D1401994

CARDIFF
CAERDYDD

ACC. No: 02891540

Africa South of the Sahara 2013

42nd Edition

LONDON AND NEW YORK

42nd edition published 2012
by Routledge
2 Park Square, Milton Park, Abingdon, Oxon, OX14 4RN

Simultaneously published in the USA and Canada by Routledge
711 Third Avenue, New York, NY10017

Routledge is an imprint of the Taylor & Francis Group, an Informa business

First published 1971

ISBN: 978-1-85743-659-4
ISSN: 0065-3896

Editor: Iain Frame

Regional Organizations Editor: Helen Canton

Senior Editor, Statistics: Philip McIntyre

Statistics Researchers: Varun Wadhawan (Team Leader), Mohd Khalid Ansari (Senior Researcher), Charu Arora (Senior Researcher), Suchi Kedia, Nirbachita Sarkar, Akshay Sharma

Directory Editorial Researchers: Arijit Khasnobis (Team Manager), Birendra Pratap Nayak (Senior Researcher), Saurav Goswami

Contributing Editors: Catriona Holman (Regional Organizations), Gareth Wyn Jones (Commodities), Gareth Vaughan (Commodities)

Senior Editor: Juliet Love

Typeset in New Century Schoolbook
by Data Standards Limited, Frome, Somerset

FOREWORD

The year's main political and economic developments in each of the 53 countries and territories of the region, are comprehensively narrated and examined in this volume, the 42nd edition of AFRICA SOUTH OF THE SAHARA . Readers' perspectives are further expanded by the General Survey, which provides an in-depth analysis of current economic trends, an assessment of aid and development initiatives over the past 100 years, an insight into the phenomenon of failed states and the repercussions of, and responses to, state failure in sub-Saharan Africa, an examination of the People's Republic of China's increasing political and economic ties with the African continent, the prospects of the East African Community, and an exploration of health and medical issues. New essays detailing the burgeoning relationship between Brazil and the African continent and investigating West Africa's security dilemmas are also featured.

In addition to contributions by specialist authors, researchers and commentators, all statistical and directory material in the new edition has been extensively updated, revised and expanded. A calendar of the key political events of 2011–12 provides convenient rapid reference to the year's main developments. Comprehensive coverage of international organizations and research bodies active in Africa, is included, together with detailed background information on the continent's major agricultural and mineral commodities. Select bibliographies of relevant books and periodicals are also provided.

The entire content of the print edition of AFRICA SOUTH OF THE SAHARA is available online at www.europaworld.com. This prestigious resource incorporates sophisticated search and browse functions as well as specially commissioned visual and statistical content. An ongoing programme of updates of key areas of information ensures currency of content, and enhances the richness of the coverage.

The year under review in sub-Saharan Africa was notable for significant unrest across the region. The world's newest nation, South Sudan, came into conflict with Sudan (from which it had seceded in July 2011) over arrangements regarding the transportation of petroleum. Tensions were compounded by an ongoing dispute over the demarcation of the common border, and in January 2012 South Sudan halted oil production, resulting in both countries' economies experiencing severe difficulties. Eastern areas of the Democratic Republic of the Congo (DRC), close to the border with Rwanda, were also affected by violence in 2012, as a result of which more than 200,000 people were reported to have been displaced. Meanwhile, in West Africa, the peaceful handover of power in Senegal in April 2012, following the defeat of Abdoulaye Wade by Macky Sall in the run-off presidential election the previous month, was in stark contrast to the military coups which took place in neighbouring Mali and Guinea-Bissau in March and April, respectively. Although interim administrations and election schedules were subsequently established in both countries, the security situation remained extremely fragile, especially in the north of Mali where separatist Islamist groups were in control of large areas of territory. The increasing number of attacks by the Islamist Boko Haram movement in Nigeria—which was believed to have been responsible for some 1,400 deaths in the country since 2010—provided further cause for concern in the sub-region.

Elsewhere in sub-Saharan Africa, the death in August 2012 of the long serving Ethiopian Prime Minister, Meles Zenawi, and the passing in July of John Evans Atta Mills, the Ghanaian President, threatened the stability of two of the continent's fastest growing economies. However, the death of the Malawian President, Bingu wa Mutharika, in April enabled his successor, Joyce Banda, to improve hitherto strained relations with the international community and to introduce necessary economic reforms. Further positive developments were observed in Somalia with the adoption of a new Provisional Constitution, which facilitated the election of Hassan Sheikh Mohamud as President and the creation of new institutions of state. Presidential elections were also successfully held in Zambia, Cameroon, Liberia, The Gambia and the DRC; in all bar the former incumbents were returned to office.

The Editors are once again thankful to all the contributors for their articles and advice, and to the numerous governments and organizations that have returned questionnaires and provided statistical and other information.

October 2012

ACKNOWLEDGEMENTS

The Editors gratefully acknowledge the interest and co-operation of the many national statistical and information offices and embassies and high commissions, whose valued assistance in updating the material contained in AFRICA SOUTH OF THE SAHARA is greatly appreciated.

We acknowledge particular indebtedness for permission to reproduce material from the following publications: the United Nations' statistical databases and *Demographic Yearbook*, *Statistical Yearbook*, *Monthly Bulletin of Statistics*, *Industrial Commodity Statistics Yearbook* and *International Trade Statistics Yearbook*; the United Nations Educational, Scientific and Cultural Organization's *Statistical Yearbook* and Institute for Statistics database; the *Human Development Report* of the United Nations Development Programme; the Food and Agriculture Organization of the United Nations' statistical database; the statistical databases of the UNCTAD/WTO International Trade Centre; the statistical databases of the World Health Organization; the International Labour Office's statistical database and *Yearbook of Labour Statistics*; the World Bank's *World Bank Atlas*, *Global Development Finance*, *World Development Report* and *World Development Indicators*; the International Monetary Fund's statistical database, *International Financial Statistics* and *Government Finance Statistics Yearbook*; the African Development Bank's *African Statistical Yearbook 2012*; the World Tourism Organization's *Compendium* and *Yearbook of Tourism Statistics*; the US Geological Survey; the International Telecommunication Union; the International Road Federation's *World Road Statistics* and *The Military Balance 2012*, a publication of the International Institute for Strategic Studies, Arundel House, 13–15 Arundel Street, London, WC2R 3DX, United Kingdom. We acknowledge *La Zone Franc* and the regular publications of the Banque Centrale des Etats de l'Afrique de l'Ouest and of the Banque des Etats de l'Afrique Centrale as the sources of some of our financial information on francophone Africa.

The articles on Saint Helena, Ascension and Tristan da Cunha make use of material from *The Commonwealth Yearbook*, with the kind permission of TSO (The Stationery Office).

HEALTH AND WELFARE STATISTICS: SOURCES AND DEFINITIONS

Total fertility rate Source: WHO Statistical Information System (part of the Global Health Observatory). The number of children that would be born per woman, assuming no female mortality at child-bearing ages and the age-specific fertility rates of a specified country and referenceperiod.

Under-5 mortality rate Source: WHO Statistical Information System. Defined by WHO as the probability of a child born in a specific year or period dying before reaching the age of five, if subject to the age-specific mortality rates of that year or period.

HIV/AIDS Source: UNAIDS. Estimated percentage of adults aged 15 to 49 years living with HIV/AIDS. < indicates 'fewer than'.

Health expenditure Source: WHO Statistical Information System.

US $ per head (PPP)

International dollar estimates, derived by dividing local currency units by an estimate of their purchasing-power parity (PPP) compared with the US dollar. PPPs are the rates of currency conversion that equalize the purchasing power of different currencies by eliminating the differences in price levels between countries.

% of GDP

GDP levels for OECD countries follow the most recent UN System of National Accounts. For non-OECD countries a value was estimated by utilizing existing UN, IMF and World Bank data.

Public expenditure

Government health-related outlays plus expenditure by social schemes compulsorily affiliated with a sizeable share of the population, and extrabudgetary funds allocated to health services. Figures include grants or loans provided by international agencies, other national authorities, and sometimes commercial banks.

Access to water and sanitation Source: WHO/UNICEF Joint Monitoring Programme on Water Supply and Sanitation (JMP) (Progress on Drinking Water and Sanitation, 2012 Update). Defined in terms of the percentage of the population using improved facilities in terms of the type of technology and levels of service afforded. For water, this includes house connections, public standpipes, boreholes with handpumps, protected dug wells, protected spring and rainwater collection; allowance is also made for other locally defined technologies. Sanitation is defined to include connection to a sewer or septic tank system, pour-flush latrine, simple pit or ventilated improved pit latrine, again with allowance for acceptable local technologies. Access to water and sanitation does not imply that the level of service or quality of water is 'adequate' or 'safe'.

Carbon dioxide emissions Source: World Bank, World Development Indicators database, citing the Carbon Dioxide Information Analysis Center (sponsored by the US Department of Energy). Emissions comprise those resulting from the burning of fossil fuels (including those produced during consumption of solid, liquid and gas fuels and from gas flaring) and from the manufacture of cement.

Human Development Index (HDI) Source: UNDP, *Human Development Report* (2011). A summary of human development measured by three basic dimensions: prospects for a long and healthy life, measured by life expectancy at birth; knowledge, measured by a combination of mean years of schooling and expected years of schooling; and standard of living, measured by GNI per head (PPP US $). The index value obtained lies between zero and one. A value above 0.8 indicates very high human development, between 0.7 and 0.8 high human development, between 0.5 and 0.7 medium human development, and below 0.5 low human development. A centralized data source for all three dimensions was not available for all countries. In some cases other data sources were used to calculate a substitute value; however, this was excluded from the ranking. Other countries, including non-UNDP members, were excluded from the HDI altogether. In total, 187 countries were ranked for 2011.

CONTENTS

THE DEMOCRATIC REPUBLIC OF THE CONGO

THE REPUBLIC OF THE CONGO

CÔTE D'IVOIRE

DJIBOUTI

EQUATORIAL GUINEA

ERITREA

ETHIOPIA

GABON

THE GAMBIA

GHANA

GUINEA

GUINEA-BISSAU

KENYA

LESOTHO

PART THREE

Regional Information

THE CONTRIBUTORS

Alexandre Abreu. Researcher, Centre of African and Development Studies, University of Lisbon, Portugal.

J. A. Allan. Former Professor of Geography, School of Oriental and African Studies, University of London, United Kingdom.

Kwesi Aning. Dean and Director, Academic Affairs and Research Department, Kofi Annan International Peacekeeping Training Centre, Accra, Ghana.

Festus Aubyn. Senior Research Fellow, Kofi Annan International Peacekeeping Training Centre, Accra, Ghana.

L. Berry. Former Professor of Geography, University of Dar es Salaam, Tanzania.

E. A. Boateng. Environmental consultant and educationalist.

Richard A. Bradshaw. Professor of History, Centre College, Kentucky, USA.

Sir Mervyn Brown. Former British Ambassador in Madagascar. Member, Académie Malgache.

Richard Brown. Former Dean, School of African and Asian Studies, University of Sussex at Brighton, United Kingdom.

Greg Cameron. Professor of Political Science and Rural Studies, Nova Scotia Agricultural College, Canada.

Marisé Castro. Researcher, Amnesty International, International Secretariat, London, United Kingdom.

Phil Clark. Lecturer in Comparative and International Politics, School of Oriental and African Studies, University of London, United Kingdom, and Advisory Board Member, Oxford Transitional Justice Research.

John I. Clarke. Professor of Geography, University of Durham, United Kingdom.

Walter S. Clarke. Senior Advisor for Civil-Military Co-operation, Global Center for Disaster Management and Humanitarian Action, College of Public Health, University of South Florida, USA.

Julian Cooke. Editor of the *Anglo-Malagasy Society Newsletter*.

Juan Fandos-Rius. Encyclopaedist and historian of the Central African Republic.

Edward George. Writer specializing in sub-Saharan African political and economic issues.

Marie Gibert. Lecturer in International Relations, Nottingham Trent University.

Pierre Gourou. Late Professor of Geography, Université Libre de Bruxelles, Belgium, and Collège de France, Paris, France.

R. J. Harrison Church. Late Professor of Geography, London School of Economics, United Kingdom.

David Hilling. Research adviser, University of Greenwich, United Kingdom.

Victoria Holligan. Economist specializing in sub-Saharan Africa and the global energy sector.

Obi Iheme. Writer and security consultant.

A. MacGregor Hutcheson. Lecturer in Geography, Aberdeen College of Education, United Kingdom.

Michael Jennings. Senior Lecturer in International Development, School of Oriental and African Studies, University of London, United Kingdom.

Warka Solomon Kahsay Graduate student, Saint Francis Xavier University, Antogonish, Canada.

Zachary D. Kaufman Adjunct Professor, Elliot School of International Affairs, George Washington University, USA.

George Kay. Head of the Department of Geography and Recreation Studies, Staffordshire University, United Kingdom.

Joseph Lake. Economist specializing in sub-Saharan Africa.

B. W. Langlands. Late Professor of Geography, Makerere University College, Kampala, Uganda.

I. M. Lewis. Emeritus Professor of Anthropology, London School of Economics and Political Science, United Kingdom.

Akin L. Mabogunje. Former Professor of Geography, University of Ibadan, Nigeria.

Hugh Macmillan. Former Professor of History, University of Transkei, South Africa.

Paul Melly. Journalist specializing in francophone Africa and Associate Fellow of the Africa Programme at the Royal Institute of International Affairs (Chatham House), United Kingdom.

Peter K. Mitchell. Honorary Senior Research Fellow, Centre of West African Studies, University of Birmingham, United Kingdom.

W. T. W. Morgan. Senior Lecturer, Department of Geography, University of Durham, United Kingdom.

Gregory Mthembu-Salter. Writer specializing in the political and economic affairs of African countries.

Katharine Murison. Editor of *Africa South of the Sahara*, 2001–04.

Quentin Outram. Senior Lecturer in Economics, Leeds University Business School, University of Leeds, United Kingdom.

René Pélissier. Author specializing in contemporary Spanish-speaking and Portuguese-speaking Africa.

Bhairav Raja. International development consultant specializing in African and Latin American political and economic issues.

Christopher Saunders. Emeritus Professor, Department of Historical Studies, University of Cape Town, South Africa.

Gerhard Seibert. Researcher, Centro de Estudos Africanos (CEA)/ ISCTE—IUL, Lisbon, Portugal.

Miles Smith-Morris. Writer specializing in developing countries.

Ana Naomi de Sousa. Journalist and writer specializing in lusophone and sub-Saharan African countries.

Donald L. Sparks. Professor of International Economics, The Citadel, Charleston, South Carolina, USA, and Visiting Professor of Economics, Innsbruck Summer Program, Austria.

Richard Synge. Writer and journalist specializing in African political and economic issues and Editor of Global (www.global-briefing.org).

Charlie Tarr. Writer specializing in sub-Saharan African political and economic issues.

Ian Taylor. Professor of International Relations, University of St Andrews, United Kingdom.

Virginia Thompson. Writer specializing in francophone Africa.

Olalekan Uthman. Research Fellow, Public Health, Epidemiology, and Biostatistics, University of Birmingham, United Kingdom.

Linda Van Buren. Writer specializing in the business and economic affairs of African countries.

Manickam Venkataraman. Associate Professor of Political Science and International Relations, Addis Ababa University, Ethiopia.

Geoffrey J. Williams. Former Professor of Geography, University of Zambia, Zambia.

Paul D. Williams. Associate Professor, Elliot School of International Affairs, George Washington University, USA.

Duncan Woodside. Journalist and analyst specializing in economics and conflict in the Great Lakes of Africa.

Ralph Young. Senior Lecturer, Department of Government, University of Manchester, United Kingdom.

ABBREVIATIONS

Acad.	Academician; Academy
ACP	African, Caribbean and Pacific (States)
AfDB	African Development Bank
ADF	African Development Fund
Adm.	Admiral
Admin.	Administration; Administrative; Administrator
AEC	African Economic Community
AG	Aktiengesellschaft (limited company)
AGOA	African Growth and Opportunity Act
a.i.	ad interim
AIDS	acquired immunodeficiency syndrome
AM	Amplitude Modulation
Apdo	Apartado (Post Box)
Apt	Apartment
ARV	advanced retroviral
Ass.	Assembly
Asscn	Association
Assoc.	Associate
Asst	Assistant
AU	African Union
Aug.	August
auth.	authorized
Av.	Avenida (Avenue)
Ave	Avenue
BCEAO	Banque Centrale des Etats de l'Afrique de l'Ouest
Bd	Board
b/d	barrels per day
BEAC	Banque des Etats de l'Afrique Centrale
Bldg(s)	Building(s)
Blvd	Boulevard
BOAD	Banque Ouest-Africaine de Développement
BP	Boîte Postale (Post Box)
br.(s)	branch(es)
Brig.	Brigadier
C	Centigrade; Cedi(s) (Ghana currency)
c.	circa
cap.	capital
Capt.	Captain
CEMAC	Communauté Economique et Monétaire de l'Afrique Centrale
Cen.	Central
CEO	Chief Executive Officer
cf.	confer (compare)
CFA	Communauté Financière Africaine; Coopération Financière en Afrique Centrale
Chair.	Chairman/woman
Cie	Compagnie
c.i.f.	cost, insurance and freight
C-in-C	Commander-in-Chief
circ.	circulation
cm	centimetre(s)
cnr	corner
c/o	care of
Co	Company; County
Col	Colonel
Comm.	Commission
Commdr	Commander
Commr	Commissioner
Conf.	Conference
Confed.	Confederation
COO	Chief Operating Officer
Corpn	Corporation
CP	Caixa Postal, Case Postale (Post Box)
Cpl	Corporal
Cttee	Committee
cu	cubic
cwt	hundredweight
Dec.	December
Del.	Delegate
Dem.	Democratic
Dep.	Deputy
dep.	deposits
Dept	Department
Devt	Development
Dir	Director
Div.	Division(al)
Dr	Doctor
Dr.	Drive
Dra	Doctora
dwt	dead weight tons
E	East; Eastern; Emalangeni (Swaziland currency)
€	Euro (currency)
EAC	East African Community
EC	European Community
ECA	Economic Commission for Africa (UN)
ECF	Extended Credit Facility
ECOWAS	Economic Community of West African States
ECU	European Currency Unit(s)
Ed.(s)	Editor(s)
EDF	European Development Fund
edn	edition
EEZ	Exclusive Economic Zone
e.g.	exempli gratia (for example)
EIB	European Investment Bank
EME	emerging market economy
Eng.	Engineer; Engineering
EP	Empresa Pública
EPZ	Export Processing Zone
ESAF	Enhanced Structural Adjustment Facility
est.	established; estimate; estimated
etc.	etcetera
EU	European Union
excl.	excluding
Exec.	Executive
exhbn(s)	exhibition(s)
Ext.	Extension
f.	founded
FAO	Food and Agriculture Organization
f.a.s.	free alongside
FDI	foreign direct investment
Feb.	February
Fed.	Federation; Federal
FG	Guinea Franc
FIDES	Fonds d'Investissement et de Développement Economique et Social
Flt	Flight
FMD	foot-and-mouth disease
FMG	Malagasy Franc
fmr(ly)	former(ly)
f.o.b.	free on board
Fr	Father
Fr.	Franc(s)
Fri.	Friday
ft	foot (feet)
FTA	free trade agreement/area
g	gram(s)
GDP	gross domestic product
Gen.	General
GMO(s)	genetically modified organism(s)
GMT	Greenwich Mean Time
GNI	gross national income
GNP	gross national product
Gov.	Governor
Govt	Government
GPO	General Post Office
grt	gross registered ton(s)
GWh	gigawatt hour(s)
ha	hectare(s)
HDI	Human Development Index
HIPC	heavily indebted poor country
HIV	human immunodeficiency virus
hl	hectolitre(s)
HLTF	High Level Task Force
HM	His/Her Majesty
HPAI	highly pathogenic avian influenza
HQ	Headquarters
HYV	high-yielding variety
ibid.	ibidem (from the same source)
IBRD	International Bank for Reconstruction and Development (World Bank)
ICT	information and communication technology
IDA	International Development Association
IDPs	Internally Displaced Persons
i.e.	id est (that is to say)
IGAD	Intergovernmental Authority on Development
ILO	International Labour Organization/Office
IMF	International Monetary Fund
in	inch (inches)
Inc	Incorporated
incl.	include, including

Ind.	Independent
Ing.	Engineer
Insp.	Inspector
Inst.	Institute
Int.	International
Is	Islands
ISIC	International Standard Industrial Classification
ISP	internet service provider
ITUC	International Trade Union Confederation
IUU	illegal, unreported and unregulated
Jan.	January
Jr	Junior
Jt	Joint
K	Kwacha (Malawi and Zambia currencies)
kg	kilogram(s)
km	kilometre(s)
kW	kilowatt(s)
kWh	kilowatt hour(s)
lb	pound(s)
Lda	Limitada (limited company)
LDCs	Least Developed Countries
Le.	Leone (Sierra Leone currency)
LLC	Limited Liability Company
LNG	Liquefied natural gas
LPG	Liquefied petroleum gas
Lt	Lieutenant
Ltd	Limited
M	Maloti (Lesotho currency)
m	metre(s)
m.	million
Maj.	Major
Man.	Manager; Managing
MB/s	megabits per second
MDG	Millennium Development Goal
MDRI	multilateral debt relief initiative
Me	Maître
mem.	member
MFA	Multi-fibre Arrangement
Mfg	Manufacturing
mfrs	manufacturers
mg	milligram(s)
Mgr	Monseigneur, Monsignor
Mil.	Military
Mlle	Mademoiselle
mm	millimetre(s)
Mme	Madame
Mon.	Monday
MP	Member of Parliament
MSS	manuscripts
Mt	Mount
MV	Motor Vessel
MW	megawatt(s); medium wave
MWh	megawatt hour(s)
N	North; Northern
₦	Naira (Nigerian currency)
NA	National Association (banking)
n.a.	not available
Nat.	National
NCO	Non-Commissioned Officer
NEPAD	New Partnership for Africa's Development
n.e.s.	not elsewhere specified
NGO	non-governmental organization
No.	number
Nov.	November
nr	near
nrt	net registered ton(s)
NV	Naamloze Vennootschap (limited company)
OAU	Organization of African Unity
Oct.	October
OECD	Organisation for Economic Co-operation and Development
OIC	Organization of the Islamic Conference, Organization of Islamic Cooperation
OMVS	Organisation pour la Mise en Valeur du Fleuve Sénégal
OPEC	Organization of the Petroleum Exporting Countries
opp.	opposite
Org.(s)	Organization(s)
oz	ounce(s)
P	Pula (Botswana currency)
p.	page
p.a.	per annum
Parl.	Parliament(ary)
Perm.	Permanent
PGM	platinum-group metals
pl.	place (square)
PLC	Public Limited CompanyPGM
PMB	Private Mail Bag
PO	Post Office
POB	Post Office Box
PPP	purchasing-power parity
Pres.	President
PRGF	Poverty Reduction and Growth Facility
Prin.	Principal
Prof.	Professor
Propr	Proprietor
Prov.	Province; Provincial
PSI	Policy Suport Instrument, Poverty Strategies Initiative
Pte	Private
Pty	Proprietary
p.u.	paid up
publ.(s)	publication(s); published
Publr	Publisher
Pvt.	Private
q.v.	quod vide (to which refer)
R	Rand (South African currency)
Rd	Road
RECs	regional economic communities
regd	registered
reorg.	reorganized
Rep.	Representative
Repub.	Republic
res	reserves
retd	retired
Rev.	Reverend
Rm	Room
RMS	Royal Mail Steamer
Rs	Rupee(s) (Mauritius currency)
Rt	Right
S	South; Southern
SA	Société Anonyme, Sociedad Anónima (limited company); South Africa
SADC	Southern African Development Community
SARL	Sociedade Anônima de Responsabilidade Limitada (limited company)
Sat.	Saturday
SDR	Special Drawing Right(s)
Sec.	Secretary
Secr.	Secretariat
Sept.	September
Sgt	Sergeant
SITC	Standard International Trade Classification
SME	small and medium-sized enterprises
Soc.	Society
Sq.	Square
sq	square (in measurements)
SR	Seychelles Rupee(s)
Sr	Senior
St	Street; Saint, San, Santo
Sta	Santa
Ste	Sainte
STI(s)	sexually transmitted infection(s)
Stn	Station
Sun.	Sunday
Supt	Superintendent
tech.	technical, technology
trans.	translator, translated
Treas.	Treasurer
TV	Television
UA	Unit(s) of Account
UEE	Unidade Económica Estatal
UEMOA	Union Economique et Monétaire Ouest-Africaine
UK	United Kingdom
ul.	ulitsa (street)
UM	Ouguiya(s) (Mauritania currency)
UN	United Nations
UNAIDS	United Nations Joint Programme on HIV/AIDS
UNCTAD	United Nations Conference on Trade and Development
UNDP	United Nations Development Programme
UNESCO	United Nations Educational, Scientific and Cultural Organization
UNHCR	United Nations High Commissioner for Refugees
Univ.	University
UNWTO	World Tourism Organization
US(A)	United States (of America)
USAID	United States Agency for International Development
USSR	Union of Soviet Socialist Republics
Vol.(s)	Volume(s)
W	West; Western
WHO	World Health Organization
WSSD	World Summit on Sustainable Development
WTO	World Trade Organization
yr(s)	year(s)

INTERNATIONAL TELEPHONE CODES

To make international calls to telephone and fax numbers listed in *Africa South of the Sahara*, dial the international code of the country from which you are calling, followed by the appropriate country code for the organization you wish to call (listed below), followed by the area code (if applicable) and telephone or fax number listed in the entry.

	Country code	+ GMT*
Angola	244	+1
Ascension Island	247	0
Benin	229	+1
Botswana	267	+2
British Indian Ocean Territory	246	+5
Burkina Faso	226	0
Burundi	257	+2
Cameroon	237	+1
Cape Verde	238	-1
The Central African Republic	236	+1
Chad	235	+1
The Comoros	269	+3
Congo, Democratic Republic	243	+1
Congo, Republic	242	+1
Côte d'Ivoire	225	0
Djibouti	253	+3
Equatorial Guinea	240	+1
Eritrea	291	+3
Ethiopia	251	+3
Gabon	241	+1
The Gambia	220	0
Ghana	233	0
Guinea	224	0
Guinea-Bissau	245	0
Kenya	254	+3
Lesotho	266	+2
Liberia	231	0
Madagascar	261	+3
Malawi	265	+2
Mali	223	0
Mauritania	222	0
Mauritius	230	+4
Mayotte	262	+3
Mozambique	258	+2
Namibia	264	+2
Niger	227	+1
Nigeria	234	+1
Réunion	262	+4
Rwanda	250	+2
Saint Helena	290	0
São Tomé and Príncipe	239	0
Senegal	221	0
Seychelles	248	+4
Sierra Leone	232	0
Somalia	252	+3
South Africa	27	+2
South Sudan	211†	+2
Sudan	249	+2
Swaziland	268	+2
Tanzania	255	+3
Togo	228	0
Tristan da Cunha	290	0
Uganda	256	+3
Zambia	260	+2
Zimbabwe	263	+2

*Time difference in hours + Greenwich Mean Time (GMT). The times listed compare the standard (winter) times. Some countries may adopt Summer (Daylight Saving) Times—i.e. + 1 hour—for part of the year.

† Some telephone numbers for South Sudan use the country code for Sudan (249) or Uganda (256).

EXPLANATORY NOTE ON THE DIRECTORY SECTION

The Directory section of each chapter is arranged under the following headings, where they apply:

THE CONSTITUTION

THE GOVERNMENT
- HEAD OF STATE
- CABINET/COUNCIL OF MINISTERS
- EXECUTIVE
- MINISTRY ADDRESSES

LEGISLATURE

ELECTION COMMISSION

POLITICAL ORGANIZATIONS

DIPLOMATIC REPRESENTATION

JUDICIAL SYSTEM

RELIGION

THE PRESS

PUBLISHERS

BROADCASTING AND COMMUNICATIONS

FINANCE
- CENTRAL BANK
- NATIONAL BANKS
- COMMERCIAL BANKS
- DEVELOPMENT BANKS
- MERCHANT BANKS
- SAVINGS BANKS
- INVESTMENT BANKS
- FINANCIAL INSTITUTIONS
- STOCK EXCHANGE
- INSURANCE

TRADE AND INDUSTRY
- GOVERNMENT AGENCIES
- DEVELOPMENT ORGANIZATIONS
- CHAMBERS OF COMMERCE
- INDUSTRIAL AND TRADE ASSOCIATIONS
- EMPLOYERS' ORGANIZATIONS
- UTILITIES
- MAJOR COMPANIES
- CO-OPERATIVES
- TRADE UNIONS

TRANSPORT
- RAILWAYS
- ROADS
- INLAND WATERWAYS
- SHIPPING
- CIVIL AVIATION

TOURISM

DEFENCE

EDUCATION

POLITICAL EVENTS IN AFRICA SOUTH OF THE SAHARA, 2011–12

SEPTEMBER 2011

3 **São Tomé and Príncipe** Dr Manuel Pinto da Costa took office as President.

7 **Malawi** President Bingu wa Mutharika appointed a new, 31-member cabinet. Minister of Finance Ken Kandodo and Minister of Foreign Affairs Prof. Etta Banda were among nine senior ministers who were not included in the new Government.

9 **Cape Verde** Jorge Carlos Fonseca was formally sworn in as President.

11 **Democratic Republic of the Congo (DRC)** President Joseph Kabila Kabange effected a major reorganization of the Government. Among the most notable appointments was that of Louis Alphonse Koyagialo Ngbase te Gerengbo as Deputy Prime Minister in charge of Posts, Telephones and Telecommunications.

12 **Niger** President Issoufou Mahamadou reorganized the Government appointing, *inter alia*, Omar Hamidou Tchiana as Minister of State, Minister of Mines and Industrial Development and Foumakoye Gado as Minister of Petroleum and Energy.

20 **Zambia** A presidential election was held, at which Michael Chilufya Sata of the Patriotic Front was declared the winner having secured 42.9% of the total votes cast. Incumbent President Rupiah Banda received 36.2% of the vote. Sata took office on 23 September and appointed a new, 19-member Cabinet on 29 September.

OCTOBER 2011

2 **Seychelles** Results were announced of the general election held between 29 September and 1 October. Parti Lepep, under the leadership of Prime Minister James Alex Michel, won all 25 directly elected seats in the National Assembly. It was also allocated an additional six proportional seats as it had secured 88.6% of the total valid votes. The election was boycotted by the main opposition party, the Seychelles National Party.

7 **Rwanda** President Paul Kagame named Pierre Damien Habumuremyi, hitherto Minister of Education, as Prime Minister, replacing Bernard Makuza.

Senegal In a government reorganization Faustin Diatta was dismissed as Minister of Sport. Responsibility for that portfolio was assumed by Abdoulaye Makhtar Diop, Minister of State, Minister of the Civil Service and Employment.

8 **Djibouti** Moussa Ahmed Hassan (hitherto Minister of Housing, Urban Planning and the Environment) was named as Minister of Education, replacing Adawa Hassan Ali, while Hassan Omar Mohamed Bourhan was appointed to Ahmed Hassan's former portfolio.

9 **Cameroon** At the presidential elections Paul Biya secured 78.0% of the total votes cast. His nearest rival, Ni John Fru Ndi, received 10.7% of the vote.

11 **Liberia** In the first round of the presidential election Ellen Johnson-Sirleaf (Unity Party) received 43.9% of the total vote, while her closest rival Winston A. Tubman (Congress for Democratic Change) secured 32.7% of the vote. In the second round of the election, held on 8 November 2011, Johnson-Sirleaf received 90.7% of the vote.

17 **Swaziland** King Mswati III effected a reorganization of the Cabinet. Most notably, Chief Mgwagwa Gamedze was appointed Minister of Justice, replacing David Matse, and Winnie Magagula became Minister of Information, Communication and Technology, in place of Neliswe Shongwe.

23 **South Africa** President Jacob Zuma named Richard Baloyi as Minister of Co-operative Governance and Traditional Affairs, and Thembelani Nxesi as Minister of Public Works.

26 **Botswana** President Seretse Khama Ian Khama announced a new Government, appointing Ramadeluka Seretse as Minister of Defence, Justice and Security, Edwin Batsu as Minister of Labour and Home Affairs, Peter Siele as Minister of Local Government, and Lebonamang Mokalake as Minister of Lands and Housing.

28 **Madagascar** Jean Omer Beriziky, a former Malagasy ambassador to the European Union, was named as Prime Minister, replacing Gen. Albert Camille Vital, who had resigned on 17 October. Subsequently, on 21 November, Beriziky named a Government of National Unity.

29 **Saint Helena, Ascension and Tristan da Cunha** Mark Capes was sworn in as Governor.

NOVEMBER 2011

7 **Burundi** President Pierre Nkurunziza effected a major reorganization of the Council of Ministers. Among those appointed were Laurent Kavakure (Minister of External Relations and International Co-operation), Pascal Barandagiye (Minister of Justice) and Côme Manirakiza (Minister of Energy and Mines).

9 **Kenya** A new Independent Electoral and Boundaries Commission was officially inaugurated, replacing the former Electoral Commission of Kenya. Ahmed Isaack Hassan was appointed Chairman.

13 **Equatorial Guinea** Several amendments to the Constitution were approved by national referendum, including the limiting of the President's tenure to two seven-year terms and the creation of the post of Vice-President.

17 **Ethiopia** In a minor government reorganization Kebede Chane was named as Minister of Trade, replacing Abdurahman Shek Mohammed.

24 **The Gambia** At a presidential election Alhaji Yahya Jammeh, representing the Alliance for Patriotic Reorientation and Construction (APRC), secured a fourth term of elected office, having taken 71.5% of the valid votes cast. His nearest rival, Ousainou Darboe, the candidate of the United Democratic Party, won 17.4% of the ballot.

DECEMBER 2011

1 **Angola** João Baptista Borges was appointed Minister of Energy and Water, replacing Emanuela Bernardeth Afronso Vieria Lopes.

9 **Cameroon** President Biya appointed a new Government, in which Philémon Yang and Amadou Ali were confirmed as Prime Minister and Deputy Prime Minister, Minister-delegate at the Presidency in charge of Relations with the Assemblies, respectively.

9 **DRC** The Commission Electorale Nationale Indépendante released preliminary results of the presidential election held on 28–29 November, according to which Kabila was declared the victor, having secured 49.0% of the valid votes cast. His closest challenger, Etienne Tshisekedi Wa Mulumba, who took 32.3% of the votes, immediately rejected the officially declared figures, and it was reported that at least six people had been killed during protests in the capital, Kinshasa.

11 **Côte d'Ivoire** At legislative elections the Rassemblement des Républicains of President Alassane Ouattara secured 127 seats out of a total 254 contested seats. The Parti Démocratique de la Côte d'Ivoire—Rassemblement Démocratique Africain was placed second winning 77 seats.

12 **Republic of the Congo** In a government reorganization the Minister of Scientific Research, Bruno Jean-Richards Itoua, and the Minister of Water and Energy, Henry Ossebi, exchanged positions.

17 **Gabon** The Parti Démocratique Gabonais secured 114 out of a total 120 seats in elections to the Assemblée nationale. The Rassemblement pour le Gabon won three seats; the Cercle des Libéraux Réformateurs, the Parti Social-Démocrate and the Union pour la Nouvelle République each won one seat each.

JANUARY 2012

9 **Guinea-Bissau** The death was announced of Malam Bacai Sanhá, President of Guinea-Bissau since 2009, following a prolonged period of illness. Under the terms of the country's Constitution, the functions of the head of state were assumed on an interim basis by the President of the Assembleia Nacional Popular, Raimundo Pereira, pending a presidential election which was required to be held within 90 days.

16 **Liberia** Johnson-Sirleaf was sworn in as President, and on 19 January she nominated a number of government ministers, including Augustine Ngafuan, Minister of Foreign Affairs; Amara Konneh, Minister of Finance; and Brownie Samukai, Minister of Defence. Further nominations were made on 23 January, notable among which were Patrick Sendolo as Minister of Lands, Mines and Energy, and Blamo Nelson as Minister of Internal Affairs.

12 **Zambia** President Michael Sata carried a reorganization of the Cabinet in which Given Lubinda was appointed Minister of Foreign Affairs, while Chishimba Kambwili became Minister of Labour, Youth and Sports. Fackson Shamenda was assigned to the Ministry of Information, Broadcasting and Tourism.

23 **International Criminal Court/Kenya** The International Criminal Court confirmed that four Kenyans, among them the Deputy Prime Minister and Minister of Finance, Uhuru Kenyatta, and the former Minister of Education, William Ruto, were to face charges of crimes against humanity relating to their roles in the nation-wide unrest that followed the disputed presidential election of December 2007. According to UN figures, approximately 1,200 people were killed and more than 600,000 displaced during ethnic and tribal violence that occurred in early 2008 after Mwai Kibaki was controversially re-elected to the presidency. Kenyatta relinquished the finance portfolio on 26 January.

25 **Ghana** President John Evans Atta Mills made changes to the composition of the Government, appointing Dr Benjamin Kunbour Attorney-General and Minister of Justice. Alban S.K. Bagbin (hitherto Minister of Water Resources, Works and Housing) became Minister of Health and was in turn replaced by Enoch Teye Mensah (previously Minister of Employment and Social Welfare). Moses Asaga was named as Minister of Employment and Social Welfare.

27 **Chad** Bedoumra Kordié was named as Minister of Planning, the Economy and International Co-operation, replacing Mahamat Ali Hassan, while Brahim Alkhali became Minister of Energy and Petroleum, replacing Eugène Tabé.

31 **Lesotho** The Prime Minister Pakalitha Mosisili dismissed two ministers and a deputy minister following a dispute within the ruling Lesotho Congress for Democracy (LCD) party.

FEBRUARY 2012

8 **Burundi** President Maj. Jean-Pierre Nkurunziza carried out a minor reorganization of the Government in which Tabu Abdallah Manirakiza was appointed Minister of Finance and Planning for Economic Development, replacing Clotilde Niragira. Issa Ngendakumana was named as Minister at the Presidency, in charge of Good Governance and Privatization.

14 **The Gambia** President Jammeh completed the reconstitution of his Cabinet following his re-election as President.

26 **Senegal** In the first round of the presidential election incumbent Abdoulaye Wade received 34.8% of the total vote, while former Prime Minister Macky Sall secured 26.6%. A run-off was scheduled for 25 March.

28 **Gabon** A new Cabinet comprising 29 members was announced by Raymond Ndong Sima, who had been appointed Prime Minister and Head of Government on 13 February.

MARCH 2012

6 **DRC** The Prime Minister, Adolphe Muzito, announced his resignation and that of his Government. The Deputy Prime Minister, Louis Koyagialo, was named acting premier.

13 **Côte d'Ivoire** The Ivorian President, Alassane Ouattara, announced the formation of a new Government, headed by Jeannot Kouadio Ahoussou, hitherto Minister of State, Keeper of the Seals, Minister of Justice. The previous day the outgoing Prime Minister, Guillaume Soro, who had announced his resignation on 8 March, was unanimously elected President of the Assemblée nationale. Ouattara personally assumed responsibility for the defence portfolio; however, almost all members of the previous administration retained their posts.

14 **Seychelles** The National Assembly approved six new ministers appointed by President James Michel. The new ministers were: Pierre Laporte (Finance, Commerce and Investment); Alain St Ange (Tourism and Culture); Christian Lionnet (Land Use and Housing); Rolph Payet (Environment and Energy); Mitcy Larue (Health); and Idith Alexander (Employment and Human Resource Development).

18 **Guinea-Bissau** In the first round of the presidential election former Prime Minister Carlos Gomes Junior received 49.0% of the vote, while former President Mohamed Yalá Embaló received 23.4%. A run-off election was scheduled for 29 April.

21–22 **Mali** A group of rebel soldiers led by Capt. Amadou Sanogo announced the ouster of Amadou Toumani Touré (President since 2002), and the suspension of the Constitution and the dissolution of the institutions of state. Sanogo, who proclaimed himself head of a Comité National pour le Redressement de la Démocratie et la Restauration de l'Etat, stated that the troops had seized power as a result of the Government's 'incompetence' in handling a rebellion by members of the Tuareg ethnic group in the north of the country. A presidential election, in which Touré was not eligible to stand owing to the constitutional expiry of his mandate, had been scheduled to take place on 29 April.

25 **Senegal** Sall won the run-off presidential election with 65.8% of the votes cast.

26 **Kenya** In a major reorganization of the Government Najib Balala was dismissed as Minister of Tourism and was replaced by Danson Mwanzo, while Eugene Wamalwa was appointed Minister for Justice, National Cohesion and Constitutional Affairs. The former Minister of Justice, Minister Mutula Kilonzo, was named as Minister of Education. Moses Wetangula (hitherto Minister of Foreign Affairs) was appointed Minister of Trade, and was in turn replaced by Sam Ongeri (formerly Minister of Education). Chirau Ali Mwakwere (hitherto Minister of Trade) became Minister of the Environment, while Njeru Githae was confirmed as Minister for Finance, the post he had held in an acting capacity since January.

29 **The Gambia** At legislative elections the ruling APRC secured 43 of the 48 available seats, while the National Reconciliation Party and independent candidates won one seat and four seats, respectively.

30 **Mauritius** President Anerood Jugnauth resigned from his post and was immediately replaced by Vice-President Monique Ohsan Bellepeau in an interim capacity.

APRIL 2012

2 **Niger** A reorganization of the Government was carried out.

3 **Senegal** Sall was sworn in as President of Senegal and later that day appointed Abdoul Mbaye as Prime Minister. On 4 April Mbaye inaugurated a new Government.

7 **Malawi** Joyce Banda was sworn in as Malawi's first female President following the death of the incumbent Bingu wa Mutharika on 5 April. President Banda named a 23-member cabinet on 26 April. Khumbo Kachali, had been appointed Vice-President on 11 April.

12 **Guinea-Bissau** Members of the military seized power and detained Pereira and Gomes Júnior. It was reported that the coup was carried out in reaction to plans by Gomes Júnior to use Angolan troops to remove certain elements of the Guinea-Bissau armed forces. A 'Military Command' (Comando Militar) was formed, under the leadership of the army Deputy Chief of Staff, Gen. Mamadu Ture Kuruma, and on 18 April the establishment of a National Transitional Council (NTC—Conselho Nacional de Transição) was announced, after 22 political parties and the military junta agreed upon a new electoral schedule.

14 **Togo** President Faure Gnassingbé announced the dissolution of his political party, the Rassemblement pour le Peuple Togolais, and the creation of a new political party in its place, the Union pour la République.

16 **The Gambia** President Jammeh effected a reorganization of the Cabinet, with Sheriff M. L. Gomez replaced by Lamin Kaba Bajo as Minister of the Interior. Mambury Njie (hitherto Minister of Finance and Economic Affairs) was appointed Minister of Foreign Affairs, while Abdou Kolley (previously Minister of Water Resources, Fisheries and National Assembly Matters) became Minister of Finance and Economic Affairs. Dr Mamadou Tangara (previously Minister of Foreign Affairs) was named as Minister of Fisheries, Water Resources and National Assembly Matters.

18 **DRC** President Kabila appointed Augustin Matata Ponyo (formerly Minister of Finance) Prime Minister following confirmation of his re-election to the presidency. Ponyo announced the formation of a new Government on 28 April.

MAY 2012

4 **Tanzania** President Jakaya Mrisho Kikwete effected a major reorganization of his Cabinet, dismissing six ministers and two deputy ministers. Among those dismissed were Mustafa Mkullo (Finance), William Ngeleja (Energy and Minerals) and Cyril Chami (Industry, Trade and Marketing).

20 **Mali** Following extensive discussions with mediators from the Economic Community of West African States (ECOWAS), it was agreed that Dioncounda Traoré, who, on 12 April, had taken office as Interim President for a period of 40 days, would remain in that post for a transitional period of one year. The announcement precipitated mass protests in the Malian capital, Bamako, during which three demonstrators were killed and Traoré was injured. He subsequently travelled to Paris, France, for medical treatment.

22–23 **Equatorial Guinea** Following the resignation of the previous Government on 18 May in line with constitutional reforms, a new Prime Minister, Ehate Tomi, was appointed, along with a new Government.

22 **Guinea-Bissau** Under the terms of an agreement brokered by ECOWAS, the military junta that had deposed the institutions of state on 12 April returned control of the country to a new, 27-member, civilian Government, headed by Prime Minister Rui Duarte de Barros. The new administration was expected to remain in power for a transitional period of one year before the holding of elections. Duarte de Barros had been named as Prime Minister on 16 May on which day Manuel Serifo Nhamadjo had, also finally accepted his appointment as Transitional President, having, in April, initially refused to take up the post. An ECOWAS military contingent comprising more than 600 troops was to be dispatched to Guinea-Bissau in order to monitor the security situation there.

26 **Lesotho** At a general election the Democratic Congress won 41 out of a total of 80 constituency seats and was allocated a further seven seats by compensatory proportional representation, bringing its total to 48 in the 120-member National Assembly. The All Basotho Convention (ABC) secured 26 constituency seats and was in turn allocated a further four compensatory seats by proportional representation. The leader of the ABC, Thomas Thabane, subsequently concluded a coalition agreement with the LCD and the Basotho National Party and was sworn in as Prime Minister on 8 June.

JUNE 2012

2 **Central African Republic** Minister of State for Finance and the Budget Lt Col. Sylvain Ndoutingaï was dismissed from the Cabinet.

10 **Kenya** The Minister of Provincial Administration and Internal Security, Prof. George Saitoti, was killed in a helicopter crash. The Minister of Defence, Yusuf Mohamed Haji, assumed responsibility for Saitoti's post on an interim basis.

12 **South Africa** President Jacob Zuma dismissed General Bheki Cele as National Police Chief on 12 June, and made several changes to the Cabinet. Sibusiso Ndebele (hitherto Minister of Transport) was assigned as Minister of Correctional Services and was in turn replaced by Ben Martins. Lindiwe Nonceba Sisulu (previously Minister of Defence) became Minister of the Public Service and Administration and Nosiviwe Mapisa-Nqakula was appointed to Sisulu's former portfolio.

JULY 2012

1 **Senegal** At the legislative elections the ruling Benno Bokk Yaakaar coalition secured 119 out of a total 150 seats, with the opposition Parti Démocratique Sénégalais won only 12 seats.

8 **Sudan** President Lt-Gen. Omar Hassan Ahmad al-Bashir effected a reorganization of his Cabinet, reducing the number of ministerial posts by merging several ministries. The Ministry of Water Resources was merged with the Ministry of Electricity, while the Ministry of Culture was consolidated with the Ministry of Information. The Ministry of International Co-operation was abolished.

10 **Zambia** President Sata reorganized the Government.

15 **African Union** Nkosazana Clarice Dlamini-Zuma, of South Africa was elected Chairperson of the African Union, making her the first woman to lead the organization.

Republic of the Congo At the legislative elections held on 15 July (with a second round on 5 August) the Parti Congolais du Travail secured 89 out of a total of 136 contested seats, while the Mouvement Congolais pour la Démocratie et le Développement Intégral and the Rassemblement pour la Démocratie et le Progrès Social each won seven seats. Voting in three constituencies in Brazzaville did not take place.

16 **Central African Republic** Minister of Justice and Moralization Firmin Findiro was dismissed from the Cabinet.

19 **Togo** Following Gilbert Houngbo's resignation as Prime Minister on 11 July, Kwesi Séléagodji Ahoomey-Zunu was appointed head of government by President Faure Gnassingbé. A new administration was formed on 31 July.

21 **Mauritius** Kailash Purryag was sworn in as President.

24 **Ghana** The death was announced of President Mills. Later that day the Vice-President, John Dramani Mahama, was sworn in as President at an emergency parliamentary session.

AUGUST 2012

15 **Uganda** In a reorganization of the Government President Yoweri Museveni reappointed several ministers, who had faced allegations of corruption. Sam Kutesakahamba returned to the Government as Minister of Foreign Affairs after stepping down in 2011 on graft charges. John Mwoono Nasasira, Minister in the Office of the Prime Minister, in charge of General Duties, and Mwesigwa Rukutana, a Minister of State of Labour, who had stepped down alongside Kutesakahamba, were also reinstated to the Cabinet. In April a court had dismissed the charges against the three ministers due to a legal technicality. Maria Kiwanuka and Tarsis Kabwegyere were also reappointed as Minister of Finance, Planning and Economic Development and Minister of Gender, Labour and Social Affairs, respectively.

19 **Sudan** The Minister of Guidance and Endowments, Minister Ghazi Al-Saddiq, died in an aeroplane crash.

20 **Ethiopia** Prime Minister Meles Zenawi died while receiving treatment in a hospital in Belgium following a long period of illness. Deputy Prime Minister Hailemariam Desalegn assumed the role of Acting Prime Minister in accordance with the Constitution, and was sworn in as Prime Minister in September.

Mali A new Government of National Unity was formed Mali in an effort to restore stability following the military coup of 22 March. The cabinet comprised 31 ministers, including five regarded as close to the coup leader, Sanogo. Cheick Modibo Diarra was also retained as Prime Minister.

23 **The Gambia** In a reorganization of the Cabinet Dr Mamadou Tangara (hitherto Minister of Higher Education, Research, Science and Technology) and Mambury Njie (hitherto Minister of Foreign Affairs, International Co-operation and Gambians Abroad) exchanged porfolios. A few days later, however, President Jammeh dismissed Mambury Njie from the Cabinet.

27 **Réunion** Jean-Luc Marx took office as Prefect.

29 **Guinea** Souleymane Cissé, Minister of Planning, and Aboubacar Sidiki Koulibaly, Minister of Auditing and Economic and Financial Control, resigned from the Government.

Nigeria President Goodluck Jonathan dismissed Bart Nnaji, Minister of Power, from the Cabinet for compromising the privatization process of the electricity sector.

31 **Angola** Legislative elections were held at which the ruling Movimento Popular de Libertação de Angola won 71.9% of the votes cast, and 175 of the 220 seats in the Assembléia Nacional, while the União Nacional para a Independência Total de Angola took 18.7% and 32 seats. The elections were the first to be conducted under the new Angolan Constitution, promulgated on 5 February 2010, according to the terms of which the leader of the party commanding a majority in the legislature is appointed President. Thus, José Eduardo dos Santos, President since 1979, was re-elected for a further five-year term.

PART ONE
General Survey

ECONOMIC TRENDS IN AFRICA SOUTH OF THE SAHARA

DONALD L. SPARKS

INTRODUCTION AND RECENT TRENDS

While the world-wide recession that began in 2008 did not bypass the economies of sub-Saharan Africa, the region continues to make a strong recovery. Indeed, the region's combined gross domestic product (GDP) grew by 4.9% in 2010 and by 5.5% in 2011. This recovery resulted in per head growth of 2.5% in 2010 and of 2.7% in 2011. Growth was led by stronger export volumes, rising commodity prices and an upturn in the global economy. None the less, the 2008–09 downturn caused considerable social dislocation and hardship, affecting millions of households. According to World Bank estimates, as many as 7m. Africans were prevented from rising above the poverty line as a result of the downturn. The slowdown has varied in extent and nature across the region, with oil exporters and middle-income countries affected more severely than low-income and less globally integrated countries.

Recent growth showed dissimilarities by sub-region (see Table 1, below). Despite suffering severe drought and famine, East Africa generally maintained its faster growth trajectory, recording 5.8% growth in 2011. Eritrea led that sub-region, with growth of 17.2%, followed by Ethiopia (7.4%), Rwanda (7.2%), Tanzania (6.4%), Uganda (5.6%) and Djibouti (4.6%). In West Africa economic activity moderated somewhat in 2011, with GDP growth falling from 6.9% in 2010 to 5.6% in 2011. Lower oil production in Nigeria and political turmoil in Côte d'Ivoire contributed to the decline, but was somewhat counterbalanced by Ghana's 12.2% growth rate. Central Africa's growth also moderated, from 5.2% in 2010 to 4.2% in 2011. Chad's reduced oil output contributed to the region's decline. In Southern Africa overall output expanded by 5.8% in 2011, compared with 3.2% in 2010. South Africa is more integrated into global markets (making it more vulnerable to external shocks) and its recovery has been slower (nevertheless, its GDP rose by 3.1% in 2011 from 2.8% in 2010). Other countries in the region achieved solid growth: Botswana, Mozambique and Zambia all recorded growth above 6%. Even Zimbabwe's economy grew by 4% in 2011.

Table 1. Regional GDP Growth Rates (annual % change, in real terms)

	1984–2004	2009	2010	2011
Central Africa	3.9	1.8	5.2	4.2
East Africa	4.1	3.8	5.8	5.8
Southern Africa	3.1	–0.8	3.2	5.8
West Africa	3.6	4.6	6.9	5.6

Sources: OECD, *African Economic Outlook 2007*; AfDB, *African Development Indicators 2008/09*; UNECA, *Africa 2009–11: Positive Signs After the Crisis*; and UNECA, *Economic Report on Africa 2012: Unleashing Africa's Potential as a Pole of Global Growth*.

A decade ago, *The Economist* labelled Africa 'The Hopeless Continent'. By 2011 the cover of *The Economist* showed the headline 'Africa Rising'. Labour productivity has been rising by an average of nearly 3% a year. Trade between Africa and the rest of the world has increased by some 200% since 2000, and, as noted above, regional growth has been impressive, certainly compared to the rest of the world. Many (although not all) states in sub-Saharan Africa were in a better position to weather the crisis than was the case 10 years ago. Many countries have much stronger macroeconomic policies—and stronger economies—than previously, owing to factors that will be discussed below. Furthermore, the region has limited (although growing) integration with global financial markets and thus has been somewhat insulated from the global financial crisis. Indeed, of the 10 fastest-growing world economies during 2001–10, according to the Economist Intelligence Unit, six were in sub-Saharan Africa: Angola, Nigeria, Ethiopia, Chad, Mozambique and Rwanda. None the less, most states will expand at a slower rate than the 6% that many economists believe to be the minimum necessary to ensure real economic growth in light of the region's high population growth.

Sub-Saharan Africa has great diversities, yet the 49 countries of the region share many common characteristics. They range significantly in terms of population, size and economic scale. Nigeria has the largest population (an estimated 171m. in 2012), while six other independent countries of the region each contain less than 1m. people. Seychelles has the smallest population, of just 90,024. The region's estimated total population in 2010 was 854m. and may reach 970m. by 2015, according to the World Bank. Indeed, Africa's population is growing more rapidly than that of any other region world-wide, and for many African countries the population is doubling each generation. One-half of the region's population is under 18 years of age. Climate and topography vary greatly and include Mediterranean, tropical and semi-tropical, desert, rain forest, savannah, mountains and plains. Most Africans (some 64% in 2009) live in rural areas, although some countries are more intensively urbanized than others. Djibouti's urban population, for example, represents some 84% of the country's total, while in Rwanda it accounts for only 18%. Generally, the region has a very low population density (36 people per sq km), which increases the cost of providing infrastructure and services. Namibia has the lowest density, with 2.5 people per sq km, and Mauritius the highest, with 622 people per sq km. Gross national income (GNI) per head in 2010 ranged from US $170 in Burundi to $14,540 in Equatorial Guinea, while the average for sub-Saharan Africa was $1,165. Educational levels also vary greatly; nearly 100% of children in the appropriate age-group were enrolled in primary schools while enrolment in secondary schools averaged only 34%. In 2009 the region's adult literacy rate was 62%, the lowest of any region globally. Zimbabwe had an adult literacy rate of 91%, while Burkina Faso's was only 29%. In 2009 only 57% of females in the region were literate, while only one-quarter of rural females attended primary school. Expenditure on education was low, at an annual average of less than $50 per pupil. Life expectancy at birth also varies, from 42 years in Mozambique to 73 years in Mauritius and Seychelles, averaging 51 years for males and 54 years for females, according to the World Bank. In many countries, particularly in those most affected by HIV/AIDS, such as Swaziland and Botswana, average life expectancy has been reduced by more than 20 years since the mid-1980s. Some sub-Saharan countries, including South Africa, the Democratic Republic of the Congo (DRC) and Zimbabwe, are relatively well endowed with natural resources, while others, for example Niger and Somalia, have few such assets.

The economies of sub-Saharan Africa are, for the most part, small and fragile, and despite its recent positive growth noted above, the region is rapidly being left behind in the global economy. The World Bank suggests that the region has been caught in a 'poverty trap': low incomes lead to low savings, which lead to low investment and consumer demand; low investment results in lower productivity and lower demand leads to less revenue, both of which lead back to poverty. In 2011 sub-Saharan Africa accounted for just 2% of world trade and only 1% of global GDP. The region is poor: according to the World Bank, its combined GNI was US $1,003,000m. in 2010, less than that of Spain ($1,462,000m.). If South Africa and Nigeria were excluded from calculations, the combined GNI would be approximately $513,000m., less than that of Belgium. In 2008 47.5% of the population lived on less than $1 per day, at that time the internationally recognized poverty line (although this was down from nearly 50% in 1990). Indeed, nearly 70% of all Africans lived on less than $2 per day in 2012. Unlike that of all the other developing areas, sub-Saharan Africa's output per head was lower in 2011 than it was 30 years earlier, having declined by about 50% in some countries. In 2012 its GNI per caput was the lowest in the world. According to the World Bank, Africa was forecast to be the only region in which the number of poor people would increase between 2001 and 2015, with the number projected to rise from 313m. to 340m. during this period. By 2015 sub-Saharan Africa was expected to be home to more very poor people than in the rest of the world combined. It was the only region in which child malnutrition was not declining as the second decade of the 21st century began.

Table 2. Population Living on Less Than US $2 per day (%)

	1990	2005	2008
East Asia and Pacific	29.6	38.7	33.2
Eastern Europe and Central Asia	0.5	8.9	2.2
Latin America and Caribbean	11.3	17.1	12.4
Middle East and North Africa	2.4	16.9	13.9
South Asia	41.3	73.9	70.9
Sub-Saharan Africa	44.6	72.9	69.2

Sources: World Bank, *World Development Indicators 2011*; and World Bank, *World Development Indicators 2012*.

Sub-Saharan Africa has the world's second most unequal distribution of income, after Latin America. The supply of food available per person, measured in daily caloric intake, fell from 2,140 calories in 1971 to 2,100 in the mid-1990s, increasing the number of malnourished people from 94m. to 210m., according to FAO; about 30% of the region's children have suffered from malnutrition during the past decade. An estimated 22.4m. people in sub-Saharan Africa were living with HIV/AIDS in 2008. By 2009 over 5% of the region's total population (aged 15–49) was infected. According to UNAIDS, the region accounts for 67% of the world's 33.4m. HIV-positive people and 86% of AIDS-infected children. Only about one-third of the region's population has access to adequate sanitation (although this is higher in urban areas), and in some nations this is as low as 8%–15%. About two-thirds now have access to clean water (up from 55% in the 1990s). The constant threat of war and civil conflict poses grave questions about the possibility of economic gain; indeed, one in five Africans currently live in a country seriously affected by war or strife.

Given this vast diversity, it is, accordingly, difficult to draw general conclusions about the continent's economic performance as a whole during any given year. Additionally, the lack of current statistics for several countries makes it difficult to make accurate assessments of economic conditions. Nevertheless, some broad comparisons can be made: while improving since the mid-1990s, the region's overall economic growth rate during the 1980s and early 1990s was dismal. Between 1975 and 1985 the region faced two oil shocks, steep declines in commodity prices, and increased conflicts. Sub-Saharan Africa recorded average annual GDP growth of 3.2% in 1961–2001; this only slightly exceeded the rate of population growth. Taking inflation and population growth into account, the region's real GDP per head actually fell by 42.5% between 1980 and 1990. Growth per head between 1960 and 2000 in sub-Saharan Africa averaged 0.8% per year, compared with an average of 2.3% for all of the world's developing countries. The region's growth rates have also been more volatile than other regions. Between 1960 and 1994 only five countries sustained real per head growth rates above 2.0% per year: Botswana; Cape Verde; Mauritius; Seychelles; and Swaziland. (In fact, Botswana had the world's fastest growing economy during the 1980s and 1990s, recording remarkable average annual GDP growth rates of 8.1% in 1980–2000 and 13.1% in 1985–89.)

Over the past decade growth has varied greatly, especially between the petroleum producers (whose growth, until the global recession, was generally much stronger) and other countries. The record growth rates for 2006 and 2007 were attributed mostly to oil and non-fuel mineral exports, and generally good growing conditions for agriculture. Domestic demand also contributed to the positive growth, and domestic investment reached 22% of GDP in 2007, an all-time high. In addition, economists noted the economic reforms by many governments, including strengthening their macroeconomic policies, as finally showing results. The impact of the recession was felt more strongly in the region's oil and mineral exporting countries than in the more diversified economies.

As suggested below, by virtually any economic or social indicator, sub-Saharan Africa performs less well than any other developing region. Since 1971 the UN has viewed Least Developed Countries (LDCs) as a category of states that are considered to be highly disadvantaged in their development process. Of the 48 LDCs, in 2012 33 were in sub-Saharan Africa. Of the 45 countries included within the 'low human development' category in the UN's 2012 *Human Development Report*, 36 were in sub-Saharan Africa. Botswana, Cape Verde, the DRC, Equatorial Guinea, Namibia, South Africa, São Tomé and Príncipe and Swaziland were ranked in the 'medium human development' category, while only Mauritius and Seychelles were included within the 'high' category; none were ranked in the 'very high' category.

Of the world's developing areas, sub-Saharan Africa has the worst record in virtually all of the most important indicators (see Table 3). The region has the lowest GNI per caput, the lowest life expectancy at birth, the lowest youth literacy rate,

Table 3. Social and Economic Indicators in the Developing World

	East Asia/ Pacific	East Europe/ Central Asia	Latin America/ Caribbean	Middle East/ North Africa	South Asia	Sub-Saharan Africa
GNI per head, Atlas method (US $, 2010)	3,691	7,214	7,802	3,839	1,213	1,165
GNI, Atlas method (US $ million, 2010)	7,249,000	2,946,700	4,505,000	1,283,500	1,920,100	1,003,600
GDP growth (% change, 2009–10)	9.7	5.7	6.2	4.3	8.1	4.8
Prevalence of undernourishment, (% of population 2005–09)	11	6	9	7	22	28
HIV prevalence (% of persons aged 15–49, 2009)	0.2	0.6	0.5	0.1	0.3	5.4
Life expectancy (years at birth, 2010)	72	71	74	72	65	54
Under-5 mortality rate (per 1,000 live births, 2009)	26	21	23	31	71	130
Youth literacy rate (% of males aged 15–24, 2005–09)	99	99	97	93	85	77
Youth literacy rate (% of females aged 15–24, 2005–09)	99	99	97	97	72	76
Access to improved water sources (% of population, 2010)	90	96	94	89	90	61
External debt (US $ million, 2010)	1,013,971	1,273,418	1,038,725	143,595	400,596	205,992
External debt (% of GNI, 2010)	13.5	43.0	21.7	14.1	19.2	20.0

Sources: World Bank, *World Development Indicators 2010*; and World Bank, *World Development Indicators 2012*.

the highest rate of adult HIV infection and the highest number of children not living past five years of age.

The factors underlying Africa's parlous economic and social condition can be broadly categorized either as 'external' or 'internal'. The major external factors include adverse movements in the terms of trade (excluding petroleum and selected non-fuel commodities) and declines in foreign aid and foreign investment. The internal factors include small, fragmented economies, high levels of ethnic diversity, poor soils, widely fluctuating and harsh climates, widespread civil strife which often spills over borders, inadequate human and physical infrastructure, the large number of landlocked states, rapid urbanization and population growth, environmental degradation, ineffective (and often corrupt) government and inappropriate public policies. Unfortunately, African governments have but limited control over many of these factors, particularly the external ones.

EXTERNAL CAUSES OF ECONOMIC DECLINE

Trade, Regional Co-operation and South-South Linkages

Sub-Saharan Africa occupies a minor role in global trade, and accounted for perhaps 1% of the world's total of merchandise exports in 2009. On the positive side, the region has consistently exported more goods than it has imported (see Table 4). In 2010 merchandise exports totalled US $332,600m. and imports amounted to $302,600m., resulting in a merchandise trade surplus of $30,000m., although this compared unfavourably with a surplus of $41,500m. in 2008. Owing to negative capital flows, the region generally has run current account deficits since the 1980s, and the 2008–09 global recession pushed current account balances further into deficit.

Table 4. Sub-Saharan Africa's Trade Data (US $'000 million at current prices)

	1980	1990	2000	2010
Merchandise exports	83.5	79.5	93.3	332.6
Merchandise imports	76.8	74.3	81.3	302.6
Visible trade balance	6.7	5.2	12.0	30.0

Sources: World Bank, *World Development Indicators 2011*; and World Bank, *World Development Indicators 2012*.

One of the most serious of the external factors underlying this decline has been Africa's inability to diversify its trade. For example, crude petroleum represents just over one-half of the value of total exports. For two-thirds of the countries in the region, 60% of their exports come from only one or two products. In 13 countries, one product constitutes 75% or more of total exports. For example, Angola's major export, oil, accounts for more than 90% of its total exports. On the other hand, South Africa's exports are the most diverse, with 39 products accounting for more than 75% of total exports, and platinum, its largest single export, accounting for only some 7% of the total. In addition, the region has seen declining traditional exports and increasing imports, both in terms of value and volume. Of total exports, manufactures is the most important component, comprising 66% of total exports, followed by fuel (11%), ores and minerals (2%), food (2%) and agriculture (1%). More than one-half of sub-Saharan Africa's exports (57.9% in 2009) generally go to the affluent Organisation for Economic Co-operation and Development (OECD) countries, from which the region traditionally purchases about 50% of its imports. Europe remains the main trade partner, although its share of trade has declined from 44% of the total in 1995 to 32% in 2005. A generation ago, Brazil, Russia, India and the People's Republic of China accounted for perhaps 1% of African trade. In 2012 they constitute 20% and by 2030 the amount is expected to be 50%. Indeed, by 2006 China had taken much of this trade and become a major trading partner, with trade between China and Africa increasing from US $3,000m. in 1995 to more than $39,000m., equivalent to about 10% of Africa's total trade, and this was expected to have doubled by 2010. Furthermore, China is now the major purchaser of the region's petroleum. Nevertheless, African countries typically produce one or two major agricultural or mineral commodities for export to the industrialized countries in the West. Primary products account for approximately 80% of the region's export revenues, about the same level as during the 1960s. Poor export performances, combined with the range of problems discussed below, have generated increased deficits in most African countries' current accounts.

The volumes and price levels for the region's primary exports have been uneven. Table 5 illustrates such fluctuations in 11 major commodities.

Table 5. Exports Prices of Major Commodities from Africa

Commodity	1980	1990	2010
Copper (US $ per metric ton)	2,690	2,586	6,248
Iron ore (US cents per dry metric ton unit)	35	32	134
Phosphate rock (US $ per metric ton)	58	39	102
Cocoa (US cents per kg)	321	123	260
Coffee (US cents per kg)	427	192	358
Cotton (US cents per kg)	252	177	189
Groundnut oil (US $ per metric ton)	1,059	947	1,164
Oil palm (US $ per metric ton)	719	282	747
Tea (US cents per kg)	224	144	212
Sugar (US cents per kg)	78	27	39
Tobacco (US $ per metric ton)	2,806	2,297	3,570

Source: World Bank, *World Development Indicators 2011*.

Prices for many of the region's most important agricultural commodities have fluctuated greatly. Using 2000 = 100, prices for cocoa increased from 233 to 260 from 1970 to 2010, while tea fell from 307 to 212, coconut oil from 1,376 to 932, groundnut oil from 1,312 to 1,164, palm oil from 901 to 747 and maize from 202 to 154. Apart from crude oil, all commodity price indices registered record highs by mid-2011. Rising demand from emerging markets continued to be the leading factor in this growth. Until quite recently the region's petroleum exporters have generally benefited the most, yet generally these gains have not resulted in sustained growth.

The import policies of the Western industrialized countries have played a major, and often negative, role in Africa's export performance. In 2000 the Cotonou Agreement replaced successive Lomé Conventions between the European Union (EU) and the group of African, Caribbean and Pacific (ACP) states. Under the new agreement, the preferential treatment currently in force was to be retained initially, but thereafter trade between ACP countries and the EU was to be gradually liberalized over a period of 12–15 years. A new generalized system of preferences introduced by the European Commission came into effect in 2005. The scheme offers duty-free access to the EU market for 80% of tariff lines from countries that adhere to international conventions on human rights, labour, good governance and the environment. In late 2007 trade talks at the EU-Africa Summit in Lisbon, Portugal, promoted a new accord, known as the Economic Partnership Agreements (EPAs), bilateral agreements to phase out the remaining preferential trade pacts. By mid-2009 19 African governments had signed EPAs. Meanwhile, in 2004 the USA extended its Africa Growth and Opportunity Act (AGOA) until 2015.

Another major trade policy change in 2004 was the World Trade Organization (WTO) phase-out of bilateral quotas on textiles and clothing. While China and India gained from this development, many African producers were no longer able to compete with them. Badly affected countries included Mauritius, Lesotho, Kenya, Madagascar, Malawi, Namibia, Nigeria, South Africa, Swaziland, Tanzania and Zambia. The International Textile, Garment and Leather Workers' Federation estimated in mid-2006 that the region had lost more than 250,000 related jobs since 2005.

Notwithstanding the above and the benefits of the Lomé Conventions, protectionism and restrictive agricultural practices, particularly in the EU and (to a lesser extent) the USA, have resulted in an oversupply of some agricultural commodities, and have thus inhibited world-wide demand and weakened world prices. Agricultural subsidies in the USA, Japan and the EU amount to some US $360,000m. annually, more than the total of sub-Saharan Africa's exports. Eliminating these supports would benefit sub-Saharan Africa greatly: a recent study suggested that incomes per head would increase by $6. The aid organization Oxfam has estimated that certain countries lose more because of these tariffs than they gain in Western aid. The annual losses for cotton producers in the developing world from US and EU price support policies are estimated at $120m.–$240m. annually. Tariff and non-tariff barriers to trade erected by the Western industrialized countries have discouraged value-added or semi-processed agricultural imports from African states. The World Bank has estimated that high tariffs, anti-'dumping' regulations and other trade barriers cost sub-Saharan Africa $20,000m. annually in lost exports. Besides the decreased demand owing to protectionism from the developed nations, as their incomes increase, consumer demand for agricultural products does not advance proportionately. Industry is increasingly turning to substitutes, such as fibre optics for copper wires in telecommunications and beet sugar for cane sugar. As agricultural prices decline, Western consumers do not increase their consumption. Furthermore, even in countries that have dynamic export sectors such as Kenya (which exports cut flowers) and Lesotho (apparel), benefits for employment and diversification of their respective economies remain low. Finally, many African nations rely on import taxes as major sources of government revenues, and are thus hesitant to reduce such barriers.

Trade between African states is low: in 2011 regional trade within sub-Saharan Africa comprised around 11% of the total. Most African states produce similar products for export, generally primary agricultural or mineral commodities, and, as most of the value added is carried out in Western industrialized countries, there is little African demand for these products. African states themselves often discourage trade by their strongly inward-orientated, import-substitution development strategies, including overvalued exchange rates and protectionist trade policies. Their transport infrastructure is geared towards export to the EU, Japan and North America, (and more recently towards China) rather than to nearby countries. Finally, since the land-locked countries' trade is principally with Europe, neighbouring countries are often viewed as competitive obstacles rather than potential markets.

African states have tried various methods of improving their trade performance, and of developing overall regional economic co-operation. Indeed, trade tariffs were reduced from 30%–40% in the early and mid-1990s to less than 15% in many countries in 2001, and to less than 10% in countries with very open economies, such as Zambia and Uganda. At mid-2011 they stood at a regional average of 8.7%. There have been several attempts to form free trade areas or customs unions, and the New Partnership for Africa's Development (NEPAD) has adopted regional integration as one of its core objectives. In November 2011 trade ministers, meeting in Kigali, Rwanda, agreed to the Pan-African Free Trade Area, which, when implemented, would eliminate tariffs on internally traded goods and services. Regional trade would then be likely to rise from a share of 11% of total trade to about 15.4% by 2022. Sub-Saharan Africa has more regional organizations than any other region. Most countries are members of overlapping arrangements ranging from joint management of shared water resources, trade corridors, irrigation and various agricultural improvements, hydropower and flood control.

In early 1997 the Organization of African Unity (OAU) inaugurated the African Economic Community, with the eventual goal of uniting the region's existing economic organizations into a single institution similar to the EU. The OAU was formally replaced by a new African Union (AU) in July 2002. None the less, the results of most regional integration efforts have been modest.

The Southern African Customs Union (SACU), comprising Botswana, Lesotho, Namibia, South Africa and Swaziland, is the world's oldest existing customs union, celebrating in 2010 the 100th anniversary of its foundation. It is also perhaps the most successful regional organization in Africa. SACU permits free trade among its members and provides a common external tariff. Customs revenue is generally collected by South Africa and allocated to individual members according to a formula based on members' share of total trade.

Table 6. Member Countries of Major Regional Groupings in Sub-Saharan Africa

Organization	Member countries
Union Economique et Monétaire Ouest-Africaine	Benin, Burkina Faso, Côte d'Ivoire, Guinea-Bissau, Mali, Niger, Senegal and Togo
Communauté Economique et Monétaire de l'Afrique Centrale	Cameroon, Central African Republic, Chad, Rep. of the Congo, Equatorial Guinea and Gabon
Common Market for East and Southern Africa	Angola, Burundi, Comoros, DRC, Djibouti, Eritrea, Ethiopia, Kenya, Madagascar, Malawi, Mauritius, Rwanda, Seychelles, Sudan, Swaziland, Uganda, Zambia and Zimbabwe
East African Community	Burundi, Kenya, Rwanda, Tanzania and Uganda
Southern African Development Community	Angola, Botswana, DRC, Lesotho, Malawi, Mauritius, Mozambique, Namibia, Seychelles, South Africa, Swaziland, Tanzania, Zambia and Zimbabwe
Southern African Customs Union	Botswana, Lesotho, Namibia, South Africa and Swaziland
Common Monetary Area (Rand Zone)	Lesotho, Namibia, South Africa and Swaziland

Source: IMF.

Two more recently established groupings, commanding good prospects, are the Southern African Development Community (SADC) and the Economic Community of West African States (ECOWAS). The latter has as its eventual goal the removal of barriers to trade, employment and movement between its 15 member states, as well as the rationalization of currency and financial payments among its members (see Part Three—Regional Information, and Table 6). Owing to the political and economic disparity of its members, it is likely to be many years before the above objectives are fully met. SADC (see Part Three—Regional Information) was established initially as the Southern African Development Co-ordination Conference (SADCC) to provide a counter, during the era of apartheid, to South Africa's economic hegemony over the region. SADCC did not initially seek an economic association or customs union, but rather to function as a sub-regional planning centre to rationalize development planning. Its reconstitution in 1992 as SADC placed binding obligations on member countries with the aim of promoting economic integration towards a fully developed common market.

Another important grouping, the Franc Zone (see Part Three—Regional Information), was formed in 1948 and now comprises, together with France, 13 former French colonies, Equatorial Guinea (a former Spanish colony), and Guinea-Bissau (a former Portuguese possession). It operates with four general principles: fixed parity exchange rates; convertibility guaranteed by the French Treasury; free movement of capital; and a central foreign exchange reserve. Excluding France, each of the Zone's members are small states, none with a population exceeding 20m., and most are poor. A few, such as Cameroon, the Republic of the Congo, Equatorial Guinea and Gabon, are heavily reliant on petroleum export revenues.

In January 1999 the French franc became one of the EU currencies linked to a single currency unit, the euro, thus effectively pegging the CFA franc to the euro. In February 2000 the Union Economique et Monétaire Ouest-Africaine (UEMOA) and ECOWAS, to which UEMOA member countries also belong, adopted an action plan aimed at harmonizing UEMOA's economic programme with that of a planned second West African monetary union (the West African Monetary Zone), to be established by the remaining—mainly anglophone—ECOWAS member states. A merger of the two complementary monetary unions, and the replacement of the CFA franc by a new single West African currency, was envisaged. In addition, a number of other bodies have been established in recent years to facilitate regional integration in such areas as business law, insurance, social affairs and statistics-gathering.

Another noteworthy development in regional co-operation was the initial participation in 1992 of 13 southern and East African and Indian Ocean states in the Cross Border Initiative (CBI), supported by the World Bank, the AfDB and the EU. This initiative is aimed at liberalizing the member countries' foreign exchange systems, deregulating cross-border investments and facilitating the movement of goods, services and people among the participating countries. The CBI is voluntary, and most states involved in it have joined the WTO and participated in the Doha Round of trade negotiations. Most economists agree that a more liberal world-wide trade regime would benefit Africa as much as anywhere.

Despite the initiatives discussed above, intra-regional trade remains low (see Table 7). In only three of the major trade groups did merchandise exports comprise over 10% of intra-bloc exports in 2008.

Table 7. Merchandise Exports within Regional Trade Blocs (% of total bloc exports)

Organization and year of establishment	2000	2008
Common Market for Eastern and Southern Africa (1994)	6.1	4.1
Communauté Economique et Monétaire de l'Afrique Centrale (1994)	1.1	1.4
Cross Border Initiative (1992)	11.8	14.0*
East African Community (1996)	22.6	17.6
Economic Community of Central African States (1983)	1.0	0.6
Economic Community of the Great Lakes Countries (1976)	0.8	1.3*
Economic Community of West African States (1975)	7.6	7.6
Indian Ocean Commission (1984)	4.4	5.1
Mano River Union (1973)	0.4	0.3*
Southern African Development Community (1992)	9.5	10.1
Union Douanière et Economique de l'Afrique Centrale (1964)	1.0	0.9*
Union Economique et Monétaire Ouest-Africaine (1994)	13.1	14.5

* 2005 figure.

Source: World Bank, *African Development Indicators 2010* and *World Development Indicators 2010*.

In recent years sub-Saharan Africa has increased its economic involvement with other developing nations in the South. Countries such as China, India and Brazil are championing new and more appropriate technologies, especially in agriculture. China has boosted its technology co-operation, organized training courses in practical technologies and has sent over 10,000 agro-technicians to train local farmers. It has pledged to establish 14 centres for agricultural research in the region. Indian companies have become major investors in agricultural schemes. Brazil's EMBRAPA (an agricultural research and training institution) has been a driving force in Ghana. Also, in 2003 India, Brazil and South Africa established the ISAB Facility Fund for the Alleviation of Poverty and Hunger in Africa.

Foreign Debt, Aid and Investment

Three of the most obvious manifestations of external difficulties are foreign debt, fluctuating levels of international aid and the difficulty of attracting outside investment. In 2010 sub-Saharan Africa's level of official (non-concessional) external debt amounted to US $278,450m., compared with $198,900m. in 2009 and $216,250m. in 2005. Debt decreased prior to the global economic crisis, owing to the effect of debt relief initiatives such as the initiative for Heavily Indebted Poor Countries (HIPC, see below) but has since risen. Nevertheless, total external debt was equivalent to 24.9% of GDP, which compared favourably with other developing regions (see Table 3). The region's ratio of debt to exports was estimated at 5.9% in 2009, down from 15.9% in 1995. This compared reasonably favourably with the ratio for all low- and middle-income economies, which was 11.3% in 2009.

The majority of the 'most debt-distressed countries' are in sub-Saharan Africa. During the past two decades there has been a continuing debate on how best to reduce poor countries' debt burdens and how to fund such reductions. Several non-governmental organizations (NGOs), led by the Jubilee Debt Campaign, Action Aid and Christian Aid, have advocated for complete debt cancellation. Those organizations issued a warning in 2005 that the UN Millennium Development Goals (MDGs, see below) would not be met unless there was complete debt relief. In 1996 the World Bank and the IMF launched an initiative for HIPC to help ensure that the world's poorest countries could reduce their debts to 'sustainable levels'. The HIPC initiative was supplemented in 2005 by the Multilateral Debt Relief Initiative, which allows for 100% relief on eligible debts by the IMF, the World Bank and the African Development Fund. The HIPC guidelines required a candidate country to complete a three-year reform programme. These reforms included economic stabilization programmes, restructuring state-owned enterprises and targeting public spending toward poverty reduction, health and education. It is then permitted a further three years to carry out further adjustments to obtain the actual debt reductions. Of the 39 countries that had have received full or partial debt relief by the end of 2011, 30 were from sub-Saharan Africa. Eritrea, Somalia and Sudan are being considered for entry into the programme. Most observers believe that the resources freed from debt repayment should be used on health, education and other social services.

Many countries in the region have been some of the largest recipients of aid, which has, in many cases, been equivalent to 10%–20% of GDP, and sometimes higher. Indeed, in 2008 official development assistance (ODA) was equivalent to 31% of the GNI of Guinea-Bissau. There is a wide variation of levels of assistance. ODA increased from US $13,108m. in 2000 to $40,516m. in 2006. In 2009 total assistance (from both bilateral and multilateral sources) amounted to $44,510m., but fell to 11,843m. in 2010. The largest recipient of bilateral ODA in 2007 was Tanzania, which received $1,800m., followed by Cameroon and Sudan, each of which received about $1,700m. Nine countries—Tanzania, Ethiopia, Sudan, Nigeria, Cameroon, Mozambique, Uganda, Kenya and the DRC—accounted for 53% of total ODA to the region in 2007. The composition of ODA has changed in recent years: less is now targeted for long-term economic development and a greater proportion is being devoted to short-term emergency food aid and peace-keeping activities. By 2008 the sub-Saharan region's major donors were the European Commission, the USA and France, accounting for about one-half of the total. These were followed by the United Kingdom, Germany, Japan, the Netherlands and China. US ODA totalled US $6,691m. in 2008, while China's assistance increased from approximately $300m. in 1989–92 to an estimated $1,500m. in 2007, doubling during 2006–09 alone. In November 2009 the Chinese Premier, Wen Jiabao, pledged $10,000m. in subsidized loans over the coming three years. China has also offered to cancel existing debts, to construct new hospitals and implement training schemes for 15,000 professionals.

It is a widely held view among economists that foreign aid is effective in stimulating growth in countries with sound macroeconomic environments, but is ineffective, and can be detrimental, in countries with weak policy environments. Also, many states have become 'aid dependent'. Sub-Saharan Africa's per caput ODA totalled US $53 in 2009, the highest among the developing world. The region also boasted the highest levels of ODA as a percentage of GNI, at 23%, compared with 4% for the Middle East and North Africa (the next highest). Aid is often given for political reasons and includes construction of physical projects, such as roads and dams, and little is provided for recurrent costs. These projects are generally carried out in an unco-ordinated way, funded by multiple donor agencies. In 2005 100 partner countries and donors endorsed the Paris Declaration on Aid Effectiveness, an attempt more successfully to co-ordinate aid to ensure more productive results. This programme also forms part of the WTO's Aid for Trade Agenda. Sub-Saharan Africa is the largest recipient of trade-related technical assistance and capacity building, receiving about one-third of the world's total.

In 2004 and 2005 the Commission for Africa called for an increase of US $25,000m. from the world's richest countries, representing 0.08% of the 22 richest donors' national income. At the Group of Eight (G8) summit of leading industrialized nations held in Gleneagles, United Kingdom, in July 2005, leaders of those nations pledged to double the amount of aid for Africa to $50,000m. per year by 2010. In June 2007 the G8 reaffirmed its pledge at the summit held in Heiligendamm, Germany, at which leaders agreed to commit $60,000m. to combat disease in Africa. However, many anti-poverty activists contended that the rich nations had not kept to their commitments and that the increase in aid had not been as large as promised. Indeed, at mid-2012 it remained unclear whether or not the complete aid pledged was forthcoming.

Foreign direct investment (FDI) can bring many benefits to developing countries, and a lack of capital can be, and has been, a major impediment to development. FDI contributes to capital formation, human capital development, technology transfer, increased managerial skills and market expansion. Generally, there is a strong correlation between higher FDI and economic growth. Since the late 1980s increased levels of FDI to developing countries have generated more intense competition for new FDI. Negotiations between host countries and potential investors generally produce an outcome more favourable to the investor, as the host country does not want to lose the deal, and often provides substantial incentives, including tax holidays or lower taxes, direct subsidies and other arrangements. In any event, sub-Saharan Africa has a poor record of attracting such investment. In 2001 the region attracted only 8% of the total FDI allocated to all developing countries and the majority of that went to petroleum-producing nations. By 2007 private capital flows into sub-Saharan Africa had more than quadrupled since 2000. In that year private capital flows reached US $48,000m. to overtake ODA (which totalled $40,000m.) for the first time. However, as a result of the global recession, FDI to the region declined to $33,651m. in 2008, to $29,096m. in 2009 and even lower in 2010, to $24,984m. The main destinations for FDI in 2009 were Nigeria ($5,787m.) and South Africa ($5,354m.). The latter, in 2007 a net exporter of capital, held the region's largest amount of FDI stock, nearly $93,000m., representing about 25% of the total FDI stock in the region. The rate of return of the region's FDI was impressive; at 12.1% it was the highest among developing host regions in 2007. FDI in the textile sector is what is termed as 'footloose', attracted by temporary conditions such as preferential market access granted through the African Growth and Opportunity Act or protections accorded under the Multifibre Arrangment before it expired in 2005.

Traditionally, over one-half of FDI to the region has come from France, the Netherlands, South Africa, the United Kingdom and the USA. However, in recent years China has become a major investor, with almost US $12,000m. invested by 2007 (and the region's major customer, purchasing over 10% of sub-Saharan Africa's exports, equating to $19,000m. in 2007). Chinese FDI increased by 80% during 2008–09, and most of China's investment has been in oil-producing states. In early 2008 three Chinese parastatals signed an agreement with the DRC for a $9,000m. mining infrastructure project, while China's ICBC Bank purchased a 20% stake in South Africa's Standard Bank in a deal valued at $5,500m. In 2008 Japan announced a $2,500m. investment fund to help Japanese firms do more business in the region. The region has also seen a growth in sovereign wealth funds over the past few years. FDI outflows from the region amounted to $6,000m., led by South Africa (investing in banking and ICT) which was responsible for 80% of the region's outflows in 2007. The other major countries with outward investments were Liberia and Nigeria.

The sub-Saharan region has yet to broaden its investment base beyond energy and mining, which remain its prime attractions. However, FDI in manufacturing, communications and infrastructure has increased since the late 2000s. Furthermore, while foreign investors are attracted by the region's vast raw materials and low-wage economies, they are fearful of internal political volatility and the uncertainty of securing the enforcement of commercial contracts. These considerations, combined with the deteriorating human and physical infrastructure, have virtually extinguished investor confidence. Investor perception is of major importance. In the World Bank's *Doing Business in Africa 2012* survey, Mauritius (23rd) and South Africa (35th) were the only sub-Saharan African countries to be ranked in the top 50 world-wide in terms of the ease of doing business. The World Economic Forum ranked South Africa as the most competitive country in the sub-Saharan region (50th out of 142 countries world-wide), followed by Mauritius (54th). The Forum's *2011–12 Competitiveness Report* (using an index of several criteria) suggested that those countries that are most serious in reforming their economic policies (such as Uganda, Tanzania and Mozambique) are also those achieving the best rates of economic growth. Countries at the bottom of the list included Burundi, Chad and Zimbabwe. Importantly, optimism appears to be increasing about the region in general. Investors appeared more confident about improvements in tariffs, the rule of law and access to financing.

African capital flight is huge. An estimated US $700,000m. fled the region between 1970–2008. Added to this capital flight is a large 'brain drain' of skilled human resources due to the lack of suitable jobs at home (or to a variety of other reasons, including personal security). Sub-Saharan African countries that invest in training doctors have ended up losing some $2,000m., as those doctors leave home to find work abroad. The IMF suggested that some 30,000 Africans with doctoral degrees were working in North America and Europe in the early 2000s. Zambia has trained over 600 physicians since its independence but only 50 remain in its health care system. Significantly, the attraction of the industrial countries is likely to grow. Nursing shortages in the USA are projected to reach 500,000 by 2015, and already the past decade has seen a dramatic increase in nurses migrating from Africa to the developed nations. Health care is but one illustration of the severe problems caused when the very skilled people trained and needed to develop a country leave for better opportunities. On the positive side, however, worker remittances are the second largest type of capital flows into the region, although the euro crisis has taken a toll, as Western Europe accounts for some 40% of the total worker remittances coming into sub-Saharan Africa. Finally, a recent UN report estimated that Africans hold as much as 40% of their financial portfolios outside Africa. If these funds returned, the region would increase its capital stock by about two-thirds.

Local equity markets remain small in the region. Although the number of stock markets had grown from five in 1989 to 18 by 2010, the majority of exchanges list only a handful of stocks. There were 944 listed domestic companies in 2011, down from 1,088 in 2000. The region's largest exchange, in Johannesburg, South Africa, listed 410 companies in 2011. Market capitalization totalled US $951,930m. in 2011, up from $217,754m. in 2000. Private portfolio flows into the region are much smaller than FDI flows, and South Africa is the principal destination, accounting for some 80% of the total. Mauritius is the most active portfolio investor in intra-African portfolio investments. Such flows are highly volatile and pro-cyclical and often referred to as 'hot money'.

INTERNAL CAUSES OF ECONOMIC DECLINE

Africa faces a number of 'internal' economic problems, which, in the view of many analysts, may outweigh the 'external' factors discussed above. Many countries in sub-Saharan Africa are still suffering from a crisis of statehood and a crisis of capability. An urgent priority is to rebuild state effectiveness through an overhaul of public institutions, the resurrection of the rule of law, and credible checks on abuse of state power. Indeed, as far back as 1989 a World Bank study on sub-Saharan Africa's quest for sustainable growth suggested that 'underlying the litany of Africa's problems is a crisis of governance'. This, unfortunately, is still the case in all too many countries.

Governance, Parastatal Organizations, the Business Environment and the Informal Sector

After independence in the 1950s and 1960s most newly formed African governments believed they had three fundamental choices for developing their economies and for encouraging industrialization in the broadest sense. They could: (i) nationalize existing entities; (ii) seek to attract private investment from abroad by offering favourable investment incentives (tax 'holidays', for example); or (iii) invest heavily in public enterprises. Most governments adopted combinations of all three, but virtually every national administration south of the Sahara opted for substantial parastatal involvement. By and large there was little indigenous involvement in the modern sector, and almost none in the industrial sphere.

Most of the early parastatal organizations operated in natural monopoly areas: large infrastructural projects (highways, railways and dams) and social service facilities (schools, hospitals and medical clinics). Government soon moved into areas that had previously been dominated by the private sector (or, at least, traditionally dominated by the colonial sector in most 'mixed' economies). The share of parastatal bodies in employment was as high as 60% of the labour force in Mozambique in the late 1980s, and accounted for more than one-third of employment in many other countries. Most analysts have generally considered parastatal organizations to have failed, at least in terms of economic efficiency criteria. After independence most African countries expanded the size of their civil service more rapidly than their economic growth justified. This expansion was designed to provide employment, but civil servants received lower and lower real wages. None the less, African élites looked to the public sector as the avenue of advancement to their careers. The region was generally slow to develop indigenous entrepreneurs. Governments became bloated and corrupt. For most states the need for better governance became critical and many governments have scaled back the role of parastatals in recent years.

The general perception is that the region has not developed an appropriate enabling environment for the private sector to grow and flourish. Indeed, it lags behind other regions in providing a quality business environment. Of the 20 countries world-wide with the most regulatory obstacles to doing business, 17 are in sub-Saharan Africa, with the Central African Republic, the DRC, Guinea-Bissau and São Tomé and Príncipe being the four lowest-ranking countries. Property transfer is difficult and costly: in 2010 it took an average of some 82 days in sub-Saharan Africa, compared with 35 days in the Middle East; in some countries it is much worse. In addition to the delays owing to excessive bureaucracy, there are often further delays caused by poor infrastructure. In conjunction with the 2005 G8 meeting, several large multinational corporations (including De Beers, Nestlé and Standard Chartered) formed Business for Africa, a new NGO that aimed to help improve overall business conditions in the region. Later in 2005 the Investment Climate Facility for Africa was launched. This facility supports the countries that are undergoing the African Peer Review Mechanism (APRM) of the NEPAD by bringing together the government sector and business to improve the investment climate. Many countries in the region rank poorly in Transparency International's corruption perception index; in 2010 only two countries, South Africa and Mauritius, ranked in the top 50 least corrupt countries. The World Bank ranks the region last on the 'average ease of doing business' scale.

The informal sector accounts for more than 70% of non-agricultural employment, and the sector comprised an average of 42% of GNI in 2000, ranging from under 30% in South Africa to 60% in Tanzania and Nigeria. Some 90% of new jobs created in sub-Saharan Africa during the 1990s were in the informal sector. Indeed, informal sector employment in Uganda and Kenya now exceeds employment in the formal sector and nearly 90% of the labour force in Ghana comes from the informal sector. Many small firms see no advantage in joining the formal sector. For example, formal employment usually entails rigid employment contracts making the recruitment and dismissal of employees difficult. Many business owners have poor proof of title, and without adequate property rights and contract enforcement, lenders are hesitant to extend credit. While the types of activities carried out in the informal sector have existed even prior to colonialism, independence brought in the distinction between informal and formal activities, as countries around the region sought to formalize or 'modernize' their economies. The focus then (and indeed to some degree today) was rapid industrialization. Now, for much of the region it is the informal sector, not the formal sector that is the growth engine. It should be noted that around the world about two-thirds of all employees work in the informal sector. Thus, how governments treat the informal sector has profound impacts on employment, growth, equity and sustainability.

Civil Strife

Social and political stability are generally associated with higher economic growth rates. Since acceding to independence, more than one-half of sub-Saharan African countries have been caught up in civil wars, uprisings, mass migrations and famine. In 2011 there were three ongoing civil wars, although fewer than the 16 that existed in the 1990s. A recent study suggests that the typical civil war in the region has lasted about seven years and caused GDP to decline by more than 2% for each year of strife. Furthermore, it typically takes a country about 14 years after the end of the conflict to recover to its pre-war growth. Many post-conflict governments continue to spend heavily on their military, thus reducing the potential peace dividend. Conflicts can be both a cause and consequence of poverty and some observers have termed this the 'conflict trap'. The Office of the UN High Commissioner for Refugees estimated that at the end of 2009 22.1% of the world's 10.4m. refugees were sub-Saharan Africans. Strife continues to plague many areas of the region, with conflicts sometimes involving neighbouring countries and thus inhibiting economic growth for the entire sub-continent.

Health, Population, Education, the Natural Environment and Climate Change

Virtually all African states face significant problems in providing health services and education, and the region spends 8.7% of its GDP on social services, the lowest rate in the world. This expenditure has been unevenly distributed among countries: for example, in 2007 the Republic of the Congo spent less than 2.4% of its GDP, while Liberia spent 10.6%. Moreover, care was unevenly distributed throughout many countries, with most health facilities concentrated in urban areas. Seychelles leads the region with 151 physicians per 100,000 people, contrasted with Ethiopia's 1.6 per 100,000. According to the UN Children's Fund (UNICEF), a number of countries, including Angola, Ethiopia and Mozambique, spent more over many years on their military requirements than on health and education. With declining export receipts and general budget austerity, many African countries have been compelled to decrease their budgetary provisions for health. Only about one-third of the region's population has access to adequate sanitation, and in some nations this is as low as 8%–15%. Just over one-half of the total population now has access to clean water (the comparable figure among the urban population is 80%). Significantly, some 80% of illness in Africa's LDCs can be associated with inadequate water supplies or poor sanitation. Between 1990 and 2004 there was an increase of some 60m. in the number of people without access to clean drinking water, and the situation is worse for sanitation. The AfDB's assessment in 2007 concluded that the problem is not a lack of water, but a distribution issue. In most cities at least one-half of the water supply is wasted or cannot be accounted for. Urban sanitation access ranges from a high of 79% of the population in Angola's cities, to 14% in Eritrea. In 2011 several states experienced outbreaks of cholera, the worst cases were in Ethiopia, Mozambique, Zimbabwe, and the DRC and Republic of Congo. Some 5,000 lives were lost in an epidemic of cholera in Zimbabwe that began in 2008. Some 28% of the total population are undernourished, with the prevalence of child malnutrition among children under the age of five at 43%.

HIV/AIDS, malaria and deaths from conflicts have contributed to a decline in life expectancy in several states, particularly those hardest hit in southern Africa. While the pandemic has slowed somewhat in the region, HIV/AIDS has become the most threatening health problem in sub-Saharan Africa (see Table 8). The prevalence of HIV as a percentage of the population aged 14–49 years in 2007 was 5%; in Botswana, Lesotho, and Swaziland, the average was over 20%. Some 22.4m. Africans were living with HIV in 2008 (of which 13.4m. were women and 1.8m. children). This figure represented 67% of estimated HIV infection world-wide (some 86% of the world's

HIV-infected children were in Africa) and more than 20m. Africans have already died from the disease. Such is the mortality rate among the young that the average life expectancy at birth in several African countries—Angola, Lesotho, Sierra Leone, Swaziland, Zambia and Zimbabwe—had fallen to around 40 years of age or below by 2006. AIDS in Africa generally affects young adults (aged 20–45 years) in their most economically productive years, and in Africa the educated, urban élite have been hardest hit. In fact, infection rates in urban areas are approximately double those of rural areas. However, the rate of new infections has showed a notable decline, from 2.2m. in 2001 to 1.9m. in 2010. This decrease was the result of heightened awareness campaigns for changing personal behaviour, and the promotion and use of prophylactics.

Owing to the AIDS pandemic there are currently more than 12m. orphans in Africa, imposing major strains on individual governments' ability to provide housing, health care and education. Before AIDS one in 50 children in the region were orphans; in some countries that rate was one in 10 by the late 1990s. Given the size of the pandemic in several African states, it is reasonable to expect that AIDS will curtail GDP growth in several countries during the 2010s. The World Bank has expressed the view that overall growth in GDP per head is unaffected if a country's overall infection rate remains below 5%. However, when the disease reaches 8% of the adult population, growth per head is 0.4% lower than it would otherwise have been. When the infection rate exceeds 25%, then the cost to growth is close to 1%.

Table 8. HIV/AIDS data, 2008 (millions, unless otherwise indicated)

	World	Africa
People living with HIV	33.4	22.4
Women living with HIV	15.7	13.4
Children living with HIV	2.1	1.8
AIDS-related deaths	2.0	1.4
AIDS-related deaths of children	0.3	0.2
New HIV infections	2.7	1.9
Newly infected children	0.4	0.4
People receiving antiretroviral treatment	4.0	2.9
People requiring antiretroviral treatment	9.5	6.7
Average adult infection rate (%)	0.8	5.2

Source: *Africa Renewal* (UN Dept of Public Information), Vol 23, No. 4, January 2010.

Additionally, the incidence of tuberculosis has risen sharply in the recent past, reaching 369 cases per 100,000 people in 2007, and claiming some 2m. deaths world-wide annually. This increase has been linked to the growing AIDS incidence, as about 50% of tuberculosis patients are HIV-infected. The International Partnership Against AIDS in Africa was launched in 1999, with the participation of African governments, the UN, international donors, and the private and community sectors. The Partnership has campaigned for, and 10 states have received, access to lower-cost generic drugs to fight HIV/AIDS and South Africa has successfully negotiated agreements with pharmaceutical companies to produce drugs domestically. In 2000 the USA agreed to allow African states to develop generic AIDS vaccines without regard to US patent protections. In June 2001 Botswana became the first African state to take advantage of lower-priced drugs and hoped to be able to provide therapies for 100,000 infected citizens. Of the 4m. Africans requiring antiretroviral treatment, fewer than 100,000 were receiving it in 2004. However, the drastic fall in prices mentioned above has subsequently enabled treatment expansion. By 2008 the number of Africans receiving antiretroviral treatment had risen to 2.9m.; however, another 6.7m. were in need.

Approximately 11% of disease-induced deaths in Africa are caused by malaria, and approximately 90% of world-wide deaths caused by malaria occur in sub-Saharan Africa. Since 2000 the number of confirmed malaria cases has declined by 50% in 11 regional countries, due to increased use of insecticide-treated bed nets and wider access to anti-malaria drugs. Nonetheless, malaria's toll is greater than that of all other tropical diseases combined. Some researchers believe that had malaria been eradicated 30 years ago, the region's GDP would now be one-third higher than it is. During 2000–06 Niger had the most deaths, recording 469 per 100,000 people. More than 25m. cases of malaria were reported in 2008. The World Bank estimates that malaria takes US $12,000m. of Africa's GDP every year.

In late 2001 the UN announced a Global AIDS and Health Fund to increase funding for AIDS, malaria and tuberculosis programmes from an annual level of less than US $2,000m. to $7,000m. African trypanosomiasis (sleeping sickness), which had been virtually eradicated in the early 1960s, reappeared in 1970, and is now widespread. Owing to a lack of screening and treatment, and regional conflict, this disease has become the greatest cause of mortality in areas of South Sudan, Angola and the DRC. None the less, there have been some successful attempts to combat disease in the region. For example, onchocerciasis (river blindness) has been virtually eliminated in West Africa; WHO estimated that its programme for the control of the disease (concluded in 2002) prevented 600,000 new cases. During the past few years there have been numerous new initiatives to improve health conditions in Africa.

Until relatively recently most African governments did not regard rapid population growth or environmental degradation as matters for concern. Indeed, until quite recently most areas of the region practised what is known as 'slash and burn' agriculture, a technique that can only succeed where land is abundant. During the past decade a succession of countries, realizing that their resources cannot service their population growth, have begun to recognize the necessity for environmental protection.

African countries have some of the highest annual rates of population growth in the world: during 2001–10 Angola, Benin, Burkina Faso, Chad, Equatorial Guinea, Eritrea, Liberia, Madagascar, Mali, Niger, Sierra Leone and Uganda all had population growth rates of 3% or greater. Over the next 30 years the population is expected to double. As it grows in size, it will also alter in shape: the median age now is 20 years, compared with 30 in Asia and 40 in Europe. Africa's dependency ratio (the ratio of working-age population to dependants) is close to 1:1, compared with East Asia's ratio of 2:1.

By 2000 about three-quarters of all African countries had family-planning programmes, and some have set targets for population growth. Stemming rapid population growth in Africa is difficult because of social as well as economic factors. Most Africans live in rural areas on farms and require large numbers of helpers. The cheapest way of obtaining such assistance is for a farmer to have more children. Owing to the high infant mortality rate (resulting from poor health and nutrition), rural couples tend to want, and have, more babies. Additionally, African countries do not have organized old-age support schemes, and children are often viewed as potential providers of support for the elderly. However, Africa now seems to be on the path toward smaller families that has occurred in much of the world, although at a very slow rate. One important success is the recent huge decline in child mortality. A recent World Bank study shows that in 16 of the 20 countries that have sufficient data, child mortality rates (the number of deaths of children under five per 1,000 live births) fell since 2005. Twelve countries demonstrated falls of over 4.4% per year, higher than in China during the early 1980s. Indeed, the top rates of decline in African child mortality are the highest in the world in the past 30 years.

There has been a direct link between education and growth—between 1960 and 1980 the African countries that had higher percentages of children enrolled in primary school also had higher economic growth rates. Low primary school enrolment hampers economic development. The percentage of malnourished children rose from 31% in 1992 to 32% in 2003, the only region in the world to witness such an increase: children who do not have enough to eat perform poorly in school. A further key factor is that of increased education for women, which is clearly associated with lower fertility rates. A recent study by the World Bank found that the three countries with declining fertility—Botswana, Kenya and Zimbabwe—had the highest levels of female schooling and the lowest rates of child mortality. The study also indicated that in the Sahel, where female schooling rates are lowest, both fertility rates and child mortality have remained high. With an average of 5.2 births per female, sub-Saharan Africa has the highest fertility rate in the world.

Shortly after independence most countries of the sub-Saharan region initiated programmes aimed at establishing universal primary education. In 2004 93% of children in the appropriate age-group were enrolled in primary schools (compared with 79% in 1999). This compared with an enrolment rate of 91% for all developing countries, and virtually 100% in Western industrialized countries. It should be noted that boys have greater access to education: 94% of boys were enrolled in primary schools in 1998–2000, compared with 81% of girls. About 30% of children in the relevant age-group in the region were enrolled in secondary schools (up from 24% in 1999), and only 7% of the poorest rural children. In addition, in 2007 some 36m. children did not attend school. Only 30% of each class graduates junior secondary school, while even fewer (12%) graduates senior secondary school. Access to tertiary education, while increasing in recent years, still remains the lowest in the world, with less than 5% of the relevant age population enrolled. In 2009 adult literacy ranged from 91.9% in Zimbabwe to 33.6% in Chad.

Rapid urbanization has also imposed stresses on many African economies. Africa is still very largely rural and agricultural. In 1980 about 75% of the region's population lived in rural areas, but that figure has declined to around 60%. However, approximately 70% of Africa's poorest live in rural areas. Urbanization has increased at an alarming pace (it is currently growing at an annual rate of 4%, the highest in the world), and it has been forecast that by 2025 Africa's urban population will be three times larger than in 2000, with more than one-half of the population living in cities. More than 45% of all urban-dwelling sub-Saharan Africans reside in cities with more than 500,000 inhabitants, compared with only 8% in 1960, when there were only two cities in the region with populations exceeding 500,000. Unemployment and under-employment are rampant in every major city of Africa. Living conditions in virtually every city have worsened over the last two decades. In addition, the cost of living is relatively more expensive in Africa than in many other developing regions. For example, the price of water (per 1,000 litres) is US $1.40 in sub-Saharan Africa, compared with less than $0.60 in Asia, the Middle East and Latin America. Cost of home ownership requires 12.5% of family income in Africa, compared with 11.3% in Asia, 10.9% in the Middle East and 5.4% in Latin America. Africans spend on average 64% of their income on food. Population growth has put additional pressure on good agricultural and grazing lands, and on fuelwood. About 80% of the region's energy needs are supplied by fuelwood gathered by rural dwellers. Furthermore, population pressures add to deforestation, soil degradation and declines in agricultural output. In the early 2000s it was estimated that some 7% of forest cover was being lost annually.

Africa's environment has been under intense pressure, especially during the past 20 years. With the increases in population discussed above, overcultivation and overgrazing have turned vast areas into virtual wastelands. Also, wood is collected for heating and cooking, supplying 70% of domestic energy needs. During 1990–2005 sub-Saharan Africa had the highest annual average rate of deforestation in the world. During 1990–2007 forest area as a percentage of total land area declined from 29.4% to 26.2%. FAO estimates that old growth forests in the region are being cut down at more than 4m. ha per year, twice the world's deforestation average. According to the World Bank, African forests are believed to contain 45% of the world's biodiversity, while forest-related activities account for at least 10% of GDP for 17 nations in the region. In addition, the region contains about 15% of the world's remaining forests, second to South America in the amount of tropical forests that are the most effective in removing carbon from the air. Across the Sahel population increases and changes in settlement patterns are putting pressure on fragile ecosystems. Fertile land is turning into dust, as people living in the transitional zone between the Sahel and the Sahara cut down trees for charcoal and send their animals further out in search of pasture. Civil wars have also contributed significantly to environmental degradation.

Many government leaders in the past suggested that the achievement of economic growth was inconsistent with environmental protection, and that African development could only advance at the expense of its environment. It has only been in the past few years that the two goals have been recognized as not mutually exclusive. Indeed, it is now generally accepted that sustained economic growth is impossible without adequate environmental protection. Specifically, many countries, such as Kenya, Tanzania and South Africa, increasingly depend on tourism based on wildlife and undisturbed natural habitats. By 1996 40 African states, with support from a number of UN and bilateral donors, had begun to develop national environmental action plans (NEAPs), which were intended to create a framework for the better integration of environmental concerns into a country's economic development. In 2010 the region received 31.6m. visitors, fewer than 1% of the world's total. None the less, recently Africa has been one of the fastest-growing regions for international tourism. The number of visitors in 2011 amounted to a 13% increase compared with 2010, and South Africa's travel receipts rose by 24%, due to the large number of foreign visitors who attended the FIFA World Cup.

Climate change will affect Africa more seriously than any other area in the world, although the region produces only about 7% of the world's greenhouse gases. Greater rainfall variability will contribute to both more flooding and droughts, and exacerbate the malaria problem. Smallholders, already often in danger, will be placed at even greater risk. In 2007 the UN's Intergovernmental Panel on Climate Change predicted a minimum increase in temperature of 2.5°C by 2030, suggesting that food security will be severely compromised. Water will become a critical problem. The warming trend could affect biodiversity and animal habitats, while rising sea levels could be a problem for low-lying regions, particularly coastal cities. It should be noted, however, that global warming could bring benefits; for example, eastern Africa could see increased rainfall in its parched highland areas.

Physical Infrastructure, the Structure of the Economies, Employment and Inflation

For most countries in the region physical infrastructure—including transportation, electricity and communications—has generally deteriorated since the achievement of independence in the early and mid-1960s. With 16 land-locked countries, high transportation costs have hampered growth. Additionally, such essential services as electric power, water, roads, railways, ports and communications have been neglected, particularly in rural areas. Indeed, the region's energy infrastructure is tiny and fragile, and service is unpredictable. The region has what the World Bank has branded an 'infrastructure deficit'.

The entire electric generation capacity (63 GW) is comparable to that of Spain. About one-quarter of the population has access to electricity, compared with 40% in low-income economies elsewhere. The region has the world's lowest per capita consumption of electricity at 511 kWh (in 2009), compared to a world average of 2,803 kWh. In 2007 electric power consumption per caput was 550 kWh, compared with the global average of 2,846 kWh. The region uses only 3% of its renewable water for electricity generation, compared with 52% in South Asia. In addition, climate change will render hydrology more difficult as water levels will probably vary more greatly than in the past.

An integrated and well-maintained road system is vital for a country's economic growth and development. However, over one-half of the roads in sub-Saharan Africa are in very poor condition and in many countries the road network is woefully inadequate. For example, the DRC, with an area one-quarter the size of the USA has just 1,736 miles of paved roads, slightly more than in the District of Columbia in the USA (with 1,500 miles). Even in countries where the road network is good, for example in South Africa, recent budgetary constraints have delayed much-needed maintenance and expansion. Poor transportation affects all facets of African life, from commerce, to health care to schooling. Some 70% of Africa's rural population lives more than a mile from an all-season road. Poor roads add to the costs of production in a region with the world's highest poverty rates. The costs of transporting goods in Africa are the highest in the world. For example, for three francophone countries (Cameroon, Côte d'Ivoire and Mali) road transport costs are 40% more expensive than in France (where labour costs are much higher than in Africa). Poor road conditions can increase fuel consumption and the need for vehicle maintenance due to damage, and reduce the life of tires and of vehicles. Owing to lower speeds, vehicles are not as efficient.

Higher transportation costs raise the costs of doing business, impede private investment and add another barrier to Africa's ability to take advantage of the rapid growth in world trade. Trade is highly sensitive to transport costs: a 10% decrease in such costs could increase Africa's trade by 25%. For Africa's land-locked countries, high transport costs means that even if they do everything else right, they will effectively remain land-locked. Of all the world's regions, intra-regional trade is lowest in sub-Saharan Africa. While there are many reasons for this (e.g. tariff and non-tariff barriers, cumbersome customs procedures, lack of product diversification, the similarity in production among neighbouring countries), poor roads play a major role. For many areas it is a lack of sufficient maintenance rather than a lack of infrastructure itself that hinders business growth and, even where the infrastructure exists, it is often of poor quality. The cost of exporting or importing a standard cargo container of goods costs about US $2,000, or twice the amount in other regions of the world. The World Bank estimates that the region requires $22,000m. annually for both capital and maintenance expenditures.

The underlying structure of sub-Saharan Africa's economies has not changed dramatically since independence. In 1965 agriculture accounted for 24% of GDP, industry 30%, and services 46%, according to the World Bank. By 2008 agriculture contributed 12% of GDP, while industry and services contributed 33% and 55%, respectively. African goals of rapid industrialization were not achieved. Manufacturing advanced rapidly in the early 1960s, but then slowed to about the same average growth rate as overall GDP. While petroleum output expanded more swiftly, only a few states—Angola, Cameroon, the Republic of the Congo, Gabon and Nigeria—benefited. Since 1990 the oil industry has invested more than US $20,000m. in exploration and production activities and the region's proven oil reserves more than doubled between 1980 and 2005, to 114,300m. barrels, according to British Petroleum. Output increased by 60% during that period, and the region now supplies about 12% of the world's petroleum. It should be noted that with the exception of Nigeria and Angola, none of the other states are members of the Organization of Petroleum Exporting Countries (OPEC), and thus are not subject to output limits. Finally, many economists note that much of the petroleum revenues have not gone toward sustainable development, and in many cases this has added to social instability and environmental degradation, resulting in what has been termed 'the oil curse'. The World Bank cited four paradoxes relative to the region's energy crisis: abundant energy but little power; higher prices but high production costs; inefficient reform in the energy sector; and inadequate financing.

By 2008 manufacturing accounted for only 15% of the region's GDP (compared with 17% in 1965). Owing to low productivity and low investment, the growth rate of the region's manufacturing sector declined from 3.8% in 1997 to 0.4% in 1998, before recovering to reach 4.2% in 2005. However, production costs in the region are generally higher than other regions. For example, indirect costs such as infrastructure result in higher prices than competition from China or India. Another problem for the region is the poor level of productivity in general, and of investment productivity in particular, as measured by a capital input-output ratio. Thus, even if Africa can attract more foreign investment, it must make that investment more productive.

The region lacks the technology available in many other parts of the world; for example, only one African per 100 people had fixed-line telephones in 2009. Mauritius had the most land lines, with 29 per 100 people. However, the use of mobile cellular telephones was approaching 33 per 100 people. Indeed, between 1999 and 2004 the region's mobile phone market grew faster than in any other region world-wide, with an annual average increase of 58%. In 2008 Seychelles and South Africa had the largest number of mobile phones in the region, with 98 and 92 phones per 100 inhabitants, respectively. Ethiopia and Eritrea had the lowest number of mobile phones, with about two and four per 100 people, respectively. Nearly one-third of all the region's inhabitants have access to wireless telephone services. Mobile phones allow access to banking to people who otherwise would be without it, and provide other important services, such as information on the weather and crop prices. Internet use is relatively low, with 11.3 internet users per 100 people in 2009 (the world average is 30.2). However, recent growth has been impressive; during 2000–08 the number of internet subscribers increased from 3m. to 32m.

As a result of decreased inflationary pressures world-wide, as reflected in the prices of petroleum and many manufactured goods, the average rate of inflation for the sub-Saharan region was 6% in 2004 and, even with significant growth in the following years, inflation averaged between 6% and 9% in 2007 (excluding the hyperinflation rates in Zimbabwe). However, inflation rates vary considerably from country to country. In 2008 24 countries had at least double-digit inflation, and Guinea and Kenya experienced high levels of inflation of 38.9% and 27%, respectively. Zimbabwe's political crisis has produced extremely high inflation in recent years, reaching 231% in late 2008. Due mostly to higher food prices, inflation rose to 8.4% in 2011, compared with 7.7% in 2010. In the Horn of Africa severe drought contributed to much of the increase. In Ethiopia, for example, inflation rose to nearly 40%, and in Uganda to about 20%. As a result of major policy reforms, most countries have now abandoned overvalued foreign exchange policies arising from inflation, whereby many governments had to limit foreign exchange, leading to 'parallel' or 'black' markets for foreign currencies. Indeed, many countries link their currency either to the South African rand or, via UEMOA and the Communauté Economique et Monétaire de l'Afrique Centrale, to the euro.

The region's total labour force in 2009 was 338m., of whom 43.3% were women. Estimates for unemployment vary so greatly that it is impossible to provide precise data, although the Economic Commission for Africa estimates that unemployment in the region was 7.9% in 2009, significantly higher than the rate for East Asia (4.4%), South Asia (4.4%) and Latin America and the Caribbean (7.7%). It is worth noting, however, that official unemployment estimates are as high as 30% in some countries, while unofficial estimates are higher still.

Agriculture, Food Security and the Urban Bias

Unquestionably, a leading factor behind the declines in African economies and the high levels of malnutrition has been the general neglect of agriculture. This sector basically comprises two components: food production for local consumption (often at the subsistence level), and export commodities. Agriculture accounts for only about one-sixth of GDP for the region as a whole, but 90% of rural workforce and two-thirds of total employment and 40% of export earnings. Agricultural labour productivity is quite low, and failure to transform agriculture has kept millions of rural Africans trapped in a cycle of underemployment, underproduction, low incomes and chronic poverty. While the region has 60% of the world's arable land, access to land (particularly by women, who produce up to 80% of all basic food products) remains a large problem, and insecure land tenure rights prevents farmers from investing in new technology that would increase output. Agricultural productivity is the lowest in the world: value-added per worker in 2010 was US $322 compared to the world average of $992.

For virtually all African economies the major agricultural exports consist of one or perhaps two or three primary products (cash crops such as coffee, tea, sugar, sisal, etc.), the prices of which fluctuate widely from year to year on the world market. For 44 sub-Saharan African countries their three leading agricultural exports comprise some 82% of their total agricultural exports. Unfortunately, Africa's share of world agricultural exports has declined since the 1970s. Food imports have increased dramatically, from US $5,433m. in 1980 to $8,352m. in 2000, averaging some $7,000m. per year during the 1990s.

By the late 2000s this figure had increased to some $40,000m. annually.

In 2006 the UN World Food Programme estimated that more than 30m. Africans were in need of food aid. Annual population growth has outpaced food production since 1993, resulting in a 20% increase in the number of hungry people, from 176m. to 210m. Between 1980 and 1990 the region's annual imports of cereals increased from 8.5m. metric tons to 18.2m. tons; by 2007 this had risen to 24m. tons. Regional production of cereals has nevertheless increased steadily since the mid-1990s. Fishing has also experienced challenges during recent years. The sector makes a major contribution to many economies, comprising more than 10% of the total value of exports in 11 countries; however, current fishing methods are causing many fisheries to reach their limits.

Food security remains a serious issue for much of the region. Sub-Saharan Africa is the world's most vulnerable area to food insecurity, and acute famine still persists in the region: since 2000 there have been four severe famines—in Ethiopia (in 2000), Malawi (2002) and Niger (2005), and in Somalia and Ethiopia in 2011–12, affecting some 10m. people. These countries (apart from Somalia) are all land-locked, impoverished and with high levels of malnutrition. They are dominated by subsistence-oriented, rain-fed agriculture. One-half of the calories consumed come from grains that are generally rain-fed and thus highly vulnerable to climatic change (which is likely to intensify). Many countries are highly dependent on imported food. Food production is the primary source of food for the very people who are most vulnerable—small farmers. These smallholders, who typically grow only one or two crops, are subject to various shocks, including weather and declining commodity prices, and even a modest decline in harvests can be devastating for household food security.

Famine can result from several factors, although production failures are perhaps the most common cause. The famine in Malawi in 2002 was triggered by erratic weather in late 2000 and 2001, which contributed to a 32% decline in the maize harvest. Another factor can be classified as a response failure by governments and the international community, and can include indifference by governments that, in any event, have a limited capacity to deliver basic services. In addition, many governments have reduced agricultural extension and research services as part of structural adjustments. Finally, poor infrastructure makes it difficult for farmers to get their crops to market, and, during times of famine, presents obstacles to the effective distribution of emergency food aid. Few governments have robust early warning systems, or food buffer stocks.

During the past few years there have been a number of new initiatives designed to boost agricultural productivity. These include the Africa Food Security Initiative launched at a G8 summit meeting in 2009 (with a commitment of US $22m. over two years), the USA's Feed the Future Program, and the New Vision for Agriculture sponsored by the World Economic Forum. The Africa Partnership Forum, members of which comprise African leaders, the G8, the OECD and other development partners, designated food security as a priority at its 2010 annual meeting.

Many governments have implemented economic policies that were designed to keep urban wages and living conditions high and farm prices low by maintaining the value of currencies at high, unrealistic rates of exchange. This is understandable and obvious: political power in Africa rests in the city, not in the village or countryside. This 'urban bias' was sometimes a deliberate strategy, at other times more a result of planned rural neglect, and on many occasions was endorsed by the international development community.

In addition to this 'urban bias', producers were often bound by prices fixed by their governments, and at times these 'producer' prices failed to cover input costs. This resulted in farmers reducing their production for sale and reverting to subsistence agriculture. Finally, it should be noted that investment in agriculture has traditionally been low. For example, agriculture typically receives less than 10% of public spending. Also, as much as three-quarters of the region's farmland has become degraded owing to erosion and other results of population pressures, resulting, for example, in grain yields stagnating at one metric ton per ha, compared with the world average of about three tons. Productivity growth will require a number of changes. For example, only 4% of the region's cultivated land is irrigated. Improvements in soil fertility, improved seeds and water and pest management have been long overdue. Spending on research, technology and extension remains low.

PRESSURES FOR ECONOMIC POLICY REFORM

African governments have responded to increasing pressure from a variety of sources to 'liberalize' their public economic policies. During the 1970s and early 1980s the IMF and other donors began to insist on 'conditionality' for support; the IMF, in particular, required specific macroeconomic policy changes, sometimes termed 'structural adjustments', usually in the area of exchange rates (i.e. devaluation), and reductions in government spending before a new loan agreement could be granted. In 1998 35 African countries launched structural adjustment programmes (SAPs) or borrowed from the IMF to support reform policies. Although these programmes (now called Poverty Reduction and Growth Facility arrangements) have many common points, they are actually varied. Additional pressures, now known as the 'Washington consensus', came from the World Bank and USAID. Specifically, a 1981 World Bank study proposed four major and basic policy changes that it felt were critical: namely, (i) the correction of overvalued exchange rates; (ii) the improvement of price incentives for exports and agriculture; (iii) the protection of industry in a more uniform and less direct way; and (iv) the reduction of direct governmental controls. Other pressures have originated and grown internally, as more people have become increasingly dissatisfied with their declining standard of living and the poor economic performance in their own countries. During the 1990s several countries, most notably Kenya, Madagascar, Malawi, Mauritius, Tanzania, Uganda and Zimbabwe, removed restrictions on external capital transactions. This effectively closed the gap between the official exchange rate and the 'parallel', or 'black market', rate. South Africa abolished its two-tier exchange rate system in 1995, and several other countries have also unified their foreign exchange systems, making foreign trade and investment less cumbersome.

OUTLOOK

Many economists believe that economic reforms have, in general, led to improved economic performance, although certain sectors in most countries have experienced sharp declines, and the gains have not been equally shared. Structural adjustment is very controversial and some studies have failed to demonstrate a definite linkage between reform and growth. If African governments implement their plans for economic liberalism, encompassing generally higher agricultural producer prices, and revised and realistic foreign exchange rates, together with other publicly unpopular policy measures, they will require increased outside support. Economic assistance to the region has been made increasingly dependent upon economic reform, and the major donor countries of OECD have generally reallocated most of their economic assistance to countries implementing reform programmes. Additionally, the major multilateral donors were also reallocating their resources on this basis.

If the world-wide economy recovers, and when (or if) peace and stability come to the more strife-ridden parts of the region, then Africa's economic growth should increase. The social and economic costs of conflicts can be significant. A recent study suggests that in countries experiencing civil wars, their GDP growth is on average 2.2% lower than in times of peace. While a return to peace has allowed some countries—Angola, Mozambique and Rwanda—to shift military resources toward reducing poverty, a World Bank report suggests that the 'peace dividend' does not necessarily immediately follow the resolution of civil war. The fact that such conflicts often do not end decisively means that armies are slow to demobilize, and military spending is not quickly reduced. Moreover, the resolution of civil conflict does not necessarily lead to increased security. Demobilization often results in former military personnel resorting to banditry to survive. None the less, some

Table 9. MDG Progress Summary 2010

Goal	Status
1. Eradicate extreme poverty and hunger	
1a. Reduce extreme poverty by half	Progress insufficient to meet target
1b. Productive and decent employment	No progress or deterioration
1c. Reduce hunger by half	Progress insufficient to meet target
2. Achieve universal primary education	
2a. Universal primary schooling	Progress insufficient to meet target
3. Promote Gender Equality and Empower Women	
3a. Equal girls' enrolment in primary schools	Progress sufficient to meet target
3b. Women's share of paid employment	Progress insufficient to meet target
3c. Women's equal representation in national parliaments	Progress insufficient to meet target
4. Reduce child mortality	
4a. Reduce mortality of under-five-year-olds by two-thirds	Progress insufficient to meet target
5. Improve maternal health	
5a. Reduce maternal mortality by three-quarters	No progress or deterioration
5b. Access to reproductive health	Progress insufficient to meet target
6. Combat HIV/AIDS, malaria and other diseases	
6a. Halt and reverse spread of HIV/AIDS	Progress insufficient to meet target
6b. Halt and reverse spread of tuberculosis	No progress or deterioration
7. Ensure environmental sustainability	
7a. Reverse loss of forests	Progress insufficient to meet target
7b. Halve % without improved drinking water	Progress insufficient to meet target
7c. Halve % without sanitation	Progress insufficient to meet target
7d. Improve the lives of slum-dwellers	Progress insufficient to meet target
8. Develop a global partnership for development	
8a. Internet users	Progress insufficient to meet target

Source: Source: Statistics Division, UN Department of Economic and Social Affairs.

recent developments may help. For example, in 2002 an international initiative, known as the Kimberley Process and involving more than 70 countries, introduced a certification scheme for rough diamonds, in an attempt to halt the trade in illicit diamonds (so-called 'conflict diamonds'). With increased security, more successful Africans living outside the region can be expected to return to their homelands (some 15m. Africans who were born in the region now live outside of it).

Globalization, the accelerated economic integration among nations, has brought benefits in terms of world-wide economic growth. However, these benefits have not been evenly distributed, and income disparities between rich and poor countries, and even within countries, have increased. This is most pronounced in sub-Saharan Africa. Recent history elsewhere, particularly in Asia, suggests that the unacceptable economic deterioration of the past 30 years can be reversed. As sub-Saharan Africa moves forward, its governments have begun to realize that, while many economic problems were inherited, responsibility must be taken for problems that are soluble. Rather than being hostile to foreign entrepreneurs, most African governments are now actively seeking foreign commercial involvement. Certainly by 2012 many, and perhaps most, African governments are presenting the appearance of reform, and acknowledging the parallel between political pluralism and economic development. The combination of liberalized economic policies, together with more political openness could signal the beginning of sub-Saharan Africa's transformation towards economic recovery and sustained long-term development. Indeed, Freedom House's 2012 ranking of the region's states in the area of political rights and civil liberties as 'free or partially free', at 62%, places it significantly ahead of the Middle East and North Africa, with 28%.

Nonetheless, an important question arises as to how sustainable these improvements are. For example, the volatility of growth in the region has been greater than any other region. In the past periods of growth were often (in some cases usually) followed by periods of significant decline. However, the region today is much different from the region of 1990 when it emerged from two oil price shocks, a plunge of commodity prices and a decade of economic stagnation. For example, during the 1970s growth was based on a commodity boom, which had come to an end by the 1980s with little to show for it. During the recent growth period, almost one-half of the growth came from the services sector, implying perhaps a more sustainable change. Significantly, even this recent high growth may not be high enough, or sustained enough, to reduce the number of people in poverty, which, according to the IMF, has actually increased by 60m. since 1990. Indeed, the proportion of people living on less than $1.25 a day remains at around 50%. The World Bank recently noted that 'it is considerably more difficult to sustain growth than to initiate it'. Sub-Saharan Africa still faces the potential of external shocks: the current global economic slowdown, weaker non-oil commodity prices, political and social strife, adverse weather, and increased world food prices. Africa's economic growth is largely driven by primary production and exports, while the benefits often go to small enclaves within the larger economies.

As noted above, countries that have launched economic policy reforms generally have outperformed those that have not put their programmes into full effect. Although these reforms have not come without costs or criticisms, more and more countries are 'reforming' in a determined manner, and investors who, only a few years ago, would have overlooked the region may now see Africa as a viable alternative. Perhaps the continent's most ambitious plan for reform, NEPAD, was launched in October 2001. Jointly formulated by the heads of state of Algeria, Egypt, Nigeria, Senegal and South Africa, NEPAD's aim was to develop a 'holistic, comprehensive, integrated, strategic framework for the socio-economic development of Africa'. Specifically, the priorities included: (i) creating peace, security and stability; (ii) investing in people; (iii) promoting industrialization; (iv) increasing information and communications technology; and (v) developing basic infrastructure. In an effort to strengthen NEPAD, the APRM was launched in 2003 to monitor the governance of participating countries. Accession to the APRM is voluntary, and the basic areas to be reviewed include political and corporate governance, economic management and respect for human rights. By mid-2010 30 countries had agreed to participate in the programme, of which 12 had completed their first reviews; however, not all countries have implemented their APRM recommendations. Another NEPAD initiative was the Comprehensive Agriculture Development Programme, initiated in 2003, with a commitment to devote at least 10% of national government budgets to agriculture. Thus far the target has generally not been met. Other important initiatives include the 'Extractive Industries Transparency Initiative' launched in 2012, which promotes voluntary standards for showing payments made by companies and revenues collected by governments related to gains from extractive resources such as oil, gas and minerals, and 'Publish What You Pay', which started in 2006 and also promotes more accountability for government revenues generated from natural resources.

Africa's path ahead is difficult and uncertain. Perhaps the best way to place sub-Saharan Africa's future in perspective is to examine the progress made towards achieving the MDGs adopted by 189 countries in 2000 (although it should be noted that most African governments had limited input in formulating them). The MDGs aim to reduce poverty by one-half and make other important improvements in the developing world by 2015. However, the overall conclusion presented in the 2011 *World Development Indicators* was not positive, noting that 'with the rate of progress on most of the goals sluggish, it is unlikely that they will be obtained'. As Table 9 illustrates, of the 17 sub-goals, only one ('Equal girls' enrolment in primary schools') has shown sufficient progress to meet the target based on current trends. Of the remaining 16, 13 show that progress is insufficient to meet the targets.

Thus, it seems certain that few, if any, countries will be able to achieve most of the important elements of the development agenda as envisaged in the MDGs. Indeed, the World Bank suggests that 23 countries in the region are not likely to meet any of the MDGs.

Sub-Saharan Africa was the fastest growing region in the world in 2011 and is likely to remain so in 2012. According to IMF projections, regional growth will reach 5.3% in 2013, down slightly from 5.4% in 2012, following 5.5% growth in 2011, with low-income countries performing somewhat better, at a projected 5.9% in 2013. Growth for 2013 is projected to be highest for West Africa (6.5%), followed by East Africa (5.8%), Southern Africa (4.2%) and Central Africa (3.7%). The recovery is likely to be led by exports, although export growth will depend on the performance of key export markets, particularly in the USA, the EU and China. The euro zone's sovereign debt crisis presents perhaps the most important risk for 2012 and 2013, as Europe has traditionally been the region's most important export destination and source of capital through trade, FDI, ODA and worker remittances. The possibility of a 'double-dip' recession in the rest of the world, applying pressure on commodity prices and undermining government revenues, presents another major risk for the region.

Table 10. Real GDP Growth (%)

	2011	2012	2013
Sub-Saharan Africa . . .	5.5	5.4	5.3
Excluding Nigeria and South Africa	5.9	n.a.	n.a.

Sources: IMF, *Regional Economic Outlook: Sub-Saharan Africa 2010*; and IMF, *Regional Economic Outlook: Sub-Saharan Africa 2012*.

In the medium term, the region faces a number of serious questions: How truly committed are its leaders to the principles of NEPAD? Will peace and stability come to Sudan, Somalia, and other strife-ridden areas? In addition, will sub-Saharan Africa continue to be marginalized, or can it find ways to integrate more successfully into the global economy? How can the negative effects of globalization be minimized? If the euro zone crisis gets worse, how badly will the region suffer? Will the industrialized countries open their markets to competition from the region? Will the region reduce its own trade barriers and find ways to improve co-operation and integrate its economies? Will the countries begin to invest in an often overlooked resource: their own people, particularly their women? Can the recent, positive signs of economic growth be sustained? At mid-2012 the outlook for long-term success remained clouded.

STATE FAILURE IN AFRICA: CAUSES, CONSEQUENCES AND RESPONSES

PAUL D. WILLIAMS

This essay addresses the following four questions: What is meant by state failure? What causes states to fail? What is the scope of this phenomenon in contemporary Africa, and how have insiders and outsiders responded to this process?

Different people find these questions important for different reasons. For the citizens whose states fail, the impacts upon their daily lives are rarely uniform: they can range from immense to negligible depending on a wide range of factors, including how much control the state previously exerted over its citizens, or how far the inhabitants happened to live from the capital city and other major urban centres. For Western governments, on the other hand, state failure in Africa is commonly viewed as both a moral catastrophe and, especially after the terrorist attacks on New York and Washington, DC, USA, of 11 September 2001, a security threat. These dual concerns were neatly elucidated by the then British Secretary of State for Foreign and Commonwealth Affairs, Jack Straw, in September 2002. When confronted with state failure, Straw suggested that 'we cannot but be concerned at the implications for the human rights and freedoms of those who are forced to live in such anarchic and chaotic conditions. Yet, the events of 11 September 2001 devastatingly illustrated a more particular and direct reason for our concern, for it dramatically showed how a state's disintegration can impact on the lives of people many thousands of miles away, even at the heart of the most powerful democracy in the world. In these circumstances, turning a blind eye to the break-down of order in any part of the world, however distant, invites direct threats to our national security and wellbeing. I believe therefore that preventing states from failing and resuscitating those that fail is one of the strategic imperatives of our times.'

After 11 September 2001 the US Government stated that it was 'now threatened less by conquering states than. . .by failing ones'. Africa was widely viewed as a particular cause for concern, since the continent was the part of the world where state failure is most widespread and deeply entrenched. As a result, the US National Security Strategy published in March 2006 acknowledged that 'our security depends upon partnering with Africans to strengthen fragile and failing states and bring ungoverned areas under the control of effective democracies'. Although the May 2010 US National Security Strategy had downgraded the issue compared with threats related to potentially hostile states armed with weapons of mass destruction, it still noted that 'failing states breed conflict and endanger regional and global security'. State failure is thus a serious concern for both insiders and outsiders, and it is on Africa that the international spotlight has most commonly fallen.

The prominence of such discourses about state failure has also generated a great deal of controversy. Stewart Patrick, for instance, recently argued that 'while failed states may be worthy of America's attention on humanitarian and development grounds, most of them are irrelevant to US national security. The risks they pose are mainly to their own inhabitants. Sweeping claims to the contrary are not only inaccurate but distracting and unhelpful, providing little guidance to policy makers seeking to prioritize scarce attention and resources.' In another line of critique, Charles Call suggested that the term 'failed state' should be abandoned because of several serious deficiencies: its tendency to aggregate diverse states and their problems; the related tendency to encourage generic prescriptions for successful states; the unfortunate tendency to distract attention from more fundamental questions about democracy and the nature of specific regimes; the tendency to conflate peacefulness with a process of state-building; the tendency to obfuscate the West's role in the contemporary condition of these states; and the patronizing assumption that Westerners know what a state is and should be. The latter point in particular has attracted supporters in the post-colonial studies literature who note that terms such as 'failed states', 'weak states' and 'quasi-states' are based on ethnocentric assumptions that depict African states as imperfect copies of Western European and North American states and judge them according to external standards in order 'to promote and justify their political and economic domination by Western states and other international actors'.[1] This essay is not intended to refute such critics, for they have raised many sensible questions about the dangers of using general terms like 'failure', 'fragility' and 'weakness' without due regard for the variation across the world's states. Rather, this essay provides an overview of the dominant discourses on state failure in Africa and attempts to understand what responses, from both insiders and outsiders, they have helped facilitate.

WHAT IS STATE FAILURE?

Discussions of state failure are essentially about the interrelationships between patterns of authority, political control and institution-building. Put another way, analysing state failure in Africa requires a keen sense of the shifting configurations of power on the continent and beyond. In most of the literature on the subject, the idea of 'failure' is invoked in two main senses, referred to in this essay as the failure to control and the failure to promote human flourishing.[2]

The Failure to Control

In the first sense, failure is understood in terms of the inability of state institutions to control actors and processes within a given territory. Robert I. Rotberg maintains that 'failed states cannot control their peripheral regions, especially those regions occupied by out-groups. . .Plausibly, the extent of a state's failure can be measured by the extent of its geographical expanse genuinely controlled (especially after dark) by the official government'. It is important to remember, however, that control and failure should not be seen as absolutes. A 'failed' state in this sense of the term might successfully control some of its territory but not all of it. Sudan, for example, is commonly classified as a failed state, yet it continues to exert effective control over large portions of its territory, even after the secession of South Sudan in 2011, and can wreak havoc and terror on some of those individuals and groups who contest its authority in those areas. In contrast, between 2006 and mid-2011 the Transitional Federal Government in Somalia could not even control its capital city.

This suggests that viewing the phenomenon of state failure in absolute terms and through solely statist lenses is not always particularly helpful. Rather, analysts need to appreciate the degrees of success and failure that can exist within a single state and recognize that so-called 'failed states' are usually made up of numerous (and often interconnected) zones where different sources of authority may dominate the local governance structures. In any given zone, the authority in question may vary. Indeed, as Rotberg noted, it may differ considerably within the same zone depending on the time of day or night. The authority structure could be an organ of the state's official government, but it may also be, among other things, an insurgency or guerrilla movement, a clan, a militia, an extended family, a spiritual leader, an international peace operation, or even a transnational corporation or a non-governmental organization.

To give one example, the collapse of the Somali central state in 1991 did not automatically exclude the possibility that zones of alternative forms of governance and authority existed within Somalia's officially recognized international borders. As Kenneth Menkhaus has observed, since 1991 'Somalia has repeatedly shown that in some places and at some times communities, towns, and regions can enjoy relatively high levels of peace, reconciliation, security and lawfulness despite the absence of central authority.' These authority structures have come in various shapes and sizes. They have included local polities comprised of coalitions of businessmen, clan elders and Muslim clergy involved in administering financial services and *Shari'a* courts, and larger-scale structures such as the administrative centres of the 'Republic of Somaliland' (1991–), 'Puntland' (1998–), the Rahanwin Resistance Army's administration of Bay and Bakool regions (1998–2002), and the Banaadir Regional Authority (1996).

When analysing state failure in Africa as a failure to control, analysts and practitioners would thus do well to reject a state-centric ontology in favour of a neo-Gramscian frame of reference, wherein the world is not simply seen as being made up of clashing states in an anarchic international system but, instead, is constituted by the complex inter-relationships between states, social forces and ideas within specific world orders.[3] Adopting this ontology is far more useful for analysing state failure, because, as Timothy Raeymaekers correctly observed, what we are witnessing in several cases of so-called 'state failure' is actually better understood as 'neopatrimonialism without the state'. That is, systems of patron-client relations that may or may not be linked to the official institutions of state power. Arguably, the closest Western officialdom has come to adopting such a perspective is the US Government's anxiety about what it terms 'ungoverned spaces', 'defined as geographic areas where governments do not exercise effective control'.[4] Unfortunately, this misses the crucial point that just because official governments do not control these areas it does not necessarily mean that they are completely lacking other structures of governance.

The Failure to Promote Human Flourishing

Failure is also commonly used in a second sense to highlight the ways in which states, either because of a lack of capacity or a lack of political will, fail to provide public goods to their entire population rather than favouring one or other particular segment of it. The idea that states have a responsibility to provide their citizens with certain basic rights has long been an issue of debate within international relations dating back at least as far as notions of popular sovereignty articulated by Jean Bodin in the 16th century. Since the publication in late 2001 of a report by the International Commission on Intervention and State Sovereignty, this line of argument is now commonly discussed under the heading of the 'responsibility to protect' after the title of the Commission's report.

Although African governments have jealously guarded traditional ideas about sovereignty and non-intervention, the responsibility to protect idea has made significant headway on the continent in recent years, and with it has come a plethora of literature speaking of 'failure' in these terms. In July 2000, for instance, the Constitutive Act of the new African Union (AU) included several clauses suggesting that sovereign states had a variety of obligations and responsibilities to their citizens. Moreover, Article 4(h) stated that one of the Union's principles was that it had the right 'to intervene in a Member State pursuant to a decision of the Assembly in respect of grave circumstances, namely war crimes, genocide and crimes against humanity'. Such obligations were confirmed in September 2005, when African states, along with the rest of the UN General Assembly, formally accepted the responsibility to protect principle.

As defined in the World Summit Outcome document: 'each individual State has the responsibility to protect its populations from genocide, war crimes, ethnic cleansing and crimes against humanity. This responsibility entails the prevention of such crimes, including their incitement, through appropriate and necessary means. We accept that responsibility and will act in accordance with it.' In subsequent years the UN Secretariat has defined the responsibility to protect as resting on three pillars. The first is the responsibility of each state to use appropriate and necessary means to protect its own population from genocide, war crimes, ethnic cleansing and crimes against humanity, as well as from their incitement. The second pillar refers to the commitment that UN member states will help each other exercise this responsibility. This includes specific commitments to help states build the capacity to protect their populations from the four crimes and to assist those that are under stress before crises and conflicts erupt. The third pillar refers to international society's collective responsibility to respond through the UN in a timely and decisive manner, using Chapters VI, VII and VIII of the UN Charter as appropriate, when national authorities are manifestly failing to protect their populations from the four crimes listed above.

Understood in these two senses, state failure on the African continent is a widespread phenomenon. It is important to note, however, that both these views of failure are based upon a particular conception of statehood: what Rotberg calls 'the fundamental tasks of a nation-state in the modern world' and what William Zartman refers to as 'the basic functions of the state'. The particular idea of statehood that dominates discussions about state failure was born in Europe and is usually associated with the Treaties of Westphalia in 1648. That year is thus commonly understood within mainstream international relations theory as representing the birth of modern interstate relations. Yet, while this specific date of origin makes for neat theory, it rests upon a dubious and mythical history. As Benno Teschke has argued, even in its European birthplace, the practice of Westphalian statehood as opposed to the ideal of Westphalian statehood did not emerge until well after 1648. Specifically, Teschke has shown how modern international relations based on the Westphalian ideal of statehood only began with the conjunction of the rise of capitalism and modern state formation in England. Thereafter, the English model influenced the restructuring of the old regimes of the European continent, a process that was incremental and highly uneven and was not completed until the First World War.

The relevant point for this discussion is that the nature of statehood itself is contested rather than obviously apparent. Specifically, as Christopher Clapham has argued, the Westphalian ideal rests on 'unsure foundations', not least because in some parts of the world 'the essential conditions for statehood cannot plausibly be met'. The 'fundamental tasks' of statehood envisaged in this Westphalian ideal revolved around the provision of security, welfare and representation. In particular, the defining characteristic of the Westphalian ideal of statehood has been the right of states to exercise five monopoly powers:

the right to monopolize control of the instruments of violence;

the sole right to tax citizens;

the prerogative of ordering the political allegiances of citizens and of enlisting their support in war;

the sovereign right to adjudicate in disputes between citizens;

the exclusive right of representation in international society, which has been linked with the authority to bind the whole community in international law.

Even in Europe, as Teschke observed, the practical acquisition of these monopoly powers sometimes took centuries of often violent turmoil and social upheaval. Compared with Europe and viewed from the perspective of the *longue durée*, it is clear that most states in Africa are still mired in the relatively early stages of state formation. Consequently, it should come as little surprise that the practical acquisition of these monopolies has been uneven across the continent.

Although it has been similarly traumatic and drawn out, the process of state-building has unfolded differently in Africa than it did in Europe. Unlike in Europe, where state borders were demarcated with reference to their neighbours, in Africa state power tended to radiate from a focal core (usually the capital city) that only rarely came into direct confrontation with its neighbouring governments. As a basic rule of thumb, the further one travelled from this core, the weaker the state's control became. This fact rendered the state borders drawn up by the European colonial powers in Berlin, Germany, in 1884–85 relatively meaningless, or at least highly porous, for many practical aspects of the local inhabitants' daily existence, including commerce or communicating with individuals who were officially 'foreigners', but who belonged to the same ethnic or tribal groups.

Understood in these terms, the issue of 'failed states' in Africa is largely about the extent to which the Westphalian ideal of statehood has taken root in the rather different, and in many ways inhospitable, conditions found on the continent. As the Organization of African Unity's (OAU, now the AU) charter made abundantly clear, the ideal of Westphalian statehood clearly attracted many advocates among Africa's first generation of post-colonial élites. It was also helped by the willingness of the great powers within international society to grant these states international recognition. The practical realization of this ideal, however, has been far more contested and uneven. As a result, from the outside, African states often looked like the Westphalian ideal, in that they were recognized members of international society and their representatives sat on the councils of various international organizations. On the inside, however, these governments were often considered illegitimate by much of the local population and wielded the institutions of state to subdue political opponents and benefit their supporters. These were, in Robert Jackson's famous phrase, 'quasi-states': legal fictions that rarely commanded much in the way of national loyalty or the power to control developments throughout their designated territory.

What this means for an analysis of state failure is simply that, depending on the local conditions, 'failure' is far more likely in certain parts of the continent than others. More specifically, as Clapham has argued, 'those areas of Africa that maintained reasonably settled and effective state structures during the period prior to colonialism are proving best able to do so as the institutional legacies of colonialism fade.' Where these structures were weak, other forms of authority (familial, spiritual, ethnic, etc.) have filled the vacuum.

WHAT CAUSES STATES TO FAIL?

There is no simple or single formula for understanding the causes of state failure in Africa. Nevertheless, the available literature on the subject often makes at least two relevant general distinctions. The first distinction is between states that fail because of a lack of relevant capacities and those that fail to promote the interests of all their inhabitants through political choice, often with the intention of benefiting the incumbent regime and its supporters at the expense of another group within the state. President Robert Mugabe's ongoing manipulation of the Zimbabwe African National Union—Patriotic Front (ZANU—PF) and state power in Zimbabwe is a paradigmatic example of a regime choosing to deny basic rights to certain segments of its population in an attempt to bolster regime security. The dynamics in this case are somewhat different from instances where a regime may well want to restore order to part of its territory but lacks the relevant capacities to do so. These dynamics are apparent in, for instance, the Ugandan Government's inability to defeat rather than displace the Lord's Resistance Army and Sudan's inability to defeat the Sudan People's Liberation Movement/Army. Such incapacity may sometimes lead to political compromises, such as the decision made by the Sudanese authorities to allow the south of the country to secede. At other times, the result is simply long-standing stalemates and the de facto partition of a state's territory. Outside of the military sphere, a government might wish to enhance the development prospects of its citizens but lack the necessary resources and instruments. The incumbent Governments in Liberia and Sierra Leone are cases in point.

A second distinction points to the differences between structural and contingent causes of state failure. In the structural category, four main arguments are commonly advanced. First, as noted above, the Westphalian ideal of statehood has not successfully taken root across all of Africa because local conditions were inhospitable to state-building and exerting high levels of state control over local societies. Although international society helped the process by granting recognition to Africa's newly independent states—many of which became the archetypal examples of Jackson's quasi-states—it could not ensure that their inhabitants invested a great deal of faith in, or commitment to, them. Not long after independence, however, Cold War politics meant that the superpowers often made genuinely national nation-building even more difficult by stoking the fires of dissent within many African states in the name of either communism or capitalism.

A second structural argument has revolved around the challenges posed by political geography, especially resources and environmental factors. In this case, the point is that some African states that were creations of the European colonial powers were not endowed with a physical environment conducive to administering an effective state. In particular, states such as those in the West African savannah suffered from extremely low densities of people, which made administration and social control both costly and difficult. The same was true for much of Africa since large areas of it have ecologies that cannot easily support high densities of population, not least because over 50% of the continent suffers from inadequate rainfall that makes inhospitable environments for both human settlement and agriculture. Indeed, it is arguably only the Great Lakes region and the Ethiopian highlands that have sustained relatively high densities of people.

A third structural argument has applied the concept of the security dilemma to explain how fear of an ungoverned future can propel the actors within states to hasten the collapse of central government once public order begins to erode and a situation of domestic anarchy seems likely to emerge. Here, the suggestion is that the Hobbesian fear that lies at the heart of the security dilemma explains why groups begin to think that their potential rivals will not be restrained by state authority once the institutions of state have started to disintegrate. Analytically speaking, the crucial focus becomes understanding the 'tipping point' beyond which actors start to behave as if domestic anarchy exists, even if that is not entirely the case. At that stage, the dynamics of the domestic security dilemma may ensure that their conviction that state collapse and anarchy is imminent becomes a self-fulfilling prophecy.

A fourth argument has suggested that when it comes to state success in Africa 'bigger isn't better'. Specifically, in 2006 the authors of *Big African States* concluded that most of Africa's large states have exhibited 'varying degrees of dysfunctionality (defined as the lack of provision of welfare and opportunity to the population) and, excluding to a degree South Africa, a sustained period of civil unrest, economic decline, state atrophy and social corrosion'.[5] In a series of case studies, the authors suggested that in Angola, the Democratic Republic of the Congo (DRC), Ethiopia, Nigeria and Sudan (all of which are in the top five African states in terms of population or landmass, or both) 'the actual size of these states is itself a problem for governance' and that, rather than being natural leaders, they 'are actually problems for their associated regions'. (It remains to be seen what will be the impact on these dynamics of the secession of the Republic of South Sudan in July 2011.)

The contingent causes of state failure in Africa are even more numerous with five main factors commonly cited within the literature. Crudely summarized, these refer to the influence of bad leaders, predatory actors such as warlords and so-called 'spoilers', bad economic policies, bad environments, and bad neighbours.

First, much of the blame for state failure has been heaped upon Africa's leaders, not least Maj.-Gen. Mohammed Siad Barre (Somalia), Dr Siaka Stevens (Sierra Leone), Mobutu Sese Seko (Zaire/the DRC), Gen. Samuel Doe and later Charles Taylor (Liberia), and Robert Mugabe (Zimbabwe). More recently, Issaias Afewerki (Eritrea) and Laurent Gbagbo (Côte d'Ivoire) might be added to the list. In many African states, such leaders and their political élites have been criticized for pursuing patrimonial politics that seek to use external sources of aid and finance to reward their supporters and weaken their opponents rather than pursuing genuinely national development strategies. Second, warlords and other 'spoilers' have been blamed for inflaming ethnic tensions and hastening state failure. The motivations of these predatory actors vary from case to case, but a common claim is that they have pursued violent strategies in order to accumulate wealth through the control of formal and/or informal markets. In this view, weak or failing state institutions provide an environment from which such warlords and 'spoilers' can profit.

The third set of contingent factors concerns the political economy of state failure, especially the adoption by governments of 'bad' macroeconomic policies resulting in fiscal deficits and balance of payments crises, and the paradoxical effects of structural adjustment policies encouraged by a variety of international donors. As Nicolas van de Walle argued, both of these factors encouraged a 'hollowing out' of the state, which, in turn, increased 'the chances that minor political incidents and disputes could cause the descent into failure'. Such political economies did not, however, automatically produce failed states. Hence, although Zaire/the DRC and Sierra Leone were both 'hollowed out' before failing, states such as the Central African Republic (CAR), Malawi and Niger were also weakened by economic failure but did not suffer a similar fate.

A fourth commonly cited factor relates to the proliferation and availability of armaments, especially small arms and light weapons, in many of Africa's weak and fragile states. An environment awash with arms makes it difficult for governments to control all of their territory or protect all of their citizens because, as Michael Klare suggested, 'anti-government formations can readily assemble sufficient weaponry to mount a revolution or insurgency'. A fifth contingent cause of state failure concerns the role played by actors within neighbouring states. These have tended to be either incumbent governments hostile to their neighbouring regimes (e.g., Taylor's destabilization of Sierra Leone throughout the 1990s), or insurgent groups that destabilize their target state with or without support from the government of their (temporary) host state (e.g., the Rwandan Patriotic Front's use of Uganda as a base for its operations before it invaded Rwanda in 1990, or Hutu genocidaires using eastern Zaire/the DRC to destabilize Paul Kagame's regime after the 1994 genocide).

All of these factors can play a role in state failure, but the current state of knowledge remains far too vague accurately to predict the tipping points in particular cases.

WHAT IS THE SCOPE OF THE PROBLEM?

As noted above, failed states raise challenges both for the great powers concerned about what threats might come out of them and for the locals who have to endure life inside them. Indeed, it has been suggested that since 'the end of the Cold War, weak and failing states have arguably become the single-most important problem for international order'.[6] Although state failure is not confined to Africa, the problem is arguably more widespread, deeply rooted and pressing here than in any other continent.

Failed states can spawn a variety of transnational security problems with terrorism, proliferation of weapons of mass destruction, crime, disease, energy insecurity, and regional instability chief among them. Not all of them, however, are equally prevalent in Africa's cases. With the notable exceptions of actors operating out of Sudan, Somalia and some parts of the Sahel, transnational terrorism has been relatively rare in sub-Saharan Africa. The same could also be said for weapons of mass destruction proliferation. In contrast, small arms and light weapons proliferation, transnational crime (especially the illicit trade in drugs, arms, minerals, petroleum, timber, wildlife and human beings), infectious diseases (including HIV/AIDS, malaria, tuberculosis, hepatitis B, Ebola, measles, and the West Nile virus), and political instability in the Horn of Africa and the Gulf of Guinea oil states do pose significant threats and challenges to both the locals and, to a lesser extent, the great powers.

It is important to note, however, that these challenges are unevenly distributed across Africa's failing states. Transnational criminals, for instance, tend not to operate in areas of complete state collapse (such as Somalia), but instead prefer areas where a basic degree of physical and financial infrastructure exists and where bureaucrats and officials are susceptible to bribery (such as Kenya, Nigeria and South Africa). Cells of transnational terrorist networks are likely to require similar levels of infrastructure and at least a degree of order if they are to use failing states for anything other than transit routes and temporary bases of operations. The major al-Qa'ida attacks against US embassies in 1998, for instance, took place in Kenya and Tanzania but were allegedly orchestrated from a partially failed state in the form of Sudan and an almost entirely collapsed state in the shape of Somalia. Viewed from a longer-term perspective, however, most terrorism in Africa has been nationally oriented and targeted against white-minority rule or in specific revolutionary settings, notably Ethiopia and Algeria.

During the early stages of the 21st century Africa provided many of the usual suspects on the lists of the world's failed states including Chad, the CAR, the DRC, Liberia, Sierra Leone, Sudan and Zimbabwe. In addition, Somalia was often classified in a league of its own as having collapsed altogether rather than simply failed. Africa's leading status in these rankings has been consistently confirmed by four popular attempts to categorize and measure different types of state failure, namely, the World Bank's Governance Matters data set, the Failed States Index, the UN Development Programme's (UNDP) Human Development Index, and Freedom House's annual surveys of political freedom.

The World Bank's *Governance Matters 2011* data ranked world-wide governance indicators, covering 213 economies (countries and territories). It defined governance as 'the set of traditions and institutions by which authority in a country is exercised. This includes (1) the process by which governments are selected, monitored and replaced, (2) the capacity of the government to effectively formulate and implement sound policies, and (3) the respect of citizens and the state for the institutions that govern economic and social interactions among them.' The 2011 report measured six dimensions of governance between 1996 and 2009: voice and accountability, political stability and absence of violence, government effectiveness, regulatory quality, rule of law, and control of corruption. The results across these different dimensions confirmed Africa's place as the global centre of state failure. In particular, the continent contained eight of the world's 22 least accountable territories, 10 of the 22 most politically unstable and potentially violent territories, 13 of the 21 least effective governments, eight of the 21 territories with the worst regulatory quality, 13 of the 22 territories where the rule of law was weakest, and 10 of the 20 territories least able to control corruption. Overall, this set of indicators suggested that, once again, the African territories with the consistently worst performing governance structures across the World Bank's different categories were Somalia, Sudan, Zimbabwe, the DRC, Equatorial Guinea, Eritrea, Guinea, Guinea-Bissau, Chad and Côte d'Ivoire.

A similar picture emerged from the *Failed States Index 2012*, compiled by *Foreign Policy* magazine and the Fund for Peace. This was the eighth annual index and measured performance along 12 political, economic, military and social indicators of instability (demographic pressures, refugees and displaced persons, group grievance, human flight, uneven development, economy, delegitimization of the state, public services, human rights, security apparatus, factionalized élites, and external intervention). This year it concluded that the world's five most failing states were all in Africa: Somalia (most failing), the DRC (second), Sudan (third), Chad (fourth) and Zimbabwe (sixth). Continuing down the scale, it suggested that Africa contained 15 of the world's 42 most failing states, one more than in the previous year.

The third popular ranking system is UNDP's *2011 Human Development Index*. It focuses on three dimensions of development (health, education and living standards) and four key indicators (life expectancy at birth, mean and expected years of schooling, and gross national income per capita). UNDP suggests that this provides a reasonable profile of the extent to which a particular state is promoting human flourishing. From a total of 187 states, UNDP's conclusion was startling: 36 of the 46 countries listed in its category of Low Human Development were exclusively African. In addition, it should be noted that the index did not include Somalia, presumably owing to the difficulty of gathering data. The 10 worst African performers on this list were the DRC (187th), Niger (186th), Burundi (185th), Mozambique (184th), Chad (183rd), Liberia (182nd), Burkina Faso (181st), Sierra Leone (180th) and the CAR (179th), and Guinea (178th),. The daily realities behind these figures included the uncomfortable facts that one-half of all Africans live on less than US $1 a day, more than one-half of them lack access to hospitals or doctors, one-third suffer from malnutrition, one in six children die before their fifth birthday, and the average African's life expectancy is just 41 years.

The final popular set of indicators is compiled by Freedom House in its annual report, *Freedom in the World*. This measures levels of political freedom, defined as people having 'the opportunity to act spontaneously in a variety of fields outside the control of the government and other centres of potential domination'. It does so by assessing the extent to which citizens enjoy political rights and civil liberties in 195 countries (now including the Republic of South Sudan) and 14 territories around the world. According to *Freedom in the World 2012*, Africa is currently home to some of the world's most repressive regimes. Specifically, Freedom House classified 21 African states as 'not free', one more than in 2010 and representing 44% of the global total. (In addition, the territory of Western Sahara was also classified as 'not free'.) A country is defined as 'not free' when Freedom House judges 'basic political rights are absent, and basic civil liberties are widely and systematically denied'. Of these 21 'not free' states, Freedom House placed four African countries—Equatorial Guinea, Eritrea, Somalia and Sudan—in its special category of 'the worst of the worst', i.e. the nine states globally given the survey's lowest possible rating. This was one better than the previous year owing to Libya's departure from 'the worst of the worst' list. The Freedom House analysis suggested that during 2011 five countries in Africa suffered reversals of significant magnitude (Djibouti, Ethiopia, Malawi, Sudan and Uganda). This was a significant improvement from the 16 significant reversals that the continent suffered during 2009, although notable improvements during 2011 occurred only in Egypt and Zambia.

Since late 2007 two new indices of state failure in Africa have appeared in the intellectual market-place. In September 2007 the Mo Ibrahim *Index of African Governance* was published. Prepared under the auspices of a team led by Robert I. Rotberg from Harvard University, USA, this project developed a new definition of governance as the delivery of key political goods in five main areas.[7] Using this definition, the index assessed the quality of governance in the 48 countries of sub-Saharan Africa against 58 individual measures using data from the years 2000, 2002, and 2005 (the former two years were used by the index as base-line indicators). In 2009 the index was updated to include 84 indicators divided into four main categories: Safety and Rule of Law; Participation and Human Rights; Sustainable Economic Opportunity; and Human Development. Data was drawn from 2009 if available and 2008 if not. In its current version, the *2011 Index of African Governance* added two additional indicators and drew its conclusions from 23 data providers giving the index some 40,000 raw data points. It is therefore best described as a 'poll of polls' on governance issues in sub-Saharan Africa. At the top end of the governance spectrum, this index listed Mauritius (first), Cape Verde (second), Botswana (third), Seychelles (fourth) and South Africa (fifth). These countries also occupied the top five places in 2007, 2008, 2009 and 2010. The bottom of the spectrum was occupied, as usual, by Somalia (53rd), Chad (52nd), Zimbabwe (51st), the DRC (50th), the CAR (49th), Sudan (48th), and Eritrea (47th).

In March 2008 the Brookings Institution added to the pool of indices when it launched its new *Index of State Weakness in the Developing World*. Led by former US Assistant Secretary of State for African Affairs Susan E. Rice (currently US Permanent Representative to the UN) and Stewart Patrick, this index defined weak states 'as countries lacking the capacity and/or will to foster an environment conducive to sustainable and equitable economic growth; to establish and maintain legitimate, transparent, and accountable political institutions; to secure their populations from violent conflict and to control their territory; and to meet the basic human needs of their population'. The Brookings Index ranked the 141 developing countries, which the World Bank classifies as low-income, lower middle-income, and upper middle-income. Each country was assessed against 20 indicators divided into four baskets: economic, political, security and social welfare. Of the 28 states in the index's bottom quintile, 22 of them were African (African states represented 37 of the 56 states in the bottom two quintiles). The worst performers were Somalia (first), the DRC (third), Burundi (fifth), Sudan (sixth), the CAR (seventh), Zimbabwe (eighth), Liberia (ninth) and Côte d'Ivoire (10th). This index has not been updated since 2008.

These ranking systems all have significant limitations and have to confront difficult methodological questions, but they do have the benefit of highlighting how unwise it is to generalize about the nature or effects of state failure in Africa. Nevertheless, they all make it abundantly clear that the continent is suffering more than most other parts of the world. Thus, the pertinent practical question is how have locals and outsiders responded?

HOW HAVE INSIDERS AND OUTSIDERS RESPONDED TO STATE FAILURE IN AFRICA?

It is possible to identify four main types of responses to state failure in Africa. First, there have been external attempts, often led by Western governments, to reassert the failing state's control over its territory. There have also been similar attempts to encourage Africa's failing governments to provide their citizens with human rights and basic public goods. A third type of response has occurred in relatively rare instances where international society has been willing to permit states to disintegrate and break into separate smaller units. Finally, there have been the responses of local Africans themselves. These have ranged from active participation in the struggle to rebuild and control state power to indifference and sometimes hostility towards the entire process.

Resurrection

Western responses to Africa's failed states have been selective and intermittent. Selectivity is part and parcel of any state's foreign policy, and the responses of Western governments to Africa's failing states have concentrated on those that are perceived to pose the greatest threats to Western security concerns. The US Government, for instance, was criticized for singling out only two African states—Ethiopia and Sudan—for its Transitional Initiative to encourage democratization in fragile and post-conflict states. (The Initiative allocated US $275m. of its $325m. budget to just four states: Afghanistan, Ethiopia, Haiti and Sudan.) This left worthy candidates such as Somalia, the DRC, Liberia, Sierra Leone, Burundi and the CAR with few funds to help democratization and civil society initiatives. However, Western responses to state failure have also been selective in a more geo-strategic sense. Despite suffering from some of the most serious examples of state failure on the planet, the African continent has not attracted a major transitional administration of the kind sponsored by Western states in Bosnia and Herzegovina, Kosovo, Timor-Leste and, to a lesser extent, Afghanistan. In this sense, state failure in Africa remains on the margins of Western concern even after the events of 11 September 2001.

The selective response of Western governments has been mirrored, and to some extent fostered, by the intermittent and transient Western media coverage given to state failure in Africa. This is usually explained by the fact that failed state stories do not meet enough of the traditional Western news criteria to keep them on the front pages of newspapers or on television screens. The United Kingdom and France appear to have more media coverage of these issues than most Western states but it remains infrequent, concentrated on their former colonies, and often involves stories that score highly in terms of drama, conflict and sensation but provide little in the way of historical background or explanation.

Given this context, when Western states have responded in concrete terms to Africa's failing states, they have usually tried to address the two different types of failure discussed above: the failure to control and the failure to promote human flourishing.

Outsiders have employed several strategies to help failing states reassert control over the actors within their territorial borders. To date, the most resource-intensive have been those designed to disarm, demobilize and reintegrate (DDR) former combatants, usually orchestrated by some kind of international peace-keeping force. These DDR programmes are then usually followed by a process of 'security sector reform', the current pseudonym for building new, usually broad-based, security institutions, notably the armed forces, police and intelligence services but also increasingly extending to cover the justice sector as well. Once again, however, and reflecting the powerful influence the Westphalian ideal of statehood exerts over the architects of these programmes, such efforts have been criticized for under-estimating the power of informal economies in Africa's failed states and the crucial roles played by private actors in such settings. As part of the reform process, Western powers have been keen to strengthen the capacity of African states to conduct complex peace operations. The most recent framework was announced at the 2004 Group of Eight industrialized countries (G8) summit, where the leaders pledged under the Global Peace Operations Initiative to support the training of some 40,000 African peace-keepers (out of a world-wide total of 75,000) to help make the much vaunted African Standby Force a reality by 2010. However, despite training over 75,000 African peace-keepers, the African Standby Force did not meet its 2010 deadline, which has now been extended to 2015, and doubts still remain about its operational capabilities and the relationship between the AU and the continent's Regional Economic Communities. In addition to training and helping to equip African peace-keepers, Western states have also deployed small numbers of their own soldiers to so-called 'hybrid' peace operations in some of Africa's failing states, including the United Kingdom in Sierra Leone, France in Côte d'Ivoire, European Union-led operations in the DRC, Chad, the CAR and Somalia, and the USA in Liberia, central Africa and Somalia. In most cases, however, it remains too early to determine whether these efforts to reassert state control have succeeded.

A similar pattern has emerged in relation to external attempts to enhance the provision of public goods in Africa's failing states. Here, the primary mechanisms have been increasing levels of foreign aid and development assistance, placing diplomatic pressure on African élites to adopt what the World Bank calls 'good governance', including the strengthening of the African Peer Review Mechanism, and more general attempts to implant the idea that states have a responsibility to protect the human rights of their own citizens.

With few exceptions, aid from most Western states has been concentrated on their traditional friends and allies in Africa. Nevertheless, both the United Kingdom and the USA have made significant increases in certain sectors, notably in funding to stem the prevalence of HIV/AIDS on the continent. On the other hand, the so-called 'global war on terror' has meant that significant amounts of Western development assistance has been allocated to states considered to be in the front line of the fight against terrorism, notably Iraq, Afghanistan and Pakistan. Efforts to encourage 'good governance' have come from a variety of sources, but since its formal adoption by the OAU in July 2001 the New Partnership for Africa's Development (NEPAD) has remained the most comprehensive framework to address this issue. However, NEPAD has suffered from several problems, most notably those relating to its élitist and market-driven design, the slow pace of implementation, and, perhaps most significantly for both Washington and London, the failure of many African states adequately to criticize Robert Mugabe's regime for plunging Zimbabwe into a crisis from which there will be no quick escape. At the same time that many African states were making excuses for the mayhem generated by Mugabe's ZANU—PF regime, they were also explaining why Article 4(h) of the AU's new charter did not apply to the war in Darfur, Sudan, in spite of clear evidence that 'grave circumstances' had existed in the region since at least mid-2003. In early 2011 it was also notable that unlike several other international organizations, including the UN Security Council and the League of Arab States, the AU did not call for military intervention to protect civilians in Libya.

Of course, these two types of response are intimately related to one another. As a result, Western powers have started to pay greater attention to co-ordinating their responses across all the relevant dimensions of state failure. They have also acknowledged that there is an urgent need to prevent state failure rather than just to manage its consequences. One prominent example in this regard is the British Government's *Investing in Prevention* report issued in 2005. This concluded that attempts to resurrect failed states and prevent their (re)occurrence should adopt a 'four S's' strategy:

appropriate scale of political attention and financial resources;

sustaining action over longer time horizons;

developing systematic approaches to action across political, development, economic, security and other dimensions;

achieving greater sophistication of understanding of long-run dynamics of instability.

Importantly, the report also emphasized the need to change élite behaviour in fragile and failing states through a series of co-ordinated incentive strategies. Given the importance of contingent causes of state failure discussed above, this is an important focus for action.

The State is Dead, Long Live the State

A third type of response has been far less prevalent in Africa. Despite the continuing problems confronting attempts to resurrect Africa's failed states, it has been rare for the great powers within international society to countenance their disintegration or what Jeffrey Herbst has called the 'let them fail' approach. Nevertheless, such a response is possible, as indicated by the belated recognition of an independent Namibia and Eritrea, Western Sahara's UN-endorsed (but currently stalled) referendum on secession from Morocco, and the secession of the new Republic of South Sudan under the terms of the 2005 Comprehensive Peace Agreement. These exceptions have usually occurred when insurgencies have succeeded in gaining and sustaining control over significant areas of territory, frequently through a military struggle. The rarity of this outcome suggests two things. First, given the relatively large number of insurgencies in Africa, the small number of secessions suggests that it is difficult for such movements to achieve decisive military victories over incumbent regimes and maintain control of sizeable territories for long periods of time when they do. Second, international society's general reluctance to countenance the 'death' of states and their breaking into smaller units demonstrates the power that the Westphalian ideal of statehood continues to exert even in the face of such implausible candidates for 'successful' state-building as Nigeria and the DRC.

In Herbst's opinion, the crucial issue is not to concentrate on resurrecting the old failed state, but to think through what the alternatives to failed states might look like and 'to increase the congruence between the way that power is actually exercised and the design of units'. As the examples in Somalia noted above suggest, it is clear that alternative units and structures already exist, but very few of them are granted official recognition by international society. The first step in this recognition process would be for international society to countenance decertifying states when they fail to meet their sovereign responsibilities (of either control or promoting basic standards of human flourishing). Indeed, the US Administration has previously indulged in this kind of activity by designating certain countries including Iraq, Iran, Libya, Syria and the Democratic People's Republic of Korea as rogue, pariah or evil states that are unfit to participate as normal members of international society. The logical next step is to decide the criteria for selecting potential new states. This will be controversial, but a reasonable place to start, as Herbst suggests, is with the question of which actors or institutions are actually providing political order in a given territory. Herbst concludes that 'the long-term aim would be to provide international recognition to the governmental units that are actually providing order to their citizens as opposed to relying on the fictions of the past'.

Local Competition and Local Indifference

Finally, it is important to analyse local responses to state failure in Africa. The first point to note is that these have not been uniform. Some locals have competed to lead the resurrection process and, hopefully, benefit from the material resources that flow from it, including foreign aid, humanitarian assistance and loans from the international financial institutions. Others, however, have tried their best to ignore the collapse of central government institutions and continue to by-pass state power in many aspects of their everyday lives. In southern Africa, for instance, states have long failed to meet the needs of the region's peoples. Given the imperial foundations of the region's states, this is hardly surprising. As a consequence, as Peter Vale has argued, ordinary southern Africans have lost faith in, and increasingly by-pass, a state system that 'neither delivers security nor satisfies a desire for community'. Instead, they have engaged in alternative forms of social intercourse related to, among other things, religious affiliations, trading associations, musicology, and migration patterns, all of which show little respect for the political borders erected by southern Africa's states. In this sense, many ordinary Africans have become adept at forming accommodation strategies in a variety of different arenas to fulfil their needs when their state has failed them.

Over time, this has produced many different attitudes to 'the state' in Africa, from squabbling élites desperate to resurrect and then control new state institutions, to ordinary people who are often either indifferent or explicitly hostile to state-building projects focused on the urban centres. In Somalia, for example, not only have certain groups carried on their lives in spite of the collapse of the central state but they are extremely suspicious of any attempts to revive it. Whereas the conventional wisdom of Western-dominated institutions such as the World Bank and the G8 dictates that an effective central state is a prerequisite for national development, many Somalis view the state as 'an instrument of accumulation and domination, enriching and empowering those who control it and exploiting and oppressing the rest'.[8] As a consequence, there have been a variety of groups hostile to international efforts to resuscitate the trappings of central government in the Somali capital, Mogadishu. This also raises the important observation made by Menkhaus that state-building and peace-building might at times be 'mutually antagonistic enterprises in Somalia'. Consequently, outsiders should not automatically assume that insiders are united on the need to resurrect failed states. Instead, they should canvass the opinion of insiders and think carefully about when alternatives to failed states should be put into practice.

THE STRANGE CASE OF SOMALIA

As discussed above, the dilemmas and challenges of state-building are exemplified by the case of Somalia, for many years the collapsed state *par excellence* and the focus of much US counter-terrorism activity. In particular, not only does any potential central government in Somalia confront huge incapacity problems, but the process of building central institutions may well exacerbate the likelihood of violent conflict within the country and, ironically, make it a more attractive destination for terrorist organizations.

Contemporary Somalia exemplifies some of the conceptual points raised earlier in this essay. First, just because Somalia was long a state without a central government, this did not mean it was devoid of various systems of governance and sources of authority. In this sense, it should not be seen as one of the US Government's 'ungoverned spaces'. Although Somalia has lacked a permanent central government since 1991, at the local, municipal and neighbourhood levels coalitions of clan elders, businessmen and Muslim clergy overseeing *Shari'a* courts have provided governance structures and become sources of authority. At the regional/provincial level, power struggles within Somalia have revolved around the capital city, Mogadishu, but also the northern regions of the 'Republic of Somaliland' (which declared itself an independent republic in 1991) and 'Puntland' (which declared itself an autonomous state within Somalia in May 1998). In addition, from 2004–05, Somalia was in the rare situation of having its recognized Transitional Federal Government (TFG) based outside its territory, in Nairobi, Kenya. The TFG moved into the Somali town of Jowhar and then Baidoa in June 2005, and in December 2006 it relocated to Mogadishu with support from an Ethiopian intervention force.

Second, coalitions of insiders and outsiders have played important roles in both keeping the state fractured and attempting to resurrect a set of central government institutions. Some insiders have asked external actors to provide a variety of peace operations to help the state-building project. In October 2004, for instance, the Somali President, Col Adbullahi Yussuf Ahmed, appealed for 20,000 peace-keepers to secure the country and disarm some 55,000 militiamen. Furthermore, in early 2005 the AU and then the Intergovernmental Authority on Development agreed to authorize the deployment of troops to facilitate the return of Somalia's TFG to Mogadishu. However, neither of these operations were carried out. It was only in early 2007, after the conflict that expelled the Union of Islamic Courts (UIC) from Mogadishu, that the AU actually deployed approximately 1,600 Ugandan troops as part of its Mission in Somalia (AMISOM). (By early 2012 the AMISOM forces had climbed to an authorized strength of 17,731, including soldiers from Uganda, Burundi, Kenya, and a small number from Djibouti.) These moves were, of course, criticized by those insiders hostile to the entire externally-driven state-building project, notably the supporters of al-Shabaab.

These developments demonstrate Menkhaus's point that there exist competing views of the state in Somalia. For most external actors, the conventional wisdom is that an effective and to some extent centralized state government is a prerequisite for development. This view is supported by those insiders who think they are likely to benefit from the resurrection of a central government. On the other hand, for many Somalis, the state is seen as an instrument of accumulation and domination, enriching and empowering those who control it and exploiting and oppressing the rest. For these insiders, state-building is something to be resisted.

Arguably, the three main external actors behind the most recent state-building project in Somalia have been Ethiopia, the USA and Kenya. For Ethiopia, the primary goal has been to avoid a situation where Islamist extremists control a unified Somalia and reawaken nationalist desires to return the Ogaden region of Ethiopia to Somali control. This explains Ethiopia's strong support for the TFG and its deep suspicion of the UIC and other Islamist radicals and irredentists. For the Kenyans, the principal concerns were how to deal with the outflow of many Somali refugees and then, in late 2011, Somali insurgents were blamed for a series of kidnappings and attacks which significantly affected Kenya's tourism industry. The result was a unilateral Kenyan military operation into the south-west of Somalia with the strategic objective of establishing an effective buffer zone and dislodging al-Shabaab forces from the port city of Kismayo. For the USA, on the other hand, the major objective is to avoid a situation where Somalia becomes a safe haven for anti-Western terrorist organizations. From the USA's perspective, the best way to secure this goal is to support a stable, moderate central government and help it build the capacity to police its borders and root out extremists within them. To this end, during the early 2000s the US authorities supported the self-styled Alliance for the Restoration of Peace and Counter-Terrorism (ARPCT), which in reality was simply a disorganized collection of warlords and opportunist militia.

The problem with the US position was two-fold. First, Somalia had not become a major safe haven for terrorist organizations in spite of the ascendance of political Islamism and the lack of effective government institutions. For example, in 2005 US intelligence-gathering in Somalia produced no evidence of al-Qa'ida bases, or that al-Ittihad al-Islam was operating as one of its subsidiaries. Indeed, it was US support for the ARPCT that helped Islamist extremists to gain ascendancy over more moderate Islamist voices in late 2006. Second, the USA's idea that establishing the institutions of a central state would help to reduce the threat of transnational terrorists using Somalia as a base was flawed, at least in the short-term.

As Menkhaus has persuasively argued, there are six main reasons that explain why terrorist organizations have not been attracted to Somalia during its period as a collapsed state. First, terrorist cells and bases are much more exposed to international counter-terrorist action in zones of state collapse where US Special Forces could violate state sovereignty regularly and with impunity. The US air-strikes in January 2007 and March 2008 against al-Qa'ida suspects in Somalia were a case in point. Second, areas of state collapse tend to be inhospitable and dangerous, particularly for foreigners. Consequently, since few foreigners choose to reside in such environments, foreign terror cells will find it very difficult to blend into the local population and retain the degree of secrecy necessary to conduct their activities. A third factor is the double-edged nature of the lawlessness that accompanies situations of state collapse: while lawlessness reduces the risk of apprehension by law enforcement agencies, it increases the likelihood that terror cells will suffer from more common crimes such as kidnapping, extortion or assassination. As Menkhaus suggests, 'it appears that lawlessness can inhibit rather than facilitate certain types of lawless behavior'.[9] A fourth problem is that any terrorists would be susceptible to betrayal by Somalis looking to ingratiate themselves with the US authorities. Fifth, Somalia represents an environment in which it is very difficult to stay neutral and outside the inter-clan rivalries. Relatively mundane activities such as hiring personnel or renting buildings will inevitably be seen as evidence of taking sides, and once this perception has been established the external actor in question becomes a legitimate target of reprisals by rival clans. Finally, the collapse of the Somali state has left it without the usual array of 'soft' Western targets such as embassies and businesses. As a result, Somalia is more likely to be used as a transit point for *materiel* than to act as a more permanent base for cells. Even terrorists, it would seem, require a degree of political order to conduct their activities. The 'security paradox' identified by Menkhaus is that, at least in the short-term, attempts to resurrect effective state institutions in Somalia may create an environment that is more, not less, conducive to terrorist cells basing themselves in the country.

On the basis of this analysis, Menkhaus concluded that Somalia poses a uniquely difficult challenge for would-be state-builders. First, the success of local adaptation to state collapse could impede state-building efforts by reducing local incentives to support a revived state. Second, state-building will continue to be a conflict-producing enterprise, due to the zero-sum view that most Somali political actors have of control of the state. Third, a major obstacle to state-building is the lack of revenues that a government can secure from taxes; as a consequence, any project will need major external funding. Menkhaus's solution was for outsiders to support the establishment of a 'mediated state' in which the government co-operates with local intermediaries and rival sources of authority to provide core functions of public security and justice. The process by which such mediation is decided can only emerge from genuine dialogue between insiders.

CONCLUSIONS

What conclusions follow from this analysis of state failure in Africa? In response to the first question, 'what is meant by state failure?', it was suggested that most of the contemporary debate is based upon a particular conception of statehood that invokes an ideal formalized at the Treaties of Westphalia in 1648. For a variety of reasons, this ideal has not successfully taken root in many parts of Africa. As a consequence, not only is state failure widespread on the continent, but significant parts of it should be understood as remaining in the early stages of the state formation process and much more turmoil should therefore be expected. In order to understand the contemporary dynamics of this process, analysts should pay closer attention to the configurations of power on the continent and move beyond state-centric and statist approaches. One plausible alternative would be to utilize the neo-Gramscian approach with its focus on the inter-relationships between states, social forces, ideas and world orders. This would provide a set of conceptual tools to help understand the phenomenon of 'neo-patrimonialism without the state'.

In terms of the causes of state failure, contemporary debates distinguish between those states that choose to fail certain segments of their populations, and those that lack the resources effectively to control their territory. In addition, although a wide array of structural and contingent factors continue to generate discussion, collective knowledge about these processes remains limited and unable to predict the tipping points in particular cases. Finally, there is the crucial practical question of responses to state failure in Africa. For outsiders at least, the most common approach has been to resurrect the institutions of state power, usually following Weberian and liberal blueprints. However, as the case of Somalia demonstrates, the processes of state-building and peace-building may sometimes be mutually exclusive enterprises. Moreover, resurrection strategies may, in the short-term at least, make collapsed states a more attractive destination for extremist organizations. In spite of such problems, it is only rarely that international society has agreed to the disintegration of existing states into smaller ones. Sometimes, some insiders have joined the competition to control these new units. In contrast, other insiders have continued to bypass a state system that has consistently failed to meet their basic needs. This suggests that the real solution to state failure in Africa lies in developing political communities that can provide for the needs of their members and gain recognition in wider global politics. How closely these communities will resemble the ideal of Westphalian statehood remains to be seen.

FOOTNOTES

[1] Hill, J. 'Beyond the Other? A postcolonial critique of the failed state thesis' in *African Identities*, Vol. 3, No. 2, pp. 139–140. Abingdon, 2005.

[2] See, for example, Dorff, Robert H. 'Failed States After 9/11: What did we know and what have we learned?' in *International Studies Perspectives*, Vol. 6, No. 1, pp. 20–34. Oxford, 2005. Dorff refers to these two conceptions of failure as 'the ungovernable state' and the 'bad government state'.

[3] The seminal statements of this perspective are R. W. Cox's 'Social Forces, States and World Orders: Beyond International Relations Theory' in *Millennium*, Vol. 10, No. 2 (1981), pp. 126–55; 'Gramsci, Hegemony and International Relations: An essay in method' in *Millennium*, Vol. 12, No. 2 (1983), pp. 162–75; and *Production, Power, and World Order*, New York, Columbia University Press, 1987. See also Barnett, M. 'Authority, intervention and the outer limits of international relations theory' in Callaghy, T., Kassimir, R. and Latham, R. (Eds). *Intervention and Transnationalism in Africa*. Cambridge, Cambridge University Press, 2001.

[4] See 'Current and Projected National Security Threats to the United States', Vice Adm. Lowell E. Jacoby, US Navy, Director, Defense Intelligence Agency. Statement for the Record Senate Select Committee on Intelligence, 24 February 2004. http://www.dia.mil/publicaffairs/Testimonies/statement12.html.

[5] Clapham, C. *et al* (Eds). *Big African States*, p. 1. Johannesburg, Wits University Press, 2006.

[6] Fukuyama, F. *State-Building: Governance and World Order in the 21st Century*, p. 92. Ithaca, NY, Cornell University Press, 2004.

[7] The five categories are: safety and security; rule of law, transparency and corruption; participation and human rights; sustainable economic development; and human development.

[8] Menkhaus, K. 'State Collapse in Somalia: Second Thoughts' in *Review of African Political Economy*, No. 97 (2003), p. 409.

[9] Menkhaus, K., 'Somalia and Somaliland' in Robert I. Rotberg (Ed.). *Battling Terrorism in the Horn of Africa*, p. 40. Washington, DC, Brookings Institution Press, 2005.

BIBLIOGRAPHY

Bates, R. H. *When Things Fell Apart: State Failure in Late-Century Africa*. Cambridge, Cambridge University Press, 2007.

Brookings Institution. *Index of State Weakness in the Developing World*. See http://www.brookings.edu/reports/2008/02_weak_states_index.aspx. Accessed on 6 August 2010.

Call, C. T. 'The Fallacy of the 'Failed State'' in *Third World Quarterly*, Vol. 29, No. 8, pp. 1491–1507. Abingdon, 2008.

Clapham, C. 'Degrees of Statehood' in *Review of International Studies*, Vol. 24, pp. 143–57. Cambridge, 1998.

'The Challenge to the State in a Globalized World' in *Development and Change*, Vol. 33, No. 5, pp. 775–795. Oxford, 2002.

'Terrorism in Africa: Problems of Definition, History and Development' in *South African Journal of International Affairs*, Vol. 10, No. 2, pp. 13–28. Braamfontein, 2003.

Clapham, C., Hersbt J., and Mills G. (Eds). *Big African States*. Johannesburg, Wits University Press, 2006.

Council on Foreign Relations. *More than Humanitarianism: A Strategic US Approach Toward Africa*. New York, Independent Task Force Report No. 56, pp. 20–101, 2006.

Englebert, P., and Tull, D. M. 'Postconflict Reconstruction in Africa: Flawed Ideas about Failed States' in *International Security*, Vol. 32, No. 4, pp. 106–139. Cambridge, MA, 2008.

Evans, G. *The Responsibility to Protect*. Washington, DC, Brookings Institution Press, 2008.

Freedom House, *Freedom in the World 2010*, available at www.freedomhouse.org.

Fukuyama, F. *State-Building: Governance and World Order in the 21st Century*. Ithaca, NY, Cornell University Press, 2004.

Giddens, A. *The Nation State and Violence*. Berkeley, CA, University of California Press, 1987.

Herbst, J. *States and Power in Africa*. Princeton, NJ, Princeton University Press, 2000.

Hobson, J. M. *The State in International Relations*. Cambridge, Cambridge University Press, 2000.

Holm, H. 'Failing Failed States: Who Forgets the Forgotten?' in *Security Dialogue*, Vol. 33, No. 4, pp. 457–471. London, 2002.

Jackson, R. H. *Quasi-States: Sovereignty, International Relations and the Third World*. Cambridge, Cambridge University Press, 1990.

Linklater, A. *The Transformation of Political Community*. Cambridge, Polity, 1998.

Menkhaus, K. 'State Collapse in Somalia: Second Thoughts' in *Review of African Political Economy*, No. 97 (2003), pp. 405–422.

'Somalia and Somaliland' in Robert I. Rotberg (Ed.), *Battling Terrorism in the Horn of Africa*. Washington, DC, Brookings Institution Press, 2005.

'Governance without Government in Somalia: Spoilers, State Building, and the Politics of Coping' in *International Security*, Vol. 31, No. 3, pp. 74–106. Cambridge, MA, 2006/07.

Milliken, J., and Krause, K. 'State Failure, State Collapse, and State Reconstruction: Concepts, Lessons and Strategies' in *Development and Change*, Vol. 33, No. 5, pp. 753–774. Oxford, 2002.

Mo Ibrahim Foundation. *The Ibrahim Index 2009.* See http://www.moibrahimfoundation.org/en/section/the-ibrahim-index. Accessed on 6 August 2010.

Patrick, S. 'Weak States and Global Threats: Fact or Fiction?' in *The Washington Quarterly*, Vol. 29, No. 2, pp. 27–53. Washington, DC, 2006.

'Why Failed States Shouldn't be our Biggest National Security Fear' in *The Washington Post*, 15 April 2011. Washington, DC, 2011.

Prime Minister's Strategy Unit (PMSU). *Investing in Prevention: An International Strategy to Manage Risks of Instability and Improve Crisis Response*. London, PMSU, February 2005.

Raeymaekers, T. *Collapse or Order? Questioning State Collapse in Africa*. Conflict Research Group, Working Paper No. 1, May 2005.

Reno, W. *Warlord Politics and African States*. Boulder, CO, Lynne Rienner Publishers, 1998.

Reus-Smit, C. 'Human rights and the social construction of sovereignty' in *Review of International Studies*, Vol. 27, No. 4, pp. 519–538. Cambridge, 2001.

Rotberg, R. I. (Ed.). *When States Fail: Causes and Consequences*. Princeton, NJ, Princeton University Press, 2004.

Spear, J. 'From Political Economies of War to Political Economies of Peace: The Contribution of DDR after Wars of Predation' in *Contemporary Security Policy*, Vol. 27, No. 1, pp. 168–189. Abingdon, 2006.

Stedman, S. J. 'Spoiler Problems and Peace Processes' in *International Security*, Vol. 22, No. 2 (1997), pp. 5–53.

Taylor, I. *NEPAD: Towards Africa's Development or Another False Start?* Boulder, CO, Lynne Rienner Publishers, 2005.

'Blind Spots in Analyzing Africa's Place in World Politics' in *Global Governance*, Vol. 10 (2004), pp. 411–417.

Teschke, B. *The Myth of 1648: Class, Geopolitics and the Making of Modern International Relations*. London, Verso, 2003.

The National Security Strategy of the United States of America (September 2002).

The National Security Strategy of the United States of America (March 2006).

The National Security Strategy of the United States of America (May 2010).

UN Development Programme. *Human Development Index 2009.* See http://hdr.undp.org/en/reports/global/hdr2009/. Accessed on 6 August 2010.

UN Secretary-General. *Implementing the Responsibility to Protect*. UN doc. A/63/677, 12 January 2009.

Vale, P. *Security and Politics in South Africa: The Regional Dimension*. Boulder, CO, Lynne Rienner Publishers, 2003.

Walter, B. F., and Snyder, J. (Eds). *Civil Wars, Insecurity, and Intervention*. New York, Columbia University Press, 1999.

Williams, P. D. *War and Conflict in Africa*. Cambridge, Polity Press, 2011.

Woods, N. 'The Shifting Politics of Foreign Aid' in *International Affairs*, Vol. 81, No. 2, pp. 393–409. Oxford, 2005.

Zartman, W. I. (Ed.). *Collapsed States: The Disintegration and Restoration of Legitimate Authority*. Boulder, CO, Lynne Rienner Publishers, 1995.

2005 World Summit Outcome. UN General Assembly: 60th Session, A/60/L.1, 20 September 2005.

THE SECURITY SITUATION IN WEST AFRICA

KWESI ANING and FESTUS AUBYN

INTRODUCTION

West Africa undoubtedly remains one of the most volatile or fragile regions on the African continent. The early 1990s and the first years of the 21st century saw many parts of the region embroiled in violent conflicts. Indeed, despite the progress made in consolidating peace and democracy over the past decade, the region continues to be fraught with multiple security challenges which are not only national in scope but cross-cutting and cross-border. Most of the security threats that existed over two decades ago have not yet receded. The region continues to be plagued by military takeovers, poor governance, corruption, undemocratic regimes, high youth unemployment and striking poverty levels. The emergence of new threats, such as the issue of trafficking in narcotics and other organized crime, terrorism, religious extremism, maritime piracy and election violence, as well as the 'traditional' threats, poses serious challenges to regional stability.

Over the past decade the security and governance situation in a number of West African states has deteriorated, highlighting the fragile nature of progress made towards democratic consolidation in the region. In particular, the 'Arab Spring' of revolutionary protests in North Africa and the Middle East during 2011, and the negative impacts of the Libyan conflict, have affected the fragile security environment in the Sahel region and West Africa. For instance, the renewed rebellion by Azawad militants in Mali, fuelled by the return of rebel leaders and by the proliferation of weapons, has contributed to the toppling of the Government of President Gen. (retd) Amadou Toumani Touré. In addition, the worsening impact of climate change and food insecurity in the area is creating a humanitarian crisis. In Guinea-Bissau, the democratic process was halted after the military seized power following the arrest of the Interim President, Raimundo Pereira, and the former Prime Minister and presidential election frontrunner, Carlos Gomes Júnior, on 12 April 2012. There is no doubt that these negative events could jeopardize the fragile peace processes under way, especially in the neighbouring countries which comprise the Mano River Union (MRU)—Côte d'Ivoire, Guinea, Liberia and Sierra Leone—and they could threaten the stability of the entire region if not well managed.

The upsurge of piracy in the Gulf of Guinea and the dangers posed by the rise of both Islamist and Christian religious fundamentalism in the region, as depicted by the terrorist activities of the Islamist sect Boko Haram in Nigeria and of al-Qa'ida in the Islamic Maghreb (AQIM), is also sending foreboding signals to regional stability. Organized crime and the drugs trade are also threatening the existence of states in West Africa with the emergence of what is termed narco-terrorism across the region. Public health issues relating to diseases, particularly HIV/AIDS, tuberculosis and malaria still persist, killing most of the affected persons. What is even more worrisome is the fact that all these challenges are happening at a time when the regional bloc, the Economic Community of West African States (ECOWAS), and the African Union are striving so hard to fine-tune their peace and security mechanisms and policies to address both the emerging and existing threats to the region.

However, it is imperative to note that despite this gloomy picture of the region, there are certainly some grounds for optimism and notable opportunities for the future. There has been a general decrease in intra-state conflicts to such an extent that the MRU region, for example, has now ceased to be the epicentre of regional conflicts. This has encouraged inward investment and a positive economic outlook in the region, with most West African economies defying the global financial and economic crisis to record gross domestic product growth rates of between 6% to 14%[1]. Furthermore, although there have been various examples of election-related violence throughout the region, many political leaders continue to win power through elections and not via the barrel of the gun. During the past two years there have been elections in Togo, Guinea, Nigeria and Côte d'Ivoire, as well as in Senegal and Liberia. These events show encouraging signs that democratic practices are continuing to take root in West Africa, albeit in a somewhat fragile manner. However, with two of the five elections scheduled to be held in the region during 2012 already being truncated by military coups (in Mali and Guinea-Bissau), West Africa seems to be on the edge once again as Ghana and Sierra Leone prepare for elections in the latter part of 2012.

Against the backdrop of these mixed developments, this essay provides a comprehensive assessment of some of the security challenges confronting West Africa, with a special focus on the key recent developments across the region. It identifies the following as the major issues that pose significant threats to regional peace and stability: unconstitutional changes of government; transnational organized crime, including trafficking in arms, drugs and people; terrorism; maritime piracy; governance challenges; and lastly, the impact of climate change and environmental degradation. It is argued that these challenges have the potential to put at risk the very foundations of states in the region and also undermine governance, the rule of law, economic development, stability and peace-building activities. The subsequent sections of this essay examine these security threats in greater detail.

GOVERNANCE CHALLENGES

In reality, the governance landscape in West Africa is seriously under threat. There is a deepening fragility of states in the region, especially in those undergoing reconstruction from years of conflict and civil war. Most government institutions and agencies, such as the security services and judiciary, continue to be ineffective and inefficient, non-functional, corrupt and subject to political manipulation and intimidation, making the state a threat to its own self. In Guinea-Bissau, for example, endemic corruption in the military, judiciary and civilian administration have made these institutions easy prey for outside criminal networks and drugs-traffickers. The country ranked 154 out of 182 countries in Transparency International's 2011 Corruption Perceptions Index.

Governance in the region has not produced the required impact on the long-standing problems of human security, transparency and accountability, endemic corruption, adherence to the rule of law, electoral credibility and economic mismanagement[2]. There is a general feeling of discontent among the public in many countries, leading to armed rebellions by some dissident or disgruntled groups. In particular, bad governance and its resultant political marginalization and unequal distribution of power and resources between groups who are divided by race, religion and ethnicity is forcing people to use violence as a means to obtain their equitable share of the national resources[3]. The threats arising from the deepening economic and political crisis in Nigeria provides a graphic case in point: most of the motivations fuelling the violent activities of Boko Haram, the Movement for the Emancipation of the Niger Delta (MEND), the Niger Delta Boys and other armed groups are just symptoms of years of economic deprivation, corruption, unequal distribution of state resources and political marginalization as a result of bad governance[4].

Another major setback in the pursuit of more representative and legitimate institutions in West Africa is the issue of election-related violence. The impressive strides made in consolidating growing democracies in the region have always been threatened by the prevalence of violence during elections. Recent polls in Côte d'Ivoire, Nigeria, Liberia, Togo and Senegal were all marred by violence, although this did not escalate to full-blown conflict. In most cases the manipulation of deep regional and ethnic cleavages, unresolved land as well as ethnic and chieftancy disputes by political élites, weakness and inadequacies in the electoral system, and an absence of political tolerance and non-compliance of rules of orderly political competition have accounted for this disturbing phenomenon[5]. The fiercely competitive nature of party politics due to a 'winner takes all' culture and the failure of the security forces and judiciary to prosecute and promptly resolve electoral problems, leading to pervasive impunity and a weak rule of law, have also served as a motivating factor for violence during elections.

The consequences of such violence has resulted in deaths and serious injuries to victims; forced migration and the wanton destruction of properties; the incremental defensive militarization of communities, leading to the proliferation of small arms and light weapons (SALWs); and a total breakdown of public law and order[6].

UNCONSTITUTIONAL CHANGES OF GOVERNMENT

West Africa remains one of the most coup-prone regions in Africa, with a long history of military coups dating back to the early 1960s. Beginning in 1963 with the first post-colonial coup in Togo, almost every five-year period has seen a mix of successful and failed coup attempts in the region. In a study entitled 'Coups and Conflicts in West Africa, 1955–2004: Part II, Empirical Findings', Patrick McGowan, for example, opines that 'from independence through to 2004, the sixteen West African States experienced forty-four successful military-led coups, forty-three often bloody failed coups and at least eighty-two coup plots.'[7] With the exception of Senegal and Cape Verde, all the West African states have experienced military coups since their independence. Benin and Nigeria appear to top the list, with six successful coups, followed by Ghana, Sierra Leone and Niger, with five coups each, and then Burkina Faso, which has experienced four.

Although the frequency of military coups declined significantly during the early years of the 21st century, perhaps due to the increasing democratization processes, there has been a resurgence of the phenomenon in recent years. This is posing a serious threat not only to peace and security, but also to the welfare and development of the region. Since 2008 there have been several military coups across the region in countries such as Mauritania, Niger, Guinea, Guinea-Bissau and Mali. However, the most recent occurrences were in Mali and Guinea-Bissau. Broadly put, the incentives that prompt or perhaps drive most of these coups have been some combination of 'greed and grievances'; thus, the capture of state resources or the so-called rectification of wrongs by the military[8]. This notwithstanding, it is also important to locate the causes of these coups within the various domestic complexities and contexts. A cursory look at the causes of the recent coups in Mali and Guinea-Bissau will suffice in this context.

In Mali the poor handling of the Tuareg rebellion in the north was cited as the reason for the overthrow of President Touré in March 2012[9]. The military junta led by Capt. Amadou Sanogo accused the Government of not providing them with enough weapons effectively to respond to the rebellion, which subsequently led to the retreat of the national army from several northern towns. However, although power has been handed back to an interim civilian government led by Mali's parliamentary speaker, Dioncounda Traoré, after the lifting of sanctions by ECOWAS, it seems that all is not well in the country. Mali ranks 175th out of 178 countries, according to the UN Development Programme's 2011 Human Development Index Report, and the political crisis has further aggravated the plague of famine and poverty. The Tuareg secessionist movement, the Mouvement national de libération de l'Azaouad (MNLA), has also seized vast tracts of Mali's desert north and the legendary city of Timbuktu, and has declared an independent 'state of Azawad' (together with other groups like the Ansar el-Din, another Tuareg-led group in the areas who are also seeking to implement an orthodox interpretation of Islamic law in Mali), though without any international recognition. The challenge for the Malian Government now is how to reclaim that part of the country from the MNLA's continued occupancy and to improve the deteriorating economic conditions. This is imperative because the current situation has created a security void, which, if not well addressed, could exacerbate regional instability and the problems of terrorism and smuggling.

In Guinea-Bissau, on the other hand, the recent coup represents another major setback in the country's quest to end its long history of misrule and political instability. Since independence from Portugal in 1974, periods of stability have been rare. Guinea-Bissau remains one of the countries in West Africa where no democratically elected president has ever completed a term in office since independence. According to the leaders of the recent coup, they intervened in the country's democratic process because they discovered a 'secret deal' between the Government and the Angolan Technical Military and Security Mission in Guinea-Bissau (MISSANG-GB), which reportedly aimed to undermine the army[10]. MISSANG-GB has been in the country under the framework of the ECOWAS-Community of Portuguese-Speaking Countries (CPLP) 'roadmap' on Defence and Security Sector Reform. However, its presence has fuelled tensions between the Government and the army, which accused Prime Minister Gomes Júnior of using MISSANG-GB to bolster his own position and weaken its leadership. As a result, the army opposed the mission's presence in the country and has persistently called for its withdrawal. Apparently, what actually motivated the coup was that during the electoral campaign, the Government reaffirmed its determination to keep MISSANG-GB. And with Gomes Júnior securing the largest number of votes in the first round of the presidential election of March 2012, the army feared that MISSANG-GB would be maintained if he were elected, hence its staging of the coup. Currently, a solution to the country's political crisis remains elusive. What is required is a critical examination of the issues that led to the crisis—namely governance deficits and drugs-trafficking—because Guinea-Bissau is the gateway for drugs into West Africa. However, looking at the factors that underlie most coups in the region, until the political economy of states change for the better, the incidence of coups are likely to continue.

THREATS OF TRANSNATIONAL CRIMINALITY

Although transnational organized crime is a universal problem, it appears that the West African region is plagued by what Susan Rice described as 'a particularly insidious version that preyed on societies that were struggling to emerge from years of civil conflicts'[11]. Transnational organized crime is nothing more than the most visible symptom of regional vulnerabilities facilitated by bad governance, the weakness of law enforcement structures and state institutions, endemic corruption, unemployment, poverty and porous borders[12]. And criminal networks and groups from both within and outside the region are exploiting these vulnerabilities to commit a range of crimes. These include trafficking in drugs, people (destined for illegal migration or the sex trade), arms, petroleum and counterfeit goods; advanced fee and internet fraud; the smuggling of cigarettes and natural resources (hardwood and diamonds); illegal manufacture of firearms; armed robbery; and theft[13]. A more worrying trend is that the impact of these criminal activities are putting at risk the very foundation of viable democratic states and undermining governance, the rule of law, economic development, stability and peace-building activities in the region. As the threats from transnational organized crime continue to intensify without any major progress towards addressing them, they have the potential seriously to challenge regional stability by fomenting conflict and undermining development. This section will examine two of these organized crimes: drugs-trafficking and arms proliferation and -trafficking, which are considered to be particularly crucial for the stability of the region.

Drugs-Trafficking

West Africa remains a transit point for drugs-traffickers operating within the region and their collaborators outside the region—the rest of Africa, South America, Europe and Asia. For most of the drugs cartels in South America and Europe especially, West Africa not only represents the shortest, but also the most cost-effective, channel for trafficking illicit drugs to Europe. The threat is spreading so rapidly throughout the region that, according to Antonio Maria Costa, West Africa is turning from the 'Gold Coast into the Coke Coast'[14]. Similarly, the UN Office on Drugs and Crime (UNODC) estimates that at least 50 metric tons of cocaine transits West Africa annually, heading north to European cities, where they have a street value of almost US $2,000m.[15]. Benin, Burkina Faso, Ghana,

Guinea-Bissau, Gambia, Mali, Niger, Sierra Leone, Togo and Guinea are some of the transit countries for cocaine-trafficking. For instance, UNODC's 2011 World Drug Report, stated that the largest seizure of cocaine in Africa in 2008/09 was registered by Ghana (841 kg), followed by Sierra Leone (703 kg), Togo (393 kg, falling to 34 kg in 2009) and Nigeria (365 kg, rising to 392 kg in 2009)[16]. These statistics demonstrate how serious and insidious the drugs-trafficking trade is in the region. The West African transit routes, which feed the European cocaine market, according to UNODC Executive Director Yuriy Fedotov, are now thought to generate some US $900m. a year[17]. In terms of its impact, Guinea-Bissau appears to be the most gravely affected country in the region. UNODC reports estimate that in 2008 the value of cocaine transported through the country was even greater than its entire national income[18]. Guinea-Bissau is fast becoming a strategic link in the transport of illegal narcotics from South America to Europe perhaps due to its geographical location, the high level of corruption and absence of any rule of law, as demonstrated by the recent military coup.

Besides cocaine, West Africa also remains a key source of cannabis in southern Europe and has become an emerging transshipment point for heroin, as well as for precursors of amphetamine-type stimulants[19]. Given the enormous amount of money that is controlled by drugs-traffickers, they are able to subvert legitimate state institutions, and corrupt high-level government and public officials and law enforcement agencies. The accusation by the US Administration in April 2010 that two high-level military officials in Guinea-Bissau—former Navy Chief of Staff Rear Adm. José Américo Bubo Na Tchuto and Air Force Chief of Staff Ibraima Papá Camara—were involved in drugs running is a testimony to this worrisome situation[20]. A more recent case in point was the scandal that involved the police and judiciary in Ghana over the trial of Nana Ama Martin, a suspect who was arrested with 1,020 g of cocaine, only for the cocaine mysteriously to turn into baking powder[21]. Such cases undermine the authority and effectiveness of state institutions and erode the rule of law. Drugs barons are also supporting rival political parties and candidates in national elections with a view to influencing the outcome of elections for personal gain[22]. There has also been an increase in the acts of violence, conflicts and terrorist activities that are being fuelled by drugs-trafficking and organized crime. This has a huge potential for disrupting the security and socio-economic stability of states in the region and the issue needs to be addressed before it takes root and poses an even greater danger.

Small Arms Proliferation and Trafficking

Arms-trafficking and the resultant arms proliferation remains one of West Africa's major security problems. There has been an influx of small arms and light weapons (SALWs) in the region due to the numerous armed conflicts that have beset countries such as Liberia, Sierra Leone, Côte d'Ivoire, Guinea, Guinea-Bissau and Nigeria over the past few decades[23]. SALWs remain the primary weapons of intra- and inter-communal feuds, local wars, armed insurrections and rebel activities, election violence and terrorism throughout West Africa in particular and in Africa as a whole[24]. Throughout the region SALWs are in the hands of states and non-state actors such as ethnic militia groups, private security companies, arms-smugglers, criminal gangs, bandits, mercenaries and vigilantes[25]. These non-state actors often act with impunity, using SALWs to wage wars and terrorize civilian populations, committing crimes, armed robberies and human rights abuses. The MRU area, which used to be the epicentre of conflict in West Africa, seems to be serving as the source of, and destination for, illicit arms in the region[26]. Again, the internal governance challenges of Nigeria—as manifested in the rising number of non-state armed groups such as Boko Haram, MEND, the Fulani herdsmen, Niger Delta Boys and kidnappers—has made the country a ready market for illicit arms proliferation and a major conduit for arms-smuggling to West Africa. It is estimated that armed conflicts cost Africa some US $18,000m. annually, with 60%–90% of deaths in these conflicts being traced to the 100m. SALWs in circulation on the continent[27]. West Africa alone accounts for about 8m. of the 100m. arms in circulation, with 40% of these arms in the hands of civilians[28]. In Ghana, for example, a study conducted by the Ghana National Commission on Small Arms in 2004 indicated that between 120,000 and 400,000 small arms were in circulation. Of this number, only 95,000 were registered, leaving a significant number of illicit guns, in circulation and over 75,000 illegally locally manufactured weapons. This presents a major concern because Ghana is preparing for elections in December 2012, and the uncontrolled movement of these arms could be used by disgruntled elements to foment violence.

More importantly, the 'Arab Spring' and the fallout from the Libyan crisis have added a dangerous element to the situation, by increasing the inflow of unspecified and unquantifiable numbers of arms and ammunition from the Libyan arsenal and outside the region[29]. The power crisis in Mali caused partly by the renewed Tuareg rebellion following the return of hundreds of armed nomadic Tuareg mercenaries from Libya illustrates this perilous condition. The effects of SALWs proliferation in the region are multiple but interconnected. They include: causing the deaths of millions of citizens and thwarting developmental efforts; obstructing humanitarian relief and development programmes; causing population displacement; exacerbating gender-based violence; and undermining peace initiatives.

TERRORISM

Security in West Africa and especially the Sahel region is becoming very tenuous, with the increasing prevalence of terrorist activities by groups such as AQIM and Boko Haram in northern Nigeria. The activities of terrorist groups have intensified following the 'Arab Spring' and the Libyan crisis, which have also unfortunately led to an influx of illegal weapons into the region. In addition, the consequences of the Libyan conflict have also led to the establishment of two new terrorist groups, namely the Ansar el-Din and the Mouvement Unicité et Jihad en Afrique de l'Ouest, both jihadist groups which are involved in the kidnapping of foreign workers in the Sahel[30].

In West Africa AQIM is the most well-known and verifiable terrorist group whose operations threaten the stability of the region. As an organization which originated in Algeria, its operations have now spread across Mali, Mauritania and Niger, exploiting the structural weaknesses of these states, the porous borders and the socio-economic discontent of the respective populations[31]. Since 2007, when AQIM changed its name from the Groupe salafiste pour la prédication et le combat to reflect its alliance with al-Qa'ida, it has undertaken opportunistic kidnappings of foreign tourists and workers of non-governmental organizations in the Sahel. In September 2010, for example, the group kidnapped seven employees and family members from the compound of the French multinational nuclear services firm Areva in Arlit, Niger. Two French nationals were also kidnapped in January 2011 from a restaurant in Niamey, Niger, and were later killed after a failed rescue attempt near the Malian border. Individual attacks against local security outposts have also been recorded in Algeria, Mauritania and Niger. Besides the kidnappings, it is believed that AQIM is working with drugs cartels and other criminal networks in the region to smuggle drugs, arms and other contraband goods to augment their resources and fund their ongoing operations. Recent reports also indicate that AQIM is now well integrated with local Sahelian communities in an effort to deepen its roots, grow its resource base and develop its operational strength. Thus, the group has taken advantage of the inability of governments in the Sahelian region to exercise effective control over their peripheral territory to advance its interests[32]. According to a recent report by a UN inter-agency assessment mission dispatched to the Sahel in December 2011, for instance, the humanitarian vacuum created by the food insecurity in the Sahelian region is now being filled by: 'AQIM and other criminal elements who are reportedly providing services and humanitarian assistance in remote areas. This situation has in turn enabled the terrorist group to 'develop recruitment and local support networks for gathering information, supplying arms and ammunition, and other logistics''[33]

With the exception of AQIM, terrorism in West Africa has manifested itself as a local phenomenon. The increased incidence of terrorism in Nigeria by Boko Haram is a vivid case in point. The group has been behind several bomb attacks in military and police installations and has also claimed responsibility for similar attacks in some northern states of Nigeria such as Borno, Kaduna, Kano and Plateau, killing hundreds of people[34]. There have also been violent clashes between the group and the security forces, with both parties sustaining severe casualties and deaths[35]. One of Boko Haram's fiercest attacks was a car bombing of the UN building in Abuja, which killed 18 people in August 2011. This exposed the operational constraints of the Nigerian security services, further raising questions regarding the ability of the Government to respond to the terrorist threat. Despite the authorities' heavy-handed response to the Islamist insurgency, the crisis continues to worsen, with many sporadic attacks causing more deaths and the destruction of property. The impact of Boko Haram's violent activities has created regional, ethnic and religious tensions between the Muslims in the north and the Christians in the south of the country.

It has been discovered that Boko Haram has established links with AQIM and that some of its members have even received training in AQIM camps in Mali. Seven members of the group were reportedly arrested while crossing Niger on their way to Mali in possession of documentation on the manufacturing of explosives, propaganda leaflets, and names and contact details of AQIM members[36]. The fact is that such alliances have the potential to further destabilize the region and reverse the democratic and peace-building achievements attained so far. Although many analyses of the underlying cause of the insurgency traces it to religious fundamentalism and fanaticism, some believe that it goes beyond that to include grievances over persistent government corruption and mismanagement, economic injustice and poverty[37]. Despite the fact that Boko Haram's activities are locally based and have not yet spread to other parts of West Africa, anything that happens to Nigeria (as the regional hegemon) will have serious security implications for the entire region. To that effect, it is important not to view the violent activities of Boko Haram as a national problem, but rather as a region-wide security crisis.

MARITIME PIRACY AND ARMED ROBBERY

The Gulf of Guinea is fast becoming a potential hotspot for piracy and armed robbery linked to illegal fishing, oil bunkering and trafficking in arms, narcotics and people due to the weak enforcement capabilities of states in the region. Although it has not reached the scale of that off the coast of Somalia or in the Gulf of Aden, it appears to be increasing, since the high-value assets such as oil reserves, cocoa and metals, which pirates target, are copious[38]. Piracy and armed robbery are thus on the rise and have become more systematic. The pirates have become more violent, resorting to sophisticated modes of operation and utilizing heavy weapons. In fact, the number of recent attacks and the damage they have caused has reached worrisome proportions and threatens regional stability as well as disrupting shipping and investment.

At the beginning of 2012 alone, 10 reports were received by the International Chamber of Commerce from Nigeria, equalling the number reported in the country for the whole of 2011[39]. Primarily, most of the oil-producing countries like Nigeria have been the target due to their high-value petroleum assets, as have countries like Benin, which rely extensively on their ports for national revenue. For example, Nigeria recorded the majority of incidents of piracy (54%) in West Africa between 2001 and 2008, according to the International Maritime Bureau[40]. The impacts of piracy are negatively affecting development, security, trade and other economic activities in the region. In Benin, for instance, fees raised from the port of Cotonou, Benin, alone generate 80% of income for the national budget[41]. A report by the UN Security Council in February 2012 also estimates that piracy has resulted in a current annual loss of US $2,000m. in revenue to West African economies, and that the number of ships docking at Cotonou has declined by 70% as a result of the attacks[42]. More significantly, the impetus behind piracy has been some combination of political and economic opportunism by existing criminal gangs in Nigeria's restive Niger Delta region, such as MEND[43]. The proliferation of arms, and high levels of youth unemployment and poverty is also contributing to this phenomenon in the Gulf of Guinea. As countries such as Liberia, Sierra Leone and Ghana discover large quantities of offshore oil resources, attacks on oil rigs and commercial vessels by pirates is bound to increase if the territorial waters are not vigorously and effectively policed by West African naval forces.

IMPACT OF CLIMATE CHANGE AND ENVIRONMENTAL DEGRADATION

The impact of climate change and other natural disasters such as droughts and flooding is causing environmental degradation leading to high poverty levels and the displacement of millions of people across the region. Countries in the Sahel regions such as Mauritania, Mali, Niger and Burkina Faso appear to be the hardest hit, with growing food insecurity rooted in drought, high food prices and conflict. The influx of an estimated 420,000 returnees from Libya to Niger, Mali, Chad and Mauritania, according to the UN, has further exacerbated the situation[44]. According to CARE International, 15.6m. people are currently at risk from the food crisis in the Sahel region of West Africa, including 1m. children who are at risk of severe malnutrition[45]. This has created a humanitarian crisis and had a negative impact on the capacity of governments, humanitarian agencies and non-governmental organizations working in the area.

Since 2005 the effects of conflict in the Sahel region and natural factors (rainfall levels have decreased and become erratic or less predictable in the region, causing poor food harvests and water shortages) have resulted in high livestock mortality rates and poor agricultural yields, leading to increased food prices of staple food such as maize, millet and sorghum. In Mali alone, more than 107,000 people have been displaced and 128,000 others have sought refuge in neighbouring countries as a result of the Tuareg rebellion in the northern cities of Gao, Kidal and Timbuktu, further exacerbating the precarious food security of host communities. In a related report, Oxfam International also indicated that over 5.4m. people (35% of the population) in Niger, 2m. in Burkina Faso and 700,000 people (over 25% of the population) in Mauritania are estimated to be vulnerable to food insecurity. This problem has the potential to trigger violent conflict, particularly between nomads and farmers, and also between locals and migrants over scarce arable lands, forest, grazing lands and water resources[46].

Another major challenge is the environmental damage caused by oil extraction and production. As a result of oil exploration, people's farmlands are being acquired by governments, destroying the livelihoods of communities in oil production areas. In Ghana, for instance, people's farmlands have been bought by oil companies and the Government for the establishment of a gas-processing plant and other industries related to the production in the Jomoro District of the Western region. This is causing displacement of human settlement and exposing communities to environmental dangers[47]. Since Ghana is an emerging oil-producer, the threats posed by a few disgruntled individuals taking up arms and causing upset in the country cannot be ruled out in the long term. Moreover, the environmental pollution caused by gas-flaring, ground oil waste dumping and oil spills is seriously affecting the inhabitants of oil-producing areas such as the Niger Delta region in Nigeria. This is deepening poverty and causing the destruction of wildlife and biodiversity, loss of fertile soil, pollution of air and drinking water, degradation of farmland and damage to aquatic ecosystems, and serious health problems in surrounding villages and towns[48].

CONCLUSION

There has been some remarkable progress made towards consolidating peace and democracy in West Africa over the past decade. However, the region continues to be plagued by both old and new threats which have the propensity to reverse the region's peace-building advances and democratic gains.

The issues of governance, unconstitutional changes of government, transnational criminality including drugs- and arms-trafficking, terrorism, piracy and armed robbery in the Gulf of Guinea, and the impact of climate change and environmental degradation have been identified in this essay as some of the major threats that have the potential to destabilize the region. These challenges have emerged as a result of regional vulnerabilities such as bad governance, a weakness of law enforcement structures and state institutions, endemic corruption, unemployment, poverty and porous borders. The impact of the 'Arab Spring' and the crisis in Libya has also worsened the already precarious situation by causing a humanitarian crisis in the Sahel region, armed rebellion in northern Mali and the proliferation of SALWs in the region. The impacts of all these threats are putting at risk the very foundation of viable democratic states and undermining governance, the rule of law, economic development, stability and peace-building activities in the region. With the deepening fragility of states and the fact that most of these threats remain largely unresolved, it is argued that the potential for instability could continue to grow and seriously challenge West Africa's long-term stability.

FOOTNOTES

[1] Keynote address by Victor Gbeho, former ECOWAS President, on 'The West African Region: Between Peace Dividends and the Road to Recovery' at the Kofi Annan International Peacekeeping Training Centre, Accra, Ghana, on 9–11 January 2012.

[2] Economic Commission for Africa. 'Perspectives on Governance in West Africa: Recommendations and Plan of Actions', the fourth African Development Forum, 2004.

[3] UUN Security Council, 'Emerging Security Threats in West Africa' in Research Report No. 1, May 2011.

[4] Amnesty International. 'Killing at Will: Extrajudicial Executions and Unlawful Killings by the Police in Nigeria', Amnesty International Publications, December 2009; Human Rights Watch. 'Nigeria Country Summary', in January 2012 Report.

[5] Omotola, S. 'Explaining Electoral Violence in Africa's New Democracies', in *African Journal of Conflict Resolution*, Vol. 10, No. 3, pp. 51–73, 2010; Hounkpe, M., and Gueye, A. B. *The Role of Security Forces in the Electoral Process: The Case of Six West African Countries*, Lagos, Friedrich-Ebert-Stiftung, 2010.

[6] Adejumobi, S. 'Elections in Africa: A Fading Shadow of Democracy?', in *International Political Science Review*, Vol. 21. No. 1, 2000.

[7] McGowan, P. J. 'Coups and Conflicts in West Africa, 1955–2004: Part II, Empirical Findings', in *Armed Forces and Society*, Vol. 32, No. 2, p. 234, 2006. This number has increased with the recent coups in Mauritania, Niger, Mali, Guinea and Guinea-Bissau.

[8] For more information see Collier, P., and Hoeffler, A. 'Coup Traps: Why does Africa have so many Coups d'Etat?' Centre for the Study of African Economies, Department of Economics, University of Oxford, 2005 (Preliminary Draft Paper).

[9] The rebellion begun when hundreds of armed nomadic Tuareg mercenaries came back to their home base in northern Mali after the death of Libyan leader Col Muammar al-Qaddafi. These mercenaries joined the MNLA on their return and began what they considered the fourth Tuareg rebellion, resuming their struggle of the past decades to establish the State of Azawad that would cover all of northern Mali down to the Niger river. See Deschamps-Laporte, L. 'Jihadism and Tuareg nationalism are not the same'. Available at: http://www.pambazuka.org/en/category/features/81475/print, accessed 10 May 2012.

[10] For more information see the report of the Chairperson of the AU Commission, Jean Ping, on the Situations in Guinea Bissau, Mali and between the Sudan and South Sudan, delivered to the AU Peace and Security Council on April 24 2012; Clottey, P. 'ECOWAS to Meet Guinea Bissau Coup Leaders', http://www.voanews.com, accessed May 7 2012.

[11] See 'Security Council Presidential Statement Calls for System-Wide UN Action to Combat Transnational Crime — Drug Trafficking, Piracy, Terrorism in West Africa, Sahel', 6,717th Meeting of the UN Security Council, 21 February 2012.

[12] UNODC, *Transnational Organized Crime in the West African Region*. Vienna, UNODC, 2005.

[13] Aning, K. 'Organized Crime in West Africa: Options for EU Engagement'. International IDEA, 2009; Aning, K. 'Africa: Confronting Complex Threats' Coping with Crises Working Paper Series, February 2007; UNODC, *Transnational Trafficking and the Rule of Law in West Africa: A Threat Assessment*. Vienna, UNODC, 2009.

[14] See http://www.un.org/en/events/tenstories/08/westafrica.shtml, accessed 10 May 2012.

[15] See 'West Africa Coast Initiative' http://www.unodc.org/westand-centralafrica/en/west-africa-coast-initiative.html, accessed 6 May 2012.

[16] UNODC, *World Drug Report 2011*. Vienna, UNODC, 2011.

[17] See 'Threats to Peace and Security in West Africa and the Sahel Region'. Available at: http://www.securitycouncilreport.org, accessed 16 May 2012.

[18] UN Security Council, 2011, op. cit.

[19] Cockayne, J. and Williams, P. 'The Invisible Tide: Towards an International Strategy to Deal with Drug Trafficking through West Africa'. IPI policy papers, 14 October 2009.

[20] The USA imposed financial sanctions on them and proscribed US citizens from doing business with them under the Foreign Narcotics Kingpin Designation Act. See UN Security Council, 'Emerging Security Threats in West Africa' in Research Report No. 1, May 2011.

[21] The suspect was arrested on 28 August 2008 with the alleged cocaine slabs, but was granted bail after the substance had been re-tested and proven to be cocaine on 27 September 2011. On 28 September, when the Defence Attorney called for another re-testing of the substance to confirm it, the next test revealed that the substance was sodium bicarbonate and not cocaine contrary to initial results. See 'Court erred in granting 'missing' cocaine suspect bail – Police' http://www.citifmonline.com/index.php?id=1.700823, accessed 10 May 2012; see also http://www.etvghana.com/index.php/primenews-articles/688-police-and-nacob-raise-red-flags-in-missing-cocaine-saga, accessed 9 May 2012.

[22] Souaré, 2010, op. cit; WANEP, 'Drug Trafficking: An Alarming Human Security Threat', Warn Policy Brief, September 12, 2007; See also Aning, K. 'Understanding the Intersection of Drugs, Politics and Crime in West Africa: An Interpretive Analysis'. GCST Policy Brief Series No. 6 April 2010.

[23] For more information see Darkwa, L. 'The Challenge of Sub-regional Security in West Africa: the case of 2006 ECOWAS Convention on Small and Light Weapons'. Nordiska AfrikaInstitutet, Uppsala, Discussion Paper 69, 2011; UNODC, 2009, op cit.

[24] For more information see Florquin, N., and Berman, E. (Eds.). *Armed and Aimless: Armed Groups, Guns, And Human Security In The ECOWAS Region*. Geneva, Small Arms Survey, 2005; Musah, A., and Fayemi, K. (Eds). *Mercenaries: An African Security Dilemma*. London, Pluto Press, 2000.

[25] Ebo. A., with Mazal, L. 'Small Arms Control in West Africa', International Alert, October 2003; Stohl, R. 'The Legacy of Illicit Small Arms: Devastation in West Africa', US Congressional Human Rights Caucus, Briefing on Small Arms in West Africa, May 20, 2004; Hutchful, E. *'African States and the Challenge of National Security in the Post-Cold War Era' in Ghana in Search of National Security Policy*. Accra, LECIA, 2007.

[26] *ibid*.

[27] Baffour Dokyi Amoa, 'The Role of Small Arms in African Civil Wars' http://www.pambazuka.org, accessed 14 May 2012.

[28] Sarjoh Bah, A., and Aning, K. 'ECOWAS and Conflict Prevention in West Africa', Centre on International Cooperation, New York University, 2008.

[29] See 'Threats to Peace and Security in West Africa and the Sahel Region' http://www.securitycouncilreport.org, accessed 16 May 2012.

[30] *ibid*.

[31] Obi, C. I. 'Terrorism in West Africa: Real, Emerging Or Imagined Threats?', in *African Security Review* 15.3, 89 (2006) Institute for Security Studies.

[32] Goita, M. 'West Africa Growing Terrorist Threat: Confronting AQIM's Sahelian Strategy', in *Africa Security Brief*, February 2011.

[33] See 'Threats to Peace and Security in West Africa and the Sahel Region' http://www.securitycouncilreport.org, accessed 16 May 2012.

[34] Campbell, J. 'To Battle Nigeria's Boko Haram, Put Down Your Guns: How to Undermine the Growing Islamist Threat', in *Foreign Affairs*, September 9, 2011.

[35] Amnesty International, 'Killing at Will: Extrajudicial Executions and Unlawful Killings by the Police in Nigeria', Amnesty International Publication, December 2009; Human Rights Watch, 'Nigeria Country Summary', January 2012 Report.

[36] See 'Threats to Peace and Security in West Africa and the Sahel Region', http://www.securitycouncilreport.org, accessed 16 May 2012.

[37] Aning, K., and Aubyn, F. 'Confronting the Threats of Boko Haram Crises in Northern Nigeria: Exploring Options for a Peaceful

Settlement' (unpublished paper); Danjibo, N. D., 'Islamic Fundamentalism and Sectarian Violence: The 'Maitatsine' and 'Boko Haram' Crises in Northern Nigeria', Paper presented at the IFRA Conference on Conflict And Violence in Nigeria, 2009.

[38] See 'Supply vessels attacked off Nigeria as piracy threat grows' http://www.defenceweb.co.za, accessed 15 May 2012.

[39] UN News Centre, 'Gulf of Guinea needs regional anti-piracy strategy, UN official stresses' http://www.un.org/apps/news/story.asp?NewsID=41390&Cr=gulf+of+guinea&Cr1, accessed 8 May 2011.

[40] International Maritime Organisation, *Reports of Acts of Piracy and Armed Robbery Against Ships: Annual Report - 2009*; UN Security Council, 'Emerging Security Threats in West Africa', in Research Report No. 1 May 2011.

[41] See http://www.un.org/News/Press/docs/2012/sc10558.doc.htm, accessed 12 May 2012.

[42] See 'Threats to Peace and Security in West Africa and the Sahel Region' http://www.securitycouncilreport.org, accessed 16 May 2012.

[43] See http://www.csmonitor.com, accessed 10 May 2012.

[44] See http://www.un.org/News/Press/docs/2012/sc10533.doc.htm, accessed 16 May 2012.

[45] See http://www.care.org/emergency/niger-sahel-west-africa-food-crisis-humanitarian-aid/index.asp#, accessed May 12 2012; see also 'Food Crises in Sahel' http://www.oxfam.org/en/sahel, accessed 10 May 2012.

[46] For more information see Atta-Asamoah, A., and Aning, K. 'Demography, Environment and Conflict in West Africa', Kofi Annan International Peacekeeping Training Centre occasional paper; Brown, O., and Crawford, A. 'Assessing the Security Implications of Climate Change for West Africa: Country Case Studies of Ghana and Burkina Faso', International Institute of Sustainable Development, 2008.

[47] See 'Gas Flaring Imminent' http://www.dailyguideghana.com/?p=18048, accessed 6 May 2012.

[48] See 'Oil Production and Environmental Damage' http://africaoil.-ning.com, accessed 7 May 2012.

THE ONGOING DEVELOPMENT OF CHINESE TIES WITH SUB-SAHARAN AFRICA

IAN TAYLOR

The People's Republic of China's trade with Africa grew rapidly in 2011, reaching US $166,300m., an increase of 31% on 2010's figure of $126,900m. and 8.4% higher than the overall growth rate of China's foreign trade. This upward trend was a continuation of the recovery in trade volume between China and Africa that had declined after the onset of the global economic crisis in the late 2000s. While China experienced its slowest pace in economic growth in three years in 2011, with growth falling below 9% for the first time since 2001, trade with Africa continued apace. In fact, between 2001 and 2010 bilateral trade between China and Africa grew at an average annual rate of 28%. With a gross domestic product (GDP) valued at approximately $7,000,000m. and growing, China is projected to become the world's largest economy (by nominal GDP) by 2017. China is currently Africa's largest bilateral trading partner and forecasts suggest that by 2015 Sino-African trade may rise to $400,000m. per year. Currently, China's largest trade partners in Africa are, in descending order, South Africa, Angola, Sudan, Nigeria and Egypt.

One way this is articulated is through the notion of China as a 'responsible great power', a state that supports and operates according to international norms and within multilateral institutions. This behaviour dovetails with the officially proposed concept, initially aired in 2003, of China's 'peaceful rise'. As some observers have focused on the inevitability of China's 'rise', rather than the 'peaceful' part of the slogan, the concept is now cast as China's 'peaceful development', as a means of reassuring other countries of Beijing's intentions. In fact, Beijing's policy-makers seem to be going out of their way not to alarm the world about China's rise, with President Hu Jintao's stated policy now merely to build a 'moderately prosperous society in all respects' along technocratic lines using the Scientific Outlook on Development. The developing world has long been an area where Beijing's foreign policy has been pursued actively, using the development of common interests with the South to raise China's global stature and increase Beijing's bargaining leverage with the USA. Africa can be said to be central to Beijing's quest to be taken seriously.

HISTORICAL CONTEXT

The links between China and Africa in the contemporary period trace their essential roots to three occurrences: the crisis in China's international relations after the Tiananmen Square incident on 4 June 1989; the incredible expansion of the Chinese economy in the 1990s and 2000s; and the desire to take advantage of numerical support in the UN granted by, in part, African states, to prevent hostile votes against China *vis-à-vis* its human rights record and to ensure that the Republic of China (Taiwan) remains an unrecognized international outcast. Prior to this period, Africa's importance in Beijing's foreign policy had declined during the 1980s as China's Socialist Modernization project appealed for massive foreign investment and technology deemed unavailable from Africa.

In addition, Chinese tensions with both the USA and the USSR lessened throughout the 1980s, further marginalizing Africa's importance in China's view. However, post-Tiananmen Square China 'rediscovered' Africa and this renewed interest has been built on every year by the huge growth in Chinese firms and corporations—as well as by ordinary Chinese entrepreneurs—who have embarked upon a concerted drive to discover markets and commercial opportunities overseas. The twin motivations of diplomacy and economics now firmly drive China's linkages with the African continent. Both of these impulses help further China's overall political ambition: to be taken seriously as a 'responsible power' and for China to be restored to its 'rightful place'. The developing world—Africa included—plays a role in this.

Chinese foreign policy is linked to the key domestic concern of the Chinese Communist Party (CCP), namely promoting China's economic development while maintaining political and social stability. This reflects a process whereby the CCP has changed from being a revolutionary party grounded in class struggle and mass mobilization to a ruling party with its attendant focus on order and security. All Chinese foreign policy is aimed at securing the country's economic development and territorial integrity. In addition, the CCP hopes to strengthen its legitimacy through a sophisticated foreign policy, putting China on the world stage as an influential player and creating stability for the nation. Domestically, the post-Mao Chinese state has been arguably based on an unwritten social contract between the party and the people, where the people do not compete with the party for political power as long as the party looks after their economic fortunes. Externally, foreign policy that sustains an international environment supportive of economic growth and stability in China serves these objectives.

RELATIONS WITH AFRICA

Although maintaining good links with Washington is central to Chinese foreign policy, Beijing has often expressed concern about the rise of an unchallenged hegemon, namely the USA. China has maintained the position that in the current international system it is imperative that China and the developing world support each other and work together to prevent over-domination by this new hegemon. Asserting that respect for each other's affairs and non-interference should be the basis of any new international order is fundamental to this stance. Today, Sino-African unity remains a focal point: '[China and Africa] support each other in international affairs, especially on major issues such as human rights, safeguard the legitimate rights of developing countries and make efforts to promote the establishment of a new just and rational international political and economic order'.[1]

Africa has been diplomatically important for China since the late 1950s, when Chinese diplomacy began to emerge from the fallout of the Korean War and the shadow of the Soviet Union. During the early period of Sino-African interaction, China's role was ideologically motivated and included support for national liberation movements as well as direct state-to-state aid, most noticeably with Tanzania. Indeed, by the mid-1970s China had a greater amount of aid projects in Africa than the USA. However, as the Socialist Modernization programme accelerated under Deng Xiaoping from the late 1970s onwards, there was a concomitant reduction of Chinese interest in the continent. This can in part be explained by the fact that Africa's failure to develop its economies efficiently and to open up to the international market militated against Chinese policy aims, and the increasingly extraneous role the continent played in global (superpower) geopolitics resulted in a halt to closer Chinese involvement. Essentially, Beijing not only viewed Africa as largely immaterial in its quest for modernization, but also saw that the rationale behind its support for anti-Soviet elements in the continent was no longer valid.

However, one event and two processes—one within Africa and the other within China—came together to stimulate the current close involvement of Chinese actors in Africa. First, the events of 4 June 1989 in and around Tiananmen Square meant that Beijing underwent a major re-evaluation of its foreign policy towards the developing world. While Tiananmen Square resulted in a crisis (albeit temporary) in China's relations with the West, Africa's reaction was far more muted, if not openly supportive. As the then Chinese Minister of Foreign Affairs, Qian Qichen, stated in his memoirs, "it was...our African friends who stood by us and extended a helping hand in the difficult times following the political turmoil in Beijing, when

Western countries imposed sanctions on China'. In fact, the events of June 1989 did not affect Chinese relations with the developing world as it did with the Western world. What changed was Beijing's attitude towards the developing world countries, which turned from one of benign neglect to one of renewed emphasis.

As a result, the developing world was elevated in Chinese thinking to become a cornerstone of Beijing's foreign policy. Post-1989 the 1970s rhetoric of China being an 'all-weather friend' of Africa was redeployed with vigour, and this stance has been maintained to the present day. This posture was a reaffirmation of the Five Principles of Peaceful Co-existence, formulated in 1954, and set out the guidelines for Beijing's foreign policy and its relations with other countries. These Five Principles were namely: mutual respect for each other's territorial integrity; non-aggression; non-interference in each other's internal affairs; equality and mutual benefit; and peaceful co-existence. Thus Chinese policy-makers have returned to their roots in reasserting what is in fact an old theme in Beijing's foreign policy.

The first of the two macroprocesses occurred as Africa's economic reform programmes gained momentum in the 1990s, and Beijing began to believe that the macroeconomic situation in Africa was taking a favourable turn with resultant opportunities for Chinese commerce. This analysis was based on the belief that African countries had adopted a set of active measures to push forward the pace of privatization, and to open up international trade and reform based on bilateral and multilateral trade agreements. An implicit proposition was that African economies had begun to copy China in its open-door policy.

Beijing has sought to take advantage of these developments in Africa and has officially encouraged joint ventures and economic co-operation at multiple levels. This is reinforced by the belief held by many Chinese manufacturers and entrepreneurs that the types of goods (household appliances, garments and other domestic products) that China produces and markets have immense potential in Africa, where the economy is not yet as developed as in Western nations and where the consumers are perceived to be more receptive to the type of inexpensive products that Chinese manufacturers typically produce. That the domestic markets of many African countries are relatively small and that there is relatively little competition means that market share can be large from the beginning of operations. Additionally, Africa is perceived by both the Chinese Government and by Chinese companies to be rich in natural resources, particularly in crude petroleum, non-ferrous metals and fisheries.

The above then links up with the second macroprocess: namely that China's rapidly developing economy in itself propels Sino-African trade. China's growth in recent years has been extraordinary; however, what is often overlooked in discussions of Sino-African ties is that the significance of China to Africa has to be appreciated in terms of Beijing's own development trajectory. China's real economic growth—on average just under 9% per year for the last 30 years—has been grounded in an average annual growth in exports of over 17%. This commerce is based on Chinese factories processing and assembling parts and materials which originate from outside China. China's leadership is dependent on this high-speed growth continuing as, with the effective abandonment of Marxist ideology, the only de facto reason that legitimates continuing CCP rule is economic growth. However, mounting saturation of China's existing export markets, as well as a rapid increase in the price of imported raw materials into China (due in the main to Chinese demand increasing prices), makes Africa more and more important to China's economy. Indeed, as the growth in the value of Chinese exports decelerates, Beijing has to maintain the growth of its economy through adding more Chinese 'content' to its exports. Discovering sources of raw materials is integral to this strategy and requirement, and is where Africa fits squarely into Chinese foreign policy and domestic necessities. Indeed, it might be avowed that the importance of Africa to China's own development cannot be overstated. Consequently, although maintaining good links with Washington is fundamental to Chinese foreign policy, Africa is becoming ever more important.

With regard to Sino-African relations, this feeds into the long-held stance by Beijing that it is the leader of the developing world. Typically, when in South Africa in early 2007, Hu Jintao remarked that while 'Africa is the continent with the largest number of developing countries, China is the biggest developing country'. This is a familiar theme in Sino-African diplomacy, as is the refrain that it was Western powers, not China, who colonized Africa and exploited the continent's resources. Similarly, as Qian Qichen stated, 'as developing regions that. . .once suffered the oppression and exploitation of imperialism and colonialism, China and the African countries. . .easily understand each other's pursuit of independence and freedom and. . .have a natural feeling of intimacy'. Such sentiments are repeatedly utilized by Beijing to argue that there are in fact no conflicts of interest between China and African countries, something that is obviously not entirely accurate.

Paradoxically, as China's leadership increasingly integrates itself into the global economy and starts tentatively to play by essentially Western rules, as exemplified by Beijing's membership of the World Trade Organization, it has sought to strengthen political ties with various African countries, arguably as, in part, a defensive mechanism to be deployed against these very same impulses if and when they threaten influential domestic interests. This irony reflects the overall tension in China's diplomatic policy of pursuing both engagement and a certain distant coolness *vis-à-vis* the global order. This, and the notion that China seeks to 'restore' its 'rightful place' in world politics by being seen as some sort of leader of the developing world, while casting itself as a 'responsible power', may be seen as important rationales influencing broader foreign policy goals.

Although it is true that there is an official Africa policy issued by Beijing, there are in fact many Chinas and equally, many Africas. Disaggregating this complex milieu is essential when talking of Sino-African relations or what 'China' is doing in 'Africa'. Because of this reality, the notion that China or the Chinese are 'colonizing' Africa—an allegation levelled both by Western and African commentators—is misleading. This is because there is an implicit assumption within some accounts of Chinese foreign policy that there exists an overarching grand strategy, centred in Beijing. It is, at best, acceptable to state that there are certain aspirations focused on quite specific facets of Sino-African ties. The most obvious example would be in Chinese state-owned oil corporations and their investments in African resource industries. This is clearly connected to China's energy needs and the domestic dynamics associated with China's rise. But even here there are rivalries and competitions between different energy companies, and these may or may not coincide with the interests of other Chinese actors'—be they state or private. Given the highly opaque nature of any energy deal signed by a Chinese corporation in Africa (and it should be noted that Chinese companies are by no means unique in this regard), untangling the impulses and motives behind such agreements is extremely problematic.

Beyond the energy sector, rivalries between different Chinese provinces, cities, municipalities and/or individuals play themselves out on a daily basis in Africa and lay bare the myth of a monolithic China relentlessly pushing forward on some sort of 'Chinese safari'. Analysis of Sino-African relations has to be more nuanced than any talk of a 'Chinese strategy' for Africa, with its associated fears of Chinese competition with Western interests. Equally, we should recognize that Sino-African relations are processes not of colonization but of globalization and the reintegration of China into the global economy—a project that has enjoyed the hitherto enthusiastic support of Western capitalism. Furthermore, it is ironic that much of this criticism comes from Western sources, given that the West taught Beijing the market economy and now criticizes Chinese actors for expanding into Africa using market principles.

PETROLEUM AND AFRICA

Where there is coherence in Sino-African relations, Beijing's foreign policies in Africa are arguably based on several key aims. As mentioned above, a principal intention is to encourage Chinese corporations to 'go global' and assist in the policy of ensuring regime security through access to crucial resources. A Chinese Ministry of Commerce statement has in fact averred that Africa is one of the most important regions for carrying out its 'go outward' strategy. The resulting hike in commodity prices has been potentially beneficial for many of Africa's economies, although the income from this is obviously uneven and dependent upon a country's resource attributes. Higher prices combined with higher production levels propelled sub-Saharan Africa's real gross domestic product (GDP) to increase by an average of 4.4% in 2001–04, compared with 2.6% in the previous three years. In 2005 Africa's economy grew by 5.5% and much of this was linked to burgeoning demands from China. Yet in terms of receipts from commodities, benefits are skewed towards certain economies. South Africa provides iron ore and platinum, while the Democratic Republic of the Congo and Zambia supply copper and cobalt. Timber is sourced from Gabon, Cameroon, the Republic of the Congo and Liberia, while various west and central African nations supply raw cotton to Chinese textile factories. It is, however, petroleum that remains China's biggest commercial interest in Africa.

Much Western concern about China's alleged 'oil safari' seems motivated by commercial rivalries, often tinged with possibly nationalist sentiments, centred on Chinese companies encroaching on territory long held to be in the Western sphere of influence. This is particularly so in West Africa. However, Chinese companies might be said to be vigorously seizing opportunities previously overlooked by longer, more established actors. Of course, Chinese oil corporations have a comparative advantage over their private, commercial competitors, in that being state-owned they are able to develop into Africa without concerning themselves with the interests of shareholders—a particular advantage when outbidding competitors for major contracts by paying over the odds, as has been alleged. In addition, because they are state-owned, the oil corporations are able to work in tandem with the Chinese state in a neo-mercantilist fashion, which has, it seems apparent, often been played out with 'sweetener' deals and packages that include generous loans and/or promises of infrastructure development in return for petroleum. Lubricating commercial deals with extras was, of course, precisely what Western powers were doing in Africa long before China became involved, and prior to the ascendancy of neo-liberalism mercantilist trade strategies were the norm. Is it the case that, having been enthusiastic in adopting and promoting neo-liberalism, Western policy-makers are now uneasy that this may, under certain circumstances, actually put Western corporations at a disadvantage when competing overseas with nations such as China which still retain state involvement in the economy?

When Western corporations in Africa have so many economic advantages and a long-established presence, it is hardly surprising that Chinese competitors use whatever advantages they might have to secure their goals. That is the nature of capitalism, surely? The hypocrisy (from a Chinese point of view) of the US Administration blocking the attempt in 2005 by the China National Offshore Oil Corporation to purchase the Union Oil Company of California (Unocal), predicated as it was on allegedly defending US national interests, exposed, in the eyes of Chinese policy-makers, much of the rhetoric regarding 'free markets' and open and fair competition for the world's petroleum resources. In fact, the decision in 2005 undoubtedly spurred on Chinese oil companies' entry into Africa's oil markets and probably further stimulated the policy of pursuing state-backed oil deals as a means to guarantee supplies. In Chinese minds, there is a question as to whether the USA is willing to play fair when it comes to energy competition. In addition, China has had much less time to get used to the often brutal world of energy politics, and has had to play 'catch-up' since 1993, when China became a petroleum-importing state. Indeed, the signals associated with the blocking of the Unocal deal are now possibly being played out in Africa and an increased Chinese presence in the continent's oil industries.

Certainly, support from Beijing lowers the political risks for Chinese energy corporations investing in certain countries, and this lower level of risk, when linked to cheap loans from state-owned banks, means that Chinese companies enjoy a lower cost of capital than Western competitors. However, because of the obscure (and often hidden) nature of many of China's petroleum deals with African economies, it remains largely unclear whether alleged overbidding on certain oil agreements by Chinese companies is because of a secure-at-all-costs (and hence conscious) strategy or because of a naivety in international oil deals. Either way, it could be argued that Africa wins—if Chinese companies want to pay African governments over the odds for their petroleum, then that is China's problem. At one level that might be true. However, there is also the issue that in locking in African governments to oil contracts—even if at the time the buying price was perhaps artificially high—African leaders may be selling their countries short by not going through an open tendering process.

Criticism of Chinese petroleum companies for engaging with such practices is often linked to concerns about the possibilities of corruption. This can be viewed in two ways. First, it can be reasonably charged that when Western oil corporations complain about the Chinese concluding petroleum agreements in the Gulf of Guinea through corrupt and opaque means, they are being deeply hypocritical, as it has long been alleged that Western companies, with the tacit approval of their home governments, have used graft to secure deals. In some cases this is not even tacit but quite open. After all, the Elf corruption scandal in France revealed that annual cash transfers totalling about £10m. were made to the former Gabonese President, El Hadj Omar Bongo Ondimba, while other huge sums were paid to leaders in Angola, Cameroon and the Republic of the Congo. The multi-million dollar payments were partly aimed at guaranteeing that it was Elf and not US or British firms that pumped the petroleum, but also to ensure the African leaders' continued allegiance to France. Damning indictments of Shell's activities in Nigeria are well-known, while in 2006 Condoleezza Rice publicly labelled Equatorial Guinea's President, Teodoro Obiang Nguema, as a 'good friend' of the USA, even though the country is characterized as a 'criminal state' elsewhere. So, constructing China's oil diplomacy as 'bad' while glossing over the Western governments' and corporations' own duplicitousness in Africa's energy industries is somewhat unpalatable. Indeed, such a stance smacks of a new 'two-tierism', this time constructed around simplistic binaries: whatever China does is wrong and whatever the West does can be rationalized away and is right. This of course should not be seen as giving a green light to Chinese companies to follow in the tarnished footsteps of the West, but rather that context is required.

CHINA'S SOFT POWER IN AFRICA

Chinese cultural, educational and media links to Africa originated in the 1950s when the goal was to promote Marxism-Leninism and Maoism. While these impulses have vanished from Chinese foreign policy, the promotion of Chinese 'soft power' continues to be a major aspect of the Sino-African relationship. Well over 30,000 African students have received scholarships to study in China and the country now offers 4,000 new scholarships each year to Africans. Beijing has also provided technical training in 20 different fields to over 30,000 Africans. A Chinese youth volunteer programme, which mirrors aspects of the US Peace Corps, has been set up, reflecting the importance China's leaders now attach to the promotion of Chinese soft power. China deployed its first medical team in 1964 at the invitation of the Algerian government and since then, Beijing has cumulatively sent over 18,000 doctors and medical personnel to more than 47 African countries. The Chinese claim to have treated as many as 200m. patients in Africa.

China has paid particular attention to developing ties with the African media. Xinhua news agency has over 20 bureaus across Africa and now competes with Reuters and Agence France Presse for the dissemination of news from the continent. Regional centres in Cairo, Egypt, and Nairobi, Kenya, demonstrate Xinhua's commitment. In January 2011 China officially launched China Central Television (CCTV) Africa in Nairobi. The channel will cover the political, economic, social and cultural aspects of the entire African region. Meanwhile,

China Radio International transmits from Nairobi in Swahili, Chinese, and English and has global rebroadcast rights. There are around 30 Confucius Institutes in Africa and more are planned. The first Institute in Africa was in Nairobi, set up in 2005. Emblematically, in 2011, it had enrolled 560 students, of which 129 are undergraduate degree students majoring in Chinese. It was announced that by 2012, the Kenyan-based Institute will open teaching centres for master's and doctoral programmes in the Chinese language in order to train local teachers in Nairobi. The plan is that Kenya's secondary and primary schools will begin to teach the Chinese language in the future, possibly displacing French.

Elsewhere, the Confucius Institute at the University of Yaounde II (Cameroon) created the model of 'One Institute with Multiple Teaching Centers'. Currently hosting nine teaching centres, including a centre certified to offer a Chinese language degree, in 2011 it had nearly 6,000 registered students, the highest among all African Confucius Institutes. In addition, it has organized 27 activities, attracting over 200,000 people. In April 2011 the President of Cameroon awarded a Presidential Knight Medal to Zhang Xiaozhen, the Institute's former Director.

NEW AFRICAN UNION HEADQUARTERS

The early 2010s saw the continuation of construction efforts on a new African Union (AU) headquarters in the Ethiopian capital, Addis Ababa. Standing on what was once Ethiopia's oldest maximum security prison, the new AU headquarters was fully funded by China as a gift to the AU at a reported cost of some US $200m. The office complex of 27 storeys, reaching almost 100 m, is Addis Ababa's tallest building by far, overlooking a vast conference centre where African heads of state are expected to meet for years to come. Most of the materials used were imported from China and even the furniture was provided by China. The building came with a promise that Chinese technicians will ensure its maintenance in coming years.

The gift of the new headquarters was announced by Chinese President Hu Jintao at the Beijing Summit on China-Africa cooperation in 2006. China described it as the largest single Chinese aid project to Africa since the construction of the Tan-Zam Railway (built between 1970 and 1975 in order to give land-locked Zambia a route to the Tanzanian port of Dar es Salaam, thus freeing it from dependence on trade routes that went through countries then ruled by white minority regimes. Construction began in January 2009 and involved 1,200 Chinese and Ethiopian workers. It was completed on schedule in December 2011.)

Critics argued that such ostentatious headquarters suggested a fresh form of dependency evolving in Africa's international relations. New commercial suitors from among emerging powers are certainly flocking to Africa, but the difference between them and the older established partners is difficult to discern. For Africa, the new headquarters and the manifest Chinese commitment at least resolved one problem which had been hovering over the AU as an institution since Col Muammar al-Qaddafi, the late Libyan leader, was killed in October 2011: who will replace Qaddafi as the new patron and provider of largesse for the AU, an institution which is perennially underfunded due to its members resolute refusal to pay their subscriptions. Currently, three-quarters of the AU's administrative costs are covered by Nigeria, South Africa, Egypt, Algeria and Libya, although Libya's future contributions are in doubt and certainly will not match Qaddafi's overly-generous pledges.

In January 2012 the AU inaugurated the newly built headquarters. The building was opened by Jia Qinglin, the Chairman of the National Committee of the Chinese People's Political Consultative Conference and Jean Ping, the Chairman of the AU Commission. At the event, Equatorial Guinea President Teodoro Obiang Nguema, praised the 'generosity of the Chinese Government', and described the building as marking 'a qualitative leap in the relations between China and Africa'. He noted that China did not hesitate to press ahead with the project, despite the international financial crisis. 'It's at difficult moments that we know who our friends are', stated Obiang. 'Through this building, China has shown that it can be considered a true friend'. Notably, on radio receivers delivering simultaneous translation in the conference hall, Mandarin occupied channel one. Despite contributing the largest part of AU project finance, the European Union was comprehensively upstaged by the Chinese in 2011–12 with regard to Africa's premier institution.

SINO-AFRICAN ECONOMIC INTERACTION

The legitimacy of China's political system is today based upon the CCP's ability to sustain economic growth. Intimately linked to this, Beijing is faced with a long-term decline in domestic petroleum production. In contrast to the past heady days of Maoist 'solidarity', China's economic dealings with most African countries are today based on a cool evaluation of their perceived economic potential. Consequently, China is actively and aggressively pursuing petroleum and other natural resources in Africa. China is currently the world's second largest petroleum importer and the second largest consumer of African resources.[2] The abundance of natural resources in Africa has led China to pursue long-term deals with African governments in order to ensure continued access to all varieties of raw materials and energy in Africa. As China is excluded from the majority of Middle East oil supplies and wishes to limit its vulnerability to the international petroleum market, it has invested heavily in Africa, deliberately courting states that the West has overlooked.

Beijing's economic interest in Africa is based on three assumptions. First, Beijing believes that the macroeconomic situation in Africa is taking a favourable turn. This analysis is based on the belief that (as the Chinese would no doubt assert), in copying China, African countries have adopted a set of active measures to push forward the pace of privatization and to open up international trade and reform based on bilateral and multilateral trade agreements.

Second, Chinese manufacturers (and shopkeepers) believe that the types of goods (household appliances, garments and other domestic products) which they produce and sell have immense potential in Africa, where the economy is not yet as developed as in Western nations.

Third, Africa is perceived by both the Chinese Government and by Chinese companies to be rich in natural resources, particularly in crude petroleum, non-ferrous metals and fisheries. Indeed, China's rapidly developing petroleum requirements have helped propel Sino-African trade in recent years. In 1993 China became a net importer of that commodity and petroleum will be the only feasible primary fuel for the foreseeable future that will be in the position to fulfil China's growing needs regarding both transportation and industry. As a result, Chinese companies have been faithfully developing linkages with oil-rich countries in Africa such as Angola, Nigeria and Sudan. China's approach towards securing access to African resources is what David Zweig and Bi Jianhai have termed a resource-based foreign policy, which by its very nature has 'little room for morality'.[3] In a resource grab in Africa, China has encouraged state-owned petroleum companies to invest heavily in Africa; in the first 10 months of 2005 alone trade between the continent and China increased by 39% largely due to oil exports.[4] In its investment in African states the Chinese Government and state-owned companies firmly emphasize the principle of non-interference in domestic affairs when justifying their involvement with leaders deplored by the West.

China's interest in ensuring its resource security and economic growth through involvement in Africa is by no means restricted to petroleum, and encompasses all natural resources. From investment in copper in Zambia and platinum interests in Zimbabwe, to supporting fishing ventures in Gabon and Namibia, China has vigorously courted and pursued the political and business élite to guarantee its continued access. One of the immediate benefits of Chinese interest in African resources was that it dramatically increased demand and revitalized industries such as Zambia's copper sector.

In October 2011 an official from the state-owned China Development Bank announced that it would provide a US $1,000m. special purpose loan to support small and medium-sized enterprises in Ethiopia, Egypt and other African countries, while the same month saw Australia-listed Sundance Resources announce that it would be acquired by China's Sichuan Hanlong Group for $1,650m., giving Hanlong access to the $4.7m. Mbalam iron mine in the Republic of the Congo and Cameroon. Meanwhile, state-owned China Petrochemical Corp (Sinopec Group) said that it had completed its acquisition of an 80% stake in Pecten Cameroon in Cameroon, from Royal Dutch Shell, gaining its first oil production assets in the African country. China Nonferrous Metal Mining Ltd, one of China's largest state-owned enterprises announced plans to invest around $2,000m. in Zambia in 2011–2015, to expand operations and begin construction of infrastructure facilities, adding that it had already injected nearly $2,000m. into the African country. In addition, a subsidiary of Shanghai Construction Group announced it would acquire 60% of Eritrea-based Zara Mining Share Company for $80m., and retain the option of further acquiring unconfirmed mines for $20m.

In January 2011 Sichuan Hongda Corporation won the tender to invest in the Mchuchuma and Liganga mining projects in southern Tanzania, a bidding exercise that attracted 48 international companies. Under the agreement, National Development Corporation (NDC) and Sichuan Hongda will form a subsidiary, Tanzania China International Mineral Resources Ltd (TCMR), to develop the two projects. NDC will hold a 20% in TCMR while Sichuan Hongda Group will hold the remaining 80%. The subsidiary will raise the money required for the projects, to be implemented in two phases. The first phase will see Mchuchuma extracting coal to be used in generating electricity while the second will involve extracting iron ore from Liganga. The Liganga project will be the second largest iron mining and smelting projects in sub-Saharan Africa, after South Africa, while the Mchuchuma coal project would provide diversity for power generation. The US $3,000m. deal to develop coal and iron ore projects in the southern part of the country is reportedly the single largest investment ventures in Tanzania thus far.

A CHINESE MODEL FOR AFRICA?

Politically, as well as economically, China's presence in Africa has been based on the premise of providing an alternative development model for African states and leaders. According to Naidu, China is seen as 'a refreshing alternative to the traditional engagement models of the West. . .African governments see China's engagement as a point of departure from Western neo-colonialism and political conditions'.[5] Yet the absolute emphasis China places on respect for state sovereignty and non-interference as an article of faith for the Chinese leadership, as well as a willingness to deal with states ostracized by the West, may appear promising to some African leaders, but it profoundly challenges the Western vision of a flourishing Africa governed by democracies that respect human rights and the rule of law, and embrace free markets. A common bond in their desire to overcome and shake off the legacy of colonialism has further united Chinese and African political interests, evinced in a portrayal of the former colonial powers as a common enemy.

In countering the Western promotion of neo-liberal reforms in Africa, Chinese sources have argued that this imposition of an essentially Western ideology on African states is a form of neo-imperialism. In what has been termed the post-Washington Consensus era, the search for a new developmental path is understandable and China's 'model' of development has been implicitly promoted as providing an appealing alternative. Joshua Cooper Ramo has cast this as the 'Beijing Consensus', consisting of three key parts: a commitment to innovation and constant experimentation, instead of a one-size-fits-all neo-liberal project; a rejection of per-head GDP as the 'be all and end all', i.e. sustainability and equality must be equally part of policy; and self-determination and opposition to any hierarchy of nations.[6] It is a 'model' within the neo-liberal paradigm, but with idiosyncratic facets. Although Chinese diplomats deny that they seek to export any model to Africa or elsewhere, it is a fact that Ramo's ideas have been promoted within China and approvingly cited by the official Xinhua news agency and elsewhere, and Chinese academics see soft power as intrinsic to building Sino-African ties.

Equally, the Chinese leadership has been politically dexterous in the stylish way in which it courts African leaders. This is notwithstanding a general and historic Chinese disdain for Africans which has caused problems for Sino-African ties in the past. Through political and business summits such as the various Sino-African forums, as well as state visits by high-ranking Chinese political officials, Beijing symbolically accords Africa equal diplomatic status with the dominant powers. For instance, as an emblematic gesture, it has become a tradition that the first overseas visit that China's Minister of Foreign Affairs undertakes each year is to Africa. Equally, African élites are deeply appreciative of receiving lavish welcomes whenever they visit Beijing. In contrast, when an African leader visits London or Washington, DC, unless they are from South Africa or Egypt or one of the few states deemed important, they are barely afforded a few minutes and even then they are more likely to be belaboured for their numerous chronic failures in governance than they are to be toasted as 'dear friends' and, importantly, credible statesmen. China's leadership realizes this and thus expends energy on massaging the egos of Africa's leaders. And this pays off. Beijing has been successful in gaining African support at institutions such as the UN, where the vote of the African bloc has allowed China to block resolutions on domestic human rights abuses. African support also of course helped Beijing in its campaign to host the 2008 Olympics.

Symbolic diplomacy, defined as the promotion of national representation abroad, has become an increasingly important component of Chinese foreign policy in Africa and elsewhere. As a developing nation, China's policy-makers are very much aware of the importance of prestige projects in asserting the power of state leaders and, as such, have been involved in large-scale projects of this nature, such as building national stadiums all over Africa. This approach has proven beneficial to both the ruling élites in Africa, who view these as projections of regime legitimacy and power (and suitably impress the local populations) and to Beijing, as it demonstrates China's rising prominence and presence. Through these kinds of project, combined with aid packages and the notion that China may be a 'model' for Africa, Beijing is very much asserting itself as an equal of Western powers as well as appealing to the African élite classes. Indeed, the 'Beijing Consensus' draws its meaning and appeal not from some coherent set of economic or political ideas à la Ramo, but from its intimation of an alternative pole, from which those opposed to Washington and, by extension, the West can draw inspiration. China's alternative path is partly attractive because of the apparent success of the experience of economic reform. Other developing states might also lean towards Beijing not just because China's leaders do not attach democratizing and liberalizing conditions to bilateral relations, but also because China is providing alternative sources of economic opportunities (with non-democratizing strings attached).

However, Africa's intellectuals must approach with caution the notion that China offers up an alternative model of development. Firstly, conceptions of Chinese 'soft power' built on the appeal of China as an economic model overstate the ability of China to project and promote an alternative economic type. It is true that although liberalizing the economy while preserving an authoritarian political system might be appealing to some African autocrats, this surely has its limits, not least to the Chinese themselves in promoting such a message, given that supporting authoritarian élites in Zimbabwe and Sudan has already provoked anti-Chinese feelings among African civil society leaders. Furthermore, China's sustained growth has taken place not only with no reference to democracy or transparency, but has also generally shunned policy reforms promoted from outside. This must seem attractive for those African leaders who have no real legitimacy or who are tired of having to fend off criticisms from the international finance institutions (IFIs) and the wider donor community.

Yet China's extraordinary economic growth has come about, certainly initially, within the broader context of a capable state and in a region that is itself economically dynamic. Rapid economic growth without democratization, as per the East

Asian model, often required a strong developmental state. Contrast this milieu with Africa. Granted even the relative declining reach of the Chinese state as liberalization progresses, the type of comparative internal strength and concomitant stability that Beijing is able to enact is beyond the ambition of most—if not all—current African leaders.

Furthermore, the irony is that those who applaud alternatives to Western-dominated IFIs often—sometimes perhaps without realizing so—end up in a position where they not only support the authoritarian status quo in some African states, but also the emerging leadership of China. Opposition to neo-liberalism—something that has considerable appeal—can result in the promotion not of social democracy, nor even Keynesian liberalism, but of illiberal authoritarianism. In fact, China's 'model' can only be defined by what it is against, rather than any coherent alternative project. China's 'model' is essentially not having a model, which is attractive to many in Africa because the ideology of neo-liberalism is so widely resented. Temporarily this is enough to garner respect and a degree of moral authority, but in the long-term promoting something rather than not promoting anything is a necessity if Beijing wishes to establish itself in its own terms rather than as a negative reactive symbol which highlights the repulsion of others towards the global hegemon.

Besides, within China itself there is a debate as to whether or not the Latin American fate of social polarization, international dependency and economic stagnation is China's future fate unless appropriate policies are implemented. These debates often question the capitalist direction of Beijing's current course, again destabilizing the notion of a 'model'. Less sanguine interpretations of China seem to have been missed by those advocating the Chinese model for Africa.

Indeed, market reforms in China have led inevitably toward a capitalist and foreign-dominated developmental path, with massive social and political implications, which have yet to be fully played out. Even though a key criteria of capitalism, i.e. private ownership of the means of production, is not wholly present in China, profit motivation, capital accumulation, free wage labour, commercialization/marketization, in other words economism (profit-making, competition and the rule of capital), is gaining priority as the determinant driving force of societal development. This has generated dislocations across the country, as well as acute uneven development, with China's 'model' actually being cast as either crony capitalism or gangster capitalism. The rapid growth figures that have been experienced in post-Mao China have arguably not been because of improvements in efficiency, but have gone hand in hand with a systematic dismantling of the social benefits that facilitated a significant level of equality during the socialist construction period. Today, the transition to a liberal market system in China has been conceivably predicated on intensified exploitation, which has attracted a mass incursion by foreign corporations, aided by a comprador cadre. Ironically, given the Chinese economy's arguably excessive dependence on exports and foreign direct investment (around three-fifths of its exports and nearly all its high technology exports are manufactured by non-Chinese firms), foreign companies are routinely denounced within Africa as 'neo-colonialists'. How such realities fit into a Chinese model for Africa is unclear.

Arguably the most we can say about China as a 'model' is that an overarching ideology, with a strong state and an élite dedicated to development but prepared to indulge in policy experimentation utilizing sub-national officials and social institutions, can stimulate growth and development. However, that is not specific to China—it is a generic developmental state model and one that Africa has long needed. The key difference between China and Africa is that the state in Beijing has promoted rapid (albeit uneven) development—this is something largely absent from most African experiences, with a few exceptions.

CONCLUDING REMARKS

Although Beijing's primary focus is naturally on East Asia and maintaining cordial links with the USA, by advancing the theme of non-interference in domestic affairs and promoting a culturally relativist notion of human rights, China has been able to secure its own position and, at the same time, appeal to numerous African leaders. Equally, the Chinese state leadership has been increasingly encouraging Chinese corporations to play a role in Sino-African ties. This emphasis on economic linkages with Africa not only enables Chinese corporations to develop their export capabilities and reach, but also empowers the Chinese state to project itself further on the continent. As a result, the state encourages corporate activity as a means to maintain its commercial and political links with Africa.

There is no question that China's increased presence in Africa is having a significant impact in both the political and economic arenas. *Realpolitik* plays a significant role in China's relationship with sub-Saharan Africa, as it has done with its Asian neighbours. The choice of focusing on infrastructure, agriculture and resource development coincides with the African élite's own desires, and Chinese 'no strings attached' policies are regarded as a welcome breath of fresh air, compared with the West's 'shock treatment' policies that have left many African countries in a dilapidated economic position.

In an attempt to offset Washington's position in the international system, Beijing has sought and will continue to seek improved relations with non-Western powers. Africa has not been an exception to this policy and this is likely to continue. Indeed, China's policies are essentially an attempt for the leadership of the developing world. China wishes to play a new international role as a champion of the developing world. Africa is fast emerging as a testing ground for this policy. As part of this strategy, China has over the last decade or so reformed its aid policies, moving away from bilateral economic co-operation schemes and the furnishing of outright aid or low interest loans to a more focused policy that aims to build up trade, investment and joint ventures in Africa. Whether this linking of aid to the construction of joint ventures with Chinese firms amounts to conditionalities is a moot point. While it is true that China has stated that it will continue to supply aid to Africa, this is couched very much within the confines and limitations of what Beijing terms China's 'capacity'. The emphasis these days is on improving the overall economic environment for Chinese trade in Africa. This produces a contradiction that China is increasingly coming to understand.

It can be seen that China's foreign policy in Africa has been based on several key aims. China has focused on ensuring its regime security through access to crucial resources. By portraying itself as an advocate for the developing world and emphasizing the rhetoric of South-South co-operation, China has arguably offered up an alternative model to Western dominance. China has in turn invested substantially in many African states and cancelled millions in debt. However, to achieve its policy goals, Beijing has been prepared to defend autocratic regimes that commit gross human rights abuses. As a repressive Government in its own right, the Chinese leadership has implicitly opposed the emergence of civil society in Africa and actively supported authoritarian regimes. The political and economic effects of China's presence in Africa can from one view thus be largely characterized as beneficial to the ruling élite but as being to the long-term disadvantage of Africa's peoples.

However, it must be emphasized that China's policies towards Africa are evolving and maturing and Beijing is experiencing a steep learning curve. Recent developments suggest that China is starting to realize that, like all other actors in Africa, Beijing needs stability and security in order for its investments to flourish and for its connections with the continent to be coherent. Prior to the 2008 global recession, China's state-owned enterprises were awash with capital and invested overseas, including in Africa, with great enthusiasm. Risk management and financial sustainability were relatively low down on the list of concerns. Weakened state control and a relative *laissez-faire* attitude by Beijing in its encouragement to Chinese corporations to 'go global' meant that a massive outflow in Chinese investment occurred. Agencies such as the IMF and World Bank were excluded as Chinese investors scrambled for deals. However, 2009 saw a change in this. China's quest for commodities in Africa has by no means stopped, but Chinese companies are now more cautious and seek to avoid some of the most chaotic parts of Africa. This has continued. Commercial deals receive much greater scrutiny and risk is now very seriously calculated. Western nations have had to learn the hard way that propping up dictators with no real coherent plan is neither sustainable nor desirable, and Chinese companies have done the same.

In fact, China is increasingly keen to place more efforts in infrastructure funding, trade, technology transfer and development in Africa. In late 2011 the East African Community (EAC) and China signed a Framework Agreement on economy, trade, investment and technical co-operation. For China, this is the first such working mechanism with a regional bloc and the first of its kind in sub-Saharan Africa. The agreement will attempt to further open up Sino-EAC investment and trade opportunities and was expected to focus on the promotion of commodity trade, exchange of visits by business people from both sides, co-operation on investment, infrastructure and human resource development and training.

China's growing business engagements in Africa can create an opportunity for local companies to move towards the production of labour-intensive manufactured goods and services, and away from the disproportionate reliance on its few raw commodities. Such engagements may lead to technology exchanges, enhanced labour skills and increased competition, all of which would ultimately make companies more efficient. Although China's modified approach to economic co-operation in Africa offers immense opportunities for countries to kick-start their economies, African countries still present several obstacles to global integration, which could potentially hinder their development. Lack of education and labour skills, along with low levels of technology and weak infrastructure, have resulted in the current inefficient business atmosphere and the continent's overall inability to experience substantial economic growth. Moreover, overwhelmingly widespread corruption and excessive bureaucracy tend to prevent businesses from engaging in sustainable and profitable global transactions.

Consequently, it is likely that China will increasingly promote transparency, and ensure strong governance without compromising China's international reputation. What is certain, however, is that China's presence in Africa is set to continue and Western actors need to be cognizant of both the opportunities and challenges that this presents to established players in the continent.

FOOTNOTES

[1] 'Sino-Africa Relations', Embassy of the People's Republic of China in the Republic of Zimbabwe, 2003.

[2] See Taylor, I. 'China's Oil Diplomacy in Africa' in *International Affairs*, Vol. 82, No. 5, September 2006, pp. 937–960.

[3] Zweig, D., and Jianhai, B. 'China's Global Hunt for Energy' in *Foreign Affairs*, Vol. 84, No. 5, September/October 2005, p. 31.

[4] Eisenman, J., and Kurlantzick, J. 'China's Africa Strategy' in *Current History*, May 2006, p. 219.

[5] Naidu, S., and Davies, M. 'China Fuels its Future with Africa's Riches' in *South African Journal of International Affairs*, Vol. 13, No. 2, Winter/Spring 2006, p. 80.

[6] Ramo, J. *The Beijing Consensus: Notes on the New Physics of Chinese Power*. London, Foreign Affairs Policy Centre, 2004.

A CENTURY OF DEVELOPMENT: POLICY AND PROCESS IN SUB-SAHARAN AFRICA

MICHAEL JENNINGS

The last 100 years have been the century of 'development' in Africa. National governments, external powers, development consultants, policy-makers and analysts have drawn up plans and implemented programmes designed to reduce poverty and improve the socio-economic lives of the continent's inhabitants. Aid policies and structures have emerged and evolved to pay for development activity. Societies have been transformed through the imposition of colonial rule, the birth of nation-states, incorporation into the global capitalist system, and by donor-imposed economic and governmental structures. Vast sums of money have been spent on developing Africa, entire professions have emerged concerned solely with poverty alleviation, and the line of politicians who have declared poverty in Africa to be the world's most pressing issue stretches back through the decades.

Yet, for all the effort, energy and words expended on development in Africa, what has been achieved? Life expectancy for someone living in sub-Saharan Africa was 58 years in 1960. By 1990 it had risen to 70 years, but by 2004 it had declined to just 46 years. The proportion of undernourished increased from 31% in 1990–92 to 32% in 1999–2001. By 2002 203m. people in sub-Saharan Africa suffered from hunger (33m. more than a decade earlier). Over one-half of all maternal deaths occur in sub-Saharan Africa. Every three seconds a child dies from a preventable disease—30,000 a day—a large proportion of these in Africa. One could be forgiven for assuming that development has achieved little in the continent. Certainly the levels of suffering are almost beyond imagination, reduced to statistics showing in stark numbers the realities of life for millions of people.

Since 2005 the issue of development in Africa has achieved unprecedented prominence on the world stage. The international community has held meeting after meeting to discuss poverty alleviation, aid policy, poor-country debt and related issues. Major reports from the United Kingdom and the UN, amongst others, have sought to highlight the immediateness of the crisis and define new approaches to development, while from the first half of 2006, a potential new major player in African development—the People's Republic of China—appeared to be emerging, raising questions about current policy paradigms.

'Development' has largely been presented as a monolithic, universally understood concept that has stood unchanging across the decades. In reality, the meaning of development, in terms of planned development, and the question of how it should be achieved has shifted during the course of the century of development. In particular, two main questions have exercised those who plan or set policy for, or analyse, development in Africa. First, which agency should be responsible for planning and implementing development? Second, what are the objectives of development, in other words, what does 'development' actually mean? The answers to these questions have changed over the past century of development in Africa, and continue to play central roles in the debates about aid and support for current and future African development.

A HISTORY OF DEVELOPMENT IN AFRICA

The Beginnings: Colonial Development to 1939

'Development' in Africa, in the sense of planned interventions in society and economy, began for much of the region with the onset of colonialism. Colonial powers were determined that the newly acquired territories not be a drain on metropolitan treasuries, and that they become sources of income. Early colonial planners regarded Africa as mired in tradition and stagnant economies, lacking in the vital accoutrements of 'civilization': capitalist social and economic structures (in particular a cash economy); modern communications and transport; and a centralized administration. The colonial task, as it liked to present itself at least, was to mould these new societies and 'develop' them, in order to create modern societies operating within a global market. 'Development' was defined by European perceptions of social organization, European economic need, and the requirements of colonial administrations to maintain power and control.

Reflecting the Victorian division of society into rigidly delineated public, private and philanthropic spheres, early colonial development planning relied on the private sector as the engine of change and development. Capitalist investment would create the required modern institutions and structures, with the state providing the rule of law and order. Welfare activities could be left to the charitable sector (in this case the missions) who would provide the bulk of health and education services to the African population. However, the failure of the anticipated private investment to arrive in the new colonies forced the state to accept responsibility for creating the infrastructure—in particular the ports and railways—essential for the colonial development vision.

For most African countries, agriculture was identified as the critical sector which would drive economic growth and expansion. Development planning, by the early 20th century, had thus become a question of how to increase agricultural output. Administrations faced two broad constraints (one real, one contrived by colonial depictions of Africans) in meeting this objective: a poor infrastructure inhibiting the movement of crops from the field to their end destination in Europe; and a belief that traditional land-use practices could not sustain a massive increase in production for the new export market. The first could be met through government investment. Over 90% of British government loans to the colonies, for example, were for the construction of the railways, largely in eastern and central Africa[1]. By the 1930s a network of roads and rail tracks integrated cash-cropping rural hinterlands to the global market. Those areas deemed unproductive were largely ignored and forced to rely on migrant labour as the main opportunity for cash generation.

The second constraint was to be met by encouraging African farmers to change their practices, adopt 'modern' (i.e. European) techniques and new crops. Colonial depictions of African peasantry as inherently conservative and unwilling to change were used to justify compulsion and, in some cases, force. In Uganda in the early 20th century, for example, farmers were forced (often with physical violence) to grow cotton in certain districts. Development was therefore regarded as a fundamentally conflictual process: means were sought to persuade people that the priorities of the colonial state ought to be respected, with such persuasion turning to force where argument alone failed.

Thus over the course of the first two decades of the 20th century, several important characteristics of 'development' had emerged. First, it was defined almost exclusively in economic terms. Welfare services would ultimately expand as national incomes rose, but it was not a priority for development planners. Second, the characterization of African societies as resistant to modernizing demands created a mindset that development implied conflict between planners and target communities. Development was to be a process of encouraging or forcing people to change, regardless of whether they accepted the logic of externally imposed values. Third, development was a process largely set and controlled by the state. However reluctantly, governments had assumed greater responsibility for development planning and financing. Nevertheless, that financing was to be the responsibility of individual territories, not a burden on the taxpayers of the European powers. Until colonial territories had sufficient incomes to pay for their development, European loans, not grants, would provide the necessary funds. Between 1896 and 1923 98% of British government funds for colonial development (across all the British Empire) were in the form of loans. Colonial assistance (or 'aid' as we would now call it) was to be extremely limited.

By the mid-1920s politicians in Europe, especially in France and the United Kingdom, were calling for an interventionist policy, and improved funding mechanisms for the required modernizations. The foundations of modern official development aid were laid at the end of the 1920s: the British Colonial Development Act (CDA) of 1929; and the French Fonds d'Investissement pour le Développement Economique et Social (FIDES) of 1931. For the first time, taxpayers of one country were to support sustained development of those in another, and largely through aid in the form of grants rather than loans. Over 60% of CDA funds were provided in the form of grants, and of the loan element, around 80% was on easy repayment terms (generally with an interest-free period of three or four years and low rates thereafter). The FIDES similarly envisaged grants being made from French national income to support development in its colonial territories.

These acts were of great significance for future development funding. The principle that development should only be funded through internal revenues was broken, and metropolitan regimes accepted that they had a responsibility to provide aid. Moreover, the types of intervention that both CDA and FIDES envisaged supporting signalled a new departure in the defining of development. The 'development as economic growth' paradigm was gradually replaced with a model that sought to include welfare concerns. Aid was increasingly understood as a social investment as much as economic. Public health schemes in particular became a significant focus of aid allocations (16% of CDA schemes by 1939, the second highest proportion after communication and transport schemes). Advisory committees reviewing project proposals came to the conclusion that living standards were as important a responsibility of colonial development as increasing productivity and, indeed, could contribute to the latter.

By the end of the 1930s the foundations of the modern development era had been laid. First, the state had gradually accepted responsibility for planning, directing and funding development, abandoning its earlier position that private investment was to be the main driving engine. Second, the definition of what constituted development had widened from almost exclusively economic dimensions to incorporate a social welfare agenda that regarded improving living standards as essential to the developmental mandate.

The Primacy of the State, 1945–70s

Global depression in the 1930s and the onset of war in 1939 impeded the efforts to implement fully the new principles underlying development planning and aid that had emerged by the end of the 1930s. Such efforts were postponed until 1945, from which point colonial and metropolitan governments began to put into effect a more interventionist development policy. Post-war development was characterized by three elements: the absolute primacy of the state in directing, implementing and managing all aspects of development policy; a fuller incorporation of social development/welfarist principles; and the rise of international organizations to prominence in policy-setting and funding of development.

The experiences of central planning at home and in their colonies during the war suggested to the European colonial powers that micro-management of colonial economies was the most efficient means of ensuring development objectives were met. Colonial administrations devised long-term development plans, used marketing boards to set producer prices and purchase entire crops, increased the number of agricultural advisers, and sought to change laws governing land-use, labour migration, urban settlement, pursuing measures designed primarily rapidly to 'modernize' (as they perceived it) colonial societies. The state was able to exert its full authority over development. Following independence from the late 1950s to the mid-1960s for the majority of sub-Saharan African states, this trend was continued.

But the role of the state in development was founded on more than inherited structures and mechanisms for enforcing control. It also rested on a consensus that development was best left to the state. The creation of a large public sphere was not only tolerated, but encouraged by donors. International overseas development assistance (ODA) was directed through government departments and treasuries across Africa. Government ministers were expected to formulate development plans. The World Bank and other Bretton Woods institutions undertook projects with governments for the large part, rather than private investors or voluntary agencies.

As the state assumed full control over development processes, the breadth of aims to which its activity was directed continued to expand. The definition of 'development' had fully accepted social welfare principles by this period, culminating in the late 1960s with the emergence of 'social development' as an objective in itself. Social welfare schemes came to dominate colonial aid spending in Africa, a trend continued following independence. The new national governments assumed responsibility for the provision of welfare services. The rise to dominance of social development at the national level reflected broader shifts in the international community: the UN International Development Strategy in 1970 which put social objectives at the heart of the developmental mandate; and the announcement by the President of the World Bank, Robert McNamara, of the 'dethronement of gross national product' as a marker for progress.

Colonial development policy had been geared towards benefiting the metropolitan economy as much as (if not more than) the colonial territories. The independent governments had no such dualistic imperatives to consider in their development policy. However, the departure of colonial administrations left a vacuum into which the emergent international development organizations could enter. While African governments to a large extent could set national policies reflecting their own interpretations of needs and priorities, the IMF, the World Bank, other UN agencies, as well as powerful new donor countries such as the USA, the USSR, non-colonial European powers, etc., were increasingly important partners in the process. African countries had since the onset of colonialism been subject to the policies of those who controlled access to funds. With the massive expansion in aid for development, particularly from the 1960s, they became subject to a broader range of interests. While economies grew, significant power over development remained at the national level in Africa. However, the apparent strength of the state in Africa masked a growing vulnerability. Should economic crisis emerge, the authority of those states could be challenged by the new masters of development.

Rolling Back the State, 1980s–90s

From the mid-1970s a global slump in trade, collapsing commodity prices, and the economic shock of successive oil crises undid the advances made by African governments and led to a fundamental reappraisal of international development policy. The weakening economic position of African governments by the late 1970s and early 1980s left them less able to meet the rising costs of social welfare and development spending. The sudden rise in interest rates led to the African debt crisis with governments now unable to meet the repayments for loans they were encouraged to take out in the more affluent 1960s and early 1970s. Unable to mitigate the effects of economic crisis themselves, African governments could not sustain internal control over development processes, and from the mid-1980s to the early 1990s they saw a gradual transfer of their power to external donors and international organizations.

The state, identified as the driver of development for over 60 years, was now regarded as its chief brake: states were too big, too unwieldy and too inflexible to the demands of the global market. International donors began to call for the public sector to downsize and to undo its network of controls over economy and society. The market was resurgent, and private investment held up as the solution to poverty and new engine of development. The structural adjustment programmes imposed upon African governments called for the state to act as a manager of development and welfare, not the deliverer. The principles of the free market were to be adopted as African regimes were encouraged to sell off parastatals, dramatically cut the number of civil servants and public officials, eliminate subsidies and price-supports and open up their economies.

The 'Washington consensus'—a phrase coined by the economist John Williamson in relation to Latin America—came to characterize the new orthodoxy underlying development policy world-wide. Amongst its key tenets, governments were to impose fiscal discipline, remove controls over interest and exchange rates, liberalize trade, and privatize uncompetitive public assets. Whilst it was never truly a 'consensus' (not all of its policy recommendations were accepted, indeed some were vigorously opposed by the emerging anti-globalization campaigners), its promulgation through organizations such as the World Bank and the IMF and major donors gave it power and authority. Individual countries were forced through economic and political crisis to accept these terms in order to receive continued ODA. In Tanzania, for example, economic crisis and the refusal of its main bilateral donors to consider increasing aid unless it negotiated with the IMF, forced it to accept structural adjustment in the mid-1980s. Almost one-half of World Bank lending in 1986–90 in Tanzania was tied to structural adjustment. The combination of a government crippled by an economic crisis, and Organisation for Economic Co-operation and Development (OECD) member countries prepared to use their aid policies to support the promotion of a new orthodoxy left many African states few options other than to cede to the demands of international donors. Aid had become a tool for control as much as for development.

The State Resurgent? The Good Governance Agenda

The hoped for massive inflow of private capital following liberalization and structural adjustment did not occur, and development indicators for much of sub-Saharan Africa during the 1990s seemed to go into reverse. As the HIV/AIDS pandemic swept across eastern, central and southern Africa, in particular, with debt levels increasingly unsustainable, along with a series of crop failures, droughts and famines associated with the El Niño effect, it was becoming increasingly clear that the power of the market alone was not sufficient to break through the development bottleneck. Just as the early colonial development planners had been forced to recognize the limits of private investment, the World Bank acknowledged that it had been overzealous in pursuing the rolling back of the state and had unwittingly undermined the ability of states to pursue development.

Governance became the new watchword of development, with the adoption in the early 1990s of the 'good governance' agenda by the World Bank and national and international donors. A 1989 World Bank report characterized Africa's development failure as the result of a crisis of governance. The 1992 World Development Report coined the phrase 'good governance' and placed it at the heart of international development policy, highlighting four key areas: public sector management; accountability; a sound legal framework for development; and transparency.

During the 1990s the technocratic model of the World Bank was refined by major donors and institutions such as the UN, focusing in particular on the democratic deficit in many African countries, the link between human rights and development and the link between effective and efficient states and the provision of equitable and universal social services. Good governance came to be defined as a democratic system, an independent judiciary, transparent systems, with a strong civil society able to participate fully in public life. Development could be achieved, the new orthodoxy suggested, through the use of aid and international development policy to reinforce good governance across the region. As the 1990s drew to a close international funds that a decade earlier had been channelled through non-official agencies, bypassing government ministries, agencies and treasuries, were now to be directed once more through state institutions. Governments across Africa were required by international donors to draw up Sector-Wide Approaches and Poverty Reduction Strategy Papers (PRSPs) to illustrate a commitment to spending their national income to improve both the developmental prospects of the country and the lives of the most vulnerable. Health ministries were to receive funds earmarked for public health projects; government agencies responsible for water and sanitation projects were once more put in charge of implementing schemes and programmes.

PRSPs also built on a growing consensus that development interventions lacked local legitimacy (linking in through this to the good governance agenda), were too short-term in their focus, and failed to build on best practice. Accordingly, PRSPs were established on five key principles: they should be country-driven (enhancing local ownership); they were to be result-oriented; they were comprehensive in their definitions of poverty and assessment of the causes of that poverty; they were to be partnership-oriented (i.e. multi-stakeholder in delivery, bringing together public, private and volunteer sectors); and they were to adopt a long-term perspective in their planning. Built into the PRSP process was pro-poor planning: interventions, plans to encourage economic growth, efforts at diversification and increasing foreign direct investment, etc., were all to take into account the needs of the poorest.

Conditions were still attached to the receipt of aid and donor support, but these conditions were designed to improve the effectiveness of the state rather than seeking to bypass it entirely. Donor aid to Kenya in the late 1990s and 2000s, for example, was tied to the Government addressing human rights issues and tackling corruption, while the US Millennium Challenge Fund with its free trade-oriented African Growth and Opportunity Act insisted that recipient governments commit to democracy, open markets, and good governance before aid in significant amounts was granted. Increasingly, aid has been tied to a raft of measures designed to promote multi-party democracy, transparency and openness in governance, and effective plans for poverty reduction.

While growing consensus around a set of developmental objectives and priorities focused around the UN Millennium Development Goals (MDGs), the good governance agenda, and pro-poor economic planning and management, donors recognized that the failure to increase aid was impeding progress in Africa. During the mid-2000s calls for an expansion in total aid flows, and improvements to the delivery mechanisms, were led by the British Government. This 'London agenda' sought to enhance recipient state capacity to manage and implement development by giving it greater direct control over the allocation of resources to specific sectors. The London agenda identified three key reforms to an improved aid system: the removal of conditionality; efforts to ensure guaranteed aid flows over the medium-term to better enable government development planning efforts; and, where possible, aid to be channelled directly to treasuries (known as 'direct budgetary support'), rather than through specific ministries, or private and voluntary sector organizations. In order to effect these reforms, it called for aid to be channelled through multilateral institutions (rather than bilateral), removing donor national self-interest; and for the creation of new delivery mechanisms that would be capable of rapidly scaling up aid levels, such as the establishment of International Finance Facilities.

However, while donors agreed to scale up aid flows to Africa (although commitments to increase aid to US $130,000m. by 2010 were not met), and many donors (including the World Bank) questioned the efficacy of tied aid, there was less willingness by some major donors to switch from bilateral to multilateral systems for delivery. Nor did all accept the need for removing (or reducing) conditionality. With the failure of donors to deliver on the promised scaling up of aid agreed at the 2005 Gleneagles Group of Eight leading industrial countries (G8) meeting, and the onset of the global financial crisis in 2008, the London agenda appeared to be weakened.

The result in the early years of the 21st century has been to revive the power of the state to manage development from its moribund condition of the late 1980s and early 1990s, but not so completely as seriously to challenge the power of those who hold the purse strings. The state has been resurgent, not victorious. Moreover, by the end of the 2000s the global financial crisis (which obliged donors to account better for aid delivery and results to an increasingly sceptical public), and perceptions of continued and growing endemic corruption in many of the so-called 'donor darlings' (such as Tanzania and Uganda) led to pressure on donors to return to more directed aid models, rather than the general budgetary support advocated so strongly at the start of the decade.

Rights, Security and Development

If the period from the late 1990s saw a partial return to earlier notions of the role of the state in promoting and directing development, the scope of what the state was supposed to manage continued to evolve. One of the most significant of these shifts was the rights-based approach. During the 1980s human rights organizations began to consider issues of development as part of their mandate. At the same time, non-governmental organizations and non-official development-sector workers began to consider how the poor and marginalized could best be guaranteed access to particular services and expectations. Gradually the two merged, creating an understanding that one central task of development was to ensure that all people had access to a range of services and opportunities to which all had a right under an emerging consensus of universal human rights. Thus the right to a certain level of education, to a particular level of health care and to a sustainable livelihood and security became not responsibilities of a national government to provide, but the right of all people to expect. By framing development objectives as 'rights', governments which had signed up to the new international treaties that were drafted throughout the 1990s could be held to account.

The 1994 UN Development Programme Human Development Report introduced the notion of human security, which was to continue the broadening of the definition of poverty. Human security, the report suggested, consisted of seven areas: economic security, food security, health security, environmental security, personal security, community security and political security. Linked into this, government and international organizations were advised to focus on meeting 'basic needs' as part of a growing emphasis on meeting the needs of the poorest of the poor. These concerns found their way into the pro-poor planning systems that emerged in the mid- to late 1990s (and encapsulated in the new PRSPs), and were incorporated into the formulation of the MDGs that were to shape development objectives from 2000.

However, at the same time, a rival construction of the link between 'security' and 'development' emerged. With the rise of the securitization of development discourse in the 1990s, poverty and global security concerns became conflated. Development became increasingly defined as a global security concern, and interventions characterized as protecting western interests from instability as much as reducing the impact of poverty on the poor and poor countries themselves. The result was that the social and economic concerns of donor agencies became increasingly intertwined with the security concerns of donor foreign policy. In the USA, the State Department became an increasingly important deliverer of aid in its own right, with control over a significant aid budget. Military forces have become used with greater frequency in delivering aid and implementing programmes. The US military command in Africa (AFRICOM), established in October 2007, will contribute to humanitarian and development activities. Non-governmental organizations have expressed concern over the conflation of humanitarian and military objectives in intervention in conflicts, a process highlighted by the experiences of working in Somalia from 1992. This process continued into the 2000s, accelerated (but not initiated) by the 11 September 2001 terrorist attacks in the USA.

It was not just poverty that was increasingly securitized: health issues too became imbued with a security prism. In 2000 the UN declared HIV/AIDS to constitute a security risk, albeit focusing mainly on the countries most affected. In 2002 the US National Intelligence Council released a report outlining the diseases presenting a potential security risk for US interests (the Central Intelligence Agency had suggested HIV/AIDS constituted such a threat as early as 1987, but for different, and as it turned out, unfounded, reasons).

To return to the two questions that have formed the basis of development debates over the course of the past century—those of agency and of objective—one can see that the argument has come full circle in the case of the former. In current debates it is the state that is dominant in managing and implementing development. There is a broad consensus, however, that it must be a particular type of state: one that is transparent and democratic; that pursues sound macroeconomic management; that puts poverty alleviation and eradication at the heart of its agenda; that guarantees the rule of law; and that protects the rights of its citizens. In terms of the objectives towards which this state is oriented, however, the definition of development has continued to widen, incorporating new ideas, notions, priorities and trends. Development no longer means economic growth from which all else will flow: it incorporates broad social objectives; notions of people's right to certain opportunities, services and levels of care; and issues of sustainability and security. Development has come to mean the creation of an entirely different society, where absolute poverty is eradicated, where all people have access to the same opportunities and where all live without fear.

AID AND DEVELOPMENT IN AFRICA TODAY

The current development environment has largely been shaped by the MDGs, and how best to meet the internationally agreed targets by 2015. At the turn of the century, reflecting on four decades of failure following the pronouncement of the 'decade of development', the international community sought to prioritize the development of the world's poorest countries, and the eradication of poverty. A set of eight goals to be achieved by 2015 was agreed by the 191 member-states of the UN:

The eradication of extreme hunger and poverty: reduce by one-half the proportion of people living on less than US $1 per day, and by one-half the number of people suffering from hunger.

Universal primary education.

Promotion of gender equality and female empowerment: eliminate gender disparity in primary and secondary education, and attain a higher proportion of female representation in parliaments.

Reduce child mortality: reduce child mortality rates for under-fives by two-thirds.

Improve maternal health: reduce maternal mortality ratio by three-quarters.

Combat HIV/AIDS, malaria and other preventable diseases: halt and begin to reverse the spread of HIV/AIDS, malaria and other diseases.

Ensure environmental sustainability: reduce by one-half the proportion of people without access to safe water, improve the lives of 100m. slum dwellers, ensure sustainable development.

Develop a partnership for development: ensure fair trade, address the problem of debt, increase access to essential medicines, make new technologies available to poor countries.

However, approaching the 2015 deadline for achieving the MDGs, prospects for meeting the targets in sub-Saharan Africa appear poor. Progress at the global level has not been matched in Africa, where movement has been slower (and has in some cases reversed). The greatest success has been in moving towards universal primary education, currently at an estimated rate of 76% across sub-Saharan Africa. However, while in countries such as Burundi, Rwanda and Tanzania primary school enrolment rates of over 95% have been estimated, almost one-quarter of children across sub-Saharan Africa remain outside the education system. Moreover, whilst enrolment has increased, there have been questions over completion rates and quality of education, and opportunities for post-primary education remain poor. The WHO and UN announced in early 2012 that the MDG relating to provision of safe drinking water had been reached. However, it emerged that the claimed success was rather more tenuous, and related to the delivery of water rather than its actual safety for drinking. Progress in meeting the targets for the reduction of child mortality (MDG 4), and for improvement in maternal health (MDG 5) is seriously inadequate. Although there has been a 28% fall in the under-five mortality rate since 1990, sub-Saharan Africa, with an overall mortality rate of 129 per 1,000 births, is lagging far behind the next worst performing region (Southern Asia, with 69 deaths per 1,000). Similarly, maternal mortality remains far above the 2015 target, with more than twice the number of deaths per 100,000 births (640) than the next worst performing region (280 in Southern Asia). Progress towards achieving the objective resulted in a 26% fall from the 1990 figures, far too slow to meet the target.[1]

Partly in response to the rise in hunger in Africa from the mid-2000s (caused in part by higher food prices, but compounded by limited increases in food production as well as droughts and food shortages in various parts of the continent), donors began to emphasise the importance of agricultural development. Private and public investment in agriculture had fallen significantly from the 1980s, along with donor support for the agricultural sector (as social infrastructure came increasingly to dominate aid spending). As a result donors and national governments pledged to reverse the decades of under-investment, although the response has been slow and not on a scale that seriously addresses the scale of the problem.

As debates began in earnest on what would replace the MDG process, attention also increasingly turned to questions of sustainability and the potential problems caused by climate change and the need for climate adaptation. Many called for this to be given a more central space in post-2015 development objectives, arguing that social, productive and other development sectors were all dependent on achieving success in this area. However, with the global community deadlocked over efforts to fund climate change mitigation and adaptation strategies, prospects for a successful adoption of sustainability as a core meaningful concept in development seem a distant hope.

AID

Since the mid-2000s aid levels have substantially risen. Levels of ODA have risen from US $69,064m. in 2003 to $128,700m. in 2010. In total, aid measured in real terms has increased by around 37% since 2004. However, in 2011 net ODA was £133,500m., a fall of 2.7% in real terms from the peak of 2010. It also represented a fall as a proportion of gross domestic income from a peak of 0.32% in 2009 to 0.31%. Total aid to Africa also fell by 0.9% to $28,000m., down from $29,300m. the previous year.[2]

While donors continued to reiterate their commitment to maintain and increase aid to Africa, there was a shortfall of some US $19,000m. on pledges made at the G8 summit in 2005, reflecting the failure of donors to meet their commitments. Divisions also remain over how best to deliver the increased level of ODA, with several major donors (in particular the USA) unwilling to commit to multilateral models or to reduce conditionality.

The economic crisis in the euro zone from 2010 also placed pressure on aid levels, with some donors freezing or reducing their commitments. The Global Fund was in crisis in 2011, after allegations of fraud led several donors to hold back their contributions leading to a serious curtailment of its funded programmes. While the official reason for donor reticence was over the corruption allegations, observers felt that in many instances donors had used this as an excuse to justify cutting back part of their aid budgets.

THE RISE OF NEW DEVELOPMENT ACTORS?

In the late 2000s a new group of donors, largely from the emerging economies and led primarily by China, began to make a greater impact on African development and aid. At the beginning of 2006 China declared its intention to extend and deepen its links with sub-Saharan Africa, in its 'Africa Policy', launched in January. China announced that it would support African economic and social development and capacity-building through increased economic assistance, debt reduction and relief, as well as through investment and a move towards the creation of a free-trade agreement between China and the African region. Japan too has increased the scale of its commitment to sub-Saharan Africa, announcing in May 2008 that it would double its aid to Africa by 2012 to US $3,500m., as well as providing access to $4,000m. of low-interest rate loans. India and Saudi Arabia have also increased aid to Africa (the latter's aid level currently stands at a little over $2,000m. dollars, but its trend generally fluctuates widely according to the price of petroleum).

The rise of new donors, and China in particular, has caused concern among OECD donors over the potential impact on its policy of linking good governance, 'pro-poor' growth and development. China's willingness to respect national sovereignty and internal political decisions is viewed in some quarters as giving rise to a 'Beijing consensus' that challenges the insistence of western donors on attaching conditions to development aid. Sudan and Zimbabwe, both recipients of significant amounts of Chinese aid, are held up as examples of how China is allegedly subverting international efforts to promote change. However, in reality, there is little prospect of China and other new donors replacing western donor aid (the Chinese Government, for example, is developing African programmes in partnership with the World Bank), and thereby fatally undermining the good governance agenda. Nevertheless, these trends perhaps mark the emergence of new global actors in international aid and development, and with it new directions in development policy.

CONCLUSION: THE CHALLENGE FOR THE FUTURE

To return to the question posed at the beginning of the essay: has development failed in Africa? It is true that many human development indicators appear to be falling: the proportion of those suffering from hunger has increased since the mid-1990s; life expectancies have fallen across the region; and the daily realities of grinding poverty continue to make their impact on millions of people. The story of development also appears to be one in which voices from Africa have been silenced by successive external powers. But, as ever, external aid and development policy devised in the USA and in Europe is but one aspect of Africa's hope for the future. Ultimately the answers lie, as they always have, within the continent itself. Development policy has too often been implemented with the interests of non-Africans at its heart. Policies have been started and abruptly stopped as trends and debates have shifted. The developed world has forced African countries to accept free markets while continuing to impose restrictions in their own. But through the constantly shifting international policies, the citizens of Africa have sought to improve their daily lives in small, incremental ways.

This essay has focused on the broad debates and shifting agendas in African development. However, it would be wrong to conclude that the sole story of development is located there. Self-help and community groups across Africa, civil society organizations, local faith and secular development groups have undertaken local schemes and projects with little, if any, external assistance. Colonial and international policies have been resisted and refined by those living with the consequences. African governments have in the recent past sought to address in concert some of the problems facing the continent. Through the establishment of the New Partnership for Africa's Development (NEPAD), the African Union, the creation of an African peace-keeping force, through free trade zones and other institutional unions, Africa is gradually restoring a measure of control over its own destiny. Of course, not all is positive. Corruption and violence continue to undermine development efforts. Violent conflict takes its toll in life and human misery. The lack of resources means many states are unable to meet their commitments, even where willing. However, should, as the past tells us is likely, the world avoid its responsibilities and once more push African poverty to the back of the international agenda, the prospects for development and poverty alleviation will continue to lie with Africans themselves.

FOOTNOTES

[1] UN, *The Millennium Development Goals Report 2011*, p.16–17. New York, NY, 2011.

[2] OECD, 'Development: Aid to developing countries falls because of global recession', Available at http://www.oecd.org/document/3/0,3746,en_2649_37413_50058883_1_1_1_37413,00.html.

BRAZIL-AFRICA RELATIONS

GERHARD SEIBERT

INTRODUCTION—THE DEVELOPMENT OF BRAZIL'S AFRICA POLICY UNDER PRESIDENT LULA DA SILVA

Former Brazilian President (2003–10) Luiz Inácio Lula da Silva's frequent official visits to Africa have often been quoted as a visible expression of Brazil's intention to strengthen bilateral relations with African countries as part of a global foreign policy. At the beginning of his presidency he declared the strengthening of South-South co-operation in general, and the renewal of relations with Africa in particular, as integral parts of Brazil's political ambitions in a new international political context. An important domestic force behind his Government's expansive Africa policy was the political demands of the Afro-Brazilian emancipation movement; to a considerable extent he owed his electoral victory in October 2002 to the votes of Afro-Brazilians. Immediately after taking office in January 2003, Lula's Government introduced African history and Afro-Brazilian history and culture into Brazilian public and private school curricula. In turn, this legislation resulted in a considerable expansion of courses on African history at Brazilian universities in order to train the necessary teachers.

During his eight-year presidency Lula made 12 official trips to Africa visiting 23 different countries, a number of which he visited more than once. He visited more African countries than all his predecessors combined and more than any other foreign head of state. President Fernando Henrique Cardoso (1995–2002) only visited Angola and South Africa, in 1996, while Itamar Franco (1992–94) made no visits to Africa at all. President José Sarney paid a single visit to Angola in 1989 and Collor de Mello (1990–92) made a four-country trip to Angola, Zimbabwe, Mozambique and Namibia in 1991. To highlight the growing importance, it was also notable that Celso Amorim, Minister of Foreign Affairs in the Lula administration, made 67 visits to 31 African countries. During the Lula presidency, to reinforce its presence in Africa, Brazil increased the number of diplomatic representations in Africa from 17 to 37, of which 35 were embassies and two were general consulates. There are only six countries in the world with greater diplomatic representation in African countries than Brazil, and among Western countries, only the USA maintains more diplomatic missions in Africa. Another visible expression of the strengthening of ties between Brazil and Africa is the number of African embassies in Brasília which increased from 16 to 33 between 2003 and 2010. At the same time, heads of state and government of 28 African countries made 48 official visits to Brazil. In recognition of his efforts in deepening the relations between Latin America and Africa Lula was invited as guest of honour at the 13th African Union (AU) Summit in Libya in July 2009. One year later, at the Economic Community of West African States summit in Sal (Cape Verde), he was officially honoured for his efforts in bringing Brazil closer to the African continent.

In the official political discourse closer relations with Africa have frequently been related to the slave trade and slavery in Brazil, which resulted in a historical, cultural and emotional debt with Africa, but a political commitment to Brazilians of African descent has also been mentioned in this context. The country's population of African origin and the supposed historical-cultural affinities with Africa are considered as striking differences between Brazil and other emerging powers such as the People's Republic of China, India and Russia. Another recurrent argument in the political discourse is the geographic proximity, with Africa located at the other margin of the South Atlantic resembling a river, which can easily be crossed. This discourse should not obscure the fact that Brazil's Africa policy is guided by a quest to secure raw materials and export markets for its own economy in order to increase domestic economic growth. Brazil requires sustainable economic growth to create jobs to fight poverty and hunger at home. Nevertheless, the main political goal of strengthening relations with African countries is ensuring the support of African governments for Brazil's global political ambitions, with its particularly aims of playing a more significant role in international politics and having a permanent seat on the UN Security Council.

A HISTORY OF AFRO-BRAZILIAN RELATIONS

As in the case of India and China, Brazil's relations with Africa are not completely new, but rather they mark the country's return to Africa, since they are the resumption of closer ties that were interrupted in the late 1980s due to Africa's economic and political problems and Brazil's own external debt crisis. However, Brazil's efforts to intensify political and economic relations with Africa, which began in the late 1970s, occurred in a different domestic and international political context than those pursued under the Lula Government. Brazil's relations with Africa date from the early 16th century when the slave trade began, and which until its abolition, gave rise to the forced migration of about 3.6m. Africans to Brazil, a former Portuguese colony. Primarily as a result of the slave trade, according to the most recent population census of 2010, 51% of Brazil's population of 191m. is at least partly of African descent. Furthermore, until Brazil's independence from Portugal in 1822 and the end of the slave trade, Brazilians served in the military and as civil servants in the Portuguese territories in Africa and were engaged in the slave and commodity trade with the continent. In the course of the 19th century thousands of former Brazilian slaves returned to Africa. These returnees settled in cities like Accra (Ghana), Lomé (Togo), Uidah, Porto Novo, and Agoué (Benin) and Lagos (Nigeria), where they created distinctive Afro-Brazilian communities with their own customs and cuisine. In recent years, Brazil has re-established ties with a few still traceable communities of former slaves who returned to West Africa.

Following the end of the slave trade, the abolition of slavery (1888) and the beginning of European colonialism in the late 19th century, Brazil practically ceased relations with the African continent. In the first half of the 20th century Brazil only maintained relations with South Africa, and trade with that country accounted for 90% of its external trade with the continent. In the second half of the 20th century Brazil's relations with Africa were characterized by varying levels of stability according to the different economic and political conjunctures of the time. In one short period, the so-called Independent Foreign Policy during the presidencies of Jânio Quadros (1961) and João Goulart (1961–64), Brazil began initiatives to establish closer relations with the newly independent African states. However, the military coup in 1964 ended this rapprochement with Africa, as the new right-wing military rulers in Brasília maintained close relations with Portugal's dictatorial regimes of Dr António de Oliveira Salazar and his successor, Dr Marcello Caetano, which categorically rejected international demands for the decolonization of its African territories; these had, since 1951, been officially considered as Portuguese overseas provinces. Indeed, Brazil was the only developing country, which did not vote in favour of the UN resolutions that condemned the Portuguese colonial policy. The first signs of a change in Brazil's Africa policy appeared in 1972 when foreign minister Mário Gibson Barboza made a trip to Zaire (now the Democratic Republic of the Congo) and eight West African countries in an attempt to increase bilateral trade and co-operation. However, at the same time the Brazilian Government continued supporting Portugal's colonial policy. In November 1973 Brazil was one of seven countries, which voted against a UN resolution that recognized the unilateral declaration of independence of Guinea-Bissau of September that year.

However, the 1973 oil crisis, which threatened Brazil's energy security and economic growth, prompted the military regime to change its African policy. In the late 1960s and early 1970s the average annual growth of Brazil's economy was 10%

during seven consecutive years, a boom that the military rulers did not wish to jeopardize. The threat to economic growth and the quest for raw materials and new export markets motivated the military regime of Gen. Ernesto Geisel (1974–79) to embark on a new foreign policy titled 'Responsible and Ecumenical Pragmatism'. The fall of the Portuguese dictatorship in April 1974 facilitated the change. To demonstrate its new African policy in July 1974 Brazil formally recognized the independence of Guinea-Bissau, before the recognition by Portugal's new Government, in August that year. In November Brazil was the first country, which diplomatically recognized the then socialist Movimento Popular de Libertação de Angola regime. In the years that followed Brazil strengthened its ties with African countries, which also resulted in a considerable increase of bilateral trade and the beginning of the engagement of large Brazilian enterprises like the petroleum company Petróleo Brasileiro (Petrobras) and the construction company Construtora Norberto Odebrecht (CNO) in Africa. During this period Brazil appeared in Africa as another developing country and a member of the G77, the group of developing countries established in 1964. The last military ruler, Gen. João Baptista de Figueiredo, (1979–85) was the first Brazilian president to make an official trip to Africa, in 1983, when he visited the five former Portuguese colonies on the continent.

In the mid-1980s Brazil's own economic crisis—provoked by unsustainable external debts left behind by the military regime—and the economic predicaments occurring in Africa at the same time resulted in a regression of Brazil's political and economic relations with the continent. In the 1980s and 1990s Brazil's average annual gross domestic product (GDP) growth declined to only 2.2% and 1.8%, respectively. Consequently, in the period from 1985 to 1990 Africa's share of Brazilian exports declined from 7.9% to 3.2%, while its share of imports slumped from 13.2% to 2.8%. Between 1992 and 1996 the total value of Brazilian exports to Africa stagnated at about US $1,500m., less than in 1985, and Africa's share in Brazil's foreign trade dropped back to the levels of the 1950s and 1960s. Due to its own economic problems Brazil was no longer able to grant import credits to African countries, while many of them were also hit by economic crises in the 1980s. Only a few large companies, including Petrobras and CNO, continued investing in Africa. Brazil's economic problems resulted in the closure of the Brazilian embassies in Ethiopia, Tanzania, Cameroon, the DRC, Togo and Zambia. Consequently, Brazil's relations with Africa became largely restricted to the Países Africanos de Língua Oficial Portuguesa (PALOP—African Countries of Portuguese Official Language) and Nigeria, an important oil supplier, although, with the exception of São Tomé and Príncipe, at the time Brazil maintained embassies in all Portuguese-speaking African countries. After 1985 Brazil's foreign policy prioritized bilateral relations with neighbouring countries in South America, the USA, the European Community and subsequently with emerging powers like Russia, China and India. Out of the 34 Brazilian diplomats based in Africa in 1983 only 24 remained in their posts in 1993, while at the same time the number of diplomats in Europe and South and North America increased. However, during the 1990s political stability and economic growth permitted Brazil to gradually change its image from a developing country to a potentially developed country.

As mentioned above, at the beginning of his presidency President Lula resumed his country's relations with Africa as part of an ambitious global foreign policy, which aimed to obtain a prominent position for Brazil in the international political arena, matching its geographic, demographic and economic importance. Meanwhile the context of Brazil's foreign policy had changed, both domestically and internationally. Whereas in the 1970s Brazil was a right-wing military dictatorship and international politics were dominated by the bipolarity of the Cold War, by the time Lula acceded to the presidency Brazil was a consolidated democracy with a fast-growing economy in a multipolar world. Lula's presidency coincided with the first decade of the 21st century, which was marked by three characteristics: a) by the emergence, in global terms, of a space conducive to the affirmation of the new polycentrism in response to the unilateralism of US President George W. Bush's (2001–09) strategy, the relative decline of the USA's power and prestige, and the impact of the international financial and economic crisis; b) in economic terms by the expansion of the global economy, followed by an acute financial crisis that particularly weakened the Western developed countries, resulting in the substitution of the G7 by the G20 in the management of the world economy; c) in Latin America by a leadership vacuum caused by the diversion of the attention of the USA, and by the temporary absence of Mexico and Argentina, and the increasing heterogeneity of the political regimes due to the populist rulers in Venezuela, Bolivia and Ecuador.

BRAZIL'S FOREIGN POLICY INITIATIVES TOWARD AFRICA

Brazil's foreign policy has frequently stressed Africa's importance as part of the country's South-South co-operation. Although after 1985 and prior to the Lula presidency Brazilian governments did not consider the Africa policy a priority, Brazil's diplomats did develop various multilateral initiatives to reinforce South-South co-operation. The Zona de Paz e Cooperação do Atlântico Sul (ZOPACAS—South Atlantic Peace and Co-operation Zone) was established in 1986 under President José Sarney (1985–90) through a UN resolution on Brazil's initiative to promote regional co-operation, peace and security, and prevent the proliferation of nuclear weapons in the South Atlantic. ZOPACAS members are Argentina, Brazil, Uruguay and 21 African coastal states. From 1988 to 1998 biannual ministerial meetings were held; however, thereafter the organization led only a shadowy existence. It was not until 2007, after an interruption of almost 10 years that ZOPACAS was reactivated during a ministerial meeting in Luanda, Angola, when it was agreed to intensify economic, political, environmental and security co-operation in the South Atlantic region. In December 2010 the Brazilian Government hosted a ZOPACAS Round Table to revitalize the organization and discuss co-operation possibilities among its members.

Another multilateral initiative to develop South-South co-operation, which Brazil has co-founded, is the Africa-South America Summit (ASA) comprising 12 Latin American and 54 African countries. On the initiative of Lula and former Nigerian President Olusegun Obasanjo the first ASA summit was held in Abuja, Nigeria, in 2006. The second ASA summit took place in Margarita Island (Venezuela) in 2009. A third ASA summit scheduled for May 2012 in Malabo (Equatorial Guinea) was postponed indefinitely without official reason at the request of the South American members.

The Comunidade dos Países de Língua Portuguesa (CPLP—Community of Portuguese-speaking Countries), proposed during a meeting of the heads of state of Brazil, Portugal and the five PALOP countries in São Luís de Maranhão (Brazil) in 1989, and formally created in 1996 in Lisbon, Portugal, has recently received more importance as an instrument to strengthen Brazil's relations with the five PALOP countries, which Brazilian diplomacy considers as closely related in terms of language and history. Angola and Mozambique have been important mediators for Brazil in southern Africa; the Brazilian presence in West Africa has remained fairly modest in comparison.

Under President Lula Brazil continued to favour a multilateral approach to its involvement in the international arena and search for a greater role in the changing global political order. In 2003 at the 5th Ministerial Conference of the World Trade Organization (WTO) in Cancun (Mexico), Brazil, together with China, India, South Africa, another four African countries and other countries of the South, created the G20 to promote the abolition of state subsidies for agriculture and trade protectionism in the framework of a new world trade agreement. In the same year, the IBSA Dialogue Forum was created by India, Brazil and South Africa with the aim of deepening political, strategic and economic co-operation between the three emerging powers, which represent populous multi-ethnic democracies in three continents, all of which are seeking to claim a permanent seat on the UN Security Council. IBSA has established 17 government-level working groups that regularly exchange know-how and experience in key areas relevant to developing countries. IBSA also operates a development fund with a modest annual contribution of US $1m. per member, which has undertaken projects in Guinea-Bissau, Cape Verde and Burundi. Since 2008 IBSA has held annual summits attended by the three members' heads of state.

Brazil also supported South Africa's integration as a representative of the African continent in the BRIC (Brazil, Russia, India, China) group of emerging powers with large economies and high economic growth rates. These countries have, however, also been characterized by significant socioeconomic inequalities resulting in low per capita income rates. In Brazil currently 8.5% of the population live in extreme poverty, although as a result of successful social policies between 2003 and 2010 20.4m. Brazilians have succeeded in escaping poverty. Between 2000 and 2009 the total value of trade between the four BRIC countries and Africa increased almost ten-fold from US $1,600m. to $157,000m., while trade with the rest of the world only tripled over the same period. The first summit of heads of state of the BRIC was held in 2009 in Yekaterinburg (Russia), at which the four countries demanded more say for emerging powers in the IMF and the UN, as well as a more stable international monetary system. The second BRIC summit, held in Brasília in April 2010, supported transformations in global governance on all relevant levels. At the third summit in Hainan, China, in April 2011, South Africa formally joined the grouping which was restyled BRICS. China has become Brazil's most important foreign investor and trading partner, but is also a major competitor with regard to manufactured goods and resources in Africa.

BRAZILIAN TRADE AND INVESTMENTS IN AFRICA

The strengthening of Brazil-Africa relations in recent years has also been mirrored by an increase in bilateral trade and investments by Brazilian companies in Africa, where currently some of the fastest growing economies are located. However, the scope of Brazil's trade and investments in Africa does not yet correspond to the country's impressive prestige diplomacy, nor does it match that of larger emerging powers like China and India. Between 2000 and 2010, Brazil's total trade (imports and exports) with Africa as a whole grew five-fold in value from US $4,254m. (representing 3.8% of the total value of Brazil's external trade) to $20,563m. (5.3%). Over the same period, Brazilian trade with the then 47 sub-Saharan countries increased from $2,000m. (1.9% of total trade) to $12,000m. (3.2%). Nevertheless, viewed proportionally, the trade with Africa did not reach the share registered in 1985. Relatively, the best year in the recent period was 2007, with Africa responsible for 7.1% of Brazil's external trade. In comparison, from 2000 to 2010 China's share of Brazil's trade increased from 2.1% to 14.7%. In 2010 Brazil was the origin of 2.1% of Africa's total imports and occupied only the 16th position in a ranking of Africa's suppliers, behind other BRICS countries such as China (1st position with 13.8% of imports), India (6th, 4.1%) and South Africa (11th, 2.8%). Brazil's principal trading partners in Africa are Algeria, Nigeria, Angola, South Africa and Egypt. Together these five countries account for two-thirds of Brazilian exports to Africa and 85% of imports from the continent. Algeria, Angola and Nigeria almost exclusively export oil to Brazil, while South Africa is predominantly a supplier of coal and ores. Brazil's main exports to Africa are sugar, vegetable and animal oils and fats, and motor vehicles.

Table 1 Brazil's External Trade with Africa (US $ million, f.o.b)

	2000	2005	2010	2011
Merchandise exports .	1,347	5,981	9,262	12,225
Merchandise imports .	2,907	6,657	11,301	15,436
Visible trade balance .	–1,560	–675	–2,041	–3,211

Source: Ministério do Desenvolvimento, Indústria e Comércio Externo.

Table 2 Africa's Share of Brazil's External Trade (%)

	2000	2005	2010	2011
Merchandise exports .	2.4	5.0	4.6	4.8
Merchandise imports .	5.2	9.0	6.2	6.8

Sources: Elaborated by the author based on the statistics of the Ministério do Desenvolvimento, Indústria e Comércio Externo.

Brazilian direct investments in Africa are concentrated in the energy, mining, construction and biofuel sectors. After the USA, Brazil is the world's second largest producer of ethanol. A study by the Brazilian Fundação Getúlio Vargas has recommended Angola and Mozambique as favourable locations for the production of ethanol and other biofuels in Africa. As a leader in biofuel technology Brazil has shown a keen interest in producing it in African countries. In late 2010 the Brazilian Government announced that it would invest US $300m. in a sugar-cane plantation in Ghana, which was expected to make ethanol the country's fourth largest export after cocoa, gold and timber. Similar biofuel deals worth hundreds of millions of dollars were signed with Mozambique, Angola, the Republic of the Congo and Nigeria.

Africa is only the fifth most important region in terms of location of the large Brazilian enterprises, after South America, Europe, Asia and North America. However, in recent years Africa has been the region with the third highest increase of Brazilian direct foreign investments. In 2009 Brazilian investments in Africa exceeded US $10,000m. and accounted for almost 6.4% of the country's total direct foreign investments of $157,000m. The principal Brazilian companies, which have invested and operate in several African countries are the oil company Petrobras, the mining company Vale, the construction companies CNO, Camargo Corrêa, Construtora Queiroz Galvão, Construtora Andrade Gutierrez (CAG, particularly through its Portuguese subsidiary Zagope) and Marcopolo, a bus manufacturer, which owns production plants in South Africa (since 2000) and Egypt (since 2008). Marcopolo's sales in Africa represent 5% of the company's annual global production. Petrobras has operated in Angola's oil sector since 1979, and the company also has interests in Benin, Gabon, Libya, Namibia, Nigeria, and Tanzania. Petrobras has engaged in oil production only in Angola, the company's operational centre in Africa, and Benin, while in the other countries the company has participated in oil exploration. Vale (formerly Companhia Vale do Rio Doce), currently the world's second largest mining company, has investments in Angola, the DRC, Guinea, Liberia, Malawi, Mozambique, South Africa and Zambia. In 2007 Vale and the Mozambican Government signed an agreement on coal mining in Moatize (Tete province). The mining complex, a $1,300m. investment, was expected to extract 11m. metric tons of coal for steel and energy production annually. Vale has involved another 20 Brazilian companies in the construction of the mining complex, which has estimated total coal reserves of 1,000m. tons. The beginning of coal extraction, expected to create 4,500 jobs, started in August 2011. In March 2009 Vale and African Rainbow Minerals (ARM) signed a joint venture agreement on a 50% stake each in the Canadian company Teal Minerals, which operates copper mines in Zambia and the DRC, as well as a gold mine in Namibia. In total Vale has invested about $2,500m. in Africa, predominantly in the mining industry.

The engineering and construction company CNO has focused its activities in Angola, but is also present in Djibouti, Ghana, Libya and Mozambique. In 1982 the company started building the Capanda hydroelectric dam in Angola with a planned electricity production capacity of 520 MW, although due to the civil war in Angola construction work was interrupted several times. Meanwhile the Brazilian Government has granted Angola additional loans to complete the dam. In addition CNO has been engaged in the construction of roads, housing and industrial plants, the extension of the drinking water supply, and urbanization projects in Angola. The Brazilian company's engagement in Angola is not limited to construction since it has established a sugar cane plantation for the production of ethanol, has stakes in diamond production companies and is a major shareholder in a supermarket chain. CNO is the largest private-sector employer in Angola, currently employing 16,000 local people. Furthermore, the company has performed mining and tunnelling work in South Africa and built a dam in Botswana. In Mozambique the company has been in charge of the infrastructure construction of the coal mine in Moatize. The company carried out oil-drilling in Gabon and the Republic of the Congo, repaired a railway line in Liberia and built a container harbour in Djibouti. In the past CNO also received large orders in Cameroon, Mauritania, Rwanda and Zaire. In 2009 Africa generated income of US $$2,420m. for CNO, about 10% of the company's total earnings.

Camargo Corrêa has also concentrated its operations in Angola, where it has been engaged in the construction of roads, schools and hospitals. In addition the company heads a consortium that has been entrusted with the construction of the Mphanda-Nkuma hydroelectric dam on the Zambezi in Mozambique. CAG has been engaged in Angola, Algeria, Cameroon, Guinea, Equatorial Guinea, Libya, Mali, Mauritania, Mozambique, and the Republic of the Congo. The company's construction projects in Africa are carried out by its subsidiary Zagope, a Portuguese company acquired in 1988. Its Portuguese origin enables Zagope access to European development funds for the financing of projects in Africa. African projects account for 27% of CAG's receipts. The number of small and medium-sized Brazilian companies doing business in Africa has also increased, particularly in Angola, the principal destination of Brazilian investments, followed by Mozambique, Libya and South Africa. Angola hosts more than 100 Brazilian companies, which is by far the largest number of all African countries. In November 2010 the Agência Brasileira de Promoção de Exportações e Investimentos (Apex-Brasil) inaugurated in Luanda its eighth business centre abroad and the first in Africa. Currently Brazilian companies operate in 19 African countries. Unlike Chinese companies, which often employ their own workers, Brazilian companies claim to use predominantly local workforce on their projects.

Brazil has identified the lack of direct sea and air links with Africa as bottlenecks for the expansion of its economic interests in Africa. There is only one single Brazilian merchant shipping line, operating a fortnightly service between Santos and Dakar (Senegal) which directly connects the country with Africa. Virtually all Brazilian exports to Africa have to be shipped through European ports where they are transshipped to vessels bound for Africa. Another alternative is to ship the goods on vessels going from Brazil to Asia with a stopover in South Africa where they are transhipped to vessels sailing from there to other African ports. Furthermore, African destinations account for only 0.4% of all international flights departing from Latin America. The three existing direct flights from Brazil to the continent are all operated by African airlines: South African Airways (São Paulo–Johannesburg), Angola's TAAG (São Paulo/Rio de Janeiro–Luanda), and TACV Cabo Verde Airlines (Fortaleza–Praia). In 2011 300,200 air passengers travelled on these flights from Brazil to Africa accounting for 2% of Brazil's international air traffic in that year. South Africa received 64% of the passengers from Brazil, while Angola and Cape Verde were the destination of 34% and 4% of these air travellers, respectively. Due to the lack of direct flights to Africa, travellers from Brazil must frequently go via European airports, which make the flights to Africa more expensive and lasting 25 hours or more.

BRAZIL'S DEVELOPMENT CO-OPERATION WITH AFRICA

The country's technical co-operation is co-ordinated by the Agência Brasileira de Cooperação (ABC—Brazilian Co-operation Agency), a department of the foreign ministry. Technical co-operation has become an important instrument of Brazil's foreign policy, since the projects contribute to Brazil's political affirmation, prestige and visibility in the recipient countries, and increase those countries' receptivity to do business with Brazilian companies. The ABC was established in 1987 to manage the international development assistance received by Brazil; however, in recent years the agency has been transformed into an institution that organizes and co-ordinates the country's technical co-operation projects in Latin America and Africa, which are carried out by dozens of different public, private and non-governmental entities. The projects of this technical co-operation have been concentrated in areas where Brazil believes it has comparative advantages, particularly in sectors such as agriculture, health, education, professional training, energy, social protection and public administration. Many of these projects are based on experiences with similar programmes, which have been successfully implanted in Brazil. It is believed that the geographic proximity between Brazil and Africa resulted in the geophysical similarities of soil and climate of certain Brazilian regions with parts of Africa, which can benefit development co-operation, especially in tropical agriculture and medicine. Brazil defines its development assistance as South-South co-operation, perceived as a horizontal relationship between equal partners, guided by the political principles of non-interference in the internal affairs of recipient countries and without any political conditionality. Brazil claims that its development co-operation is guided by solidarity and claims to be a partner rather than a donor. From this perspective Brazil and Africa are viewed as natural partners, and their co-operation entails automatically mutual benefits for both parties. Technical co-operation is decentralized, based on demands from the partner countries and provided at comparatively low costs. The bulk of Brazil's technical co-operation involves small projects with a renewable duration of two years. Brazil's development co-operation does not include the transfer of financial resources. However, Brazil's co-operation is generally conditioned by the supply of human resources, technology and equipment from Brazil.

In recent years the ABC's annual budget has increased considerably; however, in absolute terms the amounts have been rather modest. In the period from 1997 to 2006 the ABC budget allocated a total of US $7.3 million in African countries, while in 2010 the projects in Africa already accounted for $22 million, equivalent to 57% of the total annual budget. In that year the ABC implemented or programmed technical co-operation projects in 37 African countries. However, at the same time, due to the same language, shared colonial history and supposed cultural affinities, the ABC concentrated 55% of its technical co-operation in Africa in the five PALOP countries, which are also the principal destination of the development assistance provided by the former colonial power, Portugal. Besides the bilateral technical co-operation with African countries, Brazil also engaged in tripartite co-operation with member countries of the Organisation for Economic Co-operation and Development (OECD). Brazil has signed trilateral co-operation agreements with Japan, the USA, Germany, France, Italy and the United Kingdom. The aim of trilateral co-operation is to share knowledge and experiences, but also costs, since Brazil possesses limited means. Since 2008 Brazil has also begun to establish so-called structuring projects with a larger scope and duration.

ABC's most important partner in the agriculture sector is the Empresa Brasileira de Pesquisa Agropecuária (EMBRAPA—Brazilian Agricultural Research Corporation), founded in 1973 and with a total staff of 9,248 people, of whom 2,215 are researchers; it has an annual budget of about US $1,000m. In 2006 the corporation, which has an internationally recognized expertise in tropical agriculture, established a regional office in Accra (Ghana), since which time EMBRAPA has commenced three large long-term structuring projects in Africa. In 2008 it established the experimental station for the genetic improvement of cotton in Sotuba (Mali), which also includes the neighbouring cotton producing countries Burkina Faso, Chad and Benin. A technical support project for the development of agricultural innovation in Mozambique was inaugurated in 2010. In the same year EMBRAPA launched a rice-growing development project in Senegal with a budget of $2.4m. A separate unit within the corporation that provides technical training courses for African researchers and experts is the Centro de Estudos e Capacitação em Agricultura Tropical (CECAT—Centre for Strategic Studies and Capacity Building in Tropical Agriculture). Another unit administering agricultural technical training is the Serviço Nacional de Aprendizagem Rural (SENAR—National Service for Rural Learning SENAR), which since 2010 has provided capacity building for 70 trainees from 35 African countries. In 2010

EMBRAPA created the Africa-Brazil Agricultural Innovation Marketplace which aims at strengthening the co-operation between Brazilian and African experts and institutions in the tropical agricultural sector. The initiative, which is supported by several international donors, is currently running 10 projects in Burkina Faso, Ethiopia, Ghana, Mozambique, Kenya, Tanzania and Togo.

The entity that is in charge of the ABC projects in the health sector is the prestigious Fundação Oswaldo Cruz (Fiocruz), the origins of which date to the year 1900. Reformed in the 1970s, the foundation is associated with the health ministry and has more than 7,500 employees. One of Fiocruz's major projects in Africa is the anti-retroviral drugs manufacturing factory in Maputo, Mozambique, which involves an investment of US $23 million. Promised in 2003 during an official visit of President Lula to Mozambique, a country with one of the highest prevalence rates of HIV/AIDS in the world, the completion of the project suffered consecutive delays. Finally, in July 2012 the factory started operations; however, it has thus far only packaged, stored and distributed anti-retroviral drugs produced in Brazil. Another Fiocruz project is the Haemophilia and Anaemia Treatment Centre in Accra (Ghana), financed with $7 million and inaugurated in 2011.

The Serviço Nacional de Aprendizagem Industrial (SENAI—National Service of Industrial Learning), which was created in 1942, is in charge of Brazil's technical co-operation in the area of vocational training and is entirely financed with the compulsory contributions of Brazil's private sector. SENAI has 22,595 employees and provides vocational training courses in 27 areas of specialization. The organization has created vocational training centres in Angola, Cape Verde and Guinea-Bissau, and a further two centres in São Tomé and Mozambique have been in the preparation phase. Between the commencement of courses in 2000 and 2008 the vocational training centre of Cazenga in Luanda has almost trained 19,000 participants. In 2005 the Angolan authorities took over the management of this centre. During 2008–11 the vocational training centre in Bissau graduated 523 trainees. Besides the establishment of these centres, SENAI has also been involved in providing vocational training services to Brazilian companies in Africa. SENAI has provided capacity building services to CNO in Angola, Vale in Mozambique and Petrobras in Tanzania.

After Mozambique, the ABC's second major partner country in Africa, both in terms of finance and the number of projects, has been São Tomé and Príncipe, Africa's second smallest country with a population estimated at 187,000 in 2012. Considered as a perfect example of Brazil's technical co-operation in Africa, as it has received projects from all principal areas of Brazilian technical co-operation, the small archipelago has benefited from 16 projects with total ABC financing of almost US $11 million. In comparison, between 2007 and 2010, Portugal provided its former colony with average official development assistance of $12.2m. per year. The ABC projects in São Tomé all have two-year operational time frames; however, some have already been renewed for the same period more than once. Only three of the 16 projects have a local resident Brazilian co-ordinator, while the others are all managed from Brazil by the ABC and the other participating organizations, whose project supervisors pay regular visits to São Tomé.

In recent years Brazil has also significantly increased its financial co-operation with African countries. By 2007 the Banco Nacional do Desenvolvimento Econômico e Social (BNDES) had disbursed credits worth a total of US $742m. for 29 projects in Africa. In 2008 and 2009 BNDES provided loans of $265m. and $360.5m., respectively, to finance investments in Africa. BNDES extended a credit line of $3,200m. to Angola, of which $1,700m. has already been disbursed, and in 2010 provided a credit line of $3,500m. for Brazilian companies operating in Ghana and Mozambique. The principal purpose of BNDES loans is not South-South development co-operation, but the promotion of the integration of Brazilian companies in the international market. However, there have been recent cases of BNDES operations, where the Brazilian state has assumed the political risk of loans approved for investments in certain countries. Another entity of Brazil's financial co-operation is the Câmara De Comércio Exterior (CAMEX—Chamber of External Trade) of the Ministry of Development, Industry and Foreign Trade, which provided credits worth $640m. for the food security programme Mais Alimentos Africa, of which $240m. was disbursed in 2011 and $400m. in 2012. As part of this credit line Ghana and Zimbabwe received credits valued at $95m. and $98m., respectively, destined for the purchase of agricultural equipment in Brazil. This food security programme, which is co-ordinated by the Ministry of Agrarian Development, aims to assist family agriculture to increase food production and to create employment in rural areas in the participating African countries. Another instrument of Brazil's financial co-operation is the Programa de Financiamento às Exportações (PROEX—Export Financing Programme), which has existed since 1991 to finance either the Brazilian exporter or the foreign importer. In the period from 2005 to 2010 PROEX export financing for Africa decreased from $266m. (54% of the total) to merely $20.2m. (4%). In addition, Brazil has renegotiated bilateral debts with African countries worth $1,000m., almost 75% of the total of outstanding debts renegotiated by the Lula Government, an important measure to enable these countries access to new credits, to the benefit of Brazilian exports.

As part of its efforts to strengthen relations with Africa, Brazil has also extended its educational and cultural co-operation with the continent. Four Brazilian universities and four local universities participated in the creation of the Open University of Mozambique, financed with US $30m. during a nine year period. The project hopes to benefit 10,000 students during the first five years. Another ambitious project in higher education related to Africa is the Universidade da Integração Internacional da Lusofonia Afro-Brasileira (Unilab) in Redenção which was inaugurated on 25 May 2011, (Africa Day, which is celebrated annually in commemoration of the foundation of the Organization for African Unity in Addis Ababa, Ethiopia, in 1963). As well as the inauguration date, the choice of the location Redenção, a small remote town in the interior of the north-eastern federal state of Ceará, was also symbolic, since in 1883 this was the first Brazilian municipality where slavery was abolished. In an initial phase Unilab aims to admit 5,000 students, one-half of which will be Brazilians and the other 50% students from the five PALOP countries and Timor-Leste. To encourage the foreign students to apply for admission at Unilab they receive scholarships during the undergraduate courses, which is not normal practice in other Brazilian universities, since they only provide places for foreign students as part of the Programa de Estudantes Convênio-Graduação (PEC-G). Between 2000 and 2010 PEC-G provided 4,976 places for undergraduate courses at Brazilian universities for students from 20 African countries. However, during this period, two countries accounted for more than two-thirds of the beneficiaries: Cape Verde 50% and Guinea-Bissau 27%. Between 2001 and 2011 316 graduate students from 14 African countries received scholarships financed by the programme PEC-Pós-Graduação (PG) to obtain a Master's degree or doctorate at Brazilian universities. The majority of African students, who were granted such scholarships, came from Mozambique (113), Cape Verde (98) and Angola (49).

In charge of the Ministry of Foreign Affairs' cultural co-operation are the Brazilian Cultural Centres, which are directly subordinated to the country's local diplomatic representations. Of Brazil's 21 existing cultural centres abroad, six are located in Africa: in the capitals of the five PALOP countries and in Pretoria (South Africa). The principal activities of these centres involve the instruction of the Portuguese language spoken in Brazil and the dissemination and diffusion of Brazilian literature, visual arts, scenic arts, cinematography and music, as well as the organization of conferences and workshops and the distribution of information on Brazil. Since the 1980s, and independent of government cultural policies, Brazilian *telenovelas* (soap operas) have enjoyed increasing popularity in Africa. At the same time, Brazilian Pentecostal churches have expanded on the African continent, particularly the controversial Igreja Universal Reino de Deus (IURD), which has been active in another 19 African countries in addition to the five PALOP countries.

In 2010 the Instituto de Pesquisa Económica Aplicada (IPEA—Institute of Applied Economic Research) published a report on Brazil's investments in bilateral and multilateral development co-operation in the period of 2005 to 2009. According to the report, during the five-year period, Brazil disbursed a total of R$2,900m. (US $1,720m.) for international assistance, of which 75% was in the form of contributions for international organizations and regional development banks, 16.4% in humanitarian aid, 10% in scholarships and only 9% in technical co-operation. The financial co-operation was not included in the survey, since Brazil considers as development co-operation only non-refundable grants, while export-financing is officially not classified as development assistance. In a recent report the Global Health Initiatives Strategies (GHI) has estimated that in 2010 Brazil granted between €400m. and $1,200m. worth of development assistance, roughly the same amount as India or Portugal, but considerably less than China or the major donor countries organized in the Development Assistance Committee (DAC) of the OECD. However, the problem with such figures and comparisons is that Brazil and other non-DAC members do not publish official data on their international development co-operation, and consensual criteria with regard to accounting of the different modalities of development assistance do not exist either.

Table 3 Expenditure by Country on Development Co-operation in 2010, US $m.

United Kingdom	13,005
European Union	12,680
Netherlands	6,360
China	3,900
Brazil	400–1,200
India	690
Portugal	640
Russia	400–500
South Africa	143

Sources: Sources: GHI and DAC.

BIBLIOGRAPHY

Banco Mundial e Instituto de Pesquisa Económica Aplicada. *Ponte sobre o Atlântico. Brasil e África Subsaariana. Parceira Sul-Sul para o Crescimento*. Brasília, 2011.

Barbosa, A. de F., Narciso, T., and Bianclalana, M. 'Brazil in Africa: Another Emerging Power in the Continent?' in *Politikon* 36(1), pp. 59–86, 2009.

Cabral, L. (2011). 'Cooperação Brasil-África para o desenvolvimento: Caracterização, tendências e desafios' in *Textos Cindes* No. 26. CINDES, Rio de Janeiro, 2011.

da Costa, K. P., and da Motta Veiga, P. (2011). 'O Brasil frente à emergência da África; comércio e política comercial' in *Textos Cindes* No. 24. CINDES, Rio de Janeiro, 2011.

Global Health Initiatives Strategies. 'Shifting Paradigm. How the BRICS Are Reshaping Global Health and Development', www.ghsinitiatives.org/downloads/ghsi_brics_report.pdf.

Iglesias, R. 'Como aumentar a competitividade exportadora brasileira na África'. Paper presented at the Fórum Brasil–África, Fortaleza, 9–11 May 2012.

Iglesias, R., and da Costa, K. P. 'O investimento direto brasileiro na África' in *Textos Cindes* No. 27. CINDES, Rio de Janeiro, 2011.

Instituto de Pesquisa Económica Aplicada. *Cooperação Brasileira para o Desenvolvimento Internacional: 2005-2009*. Brasília, 2009.

IPAD. Ajuda Pública ao Desenvolvimento Portuguesa 2007/2010, www.ipad.mne.gov.pt/CooperacaoDesenvolvimento/AjudaPublicaDesenvolvimento/Estatísticas/Paginas/default.aspx

Itamaraty. Histórico do PEC-G, www.dce.mre.gov.br/PEC/G/historico.html.

Itamaraty. Histórico do PEC-PG, www.dce.mre.gov.br/PEC/PG/historico.html.

Ministry of External Relations. *Letters from Africa*. Brasilia, 2010.

Ribeiro, C. O. *Relações Político-Comerciais Brasil-África (1985–2006)*. Unpublished PhD thesis, Universidade de São Paulo, 2007.

'Crise e castigo: as relações Brasil-África no governo Sarney' in *Revista Brasileira da Política Internacional* 51(2), pp. 39–59, 2008.

'Adjustment Changes. A Política Africana do Brasil no Pós-Guerra Fria' in *Revista Sociologia Política (Curitiba)* 18 (35), pp. 55–79, 2010.

Ricupero, R. 'Carisma e prestígio: a diplomacia do período Lula de 2003 a 2010' in *Política Externa* 19(1), pp. 27–42, 2010.

Seibert, G. *Brazil in Africa: Ambitions and Achievements of an Emerging Regional Power in the Political and Economic Sector*. Paper presented at the 4th European Conference on African Studies, Uppsala (Sweden), 15–18 June, 2011.

Visentini, P. F. *Prestige Diplomacy, Southern Solidarity or "Soft Imperialism"? Lula's Brazil-Africa Relations (2003 Onwards)*. Paper presented at the Africa Studies Centre, Leiden, Netherlands, 10 April 2009.

White, L. 'Understanding Brazil's new drive for Africa' in *South African Journal of International Affairs* 17(2), pp. 221–242, 2010.

THE EAST AFRICAN COMMUNITY

DUNCAN WOODSIDE

INTRODUCTION—CREATION OF THE PRESENT-DAY EAST AFRICAN COMMUNITY

The East African Community (EAC)'s founding member states are Kenya, Tanzania and Uganda. The foundation stone for the Community was laid on 30 November 1993, with the signing of the Agreement for the Establishment of the Permanent Tripartite Commission for East African Co-operation by Kenya's President Daniel arap Moi, Uganda's President Gen. (retd) Yoweri Kaguta Museveni and Tanzania's President Ali Hassan Mwinyi. Just over two years later, in March 1996, political co-operation commenced, with the establishment of a Secretariat, before the Treaty for the Establishment of the East African Community came into effect on 7 July 2000, after ratification by all three member countries.

On 30 November 2001 the EAC's heads of state inaugurated the East African Legislative Assembly (EALA) and the East African Court of Justice (EACJ). A Customs Union came into force in January 2005 and a Common Market in July 2010, ahead of the planned establishment of a monetary union and a political federation thereafter.

Membership of the EAC increased from the original three member states to five on 1 July 2007, with the inclusion of Rwanda and Burundi. These two countries nominally joined the Customs Union in 2008, but were not required to start applying its policies until July 2009.

The countries comprising the EAC have all undergone significant development in recent years. However, the Common Market has so far only been partially implemented and achieving the remaining evolutionary objectives of the Community will be a challenging task. In particular, the sacrifice of economic policy-making autonomy and political sovereignty entailed by monetary union and a political federation, respectively, may prove to be two steps too far down the road of integration, especially given a tendency towards political authoritarianism among some member states.

EARLIER INTEGRATION ATTEMPTS

The regional integration attempts that began in the early 1990s were not the first such initiatives. A predecessor organization to today's EAC—also known as the East African Community—existed between 1967 and 1977. The original EAC was born out of a body called the East African Common Services Organization (EACSO). EACSO had itself replaced the British-administered East African High Commission, due to the decolonization of Kenya, Zanzibar, Uganda and Tanganyika in the early 1960s. (Tanganyika and Zanzibar merged to become Tanzania in 1964, after Zanzibar experienced a violent revolution.) EACSO maintained the moderate level of integration that had been achieved under the East African High Commission, including a regional postal system, a common external tariff, transport network and currency. The original EAC was then intended to deepen this integration. However, post-independence political turmoil caused the original EAC to disintegrate. Tensions were generated between Tanzania and Kenya, as the former embraced an autarchic form of socialism under President Julius Nyerere in 1967. This lurch to the left brought into question the EAC's trading regime, against a backdrop of resentment among the other member states towards Kenya, which formed the Community's biggest and most powerful economy.

The most significant problem for the original EAC arguably came in 1971, when Maj.-Gen. Idi Amin Dada overthrew President Milton Obote in a military coup in Uganda. Amin's erratic rule saw his country engage in border clashes with Tanzania in 1972–73, before he declared himself President for Life in 1976 and claimed parts of Kenya. After the collapse of the EAC in 1977, regional relations reached a nadir as Uganda invaded Tanzania in 1978 in an attempt to annex the Kagera region. In 1979 Tanzania retaliated by invading Uganda and bringing together various internal revolutionary factions to force Amin from power.

EAC MEMBER STATE BIOGRAPHIES

Burundi

Burundi is the least developed nation in the EAC. The country's nominal gross domestic product (GDP) reached just US $1,330m. in 2009, according to the IMF, while GDP per head stood at just $140. Over two-thirds of the population live below the World Bank's official poverty line. The tiny land-locked country, which depends heavily on modest export earnings from its tea and coffee sectors, was ravaged by a brutal ethnic civil war over the period 1993–2003. Low-level conflict has simmered since then, although the ethnic element has been solved by the introduction, in 2000, of power-sharing quotas for the two main groups, the Hutu and the Tutsi. Presently the conflict centres on the drift towards authoritarianism of the ruling Conseil National pour la Défense de la Démocratie—Forces pour la Défense de la Démocratie, since its victory in post-war legislative elections in 2005. The ruling party's closure of political space, which resulted in all opposition presidential candidates boycotting elections held in 2010, forced dissidents from both the Hutu and Tutsi communities to retreat into hiding, raising fears of a new, full-scale rebellion emerging, this time transcending ethnic boundaries.

Kenya

Kenya is the EAC's largest economy, by a considerable margin. Nominal GDP in 2009 reached US $29,500m., while GDP per head stood at around $740. Tourism, manufacturing, flower-farming and large-scale agriculture (including tea production) all feed into economic growth, which registered around 5% in real terms in 2010. However, while Kenya's middle class is burgeoning, there is a very pronounced gap between rich and poor, even by the standards of a developing country. Land grabbing—both under British colonization and in the years that followed independence—stripped many people of their subsistence plots, leading to a mass influx of people to cities and the creation of sprawling slums. This enforced urbanization, high youth unemployment and significant corruption within the police force has resulted in very high levels of crime. Violent crime is a particular problem, and is much worse than in Tanzania, Rwanda or Uganda. Further security concerns surround the country's political situation, although the outlook has improved considerably since the ethnic violence that followed a disputed presidential election in December 2007. The adoption, in August 2010, of a new Constitution, which limited presidential powers and prepared for land reform, has created hopes that the country may finally be able to begin breaking with its corruption-riddled past by pursuing meaningful reform.

Rwanda

With a nominal GDP of US $5,024m. in 2009, Rwanda is the second smallest state in the EAC, in economic terms. Like Burundi, its neighbour to the south, Rwanda is land-locked and has a history of Tutsi–Hutu ethnic conflict, the most violent expression of which came in 1994, when between 500,000 and 800,000 Tutsis and moderate Hutus were killed in a genocide perpetrated by an extremist Hutu regime. However, since the end of the genocide—and the conclusion of a civil war in July 1994—Rwanda's development, both in terms of peace and urban prosperity, has been remarkable. During just three years between 2008 and the end of 2010, the economy increased in size, in real terms, by close to one-quarter, despite the fact that the developed world was mired in recession for much of this period. In 2010 the economy expanded by 7.4%, in real terms, according to the country's Ministry of Finance and Economic Planning. The World Bank designated Rwanda as the world's leading reformer in its annual *Doing Business* report in 2009. However, the main downside is the highly authoritarian style of the country's Government, embodied by the micro-managing zeal of the President, Maj.-Gen. Paul Kagame. This has forced many opposition politicians and journalists into exile.

Tanzania

Tanzania, with a nominal GDP of US $22,600m. in 2009, is the second largest economy in the EAC, behind Kenya. Gold, coffee, tea and tobacco exports are key to foreign exchange earnings. Historically, Tanzania is the most politically stable of the five EAC member states. It has not been affected by the ethnic violence that has characterized much of Rwanda's and Burundi's histories, nor the coups suffered by Uganda in the 1970s and 1980s, or the election violence associated with Kenya. (This is the case at least on mainland Tanzania; Zanzibar has a more volatile political history.) However, of the original three member states, Tanzania is also the country most prone to negotiating 'opt-outs' from EAC commitments.

Uganda

Uganda's GDP reached US $16,900m. in 2009. Like other EAC countries, tea and coffee represent important sources of foreign currency earnings for Uganda, which has registered a strong level of economic growth in recent years. Income per head in 2009 was around $560. The discovery of significant deposits of petroleum—which, according to France's Total, could yield 300,000 barrels per day—opens up the opportunity for the country to propel itself into the 'middle-income' category much more quickly than would otherwise have been possible. However, concerns have been raised about the transparency of the Government's dealings with multinational oil companies, heightening fears that the management of future petroleum revenues may not be to the optimum benefit of communities in oil-rich areas, or to the country's wider development.

TODAY'S EAC—ORGANS AND INSTITUTIONS

The principal political organs of the EAC are the Summit, the Council of Ministers, the EALA and the EACJ. The Summit is comprised of the heads of state (i.e. Presidents) of the five member nations. Ultimate decision-making power resides with the Summit, where decisions are made on a consensual basis. There is one ordinary Summit meeting per year, while extraordinary meetings can be called by any of the heads of state. The Summit is chaired by the member states' heads of state on an annual rotational basis, with Kenya's President Mwai Kibaki mandated as Chairman for the period December 2011 until December 2012. Agendas are generally referred to the Summit by the Council of Ministers, although the Summit retains the autonomy to set its own agenda and, under the auspices of the 2000 EAC Treaty, has the authority to issue rules and orders to be followed by the other organs of the Community.

The Council of Ministers has a degree of decision-making power and is primarily comprised of member states' ministers for regional co-operation, although additional ministers can be selected at the behest of each member state. The minister for regional co-operation is usually selected by a member state as its head of delegation to the Council of Ministers. As with the Summit, decisions are made on a consensual basis, such that the agreement of all five member states' heads of delegation is required, in order for a proposal to be ratified. When consensus is not achieved—i.e. when one or more head of delegation lodges an objection to a proposal—then the matter is referred to the Summit. The Council of Ministers has the authority to set its own procedure and is chaired on a rotational basis by member states' ministers for regional co-operation. It meets twice per year, with one meeting immediately prior to the annual Summit.

The EALA is the legislative arm of the EAC. It has 52 legislators; each member state elects nine (resulting in 45 elected legislators); five legislators are comprised of each member state's minister for EAC affairs (or assistant minister for EAC affairs); and the remaining two are the Counsel and the Secretary-General to the EAC. Key functions of the EALA include debating and approving the EAC's annual budget, making recommendations to the Council of Ministers for the implementation of the EAC and overseeing specialist legislative committees. Key committees include the Committee on Agriculture, Tourism and Natural Resources; the Committee on Communication Trade and Investment; and the Committee on Regional Affairs and Conflict Resolution.

The EACJ was established under Article 9 of the 2000 EAC Treaty and its core responsibility is to ensure that intra-EAC laws are interpreted and applied in line with this Treaty. The EACJ sits in the Tanzanian town of Arusha. In April 2012 the EAC heads of state, in their 10th extraordinary meeting, directed the Council of Ministers to consider an extension of the EACJ's remit to cover crimes against humanity. This would involve proposing amendments to Article 27(2) of the EAC Treaty, in order to widen the EACJ's jurisdiction to include human rights and crimes against humanity committed by individuals and states. The changes, once proposed, would be referred to partner states for consideration and then referred back to the heads of state. This move came against a backdrop where the Hague-based International Criminal Court (ICC) in January 2012 confirmed charges against four Kenyans (including two aspiring presidential candidates, Uhuru Kenyatta and William Ruto) for alleged crimes against humanity perpetrated during Kenya's 2007–08 post election violence. The cases had been taken up by the ICC at the behest of former UN Secretary General (and official mediator during the Kenya crisis) Kofi Annan, after Kenya's government repeatedly stalled on establishing a domestic judicial mechanism to deal with alleged high-level orchestrators of crimes committed during the crisis.

The EACJ has, however, demonstrated a degree of independence from the influence of partner states' national authorities. In a ruling on 1 December 2011, a four judge panel at the EACJ's First Instance Division ruled that Lt-Col Rugigana Ngabo had been illegally detained by agents of Rwanda's Government, and ordered the latter to pay costs to the applicant's sister, Plaxeda Rugumba. The court ruled that the detention contravened Article 6(d) and Article 7(2) of the EAC Treaty, which guarantees that 'partner states shall be bound by the principles of *inter alia*, good governance and the rule of law'. It further found that the detention contravened Rwandan law, particularly in terms of a failure to bring the suspect in front of a national court within 48 hours of arrest. In 2011 and 2012, the EACJ's First Instance Division was also considering a case brought by seven alleged perpetrators of the July 2010 Kampala terror attacks, who contended that Kenya's courts failed to follow national judicial process, when they extradited the seven Kenyan citizens to Uganda.

Other key EAC organs are the Co-ordination Committee and the Secretariat. The Co-ordination Committee provides a civil service function, as it is comprised of the member states' permanent secretaries for regional co-operation and it is mandated to implement the decisions of the Council of Ministers. The Secretariat is the executive organ of the EAC and is comprised primarily of the Secretary-General, Deputy Secretaries-General and Counsel. The Secretary-General heads the Secretariat, obliging him or her to take responsibility for the accounts of the EAC and act as secretary to the Summit. The Secretary General serves a fixed five-year term and is selected by the relevant member state on a rotational basis.

The principal institutions of the EAC are the Civil Aviation Safety and Security Oversight Agency (CASSOA), the East African Development Bank (EADB), the Inter-University Council for East Africa (IUCEA), the Lake Victoria Basin Commission (LVBC) and the Lake Victoria Fisheries Organization (LVFO). The CASSOA oversees a harmonization of regional operating regulations in accordance with international civil aviation safety and security standards. To this end, the agency encourages the inter-state sharing of personnel and expertise, and takes a lead role in the development and supervision of procedures for member states' civil aviation activities. The EADB provides finance for, and advises on, development projects in the EAC. It is part-owned by four member states (Kenya, Tanzania, Rwanda and Uganda), the African Development Bank (AfDB) and a number of financial institutions in the private sector. The IUCEA facilitates the promotion—and mutual recognition among member states—of academic standards in the EAC, while also helping universities to better serve the needs of employers and regional development. The LVBC maintains responsibility for co-ordinating the sustainable development of the Victoria Basin, while the LVFO promotes sustainable fishing by communities and nation-states in Lake Victoria, which is shared by Uganda, Tanzania and Kenya.

TODAY'S EAC—CUSTOMS UNION

The protocol for the establishment of the EAC's Customs Union was signed by the then member states—Kenya, Tanzania and Uganda—on 2 March 2004 in Arusha. The objectives of the Customs Union are four-fold: to liberalize intra-EAC trade; to promote the diversification and expansion of industrial activity in the EAC; to promote intra-EAC production efficiency; and to increase foreign direct investment (FDI) in the EAC. It was envisaged that achievement of the first objective (liberalization) would help facilitate the second, third and fourth objectives.

The liberalization of trade refers to both intra-EAC trade and external trade. With regard to the latter, the Customs Union established a three-tier common external tariff. Goods entering Kenya, Uganda and Tanzania from outside the three-nation bloc would be taxed at a rate of zero (for raw materials), 10% (for intermediate products) and 25% (for fully finished goods).

With regard to intra-EAC trade, it was acknowledged by Kenya that its neighbours Tanzania and Uganda would lose out in the event that all internal tariffs were dismantled immediately, due to Kenya's relatively large and efficient manufacturing sector. It was therefore agreed that certain goods (termed 'Category B' goods) exported from Kenya to either Tanzania or Uganda (including textiles, iron, paper, plastics, steel, wood, agricultural products and construction materials) would remain subject to tariffs. These tariffs would be diminished progressively before being eliminated after five years (i.e. by 2010). Goods classified as 'Category A' were, from the start of the Customs Union, to be allowed to enter Tanzania and Uganda from Kenya exempt from tariffs. Similarly, all trade between Uganda and Tanzania, and all exports from Uganda and Tanzania to Kenya, were, from the outset, to be tariff-free. The signatories also agreed to remove all existing non-tariff barriers (for example, cumbersome inspection and documentation requirements) and pledged not to establish new barriers. In reality, however, non-tariff barriers have persisted.

Kenya's willingness to provide a transition period initially created breathing space for Tanzania's and Uganda's lagging and relatively small manufacturing sectors, enabling producers in these latter two countries to adjust gradually to heightened competition. This concession by Kenya therefore gave important impetus to the evolution of the 'reborn' EAC, as the largely successful creation of the Customs Union justified the time, money and political capital committed to the revived integration project.

Rwanda and Burundi nominally joined the Customs Union in 2008, after becoming member nations of the EAC in July 2007. However, the two new entrants were not required to start implementing the Customs Union's policies until July 2009. Important exemptions continued for some time after this date. In March 2012, Rwanda was granted a six-month extension to an existing waiver on sugar import duties.

TODAY'S EAC—COMMON MARKET

The Common Market, which came into being on 1 July 2010 after being signed by all five heads of state on 20 November 2009, has evolved as a logical extension of the Customs Union. The Customs Union, various caveats aside, allows for the free movement of goods within the EAC, while the Common Market extends this free movement (while again allowing important caveats) to the free movement of capital, services and labour.

The Common Market's rationale is to accelerate economic growth and wider development within the EAC by enabling private enterprise to expand and flourish, via the provision of greater access to funding opportunities, labour markets and service industries. Additionally, this deepening of economic integration is designed to provide greater consumer choice, since the removal of barriers to trade, capital flows, labour and services enhances competition among firms and destroys monopolies, thereby reducing consumer prices.

Capital

In the EAC's Common Market Protocol, the free movement of capital entails, in its barest essentials, the removal of 'restrictions between the Partner States, on the movement of capital belonging to persons resident in the [East African] Community' and an end to 'any discrimination based on the nationality or on the place of residence of the persons or on the place where the capital is invested'.

At the outset of the Common Market Kenya, Uganda and Rwanda maintained open capital accounts. As long-standing members of the EAC with a commitment to free market principles, it came as little surprise that Uganda and Kenya adopted such an open stance. Meanwhile, although Rwanda was a relatively late (and small) entrant to the EAC, it has placed significant emphasis on the development of its financial services sector, so felt confident that its currency and banking system would not only be able to withstand, but could actually flourish, in an environment of enhanced financial services competition in the region.

However, despite signing the Common Market Protocol in November 2009 (and officially joining the Common Market in July 2010), Burundi and Tanzania decided to maintain controls on capital account transactions with fellow EAC member states, while pledging to eliminate restrictions over the period 2010–15. The latter two countries were able to maintain capital account restrictions due to Article 25 of the Common Market Protocol, which allows four 'general exceptions' to the free movement of capital, on the grounds of prudential supervision, public policy considerations, money-laundering or financial sanctions. Although the latter two categories are very narrowly defined, the former two—'prudential supervision' and, in particular, 'public policy considerations'—are clearly open to significant interpretation.

These two broad exceptions make it easy for a member state to claim that the free movement of capital poses risks to the stability of its national banking systems and currency, thereby potentially enabling a dissenting member state to insulate its financial system (or exchange rate) against competition indefinitely. The legitimacy of recoursing to such claims has been enhanced by the global financial crisis of 2008–09, which, for the first time in decades, has brought into significant question the wisdom of allowing unrestricted capital mobility. This crisis showed how damaging large-scale capital withdrawals could be to the financial systems and national economies of even developed countries, particularly Iceland and Ireland, but also such giants as the United Kingdom.

Despite the crisis that has swept through developed markets, Rwanda, Kenya and Uganda remain committed to the free movement of capital. Rwanda opened a national stock exchange in January 2008—a market that received a significant boost from the tabling of US $80m. of bids for a January 2011 flotation of brewer BRALIRWA. However, Burundi and Tanzania are likely to retain a much more cautious stance with regard to capital market openness, with only a very incremental removal of restrictions expected over the five years to 2015. The post-conflict, pro-market reformist zeal that has been a hallmark of Rwanda over the last decade or so has not been replicated by Burundi, which has emerged from civil war only latterly and is still dogged by a very low level of economic development. Meanwhile, although Tanzania has adopted a progressively more pro-market orientation since the retirement of President Nyerere in 1985, the country's political establishment maintains a measure of suspicion of capital mobility consistent with its socialist legacy.

In the case of the EAC, the Common Market also extends to member states' harmonizing of monetary and fiscal policies. This co-ordination over macroeconomic policy is designed to minimize the divergence of national business cycles and to reduce the danger of member states over-borrowing or descending into hyperinflation. Such fiscal and monetary discipline is, moreover, an important precursor for monetary union.

Labour

The Common Market Protocol included a pledge by the EAC's five nations to 'guarantee the free movement of workers, who are citizens of the other Partner States, within their territories' and to 'ensure non discrimination of the workers of the other Partner States, based on their nationalities, in relation to employment, remuneration and other conditions of work and employment'.

However, as with the other sectors, the opening of labour markets is only partial and is unbalanced across the member states. Although Kenya committed itself to removing domestic restrictions on the employment of other EAC countries' citizens in the managerial, professional, technical, associate professional and craft categories from 1 July 2010, Burundi committed only to allowing professionals from fellow member states to work within its borders from this date. Uganda agreed to remove restrictions in the managerial, professional and craft categories from 1 July, while Rwanda opened up the professional, technical and associate professional categories. Despite its status as a founder member of the EAC, Tanzania has, as in other sub-sectors, lagged behind the majority of its peer nations in the opening of its labour market. The country committed only to opening up the professional, technical and associate professional categories, and pledged to do so only on a gradual basis over the period 2010–15 (rather than immediately in July 2010).

Alongside the opening of labour markets, the Common Market has made it easier for EAC citizens to move between the member states. A visa is not required in order to travel from a citizen's country of residence and enter another EAC member state.

Services

The Common Market Protocol, when it first came into effect in July 2010, involved only a modest cross-border opening up of member countries' service sectors. The protocol theoretically guaranteed 'the free movement of service suppliers who are nationals of the Partner States', but only seven sectors are scheduled to be opened up over the period 2010–15, and even then only on an incremental basis. The seven sectors are: communications, distribution, financial, travel and tourism, educational, transport, and business/professional services.

Progress in opening up and harmonizing the tourism sector—a key foreign exchange earner for all member states except Burundi—has been particularly slow. As of mid-2011, the member states had still to agree on the modalities of introducing a single, EAC-wide tourist visa. At this stage, all the member states maintained national systems for issuing tourist visas to visitors outside the EAC, with some countries charging more than others. For example, a three-month tourist visa cost US $25 per person for Kenya, while in Uganda it was $50. Beyond a uniform, EAC-wide fee, the member states would need to devise, and agree on, a system of sharing revenues from visas, against a backdrop where some countries receive substantially more visitors than others. Security risks provide a further complicating factor: an individual's nationality and background may be perceived to pose a risk by one (or more) member state, but not by others.

Five key sectors—health, social affairs, construction, energy and environmental services—were left out of the Common Market Protocol. The member states pledged to address these areas at an undetermined future date.

TOMORROW'S EAC—MONETARY UNION?

The construction of a monetary union has been anticipated from the EAC's outset. The EAC Treaty, which came into effect in 2000, provided for the establishment of a monetary union in Articles 5, 82, 83, 84, 85 and 86. The key objectives of East African Monetary Union (EAMU) are two-fold: to remove the costs involved in transacting business across the EAC in different currencies, and to reduce foreign exchange risks. With regard to the latter, businesses trading in multiple EAC countries are subject to the vagaries of swings in the value of member states' exchange rates. A company domiciled in Kenya but offering services or goods in Uganda, for example, can suffer in the event that the Uganda shilling suddenly depreciates sharply against the Kenya shilling, because the value of sales in Uganda when converted back into the home currency (Kenya shillings) is suddenly reduced. Monetary union would remove these risks and uncertainties, at least at the intra-EAC level.

The timeline for EAMU is ambitious. The target date for the introduction and circulation of a single currency is 2015. This ultimate aim is to be preceded by two phases of preparation. In the first phase (up to the end of 2010), the member countries were meant to meet basic economic 'convergence criteria', before a second phase (2011–14), when those criteria are to be tightened. Those criteria will be considered in detail below.

The planned adoption of monetary union is very loosely based on the European Union (EU)'s model. It may seem slightly incredible that the EAC is committed to adopting its own version of such a union. Designing, implementing and maintaining effective economic and monetary union for highly developed European nations was a very challenging exercise—and remains so, in view of the fallout from the 2008–09 financial crisis, which has seen question marks emerge about the ability of a number of member states (in particular Greece, Ireland and Portugal) to maintain the confidence of government bond markets. Considered against this backdrop, what then are the chances of economic and monetary union coming to sustainable fruition in the EAC, where some member states are perennially dependent on the largesse of the IMF's lending facilities?

In answer to this, while there are clearly risks involved in the adoption of monetary union, it is by no means an impossibly reckless exercise for the EAC countries. In fact, EAMU, if it comes into being, will not be the first regional single currency arrangement in sub-Saharan Africa: the franc de la Coopération Financière en Afrique Centrale (CFA franc) is used by 14 countries in West and Central Africa. The CFA franc even encompasses two monetary unions—the Union Economique et Monétaire Ouest-Africaine (made up of Benin, Burkina Faso, Côte d'Ivoire, Guinea-Bissau, Mali, Niger, Senegal and Togo) and the Communauté Economique et Monétaire de l'Afrique Central (comprising Cameroon, the Central African Republic, Chad, the Republic of the Congo, Equatorial Guinea and Gabon). The currency has displayed a remarkable degree of stability in recent years, with the successful maintenance of a fixed peg against the euro, despite the CFA franc zone containing some of the world's least stable countries. Central government authority in the Central African Republic and Chad, for example, is extremely tenuous and rebel groups plague large swathes of territory in these countries. Against such a backdrop, the successful maintenance of the CFA zone's euro peg must provide some confidence among EAC partner states about their own chances of forming a successful monetary union.

However, the timescale envisaged appears a little ambitious. The EAC's partner states only began negotiating a protocol for monetary union in early 2011. In April of that year delegates from the member states met in Mwanza, Tanzania, to discuss the draft preamble, interpretations, objectives, scope and principles, according to the EAC's press office. At that stage, delegates had still to begin negotiating the harmonization of financial and macroeconomic statistics, a clarification of convergence criteria, the legal and regulatory framework, the exchange rate mechanism and monetary policy. This left remarkably little time before the proposed 2015 inception of the single currency, especially in view of the fact that it took more than seven years for the EU to bring into force the euro, after establishing the convergence criteria. The 1991 Maastricht Treaty established the protocol for monetary union (including convergence criteria), before the euro effectively came into force with a fixing of exchange rates in 1999. However, the physical introduction of euro banknotes and coins did not take place until 2002, effectively translating into an additional three-year buffer period (in addition to the 1991–99 transition) to resolve outstanding issues (conceivably including, had an emergency situation required it, the opt-out of a member state before the 'point of no return').

One of the most important outstanding prerequisites for a successful introduction of EAMU is the clarification of (and adherence to) convergence criteria by the member states. The EAC commissioned the European Central Bank (ECB) to undertake a study on the preparedness of the EAC for monetary union. In a February 2010 report on this subject entitled

'Study on the establishment of a monetary union among the Partner States of the East African Community', the ECB drew attention to what it regarded as the EAC's vagueness in the drafting of convergence criteria. In the first convergence phase (to the end of 2010), the partner states of the EAC were meant to:

keep overall budget deficits to a maximum of 6% of GDP, exclusive of grants (and a maximum of 3% of GDP, inclusive of grants);

maintain an annual average inflation rate of 5% or below;

maintain external (foreign exchange) reserves equivalent to more than four months of imports;

sustain real GDP growth of at least 7% per annum;

maintain national savings of at least 20% of GDP;

maintain stable real exchange rates;

maintain market-determined interest rates;

ensure that domestic and foreign debt were sustainable.

However, the ECB study maintained that the definition of terms for many of these variables was too open to interpretation, thereby calling into question the uniformity and coherence of the yardsticks. For example, an 'overall budget deficit' is quite a loose term, without establishing what can and cannot be listed as extra-budgetary spending and revenues, according to the report's authors. Similarly, according to the ECB, confusion and data inconsistency can be caused by the interpretation of what constitutes the 'annual average inflation rate' since the convergence criteria do not specify whether consumer, retail, wholesale or some other measure of price growth should be the yardstick. Additionally, there are no statistical benchmarks for what constitutes a stable real exchange rate or a sustainable level of foreign or domestic debt.

Separately, the ECB study questioned the extent to which the achievement of a real GDP growth rate of at least 7% per annum represents a convergence yardstick. If, for example, one country achieves annual growth of 7%, while another experiences a very rapid 15%, then it would be difficult to say that business cycles and economic conditions in these two states had converged to anything like an ideal level. This is important because even moderate national divergences in cyclical economic growth make the pursuit of the 'one size fits all' regional monetary or exchange rate policy necessitated by monetary union less than ideal. The country with the higher rate of economic growth will invariably require higher interest rates than the country with lower economic growth, in order to prevent the faster-growing economy from overheating and provoking inflation. In this context, the ECB recommended that rather than stipulating a minimum rate of real GDP growth, the EAC convergence criteria should instead centre on a band of fluctuation around the mean annual average real GDP growth rate of partner states. Thus, for example, the acceptable range of real GDP growth might be +/–2.5%, around a central figure of 7%. A similar alteration might also be made to the inflation criteria: for example, instead of a maximum annual inflation rate of 5% (whether consumer, retail or otherwise), the partner states might instead be expected to achieve an inflation rate of 3%, with a +/–2% margin of fluctuation.

Some of the convergence criteria for the second phase (2011–14) are a little more stringent, although, like those for the first phase, still in need of significant clarification, according to the ECB study. Key requirements for the second phase include:

keeping overall budget deficits to a maximum of 5% of GDP, exclusive of grants (and a maximum of 2% of GDP, inclusive of grants);

maintaining external reserves equivalent to more than six months of imports;

a 'sustained pursuit of debt sustainability'.

The negotiations that began in earnest in 2011 among member states are likely to result in modifications to (and clearer definitions of) the convergence criteria. Once the criteria are finalized, the partner states may have to adjust national policies sharply in order to qualify, ahead of the 2015 target date for the circulation of the single currency.

In advance of the likely clarification of the convergence criteria, it is possible to make some observations about the level of convergence that has been achieved thus far. The year 2010 yielded an impressively small range of outcomes for national GDP growth, but substantial divergences in consumer price growth, according to IMF statistics (as of 15 May 2011). Most positively, the lowest national rate of annual real GDP growth achieved in 2010 was recorded by Burundi, at a reasonably respectable 3.8%, while Rwanda and Tanzania scored highest, both with 6.5%. This amounted to an impressive range of just 2.7% between the highest and lowest national economic growth rates. Uganda's economy expanded by 5.2% in real terms in 2010, while Kenya recorded growth of 5.0%. On the downside, national consumer price inflation ranged between 2.3% (Rwanda) and a worryingly high 10.5% (Tanzania). Consumer price growth was also high in Uganda in 2010, totalling 9.4%, before rising further in the first few months of 2011, to 14.1% year-on-year in April of that year. This surge in prices was partly attributable to the effects of high global oil prices, but also to localized droughts and, most worryingly, a significant increase in government spending that had taken place ahead of legislative elections in February. Uganda's increase in spending (much of it unbudgeted) raised concerns about fiscal discipline and meant that the IMF was, in that month, unable to complete a review of the country's economic performance in line with its Policy Support Instrument.

Despite such significant divergences in the macroeconomic trajectories of partner countries, the EAC continued its push towards monetary union in 2011. Across the course of the year, it held six separate rounds of talks on the topic, so that by the end of 2011 the High Level Task Force had negotiated 49 articles of the draft Monetary Union Protocol (more than one-half of the total number required). The key articles successfully negotiated at that stage were the scope of monetary union; the macroeconomic policy framework and convergence; monetary policy framework; exchange rate policy; co-ordination of fiscal policy and budget formulation; EAC-wide project financing; and external and domestic debt management frameworks. In February 2012 the finance ministers of the member states met in Arusha together with representatives of the IMF at a two-day regional conference, during which EAC Secretary-General Richard Sezibera re-emphasized that the regional bloc's immediate objective was the establishment of monetary union.

The reaffirmation of this goal came despite escalating problems in the euro zone, where a sovereign debt crisis was calling into question the continued viability of Europe's single currency. In particular, Greece was experiencing increasing difficulty in paying its debts, despite an earlier bailout, and its government was locked in negotiations with the EU over a new rescue package. The euro zone crisis intensified during the first half of 2012, as the Greek Government collapsed after it proved unable to agree to new bailout terms. This put pressure on the eurobonds of other highly indebted euro zone nations (including Portugal and Spain) and undermined the value of the euro on global currency markets.

As 2012 progressed important individuals within one particular EAC partner state began to question the wisdom of monetary union, particularly in terms of the timetable (inter-community negotiations on the topic were due to be completed by 2013). An adviser to President Kagame, Prof. Manasseh Nshuti, argued in two articles in the heavily state-aligned *New Times* newspaper that the East African bloc should avoid rushing the process, due both to the problems emerging in the euro zone and reservations about the EAC's own degree of economic integration. 'Even with the political misjudgement in the euro project, it took 40 years of serious testing of monetary as well as fiscal discipline before a monetary union was launched [in Europe],' he cautioned. Furthermore, the degree of fiscal and inflationary convergence attained by EAC partner states remains a long way off that achieved pre-union by euro zone countries. Inflation, Nshuti pointed out, is inevitably volatile and periodically high in emerging markets; and the EAC countries would retain the status of emerging markets for some years to come. His comments were significant, because they could be read as a reflection of Rwanda's policy position on monetary union within the EAC. Indeed, political discipline within the ruling Front Patriotique Rwandaise (FPR) is intensely strong, so Nshuti would almost certainly not have been writing without the backing of President Kagame.

Policy Objective

Member states will also have to agree on a name for the single currency, and to establish a policy objective for the regional central bank. The principal choice will be between price stability (i.e. attempting to keep intra-EAC inflation within a targeted range) or exchange rate stability. Opting for the latter might involve fixing the EAMU currency to the euro (as per the franc CFA zone), the dollar or a basket of currencies. Fixing the currency in such a way would have the advantage of reducing the foreign exchange risks of businesses conducting trade between the EAC and the eurozone and/or the USA. This would not only benefit some EAC businesses with trading partnerships in the developed world, but also, in the event of a credible and sustainable exchange rate peg, encourage greater FDI to the EAC, by dint of the reduced currency risk borne by potential inward investors. The downside of a fixed exchange rate, however, is that it would mean sacrificing optimum policy control over price growth in the EAC, since central bank operations in the foreign exchange and money markets would be geared towards maintaining the currency union's exchange rate, rather than controlling inflation *per se*.

On balance, the circulation of a common currency in the EAC appears too ambitious, especially in light of the sobering effect generated by the euro zone crisis. The EAC may yet choose to phase in the introduction of the single currency by, for example, fixing the exchange rates of member countries from 2015 and then waiting for a period of a few months or even years before withdrawing national currencies and circulating the new currency. Alternatively, it may opt for a bolder postponement, in the shape of delaying the locking of national currencies' exchange rates until after 2015. These scenarios—and other permutations, including the possibility that one or more member state may opt to join the monetary union at a later date than a 'first wave' of participants—will likely remain the subject of speculation for some time.

TOMORROW'S EAC—POLITICAL FEDERATION?

The EAC Treaty stipulates that the ultimate aim of the integration process is political union. In Article 5, paragraph 2 of the treaty (entitled 'Objectives of the Community'), it is stated that 'the Partner States undertake to establish among themselves and in accordance with the provisions of this Treaty, a Customs Union, a Common Market [and] subsequently a Monetary Union and ultimately a Political Federation'. Progress towards constructing such a political federation has been limited, in part because of limited progress towards achieving the preceding objective of monetary union.

The then heads of state of member countries in the EAC resolved at an extraordinary Summit meeting in August 2004 to establish a fast track mechanism, in order to accelerate the process of constructing a political federation, before instructing the Council of Ministers in 2005 to survey views among key stakeholders in the EAC nations on the integration process and political union. These surveys yielded significant concerns about the objective of achieving a political federation, particularly in terms of the surrender of national sovereignty that would inevitably be entailed. Subsidiary to this, fears were also expressed about the budgetary demands on member states that would be exacted by a full political federation, against a backdrop where member states remain heavily dependent on external aid just to fund their existing national budgets.

By definition, since a monetary union is scheduled to precede a political federation, the latter would require member countries to surrender powers above and beyond the conduct of monetary and exchange rate policy. The exact degree to which powers would be surrendered would depend upon the eventual outcome of negotiations on a protocol for the political federation, and upon opt-outs negotiated by individual member states.

In Article 5, Paragraph 1 of the EAC Treaty, the fields of social policy, defence and security are referred to as areas of potential future co-operation. Defence and security are national policy spheres that are likely to remain jealously guarded for some years to come.

On balance, the readiness of member states to commit to a political federation remains in considerable doubt. Pledging full commitment to this stated outcome is difficult for any sovereign country, but particularly so for the countries of East Africa, which, to varying degrees, remain bedevilled by a reluctance on the part of governing élites to open up democratic space.

The national Governments of Rwanda and Burundi are particularly authoritarian. Both countries held presidential elections in 2010; in Rwanda President Kagame secured 93.1% of the vote, while in Burundi, President Jean-Pierre Nkurunziza took 91.6%. In Rwanda the three most credible potential opposition candidates were prevented from running. That left Kagame with competition from only three candidates, none of whom actively opposed the incumbent's policies. In Burundi Nkurunziza was the sole candidate, as all opposition parties (and their leaders) boycotted the poll after alleging that local elections held earlier in the year had been rigged. Uganda held a presidential election in February 2011, which saw President Museveni, who had already served 25 years in power, returned for a third elected term, against a backdrop where the EU criticized the ruling National Resistance Movement for the widespread provision of 'gifts' to the electorate. Tanzania's presidential election in November 2010—which saw President Lt-Col (retd) Jakaya Mrisho Kikwete secure a new five-year term—was marred by allegations of electoral malpractice by opposition candidate Willibrod Peter Slaa, who claimed that police and security forces had rigged the vote. Finally, Kenya's heavily disputed presidential election in December 2007 was followed by two months of violence, which killed some 1,500 people and displaced a further 300,000, before international mediation yielded a power-sharing deal which saw Kibaki remain as President and his principal challenger, Raila Odinga, assume the newly created post of Prime Minister.

Given these region-wide democratic deficiencies—and, more particularly, the reluctance of incumbent presidents and ruling parties in some countries to allow genuine challenges to their authority—it is difficult to see EAC member states ceding significant political powers to a supranational authority in the immediate future. For the remainder of this decade (and possibly considerably beyond), the partial ceding of macroeconomic policy control (i.e. over monetary and exchange rate policy) demanded by EAMU appears to be challenge enough for the nation-states of the EAC.

There were some small advances, in terms of political and security co-operation in 2011 and 2012. In November 2011 President Kagame opened a training programme in Rwanda, involving the instruction of over 300 troops from EAC partner states. The programme, held at the Rwanda Military Academy in Nyakimana, involved training in disaster management, counter terrorism and peace support. In May 2012 the EALA passed the EAC Conflict Management Bill 2011, paving the way for the establishment of a Conflict Prevention, Management and Resolution Mechanism (CPMR). The CPMR would be tasked with identifying potential sources of regional conflict and defusing such conflicts. As of mid-2012 the EAC's draft Peace and Security Protocol—which covers areas including cross-border cattle theft, genocide, the illegal trade in small arms, peacekeeping, piracy and terrorism—was before the regional bloc's Sectoral Council on Legal and Judicial Affairs, where it was being evaluated ahead of final multilateral political approval.

Although a substantial deepening of political integration appears a long way off, a medium-term widening of the EAC is more realistic. In April 2012 the heads of state of the EAC countries directed the regional bloc's Council of Ministers to produce a report evaluating a bid for membership by South Sudan, which had officially seceded from Sudan in July 2011. The report was due to be completed and considered in November 2012. Ahead of this deadline, the EAC sent a delegation to Juba, the capital of South Sudan, in July 2012, to analyze the country's readiness. The success of the application, which was launched in November 2011, would depend, at least in part, on the resolution of conflict between Sudan and South Sudan. More than seven years after the official end of the 1983–2005 north-south civil war (which killed an estimated 2m. people), fighting broke out between the Sudan Armed Forces (SAF) and the national military of newly-independent South Sudan in March and April 2012, when the latter's troops occupied the northern reaches of the disputed Heglig oilfields. Although there had been clashes during the 2005–11 political transition—usually characterized by fighting between armed proxies—the conflict in Heglig represented arguably the most serious breach of the peace since the end of the civil war. In response, the UN Security Council in early May 2012 issued Resolution 2046, which threatened both countries with multilateral sanctions, in the event that they failed to resume negotiations on key post-secession issues, including oil sharing and the demarcation of a common border. During their April 2012 meeting the EAC Heads of State issued a communiqué, which urged the two countries to return to talks and to resolve the outstanding issues, in line with the UN Security Council's position. At that stage, it appeared likely that any failure by the two Sudans to de-escalate military tensions and make political progress could adversely impact South Sudan's application to join the EAC, particularly in view of the aggression displayed during a 10-day incursion into Heglig in April.

Sudan's own bid for EAC membership was turned down in November 2011. Officially, the reason was an absence of 'geographical proximity,' in view of South Sudan's secession resulting in Sudan having no border with an existing EAC partner state. However, Uganda objected to Sudan's membership bid, in part due to historical tensions, which had involved the two countries backing proxy forces against one another in the years before 2005. Uganda's First Deputy Prime Minister and Minister in Charge of East African Community Affairs, Eriya Kategaya, candidly stated that Sudan's rejection was motivated by 'several issues like their democracy, the way they treat women and their religious politics'.

Aside from Sudan and South Sudan, other potential EAC aspirants are the Democratic Republic of the Congo (DRC) and Somalia. Uganda's President Museveni advocated the accession of the DRC in January 2012, during the opening in Kampala of the East African Legislative Assembly (EALA). However, the DRC's accession prospects were undermined by a renewed rise in cross-border tensions with Rwanda, signalled by the start of a new mutiny by senior Congolese Tutsi officers in mineral rich Nord Kivu province in April 2012. Human Rights Watch and the UN Group of Experts on the DRC accused Rwanda's Tutsi dominated Government of backing this mutiny, allegedly through cross-border provision of arms and sanctuary for the rebels (charges denied by the Rwandan Government). Earlier, in April 2011, Rwanda's President Kagame voiced his support for Somalia joining the EAC, after meeting in Kigali with President Sheikh Sharif Sheikh Ahmed.

EXTERNAL RELATIONS

A number of influential countries appointed ambassadors or concluded draft political and trade agreements with the EAC in 2011 and 2012. Germany appointed his Excellency Klaus-Peter Brandes as its special representative to the EAC in October 2011, before the Chinese (Lv Youqing) and Australian (Geoffrey Tooth) ambassadors to Tanzania in March 2012 presented letters appointing them dually as their countries' representatives to the EAC. The People's Republic of China and the EAC signed a Framework Agreement on economy, trade, investment and technical co-operation in November 2011. Trade between the EAC and China totalled $3,890m. in 2010, while the People's Republic had invested $750m. in developing the manufacturing capacity of the five nation bloc as of September 2011, mainly in clothing and machinery production, according to Chinese data. Moving forward, the EAC's Secretary-General, Richard Sezibera, identified investment in roads (particularly the $566m. Arusha–Holili–Voi road) as a key priority. In order to facilitate the further development of Sino-EAC commercial activity, the framework agreement established a Joint Committee on Economy, Trade, Investment and Technical Co-operation. In June 2012 the EAC and the US Government resolved to establish a new trade and investment partnership, which would extend the existing African Growth and Opportunity Act (AGOA) and the Trade & Investment Framework Agreement (TIFA). Outlined by US Trade Representative Ron Kirk and Sezibera, this planned new agreement would entail a new trade deal, capacity building, a regional investment treaty and a reduction of trade barriers.

BIBLIOGRAPHY

Debrun, X., Masson, P., and Pattillo, C. *Should African Monetary Unions Be Expanded? An Empirical Investigation of the Scope for Monetary Integration in Sub-Saharan Africa*. IMF Working Paper WP/10/157. IMF, 2010.

East African Community. *Treaty for the Establishment of the East African Community*. Arusha, 1999.

East African Community Secretariat. *Protocol on the Establishment of the East African Community Customs Union*. Arusha, 2004.

Report of the Committee on Fast Tracking East African Federation. Arusha, 2007.

Protocol on the Establishment of the East African Community Common Market. Arusha, 2009.

East African Community Facts & Figures – 2010. Arusha, March 2011.

European Central Bank Staff. *Study on the Establishment of a Monetary Union Among Partner States of the East African Community*. 2010.

Kabatabaazi, W. *The EU-East African Community Economic Partnership Agreement: The Impact of EPAs on the Right to Food*. Saarbrücken, Lambert Academic Publishing, 2010.

Kasule, S. *Regionalism in Africa: A Case Study of the East African Community*. Saarbrücken, VDM Verlag, 2009.

Khorana, S., Kimbugwe, K., and Perdikis N. *The impact of tariff reductions under the East African Community Customs Union: Intra-trade effects on Uganda*. Aberystwyth University, 2007.

Kikonyogo, J. *Similar Solutions for Similar Problems: Harmonising Energy Trade and Investment Policies and Strategies in the East African Community*. Saarbrücken, Lambert Academic Publishing, 2011.

Oitamong, M. *The Revived East African Community: Fast-Tracking the Political Federation*. Saarbrücken, Lambert Academic Publishing, 2010.

HEALTH AND MEDICAL ISSUES IN SUB-SAHARAN AFRICA

OLALEKAN UTHMAN

The strong influence of socio-economic factors on health outcomes plays a central role in the discussion of health and medical issues in sub-Saharan Africa, making poverty the key focus of many initiatives to improve population health in Africa. In addition to the pervasive poverty at national levels in most sub-Saharan countries, which has led to a steady deterioration in the infrastructure and systems required to deliver health care, poverty at an individual level has, through malnutrition, poor living conditions and the inability to afford treatment, worsened the situation of many individuals and families. The increasing awareness of the links between poverty and ill health perhaps lay at the heart of initiatives in 2007 to hold leaders of the world's largest industrialized nations to the commitments that they had made towards tackling poverty and underdevelopment in Africa in the preceding two years. Increasingly, there was also an emphasis on Africans finding their own solutions to the health challenges facing the continent, with governments being encouraged to channel savings from debt relief into investments in health.

The vast majority of people living in sub-Saharan Africa have yet to benefit from the advances in medical research and public health that other regions of the world have enjoyed in terms of human development. This limited development is due to the burden of infectious diseases, particularly human immunodeficiency virus/acquired immunodeficiency syndrome (HIV/AIDS), tuberculosis (TB) and malaria. A child born in sub-Saharan Africa faces more health risks than a child born in any other part of the world. Such a child has more than a 50% chance of being malnourished and a high risk of being HIV-positive at birth, while malaria, diarrhoeal diseases and acute respiratory diseases account for 51% of deaths. A child born in the sub-Saharan African region is more likely to lose his or her mother owing to complications in childbirth or to HIV/AIDS, while that child has a life expectancy of just 47 years, and is very likely—at least once in his or her short life—to be affected by drought, famine, flood or civil war, or to become a refugee. People living in this region are more exposed to a heavy and wide-ranging burden of disease partly because of the region's unique geography and climate. These factors make malaria, for instance, more intractable in sub-Saharan Africa than it is elsewhere. People living south of the Sahel region and in parts of the Great Lakes region and southern Africa are at risk of epidemic meningitis. Forests harbour rare but headline-grabbing haemorrhagic fever viruses, such as Marburg and Ebola. By cutting down the trees surrounding a village, people can expose themselves to an outbreak of one of these highly fatal diseases. Mosquitoes that transmit malaria are capable of breeding in a footprint filled with water. Other mosquitoes transmit yellow fever and lymphatic filariasis. Non-communicable diseases (NCDs), including, but not limited to, cardiovascular diseases, cancer, mental health and diabetes, are now major sources of morbidity and mortality in sub-Saharan Africa. NCDs are projected to overtake infectious diseases as the major cause of death in the sub-Saharan African region by 2030. Over 80% of deaths from NCDs worldwide are estimated to occur in low- and middle-income countries. The World Health Organization (WHO) projects that the number of deaths from ischemic heart disease in Africa region will double by 2030. The prevalence of diabetes mellitus in Africa is predicted to increase by 80% in about 20 years. In most countries the poorest people have the highest risk of developing NCDs and are least able to cope with the resulting financial consequences. When the costs to individuals are calculated, the loss to the economy can be substantial. Furthermore, road traffic collisions place a heavy burden on households and, in turn, regional and national economies.

Nowhere has HIV/AIDS killed such large proportions of the population, nor has TB re-emerged to fuel the HIV/AIDS epidemic, as it has in sub-Saharan Africa. No other region has witnessed so many armed conflicts and other humanitarian emergencies. People living in the sub-Saharan African region face a heavy and wide-ranging burden of disease, which takes its toll on social and economic development and shortens their life expectancy. The HIV/AIDS epidemic as well as the resurgence of malaria and TB, and the effects of armed conflict, have swept away improvements in life expectancy and eradicated progress in human development made during the 1970s and 1980s by some sub-Saharan countries. In addition, countries in the region continue to suffer from other emergencies, large-scale migration, famine and economic decline, while the complications of pregnancy and childbirth claim almost 500,000 lives in the region each year.

Less than three years now remain before the 2015 deadline by which world leaders have pledged to reduce hunger and extreme poverty by one-half and to make substantial gains in education, health, social equity, environmental sustainability and international solidarity. Without stronger commitment and more rapid progress, most of those goals will not be met. All developing regions except sub-Saharan Africa, Western Asia and parts of Eastern Europe and Central Asia are expected to achieve the targets of the UN's Millennium Development Goals (MDGs). These shortfalls reflect slow growth in sub-Saharan Africa in the 1990s and the transition from planned to market economies that saw poverty increase. Nowhere are the signs more ominous than in sub-Saharan Africa, the world's poorest and least developed region. Africa entered the new millennium with the highest poverty and child mortality rates, and the lowest school enrolment figures in the world. Child mortality rates in Africa changed little during the 1990s, owing largely to the HIV/AIDS pandemic, which eroded the gains in infant and maternal health made by some countries. Much the same can be said for Africa's primary school enrolments, which rose only modestly from a world low of 56% in 1991 to 59% a decade later; this is also partly a result of HIV/AIDS, which has forced many children, particularly girls, to withdraw from education to care for sick relatives and has reduced the ability of many families to pay school fees.

Hunger and malnutrition are major causes of the deprivation and suffering targeted by all of the other MDGs. Hungry children start school later (if at all), drop out sooner and learn less while they do attend, stalling progress towards universal primary and secondary education (MDG 2). Poor nutrition for women is one of the most damaging outcomes of gender inequality. It undermines women's health, stunts their opportunities for education and employment and impedes progress towards gender equality and empowerment of women (MDG 3). As the underlying cause of more than one-half of all child deaths, hunger and malnutrition are the greatest obstacles to reducing child mortality (MDG 4). Hunger and malnutrition increase both the incidence and the fatality rate of conditions that cause a majority of maternal deaths during pregnancy and childbirth (MDG 5). Hunger and poverty compromise people's immune systems, force them to adopt risky survival strategies, and greatly increase the risk of infection and death from HIV/AIDS, malaria and other infectious diseases (MDG 6). Under the burden of chronic poverty and hunger, livestock herders, subsistence farmers, forest dwellers and fisherfolk may use their natural environment in unsustainable ways, leading to further deterioration of their livelihood conditions. Empowering the poor and hungry as custodians of land, waters, forests and biodiversity can advance both food security and environmental sustainability (MDG 7).

It is widely accepted that public services in most sub-Saharan countries have failed to deliver even the most basic services required for improving health. To compound this failure, the basic standard of living has declined for many people, leaving them trapped in a vicious cycle of ill health and poverty. Recent data indicate that while the numbers of people living on less than US $1.25 per day in other regions of the world have declined, the numbers in sub-Saharan Africa have remained static or risen. According to the World Bank, an estimated 388m. people in the region (more than one-half of the population) were living in poverty in the mid-2000s, an increase from 300m. in the early 1990s. While the 2006 *World Development Report* suggested that there were grounds for cautious optimism, identifying seven countries in the region that had achieved or were on track to achieve the target of halving poverty rates by 2015, the 2007 report warned that without renewed action, the effects of HIV/AIDS could lead to incomes in sub-Saharan Africa declining to levels not seen since the 1960s. The report also acknowledged that African economies were growing but not at a rate sufficient to meet the MDGs. However, the 2012 *World Development Report* asserted that greater gender equality can enhance economic efficiency and improve other development outcomes.

The vast majority of deaths from malaria occur in sub-Saharan Africa, where malaria also presents major obstacles to social and economic development. Malaria has been estimated to cost Africa more than US $12,000m. every year in lost gross domestic product (GDP), even though it could be controlled for a fraction of that amount. Considering the impact of malaria alone on the economic development of the region, a report in 2000 by researchers from the Center for International Development at Harvard University and the London School of Hygiene and Tropical Medicine estimated that economic growth in African countries with intense malaria was slowed by 1.3% per head per year. If the disease had been eradicated 35 years earlier, the gross domestic product (GDP) of sub-Saharan Africa in 2000 would have been some $100,000m. more. In other words, the short-term benefit from controlling malaria in the region would amount to an extra $12,000m. per year. The HIV/AIDS epidemic is having a similarly adverse effect on economic development, particularly in the agricultural sector as crop production is hampered by sickness, the time taken to look after sick relatives and loss of income. FAO estimated that by 2003 8m. agricultural workers had died because of AIDS in the 25 worst affected African countries, and that a further 16m. would die before 2020, resulting in the loss of up to one-quarter of the agricultural work-force and a consequent reduction in food production. The impact of fewer farmers is already being felt in sub-Saharan Africa, which continues to experience severe food shortages.

MAIN RISKS TO HEALTH

HIV/AIDS and TB

Sub-Saharan Africa remains the region most heavily affected by HIV. In 2010 about 68% of all people living with HIV resided in sub-Saharan Africa, a region with only 12% of the global population. Sub-Saharan Africa also accounted for 70% of new HIV infections in 2010, although there was a notable decline in the regional rate of new infections. The epidemic continues to be most severe in southern Africa, with South Africa having more people living with HIV (an estimated 5.6m.) than any other country in the world. HIV/AIDS accounts for about 20% of all deaths and disability-adjusted life years lost in Africa. The cost of the AIDS epidemic is incurred not only in dollars, but also in the suffering and death of friends and family. The loss to society is incalculable. The continent has lost productivity and creativity, as well as health and social service.

Almost one-half of the deaths from AIDS-related illnesses in 2010 occurred in southern Africa. AIDS has claimed at least 1m. lives annually in sub-Saharan Africa since 1998. Since then, however, AIDS-related deaths have steadily decreased, as free antiretroviral therapy (ART) has become more widely available in the region. A total of 2.5m. deaths have been averted in low- and middle-income countries since 1995 due to antiretroviral therapy being introduced, according to new calculations by the Joint United Nations Programme on HIV/AIDS. Much of that success has come in the past two years, when rapid improvements in access to treatment occurred; in 2010 alone, 700,000 AIDS-related deaths were averted. The total number of new HIV infections in sub-Saharan Africa has dropped by more than 26%, to 1.9m. from an estimated 2.6m. at the height of the epidemic in 1997.

HIV and TB have been described as a lethal combination, each accelerating the effects of the other. From the early stages of the HIV epidemic, a strong association with TB was apparent and HIV subsequently emerged as one key factor undermining global TB control. Despite being preventable and treatable, TB remains the most common life-threatening opportunistic infection and a leading cause of deaths among people living with HIV/AIDS. Unprecedented resources have been invested in HIV/AIDS throughout low-income countries, but without a concomitant increase in basic TB control and without a concerted response to TB and HIV co-infection. TB now threatens the successes arising from that investment. All advances in the treatment of HIV and TB have the potential to be undermined, or worse, reversed, by the widespread failure to respond to the dual TB/HIV co-epidemic in a co-ordinated and integrated way. Driven by a generalized HIV epidemic and compounded by weak health care systems, inadequate laboratories, and conditions that promote transmission of infection, this devastating situation has steadily worsened, exacerbated by the emergence of drug-resistant strains of TB. In 2010 there were still an estimated 8.8m. new cases of TB, of which 12%–14% were people also infected with HIV. The proportion of TB cases co-infected with HIV is highest in the African region, which accounted for 82% of TB cases among people living with HIV. Without proper treatment, approximately 90% of people living with HIV/AIDS die within months of developing active TB disease. With the recent spread of drug-resistant TB, this already complicated interplay between TB and HIV has only become more deadly, more costly, and more difficult to address. Because most African countries have little or no capacity to test for TB drug resistance, and because of the increased difficulty of treatment and the already high mortality associated with standard TB-HIV co-infection, drug-resistant TB has resulted in mortality rates exceeding 95% among people living with HIV/AIDS in some areas.

Water, Hygiene and Sanitation

For both water and sanitation there continue to be major disparities among regions. Sanitation coverage is lowest in sub-Saharan Africa. For water, coverage is only 61% in sub-Saharan Africa, but all other regions have coverage rates of 87% or higher. About one in three of the 1.8m. world-wide deaths estimated to be a direct result of unsafe water and sanitation occurs in sub-Saharan Africa, according to WHO, and only 36% of the population of the region has access to basic sanitation. Estimating the true impact of these deficiencies on health is difficult, owing to their effect on childhood malnutrition, which in turn contributes to a much higher risk of death from infectious disease.

A study by the World Bank in Ethiopia found that while biological factors, such as age and mother's height, and socio-economic factors, such as household wealth and mother's education, were important determinants of children's nutritional status, access to water and sanitation were an important determinant of the probability of a child being underweight. This effect was particularly marked among children living in rural areas. The findings of the study reinforced earlier suggestions that childhood stunting and poor growth has as much to do with poor hygiene, sanitation and inadequate water supply, as with food availability. Repeated childhood illnesses, and diarrhoea in particular, undermine children's growth and inhibit the absorption of nutrients. According to WHO estimates, more than 800,000 African children die every year from the 4m. episodes of diarrhoea that occur in the region.

Apart from diarrhoeal diseases and malnutrition, poor access to safe water and sanitation is linked to several infectious diseases in sub-Saharan Africa, including schistosomiasis, malaria, trachoma and hepatitis A. More recently, studies have suggested that hand-washing with soap may reduce the risk of childhood pneumonia. Improved hygiene resulting from better sanitation and improved drinking water would do much to reduce the death, disability and illness caused by these preventable diseases. A report published in 2006 investigating progress towards achieving the MDGs in the area of water and sanitation suggested that while countries such as Angola, the Central African Republic, Chad, Malawi and Tanzania had increased drinking water coverage by 50% or more, poor progress in countries like Ethiopia, Niger and Nigeria meant that sub-Saharan Africa was unlikely to meet the goal of 74% of the population having access to improved drinking water. In 2006 nearly 300m. Africans still had no access to safe drinking water. The report also found that rural-urban disparities in relation to access to water and sanitation were most marked in Africa. Similar disparities between the rich and poor were underscored by WHO in March 2010, with the Organization reporting that the richest 20% of the population in sub-Saharan African were more than twice as likely to use an improved drinking water source and almost five times more likely to use improved sanitation facilities than the poorest 20% of the region's population.

Malaria

Malaria affects 109 countries worldwide; yet, 35 countries suffer 98% of the global malaria death toll. Just five of these—Nigeria, the Democratic Republic of Congo (DRC), Uganda, Ethiopia and Tanzania—account for 50% of global deaths and 47% of all malaria cases. Beyond the suffering malaria causes individuals, families and communities, the disease also deepens and reinforces poverty in some of the poorest areas of the world. Malaria costs Africa at least US $12,000m. in direct losses and much more than that in lost economic growth each year. Malaria's apparent synergy with HIV has led to the suggestion that adults infected with HIV should join children and pregnant women as a target group for malaria prevention and treatment.

Providing comprehensive support to help high-burden countries provide universal coverage of malaria prevention and treatment is a key strategic priority of the Global Malaria Action. Up to an estimated 4.2m. lives could be saved by 2015 in the 20 highest burden African countries alone. Implementing the plan will also generate economic growth and liberate critical health care resources in regions struggling to strengthen their health systems. The universal coverage prevention consists of two parts, namely prevention and case management. First, prevention: 100% of the population at risk is provided with locally appropriate preventive interventions. Coverage is defined as follows: one long lasting insecticidal net for every two people; a household is routinely sprayed with indoor residual spraying; every pregnant woman living in a high transmission setting receives at least two doses of an appropriate antimalarial drug during her pregnancy. Second, case management: 100% of patients receive locally appropriate case management interventions. Coverage is defined as follows: prompt parasitological diagnosis by microscopy or rapid diagnostic tests; and treatment with effective drugs within 24 hours after the first symptoms appear.

Vaccine-Preventable Childhood Diseases

Sub-Saharan Africa has the lowest coverage rates for childhood immunizations in the world, a situation worsened by conflict in Sudan, Côte d'Ivoire and the DRC. In 2010 more than 6m. children in sub-Saharan Africa did not receive the full series of three doses of the diphtheria-tetanus-pertussis vaccine by one year of age. In sub-Saharan Africa, children born to mothers and fathers with no formal education; from poorest households; low maternal health-seeking behaviours; urban areas; communities with high illiteracy rates; and from countries with high fertility rates were more likely to be unimmunized. Public health programmes designed to improve coverage of childhood immunization should address people, and the communities and societies in which they live.

Nevertheless, immunization rates continue to improve. Immunization has saved over 20m. lives in the last two decades. More than 100m. infants are immunized each year, saving 2m.–3m. lives annually. Global mortality attributed to measles declined by 78% from an estimated 733,000 deaths in 2000, to 164,000 in 2008. The prevalence of polio has declined dramatically since 1988, from more than 350,000 cases to 1,410 confirmed polio cases (including 1,349 wild virus confirmed cases) in 2010. Only four countries remain endemic—Afghanistan, India, Nigeria and Pakistan—compared with more than 125 countries in 1988.

Measles remains one of the leading causes of death among young children globally, despite the availability of a safe and effective vaccine. An estimated 139,300 people died from measles in 2010—mostly children under the age of five. Measles is still common in many developing countries, particularly in parts of Africa. More than 20m. people are affected by measles each year. In 2008 WHO estimated that 1.5m. deaths among children aged under five years were due to diseases that could have been prevented by routine vaccination. This represents 17% of global total mortality in children under five years of age.

Respiratory Disease and Indoor Air Pollution

Of all infectious diseases, acute respiratory infections are the biggest killer of children in sub-Saharan Africa, often striking those who are malnourished, of low birthweight or whose immune systems are weakened. Of a total population of some 75m. children aged under five years, pneumonia kills 1.2m.–1.5m. each year, according to WHO. Pneumonia is not the only cause of respiratory disease in the region, however, and WHO estimates that between 300,000 and 500,000 deaths could be a direct result of indoor pollutants from burning biomass fuels. Sub-Saharan Africa was thought to account for 24% of these deaths and 54% of the morbidity associated with biomass fuels. An assessment by the International Energy Agency in 2004 suggested that the use of biomass fuels, such as wood, dung and agricultural residues, for domestic purposes would continue to rise. This increase is likely to be marked in sub-Saharan Africa, owing to population growth and the increasing difficulty of gaining access to alternatives such as kerosene and liquid petroleum gas. Initiatives such as the smoke hoods to reduce indoor air pollution piloted by the Intermediate Technology Development Group in Kenya hold potential for tackling this challenge.

Malnutrition in Women and Children

Poor maternal nutrition and health can be considered the hub of the vicious cycle that passes hunger from one generation to the next: from malnourished mothers to low birthweight babies who are at high risk of stunting during childhood, of reduced working and earning capacity as adults, and of giving birth to low birthweight babies themselves. Most of the maternal mortality in sub-Saharan Africa could be prevented if women in developing countries had access to adequate diets, safe water and sanitation facilities, and basic literacy and health services during pregnancy and childbirth. Women who are underweight before starting pregnancy and gain too little weight during pregnancy suffer increased risks of complications and death. Stunting during childhood leaves women particularly vulnerable to obstructed labour, in which the baby's head is too large to fit through the birth canal. Obstructed labour causes more than 40,000 maternal deaths each year and is far more common in short women. Anaemia is one of the main indirect causes blamed for 20% of maternal deaths and has also been found to heighten the risk of haemorrhage and post-delivery infection (sepsis), which together account for another 40%.

Every year, about 9.7m. children die before they reach their fifth birthday, although this figure has declined from almost 13m. According to UNICEF, were current trends to continue, sub-Saharan Africa would account for nearly 60% of all child deaths by 2015. Hunger and malnutrition are the underlying cause of more than one-half of all child deaths, but relatively few of these deaths are the result of starvation; the vast majority are caused by the impact of neonatal disorders and a handful of treatable infectious diseases (including diarrhoea, pneumonia, malaria and measles) on bodies and immune systems that have already been weakened by hunger and malnutrition. The importance of malnutrition as an underlying cause of death for children aged under five years has been recognized for many years and has recently been confirmed: 53% of all of these child deaths could be attributed to being underweight and 35% of deaths are due to the effect of undernutrition on diarrhoea, pneumonia, malaria and measles.

In 2010 an estimated 18%, or 103m., children under five years of age in developing countries were underweight (low weight-for-age according to the WHO child growth standards). Underweight is most common in Eastern, Western and Middle Africa (22%, 22% and 21%, respectively). Children in the poorest households are twice as likely to be underweight as those in the least poor households. Children living in rural areas are more likely to be underweight than those living in urban areas. Childhood malnutrition, including poor growth and micronutrient deficiencies, is an underlying cause of death in an estimated 35% of all deaths among children under five years of age. Projections suggest that the problem of malnutrition in Africa is likely to worsen in the immediate future if current trends continue. WHO estimates that being underweight contributes to the deaths of about 1.8m. people per year in sub-Saharan Africa. Deficiencies in other nutrients, such as iodine, iron, vitamin A and zinc, also contribute to increased rates of death from infectious diseases in the region.

Maternal and Child Mortality

A woman dies from complications in childbirth every minute—about 529,000 each year—the vast majority of them in developing countries. A woman in sub-Saharan Africa has a 1 in 16 chance of dying in pregnancy or childbirth, compared with a 1 in 4,000 risk in a developing country—the largest difference between poor and rich countries of any health indicator. The main causes of maternal death are severe bleeding (haemorrhage), infection (sepsis), eclampsia, obstructed labour and unsafe abortion, but increasing numbers of mothers in this region die from indirect causes, such as HIV/AIDS, TB, malaria and anaemia. Of the 20 countries with the highest maternal mortality ratios in the world, 19 are in sub-Saharan Africa and one—Afghanistan—is in Asia. Sub-Saharan Africa accounts for about one-10th of the world's population and 20% of global births, yet nearly one-half of the mothers who die globally as a result of pregnancy and childbirth are in this region. Pregnancy- and childbirth-related complications were the second leading cause of death and disability for women aged 15–49 years in this region in 2002 with an estimated 231,000 deaths, according to WHO. The leading cause was HIV/AIDS with 866,000 deaths. Sub-Saharan African women are more likely to suffer debilitating complications linked to pregnancy and childbirth. A study in West Africa showed that for each maternal death, a further 30 women may suffer long-lasting disabilities owing to a range of conditions, such as chronic anaemia, infertility and obstetric fistula. Harmful traditional practices such as female genital mutilation and nutritional taboos also contribute to poor maternal health. Female genital mutilation (the partial or total removal of external genitalia) is practised in 27 of the 46 states in the region.

Every day an estimated 12,000 children die in sub-Saharan Africa from easily preventable or treatable illnesses and conditions, such as pneumonia, diarrhoea, measles, malaria and malnutrition. Lesotho, Malawi, Mozambique and Namibia made slow progress in reducing child mortality, while under-five child mortality decreased in a further 10 countries in this region. However, the number of under-five deaths has since increased, and there has been no overall reduction in child mortality in this region.

Chronic Disease, Accidents and Injuries

According to WHO projections, over the next 10 years Africa will experience the largest increase in death rates from cardiovascular disease, cancer, respiratory disease and diabetes. Africa's chronic disease burden is attributed to multifaceted factors including increased life expectancy, changing lifestyle practices, poverty, urbanization and globalization. Rising rates of morbidity and mortality as a result of chronic diseases co-exist with an even greater burden of infectious disease, which still accounts for at least 69% of deaths on the continent.

Although undernutrition is still the most important underlying factor causing high infant and child mortality in the region, more than one-third of African women and one-quarter of African men are estimated to be overweight, and WHO predicted in 2006 that this figure would rise to 41% and 30%, respectively, by 2016. In South Africa one in three men and more than one in two adult women are overweight and obese, the same levels as in the USA. Obesity is now becoming a major disease, in line with HIV and malnutrition, and is a serious risk factor for cancer, particularly for cancers of the stomach, colon, breast, uterus and kidney; dietary factors are now estimated to account for about one-fifth of the burden of cancer in developing countries.

In 2011 tobacco use killed almost 6m. people, with nearly 80% of these deaths occurring in low- and middle-income countries. The prevalence of tobacco use was 29% in males and 7% in females in 2000, but had declined to 17.7% and 2.8%, respectively, in 2006. The Global Youth Tobacco Survey showed that the proportion of 13–15-year-olds who regularly smoke ranged from 13% in Kenya to 33% in Uganda.

Armed conflict is a frequent occurrence in many African countries and is a major cause of ill health and mortality. Five of the world's 10 most serious conflicts during the 1990s took place in the African region. In addition to the deaths and injuries incurred, there are health consequences resulting from the displacement of populations, the breakdown of health and social services, and the heightened risk of disease transmission. Even in countries that have not experienced armed conflicts, there is a heavy toll from firearm injuries and other types of interpersonal violence, which can lead to physical disability.

Injury is a leading cause of death and disability in the African region, particularly in those aged 5–29 years. Three of the top five causes of death for this age-group are injury related. Furthermore, road traffic deaths in the African region are 40% higher than in all other low- and middle-income countries and 50% higher than the world average. The epidemic of road traffic injuries in developing countries is still in its early stages, but it threatens to grow exponentially with the rapid increase in the number of vehicles.

Neglected Tropical Diseases

Neglected tropical diseases (NTDs) can be usefully considered as a group because they are concentrated almost exclusively in impoverished populations living in marginalized areas—the populations left behind by socio-economic development. Neglected diseases—such as sleeping sickness, visceral leishmaniasis and Buruli ulcer—continue to take their toll in the sub-Saharan African region, but they no longer figure on the disease control agenda. NTDs are a group of chronic disabling infections affecting more than 1,000m. people world-wide, mainly in Africa and mostly those living in remote rural areas, urban slums or conflict zones. Beyond their negative impact on health, NTDs contribute to an ongoing cycle of poverty and stigma that leaves people unable to work, go to school, or participate in family and community life. While the 'big three' infections—AIDS, TB and malaria—have caught the world's attention, these other disabling and sometimes fatal infectious diseases in Africa have, until very recently, been receiving relatively little attention from donors, policymakers and public health officials. Yet NTD control represents a largely untapped development opportunity to alleviate poverty in the world's poorest populations, and therefore has a direct impact on the achievement of the MDGs.

THE COST OF ILL HEALTH

Poor health does not just affect individuals, but restricts families and entire societies, and retards the regional development goals of sub-Saharan Africa. In fact, in the countries most affected by the HIV/AIDS epidemic the demographic structure of the country is being changed beyond all recognition.

Ill health in sub-Saharan Africa exerts a toll not just on the individual sufferer, but on families' ability to earn a living, educate their children and save money in order to purchase essential items, such as food and drugs. This, in turn, creates a vicious cycle of ill health and poverty, each fuelling the other and trapping millions of people. The poor describe poverty not as an absence of money, but as powerlessness, alienation, disease, illiteracy and death. Ill health owing to poverty directly affects children's ability to go to school, and adults' ability to work and earn a living or grow food to feed the family. For example, according to the African Medical and Research Foundation (AMREF), in Kenya schoolchildren miss 11% of school days as a result of malaria, and up to one-half of all medically related absences from school are due to the illness.

Many of the health problems in sub-Saharan Africa affect poorer people disproportionately. Until quite recently it was thought that poorer people in the region faced more ill health purely owing to their low socio-economic and nutritional status. However, recent research has demonstrated how ill health deals the poor a double blow—not only do they suffer more episodes of ill health than wealthier people, but they are much less likely to receive treatment. Surveys conducted in Côte d'Ivoire in 2005 and in Kenya in 2007 found that poorer families had higher parasite burdens, lived further away from health facilities and were less likely to seek treatment than their wealthier counterparts.

Any attempt to assess the economic impact of endemic diseases, such as malaria, must take into account not only the direct and indirect costs borne by those affected, but also wider social costs. For example, malaria changes whole families' behaviours, affecting their ability to work, send children to school, migrate to look for work and save money. However, malaria also affects income on a national level, because of its impact on trade, tourism and direct foreign investment. In the most extreme cases, the health problems in sub-Saharan Africa are not just having macroeconomic effects at regional level, but are changing the demographic structure of entire countries. In the case of malaria, Jeffrey Sachs and Pia Malaney argue that, because malaria is responsible for about one-quarter of childhood deaths, families compensate by having more children. This higher fertility rate, they maintain, has knock-on effects on future generations of children in poor families. There is less money available to pay for the education of more children, and female children tend to be less likely to be sent to school. In the long term, such factors can have a significant impact on economic growth and productivity.

Several studies have sought to quantify the macroeconomic impact of disease. The prevalence of HIV/AIDS for adults aged 15–49 years in the African region is estimated at about 7.2%. In every other WHO region the average was less than 1%. There is general agreement that the economic and social impact of HIV/AIDS in the African region has been devastating. The epidemic has drastically reduced the work-force in many countries, while the cost of caring for the growing generation of AIDS orphans could slow down long-term GDP growth by as much as 1.0%–1.5% in countries with a high prevalence of HIV/AIDS, such as Kenya and South Africa. The most extreme example of long-term demographic change is provided by countries in sub-Saharan Africa with a high prevalence of HIV/AIDS. With HIV/AIDS tending to strike people down when they are at their most productive, the entire population structure of countries such as Botswana is likely to be radically altered by 2020. In turn, fewer adults of working age will contribute less to such countries' economies, further retarding economic and social development in the region.

The HIV orphans crisis in sub-Saharan Africa will have far-reaching effects, notably on the long-term economic outlook of the region. One study in Kenya found that only 7% of the farming households headed by orphans knew how to cultivate crops and keep livestock. Rural families are losing their own internal knowledge about how to earn a living, and normal family life is being disrupted irrevocably. A study of HIV orphans in Uganda published in 2005 showed that, compared with non-orphans, orphaned children showed higher levels of anger, anxiety and depression and were more likely to have suicidal feelings and hopelessness about the future. The long-term implications of this cohort of traumatized children for Africa's development are unclear.

THE RESPONSE TO THE HEALTH EMERGENCY

Governments in sub-Saharan Africa have failed to provide the most basic health care, and health services have all but collapsed in many countries as a result of the HIV/AIDS epidemic. Such an extreme crisis clearly calls for an appropriate response, and a number of Public Private Partnerships (PPPs) have been created to manage the funds, resources and expertise required to fight the most deadly diseases. Following the summit of the G8 at Okinawa, Japan, in 2000, the Global Fund to Fight AIDS, TB and Malaria was established to channel funding to projects tackling the three biggest killers; the initial aim was to raise up to US $10,000m. annually by 2005. However, at May 2007 the contributions for 2006 stood at just $1,839m. with $2,441m. pledged for 2007. As of the same date, the Fund had disbursed $3,700m. to public and private recipients in 132 countries. Fund-raising efforts were continuing on an ongoing basis and yielding results with the G8, Spain and Thailand all pledging increased contributions to the Fund. The Fund also produced results, helping to increase the number of people receiving antiretrovirals from 130,000 in December 2004 to 770,000 by December 2006. Similar partnerships have been established for malaria (Roll Back Malaria), TB (Stop TB), polio (Global Polio Eradication Initiative) and onchocerciasis (African Programme for the Control of Onchocerciasis) with varying degrees of success. The GAVI Alliance (formerly the Global Alliance for Vaccines and Immunisation) was launched in 2000, while yet another PPP is attempting to improve access to much-needed drugs to treat HIV/AIDS (the Accelerating Access Initiative).

The GAVI Alliance is a public-private global health partnership committed to saving children's lives and protecting people's health by increasing access to immunization in poor countries. The Alliance brings together developing country and donor governments, leading multilateral organizations such as WHO, UNICEF and the World Bank, civil society organizations, public health institutes, donor and implementing country governments, major private philanthropists such as the Bill & Melinda Gates Foundation and 'la Caixa', vaccine industry representatives and the financial community. The GAVI Alliance also serves as a forum for collaboration, with partners' different skills and experience delivering new and better ways of improving routine immunization. Through active participation in GAVI task teams and working groups, the best talents in immunization bring new solutions to key questions such as how substantially to increase the amount of funding available for vaccine support and how to introduce new vaccines at prices developing countries can afford. The GAVI has prevented more than 5m. future deaths in just 10 years and raised global immunization coverage to its highest-ever level. From 2000–10, according to WHO figures, the Alliance's financial support—US $ 5,700m. in 10 years—has helped in the immunization of 288m. children, who might otherwise not have had access to vaccines. This figure includes: 267m. children protected against hepatitis B; 91m. children immunized against Haemophilus influenzae type b (Hib), the cause of deadly forms of meningitis and pneumonia; and 41.6m. children who have received the yellow fever vaccine. In addition, a series of one-off investments in vaccines that are not part of GAVI's regular programme—measles, polio and tetanus—has prevented another 1.4m. future deaths.

There is optimism too that the increased financial support to countries in sub-Saharan Africa from the Global Fund will help reverse previously disappointing progress on TB. While the 2005 WHO target of detecting at least 70% of all infectious cases and curing 85% of these was not reached, it was estimated that about 60% of all cases were detected by the end of 2005 and that 82% of these were cured. There are therefore signs that the detection and cure rates could be improved with greater funding to strengthen the infrastructure and health systems in sub-Saharan Africa. The region has been singled out by WHO as requiring a special focus to reduce the escalating incidence rates fuelled by the HIV epidemic. The Global Tuberculosis Control Report in 2007 found that the rate of growth world-wide had stabilized but that the caseload continued to grow in sub-Saharan Africa.

In 2006 governments made a historic commitment at the UN to dramatically scale up the response to AIDS. In the Political Declaration on HIV/AIDS in that year, countries committed to provide universal access to HIV prevention, treatment, care and support services to all those in need by 2010. This commitment has as its foundation the Declaration of Commitment on HIV/AIDS (2001), in which governments made a series of time-bound commitments to expand their efforts to address HIV. Both of these declarations support and generate momentum towards universal access and achieving the Millennium Development Goals, particularly Millennium Development Goal 6, which seeks to halt and reverse the spread of HIV by 2015. The year of 2011 marks 30 years since the discovery of AIDS, 10 years since the significant UN General Assembly Special Session on HIV/AIDS that declared AIDS an issue of international security, and five years since the 2006 High Level Meeting when the universal access commitment was made.

Although these are all important milestones, lives are still being lost. In the context of fiscal austerity and multiple global development challenges, the 2011 High Level Meeting provided an unparalleled opportunity to build on unprecedented progress in addressing this global health crisis and to galvanize Member States to commit to a transformative agenda that overcomes remaining barriers to effective HIV services and build effective, equitable and sustainable HIV responses. Treatment 2.0 is a WHO/UNAIDS initiative that aims to catalyze the next phase of HIV treatment scale up through promoting innovation and efficiency gains. It will help countries to reach and sustain universal access to treatment, and capitalize on the preventive benefit of antiretroviral therapy through focused work in five priority areas: 1) optimize drug regimens; 2) provide point of care diagnosis; 3) reduce costs; 4) adapt delivery systems; and 5) mobilize communities. These priority areas are interrelated and WHO/UNAIDS are working with global partners, technical experts and other UN co-sponsors to implement this initiative in countries, with short-, medium- and long-term targets and milestones.

The UN General Assembly in its resolution decided that the high-level meeting of the General Assembly on the prevention and control of non-communicable diseases would be held on 19 and 20 September 2011 in New York, USA, and that the high-level meeting would address the prevention and control of non-communicable diseases worldwide, with a particular focus on developmental and other challenges and social and economic impacts, particularly for developing countries. The Human Heredity and Health in Africa (H3Africa) Initiative is a partnership between the African Society of Human Genetics, the US National Institutes of Health (NIH) and the Wellcome Trust. The H3Africa Initiative aims to facilitate a contemporary research approach to the study of genomics and environmental determinants of common diseases, with the aim of improving the health of African populations. To achieve this, the Initiative will support the creation and development of the necessary expertise and infrastructure in Africa and establish pan-African research networks. It is envisaged that studies funded through the Initiative will inform subsequent strategies to address the health inequities in both communicable and non-communicable diseases, leading to health benefits in Africa.

There have been other success stories too, where strong government action has been carried out in a climate of openness. In Uganda, for example, one of the first countries to be seriously affected by the HIV/AIDS epidemic, the early recognition of the severity of the situation by the Government led to a decline in HIV/AIDS prevalence among certain groups from the mid-1990s. This was widely acknowledged to have been a direct result of mass education and prevention campaigns. According to UNAIDS, the percentage of adults (aged 15–49 years) living with HIV/AIDS in Uganda declined from some 14.0% in the early 1990s to 8.3% in 1999 and to 5.4% in 2007.

Non-governmental organizations (NGOs) perform an important function in facilitating health development in sub-Saharan Africa, but in the early 21st century there were signs that the traditional manner of bidding for money from donors for specific projects with limited coverage was changing. Some NGOs, such as Oxfam and Christian Aid, were playing a strong global advocacy role, appealing for increased resources from donor countries and organizing specific campaigns aimed at accelerating access to badly needed drugs, a role emphasized by the massive joint collaborative Make Poverty History campaign in 2005. Apart from lobbying governments in industrialized countries for debt relief and fairer trade for Africa, NGOs were also lobbying for trade and patent rules to be relaxed to allow poorer countries to import lower-cost versions of HIV drugs.

Some technical NGOs based in sub-Saharan Africa, such as AMREF, find that they are now viewed very much as partners by the governments in the host countries in which they work, allowing them to guide and influence national health policies in favour of the poor. In early 2003 AMREF announced that two major donors, the Canadian International Development Agency and the Swedish International Development Agency, had provided it with unrestricted funding, recognizing the organization's role in developing and testing an evidence base of proven interventions to improve the health of the poorest.

Finally, the private sector is also playing an increasingly important role in responding to sub-Saharan Africa's health emergency. In Kenya, for example, employers are being encouraged to work together with NGOs to provide malaria treatment and prevention for local workers, outwith government health services. In South Africa numerous employers have been persuaded of the need to provide antiretroviral drugs to employees and their families, partly in recognition of the devastating effect of HIV/AIDS on the work-force.

None the less, the most visible aspect of private sector involvement has been the drug donation programmes of the pharmaceutical industry to combat several diseases in sub-Saharan Africa. By the late 2000s, among others, there were PPPs covering African trypanosomiasis, HIV/AIDS, leprosy, lymphatic filariasis, malaria (including a drug donation programme for malarone), onchocerciasis, polio, trachoma, TB (Action TB) and vitamin A disorders. There were at least four PPPs aimed at accelerating the development of a vaccine against HIV/AIDS. However, reports of trials for a candidate AIDS vaccine have so far been disappointing, and prevention through education remains at the forefront of efforts to control the spread of infection. The role of PPPs in the development of new drugs for neglected diseases continues to expand. By 2006 there were over 90 of these partnerships, many of them involving major pharmaceutical companies working on a non-commercial basis.

OUTLOOK

After many decades of investment, aid and development, sub-Saharan Africa is at a crossroads. The early health gains made by governments that invested heavily in health services during the 1970s and 1980s have not been sustained, and by the late 2000s there were more poor people with poorer health in the region than at any time before. As a result, there appeared to be a greater willingness on the part of the global community to address these problems. Many governments and agencies involved in health and development have come to acknowledge that relying on economic development alone to improve health is not enough. To defeat poverty, sub-Saharan Africa's health challenges must be tackled in tandem with the economic and social development challenges of the region. To achieve this will require major investment, not only in fighting disease, but also in developing the capacity of health systems. If donor governments were to meet their undertaking to the UN to allocate 0.7% of GDP to international aid and development, a good start could be made towards reversing the decades of underinvestment.

There are other ways that governments in the region could be helped by external action. Debt relief and debt restructuring was one option pursued through the initiatives for heavily indebted poor countries (HIPCs) and multilateral debt relief. None the less, those countries that received debt relief used the savings to invest heavily in social infrastructure projects. Mozambique introduced free immunization for children, while Tanzania, Malawi and Zambia all abolished primary school fees. If the G8 countries fulfilled their promises on debt, the savings would dwarf the amounts currently being pledged to the Global Fund to Fight AIDS, TB and Malaria. In the early 21st century, there was cautious optimism that donor countries and African governments were beginning to confront the challenges more vigorously. However, the emerging economic growth trends in sub-Saharan Africa and a move towards more civil government had yet to be translated into improvement in the health of the population.

In the absence of extensively expanded preventative, treatment and care efforts, the AIDS death toll in sub-Saharan Africa was expected to continue to rise. The social and economic consequences of the disease are already widely felt, not only in the health sector but also in agriculture, education, industry, human resources, transport and the economy in general. The AIDS epidemic in sub-Saharan Africa threatens to devastate whole communities, rolling back decades of development progress. For lasting solutions to the region's health emergency, health and development workers must turn to proven public health interventions aimed firmly at preventing subsequent generations becoming affected. Most people in the region are not infected with HIV/AIDS, and the challenge during the next decade will be to change behaviours across many diverse societies in order to limit the spread of the virus. Agencies involved in economic development must recognize the critical role of ill health in holding back individuals, families, communities and countries from reaching their potential.

In mid-2010 UNAIDS began implementing Treatment 2.0, a new approach intended to simplify the way in which HIV treatment is provided and to expand access to life-saving medicines. It was hoped that this new approach would reduce treatment costs, make treatment regimens simpler and more effective, reduce the burden on health systems, and improve the quality of life for people infected with HIV and their families. It has been suggested that, compared with current treatment approaches, Treatment 2.0 could avert an additional 10m. deaths by 2025. In addition, the new platform could reduce the number of new cases of HIV by up to 1m. annually if countries provide antiretroviral therapy to all people in need, following revised WHO treatment guidelines.

Governments must continue to reform their health sectors and decentralize services, so that they are more accessible to people living in rural areas. They must also make better use of more appropriate technologies in areas such as sanitation and hygiene, if the number of people at risk of environmental health conditions is to be reduced. In addition, African governments will need to identify ways to retain health care workers, who will be crucial in any effort to improve health on the continent.

NGOs are likely to continue to play a strong role in health reform, but may move away from project implementation to more strategic work, identifying partners with which to work, including national governments.

Finally, and perhaps most crucially, if the health and poverty problems endemic to sub-Saharan Africa are to be tackled sustainably, top-level political leadership will be required. The problems are multifaceted, and involve addressing the political, economic, social and wider determinants of ill health, poverty and poor socio-economic development, not to mention the problems of environmental degradation that compound the difficulties. Sub-Saharan Africa has the largest share of health and poverty problems in the world today, but it did not reach this situation by accident. Reversing the decades of neglect and underinvestment will require commitment on a global scale never before seen, but the people of the region surely deserve nothing less.

BIBLIOGRAPHY AND REFERENCES

African Medical and Research Foundation. *Better Health for the People of Africa*. Nairobi, 2000.

African Union. 'Fight Malaria: Africa Goes from Control to Elimination by 2010' in *African Union Health Ministers Conference Report*. April 2007.

Belue, R., Okoror, T. A., Iwelunmor, J., Taylor, K. D., Degboe, A. N., Agyemang, C., and Ogedegbe, G. 'An overview of cardiovascular risk factor burden in sub-Saharan African countries: a socio-cultural perspective' in *Global Health*, Vol. 5, No. 10. 2009.

Bonnel, R. *Economic Analysis of HIV/AIDS*. Africa Development Forum 2000, Background Paper. World Bank, September 2000.

Centers for Disease Control and Prevention. 'Progress in Reducing Measles Mortality—Worldwide, 1999–2003' in *Morbidity and Mortality Weekly Report*. Atlanta, GA, 2005.

Chuma, J., Gilson, L., and Molyneux, C. 'Treatment-seeking behaviour, cost burdens and coping strategies among rural and urban households in Coastal Kenya: an equity analysis' in *Tropical Medicine and International Health*, Vol. 12, No. 5, pp. 673–686. Oxford, 2007.

Corbett, E. L., Watt, C. J., Walker, N., Maher, D., Williams, B. G., Raviglione, M. C., and Dye, C. 'The growing burden of tuberculosis: global trends and interactions with the HIV epidemic' in *Archives of internal medicine*, Vol. 163, No. 9, pp. 1009–1021. Chicago, IL, 2003.

Dalal, S., Beunza, J. J., Volmink, J., Adebamowo, C., Bajunirwe, F., Njelekela, M., Mozaffarian, D., Fawzi, W., Willett, W., Adami, H. O., and Holmes, M. D. 'Non-communicable diseases in sub-Saharan Africa: what we know now' in *International Journal of Epidemiology*, Vol. 40, pp. 885–901. 2011.

Dare, L. 'WHO and the challenges of the next decade' in *The Lancet*, Vol. 361, No. 9352, pp. 170–171. London, 2003.

De-Graft Aikins, A., Unwin, N., Agyemang, C., Allotey, P., Campbell, C., and Arhinful, D. 'Tackling Africa's chronic disease burden: from the local to the global' in *Globalization and Health*, Vol. 6, No. 5. London, 2010.

Eriksen, M., Mackay, J., and Ross, H. *The Tobacco Atlas.*, 4th edn. The American Cancer Society, Atlanta, GA, 2012.

Famine Early Warning System Network. *Executive Overview Brief, 7 July 2005*. www.fews.net/execbrief.

Filippi, V., Ronsmans, C., Campbell, O. M., Graham, W. J., Mills, A., Borghi, J., *et al*. 'Maternal health in poor countries: the broader context and a call for action' in *The Lancet*, Vol. 368, No. 9546, pp. 1535–1541. London, 2006.

Food and Agricultural Organization of the United Nations (FAO). *The State of Food Insecurity in the World 2005*. Rome, Italy.

Gallup, J. L., and Sachs, J. D. *The Economic Burden of Malaria*. Working Paper No. 52. Cambridge, MA, Center for International Development at Harvard University, July 2000.

Gwatkin, D. 'How well do health programmes reach the poor?' in *The Lancet*, Vol. 361, No. 9357, pp. 540–541. London, 2003.

Havlir, D. V., Getahun, H., Sanne, I., and Nunn, P. 'Opportunities and challenges for HIV care in overlapping HIV and TB epidemics' in *The Journal of the American Medical Association*, Vol. 300, No. 4, pp. 423–430. Chicago, IL, 2008.

Holmes, M. D., Dalal, S., Volmink, J., *et al*. 'Non-communicable diseases in sub-Saharan Africa: the case for cohort studies' in *PLoS Medicine*, Vol. 7, No. 5. San Francisco, CA, 2010.

International Development Research Centre. *Fixing Health Systems*. www.idrc.ca/tehip.

Lawn, S. D., Butera, S. T., and Shinnick, T. M. 'Tuberculosis unleashed: the impact of human immunodeficiency virus infection on the host granulomatous response to Mycobacterium tuberculosis' in *Microbes Infection*, Vol. 4, No. 6, pp. 635–646. 2002.

Luby, Stephen P., *et al*. 'Effect of handwashing on child health: a randomised controlled trial' in *The Lancet*, Vol. 366, No. 9481, pp. 225–233. London, 2005.

Mahmud Khan, M., Hotchkiss, D. R., Berruti, A. A., and Hutchinson, P. L. 'Geographic aspects of poverty and health in Tanzania: does living in a poor area matter?' in *Health Policy and Planning*, Vol. 21, No. 2, pp. 110–122. Oxford, 2005.

Médecins sans frontières. *Act now to get malarial treatment that works to Africa*. April 2003.

Moran, M. 'A Breakthrough in R&D for Neglected Diseases: New Ways to Get the Drugs We Need' in *PLoS Medicine*, Vol. 2, No. 9. San Francisco, CA, 2005.

Raso, G., *et al*. 'Disparities in parasitic infections, perceived ill health and access to health care among poorer and less poor schoolchildren of rural Côte d'Ivoire' in *Tropical Medicine and International Health*, Vol. 10, No. 1, p. 42. Oxford, 2005.

Roll Back Malaria Partnership/World Health Organization (WHO). *World Malaria Report 2005*. rbm.who.int/wmr2005/html/exsummary_en.htm.

Rosegrant, M., and Meijer, S. 'Appropriate Food Policies and Investments Could Reduce Child Malnutrition by 43% in 2020' in *The Journal of Nutrition*, Vol. 132. Pennsylvania, PA, International Food Policy Research Institute, 2002.

Sachs, J., and Malaney, P. 'The economic and social burden of malaria' in *Nature*, Vol. 415, No. 6872, pp. 680–685. London, 2002.

Schellenberg, J. A., *et al*. 'Inequities among the very poor: health care for children in rural southern Tanzania' in *The Lancet*, Vol. 361, No. 9357, pp. 561–566. London, 2003.

Silva, P. *Environmental factors and children's malnutrition in Ethiopia*. Policy Research Working Paper. World Bank, January 2005.

UN. *Towards universal access: assessment by the Joint United Nations Programme on HIV/AIDS on scaling up HIV prevention, treatment, care and support.* Geneva, Switzerland, 2006.

UNAIDS. *Report on the global AIDS epidemic 2010*. Geneva, Switzerland.

Sub-Saharan Africa AIDS epidemic update regional summary, 2008. Geneva, Switzerland.

UNAIDS World AIDS report: 2011 - How to get to zero: Faster, Smarter, Better. Geneva, Switzerland, Joint United Nations Programme on HIV/AIDS (UNAIDS), 2011.

UNICEF. *Progress for Children No. 5: A Report Card on Water and Sanitation*. September 2006.

UNICEF, WHO and World Bank. *State of the World's Vaccines and Immunization.* 2002.

Unwin, N. 'Non-communicable disease and priorities for health policy in sub-Saharan Africa' in *Health Policy Plan*, Vol. 16, pp. 351–2. 2001.

USAID, UNICEF and UNAIDS. *Children on the Brink 2002: a Joint Report on Orphan Estimates and Program Strategies*.

Wardlaw, T. *Coverage at country level for child survival interventions*. Presented at the UNICEF Tracking Progress in Child Survival Countdown to 2015 Conference held at the University of London on 13–14 December 2005. cs.server2.textor.com/alldocs/6%20-%20Tessa%20Wardlaw%20No%20photos.ppt.

WHO. *Preventing Chronic Disease. A Vital Investment.* Geneva, Switzerland, 2005.

The Health of the People: The African Regional Health Report (2006).

World Malaria Report 2010. Geneva, Switzerland.

Global tuberculosis control. Epidemiology, strategy, finance. Geneva, Switzerland, 2009.

The treatment 2.0 framework for action: catalysing the next phase of treatment, care and support. Geneva, Switzerland, 2011.

WHO, UNICEF and UNFPA. *Maternal Mortality in 2000*.

Wiysonge, C. S., Uthman, O. A., Ndumbe, P. M., and Hussey, G. D. 'Individual and contextual factors associated with low childhood immunisation coverage in sub-saharan Africa: a multilevel analysis' in *PLoS One*, Vol. 7, No. 5. 2012.

World Bank. *World Development 2012: Gender equality and development.* The International Bank for Reconstruction and Development/The World Bank. Washington, DC, 2011.

Yaoundé Call to Action. www.rollbackmalaria.org/forumV/docs/YaoundeCall_to_Action-en.pdf.

Young, F., Critchley, J. A., Johnstone, L. K., and Unwin, N. C. 'A review of co-morbidity between infectious and chronic disease in Sub Saharan Africa: TB and Diabetes Mellitus, HIV and Metabolic Syndrome, and the impact of globalization' in *Globalization and Health*, Vol. 5, No. 9. London, 2009.

EUROPEAN COLONIAL RULE IN AFRICA

RICHARD BROWN

The colonial era in Africa began with the continent's hectic partition by the European powers in the final quarter of the 19th century. It ended in circumstances of equal haste less than a century later, leaving the present states of Africa as its political legacy. However, Europe had been in direct contact with sub-Saharan Africa from the mid-15th century, following the Portuguese maritime explorations. Commercial contacts gradually became dominated by the massive and destructive trade in slaves carried on by the Portuguese, Dutch, French, British and others. In all, some 14m. Africans are estimated to have been transported to the Caribbean and the Americas or to have lost their lives as a result of the trade. Colonizing efforts were few before the 19th century, but Portugal maintained a token presence in the areas that much later were extended to become Angola and Mozambique, while the Dutch initiated European settlement from Cape Town in 1652. Elsewhere the prolonged trade contacts generated only scattered European footholds along the African coasts.

The United Kingdom was the leading trafficker in slaves in the 18th century, but after 1807, when British subjects were prohibited from further participation in the slave trade, a new era began. The subsequent campaign against the slave trade of other nations; the search for new trade products such as palm oil; the onset of geographical exploration; the outburst of Christian missionary zeal; improved communications (the telegraph and steamships); growing knowledge of tropical medicine; and Europe's new industrial might all combined to make Africa increasingly vulnerable to European colonial encroachment. The discovery of diamonds in southern Africa in 1867, and the opening of the Suez Canal two years later, further focused attention on the continent. Even before the main scramble for colonies began in the 1870s, the United Kingdom and France had been steadily increasing their commercial and political involvement in Africa.

The United Kingdom established a settlement at Freetown (Sierra Leone) as a base for freed slaves from 1808, and subsequently engaged in a series of conflicts with inland Ashanti from its outposts on the Gold Coast (Ghana), while steadily increasing its influence in the Niger delta region, in Zanzibar, and in southern Africa. In the mid-1800s Gen. Louis Faidherbe began France's expansion into the West African interior along the River Senegal from its long-held trading settlements at the river's mouth. Simultaneously, the interests of both countries grew in Madagascar, but it was France that later annexed the island (1896). During this period of colonial expansion France extended its penetration of West Africa from existing bases in the interior, as well as from enclaves on the coast. It created, too, a second colonial fiefdom in Equatorial Africa, with its administrative base in Libreville, on the Gabonese coast. The result of this strategy was the emergence of two large French colonial federations: Afrique occidentale française (AOF, 1895) eventually included Senegal, Upper Volta (Burkina Faso), Soudan (Mali), Dahomey (Benin), Guinea, Niger, Mauritania and Côte d'Ivoire; Afrique equatoriale française (AEF, 1910) comprised Gabon, Middle Congo (Republic of the Congo), Oubangui Chari (Central African Republic) and Chad. Meanwhile, in West Africa, the United Kingdom extended its foothold on the Gambian coast into a protectorate, enlarged its territorial holdings in Sierra Leone, created the Gold Coast Colony (1874, later conquering Ashanti and adding territory to the north as the scramble proceeded), and sanctioned the advance of the Royal Niger Co into the heavily populated region that subsequently, as Nigeria, became the United Kingdom's most important African colony.

The quest for colonies gained momentum as other European powers entered the field. The first of these was Belgium, whose ambitious monarch, Leopold II, created the International Association for the Exploration and Civilization of Central Africa (1876) as a means of establishing and administering a vast personal empire in the Congo basin, which in 1885 was ironically designated the Congo Free State. The Association's infamous regime of exploitation led to international outrage and eventually, in 1908, to the transfer of the territory to the Belgian state. Another late participant in the drive to colonize Africa was Germany, which had newly emerged as a major industrial power. In 1884 its Chancellor, Otto von Bismarck, declared German protectorates over Togoland, Kamerun and South West Africa (Namibia). Bismarck then moved swiftly to organize the Berlin West Africa Conference (1884–85), which created a generally agreed framework for colonial expansion in order to avert any major conflict among the European powers. Shortly afterwards Bismarck added German East Africa (Tanganyika, the mainland of modern Tanzania) to Germany's colonial possessions. (After the German defeat in the First World War, the administration of these territories passed to the victors as League of Nations mandates. South Africa obtained Namibia, Tanganyika was awarded to the United Kingdom, and Ruanda-Urundi to Belgium, while Kamerun and Togoland were each partitioned between the United Kingdom and France.)

Although the United Kingdom, as the leading European economic power, would have preferred to adhere to its traditionally gradual method of empire-building, it emerged from the scramble as the dominant colonial power, both in terms of territory and population. Apart from its West African possessions, the United Kingdom acquired substantial territorial holdings in eastern and southern Africa. The largest of these was the Sudan, a consequence of British involvement in Egypt and the importance attached to the Suez Canal. Egypt had been employing British soldier-administrators in its efforts to gain control of the Sudan, but in 1881 a Muslim cleric proclaimed himself the Mahdi (supreme spiritual leader) and declared a *jihad* (holy war). In 1885 the Mahdi's forces captured Khartoum, killing Gen. Charles Gordon and causing outrage in the United Kingdom. The Mahdist state was destroyed by Anglo-Egyptian forces led by Gen. Horatio Kitchener in 1898, just in time to forestall a parallel French expedition at Fashoda. The Sudan officially became an Anglo-Egyptian condominium, but was in effect administered as a British colony, which became highly valued for its cotton production. Fertile Uganda, supposedly a key to control of the Nile valley, had been made a protectorate in 1894, and neighbouring Kenya (as British East Africa) was added by the United Kingdom the following year in order to secure access to the sea. The offshore island of Zanzibar, long a focus of British interest and commercially significant for its cloves, was formally declared a protectorate in 1890. Further to the south, missionaries played an important part in the British acquisition of the land-locked Nyasaland protectorate (Malawi) in 1891.

In the extreme south the United Kingdom had obtained the Cape Colony by treaty at the end of the Napoleonic Wars (1814), and soon found itself in conflict both with its white settlers of mainly Dutch origin (Afrikaners, or Boers), as well as with the area's many indigenous kingdoms and chieftaincies. In 1843 the British coastal colony of Natal was founded, principally as a means of containing the Afrikaners in the interior, where they established the Orange Free State and Transvaal republics. Fatefully, these developments coincided with the discoveries of immense reserves of diamonds (1867) and gold (1886). The ensuing upheavals and an insatiable demand for 'cheap native labour' brought about the final conquest of the African peoples (most notably in the Zulu War, 1879). Acting on behalf of the United Kingdom, the mining magnate Cecil Rhodes organized from the Cape the further northward conquest and occupation of Southern Rhodesia (Zimbabwe) and Northern Rhodesia (Zambia), beginning in 1890: in 1884 Rhodes had been instrumental in the British acquisition of Bechuanaland (Botswana) as a protectorate, to safeguard the land route from the Cape into the interior, which had been threatened by German activity in South West Africa. The United Kingdom had also obtained Basutoland (Lesotho) in 1868, and formally established a protectorate over Swaziland in 1903. However, British claims to paramountcy throughout southern Africa were challenged by the two Afrikaner republics in the Boer War (1899–1902). The United Kingdom overcame the republics only with great difficulty, and then left the Afrikaners, who formed the main element of the privileged white minority, in political control of a newly fashioned Union of South Africa, which was then granted virtual independence (1910). Known as the high commission territories, Bechuanaland, Basutoland and Swaziland, however, remained under British rule. Subsequent South African ambitions to annex them were thwarted, and they eventually proceeded to independence in the 1960s.

Despite its economic weakness relative to the other European powers, Portugal obtained a major share of the colonial division of southern Africa. British diplomatic support helped Portugal to secure the vast colonies of Angola (including Portuguese Congo, later known as Cabinda) and Mozambique; in West Africa Portugal had long been in control of mainland (Portuguese) Guinea (now Guinea-Bissau), the Cape Verde archipelago and the islands of São Tomé and Príncipe. Spain, meanwhile, acquired the islands of Fernando Póo (Bioko) and Annobón (Pagalu), together with the mainland enclave of Río Muni, which now form the Republic of Equatorial Guinea.

Some African polities themselves participated in the scramble: the kingdoms of Buganda and Ethiopia both seized opportunities to expand. Indeed, Ethiopia successfully defended itself against Italian aggression by winning a famous victory at the battle of Adowa (1896). Italy had to content itself with Eritrea and the major part of Somalia, until Mussolini's armies overran Ethiopia in 1935. (Italian occupation was ended by an Anglo-Ethiopian military expedition in 1941.) Eritrea, however, was not to emerge as an independent state until 1993. Liberia, a US-inspired republic founded in 1847 and politically dominated by descendants of former slaves, remained nominally independent throughout the colonial era, but in practice became an economic dependency of US rubber-growing interests.

COLONIAL RULE

There was much resistance to the European intrusion by many of the Islamized, as well as the indigenous, cultures of West Africa. There were also major rebellions against the Germans in South West Africa and Tanganyika, and against the British in Southern Rhodesia; however, divisions within and between African ethnic groups, superior European weaponry and the widespread use of African troops enabled the colonial powers generally to secure control of their territorial acquisitions without great difficulty (although military operations continued in some areas until the 1920s). Boundaries were, in the main, effectively settled by 1900 or soon afterwards. Most colonies enclosed a varied assortment of societies, but many African groupings found themselves divided by the new frontiers (the Somali, for example, were split among British, French, Italian and Ethiopian administrations). Although in the long run colonialism did much to undermine previous patterns of life, its administrative policies and the development of written languages (mainly by missionaries) fostered ethnic identity, helping to replace pre-colonial cultural and political fluidity by modern tribalism. African reactions to colonialism also contributed to the growing sense of ethnic self-awareness. At the same time, members of the Western-educated indigenous élites were also exploring alternative identities based on the colonial territory (nationalism) or, indeed, on the broader concept of Pan-Africanism.

As military control gave way to civil administration, economic issues came to the fore. In the early decades of colonial rule a considerable amount of railway construction was carried out, and there was a marked development of the export-orientated economy. Colonial taxation was an important stimulus to peasant production and to wage-labour, but in the early period all colonies conscripted labour by force. In the more primitive and undeveloped colonies (as in the Portuguese territories) coercion of labour persisted into the 1960s. In much of West Africa and parts of East Africa export production remained mainly in indigenous hands. Elsewhere, concessionary companies (as in the Belgian Congo and AEF) or white settlers (as in South Africa and Southern Rhodesia) were the major agricultural producers. White settlers, whose interests were almost invariably given priority, were also a significant force in Kenya, as well as in Northern Rhodesia, the Belgian Congo, Angola, Mozambique, Kamerun and Côte d'Ivoire. Mining was a dominant force in a number of areas. In South Africa it provided the main impetus to the development of a strong industrial base by the late 1930s. Southern Rhodesia followed a similar pattern, although on a smaller scale. The important copper mines of the Belgian Congo (subsequently known as Zaire and now the Democratic Republic of the Congo) were later (in the 1920s) joined by those of Northern Rhodesia. Tin in Nigeria, gold in the Gold Coast and, later, diamonds and uranium in Namibia augmented the primary agricultural exports of these territories. Overall, the growth of a money economy did most to change African life, as different areas developed new production, supplied labour, stagnated, or developed the towns that were essential to the conduct of trade and, in the late colonial period, to the growth of manufacturing in some areas additional to that already established in South Africa.

Where settlers monopolized land and resources, colonialism tended to bear harshly on traditional African life. Elsewhere, however, the direct European impact was more muted. The very small number of European colonial officials in non-settler colonies necessitated reliance on African intermediaries to sustain rule. Such administrations had to limit their interventions in African life and rely on traditional and created chiefs to carry out day-to-day administration (often in arbitrary and non-traditional ways), although military power was never far away in the event of any breakdown in control. By the 1920s air power could be used to transport troops quickly to suppress uprisings. The British, in particular, favoured the policy of 'indirect rule', bolstering traditional authorities as subordinate allies, but often with new powers and resources unavailable to their predecessors. The British colonial doctrine emphasized the separateness of its colonies from the imperial power and theoretically envisaged eventual political independence. Some degree of freedom of expression was allowed (many African newspapers flourished in British West Africa), and a limited political outlet for a circumscribed few was eventually provided through the establishment of legislative councils. In contrast, the French doctrine of assimilation theoretically envisaged Africans as citizens of a greater France, but little was done to make this a reality until after the Second World War. These contrasting British and French principles were not without influence on policy, for example in the educational sphere, and they also helped to shape the later patterns of decolonization and post-colonial relationships. Whatever the theory, all colonial regimes were deeply influenced by the racist outlook that had taken hold of the European mind in the 19th century and in practice treated their colonial subjects as inferior beings.

Racial discrimination was deeply resented by the Western-educated élites. In coastal West Africa and in South Africa the existence of these élites actually pre-dated the scramble, and soon lawyers, clergy, teachers and merchants founded moderate protest associations, such as the Aborigines' Protection Society (1897) in the Gold Coast and the Native National Congress (1912), later the African National Congress, in South Africa. By the 1920s clerks and traders in Tanganyika were able to form an African Association on a territory-wide basis. In other social strata religious associations were often the chief vehicles for African assertion. These could be traditional, Christian, Islamic or syncretic in inspiration, and often aroused mass enthusiasm, to the concern of the colonial authorities. Occasionally there were violent clashes. In 1915 Rev. John Chilembwe led an armed uprising, protesting at the recruitment of Africans for service in the First World War and at conditions for tenants on European-owned estates in Nyasaland. Worker protest appeared early in towns, and on the railways and in mines. Rural protest was often about taxation (as in the 1929 riots by women in Eastern Nigeria) or commodity prices (as in the Gold Coast cocoa boycotts of the 1930s). Yet, whatever the level of discontent, prior to the Second World War the colonial grip remained unshaken.

Any complacency about the underlying state of colonial Africa had, however, already been shattered by the world economic depression beginning in 1929–30. The effects of the collapse of prices were so severe that the major European powers, the United Kingdom, France and Belgium, began to perceive the need to provide development funds and to improve social welfare and education in their colonies, if Africa's ability to export tropical products and to import finished goods was to be sustained. These ideas, however, only began to make themselves strongly felt after the Second World War, when they were to add to the ferment of change then gathering force throughout the continent.

DECOLONIZATION

Events inside and outside Africa interacted to produce the surge towards independence after 1945. The Second World War itself provided the immediate context. The war greatly weakened the colonial powers, and brought to the fore the USA, which opposed European colonial control of Africa. African troops were enrolled to fight in Asia and the Mediterranean, returning with a deep resentment at post-war conditions and the continuing colonial subordination. The victory over fascism and the enunciation of the Atlantic Charter also encouraged thoughts of liberation within the continent. Economic change intensified as both the war and its aftermath stimulated demand, and there was a surge of African migration to the towns. Economic and social grievances multiplied, especially in relation to the inadequacy of urban facilities and lack of educational opportunities. Among peasant farmers, prices, marketing arrangements and new levels of bureaucratic interference aroused intense resentment. Owing to labour migration, links between town and country were close and provided opportunities for newly militant nationalist parties in the more developed colonies, such as the Gold Coast and Côte d'Ivoire, to put pressure on the colonial authorities. For the democratic European powers the increasing African discontent raised both the moral and material costs of maintaining colonial rule. In any case, with the exception of Portugal, political control was no longer regarded as essential to the safeguarding of economic interests, particularly as capitalism was becoming increasingly internationalized and the concept of possessing colonies was beginning to appear outmoded.

In French Africa the Second World War helped directly to set in train events that were ultimately to lead to independence. Following the German defeat of France in 1940, AEF repudiated the Vichy Government and declared its support for the 'Free French' under Gen. Charles de Gaulle. The Brazzaville Conference convened by de Gaulle in 1944 spoke in general terms of a new deal for Africans, while the new French Constitution adopted in 1946 provided for direct African elections to the French Assemblée nationale. Political parties established themselves throughout francophone Africa, although their demands were for fuller rights of citizenship within the French state rather than for independence. Attempts by the French Government to thwart African political progress altogether were unsuccessful. The 1956 *loi cadre* (enabling law) introduced universal adult suffrage, but, to the dismay of many nationalist politicians, the franchise was applied individually to the separate states of the two federations, so that the structures of AOF and AEF were allowed to wither away. In 1958 de Gaulle, still attempting to salvage something of the greater France concept, organized a referendum in which only Guinea voted for full independence. By 1960, however, the remaining AOF and AEF territories, as well as Madagascar, had insisted upon receiving *de jure* independence, even if, despite outward appearances, they remained tied economically and militarily to France.

The events that ended the French empire in sub-Saharan Africa were hastened by concurrent developments in neighbouring British colonies, especially the Gold Coast. With no settler communities to placate, decolonization in British West Africa proceeded relatively smoothly, although much more rapidly than had been contemplated. Popular grievances gave a new edge to the political demands of the now sizeable educated middle classes, and the United Kingdom's cautious post-war moves towards granting internal self-government were soon perceived as inadequate even by the British themselves. When police fired on an ex-serviceman's peaceful demonstration in Accra (Gold Coast) in 1948, the resulting unrest, strikes and rural agitation led to major policy changes. Sensing the new mood, the militant nationalist Kwame Nkrumah formed the Convention People's Party (CPP) in 1949 with the slogan 'self-government now'. Its populist appeal enabled it, in 1951, to overcome the more moderate United Gold Coast Convention party (of which Nkrumah had earlier been General Secretary) in an election based on a new and more democratic Constitution. Although in gaol for sedition, Nkrumah was released and invited to become head of an independent Government. This dramatic development, followed by the granting of independence in 1957 as Ghana (whose boundaries also took in the former mandated territory of British Togoland), had repercussions throughout black Africa. (In fact, the Sudan had achieved independence in the previous year, when the Anglo-Egyptian condominium was brought to an end, but this had attracted little outside attention.) Nkrumah sought, with some success, to intensify African revolutionary sentiment still further by organizing an African Peoples' Conference in Accra in 1958. Nigeria's progress towards independence, meanwhile, was complicated by its enormous size and colonially imposed regional structure. Rival regional and ethnic nationalisms competed, and no one party could achieve the degree of overall dominance enjoyed by the CPP in the Gold Coast. None the less, a federal Nigeria became independent in 1960, followed by Sierra Leone (1961) and The Gambia (1965).

Belgium initially remained aloof from the movement towards decolonization. It appeared to believe that its relatively advanced provision for social welfare and the rapid post-war economic growth in the Belgian Congo would enable it to avoid making political concessions and to maintain the authoritarian style of government that had characterized its administration of the territory since it took over from the Belgian King. The Belgian Congo, however, could not be insulated—any more than any other part of Africa—from the anti-colonial influences at work throughout the continent. From 1955 onwards nationalist feeling spread rapidly, despite the difficulties in building effective national parties in such a huge country. Urban riots in 1959 led to a precipitate reversal in Belgian policy: at the Brussels Round Table Conference in January 1960 it was abruptly decided that independence was to follow in only six months. Not surprisingly, the disintegration of political unity and order in the country speedily followed the termination of Belgian administration. Belgian rule in the mandated territory of Ruanda-Urundi ended in 1962, and was followed by its division into the separate countries of Rwanda and Burundi.

Meanwhile, in eastern and southern Africa, the United Kingdom was also encountering difficulties in implementing decolonization. In Uganda, where its authority rested to a large extent on an alliance with the kingdom of Buganda, British policies had tended to stratify existing ethnic divisions. The deeply ingrained internal problems that preceded independence in 1962 continued to beset Uganda for the next 25 years. In contrast, however, the nationalist movement led by Julius Nyerere in Tanganyika was exceptionally united, and there was little friction prior to independence in 1961. Three years later Tanganyika united with Zanzibar (which obtained independence in 1963) as Tanzania. In Kenya, as in other colonies with significant settler minorities, the process of decolonization was troubled. During the post-war period the settlers of Kenya sought political domination and worked to suppress emergent African nationalism. African frustrations, particularly about access to land among the Kikuyu, and growing unrest among the urban poor, led in 1952 to the declaration of a state of emergency and the violent revolt the British knew as 'Mau Mau'. This was fiercely suppressed, but only with the help of troops from the United Kingdom, a factor that helped finally to destroy the settlers' political credibility. Kenya eventually achieved independence in 1963 under the leadership of the veteran nationalist, Jomo Kenyatta. Vilified by the settlers in the 1950s as a personification of evil, Kenyatta, firstly as Prime Minister and subsequently as President, in fact strove to protect the economic role of the settler population and to maintain good relations with the United Kingdom.

Settler interests were more obstructive further to the south. The whites of Southern Rhodesia had obtained internal self-government as early as 1923, but in 1953 the colony was allowed by the United Kingdom to become the dominant partner in a federation with Northern Rhodesia and Nyasaland. Conflict followed with African nationalists in the two northern territories, and the federation eventually collapsed in 1963, when the United Kingdom had to concede that its policy of decolonization could only effectively apply to the two northern territories whose Governments it still controlled. In 1964 Nyasaland became independent as Malawi and Northern Rhodesia as Zambia. When the United Kingdom then refused white-minority rule independence to Southern Rhodesia, its settler-dominated Government, led by Ian Smith, unilaterally declared independence (1965). This was resisted by the United Kingdom and condemned by the UN, but an ineffectual campaign of economic sanctions was defeated by support for the Smith regime from neighbouring South Africa and Portugal. African nationalists eventually succeeded in organizing the guerrilla war that, in the 1970s, paved the way for a negotiated settlement. With Robert Mugabe as its leader, the country became independent as Zimbabwe (1980), a development that owed much to the collapse of Portuguese rule in Africa after 1974.

During the lengthy dictatorship of Dr António de Oliveira Salazar Portugal regarded its African colonial possessions as inalienable, and in 1951 they were declared to be overseas provinces. However, intense political repression failed to prevent the emergence of armed resistance movements in Angola (1961), Guinea-Bissau (1963) and Mozambique (1964). Most successfully in Guinea-Bissau, under the leadership of Amílcar Cabral, these guerrilla movements succeeded in mobilizing rural support. Eventually, in 1974, following the military overthrow of the Portuguese regime, progress towards internal democratization was accompanied by a determination to implement an accelerated policy of decolonization. In Angola, where the divided nationalist movement provided opportunities for external intervention on opposite sides by South African and Cuban forces, independence proved difficult to consolidate. Mozambique also suffered greatly from South Africa's policy of destabilizing its newly independent neighbours.

During this period South Africa was itself conducting a colonial war in Namibia, which it continued to occupy in defiance of the UN after it had terminated the mandate in 1966. The war against the South West African People's Organisation of Namibia continued until a negotiated settlement finally led to independence in 1990, effectively concluding the colonial era in Africa.

DATES OF INDEPENDENCE OF AFRICAN COUNTRIES

In Chronological Order of Independence—Post-War

Libya	24 Dec. 1951
Sudan	1 Jan. 1956
Morocco	2 March 1956
Tunisia	20 March 1956
Ghana	6 March 1957
Guinea	2 Oct. 1958
Cameroon	1 Jan. 1960
Togo	27 April 1960
Mali	20 June 1960
Senegal	20 June 1960
Madagascar	26 June 1960
The Democratic Republic of the Congo (as the Congo)	30 June 1960
Somalia	1 July 1960
Benin (as Dahomey)	1 Aug. 1960
Niger	3 Aug. 1960
Burkina Faso (as Upper Volta)	5 Aug. 1960
Côte d'Ivoire	7 Aug. 1960
Chad	11 Aug. 1960
The Central African Republic	13 Aug. 1960
The Republic of the Congo (Congo-Brazzaville)	15 Aug. 1960
Gabon	17 Aug. 1960
Nigeria	1 Oct. 1960
Mauritania	28 Nov. 1960
Sierra Leone	27 April 1961
Tanzania (as Tanganyika)	9 Dec. 1961
Rwanda	1 July 1962
Burundi	1 July 1962
Algeria	3 July 1962
Uganda	9 Oct. 1962
Zanzibar (now part of Tanzania)	10 Dec. 1963
Kenya	12 Dec. 1963
Malawi	6 July 1964
Zambia	24 Oct. 1964
The Gambia	18 Feb. 1965
Botswana	30 Sept. 1966
Lesotho	4 Oct. 1966
Mauritius	12 March 1968
Swaziland	6 Sept. 1968
Equatorial Guinea	12 Oct. 1968
Guinea-Bissau	10 Sept. 1974
Mozambique	25 June 1975
Cape Verde	5 July 1975
The Comoros	6 July 1975*
São Tomé and Príncipe	12 July 1975
Angola	11 Nov. 1975
Seychelles	29 June 1976
Djibouti	27 June 1977
Zimbabwe	18 April 1980
Namibia	21 March 1990
Eritrea	24 May 1993
South Sudan	9 July 2011

* Date of unilateral declaration of independence, recognized by France (in respect of three of the four islands) in December 1975.

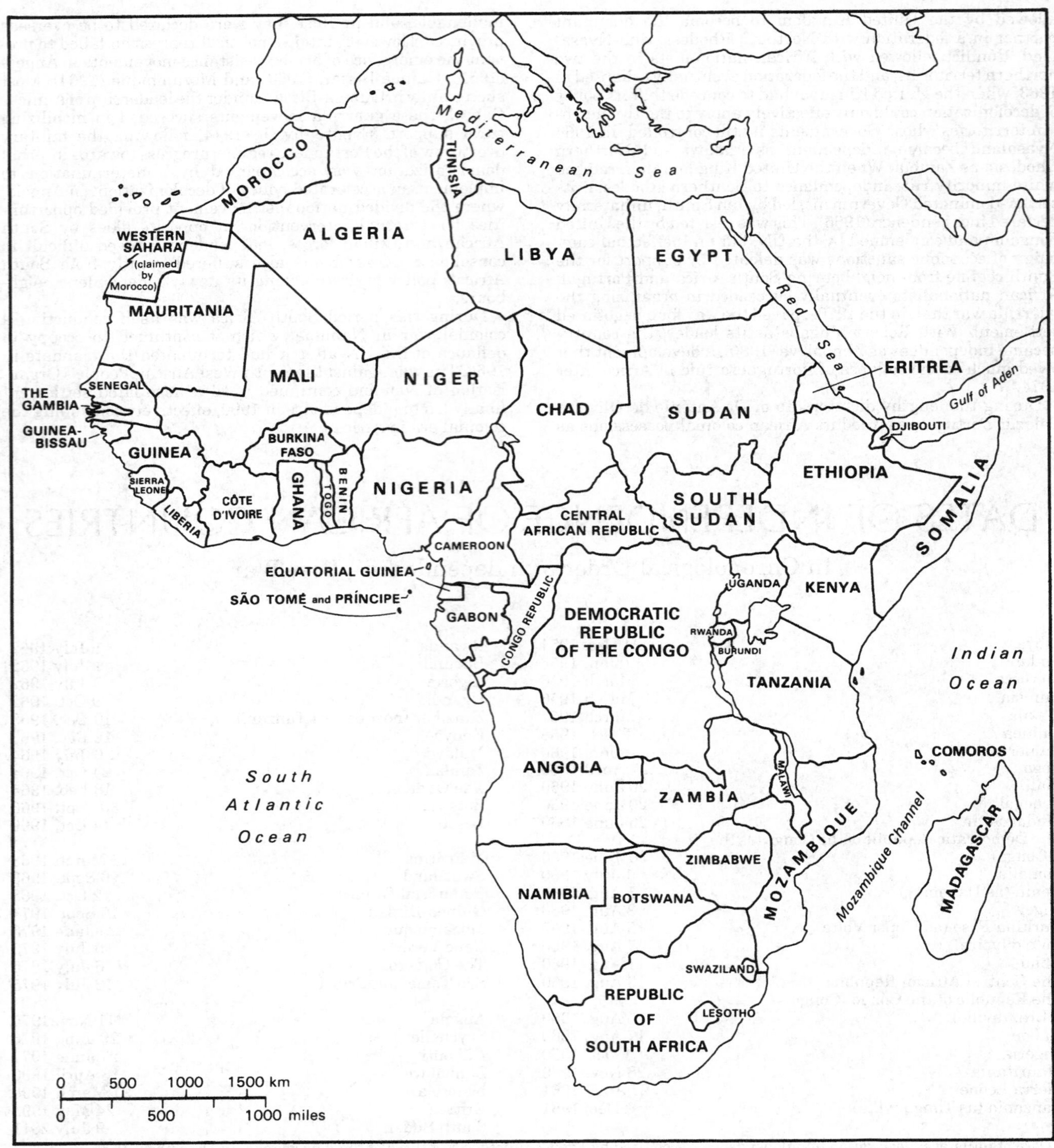

Outline Political Map of Contemporary Africa

PART TWO
Country Surveys

ANGOLA

Physical and Social Geography

RENÉ PÉLISSIER

PHYSICAL FEATURES

The Republic of Angola, covering an area of 1,246,700 sq km (481,354 sq miles), is the largest Portuguese-speaking state in Africa. It is composed of 18 provinces, one of which, Cabinda (formerly known as Portuguese Congo), is separated from the others by the oceanic outlet of the Democratic Republic of the Congo (DRC, formerly Zaire) and the delta of the River Congo. On its landward side Cabinda is surrounded by the DRC and the Republic of the Congo. Greater Angola is bordered to the north and east by the DRC, to the east by Zambia and to the south by Namibia. Excluding the Cabinda enclave, Angola extends 1,277 km from the northern to the southern border, and 1,236 km from the mouth of the Cunene river to the Zambian border.

Two-thirds of Angola is a plateau. The average elevation is 1,050 m–1,350 m above sea-level, with higher ranges and massifs reaching above 2,000 m. The highest point of Angola is Mt Moco (2,620 m) in the Huambo province. Through the central part of the inland plateau runs the watershed of Angola's rivers. The coastal plain on the Atlantic is separated from this plateau by a sub-plateau zone, which varies in breadth from about 160 km in the north to 25 km–40 km in the centre and south. The Namib desert occupies the coastal plain at a considerable height above Namibe. Towards the Cuango (Kwango) basin, in the Zaire province, a sedimentary hollow forms the Cassange depression, in which cotton is cultivated. The north-western section of the Angolan plateau has jungle-covered mountains, which are suitable for the cultivation of coffee. The Mayombe range in Cabinda is covered by equatorial jungle.

Except for the Cuanza (Kwanza) river, which is navigable up to Dondo (193 km upstream), Angolan rivers do not provide easy access to the interior from the coast. On the other hand, they are harnessed for the production of electricity and for irrigation. The main rivers are, above the Cuanza, the Chiloango (Cabinda), the Congo, the M'bridge, the Loge, the Dange and the Bengo. The Cassai (Kasai), Cuilo (Kwilu) and Cuango rivers are known more for their importance to the DRC than for their upper reaches in Angola, although many tributaries of the Kasai intersect the Angolan plateau, exposing rich deposits of alluvial diamonds in the Lunda provinces.

Angola has a tropical climate, locally tempered by altitude. The Benguela current, along the coast, influences and reduces rainfall in that part of the country, which is arid or semi-arid. The interior uplands in the Bié, Huambo and Huila provinces enjoy an equable climate.

POPULATION

According to the most recent census, held in 1970, Angola had 5,646,166 inhabitants and a population density of 4.5 persons per sq km. By mid-2012, when the population was estimated at 20,162,518, the density had risen to 16.2 persons per sq km. Angola is overwhelmingly rural and has considerable ethnic diversity, although all indigenous groups, of which the Ovimbundu and Mbundu are the most numerous, are of Bantu stock. An important characteristic of the population is its youth, as 46% are under 15 years old and only 2.5% are over 65. According to WHO estimates, the average life expectancy at birth in 2010 was 49 years for males and 52 years for females. In 2001–10 Angola's population increased at an estimated average annual rate of 3.2%.

Following the onset of civil strife in the mid-1970s, Angola experienced considerable economic dislocation, accompanied by a widespread regrouping of African populations, brought about by insecurity and massacres. The population is predominantly engaged in food-crop farming and, in the south, in cattle-raising. Only in areas where coffee, cotton and maize are cultivated are Angolans engaged to any extent in commercial agriculture. An estimated 69.5% of the economically active population were employed in the agricultural sector in 2009. Serious food shortages and periods of famine periodically beset central and southern Angola. The lengthy civil conflict created problems of 'internal' refugees (a total of 4.3m. were believed to have been displaced by the conflict), and in late 2006 it was estimated that there were some 171,393 Angolan refugees in surrounding countries, despite the return of almost 400,000 since the cease-fire of April 2002. As refugees were repatriated, resettlement was likely to alter the demography of the country significantly.

The population of the capital, Luanda (which was 480,613 at the 1970 census), was estimated to have risen to 5.1m. by mid-2011, and the city has experienced a boom in construction since 2000. Benguela and Lobito were among the most seriously damaged by the war, and the port of Lobito suffered from the disruption of traffic with the DRC and Zambia. Huambo, formerly an important centre for rail traffic to the eastern regions and to the DRC and Zambia, and for road traffic to Luanda and Namibia, was once again expected to become a focal point of economic activity. Other centres, such as Namibe, Lubango, Kuito and Luena, also suffered from the war and local disorder. The city of Cabinda has benefited from the exploitation of offshore petroleum resources, while pioneer towns such as Menongue and Saurimo may eventually assume new importance as regional centres.

Recent History

EDWARD GEORGE

INDEPENDENCE AND CIVIL WAR

The period preceding its independence in 1975 bestowed the former Portuguese colony of Angola with four competing nationalist movements, none of which was able to assert its supremacy over the others—the Movimento Popular de Libertação de Angola (MPLA), the Frente Nacional de Libertação de Angola (FNLA), the União Nacional para a Independência Total de Angola (UNITA) and the Frente para a Libertação do Enclave de Cabinda (FLEC). The divisions between the groups stemmed from a combination of factors, including the ethnic and social origins of their respective leaderships, their ideologies and the concomitant international patronage that they received.

The MPLA, a successor to the oldest Angolan anti-colonialist movement, the Partido da Luta Unida dos Africanos de Angola, was considered to be dominated by the Mbundu people, who inhabited the area around the capital, Luanda. Although it aimed to represent all Angolans, the MPLA's programme primarily reflected the views of urban intellectuals, mostly *assimilados* (the Europeanized Africans granted Portuguese citizenship) and *mestiços* (people of mixed African and European descent), as personified by its first leader, Mário de Andrade. From its inception in 1956, the MPLA displayed a strong leftist orientation as well as links with the Portuguese Communist Party. These proclivities led to substantial material support from the countries of the Soviet bloc. Being most exposed, because of its urban base, to Portuguese anti-nationalist repression, the MPLA was significantly bolstered by the appointment, as President of the movement, in 1962, of Dr Agostinho Neto, an *assimilado* Mbundu and former political prisoner.

As the name of the FNLA's predecessor, the União das Populações do Norte de Angola, indicates, the movement was established in 1962 initially to represent the interests of the Bakongo people living in the north of Angola. Although it later abandoned the phrase 'do Norte', the organization continued to retain strong links with the Bakongo of Zaire (now the Democratic Republic of the Congo—DRC), which were cemented by family ties between its leader, Holden Roberto, and the Zairean leader, Mobutu Sese Seko. Largely as a result of Mobutu's high standing among Western powers, the FNLA was able to secure US assistance, which increased as the days of the Portuguese colonial empire came to an end. Following an anti-Portuguese uprising, the FNLA formed an Angolan government-in-exile, the Governo Revolucionário de Angola no Exílio (GRAE).

The third major nationalist movement, UNITA, was formed in 1966, following the defection from the FNLA/GRAE of representatives of the Ovimbundu people, led by Jonas Savimbi. The most numerous among the Angolan tribes, the Ovimbundu populated mainly the rural areas of the country's central Bié plateau. With the two superpowers of the USSR and the USA already committed to other Angolan nationalist movements, UNITA turned for support to the People's Republic of China. As well as the receipt of arms deliveries and direct military training from China, UNITA also embraced the Maoist military doctrine and party-political structure.

The smallest of the Angolan nationalist movements, FLEC, never aspired to broaden its appeal beyond its regional base in the Cabinda enclave. Its secessionist programme precluded alliances with any of the other movements, as they all supported, at least in theory, Angola's territorial integrity. FLEC's key personalities included António Eduardo Sozinho and N'zita Henriques Tiago.

Each organization had a military wing, in the case of the MPLA entitled the Forças Armadas Populares de Libertação de Angola (FAPLA) and in the FNLA's case the Exército de Libertação Nacional de Angola (ELNA), all of which engaged in armed struggle against Portuguese colonial rule.

Angola's progress towards independence was substantially bolstered by the coup in Portugal in April 1974, itself a product of popular dissatisfaction with colonial wars in Africa. Fighting between the nationalists and the Portuguese army ceased and all nationalist organizations were permitted to operate legally. In January 1975 an agreement was reached between the representatives of the MPLA, UNITA, the FNLA and the Portuguese Government, establishing the date for Angola's independence as 11 November 1975, and allowing for the formation of a transitional Angolan Government. Headed by a Portuguese High Commissioner, the 'Government of National Unity' consisted principally of representatives of the MPLA, UNITA and the FNLA, but excluded FLEC and other smaller groups. The new administration also disregarded the interests of Angola's significant white population. By mid-1975 the fragile governing coalition had started to disintegrate, falling victim to serious internal differences as well as to the growing superpower rivalry in which the Angolans played the role of proxies. The pro-Western FNLA, viewed as the strongest of the three nationalist movements, benefited from a covert mercenary recruitment campaign directed by the US Central Intelligence Agency. In response, the USSR provided the MPLA forces with substantial military aid, which was followed by the clandestine arrival of Cuban military instructors in Angola.

In June 1975 heavy fighting erupted between MPLA and FNLA forces in Luanda, and rapidly spread to other major towns. By the end of that month the FNLA had been ejected from the capital, while the MPLA had been forced out of the northern provinces of Uíge and Zaire, with UNITA drawn into the conflict on the side of the FNLA. The pro-MPLA stance of the Portuguese administration helped to tilt the balance further between the movements. When the transitional Government in Luanda collapsed in August, the positions vacated by the FNLA and UNITA were allocated to MPLA nominees. By early October more Cuban military personnel had arrived, helping the MPLA to gain control of 12 of the country's 16 provincial capitals. Meanwhile, in August South African forces entered Angola, in support of the FNLA-UNITA alliance, and occupied the Ruacana hydroelectric complex on the boundary Cunene river. This was followed, on 23 October, by an invasion of South African-led troops, which rapidly advanced to within 100 km of Luanda. The South African intervention prompted an immediate massive inflow of Soviet arms and Cuban troops. It also resulted in a significant decline in international support for the FNLA and UNITA.

Angolan independence was declared, as originally planned, on 11 November 1975. However, the country found itself divided by two competing administrations. While the MPLA declared the creation of the People's Republic of Angola in Luanda, with Neto as President, the FNLA and UNITA proclaimed the establishment of the Democratic People's Republic of Angola in Huambo (formerly Nova Lisboa), the country's second largest city. By early 1976 the MPLA had gained the upper hand, bolstered by the support of some 36,000 Cuban troops and vast amounts of Soviet arms. By the end of February the forces of the FNLA and its mercenaries in northern Angola had been decisively defeated, and in the following month South African troops, under international pressure, withdrew into Namibia, while UNITA was forced out of Huambo.

Despite its military success, the MPLA Government faced considerable difficulties. Angola's infrastructure had been damaged by the war, the administration had ceased to function and the economy had collapsed. The exodus of the Portuguese population, which represented a significant proportion of the skilled work-force, as well as the massive internal displacement of the remaining population, served only to worsen the situation. The MPLA itself had come under severe strain from factionalism and internal dissension, exacerbated by an increasingly orthodox communist stance adopted by the dominant grouping led by Neto. At a plenum of its central committee in October 1976 the MPLA formally adopted Marxism-Leninism.

A bloody power struggle developed in May 1977, during which members of the so-called *Nitistas*, an MPLA faction opposed to the Neto group, were responsible for the deaths of a number of senior government leaders. The *Nitistas* were, however, defeated, following the intervention in support of Neto's faction of Cuban troops stationed in Angola. A thorough purge of the MPLA followed, during which the party lost more than two-thirds of its membership. In December 1977 the first party congress expanded the name of the movement to MPLA—Partido do Trabalho (MPLA—PT), and proclaimed it a vanguard party of the working classes. The posts of Prime Minister and Deputy Prime Minister were abolished in December 1978, giving Neto direct control over the Government, while the ethnic composition of the MPLA—PT political bureau was significantly altered by the appointment of several non-Mbundu members. Improved party cohesion allowed the transfer of power (as leader of the MPLA—PT and state President) to José Eduardo dos Santos following Neto's death in September 1979.

CONFLICT WITH SOUTH AFRICA

Relations between Angola and Portugal remained strained until 1978, when the two countries resolved most of their remaining differences. Angola also became an active member of the alliance of the 'front-line states', which opposed the apartheid regime in South Africa. The African National Congress of South Africa (ANC) and the South West Africa People's Organisation of Namibia (SWAPO) both opened offices in Luanda. SWAPO, fighting for the independence of South African-occupied Namibia, was allowed to establish bases on territory controlled by the MPLA—PT. These factors, combined with increasingly open South African support for UNITA, led to increasing confrontation between the MPLA—PT and South Africa.

A key element in UNITA's survival was the South African military and logistical support that it received. The South African Government felt threatened by the continuing presence of a large number of Cuban forces in Angola and resented the MPLA—PT's support for SWAPO. The South African Defence Forces (SADF) established support bases for UNITA in Kuando-Kubango province, while the South African air force provided air cover for Savimbi's headquarters in Jamba. From the late 1970s the SADF regularly launched incursions into Angola in pursuit of SWAPO guerrillas.

The advent of a new Republican Administration in the USA in 1981, led by Ronald Reagan, resulted in a change in US policy towards Africa. The US Administration adopted 'Constructive Engagement' with the South African Government, at the time an international pariah, in an effort to persuade it to accept Namibian independence. Simultaneously, the linking of Namibian independence and the withdrawal of SADF forces from Angola to the withdrawal of Cuban forces from the region was proposed. The new US Administration also reversed its policy towards UNITA. Believing that the Angolan Government needed to be weakened in order to force the Cubans' departure, the USA steadily increased military support for UNITA.

Armed incursions by South Africa were accompanied by an escalation in the activities of UNITA, which assumed a more prominent military role, expanding its operations in eastern Angola while the Government deployed its main forces in the west against the SADF. Throughout 1982 and 1983 the SADF and UNITA together intensified their activities in Angola. In August 1983 the conflict escalated when a large UNITA force attacked and destroyed the strategic town of Cangamba, in Moxico province, with the aid of intense aerial bombardment by the South African air force. Meanwhile, in July 1983 regional military councils were established in all areas affected by the fighting, concentrating all state power in the hands of military officers, directly responsible to the President. This increased the efficiency of the FAPLA, which now constituted the country's official armed forces.

In December 1983 the SADF launched an invasion of southern Angola with 2,000 troops, and, following heavy clashes around Cuvelai, the US Administration arranged a cease-fire and convened peace talks in Lusaka, Zambia. In February 1984 South Africa and Angola signed the Lusaka Accord, under which South Africa pledged to withdraw its troops from Angola in exchange for Angola curbing SWAPO's activities. The SADF officially withdrew from Angola in April 1985. In the following month, however, a unit of its special forces was captured while engaged in operations against petroleum installations in Cabinda. The SADF's 'hot-pursuit' incursions into Angola were resumed in June. In October 1987 South Africa admitted, for the first time, that it was maintaining a 'limited presence' inside Angola, and in the following month it confirmed that it was providing military support to UNITA, and had engaged in direct military action against Soviet and Cuban forces stationed there. South Africa's intensification of aggression against Angola was widely condemned, and in late November the UN Security Council demanded the unconditional withdrawal of South African troops from Angola. Despite agreeing to comply with this demand, South Africa nevertheless continued its military incursions into Angola. These were matched by a massive escalation of UNITA operations in the countryside, which led to the displacement of hundreds of thousands of peasants.

TOWARDS A REGIONAL ACCORD

In April 1987 representatives of the MPLA—PT administration and the US Government resumed efforts to solve the interlinked issues of Namibian independence and the withdrawal of third-party forces from Angola. While negotiations continued, the FAPLA, with Cuban miltary support, launched an offensive in south-eastern Angola against UNITA's forward base at Mavinga. Facing defeat, UNITA sought the help of South Africa, and in August the SADF dispatched 2,000 troops to repulse the MPLA offensive, defeating FAPLA-Cuban forces at the Lomba river. Having withdrawn, the FAPLA then instigated a counter-attack, with the support of 20,000 Cuban reinforcements, and repeatedly repelled the South African attacks, bringing the fighting in Angola to a stalemate.

Negotiations between representatives of Angola, Cuba and the USA continued throughout early 1988, as did separate negotiations between South Africa and UNITA, and the USA and the USSR. On 22 December the participants in the negotiations (with the exception of UNITA) met in New York, USA, where a bilateral agreement was signed by Angola and Cuba, and a tripartite accord by Angola, Cuba and South Africa. Under these agreements, 1 April 1989 was designated as the date of the implementation of the Namibian independence process. In addition, Cuba undertook to complete a phased withdrawal of its estimated 65,000 troops from Angola by July 1991. All prisoners of war were to be exchanged and the signatories of the tripartite accord were to refrain from supporting forces intent on undermining each other's Governments. The latter clause necessitated both the curtailment of South African aid to UNITA and the departure from Angola of an estimated 6,000 members of the ANC's military wing. In accordance with the agreements, the UN Security Council authorized the creation of a UN Angola Verification Mission (UNAVEM) to monitor the redeployment and withdrawal of Cuban troops. UNAVEM commenced operations in January 1989.

The New York accords ended South African involvement in Angolan affairs, but failed to resolve the internal conflict in Angola. The MPLA—PT Government continued to reject UNITA's appeals for a cease-fire, instead offering the rebel organization, in early February 1989, a 12-month amnesty. However, UNITA, reiterating its own aim of laying the foundations for a multi-party democracy in Angola, responded by launching a major offensive against FAPLA targets. In March, following a statement by President dos Santos declaring his willingness to find a resolution to the conflict, Savimbi announced UNITA's intention to honour a unilateral moratorium on offensive military operations until mid-July to facilitate outside mediation. In June Savimbi and dos Santos held direct negotiations at a conference in Gbadolite, Zaire, organized by President Mobutu, as a result of which they eventually signed a cease-fire accord. However, the accord was interpreted differently by each party, and in August Savimbi announced a resumption of hostilities.

THE ESTORIL PEACE AGREEMENT

Talks between UNITA and the MPLA—PT Government resumed in October 1989. In May 1990 UNITA recognized dos Santos as Head of State, and in October it accepted the MPLA—PT Government as an interim administration, pending elections. At a meeting of the MPLA—PT central committee in July, the country's evolution towards a multi-party political system was finally accepted. Further reforms, including the replacement of the party's Marxist-Leninist ideology with a commitment to 'democratic socialism', the introduction of a market economy, the legalization of political parties and the transformation of the army from a party to a state institution, were formally approved at the MPLA—PT congress in December. The legalization of political parties, which was approved by the People's Assembly in March 1991, paved the way for the final round of talks between UNITA and the Government. The legislation, however, stipulated that political parties must enjoy support in at least 14 of Angola's 18 provinces, thereby effectively excluding the Cabinda-based FLEC from the democratic process.

On 1 May 1991 a peace agreement was signed by the the MPLA—PT Government and UNITA in Estoril, Portugal. The agreement provided for a cease-fire from 15 May, which was to be monitored by a joint political and military committee comprising representatives from the MPLA—PT, UNITA, the UN, Portugal, the USA and the USSR. Immediately following the cease-fire, the provision of aid from abroad to the warring parties was to cease and a new national army was to be established, composed of equal numbers of FAPLA and UNITA soldiers. Free and democratic elections were to be held by the end of 1992, and refugees and exiles were to be allowed to return to Angola.

In September 1991 Savimbi returned to Luanda for the first time since the beginning of the civil war, and UNITA headquarters were transferred to the capital in October. At an extraordinary congress of the MPLA—PT, held in May 1992, delegates voted to remove the suffix 'Partido do Trabalho' from the party's official name. In August constitutional amendments removed the remnants of the country's former Marxist ideology, and deleted the words 'People's' and 'Popular' from the Constitution and from the names of official institutions. The name of the country was changed from the People's Republic of Angola to the Republic of Angola. In September FAPLA and UNITA forces were formally disbanded, and the new 50,000-strong national army, the Forças Armadas de Angola (FAA), was officially established.

THE 1992 ELECTIONS

Despite the appointment of FAPLA's Gen. João Baptista de Matos and UNITA's Gen. Abilo Kamalata 'Numa' as joint Supreme Commanders of the FAA in January 1992, concerns were expressed at the declining number of government and UNITA troops in the confinement areas and the reoccupation of territory by rebel forces. Evidence of serious divisions within UNITA emerged in March, adding to persistent reports of bloody purges and 'disappearances' of Savimbi's opponents or rivals. At the same time it became apparent that UNITA had deliberately slowed the process of demobilization, in protest against the formation of a new government paramilitary unit, the 'emergency police', recruited from the MPLA's own special forces.

Presidential and legislative elections took place, as scheduled, on 29–30 September 1992, with dos Santos, Savimbi and the FNLA President, Holden Roberto, among the 12 registered presidential candidates. Preliminary results indicated that the MPLA had obtained a majority of seats in the new Assembleia Nacional; however, Savimbi demanded an inquiry into alleged electoral irregularities. On 5 October UNITA withdrew from the FAA. According to the official election results, published on 17 October, dos Santos received 49.6% of the total votes cast in the presidential election, just short of the 50% required to avoid a second round against Savimbi, who secured 40.1%. In the legislative elections the MPLA won 129 of the 220 seats in the Assembleia Nacional, compared with 70 seats for UNITA.

RESUMPTION OF THE CIVIL WAR

Following the announcement of the official election results, violence erupted between MPLA and UNITA supporters in various cities, including Luanda and Huambo, and by October 1992 hostilities had spread throughout the country. While the second round of the presidential election was postponed indefinitely, the newly elected Assembleia Nacional convened in November. The UNITA parliamentarians refused to take their seats, claiming that the convention of the legislature in the absence of an elected state President was illegal. This, however, did not prevent dos Santos from nominating the Secretary-General of the MPLA, Marcolino José Carlos Moco, as the new Prime Minister.

Already in control of most of the Angolan countryside, UNITA captured a number of major cities, including Huambo and Kuito. Eventually, the FAA repulsed the UNITA forces and retook most of the towns, but at the cost of heavy casualties. Vast tracts of the country were made uninhabitable, displacing millions of Angolans, while thousands more were seriously injured as a result of the large-scale laying of landmines. Lengthy negotiations to end the conflict commenced in October 1992 in Lusaka, but gradually a view was formed among international observers that the principal reason for the failure of these talks lay with Savimbi, who was accused of continuously raising new conditions and objections to procedures that had already been agreed upon. In May 1993 the USA announced its decision to recognize the Angolan Government.

THE LUSAKA ACCORD

The UN threatened to impose a number of sanctions on the UNITA rebels, including an embargo on the sales of arms and petroleum, the freezing of foreign assets and the expulsion of UNITA representatives from Western capitals. To monitor compliance with the agreed peace measures, UNAVEM II was established by the UN in 1993. However, a lack of co-operation from the Angolan Government, as well as from UNITA, severely limited the mission's effectiveness.

In February 1995 the UN Security Council established UNAVEM III, which was to comprise a military peace-keeping force of some 7,000 troops. Its deployment, however, was conditional on the cessation of hostilities and the disengagement of government and UNITA forces. As a result of UN mediation, Savimbi and dos Santos met in May in Lusaka for direct talks. Addressing dos Santos as President of Angola, Savimbi officially accepted dos Santos' election as Head of State and pledged his full co-operation in national reconstruction. Dos Santos requested that Savimbi nominate the UNITA appointees to a new government of national unity and reconciliation. Savimbi was also offered one of two vice-presidential posts that were to be created

In March 1996, at discussions held in Libreville, Gabon, dos Santos and Savimbi agreed on terms for the establishment of a new government, in accordance with the provisions of the Lusaka Accord of May 1995. Savimbi, however, made the participation of UNITA's governmental nominees conditional on the inclusion of other opposition parties in the Government, most notably the President of the FNLA, Holden Roberto. Public protest against deteriorating economic conditions led dos Santos, in June 1996, to replace Prime Minister Moco with the President of the Assembleia Nacional, Fernando José França van-Dúnem.

Meanwhile, in September 1995 the Government signed a four-month cease-fire agreement with FLEC—Renovada (FLEC—R), a breakaway faction of the main FLEC separatist movement. In May 1996 the Government and another Cabinda secessionist faction, FLEC—Forças Armadas Cabindesas (FLEC—FAC), signed an accord outlining the terms of a cease-fire. However, following renewed fighting later that month between government troops and the secessionists, the leader of FLEC—FAC, N'zita Henriques Tiago, declared that a definitive cease-fire would only follow the withdrawal of the FAA from Cabinda.

An agreement was reached in April 1997 to confer on Savimbi the special status of official 'leader of the opposition', after his earlier rejection of the vice-presidency. Following the arrival of the full contingent of UNITA deputies and government nominees in Luanda, on 11 April the new Government of National Unity and Reconciliation was inaugurated. UNITA received four ministerial posts and seven deputy ministerial posts. A further 10 minor political parties were represented in the 87-member Government.

THE COLLAPSE OF THE LUSAKA ACCORD

In May 1997, following the recognition by Angola of the DRC and its new Government, the FAA launched an offensive against the UNITA-controlled diamond-producing provinces of Lunda-Sul and Lunda-Norte. In June the UN Security Council voted unanimously to disband UNAVEM III and replace it with a scaled-down operation, the UN Observer Mission in Angola (MONUA), to oversee the implementation of the remaining provisions of the Lusaka Accord.

In October 1997 the Angolan Government provided military support to the former President of the Republic of the Congo, Gen. Denis Sassou-Nguesso, in his military coup against the elected Government of President Pascal Lissouba. Angola's involvement was reported to have been prompted by Lissouba's support for FLEC and UNITA forces. In the same month the UN Security Council finally ordered the implementation of additional sanctions against UNITA, on the grounds that the movement had failed to meet its obligations under the terms of the peace process. In January 1998 UNITA formally transferred the important Cuango valley diamond mines in Lunda-Norte province to government control. In that month a new schedule was agreed for the implementation of the Lusaka protocol. However, Savimbi remained in the UNITA stronghold of Andulo in central Angola. In August the Government suspended UNITA's government and parliamentary representatives from office.

A group of five UNITA moderates issued a manifesto in September 1998 announcing the suspension of Savimbi and the introduction of an interim UNITA leadership, pending a party congress. However, the group, which styled itself UNITA—Renovada (UNITA—R), commanded very limited support among UNITA's leaders in Luanda. Conversely, the Government quickly recognized the faction as the sole and legitimate representative of UNITA in negotiations concerning the implementation of the Lusaka peace process, prompting several senior UNITA figures, among them Isaías Samakuva, to leave Luanda. While UNITA—R pledged to implement the Lusaka Accord, observers questioned its ability to influence UNITA members outside the capital. In late September the Government revoked the suspension of UNITA's representatives in the Government and legislature. In October the Assembleia Nacional repealed Savimbi's special status. In that month UNITA—R failed to impose its candidate to lead the UNITA parliamentary group when Abel Chivukuvuku was overwhelmingly re-elected as its Chairman. While no longer claiming allegiance to Savimbi, Chivukuvuku also opposed UNITA—R, and emerged as the informal leader of another faction of UNITA. In January 1999 UNITA—R held its first congress, in Luanda, at which Eugénio António N'Golo 'Manuvakola' was elected leader.

The ruling MPLA also succumbed to increasing factional divisions. At its congress in December 1998 dos Santos strengthened his continuing tenure of the party presidency by having his close ally João Manuel Gonçalves Lourenço elected as Secretary-General of the MPLA. In January 1999 dos Santos reorganized the Council of Ministers, assuming the responsibilities of Prime Minister, a post he had abolished, in line with the Constitution, for an 'exceptional period' in order to conduct the war.

In February 1999 the UN Security Council voted unanimously to end MONUA's mandate and withdraw its operatives from Angola by March, on the grounds that conditions had deteriorated to such an extent that UN personnel were no longer able to function. The UN also decided further to tighten its sanctions regime against UNITA. In June a UN report disclosed the contravention of sanctions by a number of African Heads of State, listing, among others, the Presidents of Togo and Burkina Faso as allegedly being involved in the trading of arms for UNITA-mined diamonds.

The ensuing furore forced the South African company De Beers, which controls the majority of international trade in diamonds, to announce a policy of purchasing only legitimately mined gems. The Angolan Government also attempted to stem the flow of illegal diamonds by introducing a strict regime of stone certification. In addition, a new state diamond company, the Sociedade de Comercialização de Diamantes (SODIAM), which was to centralize and regulate the country's diamond trade, was subsequently established.

By October 1999 the UNITA headquarters in Bailundo and the military base in Andulo had fallen to government forces. The fall of Bailundo, the traditional seat of the principal Ovimbundu *regulos* (tribal kings), significantly weakened Savimbi's claim to represent Angola's largest ethnic group. It also boosted the position of Luanda-based Chivukuvuku, himself a scion of an Ovimbundu *regulo*. By July 2000 the Angolan Government claimed that the conventional war against Savimbi was over. However, it was widely believed that without a workable final accord between dos Santos and Savimbi there was little chance of concluding Angola's civil war.

In October 2000 the mandate for the UN Office in Angola (UNOA) was extended until April 2001, although it was to remain restricted to the monitoring of human rights, capacity building and humanitarian support; the mandate was further extended in April 2001. Meanwhile, the opposition organized hunger strikes in protest against the alleged implication of dos Santos in an arms-trafficking scandal, involving a French company, Brenco International, a French businessman, Pierre Falcone, and his Russian-born associate, Arcady Gaydamak—the so-called 'Angolagate' affair. It was alleged that the company, as well as a number of French and Angolan politicians, was implicated in the unauthorized sales of arms, worth some US $790m., to the Angolan Government in 1993–2000. Investigations into the dealings were initiated in France in 1998; also under investigation was the controversial restructuring of Angola's $5,000m. debt to Russia in 1996, in which Falcone had also been involved. The Angolan Government expressed its disappointment at the holding of such an inquiry, and relations with France deteriorated considerably.

THE DEATH OF JONAS SAVIMBI

In January 2001 Gen. João Baptista de Matos was replaced as Chief of Staff of the FAA by Armando da Cruz Neto,apparently indicating a decision by dos Santos to pursue a more aggressive policy against UNITA. Fighting between UNITA and MPLA forces continued throughout early and mid-2001. The conflict also spread to neighbouring countries, with the Zambian army skirmishing with the FAA along the border and UNITA launching several attacks into Namibian territory. However, by early 2002 a substantial portion of Angola's territory had been brought under government control. On 22 February the Government announced that Savimbi had been killed in an army operation in a remote area in Moxico province, close to the Zambian border. The Government stated that hostilities would continue until UNITA complied with the Lusaka protocol.

US and other Western officials pressed for a dignified surrender of UNITA troops, given that the FAA had effectively defeated the rebel movement. In addition, in early March 2002 Savimbi's successor, António Dembo, was either killed by the FAA or died as a result of a shortage of medical supplies. On 13 March the FAA announced that it had halted all military operations against UNITA and had entered into negotiations with the remaining UNITA forces, led by their Chief-of-Staff, Gen. Abreu 'Kamorteiro' Muengo.

On 30 March 2002 UNITA finally agreed to a cease-fire, the conditions of which reflected the military victory achieved by the FAA over the rebels, and an official agreement was ratified on 4 April in Luanda; the latter involved a formal acceptance by UNITA of the terms of the Lusaka protocol. Significantly, the UN and Russian, US and Portuguese representatives were excluded from negotiations, highlighting the Government's distrust of international intervention, and especially of the UN, the presence of which was blamed for facilitating the rearmament of UNITA following the 1994 Lusaka Accord. According to the terms of the cease-fire, within nine months an estimated 50,000 UNITA fighters and 250,000 family members were to be cantoned; only some 5,000 UNITA combatants were to be integrated into the FAA; all UNITA weapons were to be handed over to the FAA; and UNITA officials were to assume the government positions allocated under the Lusaka Accord (posts currently occupied by members of UNITA—R). The demobilization process was to be supervised by a Joint Military Commission (JMC), established under the 1994 Lusaka Accord, with a minor role for the international observers.

In August 2002 UNOA was replaced by the UN Mission in Angola (UNMA). By the end of the year all UN Security Council sanctions against UNITA had been lifted. UNMA's mandate expired in February 2003, and the focus of the remaining UN presence in Angola subsequently shifted to humanitarian issues.

Following the April 2002 cease-fire, UNITA officials were gradually appointed to a number of government, diplomatic and military positions. The JMC was disbanded in November 2002; by July 2003 81,000 UNITA soldiers and 387,000 dependants had been demobilized. The full demobilization process was completed by the end of 2004. The slow integration of UNITA soldiers contributed to the precarious security situation in the country, which was plagued by acts of banditry and landmine incidents following the cease-fire.

THE POST-WAR TRANSITION

A cross-party parliamentary commission, including members of both UNITA and the MPLA, was established, following the cease-fire, to discuss the terms of a new constitution. The MPLA-controlled Constitutional Commission determined that the President should be both Head of State and Head of Government, with the power to appoint provincial governors, as well as supreme commander of the armed forces, leaving the Prime Minister with an advisory role. There was to be only one legislative chamber, and a new flag was to be adopted. The draft constitution was finally presented to the Constitutional Commission in January 2004. The MPLA published a draft election timetable in August, proposing legislative and presidential elections in September 2006.

Following the death of Savimbi in 2002, UNITA struggled to transform itself from a guerrilla movement into a national political party. The organization formed a 'management commission' in an attempt to unite its different components, namely UNITA's military forces, led by Gen. Lukamba 'Gato', UNITA members in exile, led by Samakuva, and the parliamentary UNITA, led by Chivukuvuku. UNITA—R was not included in the commission, reflecting its discredited role within the organization. A UNITA congress was held in June 2003, and Samakuva was elected as the organization's new President. The appointment of Ernesto Mulato, a non-Ovimbundu from Uíge province, as party Vice-President was seen as an attempt by Samakuva to broaden UNITA's appeal beyond its Ovimbundu base of support. In early 2005 Samakuva was presented as UNITA's candidate for the forthcoming presidential election. However, by early 2006 UNITA had failed to make an impact nationally, and its leadership complained of widespread intimidation (including an alleged assassination attempt against Samakuva while he addressed a rally in Huambo in February 2005), attempts by government officials to bribe them to agree to political concessions and the failure of the Government to deliver the administrative posts promised to UNITA under the April 2002 peace accord.

Consequently, from late 2002 the Government was in a stronger position than ever before, bolstered by crucial support from the USA, which was importing an increasing amount of petroleum from Angola. In December dos Santos took advantage of the MPLA's consolidation of power to reorganize the Government, including the appointment of a Prime Minister (the powers of the premiership had been controlled by the President since January 1999). The new Prime Minister was Fernando 'Nando' da Piedade Dias dos Santos, hitherto Minister of the Interior. In January 2003 an independent newspaper, *Angolense*, published a list of 59 Angolans with personal fortunes of more than US $50m., which included many existing and former government officials. This unwelcome publicity came at a time when the Government was under increasing scrutiny for having failed to lift the majority of ordinary Angolans out of extreme poverty, despite the country's considerable petroleum resources.

In June 2003 the Angolan Government controversially appointed Pierre Falcone as its ambassador to UNESCO in Paris, France, prompting outcry from opposition groups. Falcone had been under investigation by French courts since 1998 for his role in the 'Angolagate' affair. In December 2003 dos Santos was unanimously re-elected as Chairman of the MPLA. The Minister of Labour, Public Administration and Social Security, Dr António Domingos Pitra da Costa Neto, a little-known technocrat and loyal supporter of the President, was appointed party Vice-President, while Julião Mateus Paulo, another dos Santos loyalist, replaced Lourenço as the MPLA's Secretary-General. Lourenço had been regarded as a possible successor to dos Santos, and his demotion was viewed as an attempt by the President to thwart his ambitions.

Angolan refugees and internally displaced persons (IDPs) returned to their homes in Angola in great numbers following the end of the war. In December 2003 the UN Office for the Coordination of Humanitarian Affairs estimated that 3.8m. Angolans had returned to their place of origin in Angola, leaving a total of 500,000 IDPs in Angolan camps and temporary areas and a further 400,000 living with relatives or host families. Between late 2002 and late 2003 the Angolan Government and the office of the UN High Commissioner for Refugees (UNHCR) established separate tripartite commissions with Zambia, the DRC, Namibia, Botswana, the Republic of the Congo and South Africa, with the aim of facilitating the repatriation of Angolan refugees from these countries. According to UNHCR figures, between 2002 and 2006 a total of 410,000 refugees returned to Angola, of whom around one-third received assistance from UNHCR. In 2010 there were an estimated 118,157 Angolan refugees in the region, including 79,617 in the DRC and 25,265 in Zambia. Many returning refugees were unable to plant and harvest properly, partly owing to the presence of landmines in vast areas of Angola, and also as a result of unclear property rights in several areas. In October 2004 President dos Santos began a series of government reshuffles in an effort to improve the MPLA's image in the period preceding legislative elections (scheduled to take place in 2006). The reorganizations reflected a new MPLA policy of 'gradualism' in its attempts to reform the Government, and represented a move away from the 1990s when changes to the Government were carried out with full-scale reappointments, greatly increasing political instability. In a further move to improve the Government's image, in late 2004 a campaign was launched to combat corruption. However, in 2011 Angola was still ranked towards the bottom of Transparency International's Corruption Perceptions Index (joint 168th out of 182 countries), and many observers dismissed the Government's moves as purely cosmetic.

Although President dos Santos announced in December 2004 that elections would finally take place in 2006, he did not confirm whether legislative and presidential elections would occur at the same time, as demanded by the opposition. In April 2005 a package of new electoral laws, with provisions regarding regulations for the registration and financing of parties, and for the preparation of the electoral register, was approved by the Assembleia Nacional. An 11-member Comissão Nacional Eleitoral (CNE—National Electoral Commission) was sworn into office in August to oversee the electoral process; it comprised two members chosen by the President, six elected by the Assembleia Nacional, a Supreme Court judge, a representative of the Ministry of Territorial Administration and one from the Conselho Nacional da Comunicação Social (National Council for Social Communication). In June the Supreme Court ruled that President dos Santos was eligible to stand in the elections, and up to two more times subsequently, arguing that his current tenure in office was not covered by the new Constitution. Although dos Santos argued in favour of delaying the elections, Angola's leading opposition parties continued to insist that they be held in 2006. In January 2006 tensions within UNITA surfaced when 16 UNITA deputies in the Assembleia Nacional refused a request from Samakuva to stand down in favour of his preferred candidates.

In March Samakuva responded by expelling four members from the party.

In February 2006 Gen. Roberto Leal Ramos Monteiro 'Ngongo' was appointed Minister of the Interior, replacing Osvaldo de Jesus Serra Van-Dúnem, who had died earlier that month. Also in February, President dos Santos dismissed Gen. Fernando Garcia Miala, the director of the Serviço de Inteligência Externa (Angola's foreign intelligence service). A subsequent government investigation accused Miala of carrying out unauthorized surveillance of certain ministers and of seeking to undermine the President's authority. However, rumours that Miala had been plotting a coup against dos Santos were denied by the Government. In September 2007 Miala was sentenced to four years in prison.

POST-WAR PROGRESS IN CABINDA

The conflict in Cabinda continued following the end of the civil war in April 2002, although on a smaller scale, with the army launching several ferocious attacks against FLEC in late 2002. Despite commanding the support of the majority of the Cabinda population, FLEC was weakened by the defection of a number of its members. The Angolan Government was keen to suppress FLEC activity so that foreign companies could begin onshore petroleum exploration in Cabinda, and in August 2003 one of FLEC's most senior leaders, Ranque Franque, was invited to Luanda to commence peace negotiations with the Government. In August 2004 FLEC's two main factions, FLEC—FAC and FLEC—R, joined forces to negotiate with the Government, but a power struggle between the movement's Secretary-General, António Bento Bembe, and its leader, N'zita Henriques Tiago, slowed progress. In February 2006 a group of civil-society organizations and pro-independence factions styling itself the Fórum Cabindês para o Diálogo (FCD) held talks with the Angolan Government aimed at ending the conflict, and in March it was announced that the enclave would be granted special status.

Following the introduction of a formal cease-fire in mid-June 2006 and the creation of a special statute for Cabinda in mid-July, on 1 August the Angolan Government signed a peace agreement with Bembe on the FCD's behalf. The agreement had five key elements: the full cessation of hostilities; the demobilization of all FLEC troops and their reintegration into the national army, police or civilian society; special status for Cabinda as an autonomous region of Angola; an amnesty for all fighters who surrendered to the authorities; and a significant reduction in the number of FAA troops in Cabinda. The agreement also provided for the appointment of three FCD deputy ministers in the Government, of a deputy governor for Cabinda and the appointment of FCD members to various positions in the Cabinda office of the national oil company, Sociedade Nacional de Combustíveis de Angola (SONANGOL). However, the agreement was immediately rejected by Tiago, who questioned Bembe's authority to conclude it and vowed that fighting would continue. In January 2007 615 former FLEC fighters were incorporated into the FAA and another 113 into the national police force, but there remained as many as 1,000 FLEC fighters who had yet to demobilize. Meanwhile, sporadic attacks continued on army convoys and positions in Cabinda carried out by Tiago's faction of FLEC.

On 1 August 2007 the special statute for Cabinda came into force, granting the enclave political autonomy in the areas of finance, trade, industry and tourism. As promised, FLEC leaders were allocated a number of government positions, including Bembe, who was appointed Minister without Portfolio; Macários Romão Lembe was appointed Deputy Governor of Cabinda. In addition, FLEC military chief Maurício Amado Zulo was appointed Deputy Chief of General Staff of the Armed Forces, and other FLEC members were appointed to advisory roles on various public bodies, including SONANGOL, Angola Telecom, and the port and air authorities.

Dissident FLEC units have continued the insurgency, and since mid-2007 there have been sporadic reports of attacks on FAA units in Cabinda and raids by Angolan special forces on FLEC bases across the border in the DRC. In December 2007 a FLEC ambush killed a Brazilian employee of an oil company; FLEC's military chief warned all foreigners to leave Cabinda or suffer the same fate. In March 2008 FLEC guerrillas seriously wounded a Portuguese technician and killed two workers at an oil installation near Buco Zau. As a result of the rise in FLEC activity, SONANGOL suspended onshore seismic surveys in Cabinda. In the period preceding the September 2008 legislative elections (see below) FLEC carried out a series of attacks against the army and MPLA members. In response, the security forces launched a repressive campaign against dissidents in the enclave.

THE PRE-ELECTION PERIOD

The Council of Ministers announced in August 2006 that the registration of an estimated 7.5m.–8m. Angolan voters would begin in November, and continue until June 2007. In October 2006 the Government launched a public campaign to encourage popular participation in the elections. The CNE extended voter registration until mid-September 2007, owing to delays caused by heavy rains and poor road access to remote communities. According to the Comissão Interministerial do Processo Eleitoral (CIPE), a total of 8.1m. Angolans were eventually registered. However, more than 200,000 Angolans living abroad were not registered owing to a lack of capacity at Angolan diplomatic missions.

Meanwhile, in May 2007 Angola joined the UN Human Rights Council for the period 2007–10. However, Angola's membership drew criticism from human rights groups, which accused the Government of subjecting dissidents to torture, arbitrary detention and trial before military tribunals. In response, the Government announced that Angola would ratify four human rights protocols by 2010, including conventions on torture, racial discrimination, and the rights of migrant workers and their families.

The death of the long-serving leader of the FNLA, Holden Roberto, on 2 August 2007 sparked a lengthy struggle for the leadership of the party between Lucas Ngonda and Ngola Kabangu, both of whom claimed to be Roberto's rightful successor. In December President dos Santos announced that Angola's legislative elections would be held on 5–6 September 2008. The presidential election was expected to follow in the second half of 2009. On 1 April 2008 a final two-month phase of voter registration commenced.

In February 2008 the Government announced that it was to intensify the disarmament process, which would be implemented in three stages: raising awareness through public information campaigns; the voluntary surrender of weapons; and eventually the enforced surrender of weapons. Small firearms remained widespread among the civilian population, and during 2008 20,000 weapons were handed into the authorities.

The Assembleia Nacional approved changes to the electoral code in April 2008, extending the period within which official election results were required to be released. This decision elicited criticism from UNITA, which claimed that any delay in releasing official results could lead to a repeat of the violence and instability that followed the presidential election in Zimbabwe (see chapter on Zimbabwe). The supplementary registration of voters was completed at the end of May, adding an additional 350,000 voters to those already registered. In early June President dos Santos issued a presidential decree confirming that the legislative elections would take place on 5 September, and would be extended to a second day of voting in exceptional circumstances. However, after strong opposition from UNITA, which claimed that a second day's voting would increase the opportunity for fraud, in July the Assembleia Nacional ruled that voting would take place on a single day.

The Assembleia Nacional approved the creation of Angola's highest judicial body, the Tribunal Constitucional (Constitutional Court), which would assume certain functions of the Supreme Court, in mid-June 2008. The seven-member court comprised three judges selected by the Assembleia Nacional, three by the President, and one by the Supreme Court. The Tribunal Constitucional was expected to rule on new laws and international treaties to ensure that they complied with Angola's Constitution, as well as being the final arbitrator on electoral issues, including complaints of fraud and the eligibility of candidates.

Political parties launched their electoral campaigns in early August 2008, following approval by the Tribunal Constitucional of 5,200 candidates, one-third of whom were women, from 10 parties and four coalitions to contest the elections. During the campaign the opposition parties complained of intimidation by the authorities and of repressive action against the independent media, including the suspension of the operating licence of UNITA's radio station, Rádio Despertar.

THE 2008 LEGISLATIVE ELECTIONS

The first legislative elections to take place in Angola for some 16 years were held, as scheduled, on 5 September 2008. Turnout was high, at an estimated 87.4%, and according to foreign electoral observers voting was conducted peacefully and in an orderly manner. On 16 September the CNE announced the official results, giving the MPLA 81.6% of a total 6.5m. valid ballots cast, and an absolute majority with 191 seats in the Assembleia Nacional. In contrast, UNITA came a distant second with 10.4% of the votes; its parliamentary representation collapsed to just 16 seats. Of the remaining seats, eight were taken by the Partido de Renovação Social (PRS), three by the FNLA and two by the Nova Democracia—União Eleitoral. An unusually high number of ballots (763,000) were declared invalid, which was interpreted as protest votes against both the Government and the weakness of opposition parties. In accordance with Angola's law on political parties, the CNE announced that the five parties that had received less than 0.5% of the vote would be dissolved. Following the MPLA's election victory, in late September President dos Santos carried out a reorganization of the Council of Ministers, including the removal of UNITA members from all cabinet posts. The former Governor of Huambo province, Paulo Kassoma, replaced Fernando 'Nando' da Piedade Dias dos Santos as Prime Minister, while the latter was elected as President of the Assembleia Nacional.

President dos Santos announced in November 2008 that a new constitution would be introduced before the presidential election was held, and suggested that this could involve changing the way the President was elected from a national poll to a vote by the Assembleia Nacional. Each party with seats in the Assembleia Nacional was to present its own proposals for reforming the Constitution to the cross-party Constitutional Commission before the end of April 2009. However, in July the Constitutional Commission was granted a six-month extension to continue its work, with a deadline of January 2010 to draft a new constitution.

In November 2009 the Attorney-General launched an investigation into the illegal transfer of US $137m. of funds from the Banco Nacional de Angola (BNA) and the Ministry of Finance to 'offshore' bank accounts in 2007–09. A total of 18 BNA and finance ministry officials were arrested as a result of the investigation and $98m. was recovered. In response, President dos Santos announced a 'zero tolerance' campaign against corruption in official quarters.

ADOPTION OF A NEW CONSTITUTION

In early November 2009 the Constitutional Commission submitted three proposals for the new constitution to public consultation. The first proposed a strengthened presidential system, the second proposed a semi-presidential system, with the Prime Minister as Head of Government, and the third proposed abolishing the presidency and replacing it with a purely parliamentary system. The consultation was due to last until December, after which the Commission would present a draft of the new constitution to the Assembleia Nacional.

In mid-November 2009 UNITA formed a new opposition alliance with the PRS and the Partido Democrático para o Progresso—Aliança Nacional de Angola (PDP—ANA), known as the Fórum de Concertação Política (FCP), pledging to vote together against the MPLA in the Assembleia Nacional. In December President dos Santos was re-elected unopposed as party leader for another five years.

On 21 January 2010 the Assembleia Nacional approved the new Constitution, which established a presidential-parliamentary system (based on that in South Africa), under which the President would not be elected by popular vote but would instead be the leader of the party with a parliamentary majority. The role of Prime Minister was abolished and replaced by that of a Vice-President, who was to head the Government under the direct authority of the President. The Constitution established a two-term presidential limit, but was not retrospective, potentially enabling dos Santos to remain President until 2022. Following approval by the Tribunal Constitucional, the new Constitution came into force on 5 February 2010. President dos Santos subsequently carried out a major reorganization of the Government, including the appointment of the former Prime Minister, Dias dos Santos, as Vice-President.

In early January 2010 the Togolese national football team was attacked by unidentified gunmen as its convoy of buses entered the enclave of Cabinda ahead of the start of the 2010 Coupe d'Afrique des Nations (Africa Cup of Nations), which was being hosted by Angola. The ambush resulted in the deaths of three members of the Togo team, as well as several Angolan police and assailants. Claiming FLEC—FAC to have been responsible for the attack, the Government instigated a crack-down on opposition groups in the enclave and carried out numerous arrests. In March 2010 the Assembleia Nacional approved a new law aimed at improving transparency and preventing conflicts of interest by government officials. The legislation required members of the Assembleia Nacional to declare their assets and interests, and prohibited them from taking part in public tenders or receiving donations or gifts from third parties. However, civil-society groups criticized the law for failing to create an independent commission to monitor corruption and for not including the misappropriation of public money among its provisions.

Lucas Ngonda was elected as leader of the FNLA at the party's extraordinary congress held in Luanda in July 2010. Ngonda called the congress in order to resolve his long-running power struggle with Ngola Kabangu, who boycotted the congress. Kabangu was subsequently expelled from the party, prompting him to establish his own faction, drawing on his support base in Zaire province. In January 2011, however, the Tribunal Constitucional ruled that Ngonda's election as FNLA leader had been unconstitutional, precipitating a fresh leadership contest, with Kabangu vowing to secure command of the party.

Meanwhile, in June 2010 the Government started prosecution proceedings against four human rights activists in Cabinda for their alleged links with the FLEC faction suspected of carrying out the attack on the Togolese national football team; in August the four activists were sentenced to prison terms of three to six years for 'crimes against state security'. This provoked international outcry, as no direct link between the accused and the attack had been proven. Following a legal challenge in the Supreme Court, the charges were dismissed and all four were released. The Government's clamp-down in Cabinda was accompanied by rising concerns over freedom of speech in Angola. In September three independent newspapers that had been heavily critical of the Government were purchased by unknown private investors linked to the MPLA, and their editorial directors were changed. Attacks on Angolan journalists also increased, starting with the murder in September of a presenter on the pro-UNITA Rádio Despertar.

President dos Santos initiated a wide-ranging reorganization of the Government in September 2010, replacing several key figures over subsequent months. In October dos Santos promoted Gen. Geraldo Sachipengo Nunda, a former UNITA commander, to Chief of General Staff of the FAA, and in December the President's office for military affairs—the Casa Militar—was restructured.

An online protest movement, calling itself the Angolan People's Revolution, emerged in late February 2011, inspired by the ongoing popular protests in North Africa. Opposed to the ruling MPLA and President dos Santos, the group appealed for national protests to be held on 7 March and 2 April. In response, the Government convened its own 'solidarity march' on 5 March with 40,000 supporters and launched a clamp-down on known activists. In the event, only around 20 Angolans participated in the first protest, all of whom were quickly arrested, but a larger group of around 300 attended the 2 April protest, which the authorities allowed to proceed. In early September further demonstrations were organized in Luanda and Benguela, including a 'sit-down' by 80 people outside Luanda's court house, protesting against the arrests of the activists in March as well as against the eviction of families from land acquired by government expropriations.

In April 2011 the MPLA held its fourth extraordinary congress in Luanda, which was convened to discuss party strategy ahead of the 2012 legislative elections. Despite speculation that President dos Santos would use the opportunity to designate an official successor, no changes to the party leadership were announced. However, the President confirmed that the elections would take place before the end of 2012.

In July 2011 the Assembleia Nacional approved a new law redefining the boundaries of the province of Luanda and reducing the number of its municipalities from nine to seven. In the same month the Governor of Luanda province, José Maria Ferraz dos Santos, was removed from office amid accusations of corruption. He was replaced in November by Sebastião Francisco Bento, a leading MPLA cadre and dos Santos loyalist.

In July 2011 senior members of UNITA sent an open letter to the press demanding the removal of the party's leader, Samakuva, whom they accused of being intolerant of criticism. UNITA had been due to hold a congress earlier that year, during which a leadership election was to have taken place, but the congress had been repeatedly postponed owing to a lack of funds. In October Samakuva announced that the congress would proceed in December and that he would stand for re-election as party leader. Samakuva was duly re-elected, comfortably defeating his only challenger, José Pedro Katchiungo, with 85% of the votes cast. Following the congress, Samakuva's main rival, Abel Chivukuvuku, announced his departure from UNITA to establish a new party, Convergência Ampla de Salvação de Angola-Coligação Eleitoral (CASA-CE). The new party threatened fatally to weaken UNITA by drawing support away from it in the run-up to the 2012 legislative elections.

In October 2011 President Dos Santos announced that legislative elections would take place in the third quarter of 2012, with voter registration to be completed by the end of 2011. The Government also promised to hold the country's first municipal elections in 2013 or 2014, several years behind schedule. In December 2011 the Assembleia Nacional approved new legislation, amending the composition of the CNE. The CNE was thenceforth to comprise nine members from the ruling MPLA and seven from the opposition, and was to be headed by a non-partisan judge. However, the reappointment in January 2012 of Suzana Inglês as the CNE President, provoked strong criticism from the opposition, who complained that, as a leading member of the MPLA, Inglês was not impartial. A small demonstration held in Luanda on 10 March to protest against the reinstatement turned violent when demonstrators were attacked by pro-Government vigilantes, resulting in several injuries. In May the Supreme Court blocked Inglês' reappointment as President of the CNE, upholding opposition complaints that she was not a judge, as required by law. André da Silva Neto was subsequently appointed to head the CNE.

In January 2012 there was much media speculation that Manuel Domingos Vicente, the former CEO of SONANGOL, would succeed dos Santos as President, following his appointment to the new role of Minister of State for Economic Coordination. In June President dos Santos announced that the legislative elections would take place on 31 August, with campaigning to start on 1 August. As expected, dos Santos took first place on the party list, indicating his intention to seek another term in the presidency, while Vicente took second place, confirming his position as the likely successor to dos Santos should the latter decide to stand down mid-way through his next term. On 6 July the Tribunal Constitucional approved a total of nine parties and coalitions to contest the forthcoming elections, including the MPLA, UNITA and the newly formed CASA-CE.

THE 2012 LEGISLATIVE ELECTIONS

The MPLA secured a decisive victory at the legislative elections held on 31 August 2012, according to results released by the CNE on 7 September. Of the 220 seats in the Assembleia Nacional, the MPLA won 175, with 71.9% of the votes cast. UNITA was placed second with 32 seats (18.7%) and CASA-CE took eight seats (6.0%). The PRS took three seats and the FNLA took two. Thus, dos Santos was re-elected to serve a further five-year presidential term. The rate of voter participation was put at 62.7% of the registered electorate.

FOREIGN AFFAIRS

In October 2007 the Brazilian President, Luis Inácio Lula da Silva, made an official visit to Luanda, signing seven new bilateral co-operation accords in areas including health, education and biofuels. Da Silva also announced a US $1,000m. increase in Brazil's credit line for Brazilian companies investing in Angola.

A French delegation visited Angola in November 2007 for discussions aimed at easing tensions over the arms-trafficking scandal in the 1990s (see above). During the visit it was announced that Angolan officials who had been named in the affair would not form part of the judicial process when the case resumed in early 2008.

French President Nicolas Sarkozy's first official visit to Angola took place in May 2008. Keen to leave behind the 'Angolagate' affair, Sarkozy appealed for a new era of Franco-Angolan relations. During his visit he signed four new co-operation accords and pledged to re-open the offices of the French development agency, Agence française de développement, by the end of the year. However, relations remained strained as the trial of 42 people involved in the 'Angolagate affair' commenced in Paris in October.

After several postponements, verdicts were finally handed down in October 2009, with Falcone and Gaydamak receiving six-year prison sentences for arms-trafficking and money-laundering. Thirty-two others received two- to three-year sentences (some of which were suspended) and hefty fines for having received illicit funds from arms-trafficking, including the former French Minister of the Interior, Charles Pasqua, and Jean-Christophe Mitterrand, son of former French President François Mitterrand. Pasqua vowed to appeal, implicating another former French President, Jacques Chirac, in the scandal. The appeal was finally heard in April 2011, when all charges against Mitterrand, Pasqua, Gaydamak and Falcone were dismissed. Although no Angolans were charged with wrongdoing in the 'Angolagate' case, prosecutors claimed that many officials in that country, including dos Santos, had received tens of millions of dollars in illegal payments. The Angolan Government, in turn, denounced the trial as politically motivated.

In February 2008 Angola and the DRC resolved a long-standing dispute over the border between their offshore petroleum exploration areas, signing a protocol that created a joint interest area, equally dividing exploration rights between the two countries. Although the international press reported in November that Angolan troops had intervened in the DRC in support of President Joseph Kabila Kabange against rebel forces led by Laurent Nkunda in the eastern province of Kivu, this was strongly denied by the Angolan Government. In March 2009 the border dispute over the two countries' shared maritime border was reignited when the DRC Minister of Hydrocarbons stated that some of Angola's oilfields in the Cabinda basin would have to be surrendered to the DRC. The DRC Government also accused Angolan forces of illegally occupying three villages in Bas-Congo province, although Angolan troops subsequently withdrew into northern Angola. In April senior delegations from both Governments met in Luanda for talks and agreed to establish a joint technical commission to demarcate the maritime border; its first meeting was held in June.

In April 2008 controversy was aroused when the Angolan Government agreed to allow a Chinese ship carrying weapons for Zimbabwe to dock in Luanda. The ship had been denied permission to unload its cargo in South Africa, Namibia and Zimbabwe, and the Angolan Government officially allowed it only to refuel and unload construction materials destined for Angola. However, there were suspicions that Angola had used its regional influence to enable the cargo to be unloaded at Pointe-Noire, the Republic of the Congo, and flown to Harare,

Zimbabwe. President dos Santos made a four-day visit to China in December 2008 as part of efforts to boost bilateral relations and increase Chinese financing for infrastructure development; he signed new accords on trade, construction, technology and aviation.

The Angolan Government sought to boost ties with Russia, and in May 2009 the Angolan Minister of Foreign Affairs made an official visit to Moscow, where he signed a number of economic and financing agreements. This was followed in June by a visit to Angola by the Russian President, Dmitry Medvedev, as part of an African tour. Following talks with President dos Santos, Medvedev signed six new agreements in mining, energy, transport, telecommunications, health and education, and agreed a medium-term programme for economic, technological and trade co-operation covering the period 2009–13. The Russian Government also agreed to provide financing for the construction of two new hydroelectric power stations on the Cuanza river, as well as US $295m. for the construction of a national satellite communications system in Angola, Angosat.

In August 2009 the US Secretary of State, Hillary Rodham Clinton, visited Luanda as part of a seven-nation tour of Africa to strengthen US-African trade ties. Although Clinton appealed for greater efforts to curb corruption and human rights abuses in Cabinda, she also praised the country's economic and democratic progress since 2002 and signed a series of new co-operation accords. Later in August 2009 the South African President, Jacob Zuma, made his first state visit to Angola, accompanied by a large business delegation, during which he signed new bilateral accords on trade, industry, energy, aviation, media and sports. A protocol was also signed by the Angolan and South African oil companies, SONANGOL and Petrosa, to co-operate in oil exploration, refining and distribution.

In late 2009 renewed tensions arose between Angola and the DRC over the mutual expulsion of nationals from both countries. Following the expulsion of an estimated 160,000 Congolese (many of whom were illegal diamond miners) from Angola during 2009, in September the DRC Government started expelling over 50,000 Angolans from the Bas-Congo province into Angola's northern Zaire province. Following emergency talks in October, both Governments agreed to suspend the expulsions pending further bilateral talks in December. These led to the creation of four bilateral subcommissions to deal with refugee and border issues, infrastructure, oil sector issues and security. Further talks were held in April 2010 to settle the dispute over the countries' mutual maritime border, an area believed to hold substantial hydrocarbon reserves, and in November both parties agreed to submit the dispute to the UN for arbitration. However, in late 2010 the Angolan Government expelled a further 7,000 Congolese, many of whom, according to UNHCR, were subjected to violence, extortion and rape by Angolan soldiers. In August 2011 President Kabila visited Luanda to hold talks with the Angolan President; discussions between the two leaders reportedly covered the recent expulsions and Angolan proposals to share oil production in the disputed maritime border area.

The Chinese Vice-President, Xi Jinping, who was widely expected to become the next Chinese leader, made a two-day visit to Luanda in late November 2010, reaffirming bilateral ties and agreeing additional credit lines and loans. In December President dos Santos made his first official visit to South Africa, accompanied by a large ministerial delegation, to cement his close ties with South African President Zuma.

In March 2011 President dos Santos came under heavy international criticism for his support of Laurent Gbagbo, the embattled President of Côte d'Ivoire, who had lost a disputed election in late November 2010. Despite recognition by the UN, the African Union, the Economic Community of West African States (ECOWAS) and the international community of Gbagbo's rival, Alassane Ouattara, as the rightful winner, President dos Santos publicly supported Gbagbo, offering to mediate in the crisis and providing material and financial support to his Government. However, after Gbagbo was forcibly removed from power in early April 2011, the Angolan Minister of Foreign Affairs insisted that the Government had supported a negotiated settlement rather than Gbagbo and that it now recognized Ouattara's administration. The Angolan Government also angered the international community by strongly opposing NATO's military intervention in Libya from March 2011; this stance placed Angola in an awkward position when the regime of Col Muammar al-Qaddafi was overthrown in October.

Relations with the USA cooled in March 2011 after the Luanda authorities seized a US ship en route to Kenya. Although the vessel was carrying food aid for central Africa, the authorities impounded it following the discovery of an undeclared cargo of ammunition on board. Once it was revealed that the ammunition had been legally purchased by the Kenyan Government, the ship was allowed to leave. The incident further soured US-Angolan relations, which were already tense after several US banks had closed the accounts of the Angolan embassy in the USA (along with those of numerous other diplomatic missions) because they did not comply with new US anti-money-laundering legislation.

In July 2011 the German Federal Chancellor, Angela Merkel, became the first German Head of Government to visit Angola; during her visit to Luanda she signed a new bilateral co-operation agreement focused on Germany providing Angola with technological and training assistance. In October the new Brazilian President, Dilma Rousseff, made her first visit to Angola, reaffirming the ongoing economic, scientific and technical co-operation programme between the two countries and pledging increased Brazilian trade finance lines. The following month the Portuguese Prime Minister, Pedro Passos Coelho, visited Luanda as part of efforts to encourage Angolan investment in Portugal, one of the country's most important trading partners. In April 2012 the President of the European Commission (EC), José Manuel Durão Barroso, visited Angola, the first EC President to do so.

In April 2012 Angola suffered a setback in its African foreign policy when the Government of Guinea-Bissau was overthrown by a military coup. A 200-strong Angolan military mission (Missang) had been based in Guinea-Bissau since 2011 to retrain that country's armed forces, but it had fallen foul of the country's senior military leadership, who accused the Angolans and the long-serving Guinea-Bissau Prime Minister of plotting to destroy the Guinea-Bissau army. Following mediation by ECOWAS, a transitional government was established in Guinea-Bissau and a stabilization force comprising Nigerian troops was dispatched to the country, while Missang was withdrawn in June 2012. The failure of the mission represented a major reversal in Angolan efforts to expand the country's influence into West Africa and led to the cancellation of the Angola Bauxite project to construct a bauxite mine and deepwater port in Guinea-Bissau.

Economy

EDWARD GEORGE

INTRODUCTION

Prior to independence in 1975, Angola enjoyed a high-output economy, with a rapidly expanding manufacturing sector, near self-sufficiency in agriculture, with crop surpluses for export and abundant natural resources, such as petroleum and iron ore. The petroleum sector has continued to prosper, but almost all other sectors of the economy are operating at a fraction of pre-independence levels. The civil war that began in 1975 disrupted output, made transport and distribution increasingly difficult, and led to the displacement of a large part of the population. Resources were diverted towards defence; in the late 1980s annual defence spending absorbed as much as one-half of the Government's total budget expenditure. Following the resumption of hostilities in 1992, some analysts estimated that government expenditure on arms (including unofficial spending) amounted to around 90% of total expenditure.

After the end of the civil war in 2002, Angola underwent an economic boom, fuelled by rising foreign direct investment (FDI), increased oil production and revenue, and rising volumes of Chinese finance (which is transforming the country's decrepit infrastructure). Angola's gross domestic product (GDP), according to the IMF, increased, in real terms, by an average of 16.2% per year in 2004–08 (while population growth was 2.9%). In 2008 real GDP growth of 13.8% was recorded, the fifth year in succession that real GDP grew by more than 10%. However, the combined impact of the global economic downturn, lower oil prices and the Organization of the Petroleum Exporting Countries (OPEC) reducing quotas severely depressed real GDP growth in 2009, which grew by just 2.4%, according to the IMF. Despite the strong rebound in oil prices, the accumulation of government payment arrears to the construction sector and faltering petroleum output caused by maintenance outages restrained real GDP growth to an estimated 3.4% in both 2010 and 2011. However, the IMF expected real GDP to increase to 9.7% in 2012 as the economic recovery gained momentum. Petroleum has become the mainstay of the economy, accounting for 98.9% of export earnings in 2011. The oil sector provided an estimated 49.3% of GDP that year. Nevertheless, a majority of the economically active population is dependent on the depressed agricultural sector.

ECONOMIC POLICY

Following independence, the Government implemented a policy of state interventionism and wide-scale nationalization based on its Marxist-Leninist ideology, but also in response to the economic crisis caused by the war and the emigration of skilled Portuguese workers. In 1987, however, President José Eduardo dos Santos announced plans to implement major reforms of the economy, aimed at reducing reliance on the state sector and at increasing productivity, purchasing power and consumption levels. He also declared Angola's intention to seek membership of the IMF in order to take advantage of Western financial assistance for economic reform.

Consequently, an economic and financial restructuring programme, the Saneamento Económico e Financeiro (SEF), was implemented in January 1988. The programme involved a reduction in government control over state enterprises; redeployment of civil servants to more productive enterprises; improvements in the supply and distribution systems; and more price incentives for smaller enterprises. External financial support was needed for the success of the programme, and the Government actively encouraged joint ventures between foreign and Angolan enterprises. Angola was admitted to the IMF in September 1989. In October 1990 the ruling Movimento Popular de Libertação de Angola—Partido do Trabalho (MPLA—PT) proposed the introduction of a market economy.

A new programme of economic reforms was presented in November 1991, which included tax reductions; the abolition of price 'ceilings' on all except a few basic commodities; salary increases for public sector workers, to compensate for the withdrawal of ration cards; and a national minimum wage.

In July 1996 the Government introduced a further reform programme, *Nova Vida* ('New Life'). However, many components of the Government's economic reform objectives were never implemented, owing to the civil war. Since the end of the civil war, the Government has made substantial progress in reforming its fiscal and administrative operations, supported by rapidly rising oil revenues and huge inflows of FDI. Nevertheless, serious concerns remain about the transparency of petroleum and diamond revenues and of the national petroleum and diamond companies, the Sociedade Nacional de Combustíveis de Angola (SONANGOL) and the Empresa Nacional de Diamantes de Angola (ENDIAMA).

In December 2006 the Government created a development bank, the Banco de Desenvolvimento de Angola (BDA), which was to channel 5% of oil tax revenue and 2% of diamond tax revenue into financing for reconstruction projects and credits for private sector projects. The bank's key objectives were to support the relaunching of 'productive lines'—in particular agro-industries and factories producing construction materials—and to bolster growth outside the petroleum sector. However, there were concerns over the transparency of the BDA's operations and fears that only companies linked to Angola's political élite would benefit from funding.

In May 2008 President dos Santos outlined an ambitious economic programme for the period 2009–12; targets included annual real GDP growth of 17.1%, annual growth of revenue and spending of 18.5%, and a reduction in the unemployment rate to less than 15% by the end of 2012. Although these targets were subsequently downgraded owing to the impact of the global economic downturn and the decline in Angolan oil production in 2009–10, they were expected to be reinstated ahead of the 2012 legislative elections as the economic outlook improved.

Monetary Policy

As a result of the conflict and the Government's policy of monetizing large fiscal deficits, the rate of inflation regularly spiralled out of control from the early 1990s. From 2000, however, the annual rate of inflation declined steadily from a peak of 325% in 2000 to 12.5% in 2008. It is likely that the Government suppressed inflation through artificial measures, including deferred state payments, delays in raising regulated prices on utilities and costly intervention in the currency markets to support the exchange rate (the 'hard kwanza' policy introduced in 2003). As a result of chaotic monetary policy, the currency also suffered ongoing, and at times severe, depreciation. After the kwanza was replaced, at par, by a new kwanza in September 1990, it was devalued by more than 50% in October to US $1 = 60 new kwanza. The resumption of the war in 1992 prompted further devaluations, which brought the official exchange rate to $1 = 2,150,000 new kwanza in January 1995. In July 1995 a 'readjusted' kwanza, with a value equivalent to 1,000 new kwanza, entered into circulation. The currency continued to depreciate, but, following the introduction of the *Nova Vida* programme in 1996, the differential between the official and parallel exchange rates decreased to around 10%. By April 1999 the value of the currency had deteriorated considerably, with the official rate standing at $1 = 740,000 readjusted kwanza, compared with a free market rate of $1 = 1,620,000 readjusted kwanza.

The dual exchange rate was finally abolished in May 1999. Banking transactions were liberalized, allowing commercial banks to trade among themselves in US dollars, thus creating an interbank money market. In December a new currency, the kwanza, replaced the readjusted kwanza at a rate of 1 kwanza = 1,000,000 readjusted kwanza. Following the establishment of free floating exchange rates, the rate for the new kwanza was set at US $1 = 5.5 kwanza. The continued high level of inflation brought the currency to an average of $1 = 74.6 kwanza in 2003. In that year the central bank, the Banco Nacional de Angola (BNA), adopted the 'hard kwanza' policy, using the country's large petroleum revenues to intervene in the foreign exchange markets to prop up the value of the currency. In addition, rapidly rising foreign exchange reserves, which rose to a peak of $20,400m. in November 2008, and strong growth in deposits in national currency, supported the kwanza's strength. Coupled with the weakness of the dollar on international markets, the kwanza's depreciation against the dollar was reversed, and its value appreciated from an average of $1 = 87.2 kwanza in 2004 to $1 = 75.0 kwanza in 2008.

However, following the collapse in international oil prices and the imposition of OPEC quota reductions, foreign exchange reserves decreased sharply to US $12,500m. by the end of June 2009. This forced the BNA to take drastic measures to stem their decline, including tightening capital controls, restricting the sale of US dollars to commercial banks, raising the level of assets they must hold with the BNA from 10% to 30% and withholding $6,800m. of payments to foreign construction companies working in Angola. Although these measures helped stem the decline in reserves, they led to a wide divergence between the official and parallel exchange rates, which by late September were trading at $1 = 78 kwanza and $1 = 100 kwanza, respectively. Eventually, in October the BNA was forced to loosen the kwanza's unofficial peg to the US dollar, allowing it to depreciate to around $1 = 92.5 kwanza by mid-2010. In the mean time, foreign exchange reserves climbed again on the back of rising oil revenues, reaching $19,750m. by the end of 2010. This enabled the BNA to loosen capital controls and lower the level of assets commercial banks must hold with the BNA to 25%, while also keeping the kwanza broadly stable. Foreign exchange reserves increased to $27,955m. by the end of 2011 and reached $33,000m. in May 2012, buoyed by rising oil production and high international prices. This helped to stabilize the kwanza at around $1 = 93.5 kwanza by mid-2012.

In May 2010 the Assembleia Nacional (National Assembly) approved a new law transferring responsibility for setting monetary and exchange rate policy from the BNA to the Ministry of the Economy. A new BNA Governor was appointed in October, with a remit to reform the banking sector and review monetary policy. In November the Assembleia Nacional approved an amendment to the foreign exchange law, requiring all banks to increase their holdings in kwanza to 80% of their capital and obliging oil companies to use local banks for all payments to Angolan sub-contractors. The amended legislation was implemented in January 2012 and its provisions were to be phased in over a two-year period. In June 2011 the BNA increased efforts to reduce the 'dollarization' of Angola's economy and to encourage kwanza-based transactions by banning commercial banks from foreign currency lending. Only banks with existing foreign currency revenues or those lending for long-term investments were exempt from the new regulation. In October the BNA's monetary policy committee held its first meeting, at which it agreed to introduce a benchmark interest rate of 10.5%, which was to be used as the key instrument for the future progress of monetary policy.

Budgetary Policy

Budgets since 1993 have focused on restoring economic and financial stability and promoting economic production, although defence has remained the sector with the largest allocation of funds. In January 2000 the Government abolished the much-criticized policy of recording foreign exchange transactions in the petroleum sector as 'off-budget' items and requiring all transactions to be registered with the BNA. Moreover, the cessation of hostilities increased pressure on the Government to produce transparent and meaningful budget figures, something it had previously failed to do. During 2004–07 successive budgets resulted in substantial rises in expenditure, primarily to pay for public sector salary increases, infrastructure rehabilitation and priority sector projects. As in the past, only around 6% of the 2007 public investment programme was financed domestically, with the bulk of financing coming from oil-backed loans and new credit lines from the People's Republic of China, Brazil, Portugal and Russia.

The Government attempted to improve public expenditure management by introducing an online budget tracking system, the Sistema Integrado de Gestão Financeira do Estado, which it hoped would strengthen the unity and coherence of state finances. In late 2008 an audit of its domestic debt stock, estimated at US $7,500m., was carried out and new guidelines for improving the management of debt and public expenditure were formulated. As part of its decentralization programme, in April 2008 the Government created the Fundo de Apoio à Gestão Municipal (Fugem) to provide each of Angola's 167 municipalities with $5m. of annual funding for local services. The Government also established a national reserve fund, Conta de Reserva do Tesouro Nacional, to act as a stabilization fund to finance budgetary shortfalls when oil prices were low.

In December 2009 the Assembleia Nacional approved the 2010 budget, which was based on real GDP growth of 8.6% and a rise in oil output to 1.9m. barrels per day (b/d). Revenue was forecast to rise by 20.3%, to US $28,600m., while spending was projected to decline by 6.4%, to $31,270m., as a result of lower expenditure on government services and domestic debt repayments. This reflected the Government's commitments to the IMF to curb spending and strengthen the country's financial position after the 2009 fiscal crisis. Around one-third of expenditure was allocated to social sectors, including health, education and basic infrastructure. However, in August 2010 the Government revised the 2010 budget, increasing spending by 28% to take account of the higher oil reference price of $65.3 per barrel, but reducing fuel subsidies by 20%. A Strategic Oil Reserve Fund was also created, to be administered directly by the presidency, which was to receive the revenue from 100,000 b/d for investment in social projects.

In April 2010 the Government approved a new budget law aimed at improving fiscal transparency and efficiency, requiring all government spending and contracts with third parties to appear in the budget. A new public contracting law was also endorsed, limiting payments for public service contracts to 15% of the contract value, or 30% with prior approval from the Ministry of Finance. In May the Government announced plans to pay off the arrears accumulated for foreign construction companies in Angola during 2008–09, which were estimated to have risen to between US $6,800m. and $9,000m. by the end of 2009. An initial $850m. was paid during April–August 2010, which included down payments for the largest creditors, and a further $5,700m. in the first quarter of 2011, with the balance being repaid by the end of the year. In an effort to prevent the accumulation of fresh arrears, the Ministry of Finance introduced regular audits of domestic debt and departmental budgetary spending, stricter guidelines for public investment projects and a more transparent tender process. The Government launched a five-year programme in August 2010 to overhaul the tax system—the Projecto Executivo para a Reforma Tributária. The first reforms introduced in April 2011 included reductions to property taxes, to urban taxes on rented properties and to stamp duty, all of which were aimed at stimulating the construction of new housing.

In November 2010 the Assembleia Nacional approved the 2011 budget, which was based on real GDP growth of 7.6% in 2011, average oil output of 1.9m. b/d and a conservative average oil price of US $68 per barrel (later revised upwards to $93.4 per barrel). Revenue was forecast to rise by 6.4%, to $36,200m., while expenditure was expected to decrease by 0.3%, to $34,100m., reflecting public spending restraint. As in previous budgets, around one-third of spending was allocated to social sectors. The forecast budget surplus, equivalent to 2% of GDP, was reserved to pay down the domestic debt stock, although given the initial low oil reference price the surplus was expected to be substantially higher. In May 2010 Angola secured its first sovereign credit rating, receiving a B+ or B1 rating from Standard & Poor's (S&P), Fitch Ratings and Moody's Investors, on a par with Nigeria and Ghana. However, due to concerns about increasing domestic debt arrears in 2009–10, the country postponed the planned issue of up to $4,000m. of bonds on the international capital markets. None the less, in May 2011 the Minister of Finance announced that Angola planned to sell $500m. of bonds in September, and in late May and early June Fitch Ratings and Moody's both upgraded the country's rating by one notch, from B+ to BB– and from B1 to Ba3, respectively, reflecting the Government's progress with clearing its domestic arrears. In July S&P also raised Angola's rating, from B+ to BB–. However, owing to the ongoing turmoil in global financial markets the Government postponed indefinitely its plans to issue a first international bond.

In November 2011 the Assembleia Nacional approved the 2012 budget, which was based on real GDP growth of 12.8%, average oil output of 1.84m. b/d and a conservative average oil price of US $77 per barrel. Revenue and expenditure were forecast to be evenly balanced at $46,700m., 29% higher than the previous year, as the Government increased the level of spending following the clearing of its domestic debt arrears in 2010–11. The largest rises in expenditure were earmarked for health and education. The budget also included three new tax codes, which were to be implemented in January 2012, and there were proposals to introduce value-added tax (VAT) and wealth tax in future budgets.

Relations with Foreign Donors

Talks between the Government and the IMF have continued since 1999 regarding an economic monitoring programme that would facilitate further donor assistance and a restructuring of the country's external debt. In April 2000 an agreement with the IMF provided for the implementation of a staff-monitored programme (SMP) for a nine-month period; however, no new disbursements of funds were agreed upon.

An IMF mission to Angola in February 2002 noted that the Government remained unwilling to disclose the management of its petroleum revenue, as well as the accounts for SONANGOL. In May 2003 the Angolan Government formally requested a new IMF poverty reduction and growth facility (PRGF) programme. This seemed unlikely to occur, however, as in September the IMF published a highly critical report on Angola's economic mismanagement. Noting that little action had been taken to promote financial transparency, the report lamented Angola's continuing macroeconomic instability, poor fiscal management, stalled structural reforms and failure to tackle poverty. Nevertheless, in April 2004 Angola once again pressed the IMF for a new PRGF programme. While a formal lending agreement with the IMF remained unlikely, the IMF expressed interest in establishing a new SMP, provided the Government made significant progress with reforms.

In August 2005 the Minister of Finance indicated that the Government wanted to implement its own 'home-grown' reform programme under a new IMF monitoring mechanism, the policy support instrument. Given the Government's poor record on economic reform, the IMF insisted that an SMP be successfully implemented first. However, in March 2006 the Fund announced that it did not consider an economic programme necessary for Angola as it had access to sufficient resources to fund its reconstruction. The breakdown in negotiations was confirmed by the Angolan Government in February 2007 when it formally called off talks with the Fund on a new monitoring arrangement, insisting that it no longer required funding from the IMF and that its own 'home-grown' economic reform programme would be sufficient to ensure economic growth, macroeconomic stability and poverty reduction. However, the Angolan Government continued with the IMF's biannual Article IV consultations, and it accepted technical assistance offered by the Fund for the analysis of economic data. The IMF's 2007 Article IV consultation report showed strong macroeconomic performance in 2006, fuelled by rapid expansion of the oil and diamond sectors, and to a lesser extent by services, construction and manufacturing. The Fund estimated real GDP growth of 23.4% in 2007, driven by rising petroleum output and high international prices. However, the Fund urged the Government to adopt a medium-term fiscal framework in order to avoid the cyclical nature of growth of the past, and to foster the development of the non-oil sectors. The IMF's 2008 Article IV consultation report indicated real GDP growth at an estimated 15% in 2008, stabilizing inflation and a large current account surplus.

In the latter half of 2009 the IMF reached a preliminary agreement to award a 27-month stand-by financing arrangement (SBA) to provide immediate support in easing liquidity constraints. The SBA was endorsed by the IMF in November, with funding totalling US $1,400m., the largest IMF loan awarded to a sub-Saharan African country. The SBA focused on three areas: fiscal reform, with a priority on restraining current expenditure, boosting revenue collection and improving transparency; orderly exchange-rate adjustment, through tighter monetary policy and the managed depreciation of the kwanza; and strengthening the financial sector, primarily through improving the regulatory and supervisory capacities of the BNA. In March 2010 the IMF carried out its first review of the SBA, broadly endorsing the Government's macroeconomic management under the programme, with a return to strong economic growth and public investment. However, due to delays with reforms to fiscal, monetary and foreign exchange policy, the Fund delayed the second SBA disbursement. This finally occurred in May after the Government had enacted new laws to better the efficiency of public spending and debt management. The Fund indicated that if Angola's external outlook continued to improve the country could move to a precautionary SBA (PSBA), under which countries do not intend to draw on approved amounts but retain the option to do so if necessary. In July 2010 the IMF carried out its second review of the SBA, endorsing the Government's reform programme and reporting a return to strong economic growth. The IMF's discussions focused on formulating a plan to repay the Government's substantial stock of domestic arrears, which had risen to as high as US $9,000m. In September the IMF completed its third review of the SBA, disbursing a further $353m. of funding, and urged the Government to expedite the repayment of domestic arrears. The IMF's fourth review of the SBA was conducted in November, focusing on the near-term economic outlook, the 2011 budget and the domestic arrears repayment plan. Although the IMF praised the Government for curbing expenditure and for repaying around one-third of its arrears, the Fund reduced its projection for real GDP growth in 2010 to 2.5%, mostly as a result of oil production outages in the final quarter of the year.

In June 2011 the IMF carried out its fifth review of the SBA, commending the Government for making progress with reviving economic growth, paying off its domestic arrears and restraining expenditure. The Government was reported to be considering moving to a PBSA before the end of the current SBA, but decided to see the SBA through to its conclusion after the IMF indicated that it would allow additional spending via a supplementary budget.

In January 2012 the IMF carried out its sixth and final review of the SBA, again praising the Government for its economic performance in 2011 and judging the programme to have proved an overall success. However, the Fund warned that the Government should adopt further measures to protect against a potential future oil price shock, and it identified a discrepancy of US $31,400m. in the fiscal accounts for 2007–10, most of which was ascribed to the quasi-fiscal operations of SONANGOL, including fuel subsidies, investment in road, rail and housing projects, and external debt servicing. Although this discrepancy was later reduced to $4,000m., it once again highlighted what little progress the Government had made over the preceding decade in bringing SONANGOL's quasi-fiscal operations into the national budget. The Government did not request a successor SBA, but was expected to sign up to post-programme monitoring to ensure continued IMF expertise and assistance, as well as a biannual evaluation and report on the country's economic performance.

AGRICULTURE

Owing to its large area and variety of climate, Angola is one of the most promising agricultural countries of Southern Africa, with an estimated 35m. ha of arable land. However, only about 3% of Angola's total area has been cultivated as arable or permanent crop land, because of civil unrest, transport problems, and a lack of proper marketing facilities and incentives. As a result, shortages have been prevalent, and famine has been a frequent occurrence since independence. Less than one-half of the country's cereal requirements is produced locally. The depopulation of the countryside, as a consequence of the civil war, resulted in crops being left unharvested and in a widespread failure to replant. Following the end of the civil war in April 2002 (see Recent History), the Government made considerable efforts to effect a recovery in agricultural production. According to the World Bank, in 2010 agriculture contributed an estimated 10% of GDP. In May 2008 the Government produced its economic programme for 2009–12, which envisaged increasing the area under cultivation by 4m. ha, with the goal of producing 15m. metric tons of grain by 2013. Over this period US $1,200m. was to be invested in agricultural development, financed by a credit line from the China Development Bank. In recent years the Government has greatly increased the availability of financing for farmers. In February 2010 the Government announced a $250m. credit line for agricultural loans to small and medium-sized farmers. One of the most serious impediments to increasing the level of agricultural production is the vast number of anti-personnel mines that remain concealed about the countryside as a result of the war. It was estimated that there were some 5m.–7m. unexploded mines in Angola, which could take up to 200 years to clear completely at the current speed of demining operations. The UN has taken the lead in conducting extensive demining operations and in supporting the Central Mine Action Training School, established to instruct demobilized soldiers from both government and UNITA forces. However, despite the recent establishment of new landmine clearance teams and the extension of demining activity, landmines continue to kill and injure.

Major Crops

Cassava is the main Angolan crop in terms of volume produced, and is the staple food of the majority of the population. Most of the crop is consumed domestically. Production rose from an estimated 6.6m. metric tons in 2004 to 13.9m. tons in 2010. The cultivation of bananas is being increased in the lower reaches of the rivers north of Luanda and of the Cuvo river. Estimated output was 432,700 tons in 2010. Sisal exports reached 67,000 tons in 1974, when Angola was Africa's second most important producer. Production has since declined sharply, principally as a result of a slump in world prices and the transition from private to state ownership, amounting to only an estimated 540 tons in 2010. Sorghum and millet are important staples for Angolans, and 40,600 tons of millet were produced in 2010, the bulk of which was traded and consumed locally.

Since independence maize output has fluctuated. It improved as a result of the end of the war and better rains, rising from 428,769 metric tons in 2001 to 1.1m. tons in 2010. Good weather and increased planting resulted in a record cereal harvest in 2008/09, estimated by FAO at 1.2m. tons, compared with 738,000 tons in 2007/08. Accordingly, FAO estimated that Angola's cereal import requirement decreased from around 750,000 tons in 2007/08 to zero in 2009/10, with the exception of modest imports of wheat and rice. FAO estimated that the cereal import requirement would see a moderate increase in 2011/12, compared with the previous year, to 868,000 tons, reflecting the rising level of urban consumption. Although food security has greatly improved since the end of the war, FAO estimated that pockets of food insecurity remained in isolated areas and communities affected by localized flooding.

In the mid-1970s Angola was the second largest African coffee producer and the world's main supplier of Robusta coffee. Prior to independence, annual production of green coffee was more than 200,000 metric tons, with the USA being the main export customer. Coffee was cultivated on a variety of Portuguese plantations, ranging from substantial commercial holdings to family plantations. However, the subsequent departure of the Portuguese, neglect of the plantations, which were nationalized following independence, and civil conflict contributed to a decline, reducing production to about one-50th of pre-independence levels.

In 1983 the Government established the Empresa de Rebenefício e Exportação do Café de Angola (CAFANGOL), a state-controlled coffee-processing and trading organization. Plans to privatize CAFANGOL, together with the state-owned coffee plantations, commenced in 1997, although foreign ownership of the plantations was to be limited to 30%–40%. The Angolan National Institute of Coffee and the UN World Food Programme launched a project to provide employment for demobilized soldiers and their families on coffee plantations, and in 2002 a plantation was set up outside Huambo for UNITA returnees. Owing to the provision of subsidized fertilizers and equipment, and the granting of micro-credits to coffee growers, the Government estimated that production rose to 12,000 metric tons in 2011, and forecast that it would increase to 13,900 tons in 2012.

Following independence, the main sugar cane plantations were reorganized as workers' co-operatives, with Cuban management and assistance; however, production of sugar cane (which peaked at 967,433 metric tons in 1973) declined sharply. The withdrawal of Cuban personnel by 1991 led to further deterioration in the sector. Since the mid-1990s production of sugar cane has been broadly stable at around 360,000 tons, requiring large volumes of imports of refined sugar to meet domestic shortfalls. In September 2009 SONANGOL, Brazil's Oderbrecht and an Angolan company, Damer, formed a joint venture, Biocom, to produce sugar on a 30,000-ha plantation in Malanje province. The US $220m. investment planned to produce 280,000 tons of sugar and 30,000 cu m of ethanol per year by 2012, as well as generate 217 MW of power from waste.

Cotton was formerly one of the most promising products of Angola, and was both a concessionary and an African cultivation. In 1974 production of cotton seed and lint totalled 103,000 metric tons. The collapse of European-owned plantations reduced production of seed cotton, and in 2010 output was just 2,200 tons. In 2007 the Ministry of Agriculture and Rural Development launched a US $40m. project to plant 5,000 ha of irrigated cotton fields in Kwanza-Sul province.

Exports of palm oil totalled 4,400 metric tons in 1974, but ceased shortly after independence. However, domestic production grew steadily, totalling 23,400 tons of palm kernels and 57,000 tons of palm oil in 2010, all of which was consumed domestically. Tobacco grows well on the formerly white-owned farms in the central and southern provinces of Benguela, Huíla and Namibe, with an estimated output of 5,600 tons in 2010. Other commodities (such as rice, sorghum, beans, tropical and temperate fruit, cocoa and groundnuts) are testimony to the agricultural potential of Angola.

In addition to the Biocom venture, a number of other foreign companies are developing biofuel projects in Angola. In 2007 Afriagro announced plans to invest US $47m. in a 20,000-ha palm plantation in Bengo province, with the aim of producing biofuel for export, and in 2009 Gesterra, a subsidiary of the British company Lonrho, launched a project to develop 10,000 ha of land for biofuels in Bengo, Uíge and Zaire provinces. In response to concerns that unregulated development of biofuels could prejudice domestic food production, the Assembleia Nacional approved a new biofuel law in 2010. This required foreign investors to sell a fixed portion of their produce to SONANGOL and obliged them to form partnerships with local businesses. Biofuel projects must ensure that local populations have access to clean water, basic services and medical care, and projects are allowed to use only land that is not already under cultivation or intended for food production.

Livestock, Forestry and Fisheries

Livestock-raising is concentrated in southern and central Angola, owing to the prevalence of the tsetse fly and the poor quality of the natural pastures in the north of the country. Some two-thirds of all cattle are found in Huíla province alone. The modern ranching sector, established by the Portuguese, was nationalized following independence, and has subsequently been adversely affected by civil war and drought. Meat shortages are prevalent in all cities, and imports of meat are indispensable. In 2010, according to FAO, Angola had only 5.1m. head of cattle, 2.6m. goats, 791,000 pigs and 355,000 sheep. However, the revival of livestock-breeding has increased cattle meat production, which according to FAO reached 105,500 metric tons in 2010.

Angola possesses important forestry resources, especially in the Cabinda, Moxico, Luanda and Kwanza-Norte provinces. Cabinda, in particular, has some valuable indigenous species, such as African sandalwood, rosewood and ebony. Softwood plantations of eucalyptus and cypress are used for fuel and grow along the Benguela railway and near Benguela, where they are used for wood pulp and paper manufacture. Exports of timber, however, ceased at independence. As in other sectors, output of logs and industrial roundwood decreased sharply after independence, from over 550,000 cu m in 1973 to some 40,000 cu m in the early 1980s. Output recovered in the mid-1980s and by 2010 had risen to 1.1m. cu m, in addition to 4.0m. cu m of firewood and 293,494 metric tons of charcoal.

The fishery industry is mainly centred around Namibe, Tombua and Benguela. However, the industry suffered from the withdrawal of most Portuguese trawlers at independence. Few trawlers are currently operational, owing to lack of maintenance, while foreign trawlers operating off the coast have significantly depleted fish reserves in Angolan waters. Around two-thirds of the annual catch is made by foreign and local trawlers, with the remainder being caught by around 20,000 local artisanal fishermen. The total catch declined from an average of 450,000 metric tons per year in the early 1970s to a low of 85,000 tons in 1986, before recovering to an average of 140,000 tons per year in the 1990s and to over 200,000 tons per year in the first half of the 2000s. FAO estimated the total catch at 260,200 tons in 2010.

MINERALS

Petroleum and Gas

The petroleum industry is the principal economic mainstay of the Government, with petroleum extraction, refining and distribution constituting Angola's most important economic activity. Output of petroleum expanded rapidly during the 1980s, from an average of 155,000 b/d in late 1982 to 550,000 b/d in 1992. Following a small decline in 1993, owing to the war, production again increased consistently, reaching an average of 981,000 b/d in 2004, following the start of production, in early 2002, at the Girassol field operated by Total. Production rose from 1.25m. b/d in 2005 to an estimated 1.90m. b/d in 2008, before declining to an estimated 1.81m. b/d in 2009 as a result of quota reductions imposed by OPEC, and 1.76m. b/d in 2010 owing to technical problems. Production fell further in 2011, to an average of 1.66m. b/d, due to maintenance work being carried out on key producing fields operated by ExxonMobil and BP, but was expected to recover to over 1.80m. b/d in 2012 as these fields returned to full production capacity. The Government has long-standing plans to increase production to over 2m. b/d, but this target has been repeatedly put back owing to technical delays in Angola's ultra-deepwater fields and the maturing of older fields. Recent discoveries in Angola's ultra-deepwater 'pre-salt' formation could drive a dramatic increase in production, with the Government forecasting output to reach a potential 3.5m. b/d by 2020.

Total FDI in the sector was estimated at US $26,000m. in 2003–07, and SONANGOL expected the sector to attract over $50,000m. in FDI in 2009–13. Angola's export earnings from petroleum and petroleum products have increased steadily in recent years, peaking at an estimated $66,1119m. in 2008, before decreasing in line with international prices to $40,720m. in 2009. They subsequently recovered to an estimated $62,965m. in 2011 and, according to the IMF, were projected to reach a record $76,197m. in 2013. Hydrocarbons typically account for over 95% of total exports and around 90% of state revenues. Angola is the second largest exporter of hydrocarbons in sub-Saharan Africa, after Nigeria. The petroleum and gas sectors account for around 55% of GDP. Estimates of proven recoverable reserves of crude petroleum have more than doubled since 1997, reaching an estimated 13,500m. barrels in 2010 (although this figure declined to 10,500m. barrels in 2011, according to OPEC). On 1 January 2007 Angola was formally admitted to OPEC; this was followed by the appointment in January 2009 of Angola's Minister of Petroleum, José Maria Botelho de Vasconcelos, as OPEC President for a one-year period. In December 2007 OPEC announced a production quota for Angola of 1.95m. b/d, marginally above the country's output level that month of 1.80m. b/d. However, in the wake of the global financial crisis and the collapse in oil prices, which declined from a peak of US $147 per barrel in July 2008 to $34 per barrel in late December, OPEC imposed a series of production cuts on its members, although the exact level of Angola's new quota was not announced. It was believed to be between 1.52m. b/d and 1.66m. b/d; however, throughout 2009 Angola continued to increase production, which averaged an estimated 1.84m. b/d for the year. In July Vasconcelos requested 'special consideration' for Angola to exceed its quota, similar to that granted to Iraq and Kuwait following the 1991 Gulf War, as the country was still in a phase of post-conflict reconstruction. Although OPEC refused formally to grant this request, given the cartel's secrecy regarding quotas and its reluctance to censure publicly the worst offenders, Angola was able to continue producing well in excess of its presumed OPEC quota.

The greatest impetus to expansion of the petroleum industry came from the Cabinda Gulf Oil Company (CABGOC), which discovered petroleum off shore at Cabinda in 1966. After independence, SONANGOL was established in 1976 to manage all fuel production and distribution, and in 1978 was authorized to acquire a 51% interest in all petroleum companies operating in Angola. In the late 1970s SONANGOL divided the Angolan coast, excluding Cabinda, into 13 exploration blocks, which were leased to foreign companies under production-sharing agreements. Although CABGOC's Cabinda offshore fields (which are operated by the US Chevron Corporation) remain the core of the Angolan petroleum industry (accounting for about two-thirds of total output), production has been buoyant at other concessions close to the enclave.

A lingering maritime border dispute between Angola and the Republic of the Congo was settled in 2002, which allowed ChevronTexaco (known as Chevron from May 2005) to begin prospecting in the area. In recent years attention has focused on deep-water blocks (numbered 14–33), which have produced promising results. In 1997 Elf Aquitaine announced the discovery of one of Africa's largest ever petroleum fields, Girassol, with estimated reserves of 3,500m. barrels, off the Angolan coast. In the same year the company discovered another giant deep-sea oilfield in Block 17, Dália. Girassol started production in 2002. Production on the 1,000m.-barrel Dália oilfield started in December 2006, and rose to 240,000 b/d in mid-2007. In November 2003 Block 17's Jasmin oilfield commenced production, reaching 50,000 b/d in 2004 (raising production on the entire Girassol project to 230,000 b/d). However, Total's relations with the Government were strained by France's ongoing judicial proceedings against Pierre Falcone (see Recent History). In response, the Angolan Government rescinded the company's further exploration rights in Block 17. After lengthy negotiations, in May 2007 Total succeeded in winning back the acreages on Block 17, in return for selling SONANGOL the former assets of Petrofina. Total's next development in Block 17, the 220,000-b/d Pazflor field, started production in November 2011. Meanwhile, Total announced in September 2010 that it was proceeding with the CLOV development, which links the Cravo, Lírio, Orquídea and Violeta fields in Block 17, with the potential to produce 160,000 b/d. Drilling was due to start in 2012, with production expected to commence in the second half of 2014.

In 1998 Exxon announced a large petroleum discovery, Kizomba, in Block 15. Total reserves were estimated at 1,000m. barrels. Further discoveries were made in 1999 and 2000. Exxon began construction on the US $4,300m. project in 2002, and production on the Kizomba-A project started in 2004, with a plateau rate of 250,000 b/d. Production on Kizomba-B began in 2005. Both fields were producing 550,000 b/d from recoverable reserves estimated at 2,000m. barrels. Combined with production of 80,000 b/d from the Xikomba field in the same block, this meant that ExxonMobil overtook Chevron as Angola's largest petroleum operator. In October 2007 production started at ExxonMobil's Marimba North project in Block 15, producing 40,000 b/d, which raised the block's total output to 540,000 b/d. In December the Mondo field started production and was expected to produce 100,000 b/d.

Two new discoveries were announced in the ultra-deep maritime zone north-west of Luanda in 2003, the Gindungo-1 field in Block 32 (operated by Total) and the Saturno well on Block 31 (operated by BP). Also in 2003 ChevronTexaco awarded contracts for the development of its Benguela, Belize, Lobito and Tombôco projects in deep-water Block 14; production commenced on these four fields in 2006. Chevron forecast that the combined production from the fields would rise to 200,000 b/d by 2009. In August 2009 Chevron announced the start of production at the Tômbua and Lândana fields in Block

14, adding a further 130,000 b/d to the company's output in Angola.

In March 2005 the Ministry of Petroleum approved the transfer of SONANGOL's 50% stake in Block 18 to SONANGOL Sinopec International—a joint venture between SONANGOL and the China Petroleum Company (Sinopec). In May a group of petroleum companies paid a US $4.5m. signature bonus for shallow-water Block 10, which would be operated by Devon Energy. In October ExxonMobil announced two new discoveries in deep-water Block 15, Kakocha and Tchihumba. In November the Xikomba oilfield (with total recoverable reserves of 100m. barrels) in ExxonMobil's Block 15 began production, reaching 80,000 b/d by the end of 2005.

In an effort to maintain the increase in production, the Angolan Government decided to relicence existing oil blocks on the expiry of their concessions. In 2005 SONANGOL put up for tender exploration licences for shallow-water Blocks 1, 5 and 6, and deep-water Block 26, and relinquished acreages in deep-water Blocks 15, 17 and 18. In 2006 SONANGOL awarded exploration licences for all seven blocks.

BP was given approval in July 2008 to proceed with a US $10,000m. investment in Block 31, which would involve tying together four existing fields to produce 150,000 b/d by 2012. In October 2008 ExxonMobil started production on its Saxi and Batuque fields in Block 15, with production reaching 200,000 b/d by the end of that year. In March 2009 Brazil's national oil company, Petrobras, announced plans to invest $795m. in exploration activity in Angola during 2009–13. In April 2009 BP announced its 18th discovery on Block 31, the Oberon well, which was expected to produce more than 5,000 b/d. In June SONANGOL announced that production had started from the Morsa field in Block 2, with output expected to reach 20,000 b/d.

Since the end of the civil war in 2002 exploration activity has improved in Cabinda's onshore area, although it has been periodically disrupted by attacks by renegade elements of the separatist movement, Frente para a Libertação do Enclave de Cabinda (FLEC). Onshore exploration activity has been led by an Australian oil company, Roc Oil. In early 2009 an Argentine company, Pluspetrol, acquired a 45% stake in Roc Oil's Cabinda Onshore South block, pledging to continue the company's existing drilling programme for 2009.

In 2006 the Government created five new blocks (designated Blocks 46–50) in Angola's ultra-deep north-west maritime zone, an area west of the existing ultra-deep-water Blocks 31–34 known as 'ultra-ultra-deep-water'. A new licensing round, which had originally been initiated in 2007 before being suspended in 2009 due to the deteriorating global economic climate, finally commenced in March 2010, when SONANGOL began secret negotiations with 13 oil companies for acreages on 11 deep-water blocks where large pre-salt reserves were believed to exist. In January 2011 SONANGOL awarded stakes in the blocks to seven companies, including BP, Total, Statoil, ConocoPhillips and ENI. New entrants to Angola's oil sector included Cobalt Energy of the USA and Repsol of Spain, while SONANGOL secured minority stakes in all 11 blocks. SONANGOL had concluded production-sharing contracts with all seven companies by the end of the year. In Febuary 2012 Cobalt Energy announced that it had struck oil in one of its exploratory wells, discovering a pre-salt reservoir believed to contain 1,500m. barrels of crude petroleum. The discovery could herald the emergence of Angola's pre-salt reserves as the country's richest new source of revenue, with production potentially rivalling Brazil's huge pre-salt finds of recent years. Meanwhile, in September 2011 SONANGOL announced that it was to auction several onshore blocks in the Kwanza Basin in 2012 in an effort to revive exploration activity in the region where Angola's oil production had started in the 1950s.

The majority of Angola's petroleum is exported to the USA and China in its crude form, although the Luanda refinery processes around 38,000 b/d of crude petroleum. The Government has long-standing plans to upgrade and increase the capacity of the Luanda refinery to 100,000 b/d, and in July 2007 SONANGOL acquired a 56% stake in the refinery from Total. There were also plans to construct a new refinery, capable of processing 200,000 b/d at Lobito. After lengthy delays, in March 2006 the Government signed a consortium agreement with SONANGOL and Sinopec to build and operate the refinery, known as Sonaref. Construction of the refinery was due to be carried out by the Republic of Korea's Samsung, and to be operational by 2010. However, in March 2007 the Government announced that it had suspended negotiations with Sinopec after both parties were unable to agree on the kind of petroleum products to produce at the refinery. SONANGOL then announced that it would complete the project on its own. In November 2008 SONANGOL contracted a US company to provide engineering and design for the project, which was expected to take four years to complete, at a cost of $8,000m. However, construction was delayed owing to financing problems. In May 2010 Vasconcelos announced that the refinery would start operating in 2014 at a rate of 115,000 b/d, rising to 200,000 b/d in 2015. In July 2011 Vasconcelos announced plans to build a new refinery near Soyo with a capacity of 200,000 b/d, casting doubt on whether the resumption of work on the Sonaref refinery project, which had been due to start before the end of 2011, would actually proceed.

SONANGOL has estimated Angola's gas reserves at 11,000,000m. cu ft. In 1998 the Government announced its intention to commence the production of liquefied natural gas (LNG), from a plant in Soyo—the Angola LNG project—which would produce 7,200m. cu m of LNG for export, plus around 1,300m. cu m of fuel for domestic use. In 2002 ChevronTexaco, SONANGOL, TotalFinaElf, BP, Norsk Hydro and ExxonMobil signed an agreement for this project, in which ChevronTexaco was to hold the largest stake; Agip-ENI acquired ExxonMobil's share in 2007. The project was expected to start production in June 2012, at a rate of 5.2m. metric tons per year, eventually rising to 8.0m. tons per year. The majority of LNG was expected to be exported to a regasification plant near Pascagoula, Mississippi, USA, but, given the growth of shale gas in the USA in recent years, the Angolan Government is now considering other export markets (notably Asia where LNG prices are highest). Construction work on the LNG plant in Soyo started in 2008, and in the following year work commenced on a 500-km pipeline linking seven blocks to the plant. However, the cost of the project spiralled from the original forecast of US $4,000m. to an estimated $10,000m. As part of the LNG project, in 2010 SONANGOL formed a joint venture with Electricidade de Portugal to build a gas-powered electricity plant at an estimated cost of $500m., which would supply power mainly to the surrounding region. Two other gas projects are in development. In 2004 operations began in ChevronTexaco's US $1,900m. Sanha-Bombôco gas and condensate field in Block 0, which achieved output of 100,000 b/d of liquid hydrocarbons in 2007. In June 2007 two Spanish companies, Gas Natural and Repsol YPF, acquired the remaining stake in a second gas consortium—including Sonagás, ENI, Galp Energia and Exem—which would explore for gas in Angola in order to support a second LNG plant.

In November 2007 the Government announced plans to reform SONANGOL, transferring some of its large portfolio of interests in shipping, construction and air transport, as well as its substantial quasi-fiscal operations, to the oil and finance ministries. However, the process was expected to take at least five years to complete, with a view to listing SONANGOL on the New York Stock Exchange in the USA. In the mean time, SONANGOL continued to increase its interests, particularly in the sectors of banking, shipping, and oil and petroleum products distribution, as well as expanding its overseas petroleum exploration activities with the acquisition of stakes in oilfields in Gabon, Guinea, South Sudan, Argentina, Brazil, the Gulf of Mexico, Ecuador, Indonesia, Iraq, Venezuela and Cuba.

Diamonds

Angola is believed to be one of the richest countries in mineral reserves of Southern Africa. Angola's kimberlite pipes, first discovered in 1911, are believed to rank among the world's five richest deposits of embedded diamonds. The country's diamond reserves have been estimated at over 200m. carats, the majority of them being alluvial deposits, although there is increasing exploitation of diamond-bearing kimberlite rocks. During 1986–2000 full control of this sector was exercised by the state enterprise ENDIAMA, which instigated a new national diamond policy, whereby mining was to be divided into blocks, to be exploited under production-sharing agreements with foreign concessionaires. Annual output reached 3.8m. carats in 1999, and increased to 5.1m. carats in 2001. Several new diamond fields were explored in the early 2000s, and, according to data collected by the Kimberley Process Certification Scheme (an international initiative that aims to identify the source mine of each diamond), annual diamond production rose from an estimated 6.1m. carats in 2004 to 8.9m. carats in 2008, worth US $1,210m. This made Angola the world's fifth largest producer of rough diamonds by volume in 2008, after Australia, Botswana, the Democratic Republic of the Congo (DRC) and Russia, and the world's 11th largest diamond exporter. Angola has hopes of becoming the world's second largest diamond producer. However, the impact of the global economic downturn and financial crisis in late 2008 and early 2009 forced mining companies to suspend, defer or withdraw from major projects. None the less, due to an increase in production in the second half of the year as global demand recovered, annual output reached an estimated 9.2m. carats in 2009, with exports totalling 9.7m. carats (including some stockpiled diamonds). However, production decreased to an estimated 8.4m. carats in 2010 as global demand slackened once again, with total exports of 7.2m. carats (worth $824m.). None the less, the long-term prospects for the sector remain positive, with annual output expected to exceed 10m. carats by the end of the 2010s.

During the protracted civil war, diamond output figures were deceptive, since a significant proportion of actual production was mined and smuggled by UNITA, which partially controlled the diamond-producing area. Official sales of diamonds totalled US $250m. in 1992, but reached only one-quarter of that level following the resumption of civil war in late 1992, when diamond-mining areas again came under UNITA control. A report issued by the diamond-producing Angolan Selling Corporation (ASCORP) in mid-2002 indicated that annual profits in the diamond industry had contracted by some 87%, owing to a decline in demand. However, since UNITA surrendered control of its mines following the April 2002 peace agreement and the subsequent lifting of UN sanctions, official diamond exports have risen sharply, reaching an estimated $1,200m. in 2006, for which the Government earned $165m. in tax revenue.

The role played by the illicit diamond trade in perpetuating the civil war in Angola was highlighted in a high-profile campaign launched by the organization Global Witness, based in the United Kingdom. The resultant publicity forced De Beers to announce, in 1999, that it would only purchase diamonds bearing government certificates of origin. Pressure on the diamond industry was intensified following the publication in 2000 of a report by the UN Sanctions Committee, 'naming and shaming' the Presidents of Togo and Burkina Faso, as well as Belgian, Bulgarian and Ukrainian officials, accusing them of involvement in the illicit diamond trade and of providing military assistance to UNITA.

In April 2006 ENDIAMA entered into a five-year joint venture with Russian company Alrosa to explore for diamonds in the Cacolo area of Lunda-Sul province. By the end of 2006 there were 14 formal sector mines in operation in Angola. By the end of 2009 there were a total of 172 diamond concessions in 14 provinces, of which 45 were carrying out prospecting over an area of 107,000 sq km. The largest kimberlite mine in Catoca, Lunda-Sul, is a joint venture involving ENDIAMA, Alrosa, Brazil's Odebrecht and Israeli diamond merchant Lev Leviev. The mine produced US $527m. of diamonds in 2010, making it the richest kimberlite mine in the world. In May 2011 Leviev sold his stake in Catoca to China Sonangol International Holding for $400m. The Government has long-standing plans to develop other kimberlite resources at Camafuca and Camatchia-Camagico in Lunda-Norte.

As a result of the global financial crisis and the collapse in international diamond prices, in late 2008 most mining companies operating in Angola were forced to suspend or cancel diamond projects, prompting a major contraction in the sector, with over 1,000 jobs lost. However, due to the recovery in diamond prices in 2010, a number of new projects were implemented, including a $28m. investment in the Luana diamond mine, which was expected to produce 3,000 carats per month, and a $19.5m. investment in the Luxinge diamond concession in Lunda-Norte.

In 2006 the Government created the pan-African Association of Diamond Producing Nations (ADPA), to be headed by Angola with its headquarters in Luanda. The association's main objective was to co-ordinate the policies of Africa's diamond producers to protect international prices, boost foreign investment in Africa's mining sector and capture a greater share of profits.

Other Mining

Iron-mining began in 1956 and annual production averaged 700,000–800,000 metric tons in the 1960s from mines in the Huambo and Bié provinces. In 1981 a state-owned iron company, Empresa Nacional de Ferro de Angola (FERRANGOL), was created. Angola holds considerable ore production stockpiles, which await the eventual rehabilitation of rail links to the coast. In 2006 the Government launched a programme to encourage foreign investors to develop reserves of iron and manganese at both the Cassinga mine and at the Cassala-Kitungo deposits, which were believed to contain over 4,000m. tons of iron ore. In 2010 FERRANGOL announced that it had formed a joint venture with four Angolan companies and an unnamed foreign company to develop Cassinga's iron deposits. The US $3,000m. project was expected to involve the construction of a 650-km railway to Namibe and a steel plant using iron ore from the deposit, and would be preceded by a two-year feasibility study. FERRANGOL expected the mine to produce 5m.–10m. tons of ore in its first years of operation, subsequently rising to 20m. tons per year. In January 2012, in a joint venture between FERRANGOL and the private Angolan consortium DT Génio Mineira, exploratory drilling for iron ore and manganese commenced at the Cassala Quitono project in Kwanza-Norte. The mine was expected to produce 3m. tons of ore per year by 2013, subsequently rising to over 30m. tons per year.

Reserves of copper were identified in Uíge province, and other deposits are known to exist in the Namibe, Huíla and Moxico provinces. The copper mine in Mavoio, Uíge province, produced 30,000 metric tons of copper per year during the colonial period, but was closed down in 1972. In 2006 a British mining company, Silverpritex, started mining for copper in Cachoeiras de Binga, Kwanza-Sul province, while important deposits of feldspar have been found in the southern province of Huíla. In 2008 two Angolan companies, AP Services and Genius Mineral, started exploratory drilling for copper on the Tetelo-Mavoio licence, in Uíge province, which has proven ore reserves of 31.3m. tons. The companies planned to start mining copper in the second half of 2010, with the aim of producing 240,000 tons of copper per year. In 2005 a US-based company, Mayfair Mining and Minerals, Inc, was awarded a 70% stake in the Ucua licence in western Bengo province, where it was to prospect for emeralds, aquamarines and minerals. Exploration for precious metals, including gold, was expected to start in Mpopo, Huíla province, in 2013. Unexploited reserves of phosphate rock exist in the Zaire and Cabinda provinces, and deposits of uranium have been found along the border with Namibia.

In 2007 Angola and Guinea-Bissau signed an agreement authorizing a private Angolan company, Angola Bauxite, to develop 110m. metric tons of bauxite reserves in Guinea-Bissau's Boé region. In 2008 Angola Bauxite announced that it would invest US $500m. in the project, which would include construction of the mine (with an annual production capacity of 3m. tons of bauxite), a deep-water port at Buba and a railway linking the two. However, the project foundered owing to financing difficulties during the 2008–10 global crisis, and it was effectively abandoned following the *coup d'état* in Guinea-Bissau in April 2012, which removed the pro-Angolan Government from power and forced the withdrawal of the Angolan military training mission from the country. In July 2011 the Assembleia Nacional approved amendments to the mining code, its first revision since 1992. The amendments were aimed at stimulating exploitation of the country's diamond, iron and copper reserves. Under the new regulations, mining companies would be awarded 35-year exploration and production licences, which could be renewed for a period of 10 years a maximum of two times. In addition, ENDIAMA would have a mandatory 51% stake in all diamond mines, although the company would not be allowed to carry out mining activities but would rather act as simply a concessionaire. All informal mining—including that undertaken by thousands of *garimpeiros* in the country's Lunda provinces—would be classed as a crime against the State. The Government has also launched a tender for a new geological survey of Angolan territory, with the goal of locating undiscovered mineral reserves.

POWER

Angola's power potential exceeds its needs, with an estimated hydroelectric potential of 18,000 MW. However, since independence there have been no significant additions to Angola's power-generating capacity. As a result, power supply is erratic and the situation is exacerbated by the fragmentation of the market into several independent producers, and the absence of a national grid. In 2009 the Government estimated that only 32% of the population had access to a regular power supply, decreasing to 10.7% for the rural population. Accordingly, up to 80% of rural communities rely on biomass (in particular wood and farm residue) for cooking and heating. In 2002 Angola had 205 MW of installed hydroelectric capacity and 412 MW of thermal capacity, but by 2010 several new projects had boosted total generating capacity to 790 MW. In May 2010 the Government announced that it would invest US $18,000m. in expanding generating capacity in 2010–17, with a focus on the Cuanza, Catumbela and Cunene rivers. In June 2011 the Government pledged that $20,000m. of oil revenue would be used to fund the construction of new dams and hydroelectric plants. In December the new Minister of Energy and Water updated the Government's power investment plan, pledging $16,500m. of funding in 2012–15 with the aim of boosting generating capacity by 12%. Since 2007 work has also been under way to rehabilitate and expand the country's electricity grid, particularly into rural areas. As part of this programme, in mid-2009 a Chinese company, CMEC, started work on rehabilitating the power grids in Malanje and Cacuso, in Malanje province, and in Saurimo, Lunda-Sul province. Around two-thirds of Angola's energy output is of hydroelectric origin, and there is an impressive dam on the Cuanza river at Cambambe, constructed and operated by a Brazilian company; its generating capacity stood at 60 MW in 2007. Luanda's industries are the main beneficiaries of power from the dam. There is also an 18-MW dam at Mabubas on the Dande river. Construction of the Capanda dam in Malanje province began in 1962 but was repeatedly halted due to the war, only resuming in 2000. In 2004 two 130-MW turbines started operations, supplying power to Luanda and other large towns in north-central Angola. In 2007 a new 260-MW generating unit was completed at Capanda, which doubled the dam's generating capacity to 520 MW. Separate projects were also under way to construct new power lines linking Cambambe with Luanda and the northern province of Uíge. In January 2007 the Government approved a US $218m. 15-month project, led by Brazil's Oderbrecht, to construct new power lines between the Capanda dam and Luanda. The same month the 30-MW Caminhos de Ferro de Angola power station started supplying power to Luanda. In 2009 Oderbrecht was awarded a four-year contract to increase the height of the wall on the Cambambe dam and to install four new turbines, with the aim of boosting its output to 700 MW. The first new turbine was expected to start producing power by June 2011, and there were plans to construct an additional 80-MW plant at the dam. However, power supplies remain unreliable and in September 2011 Luanda endured periodic blackouts caused by repairs to the Capanda dam's generating and distribution network. Other power projects under way in the north of the country include the construction of a 400-MW combined cycle power station in Soyo and a 400-MW thermal power plant in Zaire province.

Prior to independence Lobito and Benguela were provided with electricity by two privately owned dams, the Lomaum and the Biópio, both on the Catumbela river. In 2009 an Angolan company, Kamzuro-Electrice, started reconstruction of the Lomaum dam at a cost of US $12.2m. The dam was due to resume generating 60 MW in 2011, which would supplement the 10 MW produced by the Biópio dam. The local authorities also planned to develop mini-hydroelectric dams in the area to meet rising power demand. The Ngove dam, located on the Cunene river 120 km south of Huambo, was partially destroyed during the war. In 2007 a Brazilian company started reconstruction and modernization of the dam, at an estimated cost of $150m. The 60-MW dam was to provide power to Huambo and Kuito-Bié, as well as regulate the flow of water to the Ruacaná dam further downstream and provide irrigation for neighbouring provinces. Further south, the 26-MW Matala dam serves Lubango, Namibe and Cassinga. Rehabilitation of the dam started in May 2010 and was expected to last three years, at an estimated cost of $255m., increasing its generating capacity to 40 MW. The Matala dam was only a very small part of an ambitious Angolan-Namibian scheme for damming the Cunene river, thus providing Namibia, which is deficient in power and water, with cheap electricity and a permanent water supply. During the colonial era a power station was built at Calueque, near the Ruacaná Falls, where the Cunene river reaches the Namibian border, which piped water to an underground power station at Ruacana in northern Namibia, producing 240 MW. However, further development of the project was impeded by instability in the region, and it never achieved its full potential. In 2009 the Namibian Government launched a feasibility study for a $750m. project, to be jointly funded by the Angolan and Namibian Governments, to build a 400-MW power station at Baynes, in northern Namibia, using water piped from a new dam on the Cunene river, close to the existing power station at Calueque. Construction could start in 2013, with the first power being produced by 2017.

In 2006 it was reported that Russia's Technopromexport planned to invest US $1,000m. in the construction of three new power stations on the Cuanza river at Njanga, Lauka and Kalulu Kabasa, each with generating capacity in excess of 500 MW. In 2007 feasibility studies were launched for all three dams, which could be operational as early as 2013. In 2009 the Russian Government announced that it would finance the construction of two new hydroelectric power stations on the Cuanza river, located at Lauca and Caculo Cabaça, with a combined generating capacity of 3,680 MW. Angola has long-standing plans to draw power from the 4,300-MW Inga III hydroelectric project in the DRC. In 2010 work started on constructing power lines from the dam to Cabinda, and the first electricity was due to be transmitted to Angola in 2012.

INDUSTRY

Angola's industrial activity is centred on construction materials, petroleum-refining, food- and drink-processing, textiles, equipment for the petroleum industry, steel, chemicals, electrical goods and vehicle assembly. Angola's manufacturing sector has considerable potential, in view of the country's abundance of raw materials, such as petroleum and iron ore. However, the high cost of operating in Angola, owing to excessive regulation, poor infrastructure and the overvalued exchange rate, has meant that only manufacturers making heavy goods, such as bottled water or cement (which are expensive to transport), are profitable. As a result, manufacturing and construction together contribute only around 7% of GDP.

Following the withdrawal of Portuguese owners, many enterprises were brought under state control and ownership, and by the mid-1980s about 80% of the industrial work-force was employed in state-owned companies. Under the SEF, introduced in January 1988, legislation was reformed, granting state enterprises autonomous control of management. A new foreign investment code was also introduced, which aimed to increase the rights of foreign companies regarding operation, transfer of profits, taxation, etc., while, in return, foreign investors were expected to expand the transfer of technical and managerial skills to Angolan industrial personnel. Under the new code, however, many sectors remained closed to foreign investment. The Government's privatization programme was approved in 2001, but little progress has been made. In 2003 the Government introduced several laws to replace the previous investment regime. The laws aimed to promote foreign investment in Angola by allowing companies to repatriate profit, and to bring the legal framework for private sector operations in the country in line with international practice. A new agency was also created to oversee private investment, Agência Nacional do Investimento Privado, and a one-stop business registration shop, Guichê Único de Empresas, in an effort to streamline procedures.

In 2003 the Government launched the Aldeia Nova project, which aimed to create an agro-industrial sector in Angola and reduce imports of food and processed food products. After initially being piloted on a 17,000-ha site in Kwanza-Sul province, the project was to be extended across Angola in 2008–12, supported by a US $400m. investment from the Government. However, progress with the project has been slow, mainly owing to the lack of electricity in rural areas to power the processing factories and the poor state of the roads to key consuming markets, notably Luanda. In 2011 Ecatema of Spain announced plans to build an agro-industrial unit to process bananas and tomatoes in Caxito, Bengo province, facilitated by a credit line from the Spanish Government.

Following the end of the civil war in 2002, a major construction boom began in Luanda. In 2006 the Government launched a project, Programa de Reestruturação do Sistema de Logística e de Distribuição de Produtos Essenciais à População, to create a network of markets and shops across Angola selling basic goods at low prices. The project, which was forecast to cost an estimated US $1,700m. over 2006–12, would involve the construction of 10,000 retail outlets, 16 municipal, suburban and rural markets, and 31 supermarkets branded as 'Nosso Super'. However, the supermarket chain struggled to establish itself, owing to poor logistics and high prices, and in September 2011 the Government transferred its management to the Brazilian company, Odebrecht.

Other projects under development included the Nova Vida project in Lunda-Sul, which commenced in 2001 and aimed to build 2,500 luxury homes for civil servants; however, the forced eviction of more than 600 families from the proposed site drew criticism from humanitarian groups. The Luanda Waterfront Corporation was carrying out the redevelopment of Luanda's waterfront boulevard as part of a US $2,000m., 13-year project (scheduled to be completed by 2014). In 2006 the Government announced that it would build 200,000 new homes by 2008 to meet the country's housing shortage. In August 2007 the Brazilian architect Oscar Niemeyer revealed that he had been invited to design a new capital city for Angola, with 2m. residents, located between Cacuaco and Barra do Dande. However, in September the Government stated that instead it planned to build a network of urban hubs, each with up to 100,000 residents. There were also plans to build a new city in Benguela's Baía Azul municipality, at an estimated cost of $2,000m. In order to meet rising visitor demand, a total of 39 hotels were planned to be constructed in Angola in 2008–12, at a cost of over $500m. As part of the Government's package of investments ahead of the 2010 association football Coupe d'Afrique des Nations (Africa Cup of Nations) tournament, which was hosted in Angola, four new stadia were built, at a cost of some $500m., and a number of airports were modernized.

However, the global downturn and the collapse in government investment in 2009 had a huge impact on the construction sector, resulting in the laying off of an estimated 20% of the work-force. In addition, the Government built up an estimated US $6,800m. of payment arrears to Brazilian and Portuguese construction companies operating in Angola, resulting in a number of projects being deferred or cancelled. Although the Government drew up a plan to repay its domestic debt arrears in May 2010, this was repeatedly delayed owing to the Government's weak fiscal position. As a result, the construction sector and property prices remained depressed throughout 2010 and into 2011 as arrears to contractors were paid off. In May 2011 the Angolan Government signed new accords with the Chinese Government, committing CITIC Construction to help to design two new municipalities in Luanda, Kilamba Kiaxi and Belas.

The spectacular growth of the construction sector following the end of the war spurred the revival of the main cement works, operated by the Empresa de Cimentos de Angola (Cimangola), in Luanda, and the sector was also expected to benefit from the Capanda dam project. Nova Cimangola, a cement company formed as a public-private partnership with a Norwegian firm, Scancem, increased production from 182,000 metric tons in 1995 to 600,000 tons in 2002. The company invested US $25m. in 2003–07, and following further investment of $21m. in 2010–11 increased production at its Luanda plant to 1.8m. tons per year. The company planned to invest $200m. in building a new facility in Cacuaco with the capacity to produce 2m. tons per year by 2013. In 2006 Portugal's second largest cement company, Secil, announced investment of $91m. in the construction of a cement factory in Lobito. Operations started in 2009 with initial production of 250,000 tons per year; a second cement factory in Lobito, which the company started building in 2009 at a cost of $131m., was expected to boost output by 240,000 tons per year. In 2007 construction started on a $200m. industrial complex in Lobito, Palanca Cimentos, which would produce 1.2m. tons per year of clinker and cement. In 2008 a Japanese company, Sojitz, commenced construction of a $500m. cement factory in Kwanza-Sul, which was expected to start producing 1.4m. tons per year in 2011.

The manufacture of beer and soft drinks has taken off since the end of the war in 2002, supported by the rising purchasing power of the population. In 2008 a new beer factory opened in Bom Jesus, following a US $200m. investment. In the same year a water-bottling plant started operations in Tchipipa, with the capacity to produce 14,000 bottles of mineral water per day. In 2009 SAB Miller announced plans to invest $125m. in the construction of a brewery and soft drinks factory in Angola, which aimed to produce 500,000 hl of beer and 200,000 hl of soft drinks per year. In 2010 the Portuguese group Unicer announced plans to invest $120m. in building a beer factory in Bengo province with a capacity of 100m.–200m. litres of beer, with first production expected in late 2011. In June 2011 Namibia's Nampak opened a $160m. drink-can manufacturing plant in Viana, in Luanda's suburbs, with the capacity to produce 750m. cans per year.

Elsewhere, development of the manufacturing sector has been uneven. In 2005 Volkswagen announced plans to construct a vehicle assembly plant and dealer network for Volkswagen and its subsidiary, Skoda, in Angola. The US $48m. project was to employ up to 2,500 people and was expected to start operations by 2007. However, at mid-2012 the project showed no sign of coming to fruition. In 2005 Troller Jeeps announced it was constructing a vehicle assembly plant in Viana. In 2008 the Export-Import Bank of India announced investment of $45m. in the rehabilitation of a textile factory in Benguela province, creating 4,000 new jobs. In 2009 Japan's Nissan, in partnership with China's Dongfeng and CSG Automóvel-Angola, opened a $30m. assembly plant in Viana with the capacity to produce 30,000 cars and 3,000 vans per year (by 2012).

TRANSPORT AND COMMUNICATIONS

Angola's colonial administration made a considerable effort to improve the communications network, and in 1974 there were 8,317 km of tarred roads in a total road network of 72,323 km, the second-largest road network in sub-Saharan Africa (after South Africa). These efforts were continued by the Government, in part to facilitate military transport. In 2010 Angola had 73,000 km of roads, of which 24,000 km were considered main roads, although only around one-half of these were paved. Bus transportation was also fairly developed following independence, but from the early 1980s guerrilla warfare dramatically curtailed most road transportation. In 1988 a US $340m. emergency programme was launched to rehabilitate the transport infrastructure (including roads, railways, seaports and airports). A substantial programme of road and bridge rehabilitation was announced in 2000, and further programmes followed in 2002 and 2005. Between 2002 and 2007 a total of 3,900 km of road were rebuilt. In April 2007 the Government announced a $2,000m. programme to expand Angola's road network. It was planned that a total of 14,000 km would be constructed by the end of 2011, in addition to 120 bridges and adjacent infrastructure destroyed during the war. In 2009 the Government purchased 1,000 new buses from the Indian company Hinduja, at a cost of $43m., to be used for public transport. In June 2011 a new bridge joining Luanda to the adjacent Ilha do Cabo was inaugurated, forming part of the $300m. Baia de Luanda regeneration project launched in 2007. The project also involved the use of reclaimed land to build a six-lane motorway, the creation of parking spaces for 30,000 vehicles and the planting of 3,000 trees along the bay.

Prior to independence the Portuguese constructed a rail network totalling 2,722 km. However, by the end of the war in 2002 the network had almost entirely ceased to function, with only small sections of line still operating along the coast. Railways served a dual purpose, to open the interior and to provide export channels for Zambia and the land-locked province of Katanga in the DRC, which export large volumes of minerals. Hence, all railway lines run towards the coast. The volume of freight handled on Angolan railways was 9.3m. metric tons in 1973, but the annual total declined to 135,000 tons in 1994, recovering only slowly from the late 1990s (reaching 242,000 tons by 2001). Heavy investment resulted in 690 km of new track being laid between 2002 and 2007.

The 479-km Luanda railway, Caminho de Ferro de Luanda, which was chiefly for local goods traffic and passengers, was the only line functioning with a degree of regularity during the late 1980s. In 1997 work was completed on the reconstruction of the 180-km rail link between Luanda and Dondo, in Kwanza-Norte province, which had been closed for seven years owing to the hostilities. Rehabilitation of the Luanda railway, which was damaged by the destruction of bridges by UNITA prior to 1991 and subsequently by further hostilities, commenced in 2005. The US $600m. project was financed by China and implemented by China Railway Construction Corporation, and involved the reconstruction of 16 stations and 40 bridges and the creation of 20 new stations. However, work on the line was delayed due to financing shortages, lack of materials and disagreements between the Chinese company working on the line and the Angolan management. As a result, the project was not completed until July 2010, with the first passenger services resuming in January 2011. The new line was shorter, at 424 km, and included three new fuel storage facilities along its length.

The 1,336-km Caminho de Ferro de Benguela was of international importance and was the strategic outlet for exports of copper and zinc from Zaire and Zambia, bypassing South Africa and providing the most direct link to the west coast. However, UNITA guerrilla attacks caused the suspension of all cross-border traffic after 1975. For the most part, the domestic Lobito–Huambo section of the railway continued to operate, although at a reduced level. In April 2002 a 45-km section of the railway was opened in Huambo province. In 2003 the Government announced that it planned to invest US $4,000m. in rebuilding the country's rail network, with the involvement of the private sector. Work began in 2005 on the 11-year project, financed in part by a $2,000m. Chinese credit line; the project involved the rehabilitation of Angola's three existing lines—from Lobito to the Zambian border, from Luanda to Malanje, and from Namibe to Menongue—as well as the construction of a new line along the coast linking Luanda, Lobito and Benguela. A feasibility study was also under way for a railway from Luanda to the northern enclave of Cabinda, via a new road bridge that was to be built over the Congo river. Reconstruction of the Benguela line was undertaken by the China Railway 20 Bureau Group Corporation, mostly using Chinese labour and credit. The project proceeded slowly and by mid-2012 the line had been completed as far as Luena, 1,000 km down the line, with irregular rail services operating as far as Huambo. The line was not expected to become fully operational until 2013 at the earliest, when it was planned to be connected to the rail network in the DRC. According to government forecasts, the rehabilitated line will carry 20m. metric tons of freight and 4m. passengers per year, reconnecting Zambia and Zimbabwe's copperbelts with the Atlantic seaboard. In 2008 the Zambian President announced plans to construct a new 288-km railway line from Zambia's Copperbelt province to the town of Cazombo in order to resume copper exports along the Benguela railway line. In the long term, the Angolan Government planned to connect Angola's rail network to those of Namibia and South Africa.

The 907-km Namibe railway, Caminho de Ferro de Moçâmedes, in the south of the country, was assuming a new importance as a carrier of iron ore from Cassinga before the security situation resulted in the closure of the mines. In 2006 work began on a US $200m. project to rehabilitate and modernize the line. The project was to involve the replacement of 856 km of track, the building of 56 new stations and the purchase of new locomotives. Following construction delays and some flooding damage, it was anticipated that the line would become fully operational in mid-2012. Once complete, the line was expected to carry 2m. passengers and 15m. metric tons of goods per year. In early 2005 the President of Namibia announced that the construction of a new railway line to connect the Namibian port of Walvis Bay with Namibe had begun. In March 2012 the Government announced plans to merge the three state-owned companies that operate Angola's railway lines into a single body, Caminhos de Ferro de Angola (CFA), prior to the privatization of the railways' commercial and operational activities. Internal air transport is well developed, with a network of good airports and rural landing strips, and has become the only moderately safe means of transportation, owing to the insecurity on road and rail routes. The Chinese Government helped finance the modernization of Luanda's 4 de Fevereiro International Airport, which was due for completion by the end of 2010. It was also carrying out the US $60m. construction of a second airport in Bom Jesus, but this encountered financing problems and was not expected to open until 2012 at the earliest. In 2008 the Government signed a contract with Tecnovia Angola to rehabilitate and extend the runways at Malanje and Cabinda airports. The Government announced in January 2009 that $400m. would be invested in modernizing 30 airports, including Luanda, Benguela and Lubango, in preparation for the 2010 Africa Cup of Nations. In January 2010 Lubango's new international airport started operations, along with the rehabilitated airports of Benguela and Catumbela. Angola's national airline, Linhas Aéreas de Angola (TAAG), operates domestic and international flights. In June 2011, as part of plans to modernize its fleet, TAAG signed an agreement to purchase several Boeing 777 aircraft under a $256m. long-term loan guarantee from the Export-Import Bank of the United States.

Angola's main harbours are Lobito, Luanda and Namibe. Cabinda has become the principal loading port, with an annual 7.6m. metric tons (mostly petroleum) handled in recent years, and started extensive rehabilitation in 2007. The port of Lobito handled 1.57m. tons in 2007, up from just 300,000 tons in 2002, most of which was construction equipment and materials for infrastructure rehabilitation, increasing its share to 10% of Angola's port activity. In 2008 construction started on a new dry port at Lobito, which was to handle the increase in traffic once the Benguela railway reopened to mineral shipments from Zambia and the DRC. In July 2009 a Dutch company, Heerema Marine Contractors, started work on the construction of a US $160m. shipyard in Sumbe, Kwanza-Sul province. The shipyard commenced operations in September 2010 and planned to provide services to offshore oil and gas exploration projects in the Gulf of Guinea. In August 2009 the Government announced plans to construct two new commercial ports, at Barra do Dande, 50 km north of Luanda, and at Caio Litoral, 18 km from Cabinda City, with both ports scheduled to be operational by 2013.

As the country exports very little except petroleum, unloaded goods account for about 85% of traffic south of Cabinda. Passenger traffic is now almost negligible. During the 2000s Angola's main general cargo terminal, Luanda Commercial Port, underwent a US $90m. modernization programme. In 2005 a fourth terminal, operated by the state-owned Unicargas, came into operation in Luanda port, handling 244,000 metric tons of cargo per year. In 2006 the Government announced that a fifth terminal supporting mining activity was to be added. In the following year Luanda port granted a 20-year concession to run its container terminal to the management company Sociedade Gestora de Terminais (Sogester), which invested $155m. in modernizing and upgrading the terminal over the following four years, including $57m. in the construction of a deep-water harbour. The port of Luanda planned to invest $350m. in 2010–15 to upgrade its infrastructure, build three new terminals and acquire modern equipment. Luanda port has steadily increased its traffic, the volume of goods handled rising from 2.6m. tons in 2002 to 5.6m. tons in 2007; the Government was keen to raise this to 11.0m. tons by 2010. However, the massive increase in imports of building materials and consumer goods from 2003 caused significant bottlenecks at the port, and by mid-2009 as many as 85 ships were waiting in Luanda harbour to unload. In 2008 the Ministry of Transport implemented a review of clearing procedures at Luanda's port, which helped to reduce waiting times for cargo ships to unload. In 2009 work started on a $1,200m. project to expand the port of Lobito (increasing its handling capacity to an annual 11m. tons), including the construction of a dry dock and mineral terminals. Following delays in 2010 caused by the global financial crisis, the new developments were to be fully operational by mid-2012. In July 2012 the Angolan Government stated that freight costs had fallen by 22% over the previous four years, from an average of $3,665 per container in 2008 to $2,850 per container in 2011, even though the annual volume of freight had increased by 10.7% to 421,000 containers over the same period. However, freight costs were still around 30% higher than the average costs in Ghana, Cameroon, Senegal, Gabon and Côte d'Ivoire.

Angola's telephone communications network, which was badly damaged during the years of war, benefited from considerable investment in the late 1990s. Angola Telecom's (AT) infrastructure investment aims for compatibility with Africa One, the fibre-optic cable system that will serve the African continent. In 2007 AT awarded the Ericsson Group a US $70m. contract to construct an undersea fibre-optic network linking Angola's six coastal provinces, which became operational in early 2009. In April 2009 AT announced plans to invest $2,400m. in expanding the fixed-line network in 2009–13, including the installation of 500,000 new lines and the linking of Angola's remaining provinces to the national fibre-optic network.

In January 2001 the state monopoly on telecommunications was ended, and in March a new cellular communications network was inaugurated. In December 2002 a second national operator, Mundo StarTel, was licensed, and in 2004 Telecom Namibia purchased a 44% stake in the company, promising to invest N $19m. (US $14m.) over the next three years to install high-speed networks. In September 2003 AT launched an ADSL broadband internet service in Luanda. A rival broadband internet service was introduced by a new cable television company in 2004. In late 2003 Movicel, the mobile cellular telephone subsidiary of AT, awarded a contract to Nortel Networks of Canada to install a new network, the code division multiple access, compatible with the mobile telephone systems used in North America. Movicel's competitor, Unitel, uses the Global System for Mobile Communications, which is common in Europe. Both companies had extended mobile telephone coverage to all 18 of Angola's provincial capitals by the end of 2005. In December 2010 Unitel had 6m. subscribers, while Movicel had around 3m. In July 2009 the Government sold its 80% stake in Movicel to a consortium of Angolan investors, the largest privatization since the end of the war in 2002. In June 2010 Unitel announced plans to install a third-generation mobile technology network in Angola at a cost of $800m. According to the International Telecommunication Union, 9.5m. Angolans—or one in two—had a mobile telephone subscription by the end of 2011, a massive increase compared with just 20,000 when the first mobile telephones were introduced in 1995. In comparison, there were only 303,200 fixed lines in operation at the end of 2011. According to the Ministry of Telecommunications and Information Technology, there were 2m. mobile internet users in Angola at the end of 2010.

TRADE AND FOREIGN PAYMENTS

According to the International Trade Centre, the principal exported commodities in 2011 were crude petroleum (which, at an estimated US $58,706m., accounted for 98.9% of total export earnings) and diamonds ($500m., or 0.8%). China was Angola's principal customer in 2011 (42.0% of total exports), followed by the USA (23.3%), Taiwan (9.5%), Canada (4.2%) and Italy (3.5%). The main sources of imports in 2011 were Portugal (21.4%), China (18.3%), the USA (9.9%) and Brazil (7.1%). In 2011 the total value of merchandise exports was $59,349m. and the value of merchandise imports was $15,181m., leaving a huge trade surplus of $44,168m., and a surplus of $16,000m. on the current account of the balance of payments. The country's large external debt was estimated by the World Bank at $12,683m. at the end of 2010 (down from $15,132m. in 2008), of which $9,223m. was medium- and long-term public debt. Angola's foreign exchange reserves peaked at $20,400m. in November 2008, before the collapse in the international oil price drove them down to a low of $12,500m. in June 2009. However, following the imposition of stringent capital controls and the loosening of the kwanza's unofficial peg to the US dollar, reserves subsequently recovered, rising to $19,750m. by the end of 2010. Buoyed by rising oil revenues, reserves had increased to $27,955m. by the end of 2011 and stood at $33,000m. in May 2012. Since the end of the civil war Angola has contracted substantial new oil-backed loans and credit lines to finance infrastructure rehabilitation and rising government expenditure on priority social sectors. In 2004 Angola agreed a US $2,000m. oil-backed credit line from China's Eximbank for infrastructure projects. Over the next three years, this Chinese credit line was extended to more than $4,500m., including $2,500m. from Eximbank and $2,000m. from the Hong Kong-based China International Fund (CIF). However, after the CIF experienced severe problems raising the promised financing, the Angolan Government was forced to issue $3,500m. of treasury bills in 2007 to fund the infrastructure works covered by the credit line. In 2009 the China Development Bank granted Angola a new credit line, worth $1,000m., to finance agricultural projects. In 2010 the World Bank estimated that China had extended loans and credit lines to Angola worth a total of $14,500m. since 2002. China's Eximbank announced in July 2010 that further credit lines would be made available to Angola, believed to be worth $6,000m., for funding agricultural, road-building and infrastructure projects.

Angola has also contracted sizeable oil-backed commercial loans. In 2004 SONANGOL agreed a US $2,350m. loan from the United Kingdom's Standard Chartered Bank, the largest loan in Angola's history up till then, for budgetary support, debt repayment and investment costs in Angola's ultra-deep-water blocks. Despite a sharp rise in oil revenues and promises to desist from the practice, the Government continued to contract new loans collateralized against future oil production. In April 2008 Angola agreed a €225m. oil-backed loan from Deutsche Bank to finance the rehabilitation of roads and other infrastructure in Luanda. In July 2008 SONANGOL contracted a $2,500m. syndicated loan, arranged by Standard Chartered Bank, to finance the company's share of the Angola LNG project.

Despite contracting substantial new debt, Angola has repaid or negotiated write-offs of much of its external debt since 2002. In September 2003 an agreement was signed with Germany to cancel one-half of Angola's US $283m. debt, while in November Poland agreed to reduce Angola's $153m. debt (from Cold War arms sales) by 60%, to $61m., with the remaining 40% to be repaid from 2006. In the same month the Brazilian Government agreed to reschedule Angola's $997m. debt, with payments stretching from 2005 to 2017.

In 2002 Portugal and Angola signed an agreement to restructure the latter's €2,200m. debt, at highly concessional interest rates, which was criticized by other donors. In 2005 Angola signed a further agreement with Portugal to reschedule its US $958m. debt, under which it repaid $258m. immediately, with the remainder to be repaid in 25 equal annual instalments from 2009 onwards. Angola also agreed to pay $195m. to Portuguese banks, representing 35% of its debts to them, with the remainder of its debt to be written off.

In December 2007 the 'Paris Club' of official creditors announced that Angola would repay its outstanding arrears in three tranches, comprising US $800m. in January 2008, $600m. in January 2009 and $400m. in January 2010. This enabled 'Paris Club' members to open new export credit lines for Angola, including $1,700m. from Germany, $1,000m. from Canada, €600m. from Spain, $120m. from the USA, and $70m. from the United Kingdom. In March 2009 the World Bank agreed to offer Angola a $1,000m. financing facility, available over four years, to finance projects aimed at economic diversification. The Portuguese Government also increased its existing credit lines to Angola to over €1,100m.

Angola's inclusion in the African, Caribbean and Pacific (ACP) group of signatories of the third and fourth Lomé Conventions not only made more funds available from the European Union (EU), but also increased both the range and volume of its trading operations. In 2003 Angola ratified the Cotonou Agreement (the successor to the fourth Lomé Convention), which had been concluded between the EU and the ACP states in 2000. Angola participates fully in the Southern African Development Community (SADC), and has special responsibility for the co-ordination of energy development and conservation. However, Angola has not joined the SADC free trade area, which came into operation in January 2008, although it could do so once the rehabilitation of its transport infrastructure has been completed. In 1999 Angola became a member of the Communauté Economique des Etats de l'Afrique Centrale, which the Angolan President, José Eduardo dos Santos, viewed as a key organization for developing Angola's international role as a central African power.

Statistical Survey

Sources (unless otherwise stated): Instituto Nacional de Estatística, Av. Ho Chi Minh, CP 1215, Luanda; tel. 222322776; e-mail ine@angonet.gn.apc.org; Ministério do Planeamento, Largo do Palácio do Povo, Rua 17 de Setembro, Luanda; tel. 222390188; fax 222339586; e-mail geral@minplan.gov.ao; internet www.minplan.gov.ao.

Area and Population

AREA, POPULATION AND DENSITY

Area (sq km)	1,246,700*
Population (census results)	
30 December 1960	4,480,719
15 December 1970	
Males	2,943,974
Females	2,702,192
Total	5,646,166
Population (UN estimates at mid-year)†	
2010	19,081,912
2011	19,618,432
2012	20,162,518
Density (per sq km) at mid-2012	16.2

* 481,354 sq miles.

† Source: UN, *World Population Prospects: The 2010 Revision*.

POPULATION BY AGE AND SEX

(UN estimates at mid-2012)

	Males	Females	Total
0–14	4,644,934	4,610,293	9,255,227
15–64	5,121,760	5,284,176	10,405,936
65 and over	223,739	277,616	501,355
Total	9,990,433	10,172,085	20,162,518

Source: UN, *World Population Prospects: The 2010 Revision*.

PROVINCES

(population estimates, 2002)

	Area (sq km)	Population	Density (per sq km)
Luanda	2,418	2,700,421	1,116.8
Huambo	34,274	1,454,352	42.4
Bié	70,314	997,860	14.2
Malanje	87,246	784,820	9.0
Huíla	75,002	1,161,410	15.5
Uíge	58,698	929,120	15.8
Benguela	31,788	1,595,193	50.2
Kwanza-Sul	55,660	744,235	13.4
Kwanza-Norte	24,110	375,316	15.6
Moxico	223,023	369,290	1.7
Lunda-Norte	102,783	386,036	3.8
Zaire	40,130	290,400	7.2
Cunene	88,342	397,750	4.5
Cabinda	7,270	192,454	26.5
Bengo	31,371	424,856	13.5
Lunda-Sul	56,985	470,072	8.2
Kuando Kubango	199,049	391,670	2.0
Namibe	58,137	281,745	4.8
Total	1,246,600	13,947,000	11.2

PRINCIPAL TOWNS

(population at 1970 census)

Luanda (capital)	480,613	Benguela	40,996
Huambo (Nova Lisboa)	61,885	Lubango (Sá da Bandeira)	31,674
Lobito	59,258	Malange	31,559

Source: Direcção dos Serviços de Estatística.

Mid-2011 ('000, incl. suburbs, UN estimate): Luanda 5,068 (Source: UN, *World Urbanization Prospects: The 2011 Revision*).

BIRTHS AND DEATHS

(annual averages, UN estimates)

	1995–2000	2000–05	2005–10
Birth rate (per 1,000)	51.0	49.0	43.5
Death rate (per 1,000)	21.1	17.6	15.3

Source: UN, *World Population Prospects: The 2010 Revision*.

Life expectancy (years at birth): 50.7 (males 49.2; females 52.1) in 2010 (Source: World Bank, World Development Indicators database).

ECONOMICALLY ACTIVE POPULATION

('000 persons, 1991, estimates)

	Males	Females	Total
Agriculture, etc.	1,518	1,374	2,892
Industry	405	33	438
Services	644	192	836
Total labour force	2,567	1,599	4,166

Source: UN Economic Commission for Africa, *African Statistical Yearbook*.

Mid-2012 (estimates in '000): Agriculture, etc. 6,193; Total (incl. others) 9,011 (Source: FAO).

Health and Welfare

KEY INDICATORS

Total fertility rate (children per woman, 2010)	5.4
Under-5 mortality rate (per 1,000 live births, 2010)	161
HIV/AIDS (% of persons aged 15–49, 2009)	2.0
Physicians (per 1,000 head, 2004)	0.08
Hospital beds (per 1,000 head, 2005)	0.1
Health expenditure (2009): US $ per head (PPP)	297
Health expenditure (2009): % of GDP	4.9
Health expenditure (2009): public (% of total)	89.9
Access to water (% of persons, 2010)	51
Access to sanitation (% of persons, 2010)	58
Total carbon dioxide emissions ('000 metric tons, 2008)	24,370.9
Carbon dioxide emissions per head (metric tons, 2008)	1.4
Human Development Index (2011): ranking	148
Human Development Index (2011): value	0.486

For sources and definitions, see explanatory note on p. vi.

Agriculture

PRINCIPAL CROPS

('000 metric tons)

	2008	2009	2010
Wheat*	4	5	5
Rice, paddy	8	14	18
Maize	702	970	1,073
Millet	27	40	41*
Potatoes	402	823	841*
Sweet potatoes	820	983	987
Cassava (Manioc)	10,057	12,828	13,859
Sugar cane*	400	360	360
Beans, dry	124	247	250*
Groundnuts, with shell	92	111	115
Palm oil†	46	55	57
Sunflower seed*	12	11	24
Oil palm fruit*	250	280	280
Cottonseed*	1	1	1
Tomatoes*	15	15	16
Onions and shallots, green*	19	19	17
Bananas*	430	432	433
Citrus fruit*	96	97	100
Pineapples*	42	42	44
Coffee, green†	3	1	2

* FAO estimate(s).

† Unofficial figures.

Aggregate production ('000 metric tons, may include official, semi-official or estimated data): Total cereals 742 in 2008, 1,030 in 2009, 1,136 in 2010; Total roots and tubers 11,279 in 2008, 14,633 in 2009, 15,687 in 2010; Total vegetables (incl. melons) 291 in 2008, 297 in 2009, 275 in 2010; Total fruits (excl. melons) 607 in 2008, 602 in 2009, 608 in 2010.

Source: FAO.

LIVESTOCK

('000 head, year ending September, FAO estimates)

	2008	2009	2010*
Cattle	4,921	5,031	5,143
Pigs*	785	788	791
Sheep*	345	350	355
Goats	2,478	2,524*	2,571
Chickens*	7,000	7,100	7,200

* FAO estimate(s).

Source: FAO.

LIVESTOCK PRODUCTS

('000 metric tons, FAO estimates)

	2008	2009	2010
Cattle meat	100.3	104.4	105.5
Goat meat	11.2	11.4	11.4
Pig meat	28.0	28.2	32.5
Chicken meat	8.0	8.1	8.1
Game meat	7.3	7.8	8.9
Sheep meat	1.3	1.3	1.3
Cows' milk	195.5	158.4	183.8
Hen eggs	4.9	4.5	4.5
Honey	26.6	25.6	22.9

Source: FAO.

Forestry

ROUNDWOOD REMOVALS

('000 cubic metres, excluding bark, FAO estimates)

	2008	2009	2010
Sawlogs, veneer logs and logs for sleepers	46	46	46
Other industrial wood	1,050	1,050	1,050
Fuel wood	3,828	3,917	4,009
Total	4,924	5,013	5,105

Source: FAO.

SAWNWOOD PRODUCTION

('000 cubic metres, including railway sleepers, FAO estimates)

	1983	1984	1985
Total	6	2	5

1986–2010: Annual production as in 1985 (FAO estimates).

Source: FAO.

Fishing

('000 metric tons, live weight)

	2008	2009	2010
Capture	305.8*	272.3	260.0*
Freshwater fishes	7.5*	5.8	10.0*
West coast sole	0.9	0.8	0.8*
West African croakers	21.9	19.1	18.4*
Dentex	26.2	33.8	32.0*
Cunene horse mackerel	44.4	13.8	13.3
Pilchards and sardinellas	70.4	74.2	71.0*
Chub mackerel	7.6	10.1	9.7*
Aquaculture*	0.2	0.2	0.2
Total catch (incl. others)*	306.0	272.5	260.2*

* FAO estimate(s).

Source: FAO.

Mining

('000 metric tons, unless otherwise indicated)

	2008	2009	2010*
Crude petroleum ('000 42-gallon barrels)	684,375	651,000	676,000
Salt (unrefined)	35	35	45
Diamonds ('000 carats)†	8,907	13,828	13,000

* Estimates.
† Reported figures, based on estimates of 10% of production at industrial grade.

Source: US Geological Survey.

Industry

SELECTED PRODUCTS
('000 metric tons unless otherwise indicated)

	2006	2007	2008
Cement*	1,373	1,400	1,780
Jet fuels	313	351	325
Motor gasoline (petrol)	98	56	68
Naphthas	155	140	118
Kerosene	5	0.5	1
Distillate fuel oils	681	513	527
Residual fuel oils	587	601	680
Electric energy (million kWh)	2,959	3,318	3,991

* Data from FAO.

Source: mainly UN Industrial Commodity Statistics Database.

Cement ('000 metric tons): 1,800 in 2009; 1,500 in 2010 (estimate) (Source: US Geological Survey).

Finance

CURRENCY AND EXCHANGE RATES

Monetary Units
100 lwei = 1 kwanza.

Sterling, Dollar and Euro Equivalents (31 May 2012)
£1 sterling = 147.812 kwanza;
US $1 = 95.338 kwanza;
€1 = 118.248 kwanza;
1,000 kwanza = £6.77 = $10.49 = €8.46.

Average Exchange Rate (kwanza per US $)
2009 79.328
2010 91.906
2011 93.741

Note: In April 1994 the introduction of a new method of setting exchange rates resulted in an effective devaluation of the new kwanza, to US $1 = 68,297 new kwanza, and provided for an end to the system of multiple exchange rates. Further substantial devaluations followed, and in July 1995 a 'readjusted' kwanza, equivalent to 1,000 new kwanza, was introduced. The currency, however, continued to depreciate. Between July 1997 and June 1998 a fixed official rate of US $1 = 262,376 readjusted kwanza was in operation. In May 1999 the Central Bank announced its decision to abolish the existing dual currency exchange rate system. In December 1999 the readjusted kwanza was replaced by a new currency, the kwanza, equivalent to 1m. readjusted kwanza.

BUDGET
('000 million kwanza)

Revenue*	2010	2011†	2012‡
Tax revenue	3,094	4,402	4,740
Petroleum	2,500	3,758	3,736
Non-petroleum	594	644	1,004
Non-tax revenue	199	223	196
Total	3,293	4,625	4,936

Expenditure	2010	2011†	2012‡
Current	2,046	2,647	2,826
Wages and salaries	714	887	1,061
Goods and services	619	842	922
Interest payments	90	62	111
Domestic	27	37	70
External	63	24	41
Transfers	624	856	732
Capital	733	785	922
Domestic financed	580	675	656
Foreign financed	154	111	266
Total	2,780	3,432	3,748

* Excluding grants received ('000 million kwanza): 2 in 2010; 4 in 2011 (estimate); 0 in 2012 (projection).
† Estimates.
‡ Projections.

Source: IMF, *Angola: Sixth Review Under the Stand-By Arrangement, Request for Waivers of Nonobservance of Performance Criteria, and Proposal for Post-Program Monitoring—Staff Report; Press Release on the Executive Board Discussion; and Statement by the Executive Director for Angola* (May 2012).

INTERNATIONAL RESERVES
(US $ million at 31 December)

	2009	2010	2011
IMF special drawing rights	425.65	410.13	393.11
Foreign exchange	13,238.45	19,339.35	27,007.91
Total	13,664.10	19,749.47	27,401.01

Source: IMF, *International Financial Statistics*.

MONEY SUPPLY
(million kwanza at 31 December)

	2009	2010	2011
Currency outside banks	169,748	171,631	208,741
Demand deposits at banking institutions	607,017	693,352	952,980
Total (incl. others)	776,770	869,391	1,161,747

Source: IMF, *International Financial Statistics*.

COST OF LIVING
(Consumer Price Index for Luanda at December; base: 1994 average = 100)

	1999	2000	2001
Food	3,551.1	11,211.2	22,494.2
Clothing	5,189.4	21,449.2	45,733.9
Rent, fuel and light	28,392.7	157,756.4	434,224.6
All items (incl. others)	5,083.6	18,723.6	40,456.1

Source: IMF, *Angola: Selected Issues and Statistical Appendix* (September 2003).

All items (Consumer Price Index for Luanda; base: 2000 = 100): 2,347.7 in 2007; 2,640.5 in 2008; 3,003.0 in 2009; 3,437.5 in 2010 (Source: ILO).

NATIONAL ACCOUNTS
(million kwanza at current prices)

Expenditure on the Gross Domestic Product

	2009	2010	2011
Government final consumption expenditure	1,442,455	1,825,639	2,241,744
Private final consumption expenditure	3,609,865	3,082,798	3,303,526
Gross fixed capital formation	918,327	1,162,277	1,427,187
Increase in stocks	48,014	60,769	74,619
Total domestic expenditure	6,018,661	6,131,483	7,047,076
Exports of goods and services	3,288,250	4,719,996	6,564,710
Less Imports of goods and services	3,318,236	3,271,931	4,304,686
GDP in purchasers' values	5,988,675	7,579,547	9,307,100

Gross Domestic Product by Economic Activity

	2009	2010	2011
Agriculture, forestry and fishing	610,970	745,993	929,250
Mining and quarrying	2,715,327	3,467,054	4,300,415
Manufacturing	371,231	473,735	604,970
Construction	449,582	601,642	714,781
Wholesale and retail trade; restaurants and hotels	978,154	1,229,626	1,459,085
Transport and communications	262,213	325,503	390,815
Public administration and defence	453,995	548,198	675,459
GDP at factor cost	5,841,472	7,391,751	9,074,775
Indirect taxes on products	147,203	187,796	232,325
GDP in purchasers' values	5,988,675	7,579,547	9,307,100

Source: African Development Bank.

BALANCE OF PAYMENTS
(US $ million)

	2008	2009	2010
Exports of goods f.o.b.	63,913.9	40,827.9	50,594.9
Imports of goods f.o.b.	–20,982.2	–22,659.9	–16,666.9
Trade balance	42,931.8	18,168.0	33,928.0
Exports of services	329.5	623.1	856.9
Imports of services	–22,139.3	–19,169.4	–18,754.4
Balance on goods and services	21,121.9	–378.2	16,030.5
Other income received	422.3	131.3	134.0
Other income paid	–14,139.8	–6,954.5	–8,305.8
Balance on goods, services and income	7,404.3	–7,201.3	7,858.7
Current transfers received	154.5	56.8	58.4
Current transfers paid	–364.5	–427.1	–496.1
Current balance	7,194.2	–7,571.7	7,421.1
Capital account (net)	6.5	4.1	0.9
Direct investment abroad	–2,569.6	–6.8	–1,340.4
Direct investment from abroad	1,679.0	2,205.3	–3,227.2
Portfolio investment assets	–1,757.5	–558.1	–273.5
Portfolio investment liabilities	—	68.0	3.0
Other investment assets	–2,709.2	–1,369.0	97.6
Other investment liabilities	6,576.1	1,784.1	3,228.9
Net errors and omissions	–1,235.9	454.7	–1,730.0
Overall balance	7,183.5	–4,989.3	4,180.3

Source: IMF, *International Financial Statistics*.

External Trade

SELECTED COMMODITIES

Imports (million kwanza)	1983	1984	1985
Animal products	1,315	1,226	1,084
Vegetable products	2,158	3,099	2,284
Fats and oils	946	1,006	1,196
Food and beverages	2,400	1,949	1,892
Industrial chemical products	1,859	1,419	1,702
Plastic materials	431	704	454
Textiles	1,612	1,816	1,451
Base metals	1,985	3,730	2,385
Electrical equipment	3,296	2,879	2,571
Transport equipment	2,762	2,240	3,123
Total (incl. others)	20,197	21,370	19,694

Exports (US $ million)	2008	2009	2010
Crude petroleum	61,666	39,271	48,629
Refined petroleum products	400	314	423
Gas (per barrel)	392	218	300
Diamonds	1,210	814	976
Total (incl. others)	63,914	40,828	50,595

Total imports (US $ million): 16,970 in 2008; 23,643 in 2009; 18,143 in 2010; 20,791 in 2011.

Total exports (US $ million): 66,427 in 2011.

Sources: Banco Nacional de Angola; African Development Bank.

PRINCIPAL TRADING PARTNERS
(US $ million)*

Imports c.i.f.	2009	2010	2011
Belgium	445.0	375.9	361.9
Brazil	1,333.0	943.9	1,073.5
Canada	71.6	189.4	124.4
China, People's Republic	2,386.0	2,003.9	2,784.2
France	752.7	841.5	813.0
Germany	414.9	349.5	348.2
Italy	709.2	298.7	333.8
Japan	178.4	131.1	142.3
Korea, Republic	325.3	158.1	218.0
Malaysia	47.3	94.0	282.6
Netherlands	369.4	333.6	353.0
Norway	146.1	459.0	221.0
Portugal	3,126.7	2,532.9	3,245.1
Singapore	330.2	319.5	250.6
South Africa	682.0	700.1	897.7
Spain	495.4	371.7	357.5
Sweden	219.7	97.1	85.1
Thailand	139.0	142.9	180.0
Turkey	151.7	109.5	220.6
United Kingdom	519.0	827.1	602.4
USA	1,422.9	1,291.6	1,500.9
Total (incl. others)	16,857.4	15,017.0	15,181.1

Exports f.o.b.	2009	2010	2011
Canada	1,207.2	1,575.9	2,469.6
China, People's Republic	14,675.8	22,815.0	24,922.2
France	3,270.5	2,126.3	1,825.6
Germany	350.8	301.6	1,229.9
Italy	36.8	348.8	2,068.4
Netherlands	1,010.8	783.6	1,139.2
Peru	220.5	222.7	700.2
Portugal	211.2	746.4	1,639.7
South Africa	1,370.6	1,998.2	1,584.8
Spain	761.0	623.5	595.8
Taiwan	1,058.6	2,859.6	5,665.3
United Kingdom	421.1	66.7	437.0
USA	9,703.1	12,281.3	13,833.0
Total (incl. others)	40,142.2	53,445.7	59,349.0

* Data are compiled on the basis of reporting by Angola's trading partners, and totals may differ to those for trade recorded by commodity as a result.

Source: Trade Map-Trade Competitiveness Map, International Trade Centre, www.intracen.org/marketanalysis.

Transport

GOODS TRANSPORT
(million metric tons)

	2002	2003	2004
Air	646.4	248.6	21,745.0
Road	7,505.7	4,635.5	19,031.0
Railway	253.6	129.3	54.0
Water	3,523.8	4,259.7	1,189.0

Source: Portais Governo de Angola.

PASSENGER TRANSPORT
(million passenger-km)

	2002	2003	2004
Air	804.9	978.4	21,229.0
Road	235,208.0	1,112,272.0	1,188,063.0
Railway	2,975.2	3,708.4	192.0
Water	—	—	1,522.0

Source: Portais Governo de Angola.

ROAD TRAFFIC
(motor vehicles in use at 31 December, estimates)

	1997	1998	1999
Passenger cars	103,400	107,100	117,200
Lorries and vans	107,600	110,500	118,300
Total	211,000	217,600	235,500

2000–02: data assumed to be unchanged from 1999 (estimates).

Source: UN, *Statistical Yearbook*.

2007 (motor vehicles in use at 31 December): Total 671,060 (Source: IRF, *World Road Statistics*).

SHIPPING

Merchant Fleet
(registered at 31 December)

	2007	2008	2009
Number of vessels	130	134	153
Total displacement (grt)	56,770	59,433	63,098

Source: IHS Fairplay, *World Fleet Statistics*.

International Sea-borne Freight Traffic
(estimates, '000 metric tons)

	1989	1990	1991
Goods loaded	19,980	21,102	23,288
Goods unloaded	1,235	1,242	1,261

Source: UN Economic Commission for Africa, *African Statistical Yearbook*.

CIVIL AVIATION
(traffic on scheduled services)

	2007	2008	2009
Kilometres flown (million)	7	7	7
Passengers carried ('000)	277	284	275
Passenger-km (million)	691	706	680
Total ton-km (million)	140	135	126

Source: UN, *Statistical Yearbook*.

2010: Passengers carried ('000) 1,283 (Source: World Bank, World Development Indicators database).

Tourism

FOREIGN TOURIST ARRIVALS

Country of origin	2007	2008	2009
Belgium	1,469	1,654	1,650
Brazil	21,749	35,231	46,866
France	13,305	26,649	21,760
Germany	1,790	2,551	3,361
Italy	2,308	3,324	4,259
Philippines	3,488	7,043	6,096
Portugal	37,905	53,568	86,330
Russia	2,241	2,477	2,694
South Africa	13,328	15,476	25,803
Spain	2,044	2,593	5,007
United Kingdom	15,440	20,425	15,870
USA	10,593	14,319	15,140
Total (incl. others)	194,730	294,258	365,784

Tourist arrivals ('000): 425 in 2010.

Tourism receipts (US $ million, incl. passenger transport, unless otherwise indicated): 293 in 2008; 554 in 2009; 719 in 2010 (excl. passenger transport).

Source: World Tourism Organization.

Communications Media

	2009	2010	2011
Telephones ('000 main lines in use)	303.2	303.2	303.2
Mobile cellular telephones ('000 subscribers)	8,109.4	8,909.2	9,491.0
Internet subscribers ('000)	320	n.a.	n.a.
Broadband subscribers ('000)	20.0	20.0	25.0

Personal computers: 110,614 (6.5 per 1,000 persons) in 2006.

Source: International Telecommunication Union.**Radio receivers** ('000 in use, 1999): 840 (Source: UN, *Statistical Yearbook*).

Daily newspapers (2004): 1 (average circulation 35,0000 copies) (Source: UNESCO Institute for Statistics).

Book production (1995): 22 titles (all books) (Source: UNESCO, *Statistical Yearbook*).

Education

(2009/10)

	Teachers	Students		
		Males	Females	Total
Pre-primary	18,032	332,182	336,176	668,358
Primary	93,379	2,361,331	1,911,675	4,273,006
Secondary:				
general	13,694	261,906	225,623	487,529
vocational	8,294	219,144	141,651	360,795
Higher	2,407	36,172	30,079	66,251

Source: mainly UNESCO Institute for Statistics.

Pupil-teacher ratio (primary education, UNESCO estimate): 45.8 in 2009/10 (Source: UNESCO Institute for Statistics).

Adult literacy rate (UNESCO estimates): 70.1% (males 82.7%; females 58.1%) in 2010 (Source: UNESCO Institute for Statistics).

Directory

The Constitution

The main provisions of the Constitution promulgated on 5 February 2010 are summarized below:

BASIC PRINCIPLES

The Republic of Angola shall be a sovereign and independent state whose prime objective shall be to build a free and democratic society of peace, justice and social progress. It shall be a democratic state based on the rule of law, founded on national unity, the dignity of human beings, pluralism of expression and political organization, respecting and guaranteeing the basic rights and freedoms of persons, whether as individuals or as members of organized social groups. Sovereignty shall be vested in the people, which shall exercise political power through periodic universal suffrage.

The Republic of Angola shall be a unitary and indivisible state. Economic, social and cultural solidarity shall be promoted between all the Republic's regions for the common development of the entire nation and the elimination of regionalism and tribalism.

Religion

The Republic shall be a secular state and there shall be complete separation of the State and religious institutions. All religions shall be respected.

The Economy

The economic system shall be based on the coexistence of diverse forms of property—public, private, mixed, co-operative and family—and all shall enjoy equal protection. The State shall protect foreign investment and foreign property, in accordance with the law. The fiscal system shall aim to satisfy the economic, social and administrative needs of the State and to ensure a fair distribution of income and wealth. Taxes may be created and abolished only by law, which shall determine applicability, rates, tax benefits and guarantees for taxpayers.

Education

The Republic shall vigorously combat illiteracy and obscurantism and shall promote the development of education and of a true national culture.

FUNDAMENTAL RIGHTS AND DUTIES

The State shall respect and protect the human person and human dignity. All citizens shall be equal before the law. They shall be subject to the same duties, without any distinction based on colour, race, ethnic group, sex, place of birth, religion, level of education, or economic or social status.

All citizens aged 18 years and over, other than those legally deprived of political and civil rights, shall have the right and duty to take an active part in public life, to vote and be elected to any state organ, and to discharge their mandates with full dedication to the cause of the Angolan nation. The law shall establish limitations in respect of non-political allegiance of soldiers on active service, judges and police forces, as well as the electoral incapacity of soldiers on active service and police forces.

Freedom of expression, of assembly, of demonstration, of association and of all other forms of expression shall be guaranteed. Groupings whose aims or activities are contrary to the constitutional order and penal laws, or that, even indirectly, pursue political objectives through organizations of a military, paramilitary or militarized nature shall be forbidden. Every citizen has the right to a defence if accused of a crime. Individual freedoms are guaranteed. Freedom of conscience and belief shall be inviolable. Work shall be the right and duty of all citizens. The State shall promote measures necessary to ensure the right of citizens to medical and health care, as well as assistance in childhood, motherhood, disability, old age, etc. It shall also promote access to education, culture and sports for all citizens.

STATE ORGANS

President of the Republic

The President of the Republic shall be the Head of State, Head of Government and Commander-in-Chief of the Angolan armed forces. The leader of the political party, or coalition of political parties, obtaining a majority vote in the general elections shall be named President of the Republic and shall be assisted by a Vice-President; the position of Vice-President shall be filled by the deputy leader of the ruling party. The President may serve a maximum of two five-year terms. The President of the Republic shall have the following powers:

to appoint and dismiss Ministers and other government officials determined by law

to appoint the judges of the Supreme Court

to preside over the Council of Ministers

to declare war and make peace, following authorization by the Assembléia Nacional

to sign, promulgate and publish the laws of the Assembléia Nacional, government decrees and statutory decrees

to preside over the National Defence Council

to decree a state of siege or state of emergency

to announce the holding of general elections

to issue pardons and commute sentences

to perform all other duties provided for in the Constitution.

Assembléia Nacional

The Assembléia Nacional is the supreme state legislative body, to which the Government is responsible. The Assembléia shall be composed of 220 deputies, elected for a term of five years. The Assembléia shall convene in ordinary session twice yearly and in special session on the initiative of the President of the Assembléia, the Standing Commission of the Assembléia or of no less than one-third of its deputies. The Standing Commission shall be the organ of the Assembléia that represents and assumes its powers between sessions.

Government

The Government shall comprise the President of the Republic, the ministers and the secretaries of state, and other members whom the law shall indicate, and shall have the following functions:

to organize and direct the implementation of state domestic and foreign policy, in accordance with the decision of the Assembléia Nacional and its Standing Commission

to ensure national defence, the maintenance of internal order and security, and the protection of the rights of citizens

to prepare the draft National Plan and General State Budget for approval by the Assembléia Nacional, and to organize, direct and control their execution.

The Council of Ministers shall be answerable to the Assembléia Nacional. In the exercise of its powers, the Council of Ministers shall issue decrees and resolutions.

Judiciary

The organization, composition and competence of the courts shall be established by law. Judges shall be independent in the discharge of their functions.

Local State Organs

The organs of state power at provincial level shall be the Provincial Assemblies and their executive bodies. The Provincial Assemblies shall work in close co-operation with social organizations and rely on the initiative and broad participation of citizens. The Provincial Assemblies shall elect commissions of deputies to perform permanent or specific tasks. The executive organs of Provincial Assemblies shall be the Provincial Governments, which shall be led by the Provincial Governors. The Provincial Governors shall be answerable to the President of the Republic, the Council of Ministers and the Provincial Assemblies.

National Defence

The State shall ensure national defence. The National Defence Council shall be presided over by the President of the Republic, and its composition shall be determined by law. The Angolan armed forces, as a state institution, shall be permanent, regular and non-partisan. Defence of the country shall be the right and the highest indeclinable duty of every citizen. Military service shall be compulsory. The forms in which it is fulfilled shall be defined by the law.

The Government

HEAD OF STATE

President: José Eduardo dos Santos.

Vice-President: Manuel Domingos Vicente.

COUNCIL OF MINISTERS

(October 2012)

President: JOSÉ EDUARDO DOS SANTOS.

Vice-President: MANUEL DOMINGOS VICENTE.

Minister of State and Head of Civil Staff: EDELTRUDE MAURÍCIO FERNANDES GASPAR DA COSTA.

Minister of State and Head of Military Staff: Gen. MANUEL HÉLDER VIEIRA DIAS, Jr.

Minister of the Economy: ABRAHÃO PIO DOS SANTOS GOURGEL.

Minister of Foreign Affairs: GEORGE REBELO CHICOTY.

Minister of National Defence: Gen. CÂNDIDO PEREIRA DOS SANTOS VAN-DÚNEM.

Minister of the Interior: ÂNGELO DE BARROS VEIGA TAVARES.

Minister of Parliamentary Affairs: ROSA LUÍS DE SOUSA MICOLO.

Minister of Territorial Administration: BORNITO DE SOUSA BALTAZAR DIOGO.

Minister of Justice: RUI JORGE CARNEIRO MANGUEIRA.

Minister of Public Administration, Labour and Social Security: Dr ANTÓNIO DOMINGOS PITRA DA COSTA NETO.

Minister of Social Communication: JOSÉ LUÍS DE MATOS.

Minister of Youth and Sports: GONÇALVES MANUEL MUANDUMBA.

Minister of Planning and Territorial Development: JOB GRAÇA.

Minister of Finance: CARLOS ALBERTO LOPES.

Minister of Commerce: ROSA PEDRO PACAVIRA DE MATOS.

Minister of Hotels and Tourism: PEDRO MUTINDI.

Minister of Agriculture, Rural Development and Fisheries: AFONSO PEDRO CANGA.

Minister of Fisheries: VITÓRIA FRANCISCO LAPAS CRISTÓVÃO DE BARROS NETO.

Minister of Geology and Mines: MANUEL FRANCISCO QUEIRÓS.

Minister of Industry: BERNARDA GONÇALVES MARTINS HENRIQUES DA SILVA.

Minister of Petroleum: JOSÉ MARIA BOTELHO DE VASCONCELOS.

Minister of the Environment: MARIA DE FÁTIMA MONTEIRO JARDIM.

Minister of Construction: FERNANDO ALBERTO SOARES DA FONSECA DE LEMOS.

Minister of Town Planning and Housing: JOSÉ ANTÓNIO DA CONCEIÇÃO E SILVA.

Minister of Transport: AUGUSTO DA SILVA TOMÁS.

Minister of Telecommunications and Information Technology: JOSÉ CARVALHO DA ROCHA.

Minister of Energy and Water: JOÃO BAPTISTA BORGES.

Minister of Science and Technology: MARIA CÂNDIDA PEREIRA TEIXEIRA.

Minister of Health: JOSÉ VIERA DIAS VAN-DÚNEM.

Minister of Education: M'PINDA SIMÃO.

Minister of Higher Education: ADÃO DO NASCIMENTO.

Minister of Culture: ROSA MARIA MARTINS DA CRUZ E SILVA.

Minister of Social Assistance and Reintegration: JOÃO BAPTISTA KUSSUMUA.

Minister of Family and the Promotion of Women: MARIA FILOMENA LOBÃO TELO DELGADO.

Minister of Former Combatants and War Veterans: KUNDI PAIHAMA.

MINISTRIES

Office of the President: Rua 17 de Setembro, Palácio do Povo, Luanda; tel. 222332939; fax 222339855; internet www.pr.ao.

Office of the Vice-President: Largo 17 de Setembro, Luanda; tel. 222396501; fax 222397071; internet www.vicepresidencia.gov.ao.

Ministry of Agriculture, Rural Development and Fisheries: Largo António Jacinto, CP 527, Luanda; tel. 222322377; fax 222320553; e-mail geral@minagri.gov.ao; internet www.minagri.gov.ao.

Ministry of Commerce: Palácio de Vidro, Largo 4 de Fevereiro 3, CP 1242, Luanda; tel. 222311191; fax 222310335; e-mail gamaarte63@yahoo.com.br; internet www.minco.gov.ao.

Ministry of Culture: Edif. Ministerial, 1° andar, Largo António Jacinto, Luanda; tel. and fax 222322070; e-mail geral@mincult.gov.ao; internet www.mincult.gov.ao.

Ministry of the Economy: Luanda; e-mail geral@minec.gov.ao; internet www.minec.gov.ao.

Ministry of Education: Largo António Jacinto, CP 1281, Luanda; tel. 222321236; fax 222321592; e-mail geral@med.gov.ao; internet www.med.gov.ao.

Ministry of Energy and Water: Rua Cónego Manuel das Neves 234, CP 2229, Luanda; tel. 222393681; fax 222393684; e-mail geral@minen.gov.ao; internet www.minerg.gov.ao.

Ministry of the Environment: Rua Frederico Engels 94, 8° andar, Luanda; tel. 222334761; fax 222394758; e-mail geral@minam.gov.ao; internet www.minam.gov.ao.

Ministry of Family and the Promotion of Women: Palácio de Vidro, 2° andar, Largo 4 de Fevereiro, Luanda; tel. and fax 222311728; e-mail geral@minfamu.gov.ao; internet www.minfamu.gov.ao.

Ministry of Finance: Largo da Mutamba, Luanda; tel. and fax 222338548; e-mail geral@minfin.gov.ao; internet www.minfin.gv.ao.

Ministry of Foreign Affairs: Rua Major Kanhangulo, Luanda; tel. 222394827; fax 222393246; e-mail geral@mirex.gov.ao; internet www.mirex.gov.ao.

Ministry of Former Combatants and War Veterans: Av. Comandante Gika 2, CP 3828, Luanda; tel. 222321648; fax 222320876; e-mail geral@macvg.gov.ao; internet www.macvg.gov.ao.

Ministry of Geology, Mines and Industry: Av. Comandante Gika, CP 1260, Luanda; tel. 222322905; fax 222321655; e-mail geral@mgm.gov.ao; internet www.mgm.gov.ao.

Ministry of Health: Rua 17 de Setembro, CP 1201, Luanda; tel. and fax 222391641; e-mail geral@minsa.gov.ao; internet www.minsa.gov.ao.

Ministry of Higher Education, Science and Technology: Av. Lenine 106/108, Maianga, Luanda; tel. 222330218; fax 222338210; e-mail geral@mct.gov.ao; internet www.mct.gov.ao.

Ministry of Hotels and Tourism: Luanda.

Ministry of the Interior: Largo do Palácio de Vidro, Rua 25 de Abril 1 R/C, CP 2723, Luanda; tel. 222335976; fax 222395133; e-mail geral@minint.gov.ao; internet www.minint.gov.ao.

Ministry of Justice: Rua 17 de Setembro, CP 2250, Luanda; tel. and fax 222336045; e-mail geral@minjus.gov.ao; internet www.minjus.gov.ao.

Ministry of National Defence: Rua 17 de Setembro, Luanda; tel. 222330354; fax 222334276; e-mail geral@minden.gov.ao; internet www.minden.gov.ao.

Ministry of Petroleum: Av. 4 de Fevereiro 105, CP 1279, Luanda; tel. and fax 222385847; e-mail geral@minpet.gov.ao; internet www.minpet.gov.ao.

Ministry of Planning: Largo do Palácio do Povo, Rua 17 de Setembro, Luanda; tel. 222390188; fax 222339586; e-mail geral@minplan.gov.ao; internet www.minplan.gov.ao.

Ministry of Public Administration, Labour and Social Security: Rua do 1° Congresso do MPLA 5, Luanda; tel. 222399506; fax 222399507; e-mail geral@mapess.gov.ao; internet www.mapess.gov.ao.

Ministry of Social Assistance and Reintegration: Av. Hoji Ya Henda 117, CP 102, Luanda; tel. 222440370; fax 222342988; e-mail geral@minars.gov.ao; internet www.minars.gov.ao.

Ministry of Social Communication: Av. Comandante Valódia 206, 1° e 2° andares, CP 2608, Luanda; tel. and fax 222443495; e-mail geral@mcs.gov.ao; internet www.mcs.gov.ao.

Ministry of Telecommunications and Information Technology: Av. 4 de Fevereiro, Rua das Alfândegas 10, Luanda; tel. and fax 222390895; e-mail geral@mtti.gov.ao; internet www.mtti.gov.ao.

Ministry of Territorial Administration: Av. Comandante Gika 8, Luanda; tel. 222321072; fax 222323272; internet www.mat.gov.ao.

Ministry of Town Planning and Construction: Av. 4 de Fevereiro, Luanda; tel. 222334429; e-mail geral@minuh.gov.ao; internet www.minuh.gov.ao.

Ministry of Transport: Av. 4 de Fevereiro 42, CP 1250-C, Luanda; tel. 222311303; fax 222311582; e-mail geral@mintrans.gov.ao; internet www.mintrans.gov.ao.

Ministry of Youth and Sports: Av. Comandante Valódia 299, 4° andar, Luanda; tel. and fax 222443521; e-mail geral@minjud.gov.ao; internet www.minjud.gov.ao.

PROVINCIAL GOVERNORS

(October 2012)

All Provincial Governors are ex officio members of the Government.

Bengo: JOÃO BERNARDO DE MIRANDA.

Benguela: ARMANDO DA CRUZ NETO.

Bié: ÁLVARO MANUEL DE BOAVIDA NETO.

Cabinda: ALBINA MATILDE BARROS DA LOMBA.

Cunene: ANTÓNIO DIDALELWA.

Huambo: FERNANDO FAUSTINO MUTEKA.

Huíla: JOÃO MARCELINO TYIPINGE.

Kuando Kubango: FRANCISCO HIGINO LOPES CARNEIRO.

Kwanza-Norte: HENRIQUE ANDRÉ JÚNIOR.

Kwanza-Sul: EUSÉBIO DE BRITO TEIXEIRA.

Luanda: BENTO SEBASTIÃO FRANCISCO BENTO.

Lunda-Norte: ERNESTO MUANGALA.

Lunda-Sul: CÂNDIDA MARIA GUILHERME NARCISO.

Malanje: NORBERTO FERNANDES DOS SANTOS.

Moxico: JOÃO ERNESTO DOS SANTOS.

Namibe: ISAAC MARIA DOS ANJOS.

Uíge: PAULO POMBOLO.

Zaire: JOSÉ JOANES ANDRÉ.

President and Legislature

PRESIDENT

Under the terms of the Constitution, the leader of the political party, or coalition of political parties, obtaining a majority vote in the legislative elections shall be named President of the Republic.

LEGISLATURE

Assembleia Nacional: CP 1204, Luanda; tel. 222334021; fax 222331118; e-mail assembleianacional@parlamento.ebonet.net; internet www.parlamento.ao.

President: FERNANDO DA PIEDADE DIAS DOS SANTOS.

General Election, 31 August 2012

Party	Votes	% of valid votes	Seats
MPLA	4,135,503	71.85	175
UNITA	1,074,565	18.67	32
CASA-CE	345,589	6.00	8
PRS	98,233	1.71	3
FNLA	65,163	1.13	2
Others	36,951	0.64	—
Total	5,756,004	100.00	220

Election Commission

Comissão Nacional Eleitoral (CNE): Av. Amílcar Cabral, 30–31, Luanda; tel. 222393825; internet www.cne.ao; f. 2005; govt agency; Pres. ANDRÉ DA SILVA NETO.

Political Organizations

In June 2010 there were 77 legally recognized political parties in Angola.

Angola Democrática—Coligação (AD): e-mail info@ad-coligacao.org; internet www.ad-coligacao.org; Pres. KENGELE JORGE (acting).

Bloco Democrático: 4° andar, 74 C, Av. de Portugal, Luanda; tel. 222397482; fax 222440556; Pres. JUSTINO PINTO DE ANDRADE; Sec.-Gen. Dr FILOMENO VIEIRA LOPES.

Convergência Ampla de Salvação de Angola-Coligação Eleitoral (CASA-CE): Sagrada Família, Rua Cabral Moncada 179, Junto ao INE Garcia Neto, Luanda; e-mail casa.inform@yahoo.com; f. 2011; Leader ABEL CHIVUKUVUKU.

Fórum Fraternal Angolano Coligação (FOFAC): Luanda; f. 1997; Leader ARTUR QUIXONA FINDA.

Frente Nacional de Libertação de Angola (FNLA): Av. Hoji Va Henda (ex Av. do Brasil) 91/306, CP 151, Luanda; e-mail contact@fnla.net; internet www.fnla.net; f. 1962; Pres. LUCAS NGONDA; Sec.-Gen. BENJAMIM MANUEL DA SILVA.

Movimento Popular de Libertação de Angola (MPLA) (People's Movement for the Liberation of Angola): Luanda; e-mail sede@mpla-angola.org; internet www.mpla-angola.org; f. 1956; in 1961–74 conducted guerrilla operations against Portuguese rule; governing party since 1975; known as Movimento Popular de Libertação de Angola—Partido do Trabalho (MPLA—PT) (People's Movement for the Liberation of Angola—Workers' Party) 1977–92; in Dec. 1990 replaced Marxist-Leninist ideology with commitment to 'democratic socialism'; absorbed the Fórum Democrático Angolano (FDA) in 2002; Chair. JOSÉ EDUARDO DOS SANTOS; Sec.-Gen. JULIÃO MATEUS PAULO.

Nova Democracia—União Eleitoral: f. 2006; a splinter group from the Partidos de Oposição Civil comprising the Frente Unida para Liberdade Democratica (FULD), the Movimento para Democracia de Angola (MPDA), the Partido Angolano Republicano (PAR), the Partido Social Independente de Angola (PSIA), the Partido Socialista Liberal (PSL) and the União Nacional para Democracia (UND); Sec.-Gen. QUINTINO DE MOREIRA.

Partido Democrático para o Progresso de Aliança Nacional Angolana (PDP—ANA): Rua n° 6, Casa n° 73, Quarterão 6, Bairro Palanca, Municipio de Kilamba Kiaxi; tel. 926013905; e-mail pdpana@pdp-ana.org; internet www.pdp-ana.org; f. 1991; Pres. SEDIANGANI MBIMBI.

Partido Democrático de Renovação Social: Luanda; f. 2009; Leader LINDO BERNARDO TITO.

Partido de Renovação Social (PRS): Rua n°1, Martires de Kifangondo n° 33D; tel. 222326293; fax 222323037; e-mail sede@prs-angola.com; internet www.prs-angola.com; Pres. EDUARDO KWANGANA; Sec.-Gen. JOÃO BAPTISTA NGANDAJINA.

Partido Renovador Democrático (PRD): internet prd-angola.org; Leader LUÍS DA SILVA DOS PASSOS.

Plataforma Política Eleitoral (PPE): nine-party coalition; Leader JOSÉ MANUEL.

União Nacional para a Independência Total de Angola (UNITA): Rua 28 de Maio, 1A Travessa 2, Maianga, Luanda; tel. and fax 222331215; e-mail info@unitaangola.org; internet www.unitaangola.com; f. 1966 to secure independence from Portugal; later received Portuguese support to oppose the MPLA; UNITA and the Frente Nacional de Libertação de Angola conducted guerrilla campaign against the MPLA Govt with aid from some Western countries, 1975–76; supported by South Africa until 1984 and in 1987–88, and by USA after 1986; obtained legal status in March 1998, but hostilities between govt and UNITA forces resumed later that year; signed cease-fire agreement with the MPLA Govt in April 2002; joined the Govt in Dec. 2002; support drawn mainly from Ovimbundu ethnic group; Pres. ISAÍAS SAMAKUVA.

Other major parties include:

Forças de Libertação do Estado de Cabinda/Posição Militar (FLEC/PM): f. 2003; a breakaway faction of FLEC seeking the secession of Cabinda province; Sec.-Gen. RODRIGUES MINGAS.

Frente para a Libertação do Enclave de Cabinda (FLEC): f. 1963; comprises several factions, claiming total forces of c. 5,000 guerrillas, seeking the secession of Cabinda province; in Sept. 2004 the Frente para a Libertação do Enclave de Cabinda—Forças Armadas Cabindesas (FLEC—FAC) and the Frente para a Libertação do Enclave de Cabinda—Renovada (FLEC—R) merged under the above name; Leader N'ZITA HENRIQUES TIAGO; Sec.-Gen. ANTÓNIO BENTO BEMBE.

Frente para a Libertação do Enclave de Cabinda—Conselho Superior Alargado (FLEC—CSA): f. 2004; political wing of FLEC; supports Cabindan independence through negotiation.

The **Fórum Cabindês para o Diálogo (FCD)** was formed in 2004 to provide a united platform for Cabindan separatists and civil-society leaders with which to negotiate with the Government. Its leader was ANTÓNIO BENTO BEMBE.

Diplomatic Representation

EMBASSIES IN ANGOLA

Algeria: Edif. Siccal, Rua Rainha Ginga, CP 1389, Luanda; tel. 222332881; fax 222334785; e-mail ambalg@netangola.com; Ambassador KAMEL BOUGHABA.

Argentina: Rua Comandante Nicolau Gomes Spencer 62, Bairro Maculusso, Luanda; tel. 222325098; fax 222324095; JUAN AGUSTÍN CABALLERO.

Belgium: Av. 4 de Fevereiro 93, 3° andar, CP 1203, Luanda; tel. 222336437; fax 222336438; e-mail luanda@diplobel.fed.be; internet www.diplomatie.be/luanda; Ambassador CHARLES DELOGNE.

Brazil: Rua Houari Boumedienne 132, Miramar, CP 5428, Luanda; tel. 222441307; fax 222444913; e-mail bras.secretariado@netcabo.co.ao; Ambassador ANA LUCY GENTIL CABRAL PETERSEN.

Cape Verde: Rua Oliveira Martins 3, Luanda; tel. 222321765; fax 222320832; Ambassador DOMINGOS PEREIRA MAGALHÃES.

China, People's Republic: Rua Houari Boumedienne 196, Miramar, CP 52, Luanda; tel. 222441683; fax 222444185; internet ao.chineseembassy.org; Ambassador GAO KOTIANG.

Congo, Democratic Republic: Rua Cesário Verde 24, Luanda; tel. 222361953; Ambassador ERIC PALUKU KAMUVU.

Congo, Republic: Av. 4 de Fevereiro 3, Luanda; tel. 222310293; Ambassador CHRISTIAN GILBERT BEMBET.

Côte d'Ivoire: Rua Eng. Armindo de Andrade 75, Miramar, CP 432, Luanda; tel. 222440878; fax 222440907; e-mail aciao@ambaci-angola

.org; internet www.ambaci-angola.org; Ambassador ASSAMOI B. DÉSIRÉ.

Cuba: Rua Che Guevara 42, Ingombotas, Luanda; tel. 222339171; fax 222339165; e-mail embcuba.ang@supernet.ao; internet emba .cubaminrex.cu/angola; Ambassador PEDRO ROSS LEAL.

Egypt: Rua Comandante Stona 247, Alvalade, CP 3704, Luanda; tel. 222321591; fax 222323285; e-mail embegipto@ebonet.net; Ambassador GAMAL ABDEL METWALY.

Equatorial Guinea: Luanda; Ambassador JOSE MICHA AKENG.

France: Rua Reverendo Pedro Agostinho Neto 31–33, CP 584, Luanda; tel. 222334841; fax 222391949; e-mail cad.luanda-amba@diplomatie.gouv.fr; internet www.ambafrance-ao.org; Ambassador PHILIPPE GARNIER.

Gabon: Av. 4 de Fevereiro 95, Luanda; tel. 222372614; Ambassador FRANÇOIS MOUELY-KOUMBA.

Germany: Av. 4 de Fevereiro 120, CP 1295, Luanda; tel. 222334516; fax 222372551; e-mail info@luanda.diplo.de; internet www.luanda .diplo.de; Ambassador JORG-WERNER WOLFGANG MARQUARDT.

Ghana: Rua Cirilo da Conceição E Silva 5, 1A, CP 1012, Luanda; tel. 222338239; fax 222338235; e-mail embassyghana@ebonet.net; Ambassador MARTIN ACHIAMPONG QUANSAH.

Holy See: Rua Luther King 123, CP 1030, Luanda; tel. 222330532; fax 222332378; Apostolic Nuncio Most Rev. NOVATUS RUGAMBWA.

India: Rua Marquês das Minas 18A, Macalusso, CP 6040, Luanda; tel. 222392281; fax 222371094; e-mail indembluanda@netcabo.co.ao; internet www.indembangola.org; Ambassador SHIRI PRADHN.

Israel: Edif. Siccal, 11° andar, Rua Rainha Ginga 34, Luanda; tel. 222331501; fax 222397331; e-mail info@luanda.mfa.gov.il; internet luanda.mfa.gov.il; Ambassador IRIT WAIDERGORN.

Italy: Rua Américo Boavida 51, Ingombotas, CP 6220, Luanda; tel. 222331245; fax 222333743; e-mail segreteria.luanda@esteri.it; internet www.ambluanda.esteri.it; Ambassador GUISEPPE MISTRELLA.

Japan: Rua Armindo de Andrade 183–185, Miramar, Luanda; tel. 222442007; fax 222449888; internet www.angola.emb-japan.go.jp; Ambassador RYOZO MYOI.

Mali: Rua Alfredo Felner 5, Nelito Souares 11, Luanda; e-mail ambamali@netangola.com; Ambassador FAROUK CAMARA.

Morocco: Edif. Siccal, 10° andar, Rua Rainha Ginga, CP 20, Luanda; tel. 222393708; fax 222338847; e-mail aluanda@supernet.ao; Ambassador EL GHALLAOUI SIDATI.

Mozambique: Rua Salvador Alende 55, Luanda; tel. and fax 222334871; e-mail embamoc.angola@minec.gov.mz; Ambassador DOMINGOS FERNANDES.

Namibia: Rua dos Coqueiros 37, CP 953, Luanda; tel. 222395483; fax 222339234; e-mail embnam@netangola.com; Ambassador CLAUDIA NDADALEKA USHONA.

Netherlands: Edif. Secil, 6°, Av. 4 de Fevereiro 42, CP 3624, Luanda; tel. 222310686; fax 222310966; e-mail lua@minbuza.nl; internet www.mfa.nl/lua-en; Ambassador SUSANNA TERSTAL.

Nigeria: Rua Houari Boumedienne 120, Miramar, CP 479, Luanda; tel. and fax 222340089; Ambassador FOLORUNSO OLUKAYODE OTUKOYA.

Norway: Rua de Benguela 17, Bairro Patrice Lumumba, CP 3835, Luanda; tel. 222449936; fax 222446248; e-mail emb.luanda@mfa.no; internet www.noruega.ao; Ambassador JON VEA.

Poland: Rua Comandante N'zagi 21–23, Alvalade, CP 1340, Luanda; tel. 222323088; fax 222323086; e-mail luanda.amb .sekretariat@msz.gov.pl; internet www.luanda.polemb.net; Ambassador MAREK ROHR-GARZTECKI.

Portugal: Av. de Portugal 50, CP 1346, Luanda; tel. 222333027; fax 222390392; e-mail embaixada.portugal@netcabo.co.ao; internet www.embaixadadeportugal-luanda.com.pt; Ambassador FRANCISCO MARIA DE SOUSA RIBEIRO TELLES.

Romania: Rua Ramalho Ortigão 30, Alvalade, Luanda; tel. and fax 222321076; e-mail ambromania@ebonet.net; Chargé d'affaires a.i. IACOB PRADA.

Russia: Rua Houari Boumedienne 170, CP 3141, Luanda; tel. 222445028; fax 222445320; e-mail rusemb@netangola.com; Ambassador SERGUEY NENÁCHEV.

São Tomé and Príncipe: Rua Armindo de Andrade 173–175, Luanda; tel. 222345677; Ambassador ARMINDO BRITO FERNANDES.

Serbia: Rua Comandante N'zagi 25–27, Alvalade, CP 3278, Luanda; tel. 222321421; fax 222321724; e-mail serbiaemb@snet.co.ao; Chargé d'affaires a.i. BRANKO NIKOLIC.

South Africa: Edif. Maianga, 1° e 2° andares, Rua Kwamme Nkrumah 31, Largo da Maianga, CP 6212, Luanda; tel. 222334187; fax 222398730; e-mail saemb.ang@netangola.com; internet www.sambangola.info; Ambassador GODFREY NGWENYA.

Spain: Av. 4 de Fevereiro 95, 1° andar, CP 3061, Luanda; tel. 222391166; fax 222332884; e-mail emb.luanda@maec.es; Ambassador JOSÉ MARÍA CASTROVIEJO Y BOLIBAR.

Sweden: Rua Garcia Neto 9, CP 1130, Miramar, Luanda; tel. 222440706; fax 222443460; e-mail ambassaden.luanda@foreign .ministry.se; internet www.swedenabroad.com/luanda; Ambassador LENA SUNDH.

Turkey: Hotel Colinas do Sol, Talatona, Luanda; tel. 914522800 (mobile); fax 222393330; e-mail embassy.luanda@mfa.gov.tr; Ambassador HAMIT OSMAR.

Ukraine: Rua Companhia de Jesus 35, Miramar, Luanda; tel. 222447492; fax 222448467; e-mail emb_ao@mfa.gov.ua; Chargé d'affaires PAVLO KOSTETESKYI.

United Kingdom: Rua Diogo Cão 4, CP 1244, Luanda; tel. 222334582; fax 222333331; e-mail ppa.luanda@fco.gov.uk; internet ukinangola.fco.gov.uk; Ambassador RICHARD WILDASH.

USA: Rua Houari Boumedienne 32, Miramar, CP 6468, Luanda; tel. 222641000; fax 222641232; e-mail ConsularLuanda@state.gov; internet angola.usembassy.gov; Ambassador CHRISTOPHER J. MCMULLEN.

Viet Nam: Rua Alexandre Peres 4, Maianga, CP 1774, Luanda; tel. 222390684; fax 222390369; e-mail dsqvnangola@netangola.com; internet www.vietnamembassy-angola.org; Ambassador BA KHOA.

Zambia: Rua Rei Katyavala 106–108, CP 1496, Luanda; tel. 222331145; Ambassador RAPHAEL CHISHETA.

Zimbabwe: Edif. Secil, Av. 4 de Fevereiro 42, CP 428, Luanda; tel. and fax 222311528; e-mail embzimbabwe@ebonet.net; Ambassador (vacant).

Judicial System

The country's highest judicial body is the Tribunal Constitucional (Constitutional Court), while there is also a Tribunal da Relação (Supreme Court) and a Court of Appeal. There are also civil, criminal and military courts.

Tribunal Constitucional (Constitutional Court): Luanda; internet www.tribunalconstitucional.ao; f. 2008; 7 judges; Pres. Dr RUI CONSTANTINO DA CRUZ FERREIRA.

Tribunal da Relação (Supreme Court): Rua 17 de Setembro, Luanda; fax 222335411; Pres. Dr CRISTIANO ANDRÉ.

Office of the Attorney-General: Rua 17 de Setembro, Luanda; tel. 222333171; fax 222333172; Attorney-General JOÃO MARIA DE SOUSA.

Religion

In 1998 it was estimated that 47% of the population followed indigenous beliefs, with 53% professing to be Christians, mainly Roman Catholic. There is a small Muslim community, which comprises less than 1% of the population.

CHRISTIANITY

In early 2005 some 85 Christian denominations were registered in Angola.

Conselho de Igrejas Cristãs em Angola (CICA) (Council of Christian Churches in Angola): Rua 15 24, Bairro Cassenda, CP 1301/1659, Luanda; tel. 222354838; fax 222356144; e-mail info@cicaangola.org; f. 1977 as Conselho Angolano de Igrejas Evangélicas; 14 mem. churches; 5 assoc. mems; 1 observer; Pres. Rev. ALVARO RODRIGUES; Gen. Sec. Rev. LUÍS NGUIMBI.

Protestant Churches

Igreja Evangélica Congregacional em Angola (Evangelical Congregational Church in Angola—IECA): CP 1552, Luanda; tel. 222355108; fax 222350868; e-mail iecageral@snet.co.ao; f. 1880; 750,000 mems; Gen. Sec. Rev. AUGUSTO CHIPESSE.

Evangelical Lutheran Church of Angola: CP 222, Lubango; tel. 22228428; e-mail iela_lubango@yahoo.com.br; 40,000 mems (2010); Pres. Rev. TOMÀS NDAWANAPO.

Missão Evangélica Pentecostal de Angola (Evangelical Pentecostal Church of Angola): CP 219, Porto Amboim; 13,600 mems; Sec. Rev. JOSÉ DOMINGOS CAETANO.

Igreja Evangélica Unida de Angola (United Evangelical Church of Angola): CP 122, Uíge; 11,000 mems; Gen. Sec. Rev. A. L. DOMINGOS.

Other active denominations include the African Apostolic Church, the Church of Apostolic Faith in Angola, the Church of Our Lord Jesus Christ in the World, the Evangelical Baptist Church, the Evangelical Church in Angola, the Evangelical Church of the Apostles of Jerusalem, the Evangelical Reformed Church of Angola, the

Kimbanguist Church in Angola, the Maná Church and the United Methodist Church.

The Roman Catholic Church

Angola comprises five archdioceses and 14 dioceses. An estimated 52% of the population were Roman Catholics.

Bishops' Conference

Conferência Episcopal de Angola e São Tomé (CEAST), CP 3579, Luanda; tel. 222443686; fax 222445504; e-mail ceast@snet.co.ao.

f. 1967; Pres. Most Rev. Gabriel Mbilingi (Archbishop of Lubango).

Archbishop of Huambo: Most Rev. José de Queirós Alves, Arcebispado, CP 10, Huambo; tel. 241220130; fax 241220133; e-mail bispado.huambo@asat.signis.net.

Archbishop of Luanda: Most Rev. Damião António Franklin, Arcebispado, Largo do Palácio 9, CP 87, 1230-C, Luanda; tel. 222331481; fax 222334433; e-mail spastoral@snet.com.ao.

Archbishop of Lubango: Most Rev. Gabriel Mbilingi, Arcebispado, CP 231, Lubango; tel. and fax 261230140; e-mail arquidiocese.lubango@netangola.com.

Archbishop of Malanje: Most Rev. Dom Benedito Roberto, CP 192, Malanje; tel. 2038421708.

Archbishop of Saurimo: Most Rev. José Manuel Imbamba, CP 52, Saurimo; tel. 761572551 (mobile); fax 761572553 (mobile).

The Press

DAILIES

Diário da República: CP 1306, Luanda; tel. 217810870; fax 213945750; e-mail dre@incm.pt; internet www.dre.pt; official govt bulletin.

O Jornal de Angola: Rua Rainha Ginga 18–24, CP 1312, Luanda; tel. 222335531; fax 222333342; e-mail jornaldeangola@nexus.ao; internet jornaldeangola.sapo.ao; f. 1975; state-owned; Dir José Ribeiro; mornings and Sun.; circ. 41,000.

PERIODICALS

Angolense: Rua Cónego Manuel das Neves 83b, Luanda; tel. 222445753; fax 222340549; e-mail angolense@netangola.com; internet www.jornalangolense.com; f. 1998; weekly; Dir Américo Gonçalves; Editor-in-Chief Suzana Mendes.

O Apostolado: Rua Comandante Bula 118, São Paulo, CP 3579, Luanda; tel. 222432641; fax 222440628; e-mail redaccao@apostolado-angola.org; internet www.apostolado-angola.org; f. 1935; current and religious affairs; Dir Maurício Agostinho Camuto.

A Capital: Rua Canego Manuel das Neves, Prédio 5, 1° andar, Luanda; tel. 222440549; e-mail info@semanarioacapital.com; internet semanarioacapital.com; f. 2003; weekly; Dir Tandala Francisco.

Chocolate: Rua Augusto Tadeu de Bastos 52, Maianga, Luanda; tel. 222398565; e-mail revistachocolate@visao.co.ao; internet www.revistachocolate.com; publ. by Media Nova; monthly; lifestyle; circ. 10,000.

Eme: Luanda; tel. 222321130; f. 1996; fortnightly; MPLA publ; Dir Fernando Fati.

EXAME Angola: Zona Residencial ZR6-B, Lote 32, Sector de Talatona, Luanda Sul; tel. 222003275; fax 222003289; e-mail info@exameangola.com; internet www.exameangola.com; publ. by Media Nova; Editor Carlos Rosado de Carvalho.

Folha 8: Rua Conselheiro Júlio de Vilhena 24, 5° andar, CP 6527, Luanda; tel. 222391943; fax 222392289; e-mail folha8@ebonet.net; internet folha8online.com; f. 1994; 2 a week; Editor William Tonet.

Jornal dos Desportos: Rua Rainha Ginga 18–24, CP 1312, Luanda; tel. 222335531; fax 222335481; e-mail jornaldosdesportos@hotmail.com; internet jornaldosdesportos.sapo.ao; f. 1994; bi-weekly; Dir Matias Adriano; Editorial Dir Policarpo da Rosa; circ. 5,000.

Lavra & Oficina: CP 2767-C, Luanda; tel. 222322421; fax 222323205; e-mail uea@uea-angola.org; internet www.uea-angola.org; f. 1975; journal of the União dos Escritores Angolanos (Union of Angolan Writers); monthly; circ. 5,000.

O País: Casa Amarela, Lote 32, Sector de Talatona, Zona Residencial 6-B, Luanda; tel. 222003275; fax 222003289; e-mail info@opais.co.ao; internet www.opais.net; f. 2008; publ. by Media Nova; weekly; Editor-in-Chief José Kaliengue.

Semanário Angolense: Rua António Feliciano de Castilho 103, Luanda; tel. 222264915; fax 222263506; e-mail info@semanarioangolense.net; internet www.semanarioangolense.net; f. 2003; independent; current affairs; Dir Felizberto Graça Campos; weekly.

Semanário Económico: Luanda; f. 2009; publ. by Media Nova; weekly; Editor Pedro Narciso.

Vida: Casa Amarela, Lote 32, Sector de Talatona, Zona Residencial 6-B, Luanda; tel. 222003275; fax 222003289; e-mail info@opais.co.ao; publ. by Media Nova; Dir-Gen. Luís Fernando.

NEWS AGENCIES

In early 2006 legislation was passed by the Assembléia Nacional ending the governmental monopoly over news agencies.

Agência Angola Press (ANGOP): Rua Rei Katyavala 120, CP 2181, Luanda; tel. 222447343; fax 222447342; e-mail angop@netangola.com; internet www.angolapress-angop.ao; f. 1975; Dir-Gen. Manuel da Conceição.

Centro de Imprensa Anibal de Melo (CIAM): Rua Cerqueira Lukoki 124, CP 2805, Luanda; tel. 222393341; fax 222393445; govt press centre; Dir Dr Olympio de Sousa e Silva.

Publishers

Chá de Caxinde: Av. do 1° Congresso do MPLA 20–24, CP 5958, Luanda; tel. 222336020; fax 222332876; e-mail chacaxinde@ebonet.net; f. 1999; Dir Jaques Arlindo dos Santos.

Editorial Kilombelombe: Luanda; Dir Mateus Volódia.

Editorial Nzila: Rua Comandante Valódia 1, ao Largo do Kinaxixi, Luanda; tel. 222447137; e-mail edinzila@hotmail.com.

Plural Editores: Rua Lucrécia Paim 16a, Bairro do Maculusso, Luanda; tel. 924351990; fax 222339107; e-mail plural@pluraleditores.co.ao; internet www.pluraleditores.co.ao; f. 2005; 100% owned by Porto Editora (Portugal); technical and educational; CEO Alexandre Alves.

Ponto Um Indústria Gráfica: Rua Sebastião Desta Vez 55, Luanda; tel. 222448315; fax 222449424.

União dos Escritores Angolanos (UEA): Luanda; tel. and fax 222323205; e-mail uea@uea-angola.org; internet www.uea-angola.org.

GOVERNMENT PUBLISHING HOUSE

Imprensa Nacional, UEE: CP 1306, Luanda; f. 1845; Gen. Man. Ana María Sousa e Silva.

Broadcasting and Communications

TELECOMMUNICATIONS

Angola Telecom (AT): Rua das Quipacas 186, CP 625, Luanda; tel. 222395990; fax 222391688; internet www.angolatelecom.com; state telecommunications co; Pres. Feliciano António.

Movicel Telecomunicações, Lda: Rua Mãe Isabel 1, Luanda; tel. 222692000; fax 222692090; internet www.movicel.co.ao; f. 2002; mobile cellular telephone operator; Chair. Manuel Avelino; Exec. Dir Carlos Brito.

Mundo StarTel: Rua Ndunduma 188, São Paulo, Município de Sambizanga, Luanda; tel. 222432417; fax 222446972; e-mail sede@startel.co.ao; internet www.startel.co.ao; f. 2004; 44% owned by Telecom Namibia; Dir-Gen. Paulo António da Motta Garcia.

Nexus Telecomunicações e Serviços SARL: Rua dos Enganos 1, 1° andar, Luanda; tel. 228740041; fax 228740741; e-mail nexus@nexus.ao; internet www.nexus.ao; began operations mid-2004; fixed-line operator.

Unitel SARL: Talatona Sector 22, Via C3, Luanda Sul; tel. 923192222 (mobile); fax 222013624; e-mail unitel@unitel.co.ao; internet www.unitel.ao; f. 1998; 25% owned by Portugal Telecom; private mobile telephone operator; Dir-Gen. Miguel F. Veiga Martins; 5.7m. subscribers.

Regulatory Authority

Instituto Angolano das Comunicações (INACOM): Av. de Portugal 92, 7° andar, CP 1459, Luanda; tel. 222338352; fax 222339356; e-mail inacom.dg@netangola.com; internet www.inacom.og.ao; f. 1999; monitoring and regulatory authority; Dir-Gen. Domingos Pedro António.

BROADCASTING

Radio

A decree on the regulation of radio broadcasting was approved in 1997. Since that time private operators had reportedly experienced difficulty in gaining permission to broadcast, although several private stations were operating in Luanda in the early 2010s.

Rádio Nacional de Angola: Av. Comandante Gika, CP 1329, Luanda; tel. 222320192; fax 222324647; e-mail dgeral@rna.ao; internet www.rna.ao; state-controlled; operates Canal A, Radio 5, Radio FM Estério, Radio Luanda and Radio N'gola Yetu; broadcasts in Portuguese, English, French, Spanish and vernacular languages (Chokwe, Kikongo, Kimbundu, Kwanyama, Fiote, Ngangela, Luvale, Songu, Umbundu); Dir-Gen. ALBERTO DE SOUSA.

Luanda Antena Comercial (LAC): Rua Luther King 5, CP 3521, Luanda; tel. 222394989; fax 222396229; e-mail lac@ebonet.net; internet www.nexus.ao/lac; popular music.

Radio CEFOJOR: Rua Luther King 123/4, Luanda; tel. 222336140; f. 2003; commercial station, provides journalistic training; Dir-Gen. JOAQUIM PAULO DA CONCEIÇÃO.

Rádio Ecclésia—Emissora Católica de Angola: Rua Comandante Bula 118, São Paulo, CP 3579, Luanda; tel. 222447153; fax 222446346; e-mail info@radioecclesia.org; internet www.radioecclesia.org; f. 1955; broadcasts mainly restricted to Luanda; coverage of politics and current affairs; Dir-Gen. MUANAMOSSI MATUMONA.

Radio Escola: Rua Luther King 123/124, Luanda; tel. 222337409; fax 222446346; educational.

Rádio Mais: Edifício Laranja, Projecto Nova Vida, Rua 40, Luanda; tel. 928818316; e-mail info@radiomais.co.ao; internet www.radiomais.co.ao; Dir-Gen. JOSÉ MARQUES VIEIRA.

Rádio Morena Comercial, Lda: Rua Comandante Kassanji, CP 537, Benguela; tel. 272232525; fax 272234242.

The Voice of America (internet www.ebonet.net/voa) also broadcasts from Luanda.

Television

In early 2006 legislation was passed by the Assembléia Nacional ending the Government's monopoly over television and simplifying the radio licensing process. A digital television system, TV Cabo Angola, began broadcasting in early 2006.

Televisão Pública de Angola (TPA): Av. Ho Chi Minh, CP 2604, Luanda; tel. 222320026; fax 222323027; e-mail gabinetedg@tpa.ao; internet www.tpa.ao; f. 1976; state-controlled; 2 channels; Coordinator of the Executive Committee HÉLDER BÁRBER.

TV Cabo Angola: Rua Comandante Che Guevara 87/89, Bairro do Maculusso, Ingombota, Luanda; tel. 222680000; fax 222680001; e-mail tvcabo@tvcabo.co.ao; internet www.tvcabo.co.ao; provider of digital television and internet services.

TV Zimbo: Av. do Talatona, Luanda Sul; tel. 222004201; e-mail info@tvzimbo.co.ao; internet www.tvzimbo.net; Dir-Gen. FILIPE CORREIA DE SÁ.

Finance

(cap. = capital; res = reserves; dep. = deposits; m. = million; brs = branches; amounts in kwanza (equivalent to 1m. readjusted kwanza), unless otherwise indicated)

BANKING

All banks were nationalized in 1975. In 1995 the Government authorized the formation of private banks. In 2011 there were 23 banks licensed to operate in Angola.

Central Bank

Banco Nacional de Angola: Av. 4 de Fevereiro 151, CP 1298, Luanda; tel. and fax 222333717; e-mail bna.cri@ebonet.net; internet www.bna.ao; f. 1976; bank of issue; cap. 5m., res –39,106m., dep. 1,291,174m. (Dec. 2008); Gov. JOSÉ DE LIMA MASSANO; 6 brs.

Commercial Banks

Banco Angolano de Negócios e Comércios SA: 126 Rua Amilcar Cabral, Luanda; tel. 222339285; fax 222394972; e-mail servicosgerais@banc.ws; internet www.banc.ws; f. 2007; cap. 930m., res 539m., dep. 6,664m. (Dec. 2009); Chair. SÉRGIO FILIPE DE SOUSA.

Banco BIC SA: Rua Major Kanhangulo 212, Luanda; tel. 222371227; fax 222395099; e-mail bancobic@bancobic.ao; internet www.bancobic.ao; f. 2005; 25% owned by Fidel Kiluange Assis Araujo; 20% owned by Fernando Mendes Teles; cap. 2,414.5m., res 25,413.2m., dep. 334,646.0m. (Dec. 2009); Chair. FERNANDO MENDES TELES.

Banco Comercial Angolano SARL (BCA): Av. Comandante Valódia 83A, CP 6900, Luanda; tel. 222449548; fax 222449516; internet www.bca.co.ao; f. 1997; 50% owned by Absa; cap. 0.9m., res 347.4m., dep. 1,799.3m. (Dec. 2002); Pres. FRANCISCO DA SILVA CRISTOVÃO; CEO MATEUS FILIPE MARTINS; 4 brs (2005).

Banco de Fomento Angola—BFA: Rua Amílcar Cabral 58, Maianga, Luanda; tel. 222638900; fax 222638925; internet www.bfa.ao; f. 1993 as Banco Fomento Exterior; name changed to above in 2001; 50.1% owned by Banco BPI, SA, Portugal; cap. 3,522.0m., res 26,183.2m., dep. 463,411.7m. (Dec. 2009); CEO EMIDIO PINHEIRO; 38 brs (2005).

Banco Millennium Angola SA: 59 Av. Lenine, Luanda; tel. 222632100; fax 222632494; e-mail comunicacao@millenniumangola.ao; internet www.millenniumangola.ao; f. 2006; 52.7% owned by Banco Comercial Português SA, 31.5% owned by Sonangol, 15.8% owned by Banco Privado Atlântico; cap. 3,809.3m., res 8,684.6m., dep. 79,727.0m. (Dec. 2009); Pres. and CEO Eng. JOSÉ REINO DA COSTA.

Banco de Poupança e Crédito SARL (BPC): Largo Saydi Mingas, CP 1343, Luanda; tel. and fax 222372529; e-mail bpc@bpc.ao; internet www.bpc.ao; f. 1956 as Banco Comercial de Angola; 99% state-owned, 1% owned by the Instituto Nacional de Segurança Social; cap. 7,507.4m., res 28,252.4m., dep. 390,946.7m. (Dec. 2009); Chair. PAIXÃO ANTÓNIO JÚNIOR.

Banco Regional do Keve SARL: Edif. Robert Hudson, Rua Rainha Ginga 77, CP 1804, Luanda; tel. 222394100; fax 222395101; e-mail sedecentral@bancokeve.ao; internet www.bancokeve.ao; f. 2003; cap. 4,000.0m., res 1,781.3m., dep. 29,681.3m. (Dec. 2009); Pres. AMILCAR AZEVEDO DA SILVA.

Banco Sol: Rua Rei Katyavala 110–112, Maculusso, Zona 8, Ingombotas, CP 814, Luanda; tel. 222394717; fax 222440226; e-mail banco.sol@ebonet.net; internet www.bancosol.ao; f. 2000; 55% owned by SANSUL; cap. 1,377.5m., res 1,914.8m., dep. 93,189.0m. (Dec. 2009); Pres. SEBASTIÃO BASTOS LAVRADOR.

Development Banks

Banco de Comércio e Indústria SARL: Rua Rainha Ginga, Largo do Atlético 73–83, POB 1395, Luanda; tel. 222330209; fax 222334924; e-mail falfredo@bci.ebonet.net; internet www.bci.ao; f. 1991; 91% state-owned; privatization pending; provides loans to businesses in all sectors; cap. 2,531.9m., res 5,078.3m., dep. 58,865.6m. (Dec. 2008); Chair. ADRIANO RAFAEL PASCOAL; 5 brs.

Banco de Desenvolvimento de Angola (BDA): Av. 4 de Fevereiro 113, Luanda; tel. 222692800; fax 222396901; e-mail bancobda@bda.ao; internet www.bda.ao; f. 2006; Pres. FRANCO PAIXÃO.

Investment Bank

Banco Angolano de Investimentos SARL (BAI): Rua Major Kanhangulo 34, CP 6022, Luanda; tel. 222693800; fax 222335486; e-mail baised@bancobai.co.ao; internet www.bancobai.co.ao; f. 1997; fmrly Banco Africano de Investimentos SARL; name changed as above in 2011; 8.95% owned by BAI Treasury Stock; 8.5% owned by SONANGOL; cap. 14,786.7m., res 21,371.7m., dep. 652,032.6m. (Dec. 2009); Chair. Dr JOSÉ CARLOS DE CASTRO PAIVA; 45 brs.

Foreign Banks

Banco Comercial Português—Atlântico SA: Rua Rainha Ginga 83, CP 5726, Luanda; tel. 222397922; fax 222397397; Gen. Man. MARIA NAZARÉ FRANCISCO DANG.

Banco Espírito Santo Angola SARL (BESA): Rua 1, Congresso No. 27, Ingombotas, Luanda; tel. 222693600; fax 222693697; internet www.besa.ao; f. 2002; 79.96% owned by Banco Espírito Santo SA (Portugal); cap. US $162.9m., res $24.4m., dep. $5,958.6m. (Dec. 2009); Pres. and Chair. ÁLVARO DE OLIVEIRA MADALENO SOBRINAO.

Banco Totta de Angola SARL: Av. 4 de Fevereiro 99, CP 1231, Luanda; tel. 222332729; fax 222333233; e-mail tottango@ebonet.net; 99.98% owned by Banco Santander Totta; cap. €15.5m. (Dec. 2003); Man. Dir Dr MÁRIO NELSON MAXIMINO; 7 brs.

NovoBanco: Rua Ndunduma 253/257, Bairro Miramar, Município Sambizanga, Luanda; tel. 222430040; fax 222430074; e-mail secretariado@novobanco.ao; internet www.novobanco.net; f. 2004; Pres. MARIO A. BARBER.

STOCK EXCHANGE

Bolsa de Valores e Derivativos do Angola (BVDA): Mutamba, Luanda; f. 2006; Pres. JOSÉ PEDRO DE MORAIS.

INSURANCE

AAA Seguros SA: Rua Lenine 58, Luanda; tel. 222691331; fax 222691342; e-mail carlos.vicente@aaa.co.ao; internet www.aaa.co.ao; f. 2000; life and non-life; Pres. Dr CARLOS MANUEL DE SÃO VICENTE.

ENSA Seguros de Angola (Empresa Nacional de Seguros e Resseguros de Angola, UEE): Av. 4 de Fevereiro 93, CP 5778, Luanda; tel. 222332990; fax 222332946; e-mail geral@ensa.co.ao; f. 1978; state-owned; to be privatized; Chair. MANUEL JOAQUIM GONÇALVES; Pres. and Dir-Gen. ALEIXO AUGUSTO.

GA Angola Seguros (Global Alliance Insurance Angola): Av. 4 de Fevereiro 79, 1° andar, Luanda; tel. 222330368; fax 222398815; e-mail blara@globalalliance.co.ao; internet www.globalalliance.co

.ao; f. 2005; owned by Global Alliance Group (United Kingdom); Gen. Man BRIAN LARA.

Nova Sociedade de Seguros de Angola S.A. (Nossa Seguros): Av. 4 de Fevereiro 111, Luanda; tel. 222399909; fax 222399153; e-mail info@nossaseguros.com; internet www.nossaseguros.com.

Trade and Industry

GOVERNMENT AGENCIES

Agência Nacional para o Investimento Privado (ANIP): Edificio do Ministerio da Industria, 9º andar, Rua Cerqueira Lukoki No. 25, CP 5465, Luanda; tel. 222391434; fax 222332965; e-mail geral@anip.co.ao; internet www.anip.co.ao; f. 2003; Co-ordinator Dr AGUINALDO JAIME.

Gabinete de Obras Especiais: Luanda; Dir MANUEL FERREIRA CLEMENTE JÚNIOR.

Gabinete de Reconstrução Nacional: Luanda; f. 2004; monitors economic and social reconstruction programmes; Dir ANTÓNIO TEIXEIRA FLOR.

Gabinete de Redimensionamento Empresarial: Rua Cerqueira Lukoki 25, 9° andar, CP 594, Luanda; tel. 222390496; fax 222392987; internet www.gare-minfin.org; privatization agency.

Instituto Angolano da Propriedade Industrial: Rua Cerqueira Lukoki 25, 6º andar, CP 3840, Luanda; tel. 222004991; fax 222336428; e-mail prudencia.iapi@hotmail.com; Dir BARROS BEBIANO JOSÉ LICENÇA.

Instituto de Desenvolvimento Agrário: Rua Comandante Gika, CP 2109, Luanda; tel. and fax 222323651; e-mail ida.canga@netangola.com; promotes agricultural devt; Dir MARCOS NHUNGA.

Instituto de Desenvolvimento Industrial de Angola (IDIA): Rua Cerqueira Lukoki 25, 8° andar, CP 594, Luanda; tel. and fax 222338492; e-mail idiadg@netangola.com; f. 1995; promotes industrial devt; Dir BENJAMIM DO ROSÁRIO DOMBOLO.

Instituto de Investimento Estrangeiro (IIE): Rua Cerqueira Lukoki 25, 9º andar, CP 594, Luanda; tel. 222392620; fax 222393381; foreign investment agency.

Instituto Nacional de Cereais (INCER): Av. 4 de Fevereiro 101, CP 1105, Luanda; tel. and fax 222331611; promotes cereal crops; Dir-Gen. BENJAMIM ALVARO CASTELO.

CHAMBER OF COMMERCE

Câmara de Comércio e Indústria de Angola (CCIA) (Angolan Chamber of Commerce and Industry): Largo do Kinaxixi 14, 1° andar, CP 92, Luanda; tel. 222444506; fax 222444629; e-mail ccira@ebonet.net; internet www.ccia.ebonet.net; Pres. ANTÓNIO JOÃO DOS SANTOS; Sec.-Gen. ANTÓNIO TIAGO GOMES.

INDUSTRIAL AND TRADE ASSOCIATIONS

Associação Comercial de Benguela: Rua Sacadura Cabral 104, CP 347, Benguela; tel. 272232441; fax 272233022; e-mail acbenguela@netangola.com; internet www.netangola.com/acb; f. 1907; Pres. AIRES PIRES ROQUE.

Associação Comercial e Industrial da Ilha de Luanda (ACIL): Largo do Kinaxixi 9, Luanda; tel. 222341866; fax 222349677; Pres. PEDRO GODHINO DOMINGOS.

Associação Industrial de Angola (AIA): Rua Manuel Fernando Caldeira 6, CP 61227, Luanda; tel. 222330624; fax 222338650; e-mail contactos@aiangola.net; internet aiangola.net; Pres. JOSÉ SEVERINO.

Associação de Mulheres Empresárias: Largo do Kinaxixi 14, 3° andar, Luanda; tel. 222346742; fax 222343088; f. 1990; asscn of business women; Sec.-Gen. HENRIQUETA DE CARVALHO.

Rede Angolana do Sector Micro-Empresarial (RASME): Luanda; asscn of small businesses; Exec. Co-ordinator BAY KANGUDI.

STATE TRADING ORGANIZATIONS

Angolan Selling Corporation (ASCORP): Edif. Soleil B, Rua Tipografia Mama Tita, Ingombotas, CP 3978, Luanda; tel. 222396465; fax 222397615; e-mail ascorpadmin@ebonet.net; f. 1999; 51% state-owned diamond-trading co; Pres. NOE BALTAZAR.

Direcção dos Serviços de Comércio (DNCI) (Dept of Trade): Palácio de Vidro, 3° andar, Largo 4 de Fevereiro 7, CP 1337, Luanda; tel. and fax 222310658; e-mail minco.dnci.gc@netangola.com; internet www.dnci.net; f. 1970; brs throughout Angola; Dir GOMES CARDOSO.

Exportang, UEE (Empresa de Exportações de Angola): Rua dos Enganos 1A, CP 1000, Luanda; tel. 222332363; co-ordinates exports.

Importang, UEE (Empresa de Importações de Angola): Calçada do Município 10, CP 1003, Luanda; tel. 222337994; f. 1977; co-ordinates majority of imports; Dir-Gen. SIMÃO DIOGO DA CRUZ.

Nova Angomédica, UEE: Rua do Sanatório, Bairro Palanca, CP 2698, Luanda; tel. 222261366; fax 222260010; f. 1981; production and distribution of pharmaceutical goods; Gen. Dir JOSÉ LUÍS PASCOAL.

Sociedade de Comercialização de Diamantes de Angola SARL (SODIAM): Edif. Endiama/De Beers, Rua Rainha Ginga 87, CP 1072, Luanda; tel. 222370217; fax 222370423; e-mail sodiamadmin@ebonet.net; f. 2000; part of the ENDIAMA group; diamond-trading org.; Man. Dir MANUEL ARNALDO DE SOUSA CALADO.

STATE INDUSTRIAL ENTERPRISES

Empresa de Obras Especiais (EMPROE): Rua Ngola Kiluange 183–185, Luanda; tel. 222382142; fax 222382143; building and civil engineering; Dir-Gen. SILVA NETO.

Empresa de Rebenefício e Exportação do Café de Angola, UEE (CAFANGOL): Rua Robert Shields 4–6, CP 342, Luanda; tel. 222337916; fax 222332840; e-mail cafangol@nexus.ao; f. 1983; nat. coffee-processing and trade org.; Dir-Gen. ISAIAS DOMINGOS DE MENEZES.

Empresa dos Tabacos de Angola: Rua Major Kanyangulu, 220, CP 1238, Luanda; tel. 222332760; fax 222331091; e-mail eta@nexus.ao; manufacture of tobacco products; Gen. Man. K. BITTENCOURT.

Empresa Nacional de Cimento, UEE (ENCIME): CP 157, Lobito; tel. 272212325; cement production.

Empresa Nacional de Diamantes de Angola (ENDIAMA), UEE: Rua Major Kanhangulo 100, CP 1247, Luanda; tel. and fax 222332718; fax 222337216; internet www.endiama.co.ao; f. 1981; commenced operations 1986; diamond mining; a number of subsidiary cos undergoing privatization; Pres. Dr MANUEL ARNALDO DE SOUSA CALADO.

Empresa Nacional de Ferro de Angola (FERRANGOL): Rua João de Barros 26, CP 2692, Luanda; tel. 222373800; iron production; Chair. DIAMANTINO PEDRO DE AZEVEDO; Dir ARMANDO DE SOUSA.

Empresa Nacional de Manutenção, UEE (MANUTECNICA): Rua 7, Av. do Cazenga 10, CP 3508, Luanda; tel. 222383646; assembly of machines and specialized equipment for industry.

Sociedade Nacional de Combustíveis de Angola (SONANGOL): Rua Rainha Ginga 22, CP 1316, Luanda; tel. 226643342; fax 2223919782; e-mail hld.gci@sonangol.co.ao; internet www.sonangol.co.ao; f. 1976; exploration, production and refining of crude petroleum, and marketing and distribution of petroleum products; sole concessionary in Angola, supervises on- and offshore operations of foreign petroleum cos; 11 subsidiaries, incl. shipping cos; holds majority interest in jt ventures with Cabinda Gulf Oil Co (CABGOC), Fina Petróleos de Angola and Texaco Petróleos de Angola; CEO MANUEL VICENTE; c. 7,000 employees.

Sonangalp, Lda: Rua Manuel Fernando Caldeira 25, 1725 Luanda; tel. 222334527; fax 222339802; e-mail geral@sonangalp.co.ao; internet www.sonangalp.co.ao/v1; f. 1994; 51% owned by SONANGOL, 49% owned by Petrogal Angola (Portugal); fuel distribution; Pres. ANTÓNIO SILVESTRE.

UTILITIES

Electricity

Empresa Nacional de Construções Eléctricas, UEE (ENCEL): Rua Comandante Che Guevara 185–187, CP 5230, Luanda; tel. 222446712; fax 222446759; e-mail encel@encel.co.ao; internet www.encel.co.ao; f. 1982; supplier of electromechanical equipment; Dir-Gen. DANIEL SIMAS.

Empresa Nacional de Electricidade, EP (ENE): Edif. Geominas 6°–7° andar, CP 772, Luanda; tel. 222321499; fax 222323382; e-mail enepdg@netangola.com; internet www.ene.co.ao; f. 1980; production and distribution of electricity; Pres. and Dir-Gen. Eng. FERNANDO BARROS C. GONGA.

Water

Empresa Provincial de Água de Luanda (EPAL): Rua Frederich Engels 3, CP 1387, Luanda; tel. 222335001; fax 222330380; e-mail epalsdg@snet.co.ao; state-owned; Pres. LEONÍDIO GUSTAVO FERREIRA DE CEITA.

MAJOR COMPANIES

Agip Angola, Lda: Rua Nicolau Gomes Spencer 140, CP 1289, Luanda; tel. 22391894; fax 22394133; e-mail africa@agip.com; subsidiary of ENI SpA, Italy; Chair. PIETRO CAVANNA; Man. Dir PIERO FRAENZI; 85 employees.

Agroquímica de Angola SARL (AGRAN): CP 67, Luanda; tel. 222333594; fax 222339499; e-mail agran@netangola.com; f. 1960; 98.7% owned by Finertec, Portugal; manufacture of agricultural chemicals.

Angola Polishing Diamond, SA: Luanda; f. 2005; 47% owned by LLD Diamonds Ltd (Israel), 48% owned by SODIAM; Dir-Gen. MIGUEL BONDO, Júnior; c. 400 employees.

BP Angola, Lda: Av. Rainha Ginga 87, Luanda; tel. 222637440; fax 222637333; subsidiary of BP PLC, UK; Man. Dir MARTYN MORRIS; over 800 employees.

Cimenfort: Catumbela; cement producer.

Chevron: Av. Lenine 77, CP 2950, Luanda; tel. 222692600; fax 222394348; e-mail Clocal@chevron.com; internet www.chevroninangola.com; owns Cabinda Gulf Oil Co (CABGOC); Man. Dir RICHARD P. COHAGAN.

Coca-Cola Bottling SARL: Rua N'Gola Kiluange 370, Luanda; tel. 222381212; fax 222383256; internet www.sabmiller.com; f. 1999; 55% owned by Coca-Cola, USA, 45% state-owned; bottling plant at Bom Jesus; Man. Dir BOYCE LLOYD.

Companhia Fabril e Comercial de Angola SARL (COMFABRIL): Av. 4 de Fevereiro 79, CP 859, Luanda; tel. 222336393; fax 222336390; manufacture and sale of chemicals; Pres. JOSÉ MANUEL DA SILVA JOSÉ MELLO.

Fina Petróleos de Angola SARL (PETRANGOL): Rua Rainha Ginga 128, CP 1320, Luanda; tel. 222336855; fax 222391031; f. 1958 for exploration, production and refining of petroleum and natural gas; operates Luanda petroleum refinery, Petrangol, with capacity of 40,000 b/d; also operates Quinfuquena terminal; 64.1% owned by Total (France); Gen. Man. CARLOS ALVES; 553 employees.

Lena Construções Engenharia Angola: Rua Comandante Kwenha 197, Bairro do Maculusso, Luanda; tel. 222395601; fax 222398828; e-mail lena.angola@lenaconstrucoes.pt.

Nova Cimangola (Empresa de Cimentos de Angola): Av. 4 de Fevereiro 42, CP 2532, Luanda; tel. 222334941; fax 222334940; f. 1994; 49% owned by Cimpor, Portugal; 39% state-owned; production of cement and plaster; CEO MANUEL VICTOR.

Petrogal Angola SA: Av. 4 de Fevereiro 3–4, Luanda; tel. 222397987; fax 222339499; 100% owned by Galpenergia (Portugal); exploration, production and distribution of petroleum; Chair. Prof. MANUEL FERREIRA DE OLIVEIRA.

Petromar UEM: Rua Rodrigo Miranda 17, CP 6328, Bairro Ingombotas, Luanda; tel. 222321600; fax 222322260; e-mail petromar@petromar.co.ao; internet www.petromar.co.ao; f. 1984; exploration and production of petroleum and gas; Dir-Gen. PHILIPPE FREDERIC.

Sociedade Angolana de Gases Comprimodos SARL (ANGASES): Travessa da Boavista, 30–32, Luanda; tel. 222392401; e-mail angases@ebonet.net; f. 1951; production of medical and industrial gases and electrodes; Gen. Man. JULIO DE MELO ARAUJO.

Sociedade de Desenvolvimento Mineiro de Angola SARL: Parque Empresarial Odebrecht, Av. Pedro de Castro Van-Dúnem 'Loy' s/n, Bloco D, Luanda Sul, CP 6551, Luanda; tel. 222678300; fax 222678315; e-mail stinfo@sdm.net; owned by Odebrecht (Brazil) and ENDIAMA; Dir-Gen. MAURÍCIO NEVES.

Sociedade Mineira de Catoca, Lda: Edif. Endiama, 4° andar, Rua Major Kanhangulo 100, Luanda; tel. 222676700; fax 222390840; e-mail contato@catoca.com; internet www.catoca.com; f. 1992; jt diamond mining and exploration operation owned by ENDIAMA, Alrosa (Russia), Odebrecht (Brazil) and Daumonty Financing BV; Dir-Gen. GANGA JÚNIOR; 2,000 employees.

Sociedade Unificada de Tabacos de Angola, Lda (SUT): Rua Deolinda Rodrigues 530–537, CP 1263, Luanda; tel. 222360180; fax 222360170; f. 1919; tobacco products; 100% owned by British American Tobacco Company; Gen. Man. Dr MANUEL LAMAS.

TRADE UNIONS

Sindicato dos Jornalistas Angolanos (SJA): CP 2805, Luanda; tel. 222334888; fax 222393445; f. by fmr mems of the União dos Jornalistas Angolanos; Sec.-Gen. Dr LUÍSA ROGÉRIO.

Sindicato Nacional de Professores (Sinprof): Rua da Missão 71, 4° andar, Luanda; tel. 222371780; e-mail sinprof@sinprof.org; teachers' union; Pres. GUILHERME SILVA; Sec.-Gen. GRAÇA MANUEL.

União dos Jornalistas Angolanos (UJA): Rua Francisco Távora 8, 1° andar, CP 2140, Luanda; tel. 222338972; fax 222332420; f. 1992; Pres. AVELINO MIGUEL; Gen. Sec. LUISA ROGÉRIO; 1,253 mems in 2003.

União Nacional das Associações de Camponeses Angolanos (UNACA): Rua Major Kanhangulo 146, 1° andar, CP 2465, Luanda; e-mail secretaria@unaca.org; peasants' asscn; Gen. Sec. PAULO UIME.

União Nacional dos Trabalhadores Angolanos (UNTA) (National Union of Angolan Workers): Av. 4 de Fevereiro 210, CP 28, Luanda; tel. 222334670; fax 222393590; e-mail untadis@netangola.com; f. 1960; Sec.-Gen. MANUEL AUGUSTO VIAGE; c. 160,000 mems (2007).

Transport

The transport infrastructure was severely dislocated by the civil war that ended in 2002. Subsequently, major rebuilding and upgrading projects were undertaken.

RAILWAYS

There are three main railway lines in Angola, the Benguela railway, which runs from the coast to the Zambian border, the Luanda–Malange line, and the Moçâmedes line, which connects Namibe and Kuando Kubango. In 2004 only 850 km out of a total of almost 3,000 km of track were operational. A plan introduced in late 2004 to rehabilitate and extend the rail network was expected to take 11 years and to cost US $4,000m. In mid-2005 a project for rebuilding and upgrading the railway system was approved by the Southern African Development Community (SADC). Some 190 km of the 424-km Luanda–Malange line became operational in 2010 when goods transport started between Luanda and Dondo. The Benguela line—a significant export route—was scheduled to reopen in mid-2013, following demining and reconstruction work by Chinese workers. The Moçamedes line was scheduled to reopen in 2012.

Direcção Nacional dos Caminhos de Ferro: Rua Major Kanhangulo, CP 1250, Luanda; tel. 222370091; f. 1975; nat. network operating 4 fmrly independent systems covering 2,952 track-km; Dir JULIO BANGO.

Benguela Railway (Caminho de Ferro de Benguela—Empresa Pública): Praça 11 Novembro 3, CP 32, Lobito, Benguela; tel. 272222645; fax 272225133; e-mail cfbeng@ebonet.net; owned by Govt of Angola; line carrying passenger and freight traffic from the port of Lobito across Angola, via Huambo and Luena, to the border of the Democratic Republic of the Congo (DRC, fmrly Zaire); 1,301 track-km; in 2004 a consortium from China (People's Republic) agreed to rehabilitate the line to the DRC; CEO JOSÉ CARLOS GOMES; 1,700 employees.

Caminho de Ferro de Moçâmedes (CFM): CP 130, Lubango; tel. 261221752; fax 261224442; e-mail gab.dir.cfm@netangola.com; f. 1905; main line from Namibe to Menongue, via Lubango; br. lines to Chibia and iron ore mines at Cassinga; 838 track-km; Chair. DANIEL KIPAXE; CEO JÚLIO BANGO JOAQUIM.

Luanda Railway (Empresa de Caminho de Ferro de Luanda, UEE): CP 1250-C, Luanda; tel. 222370061; f. 1886; serves an iron-, cotton- and sisal-producing region between Luanda and Malange; 536 track-km; CEO OSVALDO LOBO DO NASCIMENTO.

ROADS

In 2001 Angola had 51,429 km of roads, of which 7,944 km were main roads and 13,278 km were secondary roads. About 10.4% of roads were paved. It was estimated that 80% of the country's road network was in disrepair. In 2005–06 contracts were awarded to various foreign companies to upgrade the road network, including the main north–south coastal road. A government programme to rebuild some 14,000 km of the road network commenced in the late 2000s.

Direcção Nacional dos Transportes Rodoviárias: Rua Rainha Ginga 74, 1° andar, Luanda; tel. 222339390; fax 222334427.

Instituto Nacional de Estradas de Angola (INEA): Rua Amílcar Cabral 35, 3° andar, CP 5667, Luanda; tel. 222332828; fax 222335754; Dir-Gen. JOAQUIM SEBASTIÃO.

SHIPPING

The main harbours are at Lobito, Luanda and Namibe. The first phase of a 10-year SADCC (now SADC) programme to develop the 'Lobito corridor', for which funds were pledged in January 1989, was to include the rehabilitation of the ports of Lobito and Benguela. In January 2007 the Japanese authorities pledged US $9m. for the rehabilitation of the quays of Namibe and Lobito ports. The port of Luanda was due to be upgraded by the end of 2010. In December 2009 Angola's registered merchant fleet comprised 153 vessels, totalling 63,098 grt.

Instituto Marítimo e Portuário de Angola (IMPA): Rua Rainha Ginga 74, 4° andar, Luanda; tel. and fax 222390034; Dir-Gen. VICTOR DE CARVALHO.

Agenang, UEE: Rua Engracia Fragoso 47–49, CP 485, Luanda; tel. 222393988; fax 222391444; state shipping co; scheduled for privatization.

Cabotang—Cabotagem Nacional Angolana, UEE: Av. 4 de Fevereiro 83A, Luanda; tel. 222373133; operates off the coasts of Angola and Mozambique; Dir-Gen. JOÃO OCTAVIO VAN-DÚNEM.

Empresa Portuária do Lobito, UEE: Av. da Independência 16, Lobito, Benguela; tel. 272222645; fax 272222865; e-mail dop@portodolobito.com; long-distance sea transport; CEO BENTO PAIXÃO DOS SANTOS.

Empresa Portuária de Luanda: Av. 4 de Fevereiro, CP 1229, Porto de Luanda; tel. 222311753; fax 222311178; e-mail geral@portoluanda.co.ao; internet www.portoluanda.co.ao; CEO Francisco Venâncio.

Empresa Portuária de Moçâmedes—Namibe, UEE: Rua Pedro Benje 10a e c, CP 49, Namibe; tel. 264260643; long-distance sea transport; CEO Joaquim Domingos Neto.

Orey Angola, Lda: Largo 4 de Fevereiro 3, 3° andar, CP 583, Luanda; tel. 222311454; fax 222310882; e-mail orey@oreylad.ebonet.net; internet www.orey-angola.com; int. shipping, especially to Portugal; Dir João Teiga.

Sécil Marítima SARL, UEE: Edif. Secil, Av. 4 de Fevereiro 42, 1° andar, CP 5910, Luanda; tel. 222311334; fax 222311784; e-mail secilmaritima@msn.com; operates ports at Lobito, Luanda and Namibe; Gen. Man. Maria Amélia Rita.

CIVIL AVIATION

Angola's airport system is well developed, but suffered some damage in the later years of the civil war. The 4 de Fevereiro international airport in Luanda underwent modernization in the late 2000s, while a new international airport, at Lubango was opened in January 2010. During the late 2000s airports at Luanda, Lobito, Soyo, Namibe, Saurimo, Uíge, Huambo and Bié also underwent rehabilitation. In 2009 it was announced that two further international airports were to be built in Luanda and Benguela.

Direcção Nacional da Aviação Civil: Rua Frederich Engels 92, 6° andar, CP 569, Luanda; tel. 222339412.

Instituto Nacional da Aviação Civil: Rua Miguel de Melo 96, 6º andar, Luanda; tel. 222335936; fax 222390529; internet www.inavic.gv.ao; Dir-Gen. Dr Gaspar Francisco dos Santos.

Empresa Nacional de Aeroportos e Navegação Aerea (ENANA): Av. Amílcar Cabral 110, CP 841, Luanda; tel. and fax 222351267; e-mail cai_enana@snet.co.ao; administers airports; Chair. Manuel Ferreira de Ceita.

Air Nacoia: Rua Comandante Che Guevara 67, 1° andar, Luanda; tel. and fax 222395477; f. 1993; Pres. Salvador Silva.

SONAIR SARL: Aeroporto Internacional 4 de Fevereiro, Luanda; tel. 222633502; fax 222321572; e-mail commercial.sonair@sonangol.co.ao; internet www.sonairsarl.com; f. 1998; subsidiary of SONANGOL; operates direct flights between Luanda and Houston, USA; Chair. Manuel D. Vicente; CEO João Alves Andrade.

TAAG—Linhas Aéreas de Angola: Rua da Missão 123, CP 79, Luanda; tel. 222332338; fax 222390396; e-mail gci_taag@ebonet.net; internet www.nexus.ao/taag; f. 1938; internal scheduled passenger and cargo services, and services from Luanda to destinations within Africa and to Europe and South America; Chair. Dr António Luis Pimentel de Araújo.

Angola Air Charter: Aeroporto Internacional 4 de Fevereiro, CP 3010, Luanda; tel. 222321290; fax 222320105; e-mail aacharter@independente.net; f. 1992; subsidiary of TAAG; CEO A. de Matos.

Transafrik International Ltd: Aeroporto Internacional 4 de Fevereiro, Luanda; tel. 222353714; fax 222354183; e-mail info@transafrik.com; internet www.transafrik.com; f. 1986; operates int. contract cargo services; CEO Björn Näf; Chief Financial Officer Stephan Brandt.

Tourism

Angola's tourism industry is undeveloped as a result of the years of civil war, although its potential for development is great. Tourist arrivals totalled 425,000 in 2010 and receipts from tourism in that year amounted to US $719m.

National Tourist Agency: Palácio de Vidro, Largo 4 de Fevereiro, CP 1240, Luanda; tel. 222372750.

Defence

In accordance with the peace agreement concluded by the Government and the União Nacional para a Independência Total de Angola (UNITA) in May 1991, a new 50,000-strong national army, the Forças Armadas de Angola (FAA), was established, comprising equal numbers of government forces, the Forças Armadas Populares de Libertação de Angola (FAPLA), and UNITA soldiers. After elections in 1992, UNITA withdrew its troops from the FAA and hostilities resumed. Following the signing of the Lusaka Accord in November 1994, the integration of the UNITA contingent into the FAA resumed. In 1995 agreement was reached between the Government and UNITA on the enlargement of the FAA to comprise a total of 90,000 troops, and discussions began concerning the potential formation of a fourth, non-combatant branch of the FAA, which would engage in public works projects. In mid-1997 the Government estimated that UNITA maintained a residual force numbering some 25,000–30,000 troops, while UNITA claimed to have a force of only 2,963 'police'. In March 1998 UNITA issued a declaration announcing the complete demobilization of its forces and by May some 11,000 UNITA soldiers had been integrated into the FAA. However, the integration process was abandoned following the resumption of hostilities between the Government and UNITA in December 1998. Following the ratification of a cease-fire in April 2002, only 5,000 UNITA fighters were integrated into the FAA; it was estimated that 80,000 had been reintegrated into civilian life by November 2003. As assessed at November 2011, the FAA had an estimated total strength of 107,000: army 100,000, navy 1,000 and air force 6,000. In addition, there was a paramilitary force numbering an estimated 10,000.

Defence Expenditure: Budgeted at 352,000m. kwanza for 2012.

Chief of General Staff of the Armed Forces: Gen. Geraldo Sachipengo Nunda.

Chief of General Staff of the Army: Gen. Jorge Barros Ngutó.

Chief of General Staff of the National Air Force: Gen. Francisco Gonçalves Afonso.

Chief of General Staff of the Navy: Adm. Augusto da Silva Cunha.

Education

Education is officially compulsory for eight years, between seven and 15 years of age, and is provided free of charge by the Government. Primary education begins at seven years of age and lasts for six years. Secondary education, beginning at the age of 11, lasts for up to six years, comprising two cycles of three years each. As a proportion of the school-age population, the total enrolment at primary and secondary schools was equivalent to 83% in 2009/10. According to UNESCO estimates, enrolment at primary schools in 2009/10 included 86% of children in the relevant age-group (boys 93%; girls 78%), while secondary enrolment in 2009/10 included 12% of children in the relevant age-group (boys 12%; girls 13%). In 2009/10 a total of 66,251 students were enrolled in tertiary education. In November 2002 the Government announced plans for the construction of seven provincial universities, five science and technology institutes, three medical schools and a nutrition research centre. There are also four private universities. Much education is now conducted in vernacular languages rather than Portuguese. In 2004 the Government recruited 29,000 new teachers, to be trained by the UN Children's Fund (UNICEF). The 2006 budget allocated an estimated 83,500m. kwanza to education.

Bibliography

Andresen Guimarães, F. *The Origins of the Angolan Civil War: Foreign Intervention and Domestic Political Conflict.* Basingstoke, Palgrave, 2001.

Anstee, M. *Orphan of the Cold War: The Inside Story of the Collapse of the Angolan Peace Process.* London, Macmillan, and New York, St Martin's Press, 1996.

Bender, G. J. *Angola Under the Portuguese: The Myth and the Reality.* Lawrenceville, NJ, Africa World Press, 2004.

Bhagavan, M. R. *Angola's Political Economy: 1975–1985.* Uppsala, Nordic Africa Institute, 1996.

Birmingham, D. *Frontline Nationalism in Angola and Mozambique.* London, James Currey Publrs, and Trenton, NJ, Africa World Press, 1992.

Empire in Africa: Angola and its Neighbors. Columbus, OH, The Ohio State University Press, 2006.

Bridgland, F. *Jonas Savimbi: A Key to Africa.* Edinburgh, Mainstream, 1986.

Broadhead, S. H. *Historical Dictionary of Angola.* 3rd edn. Metuchen, NJ, Scarecrow Press, 1992.

Cann, J. P. *Counter-insurgency in Africa: The Portuguese Way of War 1961–1974.* Westport, CT, Greenwood Press, 1997.

Chabal, P., and Videl, N. (Eds). *Angola: The Weight of History.* New York, Columbia University Press, 2007.

Cilliers, J., and Dietrich, C. (Eds). *Angola's War Economy: The Role of Oil and Diamonds.* Pretoria, Institute for Security Studies, 2000.

Conçalves, J. *Economics and Politics of the Angolan Conflict: The Transition Re-Negotiated.* Bellville Centre for Southern Africa Studies, University of the Western Cape, 1995.

Crocker, C. A. *High Noon in Southern Africa: Making Peace in a Rough Neighbourhood.* New York, W. W. Norton, 1992.

Fish, B., and Durost Fish, B. *Angola: 1980 to the Present: Slavery, Exploitation, and Revolt (Exploration of Africa).* London, Chelsea House Publications, 2001.

Galliani, F. *Portrait of the New Angola.* Milan, Skira Editore, 2012.

George, E. *The Cuban Intervention in Angola (1965–1991), from Che Guevara to Cuito Cuanavale.* London, Frank Cass, 2005.

Gleijeses, P. *Conflicting Missions: Havana, Washington, and Africa, 1959–1976.* Chapel Hill, NC, and London, University of North Carolina Press, 2002.

Hart, K., and Lewis, J. (Eds). *Why Angola Matters.* London, James Currey Publrs, 1995.

Henderson, L. W. *Angola: Five Centuries of Conflict.* Ithaca, NY, Cornell University Press, 1979.

Heywood, L. *Contested Power in Angola, 1840s to the Present.* Rochester, NY, University of Rochester Press, 2000.

Hodges, T. *Angola: Anatomy of an Oil State.* Oxford, James Currey Publrs, 2004.

Jaime, D., and Barber, H. *Angola: Depoimentos para a História Recente, 1950–76.* Lisbon, Istoé Comunicações, 1999.

Jett, D. T. *Why Peacekeeping Fails.* Basingstoke, Palgrave, 2001.

Konczacki, Z. A., Parpart, J. L., and Shaw, T. M. (Eds). *Studies in the Economic History of Southern Africa.* Vol. I. London, Frank Cass, 1990.

MacQueen, N. *The Decolonization of Portuguese Africa: Metropolitan Revolution and the Dissolution of Empire.* Harlow, Longman, 1997.

Maier, K. *Angola: Promises and Lies.* London, Serif Books, 2007.

Marcum, J. *The Angolan Revolution.* 2 vols. Cambridge, MA, MIT Press, 1969 and 1978 (new edn).

Martin, J. W. *A Political History of the Civil War in Angola, 1974–90.* New Brunswick, NJ, Transaction Publishers, 1992.

Matz, P. *Lost in Transformation: Two Years in Angola.* Books on Demand, 2008.

Mendes, P. R. *Bay of Tigers: A journey through war-torn Angola.* London, Granta, 2004.

Minter, W. (Ed.). *Operation Timber: Pages from the Savimbi Dossier.* Trenton, NJ, Africa World Press, 1988.

Apartheid's Contras: An Inquiry into the Roots of War in Angola and Mozambique. London, Zed Press, 1994.

Mohanty, S. *Political Development and Ethnic Identity in Africa: A Study of Angola since 1960.* London, Sangham, 1992.

Moorhouse, K., and Wei, C. *No One Can Stop the Rain: A Chronicle of Two Foreign Aid Workers During the Angolan Civil War.* London, Ontario, Insomniac Press, 2005.

Pearce, J. *An Outbreak of Peace: Angola's Situation of 'Confusion'.* Cape Town, New Africa Books, 2005.

Pélissier, R. *Explorar: Voyages en Angola.* Orgeval, Editions Pélissier, 1980.

Power, M., and Alves, A. (Eds). *China and Angola: A Marriage of Convenience?* Oxford, Pambazuka Press, 2012.

Reed, K. *Crude Existence: Environment and the Politics of Oil in Northern Angola.* Berkeley, CA, University of California Press, 2009.

Shaxson, N. *Poisoned Wells: The Dirty Politics of African Oil.* London, Palgrave Macmillan, 2008.

Spikes, D. *Angola and the Politics of Intervention.* Jefferson, NC, McFarland Publishers, 1993.

Tvedten, I. *Angola: Struggle for Peace and Reconstruction.* Boulder, CO, Westview Press, 1997.

Vincenti, S. *Angola e Africa do Sul.* Luanda, Eclicas do Autor, 1994.

Weigert, S. *Angola: A Modern Military History, 1961–2002.* Basingstoke, Palgrave Macmillan, 2011.

Westad, O. *The Global Cold War: Third World Interventions and the Making of Our Times.* Cambridge, Cambridge University Press, 2007.

Wheeler, D. L., and Pélissier, R. *Angola.* London, Greenwood Press, 1978.

Wright, G. *The Destruction of a Nation: United States Policy towards Angola since 1945.* London, Pluto Press, 1997.

BENIN

Physical and Social Geography

R. J. HARRISON CHURCH

The Republic of Benin, bordered on the east by Nigeria, on the west by Togo and to the north by Burkina Faso and Niger, covers an area of 112,622 sq km (43,484 sq miles). From a coastline of some 100 km on the Gulf of Guinea, the republic extends inland about 650 km to the Niger river. The population was 6,769,914 at the census of February 2002. At mid-2012, according to UN estimates, the population was 9,351,837, giving an average population density of 83.0 inhabitants per sq km. The population of Cotonou, the political capital and major port, was estimated at 923,923 in mid-2011, and that of Porto-Novo, the official capital, was 276,993 in mid-2009. Other large cities include Abomey-Calavi (with a population of 376,993 in 2006), Djougou (207,926) and Banikoura (180,853).

The coast is a straight sandbar, pounded by heavy surf on the seaward side and backed by one or more lagoons and former shorelines on the landward side. Rivers flow into these lagoons, Lakes Ahémé and Nokoué being estuaries of two rivers whose seaward exits are obstructed by the sandbar. A lagoon waterway is navigable for barges to Lagos, Nigeria.

North of Lake Nokoué the Ouémé river has a wide marshy delta, with considerable agricultural potential. Elsewhere the lagoons are backed northward by the Terre de Barre, a fertile and intensively farmed region of clay soils. North again is the seasonally flooded Lama swamp. Beyond are areas comparable with the Terre de Barre, and the realm of the pre-colonial kingdom of Dahomey.

Most of the rest of the country is underlain by Pre-Cambrian rocks, with occasional bare domes, laterite cappings on level surfaces, and poor soils. In the north-west are the Atacora mountains, whose soils, although less poor, are much eroded. On the northern borders are primary and other sandstones; soils are extremely infertile and short of water.

Deposits of low-grade iron ores, chromium, rutile, phosphates, kaolin and gold occur in the north of the country. Extraction of petroleum from a small oilfield, off shore from Cotonou, at Sémé, ceased in late 1998, although there were attempts at rehabilitation in the early 2000s. Reserves of natural gas, estimated to total 4,000m. cu m, were also being evaluated at that time. Limestone and marble are currently mined.

Southern Benin has an equatorial climate, most typical along the coast, although with a low rainfall of some 1,300 mm. Away from the coast the dry months increase until a tropical climate prevails over the northern half of the country. The dry season alternates with a wet one, the latter being of seven months in the centre and four months in the north.

In the colonial period the Fon and Yoruba of the south enjoyed educational advantages and were prominent in administration throughout French West Africa. After independence many were expelled to Benin, where there is great unemployment or underemployment of literates. The northern peoples, such as the Somba and Bariba, are less Westernized. The Fon were the most numerous ethnic group in the country, accounting for 39.2% of the population in 2002, followed by the Adja (15.2%) and Yoruba (12.3%).

Recent History

KATHARINE MURISON

INDEPENDENCE AND ARMY RULE

Benin (then Dahomey) became a self-governing republic within the French Community in December 1958 and an independent state on 1 August 1960. Political life in the republic was extremely unstable following independence, as regionally based interests contended for power. Hubert Maga, the republic's first President, was deposed in October 1963 by a coup, and successive army-supported regimes governed the country for the ensuing decade.

In October 1972 Maj. (later Brig.-Gen.) Mathieu Kérékou, a northerner, seized power. Marxism-Leninism was introduced as the national ideology, and banking, insurance and the principal industrial sectors were nationalized; the Parti de la Révolution Populaire du Bénin became the sole authorized political party. In 1975 the country was renamed the People's Republic of Benin. In the early 1980s worsening economic conditions prompted Benin to move increasingly towards the Western bloc and the IMF. By the mid-1980s France had replaced the USSR as the principal supplier of military equipment, while also remaining predominant in trade, development assistance and other forms of co-operation. Amid rising social tensions and ethnic rivalries, Kérékou left the army in January 1987 to become a civilian Head of State. Ensuing tensions between the Government and the army culminated in attempted coups in March and June 1988.

'CIVILIAN COUP'

Although a period of repression in the aftermath of the coup attempts, in conjunction with popular dissatisfaction at IMF-stipulated austerity measures, engendered an atmosphere of increased instability, at legislative elections in June 1989 a single list of 206 candidates was approved by almost 90% of the votes cast. In August the legislature, the Assemblée Nationale Révolutionnaire (ANR), re-elected Kérékou to the presidency for a further five-year term. However, in December the abandonment of Marxism-Leninism as the state ideology was announced.

In February 1990 a national conference of the 'active forces of the nation' voted to abolish the existing structure of government and its institutions. Pending elections to a new legislature, the functions of the ANR were assumed in March by an interim Haut Conseil de la République (HCR), which included the principal opposition leaders. The President of the Republic was for the first time to be elected by universal suffrage, with a five-year mandate, renewable only once. Nicéphore Soglo, a former official of the World Bank, was designated interim Prime Minister. Kérékou was obliged to relinquish the defence portfolio to Soglo, and also to accept the conference's resolution to change the country's name to the Republic of Benin. In May the military prefects of Benin's six provinces were replaced by civilians, and in June an extensive restructuring of the armed forces was implemented. In August legislation was promulgated to permit the registration of political parties.

Benin was thus the first sub-Saharan African country to experience a 'civilian coup'. A draft constitution was submitted to a national referendum in December 1990. Voters were asked to choose between two versions of the Constitution, one of which incorporated a clause stipulating upper and lower age-limits for presidential candidates (thereby automatically disqualifying several former Presidents); 95.8% of those who voted gave their assent to one or other of the versions, with 79.7% of voters endorsing the age restrictions.

Some 24 political parties participated in legislative elections held in February 1991. A pro-Soglo alliance secured the greatest number of seats (12) in the 64-member Assemblée nationale. The first round of the presidential election, on 10 March, was contested by 13 candidates. Reflecting regional ethnic divisions, Soglo, who secured 36.2% of the vote, received his greatest support in the south of the country, while Kérékou, who was favoured in the north, took 27.3%. Soglo was elected President in a second round of voting, securing 67.7% of the total votes cast. Before its dissolution, in late March, the HCR granted Kérékou immunity from any legal proceedings arising from his years in power.

THE SOGLO PRESIDENCY, 1991–96

Soglo was inaugurated as President on 4 April 1991. He subsequently relinquished the defence portfolio. The Soglo administration intensified efforts at economic liberalization, and also began criminal proceedings against corrupt former state officials.

The President's position was strengthened by the formation, in June 1992, of Le Renouveau, a pro-Soglo majority group, comprising some 34 deputies, the absence of a majority party or coalition in the Assemblée nationale having hitherto delayed the passage of legislation. However, Soglo lost his majority support in October 1993, when 15 members withdrew from Le Renouveau. In July, meanwhile, Soglo had aligned himself with the (Parti de la) Renaissance du Bénin (RB), formed by his wife, Rosine, in 1992; he was appointed leader of the RB in July 1994.

Preparations for elections to the Assemblée nationale, scheduled for February 1995, engendered further friction between the executive and the legislature. Soglo opposed the creation of an independent electoral commission, the Commission Électorale Nationale Autonome (CENA), which the Assemblée nationale none the less approved in November 1994, and a planned increase in the number of deputies from 64 to 83. Twice postponed as a result of organizational difficulties, the elections finally took place on 28 March 1995, contested by 31 political organizations. The Constitutional Court annulled the results of voting for 13 seats owing to irregularities. Following by-elections in May, the RB held 20 seats in the Assemblée nationale, and other supporters of Soglo a total of 13. Opposition parties held 49 seats, the most prominent being the Parti du Renouveau Démocratique (PRD), with 19 seats. Bruno Amoussou, the leader of the opposition Parti Social-démocrate (PSD), was elected President of the legislature. A new Government was announced in June.

THE RETURN OF KÉRÉKOU

The first round of the presidential election was held on 3 March 1996 and contested by seven candidates. Soglo secured 35.7% of the valid votes and Kérékou 33.9%, followed by Adrien Houngbédji, the leader of the PRD (19.7%). Most of the defeated candidates, among them Houngbédji, expressed their support for Kérékou, who was victorious in a second round of voting conducted on 18 March, with 52.5% of the votes cast. Some 78.1% of those eligible had voted. Kérékou was inaugurated as President on 4 April. Having sought authorization by the Constitutional Court for the appointment of a Prime Minister (provision for such a post is not stipulated in the Constitution), Kérékou named Houngbédji as premier in a Government that included representatives of eight parties that had supported his presidential campaign.

Following several months of labour unrest, in May 1998 Houngbédji resigned as Prime Minister and withdrew the PRD from the Government. The most senior member of a new Government appointed by Kérékou in mid-May was Pierre Osho, as Minister-delegate to the Presidency, in charge of Defence and Relations with the Institutions. The new Government, which included representatives of seven parties, commanded the support of just 27 members of the Assemblée nationale.

On 30 March 1999 some 35 parties and alliances contested elections to the 83-member Assemblée nationale. The opposition parties won a narrow victory, securing 42 seats, while the pro-Kérékou parties took 41. Voting was divided on clear regional lines: the RB won 27 seats, principally in the centre and the south, while parties supporting Kérékou performed strongly in the north. The opposition was swift to reassure observers that it intended to co-operate with the President. In June Kérékou effected a minor cabinet reshuffle, as a result of which the number of parties represented in the Council of Ministers increased to 10.

Kérékou Re-elected

Of the 17 candidates permitted to contest the presidency on 4 March 2001, Soglo was, once again, widely regarded as the sole credible challenger to Kérékou. Kérékou gained the largest share of the votes, with Soglo in second place, but failed to secure an absolute majority. As campaigning for a second round, to be held on 18 March, proceeded, the Constitutional Court conducted a review of the initially declared results of the first round. According to revised provisional results, issued on 13 March, Kérékou received 45.4% of the votes cast, Soglo 27.1%, Houngbédji 12.6% and Amoussou 8.6%. The revised results indicated an increase in the electoral roll of some 300,000, and measured turn-out at around 80%.

On 16 March 2001, following the rejection of his appeal to the Constitutional Court for a re-run of the election, Soglo withdrew his candidacy and urged his supporters to abstain from voting in the second round. Polling was postponed, initially until 19 March, and subsequently until 22 March, in order to permit Houngbédji to campaign. However, on 19 March Houngbédji also declared his dissatisfaction with the conduct of the election and withdrew. Despite having previously declared his support for Kérékou, Amoussou agreed to challenge him for the presidency. The second round of the election duly took place on 22 March. Voter participation was, at approximately 55%, notably lower than in the first round. Two days after the poll, the CENA announced that Kérékou had been re-elected, with 84.1% of the valid votes cast.

Kérékou formed a new Government in May 2001. Amoussou retained his post as Minister of State, responsible for the Co-ordination of Government Action, Future Planning and Development. In July it was announced that proposed municipal elections had been cancelled, as a result of overspending on the presidential election.

The delayed municipal and local elections were held in two rounds in December 2002 and January 2003. Although supporters of Kérékou, who formed an electoral alliance known as the Union pour le Bénin du Futur (UBF), were the most successful grouping overall, the RB gained the majority of seats in Cotonou, where Nicéphore Soglo was elected mayor, while the PRD secured control of Porto-Novo. Following the municipal elections, the UBF formally constituted itself as a party, under the leadership of Amoussou; the PSD merged into the UBF.

Elections to the Assemblée Nationale, 2003

The legislative elections held on 30 March 2003 were contested by 14 political groups, and were marked by an appreciably lower turn-out than previous legislative elections, estimated at around 50%. The elections resulted in the establishment of a clear pro-presidential majority in the Assemblée nationale for the first time since the introduction of multi-party elections, with supporters of Kérékou securing 52 of the 83 elective seats. The UBF emerged as the largest single party, with 31 seats, and the pro-presidential Mouvement Africain pour la Démocratie et le Progrès (MADEP) won nine seats. The representation of the RB, the largest party in the outgoing assembly, was reduced from 27 to 15 seats. On 10 April Houngbédji announced that the PRD, which secured 11 seats in the elections, would henceforth support the Government, as a result of which the pro-presidential bloc in the Assemblée nationale held 63 seats.

In April 2003 Antoine Kolawolé Idji of the MADEP, hitherto Minister of Foreign Affairs and African Integration, was elected as President of the Assemblée nationale. After lengthy consultations, the formation of a new Government was finally announced in June. Amoussou was appointed to the most senior ministerial position, as Minister of State, responsible for Planning and Development.

PRESIDENTIAL ELECTION OF 2006

By early 2005 there was already much discussion regarding possible contenders for the presidency at the election due in March 2006, which Kérékou was constitutionally barred from contesting, having served two consecutive terms of office and having exceeded the 70-year age limit for candidates. Nicéphore Soglo was also ineligible to stand again owing to his age. In February 2005 Kérékou effected a major reshuffle of the Council of Ministers, notably dismissing Amoussou and the Minister of Finance and the Economy, Grégoire Laourou, who were replaced, respectively, by Zul Kifl Salami and Cosme Sèhlin. Pierre Osho, a close ally of the President, was retained as Minister of State, responsible for National Defence. It was suggested that Amoussou, who was regarded as a potential candidate for the presidency, had been removed from the Government to allow him to concentrate on preparing for the forthcoming election. In November Sèhlin suggested that the Government did not have sufficient resources to fund the presidential election, which was scheduled for 5 March 2006. In the following month the Assemblée nationale approved the cancellation of a planned electoral census, in an apparent attempt to reduce costs. In January 2006 Osho resigned from the Council of Ministers in protest at the management of the election.

Despite the financial difficulties, the first round of the presidential election, contested by 26 candidates, was held on 5 March 2006, as scheduled. Dr Boni Yayi, until recently President of the Banque Ouest-Africaine de Développement (BOAD) and standing as an independent, received the largest share of the votes cast, with 35.6%, followed by Houngbédji, with 24.1%, Amoussou, with 16.2%, and Léhadi Soglo, the eldest son of Nicéphore and Rosine Soglo, with 8.4%. Some 76% of the electorate participated in the first round. International observers were largely satisfied with the conduct of the poll, despite concerns regarding the high number of registered voters, which was widely regarded to be excessive considering the size of the population.

A second round of voting was contested by Yayi and Houngbédji on 19 March 2006. Of the 24 candidates defeated in the first round, 11 urged their supporters to vote for Yayi, including Amoussou and Soglo. Yayi won a decisive victory in the second round, securing 74.5% of the votes cast. A lower turnout, of around 67%, was recorded.

YAYI'S FIRST TERM, 2006–11

Yayi was inaugurated to succeed Kérékou as Head of State on 6 April 2006. The new President pledged to reduce poverty, to combat corruption and to revive the economy, with the aim of achieving a double-digit rate of annual growth by 2010. Two days later the President announced the formation of a new Council of Ministers dominated by technocrats and comprising 22 members, none of whom had served in the outgoing Government. Pascal Koupaki, a former official at the Banque Centrale des Eats de l'Afrique de l'Ouest (BCEAO), was appointed as Minister of Development, the Economy and Finance, the most senior position in the Government.

Organizational difficulties, mainly resulting from internal divisions within the CENA, forced the postponement of legislative elections from 25 March 2007 to 31 March. The 83 seats in the Assemblée nationale were contested by 2,158 candidates representing 24 parties and alliances. The Force Cauris pour un Bénin Émergent (FCBE), a pro-presidential coalition of some 20 parties, became the largest grouping in the legislature, securing 35 seats, followed by the Alliance pour une Dynamique Démocratique (comprising the RB, the MADEP and the PSD, among others), which won 20 seats, and the PRD, which took 10. The remaining seats were shared by nine other parties or alliances. It was reported that only 20 deputies from the outgoing legislature had succeeded in retaining their seats. The CENA estimated voter turn-out at 58.7%. In May Mathurin Nago of the FCBE, hitherto Minister of Higher Education and Professional Training, was elected as President of the Assemblée nationale, defeating Amoussou.

President Yayi announced a comprehensive reorganization of the Council of Ministers in June 2007, in which the number of portfolios was increased to 26. Of the 17 new appointees included in the Government, some of the most notable were Soulé Mana Lawani as Minister of Finance and Ganiou Soglo, the youngest son of Nicéphore and Rosine Soglo and a member of the RB, as Minister of Youth, Sports and Leisure. Koupaki remained the most senior minister, in the position of Minister of State, in charge of the Economy, Planning, Development and the Evaluation of Public Action, while Issifou Kogui N'Douro, the Minister of National Defence, was also promoted to the rank of Minister of State. A minor government reorganization was effected in November, entailing the transfer of responsibility for the economy from Koupaki to Lawani and the division of the Ministry of Primary Education, Literacy and National Languages into two separate ministries.

In early 2008 13 deputies from minor parties that had hitherto participated in a pro-Yayi grouping in the legislature announced the withdrawal of their support for the President and the formation of a new movement, G13. In March, moreover, the MADEP, the PRD, the PSD and the RB, allied as G4, signed a declaration containing wide-ranging criticisms of the Government, which they accused of undermining democracy in Benin. Elections to select 1,435 communal and municipal councillors, as well as thousands of other local representatives, took place on 20 April, contested by some 26,000 candidates. However, polling was marred by severe organizational difficulties, particularly in the south of the country, which led to the elections in Abomey-Calavi, Ouidah, Glazoué and Dogbo being conducted on 1 May. Observers from the Economic Community of West African States (ECOWAS) recommended the computerization of the electoral register and the establishment of a permanent CENA. Following several delays, the CENA finally announced the results of the elections in late May. It was reported that the FCBE had secured the largest number of council seats, winning 701, while G13 had taken 189, the PRD 117, the RB 105, the PSD 85, Force Clé 66 and the MADEP 41. None the less, opposition parties obtained a majority of seats in many of the larger towns, with the RB and the PRD retaining control of Cotonou and Porto-Novo, respectively.

Political uncertainty increased in the following months, as deputies belonging to G4, G13 and Force clé disrupted the activities of the Assemblée nationale (in which the Government now lacked a majority), prompting President Yayi to adopt several pieces of legislation by decree from late July 2008. In an apparent attempt to regain the support of his erstwhile allies, Yayi appointed a number of opposition members to the Government in a major reorganization announced in October. However, G13 refused to participate in the enlarged 30-member administration, forcing Yayi to replace two appointees from that movement. Notable changes included the appointment of Jean-Marie Ehouzou, Benin's Permanent Representative to the UN since 2006, as Minister of Foreign Affairs, African Integration, Francophone Affairs and Beninois Abroad, and the promotion of Armand Zinzindohoué, hitherto Minister-delegate at the Presidency, in charge of Transport and Public Works, to the position of Minister of the Interior and Public Security.

A commission charged by President Yayi in February 2008 with reviewing the Constitution presented its report in January 2009, recommending relatively minor amendments, including the establishment of a Court of Accounts (to replace the Chamber of Accounts of the Supreme Court) and the introduction of provisions on the CENA and the office of Mediator of the Republic, which had been created in 2006 to resolve disputes arising between state or public institutions and citizens. (Albert Tévoédjrè was formally inaugurated as the country's first Mediator in August.) Also in January 2009 a commission established by Yayi three months earlier to examine the country's territorial divisions proposed an increase in the number of departments from 12 to 21. In May the Assemblée nationale adopted legislation on the creation of a permanent, computerized electoral register; the vote revealed divisions within the opposition alliance of G4, G13 and Force Clé, with some constituent parties, including the RB, supporting the legislation, while a number of deputies of the PRD and Force Clé reportedly abstained. Substantial financial and technical assistance for the establishment of the register was pledged by international donors, and a national electoral census was initiated in November. None the less, the issue continued to prove divisive, with opposition parties claiming that the process for compiling the new register lacked transparency.

Yayi effected several government changes in mid-2009. In June Roger Dovonou, the Minister of Agriculture, Stockbreeding and Fisheries, and Grégoire Akofodji, the Minister of Industry, exchanged portfolios, while Idrissou Daouda, hitherto the Managing Director of the BCEAO, was appointed as Minister of the Economy and Finance to replace Soulé Mana Lawani, who had been dismissed following her implication in alleged financial irregularities related to the construction of infrastructure for a summit of the Community of Sahel-Saharan States (CEN-SAD) held in Cotonou in June 2008.

Meanwhile, the presidential election due in 2011 was the subject of much speculation throughout 2009 and into 2010. In May 2009 a new movement supportive of Yayi, the Union pour la Majorité Présidentielle Plurielle, was established. However, the President continued to struggle to secure legislative approval for government proposals and imposed his budget for 2010 by decree, following its rejection by the Assemblée nationale in December 2009. Meanwhile, in September G4 and Force Clé agreed to contest the presidential election jointly, and in April 2010, grouped in the Union Fait la Nation (UN), the parties designated Adrien Houngbédji, the leader of the PRD, as their single candidate.

Yayi announced the formation of a new Government in June 2010; eight new ministers were appointed, including Modeste Kérékou, the son of former President Kérékou, as Minister of Youth, Sports and Leisure, although the most senior positions remained unchanged. However, Zinzindohoué was dismissed as Minister of the Interior and Public Security in early July owing to his alleged involvement in a financial scheme that was believed to have defrauded its depositors. Later that month, following demonstrations by investors in the scheme, who accused government officials of having effectively endorsed the company involved, a group of some 50 deputies signed a letter addressed to Nago, the President of the Assemblée nationale, demanding the initiation of legal proceedings against President Yayi in connection with the scandal. Nago dismissed the letter, stating that it contained no evidence that warranted mounting a case against Yayi. The collapse of the scheme, investors in which numbered at least 70,000, had reportedly resulted in the loss of more than 100,000m. francs CFA.

In September 2010 the Constitutional Court nullified legislation adopted by the Assemblée nationale in the previous month that had provided for an increase in the number of deputies in the Assemblée nationale from 83 to 99 and the introduction of a 20% quota for the representation of women on party lists for parliamentary elections. The Court asserted that financial resources were insufficient to support an additional 16 deputies and that the quota for female candidates violated constitutional guarantees regarding gender equality, noting that such a quota would only be justifiable if it applied to both sexes or was higher, given that women account for more than 50% of Benin's population.

2011 ELECTIONS: YAYI RETURNED TO OFFICE

The presidential election took place on 13 March 2011, having been postponed twice owing to delays in the registration of voters under the new computerized system and in the distribution of voting cards. Yayi was re-elected in a first round of voting, securing 53.1% of the valid votes cast, according to provisional official results. Of the 13 other candidates, his nearest rival was Houngbédji, who received 35.6% of the votes, followed, with 6.1%, by Abdoulaye Bio Tchané, a former Minister of the Economy and Finance in Kérékou's administration, who had resigned as President of BOAD in order to contest the ballot. Houngbédji disputed the results, alleging widespread irregularities, and declared himself the rightful winner. However, the Constitutional Court confirmed the results at the end of March, rejecting challenges by all three leading candidates (Yayi having claimed a greater margin of victory). A turn-out of 84.8% was recorded. In a ceremony boycotted by the main opposition leaders, President Yayi was inaugurated to serve a second term in office on 6 April.

Legislative elections were held on 30 April 2011 and contested by some 1,600 candidates representing 19 parties and alliances. According to final results validated by the Constitutional Court on 9 May, the FCBE secured 41 seats, while the UN obtained 30. The remaining 12 seats were divided between six minor political movements, four of which were deemed to be loyal to Yayi, who could thus anticipate the support of a total of 49 of the 83 members of the new Assemblée nationale. The rate of voter participation was notably low, at an estimated 48%. Nago was re-elected as President of the Assemblée nationale later in May.

Yayi announced the formation of a new Government on 28 May 2011, appointing Koupaki as Prime Minister. The creation of such a position (provision for which did not exist in the Constitution) had been one of Yayi's election campaign pledges. Other notable appointees to the Council of Ministers, which was reduced from 35 to 26 members (eight of whom were women), included Adidjatou Mathys as the first female Minister of the Economy and Finance, Benoît Assouan Dègla, a former presidential adviser, as Minister of the Interior and Public Security, and Blaise Ahanhanzo-Glèlè, a member of the RB, as Minister of the Environment, Housing and Town Planning. Yayi's parliamentary support increased to 61 of the Assemblée nationale's 83 deputies, following the defection from the opposition to the presidential majority of several parties, most significantly the RB, which held nine seats.

The decision to award a 25% pay increase to civil servants at the Ministry of the Economy and Finance (who had been observing a three-day strike every week for nearly eight months) prompted expressions of concern from international donors regarding the rising wage bill in late May 2011, as well as industrial action by employees at 24 other ministries demanding a similar raise. Civil servants at the Ministry of the Economy and Finance also subsequently renewed their partial strike, after their salary increase was rescinded in response to a ruling by the Constitutional Court in June that it violated constitutional provisions regarding equality. The dispute was resolved in July, when the Government agreed to a 25% pay rise for all civil servants, to be implemented in 2011 for those employed by the Ministry of the Economy and Finance and in stages during 2011–14 for the others. Following a 48-hour strike by customs officers in mid-September 2011, which paralysed operations at the port of Cotonou, the Assemblée nationale adopted legislation removing the right to strike from so-called 'paramilitary' personnel (including customs officers and officials employed in the forestry and water industries), in addition to soldiers and members of the security forces. Trade union leaders and the UN condemned the new law.

Constitutional reform was under consideration in 2011–12. However, in October 2011 the Constitutional Court ruled that certain articles of the Constitution, including those related to the presidential term and the age limit for presidential candidates, could not form part of a proposed referendum on constitutional amendments.

President Yayi assumed personal responsibility for the defence portfolio as part of a government reorganization effected in April 2012, with Issifou Kogui N'Douro, hitherto Minister of State, in charge of National Defence, appointed as Minister of State, in charge of Presidential Affairs. Among other changes, Mathys was dismissed as Minister of the Economy and Finance, being replaced by Jonas Gbian, hitherto Minister of Energy, Mining and Petroleum Research, Water and the Development of Renewable Energy Sources, who was in turn succeeded by Sofiatou Onifade Babamoussa. Gbian's greatest challenge in his new post was to reverse a sharp decline in government revenue, notably through implementing a reform of the customs system.

EXTERNAL AFFAIRS

Benin has contributed to several regional peace-keeping operations in recent years. Troops from Benin participated in ECOWAS peace-keeping missions in Côte d'Ivoire from early 2003 and in Liberia from September of that year, and were subsequently incorporated into the UN operations that followed in both countries. Beninois soldiers were also involved in the UN Mission in Sudan that was authorized in March 2005 and the UN Mission in the Republic of South Sudan that succeeded it following the independence of South Sudan in July 2011, as well as in UN peace-keeping operations in the Democratic Republic of the Congo from April 2005, and in the UN mission that was conducted in the Central African Republic and Chad from September 2007 to December 2010.

Benin maintains generally good relations with neighbouring countries, and joined CEN-SAD in March 2002; the country hosted the 10th CEN-SAD summit in Cotonou in June 2008, when President Yayi assumed the chairmanship of the organization. None the less, in mid-2000 a long-term dispute between Benin and Niger over the ownership of various small islands in the Niger river erupted once more after Nigerien soldiers reportedly sabotaged the construction of a Beninois administrative building on Lété Island. Meetings between representatives of Benin and Niger, and subsequent arbitration by the Organization of African Unity (now the African Union), failed to resolve the dispute, and in April 2002 the two countries officially ratified an agreement (signed in June 2001) to refer the dispute to the International Court of Justice (ICJ) at The Hague, Netherlands, for arbitration. In July 2005 the Chamber of the ICJ issued its judgment on the delineation of the border between Benin and Niger, ruling that 16 of the 25 islands, including Lété, belonged to Niger; both countries' Governments accepted the ruling. Meanwhile, in November 2004 Nigerien traders and haulage contractors commenced a boycott of the port of Cotonou in response to the fatal shooting in the city of two Nigeriens by Beninois gendarmes in September. President Kérékou visited Niger in December in an attempt to ease tensions resulting from the shooting. The boycott was ended in January 2005 following a meeting between the Nigerien President, Mamadou Tandja, and the Beninois Minister of Foreign Affairs and African Integration, Rogatien Biaou, in Niamey, the capital of Niger, during which Biaou announced that the Beninois Government would pay compensation to the families of the victims.

Benin and Nigeria launched joint police patrols along their common border in August 2001, following concerns about cross-border crime and the reported import of small arms from Benin to Nigeria. Renewed concerns about cross-border crime prompted the Nigerian authorities to close the border unilaterally in August 2003. Following a meeting between the Presidents of the two countries later in the month, the frontier was reopened and measures aimed at enhancing co-operation to combat cross-border crime were announced. In July 2004 it was reported that a joint commission had amicably resolved a dispute over the land and maritime boundary between Benin and Nigeria. None the less, tensions remained over the smuggling of goods, particularly fuel, from Nigeria to Benin, and in January 2005 enhanced joint patrols of the common border were launched. In April Presidents Obasanjo and Kérékou signed a bilateral trade agreement aimed at curbing smuggling and other cross-border crime, as well as enhancing trade relations. Shortly after his inauguration in April 2006, President Yayi's first official foreign visit was to Nigeria, where he held discussions with Obasanjo. In August Yayi and Obasanjo signed a treaty on the maritime boundary between Benin and Nigeria, while the two countries' Ministers of Foreign Affairs signed a memorandum of understanding on the establishment of a joint standing committee to delineate the land boundary. At a summit meeting held in the Nigerian capital, Abuja, in February 2007, Yayi, Obasanjo and the President of Togo, Faure Gnassingbé, announced the formation of a 'co-prosperity zone', aimed at accelerating the integration of their national economies and promoting peace, stability and development in West Africa. Later that month the electricity networks of Benin and Nigeria were officially connected, enabling energy to be supplied from Nigeria to Benin (and also to Togo) at a lower cost. Furthermore, a pipeline to transport natural gas from Nigeria to Benin, Togo and Ghana commenced operations in 2010.

In response to mounting concern regarding piracy in the Gulf of Guinea, at the beginning of August 2011 President Yayi announced that he had sought UN assistance to counter attacks, while a group of international maritime insurers added the waters of Benin to a list of areas deemed to be of high risk. Later that month a French frigate, in co-operation with Benin's naval forces, conducted a surveillance mission in the area as part of efforts to combat piracy. Meanwhile, at a meeting in Abuja, Yayi and his Nigerian counterpart, Goodluck Jonathan, agreed to take co-ordinated action against piracy, as well as cross-border banditry and terrorism, and in September Benin and Nigeria commenced joint naval patrols in the Gulf of Guinea. Also in September, during an official visit by Yayi to the People's Republic of China, where he held talks with President Hu Jintao, Chinese financial support offered to Benin notably included funding of 2,800m. francs CFA for a patrol boat to enhance maritime security. In October the UN Security Council adopted a resolution condemning piracy in the Gulf of Guinea. In the following month, as UN experts conducted an assessment into the threat of piracy in the area, it was reported that the number of vessels entering the port of Cotonou had declined by some 70% since piracy had begun to affect the waters off Benin, owing not only to fear of attack but also to higher insurance premiums. In a report submitted in January 2012, the UN assessment mission concluded that a failure to act against piracy in the Gulf of Guinea would be 'catastrophic'—noting, *inter alia*, Benin's heavy reliance on port activities (which provide some 80% of national fiscal revenue)—and, while praising existing regional anti-piracy efforts, in particular the joint patrols by Benin and Nigeria, emphasized the need for a longer-term strategy, supported by substantial international assistance. According to the International Maritime Bureau, there were 20 attacks off Benin's coast in 2011, eight of which resulted in successful hijackings.

From late April 2005 thousands of Togolese sought refuge in Benin, having fled the violence that followed a presidential election in their country. The Beninois Government appealed for some US $5m. in international aid to support its efforts to assist the refugees. By the end of the year the office of the UN High Commissioner for Refugees (UNHCR) had registered 26,632 Togolese refugees in Benin, many of whom were living with family and friends. Many refugees subsequently returned to Togo, following the restoration of stability in that country; by the end of 2006 9,444 remained in Benin, according to UNHCR. In April 2007 Benin, UNHCR and Togo signed an agreement on the voluntary repatriation of the remaining refugees; at the end of 2011 5,883 Togolese refugees were registered with UNHCR in Benin.

In May 2009 it was announced that the Presidents of Benin and Burkina Faso had decided to refer a long-running border dispute to the ICJ; an agreement to this effect was signed in September and was ratified by Benin's Assemblée nationale in May 2010, although the case had not been formally submitted to the Court by April 2012. Pending a verdict by the Court, the disputed 68-sq km area was to remain neutral and to be administered and financed jointly.

Economy

PAUL MELLY

INTRODUCTION

Like most West African countries, Benin is heavily reliant on agriculture, with cotton being the principal cash crop, particularly in the north. There is some industrial activity and plantation forestry in the south. With average gross domestic product (GDP) per head of US $360 in 2011, Benin is not among the poorest West African countries. It lacks major energy or mineral resources, but the economic base is relatively diverse, particularly in the south, where business activity is well developed. Commerce and services related to trade account for two-thirds of GDP.

Benin is distinguished from most other members of the Economic Community of West African States (ECOWAS) and the Union Economique et Monétaire Ouest-Africaine (UEMOA) by the large scale of its economic activity related to Nigeria. As by far the largest market in the region, with 155m. people, this giant eastern neighbour exercises a huge influence on Benin (with a population of only 9m.): trade with Nigeria accounts for more than one-third of GDP. Cotonou, Benin's main city and port, is an important channel for Nigerian external trade flows and in 2003 a temporary Nigerian ban on certain imports produced a decline of more than 25% in Benin's export revenues. However, much cross-border activity is unregulated; for example, fuel smuggled in from Nigeria is widely sold in the informal market. Benin is also an important trade gateway to landlocked Niger and Burkina Faso, and migrants from Niger work in Cotonou.

Since its economy is more externally oriented than in West Africa, Benin was more sharply affected by the global economic crisis than other UEMOA states. Activity was also damaged by the weakness of the global market for cotton, a principal cash crop in central-northern regions.

Benin's modern economic transformation followed the abandonment of one-party Marxist rule in 1990–91 and the pursuit of a gradual transition to the market system. The first democratically elected head of state, Nicéphore Soglo, a former IMF and World Bank official, sought to liberalize economic activity and stabilize national finances. His reform programme was supported by international partners through an IMF programme, enhanced aid flows and debt relief.

A crucial stimulus to growth was produced by the devaluation of the CFA franc—the common currency of the UEMOA countries—in 1994. Pegged to the French franc, the CFA had strengthened against the US dollar, hindering the competitiveness of Benin and other franc zone states. Devaluation of the currency to a new fixed rate at one-half of the old value increased the cost of living for urban populations that consumed imported consumer goods—including bread, made from imported wheat flour. The cost of industrial components and imported fuel also rose sharply. However, devaluation dramatically boosted the competitiveness of the rural economy, upon which most of the population depends; this stimulated both the export sector and domestic demand for locally produced food.

Nevertheless, the reduction in urban household purchasing power undermined Soglo's popularity and he was defeated in the 1996 election. Former President Mathieu Kérékou returned to power (from 1996 to 2006), but continued Soglo's economic policies of monetary and fiscal discipline, and economic liberalization, in close partnership with the IMF and international donors.

Benin secured large reductions in its external debt service burden under the Heavily Indebted Poor Countries (HIPC) initiative and the Multilateral Debt Relief Initiative (MDRI), accompanied by increased policy emphasis on poverty reduction and grassroots development. Yet, Benin has made less progress in reducing poverty than almost any other peaceful and stable low income sub-Saharan country. Real GDP per head rose by only 0.9% between 2004 and 2008, and has since almost stagnated, although there were signs of greater progress in 2012.

The progress of liberalization has been uneven, impeded by administrative and political obstacles. Public scepticism about privatization has been heightened by allegations of corruption, notably in relation to the disposal of the fuel distributor SONACOP (the Société Nationale de Commercialisation des Produits Pétroliers); in 2008 the state reclaimed a 55% stake in the company that had been sold to a private company in 1999. The Government began to instigate reforms in the cotton sector in 2000, ending the monopsony of the Société Nationale pour la Promotion Agricole (SONAPRA), but the reform process has been prolonged. In late 2007 the Government suspended the privatization of SONAPRA and the formation of the Société de Développement du Coton (SODECO)—in which the Government held only a 35% stake—because of reported irregularities. Eventually, the Government proceeded with the establishment of SODECO, but the company soon experienced serious difficulties, and by 2010 cotton production was falling.

Planned reforms in other sectors also suffered delays. A telecommunications regulator and a new national operator, Bénin Télécoms (BT), were established in 2003–04, but government hopes of selling the heavily indebted company to Maroc Télécom or Orange were not realized. Water and energy services were separated in 2003, but the Société Nationale des Eaux du Bénin (SONEB—water) and the Société Béninoise d'Énergie Électrique (SBEE—power) remain parastatal entities; the latter has serious financial problems, with estimates of its debts ranging from 17,000m. francs CFA to 30,000m. francs CFA, and has been accused of focusing investment on the home regions of its senior managers. Generating capacity has failed to keep pace with demand and power cuts are frequent. The Government aims to stimulate investment in the power sector with plans to create a regulatory structure.

Despite these reverses, the administration of President Boni Yayi, who succeeded Kérékou in 2006 and was re-elected in 2011, has maintained Benin's commitment to the long-term process of economic liberalization. The operation of the container terminal at Cotonou port was transferred to the French group Bolloré in 2009 and the Government has also sought to reduce state involvement in the textiles, petroleum, cement, hotels and brewing sectors. The banking sector is already largely owned by commercial interests: Banque Internationale du Bénin is Nigerian-owned, while Financial Bank Bénin is mainly Swiss-owned; the Moroccan-based Banque Marocaine du Commerce Extérieur is a major shareholder in the Bank of Africa group, of which the Benin bank has 38 branches. The pan-African Ecobank group also operates in the country.

Like most other West African countries, Benin has managed to sustain a positive rate of real GDP growth in recent years, despite the global financial crisis and rising world prices for food and energy. GDP growth declined from 5% in 2008 to 2.7% the following year and 2.5% in 2010, as the global crisis had a negative impact on activity. Benin also suffered from a poor cotton harvest in 2009 and a dramatic contraction in foreign direct investment in 2008 and 2009. However, real GDP growth rebounded to 3.1% in 2011 and to an estimated 3.5% in 2012. Benin has been adversely affected by the impact of an increase in domestic fuel prices in Nigeria, from where large volumes of fuel flow into the Beninois market. This has resulted in a sharp rise in inflation, to an estimated 7% in 2012.

In June 2010 the IMF approved a three-year Extended Credit Facility (ECF) of US $109m. for Benin. Initial progress under the programme was hindered by weak domestic demand, the impact of the global economic crisis and unexpected spending pressures, particularly after Benin suffered its worst floods in five decades in late 2010. The floods caused many deaths and left 150,000 people homeless. Flood damage cost Benin's economy and society 125,000m. francs CFA ($250m.), equivalent to 4% of GDP; agricultural sector losses were estimated at 30,000m. francs CFA, while damage to infrastructure was estimated at 56,000m. francs CFA. The quality of bank loan portfolios weakened. However, the IMF consequently agreed to postpone key programme targets and

Benin has since made a significant recovery, with resurgent growth, progress in increasing rates of government revenue collection and the launch of customs reforms. In July 2012 the Fund judged that sufficient progress had been made for the release of a fourth tranche of funding under the ECF arrangement.

POPULATION AND EMPLOYMENT

Almost three-quarters of Benin's approximately 9.4m. (according to 2012 UN estimates) inhabitants live in the southern regions, where there is a population density of more than 200 people per sq km, one of the highest in West Africa. Population density is lower in the less fertile and more arid north of the country. The past two decades have seen a marked drift of population into the main urban areas, which were home to 42% of all Beninois by 2010, around double the level of 1990. While the national rate of population growth is projected to average 2.7% annually over 2010–15, urban population has been rising by 4.1% per year. Official figures reported the population of Cotonou at more than 760,000 in 2006, but some estimates suggest that in fact the conurbation may now be home to as many as 1.2m.

Benin has a strong cultural identity, exemplified by the Dan Homey kingdom and the continuing importance of the Vodoun religion, and long-standing educational and intellectual traditions; the latter contribute to the vigour of modern democratic and media culture. Educational standards are relatively high and the country is host to a number of research institutions. However, there is a shortage of appropriate employment opportunities for graduates.

While agriculture, livestock and fishing engage around one-half of the work-force, the public sector has also traditionally been a significant source of employment. It accounted for about one-half of wage and salary earners in the early 1990s, although this proportion later declined as the Soglo and Kérékou administrations sought to contain public expenditure and reduce the state's role in the economy: the number of civil servants declined from 40,053 in 1990 to 30,619 in 1999. However, the effectiveness of the administration has been undermined by the poor and erratic remuneration of civil servants. For much of the 1990s the levels of salary actually paid to staff fell behind the official grade-based salary structure, and by the end of 2006 the accumulated wage arrears were equal to 7.1% of GDP. The problem has since persisted, even affecting Benin's diplomatic missions abroad.

AGRICULTURE, FORESTRY AND FISHERIES

The economy is largely dependent on the agricultural sector, which accounts for 32% of GDP but provides the livelihood for a much greater share of the workforce. Since a drought in the early 1980s, output of the major food crops has risen strongly, reflecting both improved climatic conditions and a transfer of emphasis from cash crops to the cultivation of staple foods. In 2005 the Government finalized a food security strategy prepared with the support of FAO, which stressed issues such as improved use of water resources, arrangements for stocking food reserves, small-scale livestock-raising and farming in urban fringe areas. Benin is now broadly self-sufficient in basic foods. However, 12% of the population is still undernourished, and 38% of children suffer from stunted growth because of malnutrition. Output of most key food crops fluctuates, with cassava production increasing from 2.3m. metric tons in 2007/08 to 3.6m. tons in 2008/09, but falling back to 2.3m. tons in 2010/11, while the yam harvest rose from 1.7m. tons in 2007/08 to 2.5m. tons the following year, but then stagnated. Output of paddy rice increased from 73,000 tons in 2007/08 to 109,400 tons in 2008/09, before slipping back to a level of just over 80,000 tons a year; production of maize fell, to only 920,000 tons in 2010/11, from 1m. tons the previous year, while output of millet and sorghum also declined sharply in 2010/11, to 130,200 tons, from 162,300 tons the previous year. Crops that are grown in the northern Sahel and savannah regions are vulnerable to periodic droughts, which can dramatically reduce output from the levels experienced in years of good harvests. The area of land planted with food crops rose from 1.7m. ha in 2008 to more than 2m. ha in 2009. In part, this may reflect the troubled condition of the world cotton market, which might lead some farmers to switch land from cotton to the production of food crops for sale in local markets. Benin has been importing around 200,000 tons of rice each year, leaving the country exposed to the high level of global grain prices; however, FAO is supporting a project to hugely expand domestic production.

In the past the major cash crop was oil palm, which remains the principal tree crop. Output of palm products, which was formerly based on natural plantations, covering 400,000 ha, benefited in the 1970s from intensive cultivation on some 30,000 ha of industrial plantations, partly financed by French aid. Production of palm kernels was estimated at 50,000 metric tons in 1976, palm kernel oil at more than 21,000 tons, and palm oil at almost 50,000 tons. However, output subsequently fell, owing to low producer prices and the overvaluation of the CFA franc. By the mid-1990s combined marketed production of palm oil and palm kernel oil had sunk to an average of only 15,000–20,000 tons per year, but it later rebounded, reaching 46,800 tons in 2005. The figure for marketed production is distorted by the incidence of smuggling from Nigeria (in order to secure payment in the 'hard currency' CFA franc, rather than naira).

Today the most valuable commercial crop is cotton: exports were worth an estimated 60,100m. francs CFA (US $135m.) in 2010—some 11% of domestically produced exports (excluding goods imported for re-export to neighbouring states). The 1980s and early 1990s saw steady growth in cotton output, but in recent years the crop has been in decline. This is largely due to difficult international circumstances. The strength of the CFA franc, which is pegged to the euro, hampers the competitiveness of the Beninois cotton sector, particularly following the world liberalization of world textiles trade, which has left poor African producers struggling to compete against large industrial producers from Asia. Problems are compounded by the lack of progress in world trade talks, where West African countries have so far failed in their campaign to secure an end to the subsidization of cotton production in developed countries, particularly the USA. However, the cotton sector has also been affected by local issues in Benin, including management problems at the cotton-marketing board, a lack of timely and effective distribution of inputs, disputes over cotton seed prices, the diversion of fertilizers and late planting. In 2002 the restructuring of SONAPRA contributed to a record output of 485,522 tons. However, the crop has since suffered a dramatic decline, with output of only 268,600 tons in 2007/08, sinking further each year, to a mere 134,900 tons in 2010/11. While cotton output has declined, production of groundnuts—another dryland cash crop—has been rising, from 114,500 tons in 2007/08 to an estimated 166,400 tons in 2010/11. Some farmers may have switched from cotton to groundnuts. However, in 2010 the Government launched a new programme of support for cotton growers, which raised the producer price to 250 francs CFA per kg (from 190 francs CFA per kg hitherto). This led to a 30,000 ha increase in the area planted with cotton, reaching 175,000 ha by the end of July 2010, suggesting that a significant recovery in cotton output may be feasible.

Whereas cotton is grown mainly in the more arid north, the climate of the south, with two rainy seasons, permits the cultivation of other cash crops including coffee and cocoa. The marketed production of cocoa and coffee tends to vary widely, since much of the recorded production originates in Nigeria. Groundnuts and karité nuts (sheanuts) are also grown. In 2010 the Government launched a farm sector recovery programme, which was partly intended to encourage the growth of small businesses related to agriculture.

In 2010, according to FAO estimates, cattle herds numbered 2.0m. head, sheep and goats 2.4m., and pigs (kept mainly in the south) 368,000. Livestock farming is practised in its traditional form in the north.

Exploitation of timber resources (mainly for fuel) is still limited, although rising, with annual roundwood production for sale as timber products amounting to 427,000 cu m in 2010, according to FAO estimates. There are plantations of teak in the centre-south of the country. Roundwood production for sale as timber and veneer is dwarfed by the cutting of firewood, which was estimated at 6.3m. cu m in 2010. The environmental impact of firewood-cutting is partly offset by a programme of reafforestation around populated areas.

Food supply is also supplemented by fishing, the majority of which takes place in inland waters, although in recent years the traditional sector has been in decline, owing to salination of the lagoons around Cotonou. Fishing is mainly based on artisanal fishing, with the annual total catch recorded at just over 40,000 metric tons in 2010. Additionally, in the late 1990s many instances of unregulated fishing vessels, including Nigerian artisanal and semi-industrial vessels and other foreign vessels, operating illicitly within Benin's exclusive economic zone were reported.

MINING AND POWER

Although phosphates, kaolin, chromium, rutile, gold and iron ore have been located in the north, the only minerals so far exploited are limestone (for cement), marble, petroleum and natural gas, and mining contributed only a projected 0.3% of GDP in 2009. Production of petroleum in Benin began in the Sémé oilfield, 15 km off shore from Cotonou, in 1982, with initial output averaging 4,000 barrels per day (b/d). Production reached a peak of 9,000 b/d in 1985, with the entry into operation of a third well and of water-injection facilities, but ceased at the end of 1998, as a result of declining reserves, combined with low world prices for crude petroleum. In October 1999, however, Zetah Oil signed a contract to rehabilitate the oilfield, and subsequently signed a 25-year production contract for the field, which was estimated to retain petroleum reserves of some 22m. barrels. Exploration for oil and gas was accelerated in late 2002, with concessions being granted to Canadian and US companies. However, by the late 2000s output was negligible.

Electricity supply (512.8m. kWh in 2003) comes largely from the Akosombo hydroelectric dam in Ghana, as operations at the 62-MW installation on the frontier with Togo at Nangbeto, on the Mono river, which began in 1988, have tended to be sporadic. A second dam, with 104 MW capacity, was under construction at Adjarala, with the aim of achieving eventual self-sufficiency in power for both Benin and Togo. Benin has energy coverage of 30%, according to the SBEE. In 2006 Benin experienced energy problems when the Ghana Volta River Authority and Compagnie Ivoirienne d'Électricité, which together provided over 70% of Benin's energy supply, reduced their exports due to low water levels. This was compounded by the cessation of energy production at the Nangbeto Dam in 2007, which also affected exports to Benin. In February 2007, meanwhile, an electrical interconnection linking Communauté Electrique du Bénin, which delivers power to Benin and Togo, and the Nigerian Electricity Power Authority, was inaugurated by the heads of state of Benin, Ghana, Togo and Nigeria. This interconnection was to ensure continuity between the power grids of Nigeria, Benin, Togo, Côte d'Ivoire, Niger and Burkina Faso, and would consequently, it was hoped, serve to decrease future instances of power shortages. Nevertheless, and despite Government pledges to implement reforms in the energy sector (including the long-anticipated privatization of SBEE) in order to increase the sector's efficiency, power shortages were expected to remain an issue.

The 678-km West African Gas Pipeline, which supplies Nigerian natural gas to Benin, Togo and Ghana, became operational in 2009. Imports of petroleum products accounted for 11.2% of the value of Benin's total imports in 2010, but are supplemented by smuggled imports from Nigeria.

MANUFACTURING

Manufacturing activity is still small-scale and, apart from the construction materials, beer and soft drinks industries, is mainly confined to the processing of primary products for export (cotton-ginning, oil palm-processing), or import substitution of simple consumer goods. The secondary sector contributed only 0.3% to overall GDP growth in 2010, because of cuts in expenditure on public works projects. The index of industrial production contracted by 21.1% in 2009 and a further 1% in 2010, reflecting the decline in cotton output. Cotton-processing has been the most important activity since the late 1980s. With capacity at 560,000 metric tons, there is excess capacity over national cotton production and almost all cotton exports now take the form of ginned cotton or other downstream products. Other agricultural processing plants—for maize, cashew nuts and vegetables—have been rehabilitated to supply the stronger domestic and foreign markets. Two major cotton-oil processing plants ceased operations in early 2005.

Cement and sugar joint ventures established with Nigeria in the early 1980s proved unprofitable, and their management was leased out to overseas investors in 1999. The cement plant at Onigbolo began production in 1982, but plans to sell one-half the scheduled output of 600,000 tons per year to Nigeria failed to materialize. Despite pressure from international donors, successive governments were slow to implement plans for the privatization of Onigbolo; but a transfer of ownership was finally completed in 2010, after a transitional period under leased commercial management. This left France's Lafarge with a 51% stake, while the Nigerian group Dangote took 43%. Cement imports and prices were liberalized with effect from August 2002. Annual output of hydraulic cement of 200,000–250,000 tons was recorded in 1999–2006. The Senegalese group Ciments du Sahel is developing a 170,000m. francs CFA plant at Massé, which is claimed to be one of the largest private sector projects in Benin.

The Savé sugar complex has also had a troubled history; a 2001 estimate suggested that rehabilitation of the complex, under the management of a Mauritian company, would cost 16,000m. francs CFA. Chinese investors expressed some interest in the plant, but later expressed doubts. Conditions attached to the resumption of Benin's IMF programme in 1999 included the privatization of the petroleum company, SONACOP, and the Société Industrielle des Textiles. A 55% stake in SONACOP was sold, but was subsequently reclaimed by the Government (see above).

THE SERVICES SECTOR

The services sector is the largest sector in economic terms, accounting for a projected 50.5% of GDP in 2009; the tertiary sector as a whole contributed 1.4% of real GDP growth in 2010 (compared with 1.3% the previous year). The sector consists mainly of trade and commerce (which contributed a projected 35.9% of the GDP of the tertiary sector in 2006), transport, telecommunications and other personal services, as well as the relatively large public administration. Five private banks were established in the 1990s, and a small regional stock exchange (the Bourse Régionale des Valeurs Mobilières, with its head office in Abidjan, Côte d'Ivoire) was founded in 1998. Transport and port services are an important activity, owing to Cotonou's role as a trade gateway for Nigeria and for land-locked Sahelian countries (see below). Tourism still remains underdeveloped in Benin, with most infrastructure being concentrated in Cotonou. Receipts from tourism (including passenger transport) amounted to US $216.0m. in 2008. According to the World Bank, the GDP of the services sector increased at an average annual rate of 4.0% in 2000–07; output of the sector grew by 4.6% in 2007. However, services activity has been affected by the general trading slowdown over recent years, as a result of troubled international conditions. In 2010 a number of illegal and fraudulent microfinance schemes collapsed, having accumulated savings from 150,000 depositors equivalent to about 5% of GDP; the Government seized the assets of these entities and launched a scheme to reimburse small depositors from the assets. The crisis did not cause serious damage to the formal banking system.

Transport Infrastructure

Benin's transport infrastructure is comparatively good. Most internal transportation uses the country's road network: in 2011 the classified road network totalled some 30,000 km, about 6% of which was paved. A number of major road construction schemes, including the upgrading of the 222-km Dassa–Parakou link of the Cotonou–Niger highway, have been implemented, with financial support from the European Community (now European Union—EU), the African Development Bank (AfDB) and the Arab Bank for Economic Development in Africa. By the construction of new roads and the upgrading of existing routes, it is hoped to develop the country's status as an entrepôt for regional trade. Benin's foreign earnings benefit from the transit trade from Niger via the 579-km Benin–Niger railway. There have long been plans to extend the line from Parakou to Niamey, but the project's implementation has been hampered by Niger's economic circumstances and strained budget resources, and the two cities remain at present linked only by road. However, in 2010 Niger announced that it would commission studies for the project.

The port of Cotonou handles 3.0m.–5.4m. metric tons of freight per year, of which up to 1m. tons has typically been transit trade with Niger and Burkina Faso, and some 300,000 second-hand motor vehicles, nearly all of which are destined for Burkina Faso, Chad, Mali, Niger and Nigeria. In August 2009 the Government awarded a 25-year concession to rehabilitate and manage the port to Société de Manutention du Terminal à Conteneurs de Cotonou, part of the French Bolloré Group. Despite strong competition from Lomé in Togo, freight traffic through Cotonou still grew by 4.5% in 2010, reaching 7m. tons; container traffic rose by 2.7%, to 200,000 20-ft (6-m) equivalent units (TEU). The construction of a new deepwater quay was expected to double container throughput capacity, while the launch of an electronic single administrative window in March 2011 should accelerate the processing of cargo. The retail and small trading sector has suffered two years of contraction, with activity falling by 17.7% in 2009 and a further 3.2% in 2010.

In 2006 the EU, under the eighth European Development Fund, awarded Benin a grant of €23m. for the building of a new road network in Banikoara-Kandi (located in the Benin cotton belt), and it was anticipated that the building of the network would improve conditions for the transport of cotton to the processing facilities and to producers. In December 2007 the Government assigned 6,670m. francs CFA to the expansion of facilities at Cotonou international airport, and in February 2008 President Boni Yayi laid the foundation stone for a second international airport at Parakou.

FINANCE

In 1989–90 political turmoil combined with social and financial pressures to force the downfall of the old one-party system. But four years later Benin's new democracy weathered the urban social strains resulting from devaluation of the CFA franc in 1994 and, since that time, successive governments have managed to advance the process of financial and economic reform without fundamentally endangering political stability. Economic discontents have sometimes contributed to the electoral defeat of an incumbent government in Benin; however, they have not put the functioning of the political system in question.

Benin has benefitted from a broad range of donor assistance. The IMF has been a consistent source of support: while the volume of money that it provides is fairly small, its programmes catalyze aid from other sources because they are taken by other partners as an endorsement of Benin's policies. Benin has received substantial debt relief under the HIPC initiative and, since 2006, the MDRI. This has eased the strain that debt service imposes on government finances: in 2006–09 annual interest payments on government external debt were less than 8,000m. francs CFA (US $17.2m.) each year. Donors who have supported Benin in recent years include the World Bank (for project sectors including education, the national HIV/AIDS programme, food security, the environment, poverty reduction and the restructuring of the cotton sector), the AfDB (for road improvements, rural electrification and debt relief), the Banque Ouest-Africaine de Développement (BOAD—for urban regeneration) and the World Food Programme (in the form of food aid). There have also been a number of bilateral initiatives, including finance from France (for poverty reduction, support of the cotton sector, decentralization, language training, development of the national parks, road rehabilitation and the development of the media), Denmark (for transport infrastructure, health care, the agricultural sector, the promotion of democracy, and water supply and treatment) and Germany (for infrastructure and health care projects). Non-EU countries that have provided financial assistance to Benin include Switzerland (to fund a population census), Canada (in support of the HIV/AIDS programme), the USA (for education, the promotion of democracy and good governance), the People's Republic of China (for rural development projects) and Japan (for equipment finance, healthcare and food aid).

Despite this external support, the Government's increased expenditure on poverty reduction programmes, support for the cotton sector and the impact on revenue of the economic slowdown in certain business sectors has exerted continuing strain on state finances. The budget deficit was equivalent to 1.1% of GDP in 2008, but rose dramatically to 4.8% the following year, before sinking back to 0.7% in 2010. The cost of flood damage is believed to have resulted in a further increase in the deficit in 2011. According to IMF estimates, the overall fiscal deficit represented 3.1% of GDP in 2010, widening to 4.3% in 2011; the deficit was projected at 3.6% in 2012.

FOREIGN TRADE AND PAYMENTS

Official data have traditionally shown Benin recording a large external trade deficit, but it is hard to gauge the true balance of trade flows in the economy because of the large volumes of goods that pass through informal channels to and from Nigeria without being reported to the authorities. There is also a huge volume of official re-export trade: in 2009 re-exports of imported goods accounted for 241,000m. francs CFA of Benin's total exports of 301,000m. francs CFA. In 2010 re-exports rose to 293,400m. francs CFA (of total exports amounting to 687,600m. francs CFA). The sharp depreciation of the currency in 1994 temporarily narrowed the gap between exports and imports, but this situation did not continue. By 2007 the deficit in trade in goods and services had reached 15.5% of GDP. It has subsequently declined, but still remains in double digits, at 13.2% of GDP in 2009 and an estimated 11.6% in 2010. The main elements of the export account are re-exports and cotton; exports of the latter reached 60,100m francs CFA in 2010. Imports were valued at 901,000m. francs CFA in that year. The principal elements of the import account are capital equipment, petroleum products and food. China is a major source of Benin's imports, accounting for 16.3% of the total in 2010; however, much of this trade is re-exported. Other major suppliers included France, Togo and the Netherlands. The principal market for exports in 2010 was Nigeria. Other major customers were China, India, Chad and Indonesia and.

Historically, the deficit on merchandise trade has been partly covered by remittances from Benin nationals overseas, which were estimated at an annual average of US $60m.–$70m. by the early 2000s. Remittances from Europe to West African countries have generally been adversely affected by the impact of economic slowdown in EU economies since 2008. The deficit on the current account of the balance of payments stood at 277,600m. francs CFA in 2009, falling to 233,600m. francs CFA in 2010; it rebounded to 270,700m. francs CFA in 2011, but is estimated to have declined again, to around 230,000m. francs CFA, in 2012. The inflow of overseas development aid is an important contribution to the current balance. Annual totals can fluctuate due to the phasing of disbursements for one-off projects. However, budget assistance grants remain consistently important, contributing 348,800m. francs CFA in 2009, 262,500m. francs CFA in 2010 and 281,000m. francs CFA in 2011. The principal donors are France, the World Bank (IDA concessional arrangement), the AfDB, the European Commission, the USA, Denmark and Germany.

The devaluation of the CFA franc in January 1994 greatly increased the burden of servicing foreign debt. However, the IMF, the World Bank and the EU implemented a special programme of support for Benin and the other Franc Zone states. Benin subsequently benefited from further waves of debt relief for low-income countries pursuing economic reforms endorsed by the IMF; these culminated in the HIPC and MDRI initiatives which aimed to bring debt service costs down to affordable levels, to leave the Government with more money to spend on poverty reduction, health and education; these basic development concerns were given increased priority in the public expenditure strategies negotiated between the Government and the IMF as part of the HIPC process.

In July 2000, as part of the HIPC initiative, the IMF and the World Bank announced the eventual cancellation of some US $460m. of Benin's debt and announced a further three-year enhanced HIPC programme for 2000–03. Benin became the eighth country to reach 'completion point' under the enhanced HIPC initiative, in March 2003, with the consequence that its creditors became firmly committed to the debt relief provisionally agreed in 2000. In June 2005 Benin was among 18 countries to be granted 100% debt relief on multilateral debt, under the MDRI programme introduced by major multilateral development agencies (with the support of the Group of Eight leading industrialized nations—G8). The country's total external debt at the end of 2009 was $1,100m., most of which was public or publicly guaranteed debt. However, much of the debt is development credit on highly concessional terms and the cost of debt service in 2009 was equivalent to only 2.5% of goods and services export income.

ECONOMIC PROSPECTS

The peaceful transfer of power to President Boni Yayi, the former head of the BOAD, in elections held in March 2006, demonstrated Benin's continued adherence to the democratic process, and the majority achieved in the legislative elections of March 2007 provided Yayi with favourable conditions in which to pursue the continued restructuring of both the public and private sectors and to implement his stated economic vision for accelerating growth and reducing poverty. The re-election of Yayi in March 2011, despite difficult economic circumstances, will enable the Government to maintain a steady economic policy course.

However, corruption poses a serious threat to the effective implementation of reform plans and the delivery of public services. Despite the establishment in September 2004 of a monitoring body, the Observatoire de Lutte Contre la Corruption, the formulation of anti-graft legislation and other initiatives, a survey carried out in 2006 by the AfDB and the World Bank found that 58% of Benin's population considered corruption to be a serious problem. The customs authorities, the legal system, the highway patrol force and the tax authorities were regarded as being particularly corrupt.

The problem of combating corruption is complicated by the scale of cross-border trade. In 2010 there was a marked rise in formal transit trade and a fall in the officially declared volume of imports for home consumption; however, the IMF fears that these official figures may reflect an attempt by traders to circumvent the payment of customs tariffs on imports. Curbing fraud of this type will continue to pose a serious challenge.

In the long term, regional trade liberalization may reduce tariffs and the scope for fraud, but it will also reduce government revenue. The Government therefore needs to extend the tax base into new areas in order to ensure that it has sufficient revenues in the future; it aims to increase fiscal receipts to 18% of GDP by 2014. Benin will also continue to face occasional economic shocks, such as the rise in world food prices in 2008 and the floods of 2010. The 2008 food price crisis forced the Government to buy buffer food stocks and to reduce import duties on nine staple products, including rice, milk, sugar and flour. The Government was obliged to offset the cost of these measures by curbing other expenditure.

For a small economy such as Benin, regional integration and partnerships within West Africa are a key priority. In February 2007, following an initiative of President Yayi and the then Nigerian President, Olusegun Obasanjo, a 'co-prosperity zone' was established encompassing Benin, Nigeria and Togo (with possible membership envisaged for Ghana). It was hoped that this scheme, which aimed to achieve greater integration of the countries' markets in energy, telecommunications and transport, would increase trade and thereby contribute positively to Benin's economic growth. Despite the sharp reduction in GDP growth in 2009 resulting from the global economic crisis (see above), significant progress in structural reforms was made in that year: a concession for management of the port of Cotonou was awarded to a private operator and the restructuring of the state electricity utility began. However, the prospects for privatization in the telecommunications sector remain difficult.

Benin will continue to be heavily dependent on the wider economic climate in West Africa, particularly Nigeria and the Sahelian states. The sharp upturn in inflation, following the rise in Nigerian domestic fuel prices, is a reminder of the country's exposure to economic developments in its giant eastern neighbour. It will also remain vulnerable to global conditions, notably the patterns of remittance flows from Europe and the international market price of cotton.

Statistical Survey

Source (unless otherwise stated): Institut National de la Statistique et de l'Analyse Economique, BP 323, Cotonou; tel. 21-30-82-43; fax 21-30-82-46; e-mail insae@insae-bj.org; internet www.insae-bj.org.

Area and Population

AREA, POPULATION AND DENSITY

Area (sq km)	112,622*
Population (census results)	
15–29 February 1992	4,915,555
11 February 2002	
Males	3,284,119
Females	3,485,795
Total	6,769,914
Population (UN estimates at mid-year)†	
2010	8,849,892
2011	9,099,924
2012	9,351,837
Density (per sq km) at mid-2012	83.0

* 43,484 sq miles.

† Source: UN, *World Population Prospects: The 2010 Revision*.

POPULATION BY AGE AND SEX

(UN estimates at mid-2012)

	Males	Females	Total
0–14	2,039,460	2,013,366	4,052,826
15–64	2,464,787	2,550,250	5,015,037
65 and over	113,299	170,675	283,974
Total	4,617,546	4,734,291	9,351,837

Source: UN, *World Population Prospects: The 2010 Revision*.

ETHNIC GROUPS

2002 (percentages): Fon 39.2 (incl. Fon 17.6; Goun 6.3; Aïzo 4.3; Mahi 3.5; Ouémè 2.5; Torri 2.4; Kotafon 1.4; Tofin 1.3); Adja 15.2 (incl. Adja 8.7; Sahouè 2.6; Xwla 1.4; Mina 1.2); Yoruba 12.3 (incl. Nagot 6.8; Yoruba 1.8; Idaasha 1.5; Holli-Djè 1.4); Bariba 9.2 (incl. Bariba 8.3); Peulh 6.9 (incl. Peulh Fulfuldé 5.5); Otamari 6.1 (incl. Berba 1.4; Ditamari 1.3; Waama 1.0); Yoa Lokpa 4.5 (incl. Yoa 1.8; Lokpa 1.2); Dendi 2.5 (incl. Dendi 2.4); Others 2.7.

ADMINISTRATIVE DIVISIONS
(2012, official projections)

Département	Area (sq km)	Population	Population density (per sq km)
Alibori	25,683	720,812	28.1
Atacora	20,459	759,992	37.1
Atlantique	3,233	1,108,944	343.0
Borgou	25,310	1,001,724	39.6
Collines	13,561	741,326	54.7
Couffo	2,404	725,644	301.8
Donga	10,691	484,230	45.3
Littoral	79	920,013	11,645.7
Mono	1,396	498,028	356.8
Ouémé	2,835	1,010,855	356.6
Plateau	1,865	563,151	302.0
Zou	5,106	829,898	162.5
Total	112,622	9,364,617	83.2

PRINCIPAL TOWNS
(Communes, 2007)

Cotonou	781,902	Bohicon	132,953
Porto-Novo (capital)	262,808	Tchaourou	125,614
Djougou	213,833	Savalou	123,151
Banikoara	178,726	Malanville	119,475
Parakou	176,106	Ketou	118,153
Aplahoue	137,533	Kalale	117,591
Seme-Kpodji	135,473		

Mid-2011 (incl. suburbs, UN estimate): Cotonou 923,923 (Source: UN, *World Urbanization Prospects: The 2011 Revision*).

BIRTHS AND DEATHS
(annual averages, UN estimates)

	1995–2000	2000–05	2005–10
Birth rate (per 1,000)	44.0	42.2	40.7
Death rate (per 1,000)	14.6	13.4	12.4

Source: UN, *World Population Prospects: The 2010 Revision*.

2011: Birth rate 40.5 per 1,000; Death rate 8.7 per 1,000 (Source: African Development Bank).

Life expectancy (years at birth): 55.6 (males 53.8; females 57.5) in 2010 (Source: World Bank, World Development Indicators database).

ECONOMICALLY ACTIVE POPULATION
(persons aged 10 years and over, 1992 census)

	Males	Females	Total
Agriculture, hunting, forestry and fishing	780,469	367,277	1,147,746
Mining and quarrying	609	52	661
Manufacturing	93,157	67,249	160,406
Electricity, gas and water	1,152	24	1,176
Construction	50,959	696	51,655
Trade, restaurants and hotels	36,672	395,829	432,501
Transport, storage and communications	52,228	609	52,837
Finance, insurance, real estate and business services	2,705	401	3,106
Community, social and personal services	126,122	38,422	164,544
Sub-total	1,144,073	870,559	2,014,632
Activities not adequately defined	25,579	12,917	38,496
Total employed	1,169,652	883,476	2,053,128
Unemployed	26,475	5,843	32,318
Total labour force	1,196,127	889,319	2,085,446

Source: ILO, *Yearbook of Labour Statistics*.

2002 (census results): Total employed 2,811,753 (males 1,421,474, females 1,390,279); Unemployed 19,123 (males 12,934, females 6,189); Total labour force 2,830,876 (males 1,434,408, females 1,396,468).

Mid-2012 (estimates in '000): Agriculture, etc. 1,630; Total labour force 3,846 (Source: FAO).

Health and Welfare

KEY INDICATORS

Total fertility rate (children per woman, 2010)	5.3
Under-5 mortality rate (per 1,000 live births, 2010)	115
HIV/AIDS (% of persons aged 15–49, 2009)	1.2
Physicians (per 1,000 head, 2008)	0.06
Hospital beds (per 1,000 head, 2010)	0.5
Health expenditure (2009): US $ per head (PPP)	69
Health expenditure (2009): % of GDP	4.3
Health expenditure (2009): public (% of total)	53.8
Access to water (% of persons, 2010)	75
Access to sanitation (% of persons, 2010)	13
Total carbon dioxide emissions ('000 metric tons, 2008)	4,066.7
Carbon dioxide emissions per head (metric tons, 2008)	0.5
Human Development Index (2011): ranking	167
Human Development Index (2011): value	0.427

For sources and definitions, see explanatory note on p. vi.

Agriculture

PRINCIPAL CROPS
('000 metric tons)

	2008	2009	2010
Rice, paddy	109.4	150.6	167.0*
Maize	978.1	1,205.2	1,132.7*
Millet	36.3	27.4	26.9
Sorghum	142.0	124.0	127.5†
Sweet potatoes	72.9	63.7	77.3
Cassava (Manioc)	3,611.2	3,996.4	4,147.4†
Yams	2,527.3	2,370.9	3,596.0*
Sugar cane	40.9	48.5*	48.0*
Beans, dry	143.6	127.5*	160.0*
Cashew nuts, with shell†	86.0	117.0	69.7
Groundnuts, with shell	115.6	121.0*	117.0*
Coconuts	20.3*	17.5*	17.2†
Oil palm fruit†	255	260	260
Seed cotton	244.6	229.0†	224.9†
Cottonseed*	135	120	110
Tomatoes	184.5	159.0	182.3†
Chillies and peppers, green	46.1	25.8	25.0†
Okra	48.1	49.1†	39.9†
Pineapples	135.0	222.2	220.8†
Cotton (lint)†	100.0	91.5	76.3

* Unofficial figure(s).
† FAO estimate(s).

Aggregate production ('000 metric tons, may include official, semi-official or estimated data): Total cereals 1,268 in 2008, 1,508 in 2009, 1,455 in 2010; Total roots and tubers 6,214 in 2008, 6,434 in 2009, 6,065 in 2010; Total pulses 191 in 2008, 166 in 2009, 203 in 2010; Total vegetables (incl. melons) 389 in 2008, 376 in 2009, 342 in 2010; Total fruits (excl. melons) 283 in 2008, 386 in 2009, 399 in 2010.

Source: FAO.

LIVESTOCK
('000 head, year ending September)

	2008	2009	2010
Cattle	1,908	1,954	2,005
Sheep	781	791	808
Goats	1,549	1,523	1,605
Pigs	340	357	368
Chickens	15,286	15,999	16,550

Source: FAO.

LIVESTOCK PRODUCTS
('000 metric tons, FAO estimates)

	2008	2009	2010
Cattle meat	24.0	24.2	28.7
Goat meat	4.9	5.0	5.1
Pig meat	4.3	4.4	4.6
Chicken meat	21.1	19.7	19.7
Game meat	6.8	7.3	7.8
Cows' milk	29.7	30.5	32.0
Goats' milk	7.7	7.9	8.2
Hen eggs	13.8	13.1	14.0

Source: FAO.

Forestry

ROUNDWOOD REMOVALS
('000 cubic metres, excl. bark)

	2007	2008	2009
Sawlogs, veneer logs and logs for sleepers	130	130*	130*
Other industrial wood*	297	297	297
Fuel wood*	6,141	6,184	6,228
Total*	6,568	6,611	6,655

* FAO estimate(s).

2010–11: Production assumed to be unchanged from 2009 (FAO estimates).

Source: FAO.

SAWNWOOD PRODUCTION
('000 cubic metres, incl. railway sleepers)

	2005	2006	2007
Total (all broadleaved)	31*	146	84

* FAO estimate.

2008–11: Production assumed to be unchanged from 2007 (FAO estimates).

Source: FAO.

Fishing

('000 metric tons, live weight)

	2008	2009	2010
Capture*	37.5	38.9	39.8
Tilapias*	12.8	13.4	13.7
Black catfishes*	1.8	1.9	1.9
Torpedo-shaped catfishes*	1.8	1.9	1.9
Mullets	2.6	2.7	2.8
Sardinellas	0.4	0.8	1.3
Bonga shad	0.9	0.5	0.3*
Freshwater crustaceans*	2.8	2.3	2.0
Penaeus shrimps*	1.5	1.2	1.0
Aquaculture	0.2*	0.4	0.5
Total catch (incl. others)*	37.7	39.3	40.3

* FAO estimate(s).

Note: Figures exclude catches by Beninois canoes operating from outside the country.

Source: FAO.

Mining

	2006	2007	2008
Clay ('000 metric tons)	72.2	77.3	77.0
Gold (kg)	24	19	20
Gravel ('000 cu m)	10.6	25.3	25.0

2009–10: Production assumed to be unchanged from 2008 (estimates).

Source: US Geological Survey.

Industry

SELECTED PRODUCTS
('000 metric tons unless otherwise indicated)

	2008	2009	2010
Cement (hydraulic)	1,500	1,500	1,500
Beer of barley*	76.5	57.0	136.0
Palm oil†	42	44	46
Palm kernel oil†	12.4	13.2	13.2

* Estimates.

† Unofficial figures.

Beer of sorghum ('000 metric tons): 32.8 in 2000; 35.0 in 2001; 41.8 in 2002 (Source: FAO).

Salted, dried or smoked fish ('000 metric tons): 2.0 in 2001; 2.0 in 2002; 2.4 in 2003 (Source: FAO).

Electric energy (million kWh): 128 in 2006; 132 in 2007; 136 in 2008.

Sources: US Geological Survey; FAO; UN Industrial Commodity Statistics Database.

Finance

CURRENCY AND EXCHANGE RATES

Monetary Units

100 centimes = 1 franc de la Communauté Financière Africaine (CFA).

Sterling, Dollar and Euro Equivalents (31 May 2012)

£1 sterling = 819.959 francs CFA;
US $1 = 528.870 francs CFA;
€1 = 655.957 francs CFA;
10,000 francs CFA = £12.20 = $18.91 = €15.24.

Average Exchange Rate (francs CFA per US $)

2009 472.186
2010 495.277
2011 471.866

Note: An exchange rate of 1 French franc = 50 francs CFA, established in 1948, remained in force until January 1994, when the CFA franc was devalued by 50%, with the exchange rate adjusted to 1 French franc = 100 francs CFA. This relationship to the French currency remained in effect with the introduction of the euro on 1 January 1999. From that date, accordingly, a fixed exchange rate of €1 = 655.957 francs CFA has been in operation.

BUDGET
('000 million francs CFA)

Revenue	2009	2010*	2011†
Tax revenue	500.4	525.9	578.0
Taxes on international trade and transactions‡	259.3	278.4	304.0
Direct and indirect taxes	241.2	247.5	273.9
Non-tax revenue	75.4	77.1	72.0
Total	575.8	603.0	650.0

Expenditure	2009	2010*	2011†
Salaries	225.9	238.7	270.0
Pensions and scholarships	39.8	43.6	53.0
Other expenditure and current transfers	212.7	204.4	211.6
Investment	302.3	177.2	233.0
Budgetary contribution	221.6	101.2	133.0
Financed from abroad	80.7	76.0	100.0
Interest due	15.6	17.7	29.9
External debt	8.2	8.1	7.6
Net lending	12.7	20.6	—
Total	809.0	702.2	797.5

* Preliminary figures.
† Projections.
‡ Including value-added taxes on imports.

2012 (projections): Total revenues 710.0; Total expenditure (incl. net lending) 843.9 (Current expenditure 614.2, Capital expenditure and net lending 229.7).

Source: IMF, *Benin: Second Review Under the Three-Year Arrangement Under the Extended Credit Facility and Request for a Waiver of the Nonobservances of a Continuous Performance Criterion — Staff Report; Staff Supplement; Press Release; and Statement by the Executive Director for Benin* (September 2011).

INTERNATIONAL RESERVES
(excluding gold, US $ million at 31 December)

	2009	2010	2011
IMF special drawing rights	77.9	76.6	76.3
Reserve position in IMF	3.4	3.4	3.4
Foreign exchange	1,148.5	1,120.1	807.7
Total	1,229.8	1,200.1	887.4

Source: IMF, *International Financial Statistics*.

MONEY SUPPLY
('000 million francs CFA at 31 December)

	2009	2010	2011
Currency outside banks	339.7	347.6	376.8
Demand deposits at deposit money banks	415.2	449.0	483.4
Checking deposits at post office	8.9	9.1	8.3
Total money (incl. others)	764.3	806.2	869.5

Source: IMF, *International Financial Statistics*.

COST OF LIVING
(Consumer Price Index in Cotonou; base: 2000 = 100)

	2007	2008	2009
Food, beverages and tobacco	112.6	132.9	140.3
Clothing	102.0	102.2	102.1
Rent*	131.4	137.7	141.5
All items (incl. others)	120.8	130.3	133.2

* Including water, electricity, gas and other fuels.

2010: Food, beverages and tobacco 141.6; All items (incl. others) 133.7.

2011: Food, beverages and tobacco 149.6; All items (incl. others) 137.4.

Source: ILO.

NATIONAL ACCOUNTS
('000 million francs CFA at current prices)

Expenditure on the Gross Domestic Product

	2009	2010	2011
Government final consumption expenditure	374.5	385.4	412.2
Private final consumption expenditure	2,365.0	2,489.1	2,604.4
Gross fixed capital formation	651.6	666.0	743.8
Change in inventories	8.1	17.5	32.7
Total domestic expenditure	3,399.2	3,558.0	3,793.1
Exports of goods and services	490.8	490.8	502.3
Less Imports of goods and services	780.6	800.7	852.5
GDP in purchasers' values	3,109.4	3,248.2	3,442.8

Gross Domestic Product by Economic Activity

	2009	2010	2011
Agriculture	1,006.9	1,053.8	1,128.2
Mining and quarrying	7.3	7.4	8.0
Manufacturing	232.0	250.6	272.9
Electricity, gas and water	31.0	33.7	36.2
Construction	135.0	137.7	148.8
Wholesale and retail trade, restaurants and hotels	526.7	537.0	559.0
Finance, insurance and real estate	343.7	361.6	385.0
Transport and communication	256.4	263.9	275.1
Public administration and defence	320.2	330.9	357.7
Sub-total	2,859.2	2,976.6	3,170.9
Indirect taxes	305.3	328.8	333.7
Less Imputed bank service charge	55.2	57.1	61.8
GDP in purchasers' values	3,109.4	3,248.2	3,442.8

Source: African Development Bank.

BALANCE OF PAYMENTS
('000 million francs CFA)

	2008	2009	2010*
Exports of goods f.o.b.	290.1	348.9	405.7
Imports of goods f.o.b.	–696.5	–699.9	–701.4
Trade balance	–406.4	–351.0	–295.7
Exports of services	237.8	171.0	180.6
Imports of services	–228.5	–234.2	–245.2
Balance on goods and services	–397.1	–414.2	–360.4
Income (net)	–5.1	–15.5	–8.9
Balance on goods, services and income	–402.2	–429.7	–369.3
Private unrequited transfers	73.4	32.4	45.8
Public unrequited transfers	88.6	119.7	98.8
Current balance	–240.2	–277.6	–224.7
Capital account (net)	21.6	28.8	19.2
Medium- and long-term public capital	66.4	46.6	68.3
Medium- and long-term private capital	45.0	5.0	30.0
Foreign direct investment	77.8	48.7	58.2
Portfolio investment	9.4	37.6	30.1
Deposit money banks	16.9	–40.2	–57.5
Short-term capital	34.1	27.8	90.0
Net errors and omissions	16.9	38.7	11.4
Statistical discrepancy	—	33.3	—
Overall balance	47.9	–51.3	25.0

* Estimates.

Source: IMF, *Benin: Second Review Under the Three-Year Arrangement Under the Extended Credit Facility and Request for a Waiver of the Nonobservances of a Continuous Performance Criterion — Staff Report; Staff Supplement; Press Release; and Statement by the Executive Director for Benin* (September 2011).

External Trade

PRINCIPAL COMMODITIES

(distribution by HS, US $ million)

Imports c.i.f.	2008	2009	2010
Meat and meat products	123.8	144.9	139.4
Meat and edible offal	123.5	144.6	138.8
Cereals	193.7	95.4	80.4
Rice	184.7	91.5	78.6
Animal and vegetable oils	85.9	74.5	92.4
Palm oil	76.9	67.2	72.6
Salt, sulphur, earth, stone, plaster, lime and cement	36.5	47.5	52.9
Cement, etc.	27.0	39.5	45.7
Mineral fuels, oils, distillation products, etc.	253.9	258.1	308.9
Petroleum oils	170.2	153.2	182.1
Iron and steel	105.3	75.2	64.5
Bars, rods, coils of iron and steel	82.3	58.0	39.7
Pharmaceutical products	60.5	60.8	65.1
Medicament mixtures	50.3	57.1	56.9
Clothing, textile articles, etc.	62.3	57.2	54.2
Warm clothes and articles	58.2	51.6	52.0
Nuclear reactors, boilers, machinery, etc.	73.5	68.2	54.6
Electrical, electronic equipment	63.9	56.4	39.3
Vehicles other than railway, tramway	111.8	114.3	118.6
Cars (incl. station wagons)	53.9	50.4	48.0
Total (incl. others)	1,713.6	1,545.0	1,494.3

Exports f.o.b.	2008	2009	2010
Edible fruit, nuts, peel of citrus fruit, melons	37.4	33.4	30.7
Animal and vegetable oils	39.8	32.5	16.7
Sunflower, cotton-seed oil	1.6	0.4	6.1
Palm oil	10.3	15.8	5.1
Cereals	11.3	38.1	100.3
Rice	11.2	38.1	90.6
Tobacco and manufactured tobacco substitutes	14.1	15.0	n.a.
Cotton	167.8	135.4	105.1
Woven cotton fabrics	8.8	6.0	4.9
Iron and steel	58.9	41.4	27.8
Nuclear reactors, boilers, machinery, etc.	4.8	13.2	7.2
Total (incl. others)	421.1	425.3	434.5

Source: Trade Map-Trade Competitiveness Map, International Trade Centre, www.intracen.org/marketanalysis.

PRINCIPAL TRADING PARTNERS

(US $ million)

Imports c.i.f.	2008	2009	2010
Belgium	75.0	63.4	60.9
Brazil	45.4	44.5	21.9
China, People's Repub.	227.4	208.2	188.7
Côte d'Ivoire	47.5	44.7	37.7
France	288.2	271.7	243.1
Germany	22.5	48.6	53.9
Ghana	25.7	3.3	7.0
Hong Kong	19.6	22.3	8.7
India	17.1	15.6	15.0
Italy	34.4	21.4	22.4
Japan	29.6	21.2	14.8
Malaysia	48.6	50.3	69.1
Netherlands	66.0	77.6	106.0
Nigeria	61.9	48.5	56.2
Norway	12.2	18.2	14.9
Singapore	20.7	13.1	16.1
South Africa	30.3	20.0	16.9
Spain	34.4	33.1	36.0
Sweden	22.7	18.3	7.8
Switzerland	68.2	26.1	22.6
Thailand	102.3	42.8	44.5
Togo	120.4	168.8	162.2
Turkey	4.9	5.9	15.6
Ukraine	35.4	1.2	3.5
United Arab Emirates	31.5	27.2	26.7
United Kingdom	50.3	59.8	52.8
USA	34.9	38.3	36.3
Total (incl. others)	1,713.6	1,549.0	1,494.3

Exports f.o.b.	2008	2009	2010
Burkina Faso	4.9	2.6	1.5
Cameroon	0.2	1.9	4.7
Chad	19.5	22.9	17.7
China, People's Repub.	70.1	78.7	50.6
Côte d'Ivoire	9.8	11.0	2.8
Denmark	9.2	3.8	7.0
France	4.3	2.5	1.2
Ghana	6.5	1.4	2.1
India	38.4	35.0	22.5
Indonesia	24.6	8.7	14.7
Italy	1.5	0.4	5.1
Mali	5.2	5.0	0.1
Malaysia	10.7	5.2	7.6
Morocco	5.6	3.4	3.0
Netherlands	0.7	0.7	7.0
Niger	4.6	8.8	14.0
Nigeria	88.4	169.7	210.8
Pakistan	10.0	3.5	3.0
Portugal	8.7	10.7	7.8
Singapore	1.1	0.7	4.4
Thailand	11.9	6.4	4.1
Togo	6.0	10.4	8.8
Viet Nam	13.4	13.3	10.0
Total (incl. others)	421.1	425.3	434.5

Source: Trade Map-Trade Competitiveness Map, International Trade Centre, www.intracen.org/marketanalysis.

Transport

RAILWAYS

(traffic)

	1998	1999	2000
Passengers carried ('000)	699.8	n.a.	n.a.
Passenger-km (million)	112.0	82.2	156.6
Freight ton-km (million)	218.7	269.0	153.2

Source: mainly IMF, *Benin: Statistical Appendix* (August 2002).

2001 (traffic, million): Passenger-km 101; Net ton-km 316 (Source: UN, *Statistical Yearbook*).

2002 (traffic, million): Net ton-km 482 (Source: UN, *Statistical Yearbook*).

ROAD TRAFFIC

(motor vehicles in use)

	1994	1995	1996
Passenger cars	26,507	30,346	37,772
Buses and coaches	353	405	504
Lorries and vans	5,301	6,069	7,554
Road tractors	2,192	2,404	2,620
Motorcycles and mopeds	220,800	235,400	250,000

2007: Passenger cars 149,310; Buses and coaches 1,114; Lorries and vans 35,656; Motorcycles and mopeds 15,600.

Source: IRF, *World Road Statistics*.

SHIPPING

Merchant Fleet
(registered at 31 December)

	2007	2008	2009
Number of vessels	6	6	7
Total displacement (grt)	1,003	1,003	1,271

Source: IHS Fairplay, *World Fleet Statistics*.

International Sea-borne Freight Traffic
(at Cotonou, including goods in transit, '000 metric tons)

	2004	2005	2006
Goods loaded	488.2	596.1	514.3
Goods in transit	n.a.	n.a.	2.1
Goods unloaded	3,520.6	4,556.8	4,854.8
Goods in transit	n.a.	n.a.	2,462.1

Source: IMF, *Benin: Selected Issues and Statistical Appendix* (August 2008).

CIVIL AVIATION

(traffic on scheduled services, domestic and international)*

	1999	2000	2001
Kilometres flown (million)	3	3	1
Passengers carried ('000)	84	77	46
Passenger-km (million)	235	216	130
Total ton-km (million)	36	32	19

* Including an apportionment of the traffic of Air Afrique.

Source: UN, *Statistical Yearbook*.

Tourism

FOREIGN VISITORS BY COUNTRY OF ORIGIN*

	2007	2008	2009
Angola	10,921	3,504	609
Austria	1,745	295	222
Belgium	3,900	1,910	2,162
Burkina Faso	4,470	10,600	9,700
Burundi	1,240	74	31
Cameroon	11,600	7,244	5,357
Central African Republic	1,047	1,445	840
Chad	1,932	1,481	1,900
Congo, Republic	33,896	12,468	6,839
Côte d'Ivoire	14,745	12,940	7,550
France	14,641	15,846	2,519
Gabon	4,244	10,287	8,313
Germany	2,000	2,718	1,992
Ghana	8,300	4,196	5,126
Guinea	1,967	1,740	422
Madagascar	1,148	332	239
Malawi	890	12	35
Mali	1,400	1,729	1,273
Niger	7,700	5,240	5,900
Nigeria	22,900	21,150	13,184
Senegal	2,880	4,111	3,059
Togo	9,988	6,667	11,551
Tunisia	1,500	1,342	917
USA	1,200	1,448	2,684
Total (incl. others)	186,394	188,000	190,000

* Arrivals of non-resident tourists at national borders, by country of residence.

Total foreign visitors ('000): 199 in 2010.

Receipts from tourism (US $ million, excl. passenger transport): 131 in 2009; 133 in 2010.

Source: World Tourism Organization.

Communications Media

	2009	2010	2011
Telephones ('000 main lines in use)	127.1	133.4	152.7
Mobile cellular telephones ('000 subscribers)	5,033.3	7,074.9	7,765.2
Internet subscribers ('000)	19.4	n.a.	n.a.
Broadband subscribers	1,800	3,600	3,900

Personal computers 60,000 (7.1 per 1,000 persons) in 2007.

Source: International Telecommunication Union.

Television receivers ('000 in use): 272 in 2000 (Source: UNESCO, *Statistical Yearbook*).

2004: Daily newspapers 34 (average circulation 3,000 copies); Non-daily newspapers 24 (average circulation 2,000 copies) (Source: UNESCO Institute for Statistics).

1999: Radio receivers ('000 in use): 2,661; Periodicals 106 (average circulation 110,000 copies) (Sources: UNESCO, *Statistical Yearbook* and Institute for Statistics).

Book production: 84 titles (42,000 copies) in 1994 (first editions only); 9 titles in 1998. (Sources: UNESCO, *Statistical Yearbook*, UNESCO Institute for Statistics.).

Education

(2009/10 unless otherwise indicated)

			Students ('000)		
	Institutions	Teachers	Males	Females	Total
Pre-primary	283[1]	2,928	48.1	49.2	97.3
Primary	4,178[2]	38,540	957.1	830.8	1,787.9
Secondary	145[3]	14,410[4]	281.2[5]	154.3[5]	435.4[5]
Tertiary	n.a.	955[6]	n.a.	n.a.	42.6[7]

[1] 1995/96.
[2] 1999/2000.
[3] 1993/94.
[4] 2003/04.
[5] 2004/05.
[6] 2000/01.
[7] 2005/06.

Source: UNESCO, *Statistical Yearbook* and Institute for Statistics.

Pupil-teacher ratio (primary education, UNESCO estimate): 46.4 in 2009/10 (Source: UNESCO Institute for Statistics).

Adult literacy rate (UNESCO estimates): 42.4% (males 55.2%; females 30.3%) in 2010 (Source: UNESCO Institute for Statistics).

Directory

The Constitution

A new Constitution was approved in a national referendum on 2 December 1990. Its main provisions are summarized below:

PREAMBLE

The Beninois People reaffirm their opposition to any political regime founded on arbitrariness, dictatorship, injustice and corruption, reassert their attachment to the principles of democracy and human rights, as defined in the United Nations Charter, the Universal Declaration of Human Rights and the African Charter of the Rights of Man and Peoples, proclaim their attachment to the cause of African Unity and solemnly adopt this new Constitution as the supreme Law of the State.

I. THE STATE AND SOVEREIGNTY

Articles 1–6: The State of Benin is an independent, sovereign, secular, democratic Republic. The capital is Porto-Novo. The official language is French. The principle of the Republic is 'government of the People, by the People and for the People'. National sovereignty belongs to the People and is exercised through elected representatives and by referendums. Political parties operate freely, as determined by the Charter of Political Parties, and must respect the principles of national sovereignty, democracy, territorial integrity and the secular basis of the State. Suffrage is universal, equal and secret.

II. RIGHTS AND DUTIES OF THE INDIVIDUAL

Articles 7–40: The State is obliged to respect and protect the sacred and inviolable rights of the individual, and ensures equal access to health, education, culture, information, vocational training and employment. Primary education is compulsory. The State progressively assures the provision of free public education. Private schools are permitted. Torture and the use of cruel or degrading punishment are prohibited, and detention is subject to strict limitations. All persons have the right to property ownership, to freedom of conscience and expression. The State guarantees the freedoms of movement and association. All are equal before the law. The State recognizes the right to strike. Military service is compulsory.

III. THE EXECUTIVE

Articles 41–78: The President of the Republic is the Head of State. Candidates for the presidency must be of Beninois nationality by birth or have been naturalized for at least 10 years, and must be aged 40–70 years. The President is elected for a mandate of five years, renewable only once, by an absolute majority of votes cast. If no candidate receives an absolute majority, a second round is to be held between the two highest placed candidates. The Constitutional Court oversees the regularity of voting and announces the results. No President may serve more than two mandates.

The President of the Republic holds executive power. Following consultation with the Bureau of the Assemblée nationale, he names the members of the Government, who may not hold any parliamentary mandate. The President of the Republic chairs the Council of Ministers and has various defined powers of appointment.

The President of the Republic promulgates laws adopted by the Assemblée nationale, and may demand the resubmission of a law to the Assemblée nationale prior to its promulgation. In the event that the President of the Republic fails to promulgate a law, the Constitutional Court may, in certain circumstances, declare the law as binding.

After consultation with the President of the Assemblée nationale and the President of the Constitutional Court, the President of the Republic may call a referendum on matters pertaining to human rights, sub-regional or regional integration or the organization of public powers. The President of the Republic is the Supreme Chief of the Armed Forces.

The President of the Republic may delegate certain specified powers to ministers. The President of the Republic or any member of his Government may be called to account by the Assemblée nationale.

IV. THE LEGISLATURE

i. The Assemblée Nationale

Articles 79–93: Parliament exercises legislative power and controls the activities of the Government. Deputies of the Assemblée nationale, who must be civilians, are elected by direct universal suffrage for four years, and may be re-elected. The Assemblée nationale elects its President and a Bureau. Deputies enjoy various conditions of immunity from prosecution.

ii. Relations between the Assemblée Nationale and the Government

Articles 94–113: Members of the Government may attend sessions of the Assemblée nationale. Laws are approved by a simple majority, although organic laws require an absolute majority and approval by the Constitutional Court. The Assemblée nationale authorizes any declaration of war. States of siege and of emergency are declared in the Council of Ministers, although the Assemblée nationale must approve the extension of any such state beyond 15 days.

Deputies may, by a three-quarters' majority, decide to submit any question to referendum. If the Assemblée nationale has not approved a balanced budget by 31 December of any year, the measures foreseen by the finance law may be implemented by ordinance.

V. THE CONSTITUTIONAL COURT

Articles 114–124: The Constitutional Court is composed of seven members, of which four are named by the Bureau of the Assemblée nationale and three by the President of the Republic, each for a mandate of five years, renewable only once. The President of the Constitutional Court is elected by his peers for a period of five years and is a senior magistrate or lawyer. The decisions of the Constitutional Court are not subject to appeal.

VI. THE JUDICIARY

Articles 125–130: The judiciary is independent of the legislature and of the executive. It consists of the Supreme Court, and other courts and tribunals created in accordance with the Constitution. Judges may not be removed from office. The President of the Republic appoints magistrates and is the guarantor of the independence of the judiciary, assisted by the Higher Council of Magistrates, the composition, attributes, organization and function of which are fixed by an organic law.

i. The Supreme Court

Articles 131–134: The Supreme Court is the highest jurisdiction of the State in administrative and judicial matters, and with regard to the accounts of the State and to local elections. The decisions of the Court are not subject to appeal. The President of the Supreme Court is appointed for five years by the President of the Republic. The President of the Supreme Court may not be removed from office during his mandate, which is renewable only once.

ii. The High Court of Justice

Articles 135–138: The High Court of Justice comprises the members of the Constitutional Court (other than its President), six deputies of the Assemblée nationale and the President of the Supreme Court. The High Court of Justice elects a President from among its members and is competent to try the President of the Republic and members of the Government in cases of high treason, crimes committed during the exercise of their functions and plots against state security. In the event of an accusation of high treason or of contempt of the Assemblée nationale, and in certain other cases, the President of the Republic and members of the Government are to be suspended from their functions. In the case of being found guilty of such charges, they are dismissed from their responsibilities.

VII. THE ECONOMIC AND SOCIAL COUNCIL

Articles 139–141: The Economic and Social Council advises on proposed laws, ordinances or decrees that are submitted to it. Proposed laws of an economic or social nature must be submitted to the Council.

VIII. THE HIGH AUTHORITY FOR BROADCASTING AND COMMUNICATION

Articles 142–143: The High Authority for Broadcasting and Communication assures the freedom of the press and all other means of mass communication. It oversees the equitable access of political parties, associations and citizens to the official means of communication and information.

IX. INTERNATIONAL TREATIES AND ACCORDS

Articles 144–149: The President of the Republic negotiates and ratifies international treaties and accords. Peace treaties, those relating to international organization or territorial changes and to certain other matters must be ratified by law.

X. LOCAL AUTHORITIES

Articles 150–153: The local authorities of the Republic are created by law and are freely administered by elected councils. Their development is overseen by the State.

XI. ON REVISION

Articles 154–156: The initiative for the revision of the Constitution belongs jointly to the President of the Republic, after a decision has been taken in the Council of Ministers, and to the Assemblée nationale, given a majority vote of three-quarters of its members. A revision requires approval by referendum, unless it is supported by a majority of four-fifths of the members of the Assemblée nationale. The republican and secular basis of the State may not be the subject of any revision.

The Government

HEAD OF STATE

President: Dr BONI YAYI (inaugurated 6 April 2006; re-elected 13 March 2011).

COUNCIL OF MINISTERS

(September 2012)

President, Head of Government, in charge of National Defence: Dr BONI YAYI.

Prime Minister, responsible for the Co-ordination of Government Action, the Evaluation of Public Policy, Denationalization and Social Dialogue: PASCAL IRÉNÉE KOUPAKI.

Minister of State, in charge of Presidential Affairs: ISSIFOU KOGUI N'DOURO.

Minister of the Interior and Public Security: BENOÎT ASSOUAN DÈGLA.

Keeper of the Seals, Minister of Justice, Legislation and Human Rights, and Government Spokesperson: MARIE-ELISE GBÉDO.

Minister of Decentralization, Local Government, Administration and Land Settlement: RAPHAËL EDOU.

Minister of Foreign Affairs, African Integration, Francophone Affairs and Beninois Abroad: NASSIROU ARIFARI BAKO.

Minister of Economic Analysis, Development and Planning: MARCEL DE SOUZA.

Minister of the Economy and Finance: JONAS GBAIN.

Minister of Agriculture, Stockbreeding and Fisheries: KATÉ SADAÏ.

Minister of Industry, Commerce and Small and Medium-sized Enterprises: MADINA SÉPHOU.

Minister of Energy, Mining and Petroleum Research, Water and the Development of Renewable Energy Sources: SOFIATOU ONIFADE BABAMOUSSA.

Minister of Health: AKOKO KINDÉ GAZARD.

Minister of Nursery and Primary Education: ERIC N'DAH.

Minister of Secondary Education, Technical and Professional Training and the Integration of Youths: ALASSANE SOUMANOU.

Minister of Higher Education and Scientific Research: FRANÇOIS ADÉBAYO ABIOLA.

Minister of Labour and the Civil Service: MAÏMOUNA KORA ZAKI.

Minister of Youth, Sports and Leisure: DIDIER APLOGAN.

Minister of Microfinance and Youth and Women's Employment: RECKYA MADOUGOU.

Minister of the Environment, Housing and Town Planning: BLAISE AHANHANZO-GLÈLÈ.

Minister in charge of Relations with the Institutions: SAFIATOU BASSABI.

Minister of Public Works and Transport: LAMBERT KOTY.

Minister-delegate at the Presidency, in charge of the Maritime Economy and Ports: VALENTIN DJÈNONTIN.

Minister of Information and Communication Technology: MAX AHOUÈKÈ.

Minister of Culture, Literacy, Crafts and Tourism: JEAN-MICHEL ABIMBOLA.

Minister of Administrative and Institutional Reform: MARTIAL SOUNTON.

Minister of the Family, Social Affairs, National Solidarity, the Disabled and Senior Citizens: FATOUMA AMADOU DJIBRIL.

MINISTRIES

Office of the President: BP 1288, Cotonou; tel. 21-30-00-90; fax 21-30-06-36; internet www.gouv.bj.

Ministry of Administrative and Institutional Reform: rue du Collège Père Aupiais, BP 3010, Cotonou; tel. 21-30-80-14; fax 21-30-18-51; e-mail mrai@reforme.gouv.bj; internet www.reforme.gouv.bj.

Ministry of Agriculture, Stockbreeding and Fisheries: 03 BP 2900, Cotonou; tel. 21-30-04-10; fax 21-30-03-26; e-mail sgm@agriculture.gouv.bj; internet www.agriculture.gouv.bj.

Ministry of Culture, Literacy, Crafts and Tourism: Cotonou.

Ministry of Decentralization, Local Government, Administration and Land Settlement: Cotonou; tel. 21-30-40-30.

Ministry of the Economy and Finance: BP 302, Cotonou; tel. 21-30-02-81; fax 21-31-18-51; e-mail sgm@finance.gouv.bj; internet www.finances.bj.

Ministry of Energy, Mining and Petroleum Research, Water and the Development of Renewable Energy Sources: Cotonou.

Ministry of the the Environment, Housing and Town Planning: 01 BP 3621, Cotonou; tel. 21-31-55-96; fax 21-31-50-81; e-mail sg@environnement.gouv.bj.

Ministry of the Family, Social Affairs, National Solidarity, the Disabled and Senior Citizens: 01 BP 2802, Cotonou; tel. 21-31-67-08; fax 21-31-64-62.

Ministry of Foreign Affairs, African Integration, Francophone Affairs and Beninois Abroad: Zone Résidentielle, route de l'Aéroport, 06 BP 318, Cotonou; tel. 21-30-09-06; fax 21-38-19-70; e-mail infos@maebenin.bj; internet www.maebenin.bj.

Ministry of Health: Immeuble ex-MCAT, 01 BP 882, Cotonou; tel. 21-33-21-41; fax 21-33-04-64; e-mail sgm@sante.gouv.bj; internet www.ministeresantebenin.com.

Ministry of Higher Education and Scientific Research: 01 BP 348, Cotonou; tel. 21-30-06-81; fax 21-30-57-95; e-mail sgm@recherche.gouv.bj; internet www.mesrs.bj.

Ministry of Industry, Commerce and Small and Medium-sized Enterprises: BP 363, Cotonou; tel. and fax 21-30-30-24; e-mail mic@mic.bj; internet www.mic.bj.

Ministry of Information and Communication Technology: Cotonou.

Ministry of the Interior and Public Security: BP 925, Cotonou; tel. 21-30-11-06; fax 21-30-01-59.

Ministry of Justice, Legislation and Human Rights: BP 2493, Cotonou; tel. 21-30-08-90; fax 21-30-18-21; e-mail sgm@justice.gouv.bj; internet www.justice.gouv.bj.

Ministry of Labour and the Civil Service: BP 907, Cotonou; tel. 21-31-26-18; fax 21-31-06-29; e-mail sgm@travail.gouv.bj; internet www.travail.gouv.bj.

Ministry of Microfinance and Youth and Women's Employment: BP 302, Cotonou; tel. 21-30-02-81; fax 21-30-18-51.

Ministry of National Defence: BP 2493, Cotonou; tel. 21-30-08-90; fax 21-30-18-21.

Ministry of Nursery and Primary Education: 01 BP 10, Porto-Novo; tel. 20-21-33-27; fax 20-21-50-11; e-mail sgm@enseignement.gouv.bj; internet www.enseignement.gouv.bj.

Ministry of Planning, Development and the Evaluation of Public Action: Cotonou; internet www.developpement.bj.

Ministry of Public Works and Transport: Cotonou.

Ministry of Secondary Education, Technical and Professional Training and the Integration of Youths: 10 BP 250, Cotonou; tel. and fax 21-30-56-15.

Ministry of Small and Medium-sized Enterprises and the Promotion of the Private Sector: Cotonou.

Ministry of Town Planning, Housing, Land Reform and the Fight against Coastal Erosion: Cotonou.

Ministry of Trade: BP 363, Cotonou; tel. 21-30-76-46; fax 21-30-30-24; e-mail sgm@commerce.gouv.bj; internet www.commerce.gouv.bj.

Ministry of Youth, Sports and Leisure: 03 BP 2103, Cotonou; tel. 21-30-36-14; fax 21-38-21-26; internet www.mjsl.bj.

President and Legislature

PRESIDENT

Presidential Election, 13 March 2011

Candidate	Votes	% of votes
Boni Yayi	1,579,550	53.14
Adrien Houngbédji	1,059,396	35.64
Abdoulaye Bio Tchané	182,484	6.14
Issa Salifou	37,219	1.25
Christian Eunock Lagnidé	19,221	0.65
François Janvier Yahouédéhou	16,591	0.56
Others*	77,984	2.62
Total	2,972,445	100.00

* There were eight other candidates.

LEGISLATURE

Assemblée nationale

BP 371, Porto-Novo; tel. 20-21-22-19; fax 20-21-36-44; e-mail assemblee.benin@yahoo.fr; internet www.assembleebenin.org.

President: MATHURIN NAGO.

General Election, 30 April 2011

Party	Seats
Force Cauris pour un Bénin Émergent (FCBE)	41
Union Fait la Nation (UN)	30
Alliance G13 Baobab	2
Alliance Amana	2
Alliance Cauris	2
Alliance Forces dans l'Unité (AFU)	2
Union pour la Bénin (UB)	2
Union pour la Relève-Force Espoir (UPR-FE)	2
Total	83

Election Commission

Commission Électorale Nationale Autonome (CENA): 01 BP 443, Cotonou; tel. 21-31-69-90; e-mail info@cena-benin.org; internet www.cena-benin.org; f. 1994; 25 mems, of whom 18 are appointed by the Assemblée nationale, 2 by the President of the Republic, 2 by civil society; there are additionally 4 members of the Commission's permanent administrative secretariat; Chair. PASCAL TODJINOU.

Advisory Council

Conseil Économique et Social (CES): ave Jean-Paul II, 08 BP 679, Cotonou; tel. 21-30-03-91; fax 21-30-03-13; e-mail noc@ces-benin.org; internet www.ces-benin.org; f. 1994; 30 mems, representing the executive, legislature and 'all sections of the nation'; reviews all legislation relating to economic and social affairs; competent to advise on proposed economic and social legislation, as well as to recommend economic and social reforms; Pres. RAPHIOU TOUKOUROU.

Political Organizations

The registration of political parties commenced in August 1990. Some 19 political parties or alliances contested the 2011 legislative elections.

Alliance pour une Dynamique Démocratique (ADD): Leader NICÉPHORE SOGLO.

Mouvement Africain pour la Démocratie et le Progrès (MADEP): BP 1509, Cotonou; tel. 21-31-31-22; f. 1997; Leader El Hadj SÉFOU L. FAGBOHOUN.

Parti Social-Démocrate (PSD): Leader BRUNO AMOUSSOU.

La Renaissance du Bénin (RB): BP 2205, Cotonou; tel. 21-31-40-89; f. 1992; Chair. ROSINE VIEYRA SOGLO.

Union des Forces Démocratiques (UFD): Parakou; f. 1994; Leader SACCA GEORGES ZIMÉ.

Alliance Étoile: f. 2002; Leader SACCA LAFIA.

Union pour la Démocratie et la Solidarité Nationale (UDS): BP 1761, Cotonou; tel. 21-31-38-69; Pres. SACCA LAFIA.

Les Verts du Bénin—Parti Écologiste du Bénin: 06 BP 1336, Cotonou; tel. and fax 21-35-19-47; e-mail greensbenin@yahoo.fr; internet www.greensbenin.org; f. 1995; Pres. TOUSSAINT HINVI; Sec. PIERRE AHOUANOZIN.

Alliance des Forces du Progrès (AFP): Assemblée nationale, BP 371, Porto-Novo; Leader VALENTIN ADITI HOUDE.

Alliance du Renouveau (AR): Leader MARTIN DOHOU AZONHIHO.

Force Cauris pour un Bénin Émergent (FCBE): tel. 95-86-11-00; e-mail fcbe@gmail.com; internet www.fcbe2007.org; Pres. EXPÉDIT HOUESSOU; Sec.-Gen. DAVID NAHOUAN.

Force Clé: Carré 315, ScoaGbéto, 01 BP 1435, Cotonou; tel. 21-35-09-36; f. 2003 on basis of Mouvement pour une Alternative du Peuple; Leader LAZARE SÈHOUÉTO.

Force Espoir (FE): Leader ANTOINE DAYORI.

G13: f. 2008 by fmr supporters of President Yayi; Leader ISSA SALIFOU.

Mouvement pour le Développement et la Solidarité (MDS): BP 73, Porto-Novo; Leader SACCA MOUSSÉDIKOU FIKARA.

Nouvelle Alliance: Cotonou; f. 2006; Leader CORENTIN KOHOUE.

Parti pour la Démocratie et le Progrès Social (PDPS): Leader EDMOND AGOUA.

Parti du Renouveau Démocratique (PRD): Immeuble Babo Oganla, 01 BP 1157, Porto-Novo; tel. 21-30-07-57; f. 1990; Leader ADRIEN HOUNGBÉDJI.

Rassemblement pour la Démocratie et le Panafricanisme (RDP): 03 BP 1050, Cotonou; tel. 21-32-02-83; fax 21-32-35-71; e-mail cotrans@leland.bj; f. 1995; Pres. DOMINIQUE O. HOUNGNINOU; Treas. JANVIER SETANGNI.

Restaurer l'Espoir (RE): Leader CANDIDE AZANNAÏ.

Union pour le Bénin du Futur (UBF): 03 BP 1972, Cotonou; tel. 21-33-12-23; e-mail amoussou@avu.org; f. 2002 by supporters of then Pres. Kérékou; separate faction, UBF 'Aller Plus Loin', formed Oct. 2004 under leadership of JOSEPH GANDAHO, comprising more than 30 pro-presidential parties and assens; further, smaller, faction, the 'Alliance UBF' formed April 2005, led by ALAIN ADIHOU; Co-ordinator BRUNO AMOUSSOU.

Front d'Action pour le Renouveau, la Démocratie et le Développement—Alafia (FARD—Alafia): 01 BP 3238, Cotonou; tel. 21-33-34-10; f. 1994; Sec.-Gen. DANIEL TAWÉMA.

Union pour la Relève (UPR): Gbégamey; internet www.uprbenin.org; Leader ISSA SALIFOU.

Diplomatic Representation

EMBASSIES IN BENIN

China, People's Republic: 2 route de l'Aéroport, 01 BP 196, Cotonou; tel. 21-30-07-65; fax 21-30-08-41; e-mail prcbenin@serv.eit.bj; internet bj.chineseembassy.org; Ambassador TAO WEIGUANG.

Congo, Democratic Republic: Carré 221, Ayélawadjè, Cotonou; tel. 21-30-00-01.

Cuba: ave de la Marina, face Hôtel du Port, 01 BP 948, Cotonou; tel. 21-31-52-97; fax 21-31-65-91; e-mail embacuba@benin.cubaminrex.cu; internet emba.cubaminrex.cu/benin; Ambassador OSCAR GENARO COET BLACKSTOCK.

Denmark: Lot P7, Les Cocotiers, 04 BP 1223, Cotonou; tel. 21-30-38-62; fax 21-30-38-60; e-mail cooamb@um.dk; internet www.ambcotonou.um.dk; Ambassador GERT MEINECKE.

Egypt: Lot G26, route de l'Aéroport, BP 1215, Cotonou; tel. 21-30-08-42; fax 21-30-14-25; Ambassador RAMADAN MOHAMED E. BAKR.

France: ave Jean-Paul II, BP 966, Cotonou; tel. 21-30-02-25; fax 21-30-15-47; e-mail ambafrance.cotonou@diplomatie.gouv.fr; internet www.ambafrance-bj.org; Ambassador JEAN-PAUL MONCHAU.

Germany: 7 ave Jean-Paul II, 01 BP 504, Cotonou; tel. 21-31-29-67; fax 21-31-29-62; e-mail info@cotonou.diplo.de; internet www.cotonou.diplo.de; Ambassador HANS JÖRG NEUMANN.

Ghana: route de l'Aéroport, Lot F, Les Cocotiers, BP 488, Cotonou; tel. 21-30-07-46; fax 21-30-03-45; e-mail ghaemb02@leland.bj; Ambassador MODESTUS AHIABLE.

Holy See: 08 BP 400, Cotonou; tel. 21-30-03-08; fax 21-30-03-10; e-mail nonciaturebenin@gmail.com; Apostolic Nuncio Archbishop MICHAEL AUGUST BLUME (Titular Archbishop of Alexanum).

Japan: Villa A2, Complexe CEN-SAD, Laico-Benin, blvd de la Marina, Cotonou; tel. 21-30-59-86; fax 21-30-59-94.

Korea, Democratic People's Republic: Cotonou; Ambassador KIM PYONG GI.

Kuwait: Cotonou; Ambassador FAEYEZ MISHARI AL-JASSIM.

Libya: Carré 36, Cotonou; tel. 21-30-04-52; fax 21-30-03-01; Ambassador TOUFIK ASHOUR ADAM.

Netherlands: ave Pape Jean Paul II, route de l'Aéroport, derrière le Tri Postal, 08 BP 0783, Cotonou; tel. 21-30-04-39; fax 21-30-41-50; e-mail cot@minbuza.nl; internet www.ambassadehollande-cotonou.org; Ambassador W. WOUTER PLOMP.

Niger: derrière l'Hôtel de la Plage, BP 352, Cotonou; tel. 21-31-56-65; Ambassador LOMPO SOULEYMANE.

Nigeria: ave de France, Marina, BP 2019, Cotonou; tel. 21-30-11-42; fax 21-30-11-13; Ambassador LAWRENCE LAWRENCE OBISAKIN.

South Africa: Marina Hotel, blvd de la Marina, 01 BP 1901, Cotonou; tel. 21-30-72-17; fax 21-30-70-58; e-mail foreign@intnet.bj; Chargé d'affaires a.i. KGOSIETSILE CHARLES KEEPILE.

Russia: Zone résidentielle, ave de la Marina, face Hôtel du Port, BP 2013, Cotonou; tel. 21-31-28-34; fax 21-31-28-35; e-mail ambrusben@mail.ru; internet www.benin.mid.ru; Ambassador YURII GRASHCHENKOV.

USA: rue Caporal Anani Bernard, 01 BP 2012, Cotonou; tel. 21-30-06-50; fax 21-30-03-84; e-mail irccotonou@state.gov; internet cotonou.usembassy.gov; Chargé d'affaires SUSAN TULLER.

Judicial System

Constitutional Court: BP 2050, Cotonou; tel. 21-31-16-10; fax 21-31-37-12; e-mail cconstitutsg@yahoo.fr; internet www.gouv.bj/institutions/cour_constitutionnelle/presentation.php; f. 1990; inaug. 1993; 7 mems; 4 appointed by the Assemblée nationale, 3 by the President of the Republic; exercises highest jurisdiction in constitutional affairs; determines the constitutionality of legislation, oversees and proclaims results of national elections and referendums, responsible for protection of individual and public rights and obligations, charged with regulating functions of organs of state and authorities; Pres. ROBERT DOSSOU; Sec.-Gen. MARCELLINE-CLAIRE GBÈHA AFOUDA.

High Court of Justice: 01 BP 2958, Porto-Novo; tel. 20-21-26-81; fax 20-21-27-71; tel. hcjbenin@intnet.bj; internet www.gouv.bj; f. 1990; officially inaugurated in 2001; comprises the 6 members of the Constitutional Court (other than its President), 6 deputies of the Assemblée nationale and the First President of the Supreme Court; competent to try the President of the Republic and members of the Government in cases of high treason, crimes committed in, or at the time of, the exercise of their functions, and of plotting against state security; Pres. Prof. THÉODORE HOLO.

Supreme Court: 01 BP 330, Cotonou; tel. and fax 20-21-26-77; fax 20-21-32-08; e-mail info@coursupreme.gouv.bj; internet www.coursupreme.gouv.bj; f. 1960; highest juridical authority in administrative and judicial affairs and in matters of public accounts; competent in disputes relating to local elections; advises the executive on jurisdiction and administrative affairs; comprises a President (appointed by the President of the Republic, after consultation with the President of the Assemblée nationale, senior magistrates and jurists), presidents of the component chambers, a public prosecutor, 4 assistant procurators-fiscal, counsellors and clerks; Pres. OUSMANE BATOKO; Attorney-Gen. JEAN-BAPTISTE MONSI; Pres. of the Judicial Chamber JACQUES MAYABA; Pres. of the Administrative Chamber GRÉGOIRE Y. ALAYÈ; Pres. of the Chamber of Accounts JUSTIN BIOKOU; Chief Clerk FRANÇOISE TCHIBOZO-QUENUM.

Religion

Religious and spiritual cults, which were discouraged under Kérékou's military regime, re-emerged as a prominent force in Beninois society during the 1990s. At the time of the 2002 census it was estimated that some 38% of the population were Christians (mainly Roman Catholics), 24% were Muslims, and 17% followed the traditional *vodoun* religion, with a further 6% being adherents of other traditional religions.

CHRISTIANITY

The Roman Catholic Church

Benin comprises two archdioceses and eight dioceses. An estimated 27.6% of the population were Roman Catholics.

Bishops' Conference

Conférence Episcopale du Bénin, Archevêché, 01 BP 491, Cotonou; tel. 21-30-66-48; fax 21-30-07-07; e-mail cepiscob@usa.net; Pres. Most Rev. ANTOINE GANYÉ (Bishop of Dassa-Zoumé).

Archbishop of Cotonou: Most Rev. ANTOINE GANYÉ, Archevêché, 01 BP 491, Cotonou; tel. 21-30-01-45; fax 21-30-07-07; e-mail mhlagbot@yahoo.fr.

Archbishop of Parakou: PASCAL N'KOUÉ, Archevêché, BP 75, Parakou; tel. 23-61-02-54; fax 23-61-01-09; e-mail archeveche@borgou.net.

Protestant Church

There are an estimated 257 Protestant mission centres in Benin.

Eglise Protestante Méthodiste en République du Bénin (EPMB): 54 ave Mgr Steinmetz, 01 BP 34, Cotonou; tel. and fax 21-31-11-42; e-mail epmbenin@intnet.bj; f. 1843; Pres. Rev. Dr SIMON K. DOSSOU; Sec. Rev. Dr CÉLESTIN GB. KIKI; 101,000 mems (1997).

VODOUN

The origins of the traditional *vodoun* religion can be traced to the 14th century. Its influence is particularly strong in Latin America and the Caribbean, owing to the shipment of slaves from the West African region to the Americas in the 18th and 19th centuries.

Communauté Nationale du Culte Vodoun (CNCV): Ouidah; Pres. HOUNGUÈ TOWAKON GUÈDÉHOUNGUÈ II.

ISLAM

Union Islamique du Bénin (UIB): Cotonou; Pres. Imam El Hadj MOHAMED AMED SANNI; Sec.-Gen. FAÏSSOU ADÉGBOLA.

BAHÁ'Í FAITH

National Spiritual Assembly: BP 1252, Cotonou.

The Press

In 2010 there were some 75 dailies and periodicals recognized by the Haute Autorité de l'Audiovisuel et de la Communication in Benin.

DAILIES

Actu-Express: 01 BP 2220, Cotonou; tel. 97981047 (mobile); internet www.actuexpress.com; Dir of Publication MÉDÉRIC FRANÇOIS GOHOUNGO.

L'Adjinakou: Lot AC, Parcelle 1 Avakpa-Tokpa, Immeuble Radio école APM, 03 BP 105, Porto-Novo; tel. 20-22-06-76; e-mail adjinakou2004@yahoo.com; internet www.journal-adjinakou-benin.info; f. 2003; Dir of Publication MAURILLE AGBOKOU.

L'Araignée: siège du cyber DOPHIA, face Cité Houeyiho, 01 BP 1357, Cotonou; tel. 21-30-64-12; fax (44) 21-32-18-84; e-mail info@laraignee.org; internet www.laraignee.org; f. 2001; online only; politics, public affairs, culture, society, sport; Dir of Publishing FÉLIX ANIWANOU HOUNSA; Editor-in-Chief WILLÉANDRE HOUNGBÉDJI.

L'Aurore: face Clinique Boni, 05 BP 464, Cotonou; tel. 21-33-70-43; e-mail laurore1998@yahoo.fr; Dir PATRICK ADJAMONSI; circ. 1,500.

L'Autre Quotidien: Lot 115 Z, rue Capitaine Anani, Face PNUD, Zone Résidentielle, 01 BP 6659, Cotonou; tel. 21-31-01-99; fax 21-31-02-05; e-mail lautreredaction@yahoo.fr; internet www.lautrequotidien.com; Dir ROMAIN TOÏ; Editor-in-Chief LÉON BRATHIER.

Bénin-Presse Info: 01 BP 72, Cotonou; tel. 21-31-26-55; fax 21-31-13-26; e-mail abpben@bow.intnet.bj; internet www.gouv.bj/presse/abp/index.php; bulletin of Agence Bénin-Presse; Dir YAOVI R. HOUNKPONOU; Editor-in-Chief JOSEPH VODOUNON.

Le Confrère de la Matinée: Esplanade du Stade de l'Amitié, Cotonou; tel. 21-04-20-14; e-mail info@leconfrere.com; internet www.leconfrere.com; Dir of Publication FAUSTIN BABATOUNDÉ ADJAGBA.

Djakpata: Quartier Todote C/410, Maison Bokononhui, 02 BP 2744, Cotonou; tel. 21-32-43-73; e-mail quotidiendjakpata@yahoo.fr; internet djakpata.info; Editor CYRILLE SAÏZONOU.

Les Echos du Jour: Carré 136, Sodjatimè, 08 BP 718, Cotonou; tel. 21-33-18-33; fax 21-33-17-06; e-mail echos@intnet.bj; independent; Dir MAURICE CHABI; Editor-in-Chief SÉBASTIEN DOSSA; circ. 3,000.

Fraternité: face Station Menontin, 05 BP 915, Cotonou; tel. 21-38-47-70; fax 21-38-47-71; e-mail fraternite@yesouikend.com; internet yesouikend.com/fraternite; Dir of Publication BRICE U. HOUSSOU; Editor-in-Chief GÉRARD GANSOU.

L'Informateur: Etoile Rouge, Bâtiment Radio Star, Carré 1072C, 01 BP 5421, Cotonou; tel. and fax 21-32-66-39; f. 2001; Dir CLÉMENT ADÉCHIAN; Editor-in-Chief BRICE GUÈDÈ.

Le Matin: Carré 54, Tokpa Hoho, 06 BP 2217, Cotonou; tel. 21-31-10-80; fax 21-33-42-62; e-mail lematinonline@moncourrier.com; f. 1994; independent; Dir MOÏSE DATO; Editorial Dir IGNACE FANOU.

Le Matinal: Carré 153–154, Atinkanmey, 06 BP 1989, Cotonou; tel. 90-94-83-32; e-mail infodumatinal@yahoo.fr; internet www.actubenin.com; f. 1997; daily; Dir-Gen. MAXIMIN TCHIBOZO; Editor-in-Chief NAPOLÉON MAFORIKAN; circ. 5,000.

La Nation: Cadjèhoun, 01 BP 1210, Cotonou; tel. 21-30-02-99; fax 21-30-34-63; e-mail onipben@intnet.bj; internet www.gouv.bj/presse/lanation/index.php; f. 1990; official newspaper; Dir AKUÉTÉ ASSEVI; Editor-in-Chief HUBERT O. AKPONIKPE; circ. 4,000.

La Nouvelle Tribune: Immeuble Zonon, Lot 1498, P Quartier Missogbè à Vêdoko, 09 BP 336, Cotonou; tel. 21-38-34-88; e-mail redaction@lanouvelletribune.info; internet www.lanouvelletribune.info; f. 2001; Dir-Gen. and Dir of Publication VINCENT FOLY; Editorial Dir EMMANUEL S. TACHIN.

L'Oeil du Peuple: Carré 743, rue PTT, Gbégamey, 01 BP 5538, Cotonou; tel. 21-30-22-07; e-mail loeildupeuple@yahoo.fr; Dir CELESTIN ABISSI; Editor-in-Chief PAUL AGBOYIDOU.

Le Point au Quotidien: 332 rue du Renouveau, 05 BP 934, Cotonou; tel. 90-91-69-45; fax 21-32-25-31; e-mail info@lepointauquotidien.com; independent; Dir and Editor-in-Chief FERNANDO HESSOU; circ. 2,000.

La Presse du Jour: 01 BP 1719, Cotonou; tel. 21-30-51-75; internet www.lapressedujour.net; Dir of Publication PASCAL HOUNKPATIN.

Le Progrès: 05 BP 708, Cotonou; tel. 21-32-52-73; e-mail journalprogres@hotmail.com; internet www.leprogres.info; f. ; Dir of Publication LUDOVIC AGBADJA.

Le Républicain: Les Presses d'Afrique, Carré 630, Tanto, 05 BP 1230, Cotonou; tel. and fax 21-33-83-04; e-mail lerepublicain@lerepublicain.org; independent; Editor-in-Chief ISIDORE ZINSOU.

La Tribune de la Capitale: Lot 03-46, Parcelle E, Houinmè, Maison Onifadé, Catchi, 01 BP 1463, Porto-Novo; tel. 20-22-55-69; e-mail latribunedelacapitale@yahoo.fr; internet www.latribunedelacapitale.com; Dir of Publication SETH EVARISTE HODONOU; Editor-in-Chief KPAKOUN CHARLES.

PERIODICALS

Agri-Culture: 03 BP 0380, Cotonou; tel. and fax 21-36-05-46; e-mail agriculture@uva.org; f. 1999; monthly; Editor-in-Chief JOACHIM SAÏZONOU; circ. 1,000.

L'Autre Gazette: 02 BP 1537, Cotonou; tel. 21-32-59-97; e-mail collegi@beninweb.org; Editor-in-Chief WILFRIED AYIBATIN.

L'Avenir: Carré 911, 02 BP 8134, Cotonou; tel. 21-32-21-23; fortnightly; political analysis; Dir CLAUDE FIRMIN GANGBE.

Le Canard du Golfe: Carré 240, Midombo, Akpakpa, 06 BP 59, Cotonou; tel. 21-32-72-33; e-mail lecanardugolfe@yahoo.fr; satirical; weekly; Dir F. L. TINGBO; Editor-in-Chief EMMANUEL SOTIKON.

Le Continental: BP 4419, Cotonou; tel. 21-30-04-37; fax 21-30-03-21; Editor-in-Chief ARNAULD HOUNDETE.

La Croix du Bénin: Centre Paul VI, 01 BP 105, Cotonou; tel. and fax 21-32-11-19; e-mail andrequenum@yahoo.com; internet www.lacroixdubenin.com; f. 1946; twice a week; Roman Catholic; Editor Rev. Dr ANDRÉ S. QUENUM.

Emotion Magazine: 06 BP 1404, Cotonou; tel. 95-40-17-07; fax 21-32-21-33; e-mail emomagazine@yahoo.fr; f. 1998; every 2 months; cultural and social affairs; Dir of Publication ERIC SESSINOU HUANNOU; Editor-in-Chief BERNARD HERMANN ZANNOU; circ. 3,000 (2006).

La Gazette du Golfe: Immeuble La Gazette du Golfe, Carré 902E, Sikècodji, 03 BP 1624, Cotonou; tel. 21-32-68-44; fax 21-32-52-26; e-mail gazettedugolfe@serv.eit.bj; f. 1987; weekly; Dir ISMAËL Y. SOUMANOU; Editor MARCUS BONI TEIGA; circ. 18,000 (nat. edn), 5,000 (int. edn).

Le Gongonneur: 04 BP 1432, Cotonou; tel. 90-90-60-95; fax 21-35-04-22; e-mail dahoun@yahoo.com; f. 1998; owned by Prix Etoile Internationale à la Qualité; Dir MATHIAS C. SOSSOU; Editor-in-Chief GAFFAROU RADJI.

Le Héraut: 03 BP 3417, Cotonou; tel. 21-36-00-64; e-mail franck.kouyami@auf.org; internet leheraut.org; monthly; current affairs; analysis; produced by students at Université nationale du Bénin; Dir GEOFFREY GOUNOU N'GOYE; Editor-in-Chief GABRIEL DIDEH.

Initiatives: 01 BP 2093, Cotonou; tel. 21-31-22-61; fax 21-31-59-50; e-mail cepepe@firstnet1.com; 6 a year; journal of the Centre de Promotion et d'Encadrement des Petites et Moyennes Entreprises.

Journal Officiel de la République du Bénin: BP 59, Porto-Novo; tel. 20-21-39-77; f. 1890; present name adopted 1990; official govt bulletin; fortnightly; Dir AFIZE DÉSIRÉ ADAMO.

Madame Afrique: Siège Mefort Inter Diffusion, Carré 1066, quartier Cadjehoun, 05 BP 1914, Cotonou; tel. 97-68-22-90; e-mail madafric@yahoo.fr; f. 2000; monthly; women's interest; Dir of Publication BERNARD G. ZANKLAN.

Le Magazine de l'Entreprise: BP 850, Cotonou; tel. 21-30-80-79; fax 21-30-47-77; e-mail oliviergat@hotmail.com; f. 1999; monthly; business; Dir A. VICTOR FAKÈYÈ.

Le Perroquet: Carré 478, Quartier Bar-Tito, 03 BP 880, Cotonou; tel. 21-32-18-54; e-mail leperroquet2003@yahoo.fr; internet www.leperroquet.fr.gd; f. 1995; 2 a month; independent; news and analysis; Dir DAMIEN HOUESSOU; Editor-in-Chief CHARLES RICHARD NZI; circ. 4,000 (2004).

Press Association

Union des Journalistes de la Presse Privée du Bénin (UJPB): blvd de la République, près Cadmes Plus, 03 BP 383, Cotonou; tel. 21-32-52-73; e-mail ujpb@h2com.com; internet www.h2com.com/ujpb; f. 1992; asscn of independent journalists; Pres. AGAPIT N. MAFORIKAN.

NEWS AGENCY

Agence Bénin-Presse (ABP): BP 72, Cotonou; tel. and fax 21-31-26-55; e-mail abpben@intnet.bj; internet www.abp.gouv.bj; f. 1961; nat. news agency; Dir YAOVI R. HOUNKPONOU.

Publishers

AFRIDIC: 01 BP 269, 01 Porto-Novo; tel. 20-22-32-28; f. 1996; poetry, essays, fiction; Dir ADJIBI JEAN-BAPTISTE.

Editions de l'ACACIA: 06 BP 1978, Cotonou; tel. 21-33-04-72; e-mail zoundin@yahoo.fr; f. 1989; fmrly Editions du Flamboyant; literary fiction, history, popular science; Dir OSCAR DE SOUZA.

Editions des Diasporas: 04 BP 792, Cotonou; e-mail camouro@yahoo.fr; poetry, essays; Editor CAMILLE AMOURO.

Editions Ruisseaux d'Afrique: 04 BP 1154, Cotonou; tel. and fax 90-94-79-25; fax 21-30-31-86; e-mail ruisseau@leland.bj; f. 1992; children's literature; Dir BÉATRICE GBADO.

Graphitec: 04 BP 825, Cotonou; tel. and fax 21-30-46-04; e-mail lewado@yahoo.com.

Imprimerie Notre Dame: BP 109, Cotonou; tel. 21-32-12-07; fax 21-32-11-19; f. 1974; Roman Catholic publs; Dir BARTHÉLÉMY ASSOGBA CAKPO.

Société Tunde: 06 BP 1925, Cotonou; tel. 21-30-15-68; fax 21-30-42-86; e-mail tunde.sa@tunde-sa.com; internet www.tunde-sa.com; f. 1986; economics, management; Pres. BABATOUNDÉ RASAKI OLLOFINDJI; Dir-Gen. ALFRED LAMBERT SOMA.

Star Editions: 01 BP 367, Recette principale, Cotonou; tel. 90-94-66-28; fax 21-33-05-29; e-mail star_editions@yahoo.fr; business, economics, science, poetry; Editor JOACHIM ADJOVI.

GOVERNMENT PUBLISHING HOUSE

Office National d'Edition, de Presse et d'Imprimerie (ONEPI): 01 BP 1210, Cotonou; tel. 21-30-02-99; fax 21-30-34-63; f. 1975; Dir-Gen. INNOCENT ADJAHO.

Broadcasting and Communications

TELECOMMUNICATIONS

Benin's fixed-line telephone sector is dominated by the state operator, Bénin Télécoms. In 2011 there were five providers of mobile cellular telephone services, of which four were privately owned and one, Libercom, was state-owned. At December 2007 there were 110,254 subscribers to fixed-line telephone services, while at June 2010 there were 6.3m subscribers to mobile telephone services.

Autorité Transitoire de Régulation des Postes et Télécommunications (ATRPT): ave Steinmetz, Von opposé ancien Air Gabon, Immeuble Suzanne Loko, 01 BP 2034, Cotonou; tel. 21-31-72-76; fax 21-31-72-76; e-mail infos@atrpt.bj; internet www.atrpt.bj; f. 2007; Pres. FIRMIN DJIMENOU.

Bénin Télécoms: Ganhi, 01 BP 5959, Cotonou; tel. 21-31-20-45; fax 21-31-38-43; e-mail sp.dgbttelecoms@intnet.bj; internet www.benintelecoms.bj; f. 2004; Dir-Gen. URBAIN FADÉGNON (acting); 110,254 subscribers (Dec. 2007).

Bell Bénin Communications (BBCOM): 02 BP 1886, Gbégamey; tel. 21-30-52-84; fax 21-30-84-84; internet www.bellbenin.net; f. 2002; mobile cellular telephone operator; Chief Exec. ISSA SALIFOU; 443,550 subscribers (2008).

Glo Mobile Bénin: Aïdjèdo, Lot 817 Parcelle C, ave de la Libération, 01 BP 8050, Cotonou; tel. 21-32-44-56; Dir-Gen. FEMMY OGUNLUSI; 560,090 subscribers (2008).

Libercom: blvd Saint-Michel, face Hall des Arts et de la Culture, 01 BP 5959, Cotonou; tel. 21-31-46-48; fax 21-31-49-42; e-mail renseignements@libercom.bj; internet www.libercom.bj; f. 2000; mobile cellular telephone operator in Cotonou and Porto-Novo; Dir-Gen. ISIDORE DÉGBÈLO; 194,888 subscribers (2008).

MTN Bénin: 01 BP 5293, Cotonou; tel. 21-31-66-41; internet www.mtn.bj; f. 2000 as BéninCell; renamed as Areeba in 2005; mobile cellular telephone operator in Cotonou, Porto-Novo and Parakou under network name Areeba; owned by Mobile Telephone Network International (South Africa); CEO MOHAMAD BADER; 267,583 subscribers (2005).

Moov Bénin: Immeuble Kougblenou, 5è étage, ave Mgr Steinmetz, Cotonou; e-mail moov@moov.bj; internet www.moov.bj; f. 2000 as Telcel Bénin; mobile cellular telephone operator in Cotonou, Porto-Novo, Abomey, Lokossa, other regions of southern Benin and in Parakou; Dir-Gen. TALIBI HAÏDRA; 950,584 subscribers (2008).

BROADCASTING

Since 1997 the Haute Autorité de l'Audiovisuel et de la Communication has issued licences to private radio and television stations.

Haute Autorité de l'Audiovisuel et de la Communication (HAAC): 01 BP 3567, Cotonou; tel. 21-31-17-45; fax 21-31-17-42; e-mail infohaac@haacbenin.org; internet www.haacbenin.org; f. 1994; Pres. THÉOPHILE NATA.

Radio

Office de Radiodiffusion et de Télévision du Bénin (ORTB): 01 BP 366, Cotonou; tel. 21-30-46-19; fax 21-30-04-48; e-mail drp@ortb.bj; internet www.ortb.bj; state-owned; radio programmes broadcast from Cotonou and Parakou in French, English and 18 local languages; Dir-Gen. JULIEN PIERRE AKPAKI; Dir of Radio CHRISTIAN DE SOUZA.

Atlantic FM: 01 BP 366, Cotonou; tel. 21-30-20-41; Dir JOSEPH OGOUNCHI.

Radiodiffusion nationale du Bénin: BP 366, Cotonou; tel. 21-30-10-96; f. 1953; Dir MOUFALIOU LIADY.

Radio Régionale de Parakou: BP 128, Parakou; tel. 23-61-07-73; Dir SÉNI SOUROU.

Bénin-Culture: BP 21, Association pour l'Institutionnalisation de la Mémoire et de la Pensée Intellectuelle Africaine, 01 BP 21, Porto-Novo; tel. 20-22-69-34; Head of Station ARMAND COVI.

Golfe FM-Magic Radio: 03 BP 1624, Cotonou; tel. 21-32-42-08; fax 21-32-42-09; e-mail golfefm@serv.eit.bj; internet www.eit.bj/golfefm.htm; Dir ISMAËL SOUMANOU.

Radio Afrique Espoir: Carré 123, 03 BP 203, Porto-Novo; tel. 20-21-34-55; fax 20-21-32-63; e-mail afespoir@intnet.bj; Dir RAMANOU KOUFERIDJI.

Radio Carrefour: 03 BP 432, Cotonou; tel. 21-32-70-50; fax 22-51-16-55; e-mail chrisdavak@yahoo.fr; f. 1999; production and broadcast of radio and television programmes; Dir-Gen. CHRISTOPHE DAVAKAN.

Radio FM-Ahémé: BP 66, Bopa, Mono; tel. 95-05-58-18; f. 1997; informative, cultural and civic education broadcasts; Dir AMBROISE COKOU MOUSSOU.

Radio Immaculée Conception: BP 88, Allada; tel. 21-36-80-97; e-mail satric@immacolata.com; internet www.immacolata.com; operated by the Roman Catholic Church of Benin; broadcasts to Abomey, Allada, Bembéréke, Cotonou, Dassa-Zoume, Djougou and Parakou; Dir Fr ALFONSO BRUNO.

Radio Maranatha: 03 BP 4113, Cotonou; tel. and fax 21-32-58-82; e-mail maranatha.fm@serv.eit.bj; internet www.eit.to/RadioMaranatha.htm; operated by the Conseil des Eglises Protestantes Evangéliques du Bénin; Dir Rev. CLOVIS ALFRED KPADE.

Radio Planète: 02 BP 1528, Immeuble Master Soft, Cotonou; tel. 21-30-30-30; fax 21-30-24-51; internet www.planetefm.com; Dir JANVIER YAHOUEDEHOU.

Radio Solidarité FM: BP 135, Djougou; tel. 23-80-11-29; fax 23-80-15-63; Dir DAOUDA TAKPARA.

Radio Tokpa: Dantokpa, Cotonou; tel. 21314532; internet www.radiotokpa.net; Dir-Gen. GUY KPAKPO.

La Voix de la Lama: 03 BP 3772, Cotonou; tel. 21-37-12-26; fax 21-37-13-67; e-mail voix_delalama@yahoo.fr; f. 1998; non-commercial FM station, broadcasting on 103.8 Mhz from Allada; Dir SÉRAPHINE DADY.

La Voix de l'Islam: 08 BP 134, Cotonou; tel. 21-31-11-34; fax 21-31-51-79; e-mail islamben@leland.bj; operated by the Communauté musulmane de Zongo; Dir El Hadj MAMAN YARO.

Radio Wêkê: 05 BP 436, Cotonou; tel. 20-21-38-40; fax 20-21-37-14; e-mail issabadarou@hotmail.com; Promoter ISSA BADAROU-SOULÉ.

Benin also receives broadcasts from Africa No. 1, the British Broadcasting Corporation World Service and Radio France International.

Television

ORTB: (see Radio); Dir of Television STÉPHANE TODOME.

ATVS: BP 7101, Cotonou; tel. 21-31-43-19; owned by African Television System-Sobiex; Dir JACOB AKINOCHO.

LC2 Media (LC2): 05 BP 427, Cotonou; tel. 21-33-47-49; fax 21-33-46-75; e-mail lc2@lc2tv.com; internet www.lc2tv.com; commenced broadcasts 1997; CEO CHRISTIAN LAGNIDE; Man. NADINE LAGNIDE WOROU.

Telco: 44 ave Delorme, 01 BP 1241, Cotonou; tel. 21-31-34-98; e-mail telco@serv.eit.bj; relays 5 int. channels; Dir JOSEPH JÉBARA.

TV+ International/TV5: 01 BP 366, Cotonou; tel. 21-30-10-96; Dir CLAUDE KARAM.

Finance

(cap. = capital; res = reserves; dep. = deposits; m. = million; br(s). = branch(es); amounts in francs CFA)

BANKING

In 2009 there were 12 banks and one financial institution in Benin.

Central Bank

Banque Centrale des Etats de l'Afrique de l'Ouest (BCEAO): ave Jean-Paul II, BP 325, Cotonou; tel. 21-31-24-66; fax 21-31-24-65; e-mail akangni@bceao.int; internet www.bceao.int; HQ in Dakar, Senegal; f. 1962; bank of issue for the mem. states of the Union Economique et Monétaire Ouest-Africaine (UEMOA, comprising Benin, Burkina Faso, Côte d'Ivoire, Guinea-Bissau, Mali, Niger, Senegal and Togo); cap. 134,120m., res 1,474,195m., dep. 2,124,051m. (Dec. 2009); Gov. KONÉ TIÉMOKO MEYLIET; Dir in Benin ALAIN FAGNON KOUTANGNI; br. at Parakou.

Commercial Banks

Bank of Africa—Bénin (BOAB): ave Jean-Paul II, 08 BP 0879, Cotonou; tel. 21-31-32-28; fax 21-31-31-17; e-mail information@boabenin.com; internet www.boabenin.com; f. 1990; cap. 9,000m., res 19,285m., dep. 429,487m. (Dec. 2009); Chair. PAULIN L. COSSI; Dir-Gen. CHEIKH TIDIANE N'DIAYE; 28 brs.

Banque Atlantique du Bénin: rue du Gouverneur Bayol, 08 BP 0682 Cotonou; tel. 21-31-10-18; fax 21-31-31-21; e-mail babn_support@banqueatlantique.net; internet www.banqueatlantique.net; cap. 6,500m., res –1,324m., dep. 74,079m. (2009); Chair. DOSSONGUI KONÉ; 6 brs.

Banque Internationale du Bénin (BIBE): carrefour des Trois Banques, ave Giran, 03 BP 2098, Jéricho, Cotonou; tel. 95-07-01-02; fax 21-31-23-65; e-mail bibedi@leland.bj; internet www.bibebank.net; f. 1989; owned by Nigerian commercial interests; cap. 9,000m., dep. 48,577m. (Dec. 2002); Chair. Dr G. A. T. OBOH; Man. Dir JEAN-PAUL K. AIDDO; 4 brs.

Continental Bank—Bénin (La Continentale): ave Jean-Paul II, carrefour des Trois Banques, 01 BP 2020, Cotonou; tel. 21-31-24-24; fax 21-31-51-77; e-mail contact@cbankbenin.com; f. 1993 to assume activities of Crédit Lyonnais Bénin; 43.61% state-owned; full transfer to private sector ownership proposed; cap. 3,600m., res 2,720m., dep. 43,407m. (Dec. 2007); Pres. FOGAN SOSSAH; Dir-Gen. GWEN OLOKÉ-ABIOLA; 13 brs.

Diamond Bank Bénin: 308 rue du Révérend Père Colineau, 01 BP 955, Cotonou; tel. 21-31-79-27; fax 21-31-79-33; e-mail info@benin.diamondbank.com; internet www.benin.diamondbank.com; f. 2001; 80% owned by Diamond Bank (Nigeria); cap. and res 1,939m., total assets 20,645m. (Dec. 2003); Chair. PASCAL GABRIEL DOZIE; Dir-Gen. BENEDICT IHEKIRE; 9 brs.

Ecobank Bénin: rue du Gouverneur Bayol, 01 BP 1280, Cotonou; tel. 21-31-40-23; fax 21-31-33-85; e-mail ecobankbj@ecobank.com; internet www.ecobank.com; f. 1989; 79% owned by Ecobank Transnational Inc (operating under the auspices of the Economic Community of West African States); total assets 600,067m., dep. 259,943.6m. (Dec. 2008); Pres., Chair. and Dir RAPHIOU TOUKOUROU; Man. Dir CHEIKH TRAVALY; 6 brs.

Orabank Bénin SA (FBB): ave du Gouverneur Général Ponty, 01 BP 2700, Cotonou; tel. 21-31-31-00; fax 21-31-31-02; e-mail secretariat.fbbj@financial-bank.com; internet benin.financial-bank.com; f. 1996; 93.18% owned by Oragroup (Togo), 5.11% owned by Caisse Nationale de Sécurité Sociale; cap. 2,500.0m., dep. 58,661.8m., total assets 61,862.0m. (Dec. 2006); Pres. GABRIEL OUSMANE MOUSSA; Dir-Gen. RIZWAN HAÏDER; 8 brs.

Finadev: ave du Commandant Decoeur, 01 BP 6335, Cotonou; tel. 21-31-40-81; fax 21-31-79-22; e-mail info.bj@finadev-groupe.com; f. 1998; 25% owned by Financial Bank Bénin, 25% owned by FMO (Netherlands); cap. and res 1,016.0m., total assets 6,254.6m. (Dec. 2005); Pres. RÉMY BAYSSET; Dir-Gen. CHRISTINE WESTERCAMP; 4 brs.

Société Générale de Banques au Bénin (SGBBE): ave Clozel, Quartier Ganhi, 01 BP 585, Cotonou; tel. 21-31-83-00; fax 21-31-82-95; e-mail hotline.sogebenin@socgen.com; internet www.sogebenin.com; f. 2002; 67% owned by Genefitec, a wholly owned subsidiary of Groupe Société Générale (France); cap. and res 2,044.0m., total assets 25,503.0m. (Dec. 2003); Pres. GILBERT MEDJE; Dir-Gen. CHRISTIAN METAUX; 4 brs.

Savings Bank

Caisse Nationale d'Epargne: Cadjèhoun, route Inter-Etat Cotonou-Lomé, Cotonou; tel. 21-30-18-35; fax 21-31-38-43; e-mail fdossou@opt.bj; internet www.cne.opt.bj; state-owned; Pres. CHARLES PRODJINOTHO; Dir ZAKARI BOURAHIMA.

Credit Institutions

Crédit du Bénin: 08 BP 0936, Cotonou; tel. 21-31-30-02; fax 21-31-37-01; Man. Dir GILBERT HOUNKPAIN.

Crédit Promotion Bénin: 03 BP 1672, Cotonou; tel. 21-31-31-44; fax 21-31-31-66; wholly owned by private investors; Pres. BERNARD ADIKPETO; Man. Dir DÉNIS OBA CHABI.

Equipbail Bénin: blvd Jean-Paul II, 08 BP 0690, Cotonou; tel. 21-31-11-45; fax 21-31-46-58; e-mail equip.be@bkofafrica.com; internet www.bkofafrica.net/equipbail.htm; f. 1995; 58.7% owned by Bank of Africa—Bénin; cap. and res 1,229.2m., total assets 5,966.3m. (Dec. 2006); Pres. PAUL DERREUMAUX.

Financial Institution

Caisse Autonome d'Amortissement du Bénin: BP 59, Cotonou; tel. 21-31-47-81; fax 21-31-53-56; e-mail caa@firstnet.bj; f. 1966; govt owned; manages state funds; Man. Dir Adam Dende Affo.

STOCK EXCHANGE

Bourse Régionale des Valeurs Mobilières (BRVM): Antenne Nationale des Bourses du Bénin, Immeuble Chambre de Commerce et d'Industrie du Bénin, ave Charles de Gaulle, 01 BP 2985, Cotonou; tel. 21-31-21-26; fax 21-31-20-77; e-mail patioukpe@brvm.org; internet www.brvm.org; f. 1998; nat. branch of BRVM (regional stock exchange based in Abidjan, Côte d'Ivoire, serving the member states of UEMOA); Man. in Benin Pauline Atioukpe.

INSURANCE

In 2008 there were 13 insurance companies in Benin.

Allianz Bénin Assurances: Carré 5, ave Delorme, 01 BP 5455, Cotonou; tel. 21-31-67-35; fax 21-31-67-34; e-mail allianz.benin@allianz-bj.com; internet www.allianz-africa.com/benin; f. 1998; Dir-Gen. Cyril Choppin de Janvry.

A&C Bénin: Carré 21, 01 BP 3758, ave Delorme, Cotonou; tel. 21-31-09-32; fax 21-31-08-70; e-mail info@acbenin.com; internet www.acbenin.com; f. 1996; broker specializing in all branches of insurance; Man. Dir Justin Hubert Agboton.

Africaine des Assurances: Place du Souvenir, 01 BP 3128, Cotonou; tel. 21-30-04-83; fax 21-30-14-06; e-mail assuraf@intnet.bj; internet www.africaine-assur.com; Pres. Antoine Zounon; Dir-Gen. Vincent Maforikan.

Africaine Vie Bénin: 01 BP 2040, Cotonou; tel. 21-30-39-93; fax 21-30-02-91; e-mail trmetinhoue@yahoo.fr; f. 2006; Dir-Gen. Roland Mêtinhoué.

ASA Bénin: 01 BP 5508, Cotonou; tel. and fax 21-30-00-40; internet asabenin.org; fmrly Société Nationale d'Assurance; Sec.-Gen. Armand Yehouenou.

Assurances et Réassurance du Golfe de Guinée (ARGG): 04 BP 0851, Cadjehoun, Cotonou; tel. 21-30-56-43; fax 21-30-55-55; e-mail argg@intnet.bj; internet arggbenin.org; non-life insurance and re-insurance; Man. Dir Paulin Houechenou.

Avie Assurances: Immeuble Notre-Dame, ave Clozel, 01 BP 7061, Cotonou; tel. 21-31-83-55; fax 21-31-83-57; e-mail contact@avieassur.com; f. 2004; Dir-Gen. Evelyne Marie S. Fassinou.

Colina Vie Bénin: Lot 636, Quartier Les Cocotiers, 04 BP 1419, Cotonou; tel. 21-30-85-23; fax 21-30-55-46; e-mail benin@groupecolina.com; Dir-Gen. Mariam Nassirou.

Fédérale d'Assurances (FEDAS): 01 BP 4201, Cotonou; tel. 21-31-56-77; fax 21-31-49-79; e-mail fedasbenin@yahoo.fr; f. 1998; Dir-Gen. Faissou Adeyeman.

Gras Savoye Bénin: Immeuble Aboki Hounkpehedji, 1er étage, ave Mgr Steinmetz, face de l'Immeuble Kougblenou, 01 BP 294 RP Cotonou; tel. 21-31-69-22; fax 21-31-69-79; e-mail gsbenin@leland.bj; affiliated to Gras Savoye (France); Man. Guy Bihannic.

Nouvelle Société Interafricaine d'Assurances du Bénin: Immeuble Kougblénou, ave Mgr Steinmetz, 08 BP 0258, Cotonou; tel. 21-31-33-69; fax 21-31-35-17; e-mail nsab@nsiabenin.com; f. 1997; Dir-Gen. Alain Lath Houngue.

SOBAC: Carré 5, ave Delorme, 01 BP 544, Cotonou; tel. 21-31-67-35; fax 21-31-67-34; e-mail sobac@intnet.bj; affiliate of AGF (France).

Union Béninoise d'Assurance-Vie: Place du Souvenir, 08 BP 0322, Cotonou; tel. 21-30-02-12; fax 21-30-07-69; e-mail uba@ubavie.com; f. 1994; cap. 500m.; 53.5% owned by Groupe SUNU (France); Man. Dir Venance Amoussouga.

Trade and Industry

GOVERNMENT AGENCIES

Centre Béninois du Commerce Extérieur (CBCE): pl. du Souvenir, BP 1254, Cotonou; tel. 21-30-13-20; fax 21-30-04-36; e-mail cbce@bow.intnet.bj; internet www.cbce.africa-web.org; f. 1988; provides information to export cos.

Centre Béninois de la Recherche Scientifique et Technique (CBRST): 03 BP 1665, Cotonou; tel. 21-32-12-63; fax 21-32-36-71; e-mail cbrst@yahoo.fr; internet www.cbrst-benin.org; f. 1986; promotes scientific and technical research and training; 10 specialized research units; Dir-Gen. Biaou Fidèle Dimon.

Centre de Promotion de l'Artisanat: à côté du Hall des Arts et de la Culture, 01 BP 2651, Cotonou; tel. 21-30-34-32; fax 21-30-34-91; e-mail cpainfos@ifrance.com; internet www.cpabenin.bj; f. 1987; Dir Latifou Alassane.

Centre de Promotion et d'Encadrement des Petites et Moyennes Entreprises (CEPEPE): face à la Mairie de Xlacondji, 01 BP 2093, Cotonou; tel. 21-31-22-61; fax 21-31-59-50; e-mail cepepe@firstnet.bj; internet www.cepepe.org; f. 1989; promotes business and employment; offers credits and grants to small businesses; undertakes management training and recruitment; publishes bi-monthly journal, *Initiatives*; Dir-Gen. Théophile Capo-Chichi.

Conseil d'Analyse Economique: Palais de la Marina, 01 BP 2028, Cotonou; tel. 21-30-08-07; fax 21-30-18-03; e-mail contact@caebenin.org; internet www.caebenin.org/web; f. 2006; Pres. Fulbert Amoussouga Gero.

Institut National de Recherches Agricoles du Bénin (INRAB): 01 BP 884, Cotonou; tel. 21-30-02-64; fax 21-30-37-70; e-mail inrabdg4@intnet.bj; internet www.inrab.bj.refer.org; f. 1992; undertakes research into agricultural improvements; publicizes advances in agriculture; Dir David Yao Arodokoun.

Office Béninois de Recherches Géologiques et Minières (OBRGM): 04 BP 1412, Cotonou; tel. 21-31-03-09; fax 21-31-41-20; e-mail nestorved@yahoo.fr; internet www.energie.gouv.bj/obrgm/index.htm; f. 1996 as govt agency responsible for mining policy, exploitation and research; Dir-Gen. Cyriaque Tossa.

Office National d'Appui à la Sécurité Alimentaire (ONASA): PK3, route de Porto-Novo, 06 BP 2544, Cotonou; tel. 21-33-15-02; fax 21-33-02-93; e-mail onasa@onasa.org; internet www.onasa.org; f. 1992; distribution of cereals; Pres. Imarou Salé; Dir-Gen. Irenée Bio Aboudou.

Office National du Bois (ONAB): PK 3,5 route de Porto-Novo, 01 BP 1238, Cotonou; tel. 21-33-16-32; fax 21-33-39-83; e-mail contact@onab-benin.net; internet www.onab-benin.net; f. 1983; reorganized and partially privatized in 2002; forest devt and management, manufacture and marketing of wood products; industrial activities privatized in 2009; Dir-Gen. Dr Clement Kouchade.

DEVELOPMENT ORGANIZATIONS

Agence Béninoise pour la Réconciliation et le Développement: 04 BP 0409, Cotonou; tel. 21-30-68-82; Amonkè Ayichatou Been Fafoumi.

Agence Française de Développement (AFD): blvd de France, 01 BP 38, Cotonou; tel. 21-31-35-80; fax 21-31-20-18; e-mail afdcotonou@groupe-afd.org; internet www.afd.fr; fmrly Caisse Française de Développement; Country Dir Fulvio Mazzeo.

Conseil des Investisseurs Privés au Bénin (CIPB): Carré 85 ave Stenmetz, Tokpa Hoho, 03 BP 4304, Cotonou; tel. 21-31-47-67; fax 21-31-65-29; e-mail info@cipb.bj; internet cipb.bj; f. 2002; Pres. Roland Riboux; Sec.-Gen. Marius Elegbede.

France Volontaires: BP 344, Recette Principale, Cotonou; tel. 21-30-06-21; fax 21-30-07-78; e-mail afvpbn@intnet.bj; internet www.france-volontaires.org; f. 1964; name changed as above in 2009; Nat. Delegate Rémi Hallegouët.

Mission de Coopération et d'Action Culturelle (Mission Française d'Aide et de Coopération): BP 476, Cotonou; tel. 21-30-08-24; administers bilateral aid from France; Dir Bernard Hadjadj.

Projet d'Appui au Développement des Micro-entreprises (PADME): C/647 Cadjehoun, rue de la Polyclinique les Cocotiers, 08 BP 712, Cotonou; tel. 21-30-30-47; fax 21-30-23-78; internet www.padmebenin.org; f. 1994; Dir-Gen. René Azokli.

SNV Bénin (Société Néerlandais de Développement): 01 BP 1048, Carré 107, Zone Résidentielle, Rue du PNUD, Cotonou; tel. 21-31-21-22; fax 21-31-35-59; e-mail benin@snvworld.org; internet www.snvbenin.bj; Country Dir Dellaphine B. Rauch-Houekpon.

CHAMBER OF COMMERCE

Chambre de Commerce et d'Industrie du Bénin (CCIB): ave du Général de Gaulle, 01 BP 31, Cotonou; tel. 21-31-20-81; fax 21-31-32-99; e-mail ccib@bow.intnet.bj; internet www.ccibenin.org; f. 1908; present name adopted 1962; Pres. Ataou Soufiano; brs at Parakou, Mono-Zou, Natitingou and Porto-Novo.

EMPLOYERS' ORGANIZATIONS

Conseil National des Chargeurs du Bénin (CNCB): 06 BP 2528, Cotonou; tel. 21-31-59-47; fax 21-31-59-60; e-mail cncb@intnet.bj; internet www.cncbenin.com; f. 1983; represents interests of shippers; Dir-Gen. Pierre Gansaré.

Conseil National du Patronat du Bénin (CNP–Bénin): 01 BP 1260, Cotonou; tel. 21-30-74-06; fax 21-30-83-22; e-mail cnpbenin@yahoo.fr; internet www.cnpbenin.org; f. 1984 as Organisation Nationale des Employeurs du Bénin; Pres. Sébastien Ajavon; Sec.-Gen. Victor Fakeye.

Fédération des Unions de Producteurs du Bénin (FUPRO): Quartier Zakpo Houdanou, Immeuble Tossou Lazard, SACLO, BP 372, Bohicon; tel. 22-11-18-51; fax 22-51-09-46; e-mail fuproben@

yahoo.fr; internet www.fupro.org; f. 1994; Pres. LIONEL GUEZODJE; Sec.-Gen. JUSTIN SEKOU KOUNOU.

Fondation de l'Entrepreneurship du Bénin (FEB): pl. du Québec, 08 BP 1155, Cotonou; tel. 21-31-35-37; fax 21-31-37-26; e-mail fonda@intnet.bj; internet www.placequebec.org; non profit-making org.; encourages the devt of the private sector and of small and medium-sized businesses; Dir PIERRE DOVONOU LOKOSSOU.

UTILITIES

Communauté Electrique du Bénin (CEB): Vedoko, BP 537, Cotonou; tel. 21-30-06-75; f. 1968; jt venture between Benin and Togo to exploit energy resources in the 2 countries; Dir-Gen. DJIBRIL SALIFOU.

Société Béninoise d'Énergie Électrique (SBEE): 01 BP 2047, Cotonou; tel. 21-31-21-45; fax 21-31-50-28; f. 1973; state-owned; production and distribution of electricity and water; separation of electricity and water sectors pending, prior to proposed privatization of electricity operations; Dir-Gen. MARIUS Z. HOUNKPATIN.

Société Nationale des Eaux du Bénin (SONEB): 92 ave Pope Jean-Paul II, 216 RP Cotonou; tel. 21-31-20-60; fax 21-31-11-08; e-mail info@soneb.com; internet www.soneb.com; f. 2003 to assume water activities of Société Béninoise d'Electricité et d'Eau; operates under supervision of ministry responsible for water resources; utilises about 60 systems of drinkable water adductions, feeding 69 municipalities; Pres. EMILE LOUIS PARAÏSO; Dir-Gen. ADRIEN TODOMÈ DOSSOU.

MAJOR COMPANIES

The following are among the largest companies in terms of either capital investment or employment.

Agence d'Exécution des Travaux Urbains SA (AGETUR): 01 BP 2780, Cotonou; tel. 21-30-39-21; fax 21-30-51-30; e-mail agetur@intnet.bj; internet www.agetur.bj; civil construction; Pres. and Dir-Gen. LAMBERT KOTY.

Agence Privé d'Investigations et d'Analyses Stratégiques (APIAS): 01 BP 6468, Cotonou; tel. 95-95-98-54; e-mail apias@apiasbenin.com; internet www.apiasbenin.com; financial and information technology solutions; Dir-Gen. HUGUETTE TONOUEWA.

AGETIP Benin: lot H16, Les Cocotiers, rue 966, Recette Principale, 01 BP 413, Cotonou; tel. 21-30-13-05; fax 21-30-04-54; e-mail agetipbn@agetip-benin.com; internet www.agetip-benin.com; civil construction; Dir-Gen. RAYMOND ADEKAMBI.

Bio-Benin: 04 BP 1227, Cotonou; tel. 21-30-14-20; fax 21-30-12-76; f. 1984; 99.9% state-owned; mfrs and wholesalers of pharmaceutical preparations; cap. 300m. francs CFA; Dir ALI ASSANI.

British American Tobacco Benin (BAT-Bénin): BP 07, Ouidah; tel. 21-34-13-04; fax 21-34-12-83; f. 1984; fmrly Société Béninoise des Tabacs et Allumettes (SOBETA); mfrs of tobacco products; Man. Dir JEAN PIERRE QUADRI.

Cajaf Comon: PK 16, 5 Autoroute du Nigeria, Djeffa, Seme Kpodji, 03 BP 0879 Cotonou; tel. 20-24-02-41; fax 20-24-01-43; e-mail comon.cajaf@laposte.net; importer and distributor of food items; Dir-Gen. SÉBASTIEN ADJAVON.

CAMIN SA—Centrale de l'Automobile et de Matériel Industriel: PK3,5, Akpakpa, route de Porto-Novo, Zone Industrielle, 01 BP 2636, Cotonou; tel. 21-33-01-95; fax 21-33-12-55; e-mail societe_camin@yahoo.fr; f. 1986; import and export of motorcycles, vehicles, components and parts, and agricultural and industrial equipment; Chair. and Man. Dir RÉMY GAUDENS YESSOUFOU; 93 employees (2010).

CIMBENIN SA—Cimenterie du Bénin: PK8, route de Porto Novo, BP 1224, Cotonou; tel. 21-33-07-32; fax 21-33-02-45; e-mail cimbenin@hcafrica.com; internet www.heidelbergcement.com; f. 1991; cap. 1,950m. francs CFA; mfrs of cement and wholesalers of bldg materials; 54% owned by HeidelbergCement Group (Germany); Man. Dir ALPHONSO RODRIGUEZ; 129 employees (2011).

Colas-Bénin: PK4, route de Porto-Novo, 01 BP 228, Cotonou; tel. 21-33-40-10; fax 21-33-06-98; e-mail secretariat@colasbenin.bj; internet www.colas.com; construction; mem. of Groupe Colas (France); Dir STÉPHANE KNEBEL; 600 employees (2011).

Compagnie Béninoise de Négoce et de Distribution (CBND): ave Pierre Delorme, 01 BP 07, Cotonou; tel. 21-31-34-61; fax 21-31-34-63; e-mail cbnd@intnet.bj; internet www.groupecbnd.com; f. 1973; fmrly CFAO Bénin; import, export and distribution of consumer goods; sales 120,000 francs CFA (2000); Pres. and Dir-Gen. EMMANUEL KOUTON; 75 employees (2002).

Complexe Textile du Bénin (COTEB): Route inter Etats Parakou-Djougou, BP 231, Parakou; tel. 23-61-09-49; fax 23-61-11-99; e-mail direction@coteb.net; internet coteb.net; production of textiles and garments; Man. Dir D. LENAERTS.

Fludor Benin SA: Immeuble Kougblénou, ave Steinmetz, 03 BP 4304, Cotonou; tel. 21-31-65-31; fax 21-31-65-29; e-mail info@fludorbenin.com; internet www.fludorbenin.com; f. 1996; agro-based; Pres. and Dir-Gen. ROLAND RIBOUX; 257 permanent and 300 temporary employees.

Grands Moulins du Bénin (GMB): Zone Industrielle d'Akpakpa, 01 BP 949, Cotonou; tel. 21-33-08-17; internet www.chagourygroup.com/grandmoulins.html; f. 1971; cap. 438m. francs CFA; owned by Chagoury Group (Nigeria); wheat-milling; Chair. GILBERT RAMEZ CHAGOURY; Chief Exec. RONALD CHAGOURY.

Groupe la Tour: Carré 161, carrefour de l'Eglise, Sacré-Coeur, Akpakpa, 01 BP 3900, Cotonou; tel. 21-33-47-56; fax 21-33-55-97; e-mail latour@latourafrique.com; distribution of construction materials, household and office equipment, electrical goods, clothing.

Industrie Béninoise des Corps Gras (IBCG-SA): 06 BP 2548, Cotonou; tel. 21-33-07-78; fax 21-33-04-60; e-mail ibcg@groupe-aiglon.com; f. 2000 following the privatization of Société Nationale pour l'Industrie des Corps Gras, f. 1962; processes sheanuts (karité nuts), palm kernels and cottonseed; Man. Dir GEORGES ORSONI.

SCB—Société des Ciments du Bénin: Xwlacodji, rue 657, 01 BP 448, Cotonou; tel. 21-31-37-03; fax 21-31-50-74; e-mail scb@serv.eit.bj; produces and distributes cement; owned by Amida Group (France); Pres. PIERRE AMIDA.

SCB-Lafarge: Résidence des Cocotiers 01 BP 1557, Cotonou; tel. 20-30-61-81; fax 20-30-61-83; e-mail scb.lafarge@scb-lafarge.bj; f. 1999 to replace Société des Ciments d'Onigbolo; 50% owned by Société des Ciments du Bénin, 50% by Société Financière Lafarge (France); produces and markets cement; cap. 10,000m. francs CFA; Pres. TONY HADLEY; Man. Dir MARIUS ELÉGBÉDÉ.

Société Béninoise de Brasserie (SOBEBRA): route de Porto-Novo, BP 135, Cotonou; tel. 21-33-10-61; fax 21-33-01-48; e-mail contact@sobebra-bj.com; internet sobebra-bj.com; f. 1957; cap. 3,200m. francs CFA; production and marketing of beer, soft drinks and ice; Pres. BARNABÉ BIDOUZO; Dir-Gen. PATRICK CROUZET.

Société Béninoise de Textiles (SOBETEX): BP 208, Cotonou; tel. 21-33-10-94; f. 1968; cap. 500m. francs CFA; 49% state-owned; bleaching, printing and dyeing of imported fabrics; Pres. FRANÇOIS VRINAT; Dir EMILE PARAÏSO.

Société de Commerce d'Automobile et de Réprésentation (SOCAR Bénin): PK3, route de Porto-Novo, 01 BP 6, Cotonou; tel. 21-33-11-81; fax 21-33-11-84; e-mail louis.besancenot@socar-benin.com; internet www.socar-benin.com; wholesale trade in motor vehicles and spare parts; Dir-Gen. GEOFFREY FADOUL.

Société Nationale de Commercialisation des Produits Pétroliers (SONACOP): ave Jean Paul II, 01 BP 245, Cotonou; tel. 21-31-22-90; fax 21-31-24-85; e-mail dirgene@sonacop.net; internet www.sonacop.net; f. 1974; 55% owned by La Continentale des Pétroles et d'Investissements (CPI), 35% state-owned; imports and distributes petroleum products; cap. 1,500m. francs CFA; Dir-Gen. EXPÉDIT CODJO HOUESSOU; 310 employees (2005).

Société Nationale pour la Promotion Agricole (SONAPRA): 01 BP 933, Cotonou; tel. 21-33-08-20; fax 21-33-19-48; f. 1983; state-owned; manages 10 cotton-ginning plants; distributes and markets cotton fibre and cotton seed; sales of cotton US $75m. (2004/05); Dir-Gen. IDRISSOU BAKO.

Total Bénin: ave Jean Paul II, 08 BP 701, Cotonou 08; tel. 21-30-65-47; distribution of petroleum; Dir-Gen. OLIVIER LASSAGNE.

TRADE UNIONS

Centrale Syndicale des Travailleurs du Bénin (CSTB): 03 BP 0989, Cotonou; tel. 21-30-13-15; fax 21-33-26-01; actively opposes privatization and the influence of the international financial community; linked to the Parti Communiste du Bénin; Sec.-Gen. GASTON AZOUA.

Centrale des Syndicats Autonomes du Bénin (CSA—Bénin): 1 Blvd St Michel, Bourse du Travail, 04 BP 1115, Cotonou; tel. 21-30-31-82; fax 21-30-23-59; e-mail csabenin@intnet.bj; internet csa-benin.org; principally active in private sector enterprises; Sec.-Gen. DIEUDONNÉ LOKOSSOU.

Centrale des Syndicats du Secteur Privé et Informel du Bénin (CSPIB): 03 BP 2961, Cotonou; tel. 21-33-53-53; Sec.-Gen. CHRISTOPHE C. DOVONON.

Centrale des Syndicats Unis du Bénin (CSUB): Cotonou; tel. 21-33-10-27; Sec.-Gen. JEAN SOUROU AGOSSOU.

Confédération Générale des Travailleurs du Bénin (CGTB): 06 BP 2449, Cotonou; tel. 21-31-73-11; fax 21-31-73-10; e-mail cgtbpdd@bow.intnet.bj; principally active in public administration; Sec.-Gen. PASCAL TODJINOU; 33,275 mems (2002).

Confédération des Organisations Syndicales Indépendantes du Bénin (COSI—Benin): Bourse du Travail, 03 BP 1218, Cotonou; tel. 21-30-39-65; fax 21-33-27-82; e-mail cosibenin@intnet.bj; Sec.-Gen. GOERGES KAKAÏ GLELE.

Union Nationale des Syndicats de Travailleurs du Bénin (UNSTB): 1 blvd Saint-Michel, BP 69, Recette Principale, Cotonou; tel. and fax 21-30-36-13; e-mail unstb@unstb.org; internet www.unstb.org; principally active in public administration; sole officially recognized trade union 1974–90; 40,000 members in 2005, of which 25,000 in the informal sector; Sec.-Gen. EMMANUEL ZOUNON.

Transport

RAILWAYS

In 2006 there were 758 km of railway track in operation. There are plans to extend the 438-km Cotonou–Parakou line to Dosso, Niger.

Organisation Commune Bénin-Niger des Chemins de Fer et des Transports (OCBN): BP 16, Cotonou; tel. 21-31-28-57; fax 21-31-41-50; e-mail ocbn@intnet.bj; f. 1959; 50% owned by Govt of Benin, 50% by Govt of Niger; total of 579 track-km; main line runs for 438 km from Cotonou to Parakou in the interior; br. line runs westward via Ouidah to Segboroué (34 km); also line of 107 km from Cotonou via Porto-Novo to Pobé (near the Nigerian border); extension to the Republic of Niger proposed; Dir-Gen. RIGOBERT AZON.

ROADS

In 2011 there were some 30,000 km of roads, including 1,823 km of paved roads.

Agence Générale de Transit et de Consignation (AGETRAC): blvd Maritime, BP 1933, Cotonou; tel. 21-31-32-22; fax 21-31-29-69; e-mail agetrac@leland.bj; f. 1967; goods transportation and warehousing.

Compagnie de Transit et de Consignation du Bénin (CTCB Express): Cotonou; f. 1986; Pres. SOULÉMAN KOURA ZOUMAROU.

Fonds Routier du Bénin: Cotonou; internet www.fondsroutier.bj; Dir-Gen. SYLVESTRE KOCHOFA.

SHIPPING

The main port is at Cotonou. In 2006 the port handled some 5.4m. metric tons of goods. In 2009 the merchant fleet of Benin comprised seven vessels, with a total displacement of 1,271 grt.

Port Autonome de Cotonou (PAC): BP 927, Cotonou; tel. 21-31-28-90; fax 21-31-28-91; e-mail pac@leland.bj; internet www.portdecotonou.com; f. 1965; state-owned port authority; Chief Exec. (vacant).

Compagnie Béninoise de Navigation Maritime (COBENAM): pl. Ganhi, 01 BP 2032, Cotonou; tel. 21-31-27-96; fax 21-31-09-78; e-mail cobenam@elodia.intnet.bj; f. 1974 by Govts of Algeria and Dahomey (now Benin); 100% state-owned; Pres. ABDEL KADER ALLAL; Man. Dir ARMAND PRIVAT KANDISSOUNON.

Maersk Bénin: Maersk House, Zone OCBN Lot 531, Parcelle B, 01 BP 2826, Cotonou; tel. 21-31-39-93; fax 21-31-56-60; e-mail coocuscal@maersk.com; internet www.maerskline.com/bj; subsidiary of Maersk Line (Denmark); Dir DAVID SKOV.

Société Béninoise d'Entreprises Maritimes (SBEM): BP 1733, Cotonou; tel. 21-31-23-57; fax 21-31-59-26; warehousing, storage and transportation; Dir RÉGIS TISSER.

Société Béninoise des Manutentions Portuaires (SOBEMAP): blvd de la Marina, BP 35, Cotonou; tel. 21-31-41-45; fax 21-31-53-71; e-mail infos@sobemap.com; internet www.sobemap.com; f. 1969; state-owned; Dir-Gen. SOUMANOU SÉIBOU TOLÉBA.

Société Béninoise Maritime (SOBEMAR): Carré 8, Cruintomé, 08 BP 0956, Cotonou; tel. 21-31-49-65; fax 21-31-52-51; e-mail adm@sobemar-benin.com; internet www.navitrans.fr; f. 1992; Pres. RODOLPHE TORTORA.

CIVIL AVIATION

There is an international airport at Cotonou-Cadjehoun and there are secondary airports at Parakou, Natitingou, Kandi, Savè, Porga and Djougou.

Aviation Civile du Bénin: 01 BP 305, Cotonou; tel. 21-30-92-17; fax 21-30-45-71; e-mail anacaero@anac.bj; internet www.anac.bj; Dir-Gen. ARISTIDE DE SOUZA.

Trans Air Bénin (TAB): ave Jean Paul II, Lot No 14, Les Cocotiers, Cotonou; tel. 21-00-61-65; fax 21-30-92-75; e-mail transairbenin@aol.com; f. 2000; regional flights; Dir BRICE KIKI.

Tourism

Benin's rich cultural diversity and its national parks and game reserves are the principal tourist attractions. About 199,000 tourists visited Benin in 2010. Receipts from tourism were estimated at US $133.0m. in that year.

Direction de la Promotion et des Professions Touristiques: BP 2037, Cotonou; tel. 21-32-68-24; fax 21-32-68-23; internet www.benintourism.com.

Defence

As assessed at November 2011, the Beninois Armed Forces numbered an estimated 4,750 active personnel (land army 4,300, navy about 200, air force 250). Paramilitary forces comprised a 2,500-strong gendarmerie. Military service is by selective conscription, and lasts for 18 months.

Defence Expenditure: Estimated at 34,900m. francs CFA in 2011.

Chief of Defence Staff: Brig.-Gen. CHABI A. BONI.

Chief of Staff of the Army: Col DOMINIQUE M. AHOUANDJINOU.

Chief of Staff of the Navy: Capt. FERNAND MAXIME AHOYO.

Chief of Staff of the Air Force: Col CAMILLE MICHODJEHOUN.

Education

The Constitution of Benin obliges the state to make a quality compulsory primary education available to all children. Primary education was declared free of charge in 2006. Primary education begins at six years of age and lasts for six years. Secondary education, beginning at 12 years of age, lasts for up to seven years, comprising a first cycle of four years and a second of three years. According to UNESCO estimates, primary enrolment in 2009/10 included 94% of children in the appropriate age-group, while enrolment at secondary schools in 2000/01 included 20% of children in the appropriate age-group (males 26%; females 13%). In the 1990s the Government sought to extend the provision of education. In 1993 girls in rural areas were exempted from school fees, and in 1999 the Government created a 500m. francs CFA fund to increase female enrolment. The Université Nationale du Bénin, at Cotonou, was founded in 1970 and a second university, in Parakou, opened in 2001. In 2005/06 a total of 42,600 students were enrolled at tertiary education institutes. According to UNESCO estimates, in 2007 spending on education represented 15.9% of total budgeted government expenditure.

Bibliography

Adamon, A. D. *Renouveau démocratique au Bénin: la Conférence nationale des forces vives et la période de transition*. Paris, L'Harmattan, 1995.

Adekounte, F. L. *Entreprises publiques Béninoises: la descente aux enfers*. Cotonou, Les Editions du Flamboyant, 1996.

Adjovi, V. E. *Une élection libre en Afrique: la présidentielle du Bénin, 1996*. Paris, Editions Karthala, 1998.

Albert, I. *Des femmes. Une terre: une nouvelle dynamique sociale au Bénin*. Paris, L'Harmattan, 1993.

Alpern, S. B. *Amazons of Black Sparta: The Women Warriors of Dahomey*. New York, New York University Press, 1998.

Banégas, R. *La démocratie à pas de caméléon. Transition et imaginaires politiques au Bénin*. Paris, Editions Karthala, 2003.

Bio Tchané, A., and Montigny, P. *Lutter contre la corruption: un impératif pour le développement du Bénin dans l'économie internationale*. Paris, L'Harmattan, 2000.

Campbell, W. D. *The Emergent Independent Press in Benin and Côte d'Ivoire*. Westport, CT, Praeger Publishers, 1998.

Cornevin, R. *La République populaire du Bénin, des Origines dahoméennes à nos jours*. Paris, Académie des Sciences d'Outremer, 1984.

Decalo, S. *Historical Dictionary of Benin*. Metuchen, NJ, Scarecrow Press, 1995.

Dissou, M. *Le Bénin et l'épreuve démocratique: leçons des élections de 1991 à 2001*. Paris, L'Harmattan, 2002.

Dovenon, N. *Bénin: Quelles solutions pour un développement durable?* Paris, L'Harmattan, 2010.

Dunn, J. (Ed.). *West African States: Failure and Promise*. Cambridge, Cambridge University Press, 1978.

Eades, J. S., and Allen, C. *Benin*. Oxford, Clio, 1996.

Garcia, L. *Le royaume du Dahomé face à la pénétration coloniale*. Paris, Editions Karthala, 1988.

Gbago, B. G. *Le Bénin et les droits de l'homme*. Paris, L'Harmattan, 2001.

Hado, P., and Opoubor, A. *Boni Yayi, société civile et dynamique du changement au Bénin*. Paris, L'Harmattan, 2007.

Harding, L. *Das Königreich Benin: Geschichte, Kultur, Wirtschaft*. München, Oldenbourg Wissenschaftsverlag, 2010.

Harrison Church, R. J. *West Africa*. 8th edn. London, Longman, 1979.

Heilbrunn, J. R. *Markets, Profits and Power: The Politics of Business in Benin and Togo*. Bordeaux, Centre d'étude d'Afrique noire, 1996.

Houngnikpo, M. C. *Determinants of Democratization in Africa: A Comparative Study of Benin and Togo*. Lanham, MD, University Press of America, 2001.

Manning, P. *Slavery, Colonialism and Economic Growth in Dahomey, 1640–1960*. Cambridge, Cambridge University Press, 1982.

Noudjenoume, P. *La démocratie au Bénin, 1988–1993: bilans et perspectives*. Paris, L'Harmattan, 1999.

Les Frontières Maritimes du Bénin. Paris, L'Harmattan, 2004.

Okunlola, O., and Laleye, M. *La Décentralisation et le Développement des Territoires au Bénin*. Paris, L'Harmattan, 2003.

Onibon, Y. O. *Les Femmes Béninoises: de l'étalage a la conquête du marché international*. Paris, Université de Paris, 1995.

Padonou, O., and Quenum, E. C. *Le Bénin et les operations de paix. Pour une capitalisation des expériences*. Paris, L'Harmattan, 2012.

Passot, B. *Le Bénin: guide pratique*. Paris, L'Harmattan, 2005.

Topanou, P. V. *Boni Yayi ou le grand malentendu*. Paris, L'Harmattan, 2012.

Van Ufford, P. Q. *Trade and Traders: The Making of the Cattle Market in Benin*. Amsterdam, Thela Thesis, 1999.

Pfeiffer, V. *Agriculture au Sud Bénin*. Paris, L'Harmattan, 1988.

Pliya, J. *L'histoire de mon pays le Bénin*. Librairie Notre Dame, Cotonou, 1997.

BOTSWANA

Physical and Social Geography

A. MacGREGOR HUTCHESON

PHYSICAL FEATURES

The Republic of Botswana is a land-locked country, bordered by Namibia to the west and north, by the latter's Caprivi Strip to the north, by Zimbabwe to the north-east, and by South Africa to the south and south-east. Botswana occupies 581,730 sq km (224,607 sq miles) of the downwarped Kalahari Basin of the great southern African plateau, which has here an average altitude of 900 m above sea-level. Gentle undulations to flat surfaces, consisting of Kalahari sands overlying Archean rocks, are characteristic of most of the country but the east is more hilly and broken. Most of southern Botswana is without surface drainage and, apart from the bordering Limpopo and Chobe rivers, the rest of the country's drainage is interior and does not reach the sea. Flowing into the north-west from the Angolan highlands, the perennial Okavango river is Botswana's major system. The Okavango drains into a depression in the plateau, 145 km from the border, to form the Okavango swamps and the ephemeral Lake Ngami. From this vast marsh, covering 16,000 sq km, there is a seasonal flow of water eastwards along the Botlete river 260 km to Lake Xau and thence into the Makarakari salt pan. Most of the water brought into Botswana by the Okavango is lost through evaporation and transpiration in the swamps.

The Kalahari Desert dominates southern and western Botswana. From the near-desert conditions of the extreme southwest with an average annual rainfall around 130 mm, there is a gradual increase in precipitation towards the north (635 mm) and east (380 mm–500 mm). There is an associated transition in the natural vegetation from the sparse thornveld of the Kalahari Desert to the dry woodland savannah of the north and east, and the infertile sands give way eastwards to better soils developed on granitic and sedimentary rocks.

POPULATION AND RESOURCES

The eastern strip, the best-endowed and most developed region of Botswana, possesses about 80% of the population, which totalled 2,024,904, according to the census of August 2011. Seven of the eight Batswana tribes, and most of the Europeans and Asians, are concentrated in the east. A substantial number of Batswana (the figure is unrecorded, but estimated to be at least 50,000) are employed in South Africa, many of them (an estimated 5,867 at the end of 2000) in mining, although this figure declined dramatically in the 2000s. The absence of these workers helps to ease pressure on resources and contributes to the country's income through deferred pay and remittances sent home to their families. However, as a large proportion of the population is less than 15 years of age, there is a pressing need for improvements in agricultural productivity and in other sectors of the economy to provide work for the growing number of young people who are entering the labour market.

Shortage of water, resulting from the low annual rainfall and aggravated by considerable fluctuations in the monthly distribution and total seasonal rainfall, is the main hindrance to the development of Botswana's natural resources, although a number of projects have improved water supply to the main centres of economic activity. Limitations imposed by rainfall make much of the country more suitable for the rearing of livestock, especially cattle, but it has been estimated that in eastern Botswana 4.45m. ha are suitable for cultivation, of which only about 10% is actually cultivated. Although in the east the irrigation potential is limited, the Okavango-Chobe swamps offer substantial scope for irrigation (as much as an estimated 600,000 ha).

In recent years Botswana's economic base has been considerably widened. Exploitable deposits of diamonds (of which Botswana is the world's largest producer by value), gold, silver, uranium, copper, nickel, coal, manganese, asbestos, common salt, potash, soda ash and sodium sulphate have been identified, and some of these minerals are currently being mined. In particular, the major developments of diamond mining at Orapa, Letlhakane and Jwaneng, and copper-nickel mining focused on Selebi-Phikwe, with their attendant infrastructural improvements, are assisting in the diversification of the predominantly agricultural economy.

Recent History

CHRISTOPHER SAUNDERS

What today is the Republic of Botswana was the northern portion of the territory that the British Government declared a protectorate in 1885, at the request of local Tswana rulers who wished to deter Boer encroachment from the Transvaal in the east. In 1895 the southern portion was incorporated into the Cape Colony, but the large northern protectorate continued to be ruled directly by Britain through the High Commissioner. There was some expectation that the Bechuanaland protectorate would be incorporated in the new Union of South Africa after 1910, but the Tswana made clear their opposition to this, and the sparsely populated territory remained under direct British rule until it gained its independence as Botswana in 1966, with over 80% of its land still under tribal control.

It was not until 1960 that the first nationalist party, the Bechuanaland People's Party, was founded, with links to the African National Congress of South Africa (ANC). Two years later the most influential figure in the country, Seretse (later Sir Seretse) Khama, paramount chief of the Ngwato, the largest Tswana grouping, formed the Bechuanaland (later Botswana) Democratic Party (BDP). In the territory's first direct general election under universal adult suffrage, held in 1965, the BDP won 28 of the 31 seats; Khama became Prime Minister. Independence followed on 30 September 1966, when Bechuanaland became the Republic of Botswana, with Khama as the first President. Diamonds were then discovered and independent Botswana became the world's largest supplier to the global market. As a result, in the decades that followed the country achieved a rate of economic growth unmatched anywhere else in Africa. Botswana became known as the continent's most stable democracy, with the BDP remaining the ruling party from independence to the present.

When Khama died in July 1980, his Vice-President, Dr Quett (later Sir Quett) Ketumile Masire, succeeded to the presidency. As Minister of Finance and Development Planning, Masire had played an important role in the country's economic development and he was to remain in office for 18 years.

In March 1992 the Vice-President, Peter Mmusi, and the Minister of Agriculture, Daniel Kwelagobe, resigned after being implicated by a commission of inquiry in a corruption scandal involving the illegal transfer of land. Festus Mogae, who as Minister of Finance and Development Planning had developed a reputation for fiscal prudence and sound economic management, was appointed Vice-President and allocated the portfolio of local government and lands. Mmusi and Kwelagobe remained in the BDP but opposed the Government's economic liberalization policy, and sought to overturn the findings of the commission on illegal land dealings. Uncertainty about the future leadership of the BDP and the President's silence on this matter added to the divisions within the ruling party before the general election of October 1994. Although the Government rejected the demands of the leading opposition party, the Botswana National Front (BNF), for the appointment of an independent electoral commission and for the reduction of the voting age to 18 years, the party abandoned its threat to boycott the election and sought, instead, to mobilize popular support on the issues of government corruption and economic recession. The BNF fared unexpectedly well in the election, winning 37.7% of the votes and increasing its representation to 13 seats. The BDP, however, with 53.1% of the vote, won 26 seats. Only three ministers (among them Mogae) retained their portfolios in the new Cabinet, which included Kwelagobe, who had been acquitted by the High Court on charges relating to the corruption allegations made against him and was reinstated as Minister of Agriculture.

A number of constitutional amendments were adopted in mid-1997. The President was henceforth limited to two terms of office, and provision was made for the Vice-President to succeed automatically in the event of the death or resignation of the President. The electoral system was reformed, the age of eligibility to vote was reduced to 18 years and an independent electoral commission was established. In November 1997 Masire announced that he would retire the following year. A ceremony to mark his retirement was held on 31 March 1998 and the following day Mogae was inaugurated as President.

THE MOGAE PRESIDENCY

The only new minister in Mogae's Cabinet was Lt-Gen. Seretse Khama Ian Khama, the oldest son of Sir Seretse Khama, and paramount chief of the Ngwato, the largest tribal group in the country. A military man, he was Commander of the Botswana Defence Force (BDF), but now received the portfolio of presidential affairs and public administration, and was designated as Vice-President, subject to his election to the National Assembly. In July 2003 he was elected Chairman of the BDP. Ponatshego Kedikilwe, who had been favoured for the vice-presidency by certain prominent members of the BDP leadership, was appointed Minister of Finance and Development Planning.

Meanwhile, hostility between Kenneth Koma, founder and long-time leader of the BNF, and his deputy, Michael Dingake, resulted in a split within that party. At the BNF's annual congress in April 1998 Koma, supported by dissident members who had been expelled from the party, ordered the expulsion of leading members, some of whom then formed the Botswana Congress Party (BCP). This became the official opposition in mid-July, after 11 of the BNF's 13 deputies decided to join the new party. Despite discontent in the BDP over corruption and the conduct of the primary ballot to select candidates for the October 1999 general election, the BDP won 33 of the 40 seats in that election, the BNF six and the BCP only one. BCP leader Dingake was defeated in the capital, Gaborone.

In February 2000 eastern Botswana suffered the worst floods ever recorded in the country, and more than 11,000 houses were destroyed, leaving over 60,000 people homeless. However, of much greater long-term significance was the HIV/AIDS pandemic, which had by 2000 become the Government's primary health concern. Botswana was the first country in Africa to distribute antiretroviral drugs for those with HIV through its public health system under the Masa (New Dawn) programme, but by 2003 it was estimated that 300,000 people in Botswana were HIV-positive, with some 37% of 15–49-year-olds infected, the highest proportion anywhere in the world. As a result, life expectancy declined to 40 years by early 2006, although this figure was subsequently revised upwards, and was estimated at 61 years in 2008, by which time HIV was being managed as a chronic disease. The Masa programme provided free antiretrovirals and counselling, targeting priority groups of HIV-positive people, including pregnant women, children older than six months and patients with tuberculosis. District and village AIDS committees and voluntary test centres were established and began to roll out antiretrovirals to additional sites. HIV prevalence among pregnant women began to decline, HIV transmission from mother to child dropped dramatically, and by the end of 2007 over 90,000 people were receiving antiretroviral drugs. Yet, while Botswana had one of the most progressive and comprehensive programmes anywhere for tackling the disease, people remained reluctant to discover their HIV status, and it seemed unlikely that the aim of preventing new infections by 2016 would be achieved. By 2009 one-quarter of the population aged 15 years and over (an estimated 300,000 adults) was living with HIV—the second highest rate of HIV prevalence in the world after Swaziland. With US funding for antiretroviral drugs declining, the burden fell on Botswana itself. In October 2011 former President Mogae, who had won the Mo Ibrahim Prize for good governance in Africa in 2008 and who headed the government-supported Aids Council, argued that it was difficult to promote safe sex when homosexuality and prostitution were illegal. Homosexuality remained punishable by up to seven years' imprisonment.

Following the recommendations of a commission established in July 2000 to investigate allegations of discrimination against minority ethnic groups, the Government presented a number of draft constitutional amendments to Parliament in 2002. Under the proposals, the House of Chiefs, Botswana's second legislative chamber, was to be renamed the Ntlo ya Dikgosi, and its membership increased from 15 to 35, comprising 30 members elected every five years by senior tribal authorities and five specially appointed members. In April 2002 the draft amendments were revised to allow the eight paramount chiefs from the Setswana-speaking 'principal tribes' to retain their ex officio status in the chamber, prompting criticism from opposition parties and from those who believed that discrimination was continuing against minority ethnic groups, including the indigenous San (Bushmen) people. Long before the matter was resolved, the National Assembly approved legislation providing for the expansion of its membership from 40 to 57, with effect from the 2004 general election. The constitutional changes to the Ntlo ya Dikgosi came into effect in December 2005.

From the late 1990s the Botswana Government provoked much international criticism for its attempts to relocate some 3,000 San, often referred to by the derogatory terms Basarwa, meaning people without cattle, from their ancestral lands in the Central Kalahari Game Reserve (CKGR) to new settlements outside the reserve. A government study conducted in 1985 found that the San in the CKGR were abandoning their traditional means of hunting on foot in favour of guns, horses and even four-wheel drive vehicles. Permanent, settled agricultural communities, grazing livestock, were being established that were not consistent with the land-use patterns envisaged when the CKGR was formed. In an attempt to persuade the San to move out of the reserve, the Government began to disconnect water supplies, and offered them compensation if they relocated. The London-based minority-rights group Survival International (SI), which took up the case of the San, claimed that the policy of resettlement had been devised to allow diamond mining to take place in the reserve, where a number of diamond companies had licences to prospect.

The issue of the forced removal of the San from the CKGR came to the fore again in January 2002, when the Government cut off water supplies to those who had refused to leave the reserve. In April that year 243 San, assisted financially by SI and the First People of the Kalahari movement, began legal action, requesting a ruling that the termination of basic services was illegal and that they had been deprived of their land by force. The case was initially dismissed on a technicality but was subsequently taken to the High Court. In December 2006 that court ruled that the Government's refusal to issue San with hunting licences for the reserve was unlawful and that the San had the right to remain on their ancestral land. Although it accepted the judgment, the Government declared that it would not help the San to return, and San continued to be detained for hunting in the reserve. SI remained actively involved, and continued to claim that the Government sought to drive out the San. In June 2008 newly appointed President Khama reasserted the Government's position and that the authorities would not provide the San with any amenities in the reserve. Meanwhile, diamond companies had begun prospecting and in early 2009 the Government admitted that diamond mining would in future take place in the reserve. In 2012 SI continued to claim that the security forces were arresting and intimidating San in the CKGR, and in that year the San of Botswana joined other San communities in Namibia and South Africa in petitioning the UN to force their respective governments to recognize their land and resource rights.

In 2005 the Government tabled legislation in the National Assembly to make the Constitution 'tribally neutral'. This removed a clause giving protection to the San and other minorities, and critics argued that the amendment was designed to undermine the court challenge. When further evictions of San were threatened, an urgent application was made to the High Court to prevent them. In February 2005 Professor Kenneth Good, an Australian-born lecturer in political science at the University of Botswana, was given 48 hours to leave the country owing to the widespread belief that he had supported SI's attempt to have Botswana's diamonds labelled 'blood diamonds' (diamonds obtained in situations of conflict) because of the removal of the San from the CKGR. (When those San who returned to the CKGR were prevented from drawing water from a well there, they lodged a formal complaint at the High Court, which in 2010 rejected their right to the water. In a setback to the Government, the Court of Appeal overturned this decision in January 2011. The Government accepted the judgment and pledged to continue efforts to resolve the issue with the San through dialogue.)

President Mogae and his Government were strong supporters of the Kimberley Process Certification Scheme (see Economy), which regulated the trade in rough diamonds, and Botswana maintained that the country could account for the origin of all its diamonds. Good, who rejected the notion that Botswana was a 'model democracy', had also criticized the President's nomination of Khama as his designated successor. He alleged that Khama had awarded tenders to family members when head of the army and had commandeered military helicopters to aid the BDP's election campaign. Although Good challenged his deportation order in court, he failed to have the decision overturned. The Attorney-General stated that the matter was beyond judicial review. Appeals to Mogae by Good's supporters were unsuccessful and he settled abroad.

The 2004 Election

In the legislative elections held on 30 October 2004, 75% of those registered voted and the ruling BDP won 44 of the 57 seats with 51.7% of the vote. The BNF increased its number of seats to 12, but its President, Otsweletse Moupo, lost his seat. The party's Secretary-General, Akanyang Magama, took over as leader of the opposition. As in the 1999 election, the BCP won only one seat, but its share of the vote increased from 11.9% to 16.6% and its victory in Gaborone Central was the main surprise of the election. Re-elected President by the National Assembly for a second and final term, Mogae was sworn in on 2 November. In an extensive reorganization of his Cabinet, Mogae appointed 11 new ministers, nine of whom were new members of the National Assembly. Those appointed tended to support Khama, while supporters of Kedikilwe were excluded. Among those removed from the Cabinet was Kwelagobe, the Secretary-General of the BDP, who had held ministerial office since 1973. The President was also able to appoint four members of the National Assembly and his decision to select two defeated BDP candidates was criticized for breaking an unwritten rule that defeated candidates should not be appointed.

In the concurrently held local elections, most of the seats in the capital and in Lobatse, the hub of the beef industry, were secured by the opposition, while the majority of the seats in Francistown, the second largest city, were won by the BDP. For some observers the election reinforced Botswana's reputation as a stable, liberal democracy, but the continued weakness of the opposition was the cause of much comment. The BCP claimed that the state media had given the ruling party unfair advantage and not allowed the opposition to present its case. Others argued for proportional representation as a way to give the opposition a larger presence in the National Assembly.

That the BDP remained so politically dominant was in part a consequence of the very divided opposition. In February 2006 representatives of the four main opposition parties met to try to agree on how to co-operate in the run-up to the next general election. For some time it appeared that progress was being made, but by early 2007 the talks had collapsed.

In late 2006 controversy surrounded the Government's Intelligence and Security Bill, which proposed that a new security directorate be established. Non-governmental organizations were concerned that there would be no parliamentary oversight of this, nor adequate means for recourse in cases of abuse. Critics of the Government pointed to the legislation as further evidence that the country was moving in an authoritarian direction. Further evidence brought forward included the proposed selection procedure for BDP candidates for the 2009 legislative elections, and the announcement by the Government in March 2007 that 17 individuals from the United Kingdom, the USA, Australia and Canada—mainly human rights campaigners, journalists and academics—would henceforth require visas to visit Botswana.

In early 2008, as Mogae approached the end of his second term as President, the BDP rejected the idea of a direct election to the presidency. Mogae relinquished the presidency on 31 March and the following day Khama was inaugurated as Head of State. Some observers feared that his leadership style would be authoritarian, given his military background. However, although he spoke of the importance of discipline in his inaugural address, most commentators were impressed by the peaceful nature of the handover, a stark contrast to neighbouring Zimbabwe, where Robert Mugabe was increasingly resorting to the use of force to retain power.

THE PRESIDENCY OF IAN KHAMA

In September 2007 Botswana was ranked first in Africa for the rule of law, transparency and lack of corruption according to the *Index of African Governance*, produced by the Mo Ibrahim Foundation, which was established as a vehicle for discussing good governance across sub-Saharan Africa and world-wide. The Global Peace Index, as produced by Vision of Humanity, a focus group for global peace initiatives, rated it the most peaceful country on the continent, while the Heritage Foundation's 2008 *Index of Economic Freedom* ranked it second in sub-Saharan Africa, with its economy rated as 68.6% free. According to the civil society organization Transparency International, Botswana was the least corrupt African country.

However, in 2008 the Director of Public Prosecutions brought corruption charges against the former Managing Director of Debswana Diamond Co (Pty) Ltd, Louis Nchindo, and a number of that company's senior employees. Debswana, a 50:50 joint venture between the Government of Botswana and De Beers Centenary AG of Switzerland, contributed more than 80% of Botswana's foreign earnings through its diamond sales and 50% of the country's public revenue. Furthermore, by late 2009 there was rising concern over a number of extra-judicial killings of people whom the state referred to as suspected criminals. In September a report by the Bench Marks Foundation, a faith-based organization which monitors corporate social responsibility, revealed that Debswana had long had close links with the ruling BDP. In February 2010 Nchindo was found dead in a remote game reserve, shortly before the much-delayed case against him was to be heard. Former President Mogae was to have given evidence for the prosecution, amid allegations that De Beers had funded the BDP over many years. Nchindo's death was officially declared to have been suicide, although some believed that he might have been murdered to prevent the case from going ahead.

In 2009, as a result of the global economic crisis, diamond mining was suspended for a time and Debswana only produced 17m. carats from its diamond mines, compared with 32m. carats in 2008, while sales of diamonds were 39% lower, at US $1,700m. Standard and Poor's downgraded the country's credit rating from A to A–. Nevertheless, in November the head of De Beers announced that Debswana would proceed with a major extension at the world's richest diamond mine, Jwaneng, in what would be, at $3,000m., the largest ever single capital investment in Botswana's private sector. This would extend the life of the mine, which in 2009 contributed 70% of Debswana's total revenue, to at least 2025. In April 2010 the company announced that it was ready to increase production if market conditions improved, but that it was also considering diversifying further into coal and energy. The decision by the De Beers Diamond Trading Company to move from London to Gaborone by 2013 was expected to lead to an inflow of expertise and technology.

In the run-up to the general election of 16 October 2009 there was much dissension in the BDP, with the Barata-Phathi ('We Love the Party') faction accusing President Khama of acting dictatorially. At the general election Khama retained widespread support, especially in the rural areas, and as a result secured his first full five-year presidential term. The BDP won 45 of the 57 seats in the National Assembly, one more than in 2004, though only 53.3% of the vote; the BNF secured only six seats, with 21.9% of the vote; and the BCP won four seats with 19.2% of the vote. It was widely accepted that the election had been free and fair. Nevertheless, tensions within the BDP remained, and in April 2010 prominent members of the Barata-Phathi faction announced that they were leaving the ruling party and forming a new party, the Botswana Movement for Democracy (BMD), which four members of the National Assembly joined.

In April 2011 public sector workers commenced industrial action demanding higher wages, their salaries having remained stagnant since 2008. President Khama contended that the Government, which remained the single largest employer in the country, could not afford to meet the workers' demands owing to the budgetary deficit; the deficit was forecast to increase to 7,000m. pula (US $1,100m.) in the 2011/12 fiscal year, largely owing to the impact of the global recession on state revenues and also to reduced revenues from the Southern African Customs Union (SACU). Almost 1,500 government employees in essential services were dismissed, and a number of hospitals and schools were closed. The trade unions demanded the unconditional reinstatement of those dismissed and stated that the strike would continue indefinitely until the workers' demands were met. While the BDP accused opposition parties of promoting the strike to try to bring about a popular uprising similar to those that had occurred earlier in the year in North Africa, the trade unions were very critical of the state-run media for carrying so little news of the strike. By mid-May 2011 over 90,000 workers were involved, and the strike was threatening to undermine the country's image as an African success story. President Khama held firm, however, and the strike ended after eight weeks with a victory for the Government, which then proceeded to enlarge the areas of work regarded as essential and in which workers could not go on strike (These included teachers and diamond workers). Following legal action by the labour unions, the Government reinstated most of the public sector workers who had been dismissed during the strike.

The opposition parties failed to capitalize on the opportunity that the strike provided, and the leading public sector trade union threatened to withdraw its support in the 2014 general election if they did not agree to an electoral alliance. The BMD, the BNF (which received a boost when the former BDP Secretary-General joined the party), the BCP and the Botswana People's Party signed a memorandum of understanding on electoral co-operation, but in December 2011 the BCP withdrew from unity talks among the opposition parties, the so-called 'Umbrella project', due to a dispute over the allocation of parliamentary constituencies ahead of the election. In February 2012 Botsalo Ntuane of the BMD was removed as Leader of the Opposition in Parliament; however, the position remained vacant, as the opposition parties were unable to agree upon a replacement, further damaging their reputation among the electorate. A report issued by a South Africa-based think tank, the Institute for Democracy in Southern Africa, was critical of the state of democracy in Botswana, citing the weakness of the legislature in relation to the executive, the lack of public participation and the absence of an institutional framework to promote political accountability. Meanwhile, following the execution of a convicted murderer in January, there had been appeals, from within the country and without, for the Government to suspend the implementation of the death penalty, but they went unheeded. Khama's leadership style continued to show authoritarian tendencies, and the BDP maintained its presentation of itself as the natural party of government. In February the BDP celebrated its 50th anniversary, and few observers expected that it would not continue to rule for many years to come.

EXTERNAL RELATIONS

Following the unilateral declaration of independence by Rhodesia (now Zimbabwe) in 1965, Seretse Khama voiced his opposition to the illegal regime, but his country remained dependent on the Rhodesian-owned railways for its economic survival. Khama nevertheless played an important role in forging the alliance of 'front-line' states against the apartheid regime in South Africa in the mid-1970s, and Botswana was also a founder member of the Southern African Development Co-ordination Conference (SADCC) in 1980, reorganized in 1992 as the Southern African Development Community—SADC. SADCC was formed to encourage regional development and reduce its members' economic dependence on South Africa. In the 1970s and 1980s it was Botswana's policy to accommodate South African refugees, while not allowing them to use the country as a base for attacks on South Africa. With the relaxation of the political climate within South Africa from 1990 there was a gradual improvement in relations between the two countries; full diplomatic relations were established in June 1994, after which the two countries worked closely together in SADC.

Full diplomatic relations were established between Botswana and Zimbabwe in May 1983, although by the mid-1990s the Government had become concerned at the growing number of illegal immigrants in the country, the majority of whom were from Zimbabwe. With the worsening of Zimbabwe's economic crisis, considerable numbers of Zimbabweans again moved into Botswana, and a number of violent incidents took place along the border. In July 2003 Botswana and Zimbabwe began operating joint patrols intended to prevent the passage of refugees into Botswana, and by 2004 Botswana was repatriating some 2,500 illegal immigrants—mainly Zimbabweans—each month. It was not known how many remained within the country. Although President Mogae stated that Zimbabwe suffered from a 'drought of leadership', his Government hesitated to criticize its neighbour openly, either in SADC or in bilateral talks.

Shortly after Khama took office as President, and in the context of record oil prices, the Botswana Government banned the export of bulk fuel to Zimbabwe and Khama requested that the media expose the plight of refugees from Zimbabwe, for whom a temporary refugee camp had been set up in Francistown. Following the disputed presidential election in Zimbabwe in March 2008, Morgan Tsvangirai, the leader of the opposition Movement for Democratic Change, who claimed to have secured victory in the poll, was granted temporary refuge in Gaborone, where he was provided with state security. Khama announced that he would not attend SADC meetings to which Mugabe had been invited. In June 2008 the Botswana Government condemned the Mugabe regime's campaign of violence and intimidation against opposition supporters ahead of the run-off election, although reluctantly supported the power-sharing arrangement reached there subsequently. Tensions with Zimbabwe continued, with some arguing that Botswana should take a stronger line against the Zimbabwe regime within SADC.

Following the achievement of independence by Namibia in March 1990, presidential visits were exchanged by Botswana and Namibia, and steps were taken to ensure bilateral co-operation. However, in 1992 a border dispute developed between the two countries regarding their rival territorial claims over a small island in the Chobe river, which Namibia called Kasikili and Botswana Sedudu. In early 1995 Botswana and Namibia agreed to present the case for arbitration at the International Court of Justice (ICJ) in the Hague,

Netherlands, and in February 1996 the two countries signed an agreement committing themselves in advance to the court's eventual judgment. What were perceived as attempts by Botswana to extend the role and capabilities of its armed forces (most notably the completion of a large new airbase at Molepolole in 1995 and efforts during 1996–97 to procure military tanks) were, for a time, a source of friction between the two countries, although Botswana emphasized that it only sought to enable its military to fulfil a wider regional and international peace-keeping role. A Namibian proposal to construct a pipeline to take water from the Okavango river, which feeds the Okavango delta, an important habitat for Botswana's varied wildlife and a major tourist attraction, created further tension.

In early 1997 it was reported that Namibia had been angered by Botswana's erection of a fence along Namibia's Caprivi Strip, which separates the two countries to the north. Botswana insisted that the fence was simply a measure to control the spread of livestock diseases. In January 1998 an emergency meeting of the Botswana-Namibia Joint Commission on Defence and Security was held to discuss ownership of an island named Situngu in the Chobe river. The two countries agreed to set up a joint technical commission to demarcate the shared border and confirmed that they would accept the judgment of the ICJ on Sedudu-Kasikili. In December the ICJ awarded the island to Botswana. A joint commission was subsequently established to investigate other demarcation disputes along the Chobe and two other rivers.

Towards the end of 1998 relations between the two countries were further strained by the arrival in Botswana of more than 300 refugees from the Caprivi Strip in Namibia. These included Mishake Muyongo, who had been suspended as President of the Democratic Turnhalle Alliance (the leading Namibian opposition party) in August, and other leading Caprivians who had been campaigning for the secession of their region from Namibia. Other refugees followed, claiming intimidation and harassment by the Namibian army, and by early 1999 more than 2,000 were living in a camp north of Gaborone. Demands by Namibia for their extradition were refused, although it was agreed by the two Governments in March 1999 that prominent dissidents among the refugees would be allowed to leave Botswana for another country, and that an amnesty was to be extended to other refugees returning to Namibia. A formal agreement to this effect was signed in May under the auspices of the office of the UN High Commissioner for Refugees (UNHCR), after which Muyongo and two others were granted asylum in Denmark. However, the programme to repatriate others to Namibia was suspended in August 1999, and some 2,400 refugees remained in Botswana. A new agreement for their repatriation to the Caprivi Strip was signed by UNHCR and the two countries in April 2002, and in August of that year those refugees who had registered for repatriation began to return to Namibia. Between August and October some 800 refugees were repatriated to Namibia, leaving some 1,200 in Botswana, who remained reluctant to return.

Botswana's principled stand on apartheid, its political stability and democratic record, and its reputation for moderation, gave the country a minor but effective voice in many international deliberations. The SADC Secretariat, located in Gaborone, was opened by Masire in 1990, and after he left office Masire acted as facilitator in efforts to achieve peace in the Democratic Republic of the Congo. Botswana joined with South Africa in a military operation in Lesotho in 1998 to restore stability there. In 2004 SADC agreed that an early-warning centre to collect information on developing crises in the region would be located in Botswana, and the headquarters of the planned SADC military force, part of the African Union's African Standby Force, was to be stationed there because of the country's stability and its central geographical position in the southern African region. Meanwhile, Botswana and Zambia continued to seek funding for the proposed Kazungula Bridge, which would directly link the two countries across the Zambezi river. President Michael Chilufya Sata of Zambia made his first state visit to Botswana in March 2012; this followed a decision by the African Development Bank the previous month in which it agreed to provide a loan to finance the construction of the bridge, estimated to cost US $260m.

The signing by Botswana of an interim Economic Partnership Agreement with the European Union (EU) in June 2009 provoked tension within SACU. South Africa and Namibia refused to sign similar agreements. Although the Botswana Government stated that it had no choice but to sign the accord if it wanted to retain market access to the EU, in 2010 it agreed to seek to work together with the other SACU countries in order to present a united front to the EU. In mid-2012 the issue was still unresolved.

Relations with South Africa suffered when in late 2011 Julius Malema, President of the ANC Youth League, appealed for regime change in Botswana, claiming that the Botswana Government was a 'puppet' of US 'imperialism' and was out of line with other countries in Southern Africa on Zimbabwe and other regional matters. The ANC Youth League declared that it would establish a Botswana Command Team to work towards uniting the opposition in Botswana against the BDP. South African President Jacob Zuma and the ANC criticized Malema, who was brought before a disciplinary committee. Despite issuing an apology, Malema was expelled from the ANC in March 2012.

Botswana, largely semi-arid with limited water resources, imported 90% of its food, most of it from South Africa. Climate change seemed likely to exacerbate food supply problems, and rising food prices threatened to produce social unrest in a country with one of the most inequitable income distributions in the world: though Botswana was a middle income country, the median per head household income in Gaborone was only US $2 per day. Botswana also remained highly dependent on the transfer payments it received from SACU, the terms of which were in 2012 being renegotiated, with South Africa demanding a much-increased share of the revenues.

Economy

LINDA VAN BUREN

Revised for this edition by DUNCAN WOODSIDE

INTRODUCTION

Classed as an 'upper middle-income country' by the World Bank, in 2010 Botswana had a gross national income per head of US $6,890, one of the highest in Africa, where the average was $1,165; the world average was $9,097. Diamonds have transformed Botswana's economy, providing a level of financial stability that is rare in Africa. Over the years this precious commodity has significantly alleviated the effects of regional problems in other sectors, such as livestock and tourism. Botswana promotes its output as 'diamonds for development', as an alternative to so-called 'conflict diamonds' (see below), and much of the country's diamond revenue has funded, and continues to fund, its development.

The National Development Plan 10 (NDP 10), which covers the seven-year period 1 April 2009–31 March 2016, set the real GDP growth target at 3.1% per annum. After a contraction of 4.9% in 2009 (owing to a recession in developed countries and the impact of this on global diamond prices), real GDP rose by 7.2% in 2010 (bolstered by the mining sector, which grew by

7%). NDP 10 targeted inflation of between 3% and 6% per annum. Year-on-year inflation stood at 6.9% in 2010, down from 8.2% in 2009. Botswana's inflation figures—although comparing very favourably with many other African economies, especially in view of the hyperinflation that prevailed in neighbouring Zimbabwe in the late 2000s—have been higher than the country's economic planners and consumers would wish. For this reason, parastatals have been directed to exercise restraint in pricing and to achieve their revenue targets through improved productivity rather than through price increases.

According to the IMF, real GDP growth slowed to 5.0% in 2011, due in large part to subdued international diamond demand late in the year. The Fund predicted that the economy would grow by just 3.3% in real terms in 2012, due to a combination of domestic and international factors. Externally, the first half of 2012 proved largely subdued for the diamond trade, as an intensifying sovereign debt crisis in the euro area generated fears of extended recessions in many developed countries. Domestically, the IMF cautioned that a number of infrastructure projects were nearing maturity, with the end of such activity likely to exert a drag on economic output. Nevertheless, the Fund envisaged a moderate recovery during 2013, with growth rising to 4.6%. The IMF remained sceptical in mid-2012 about the central bank's ability to bring inflation within its target range and predicted that consumer prices would rise by 7.8% in 2012 and 6.7%, in 2013.

The Bank of Botswana must execute a delicate balancing act in setting the value of the pula. On the one hand, its rate against the US dollar is crucial, as global diamond sales are denominated in dollars; on the other hand, the pula's rate against the South African rand is also important, because South Africa is Botswana's main supplier. After several years during which the trends of the US dollar and the South African rand were at odds with each other, the Bank of Botswana introduced a new exchange rate regime in 2005, termed the 'crawling band'. This broadened the margins between the buy rate and the sell rate of the pula by the Bank of Botswana, the effect of which was to spur a significant increase in inter-bank trading, thereby fostering considerably more competition among banks in the foreign exchange market. During the year to 18 May 2011 the pula appreciated by 5% against the US dollar, but it depreciated by 3.3% against the rand.

At 30 November 2010 Botswana's foreign exchange reserves stood at US $8,280m., down from $9,300m. one year earlier. Forward import cover shortened from 30 months in November 2006 to 21 months in 2009, and further to 19 months in 2010. Nevertheless, Botswana still had the longest forward import cover in the world by a wide margin, a distinction it achieves consistently. The Government regards the high level of foreign exchange reserves as essential to sustain Botswana's future economic development as diamond earnings level out and indeed decline. The 2009 recession gave Botswana cause to rely on its cushion of reserves. The global economic downturn severely depressed demand for diamonds leading even to the temporary closure of diamond mines in the country. With the resultant steep decline in export revenue, the trade balance worsened, and the balance of payments suffered; however, the overall balance of payments was protected by the cushion of foreign exchange reserves.

In his budget speech given in February 2011, Minister of Finance and Development Planning Kenneth Matambo identified a 'mismatch between what our education system provides and what the labour market requires' as one of the biggest challenges facing Botswana's economic planners. The World Bank acknowledges that, at 10% of GDP, Botswana's educational expenditure is high, and that 'significant educational achievements have been attained', not least 'nearly universal and free education' and a literacy rate of 83%. However, this 'mismatch' persists. To address it, in 2010 the Government set up an employment exchange service to help to bring potential employers together with job seekers, and established a Labour Market Observatory (LMO) within the Ministry of Finance and Development Planning, to identify the nature of these 'mismatches' and to enable the Government to alleviate them.

Another major factor affecting Botswana's labour force is the high incidence of HIV/AIDS; 24.8% of the adult population (aged 15 years and over) is HIV positive, rendering Botswana's adult HIV/AIDS prevalence rate the second highest in the world, behind only that of Swaziland. To address this situation, the Botswana Government introduced the Prevention of Mother-to-Child Transmission (PMTCT) programme, and became the first African government to aim to provide anti-retroviral treatment (ART) drugs to all citizens who need them. By December 2009 Botswana had achieved 'universal treatment access'—defined by the World Health Organization (WHO) as a situation in which 'at least 80% of those who need HIV treatment are receiving it'; by comparison, the rate for sub-Saharan Africa as a whole stood at 37%.

AGRICULTURE

Botswana's agricultural sector employed about 44% of the economically active population in December 2010 (a level that has changed little for more than a decade), yet contributed just 2.5% of total GDP in 2011. Composed partly of semi-desert and partly of a savannah area, with erratic rainfall and relatively poor soils, the country is more suited to grazing than to arable production. Agriculture remains dominated by the livestock sector generally and by the cattle industry in particular. Botswana has 325,000 ha of arable land. Of the country's total annual cereal requirement of about 325,000 metric tons per annum, Botswana's farmers are able to supply about 25% in good years, and the Government is sufficiently solvent to be able to pay for grain imports to address the shortfall. In the arable sector, commercial farmers provide a disproportionate share of crop production. Of the 85% of small-scale farms producing crops, almost one-third cover less than 3 ha, and only 6.8% cover more than the 10-ha minimum necessary for household self-sufficiency, even in years of adequate rains. As a result, two-thirds of rural households are reported to depend for as much as 40% of their income on members employed in the formal, predominantly commercial, agricultural sector.

Botswana is considered to have substantial irrigation potential, particularly in the Okavango delta and Chobe areas. In view of the unique and fragile nature of the Okavango, especially, there are also significant possible environmental risks in realizing this potential, which became the subject of considerable study in the 1990s. Some experimentation, using flood recession irrigation, was initiated at Molapo, on the eastern fringe of the Okavango. Three major dams were under construction in 2011. The largest—the 400m.-cu m Dikgatlhong Dam, at the confluence of the Shashe and Tati rivers in north-eastern Botswana—was being built by Sinohydro Corporation of the People's Republic of China, at a projected cost of P1,200m.; the dam was reported to be eight months behind schedule and was due for completion in February 2012. The smallest, the 42m.-cu m Lotsane Dam, which was also being constructed by Sinohydro, was expected to come on stream in October 2011. The 90m.-cu m Thune Dam was scheduled to be commissioned in March 2013. According to government figures, even though Botswana is by and large an arid country, the proportion of the population who have sustainable access to safe drinking water is 98%, and the Government is continuing its efforts to bring this figure up to 100%. In contrast to this impressive figure is the less commendable percentage of people with access to good sanitation, which is 40%, with an NDP 10 target of 55% by 2016.

The improved management of the agricultural sector is a government priority, especially owing to its key role in providing employment. Notably, however, although drought and HIV/AIDS affected the entire southern African region, in 2009 and 2010 the UN World Food Programme (WFP) deemed South Africa and Botswana to be the only countries in the region capable of coping without WFP assistance.

A major study of the livestock sector completed in 2005 recommended significant reforms of the sector, including a reduction in the 'excess regulatory burden' and a restructuring of the Botswana Meat Commission (BMC). This huge parastatal is headquartered in Lobatse, where its main abattoir can handle 800 head of cattle per day. The abattoir is fully integrated with a cannery, a tannery and a by-products unit. The Government insisted that the BMC divest some of its non-core business and assets, including houses and land. The BMC responded by removing utility subsidies for its employees and by placing non-core businesses, such as Mainline Couriers in Gaborone and Botswana Road Services in Francistown, on the market. The reforms soon bore fruit: the BMC's annual profits rose from P19.8m. in 2005 to P84.2m. in 2008. However, by raising producer prices at a time of falling international beef prices, the BMC suffered a pre-tax loss of P187.5m. in 2009, prompting renewed appeals for a restructuring of the meat sector. The BMC is responsible for slaughtering all the country's cattle and is capable of handling the high levels of throughput that occur in times of drought, although in the absence of drought conditions, when owners are replenishing their herds, the BMC has excess capacity. The country's third abattoir, at Maun, was due to reopen in 2010, but in June of that year plans to privatize the abattoir were announced. From late 2010 investment partners were being sought as cash flow problems at the BMC rendered the parastatal unable to reopen the Maun abattoir on its own. However, in February 2011 the European Union banned imports of beef from Botswana after an inspection of facilities in the country. This generated an 89% month-on-month reduction in beef exports in February, according to the central bank. The industry was also affected in that year by incidences of foot-and-mouth disease in the north of the country. The Ministry of Agriculture sought to find new outlets for the country's beef production in Zimbabwe and Angola.

Botswana's cattle sector is very strongly focused on beef production rather than dairy output, and milk has to be imported. A government study found that Botswana has the potential to increase local production of milk through increased dairy herd size and more modern farm management techniques. The BMC also processes cowhides to the wet-blue stage, thereby increasing the value of the hides by 125%. The hides are then marketed globally under tender. The BMC has the capability of tanning the hides all the way through to finished leathers, but it stops at the wet-blue stage because further processing would not offer a sufficient return, owing to the small size of the local market for leather products. Tanning to finished leathers does take place in Botswana, but on a smaller scale.

In contrast to the cattle sector, sheep and goat numbers have withstood the periodic droughts reasonably well. Principally a subsistence sector resource, the national herd of sheep and goats increased from 776,000 head in 1982 to 2.25m. in 2010. Of the 2009 total, 2.1m. were goats and 153,000 were sheep. The main commercial development other than beef has been in urban poultry farming; Botswana had about 5.1m. chickens in 2009, 2.3m. more than in 1999. Efforts have also been made to improve the availability of eggs and chickens in rural areas and to improve local production of milk and fish. Diversification efforts have focused on ostrich- and fish-farming, and on improving the infrastructure for the marketing of fresh milk.

MINERALS AND MINING

In 2010 Botswana was the world's largest diamond producer by value, yet it was only after independence, in 1966, that the country was found to possess abundant reserves of diamonds, coal, copper-nickel, soda ash, potash and sodium sulphate. Substantial deposits of salts and plutonium, as well as smaller reserves of gold, silver and a variety of industrial minerals, were also identified. The mining sector contributed 33.9% of GDP in 2011, compared with 32.9% in 2010 and 27.4% in 2009; in the latter year performance was inhibited by the temporary closure of all four of the country's diamond mines in February and by a sharp decline in global demand for diamonds because of the world economic recession. Three of the mines reopened in April, but the Damtshaa mine was to remain closed until 2012. The GDP of the mining and quarrying sector increased, in real terms, at an average annual rate of 3.4% in 2000–08. The country's diamond mines are owned and operated by the Debswana Diamond Co (Pty), a joint venture owned equally by the Botswana Government and De Beers Centenary AG of Switzerland, which employed more than 6,000 people in the mid-2000s. In 2010 the diamond industry accounted for 30% of Botswana's GDP and 80% of export earnings, and provided around a fifth of global output.

Large-scale mineral exploitation began in 1971, when the 117-ha Orapa diamond mine (the world's second largest) began production, and Botswana proceeded to develop a relatively diverse mining sector, with three major diamond mines, coal exploitation and copper-nickel production, as well as the mining of gold, industrial minerals and semi-precious stones. The Letlhakane pipe, near Orapa, began producing diamonds in 1977. Jwaneng, 125 km west of Gaborone, came on stream in 1982 and is the world's most productive diamond mine by value. The Damtshaa mine, comprising four small diamond pipes 20 km east of Orapa, was formally commissioned in October 2003 and was forecast to produce 5m. carats from 39m. metric tons of ore over the 31-year projected life of the mine. Although all current diamond-mining operations are carried out by Debswana, a number of other companies have become involved in diamond exploration, conducting extensive ground surveys.

From the mid-1980s until the start of the global recession of 2008, the diamond industry continued to strengthen its role as the mainstay of Botswana's vigorous economic performance. In 2001 a UN initiative to boycott so-called 'conflict diamonds' gave a further boost to Botswana's diamond industry, when overseas officials visited the country and proclaimed Botswana's diamonds to be 'blood-free'. The enforcement mechanism is a certification scheme aimed at excluding diamonds from the world market that have been traded for arms by rebel movements in conflict zones. Botswana rapidly became one of the major beneficiaries of this initiative, known as the Kimberley Process Certification Scheme. Botswana was elected to the position of Vice-Chair of the Kimberley Process for 2005, a post which led automatically to the Chair position in 2006.

After more than two years of negotiations, an agreement was signed in May 2006 that renewed the license for 25 years on the world's most valuable diamond mine, Jwaneng, belonging to Debswana. As part of the agreement Botswana increased its share in De Beers from 7.5% to 15%. A new extension at Jwaneng was announced that, it was envisaged, would deepen the mine from 330 m to 625 m, thereby enabling access to a further 95m. carats of diamonds, and would extend the life of the mine until at least 2025; the so-called Cut 8 project was to receive an initial investment of US $500m. from Debswana, with a further $2,500m. to be disbursed subsequently. The Government and De Beers also agreed to launch a new joint venture, the Diamond Trading Company Botswana (DTCB), to help the country to diversify from its heavy reliance on the mining of diamonds. The DTCB was to sort, polish and value rough diamonds, and the process of aggregation, by which the best sales parcels of diamonds are arranged, was to be moved from London, United Kingdom, to Gaborone, where a large building housing the DTCB was opened in 2008. Licences were granted to 16 diamond-cutting companies with the aim of processing an estimated 34m. carats a year (22% of world output and $6,000m. in value) in Botswana by 2009, before being exported. However, the founding of the DTCB coincided with the world's most serious economic crisis since the 1930s. This development and the creation of numerous diamond factories is an indication of a subtle but unmistakable shift in the power ratio of the two 50:50 partners in Debswana. Previously, De Beers would have simply vetoed any efforts towards vertical development or greater value added within Botswana in favour of the status quo—shipping all the diamonds off in rough form into Central Selling Organization coffers. However, Botswana is now exercising much more control over this commodity and is emerging as a global player in the diamond market. Furthermore, in 2006 the Government granted a licence to a company other than Debswana to mine diamonds in Botswana. DiamonEx (Pty) Ltd of Botswana, whose parent was DiamonEx of Australia, owned 100% of the 3.7m.-carat Lerala diamond mine in eastern Botswana. Reaching full production in 2008, the mine was expected to produce 330,000 carats per year over the 10 years to 2018. However, Lerala came on stream just in time to suffer from the global economic recession, and, as a result, DiamonEx of Botswana was, at its own request, placed under judicial management in January 2009. In March DiamonEx sold 80% of Lerala to Fleming Asset Management Botswana. The mine remained closed throughout 2009 and 2010. Capital investment partners were being sought in 2011 to enable the mine to reopen. Meanwhile, Firestone Diamonds plc began exploring 83 kimberlite pipes in the Tsabong area of south-western Botswana in 2007. The company is also exploring the BK11 kimberlite, near Orapa, and is participating in joint venture exploration projects with Debswana at Orapa and Jwaneng.

World-wide diamond prices declined by 16% during the 2008–09 global economic recession, and, as a result, De Beers massively reduced the number of stones offered for auction. Large gemstones, in which Botswana excels, were particularly badly affected. Debswana was not able to sell any diamonds in November 2008 and sold very small quantities in December 2008 and January 2009. The Government therefore received no royalties and no dividends from its 50% stake in Debswana during that period. Botswana's total diamond production fell by 3.5%, from 33.8m. carats in 2007 to 32.6m. carats in 2008, while its total diamond sales fell by 17%, to 28.9m. carats. In 2009 diamond revenue declined by 49%. However, diamond exports recovered strongly in 2010, exceeding US $3,010m. in that year.

In a boost to the local diamond industry, De Beers announced in September 2011 that it planned to relocate its trading and sorting activities for the mineral from London to Botswana by the end of 2013, which would allow the direct sale of local output onto the international market for the first time. The development formed part of a 10-year agreement signed between the company and the Botswana Government, which remained a minority shareholder in the firm. The deal would guarantee De Beers continued access to Botswana's diamond deposits. Minister of Minerals, Energy and Water Resources Ponatshego Kedikilwe underlined that the relocation would allow the country to verify prices at source. De Beers also announced that it would increase the value of diamonds it offered to companies in Botswana from US $550m. to $800m. per year.

In another major development, in November 2011 British mining corporation Anglo American announced that it was purchasing a controlling stake in De Beers for US $5,100m. Anglo American professed itself to be confident about the long-term health of the diamond-mining industry, given tight global supply and rising overall demand from emerging economies, particularly China and India. The acquisition was not expected to jeopardize Botswana's position in the global diamond trade. The country maintained a 15% stake in De Beers, and Anglo American acknowledged that the Government would retain an option to increase its holdings in the acquired entity to 25%. Moreover, Kedikilwe stated that Anglo American's acquisition would not adversely affect the sales agreement it signed with De Beers in September, and added that the Government would explore its options with regard to increasing its own stake ahead of the expected completion of Anglo American's purchase in late 2012. In March the Government announced that it would terminate a ban on issuing new diamond-cutting licences. The move, expected to take effect from April, came amid an increase in the local supply of diamonds following the September 2011 sales agreement between the Government and De Beers. It was expected that the development would boost employment; the country's diamond cutting and polishing sector accounted, at that stage, for around 3,000 local jobs.

United Kingdom-based Gem Diamonds announced in June 2012 that it was delaying the start of extraction at its Ghangoo mine from 2013 to early 2014 due to an accident at the site that killed two contractors. Production was envisaged to start at a relatively low rate, of 100,000 carats in 2013, before an eventual rise to 780,000 carats per year.

Production of copper-nickel matte at Selebi-Phikwe began in 1974, and output rose steadily, reaching some 50,000 metric tons per year by the late 1980s. However, the value of sales of matte per ton declined consistently during the 1980s, owing to depressed international prices for nickel and copper. These low prices created acute financial problems for the operating company, Bamangwato Concessions Ltd (BCL), and for its parent group, Botswana Roan Selection Trust. By 2005, however, the company had returned to profitability, to the extent that in 2005 and 2006 it covered all its current operating costs. In 2007 BCL was again in profit and refurbished its smelter plant. Another copper-nickel mine, at Selkirk, east of Francistown, was opened at the end of 1988 by a consortium of Swiss and British investors, with an annual production capacity of 60,000 tons of high-grade ore. Plans to develop the adjacent, and larger, Phoenix deposit came to fruition, and the Phoenix expansion—making it the largest nickel mine in Africa—helped to raise BCL's output from 2m. tons in 2002 to 2.5m. tons in 2003. The open-pit Phoenix and underground Selkirk operations, as well as the US $620m. new-technology Botswana Metal Refinery (BMR), were subsequently owned 85% by Tati Nickel and 15% by the Botswana Government. In 2007 they became majority Russian-owned, when MMC Norilsk Nickel of Russia acquired Tati Nickel's parent company, Lion Ore International. Construction of the BMR plant began in October 2007, with completion scheduled for the third quarter of 2009. However, the global recession caused demand for copper and nickel to fall dramatically, and the capital cost of constructing the BMR increased to three times that which had been envisaged by the feasibility study. It was decided in May 2008 to suspend the BMR project.

Copper- and silver-mining prospects suffered a set-back in May 2012, when Canadian mineral exploration firm Hana Mining revised downwards its assessment of its Ghanzi copper and silver development. The company announced that the project would likely cost an initial US $300.5m. to bring into production and that it would yield an average of 30,119 metric tons of copper and 878,000 oz of silver per year. The estimated average cost of copper extraction was $1.96 per pound for the first five years, declining to $1.75 subsequently.

Plans to exploit Botswana's coal reserves have been restricted by the low level of international prices and by the great distance to major coal markets. Some 17,000m. metric tons of steam coal suitable for use in power plants have been identified in the east, and coal is extracted at Morupule Colliery (a subsidiary of Debswana). Most of the coal extracted is used to generate electricity to service the mining industry and the soda ash plant at Sua Pan. The Government has also encouraged domestic coal use, in order to conserve fuel wood. Production of coal at Morupule reached 962,427 tons in 2006, but declined to 832,007 tons in 2007. A new P87m. coal-washing plant was commissioned in 2008 to improve the calorific value of Morupule coal. Studies have revealed that substantial exploitable coal bed methane reserves exist at Kodibeleng, and pilot production wells were spudded in 2006. Construction was to have begun in early 2008 on a combined coal mine, coal-fired power station and coal-to-hydrocarbons operation at Mmamabula, the output of which was to have been exported mainly to the Electricity Supply Commission (ESKOM) of South Africa, with a target delivery date of early 2011. However, in May 2008 project leader Meepong Resources, a subsidiary of CIC Energy Corpn of Canada, revised its risk assessment in a 'tightening' economic climate and indicated that the changed risk allocations for other participating companies would necessitate renegotiations that 'may impact on the schedule'. In November CIC confirmed that construction of the plant would go ahead, starting in 2009, and with a target completion date of early 2013; however, total output would amount to just 1,320 MW instead of 3,600 MW. The US $6,000m. Phase I would create 6,000 temporary construction jobs over a four-year period as well as 1,350 permanent jobs after start-up. The scheme's capacity is significantly higher than the national power requirement of Botswana and power exports are forecast to earn $850m. per year over 40 years. Ensuring that South Africa would be an important client was widely considered essential to the project's success; however, that country has proven more reluctant to make a commitment than BMR backers had hoped.

In January 2012 President Lt-Gen. Seretse Khama Ian Khama announced that his Government had repealed a ban on issuing new coal-mining licences. A moratorium had been imposed in June 2011 to give the Government time to conclude a new national strategy for coal exploitation. The ban had also been introduced to counteract speculation while the Government formulated a plan to ensure that purchasers of licences were sufficiently capitalized and possessed enough expertise to develop coal mines and associated infrastructure. The completed study indicated that the country had an annual capacity to extract up to 90m. tons of coal, which would largely be exported to Asia, particularly China and India.

For many years gold was mined in Botswana on a small scale. In 1987 the Botswana Government and private US and Canadian interests formed a joint venture, Shashe Mines, to explore gold deposits at Map Nora near Francistown; exploitation of the mineral commenced in 1989. The Bonanza gold mine in Tati Schist, 40 km from Francistown, has proven reserves of 2,040 metric tons, with a gold content of 14.8 g per ton, in association with silver and other minerals. Kudu Mining also operates the Rainbow gold mine, some 60 km from Francistown. A new gold mine at Mupane, 30 km south-east of Francistown, commenced production in 2004, with Gallery Gold as its parent. Iamgold of Canada acquired Mupane when it acquired Gallery Gold in 2006. Mupane produced 101,000 oz of gold at a cash cost of US $367 per oz in 2008; the forecast for 2009 was for output of 80,000 oz, but actual output stood at 51,000 oz at a cash cost of $735 per oz.

MANUFACTURING

The manufacturing sector contributed 4.2% of GDP in 2011. The largest factor inhibiting growth has been the small size of the Botswana market, while trade barriers are another inhibiting factor, restricting Botswana-based manufacturers from operating in neighbouring, larger markets, particularly South Africa. Nevertheless, 2005 saw the establishment of a number of new ventures, albeit on a modest scale, including companies producing lead ingots, asphalt and bitumen, sewerage pipes, leather, t-shirts, pasta, biscuits, float glass and bone china. A can-manufacturing company at Lobatse began production in 2007. Import dependence remains a problem, however; the low percentage of value added to some products in Botswana is used by neighbouring states as an excuse to maintain trade barriers, although as the labour force becomes more skilled, there will be greater potential for higher proportions of value to be added.

The manufacturing sector is regarded as the primary stimulus for job creation, which is often cited as the Botswana economy's most serious challenge. Past performance indicates that the sector does hold considerable potential for creating employment opportunities. Formal employment in manufacturing increased from 4,400 jobs in 1978 to more than 27,500 jobs in 1991. As of September 2008 a total of 315,800 people held formal sector jobs in Botswana, 61% of whom were employed in the private sector. The manufacturing sector's generally strong performance can be attributed to a number of government policies, based on the Financial Assistance Policy, which provided a wide range of subsidies to potential entrepreneurs, particularly in the small-scale sector, and a highly attractive foreign investment code.

The Government's current diversification programme also places priority on the country's need to develop manufacturing. The parastatal Botswana Development Corporation (BDC) has for four decades supported more than 100 enterprises, including companies involved in brewing, sugar-packaging, furniture-making, clothing manufacture, tourism, milling and concrete products. Investments in 2008 were in can-manufacturing, glass-making and the production of Italian-style ceramic floor tiles, while ventures in 2009 included coffee-processing, pharmaceutical manufacture and footwear manufacture. Can Manufacturers Botswana, 100% owned by the BDC, entered production in August 2008 in Lobatse, while Fengyue Glass Manufacturing opened in 2008 in Palapye, producing float glass, as a joint venture between the BDC and Fengyue of China.

The Botswana Export Development and Investment Authority (BEDIA) was established in 1997 to promote exports of the country's manufactured goods. BEDIA also seeks ways to add value locally to Botswana's own raw materials; schemes under consideration to this end range from jewellery to textiles, garment manufacture, glass-making, tanneries, leather goods manufacture and even information technology products. The Botswana International Financial Services Centre (IFSC) was established in 2003. Together with the BDC and BEDIA, it was involved in attracting foreign direct investment (FDI) into Botswana. However, NDP 10 acknowledged that the inflow of FDI had been 'low' and that one of the reasons was that 'the role of attracting foreign investment remains fragmented'. Having the BDC, IFSC and BEDIA constituted 'too many role players', according to NDP 10, and the Government aimed to 'rationalize the functions of these institutions by assigning their role in attracting investment to one entity'.

ENERGY, UTILITIES AND TRANSPORT INFRASTRUCTURE

Rapid growth in the economy and of the population resulted in an equally rapid expansion in the demand for energy and water. The Botswana Power Corporation (BPC) has implemented a continuing programme of capacity expansion, of which a major project was the Morupule power station. Using coal mined at Morupule, the station became the focus of a new national grid system linking the existing northern and southern networks, based on the Selebi-Phikwe and Gaborone power stations, with six 30-MW units in operation. However, during the six years to March 2009 Botswana's level of electricity self-sufficiency remained 'very low', according to NDP 10. Against a demand of 530 MW, Morupule was able to supply only 120 MW. In 2008 almost all of the 75% of Botswana's electricity that needed to be imported was still brought in from South Africa. This figure did, however, include power that had originally been sourced in Mozambique and had arrived in Botswana through South Africa.

In 2006 the BPC embarked upon a US $600m. expansion of generating capacity at Morupule power station; this project, dubbed Morupule B, was to quadruple generating capacity from 120 MW in 2009 to 600 MW, with commercial operations expected to commence in 2012. This upgrade was intended to replace 100% of the country's power imports, rendering Botswana completely self-sufficient in electricity generation. The Government announced in May 2012 that it would issue tenders later that year for two coal-fired power stations, each capable of generating 300 MW. The project would involve the expansion of the existing Morupule complex by 2015–16 and the construction of a new plant at an undefined location by 2018–19.

For an arid country such as Botswana, the provision of water is a formidable challenge and one that has been largely achieved; no less than 98% of the population has access to clean drinking water. Water development efforts are laid out in the National Water Master Plan (NWMP), which in 2004 underwent an extensive review. Beyond the remote Okavango and Chobe areas, the country has only minimal surface water supplies, and 80% of national demand is met from groundwater sources. Although not fully assessed, groundwater supplies are not expected to exceed 4,000m. cu m per year, and intense competition for water resources has emerged in the main urban and mining areas in the east, leading to the postponement of plans for the development of industrial sites, particularly in Gaborone. The situation has been further exacerbated by recurrent drought. Aid from overseas is currently being used to develop water resources. Now part of the NWMP, the Ntimbale Dam was completed in 2006, and its treatment works and pipeline were completed one year behind schedule in 2008. The construction of three more dams was under way in 2011 (see above). Other water projects include the Maun Water Supply and Sanitation Design, the Kanye/Molepolole Emergency Water Supply Plan, the Tonota Emergency Water Supply Plan and the construction of a booster pump station for the Ramotswa water supply system.

By regional standards, Botswana had a relatively well-developed transport infrastructure. There were just over 8,400 km of paved roads in the country in 2005. However, there was a set-back for the development of road infrastructure in early 2012, when Zambia's Ministry of Transport, Works, Supply and Communications announced that there was a US $130m. shortfall in funding for the construction of the Kazungula Bridge, which would link the two countries. Upon completion, the bridge would cross the Zambezi river, providing a vital trade route for both countries.

FOREIGN TRADE AND BALANCE OF PAYMENTS

Diamonds have been Botswana's principal export by value since the mid-1970s, accounting for as much as 88% of total earnings and for more than 50% of government revenue in some years; however, diamond export revenue plunged from P20,793m. in 2008 to just P15,234m. in 2009. A significant recovery took place in 2010, when diamond export revenue grew by 33%, and diamond production rose by 36% to an estimated 24m. carats. Further increases were forecast for 2011 and beyond, with a full recovery to pre-recession levels expected by 2013. Other exports include copper-nickel matte, textiles, meat and meat products, soda ash and salt. Botswana's principal imports are machinery and electrical equipment, fuel, food, beverages and tobacco, vehicles and transport equipment, chemical and rubber products, and diamonds. (The world's largest diamond producer does indeed import diamonds—an indication that the diamond-cutting and -polishing operations established recently in Botswana are attracting overseas custom.) The United Kingdom is generally the principal client, purchasing 53.1% by value of all exports in 2009. Other major clients include South Africa, Norway, Zimbabwe (where the replacement of the worthless Zimbabwe dollar by the US dollar improved payment prospects), Belgium and Israel. Botswana's main supplier is the Common Customs Area (primarily South Africa), which in 2009 provided 76% of Botswana's imports by value.

Total exports of goods on a free-on-board (f.o.b.) basis declined from US $5,053m. in 2007 to $4,789m. in 2008, falling further to $3,462m. in 2009, but with a recovery to $4,112m. expected for 2010 and further steady recoveries projected for 2011 and beyond. Diamond exports accounted for $2,139m., or 61.8% of total export revenue, in 2009. Total imports of goods on a f.o.b. basis increased from $3,444m. in 2007 to $4,458m. in 2008, before declining moderately to $4,121m. in 2009, but with steady increases expected thereafter. The visible trade balance, which has been traditionally in surplus, carried deficits in 2008 and 2009, the shortfall amounting to $659m. in the latter year. The deficit was projected to decline to $484m. in 2010, to $245m. in 2011, to $196m. in 2012 and to $73m. in 2013, before a forecast return to surplus in 2014. The current account of the balance of payments, which is also traditionally in surplus, turned negative with a $243m. deficit, and a further shortfall, of $35m., was expected for 2010; a surplus of $94m. was forecast in 2011, with steadily rising surpluses anticipated thereafter. Following a surplus of $1,503m. in 2009, the overall balance of payments is widely considered to have entered a prolonged period of deficit, with deficits projected each year through to 2015. Botswana's policy of maintaining a high level of international reserves cushioned the effects of these negative balance of payments results. Even at their lowest point, at 30 November 2010, reserves of $8,279m. were sufficient to cover 18.6 months' worth of imports of goods and services. The forward reach of import cover was forecast to rise steadily to more than 30 months' worth by 2015.

Botswana operates an open economy, with combined import and export values exceeding GDP, making both the domestic economy and the external account vulnerable to fluctuations in the terms of trade and exchange rates. The Government has maintained a flexible, trade-orientated exchange rate policy since the pula was established in 1976 as the national currency. For an economy as open as Botswana's, even in years of considerable global upheaval, such as 1998, 2008 and 2009, the rate of inflation remained remarkably stable. Botswana's balance of payments situation was also helped by its low debt burden. Botswana's total external debt could be paid off completely out of the country's foreign reserves 21 times over in 2007 and 2008. Even with this commendable track record on lack of indebtedness, Botswana did indicate in NDP 10 that a debt management strategy was being developed 'to avoid Botswana getting into a debt trap'. The level of total external debt did dramatically increase from 3.2% of GDP in 2008 to 15.4% of GDP in 2009, but this level remained well below the value of Botswana's foreign reserves.

GOVERNMENT FINANCE

At independence about one-half of Botswana's public expenditure was financed directly by the Government of the United Kingdom. This extreme level of reliance on external support was altered by Botswana's accession to SACU in 1969, and the country had become financially independent of the United Kingdom by 1972/73. From 1977/78 until 1982/83 customs revenue from SACU constituted the principal component of government income, but since then this source has been overtaken by mineral revenue, which in 2006/07 accounted for an estimated 40.6% of total revenue (excluding grants), compared with 27.5% for customs and excise revenue. Owing to an estimated 49% decrease in total diamond export revenue, of which one-half goes to the Government as a 50% shareholder, government revenue also experienced a severe decline in 2008/09. In 2002 Botswana introduced a value-added tax (VAT), which replaced the old sales tax. The 2010/11 budget raised the VAT rate from 10% to 12% with effect from 1 April 2010. A new SACU agreement was signed in October 2002, and in June 2003 negotiations began towards the creation of a SACU-USA Free Trade Area (FTA); these negotiations continued into 2006, protracted by the inability to reach agreement over intellectual property rights that would have hindered SACU member states' ability to import drugs needed to treat HIV/AIDS, and talks stalled in April. The two parties then negotiated a less comprehensive Trade, Investment, Development and Co-operation Agreement, which was signed in 2008. It was envisaged that talks on a full FTA would eventually be resumed. An FTA between SACU and the European Free Trade Area came into force on 1 May 2008, granting SACU exporters free access to markets in Iceland, Liechtenstein, Norway and Switzerland.

After many years of balanced budgeting, Botswana experienced budgetary deficits for three consecutive years in the late 2000s, with a fourth successive deficit forecast for 2011/12. Revised out-turn estimates indicate that the 2010/11 budgetary deficit was equivalent to 10.1% of GDP, well outside the IMF's preferred ceiling of 5% of GDP. The 2011/12 budget envisaged total expenditure of P41,120m., of which P30,350m. was recurrent spending and P10,770m. was for development. Total revenue and grants were projected at P34,100m., of which mineral revenues were to contribute 33% and customs revenues were to provide 25%. The resultant budgetary deficit of P6,930m. was equivalent to 6.3% of forecast GDP. As Botswana is not a debtor to the IMF (and indeed carries little debt of any kind), it is free to make its own financial decisions. Furthermore, the Government possesses the ability to finance 100% of the budgetary deficit by simply drawing down its foreign reserves. Obviously, however, if the Government were to continue with deficit spending at this level, indebtedness would inevitably follow.

In June 2012 the IMF commended the Government for targeting a small fiscal surplus in the 2012/13 budget and for maintaining 'expenditure restraint'. However, the Fund continued to appeal for a widening of the tax base, as a means of preparing for the eventual inevitable decline in diamond revenues. It also recommended a reduction of tax exemptions and an improvement in administrative collection capacity.

Statistical Survey

Source (unless otherwise stated): Central Statistics Office, Private Bag 0024, Gaborone; tel. 352200; fax 352201; e-mail csobots@gov.bw; internet www.cso.gov.bw.

Area and Population

AREA, POPULATION AND DENSITY

Area (sq km)	581,730*
Population (census results)	
17 August 2001	1,680,863†
9-18 August 2011	
Males	989,128
Females	1,035,776
Total	2,024,904
Density (per sq km) at 2011 census	3.5

* 224,607 sq miles.

† Excluding 60,716 non-Batswana enumerated at the time of the census.

POPULATION BY AGE AND SEX

(UN estimates at mid-2012)

	Males	Females	Total
0–14	330,388	325,115	655,503
15–64	671,019	641,202	1,312,221
65 and over	36,387	49,126	85,513
Total	1,037,794	1,015,443	2,053,237

Note: Estimates not adjusted to take account of results of 2011 census.

Source: UN, *World Population Prospects: The 2010 Revision*.

DISTRICTS AND SUB-DISTRICTS

(population at 2011 census)

Central		Kweneng West	47,797
Bobonong	71,936	*North-East*	
Boteti	57,376	Francistown	98,961
Mahalapye	118,875	North-East	60,264
Orapa	9,531	*North-West*	
Selebi-Phikwe	49,411	Chobe	23,347
Serowe/Palapye	180,500	Ngamiland West	59,421
Sowa Town	3,598	Ngamiland East†	92,863
Tutume	147,377	*South-East*	
Ghanzi		Gaborone	231,592
Ghanzi*	43,355	Lobatse	29,007
Kgalagadi		South-East	85,014
Kgalagadi North	20,476	*Southern*	
Kgalagadi South	30,016	Barolong	54,831
Kgatleng		Jwaneng	18,008
Kgatleng	91,660	Ngwaketse	129,247
Kweneng		Ngwaketse West	13,689
Kweneng East	256,752	**Total**	2,024,904

* Including Central Kalahari Game Reserve (CKGR) sub-district.

† Including Delta sub-district.

PRINCIPAL TOWNS

(population at 2011 census)

Gaborone (capital)	231,592	Serowe	50,820
Francistown	98,961	Selebi-Phikwe	49,411
Molepolole	66,466	Kanye	47,007
Maun	60,263	Mochudi	44,815
Mogoditshane	58,079	Mahalapye	43,289

BIRTHS AND DEATHS

(annual averages, UN estimates)

	1995–2000	2000–05	2005–10
Birth rate (per 1,000)	28.6	25.5	24.2
Death rate (per 1,000)	11.0	14.9	12.6

Source: UN, *World Population Prospects: The 2010 Revision*.

2006 (Health Statistics Report estimates): Live births 44,709; deaths 11,075 (Source: UN, *Population and Vital Statistics Report*).

Marriages: 4,521 (marriage rate 5.0) in 2009.

Life expectancy (years at birth): 53.1 (males 54.0; females 52.2) in 2010 (Source: World Bank, World Development Indicators database).

EMPLOYMENT

(number of persons aged 7 years and over, 2006 labour force survey)

	Males	Females	Total
Agriculture, hunting, forestry and fishing	98,805	62,561	161,367
Mining and quarrying	12,457	1,716	14,173
Manufacturing	16,010	19,962	35,973
Electricity, gas and water supply	2,626	1,537	4,163
Construction	23,111	4,476	27,587
Wholesale and retail trade; repair of motor vehicles, motorcycles and personal and household goods	27,924	49,478	77,401
Hotels and restaurants	3,770	10,898	14,667
Transport, storage and communications	10,496	5,555	16,050
Financial intermediation	3,018	5,406	8,424
Real estate, renting and business services	15,554	9,701	25,255
Public administration and defence; compulsory social security	34,539	25,618	60,157
Education	15,182	28,063	43,245
Health and social work	5,393	8,609	14,002
Other community, social and personal service activities	5,213	5,342	10,554
Private households with employed persons	7,208	18,027	25,235
Extra-territorial organizations and bodies	456	439	895
Total employed	281,762	257,388	539,150

Mid-2012 ('000 persons, FAO estimates): Agriculture, etc. 326; Total labour force 783 (Source: FAO).

Health and Welfare

KEY INDICATORS

Total fertility rate (children per woman, 2010)	2.8
Under-5 mortality rate (per 1,000 live births, 2010)	48
HIV/AIDS (% of persons aged 15–49, 2009)	24.8
Physicians (per 1,000 head, 2006)	0.3
Hospital beds (per 1,000 head, 2008)	1.8
Health expenditure (2009): US $ per head (PPP)	1,296
Health expenditure (2009): % of GDP	10.0
Health expenditure (2009): public (% of total)	76.0
Access to water (% of persons, 2010)	96
Access to sanitation (% of persons, 2010)	62
Total carbon dioxide emissions ('000 metric tons, 2008)	4,840.4
Carbon dioxide emissions per head (metric tons, 2008)	2.5
Human Development Index (2011): ranking	118
Human Development Index (2011): value	0.633

For sources and definitions, see explanatory note on p. vi.

Agriculture

PRINCIPAL CROPS
('000 metric tons)

	2008	2009	2010*
Maize	9.0	13.2	14.1
Sorghum	23.6	37.6	41.0
Sunflower seed	8.1	6.0†	3.7
Roots and tubers	99.7*	87.6*	99.4
Pulses	2.3	2.5*	2.3

* FAO estimate(s).
† Unofficial figure.

Aggregate production ('000 metric tons, may include official, semi-official or estimated data): Total cereals 35.9 in 2008, 55.9 in 2009, 60.5 in 2010; Total vegetables (incl. melons) 31.7 in 2008, 25.8 in 2009, 28.0 in 2010; Total fruits (excl. melons) 7.9 in 2008, 6.0 in 2009, 5.9 in 2010.

Source: FAO.

LIVESTOCK
('000 head, year ending September)

	2008	2009	2010*
Cattle	2,222	2,467	2,550
Horses	38	38	38
Asses	330*	330*	330
Sheep	188	170	153
Goats	1,880	2,000*	2,100
Pigs	14	13	13
Poultry	4,800*	5,000*	5,100

* FAO estimate(s).

LIVESTOCK PRODUCTS
('000 metric tons)

	2008	2009	2010
Cattle meat*	36.0	36.0	37.0
Goat meat	5.5	5.5	5.5*
Chicken meat*	6.6	5.8	6.8
Other meat*	8.0	8.5	9.1
Cows' milk*	108.2	112.4	114.2
Goats' milk*	4.8	3.9	4.1
Hen eggs*	4.5	4.3	4.5

* FAO estimate(s).

Source: FAO.

Forestry

ROUNDWOOD REMOVALS
('000 cubic metres, excl. bark, FAO estimates)

	2008	2009	2010
Industrial wood	105.0	105.0	105.0
Fuel wood	673.9	678.6	683.3
Total	778.9	783.6	788.3

Source: FAO.

Fishing

(capture in metric tons, live weight)

	2008	2009*	2010
Tilapias	61	52	43
Torpedo-shaped catfishes	23	19	16
Other freshwater fishes	2	2	1
Total catch	86	73	60

* FAO estimates.

Source: FAO.

Mining

(metric tons, unless otherwise indicated)

	2009	2010	2011
Hard coal	737,798	988,240	787,729
Copper ore*†	24,382	20,833	14,231
Nickel ore†	29,616	23,053	13,842
Gold (kg)	1,626	1,774	1,562
Cobalt*†	342	252	129
Salt	241,114	346,761	446,525
Diamonds ('000 carats)	17,733	22,019	22,903
Soda ash (natural)	215,188	240,898	257,851
Sand and gravel ('000 cu m)‡	3,000	3,000§	n.a.

* Figures refer to the metal content of matte; product smelted was granulated nickel-copper-cobalt matte.
† Figures refer to the nickel content of matte and include some product not reported as milled.
‡ Source: US Geological Survey.
§ Estimate.

Source (unless otherwise stated): Bank of Botswana, *Annual Report 2011*.

Industry

SELECTED PRODUCTS

	2001	2002	2003
Beer ('000 hl)	1,692	1,396	1,198
Soft drinks ('000 hl)	431	389	405
Electric energy (million kWh)	1,010	1,060	1,133

Electric energy (million kWh): 991 in 2004; 971 in 2005; 1,042 in 2006; 721 in 2007; 631 in 2008.

Source: UN Industrial Commodity Statistics Database.

Finance

CURRENCY AND EXCHANGE RATES

Monetary Units
100 thebe = 1 pula (P).

Sterling, Dollar and Euro Equivalents (31 May 2012)
£1 sterling = 12.174 pula;
US $1 = 7.852 pula;
€1 = 9.739 pula;
100 pula = £8.21 = $12.74 = €10.27.

Average Exchange Rate (pula per US $)

2009	7.1551
2010	6.7936
2011	6.8382

BUDGET
(million pula, year ending 31 March)

Revenue*	2009/10	2010/11	2011/12†
Taxation	26,773.9	29,615.7	35,099.6
Mineral revenue	9,088.4	12,059.9	12,974.0
Customs and excise	7,931.0	6,206.6	8,441.0
Non-mineral income taxes	5,560.6	6,413.4	7,138.0
Other taxes	4,193.8	4,935.9	6,546.6
General sales tax/VAT	3,943.5	4,637.7	6,212.0
Other current revenue	2,480.4	1,964.4	2,584.4
Interest	32.1	36.7	31.3
Other property income	1,107.7	760.6	605.4
Fees, charges, etc.	1,237.1	1,096.5	1,870.2
Sales of fixed assets and land	103.6	70.6	77.4
Total	29,254.3	31,580.1	37,684.0

Expenditure‡	2009/10	2010/11	2011/12†
General services (incl. defence)	9,737.0	9,685.1	10,561.6
Social services	17,969.2	17,110.2	19,401.1
Education	9,299.9	9,294.9	9,566.4
Health	3,372.1	3,384.0	4,848.9
Housing, urban and regional development	3,480.4	2,741.1	3,309.4
Food and social welfare programme	727.1	675.1	732.3
Other community and social services	1,089.8	1,015.1	944.0
Economic services	8,388.5	8,330.4	8,684.3
Agriculture, forestry and fishing	1,185.0	1,107.1	1,252.8
Mining	768.6	619.2	683.3
Electricity and water supply	1,857.2	2,832.9	2,730.1
Roads	1,900.5	1,917.9	2,119.2
Others	2,677.3	1,853.2	1,898.9
Transfers	3,394.6	3,291.8	3,106.4
Deficit grants to local authorities	3,024.8	2,768.2	2,548.9
Interest on public debt	369.8	523.5	557.5
Total	39,489.2	38,417.5	41,753.3

* Excluding grants received (million pula): 768.8 in 2009/10; 329.4 in 2010/11; 310.3 in 2011/12 (estimate).

† Estimates.

‡ Including net lending (million pula): 751.7 in 2009/10; –43.6 in 2010/11; –114.5 in 2011/12 (estimate).

Source: Bank of Botswana, *Annual Report 2011*.

INTERNATIONAL RESERVES
(US $ million at 31 December)

	2009	2010	2011
IMF special drawing rights	145.57	143.19	133.57
Reserve position in IMF	17.79	20.86	41.88
Foreign exchange	8,540.60	7,721.16	7,906.44
Total	8,703.96	7,885.21	8,081.89

Source: IMF, *International Financial Statistics*.

MONEY SUPPLY
(million pula at 31 December)

	2009	2010	2011
Currency outside depository corporations	1,145	1,241	1,431
Transferable deposits	5,963	8,023	7,244
Other deposits	31,609	33,596	36,088
Broad money	38,717	42,860	44,763

Source: IMF, *International Financial Statistics*.

COST OF LIVING
(Consumer Price Index; base: 2000 = 100)

	2008	2009	2010
Food (incl. beverages)	207.7	237.4	246.1
Clothing (incl. footwear)	122.2	132.6	143.2
Fuel	288.9	284.6	320.6
All items (incl. others)	196.6	212.5	227.3

2011: Food (incl. beverages) 263.0; All items (incl. others) 246.4.

Source: ILO.

NATIONAL ACCOUNTS
(million pula at current prices, provisional figures)

Expenditure on the Gross Domestic Product

	2009	2010	2011
Government final consumption expenditure	20,077	21,141	23,991
Private final consumption expenditure	36,977	42,773	54,243
Increase in stocks	2,493	2,396	3,350
Gross fixed capital formation	23,789	27,456	33,620
Total domestic expenditure	83,335	93,766	115,204
Exports of goods and services	26,798	33,402	46,379
Less Imports of goods and services	35,306	40,465	52,529
Statistical discrepancy	7,721	14,555	11,486
GDP in purchasers' values	82,548	101,258	120,541
GDP at constant 1993/94 prices	24,274	25,977	27,289

Gross Domestic Product by Economic Activity

	2009	2010	2011
Agriculture, hunting, forestry and fishing	2,326	2,385	2,843
Mining and quarrying	21,538	31,638	38,878
Manufacturing	3,343	3,857	4,762
Water and electricity	2,409	2,824	3,416
Construction	4,313	5,169	6,884
Trade, restaurants and hotels	11,328	13,154	15,130
Transport, post and telecommunications	4,050	4,597	5,263
Finance, insurance and business services	10,302	11,598	13,092
Government services	15,364	16,782	19,399
Social and personal services	3,765	4,194	4,937
Sub-total	78,737	96,197	114,604
Less Imputed bank service charge	4,563	4,835	5,407
GDP at basic prices	74,174	91,362	109,197
Import duties	4,610	5,183	6,148
Taxes on products	4,204	5,212	5,742
Less Subsidies on products	439	499	547
GDP in purchasers' values	82,548	101,258	120,541

Source: Bank of Botswana, *Annual Report 2011*.

BALANCE OF PAYMENTS
(US $ million)

	2008	2009	2010
Exports of goods f.o.b.	4,800.1	3,435.0	4,633.3
Imports of goods f.o.b.	–4,364.9	–4,003.2	–4,841.7
Trade balance	435.1	–568.3	–208.5
Exports of services	871.8	496.0	394.5
Imports of services	–783.0	–952.2	–876.6
Balance on goods and services	524.0	–1,024.5	–690.6
Other income received	474.7	352.4	413.0
Other income paid	–1,171.3	–455.0	–655.6
Balance on goods, services and income	–172.7	–1,127.1	–933.2
Current transfers received	1,399.3	1,153.5	1,396.2
Current transfers paid	–358.9	–547.6	–417.2
Current balance	867.8	–521.3	45.9
Capital account (net)	76.3	89.2	19.0
Direct investment abroad	91.1	–65.2	–0.3
Direct investment from abroad	902.4	824.1	265.0
Portfolio investment assets	322.9	347.8	396.8
Portfolio investment liabilities	–29.5	17.7	17.8
Other investment assets	–1,194.6	–1,142.6	–1,217.8
Other investment liabilities	–9.3	38.6	–96.2
Net errors and omissions	144.0	699.9	609.5
Overall balance	1,171.0	288.5	39.8

Source: IMF, *International Financial Statistics*.

External Trade

PRINCIPAL COMMODITIES
(million pula)

Imports c.i.f.	2009	2010	2011
Food, beverages and tobacco	4,436.2	4,812.5	5,235.1
Fuels	4,515.9	5,520.7	8,289.4
Chemicals and rubber products	3,754.4	4,206.6	4,558.7
Wood and paper products	1,334.2	1,314.9	1,412.0
Textiles and footwear	1,504.0	1,562.5	1,787.4
Metals and metal products	2,392.3	2,855.2	3,703.9
Machinery and electrical equipment	5,798.4	6,765.6	11,459.6
Vehicles and transport equipment	4,222.0	3,706.1	4,567.0
Total (incl. others)	33,572.8	38,458.8	49,715.3

Exports f.o.b.	2009	2010	2011
Meat and meat products	808.4	1,084.0	333.1
Diamonds	15,234.1	21,779.9	30,247.7
Copper-nickel matte	3,621.2	4,240.2	2,940.3
Textiles	1,417.6	1,118.5	1,817.7
Vehicles and parts	492.1	501.7	749.8
Total (incl. others)	24,318.9	32,052.0	40,081.3

PRINCIPAL TRADING PARTNERS
(million pula)

Imports c.i.f.	2009	2010	2011
SACU*	25,761.1	28,308.0	33,159.9
Zimbabwe	272.2	258.5	330.6
United Kingdom	2,042.7	3,563.3	4,915.0
Other Europe	19.5	16.7	32.1
China, People's Republic	1,097.7	2,075.1	5,429.5
Korea, Repub.	46.9	55.2	83.0
USA	727.0	506.9	1,068.8
Total (incl. others)	33,572.8	38,458.8	49,715.3

Exports f.o.b.	2009	2010	2011
SACU*	3,573.9	4,382.7	5,708.2
Zimbabwe	1,085.4	1,195.1	1,188.1
Other Africa	18.3	3.3	10.4
United Kingdom	13,061.8	17,710.1	24,961.1
Other Europe	1.0	4.6	5.3
USA	321.5	385.1	426.5
Total (incl. others)	24,318.9	32,052.0	40,081.3

* Southern African Customs Union, of which Botswana is a member; also including Lesotho, Namibia, South Africa and Swaziland.

Transport

RAILWAYS
(traffic)

	2007	2008	2009
Number of passengers ('000)	382.8	415.9	97.6*
Freight ('000 metric tons)	1,750.7	1,759.5	1,927.5

* Preliminary figure.

Freight carried ('000 metric tons): 2,010.8 in 2010; 2,034.8 in 2011.

ROAD TRAFFIC
(registered vehicles)

	2008	2009*	2010*
Cars	120,783	135,334	174,781
Light duty vehicles	88,547	91,826	95,750
Trucks	15,324	17,209	21,238
Buses	10,889	11,590	n.a.
Tractors	3,371	4,057	n.a.
Others (incl. trailers, motorcycles and tankers)	17,584	20,623	n.a.
Total	256,498	280,639	333,451

* Estimates.

CIVIL AVIATION
(traffic on scheduled services, million)

	2007	2008	2009
Kilometres flown	4	4	4
Passenger-km	116	118	113
Total ton-km	10	11	10

Source: UN, *Statistical Yearbook*.

Passengers carried: 772,186 in 2009; 774,771 in 2010; 788,461 in 2011.

Freight carried (metric tons): 1,098.2 in 2007; 1,067.8 in 2008; 936.9 in 2009.

Tourism

FOREIGN TOURIST ARRIVALS

Country of origin	2004*	2006	2007
Namibia	57,542	78,530	64,298
South Africa	626,207	516,329	479,473
United Kingdom	24,069	23,860	19,690
Zambia	72,492	126,201	80,592
Zimbabwe	576,328	499,869	652,292
Total (incl. others)	1,522,807	1,425,994	1,455,151

* Data for 2005 were not available.

Total tourist arrivals ('000): 1,500 in 2008; 2,103 in 2009; 2,145 in 2010.

Receipts from tourism (US $ million, excl. passenger transport): 553 in 2008; 228 in 2009; 218 in 2010.

Source: World Tourism Organization.

Communications Media

	2008	2009	2010
Telephones ('000 main lines in use)	142.3	137.4	137.4
Mobile cellular telephones ('000 subscribers)	1,485.8	1,874.1	2,363.4
Internet subscribers ('000)	10.0	12.0	n.a
Broadband subscribers ('000)	8.9	10.0	12.0

Personal computers: 120,000 (62.5 per 1,000 persons) in 2008.

Source: International Telecommunication Union.

Television receivers ('000 in use): 40 in 2000 (Source: UNESCO, *Statistical Yearbook*).

Radio receivers ('000 in use): 237 in 1997 (Source: UNESCO, *Statistical Yearbook*).

Book production (first editions only): 158 titles in 1991, including 61 pamphlets (Source: UNESCO, *Statistical Yearbook*).

Daily newspapers: 2 in 2004 (average circulation 75,278) (Source: UNESCO, *Statistical Yearbook*).

Non-daily newspapers: 3 in 1996 (average circulation 51,000 copies); 9 in 2004 (Source: UNESCO, *Statistical Yearbook*).

Other periodicals: 14 titles in 1992 (average circulation 177,000 copies) (Source: UNESCO, *Statistical Yearbook*).

Education

(2011 unless otherwise indicated)

	Institutions	Teachers	Students
Primary	810	13,509	332,971
Secondary	265*	11,910*	171,986†
General programmes	n.a.	11,910‡	168,220*
Technical and vocational programmes*	43	992	9,395
Tertiary	2§	529‖	16,239¶

* 2007.

† 2009.

‡ 2006/07.

§ 2001; number of colleges of education.

‖ 2004/05.

¶ 2005/06.

Source: Ministry of Education, Gaborone; UNESCO Institute for Statistics.

Agricultural college (2006): Teachers 106; students 960.

University (2010/11): Teachers 813; students 15,731 (Source: University of Botswana).

Pupil-teacher ratio (primary education, UNESCO estimate): 25.4 in 2008–09 (Source: UNESCO Institute for Statistics).

Adult literacy rate (UNESCO estimates): 84.5% (males 84.0%; females 84.9%) in 2010 (Source: UNESCO Institute for Statistics).

Directory

The Constitution

The Constitution of the Republic of Botswana took effect at independence on 30 September 1966; it was amended in August and September 1997. Its main provisions, with subsequent amendments, are summarized below:

EXECUTIVE

President

Executive power lies with the President of Botswana, who is also Commander-in-Chief of the armed forces. Election for the office of President is linked with the election of members of the National Assembly. The President is restricted to two terms of office. Presidential candidates must be over 30 years of age and receive at least 1,000 nominations. If there is more than one candidate for the Presidency, each candidate for office in the Assembly must declare support for a presidential candidate. The candidate for President who commands the votes of more than one-half of the elected members of the Assembly will be declared President. In the event of the death or resignation of the President, the Vice-President will automatically assume the Presidency. The President, who is an ex officio member of the National Assembly, holds office for the duration of Parliament. The President chooses four members of the National Assembly.

Cabinet

There is also a Vice-President, whose office is ministerial. The Vice-President is appointed by the President and deputizes in the absence of the President. The Cabinet consists of the President, the Vice-President and other Ministers, including Assistant Ministers, appointed by the President. The Cabinet is responsible to the National Assembly.

LEGISLATURE

Legislative power is vested in Parliament, consisting of the President and the National Assembly, acting after consultation in certain cases with the Ntlo ya Dikgosi. The President may withhold assent to a Bill passed by the National Assembly. If the same Bill is again presented after six months, the President is required to assent to it or to dissolve Parliament within 21 days.

Ntlo ya Dikgosi

Formerly known as the House of Chiefs, the Ntlo ya Dikgosi comprises the Chiefs of the eight principal tribes of Botswana as ex officio members, four members elected by sub-chiefs from their own number, and three members elected by the other 12 members of the Ntlo ya Dikgosi. Bills and motions relating to chieftaincy matters and alterations of the Constitution must be referred to the Ntlo ya Dikgosi, which may also deliberate and make representations on any matter. Following a review, in December 2005 the membership of the Ntlo ya Dikgosi was increased from 15 to 35.

National Assembly

The National Assembly consists of 40 members directly elected by universal adult suffrage, together with four members who are elected by the National Assembly from a list of candidates submitted by the President; the President, the Speaker and the Attorney-General are also ex officio members of the Assembly. The life of the Assembly is five years. In June 2002 the National Assembly voted to increase its membership from 40 directly elected members to 57, with effect from the following general election.

The Constitution contains a code of human rights, enforceable by the High Court.

The Government

HEAD OF STATE

President: Lt-Gen. SERETSE KHAMA IAN KHAMA (took office 1 April 2008).

Vice-President: Dr PONATSHEGO H. KEDIKILWE.

CABINET

(October 2012)

The Government is formed by the Botswana Democratic Party.

President: Lt-Gen. SERETSE KHAMA IAN KHAMA.

Vice-President: Dr PONATSHEGO H. KEDIKILWE.

Minister of Defence, Justice and Security: RAMADELUKA SERETSE.

Minister of Presidential Affairs and Public Administration: MOKGWEETSI ERIC MASISI.

Minister of Foreign Affairs and International Co-operation: PHANDU T. C. SKELEMANI.

Minister of Finance and Development Planning: KENNETH O. MATAMBO.

Minister of Infrastructure, Science and Technology: JOHNNIE K. SWARTZ.

Minister of Lands and Housing: LEBONAMANG MOKALAKE.

Minister of Labour and Home Affairs: EDWIN BATSU.

Minister of Youth, Sports and Culture: SHAW KGATHI.

Minister of Trade and Industry: DORCAS MAKGATO-MALESU.

Minister of Local Government: PETER SIELE.

Minister of Agriculture: CHRISTIAN DE GRAAF.

Minister of Transport and Communications: NONOFO MOLEFHI.

Minister of Minerals, Energy and Water Resources: ONKOKAME KITSO MOKAILA.

Minister of Education and Skills Development: PELONOMI VENSON-MOITOI.

Minister of Environment, Wildlife and Tourism: TSHEKEDI KHAMA.

Minister of Health: JOHN SEAKGOSING.

Attorney-General: Dr ATHALIAH MOLOKOMME.

Secretary to the Cabinet: ERIC MOLALE.

In addition, there were eight Assistant Ministers.

MINISTRIES

Office of the President: PMB 001, Gaborone; tel. 3950825; fax 3950858; e-mail op.registry@gov.bw; internet www.gov.bw/government/ministry_of_state_president.html#office_of_the_president.

Ministry of Agriculture: PMB 003, Gaborone; tel. 33689000; fax 3975805; e-mail mkojane@gov.bw; internet www.moa.gov.bw.

Ministry of Education and Skills Development: Chief Education Officer, Block 6 Bldg, 2nd Floor, Government Enclave, Gaborone; Private Bag 005, Gaborone; tel. 3655400; fax 3655458; e-mail cde.registry@gov.bw; internet www.moe.gov.bw.

Ministry of Environment, Wildlife and Tourism: PMB BO199, Standard House, 2nd Floor, Main Mall, Bontleng, Gaborone; tel. 3914955; fax 3191346; internet www.mewt.gov.bw.

Ministry of Finance and Development Planning: Government Enclave, Khama Cres., Blk 25, State Dr., PMB 008, Gaborone; tel. 3950100; fax 3905742; e-mail kmutasa@gov.bw; internet www.finance.gov.bw.

Ministry of Foreign Affairs and International Co-operation: Government Enclave, Private Bag 00368, Gaborone; tel. 3600700; fax 3913366; e-mail mofaic-admin@lists.gov.bw; internet www.mofaic.gov.bw.

Ministry of Health: PMB 0038, Gaborone; tel. 3170585; e-mail moh-webmaster@gov.bw; internet www.moh.gov.bw.

Ministry of Infrastructure, Science and Technology: PMB 007, Gaborone; tel. 3958500; fax 3913303; internet www.mist.gov.bw.

Ministry of Labour and Home Affairs: PMB 002, Gaborone; tel. 3611100; fax 3913584; e-mail msetimela@gov.bw; internet www.gov.bw/government/ministry_of_labour_and_home_affairs.html.

Ministry of Lands and Housing: PMB 00434, Gaborone; tel. 3904223; fax 3911591.

Ministry of Local Government: PMB 006, Gaborone; tel. 3658400; fax 3952382; internet www.mlg.gov.bw.

Ministry of Minerals, Energy and Water Resources: Khama Cres., PMB 0018, Gaborone; tel. 3656600; fax 3972738.

Ministry of Trade and Industry: PMB 004, Gaborone; tel. 3601200; fax 3971539; internet www.mti.gov.bw.

Ministry of Transport and Communications: PMB 0044, Gaborone; tel. 3907230; fax 3907236.

Ministry of Youth, Sports and Culture: Plot 50626, Samora Machel Dr., next to Cresta Lodge, PMB 00514, Gaborone; tel. 3682600; fax 3913473; e-mail mysc_pro@gov.bw; internet www.mysc.gov.bw.

Legislature

NTLO YA DIKGOSI

Following a review, in December 2005 the membership of the Ntlo ya Dikgosi was increased from 15 to 35 members.

Chairperson: Chief MOSADI SEBOKO.

NATIONAL ASSEMBLY

Speaker: Dr MARGARET NASHA.

General Election, 16 October 2009

Party	Votes	% of votes	Seats
Botswana Democratic Party	290,099	53.26	45
Botswana National Front	119,509	21.94	6
Botswana Congress Party	104,302	19.15	4
Botswana Alliance Movement	12,387	2.27	1
Independents	10,464	1.92	1
Botswana People's Party	7,554	1.39	–
MELS Movement of Botswana	292	0.05	–
Botswana Tlhoko Tiro Organisation	40	0.01	–
Total	544,647	100.00	57†

† The President and the Attorney-General are also ex officio members of the National Assembly.

Election Commission

Independent Electoral Commission (IEC): Government Enclave, Block 8, 7th Floor, Private Bag 00284, Gaborone; tel. 3612400; fax 3900581; e-mail iecwebmaster@gov.bw; internet www.iec.gov.bw; f. 1997; Chair. M. S. GAONGALELWE.

Political Organizations

Botswana Alliance Movement (BAM): POB 1869, Francistown; tel. and fax 2413167; f. 1998 as an alliance of opposition parties—the Botswana Labour Party, United Socialist Party (PUSO), Botswana People's Party (BPP), Botswana Progressive Union, United Action Party and Independence Freedom Party—to contest the 1999 general election; the BPP withdrew in July 2000; Pres. EPHRAIM LEPETU SETSHWAELO; Chair. MOTSAMAI K. MPHO; Sec.-Gen. MATLHOMOLA MODISE.

Botswana Congress Party (BCP): Plot 364, Extension 4, Independence Ave, Gaborone; POB 2918, Gaborone; tel. and fax 3181805; internet www.bcp.org.bw; f. 1998 following split from the BNF; Pres. GILSON SALESHANDO; Nat. Chair. BATISANI MASWIBILI; Sec.-Gen. TAOLO LUCAS.

Botswana Democratic Party (BDP) (Domkrag): Plot 695, behind Tsholetsa House, POB 28, Gaborone; tel. 3952564; fax 3913911; e-mail bserema@bdp.org.bw; internet www.bdp.org.bw; f. 1962 as the Bechuanaland Democratic Party; Pres. SERETSE KHAMA IAN KHAMA; Chair. DANIEL K. KWELAGOBE; Sec.-Gen. THATO KWEREPE.

Botswana National Front (BNF): POB 40065, Gaborone; tel. and fax 3182921; e-mail botswananationalfront@yahoo.com; f. 1966; incl. fmr mems of the United Socialist Party (PUSO), which split from the BNF in 1994 later to re-affiliate in 2005; Pres. OTSWELETSE MOUPO; Chair. NEHEMIAH MODUBULE; Sec.-Gen. MOHAMMED KHAN.

Botswana Movement for Democracy (BMD): Gaborone; f. 2010 by fmr mems of the Botswana Democratic Party; Chair. GOMOLEMO MOTSWALEDI (acting).

Botswana People's Party (BPP): POB 685, Francistown; tel. 72610603; f. 1960; Pres. WHYTE MAROBELA.

Botswana Workers' Front (BWF): Private Bag 00704, Jwaneng; tel. 3552877; fax 3956866; f. 1993 following split from the BNF; mems may retain dual membership of the BNF; Leader SHAWN NTHAILE.

MELS Movement of Botswana: POB 501818, Gaborone; tel. 3933140; fax 3933241; e-mail joinaandass@botsnet.bw; f. 1984; Marxist-Leninist; Leader THEMBA JOINA; Vice-Pres. EPHRAIM MAKGETHO.

New Democratic Front (NDF): Gaborone; f. 2003 following split from the BNF; affiliated to the BCP since mid-2006; Leader DICK BAYFORD.

Diplomatic Representation

EMBASSIES AND HIGH COMMISSIONS IN BOTSWANA

Angola: Plot 13232, Khama Cres., Nelson Mandela Rd, PMB BR 111, Gaborone; tel. 3900204; fax 3975089; Ambassador JOSÉ AGOSTINHO NETO.

Brazil: Plot 11245, Main Mall, Standard House, 3rd Floor, PMB 475, Gaborone; tel. 3951061; fax 3972581; e-mail main.mail@embassyofbrazil.co.bw; internet www.embassyofbrazil.co.bw; Ambassador JOÃO INÁCIO PADILHA.

China, People's Republic: Plot 3096 North Ring Rd, POB 1031, Gaborone; tel. 3952209; fax 3900156; e-mail chinaemb_bw@mfa.gov.cn; internet bw.china-embassy.org; Ambassador LIU HUANXING.

Cuba: Plot 5198, The Village, POB 40261, Gaborone; tel. 3951750; e-mail cubanembassy@botsnet.bw; internet emba.cubaminrex.cu/botswana; Ambassador RAMÓN ALONSO MEDINA.

France: 761 Robinson Rd, POB 1424, Gaborone; tel. 3973863; fax 3971733; e-mail frambbots@info.bw; internet www.ambafrance-bw.org; Ambassador GENEVIÈVE IANCU.

Germany: Professional House, 3rd Floor, Segoditshane Way, Broadhurst, POB 315, Gaborone; tel. 3953143; fax 3953038; e-mail info@gaborone.diplo.de; internet www.gaborone.diplo.de; Ambassador ULF HANEL.

India: Plot 5375, President's Dr., PMB 249, Gaborone; tel. 3972676; fax 3974636; e-mail administration@hci.org.bw; internet www.highcommissionofindia.org.bw; High Commissioner V. N. HADE.

Kenya: Plot 2615, Zebra Way, off Chuma Dr., PMB 297, Gaborone; tel. 3951408; fax 3951409; e-mail info@khcbotswana.org.bw; internet www.khcbotswana.com; High Commissioner DANIEL SIDINGA.

Libya: Plot 8851, Government Enclave, POB 180, Gaborone; tel. 3952481; fax 356928; Chargé d'affaires ASSED MOHAMED ALMUTAA.

Mozambique: 69 State House Dr., POB 00215, Gaborone; tel. 3191251; fax 3191262; e-mail anuvunga@info.bw; High Commissioner BELMIRO JOSÉ MALATE.

Namibia: Plot 186, Morara Close, POB 987, Gaborone; tel. 3902181; fax 3902248; e-mail namibhc@botsnet.bw; High Commissioner H. T. HISHONGWA.

Nigeria: Plot 1086–92, Queens Rd, The Mall, POB 274, Gaborone; tel. 3913561; fax 3913738; High Commissioner ISAAC ONUH.

Russia: Plot 4711, Tawana Close, POB 81, Gaborone; tel. 3953389; fax 3952930; e-mail embrus@info.bw; internet www.botswana.mid.ru; Ambassador ANATOLY NIKOLAEVICH KORSUN.

South Africa: Plot 29, Queens Rd, PMB 00402, Gaborone; tel. 3904800; fax 3905501; e-mail sahcgabs@botsnet.bw; High Commissioner L. SHOPE.

United Kingdom: Plot 1079–1084, Main Mall, off Queens Rd, PMB 0023, Gaborone; tel. 3952841; fax 3956105; e-mail bhc@botsnet.bw; internet ukinbotswana.fco.gov.uk; High Commissioner JENNIFER ANDERSON.

USA: Embassy Enclave, off Khama Cres., POB 90, Gaborone; tel. 3953982; fax 3956947; internet botswana.usembassy.gov; Ambassador MICHELLE D. GAVIN.

Zambia: Plot 1120, Queens Rd, The Mall, POB 362, Gaborone; tel. 3951951; fax 3953952; High Commissioner MARINA MALOKOTA NSINGO.

Zimbabwe: Plot 8850, POB 1232, Gaborone; tel. 3914495; fax 3905863; e-mail zimembassy@zimgaborone.gov.zw; Ambassador THOMAS MANDIGORA.

Judicial System

There is a High Court at Lobatse and a branch at Francistown, and Magistrates' Courts in each district. Appeals lie to the Court of Appeal of Botswana. The Chief Justice and the President of the Court of Appeal are appointed by the President.

Chief Justice: MARUPING DIBOTELO.

High Court

Private Bag 1, Lobatse; tel. 5330396; fax 5332317.

Judges of the High Court: ISAAC K. B. LESETEDI, MARUPING DIBOTELO, UNITY DOW, MOATLHODI MARUMO, STANLEY SAPIRE, LEATILE DAMBE, LOT MOROKA.

President of the Court of Appeal: PATRICK TEBBUTT.

Justices of Appeal: STANLEY MOORE, JULIAN NGANUNU, HEIN GROSSKOPF, NEVILLE ZIETSMAN, NICHOLAS JOHN MCNALLY, RODGER KORSAH, CHRIS PLEWMAN.

Registrar and Master: GODFREY NTHOMIWA.

Office of the Attorney-General

Private Bag 009, Gaborone; tel. 3954700; fax 3957089.

Attorney-General: Dr ATHALIAH MOLOKOMME.

Religion

In 2006, according to official figures, the majority of the population aged 10 years and above were Christians (approximately 62%); an estimated 2% held animist beliefs. There are Islamic mosques in Gaborone and Lobatse. Hinduism and the Bahá'í Faith are also represented.

CHRISTIANITY

Botswana Council of Churches (Lekgotla la Dikereke mo Botswana): POB 355, Gaborone; tel. and fax 3951981; e-mail bots.christ.c@info.bw; f. 1966; Pres. Rev. MPHO MORUAKGOMO; Gen. Sec. DAVID J. MODIEGA; 24 mem. churches and orgs.

The Anglican Communion

Anglicans are adherents of the Church of the Province of Central Africa, covering Botswana, Malawi, Zambia and Zimbabwe. The Church comprises 15 dioceses, including one in Botswana. The current Archbishop of the Province is the Bishop of Northern Zambia. The Province was established in 1955, and the diocese of Botswana was formed in 1972. There were some 10,500 adherents at mid-2000.

Bishop of Botswana: Rt Rev. MUSONDA TREVOR S. MWAMBA, POB 769, Gaborone; tel. 3953779; fax 3952075; e-mail info@anglicanbotswana.org.bw.

Protestant Churches

There were an estimated 178,000 adherents in the country at mid-2000.

African Methodist Episcopal Church: POB 141, Lobatse; tel. 5407520; e-mail mobeat@bpc.bw; Presiding Elder Rev. MOSES P. LEKHORI.

Evangelical Lutheran Church in Botswana (Kereke ya Luthere ya Efangele mo Botswana): POB 1976, Serotologane St, Plot 28570, Gaborone; tel. 3164612; fax 3164615; e-mail elcb@info.bw; f. 1979; Bishop Dr COSMOS MOENGA; 43 congregations; 18,650 mems (2010).

Evangelical Lutheran Church in Southern Africa (Botswana Diocese): Bontleng, POB 201012, Gaborone; tel. and fax 302144; f. 1982; Bishop Rev. G. EKSTEEN.

Methodist Church of Southern Africa (Gaborone Circuit): POB 260, Gaborone; tel. 3167627; Circuit Supt Rev. ODIRILE E. MERE.

United Congregational Church of Southern Africa (Synod of Botswana): POB 1263, Gaborone; tel. 3952491; synod status since 1980; Chair. Rev. D. T. MAPITSE; Sec. Rev. M. P. P. DIBEELA; c. 24,000 mems.

Other denominations active in Botswana include the Church of God in Christ, the Dutch Reformed Church, the Mennonite Church, the United Methodist Church and the Seventh-day Adventists.

The Roman Catholic Church

Botswana comprises one diocese and one apostolic vicariate. The metropolitan see is Bloemfontein, South Africa. The church was established in Botswana in 1928, and adherents comprised some 5% of the total population. The Bishop participates in the Southern African Catholic Bishops' Conference, currently based in Pretoria, South Africa.

Bishop of Gaborone: Rt Rev. VALENTINE TSAMMA SEANE, POB 218, Bishop's House, Plot 162, Queens Rd, Gaborone; tel. 3912958; fax 3956970; e-mail gabs.diocese@botsnet.bw.

Vicar Apostolic of Francistown: Rt Rev. FRANKLYN NUBUASAH, POB 702, Tsane Rd, 14061 Area W, Francistown; tel. 2413601; fax 2417183; e-mail catholicoffice@botsnet.bw.

The Press

DAILY NEWSPAPERS

Dikgang tsa Gompieno (Daily News): 37795 Wellie Seboni Dr., Private Bag BR 139, Gaborone; tel. 3653500; fax 3901675; e-mail dailynews@gov.bw; internet www.dailynews.gov.bw; f. 1964; Mon.–Fri.; publ. by Dept of Information and Broadcasting; Setswana and English; Acting Editor THEBEYAME RAMOROKA; circ. 60,000.

Mmegi/The Reporter: Segogwane Way, Plot 8901, Broadhurst, Private Bag BR 50, Gaborone; tel. 3974784; fax 3905508; e-mail dikgang@mmegi.bw; internet www.mmegi.bw; f. 1984 as *Mmegi wa Dikgang*; daily; publ. by Dikgang Publishing Co; Setswana and English; Man. Editor TITUS MBUYA; circ. 20,000; also publishes the weekly *Mmegi Monitor* (f. 2000, Monday, circ. 16,000).

PERIODICALS

Botswana Advertiser/Northern Advertiser: 5647 Nakedi Rd, Broadhurst Industrial, POB 130, Gaborone; tel. 3914788; fax 3182957; e-mail sales@northernadvertiser.co.bw; internet www.theadvertiser.co.bw; f. 1971; owned by Screen Print (Pty) Ltd; weekly; English; circ. 90,000 (*Botswana Advertiser*), 35,000 (*Northern Advertiser*); Gen. Man. MARTIN CHIBANDA.

The Botswana Gazette: 125 Sedimosa House, Millennium Park, Kgale View, POB 1605, Gaborone; tel. 3912833; fax 3972283; e-mail editor@gazette.com; internet www.gazette.bw; f. 1985; publ. by News Co Botswana; weekly; Man. Dir CLARA OLSEN; Editor OARABILE MOTSETA; circ. 23,500.

Botswana Guardian: Plot 14442, Kamushungo Rd, G-West Industrial Site, POB 1641, Gaborone; tel. 3908432; fax 3908457; internet www.botswanaguardian.co.bw; f. 1983; weekly; publ. by Pula Printing & Publishing (Pty) Ltd; English; Editor OUTSA MOKONE; circ. 21,505.

Business and Financial Times: Unit 9, Plot 64, Gaborone International Commerce Park, POB 402396, Gaborone; tel. 3939911; fax 3939910; e-mail businesstimes@botsnet.bw; internet www.businesstimes.co.bw; Publr JAFFAR KATERYA MBUI; Editor JIMMY SWIRA.

Francistown News and Reviews: POB 632, Francistown; tel. and fax 2412040; weekly; English.

Kutlwano: Willie Sebonie Rd, Private Bag BR 139, Gaborone; tel. 3653500; fax 3653630; e-mail kutlwano@gov.bw; monthly; publ. by Dept of Information Services; Setswana and English; Editor BOME MATSHABA; circ. 15,000.

The Midweek Sun: Plot 14442, Kamushungo Rd, G-West Industrial Site, POB 00153, Gaborone; tel. 3908408; fax 3908457; internet www.midweeksun.co.bw; f. 1989; weekly; English; Editor MIKE MOTHIBI; circ. 17,971.

Mokgosi Newspaper: Plot 134, Madirelo, Tlokweng, POB 46530, Gaborone; tel. 3936868; fax 3936869; e-mail mokgosi@mmegi.bw.

The Ngami Times: Mabudutsa Ward, Private Bag BO 30, Maun; tel. 6864807; fax 6860257; e-mail tnt@info.bw; internet www.ngamitimes.com; f. 1999; owned by The Ngami Times Printing and Publishing Co Botswana (Pty) Ltd; weekly; English; Editor NORMAN CHANDLER.

The Oriental Post: Gaborone; f. 2009; weekly; Chinese; Dir MILES NAN.

Sunday Standard: Postnet Kgale View, Private Bag 351, Suite 287, Gaborone; tel. 3188784; fax 3188795; internet www.sundaystandard.info; Editor OUTSA MOKONE.

Sunday Tribune: POB 41458, Gaborone; tel. and fax 3926431; weekly.

Tautona Times: Office of the President, PMB 001, Gaborone; tel. 71318598; e-mail jramsay@gov.bw; f. 2003; weekly; electronic press circular publ. by the Office of the Pres; Communications Co-ordinator Dr JEFF RAMSAY.

The Voice: Plot 170, Unit 7, Commerce Park, POB 40415, Gaborone; tel. 3161585; fax 3932822; e-mail voicebw@yahoo.com; internet www.thevoicebw.com; f. 1992 as *The Francistowner*; weekly; Publr BEATA KASALE; Man. Editor DONALD MOORE; Editor EMANG BOKHUTLO; circ. 30,000.

Wena Magazine: POB 201533, Gaborone; tel. and fax 3907678; e-mail environews@it.bw; f. 1998; 6 a year; English and Setswana; environmental issues; Editor and Publr FLORA SEBONI-MMEREKI; circ. c. 8,000.

The Zebra's Voice: National Museum, 331 Independence Ave, Private Bag 00114, Gaborone; tel. 3974616; fax 3902797; e-mail bemotswakhumo@gov.bw; internet www.botswana-museum.gov.bw; f. 1980; twice a year; cultural affairs; Editor BERLINAH MOTSWAKHUMO; circ. 5,000.

NEWS AGENCY

Department of Information Services, Botswana Press Agency (BOPA): Private Bag BR 139, Gaborone; tel. 3653525; fax 3653626; e-mail bopa@gov.bw; f. 1981; News Editor MABEL KEBOTSAMANG.

PRESS ORGANIZATIONS

Botswana Journalists' Association (BOJA): POB 60518, Gaborone; tel. 3974435; e-mail penlite@info.bw; internet www.botswanamedia.bw/boja.htm; f. 1977; represents professional journalists; Chair. SECHELE SECHELE; Sec.-Gen. RAMPHOLO MOLEFHE; 55 mems (1999).

Botswana Media Consultative Council (BMCC): POB 2679, Gaborone; tel. 71624382; e-mail botswanamedia@info.bw; internet www.botswanamedia.bw; f. 1998; promotes the devt of a democratic media; Chair. Dr JEFF RAMSAY; Exec. Sec. ANTOINETTE O. CHIGODORA; 40 mem. orgs (1999).

Publishers

A. C. Braby (Botswana) (Pty) Ltd: Unit 3/A/2, Western Industrial Estate, 22100 Phase 4 Industrial, POB 1549, Gaborone; tel. 3971444; fax 3973462; e-mail customercare@brabys.co.za; internet www.brabys.com/bw/; business directories.

Bay Publishing: POB 832, Gaborone; tel. and fax 3937882; e-mail baybooks@orangemail.co.bw; f. 1994; Dir LENE BAY.

Botsalo Books: Gaborone International Commerce Park, Kgale, Plot 59/60, Unit 5, POB 1532, Gaborone; tel. 3912576; fax 3972608; e-mail botsalo@botsnet.bw; internet www.abcdafrica.com/botsalobooks.

The Botswana Society (BotSoc): Kgale Siding Office 1A, Kgale, POB 71, Gaborone; tel. and fax 3919745; fax 3919673; e-mail botsoc@info.bw; internet www.botsoc.org.bw; f. 1968; archaeology, arts, history, law, sciences; Chair. JOSEPH TSONOPE.

Heinemann Educational Botswana (Pty) Ltd: Plot 20695, Unit 4, Magochanyana Rd, POB 10103, Village Post Office, Gaborone; tel. 3972305; fax 3971832; e-mail hein@info.bw; internet www.heinemann.co.za; Man. Dir LESEDI SEITEI.

Lentswe la Lesedi (Pty): POB 2365, Gaborone; tel. 3903994; fax 3914017; e-mail publisher@lightbooks.net; f. 1992; Publr CHARLES BEWLAY.

Lightbooks Publishers: Digitec House, 685 Botswana Rd, The Mall, POB 2365, Gaborone; tel. 3903994; fax 3914017; e-mail publisher@lightbooks.net; internet www.lightbooks.net; f. 1992; commercial publishing division of Lentswe la Lesedi (Pty); scholarly, research, women's issues, journals, reports; Publr CHARLES BEWLAY.

Longman Botswana (Pty) Ltd: Plot 14386, West Industrial Site, New Lobatse Rd, POB 1083, Gaborone; tel. 3922969; fax 3922682; e-mail connie.burford@pearsoned.com; f. 1981; subsidiary of Pearson Education, UK; educational; Man. Dir J. K. CHALASHIKA.

Macmillan Botswana Publishing Co (Pty) Ltd: Plot 50635, Block 10, Airport Rd, POB 1155, Gaborone; tel. 3911770; fax 3911987; e-mail uiterwijkw@macmillan.bw; Man. Dir WIM UITERWIJK.

Medi Publishing: Phakalane Phase 1, Medie Close, Plot No. 21633, POB 47680, Gaborone; tel. 3121110; e-mail medi@it.bw; f. 1995; scholarly; Publishing Dir PORTIA TSHOAGONG.

Mmegi Publishing House (MPH): Plot 8901, Segogwane Way, Broadhurst, Private Bag BR 50, Gaborone; tel. 3952464; fax 3184977; e-mail editor@mmegi.bw; internet www.mmegi.bw; owned by Dikgang Publishing Co; academic and general.

Printing and Publishing Co (Botswana) (Pty) Ltd (PPCB): Plot 5634 Nakedi Rd, Broadhurst Industrial, POB 130, Gaborone; tel. 3912844; fax 3913054; e-mail ppcb@info.bw; internet www.ppcb.co.bw; educational; Man. Dir Y. MUSSA; Gen. Man. GAVIN BLAMIRE.

GOVERNMENT PUBLISHING HOUSE

Department of Government Printing and Publishing Service: Private Bag 0081, Gaborone; tel. 353202; fax 312001; Dir O. ANDREW SESINYI.

Broadcasting and Communications

TELECOMMUNICATIONS

Botswana Telecommunications Authority (BTA): 206–207 Independence Ave, Private Bag 00495, Gaborone; tel. 3957755; fax 3957976; e-mail pro@bta.org.bw; internet www.bta.org.bw; f. 1996; independent regulator for the telecommunications industry; Chair. Dr BOTSWIRI OUPA TSHEKO; CEO THARI G. PHEKO.

Botswana Telecommunications Corpn (BTC): POB 700, Gaborone; tel. 3958000; fax 3913355; internet www.btc.bw; f. 1980; state-owned; privatization pending; fixed-line telecommunications provider; Chair. LEONARD MUSA MAKWINJA; CEO PAUL TAYLOR.

Mascom: Tsholetsa House, Plot 4705/6, Botswana Rd, Main Mall, Private Bag BO298, Bontleng, Gaborone; tel. 3903396; fax 3903445; e-mail backoffice@mascom.bw; internet www.mascom.bw; f. 1998; 60% owned by DECI; 40% owned by Econet Wireless; mobile cellular telecommunications provider; CEO JOSE VIEIRA COUCEIRO.

Orange Botswana: Camphill Bldg, Plot 43002/1, Private Bag BO64, Bontleng, Gaborone; tel. 3163370; fax 3163372; internet www.orange.co.bw; f. 1998 as Vista Cellular; present name adopted in 2003; 49% owned by Orange SA, France; 46% owned by Mosokelatsebeng Cellular; mobile cellular telecommunications provider; CEO ELISABETH MEDOU BADANG.

BROADCASTING

The Department of Information and Broadcasting operates 21 radio stations across the country from bureaux in Gaborone, Kanye, Serowe and Francistown. The National Broadcasting Board was preparing to issue three further licences for private commercial radio stations in addition to those already held by Yarona FM and GABZ FM.

Department of Information and Broadcasting: Private Bag 0060, Gaborone; tel. 3658000; fax 564416; e-mail otsiang@btv.gov.bw; internet www.dib.gov.bw; f. 1978 following merger between Information Services and Radio Botswana; Dir O. ANDREW SESINYI.

Radio

Radio Botswana (RB1): Private Bag 0060, Gaborone; tel. 3952541; fax 3957138; e-mail rbeng@info.bw; state-owned; f. 1965; fmrly Radio Bechuanaland; culture, entertainment, news and current affairs programmes; broadcasts 18 hours daily in Setswana and English; Dir ANDREW SESINYI; Head of Programmes M. GABAKGORE.

Radio Botswana (RB2) (FM 103): Private Bag 0060, Gaborone; tel. 3653000; fax 3653346; e-mail mmphusu@gov.bw; f. 1992; contemporary entertainment; Head of Programmes MONICA MPHUSU.

GABZ FM 96.2: Private Bag 319, Gaborone; tel. 3956962; fax 3181443; e-mail feedback@gabzfm.co.bw; internet www.gabzfm.com; f. 1999; owned by Thari Investment; entertainment, news and politics; broadcasts in Setswana and English; Man. Dir KENNEDY OTSHELENG.

Yarona FM 106.6: POB 1607, Gaborone; tel. 3912305; fax 3901063; e-mail info@yaronafm.co.bw; internet www.yaronafm.co.bw; f. 1999; owned by Copacabana Investment; Station Man. DUMI LOPANG.

Television

Botswana Television (BTV): Private Bag 0060, Gaborone; tel. 3658000; fax 3900051; e-mail marketing@btv.gov.bw; internet www.btv.gov.bw; f. 2000; broadcasts local and international programmes 8 hours daily (Mon.–Fri.) and 10 hours (Sat.–Sun.); 60% local content; Gen. Man. MOLEFHE SEJOE.

E-Botswana: Plot 53996, Mogochama St, opposite Coca Cola, POB 921, Gaborone; tel. 3957654; fax 3901875; e-mail info@ebotswana.co.bw; internet www.ebotswana.co.bw; f. 1988; present name adopted 2010; operated by Gaborone Broadcasting Co (Pty) Ltd; 49% owned by Sabido (South Africa); Setswana and English; rebroadcasts foreign TV programmes; Man. Dir MIKE KLINCK.

Finance

(cap. = capital; res = reserves; dep. = deposits; m. = million; brs = branches; amounts in pula, unless otherwise stated)

In 2010 there were 10 commercial banks, 1 investment bank and 4 financial institutions in Botswana.

BANKING

Central Bank

Bank of Botswana: POB 712, Private Bag 154,17938 Khama Cres., Gaborone; tel. 3606301; fax 3974859; e-mail selwej@bob.bw; internet www.bankofbotswana.bw; f. 1975; bank of issue; cap. 25m., res 34,609.1m., dep. 20,898.3m. (Dec. 2009); Gov. LINAH MOHOHLO.

Commercial Banks

ABN AMRO Bank (Botswana) Ltd: Private Bag 254, Gaborone; tel. 3692911; fax 3692933; f. 2009; Man. Dir MAXIMILIAAN TERWINDT.

BancABC: ABC House, Tholo Office Park, Plot 50669, Fairground Office Park, POB 00303, Gaborone; tel. 3905455; fax 3902131; e-mail abcbw@africanbankingcorp.com; internet www.africanbankingcorp.com; f. 1989 as ulc (Pty) Ltd; name changed to African Banking Corpn (Pty) Ltd in 2001; present name adopted in 2009; subsidiary of ABC Holdings Ltd; financial services and investment banking; operates in Botswana, Mozambique, Tanzania, Zambia and Zimbabwe; cap. 34.1m., res 6.1m., dep. 1,405.0m. (Dec. 2009); Chair. HOWARD BUTTERY; CEO DOUGLAS MUNATSI.

Bank Gaborone Ltd: Plot 5129, Pilane/Queens Rd, The Mall, Private Bag 00325, Gaborone; tel. 3671500; fax 3904007; e-mail info@bankgaborone.co.bw; internet www.bankgaborone.co.bw; f. 2006; Chair. J. C. BRANDT; Man. Dir ANDRÉ BARNARD.

Bank of Baroda (Botswana) Ltd: AKD House, Plot 1108, Queens Rd, The Main Mall, Bontleng, POB 21559, Gaborone; tel. 3188878; fax 3188879; e-mail botswana@barodabank.co.bw; internet www.bankofbaroda.co.bw; f. 2001; subsidiary of the Bank of Baroda, India; Man. Dir DEBABROTO MITRA; Chief Man. R. N. BOKADE.

Barclays Bank of Botswana Ltd: Barclays House, 6th Floor, Plot 8842, Khama Cres., POB 478, Gaborone; tel. 3952041; fax 3913672; e-mail botswana.customerservice@barclays.com; internet www.barclays.com/africa/botswana; f. 1975 as local successor to Barclays Bank Int. Ltd; 74.9% owned by Barclays Bank PLC, UK; cap. 17.1m., res 71.4m., dep. 10,541.0m. (Dec. 2009); Chair. BLACKIE MAROLE; Man. Dir THULISIZWE JOHNSON; 52 brs.

Capital Bank Ltd: Plot 17954, Old Lobatse Rd, POB 5548, Gaborone; tel. 3907801; fax 3922818; internet www.capitalbank.co.bw; f. 2007; cap. 58.5m., dep. 518.9m. (Dec. 2009); CEO SRIRAM GADE.

First National Bank of Botswana Ltd: Finance House, 5th Floor, Plot 8843, Khama Cres., POB 1552, Gaborone; tel. 3642600; fax 3906130; e-mail ddesilva@fnbbotswana.co.bw; internet www.fnbbotswana.co.bw; f. 1991; 69.5% owned by First Nat. Bank Holdings Botswana Ltd; cap. 51.0m., res 1,107.4m., dep. 10,566.6m. (June 2010); Chair. PREMCHAND DEPAL SHAH; CEO LORATO BOAKGOMO-NTAKHWANA; 18 brs.

Kingdom Bank Africa Limited: Plot 115, Unit 23, Kgale Mews International Financial Park, POB 45078, Riverwalk, Gaborone; tel. 3906926; fax 3906874; e-mail kbal@kingdombotswana.co.bw; internet www.kingdombotswana.com; f. 2003; 52.57% owned by Brotherhood Holdings Ltd; cap. US $5.1m., res. –1.9m., dep. $6.6m. (Dec. 2009); Chair. MICHAEL MCNAUGHT; Man. Dir SIBONGINKOSI MOYO.

Stanbic Bank Botswana Ltd: Stanbic House, 1st Floor, Plot 50672, Fairground (off Machel Dr.), Private Bag 00168, Gaborone; tel. 3901600; fax 3900171; e-mail stanbic@mega.bw; internet www.stanbic.co.bw; f. 1992; subsidiary of Standard Bank Investment Corpn Africa Holdings Ltd; cap. 23.1m., res 9.6m., dep. 3,617.4m. (Dec. 2006); Man. Dir D. W. KENNEDY; Exec. Dir T. FERREIRA; 6 brs.

Standard Chartered Bank Botswana Ltd: Standard House, 5th Floor, Plots 1124–1127, The Mall, POB 496, Gaborone; tel. 3601500; fax 3918299; internet www.standardchartered.com/bw; f. 1975; 75% owned by Standard Chartered Holdings (Africa) BV, Amsterdam; cap. 44.5m., res 60.0m., dep. 7,512.6m. (Dec. 2009); Man. Dir DAVID CUTTING; 11 brs; 5 agencies.

Other Banks

Botswana Savings Bank: Tshomarelo House, POB 1150, Gaborone; tel. 3912555; fax 3952608; e-mail marketing@bsb.bw; internet www.bsb.bw; f. 1992; cap. and res 48.4m., dep. 101.5m. (March 2000); Chair. F. MODISE; Man. Dir LANDRICK OTENG SIANGA.

Letshego: POB 318, Gaborone; tel. 3180635; fax 3957949; e-mail letshego@info.bw; internet www.letshego.co.bw; f. 1998; microfinance; 43.8% owned by Micro Provident Ltd; 34.9% owned by the Int. Finance Corpn, Netherlands Devt Finance Co, Pan-African Investment Partners and Pan-Commonwealth African Partners; total assets 328.0m. (Oct. 2005); Chair. LEGODILE E. SEREMA; Man. Dir FREDRICK MMELESI.

National Development Bank: Development House, Plot 1123, The Mall, POB 225, Gaborone; tel. 3952801; fax 3974446; e-mail bmojalemotho@ndb.bw; internet www.ndb.bw; f. 1963; cap. 77.7m., res 49.8m. (March 2009); Chair. LESEDI SEITEI (acting); CEO LORATO C. MORAPEDI; 3 brs.

STOCK EXCHANGE

Botswana Stock Exchange: Exchange House, Office Block 6 Plot 64511, Fairgrounds, PMB 00417, Gaborone; tel. 3180201; fax 3180175; e-mail enquiries@bse.co.bw; internet www.bse.co.bw; f. 1989; commenced formal functions of a stock exchange in 1995; Chair. LIPALESA SIWAWA; CEO Dr HIRAN MENDIS; 27 cos and 32 securities firms listed in 2004.

INSURANCE

In 2010 there were 15 insurance companies in Botswana.

Botswana Eagle Insurance Co Ltd: Eagle House, Plot 54479, Fairgrounds, POB 1221, Gaborone; tel. 3188888; fax 3188911; e-mail john.main@botswanaeagle.co.za; f. 1976; subsidiary of Zurich Insurance Co South Africa Ltd, fmrly South African Eagle Insurance Co Ltd; Man. JOHN MAIN.

Botswana Insurance Co. Ltd: BIC House, Gaborone Business Park, Plot 50372, Gaborone Show Grounds, POB 715, Gaborone; tel. 3600500; fax 3972867; internet www.bic.co.bw; f. 1975; Man. Dir DZIKAMANI NGANUNU.

Botswana Insurance Holdings Ltd (BIHL): Block A, Fairground Office Park, POB 336, Gaborone; tel. 3645100; fax 3905884; f. 1975; 54% owned by African Life Assurance Co Ltd (Aflife), South Africa; total assets 80.8m. (Dec. 2006); Chair. BATSHO DAMBE-GROTH; CEO REGINA SIKALESELE-VAKA.

Botswana Life Insurance Ltd: Block A, Fairground Office Park, Plot 50676, Gaborone; tel. 3645100; fax 3905884; e-mail Webmaster@blil.co.bw; internet www.botswanalifeinsurance.com; subsidiary of BIHL; life insurance; CEO CATHERINE LESETEDI-LETEGELE.

General Insurance Botswana (GIB): 767 Tati Rd, Private Bag 00315, Gaborone; tel. 3184310; fax 3950008; internet www.gib.co.bw; Man. Dir SOPHIE K. TSHEOLE.

Hollard Insurance Botswana: Plot 50676, 2nd Floor, Block A, BIFM Bldg, Fairgrounds Business Park, POB 45029, Gaborone; tel.

3958023; fax 3958024; internet www.hollard.co.bw; Man. THEMBA MPOFU.

Metropolitan Life of Botswana Ltd: Standard House, 1st Floor, Queens Rd, Main Mall, Private Bag 231, Gaborone; tel. 3624300; fax 3624423; e-mail omothibatsela@metropolitan.co.bw; internet www.metropolitan.co.bw; f. 1996; 75% owned by Metropolitan South Africa, 25% owned by the Botswana Devt Corpn; Man. Dir OUPA MOTHIBATSELA.

Mutual and Federal Insurance Co of Botswana Ltd: Bldg B, Fairground Office Park, Private Bag 00347, Gaborone; tel. 3903333; fax 3903400; e-mail jbekker@mf.co.za; f. 1994; subsidiary of Mutual and Federal, South Africa; Man. Dir JACK BEKKER.

Regent Insurance Botswana: Plot 50370, Twin Towers, East Wing Fairgrounds Office Park, Private Bag BR 203, Gaborone; tel. 3188153; fax 3188063; Man. Dir A. A. BOTES; also **Regent Life Botswana**, life insurance.

Trade and Industry

GOVERNMENT AGENCIES

Botswana Housing Corpn (BHC): Plot 4773, cnr Mmaraka and Station Rds, POB 412, Gaborone; tel. 3605100; fax 3952070; e-mail info@bhc.bw; internet www.bhc.bw; f. 1971; provides housing for central govt and local authority needs and assists with private sector housing schemes; Chair. MACLEAN C. LETSHWITI; CEO MOOTIEMANG R. MOTSWAISO.

Citizen Entrepreneurial Development Agency (CEDA): Leseding House, 1st Floor, Plot 204, Independence Ave, Private Bag 00504, Gaborone; tel. 3170895; fax 3170896; e-mail info@ceda.co.bw; internet www.ceda.co.bw; f. 2001; develops and promotes citizen-owned enterprises; provides business training and financial assistance; Chair. LUCAS PHIRIE GAKALE; CEO THABO PRINCE THAMANE.

Competition Authority: Private Bag 00101, Gaborone; tel. 3934278; e-mail competitionauthority@gmail.com; f. 2011; monitors, controls and prohibits anti-competitive trade or business practices; CEO THULA GILBERT KAIRA.

Department of Town and Regional Planning: Private Bag 0042, Gaborone; tel. 3658596; fax 3913280; e-mail rchephethe@gov.bw; f. 1972; responsible for physical planning policy and implementation; Dir R. CHEPHETHE.

Public Enterprises Evaluation and Privatisation Agency (PEEPA): Twin Towers, East Wing, 2nd Floor, Fairground Office Park, Private Bag 00510, Gaborone; tel. 3188807; fax 3188662; e-mail peepa@peepa.co.bw; internet www.peepa.co.bw; f. 2001; responsible for commercializing and privatizing public parastatals; Acting CEO KGOTLA RAMAPHANE.

DEVELOPMENT ORGANIZATIONS

Botswana Council of Non-Governmental Organisations (BOCONGO): Bonokopila House, Plot 53957, Machel Dr., Private Bag 00418, Gaborone; tel. 3911319; fax 3912935; e-mail bocongo@bocongo.org.bw; internet www.bocongo.org.bw; Chair. Rev. BIGGIE BUTALE; 84 mem. orgs.

Botswana Development Corpn Ltd: Moedi, Plot 50380, Gaborone International Showgrounds (off Machel Dr.), Private Bag 160, Gaborone; tel. 3651300; fax 3904193; e-mail enquiries@bdc.bw; internet www.bdc.bw; f. 1970; Chair. SOLOMON. M. SEKWAKWA; Man. Dir MARIA M. NTHEBOLAN.

Botswana Export Development and Investment Authority (BEDIA): Plot 28, Matsitama Rd, The Main Mall, POB 3122, Gaborone; tel. 3181931; fax 3181941; e-mail bedia@bedia.bw; internet www.bedia.co.bw; f. 1997; promotes and facilitates local and foreign investment; Chair. MORAGO NGIDI; CEO JACOB NKATE.

Botswana International Financial Services Centre (Botswana IFSC): Plot 50676, Block B, Fairground Office Park, Private Bag 160, Gaborone; tel. 3605000; fax 3913075; e-mail ifsc@ifsc.co.bw; internet www.botswanaifsc.com; f. 2003; govt-owned; facilitates and promotes the devt of cross-border financial services based in Botswana; CEO ALAN P. BOSHWAEN.

RETENG: the Multicultural Coalition of Botswana: POB 402786, Gaborone; tel. 71654345; fax 3937779; f. 2003; umbrella org. composed of human rights advocacy and conservation groups, and public service and private sector unions; Sec.-Gen. Prof. LYDIA NYATHI-RAMAHOBO.

CHAMBER OF COMMERCE

Botswana National Chamber of Commerce and Industry: POB 20344, Gaborone; tel. 3952677; Dir MODIRI J. MBAAKANYI.

INDUSTRIAL AND TRADE ASSOCIATIONS

Botswana Agricultural Marketing Board (BAMB): Plot 130, Unit 3–4, Gaborone International Finance Park, Private Bag 0053, Gaborone; tel. 3951341; fax 3952926; internet www.bamb.co.bw; Chair. D. TIBE; CEO MASEGO MPHATHI.

Botswana Meat Commission (BMC): Plot 621, 1 Khama Ave, Private Bag 4, Lobatse; tel. 5330321; fax 5332228; internet www.bmc.bw; f. 1966; slaughter of livestock, export of hides and skins, carcasses, frozen and chilled boneless beef; operates tannery and beef products cannery; CEO DAVID FELAPAU; Gen. Man. JOHNSON BOJOSI.

EMPLOYERS' ORGANIZATIONS

Botswana Confederation of Commerce, Industry and Manpower (BOCCIM): BOCCIM House, Old Lobatse Rd, Plot 5196, POB 432, Gaborone; tel. 3953459; fax 3973142; e-mail publicrelations@boccim.co.bw; internet www.boccim.co.bw; f. 1971; Pres. ALEX LETLHOGONOLO MONCHUSI; CEO MARIA MACHAILO-ELLIS; 2,000 mems.

Botswana Teachers' Union (BTU): Plot 0019, BTU Rd, Mogoditshane; BTU Centre, Private Bag 0019, Mogoditshane; tel. 3906774; fax 3909838; e-mail btu@it.bw; internet www.btu.co.bw; f. 1937 as the Bechuanaland Protectorate African Teachers' Asscn; present name adopted 1966; Pres. SIMON MAPULELO; Sec.-Gen. IBO NANA KENOSI; 13,000 mems.

UTILITIES

Electricity

Botswana Power Corpn (BPC): Motlakase House, Macheng Way, POB 48, Gaborone; tel. 3603000; fax 3973563; e-mail contact@bpc.bw; internet www.bpc.bw; f. 1971; parastatal; operates power station at Morupule (132 MW); Chair. EWETSE RAKHUDU; Acting CEO JACOB N. RALERU.

Water

Department of Water Affairs: Khama Cres., Private Bag 0018, Gaborone; tel. 3656600; fax 3972738; e-mail dwa@global.bw; provides public water supplies for rural areas.

Water Utilities Corpn: Private Bag 00276, Gaborone; tel. 3604400; fax 3973852; e-mail metsi@wuc.bw; internet www.wuc.bw; f. 1970; 100% state-owned; supplies water to main urban centres; Chair. NOZIPHO MABE; Chief Exec. FRED MAUNGE.

MAJOR COMPANIES

The following are among the leading companies in Botswana in terms of capital investment and employment. Amounts are in pula.

Bamangwato Concessions Ltd (BCL): BCL Mine, Box 3, Selebi Phikwe; tel. 2621200; fax 2610441; e-mail bcl@bcl.bw; internet www.bcl.bw; f. 1956; 85% owned by Botswana RST Ltd (Botrest); 7.5% owned by Lion Ore Mining Int. Ltd Group, Canada; 7.5% state-owned; sole copper mining co; copper mining, smelting and processing; Gen. Man. MONTWEDI MPHATHI; 4,000 employees (2006).

Botswana RST Ltd (Botrest): POB 3, Selebi-Phikwe; tel. 810211; fax 810441; e-mail bcl@bcl.bw; f. 1967 as Botswana Roan Selection Trust Ltd; holding co with 85% shareholding in copper-nickel producers, BCL Ltd; Chair. D. C. BAILEY; Gen. Man. MONTWEDI MPHATHI; 4,800 employees.

BP Botswana (Pty) Ltd: Plot 682/3, Botswana Rd, Main Mall, POB 183, Gaborone; tel. 3951077; fax 3912836; f. 1975; petroleum exploration and production.

Chobe Holdings Ltd: Chobe National Park, POB 32, Kasane; tel. 6250340; fax 6250280; e-mail info@chobeholdings.co.bw; internet www.chobeholdings.co.bw; f. 1983; eco-tourism; interests in Botswana and Namibia; revenue 129m. (2012); Chair. Justice JULIAN NGANUNU; Man. Dir JONATHAN M. GIBSON.

Debswana Diamond Co (Pty) Ltd: Debswana House, The Mall, POB 329, Gaborone; tel. 3614200; fax 3180778; internet www.debswana.com; owned equally by the Botswana Govt and De Beers Centenary AG, Switzerland; sole diamond-mining interest in Botswana; operates three mines in Orapa and one at Jwaneng; Chair. Dr GARETH PENNY; Man. Dir JIM GOWANS; 6,000 employees.

Engen Botswana Ltd: Plot 54026, Western Bypass, Gaborone West, POB 867, Gaborone; tel. 3922210; fax 3922284; e-mail info.botswana@engenoil.com; internet www.engen.co.bw; fmrly Mobil; subsidiary of Engen Petroleum Ltd, South Africa; suppliers of petroleum-based fuels and lubricants; revenue 680.2m. (March 2006); Chair. Dr S. NDZINGE; Man. Dir D. MURASHIKI.

Furnmart Ltd: Plot 20573/4, Magochanyama Rd, Private Bag BR 60, Gaborone; tel. 3905463; e-mail ramani@cashb.bw; furniture and appliance retail; operates in Botswana, Namibia and Zimbabwe; revenue 133.7m. (July 2005); Chair. JOHN T. MYNHARDT; Man. Dir T. L. J MYNHARDT; 39 stores in Botswana; c. 1,000 employees.

G4S Security Services (Botswana) Ltd: POB 1488, Gaborone; tel. 3912211; fax 3972779; f. 2003 following acquisition of Inco Group; subsidiary of Group 4 Securicor PLC, UK; fmrly Securicor Botswana Ltd; security and cash transportation services; revenue 59.2m. (Dec. 2005); Chair. L. M. MPOTOKWANE; Man. Dir P. S. RADITLADI; 1,456 employees.

MRI Botswana: Plot 20623, Block 3, cnr Samedupe Rd and Ramakukane Way, Broadhurst Industrial Estate, Private Bag BR 256, Gaborone; tel. 3903066; fax 3164728; e-mail enquiries@mri.co.bw; internet www.mri.co.bw; f. 1992; suppliers of medical and rescue services; revenue 17.9m. (June 2005); Chair. DENNIS J. ALEXANDER; Man. Dir Dr KHUMOETSILE MAPITSE (acting).

Northern Textile Mills (Pty) Ltd: Plot 9807, Phase 4 Industrial Area, POB 1508, Francistown; tel. 2414773; fax 2414947; e-mail sales@nortex.info.bw; internet www.nortex.co.za; f. 1990; mfrs of household textiles; exports to Mauritius, South Africa, Tanzania, Zimbabwe and the USA; Man. Dir MUKESH JOSH; 382 employees.

RDC Properties Ltd: POB 1415, Gaborone; tel. 3901654; fax 373441; tel. rdc@rdc.bw; f. 1996; property management, devt and retail; interests in Botswana, Madagascar and South Africa; revenue 18.7m. (Dec. 2005); Chair. M. A. GIACHETTI; Man. Dir GUIDO R. GIACHETTI.

RPC Data Ltd: Plot 39, Unit 5, International Commerce Park, Private Bag BR 42, Gaborone; tel. 3903644; fax 3903645; e-mail info@rpcdata.com; internet www.rpcdata.com; f. 1989 as Rob Pool Computing (Pty) Ltd; present name adopted in 1994; management consultancy and information technology services; operates in Botswana, South Africa, Uganda and Zambia; revenue 28.8m. (May 2003); Chair. T. SERETSE; Man. Dir MOMPATI NWAKO.

Sechaba Brewery Holdings Ltd (SBHL): Kgalagadi Breweries (Pty) Ltd, cnr Kubu Rd and Nelson Mandela Dr., Broadhurst Industrial Estate, POB 631, Gaborone; tel. 3971598; fax 3971594; e-mail birkholtzd@kbl.bw; 25.6% owned by Botswana Devt Corpn, 16.8% owned by SABMiller Africa BV, Netherlands; SABMiller controls 40% of KBL and BBL; mfrs of clear beer and soft drinks; distributors of wines and spirits (Kgalagadi Breweries Ltd) and traditional beers (Botswana Breweries Ltd); sales 920.4m. (March 2006); Chair. EDWARD W. KOMANYANE; Man. Dir L. J. MATSELA; 1,000 employees.

Sefalana Holding Co Ltd: Plot 117, Kwena House, Unit 3, Kgale, Private Bag 0080, Gaborone; tel. 3913661; fax 3907613; miller, processor and distributor of cereals (Foods Botswana); motor vehicle dealership and travel agency (M. F. Holdings Ltd); soap production (Kgalagadi Soap Industries Ltd); revenue 70.6m. (April 2006); Chair. MODIRI J. MBAAKANYI; Man. Dir BRIAN FROHKICH; 869 employees.

Sefalana Cash and Carry Ltd (SEFCASH): Plot 10235. cnr Lejara and Moporoporo Rds. Broadhurst Ext 20, Private Bag 00422, Gaborone; tel. 3681700; fax 3907614; f. 1994; wholesale retailer; 80% owned by Sefalana Holding Co Ltd; revenue 990.9m. (April 2005); Man. Dir H. KAMPMANN; 23 brs.

Turnstar Holdings Ltd: Acumen Park, Plot 50370, Fairground Office Park, POB 1172, Gaborone; tel. 3180156; fax 3180921; e-mail frabie@khumopam.co.bw; f. 2002; property investment; revenue 96.0m. (Jan. 2009); Chair. C. M. LEKAUKAU; Man. Dir G. H. ABDOOLA.

CO-OPERATIVES

Department for Co-operative Development: POB 86, Gaborone; tel. 3950500; fax 3951657; e-mail vmosele@gov.bw; f. 1964; promotes marketing and supply, consumer, dairy, horticultural and fisheries co-operatives, thrift and loan societies, credit societies, a co-operative union and a co-operative bank; Commissioner VIOLET MOSELE.

TRADE UNIONS

Botswana Federation of Trade Unions (BFTU): POB 440, Gaborone; tel. and fax 3952534; f. 1977; Pres. ALLEN KEITSENG; Sec.-Gen. GAZHANI MHOTSHA; 25,000 mems (2001).

Affiliated Unions

Other affiliated unions include: the Air Botswana Employees' Union; the Botswana Bank Employees' Union; the Botswana Beverages and Allied Workers' Union; the Botswana Central Bank Staff Union; Botswana Construction Workers' Union; the Botswana Diamond Sorters and Valuators' Staff Union; the Botswana Hotel, Wholesalers, Furniture, Agricultural and Commercial General Workers' Union; the Botswana Housing Corpn Staff Union; the Botswana Institute of Development Management Workers' Union; the Botswana Manufacturing and Packaging Workers' Union; the Botswana Meat Industry Union; the Botswana Mining Workers' Union; the Botswana National Development Bank Staff Union; the Botswana Postal Services Workers' Union; the Botswana Power Corpn Workers' Union; the Botswana Private Medical and Health Services Workers' Union; the Botswana Railways Amalgamated Workers' Union; the Botswana Savings Bank Employees' Union; the Botswana Telecommunications Employees' Union; the Botswana Vaccine Institute Staff Union; the National Amalgamated Local and Central Government, Parastatal, Statutory Body and Manual Workers' Union; and the Rural Industry Promotions Co Workers' Union.

Principal Non-affiliated Unions

Botswana Landboard and Local Authority Health Union (BLLAHU): Private Bag 40, Francistown; tel. and fax 2413312; internet www.bulgsa.org.bw; fmrly the Botswana Unified Local Govt Service Assen; renamed in 2007 on achieving union status; Pres. PELOTSHWEU A. D. S. BAENG; Sec.-Gen. MOSHE NOGA.

Botswana Sectors of Educators Trade Union (BOSETU): Unit 5, Commerce Park, Broadhurst, POB 404341, Gaborone; tel. 3937472; fax 3170845; f. 1986 as Botswana Fed. for Secondary School Teachers; Pres. SHANDUKANI HLABANO; Sec.-Gen. TOBOKANI RARI.

The BLLAHU, the BOSETU and three other unions (the Botswana Public Employees Union, the Botswana Teachers Union and the National Amalgamated Local Government, and Central Government and Parastatals Union) form the Botswana Federation of Public Service Unions (BOFEPUSU).

Transport

RAILWAYS

The 960-km railway line from Mafikeng, South Africa, to Bulawayo, Zimbabwe, passes through Botswana and has been operated by Botswana Railways (BR) since 1987. In 2010 there were 888 km of 1,067-mm-gauge track within Botswana, including three branches serving the Selebi-Phikwe mining complex (56 km), the Morupule colliery (16 km) and the Sua Pan soda-ash deposits (175 km). Through its links with Transnet, which operates the South African railways system, and the National Railways of Zimbabwe, BR provides connections with Namibia and Swaziland to the south, and an uninterrupted rail link to Zambia, the Democratic Republic of the Congo, Angola, Mozambique, Tanzania and Malawi to the north. However, freight traffic on BR was severely reduced following Zimbabwe's construction, in 1999, of a rail link from Bulawayo to Beitbridge, on its border with South Africa. In April 2009 BR suspended all passenger services owing to continuing losses. In 2010 plans were under way for the construction of a trans-Kalahari railway linking the Mmamabula coal deposits in Botswana with the port of Walvis Bay, Namibia. A 1,100-km railway project linking Botswana with a new port in southern Mozambique was also under consideration.

Botswana Railways (BR): Private Bag 52, Mahalapye; tel. 4711375; fax 4711385; e-mail info@botrail.bw; internet www.botswanarailways.co.bw; f. 1986; Chair. RAYMOND WATSON; CEO TAOLO SEBONEGO.

ROADS

In 2011 there were 25,798 km of roads, including 8,916 km of secondary roads. Some 33% of the road network was paved, including a main road from Gaborone, via Francistown, to Kazungula, where the borders of Botswana, Namibia, Zambia and Zimbabwe meet. The construction of a 340-km road between Nata and Maun was completed in the late 1990s. Construction of the 600-km Trans-Kalahari Highway, from Jwaneng to the port of Walvis Bay on the Namibian coast, commenced in 1990 and was completed in 1998. A car-ferry service operates from Kazungula across the Zambezi river into Zambia.

Department of Road Transport and Safety: Private Bag 0054, Gaborone; tel. 3905442; e-mail amotshegwe@gov.bw; internet www.roadtransport.gov.bw; responsible for national road network; responsible to the Ministry of Works and Transport; Dir O. M. B. MOSIGI (acting).

CIVIL AVIATION

The main international airport is at Gaborone. Four other major airports are located at Kasane, Maun, Francistown and Ghanzi. In 2000 there were also 108 airfields throughout the country. Scheduled services of Air Botswana are supplemented by an active charter and business sector. In 2011 there were some 14 non-scheduled air operators in Botswana.

Civil Aviation Authority of Botswana (CAAB): Plot 61920, Letsema Office Park, POB 250, Fairgrounds, Gaborone; tel. 3688200; fax 3931883; e-mail caab@caab.co.bw; internet www.caab.co.bw; f. 2009; Chair. MARK SAMPSON; CEO MAJ. GEN. (RETD) JEFFERSON G.TLHOKWANE.

Air Botswana: POB 92, Sir Seretse Khama Airport, Gaborone; tel. 3952812; fax 3974802; internet www.airbotswana.co.bw; f. 1972; 45% state-owned; transfer to private sector suspended in October 2007; domestic services and regional services to countries in eastern and southern Africa; Chair. G. N. THIPE; Gen. Man. SAKHILE NYONI-REILING; 150,000 passengers per year.

Moremi Air: 1st Floor, Maun Airport Bldg, Private Bag 187, Maun; tel. 6863632; fax 6862078; e-mail info@moremiair.com; internet www.moremiair.com; air charter operator; Gen. Man. KELLY SEROLE.

Tourism

There are five game reserves and three national parks, including Chobe, near Victoria Falls, on the Zambia–Zimbabwe border. Efforts to expand the tourism industry include plans for the construction of new hotels and the rehabilitation of existing hotel facilities. In 2008 foreign tourist arrivals were estimated at 2.1m. Receipts from tourism totalled $218m. in that year.

Botswana Tourism Board: Plot 50676, Fairground Office Park, Block B, Ground Floor, Gaborone; tel. 3913111; fax 3959220; e-mail board@botswanatourism.co.bw; internet www.botswanatourism.co.bw; f. 2003; CEO MYRA SEKGOROROANE.

Department of Wildlife and National Parks: POB 131, Gaborone; tel. 3971405; fax 3912354; e-mail dwnp@gov.bw; Dir J. MATLHARE.

Hospitality and Tourism Association of Botswana (HATAB): Private Bag 00423, Gaborone; tel. 3957144; fax 3903201; internet www.hatab.bw; f. 1982; fmrly Hotel and Tourism Asscn of Botswana; CEO MORONGOE NTLOEDIBE-DISELE.

Defence

Military service is voluntary. Botswana established a permanent defence force in 1977. As assessed at November 2011, the total strength of the Botswana Defence Force (BDF) was some 9,000, comprising an army of 8,500 and an air force of 500. In addition, there was a paramilitary police force of 1,500. There are plans to enlarge the strength of the army to 10,000 men. In March 2007 Botswana began recruiting women into the BDF for the first time.

Defence Expenditure: Budgeted at P3,680m. in 2012.

Defence Force Commander: Maj.-Gen. TEBOGO H. C. MASIRE.

Education

Although education is not compulsory, enrolment ratios are high. Primary education begins at six years of age and lasts for up to seven years. Secondary education, beginning at the age of 13, lasts for a further five years, comprising a first cycle of three years and a second of two years. In 2010 a total of 331,196 pupils were enrolled in primary education, while in 2009 a total of 171,986 pupils were enrolled in secondary education. A total of 16,239 pupils were enrolled in tertiary education in 2005/06. According to UNESCO estimates, enrolment at primary schools in 2006/07 included 86% of children in the relevant age-group (boys 85%; girls 86%), while the ratio for secondary enrolment in the same year was 59% (boys 55%; girls 63%). The Government aims to provide universal access to 10 years of basic education. Botswana has the highest teacher-pupil ratio in Africa, but continues to rely heavily on expatriate secondary school teachers. School fees were abolished in 1987. However, in October 2005 legislation was approved to reintroduce fees for secondary education from January 2006. Tertiary education is provided by the University of Botswana (which was attended by 14,676 students in 2009/10) and the affiliated College of Technical and Vocational Education. There are also more than 40 other technical and vocational training centres, including the Institutes of Health Sciences, the Botswana College of Agriculture, the Roads Training College, the Colleges of Education (Primary and Secondary), and the Botswana Institute of Administration and Commerce. Expenditure on education by the central Government in 2010/11 was budgeted at P9,566.4m. (representing 22.9% of total expenditure by the central Government).

Bibliography

Alexander, K., and Kaboyakgosi, G. (Eds). *A Fine Balance. Assessing the Quality of Governance in Botswana*. Pretoria, Institute for Democracy in South Africa, 2012.

Amanze, J. N. (Ed.). *African Christianity in Botswana*. Gweru, Mambo Press, 1998.

Bolaane, M., and Mgadla, P. T. *Batswana*. New York, Rosen Publishing Group Inc., 1997.

Botswana Society. *Settlement in Botswana*. London, Heinemann Educational, 1982.

Chilisa, B., Mafela, L., and Preece, J. (Eds). *Educational Research for Sustainable Development*. Gaborone, Lightbooks Publishers, 2005.

Dale, R. *Botswana's Search for Autonomy in Southern Africa*. Westport, CT, Greenwood Press, 1995.

Dingake, M. *The Politics of Confusion: The BNF Saga 1984–1998*. Gaborone, Bay Publishing (Pty) Ltd, 2004.

Düsing, S. *Traditional Leadership and Democratisation in Southern Africa: A Comparative Study of Botswana, Namibia, and Southern Africa*. London, Lit, 2002.

Good, K. *Diamonds, Dispossession & Democracy in Botswana*. Woodbridge, Suffolk, James Currey, 2008.

Hassan, Z. E. *Livelihood Diversification in Drought-prone Rural Botswana*. Kiel, Wissenschaftsverlag Vauk Kiel, 2002.

Jackson, A. *Botswana, 1939–1945: An African Country at War*. Oxford, Clarendon Press, 1999.

Leith, J. C. *Why Botswana Prospered*. Montreal, McGill-Queen's University Press, 2005.

Livingston, J. *Debility and the Moral Imagination in Botswana*. Bloomington, IN, Indiana University Press, 2005.

Makgatla, J. *Elite Conflict in Botswana: A History*. Pretoria, Africa Institute of South Africa, 2006.

Masire, K. *Very Brave or Very Foolish? Memoirs of an African Democrat*. Gaborone, Macmillan Botswana, 2006.

Maundeni, Z. *40 Years of Democracy in Botswana, 1965-2005*. Gaborone, Mmegi Publishing House, 2005.

Mazonde, I. N. (Ed.). *Minorities in the Millennium: Perspectives from Botswana*. Gaborone, Lightbooks, 2002.

Molomo, M. G., and Mokopakgosi, B. T. *Multi-Party Democracy in Botswana*. Harare, SAPES Trust, 1991.

Morton, F., *et al. Historical Dictionary of Botswana*, 4th edn. Methuen, NJ, Scarecrow Press, 2008.

Motzafi-Haller, P. *Fragmented Worlds, Coherent Lives: The Politics of Difference in Botswana*. Westport, CT, Bergin and Garvey, 2002.

Ntanda Nsereko, D. *Constitutional Law in Botswana*. Gaborone, Pula Press, 2002.

Peters, P. E. *Dividing the Commons: Politics, Policy and Culture in Botswana*. London, University Press of Virginia, 1994.

Preece, J., and Mosweunyane, D. *Perceptions of Citizenship Responsibility Amongst Botswana Youth*. Gaborone, Lightbooks Publishers, 2004.

Rakner, L. *Botswana: 30 Years of Economic Growth, Democracy and Aid*. Bergen, CMI, 1996.

Saugestad, S. *The Inconvenient Indigenous: Remote Area Development in Botswana*. Uppsala, Nordic Africa Institute, 2001.

Schmidt, D. A. *The Bechuanaland Pioneers and Gunners*. Westport, CT, Praeger, 2006.

Seidman, J. *In Our Own Image*. Gaborone, Foundation for Education with Production, 1990.

Selolwane, O., and Shale, V. *Inter-party relations and democracy in Botswana*. Johannesburg, EISA, 2008.

Siphambe, H. K., *et al. Economic Development of Botswana: Facets, Policies, Problems and Prospects*. Gaborone, Bay Publishing (Pty) Ltd, 2005.

Stedman, S. J. *Botswana: The Political Economy of Democratic Development*. Boulder, CO, Lynne Rienner Publishers, 1993.

Tlou, T., *et al. Seretse Khama, 1921–1980*. Johannesburg, Macmillan, 1995.

Vanqa, T. P. *The Development of Education in Botswana*. Gaborone, Lightbooks Publishers, 2001.

Vaughn, O. *Chiefs, Power and Social Change: Chiefship and Modern Politics in Botswana, 1880s–1990s*. Trenton, NJ, Africa World Press, 2003.

Werbner, R. P. *Reasonable Radicals and Citizenship in Botswana* Bloomington, IN, Indiana University Press, 2004.

Williams, A. S. *Colour Bar: The Triumph of Seretse Khama and His Nation*. London; New York, Allen Lane, 2006.

Wiseman, J. *Botswana*. Oxford, ABC Clio, 1992.

THE BRITISH INDIAN OCEAN TERRITORY (BIOT)

The British Indian Ocean Territory (BIOT) was formed in November 1965, through the amalgamation of the former Seychelles islands of Aldabra, Desroches and Farquhar with the Chagos Archipelago, a group of islands 1,930 km north-east of Mauritius, previously administered by the Governor of Mauritius. Aldabra, Desroches and Farquhar were ceded to Seychelles when that country was granted independence in June 1976. Since then BIOT has comprised only the Chagos Archipelago, including the coral atoll Diego Garcia, with a total land area of 60 sq km (23 sq miles).

BIOT was established to meet British and US defence requirements in the Indian Ocean. Following the purchase of the islands by the British Crown in 1967, the coconut plantations (production of copra was previously the principal economic function of the islands) ceased to operate and the inhabitants were offered the choice of resettlement in Mauritius or in Seychelles. The majority (which numbered about 1,200) went to Mauritius, the resettlement taking place during 1969–73, prior to the construction of the military facility. Mauritius subsequently campaigned for the immediate return of the territory, and received support from the Organization of African Unity (now the African Union) and from India. A protracted dispute with the United Kingdom over compensation for those displaced ended in 1982 when the British Government agreed to an *ex gratia* payment of £4m. In July 2000 a judicial review of the validity of the Immigration Ordinance of 1971, under which the islanders were removed from BIOT, and which continued to prevent them from resettling in the territory, was instigated.

In November 2000 the British High Court ruled that the Chagos islanders (Ilois) had been illegally evicted from the Chagos Archipelago, and quashed Section 4 of the 1971 Ordinance, which prevented the return of the Ilois to BIOT. During the case it transpired that the British Government had received a subsidy of US $11m. on the purchase of Polaris submarines in the 1960s from the USA, in return for the lease of Diego Garcia for the US military. Furthermore, the Government had apparently termed the Ilois 'contract workers' in order to persuade the UN that the islanders were not an indigenous population with democratic rights. However, memoranda of the Foreign and Commonwealth Office (FCO) revealed government knowledge of some of the Ilois living in the Chagos Archipelago for two generations. The British Secretary of State for Foreign and Commonwealth Affairs declined an appeal, thereby granting the islanders an immediate right to return to BIOT. Despite this, a new ordinance, issued in January 2001, allowed the residents to return to any of the islands in the Archipelago, except Diego Garcia. The British Overseas Territories Act came into effect in May 2002, allowing the displaced islanders to apply for British citizenship. In October 2003 the High Court ruled that although the islanders could claim to have been ill-treated, the British Government had not known at the time that its actions were unlawful and their claims for compensation were dismissed. Many of the islanders subsequently moved to the United Kingdom.

In June 2004 the British Government issued two decrees explicitly stating the country's control of immigration services within the archipelago and banning the Ilois from returning. In May 2006 the British High Court ruled that the exclusion of the islanders from their territory was irrational and unlawful. The British Government commenced proceedings to overturn the May ruling at the Court of Appeal in February 2007; however, in May that court confirmed that the residents of the Chagos Archipelago had been unlawfully removed and upheld the displaced islanders' immediate right to return. In November the House of Lords granted the British Government the right to appeal against the Court of Appeal's decision, on the condition that the Chagossians' costs were met by the British Government. The appeal was heard in mid-2008 and in November the House of Lords ruled in favour of the British Government, thus denying the Chagossians the right to return, and citing as its main reason the fact that the United Kingdom would have been obliged to meet the costs of economic, social and educational advancement of the residents. The ruling also stated that fair compensation had been agreed and paid, and that the British Government had no further obligations towards the Chagossians. Having exhausted the appeals process in the United Kingdom, the Chagossians announced that they would take their case to the European Court of Human Rights (ECHR); however, it was estimated that only approximately 700 of the 2,000 deported during the 1960s and 1970s were still alive.

In April 2010 the British Government announced that it had designated the Chagos archipelago a marine protection area (MPA), within which all fishing and other activities were to be prohibited. The conservation area, covering some 544,000 sq km, was to be patrolled by a ship vested with the powers to arrest fleets caught fishing illegally, to impose fines of up to £100,000 and to confiscate boats and fishing equipment. These plans were expected to have an impact on the Chagossians' hearing at the ECHR as the ban on fishing would remove the legal means by which they could sustain their standard of living. In December the Mauritian Government announced that it had taken a case against the United Kingdom to the UN International Tribunal for the Law of the Sea on the grounds that the MPA was not compatible with the UN Convention on the Law of the Sea. Furthermore, the Chagossians also appealed for a judicial review of the decision to create the MPA, although this was not to take place until after the ECHR had delivered its verdict. The British Government requested a further delay to the ECHR hearing in September 2011 and no decision had been taken by that body by mid-2012.

A 1966 agreement between the United Kingdom and the USA provided for BIOT to be used by both countries over an initial period of 50 years, with the option of extending this for a further 20 years. The United Kingdom undertook to cede the Chagos Archipelago to Mauritius when it was no longer required for defence purposes. Originally the US military presence was limited to a communications centre on Diego Garcia. In 1972, however, construction of a naval support facility was begun, apparently in response to the expansion of the Soviet maritime presence in the Indian Ocean. Diego Garcia has frequently been used as a base for US aircraft carrying out air strikes on Iraq and Afghanistan. In March–April 2003 the base was used to launch bombing raids on Iraq in the US-led military campaign to oust the regime of Saddam Hussain. In February 2008 the British Secretary of State for the Foreign and Commonwealth Office admitted that, contrary to previous government statements, a number of so-called rendition flights (the transfer of detainees, in particular terrorist suspects, by the US Central Intelligence Agency to third countries where it was possible that they might be subjected to torture during interrogation) had used facilities at Diego Garcia.

In December 2000, following the British High Court's ruling, Mauritius again staked its claim for sovereignty over the Chagos Archipelago. In April 2004 Paul Bérenger, the recently installed Prime Minister of Mauritius, renewed the campaign to reclaim sovereignty after specialists in international law advised him that the decree by which the United Kingdom separated the Chagos Archipelago from Mauritius was illegal. An attempt was made to block the Mauritian Government from pursuing the case at the International Court of Justice on the basis of a long-standing ruling, whereby members of the Commonwealth could not take the United Kingdom to court; in July the ruling was extended to former members of the Commonwealth, in order to prevent Mauritius from circumventing the obstacle by withdrawing from that organization. Mauritius announced that it would pursue the matter at the General Assembly of the UN.

The civil administration of BIOT is the responsibility of a non-resident commissioner in the FCO in London, United Kingdom, represented on Diego Garcia by a Royal Navy commander and a small British naval presence. A chief justice, a senior magistrate and a principal legal adviser (who performs the functions of an attorney-general) are resident in the United Kingdom.

Land Area: about 60 sq km.

Population: There are no permanent inhabitants. In February 2012 there were about 2,800 US and British military personnel and civilian support staff stationed in the territory.

Currency: The official currency is the pound sterling, but the US dollar is also accepted.

Commissioner: COLIN ROBERTS, Head of Overseas Territories Dept, Foreign and Commonwealth Office, King Charles St, London, SW1A 2AH, United Kingdom; tel. (20) 7008-2890.

Administrator: JOHN MCMANUS, Overseas Territories Dept, Foreign and Commonwealth Office, King Charles St, London, SW1A 2AH, United Kingdom; tel. (20) 7008-2890.

Commissioner's Representative: Commdr RICHARD G. C. MARSHALL, RN, Diego Garcia, c/o BFPO Ships.

BURKINA FASO

Physical and Social Geography

R. J. HARRISON CHURCH

Burkina Faso (formerly the Republic of Upper Volta) is a land-locked state of West Africa and is situated north of Côte d'Ivoire, Ghana and Togo. Burkina has an area of 274,200 sq km (105,870 sq miles). The December 2006 census recorded a total population of 14,017,262, giving an average density of 50.1 inhabitants per sq km. In 2012, according to UN estimates, this had risen to 17,481,982 and a density of 63.8 inhabitants per sq km. In the early 2000s there was large-scale emigration to neighbouring Côte d'Ivoire and Ghana by people seeking work on farms, in industries and in the service trades, although economic and political difficulties in these host countries (particularly the former) prompted the return of large numbers of migrant workers to Burkina. The main ethnic groups are the Mossi in the north and the Bobo in the south-west. Along the northern border are the semi-nomadic Fulani, who are also present in the east of the country. The capital city, Ouagadougou, had a population of 1,475,223 in 2006; the second city, Bobo-Dioulasso, had 489,967 inhabitants at that time.

Towards the south-western border with Mali there are primary sandstones, terminating eastward in the Banfora escarpment. As in Guinea, Mali and Ghana, where there are also great expanses of these rocks, their residual soils are poor and water percolates deep within them. Although most of the rest of the country is underlain by granite, gneisses and schists, there is much loose sand or bare laterite; consequently, there are extensive infertile areas. Moreover, annual rainfall is only some 635 mm–1,145 mm, and comes in a rainy season of at the most five months. Water is scarce except by the rivers or in the Gourma swampy area; by the former the simulium fly, whose bite leads to blindness, has been the target of extensive eradication projects, while in the latter the tsetse, a fly that can cause sleeping-sickness, is found. Given the grim physical environment, the density of population in the north-central Mossi area is remarkable. The area is, in fact, one of the oldest indigenous kingdoms of West Africa, dating back to the 11th century. Islam first penetrated the area during the 14th–16th centuries. At the end of the 18th century some local rulers, notably the leader of the Mossi, adopted Islam, but traditional religious practices among the population remained strong. Islam's expansion was facilitated by the circumstances of French rule, and by the time of the 2006 census, more than 60% of the population were Muslims.

Burkina Faso has valuable deposits of gold, manganese and zinc, industrial exploitation of which is in progress or is planned. Reserves of silver, nickel, lead, phosphates and vanadium have also been identified.

Recent History

KATHARINE MURISON

Burkina Faso (then Upper Volta) became a self-governing republic within the French Community in December 1958. Full independence followed on 5 August 1960, with Maurice Yaméogo, the leader of the Union Démocratique Voltaïque (UDV), as President. Yaméogo's administration was autocratic in style. Opposition parties were banned, and popular support for the Government receded as the country's economic condition worsened. In January 1966 Yaméogo was deposed in an army coup, led by Lt-Col Sangoulé Lamizana. An elected civilian administration took office in December 1970, although effective power remained with the army. Further elections took place in May 1978, but all political parties except the UDV, the Union Nationale pour la Défense de la Démocratie, led by Hermann Yaméogo, the son of the country's first President, and Prof. Joseph Ki-Zerbo's Union Progressiste Voltaïque were suppressed.

ARMY REGIMES, 1980–87

In November 1980 Lamizana was overthrown in a bloodless coup led by Col Saye Zerbo, who formed a governing Comité Militaire de Redressement pour le Progrès National (CMRPN) and banned political activity. In November 1982 Zerbo and the CMRPN were supplanted by a military Conseil du Salut du Peuple (CSP), led by Maj. Jean-Baptiste Ouédraogo. Capt. Thomas Sankara, who had resigned from the CMRPN in 1981, was appointed Prime Minister.

It became increasingly apparent that Ouédraogo was presiding over a divided regime. In May 1983 Ouédraogo ordered the arrest of Sankara and his supporters in the CSP. Members of Sankara's commando unit, led by Capt. Blaise Compaoré, mutinied, and in August Sankara deposed Ouédraogo in a military coup. Sankara installed a Conseil National de la Révolution (CNR) and formed a new Government, with himself as Head of State and Compaoré as Minister of State at the Presidency.

The CNR swiftly reorganized the country's public administration and installed 'revolutionary people's tribunals' to try former public officials charged with corruption. In August 1984 Sankara renamed the country Burkina Faso ('Land of the Incorruptible Men'). The army was purged, thorough reform of the judicial and education systems was conducted, and economic austerity measures implemented.

During 1987 divisions between Sankara and the three other leaders of the CNR became increasingly evident. In October a commando unit loyal to Compaoré opened fire on Sankara, killing him and 13 allies. A Front Populaire (FP) was proclaimed as successor to the CNR, and Compaoré, the Chairman of the FP, became Head of State. (In August 2008, testifying before Liberia's Truth and Reconciliation Commission, Prince Yormie Johnson, a Liberian senator who had led one of the warring factions in the 1989–96 Liberian civil war, claimed that both he and former Liberian President Charles Taylor were involved in the assassination of Sankara; in October a further allegation by Johnson, made in an interview with the French news agency Agence France Presse, that the killing had been ordered by Compaoré was vehemently denied by the Burkinabè Government.)

THE FRONT POPULAIRE

While the FP pledged a continuation of the CNR's revolutionary politics, a phase of 'rectification', to incorporate economic liberalization, was announced. Negotiations for financial assistance with the IMF and the World Bank were instigated. In April 1989 the formation was announced of a new political grouping, the Organisation pour la Démocratie Populaire/ Mouvement du Travail (ODP/MT), under the leadership of a prominent supporter of Compaoré, Clément Oumarou Ouédraogo. Leading members of groups that had refused to affiliate to the ODP/MT were removed from political office, while Ouédraogo was appointed as Minister-delegate to the Co-ordinating Committee of the FP. In September four leaders associated with the 1983 revolution were summarily executed, following the alleged discovery of a coup plot. Compaoré subsequently assumed the defence and security portfolio.

At the first congress of the FP in March 1990, delegates appointed a commission to draft a new constitution that would define a process of 'democratization'. In April Clément Oumarou Ouédraogo was dismissed from the leadership of the ODP/MT and subsequently removed from the Government. Roch Marc Christian Kaboré, whose political orientation was closer to that of Compaoré, assumed both the leadership of the ODP/MT and a senior position within the FP. Kaboré was promoted to the rank of Minister of State in September.

In March 1991 a congress of the ODP/MT adopted Compaoré as the party's official candidate for the forthcoming presidential election and abolished its adherence to Marxist-Leninist ideology. In May an appeal was made to political exiles to return to Burkina, and in August Compaoré declared an amnesty for all 'political crimes' committed since independence.

THE FOURTH REPUBLIC

The draft Constitution, which provided for a multi-party political system in what was to be designated the Fourth Republic, was endorsed by 93% of those who voted (reportedly one-half of the electorate) in a national referendum on 2 June 1991. The Constitution took effect on 11 June, whereupon the functions of the FP were separated from the organs of state. Compaoré remained Head of State, pending a presidential election, while the most senior member of the new transitional Council of Ministers was Kaboré. A reorganized Government, appointed in July, included several opposition members, among them Hermann Yaméogo. (Yaméogo, himself now a presidential candidate, had been appointed to the FP in March 1990, only to be expelled three months later.) In August 1991, however, Yaméogo and two other members of his Alliance pour la Démocratie et la Fédération (ADF) resigned their government posts in protest against proposed electoral procedures. In September opposition parties established a Coordination des Forces Démocratiques (CFD), and the remaining opposition members resigned from the transitional Government. In October five CFD representatives withdrew their presidential candidatures.

Compaoré (who had resigned his army commission in order to contest the presidency as a civilian) was the sole candidate in the presidential election, which took place, as scheduled, on 1 December 1991. He secured the support of 90.4% of those who voted, but an appeal by the CFD for a boycott of the poll was widely heeded, and an abstention rate of 74.7% was recorded. Compaoré was sworn in as President of the Fourth Republic on 24 December. In February 1992 the Government was reorganized to include Hermann Yaméogo and three other opposition members.

Some 27 parties contested postponed elections to the 107-seat Assemblée des Députés Populaires (ADP), which were held on 24 May 1992. The ODP/MT won 78 seats, while the Convention Nationale des Patriotes Progressistes—Parti Social-démocrate (CNPP—PSD) secured 12 seats, and the ADF four. An abstention rate of 64.8% was recorded. Compaoré appointed an economist, Youssouf Ouédraogo, as Prime Minister; the new Government included representatives of seven political organizations, although the ODP/MT retained control of most strategic ministries. In May 1993, following a split in the CNPP—PSD, six of the party's deputies joined Joseph Ki-Zerbo's newly formed Parti pour la Démocratie et le Progrès (PDP).

Following the 50% devaluation of the CFA franc, in January 1994, the Government introduced emergency measures intended to offset the immediate adverse effects of the currency's depreciation. Negotiations between trade unions, which denounced the measures as inadequate, and the Government failed to reach a compromise, and in March Youssouf Ouédraogo resigned. Kaboré was subsequently appointed Prime Minister.

At municipal elections in February 1995 the ODP/MT won control of 26 of Burkina's 33 major towns, although less than 10% of those eligible were reported to have registered to vote. In December members were appointed to serve a three-year term in Burkina's second legislative chamber, the 178-member Chambre des Représentants, which was to function in an advisory capacity.

In February 1996 Kadré Désiré Ouédraogo, hitherto Deputy Governor of the Banque Centrale des Etats de l'Afrique de l'Ouest, was appointed to succeed Kaboré as Prime Minister. Meanwhile, the Congrès pour la Démocratie et le Progrès (CDP) was formed, grouping the ODP/MT and 10 other parties. Ouédraogo assumed personal responsibility for the economy and finance portfolio in September.

Constitutional amendments and a new electoral code were approved by the ADP in January 1997: among the changes were the removal of restrictions on the renewal of the presidential mandate (which hitherto had been renewable only once) and an increase in the number of parliamentary seats to 111. The number of administrative provinces was also increased from 30 to 45. Elections to the enlarged legislature, now renamed the Assemblée nationale, took place on 11 May, at which the CDP won an overwhelming majority, with a total of 101 seats. The PDP secured six seats, and the Rassemblement Démocratique Africain (RDA) and the ADF each took two seats. Kadré Désiré Ouédraogo retained the premiership in the new Government appointed in June. In July 1998 an independent electoral body, the Commission Électorale Nationale Indépendante (CENI), comprising representatives of the legislative majority (the CDP and its allies), the opposition and civil society, was inaugurated.

Political Instability

Principal opposition leaders, including Ki-Zerbo and Hermann Yaméogo, the latter now leading the Alliance pour la Démocratie et la Fédération—Rassemblement Démocratique Africain (ADF—RDA), refused to participate in the presidential election held on 15 November 1998, and Compaoré secured a decisive victory, with 87.5% of the valid votes cast. A new Government, again headed by Kadré Désiré Ouédraogo, was appointed in January 1999.

In December 1998 Norbert Zongo, an investigative journalist and managing editor of the newspaper *L'Indépendant*, was found dead, together with three colleagues, precipitating a major political crisis. Zongo, a frequent critic of Compaoré, had been investigating the death of David Ouédraogo, a chauffeur (employed by François Compaoré, the President's brother), who had allegedly been tortured to death by members of the presidential guard. Several opposition groups, demanding a full investigation into the matter, subsequently formed the Collectif d'Organisations Démocratiques de Masse et de Partis Politiques. In January 1999 the formation of an independent commission of inquiry was announced. In early May the commission of inquiry (in which the Collectif refused to participate) submitted its final report, which suggested that members of the presidential guard implicated in the death of David Ouédraogo were also responsible for the murders of Zongo and his colleagues. In May Compaoré announced that the presidential guard was to be reorganized, and that the state would pay compensation to the families of David Ouédraogo, Norbert Zongo and their associates.

In early June 1999 Compaoré established a Collège des Sages, composed of state elders, religious and ethnic leaders, and other respected citizens, which was to work towards national reconciliation and to investigate unpunished political crimes committed since 1960. In mid-June 1999 the Collège ordered the arrest of three members of the presidential guard, accused of the murder of David Ouédraogo, and further implicated in the murder of Zongo. The Collège published its report in August, recommending that a government of national unity be formed, in addition to a 'commission of truth and justice', which would oversee the transition to a truly plural political system and investigate unresolved political murders, including that of former President Sankara. The Collège also suggested that amnesty be granted to those implicated during the commission's investigations, and that compensation be paid to the families of victims. The Collège further recommended that Compaoré not seek re-election and that fresh legislative elections be held. Although Compaoré praised the conclusions of the report, the opposition rejected the proposed amnesty and the requirement that Compaoré assent to the proposed reforms.

Only two members of the opposition were included in the new Council of Ministers announced in October 1999, most political leaders having indicated that they would not participate in a government of national unity until legal proceedings were expedited against those suspected of the murders of Ouédraogo and Zongo. In November, in accordance with the recommendations of the Collège des Sages, two advisory commissions were inaugurated, one of which was to examine clauses of the Constitution and to formulate rules governing political parties, while the other was to promote national reconciliation. Many opposition parties refused to participate in the commissions.

In January 2000 the ruling CDP organized a public demonstration in favour of the proposals of the advisory commission on political reform, which had recommended the modification of the electoral code and the reform of the judiciary and the Constitution, most notably to restrict the presidential mandate to two successive terms. In February the advisory commission on national reconciliation published its report; among its demands were the prosecution of those suspected of involvement in so-called political killings, the granting of official apologies, compensation and a guarantee regarding the future security of victims of political violence or their relatives. The commission also called for greater freedom of speech and of assembly, the resolution of legal proceedings in the Ouédraogo and Zongo cases, the introduction of an amnesty law, and the construction of a monument to Sankara.

Constitutional and Electoral Reform

In April 2000 the Assemblée nationale adopted legislation revising the electoral code; under the new regulations, 90 deputies were to be elected from regional lists, while 21 would be elected from a national list. The Assemblée also approved a constitutional amendment reducing the presidential mandate from seven to five years, renewable only once. (However, as the new limits were to take effect from the next election, Compaoré would be able to stand again in 2005 and 2010.)

Hermann Yaméogo was expelled from the Groupe du 14 Février (G-14f) opposition group in April 2000 for having criticized the group's policy of not co-operating with the Government on reform until the David Ouédraogo and Zongo cases had been resolved. The CDP won a clear victory in delayed municipal elections on 24 September, retaining outright control of 40 of the 49 municipalities. Although the G-14f and the PDP boycotted the poll, some 25 parties contested the elections, at which a turn-out of 68.4% was reported, and 14 parties gained representation. Three parties, including the ADF—RDA, had been expelled from the Collectif and the G-14f after they nominated their own election candidates.

The trial of the soldiers accused of murdering David Ouédraogo began in August 2000. Two of the defendants were acquitted by the military tribunal, but two members of the presidential guard, including Marcel Kafando, its head at the time of Ouédraogo's death, were sentenced to 20 years' imprisonment, with a third member sentenced to 10 years'. In February 2001 Kafando was charged additionally with arson and with the murder of Zongo and three others. However, the remaining charges against Kafando were dismissed in mid-2006 on the grounds of lack of evidence, prompting criticism from international press freedom groups and human rights organizations.

Meanwhile, in November 2000, amid heightened social unrest, Kadré Désiré Ouédraogo resigned as Prime Minister and was replaced by Paramanga Ernest Yonli, hitherto Minister of the Civil Service and Institutional Development. Compaoré subsequently formed a 36-member Council of Ministers, including 12 opposition members. The new appointments resulted from an accord reached by Yonli and representatives of seven political parties, including the CDP and the ADF—RDA.

In June 2001 several thousand people participated in a demonstration in Ouagadougou, led by the Collectif, demanding that those whom they believed to have ordered the killing of Zongo, including François Compaoré, be brought to justice. Meanwhile, the PDP merged with the Parti Socialiste Burkinabè (PS), to form the PDP—PS. In February 2002 the Assemblée nationale adopted a constitutional amendment providing for the abolition of the Chambre des représentants, following the failure to appoint replacement representatives for those whose terms had expired in December 2001.

Legislative Elections, 2002

Some 30 parties contested elections to the Assemblée nationale on 5 May 2002. The CDP narrowly retained its majority, securing 57 of the 111 seats, although its representation was much reduced. The ADF—RDA won 17 seats and the PDP—PS 10 seats; 10 other parties were represented in the new legislature. Kaboré was elected as President of the Assemblée in June, prior to the reappointment of Yonli as Prime Minister. The new 31-member Government did not include any representatives of the opposition.

In June 2003 Hermann Yaméogo resigned from the ADF—RDA and formed a new party, the Union Nationale pour la Démocratie et le Développement (UNDD); In October the Government announced that the authorities had prevented a planned coup. By January 2004 15 members of the armed forces, including several members of the presidential guard, and two civilians had been arrested on suspicion of involvement in the alleged plot. It was announced that the detainees were to be charged with threatening state security. The alleged leader of the group, Capt. Luther Ouali, was additionally to be charged with treason and complicity with a foreign power; reports, denied by the Governments of both countries, stated that Ouali had made contact with prominent officials in Côte d'Ivoire and Togo. In mid-January President Compaoré dismissed the Minister of Defence, Gen. Kouamé Lougué, appointing in his place Yéro Boly, hitherto head of the presidential administration. Ouali, was sentenced to 10 years' imprisonment by a military court in April; six other defendants received lesser sentences.

In April 2004 the Assemblée nationale approved an amendment to the electoral code, changing the electoral unit from the region, which number 15, to the province, of which there are 45. The vote was boycotted by most opposition parties, which claimed that they would be disadvantaged by the revised electoral code as they would be unable to field candidates in all 45 electoral units. The amendment represented a return to the system in place prior to the reforms adopted in 2000: these were regarded as having contributed to the opposition's success in significantly increasing its legislative representation in the 2002 elections.

Presidential Election, 2005

In March 2005 it was announced that the first round of the presidential election would take place on 13 November. Local elections, which had previously also been expected to be held in November, just before the presidential poll, were postponed until 12 February 2006. In June 2005 Compaoré announced his intention to seek a third term as the presidential candidate of the CDP. The legitimacy of Compaoré's candidacy was disputed by several opposition parties, which claimed that the constitutional amendment approved in 2000 that limited a President to serving only two terms of office should be applied retroactively, and five opposition candidates subsequently lodged an appeal with the Constitutional Council to that effect. However, the Council rejected this appeal.

The presidential election was held on 13 November 2005, as scheduled, contested by 13 candidates. With the opposition divided, Compaoré was re-elected by an overwhelming majority of the votes cast, securing 80.4%, compared with the 4.9% won by his nearest rival, Bénéwendé Stanislas Sankara of the Union pour la Renaissance—Mouvement Sankariste (UNIR—MS). An electoral turn-out of 57.7% was reported. Compaoré was inaugurated on 20 December and a new Government was formed in January 2006, again headed by Prime Minister Yonli. A number of new ministers were appointed from parties that had supported Compaoré in the presidential election, with the entry into government of Gilbert Ouédraogo, the President of the ADF—RDA, as Minister of Transport, particularly notable.

Compaoré and the CDP Consolidate Power

Following two further postponements, the municipal elections were finally held on 23 April 2006 in Burkina Faso's 351 municipalities (302 new communes having been created in rural areas since the last elections in 2000). Of the 73 political parties that contested the elections, around 30 secured municipal representation, although the CDP retained control of most principal towns and won 72% of the available council seats. Only 49.1% of the electorate participated in the polls.

Heavy fighting between the police and the army in December 2006, in which three soldiers and two police officers were killed, prompted the Government to postpone summits of the Economic Community of West African States (ECOWAS) and the Union Economique et Monétaire Ouest-Africaine, which had been due to take place in Ouagadougou. The military and the police agreed to end hostilities after a week, and the summits were held in the Burkinabè capital in the following month. A committee, comprising military leaders, officials from the Ministry of Defence and soldiers' representatives, was subsequently established to examine the soldiers' complaints. In October 2007, however, around 100 soldiers demonstrated in Ouagadougou, following the collapse of talks with the committee.

Elections to the Assemblée nationale took place on 6 May 2007, contested by 47 parties. The CDP strengthened its majority, securing 73 of the 111 seats, while the ADF—RDA took 14 seats. The remaining 24 seats were shared by 11 parties. The PDP—PS, whose founder, Ki-Zerbo, had died in December 2006, performed particularly poorly, its representation declining to two seats (from 10). A turn-out of 56.4% was reported. Kaboré was re-elected as President of the Assemblée nationale in June 2007.

Tertius Zongo, ambassador to the USA since 2002 and a former government minister, was appointed as Prime Minister in June 2007, following the resignation of Yonli and his Government. Although many ministers who had served under Yonli were retained in Zongo's new Council of Ministers, notable changes included the appointment of Djibril Bassolet, hitherto Minister of Security, as Minister of Foreign Affairs and Regional Co-operation, and his replacement by Assane Sawadogo.

Significant rises in prices of foodstuffs and fuel provoked public unrest in late February 2008. Protests took place in Ouahigouya, Banfora and Bobo-Dioulasso (the country's second largest town), where more than 200 people were detained after violence erupted, subsequently spreading to Ouagadougou, where rioting led to further arrests. Earlier that month the Government had declared its intention to introduce measures aimed at stabilizing prices, with those of some basic goods having increased by more than 60% in recent weeks; following the initial demonstrations, the Government ordered the suspension of import duties on certain products for a period of three months, and later announced reductions of 5%–15% in the prices of a number of staple foodstuffs. In early March it was reported that 29 people had been sentenced to between three and 36 months' imprisonment in connection with the disturbances in Bobo-Dioulasso. Thibault Nana, the leader of a minor opposition party, the Rassemblement Démocratique et Populaire, was sentenced to three years' imprisonment in mid-March, having been found guilty of organizing the protest in the capital, while 44 others received one-year custodial sentences. Meanwhile, several trade unions and civil society organizations formed the Coalition nationale contre la vie chère to demand, *inter alia*, a 25% increase in salaries and pensions for both public and private sector workers, a reduction in the prices of essential goods and the introduction of price controls. Several thousand people participated in peaceful marches organized by the coalition in Ouagadougou and other towns in mid-March. Although the Government agreed to lower electricity and water prices for the most impoverished citizens and to extend the suspension of import duties on certain products for a further three months, the coalition deemed these measures inadequate and called a two-day general strike in April and a three-day strike in May, both of which were partially observed.

In June 2008 a new anti-corruption authority, the Autorité Supérieure de Contrôle de l'Etat, with the power to refer cases directly to the courts, was created by the Government to replace three existing bodies. Government changes made in September included the appointment of Bédouma Alain Yoda, hitherto Minister of Health, as Minister of State, Minister of Foreign Affairs and Regional Co-operation, to replace Bassolet, who had recently become the joint chief mediator of the UN and the African Union (AU) in their efforts to resolve the conflict in the Sudanese region of Darfur. Also notable was the dismissal of Assane Sawadogo, after only 15 months in office; Emile Ouédraogo was allocated the security portfolio.

In March 2009 UNIR—MS formally merged with two smaller Sankarist parties to form the Union pour la Renaissance—Parti Sankariste (UNIR—PS). The Assemblée nationale adopted several amendments to the electoral system in April and May, including a reduction in the percentage of votes that parties are required to secure in elections to be eligible for state funding from 5% to 3%. Also approved was a specification that the official leader of the parliamentary opposition should not come from a party supportive of the Government (the ADF—RDA had hitherto provided the holder of this position, being the second largest party in the legislature, despite its support for Compaoré's administration). Bénéwendé Sankara, the President of the UNIR—PS, was designated as the official leader of the parliamentary opposition in September.

Internal divisions continued to damage the ruling CDP in 2009–10. In July 2009 Salif Diallo, who had been appointed as ambassador to Austria some months after his dismissal from the Government in March 2008, was suspended from the CDP, in which he occupied the post of First Vice-President, after he criticized the Burkinabè political system in a newspaper interview; he was readmitted to the party in February 2010. Meanwhile, a new opposition party, the Convention Nationale du Progrès du Burkina, was created in August 2009 by several former senior members of the CDP. In March 2010, moreover, Zéphirin Diabré, a former government minister in Compaoré's regime, announced the formation of another new opposition organization, the Union pour le Progrès et le Changement.

Compaoré's Fourth Elected Term

In February 2010 it was announced that a presidential election would be held on 21 November. A further five-year term for Compaoré would be his last under current constitutional provisions. However, several allies of the President had proposed amending the Constitution to abolish the two-term limit introduced in 2000. This plan, aimed at extending Compaoré's rule indefinitely, prompted criticism from opposition leaders, Roman Catholic bishops and civil society groups, among others. In April 2010 a number of opposition parties established Coalition 37 (named after the relevant article of the Constitution) to resist any such revision. None the less, at an extraordinary party congress held in early August, the CDP formally advocated the removal of the limit on presidential mandates and, in his absence, approved Compaoré as its candidate in the forthcoming election. In addition, the party declared its support for the creation of an upper legislative chamber, the Sénat, although it did not indicate when it intended to seek approval for its proposed constitutional reforms. Compaoré confirmed his presidential candidacy later in August. In October it was announced that municipal elections due to take place in April 2011 had been postponed and would be conducted concurrently with legislative polls in May 2012.

Seven candidates contested the presidential election, which was held, as scheduled, on 21 November 2010. Compaoré again secured a decisive victory, winning 80.2% of the valid votes cast. His nearest rivals, receiving 8.2% and 6.3% of the vote, respectively, were Hama Arba Diallo, the mayor of the north-eastern commune of Dori, representing the Parti pour la Démocratie et le Socialisme, and Bénéwendé Sankara, of the UNIR—PS. A turn-out of 54.9% was recorded. Challenges to the results from Diallo and Sankara and two other defeated candidates, who cited serious electoral irregularities (particularly related to errors on voting cards), were rejected by the

Constitutional Council, while observers from the AU and ECOWAS declared the election to have been 'transparent'. Compaoré was inaugurated to serve a fourth elected term of office on 21 December. A new Government, again headed by Prime Minister Zongo, was appointed in January 2011. The most notable new appointee was Bongnessan Arsène Yé, a former President of the Assemblée nationale, who was named Minister of State, Minister at the Presidency, in charge of Political Reform, in which post he was to introduce planned amendments to the Constitution.

Despite President Compaoré's comfortable re-election in November 2010, his administration was threatened by severe unrest during the first half of 2011. The death of a student in uncertain circumstances in police custody in the town of Koudougou, some 75 km west of Ouagadougou, provoked violent protests in late February, in which six people were reportedly killed. (Three police officers were sentenced to eight–10 years' imprisonment in August for their involvement in the student's death.) The Governor of the Centre-ouest region, of which Koudougou is the capital, was subsequently dismissed. Military strife followed in late March, when troops from two army camps protested in Ougadougou, firing into the air and looting businesses, following the conviction of five soldiers on charges of assaulting a civilian; the five were released from prison shortly afterwards. Tensions escalated on 14 April, when a mutiny by members of the presidential guard, over unpaid housing and food allowances, prompted Compaoré to flee Ouagadougou for several hours. On his return the following day, the President attempted to restore calm by dismissing his Government, replacing the Chief of the General Staff of the Armed Forces and the head of the presidential guard, imposing an overnight curfew in the capital and ordering the payment of allowances to soldiers. However, business owners whose properties had been damaged by the mutinous troops attacked several public buildings in Ouagadougou, notably setting fire to the headquarters of the CDP, and the mutiny spread to other towns, with soldiers being joined by police officers in Kaya. Meanwhile, thousands of people participated in protests against high food and fuel prices. On 18 April Luc Adolphe Tiao, hitherto ambassador to France, was appointed as the new Prime Minister. Three days later the composition of the new Government was announced, the number of ministers having been reduced from 38 to 29. Bassolet resigned from his UN-AU role to return to the post of Minister of Foreign Affairs and Regional Co-operation, while Compaoré himself assumed responsibility for the defence portfolio.

Disturbances continued in late April 2011, however, involving, among others, traders in Koudougou, farmers in Bobo-Dioulasso and police officers in Ouagadougou, and an opposition rally was held in support of demands for Compaoré to stand down. A day earlier the President had announced that soldiers had agreed to end their protests. In early May the Government introduced a series of emergency measures aimed at allaying public discontent over the high cost of living, including a reduction in the prices of certain staple foodstuffs and a 10% cut in taxes on salaries. None the less, on 14 May soldiers in the town of Po, some 140 km from Ouagadougou, fired their weapons for several hours before returning to barracks, while thousands of women participated in an anti-Government demonstration in the capital. The curfew in Ouagadougou was lifted two days later. Further protests by soldiers demanding the payment of allowances took place in Dori and other towns in late May. In early June forces loyal to Compaoré intervened for the first time since the unrest began to quell a mutiny by soldiers in Bobo-Dioulasso, following several days of looting and shooting. Calm was restored, but six soldiers and a teenage girl were killed in an exchange of fire; at least 109 people were initially arrested for involvement in the rebellion and looting. Later that month, in response to the disorder of the preceding few months, all 13 regional governors were replaced, and in July 566 soldiers were discharged from the armed forces and 217 were detained on charges of rebellion, desertion and looting. Meanwhile, the European Union announced that it would provide €8m. in funding in 2012 in support of judicial, security and defence reforms in Burkina Faso, as well as measures to combat corruption. President Compaoré effected changes to the armed forces in September 2011, notably replacing the military commanders in Bobo-Dioulasso and Kaya and reorganizing army regiments. Economic measures seemingly aimed at averting further social unrest were announced in November, including a pledge to create 54,200 new jobs for young people during 2012–14, the allocation of more than 9,600m. francs CFA to assist those who had suffered looting or damage to property, and a 5% rise in the pay and pensions of public sector employees (although trade unions had demanded an increase of 30%).

Meanwhile, political reforms remained under consideration: an advisory body created in April 2011 to discuss and make recommendations on the issue, the 66-member Conseil Consultatif sur les Réformes Politiques (CCRP), commenced work in June, but was boycotted by several opposition parties and civil society organizations. The opposition withdrew its members from the CENI in June, accusing the commission's President, Moussa Michel Tapsoba, a human rights activist and one of the five civil society representatives, of being incapable of organizing transparent legislative and municipal elections in May 2012, following problems experienced during the 2010 presidential election. The CDP and Prime Minister Tiao had also sought Tapsoba's resignation, which he had refused to tender. In July 2011 the Assemblée nationale approved a government proposal for the early replacement of the CENI, the mandate of its current members not being due to expire until September. Barthélemy Kéré, a lawyer representing the Roman Catholic community and a member of the previous commission, was elected as the President of the new CENI at the beginning of August. In October Kéré announced the postponement of the legislative and municipal elections until late 2012, in order to allow the introduction of biometric voter cards intended to enhance the transparency of future polls, which had been demanded by the opposition. Regional and national conferences took place in October and December 2011, respectively, to discuss the CCRP's proposals for political reform, which included the establishment of a Sénat, an increase in the number of deputies, the creation of a constitutional status for traditional leaders and the imposition of minimum and maximum ages for presidential candidates of 35 and 75 years, but not the abolition of the limit on presidential terms. In March 2012 the Council of Ministers adopted a decree creating a committee charged with monitoring the implementation of reforms on which consensus had been reached.

Ousmane Guiro, the head of the customs department, was dismissed and charged with embezzlement in January 2012, after suitcases allegedly belonging to him, and containing nearly 2,000m. francs CFA, were seized by police. Compaoré dismissed the Minister of Justice and the Promotion of Human Rights, Keeper of the Seals, Jérôme Traoré, in February, amid public anger over allegations that he ordered the beating and arrest of a mechanic following a traffic-related incident. In the ensuing government reorganization, Salamata Sawagogo Tapsoba was designated Minister of Justice, Keeper of the Seals, while Albert Ouédraogo, hitherto Minister of Secondary and Higher Education, was appointed to head a new Ministry of Human Rights and Civic Promotion, being replaced in the education portfolio by Moussa Ouattara.

Major changes to the leadership of the ruling CDP were effected at a party congress held in March 2012. A new ruling body, the Secrétariat Exécutif National (SEN), was established, with the head of the presidential administration, Assimi Kouanda, who had directed Compaoré's re-election campaign in 2010, replacing Roch Marc Christian Kaboré as party leader, in the post of National Executive Secretary (as the party presidency had been renamed). The SEN comprised 38 members, 21 of whom had not previously held senior party leadership positions. This renewal of the party was attributed to its desire to improve its standing ahead of the elections due later in the year. However, observers also noted that many of the new SEN members were close allies of Compaoré (most notably his brother, François Compaoré), suggesting that the President was seeking to exert greater influence over the party. In early April 2012 the Assemblée nationale approved an increase in the number of deputies from 111 to 127 with effect from the forthcoming elections, which were subsequently scheduled for 2 December.

FOREIGN RELATIONS

Compaoré has gained considerable respect as a regional mediator in recent years, although during the 1990s some regional and Western governments expressed concern at his perceived role in the conflicts in Liberia, Sierra Leone and Angola.

Following the escalation of the civil conflict in Liberia after early 1990, Burkina's relations with some members of ECOWAS deteriorated as a result of the Compaoré Government's open support for Charles Taylor's rebel National Patriotic Front of Liberia and refusal to contribute troops to the ECOWAS force (ECOMOG) that was sent to Liberia in mid-1990. In September 1995, however, the Compaoré administration announced that Burkina would contribute troops to ECOMOG. In February 1997 Burkinabè troops assisted in the preparations for elections in Liberia; members of the Burkinabè military subsequently remained in Liberia to assist in training new armed forces.

In early 1999 President Ahmed Tejan Kabbah of Sierra Leone and the Government of Nigeria alleged that Burkina and Liberia were co-operating to provide support and supply arms to the rebel fighters of the Revolutionary United Front (RUF) in Sierra Leone. In early 2000 a report to the UN Security Council accused Burkina Faso of having on several occasions supplied weapons to the RUF in exchange for diamonds. It was also alleged that Burkina Faso had supplied weapons to Liberia and to Angolan rebel groups, despite international embargoes on the supply of weapons to those countries. The claims were strenuously denied by the Burkinabè Government. Although Compaoré, in May 2001, criticized a UN decision to impose travel restrictions on Liberian officials, subsequent relations with the Taylor Government were more distant, and Compaoré welcomed Taylor's resignation as President of Liberia in August 2003.

In November 1999 a dispute over land rights between Burkinabè settlers in the south-west of Côte d'Ivoire and the indigenous Krou population led to the violent and systematic expulsion from the region of several hundred Burkinabè plantation workers. Several deaths were reported, and it was estimated that up to 20,000 expatriates subsequently returned to Burkina. Following the coup in Côte d'Ivoire in December, the military authorities assured the Government of Burkina that the expulsions would cease and that measures would be taken in order to allow workers to return. None the less, tensions between the two countries heightened as the former Prime Minister of Côte d'Ivoire, Alassane Ouattara, was excluded from participation in the Ivorian presidential election of October 2000 because of his Burkinabè origins. Following a coup attempt in Abidjan, Côte d'Ivoire, in January 2001, which the Ivorian Government attributed to the influence of unnamed, neighbouring states, attacks on Burkinabè expatriates in Côte d'Ivoire reportedly increased; by late January it was reported that up to 10,000 Burkinabè were returning to Burkina each week. In June the two countries announced that they would commence joint patrols of their common border. In July a meeting between Compaoré and the democratically elected Ivorian President, Laurent Gbagbo, in Sirte, Libya, was reported to have helped defuse tensions between the two countries, and Gbagbo made his first official visit to Burkina in December.

Following the outbreak of further unrest in Côte d'Ivoire in September 2002, Gbagbo again alleged that an unnamed, neighbouring country (widely regarded as a reference to Burkina) was implicated in the rebellion. However, in November, following an attack on the residence of the Burkinabè President in Abidjan, the Ivorian Government expressed its regret for the attack. As a result of the upsurge in violence in Côte d'Ivoire, at least 350,000 Burkinabè citizens reportedly fled Côte d'Ivoire for Burkina. Compaoré welcomed the peace agreement signed in France in January, known as the Marcoussis Accords, which provided for a government of national reconciliation in Côte d'Ivoire, although at the end of the month the Burkinabè embassy in Abidjan was attacked and set on fire by opponents of the agreement. The common border of the two countries, closed since the onset of the rebellion, was reopened in September as greater stability appeared to return to Côte d'Ivoire. In October the Government of Côte d'Ivoire denied suggestions of Ivorian involvement in the alleged coup plot in Burkina (see above). In late 2003 Compaoré hosted meetings with several prominent Ivorian leaders, emphasizing the need to develop bilateral co-operation.

Bilateral relations subsequently improved, and in early 2007 Compaoré mediated direct talks between Gbagbo and former rebel leader Guillaume Soro, which resulted in the signing of a new political agreement between the two sides in Ouagadougou in March. Compaoré made his first visit to Côte d'Ivoire in seven years in June to attend the inaugural meeting of a committee charged with monitoring the implementation of the agreement. In September Compaoré appointed the former Burkinabè Minister of Justice, Boureima Badini, to be his special representative in efforts to accelerate the peace process in Côte d'Ivoire, although the President continued personally to facilitate negotiations between the main protagonists. Relations between Burkina Faso and Côte d'Ivoire were further strengthened in July 2008 by an official visit to Burkina by President Gbagbo, during which bilateral agreements on defence, security, infrastructure and energy were signed. In September 2009 Compaoré and Gbagbo presided over a joint meeting of their Governments in Yamoussoukro, Côte d'Ivoire, but in the following month a UN panel of experts claimed that weapons were being transferred from Burkina Faso to Ivorian rebel forces. Meanwhile, Compaoré continued in his role as 'facilitator' in Côte d'Ivoire as the country prepared to hold a repeatedly delayed presidential election. The election finally took place in October and November 2010, but its outcome was disputed by the two run-off candidates, Gbagbo and Alassane Ouattara. Compaoré formed part of a mediation panel of regional heads of state charged by the AU in January 2011 with attempting to seek a resolution to the political crisis, as Gbagbo refused to concede defeat, but mediatory efforts failed and violence ensued. Having been officially declared as Ivorian President in early May, Ouattara visited Burkina Faso some 11 days later, holding cordial discussions with Compaoré.

Meanwhile, Compaoré chaired the negotiations that led to the conclusion of a political accord between Togo's Government and main opposition parties in August 2006, and subsequently presided over a committee established to monitor its implementation. Burkina Faso contributed some 800 troops to the AU-UN peace-keeping mission in Darfur established in July 2007, its largest ever deployment in a foreign country. In October 2009, following the violent suppression of a pro-democracy rally in Guinea in the previous month, the Burkinabè President was designated by ECOWAS to mediate in efforts to resolve the political crisis in that country, while Compaoré and Djibril Bassolet, Burkina Faso's Minister of Foreign Affairs and Regional Co-operation, also acted as ECOWAS mediators in Mali after the Malian President was deposed in March 2012. Violence in northern Mali prompted more than 253,000 Malians to flee into neighbouring countries by late July that year, with nearly 108,000 having entered Burkina Faso. Burkinabè troops were dispatched to Guinea-Bissau in May as part of a planned deployment of a 600-strong ECOWAS peace-keeping force following a coup in that country in the previous month.

Links with Libya have generally been strong under the Compaoré regime; Burkina was, notably, a founder member of the Libyan-sponsored Community of Sahel-Saharan States, established in 1997. Despite Compaoré's long-standing close relationship with Libyan leader Col Muammar al-Qaddafi, in August 2011 Burkina Faso officially recognized the opposition National Transitional Council as the sole legitimate authority in Libya, while at the same time reportedly offering Qaddafi exile (although this was subsequently refuted), prior to his death in October.

Burkina Faso sought amicably to resolve a long-running border dispute with Benin in March 2008, both countries pledging not to make any 'visible sovereignty act' in a 68-sq km area and to allow residents of the zone to vote in the country of their choice. In May 2009 it was announced that the two countries' Presidents had decided to refer the case to the International Court of Justice (ICJ), based at The Hague,

Netherlands; an agreement to this effect was signed in September, although the case had not been formally submitted to the Court by April 2012. Pending a verdict by the Court, the disputed 68-sq km area was to remain neutral and to be administered and financed jointly. Meanwhile, in February 2009 the Governments of Burkina and Niger signed an agreement on seeking arbitration by the ICJ over the demarcation of part of their common border; the dispute was jointly submitted to the Court in July 2010, with public hearings in the case due to be held in October 2012.

Economy

PAUL MELLY

INTRODUCTION

A land-locked country in the savannah lands of the West African Sahel, Burkina Faso has been continually challenged in its efforts to ensure the survival of its largely agricultural and pastoral economy; desertification and soil erosion are ever-present threats. Although mining now makes a significant contribution to output and exports, the prospects for economic diversification and industrial development are hampered by high transport costs, low consumer buying power and the narrowness of the natural resource base. For many years the Government lacked a coherent overall strategy for rural development, but recently there has been an attempt to tackle rural poverty in a more comprehensive manner. Furthermore, Burkina Faso has a proven long-term record of effective grass-roots service provision, and stable macroeconomic and fiscal policy.

However, some underlying economic strains have persisted, such as soldiers' discontent at their pay and conditions, a point highlighted by the army mutinies of 2011. Meanwhile, like other Sahelian countries, Burkina Faso suffered a poor rainy season in 2011; this placed domestic food production under pressure and severely damaged nutrition and levels of income in some rural communities. Additionally, in the first half of 2012 the north of the country saw an influx of refugees from the conflict in Mali; although donors have provided humanitarian assistance, this has put an inevitable further strain on grazing and food supply in a number of already vulnerable rural communities.

Around 80% of Burkina Faso's 17.5m. people (as estimated in 2012) live in rural areas, reliant on traditional farming methods for subsistence, supplemented with modest earnings from the sale of cash crops, fruit, vegetables, livestock or firewood. The climate is arid, and the rivers mostly seasonal, so supplies of water can run low during the long dry period, and the economy is vulnerable to weather patterns. Outside the rainy season, economic activity in rural areas declines; there are a lack of alternative employment opportunities. During recent years the rural economy has suffered from the problems facing the cotton sector: franc zone producers have suffered from intense global competition, caused both by the 2005 liberalization of world textiles trade and the continued subsidizing of cotton production in many developed countries, particularly the USA.

Owing to its land-locked location, Burkina Faso is dependent on good relations with its coastal neighbours, and on the economic and political conditions in these countries. Between 2m. and 4m. Burkinabè work abroad, some seasonally and some permanently, primarily in Côte d'Ivoire, where they account for much of the manual labour force in the cocoa sector, and in Ghana and Mali, where they primarily work in the services sector. In Côte d'Ivoire the December 1999 coup and the September 2002 outbreak of civil war left Sahelian migrants facing a risk of ethnically motivated violence; some 500,000 Burkinabè migrants fled home. This imposed strains on Burkina Faso's domestic labour market and social climate, and many migrants eventually chose to return to Côte d'Ivoire as conditions there improved. The early 2011 conflict over the Ivorian presidency briefly revived fears among migrant communities, but movements of people were on a more limited scale and conditions have gradually returned to a fragile normality. The partition of Côte d'Ivoire for much of the period from 2008–10 frequently impeded the flow of goods to its principal port of Abidjan, forcing Burkina Faso to channel much of its external trade through Senegal (via Mali), Ghana, Togo and Benin.

The tradition of worker migration reinforces Burkina Faso's commercial contacts with its southern neighbour countries, where many consumer goods are purchased for resale in the country. Many Burkinabè also migrate to work in Europe, particularly France. Migrant remittances contribute to the national balance of payments. However, largely owing to the prolonged crisis in Côte d'Ivoire, remittance inflows have declined from 50,000m. francs CFA in 1999 to an estimated 3,400m. francs CFA in 2009; since 2009 they have also been dampened by the depressed state of the European labour markets.

Manufacturing activity is restricted to small units, mainly in the second city, Bobo-Dioulasso, and, to a lesser extent, in Banfora, Koudougou and the capital, Ouagadougou. It takes the form of import substitution and the processing of local agricultural commodities; cotton-ginning is the only industrial activity that makes a significant contribution to exports. As in most West African countries, the informal sector is an important provider of jobs and income. Fewer than 500,000 Burkinabè work in formal employment (80,000 in the public sector, and 400,000 in the private sector); the vast majority live from agriculture, pastoralism or the informal sector. Mining is gaining in importance; the production of gold has almost doubled since 2009, owing to the opening of a new mine at Essakane, and zinc and manganese are also produced. The Government has had some success in promoting Ouagadougou as a cultural centre, notably through the biennial Fespaco—the Pan-African Film and Television Festival—the most important such event south of the Sahara.

The economy's dependence on agriculture and on migrant remittances results in wide fluctuations in performance from year to year; in the late 1980s and early 1990s growth in gross domestic product (GDP) barely kept pace with the steady increase in population. The 50% devaluation of the CFA franc in January 1994 increased the cost of imports, but also gave a sharp boost to the competitiveness of local production, principally benefiting the rural economy, including the cotton sector. During 1996–2006 annual GDP growth averaged 4.9%, and over the first six years of the 2000s it averaged more than 6%. GDP growth slowed to 5.5% in 2006 and 3.6% in 2007, before rebounding to 5.2% in 2008. Burkina Faso felt the impact of the global economic crisis, with real growth of only 3.2% in 2009. However, the launch of new mining projects and a surge in gold output resulted in GDP increasing by 7.9% in 2010 in real terms. Economic activity appears to have been consolidated at this higher base, with real GDP growth of 5.6% in 2011 and an estimated 5.0% in 2012; the IMF projects a growth rate of 6.0% for 2013. The resurgence has been driven not only by mining but also by agriculture and services; the flow of credit to the economy has expanded and the terms of external trade have also improved, strengthening Burkina Faso's balance of payments. Although the first half of 2011 was troubled, with demonstrations and unrest, and a series of mutinies in military units, the Government sought to restore calm with extra spending, equivalent to 0.5% of GDP.

Despite stronger economic growth, Burkina Faso remains one of the world's poorest countries: in 2011 real GDP was only US $322 per caput—much higher than Niger but still markedly less than that of neighbouring Benin. Despite a sustained drive to improve grassroots service provision, the country's development indicators are also among the lowest in the world. In the UN Development Programme's *Human Development Index* for 2011 Burkina ranked 181st out of 187. Some 68% of boys and 61% of girls attend primary school, but only 18% and 14%, respectively, continue to secondary school, and only 11% of Burkinabè have access to improved sanitation. However, there has been progress in some respects: the infant mortality rate among children under five has improved to 166 per 1,000 live births, while average life expectancy has risen to 55.4 years. Among adults aged 15–49, the rate of HIV infection is 1.2%; this may reflect the fact that many Burkinabè men migrate to work in Côte d'Ivoire, where prevalence rates are much higher.

The post-revolutionary Government of Capt. Thomas Sankara (1983–87) nationalized areas of economic activity. However, the past two decades have been characterized by a sustained programme of economic liberalization and a close policy partnership with the IMF. The Government and the Fund have agreed a target of reducing the number of people living below the poverty line from 46% in 2003 to less than 35% by 2015, and improving access to education and health services.

The business environment for investors has improved considerably and the World Bank's indicators on the ease of doing business, measured in mid-2011, ranked Burkina Faso 24th of 46 sub-Saharan countries. The best prospects for modernization and economic growth appear to lie in the development of a range of activities: mining, light industry, such as the production of garments using local hand-picked cotton, as well as livestock exports, cultural tourism, the export of horticultural products to Europe and trade with neighbouring countries. As in most countries using the CFA franc currency, inflation has remained in low single figures.

AGRICULTURE

Agriculture, livestock-rearing, forestry and fishing accounted for 34.8% of Burkina Faso's GDP in 2009 and employed some 84% of the labour force in 2008. Growth in output is driven by an extension of the areas under cultivation, rather than the improvement of yields. For five years the area under crops expanded by an annual average of 2.3%, reaching 4.1m. ha by 2008—some 45% of the potential cultivable land in the country; this prompted the Ministry of Agriculture to warn that if agricultural growth continued at that level, the supply of land would be exhausted by 2030. The rate of population growth has fallen but is still 3% per year. Thus, it will be essential to improve crop yields and promote farming practices that conserve soil fertility, if farming output is to keep pace with the rise in local demand.

The farming year runs from June to May and levels of cereal production are largely determined by the weather; Burkina Faso has a Sahelian climate—with most rainfall between June and September, and the main cereal crops harvested mostly during the final four months of the year. Severe droughts are not uncommon. Food crop production rose by 20% in 2010, but rainfall was disappointing in 2011, exerting severe downward pressure on output. In years of good rainfall, the country rebuilds food stocks to last through periods of drought. However, poor transport and storage facilities hinder the effective availability of supplies. Conditions in the cotton market also have an impact on food production: when cotton prices are weak farmers switch more land to the cultivation of cereals for sale to domestic consumers. In 2009/10 Burkina Faso produced more than 4m. tons of cereals, including 1.5m. tons of sorghum, 970,000 tons of millet and 895,000 tons of maize, despite suffering severe floods in September 2009. Rice output rose by 9.5%. 2010 saw further production growth, with millet and sorghum output rising to 3.1m. tons, a maize crop of 1.1m. tons, and rice output of 233,000 tons. However, the poor rainfall of 2011 produced a serious reverse, with output falling sharply and pressure on food supply throughout the 2011/12 crop marketing year. Some northern and eastern areas were reported to be suffering 'critical' food supply pressures, although the position was much better in the south and west.

Burkina Faso produces some cash crops as the surplus of subsistence cultivation, mainly karité nuts (sheanuts—70,000 tons in 2007), and sesame (18,802 tons in 2007). Since the 1990s, there has considerable government investment in cotton, groundnuts, sugar, cashew nuts and fruit and market gardening, with financial aid from, among others, the European Development Fund (EDF). For example, Burkina Faso now exports organic mangoes to Europe.

The most important cash crop is cotton. An estimated 4m. rural Burkinabè depend directly or indirectly on this for their livelihood, in 12 cotton-growing regions. The devaluation of the CFA franc in January 1994 boosted competitiveness and a major investment programme for the cotton sector parastatal, Société Burkinabè des Fibres Textiles (SOFITEX), was announced in 1996. Over the past 10 years, however, conditions have been much more difficult: with its strong CFA franc currency, which is pegged to the euro, Burkina Faso has struggled to compete in a world market where prices are heavily influenced by low-cost output from Asia and major US government subsidies for American cotton production.

On the advice of the IMF, the Government ended the SOFITEX monopoly on the collection and marketing of seed cotton and partially privatized the company: a 30% stake went to the cotton farmers' union, the Union Nationale des Producteurs de Coton du Burkina (UNPCB) and 34% to the French company Dagris; the state retained a 35% stake. In addition, two private cotton-ginning companies were established: Faso Coton in the central region and the Société Cotonnière du Gourma in the east.

As a result of these reforms and significant investment in new cotton-producing areas, by 2003 Burkina Faso had become the largest cotton producer in sub-Saharan Africa, with a record crop, of 760,000 metric tons, harvested in 2006. However, a subsequent decline in world prices and a rise in input costs plunged the sector into financial crisis. Producer prices were reduced—from 175 francs CFA per kg in 2005 to just 145 francs CFA per kg in 2007. As a result, some 50,000 cotton farmers abandoned cotton and switched to food crops. In response, SOFITEX introduced a cash reserve fund (*fonds de lissage*) to help to protect farmers from fluctuations in the cotton price and encourage them to diversify into oil crops. The new mechanism bases producer prices on world levels but makes compensatory payments to growers when prices are low; when world prices are high the extra income is used to replenish the fund. In 2007 SOFITEX was recapitalized at a cost of 1% of GDP. Dagris did not participate this time, which resulted in the Government's stake rising to 60%. In 2009 financial and operational audits were undertaken to prepare for the eventual sale of 30% to a strategic investor, although the pace of privatization is being phased.

In this difficult domestic and international context, cotton production has fluctuated sharply: from 713,400 metric tons in 2005/06, it fell sharply to just 355,700 tons in 2007/08. There was a fresh recovery in 2008/09, with output reaching 720,700 tons, before a renewed slide in output, to 483,900 tons in 2009/10. In 2010/11 farmers were encouraged by a rise of more than 10% in the producer price, to 182 francs CFA per kg; this stimulated a gentle rebound in output, to 529,600 tons. The Government has been promoting the cultivation of genetically modified strains, in an effort to improve output; the area planted with these strains doubled between 2009 and 2011.

A reduction in the subsidies through which developed countries support their cotton farmers has been on the agenda of world trade talks for most of the 21st century, but there has been little progress towards an agreement, owing to the political sensitivity of the issue in southern US states, and the main world trade negotiations have reached an impasse. West African cotton producers estimate that they have lost US $150m. per year in export earnings since 1997 as a result of US government subsidies to 25,000 US cotton farmers, which were estimated at more than $4,500m. in 2006. In 2009 cotton accounted for only 111,000m. francs CFA of Burkina Faso's total 712,800m. francs CFA exports.

The production of groundnuts has roughly tripled since the mid-1980s. Output fluctuated in the 300,000–350,000 ton range over the three seasons to 2010/11. Production of sugar cane began in 1974/75 and has risen sharply in recent years, driven by buoyant global demand, reaching an estimated 455,000 tons in 2010. Nevertheless, the sugar sector has experienced financial difficulties, due to mismanagement and low sales of domestic sugar, which has struggled to compete with cheaper imports of sugar beet.

Stock-rearing is practised by the semi-nomadic Fulani (Peulh) in the sparsely populated areas of the north and east, although a large-scale programme is redeveloping livestock production in the west of the country. An FAO-supported West African regional development project for those areas affected by trypanosomiasis (sleeping-sickness) includes Burkina Faso. In 2008 there were an estimated 8.4m. cattle, 8.2m. sheep and 12.3m. goats in the country. Livestock production (including live animals and livestock products, hides and skins) contributed an estimated 12.5% of the country's export earnings in 2006. Animals are often exported to West African coastal markets, and there may be substantial informal and unrecorded cross-border exports of livestock.

The small fish catch from rivers and lakes (some 9,000–10,000 metric tons per year, according to FAO) is consumed locally. Timber production is insignificant, although almost one-quarter of Burkina Faso's national territory is categorized as forest; however, foreign agencies are now funding timber development projects in the Kompienga and Bagré Dam regions. In 2003 the Government launched a 10-year plan to combat desertification and land erosion through afforestation programmes covering 350 districts; it was anticipated that some 17,500 ha of forest would be developed as a result.

MINING

The administration of President Blaise Compaoré has accelerated the exploitation of Burkina Faso's mineral resources, which include gold, manganese, zinc and silver. In recent years the sector has grown dramatically. Liberalization of the outdated mining code, and strong international demand and prices for minerals, have persuaded foreign mining firms to increase their exploration activities in Burkina Faso.

A series of new projects has produced a steady upward trend in gold production, rising from 209 kg in 2002 to 1,571 kg in 2006, to 5,380 kg in 2008 and 12,149 kg in 2009. Consequently, the value of gold exports has soared, from just 4,600m. francs CFA in 2007 to 55,600m. francs CFA in 2008, some 179,800m. francs CFA in 2009 and 448,700m. francs CFA in 2010. Gold has overtaken cotton as Burkina Faso's main export, accounting for more than one-half of total exports—although cotton remains much more important as a source of cash income for the country's rural families.

In 1999 the state-owned Poura gold mine, then Burkina Faso's only industrial pit, was closed. The revival of the sector was led by the Canadian company High River Gold Mines, with a new pit at Taparko, in the Centre-North region, as well as a mill and the infrastructure to process ore from both Taparko and the nearby Bouroum deposits. Commercial production began in October 2007. In 2008 three more significant gold mines commenced operations, at Kalsaka, Youga and Mana. Construction of the Kalsaka mine, located 150 km north-west of Ouagadougou, began in June 2005. The project was developed by the British-based Cluff Mining, which held a 78% stake, with the Government and private investors holding the remaining shares. Completed in November 2008, the mine was expected to produce 22 metric tons of gold over 20 years. In early 2005 Etruscan Resources of Canada began development of a US $94m. open-cast mine at Youga, 180 km south-east of Ouagadougou. Opening in July 2008, the mine produced 29,305 troy oz of gold in its first year of operation. In 1998 the Canadian mining company Société d'Exploitation Minière en Afrique de l'Ouest (SEMAFO) started prospecting at Mana, near the Malian border. In February 2007 SEMAFO was issued with a permit to develop a mine, at a projected cost of $72m., with potential output estimated at 25 tons of gold per year over eight years; production began in 2008. The Belahouro and Inata permits, north-east of Ouagadougou, are being developed by Goldbelt Resources of Canada; Riverstone Resources, of Canada, is developing the Bissa prospect, 220 km west of Ouagadougou. Ampella Mining, of Australia, has also been engaged in exploration, and now has projects at Madougou, Doulnia, Batié West and Donko. However, the most significant breakthrough has come with the development, by another Canadian company, Orezone Resources, of the Essakane prospect in the north-east. This potentially holds Burkina Faso's richest deposits, with estimated reserves of 84m. tons of ore. Production commenced ahead of schedule in July 2010, and was expected to yield 315,000 oz of gold per year.

The latest major leap forward came with the opening of another new pit, Essakane, in the north, in which Canada's IAM Gold has invested US $450m. As a result, between 2009 and 2010 Burkina's total gold production almost doubled, to 23,100 kg. Essakane is expected to produce 10 metric tons of gold per annum for about 10 years.

In November 2004 AIM Resources of Australia acquired a majority stake in a project to produce zinc at Perkoa, in central Burkina Faso; in February 2007 the Government authorized a start to mining operations. Construction began in March, at an investment cost of 75,000m. francs CFA, with output projected to reach 500,000 metric tons of ore per year over 17 years. Reserves were estimated at 6m. tons at 14.5% grade of zinc. The mine is now run by Blackthorn Resources of Australia.

Burkina Faso's other mineral prospects include titanium, vanadium, nickel, bauxite, copper, lead and phosphates, although none of these are considered to be commercially viable at present. A more immediate development prospect is for the quarrying of limestone deposits at Tin Hrassan, near Tambao, which can be developed for cement production.

POWER

Electricity generating capacity was considerably expanded in the 1990s, with growth continuing in the early 2000s. Total production of electricity by the national power company, Société Nationale Burkinabè d'Électricité (SONABEL), increased from 216m. kWh in 1993 to an estimated 700m. kWh by 2009. A further 145m. kWh was imported. Industry, government and business accounts for much of the power consumption. The national grid is poorly developed and in 2009 SONABEL had only 337,155 low voltage customers; the company announced that only 104 communities in Burkina Faso were supplied with electric power. (Some villages may have limited off-grid supply, such as local solar installation, to meet priority community uses.) As a result, more than 90% of domestic fuel needs are met with firewood. However, the growth in urban population is expected to increase domestic demand for grid supplies to 168 MW by 2015. In early 2010 the African Development Bank (AfDB) approved a US $38m. loan for extensions to the rural power network as well as improved interconnections with both Côte d'Ivoire and Ghana.

The majority of electricity output (around 60%–85%) is thermal, with the remainder largely provided by two hydroelectric stations, on the Kompienga and Bagré rivers, with a combined capacity of 31 MW. In the late 1990s ambitious plans were drawn up to connect Burkina Faso to the West African Power Pool (WAPP), routing power from Côte d'Ivoire through Burkina Faso to neighbouring countries. In April 2001 a power line from Côte d'Ivoire to Bobo-Dioulasso was completed, and in 2009 an onward connection from Bobo-Dioulasso to Ouagadougou was brought into service. The WAPP is considering building a 700-km power line linking Mali, Ouagadougou and Nigeria. There are also plans for electricity interconnection with Ghana, which will be financed by France and the European Investment Bank. Construction of the first phase of a US $540m. hydroelectric dam at Samendéni, in the west of the country, began in January 2008. The dam reservoir will have a capacity of 5,000m. cu m, which should be sufficient to irrigate 21,000 ha of new farmland, and generate 16 GWh of power. However, Burkina has to stimulate increased private investment in the energy sector. The Government has drafted plans to end its monopoly on production and distribution by privatizing SONABEL and the petroleum-importing company, Société Nationale Burkinabè d'Hydrocarbures (SONABHY), although this process has been repeatedly postponed. The Government and the IMF have also agreed on a new mechanism to end petroleum product subsidies and ensure that domestic fuel prices reflect international oil prices.

MANUFACTURING

Manufacturing accounted for 12.0% of GDP in 2008, according to the AfDB, and is concentrated in Ouagadougou, Bobo-

Dioulasso, Koudougou and Banfora. Growth of the sector has been hampered by the small size of the domestic market, the lack of indigenous raw materials, and shortages of finance and management skills. The introduction at the beginning of 2000 of duty-free trade in industrial goods within the regional grouping, the Union Economique et Monétaire Ouest-Africaine (UEMOA), brought stiff competition, which most local manufacturers were not well placed to counter. The AfDB estimates that manufacturing GDP increased at an average annual rate of 8.8% over 2000–07; growth then slowed, to 4.5% in 2007 and 2.5% in 2008, owing to a steep decline in cotton production, coupled with a lack of competitiveness due to the strength of the euro.

Agricultural-processing (in particular, cotton, leather and sugar), represents more than one-half of the sector's output; in 2005 Burkina Faso had 14 cotton-ginning factories. The manufacture of consumer goods for import substitution is also significant. The first industrial plant of any size was the textile plant at Koudougou, which opened in 1970. However, textile production has collapsed in recent years, and by 2006 only around 1.5% of SOFITEX's annual output was being made into textiles in Burkina Faso. However, that year also saw the completion of rehabilitation work at the Faso Fani textile mill of the renamed Société des Textiles du Faso (FASOTEX), which had closed in 2001.

Despite a 30,000m. francs CFA investment programme, the Brafaso brewing company has suffered serious difficulties: it was formally liquidated in 2011, but was saved in early 2012 when the Government agreed to clear its debts. The Compaoré administration has implemented an extensive divestment programme, aiming to reduce the Government's equity in industrial concerns to a maximum of 25%. By September 2002 a total of 26 enterprises had been transferred to the private sector, while a further 16 had been liquidated or were in the process of liquidation. In 2005 14 enterprises remained state-owned. The Government has plans to resume production at the country's largest flour mill, Grands Moulins du Burkina, which was forced to close after the war in Côte d'Ivoire disrupted its supply of wheat.

TRANSPORT AND COMMUNICATIONS

The transport network has received considerable investment in recent years. The 1,260-km rail line from Abidjan through Bobo-Dioulasso, Koudougou and Ouagadougou to Kaya is a key international artery for economic activity. The Government hopes that development of the Tambao manganese deposits in the far north will facilitate the extension of the railway from Kaya to Tambao. Until 1987 the line was run as a joint partnership between Burkina and Côte d'Ivoire; the two countries then established separate rail companies before opting to transfer the service to a private sector operator. SITARAIL, a consortium of French, Belgian, Ivorian and Burkinabè interests, assumed management of operations in 1995. The outbreak of civil war in Côte d'Ivoire in September 2002 forced the line to close for a year, and by the time it was reopened much of Burkina Faso's trade had been re-routed through ports in Ghana, Togo and Benin. There are plans for an 800-km railway from Ouagadougou to the Ghanaian port of Tema, projected to cost US $750m., and for connections from the Burkina Faso rail network to Benin, Niger and Togo, as part of the Africarail project.

Burkina Faso has a total road network of more than 90,000 km, including just over 15,000 km of highways. Since the late 1990s there has been heavy investment in repairs and expansion. In late 2000 the Government announced a three-year plan to build 6,000 km of rural roads, and a further 1,000-km rural roads programme followed in September 2005. In 2008 work began on a major programme of road upgrades funded by the US Government's Millennium Challenge Account (MCA), and in February 2009 the AfDB and the German development bank, KfW Bankengruppe, provided 53,200m. francs CFA in loans and grants for road rehabilitation; this latter project included the route from Koupéla to Togo, via Bittou and Cinkanse.

The country has two international airports (at Ouagadougou and Bobo-Dioulasso); infrastructure at Ouagadougou airport was updated, with financial assistance from France, in the 1990s. In late 2006 the Government announced plans to build a new international airport, at a cost of US $450m. Sited 35 km north-east of Ouagadougou, at Donsin, this will have capacity to handle 1.5m. passengers per year (compared with 250,000 per year at the old airport).

The fixed-line telephone network had only seven fixed telephone lines per 1,000 people in 2007. However, mobile phone usage has grown dramatically, from just 25,200 subscribers in 2000 to 2.6m. in 2008. In December 2006 the Government sold its 51% stake in the national telephone company, the Office National des Télécommunications (ONATEL), to Maroc Télécom; ONATEL set up a mobile telephone subsidiary, TELMOB, in 1996. Two other companies also operate in Burkina Faso—Telecel and Airtel (formerly Zain)—the Government has drawn up plans to issue a fourth licence. To promote the development of fixed-line and internet connections it has also drawn up plans to reissue all licences as multi-service licences, covering mobile, fixed-line and internet.

ECONOMIC POLICY

The foundations of economic policy over the past two decades have been a combination of monetary discipline, fiscal stability and economic liberalization—implemented in close partnership with the IMF and World Bank—and a sustained drive to reduce poverty and bolster development at the grassroots. The low taxable capacity of the economy has hampered efforts to contain the budget deficit, although some progress has been made through spending discipline and enhanced revenue from taxation, including value-added tax (VAT). The Government has reduced its liabilities to some extent by privatizing some loss-making state enterprises and restructuring those that remain under state ownership. However, the Government remains heavily dependent on external aid to finance capital spending.

At several points, the state has had to weather episodes of increased financial pressure. The civil war in Côte d'Ivoire squeezed Burkinabè government revenues, owing to a decline in customs and excise revenue from trade with Côte d'Ivoire, and a reduction in remittances from Burkinabè workers based there. In 2009 the Government compensated for a marked slowdown in economic activity, resulting in part from the impact of the global financial crisis, by adopting an expansionary fiscal strategy. This deepened the fiscal deficit to 10.7% of GDP, compared with 8.3% the preceding year. The 2009 deficit would have been much deeper but for the success of a drive to strengthen revenue collection: budget receipts rose by 22%, reaching 13.7% of GDP (from 13.1% in 2008). However, the growth of gold sector fiscal revenues and dividend income (from mines where the state is a shareholder) is a major bonus; in 2010 fiscal revenues rose by 14% and overall budget receipts increased by 26%; grant aid also rose by 14.1%. These factors gave the Government the confidence to increase spending, by 8.1%. However, the tax base remains narrow and there are few potential new fiscal revenue streams, other than the mining sector. In 2007 the Government started a comprehensive reform of tax policy, aiming to modernize tax and customs administration and to improve tax collection through the introduction of a simplified tax code. However, fiscal policy has at times been restrained by pressure from the country's six largest trade union federations.

In recent years Burkina Faso has experienced several bouts of tension related to economic issues. Between May 2005 and March 2008 the country's trade unions held 10 national strikes in protest against the rising cost of living and poor working conditions. In early 2008 a doubling in the price of maize—partly as a result of high global prices—provoked unrest; the Government responded with emergency action to alleviate the cost of living, suspending taxes and duties on goods such as rice, flour and cooking oil, and suspending the oil price mechanism, for six months. However, while such general subsidy measures ease political pressures, they do not target the poor specifically and the IMF has encouraged the Government to explore alternative means of helping the urban poor. In 2011, despite military mutinies that were a result of grievances about their allowances, and civilian demonstrations demanding political reforms, the Government remained committed to plans to reform fuel-pricing, even though this will leave domestic consumers exposed to high world oil prices.

The Government has sometimes used expenditure as an active support to economic activity and living standards: in 2009, for instance, it increased total expenditure by 21.2%, with a 9.6% rise in current spending. The key elements of this aggressive counter-cyclical spending strategy were public service pay (with the salary bill having increased by 14.8%), subsidies for cotton-farming inputs (11,500m. francs CFA), the payment of 4,400m. francs CFA in arrears owed to cotton growers and 16,700m. francs CFA in public sector debt arrears owed to domestic business creditors. The cotton company SOFITEX was recapitalized (18,500m. francs CFA) and the Government paid off 8,800m. francs CFA that the firm owed to local banks. The Government also implemented a 50,000m. francs CFA programme of capital spending, including repairs to infrastructure damaged in flooding in September 2009. Burkina Faso's ability to pursue this aggressive counter-cyclical spending programme owed much to the strong support of international donors, who increased grant aid by 58% in 2009; indeed, grants accounted for 43% of budget receipts.

Economic conditions during 2010 were more favourable and the Government was able to stick with a strong fiscal stance. Expenditure was contained below IMF targets and revenue collection was strengthened. Capital spending, mainly on infrastructure, was increased again, but the salaries bill, which accounts for more than 40% of the budget, was slightly reduced from 2009 levels. The basic primary deficit, which had reached 5.3% of GDP in 2009, was reduced to 5% of GDP. This has meant that the Government had a stable base upon which to act when it came under renewed pressure to further boost spending in 2011, as a result of a flare-up of domestic unrest, and a temporary renewal of the crisis in Côte d'Ivoire (the key regional trade partner and home to many migrant Burkinabè workers). The Government responded with further social measures, costing about 0.5% of GDP.

Burkina has pursued a series of IMF programmes. The current arrangement is a US $67.7m. three-year Extended Credit Facility (ECF), approved in June 2010. Targets under the programme have been relaxed slightly, to allow for the extra social spending in 2011, but the overall fiscal stance remains prudent. Further progress in bolstering revenues and reducing fuel subsidies has helped to consolidate the fiscal position and this helped the country cope with the renewed pressures imposed by the drought and poor harvest of late 2011 and, in 2012, the influx of refugees from areas of northern Mali that had been taken over by rebels.

Through successive programmes the Fund has encouraged Burkina Faso to encourage private sector growth and liberalization, with plans for the privatization of ONATEL, SONABEL and SONABHY. Over recent years the Government has sold a 51% stake in ONATEL to Maroc Télécom and sold a 90% stake in the Banque Agricole et Commerciale du Burkina to the regional banking group Ecobank. It has also privatized the Hotel Silmande in Ouagadougou, the Comptoir Burkinabè des Métaux Précieux, the Centre National de Traitement de l'Information and the Société Nationale du Cinéma du Burkina, while the Bureau des Mines et de la Géologie du Burkina has been prepared for divestment. In December 2010 the Government decided that SONABEL and the Office National de l'Eau et de l'Assainissement (ONEA—water and sanitation) would not actually be sold, but would be placed under commercial management, governed by performance contracts.

In December 2010 the Government adopted a Strategy for Accelerated Growth and Sustained Development (SCADD) for 2011–15, which was projected to cost US $15,000m. It was reviewed by the IMF and the World Bank in mid-2011. The new strategy seeks to build on past poverty reduction efforts that have been underway since the 1990s, but it lays increased stress on implementation, effectiveness and regular assessments of progress. Past experience has shown that even with sustained effort, it is difficult to actually reduce levels of poverty. The SCADD therefore tries to break this pattern by acting across a wide range of issues, including private sector development, the investment climate, rural development, gender, population, and the environment. However, the strategy was prepared prior to the unrest of 2011. After these upheavals, the IMF and the World Bank subsequently warned that there was a need for more emphasis on good governance, accountability and inclusive growth; greater efforts to promote transparency and combat corruption were required. Poverty levels have been falling, but only slowly: a household welfare survey in 2009 found that 43.9% of Burkinabè still live in poverty. While deprivation has decreased in rural areas it appears to have increased in urban communities; this may be because urban consumers are more directly effected by rises in the cost of cereals and imported fuel

The SCADD does emphasize agricultural development, which is crucial to tackling poverty among farmers. However, the IMF and the World Bank have recently argued that action is needed to improve farmers' access to inputs and credit; they have also pressed for the decentralization of services. Progress has been made in improving access to education: since 2006/07, the number of schools has grown from 8,182 to 10,198, and the gross rate of primary school enrolment has risen by 10 percentage points since 2005. There has also been good progress in health provision and by 2010 some 70% of births were attended by trained personnel. The Government has taken steps to improve the targeting of action to combat HIV/AIDS; the rate of HIV infection is stabilizing and, in some urban areas, is now in decline. Burkina Faso's social safety net remains limited and the IMF and the World Bank point out that universal fuel subsidies have had only limited benefits for the poorest people; they are pressing for more targeted measures, such as a youth employment strategy, and action to combat the social and economic obstacles facing women and girls.

FOREIGN TRADE AND PAYMENTS

Burkina Faso has suffered from a chronic and substantial trade deficit. Its export capacity has in the past been highly vulnerable to weather conditions and trends in international prices for cotton. However, the surge in gold exports over the past three years has substantially strengthened exports: these rose by 37% in 2009, to reach 425,200m. francs CFA, and by more than 65% in 2010, reaching 712,800m. francs CFA (about 17% of GDP). Burkina Faso's import bill reflects a range of factors: the domestic food balance; international prices for petroleum; and the level of investment spending, both public and private. Annual fluctuations in the size of the deficit have therefore been substantial. The total import bill fell back to 652,800m. francs CFA in 2009 (from 711,700m. francs CFA in 2008), as the international cost of fuel and food eased; but imports rebounded in 2010, to reach 845,900m. francs CFA. However, overall, the rise in gold exports has largely offset the impact of higher food and fuel costs and the trade deficit has shrunk—from 401,400m. francs CFA in 2008 to 227,600m. francs CFA in 2009, and just 133,000m. francs CFA in 2010. Moreover, privatization revenues, inward aid flows and a reduced level of debt payments to external creditors have combined to strengthen the overall balance of payments: the current account deficit has reduced from 179,400m francs CFA in 2009 to an estimated 143,000m. francs CFA in 2010. The deficit was estimated to have deepened slightly, to 164,300m. francs CFA in 2011, but was forecast to have doubled, to about 350,000m. francs CFA, in 2012; this probably reflects an increased need to import food, after the poor harvest of 2011. If official aid transfers are excluded, these increased costs show up even more clearly: with the positive impact of aid excluded, the current account shrank from 540,900m. francs CFA in 2008 to an estimated 326,000m. francs CFA in 2010, but rebounded to 385,600m. francs CFA in 2011, and to a projected 505,900m. francs CFA in 2012.

The recent development of gold exports has radically altered the geographical balance of Burkina Faso's exports over the past three years. In 2007 the People's Republic of China was still the main export market, taking 29.6% of the total, mostly cotton; Singapore, another key Asian partner, ranked second (15.7%). However, more recent figures record Switzerland as the main export market, accounting for more than 55% of all exports—data that if confirmed would indicate that much of Burkina Faso's gold output is being traded through Switzerland. These provisional figures indicated that the EU (14.9% of exports) and Singapore (11.8%) remain important markets, probably for cotton and traditional exports. Significant regional markets are Ghana—probably for livestock—and Niger; the return of peace in Côte d'Ivoire is likely to facilitate the revival of livestock exports, to meet demand for meat in Abidjan. The figures suggested that the traditional pattern of import trade remains largely unchanged: the EU (accounting for 32.7% of the total) remains the main source of manufactured goods and technology, and France has traditionally been the key EU supplier. Côte d'Ivoire (14.5% of the total) also remains an important supplier. China (9.8%) is an important supplier of consumer goods; India (4.4%) and Thailand, for rice, are also significant suppliers of food. The USA (4.9%) has emerged as a significant source of imports, possibly reflecting the supply of mining equipment.

Traditionally, cotton has been the principal export, valued at 96,800m. francs CFA in 2009 and an estimated 111,000m. francs CFA in 2010. However, sales of gold have risen dramatically over the past three years, from only 4,600m. francs CFA in 2007 to 448,700m. francs CFA in 2010. Shea products (18,600m. francs CFA in 2010) provide export earnings for rural communities, and shipments to Europe of high-value fruit such as mangoes are a further source of farm income with potential for future growth. The major imports in recent years have been oil or petroleum products—179,700m. francs CFA in 2009 and 220,500m. francs CFA in 2010—and capital equipment (179,700m. francs CFA in 2009 and 298,700m. in 2010) and food (67,600m. in 2009 and 68,100m. francs CFA in 2010). The upsurge in capital equipment imports probably reflects the pace of new development in the mining sector.

The deficit on merchandise trade has been reduced by the growth of gold exports. Although freight and insurance costs (an estimated 193,200m. francs CFA in 2010) are a heavy burden on the balance of payments, remittances from Burkinabè migrants abroad, and aid inflows, make a substantial positive contribution to the current account. Remittances fluctuate as a result of economic conditions in host countries and may have been depressed by the economic slowdown in Europe; initial indications suggest that remittances may have risen from a net 600m. francs CFA in 2009 to 8,200m. francs CFA in 2010.

The overall flow of official development assistance from multilateral institutions and bilateral donors fluctuates from year to year, owing to the timing of individual capital projects. However, the underlying level of support remains solid and stable, allowing the Government to plan ahead for both its ongoing current expenditure and individual capital investments. Official grant transfers under the current account were 173,500m. francs CFA in 2009 and an estimated 170,200m. francs CFA in 2010, whereas project grants amounted to 86,900m. francs CFA in 2009 but fell to an estimated 51,100m. francs CFA in 2010. For countries such as Burkina Faso that have a strong and long-standing policy partnership with the IMF and donors, there is a trend for donors to provide a growing proportion of aid in the form of general balance of payments support, leaving the Government to decide on detailed spending priorities.

Burkina Faso's key donor partners include the EU, which approved a €423m. (US $575m.) programme of support under the Tenth EDF (2008–13), the World Bank, the African Development Bank, Islamic and Arab institutions, and a range of bilateral partners, notably the USA and France. In 2011 the World Bank approved seven projects prioritizing poverty reduction and rural development, at a cost of $309m.

Burkina Faso benefited from the Heavily Indebted Poor Countries (HIPC) initiative and the Multilateral Debt Relief Initiative (MDRI), of which the purpose was to bring the cost of servicing its external debt down to levels that were sustainable in economic terms and that would leave the Government in a position to expand its action to combat poverty, improve basic health and education, and advance the country towards the Millennium Development Goals. Burkina Faso became the fifth country to reach completion point under the enhanced HIPC initiative in April 2002 and it was among 18 countries to be granted 100% relief on multilateral debts, under the MDRI, in June 2005. After these relief measures, external debt amounted to only US $700m. at the end of 2006, and was equivalent to 19.8% of GDP in 2007. By 2011 it had risen to 24.9% of GDP.

Statistical Survey

Source (except where otherwise stated): Institut National de la Statistique et de la Démographie, 555 blvd de la Révolution, 01 BP 374, Ouagadougou 01; tel. 50-32-49-76; fax 50-32-61-59; e-mail insd@cenatrin.bf; internet www.insd.bf.

Area and Population

AREA, POPULATION AND DENSITY

Area (sq km)	274,200*
Population (census results)	
10 December 1996	10,312,609
9–23 December 2006	
Males	6,768,739
Females	7,248,523
Total	14,017,262
Population (UN estimates at mid-year)†	
2010	16,468,714
2011	16,967,845
2012	17,481,982
Density (per sq km) at mid-2012	63.8

* 105,870 sq miles.

† Source: UN, *World Population Prospects: The 2010 Revision.*

POPULATION BY AGE AND SEX

(UN estimates at mid-2012)

	Males	Females	Total
0–14	4,014,128	3,873,958	7,888,086
15–64	4,515,626	4,682,298	9,197,924
65 and over	156,291	239,681	395,972
Total	8,686,045	8,795,937	17,481,982

Source: UN, *World Population Prospects: The 2010 Revision.*

ETHNIC GROUPS

1995 (percentages): Mossi 47.9; Peul 10.3; Bobo 6.9; Lobi 6.9; Mandé 6.7; Sénoufo 5.3; Gourounsi 5.0; Gourmantché 4.8; Tuareg 3.1; others 3.1 (Source: La Francophonie).

PROVINCES
(population at 2006 census)

	Population	Capital	Population of capital
Balé	213,423	Boromo	29,849
Bam	275,191	Kongoussi	70,840
Banwa	269,375	Solenzo	121,819
Bazèga	238,425	Kombissiri	67,964
Bougouriba	101,479	Diébougou	42,067
Boulgou	543,570	Tenkodogo	124,985
Boulkiemdé	505,206	Koudougou	138,209
Comoé	407,528	Banfora	109,824
Ganzourgou	319,380	Zorgho	48,096
Gnagna	408,669	Bogandé	84,838
Gourma	305,936	Fada N'Gourma	124,577
Houet	955,451	Bobo-Dioulasso (rural)	64,075
Ioba	192,321	Dano	46,469
Kadiogo	1,727,390	Ouagadougou	1,475,223
Kénédougou	285,695	Orodara	31,632
Komandjari	79,507	Gayéri	48,757
Kompienga	75,867	Pama	37,296
Kossi	278,546	Nouna	73,006
Koulpélogo	258,667	Ouargaye	32,658
Kouritenga	329,779	Koupéla	58,411
Kourwéogo	138,217	Boussé	43,352
Léraba	124,280	Sindou	18,280
Loroum	142,853	Titao	66,717
Mouhoun	297,350	Dédougou	86,965
Nahouri	157,071	Pô	51,552
Namentenga	328,820	Boulsa	81,967
Nayala	163,433	Toma	29,451
Noumbiel	70,036	Batié	31,963
Oubritenga	238,775	Ziniaré	62,972
Oudalan	195,964	Gorom-Gorom	106,346
Passoré	323,222	Yako	80,926
Poni	256,931	Gaoua	52,733
Sanguié	297,036	Réo	61,960
Sanmatenga	598,014	Kaya	117,122
Séno	264,991	Dori	106,808
Sissili	208,409	Léo	51,037
Soum	347,335	Djibo	60,042
Sourou	220,622	Tougan	67,589
Tapoa	342,305	Diapaga	32,620
Tuy	228,458	Houndé	76,998
Yagha	160,152	Sebba	32,374
Yatenga	553,164	Ouahigouya	125,030
Ziro	175,915	Sapouy	55,968
Zondoma	166,557	Gourcy	81,226
Zoundwéogo	245,947	Manga	33,042
Total	14,017,262		

PRINCIPAL TOWNS
(population at 2006 census)

Ouagadougou (capital)	1,475,223	Kaya	54,365
Bobo-Dioulasso	489,967	Tenkodogo	44,491
Koudougou	88,184	Fada N'gourma	41,785
Banfora	75,917	Dédougou	38,862
Ouahigouya	73,153	Houndé	34,669

Mid-2011 (incl. suburbs, UN estimate): Ouagadougou 2,052,530 (Source: UN, *World Urbanization Prospects: The 2011 Revision*).

BIRTHS AND DEATHS
(annual averages, UN estimates)

	1995–2000	2000–05	2005–10
Birth rate (per 1,000)	45.8	44.9	43.9
Death rate (per 1,000)	15.6	14.2	12.6

Source: UN, *World Population Prospects: The 2010 Revision*.

Life expectancy (years at birth): 54.9 (males 54.0; females 55.9) in 2010 (Source: World Bank, World Development Indicators database).

ECONOMICALLY ACTIVE POPULATION
(1996 census, persons aged 10 years and over)

	Males	Females	Total
Agriculture, hunting, forestry and fishing	2,284,744	2,229,124	4,513,868
Mining and quarrying	2,946	1,033	3,979
Manufacturing	46,404	25,161	71,565
Electricity, gas and water	2,279	534	2,813
Construction	20,678	398	21,076
Trade, restaurants and hotels	98,295	126,286	224,581
Transport, storage and communications	20,024	556	20,580
Finance, insurance, real estate and business services	10,466	2,665	13,131
Community, social and personal services	76,690	27,236	103,926
Sub-total	2,562,526	2,412,993	4,975,519
Activities not adequately defined	15,104	13,712	28,816
Total employed	2,577,630	2,426,705	5,004,335
Unemployed	51,523	19,757	71,280
Total labour force	2,629,153	2,446,462	5,075,615

Mid-2012 ('000, estimates): Agriculture, etc. 7,394; Total labour force 8,035 (Source: FAO).

Health and Welfare

KEY INDICATORS

Total fertility rate (children per woman, 2010)	5.3
Under-5 mortality rate (per 1,000 live births, 2010)	176
HIV/AIDS (% of persons aged 15–49, 2009)	1.2
Physicians (per 1,000 head, 2008)	0.06
Hospital beds (per 1,000 head, 2010)	0.4
Health expenditure (2009): US $ per head (PPP)	89
Health expenditure (2009): % of GDP	6.6
Health expenditure (2009): public (% of total)	49.7
Access to water (% of persons, 2010)	79
Access to sanitation (% of persons, 2010)	17
Total carbon dioxide emissions ('000 metric tons, 2008)	1,855.5
Carbon dioxide emissions per head (metric tons, 2008)	0.1
Human Development Index (2011): ranking	181
Human Development Index (2011): value	0.331

For sources and definitions, see explanatory note on p. vi.

Agriculture

PRINCIPAL CROPS
('000 metric tons)

	2008	2009	2010
Rice, paddy	195.1	213.6	270.7
Maize	1,013.6	894.6	1,133.5
Millet	1,255.2	970.9	1,147.9
Sorghum	1,875.1	1,521.5	1,990.2
Sweet potatoes	73.2	81.5	92.5
Yams	42.3	80.9	97.6
Sugar cane*	455	455	455
Cow peas, dry*	537.7	453.6	626.1
Bambara beans	55.6	44.7	59.5
Groundnuts, with shell	346.3	330.6	340.2
Okra*	22	18	21
Cotton lint*	266.0	183.0	190
Cottonseed†	315	265	250
Seed cotton	720.7	483.9	529.6

* FAO estimates.
† Unofficial figures.

Aggregate production ('000 metric tons, may include official, semi-official or estimated data): Total cereals 4,358.5 in 2008, 3,626.6 in 2009, 4,560.5 in 2010; Total pulses 613.3 in 2008, 514.4 in 2009, 707.0 in 2010; Total roots and tubers 121.9 in 2008, 168.0 in 2009, 196.4 in 2010; Total vegetables (incl. melons) 275.3 in 2008, 217.4 in 2009, 281.3 in 2010; Total fruits (excl. melons) 90.2 in 2008, 100.0 in 2009, 96.5 in 2010.

LIVESTOCK
('000 head, year ending September)

	2008	2009	2010*
Cattle	8,072	8,234	8,399
Sheep	7,770	8,003	8,243
Goats	11,634	11,983	12,343
Pigs	2,083	2,125	2,167
Chickens	35,359	37,000*	39,000
Horses	38	38	39
Asses	1,009	1,030	1,050
Camels	16*	17	17

* FAO estimate(s).

Source: FAO.

LIVESTOCK PRODUCTS
('000 metric tons, FAO estimates)

	2008	2009	2010
Cattle meat	106.6	110.5	133.5
Sheep meat	18.0	18.3	19.0
Goat meat	30.8	31.8	32.6
Pig meat	30.0	30.6	27.7
Chicken meat	33.8	35.4	35.4
Cows' milk	201.7	209.0	219.4
Goats' milk	42.5	43.8	45.6
Hen eggs	48.7	51.1	52.0

Source: FAO.

Forestry

ROUNDWOOD REMOVALS
('000 cubic metres, excluding bark, FAO estimates)

	2008	2009	2010
Sawlogs, veneer logs and logs for sleepers	73	73	73
Other industrial wood	1,098	1,098	1,098
Fuel wood	12,418	12,600	12,785
Total	13,589	13,771	13,956

2011: Production assumed to be unchanged from 2010 (FAO estimates).

Source: FAO.

SAWNWOOD PRODUCTION
('000 cubic metres)

	2005	2006	2007
Total (all broadleaved)	1.1	0.7	5.2

2008–11: Production assumed to be unchanged from 2007 (FAO estimates).
Source: FAO.

Fishing

(metric tons, live weight)

	2008	2009	2010*
Capture	11,093	11,800*	14,520
Freshwater fishes	11,093	11,800	14,520
Aquaculture	405*	205	300
Total catch*	11,498	12,005	14,820

* FAO estimate(s).

Source: FAO.

Mining

(estimates)

	2008	2009	2010
Cement (metric tons)	30,000	30,000	30,000
Gold (kg)*	7,633	13,181	24,104

* Includes artisanal mining, which was estimated at 1,600 kg annually.

Source: US Geological Survey.

Industry

SELECTED PRODUCTS
(metric tons, unless otherwise indicated)

	2000	2001	2002
Edible oils	17,888	19,452	19,626
Shea (karité) butter	186	101	21
Flour	12,289	13,686	10,005
Pasta	211	n.a.	n.a.
Sugar	43,412	46,662	47,743
Beer ('000 hl)	494	500	546
Soft drinks ('000 hl)	221	222	250
Cigarettes (million packets)	85	78	78
Printed fabric ('000 sq m)	275	n.a.	n.a.
Soap	12,079	9,240	9,923
Matches (cartons)	9,358	4,956	3,009
Bicycles (units)	22,215	17,718	20,849
Mopeds (units)	16,531	19,333	19,702
Tyres ('000)	397	599	670
Inner tubes ('000)	2,655	3,217	2,751
Electric energy ('000 kWh)	390,352	365,503	364,675

Electric energy ('000 kWh): 612,712 in 2007; 619,400 in 2008; 699,790 in 2009.

Source: mainly IMF, *Burkina Faso: Selected Issues and Statistical Appendix* (September 2005).

Raw sugar ('000 metric tons): 40 in 2006–08 (Source: UN Industrial Commodity Statistics Database).

Finance

CURRENCY AND EXCHANGE RATES

Monetary Units
100 centimes = 1 franc de la Communauté Financière Africaine (CFA).

Sterling, Dollar and Euro Equivalents (31 May 2012)
£1 sterling = 819.959 francs CFA;
US $1 = 528.870 francs CFA;
€1 = 655.957 francs CFA;
10,000 francs CFA = £12.20 = $18.91 = €15.24.

Average Exchange Rate (francs CFA per US $)
2009 472.186
2010 495.277
2011 471.866

Note: An exchange rate of 1 French franc = 50 francs CFA, established in 1948, remained in force until January 1994, when the CFA franc was devalued by 50%, with the exchange rate adjusted to 1 French franc = 100 francs CFA. This relationship to French currency remained in effect with the introduction of the euro on 1 January 1999. From that date, accordingly, a fixed exchange rate of €1 = 655.957 francs CFA has been in operation.

BUDGET

('000 million francs CFA)

Revenue*	2009	2010†	2011‡
Tax revenue	494.6	565.7	661.5
Income and profits	106.7	133.6	187.1
Domestic goods and services	282.9	318.4	352.7
International trade	89.7	96.8	106.2
Non-tax revenue	44.5	115.5	83.3
Total	539.1	681.3	744.7

Expenditure§	2009	2010†	2011‡
Current expenditure	499.1	530.9	633.4
Wages and salaries	228.4	245.8	281.5
Goods and services	95.1	90.8	100.8
Interest payments	16.9	21.4	22.0
Current transfers	158.8	172.9	229.05
Capital expenditure	457.4	531.2	584.6
Expenditure carried forward from previous year	0.0	67.7	46.6
Total	956.4	1,129.8	1,264.6

* Excluding grants received ('000 million francs CFA): 232.4 in 2009; 198.9 in 2010 (estimated); 328.9 in 2011 (programmed).

† Estimated figures.

‡ Programmed figures.

§ Excluding net lending ('000 million francs CFA): 3.2 in 2009; –6.2 in 2010 (estimated); –6.6 in 2011 (programmed).

Source: IMF, *Burkina Faso: Fourth Review Under the Three-Year Arrangement Under the Extended Credit Facility and Request for Modification of Performance Criteria and Augmentation of Access—Staff Report; Debt Sustainability Analysis; Press Release on the Executive Board Discussion; and Statement by the Executive Director for Burkina Faso* (June 2012).

INTERNATIONAL RESERVES

(excluding gold, US $ million at 31 December)

	2009	2010	2011
IMF special drawing rights	75.4	74.2	73.9
Reserve position in IMF	11.7	11.5	11.6
Foreign exchange	1,208.8	982.5	871.5
Total	1,295.8	1,068.2	957.0

Source: IMF, *International Financial Statistics*.

MONEY SUPPLY

('000 million francs CFA at 31 December)

	2009	2010	2011
Currency outside banks	251.8	215.1	189.6
Demand deposits at deposit money banks*	356.0	437.9	593.5
Checking deposits at post office	5.5	3.9	5.5
Total money (incl. others)	615.1	659.2	790.7

* Excluding the deposits of public establishments of an administrative or social nature.

Source: IMF, *International Financial Statistics*.

COST OF LIVING

(Consumer Price Index; base: 2000 = 100)

	2008	2009	2010
Food, beverages and tobacco	145.4	149.2	152.7
Clothing	118.4	122.5	118.5
Housing, water, electricity and gas	128.7	142.6	131.5
All items (incl. others)	131.1	134.6	131.4

2011: Food (incl. beverages) 162.0; All items (incl. others) 135.0.

Source: ILO.

NATIONAL ACCOUNTS

('000 million francs CFA in current prices)

Expenditure on the Gross Domestic Product

	2009	2010	2011
Government final consumption expenditure	735	762	833
Private final consumption expenditure	2,881	2,647	3,216
Gross fixed capital formation	883	1,002	1,065
Change in stocks	–55	232	137
Total domestic expenditure	4,444	4,643	5,251
Exports of goods and services	443	798	958
Less Imports of goods and services	949	1,072	1,579
GDP in purchasers' values	3,938	4,369	4,629

Gross Domestic Product by Economic Activity

	2009	2010	2011
Agriculture, livestock, forestry and fishing	1,286	1,410	1,538
Mining	184	409	550
Manufacturing	357	361	405
Electricity, gas and water	46	48	50
Construction and public works	182	206	222
Wholesale and retail trade, restaurants and hotels	481	525	546
Finance, insurance and real estate	282	292	303
Transport and communications	191	154	160
Public administration and defence	611	641	680
Sub-total	3,620	4,046	4,454
Indirect taxes	372	380	283
Less Imputed bank service charge	55	56	107
GDP in purchasers' values	3,938	4,369	4,629

Source: African Development Bank.

BALANCE OF PAYMENTS

('000 million francs CFA)

	2009	2010*	2011*
Exports of goods f.o.b.	417.2	698.3	1,035.7
Imports of goods f.o.b.	–652.8	–845.9	–1,166.5
Trade balance	–235.6	–147.6	–130.8
Services (net)	–192.1	–249.0	–328.5
Balance on goods and services	–427.7	–396.6	–459.3
Income (net)	17.1	8.7	8.9
Balance on goods, services and income	–410.6	–387.9	–450.4
Private unrequited transfers (net)	62.5	61.9	64.8
Official unrequited transfers (net)	173.5	170.2	221.3
Current balance	–174.6	–155.8	–164.3
Capital account (net)	132.9	77.9	157.2
Financial account†	272.8	182.6	173.6
Net errors and omissions	–41.7	–25.4	0.0
Overall balance	189.3	79.3	166.4

* Projections.

† Including portfolio investment and direct foreign investment.

Source: IMF, *Burkina Faso: Staff Report for the 2011 Article IV Consultation and the Third Review Under the Extended Credit Facility—Staff Report; Staff Supplement; Public Information Notice and Press Release on the Executive Board Discussion; and Statement by the Executive Director for Burkina Faso* (June 2012).

External Trade

PRINCIPAL COMMODITIES
(distribution by HS, US $ million)

Imports f.o.b.	2009	2010	2011
Cereals	94.4	83.8	124.5
Rice	69.6	63.7	95.0
Mineral fuels, lubricants and related materials	441.6	453.6	588.7
Petroleum oils	419.8	424.8	546.5
Salt, sulphur, earth, stone, plaster, lime and cement	80.8	89.1	91.6
Cement, etc.	69.7	73.7	74.3
Fertilizers	59.3	82.4	82.2
Pharmaceutical products	114.7	96.0	143.2
Medicament mixtures	89.6	80.2	119.7
Iron and steel	62.9	85.9	91.4
Iron and steel articles	63.5	71.0	76.1
Nuclear reactors, boilers, machinery, etc.	150.5	182.4	196.4
Electrical, electronic equipment	121.1	114.1	146.7
Vehicles other than railway, tramway	147.2	171.7	177.7
Total (incl. others)	1,870.3	2,048.2	2,458.0

Exports f.o.b.	2009	2010	2011
Edible fruit, nuts, peel of citrus fruit, melons	6.8	13.9	71.0
Cotton	252.1	228.1	278.3
Oil seed, oleagic fruits, grain, seed, fruit, etc.	61.2	71.6	91.0
Oil seeds	60.4	71.1	90.2
Pearls, precious stones, metals, coins, etc.	379.8	883.7	1,828.2
Total (incl. others)	795.5	1,288.1	2,362.0

Source: Trade Map-Trade Competitiveness Map, International Trade Centre, www.intracen.org/marketanalysis.

PRINCIPAL TRADING PARTNERS
(US $ million)

Imports c.i.f.	2009	2010	2011
Belgium	60.7	43.6	41.6
Benin	5.6	2.5	27.7
Brazil	31.1	20.2	36.6
Canada	12.4	50.1	30.0
China, People's Repub.	183.9	198.2	241.4
Côte d'Ivoire	271.5	328.0	262.5
France	239.9	211.5	297.2
Germany	60.5	81.3	96.2
Ghana	53.3	56.0	67.3
India	83.0	57.4	91.5
Italy	22.7	23.7	33.5
Japan	55.3	53.9	59.5
Mali	22.4	20.5	52.0
Netherlands	98.8	90.4	98.3
Nigeria	23.6	26.4	84.9
Russia	13.6	31.2	50.1
Senegal	16.2	21.9	41.7
South Africa	67.7	54.8	37.8
Spain	36.8	31.4	33.6
Sweden	10.4	11.0	30.5
Thailand	33.2	21.0	38.4
Togo	79.6	91.9	95.2
Turkey	8.6	22.8	25.6
Ukraine	12.9	25.4	25.2
United Kingdom	35.6	75.9	108.1
USA	90.9	82.9	106.3
Total (incl. others)	1,870.3	2,048.2	2,458.0

Exports f.o.b.	2009	2010	2011
Belgium	32.4	18.0	52.4
Benin	16.5	8.5	7.8
Côte d'Ivoire	15.9	18.9	24.4
Denmark	2.9	3.5	14.6
France	41.0	29.9	56.7
Ghana	33.6	35.1	49.2
Mali	9.6	12.0	9.8
Netherlands	2.1	20.4	42.0
Niger	23.5	23.4	15.3
Singapore	93.5	62.8	110.5
South Africa	0.2	144.3	242.1
Switzerland	441.0	817.3	1,633.9
Togo	6.3	14.3	13.3
United Kingdom	31.1	38.1	19.8
Total (incl. others)	795.5	1,288.1	2,362.0

Source: Trade Map-Trade Competitiveness Map, International Trade Centre, www.intracen.org/marketanalysis.

Transport

RAILWAYS

	2007	2008	2009
Freight carried ('000 metric tons)	907.4	832.7	871.6
Freight ton-km ('000)	840,374	779,620	820,784
Passengers ('000 journeys)	500*	n.a.	n.a.

* Estimate.

ROAD TRAFFIC
('000 motor vehicles in use)

	2007	2008	2009
Passenger cars	97.1	103.6	110.9
Vans	23.0	24.6	26.1
Trucks	14.2	15.0	15.8
Tractors, trailers and semi-trailers	17.2	17.7	18.6
Motorbikes and mopeds	356.5	447.4	551.3

CIVIL AVIATION
(traffic on scheduled services)*

	2003	2004	2005
Kilometres flown (million)	1	1	1
Passengers carried ('000)	54	61	66
Passenger-km (million)	29	33	37
Total ton-km (million)	3	3	3

* Including an apportionment of the traffic of Air Afrique.

Source: UN, *Statistical Yearbook*.

Passengers carried ('000): 80.5 in 2008; 79.3 in 2009; 253.7 in 2010 (Source: World Bank, World Development Indicators database).

Tourism

FOREIGN VISITORS BY COUNTRY OF ORIGIN*

	2007	2008	2009
Belgium	8,345	7,889	7,806
Benin	10,442	11,005	11,138
Canada	7,025	6,695	6,434
Côte d'Ivoire	18,009	18,176	18,090
France	80,054	75,528	67,866
Germany	6,562	7,524	7,193
Ghana	6,359	7,996	8,412
Guinea	3,707	4,046	4,747
Italy	7,405	7,260	6,726
Mali	12,512	12,258	14,474

—continued	2007	2008	2009
Mauritania	2,022	2,213	1,943
Netherlands	3,657	4,656	4,536
Niger	11,406	11,811	14,888
Nigeria	4,010	5,079	5,561
Senegal	9,584	10,481	9,875
Switzerland	3,869	4,974	5,191
Togo	7,664	9,543	9,110
United Kingdom	3,942	5,253	4,712
USA	10,250	9,434	8,592
Total (incl. others)	288,965	271,796	269,227

* Arrivals at hotels and similar establishments.

Total visitor arrivals ('000): 274 in 2010.

Receipts from tourism (US $ million, excl. passenger transport): 64 in 2009; 72 in 2010.

Source: World Tourism Organization.

Communications Media

	2009	2010	2011
Telephones ('000 main lines in use)	152.5	144.0	141.5
Mobile cellular telephones ('000 subscribers)	3,823.6	5,707.8	7,682.1
Internet subscribers ('000)	23.4	28.7	n.a.
Broadband subscribers ('000)	11.9	13.7	14.1

Personal computers: 90,000 (6.3 per 1,000) in 2006.

Source: International Telecommunication Union.

Television receivers ('000 in use): 140 in 2000 (Source: UNESCO, *Statistical Yearbook*).

Radio receivers ('000 in use): 370 in 1997 (Source: UNESCO, *Statistical Yearbook*).

Daily newspapers (national estimates): 4 (average circulation 14,200 copies) in 1997; 4 (average circulation 14,500 copies) in 1998; 5 in 2004 (Source: UNESCO Institute for Statistics).

Non-daily newspapers: 9 (average circulation 42,000 copies) in 1995 (Source: UNESCO, *Statistical Yearbook*).

Book production: 12 titles (14,000 copies) in 1996 (first editions only); 5 in 1997 (Sources: UNESCO, *Statistical Yearbook*, UNESCO Institute for Statistics).

Education

(2010/11 unless otherwise indicated)

	Institutions	Teachers	Students ('000)		
			Males	Females	Total
Pre-primary	147*	2,097	24.8	24.1	48.9
Primary	9,726†	45,739	1,163.8	1,041.5	2,205.3
Secondary (general)	922†	19,810	330.5	247.8	578.3
Secondary (technical and vocational)	119†	2,999	14.0	11.9	25.9
Tertiary	52†	2,889‡	34.9‡	16.3‡	51.2‡

* 1997/98.
† 2008/09.
‡ 2009/10.

Source: mostly UNESCO Institute for Statistics.

Pupil-teacher ratio (primary education, UNESCO estimate): 48.2 in 2010/11 (Source: UNESCO Institute for Statistics).

Adult literacy rate (UNESCO estimates): 28.7% (males 36.7%; females 21.6%) in 2007 (Source: UNESCO Institute for Statistics).

Directory

The Constitution

The present Constitution was approved in a national referendum on 2 June 1991, and was formally adopted on 11 June. The following are the main provisions of the Constitution, as amended in January 1997, April 2000 and February 2002:

The Constitution of the 'revolutionary, democratic, unitary and secular' Fourth Republic of Burkina Faso guarantees the collective and individual political and social rights of Burkinabè citizens, and delineates the powers of the executive, legislature and judiciary.

Executive power is vested in the President, who is Head of State, and in the Government, which is appointed by the President upon the recommendation of the Prime Minister. With effect from the November 2005 election, the President is elected, by universal suffrage, for a five-year term, renewable only once (previously, a seven-year term had been served).

Legislative power is exercised by the multi-party Assemblée nationale. Deputies are elected, by universal suffrage, for a five-year term. The number of deputies and the mode of election is determined by law. The President appoints a Prime Minister and, at the suggestion of the Prime Minister, appoints the other ministers. The President may, having consulted the Prime Minister and the President of the Assemblée nationale, dissolve the Assemblée nationale. Both the Government and the Assemblée nationale may initiate legislation.

The judiciary is independent and, in accordance with constitutional amendments approved in April 2000 (see Judicial System), consists of a Court of Cassation, a Constitutional Council, a Council of State, a National Audit Court, a High Court of Justice, and other courts and tribunals instituted by law. Judges are accountable to a Higher Council, under the chairmanship of the Head of State, who is responsible for guaranteeing the independence of the judiciary.

The Constitution also makes provision for an Economic and Social Council, for a Higher Council of Information, and for a national ombudsman.

The Constitution denies legitimacy to any regime that might take power as the result of a *coup d'état*.

The Government

HEAD OF STATE

President: BLAISE COMPAORÉ (assumed power as Chairman of the Front populaire 15 October 1987; elected President 1 December 1991; re-elected 15 November 1998, 13 November 2005 and 21 November 2010).

COUNCIL OF MINISTERS

(September 2012)

President and Minister of National Defence and War Veterans: BLAISE COMPAORÉ.

Prime Minister: LUC ADOLPHE TIAO.

Minister of State, Minister in charge of Parliamentary Affairs and Political Reform: BONGNESSAN ARSÈNE YE.

Minister of Foreign Affairs and Regional Co-operation: YIPÈNÈ DJIBRIL BASSOLET.

Minister of the Economy and Finance: LUCIEN MARIE NOËL BEMBAMBA.

Minister of Agriculture, Water Resources and Fisheries: LAURENT GOUINDÉ SÉDEGO.

Minister of Transport, Posts and the Digital Economy: GILBERT G. NOËL OUÉDRAOGO.

Minister of Justice, Keeper of the Seals: SALAMATA SAWAGOGO TAPSOBA.

Minister of Territorial Administration, Decentralization and National Security: JÉRÔME BOUGOUMA.

Minister of Mines, Quarries and Energy: ABDOULAYE LAMOUSSA SALIF KABORÉ.

Minister of Culture and Tourism: BABA HAMA.

Minister of Communication and Government Spokesperson: ALAIN EDOUARD TRAORÉ.

Minister of Housing and Town Planning: YACOUBA BARRY.

Minister of Industry, Trade and Crafts: PATIENDÉ ARTHUR KAFANDO.

Minister of Infrastructure and Improving Access to Isolated Regions: JEAN BERTIN OUÉDRAOGO.

Minister of Health: ADAMA TRAORÉ.

Minister of Secondary and Higher Education: Prof. MOUSSA OUATTARA.

Minister of Scientific Research and Innovation: GNISSA ISAÏE KONATÉ.

Minister of National Education and Literacy: KOUMBA BOLY BARRY.

Minister of the Civil Service, Labour and Social Security: SOUNGALO APPOLINAIRE OUATTARA.

Minister of the Environment and Sustainable Development: JEAN COULDIATY.

Minister of Youth, Professional Training and Employment: ACHILLE MARIE JOSEPH TAPSOBA.

Minister of Social Action and National Solidarity: CLÉMENCE TRAORÉ SOME.

Minister of Human Rights and Civic Promotion: ALBERT OUÉDRAOGO.

Minister of Animal Resources: JÉRÉMIE OUÉDRAOGO.

Minister for the Promotion of Women: NESTORINE SANGARÉ COMPAORÉ.

Minister of Sport and Leisure: YACOUBA OUÉDRAOGO.

Minister-delegate to the Minister of Agriculture, Water Resources and Fisheries, responsible for Agriculture: ABDOULAYE COMBARY.

Minister-delegate to the Minister of the Economy and Finance, responsible for the Budget: FRANÇOIS MARIE DIDIER ZOUNDI.

Minister-delegate to the Minister of Territorial Administration, Decentralization and National Security, responsible for Local Communities: TOUSSAINT ABEL COULIBALY.

Minister-delegate to the Minister of Foreign Affairs and Regional Co-operation, responsible for Regional Co-operation: VINCENT ZAKANÉ.

Minister-delegate to the Minister of National Education and Literacy, responsible for Literacy: ZAKARIA TIEMTORÉ.

MINISTRIES

Office of the President: 03 BP 7030, Ouagadougou 03; tel. 50-30-66-30; fax 50-31-49-26; e-mail info@presidence.bf; internet www.presidence.bf.

Office of the Prime Minister: 03 BP 7027, Ouagadougou 03; tel. 50-32-48-89; fax 50-33-05-51; e-mail webmaster@primature.gov.bf; internet www.gouvernement.gov.bf.

Ministry of Agriculture, Water Resources and Fisheries: 03 BP 7005, Ouagadougou 03; tel. 50-32-41-14; fax 50-31-08-70; internet www.agriculture.gov.bf.

Ministry of Animal Resources: 03 BP 7026, Ouagadougou 03; tel. 50-39-96-15; fax 50-31-84-75; e-mail pinidie.banaon@mra.gov.bf; internet www.mra.gov.bf.

Ministry of the Civil Service and State Reform: Immeuble de la Modernisation, 922 ave Kwamé N'Krumah, 03 BP 7006, Ouagadougou 03; tel. 50-30-19-52; fax 50-30-19-55; internet www.fonction-publique.gov.bf.

Ministry of Communication and Government Spokesperson: 387 ave Georges Conseiga, 01 BP 5175, Ouagadougou 01; tel. 50-49-00-00; fax 50-33-73-87; internet www.mptic.gov.bf.

Ministry of Culture and Tourism: 11 BP 852, CMS, Ouagadougou 11; tel. 50-33-09-63; fax 50-33-09-64; e-mail mctc@cenatrin.bf; internet www.culture.gov.bf.

Ministry of Defence and War Veterans: 01 BP 496, Ouagadougou 01; tel. 50-30-72-14; fax 50-31-36-10; internet www.defense.gov.bf.

Ministry of the Economy and Finance: 395 ave Ho Chi Minh, 01 BP 7008, Ouagadougou 01; tel. 50-32-42-11; fax 50-31-27-15; e-mail webmaster@finances.gov.bf; internet www.finances.gov.bf.

Ministry of the Environment and Sustainable Development: 565 rue Agostino Neto, Koulouba, 03 BP 7044, Ouagadougou 03; tel. 50-32-40-74; fax 50-30-70-39; internet www.environnement.gov.bf.

Ministry of Foreign Affairs and Regional Co-operation: rue 988, blvd du Faso, 03 BP 7038, Ouagadougou 03; tel. 50-32-47-34; fax 50-30-87-92; e-mail webmaster.mae@mae.gov.bf; internet www.mae.gov.bf.

Ministry of Health: 03 BP 7009, Ouagadougou 03; tel. 50-32-63-40; internet www.sante.gov.bf.

Ministry of Housing and Town Planning: Ouagadougou; tel. and fax 50-30-57-86.

Ministry of Industry, Trade and Crafts: 01 BP 514, Ouagadougou 01; tel. 50-32-48-28; fax 50-31-70-53; internet www.commerce.gov.bf.

Ministry of Infrastructure and Improving Access to Isolated Regions: 03 BP 7011, Ouagadougou 03; tel. 50-30-73-33; fax 50-31-84-08; internet www.mith.gov.bf.

Ministry of Justice and the Promotion of Human Rights: 01 BP 526, Ouagadougou 01; tel. 50-32-48-33; fax 50-31-71-37; e-mail webmestre@justice.bf; internet www.justice.gov.bf.

Ministry of Labour and Social Security: 01 BP 7016, Ouagadougou 01; tel. 50-30-09-60; fax 50-31-88-01; e-mail emploi@metss.gov.bf; internet www.emploi.gov.bf.

Ministry of Mines, Quarries and Energy: 01 BP 644, Ouagadougou 01; tel. 50-31-84-29; fax 50-31-84-30; internet www.mines.gov.bf.

Ministry of National Education and Literacy: 03 BP 7032, Ouagadougou 03; tel. 50-30-66-00; fax 50-31-42-76; internet www.meba.gov.bf.

Ministry of Parliamentary Affairs and Political Reform: 01 BP 2079, Ouagadougou 01; tel. 50-32-40-70; fax 50-30-78-94; e-mail cab_mrp@yahoo.fr; internet www.mrp.gov.bf.

Ministry for the Promotion of Women: 01 BP 303, Ouagadougou 01; tel. 50-30-01-04; fax 50-30-01-02; e-mail secretariat@mpf.gov.bf; internet www.mpf.gov.bf.

Ministry of Scientific Research and Innovation: Ouagadougou.

Ministry of Secondary and Higher Education: 03 BP 7047, Ouagadougou 03; tel. 50-33-73-34; fax 50-30-02-32; e-mail messrsxxsg@yahoo.ca; internet www.messrs.gov.bf.

Ministry of Security: 01 BP 6466, Ouagadougou 01; tel. 50-31-68-91; fax 50-33-02-97; e-mail infos@secu.gov.bf; internet www.securite.gov.bf.

Ministry of Social Action and National Solidarity: 01 BP 515, Ouagadougou 01; tel. 50-30-68-75; fax 50-31-67-37; internet www.action-sociale.gov.bf.

Ministry of Sport and Leisure: 03 BP 7035, Ouagadougou 03; tel. 50-32-47-86; fax 50-33-08-18; internet www.sports.gov.bf.

Ministry of Territorial Administration, Decentralization and National Security: 01 BP 526, Ouagadougou 01; tel. 50-32-48-33; fax 50-31-72-00; internet www.matd.gov.bf.

Ministry of Transport, Posts and the Digital Economy: 03 BP 7011, Ouagadougou 03; tel. 50-30-73-33; fax 50-31-84-08.

Ministry of Youth, Professional Training and Employment: 01 BP 7016, Ouagadougou 01; tel. 50-30-09-60; fax 30-31-84-80; internet www.emploi.gov.bf.

President and Legislature

PRESIDENT

Presidential Election, 21 November 2010

Candidate	Votes	% of votes
Blaise Compaoré	1,357,315	80.15
Hama Arba Diallo	138,975	8.21
Bénéwendé Stanislas Sankara	107,310	6.34
Boukary Kaboré	39,186	2.31
Maxime Kaboré	25,077	1.48
Pargui Emile Paré	14,560	0.86
Ouampoussoga François Kaboré	10,962	0.65
Total	1,693,385	100.00

LEGISLATURE

Assemblée nationale

01 BP 6482, Ouagadougou 01; tel. 50-31-46-84; fax 50-31-45-90.

President: Roch Marc Christian Kaboré.

General Election, 6 May 2007

Parties	% of total votes*	National list seats	Total seats†
CDP	58.85	9	73
ADF—RDA	10.70	2	14
UPR	4.30	1	5
UNIR—MS	3.89	1	4
CFD/B‡	2.34	1	3
PDS	3.28	1	2
PDP—PS	2.51	—	2
RDB	2.09	—	2
UPS	1.74	—	2
PAREN	1.29	—	1
RPC	1.15	—	1
UDPS	1.03	—	1
PAI	0.83	—	1
Total (incl. others)	100.00	15	111

* Including votes from regional and national party lists.
† Including seats filled by voting from regional lists, totalling 96.
‡ The Coalition des Forces Démocratiques du Burkina, an electoral alliance of six parties.

Election Commission

Commission Électorale Nationale Indépendante (CENI): 01 BP 5152, Ouagadougou 01; tel. 50-30-00-52; fax 50-30-80-44; e-mail ceni@fasonet.bf; internet www.ceni.bf; f. 2001; 15 mems; Pres. Barthélemy Kéré.

Advisory Council

Conseil Économique et Social: 01 BP 6162, Ouagadougou 01; tel. 50-32-40-91; fax 50-31-06-54; e-mail ces@ces.gov.bf; internet www.ces.gov.bf; f. 1985; present name adopted in 1992; 90 mems; Pres. Thomas Sanon.

Political Organizations

A total of 47 political parties contested the legislative elections held in May 2007.

Alliance pour la Démocratie et la Fédération—Rassemblement Démocratique Africain (ADF—RDA): 01 BP 1991, Ouagadougou 01; tel. 50-30-52-00; f. 1990 as Alliance pour la Démocratie et la Fédération; absorbed faction of Rassemblement Démocratique Africain in 1998; several factions broke away in 2000 and in mid-2003; Pres. Gilbert Noël Ouédraogo.

Congrès pour la Démocratie et le Progrès (CDP): 1146 ave Kwamé N'Krumah, 01 BP 1605, Ouagadougou 01; tel. 50-31-50-18; fax 50-31-43-93; e-mail contact@cdp-burkina.org; internet www.cdp-burkina.org; f. 1996 by merger, to succeed the Organisation pour la Démocratie Populaire/Mouvement du Travail as the principal political org. supporting Pres. Compaoré; social democratic; Nat. Exec. Sec. Assimi Kouanda.

Convention Nationale du Progrès du Burkina: f. 2009; Pres. Moussa Boly.

Convention Panafricaine Sankariste (CPS): BP 44, Bokin; tel. 40-45-72-93; f. 1999 by merger of 4 parties, expanded in 2000 to include 2 other parties; promotes the policies of fmr Pres. Sankara; Pres. Nongma Ernest Ouédraogo.

Mouvement du Peuple pour le Socialisme—Parti Fédéral (MPS—PF): BP 3448, Ouagadougou; tel. 50-36-50-72; f. 2002 by split from PDP—PS; Leader Dr Pargui Emile Paré.

Parti Africain de l'Indépendance (PAI): Ouagadougou; tel. 50-33-46-66; f. 1999; Sec.-Gen. Soumane Touré.

Parti pour la Démocratie et le Progrès—Parti Socialiste (PDP—PS): 11 BP 26, Ouagadougou 11; tel. and fax 78-04-12-53; e-mail pdp-ps@fasonet.bf; f. 2001 by merger of the Parti pour la Démocratie et le Progrès and the Parti Socialiste Burkinabè; Nat. Pres. Dr François Kaboré.

Parti pour la Démocratie et le Socialisme (PDS): Ouagadougou; tel. 50-34-34-04; Pres. Ba Sambo.

Parti de la Renaissance Nationale (PAREN): Ouagadougou; tel. 50-43-12-26; f. 2000; social-democratic; Pres. Kilachia Laurent Bado.

Rassemblement Démocratique et Populaire (RDP): Ouagadougou; tel. 50-36-02-98; Pres. Thibaut Nana.

Rassemblement pour le Développement du Burkina (RDB): Pres. Célestin Seydou Compaoré.

Rassemblement Populaire des Citoyens (RPC): Ouagadougou; f. 2006; promotes an alternative style of politics; Pres. Antoine Ouaré.

Union pour la Démocratie et le Progrès: f. 2010; Pres. Zéphirin Diabré; Sec.-Gen. Denis Nikièma.

Union Nationale pour la Démocratie et le Développement (UNDD): 03 BP 7114, Ouagadougou 03; tel. 50-31-15-15; internet www.undd.org; f. 2003 by fmr mems of the ADF—RDA (q.v.); liberal; Pres. Me Hermann Yaméogo.

Union des Partis Sankarist (UPS).

Union pour le Progrès et le Changement (UPC): Ouagadougou; f. 2010; Pres. Zéphirin Diabré.

Union pour la Renaissance—Parti Sankariste (UNIR—PS): Ouagadougou; tel. 50-36-30-45; f. 2000 as Union pour la Renaissance—Mouvement Sankariste; renamed as above in 2009; Pres. Bénéwendé Stanislas Sankara.

Diplomatic Representation

EMBASSIES IN BURKINA FASO

Algeria: Secteur 13, Zone du Bois, 295 ave Babanguida, 01 BP 3893, Ouagadougou 01; tel. 50-36-81-81; fax 50-36-81-79; Ambassador Abdelkrim Benchiah.

Belgium: Immeuble Me Benoit Sawadogo, 994 rue Agostino Neto, Koulouba, 01 BP 1624, Ouagadougou 01; tel. 50-31-21-64; fax 50-31-06-60; e-mail ouagadougou@diplobel.fed.be; internet www.diplomatie.be/ouagadougou; Ambassador Adrien Théatre.

Canada: rue Agostino Neto, 01 BP 548, Ouagadougou 01; tel. 50-31-18-94; fax 50-31-19-00; e-mail ouaga@dfait-maeci.gc.ca; internet www.dfait-maeci.gc.ca/burkina_faso; Ambassador Ivan Roberts.

Chad: Ouagadougou; Ambassador Brahim Mahamat Imam.

Côte d'Ivoire: pl. des Nations Unies, 01 BP 20, Ouagadougou 01; tel. 50-31-82-28; fax 50-31-82-30; Ambassador Abdou Touré.

Cuba: rue 4/64, La Rotonde, Secteur 4, Ouagadougou; tel. 50-30-64-91; fax 50-31-73-24; e-mail embacuba.bf@fasonet.bf; Ambassador Ana Maria Rovira Ingidua.

Denmark: 316 ave Pr. Joseph Ki-Zerbo, 01 BP 1760, Ouagadougou 01; tel. 50-32-85-40; fax 50-32-85-77; e-mail ouaamb@um.dk; internet burkinafaso.um.dk; Ambassador Bo Jensen.

Egypt: Zone du Conseil de L'Entente, blvd du Faso, 04 BP 7042, Ouagadougou 04; tel. 50-30-66-39; fax 50-31-38-36; Ambassador Ahmad Abdel Wahed Zain.

France: ave du Trésor, 01 BP 504, Ouagadougou 01; tel. 50-49-66-66; fax 50-49-66-09; e-mail ambassade@ambafrance-bf.org; internet www.ambafrance-bf.org; Ambassador Gen. Emmanuel Beth.

Germany: 399 ave Joseph Badoua, 01 BP 600, Ouagadougou 01; tel. 50-30-67-31; fax 50-31-39-91; e-mail amb.allemagne@fasonet.bf; Ambassador Ulrich Hochschild.

Ghana: 22 ave d'Oubritenga, 01 BP 212, Ouagadougou 01; tel. 50-30-76-35; e-mail embagna@fasonet.bf; Ambassador Chief Mandeaya Bawumia.

Holy See: Tange Saabé, BP 1902, Ouagadougou 01; tel. 50-31-63-56; fax 50-31-63-55; e-mail nuntiusapbn@yahoo.it; Ambassador VITO RALLO (Titular Archbishop of Alba).

Korea, Democratic People's Republic: Ouagadougou; Ambassador KIL MUN YONG.

Libya: 01 BP 1601, Ouagadougou 01; tel. 50-30-67-53; fax 50-31-34-70; Ambassador ABD AL-NASSER SALEH MUHAMMAD YOUNES.

Mali: 2569 ave Bassawarga, 01 BP 1911, Ouagadougou 01; tel. 50-38-19-22; Ambassador (vacant).

Mauritania: Ouagadougou; Ambassador MOHAMED OULD SID AHMED LEKHAL.

Morocco: Ouaga 2000 Villa B04, pl. de la Cotière, 01 BP 3438, Ouagadougou 01; tel. 50-37-40-16; fax 50-37-41-72; e-mail maroc1@fasonet.bf; Ambassador FARHAT BOUAAZA.

Netherlands: 415 ave Dr Kwamé N'Krumah, 01 BP 1302, Ouagadougou 01; tel. 50-30-61-34; fax 50-30-76-95; e-mail oua@minbuza.nl; internet burkinafaso.nlambassade.org; Ambassador ERNST ALBERT NOORMAN.

Nigeria: rue de l'Hôpital Yalgado, 01 BP 132, Ouagadougou 01; tel. 50-36-30-15; Ambassador DAVID BALA.

Saudi Arabia: Ouaga 2000, rue de la Francophonie, Villa M05, 01 BP 2069, Ouagadougou 01; tel. 50-37-42-06; fax 50-37-42-10; e-mail saudiembassy@liptinfor.bf; Ambassador DAHIR MOOTISH ALANZI.

Senegal: Immeuble Espace Fadima, ave de la Résistance du 17 Mai, 01 BP 3226, Ouagadougou 01; tel. 50-31-14-18; fax 50-31-14-01; Ambassador MAMADOU MAKHTAR GUEYE.

South Africa: Villa 1110, Hotel Sofitel, Ouagadougou; tel. 50-37-60-98; fax 50-37-60-97; e-mail ouagadougou@foreign.gov.za; Ambassador L. S. GANTSHO.

Sweden: 11 BP 755, CMS, Ouagadougou; tel. 50-49-61-70; e-mail ambassaden.ouagadougou@sida.se; internet www.swedenabroad.com/ouagadougou; Ambassador CARIN WALL.

Taiwan (Republic of China): 994 rue Agostino Neto, 01 BP 5563, Ouagadougou 01; tel. 50-31-61-95; fax 50-31-61-97; e-mail ambachine@fasonet.bf; Ambassador ZHANG MING-ZHONG.

Turkey: Ouagadougou; Ambassador AYDIN SEFA AKAY.

USA: ave Sembene Ousmane, Ouaga 2000, Secteur 15, Ouagadougou; tel. 50-49-53-00; fax 50-49-56-28; e-mail amembouaga@state.gov; internet ouagadougou.usembassy.gov; Ambassador THOMAS DOUGHERTY.

Judicial System

In accordance with constitutional amendments approved by the Assemblée nationale in April 2000, the Supreme Court was abolished; its four permanent chambers were replaced by a Constitutional Council, a Council of State, a Court of Cassation and a National Audit Court, all of which commenced operations in December 2002. Judges are accountable to a Higher Council, under the chairmanship of the President of the Republic, in which capacity he is officially responsible for ensuring the independence of the judiciary. A High Court of Justice is competent to try the President and members of the Government in cases of treason, embezzlement of public funds, and other crimes and offences.

Constitutional Council: 40 ave de la Nation, 11 BP 1114, Ouagadougou 11; tel. 50-30-05-53; fax 50-30-08-66; e-mail conseil@conseil-constitutionnel.gov.bf; internet www.conseil-constitutionnel.gov.bf; f. 2002 to replace Constitutional Chamber of fmr Supreme Court; Pres. DÉ ALBERT MILLOGO; Sec.-Gen. HONIBIPÈ MARIAM MARGUERITE OUÉDRAOGO.

Council of State: 01 BP 586, Ouagadougou 01; tel. 50-30-64-18; e-mail webmaster@conseil-etat.gov.bf; internet www.conseil-etat.gov.bf; f. 2002 to replace Administrative Chamber of fmr Supreme Court; comprises 2 chambers: a Consultative Chamber and a Chamber of Litigation; First Pres. HARIDIATA SERE DAKOURÉ; Pres. of Consultative Chamber THÉRÈSE SANOU TRAORÉ; Pres. of Chamber of Litigation VENANT OUEDRAOGO.

Court of Cassation: 05 BP 6204, Ouagadougou 05; tel. 50-31-20-47; fax 50-31-02-71; e-mail webmaster@courcassation.bf; internet www.cour-cassation.gov.bf; f. 2002 to replace Judicial Chamber of fmr Supreme Court; First Pres. CHEICK DIMKINSEDO OUÉDRAOGO.

High Court of Justice: Ouagadougou; f. 1998; comprises 6 deputies of the Assemblée nationale and 3 magistrates appointed by the President of the Court of Cassation; Pres. DIM-SONGDO BONAVENTURE OUÉDRAOGO; Vice-Pres. SIBILA FRANCK COMPAORÉ.

National Audit Court: 01 BP 2534, Ouagadougou 01; tel. 50-30-36-00; fax 50-30-35-01; e-mail infos@cour-comptes.gov.bf; internet www.cour-comptes.gov.bf; f. 2002 to replace Audit Chamber of fmr Supreme Court; comprises 3 chambers, concerned with: local government organs; public enterprises; and the operations of the State; First Pres. NOUMOUTIÉ HERBERT TRAORÉ; Procurator-Gen. THÉRÈSE TRAORÉ SANOU; Pres of Chambers PASCAL SANOU, SÉNÉBOU RAYMONDD MANUELLA OUILMA TRAORÉ, SABINE OUEDRAOGO YETA.

Religion

The Constitution provides for freedom of religion, and the Government respects this right in practice. The country is a secular state. Islam, Christianity and traditional religions operate freely without government interference. According to the 2006 census, some 60.5% of the population are Muslims, 23.2% are Christians and 15.3% follow animist beliefs, with the remaining population being adherents of other religions or practising no religion.

ISLAM

Association Islamique Nouroul Islam: BP 262, Ouagadougou; tel. 50-31-28-88.

CHRISTIANITY

The Roman Catholic Church

Burkina Faso comprises three archdioceses and 12 dioceses. Some 19% of the total population are Roman Catholics.

Bishops' Conference

Conférence des Evêques de Burkina Faso et du Niger, 01 BP 1195, Ouagadougou 01; tel. 50-30-60-26; fax 50-31-64-81; e-mail ccbn@fasonet.bf; internet www.egliseduburkina.org.

f. 1966; legally recognized 1978; Pres. Most Rev. SÉRAPHIN FRANÇOIS ROUAMBA (Archbishop of Koupéla).

Archbishop of Bobo-Dioulasso: Most Rev. PAUL YEMBOARO OUÉDRAOGO, Archevêché, Lafiaso, 01 BP 312, Bobo-Dioulasso; tel. 20-97-00-35; fax 20-97-19-50; e-mail lafiaso@fasonet.bf.

Archbishop of Koupéla: Most Rev. SÉRAPHIN FRANÇOIS ROUAMBA, Archevêché, BP 51, Koupéla; tel. 40-70-00-30; fax 40-70-02-65; e-mail ardiokou@fasonet.bf.

Archbishop of Ouagadougou: Most Rev. PHILIPPE OUÉDRAOGO, Archevêché, 01 BP 1472, Ouagadougou 01; tel. 50-30-67-04; fax 50-30-72-75; e-mail untaani@fasonet.bf.

Protestant Churches

Some 4.2% of the population are Protestants.

Assemblées de Dieu du Burkina Faso: 01 BP 458, Ouagadougou 01; tel. 50-34-35-45; fax 50-34-28-71; e-mail adlagengo@fasonet.bf; f. 1921; Pres. Pastor MICHEL OUÉDRAOGO.

Fédération des Eglises et Missions Evangéliques (FEME): BP 108, Ouagadougou; tel. 50-36-14-26; e-mail feme@fasonet.bf; f. 1961; 10 churches and missions, 82,309 adherents; Pres. Pastor SAMUEL YAMÉOGO.

BAHÁ'Í FAITH

Assemblée Spirituelle Nationale: 01 BP 977, Ouagadougou 01; tel. 50-34-29-95; e-mail gnampa@fasonet.bf; Nat. Sec. JEAN-PIERRE SWEDY.

The Press

Direction de la Presse Écrite: Ouagadougou; govt body responsible for press direction.

DAILIES

24 Heures: 01 BP 3654, Ouagadougou 01; tel. 50-31-41-08; fax 50-30-57-39; f. 2000; privately owned; Dir BOUBAKAR DIALLO.

Bulletin de l'Agence d'Information du Burkina: 01 BP 2507, Ouagadougou 01; tel. 50-32-46-40; fax 50-33-73-16; e-mail infos@aib.bf; internet www.aib.bf; f. 1964 as L'Agence Voltaïque de Presse; current name adopted in 1984; Dir JAMES DABIRÉ.

L'Express du Faso: 01 BP 1, Bobo-Dioulasso 01; tel. 50-33-50-27; e-mail lexpress.faso@yahoo.fr; internet www.lexpressdufaso.com; f. 1998; privately owned; Dir of Publication JACQUES; Editor-in-Chief KANI MOUNTAMOU; circ. 2,000 (2010).

L'Observateur Paalga (New Observer): 01 BP 584, Ouagadougou 01; tel. 50-33-27-05; fax 50-31-45-79; e-mail lobs@fasonet.bf; internet www.lobservateur.bf; f. 1973; privately owned; also a Friday edn *L'Observateur Dimanche*; Dir EDOUARD OUÉDRAOGO; circ. in 2012 10,000 (daily), 5,000 (weekly).

Le Pays: Cité 1200 logements, 01 BP 4577, Ouagadougou 01; tel. 50-36-20-46; fax 50-36-03-78; e-mail lepays91@yahoo.fr; internet www.lepays.bf; f. 1991; independent; Dir-Gen. BOUREIMA JÉRÉMIE SIGUE; Editor-in-Chief MAHOROU KANAZOE; circ. 12,000 (2010).

Sidwaya Quotidien (Daily Truth): 5 rue du Marché, 01 BP 507, Ouagadougou 01; tel. 50-31-22-89; fax 50-31-03-62; e-mail daouda.ouedraogo@sidwaya.bf; internet www.sidwaya.bf; f. 1984; state-owned; Dir-Gen. RABANKHI ABOU-BÂKR ZIDA; Editor-in-Chief VICTORIEN AIMAR SAWADOGO; circ. 5,000 (2010).

PERIODICALS

Bendré (Drum): 16.38 ave du Yatenga, 01 BP 6020, Ouagadougou 01; tel. 50-33-27-11; fax 50-31-28-53; e-mail bendrekan@hotmail.com; internet www.journalbendre.net; f. 1990; weekly; current affairs; Dir SY MOUMINA CHERIFF; circ. 2,000 (2010).

Evasion: Cité 1200 logements, 01 BP 4577, Ouagadougou 01; tel. 50-36-17-30; fax 50-36-03-78; e-mail lepays91@yahoo.fr; internet www.lepays.fr; f. 1996; publ. by Editions le Pays; weekly; current affairs; Dir-Gen. BOUREIMA JÉRÉMIE SIGUE; Editor-in-Chief CHRISTINE SAWADOGO.

L'Evènement: 01 BP 1860, Ouagadougou 01; tel. and fax 50-36-33-03; e-mail bangreib@yahoo.fr; internet www.evenement-bf.net; f. 2001; bimonthly; Dir of Publication GERMAIN BITTIOU NAMA; Editor-in-Chief NEWTON AHMED BARRY; circ. 6,000 (2010).

Fasozine: Ouagadougou; tel. 50-30-76-01; fax 50-31-69-73; e-mail ecrire@fasozine.com; internet www.fasozine.com; f. 2005; Dir of Publication MORIN YAMONGBE.

L'Hebdomadaire: Ouagadougou; tel. 50-31-47-62; e-mail hebdcom@fasonet.bf; internet www.hebdo.bf; f. 1999; Fridays; Dir ZÉPHIRIN KPODA; Editor-in-Chief DJIBRIL TOURÉ.

L'Indépendant: 01 BP 5663, Ouagadougou 01; tel. 50-33-37-75; e-mail sebgo@fasonet.bf; internet www.independant.bf; f. 1993 by Norbert Zongo; weekly, Tuesdays; Dir LIERMÉ DIEUDONNÉ SOMÉ; Editor-in-Chief TALATO SIID SAYA; circ. 5,000 (2010).

Le Journal du Jeudi (JJ): 01 BP 3654, Ouagadougou 01; tel. 50-31-41-08; fax 50-30-01-62; e-mail info@journaldujeudi.com; internet www.journaldujeudi.com; f. 1991; weekly; satirical; Dir BOUBAKAR DIALLO; Editor-in-Chief DAMIEN GLEZ; circ. 10,000.

Laabaali: Association Tin Tua, BP 167, Fada N'Gourma; tel. 40-77-01-26; fax 40-77-02-08; e-mail info@tintua.org; internet www.tintua.org/Liens/Laabali.htm; f. 1988; monthly; promotes literacy, agricultural information, cultural affairs; Gourmanche; Dir of Publishing BENOÎT B. OUOBA; Editor-in-Chief SUZANNE OUOBA; circ. 4,000.

Le Marabout: 01 BP 3564, Ouagadougou 01; tel. 50-31-41-08; e-mail info@marabout.net; f. 2001; monthly; publ. by the Réseau Africain pour la Liberté d'Informer; pan-African politics; satirical; Dir BOUBAKAR DIALLO; Editor-in-Chief DAMIEN GLEZ.

L'Opinion: 01 BP 6459, Ouagadougou 01; tel. and fax 50-30-89-49; e-mail zedcom@fasonet.bf; internet www.zedcom.bf; weekly; Dir of Publishing ISSAKA LINGANI.

San Finna: Immeuble Photo Luxe, 12 BP 105, Ouagadougou 12; tel. and fax 50-35-82-64; e-mail sanfinna@yahoo.fr; internet www.sanfinna.com; f. 1999; Mondays; independent; current affairs, international politics; Editor-in-Chief MATHIEU N'DO.

Sidwaya Hebdo (Weekly Truth): 5 rue du Marché, 01 BP 507, Ouagadougou 01; tel. 50-31-22-89; fax 50-31-03-62; e-mail daouda.ouedraogo@sidwaya.bf; internet www.sidwaya.bf; f. 1997; state-owned; weekly; Editor-in-Chief DAOUDA E. OUÉDRAOGO.

Sidwaya Magazine (Truth): 5 rue du Marché, 01 BP 507, Ouagadougou 01; tel. 50-31-22-89; fax 50-31-03-62; e-mail daouda.ouedraogo@sidwaya.bf; internet www.sidwaya.bf; f. 1989; state-owned; monthly; Editor-in-Chief DAOUDA E. OUÉDRAOGO; circ. 2,500.

La Voix du Sahel: 01 BP 5505, Ouagadougou 01; tel. 50-33-20-75; e-mail voixdusahel@yahoo.fr; privately owned; Dir of Publication PROMOTHÉE KASSOUM BAKO.

Votre Santé: Cité 1200 logements, 01 BP 4577, Ouagadougou 01; tel. 50-36-20-46; fax 50-36-03-78; e-mail lepays91@yahoo.fr; internet www.lepays.fr; f. 1996; publ. by Editions le Pays; monthly; Dir-Gen. BOUREIMA JÉRÉMIE SIGUE; Editor-in-Chief ALEXANDRE LE GRAND ROUAMBA.

NEWS AGENCY

Agence d'Information du Burkina (AIB): 01 BP 2507, Ouagadougou 01; tel. 50-32-46-39; fax 50-33-73-16; e-mail aib.redaction@mcc.gov.bf; internet www.aib.bf; f. 1964; fmrly Agence Voltaïque de Presse; state-controlled; Dir JOLIVET EMMAÜS.

PRESS ASSOCIATIONS

Association Rayimkudemdé—Association Nationale des Animateurs et Journalistes en Langues Nationales du Burkina Faso (ARK): Sigh-Noghin, Ouagadougou; f. 2001; Pres. RIGOBERT ILBOUDO; Sec.-Gen. PIERRE OUÉDRAOGO.

Centre National de Presse—Norbert Zongo (CNP—NZ): 04 BP 8524, Ouagadougou 04; tel. and fax 50-34-37-45; internet www.cnpress-zongo.net; f. 1998 as Centre National de Presse; centre of information and documentation; provides journalistic training; incorporates Association des Journalistes du Burkina (f. 1988); Dir ABDOULAYE DIALLO.

Publishers

Editions Contact: 04 BP 8462, Ouagadougou 04; tel. 76-61-28-72; e-mail contact.evang@cenatrin.bf; f. 1992; evangelical Christian and other books in French.

Editions Découvertes du Burkina (ADDB): 06 BP 9237, Ouagadougou 06; tel. 50-36-22-38; e-mail jacques@liptinfor.bf; human and social sciences, poetry; Dir JACQUES GUÉGANÉ.

Editions Firmament: 01 BP 3392, Ouagadougou 01; tel. 50-38-44-25; e-mail brkabore@uemoa.int; f. 1994; literary fiction; Dir ROGER KABORÉ.

Editions Flamme: 04 BP 8921, Ouagadougou 04; tel. 50-34-15-31; fax 70-21-10-28; e-mail flamme@fasonet.bf; f. 1999; owned by the Assembleés de Dieu du Burkina Faso; literature of Christian interest in French, in Mooré and in Dioula; Dir Pastor ZACHARIE DELMA.

Editions Gambidi: 01 BP 5743, Ouagadougou 01; tel. 50-36-59-42; politics, philosophy; Dir JEAN-PIERRE GUINGANÉ.

Graphic Technic International & Biomedical (GTI): 01 BP 3230, Ouagadougou 01; tel. and fax 50-31-67-69; medicine, literary, popular and children's fiction, poetry; Dir-Gen. SAWADOGO N. TASSERE.

Editions Hamaria: 01 BP 6788, Ouagadougou 01; tel. 50-34-38-04; sciences, fiction.

Presses Africaines SA: 01 BP 1471, Ouagadougou 01; tel. 50-30-71-75; general fiction, religion, primary and secondary textbooks; Man. Dir A. WININGA.

Editions Sankofa et Gurli: 01 BP 3811, Ouagadougou 01; tel. 70-24-30-81; e-mail sankogur@hotmail.com; f. 1995; literary fiction, social sciences, African languages, youth and childhood literature; in French and in national languages; Dir JEAN-CLAUDE NABA.

Editions Sidwaya: BP 507, Ouagadougou 01; tel. 50-31-22-89; fax 50-31-03-62; internet www.sidwaya.bf; f. 1998 to replace Société Nationale d'Editions et de Presse; state-owned; transfer to private ownership proposed; general, periodicals; Dir IBRAHIMAN SAKANDÉ.

Broadcasting and Communications

TELECOMMUNICATIONS

Regulatory Authority

Autorité de Régulation des Communications Électroniques et des Postes (ARCEP): ave Dimdolobsom, porte 43, rue 3 angle rue 48, 01 BP 6437, Ouagadougou 01; tel. 50-37-53-60; fax 50-37-53-64; e-mail secretariat@arcep.bf; internet www.arce.bf; f. 2009 to replace Autorité Nationale de Régulation des Télécommunications (ARTEL); Pres. of the Council of Administration BÉLI MATHURIN BAKO; Dir-Gen. SIBIRI OUATTARA.

Service Providers

Airtel Burkina Faso: ave du Président Aboubacar Sangoulé Lamizana, 01 BP 6622, Ouagadougou 01; tel. 50-33-14-00; fax 50-33-14-06; e-mail info@bf.airtel.com; internet africa.airtel.com/burkina; f. 2001; fmrly Zain Burkina Faso, present name adopted 2010; mobile cellular telephone operator in Ouagadougou, Bobo-Dioulasso and 235 other towns; acquired by Bharti Airtel (India) in 2010; Dir-Gen. JOHN NDEGO; 1m. subscribers (Feb. 2008).

Office National des Télécommunications (ONATEL): ave de la Nation, 01 BP 10000, Ouagadougou 01; tel. 50-49-44-02; fax 50-31-03-31; e-mail dcrp@onatel.bf; internet www.onatel.bf; 51% owned by Maroc Telecom (Morocco, Vivendi); 23% state owned; Pres. PAUL BALMA; Dir-Gen. MOHAMMED MORCHID.

TELMOB: tel. 49-42-41; fax 50-49-42-78; e-mail wema.d@onatel.bf; internet www.telmob.bf; f. 2002; mobile cellular telephone operator in 19 cities; Dir DIEUDONNÉ WEMA; 400,000 subscribers (Dec. 2006).

Telecel-Faso: 396 ave de la Nation, 08 BP 11059, Ouagadougou 086; tel. 50-33-35-56; fax 50-33-35-58; e-mail infos@telecelfaso.bf; internet www.telecelfaso.bf; f. 2000; mobile cellular telephone operator in Ouagadougou, Bobo-Dioulasso and 19 other towns; 80% owned by Orascom Telecom (Egypt); Dir-Gen. DIMITRI W. OUÉDRAOGO; 80,000 subscribers (Dec. 2003).

BROADCASTING

In 2010 there were some 112 radio stations and 14 television stations operating in Burkina Faso.

Regulatory Authority

Conseil Supérieur de la Communication (Higher Council of Communication): 290 ave Ho Chi Minh, 01 BP 6618, Ouagadougou 01; tel. 50-30-11-24; fax 50-30-11-33; e-mail info@csi.bf; internet www.csi.bf; f. 1995 as Higher Council of Information, present name adopted 2005; Pres. MARIE NOËLLIE BÉATRICE DAMIBA; Sec.-Gen. JEAN-PAUL KONSEIBO.

Radio

Radiodiffusion-Télévision du Burkina (RTB): 01 BP 2530, Ouagadougou 01; tel. 50-31-83-53; fax 50-32-48-09; internet www.rtb.bf; f. 2001; Dir-Gen. YACOUBA TRAORÉ.

Horizon FM: 01 BP 2714, Ouagadougou 01; tel. 50-33-23-23; fax 50-30-21-41; e-mail hfm@grouphorizonfm.com; internet www.grouphorizonfm.com; f. 1990; private commercial station; broadcasts in French, English and 8 vernacular languages; operates 10 stations nationally; Dir JUDITH IDA SAWADOGO.

Ouaga FM: blvd France-Afrique, Ouagadougou; tel. 50-37-51-21; fax 50-37-61-77; internet www.ouagafm.bf; Pres. JOACHIM BAKY; Dir-Gen. ZAKARIDJA GNIENHOUN.

Radio Nationale du Burkina (La RNB): 03 BP 7029, Ouagadougou 03; tel. 50-32-43-02; fax 50-31-04-41; e-mail radio@rtb.bf; internet www.radio.bf; f. 1959; state radio service; comprises national broadcaster of informative and discussion programmes, music stations *Canal Arc-En-Ciel* and *Canal Arc-en-Ciel Plus*, and 2 regional stations, broadcasting in local languages, in Bobo-Dioulasso and Gaoua; Dir OUÉZIN LOUIS OULON.

Radio Evangile Développement (RED): 04 BP 8050, Ouagadougou 04; tel. 50-43-51-56; e-mail redbf@laposte.net; internet www.red-burkina.org; f. 1993; broadcasts from Ouagadougou, Bobo-Dioulasso, Ouahigouya, Léo, Houndé, Koudougou, Yako and Fada N'Gourma; evangelical Christian; Dir-Gen. ETIENNE KIEMDE.

Radio Locale-Radio Rurale: 03 BP 7029, Ouagadougou 03; tel. 50-31-27-81; fax 40-79-10-22; f. 1969; community broadcaster; local stations at Diapaga, Djibasso Gasson, Kongoussi, Orodara and Poura; Dir-Gen. BÉLIBIÉ SOUMAÏLA BASSOLE.

Radio Maria: BP 51, Koupela; tel. and fax 40-70-00-10; e-mail administration.bur@radiomaria.org; internet www.radiomaria.org; f. 1993; Roman Catholic; Dir BELEMSIGRI PIERRE CLAVER.

Radio Pulsar: Ave Léo Frobenius, 01 BP 5976, Ouagadougou 01; tel. 50314199; e-mail info@monpulsar.com; internet www.monpulsar.com; f. 1996; Dir FRANÇOIS YESSO.

Radio Salankoloto-Association Galian: 01 BP 1095, Ouagadougou 01; tel. 50-31-64-93; fax 50-31-64-71; e-mail radiosalankoloto@cenatrin.bf; f. 1996; community broadcaster; Dir ROGER NIKIÉMA.

Radio Vive le Paysan: BP 75, Saponé; tel. 50-40-56-21; fax 50-30-52-80; e-mail a2oyigde@yahoo.fr; f. 1995; Dir ADRIEN VITAUX.

Radio la Voix du Paysan: BP 100, Ouahigouya; tel. 40-55-04-11; fax 40-55-01-62; community broadcaster; f. 1996; Pres. BERNARD LÉDÉA OUÉDRAOGO.

Savane FM: 10 BP 500, Ouagadougou 10; tel. 50-43-37-43; internet www.savanefm.bf; Dir-Gen. CHARLEMAGNE ABISSI.

Television

BF1: Ouagadougou; f. 2010; Dir-Gen. LÉOPOLD KOHOUN.

La Télévision Nationale du Burkina: 955 blvd de la Révolution, 01 BP 2530, Ouagadougou 01; tel. 50-31-83-53; fax 50-32-48-09; e-mail television@rtb.bf; internet www.tnb.bf; branch of Radiodiffusion-Télévision du Burkina (q.v.); broadcasts 75 hours per week; Dir PASCAL YEMBOINI THIOMBIANO.

Télévision Canal Viim Koéga—Fréquence Lumière: BP 108, Ouagadougou; tel. 50-30-76-40; e-mail cvktv@cvktv.org; internet www.cvktv.org; f. 1996; operated by the Fédération des Eglises et Missions Evangéliques; broadcasts 6 hours daily (Mon.–Fri.).

TV Canal 3: ave Kwamé N'Krumah, 11 BP 340, Ouagadougou 11; tel. 50-30-06-55; e-mail info@tvcanal3.com; internet www.tvcanal3.com; f. 2002.

TV Maria: Ouagadougou; f. 2009; Roman Catholic; Dir RACHEL ZONGO.

TVZ Africa: 145 ave de Kossodo, 01 BP 70170, Ouagadougou 01; tel. 70-26-28-20; internet www.tvzafrica.com; commercial broadcaster; Pres. and Dir-Gen. MOUSTAPHA LAABLI THIOMBIANO.

Finance

(cap. = capital; res = reserves; dep. = deposits; m. = million; br(s). = branch(es); amounts in francs CFA)

BANKING

In 2009 there were 11 banks and 5 financial institutions in Burkina Faso.

Central Bank

Banque Centrale des Etats de l'Afrique de l'Ouest (BCEAO): ave Bassawarga, BP 356, Ouagadougou; tel. 50-30-60-15; fax 50-31-01-22; e-mail webmaster@bceao.int; internet www.bceao.int; HQ in Dakar, Senegal; f. 1962; bank of issue for the mem. states of the Union Economique et Monétaire Ouest-Africaine (UEMOA, comprising Benin, Burkina Faso, Côte d'Ivoire, Guinea-Bissau, Mali, Niger, Senegal and Togo); cap. 134,120m., res 1,474,195m., dep. 2,124,051m. (Dec. 2009); Gov. KONÉ TIÉMOKO MEYLIET; Dir in Burkina Faso BOLO SANOU; br. in Bobo-Dioulasso.

Other Banks

Bank of Africa—Burkina Faso (BOA—B): 770 ave du Président Sangoule Lamizana, 01 BP 1319, Ouagadougou 01; tel. 50-30-88-70; fax 50-30-88-74; e-mail boadg@fasonet.bf; internet www.boaburkinafaso.com; f. 1998; cap. 5,000.0m., res 2,428.8m., dep. 158,062.3m. (Dec. 2009); Chair. MICHEL F. KAHN; 20 brs.

Banque Agricole et Commerciale du Burkina (BAC-B): 2 ave Gamal Abdel Nasser, Secteur 3, 01 BP 1644, Ouagadougou 01; tel. 50-33-33-33; fax 50-31-43-52; e-mail bacb@bacb.bf; internet www.bacb.bf; f. 1980; fmrly Caisse Nationale de Crédit Agricole du Burkina (CNCA-B); present name adopted 2002; 25% state-owned; cap. 3,500m., res 898m., dep. 70,108m. (Dec. 2006); Pres. TIBILA KABORE; Chair. and Gen. Man. LÉONCE KONÉ; 4 brs.

Banque Commerciale du Burkina (BCB): 653 ave Kwamé N'Krumah, 01 BP 1336, Ouagadougou 01; tel. 50-30-78-78; fax 50-31-06-28; e-mail bcb@bcb.bf; internet www.bcb.bf; f. 1988; 50% owned by Libyan Arab Foreign Bank, 25% state-owned, 25% owned by Caisse Nationale de Sécurité Sociale; cap. 26,125m., res –6,555m., dep. 73,391m. (Dec. 2009); Pres. JACQUES ZIDA; Gen. Man. ABDULLA EL MOGADAMI; 4 brs.

Banque Internationale pour le Commerce, l'Industrie et l'Agriculture du Burkina (BICIA—B): 479 ave Kwamé N'Krumah, 01 BP 08, Ouagadougou 01; tel. 50-31-31-31; fax 50-31-19-55; e-mail biciabq@fasonet.bf; internet www.biciab.bf; f. 1973; affiliated to BNP Paribas (France); 25% state-owned; cap. 5,000m., res 7,338m., dep. 127,687m. (Dec. 2008); Pres. MICHEL KOMPAORÉ; Dir-Gen. LUC VIDAL; 11 brs.

Ecobank Burkina: Immeuble espace Fadima, 633 rue Ilboudo Waogyande, 01 BP 145, Ouagadougou 01; tel. 50-32-83-28; fax 50-31-89-81; e-mail ecobankbf@ecobank.com; internet www.ecobank.com; f. 1996; 82% owned by Ecobank Transnational Inc; dep. 108,167.5m. (Dec. 2008); Chair. ANDRÉ BAYALA; Dir-Gen. ROGER DAH-ACHINANON.

Société Générale de Banques au Burkina (SGBB): 248 rue de l'Hôtel de Ville, 01 BP 585, Ouagadougou 01; tel. 50-32-32-32; fax 50-31-05-61; e-mail sgbb.burkina@socgen.com; internet www.sgbb.bf; f. 1998; 50% owned by Partie Burkinabè, 44% owned by Société Générale (France), 6% owned by FINADEI; cap. and res 5,510m., total assets 95,927m. (Dec. 2004); Dir-Gen. PATRICK DELAILLE.

United Bank for Africa Burkina: 1340 ave Dimdolobsom, 01 BP 362, Ouagadougou 01; tel. 75-35-20-95; fax 75-35-20-94; e-mail info@bibburkinafaso.net; internet www.bibburkinafaso.net; f. 1974; 25% owned by Fonds Burkina de Développement Economique et Social, 24.2% owned by Holding COFIPA (Mali), 22.8% state-owned; fmrly Banque Internationale du Burkina; cap. 12,000.0m., res –4,761.3m., dep. 156,775.9m. (Dec. 2009); Pres. and Dir-Gen. GASPARD-JEAN OUÉDRAOGO; 21 brs.

Credit Institutions

Burkina Bail, SA: 1035 ave du Dr Kwamé N'Krumah, Immeuble SODIFA, 01 BP 1913, Ouagadougou 01; tel. 50-33-26-33; fax 50-30-70-02; e-mail courrierdg@burkinabail.bf; internet www.burkinabail.bf; f. 1998; 47% owned by BIB, 34% owned by FMO and 18% owned by Cauris Investissement; total assets 6,326m. (Dec. 2011); CEO KOUAFILANN ABDOULAYE SORY.

Réseau des Caisses Populaires du Burkina (RCPB): Ouagadougou; tel. 50-30-48-41; internet www.rcpb.bf; f. 1972; Dir-Gen. DAOUDA SAWADOGA; 450,000 mems (2006), 104 co-operatives.

Société Burkinabè de Financement (SOBFI): Immeuble Nassa, 1242 ave Dr Kwamé N'Krumah, 10 BP 13876, Ouagadougou 10; tel. 50-31-80-04; fax 50-33-71-62; e-mail sobfi@fasonet.bf; f. 1997; cap. 500.0m., total assets 2,850.9m. (Dec. 2002); Pres. DIAWAR DIACK.

Bankers' Association

Association Professionnelle des Banques et Etablissements Financiers du Burkina (APBEF-B): 1021 ave de la Cathédrale, 01 BP 6215, Ouagadougou 01; tel. 50-31-20-65; fax 50-31-20-66; e-mail apbef@fasonet.bf; f. 1967; Vice-Pres. MAMADI NAPON.

STOCK EXCHANGE

Bourse Régionale des Valeurs Mobilières (BRVM): s/c Chambre de Commerce, d'Industrie et d'Artisanat du Burkina, 01 BP 502, Ouagadougou 01; tel. 50-30-87-73; fax 50-30-87-19; e-mail louedraogo@brvm.org; internet www.brvm.org; f. 1998; national branch of BRVM (regional stock exchange based in Abidjan, Côte d'Ivoire, serving the member states of UEMOA); Man. LÉOPOLD OUÉDRAOGO.

INSURANCE

In 2008 there were 10 insurance companies in Burkina Faso.

Allianz Burkina Assurances: 99 ave Léo Frobénius, 01 BP 398, Ouagadougou 01; tel. 50-30-62-04; fax 50-31-01-53; e-mail allianz.burkina@allianz-bf.com; internet www.allianz-burkina.com; f. 1978; name changed as above in 2009; subsidiary of Allianz (France); non-life insurance and reinsurance; cap. 400m.; Dir-Gen. PHILIPPE AUDOUIN; also **Allianz Burkina Assurances Vie**, life insurance; Dir-Gen. PHILIPPE AUDOUIN.

Générale des Assurances: 01 BP 6275, Ouagadougou 01; tel. 50-30-06-40; fax 50-30-87-17; e-mail g.assur@fasonet.bf; Dir-Gen. (life insurance) SIMON PIERRE GOUEM; Dir-Gen. (non-life insurance) JEAN-PAUL OUÉDRAOGO.

Gras Savoye Burkina Faso: ave de la Résistance du 17 mai, 01 BP 1304, Ouagadougou 01; tel. 50-30-51-69; fax 50-30-51-73; affiliated to Gras Savoye (France); Dir-Gen. LAURENT SAWADOGO.

Raynal SA: ave du Kwamé N'Krumah, 01 BP 6131, Ouagadougou 01; tel. 50-30-25-12; fax 50-30-25-14; e-mail raynal-sa@raynal-sa.com; Dir-Gen. REYNATOU ELÉONOR BADO YAMEOGO.

Société Nationale d'Assurances et de Réassurances (SONAR): 284 ave de Loudun, 01 BP 406, Ouagadougou 01; tel. 50-33-46-66; fax 50-30-89-75; e-mail sonarinfo@sonar.bf; internet www.sonar.bf; f. 1974; 42% owned by Burkinabè interests, 33% by French, Ivorian and US cos, 22% state-owned; life and non-life; cap. 720m. (SONAR-IARD, non-life), 500m. (SONAR-Vie, life); Dir-Gen. ANDRÉ B. BAYALA; 9 brs and sub-brs.

Union des Assurances du Burkina (UAB): 08 BP 11041, Ouagadougou 08; tel. 50-31-26-15; fax 50-31-26-20; e-mail uab@fasonet.bf; f. 1991; 11% owned by AXA Assurances Côte d'Ivoire; cap. 1,000m.; Pres. APPOLINAIRE COMPAORÉ; Dir-Gen. (non-life insurance) JEAN DASMASCÈNE NIGNAN; Dir-Gen. (life insurance) SOUMAÏLA SORGHO.

Trade and Industry

GOVERNMENT AGENCIES

Bureau des Mines et de la Géologie du Burkina (BUMIGEB): 4186 route de Fada N'Gourma, 01 BP 601, Ouagadougou 01; tel. 50-36-48-02; fax 50-36-48-88; e-mail bumigeb@cenatrin.bf; internet www.bumigeb.bf; f. 1978; restructured 1997; research into geological and mineral resources; Pres. BOURI ROGER ZOMBRE; Dir-Gen. PASCALE DIENDÉRÉ.

Commission de Privatisation: 01 BP 6451, Ouagadougou 01; tel. 50-33-58-93; fax 50-30-77-41; Pres. PLACIDE SOME.

Comptoir Burkinabè des Métaux Précieux (CBMP): Ouagadougou; tel. 50-30-75-48; fax 50-31-56-34; promotes gold sector, liaises with artisanal producers; transfer to private management pending; Dir-Gen. YACOUBA BARRY.

Office National d'Aménagement des Terroirs (ONAT): 01 BP 3007, Ouagadougou 01; tel. 50-30-61-10; fax 50-30-61-12; f. 1974; fmrly Autorité des Aménagements des Vallées des Voltas; integrated rural devt, incl. economic and social planning; Man. Dir ZACHARIE OUÉDRAOGO.

Office National des Barrages et des Aménagements Hydro-agricoles (ONBAH): 03 BP 7056, Ouagadougou 03; tel. 50-30-89-82; fax 50-31-04-26; f. 1976; control and devt of water for agricultural use, construction of dams, water and soil conservation; state-owned; Dir-Gen. AÏZO TINDANO.

Office National du Commerce Extérieur (ONAC): 30 ave de l'UEMOA, 01 BP 389, Ouagadougou 01; tel. 50-31-13-00; fax 50-31-14-69; e-mail info@onac.bf; internet www.tradepoint.bf; f. 1974; promotes and supervises external trade; Man. Dir BAYA JUSTIN BAYILI; br. at Bobo-Dioulasso.

DEVELOPMENT ORGANIZATIONS

Agence Française de Développement (AFD): 52 ave de la Nation, 01 BP 529, Ouagadougou 01; tel. 50-30-60-92; fax 50-31-19-66; e-mail afdouagadougou@bf.groupe-afd.org; internet www.afd.fr; Country Dir PATRICE TRANCHANT.

Autorité de Régulation des Marchés Publics: 01 BP 2080, Ouagadougou 01; tel. 50-30-69-01; e-mail armp@armp.bf; internet www.armp.bf; f. 2007; Perm. Sec. MAMADOU GUIRA.

Bureau d'Appui aux Micro-entreprises (BAME): BP 610, Bobo-Dioulasso; tel. 20-97-16-28; fax 20-97-21-76; f. 1991; supports small business; Dir FÉLIX SANON.

Cellule d'Appui à la Petite et Moyenne Entreprise d'Ouagadougou (CAPEO): 01 BP 6443, Ouagadougou 01; tel. 50-31-37-62; fax 50-31-37-64; internet www.spid.com/capeo; f. 1991; supports small and medium-sized enterprises.

France Volontaires: 01 BP 947, Ouagadougou 01; tel. 50-30-70-43; fax 50-30-10-72; internet www.france-volontaires.org; f. 1973 as Association Française des Volontaires du Progrès; name changed as above in 2009; supports small business; Nat. Delegate EUGÈNE SOME.

Promotion du Développement Industriel, Artisanal et Agricole (PRODIA): Secteur 8, Gounghin, 01 BP 2344, Ouagadougou 01; tel. 50-34-31-11; fax 50-34-71-47; f. 1981; supports small business; Dir MAMADOU OUÉDRAOGO.

CHAMBERS OF COMMERCE

Chambre de Commerce, d'Industrie et d'Artisanat du Burkina Faso: 118/220 ave de Lyon, 01 BP 502, Ouagadougou 01; tel. 50-30-61-14; fax 50-30-61-16; e-mail ccia-bf@ccia.bf; internet www.ccia.bf; f. 1948; Pres. ALIZÈTA OUÉDRAOGO; Dir-Gen. FRANCK TAPSOBA; brs in Bobo-Dioulasso, Koupéla and Ouahigouya.

Chambre des Mines du Burkina (CMB): Ouagadougou; f. 2011; Pres. ELIE OUÉDRAOGO.

EMPLOYERS' ORGANIZATIONS

Club des Hommes d'Affaires Franco-Burkinabé: Ambassade de France au Burkina Faso, 01 BP 4382, Ouagadougou 01; tel. 50-31-32-73; fax 50-31-32-81; internet www.chafb.bf; f. 1990; represents 65 major enterprises and seeks to develop trading relations between Burkina Faso and France; Pres. EDDIE KOMBOIGO.

Conseil National du Patronat Burkinabè (CNPB): 1221 ave du Dr Kwame N'Krumah, 01 BP 1482, Ouagadougou 01; tel. 50-33-03-09; fax 50-30-03-08; e-mail cnpb@liptinfor.bf; f. 1974; comprises 70 professional groupings; Pres. El Hadj OUMAROU KANAZOE; Sec.-Gen. PHILOMÈNE YAMEOGO.

Groupement Professionnel des Industriels (GPI): Immeuble CBC, 641 ave Koubemba, 01 BP 5381, Ouagadougou 01; tel. and fax 50-30-11-59; e-mail gpi@fasonet.bf; internet www.gpi.bf; f. 1974; Pres. (vacant).

Fédération Nationale des Exportateurs du Burkina (FENEB): 01 BP 389, Ouagadougou 01; tel. 50-31-13-00; fax 50-31-14-69; e-mail fofseydou@hotmail.com; Permanent Sec. SEYDOU FOFANA.

Jeune Chambre Internationale du Burkina Faso: Immeuble Kanazoe, ave du Travail, 11 BP 136, Ouagadougou; tel. 78-85-40-41; e-mail kroser73@yahoo.fr; internet www.jci.cc/local/burkina; f. 1976; org. of entrepreneurs aged 18–40; affiliated to Junior Chambers International, Inc; Exec. Pres. K. RODOLPHE S. DJIGUIMDE.

Maison de l'Entreprise du Burkina Faso (MEBF): rue 3-1119, porte 132, 11 BP 379, Ouagadougou 11; tel. 50-39-80-60; fax 50-39-80-62; e-mail info@me.bf; internet www.me.bf; f. 2002; promotes devt of the private sector; Pres. ALAIN ROGER COEFE; Dir-Gen. ISSAKA KARGOUGOU.

Syndicat des Commerçants Importateurs et Exportateurs du Burkina (SCIMPEX): ave Kadiogo, Secteur 2, Immeuble CBC, 1er étage, 01 BP 552, Ouagadougou 01; tel. 50-31-18-70; fax 50-31-30-36; e-mail scimpex@fasonet.bf; internet www.scimpex-bf.com; f. 1959; Pres. LASSINÉ DIAWARA.

Union Nationale des Producteurs de Coton du Burkina Faso (UNPCB): 02 BP 1677, Bobo-Dioulasso 02; tel. 20-97-33-10; fax 20-97-20-59; e-mail unpcb@fasonet.bf; internet www.abcburkina.net/unpcb/unpcb_index.htm; f. 1998; Pres. KARIM TRAORÉ.

UTILITIES

Electricity

Société Générale de Travaux et de Constructions Electriques (SOGETEL): Zone Industrielle, Gounghin, 01 BP 429, Ouagadougou 01; tel. 50-30-23-45; fax 50-34-25-70; e-mail sogetel@cenatrin.bf; internet www.cenatrin.bf/sogetel; transport and distribution of electricity.

Société Nationale Burkinabè d'Électricité (SONABEL): 55 ave de la Nation, 01 BP 54, Ouagadougou 01; tel. 50-30-61-00; fax 50-31-

03-40; e-mail courrier@sonabel.bf; internet www.sonabel.bf; f. 1984; state-owned; production and distribution of electricity; Dir-Gen. SIENGUI APOLLINAIRE KI.

Water

Office National de l'Eau et de l'Assainissement (ONEA): 01 BP 170, Ouagadougou 01; tel. 50-43-19-00; fax 50-43-19-11; e-mail onea@fasonet.bf; internet www.oneabf.com; f. 1977; storage, purification and distribution of water; transferred to private management (by Veolia Water Burkina Faso) in 2001; Dir-Gen. HAROUNA YAMBA OUIBIGA.

Veolia Water Burkina Faso: 06 BP 9525, Ouagadougou 06; tel. and fax 50-34-03-00; manages operation of water distribution and sewerage services; subsidiary of Veolia Environnement (France).

CO-OPERATIVE

Union des Coopératives Agricoles et Maraîchères du Burkina (UCOBAM): 01 BP 277, Ouagadougou 01; tel. 50-30-65-27; fax 50-30-65-28; e-mail ucobam@zcp.bf; internet www.ucobam.bf; f. 1968; comprises 8 regional co-operative unions (6,500 mems, representing 35,000 producers); production and marketing of fruit, vegetables, jams and conserves; Dir-Gen. YASSIA OUEDRAOGO.

MAJOR COMPANIES

The following are some of the largest companies in terms of either capital investment or employment.

Brasseries du Burkina (BRAKINA—BGI): 01 BP 519, Ouagadougou 01; tel. 50-32-55-00; fax 50-35-60-22; e-mail g.lecluse@liptinfor.bf; f. 1960; cap. 2,530m. francs CFA; brewers, bottlers and mfrs of soft-drinks; 99% owned by BGI/CASTEL; Man. Dir GEORGES LECLUSE; 300 employees (2004).

Burkina Moto: 01 BP 1871, Ouagadougou 01; tel. 50-30-61-27; fax 50-30-84-96; e-mail bmoto@fasonet.bf; f. 1985; import and distribution of bicycles, motorcycles and tyres; private co; Pres. and Dir-Gen. APPOLINAIRE T. CAMPAORÉ; 109 employees (2002).

Burkina et Shell: 01 BP 569, Ouagadougou 01; tel. 50-30-22-06; fax 50-33-39-36; f. 1976; marketing and distribution of petroleum products; cap. US $362,829, sales US $54m. (2001); Dir-Gen. SILMIRAOGO NABALMA; 61 employees (2002).

Comptoir Burkinabè de Papier (CBP): 907 ave Yennenga, 01 BP 1338, Ouagadougou 01; tel. 50-31-16-21; fax 50-31-37-06; e-mail cbp@fasonet.bf; f. 1989; paper producer; private co; Pres. and Dir-Gen. JOSEPH BAAKLINI.

Etablissement Tiko-Tamou: 08 BP 11244, Ouagadougou 08; tel. 50-31-37-73; fax 50-31-78-61; f. 1986; mfrs of traditional woven clothing, handicrafts and musical instruments; private co; sales US $0.3m. (1999); Pres. and Dir-Gen. SATA TAMINI.

FASOPLAST—Société des Plastiques du Faso: Zone Industrielle de Youghin, 01 BP 534, Ouagadougou 01; tel. 50-34-31-51; fax 50-34-20-67; e-mail fasoplast@fasoplast.bf; f. 1986; cap. 681m. francs CFA (2001); mfrs of plastics; Man. Dir MAMADY SANOH; 300 employees (2003).

Groupe Aliz: 01 BP 2069, Ouagadougou 01; tel. 50-35-74-94; fax 50-35-74-96; e-mail grpaliz@cenatrin.bf; internet www.groupealiz.bf; f. 1986; processing and export of animal hides and skins; 2m. hides and skins processed, 600,000 raw hides exported annually; acquired Société Burkinabè de Manufacture de Cuir in 2001; Pres. and Dir-Gen. ALIZÈTA OUÉDRAOGO; 275 employees (2000).

Manufacture Burkinabè de Cigarettes (MABUCIG): 55 rue 19, 14 BP 94, Bobo-Dioulasso 14; e-mail mabucig.bobo@fasonet.bf; f. 1966; cap. 935m. francs CFA; cigarette production of 1,000 metric tons per year; Pres. LASSINE DIAWARA; Man. Dir JEAN-CLAUDE STARCZAN.

Perkoa Zinc Project: 01 BP 1463, Ouagadougou 01; tel. 50-31-66-35; f. 1999; zinc mining and exploration at Perkoa, Sanguié province; majority owned by Blackthorn Resources Ltd (Australia) since Nov. 2004.

Société Burkinabè des Fibres Textiles (SOFITEX): 2744 ave William Ponty, 01 BP 147, Bobo-Dioulasso 01; tel. 20-97-00-24; fax 20-97-00-23; e-mail sg@sofitex.bf; internet www.sofitex.bf; f. 1979; 36% state-owned; devt and processing of cotton and other fibrous plants; offers technical and financial support to growers; cap. 4,400m. francs CFA, sales US $173.1m. (2001); Dir-Gen. JEAN-PAUL SAWADOGO; 1,500 employees (2002).

Société de Construction et de Gestion Immobilière du Burkina (SOCOGIB): 01 BP 1646, 01 Ouagadougou; tel. 50-30-01-97; fax 50-31-19-20; e-mail socogib@liptinfor.bf; internet www.socogib.bf; f. 1961; construction and housing management; cap. 1,843m. francs CFA; Man. Dir EUGÈNE ZAGRÉ; 35 employees (2001).

Société Nationale Burkinabè d'Hydrocarbures (SONABHY): 01 BP 4394, Ouagadougou 01; tel. 50-43-00-01; fax 50-43-01-74; e-mail sonabhy@sonabhy.bf; internet www.sonabhy.bf; f. 1985; import, transport and distribution of refined hydrocarbons; state-owned; privatization proposed; sales US $133.7m. (2001); Pres. SÉRIBA OUATTARA; Man. Dir PAUL MARIE COMPAORÉ; 229 employees (Dec. 2005).

Société Nouvelle des Grands Moulins du Burkina (SN-GMB): BP 64, Banfora; f. 1970; 25% state-owned; cap. 865m. francs CFA; flour-millers and mfrs of animal feed; Pres. SALIF KOSSOUKA OUEDRAOGO; 140 employees (2002).

Société Nouvelle Huilerie et Savonnerie-Compagnie Industrielle du Textile et du Coton (SN-Citec): 01 BP 1300, Bobo-Dioulasso 01; tel. 20-97-77-89; fax 20-97-27-01; e-mail sncitec@fasonet.bf; internet www.dagris.fr/implantations/SN%20Citec.html; f. 1995; affiliated to Geocoton (France); cap. 3,445m. francs CFA; production of groundnut oil; mfrs of karité (shea) butter, soap and animal feed; Pres. FULGENCE TOE; Man. Dir BINTOU DIALLO; 360 employees (2005).

Société Nouvelle Sucrière de la Comoé (SN-SOSUCO): BP 13, Banfora; e-mail sosucodg@liptinfor.bf; f. 1972; cap. 6,031m. francs CFA (2002); 52% owned by Groupe IPS (Côte d'Ivoire); sugar refining; Pres. DIANGUINABA BARRO; Man. Dir DIDIER VANDERBON; 3,700 employees (2000).

Société de Promotion des Filières Agricoles (SOPROFA): Bobo-Dioulasso; f. 2001; 75% owned by Aiglon Holding Cheikna Kagnassi (Switzerland), 25% state-owned; promotion of agricultural products, including sesame, mangoes, strawberries, soybeans and oleaginous products for export; cap. 500m. francs CFA; Dir ABDOULAYE KAGNASSI.

Total Burkina: 1080 ave Kwamé N'Krumah, 01 BP 21, Ouagadougou 01; tel. 50-30-50-00; fax 50-32-50-01; e-mail total@total.bf; internet www.total.bf; petroleum distribution; fmrly Elf Oil Burkina, subsequently renamed TotalFinaElf Burkina; present name adopted 2003; Dir-Gen. THIBAULT FLICHY.

TRADE UNIONS

Confédération Générale du Travail Burkina (CGTB): 01 BP 547, Ouagadougou 01; tel. and fax 50-31-36-71; e-mail info@cgtb.bf; internet www.cgtb.bf; f. 1988; confed. of several autonomous trade unions; Sec.-Gen. TOLÉ SAGNON.

Confédération Nationale des Travailleurs Burkinabè (CNTB): BP 445, Ouagadougou; tel. 50-31-23-95; e-mail cntb@fasonet.bf; f. 1972; Sec.-Gen. AUGUSTIN BLAISE HIEN; 10,000 mems.

Confédération Syndicale Burkinabè (CSB): 01 BP 1921, Ouagadougou 01; tel. and fax 50-31-83-98; e-mail cosybu2000@yahoo.fr; f. 1974; mainly public service unions; Sec.-Gen. JEAN MATHIAS LILIOU.

Organisation Nationale des Syndicats Libres (ONSL): 01 BP 99, Ouagadougou 01; tel. and fax 50-34-34-69; e-mail onslbf@yahoo.fr; f. 1960; Sec.-Gen. PAUL NOBILA KABORÉ; 6,000 mems.

Union Syndicale des Travailleurs Burkinabè (USTB): BP 381, Ouagadougou; tel. and fax 50-33-73-09; f. 1958; Sec.-Gen. MAMADOU NAMA; 35,000 mems in 45 affiliated orgs.

Transport

RAILWAY

In 2010 the total length of track in operation was 622 km.

SITARAIL—Transport Ferroviaire de Personnes et de Marchandises: rue Dioncolo, 01 BP 5699, Ouagadougou 01; tel. 50-31-07-35; fax 50-30-85-21; 67% owned by Groupe Bolloré, 15% state-owned, 15% owned by Govt of Côte d'Ivoire; national branch of SITARAIL (based in Abidjan, Côte d'Ivoire); responsible for operations on the railway line between Kaya, Ouagadougou and Abidjan (Côte d'Ivoire); Regional Dir MOURAMANE FOFANA.

Société de Gestion du Patrimoine Ferroviaire du Burkina (SOPAFER—B): 93 rue de la Culture, 01 BP 192, Ouagadougou 01; tel. 50-31-35-99; fax 50-31-35-94; e-mail dgsopafer@liptinfor.bf; f. 1995; railway network services; Dir-Gen. AHAMADO OUÉDRAGO.

ROADS

In 2004 there were an estimated 92,495 km of roads, including 15,271 km of highways.

Fonds d'Entretien Routier du Burkina (FER): 01 BP 2517, Ouagadougou 01; Dir-Gen. MAMADOU OUATTARA.

Société Africaine de Transports Routiers (SATR): 01 BP 5298, Ouagadougou 01; tel. 50-34-08-62.

Société Nationale du Transit du Burkina (SNTB): 474 rue Ilboudo Waogyandé, 01 BP 1192, Ouagadougou 01; tel. 50-49-30-00; fax 50-30-85-21; f. 1977; 82% owned by Groupe SAGA (France), 12% state-owned; road haulage and warehousing; Dir-Gen. RÉGIS TISSIER.

Société de Transport en Commun de Ouagadougou (SOTRACO): 2257 ave du Sanematenga, 01 BP 5665 Ouagadougou

01; tel. 50-35-67-87; fax 50-35-66-80; e-mail sotraco@fasonet.bf; internet sotraco-bf.net; f. 2003; Dir-Gen. BOUREIMA TARNAGDA.

CIVIL AVIATION

There are international airports at Ouagadougou and Bobo-Dioulasso, 49 small airfields and 13 private airstrips. Plans were announced in 2006 for the construction of a new international airport at Donsin, 35 km north-east of the capital; the first phase of the project from 2007–11 was to cost some 115,000m. francs CFA. Two subsequent phases were projected to extend until 2023. Ouagadougou airport handled an estimated 2,756,367 passengers and 4,105 metric tons of freight in 2005.

Air Burkina: 29 ave de la Nation, 01 BP 1459, Ouagadougou 01; tel. 50-49-23-70; fax 50-31-31-65; e-mail resa@airburkina.bf; internet www.air-burkina.com; f. 1967 as Air Volta; 56% owned by Aga Khan Group, 14% state-owned; operates domestic and regional services; Dir MOHAMED GHELALA.

Tourism

Burkina Faso, which possesses some 2.8m. ha of nature reserves, is considered to provide some of the best opportunities to observe wild animals in West Africa. Some big game hunting is permitted. Several important cultural events are also held in Burkina Faso: the biennial pan-African film festival, FESPACO, is held in Ouagadougou, as is the biennial international exhibition of handicrafts, while Bobo-Dioulasso hosts the biennial week of national culture. In 2010 there were 274,000 foreign visitors and receipts from tourism were estimated at US $72m.

Office National du Tourisme Burkinabè (ONTB): ave Frobénius, BP 1318, Ouagadougou; tel. 50-31-19-59; fax 50-31-44-34; e-mail ontb@ontb.bf; internet www.ontb.bf; Dir-Gen. SOULÉMANE OUEDRAOGO.

Defence

National service is voluntary, and lasts for two years on a part-time basis. As assessed at November 2011, the armed forces numbered 11,200 (army 6,400, air force 600, paramilitary gendarmerie 4,200). There was also a 'security company' of 250 and a part-time people's militia of 45,000.

Defence Expenditure: Estimated at 62,400m. francs CFA in 2010.

Chief of the General Staff of the Armed Forces and Chief of Staff of the Army: Col-Maj. HONORÉ NABÉRÉ TRAORÉ.

Education

Education is provided free of charge, and is officially compulsory for 10 years between the ages of six and 16. Primary education begins at six years of age and lasts for six years, comprising three cycles of two years each. Secondary education, beginning at the age of 13, lasts for a further seven years, comprising a first cycle of four years and a second of three years. Enrolment levels are among the lowest in the region. According to UNESCO estimates, in 2008/09 primary enrolment included 60% (boys 64%; girls 57%) of children in the relevant age-group, while in 2009/10 secondary enrolment included only 16% of children in the appropriate age-group (boys 18%; girls 14%). There are three state-owned higher education institutions: a university in Ouagadougou, a polytechnic university at Bobo-Dioulasso and an institute of teacher training at Koudougou. There are also 11 private higher education institutions. The number of students enrolled at tertiary-level institutions in 2009/10 was 51,200. In 2011 spending on education was budgeted at 23.3% of total budgeted government expenditure.

Bibliography

Anderson, S. (Ed. and Trans.). *Thomas Sankara Speaks: The Burkina Faso Revolution 1983–87*. New York, and London, Pathfinder Press, 1988.

Asche, H. *Le Burkina Faso contemporain: L'expérience d'un auto-développement*. Paris, L'Harmattan, 2000.

Balima, S. T., and Frère, M.-S. *Médias et Communications sociales au Burkina Faso: Approche socio-économique de la circulation de l'information*. Paris, L'Harmattan, 2003.

Bila Kaboré, R. *Histoire politique du Burkina Faso 1919–2000*. Paris, L'Harmattan, 2002.

Burton, J.-D. *Nabaas: Traditional Chiefs of Burkina Faso*. Leuven, Snoeck-Ducaji & Zoon, 2006.

Chaigne, R. *Burkina Faso, l'imaginaire du possible: témoignage*. Paris, L'Harmattan, 2002.

Emerging Markets Investment Center. *Burkina Faso Investment and Business Guide*. 2nd edn. USA, International Business Publications, 1999.

Engberg-Pedersen, L., *Endangering Development: Politics, Projects and Environment in Burkina Faso*. Westport, CT, Praeger, 2003.

Guion, J. R. *Blaise Compaoré: Réalisme et intégrité*. Paris, Mondes en devenir, 1991.

Guirma, F. *Comment perdre le pouvoir?: Le cas de Maurice Yaméogo*. Paris, Chaka, 1991.

Guissou, B. *Burkina Faso, un espoir en Afrique*. Paris, L'Harmattan, 1995.

Jaffré, B. *Burkina Faso: les années Sankara de la révolution à la rectification*. Paris, L'Harmattan, 1989.

Konseiga, A., *et al*. *Regional Integration Beyond the Traditional Trade Benefits: Labor Mobility Contribution: The Case of Burkina Faso and Cote D'Ivoire*. Oxford, Peter Lang Publishing Group, 2005.

Kuba, R., Lentz, C., and Nurukyor Somda, C. *Histoire du peuplement et relations interethniques au Burkina Faso*. Paris, Editions Karthala, 2004.

Lachaud, J.-P. *Pauvreté, vulnerabilité et marché du travail au Burkina Faso*. Pessac, Université de Bordeaux, 1997.

Madiega, G., and Nao, O. (Eds). *Burkina Faso: Cent ans d'histoire, 1895-1995*. 2 vols, Paris, Editions Karthala, 2003.

Martens, L., and Meesters, H. *Sankara, Compaoré et la révolution Burkinabè*. EPO, Antwerp, 1989.

Massa, G., and Madiéga, Y. G. (Eds). *La Haute-Volta coloniale: témoignages, recherches*. Paris, Editions Karthala, 1995.

McFarland, D. M., and Rupley, L. A. *Historical Dictionary of Burkina Faso*. 2nd edn. Lanham, MD, Scarecrow Press, 1998.

Meijenfeldt, R. von, Santiso, C., and Otayek, R. *La démocratie au Burkina Faso*. Stockholm, International Institute for Democracy and Electoral Assistance, 1998.

Obinwa Nnaji, B. *Blaise Compaoré: The Architect of Burkina Faso Revolution*. Ibadan, Spectrum Books, 1989.

Sankara, T. *Thomas Sankara Speaks: The Burkina Faso Revolution 1983–87*. Havana, Editora Politica, 2007.

Savadogo, K., and Wetta, C. *The Impact of Self-Imposed Adjustment: The Case of Burkina Faso 1983–1989*. Florence, Spedale degli Innocenti, 1991.

Sawadogo, A. Y. *Le Président Thomas Sankara, chef de la revolution Burkinabè 1983–1987: portrait*. Paris, L'Harmattan, 2001.

BURUNDI

Physical and Social Geography

The Republic of Burundi, like its neighbour Rwanda, is exceptionally small in area, comprising 27,834 sq km (10,747 sq miles), but with a relatively large population of 8,749,386 at mid-2012, according to UN estimates. The result is a high population density, of 314.3 persons per sq km. The principal towns are the capital, Bujumbura (population estimated at 429,000 at mid-2007), and Gitega.

Burundi is bordered by Rwanda to the north, by the Democratic Republic of the Congo (DRC) to the west and by Tanzania to the south and east. The natural divide between Burundi and the DRC is formed by Lake Tanganyika and the Ruzizi river on the floor of the western rift-valley system. To the east, the land rises sharply to elevations of around 1,800 m above sea-level in a range that stretches north into the much higher, and volcanic, mountains of Rwanda. Away from the edge of the rift valley, elevations are lower, and most of Burundi consists of plateaux of 1,400 m–1,800 m. Here the average temperature is 20°C and annual rainfall 1,200 mm. In the valley the temperature averages 23°C, while rainfall is much lower, at 750 mm.

Population has concentrated on the fertile, volcanic soils at 1,500 m–1,800 m above sea-level, away from the arid and hot floor and margins of the rift valley. The consequent pressure on the land, together with recurrent outbreaks of intense internal unrest, has resulted in extensive migration, mainly to Tanzania, the DRC and Uganda. The ethnic composition of the population is much the same as that of Rwanda: about 85% Hutu, 14% Tutsi and less than 1% Twa, pygmoid hunters. Historically, the kingdoms of Urundi and Ruanda had a strong adversarial tradition, and rivalry between the successor republics remains strong. The national language is Kirundi, while French is also officially used.

Recent History

GREGORY MTHEMBU-SALTER

Burundi and neighbouring Rwanda to the north, unlike most African states, were not entirely artificial creations of colonial rule. At the time of their absorption into German East Africa in 1899, most of the territory that now comprises Burundi and Rwanda had already been incorporated into two kingdoms for at least a century. When, in 1916, Belgium occupied Ruanda-Urundi (as the League of Nations-mandated territory encompassing both Rwanda and Burundi was designated), it continued the system of 'indirect rule' operated by the German authorities. The policy had a strong impact, since an ethnic minority, the Tutsi (comprising 14% of the population, according to an unreliable colonial census), had by then established a complex dominance over the majority Hutu (85%, according to the same census) and a hunter-gatherer group, the Twa (1%). However, the potential for conflict between Hutu and Tutsi in Burundi was contained to an extent by the existence of the *ganwa*, a princely class whose clans comprised both ethnic groups. Relations between the ordinary Tutsi and the Hutu were more equal than they later became, and intermarriage was fairly common.

Rivalry within the *ganwa* was intense, and especially so from the mid-19th century onwards between those of the Batare and Bezi clans. The Bezi *ganwa* controlled the crown when German colonists arrived, the latter permitting the clan to retain it in return for submission to German rule. The Belgian colonial authorities continued the policy, with the result that Bezi predominated in 'native' administrative posts during the first part of Belgian rule. After the Second World War, however, relations between the Bezi *Mwami* (king) and the Belgian administration worsened due to growing Bezi demands for Burundi's national independence, while relations between the administration and the Batare *ganwa* improved. Reluctantly, but in order to meet demands imposed by a UN Trusteeship Council after 1948, the Belgian administration moved towards democratization. Two main parties came to the fore. The Union pour le Progrès National (UPRONA), led by Prince Louis Rwagasore (a Bezi *ganwa* and eldest son of the *Mwami*), was a progressive nationalist movement, with wide support. The rival Parti démocrate chrétien (PDC), dominated by Batare *ganwa*, was more conservative, seeking internal reforms to improve Batare status relative to the Bezi before independence. The Belgian administration strongly favoured the PDC. At legislative elections, held in September 1961, prior to the granting of internal self-government in January 1962, UPRONA won 58 of the 64 seats in the new Assemblée nationale. Rwagasore became Prime Minister after the elections, but was assassinated in October 1961 by a Greek agent of the PDC, reportedly with Belgian assistance. Rwagasore's assassination proved a crucial event in the subsequent history of Burundi; the absence of his unifying influence led to the division of UPRONA and, more importantly, helped foster the emergence of open conflict between Hutu and Tutsi.

MICOMBERO AND BAGAZA

UPRONA proved unable to contain the ethnic tensions that followed the attainment of independence on 1 July 1962. Stepping into the vacuum, the *Mwami*, Mwambutsa IV, played an active role in the composition of four short-lived post-independence governments between 1963 and 1965. Ethnic tensions worsened when Hutu Prime Minister Pierre Ngendandumwe was assassinated in January 1965, only one week after taking office. Hutu candidates won a decisive victory in parliamentary elections held in May, but Mwambutsa appointed a Tutsi *ganwa* as the new Prime Minister. Incensed, in October a faction of the Hutu-dominated gendarmerie attempted a coup. Tutsi armed forces retaliated by massacring almost the entire Hutu political establishment, and thousands of rural Hutu who had supported the revolt.

In July 1966 Mwambutsa was deposed by his son, who took the title of Ntare V, and appointed Capt. (later Lt-Gen.) Michel Micombero as Prime Minister. In November Ntare was removed from power by Micombero, who declared Burundi a republic and himself President. Following an abortive coup attempt by Hutu soldiers in April 1972, which degenerated into indiscriminate killings of Tutsi near the capital, the Tutsi military retaliated with massacres of unprecedented size and brutality. An estimated 100,000–200,000 Hutus were killed, and a further 200,000 fled the country, mainly to Zaire (now the Democratic Republic of the Congo—DRC), Tanzania and Rwanda. Nearly all Hutu elements were eliminated from the armed forces.

In November 1976 Col Jean-Baptiste Bagaza seized power from Micombero in a bloodless coup. Although the army remained the dominant force in Burundi's politics, Bagaza's regime made a limited attempt to increase democracy. The first legislative elections under universal adult suffrage were held in October 1982, and in August 1984 Bagaza, the sole candidate, was elected head of state, for the first time by direct suffrage.

There followed during the mid-1980s a sharp deterioration in the Government's observance of human rights. This was particularly marked in relation to religious freedom, and led Bagaza's regime into conflict with several Christian denominations. The number of political prisoners rose considerably, and many detainees were subjected to torture. The intensification of authoritarian rule strained relations with most donor countries, which sought to exert pressure on Bagaza by withholding development aid.

THE BUYOYA REGIME, 1987–93

In September 1987 Bagaza was deposed by an army-led coup instigated by his cousin, Maj. Pierre Buyoya, who accused him of corruption and formed a 31-member ruling Military Committee for National Salvation (CMSN). UPRONA was dissolved and the 1981 Constitution was suspended. Apart from its greater tolerance of religious freedom of expression, and the release of hundreds of political prisoners, the new regime did not differ much from Bagaza's, and was equally reliant on the support of a small Tutsi-Hima élite from Bururi province.

Hutu–Tutsi Tensions

In August 1988 groups of Hutu, claiming Tutsi provocation, slaughtered hundreds of Tutsi in the northern towns of Ntega and Marangara. The army then massacred an estimated 20,000 Hutus, and more than 60,000 Hutu refugees fled to neighbouring Rwanda. After initially resisting Hutu demands for an inquiry into the killings, and for political reform, in October Buyoya appointed Adrien Sibomana, a Hutu, as Prime Minister, and brought a number of other Hutus into the Government. In the same month a commission (comprising an equal number of Tutsi and Hutu) was established to investigate the massacres and to make recommendations for national reconciliation.

These reforms alarmed many Tutsis, and during the first half of 1989 there were several attempted coups by hardline Tutsi activists and Bagaza supporters. Following the publication in April of the report of the national unity commission, Buyoya announced plans to combat all forms of discrimination against Hutus, but inter-ethnic tension remained high. In November 1991 violent confrontations occurred in Bujumbura and the north of the country, resulting in large numbers of casualties. In April 1992 there were further violent disturbances along the border with Rwanda, blamed by the Government on the Parti de Libération du Peuple Hutu (PALIPEHUTU), which, the authorities claimed, had been trained and armed in Rwanda.

Constitutional Transition

In April 1990 the national unity commission produced a draft charter, which was submitted to extensive national debate. Public discussion, however, was closely directed and monitored by the re-established UPRONA, and failed to satisfy opposition groups. Political tensions were renewed in August, when the exiled leader of PALIPEHUTU died in prison in Tanzania, and the leader of a smaller dissident group was killed in a motor accident in Rwanda. Opponents of UPRONA alleged that Buyoya's agents had assassinated both men.

UPRONA dissolved the CMSN in December 1990, and transferred its functions to an 80-member central committee of UPRONA, with a Hutu, Nicolas Mayugi, as its Secretary-General. The draft charter on national unity, overwhelmingly approved in a referendum in February 1991, was rejected by PALIPEHUTU and other exiled opposition groups. A government reorganization later that month, in which Hutus were appointed to 12 of the 23 ministerial portfolios, was viewed with scepticism by political opponents. In March a commission was established to prepare a report on the 'democratization' of national institutions and political structures, in preparation for the drafting of a new constitution. Among the recommendations of the report, presented by Buyoya in September, were: an increase in parliamentary powers; the introduction of a once-renewable five-year presidential mandate; proportional representation; press freedom; guarantees of human rights; and a system of 'controlled multi-partyism' whereby political groupings seeking legal recognition would be required to comply with certain requirements, including ethnic, regional and religious 'impartiality'.

A referendum held in March 1992 resulted in a vote of 90% in support of the proposed new Constitution, which was promulgated on 13 March. Buyoya legalized multi-partyism in April, and by October eight political parties had received legal recognition. Among them was the Front pour la Démocratie au Burundi (FRODEBU), established by Hutu former political exiles, which rapidly gained prominence, often with the support of PALIPEHUTU activists. In the presidential poll, conducted on 1 June, Melchior Ndadaye, the FRODEBU candidate, secured victory with 64.8% of votes cast, supported by the Rassemblement du Peuple Burundien (RPB), the Parti du Peuple (PP) and the Parti Libéral (PL). Buyoya, the UPRONA candidate, received only 32.4% of the votes, with support from the Rassemblement pour la Démocratie et le Développement Économique et social (RADDES) and the Parti Social Démocrate (PSD). Elections for 81 seats in the new legislature were held on 29 June. FRODEBU won the largest share of votes cast (71%), and 65 of the 81 seats in the new legislature. UPRONA, with 21.4% of the votes, secured the remaining 16 seats. The Parti de Réconciliation du Peuple (PRP), the PP, the RADDES and the RPB all failed to attract the minimum 5% of votes needed for representation in the legislature. Ndadaye assumed the presidency on 10 July, becoming Burundi's first ever Hutu head of state. A new 23-member Council of Ministers was subsequently announced; the new Prime Minister, Sylvie Kinigi, was one of seven newly appointed Tutsis.

NDADAYE, NTARYAMIRA AND THE RESURGENCE OF ETHNIC UNREST

Ndadaye's Government immediately began bringing FRODEBU supporters into the civil service and drafted plans for extensive reform of the armed forces. The plans alarmed a number of senior UPRONA members and some military commanders, and on 21 October 1993 more than 100 army paratroopers occupied the presidential palace and the headquarters of the national broadcasting company. The insurgents detained and killed a number of prominent Hutu politicians and officials, including President Ndadaye and the parliamentary Speaker, Giles Bimazubute; François Ngeze, one of the only senior Hutu members of UPRONA, and a minister in the Government of former President Buyoya, was later proclaimed as head of a National Committee for Public Salvation (CPSN). However, immediate and unanimous international condemnation of the coup, together with the scale and ferocity of renewed inter-ethnic massacres, undermined support for the insurgents from within the armed forces, and precipitated the collapse of the CPSN, which was disbanded on 25 October. On 28 October the FRODEBU Government regained control of the country. Ngeze and 10 coup leaders were arrested, although at least 40 other insurgents had fled. In December a commission of judicial inquiry was created to investigate the insurgency.

In January 1994 FRODEBU deputies in the Assemblée nationale approved a draft amendment to the Constitution, enabling the republican President to be elected by the Assemblée nationale. After intense inter-party negotiations, the Assemblée nationale elected the former Minister of Agriculture, Cyprien Ntaryamira, as President. Ntaryamira assumed office on 5 February. Anatole Kanyenkiko of UPRONA was appointed Prime Minister, while the composition of a new multi-party Council of Ministers was finally agreed in mid-February.

Following repeated requests by the Government for an international force to protect its ministers, in November 1993 the Organization of African Unity (OAU, now the African Union—AU) agreed to the deployment of a protection force of 180 military personnel.

On 11 February 1994 an international commission of inquiry, established by a number of human-rights organizations, concluded that the majority of members of the armed forces were involved in or had supported the October coup attempt. In March, responding to Tutsi opposition to the deployment of a foreign military force, the Government convinced the OAU to reduce the strength of the mooted Mission d'Observation au Burundi (MIOB) from 180 to only 47 officers. (MIOB was finally deployed in Burundi in February 1995.) Clashes between the armed forces and Hutu militia worsened divisions between FRODEBU's moderate faction, led by Ntaryamira (who supported the forced disarmament of both Hutu and Tutsi militia groups), and Léonard Nyangoma's hardline faction, which opposed further military action against Hutu militias.

POLITICAL MANOEUVRES AND COALITION GOVERNMENT

On 6 April 1994, returning from a regional summit meeting in Dar es Salaam, Tanzania, Ntaryamira was killed (together with two government ministers), when the aircraft of Rwandan President Juvénal Habyarimana, in which the Burundi delegation was travelling, was brought down by a rocket attack above Kigali airport, and crashed on landing. (Habyarimana, who was also killed in the crash, was widely acknowledged to have been the intended victim of the attack.) Sylvestre Ntibantunganya was confirmedas interim national President on 8 April for a three-month period, after which a presidential election was to be held.

In May 1994 Nyangoma was dismissed from the Government, and almost immediately established a new party, the Conseil National pour la Défense de la Démocratie (CNDD), with an armed wing called the Forces pour la Défense de la Démocratie (FDD), with the aim of restoring by force the power FRODEBU had won in the 1993 elections. During May 1994 UPRONA elected as its new leader a Hutu, Charles Mukasi, who was radically opposed to Hutu political parties, particularly FRODEBU, which he accused of perpetrating genocide. In the same month former President Bagaza resumed political activity, at the head of a new party, the Parti pour le Redressement National.

Having discounted the possibility of organizing a general election, owing to security concerns, in June 1994 the major political parties engaged in lengthy negotiations, with UN mediation, to establish a procedure for the restoration of an elected presidency; a new power-sharing agreement was announced on 10 September. This 'Convention of Government', which detailed the terms of government for a four-year transitional period (including the allocation of nearly one-half of cabinet posts to opposition parties), was incorporated into the Constitution on 22 September. The Convention also provided for the creation of a National Security Council (formally inaugurated on 10 October) to address the security crisis. On 30 September the Convention elected Ntibantunganya to the presidency and he was formally inaugurated on 1 October. Anatole Kanyenkiko was reappointed as Prime Minister on 3 October, and two days later a coalition Government was formed.

In February 1995 Kanyenkiko was forced out of UPRONA for having failed to support the party's earlier temporary withdrawal from Government in protest at the appointment of FRODEBU's Jean Minani to the post of Speaker of the Assemblée nationale. Many UPRONA members alleged that Minani had incited genocide against Tutsis in 1993. Kanyenkiko was replaced as Prime Minister on 1 March 1995 by Antoine Nduwayo, a UPRONA candidate selected in consultation with other Tutsi opposition parties, amid allegations of extremist Tutsi militia intimidation. Meanwhile, ethnic tension persisted in the second half of 1994, exacerbated first by the scale and proximity of the violence in Rwanda, and then by the arrival in the country of an estimated 200,000 Rwandan Hutu refugees fleeing the advancing Front Patriotique Rwandais (FPR).

ETHNIC CONFRONTATION

In late 1995, as atrocities perpetrated against both Hutu and Tutsi civilians by the armed forces continued, the UN Secretary-General, Boutros Boutros-Ghali, requested that the Security Council authorize international military intervention. No action was taken, however. In February 1996 Boutros-Ghali asked the Council again, following publication of a UN report on human rights, which concluded that a state of near civil war existed in many areas of the country. Yet the Government (and Tutsi political opinion) remained fiercely opposed to a foreign military presence, and persuaded the UN Security Council that a negotiated settlement to the conflict was still attainable. Reports delivered by representatives of the US Agency for International Development and the Humanitarian Office of the European Union (EU), following an official visit undertaken in April, expressed doubts that effective power-sharing could be achieved within the terms of the 1994 Convention of Government, particularly under the leadership of a powerful Tutsi premier. The USA and the EU announced the immediate suspension of aid.

At a conference of regional heads of state in Arusha, Tanzania, in late June 1996, Nduwayo made a startling concession, when both he and Ntibantunganya (following strong pressure from former Tanzanian President Julius Nyerere) requested international troop deployment in Burundi. However, fundamental differences of interpretation regarding the purpose and mandate of the intervention force swiftly emerged between Ntibantunganya and Nduwayo, with the latter accusing the President of attempting to neutralize the country's military capability. At a mass rally of Tutsi-dominated opposition parties, organized in the capital on 5 July, Nduwayo joined other political leaders in rejecting foreign military intervention and denouncing Ntibantunganya. Some days later, however, full endorsement of the Arusha proposal for intervention was recorded by OAU member states at a summit meeting convened in Yaoundé, Cameroon.

Tensions intensified still further when reports emerged of a massacre of more than 300 Tutsi civilians at Bugendana, allegedly committed by Hutu militia, including heavily armed Rwandan Hutu refugees. FRODEBU made an urgent appeal for foreign military intervention to contain the increasingly violent civil and military reaction to these events, while Bagaza urged (Tutsi) civil resistance to foreign intervention. On 23 July 1996 Ntibantunganya was forced to abandon an attempt to attend the funeral of the victims of the Bugendana massacre, following attacks on the presidential helicopter by rioting mourners. On the following day he fled from the presidential office, seeking refuge in the US embassy. Several government ministers and the Speaker of the Assemblée nationale withdrew to the German embassy compound, and Minani fled the country.

THE RETURN OF BUYOYA

With the FRODEBU members of government in hiding, the armed forces seized power on 25 July 1996, subsequently declaring Buyoya as the interim President of a 'transitional' republic. Ntibantunganya refused to relinquish office, but Nduwayo immediately resigned.

Buyoya announced that a largely civilian, broadly based government of national unity would be promptly installed, and that future negotiations with all Hutu groups would be considered. Echoing his political strategy of the early 1990s, Buyoya appointed Pascal-Firmin Ndimira, a Hutu member of UPRONA, as Prime Minister, but failed to secure support for the Government from the rest of the region. A summit of regional heads of state, convened in Arusha on 31 July 1996, declared its intention to impose severe economic sanctions against the new regime, failing the immediate restoration of constitutional government. Western countries distanced themselves from this initiative. In early August Buyoya appointed a new multi-ethnic Council of Ministers and, shortly afterwards, an expanded transitional Assemblée nationale, incorporating existing elected deputies but with more limited powers, which he said would operate for a three-year period. Party political activity remained banned.

In the months following August 1996, conflict in eastern Zaire temporarily disrupted FDD operations in the area, and prompted the repatriation of at least 30,000 Burundians. Most militia fighters crossed into Tanzania, from where they staged frequent incursions into Burundi's southern provinces. The conflict weakened the impact of regional sanctions, enabling

Burundian exports to be transported via Uvira and Bukavu in the DRC's Sud-Kivu province, and a limited amount of imports from East Africa to reach Burundi.

In August 1996 Buyoya met Nyerere in Tanzania, and tried, unsuccessfully, to persuade him to suspend sanctions. In the following month the Regional Sanctions Co-ordinating Committee (RSCC) held its first meeting, at which it agreed to ease restrictions on the importation of emergency relief supplies; however, it emphasized that economic sanctions would remain in force until the Assemblée nationale was restored, political parties legalized and unconditional negotiations opened with Hutu militias, including the FDD.

On 12 September 1996 some powers of the Assemblée nationale were restored, excluding its authority to dismiss the Government, and exiled members of parliament were invited to return to the country. This earned Buyoya an invitation to a meeting of regional heads of state, though with the status of factional leader rather than as Burundi's President. Neither Buyoya nor Nyangoma, who was also approached by the RSCC, attended the meeting, at which the RSCC set a deadline of 31 October for the commencement of negotiations between the Government and Hutu militias. Buyoya subsequently rejected the deadline, stating that he would not start talks until economic sanctions were eased. The RSCC did ease sanctions slightly, granting further exemptions for aid agencies in October. In December there were more discussions in Arusha, at which Nyerere unsuccessfully sought to bring together the Government, FRODEBU, the CNDD and UPRONA. A meeting of regional heads of state also took place, at which it was agreed to retain economic sanctions, pending the opening of negotiations by the contending forces.

At a further meeting of regional heads of state in April 1997 at Arusha, Buyoya was invited to attend as President, and the heads of state agreed to permit the import to Burundi of most goods except fuel, which remained at the discretion of the aid agencies. However, the export of goods through countries participating in the sanctions programme remained officially prohibited.

Armed incursions by Hutu militias from refugee camps in Tanzania increased tensions in border regions, and in September and October 1997 there was sporadic fighting between Tanzanian and Burundian troops. The Burundian Government accused the Tanzanian authorities of complicity in the militia attacks. The Tanzanian Government denied this claim, retorting that Burundi was attempting to deflect international opinion from the internal nature of the conflict. At a meeting of regional foreign ministers, held in Kampala, Uganda, in August 1997, it was decided to maintain the export embargo on Burundi, despite vigorous appeals from the Burundian Government, which subsequently withdrew from all-party talks, organized by Nyerere, which took place in Arusha later that month.

By the end of 1997 national courts had imposed 220 death sentences on Hutus found guilty of committing genocide in 1993. The trial of the Tutsis accused of involvement in the 1993 coup attempt, and of assassinating President Ndadaye and six others, however, was subject to repeated adjournments, and verdicts were not delivered until May 1999. Five members of the armed forces were sentenced to death and a number of others received prison terms; however, Hutu political parties complained that all the senior officers implicated in the coup attempt were acquitted. In January 1998 the Minister of National Defence, Firmin Sinzoyiheba, was killed in a helicopter crash; he was replaced by Alfred Nkurunziza, Buyoya's chief military adviser.

On 21 February 1998 a meeting of regional heads of state in Kampala again opted to maintain sanctions. Meanwhile, tensions on the border with Tanzania began to ease, and on 12 March formal tripartite discussions were held between Burundi, Tanzania and the office of the UN High Commissioner for Refugees (UNHCR). The CNDD split on 8 May, leaving Nyangoma in charge of one faction (which retained the name CNDD), while the FDD Chief of Staff, Jean-Bosco Ndayikengurukiye, assumed leadership of the greater part of the party, including most of its armed forces, which became known as the CNDD—FDD.

POWER-SHARING AND A NEW TRANSITIONAL CONSTITUTION

With the imminent expiry of FRODEBU's electoral mandate, in March 1998 the Government initiated negotiations with the Assemblée nationale concerning the required course of action. FRODEBU demanded a return to the 1992 Constitution, while the Government proposed a continuation of the terms of office introduced by Buyoya after the July 1996 coup. A compromise was eventually reached, which Buyoya described as a 'new partnership' between the Government and the Assemblée nationale. The partnership exacerbated division within FRODEBU, particularly between those in the leadership in exile and those still based in Burundi, with the former insisting that the Arusha discussions were the only legitimate negotiating forum. On 6 June 1998 the transitional Constitution, which combined elements of both the 1992 Constitution and the 1996 decree adopted by Buyoya after the July coup, was promulgated. Under this Constitution, the Assemblée nationale was expanded, the size of the Council of Ministers was reduced and two vice-presidential posts were created. On 11 June 1998 Buyoya was sworn in as head of state, and two days later a new Council of Ministers was announced. Several rounds of talks in Arusha in mid-1998 achieved limited progress.

In October 1998 Charles Mukasi, an opponent of the Arusha negotiations, was replaced, allegedly by improper means, as UPRONA President by the Minister of Information and Government Spokesman, Luc Rukingama (a Buyoya loyalist). Rukingama was more enthusiastic about the Arusha process than Mukasi, and at the next round of discussions later that month, three of the planned commissions were successfully constituted. The briefs of the three commissions were to examine the nature of the conflict, democracy and good governance, and peace and security, respectively. Other commissions, once constituted, examined the rehabilitation of refugees and economic development, transitional institutions, and the guarantees for the implementation of the eventual peace agreement.

The CNDD—FDD and PALIPEHUTU continued attacks throughout 1998 and early 1999 on camps for the internally displaced, particularly prior to each round of talks in Arusha. In late 1998 the armed forces increased their involvement in the civil war in the DRC, and by May 1999 at least 3,000 troops were believed to have been deployed in the east, attempting to destroy CNDD—FDD camps. The effort largely failed. In August 1998 war broke out in the DRC, and the CNDD—FDD increased its presence there, supporting Congolese government troops in Sud-Kivu and Katanga. The DRC Government objected to the presence of Burundian troops in the DRC and in May 1999 threatened to launch a retaliatory attack on Bujumbura. The Burundi Government responded that the presence of its troops in the DRC was necessary to confront the security threat posed by CNDD—FDD forces, and that it would respond to any attack on its territory.

A fourth round of discussions was held at Arusha in January 1999, with the CNDD—FDD again absent. Regional heads of state decided at a meeting on 21–23 January to suspend the economic embargo, in the hope that this measure would strengthen the Arusha peace process. The decision was welcomed both internally and abroad, but dismissed by the CNDD—FDD as premature.

On 18 March 1999 FRODEBU Secretary-General Augustin Nzojibwami suspended former President Ntibantunganya from the party's executive committee, together with other senior members, for alleged ethnicism and ill discipline. In response, Minani ordered Nzojibwami's expulsion from the party. However, Nzojibwami refused to recognize the expulsion and by June two factions had developed within FRODEBU, centred around Minani and Nzojibwami.

Strongly encouraged by Nyerere, in early May 1999 seven predominantly Hutu parties, including the CNDD and the external wing of FRODEBU, met in Moshi, Tanzania, to negotiate a common position prior to the commissions convening in mid-May. The parties assumed a joint stance on most issues and became known as G7. The Government and the internal wing of FRODEBU condemned G7 for allegedly encouraging ethnic polarization, while Nyerere insisted that it facilitated the talks by minimizing differences between parties. In response to the formation of G7, predominantly Tutsi parties formed a negotiating bloc (known initially as G8, and later as G10). At the end of May Buyoya proposed a 10-year political transition, including plans for the establishment of an upper legislative chamber, the Sénat, and for the enlargement of the Assemblée nationale. Buyoya proposed that he rule for five years and a FRODEBU representative for the remaining five years. The proposals were rejected by all externally based political forces.

Commission meetings in Arusha resumed in early July 1999 for a fifth round, but made little progress. The negotiations ended on 17 July, with Nyerere blaming the failure to reach agreement on a political settlement on alleged government intransigence. The Government, meanwhile, stated that the talks could not succeed without the presence of the CNDD—FDD and a faction of PALIPEHUTU's armed wing, which had split from the party and was known as PALIPEHUTU—Forces Nationales de Libération (FNL), and blamed their absence on Nyerere. A sixth round of discussions at Arusha was due to commence in September, but was postponed, owing to Nyerere's ill health. Nyerere subsequently died in London, United Kingdom, on 14 October. His death resulted in the suspension of the Arusha process.

MANDELA BECOMES MEDIATOR

Buyoya visited the South African President, Thabo Mbeki, in Pretoria, South Africa, in August 1999, requesting that South Africa play an active role in the peace process. In December regional heads of state, meeting in Arusha, unanimously selected the former South African President, Nelson Mandela, as the new Burundi mediator. The appointment received international support as well as the endorsement of the Burundi Government. Mandela immediately urged Hutu militia leaders to join the peace process, and made his first official visit to Arusha in January 2000. Mandela subsequently attended a meeting at the UN Security Council, which condemned the Burundi Government's controversial regroupment policy, but resolved to encourage donors to resume substantial assistance.

When Mandela attended the seventh round of Arusha discussions in February 2000, he prompted contention among delegates by criticizing Tutsi domination of public life, urging equal representation of Hutu and Tutsi in the armed forces, and referring to Hutu rebel attacks on civilians as 'terrorism'. Mandela criticized Buyoya for his imprisonment of political opponents, and denounced regroupment, describing the camps as unfit for human habitation. Mandela met senior army commanders and the Minister of National Defence, Col Cyrille Ndayirukiye, in Johannesburg, South Africa, in mid-March and later met the leadership of the CNDD—FDD and PALIPEHUTU—FNL. The next Arusha round of negotiations, which commenced in late March, focused on the issue of army integration, despite the continued absence of these two parties.

Mandela arrived in Burundi for the first time in April 2000 for a brief visit that had been preceded by increased violence, particularly near Bujumbura. Mandela met with Buyoya in Johannesburg in early June, and subsequently announced that Buyoya had agreed to ensure equal representation of Hutu and Tutsi in the army and had guaranteed the closure of regroupment camps by the end of that month.

In early July 2000 the CNDD—FDD stated that it would for the first time attend, but not negotiate at, peace discussions under Mandela's mediation, which were to commence on 19 July. PALIPEHUTU—FNL maintained its boycott. Prior to the discussions, the mediators presented a draft peace accord, which brought together the positions previously agreed by the negotiating parties, but remained vague on main issues (including who should lead the transition, the nature of the electoral system and how to achieve a cease-fire), owing to a lack of consensus. The CNDD—FDD outlined its preconditions for a cease-fire and further talks with the Government, but Mandela's hopes that the parties might reach agreement on the key issues during the July discussions were disappointed.

THE ARUSHA AGREEMENT

Mandela announced that a further Arusha negotiating round would take place in late August 2000, and in the brief intervening period conducted intense bilateral discussions with political party leaders to persuade them to commit to signing an accord. To increase the pressure, Mandela invited heads of state, including the US President, Bill Clinton, and other senior international political figures to the August discussions. The round culminated on 28 August, with the signing of an agreement by all but three parties, with the remainder signing in September. The agreement included arrangements for a pre-transitional, and then transitional, period, which would be followed by democratic elections, the creation of a Sénat and amendments to the Assemblée nationale, judicial reform, the establishment of an international force to assist during the transition, and an independent investigation into alleged crimes of genocide. The agreement did not, however, cover the main issues listed above.

The CNDD—FDD and PALIPEHUTU—FNL rejected the Arusha accord and Ndayikengurukiye declined to attend a meeting arranged by Mandela in Nairobi, Kenya, in mid-September 2000 between the militia leadership, the Government and regional heads of state. The PALIPEHUTU—FNL leader, Kossan Kabura, was present, but refused to engage in discussions with Buyoya, talking only with the regional heads of state, who instructed his forces and the CNDD—FDD to observe a cease-fire within 30 days. South Africa's Deputy President, Jacob Zuma, subsequently took over an increasing amount of the Burundi mediation work from Mandela, who had earlier announced that, with the peace agreement signed, his involvement was largely over.

On 23 February 2001 a political committee within PALIPEHUTU—FNL announced that it had deposed Kabura from the post of party President and installed Agathon Rwasa in his place. Kabura insisted, however, that he remained the militia's President.

A further round of discussions in Arusha on 27–28 February 2001, arranged by Mandela, and with the regional heads of state once again in attendance, failed to resolve the principal remaining issues of disagreement. However, Mandela's proposal that the leadership of the transition should be shared, with a Tutsi as Head of Government in the first period and a Hutu in the second, was eventually accepted by the delegations. After the talks Buyoya stated that there would be no transition without a cease-fire, prompting accusations from some parties, including FRODEBU's external wing, that this amounted to a coup. Meanwhile, there were renewed clashes between the CNDD—FDD and Forces armées burundais in southern Burundi. Zuma met Ndayikengurukiye and the new Congolese President, Joseph Kabila, on 9 April in Kinshasa, DRC, and again, with Buyoya, in Libreville, Gabon, later that month.

On 23 July 2001 Mandela convened a regional summit meeting in Arusha to resolve the impasse in the peace process, and announced two days later that Buyoya would remain in the office of President for a period of 18 months, after which time he would be replaced by a Hutu leader for the following 18 months. In October Mandela convened a summit meeting in Pretoria on Burundi, and announced that a South African military force was to be deployed in the country to protect politicians returning from exile to participate in the forthcoming transitional Government and other transitional institutions. Ndayikengurukiye also attended a summit meeting, but hopes that this might mean a cease-fire could result were disappointed when the CNDD—FDD split after the Pretoria summit meeting, resulting in the emergence of a new faction, led by Pierre Nkurunziza, supported by nearly all CNDD—FDD combatants.

NEW TRANSITIONAL GOVERNMENT INSTALLED

The 700-member South African protection force was deployed in late October 2001, and, under the terms of the August 2000 agreement, a new 26-member transitional Government was installed on 1 November. Buyoya remained as head of state, the Secretary-General of FRODEBU, Domitien Ndayizeye, became Vice-President, and the Council of Ministers included members from all the signatory parties to the Arusha agreement but was dominated by UPRONA and FRODEBU.

The new transitional Assemblée nationale was inaugurated on 4 January 2002. In addition to 121 deputies from the previous Assemblée nationale, 57 new representatives had been nominated, most of them by parties that signed the Arusha agreement. FRODEBU was the largest party in the Assemblée, and Minani, its Chairman, was elected President (Speaker) of the Assemblée on 10 January. In early February the transitional Sénat commenced operations, with Libère Bararunyeretse, a close associate of Buyoya and a senior UPRONA negotiator in Arusha, as its President.

Peace negotiations, convened in Dar es Salaam on 12 August 2002, were boycotted once more by Rwasa, but attended for the first time by a newly emerged minority faction of PALIPEHUTU—FNL, headed by Alain Mugabarabona, as well as both CNDD—FDD factions. Nkurunziza's CNDD—FDD faction finally agreed to negotiate with the Government, rather than the armed forces, at the Dar es Salaam talks, but only on condition that the Government accepted responsibility for the military coup against Ndadaye in 1993. The government delegation refused, and the discussions were suspended. Fearing a permanent impasse, Zuma scheduled a regional summit meeting for 7 October 2002. The regional heads of state attended the discussions with the intention of imposing sanctions on the CNDD—FDD and PALIPEHUTU—FNL, but in the end granted a request by Zuma that they give the parties a further 30 days to negotiate. Also on 7 October Mugabarabona's faction of PALIPEHUTU—FNL signed a cease-fire agreement with the Government (despite uncertainty as to whether Mugabarabona actually commanded any forces), and Ndayikengurukiye's faction of the CNDD—FDD signed a memorandum of understanding, which later resulted in a cease-fire agreement. Despite this agreement, there was heavy fighting between government forces and CNDD-FDD combatants throughout the duration of the peace talks. Further discussions between the Government and Nkurunziza, beginning in Dar es Salaam on 26 October, also failed to secure a cease-fire agreement.

However, Nkurunziza and Buyoya attended a summit of regional heads of state on Burundi, which commenced in Arusha on 1 December 2002 and resulted in the signing of the long-awaited cease-fire agreement on 3 December. The agreement stipulated that a cease-fire should be in effect by the end of that month. CNDD—FDD combatants were to be assembled in camps, but not disarmed, and this was to be verified and monitored by an AU force. It was also agreed that a new national army, which would include combatants from the CNDD—FDD and other armed groups, would be established. Rukingama resigned as President of UPRONA on 7 December, and was replaced by Alphonse Kadege, also a Buyoya loyalist. Buyoya and Nkurunziza met in Pretoria on 27 January 2003 to discuss the implementation of the cease-fire agreement, and agreed that CNDD—FDD combatants should assemble in camps in Bubanza and Ruyigi provinces. This agreement immediately worsened the conflict in both provinces, however, as the CNDD—FDD intensified its efforts to capture territory and the armed forces fought to retain it. Regional heads of state, Buyoya and the CNDD—FDD's Secretary-General, Hassan Rajabu, met in Dar es Salaam on 1 March. Both Buyoya and Rajabu reiterated their commitment to the cease-fire agreement, but on the ground the conflict between their forces continued unabated.

NDAYIZEYE SECURES AGREEMENT WITH THE CNDD—FDD

Buyoya failed to persuade the South African Government that he should remain as head of state until the cease-fire was in place, and on 28 March 2003 announced that he would transfer the presidency to Ndayizeye when his 18-month period of office expired at the end of April. On 30 April Ndayizeye became President for the scheduled 18 months, and Kadege became Vice-President. Contingents of the AU force, known as the African Mission in Burundi (AMIB), commenced deployment in that month. (Meanwhile, in April the legislature adopted a bill providing for the establishment of an international judicial commission of inquiry into war crimes committed since mid-1962.) Ndayizeye announced his first, largely unchanged, Government in May.

Ndayizeye and Nkurunziza finally signed a power-sharing agreement in Pretoria on 8 October 2003. The CNDD—FDD agreed to abandon hostilities and order its combatants to assemble in camps, in return for substantial representation in the Government and the armed forces. By that time AMIB had reached its maximum authorized strength of 3,128 troops (of which South Africa contributed 1,629, and the remainder were contributed by Mozambique and Ethiopia).

Ndayizeye and Nkurunziza returned to Pretoria in late October 2003, where the CNDD—FDD secured a key concession: a government promise of immunity from prosecution for its combatants, which was also extended to members of the armed forces. The granting of immunity for crimes against humanity was denounced by Tutsi parties and also by some international human rights groups. Nkurunziza's CNDD—FDD officially ended hostilities on 10 November, and fighting ceased soon after throughout most of the country, with the exception of Bujumbura Rural and Cibitoke provinces, where PALIPEHUTU—FNL forces remained active. On 16 November the peace agreement was formally signed at a summit of regional heads of state in Dar es Salaam, and on 23 November Ndayizeye announced the establishment of a new Government of national unity, incorporating CNDD—FDD representatives. Nkurunziza was appointed to the newly created post of Minister of State for Good Governance and State Inspection.

Despite the terms of the peace agreement requiring CNDD—FDD combatants to assemble in camps in preparation for disarmament, many began instead to participate in joint operations with members of the armed forces against PALIPEHUTU—FNL in Bujumbura Rural and Cibitoke. On 29 December 2003 PALIPEHUTU—FNL forces ambushed and killed the papal envoy in Burundi, attracting widespread international condemnation. Clashes were also reported in Bururi province between supporters of Nkurunziza and those loyal to Léonard Nyangoma.

In January 2004 Ndayizeye appointed a new Joint Military High Command, comprising 21 members selected from the armed forces and 13 from Nkurunziza's faction of the CNDD—FDD. Ndayizeye announced that this measure would be followed by the establishment of a new and reconstituted armed forces, the Forces de défense nationales (FDN). In subsequent months heavy fighting between PALIPEHUTU—FNL and the CNDD—FDD, allied with members of the armed forces, caused the displacement of some 50,000 civilians.

HUTU AND TUTSI REPRESENTATION IN GOVERNMENT

During February and March 2004 Ndayizeye failed to secure agreement with members of parties represented in the Government on key unresolved issues, including the contents of a new draft constitution and electoral code. Amid additional concern about the ongoing civil war, he supported a postponement in elections. In April Nkurunziza withdrew the CNDD—FDD from the Government until July, alleging that Ndayizeye was not respecting the power-sharing accord. Nevertheless, in May Ndayizeye presented a new draft electoral timetable, postponing for a year the presidential poll, which was originally due to be held by the end of October. FRODEBU and the CNDD—FDD rejected the proposed extension, which was, however, supported by predominantly Tutsi parties. After a meeting of political parties, convened by Zuma in Pretoria, failed to reach agreement on the issue, a summit of regional heads of state in Dar es Salaam on 5–6 June ruled that elections must proceed according to the original schedule. Despite renewed contact between PALIPEHUTU—FNL and Zuma just before the summit, the heads of state condemned the militia for remaining outside the peace process and imposed sanctions on its leadership.

Six months after Zuma made the initial request, on 21 May 2004 the UN Security Council approved the replacement of the AMIB mission with the Opération des Nations Unies au Burundi (ONUB), which officially commenced deployment on 1 June for an initial six-month period.

Following prolonged discussions during July 2004, a draft power-sharing accord specifying 60% Hutu and 40% Tutsi representation in the Government and Assemblée nationale was signed on 6 August by the main Hutu parties, but was rejected by predominantly Tutsi parties, which objected to a definition of representation in ethnic, rather than party political, terms. Hutu parties refused to compromise and were supported by the increasingly impatient South African Government and the regional heads of state. On 13 August PALIPEHUTU—FNL, allegedly with the support of Rwandan Hutu militia and elements within the Congolese armed forces, massacred 152 Congolese Banyamulenge refugees at the Gatumba refugee camp near Bujumbura. A subsequent UN report stated that there was insufficient evidence to establish with certainty who had perpetrated the killings, although a report by Human Rights Watch unequivocally attributed responsibility to PALIPEHUTU—FNL. The Gatumba massacre took place despite a significant presence of members of the armed forces nearby. The impact of the massacre reverberated across the region, with one faction of the DRC Government temporarily suspending its participation in the political transition and the Rwandan Government threatening to reinvade the DRC if the perpetrators were not penalized. Many of the Banyamulenge refugees in Bujumburu subsequently fled to refugee camps in Rwanda. A five-member independent electoral commission was established at the end of August. In continuing protests against the agreement signed in Pretoria, Tutsi parties boycotted government meetings throughout September. Undeterred, remaining Hutu party ministers approved a new draft Constitution incorporating the Pretoria accord, which was to be submitted to a referendum and adopted prior to national elections.

On 15–17 September 2004 Ndayizeye called an extraordinary joint session of the Assemblée nationale and the Sénat to ratify the draft Constitution. With delegates from Tutsi parties absent, Hutu delegates approved the constitutional text. However, the Constitutional Court declined to conduct a scheduled hearing to endorse the text, later declaring that its role was to interpret the Constitution, not rule on its legality. Insisting that this implied the Court's endorsement of the text, Ndayizeye announced that a referendum would be conducted on 20 October, which was later rescheduled for 26 November. Since the interim Constitution was, however, due to expire on 1 November, the regional heads of state ruled that the disputed draft Constitution approved by the Sénat and Assemblée nationale replace it on this date. The regional heads of state further ruled that Ndayizeye's mandate, which was also due to expire at this time, be extended until 22 April 2005, which became the rescheduled date for national elections.

NKURUNZIZA AND THE CNDD—FDD'S ELECTORAL TRIUMPH

On 31 October 2004 the transitional Government's mandate was extended for a further six months, and the new Constitution came into effect. In mid-November Ndayizeye dismissed the Vice-President, Alphonse Kadege, owing to his alleged obstruction of government policy, and replaced him with another Tutsi member of UPRONA, Frédéric Ngenzebuhoro. The referendum did not take place as scheduled on 26 November, and the next deadline in mid-December was also missed, with the electoral commission each time citing technical constraints. The long-awaited national military demobilization programme began on 2 December; about 55,000 combatants from Hutu militia and the mainly Tutsi existing armed forces were to be demobilized under the process within five years, leaving around 30,000 combatants to form the new FDN, which was formally established on 31 December.

The referendum finally took place on 28 February 2005, with the results indicating that 90.1% of voters had endorsed the new Constitution. Despite allegations of fraud and electoral malpractice, the overall consensus of local and national observers was that the vote was generally free and fair. Ndayizeye signed the Constitution into law on 19 March, thereby enabling legislative elections to proceed. PALIPEHUTU—FNL observed a truce during the referendum period, and a meeting between its leadership and the Tanzanian President, Benjamin Mkapa, in early April resulted in a declaration from the militia that it was prepared to negotiate with the Government and would end fighting when talks began. The militia further undertook not to disrupt the electoral process. The next pre-election stage in the transitional process was for the legislature to agree on an electoral code. This took until late April, when the transitional period was scheduled to end. Regional heads of state were consequently obliged, at a meeting in Kampala, to extend the transitional period once again, until 26 August. According to this schedule, there were to be local elections in June, legislative elections in July, and subsequently, on 19 August, the new Assemblée nationale and Sénat members were to elect a new President, who was to be inaugurated one week later.

In June 2005 the Government approved a UN proposal for the establishment of a truth and reconciliation commission to investigate crimes perpetrated during the conflict from 1993. Elections to a reduced, 100-seat Assemblée nationale took place on 4 July 2005, and were judged 'reasonably free and fair' by international observers. The results showed the CNDD—FDD had won 59 seats, FRODEBU 25 and UPRONA 10. A further 18 deputies were subsequently nominated in accordance with the constitutional requirements of balance of ethnic representation (60% Hutu and 40% Tutsi) and a minimum 30% representation of women, with the result that representatives from the Twa ethnic group were allocated three seats, while the CNDD—FDD, FRODEBU and UPRONA each received five additional seats, leaving the CNDD—FDD with an absolute majority in the Assemblée of 13. Communal councillors participated in Sénat elections on 29 July. The CNDD—FDD won 30 of the 34 contested seats, and FRODEBU the remaining four. Four former Presidents were subsequently allocated seats, and Twa representatives were designated three seats. Eight further senators were later added in order to achieve the constitutionally stipulated minimum representation of women; the four political parties with the highest votes each nominated two women to the additional seats. Nkurunziza resigned as President of the CNDD—FDD on 28 July (he was replaced by the party's former Secretary-General, Hussein Radjabu) and officially presented himself as the party's presidential candidate. On 19 August a joint session of the Assemblée nationale and the Sénat elected Nkurunziza as President. Nkurunziza was the only candidate, and won more than 81.5% of votes cast. On 26 August Nkurunziza was sworn in as President in Bujumbura.

THE BEGINNING OF CNDD—FDD RULE

Nkurunziza appointed a 20-member Council of Ministers on 30 August 2005, including Martin Nduwimana of UPRONA as First Vice-President, and the Tutsi former Chief of Staff, Maj. Germain Niyoyanka, as Minister of National Defence. The establishment of the new Government was warmly welcomed by the international community, but denounced by PALIPEHUTU—FNL as illegitimate. PALIPEHUTU—FNL increased its military campaign after Nkurunziza's election, leading the new President, in October, to intensify the counter-insurgency against it. This resulted in a worsening of human rights abuses by both sides.

In January 2006 Nkurunziza made new appointments to senior civil service and parastatal positions, almost all of which were awarded to CNDD—FDD supporters. Frustrated by the party's weak representation in the new Government and angered at alleged human rights abuses, in mid-March FRODEBU President Léonce Ngendekumana ordered its representatives to withdraw from the Government. The ministers in question, however, refused to do so, and the strategy was denounced by Ngendekumana's rival in the party, Jean Minani. Raising international concerns about the stability of the administration, on 7 March Nkurunziza announced that senior members of the armed and security forces had planned a coup attempt against him. No arrests were made, however, and the allegations were dismissed as scaremongering by opposition parties. In his first ministerial reorganization on 17 March, Nkurunziza removed two CNDD—FDD ministers for alleged corruption and mismanagement.

Rwasa announced in Dar es Salaam in mid-March 2006 that PALIPEHUTU—FNL would accept unconditional negotiations with the Government to end hostilities. The Government responded positively a few days later. In mid-May, following a request from Nkurunziza that South Africa assist in the negotiations, Mbeki appointed the South African Minister of Safety and Security, Charles Nqakula, as mediator. (Zuma, who had mediated in previous discussions, had been dismissed from the South African Government in 2005, after being charged with corruption.)

In August 2006 the security forces arrested several prominent opposition politicians, including Ndayizeye and Kadege, on suspicion of involvement in the alleged coup plot announced by the Government in March. Despite protests from donors and human rights organizations that those detained be charged or released, they remained in detention without charge throughout September and October. On 5 September Second Vice-President Alice Nzomukunda of the CNDD—FDD resigned her post, citing as her reason the allegedly divisive role played in the Government by Radjabu. A week later Nzomukunda was replaced by Marina Barampana, a close ally of Radjabu.

Following further talks between the Government and PALIPEHUTU—FNL, on 7 September 2006 the two parties signed a cease-fire agreement despite having failed to resolve several key issues, including the future composition of the Government and the armed forces. A month later, in Bujumbura, Nqakula formally inaugurated a cease-fire verification commission, but this was boycotted by PALIPEHUTU—FNL, which demanded the release of its leaders from detention before it would agree to cease hostilities.

THE RULING PARTY SPLITS

The trial of Ndayizeye, Kadege and others charged with involvement in the coup plot began on 24 November 2006 but was immediately adjourned, resuming in late December. The prosecution alleged that the accused were part of a regional plot to overthrow the Government, also apparently involving the General Chief of Staff of the Rwandan armed forces Gen. James Kabarebe, Salim Saleh (the half-brother of Ugandan President Gen. (retd) Yoweri Kaguta Museveni), former Burundian President Buyoya and renegade Congolese General Laurent Nkunda. On 15 January 2007 the Constitutional Court acquitted Ndayizeye and Kadege, citing a lack of evidence.

One week after the Constitutional Court decision, Radjabu took temporary refuge in the South African embassy in Bujumbura, stating that he feared for his life. On 7 February 2007 in Ngozi there followed an extraordinary congress of the CNDD—FDD, convened by Nkurunziza but boycotted by Radjabu and his supporters, at which Radjabu was replaced as party Chairman by Col Jérémie Ngendakumana (formerly Burundi's ambassador to Kenya and viewed as a loyal supporter of Nkurunziza). Radjabu denounced the congress as illegal, but in early April the Supreme Court ruled against an annulment of the decision. Shortly after the CNDD—FDD congress, meanwhile, Nkurunziza dismissed Barampana for alleged insubordination; she was subsequently arrested and charged with fraud. Nkurunziza then dismissed other Radjabu supporters from prominent positions in the Government, including First Vice-President Yolande Nzikoruriho, who was replaced by Anatole Manirakiza, a Nkurunziza loyalist. On 27 April the Assemblée nationale voted to strip Radjabu of his immunity from prosecution, and he was immediately arrested and detained. Meanwhile, in mid-February the Government released several PALIPEHUTU—FNL leaders from detention. However, on 23 July PALIPEHUTU—FNL withdrew from the cease-fire agreement, citing security concerns.

The President's purge of Rajabu's supporters resulted in a bloc of 22 CNDD—FDD members of the Assemblée nationale withdrawing support for the Government, ending its parliamentary majority. In a bid to restore his majority, Nkurunziza formed a new Government on 13 July 2007, incorporating more FRODEBU and UPRONA ministers than previously, and including two erstwhile Rajabu supporters. The gesture proved insufficient, with neither party, nor Rajabu's faction, supporting the Government in parliament. Government legislation thus remained blocked in the Assemblée nationale, and as political tensions rose, a number of opposition members reported attacks on their residences. Meanwhile, on 27 September Nkurunziza agreed to give FRODEBU candidates five posts in a new administration. He concluded a similar agreement with UPRONA, resulting in the formation of a fragile new coalition administration in November. In December the Assemblée held a highly critical debate on the Government's negotiation strategy with PALIPEHUTU—FNL, in which members agreed to establish their own committee to improve it. Nqakula was also widely denounced as an obstacle to a settlement. Nkurunziza later rejected the Assemblée nationale's decision, claiming that it was beyond parliament's remit.

FRODEBU and UPRONA withdrew their parliamentary support for the Government in February 2008, in protest at Nkurunziza's removal of Nzomukunda from her position as First Vice-President of the Assemblée nationale. At the end of February 46 members of the Assemblée nationale wrote to the UN Secretary-General, Ban Ki-moon, alleging that they were under threat and requesting UN protection.

On 4 April 2008 the Supreme Court convicted Rajabu of plotting against the state and sentenced him to 13 years' imprisonment. Five others accused of the same offence received shorter sentences, including the former Minister of Planning, Jean Bigirimana. Fighting intensified between government forces and PALIPEHUTU—FNL in that month, resulting in hundreds of civilian casualties. On 4 May the Ugandan and Tanzanian ministers responsible for foreign affairs demanded that PALIPEHUTU—FNL end the military offensive within 10 days, and its leadership return to Bujumbura, or face expulsion from Dar es Salaam. Accordingly, although fighting between the FDN and PALIPEHUTU—FNL subsequently continued, in late May the militia leadership, including Rwasa, returned to Bujumbura, raising hopes that an end to the civil war was close. The regroupment of PALIPEHUTU—FNL's combatants began in June, but was soon suspended, in protest at the Government's refusal to allow the militia first to be allowed to register as a political party, and to receive government and military posts.

In June 2008 the Constitutional Court controversially supported a petition from Nkurunziza, who had requested that the 22 Assemblée nationale CNDD—FDD members who supported Radjabu and had been voting against the Government be expelled from the legislature. Immediately afterwards all 22 were replaced by Nkurunziza loyalists, despite claims by opposition parties that their replacement was illegal and unconstitutional. Following strong pressure from regional heads of state, PALIPEHUTU—FNL resumed participation in the regroupment programme in late July, its demands still unmet. At the end of the month the Supreme Court postponed indefinitely Radjabu's appeal against his sentence, prompting concerns about an apparent erosion of judicial independence.

Alexis Sinduhije, founder of Radio Publique Africaine, a private radio station, and latterly the founder of the Mouvement pour la sécurité et la démocratie (MSD), was arrested along with 37 other party members in early November 2008, accused of holding illegal political meetings. Sinduhije had stated his intention to contest the presidency in 2010, but the authorities refused to register his party, claiming that it was illegal to have the word 'security' in the party name. Sinduhije appeared in court in mid-November 2008 to hear the charges and was then returned to detention, leading to widespread protest from the international community; Sinduhije was acquitted in March 2009 and released.

In December 2008 Rwasa agreed at a regional summit to change PALIPEHUTU—FNL's name to the FNL, thereby meeting a government demand that it remove all ethnic reference from its name before being allowed to register as a political party. The name change was effected in January 2009. Rwasa symbolically surrendered his weapons at a special ceremony in Bubanza on 18 April, marking the start of the demobilization of FNL combatants. The FNL and the Government had earlier agreed that 3,500 FNL combatants would, during the first half of 2009, be integrated into the national army and police force, a further 5,000 would be demobilized, and another 12,500 people (later reduced to 10,500) claimed by the FNL as combatants but whose status has been contested by the Government would be sent back to civilian life with a small cash payment. The FNL was formally registered as a political party on 21 April.

TOWARDS THE 2010 ELECTIONS

The electoral commission was appointed on 9 April 2009, comprising two civil society activists and three political appointees from the CNDD—FDD, FRODEBU and UPRONA. Earlier attempts by Nkurunziza to form the commission exclusively of his own supporters had been rejected by the Assemblée nationale. In a move that generated considerable international coverage, Nkurunziza approved legislation in late April that banned the death penalty; an earlier version of the law had been rejected by the Sénat, despite being overwhelmingly approved by the Assemblée nationale.

The South African National Defence Force (SANDF) formally ended its mission to Burundi on 31 May 2009. A total of 1,100 SANDF troops subsequently returned to South Africa, while 100 remained in Burundi to provide protection for FNL politicians. In early June the Government announced that it would appoint 24 senior FNL members to government posts, although these did not include cabinet and armed force command positions, as the FNL had previously demanded. Among the appointments, Rwasa was made Director of the Institut national de sécurité sociale. The Government, in addition, released 385 FNL prisoners.

In late August 2009 Rwasa expelled several senior FNL members, including its spokesperson, Pasteur Habimana, and Jacques Kenese, the party's head of foreign relations, accusing them of disloyalty. Kenese and Habimana subsequently obtained government permission to hold a congress for the FNL in Bujumbura, which deposed Rwasa as leader and replaced him with Kenese. Rwasa, however, rejected the legality of the congress, claiming that it was an attempt by the ruling party to weaken the FNL.

The Assemblée nationale approved a new electoral code on 11 September 2009, several months later than had originally been planned, thereby paving the way for national elections to be held the following year. The code had been the subject of intense political debate, particularly regarding the form ballot papers would take, and the sequencing of the presidential, local and national legislative polls, with the CNDD—FDD's view ultimately prevailing concerning both matters. The electoral timetable was finally released on 18 December, announcing voter registration in January 2010, local elections in May, the presidential poll in June, and elections to the Assemblée nationale and Sénat in July.

On 26 December 2009 the Government formally requested the replacement of the UN Secretary-General's Special Representative in the country, Youssef Mahmoud, accusing him of inappropriately close relations with opposition parties. Mahmoud was replaced in March 2010 by Charles Petrie, who himself resigned in October. Meanwhile, accusations multiplied within Burundi that the youth wing of the CNDD—FDD, named Imbonerakure, and that of the FNL, named Ivyuma—FNL, were becoming increasingly militarized, with the former being suspected by many of receiving weapons from the national armed forces.

In late December 2009 a report was released by a UN panel of experts on the DRC which claimed that the Government was allowing the Forces Démocratiques pour la Libération du Rwanda (FDLR), a militia opposed to the Rwandan Government, to use Burundian territory as a base and to recruit new combatants. The panel's report further alleged that gold mined in eastern DRC and taxed by the FDLR was entering Burundi in large quantities, purchased by a dealer close to Gen. Adolphe Nshimirimana, the Director-General of national intelligence. The Government angrily denied all the allegations.

Voter registration went ahead as planned in January 2010, amid opposition party allegations that the CNDD—FDD had illegally distributed national identity documents to thousands of people who either possessed the documents already or were ineligible to receive them, thereby enabling them to register and subsequently, the opposition claimed, vote for the ruling party. The FNL selected Rwasa as its presidential candidate in that month, while FRODEBU chose Ndayizeye. Nkurunziza was elected as the presidential candidate by the CNDD—FDD at a special congress in late April. Earlier, despite strong opposition from the FNL, the Ministry of the Interior allowed Kenese's FNL faction to register as a party, to be named FNL iragi rya Gahutu.

Communal elections were held on 24 May 2010, resulting in a triumph for the CNDD—FDD, which secured 64% of the vote. The FNL came second, with 14%, UPRONA third, with 6%, and FRODEBU fourth, with 5%. All political parties except the CNDD—FDD denounced the result as fraudulent, although an EU electoral observer mission reported that the election had proceeded in accordance with international standards.

NKURUNZIZA'S SECOND TERM

The presidential election was held as scheduled on 28 June 2010. According to the official results confirmed by the Constitutional Court on 8 July, Nkurunziza received 91.6% of the valid votes cast. He had contested the election as the sole candidate, after the political opposition, which had joined together in June to form the Alliance des démocrates pour le changement au Burundi (ADC-Ikibiri), boycotted the poll in protest against the alleged manipulation of the results of May's communal elections. On 23 July elections to the Assemblée nationale took place. The CNDD—FDD increased its number of seats to 81, while UPRONA took 17 and FRODEBU Nyakuri (a small, pro-Government, breakaway faction of FRODEBU) just five. FRODEBU, meanwhile, boycotted the polls. A further three deputies from the Twa ethnic group were subsequently nominated in accordance with the constitutional requirements of balance of ethnic representation. At elections to the Sénat on 28 July the CNDD—FDD secured 32 of the 34 available seats; the remaining two seats were won by UPRONA. A further four seats were allocated to former Presidents and three to the Twa ethnic group, increasing the total number of senators to 41.

Rwasa fled the country in June 2010, stating that he feared for his life, and was subsequently reported to have moved to the DRC's Sud-Kivu province, where he allegedly began recruiting combatants for a planned resumption of hostilities against the Government. Nyangoma of the CNDD left Burundi in late July, following appeals for his arrest from government members, and Sinduhije left the country around the same time. In early August a congress of the FNL voted to replace Rwasa as party Chairman with Emmanuel Miburo, a former presidential adviser. Speaking from exile, Rwasa denounced the congress as illegitimate; however, the Government formally recognized Miburo as the FNL's legal representative.

On 30 August 2010 Nkurunziza appointed a new Government, including 10 new members; however, the most senior portfolios remained unchanged. In November the Government sent further troops to the African Union Mission in Somalia (AMISOM), bringing the total number of Burundian troops there to an estimated 4,000, one-half of AMISOM's total. The deployment came despite a warning from Somalia's al-Shabaab militia that it would attack Burundi in retaliation. A further 1,000 Burundian troops were sent to Somalia in March 2011.

A committee appointed by the Government in 2007 to investigate popular sentiment regarding the establishment of a Truth and Reconciliation Commission (TRC), as well as a special tribunal to prosecute crimes against humanity, reported in December 2010 that over 80% of those surveyed had said that they were in favour. The committee had originally been due to report within six months of its establishment, and was widely viewed as a ruse by the Government to delay moving forward with a TRC and tribunal.

In February 2011 Manasse Nzobonimpa, the Executive Secretary of the CNDD—FDD's 'council of the wise' and a member of the East African Legislative Assembly, publicly accused senior members of the ruling party of corruption, including Minister of Finance Clotilde Nizigama, party Chairman Jérémie Ngendakumana and Minister of Transport, Public Works and Equipment Dr Saidi Kibeya. All the accused subsequently denied any wrongdoing. In June Nzobonimpa was the subject of a failed assassination attempt in Kampala.

There were several attacks on police posts during the first half of 2011. The Government blamed the attacks on bandits, but many commentators attributed them to the FNL. The police have arrested and detained hundreds of FNL activists since the 2010 elections; many have since been tortured, and some executed extrajudicially. In June 2011 ambassadors from the EU, the USA, the Vatican, Switzerland and Norway wrote an open letter to the Burundian Government expressing 'deep concern' over the issue, demanding that the authorities end this 'intolerable practice' and prosecute suspected perpetrators. This was followed in December by the adoption of UN Security Council Resolution 2027, which also called on the Government to halt extrajudicial killings. Earlier, on 19 May, the Assemblée nationale had appointed a seven-member national human rights commission, which was welcomed by Fatsah Ouguergouz, the UN's expert on human rights in Burundi, but criticized by domestic civil society organizations on the grounds that the commission, so they alleged, was dominated by ruling party loyalists. On 18 September armed men stormed a bar in Gatumba, near the Uvira border with the DRC, killing 36 people. The FNL was widely accused of involvement in the attack, but denied any responsibility. In early October the findings of an inquiry by the national intelligence services into the massacre, which blamed the FNL for the attack, were divulged to news media.

Meanwhile, in late July 2011 Nkurunziza announced that the much-delayed TRC would be established in January 2012. The President also promised to set up a special tribunal to investigate crimes against humanity committed during the country's civil war. However, at mid-2012 neither of these bodies had yet been formed.

At least 51 Burundian soldiers serving in AMISOM were killed during clashes with Islamist al-Shabaab combatants in Somalia during October 2011, according to relatives of the victims. The AU reported lower casualty figures. Burundi's Ministry of National Defence and War Veterans announced plans in December to deploy a further 1,000 troops in Somalia, in addition to the 4,900 already stationed there.

Nkurunziza reorganized the Government on 7 November 2011, replacing six of the 21 ministers, including the Minister of Public Security, Guillaume Bunyoni, whom a government spokesman had accused of failing adequately to contain the threat posed by 'armed bandits'. Bunyoni was replaced by Gabriel Nizigama. Nkurunziza carried out another, limited, reorganization of the Council of Ministers on 8 February 2012. The main change was the replacement of the Minister of Finance and Planning for Economic Development, Clothilde Nizigama, by Tabu Abdallah Manirakiza.

In the mean time, the 2011 report of the UN panel of experts on the DRC, published in December, found that the FNL had a military leadership based in the Ruzizi Plain, south of Bujumbura, and used at least five unofficial border crossings with Sud-Kivu to link up with FNL combatants in the Fizi district of this DRC province. The report stated that many of these combatants claimed to be loyal to both the FNL and ADC-Ikibiri. According to the report, the FNL's military commander was 'General' Antoine Baranyanka, and Sinduhije was an active supporter of FNL combatants and armed rebellion, although relations between him and Baranyanka were strained. Both the Burundi Government and ADC-Ikibiri rejected the report's findings.

Sinduhije was arrested by the Tanzanian authorities in Dar es Salaam on 11 January 2012. The ADC-Ikibiri coalition immediately accused the Burundian Government of having requested Sinduhije's arrest, a charge which it denied. However, documents subsequently disclosed to the media provided evidence that the allegation was true. Sinduhije was released two weeks later, after Tanzania's Director of Public Prosecutions, Eliezer Feleshi, admitted that he had no case against him. Sinduhije was then deported to Kampala.

FORCED POPULATION MOVEMENTS

The cross-border movement of vast numbers of refugees, provoked by regional ethnic and political violence, has for decades been a key factor in Burundi's relations with all neighbouring states. Nearly all Burundi's refugees are, and historically have been, Hutu. Most of these refugees have gone to Tanzania, and while numbers fluctuated over the years, these have never totalled fewer than 200,000 from the time of the first major influx of refugees after the killings of 1972. The substantial Burundian refugee presence has been an important motivation for the Tanzanian Government's involvement in Burundian politics, and in 2002 it began a concerted drive to repatriate them. By early 2010 UNHCR assessed that nearly 500,000 Burundian refugees had returned home, and in April the Tanzanian Government announced that it would be granting Tanzanian citizenship to 162,000 Burundians who did not wish to return. This left around 40,000 refugees whose future remained unclear.

After the abortive coup in October 1993, while many of the Hutu refugees who subsequently fled the country went to Tanzania, at least 500,000 crossed into Rwanda and the DRC. The arrival of Burundian Hutu refugees fleeing persecution from the Tutsi military into Rwanda was an important factor in radicalizing Hutu sentiment prior to the Rwandan genocide. Following the genocide and subsequent victory of the FPR, thousands of Rwandan Hutus sought refuge in Burundi, while the majority of the Burundian refugees in Rwanda were repatriated. During 1995 and 1996 most of the Rwandan refugees returned home. Since 2004 the two countries have again exchanged refugees, with thousands of Rwandan Hutus fleeing to Burundi to escape the *gacaca* (traditional justice) process, which threatened to implicate them in the 1994 genocide, and Burundian Tutsis taking refuge from what they feared was a fast-approaching period of vengeful Hutu hegemony. Reassured, however, by the accommodating stance adopted by Nkurunziza's Government, almost all these Tutsi refugees have since returned. Rwandan Hutu refugees, by contrast, have often been determined to stay in Burundi, despite exhortations by both Governments for them to return. Most Burundian refugees from the 1993 conflict living in the DRC were forced to leave during 1997–98 by DRC government forces and the Burundian armed forces. Fighting between the main Goma faction of the Rassemblement Congolais pour la Démocratie (RCD—G), Mai-Mai and Banyamulenge militia in the DRC's Sud-Kivu province from 2002 caused substantial movements of Banyamulenge refugees from the DRC into Burundi. Clashes during mid-2004 between opposing factions of the Congolese government forces generated a further flow of Banyamulenge refugees into both Burundi and Rwanda. Following the massacre of Banyamulenge refugees in Burundi's Gatumba camp in August, many other Banyamulenge refugees fled the country to Rwanda, although over 27,000 remained. In March 2007 the first refugees of a group of 500 Banyamulenge survivors of the Gatumba massacre were relocated to the USA under a resettlement programme, and more have since followed. UNHCR announced in November 2010 that it had resumed the assisted repatriation of Congolese refugees from Burundi after a two-year hiatus, and that it envisaged the return of at least 12,000 refugees during the course of 2011.

Economy

DUNCAN WOODSIDE

INTRODUCTION

Burundi's recent economic history has been bedevilled by civil war, which took a particularly severe toll during 1993–2003, before subsequently lingering at a lower and intermittent intensity. Despite the country's main rebel group, the Conseil National pour la Défense de la Démocratie—Forces pour la Défense de la Démocratie (CNDD—FDD) giving up its armed struggle in late 2003 (before winning a landslide electoral victory in 2005), a full economic revival has been impeded by significant, and persistent, security problems. The last remaining rebel group, the Forces Nationales de Libération (FNL), stayed outside the political process for many years. While it eventually signed a power-sharing deal with the Government in December 2008 and finalized its political integration in 2009, a subsequent breakdown in the political process and signs of a return to rebellion have postponed the arrival of a full peace dividend for the country.

Although elections in 2010 provided an ideal chance to persuade investors and donors that the country had finally made a decisive break with its unstable past, this opportunity was spurned. All opposition contenders, including the challenger put forward by the FNL, decided to boycott the presidential election in June, after alleging that communal elections in May had been marred by fraud. As such, the presidential poll turned into a farcical one-horse race, and the seeds of a new rebellion may well have been sown, as disaffected elements (including the FNL, but also other, formerly non-militant, entities) retreated to the bush from the second half of 2010 and sporadic clashes with the army were reported.

The renewed deterioration in the political situation has been accompanied by an apparent lack of commitment on the part of the CNDD—FDD in tackling corruption. One year after the party came to power, Burundi was ranked joint 130th (along with seven other nations) out of 163 countries in Transparency International's 2006 Corruption Perceptions Index. Five years later, the 2011 index ranked Burundi a lowly 172nd of 182 countries, in large part reflecting the increasing difficulties of pursuing business opportunities in the absence of connections to the ruling party. Burundi remained one of the poorest states in the world, with annual gross domestic product (GDP) per head estimated by the IMF at US $269 in 2011, leaving the majority of citizens living on substantially less than $1 per day.

As a tiny landlocked country with few natural resources, there are limited prospects for substantial near-term improvement, even with a significant amelioration in the security situation. Low levels of education and per caput productivity also hold back Burundi's economy. According to the UN Development Programme's (UNDP) *Human Development Report 2010*, life expectancy in Burundi stood at 51.4 years, while less than 60% of the adult population was literate.

The rate of real GDP growth picked up—albeit from a very low base—following the official return to democracy. During 2006–10 real GDP growth averaged 4.1% per annum, compared with an average of just 1.7% per annum over the period 2003–05. However, real growth peaked in 2006, at 5.1%, and stood at a disappointing 3.8% in 2010. Fluctuations in the rate of real economic growth during recent years have been partly driven by the fortunes of the volatile tea and coffee sectors. Around 10% of Burundi's population of 8.7m. people work directly in the coffee industry, but the sector's importance is magnified by its status as the country's principal source of foreign currency earnings. Overall economic performance was again disappointing in 2011. Real GDP growth totalled 4.2%, according to preliminary IMF figures, amid high fuel and food prices, persistent power blackouts and a poor coffee harvest. Meanwhile, inflation increased again, reaching 13.3% year-on-year in October 2011, up from a commendable 4.1% at the end of 2010.

Beyond its meagre mineral resources and landlocked status, Burundi suffers as a result of poor power infrastructure, appalling roads and low levels of mobile cellular telephone network penetration, which reached 1.67m. people at the end of 2010, or just over 20% of the population. A development strategy released by the Government and the African Development Bank (AfDB) in 2010 therefore placed upgrading the country's infrastructure at the top of the agenda, and included proposals to pave Burundi's entire road network and to boost the supply of electricity to cover 25% of the population by 2020 (at the time of the report, only 2% of Burundians had access to power). The strategy would necessitate an increase in foreign aid, but, if successful, would result in annual economic growth rates approximately doubling from recent historical levels, to around 6%–7% per annum, according to the Government and the AfDB.

In a letter of intent to the IMF in February 2012, Burundi's Government set out a policy framework designed to achieve a rise in real economic growth to 4.8% in 2012, before a sustained acceleration to 6.0% in 2014. Over this period foreign investment in the undercapitalized tourism sector, together with a diversification of agricultural production, were earmarked as the key initial engines of improved growth.

However, it remained uncertain as to whether Burundi would be able either to improve domestic governance or to attract sufficient levels of aid and investment in order to implement its evolving development strategy successfully. During the 2005–10 administration of President Pierre Nkurunziza, the economic reform drive was frequently paralysed by governance crises. The Government was unable to adopt legislation for much of 2007–08, owing to a split in the ruling party and the opposition's parliamentary boycott. Further ensuing political crises not only postponed much needed economic reforms, but also discouraged private investment, with foreign direct investment (FDI) declining by 27% during 2007 to an estimated US $11m. Since then, however, there has been a significant resumption of private overseas investment. FDI quintupled over the following four years, to reach $104m. in 2011, according to the Burundi Investment Agency. The country's World Bank ranking in terms of ease of doing business rose from 181st (out of 183 countries) in 2011 to 169th in 2012. However, Burundi remains one of the smallest recipients of global investment flows, and its performance is way below that of neighbouring Rwanda, a country with a similarly low basic natural resource base and a history of ethnic conflict. Rwanda attracted FDI totalling $626m. in 2011.

Burundi's population density, estimated at 314.3 persons per sq km in mid-2012, is one of the highest in Africa and has been subject to significant fluctuation since mid-1993, as a result of the cross-border movement of vast numbers of refugees. The office of the UN High Commissioner for Refugees (UNHCR) estimated that 490,000 refugees returned to Burundi between 2002 and 2009, creating a number of land disputes. Large numbers of Burundians were also relocated under government plans aimed at removing them from areas of conflict.

According to the Joint UN Programme on HIV/AIDS, in 2006 some 150,000 Burundians were infected with HIV/AIDS, with an infection rate of 3.3% of adults aged between 15 and 49. In that year 70,000 people were tested at 135 voluntary centres around the country (a figure that had increased significantly from just 80 in 2003), while the rate of mother to child transmission had also decreased. The infection rate was reported to have declined to 2.0% of adults aged 15–49 in 2007.

AGRICULTURE

At mid-2011, according to FAO, an estimated 89.1% of the labour force were engaged in agriculture (including forestry and fishing), mainly at subsistence level, and the sector provided an estimated 45.5% of GDP in 2009, according to the AfDB. According to the same source, agricultural GDP increased at an average annual rate of 1.4% during 2000–07, and grew by 3.5% in 2009.

With the end of the main phase of the civil war in 2003, followed by the FNL's rejection of violence in 2008, the way should be open to a sustained long-term expansion of agricultural production and a shift from subsistence farming towards larger-scale production, in what is one of Africa's most fertile countries. In a further boost for Burundi's food production potential, the Mines Advisory Group, a British non-governmental organization (NGO) that undertakes demining in former conflict zones, declared in December 2011 that Burundi was finally 'mine-free' after seven years of clearance activities, mainly in the north-west of the country. However, the process of achieving economies of scale will probably be a slow one, given a lack of state capacity and expertise, together with persisting pockets of insecurity.

FAO estimated in February 2012 that total cereals output in Burundi reached 311,000 metric tons in 2011, a rise of 2% from 2010. Two key factors supported production: a good second rainy season and an expansion of land under cultivation, which helped to offset the negative impact of relatively poor rains in the east of the country and over-heavy rains in parts of the north. Despite the increase in production, maize and rice prices were substantially higher in the capital, Bujumbura, than they had been the previous year, rising by 15% and 28% year-on-year, respectively, in October. This was largely due to a ban on exports of food staples being imposed by Tanzania, which constrained Burundi's net food supply. Meanwhile, the 2011 banana and cassava crops were damaged by disease in many provinces. 'Banana wilt' affected production in Bubanza, Makamba, Rutana, Gitega, Mwaro, Kirundo, Muyinga and Cankuzo, while mosaic caused problems for cassava production. The impact of such diseases on subsistence agriculture, together with a resurgence of political insecurity in some areas, meant that around 10% of Burundi's population of 8.6m. people were categorized by FAO as 'food insecure' in 2011, while the UN's World Food Programme (WFP) was distributing aid to nearly 300,000 people in that year.

The governments of three of the Great Lakes countries—Burundi, Rwanda and the Democratic Republic of the Congo (DRC)—agreed in March 2012 to re-establish the dormant Institute of Agricultural and Zootechnical Research, in a bid to find a solution to banana wilt, cassava mosaic and other crop diseases. The organization, based in Lubumbashi, DRC, had not operated since 2009, due to a lack of funding, but, according to the DRC's Ministry of Agriculture and Rural Development, funding amounting to US $1.2m. every three years would henceforth be provided by each of the three countries.

In January 2009 the northern province of Kirundo was blighted by a food crisis, amid insufficient rains. The provincial governor stated that nearly 1,400 families had fled to Rwanda or Tanzania in their quest to find food. The crisis prompted WFP to dispatch an emergency mission to the area. The eastern province of Ruyigi was also affected (this time by a mixture of excessively heavy rains in some areas, and a lack of rain in others), with local media claiming that 8,000 people had fled to Tanzania.

In January 2012 Burundi's Second Vice-President, Gervais Rufyikiri, announced that the Government's agriculture budget would increase to 45,900m. Burundian francs (US $33.4m.) in 2012, from 43,200m. Burundian francs in 2011. The enlarged budget would help fund an expansion of palm oil production; an increase in irrigation schemes; the provision of 5,500 metric tons of fertilizers to farmers; a 2,000m. Burundian franc per week subsidy for the country's Strategic Food Security Fund; and an undisclosed level of loans to farmers.

Burundi's dominant cash crop is coffee, which is also a key employer (accounting for around 800,000 jobs, or 10% of the population). The annual coffee season runs from 1 April to 31 March. A poor crop in 2007/08, the yield being around 8,000 metric tons, was partly the result of a heavy reliance on mature trees during the previous season, with many of these trees being replaced (young trees have a low initial yield). More important, however, was the impact of unfavourable weather. Accordingly, coffee earnings fell from US $58.2m. in 2006/07 to $18.6m. in 2007/08, despite high coffee prices on international markets. In early 2008 the Burundian authorities announced a four-fold increase in expenditure on coffee during the 2008/09 season, to $55m. The money was to be targeted at improving processing facilities, enhancing farmer payments and incentives, and renovating coffee-washing stations. Total revenues from the 2008/09 coffee crop registered $58.9m., from output of 24,015 tons. This was followed by a very poor year in 2009/10, when output plunged to 6,381 tons and earnings fell to $16.7m. In explaining the severity of this decline, the industry regulatory authority, the Autorité de Régulation de la Filière Café du Burundi (ARFIC), blamed the highly cyclical nature of the coffee industry, but also conceded that a delay in importing pesticides and fertilizers had undermined output.

Ambitiously, ARFIC predicted that there would be a rebound in coffee output to 30,000 metric tons in 2010/11, while conceding that this would be contingent on good rains and the effective use of fertilizer. Burundi has to import fertilizer by road from the port of Mombasa in Kenya, a long and laborious process which leaves the supply of such goods vulnerable to security- and corruption-related delays. According to an AfDB estimate released in 2010, given that Burundi is situated in the middle of the continent, it costs an average of US $230 to transport 1 ton of fertilizer from Mombasa to the country, compared with an average of $130 for East African countries. In the event, the 2010/11 crop fell below the targeted level, totalling 24,000 tons, but still substantially above that achieved in 2009/10. The 2010/11 crop accumulated revenue totalling a healthy $82.8m. Coffee output then decreased drastically once again in 2011/12—an estimate in March 2012 put the annual crop at 14,000 tons. However, ARFIC claimed that a favourable outlook for rainfall put the country on course for a yield of 29,000 tons in 2012/13. Over the coming five-year period, ARFIC was, at this stage, targeting an increase in coffee output to between 40,000 and 50,000 tons per year, largely by replacing old trees (some of which dated back to the 1930s) with a fresh, higher-yielding variety.

In 2005 the authorities aimed to reform the Office des Cultures Industrielles du Burundi (OCIBU, later renamed ARFIC—see above) parastatal, which fixed the coffee price, provided agronomic expertise to farmers and carried out market prospection activities. These prerogatives were henceforth to be transferred to the farmers' associations. In early 2005 the Ministry of Agriculture and Livestock created a new body, the Observatoire des Filières au Burundi, to assist Burundi's Confédération Nationale des Caféculteurs in, inter alia, the commercialization of fertilizers, outside market prospection and establishment of the producer price. These measures were expected to contribute to curbing the smuggling of coffee to neighbouring countries. In mid-2006 the continuation of the coffee reform strategy, supported by the European Union (EU) and the World Bank, was considered to be essential to poverty reduction, especially for some 800,000 small rural producers. According to the Government, a new regulatory, legal and institutional framework for the coffee sector, including restructuring of OCIBU, was to be implemented prior to the 2007/08 harvest. However, by early 2008 this reform strategy had made little progress, in part owing to the country's political crisis in 2007. Although a competitiveness study of the coffee sector had been undertaken, the new regulatory body had still to be established, and the privatization of key assets had not been carried out. In fact, a privatization strategy had yet to be identified. The sector's privatization programme continued to stall in 2009, in part owing to the negative effects of the global financial crisis and wider economic downturn on foreign investor demand for assets in emerging markets. While investors were invited to bid for 117 Burundian coffee-washing stations in June, bidding was extremely limited, resulting in the sale of only 13 stations.

Tea is Burundi's second most important crop, and accounts for around 300,000 jobs. In December 2003 the State announced its intention to privatize the management of the Office du Thé du Burundi (OTB). It also declared that the five tea estates and plants of Ijenda, Rwegura, Teza, Tora and Buhoro would be transferred to the private sector. However, by the late 2000s, despite government assurances that it remained committed to implementing significant reform of the tea sector, this had still to be achieved, in part owing to the collapse of the Government's legislative majority.

In February 2008 the OTB predicted that tea output in 2008 would rise by 16% to 8,250 metric tons, partly owing to enhanced use of fertilizers, after financial problems had forced the regulator to suspend the distribution of fertilizers during the previous four years. Adding to the atmosphere of cautious optimism about the tea industry's prospects, the OTB underlined in April that the quality of output was improving. After upgrading three out of the country's five tea factories, prices for the top grade tea stood at US $2.18 per kg during the first quarter of 2008, compared with a price average of $1.52 per kg during the same period of 2007. The authorities' confidence proved well placed: for 2008 as a whole Burundi recorded a rise in tea earnings of nearly 40%, to $13.7m. The volume of output was similar to 2007, with a yield of 7,000 tons. In 2009 tea output rose further, to 7,500 tons, achieving earnings of $16.0m. Output increased again in 2010, to 8,016 tons (and $18.2m.), and export revenues further rose, to $22.2m., in 2011.

The high quality of Burundi's cotton is much appreciated both by the domestic textile industry and by foreign clients, and in the long term the Compagnie de Gérance du Coton expected to increase the area of cotton fields by as much as 12,000 ha. Cotton output was hampered by growing insecurity in the Imbo plain in 2003, when production was only some 2,163 metric tons, and it remained at about that level in 2005.

Burundi has obtained foreign assistance for the development of other crops. On the Imbo plain, land is being reclaimed for the cultivation of cotton and rice in an integrated rural development scheme that is assisted by the UNDP and FAO. In 2007 rice production increased to 70,900 metric tons, according to FAO. An integrated sugar scheme was established in the south-east of the Mosso region, with finance provided mainly by the AfDB, the Fund of the Organization for the Petroleum Exporting Countries and the Arab Bank for Economic Development in Africa (BADEA). Plantations of sugar cane have been established on the Mosso plain, near Bujumbura, in association with a refinery, which was projected to meet 90% of Burundi's demand for sugar by the early 1990s, with further potential for exports. The country has become a net sugar exporter in recent times, albeit an irregular one, and exports fluctuate considerably. In 2004 sugar exports amounted to 8,378 tons and sugar export revenue to 3,272m. Burundian francs (6.2% of total export revenue). However, in 2006 sugar exports amounted to just 1,000 tons and sugar export revenue to 466m. Burundian francs (0.8% of total export revenue). These exports and the smuggling of sugar to neighbouring Rwanda and the DRC contributed to chronic shortages on the domestic market. In May 2005 the Minister of Commerce and Industry acknowledged that the domestic production of 20,000 tons was insufficient to meet the requirements of the Burundian market, estimated at 23,000 tons. Bananas, sweet potatoes, cassava, pulses and maize are other important, but mainly subsistence, crops.

Although potentially self-sufficient in food production, civil disturbances and inclement weather have disrupted the country's infrastructure and prevented supplies from reaching urban centres. In 2006 heavy rains destroyed a number of homes and farms, particularly in the Makamba province, where 1,500 people were left homeless. Continued flooding destroyed 50%–80% of November's harvest, according to WFP. In 2008 WFP estimated that, while the country's population had grown by 33% from 6m. to more than 8m. between 1998 and 2008, the average annual food production per caput had fallen by 41%. On a per crop basis, the decline was 28% for cereals, 74% for pulses and 15% for bananas and plantains. Given that the main rebel group had joined the political process as long ago as early 2004, these figures generated significant concern, all the more so given that refugees were beginning to return in significant numbers from Tanzania, where more than 240,000 Burundians were still estimated to be residing at the end of 2008. A tripartite commission consisting of the Tanzanian and Burundian governments and UNHCR agreed in 2007 that Burundian refugees who arrived in Tanzania after 1992 must be repatriated. WFP stated in March 2008 that it required a further US $6m. to continue feeding 90,000 returning refugees during the second half of the year. Furthermore, WFP required an additional $20m. in order to sustain assistance for 600,000 people who were receiving help from its existing programmes (these people included Congolese refugees and families affected by HIV/AIDS) during the second quarter of 2008. For the 2007/08 harvest, WFP estimated that food production rose by 2%, which was below the rate of population growth, even ignoring the effect of the returning refugees. In a joint analysis undertaken with Burundi's Ministry of Agriculture and Livestock and other UN agencies, it was estimated that there was a shortfall of 486,000 metric tons of grain.

One of the main structural problems facing agriculture in Burundi is the fragmentation of rural land, with farms averaging 0.8 ha per household and soil problems reducing productivity. The return of refugees could exacerbate this fragmentation, but the biggest problem remains the high birth and population growth rates, so that more and more people compete for parcels of land and then over-cultivate whatever land they plant on. Furthermore, rates of fertilizer use are among the lowest in Africa. Another important challenge has been deforestation and soil erosion, which the Government and NGOs attempted to contain, with a programme of reforestation, which envisaged the planting of 45m. trees during 2001–02. (By mid-2005, however, the Burundian authorities were expressing particular concern about deforestation in the Kibira region, in the north of the country.)

In early 2002 the new Government initiated a policy of land redistribution, aimed specifically at meeting the needs of returned refugees and internally displaced persons. The authorities warned that unused land, particularly in the Gihanga and Mutinbuzi communes, would be redistributed. At the same time the Government announced plans to redistribute land that had been acquired or occupied illegally. In order to provide credit to farmers, in mid-2001 the Burundian authorities also created a Rural Fund of 2,000m. Burundian francs. These efforts were expected to be supplemented by donor contributions, directed both at supporting the rural sector and at creating revenue for returned refugees, internally displaced persons and demobilized combatants. In December the Government announced a three-year plan of action to combat soil degradation, at a projected cost of 10,300m. Burundian francs.

The development of livestock is hindered by the social system, which encourages the maintenance of cattle herds that are both too large and under-exploited. As with other subsectors, livestock-rearing has been adversely affected by civil unrest, and in 1995 and early 1996 cattle rustlers removed entire herds. In early 2003 the Agence française de développement announced a 70m.-Burundian francs programme to assist 40 peasant communities in developing new ovine and bovine herds. In February 2004 the Ministry of Agriculture and Livestock announced co-operation with veterinary laboratories in Kenya, Malawi and South Africa in their quest to find a vaccine to eradicate the foot-and-mouth epidemic in the region.

MINERALS

Small quantities of bastnaesite and cassiterite have been exploited by the Karongo Mining Co. Cassiterite exports increased to 67 metric tons in 2002, before decreasing to 24 tons in 2003 and 16 tons in 2004. The rise in international prices of columbo-tantalite (of which niobium was a by-product) in 2000–01 significantly stimulated revenue from the country's mineral exports, which increased from 219.6m. Burundian francs in 2000 to 1,635.4m. Burundian francs in 2001. In 2002 niobium exports amounted to 72 tons, but, owing to the collapse of international prices, export earnings of this product totalled only 755m. Burundian francs. As columbo-tantalite is mined in only small quantities in Burundi, the sharp increase in export volume prompted UN officials to suspect that part of the total might be illicitly traded ore from the neighbouring DRC. In 2003 niobium ore exports amounted to 32 tons, valued at 161m. Burundian francs, about one-half of the quantity of 2001 exports, but hardly more than one-10th of their value. In 2004 exports remained at about the same level, reaching 28 tons, valued at 91.8m. Burundian francs, by October. In April 2005 the Ministry of Energy and Mines admitted that these statistics failed to reflect the real situation, since some three-quarters of Burundian minerals were smuggled to Rwanda, where they could be sold at much higher prices (double in the case of cassiterite). In 2006 niobium extraction produced 3,200 kg of concentrate, down from 8,384 kg in 2005. The extraction of tantalum concentrate fell to 2,868 kg in 2006, from 9,188 kg in 2005.

Tin and tungsten extraction followed a steady upward trend until 2006: production of tin increased from 5 kg of concentrate in 2003 to 46 kg in 2006, while production of tungsten concentrate reached 238 kg in 2006, up from 8 kg in 2004. However, in 2007 production of tin declined significantly, to 2 kg, before recovering in 2008, to 21 kg. Similarly, production of tungsten decreased to 144 kg in 2007 before increasing slightly in 2008, to 194 kg.

Yields from gold-mining have been on a steadily increasing trajectory since the early 2000s, with the State having long pursued foreign funding and partnerships in this area. In March 1999 the Preferential Trade Area Bank agreed to disburse a loan of US $297,500 to allow the state-owned Burundi Mining Corpn (BUMINCO) to purchase equipment for a gold-processing plant (which was to have a monthly capacity of 10 kg), pending completion of a feasibility study on an industrial project at Masaka. Initial prospecting on the Masaka site by BUMINCO was completed in May, and further exploration commenced during that month on sites at Rugomero and Butihinda. Production of gold remained steady at an estimated 750 kg per year in 2004–08. According to the US Geological Survey, gold exports from Burundi amounted to 2,170 kg in 2008, as much as 1,000 kg of which was produced locally by artisanal miners. The remainder of the export total was re-exported primarily from the DRC. Additional foreign participation in the gold sector bodes well, however, with Sweden's International Gold Exploration acquiring an exploration license for a deposit in Mabayi-Butara in north-western Burundi during 2006.

Burundi has estimated reserves of 15m. metric tons of phosphate rock, and sufficient reserves of carbonatite (7.3m. tons) to satisfy the domestic demand for cement have also been identified, near Gatara.

Petroleum has been detected beneath Lake Tanganyika and in the Ruzizi valley, for which test drillings were carried out in the late 1980s by US petroleum interests, in association with the Burundian Government. However, petroleum experts stated that complete seismic surveys in Lake Tanganyika would also require prospecting in the DRC and Tanzanian parts of the lake. Stability in the DRC would consequently be an additional precondition to relaunching the project.

There is also potential for oil extraction in other parts of the country. In February 2011 British-based oil exploration company Surestream Petroleum announced that it was to begin full seismic surveys in two 700-sq-km blocks in June of that year. This followed initial surveys in the two locations—Block B, in the centre of Burundi; and Block D, in the south of the country—during the preceding two years, which had left the company 'almost' ready to start drilling.

The AfDB estimated in 2010 that Burundi's nickel deposits amounted to about 260m. metric tons, containing 4m. tons of metal. In March 1999 an agreement, known as the Mining Convention, was signed between the Burundian Government and an Australian company, Andover Resources (which subsequently became a subsidiary of the Canadian enterprise Argosy Minerals Inc.), for the exploitation of nickel deposits at Musongati. Andover Resources was to complete a feasibility study to assess the economic viability of the project, which envisaged the construction of a plant with an annual capacity of 45,000 tons of nickel by 2002, at a total estimated cost of US $700m.; the project was also to include the construction of employee housing and of a 35-MW power station. Following a number of delays to the project, the Burundian Minister of Energy and Mines and Argosy Minerals agreed on a new programme, including feasibility studies on the cost of access infrastructure to the Musongati mine, which was also believed to contain some platinum group metal reserves. In December 2003 the Minister of Energy and Mines announced that work would resume soon on the site. One year later, however, he informed the legislature that little progress had been made and expressed concern about Argosy Minerals' financial capacity to develop the Musongati project. With the end of the transitional period in 2005, the election of the main former rebel faction to set up a new post-war Government caused further complications for Argosy Minerals and its subsidiary. As part of a regulatory disclosure in early 2008, Argosy Minerals underlined that Andover Resources was pursuing a claim for damages against the Burundian Government for terminating the Mining Convention. In this regard, the Minister of Energy and Mines had recommended to the Council of Ministers in June 2007 that the Convention be terminated; this recommendation was accepted, despite the fact that an Inter-Ministerial Commission had already recommended in December 2005 that Andover be allowed to continue with exploration and feasibility work. Andover instructed its legal counsel to start arbitral proceedings under the Rules of the International Court of Arbitration of the International Chamber of Commerce in June 2007; these proceedings against the Burundian Government were carried out during the late 2000s.

Despite this dispute, the then Minister of Energy and Mines, Samuel Ndyiragije, announced in February 2008 that the Government was awarding high priority to the exploration of mineral resources within its overall economic strategy. However, he acknowledged that a key problem was the country's shortage of electricity, and stated that connection to the grid run by Tanzania and Uganda should help to alleviate the problem; however, no timescale for this was offered. In April 2011 Minister of Energy and Mines Moïse Bucumi claimed that extraction of nickel at the Musongati reserve, which was estimated to hold 180m. metric tons of deposits, was on course to begin in 2017. By this stage, South Africa's Samancor had replaced Andover as the operator for this reserve, and would be responsible for generating an electricity supply for the extraction process, according to Bucumi.

INDUSTRY, SERVICES AND FOREIGN INVESTMENT

There is little industrial activity in Burundi, apart from the processing of agricultural products, such as cotton, coffee, tea and vegetable oil, and small-scale wood mills. Industry contributed an estimated 16.8% of GDP in 2007, according to the AfDB. Industrial GDP declined at an average annual rate of 6.2% in 2000–07, according to the AfDB. By 2011 the industrial sector accounted for 21.5% of GDP, having received a modest boost from several years of peace.

Aside from the obvious complications caused by civil war, one of the key problems that has held back the development of industry and manufacturing is the lack of a fully functioning banking sector, which has been hampered by a legacy of bad loans (largely to bankrupt state companies). Without access to credit, very few small and medium-sized private enterprises can establish themselves. High levels of state wages (equivalent to 10.5% of GDP in 2007) have also crowded out private sector investment and growth. Nevertheless, private investment rose from 8.0% of GDP in 2006 to 9.0% of GDP in 2007, according to preliminary estimates.

In recent years there has been a significant increase in investment from overseas, which reached US $104m. in 2011, up from a mere $11m. in 2007. The Burundi Investment Agency has carried out various measures aimed at attracting higher inflows, including the reduction of the number of days required to establish a business from 32 to two. In August 2011 South Africa's President, Jacob Zuma, announced that his country intended to invest in Burundi's services and utilities sectors. During a trip by Zuma to Bujumbura, the two countries signed an economic partnership agreement, which the South African President said would involve investment in Burundi's tourism, energy and financial services sectors. In April 2012 regional supermarket chain Nakumatt, which has its headquarters in Kenya, announced that it would open an outlet in Burundi. The company declared that it had identified a suitable location and that opening a supermarket there formed a core part of its expansion strategy for the following 12 to 18 months.

However, while foreign investment has risen impressively from a very low base, domestically generated investment has remained extremely low, totalling just US $69.5m. in 2011. In an attempt to boost local capital markets, from 2010 the

Government co-ordinated closely with the World Bank regarding the introduction of electronic banking services, the enhancement of the regulation of commercial banks and microfinance organizations, the establishment of a system that can rigorously evaluate potential borrowers' creditworthiness, and the development of domestic financial markets. The absence of such mechanisms and services has proved a significant impediment to the development of the private sector, particularly in terms of slowing the emergence of a successful entrepreneurial class.

The manufacturing sector accounted for some 9.7% of GDP in 2009. By the mid-1980s several small enterprises, including glass, cement, footwear, insecticide factories, a flour mill and a brewery, had been established. A textile industry was also developed, with aid from the People's Republic of China, which exported fabrics to neighbouring Rwanda. However, the decrease of domestic cotton production forced the main company, Complexe Textile du Bujumbura (COTEBU), to rely mainly on imports.

The commission of 50,000 uniforms by the national police and armed forces in 2005 raised fresh expectations among COTEBU's management. In addition, China, which had supported the construction of the textile plant, extended a US $2m. loan to enable the company to purchase modern printing equipment. COTEBU's difficulties in the early 2000s were partially compensated for by a 9.9% increase in the output of the Brarudi beer factory in 2004, which, nevertheless, had to import soft drinks and Amstel beer from its Rwandan holding company, BRALIRWA, to meet the rising demand. In 2004 Brarudi achieved a record 10,000m. Burundian francs profit and doubled the value of its exports (1,106m. Burundian francs in 2003), which represented 4.6% of the country's export revenues.

In September 2007 Brarudi announced that it was investing US $24.5m. to increase production, as it sought to extend its regional influence. The investment was targeted at modernizing storage capacity and increasing fermenting capacity, which would allow the company to raise the volume of bottles produced each day. Indeed, the brewer planned to increase production by three or four times its existing capacity of 700,000 bottles of beer and soft drinks per day. The company was largely concentrating on augmenting its external market share, targeting expansion into Tanzania and Kenya. Brarudi's production of Amstel had already proved popular in eastern DRC, where the existence of a large number of foreign workers, government officials and local businessmen employed in mineral extraction had created substantial demand for the product. The brewer's strong regional performance, in tandem with a near-monopoly on the Burundian market (where Primus and Amstel predominate), enabled it to generate a net profit of $13m. in 2006, and retain its status as the Government's largest contributor to tax revenue. In 2010 Brarudi registered a 21% rise in sales of soft drinks and beer to 1.99m. hectolitres. The increase was partly attributed to the 2010 elections, with political parties (especially the ruling CNDD—FDD) spending campaign funds on refreshments at rallies.

Following chronic power shortages throughout 2003, the situation deteriorated further in 2004, with a decline in electricity production, to 91.6m. kWh. In January 2004 the state water and electricity company, Régie de Distribution d'Eau et d'Electricité (REGIDESO), increased its prices by 20% and 25%, respectively. However, Burundi's capacity to hold a referendum in February 2005 and the prospect of peace negotiations with the FNL rebels prompted the EU to proceed rapidly with plans to rehabilitate the country's electricity network. It decided to accelerate the disbursement of funds that it had pledged to finance the country's Rehabilitation Programme since 2000, comprising €9.3m. for the rehabilitation of the REGIDESO electricity infrastructure, the repair of hydroelectric power stations and the improvement of transport and distribution lines, which had suffered much damage during the conflict since 1993.

The most promising opportunity to improve electricity supply was the commitment made in July 2004 by the EU, Belgium and the Netherlands to support the resumption of co-operation projects in the framework of the Economic Community of the Great Lakes Countries (CEPGL), which grouped Burundi, Rwanda and the DRC in the areas of energy, water, telecommunications, agriculture and customs. These projects included the rehabilitation of the Ruzizi I hydroelectric power station and its upgrading from 28.2 MW to 39.6 MW, and the interconnection of the Ruzizi I and Ruzizi II (40 MW) power dams. Ongoing border security issues, however, generated tensions between the DRC and its two neighbouring countries, which prevented further meetings from taking place during 2004. Nevertheless, in March 2005 the DRC expressed new interest in reviving co-operation within the CEPGL framework. The International Development Association (IDA) was contributing towards financing a long-term programme to develop basic forestry services and promote tree-planting for the supply of wood for fuel, building-poles and timber. Industrial development is hampered by Burundi's distance from the sea (about 1,400 km to Dar es Salaam, Tanzania, and 2,000 km to Mombasa, Kenya), as a result of which only manufactures capable of absorbing the high costs of transport can be developed.

In April 2011 Minister of Energy and Mines Bucumi declared that Burundi would need to have access to 270 MW in generating capacity in order to meet power demand by 2020, compared with the existing supply of 45 MW. Power demand in Burundi at mid-2011 stood at an estimated 120 MW. The future expansion of demand was anticipated to arise in part from the development of industrial-scale mineral exploitation in the country, with coltan, oil, nickel, gold and cassiterite all providing opportunities in the post-war environment. Despite the supply deficit, the Ministry of Energy and Mines estimated that the country possessed 300 MW of viable power generation potential, and that participation in regional projects could potentially raise this to 1,700 MW.

A key source of future power supply was expected to come from further development of the hydroelectric sector. Potential regional projects included a 61.5-MW station at the Rusumo Falls on the Kagera river, at the border between Rwanda and Tanzania. An even bigger potential project was a third Ruzizi facility (Ruzizi III), with a planned generating capacity of 147 MW, for equitable tripartite exploitation with the DRC and Rwanda. In February 2011 Gedeon Nizeye, Director of Geology at Burundi's Ministry of Energy and Mines, stated that construction of the US $500m. project could commence in 2013, with completion scheduled for 2015. The AfDB, the German Government and the European Investment Bank all expressed an interest in funding the Ruzizi III project.

FOREIGN AID AND DEVELOPMENT PLANNING

Burundi is heavily dependent on foreign assistance, both for capital projects and for budgetary support. External grants accounted for an estimated 26% of GDP in 2008. The country has also benefited from significant debt relief, albeit several years later than many of its African peers. The 'Paris Club' of sovereign creditors wrote off all the debt owed to it by Burundi in the first quarter of 2009. The collective agreed to cancel US $129.5m. of debt, amounting to 96% of the country's sovereign obligations, while bilateral creditors agreed to write off the remaining $4.8m. As part of the debt relief deal, Burundi committed to continue prioritizing its IMF-stewarded poverty reduction strategy.

Aside from the IMF and the World Bank, Burundi has found significant favour from the EU, particularly under the auspices of the European Development Fund (EDF). Under the framework of the country's 10th EDF, €212m. in financial aid was pledged, including €48m. in direct budgetary aid over the period 2009–11.

The USA is an increasingly important bilateral donor to Burundi. Under the auspices of the US Agency for International Development (USAID), the US Government provided US $26.1m. to the central African nation in the 2007/08 fiscal year and $35.2m. in 2008/09. In the latter period, the provision of aid by the US Government could be broken down as follows: $6.5m. for long-term development assistance, $12.1m. for health and 'child survival', $16m. for food aid, $275,000 for military education and training, and $373,000 for non-proliferation, anti-terrorism, demining and other security-related programmes.

However, aid provision was significantly affected in early 2012, when the British Government's Department for International Development (DfID) announced that it was terminating its aid programme for Burundi. The United Kingdom provided £13.7m. (around US $22m.) in aid to the country in 2011, mainly for the health, education and justice sectors. DfID's termination of its assistance came as a result of a spending review by the British Government, which saw the number of developing countries receiving bilateral aid fall from 43 to 27. EU ambassador to Burundi Stephane de Loecker announced in February 2012 that the multilateral body would maintain aid to Burundi at close to €100m. (US $130m.) per year, underlining that the country retained 'priority' status due to its extremely high levels of poverty, although he warned that the continuing extrajudicial killings were 'intolerable'. This followed the UN Security Council's statement of 'grave concern' in December 2011 with regard to the same issue. Further underlining the long-term threat posed to aid by poor domestic governance in Burundi, the International Crisis Group released a report in March 2012 detailing the emergence of what it described as 'a deepening corruption crisis', involving manipulation by the ruling CNDD—FDD of the country's long-standing patrimonial culture to a level 'hitherto unknown'.

In August 2005 the IMF and IDA issued a joint statement agreeing that Burundi had taken the measures necessary to qualify for interim debt relief under the enhanced initiative for heavily indebted poor countries (HIPC), against a backdrop where total external debt had reached US $1,351m. This decision enabled Burundi to reduce its average debt-servicing payments by 80%; the Government announced that savings, which were equivalent to 35% of the national budget, were to be used to improve living standards. In November the AfDB also declared Burundi to be eligible for external debt assistance. The IMF urged the authorities to seek debt relief from non-'Paris Club' creditors that had not provided relief under the enhanced HIPC initiative on terms comparable to those obtained from 'Paris Club' creditors. In early 2007 the World Bank released a further $150m. to support social and economic projects over the following three years. A full Country Assistance Strategy was being prepared, but during 2008 the World Bank continued to run an Interim Strategy Note aimed at addressing the country's social needs and generating sustained economic growth.

Two agreements were signed with Germany in early 2007 to provide 23,000m. Burundian francs; over two-thirds of that amount was set aside for water purification projects, with the remainder to be spent on reintegration of returning refugees. Belgium, meanwhile, had already granted €10m. in late 2006 for education, rural water projects and road works. Donor nations are, however, wary of how their money is spent. Thus, in June 2007 a conference to address this concern was held in Bujumbura and was attended by major donors, namely Belgium, France, the Netherlands and the World Bank. Burundian authorities pledged their commitment to transparency, promising to spend the aid responsibly.

Complications were caused in 2007 to the Government's Poverty Reduction and Growth Facility (PRGF) with the IMF, with potential implications for the country's HIPC initiative. The sixth review of the PRGF was delayed by what the IMF termed 'a governance incident', whereby illegal payments amounting to 1.6% of GDP were made to a petrol distribution firm, INTERPETROL. The Inspector General's office stated that the payment was fraudulent, with state auditors implicating a former Minister of Finance and a former Governor of the central bank in the scandal. The sixth review of the PRGF was eventually completed before the end of 2007 with the Fund praising the authorities for their attempts to improve fiscal performance after the 'governance incident'. However, despite this, the Fund warned that progress toward HIPC completion point had been 'uneven', indicating that significant further work (particularly concerning the privatization of coffee-washing stations and development of a legal framework for the sector) would be needed for the country to receive the full benefits of debt relief.

The IMF underlined in early 2008 that the Burundian economy remained highly vulnerable to shocks and debt distress, even if it were to reach HIPC completion point smoothly. HIPC completion would be expected to take the net present value of debt to below 100% of exports, but the volatility of coffee output and prices provided little room for manoeuvre. The Fund therefore urged the Burundian Government to limit its external financing to grants and borrowing at concessional rates, urging against borrowing on international markets at market rates.

Key strides in fiscal reform included the introduction of a value-added tax and a common external tariff on 1 July 2009, in line with the requirements of Burundi's membership of the East African Community (EAC). A new, centralized revenue collection agency, the Office Burundais des Recettes (OBR, Burundi Revenue Authority—BRA), commenced operations in mid-2010. Meanwhile, during 2009 the Government streamlined its fiscal accounts, closing 254 accounts, according to the IMF. There were also significant reforms of central bank operations, as well as regulation of the wider banking industry. Moreover, a symmetrical foreign exchange market was introduced, while ceilings on interest rates were removed, enabling the more efficient operation of currency transactions, lending and borrowing. There was also close co-operation with EAC banking supervisors, culminating in the signing of a memorandum of understanding (MOU), in line with a drive for regional financial convergence and the planned eventual adoption of a single currency. In the commercial banking sector, prudential (i.e. capital adequacy) ratios were enhanced, both with regard to foreign exchange and domestic liquidity. These developments boded well for continued positive relationships with key donors.

A significant consolidation of revenue collection by the central Government was evident in 2010. Domestic revenues rose by 20%, to 362,000m. Burundian francs, according to the Ministry of Finance (IMF figures showed annual local price growth of 7.2% in 2010). Government spending in 2010 totalled 863,100m. Burundian francs, according to the Minister of Finance, Clotilde Nizigama. The shortfall between spending and revenues was largely covered by donor funding, which consistently accounts for close to one-half of the budget.

The 2011 budget envisaged spending of 1,030,000m. Burundian francs (US $835m.), a 19.3% increase from 2010, against a backdrop where inflation remained in single digits in percentage terms during the early months of 2011. However, final data from the Ministry of Finance showed that revenue collection surpassed its target of 432,600m. Burundian francs in 2011, owing to improvements instigated by the OBR: collections reached 471,000m. Burundian francs, a rise of 30% compared with the previous year.

The IMF completed its fifth review of Burundi's Extended Credit Facility (ECF)—formerly known as the PRGF—in March 2011. This entitled the Burundian Government to draw on a loan tranche equivalent to US $10.4m., from a three-year borrowing arrangement worth a total of $75.6m. The Fund commended the progress made by the authorities in implementing important structural, fiscal and monetary reforms.

Meanwhile, in April 2010 the Burundian Government and the AfDB concluded a new development strategy, which prioritized modernization of the country's power, transport and telecommunications infrastructure. The strategy, which, among other long-term targets, included establishing a national power grid by 2015 and providing 40% of the population with electricity by 2030, would require funding of US $5,800m. It was envisaged that the Government would provide 27% ($1,600m.) of this amount, aided by the development of nickel-mining potential, which would help to provide the country with an estimated $200m. in annual mining taxes. Foreign donors would be relied upon to provide 56% ($3,200m.) of the funding, while the remaining 17% ($1,000m.) was expected to come from FDI.

The process of privatizing the Office National des Télécommunications (ONATEL), which began in the early 2000s, has proved protracted. The Government planned to retain a 35% share in the company, while a 14% share was to be distributed among ONATEL's employees. REGIDESO was also designated for transfer to the private sector. In July 2001 ONATEL commissioned a telecommunications centre with a total capacity of 50,000 lines, at a cost of US $40m. In

November of that year ONATEL and the private mobile cellular telephone operator Téléphonie Cellulaire du Burundi (TELECEL) agreed to interconnect their respective networks. However, by mid-2011 the privatization of ONATEL, which had lost 50,000 subscribers during 2010 owing to competition from private operators, had yet to be completed. By this stage the privatization process was being handled by a World Bank-funded organization, Projet de Development des Secteurs Financier et Prive (PDSFP), with completion of a sale anticipated by the end of 2011.

Burundi's mobile cellular telephone market has expanded considerably in recent years, reaching 1.67m. users at the end of 2010, a rise of 55% from the end of 2009. The biggest market player is U-com, a subsidiary of Egypt's Orascom. U-com's subscriber base reached 1.1m. at the end of September 2011, up from 750,000 in March 2010. The mobile phone sector has become reasonably competitive, with state-owned ONAMOB, South Africa's Econet Wireless International, Nepal's Lacell SU and Africell (a unit of Dubai's VTL Holdings) all operating on the local market.

FOREIGN TRADE

With rampant global fuel price inflation ensuring that imports rose faster than annual export revenues, Burundi's trade deficit increased from US $242.0m. in 2007 to $281.3m. in 2008. The deficit widened further over the next three years—to $384.6m. in 2009, $424.6m. in 2010 and $458.4m. in 2011, according to preliminary IMF figures. High international petroleum prices have again been a key driver of the persistent deficit in recent years, as the country has to import its fuel. Total imports rose from $453.0m. in 2009 (when petroleum imports amounted to $57.4m.) to $525.9m. in 2010 (with the petroleum component increasing to $98.4m.), before reaching an estimated $561.1m. in 2011, when petroleum imports totalled a provisional $133.7m. Exports have risen over the same period, but have lagged behind imports. Total exports increased from $68.4m. in 2009 to $101.2m. in 2010, before rising further, to $102.7m., in 2011. The principal imports are chemical products, gas oil, motor cars, motor petroleum, trucks, and mechanical devices and parts. The country's primary sources of imports in 2010 were Saudi Arabia (which accounted for 15.8% of imports by value), Uganda (7.8%), Belgium (7.6%), China (7.5%), Kenya (6.9%) and Zambia (6.4%). In 2010 Burundi's leading export destinations were Germany (which received 27.5% of the country's exports by value), Pakistan (10.3%), Belgium (5.7%) and Rwanda (5.0%). Principal exports are coffee, tea, sugar, beer and minerals.

In January 2010 a full customs union came into force throughout the EAC, comprising Burundi, Kenya, Rwanda, Tanzania and Uganda. In effect, this meant that tariffs between member states were eliminated, thus creating a free trade area and completing a phased, incremental reduction that was begun in 2005. Burundi (and Rwanda) signed an MOU for membership of the EAC in November 2006, but did not sign the full accession treaties until June 2007. As a result, while Tanzania and Uganda were given five years to adjust to full competition with Kenya (the region's most competitive exporter), Rwanda and Burundi were faced with a sharper adjustment, with implications for the terms of trade. In November 2009 the member states of the EAC signed a common market protocol, seeking to build on the existing customs union. The common market came into force on 1 July 2010 and would, upon completion of its phased implementation (due by 2015), entail the free circulation of services, citizens and capital.

In 1985 Burundi became a full member of the Preferential Trade Area for Eastern and Southern African States (superseded in 1993 by the Common Market for Eastern and Southern Africa—COMESA). Burundi was integrated into COMESA's free trade area in January 2004. Meanwhile, a special compensation fund was to assist the economy in adapting to the consequences of the forthcoming ending of the tariff system. While Burundian businesses claimed that strong support was required to increase their competitiveness and prevent closures, the Government insisted that compensation was necessary to balance the projected losses in its customs revenue. In April 2003 the authorities announced measures to assist the textile sector in addressing the consequences of the dismantling of tariffs within COMESA. On 1 January 2004 Burundi began to implement a zero tariff on all imports from other COMESA member states, to the concern of the local private sector, which claimed that the Burundian companies were less advanced in many aspects, particularly in terms of equipment and of technology, but also in marketing expertise. Meanwhile, in September 2003 Burundi submitted a formal request to become eligible for the US African Growth and Opportunity Act initiative, which was designed to promote bilateral trade and improved market access to sub-Saharan African countries. Burundi is also a full member of the Communauté économique des états d'Afrique centrale.

TRANSPORT

The network of roads is dense, but few of the 12,322 km of routes are paved, and these are the roads that connect Bujumbura with Gitega, Kayanza and Nyanza-Lac. In 2001 the World Bank allocated US $40m. to finance the rehabilitation of the road linking Bujumbura and the Tanzanian border town of Mugina, the maintenance of the Rugombo–Kayanza road in the north-west and the construction of the Nyakararo–Mwaro–Gitega road in the centre of the country. The reform of the National Road Fund was a condition attached by the World Bank for the disbursement of these funds. The EDF announced plans for the construction of roads linking Gitega and Muyinga, Muyinga and Cankuzo, and Cankuzo and Ruyigi. BADEA also announced in 2001 that it would fund feasibility studies for the construction of the Makamba–Bururi road in the southern part of the country and of the Rumonge–Bururi–Gitega road, between Lake Tanganyika and the centre. In December 2004 the European Commission announced that it would finance the rehabilitation of the Gitega–Karusi–Muyinga road by up to €24m. and the roads in Bujumbura by up to €15.5m. The AfDB approved a grant of $150m. to Burundi and Rwanda for a road project linking Nyamitanga, Ruhwa, Ntendezi and Mwityazo. This project, scheduled for completion by the end of 2012, formed part of a wider programme to link Mugina, Bujumbura, Nyamitanga, Ruhwa, Ntendezi, Mwityazo and Gisenyi, involving Rwanda, Burundi and Tanzania in a 497.5-km regional transport corridor.

A new development strategy spearheaded by the AfDB in 2010 heralded ambitious new plans for the long-term development of the country's road network. The goal was to pave the entire existing road network and add 1,000 km of new roads to major urban centres by 2020.

Lake Tanganyika (of which Burundi has about 8% sovereignty) is a crucial component in Burundi's transport system, since most of the country's external trade is conducted along the lake between Bujumbura and Tanzania and the DRC. In 2005 the Burundian authorities expressed concern that the falling water levels of Lake Tanganyika (resulting from deforestation and climate change) had severely affected activities at the port of Bujumbura, making large amounts of dock space unusable.

Plans to construct a railway linking Burundi with Uganda, Rwanda and Tanzania were announced in 1987. The proposed line would connect with the Kigoma–Dar es Salaam line in Tanzania, substantially improving Burundi's isolated trade position. The civil unrest in Burundi caused these plans to be postponed, although they were revived with the end of the transition period. In 2006 China pledged to fund a feasibility study aimed at building a rail link from Kigali, the Rwandan capital, to Bujumbura, and thence into Tanzania. At a donor conference hosted in Tunisia in March 2009, the project was deemed 'technically and financially viable'. However, with the total cost of the project calculated at US $3,500m. (and given the feasibility study's recommendation that it be funded by a public-private partnership), construction appeared to be a long way off at that stage. With a global financial crisis and economic downturn paralyzing international capital markets, private financing for the project seemed unlikely to materialize in the short term. In March 2011 Tanzanian President Jakaya

Kikwete announced that Tanzania, Rwanda and Burundi were redoubling their joint search for project finance and stated that the financing model could be a 'build-operate-transfer' (BOT) arrangement or a joint venture. Funding from concessional sources would be prioritized, he stated, underlining the countries' desire for multilateral assistance. There have also been proposals to build a railway connecting Kigali, Bujumbura and Bukavu, which is a key port on Lake Kivu on the other side of the border with the DRC.

There is an international airport at Bujumbura. In September 2004 Rwandair Express inaugurated its first flight between Kigali and Bujumbura, under the conditions of an MOU with Air Burundi, and commenced direct flights from Bujumbura to South Africa, Kenya, Uganda and Europe.

Statistical Survey

Area and Population

AREA, POPULATION AND DENSITY

Area (sq km)	27,834*
Population (census results)†	
16–30 August 1990	5,139,073
16–31 August 2008	
Males	3,838,045
Females	4,039,683
Total	7,877,728
Population (UN estimates at mid-year)‡	
2010	8,382,849
2011	8,575,172
2012	8,749,386
Density (per sq km) at mid-2012	314.3

* 10,747 sq miles.

† Excluding adjustment for underenumeration.

‡ Source: UN, *World Population Prospects: The 2010 Revision*.

POPULATION BY AGE AND SEX
(UN estimates at mid-2012)

	Males	Females	Total
0–14	1,633,838	1,627,731	3,261,569
15–64	2,565,574	2,670,233	5,235,807
65 and over	99,329	152,681	252,010
Total	4,298,741	4,450,645	8,749,386

Source: UN, *World Population Prospects: The 2010 Revision*.

Principal Towns: Bujumbura (capital), population 235,440 (census result, August 1990). *1978:* Gitega 15,943 (Source: Banque de la République du Burundi). *Mid-2011* (urban population, incl. suburbs, UN estimate): Bujumbura 604,732 (Source: UN, *World Urbanization Prospects: The 2011 Revision*).

BIRTHS AND DEATHS
(UN estimates, annual averages)

	1995–2000	2000–05	2005–10
Birth rate (per 1,000)	40.0	36.0	34.3
Death rate (per 1,000)	17.9	16.1	14.8

Source: UN, *World Population Prospects: The 2010 Revision*.

Life expectancy (years at birth): 49.9 (males 48.5; females 51.3) in 2010 (Source: World Bank, World Development Indicators database).

ECONOMICALLY ACTIVE POPULATION*
(persons aged 10 years and over, 1990 census)

	Males	Females	Total
Agriculture, hunting, forestry and fishing	1,153,890	1,420,553	2,574,443
Mining and quarrying	1,146	39	1,185
Manufacturing	24,120	9,747	33,867
Electricity, gas and water	1,847	74	1,921
Construction	19,447	290	19,737
Trade, restaurants and hotels	19,667	6,155	25,822
Transport, storage and communications	8,193	311	8,504
Financing, insurance, real estate and business services	1,387	618	2,005
Community, social and personal services	68,905	16,286	85,191
Sub-total	1,298,602	1,454,073	2,752,675
Activities not adequately defined	8,653	4,617	13,270
Total labour force	1,307,255	1,458,690	2,765,945

* Figures exclude persons seeking work for the first time, totalling 13,832 (males 9,608, females 4,224), but include other unemployed persons.

Source: UN, *Demographic Yearbook*.

Mid-2012 (estimates in '000): Agriculture, etc. 3,852; Total labour force 4,333 (Source: FAO).

Health and Welfare

KEY INDICATORS

Total fertility rate (children per woman, 2010)	4.3
Under-5 mortality rate (per 1,000 live births, 2010)	142
HIV/AIDS (% of persons aged 15–49, 2009)	3.3
Physicians (per 1,000 head, 2004)	0.03
Hospital beds (per 1,000 head, 2006)	0.70
Health expenditure (2009): US $ per head (PPP)	45
Health expenditure (2009): % of GDP	11.4
Health expenditure (2009): public (% of total)	36.0
Access to water (% of persons, 2010)	72
Access to sanitation (% of persons, 2010)	46
Total carbon dioxide emissions ('000 metric tons, 2008)	179.7
Carbon dioxide emissions per head (metric tons, 2008)	0.0
Human Development Index (2011): ranking	185
Human Development Index (2011): value	0.316

For sources and definitions, see explanatory note on p. vi.

Agriculture

PRINCIPAL CROPS

('000 metric tons)

	2008	2009	2010
Wheat	8.1	8.6	9.0
Rice, paddy	74.5	78.4	83.0
Maize	117.7	120.4	126.4
Millet*	11.0	11.2	11.7
Sorghum	79.8	81.2	83.0
Potatoes	28.9	10.6	9.3
Sweet potatoes	900.4	484.2	303.4
Cassava (Manioc)	577.1	235.4	187.9
Taro (Coco yam)	58.3	44.5	18.5
Yams	9.9	5.6	3.1
Sugar cane	189.2	132.8	131.7
Beans, dry	189.7	202.9	201.6
Peas, dry	30.9	37.3	31.5
Groundnuts, with shell*	8.8	8.0	10.2
Oil palm fruit*	16.5	15.5	15.5
Bananas	1,760.0	620.0	136.6
Coffee, green	7.3	25.1	6.8
Tea	6.7	6.7	8.0

* FAO estimates.

Aggregate production ('000 metric tons, may include official, semi-official or estimated data): Total cereals 291.1 in 2008, 299.8 in 2009, 313.2 in 2010. Total roots and tubers 1,574.6 in 2008, 780.3 in 2009, 522.2 in 2010. Total vegetables (incl. melons) 372.8 in 2008, 442.0 in 2009, 403.0 in 2010. Total fruits (excl. melons) 1,873.8 in 2008, 733.8 in 2009, 238.5 in 2010.

Source: FAO.

LIVESTOCK

('000 head, year ending September)

	2008	2009	2010
Cattle	472	554	596
Pigs	167	203	245
Sheep	281	292	296
Goats	1,617	1,687	2,163
Chickens*	4,950	5,000	5,050

* FAO estimates.

Source: FAO.

LIVESTOCK PRODUCTS

('000 metric tons, FAO estimates)

	2008	2009	2010
Cattle meat	13.0	15.2	15.6
Sheep meat	0.6	0.7	0.7
Goat meat	6.1	6.4	6.4
Pig meat	9.8	12.0	12.0
Chicken meat	6.9	6.9	6.9
Cows' milk	22.0	26.0	25.6
Sheep's milk	0.7	0.8	0.8
Goats' milk	16.1	16.9	17.6
Hen eggs	3.1	2.8	3.0

Source: FAO.

Forestry

ROUNDWOOD REMOVALS

('000 cubic metres, excl. bark, FAO estimates)

	2007	2008	2009
Sawlogs, veneer logs and logs for sleepers	307	307	307
Other industrial wood	576	576	576
Fuel wood	8,822	8,965	9,111
Total	9,705	9,848	9,994

2010: Production assumed to be unchanged from 2009 (FAO estimates).

Source: FAO.

SAWNWOOD PRODUCTION

('000 cubic metres, incl. railway sleepers)

	2005	2006	2007
Coniferous (softwood)	18.0*	17.8	18.3
Broadleaved (hardwood)*	65.0	65.0	65.0
Total*	83.0	82.8	83.3

* FAO estimate(s).

2008–10: Production assumed to be unchanged from 2007 (FAO estimates).

Source: FAO.

Fishing

(metric tons, live weight)

	2007	2008	2009
Capture	16,700	17,766	17,700
Freshwater perches	3,600	3,169	3,160
Dagaas	12,000	13,181	13,130
Aquaculture	200	200	200
Total catch (incl. others)	16,900	17,966	17,900

2010: Figures assumed to be unchanged from 2009 (FAO estimates).

Source: FAO.

Mining

(metric tons unless otherwise indicated)

	2008	2009	2010
Gold (kg)*†	750	750	750
Tin ore†	40	8	12
Tantalum and niobium (columbium) concentrates‡	91.3	24.4	67.4
Peat	9,764	11,352	13,111

* Estimates.

† Figures refer to the metal content of ores.

‡ The estimated tantalum content (in metric tons) was 17.8 in 2008, 4.8 in 2009 and 13.1 in 2010.

Source: US Geological Survey.

Industry

SELECTED PRODUCTS

('000 metric tons unless otherwise indicated)

	2009	2010	2011
Beer ('000 hl)	1,366.5	1,665.2	1,748.8
Soft drinks ('000 hl)	287.1	319.9	331.9
Cottonseed oil ('000 litres)	31.5	26.5	43.6
Sugar	14.3	18.9	20.7
Cigarettes (million)	514.2	457.8	510.4
Paint	0.5	0.5	0.6
Polyethylene film (metric tons)	17.5	1.6	—
Soap (metric tons)	6,000.8	5,418.9	8,767.9
Plastic racks ('000)	361.1	393.2	322.4
Moulds (metric tons)	26.7	39.1	27.7
PVC tubing (metric tons)	139.9	143.2	174.2
Electric energy (million kWh)	121.1	142.0	167.9

Steel tubing (metric tons): 68.5 in 2008.

Source: Banque de la République du Burundi.

Finance

CURRENCY AND EXCHANGE RATES

Monetary Units

100 centimes = 1 Burundian franc.

Sterling, Dollar and Euro Equivalents (30 March 2012)

£1 sterling = 2,239.9 francs;
US $1 = 1,399.2 francs;
€1 = 1,868.7 francs;
10,000 Burundian francs = £4.46 = $7.15 = €5.35.

Average Exchange Rate (Burundian francs per US dollar)

2009 1,230.179
2010 1,230.748
2011 1,261.074

GOVERNMENT FINANCE

(central government operations, '000 million Burundian francs)

Summary of balances	2006	2007*	2008†
Revenue	178.8	197.6	249.8
Less Expenditure and net lending	361.0	407.9	558.0
Overall balance (commitment basis)	–182.2	–210.4	–308.2
Change in arrears	–13.7	–21.9	–17.5
External (interest)	–1.8	–0.4	—
Domestic	–11.9	–21.5	–17.5
Overall balance (cash basis)	–195.9	–232.3	–325.7
Grants	169.0	221.5	302.2
Overall balance after grants‡	–30.8	–16.3	–23.4

Revenue	2006	2007*	2008†
Tax revenue	163.4	182.6	232.0
Income tax	45.9	53.5	60.3
Taxes on goods and services	83.9	92.3	124.3
Taxes on international trade	29.7	33.7	43.2
Non-tax revenue	15.4	15.0	17.8
Total	178.8	197.6	249.8

Expenditure and net lending	2006	2007*	2008†
Current expenditure	221.5	261.2	330.2
Compensation of employees	93.9	114.0	141.2
Goods and services	63.8	70.7	93.1
Transfers and subsidies	39.5	46.7	65.6
Interest payments	24.3	29.9	30.3
DDR project§	23.5	12.2	23.5
Capital expenditure	116.8	134.8	208.8
Net lending	–0.8	–0.3	–4.5
Total	361.0	407.9	558.0

* Estimates.
† Budget forecast.
‡ Including errors and omissions.
§ Demobilization, disarmament and reintegration.

Source: IMF, *Burundi: 2008 Article IV Consultation and Request for Three-Year Arrangement Under the Poverty Reduction and Growth Facility - Staff Report; Public Information Notice and Press Release on the Executive Board Discussion; and Statement by the Executive Director for Burundi* (August 2008).

2009 (central government operations, '000 million Burundian francs): *Revenue:* Tax revenue 278.7 (Income tax 84.7, Taxes on goods and services 147.3, Taxes on international trade 44.5, Other taxation 2.2); Non-tax revenue 25.9; Exceptional revenue 7.9; Total 312.5. *Expenditure:* Current expenditure 415.9 (Compensation of employees 185.0); Capital expenditure and net loans 93.2; Total 510.1 (Source: IMF, *Burundi: Poverty Reduction Strategy Paper—Progress Report* (February 2011)).

2010 (central government operations, '000 million Burundian francs): Revenue and grants 930.6; Total expenditure 1,021.7 (Source: IMF (see below)).

2011 (central government operations, '000 million Burundian francs, projections): Revenue and grants 1,111.9; Total expenditure 1,185.4 (Source (2010–2011): IMF, *Burundi: Seventh Review Under the Three-Year Arrangement Under the Extended Credit Facility and Request for a New Three-Year Arrangement Under the Extended Credit Facility—Staff Report; Staff Supplement; Press Release on the Executive Board Discussion; and Statement by the Executive Director for Burundi* (February 2012)).

INTERNATIONAL RESERVES

(US $ million at 31 December)

	2009	2010	2011
Gold*	1.06	1.36	1.50
IMF special drawing rights	104.48	112.77	121.31
Reserve position in IMF	0.56	0.55	0.55
Foreign exchange	217.00	217.41	172.12
Total	323.10	332.09	295.48

* Valued at market-related prices.

Source: IMF, *International Financial Statistics*.

MONEY SUPPLY

(million Burundian francs at 31 December)

	2009	2010	2011
Currency outside depository corporations	120,916	139,103	153,214
Transferable deposits	365,048	435,553	373,235
Other deposits	128,426	155,472	183,918
Broad money	614,389	730,128	710,367

Source: IMF, *International Financial Statistics*.

COST OF LIVING

(Consumer Price Index for Bujumbura; base: January 2000 = 100)

	2005	2006	2007
Food	139.4	139.5	151.6
Clothing	126.7	125.9	119.1
Rent	163.2	176.6	195.5
All items (incl. others)	144.8	148.6	161.0

Source: ILO.

NATIONAL ACCOUNTS

('000 million Burundian francs at current prices)

Expenditure on the Gross Domestic Product

	2007	2008	2009*
Government final consumption expenditure	288	576	601
Private final consumption expenditure	945	1,097	1,210
Gross fixed capital formation	186	310	362
Change in inventories	0	0	0
Total domestic expenditure	1,419	1,983	2,173
Exports of goods and services	91	125	120
Less Imports of goods and services	512	831	786
GDP in purchasers' values	997	1,278	1,507

Gross Domestic Product by Economic Activity

	2007	2008	2009*
Agriculture, hunting, forestry and fishing	323	426	488
Mining and quarrying	0	0	0
Manufacturing	124	162	192
Electricity, gas and water	12	15	17
Construction	54	73	90
Trade, restaurants and hotels	60	77	91
Finance, insurance and real estate	33	44	53
Transport and communications	64	85	106
Public administration and defence	231	277	331
Other services	0	0	0
GDP at factor cost	902	1,159	1,367
Indirect taxes	96	118	140
GDP in purchasers' values	997	1,278	1,507

* Provisional figures.

Source: African Development Bank.

BALANCE OF PAYMENTS

(US $ million)

	2008	2009	2010
Exports of goods f.o.b.	69.6	66.0	101.2
Imports of goods f.o.b.	–335.5	–343.0	–438.4
Trade balance	–265.8	–277.0	–337.2
Export of services	83.3	49.9	79.5
Import of services	–258.8	–176.6	–168.2
Balance on goods and services	–441.3	–403.7	–425.9
Other income received	10.9	1.4	1.1
Other income paid	–15.2	–18.4	–12.0
Balance on goods, services and income	–445.6	–420.7	–436.8
Current transfers received	94.3	162.1	127.2
Current transfers paid	–2.0	–3.2	–13.6
Current balance	–353.3	–261.9	–323.1
Capital account (net)	67.0	82.2	75.7
Direct investment abroad	–0.6	—	—
Direct investment from abroad	3.8	0.3	0.8
Other investment assets	–30.8	–28.9	–43.6
Other investment liabilities	20.0	–718.8	106.2
Net errors and omissions	57.8	–103.6	8.1
Overall balance	–236.1	–1,030.6	–175.9

Source: IMF, *International Financial Statistics*.

External Trade

PRINCIPAL COMMODITIES

(US $ million)

Imports c.i.f.	2008	2009	2010
Food and live animals	27.1	38.8	98.0
Maize, unmilled	1.8	0.1	1.5
Beverages and tobacco	2.8	2.0	8.6
Beverages	2.0	2.0	4.4
Mineral fuels, lubricants and related materials	10.4	8.0	17.6
Chemicals and related products	52.6	55.3	142.4
Medicinal and pharmaceutical products	32.0	29.7	83.2
Basic manufactures	76.4	87.0	220.0
Machinery and transport equipment	107.4	112.1	250.1
Road vehicles	34.0	36.7	102.4
Miscellaneous manufactured articles	25.8	26.7	68.5
Total (incl. others)	315.2	344.8	832.5

Exports f.o.b.	2008	2009	2010
Food and live animals	48.9	53.8	191.7
Coffee and coffee substitutes	39.5	39.7	164.2
Sugars, molasses and honey	1.4	1.8	1.2
Beverages and tobacco	3.4	2.9	7.6
Beer made from malt	1.5	1.4	4.2
Crude materials (inedible), except fuels	12.1	8.1	24.7
Hides and skins	2.8	1.6	7.8
Mineral fuels, lubricants and related materials	1.1	1.6	5.7
Petroleum	1.1	1.6	5.7
Basic manufactures	1.2	1.0	2.2
Machinery and transport equipment	11.4	13.0	6.4
Road vehicles	7.9	9.5	3.7
Miscellaneous manufactured articles	0.8	2.0	2.5
Total (incl. others)	141.8	112.9	275.5

Source: UN, *International Trade Statistics Yearbook*.

PRINCIPAL TRADING PARTNERS

(US $ million)

Imports c.i.f.	2008	2009	2010
Belgium	54.6	46.5	100.1
Canada	2.8	4.7	2.2
China, People's Repub.	23.2	32.3	100.1
Denmark	3.8	8.3	13.3
Egypt	8.5	14.0	23.1
France (incl. Monaco)	28.8	18.4	59.6
Germany	21.1	6.2	13.2
India	15.9	19.4	50.1
Italy	6.7	12.9	11.1
Japan	15.2	17.3	78.0
Kenya	27.6	32.1	60.8
Netherlands	5.1	3.9	9.5
Rwanda	3.5	1.8	5.3
Saudi Arabia	1.5	4.4	4.7
South Africa	10.2	4.6	13.6
Tanzania	15.7	15.2	49.7
Uganda	30.3	29.7	56.9
United Arab Emirates	13.8	16.6	38.5
United Kingdom	4.1	4.1	10.5
USA	2.8	9.3	12.4
Zambia	3.0	11.7	70.1
Total (incl. others)	315.2	344.8	832.5

Exports f.o.b.	2008	2009	2010
Belgium	8.6	6.3	35.8
Chad	5.2	0.1	0.0
China, People's Repub.	1.5	1.3	5.2
Congo, Democratic Repub.	5.9	7.0	17.0
Germany	5.7	8.4	5.7
Italy	0.3	0.6	2.8
Kenya	7.6	7.3	24
Oman	1.3	1.5	4.2
Rwanda	4.5	4.7	7
Singapore	1.6	2.5	16.9
Swaziland	2.2	1.4	3.1
Switzerland and Liechtenstein	21.7	20.7	74.2
Tanzania	2.2	9.5	4.1
Uganda	3.0	6.4	6.7
United Arab Emirates	61.7	28.9	24.4
United Kingdom	0.2	0.6	36.8
Total (incl. others)	141.8	112.9	275.5

Source: UN, *International Trade Statistics Yearbook*.

Transport

ROAD TRAFFIC
('000 motor vehicles in use, estimates)

	1998	1999	2000
Passenger cars	6.6	6.9	7.0
Commercial vehicles	9.3	9.3	9.3

2001–03 ('000 motor vehicles in use): Figures assumed to be unchanged from 2000.

Source: UN, *Statistical Yearbook*.

2007 (motor vehicles in use at 31 December): Passenger cars 15,466; Vans and lorries 32,717; Motorcycles and mopeds 11,302 (Source: IRF, *World Road Statistics*).

LAKE TRAFFIC
(Bujumbura, '000 metric tons)

	2009	2010	2011
Goods:			
arrivals	167.6	222.8	224.2
departures	5.8	22.8	9.5

Source: Banque de la République du Burundi.

CIVIL AVIATION
(traffic on scheduled services)

	1996	1997	1998
Passengers carried ('000)	9	12	12
Passenger-km (million)	2	8	8

Source: UN, *Statistical Yearbook*.

Tourism

TOURIST ARRIVALS BY REGION*

	2004	2005	2006
Africa	1,333	49,473	140,868
Americas	5,908	9,956	4,025
Asia	4,528	4,023	10,062
Europe	29,409	29,486	32,199
Unspecified	92,050	55,480	14,087
Total	133,228	148,418	201,241

* Including Burundian nationals residing abroad.

Tourism receipts (US $ million, incl. passenger transport): 1.6 in 2006; 2.3 in 2007; 1.6 in 2008; 1.7 in 2009.

Source: World Tourism Organization.

Communications Media

	2008	2009	2010
Telephones ('000 main lines in use)	30.4	31.5	32.6
Mobile cellular telephones ('000 subscribers)	480.6	838.4	1,150.5
Internet subscribers ('000)	4.0	5.0	n.a.
Broadband subscribers	200	200	200

Personal computers: 65,000 (8.5 per 1,000 persons) in 2006.

Television receivers ('000 in use): 200 in 2001.

Radio receivers ('000 in use): 140 in 1997.

Daily newspapers: 1 in 2004.

Non-daily newspapers: 5 in 1998 (circulation 8,000 copies).

Sources: mainly International Telecommunication Union; UNESCO, *Statistical Yearbook*.

Education

(2009/10)

	Teachers	Students		
		Males	Females	Total
Pre-primary	1,617	27,581	27,522	55,103
Primary	36,557	931,034	918,827	1,849,861
Secondary:				
General	10,143	186,342	135,770	322,112
Technical and vocational	1,132	9,893	5,572	15,465
Higher	1,784	18,917	10,352	29,269

Institutions (1988/89): Primary 1,512; Secondary 400.

Source: UNESCO Institute for Statistics.

Pupil-teacher ratio (primary education, UNESCO estimate): 50.6 in 2009/10 (Source: UNESCO Institute for Statistics).

Adult literacy rate (UNESCO estimates): 67.2% (males 72.9%; females 61.8%) in 2010 (Source: UNESCO Institute for Statistics).

Directory

The Constitution

On 20 October 2004 a 'post-transitional' Constitution was officially adopted by the President, after its approval by both chambers of the legislature. The new Constitution, was endorsed at a national referendum on 28 February 2005 (replacing the Constitution of 28 October 2001). The main provisions of the Constitution are summarized below:

PREAMBLE

The Constitution upholds the rights of the individual, and provides for a multi-party political system. The Government is based on the will of the people, and must be composed in order to represent all citizens. The function of the political system is to unite and reconcile all citizens and to ensure that the established Government serves the people. The Government must recognize the separation of powers, the primacy of the law and the principles of good governance and transparency in public affairs. All citizens have equal rights and are assured equal protection by the law. The civic obligations of the individual are emphasized.

POLITICAL PARTY SYSTEM

Political parties may be established freely, subject to conformity with the law. Their organization and activities must correspond to democratic principles and membership must be open to all civilians. They are not permitted to promote violence, discrimination or hate on any basis, including ethnic, regional or religious or tribal affiliation. Members of defence and security bodies, and acting magistrates are prohibited from joining political parties. A five-member Commission électorale nationale indépendante guarantees the freedom, impartiality and independence of the electoral process.

EXECUTIVE POWER

Executive power is vested in the President, who is the Head of State. The President is elected by universal direct suffrage for a term of five years, which is renewable once. (The first post-transitional President is to be elected by a majority of two-thirds of members in both legislative chambers.) The President is assisted in the exercise of his powers by two Vice-Presidents, whom he appoints, and presides over the Government.

GOVERNMENT

The President appoints the Government in consultation with the Vice-Presidents. The Government is required to comprise a 60% proportion of Hutu ministers and deputy ministers and 40% of Tutsi ministers and deputy ministers, and to include a minimum 30% of women. Political parties that secured more than 5% of votes cast in legislative elections are entitled to nominate a proportionate number of representatives to the Government. The President is obliged to replace a minister in consultation with the political party that the minister represents.

LEGISLATURE

Legislative power is vested in the bicameral legislature, comprising a lower chamber, the Assemblée nationale, and an upper chamber, the Sénat. The Assemblée nationale has a minimum of 100 deputies, with a proportion of 60% Hutu and 40% Tutsi representatives, and including a minimum 30% of women. Deputies are elected by direct universal suffrage for a term of five years, while the Twa ethnic group nominates three representatives. If the election results fail to conform to the stipulated ethnic composition, additional deputies may be appointed in accordance with the electoral code. The Sénat comprises a minimum of two senators elected by ethnically balanced colleges from each of the country's provinces, and three Twa representatives, and includes a minimum 30% of women. Both chambers have a President and Vice-Presidents.

JUDICIARY

The President guarantees the independence of the judiciary, with the assistance of the Conseil Supérieur de la Magistrature. The highest judicial power is vested in the Cour Suprême. All appointments to these organs are made by the President, on the proposal of the Minister of Justice and in consultation with the Conseil Supérieur de la Magistrature, and are endorsed by the Sénat. The Cour Constitutionnelle interprets the provisions of the Constitution and ensures the conformity of new legislation. The Cour Constitutionnelle comprises seven members, who are appointed by the President, subject to the approval of the Sénat, for a six-year renewable term.

DEFENCE AND SECURITY FORCES

The establishment and operations of defence and security forces must conform to the law. Members of defence and security forces are prohibited from belonging to, participating in the activities of, or demonstrating prejudice towards, any political parties. All citizens are eligible to join the defence and security forces. During a period to be determined by the Sénat, defence and security forces are not permitted to comprise more than 50% of one single ethnic group, in order to ensure an ethnic balance and guard against acts of genocide and military coups.

The Government

HEAD OF STATE

President: Maj. JEAN-PIERRE NKURUNZIZA (inaugurated 26 August 2005; re-elected 28 June 2010).

First Vice-President: THÉRENCE SINUNGURUZA.

Second Vice-President: GERVAIS RUFYIKIRI.

COUNCIL OF MINISTERS

(September 2012)

The Government comprises members of the Conseil National pour la Défense de la Démocratie—Forces pour la Défense de la Démocratie (CNDD—FDD), the Front pour la Démocratie au Burundi (FRODEBU-Nyakuri), the Union pour le Progrès National (UPRONA) and independents.

Minister of the Interior: EDOUARD NDUWIMANA (CNDD—FDD).

Minister of Public Security: GABRIEL NIZIGAMA (CNDD—FDD).

Minister of External Relations and International Co-operation: LAURENT KAVAKURE (CNDD—FDD).

Minister at the Presidency, in charge of Good Governance and Privatization: ISSA NGENDAKUMANA.

Minister at the Presidency, in charge of East African Community Affairs: HAFSA MOSSI (CNDD—FDD).

Minister of Justice, Keeper of the Seals: PASCAL BARANDAGIYE (CNDD—FDD).

Minister of Finance and Planning for Economic Development: TABU ABDALLAH MANIRAKIZA (CNDD—FDD).

Minister of Communal Development: MARTIN MANIRAKIZA.

Minister of National Defence and War Veterans: Maj.-Gen. PONTIEN GACIYUBWENGE (Ind.).

Minister of Public Health and the Fight against AIDS: Dr SABINE NTAKARUTIMANA (CNDD—FDD).

Minister of Higher Education and Scientific Research: Dr JULIEN NIMUBONA (UPRONA).

Minister of Primary and Secondary Education, Professional and Vocational Training and Literacy: SÉVERIN BUZINGO (CNDD—FDD).

Minister of Agriculture and Livestock: ODETTE KAYITESI (CNDD—FDD).

Minister of Telecommunications, Information, Communications and Relations with Parliament: CONCILIE NIBIGIRA (UPRONA).

Minister of Water, the Environment, Territorial Development and Town Planning: JEAN-MARIE NIBIRANTIJE (CNDD—FDD).

Minister of Commerce, Industry, Posts and Tourism: VICTOIRE NDIKUMANA (UPRONA).

Minister of Energy and Mines: CÔME MANIRAKIZA (CNDD—FDD).

Minister of Civil Service, Labour and Social Security: ANNONCIATE SENDAZIRASA (CNDD—FDD).

Minister of Transport, Public Works and Equipment: MOÏSE BUKUMI.

Minister of Youth, Sports and Culture: JEAN-JACQUES NYENIMIGABO.

Minister of National Solidarity, Human Rights and Gender: CLOTILDE NIRAGIRA.

MINISTRIES

Office of the President: Bujumbura; tel. 22226063; internet www.presidence.bi.

Ministry of Agriculture and Livestock: Bujumbura; tel. 22222087.

Ministry of Civil Service, Labour and Social Security: BP 1480, Bujumbura; tel. 22225645; fax 22228715.

Ministry of Commerce, Industry, Posts and Tourism: BP 492, Bujumbura; tel. 22225330; fax 22225595.

Ministry of Energy and Mines: BP 745, Bujumbura; tel. 22225909; fax 22223337.

Ministry of External Relations and International Co-operation: Bujumbura; tel. 22222150.

Ministry of Finance: ave des Non-Aligens, BP 1830, Bujumbura; tel. 22225142; fax 22223128; internet www.finances.gov.bi.

Ministry of Higher Education and Scientific Research: Bujumbura.

Ministry of the Interior: Bujumbura.

Ministry of Justice: ave des Palmiers, Bujumbura; tel. 22222148.

Ministry of National Defence and War Veterans: Bujumbura.

Ministry of National Solidarity, Human Rights and Gender: BP 224, Bujumbura; tel. 22225394; fax 22224193; e-mail ministre@miniplan.bi; internet www.cslpminiplan.bi.

Ministry of Planning and Communal Development: Bujumbura; internet www.miniplan.bi.

Ministry of Primary and Secondary Education, Professional and Vocational Training and Literacy: Bujumbura.

Ministry of Public Health and the Fight against AIDS: rue Pierre Ngendandumwe, Bujumbura.

Ministry of Public Security: Bujumbura.

Ministry of Telecommunications, Information, Communications and Relations with Parliament: BP 2870, Bujumbura.

Ministry of Transport, Public Works and Equipment: BP 2000, Bujumbura; tel. 22222923; fax 22226900.

Minister of Water, the Environment, Territorial Development and Town Planning: BP 631, Bujumbura; tel. 22224976; fax 22228902; e-mail nduwi_deo@yahoo.fr.

Ministry of Youth, Sports and Culture: Bujumbura; tel. 22226822.

President and Legislature

PRESIDENT

A presidential election was held on 28 June 2010 at which Jean-Pierre Nkurunziza, representing the Conseil National pour la Défense de la Démocratie—Forces pour la Défense de la Démocratie, was the sole candidate. According to results confirmed by the Constitutional Court on 8 July, Nkurunziza secured 2,482,219 of the 2,709,941 votes cast, equating to 91.60%. (There were 29,195 invalid votes cast.)

SÉNAT

President: GABRIEL NTISEZERANA (CNDD—FDD).

First Vice-President: PERSILLE MWIDOGO (CNDD—FDD).

Second Vice-President: PONTIEN NIYONGABO (UPRONA).

Elections, 28 July 2010

Party	Seats*
CNDD—FDD	32
UPRONA	2
Total	34

* In accordance with constitutional requirements for balance of ethnic representation and a minimum 30% representation of women, a further four seats were allocated to former Presidents and three to the Twa ethnic group, increasing the total number of senators to 41.

ASSEMBLÉE NATIONALE

President: PIE NTAVYOHANYUMA (CNDD—FDD).

First Vice-President: MO-MAMO KARERWA (CNDD—FDD).

Second Vice-President: FRANÇOIS KABURA (UPRONA).

Elections, 23 July 2010

Party	Seats*
CNDD—FDD	81
UPRONA	17
FRODEBU-Nyakuri	5
Total	103

* In accordance with constitutional requirements for balance of ethnic representation and a minimum 30% representation of women, a further three seats were allocated to the Twa ethnic group, increasing the total number of deputies to 106. The CNDD—FDD, FRODEBU-Nyakuri and UPRONA each received an additional seat.

Election Commission

Commission électorale nationale indépendante (CENI): BP 1128, Bujumbura; tel. 22274464; tel. info@ceniburundi.bi; internet www.ceniburundi.bi; f. 2004; independent; 5 mems; Chair. PIERRE CLAVER NDAYICARIYE; Vice-Chair. MARGUERITTE BUKURU.

Political Organizations

Political parties are required to demonstrate firm commitment to national unity, and impartiality with regard to ethnic or regional origin, gender and religion, in order to receive legal recognition. By 2009 the number of registered political parties had increased to 42; these included former rebel organizations.

Alliance Burundaise-Africaine pour le Salut (ABASA): Bujumbura; f. 1993; Tutsi; Leader TÉRENCE NSANZE.

Alliance Démocratique pour le Changement au Burundi (ADC—Ikibiri): Bujumbura; f. 2010; coalition of 12 opposition parties, including Front pour la démocratie au Burundi (FRODEBU); Pres. LÉONCE NGENDAKUMANA.

Alliance Libérale pour le Développement (ALIDE): f. 2001; Leader JOSEPH NTIDENDEREZA.

Alliance des Vaillants (AV—Intware) (Alliance of the Brave): Bujumbura; f. 1993; Tutsi; Leader ANDRÉ NKUNDIKIJE.

Conseil National pour la Défense de la Démocratie (CNDD): Bujumbura; e-mail cndd_bur@usa.net; internet www.club.euronet.be/pascal.karolero.cndd.burundi; f. 1994; Hutu; Pres. LÉONARD NYANGOMA.

Conseil National pour la Défense de la Démocratie—Forces pour la Défense de la Démocratie (CNDD—FDD): fmr armed wing of the Hutu CNDD; split into 2 factions in Oct. 2001, one led by JEAN-BOSCO NDAYIKENGURUKIYE and the other by JEAN-PIERRE NKURUNZIZA; Nkurunziza's faction incl. in Govt Nov. 2003, following peace agreement; registered as political org. Jan. 2005; Chair. JÉRÉMIE NGENDAKUMANA; Sec.-Gen. GÉLASE NDABIRABE.

Forces Nationales de Libération (FNL): fmr armed wing of Hutu Parti de libération du peuple hutu (PALIPEHUTU, f. 1980); split in Aug. 2002 and in Dec. 2005; cease-fire with Govt announced Sept. 2006; formally registered as a political organization in 2009; Chair. EMMANUEL MIBURO.

Forces Nationales de Libération—Iragi rya Gahutu: f. 2009; Leader JACQUES KENESE.

Front National de Libération Icanzo (FNL Icanzo): reconstituted Dec. 2002 from fmr faction of Forces nationales de libération; Leader Dr ALAIN MUGABARABONA.

Front pour la Démocratie au Burundi (FRODEBU): Bujumbura; internet www.frodebu.bi; f. 1992; split in June 1999; Hutu; Chair. LÉONCE NGENDAKUMANA.

FRODEBU-Nyakuri: Bujumbura; f. 2008; Leader JEAN MINANI.

KAZE—Force pour la Défense de la Démocratie (KAZE—FDD): f. May 2004; reconstituted as a political party from a faction of the armed CNDD—FDD (see above); Leader JEAN-BOSCO NDAYIKENGURUKIYE.

Mouvement pour la Réhabilitation du Citoyen—Rurenzangemero (MRC—Rurenzangemero): Bujumbura; f. June 2001; regd Nov. 2002; Leader Lt-Col EPITACE BAYAGANAKANDI.

Mouvement pour la Sécurité et la Démocratie: tel. 29550803; e-mail msdburundi@yahoo.fr; internet msdburundi.org; ALEXIS SINDUHIJE; Sec.-Gen. ODETTE NTAHIRAJA.

Mouvement Socialiste Panafricaniste—Inkinzo y'Ijambo Ry'abarundi (MSP—Inkinzo) (Guarantor of Freedom of Speech in Burundi): Bujumbura; f. 1993; Tutsi; Chair. TITE BUCUMI.

Parti Libéral (PL): BP 2167, Bujumbura; tel. 22214848; fax 22225981; e-mail liberalburundi@yahoo.fr; f. 1992; Hutu; Leader GAËTAN NIKOBAMYE.

Parti pour le Développement et la Solidarité des Travailleurs (PML-Abanyamwete): Bujumbura; f. Oct. 2004; Leader PATRICIA NDAYIZEYE.

Parti pour la Réconciliation du Peuple (PRP): Bujumbura; f. 1992; Tutsi; Leader MATHIAS HITIMANA.

Parti pour le Redressement Intégral du Burundi (PARIBU): Bujumbura; f. Sept. 2004; Leader BENOÎT NDORIMANA.

Parti pour le Redressement National (PARENA): Bujumbura; f. 1994; Leader JEAN-BAPTISTE BAGAZA.

Parti Social Démocrate (PSD): Bujumbura; f. 1993; Tutsi; Leader GODEFROID HAKIZIMANA.

Rassemblement pour la Démocratie et le Développement Économique et Social (RADDES): Bujumbura; f. 1992; Tutsi; Chair. JOSEPH NZEYZIMANA.

Union pour la Paix et le Développement (Zigamibanga): f. Aug. 2002; Leader ZEDI FERUZI.

Union pour le Progrès National (UPRONA): BP 1810, Bujumbura; tel. 22225028; f. 1958 following the 1961 elections; the numerous small parties which had been defeated merged with UPRONA, which became the sole legal political party in 1966; party activities were suspended following the coup of Sept. 1987, but resumed in 1989; Chair. ALOYS RUBUKA.

Diplomatic Representation

EMBASSIES IN BURUNDI

Belgium: 9 blvd de la Liberté, BP 1920, Bujumbura; tel. 22226176; fax 22223171; e-mail bujumbura@diplobel.fed.be; internet www.diplomatie.be/bujumbura; Ambassador JOZEF SMETS.

China, People's Republic: 675 sur la Parcelle, BP 2550, Bujumbura; tel. 22224307; fax 22213735; e-mail chinaemb_bi@mfa.gov.cn; Ambassador YU XUZHONG.

Congo, Democratic Republic: BP 872, Bujumbura; tel. 22229330; e-mail ambardcbujumbura@yahoo.fr; Ambassador SALOMON BANAMUHERE BALIÈNE.

Egypt: 31 ave de la Liberté, BP 1520, Bujumbura; tel. 22223161; fax 22222918; Ambassador ABDEL MONE'M OMAR ABDEL MONE'M.

France: 60 ave de l'UPRONA, BP 1740, Bujumbura; tel. 22203000; fax 22203010; e-mail cad.bujumbura-amba@diplomatie.gouv.fr; internet www.ambafrance-bi.org; Ambassador JOËL LOUVET.

Germany: 22 rue 18 septembre, BP 480, Bujumbura; tel. 22257777; fax 22221004; e-mail info@buju.diplo.de; Ambassador JOSEPH WEISS.

Holy See: 46 ave des Travailleurs, BP 1068, Bujumbura; tel. 22225415; fax 22223176; e-mail na.burundi@diplomat.va; Apostolic Nuncio FRANCO COPPOLA (Titular Archbishop of Vinda).

Kenya: PTA Bank Bldg, 2nd Floor, West Wing Chaussée du Prince Louis Rwagasore, BP 5138, Mutanga, Bujumbura; tel. 22258160; fax 22258161; e-mail information@kenyaembassy.bu; Ambassador BENJAMIN A. W. MWERI.

Nigeria: Bujumbura; tel. 22257076; Ambassador OKWUDILI OBIDIGBO NWOSU.

Russia: 78 blvd de l'UPRONA, BP 1034, Bujumbura; tel. 22226098; fax 22222984; e-mail ustas@cbinf.com; Ambassador VLADIMIR TIMOFEEV.

Rwanda: 40 ave de la RDC, BP 400, Bujumbura; tel. 22228755; fax 22215426; e-mail ambabuja@minaffet.gov.rw; internet www.burundi.embassy.gov.rw; Ambassador AUGUSTIN HABIMANA.

South Africa: ave de la Plage, Quartier Asiatique, BP 185, Bujumbura; tel. 22248220; fax 22248219; e-mail bujumbura@foreign.gov.za; Ambassador MDU LEMBEDE.

Tanzania: 855 rue United Nations, BP 1653, Bujumbura; tel. 22248632; fax 22248637; e-mail tanzanrep@usan-bu.net; Ambassador Dr JAMES NZAGI.

USA: ave des Etats-Unis, BP 1720, Bujumbura; tel. 22223454; fax 22222926; e-mail jyellin@bujumbura.us-state.gov; internet burundi.usembassy.gov; Ambassador PAMELA JO HOWELL SLUTZ.

Judicial System

Constitutional Court: BP 151, Bujumbura; comprises a minimum of 7 judges, who are nominated by the President for a 6-year term; Pres. CHRISTINE NZEYIMANA.

Supreme Court: BP 1460, Bujumbura; tel. and fax 22213544; court of final instance; 3 divisions: ordinary, cassation and administrative; Pres. (vacant).

Courts of Appeal: Bujumbura, Gitega and Ngozi.

Tribunals of First Instance: There are 17 provincial tribunals and 123 smaller resident tribunals in other areas.

Religion

Some 70% of the population are Christians, the majority of whom are Roman Catholics. Anglicans number about 60,000. There are about 200,000 other Protestant adherents, of whom about 160,000 are Pentecostalists. About 23% of the population adhere to traditional beliefs, which include the worship of the god Imana. About 10% of the population are Muslims. The Bahá'í Faith is also active in Burundi.

CHRISTIANITY

Conseil National des Eglises Protestantes du Burundi (CNEB): BP 17, Bujumbura; tel. 22224216; fax 22227941; e-mail cneb@cbninf.com; f. 1935; 10 mem. churches; Pres. Rt Rev. ISAAC BIMPENDA (Anglican Bishop of Gitega); Gen. Sec. Rev. NOAH NZEYIMANA.

The Anglican Communion

The Church of the Province of Burundi, established in 1992, comprises five dioceses.

Archbishop of Burundi and Bishop of Matana: Most Rev. BERNARD NTAHOTURI, BP 447, Bujumbura; tel. 22924595; fax 22229129; e-mail ntahober@cbinf.com.

Provincial Secretary: Rev. PEDACULI BIRAKENGANA, BP 447, Bujumbura; tel. 22270361; fax 22229129; e-mail peab@cbinf.com.

The Roman Catholic Church

Burundi comprises two archdioceses and six dioceses. Some 69% of the total population are Roman Catholics.

Bishops' Conference

Conférence des Evêques Catholiques du Burundi, 5 blvd de l'UPRONA, BP 1390, Bujumbura; tel. 22223263; fax 22223270; e-mail cecab@cbinf.com.

f. 1980; Pres. Rt Rev. EVARISTE NGOYAGOYE (Archbishop of Bujumbura).

Archbishop of Bujumbura: Rt Rev. EVARISTE NGOYAGOYE, BP 690, Bujumbura; tel. 22231476; fax 22231165; e-mail dicabu@cni.cbinf.com.

Archbishop of Gitega: Most Rev. SIMON NTAMWANA, Archevêché, BP 118, Gitega; tel. 22402160; fax 22402620; e-mail archigi@bujumbura.ocicnet.net.

Other Christian Churches

Union of Baptist Churches of Burundi: Rubura, DS 117, Bujumbura 1; 87 mem. churches; Pres. PAUL BARUHENAMWO; mems 25,505 (2005).

Other denominations active in the country include the Evangelical Christian Brotherhood of Burundi, the Free Methodist Church of Burundi and the United Methodist Church of Burundi.

BAHÁ'Í FAITH

National Spiritual Assembly: BP 1578, Bujumbura; tel. 79955840; e-mail bahaiburundi@yahoo.fr; Sec. DENIS NDAYIZEYE.

The Press

Conseil National de la Communication (CNC): Immeuble Marcoil, blvd de l'UPRONA, Bujumbura; tel. 22259064; fax 22259066; e-mail info@cnc-burundi.org; internet cnc-burundi.org; f. 2001 under the terms of the transitional Constitution; responsible for ensuring press freedom; Pres. PIERRE BAMBASI; Sec. ESPÉRANCE NDAYIZEYE.

NEWSPAPER

Le Renouveau du Burundi: BP 2573, Bujumbura; tel. 22225411; e-mail lerenouveaubdi@yahoo.fr; f. 1978; daily; French; govt-owned; Dir of Publication THADDÉE SIRYUYUMUNSI; Editor-in-Chief ALICE KWIGIZÉ; circ. 1,200 (2011).

PERIODICALS

Arc-en-Ciel: Bujumbura; weekly; French; Editor-in-Chief THIERRY NDAYISHIMIYE.

Au Coeur de l'Afrique: Association des conférences des ordinaires du Rwanda et Burundi, BP 1390, Bujumbura; fax 22223027; e-mail cnid@cbinf.com; bimonthly; education; circ. 1,000.

Bulletin Économique et Financier: BP 482, Bujumbura; bimonthly.

Bulletin Mensuel: Banque de la République du Burundi, Service des études, BP 705, Bujumbura; tel. 22225142; monthly.

Iwacu: ave de France 6, BP 1842, Bujumbura; tel. 22258957; fax 79991474; internet www.iwacu-burundi.org; f. 2008; weekly; publ. by the Union Burundaise des Journalistes; Editor-in-Chief ANTOINE KABURAHE.

In-Burundi: c/o Cyber Média, BP 5270, ave du 18 septembre, Bujumbura; tel. 2244464; current affairs internet publication; Editor-in-Chief EDGAR C. MBANZA.

Ndongozi Y'uburundi: Catholic Mission, BP 690, Bujumbura; tel. 22222762; fax 22228907; fortnightly; Kirundi.

Revue Administration et Juridique: Association d'études administratives et juridiques du Burundi, BP 1613, Bujumbura; quarterly; French.

Ubumwe: Bujumbura; tel. 22225654; e-mail ubumwebdi@yahoo.fr; weekly; Editor-in-Chief PACIFIQUE NKESHIMANA; circ. 2,500 (2011).

PRESS ASSOCIATIONS

Association Burundaise des Femmes Journalistes (AFJO): ave Kunkiko, BP 2414, Bujumbura; tel. 79949460; fax 22254920; e-mail nijembazi@yahoo.fr; Pres. ANNICK NSABIMANA.

Union Burundaise des Journalistes (UBJ): Bujumbura; fmrly Association Burundaise des Journalistes (ABJ), present name adopted 2009; Pres. ALEXANDRE NIYUNGEKO; Sec.-Gen. BERTRAND BIHIZI.

NEWS AGENCY

Agence Burundaise de Presse (ABP): ave Nicolas Mayugi, BP 2870, Bujumbura; tel. 22213083; fax 22222282; e-mail abp@cbinf.com; internet www.abp.info.bi; f. 1975; publ. daily bulletin.

Publishers

Editions Intore: 19 ave Matana, BP 2524, Bujumbura; tel. 22223499; e-mail anbirabuza@yahoo.fr; f. 1992; philosophy, history, journalism, literature, social sciences; Dir Dr ANDRÉ BIRABUZA.

IMPARUDI: ave du 18 septembre 3, BP 3010, Bujumbura; tel. 22223125; fax 22222572; e-mail imparudi.1982@yahoo.fr; f. 1950; Dir-Gen. THÉONESTE MUTAMBUKA.

Imprimerie la Licorne: 29 ave de la Mission, BP 2942, Bujumbura; tel. 22223503; fax 22227225; f. 1991.

Les Presses Lavigerie: 5 ave de l'UPRONA, BP 1640, Bujumbura; tel. 22222368; fax 22220318.

Régie de Productions Pédagogiques: BP 3118, Bujumbura II; tel. 22226111; fax 22222631; e-mail rpp@cbinf.com; f. 1984; school textbooks; Dir ABRAHAM MBONERANE.

GOVERNMENT PUBLISHING HOUSE

Imprimerie Nationale du Burundi (INABU): BP 991, Bujumbura; tel. 22224046; fax 22225399; f. 1978; Dir NICOLAS NIJIMBERE.

Broadcasting and Communications

In 2011 there were five providers of cellular mobile telephone communications services. The state-owned ONATEL provided fixed-line services. In 2010 there were some 1.7m. mobile telephone subscribers.

TELECOMMUNICATIONS

Agence de Régulation et de Contrôle des Télécommunications (ARCT): 360 ave Patrice Lumumba, BP 6702, Bujumbura; tel. 22210276; fax 22242832; Dir-Gen. JOSEPH NSEGANA.

Direction Générale des Transports, Postes et Télécommunications: BP 2390, Bujumbura; tel. 22225422; fax 22226900; govt telecommunications authority; Dir-Gen. VITAL NARAKWIYE.

Econet Wireless Burundi: 21 blvd du 28 Novembre, BP 431, Bujumbura; tel. 22243131; fax 22243535; internet www.econet.bi; formerly Spacetel; mobile and fixed telecommunications services and products, satellite services and internet solutions; Dir-Gen. DARLINGTON MANDIVENGA.

Leo Burundi: 1 pl. de l'Indépendance, BP 5186, Bujumbura; e-mail feliciten@leo.bi; internet www.leo.bi; f. 1993; fmrly Telecel Burundi, Leo Burundi is the trade name of U-Com Burundi; mobile telephone service provider; a subsidiary of Orascom Telecom Holding; Dir-Gen. RAYMOND LAFORCE.

Office National des Télécommunications (ONATEL): ave du Commerce, BP 60, Bujumbura; tel. 22223196; fax 22226917; e-mail onatel@cbinf.com; f. 1979; Dir-Gen. SALVATOR NIZIGIYIMANA.

ONAMOB: Bujumbura; mobile cellular telephone operator owned by ONATEL.

Smart Mobile: Immeuble White Stone, blvd de l'Uprona Centre, BP 3150, Bujumbura; internet lacellsu.com; f. 2010; trade name of Lacell SU; Dir-Gen. BHUPENDRA BHANDARI.

Tempo Africell: ave de la RDC, Bujumbura; tel. 78872872; e-mail africell@cbinf.com; internet www.tempo.bi; f. 1999 as Africell; name changed as above in 2008 following acquisition by VTEL Holdings (United Arab Emirates); mobile cellular telephone service provider; CEO YANAL ABZACK.

BROADCASTING

In 2010 there were some 15 private radio stations and one private television channel operating in Burundi, in addition to the state-run Radiodiffusion et Télévision Nationale du Burundi.

Radio

Radio Bonesha FM: BP 5314, Bujumbura; tel. 22217068; e-mail umwizero@cbinf.com; f. 1996 as Radio Umwizero; EU-funded, private station promoting national reconciliation, peace and devt projects; broadcasts 9 hours daily in Kirundi, Swahili and French; Dir HUBERT VIEILLE.

Radio Isanganiro: 27 ave de l'Amitié, BP 810, Bujumbura; tel. 22246595; fax 22246600; e-mail isanganiro@isanganiro.org; internet www.isanganiro.org; f. Nov. 2002; controlled by Association Ijambo, f. by Studio Ijambo (see below); broadcasts on 89.7 FM frequency, in Kirundi, French and Swahili; services cover Bujumbura area, and were to be extended to all Great Lakes region; Dir VINCENT NKESHIMANA.

Radio Publique Africaine (RPA): Bujumbura; tel. 79920704; e-mail nfo@rpa-radioyacu.org; internet www.rpa-radiyoyacu.org; f. 2001 with the aim of promoting peace; independent; Dir ALEXIS SINDUHIJE.

Radio Renaissance FM: Bujumbura; f. 2003; Dir-Gen. INNOCENT MUHOZI.

Radio Sans Frontières Bonesha FM: Association Radio Sans Frontières 47, Chemin P. L. Rwagasore, BP 5314, Bujumbura; internet www.bonesha.bi; Dir CORNEILLE NIBARUTA.

Rema FM: Bujumbura; f. 2008.

Studio Ijambo (Wise Words): 27 ave de l'Amitié, BP 6180, Bujumbura; tel. 22219699; e-mail burundi@sfcg.org.bi; internet www.studioijambo.org; f. 1995 by Search for Common Ground; promotes peace and reconciliation.

Voix de la Révolution/La Radiodiffusion et Télévision Nationale du Burundi (RTNB): BP 1900, Bujumbura; tel. 22223742; fax 22226547; internet www.rtnb.bi; f. 1960; govt-controlled; daily radio broadcasts in Kirundi, Swahili, French and English; Pres. SALVATOR NIZIGIYIMANA; Dir-Gen. CHANNEL SABIMBONA.

Television

Télé Renaissance: Bujumbura; f. 2008; Dir-Gen. INNOCENT MUHOZI.

Voix de la Révolution/La Radiodiffusion et Télévision Nationale du Burundi (RTNB): BP 1900, Bujumbura; tel. 22223742; fax 22226547; internet www.rtnb.bi; f. 1960; govt-controlled; television service in Kirundi, Swahili, French and English; Pres. SALVATOR NIZIGIYIMANA; Dir-Gen. CHANNEL SABIMBONA.

Finance

(cap. = capital; res = reserves; dep. = deposits; m. = million; brs = branches; amounts in Burundian francs)

BANKING

In 2010 there were 10 commercial banks and 22 microfinancial institutions in Burundi.

Central Bank

Banque de la République du Burundi (BRB): ave du Gouvernement, BP 705, Bujumbura; tel. 22225142; fax 22223128; e-mail brb@brb.bi; internet www.brb-bi.net; f. 1964 as Banque du Royaume du Burundi; state-owned; bank of issue; cap. 11,000m., res 21,780m., dep. 169,043m. (Dec. 2009); Gov. GASPARD SINDAYIGAYA; First Vice-Gov. MELCHIOR WAGARA; 2 brs.

Commercial Banks

Banque Burundaise pour le Commerce et l'Investissement SARL (BBCI): blvd du Peuple Murundi, BP 2320, Bujumbura; tel. 22223328; fax 22223339; e-mail bbci@cbinf.com; f. 1988; cap. and res 2,645.8m., total assets 14,016.2m. (Dec. 2003); Pres. CELESLIN MIZERO; Dir-Gen. CHARLES NIHANGAZA.

Banque Commerciale du Burundi SM (BANCOBU): 84 chaussée Prince Louis Rwagasore, BP 990, Bujumbura; tel. 22222317; fax 22221018; e-mail info@bancobu.com; internet www.bancobu.com; f. 1960; cap. 6,820.0m., res 7,065.4m., dep. 82,091.1m. (Dec. 2009); Pres. ALEXIS NTACONZOBA; Dir-Gen. JEAN CIZA; 8 brs.

Banque de Crédit de Bujumbura SM: ave Patrice Emery Lumumba, BP 300, Bujumbura; tel. 22201111; fax 22201115; e-mail info@bcb.bi; internet www.bcb.bi; f. 1964; cap. 7,000.0m., res 3,949.6m., dep. 144,333.8m. (Dec. 2009); Pres. CLOTILDE NIRAGIRA; Gen. Man. THARCISSE RUTUMO; 8 brs.

Banque de Financement et de Leasing S.A.: blvd de la Liberté, BP 2998, Bujumbura; tel. 22243206; fax 22225437; e-mail finalease@cbinf.com; cap. and res 1,400.5m., total assets 8,578.4m. (Dec. 2003); Pres. AUDACE BIREHA; Dir-Gen. ERIC BONANE RUBEGA.

Banque de Gestion et de Financement SA: 1 blvd de la Liberté, BP 1035, Bujumbura; tel. 22221349; fax 22221351; e-mail bgf@onatel.bi; f. 1996; cap. 1,029.0m., res 986.1m., dep. 19,791.7m. (Dec. 2006); Pres. BÉDE BEDETSE; Gen. Man. MATHIAS NDIKUMANA.

Ecobank Burundi: 6 rue de la Science, BP 270, Bujumbura; tel. 22226351; fax 22225437; e-mail ecobankbi@ecobank.com; internet www.ecobank.com; cap. 7,000.1m., res 564.4m., dep. 38,044.6m. (Dec. 2009); Chair. ISAAC BUDABUDA; Man. Dir STEPHANE DOUKOURE.

Interbank Burundi SARL: 15 rue de l'Industrie, BP 2970, Bujumbura; tel. 22220629; fax 22220461; e-mail info@interbankbdi.com;

internet www.interbankbdi.com; f. 1993; cap. and res 9,385.1m., total assets 117,387.0m. (Dec. 2006); Pres. GEORGES COUCOULIS; Dir-Gen. CALLIXTE MUTABAZI.

Development Bank

Banque Nationale pour le Développement Economique SARL (BNDE): 3 ave du Marché, BP 1620, Bujumbura; tel. 22222888; fax 22223775; e-mail bnde@cbinf.com; internet www.bndesm.com; f. 1966; 40% state-owned; cap. 6,190.1m., res 811.3m., dep. 6,526.1m. (Dec. 2009); Chair. and Man. Dir DONATIEN NIJIMBERE.

Co-operative Bank

Banque Coopérative d'Epargne et de Crédit Mutuel (BCM): BP 1340, Bujumbura; operating licence granted in April 1995; Vice-Pres. JULIEN MUSARAGANY.

Financial Institutions

Fonds de Promotion de L'Habitat Urbain (FPHU): ave de la Liberté, BP 1996, Bujumbura; tel. 22224986; fax 22223225; e-mail info@fphu.bi; internet www.fphu.bi; cap. 818m. (2005); Dir-Gen. AUDACE BUKURU.

Société Burundaise de Financement: 6 rue de la Science, BP 270, Bujumbura; tel. 22222126; fax 22225437; e-mail sbf@cbinf.com; cap. and res 2,558.9m., total assets 11,680.4m. (Dec. 2003); Pres. ASTÈRE GIRUKWIGOMBA; Dir-Gen. DARIUS NAHAYO.

INSURANCE

In 2010 there were six insurance companies in Burundi.

Société d'Assurances du Burundi (SOCABU): 14–18 rue de l'Amitié, BP 2440, Bujumbura; tel. 22226520; fax 22226803; e-mail socabu@socabu.bi; internet www.socabu-assurances.com; f. 1977; cap. 180m.; Man. Dir ONÉSIME NDUWIMANA.

Société Générale d'Assurances et de Réassurance (SOGEAR): BP 2432, Bujumbura; tel. 22222345; fax 22229338; f. 1991; Pres. BENOÎT NDORIMANA; Dir-Gen. L. SAUSSEZ.

Union Commerciale d'Assurances et de Réassurance (UCAR): BP 3012, Bujumbura; tel. 22223638; fax 22223695; e-mail ucar@cbinf.com; f. 1986; cap. 150m.; Chair. Lt-Col EDOUARD NZAMBIMANA; Dir-Gen. PASCAL NTAMASHIMIKIRO.

Trade and Industry

GOVERNMENT AGENCIES

Agence Burundaise de Promotion des Investissements: Quartier Kigobe, BP 7057, Bujumbura; tel. 22275996; e-mail info@burundi-investment.com; internet www.burundi-investment.com; f. 2009; Dir-Gen. LIBÉRAT MFUMUKEKO.

Agence de Promotion des Echanges Extérieurs (APEE): 27 rue de la Victoire, BP 3535, Bujumbura; tel. 22225497; fax 22222767; e-mail apee@cbinf.com; promotes and supervises foreign exchanges.

Agence Régulateur de la Filière Café (ARFIC): 279 blvd de Tanzanie, BP 450, Bujumbura; tel. 22223193; fax 22225532; f. 2009 to replace the Office du Café du Burundi, f. 1964; contributes to policy formulation for the coffee sector and supervises coffee plantations and coffee exports; Dir EVARISTE NGAYEMPORE.

Office National du Commerce (ONC): Bujumbura; f. 1973; supervises international commercial operations between the Govt of Burundi and other states or private orgs; also organizes the import of essential materials; subsidiary offices in each province.

Office National du Logement (ONL): BP 2480, Bujumbura; tel. 22226074; f. 1974 to supervise housing construction.

Office du Thé du Burundi (OTB): 52 blvd de l'UPRONA, Bujumbura; tel. 22224228; fax 22224657; e-mail otb@cbinf.com; f. 1979; supervises production and marketing of tea; Man. Dir ALEXIS NZOHABONIMANA.

DEVELOPMENT ORGANIZATIONS

Agence Française de Développement (AFD): Immeuble Old East, BP 2740, Bujumbura; tel. 222255931; internet www.afd.fr; Gen. Man. CLEMENCE VIDAL DE LA BLACHE.

Compagnie Financière pour le Développement SA: Bldg INSS, 1 route Nationale, BP 139, Ngozi; tel. 22302279; fax 22302296; Pres. ABBÉ EPHREM GIRUKWISHAKA.

Fonds de National d'Investissement Communal (FONIC): blvd du 28 Novembre, BP 2799, Bujumbura; tel. 22221963; fax 22243268; e-mail fdc@cbinf.com; internet www.fonic.bi; f. 2007 to replace Fonds de Développement Communal; Pres. DOMITIEN NDIHOKUBWAYO.

Fonds de Promotion de l'Habitat Urbain: 6 ave de la Liberté, BP 1996, Bujumbura; tel. 22227676; fax 22223225; e-mail info@fphu.bi; internet www.fphu.bi; cap. 818m. Burundian francs; Pres. IDI KARIM BUHANGA; Dir-Gen. BUKURU AUDACE.

Institut des Sciences Agronomiques du Burundi (ISABU): BP 795, Bujumbura; tel. 22227349; fax 22225798; e-mail dgisabu@cbinf.com; f. 1962 for the scientific development of agriculture and livestock; Dir-Gen. MARIE GORETTI MIREREKANO.

Observatoire des Filières Agricoles du Burundi (OFB): 7 ave Imbo, Quartier Asiatique, BP 5, Bujumbura; tel. 22251865; fax 22250567; e-mail info@ofburundi.org; internet www.ofburundi.org; f. 2004; provides information on Burundi's agricultural sector and facilitates dialogue between key figures and orgs; Co-ordinator PATRICE NTAHOMPAGAZE.

Office National de la Tourbe (ONATOUR): route de l'aéroport, BP 2360, Bujumbura; tel. 22226480; fax 22226709; e-mail kariyo@yahoo.fr; f. 1977 to promote the exploitation of peat deposits; Dir-Gen. YVETTE KARIYO.

Société d'Economie pour l'Exploitation du Quinquina au Burundi (SOKINABU): 16 blvd Mwezi Gisabo, BP 1783, Bujumbura; tel. 22223469; fax 22218160; e-mail chiastos@yahoo.fr; f. 1975 to develop and exploit cinchona trees, the source of quinine; Dir CHRISTIAN REMEZO.

INDUSTRIAL AND TRADE ASSOCIATIONS

Association des Commerçants du Burundi (ACOBU): 254 ave du Commerce, Rohero, BP 6373, Bujumbura; tel. 22248663; Pres. CONSTANTIN NDIKUMANA.

Association des Employeurs du Burundi (AEB): 187 rue de la Mission, BP 141, Bujumbura; tel. 221119; fax 248190; e-mail assoaeb64@yahoo.fr; Pres. ALOYSE KIRAHUZI; Exec. Sec. GASPARD NZISABIRA.

Association des Femmes Entrepreneurs du Burundi (AFAB): 127 ave Kunkiko, Rohero II, BP 1628, Bujumbura; tel. 22242784; Pres. CONSOLATA NDAYISHIMIYE.

Association des Industriels du Burundi (AIB): 187 rue de la mission, Rohero, BP 141, Bujumbura; tel. 22221119; fax 22220643; e-mail aib.burundi@yahoo.fr; Pres. ECONIE NIJEMBERE; Exec. Sec. JEAN PAUL NTUHURUMURYANGO.

CHAMBER OF COMMERCE

Chambre Fédérale de Commerce et d'Industrie du Burundi (CFCIB): ave du 18 Septembre, BP 313, Bujumbura; tel. 22222280; fax 22227895; e-mail ccib@ccib.bi; internet www.cfcib.org; f. 2010 to replace Chambre de Commerce, d'Industrie, d'Agriculture et d'Artisanat du Burundi (CCIB; f. 1923); Pres. CONSOLATA NDAYISHIMIYE; 130 mems.

UTILITIES

Régie de Distribution d'Eau et d'Electricité (REGIDESO): Ngozi, Bujumbura; tel. 22302222; state-owned distributor of water and electricity services; Dir PASCAL NDAYISHIMIYE.

MAJOR COMPANIES

Brarudi: blvd du 1er Novembre, BP 540, Bujumbura; tel. 22215360; fax 22222948; internet web.brarudi.net; f. 1955; production of beer and soft drinks; Dir MAARTEN SCHUURMAN.

Burundi Mining Corpn (BUMINCO): BP 648, Bujumbura; tel. 22223299; f. 1986; part state-owned; mineral exploitation.

Compagnie de Gérance du Coton (COGERCO): BP 2571, Bujumbura; tel. 22222208; fax 22224370; e-mail cogerco@cbinf.com; f. 1984; development of cotton industry; Pres. SÉBASTIEN NDAVIZEYE; Dir-Gen. LÉOPOLD MANIRAKIZA.

Engen Petroleum Burundi SA: 10 pl. de l'Indépendance, BP 15, Bujumbura; tel. 22222848; fax 22226625; e-mail info@engen.co.bi; internet www.engen.co.bi; fmrly Fina BP Burundi; Dir-Gen. CHARLES NIKOBASA.

Société Sucrière du Moso (SOSUMO): BP 835, Bujumbura; tel. 22221662; fax 22223028; e-mail directeurgeneral@sosumo.net; internet www.sosumo.net; f. 1982 to develop and manage sugar cane plantations; Dir-Gen. AUDACE BUKURU.

TRADE UNIONS

Confédération des Syndicats du Burundi (COSYBU): ave du 18 Septembre, Ex Hôtel Central 8, BP 220, Bujumbura; tel. and fax 22248190; e-mail cosybu@yahoo.fr; Pres. THARCISSE GAHUNGU; 32 mem. asscns.

Confédération des Syndicats libres du Burundi (CSB): BP 1570, Bujumbura; tel. 222229; e-mail csb sq2001@vahoo.fr; Pres. THARCISSE NIBOGORA; Sec.-Gen. MATHIAS RUVARI.

Transport

RAILWAYS

There are no railways in Burundi. Plans have been under consideration since 1987 for the construction of a line passing through Uganda, Rwanda and Burundi, to connect with the Kigoma–Dar es Salaam line in Tanzania. This rail link would relieve Burundi's isolated trade position.

ROADS

In 2004 Burundi had a total of 12,322 km of roads, of which 5,012 km were national highways and 282 km secondary roads. In 2008 some 31.7% of all roads were paved.

Office des Transports en Commun (OTRACO): BP 1486, Bujumbura; tel. 22231313; fax 22232051; 100% govt-owned; operates public transport; Dir-Gen. NICODÈME NIZIGIYIMANA.

INLAND WATERWAYS

Bujumbura is the principal port for both passenger and freight traffic on Lake Tanganyika, and the greater part of Burundi's external trade is dependent on the shipping services between Bujumbura and lake ports in Tanzania, Zambia and the Democratic Republic of the Congo.

Société Concessionnaire de l'Exploitation du Port de Bujumbura (EPB): BP 59, Bujumbura; tel. 22226036; e-mail bujaport@cbinf.com; f. 1967; 43% state-owned; controls Bujumbura port; Dir-Gen. MÉTHODE SHIRAMBERE.

CIVIL AVIATION

The international airport at Bujumbura is equipped to take large jet-engined aircraft.

Air Burundi: 40 ave du Commerce, BP 2460, Bujumbura; tel. 22223460; fax 22223452; e-mail reservation@airburundi.com; internet www.airburundi.org; f. 1971 as Société de Transports Aériens du Burundi; state-owned; operates charter and scheduled passenger services to destinations throughout central Africa; CEO MELCHIOR NAHIMANA; Man. Dir ELIE NTACORIGIRA.

Tourism

Tourism is relatively undeveloped. The annual total of tourist arrivals declined from 125,000 in 1991 to only 10,553 in 1997. Total arrivals increased gradually thereafter, reaching 74,116 in 2003 and rising to an estimated 201,241 in 2006. Tourism receipts amounted to an estimated US $1.7m. in 2009.

Office National du Tourisme (ONT): 2 ave des Euphorbes, BP 902, Bujumbura; tel. and fax 22224208; e-mail info@burunditourisme.net; internet www.burunditourisme.net; f. 1972; responsible for the promotion and supervision of tourism; Dir DÉO NGENDAHAYO.

Defence

Burundi's armed forces, as assessed at November 2011, comprised an army of 20,000 and a paramilitary force of 31,050 gendarmes (including a 50-strong marine police force). At the end of 2004 the Government had officially established a reconstituted armed forces (Forces de défense nationales—FDN—comprising equal proportions of Hutus and Tutsis), which incorporated some 23,000 former rebel combatants, and a new police force. In April 2003 the deployment of the first members of an AU Mission in Burundi (AMIB) commenced; the contingent (which comprised mainly South African troops, with reinforcements from Ethiopia and Mozambique) was mandated to assist in the enforcement of the cease-fire between the Government and rebel factions. In May 2004 the UN Security Council approved the deployment of a Opération des Nations Unies au Burundi (ONUB—with a maximum authorized strength of 5,650 military personnel), to replace AMIB. Under a resolution of 30 June 2006, the UN Security Council ended the mandate of ONUB at the end of December, when it was replaced by a UN office, the Bureau Intégré des Nations Unies au Burundi (BINUB). BINUB was established for an initial period of one year, with authorization to continue peace consolidation, including support for the demobilization and reintegration of former combatants and reform of the security sector. BINUB's mandate was subsequently extended until 31 December 2010. In mid-December the Security Council replaced BINUB with the United Nations Office in Burundi, with effect from 1 January 2011 and with an initial mandate of 12 months (subsequently extended until 15 February 2013). Meanwhile, some 100 Burundian troops were sent to Somalia in December 2007 as part of the African Union Mission to Somalia (AMISOM), a peace-keeping force established at the beginning of that year in an attempt to stabilize the war-torn country. By mid–2012 the AU force comprised 15,541 soldiers, including 4,400 from Burundi. In 2012 a total of 4,411 troops were stationed abroad, of whom five were observers.

Defence Expenditure: Budgeted at 79,700m. Burundian francs in 2011.

Chief of Staff of the Forces de défense nationales: Maj.-Gen. GODEFROID NIYOMBARE.

Chief of Staff of the Gendarmerie: Col SALVATOR NDAYIYUNVIYE.

Education

Education is provided free of charge. Kirundi is the language of instruction in primary schools, while French is used in secondary schools. Primary education, which is officially compulsory, begins at seven years of age and lasts for six years. Secondary education begins at the age of 13 and lasts for up to seven years, comprising a first cycle of four years and a second of three years. In 2005 it was announced that primary education would be provided for free by the State, vastly increasing enrolment in the following years. In 2008/09, according to UNESCO estimates, 99% of children in the relevant age-group (males 98%; females 100%) were enrolled at primary schools. Enrolment at secondary schools in 2009/10 was equivalent to only an estimated 16% of the population (males 18%; females 15%). In 2002/03 11,915 students were enrolled at the University of Bujumbura. There are also private universities at Ngozi and Bujumbura, the Université de Ngozi, the Université Lumière de Bujumbura, the Université du Lac Tanganyika and Hope Africa University. The total number of students enrolled in higher education in 2009/10 was 29,269. Public expenditure on education in 2008 was equivalent to 22.3% of total government expenditure.

Bibliography

Brennan, K. *Burundi.* Broomall, PA, Mason Crest Publishers, 2004.

Chrétien, J.-P. 'La société du Burundi : Des mythes aux réalités', in *Revue Française d'Etudes Politiques Africaines,* Nos. 163–164 (pp. 94–118). July–August 1979.

Histoire rurale de l'Afrique des Grands Lacs. Paris, Editions Karthala, 1983.

Chretien, J.-P. *The Great Lakes of Africa: Two Thousand Years of History*. New York, Zone Books, 2003.

Chrétien, J.-P., Guichaoua, A., and Le Jeune, G. *La crise d'août 1988 au Burundi.* Paris, Editions Karthala, 1989.

Eggers, E. *Historical Dictionary of Burundi*. 2nd edn. Metuchen, NJ, Scarecrow Press, 1997.

Emerging Markets Investment Center. *Burundi Investment and Business Guide.* Washington, DC, International Business Publications, 1999.

Ewusi, K., and Akwanga, Jr, K. *Burundi's Negative Peace: The Shadow of a Broken Continent in the Era of NEPAD.* Bloomington, IN, Trafford Publishing, 2010.

Gahama, J. *Le Burundi sous administration belge.* Paris, Editions Karthala, 1983.

Guichaoua, A. (Ed.). *Les crises politiques au Burundi et au Rwanda (1993–1994)*. Paris, Editions Karthala, 1995.

Guillet, C., and Ndayishinguje, P. *Légendes historiques du Burundi.* Paris, Editions Karthala, 1987.

Hakizimana, A. *Naissances au Burundi : Entre Tradition et Planification*. Paris, L'Harmattan, 2002.

International Business Publications. *Burundi Foreign Policy and Government Guide.* Washington, DC, 2004.

Krueger, R., and Krueger, K. *From Bloodshed to Hope in Burundi: Our Embassy Years During Genocide*. Austin, TX, University of Texas Press, 2007.

Lambert, M. Y. *Enquête démographique Burundi (1970–1971).* Bujumbura, Ministère du Plan, 1972.

Lemarchand, R. *Rwanda and Burundi.* London, Pall Mall, 1970.

Ethnocide as Discourse and Practice. Washington, DC, Woodrow Wilson Center Press and Cambridge, Cambridge University Press, 1994.

Burundi: Ethnic Conflict and Genocide. Cambridge, Cambridge University Press, 1996.

The Dynamics of Violence in Central Africa. Philadelphia, PA, University of Pennsylvania Press. 2009.

Longman, T. P. *Burundi—Proxy Target: Civilians in the War on Burundi.* New York, Human Rights Watch, 1998.

Malkii, L. *Purity and Exile: Violence, Memory and National Cosmology among Hutu Refugees in Tanzania.* Chicago, IL, University of Chicago Press. 1995.

Mwakikagile, G. *Civil Wars in Rwanda and Burundi: Conflict Resolution in Africa.* New York, Nova Science Publishers, 2004.

Mworoha, E. *Histoire du Burundi*. Paris, Hatier, 1987.

Nsanzé, T. *Le Burundi au carrefour de l'Afrique.* Brussels, Remarques africaines, 1970.

Ntahombaye, P. *Des noms et des hommes. Aspects du nom au Burundi.* Paris, Editions Karthala, 1983.

Ould Abdallah, A. *Burundi on the Brink 1993–95: A UN Special Envoy Reflects on Preventative Diplomacy (Perspectives Series).* Washington, DC, United States Institute of Peace, 2000.

Reyntjens, F. *Burundi 1972–1988. Continuité et changement.* Brussels, Centre d'étude et de documentation africaines (CEDAF—ASDOC), 1989.

Small States in an Unstable Region—Rwanda and Burundi 1999–2000 (Current African Issues, 23). Uppsala, Nordiska Afrikainstitutet, 2001.

Again at the Crossroads—Rwanda and Burundi, 2000–2001. Uppsala, Nordiska Afrikainstitutet, 2001.

Sommers, M. *Fear in Bongoland: Burundi Refugees in Urban Tanzania (Studies in Forced Migration, Vol. 8).* New York, Berghahn Books, 2001.

Southall, R., and Bentley, K. *African Peace Process: Mandela, South Africa, and Burundi.* Pretoria, Human Sciences Research Council, 2005.

Tuhabonye, G., and Brozek, G. *This Voice in My Heart: A Genocide Survivor's Story of Escape, Faith, and Forgiveness.* New York, Amistad, 2006.

Uvin, P. *Life After Violence: A People's Story of Burundi*. London, Zed Books, 2008.

Watt, N. *Burundi: The Biography of a Small African Country*. New York, Columbia University Press, 2008.

CAMEROON

Physical and Social Geography

JOHN I. CLARKE

PHYSICAL FEATURES

The Republic of Cameroon covers an area of 475,442 sq km (183,569 sq miles) and contains exceptionally diverse physical environments. The country occupies a fairly central position within the African continent, with the additional advantage of a 200-km coastline. Its environmental diversity arises from various factors, including the country's position astride the volcanic belt along the hinge between west and central Africa, together with its intermediate location between the great basins of the Congo, the Niger and Lake Chad, its latitudinal extent between 2° and 13°N, its altitudinal range from sea-level to more than 4,000 m, and its spread from coastal mangrove swamp to remote continental interior.

In the south and centre of the country a large undulating and broken plateau surface of granites, schists and gneisses rises northwards away from the Congo basin to the Adamawa plateau (900 m–1,520 m above sea-level). North of the steep Adamawa escarpment, which effectively divides northern from southern Cameroon, lies the basin of the Benue river, a tributary of the Niger, which is floored by sedimentary rocks, interspersed with inselbergs and buttes. In the west of the country a long line of rounded volcanic mountains and hills extends from Mt Cameroun (4,095 m), the highest mountain in west and central Africa, north-eastwards along the former boundary between East and West Cameroon and then along the Nigerian border. Volcanic soils derived from these mountains are more fertile than most others in the country and have permitted much higher rural population densities than elsewhere.

Cameroon has a marked south-north gradation of climates, from a seasonal equatorial climate in the south (with two rainy seasons and two moderately dry seasons of unequal length), to southern savannah and savannah climates (with one dry and one wet season), to a hotter drier climate of the Sahel type in the far north. Rainfall thus varies from more than 5,000 mm in the south-west to around 610 mm near Lake Chad. Corresponding to this climatic zonation is a south-north gradation of vegetal landscapes: dense rain forest, Guinea savannah, Sudan savannah and thorn steppe, while Mt Cameroun incorporates a vertical series of sharply divided vegetation zones.

POPULATION

The population of Cameroon was enumerated at 17,052,134 at the census of November 2005, and was estimated to have risen to 20,468,945 in mid-2012, giving an average density of 43.1 inhabitants per sq km. Population growth has been rapid (an average rate of 2.3% per year in 2001–10) and the composition and distribution of the population are extremely diverse. In the southern forest regions Bantu peoples predominate, although there are also pygmy groups in some of the more remote areas. North of the Bantu tribes live many semi-Bantu peoples including the ubiquitous Bamileke. Further north the diversity increases, with Sudanese Negroes, Hamitic Fulani (or Foulbe) and Arab Choa.

The distribution of population is uneven, with concentrations in the west, the south-central region and the Sudan savannah zone of the north. An important religious and social divide lies across the country. While the peoples of the south and west have been profoundly influenced by Christianity and by the European introduction of an externally orientated colonial-type economy, the peoples of the north are either Muslim or animist and have largely retained their traditional modes of life. Consequently, the population of the south and west is much more developed, economically and socially, than that of the north, although the Government has made efforts to reduce this regional disparity.

One aspect of this disparity is the southern location of the capital, Yaoundé (estimated population 2,432,000 in 2011), and the main port of Douala (2,125,000 in 2010), as well as most of the other towns. Much of their growth results from rural–urban migration; many of the migrants come from overcrowded mountain massifs in the west, and the Bamileke constitute more than one-third of the inhabitants of Douala. Nevertheless, about two-thirds of all Cameroonians remain rural village-dwellers.

One other major contrast in the social geography of Cameroon is between anglophone north-west and south-west Cameroon, with less than one-10th of the area and just over one-fifth of the population, and the much larger, more populous francophone area of former East Cameroon. The contrasting influences of British and French rule remain evident in education, commerce, law and elsewhere, although unification of the civil services since 1972, official bilingualism and the integration of transport networks and economies have helped to reduce the disparities between the two zones.

Recent History

KATHARINE MURISON

The German protectorate of Kamerun, of which the Republic of Cameroon was formerly a part, was established in 1884. In 1916 the German administration was overthrown by combined French-British-Belgian military operations during the First World War, and in 1919 the territory was divided into British and French spheres of influence. In 1922 both zones became subject to mandates of the League of Nations, which allocated four-fifths of the territory to French administration as French Cameroun, and the other one-fifth, comprising two long, non-contiguous areas along the eastern Nigerian border, to British administration as the Northern and Southern Cameroons.

In 1946 the mandates were converted into UN trust territories, still under their respective French and British administrations. However, growing anti-colonial sentiment made it difficult for France and Britain to resist the UN Charter's promise of eventual self-determination for all inhabitants of trust territories. In 1957 French Cameroun became an autonomous state within the French Community, and on 1 January 1960 proceeded to full independence as the Republic of Cameroon. Ahmadou Ahidjo, the leader of the Union camerounaise, who had served as Prime Minister since 1958, was elected as the country's first President.

In the British Cameroons, which were attached for administrative purposes to neighbouring Nigeria, a UN-supervised plebiscite was held in 1961 in both parts of the trust territory. Voters in the Southern Cameroons opted for union with the

Republic of Cameroon, while northern Cameroon voters chose to merge with Nigeria (becoming the province of Sardauna). The new Federal Republic of Cameroon thus comprised two states: the former French zone became East Cameroon, while the former British portion became West Cameroon. Ahidjo assumed the presidency of the federation. In June 1972 the country was officially renamed the United Republic of Cameroon. The sole legal party, the Union Nationale Camerounaise (UNC), assumed full supervision of Cameroon's organized political and social affairs. In its foreign policy, the UNC Government adopted a non-aligned stance and sought to reduce its dependence on France and the Western bloc.

Despite dissatisfaction in some quarters with the single-party system and discontent among English-speaking politicians about their relatively low representation in government, Ahidjo and the UNC retained popular support in subsequent single-list elections. In 1980 Ahidjo was again re-elected as sole candidate for a further five-year term.

THE BIYA PRESIDENCY

In November 1982 Ahidjo resigned on the grounds of ill health, and transferred the presidency to Paul Biya, the country's Prime Minister since 1975. In January 1984 Biya was re-elected President, as sole candidate, and the country's original official name, the Republic of Cameroon, was subsequently restored. In March 1985 the UNC was renamed the Rassemblement Démocratique du Peuple Camerounais (RDPC). Legislative and presidential elections were held in April 1988. Voters in the legislative elections were presented with a choice of RDPC-approved candidates. Biya, the sole candidate for the presidency, obtained 98.8% of the votes cast.

Opposition and the Pro-democracy Movement

In February 1990 12 people were imprisoned, having been found guilty of subversion as a result of their alleged involvement in an unofficial opposition organization, the Social Democratic Front (SDF), led by John Fru Ndi. In May six deaths were reported, after security forces violently suppressed a demonstration organized by the SDF, which took place in Bamenda (in the English-speaking north-west of the country) and was attended by at least 20,000 people. In June, in response to continued civil unrest, Biya stated that the adoption of a multi-party system was envisaged, and subsequently announced the abolition of laws governing subversion, the relaxation of restraints on the press, and the reform of legislation prohibiting political associations. In December the National Assembly approved a constitutional amendment providing for the establishment of a multi-party system.

During 1991 pressure for political reform intensified. In January anti-Government demonstrators protested at Biya's failure (despite previous undertakings) to grant an amnesty to prisoners implicated in the April 1984 coup attempt. In April 1991 the National Assembly formally granted a general amnesty to all political prisoners, and reintroduced the post of Prime Minister. Sadou Hayatou, hitherto Secretary-General to the presidency, was appointed to the position. In late April a newly established alliance of 11 leading opposition groups, the National Co-ordination Committee of Opposition Parties (NCCOP), demanded an unconditional amnesty for all political prisoners (the existing arrangements for an amnesty excluded an estimated 400 political prisoners jailed ostensibly for non-political offences), and the convening of a national conference before 10 May. The continuing reluctance of the Government to set a date for the national conference prompted the NCCOP to initiate a campaign of civil disobedience and to demand the resignation of the Cabinet. In June the NCCOP orchestrated a general strike. In response, the Government prohibited opposition gatherings, and, following continued civil disturbances, banned the NCCOP. The effect of the general strike declined in subsequent months.

In November 1991 the Government and about 40 of the 47 registered opposition parties signed an agreement providing for the establishment of a 10-member committee to draft constitutional reforms. The opposition pledged to suspend the campaign of civil disobedience, while the Government agreed to end the ban on opposition meetings and to release all prisoners who had been arrested during the demonstrations earlier that year. However, several parties within the NCCOP, including the SDF, subsequently rejected the agreement.

At legislative elections on 1 March 1992 the RDPC won 88 of the 180 seats in the National Assembly; the Union Nationale pour la Démocratie et le Progrès (UNDP) secured 68 seats, the Union des Populations Camerounaises (UPC) 18, and the Mouvement pour la Défense de la République (MDR) six seats. The opposition parties that had not accepted the agreement in November 1991, grouped in the Alliance pour le Redressement du Cameroun (ARC), boycotted the elections, in which an estimated 61% of registered voters took part. The RDPC formed an alliance with the MDR after the elections, thereby securing an absolute majority in the National Assembly. In April Biya announced a new Cabinet, headed by Simon Achidi Achu, an anglophone member of the RDPC, as Prime Minister.

In August 1992 Biya announced that the forthcoming presidential election, due to take place in May 1993, was to be brought forward to October 1992. This measure was widely believed to benefit the Government, following the failure of a large number of opposition supporters to register earlier that year, as a result of the SDF boycott of the legislative elections. Later that month the Government introduced legislation regulating the election of the President, which prohibited political parties from forming electoral alliances. Following protracted negotiations, two of the seven opposition candidates withdrew in favour of the leader of the SDF, John Fru Ndi, who received the endorsement of the ARC.

At the presidential election, which took place on 11 October 1992, Biya was re-elected by 39.9% of votes cast, while Fru Ndi secured 35.9% and Bello Bouba Maigari, the Chairman of the UNDP, 19.2%. A number of demonstrations ensued, particularly in the North-West Province and in Douala. However, the Supreme Court ruled against a petition by Fru Ndi to invalidate the election results, despite confirmation from a US monitoring organization that it had detected widespread electoral irregularities. At the end of October, in response to continued unrest, the Government placed Fru Ndi and a number of his supporters under house arrest.

Pressure for Constitutional Reform

Biya was inaugurated for a third term as President in November 1992. His new Cabinet included representatives of the UPC, the UNDP and the Parti national du progrès. Although Biya undertook to carry out further constitutional reforms, the USA and Germany suspended economic aid in protest at the suppression of opposition activity and the continued enforcement of the state of emergency.

In March 1993, in response to international pressure, the Government announced that a national debate on constitutional reform was to take place. In April a meeting organized by the Cameroon Anglophone Movement (CAM) in Buéa, the capital of the South-West Province, issued demands for the restoration of a federal system of government, as a counter to the dominance of the French-speaking section of the population in the country. In May Biya announced that the planned debate on the revision of the Constitution was to take place in early June. Instead of the envisaged national conference, however, a technical commission was established to prepare recommendations based on proposals from all sectors of the population. Later in May the Government published draft constitutional amendments, which provided for a democratic system of government, including the establishment of an upper legislative chamber, a council of supreme judiciary affairs, a council of state, and a high authority to govern the civil service. The constitutional provisions also limited the tenure of the President to two five-year terms of office. Elections were to comprise two rounds of voting (a system more favourable to the opposition). The draft legislation retained a unitary state, but, in recognition of demands by supporters of federalism, introduced a more decentralized system of government. The constitutional proposals were subject to amendment, following the recommendations of the technical commission. However, three representatives of the English-speaking community subsequently resigned from the technical commission, in protest at the Government's alleged control of the constitutional debate.

In November 1994 Biya announced that discussions on the revision of the Constitution were to resume, following the establishment of a 'consultative constitutional review committee' and that municipal elections were to take place in 1995. Constitutional discussions in December 1994 were boycotted by the opposition, which objected to limitations in the agenda of the debate. In early 1995 revised constitutional amendments were submitted to Biya for consideration. In April Biya announced the creation of 64 new local government districts, in preparation for the forthcoming municipal elections.

In early July 1995 members of a newly emerged anglophone organization, the Southern Cameroons National Council (SCNC, which demanded that the former portion of the British Cameroons that had amalgamated with the Republic of Cameroon in 1961 be granted autonomy), staged a demonstration in Bamenda, subsequently clashing with security forces. Later that month English-speaking representatives of the Government criticized the demands for the establishment of an anglophone republic (which would be known as Southern Cameroons); the SCNC apparently intended to proclaim formally the independence of Southern Cameroons on 1 October 1996, following the adoption of a separate constitution for the new republic. In August 1995 representatives of anglophone movements, including the SCNC and the CAM, presented their demands for the establishment of an independent republic of Southern Cameroons at the UN, and urged the international community to assist in resolving the issue in order to avert civil conflict in Cameroon; the organizations claimed that the plebiscite of 1961, whereby the former southern portion of British Cameroons had voted to merge with the Republic of Cameroon on terms of equal status, had been rendered invalid by subsequent francophone domination.

Cameroon's pending application for membership of the Commonwealth (see below) prompted further controversy in 1995; opposition movements urged the Commonwealth to refuse admission to Cameroon on the grounds that no progress had been achieved with regard to Commonwealth stipulations on human rights and the democratic process, while the SCNC submitted a rival application for membership on behalf of the proposed independent republic of Southern Cameroons. (Nevertheless, Cameroon was admitted to the organization in November.) In December the National Assembly formally adopted the revised constitutional amendments, which increased the presidential mandate from five to seven years (while restricting the maximum tenure of office to two terms) and provided for the establishment of an upper legislative chamber, to be known as the Senate, and a Constitutional Council.

Some 38 political parties participated in the municipal elections, which finally took place in January 1996. The RDPC retained about 56% of the 336 local government areas, while the SDF secured 27%, principally in the west of the country. In March the SDF and the UNDP (which had also achieved some success in the municipal elections, principally in the north) urged a campaign of civil disobedience in protest at the Government's appointment by decree of representatives to replace the elected mayors in principal towns.

In September 1996 Biya appointed Peter Mafany Musonge, hitherto the manager of the Cameroon Development Corporation, to the office of Prime Minister, replacing Achidi Achu. Legislative elections were contested on 17 May 1997 by 46 political parties. The announcement later that month of provisional election results (which attributed a large majority of seats to the RDPC) prompted claims from the opposition parties of widespread electoral malpractice. In June the Supreme Court announced the official election results: the RDPC had secured 109 of the 180 seats in the legislature, while the SDF had won 43, the UNDP 13 and the Union démocratique du Cameroun (UDC) five seats. On 3 August further polls were conducted in seven constituencies where the results had been annulled owing to alleged irregularities; the RDPC won all of the seats, thus increasing its level of representation in the National Assembly to 116 seats.

A presidential election was held on 12 October 1997, contested by seven candidates. The SDF, the UNDP and the UDC boycotted the election in protest at the absence of an independent electoral commission. While official sources asserted that a record 81.4% of the electorate participated in the election, opposition leaders claimed that the abstention rate was higher than 80%. Biya was re-elected, obtaining a reported 92.6% of the votes cast. On 3 November Biya was formally inaugurated, beginning, in accordance with the revised Constitution, a seven-year term in office. Biya reappointed Musonge as Prime Minister.

In September 1998 it was reported that, following attacks on police premises, more than 40 anglophone Cameroonians, who were alleged to be secessionists campaigning for the independence of southern Cameroon, were being detained without trial and tortured in Yaoundé. The opposition suggested, however, that the raids had been staged by government agents as a pretext for further suppression of demands for increased decentralization. The trial of the alleged anglophone secessionists (the majority of whom had been arrested in 1997) began in June 1999. The defendants claimed that confessions that they were members of the separatist SCNC had been extracted under torture and threats of summary execution. In August the accused formally denied all the charges against them, although several individuals admitted to being members of a cultural association linked to the SCNC. In October three of the defendants were sentenced to life imprisonment, while 29 were acquitted. (In December 2005 the prison sentences of six of the convicted secessionists were reduced on appeal, while a further two detainees were acquitted.) The UN's Human Rights Committee subsequently criticized Cameroon for its alleged failure to protect and to respect fundamental human rights.

In November 2000 deputies staged a sit-down outside the National Assembly building after the security forces prevented the holding of a protest march from the legislative building to the presidential palace. The march had been organized by the SDF in support of demands for the creation of an independent electoral commission. In the following month the National Assembly adopted legislation on the establishment of a National Elections Observatory and on the regulation of state funding for political parties and electoral campaigns. However, five opposition parties boycotted the vote on the new body, claiming that it would be unconstitutional, as it would perform the same functions as the Constitutional Council (the functions of which were being fulfilled by the Supreme Court, pending its creation). The President's role in appointing its 11 members was also criticized.

At elections to the National Assembly, held on 30 June 2002, the RDPC increased its representation to 133 seats, while the SDF won 21 seats, the UDC five, the UPC three and the UNDP only one seat. However, the Supreme Court cancelled voting in nine constituencies, where 17 seats were at stake, because of voters' complaints. The rate of voter participation was estimated at less than 50%. Opposition parties claimed that widespread electoral irregularities had taken place and demanded that the results be annulled. Six opposition parties, including the SDF, subsequently refused to participate in the new legislature. However, the SDF's resolve was weakened by internal divisions, which were exacerbated in July, when Fru Ndi's unilateral decision to end the SDF boycott of the legislative institutions prompted allegations that he was in covert negotiations to secure a role in government. In August there was an extensive cabinet reorganization, in which 18 new members of government were appointed. On 15 September voting took place for the 17 legislative seats that had remained vacant since June; the RDPC secured a further 16 seats, increasing its majority to 149 of the 180 seats in the National Assembly, while the SDF won the remaining seat.

Presidential Election of 2004

In November 2003 the SDF, the UDC and three other opposition parties formed a coalition to contest the forthcoming presidential election. A further four parties later joined the grouping, named the Coalition Nationale pour la Réconciliation et la Reconstruction (CNRR). In July 2004 several people were injured in Yaoundé when the police intervened to suppress a protest march organized by the CNRR in support of its demand for the computerization of the electoral register. Further opposition demonstrations were staged in the capital on a weekly basis during the following months, and were similarly dispersed by the security forces.

Opposition attempts to unite behind a single presidential candidate failed in September 2004, when Fru Ndi refused to stand aside for Adamou Ndam Njoya, the leader of the UDC, who had been selected to represent the CNRR. A total of 16 candidates successfully registered to contest the election, which was held on 11 October, although three withdrew their candidatures on the eve of the poll. Biya was re-elected for a further seven-year term in office, securing 70.9% of the votes cast. His two main opponents, Fru Ndi and Njoya, received 17.4% and 4.5% of the vote, respectively. A turn-out of 82.2% was officially recorded. Opposition parties alleged widespread electoral fraud, but observers from the Commonwealth and the Organisation Internationale de la Francophonie declared themselves broadly satisfied with the conduct of the election, although they acknowledged shortcomings in its organization, in particular the exclusion of large numbers of eligible voters from the electoral roll. It was reported that only around 4.6m. voters of an adult population of some 8m. had been registered.

In December 2004 Biya appointed a new Cabinet, headed by Prime Minister Ephraim Inoni (hitherto Assistant Secretary-General of the Presidency). Inoni was an anglophone, like his predecessor, Musonge. Five political parties were represented in the new administration, although a large majority of positions were allocated to RDPC members. Inoni announced that economic reform would be his priority.

The initiation by the Government of an anti-corruption campaign in January 2006 coincided with the dismissal of around 20 heads of public enterprises, a number of whom were subsequently arrested and charged with misappropriating public funds. A new national commission with a directive to combat corruption was created by presidential decree in March, and further arrests followed. In April the National Assembly adopted legislation requiring government members and other senior state officials involved in the management of public funds to declare to a nine-member commission their assets and property at the beginning and end of their tenures of office. The SDF expressed doubts regarding the independence of the commission, but the party's proposal that the declarations be made public was rejected.

Internal divisions within the SDF intensified in February 2006, when Clément Ngwasiri, the President of the party's National Advisory Council (NAC), was expelled from the party for conducting 'anti-party activities'. The NAC had recently declared that it was assuming the leadership of the party, claiming that the mandate of the SDF's National Executive Committee (NEC) had expired in April 2003. The NAC had also announced that the next congress of the party, scheduled for 26 May 2006, at which a new NEC was to be elected, would be held in Yaoundé rather than Bamenda, as arranged by the current NEC. In May the NEC dismissed Bernard Muna, a candidate for the chairmanship of the SDF, and some 20 other activists apparently allied to Ngwasiri from the party. SDF congresses were held in both Bamenda and Yaoundé on 26 May, despite an earlier court order suspending their organization. In Bamenda Fru Ndi was re-elected as national Chairman of the SDF, while in Yaoundé dissident party members elected Muna to this position. Prior to the Yaoundé congress Grégoire Diboulé, a pro-Ngwasiri regional leader of the SDF, was killed in violent clashes between the two rival factions of the party. More than 20 members of the SDF were subsequently charged with involvement in Diboulé's murder, and were held in detention until November 2008, when most were provisionally released; two of the detainees had died in custody in the mean time. Fru Ndi was charged with complicity in the murder, but was not detained. The trial of Fru Ndi and the other SDF members finally commenced in August 2008, but was postponed indefinitely in July 2009; the SDF had claimed that the trial was politically motivated and intended to disqualify its leader from contesting the presidential election due in 2011. Meanwhile, a court in Bamenda ruled that Fru Ndi was the sole legitimate leader of the SDF in November 2006.

At an RDPC congress, held in July 2006, Biya was re-elected party leader and pledged to organize elections to a new Senate (provision for which had been made in constitutional amendments adopted in December 1995) before the end of his presidential mandate in 2011. In September 2006 Biya effected a minor cabinet reshuffle, retaining Inoni as Prime Minister.

Legislation providing for the creation of a new independent electoral commission, Elections Cameroon (ELECAM), was approved in December 2006, following a commitment made by the Government to the Commonwealth at a meeting in February. The SDF boycotted the vote, expressing dissatisfaction that members of ELECAM would be appointed by the President and that there would be a delay before the new body became operational. Pending ELECAM's establishment (which was to be achieved within 18 months), the National Elections Observatory and the Ministry of Territorial Administration and Decentralization would remain responsible for organizing and supervising elections.

Biya and the RDPC Consolidate Power

Legislative and municipal elections were held on 22 July 2007, contested by 45 political parties. Provisional results indicated that the RDPC had increased its majority in the National Assembly, as well as securing 303 of the 363 council seats available. Voter turn-out was estimated at 62%. Amid opposition allegations of widespread fraud, the Supreme Court subsequently annulled the results in five constituencies, comprising 17 seats, where voting was repeated on 30 September. Following these polls, the RDPC held a total of 153 seats in the 180-seat National Assembly, the SDF 16 seats (five fewer than after the 2002 elections), the UNDP, which remained allied to the RDPC, six (an increase of five), the UDC four and the opposition Mouvement Progressiste (MP) one. Earlier in September President Biya had effected a cabinet reorganization. Inoni was retained as Prime Minister, while Jean Nkuété, Minister of State in charge of Agriculture and Rural Development, was promoted to the rank of Deputy Prime Minister. Notable new appointees included Louis Paul Motaze as Minister of the Economy, Planning and Land Settlement, Lazare Essimi Menye as Minister of Finance, and Henri Eyebe Ayissi as Minister of External Relations.

In January 2008 it was reported that public meetings and demonstrations had been prohibited in the province of Littoral, including its capital, Douala, where several opposition parties and civil society organizations had been intending to organize protests against government plans to seek the abolition of the constitutional limitation on presidential terms in order to allow Biya to stand for re-election in 2011. The SDF declared that it would ignore the ban, and the police used tear gas to disperse opposition members attempting to stage rallies in Douala in mid-February. Later that month rioting erupted in Douala as a nation-wide strike by transport workers staged in protest against recent significant rises in the prices of fuel and basic products coincided with political opposition to constitutional reform. Despite a decision to end the strike after two days, following a slight reduction in fuel prices, the unrest spread to other cities, including Yaoundé, with some protesters demanding Biya's resignation. By the end of the month order had been restored in Douala and Yaoundé, where large numbers of heavily armed troops had been deployed, although three people were reportedly killed in clashes with the security forces in the western towns of Bamenda and Bafang. According to official figures, a total of 40 people died and more than 1,500 were arrested during the violence, although one human rights group claimed that more than 100 people had been killed. During March the Government announced a series of measures intended to allay popular discontent, including a 15% increase in the salaries of civil servants and military employees, the suspension of duties on imports of certain basic foodstuffs and a reduction in electricity tariffs.

Several former public officials were arrested in March 2008 as part of the authorities' ongoing anti-corruption campaign; the most high-profile detainees were Polycarpe Abah Abah, the former Minister of the Economy and Finance, Urbain Olanguena Awono, the former Minister of Health, and Paulin Abono Moampamb, the former Secretary of State for Public Works, all of whom had been dismissed from the Government in the September 2007 reorganization and were accused of misappropriating state funds. In August 2008 a further senior member of the RDPC, Jean-Marie Atangana Mebara, who had been Minister of State in charge of External Relations until

September 2007, was detained, after several months under house arrest, on charges of embezzling public funds in connection with the purchase in 2004 (when he was serving as Secretary-General of the Presidency) of a presidential aircraft that proved to be faulty; several other officials were alleged to be implicated in the scandal, and further arrests were made in April 2012 (see below).

Meanwhile, in mid-April 2008 the National Assembly adopted a number of constitutional amendments, including the controversial removal of the restriction on presidential terms, in a vote boycotted by SDF deputies, who denounced the revisions as a 'constitutional coup'. However, a 'day of mourning' staged by the SDF later that month in protest against the constitutional changes was reportedly not widely observed. In June opposition parties, as well as civil society organizations, also criticized the approval by the Assembly of a six-month delay in the establishment of ELECAM, which had been due to take place on 1 July. ELECAM's 12 members were finally appointed by Biya in December. However, the majority of the appointees were affiliated to the RDPC, raising serious doubts about the commission's impartiality and prompting expressions of concern both domestically (including within the ruling party itself) and internationally, notably from the European Union, which was to provide funding for the body.

In January 2009 the human rights organization Amnesty International released a report accusing Cameroon's Government of serious human rights violations, mainly related to the repression of political dissent, and condemning prison conditions in the country. (Similar concerns were expressed in a report published by a local human rights group in August.) In April some 50 people, mostly members of the SCNC, were arrested in Bamenda for allegedly participating in an illegal public meeting. (In July 2010 the SCNC claimed that 50 of its members remained imprisoned without trial.)

President Biya effected a major government reorganization in June 2009, appointing Philémon Yang, an anglophone and hitherto the Assistant Secretary-General at the Presidency, to succeed Inoni as Prime Minister. A total of nine ministers were replaced, including Rémy Zé Meka, the Minister-delegate to the President, in charge of Defence, whose portfolio was allocated to Edgar Alain Mebe Ngo, hitherto Chief of Police. Bouba Maigari, the Chairman of the UNDP, became Minister of State in charge of Transport.

The Government's anti-corruption campaign continued in 2009. Notable arrests included those, in August, of seven officials from Douala, who were accused of misappropriating public funds amounting to a reported 2,000m. francs CFA. Nevertheless, a World Bank report published in September noted that corruption remained a major deterrent to investment in Cameroon. President Biya was widely criticized in the French media that month, following revelations regarding the cost of a recent visit to France, while a scandal emerged involving the embezzlement, during 2004–09, of an estimated 16,500m. francs CFA by officials of the Banque des Etats de l'Afrique Centrale, both at its headquarters in Yaoundé and at its office in Paris, France. In January 2010 several former government officials, including Haman Adama, Minister of Basic Education until June 2009, were arrested on suspicion of corruption.

Complaints regarding the composition of ELECAM were renewed in March 2010, after the National Assembly adopted legislation increasing the involvement of the authorities in the organization of elections. Fru Ndi threatened to boycott the forthcoming presidential election if the Government did not agree to restructure ELECAM, and in the following month 10 political parties, including the SDF, the MP and the UDC, and 10 civil society organizations demanded the dissolution of the commission.

Voter registration for the presidential election due in late 2011 commenced in August 2010, amid continued criticism of ELECAM by the SDF, which claimed that the body was not qualified to organize the election, repeating demands for its reform and urging a boycott of the registration process. The party announced that it would seek to prevent the presidential election from taking place if 11 conditions were not met: these included the introduction of a second round of voting; the granting of suffrage to Cameroonians living abroad; the inclusion of biometric data on voters' cards and registers; financial independence for ELECAM; and the complete exclusion of the Ministry of Territorial Administration and Decentralization from the electoral process. However, this hardline stance provoked divisions within the SDF in the following months, leading to the resignation from the party of several senior members, including Edith Kah Walla, who declared her intention to contest the presidential ballot (later being selected as the candidate of the Cameroon People's Party, of which she became President), and former party Vice-President, Pierre Kwemo, who subsequently formed a new political organization, the Union des Mouvements Socialistes. In October the RDPC's Secretary-General, René Sadi, confirmed that the ruling party would support Biya's re-election, although the President himself had yet to declare his candidacy. Meanwhile, the replacement of senior security and intelligence officials at the end of August was linked by the media to recent rumours of a coup plot against Biya.

Biya and Fru Ndi held their first ever talks in December 2010, discussing the forthcoming presidential election among other issues. The meeting took place in Bamenda, during the President's first visit to the opposition-dominated North-West Province in nearly 20 years. In January 2011 Biya's sole challenger for the RDPC presidential nomination, Paul Abine Ayah (an RDPC deputy who had notably voted against the 2008 abolition of the constitutional limitation on presidential terms), resigned from the party, citing death threats, but stated that he still aimed to contest the presidency either as an independent or as the representative of an opposition party. Legislation increasing the deposit to be paid by presidential candidates from 1.5m. francs CFA to 5m. francs CFA was adopted in April 2011, despite opposition from the SDF, which had sought a reduction to 0.5m. francs CFA. However, also approved was an expansion in the membership of ELECAM from 12 to 18, as advocated by the opposition, with the six additional members, most of whom were representatives of civil society, being named in July. Also in July, one of the opposition's conditions for not disrupting the presidential election was fulfilled, when the Assemblée nationale approved legislation allowing citizens living abroad to vote in presidential elections and referendums. Despite most of its other demands not being met, in early August the SDF confirmed that it would participate in the presidential election, which later that month was scheduled for 9 October. In early September Fru Ndi and Biya were confirmed as the candidates of their respective parties, the SDF and the RDPC.

In late September 2011, some 10 days before the presidential election, it was reported that armed men wearing military attire and carrying placards demanding that Biya step down had opened fire in Douala and blockaded a bridge for several hours. A disqualified presidential candidate, Bertin Kisob, subsequently claimed responsibility for the incident, on behalf of the previously unknown Cameroonian People's Liberation Army. A few days later more than 200 SCNC supporters were arrested for attempting to stage an unauthorized rally in Buéa.

Biya Re-elected, 2011

The presidential ballot took place, as scheduled, on 9 October 2011. Biya was re-elected to a further seven-year term in office with 78.0% of the votes cast, while Fru Ndi, who had notably advocated a reduction in the presidential term to three years during the electoral campaign, secured 10.7%, and Garga Haman Adji of the Alliance pour la Démocratie et le Développement 3.2%. UDC leader Njoya won 1.7% of the votes cast and Paul Abine Ayah, representing the People's Action Party, took 1.3%, with the remaining 18 candidates all receiving less than 1% of the vote. Polling day was marred by the deaths of one opposition member and two police officers in isolated violent incidents, while seven opposition candidates, including Fru Ndi and Njoya, formed a coalition, prior to the announcement of the results, demanding the annulment of the election on the grounds of multiple irregularities. However, the Supreme Court, acting as the Constitutional Council, rejected their complaints and those lodged by three other candidates. A relatively low turn-out, of 65.8%, could be attributed to the perception that Biya's victory was inevitable, particularly given the multitude of opposition candidates. Biya was inaugurated to serve his sixth elected term of office on 3 November, pledging to implement major agricultural, mining, energy and infrastructure projects to transform the economy. He also promised to establish the long-awaited Senate, regional councils and Constitutional Council, provision for all of which was contained in the constitutional amendments approved by the National Assembly in December 1995.

The National Anti-Corruption Commission, which was created in March 2006 and commenced operations a year later, issued a report on its activities in November 2011, detailing numerous incidences of wrongdoing in government ministries during 2008–10. In response to the report, President Biya ordered that all ministers and managers of state corporations accused of corruption be held to account for their alleged abuses. One of those implicated in the report was the Minister of Public Works, Bernard Messengue Avom, who was accused of embezzling some 15,000m. francs CFA in the execution of road construction projects. Legislation on the creation of a special criminal court to try those accused of misappropriating large sums of public funds was adopted in December 2011.

A cabinet reorganization was effected in December 2011, in which some 16 ministers left the Government. Among the departures was that of Messengue Avom, who was replaced by Patrice Amba Salla. Alamine Ousmane Mey, hitherto General Manager of Afriland First Bank, joined the Cabinet as Minister of Finance, suceeding Essimi Menye, who was allocated the agriculture and rural development portfolio, while Deputy Prime Minister Amadou Ali, became Minister-delegate at the Presidency in charge of Relations with the Assemblies, relinquishing the justice portfolio to Minister of State Laurent Esso. Yang was retained as Prime Minister

In early April 2012 the National Assembly approved the postponement of the legislative and municipal elections, due to be held in July, by at least six months to allow the revision of the voters' register using biometric identification techniques. A new electoral code was adopted later that month; opposition parties criticized further increases in the deposits to be paid by election candidates. Also in April, former Prime Minister Inoni and Marafa Hamidou Yaya, Minister of Territorial Administration and Decentralization until the reorganization implemented four months earlier, were arrested in connection with the allegedly fraudulent purchase of a presidential aircraft in 2004. Yaya, who had been replaced in the Cabinet by René Sadi, the Secretary-General of the RDPC, had been widely considered to be a potential successor to President Biya.

REGIONAL CONCERNS

During 1989–93 President Biya actively sought Cameroon's admission to the Commonwealth, which, following the Government's agreement to comply with certain democratic conditions, was approved in 1993. Its membership took effect in November 1995. Apart from a border dispute with Nigeria (see below), relations with neighbouring countries are generally harmonious. In March 2001 tensions arising from a series of incursions into Cameroonian territory by heavily armed troops from the Central African Republic (CAR) were defused following a negotiated withdrawal. In December 2005 the first meeting was held of a bilateral commission charged with addressing security concerns at the border between Cameroon and the CAR; insecurity at the border persisted, however. In November 2006 the office of the UN High Commissioner for Refugees (UNHCR) reported that some 30,000 people from the CAR were seeking refuge in Cameroon, having fled attacks by bandits and former rebels in their own country; the refugees were mainly nomadic cattle breeders, belonging to the Mbororo ethnic group. The number of CAR refugees residing in Cameroon increased in subsequent years, according to UNHCR, reaching 90,176 by the end of 2011. In May 2008 Cameroon contributed troops to a peace-keeping force in the CAR that had been authorized by the Communauté Economique et Monétaire d'Afrique Centrale in 2002. In early February 2008 some 30,000 Chadians fled across the Chari river to the northern Cameroonian town of Kousséri to escape heavy fighting between rebels and government forces in the Chadian capital, N'Djamena. Some returned to Chad later that month, following an improvement in the security situation, but around 20,000 registered with UNHCR; the number of Chadian refugees remaining in Cameroon declined from 8,492 at the end of 2010 to 5,251 at the end of 2011.

The Bakassi Dispute

In June 1991 the Nigerian Government claimed that Cameroon had annexed nine Nigerian fishing settlements, following a long-standing border dispute, based on a 1913 agreement between Germany and the United Kingdom that ceded the Bakassi peninsula in the Gulf of Guinea (a region of strategic significance) to Cameroon. Subsequent attempts to negotiate the dispute achieved little progress. In January 1994 it was reported that members of the Cameroonian security forces had entered Nigeria and raided villages, killing several Nigerian nationals. Nigeria subsequently occupied the two nominally Cameroonian islands of Diamant and Jabane in the Gulf of Guinea. Cameroon also dispatched troops to the region. In February the Cameroon Government announced that it was to submit the matter to adjudication by the UN Security Council, the Organization of African Unity (OAU, now the African Union) and the International Court of Justice (ICJ), based in The Hague, Netherlands. Despite a resumption of negotiations between Cameroon and Nigeria in May, mediated by the Togolese Government, sporadic clashes between their armed forces continued, causing several deaths.

In February 1996 Cameroon and Nigeria agreed to refrain from further military action, and delegations from the two countries resumed discussions, again with Togolese mediation. In March the ICJ ordered both nations to cease military operations in the region, to withdraw troops to former positions, and to co-operate with a UN investigative mission. In April, however, clashes continued. Claims by Nigeria that the Cameroonian forces were supported by troops from France were denied by the French Government. In September both Governments assured the UN investigative mission of their commitment to a peaceful settlement of the dispute. In December and May 1997, however, the Nigerian authorities claimed that Cameroonian troops had resumed attacks in the region. Renewed fighting between Cameroonian and Nigerian forces was reported in December and February 1998.

From late 1998 relations between the two countries began to improve, and in November the International Committee of the Red Cross organized a prisoner exchange between the two sides. In April 1999 the President-elect of Nigeria, Gen. Olusegun Obasanjo, visited Cameroon, the first such visit since the beginning of the border conflict in 1994. The two countries were reported to have agreed to resolve the dispute 'in a fraternal way'. It was, however, announced that the ICJ proceedings would continue.

In October 2002 the ICJ issued its final verdict on the demarcation of the land and maritime boundary between Cameroon and Nigeria, notably ruling in favour of Cameroon's sovereignty over the Bakassi peninsula, citing the 1913 Anglo-German partition agreement. Despite having no option to appeal, Nigeria refused to accept the Court's decision, ostensibly in view of claims that some 90% of the peninsula's residents were Nigerian citizens. Troop deployments began to increase on both sides of the border, prompting fears of a full-scale armed conflict between the two countries. In November, however, at a meeting in Geneva, Switzerland, mediated by the Secretary-General of the UN, Kofi Annan, the Presidents of Cameroon and Nigeria signed a joint communiqué announcing the creation of a bilateral 12-member commission, to be headed by a UN Special Representative, with a mandate to achieve a peaceful solution to the Bakassi peninsula dispute. At its inaugural meeting in Yaoundé in December, the commission agreed on a 15-point peace agenda and decided to establish a sub-committee to undertake the demarcation of the boundary.

In August 2003 Nigeria and Cameroon adopted a framework agreement for the implementation of the ICJ's judgment, providing for the withdrawal of all military and administrative personnel from the Bakassi region; the process of demarcation of boundaries between the two countries was expected to take up to three years to complete. In December the Nigerian Government ceded control of 33 villages on its north-eastern border to Cameroon, but sovereignty over the disputed territory with petroleum resources remained under discussion.

Following an amicable meeting in Yaoundé in July 2004 between Presidents Biya and Obasanjo, it was confirmed that Nigerian troops would withdraw from Bakassi by 15 September. However, just days before the expiry of the deadline the Nigerian Government announced that the transfer of authority in the peninsula had been delayed by technical difficulties in demarcating the maritime border. In April 2005 Cameroon and Nigeria signed an agreement with UNHCR providing for the voluntary repatriation of some 10,000 Nigerians who had entered Cameroon in 2002, fleeing inter-ethnic conflict in Taraba State, in eastern Nigeria.

In May 2005, at talks in Geneva, again mediated by Annan, Presidents Biya and Obasanjo agreed to accelerate the negotiation of a new programme for the withdrawal of Nigerian troops from Bakassi. In July the bilateral commission resumed its activities in Yaoundé, establishing a joint working group to draft a new timetable for the withdrawal of Nigerian troops from the peninsula. At a meeting in the Nigerian capital, Abuja, in October, the bilateral commission reached agreement on a new programme for Nigeria's withdrawal, based on the report of the joint working group. On 12 June 2006, at bilateral talks mediated by Annan in New York, USA, Obasanjo signed an agreement to withdraw Nigerian troops from Bakassi within 60–90 days. The deadline for the withdrawal was met, with Nigerian troops leaving the peninsula on 14 August. Pending a full transfer of authority in Bakassi, which was to be completed within two years, the southern part of the peninsula was to remain under Nigerian administrative control. In May 2007 the bilateral commission agreed on the demarcation of the maritime border between Cameroon and Nigeria. However, in November 21 Cameroonian soldiers were killed, and a further 10 injured, in the Bakassi peninsula in an attack apparently launched from Nigerian territory; a hitherto unknown group, the Liberators of Southern Cameroon, subsequently claimed responsibility.

The demarcation of the maritime boundary between Cameroon and Nigeria was finally completed in March 2008. Security in the Bakassi peninsula was heightened in June, after five Cameroonian soldiers and a local government official were abducted and killed by unknown assailants. Further raids on Cameroonian security forces occurred in the following month. During one of the attacks Cameroonian forces captured two members of the Niger Delta Defence and Security Council (NDDSC), a group opposed to the cession of the Bakassi peninsula to Cameroon, and in another claimed to have killed 10 NDDSC rebels. Despite the violence and legal challenges in Nigeria, the full transfer of administrative authority over Bakassi took place, as scheduled, on 14 August. In October the Governments of Cameroon and Nigeria signed an agreement on co-operation in improving security at their common border. A few days later NDDSC rebels and government troops were involved in a further violent confrontation. The NDDSC demanded the release of two fighters detained in July and compensation for Nigerians forced to leave Bakassi. At the end of the month a militant group linked to the NDDSC, the Bakassi Freedom Fighters, abducted 10 workers in the petroleum industry (seven French nationals, two Cameroonians and a Tunisian) from a French vessel off the coast of Cameroon; all 10 were released after nearly two weeks, with the rebels claiming that they had been freed in exchange for 13 militants held by the Cameroonian authorities.

In March 2009 it was reported that the USA was to provide Cameroon with a radar surveillance system to monitor its coastline, particularly around the Bakassi peninsula, amid increasing concerns regarding piracy. Five Chinese fishermen were reportedly abducted in the waters off the peninsula in July, and in October the Cameroonian Ministry of Defence announced that its forces had killed four pirates who had attacked a fishing vessel in the area. The first of more than 3,000 planned border markers was laid between Cameroon and Nigeria in December. However, there were reports of alleged deaths and harassment of Nigerian nationals by Cameroonian security forces in the peninsula. In March 2010 seven Chinese fishermen were kidnapped by a previously unknown group, Africa Marine Commando (AMC), but were released less than a week later as a result of negotiations. In September the Bakassi-based AMC, which was reported to be a splinter group of the Bakassi Freedom Fighters, claimed responsibility for the abduction of six foreign sailors from a vessel off the coast of Cameroon; the hostages were released some two weeks later. The AMC also professed responsibility for an attack on a boat en route to a French-operated oil platform in the Gulf of Guinea in November, in which three soldiers, a mechanic and a pilot (all Cameroonian) were killed, together with one of the militants. In a further incident in February 2011, the AMC kidnapped 13 people in Bakassi, freeing them after 10 days, reportedly in return for payment of a ransom and the release of several pirates being held in Buéa.

At a meeting in Abuja in July 2011, the bilateral commission urged its sub-committee on border demarcation to resolve the remaining 350 km of border still to be settled; the exploitation of hydrocarbons along the border was also discussed. Cameroon and Nigeria reiterated their commitment to complete the demarcation by the end of 2012. Cameroon deployed some 600 soldiers in strategic locations close to the joint border in January 2012 in an attempt to prevent the infiltration into Cameroonian territory of Boko Haram, a militant Islamist group active in Nigeria. In the following month the Governments of Cameroon and Nigeria signed an agreement on the creation of a trans-border security committee.

Economy

DUNCAN WOODSIDE

INTRODUCTION

Compared with those of its regional peers, Cameroon's economy has consistently underperformed in recent years, despite an abundance of natural resources. At a time when many economies across sub-Saharan Africa have earned the accolade of being frontier markets, with high economic growth and buoyant investor confidence, Cameroon has lagged behind. The country's economy expanded by an average of just 2.8% per year in real terms during 2005–10. Although the period from mid-2008 to the end of 2009 was characterized by a severe global economic downturn, there had been an extended boom between 2005 and mid-2008. Moreover, growth in real global economic output recovered to 5.0% in 2010, due largely to a strong recovery in levels of production in emerging markets, which expanded by 7.1% in real terms. Cameroon's real level of economic output expanded by just 3.2% in 2010, according to the IMF, while there was zero growth in per caput income during 2005–10. Endemic corruption is one of the key factors behind Cameroon's consistently weak gross domestic product (GDP) growth. In Transparency International's 2011 Corruption Perceptions Index, the country was ranked 134th out of 183 countries. An additional factor that has constrained growth is the limited availability of credit to the private sector. A long-standing tendency on the part of the Government to fall into arrears on debt payments to local creditor banks has taken its toll on the underdeveloped domestic banking sector's ability to lend to private sector enterprises. With so much government debt on their books, the capacity for banks to add to their risk profile by lending to non-state borrowers is extremely limited. Additional constraints on economic output include a highly inefficient public sector and inadequate utilities and transport infrastructure.

The persistence of corruption means that the majority of Cameroon's population remains deprived of the benefits of the country's natural resources. The proportion of the population living in poverty was 39.9% in 2009 (down only marginally from 40.2% in 2001), according to World Bank estimates. Moreover, the UN's 2011 Human Development Index (which takes account of national income, life expectancy and access to education) ranked Cameroon 150th out of a total of 187 countries.

However, Cameroon's economic potential remains significant. If the Government of long-serving President Paul Biya—who was officially re-elected with 78% of the vote in a presidential election held in October 2011—is able to address corruption and to retrench the bloated public sector, then the country could yet move onto a significantly higher growth path, in view of the strong long-term outlook for natural resources. Major planned foreign investments include more than US $3,000m. by France's GDF Suez in a liquefied natural gas (LNG) plant, development of the $3,400m. Mbalam iron ore mine by Australia's Sundance Resources, and a $410m. investment by a unit of Singapore's GMG Global Ltd (see Agriculture) in a new rubber and palm oil plantation.

AGRICULTURE

Agriculture, forestry and fishing contributed 23.3% to Cameroon's GDP in 2009, according to the African Development Bank (AfDB), and, according to FAO estimates, provided a livelihood for an estimated 46.4% of the labour force in mid-2011. The sector's share of GDP represented a significant decline from its 32% contribution in 1978/79, when the petroleum sector was not yet developed. Small-scale farmers dominate agricultural export production, with the exception of rubber, palm oil and timber. The rubber and palm oil sectors received a significant boost in December 2011, when Sud Cameroun Hevea SA., a unit of GMG Global Ltd, announced that it had signed a US $410m. agreement with the Cameroonian Government to develop 45,200 ha of plantations. The firm expected that the export-oriented plantations would be operating at full capacity within four years. By 2011 annual production of palm oil in Cameroon was 175,000 metric tons, while annual rubber output was 60,000 tons. Timber production also remains the domain of large foreign firms, despite efforts to enhance Cameroonian participation. In the early 1980s the role of the national agricultural marketing board, the Office National de Commercialisation des Produits de Base, was reduced, and responsibility for marketing was gradually transferred to the private sector.

The agricultural sector is well diversified, reflecting the country's varied ecology. The export crop sector includes coffee, cocoa, palm oil, bananas and sugar cane. The food crop sector includes maize, millet, sorghum and rice. Cameroon is a significant world producer of cocoa, ranking fourth in recent years. Cocoa was grown on an estimated 400,000 ha in 2005, according to FAO. Coffee is also cultivated on some 250,000 ha, predominantly in the west and south, and 90% of the coffee crop is of the Robusta variety. Coffee and cocoa output can fluctuate widely from year to year, reflecting climatic and vegetative circumstances and alternations in international prices. Both yields have suffered as a result of the failure of replanting programmes to keep pace with the ageing of plantations. Cocoa farmers in Cameroon benefited from the political crisis in Côte d'Ivoire (traditionally the world's leading producer) and rising international cocoa prices in the early 2000s, and cocoa producers in Cameroon's South-West Province, the main cocoa-growing area of the country, reported record prices for their product in July 2007, as a result of improved quality and increased demand.

Cocoa production was estimated to have reached 187,475 tons in 2007/08, aided by tighter regulations in the industry. In the 2008/09 season the country produced 205,032 tons of cocoa. There was a slight fall in output in 2009/10, to 198,000 tons, before a substantial increase in 2010/11, to 236,690 tons, according to the Ministry of Agriculture and Rural Development. However, while the Société de Développement du Cacao (SODECAO) initially targeted a further increase to 250,000 tons for 2011/12, evidence from farms in the south-west and elsewhere indicated that a renewed fall in output was likely. Exports for the first five months of the crop year (which runs from August to the end of July) were down by 11% year on year, due to insufficient rains, while crops in late 2011 and early 2012 were increasingly being affected by an invasion of capsid bugs. The pests attack cocoa trees by feeding on branches. The Organisation Nationale des Producteurs de Cacao et du Café du Cameroon (ONPCCC) was, by late January 2012, predicting a fall in country-wide cocoa output of 20%–25% year on year for the 2011/12 crop. The crisis in the sector gathered further pace in early April 2012, when caterpillars attacked 2,000 ha of plantations in the south in just one week, reportedly destroying about 50% of plants.

In July 2011 US agricultural firm Cargill announced plans to train cocoa farmers in Cameroon, as part of a joint initiative with local exporter Telcar Cocoa Ltd to improve quality and increase production. The four-year programme will involve around 500 farmers being trained in methods designed to increase yields in the south-west of the country. In another bid to boost output, the ONPCCC announced in August that it would build 2,500 ovens to dry cocoa beans, again in the south-west. The drying process in this region is often complicated by heavy rains. The new devices would replace old ones, which had, in some cases, fallen into disrepair, with about 600,000 farmers likely to benefit, as a result of financial backing for the initiative by the Cocoa and Coffee Development Fund.

In early 2012 a multi-agency regulatory drive was launched to reduce the level of illicit purchases of cocoa beans from farmers by unregulated buyers. The Cocoa and Coffee Interprofessional Council, together with the Office National du Cacao at du Café (ONCC), announced the scheme in January, at a time when these authorities estimated that over 250 unlicensed buyers existed in the country, compared to just 92 that had permits. The crackdown involved seizing beans from buyers who were not registered and who had been unable to produce legitimate paperwork detailing their transactions with farmers. In order to qualify for permits, cocoa purchasers have to be able demonstrate that they have financial liquidity and adequate facilities (both for warehousing and transportation). The unregulated buyers tend to purchase undried cocoa from farmers who are financially desperate, which generates quality problems. Moreover, the authorities underlined that it was difficult to keep track of the real level of national production, with such a significant proportion of cocoa sales falling below the radar.

The performance of the coffee sector has been impressive in recent years. During the 2008/09 Robusta coffee season (December to November), Cameroon produced 44,378 metric tons of this variety, according to the ONCC. During the 2008/09 Arabica coffee season (October to September), Cameroon produced 3,744 tons of this premium variety. Exports of Arabica decreased to 533 tons in the first six months of the 2009/10 crop (to the end of March), down from 839 tons in the same period of 2008/09. Exports of Robusta, meanwhile, more than doubled in the first five months of the 2009/10 season (to the end of April) to 19,559 tons, up from 9,172 tons in the same period of 2008/09. The ONCC announced in April 2010 that it hoped to more than double aggregate coffee exports by 2015, from an annual 32,000 tons to 80,000 tons. The body is targeting a rise in Robusta exports to 65,000 tons and an increase in Arabica exports to 15,000 tons, through improved availability of fertilizer to commercial producers.

Bananas became a leading agricultural export, following the transfer to the private sector of the state-owned enterprise Organisation Camerounaise de la Banane in the late 1980s. However, the sector's prospects have since deteriorated with the end of the banana quota scheme operated by the European Union (EU), of which Cameroon was a beneficiary. The erosion in trade preferences from the EU has resulted in a decline in banana production. FAO estimated total production of 950,000 metric tons in 2010.

Cotton production, which is concentrated in the north, totalled 306,000 metric tons in 2004/05. Output of palm oil averaged 100,000 tons per year in the mid-1990s, but production was estimated at 185,000 tons in 2008. Rubber has good prospects, with yields competing with those of the major Asian producers. Output was estimated at 52,000 tons in 2009. Commercial production of cane sugar began in 1966, and output of sugar cane stood at an estimated 1.45m. tons in 2010.

Cameroon's food production has advanced at a higher rate than population growth, and the country is generally self-sufficient. In 2010 output of millet and sorghum reached an estimated 955,000 metric tons, while maize production amounted to an estimated 1.67m. tons. According to FAO, production of paddy rice was an estimated 175,000 tons in 2010. Livestock, mainly raised by traditional methods, makes a significant contribution to the food supply. In 2010 the national herd was estimated at 5.7m. cattle, 3.8m. sheep, 4.4m. and goats and 1.7m. pigs, while commercial poultry farms had an estimated 45m. chickens. Poultry production increased markedly following the introduction of an import ban on frozen chickens in 2004. The development of the fisheries industry has been constrained by the relatively small area available for exploitation (because of boundary disputes and the presence of the offshore island of Bioko, part of Equatorial Guinea) and the poor level of fish stocks in these waters. In 2010 the total catch was estimated at some 140,800 tons by FAO, with industrial fishing accounting for less than one-10th of the total.

However, despite a rich array of agricultural resources, Cameroon did not escape unscathed from the international food crisis in 2008. A global surge in the price of basic foodstuffs was exacerbated in Cameroon by inefficient agricultural marketing mechanisms and incentives. This provoked riots in the country in February 2008. Furthermore, despite a correction in international food prices in the second half of 2008, Cameroon continued to grapple with significant problems. It was claimed in 2009 that agricultural subsidies promised by the Government were failing to reach farmers, leaving the country with a maize shortage.

Overall, Cameroon's agricultural diversity has not prevented the persistence of food insecurity for elements of the population, particularly in the far north of the country, which was afflicted by droughts in 2009 and 2011, and flooding in 2010. According to the UN's Office for the Co-ordination of Humanitarian Affairs, provisional data from a 2011 survey put the rate of chronic malnutrition in the 'far north' at 44.9%, while that in the 'north' region was also very high, at 40.2%. Against this backdrop, the UN's Central Emergency Response Fund provided US $4.8m. to four UN agencies, to spend on projects designed to reduce food insecurity and the effects of drought in these northern areas in 2012.

Almost one-half of the country is covered by forest (22.5m. ha, according to the Ministry of Forests and Wildlife), but an inadequate transport system has impeded the sector's development, and only around one-third of the area has been exploited. None the less, forestry is Cameroon's second most important source of export earnings after oil, with roundwood and sawnwood exports amounting to roughly 15% of total export receipts. The Government implemented forestry legislation in 1999, according to which unprocessed log exports of 23 endangered hardwood species, including mahogany and sapele, were banned. As a result, log production officially declined from 3.4m. cu m in 2000/01 to 1.7m. cu m in 2003/04. At the same time, processed wood production has increased, with national sources estimating the 2003 growth at 12.5%. According to IMF and government estimates, production declined in 2005, as reforms to foster sustainable forestry production led to decreased utilization of forestry permits.

The country reached an agreement with the EU to certify its exports of hardwood in May 2010, in a bid to ensure that the exploitation of this resource is managed in a sustainable manner. The agreement means that Cameroonian hardwood products can only be legitimately sold in the EU if that they are certified as being legally harvested and produced. Around 80% of Cameroon's sawnwood is sold to EU countries, which (inclusive of timber-related products) earns the country around US $480m. per year. However, the new regulation will have no impact on the bulk of the country's unprocessed timber exports, given that the majority of uncut log shipments is sold to non-EU destinations, with the People's Republic of China receiving 60% of these exports.

The Malaysian-based multinational company Sime Darby announced in February 2011 that it was considering investing in a new palm oil plantation in Cameroon, which could reach up to 300,000 ha in size. If implemented, the scheme would begin with the annual planting of around 5,000 ha, rising to a maximum of 15,000 ha. According to the company, if a full 300,000 ha were planted, then investment in the project would total an estimated US $2,500m. and create 30,000 jobs.

MINING AND UTILITIES

While by far the largest source of foreign exchange earnings, mining (including petroleum production) contributed a relatively modest 7.9% of GDP in 2009. In 1976 the French petroleum company Elf (now part of Total) established a commercial oilfield in shallow water near the Nigerian border, and four fields came on stream in 1977–78. Production of crude petroleum reached a peak of 9.2m. metric tons in 1985, but declined to 5.4m. tons in 1995. A recovery was recorded in 1998, when output totalled 6.0m. tons, in response to improved incentives for the development of marginal fields; however, output has since declined continuously, as a result of the maturation of the main fields. Crude petroleum production decreased to 3.0m. tons in 2005, although it rose to an estimated 3.2m. tons in 2006, as new minor oilfields came on stream. Transparency in the management of oil revenues has meanwhile recently increased, with Cameroon joining the Extractive Industry Transparency Initiative.

In October 2002 the International Court of Justice granted Cameroon sovereignty over the oil-rich Bakassi peninsula, settling a dispute with Nigeria. This, combined with new tax incentives introduced by the Cameroonian Government in that year, was expected to open new development prospects in the petroleum sector. Nigeria completed the withdrawal of its troops from Bakassi on 14 August 2006, and the full transfer of administrative authority over the peninsula took place on 14 August 2008 (see Recent History). Meanwhile, in July 2003 a consortium, involving Petronas of Malaysia and the US companies ExxonMobil and ChevronTexaco, completed construction of a 1,070-km subterranean pipeline to transport oil from the Doba basin in southern Chad to a marine export terminal off the southern Cameroonian port of Kribi. Royalties from the new terminal were projected to total an estimated US $550m. over a 28-year period, which would partially offset the decline in direct revenue from petroleum-mining. Exploration has, meanwhile, continued in the Río del Rey basin and the Douala basin, with the announcement of minor oil discoveries and the signing of two new production-sharing agreements in 2005 and 2006. Total proven petroleum reserves in Cameroon were estimated at 250m. barrels in early 2007.

British oil exploration company BowLeven announced in November 2010 that it was considering upscaling exploitation in the offshore MLHP 5 block. In April 2011 the firm estimated that the block's Sapele-1 Deep and Lower Omicron reservoirs could potentially hold 1,000m. barrels of oil equivalent. BowLeven announced in October 2011 that it had made a significant discovery at the Deep Omicron reservoir, stating that the discovery, at the Sapele-3 exploration well, extended considerably beyond its previously confirmed hydrocarbons estimate, which meant that it would revise upwards its estimates for oil production. Discoveries had thus been made at all four of the Sapele wells that BowLeven had drilled. In January 2012 the USA's Kosmos Energy signed a deal with state-run Société Nationale des Hydrocarbures (SNH) to prospect for oil at Cameroon's Fako block. The company, with funding from Warburg Pincus and Blackstone Group, pledged to invest US $18m. in exploring the 1,300 sq km offshore bloc, according to SNH.

Oil output in Cameroon averaged 59,178 barrels per day (b/d) in Cameroon in 2011, a decline of 7.3% from the 63,900 b/d produced in 2010, according to SNH. However, state earnings from the industry rose from 420,000m. francs CFA to 527,700m. francs CFA, due to higher international oil prices. SNH was targeting an increase in national output to 100,000 b/d in 2012, as a result of the expected start of extraction at two new wells and higher output at existing wells. With regard to output from new concessions, Perenco, the country's leading oil exporter, expected to start producing at two locations in the Dissoni oil field onshore (in the Río del Rey basin) in the second half of 2012. The exploitation of these two assets alone was predicted by the company to raise output by 25,000 b/d, taking its total production in Cameroon to over 75,000 b/d (three-quarters of expected national output). Amid this environment of moderate new oil discoveries in Cameroon, resource-hungry China has sought to establish a footprint. In November 2011 Royal Dutch Shell sold an 80% stake in Pecten Cameroon to the state-owned China Petroleum Corpn (also known as Sinopec Group) for US $538m. The acquisition was completed by Addax Petroleum, a subsidiary of Sinopec, thereby providing the People's Republic with its first hydrocarbon interests in Cameroon. Pecten Cameroon has interests in 12 offshore blocs, operating two of them. The remaining 20% of the firm continued to be held by SNH.

Natural gas reserves have only recently begun to be exploited. In June 2002 nine companies were invited to consider developing the Sanaga Sud gasfield; six bids were received, and in 2006 SNH signed a production-sharing agreement with the French company Perenco to develop and exploit the offshore gasfield. The Punta Europa natural gas plant, operated by the US-based company Marathon Oil, began production in 2007 with a capacity of 3.4m. metric tons per year. As Cameroon's potential as a gas producer developed, in May 2008 SNH signed an agreement pledging to supply 250m. cu ft of gas per day to Equatorial Guinea from 2010. The country's natural gas deposits were estimated by SNH at 8,700m. cu ft in 2008.

GDF Suez announced in December 2010 that it planned to invest US $3,000m. in an LNG plant, to be located 20 km south of the coastal town of Kribi, with construction due to start in 2014–15. According to the company, the plant would have an output capacity of 3.5m. metric tons of LNG per year and could create up to 5,000 jobs.

Perenco's local subsidiary signed a production-sharing and exploration agreement with the Cameroonian Government in March 2010 for the 2,405-sq km offshore Elombo oil block. The agreement covered exploration of the block over a three-year period, and was expected to cost US $50m. In April SNH stated that the country was to begin soliciting bids for oil extraction licences for the Mamfe basin and Bakassi peninsula in late 2010 and early 2011. This followed significant discoveries in the Gulf of Guinea, in which the Mamfe basin and Bakassi peninsula are situated. Large-scale extraction from Cameroon's part of the Gulf of Guinea promised to catalyse a continued revival of national oil production. The country produced an estimated 84,000 b/d in 2008, according to BP's Statistical Review of World Energy, up from a low of 66,300 b/d in 2004, but still considerably below the level of 185,000 b/d reached in 1985. In December 2009 the Société Nationale de Raffinage secured a 45,000m. francs CFA loan from Afriland First Bank to modernize its refinery at Limbé. It was hoped that the funding would enable the state-owned refinery to process the heavy crude petroleum that Cameroon produces. Moreover, the upgrade would allow the refinery to reach a refining capacity of 70,300 b/d, up from 42,200 b/d.The Limbé refinery not only serves the domestic market, but also neighbouring sub-Saharan countries, the USA and France.

Major bauxite deposits, at Minim Martap (900m. metric tons) and Ngoundal (200m. tons), have yet to be exploited, owing partly to their distance from any seaport. In January 2006, however, the US company Hydromin signed an agreement with the Cameroonian Government to undertake the necessary investments in transport infrastructure and begin to exploit the bauxite deposits. Their development would enable the Edéa smelter, which produces some 95,000 tons of aluminium annually, but is dependent on imports of bauxite from Guinea, to be supplied locally.

Initial construction work had been scheduled to commence at the Nkamouna manganese, cobalt and nickel project, in East Province, in November 2008, and output to begin in 2010. A 40:60 joint venture between local firms (led by the Société Nationale d'Investissement du Cameroun—SNI) and the USA's Geovic Mining was established to exploit 54.7m. metric tons of ore, with the aim of achieving annual production of some 4,200 tons of cobalt and 2,100 tons of nickel for at least 21 years. However, in March 2009 Geovic announced that the global economic downturn and a funding shortfall had forced it to reduce the scale and costs of the project, while also delaying the start of work by at least one year. In June 2009 Geovic Cameroon, a subsidiary of Geovic Mining, announced that production would not begin until 2012, following a decline in cobalt prices from a high of US $52 per lb to $14.50 per lb. The company stressed that the long-term viability of the project was not in question, as it would still be profitable even if cobalt prices were to decrease to as low as $8 per lb. However, in December 2010 Geovic revised the cost of the Nkamouna project up to between $600m. and $650m., compared with a 2008 estimate of $417m. The company attributed the revision to the need to employ a more complicated metallurgical process than earlier anticipated, as well as to a general rise in global mining costs. Furthermore, Geovic underlined that the revised estimate did not include the cost of building a refinery, which, it stated, would entail an additional $150m.

Cameroon also possesses diamond reserves. In July 2010 the Republic of Korea (South Korea)'s C&K Mining signed a convention with the Government for the exploitation of the Mobilong concession, which contained provable reserves of 736m. carats of gem and industrial diamonds. A licence was awarded to C&K Mining in January 2011, which obliged the company to commence operations at the concession within a year. C&K Mining anticipated that output would begin at a rate of 50,000 carats per year, before subsequently increasing to 800,000 carats per year.

Extensive limestone deposits near Garoua supply clinker and cement plants. In mid-2003 new regulations were approved, replacing the somewhat restrictive mining law of 1964, and appearing to allow wider commercial exploitation of the country's non-oil mineral resources. An Australian company, Sundance Resources Limited, was working in collaboration with a private Cameroonian company, CAMIRON, to extract iron ore at Mbalam, north of Ngoila in East Province. Construction at the site, believed at that stage to hold deposits of 220m. metric tons, was due to begin in 2009. However, Sundance announced in October 2009 that it had been forced to postpone extraction until 2013, owing to the global financial crisis. This followed Sundance's submission of a feasibility project to the Cameroonian Government earlier that month, which forecast that the state would receive US $5,000m. in total earnings from the project over a period of 25 years. Sundance announced in March 2011 that the level of indicated high-grade resources had risen to 417.7m. tons, equivalent to an annual yield of 35m. tons of high-quality ore over a period of 25 years or more. The company said in February 2012 that it was hopeful that Cameroon's Government would soon confirm a permit for extraction at the mine, after a special ministerial committee was established to oversee the process.

In early 2006 total installed generating capacity in Cameroon amounted to 933 MW, consisting of 721 MW of hydroelectric capacity and 212 MW of thermal capacity. Heavy industry is the major consumer, with the aluminium plant, Alucam, taking nearly 50% of the total generation. The principal installations, at Edéa and Song-Loulou, supply the network linking Yaoundé, Edéa, Douala and the west. The other major network supplies the north and draws principally on the 72-MW hydroelectric station at Lagdo. In 2001 the US company AES bought a majority share in the electricity provider, Société Nationale d'Electricité du Cameroun (SONEL). In August 2004 AES-SONEL completed the construction of a new 85-MW oil-fired plant at Limbé. In September 2006 the company published an invitation for tenders for the construction of a natural gas-fired, 150-MW plant at Kribi. Construction work commenced in March 2010. It was envisaged that the plant would be completed in September 2012, at a total cost of US $342.9m. South Korea's Hyundai Engineering and Construction was to invest $162.3m. in the construction of a 232-MW gas-fired plant in Logbaba, in a bid to increase electricity supply to the country's Southern Interconnected Network, according to reports in July 2009. The plant was expected to be functional by September 2010, with a view to expanding generating capacity by a further 123 MW to 355 MW by 2012. In January 2012 SONEL announced that it would invest 30,000m. francs CFA ($58m.) to improve the power distribution network in outlying parts of Cameroon. The company planned to build a 225-kV line between Nkongsamba, in the north-west, and Bekoko, in the south-west, while an additional line was planned for Kousséri in the far north of the country.

Meanwhile, Victoria Oil & Gas of the United Kingdom, having planned an application for a 35-year exploitation and production licence, announced in November 2009 the discovery of 27.4m. of gas sands in its La-105 well at Logbaba. The company secured an exploration licence in April 2011 and, following installation of a pipeline and processing network (to honour 11 prearranged gas sale deals), began delivering output in December. By 2011 it was estimated that Logbaba had proven gas reserves totalling 212,000m. cu ft.

Cameroon has continued to suffer from power shortages. In 2009 multinational mining company Rio Tinto announced that its aluminium output at the Alucam joint venture in Cameroon had been reduced by nearly 40%, owing to the power supply to its industrial operations being restricted to just 120 MW (compared with a required level of 180 MW). Alucam is key to Cameroon's industrial sector, accounting for 7% of sector output and 5% of the country's export revenues, according to Rio Tinto. Alucam's output of aluminium was therefore expected to amount to just 55,000 metric tons in 2009, compared with an earlier projected level of 88,000 tons.

Efforts were increased in 2010–11 to address the deficient power supply. In March 2010 China's Sinohydro began construction of the 200-MW Memve'ele hydroelectric power project in South Province. The estimated cost of the project was US $795m. and it was expected to be completed by 2015. China International Water and Electric Corpn secured a contract, worth nearly 75,000m. francs CFA, to build the Lom Pangar dam, according to reports in May 2011. Construction of the dam was crucial to Cameroon achieving a targeted increase in power supply from 1,000 MW to 3,000 MW by 2020. Most of this increase in capacity was contingent upon controlling the flow of the Sanaga river, which would enable the modernization of existing downstream hydroelectric facilities and the construction of new dams. The Lom Pangar dam was designed to achieve the necessary control over river flows, partly by being located 4 km downstream from the confluence of the Pangar river and Lom river, and 13 km upstream from the Sanaga river. The World Bank, the European Investment Bank and the Agence Française de Développement all offered funds for the project, which was expected to take just over three years to build. Also in May 2011, the Government announced that it had secured a $542m. loan from the Export and Import Bank of China to finance construction of a 201-MW hydroelectric dam on the Ntem river.

There were several further investment developments in Cameroon's hydroelectric power sector in late 2011 and early 2012. China Three Gorges Project Corpn secured a US $196m. contract in August 2011 to build a hydropower facility. In December the Cameroonian Government announced that the Organization of the Petroleum Exporting Countries (OPEC) Fund for International Development, together with the Development Bank of Central African States, was providing a $51m. loan, most of which would be used to help construct the Lom Pangar hydroelectric facility. Finally, in March 2012, Joule Africa, a subsidiary of US-based Joule Investments, pledged a two-year feasibility study for a 450 MW hydroelectric facility, on the Katsina Ala river.

In May 2010 the AfDB approved a US $33.7m. loan for an 86-MW thermal power plant in Dibamba, as well as a 2-km 90-kV transmission line. The plant would be connected to the country's Southern Interconnected Grid. Earlier in the year China granted a 20-year loan amounting to $49.4m. to Cameroon for the construction of a 12-MW hydroelectric thermal power plant. The project was to include the building of a dam on the River Dja at Mekin and a 63-kV evacuation line.

The Export and Import Bank of China was reported in December 2010 to have pledged a 365,000m. francs CFA (US $736m.) loan for the construction of a water supply system for Yaoundé, drawing on reserves from the Sanaga river. The work would involve building a pumping station and 100 km of pipeline between the capital city and the river. The loan would cover most of the total cost of the project, estimated by Cameroon's Ministry of Water and Energy at 430,000m. francs CFA. The planned completion date was early 2013. In addition, the International Development Association (IDA) pledged a 14,000m. francs CFA loan, to fund the provision of clean water for both Yaoundé and Douala.

MANUFACTURING

Manufacturing contributed 16.1% of GDP in 2009. The sector is dominated by the processing of agricultural goods and raw materials, and the assembly of imported raw materials and components. The bulk of manufacturing industry is of post-independence origin, when the Government began to give priority to industrial development aimed at national and regional markets. To this end, extensive tax and financing incentives were made available, while the state took substantial shareholdings in major ventures, held through the SNI. A number of projects initiated at the beginning of the 1980s were not generally successful. Ageing plants and electricity rationing explained why the industrial sector worked roughly 30% below capacity in 2000–01. However, public works performed particularly well over this period, primarily as a result of the construction of the Chad–Cameroon pipeline.

The economic crisis in the 1980s prompted a reversal in government policies, with a programme for the privatization of state-owned companies and a tightening up or liquidation of those running at a loss. However, resistance from adversely affected interests meant that little progress was made until late 1990, when 15 companies were transferred to the private sector. Privatization continued in subsequent years, although the programme was constantly behind target, owing in part to the poor financial situation of the enterprises. Following renewed pressure from its multilateral creditors, the Government expanded the programme from mid-1994, and by late 2003 some major disposals had been effected in manufacturing, including the sugar and palm oil companies, the tea component of the Cameroon Development Corporation (CAMDEV), and SONEL. In October 2007 a leasing contract to operate the water utility, Société Nationale des Eaux du Cameroun (SNEC), was awarded to a consortium headed by Morocco's national water company. The Government has repeatedly renewed its commitment to privatization, in an effort to comply with IMF recommendations (see Foreign Trade and Aid). However, the sales of the largest single state enterprise, the CAMDEV (with remaining interests in rubber, palm oil, and bananas), Cameroon Postal Service (CAMPOST) and the state cotton company, Société de Développement du Coton, had made little progress by the late 2000s.

One of the key players in Cameroon's heavy manufacturing sector is Cimenteries du Cameroun (CIMENCAM). By 2011 local cement consumption was growing at 8% annually, and demand was expected to rise further, given the country's planned construction of a new deep-water port and two hydroelectric power facilities. Against this backdrop, in September CIMENCAM began constructing a new cement plant (the company's third), which would raise its annual production by between 600,000 and 700,000 metric tons per year. The firm expected the US $103m. plant to open in 2014, bringing its annual cement production in Cameroon to 1.5m. tons. However, after long dominating the Cameroonian market, CIMENCAM was finally having to face up to the prospect of local competition from Nigeria's Dangote, which began work on its first cement plant in Cameroon, a $115m. factory in Douala, in September 2011. It was planned that the plant would generate 1.5m. tons of cement per year and would be followed by a further $585m. of investments by Dangote in the local market. However, Dangote's plans came under threat in March 2012, when a Cameroonian government official stated that the land on which the firm was building its proposed plant was jointly owned by the municipal council and two cultural associations. Work was therefore halted at the construction site, although Cameroon's Prime Minister, Philémon Yang, publicly reassured Dangote that his Government remained committed to the project being completed as planned.

Two other foreign firms seeking to tap into the opportunities generated by Cameroon's expanding infrastructure market were South Africa's Megatron Federal and South Korea's state-controlled Pohang Iron and Steel Co (POSCO). Megatron Federal announced in August 2011 that it was planning to build an electrical equipment factory in Douala, which would manufacture goods including transformers, generators, solar energy equipment and electricity meters. In December it was reported that POSCO, the sixth largest steelmaker in the world, was planning to build a steel mill in the central African country, alongside a hydroelectric plant, with the latter powering the former. The project would use locally extracted iron ore for its steelmaking process. The announcement of the project came as output at Cameroon's 10,000m.-ton Mbalam iron ore project was expected to come online in 2014.

TRANSPORT AND TELECOMMUNICATIONS

The transport infrastructure suffers from inadequate investment and maintenance, although major divestitures—including the shipping line, the state railway and Douala harbour—have taken place in the past decade or so. The rail network, totalling some 1,100 km, forms the most important component. The main line is the 885-km Transcameroon, from Douala to Ngaoundere. There are plans to connect the line with the proposed new port at Grand Batanga (see below) and, in the long term, to construct a 1,000-km line from Kribi to the Central African Republic (CAR). In early 2008 Sundance Resources Limited, engaged in iron ore extraction at Mbalam, 450 km from Kribi, announced that it would build a railway to Kribi in order to facilitate the movement of the extracted ore.

According to the Organisation for Economic Co-operation and Development (OECD), the road network totalled some 51,346 km in 2011, of which only 8.4% was paved. According to the Ministry of Public Works in September, the Government planned to spend 175,000m. francs CFA (US $379m.) over the next decade on improving and extending the dilapidated network. It was estimated that nation-wide traffic volumes were rising by 5% per year. The investment would be spread across Cameroon's eastern, western and southern regions, with a partial focus on cocoa-growing areas, where poor roads hinder the efficiency of bringing the export crop to market. At that time the Ministry estimated that only 6% of the country's roads—i.e. not even the whole of the paved network—were in good condition, while 21% were categorized as normal, 70% as mediocre and 3% as very poor.

The privatization of road maintenance works, and strong foreign donor support, notably from the EU, has supported progress in this sub-sector since the late 1990s. Roads in the north have been improved to give access to the Ngaoundere railhead, and there are long-term plans to upgrade the east–west road linking Nigeria with the CAR. Work to rehabilitate the Wouri bridge in Douala was completed in 2006. In December a memorandum of understanding was signed enacting the Nigeria–Cameroon Highway Project, which envisioned the construction and rehabilitation of a highway from Enugu in Nigeria to Batibo in Cameroon. In June 2007 the World Bank pledged US $201m. in credits and grants to improve road and rail links between Cameroon and both Chad and the CAR, with a particular view to facilitating the export of goods from the latter two landlocked countries via the port at Douala. In early 2008 the AfDB announced that it would provide funding for the Highway Project, which was due to commence in June 2010. AfDB funding totalling $190m. was confirmed for the construction of a 1,612-km highway connecting Yaoundé with Brazzaville, the capital of the Republic of the Congo, in September 2009.

Cameroon has seaports at Douala-Bonabéri, Kribi and Limbé-Tiko (although the latter is now almost completely unusable), and a river port at Garoua. Total handling capacity is 7m. metric tons annually. Feasibility studies have been conducted for deep-water ports at Cap Limboh (near Limbé and the oil refinery) and Grand Batanga, south of the existing port handling wood and minerals at Kribi. However, the latter is dependent on the exploitation of the offshore gas and iron ore reserves, neither of which seems likely in the near future.

The poor state of the road network has encouraged the development of internal air travel and of small domestic airports. There are international airports at Douala, Garoua and Yaoundé.

The telecommunications company Cameroon Telecommunications (CAMTEL) was the sole fixed-line company operating in the country. Created in 1999, it had 110,000 subscribers in 2008. After an abortive attempt to sell a majority share in the company in 1999, the Government issued a tender for prequalification in early 2006. Privatization was further delayed in 2006 to allow more time for preparation of the final documents, and by early 2012 the process had yet to reach completion. In 2012 there were three mobile telephone providers in Cameroon: MTN Cameroon Limited; Orange; and Cameroon Mobile Telecommunications Corporation (launched by CAMTEL in March 2006).

Cameroon arranged a 26,000m. francs CFA (US $57m.) loan from the Export and Import Bank of China in December 2009 to finance a 3,200-km fibre optic network, which would also connect to neighbouring Equatorial Guinea and Gabon. The loan was expected to cover the cost of about 68% of the project.

FINANCE, AND MONETARY AND EXCHANGE RATE POLICY

Revenue from petroleum production profoundly changed Cameroon's fiscal position, and allowed a rapid rise in both current and capital spending during the early 1980s. The situation was transformed by the collapse of international oil prices in 1986, which led to diminished petroleum royalties, and was followed by a general contraction in the economy. The Government of Paul Biya was obliged to introduce austerity programmes, involving reductions in both current and capital expenditure. With the support of the World Bank, the AfDB and France, the Government commenced an extensive, five-year programme of economic restructuring in 1989/90. This entailed the reform of the country's parastatal organizations and of the inefficient administrative structure. At the same time, the Government sought to impose strict controls on public spending and introduced measures to expand the tax base.

IMF support resumed in the wake of the devaluation of the CFA franc in January 1994, but disbursements were repeatedly suspended as the Government failed to comply with performance criteria. In August 1997, however, with a new Government showing convincing commitment to structural reform, the IMF extended a US $220m. enhanced structural adjustment facility (ESAF). In 1999/2000 the Government turned the fiscal balance (on a commitment basis) into a surplus of 81,000m. francs CFA (equivalent to 1.4% of GDP). An increase in, and extension of, the sales tax also helped to improve the balance (a value-added tax was introduced in 1999), while the privatization or liquidation of parastatal companies further contributed to boosting non-oil revenues. However, by 2002–03 non-oil revenue collection began declining, as a result of lower tax compliance and continuous delays in structural reforms. At the same time, petroleum revenue failed to increase (despite higher international prices for that commodity) owing to a decline in production volumes, a rise in the discount for lower-quality petroleum and the appreciation of the CFA franc against the US dollar. The financial situation of state-owned enterprises also deteriorated, primarily as a result of growing payment arrears by the Government and delays in financial restructuring. However, fiscal performance improved in 2005, prompting the IMF to approve a new three-year Poverty Reduction and Growth Facility (PRGF), worth $26.8m., in October. An IMF review under the PRGF programme in late 2007 concluded that fiscal and financial targets were being adequately met, but voiced concerns that public expenditure required greater discipline, while corruption remained a significant problem and public sector reformscontinued to suffer delays.

An important element of the structural adjustment programme in 1989–92 was a restructuring of the financial sector, with banks being liquidated or, in a few cases, merging. Yet, the banking sector remains dominated by three main banks (including the Société Générale de Banques au Cameroun and the Banque Internationale du Cameroun pour l'Epargne et le Crédit). In April 2003 Cameroon's first stock exchange opened in Douala; it was hoped that this might drive the expansion of the private sector by improving its access to finance. However, concerns remained over relatively weak regulations, potential corruption and competition from the regional stock exchange in Libreville, Gabon. Trading started a year later, with the listing of shares from the company SNEC. By mid-2009 only two other companies had been listed: the Société Africaine Forestière et Agricole du Cameroun and the Société Camerounaise de Palmeraies.

Inflation stood at 5.1% in 2006, driven by rising prices in food, beverages, tobacco, transport and communications, but it declined to 1.7% in 2007. The 2008 budget introduced tax exemptions on construction materials and agricultural products, and predicted inflation of approximately 3% for 2008. This proved to be overly optimistic, as high food prices pushed consumer inflation to an annual average of 4.5%, according to the IMF. However, inflation declined to 3.0%, in 2009, owing to a slump in global demand.

The IMF continued to press for reform to Cameroon's financial sector, as the country lobbied for a new PRGF in the first half of 2009. The Government prepared a financial sector development strategy in a bid to modernize the sector. Although the low level of development of Cameroon's financial industry had shielded its banking sector from direct exposure to the financial crisis that engulfed developed nations in the second half of 2008, the Fund continued to view modernization as crucial for a number of reasons. Key aims were to improve access to credit for small and medium-sized private companies, and to develop a domestic bond market, which would enable Cameroon's Government to finance some of its activities via domestic borrowing rather than depending so heavily on multilateral support. In 2010 the IMF expressed renewed concerns about Cameroon's fiscal policy and the persisting need for reform. In April the Fund urged the Government to prioritize strengthening the management of the treasury and public spending. It also cautioned that the feasibility of the 2010 budget depended on ensuring sufficient demand for local currency-denominated government bonds, given that such demand might be constrained by the authorities' track record of late payments.

International credit rating agency Standard & Poor's affirmed its BB long- and short-term sovereign credit ratings on Cameroon in May 2010. The affirmation underlined Cameroon's continued sovereign status in the 'junk bond' category, due to its moderate levels of debt, problems with domestic fiscal arrears and poor local infrastructure. This continued poor rating was in all probability expected to limit the country's access to cost-effective funding on international capital markets for many years to come.

Bank deposits decreased slightly in the year to the end of June 2009, to 1,960,000,000m. francs CFA from 1,990,000,000m. francs CFA, the Ministry of Finance announced in December. Given the financial crisis that engulfed developed markets (and the concomitant global economic downturn) over this period, these figures show a remarkable degree of deposit stability. Moreover, lending actually increased over this period, to 1,300,000,000m. francs CFA, up from 1,110,000,000m. francs CFA. Even more encouragingly, this rise in lending was overwhelmingly concentrated in the private sector, as bank lending to the Government decreased, to 108,000m. francs CFA from 115,000m. francs CFA. This represented a remarkable improvement in banking performance, given that private sector credit expansion in Cameroon has often been hampered by high public sector demand for loans (and late payments by the Government on its debt obligations).

However, despite the overall health of Cameroon's banking sector, the Government announced in November 2009 that it would need to inject money into the Commercial Bank Cameroon, in order to prevent it from filing for bankruptcy. The precise level of funding remained uncertain and would depend on the development of a restructuring plan for the CBC, which maintained six branches in Cameroon, with further branches in four other African countries. In November 2010, however, the banking commission of the Banque des Etats de l'Afrique Centrale (BEAC)—of which Cameroon is a member—rejected a restructuring plan for the ailing lender, according to the Ministry of Finance, because the proposal did not comply with regulations.

Cameroon is also a member of the Communauté Economique et Monétaire de l'Afrique Centrale, which is part of the franc CFA zone. At July 2010 the exchange rate remained fixed at €1 = 656 francs CFA. The inability of national central banks to manipulate the value of the CFA franc (monetary policy is set by the BEAC, which focuses on maintaining the fixed exchange rate against the euro) has acted as a powerful disciplinary force on member states. The inability of governments to fund spending by printing money has thus helped to contain inflation, and has enabled trade to be conducted at stable exchange rates. In this context, consumer price inflation in Cameroon was just 1.3% in 2010, before rising to 2.6% in 2011, according to the IMF. In view of low inflation prevailing across the CFA franc area, the BEAC reduced its key rate by 0.25% in July 2010, to 4.0%.

The BEAC held its key rate steady at 4.0% throughout 2011 and there was still no change as of May 2012. However, the central bank's currency peg against the euro was translating into a de facto monetary easing via the exchange rate, as the European single currency came under sustained pressure on global currency markets in the first half of 2012, due to the ongoing debt crisis in the euro zone. There was even speculation that the euro might have to be abandoned by the EU and that member states would revert to maintaining national currencies, which would necessitate the BEAC finding a new monetary anchor for its exchange rate (or else resort to a currency float). By mid 2012 a partial collapse of the euro zone was an increasingly significant danger, given the inability of debt-wracked Greece to form a government and opposition in Germany to the continued subsidizing of fiscally weak member states.

FOREIGN TRADE AND AID

The emergence of petroleum as a leading export in the late 1970s resulted in a considerable and growing surplus on foreign trade, despite significant increases in the level of import spending. A trade surplus of approximately 2% of GDP, aided by high oil prices and exports of wood, coffee, cocoa and aluminium, was recorded in 2006 and 2007. The current account deficit (including grants) was projected by the IMF to decrease to just 0.4% of GDP in 2006. In that year receipts from petroleum were estimated to amount to 54% of total exports. The current account displayed a surplus of 0.2% of GDP in 2007, according to OECD.

With global oil prices reaching new peaks in July 2008, the trade account remained in comfortable surplus for 2008 as a whole, despite the correction in commodities that occurred later in the year. The trade surplus was 329,000m. francs CFA (3.1% of GDP) in 2008, according to IMF estimates, leading to a current account surplus (including grants) of some 0.8% of GDP. Exports in 2009 totalled 1,926,000m. francs CFA, thanks to higher-than-expected oil prices, while imports reached 2,080,000m. francs CFA, resulting in a trade deficit of 154,000m. francs CFA. The current account deficit, meanwhile, reached 393,000m. francs CFA. In 2010 a 29,000m. franc CFA trade surplus was recorded, according to preliminary IMF figures, with a continued increase in oil prices bringing exports to 2,309,000m. francs CFA, offsetting a significant rise in imports, to 2,280,000m. francs CFA. The annual current account deficit also narrowed, to 309,000m. francs CFA. Cameroon's principal export destinations in 2010 were Spain, which took 15.1% of the country's shipments by value, followed by the Netherlands (12.8%), China (9.4%), Italy (9.3%), France (6.5%) and the USA (6.4%). Meanwhile, Cameroon took the biggest proportion of its 2010 imports from France, which accounted for 19.1% of its external goods purchases, followed by China (13.3%), Nigeria (12.4%) and Belgium.

The high level of earnings from the petroleum sector during the early 1980s enabled development expenditure to be financed without a substantial increase in the foreign debt. Servicing of the foreign debt was thus manageable, representing about 15% of export earnings in most years during the first half of the decade. However, the January 1994 devaluation of the CFA franc doubled overnight the local currency value of the foreign debt, and special debt relief measures were agreed. A 'Paris Club' rescheduling agreement was suspended in 1995, as a result of policy shortcomings and withheld payments by the IMF and the World Bank. The external debt continued to rise, to $9,917m. by the end of 1998, but declined in subsequent years, reaching $8,367m. at the end of 2001, equivalent to 103% of gross national income (GNI); the debt-service ratio in that year was 12.6%, compared with 20.4% at the end of 2000.

In October 2000 the IMF and World Bank agreed to grant Cameroon a debt-service relief package under the enhanced initiative for heavily indebted poor countries (HIPC), worth US $2,000m. This included $1,300m. of bilateral debt relief, as later formally agreed by the 'Paris Club' in December. Interim HIPC debt relief began in 2001, and in August 2002 the British Government agreed to cancel 90% of Cameroon's external debt (worth 40,000m. francs CFA) and to reschedule the remaining 10% over a period of 23 years. External debt decreased to $8,555m. (equivalent to 92.8% of GNI) by the end of 2002. In June 2003 the World Bank announced a 'soft' loan of $49.7m. to assist the country in buying back some $935m. of unpaid debt to commercial creditors. Cameroon's external debt stock was estimated at $7,000m. at the end of 2004, equivalent to 44% of GDP. After more than one year's delay resulting from policy slippages, Cameroon reached completion point under HIPC II in May 2006. This was expected to help reduce Cameroon's future debt-service payments by about $4,900m. in nominal terms. The 'Paris Club' subsequently negotiated a generous debt relief deal with the Government, leading to a reduction in Cameroon's bilateral debt stock from $3,500m. to only $27m. Upon reaching the HIPC completion point, Cameroon also became eligible for further debt relief from the IMF, IDA and the African Development Fund under the Multilateral Debt Relief Initiative. The stock of external debt as a percentage of GDP was projected to contract from 33.2% in 2005 to 3.1% in 2006 as the Government finalized the signing of bilateral agreements with its creditors. In May 2007 France cancelled €311m. of commercial debt owed by Cameroon. Cameroon's total external debt in 2009 was US $2,941m., of which $2,128m. was public and publicly guaranteed debt. In 2009 the cost of servicing long-term public and publicly guaranteed debt and repayments to the IMF was equivalent to 1.4% of the value of exports of goods, services and income (excluding workers' remittances).

Inflows of official development assistance (ODA), which had been declining in most years since 1994, when they had reached a peak of US $730.3m. (net of repayment), recovered in the late 1990s, after the currency devaluation made Cameroon eligible for multilateral funds on concessionary terms. Net ODA receipts decreased to $572m. in 2004 and $335m. in 2005, although they totalled $649.4m. in 2009. Despite great potential, Cameroon has failed to attract any significant flows in foreign direct investment (FDI) outside the petroleum sector. It was hoped that Cameroon's accession to the Fonds Africain de Garantie et de Co-opération Economique in April 2006 would promote foreign investment in the country. FDI inflows totalled $270m. in 2008 and $337m. in 2009. An agreement signed between China and Cameroon in March 2010 heralded the prospect of greater Chinese investment in the country. The agreement involved eight projects, spread across the energy, roads, ICT, postal and agriculture sectors, and included interest-free loans totalling 3,200m. francs CFA.

Statistical Survey

Source (unless otherwise stated): Institut National de la Statistique du Cameroun, BP 134, Yaoundé; tel. 2222-0445; fax 2223-2437; internet www.statistics-cameroon.org.

Area and Population

AREA, POPULATION AND DENSITY

Area (sq km)	
Continental	466,050
Maritime	9,600
Total	475,650*
Population (census results)	
9 April 1987	10,493,655
11 November 2005	
Males	8,408,495
Females	8,643,639
Total	17,052,134
Population (UN estimates at mid-year)†	
2010	19,598,889
2011	20,030,359
2012	20,468,945
Density (per sq km) at mid-2012	43.9‡

* 183,649 sq miles.
† Source: UN, *World Population Prospects: The 2010 Revision*.
‡ Continental area only.

POPULATION BY AGE AND SEX
(UN estimates at mid-2012)

	Males	Females	Total
0–14	4,154,615	4,099,424	8,254,039
15–64	5,738,378	5,755,453	11,493,831
65 and over	327,700	393,375	721,075
Total	10,220,693	10,248,252	20,468,945

Source: UN, *World Population Prospects: The 2010 Revision*.

PROVINCES
(official population projections, 2010)

	Area (sq km)*	Population	Density (per sq km)
Centre	68,953	3,442,597	49.9
Littoral	20,248	2,789,445	137.8
West	13,892	1,911,344	137.6
South-West	25,410	1,462,448	57.6
North-West	17,300	1,921,241	111.1
North	66,090	1,875,688	28.4
East	109,002	857,587	7.9
South	47,191	705,239	14.9
Adamaoua	63,701	982,636	15.4
Far North	34,263	3,457,874	100.9
Total	466,050	19,406,100	41.6

* Continental area only.

PRINCIPAL TOWNS
(population at 1987 census)

Douala	810,000	Bamenda	110,000
Yaoundé (capital)	649,000	Nkongsamba	85,420
Garoua	142,000	Kumba	70,112
Maroua	123,000	Limbé	44,561
Bafoussam	113,000		

Mid-2011 ('000, incl. suburbs, UN estimate): Yaoundé 2,432 (Source: UN, *World Urbanization Prospects: The 2011 Revision*).

BIRTHS AND DEATHS
(annual averages, UN estimates)

	1995–2000	2000–05	2005–10
Birth rate (per 1,000)	38.0	38.0	37.2
Death rate (per 1,000)	14.6	15.3	15.0

Source: UN, *World Population Prospects: The 2010 Revision*.

Life expectancy (years at birth): 51.1 (males 50.1; females 52.1) in 2010 (Source: World Bank, World Development Indicators database).

ECONOMICALLY ACTIVE POPULATION
(persons aged six years and over, mid-1985, official estimates)

	Males	Females	Total
Agriculture, hunting, forestry and fishing	1,574,946	1,325,925	2,900,871
Mining and quarrying	1,693	100	1,793
Manufacturing	137,671	36,827	174,498
Electricity, gas and water	3,373	149	3,522
Construction	65,666	1,018	66,684
Trade, restaurants and hotels	115,269	38,745	154,014
Transport, storage and communications	50,664	1,024	51,688
Financing, insurance, real estate and business services	7,447	562	8,009
Community, social and personal services	255,076	37,846	292,922
Sub-total	2,211,805	1,442,196	3,654,001
Activities not adequately defined	18,515	17,444	35,959
Total in employment	2,230,320	1,459,640	3,689,960
Unemployed	180,016	47,659	227,675
Total labour force	2,410,336	1,507,299	3,917,635

Source: ILO, *Yearbook of Labour Statistics*.

Mid-2012 ('000, estimates): Agriculture, etc. 3,574; Total labour force 7,914 (Source: FAO).

Health and Welfare

KEY INDICATORS

Total fertility rate (children per woman, 2010)	4.5
Under-5 mortality rate (per 1,000 live births, 2010)	136
HIV/AIDS (% of persons aged 15–49, 2009)	5.3
Physicians (per 1,000 head, 2004)	0.2
Hospital beds (per 1,000 head, 2006)	1.5
Health expenditure (2009): US $ per head (PPP)	117
Health expenditure (2009): % of GDP	4.9
Health expenditure (2009): public (% of total)	25.9
Access to water (% of persons, 2010)	77
Access to sanitation (% of persons, 2010)	49
Total carbon dioxide emissions ('000 metric tons, 2008)	4,070.7
Carbon dioxide emissions per head (metric tons, 2008)	0.2
Human Development Index (2011): ranking	150
Human Development Index (2011): value	0.482

For sources and definitions, see explanatory note on p. vi.

Agriculture

PRINCIPAL CROPS
('000 metric tons)

	2008	2009	2010
Rice, paddy	72	115*	175*
Maize	1,395	1,450*	1,674
Millet	75†	65*	55†
Sorghum	931†	980*	900†
Potatoes	145	147*	151
Sweet potatoes	236	230*	242*
Cassava (Manioc)	2,883	2,950*	3,024
Yams	400	400*	410
Taro (Coco yams)	1,482	1,450*	1,470
Sugar cane*	1,450	1,450	1,450
Beans, dry	271	275*	285
Groundnuts, with shell	484	457†	460†
Oil palm fruit*	1,555	1,600	1,575
Melonseed*	62	60	62
—continued			
Tomatoes	572	570*	576
Pumpkins, squash and gourds*	142	145	146
Onions, dry	112	113*	115
Bananas	1,078	1,000*	950
Plantains	2,501	2,450*	2,604
Avocados*	55	54	56
Pineapples	126	127	137
Coffee, green	51	48†	67
Cocoa beans	229	236	264
Natural rubber	53	52	55

* FAO estimate(s).
† Unofficial figure.

Aggregate production ('000 metric tons, may include official, semi-official or estimated data): Total cereals 2,474 in 2008, 2,531 in 2009, 2,805 in 2010; Total roots and tubers 5,183 in 2008, 5,215 in 2009, 5,336 in 2010; Total vegetables (incl. melons) 1,829 in 2008, 1,846 in 2009, 1,865 in 2010; Total fruits (excl. melons) 3,886 in 2008, 3,760 in 2009, 3,879 in 2010.

Source: FAO.

LIVESTOCK
('000 head, year ending September)

	2008	2009	2010*
Horses	15	17	17
Asses	40	40	40
Cattle	5,046	5,000	5,700
Pigs	1,500	1,630	1,680
Sheep*	3,800	3,800	3,800
Goats*	4,400	4,400	4,400
Chickens	44,929	44,754	45,000

* FAO estimate(s).

Source: FAO.

LIVESTOCK PRODUCTS
('000 metric tons)

	2008	2009	2010
Cattle meat	109.6	109.6	124.0*
Sheep meat	13.3	12.7	16.5
Goat meat	17.7	16.9	20.1
Pig meat	32.6	31.1	37.8*
Chicken meat	67.7	63.9	68.0*
Game meat*	62.1	66.2	66.5
Cows' milk	170.0	170.1	175.0
Sheep's milk*	17.7	18.3	18.6
Goats' milk*	45.3	47.2	48.0
Hen eggs*	14.9	14.9	15.0
Honey*	3.8	4.2	4.2

* FAO estimate(s).

Source: FAO.

Forestry

ROUNDWOOD REMOVALS
('000 cubic metres, excl. bark, FAO estimates, unless otherwise indicated)

	2007	2008	2009
Sawlogs, veneer logs and logs for sleepers	2,274*	2,266	2,266
Other industrial wood	350	350	350
Fuel wood	9,648	9,733	9,818
Total	12,272	12,349	12,434

* Unofficial figure.

2010: Production assumed to be unchanged from 2009 (FAO estimates).

Source: FAO.

SAWNWOOD PRODUCTION
('000 cubic metres, incl. railway sleepers)

	2006	2007	2008
Total (all broadleaved)	702*	773†	773†

* FAO estimate.
† Unofficial figure.

2009–10: Production assumed to be unchanged from 2008 (FAO estimates).

Source: FAO.

Fishing

('000 metric tons, live weight)

	2008*	2009	2010*
Capture*	139.2	140.0	140.0
Freshwater fishes	74.7	75.0	75.0
Cassava croaker	0.5	0.9	0.9
Sardinellas*	2.1	2.1	2.1
Bonga shad*	41.4	41.4	41.4
Aquaculture*	0.6	0.7	0.8
Total catch*	139.8	140.7	140.8

* FAO estimates.

Source: FAO.

Mining

	2007	2008	2009
Crude petroleum (million barrels)	30.4	29.7	30.0
Gold (kg)*	2,000	1,800	1,800
Pozzolan ('000 metric tons)	600	600	600
Limestone ('000 metric tons)	100	100	100

* From artisanal mining.

Source: US Geological Survey.

Industry

SELECTED PRODUCTS
('000 metric tons unless otherwise indicated)

	2006	2007	2008
Palm oil	193	172*	185†
Raw sugar	126	100	100
Veneer sheets ('000 cu m)	47†	85*	85†
Plywood ('000 cu m)	40†	32*	32†
Jet fuels	71	73	85
Motor spirit (petrol)	320	390	399
Kerosene	300	331	261
Gas-diesel (distillate fuel) oil	569	694	658
Residual fuel oils	354	387	380
Lubricating oils	0	0	0
Petroleum bitumen (asphalt)	0	0	0
Liquefied petroleum gas	22	19	17
Cement	1,127	1,209	982
Aluminium (unwrought)	91	90	n.a.
Electric energy (million kWh)	5,106	5,753	5,551

* Unofficial figure.
† FAO estimate.

2009 ('000 cu metres unless otherwise indicated, unofficial figures): Veneer sheets 79; Plywood 24; Palm oil ('000 metric tons) 182.

2010 ('000 cu metres): Veneer sheets 85 (FAO estimate); Plywood 24 (FAO estimate), Palm oil ('000 metric tons) 111.

Sources: UN Industrial Commodity Statistics Database; FAO.

Finance

CURRENCY AND EXCHANGE RATES

Monetary Units

100 centimes = 1 franc de la Coopération Financière en Afrique Centrale (CFA).

Sterling, Dollar and Euro Equivalents (31 May 2012)

£1 sterling = 819.959 francs CFA;
US $1 = 528.870 francs CFA;
€1 = 655.957 francs CFA;
10,000 francs CFA = £12.20 = $18.91 = €15.24.

Average Exchange Rate (francs CFA per US $)

2009	472.186
2010	495.277
2011	471.866

Note: An exchange rate of 1 French franc = 50 francs CFA, established in 1948, remained in force until January 1994, when the CFA franc was devalued by 50%, with the exchange rate adjusted to 1 French franc = 100 francs CFA. This relationship to French currency remained in effect with the introduction of the euro on 1 January 1999. From that date, accordingly, a fixed exchange rate of €1 = 655.957 francs CFA has been in operation.

BUDGET
('000 million francs CFA)

Revenue*	2010	2011†	2012‡
Petroleum revenue	497	415	663
Non-petroleum revenue	1,372	1,576	1,665
Direct taxes	343	—	404
Special tax on petroleum products	83	89	95
Taxes on international trade	253	—	300
Other taxes on goods and services	612	—	768
Non-tax revenue (excluding privatization proceeds)	81	97	97
Total	1,869	1,991	2,328

Expenditure	2010	2011†	2012‡
Current expenditure	1,611	1,565	1,750
Wages and salaries	634	665	734
Other goods and services	613	479	534
Interest on public debt	33	45	48
Subsidies and transfers	331	376	434
Capital expenditure	456	680	702
Externally financed investment	100	206	196
Domestically financed investment	315	429	441
Restructuring	42	45	65
Total	2,067	2,245	2,452

* Excluding grants received ('000 million francs CFA): 71 in 2010; 104 in 2011 (budget figure); 88 in 2012 (projected figure).
† Budget figures.
‡ Projected figures.

Source: IMF, *Cameroon: 2011 Article IV Consultation—Staff Report; Debt Sustainability Analysis; Informational Annex; Public Information Notice on the Executive Board Discussion; and Statement by the Executive Director for Cameroon* (September 2011).

INTERNATIONAL RESERVES*
(US $ million at 31 December)

	2009	2010	2011
IMF special drawing rights	243.71	27.13	24.92
Reserve position in IMF	1.32	1.34	1.38
Foreign exchange	3,430.49	3,614.17	3,172.42
Total	3,675.52	3,642.64	3,198.72

* Excluding reserves of gold (30,000 troy ounces in 2008).

Source: IMF, *International Financial Statistics*.

MONEY SUPPLY
('000 million francs CFA at 31 December)

	2009	2010	2011
Currency outside depository corporations	477.87	541.75	550.26
Transferable deposits	834.44	907.34	1,102.07
Other deposits	881.33	1,026.38	1,092.91
Broad money	2,193.63	2,475.46	2,745.24

Source: IMF, *International Financial Statistics*.

COST OF LIVING
(Consumer Price Index; base: 2000 = 100)

	2006	2007	2008
Food	117.9	119.1	130.0
Clothing	100.4	100.3	100.8
Electricity, gas and other fuels	119.3	120.4	124.6
All items	116.2	117.2	123.5

All items: 127.2 in 2009; 128.9 in 2010; 132.7 in 2011.

Source: ILO.

NATIONAL ACCOUNTS
('000 million francs CFA at current prices)

Expenditure on the Gross Domestic Product

	2008	2009	2010*
Government final consumption expenditure	1,127	1,243	1,358
Private final consumption expenditure	7,840	8,304	8,776
Gross capital formation	1,842	1,965	2,220
Change in inventories	60	80	8
Total domestic expenditure	10,869	11,592	12,362
Exports of goods and services	2,520	1,770	2,030
Less Imports of goods and services	2,946	2,322	2,693
GDP in purchasers' values	10,444	11,040	11,700

Gross Domestic Product by Economic Activity

	2008	2009	2010*
Agriculture	2,257	2,391	2,535
Mining and quarrying	926	807	778
Manufacturing	1,447	1,653	1,757
Electricity, gas and water	102	100	110
Construction	315	485	598
Wholesale and retail trade, restaurants and hotels	2,053	2,059	2,107
Finance, insurance and real estate	1,069	1,117	1,245
Transport and communication	641	659	758
Public administration and defence	769	845	879
Other services	114	128	135
Sub-total	9,693	10,244	10,902
Indirect taxes	811	856	864
Less Imputed bank service charge	61	60	64
GDP in purchasers' values	10,444	11,040	11,700

* Provisional figures.

Source: African Development Bank.

BALANCE OF PAYMENTS
(US $ million)

	2008	2009	2010
Exports of goods f.o.b.	5,890.0	4,169.9	4,485.2
Imports of goods f.o.b.	–5,424.0	–4,559.0	–4,662.6
Trade balance	466.0	–389.2	–177.4
Exports of services	1,483.7	1,248.9	1,159.3
Imports of services	–2,668.3	–1,779.9	–1,745.6
Balance on goods and services	–718.6	–920.2	–763.7
Other income received	65.8	131.4	93.1
Other income paid	–394.5	–608.5	–331.7
Balance on goods, services and income	–1,047.3	–1,397.2	–1,002.3
Current transfers received	774.6	532.0	334.3
Current transfers paid	–177.0	–253.5	–188.3
Current balance	–449.7	–1,118.7	–856.3
Capital account (net)	146.5	184.1	147.0
Direct investment abroad	47.3	140.8	35.8
Direct investment from abroad	–24.2	668.3	–0.6
Portfolio investment assets	–39.3	–97.2	–10.8
Portfolio investment liabilities	–1.4	–0.7	85.2
Other investment assets	–66.4	–100.9	550.6
Other investment liabilities	449.2	394.4	–132.8
Net errors and omissions	205.1	159.7	188.8
Overall balance	267.0	229.8	6.8

Source: IMF, *International Financial Statistics*.

External Trade

PRINCIPAL COMMODITIES
(US $ million)

Imports c.i.f.	2008	2009	2010
Food and live animals	902.7	928.4	831.3
Cereals and cereal preparations	528.1	489.3	417.6
Mineral fuels, lubricants, etc.	120.6	134.0	1,421.0
Petroleum, petroleum products and related materials	96.2	113.4	1,386.4
Crude petroleum and oils	0.0	0.0	1,231.8
Chemicals and related products	496.9	511.6	536.8
Manufactured goods	672.8	601.9	676.3
Iron and steel	171.8	109.1	152.2
Tubes, pipes and fittings	44.7	26.9	26.0
Machinery and transport equipment	1,438.7	1,124.9	1,160.3
Road vehicles	60.6	40.9	55.1
Total (incl. others)	4,137.9	3,788.6	5,133.3

Exports f.o.b.	2008	2009	2010
Food and live animals	649.5	800.4	926.2
Coffee, tea, cocoa, spices, etc.	521.0	672.3	784.8
Cocoa and cocoa products	444.6	611.2	707.4
Cocoa beans (raw, roasted)	400.3	543.4	611.0
Crude materials, inedible, except fuels	741.2	505.3	602.1
Textile fibres and wastes	61.0	90.3	81.7
Raw cotton (not carded or combed)	60.8	89.9	81.3
Mineral fuels, lubricants, etc.	26.5	16.4	1,921.7
Petroleum, petroleum products and related materials	26.5	16.2	1,921.5
Crude petroleum and oils	0.0	0.0	1,415.7
Petroleum products (refined)	3.0	4.8	496.8
Manufactured goods	318.1	196.0	216.8
Aluminium	181.0	80.5	109.5
Total (incl. others)	2,126.7	1,732.4	3,878.4

Source: UN, *International Trade Statistics Yearbook*.

PRINCIPAL TRADING PARTNERS
(US $ million, estimates)

Imports c.i.f.	2008	2009	2010
Belgium	167.0	173.1	152.7
Brazil	152.0	86.4	89.3
Canada	43.4	46.2	35.0
China, People's Repub.	399.6	442.0	543.0
Côte d'Ivoire	30.1	50.9	47.9
Equatorial Guinea	9.3	7.8	124.0
France (incl. Monaco)	804.6	714.8	748.1
Germany	188.4	175.2	190.6
Greece	22.1	115.6	21.0
India	103.7	112.7	121.0
Italy	137.7	115.7	124.4
Japan	159.6	138.1	155.0
Korea, Republic	28.8	26.2	55.1
Mauritania	79.1	98.0	80.4
Netherlands	235.5	87.1	83.9
Nigeria	13.5	9.7	933.7
South Africa	129.8	89.1	109.9
Spain	79.7	84.9	74.9
Thailand	154.9	170.0	155.2
Turkey	0.1	50.2	54.4
United Kingdom	71.0	0.0	73.0
USA	261.3	149.3	169.4
Viet Nam	58.7	66.8	44.2
Total (incl. others)	4,137.9	3,788.6	5,133.3

Exports f.o.b.	2008	2009	2010
Belgium	73.6	67.8	73.4
Central African Republic	19.1	20.0	53.7
Chad	43.4	52.4	337.8
China, People's Repub.	160.2	136.3	329.6
Congo, Democratic Repub.	0.2	4.9	173.0
Congo, Repub.	36.5	29.0	0.0
Equatorial Guinea	51.8	33.8	36.2
France (incl. Monaco)	325.4	230.5	242.7
Gabon	227.8	62.6	57.6
Germany	35.0	25.3	63.1
Greece	77.4	60.4	3.7
India	17.4	11.8	138.4
Italy	205.1	116.1	376.6
Malaysia	38.6	40.5	63.5
Netherlands	394.8	493.9	508.6
Nigeria	32.1	24.5	28.3
Portugal	17.0	11.4	73.1
Spain	84.6	42.4	716.6
Togo	2.6	37.9	22.1
Turkey	12.6	17.2	23.5
United Kingdom	0.0	0.0	51.1
USA	46.3	48.1	219.7
Viet Nam	28.5	35.4	34.9
Total (incl. others)	2,126.7	1,732.4	3,878.4

Source: UN, *International Trade Statistics Yearbook*.

Transport

RAILWAYS
(traffic, year ending 30 June)

	2001	2002	2003
Freight ton-km (million)	1,159	1,179	1,090
Passenger-km (million)	303	308	322

Source: UN, *Statistical Yearbook*.

2006 (million): Passengers carried 1.1; Passenger-km 357; Freight ton-km 1,076 (Source: World Bank, World Development Indicators database).

ROAD TRAFFIC
('000 motor vehicles in use, estimates)

	2001	2002	2003
Passenger cars	134.5	151.9	173.1
Commercial vehicles	51.1	37.4	57.4

Source: UN, *Statistical Yearbook*.

2007 (motor vehicles in use): Passenger cars 190,341; Buses and coaches 17,287; Vans and lorries 51,842; Motorcycles and mopeds 72,351 (Source: IRF, *World Road Statistics*).

SHIPPING

Merchant Fleet
(registered at 31 December)

	2007	2008	2009
Number of vessels	66	64	64
Total displacement ('000 grt)	55.3	16.5	16.2

Source: IHS Fairplay, *World Fleet Statistics*.

International Sea-borne Freight Traffic
(freight traffic at Douala, '000 metric tons)

	2006	2008	2009
Goods loaded	6,468	2,160	1,824
Goods unloaded	13,416	4,848	5,352

Note: Data for 2007 were not available.

Source: UN, *Monthly Bulletin of Statistics*.

CIVIL AVIATION
(traffic on scheduled services)

	2006	2007	2008
Kilometres flown (million)	12	13	13
Passengers carried ('000)	425	453	471
Passenger-km (million)	861	910	930
Total ton-km (million)	108	111	113

Source: UN, *Statistical Yearbook*.

Passengers carried ('000): 466.1 in 2009 (Source: World Bank, World Development Indicators database).

Tourism

FOREIGN VISITORS BY COUNTRY OF ORIGIN*

	2004	2005	2006
Belgium	3,885	3,046	3,129
Canada	2,399	2,760	1,969
France	40,611	33,650	32,362
Italy	4,426	4,211	3,329
Netherlands	4,217	2,951	2,724
Switzerland	5,668	3,715	2,089
United Kingdom	5,818	5,076	4,146
USA	9,194	7,242	7,030
Total (incl. others)	189,856	176,372	184,549

* Arrivals at hotels and similar establishments.

Receipts from tourism (US $ million, incl. passenger transport): 231 in 2006; 254 in 2007; 167 in 2008.

Source: World Tourism Organization.

Communications Media

	2008	2009	2010
Telephones ('000 main lines in use)	255.3	435.4	539.5
Mobile cellular telephones ('000 subscribers)	6,160.9	8,004.1	8,636.7
Internet users ('000)	725.0	749.6	n.a.
Broadband subscribers	900	900	1,000

Personal computers: 200,000 (11.2 per 1,000 persons) in 2005.

Radio receivers ('000 in use): 2,270 in 1997.

2004: Daily newspapers 10; Non-daily newspapers 250.

Sources: mainly UNESCO, *Statistical Yearbook*; International Telecommunication Union.

Education

(2009/10 unless otherwise indicated)

			Students ('000)		
	Institutions	Teachers	Males	Females	Total
Pre-primary	1,371*	14,522	157.8	158.9	316.7
Primary	9,459*	77,098	1,895.5	1,614.9	3,510.4
Secondary:					
general	700*	21,650†	539.5	481.8	1,021.3
technical/vocational	324*	21,543†	163.6	98.2	261.8
Universities	6‡	4,235	121.8	98.5	220.3

* 1997/98.

† 2005/06.

‡ 1996/97.

Source: UNESCO Institute for Statistics.

Pupil-teacher ratio (primary education, UNESCO estimate): 45.5 in 2009/10 (Source: UNESCO Institute for Statistics).

Adult literacy rate (UNESCO estimates): 75.9% (males 84.0%; females 67.8%) in 2008 (Source: UNESCO Institute for Statistics).

Directory

The Constitution

In December 1995 the National Assembly formally adopted amendments to the 1972 Constitution that provided for a democratic system of government, with the establishment of an upper legislative chamber (to be known as the Senate), a Council of Supreme Judiciary Affairs, a Council of State, and a Civil Service High Authority, and restricted the power vested in the President, who was to serve a maximum of two seven-year terms. The restoration of decentralized local government areas was also envisaged. In April 2008 further amendments to the Constitution were adopted, the most notable of which was the abolition of the presidential two-term limit. At that time, the Senate had yet to be established, nor had there been any progress with regard to the restoration of decentralized local government. The main provisions of the 1972 Constitution, as amended, are summarized below:

The Constitution declares that the human being, without distinction as to race, religion, sex or belief, possesses inalienable and sacred rights. It affirms its attachment to the fundamental freedoms embodied in the Universal Declaration of Human Rights and the UN Charter. The State guarantees to all citizens of either sex the rights and freedoms set out in the preamble of the Constitution.

SOVEREIGNTY

1. The Republic of Cameroon shall be one and indivisible, democratic, secular and dedicated to social service. It shall ensure the equality before the law of all its citizens. Provisions that the official languages be French and English, for the motto, flag, national anthem and seal, that the capital be Yaoundé.

2–3. Sovereignty shall be vested in the people who shall exercise it either through the President of the Republic and the members returned by it to the National Assembly or by means of referendum. Elections are by universal suffrage, direct or indirect, by every citizen aged 21 or over in a secret ballot. Political parties or groups may take part in elections subject to the law and the principles of democracy and of national sovereignty and unity.

4. State authority shall be exercised by the President of the Republic and the National Assembly.

THE PRESIDENT OF THE REPUBLIC

5. The President of the Republic, as Head of State and Head of the Government, shall be responsible for the conduct of the affairs of the Republic. He shall define national policy and may charge the members of the Government with the implementation of this policy in certain spheres.

6–7. Candidates for the office of President must hold civic and political rights, be at least 35 years old and have resided in Cameroon for a minimum of 12 consecutive months, and may not hold any other elective office or professional activity. The President is elected for seven years, by a majority of votes cast by the people; there is no limit on the number of terms that may be served. Provisions are made for the continuity of office in the case of the President's resignation.

8–9. The Ministers and Vice-Ministers are appointed by the President to whom they are responsible, and they may hold no other appointment. The President is also head of the armed forces, he negotiates and ratifies treaties, may exercise clemency after consultation with the Higher Judicial Council, promulgates and is responsible for the enforcement of laws, is responsible for internal and external security, makes civil and military appointments, provides for necessary administrative services.

10. The President, by reference to the Supreme Court, ensures that all laws passed are constitutional.

11. Provisions whereby the President may declare a state of emergency or state of siege.

THE NATIONAL ASSEMBLY

12. The National Assembly shall be renewed every five years, though it may at the instance of the President of the Republic legislate to extend or shorten its term of office. It shall be composed of 180 members elected by universal suffrage.

13–14. Laws shall normally be passed by a simple majority of those present, but if a bill is read a second time at the request of the President of the Republic a majority of the National Assembly as a whole is required.

15–16. The National Assembly shall meet twice a year, each session to last not more than 30 days; in one session it shall approve the budget. It may be recalled to an extraordinary session of not more than 15 days.

17–18. Elections and suitability of candidates and sitting members shall be governed by law.

RELATIONS BETWEEN THE EXECUTIVE AND THE LEGISLATURE

19. Bills may be introduced either by the President of the Republic or by any member of the National Assembly.

20. Reserved to the legislature are the fundamental rights and duties of the citizen; the law of persons and property; the political, administrative and judicial system in respect of elections to the National Assembly, general regulation of national defence, authorization of penalties and criminal and civil procedure etc., and the organization of the local authorities; currency, the budget, dues and taxes, legislation on public property; economic and social policy; the education system.

21. The National Assembly may empower the President of the Republic to legislate by way of ordinance for a limited period and for given purposes.

22–26. Other matters of procedure, including the right of the President of the Republic to address the Assembly and of the Ministers and Vice-Ministers to take part in debates.

27–29. The composition and conduct of the Assembly's programme of business. Provisions whereby the Assembly may inquire into governmental activity. The obligation of the President of the Republic to promulgate laws, which shall be published in both languages of the Republic.

30. Provisions whereby the President of the Republic, after consultation with the National Assembly, may submit to referendum certain reform bills liable to have profound repercussions on the future of the nation and national institutions.

THE JUDICIARY

31. Justice is administered in the name of the people. The President of the Republic shall ensure the independence of the judiciary and shall make appointments with the assistance of the Higher Judicial Council.

THE SUPREME COURT

32–33. The Supreme Court has powers to uphold the Constitution in such cases as the death or incapacity of the President and the admissibility of laws, to give final judgments on appeals on the Judgment of the Court of Appeal and to decide complaints against administrative acts. It may be assisted by experts appointed by the President of the Republic.

IMPEACHMENT

34. There shall be a Court of Impeachment with jurisdiction to try the President of the Republic for high treason and the Ministers and Vice-Ministers for conspiracy against the security of the State.

THE ECONOMIC AND SOCIAL COUNCIL

35. There shall be an Economic and Social Council, regulated by the law.

AMENDMENT OF THE CONSTITUTION

36–37. Bills to amend the Constitution may be introduced either by the President of the Republic or the National Assembly. The President may decide to submit any amendment to the people by way of a referendum. No procedure to amend the Constitution may be accepted if it tends to impair the republican character, unity or territorial integrity of the State, or the democratic principles by which the Republic is governed.

The Government

HEAD OF STATE

President: PAUL BIYA (took office 6 November 1982; elected 14 January 1984; re-elected 24 April 1988, 11 October 1992, 12 October 1997; 11 October 2004; and 9 October 2011).

CABINET

(September 2012)

The Government is a coalition of the Rassemblement Démocratique du Peuple Camerounais (RDPC), the Front Pour le Salut National du Cameroun (FSNC), the Union Nationale pour la Démocratie et le Progrès (UNDP) and the Alliance Nationale pour la Démocratie et le Progrès (ANDP).

Prime Minister: PHILÉMON YANG (RDPC).

Deputy Prime Minister, Minister-delegate at the Presidency in charge of Relations with the Assemblies: AMADOU ALI (RDPC).

Ministers of State

Minister of State, Minister of Tourism and Leisure: MAIGARI BELLO BOUBA (UNDP).

Minister of State, Minister of Justice and Keeper of the Seals: LAURENT ESSO.

Ministers

Minister of Territorial Administration and Decentralization: RENÉ EMMANUEL SADI.

Minister of Social Affairs: CATHERINE LOUISE MARINETTE BAKANG MBOCK (RDPC).

Minister of Agriculture and Rural Development: LAZARE ESSIMI MENYE.

Minister of Art and Culture: AMA TUTU MUNA (RDPC).

Minister of Trade: LUC MAGLOIRE MBANGA ATANGANA.

Minister of Communication: BAKARY ISSA TCHIROMA.

Minister of Estates and Land Affairs: JACQUELINE KOUNG A. BISSIKE.

Minister of Water and Energy: BASILE ATANGANA KOUNA.

Minister of the Economy, Planning and Land Settlement: EMMANUEL NGANOU DJOUMESSI (RDPC).

Minister of Basic Education: YOUSSOUF ADIDJA ALIM.

Minister of Livestock, Fisheries and Animal Industries: DR TAIGA.

Minister of Employment and Professional Training: ZACHARIE PÉRÉVET (RDPC).

Minister of Secondary Education: LOUIS BAPES BAPES (RDPC).

Minister of Higher Education: JACQUES FAME NDONGO (RDPC).

Minister of the Environment, the Protection of Nature and Sustainable Development: PIERRE HÉLÉ (RDPC).

Minister of Finance: ALAMINE OUSMANE MEY.

Minister of Public Service and Administrative Reform: MICHEL ANGE ANGOUIN (RDPC).

Minister of Forests and Wildlife: PHILIP NGWESE NGOLE (RDPC).

Minister of Housing and Urban Development: JEAN CLAUDE MBWETCHOU (RDPC).

Minister of Youth and Civic Education: ISMAËL BIDOUNG KPWATT.

Minister of Mines, Industry and Technological Development: EMMANUEL BONDE.

Minister of Small and Medium-Sized Enterprises, Social Economy and Crafts: LAURENT SERGE ETOUNDI NGOA (RDPC).

Minister of Posts and Telecommunications: JEAN-PIERRE BYITI BI ESSAM.

Minister of Women's Affairs and the Family: MARIE THÉRÈSE ABENA ONDUA.

Minister of Scientific Research and Innovation: MADELEINE TCHUENTÉ (RDPC).

Minister of External Relations: PIERRE MOUKOKO MBONJO.

Minister of Public Health: ANDRÉ MAMA FOUDA (RDPC).

Minister of Sports and Physical Education: ADOUM GAROUA.

Minister of Transport: ROBERT NKILI.

Minister of Labour and Social Security: GRÉGOIRE OWONA.

Minister of Public Works: PATRICE AMBA SALLA.

Ministers-delegate

Minister-delegate at the Presidency, in charge of Defence: EDGARD ALAIN MEBE NGO'O.

Minister-delegate at the Presidency, in charge of the Contrôle Superieur de l'État: HENRI EYEBE AYISSI.

Minister-delegate at the Presidency, in charge of Public Markets: ABBA SADOU.

Minister-delegate at the Ministry of Territorial Administration and Decentralization, in charge of Decentralized Territorial Collectivities: JULES DORET NDONGO (RDPC).

Minister-delegate at the Ministry of Agriculture and Rural Development, in charge of Rural Development: CLÉMENTINE ANTOINETTE ANANGA MESSINA.

Minister-delegate at the Ministry of the Environment, the Protection of Nature and Sustainable Development: NANA ABOUBAKAR DJALLOH (UNDP).

Minister-delegate at the Ministry of the Economy, Planning and Land Settlement, in charge of Planning: ABDOULAYE YAOUBA.

Minister-delegate at the Ministry of Finance: PIERRE TITTI.

Minister-delegate at the Ministry of Justice, Keeper of the Seals: JEAN PIERRE FOGUI.

Minister-delegate at the Ministry of External Relations, in charge of Relations with the Commonwealth: JOSEPH DION NGUTÉ (RDPC).

Minister-delegate at the Ministry of External Relations, in charge of Relations with the Islamic World: ADOUM GARGOUM (RDPC).

Minister-delegate at the Ministry of Transport: MEFIRO OUMAROU.

Secretaries of State

Secretary of State for Defence, in charge of the National Gendarmerie: JEAN BAPTISTE BOKAM.

Secretary of State for Defence, in charge of Former Combatants and War Victims: ISSA KOUMPA.

Secretary of State for Basic Education: BENOÎT NDONG SOUMHET.

Secretary of State for Secondary Education, in charge of Normal Education: MOULOUNA FOUTSOU.

Secretary of State for Forests and Wildlife: ALHADJI KOULSOUMI BOUKAR.

Secretary of State for Housing and Urban Development, in charge of Urban Development: MARIE ROSE DIBONG.

Secretary of State for Justice, in charge of Prisons: JÉRÔME PENBAGA DOOH.

Secretary of State for Industry, Mines and Technological Development: CALISTUS GENTRY FUH.

Secretary of State for Public Health, in charge of the Fight Against Epidemics and Pandemics: ALIM HAYATOU (RDPC).

Secretary of State for Public Works, in charge of Roads: HANS NYETAM NYETAM.

Other Officials with the Rank of Minister

Ministers, Chargés de Mission at the Presidency: HAMADOU MOUSTAPHA, PAUL ATANGA NJI, VICTOR MENGOT ARREY NKONGHO, PHILIPPE MBARGA MBOA.

MINISTRIES

Correspondence to ministries not holding post boxes should generally be addressed c/o the Central Post Office, Yaoundé.

Office of the President: Palais de l'Unité, Yaoundé; tel. 2223-4025; internet www.camnet.cm/celcom/homepr.htm.

Office of the Prime Minister: Yaoundé; tel. 2223-8005; fax 2223-5735; e-mail spm@spm.gov.cm; internet www.spm.gov.cm.

Ministry of Agriculture and Rural Development: Quartier Administratif, Yaoundé; tel. 2223-1190; fax 2222-5091.

Ministry of Art and Culture: Quartier Hippodrome, Yaoundé; tel. 2222-6579; fax 2223-6579.

Ministry of Basic Education: Quartier Administratif, Yaoundé; tel. 2223-4050; fax 2223-1262.

Ministry of Communication: Quartier Hippodrome, Yaoundé; tel. 2223-3974; fax 2223-3022; e-mail mincom@mincom.gov.cm; internet www.mincom.gov.cm.

Ministry of Defence: Quartier Général, Yaoundé; tel. 2223-4055.

Ministry of the Economy, Planning and Land Settlement: Yaoundé; e-mail lecinfosminepat@gmail.com; internet www.minepat.info.

Ministry of Employment and Professional Training: Yaoundé; tel. 2222-0186; fax 2223-1820.

Ministry of the Environment, the Protection of Nature and Sustainable Development: Yaoundé.

Ministry of Estates and Land Affairs: Yaoundé.

Ministry of External Relations: Yaoundé; tel. 2220-3850; fax 2220-1133; internet www.diplocam.gov.cm.

Ministry of Finance: BP 13750, Quartier Administratif, Yaoundé; tel. and fax 7723-2099; internet www.camnet.cm/investir/minfi/.

Ministry of Forests and Wildlife: BP 1341, Yaoundé; tel. 2220-4258; fax 2222-9487; e-mail onadef@camnet.cm; internet www.camnet.cm/investir/envforet/index.htm.

Ministry of Higher Education: 2 ave du 20 mai, BP 1457, Yaoundé; tel. 2222-1770; fax 2222-9724; e-mail aowono@uycdc.uninet.cm; internet www.mineup.gov.cm.

Ministry of Justice: Quartier Administratif, Yaoundé; tel. 2223-4292; fax 2223-0005; e-mail jpouloumou@yahoo.fr.

Ministry of Labour and Social Security: Yaoundé.

Ministry of Livestock, Fisheries and Animal Industries: Yaoundé; tel. 2222-3311.

Ministry of Mines, Industry and Technological Development: Quartier Administratif, BP 955, Yaoundé; tel. 2223-3404; fax 2223-3400; e-mail minmee@camnet.cm; internet www.camnet.cm/investir/minmee.

Ministry of Posts and Telecommunications: Quartier Administratif, Yaoundé; tel. 2223-0615; fax 2223-3159; internet www.minpostel.gov.cm.

Ministry of Public Health: Quartier Administratif, Yaoundé; tel. and fax 2222-0233; internet www.minsante.gov.cm.

Ministry of Public Service and Administrative Reform: Yaoundé; tel. 2222-0356; fax 2223-0800.

Ministry of Public Works: Quartier Administratif, Yaoundé; tel. 2222-1916; fax 2222-0156.

Ministry of Secondary Education: Yaoundé.

Ministry of Scientific Research and Innovation: Yaoundé; tel. 2222-1334; fax 2222-1336; internet www.minresi.net.

Ministry of Small and Medium-Sized Enterprises, Social Economy and Crafts: BP 6096, Yaoundé; tel. 2223-2388; fax 2223-2180; e-mail enngoal1@yahoo.fr; internet www.minpmeesa.cm.

Ministry of Social Affairs: Quartier Administratif, Yaoundé; tel. 2222-5867; fax 2222-1121.

Ministry of Sports and Physical Education: POB 1016, Yaoundé; tel. 2223-1201; fax 2223-2610; e-mail minsepinfos@yahoo.fr.

Ministry of Technical and Professional Training: Yaoundé.

Ministry of Territorial Administration and Decentralization: Quartier Administratif, Yaoundé; tel. 2223-4090; fax 2222-3735.

Ministry of Tourism and Leisure: BP 266, Yaoundé; tel. 2222-4411; fax 2222-1295; e-mail mintour@camnet.cm; internet www.mintour.gov.cm.

Ministry of Trade: Yaoundé; tel. 2223-0216.

Ministry of Transport: Quartier Administratif, Yaoundé; tel. 2222-8709; fax 2223-2238; e-mail minetatcam@gmail.com; internet www.mint.gov.cm.

Ministry of Urban Development and Housing: Yaoundé; tel. 2223-2282.

Ministry of Water and Energy: Quartier Administratif, BP 955, Yaoundé; tel. 2223-3404; fax 2223-3400; e-mail minmee@camnet.cm; internet www.camnet.cm/investir/minmee.

Ministry of Women's Affairs and the Family: Quartier Administratif, Yaoundé; tel. 2223-2550; fax 2223-3965; e-mail cab_minproff@yahoo.fr; internet www.minproff.gov.cm.

Ministry of Youth and Civic Education: Quartier Administratif, Yaoundé; tel. 2223-3257; e-mail minjes@minjes.gov.cm; internet www.minjes.gov.cm.

President and Legislature

PRESIDENT

Election, 9 October 2011

Candidate	Votes	% of votes
Paul Biya (RDPC)	3,772,527	77.99
Ni John Fru Ndi (SDF)	518,175	10.71
Garga Haman Adji (ADD)	155,348	3.21
Adamou Ndam Njoya (UDC)	83,860	1.73
Ayah Paul Abine (PAPE)	61,158	1.26
Others*	246,181	5.09
Total	4,837,249	100.00

* There were 18 other candidates.

NATIONAL ASSEMBLY

President: CAVAYE YÉGUIÉ DJIBRIL.

General Election, 22 July 2007

Party	Seats
Rassemblement Démocratique du Peuple Camerounais (RDPC)	140
Social Democratic Front (SDF)	14
Union Démocratique du Cameroun (UDC)	4
Union Nationale pour la Démocratie et le Progrès (UNDP)	4
Mouvement Progressiste (MP)	1
Total	163*

* The results of voting in five constituencies (for 17 seats) were annulled, owing to irregularities. By-elections were held on 30 September 2007 at which the RDPC won 13 seats; the SDF and the UNDP each secured two seats.

Election Commission

Elections Cameroon (ELECAM): BP 13506, Yaoundé; tel. 2221-2540; fax 2221-2539; e-mail elecam@elecam.cm; internet www.elecam.cm; f. 2006 to replace Observatoire National des Élections/National Elections Observatory; 12 mems appointed by the Head of State in consultation with political parties represented in the National Assembly and civil society; Pres. SAMUEL FONKAM AZU'U; Sec.-Gen. MOHAMAN SANI TANIMOU.

Political Organizations

At December 2011 a total of 271 political parties were registered with the Minister of Territorial Administration and Decentralization, of which the most important are listed below:

Action for Meritocracy and Equal Opportunity Party (AMEC): BP 20354, Yaoundé; tel. 9991-9154; fax 2223-4642; e-mail Tabijoachim@yahoo.fr; Leader JOACHIM TABI OWONO.

Alliance pour la Démocratie et le Développement (ADD): BP 231, Garoua; Sec.-Gen. GARGA HAMAN ADJI.

Alliance des Forces Progressistes (AFP): BP 4724, Douala; f. 2002; Leader BERNARD MUNA.

Alliance Nationale pour la Démocratie et le Progrès: BP 5019, Yaoundé; tel. and fax 220-9898; Pres. HAMADOU MOUSTAPHA.

Cameroon Anglophone Movement (CAM): advocates a federal system of govt.

Front pour le Salut National du Cameroun (FSNC): Yaoundé; f. 2007; Pres. BAKARY ISSA TCHIROMA.

Mouvement Africain pour la Nouvelle Indépendance et la Démocratie (MANIDEM): BP 10298, Douala; tel. 3342-0076; fax 9996-0229; f. 1995; fmrly a faction of the UPC; Leader ANDRÉ BANDA KANI.

Mouvement pour la Défense de la République (MDR): BP 6438, Yaoundé; tel. 2220-8982; f. 1991; Leader DAKOLE DAÏSSALA.

Mouvement des Démocrates Camerounais pour la Paix (MDCP): BP 3274, Yaoundé; tel. 2220-8173; f. 2000; Leader GAMEL ADAMOU ISSA.

Mouvement pour la Démocratie et le Progrès (MDP): BP 8379, Douala; tel. 2239-1174; f. 1992; Pres. ARON MUKURI MAKA; Sec.-Gen. RENÉ MBANDA MANDENGUE.

Mouvement pour la Jeunesse du Cameroun (MLJC): BP 26, Eséka; tel. 7714-8750; fax 2228-6019; Pres. DIEUDONNÉ TINA; Sec.-Gen. JEAN LÉONARD POM.

Mouvement pour la Libération et le Développement du Cameroun (MLDC): BP 886, Edéa; tel. 3346-4431; fax 3346-4847; f. 1998 by a breakaway faction of the MLJC; Leader MARCEL YONDO.

Mouvement Progressiste (MP): BP 2500, Douala; tel. 9987-2513; e-mail djombyves@yahoo.fr; f. 1991; Pres. JEAN JACQUES EKINDI.

Nouvelle Force Populaire (NFP): BP 1139, Douala; f. 2002; Leader LÉANDRE DJINO.

Parti des Démocrates Camerounais (PDC): BP 6909, Yaoundé; tel. 2222-2842; f. 1991; Leader LOUIS-TOBIE MBIDA; Sec.-Gen. GASTON BIKELE EKANI.

Parti Libéral-Démocrate (PLD): BP 4764, Douala; tel. 3337-3792; f. 1991; Pres. JEAN ROBERT LIAPOE; Sec.-Gen. JEAN TCHUENTE.

Parti Républicain du Peuple Camerounais (PRPC): BP 6654, Yaoundé; tel. 2222-2120; f. 1991; Leader ANDRÉ ATEBA NGOUA.

Rassemblement Camerounais pour la République: BP 452, Bandjoun; tel. 3344-1349; f. 1992; Leader SAMUEL WAMBO.

Rassemblement Démocratique du Peuple Camerounais (RDPC): Palais des Congrès, 2e étage, BP 867, Yaoundé; tel. and fax 2221-2417; fax 2221-2508; e-mail rdpcpdm@rdpcpdm.cm; internet www.rdpcpdm.cm; f. 1966 as Union nationale camerounaise by merger of the Union camerounaise, the Kamerun National Democratic Party and four opposition parties; adopted present name in 1985; sole legal party 1972–90; Pres. PAUL BIYA; Sec.-Gen. RENÉ EMMANUEL SADI.

Social Democratic Front (SDF): BP 490, Mankon, Bamenda; tel. 3336-3949; fax 3336-2991; e-mail webmaster@sdfparty.org; internet www.sdfparty.org; f. 1990; Chair. NI JOHN FRU NDI; Sec.-Gen. Dr ELIZABETH TAMAJONG.

Social Democratic Movement (SDM): BP 7655, Yaoundé; tel. 9985-9372; f. 1995; breakaway faction of the Social Democratic Front; Leader SIGA ASANGA.

Southern Cameroons National Council (SCNC): BP 131, Eyumojock; tel. 796-4888; e-mail scnc@scncforsoutherncameroons.net; internet www.scncforsoutherncameroons.net; f. 1995; supports the establishment of an independent republic in anglophone Cameroon; Chair. Chief ETTE OTUN AYAMBA.

Union Démocratique du Cameroun (UDC): BP 1638, Yaoundé; tel. 2222-9545; fax 2222-4620; f. 1991; Leader ADAMOU NDAM NJOYA.

Union des Forces Démocratiques du Cameroun (UFDC): BP 7190, Yaoundé; tel. 2223-1644; f. 1991; Leader VICTORIN HAMENI BIELEU.

Union des Mouvements Socialistes: f. 2011; Leader PIERRE KWEMO.

Union Nationale pour la Démocratie et le Progrès (UNDP): BP 656, Douala; tel. 2220-9898; f. 1991; split in 1995; Chair. MAIGARI BELLO BOUBA; Sec.-Gen. PIERRE FLAMBEAU NGAYAP.

Union Nationale pour l'Indépendance Totale du Cameroun (UNITOC): BP 1301, Yaoundé; tel. 2222-8002; f. 2002; Pres. DANIEL TATSINFANG; Sec.-Gen. JEAN CLAUDE TIENTCHEU FANSI.

Union des Populations Camerounaises (UPC): BP 1348, Yaoundé; tel. 2745-5043; f. 1948; Pres. Dr SAMUEL MACH-KIT; Sec.-Gen. MOUKOKO PRISO.

Diplomatic Representation

EMBASSIES AND HIGH COMMISSIONS IN CAMEROON

Algeria: 433 rue 1828, Quartier Bastos, BP 1619, Yaoundé; tel. 2221-5351; fax 2231-5354; Ambassador TOUFIK MILAT.

Brazil: rue 1828, Quartier Bastos, BP 16227, Yaoundé; tel. 2220-1085; fax 2220-2048; e-mail embiaunde@cameroun-online.com; Ambassador ROBERTO PESSOA DACOSTA.

Canada: Immeuble Stamatiades, pl. de l'Hôtel de Ville, BP 572, Yaoundé; tel. 2223-2311; fax 2222-1090; e-mail yunde@international.gc.ca; internet www.cameroon.gc.ca; High Commissioner BENOÎT-PIERRE LARAMÉE.

Central African Republic: 41 rue 1863, Quartier Bastos, Montée du Carrefour de la Vallée Nlongkak, BP 396, Yaoundé; tel. and fax 2220-5155; Chargé d'affaires a.i. JEAN WENZOUÏ.

Chad: Quartier Bastos, BP 506, Yaoundé; tel. 2221-0624; fax 2220-3940; e-mail ambatchad_yaounde@yahoo.fr; Ambassador ANDRÉ SEKIMBAYE BESSANE.

China, People's Republic: Nouveau Bastos, BP 1307, Yaoundé; tel. 2221-0083; fax 2221-4395; e-mail chinaemb_cm@mfa.gov.cn; Ambassador WO RUIDI.

Congo, Democratic Republic: BP 632, Yaoundé; tel. 2220-5103; Chargé d'affaires a.i. FRANÇOIS LUAMBO.

Congo, Republic: Rheinallée 45, BP 1422, Yaoundé; tel. 2221-2458; fax 2221-1733; Ambassador ERIC EPENI OBONDZO.

Côte d'Ivoire: rue 1983, Résidence 140, Quartier Bastos, BP 1715, Yaoundé; tel. 2221-3291; fax 2221-3592; e-mail contact@ambaci-cam.org; internet www.ambacicam.org; Ambassador DOSSO ADAMA.

Egypt: 718 rue 1828, Quartier Bastos, BP 809, Yaoundé; tel. 2220-3922; fax 2220-2647; Ambassador IBRAHIM MOUSTAPHA HAFEZ.

Equatorial Guinea: 82 rue 1851, Quartier Bastos, BP 277, Yaoundé; tel. and fax 2221-0804; Ambassador PEDRO ELA NGUEMA BUNA.

France: Plateau Atémengué, BP 1631, Yaoundé; tel. 2222-7900; fax 2222-7909; e-mail chancellerie.yaounde-amba@diplomatie.gouv.fr; internet www.ambafrance-cm.org; Ambassador BRUNO GAIN.

Gabon: Quartier Bastos, Ekoudou, BP 4130, Yaoundé; tel. 2220-2966; fax 2221-0224; Ambassador MICHEL MANDOUGOUA.

Germany: Nouvelle Route Bastos, Bastos-Usine, BP 1160, Yaoundé; tel. 2221-0056; fax 2221-6211; e-mail info@jaun.diplo.de; internet www.jaunde.diplo.de; Ambassador REINHARD BUCHHOLZ.

Holy See: rue du Vatican, BP 210, Yaoundé (Apostolic Nunciature); tel. 2220-0475; fax 2220-7513; e-mail nonce.cam@sat.signis.net; Apostolic Pro-Nuncio Most Rev. PIERO PIOPPO (Titular Archbishop of Torcello).

Israel: rue du Club Olympique à Bastos 154, Longkak, BP 5934, Yaoundé; tel. 2221-1291; fax 2221-0823; e-mail info@yaounde.mfa.gov.il; internet yaounde.mfa.gov.il; Ambassador MICHAEL ARBEL.

Italy: Plateau Bastos, BP 827, Yaoundé; tel. 2220-3376; fax 2221-5250; e-mail ambasciata.yaounde@esteri.it; internet www.ambyaounde.esteri.it; Ambassador STEFANO PONTESILLI.

Japan: 1513 rue 1828, Quartier Bastos, Ekoudou, BP 6868, Yaoundé; tel. 2220-6202; fax 2220-6203; Ambassador TSUTOMU ARAI.

Korea, Democratic People's Republic: Yaoundé; Ambassador KIM RYONG YONG.

Korea, Republic: BP 13286, Yaoundé; tel. 2220-3756; fax 2220-3757; e-mail korean.embassy.yaounde@gmail.com; Ambassador CHO JUNE-HYUCK.

Liberia: Quartier Bastos, Ekoudou, BP 1185, Yaoundé; tel. 2221-1296; fax 2220-9781; Ambassador MASSA JAMES.

Libya: Quartier Nylon Nlongkak, Quartier Bastos, BP 1980, Yaoundé; tel. 2220-4138; fax 2221-4298; Chargé d'affaires a.i. IBRAHIM O. AMAMI.

Morocco: 32 rue 1793, Quartier Bastos, BP 1629, Yaoundé; tel. 2220-5092; fax 2220-3793; e-mail ambmaroccam@yahoo.fr; Ambassador LAHCEN SAIL.

Nigeria: Quartier Bastos, BP 448, Yaoundé; tel. 2222-3455; fax 2223-5551; e-mail nhc_yde@yahoo.com; High Commissioner HADIZA MUSTAPHA.

Russia: Quartier Bastos, BP 488, Yaoundé; tel. 2220-1714; fax 2220-7891; e-mail consrusse@camnet.cm; Ambassador AKHMEDOV STANISLAS.

Saudi Arabia: rue 1951, Quartier Bastos, BP 1602, Yaoundé; tel. 2221-2675; fax 2220-6689; Ambassador MAHMOOD BIN HOSAIN QATTAN.

South Africa: rue 1801, Quartier Bastos, BP 1636, Yaoundé; tel. 2220-0438; fax 2220-0995; e-mail yaounde@foreign.gov.za; High Commissioner N. M. TSHEOLE.

Spain: blvd de l'URSS, Quartier Bastos, BP 877, Yaoundé; tel. 2220-3543; fax 2220-6491; e-mail embespcm@mail.mae.es; Ambassador ARTURO SPIEGELBERG DE ORTUETA.

Switzerland: BP 1169, Yaoundé; tel. 2220-5067; fax 2220-9386; Ambassador URS BERNER.

Tunisia: rue de Rotary, Quartier Bastos, BP 6074, Yaoundé; tel. 2220-3368; fax 2221-0507; e-mail at.yaounde@camnet.cm; Ambassador ABDERRAZAK LANDOULSI.

Turkey: blvd de l'URSS 1782, Quartier Bastos, BP 35155, Yaoundé; tel. 2220-6775; fax 2220-6778; Ambassador OMER FARUK DOGAN.

United Kingdom: ave Winston Churchill, BP 547, Yaoundé; tel. 2222-0545; fax 2222-0148; e-mail BHC.yaounde@fco.gov.uk; internet ukincameroon.fco.gov.uk; High Commissioner BHARAT JOSHI.

USA: ave Rosa Parks, BP 817, Yaoundé; tel. and fax 2220-1500; internet yaounde.usembassy.gov; Ambassador ROBERT PORTER JACKSON.

Judicial System

The independence of the judiciary is enshrined in the Constitution and judicial power is exercised by the Supreme Court, courts of appeal and tribunals. The President of the Republic guarantees the independence of the judicial power and appoints members of the bench and of the legal department. He is assisted in this task by the Higher Judicial Council (HJC), which gives him its opinion on all nominations for the bench and on disciplinary action against judicial and legal officers. The HJC is composed of six members who serve five-year terms. Justice is rendered in Cameroon by: courts of first instance; high courts; military courts; courts of appeal and the Supreme Court.

Supreme Court

Yaoundé; tel. 2222-0164; fax 2222-0576; internet www.coursupreme.cm.

Consists of a president, 9 titular and substitute judges, a procureur général, an avocat général, deputies to the procureur général, a registrar and clerks.

President: ALEXIS DIPANDA MOUELLE.

Attorney-General: MARTIN RISSOUCK MOULONG.

Religion

It is estimated that 53% of the population are Christians (an estimated 26% of those are Roman Catholics), 25% adhere to traditional religious beliefs, and 22% are Muslims.

CHRISTIANITY

Protestant Churches

Conseil des Eglises Protestantes du Cameroun (CEPCA): BP 491, Yaoundé; tel. and fax 2223-8117; e-mail femec_org@yahoo.fr; f. 1968; name changed as above in 2005; 11 mem. churches; Pres. Rev. Dr ROBERT NGOYECK; Admin. Sec. Rev. Dr PHILIPPE NGUETE.

Church of the Lutheran Brethren of Cameroon: POB 16, Garoua; tel. and fax 2227-2573; e-mail eflcsynode@yahoo.fr; Pres. Rev. ROBERT GOYEK DAGA; 105,994 mems (2010).

Eglise Évangélique du Cameroun (Evangelical Church of Cameroon—EEC): 13 rue Alfred Saker, Akwa, Centenaire, BP 89, Douala; tel. 3342-3611; fax 3342-4011; e-mail eec@eeccameroun.org; internet www.eeccameroun.org; f. 1957; 2m. mems; Pres. Rev. ISAAC BATOMEN HENGA; Sec. Rev. JEAN SAMUEL HENDJE TOYA.

Eglise Presbytérienne Camerounaise (Presbyterian Church of Cameroon): BP 519, Yaoundé; tel. 3332-4236; independent since 1957; comprises 4 synods and 16 presbyteries; Gen. Sec. Rev. Dr MASSI GAM'S.

Eglise Protestante Africaine (African Protestant Church): BP 26, Lolodorf; e-mail epacameroun@yahoo.fr; f. 1934; Pres. Rev. FRANÇOIS PUASSE.

Evangelical Lutheran Church of Cameroon: POB 6, Ngaoundere-Adamaoua; tel. 2225-2066; fax 2225-2299; e-mail evequenational_eelc@yahoo.fr; Pres. Rev. Dr THOMAS NYIWE; 253,000 mems (2010).

Presbyterian Church in Cameroon: BP 19, Buéa; tel. 3332-2487; fax 332-2754; e-mail pcc_modoffice19@yahoo.com; 1.8m. mems; 302 ministers; Moderator Rt Rev. Dr NYANSAKO-NI-NKU.

Union des Eglises Baptistes du Cameroun (Union of Baptist Churches of Cameroon): New Bell, BP 6007, Douala; tel. 3342-4106; e-mail mbangueeboa@yahoo.fr; autonomous since 1957; Gen. Sec. Rev. EMMANUEL MBANGUE EBOA.

Other Protestant churches active in Cameroon include the Cameroon Baptist Church, the Cameroon Baptist Convention, the Presbyterian Church in West Cameroon and the Union of Evangelical Churches of North Cameroon. The Eglise Evangélique du Cameroun (EEC) et Union des Eglises Baptistes du Cameroun (UEBC) have also formed a Conseil des Eglises Baptistes et Evangéliques du Cameroun (CEBEC).

The Roman Catholic Church

Cameroon comprises five archdioceses and 20 dioceses. Some 26% of the total population are Roman Catholics.

Bishops' Conference

Conférence Episcopale Nationale du Cameroun, BP 1963, Yaoundé; tel. 2231-1592; fax 2231-2977; e-mail cenc20042003@yahoo.ca.

f. 1989; Pres. Most Rev. JOSEPH ATANGA (Archbishop of Bertoua); Sec.-Gen. SÉBASTIEN MONGO BEHONG.

Archbishop of Bamenda: Most Rev. CORNELIUS FONTEM ESUA, Archbishop's House, BP 82, Bamenda; tel. 3336-1241; fax 3336-3487; e-mail archbishopshouse@yahoo.com.

Archbishop of Bertoua: Most Rev. JOSEPH ATANGA, Archevêché, BP 40, Bertoua; tel. 2224-1748; fax 2224-2585.

Archbishop of Douala: SAMUEL KLEDA, Archevêché, BP 179, Douala; tel. 3342-3714; fax 3343-1837; e-mail mikjp2004@yahoo.fr.

Archbishop of Garoua: Most Rev. ANTOINE NTALOU, Archevêché, BP 272, Garoua; tel. 2227-1353; fax 2227-2942; e-mail archigaroua@yahoo.fr.

Archbishop of Yaoundé: Most Rev. SIMON-VICTOR TONYÉ BAKOT, Archevêché, BP 207, Yaoundé; tel. 2201-1048; fax 2221-9735; e-mail simonvita2000@yahoo.fr.

BAHÁ'Í FAITH

National Spiritual Assembly: 4230 Yaoundé; tel. 2223-0575; e-mail nsacameroon@yahoo.com; mems in 1,744 localities.

The Press

DAILIES

Cameroon Tribune: route de l'Aéroport, BP 1218, Yaoundé; tel. 2230-4147; fax 2230-4362; e-mail cameroon-tribune@cameroon-tribune.cm; internet www.cameroon-tribune.cm; f. 1974; publ. by the Société de Presse et d'Editions du Cameroun (SOPECAM), which also publishes a weekly *Weekend*, a monthly *Nyanga* and a fortnightly *Alter Ego*; govt-controlled; French and English; Publr MARIE CLAIRE NNANA; Man. Editor RAOUL DIEUDONNÉ LEBOGO NDONGO; circ. 25,000.

Mutations: South Media Corporation, 183 rue 1,055, Pl. Repiquet, BP 12348, Yaoundé; tel. 2230-6680; fax 2222-9635; e-mail journalmutations@yahoo.fr; internet quotidienmutations.info; daily; French; independent; Publr ALAIN BLAISE BATONGUÉ.

The Post: POB 91, Buéa; tel. 3332-3287; fax 7773-8904; e-mail thepostnp@yahoo.com; internet www.thepostwebedition.com; bi-weekly; independent; English; Publr FRANCIS WACHE; Editor CHARLY NDI CHIA.

PERIODICALS

Accord Magazine: BP 3696, Messa, Yaoundé; tel. 9969-0600; e-mail accordmag@hotmail.com; popular culture.

L'Anecdote: face collège Vogt, BP 25070, Yaoundé; tel. 2231-3395; e-mail journalanecdote@yahoo.com; weekly; conservative; Editor-in-Chief FRANÇOIS BIKORO.

Aurore Plus: BP 7042, Douala; tel. 3342-9261; fax 3342-4917; e-mail jouraurplus@yahoo.fr; 2 a week; Dir MICHEL MICHAUT MOUSSALA.

Les Cahiers de Mutations: South Media Corporation, 183 rue 1,055, Pl. Repiquet, BP 12348, Yaoundé; tel. 2222-5104; fax 2222-9635; monthly; Dir ROGER ALAIN TAAKAM.

Cameroon Outlook: BP 124, Limbé; f. 1969; 3 a week; independent; English; Editor JÉRÔME F. GWELLEM; circ. 20,000.

Cameroon Panorama: BP 46, Buéa; tel. 3332-2240; e-mail cainsbuea@yahoo.com; f. 1962; monthly; English; Roman Catholic; Editor Rev. Fr MOSES TAZOH; circ. 4,500.

Cameroon Review: BP 408, Limbé; monthly; Editor-in-Chief JÉRÔME F. GWELLEM; circ. 70,000.

Cameroon Times: BP 408, Limbé; f. 1960; weekly; English; Editor-in-Chief JÉRÔME F. GWELLEM; circ. 12,000.

Dikalo: BP 4320, Douala; tel. 3337-2122; fax 3337-1906; f. 1991; independent; 2 a week; French; Publications Dir TETTEH M. ARMAH; Editor HENRI EPEE NDOUMBE.

Ecovox: BP 1256, Bafoussam; tel. 3344-6668; fax 3344-6669; e-mail ecovox@cipcre.org; internet www.cipcre.org/ecovox; 2 a year; French; ecological news.

L'Effort Camerounais: BP 15231, Douala; tel. 3343-2726; fax 3343-1837; e-mail leffortcamerounais@yahoo.com; internet www.leffortcamerounais.com; bi-monthly; Catholic; f. 1955; Editor-in-Chief IRENEAUS CHIA CHONGWAIN.

The Herald: BP 1218, Yaoundé; tel. 2231-5522; fax 2231-8497; 3 a week; English; Dir Dr BONIFACE FORBIN; circ. 1,568.

Al Houda: BP 1638, Yaoundé; quarterly; Islamic cultural review.

Le Jeune Observateur: Yaoundé; f. 1991; Editor JULES KOUM KOUM.

J'informe: Yaoundé; tel. 9993-6605; fax 2220-5336; f. 2002; weekly; French; Editor DELOR MAGELLAN KAMGAING.

Journal Officiel de la République du Cameroun: BP 1603, Yaoundé; tel. 2220-1719; fax 2220-2959; weekly; official govt notices; Man. Editor JOSEPH MARCEL; circ. 4,000.

Le Messager: rue des Écoles, BP 5925, Douala; tel. 3342-0214; fax 3342-0439; internet www.lemessager.net; f. 1979; 3 a week; independent; Man. Editor (vacant); circ. 20,000.

The Messenger: BP 15043, Douala; English-language edn of *Le Messager*; Editor HILARY FOKUM.

Nleb Ensemble: Imprimerie Saint-Paul, BP 763, Yaoundé; tel. 2223-9773; fax 2223-5058; f. 1935; fortnightly; Ewondo; Dir Most Rev. JEAN ZOA; Editor JOSEPH BEFE ATEBA; circ. 6,000.

La Nouvelle Expression: 12 rue Prince de Galles, BP 15333, Douala; tel. 3343-2227; fax 3343-2669; internet www.lanouvelleexpression.net; 3 a week; independent; French; Man. Editor SÉVERIN TCHOUNKEU.

La Nouvelle Presse: face mairie de Yaoundé VIème/Biyem-Assi, BP 2625, Messa, Yaoundé; tel. 9996-6768; e-mail lanvellepresse@iccnet.cm; f. 2001; weekly; Publications Dir JACQUES BLAISE MVIE.

Nyanga: route de l'Aéroport, BP 1218, Yaoundé; tel. 2230-4147; fax 2230-4362; publ. by the Société de Presse et d'Editions du Cameroun (SOPECAM); Dir EMMANUEL TATAW.

Ouest Echos: BP 767, Bafoussam; tel. and fax 3344-1091; e-mail ouechos@wagne.net; internet www.wagne.net/ouestechos; weekly; regional; Dir MICHEL ECLADOR PÉKOUA.

La Sentinelle: BP 24079, Douala; tel. and fax 3339-1627; weekly; lifestyle; circ. 3,200.

Situations: Yaoundé; weekly.

Le Travailleur/The Worker: BP 1610, Yaoundé; tel. 2222-3315; f. 1972; monthly; French and English; journal of Organisation Syndicale des Travailleurs du Cameroun/Cameroon Trade Union Congress; Sec.-Gen. LOUIS SOMBES; circ. 10,000.

Le Triomphe: BP 1862, Douala; tel. 3342-8774; f. 2002; weekly; Publications Dir SIPOWA CONSCIENCE PARFAIT.

Weekly Post: BP 30420, Yaoundé; tel. 2206-7649; e-mail weeklyp@yahoo.com; internet weeklypost1.tripod.com; English; f. 1992; independent; Editor-in-Chief BISONG ETAHOBEN.

NEWS AGENCY

CamNews: c/o SOPECAM, BP 1218, Yaoundé; tel. 2230-3830; fax 2230-4362; Dir JEAN NGANDJEU.

PRESS ASSOCIATIONS

Conseil Camerounais des Médias (CCM): Yaoundé; internet www.ccm-info.org; f. 2005; created by the UJC to strengthen the quality and independence of journalism in Cameroon; 9 mems; Pres. PIERRE ESSAMA ESSOMBA; Sec.-Gen. PIERRE-PAUL TCHINDJI.

Union des Journalistes du Cameroun (UJC): Yaoundé; Pres. CÉLESTIN LINGO.

Publishers

AES Presses Universitaires d'Afrique: BP 8106, Yaoundé; tel. 2222-0030; fax 2222-2325; e-mail aes@iccnet.cm; internet www.aes-pua.com; f. 1986; literature, social sciences and law; Dir-Gen. SERGE DONTCHUENG KOUAM.

Editions Akoma Mba: ave Germaine Ahidjo 20189, Yaoundé; tel. 9992-2955; fax 2222-4343; e-mail akomamba@hotmail.com; educational; Dir EDMOND VII MBALLA ELANGA.

Editions Clé (Centre de Littérature Evangélique): BP 1501, ave Maréchal Foch, Yaoundé; tel. 2222-3554; fax 2223-2709; e-mail editionscle@yahoo.fr; internet www.wagne.net/cle; f. 1963; African and Christian literature and studies; school textbooks; medicine and science; general non-fiction; Dir Dr MARCELIN VOUNDA ETOA.

Editions Ndzé: BP 647, Bertoua; tel. 9950-9295; fax 2224-2585; e-mail editions@ndze.com; internet www.ndze.com; fiction; Commercial Dir ALEXIS LIMBONA.

Editions Semences Africaines: BP 5329, Yaoundé-Nlongkak; tel. 9917-1439; e-mail renephilombe@yahoo.fr; f. 1974; fiction, history, religion, textbooks; Man. Dir RÉNÉ LÉA PHILOMBE.

New Times Publishing House: Presbook Compound, BP 408, Limbé; tel. 3333-3217; f. 1983; publishing and book-trade reference; Dir and Editor-in-Chief JÉRÔME F. GWELLEM.

Presses de l'Université Catholique d'Afrique Centrale (PUCAC): BP 11628, Yaoundé; tel. 2230-5508; fax 2230-5501; e-mail p_ucac@yahoo.fr; internet www.pucac.com; Man. GABRIEL TSALA ONANA.

GOVERNMENT PUBLISHING HOUSES

Centre d'Edition et de Production pour l'Enseignement et la Recherche (CEPER): BP 808, Yaoundé; tel. 7723-1293; f. 1967; transfer pending to private ownership; general non-fiction, science and technology, tertiary, secondary and primary educational textbooks; Man. Dir JEAN CLAUDE FOUTH.

Imprimerie Nationale: BP 1603, Yaoundé; tel. 2223-1277; Dir AMADOU VAMOULKE.

Société de Presse et d'Editions du Cameroun (SOPECAM): route de l'Aéroport, BP 1218, Yaoundé; tel. 2230-4147; fax 2230-4362; e-mail mclairennana@yahoo.fr; internet cameroon-tribune.cm; f. 1977; under the supervision of the Ministry of Communication; Pres. JOSEPH LE; Dir-Gen. MARIE CLAIRE NNANA.

Broadcasting and Communications

TELECOMMUNICATIONS

In early 2011 there were three operators of telecommunication services in Cameroon: one fixed-line and two mobile cellular. In mid-2011 the Government was planning to issue licences to three new mobile operators. In December 2011 a new company, Eto'o Télécom, announced that it was to commence operations under the brand name Set Télécom.

Agence de Régulation des Télécommunications (ART): Immeuble Balanos, rue Valéry Giscard d'Estaing, BP 6132, Yaoundé; tel. 2223-0380; fax 2223-3748; e-mail art@art.cm; internet www.art.cm; f. 1998; regulatory authority; Dir-Gen. JEAN LOUIS BEH MENGUE.

Cameroon Telecommunications (CAMTEL): BP 1571, Yaoundé; tel. 2223-4065; fax 2223-0303; e-mail camtel@camnet.cm; internet www.camtel.cm; f. 1999 by merger of INTELCAM and the Dept of Telecommunications; 51% privatization pending; Pres. NFON VICTOR MUKETE; Dir-Gen. DAVID NKOTO EMANE.

Mobile Telephone Networks (MTN) Cameroon Ltd: 360 rue Drouot, Bonamouti, Akwa, BP 15574, Douala; tel. 7900-9000; fax 7900-9040; internet www.mtncameroon.net; f. 1999 as CAMTEL Mobile; acquired by MTN in 2000; mobile cellular telephone operator; 70% owned by MTN Ltd, 30% owned by Broadband Telecom Ltd; CEO KARL OLUTOKUN TORIOLA.

Orange: Immeuble CBC, ave Kennedy, Yaoundé; tel. 2222-4956; e-mail contact@orange.cm; internet www.orange.cm; mobile cellular telephone and internet operator; Dir-Gen. JEAN BARDET.

BROADCASTING

Radio

Office de Radiodiffusion-Télévision Camerounaise (CRTV): BP 1634, Yaoundé; tel. 2221-4077; fax 2220-4340; e-mail infos@crtv.cm; internet www.crtv.cm; f. 1987; broadcasts in French and English; satellite broadcasts commenced in Jan. 2001, reaching some 80% of the national territory; Pres. of Council of Administration BAKARY ISSA TCHIROMA (Minister of Communication); Dir-Gen. AMADOU VAMOULKE.

Radio Yaoundé FM 94: BP 1634, Yaoundé; tel. 2220-2089; fax 2220-4340; e-mail fm94@crtv.cm; Head of Station LOUISE POM.

Television

Television programmes from France were broadcast by the Office de Radiodiffusion-Télévision Camerounaise from early 1990.

Office de Radiodiffusion-Télévision Camerounaise (CRTV): see Radio.

Finance

(cap. = capital; res = reserves; dep. = deposits; m. = million; brs = branches; amounts in francs CFA)

BANKING

In 2010 there were 12 licensed banks in Cameroon.

Central Bank

Banque des Etats de l'Afrique Centrale (BEAC): 736 ave Monseigneur Vogt, BP 1917, Yaoundé; tel. 2223-4060; fax 2223-3329; e-mail beac@beac.int; internet www.beac.int; f. 1973; bank of issue for mem. states of the Communauté Economique et monétaire de l'Afrique Centrale (CEMAC, fmrly Union Douanière et Economique de l'Afrique Centrale): Cameroon, the Central African Repub., Chad, the Repub. of the Congo, Equatorial Guinea and Gabon; cap. 88,000m., res 227,843m., dep. 4,110,966m. (Dec. 2007); Gov. LUCAS ABAGA NCHAMA; Dir in Cameroon JEAN-MARIE BENOÎT MANI (acting); 5 brs in Cameroon.

Commercial Banks

Afriland First Bank: 1063 pl. de l'Indépendance, BP 11834, Yaoundé; tel. 2223-3068; fax 2222-1785; e-mail firstbank@afrilandfirstbank.com; internet www.afrilandfirstbank.com; formerly Caisse Commune d'Epargne et d'Investissement (CCEI); SBF & Co (36.62%), FMO (19.80%), private shareholders (43.58%); cap. and res 10,017m., total assets 161,293m. (Dec. 2003); Pres. Dr PAUL KAMMOGNE FOKAM; Gen. Man. ALAMINE OUSMANE MEY.

Banque Internationale du Cameroun pour l'Epargne et le Crédit (BICEC): ave du Général de Gaulle, BP 1925, Douala; tel. 3343-6000; fax 3343-1226; e-mail bicec@bicec.banquepopulaire.com; internet www.bicec.com; f. 1962 as Banque Internationale pour le Commerce et l'Industrie du Cameroun; name changed as above in 1997, following restructuring; 52.5% owned by Groupe Banques Populaires (France); cap. 6,000m., res 37,729m., dep. 438,081m. (Dec. 2009); Pres. JEAN-BAPTISTE BOKAM; Gen. Man. PASCAL REBILLARD; 32 brs.

Citibank N.A. Cameroon: 96 rue Flatters, Bonanjo, BP 4571, Douala; tel. 3342-2777; fax 3342-4074; internet www.citigroup.com; f. 1997; Dir-Gen. ASIF ZAIDI; COO WILSON CHOLA.

Commercial Bank Cameroon SA (CBC): ave du Général de Gaulle, BP 59, Douala; tel. 3342-0202; fax 3343-3800; e-mail cbcbank@cbc-bank.com; internet www.cbc-bank.com; f. 1997; cap. 7,000.0m., res 4,596.2m., dep. 156,758.3m. (Dec. 2005); Pres. YVES MICHEL FOTSO.

Ecobank Cameroun SA (Togo): blvd de la Liberté, BP 582, Douala; tel. 3343-8251; fax 3343-8609; e-mail ecobankcm@ecobank.com; internet www.ecobank.com; f. 2001; cap. 6,250.0m., res 2,171.2m., dep. 206,611.9m. (Dec. 2009); Chair. ANDRÉ FOTSO; Man. Dir ASSIONGBON EKUE; 24 brs.

Highland Corporation Bank SA: Immeuble Hôtel Hilton, blvd du 20 mai, BP 10039, Yaoundé; tel. 2223-9287; fax 2232-9291; e-mail atnjp@camnet.cm; internet pcnet.ifrance.com/pcnet/hcb; f. 1995; 100% privately owned; cap. 1,500m. (Dec. 1999); Exec. Pres. PAUL ATANGA NJI; Asst Dir-Gen. JOHANES MBATI.

Société Commerciale de Banque Cameroun SA: 530 rue du Roi George, BP 300, Douala; tel. 3343-5400; fax 3342-5413; e-mail ca_scb@scbcameroun.com; f. 1989 as Société Commerciale de Banque—Crédit Lyonnais Cameroun; renamed Crédit Lyonnais Cameroun SA in 2002, and as above in 2007; 35% state-owned; cap. 6,000.0m., res 13,131.1m., dep. 294,167.7m. (Dec. 2009); Pres. MARTIN ARISTIDE OKOUDA; Gen. Man. FRANCIS DUBUS.

Société Générale de Banques au Cameroun (SGBC): 78 rue Joss, BP 4042, Douala; tel. 3342-7010; fax 3343-0353; e-mail sgbcdla@camnet.cm; internet www.sgbc.cm; f. 1963; 25.6% state-owned; cap. 6,250m., res 26,524m., dep. 389,967m. (Dec. 2009); Chair. MATHURIN NDOUMBÉ EPÉE; Dir-Gen. ALEXANDRE MAYMAT; 15 brs.

Standard Chartered Bank Cameroon SA: blvd de la Liberté, BP 1784, Douala; tel. 3343-5200; fax 3342-2789; e-mail Paul.Sagnia@cm.standardchartered.com; internet www.standardchartered.com/cm; f. 1980 as Boston Bank Cameroon; name changed 1986; 100% owned by Standard Chartered Bank (United Kingdom); cap. 7,000m., res 5,797m., dep. 127,823m. (June 2005); CEO MATHIEU MANDENG; 2 brs.

Union Bank of Cameroon, Ltd (UBC): NWCA Ltd Bldg, 2nd Floor, Commercial Ave, BP 110, Bamenda, Douala; tel. 3336-2316; fax 3336-2314; e-mail ubc@unionbankcameroon.com; internet www.unionbankcameroon.com; f. 2000; share cap. 5,000m. (2005); Pres. GABRIEL IKOMÉ NJOH; Gen. Man. ABRAHAM NDOFOR.

United Bank for Africa Cameroon: blvd de la Liberté-Akwa, BP 2088, Douala; tel. 3343-3683; fax 3343-3707; e-mail ubacameroon@ubagroup.com; internet www.ubagroup.com/ubacameroon; Dir-Gen. EMEKE E. IWERIEBOR.

Development Banks

Banque de Développement des États de l'Afrique Centrale: see Franc Zone.

Crédit Foncier du Cameroun (CFC): 484 blvd du 20 mai 1972, BP 1531, Yaoundé; tel. 2223-5216; fax 2223-5221; f. 1977; 75% state-owned; cap. 6,000m. (Dec. 2007); provides assistance for low-cost housing; Chair. JULES DORET NDONGO; Gen. Man. CAMILLE EKINDI; 10 brs.

Société Nationale d'Investissement du Cameroun (SNI): pl. Ahmadou Ahidjo, BP 423, Yaoundé; tel. 2222-4422; fax 2223-1332; e-mail sni@sni.cm; internet www.sni.cm; f. 1964; state-owned investment and credit agency; cap. 22,000m., total assets 33,341m. (June 2003); Chair. SIMON ACHIDI ACHU; Dir-Gen. YAOU AISSATOU.

Financial Institutions

Caisse Autonome d'Amortissement du Cameroun: BP 7167, Yaoundé; tel. 2222-2226; fax 2222-0129; e-mail caa@caa.cm; internet www.caa.cm; f. 1985; cap. 5,000m. (1998); Dir-Gen. EVOU MEKOU DIEUDONNÉ.

National Financial Credit Company Cameroon (NFCC): BP 6578, Yaoundé; tel. 2222-4806; fax 2222-8781; e-mail national_financial_credit@yahoo.com; cap. and res 2,350m., total assets 9,338m.; Pres. ABEY JEROME ONGHER; Gen. Man. AWANGA ZACHARIA.

Société Camerounaise de Crédit Automobile (SOCCA): rue du Roi Albert, BP 554, Douala; tel. 3342-7478; fax 3342-1219; e-mail socca@socca-cm.cm; internet www.giefca.com/english/cameroun.htm; f. 1959; cap. and res 4,770m., total assets 23,748m. (Dec. 2003); Dir-Gen. JOHANN BAUDOT.

Société Camerounaise de Crédit-Bail (SOCABAIL): rue du Roi Albert, BP 554, Douala; tel. 3342-7478; fax 3342-1219; e-mail soccabail@camnet.cm; cap. 500m., res 1,343m., total assets 5,880m. (June 1999); Pres. ALAIN GUYON.

STOCK EXCHANGE

Bourse des Valeurs de Douala (Douala Stock Exchange): 1450 blvd de la Liberté, BP 442, Douala; tel. 3343-8583; fax 3353-8584; e-mail dsx@douala-stock-exchange.com; internet www.douala-stock-exchange.com; f. 2003; 23% state-owned; Chair. BÉNÉDICT BELIBI; Dir-Gen. PIERRE EKOULÉ MOUANGUÉ.

INSURANCE

In 2010 there were 24 insurance companies in Cameroon.

Activa Assurances: rue du Prince du Galles 1385, BP 12970, Douala; tel. 3343-4503; fax 3343-4572; e-mail activa.assur@camnet.cm; f. 1999; all branches except life insurance; cap. 400m.; 66% owned by Cameroonian investors, 33% by Ivorian investors; Chair. JEAN KACOU DIAGOU; Gen. Man. RICHARD NZONLIÉ LOWE; also **Activa Vie**, life insurance.

Allianz Cameroun: rue Manga Bell, BP 105, Douala; tel. 3350-2000; fax 3350-2001; e-mail allianz.cameroun@allianz-cm.com; internet www.allianz-africa.com/cameroun; formerly AGF Cameroun Assurances; all classes of insurance; Dir-Gen. BERNARD GIRARDIN (life insurance).

Association des Sociétés d'Assurances du Cameroun (ASAC): BP 1136, Douala; tel. and fax 3342-0668; e-mail contact@asac-cameroun.org; internet asac-cameroun.org; Pres. MARTIN N. FONCHA; Sec.-Gen. GEORGES MANDENG LIKENG.

AXA Assurances Cameroun: 309 rue Bebey-Eyidi, BP 4068, Douala; e-mail axa.cameroun@axacameroun.com; internet www.axacameroun.com; tel. 3342-6772; fax 3342-6453; f. 1974 as Compagnie Camerounaise d'Assurances et de Réassurances; renamed as above in June 2000; Pres. SANDA OUMAROU; Dir-Gen. THIERRY KEPEDEN.

Beneficial Life Insurance SA: BP 2328, Douala; tel. 3342-8408; fax 3342-7754; e-mail beneficial@iccnet.cm; f. 1974; Dir-Gen. ALLEN ROOSEVELT BROWN.

Chanas Assurances: BP 109, Douala; tel. 3342-1474; fax 3342-9960; e-mail chanas@iccnet2000.com; internet www.chanas-assurances.com; f. 1999; Pres. and Dir-Gen. JACQUELINE CASALEGNO.

Colina All Life: blvd de la Liberté, BP 267, Douala; tel. 3343-0904; fax 3343-1237; e-mail colinaalllife@groupecolina.com; internet www.groupecolina.com; f. 1996; life insurance; Dir-Gen. MARTIN FONCHA.

Colina La Citoyenne Cameroun: 34 rue Dinde, BP 12125, Douala; tel. 3342-4446; fax 3342-4727; e-mail citoyenne@groupecolina.com;

internet colina.cawad.com; f. 1986; non-life insurance; Dir-Gen. PROTAIS AYANGMA AMANG.

Compagnie Nationale d'Assurances (CNA): BP 12125, Douala; tel. 3342-4446; fax 3342-4727; f. 1986; all classes of insurance; cap. 600m.; Chair. THÉODORE EBOBO; Man. Dir PROTAIS AYANGMA AMANG.

General and Equitable Assurance Cameroon Ltd (GEACAM): 56 blvd de la Liberté, BP 426, Douala; tel. 3342-5985; fax 3342-7103; cap. 300m.; Pres. V. A. NGU; Man. Dir J. CHEBAUT.

Société Africaine d'Assurances et Réassurances (SAAR): BP 1011, Douala; tel. 3343-1765; fax 3343-1759; internet www .saar-assurances.com; f. 1990; Pres. Dr PAUL K. FOKAM; Dir-Gen. GEORGES LÉOPOLD KAGOU; also **SAAR-Vie**, life insurance; Dir-Gen. FERDINAND MENG.

Société Camerounaise d'Assurances et de Réassurances (SOCAR): 1450 blvd de la Liberté, BP 280, Douala; tel. 3342-5584; fax 3342-1335; f. 1973; cap. 800m.; Chair. J. YONTA; Man. Dir R. BIOUELE.

Trade and Industry

GOVERNMENT AGENCY

Conseil Économique et Social: BP 1058, Yaoundé; tel. 2223-2474; advises the Govt on economic and social problems; comprises 150 mems, who serve a 5-year term, and a perm. sec.; Pres. LUC AYANG; Sec.-Gen. ESSOME BIKOU RENÉ.

DEVELOPMENT ORGANIZATIONS

Agence Française de Développement (AFD): Immeuble Flatters, rue de la Radio, BP 2283, Douala; tel. 3342-9959; fax 3342-9959; e-mail afddouala@groupe-afd.org; internet www.afd.fr; fmrly Caisse Française de Développement; Man. GILLES CHAUSSE.

Cameroon Development Corporation (CAMDEV): Bota Area, Limbé; tel. 3333-2251; fax 3333-2680; e-mail info@cdc-cameroon .com; internet www.cdc-cameroon.com; f. 1947; reorg. 1982; cap. 15,626m. francs CFA; statutory corpn established to acquire and develop plantations of tropical crops for local and export markets; operates 3 palm oil mills and 5 rubber factories; Chair. Chief OKIAH NAMATA ELANGWE; Gen. Man. HENRY NJALLA QUAN.

Direction Générale des Grands Travaux du Cameroon (DGTC): BP 6604, Yaoundé; tel. 2222-1803; fax 2222-1300; f. 1988; commissioning, implementation and supervision of public works contracts; Chair. JEAN FOUMAN AKAME; Man. Dir MICHEL KOWALZICK.

Hévéa-Cameroun (HEVECAM): BP 1298, Douala and BP 174, Kribi; tel. 3346-1919; f. 1975; state-owned; devt of 15,000 ha rubber plantation; 4,500 employees; transferred to private ownership in 1997; Pres. ELIE C. NYOKWEDI MALONGA; Man. Dir JEAN-MARC SEYMAN.

Institut de Recherche Agricole pour le Développement (IRAD): BP 2067, Yaoundé; tel. and fax 2222-3538; e-mail contact@irad-cameroun.org; internet www.irad-cameroon.org; Dir-Gen. NOÉ WOIN.

Institut de Recherche pour le Développement (IRD): 1095 rue Joseph Essono Mballa, Quartier Elig Essono, BP 1857, Yaoundé; tel. 2220-1508; fax 2220-1854; e-mail cameroun@ird.fr; internet www .cameroun.ird.fr; f. 1944; Rep. in Cameroon BRUNO BORDAGE.

Mission d'Aménagement et d'Equipement des Terrains Urbains et Ruraux (MAETUR): 716 ave Winston Churchill, Quartier Hippodrome, BP 1248, Yaoundé; tel. 2222-3113; fax 2223-3190; e-mail maetur@maetur.cm; internet www.maetur.cm; f. 1977; Pres. ABDOULAYE ABOUBAKARY; Dir-Gen. EMMANUEL ETOUNDI OYONO.

Mission d'Aménagement et de Gestion des Zones Industrielles: BP 1431, Yaoundé; tel. and fax 2231–8440; e-mail magzicameroun@yahoo.fr; internet www.magzicameroun.com; f. 1971; state-owned industrial land authority; Dir CHRISTOL GEORGES MANON.

Mission de Développement de la Province du Nord-Ouest (MIDENO): BP 442, Bamenda; Gen. Man. JOHN B. NDEH.

Office Céréalier dans la Province du Nord: BP 298, Garoua; tel. 2227-1438; f. 1975 to combat effects of drought in northern Cameroon and stabilize cereal prices; Pres. Alhadji MAHAMAT; Dir-Gen. GILBERT GOURLEMOND.

Office National du Cacao et du Café (ONCC): BP 3018, Douala; tel. 3342-9482; fax 3342-0002; Dir-Gen. MICHAËL NDOPING.

Service de Coopération et d'Action Culturelle: BP 1616, Yaoundé; tel. 2223-0412; fax 2222-5065; e-mail mission.coop@ camnet.cm; administers bilateral aid from France; Dir YVON ALAIN.

Société de Développement du Cacao (SODECAO): BP 1651, Yaoundé; tel. 2230-4544; fax 2230-3395; e-mail sodecaodg@gmail .com; internet www.sodecao.cm; f. 1974; reorg. 1980; cap. 425m. francs CFA; devt of cocoa, coffee and food crop production in the Littoral, Centre, East and South provinces; Pres. JOSEPH-CHARLES DOUMBA; Dir-Gen. JÉRÔME MVONDO.

Société de Développement du Coton (SODECOTON): BP 302, Garoua; tel. 2227-1556; fax 2227-2026; f. 1974; Chair. HAOUNAYE GOUNOKO; Man. MOHAMMED IYA.

Société de Développement de l'Elevage (SODEVA): BP 50, Kousseri; cap. 50m. francs CFA; Dir Alhadji OUMAROU BAKARY.

Société de Développement et d'Exploitation des Productions Animales (SODEPA): BP 1410, Yaoundé; tel. 2220-0810; fax 2220-0809; e-mail courrier@sodepa.org; internet www.sodepa.org; f. 1974; cap. 375m. francs CFA; devt of livestock and livestock products; Man. Dir DIEUDONNÉ BOUBA NDENGUE.

Société de Développement de la Haute-Vallée du Noun (UNVDA): BP 25, N'Dop, North-West Province; f. 1970; cap. 1,380m. francs CFA; rice, maize and soya bean cultivation; Dir-Gen. SAMUEL BAWE CHI WANKI.

Société d'Expansion et de Modernisation de la Riziculture de Yagoua (SEMRY): BP 46, Yagoua; tel. 2229-6213; internet semry .com; f. 1971; cap. 4,580m. francs CFA; commercialization of rice products and expansion of rice-growing in areas where irrigation is possible; Pres. AHMADOU TIDJANI; Dir-Gen. MARC ATANA.

Société Immobilière du Cameroun (SIC): ave de l'Indépendance, BP 387, Yaoundé; BP 924, Douala; BP 94, Garoua; tel. 2223-3411; fax 2222-5119; e-mail sic@sicameroun.com; internet www.sicameroun .com; f. 1952; cap. 1,000m. francs CFA; housing construction and devt; Pres. ABDOULAYE HAMAN ADJI; Dir-Gen. BONIFACE NGOA NKOU.

CHAMBERS OF COMMERCE

Chambre d'Agriculture, des Pêches, de l'Élevage et des Forêts du Cameroun (CAPEF): BP 6620, Yaoundé; tel. 2222-0441; fax 2222-2025; e-mail cfe_cameroun@yahoo.fr; f. 1955; 120 mems; Pres. JANVIER MONGUI SOSSOMBA; Sec.-Gen. BERNARD NWANA SAMA; other chambers at Ebolowa, Bertoua, Douala, Ngaoundere, Garoua, Maroua, Buéa, Bamenda and Bafoussam.

Chambre de Commerce, d'Industrie, des Mines et de l'Artisanat du Cameroun (CCIMA): rue de Chambre de Commerce, BP 4011, Douala; also at BP 36, Yaoundé; BP 211, Limbé; BP 59, Garoua; BP 944, Bafoussam; BP 551, Bamenda; BP 824, Ngaoundere; BP 86, Bertoua; tel. 3342-6855; fax 3342-5596; e-mail siege@ccima.net; internet www.ccima.net; f. 1921; 160 mems; Pres. CHRISTOPHE EKEN; Sec.-Gen. SAÏDOU ABDOULAYE BOBBOY.

EMPLOYERS' ORGANIZATIONS

Association Professionnelle des Établissements de Crédit du Cameroun (APECCAM): BP 133, Yaoundé; tel. 2223-5401; fax 2223-5402; Pres. FRANCIS DUBUS; Sec.-Gen. BÉNÉDICT BELIBI.

Groupement des Femmes d'Affaires du Cameroun (GFAC): BP 1940, Douala; tel. 2223-4059; fax 2221-1041; e-mail gfacnational@yahoo.fr; f. 1985; Pres. FRANÇOISE FONING.

Groupement Inter-Patronal du Cameroun (GICAM): rue des Ministres, Bonanjo, BP 829, Douala; tel. 3342-3141; fax 3342-4591; e-mail gicam@legicam.org; internet www.legicam.org; Pres. OLIVIER BEHLE.

Mouvement des Entrepreneurs du Cameroun (MECAM): BP 12443, Douala; tel. 3339-5000; fax 3339-5001; Pres. DANIEL CLAUDE ABATÉ.

Syndicat des Commerçants Importateurs-Exportateurs du Cameroun (SCIEC): 16 rue Quillien, BP 562, Douala; tel. 3342-0304; Pres. EMMANUEL UGOLINI; Treas. MICHEL CHUPIN.

Syndicat des Industriels du Cameroun (SYNDUSTRICAM): BP 673, Douala; tel. 3342-3058; fax 3342-5616; e-mail syndustricam@camnet.cm; f. 1953; Pres. CHARLES METOUCK; Sec.-Gen. BEKE BIHEGE.

Syndicat des Producteurs et Exportateurs de Bois du Cameroun: BP 570, Yaoundé; tel. 2220-2722; fax 2220-9694; f. 1939; Pres. CARLO ORIANI.

Syndicat Professionnel des Entreprises du Bâtiment, des Travaux Publics et des Activités Annexes: BP 1134, Yaoundé; BP 660, Douala; tel. and fax 2220-2722; Sec.-Gen. FRANCIS SANZOUANGOU.

UTILITIES

Electricity

Electricity Development Corpn: Immeuble Stamatiadès, BP 15111, Yaoundé; tel. 2223-1930; fax 2223-1113; e-mail info@ edc-cameroon.org; internet edc-cameroon.org; f. 2006; state-owned; Pres. VICTOR MENGOT; Dir-Gen. Dr THÉODORE NSANGOU.

Société Nationale d'Electricité du Cameroun (AES-SONEL): BP 4077, 63 ave de Gaulle, Douala; tel. 3342-1553; fax 3342-2235;

e-mail sonel@camnet.cm; internet www.aessoneltoday.com; f. 1974; 56% owned by AES Sirocco, 44% state-owned; Pres. SERAPHIN MAGLOIRE FOUDA; Gen. Man. JEAN-DAVID BILÉ.

Water

Cameroon Water Utilities Corpn (Camwater): BP 4077, Douala; tel. 3342-5444; fax 3342-2247; f. 1967; 73% state-owned; Pres. AMADOU ALI; Dir-Gen. BASILE ATANGANA KOUNA.

MAJOR COMPANIES

The following are some of the largest companies in terms of either capital investment or employment:

ALUCAM, Compagnie Camerounaise de l'Aluminium: BP 1090, Douala; tel. 3342-2930; fax 3342-7669; f. 1984; 39% state-owned; manufacture of aluminium by electrolysis using imported alumina; Pres. and Man. Dir ALAIN MALONG.

Bolloré Africa Logistics: BP 4057, Yaoundé; tel. 3350-1283; fax 2221-3722; e-mail doris.happi@bollore.com; internet www.bollore-africa-logistics.com; f. 2008; group includes, *inter alia*, fmr entities SAGA Cameroun and TRANSINTRA; transport services; Pres. CHRISTOPHE PUJALTE; 620 employees.

Cameroon Oil Transportation Co. (COTCO): 179 rue de la Motte Piquet-Bonanjo, BP 3738, Douala; tel. 7074-1439; fax 7074-1411.

Cameroon Sugar Co, PLC (CAMSUCO): rue de l'Independence, BP 1066 Douala; tel. 2237-0017; internet camsuco.diytrade.com; f. 1972; sugar plantations, refining and marketing; transferred to private ownership in 1999; Pres. SALOMON ELOGO METOMO; Man. Dir AMOUGOU MBEDJA.

Camlait SA: rue des Industries, BP Douala; tel. 3337-4460; fax 3337-2190; dairy products.

Cimenteries du Cameroun (CIMENCAM): BP 1323, Douala; tel. 3339-1119; fax 3339-0489; e-mail sat.cim@camnet.cm; internet www.cimencam.com; f. 1965; cement works at Figuil, clinker-crushing plant at Douala-Bonabéri, factory at Garoua; 54.73% owned by Lafarge (France); Pres. PIERRE MOUKOKO MBONJO; Dir-Gen. RAVI IYER.

Contreplaqués du Cameroun (COCAM): BP 154, Mbalmayo; tel. 2228-1120; fax 2228-1420; f. 1966; cap. 2,489m. francs CFA; 89% state-owned, of which 49% by Société nationale d'investissement du Cameroun; devt of forest resources, production of plywood and slatted panels; Pres. PATRICE MANDENG; Dir-Gen. RAYMOND VINCENT ATAGANA ABENA.

Cotonnière Industrielle du Cameroun (CICAM): BP 7012, Douala-Bassa; tel. 3340-6215; fax 3340-7431; e-mail cicam@camnet.cm; f. 1967; 100% owned by Société Nationale d'Investissement du Cameroun (q.v.); factory for bleaching, printing and dyeing of cotton at Douala; Dir-Gen. MICHEL POLIDORI; 1,340 employees.

Del Monte Cameroon Ltd: BP 13275, Douala; tel. 3342-4934; fax 3342-5482; f. 1938; technical food services; Gen. Man. J. A. PELÁEZ.

Les Grandes Huileries Camerounaises: Zone Industrielle de Bassa, Douala; f. 1982; cap. 1,400m. francs CFA; 50% state-owned; Pres. Alhadji BACHIROU; Man. Dir ERIC JACOBSEN.

Guinness Cameroun SA: BP 1213, Douala; tel. 3340-7000; fax 3340-7182; e-mail enquiries@guinness.com; f. 1967; cap. 6,410m. francs CFA; production and marketing of beers; Man. Dir BRIAN JOHNSON; 900 employees.

Nouvelles Brasseries Africaines (NOBRA): rue Tamaris 5, Douala; tel. 3342-8503; f. 1979; cap. 7,000m. francs CFA; manufacturers of soft drinks; Pres. PIERRE TCHANQUE; Dir-Gen. ANDERS ANDERSEN.

Perenco Cameroun: Immeuble Saticam-Bata, blvd du President Ahidjo, BP 1225, Douala; tel. 3342-3291; fax 3342-4359; f. 1993; Dir-Gen. DÉNIS CLERC-RENAUD.

Plasticam: Zone Industrielle de Bassa, 2060 rue 3W854, BP 4071, Douala; tel. 3337-5057; fax 3337-1877; e-mail plasticamsg@iccnet2000.com; f. 1962; plastic packaging producers; Chair. DANIEL FORGET; Gen. Man. BERNARD GUILPIN.

Société Africaine Forestière et Agricole du Cameroun (SAFA Cameroun): BP 100, Douala; tel. 3342-9758; fax 3342-7512; f. 1897; plantation of natural rubber and production of rubber and latex; rubber and palm plantations at Dizangué; Pres. LUC BOEDT; Man. Dir GILBERT SUJET; 1,571 employees.

Société Anonyme des Brasseries du Cameroun (SABC): 77 rue Prince Bell, BP 4036, Douala; tel. 3342-9133; fax 3342-7945; e-mail siege@sabc-cm.com; internet www.lesbrasseriesducameroun.com; f. 1948; production of beer and soft drinks; Dir-Gen. ANDRÉ SIAKA; 1,651 employees.

Société Camerounaise des Dépôts Pétroliers (SCDP): rue de la Cité Chardy, BP 2272, Douala; tel. 3340-5445; fax 3340-4796; e-mail courrier@scdp.cm; internet www.scdp.cm; f. 1978; storage and distribution of petroleum; Dir-Gen. GASTON ELOUNDOU-ESSOMBA.

Société Camerounaise de Fabrication de Piles Electriques (PILCAM): BP 1916, Douala; tel. 3342-2628; f. 1970; cap. 1,472m. francs CFA; Pres. VICTOR FOTSO; Dir ANDRÉ FONTANA; 745 employees.

Société Camerounaise de Palmeraies (SOCAPALM): rue du Général Leman, BP 691, Douala; tel. 3343-7783; fax 3343-8734; f. 1968; 78% privatized; management of palm plantations and production of palm oil and manufactured products; Chair. JUIMO MONTHE; Gen. Man. JEAN-PIERRE CHARBON; 1,380 employees.

Société Camerounaise de Sacherie (SCS): Zone Industrielle de Bassa, BP 398, Douala; tel. 3342-3104; f. 1971; cap. 2,075m. francs CFA; 39% owned by ONCPB; production of sacks; Pres. GUILLAUME NSEKE; Dir THOMAS DAKAYI KAMGA.

Société Camerounaise de Transformation de l'Aluminium (SOCATRAL): BP 291, Edéa; tel. 3346-4024; fax 3346-4774; e-mail socalu1@yahoo.fr; f. 1960; 49% owned by ALUCAM (q.v.); production of corrugated sheets, aluminium strips and rolled discs; Pres. and Man. Dir RAFAËL TITIMANYAKA.

Société Camerounaise de Verrerie (SOCAVER): rue de Ndogbong Bassa, BP 1456, Douala; tel. 3340-0506; fax 3340-6403; e-mail socaver@camnet.cm; f. 1966; 52.9% owned by SABC (q.v.); mfrs of glassware; Pres. MICHEL PALU; Gen. Man. JEAN PIERRE KAMGNA.

Société des Eaux Minérales du Cameroun (SEMC): 77 rue du Prince Bell, BP 4036, Douala; tel. 3342-7919; fax 9950-5952; subsidiary of the Société Anonyme des Brasseries du Cameroun (SABC); producer of mineral water; Dir-Gen. PIERRE PROUVEU.

Société Forestière et Industrielle de Belabo (SOFIBEL): Yaoundé; tel. 2223-2657; f. 1975; cap. 1,902m. francs CFA; 39% state-owned; sawmill; manufacturers of plywood; Pres. SADOU DAOUDOU; Man. Dir DENIS KEEDI ATOK.

Société Industrielle Camerounaise des Cacaos (SIC CACAOS): route de Deido, BP 570, Douala; tel. 3340-3795; fax 3340-3931; e-mail siccacaos@barry-callebaut.com; f. 1949; cap. 1,147.5m. francs CFA; production of cocoa and cocoa butter; Pres. BENOIT VILLERS; Man. Dir DIDIER BUÉCHER.

Société Industrielle des Tabacs du Cameroun (SITABAC): BP 1105, Douala; tel. 3342-4919; fax 3342-5949; e-mail sitabac@camnet.cm; cap. 4,556.6m. francs CFA; manufacture and sale of cigarettes; Pres. and Dir-Gen. JAMES ONOBIONO.

La Société les Minotiers du Cameroun: BP 785, Douala; tel. 3337-7501; fax 3337-1761; f. 1986; cap. 1,010m. francs CFA; flour mill; Pres. BABA AHMADOU; Dir-Gen. ANDRÉ NGANDEU.

Société Nationale des Hydrocarbures (SNH): BP 955, Yaoundé; tel. 2220-1910; fax 2220-4651; e-mail info@snh.cm; internet www.snh.cm; f. 1980; national petroleum co; Pres. JEAN-MARIE ATANGANA; Dir-Gen. ADOLPHE MOUDIKI.

Société Nationale de Raffinage (SONARA): BP 365, Cap Limboh, Limbé; tel. 3342-3815; fax 3342-3444; e-mail sonara.coh@camnet.cm; f. 1976; cap. 17,800m. francs CFA; 66% state-owned; establishment and operation of petroleum refinery at Cap Limboh; Chair. JOHN EBONG NGOLE; Dir-Gen. CHARLES METOUCK; 620 employees.

Société des Plantations du Haut Penja: BP 05, Nyombé; tel. 7773-1121; fax 7799-2347; e-mail j.tchoumba@phpcam.com; Dir-Gen. FRANÇOIS ARMEL.

Société des Plantations de Mbanga: Immeuble TMC, 1871 blvd de la Liberté, BP 711, Douala; tel. 3343-4078; fax 3343-4074; e-mail douala_spm@hotmail.com; Pres. and Dir-Gen. JEAN-YVES BRETHES.

Société de Recherches et d'Exploitation des Pétroles du Cameroun (SEREPCA): 83 blvd de la Liberté, BP 2214, Douala-Bassa; tel. 3342-1785; fax 3342-1366; f. 1951; cap. 1,000m. francs CFA; 20% state-owned; prospecting and exploitation of offshore petroleum; Pres. JEAN-LOUIS VERMEULEN; Dir-Gen. MICHEL CHARLES; 600 employees.

Société Shell du Cameroun: BP 4082, Douala; tel. 3342-2415; fax 3342-6031; f. 1954; cap. 1,600m. francs CFA; import and distribution of petroleum products; Dir-Gen. BANJI OGUNGBEMI.

Société Sucrière du Cameroun (SOSUCAM): BP 875, Yaoundé; tel. and fax 2223-0585; e-mail sosucam@camnet.cm; f. 1965; cap. 13,925m. francs CFA (2003); 24% state-owned; sugar refinery at M'bandjock; owned by Vilgrain group of France; Pres. and Man. Dir LOUIS YINDA; more than 7,000 employees.

Summit Motors Cameroon, SA (SUMOCA): BP 4181, Douala; tel. 3337-2286; fax 3337-0558; e-mail sumoca@sumoca.com; internet www.sumoca.com; state-owned; Man. Dir ICHIRO TOMINO.

Texaco Cameroun, SA: blvd de la Liberté, POB 214, Douala; tel. 3342-3028; fax 3342-8312; e-mail jbya@chevron.com; f. 1947; Man. Dir WILLIAM C. BENNETT.

TotalFinaElf Cameroun: BP 4048, Douala-Bassa; tel. 3342-6341; fax 3342-6871; e-mail total@camnet.cm; f. 1977; 75.8% owned by Total (France); 20% owned by Société Nationale des Hydrocarbures (q.v.); exploration for, exploitation and distribution of petroleum reserves; Dir-Gen. BRUNO VINCENT.

PRINCIPAL CO-OPERATIVE ORGANIZATIONS

Centre National de Développement des Entreprises Coopératives (CENADEC): Yaoundé; f. 1970; promotes and organizes the co-operative movement; bureaux at BP 43, Kumba and BP 26, Bamenda; Dir JACQUES SANGUE.

Union Centrale des Coopératives Agricoles de l'Ouest (UCCAO): ave Samuel Wanko, BP 1002, Bafoussam; tel. 3344-4296; fax 3344-1845; e-mail uccao@uccao-cameroun.com; internet www.uccao-cameroon.com; f. 1958; marketing of cocoa and coffee; 120,000 mems; Pres. JACQUES FOTSO KANKEU; Gen. Man. FRANÇOIS MEFINJA FOKA.

West Cameroon Co-operative Association Ltd: BP 135, Kumba; founded as central financing body of the co-operative movement; provides short-term credits and agricultural services to mem. socs; policy-making body for the co-operative movement in West Cameroon; 142 mem. unions and socs representing c. 45,000 mems; Pres. Chief T. E. NJEA.

TRADE UNION FEDERATIONS

Confederation of Cameroon Trade Unions (CCTU): BP 1610, Yaoundé; tel. 2222-3315; f. 1985; fmrly the Union Nationale des Travailleurs du Cameroun (UNTC); Pres. JEAN-MARIE ZAMBO AMOUGOU.

Confédération des Syndicats Autonomes du Cameroun (CSAC): Yaoundé; Pres. COLLINS VEWESSEE; Sec.-Gen. PIERRE LOUIS MOUANGUE.

Union des Syndicats Libres du Cameroun (USLC): BP 13306, Yaoundé; tel. 2234196; Pres. FLAUBERT MOUSSOLÉ.

Other trade union federations include the Union Générale des Travailleurs du Cameroun (UGTC), the Confédération Camerounaise du Travail (CCT), the Confédération générale du travail-Liberté du Cameroun (CGT-L), the Confédération des Syndicats Indépendants du Cameroun (CSIC) and the Confédération des Travailleurs Unis du Cameroun (CTUC).

Transport

RAILWAYS

In 2010 there were some 1,103 km of track—the West Line running from Douala to Nkongsamba (166 km), with a branch line leading south-west from Mbanga to Kumba (29 km), and the Transcameroon railway, which runs from Douala to Ngaoundere (885 km), with a branch line from Ngoumou to Mbalmayo (30 km). There were also plans for the construction of a 450-km railway linking Mbalam with Kribi.

CAMRAIL: Gare Centrale de Bessengué, blvd de la Réunification, BP 766, Douala; tel. 3340-6045; fax 3340-8252; e-mail didier.vandenbon@camrail.net; internet www.camrail.net; f. 1999; passenger and freight transport; Pres. HAMADOU SALI; Dir-Gen. QUENTIN GÉRARD.

Office du Chemin de Fer Transcamerounais: BP 625, Yaoundé; tel. 2222-4433; supervises the laying of new railway lines and improvements to existing lines, and undertakes relevant research; Dir-Gen. LUC TOWA FOTSO.

ROADS

In 2011 there were an estimated 52,743 km of roads, of which 8.4% were paved. In August of that year the Government stated its intention to pave 3,500 km of new roads by 2020.

Fonds Routier du Cameroun: BP 6221, Yaoundé; tel. 2222-4752; fax 2222-4789; e-mail contact@fonds-routier.cm; f. 1996; Dir-Gen. PIERRE TITTI.

Société Camerounaise de Transport Urbain (SOCATUR): BP 1347, Douala; tel. 3340-1297; fax 3340-1297; f. 2000; bus operator in Douala; Dir-Gen. JEAN ERNEST NGALLÉ BIBEHE.

SHIPPING

There are seaports at Kribi and Limbé-Tiko, a river port at Garoua, and an estuary port at Douala-Bonabéri, the principal port and main outlet, which has 2,510 m of quays and a minimum depth of 5.8 m in the channels and 8.5 m at the quays. Total handling capacity is 7m. metric tons annually. The first phase of the Kribi Deep Sea Port commenced in December 2010 after a concessionary loan of CFA 207,000m. was granted by the Export and Import Bank of China. Plans for a similar deep sea port project at Limbé-Tiko were under way in 2011.

Autorité Portuaire Nationale (APN): BP 11538 Yaoundé; tel. 2223-7316; fax 2223-7314; Dir-Gen. JOSUÉ YOUMBA.

Port Autonome de Douala (PAD): 81 rue de la Chambre de Commerce, BP 4020, Douala; tel. 3342-0133; fax 3342-6797; e-mail portdouala@iccnet2000.com; Chair. SHEY JONES YEMBE; Dir-Gen. EMMANUEL ETOUNDI OYONO.

Camtainer: Para-maritime Area, Douala Port, BP 4993, Douala; tel. 3342-7704; fax 3342-7173; e-mail camtainer@douala1.com; internet www.camnet.cm/investir/transpor/camtenair/sommaire.htm; f. 1984; Chair. JOSEPH TSANGA ABANDA; Man. ZACHARIE KUATE.

Conseil National des Chargeurs du Cameroun (CNCC): BP 1588, Douala; tel. 3343-6767; fax 3343-7017; e-mail info@cncc-cam.org; internet www.cncc-cam.org; f. 1975; promotion of the maritime sector; Gen. Man. AUGUSTE MBAPPE PENDA.

Consignation et Logistique du Golfe de Guinée (CLGG): BP 4054, Douala; tel. 3342-0064; fax 3342-2181; e-mail agencies@camshipinc.com; f. 1975; privatized Feb. 1997; 6 vessels trading with Western Europe, USA, Far East and Africa; Chair. RENÉ MBAYEN; Man. Dir PAUL VAN DYCK.

MAERSK CAMEROUN SA—Douala: BP 12414, Douala; tel. 3342-1185; fax 3342-1186; Dir-Gen. DAVID WARE.

Société Africaine de Transit et d'Affrètement (SATA): Douala; tel. 3342-8209; f. 1950; Man. Dir RAYMOND PARIZOT.

Société Agence Maritime de l'Ouest Africain Cameroun (SAMOA): 5 blvd de la Liberté, BP 1127, Douala; tel. 3342-1680; f. 1953; shipping agents; Dir JEAN PERRIER.

Société Camerounaise de Manutention et d'Acconage (SOCAMAC): BP 284, Douala; tel. 3342-4051; e-mail socamac@camnet.cm; internet www.camnet.cm/investir/transpor/socamac/socamac.htm; f. 1976; freight handling; Pres. MOHAMADOU TALBA; Dir-Gen. HARRY J. GHOOS.

Société Camerounaise de Transport et d'Affrètement (SCTA): BP 974, Douala; tel. 3342-1724; f. 1951; Pres. JACQUES VIAULT; Dir-Gen. GONTRAN FRAUCIEL.

Société Camerounaise de Transport Maritime: BP 12351, Douala; tel. 3342-4550; fax 3342-4946.

Société Ouest-Africaine d'Entreprises Maritimes—Cameroun (SOAEM—Cameroon): 5 blvd de la Liberté, BP 4057, Douala; tel. 3342-5269; fax 3342-0518; f. 1959; Pres. JACQUES COLOMBANI; Man. Dir JEAN-LOUIS GRECIET.

SOCOPAO Cameroun: BP 215, Douala; tel. 3342-6464; f. 1951; shipping agents; Pres. VINCENT BOLLORE; Man. Dir E. DUPUY.

CIVIL AVIATION

There are international airports at Douala, Garoua and Yaoundé; there are, in addition, 11 domestic airports, as well as a number of secondary airfields.

Cameroon Civil Aviation Authority (CCAA): BP 6998 Yaoundé; tel. 2230-3090; fax 2230-3362; e-mail contact@ccaa.aero; internet www.ccaa.aero; Pres. MAXIMIN PAUL NKOUE NKONGO; Dir-Gen. PIERRE TANKAM.

Aéroports du Cameroun (ADC): Nsimalen, BP 13615, Yaoundé; tel. 2223-4521; fax 2223-4520; e-mail adc@iccnet.cm; internet aeroportsducameroun.com; f. 1999; manages major airports; 63% state-owned; Dir-Gen. ROGER NTONGO ONGUENE.

Cameroon Airlines Corpn (CAMAIRCO): f. 2008 to replace Cameroon Airlines; commenced operations in March 2011; Chair. PHILEMON YANG; Dir-Gen. ALEX VAN ELK.

Tourism

Tourists are attracted by Cameroon's cultural diversity and by its national parks, game reserves and sandy beaches. In 2006 184,549 tourists visited Cameroon. In 2008 receipts from tourism totalled US $165m.

Ministry of Tourism and Leisure: see Ministries.

Defence

As assessed at November 2011, Cameroon's armed forces were estimated to total 14,200 men (army 12,500, navy 1,300, air force 400). There was also a 9,000-strong paramilitary force.

Defence Expenditure: Estimated at 164,000m. francs CFA in 2011.

Commander-in-Chief of the Armed Forces: PAUL BIYA.

Education

Since independence, Cameroon has achieved one of the highest rates of school attendance in Africa, but provision of educational facilities varies according to region. Education, which is bilingual, is provided by the Government, missionary societies and private concerns.

Primary education in state schools is available free of charge, and the Government provides financial assistance for other schools. It begins at six years of age, and lasts for six years. Secondary education, beginning at the age of 12, lasts for a further seven years, comprising two cycles of four years and three years in the Francophone sub-system and of five years and two years in the Anglophone sub-system. In 2009/10, according to UNESCO estimates, 94% were enrolled at primary schools. In 2008/09 the number of pupils enrolled at secondary schools totalled some 1.3m. There are seven universities, six of which are state-owned. There were 220,300 students enrolled at the state-owned universities in 2009/10 and they employed a total of 3,020 teachers in that year. In 2008/09 expenditure on education was budgeted at 15.5% of total government spending.

Bibliography

Ardener, E., and Ardener, S. *Kingdom on Mount Cameroon: Studies in the History of the Cameroon Coast 1500–1960*. Oxford, Berghahn Books, 2002.

Asuagbor, G. O. *Democratization and Modernization in a Multilingual Cameroon*. Edwin Mellin Press, 1998.

Bayart, J.-F. *L'état au Cameroun*. Paris, Presses de la Fondation Nationale des Sciences Politiques, 1985.

Belinga, E. *Cameroun: La Révolution pacifique du 20 mai*. Yaoundé, 1976.

Beti, M. *Lutte ouverte aux camerounais*. Rouen, Editions des Peuples Noirs, 1986.

Bieleu, V. *Politique de défense et sécurité nationale du Cameroun*. Paris, L'Harmattan, 2012.

Biya, P. *Communal Liberalism*. London, Macmillan, 1987.

Biyita bi Essam, J.-P. *Cameroun: Complots et Bruits de Bottes*. Paris, L'Harmattan, 1984.

Biyong, M. I. N. *Cameroun: combats pour l'independance*. Paris, L'Harmattan, 2009.

Bjornson, R. *The African Quest for Freedom and Identity: Cameroonian Writing and the National Experience*. Bloomington, IN, Indiana University Press, 1994.

Chem-Langhëë, B. *The Paradoxes of Self-Determination in the Cameroons under United Kingdom Administration: The Search for Identity, Well-Being and Continuity*. Lanham, MD, University Press of America, 2004.

Chiabi, E. M. *The Making of Modern Cameroon*. Lanham, MD, University Press of America, 1997.

De Lancey, M. W. *Cameroon: Dependence and Independence*. Boulder, CO, Westview Press, 1989.

De Lancey, M. W., and Schrader, P. J. *Cameroon*. Oxford, Clio, 1986.

Epale, S. J. *Plantations and Development in Western Cameroon 1875–1975: A Study in Agrarian Capitalism*. New York, Vantage Press, 1985.

Eyelom, F. *L'impact de la première guerre mondiale sur le Cameroun*. Paris, L'Harmattan, 2007.

Eyinga, A. *Introduction à la politique camerounaise*. Paris, L'Harmattan, 1984.

Fon, L., and Balgah, S. N. *The Urbanisation Process in Cameroon: Patterns, Implications and Prospects*. New York, Nova Publishers, 2010.

Fonge, F. *Modernization Without Development: Patterns of Change and Continuity in Post-independence Cameroonian Public Service*. Trenton, NJ, Africa World Press, 1998.

Gabriel, R. *L'Administration publique camerounaise*. Paris, Librairie Générale de Droit et de Jurisprudence, 1986.

Gaillard, P. *Le Cameroun*. Paris, L'Harmattan, 1989.

Goheen, M. *Men Own the Fields, Women Own the Crops: Gender and Power in the Cameroon Grassfields*. Madison, WI, University of Wisconsin Press, 1996.

Gros, J.-G. *Cameroon: Politics and Society in Critical Perspective*. Lanham, MD, University Press of America, 2003.

Hugon, P. *Analyse du sous-développement en Afrique noire: L'example de l'économie du Cameroun*. Paris, Presses Universitaires de France, 1968.

Ignatowski, C. *Journey of Song: Public Life and Morality in Cameroon*. Bloomington, IN, Indiana University Press, 2006.

Joseph, R. A. *Radical Nationalism in Cameroon*. London, Oxford University Press, 1977.

Kengne-Pokam, E. *La France et les Etats-Unis au Cameroun: le processus démocratique national en question*. Paris, L'Harmattan, 2009.

Manga, E. J. *The African Economic Dilemma: The Case of Cameroon*. Lanham, MD, University Press of America, 1998.

Mbaku, J. M., and Takougang, J. (Eds). *The Leadership Challenge in Africa: Cameroon Under Paul Biya*. Trenton, NJ, Africa World Press, 2004.

Mehler, A. *Kamerun in der Ära Biya: Bedingungen, erste Schritte und Blockaden einer demokratischen Transition*. Hamburg, Institut für Afrika-Kunde, 1993. (Hamburger Beiträge zur Afrika-Kunde; 42).

Ndongko, W. A., and ViveKananda, F. *Economic Development of Cameroon*. Stockholm, Bethany Books, 1990.

Ngoh, V. J. *Cameroon 1884–1985: A Hundred Years of History*. Yaoundé, Imprimerie Nationale, 1988.

Southern Cameroons 1922–1961: A Constitutional History. Hampshire, Ashgate Publishing Ltd, 2001.

Owona, A. *La naissance du cameroun 1884-1914*. Paris, L'Harmattan, 2003.

Pingeaud, F. *Au Cameroun de Paul Biya*. Paris, Editions Karthala, 2011.

Previtali, S. *Le Cameroun par les ponts et par les routes*. Paris, Editions Karthala, 1988.

Regis, H. *Fulbe Voices: Marriage, Islam, and Medicine in Northern Cameroon*. Boulder, CO, Westview Press, 2002.

Sindjoun, L. *Comment Peut-On Etre Opposant au Cameroun?: Politique Parlementaire et Politique Autoritaire*. Dakar, Council for the Development of Social Science Research in Africa, 2005.

Stoecker, H. (Ed.). *German Imperialism in Africa*. London, Hurst Humanities, 1986.

Takougang, J., and Krieger, M. H. *African State and Society in the 1990s: Cameroon's Political Crossroads*. Boulder, CO, Westview Press, 1998.

Tamuedjon, J-C. *La colonisation et le Cameroun contemporain: Cinquante ans après l'indépendance et la réunification*. Paris, L'Harmattan, 2012.

Weiss, L. T. *Migrants nigérians, la diaspora dans le sud-ouest du Cameroun*. Paris, L'Harmattan, 1998.

CAPE VERDE

Physical and Social Geography

RENÉ PÉLISSIER

The island Republic of Cape Verde, comprising 10 islands, of which nine are inhabited, and five islets, lies in the Atlantic Ocean, about 500 km west of Dakar, Senegal. The archipelago comprises the windward islands of Santo Antão (754 sq km), São Vicente (228 sq km), Santa Luzia (34 sq km), São Nicolau (342 sq km), Boavista (622 sq km) and Sal (215 sq km) to the north, while to the south lie the leeward islands of Maio (267 sq km), Santiago (992 sq km), Fogo (477 sq km) and Brava (65 sq km).

The total area is 4,033 sq km (1,557 sq miles) and the administrative capital is Praia (population of 131,719 in 2010) on Santiago island. The other main centre of population is Mindelo (São Vicente), which is the principal port and, with Praia, the economic centre of the archipelago. The 2010 census recorded a total population of 491,875 (122.0 inhabitants per sq km). Santiago is the most populous of the inhabited islands, with an estimated population of 273,919 in 2010, followed by São Vicente (76,107), Santo Antão (43,915) and Fogo (37,051). Santa Luzia has no permanent inhabitants.

Except for the low-lying islands of Sal, Boavista and Maio, the archipelago is mountainous, craggy and deeply indented by erosion and volcanic activity. The highest point is Mt Fogo (2,829 m), an active volcano. Located in the semi-arid belt, the islands have an anaemic hydrography, and suffer from chronic shortages of rainfall, which, combined with high temperatures (yearly average 22°C–26°C at Praia), cause intense periodic droughts. These droughts have an economically devastating effect on the islands and necessitate heavy dependence on international food aid, which provides most of Cape Verde's food requirements. A desalination plant on São Vicente serves the needs of Mindelo, which is otherwise without drinkable water.

Ethnically, about 71% of the inhabitants are of mixed descent, except on Santiago, where the majority is of pure African stock. Whites represent about 1% of the population. The two official languages are Portuguese and Crioulo, a creole Portuguese, which is influenced by African vocabulary, syntax and pronunciation. Illiteracy is still widespread. In 2011 the average life expectancy at birth was 69.1 years for men and 76.7 years for women.

Since independence, a significant number of islanders have emigrated, principally to the USA, the Netherlands, Italy and Portugal, where Cape Verdeans have replaced Portuguese migrants to other countries of the European Union. At least 700,000 Cape Verdeans live outside the country, and their remittances provide an important source of development capital.

Recent History

EDWARD GEORGE

The Cape Verde islands were colonized by Portugal in the 15th century. In the movement for independence from Portuguese rule during the 1950s, Cape Verde aligned itself with the mainland territory of Portuguese Guinea (now Guinea-Bissau) in a unified nationalist movement, the Partido Africano da Independência do Guiné e Cabo Verde (PAIGC). At Guinea-Bissau's independence in September 1974, however, the PAIGC leadership in Cape Verde decided to pursue its claims separately, rather than to seek an immediate federation with Guinea-Bissau. In December the Portuguese Government and representatives of the islands' PAIGC formed a transitional administration. Elections to the Assembleia Nacional Popular (ANP—National People's Assembly) took place in June 1975, with independence, as the Republic of Cape Verde, following on 5 July.

Aristides Pereira, the Secretary-General of the PAIGC, became the country's first President. Pedro Pires was appointed Prime Minister. In 1980 the PAIGC was constitutionally established as the sole legal party, and in November of that year prospects of unification with Guinea-Bissau receded when Luis Cabral, the President of Guinea-Bissau (and himself a Cape Verdean), was removed in a coup. In 1981 the Cape Verdean branch of the PAIGC renamed itself the Partido Africano da Independência de Cabo Verde (PAICV). Although Cape Verde was until September 1990 a one-party state, government policies were generally pragmatic and sensitive. In the mid-1980s non-PAICV members began to take an increasingly prominent role in public and political life. Central control of the economy was eased, and in 1989 the Government introduced legislation to encourage Cape Verdeans abroad to become involved in the process of development.

DEMOCRATIC CHANGE

Moves towards a relaxation of the PAICV's political monopoly began to emerge in early 1990, as Cape Verde became affected by political changes in West Africa and Eastern Europe. In February the PAICV announced the convening of an emergency congress to discuss the possible abolition of the constitutional provision that guaranteed its political monopoly. In April a newly formed opposition group, the Movimento para a Democracia (MpD), demanded the immediate introduction of a multi-party system. In the same month Pereira announced that the next presidential election, scheduled for December 1990, would be held, for the first time, on the basis of universal adult suffrage.

In June 1990 the MpD's co-ordinator, Carlos Veiga, stated that the movement was prepared to negotiate with the PAICV for a transition to political plurality. In July Pereira announced that legislative elections would be held on a multi-party basis before the end of the year, and in September the ANP approved a constitutional amendment abolishing the PAICV's monopoly of power. The MpD duly obtained registration and held its first congress in Praia in November, at which Veiga was elected party Chairman. The MpD subsequently declared its support for the candidacy of António Manuel Mascarenhas Gomes Monteiro, a former Supreme Court judge, in the forthcoming presidential election.

The legislative elections held in January 1991 resulted in a clear victory for the MpD, which secured 56 of the 79 seats in the ANP. The PAICV held the remaining 23 seats. In the same month Veiga was sworn in as Prime Minister at the head of an interim Government, pending the result of the presidential election in February. This resulted in a decisive victory for Mascarenhas against Pereira, with the former securing 73.5%

of the votes cast. Mascarenhas took office in March, and a new Government was formed in April.

THE SECOND REPUBLIC

A new Constitution, enshrining the democratic basis of the 'Second Republic', took effect in September 1992, when a new national flag and emblem were adopted. At an extraordinary convention of the MpD in February 1994, increasing internal dissent prompted about 15 senior members of the party, led by Dr Eurico Correia Monteiro, to leave the MpD and form a new opposition group, the Partido da Convergência Democrática (PCD).

At legislative elections held in December 1995 the MpD secured 50 seats in a smaller Assembleia Nacional (AN—as the ANP had been renamed), reduced from 79 seats to 72 under legislation approved in 1994. The PAICV gained 21 seats and the PCD won the remaining seat. At the presidential election held in February 1996, Mascarenhas was re-elected unopposed.

In March 1999 Veiga confirmed speculation that he would not seek re-election as the Chairman of the MpD at the next party convention. António Gualberto do Rosário, the Deputy Prime Minister, and the Mayor of Praia, Jacinto Santos, subsequently announced their candidacies for the MpD chairmanship, and thus the premiership. The contest seriously weakened the ruling party and was followed by substantial losses in municipal elections held in February 2000. Following the resignation of Pedro Pires, who announced his candidacy for the presidential election, the PAICV elected José Maria Pereira Neves as its new President in June. At the MpD convention in July do Rosário was elected party Chairman. Meanwhile, Veiga announced his resignation from the premiership and declared his intention to contest the forthcoming presidential election. Do Rosário succeeded him as Prime Minister.

The Return of the PAICV

At legislative elections, held on 14 January 2001, the PAICV won an absolute majority of 40 seats (and 49.5% of the vote) against 30 seats (40.5%) for the MpD. A new political force, the Aliança Democrática para a Mudança, formed in October 2000 by the PCD, the Partido de Trabalho e Solidariedade and the União Caboverdiana Independente e Democrática (UCID), obtained the remaining two seats.

Shortly afterwards Neves was appointed Prime Minister. His Government, inaugurated in February 2001, stated that its priority would be the reduction of unemployment and the rehabilitation of public finances. A respected economist, Carlos Augusto Duarte de Burgo, was appointed as Minister of Finance and Planning. The first round of the presidential election, held on 11 February, was inconclusive and a second round, in which Pires narrowly defeated Veiga, securing 50.0% of votes cast, was held on 25 February. Official results eventually confirmed that Pires had defeated Veiga by a margin of only 17 votes. Appeals against the results by Veiga (citing voting irregularities) were rejected by the Supreme Court in March, which confirmed Pires as the new President.

The defeat of the MpD prompted do Rosário to resign from the party leadership in August 2001. Agostinho Lopes, one of the MpD's founding members, was elected Chairman in December. Following Lopes' appointment, the party adopted a more confrontational stance towards the Government. It established a newspaper, *Expresso das Ilhas*, to counter the perceived dominance of the media by the PAICV, and successfully opposed tax changes in the 2002 budget, which were subsequently declared unconstitutional by the Supreme Court. This prompted the Government, which did not have the parliamentary two-thirds' majority required for constitutional amendments, to propose a national consensus, a *pacto de regime*, on important political and economic themes. However, the MpD continued to obstruct the passage of legislation.

Prime Minister Neves reorganized his cabinet in April 2004. Three ministries and four secretariats of state were abolished and replaced with a new structure of 13 ministries and four secretariats of state. (In September this was changed to 14 ministries and three secretariats of state, following the creation of the Ministry of Social Communication.) In December 2005 Pires announced that he would stand for re-election, while the MpD, as expected, nominated Veiga as its official candidate. Concerns about unemployment and the recent crime wave on Santiago island dominated the election campaign, with little distinction between the two main parties' platforms.

On 6 February 2006 the Comissão Nacional de Eleições (CNE—National Elections Commission) announced that the PAICV had won a convincing victory in the legislative elections, securing 52.3% of the national vote and winning 41 out of 72 seats in the AN. The MpD received 44.0% of the vote and won 29 seats, with the remaining two seats taken by the UCID. Later that month Pires was re-elected to the presidency after securing 51.0% of the votes cast, winning by a narrow majority of 3,342 votes; he secured an estimated two-thirds of the diasporan vote. The MpD complained of electoral fraud; however, their challenges were dismissed, prompting the resignation of Lopes as Chairman. On 10 September Jorge Santos was elected as the new MpD leader, and pledged to modernize the party. Santos was a founding member of the MpD and a former mayor of Ribeira Grande (Santiago) who had narrowly been defeated by Lopes for the party leadership in 2005.

Domestic Developments

In February 2007 the PAICV and the MpD established a 14-member commission (comprising seven deputies from each party) charged with reaching consensus on issues such as revisions to the Constitution and the creation of a parliamentary auditing commission that would require a two-thirds' majority in the AN to become law. The remit of the cross-party commission included agreeing changes to the electoral code, in particular regarding the membership and structure of the CNE. The AN finally approved the new electoral code in June. The key changes included strengthening the CNE's powers and changing its membership to make it less partisan; creating single electoral regions for each island, with the exception of Santiago (which was split into two); and holding a new electoral census in the last quarter of 2007 to replace the voter register compiled in 1995. However, disagreement between the PAICV and MpD over the new membership of the CNE delayed its restructuring until November and the start of the electoral census until December. This forced the Government to seek the MpD's approval to extend the registration deadline, which prompted the resignation of the Minister of Internal Administration, Júlio Lopes Correia, in protest. Nevertheless, the registration of voters was completed by March 2008, with a total of 260,000 voters registered.

Meanwhile, in December 2007 Neves appointed Lívio Lopes, the PAICV deputy leader, as the new Minister of Internal Administration. In January 2008 Correia was appointed First Vice-President of the AN, replacing Mário Matos, the PAICV Secretary-General, who resigned owing to ill health. Matos was replaced as PAICV Secretary-General by the Minister of State and of Health, Basílio Mosso Ramos.

In June 2008 Neves announced a major reorganization of the Government. The new cabinet contained eight women, the most senior of whom was the new Minister of the Economy, Growth and Competitiveness, Fátima Fialho. Following the cabinet's inauguration on 30 June, Neves pledged to resolve the power crisis affecting the archipelago, to introduce additional measures to reduce the tax burden and increase household incomes, and tougher action to combat crime.

Cape Verde's third largest party, the UCID, split into two factions following a mutiny in July 2008 by the party's Santiago wing under the leadership of Osvaldino Andrade. The following month the Santiago wing held a rebel congress, electing Mário Moniz as President. However, the congress was dismissed as illegal by the UCID leader, António Monteiro, and both factions launched legal challenges with the Supreme Court in an effort to declare their rivals illegal.

In November 2008 the Government was embroiled in a corruption scandal involving a Portuguese bank, Banco Português de Negócios (BPN), and its offshore subsidiary in Cape Verde, Banco Insular de Cabo Verde (BICV). BPN was nationalized by the Portuguese Government after amassing losses of €700m. Of this amount, €320m. was sustained by BICV, which was used by BPN as a 'virtual branch' for its riskiest lending, transferring over €300m. to Brazilian bank accounts in 2004–07. Responding to the scandal, the MpD leader, Jorge Santos, accused the Government of opening up Cape Verde to money-laundering and called on Neves to reveal his ties with the banks. Denying any involvement in the scandal, in December Neves comfortably won a vote of confidence in his Government. However, the Government's reputation was severely damaged, given its strong promotion of Cape Verde's 'offshore' banking sector.

In January 2009 the AN created a bipartisan commission to draw up proposals for revising the Constitution. Both the PAICV and MpD agreed to expand the Supreme Court from five to seven judges, but differed on other proposed changes. The commission's recommendations were due to be debated by the AN in July, but disagreements between its PAICV and MpD members resulted in deadlock on several key issues.

The MpD announced in early 2009 that its leadership election would take place on 11 October, to be followed by the party congress. Santos, was expected to face a strong challenge for the leadership from former Prime Minister Veiga. However, in September Santos announced that he would not seek re-election, citing his wish to avoid provoking an internal split in the party, and gave his backing to Veiga to assume his role. Veiga was duly elected as party leader on 12 October. During the MpD congress on 30 October–1 November Santos and Correia e Silva were elected as the party's two deputy leaders and Agostinho Lopes as Secretary-General. Later in November the PAICV held its party congress in Praia, re-electing José Maria Neves as party leader unopposed.

In late September 2009 an outbreak of dengue fever spread across the archipelago, causing a state of emergency. The outbreak was centred on the most populous island, Santiago, but also affected the neighbouring islands of Fogo, Maio and Brava, and was declared an epidemic by the Government on 21 October. The epidemic peaked at 1,100 cases per day in early November, but by mid-December was under control, following assistance from the World Health Organization. In total there were 21,000 recorded cases of dengue, of which 174 resulted in haemorrhagic fever. The Government was heavily criticized for its slow response to the outbreak, which it originally believed was swine flu, and several Western European governments temporarily imposed travel warnings on Cape Verde, affecting tourism arrivals.

On 24 November 2009, following emergency talks to break the deadlock, the leaders of the PAICV and MpD, Neves and Veiga, signed a draft amendment to the Constitution to be presented to the AN for ratification. Amendments included the creation of a new Supreme Court, authorization for the police to carry out night raids on properties linked to organized crime, authorization for Cape Verdean citizens to be extradited for international crimes, and recognition of the International Criminal Court. However, there was no agreement on the divisive issue of whether Crioulo should be made the country's second official language. The amendments to the Constitution were ratified by the AN on 9 February 2010.

Neves carried out a government reorganization in February 2010, abolishing the Ministry of Economy, Growth and Competitiveness and moving its Minister, Fátima Fialho, to the Ministry of Tourism, Industry and Energy. Neves also created a new Minister for Cape Verdeans Abroad, appointing the former Minister of Youth and Sports, Dr Sidónio Fontes Lima Monteiro, to the role. The Ministers of Culture, Manuel Monteiro da Veiga, and of Education, Vera Duarte, left the Government, and a new Ministry of Higher Education, Science and Culture was created from their departments and placed under Fernanda Marques. Overall, there was little change to the Government's main policy team, prompting criticisms from the opposition that the entire exercise had been designed to improve the PAICV's chances ahead of legislative elections due in early 2011.

Opinion polls in August and September 2010 indicated that the PAICV was well ahead of the MpD and would win re-election if a snap general election was held. However, over one-third of those polled were undecided or did not intend to vote, indicating that the outcome was still uncertain. Voter registration officially ended on 3 December, with a total of 309,617 voters on the electoral roll, including 37,645 from the diaspora. Shortly afterwards President Pires announced that the legislative elections would be delayed by one month until February 2011, with the presidential election to follow in August. Pires blamed the delay on logistical difficulties with compiling the new voter register.

The 2011 Elections

The legislative elections took place on 6 February 2011, with voting in 13 constituencies—reduced from 20 in previous elections—comprising 10 in the archipelago and three diaspora seats in the Americas, Europe and the rest of the world. As had been expected, the PAICV won convincingly, securing 52.7% of the national vote and 38 seats in the AN. In contrast, the MpD secured 42.3% of the vote and 32 seats, three more than in the 2006 election but not enough to deny the PAICV its second successive parliamentary majority. Among the other three parties contesting the election, only the UCID managed to hold onto its two parliamentary seats, with the others failing to win a single seat.

The PAICV's victory, on an impressive turn-out of 76% of the electorate, was viewed as a strong endorsement of the leadership of Prime Minister Neves, who was immediately invited by Pires to form a new cabinet. This was duly announced in March 2011 and involved a substantial restructuring of government ministries. A new Ministry of Youth, Employment and Human Resources Development was created under the previous Minister of Youth, Janira Hopffer Almada Monteiro, with a remit to tackle the high level of youth unemployment. In addition, the Ministries of Labour, Transport and Telecommunications were abolished and their responsibilities incorporated into other ministries. The respected Minister of Finance and Planning, Cristina Duarte, retained her post, while José Brito was replaced as Minister of Foreign Affairs by Jorge Borges and Marisa Helena do Nascimento Morais was moved from the Ministry of Justice to that of Internal Administration.

In June 2011 President Pires announced that the presidential election would take place on 7 August, at which point he would stand down after having served the two consecutive terms permitted under the Constitution. The election was expected to be a contest between Jorge Carlos Fonseca, a former Minister of Foreign Affairs supported by the MpD, and Manuel Inocêncio Sousa, the former Minister of Infrastructure backed by the PAICV. Two independent candidates, the former Speaker of the AN, Aristides Lima, and Joaquim Monteiro, a veteran of the liberation war, also registered to stand in the election, although neither was expected to mount a serious challenge.

The presidential election duly took place on 7 August 2011: Fonseca won 37.8% of the total votes cast, while Sousa took 32.5% and Lima 27.8%. As no candidate won more than 50% of the votes, a run-off ballot was held on 21 August at which Fonseca secured 54.2% of votes cast. Turn-out was poor, averaging 46% in both rounds, partly owing to heavy rains during voting. Fonseca was inaugurated as President on 7 September, becoming the first non-PAICV head of state in the country's history. In October Pires was awarded the Mo Ibrahim Prize for Achievement in African Leadership, reflecting his contribution to the mediation of Côte d'Ivoire's political crisis.

In June 2012 campaigning began for local elections in Cape Verde's 22 municipalities. Voting took place on 1 July, and the MpD emerged as the clear victor, increasing the number of municipalities under its control from 12 to 13, while the PAICV saw its total decrease from 10 to eight constituencies. The municipality of Sal was won by an independent, Jorge Figueiredo, supported by the MpD. The ruling party's poor performance in the presidential and local elections was regarded by many analysts as having damaged Prime Minister Neves' reputation.

EXTERNAL AFFAIRS

The MpD Government successfully sought to expand Cape Verde's range of international contacts, with special emphasis on potential new sources of development aid, including Israel, Cuba, the People's Republic of China and states of the Persian (Arabian) Gulf. However, Cape Verde has also maintained particularly good relations with the former colonial power,

Portugal, and countries with large Cape Verdean expatriate communities, such as Luxembourg and the Netherlands. In 2009 the Cape Verdean diaspora was estimated at 518,000, compared with a domestic population of 491,000. Ties have been developed with the neighbouring autonomous regions of the Canary Islands (Spain), the Azores (Portugal) and Madeira (Portugal), with official visits resulting in the signing of protocols aimed at promoting co-operation. In February 2003 Portugal announced its support for Cape Verde's plan to seek 'special status' within the European Union (EU), and was followed by Spain and Luxembourg. During a visit to Portugal in May 2005, Prime Minister Neves announced that Cape Verde's long-term aim was to secure full EU membership, but this was likely to take many years. In February 2007 officials from the Cape Verdean and Portuguese Governments met with the European Commission and agreed to draw up an action plan for attaining 'special status'. Following prolonged negotiations, in November 2007 the EU agreed to grant Cape Verde special partnership status, under which the two would co-operate in seven key areas, including governance, security, regional integration and poverty reduction. In recent years the Government has strengthened co-operation with the EU on preventing illegal immigrants, drugs and criminal funds flowing into the EU via Cape Verde, and in August 2006 the EU agreed to extend operations under the auspices of the European Agency for the Management of Operational Co-operation at the External Borders of the European Union to the archipelago. In June 2008 Cape Verde and the EU signed a mobility partnership convention, covering the period 2009–11, aimed at facilitating circular migration to the EU and preventing illegal immigration.

Cape Verde has maintained good relations with the USA, where 400,000 expatriate Cape Verdeans live. In August 2009 the US Secretary of State, Hillary Clinton, visited Cape Verde for talks with Prime Minister Neves, re-emphasizing the archipelago's strategic importance to the USA given its proximity to the hydrocarbon deposits in the Gulf of Guinea and its location at the nexus of trade routes between Africa, Europe and the Americas. Clinton revisited Cape Verde in January 2012. Cape Verde has also maintained historically close relations with Brazil, and with other lusophone countries, in particular Angola. In 2003 the Cape Verdean and Angolan Governments announced that they had formed a 'strategic partnership'. In recent years Cape Verde has sought to strengthen bilateral ties with China, which has become an increasingly important trade partner and source of funding. The Minister of Foreign Affairs, Co-operation and Communities, Víctor Manuel Barbosa Borges, visited China in May 2007 to discuss Cape Verde's suitability for hosting one of six special economic zones, which China planned to establish in Africa. In August 2011 the Chinese Vice-Minister of Commerce, Jiang Yaoping, visited Cape Verde, signing agreements on trade, education, energy, water and health, and pledging US $1.7m. in aid to rehabilitate the main hospital in Praia.

Cape Verde maintains close relations with Portugal's other former African colonies, Guinea-Bissau, Mozambique and São Tomé and Príncipe, known collectively, with Cape Verde and Angola, as the Países Africanos de Língua Oficial Portuguesa (PALOP). In July 1996 the Comunidade dos Países de Língua Portuguesa (CPLP), comprising the five PALOP countries together with Portugal and Brazil, was formed with the intention of benefiting each member state through joint co-operation on technical, cultural and social matters. In June 2010 the President of Equatorial Guinea, Gen. Teodoro Obiang Nguema Mbasogo, made a two-day visit to Cape Verde to discuss bilateral ties, provoking controversy because of his country's poor human rights record. However, the Cape Verdean President, Pedro Pires, gave strong endorsement to Equatorial Guinea's bid to join the CPLP, and signed a series of technical co-operation agreements. In December 1996 Cape Verde also became a full member of the Sommet Francophone, a commonwealth comprising the world's French-speaking countries, having been an observer at its annual meetings since 1977. Cape Verde is a member of the African Union (formerly the Organization of African Unity), the Economic Community of West African States, the African Development Bank and the UN, and was a signatory to the Lomé Conventions, which promoted co-operation between the EU and African, Caribbean and Pacific countries. In October 2002 Cape Verde ratified the successor to the Lomé Conventions, the Cotonou Agreement.

In May 2006 Cape Verde hosted the first North Atlantic Treaty Organization (NATO) military exercise in Africa, known as Steadfast Jaguar 2006, which was designed as the first full test of the NATO Response Force. Much of the equipment used in the exercise was subsequently transferred to the Cape Verdean military. Since 2007 Cape Verde has signed accords with Portugal, Spain and the United Kingdom to carry out joint naval exercises and patrols in Cape Verde's maritime waters, with a focus on intercepting drugs-traffickers and illegal migrant flows. In May 2010 the US Government gave US $3m. to Cape Verde to purchase new maritime surveillance equipment used in interdicting drugs-trafficking operations.

Economy

EDWARD GEORGE

INTRODUCTION

According to the World Bank, Cape Verde's estimated gross national income (GNI) was US $1,846m. in 2011, equivalent to about $4,100 per head (or $3,560 per head on an international purchasing-power parity basis). Cape Verde's GNI per head is therefore the second highest of the former Portuguese African colonies after Angola. Due to far higher social and macroeconomic indicators than Angola, however, Cape Verde is the only lusophone African nation to be classified by the World Bank as a medium developed country (MDC), graduating from least developed country (LDC) status in 2008. Heavy government investment in social sectors has reduced the level of poverty. According to a survey of household incomes in 2007, the percentage of the population living below the poverty line (defined as $1.69 per day) fell from 36.7% in 2002 to 26.6% in 2007. The survey estimated that gross domestic product (GDP) per head grew by 26.9% in 2002–07. However, during the same period the percentage of poor households in rural areas rose from 63% to 72%, whereas in urban areas it fell from 37% to 28%. In 2009 unemployment was estimated to affect 13.1% of the labour force, although unemployment rates vary enormously between regions, from as low as 6.7% on Santiago and 10% on Sal to as high as 17% in the capital, Praia, and 19.2% on the western island of São Vicente. Moreover, youth unemployment is unusually high, at an estimated 30.6% in 2009. In October 2011 the central bank estimated that unemployment had decreased to 9%.

Despite the country's physical disadvantages, the economy has grown fairly steadily since independence in 1975, benefiting from the considerable provision of official aid on very favourable terms, economic reforms since the 1990s, and the substantial remittances of Cape Verdean émigrés, whose number was estimated at 518,000 in 2009, compared with a domestic population of around 500,000. According to the World Bank, officially recorded remittances from émigrés totalled US $152m. in 2011, equivalent to 9.9% of GDP, mostly from Portugal, France, the USA and the Netherlands. Remittances had declined to $133m. in 2010, reflecting the economic downturn in the euro zone. In 2001–10 Cape Verde's GDP increased, in real terms, at an average annual rate of 6.1%, compared with 6.8% in 1991–2000 and 1.3% in 1983–92. In comparison, the population increased by an average of 1.1% per year in 2000–10. According to the World Bank, real GDP growth peaked at 10.1% in 2006, driven by rising private investment, exports of goods and services, and private consumption. Real GDP growth moderated to an estimated 8.6% in 2007, 6.2% in 2008 and 3.7% in 2009, owing to the impact of the global economic downturn, but recovered to an estimated 5.2% in 2010 and 5.0% in 2011, buoyed by a rise in tourist arrivals and remittance inflows. According to the UN Conference on Trade and Development, foreign direct investment (FDI) reached $209m. in 2008, accounting for 12.3% of GDP, before decreasing to $93m. in 2011. The annual rate of inflation has declined in recent years from an average annual rate of 6% in 1991–2000 to 2.4% in 2001–10. After contracting in 2004–05, inflation rose to a peak of 6.8% in 2008, owing to a series of poor harvests and sharp increases in international cereal and oil prices, before decreasing to 1.0% in 2009. Inflation rose to 2.1% in 2010 and 4.5% in 2011 as recovering international commodity markets drove up the price of food and fuel imports. According to official data, inflation moderated to an average of 3.5% during the first five months of 2012 due to lower food and telecommunications prices.

The Government has improved its fiscal situation through reforms to tax collection and public expenditure management. In 2004 the authorities introduced value-added tax (VAT) and reformed the tariff system. Higher VAT and import duty revenues helped offset a fall in grants, and gradually reduced the fiscal deficit from 5.7% of GDP in 2006 to an estimated 1.4% in 2008. However, owing to fiscal stimulus measures implemented by the Government and a decrease in tourism revenues, the fiscal deficit rose to an estimated 6.3% of GDP in 2009 and 10.6% in 2010, before moderating to 8.9% in 2011. In that year the current account deficit (including official transfers) stood at an estimated 12.5% of GDP. At the end of December 2011 gross international reserves totalled US $339m., well below the peak of $398m. achieved at the end of 2009.

TRANSPORT AND COMMUNICATIONS

Cape Verde is strategically located between Africa, Europe and the Americas. International maritime and air transport, including transshipment, were identified as an important source of foreign exchange by both the Partido Africano da Independência de Cabo Verde (PAICV) and the Movimento para a Democracia (MpD) administrations. Cape Verde has three international ports at Porto Grande (São Vicente), Praia (Santiago) and Palmeira (Sal), as well as smaller commercial ports at Porto Novo (Santo Antão), Tarrafal (São Nicolau), Cavaleiros (Fogo), Porto Inglês (Maio), Furna (Brava) and Sal Rei (Boavista). According to the port operator, Empresa Nacional de Administração dos Portos (ENAPOR), Cape Verde's nine commercial ports were visited by a total of 5,711 ships in 2010, 1.1% higher than in 2009, and together handled 1.8m metric tons of merchandise, slightly lower than in the previous year.

Strong growth in trade is being accompanied by large-scale investment to upgrade existing port facilities. New port facilities were opened on Maio and Boavista in 1997, on Fogo in 1999, and on Brava in 2000. In June 2005 the US Millennium Challenge Account (MCA) agreed to fund a US $53m. project to further modernize and expand the port of Praia. In August 2007 the first phase of work began, involving reconstruction of the main breakwater. A second phase started in March 2008, involving the construction of a freight terminal and the lengthening of the dock's quayside; this was completed in October 2010. In September 2007 the Japanese Government pledged €2m. for a project to expand Mindelo's fishing port with the aim of increasing exports of frozen fish to the European Union (EU). In 2008 ENAPOR started major works on expanding and modernizing the ports of Praia, Palmeira, Sal Rei and Porto Novo. In February 2010 the Government contracted DRHT of Portugal and Empreitel Figueiredo of Cape Verde to modernize the port at Porto Novo (Santo Antão). Work on the project, which had an estimated cost of $31m., was completed in late 2011. In March 2010 ENAPOR announced that the Government would invest €300m. in the next phase of modernizing the archipelago's port facilities in 2010–15. Meanwhile, work was completed on a new maritime station at Vale dos Cavaleiros (Fogo), and a new fishing dock and customs building was under construction. In late 2010 expansion work commenced at the port of Sal Rei, including the construction of a new container port, which was due for completion by the end of 2012. The Government has repeatedly postponed plans to privatize ENAPOR; however, the new administration formed after the legislative elections of February 2011 pledged to complete the process by the end of 2012. As part of its liberalization plans, the Government intended to open up the archipelago's port operations to private companies, starting with the three largest ports.

In 1997 investors from the USA, Saudi Arabia and Pakistan founded an international ship registration agency in Mindelo, establishing the Cape Verdean flag as a 'flag of convenience'. The state ferry company, Arca Verde, was liquidated in 2003, and a maritime transport company, Transnacional, has subsequently operated a passenger ferry service between the islands of Santiago, Maio, Boavista, Fogo and Brava. In 2008 a Canadian company, Polar Star, also started providing inter-island passenger ferry services. In May 2009 a new company, Cabo Verde Fast Ferry, was launched to provide ferry services from Brava to other islands in the archipelago. The first services started in December 2010.

There are 2,250 km of roads in Cape Verde, of which 1,750 km are paved (mostly with cobblestones). In June 2003 the Government established a US $1.1m. National Road Fund, to be administered by the Instituto das Estradas (Road Institute), to build, rehabilitate and maintain the archipelago's road network. In support of this fund, in 2008 the Government introduced a new road tax, which it hoped would raise 300m. escudos per year for national road maintenance. The remote island of Santo Antão received the Government's special attention because of its potential as an ecotourism resort, and in July 2003 Prime Minister Neves laid the first stone of the Paul–Janela road, an internationally funded project to link the communities of Paul and Porto Novo on the island. In 2005 the Government launched a five-year programme, supported with $46m. in funding from the MCA, to upgrade and expand the road and bridge network in Santiago and Santo Antão. Major projects include the €20m. São Domingos–Assomada road and the €25m. ring road project on Santiago island, both of which were financed by Portugal. In March 2009 work was completed on the 22-km Porto Novo–Janela road on Santo Antão, which was funded by the EU, Luxembourg and Italy. In June the new Orgãos–Pedra Badejo road was inaugurated on Santiago island, which was rehabilitated with $3m. of funding from the MCA; the next phase of the project was to involve rehabilitation of the Assomada–Rincão and Cruz Grande–Calhetona roads. In July work started on Fogo's 80-km ring road, linking the island's three municipalities. The $36.1m. project was 40% funded by the Government and 60% by the Arab Bank for Economic Development of Africa and the Saudi Fund for Development.

The Government has pledged to improve air transport infrastructure on the islands, with the apparent objective of turning Cape Verde into a regional transport hub. The Amílcar Cabral international airport on Sal has a throughput capacity of 1m. passengers per year (it currently handles more than 300,000 passengers per year) and can accommodate aircraft of up to 50 metric tons. The domestic and international flights terminals have been further improved since 1998, and in May 2004 a new air traffic control system was inaugurated, giving Cape Verde the most sophisticated system currently in operation in Africa. The airport's facilities have been used as a strategic refuelling point, chiefly by South African Airways and Aeroflot (Russia), as well as a number of cargo transportation airlines, which account for around 30% of all landings.

A new international airport in Praia, designed to accommodate large aircraft, became operational in November 2005. In 2000 the airport on São Vicente was also upgraded, and in June 2005 work began on an additional 1.7-km runway for the airport, as well as on a new international airport on Boavista, at a cost of US $30m., which became operational in October 2007. In May 2008 expansion work on Maio's existing aerodrome was completed, and there are plans to build an international airport on the island. In December 2009 a fourth international airport on São Vicente, located at São Pedro, 8 km from the capital, Mindelo, started operations. Work also started on expanding the aerodrome at São Filipe (Fogo), extending its runway and upgrading its passenger terminal. There are also plans to build new international airports on Brava, in the south-west, and on Santo Antão, close to the capital, Porto Novo, to replace the aerodrome at Ponta do Sol that closed in 1999. In the first nine months of 2011 Cape Verde's airports handled 1.3m. passengers, an increase of 10.3% compared with the same period in the previous year, boosted by a 16.7% surge in international traffic.

The national airline, Transportes Aéreos de Cabo Verde (TACV), operates a regular inter-island service as well as flights to most West African airports, major European cities, Brazil and the USA. In December 2006 the company came under private management while a rescue plan was drawn up prior to its formal privatization. However, the Government subsequently announced that the privatization would be delayed indefinitely to give TACV more time to restructure its operations and reschedule its substantial debts. In April 2009 the company declared 'technical insolvency', owing to the accumulation of losses, and urged the Government to increase assistance to the airline while it underwent restructuring. In December the airport authority, Empresa Nacional de Aeroportos e Segurança AEREA (ASA), temporarily blocked TACV flights from leaving Praia International Airport until TACV agreed a restructuring deal for 1,300m. escudos of debt owed to ASA. The Minister of Finance and Planning, Cristina Duarte, announced in June 2011 that TACV's privatization would be delayed until at least 2012 while the company completed its restructuring and a strategic partner was sought by the Government. In June 2012 the Government signed an 'open skies' agreement with the United Arab Emirates (UAE), which could lead to direct flights between Cape Verde and Dubai and Abu Dhabi.

In 1995 40% of the state telecommunications company, Cabo Verde Telecom (CVT), was sold to Portugal Telecom International for US $20m., and a further 50% of CVT was divested in 1997–98. The network has expanded from 21,500 main lines in use in 1995 to 74,500 in 2011, yielding the third highest density of fixed telephone lines in sub-Saharan Africa, at 14.9 per 100 inhabitants, after Mauritius and Seychelles. In 2007 the Government formally ended CVT's monopoly on fixed-line services. In April 2009 CVT and Portugal Telecom launched a $50m. project to install a new undersea cable linking Cape Verde to the West African Cable System from 2011. CVT also introduced a mobile cellular telephone network, Telemóvel, which in September 2007 had an estimated 134,000 subscribers. In December a second mobile telephone operator, T+, launched its services in Praia. The company had extended its services across the entire country by the end of 2008. In March 2010 the national telecoms regulator, the Agência Nacional das Comunicações (ANAC), launched a tender for 3G and 4G networks. According to the International Telecommunication Union, in 2010 there were an estimated 396,400 mobile phone users in Cape Verde (the equivalent of over three-quarters of the population), 150,000 internet users and 16,700 broadband subscriptions.

The state-owned radio and television company, Rádio Televisão de Cabo Verde (RTC), is the only national television station, although a licence has been granted to a private channel. In June 2003 a group of senior French media experts arrived in Praia to modernize Cape Verde's national television network, which currently reaches only 65% of the population. In September 2006 the Government launched a tender for new licences for independent television stations. In May 2005 CVT and the Chinese Xiamen Xinouli secured an international tender to operate the first cable television network in Cape Verde. CVT launched its cable television service, ZAP TV, in June 2006, and was followed by CVXTV, a subsidiary of Xiamen Xinouli, which launched a wireless television service in April 2007. According to ANAC, there were 7,000 cable television subscribers by the end of 2009.

AGRICULTURE AND FISHERIES

The Cape Verde archipelago is situated in the Sahelian climatic zone and thus suffers from severe periodic droughts. Less than 10% (39,000 ha) of Cape Verde's total surface area is cultivable (one-half of this is on Santiago). In the absence of the necessary infrastructure to combat the effects of droughts, Cape Verde has not been able to achieve self-sufficiency in food production. Cereal production covers on average only 15% of Cape Verde's annual food requirements, and the remainder, varying from 28,000 metric tons to 70,000 tons, needs to be imported. Erratic rains, upon which most agriculture depends, have led to unpredictable harvests. After average cereal harvests in 2008 and 2009, a good harvest was achieved in 2010 after plentiful rains in the planting season. Agriculture (including forestry and fishing) contributed just 8.5% of GDP in 2011, although the sector is an important source of employment, involving 23% of the total labour force. About 54% of farms on cultivated land are smaller than 1 ha and fewer than 3% exceed 5 ha. During 2000–09 the GDP of the agricultural sector increased, in real terms, at an average annual rate of 1.8%, according to the World Bank; it increased by 4.4% in 2009.

In November 2009 the Government launched a national agricultural investment plan, covering the period 2010–15, which aimed to halve rural poverty by 2015, with a focus on improving irrigation and developing the raising of livestock. Since independence, re-afforestation plans have been put into effect with assistance from FAO. Some 23m., mostly drought-resistant, trees (American acacias) have been planted, in order to reduce soil erosion and increase groundwater levels. In addition, about 7,200 rainwater dykes have been built, new wells have been sunk and a more efficient system of irrigation has been adopted. About 3,000 ha are currently irrigated. Estimates suggest that the total potentially exploitable groundwater and surface water resources of Cape Verde are around 150m. cu m per year. In July 2006 a reservoir was opened at Poilão (Santiago island), with a storage capacity of 1.7m. cu litres irrigating an area of 65 ha; the Chinese Government had provided US $4m. of funding. In January 2010 Cape Verde's Government launched a tender for a €100m. project, funded by the Portuguese Government, to construct three new reservoirs on Santiago island to capture rainwater, at Salinero (Ribeira Grande), Tabugal (Santa Catarina) and Faveta (São Salvador); the first two were expected to be completed by the end of 2012. In addition, the project aimed to build new flood-control dykes and 70 bore wells. In March 2011 Portugal granted Cape Verde a $72m. credit line to construct the three dams, which were expected to distribute 75m. cu m of water per year, mostly for agriculture and livestock-raising.

Santiago is the main agricultural producer (contributing about one-half of total production), followed by Santo Antão and São Nicolau. Food crops are maize, beans, cassava and sweet potatoes, supplemented (wherever soils, terrain and rainfall permit) with bananas, vegetables, sugar cane and fruits. The main staples are beans and maize, which are intercropped. Poor rains in 2007 reduced the maize harvest to 3,068 metric tons from 4,116 tons in 2006. However, good rains and an expanded planting area boosted the harvest to 11,584 tons in 2008, although production moderated to around 7,500 tons in 2009 and 2010. The country produced 3,700 tons of cassava and 2,800 tons of beans in 2010. Cape Verde's overall annual cereal requirement is estimated at around 110,000 tons. More than one-half of Cape Verde's total irrigated land is used for sugar cane (production totalled an estimated 28,500 tons in 2010), most of which is used in the production of a popular alcoholic beverage, grogue, for local consumption. The Government is seeking to reallocate this land to staple and cash crops by encouraging the manufacture (and future export) of an alternative liquor using imported molasses.

Cash crops, such as bananas, Arabica coffee, groundnuts, castor beans and pineapples, are encouraged, but poor inter-island communications, low educational attainment, the shortage of government funds, lack of suitable available land and adverse climatic conditions hinder the development of a thriving agricultural sector. As a result, the islands' only significant export crops are bananas (with production of 8,900 metric tons in 2010) and mangoes (6,500 tons). Cape Verde has a 4,800-ton banana quota with the EU, and bananas are mainly shipped to Portugal. An exotic commodity, locally known as purgueira (*Jatropha curcas*), which grows wild, is also exported (for soap-making). A small quantity of coffee, castor beans and tomatoes is produced on Fogo for national consumption. Wine production, mostly for local consumption in tourism resorts, has been encouraged on Fogo, the volcanic terrain of which is suitable for viniculture.

Livestock herds have been reduced to one-quarter, or even one-10th, of their pre-drought level, but are recovering. According to FAO, in 2010 46,000 cattle, 231,400 goats, 20,370 sheep and 238,600 pigs were raised for food and milk. About 16,500 asses and horses provide the main form of transport in mountainous rural areas. Fishing offers great development potential. Cape Verde's exclusive economic zone comprises 734,265 sq km and contains one of the last significantly under-used fishing grounds in the world, with a total sustainable yield estimated at about 35,000 metric tons per year. Fishing's contribution to merchandise exports reached 37.8% (US $26m.) in 2011. The Government, which privatized the state-owned fishing company, the Empresa Caboverdiana de Pescas, has sought to encourage private entrepreneurs by means of credit facilities, training and research. The privatization of the loss-making Interbase fish-freezing plant was completed in April 2005, when the company was taken over by a Spanish-Cape Verdean consortium. In 2008 work started on a Spanish-funded project to modernize and expand Interbase's facilities, with the aim of providing refrigeration facilities for the storage and preservation of fish from the industrial fleet operating in the Atlantic. However, in September a fire destroyed Interbase's fish-freezing facilities and offices. In March 2010 the Government awarded the contract to rebuild the company's processing, storage and freezing facilities to Spain's Ramon Vizcaíno Internacional. Construction was completed in September 2011 at a cost of €1.3m., and the facilities, managed by ENAPOR, started operating in early 2012.

Fishing exports consist primarily of tuna. Although local fishing catches have increased, since 2005 the total catch has fluctuated, peaking at 24,590 tons in 2006 before falling back to 16,828 tons in 2009, according to FAO. In December 2005 Cape Verde signed a new fishing accord with the EU, covering the period September 2006–August 2011. Under the agreement, 84 EU ships would be allowed to catch 5,000 tons of fish each year in Cape Verde's territorial waters in return for an annual payment of €325,000 and a grant of €60,000 to promote sustainable fishing activities. In December 2010 the EU renewed the accord for another three years (November 2011–August 2014). Under the new accord, the number of ships would be reduced to 74, the annual quota would remain at 5,000 tons of tuna, and the compensation would be increased to €435,000, which included a grant of €110,000 to support Cape Verde's fishing sector. In 2008 Cape Verde signed a fishing protocol with the Spanish Government, which included investment in improving the fishing infrastructure in São Vicente's port, technical training and local private enterprise initiatives. In September 2009 the Brazilian organization, Serviço de Apoio às Micro e Pequenas Empresas do Ceará, and Cape Verdean businessmen launched a €1.5m. project to farm prawns in Cape Verde. The Government signed an agreement with two US companies, Peer Fish and Carlos Seaford, in July 2011 to export fresh and frozen fish from Cape Verde to the USA, creating 150 local jobs. In August 2012 the China National Fisheries Corpn was awarded a contract to build a new refrigerated warehouse in Mindelo to support local fishing and export activities.

MANUFACTURING

The industrial sector (including construction and power) remains largely undeveloped, accounting for 15.0% of GDP in 2009. According to the African Development Bank (AfDB), in 1997–2006 manufacturing GDP grew at an average annual rate of 4.1%, and by 1.8% in 2006. Manufacturing consists primarily of fish-canning, clothing, footwear, rum-distilling and bottling plants, contributing 6.8% to GDP in 2009 and employing around 6% of the total labour force. In order to attract foreign investment and promote the expansion of industrial exports, the free-zone enterprise law was enacted in 1993. This permitted enterprises producing goods and services exclusively for export, and new firms specializing in transshipment, to benefit from exemptions on tax and customs duties for a period of 10 years. Legislation enacted in 1999 provided for the transformation of industrial parks at Mindelo and Praia into free-trade zones and for the establishment of a further free-trade zone on Sal island. The free-trade zone in Mindelo is currently being extended with support from Portugal.

EXTRACTIVE INDUSTRIES

Cape Verde has no known hydrocarbon resources, although the Government has encouraged petroleum companies to prospect in its waters. In 2010 the Brazilian oil company Petróleo Brasileiro signed an accord with the Government to explore for petroleum and gas in Cape Verde's offshore area. Until recently, mining was of little significance, representing less than 1% of GDP in 2001, with pozzolana, a volcanic ash used in cement manufacture (an estimated 160,000 metric tons in 2010), and unrefined salt (an estimated 1,600 tons in 2010) traditionally being the main products. Small quantities of clay, gypsum and limestone were also produced. However, in January 2004 construction began on a pozzolana cement factory in Porto Novo (Santo Antão), projected to produce 40,000 tons per year. The US $5m. plant was financed by a consortium of Italian and Cape Verdean investors and started production in late 2005. Moreover, in 2007 construction started on a $55m. cement plant in Santa Cruz (Santiago), funded by the Chinese Government. The new plant will have a production capacity of 350,000 tons per year, easily meeting Cape Verde's domestic demand and enabling the country to export the surplus.

POWER

Cape Verde imports all of its fuel, which keeps costs for transport and electricity high. The country also provides refuelling services for ships and aircraft, and re-exports of fuel (bunkering) represented 80% of merchandise exports in 2006. Fuel is distributed by Royal Dutch/Shell and the state-owned utility, Empresa Nacional de Combustíveis (ENACOL), which was partially privatized in 2000. In 2007 the Government sold its remaining 27.4% stake in ENACOL on Cape Verde's stock exchange, but retained a 'golden share' of 2.1%. GALP Energia of Portugal and SONANGOL of Angola are the largest single investors in ENACOL, with 45.0% and 38.1%, respectively. In September 2009 the Government signed an accord with Venezuela to construct a refinery and fuel entrepot in Cape Verde, which will serve both domestic needs and international shipping. In February 2011 Royal Dutch Shell agreed to sell controlling stakes in all of its 19 African subsidiaries, including that in Cape Verde, to Swiss oil trader Vitol and its partner, Helios Investment Partners.

Electricity is generated by the national electricity and water utility, Empresa de Electricidade e Água (Electra), which has struggled to meet rising demand in recent years, leading to frequent power and water shortages. In 2008 work was due to start on a US $5.7m. project to increase power provision on Santiago, funded by Japan's development bank, the AfDB and the Government. The project will boost output at the Palmarejo plant by 25 MW and construct a new high-tension power line to the island's interior. In March 2010 the Government contracted a Finnish company to install two new 10-MW generators at the Palmarejo plant, at a cost of €22.5m.; these were due to be operational by the end of 2011. In May 2009 Electra launched a programme to reduce illegal power connections in Praia, which the company estimated consumed 12% of national output and in 2007 cost 308m. escudos in lost revenues. The company aimed to legalize existing illegal connections and fine those continuing to break the law. In May 2009 two new desalination units started operations in Palmarejo, increasing the plant's pumping capacity from 5,000 cu m/day to 6,200 cu m/day. Electra planned to open a third desalination plant, with a capacity of 5,000 cu m/day, with the aim of reducing the chronic water shortages affecting Praia.

The Government has long-standing plans to privatize Electra, but has been repeatedly thwarted by the company's organizational and financial problems. An attempt to part-privatize Electra by selling a 51% stake to Electricidade de Portugal and Águas de Portugal was reversed in September 2006, after the company had amassed huge losses. With power supply remaining erratic, in 2010 the Council of Ministers approved plans to split Electra into two companies, one covering the Barlavento islands (Electra Norte) and another covering the Sotavento islands (Electra Sul). However, in June 2011 Minister of Finance and Planning Duarte announced that Electra's privatization would be delayed until at least 2012 while the company underwent further restructuring, having amassed debts worth 10,000m. escudos by the end of 2010. In December the company was saved from bankruptcy by an emergency capital injection worth 525,000m. escudos by the national pension fund, Instituto Nacional de Previdência Social, and in early 2011 the Government started negotiations with Angola's Banco Africano de Investimento to inject 700,000m. escudos into Electra in return for shares. By the end of 2011 Electra had total estimated debts of 10,700m. escudos, and in June 2012 it was forced to issue a new bond. The company was undergoing further restructuring in 2012 with the assistance of the World Bank and US $41.4m. in funding from the MCA. As a result, privatization was expected to be delayed until at least 2013.

According to the Government, 87% of the population had access to electricity in 2009. However, the provision of electricity in rural communities remains poor, and around 40% of the population relies on firewood for fuel. In 2009 the Government launched a national energy plan, Plano Nacional para as Energias Domésticas de Cabo Verde, covering the period 2010–14, which aimed to increase the use of butane gas in rural communities. The Government also supported efforts to develop renewable energy by drawing on the archipelago's wind and solar power in order to reduce its dependence on petroleum imports. In December 2009 the Government contracted the Cabeólica consortium to construct four wind farms on Santiago, São Vicente, Sal and Boavista. The US $84m. project aims to produce 28 MW of power, with the first generation starting by the end of 2011. In December 2010 the European Investment Bank and the AfDB awarded Cape Verde a grant of $59m. to finance the project. In early 2010 a Spanish company, Martifer Solar, started construction of two solar energy plants on Santiago and Sal, at an estimated cost of $36.5m., which together will produce 7.5 MW. The Government aimed to meet 25%–50% of the archipelago's energy needs from renewable sources by 2020, compared with just 4% in 2010.

TOURISM

Tourism has been identified as the area with the most potential for economic development. Cape Verde benefits from its proximity to the European market, enjoys a favourable climate for most of the year and offers white sandy beaches and some spectacular mountain scenery. Tourism has been the sector to benefit most from foreign investment, accounting for more than 90% of FDI inflows. Consequently, the tourism industry's contribution to national GDP increased from 4.0% in 1998 to 29.8% in 2011. The number of hotel beds in Cape Verde grew from 5,239 in 2000 to 11,420 in 2008. By 2010 there were 178 tourist lodgings in Cape Verde (including hotels and hostels), employing more than 4,000 workers. The number of tourists has also increased dramatically, from around 60,000 in 1998 to 382,831 in 2010, mainly from the United Kingdom (26.1%), Germany (15.8%), Portugal (12.8%) and Italy (11.9%). Tourists were concentrated in Sal (40.5%), followed by the country's fastest growing tourism islands, Boavista (32.9%) and Santiago (13.6%). Tourism arrivals rose by 27.1% in 2011, to 427,000, again dominated by nationals from the EU, and there was a further 25.4% increase, year on year, in the first quarter of 2012. The Government aims to attract 1m. tourists to Cape Verde by 2015. According to the IMF, earnings from tourism totalled €230m. in 2008, compared with just US $40m. in 2000. Cruise liners are becoming increasingly important to the sector, and in 2010 the Government announced plans to develop a €19m. cruise ship terminal in Mindelo, São Vicente. In 2007 Cape Verde received 52 liners, and this figure was expected to rise in future years, bringing 20,000 additional tourists.

In September 2005 the Government began revising the foreign investment law in order to attract more FDI to the tourism sector. By 2007 over 90% of FDI inflows were directed towards the sector, with inflows heavily concentrated on Sal, Santiago, São Vicente and Boavista. In June 2011 the Government introduced new legislation permitting gambling and the building of casinos in Cape Verde, which could result in the realization of long-standing plans to build a casino and luxury hotel on a small island in Praia harbour.

FINANCIAL SECTOR

In 1993 the first commercial bank was established, the Banco Comercial do Atlântico (BCA), while new legislation provided for the creation of financial institutions to offer loans and credit to small and medium-sized entrepreneurs. Although its capital was raised solely from state funds provided by the Banco de Cabo Verde (BCV), BCA enjoyed relative independence from the central bank. The state's shares in BCA were sold in 1999 to a consortium led by the Portuguese Caixa Geral de Depósitos. BCV now functions solely as a central bank. The principal savings institutions are the Fundo de Solidariedade Nacional, which handles public investment, and the Instituto Caboverdiano de Solidariedade, which handles international aid. The establishment of Portuguese banks in Cape Verde was expected to raise the level of available credit lines through Portugal, and subsequently increase the level of Portuguese investment and imports.

Cape Verde's financial sector is well developed by regional standards, with an estimated 89.1% of the population having a bank account, one of the highest rates in sub-Saharan Africa. By the end of 2010 there were six commercial banks, three of which were Portuguese subsidiaries, and a total of 91 branches in all but two of Cape Verde's 22 municipalities. In 2009 BCA was the country's largest bank, with over one-half of the banking system's capital, followed by Caixa Económica de Cabo Verde, Banco Caboverdeano de Negócios, Banco Interatlântico, Angola's BAI and Ecobank. In March 2010 the Government created a socially focused bank, Novo Banco, to provide credit to low-income households and small and medium-sized businesses. In 2010 there were 13 micro-finance institutions operating in the archipelago, with a combined portfolio of 55,000 loans worth a total of 3,000m. escudos.

Concerns that Cape Verde's financial system has become the target for money-laundering led to the introduction of a new law in 2008, which required notaries, lawyers, solicitors, auditors and accountants to co-operate with the authorities in identifying criminals suspected of money-laundering. Following a scandal involving the transfer of illicit funds through the Cape Verdean offshore subsidiary of Banco Português de Negócios in 2009, the Government agreed to wind down its offshore banking sector and to regulate all banks under a single code based on EU standards.

A stock exchange, Bolsa de Valores de Cabo Verde, which was founded in 1999, finally started operations in December 2005. In June 2009 nine companies were listed on the exchange, with total market capitalization of €188.6m., the equivalent of 20% of GDP.

TRADE

Cape Verde's principal merchandise exports are clothing and footwear, canned tuna and mackerel, frozen fish and lobster. Small amounts of salt and pozzolana are exported. Among cash crops, only bananas are exported in significant quantities. Cape Verde also re-sells fuel (bunkering) to passing ships and aircraft, earning US $51.8m. in 2009. Exports of processed fish and light-manufactured goods are expected to increase substantially in the future, as new freezing and canning plants come into operation, as well as free-trade zones at Praia and Mindelo. Cape Verde traditionally operates a substantial trade deficit, which stems from the need to import some 85% of its food requirements, as well as manufactured goods, fuel and other essential goods. Although merchandise exports, including fuel (bunkering), increased from US $9m. in 1993 to $135.3m. in 2010, merchandise imports rose even more, reaching $814.2m. in 2010, thus widening the trade deficit to $678.9. According to the central bank, the trade balance widened further in 2011, as the volume of import growth outpaced that of exports.

In recent years Portugal has significantly increased its trading with Cape Verde. In 1989 Portugal exported goods worth US $34m. (32% of imports) to Cape Verde, but by 2011 the value of these transactions had reached $363.7m. (37.0% of imports). Other important sources of imports in 2011 were the Netherlands (25.4%), Spain (7.0%) and Italy (5.2%). Spain was the principal market for exports in that year, accounting for 65.9% of the total, followed by Portugal (18.9%), Bermuda (2.2%) and the USA (2.2%). In 2011 exports of services provided revenue of $599m., while imports reached $316m. Around one-half of services earnings came from tourism, with the remainder comprising the servicing of foreign aircraft and ships visiting or transiting the archipelago.

In July 2008 Cape Verde became the 153rd member of the World Trade Organization (WTO), the first African country to successfully negotiate entry since the WTO's founding in 1995. Cape Verde was granted until 2018 to meet all of its WTO convergence targets, which will include introducing new legislation on commercial, customs and copyright law.

AID AND INVESTMENT

Historically, total FDI inflows have been low, averaging US $20m. per year in 1999–2004. However, with strong investment in tourism and infrastructure development, FDI inflows rose from $82m. in 2005 to a peak of $209m. in 2008, increasing the total FDI stock to $909m., according to data from the UN Conference on Trade and Development. However, due to the impact of the global financial crisis, FDI inflows declined to $119m. in 2009, $111m. in 2010 and $93m. in 2011, bringing the total FDI stock to $1,232m. at the end of 2011. Tourism continues to receive the largest share of FDI in Cape Verde, most of which has been concentrated on the traditional tourism islands of Sal, Boavista and São Vicente, and more recently Santiago. According to Cabo Verde Investimentos, FDI inflows could reach $3,200m. in 2009–13, if all projects that have been approved go ahead, although the impact of the global economic downturn was likely to result in the more speculative projects being postponed or cancelled. The main sources of FDI are the United Kingdom, France, Portugal, Italy and the UAE. The Government expected FDI-funded projects to create at least 15,000 new jobs in the civil construction, transport and tourism sectors.

Cape Verde receives one of the highest levels of foreign aid per head in the world (US $392 per head in 2009). According to the Organisation for Economic Cooperation and Development, total official development assistance was $196m. in 2009, with Portugal, the USA, the EU and Spain being the largest bilateral donors. In May 2004 Cape Verde was selected, along with five other African countries, for generous development assistance from the MCA. Established to support countries deemed to have embraced reform, good governance and economic freedom, the MCA provided $110m. of funding for 2005/06 for a range of projects, including the upgrade of Praia's port, improvements to the road network on Santo Antão and Santiago, and water, irrigation and micro-finance programmes. In December 2009 Cape Verde became the first country to be awarded a second MCA programme, worth $66.2m. over five years, which was to focus on upgrading the country's water and sanitation infrastructure, stabilizing Electra's financial position, and improving land management. In January 2010 Portugal granted Cape Verde a €200m. credit line to finance a national housing programme, which aimed to build 8,000 new homes and rehabilitate 15,000 existing homes by 2011. In October 2011 the Chinese Government granted Cape Verde a $4.7m. loan to finance priority social infrastructure projects, and in January 2012 it approved a further $51m. loan to fund the construction of 1,600 new homes.

In January 2008 the UN formally upgraded Cape Verde's status from an LDC to an MDC. The change reflected the country's steady progress in social development, training of the workforce, poverty reduction and economic growth since the mid-1990s. The change in categorization meant that Cape Verde lost access to the highly preferential loans from multilateral sources that are available to less-developed countries. However, given the Government's strong track record in macroeconomic management, donors have pledged to continue to provide funding and budget support for Cape Verde's development projects over the coming years.

DEBT

According to the World Bank, Cape Verde's total external debt at the end of 2010 reached US $857.3m. (51.6% of GDP), a 37.2% rise compared with the end of 2008, reflecting the contracting of new concessional debt to finance infrastructure development as well as the depreciation of the euro against the US dollar. However, the Government has managed to keep debt-servicing costs to a minimum, thanks to the concessional terms on much of its debt stock and the low level of principal and interest arrears, which totalled just $3.8m. in 2008. As a proportion of the value of exports of goods and services, the debt-service ratio was just 3.5% in that year. In addition, concessional debt from bilateral and multilateral lenders made up around 90% of Cape Verde's total debt stock at the end of 2008. Public domestic debt increased from about $40m. in 1992 to $180m. at the end of 1998, but was to be converted into lower-interest bonds to be managed by the central bank of Portugal in an 'offshore' trust fund, from which 95% of the interest earned would be used to repay the national debt, with the remainder placed in a special development fund. The Government was to contribute $80m. in revenue from the accelerated privatization programme, and international donors the remaining $100m. However, the debt-conversion operation only commenced in 1999, while a deterioration of public finances prompted the Government to resort to domestic financing. Only $37m. in privatization revenue had been used to support the trust fund by mid-2002. The larger portion, $52m., was used for budgetary support. As a result, public domestic debt increased again, to $140m., at the end of 2001, equivalent to 26% of GDP. During 2003 Cape Verde cleared its arrears with all of its multilateral creditors, and by 2005 had successfully rescheduled those with all of its bilateral creditors. In March 2009 Brazil agreed to convert $4m. of external debt into development aid for the education sector.

ECONOMIC POLICY

In recent years the Government has implemented large increases in priority sector spending, much of it funded through direct budget support by donors, reflecting their increased confidence in the Government's economic management. In December 2011 the Assembleia Nacional approved the 2012 budget, based on expected real GDP growth of 6%–7%. Total government expenditure was forecast to be 3.8% lower than in the revised 2011 budget, at 57,100m. escudos (US $660m.), of which 46.3% was allocated to capital expenditure, reflecting Government investment in port expansion and increasing power generation. The largest spending allocations went to infrastructure (46%), social cohesion (15%), good governance (13%), competitiveness (12%) and human capital (12%). Public sector salaries were set to rise by 1,000m. escudos, in line with the Government's IMF commitments, despite demands from unions for a higher pay increase. Total revenue was projected to decline by 7%, to 40,700m. escudos, leaving a fiscal deficit of 16,400m. escudos, equivalent to 8.6% of GDP. This was lower than the estimated 13.6% deficit in 2010, but still more than double the 2008 deficit. The financing gap was expected to be met 78% by foreign funding and 22% through domestic borrowing.

In July 2006 the IMF granted Cape Verde a policy support instrument (PSI), a new monitoring programme designed for low-income countries that no longer need IMF financial assistance, but still require its technical assistance and endorsement of their policies. Cape Verde's PSI was focused on completing the Government's reform agenda, and was to support its medium-term expenditure framework for 2006–09. In January 2008 the IMF completed its third PSI review, praising the country's strong macroeconomic performance and significant growth in tourism and FDI. However, the Fund expressed concern with delays in reforming the energy sector, which suffers from power cuts, and the failure to introduce a mechanism for automatically adjusting fuel and utility prices; this was eventually introduced in late 2008. In April 2008 a new labour code came into force, aimed at modernizing existing legislation, improving working conditions and stimulating competitiveness. The code included new provisions for paid holidays, insurance cover, pensions and maternity leave, and guaranteed workers a full-time contract after five years of service.

In May 2008 the Government implemented emergency measures to alleviate the impact of high food and fuel prices, by reducing the import duty on wheat from 20% to 10%, and temporarily exempting basic staple foods from VAT. In June the IMF carried out its fourth PSI review, commending the Government's macroeconomic performance, in particular its success in reducing domestic debt to less than 20% of GDP two years early, restraining spending on public sector wages and improving tax administration. The Fund urged further efforts to improve the competitiveness of the private sector. In September the IMF completed its fifth PSI review, noting strong growth in the first half of 2008, but warning of the impact of the global downturn in the second half of the year.

The IMF completed its sixth PSI review in June 2009, reporting that Cape Verde was managing the impact of the global downturn well, by means of a fiscal stimulus programme made possible by prudent macroeconomic management over previous years. The Fund agreed to the Government's request to extend the PSI to July 2010, in order to allow the country more time to adjust to the impact of the downturn before drawing up a successor PSI. In July 2009 the tax authority launched a campaign to address tax fraud, collect an estimated 2,000m. escudos of unpaid taxes from 8,000 Cape Verdean businesses, and bring more small and medium-sized enterprises into the system. In August the Government amended the mechanism for automatically adjusting fuel and utility prices, giving more flexibility to distributors and ending the system of state fuel subsidies; this led to sharp increases in petrol and diesel prices.

In September 2009 the IMF carried out its seventh PSI review, commending the Government's economic performance despite the adverse global environment, with strong real GDP growth, subdued inflation and falling domestic debt. The Fund endorsed the expansionary 2010 budget with the proviso that the large projected deficit would be funded by concessional loans. In May 2010 the IMF carried out its eighth and final PSI review, again praising the Government's policy performance and forecasting a return to strong real GDP growth, from 4.1% in 2010 to 7.7% by 2014. The Fund endorsed the Government's next phase of infrastructure investment, which was aimed at easing bottlenecks in the road and port network, but urged it not to take on an unsustainable debt burden in order to achieve this.

In November 2010 the IMF awarded a successor PSI to Cape Verde, covering a period of 15 months and aimed at promoting economic growth and diversification, as well as boosting spending on social sectors. Key targets included increasing the level of foreign exchange reserves, reducing the fiscal deficit while safeguarding social sector spending, phasing out water and energy subsidies, and lowering the level of external debt. In May 2011 the Fund carried out its first review of the new PSI, reporting a return to healthy economic growth in line with the revival of the tourism sector and encouraging progress with containing the level of public debt. The IMF forecast real GDP growth of 6% in 2012 and 2013, buoyed by strong private sector expansion. However, the Fund urged the Government to increase labour market flexibility in order to boost competitiveness and job creation, and warned the country to prepare for the impact of the euro area crisis.

In February 2012 the IMF published its second review of the PSI, commending the Government's fiscal restraint, particularly a planned reduction in spending in the 2012 budget, but urging more action as the euro area crisis deepened, weakening the country's main export market and source of remittances and investment. As a result, the Fund lowered its 2012–13 growth projection to 5%. The IMF also appealed for renewed efforts to restructure state-owned enterprises, notably Electra and TACV, where progress had stalled.

In July 1998 Cape Verde and Portugal linked their respective currencies through a fixed exchange rate. This new development not only transformed the Cape Verde escudo into a convertible currency, but also established a firm monetary link to the single European currency, the euro, following its introduction in January 1999. Furthermore, it was expected to encourage trade with West African countries in the CFA franc zone, which is linked to the euro. Portugal agreed to underwrite the link with some US $50m. to augment Cape Verde's foreign currency reserves. The IMF advised the Government that stronger reserves were necessary to maintain the country's currency peg with the euro (set at a rate of 110.27 escudos = €1), but there was concern among some economists that the cost of maintaining the peg would harm economic competitiveness by preventing devaluation. Nevertheless, the Government was strongly committed to the peg as part of its efforts to promote closer integration with the EU. Since 2001 the escudo has progressively strengthened against the US dollar, in line with the euro, appreciating from an average of 123.2 escudos = $1 in 2001 to an average of 79.3 escudos = $1 in 2011.

Statistical Survey

Sources (unless otherwise stated): Instituto Nacional de Estatística, Av. Amílcar Cabral, CP 116, Praia, Santiago; tel. 613960; e-mail inecv@mail.cvtelecom.cv; internet www.ine.cv; Statistical Service, Banco de Cabo Verde, Av. Amílcar Cabral 117, CP 101, Praia, Santiago; tel. 2607060; fax 2614447; e-mail apericles@bcv.cv; internet www.bcv.cv.

AREA AND POPULATION

Area: 4,033 sq km (1,557 sq miles).

Population: 436,863 (males 211,479, females 225,384) at census of 16 June 2000; 491,875 (males 243,593, females 248,282) at census of 16–30 June 2010. *By Island* (2010 census): Boavista 9,162; Brava 5,995; Fogo 37,051; Maio 6,952; Sal 25,765; Santo Antão 43,915; São Nicolau 12,817; Santiago 273,919; São Vicente 76,107; Total 491,875 (incl. 192 homeless persons).

Density (2010 census): 122.0 per sq km.

Population by Age and Sex (2010 census): *0–14:* 155,635 (males 78,159, females 77,476); *15–64:* 304,527 (males 152,833, females 151,694); *65 and over:* 31,713 (males 12,601, females 19,112); *Total* 491,875 (males 243,593, females 248,282). Note: Total includes 364 persons (216 males, 148 females) of undeclared age.

Municipalities (population at 2010 census): Boavista 9,162; Brava 5,995; Maio 6,952; Mosteiros 9,524; Paúl 6,997; Porto Novo 18,028; Praia 131,719; Ribeira Brava 7,580; Ribeira Grande 18,890; Ribeira Grande Santiago 8,325; Sal 25,779; Santa Catarina 43,297; Santa Catarina Fogo 5,299; Santa Cruz 26,617; São Domingos 13,808; São Filipe 22,248; São Lourenço Orgaos 7,388; São Miguel 15,648; São Salvador Mundo 8,677; São Vicente 76,140; Tarrafal 18,565; Tarrafal São Nicolau 5,237; *Total* 491,875.

Births and Deaths (official estimates, 2011): Live births 13,674 (birth rate 25.9 per 1,000); Deaths 2,932 (death rate 5.6 per 1,000).

Life Expectancy (years at birth, official estimates): 73.0 (males 69.1; females 76.7) in 2011.

Economically Active Population (persons aged 10 years and over, 1990 census): Agriculture, hunting, forestry and fishing 29,876; Mining and quarrying 410; Manufacturing 5,520; Electricity, gas and water 883; Construction 22,722; Trade, restaurants and hotels 12,747; Transport, storage and communications 6,138; Financial, insurance, real estate and business services 821; Community, social and personal services 17,358; *Sub-total* 96,475; Activities not adequately defined 24,090; *Total labour force* 120,565 (males 75,786, females 44,779), including 31,049 unemployed persons (males 19,712, females 11,337) (Source: ILO). *2000 Census* (persons aged 10 years and over): Total employed 144,310; Unemployed 30,334; Total labour force 174,644. *Mid-2012* (FAO estimates): Agriculture, etc. 31,000; Total (incl. others) 197,000 (Source: FAO).

HEALTH AND WELFARE

Key Indicators

Total Fertility Rate (children per woman, 2010): 2.4.

Under-5 Mortality Rate (per 1,000 live births, 2010): 36.

Physicians (per 1,000 head, 2008): 0.6.

Hospital Beds (per 1,000 head, 2010): 2.1.

Health Expenditure (2009): US $ per head (PPP): 174.

Health Expenditure (2009): % of GDP: 3.9.

Health Expenditure (2009): public (% of total): 74.1.

Access to Water (% of persons, 2010): 88.

Access to Sanitation (% of persons, 2010): 61.

Total Carbon Dioxide Emissions ('000 metric tons, 2008): 308.0.

Carbon Dioxide Emissions Per Head (metric tons, 2008): 0.6.

Human Development Index (2011): ranking: 133.

Human Development Index (2011): 0.568.

For sources and definitions, see explanatory note on p. vi.

AGRICULTURE, ETC.

Principal Crops ('000 metric tons, 2010, FAO estimates): Maize 7.6; Potatoes 4.7; Sweet potatoes 5.1; Cassava 3.7; Sugar cane 28.5; Pulses 2.8; Coconuts 5.3; Cabbages 4.9; Tomatoes 5.5; Onions, dry 2.4; Beans, green 2.8; Cucumbers and gherkins 1.3; Bananas 8.9; Guavas, mangoes and mangosteens 6.5. *Aggregate Production* ('000 metric tons, may include official, semi-official or estimated data): Vegetables (incl. melons) 20.6; Fruits (excl. melons) 20.8; Roots and tubers 13.5.

Livestock ('000 head, 2010, FAO estimates): Cattle 46.0; Pigs 238.6; Sheep 20.4; Goats 231.4; Horses 0.5; Asses 14.5; Mules 1.9; Chickens 640.

Livestock Products ('000 metric tons, 2010, FAO estimates): Pig meat 8.3; Cattle meat 0.9; Cows' milk 11.9; Goats' milk 11.4; Hen eggs 2.1.

Fishing (metric tons, live weight, 2010): Total catch 19,500 (Skipjack tuna 6,032; Yellowfin tuna 4,492).

Source: FAO.

MINING

Production (metric tons, 2010): Salt (unrefined) 1,600. Clay, gypsum, limestone and volcanic rock were also produced, at unreported levels. Source: US Geological Survey.

INDUSTRY

Production (metric tons, 2003, unless otherwise indicated): Canned fish 200; Frozen fish 900; Flour 15,901 (1999); Beer 4,104,546 litres (1999); Soft drinks 922,714 litres (1996); Cigarettes and tobacco 77 kg (1999); Paint 628,243 kg (1997); Cement 160,000 (2010); Footwear 670,676 pairs (1996); Soap 1,371,045 kg (1999); Electric energy 286m. kWh (2008). Sources: mainly UN Industrial Commodity Statistics Database, US Geological Survey and IMF, *Cape Verde: Statistical Appendix* (October 2001).

FINANCE

Currency and Exchange Rates: 100 centavos = 1 Cape Verde escudo; 1,000 escudos are known as a conto. *Sterling, Dollar and Euro Equivalents* (31 May 2012): £1 sterling = 137.840 escudos; US $1 = 88.906 escudos; €1 = 110.270 escudos; 1,000 Cape Verde escudos = £7.25 = $11.25 = €9.07. *Average Exchange Rate* (escudos per US dollar): 79.377 in 2009; 83.259 in 2010; 79.323 in 2011.

Central Government Budget (million escudos, 2011, preliminary figures): *Revenue:* Taxation 29,864 (Taxes on income and profits 9,126, Taxes on international trade 5,921, Consumption taxes 13,814, Other tax revenue 1,003); Non-tax revenue 3,992; Grants 7,849; Total 41,705. *Expenditure:* Recurrent 30,604 (Wages and salaries 17,399, Acquisition of goods and services 2,852, Transfers and other subsidies 5,612, Interest payments 2,833, Other recurrent expenditure 1,907); Capital 26,109; Total 56,713. Source: IMF, *Cape Verde: Second Review Under the Policy Support Instrument and Requests for Waivers of Nonobservance of Assessment Criteria—Staff Report; Staff Supplements; Press Release on the Executive Board Discussion; and Statement by the Executive Director for Cape Verde* (February 2012).

International Reserves (excluding gold, US $ million at 31 December 2011): IMF special drawing rights 7.67; Reserve position in the IMF 0.02; Foreign exchange 330.93; Total 338.62. Source: IMF, *International Financial Statistics*.

Money Supply (million escudos at 31 December 2011): Currency outside depository corporations 8,493.3; Transferable deposits 35,462.4; Other deposits 69,525.6; *Broad money* 113,481.3. Source: IMF, *International Financial Statistics*.

Cost of Living (Consumer Price Index; base: 2005 = 100): All items 118.6 in 2009; 121.1 in 2010; 126.5 in 2011. Source: IMF, *International Financial Statistics*.

Expenditure on the Gross Domestic Product (million escudos at current prices, 2011 estimates): Government final consumption expenditure 26,656.0; Private final consumption expenditure 105,786.9; Gross fixed capital formation 58,670.5; Increase in stocks 572.8; *Total domestic expenditure* 191,686.2; Exports of goods and services 30,315.3; *Less* Imports of goods and services 90,204.9; *GDP in purchasers' values* 131,796.6.

Gross Domestic Product by Economic Activity (million escudos at current prices, 2011, estimates): Agriculture and forestry 6,010.7; Fishing 935.8; Construction 8,794.6; Other industry 9,403.6; Services 101,455.4; *Sub-total* 126,600.1; Indirect taxes (net) 5,196.5; *Total* 131,796.6.

Balance of Payments (US $ million, 2010): Exports of goods f.o.b. 135.34; Imports of goods f.o.b. –814.16; *Trade balance* –678.83; Exports of services 518.25; Imports of services –296.10; *Balance on goods and services* –456.68; Other income received 13.99; Other income paid –82.11; *Balance on goods, services and income* –524.80; Current transfers received 409.65; Current transfers paid –69.14; *Current balance* –184.29; Capital account (net) 39.85; Direct investment abroad 0.15; Direct investment from abroad 111.70; Portfolio investment liabilities 0.01; Other investment assets –6.20; Other investment liabilities 138.20; Net errors and omissions –70.30; *Overall balance* 29.12. Source: IMF, *International Finance Statistics*.

EXTERNAL TRADE

Principal Commodities (million escudos, 2011): *Imports c.i.f.:* Consumer goods 24,454.7 (Manufactured food products 13,975.2); Intermediate goods 15,961.6 (Construction materials 7,455.4); Capital goods 14,154.4 (Machines 8,532.4; Transportation 2,969.6); Fuel imports 14,106.4 (Fuel oil 3,750.9; Diesel oil 8,478.8); Other imports 6,472.9; Total 75,149.9. *Exports f.o.b.:* Fish and crustaceans 4,473.4 (Frozen 1,946.6); Clothing 464.1; Footwear 380.0; Total (incl. others) 5,430.7;.

Principal Trading Partners (million escudos, 2011): *Imports c.i.f.:* Brazil 2,056.1; ECOWAS 1,308.7; Germany 391.9; Italy 3,345.1; Netherlands 14,391.1; Portugal 33,606.1; Spain 7,421.8; USA 713.1; Total (incl. others) 75,149.9. *Exports f.o.b.:* ECOWAS 13.3; France 337.4; Netherlands 8.4; Portugal 977.1; Spain 3,810.6; USA 29.7; Total (incl. others) 5,430.7.

TRANSPORT

Road Traffic (motor vehicles in use at 31 December 2007): Passenger cars 35,738; Buses and coaches 542; Vans and lorries 13,540; Motorcycles and mopeds 4,333 (Source: IRF, *World Road Statistics*).

Shipping: *Merchant Fleet* (registered at 31 December 2009): Number of vessels 47; Total displacement ('000 grt) 32.0 (Source: IHS Fairplay, *World Fleet Statistics*). *International Sea-borne Freight Traffic* (estimates, '000 metric tons, 1993): Goods loaded 144, goods unloaded 299 (Source: UN Economic Commission for Africa, *African Statistical Yearbook*).

Civil Aviation (traffic on scheduled services, 2009): Kilometres flown (million) 12; Passengers carried ('000) 777; Passenger-km (million) 1,216; Total ton-km (million) 115. Sources: UN, *Statistical Yearbook*.

TOURISM

Tourist Arrivals by Country of Residence (2009): Belgium and Netherlands 2,091; France 22,676; Germany 40,138; Italy 42,628; Portugal 50,617; Spain 5,646; Switzerland 2,277; United Kingdom 57,011; USA 3,935; Total (incl. others) 287,183. *2010:* Total tourist arrivals 336,000. *2011:* Total tourist arrivals 428,000 (provisional).

Tourism Receipts (US $ million, excl. passenger transport): 285 in 2009; 278 in 2010; 369 in 2011 (provisional).

Source: World Tourism Organization.

COMMUNICATIONS MEDIA

Radio Receivers* (1997): 73,000 in use.

Television Receivers† (2000): 2,000 in use.

Telephones† (2011): 74,500 main lines in use.

Mobile Cellular Telephones† (2011): 396,400 subscribers.

Personal Computers†: 69,000 (140.3 per 1,000 persons) in 2007.

Internet Subscribers† (2010): 16,700.

Broadband Subscribers† (2011): 21,700.

Non-daily Newspapers* (2004): 5 titles.

Book Production* (1989): 10 titles.

* Source: UNESCO, *Statistical Yearbook*.

† Source: International Telecommunication Union.

EDUCATION

Pre-primary (2009/10 unless otherwise stated): 465 schools (2003/04); 1,093 teachers; 21,632 pupils.

Primary (2009/10 unless otherwise stated): 425 schools (2002/03); 3,009 teachers; 71,134 pupils.

Total Secondary (2009/10 unless otherwise stated): 33 schools (2003/04); 3,522 teachers; 61,677 pupils.

Higher (2009/10): 926 teachers; 10,144 pupils. Note: In 2002/03 a further 1,743 pupils were studying abroad.

Teacher Training (2003/04): 3 colleges; 52 teachers; 948 pupils.

Pupil-teacher Ratio (primary education, UNESCO estimate): 23.6 in 2009/10.

Adult Literacy Rate (UNESCO estimates): 84.3% (males 89.3%; females 79.4%) in 2010.

Sources (unless otherwise indicated): Comunidade dos Países de Língua Portuguesa; UNESCO Institute for Statistics.

Directory

The Constitution

A new Constitution of the Republic of Cape Verde ('the Second Republic') came into force on 25 September 1992. The Constitution defines Cape Verde as a sovereign, unitary and democratic republic, guaranteeing respect for human dignity and recognizing the inviolable and inalienable rights of man as a fundament of humanity, peace and justice. It recognizes the equality of all citizens before the law, without distinction of social origin, social condition, economic status, race, sex, religion, political convictions or ideologies and promises transparency for all citizens in the practising of fundamental liberties. The Constitution gives assent to popular will, and has a fundamental objective in the realization of economic, political, social and cultural democracy and the construction of a society that is free, just and in solidarity.

The Head of State is the President of the Republic, who is elected by universal adult suffrage and must obtain two-thirds of the votes cast to win in the first round of the election. If no candidate secures the requisite majority, a new election is held within 21 days and contested by the two candidates who received the highest number of votes in the first round. Voting is conducted by secret ballot. Legislative power is vested in the Assembléia Nacional, which is also elected by universal adult suffrage. The Prime Minister is nominated by the Assembléia, to which he is responsible. On the recommendation of the Prime Minister, the President appoints the Council of Ministers, whose members must be elected deputies of the Assembléia. There are 22 local government councils, elected by universal suffrage for a period of five years.

A constitutional revision, adopted in July 1999, gave the President the right to dissolve the Assembléia Nacional, created a new advisory chamber (Conselho Económico e Social), and gave the State the right to adopt Crioulo as the country's second official language.

A series of further amendments to the Constitution were approved by the Assembléia Nacional on 9 February 2010.

The Government

HEAD OF STATE

President: JORGE CARLOS FONSECA (elected 21 August 2011; took office 9 September).

COUNCIL OF MINISTERS
(September 2012)

The Government is composed of members of the Partido Africano da Independência de Cabo Verde and independents.

Prime Minister: JOSÉ MARIA PEREIRA NEVES.

Minister of State and of Health: MARIA CRISTINA LOPES DE ALMEIDA FONTES LIMA.

Minister of Finance and Planning: CRISTINA DUARTE.

Minister of the Presidency of the Council of Ministers and of National Defence: JORGE HOMERO TOLENTINO ARAÚJO.

Minister of Foreign Affairs: JORGE ALBERTO DA SILVA BORGES.

Minister of Parliamentary Affairs: RUI MENDES SEMEDO.

Minister of Internal Administration: MARISA HELENA DO NASCIMENTO MORAIS.

Minister of Justice: JOSÉ CARLOS LOPES CORREIA.

Minister of Infrastructure and the Maritime Economy: JOSÉ MARIA FERNANDES DA VEIGA.

Minister of the Environment, Housing and Spatial Planning: SARA MARIA DUARTE LOPES.

Minister of Youth, Employment and Human Resources Development: JANIRA ISABEL FONSECA HOPFFER ALMADA.

Minister of Tourism, Industry and Energy: HUMBERTO SANTOS DE BRITO.

Minister of Education and Sport: FERNANDA MARIA DE BRITO MARQUES.

Minister of Rural Development: EVA VERONA TEIXEIRA ORTET.

Minister of Higher Education, Science and Innovation: ANTÓNIO LEÃO DE AGUIAR CORREIA E SILVA.

Minister of Communities: MARIA FERNANDA TAVARES FERNANDES.

Minister of Culture: MÁRIO LÚCIO MATIAS DE SOUSA MENDES.

Secretary of State for Foreign Affairs: JOSÉ LUÍS ROCHA.

Secretary of State for Public Administration: ROMEU FONSECA MODESTO.

Secretary of State for Marine Resources: ADALBERTO FILOMENO CARVALHO SANTOS VIEIRA.

MINISTRIES

Office of the President: Presidência da República, Palácio do Plateau, CP 100, Plateau, Praia, Santiago; tel. 2616555; fax 2614356; internet www.presidenciarepublica.cv.

Office of the Prime Minister: Gabinete do Primeiro Ministro, Palácio do Governo, Várzea, CP 16, Praia, Santiago; tel. 2610411; fax 2613099; e-mail gab.imprensa@gpm.gov.cv; internet www.primeirominstro.cv.

Ministry of Communities: Praia, Santiago; tel. 2616744; e-mail comunidades@mdc.gov.cv; internet www.mdc.gov.cv.

Ministry of Culture: Praia, Santiago; internet www.cultura.gov.cv.

Ministry of Education and Sport: Palácio do Governo, Várzea, CP 111, Praia, Santiago; tel. 2610232; fax 2610260; internet www.minedu.cv.

Ministry of the Environment, Housing and Spatial Planning: Ponta Belém, CP 115, Praia, Santiago; tel. 2615716; fax 2614054; internet www.maap.cv.

Ministry of Finance and Planning: 107 Av. Amílcar Cabral, CP 30, Praia, Santiago; tel. 2607400; e-mail aliciab@gov1.gov.cv; internet www.minfin.cv.

Ministry of Foreign Affairs: Palácio das Comunidades, Achada de Santo António, CP 60, Praia, Santiago; tel. 2607853; fax 2619270.

Ministry of Health: Largo Desastre da Assistência, Chã d'Areia, CP 719, Praia, Santiago; tel. 2612167; fax 2613112; e-mail cndsanitario@cvtelecom.cv; internet www.minsaude.gov.cv.

Ministry of Higher Education, Science and Innovation: Praia, Santiago; tel. 2610567.

Ministry of Infrastructure and the Maritime Economy: Ponta Belém, Praia, Santiago; tel. 2615709; fax 2611595; e-mail GSoares@mih.gov.cv.

Ministry of Internal Administration: Praia, Santiago.

Ministry of Justice: Rua Cidade do Funchal, CP 205, Praia, Santiago; tel. 2609900; fax 2623262; e-mail minjus@govcv.gov.cv; internet www.mj.gov.cv.

Ministry of Parliamentary Affairs: Praia, Santiago.

Ministry of the Presidency of the Council of Ministers and of National Defence: Praia, Santiago.

Ministry of Rural Development: Praia, Santiago.

Ministry of Social Development and Families: Edifício do Ministério das Finanças, 2º Esquerdo, CP 453, Plateau, Praia, Santiago; tel. 2603260; fax 2618866; e-mail madalena.neves@govcv.gov.cv; internet www.mtfs.gov.cv.

Ministry of Tourism, Industry and Energy: Praia, Santiago.

Ministry of Youth, Employment and Human Resources Development: Praia, Santiago.

President and Legislature

PRESIDENT

Presidential Election, First Round, 7 August 2011

Candidate	Votes	% of votes
Jorge Carlos Fonseca (MpD)	60,438	37.76
Manuel Inocêncio Sousa (PAICV)	51,970	32.47
Aristides Lima (Ind.)	44,500	27.80
Joaquim Monteiro (Ind.)	3,169	1.98
Total	160,077*	100.00

* The total number of votes cast declared by the CNE was 162,229, which included 964 blank votes and 885 spoiled ballots.

Presidential Election, Second Round, 21 August 2011

Candidate	Votes	% of votes
Jorge Carlos Fonseca (MpD)	97,643	54.18
Manuel Inocêncio Sousa (PAICV)	82,634	45.85
Total	180,227*	100.00

* Excluding 1,489 blank votes and 831 spoiled ballots.

LEGISLATURE

Assembleia Nacional: Achada de Santo António, CP 20A, Praia, Santiago; tel. 2608000; fax 2622660; e-mail an-cv@cvtelecom.cv; internet www.parlamento.cv.

Speaker: BASÍLIO RAMOS.

Legislative Elections, 6 February 2011

Party	Votes	% of votes	Seats
PAICV	117,967	52.68	38
MpD	94,674	42.27	32
UCID	9,842	4.39	2
PSD	1,040	0.46	—
PTS	429	0.19	—
Total	223,952*	100.00	72

* Excluding 1,248 blank votes and 1,742 invalid votes.

Election Commission

Comissão Nacional de Eleições (CNE): Achada de Santo António, Praia, Santiago; tel. 2624323; e-mail cne@cne.cv; internet www.cne.cv; Pres. ROSA CARLOTA MARTINS BRANCO VICENTE.

Political Organizations

Grupo Independente para Modernizar Sal (GIMS): Leader JORGE FIGUEIREDO.

Movimento para a Democracia (MpD): Av. Cidade Lisboa, 4° andar, CP 90A, Praia, Santiago; tel. 2614122; e-mail mpd@mpd.cv; internet www.mpd.cv; f. 1990; advocates administrative decentralization; governing party from 1991 to 2001; formed alliance with the PCD to contest 2006 legislative and presidential elections; Chair. CARLOS VEIGA; Sec.-Gen. AGOSTINHO LOPES.

Partido Africano da Independência de Cabo Verde (PAICV): Av. Amílcar Cabral, CP 22, Praia, Santiago; tel. 2612720; fax 2611410; internet www.paicv.cv; f. 1956 as the Partido Africano da Independência do Guiné e Cabo Verde (PAIGC); name changed in 1981, following the 1980 coup in Guinea-Bissau; sole authorized political party 1975–90; governing party since 2001; Pres. JOSÉ MARIA PEREIRA NEVES; Sec.-Gen. ARMINDO MAURICIO.

Partido da Renovação Democrática (PRD): Praia, Santiago; f. 2000 by fmr mems of the MpD; Pres. JOSÉ LUÍS BARBOSA.

Partido Socialista Democrático (PSD): Praia, Santiago; f. 1992; Sec.-Gen. JOÃO ALÉM.

Partido de Trabalho e Solidariedade (PTS): Praia, Santiago; f. 1998; Interim Leader ISAÍAS RODRIGUES.

União Cristã, Independente e Democrática (UCID): Achada Santo António-Frente, Restaurante 'O Poeta', Praia, Santiago; tel. 2608134; fax 2624403.

Diplomatic Representation

EMBASSIES IN CAPE VERDE

Angola: Av. OUA, Achada de Santo António, CP 78A, Praia, Santiago; tel. 2623235; fax 2623234; e-mail emb.angola@cv.telecom.cv; Ambassador JOSEFINA GUILHERMINA COELHO DA CRUZ.

Brazil: Chã de Areia 2, CP 93, Praia, Santiago; tel. 2615607; fax 2615609; e-mail contato@embrasilpraia.org; internet www.embrasilpraia.org; Ambassador MARIA DULCE SILVA BARROS.

China, People's Republic: Achada de Santo António, CP 8, Praia, Santiago; tel. 2623029; fax 2623047; e-mail chinaemb_cv@mfa.gov.cn; Ambassador LI CHUNHUA.

Cuba: Achada de Santo António, Praia, Santiago; tel. 2619408; fax 2617527; e-mail ecubacpv@cvtelecom.cv; internet emba.cubaminrex.cu/caboverdepor; Ambassador PEDRO EVELIO DORTA GONZÁLEZ.

France: Achada de Santo António, CP 192, Praia, Santiago; tel. 2615591; fax 2615590; internet www.ambafrance-cv.org; Ambassador MARIE-CHRISTINE GLAS.

Korea, Democratic People's Republic: Praia; Ambassador RI IN SOK.

Portugal: Av. OUA, Achada de Santo António, CP 160, Praia, Santiago; tel. 2623037; fax 2623222; e-mail embportpraia@gmail.com; internet www.secomunidades.pt/web/praia; Ambassador MARIA DA GRAÇA REYNAUD CAMPOS TROCADO ANDERSEN GUIMARÃES.

Russia: Achada de Santo António, CP 31, Praia, Santiago; tel. 2622739; fax 2622738; e-mail embrus@cvtelecom.cv; internet www.capeverde.mid.ru; Ambassador ALEXANDER R. KARPUSHIN.

Senegal: Rua Abílio Macedo, Plateau, CP 269, Praia, Santiago; tel. 2615621; fax 2612838; e-mail silcarneyni@hotmail.com; Ambassador MAMADOU FALL.

USA: Rua Abílio Macedo 6, Praia, Santiago; tel. 2608900; fax 2611355; internet praia.usembassy.gov; Ambassador MARIANNE M. MYLES.

Judicial System

Supremo Tribunal de Justiça (STJ)

Gabinete do Juiz Presidente, Edif. dos Correios, Rua Cesário de Lacerda, CP 117, Praia, Santiago; tel. 2615810; fax 2611751; e-mail stj@supremo.gov.cv; internet www.stj.cv.

f. 1975; Pres. ARLINDO ALMEIDA MEDINA.

Attorney-General: FRANKLIN AFONSO FURTADO.

Religion

CHRISTIANITY

An estimated 95% of the population are believed to be adherents of the Roman Catholic Church. Protestant churches, among which the Church of the Nazarene is the most prominent, represent about 1% of the population.

The Roman Catholic Church

Cape Verde comprises two dioceses, directly responsible to the Holy See. The Bishops participate in the Episcopal Conference of Senegal, Mauritania, Cape Verde and Guinea-Bissau, currently based in Senegal.

Bishop of Mindelo: Rt Rev. ILDO AUGUSTO DOS SANTOS LOPES FORTES, CP 447, 2110 Mindelo, São Vicente; tel. 2318870; fax 2318872; e-mail diocesemindelo@cvtelecom.cv.

Bishop of Santiago de Cabo Verde: Rt Rev. ARLINDO GOMES FURTADO, Av. Amílcar Cabral, Largo 5 de Outubro, CP 46, Praia, Santiago; tel. 2611119; fax 2614599; e-mail diocesecv@cvtelecom.cv.

The Anglican Communion

Cape Verde forms part of the diocese of The Gambia, within the Church of the Province of West Africa. The Bishop is resident in Banjul, The Gambia.

Other Christian Churches

Church of the Nazarene: District Office, Av. Amílcar Cabral, Plateau, CP 96, Praia, Santiago; tel. 2613611.

Other churches represented in Cape Verde include the Church of the Assembly of God, the Church of Jesus Christ of Latter-day Saints, the Evangelical Baptist Church, the Maná Church, the New Apostolic Church, the Seventh-day Adventist Church and the Universal Church of the Kingdom of God.

BAHÁ'Í FAITH

National Spiritual Assembly: Rua Madragoa, Plateau, Praia, Santiago; tel. 2617739; f. 1984.

The Press

Boletim Oficial da República de Cabo Verde: Imprensa Nacional, Av. Amílcar Cabral, Calçada Diogo Gomes, CP 113, Praia, Santiago; tel. 2614150; fax 2614209; e-mail incv@gov1.gov.cv; weekly; official announcements.

O Cidadão: Praça Dr António Aurélio Gonçalves 2, Mindelo, São Vicente; tel. 2325024; fax 2325022; e-mail cidadao@caboverde.zzn.com; weekly; Editor JOSÉ MÁRIO CORREIA.

Expresso das Ilhas: Achada de Santo António, OUA Nº 21, R/C, CP 666, Praia, Santiago; tel. 2619807; fax 2619805; e-mail jornal@expressodasilhas.cv; internet www.expressodasilhas.sapo.cv; f. 2001 by the MpD; daily; Dir JOÃO DO ROSÁRIO; Editor-in-Chief JORGE MONTEZINHO.

Jornal de Cabo Verde: Prédio Gonçalves, 6º piso, Av. Cidade de Lisboa, CP 889, Praia; tel. 2601414; e-mail jornal@liberal-caboverde.com; print version of online news website O Liberal; Dir DANIEL MEDINA; circ. 7,000.

A Nação: CP 690, Palmarejo, Praia; tel. 2628677; fax 2628505; e-mail geral@anacao.cv; internet www.anacao.cv; f. 2007; weekly; independent; Dir ALEXANDRE SEMEDO; circ. 1,000.

Raízes: CP 98, Praia, Santiago; f. 1977; quarterly; cultural review; Editor ARNALDO FRANÇA; circ. 1,500.

A Semana: Rotunda do Palmarejo, Av. Santiago 59, CP 36C, Praia, Santiago; tel. 2629860; fax 2628661; e-mail asemana@cvtelecom.cv; internet www.asemana.publ.cv; f. 1991; weekly; independent; Editor FILOMENA SILVA; circ. 5,000.

Terra Nova: Rua Guiné-Bissau 1, CP 166, Mindelo, São Vicente; tel. 2322442; fax 2321475; e-mail terranova@cabonet.cv; f. 1975; quarterly; Roman Catholic; Editor P. ANTÓNIO FIDALGO BARROS; circ. 3,000.

There is also an online newspaper, **Visão News** (www.visaonews.com), based in the USA. Further news websites include **O Liberal** (liberal.sapo.cv), **AllCaboVerde.com** (www.noscaboverde.com), **Cabonet** (www.cabonet.org), **Sport Kriolu** (www.sportkriolu.com), dedicated to sport, and **Voz di Povo Online** (arquivo.vozdipovoonline.com).

NEWS AGENCY

Inforpress: Achada de Santo António, CP 40A, Praia, Santiago; tel. 2624313; fax 2622554; e-mail inforpress@mail.cvtelecom.cv; internet www.inforpress.publ.cv; f. 1988 as Cabopress; Pres. JOSÉ AUGUSTO SANCHES.

PRESS ASSOCIATION

Associação de Jornalistas de Cabo Verde (AJOC): Rua João Chapuzet (Travessa do mercado), CP 350A, Praia, Santiago; tel. and fax 2622121; e-mail ajoc@ajoc.org.cv; internet www.ajoc.org.cv; f. 1993; Pres. HULDA MOREIRA; 11 media cos and 159 individual mems.

Publishers

Instituto Caboverdeano do Livro e do Disco (ICL): Centro Cultural, CP 158, Praia, Santiago; tel. 2612346; books, journals, music.

GOVERNMENT PUBLISHING HOUSE

Imprensa Nacional: Av. Amílcar Cabral, Calçada Diogo Gomes, CP 113, Praia, Santiago; tel. 2612145; fax 2614209; e-mail incv@gov1.gov.cv; internet www.incv.gov.cv; Admin. JOÃO DE PINA.

Broadcasting and Communications

TELECOMMUNICATIONS

Cabo Verde Telecom (CVTelecom): Rua Cabo Verde Telecom, Várzea, CP 220, Praia, Santiago; tel. 2609200; fax 2613725; e-mail cvtelecom@cvtelecom.cv; internet www.cvtelecom.cv; f. 1995; 40% owned by Portugal Telecom; Chief Exec. ANTÓNIO PIRES CORREIA.

CVMóvel: Chã de Areia, Praia, Santiago 126-A; fax 2622509; e-mail marketing@cvt.cv; internet www.cvmovel.cv; wholly owned subsidiary of Cabo Verde Telecom providing cellular mobile services.

T+ Telecomunicações: Santiago; f. 2007; Pres. MARCO BENTO.

Regulatory Authority

Agência Nacional das Comunicações (ANAC): Edifício do MIT, Ponta Belém, CP 892, Praia, Santiago; tel. 2604400; fax 2613069; e-mail info.anac@anac.cv; internet www.anac.cv; f. 2006; Pres. DAVID GOMES.

BROADCASTING

Rádiotelevisão Caboverdiana (RTC): Rua 13 de Janeiro, Achada de Santo António, CP 1A, Praia, Santiago; tel. 2605200; fax 2605256; e-mail rtc.infos@rtc.cv; internet www.rtc.cv; govt-controlled; 40 transmitters and relay transmitters; FM transmission only; radio broadcasts in Portuguese and Creole for 24 hours daily; 1 television transmitter and 7 relay television transmitters; television broadcasts in Portuguese and Creole for 8 hours daily with co-operation of RTP Africa (Portugal) and TV5 Honde; Pres. HORÁCIO MOREIRA SEMEDO; Dir of Radio JOANA OLINDA MIRANDA; Dir of Television ÁLVARO LUDGERO ANDRADE.

Televisão de Cabo Verde: Praia, Santiago; sole television broadcaster; part of RTC; Dir ÁLVARO ANDRADE.

Praia FM: Rua Visconde de S. Januario 19, 4° andar, CP 276C, Praia, Santiago; tel. 2616356; fax 2613515; e-mail atendimento@praiafm.biz; internet praiafm.sapo.cv; f. 1999; Dir GIORDANO CUSTÓDIO.

Rádio Comercial: Av. Liberdade e Democradia 6, Prédio Gomes Irmãos, 3° esq., CP 507, Praia, Santiago; tel. 2623156; fax 2622413; e-mail multimedia.rc@cvtelecom.cv; f. 1997; Admin. HENRIQUE PIRES; Dir CARLOS FILIPE GONÇALVES.

Rádio Educativa de Cabo Verde: Achada de Santo António, Praia, Santiago; tel. 2611161; Dir LUÍS LIMA.

Rádio Morabeza: Rua São João 16, 2º andar, CP 456, Mindelo, São Vicente; tel. 2324429; fax 2324431; e-mail radiomorabeza@cvtelecom.cv; f. 1999; Editor-in-Chief NUNO FERREIRA.

Rádio Nacional de Cabo Verde (RNCV): CP 26, Praia, Santiago; tel. 2613729; Dir CARLOS SANTOS.

Rádio Nova—Emissora Cristã de Cabo Verde: CP 166, Mindelo, São Vicente; tel. 2322082; fax 2321475; internet www.radionovaonline.com; f. 2002; Roman Catholic station; Dir ANTÓNIO FIDALGO BARROS.

Voz de São Vicente: CP 29, Mindelo, São Vicente; fax 2311006; f. 1974; govt-controlled; Dir JOSÉ FONSECA SOARES.

Finance

(cap. = capital; res = reserves; dep. = deposits; m. = million; brs = branches; amounts in Cape Verde escudos, unless otherwise indicated)

BANKING

In early 2011 there were nine commercial banks and 14 international offshore financial institutions in Cape Verde.

Central Bank

Banco de Cabo Verde (BCV): Av. Amílcar Cabral 117, CP 101, Praia, Santiago; tel. 2607000; fax 2607095; e-mail avarela@bcv.cv; internet www.bcv.cv; f. 1976; bank of issue; cap. 200.0m., res –288m., dep. 28,470m. (Dec. 2009); Gov. CARLOS AUGUSTO DUARTE DE BURGO.

Other Banks

Banco Africano de Investimentos Cabo Verde SA: Edifício Santa Maria, R/C-Chã DAreia, CP 459, Praia; tel. 2601224; fax

2622810; e-mail bai@bancobai.cv; internet www.bancobai.cv; f. 2008; Pres. Dr José de Lima Massano; Dir-Gen. Dr David Ricardo Teixeira Palege Jasse.

Banco Caboverdiano de Negócios (BCN): Av. Amílcar Cabral 97, CP 593, Praia, Santiago; tel. 2604250; fax 2614006; e-mail bcn@bcdenegocios.cv; internet www.bcncv.com; f. 1996 as Banco Totta e Açores (Cabo Verde); renamed as above in 2004; 46% owned by Banif (Portugal); cap. 900,000 escudos (Dec. 2008); 3 brs; Pres. Manuel J. Chantre.

Banco Comercial do Atlântico (BCA): Praça Alexandre Albuquerque, Av. Amílcar Cabral, CP 474, Praia, Santiago; tel. 2600900; fax 2613235; e-mail bca@bca.cv; internet www.bca.cv; f. 1993; privatized in 2000; main commercial bank; cap. 1,318.6m., res 995.2m., dep. 53,688.1m. (Dec. 2009); Pres. and Gen. Man. António Joaquim de Sousa; 25 brs.

Banco Espírito Santo Cabo Verde SA: Av. Cidade de Lisboa-Fazenda, CP 35, Praia, Santiago; tel. 2602626; fax 2602630; e-mail geral@bescv.cv; f. 2010; Pres. Pedro Roberto Menéres Cudell.

Banco Interatlântico: Av. Cidade de Lisboa, CP 131A, Praia, Santiago; tel. 2614008; fax 2614752; e-mail bi@bi.cv; internet www.bi.cv; f. 1999; cap. 600m., res 261m., dep. 14,198m. (Dec. 2009); Pres. of Exec. Comm. Dr Fernando Marques Pereira.

Caixa Económica de Cabo Verde, SA (CECV): Av. Cidade de Lisboa, CP 199, Praia, Santiago; tel. 2603603; fax 2612055; e-mail antonio.moreira@caixa.cv; internet www.caixa.cv; f. 1928; privatized in 1999; commercial bank; cap. 1,392.0m., res 1,522.8m., dep. 29,229.9m. (Dec. 2009); Pres. Emanuel Jesus da Veiga Miranda; 11 brs.

Ecobank Cabo Verde: Praça Infante Dom Henrique 18, Palmarejo, CP 374c, Praia; tel. 2603660; fax 2611090; e-mail ecobankcv@ecobank.com; internet www.ecobank.com; f. 2010; Pres. Eveline Tall; Man. Dir Mamadou Moctar Sall.

STOCK EXCHANGE

Bolsa de Valores de Cabo Verde, Sarl (BVC): 16 Achada de Santo António, CP 115 A, Praia, Santiago; tel. 2603030; fax 2603038; e-mail bcv@bvc.cv; internet www.bvc.cv; f. 1998; reopened December 2005; Pres. Veríssimo Pinto.

INSURANCE

Companhia Caboverdiana de Seguros (IMPAR): Sq. Amílcar Cabral, CP 344, Mindelo, S.Vicente; tel. and fax 2603134; fax 2616025; e-mail comercial@impar.cv; internet www.impar.cv; f. 1991; Pres. Dr Luís Vasconcelos Lopes.

Garantia Companhia de Seguros: Chã d'Areia, CP 138, Praia, Santiago; tel. 2608600; fax 2616117; e-mail garantia@garantia.cv; internet www.garantia.cv; f. 1991; privatized in 2000; Pres. Dr António Joaquim de Sousa.

Trade and Industry

GOVERNMENT AGENCIES

Agência Caboverdiana de Promoção de Investimentos e das Exportações (CI—Cabo Verde Investimentos): Rotunda da Cruz do Papa 5, CP 89C, Praia, Santiago; tel. 2604110; fax 2622657; e-mail Presidente@cvinvest.cv; internet www.cvinvest.cv; f. 2004; promotes public-private investment partnerships in infrastructure, export and tourism; Pres. and CEO José Armando Duarte.

Agência Nacional de Segurança Alimentar (ANSA): Início Rampa Chã d'Areia à Terra Branca, 3º andar Prédio Laranja, CP 262, Praia, Santiago; tel. 2626290; fax 2626297; e-mail ansa@cvtelecom.cv; internet www.ansa.cv; food security agency; Pres. Miguel Monteiro.

Agência de Regulação e Supervisão dos Produtos Farmacêuticos e Alimentares (ARFA): Achada de Santo António, CP 296A, Praia, Santiago; tel. 2626457; fax 2624970; e-mail arfa@arfa.gov.cv; internet www.arfa.cv; Pres. Dr Carla Djamila Monteiro Reis.

Comissão de Investimento Externo e Empresa Franca (CIEF): Praia, Santiago; foreign investment commission.

Gabinete de Apoio à Reestruturação do Sector Empresarial do Estado (GARSEE) (Cabo Verde Privatization): Largo do Tunis, Cruzeiro, CP 323, Praia, Santiago; tel. 2614748; fax 2612334; bureau in charge of planning and supervising restructuring and divestment of public enterprises; Project Dir Dr Sérgio Centeio.

DEVELOPMENT ORGANIZATION

Instituto Nacional de Investigação e Desenvolvimento Agrário (INIDA): CP 84, Praia, Santiago; tel. 2711147; fax 2711133; f. 1979; research and training on agricultural issues.

TRADE ASSOCIATION

Associação para a Promoção dos MicroEmpresários (APME): Fazenda, Praia, Santiago; tel. 2606056; f. 1988.

CHAMBERS OF COMMERCE

Câmara de Comércio, Indústria e Serviços de Barlavento (CCISB): Rua da Luz 31, CP 728, Mindelo, São Vicente; tel. 2328495; fax 2328496; e-mail camara.com@cvtelecom.cv; internet www.cciasb.org; f. 1996; Pres. Manuel J. Monteiro.

Câmara de Comércio, Indústria e Serviços de Sotavento (CCISS): Rua Serpa Pinto 160, CP 105, Praia, Santiago; tel. 2617234; fax 2617235; e-mail cciss@cvtelecom.cv; internet www.faroldacciss.org; Pres. Paulo Lima; Sec.-Gen. Rosário Luz.

STATE INDUSTRIAL ENTERPRISES

Empresa Nacional de Avicultura, SARL (ENAVI): Tira Chapéu Zona Industrial, CP 135, Praia, Santiago; tel. 2627268; fax 2628441; e-mail enavi@cvtelecom.cv; poultry-farming.

Empresa Nacional de Combustíveis, SARL (ENACOL): Largo John Miller's, CP 1, Mindelo, São Vicente; tel. 2306060; fax 2323425; e-mail enacolsv@enacol.cv; internet www.enacol.cv; f. 1979; supervises import and distribution of petroleum; Pres. Dr Adalberto Leite Pereira de Sena; Dir Carlitos Fortes.

Empresa Nacional de Produtos Farmacêuticos, SARL (EMPROFAC): Tira Chapéu Zona Industrial, CP 59, Praia, Santiago; tel. 2627895; fax 2627899; e-mail emprofac@cvtelecom.cv; f. 1979; state monopoly of pharmaceuticals and medical imports; Dir-Gen. Óscar Baptista.

UTILITIES

Electricity and Water

Empresa de Electricidade e Água, SARL (Electra): Av. Baltasar Lopes Silva 10, CP 137, Mindelo, São Vicente; tel. 2303030; fax 2324446; e-mail comercial@electra.cv; internet www.electra.cv; f. 1982; 51% govt-owned; Pres. Antão Fortes.

MAJOR COMPANIES

Cimentos de Cabo Verde (CCV): Tira Chapéu, CP 14A, Praia, Santiago; tel. 2603110; fax 2612086; internet www.cimentoscv.com; f. 1994; 86.6% owned by Cimpor (Portugal); imports and distributes construction materials.

Companhia dos Tabacos de Cabo Verde, SARL: CP 67, São Vicente; tel. 2314400; manufacture of tobacco and tobacco products.

Construções de Cabo Verde, SA (CVC): Achada Grande, CP 242, Praia, Santiago; tel. 2633879; fax 2633221; e-mail cvc@cvc.cv; 90% owned by Grupo SOMAGUE (Portugal); construction, mainly on govt infrastructure and building projects; Pres. José Ferreira Teixeira.

Empresa Caboverdiana de Pescas (Pescave): Mindelo, São Vicente; tel. 6313118; formerly govt-owned; fishing company.

Maripesca, Lda: Rua de S. João, CP 696, Mindelo, São Vicente; tel. 2316542; fax 2316582; e-mail maripesca@cvtelecom.cv; fishing equipment.

Sociedade Caboverdiana de Tabacos, Lda (SCT): Av. 5 de Julho, CP 270, São Vicente; tel. 2323349; fax 2323351; e-mail sctabacos@cvtelecom.cv; internet www.sct.cv; f. 1996; Pres. Euclides Jesus Marques Oliveira; 41 employees.

Sociedade Industrial de Calçado, SARL (SOCAL): CP 92, Mindelo, São Vicente; tel. 2315059; fax 2312061; industrial shoe factory.

CO-OPERATIVE

Instituto Nacional das Cooperativas: Achada de Santo António, Praia, Santiago; tel. 2616376; central co-operative org.

TRADE UNIONS

Confederação Caboverdiana dos Sindicatos Livres (CCSL): Rua Dr Júlio Abreu, CP 155, Praia, Santiago; tel. 2613928; fax 2616319; e-mail ccsl@cvtelecom.cv; f. 1992; Pres. José Manuel Vaz.

Federação Nacional dos Sindicatos dos Trabalhadores da Administração Pública (FNSTAP): CP 123, Praia; tel. 2614305; fax 2613629; Pres. Miguel Horta da Silva.

Sindicato dos Transportes, Comunicações e Turismo (STCT): Praia, Santiago; tel. 2616338.

União Nacional dos Trabalhadores de Cabo Verde—Central Sindical (UNTC—CS): Av. Cidade de Lisboa, CP 123, Praia, Santiago; tel. 2614305; fax 2613629; e-mail untc@cvtelecom.cv; internet www.untc-cs.cv; f. 1978; Chair. Júlio Ascenção Silva.

Transport

ROADS

In 2004 there were an estimated 2,250 km of roads, of which 1,750 km were paved.

Associação Apoio aos Reclusos e Crianças de Rua (AAPR): Achada de Santo António, CP 205A, Praia, Santiago; tel. 2618441; fax 2619017; e-mail aapr@cvtelecom.cv; road devt agency.

SHIPPING

Cargo-passenger ships call regularly at Porto Grande, Mindelo, on São Vicente, and Praia, on Santiago. There were plans to upgrade the ports at Praia, Sal, São Vicente and Porto Novo (Santo Antão). There are small ports on the other inhabited islands. Cape Verde's registered merchant fleet at 31 December 2009 consisted of 47 vessels, totalling 32,000 grt.

Arca Verde (Companhia Nacional de Navegação): Rua 5 de Julho, Plateau, Santiago; tel. 2615497; fax 2615496; e-mail cnnarcaverdepra@cvtelecom.cv; shipping co; undergoing privatization.

Cabo Verde Fast Ferry (CVFF): CP 796, Chã d'Areia, Praia; tel. 2617552; fax 2617553; e-mail cvff.info@cvfastferry.com; internet www.cvfastferry.com; f. 2009; Pres. ANDY DE ANDRADE.

Cape Verde National Shipping Line, SARL (Cs Line): Rua Baltasar Lopez da Silva, CP 238, Mindelo, São Vicente.

Comissão de Gestão dos Transportes Marítimos de Cabo Verde: CP 153, São Vicente; tel. 2314979; fax 2312055.

Companhia Caboverdiana de Navegação: Rua Cristiano Sena Barcelos 3–5, Mindelo, São Vicente; tel. 2322852.

Companhia de Navegação Estrela Negra: Av. 5 de Julho 17, CP 91, Mindelo, São Vicente; tel. 2325423; fax 2315382.

Empresa Nacional de Administração dos Portos, SA (ENAPOR, SA): Av. Marginal, CP 82, Mindelo, São Vicente; tel. 2307500; fax 2324337; e-mail info@enapor.cv; internet www.enapor.cv; f. 1982; Chair. and Man. Dir FRANKLIM DO ROSÁRIO SPENCER.

Linhas Marítimas Caboverdianas (LINMAC): CP 357, Praia, Santiago; tel. 2614352; fax 2613715; Dir ESTHER SPENCER.

Seage Agência de Navegação de Cabo Verde: Av. Cidade de Lisboa, CP 232, Praia, Santiago; tel. 2615758; fax 2612524; f. 1986; Chair. CÉSAR MANUEL SEMEDO LOPES.

Transnacional, a shipping company, operates a ferry service between some islands.

CIVIL AVIATION

The Amílcar Cabral international airport, at Espargos, on Sal island, can accommodate aircraft of up to 50 tons and 1m. passengers per year. The airport's facilities were expanded during the 1990s. A second international airport, Aeroporto da Praia (renamed Aeroporto Nelson Mandela in 2012), was opened in late 2005, and São Pedro Airport, on the island of São Vicente, received its first international arrival in December 2009. There is also a small airport on each of the other inhabited islands.

Agência de Aviação Civil (AAC): 34 Av. Cidade de Lisboa, CP 371, Praia, Santiago; tel. 2603430; fax 2611075; e-mail dgeral@acivil.gov.cv; internet www.aac.cv; f. 2005; regulatory agency; Pres. VALDEMAR CORREIA.

Empresa Nacional de Aeroportos e Segurança AEREA, SA (ASA): Aeroporto Amílcar Cabral, CP 58, Ilha do Sal; tel. 2412626; fax 2411570; e-mail pca@asa.cv; internet www.asa.cv; f. 1984; state-owned; airports and air navigation; Pres. MÁRIO LOPES.

Halcyon Air: CP 142, Ilha do Sal; tel. 2412948; fax 2412362; e-mail comercial@halcyonair.com; internet flyhalcyonair.com; f. 2005; inter-island carrier; Dir-Gen. FERNANDO GIL EVORA.

Transportes Aéreos de Cabo Verde (TACV): Av. Amílcar Cabral, CP 1, Praia, Santiago; tel. 2608200; fax 2617275; e-mail pferreira@tacv.aero; internet www.tacv.cv; f. 1958; internal services connecting the 9 inhabited islands; also operates regional services to Senegal, The Gambia and Guinea-Bissau, and long-distance services to Europe and the USA; scheduled for privatization; Pres. and CEO JOÃO HIGINO SILVA; Gen. Man. PAULO FERREIRA.

A private company, Inter Island Airlines, also offers flights between the islands of Cape Verde.

Tourism

The islands of Santiago, Santo Antão, Fogo and Brava offer attractive mountain scenery. There are extensive beaches on the islands of Santiago, Sal, Boavista and Maio. Some 428,000 tourists visited Cape Verde in 2011, and in that year tourism receipts totalled some US $369m. The sector is undergoing rapid expansion, with development in a number of Zonas de Desenvolvimento Turístico Integral. In late 2003 the Government began steps to have Fogo, which contains the only live volcano on Cape Verde, designated a UNESCO World Heritage Site. Plans were unveiled in March 2004 to promote the island of Santa Luzia as an ecotourism destination. Construction of a large tourist resort on Santiago, expected to cost €550m., commenced in early 2005. Tourist arrivals were projected to increase to about 1m. annually by 2015.

Defence

The armed forces numbered about 1,200 (army 1,000, air force less than 100, coastguard 100), as assessed at November 2011. There is also a police force, the Police for Public Order, which is organized by the local municipal councils. National service of two years is by selective conscription. In October 2002 the Government announced a programme of reform, involving the coastguard, the military police and special forces dealing with drugs-trafficking and terrorism offences.

Defence Expenditure: Budgeted at 722m. escudos in 2011.

Chief of Staff of the Armed Forces: Col ANTERO DE MATOS.

Education

Compulsory primary education begins at six or seven years of age and lasts for six years. Secondary education, beginning at 13 years of age, is divided into two cycles, the first comprising a three-year general course, the second a two-year pre-university course. There are three teacher-training units and two industrial and commercial schools of further education. According to UNESCO estimates, primary enrolment in 2009/10 included 93% of children in the relevant age-group (males 94%; females 92%), while secondary enrolment included 66% of children in the relevant age-group (males 61%; females 71%). In 2002/03 there were 1,743 Cape Verdean students studying at overseas universities. In 2002 a private university, the Universidade Jean Piaget de Cabo Verde, opened in Praia. According to UNESCO estimates, in 2005 spending on education represented 25.4% of total budgetary expenditure.

Bibliography

Almeida, R., and Nyhan, P. *Cape Verde and its People: A Short History*. Boston, MA, TCHUBA—American Committee for Cape Verde, 1978.

Amaral, I. *Santiago de Cabo Verde*. Lisbon, 1964.

Bigman, L. *History and Hunger in West Africa: Food Production and Entitlement in Guinea-Bissau and Cape Verde*. Santa Barbara, CA, Greenwood Press, 1993.

Cabral, A. *Unity and Struggle*. New York, Monthly Review Press, 1979.

Cabral, I., and Furtado, C. *Les Etats-nations face à l'intégration régionale en Afrique de l'Ouest. Le cas du Cap-Vert*. Paris, Editions Karthala, 2010.

Carreira, A. *Cabo Verde, Formação e Extinção de uma Sociedade Escravocrata*. Bissau, 1972.

Migrações nas Ilhas de Cabo Verde. Lisbon, Universidade Nova, 1977.

Cabo Verde: Classes sociais, estructura familiar, migrações. Lisbon, Ulmeiro, 1977.

The People of the Cape Verde Islands: Exploitation and Emigration (trans. and edited by C. Fyfe). London, Hurst, and Hamden, CT, Archon Books, 1983.

da Graça, A. *Cape Verdean Culture: An Interactive / Cooperative Approach*. New Bedford, MA, 1995.

Davidson, B. *The Fortunate Isles: A Study of Cape Verde*. London, Hutchinson, and Trenton, NJ, World Press, 1989.

de Pina, M.-P. *Les îles du Cap-Vert.* Paris, Editions Karthala, 1987.

Fobanjong, J., and Ranuga, T. *The Life, Thought, and Legacy of Cape Verde's Freedom Fighter Amilcar Cabral: Essays on His Liberation Philosophy.* Lewiston, NY, Edwin Mellen Press, 2006.

Fonseca dos Santos, I., da Costa Esteves, J., and Rolland, D. *Les îles du Cap-Vert : Langues, mémoires, histoire.* Paris, L'Harmattan, 2007.

Foy, C. *Cape Verde: Politics, Economics and Society.* London, Pinter Publishers, Marxist Regimes Series, 1988.

Halter, M. *Between Race and Ethnicity: Cape Verdean American Immigrants, 1860–1965.* Champaign, IL, University of Illinois Press, 1993.

Langworthy, M., and Finan, T. J. *Waiting for Rain: Agriculture and Ecological Imbalance in Cape Verde.* Boulder, CO, Lynne Rienner, 1997.

Lesourd, M. *État et société aux îles du Cap-Vert: Alternatives pour un petit état insulaire.* Paris, Editions Karthala, 1995.

Lima, A. *Reforma Política em Cabo Verde: do Paternalismo à Modernização do Estado.* Praia, 1992.

Lobban, R. *Historical Dictionary of Cape Verde.* 4th edn. Metuchen, NJ, Scarecrow Press, 2007.

Cape Verde: Crioulo Colony to Independent Nation. Boulder, CO, Westview Press, 1998.

May, S. *Tourismus in der Dritten Welt: Das Beispiel Kapverde.* Frankfurt am Main, Campus Verlag, 1985.

Meintel, D. *Race, Culture and Portuguese Colonialism in Cabo Verde.* Syracuse, NY, Syracuse University Press, 1985.

Pereira, D. *The Challenges of the Small Insular Developing States: Are the Mauritius and the Seychelles examples for Cape Verde?* Saarbrücken, VDM Verlag, 2009.

Silva Andrade, E. *Les îles du Cap-Vert de la "découverte" à l'indépendance nationale, 1460-1975.* Paris, L'Harmattan, 1996.

Soares, J. B. *Cabo Verde: Um País em Transição.* Boston, MA, Praia Branca Production, 1993.

Ying, Q. *The Institutional Influence on a Developing Country's Economy: A Case of Cape Verde.* Saarbrücken, VDM Verlag, 2009.

THE CENTRAL AFRICAN REPUBLIC

Physical and Social Geography

DAVID HILLING

Bordered to the north by Chad, to the east by Sudan and South Sudan, to the south by the Republic of the Congo and the Democratic Republic of the Congo, and to the west by Cameroon, the Central African Republic forms a geographic link between the Sudano-Sahelian zone and the Congo basin. The country consists mainly of plateau surfaces at 600 m–900 m above sea-level, which provide the watershed between drainage northwards to Lake Chad and southwards to the Oubangui-Congo river system. There are numerous rivers, and during the main rainy season (July–October) much of the south-east of the country becomes inaccessible as a result of extensive inundation. The Oubangui river to the south of Bangui provides near-year-round commercial navigation and is the main outlet for external trade. However, development of the country is inhibited by its land-locked location and the great distance (1,815 km) to the sea by way of the fluvial route from Bangui to Brazzaville, in the Republic of the Congo, and thence by rail to Pointe-Noire.

The Central African Republic covers an area of 622,984 sq km (240,535 sq miles). At the census of December 2003 the population was 3,151,072. According to UN estimates, the population numbered 4,575,585 in mid-2012, giving an average density of 7.3 inhabitants per sq km. The greatest concentration of population is in the western part of the country; large areas in the east are virtually uninhabited. Of the country's numerous ethnic groups, the Banda and Baya jointly comprise more than 50% of the population. Sango, a lingua franca, has been adopted as the national language.

Only in the south-west of the country is the rainfall sufficient (1,250 mm) to sustain a forest vegetation. The south-western Lobaye region is a source of coffee (the main cash crop), cocoa, rubber, palm produce and timber. Cotton, also an important cash crop, is cultivated in a belt beyond the forest. This area could benefit substantially from a proposed rail link with the Transcameroon railway.

Alluvial deposits of diamonds occur widely and are exploited, but uranium is potentially of much greater economic importance. The exploitation of ore-rich deposits at Bakouma, 480 km east of Bangui, which had previously been inhibited by inadequate access routes and by technical problems, commenced in the late 2000s.

Recent History

RICHARD A. BRADSHAW and JUAN FANDOS-RIUS

INTRODUCTION

In 1958 the French-administered territory of Oubangui-Chari was granted internal self-government and became the Central African Republic (CAR). The leader of the independence movement, Barthélémy Boganda, died in an unexplained plane crash in March 1959, and David Dacko became the republic's first President at independence on 13 August 1960. On 1 January 1966 Col Jean-Bédel Bokassa, the Commander-in-Chief of the Armed Forces, seized power in a coup. Bokassa's regime became increasingly despotic, corrupt and brutal. Several external opposition groups were formed, including the Mouvement pour la libération du peuple centrafricain (MLPC), led by Ange-Félix Patassé, who had been dismissed as Prime Minister in 1978 and had fled to France. In September 1979 Bokassa, while in Libya, was deposed in a bloodless coup carried out by French troops, who returned Dacko to power. A multi-party system was restored in February 1981 and in March Dacko was elected President with 50% of the votes cast. Nevertheless, political opposition to Dacko increased during 1981 and in September Army Chief of Staff Gen. André Kolingba took power in a bloodless coup.

Kolingba banned political activity and disenchantment with the military regime soon became evident. In March 1982 an unsuccessful coup attempt was staged by Patassé; he subsequently took refuge in the French embassy, which arranged for his transport to exile in Togo. Kolingba then sought reconciliation with opponents of his regime by inviting Gen. François Bozizé Yangouvonda, a participant in the 1982 coup attempt, to return from exile; however, Bozizé chose to remain in Benin.

Patassé secured victory at the presidential election held in August–September 1993, and was sworn in as President in October. The Government's repeated failure to pay the salaries of public sector employees and members of the armed forces provoked frequent strikes and mounting political unrest during the mid-1990s. In April 1996 part of the national army mutinied in the capital demanding the immediate payment of all arrears. Faced with the presence of French troops (the Eléments Français d'Assistance Opérationelle—EFAO) in Bangui who were ready to protect the presidential palace and other key installations, the rebellion swiftly collapsed.

A protocol was signed by the Government in June 1996 that provided for the establishment of a government of national unity under the leadership of a civilian Prime Minister with no official party ties. The Bangui Accords signed at the end of January 1997 granted an amnesty to the mutineers and led to the formation of a new national unity government and the replacement of the EFAO troops. In mid-February Gen. Bozizé replaced Col Maurice Regonessa as Chief of Staff of the Armed Forces. During that month peace-keeping operations were transferred to the Mission Interafricaine de Surveillance des Accords de Bangui (MISAB), which included some 700 soldiers from Burkina Faso, Chad, Gabon, Mali, Senegal and Togo.

A National Reconciliation Conference held in Bangui in February 1998 led to the signing on 5 March of a National Reconciliation Pact by Patassé and 40 representatives of all the country's political and social groups. The pact restated the main provisions of the Bangui Accords and facilitated the authorization in March by the UN Security Council of the establishment of a peace-keeping mission, the UN Mission in the Central African Republic (MINURCA), to replace MISAB. MINURCA comprised 1,345 mostly African troops, who were to remain in the country for at least three months, but its mission was subsequently extended until the end of February 1999 in order to support and verify the legislative elections held in late 1998.

In February 1999 the UN Security Council extended MINURCA's mandate until November of that year, but the force was to be gradually reduced after the successful conclusion of a presidential election. France opposed the extension of MINURCA's mandate and withdrew its troops from the CAR in February. The presidential election took place on 19 September, and Patassé was re-elected, with 51.6% of the votes cast; he was inaugurated for a further six-year term in October.

Also in October 1999 the UN Security Council authorized the gradual withdrawal of MINURCA from the CAR, but in December the UN announced proposals to establish a Bureau de Soutien à la Consolidation de la Paix en Centrafrique (BONUCA), in Bangui. BONUCA began its operation on the same day as the final withdrawal of MINURCA, 15 February 2000, with a one-year mandate. In September BONUCA's mandate was extended until the end of 2001, and in September of that year, following continued unrest, it was extended for another one-year period.

Following Patassé's dismissal of Prime Minister Anicet Georges Dologuélé and the appointment of Martin Ziguélé to the premiership in April 2001, rebel soldiers attacked Patassé's official residence in an attempted coup. However, the insurgency was quickly suppressed and order restored by troops loyal to Patassé. Libyan troops and helicopters and a contingent of rebels from the Democratic Republic of the Congo (DRC) arrived to support the Patassé regime. In August 2002 Kolingba and 20 associates were sentenced to death *in absentia* for involvement in the attempted coup; a further 500 defendants were reported to have received prison terms of 10–20 years.

Gen. Bozizé was dismissed from the post of Chief of Staff of the Armed Forces in October 2001, and in November, after attempts were made to arrest him, violence erupted in Bangui between supporters of Bozizé and the presidential guard supported by forces from Libya. Bozizé soon fled to southern Chad, where he and some 300 of his armed supporters were granted asylum.

In October 2002 the northern suburbs of Bangui were invaded by forces loyal to Bozizé. Following heavy fighting, pro-Government forces, supported by Libyan troops and about 1,000 soldiers from a DRC rebel grouping, the Mouvement pour la Libération du Congo (MLC), succeeded in repelling the insurgents. The Patassé Government failed fully to suppress the forces allied to Bozizé, and by December the CAR was divided between loyalist areas in the south and east and rebel-held northern regions between the Chadian border and Bangui.

The first contingent of a Communauté Economique et Monétaire de l'Afrique Centrale (CEMAC) peace-keeping force (eventually to number 350) arrived in Bangui in December 2002, and in January 2003 Libyan forces were withdrawn. The CEMAC forces were mandated to protect the President, enforce security along the CAR–Chad border, and help to restructure the military. In February MLC fighters began to withdraw from the CAR, in response to international pressure on the Patassé Government.

BOZIZÉ ASSUMES POWER

Armed supporters of Bozizé and mercenaries from Chad converged on Bangui in March 2003, but encountered little resistance from government troops. President Patassé, returning from a regional summit in Niger, was forced to fly on to the Cameroonian capital, Yaoundé, after shots were fired at his plane as it approached Bangui. After the surrender of security forces in the capital and a lack of resistance from CEMAC troops, Bozizé declared himself Head of State, dissolved the Assemblée nationale and suspended the Constitution. Although the coup was officially condemned by France, the African Union (AU), the UN, CEMAC and the USA, it was alleged to have had the covert support of France, Gabon and Chad. Bozizé announced that a new consensus government would be formed in consultation with the former opposition, human rights groups and development agencies and soon secured the approval of the Governments of Gabon and the Republic of the Congo. Bozizé also gained the support of opposition parties, which pledged to oppose any attempt by Patassé to return to power.

Later in March 2003 Abel Goumba, leader of the Front Patriotique pour le Progrès, was appointed as Prime Minister. A new, broadly based transitional Government was then formed. Despite receiving only two positions in the new Council of Ministers, in mid-April the MLPC declared that it would adhere to the transitional arrangements decreed by Bozizé. Public support for the new regime increased following the payment of public sector salaries for the first time in more than two years. In April an amnesty for those convicted of involvement in the coup attempt of May 2001 was proclaimed. On 30 May 2003 Bozizé inaugurated a 98-member advisory Conseil National de Transition (CNT), which included representatives of political parties, trade unions, religious organizations and human rights groups, in order to assist him in exercising legislative power during the transitional period, which was to last 18–30 months. The CNT subsequently elected Nicolas Tiangaye, a prominent human rights activist, as its speaker. Bozizé confirmed his intention to return the country to civilian rule in January 2005, after presidential and legislative elections and the approval of a new constitution, to be drafted by the CNT.

In mid-2003 the Bozizé regime gained increasing international recognition for its efforts to reform the country's institutions and to promote reconciliation. Several prominent political figures agreed to participate in the long-delayed national dialogue which was to take place in September, including former Presidents Kolingba and Dacko. In August the state prosecutor issued an international arrest warrant for Patassé, now in exile in Togo, on charges including murder and embezzlement. In September BONUCA's mandate was extended until December 2004.

Some 350 delegates, representing the Government, political organizations, trade unions, civil society and ethnic groups, participated in the national dialogue, which ended in late October 2003, and a panel was created to oversee the implementation of the delegates' recommendations. In December Prime Minister Goumba was appointed Vice-President and a former financier, Célestin-Leroy Gaombalet, was named Prime Minister. In early December 2004 the newly appointed Transitional Constitutional Court oversaw the planned referendum on a new constitution, which was approved by 87.2% of those who voted. The new Constitution provided for a presidential term of five years, renewable only once, and increased powers for the Prime Minister.

THE 2005 ELECTIONS

Presidential and legislative elections were held concurrently on 13 March 2005. The pro-Bozizé Convergence 'Kwa na kwa' (KNK—meaning 'Work and Only Work' in Sango) coalition secured 42 of the 105 seats in the new Assemblée nationale, while the MLPC (supporting former Prime Minister Martin Ziguélé) won 11 seats; 34 independent candidates were also elected. In the presidential election Bozizé secured 43.0% of the votes cast, while Ziguélé obtained 23.5% and Kolingba 16.4%. Since no candidate had won an absolute majority, Bozizé and Ziguélé contested a second round of voting on 8 May; Bozizé was elected with some 64.7% of the total votes. The new Assemblée nationale convened on 9 June and Bozizé was sworn in as President two days later. Elie Doté was appointed Prime Minister and presented a new Council of Ministers composed primarily of KNK members, although also including two members of both the MLPC and the Rassemblement Démocratique Centrafricain (RDC).

In December 2005 the AU reported that criminal gangs were recruiting pro-Patassé soldiers from groups such as the Union des forces républicaines, led by Lt François-Florian N'Djadder-Bedaya, and the Armée Populaire pour la Restauration de la République et la Démocratie (APRD). Also in December the Assemblée granted Bozizé's request to rule by decree for nine months, a move criticized by the CAR Human Rights League. Bozizé formed a new Government in September 2006, with Doté retained as Prime Minister and also assuming the position of Minister of Finance and the Budget. Later that month Ziguélé was elected President of the MLPC.

REBEL INSURGENCIES

During mid-2006 rebel activity in the north of the country became President Bozizé's most serious problem. In August Jean-Jacques Larmassoum, a rebel leader of the APRD, was sentenced to life in prison, and former President Patassé—who was reported to be financing the training of mercenaries—was sentenced to 20 years of forced labour *in absentia*.

The village of Birao in the north-east of the country was taken in October 2006 by rebels of the Union des Forces Démocratiques pour le Rassemblement (UFDR), a coalition created in Kigali, Rwanda, in September by the Groupe d'Action Patriotique de la Libération de Centrafrique, led by Michel Am Nondroko Djotodia, the Mouvement des Libérateurs Centrafricains pour la Justice (MLCJ), led by Capt. Abakar Sabone, and the Front Démocratique Centrafricain, led by Commdt Justin Hassan. Within one week the UFDR rebels had seized control of most of the prefecture of Vakaga; however, in late November government forces and French troops regained control.

In November 2006 UN aid began to reach the devastated region around Kaga-Bandoro, which had been raided by road bandits known as *zaraguinas*, and from where thousands of local residents had fled to the prefecture of Nana-Gribizi. The Fédération internationale des droits de l'homme estimated that at least 70,000 people also fled to neighbouring Cameroon and Chad to escape fighting in the region between APRD rebels and government troops.

President Omar Bongo Ondimba of Gabon announced in mid-November 2006 that troops from that country were to be deployed to the CAR to serve as part of the Force Multinationale de la CEMAC (FOMUC). Days later humanitarian organizations decided to suspend their operations in the Paoua region due to ongoing conflict there. Later that month the Forces Armées Centrafricaines (FACA), assisted by French troops, regained control of Birao, but UFDR rebels took control of Ndélé and Bamingui. In early December French troops forced the UFDR rebels to abandon Ndélé and attacked rebels in Ouanda-Djallé. Bozizé then visited Birao to demonstrate government control of the region.

In January 2007 the UFDR announced that the Front Démocratique de Libération du Peuple Centrafricain (FDPC), led by Abdoulaye Miskine, was not part of its coalition. APRD rebels attacked Paoua in mid-January, but were unable to retain control of the town. On 25 January and 1 February in Sirte, Libya, President Bozizé met with Miskine and the APRD supporter André Ringui Le Gaillard, a former minister under Patassé. A peace agreement was signed on 2 February between the CAR Government, the FDPC and the APRD, and the following day Bozizé returned to Bangui with Miskine, who was accused of war crimes by human rights organizations.

Bozizé and Miskine subsequently returned to Libya, where Revolutionary Leader Col Muammar al-Qaddafi asked Miskine to persuade UFDR leaders to sign the Sirte Agreement calling for the withdrawal of foreign forces from the DRC. However, in March 2007 rebels launched further attacks on Birao and FACA forces were obliged to assist the CAR to regain control of the region. Later that month Bozizé appealed to all rebel groups to sign the Sirte accord. In mid-April Gen. Raymond Ndougou of the CAR armed forces and the UFDR leaders signed a new 10-point peace agreement at Birao. Both sides agreed to end their confrontation and the UFDR was granted permission to engage in politics. Sabone announced in mid-May that he did not accept the Birao agreement and that his MLCJ military front and the UFDR intended to continue their struggle.

INCLUSIVE POLITICAL DIALOGUE

Miskine and Zakaria Damane were appointed advisers to the presidency in July 2007, but in early August Miskine refused the appointment owing to doubts that the peace agreement brokered in February between the Government and the FDPC would be implemented. Nevertheless, on 23–25 August, at a meeting organized by BONUCA in Bangui, representatives from the Government, the opposition, rebel groups and civil society agreed to establish a preparatory committee (PC) for the national dialogue. An agreement was signed by all parties in early October establishing a 23-member committee to represent both the ruling KNK coalition and the opposition Union des Forces Vives de la Nation (UFVN). Representatives from civil society and the Government were allotted five seats each, while three seats were reserved for each major rebel group: the UFDR, the FDPC and the APRD. Patassé and the former Minister of National Defence, Jean-Jacques Démafouth, were both invited to participate. The UFVN only agreed to take part in the dialogue after Bozizé had agreed to increase the number of opposition representatives on the committee. On 30 November President Bozizé inaugurated the PC and in December Abebe Berhanu of the Centre for Humanitarian Dialogue (an independent organization based in Switzerland) was sworn in as Chairman.

Prime Minister Doté resigned on 18 January 2008 following a national strike organized by the country's main trade unions, including the Union Syndicale des Travailleurs de Centrafrique, over non-payment of public sector salary arrears. On 22 January Bozizé appointed a non-political figure, the rector of the University of Bangui, Prof. Faustin-Archange Touadéra, as the new Prime Minister. Touadéra subsequently named a 29-member administration; of the 15 new ministers, nine were from Bozizé's KNK. The Minister for Rural Development and Agriculture, Charles Massi, and the Minister of Foreign and Francophone Affairs and Regional Integration, Côme Zoumara, were replaced by close allies of Bozizé, Jean-Eudes Teya and Dieudonné Kombo Yaya, respectively. The President's brothers-in-law, Brig.-Gen. Raymond Paul Ndougou and Emmanuel Bizot, were named as Minister of the Interior and Public Security and Minister of Finance and the Budget, respectively. Thus, Bozizé and his associates retained control over most key ministries.

In February 2008 Benin released two leaders of the rebel UFDR, Djotodia and Abakar Sabone, who had been held in detention in Cotonou since November 2006. They were expected to return to the CAR immediately to attend the talks. Also in February 2008 the UN Secretary-General's Special Representative to the CAR, François Lonsény Fall, met with APRD leaders in the north-western town of Paoua in an effort to persuade them to participate in the negotiations. Démafouth was appointed as the APRD's new political leader in March 2008; he subsequently announced that his party would take part in the political dialogue.

There were reports of clashes between government and APRD forces in the Bocaranga region in March–April 2008, and rebels claimed to have killed more than a dozen soldiers. Following months of negotiations, on 9 May the Government signed a cease-fire agreement with the APRD in Libreville, Gabon, completing a process that began in early 2007. The Libreville agreement included provisions for an immediate cease-fire; the cantonment of rebel fighters prior to their demobilization and integration into the regular army; a general amnesty for all APRD members; the release of all prisoners held by the APRD; and the rehabilitation of areas affected by the conflict. It remained unclear, however, whether certain key APRD members were covered by the amnesty, including Démafouth, who was charged with the murder of several rivals in 2004, and the former APRD military commander, Larmassoum, who was sentenced to life imprisonment in August 2006. The amnesty was not expected to apply to Patassé, who was under investigation by the International Criminal Court (ICC), based in The Hague, Netherlands, over alleged human rights abuses committed during the 2002–03 rebellion. Patassé's ally, Jean-Pierre Bemba Gombo, the leader of the MLC and former DRC Vice-President, was arrested in Belgium in May 2008 on charges including human rights abuses committed by his forces in the CAR.

In May 2008 the UFDR leader, Djotodia, appointed Charles Massi, President of the Forum démocratique pour la modernité (FODEM), as political co-ordinator for the party; however, FODEM's political bureau opposed this and announced Massi's dismissal. On 16 May the UFDR Chief of Staff, Zakaria Damane, denounced both Djotodia and Massi.

Despite the Government's peace accord with the APRD, violence continued in the remote border regions of the CAR. From early 2008 there was an upsurge in attacks and kidnappings by *zaraguinas*. In June President Bozizé established a 15-member committee to help mobilize financial and material resources for the national dialogue. Later that month the Government signed a new 'comprehensive peace agreement' (CPA) with rebel groups in Libreville, which reaffirmed the individual cease-fires previously negotiated, and provided an amnesty for the rebel fighters and for the demobilization and reintegration of the rebels into either the national army or civilian life. The agreement was signed by leaders of the APRD and the UFDR; however, the leader of the FDPC, Miskine, was unable to attend the signing ceremony.

Bemba was transferred to the ICC at The Hague on 3 July 2008, and an initial court hearing against him took place on the following day. In July Abakar Sabone, President of the MLCJ, announced his group's withdrawal from the UFDR, and in mid-August Massi also confirmed his withdrawal from the UFDR due to disagreements over procedures for appointments within the organization.

The monitoring committee for the CPA met in mid-September 2008 in Libreville, where representatives of Gabon, the CAR, the APRD, the FDPC, the Mission de Consolidation de la Paix (MICOPAX) and the UN discussed implementation of the agreement. In late September Lt Robert Yékoua Kétté was elected President of the MLCJ, which dismissed Abakar Sabone and announced the MLCJ's reintegration into the UFDR after Yékoua Kétté was appointed its spokesperson. On 13 October President Bozizé signed an amnesty law passed by the Assemblée nationale on 29 September, despite the opposition of rebel army groups that did not approve of certain provisions therein.

The frequently postponed political dialogue was finally held in Bangui from 8–20 December 2008. Former President Patassé and his former Minister of National Defence, Démafouth, returned to the CAR capital to take part in the conference. Djotodia disclosed that the UFDR would not attend the national conference for various reasons, including a lack of guarantees with regard to their security. On 16 December the adoption of recommendations made by the CAR Politics and Governance Committee was welcomed by opposition parties. The dialogue resulted in several agreements, including the establishment of a broad-based government; a commitment to hold municipal, legislative and presidential elections in 2009 and 2010; and the setting up of an independent electoral commission, a commission to supervise the implementation of the accord and a commission to verify reconciliation.

Prime Minister Touadéra, who had resigned from his post some 10 days earlier, was again reappointed to the premiership by President Bozizé on 19 January 2009 and immediately formed a new Government. In the following month a FACA unit at Bossembélé was attacked by Convention des Patriotes pour la Justice et la Paix (CPJP) soldiers in an attempt to free rebel army prisoners held at the Bossembélé prison. On 26 February Massi was appointed Deputy Co-ordinator General for the CPJP, which subsequently convened a general assembly at Bocaranga and elected him President of its political council.

In June 2009 Chad announced that its troops had arrested Massi on his way from Sahr to Gonde, near the CAR border, and accused him of attempted subversion against a neighbouring country, namely the CAR. Also in June former President Patassé announced that he would contest the presidential election scheduled to be held in 2010. However, he was subsequently expelled from the MLPC, and Martin Ziguélé was confirmed as the party's President and declared to be its candidate in the presidential election.

In late June 2009 the ICC announced its decision to commit Bemba to trial for war crimes and crimes against humanity, including murder and rape, although there was insufficient evidence to confirm torture charges against him. In early July the FDPC leader, Abdoulaye Miskine, signed the CPA with the CAR Government in Libya. Some 20 FDPC members returned to Bangui, while Miskine remained in Libya and asked to be assigned abroad to a CAR embassy.

POSTPONEMENT AND RESCHEDULING OF THE 2010 ELECTIONS

The pro-Bozizé KNK coalition was recognized as a formal political party at a congress held in Mbaïki in October 2009. Joseph Kitiki-Kouamba, Bozizé's diplomatic advisor, was elected President of the reconstituted KNK, and former Minister of Social Affairs Marie-Solange Pagonendji-Ndakala was chosen as Vice-President. In accordance with a new electoral law adopted by the Assemblée nationale on 3 August 2009, a Commission Électorale Indépendante (CEI—Independent Electoral Commission) was established by President Bozizé on 27 August in order to conduct, organize and oversee presidential and legislative elections in 2010. Patassé returned to the CAR on 30 October 2009 and reaffirmed, in early November, that he would contest the presidency. In January 2010 former ambassador to Senegal and Deputy Minister of Regional Development Marie-Reine Hassen also announced her candidacy in the forthcoming presidential election.

It was reported on 16 January 2010 that CPJP leader Charles Massi had died earlier that month, after being subjected to torture while in detention at the western town of Bossembélé. In a statement the Ministry of National Defence formally denied killing Massi and claimed that the Government did not know his whereabouts. On 30 January President Bozizé acknowledged that Massi had been killed, but provided no details. However, in August Firmin Féindiro, the CAR Attorney-General, announced that, in the absence of evidence of Massi's death in a state prison and knowledge of his whereabouts, in accordance with CAR law he could not officially be regarded as deceased for a further 10 years.

In mid-February 2010 the CAR army announced that forces of the Ugandan rebel movement, the Lord's Resistance Army (LRA) of Joseph Kony (which had been active in the CAR since early 2008), had abducted about 10 civilians at the village of Kamandaré, in the south-east of the country, and had then attacked the nearby village of Gbangomboro. On 18 February a Ugandan army unit arrived in the region to pursue the LRA combatants. Fearing another attack by the LRA, many local civilians fled. LRA activities continued in south-eastern CAR in mid-2010.

President Bozizé announced in February 2010 that concurrent presidential and legislative elections would take place on 25 April. Nicolas Tiangaye, the spokesman for the Collectif des Forces du Changement (CFC—Collective Forces of Change), a coalition of opposition parties including the UFVN and former rebels, criticized the chosen date and requested that the elections be postponed until January 2011. On 13 March 2010 the Minister of National Security and Public Order, Gen. Jules Bernard Ouandé, announced on Radio Centrafrique that the Government had discovered plans to carry out an imminent coup, and that several undisclosed military officers and politicians were involved in the conspiracy. On 15 March President Bozizé formally declared his candidacy to seek re-election.

After widespread criticism by the opposition that preparations for the elections were incomplete, President Bozizé, with the support of the UN, the European Union (EU), France and the USA, agreed on 30 March 2010 to reschedule the first round of the elections for 16 May, and announced that the legal date for the expiry of his term, 11 June, would be respected. The procedure for registering presidential candidates was completed on 9 April, but the opposition refused to recognize the results, since only two applicants—President Bozizé and former President Patassé—had obtained registration, even though at least three others (including Hassen and Zinguélé) had declared their candidacy.

On 20 April 2010 President Bozizé dismissed Cyriaque Gonda, the Minister of Communication, Community Involvement, Dialogue and National Reconciliation, and Elié Ouéfio, the Minister of Territorial Administration and Decentralization. Ouéfio, who was also Secretary-General of the KNK, was to devote his attention to the forthcoming elections, but no explanation for Gonda's dismissal was offered. On 30 April the CEI announced that the first round of the elections could not be held on 16 May as scheduled, and both presidential and legislative elections were again postponed. Consequently, on 10 May the Assemblée nationale amended the Constitution to extend its term in office and that of the President 'for an undetermined time'. This decision was then validated by the Constitutional Court on 25 May. Finally, in mid-June the CEI announced that the twice-postponed elections would be conducted on 24 October. However, President Bozizé announced on 30 July that the joint presidential and legislative elections would not be held until 23 January 2011. A few days later the Government met with the opposition, rebels and other inclusive political dialogue representatives and agreed that the first round of elections would be held on that date, and the second round on 27 March.

The CEI announced on 9 November 2010 that six presidential candidates had been approved: Bozizé (KNK), Patassé (non-affiliated), Démafouth (APRD), Emile Gros Raymond Nakombo (RDC), Ziguélé (MLPC) and Justin Innocent Wilité (Congrès Centrafricain de la Renaissance). However, Wilité's candidacy was later rejected when he failed to pay the required deposit to take part in the election. On 14 December 29 parties loyal to Bozizé (the so-called Majorité Présidentielle) signed a joint agreement with the KNK to rally support for Bozizé, thus strengthening the incumbent's position.

BOZIZÉ RE-ELECTED

The first round of the presidential and legislative elections duly took place on 23 January 2011, supervised by an EU Election Observation Mission and an observer mission from the South African-based Electoral Institute for the Sustainability of Democracy in Africa. On 12 February the Constitutional Court published the final results, according to which 54% of all eligible voters had cast their ballot, with Bozizé winning 64.4% of the votes, Patassé 21.4%, Ziguélé 6.8%, Nakombo 4.6% and Démafouth 2.8%. Bozizé was thus re-elected President without the need for a run-off election, and on 15 March was sworn in for a second five-year term. In the first round of the legislative elections 35 of the 105-member Assemblée nationale were elected. Bozizé's KNK party won 26 seats, while the MLPC secured only one. The remaining eight seats were won by non-affiliated candidates, five of whom were reported to be close to Bozizé.

However, on 24 January 2011 the CFC, led by Tiangaye and representing eight opposition parties, announced that it regarded the election results as illegitimate due to widespread irregularities. As a result, on 17 February the CFC decided to withdraw its candidates from the legislative run-off elections. Patassé also called for a boycott of the elections. The run-off elections nevertheless proceeded as scheduled on 27 March; the KNK won a further 36 seats, while 17 were secured by non-affiliated candidates. The Parti d'Action pour le Développement (PAD) won three seats, the Mouvement pour la Démocratie et le Développement obtained two, and the Union Nationale des Démocrates Republicains, the Parti National pour un Centrafrique Nouveau, the Parti Démocratique Centrafricain, the Mouvement pour la Démocratie, l'Indépendance et le Progrès Social and the RDC each won a single seat.

Meanwhile, in an attempt to overcome the long-running dispute over the MLPC leadership, Ziguélé and Patassé met in Bangui on 4 February 2011 and announced their reconciliation. On 4 March Patassé and the MLPC and the RDC established the Front pour l'Annulation et la Reprise des Elections de 2011 (FARE-2011), a coalition devoted to the cancellation of the results of the allegedly illegitimate elections and to the holding of new elections. Soon afterwards, Patassé's health deteriorated, but the Government denied him permission to fly to Equatorial Guinea for medical treatment. On 2 April he was finally allowed to fly to Douala, Cameroon, where he died three days later. President Bozizé denied any responsibility for Patassé's death, despite being accused to the contrary, and agreed to hold an official funeral for him.

On 18 March 2011 Prime Minister Touadéra resigned. One month later President Bozizé reappointed Touadéra as premier, and members of his new Government were appointed on 22 April. Controversially, on 3 May the inaugural session of the new Assemblée nationale was held, despite the fact that the Constitutional Court had invalidated 13 of the 35 seats won in the first round of voting, and had yet to reach a decision regarding the seats disputed in the second round.

Clashes between Christians and Muslims in Bangui leading to the deaths of 11 people—eight Chadians and three Central Africans—occurred on 31 May 2011, following the discovery of the bodies of two young children. An angry mob attacked Muslims, especially small business owners, who were blamed for the children's deaths. The CAR Government imposed a curfew on three districts in north-western Bangui and a few days later, following a meeting with a member of the Chadian Government, the two countries agreed to expedite investigations into the children's murders in order to defuse tensions, release people incarcerated during the unrest and to compensate victims of the violence. On 2 June tensions increased in the north of the country when it was announced that the Catholic Bishop of Bambari, had been briefly hijacked at Ngerengou, north of Bria, and that his captors had not been identified.

On 12 June 2011 the CAR's last remaining rebel group, the CPJP, signed a cease-fire accord with the Government, which included an agreement that the rebel soldiers be confined to their barracks while talks on a final peace deal were being held. Earlier that month negotiations had taken place in the northern town of Ndélé, where the CPJP accepted a disarmament, demobilization and reintegration (DDR) accord as well as the CPA, which had been signed by most of the country's former rebel groups in Libreville in 2008. On 8 July 2011 a draft of the national strategy for the reintegration of former combatants was completed with the support of the Bureau Intégré de l'Organisation des Nations Unies en Centrafrique (BINUCA), which had replaced BONUCA in January 2010.

Faustin Bambou and Cyrus Emmanuel Sandy, two newspaper editors charged with inciting hatred and endangering state security, were imprisoned at Ngaragba prison in Bangui in June 2011. However, both were fined and released on 11 July. Bambou had written a series of articles in February and March concerning demonstrations by former soldiers, which included a suggestion that the President's son, the Minister-delegate at the Presidency, in charge of National Defence, War Veterans, War Victims and the Restructuring of the Armed Forces, Jean-Francis Bozizé, had embezzled funds donated to the CAR by the EU. Sandy had written two stories about protests in April and May.

On 14 July 2011 the CAR Government established the Comité Transitoire des Élections (CTE) to monitor the by-election that needed to be held owing to the decision of the Constitutional Court in April to annul the results in 14 districts of the recently held legislative elections. On 9 August this by-election was scheduled for 4 September, and members of the CTE were appointed on 15 August, with the Minister of Territorial Administration and Decentralization, Josué Binoua, as its President. In August tensions arose after an opposition party rally was violently disrupted by supporters of President Bozizé's KNK. The demonstration was held to encourage a boycott of the September by-election since the opposition did not accept the legitimacy of the CTE and demanded that a new committee be appointed. Yet despite the fact that the opposition, including FARE-2011, boycotted the ballot, the by-election proceeded peacefully. According to official results, the KNK won eight seats, non-affiliated deputies took three, and PAD and the Parti Social Démocrate secured one seat each.

Two government ministers, Minister of Agriculture and Rural Development Fidèle Gouandjika and Minister of State for Posts, Telecommunications and New Technologies Thierry Maléyombo, were dismissed by President Bozizé in late August 2011; the Minister-delegate at the Presidency, in charge of Finance, Abdallah Kadre, was dismissed shortly thereafter. All three men were charged with the misappropriation of funds belonging to a telephone company, in what became known as the 'Telsoft affair'. Despite the scandal, Gouandjika and Kadre subsequently resumed government posts.

At Birao in early September 2011, Gen. Adoum Rakiss, an MLCJ rebel leader, issued a press release declaring his acceptance of the Government's disarmament and reconciliation policy. The situation in north-eastern CAR deteriorated on 9 September, after CPJP rebels attacked UFDR troops at Boromata and then Bria; however, on 8 October the Government announced that a cease-fire agreement had been signed by the CPJP and the UFDR following mediation by the Médiateur de la République (National Ombudsman), former Catholic Archbishop of Bangui Paulin Pomodimo, and representatives of the UN, the AU, MICOPAX and the Government of Chad.

In mid-September 2011 Guy Simplice-Kodégué, a former spokesman for Ange Félix Patassé, announced the presence in the CAR of a new political party, the Mouvement Libéral Démocrate (MLD), which had been founded on 15 July and which reportedly represented the views of the deceased former President. In September, following an internal crisis in the MLPC, another new political party, the Union Démocratique du Peuple pour le Progrès, was established by Maitar Ndjim-Marem. A further new party, the Parti pour la Gouvernance Démocratique, led by former MLPC member Jean-Michel Mandaba, was set up in April 2012. Mandaba had been expelled from the MLPC in mid-June 2011 for contravening official party policy by accepting a ministerial post in the Government of President Bozizé.

On 6 January 2012 the APRD's leader and Vice-President of the DDR steering committee, Démafouth, was charged with endangering state security and conspiring with various rebel groups, and was placed in custody in Bangui. Three members of the UFDR were also detained. Following Démafouth's arrest, the APRD announced its decision temporarily to withdraw from the CPA. Démafouth was indicted and imprisoned in Ngaragba on 15 February, but was released on bail on 11 April. On 16 May Démafouth announced the dissolution of the APRD at a ceremony in Kaga-Bandoro, thus completing the DDR process of the former rebel group.

Meanwhile, serious allegations of corruption involving senior CAR officials continued during early 2012. On 9 March Michel Koyt, Minister in charge of the General Secretariat and Institutional Relations, and Abdallah Kadre, Minister-delegate to the Prime Minister in charge of Good Governance, were accused of engaging in large-scale fraud by using a 'shell company' (a company that exists but does not actually undertake any business activities) to misappropriate US $5m. from a development loan from India. A week later President Bozizé dismissed both ministers.

President Bozizé's nephew, Minister of State for Finance and the Budget Lt-Col Sylvain Ndoutingai, was dismissed on 2 June 2012 and replaced by Albert Besse, Bozizé's finance adviser. Two months previously Ndoutingai had been accused of plotting to overthrow the President.

EXTERNAL RELATIONS

In late December 2005 the mandate of FOMUC (CEMAC's peace-keeping force) was again extended to help restore security and stability in the CAR, especially in the north. At a meeting of the Economic Community of Central African States (ECCAS) Council of Ministers held in Libreville in February 2008, it was decided that the FOMUC command would be transferred from the CEMAC to ECCAS. In July 2008 FOMUC became MICOPAX under ECCAS command. It was planned to deploy the troops until about 2013–15, but the mandate would be reviewed and renewed, if necessary, every six months.

President Bozizé visited the EU headquarters in Brussels, Belgium, in January 2009 and discussed the economic and social situation in the CAR and the priorities of EU funding for the coming years under the 10th development fund. In April it was announced that the CAR would receive US $37.8m. (€28m.) from the World Bank to implement an emergency plan proposed in December 2008 by the Comité du Fonds Catalytique de l'Initiative Éducation pour Tous (Catalytic Fund Committee for the Education of Everyone Initiative) in Oslo, Norway. The plan envisaged the construction of 1,000 schoolrooms within a three-year period and the construction of latrines. In October 2009 Guy Samzun was welcomed by President Bozizé as the new head of the EU delegation in Bangui.

President Bozizé arrived in Ho Chi Minh City, Viet Nam, in May 2009 for an official visit to that country. This followed a joint statement signed by the two countries on the establishment of diplomatic ties in November 2008. Bozizé then travelled on to Doha, Qatar, where he held talks with the Amir of Qatar and several senior members of the Government. Bozizé also met a number of Qatari business leaders to discuss investment opportunities available in the CAR and the prospect of promoting such co-operation to boost bilateral relations.

In February 2010 the UN granted the CAR US $20m. (€14.6m.), mainly for security service reform and assistance for refugees. This financial aid was from the Fonds pour la Consolidation de la Paix à la République Centrafricaine (CAR Peace Consolidation Fund), which had been set up in 2006.

In April 2010 the CAR became the first African country to ratify the International Labour Organization Convention 169 on Indigenous and Tribal Peoples, which was expected to focus government attention on prospective legislation regarding the CAR's forest communities, such as the Aka pygmy ethnic group.

The CAR's relations with France remain important. France continues to be the principal source of foreign aid and French advisers supervise the CAR's security services. In May 2010, in support of the Heavily Indebted Poor Countries (HIPC) initiative, the French ambassador and the CAR Minister of State for Finance and the Budget signed three agreements cancelling €5.14m. of the CAR's national debt. In February 2012 the CAR received US $24.9m. from the French Government for general budget support.

In June 2011 three US human rights organizations (Enough Project, Resolve Uganda and Invisible Children) criticized the efforts of the Administration of US President Barack Obama to end violence and help affected communities to rebuild their lives in the CAR, the DRC and Sudan border area. This criticism coincided with the first anniversary of President Obama signing into law the Lord's Resistance Army (LRA) Disarmament and Northern Uganda Recovery Act, which was intended to prevent LRA violence in the region.

In mid-August 2010 the CAR Government and the Office of the UN High Commissioner for Refugees (UNHCR) relocated 8,000 of 18,000 Congolese refugees in the Mongoumba camp in south-western CAR to a new site in Batalimo, west of Mongoumba, approximately 22 miles from the DRC border, a camp with a capacity for 20,000 people. In late August UNHCR began transferring an estimated 1,500 Central African refugees scattered along a remote part of the DRC border with the CAR to a newly constructed refugee camp, some 44 miles inside the DRC. These refugees had fled from attacks by the LRA between March and May, and found shelter in several isolated border villages in the Bas-Uélé district in northern DRC. LRA attacks on civilians in the CAR, the DRC and southern Sudan intensified in September. In mid-November UNHCR and the CAR Government began relocating by air some 3,500 Sudanese refugees from a camp in Sam Ouandja, north-eastern CAR, to Bambari, in the centre of the country.

In March 2011 President Abdoulaye Wade of Senegal arrived in Bangui on a two-day official visit. In early April President Bozizé visited Porto-Novo, Benin, for the investiture of that county's President, Boni Yayi. In the following month Bozizé addressed the fourth UN Conference on the Least Developed Countries in İstanbul, Turkey.

In June 2011 the Government of the People's Republic of China urged Chinese citizens and companies based in the CAR to exercise caution owing to growing insecurity, and encouraged Chinese companies to tighten their security procedures. This statement followed reports that several Chinese individuals in Bangui had been robbed.

On 17 June 2011 a round-table discussion held in Brussels about a second Poverty Reduction Strategy Paper concerning the CAR was attended by the Belgian Government, the UN Peacebuilding Commission, the World Bank, the African Development Bank and the UN Development Programme. On 23 June Charles Armel Doubane, a former Minister of National Education, presented his credentials as the new permanent representative of the CAR to the UN to UN Secretary-General Ban Ki-Moon. On 27 June the Japanese Government donated US $12m. to the UN Children's Fund (UNICEF) to enable the rehabilitation, over a three-year period, of basic social services in the northern and south-eastern regions of the CAR, which had been worst affected by conflict.

An IMF mission visited the CAR during 30 June–13 July to assess the economic situation in the country and to discuss the possibility of a medium-term programme supported by the Extended Credit Facility. The IMF reported that economic activity had increased in 2010 partly owing to a rise in agricultural production. Real gross domestic product (GDP) was estimated to have risen by 3.3%, compared with 1.7% in 2009. Average inflation fell from 3.5% in 2009 to 1.5% in 2010. However, despite an increase in forestry and diamond exports, the external current account in 2010 was affected by a deterioration in the terms of trade as a result of high international petroleum prices.

The UN's Special Representative for Children and Armed Conflict, Rahika Coomaraswamy, visited the CAR in

November 2011 to assess the situation of children in the country, to investigate violations of pledges made by the LRA, and to sign an action plan with the CPJP for the release of child soldiers. On 21 December the UN Security Council extended the mandate of BINUCA until 31 January 2013.

At a meeting of ECCAS representatives held on 15 January 2012 it was decided to launch an attack on Chadian rebels belonging to the Front Populaire pour le Redressement (FPR), led by Abdel Kader Baba Laddé. Later that month troops from the CAR and Chad mounted a joint assault on rebel positions in Gondava and Ouandago. Both of these locations were subsequently monitored by the FACA, and humanitarian organizations provided aid to an estimated 16,000 displaced persons. In mid-March several attacks attributed to the FPR were reported in south-central CAR, in Bakala, Grimari, Ippy and Kouango.

Since early 2008 attacks carried out by the LRA in Haut Mbomou and Mbomou prefectures have led to the displacement of nearly 25,000 people. In May 2012 it was reported that the Uganda People's Defence Forces (UPDF) had captured one of the LRA's most senior military leaders, Caesar Acellam Otto, in the CAR. Together with LRA leader Kony and a number of other senior rebel commanders, Otto was believed to have been responsible for the most serious violations committed against children in the Central African region.

In early May 2012 President Idriss Deby Itno of Chad paid an official visit to President Bozizé in Bangui. The two Presidents discussed security issues and the free movement of people and trade between their countries. The meeting was attended by the former President of Burundi, Pierre Buyoya, in his capacity as the Médiateur (Ombudsman) de la Francophonie.

Economy

DUNCAN WOODSIDE

In theory, the Central African Republic (CAR) should be a reasonably wealthy nation. While the country is constrained by its landlocked location and its small population, it has a good primary resource base, notably diamonds and rainforest timber, and fertile soils, which are ideal for a wide range of crops. However, the country's post-independence history has been littered with coups, ethnically based governments and corruption. Such problems have resulted in a poor education system, weak enforcement of the rule of law and consequent concerns over property rights, making it difficult for both domestic entrepreneurs and foreign investors to establish durable and successful enterprises in the country. As such, the CAR's economy remains one of the least developed and most unattractive in the world, with the majority of the population surviving through subsistence farming and foreign investors largely shunning the country. The CAR was ranked 182nd out of 183 countries in the World Bank's 2011 *Doing Business* report, with only neighbouring Chad ranked lower. Additionally, the country was placed 179th out of 187 countries in the UN Development Programme (UNDP)'s 2011 Human Development Index (which ranks nations according to literacy, income and life expectancy).

Gen. François Bozizé seized power in a coup in early 2003. Early threats to his regime appeared to have dissipated in strength, with various rebel groups making their peace with his Government during 2006–08. The improvement in security conditions, a resumption of donor support and expansion across most sectors of the economy contributed to a modest recovery in economic growth, with gross domestic product (GDP) rising by 3.8% in 2006 and 3.7% in 2007, according to the IMF.

However, the global financial crisis in 2008, which particularly affected resource-dependent emerging markets such as the CAR, caused a slowdown in the country's mining and forestry sectors, resulting in a decline in the rate of real GDP growth to 2.0% in 2008, according to the IMF. Food price increases, fuel price volatility and power cuts also had a negative impact on growth. The rate of real economic growth fell again, to just 1.7% in 2009, as exports continued to contract. Real economic growth reached 3.3% in 2010, owing largely to an improved external environment (including a rebound in global commodity prices, which buoyed exports), and growth of 3.1% was achieved in 2011, according to preliminary estimates released by the IMF in January 2012. In May of that year the IMF revised its calculation for real GDP growth in 2011 upwards, but only very marginally, to 3.3%, on the back of a slightly better than expected performance by the mining sector, where output of precious minerals was higher than initially recorded. Overall, the growth performance in the past few years has been undermined by renewed fiscal slippage, a suspension of donor funding and delays in the implementation of mining projects. Non-performing loans have also been on a rising trend, and although local banks remain well capitalized, the provision of credit to small and medium-sized enterprises remains highly constrained.

The outlook for the CAR economy thus remains uncertain. Even the improved rate of economic growth experienced in 2010 was barely sufficient to raise overall living standards in a country where the rate of population growth is close to 2% per year. If the CAR is to move onto a higher growth trajectory, then the regime will need to make huge changes to the way it governs, by tackling the endemic culture of corruption and encouraging more open political dialogue in order to dissuade disaffected groups from resorting to armed rebellion. Failure to make headway in power-sharing talks, accompanied by a renewed upsurge in rebel activity from 2008, generated fresh scepticism among donors. Moreover, delays in the holding of the presidential and legislative elections, which had been scheduled to take place in April 2010, added to concerns that the Government was not serious about entering into political dialogue or creating a conducive environment for a definitive end to civil conflict. When the elections did eventually take place, in January 2011, the European Union (EU) raised concerns about irregularities and opposition representatives on a cross-party election body stood down in protest at the way in which the elections had been conducted. Until substantial progress is made to resolve such political issues, it is difficult to envisage a significant increase in donor support, or a wider germination of economic confidence.

In its January 2012 review of economic performance, the IMF forecast long-term real GDP growth of 5.0% per annum. However, this was contingent on a renewed improvement in government revenue collection, a resumption of donor support and a revival of foreign activity in the mining sector. The latter would be an uphill struggle, given that the French nuclear company Areva suspended operations at the CAR's Bakouma uranium mine in late 2011, owing to a dramatic decline in global uranium prices. External obstacles posed a further threat to the CAR's economic growth profile. Adding to the gloom, the country's dependence on the eurozone for investment, donor support and exports, left it vulnerable to the effects of the eurozone debt crisis, which continued to undermine developed European economies in 2011 and 2012.

AGRICULTURE

Agriculture, forestry and fishing dominate the economy, contributing an estimated 53.5% of GDP in 2009, according to the African Development Bank (AfDB), and employing 61.2% of the economically active population in mid-2012, according to FAO estimates. According to the World Bank, agricultural GDP increased at an average annual rate of 1.4% during 2000–08. The sector's GDP decreased by 8.9% in 2009, according to the AfDB. Agriculture is concentrated in the tropical rainforest area of the south-west and the savannah lands in the central region and north-west. Output of the major food crops (cassava, maize, millet, sorghum, groundnuts and rice) increased in the late 1990s, as the Government placed greater emphasis on this sector in its regional development programmes. As a result, the CAR reached near self-sufficiency in staple foods, mostly cassava, sorghum and millet. Agricultural diversification was also promoted, mainly to substitute imports. This notably involved a palm oil complex at Bossongo, with an annual capacity of 7,500 metric tons, servicing 2,500 ha of plantations, and a sugar refinery at Ouaka, supplied from 1,300 ha of new plantations. The Government also encouraged the cultivation of vegetables for export to the European market, with peppers and green beans cultivated in an area within easy reach of the country's international airport at Bangui.

Performance in agriculture has been particularly uneven in recent years. As a consequence of the fighting, agricultural production and supply declined sharply during 2003, especially in the north-west of the country. It recovered in 2004, supported by an improved security situation and increased planting, reaching 1.02m. metric tons in 2007, according to the Banque des Etats de l'Afrique Centrale (BEAC), a regional central bank that controls the monetary policy of the CAR and five other Central African countries. However, improved production did not prevent severe localized food shortages, a result of continued instability in the north of the country that had already caused the displacement of thousands of people. Given the importance of the agriculture sector, the Government has tried in recent years to revive it; in particular, a three-year recovery plan for cotton, coffee and tobacco was presented in early 2007.

The food security situation deteriorated significantly in some rural areas from 2008, owing to the incursion into the CAR of the Lord's Resistance Army (LRA), a rebel group exiled from northern Uganda. The arrival and spread of the LRA insurgency in the CAR created significant internal displacement in the south of the country, as civilians fled their fields to gather in urban centres, due to the rebel group's policy of kidnapping children and mutilating and massacring villagers. The World Food Programme reported in April 2011 that the number of internally displaced persons in the CAR amounted to 192,000, while 30% of the country's 4m. inhabitants were categorized as 'food insecure'. The LRA insurgency notwithstanding, a re-escalation of activity by local rebel groups in the north-west of the country from 2008 also hampered food security.

Coffee was superseded by cotton as the CAR's major export crop from the mid-1990s, as declining international prices led to a reduction in coffee output; coffee export earnings slumped from 10.2% of recorded export earnings in 1999 to less than 2% in 2001. Formerly produced on large, European-owned plantations, coffee production is now the domain of smallholders. The crop is cultivated mainly in the south-western and central-southern regions of the country, and more than 90% is of the Robusta variety. The Agence de Développement de la Zone Caféière is the parastatal organization responsible for the purchase, transportation and marketing of this commodity. After reaching a peak of 18,000 metric tons in 1996, production levels rapidly declined, reflecting poor growing conditions, a decrease in world prices and continued insecurity, which hampered farming activities. Coffee production declined from 5,520 tons in 2002/03 to 2,760 tons in 2005/06, according to the International Coffee Organization, before more than doubling to 6,988 tons in 2006/07, according to the BEAC. High global prices in 2006/07 significantly increased the value of coffee exports to some 4,049m. francs CFA, compared with 777m. francs CFA in the previous year. Poor rainfall, coupled with the damaging effects of the Darfur crisis in neighbouring Sudan, resulted in production decreasing to 1,930 tons in 2008/09. Coffee exports also declined by 75.2% in volume and 72.2% in value in that year, according to the BEAC.

Cotton is also cultivated by smallholders, principally in the north-east of the country. Cotton export earnings declined dramatically during 1998–2006. In 2006 cotton contributed 0.8% of total exports, compared with 17.5% in 1997, when a record crop of 46,037 metric tons was harvested. Although the sector subsequently encountered difficulties, the long-term outlook for the CAR's cotton crop is favourable, particularly as it is less vulnerable to drought than some other crops. In May 2002 the cotton utility, Société Cotonnière Centrafricaine (SOCOCA), was liquidated and replaced by the partly state-owned Société Centrafricaine de Développement des Textiles (SOCADETEX). The reconstruction of ginneries enabled production to recover to 6,100 tons in 2006/07, according to the BEAC. Meanwhile, the Government stepped up efforts to revive the sector further. In July 2007, following the liquidation of SOCADETEX, a new state company Société des Fibres Centrafricaines (SOFICA) was created. Operating in line with the Organization for the Harmonization of Business Law in Africa Act, SOFICA planned to develop a strategic partnership with the French company Diagris and secure funding from the World Bank and the EU. However, by mid-2010 SOFICA was still not operational. Cotton seed and fibre exports increased to 5,575 tons and 1,781 tons, respectively, in 2008, with total sales of 927m. francs CFA, according to the BEAC.

For decades, efforts have been made to develop the livestock industry, and the number of cattle has increased substantially, despite the problems caused by droughts, the limitations of available fodder and the prevalence of the tsetse fly. Efforts are being made to improve marketing, and to encourage the sedentary raising of cattle to allow for treatment against disease. The herd has also grown as a result of migration from Chad and Sudan. FAO estimated a total of 16.6m. head of livestock in 2010, compared with 15.9m. in 2009. Nevertheless, domestic meat production fails to satisfy demand, and development of the sector is hindered by widespread land disputes between livestock producers and crop producers.

In 2011 FAO aimed to provide support to 22,500 households in the CAR. In April of that year, the World Food Programme estimated that there were some 192,000 internally displaced people in the country, while nearly two out of three people were living below the official global poverty threshold of US $1.25 per day. This large number of displaced people, who overwhelmingly originated from rural areas, constrained agricultural activity. Moreover, many of the displaced were unable to engage in subsistence agriculture, further limiting their livelihoods and leaving them desperately dependent on international aid. Further exacerbating food insecurity, the price of cassava nearly trebled in just one month in 2011, at one stage rising from 1,000 francs CFA to 2,800 francs CFA for 15 kg, with regional disruptions (including cassava mosaic disease in neighbouring countries) compounding the effect of the local supply constraints brought about by displacement.

The CAR's large forest resources (an estimated 102,000 sq km of tropical rainforest) are at present under-exploited commercially, largely as a result of a lack of adequate roads and low-cost means of transportation to the coast. Only about 10% of the forest area is accessible to river transport. In addition, large areas are held as private hunting reserves. Nevertheless, timber exploitation expanded considerably from the late 1960s, following the formation of new companies geared towards export and the establishment of new sawmills. The forestry sector continues to suffer from major constraints, including low water levels on the traditional transport route along the Congo river and smuggling. In mid-2003 the new Government of Gen. Bozizé suspended all licences awarded under the previous administration, pending the results of a review of the sector. According to the BEAC, wood production was 500,744 cu m in 2006 and increased slightly, to 506,509 cu m, in 2007, while there were plans to improve the road network in the logging areas. Exports, mostly to Europe and neighbouring countries, increased by 7.5% from 202,212 cu m in 2006 to 217,289 cu m in 2007. In that year the Government launched invitations to tender the remaining forest-harvesting licences. The global financial crisis of 2008–09 reduced timber production and exports. In 2008 production of plywood decreased by 69.3%, while timber exports declined by 17%. Nevertheless, wood products still contributed 48% of export earning in 2008. In 2009 wood production totalled 408,725 cu m. Between 1990 and 2010 the CAR lost approximately 598,000 ha of woodland, equivalent to 2.6% of its forest cover. The rate of attrition averaged an annual 29,900 ha, or 0.13% of total forest cover per year.

An outline Responsible Procurement Programme (R-PP) was preliminarily approved by the multilateral Forest Carbon Partnership Facility (FCPF) for the CAR in Berlin, Germany, in October 2011. According to the FCPF, the CAR Government requested that it work in partnership with the UNDP in order to establish the programme. The World Bank, the principal trustee of the FCPF, was therefore reported to be making preparations for a transfer of the CAR's R-PP mandate to the UNDP. The EU was designated as a potential funder of this forestry initiative in the CAR, although other funding avenues were also being pursued.

MINING

The contribution of mining and quarrying to GDP was likely to be much greater than the AfDB estimate of 2.6% in 2009, since an estimated one-half of the output of diamonds, the leading mineral, was thought to be smuggled out of the country, escaping the official record. In the CAR, diamonds are found in widely scattered alluvial deposits (mainly in the south-west and west of the country), rather than kimberlite deposits, which are concentrated and, thus, more easily exploited and policed. The decline in recorded output, from a peak of 609,000 carats in 1968 to 416,400 carats in 2002, was partly attributable to increased smuggling, a consequence of which was a decline in the quality of officially traded stones. Independent observers have estimated illegal exports at some 500,000 carats per year. The Government aims to encourage the development of local cutting and polishing industries; by the early 2000s, however, there was still only one diamond-cutting centre and exports of diamonds remained almost entirely in uncut form. In mid-2003 the new Bozizé Government initiated a thorough review of the CAR's mining code, suspended all mining permits and closed mining interests controlled by former President Ange-Félix Patassé. (It was estimated that 50% of potential revenue from taxes on diamond exports were lost to smuggling and corruption under the Patassé administration.) Furthermore, in July the CAR became a participant in the Kimberley Process, an international certification scheme aimed at excluding from the world market diamonds that have been traded for arms by rebel movements in conflict zones.

A new mining code was adopted in December 2003, with new measures allowing for greater transparency in the issuing of licences and greater control over diamond-smuggling. This code enabled the State to gain at least 10% interest capital in mining companies holding prospecting or exploration permits. Efforts to combat fraud in the sector have continued in recent years, notably with the introduction of new export rules in November 2005. Overall diamond production rose to 585,600 carats in 2004, but decreased to 310,468 carats in 2009, according to the BEAC. The decline in official diamond production was a result of insecurity and interference from authorities in the production and marketing of diamonds. The fall in global diamond demand, coupled with the administrative closure of buying offices for non-compliance with the mining code, meant that production of rough diamonds contracted by 9.7% in the first half of 2009. According to the US Geological Survey, official diamond production decreased to 301,600 carats in 2010. Overall, the diamond industry employs about 80,000 artisan miners, providing a source of income for 600,000 people in mining zones, according to the World Trade Organization. Exports of diamonds provided some 61.9% of total export revenue in 2009, according to UN figures.

Gold is also mined, although production levels have fluctuated sharply, from a peak of 538 kg in 1980 to 43 kg in 2008, although production recovered somewhat, to 61 kg, in 2009. The signing of a first 25-year gold-mining convention in January 2006 with Aurafrique, a subsidiary of the Canadian company Axim, was expected to increase gold production in the long term. Uranium has been discovered near Bakouma, 480 km east of Bangui. Reserves are estimated at 20,000 metric tons, with a concentration ratio of some 50%. In recent years rising uranium prices and declining world stock have resulted in renewed interest from foreign companies in the Bakouma site, and a licence to mine uranium was eventually awarded to South Africa's Uramin in 2006. The Bakouma uranium-mining project was officially inaugurated in October with the State owning a 10% interest. Reserves of iron ore, copper, tin, lignite and limestone have also been located, although the inadequacy of the country's transport infrastructure has deterred mining companies from attempting their commercial exploitation. Despite potentially drillable petroleum prospects along the Chad–CAR border, energy requirements are currently satisfied through imports. The Canadian firm United Reef obtained a petroleum exploration permit through a farm-in agreement with USA-based RSM Production Corporation in 2004; however, they were unable to continue exploration activities in 2006, declaring *force majeure* due to a lack of progress in resolving a contract dispute between RSM and the Government.

The mining sector suffered a significant reverse in late 2011, when the French nuclear company Areva halted uranium extraction at the Bakouma plant. It was reported that the company suspended operations in response to reduced demand for the commodity in global markets, sparked by the Fukushima disaster in Japan in March 2011, when a tsunami caused the overheating of a nuclear reactor and a consequent fuel leak. The shutdown of Japan's nuclear facilities, together with a rise in nuclear risk aversion elsewhere in the world, led to a 30% fall in the global price of uranium over the six months from March to November 2011. As a result, Areva announced that it was suspending extraction at the Bakouma facilities for one to two years, although it reassured investors and concerned local parties that it had no intention of abandoning the project entirely, having reportedly invested US $147m. in the project to date. The company added that it would, during the planned hiatus in operations, continue to process ore that it had already extracted, thereby ensuring that staff would remain employed.

MANUFACTURING AND POWER

Manufacturing is based on the processing of primary products and is relatively undeveloped, contributing an estimated 6.3% of GDP in 2009, according to the AfDB. In the mid-1990s the major activities were the processing of foods, beverages and tobacco, furniture, fixtures, and paper and textiles. Out of 250 enterprises that were in operation before the 1996 mutiny, only a dozen, often involving foreign participation, have survived: these include the Société Centrafricaine de Cigarettes (SOCACIG—tobacco, reopened in 2000), the Société de Gestion des Sucreries Centrafricaines (SOGESCA—sugar, privatized in 2003), MOCAF (beverages), Centrafricaine des Palmeraies (CENTRAPALM—palm oil, mooted for privatization), and a number of sawmills. Manufacturing activities suffered greatly from the political and civil disruption during October 2002 and March 2003, notably ginning activities, as SOCADETEX (now SOFICA) suspended operations and several ginneries were destroyed. In real terms, the GDP of the manufacturing sector declined by 9.5% in 2002 and by 21.2% in 2003. Many public and private enterprises and public administration buildings operating around Bangui were looted, contributing to a significant decrease in production capacity not only in goods, but also in services. However, manufacturing activity has since recovered: it grew by around 8% in both 2005 and 2006, according to the BEAC. In 2008 sugar production alone increased by 15.3%, contributing to an expansion in manufacturing turnover of 8.4%. However, the sugar sector was negatively affected by power cuts at the hydroelectric power stations and by the significant increase in the cost of the alternative energy supplies, and in 2009 production declined by 28.5%, to 13,775 metric tons. In that year the GDP of the manufacturing sector contracted by 0.1%.

The main source of power supply is hydroelectric, from the two stations at the Boali Falls. Electricity coverage is low, at approximately 3% of the total population. Plans have been under way for several years to construct a new hydroelectric plant at Kembe, but no progress has been made owing to the lack of funding. The Government has proposed several projects in recent years to increase the country's hydroelectric capacity and reduce electricity shortages, but their implementation will depend on the Government's ability to secure sufficient funding. A significant element of the Patassé Government's privatization programme was the divestment of its holdings in the state power utility, the Société Énergie de Centrafrique

(ENERCA), and the petroleum distribution company, the Société Centrafricaine des Pétroles (PETROCA). The latter was privatized in 1999, with the network taken over by Elf and Total of France (now Total) and Shell, while ENERCA's power distribution division was put out to tender in early 2000. In July 2003 the Bozizé Government announced that corruption and mismanagement at ENERCA, the Société de Distribution d'Eau en Centrafrique (SODECA) and at the state-owned telephone company over the previous two years had resulted in a total loss of 15,000m. francs CFA for the Government. There was little progress made in redressing the financial situation of the three state-owned companies, although the Government held discussions in order to establish a roadmap regarding the electricity sector's full liberalization. Given the company's parlous finances, the first step would be to restructure ENERCA's debts. In 2008 electricity production declined by 8.3% due to major breakdown at the Boali Falls hydropower plants caused by years of underinvestment and poor management. However, in 2009 production recovered, increasing by 8.2%, to 136,619 MW.

TRANSPORT AND TELECOMMUNICATIONS

The transport infrastructure is underdeveloped and is a major constraint on the country's economic development. There is an extensive network of roads (an estimated 24,307 km in 2000), but only about 3% of the system is paved. The road network has suffered serious deterioration, owing to lack of maintenance. However, international development organizations and bilateral donors have extended funds for road rehabilitation projects. There is no railway, but there are long-standing plans to extend the Transcameroon line to Bangui and also to link the CAR with the rail systems in Sudan and Gabon. A large volume of freight is carried by river; of a total of 7,000 km of inland waterways, some 2,800 km are navigable, most importantly the Oubangui river south of Bangui, which is the country's main outlet for external trade, and the Sangha and Lobaye rivers. Port facilities are being improved, with assistance from France and the EU.

The principal route for the import and export trade has traditionally been the trans-equatorial route, which involves 1,800 km by river from Bangui to Brazzaville, in the Republic of the Congo, and then rail from Brazzaville to Pointe-Noire. However, instability in the Republic of the Congo from 1997, and in the neighbouring Democratic Republic of the Congo (DRC) from 2000, led to periodic suspension of this service. River traffic therefore declined, as importers and exporters turned to the new land route through Cameroon, although the outlet via Pointe-Noire remained important for timber shipments. In recent years, improved security conditions in the CAR and the rest of the region, coupled with the Government's commitment to reduce the number of road blocks, have enhanced transport. The Government plans to improve rural tracks and roads in agricultural areas as well as access to isolated areas of the country. The Communauté Economique et Monétaire de l'Afrique Centrale (CEMAC) Transport and Transit Facilitation project aims to pave part of the key Douala–Bangui corridor. In 2007/08 river, road and air traffic increased by 27.6%, 19.1% and 15.7%, respectively, according to the BEAC. There is an international airport at Bangui-M'Poko, and there are also 37 small airports for internal services. However, internal services are irregular, underserviced and dependent on the availability of fuel.

The telecommunications sector has grown rapidly in recent years, driven by mobile cellular telephone services. Société Centrafricaine de Télécommunications (SOCATEL) is 60% owned by the State and the remainder by France Câbles et Radio (France Télécoms). Four mobile telephone companies, Telecel (since 1996, with an estimated 239,000 subscribers in 2009), Azur RCA (since 2004, when it was known as Nationlink, with an estimated 96,000 subscribers in 2009), Atlantique Telecom Centrafrique (with an estimated 248,000 subscribers in 2009) and Orange Centrafrique (since 2007, with an estimated 212,000 subscribers in 2009), operate in the country. Most mobile phone services have been concentrated around Bangui; however, Atlantique Telecom, Nationlink/Azur RCA and Orange extended their network outside the capital during 2007–08. Overall, competition between operators, expansion of networks and improvements in the network enabled returns from telecommunication firms to increase by 29.1%, to 11,987m. francs CFA, in 2007/08, and by an estimated 28.2% in 2008/09, according to the BEAC.

PUBLIC FINANCE

The CAR's fiscal position remains precarious, a situation compounded by continued political instability. The narrow tax base is vulnerable to adverse trends in international prices for coffee and cotton and prone to erosion as a result of tax evasion and smuggling, while losses incurred by the parastatal organizations and personnel expenditure for the cumbersome civil service have put constant pressure on public spending. Yet improvements in public financial management began to alleviate the budget deficit, following Bozizé's seizure of power in 2003. The Government's annual deficit, exclusive of grants, declined steadily, from 8.7% of GDP in 2005 to 2.8% in 2007, although it rose to 5.1% in 2008, before decreasing to an estimated 3.0% in 2009, according to the IMF. Inclusive of grants, however, the year-to-year performance remained reasonable, with a deficit of 4.5% of GDP in 2005 being followed by surpluses of 9.0% in 2006 and 1.3% in 2007, before a deficit of 0.4% in 2008 and a surplus of 2.3% of GDP in 2009. Fiscal performance was therefore better than the IMF forecast for 2009 (the target being a deficit of 4.6% of GDP, excluding grants, and a surplus of 0.1% of GDP, including grants), despite a very low rate of real GDP growth (the economy expanded by just 1.7% that year). The Government's revenues stood at 10.8% of GDP in 2009, 0.3 percentage points above the predicted level.

The Government made a number of advances in terms of fiscal reform in 2009 and the first half of 2010, according to the IMF's Extended Credit Facility (ECF) review in October 2010. Building on a reduction of customs exemptions in 2009, a new financial management system was implemented across all spending and payment categories by mid-January 2010, while domestic arrears on debt payments (up to 2007 and including the debts of state-owned enterprises) were collated and integrated into a centralized debt database. In April 2010 the Government reconciled the complex web of assets and liabilities between it and state-owned enterprise counterparties. A clearance plan was formulated and approved for these debts. However, the IMF cautioned that an accurate measurement of debt arrears was constrained by 'technical and organizational difficulties'. The IMF also noted that the Government had missed an end-of-2009 deadline for the payment of value-added tax (VAT) refunds, after the authorities discovered inconsistencies in the process for approving rebate requests.

However, in January 2012 the IMF stated that renewed fiscal slippage had occurred in the second half of 2010 and in 2011, resulting in the earlier improvements in revenue collection being largely reversed. New payment arrears to both domestic and external creditors (including the 'Paris Club' of sovereign lenders) had accrued and there had been slippage on the spending side, partly as a result of the presidential and legislative elections that took place in early 2011. Thus, the budget deficit reached 7.7% of GDP, excluding grants, in 2010. The IMF pointed to a 'lack of transparency and due process' in budget execution, which created 'serious governance concerns' and led to a suspension of donor support. There was a slight improvement in the budget deficit in 2011, which, inclusive of grants, stood at 2.4% of GDP; however, the shortfall (before grants) remained high, at 6.5% of GDP. Following a visit to the CAR by an IMF delegation in April 2012, the Fund was slightly more optimistic regarding the country's medium-term fiscal outlook, expressing its hope that a specially convened National Forum on Public Finances held in late 2011 would precipitate a rise in revenue collection. With regard to expenditure, the IMF called for the elimination of consumer fuel subsidies, while suggesting a mitigation of the adverse implications of this action through 'targeted measures to protect the most vulnerable groups of the population'. In addition, the Fund discussed with the Government the possibility of a new three-year ECF, after a hiatus in budgetary support, and predicted that the overall fiscal balance could revert to a modest surplus in 2012 (inclusive of donor grants).

MONETARY AND EXCHANGE RATE POLICY

The CAR is a member of the BEAC, along with Cameroon, the Republic of the Congo, Gabon, Equatorial Guinea and Chad. It is also a member of CEMAC, which forms part of the CFA zone, which in turn also encompasses all eight countries operating under the auspices of the Banque Centrale des États de l'Afrique de l'Ouest (BCEAO). At July 2012 the exchange rate remained fixed at €1 = 656 francs CFA.

The inability of national central banks to manipulate the value of the CFA (monetary policy is set by the BEAC and the BCEAO, which focus on maintaining the fixed exchange rate against the euro) has acted as a powerful disciplinary force on member states. This has been particularly important for the CAR, where democratic accountability has often been undermined by a tendency towards military rule, corruption and coups. The inability of governments to fund spending by printing money has thus helped to restrain inflation, and has enabled trade to be conducted at stable rates of exchange. In this context, consumer price inflation in the CAR for 2009 was just 3.5%, according to the IMF, declining from 9.3% in the previous year, at the height of the global commodity boom. In view of the low level of inflation in the CAR in 2009 (mirrored by subdued price growth in other CEMAC countries), the BEAC maintained the interest rate at 4.25% at its final monetary policy meeting of the year in December. However, with economic growth starting to pick up after the downturn, the BEAC stressed that its easing cycle—which had seen the cost of borrowing reduced by 1.25% from a high of 5.5%—was over, with the next move in interest rates likely to be an increase. In the event, however, the sluggish global economic recovery and a continuation of manageable inflation levels allowed the regional central bank to maintain an accommodative monetary policy for rather longer. In fact, the BEAC reduced its key rate by a further 0.25% in July 2010, to 4.0%, and at mid-2011 showed no immediate appetite for embarking on a tightening cycle. A large interest rate differential with the European Central Bank (ECB) also contributed to the lack of pressure on the BEAC to constrict monetary policy. At May 2011 the ECB's key policy rate stood at 1.25%, a negative differential of some 2.75%. The CFA franc zone's relatively high interest rates helped to maintain confidence in the CFA/euro peg.

Despite providing a restraint on excesses at the country level, the credibility of the BEAC itself has come under scrutiny. In July 2010 it was reported that the IMF had halted disbursements to the central bank due to allegations of fraud. This followed a letter sent by the IMF in May questioning a 'lack of receipts for transactions', amid concerns that BEAC had failed to address 'underlying issues' uncovered by a 2009 investigation into the alleged disappearance of €40m. at the bank's Paris office. The World Bank subsequently announced that it had also frozen payments to the monetary authority 'until concerns over BEAC's accounts have been resolved'.

The BEAC held its key rate steady at 4.0% throughout 2011, although it appeared likely that there would be monetary tightening in 2012, as the regional central bank predicted in early 2011 an annual real GDP growth rate across its monetary area of 6.0%. This was rather higher than that prevailing in the CAR, where the economy expanded by 3.3% in 2011 and inflation averaged only 1.2%, albeit rising faster towards the end of the year. The low growth rate increased the risk that monetary conditions would be too tight to correspond with the CAR's own specific needs. However, partially offsetting these concerns, the BEAC's currency peg against the euro represented a de facto monetary easing via the exchange rate, as the euro came under sustained pressure on global currency markets in the first half of 2012, due to the ongoing debt crisis in the eurozone. There was even speculation that the European single currency might have to be abandoned by the EU and that member states would revert to maintaining national currencies, which would necessitate the BEAC finding a new monetary anchor for its exchange rate (or else resorting to a currency float). By mid-2012 a partial collapse of the eurozone appeared an increasingly significant danger, given the doubts concerning the long-term stability of the new Government of debt-ridden Greece and opposition in Germany to the continued subsidizing of fiscally weak member states. Spain's finances were also coming under pressure, amid rumours of deposit runs having taken place at several of its banks.

FOREIGN TRADE AND THE BALANCE OF PAYMENTS

The CAR's foreign trade balance turned from small surpluses from the mid-1990s to deficits from 2003. Structural weaknesses (especially in transport), political instability, power shortages and fluctuations in the international prices for diamonds, coffee, timber and cotton have prevented the CAR's exports from reaching their full potential. In addition, a large proportion of diamond and wood exports are believed to be unrecorded. The trade deficit in 2009 was 63,900m. francs CFA (US $136m.), a moderate decrease from 72,300m. francs CFA ($162m.) in 2008, according to IMF figures published in October 2010. The 2009 trade deficit comprised export earnings totalling 57,500m. francs CFA ($122m.) and imports totalling 121,400m. francs CFA ($258m.). The most significant export in 2009 in terms of value was timber, which earned 23,600m. francs CFA ($50.1m.), closely followed by diamonds, which yielded 23,300m. francs CFA ($49m.). The principal destination in 2010 for exports was Belgium, which received 25.6% of the country's shipments, followed by the People's Republic of China (17.5%), Morocco (12.1%), the DRC (8.1%), France (6.1%) and Indonesia (4.9%). The primary source of imports in 2010 was the Netherlands (27.8%), France (11.9%), Cameroon (8.3%) and China (5.1%).

The CAR has traditionally recorded a large net outflow on the services account. As a result, the country's current account balance has remained in deficit, and the shortfall has become more pronounced in recent years, due to the emergence of the above-mentioned structural trade deficit. The current account deficit (including grants) represented 2.7% of GDP in 2006, before increasing to 4.1% of GDP in 2007. In 2008 the current account deficit (including grants) widened to 10.2% of GDP due to rising fuel imports and lower export volumes of timber and diamonds, before it declined slightly in 2009, to (a none the less substantial) 7.7% of GDP, largely owing to the modest improvement in the trade deficit that year. Although the size of the current account deficit has caused concern, donor support—and consequent inflows to the capital account—has offset some of this apprehension. The capital account recorded a surplus of 29,700m. francs CFA in 2008 and 406,000m. francs CFA in 2009, according to the IMF. The 2009 capital account surplus was buoyed by the substantial external debt relief that arrived in that year.

DEVELOPMENT AID AND DEBT RELIEF

The CAR has traditionally received moderate inflows of aid in grant form. However, the country has not proved particularly attractive to foreign private investors (other than in the diamond, timber and telecommunications sectors). The total external debt consequently rose over a long period, reaching US $946m. in 1995. The Government benefited from two successive debt relief packages from bilateral creditors in 1994 and 1998, which helped to clear payment arrears and reduce the stock of external debt to $821.9m. by the end of 2001. Total debt stock stood at $1,082m. by the end of 2004, equivalent to 83% of gross national income (GNI), and at $1,016m. at the end of 2005, equivalent to 47.3% of GNI. In 2006 outstanding debt increased to $1,100m. or $856m. in net present value (NPV) terms. 'Paris Club' creditors agreed in April 2007 to restructure $36.1m. of debt. Furthermore, China cancelled two loans in January 2007, while South Africa cancelled all remaining debt.

The continued efforts by the Government to improve economic management and the fiscal position contributed to the approval by the IMF of a three-year (2007–09) poverty reduction and growth facility (PRGF) in December 2006, providing for US $54.5m. in funding. In June 2009 the IMF completed the fourth review of the CAR's economic performance under the PRGF, approving a six-month extension and access to $38.7m.

in funding. Also in that month the CAR reached completion point under the initiative for heavily indebted poor countries (HIPC) as key reforms aiming for macroeconomic stability and poverty reduction were introduced. According to the IMF, the authorities made good progress in implementing measures in the areas of transparency, structural reforms in the forestry and mining sectors, civil service reform, public debt management, social sectors and HIV. Debt relief has reduced the CAR's debt burden significantly; in NPV terms, relief from the World Bank's International Development Association (IDA) amounted to $207m. and relief from the IMF totalled $26.8m. Meanwhile, the NPV of external public and guaranteed debt was reduced from 36.2% of GDP in 2008 to 10.7% in 2009, according to the IMF.

The fiscal deficit, inclusive of grants, was close to zero in 2009, according to initial estimates, and in January 2010 the IMF reported that programme implementation remained 'broadly satisfactory' and stated that it supported a waiver for a failure to meet a target on reducing commercial bank lending to the Government, in light of corrective action taken to reduce dependence on this expensive source of credit (interest charged by commercial banks to the Government in the CAR was around 15% per annum in 2009). However, IMF funding was subsequently disrupted due to concerns over alleged fraud at the BEAC (see above). IMF assistance to the CAR is routinely provided via the BEAC, so the IMF's suspension of payments to the regional central bank blocked the CAR's access to US $12.9m. in multilateral funds. However, in August 2010 the IMF announced that it had approved the disbursement of $13.1m. to the CAR, bringing total disbursements to $104.9m. under the country's ECF. This followed the Fund's completion of a sixth review under the four-year ECF, which commended the Government for its satisfactory implementation of reforms 'against the backdrop of difficult domestic and external challenges'. In particular, the IMF congratulated the Government on improving revenue collection and budget execution, while also reducing domestic arrears.

The EU has been an important source of donor support for the CAR. Its Country Strategy Paper for the period 2008–13 envisaged the provision of €142.8m. to the impoverished country, to be distributed via the European Development Fund. The core areas of donor support for the five-year period were specified by the EU as follows: governance, social and economic rehabilitation, and infrastructure development. Macroeconomic budgetary support for the five-year period was set at €34m. The preceding EU programme, which covered the period 2002–07, had focused largely on infrastructural and transport spending. A total of €55m. was provided for the construction of a road to connect Bouar, in the CAR, with the settlement of Garoua-Boulaï, in neighbouring Cameroon.

Significant financial support has continued to be provided by the World Bank. In May 2012 the multilateral lender's Board of Executive Directors approved a US $28.2m. grant targeted at improving the CAR's provision of health care. The programme was to focus on rural areas and aimed to benefit at least 2.5m. people over four years. The Bank stated that work would be sub-contracted to third-party providers, with contracts stipulating the achievement of performance targets, in order for these commissioned service providers to qualify for full payment. Part of the overall programme funding would be disbursed to rationalize the workings of the Ministry of Public Health, Population and the Fight against AIDS, particularly in terms of improving in-house expertise in performance evaluation, in order to enable the Government better to assess the quality of its contracted service providers. The programme was agreed against a backdrop where the CAR has some of the worst health statistics in the world, including a death rate for children under the age of five standing at 17.6%.

Statistical Survey

Source (unless otherwise stated): Division des Statistiques et des Etudes Economiques, Ministère de l'Economie, du Plan et de la Coopération Internationale, Bangui.

Area and Population

AREA, POPULATION AND DENSITY

Area (sq km)	622,984*
Population (census results)	
8 December 1988	2,463,616
8 December 2003†	
Males	1,569,446
Females	1,581,626
Total	3,151,072
Population (UN estimates at mid-year)‡	
2010	4,401,051
2011	4,486,833
2012	4,575,585
Density (per sq km) at mid-2012	7.3

* 240,535 sq miles.

† Source: UN, Population and Vital Statistics Report.

‡ Source: UN, *World Population Prospects: The 2010 Revision*.

POPULATION BY AGE AND SEX

(UN estimates at mid-2012)

	Males	Females	Total
0–14	907,131	915,170	1,822,301
15–64	1,268,040	1,304,429	2,572,469
65 and over	79,376	101,439	180,815
Total	2,254,547	2,321,038	4,575,585

Source: UN, *World Population Prospects: The 2010 Revision*.

PRINCIPAL TOWNS

(estimated population at mid-1994)

Bangui (capital)	524,000	Carnot	41,000
Berbérati	47,000	Bambari	41,000
Bouar	43,000	Bossangoa	33,000

Mid-2009 (incl. suburbs, UN estimate): Bangui 701,597 (Source: UN, *World Urbanization Prospects: The 2009 Revision*).

BIRTHS AND DEATHS

(annual averages, UN estimates)

	1995–2000	2000–05	2005–10
Birth rate (per 1,000)	39.8	38.3	35.6
Death rate (per 1,000)	19.2	19.5	17.6

Source: UN, *World Population Prospects: The 2010 Revision*.

Life expectancy (years at birth): 47.6 (males 46.1; females 49.2) in 2010 (Source: World Bank, World Development Indicators database).

ECONOMICALLY ACTIVE POPULATION
(persons aged 6 years and over, 1988 census)

	Males	Females	Total
Agriculture, hunting, forestry and fishing	417,630	463,007	880,637
Mining and quarrying	11,823	586	12,409
Manufacturing	16,096	1,250	17,346
Electricity, gas and water	751	58	809
Construction	5,583	49	5,632
Trade, restaurants and hotels	37,435	54,563	91,998
Transport, storage and communications	6,601	150	6,751
Financing, insurance, real estate and business services	505	147	652
Community, social and personal services	61,764	8,537	70,301
Sub-total	558,188	528,347	1,086,535
Activities not adequately defined	7,042	4,627	11,669
Total employed	565,230	532,974	1,098,204
Unemployed	66,624	22,144	88,768
Total labour force	631,854	555,118	1,186,972

Source: ILO.

Mid-2012 (estimates in '000): Agriculture, etc. 1,275; Total labour force 2,084 (Source: FAO).

Health and Welfare

KEY INDICATORS

Total fertility rate (children per woman, 2010)	4.6
Under-5 mortality rate (per 1,000 live births, 2010)	159
HIV/AIDS (% of persons aged 15–49, 2009)	4.7
Physicians (per 1,000 head, 2004)	0.1
Hospital beds (per 1,000 head, 2006)	1.2
Health expenditure (2009): US $ per head (PPP)	30
Health expenditure (2009): % of GDP	4.0
Health expenditure (2009): public (% of total)	34.2
Access to water (% of persons, 2010)	67
Access to sanitation (% of persons, 2010)	34
Total carbon dioxide emissions ('000 metric tons, 2008)	260.4
Carbon dioxide emissions per head (metric tons, 2008)	0.1
Human Development Index (2011): ranking	179
Human Development Index (2011): value	0.343

For sources and definitions, see explanatory note on p. vi.

Agriculture

PRINCIPAL CROPS
('000 metric tons)

	2008	2009	2010
Maize	146.8	151.2	150.0
Millet*	10.0	10.0	10.0
Sorghum*	40.8	50.4	40.0
Cassava (Manioc)	621.8	642.9	679.0
Taro (Coco yam)†	109.9	113.7	118.0
Rice, paddy	38.0	39.1	39.0
Yams†	402.2	415.9	435.0
Sugar cane†	95.0	95.0	95.0
Groundnuts, with shell	159.5	162.7	140.0
Oil palm fruit	14.4	9.2	4.7
Sesame seed	49.0	50.0	50.0

—*continued*	2008	2009	2010
Melonseed†	32.4	34.1	31.1
Pumpkins, squash and gourds	32.3	32.9	30.0
Bananas†	124.9	125.0	126.0
Plantains†	82.1	85.0	88.0
Oranges†	22.0	20.9	24.0
Pineapples†	14.0	14.2	14.5
Coffee, green*	3.3	3.6	1.6
Seed cotton	2.3	7.5	10.5

* Unofficial figures.
† FAO estimates.

Aggregate production ('000 metric tons, may include official, semi-official or estimated data): Total cereals 235.5 in 2008, 250.7 in 2009, 239.0 in 2010; Total roots and tubers 1,135.0 in 2008, 1,173.6 in 2009, 1,233.2 in 2010; Total pulses 31.2 in 2008, 30.8 in 2009, 31.3 in 2010; Total vegetables (incl. melons) 97.3 in 2008, 99.2 in 2009, 95.0 in 2010; Total fruits (excl. melons) 263.9 in 2008, 268.8 in 2009, 274.6 in 2010.

Source: FAO.

LIVESTOCK
('000 head, year ending September)

	2008	2009	2010
Cattle	3,723	3,807	3,893
Goats	4,347	4,599	4,862
Sheep	351	369	388
Pigs	997	1,041	1,087
Chickens	5,869	6,117	6,376

Source: FAO.

LIVESTOCK PRODUCTS
('000 metric tons, FAO estimates)

	2008	2009	2010
Cattle meat	81.0	82.5	85.0
Sheep meat	2.0	2.1	2.2
Goat meat	16.1	17.0	18.0
Pig meat	13.5	14.3	16.0
Chicken meat	5.2	5.5	5.7
Game meat	15.8	15.9	19.7
Cows' milk	71.0	72.0	75.0
Hen eggs	1.9	1.9	1.9
Honey	15.5	16.3	14.8

Source: FAO.

Forestry

ROUNDWOOD REMOVALS
('000 cubic metres, excluding bark)

	2006	2007	2008
Sawlogs, veneer logs and logs for sleepers	524*	533†	533†
Other industrial wood*	308	308	308
Fuel wood*	2,000	2,000	2,000
Total	2,832	2,841	2,841

* FAO estimate(s).
† Unofficial figure.

2009–10: Production assumed to be unchanged from 2008 (FAO estimates).

Source: FAO.

SAWNWOOD PRODUCTION
('000 cubic metres, including railway sleepers)

	2006	2007	2008
Total (all broadleaved)	69*	95†	95†

* FAO estimate.
† Unofficial figure.

2009–10: Production assumed to be unchanged from 2008 (FAO estimate).

Source: FAO.

Fishing

('000 metric tons, live weight of capture, FAO estimates)

	2008	2009	2010
Total catch (freshwater fishes)	31.0	33.0	35.0

Source: FAO.

Mining

	2008	2009	2010
Gold (kg)	43	61	60
Diamonds ('000 carats)*	377.2	311.8	301.6
Limestone ('000 metric tons)	85	n.a.	n.a.

* Production is approximately 70% to 80% gem quality.

Source: US Geological Survey.

Industry

SELECTED PRODUCTS
('000 metric tons, unless otherwise indicated)

	2004	2005	2006
Beer ('000 hectolitres)	118.7	118.9	123.1
Sugar (raw, centrifugal)*	12	12	n.a.
Soft drinks ('000 hectolitres)	41.4	46.7	51.8
Cigarettes (million packets)	16.0	n.a.	n.a.
Palm oil*	1.7	1.7	1.7
Groundnut oil*	33.2	33.2	33.2
Plywood ('000 cubic metres)*	2.0	2.0	2.0

* FAO estimates.

Sources: IMF, *Central African Republic: Selected Issues and Statistical Appendix* (January 2008); FAO.

Groundnut oil ('000 metric tons, FAO estimates): 37.5 in 2008; 39.4 in 2009; 33.7 in 2010 (Source: FAO).

Electric energy (million kWh, estimates): 110 in 2003; 110 in 2004; 110 in 2005 (Source: UN, *Industrial Commodity Statistics Yearbook*).

Palm oil ('000 metric tons, FAO estimates): 1.1 in 2008; 0.7 in 2009; 0.4 in 2010 (Source: FAO).

Plywood ('000 metric tons, FAO estimates): 2.0 in 2008–10 (Source: FAO).

Finance

CURRENCY AND EXCHANGE RATES

Monetary Units

100 centimes = 1 franc de la Coopération Financière en Afrique Centrale (CFA).

Sterling, Dollar and Euro Equivalents (31 May 2012)

£1 sterling = 819.959 francs CFA;
US $1 = 528.870 francs CFA;
€1 = 655.957 francs CFA;
10,000 francs CFA = £12.20 = $18.91 = €15.24.

Average Exchange Rate (francs CFA per US $)

2009 472.186
2010 495.277
2011 471.866

Note: An exchange rate of 1 French franc = 50 francs CFA, established in 1948, remained in force until January 1994, when the CFA franc was devalued by 50%, with the exchange rate adjusted to 1 French franc = 100 francs CFA. This relationship to French currency remained in effect with the introduction of the euro on 1 January 1999. From that date, accordingly, a fixed exchange rate of €1 = 655.957 francs CFA has been in operation.

BUDGET
('000 million francs CFA)

Revenue*	2009†	2010‡	2011‡
Tax revenue	81.1	89.2	97.3
Taxes on profits and property	18.4	20.3	22.5
Taxes on goods and services	62.7	68.8	74.9
Taxes on international trade	18.2	20.8	23.6
Non-tax revenue	19.8	18.0	17.3
Total	100.9	107.2	114.6

Expenditure§	2009†	2010‡	2011‡
Current primary expenditure	79.8	103.4	98.6
Wages and salaries	39.6	46.0	49.0
Other goods and services	22.8	32.3	27.9
Transfers and subsidies	17.5	25.0	21.7
Interest payments	8.7	5.7	4.2
Capital expenditure	40.3	59.2	65.9
Domestically financed	7.4	18.4	15.4
Externally financed	32.8	40.8	50.5
Total	128.8	168.2	168.8

* Excluding grants received ('000 million francs CFA): 49.4 in 2009 (preliminary figure); 54.2 in 2010 (projected figure); 50.3 in 2011 (projected figure).
† Preliminary figures.
‡ Projections.
§ Excluding adjustment for payment arrears ('000 million francs CFA): 19.2 in 2009 (preliminary figure); 20.0 in 2010 (projected figure); 15.0 in 2011 (projected figure).

Source: IMF, *Central African Republic: Sixth Review Under the Arrangement Under the Extended Credit Facility and Financing Assurances Review—Staff Report; Debt Sustainability Analysis; Staff Supplement; Press Release on the Executive Board Discussion; and Statement by the Executive Director for Central African Republic* (October 2010).

INTERNATIONAL RESERVES
(US $ million at 31 December)

	2009	2010	2011
Gold (national valuation)	—	4.78	17.01
IMF special drawing rights	4.33	4.28	4.23
Reserve position in IMF	0.32	0.36	0.40
Foreign exchange	205.94	176.54	149.88
Total	210.59	185.96	171.52

Source: IMF, *International Financial Statistics*.

MONEY SUPPLY
('000 million francs CFA at 31 December)

	2009	2010	2011
Currency outside banks	78.02	94.41	105.43
Demand deposits at commercial and development banks	51.34	55.02	61.69
Total money	129.36	149.43	167.12

Source: IMF, *International Financial Statistics*.

COST OF LIVING
(Consumer Price Index for Bangui; base: 2000 = 100)

	2006	2007	2008
Food	118.9	121.1	134.9
Fuel and light	104.9	104.9	111.5
Clothing	131.0	128.1	130.6
All items (incl. others)	119.1	120.3	131.5

2009: All items 136.1.

2010: All items 138.1.

Source: ILO.

NATIONAL ACCOUNTS
(million francs CFA at current prices)

Expenditure on the Gross Domestic Product

	2007	2008	2009*
Government final consumption expenditure	69,577	69,577	78,995
Private final consumption expenditure	724,009	806,019	856,034
Gross capital formation	81,450	103,163	105,631
Total domestic expenditure	875,036	978,759	1,040,660
Exports of goods and services	123,143	103,995	95,579
Less Imports of goods and services	184,544	194,447	200,492
GDP in purchasers' values	813,635	888,307	935,747

Gross Domestic Product by Economic Activity

	2007	2008	2009*
Agriculture, hunting, forestry and fishing	416,632	466,830	478,376
Mining and quarrying	21,182	13,870	16,218
Manufacturing	50,992	56,271	59,466
Electricity, gas and water	6,802	5,959	6,173
Construction	31,289	36,080	38,090
Wholesale and retail trade, restaurants and hotels	98,815	108,425	114,135
Finance, insurance and real estate	49,541	54,359	57,221
Transport and communication	42,482	46,613	49,068
Public administration and defence	36,300	36,900	39,500
Other services	13,200	12,600	16,700
GDP at factor cost	767,235	837,907	874,947
Indirect taxes	46,400	50,400	60,800
GDP in purchasers' values	813,635	888,307	935,747

* Provisional figures.

Note: Deduction for imputed bank service charge assumed to be distributed at origin.

Source: African Development Bank.

BALANCE OF PAYMENTS
('000 million francs CFA)

	2007	2008*	2009†
Exports of goods	85.4	65.9	57.5
Imports of goods	–120.0	–138.2	–121.4
Trade balance	–34.6	–72.3	–63.9
Services (net)	–41.5	–43.5	–43.3
Balance on goods and services	–76.1	–115.8	–107.2
Income (net)	–5.1	–9.9	–3.4
Balance on goods, services and income	–81.2	–125.7	–110.6
Current transfers (net)	30.5	34.1	38.1
Current balance	–50.7	–91.6	–72.4
Capital account (net)	25.4	29.7	406.0
Project grants	20.2	29.7	32.8
Capital grants and transfers	5.2	0.0	373.2
Financial account	–3.1	56.2	–305.4
Public sector (net)	–12.4	–17.3	–336.4
Private sector (net)	9.3	73.5	31.0
Overall balance	–28.5	–5.7	28.2

* Preliminary figures.

† Estimates.

Source: IMF, *Central African Republic: Sixth Review Under the Arrangement Under the Extended Credit Facility and Financing Assurances Review—Staff Report; Debt Sustainability Analysis; Staff Supplement; Press Release on the Executive Board Discussion; and Statement by the Executive Director for Central African Republic* (October 2010).

External Trade

PRINCIPAL COMMODITIES
(distribution by SITC, US $ million)

Imports c.i.f.	2007	2008	2009
Food and live animals	29.6	38.6	69.2
Cereals and cereal preparations	15.9	23.0	27.2
Flour of wheat or meslin	7.3	12.3	13.1
Beverages and tobacco	4.4	6.1	6.9
Tobacco and tobacco manufactures	3.1	4.5	5.5
Crude materials (inedible) except fuels	33.9	5.9	6.1
Textile fibres (excl. wool tops) and waste	2.7	4.0	4.5
Mineral fuels, lubricants, etc.	1.7	2.5	1.3
Petroleum, petroleum products, etc.	1.6	2.5	2.5
Chemicals and related products	22.6	24.9	30.8
Medicinal and pharmaceutical products	17.5	17.1	23.3
Medicaments	16.6	16.2	20.7
Manufactured goods	42.6	32.7	29.8
Non-ferrous metals	2.1	2.2	2.3
Non-metallic mineral manufactures	25.5	6.3	7.5
Machinery and transport equipment	49.8	55.5	46.5
Machinery specialized for particular industries	3.6	6.5	3.2

Imports c.i.f.—*continued*	2007	2008	2009
Civil engineering and contractors' plant and equipment	2.7	4.4	2.2
General industrial machinery, equipment and parts	4.5	4.4	5.2
Telecommunications and sound equipment	10.7	9.9	10.0
Road vehicles and parts*	18.0	15.5	15.3
Passenger motor cars (excl. buses)	4.0	3.9	1.4
Motor vehicles for goods transport and special purposes	6.9	3.2	5.7
Goods vehicles (lorries and trucks)	1.8	2.3	5.0
Parts and accessories for cars, buses, lorries, etc.*	1.2	2.0	1.8
Miscellaneous manufactured articles	10.3	15.4	13.6
Total (incl. others)	197.8	185.0	211.7

* Excluding tyres, engines and electrical parts.

Exports f.o.b.	2007	2008	2009
Food and live animals	3.5	1.6	2.5
Crude materials (inedible) except fuels	98.8	99.2	74.9
Cork and wood	62.8	56.7	24.9
Textile fibres (excl. wool tops) and waste	1.0	1.7	0.4
Industrial diamonds (sorted)	34.8	40.2	49.6
Basic manufactures	27.7	9.3	0.3
Diamonds (excl. sorted industrial diamonds), unmounted	27.6	9.2	0.1
Sorted non-industrial diamonds, rough or simply worked	1.6	—	0.1
Machinery and transport equipment	0.7	3.3	0.7
Road vehicles	0.7	2.4	0.3
Total (incl. others)	131.1	114.2	80.5

Source: UN, *International Trade Statistics Yearbook*.

PRINCIPAL TRADING PARTNERS
(US $ million)

Imports c.i.f.	2007	2008	2009
Belgium	10.7	7.9	9.6
Brazil	3.4	4.8	5.9
Cameroon	17.5	24.4	18.6
China, People's Repub.	11.3	14.7	16.8
France (incl. Monaco)	48.7	58.5	48.0
Germany	3.2	4.1	2.9
Italy	4.1	2.0	4.2
Japan	5.2	5.4	8.3
Netherlands	3.4	9.8	13.5
South Africa	4.5	5.0	4.5
USA	5.0	5.7	33.0
Total (incl. others)	197.8	185.0	211.7

Exports f.o.b.	2007	2008	2009
Belgium	24.9	34.6	47.1
Cameroon	1.6	2.7	1.1
China, People's Repub.	14.6	19.8	7.5
France (incl. Monaco)	9.8	11.4	7.5
Germany	11.0	12.6	6.8
Israel	18.2	6.2	0.1
Italy	3.9	3.6	1.3
Portugal	1.7	1.1	0.2
Spain	1.2	1.8	0.9
Switzerland (incl. Liechtenstein)	11.9	4.1	0.8
Turkey	2.5	3.2	1.2
USA	0.4	0.3	0.8
Total (incl. others)	131.1	114.2	80.5

Source: UN, *International Trade Statistics Yearbook*.

Transport

ROAD TRAFFIC
(motor vehicles in use)

	1999	2000	2001
Passenger cars	4,900	5,300	5,300
Commercial vehicles	5,800	6,300	6,300

Source: UN, *Statistical Yearbook*.

2007 (motor vehicles in use at 31 December): Passenger cars 1,225; Vans and lorries 58; Motorcycles and mopeds 4,492; Total 5,775 (Source: IRF, *World Road Statistics*).

SHIPPING
(international traffic on inland waterways, metric tons)

	1996	1997	1998
Freight unloaded at Bangui	60,311	56,206	57,513
Freight loaded at Bangui	5,348	5,907	12,524
Total	65,659	62,113	70,037

Source: Banque des Etats de l'Afrique Centrale, *Etudes et Statistiques*.

CIVIL AVIATION
(traffic on scheduled services)*

	1999	2000	2001
Kilometres flown (million)	3	3	1
Passengers carried ('000)	84	77	46
Passenger-km (million)	235	216	130
Total ton-km (million)	36	32	19

* Including an apportionment of the traffic of Air Afrique.

Source: UN, *Statistical Yearbook*.

Tourism

FOREIGN VISITORS BY COUNTRY OF ORIGIN*

	2007	2008	2009
Cameroon	1,604	2,895	4,125
Chad	740	1,275	3,221
Congo, Democratic Rep.	300	795	588
Congo, Republic	622	1,107	734
Côte d'Ivoire	418	1,024	1,116
France	4,096	6,975	4,431
Gabon	306	912	695
Italy	759	788	2,017
Senegal	564	1,127	1,662
Total (incl. others)	17,117	30,611	52,429

* Arrivals at hotels and similar establishments.

Receipts from tourism (US $ million, incl. passenger transport, unless otherwise indicated): 11.8 in 2008; 6.0 in 2009; 6.0 in 2010 (excl. passenger transport).

Total tourist arrivals ('000): 54 in 2010.

Source: World Tourism Organization.

Communications Media

	2008	2009	2010
Telephones ('000 main lines in use)	12.0	3.6	5.3
Mobile cellular telephones ('000 subscribers)	250.0	679.7	979.2
Internet subscribers ('000)	—	0.1	0.1

Source: International Telecommunication Union.

Personal computers: 12,000 (2.9 per 1,000 persons) in 2005 (Source: International Telecommunication Union).

Radio receivers: 283,000 in use in 1997 (Source: UNESCO, *Statistical Yearbook*).

Daily newspapers: 3 in 1996 (average circulation 6,000) (Source: UNESCO, *Statistical Yearbook*).

Non-daily newspapers: 1 in 1995 (average circulation 2,000) (Source: UNESCO, *Statistical Yearbook*).

Education

(2009/10 unless otherwise indicated)

			Students		
	Institutions*	Teachers	Males	Females	Total
Pre-primary	162	300	7,036	7,219	14,255
Primary	930	7,553	370,173	266,698	636,871
Secondary:					
general	46	1,466	51,195	30,486	81,681
vocational	n.a.	257	3,079	1,583	4,662
Tertiary	n.a.	340†	8,422	2,736	11,158

* 1990/91 figures.
† 2008/09 figure.

Source: UNESCO Institute for Statistics.

Pupil-teacher ratio (primary education, UNESCO estimate): 81.3 in 2010/11 (Source: UNESCO Institute for Statistics).

Adult literacy rate (UNESCO estimates): 56.0% (males 69.3%; females 43.2%) in 2010 (Source: UNESCO Institute for Statistics).

Directory

The Constitution

Following the overthrow of President Ange-Félix Patassé in March 2003, the Constitution of January 1995 was suspended. The new Constitution, approved by 87.2% of the electorate at a referendum in December 2004, provides for a presidential term of five years, renewable only once. Executive authority is held by the President, who is elected by direct popular vote and who, in turn, appoints a Council of Ministers (headed by a Prime Minister). The legislature comprises a directly-elected 105-member Assemblée nationale (National Assembly), which remains in office for a five-year term.

The Government

HEAD OF STATE

President of the Republic and Minister of National Defence, War Veterans, War Victims and the Restructuring of the Armed Forces: Gen. FRANÇOIS BOZIZÉ YANGOUVONDA (assumed power 16 March 2003; elected by direct popular vote 8 May 2005; re-elected 23 January 2011).

COUNCIL OF MINISTERS

(September 2012)

Prime Minister and Head of Government: Prof. FAUSTIN-ARCHANGE TOUADÉRA.

Minister of State for Finance and the Budget: ALBERT BESSE.

Minister of State for Planning and the Economy: SYLVAIN MALICKO.

Minister of State for the Development of Transport: Col PARFAIT-ANICET M'BAYE.

Minister of State for Higher Education and Scientific Research: JEAN WILIBIRO-SACKO.

Minister of State for Posts, Telecommunications and New Technologies: ABDOU KARIM MECKASSOUA.

Minister of Agriculture and Rural Development: FIDÈLE GOUANDJIKA.

Minister of Water Resources, Forests, Hunting and Fishing: EMMANUEL BIZOT.

Minister of Foreign Affairs and Central Africans Abroad: Gen. ANTOINE GAMBI.

Minister of the Environment and Ecology: FRANÇOIS NAOUEYAMA.

Minister of Housing and Living Conditions: GONTRON DJONO-DJIDOU-AHABO.

Minister in charge of the Secretariat-General of the Government and Relations with the Institutions: MICHEL KOYT.

Minister of Professional and Technical Education and Training: DJIBRINE SALL.

Minister of Territorial Administration and Decentralization: JOSUÉ BINOUA.

Minister of Public Health, Population and the Fight against AIDS: JEAN-MICHEL MANDABA.

Minister of the Civil Service, Labour and Social Security: NOËL RAMANDAN.

Minister of National Security, Emigration-Immigration and Public Order: CLAUDE RICHARD GOUANDJA.

Minister of Trade and Industry: MARLYN MOULIOM ROOSALEM.

Minister of Equipment, Public Works and Promotion of the Regions: JEAN PROSPER WODOBODÉ.

Minister of Primary and Secondary Education and Literacy: GISÈLE ANNIE NAM.

Minister of Justice and Moralization, Keeper of the Seals: (vacant).

Minister of International Co-operation, Regional Integration and Francophone Affairs: DOROTHÉRE AIMÉE MALÉNZAPA.

Minister of Communication and Democratic and Civic Education: ALFRED TAÏNGA POLOKO.

Minister of Social Affairs, National Solidarity and the Promotion of Gender Equality: MARGUÉRITE PÉTRO KONI ZEZÉ ZARAMBAUD.

Minister of Energy and Hydraulics: LÉOPOLD MBOLI FATRAN.

Minister of Town Planning and the Reconstruction of Public Buildings: PASCAL KOYAMÉNÉ.

Minister of Tourism Development and Artisanal Industries: SYLVIE ANNICK MAZOUNGOU.

Minister of Youth, Sports, Arts and Culture: JEAN-SERGE BOKASSA.

Minister of the Promotion of Small and Medium-sized Enterprises, the Informal Sector and the Guichet Unique: ALBERTINE AGOUNDOUKOUA MBISSA.

Minister-delegate to the Minister of State for Agriculture and Rural Development, responsible for Stockbreeding and Animal Health: YOUSSOUFA YÉRIMA MANDJO.

Minister-delegate at the Presidency, in charge of National Defence, War Veterans, War Victims and the Restructuring of the Armed Forces: Col JEAN-FRANCIS BOZIZÉ.

Minister-delegate at the Presidency, in charge of Development Centres: DAVID BANZOUKOU.

Minister-delegate at the Presidency, in charge of Mines: OBED NAMSIO.

Minister-delegate at the Presidency, in charge of Civil Aviation: THÉODORE JOUSSO.

Minister-delegate at the Presidency, in charge of the Disarmament, Demobilization and Rehabilitation of Former Combatants and the National Youth Pioneers: Brig. SYLVESTRE YANGONGO.

MINISTRIES

Office of the President: Palais de la Renaissance, Bangui; tel. 21-61-46-63; internet presidencerca.com.

Ministry of Agriculture and Rural Development: Bangui; tel. 21-61-28-00.

Ministry of the Civil Service, Labour and Social Security: Bangui; tel. 21-61-21-88; fax 21-61-04-14.

Ministry of Communication and Democratic and Civic Education: Bangui.

Ministry of the Development of Transport: BP 941, Bangui; tel. 21-61-70-49; fax 21-61-46-28.

Ministry of Energy and Hydraulics: Bangui; tel. 21-61-20-54; fax 21-61-60-76.

Ministry of the Environment and Ecology: Bangui.

Ministry of Equipment, Public Works and Promotion of the Regions: Bangui.

Ministry of Finance and the Budget: BP 696, Bangui; tel. 21-61-38-05.

Ministry of Higher Education and Scientific Research: BP 791, Bangui; tel. 21-61-08-38.

Ministry of Housing and Living Conditions: Bangui.

Ministry of International Co-operation, Regional Integration and Francophone Affairs: Bangui; tel. 21-61-54-67; fax 21-61-26-06.

Ministry of Justice and Moralization: Bangui; tel. 21-61-52-11.

Ministry of National Defence, War Veterans, War Victims and the Restructuring of the Armed Forces: Bangui; tel. 21-61-00-25.

Ministry of National Security, Emigration-Immigration and Public Order: Bangui; tel. 21-61-14-77.

Ministry of Planning and the Economy: BP 912, Bangui; tel. 21-61-70-55; fax 21-61-63-98.

Ministry of Posts, Telecommunications and New Technologies: Bangui; tel. 21-61-29-66.

Ministry of Primary and Secondary Education and Literacy: Bangui.

Ministry of Professional and Technical Education and Training: Bangui.

Ministry of the Promotion of Small and Medium-sized Enterprises, the Informal Sector and the Guichet Unique: Bangui.

Ministry of Public Health, Population and the Fight against AIDS: Bangui; tel. 21-61-16-35.

Ministry of Social Affairs, National Solidarity and the Promotion of Gender Equality: Bangui; tel. 21-61-55-65.

Ministry of Territorial Administration and Decentralization: Bangui.

Ministry of Tourism Development and Artisanal Industries: Bangui; tel. 21-61-04-16.

Ministry of Town Planning and the Reconstruction of Public Buildings: Bangui; tel. 21-61-69-54.

Ministry of Trade and Industry: Bangui; tel. 21-61-10-69.

Ministry of Water Resources, Forests, Hunting and Fishing: Bangui; tel. 21-61-79-21.

Ministry of Youth, Sports, Arts and Culture: Bangui; tel. 21-61-39-69.

President and Legislature

PRESIDENT

Presidential Election, 23 January 2011

Candidate	Votes	% of votes
Gen. François Bozizé Yangouvonda	718,801	64.37
Ange-Félix Patassé	239,279	21.43
Martin Ziguélé	75,939	6.80
Emile Gros-Raymond Nakombo	51,469	4.61
Jean-Jacques Démafouth	31,184	2.79
Total	1,116,672	100.00

ASSEMBLÉE NATIONALE

Speaker: CÉLESTIN-LEROY GAOMBALET.

General Election, 23 January and 27 March 2011

Party	Seats
Kwa na Kwa	61
Majorité Présidentielle	11
L'Opposition	2
Independents	26
Total	100*

* Following the second round of elections, five seats remained undeclared.

Election Commission

Autorité Nationale des Elections (ANE): Bangui; f. 2012; 7 mems.

Political Organizations

Alliance pour la Démocratie et le Progrès (ADP): Bangui; internet alliance-democratie-progres.over-blog.com; f. 1991; progressive; Nat. Pres. EMMANUEL OLIVIER GABIRAULT.

Armée Populaire pour la Restauration de la République et la Démocratie (APRD): Bangui; armed insurrectionary group; Leader JEAN-JACQUES DÉMAFOUTH.

Concertation des Partis Politiques d'Opposition (CPPO): Bangui; umbrella org. of 12 parties opposed to former President Patassé.

Convention Nationale (CN): Bangui; f. 1991; Leader DAVID GALIAMBO.

Coordination des Patriotes Centrafricains (CPC): Paris (France) and Bangui; f. 2003; umbrella org. for groups opposed to former President Patassé and affiliated to the uprising of March 2003; Sec.-Gen. ABDOU KARIM MÉCKASSOUA.

Forum Démocratique pour la Modernité (FODEM): ave Dejean, Sicai, Bangui; tel. 21-61-29-54; e-mail eric.neris@fodem.org; internet www.fodem.org; f. 1997; Pres. (vacant).

Front Démocratique de Libération du Peuple Centrafricain (FDPC): e-mail miskinedardar@yahoo.fr; internet www.centrafriquefdpc.com; Leader ABDOULAYE MISKINE.

Front Patriotique pour le Progrès (FPP): BP 259, Bangui; tel. 21-61-52-23; fax 21-61-10-93; f. 1972; aims to promote political education and debate; Leader ALEXANDRE GOUMBA.

Kwa na Kwa (KNK): Bangui; f. 2004; formally constituted as a political party in 2009; Sec.-Gen. ELIÉ OUÉFIO.

Mouvement National pour le Renouveau: Bangui; Leader PAUL BELLET.

Mouvement pour la Démocratie et le Développement (MDD): Bangui; f. 1993; aims to safeguard national unity and the equitable distribution of national wealth; Leader LOUIS PAPENIAH.

Mouvement pour la Démocratie, l'Indépendance et le Progrès Social (MDI-PS): BP 1404, Bangui; tel. 21-61-18-21; e-mail mdicentrafrique@chez.com; internet www.chez.com/mdicentrafrique; Sec.-Gen. DANIEL NDITIFEI BOYSEMBE.

Mouvement pour la Libération du Peuple Centrafricain (MLPC): Bangui; internet www.lemlpc.net; f. 1979; leading party in govt Oct. 1993–March 2003; Pres. MARTIN ZIGUÉLÉ; Sec.-Gen. JEAN-MICHEL MANDABA.

Nouvelle Alliance pour le Progrès (NAP): Bangui; internet www.centrafrique-nap.com; Leader JEAN-JACQUES DÉMAFOUTH.

Parti Social-Démocrate (PSD): BP 543, Bangui; tel. 21-61-59-02; fax 21-61-58-44; Leader ENOCH DERANT LAKOUÉ.

Rassemblement Démocratique Centrafricain (RDC): BP 503, Bangui; tel. 21-61-53-75; f. 1987; sole legal political party 1987–91; Leader (vacant).

Union des Forces Démocratiques pour le Rassemblement (UFDR): Bangui; f. 2006; Chief of Staff ZAKARIA DAMANE.

Front Démocratique Centrafricain (FDC): Bangui; Leader Commdt JUSTIN HASSAN.

Groupe d'Action Patriotique de la Libération de Centrafrique (GAPLC): Bangui; Leader MICHEL AM NONDROKO DJOTODIA.

Mouvement des Libérateurs Centrafricains pour la Justice (MLCJ): Bangui; Leader Capt. ABAKAR SABONE.

Union des Forces Républicaines de Centrafrique: Bangui; f. 2006; armed insurrectionary group; Leader Lt FRANÇOIS-FLORIAN N'DJADDER-BEDAYA.

Union pour un Mouvement Populaire de Centrafrique (UMPCA): Pres. YVONNE M'BOÏSSONA.

Diplomatic Representation

EMBASSIES IN THE CENTRAL AFRICAN REPUBLIC

Cameroon: rue du Languedoc, BP 935, Bangui; tel. 77-59-31-80 (mobile); e-mail ambacambangui@yahoo.fr; Chargé d'affaires a.i. NICOLAS NZOYOUM.

Chad: ave Valéry Giscard d'Estaing, BP 461, Bangui; tel. 21-61-46-77; fax 21-61-62-44; Ambassador ABDERAHIM YACOUB N'DIAYE.

China, People's Republic: ave des Martyrs, BP 1430, Bangui; tel. 21-61-27-60; fax 21-61-31-83; e-mail chinaemb_cf@mfa.gov.cn; Ambassador SUN HAICHAO.

Congo, Democratic Republic: Ambassador EMBE ISEA MBAMBE.

Congo, Republic: ave Boganda, BP 1414, Bangui; tel. 21-61-03-09; e-mail diplobrazzabangui@yahoo.fr; Ambassador GABRIEL ENTCHA-EBIA.

Egypt: angle ave Léopold Sédar Senghor et rue Emile Gentil, BP 1422, Bangui; tel. 21-61-46-88; fax 21-61-35-45; e-mail ambassadedEgypt_Centreafrique@excite.com; Ambassador AZZA EL-GUIBALI.

France: blvd du Général de Gaulle, BP 884, Bangui; tel. 21-61-30-05; fax 21-61-74-04; e-mail contact@ambafrance-cf.org; internet www.ambafrance-cf.org; Ambassador JEAN-PIERRE VIDON.

Holy See: ave Boganda, BP 1447, Bangui; tel. 75041492 (mobile); e-mail nonciature.rca@hotmail.com; Apostolic Nuncio JUDE THADDEUS OKOLO (Titular Archbishop of Novica).

Japan: Temporarily closed; affairs handled through the embassy of Japan, Yaoundé, Cameroon, since October 2003.

Libya: Bangui; tel. 21-61-46-62; fax 21-61-55-25; Ambassador OMAR ISSA BARUNI.

Morocco: ave de l'indépendence, BP 1609, Bangui; tel. 21-61-39-51; fax 21-61-35-22; e-mail sifama-bg@intnet.cf; Ambassador MUSTAPHA EL-HALFAOUI.

Nigeria: ave des Martyrs, BP 1010, Bangui; tel. 21-61-07-44; fax 21-61-12-79; e-mail jimgom7@yahoo.com; Ambassador ROLAND OMOWA.

Russia: ave du Président Gamal Abdel Nasser, BP 1405, Bangui; tel. 21-61-03-11; fax 21-61-56-45; e-mail rusconsrca@yandex.ru; internet www.rca.mid.ru; Ambassador ALEKSANDR V. KASPAROV.

Sudan: ave de France, BP 1351, Bangui; tel. 21-61-38-21; Ambassador OMAR SALIH ABU BAKR.

USA: ave David Dacko, BP 924, Bangui; tel. 21-61-02-00; fax 21-61-44-94; internet bangui.usembassy.gov; Ambassador LAURENCE D. WOHLERS.

Judicial System

Supreme Court: BP 926, Bangui; tel. 21-61-41-33; highest judicial organ; acts as a Court of Cassation in civil and penal cases and as Court of Appeal in administrative cases; comprises four chambers: constitutional, judicial, administrative and financial; Pres. TAGBIA SANZIA.

Constitutional Court: BP 2104, Bangui; tel. 21-61-99-58; fax 21-61-99-52; f. 1995; Pres. MARCEL MALONGA.

There is also a Court of Appeal, a Criminal Court, 16 tribunaux de grande instance, 37 tribunaux d'instance, six labour tribunals and a permanent military tribunal.

Religion

It is estimated that 24% of the population hold animist beliefs, 50% are Christians (25% Roman Catholic, 25% Protestant) and 15% are Muslims. There is no official state religion.

CHRISTIANITY

The Roman Catholic Church

The Central African Republic comprises one archdiocese and eight dioceses. An estimated 25% of the population are Roman Catholics.

Bishops' Conference

Conférence Episcopale Centrafricaine, BP 1518, Bangui; tel. 21-61-70-72; fax 21-61-46-92; e-mail ceca_rca@yahoo.fr.

f. 1982; Pres. Most Rev. EDOUARD MATHOS.

Archbishop of Bangui: Most Rev. DIEUDONNÉ NZAPALAINGA, Archevêché, BP 1518, Bangui; tel. 21-61-08-98; fax 21-61-46-92; e-mail archbangui@yahoo.fr.

Protestant Church

Eglise Évangélique Luthérienne de la République Centrafricaine: BP 100, Bouar; tel. 70-80-73-36; fax 21-31-41-70; e-mail eelrca@skyfile.com; Pres. Rev. ANDRÉ GOLIKE; 55,000 mems (2010).

Eglise Protestante du Christ Roi: rue des Missions, BP 608, Bangui; tel. 21-61-14-35; fax 21-61-35-61; e-mail sgudeac@intnet.cf; f. 1968.

The Press

The independent press is highly regulated. Independent publications must hold a trading licence and prove their status as a commercial enterprise. They must also have proof that they fulfil taxation requirements. There is little press activity outside Bangui.

DAILIES

Le Citoyen: BP 974, Bangui; tel. 21-61-89-16; e-mail ltdc@yahoo.fr; independent; Dir MAKA GBOSSOKOTTO; circ. 1,000.

Le Confident: BP 427, Bangui; tel. 75-04-64-14; e-mail leconfident2000@yahoo.fr; internet www.leconfident.net; f. 2001; Mon.–Sat; Dir MATHURIN C. N. MOMET; circ. 500.

Le Démocrate: BP 427, Bangui; Dir of Publication FERDINAND SAMBA; circ. 500.

L'Hirondelle: Bangui; independent; Editor-in-Chief JULES YANGANDA; circ. 500.

PERIODICALS

Bangui Match: Bangui; monthly.

Centrafrique-Presse: BP 1058, Bangui; tel. and fax 21-61-39-57; e-mail info@centrafrique-presse.com; weekly; Publr PROSPER N'DOUBA.

Demain le Monde: BP 650, Bangui; tel. 21-61-23-15; f. 1985; fortnightly; independent; Editor-in-Chief NGANAM NOËL.

Journal Officiel de la République Centrafricaine: BP 739, Bangui; f. 1974; fortnightly; economic data; Dir-Gen. GABRIEL AGBA.

Nations Nouvelles: BP 965, Bangui; publ. by Organisation Commune Africaine et Mauricienne; politics and current affairs.

Le Patriote: Bangui; Dir of Publication AMBROISE YALIMA.

Le Peuple: BP 569, Bangui; tel. 21-61-76-34; f. 1995; weekly; Editor-in-Chief VERMOND TCHENDO.

Le Progrès: BP 154, Bangui; tel. 21-61-70-26; f. 1991; monthly; Editor-in-Chief BELIBANGA CLÉMENT; circ. 2,000.

Le Rassemblement: Bangui; organ of the RDC; Editor-in-Chief MATHIAS GONEVO REAPOGO.

La Tortue Déchainée: Bangui; independent; satirical; Publr MAKA GBOSSOKOTTO.

PRESS ASSOCIATION

Groupement des Editeurs de la Presse Privée Indépendante de Centrafrique (GEPPIC): Bangui; Pres. PATRICK AGOUNDOU.

Observatoire des Médias Centrafricains (OMCA): Bangui; Pres. PIERRE DÉBATO, II.

Union des Journalistes de Centrafrique (UJCA): Bangui; Pres. MAKA GBOSSOKOTO.

NEWS AGENCY

Agence Centrafrique Presse (ACAP): BP 40, Bangui; tel. 21-61-22-79; e-mail infoacap@yahoo.fr; internet www.acap-cf.info; f. 1960; Gen. Man. ALAIN BERTRAND KOGALAMA.

Publisher

GOVERNMENT PUBLISHING HOUSE

Imprimerie Centrafricaine: ave David Dacko, BP 329, Bangui; tel. 21-61-72-24; f. 1974; Dir-Gen. SERGE BOZANGA.

Broadcasting and Communications

In 2011 there were four mobile cellular telephone operators and one fixed-line telephone operator in the country. In 2010, according to the International Telecommunication Union, there were 979,200 subscribers to mobile telephone services and 5,300 subscribers to fixed-line services.

TELECOMMUNICATIONS

Agence de Régulation des Télécommunications (ART): Immeuble de la Poste, BP 1046, Bangui; tel. 21-61-56-51; fax 21-61-05-82; e-mail art-rca@art-rca.org; internet www.art-rca.org; regulatory authority; Dir-Gen. JOSEPH NGANAZOUI.

Atlantique Telecom Centrafrique SA: Immeuble Moov, ave du Président Mobutu, BP 2439 Bangui; tel. and fax 21-61-23-85; internet www.moov-rca.com; operates mobile cellular telephone services under Moov network; Dir-Gen. SOULEYMANE DIALLO (Moov Centrafrique); 248,063 subscribers.

Azur RCA: ave de l'Indépendance, Ex FNUAP, BP 1418, Bangui; tel. 21-61-33-97; fax 21-61-33-07; e-mail contact@azur-rca.com; internet www.azur-rca.com; f. 2004; fmrly Nation Link Telecom; mobile cellular telephone operator; Dir-Gen. YANNICK BOURDEU; 96,499 subscribers (2009).

Orange Centrafrique: Imeuble SODIAM, ave Bathélemy Boganda, BP 863, Bangui; tel. 72-27-08-00; e-mail serviceclient@orange.cf; internet www.orange.cf; f. 2007; mobile cellular telephone operator; Pres. MICHEL BARRÉ; Dir-Gen. BRUNO ALLASSONNIÈRE; 211,657 subscribers (2009).

Société Centrafricaine de Télécommunications (SOCATEL): BP 939, Bangui; tel. 21-61-42-68; fax 21-61-44-72; e-mail dg-socatel@socatel.cf; internet www.socatel.cf; f. 1990; 60% state-owned; 40% owned by France Câbles et Radio (France Télécoms); further privatization suspended March 2003; Dir-Gen. SIMON SERGE BOZANGA; 10,000 subscribers (2009).

Telecel: BP 939, Bangui; tel. 21-61-19-30; fax 21-61-16-99; f. 1996; mobile cellular telephone operator; Dir-Gen. LIONEL GOUSSI; 238,868 subscribers (2009).

BROADCASTING

Radiodiffusion-Télévision Centrafricaine: BP 940, Bangui; tel. 21-61-25-88; f. 1958 as Radiodiffusion Nationale Centrafricaine; govt-controlled; broadcasts in French and Sango.

Radio Centrafrique: Bangui; tel. 75-50-36-32; e-mail yakanet.rca@gmail.com; internet www.radiocentrafrique.org; Dir-Gen DAVID GBANGA.

Radio Ndeke Luka: community station operated by UN.

Radio Nostalgie: commercial radio station in Bangui.

Radio Notre-Dame: radio station operated by Roman Catholic Church.

Radio Rurale: community stations operating in Bouar, Nola, Berbérati and Bambari.

TELEVISION

Télévision Centrafricaine (TVCA): Bangui; tel. 21-61-61-02; Dir-Gen. MICHEL OUAMBÉTI.

Finance

(cap. = capital; res = reserves; dep. = deposits; m. = million; br. = branch; amounts in francs CFA)

BANKING

In 2010 there were four commercial banks in the country.

Central Bank

Banque des Etats de l'Afrique Centrale (BEAC): BP 851, Bangui; tel. 21-61-24-00; fax 21-61-19-95; e-mail beacbgf@beac.int; internet www.beac.int; headquarters in Yaoundé, Cameroon; f. 1973; bank of issue for mem. states of the Communauté économique et monétaire de l'Afrique centrale (CEMAC, fmrly Union douanière et économique de l'Afrique centrale), comprising Cameroon, the CAR, Chad, the Repub. of the Congo, Equatorial Guinea and Gabon; cap. 88,000m., res 227,843m., dep. 4,110,966m. (Dec. 2007); Gov. LUCAS ABAGA NCHAMA; Dir in CAR CAMILLE KELEFIO.

Commercial Banks

Banque Populaire Maroco-Centrafricaine (BPMC): rue Guérillot, BP 844, Bangui; tel. 21-61-31-90; fax 21-61-62-30; e-mail bpmc@intnet.cf; f. 1991; 57.5% owned by Groupe Banque Populaire (Morocco); cap. and res 4,183m., total assets 13,331m. (Dec. 2003); Gen. Man. MOHAMMED BENZIANI.

Commercial Bank Centrafrique (CBCA): rue de Brazza, BP 59, Bangui; tel. 21-61-29-90; fax 21-61-34-54; e-mail cbcabank@cbc-bank.com; internet www.cbc-bank.com/cb_centrafrique/page.php?langue=fr; f. 1999; 54.5% owned by Groupe Fotso; 40.5% owned by CAR private shareholders; 5% owned by Commercial Bank Cameroon SA; cap. 1,500.m., res 1,856.3m., dep 22,941.2m. (Dec. 2005); Pres. SERGE PSIMHIS; Dir-Gen. THÉODORE DABANGA; 1 br.

Ecobank Centrafrique: pl. de la République, BP 910, Bangui; tel. 21-61-00-42; fax 21-61-34-38; e-mail ecobankcf@ecobank.com; internet www.ecobank.com; f. 1946 as BAO; cap. 5,000m., res 845m., dep. 53,621m. (Dec. 2009); Pres. KASSIMOU ABOU KABASSI; Man. Dir CHRISTIAN ASSOSSOU.

Development Bank

Banque de Développement des Etats de l'Afrique Centrale: see Franc Zone.

Financial Institutions

Caisse Autonome d'Amortissement de la République Centrafricaine: Bangui; tel. 21-61-53-60; fax 21-61-21-82; management of state funds; Dir-Gen. JOSEPH PINGAMA.

Caisse Nationale d'Epargne (CNE): Office national des postes et de l'épargne, Bangui; tel. 21-61-22-96; fax 21-61-78-80; Pres. SIMONE BODEMO-MODOYANGBA; Dir-Gen. AMBROISE DAOUDA; Man. ANTOINE BEKOUANEBANDI.

Bankers' Association

Association Professionnelle des Banques: Bangui.

Development Agencies

Agence Française de Développement: route de la Moyenne Corniche, BP 817, Bangui; tel. 21-61-45-78; fax 21-61-03-06; e-mail afdbangui@groupe-afd.org; internet www.afd.fr; administers economic aid and finances specific development projects; Man. JOCELYN LEVENEUR.

Mission Française de Coopération et d'Action Culturelle: BP 934, Bangui; tel. 21-61-63-34; fax 21-61-28-24; administers bilateral aid from France; Dir HERVÉ CRONEL.

INSURANCE

Agence Centrafricaine d'Assurances (ACA): BP 512, Bangui; tel. 21-61-06-23; f. 1956; Dir R. CERBELLAUD.

Allianz Centrafrique Assurances: blvd Général de Gaulle, BP 343, Bangui; tel. 21-61-36-66; fax 21-61-33-40; e-mail allianz.centrafrique@allianz-cf.com; internet www.allianz-africa.com; f. 1988; Dir of Operations BRUNO RIBEYRON.

Assureurs Conseils Centrafricains (ACCAF): ave Barthélemy Boganda, BP 743, Bangui; tel. 21-61-19-33; fax 21-61-44-70; e-mail centrafrique@ascoma.com; internet www.ascoma.com; f. 1968; owned by Ascoma (Monaco); Man. VENANT EBELA; Dir-Gen. SYLVAIN COUSIN.

Entreprise d'Etat d'Assurances et de Réassurances (SIRIRI): Bangui; tel. 21-61-36-55; f. 1972; Pres. EMMANUEL DOKOUNA; Dir-Gen. MARTIN ZIGUÉLÉ.

Union des Assurances Centrafricaine (UAC): rue de la Victoire, BP 896, Bangui; tel. 21-61-31-02; fax 21-61-18-48; e-mail uac02@yahoo.fr; f. 1999; non-life insurance; Dir-Gen. PATHÉ DIONE.

Trade and Industry

DEVELOPMENT ORGANIZATION

Agence Centrafricaine de Développement Agricole (ACDA): ave David Dacko, BP 997, Bangui; tel. 21-61-54-85; e-mail acda_2010@yahoo.fr; internet www.acda-rca.org; f. 1993; purchasing, transport and marketing of cotton, cotton-ginning, production of cottonseed oil and groundnut oil; Pres. HONORÉ FEIZOURE.

INDUSTRIAL AND TRADE ASSOCIATIONS

Agence de Développement de la Zone Caféière (ADECAF): BP 1935, Bangui; tel. 21-61-47-30; coffee producers' asscn; assists coffee marketing co-operatives; Dir-Gen. J. J. NIMIZIAMBI.

Agence Nationale pour le Développement de l'Elevage (ANDE): BP 1509, Bangui; tel. 21-61-69-60; fax 21-61-50-83; assists with development of livestock; Dir-Gen. EMMANUEL NAMKOISSÉ.

Bourse Internationale de Diamant de Bangui: BP 26, Bangui; tel. 21-61-58-63; fax 21-61-60-76; diamond exchange; supervised by the Ministry of Energy and Hydraulics.

Caisse de Stabilisation et de Pérequation des Produits Agricoles (CAISTAB): BP 76, Bangui; tel. 21-61-08-00; supervises marketing and pricing of agricultural produce; Dir-Gen. M. BOUNANDELE-KOUMBA.

Fédération Nationale des Eleveurs Centrafricains (FNEC): ave des Martyrs, BP 588, Bangui; tel. 21-61-23-97; fax 21-61-47-24; Pres. BI AMADOU SOUAIBOU; Sec.-Gen. YOUSSOUFA MANDJO.

Groupement des Industries Centrafricaines (GICA): BP 804, Bangui; umbrella group representing 12 principal companies of various industries; Pres. PATRICK DEJEAN.

Office National de la Forêts (ONF): BP 915, Bangui; tel. 21-61-38-27; f. 1969; afforestation, development of forest resources; Dir-Gen. C. D. SONGUET.

CHAMBERS OF COMMERCE

Chambre d'Agriculture, d'Elevage, des Eaux, Forêts, Chasses, Pêches et du Tourisme: BP 850, Bangui; tel. 21-61-06-38; e-mail chagri_rca@hotmail.com; f. 1964; Sec.-Gen. HENRI OUIKON.

Chambre de Commerce, d'Industrie, des Mines et de l'Artisanat (CCIMA): blvd Charles de Gaulle, BP 823, Bangui; tel. 21-61-16-68; fax 21-61-35-61; e-mail ccima@intnet.cf; internet ccima-rca.com; f. 1935; Pres. ROBERT NGOKI; Treas. THÉODORE LAWSON.

EMPLOYERS' ORGANIZATION

Union Nationale du Patronat Centrafricain (UNPC): Immeuble Tropicana, 1°, BP 2180, Bangui; tel. and fax 21-61-16-79; e-mail unpc-rca@intnet.cf; Pres. GILLES GILBERT GRESENGUET.

UTILITIES

Electricity

Société Energie de Centrafrique (ENERCA): ave de l'Indépendance, BP 880, Bangui; tel. 21-61-20-22; fax 21-61-54-43; e-mail enerca@intnet.cf; f. 1967; state-owned; production and distribution of electric energy; 119.1 GWh produced for the Bangui grid in 2003; Dir-Gen. SAMUEL TOZOUI.

Water

Société de Distribution d'Eau en Centrafrique (SODECA): BP 1838, Bangui; tel. 21-61-59-66; fax 21-61-25-49; e-mail sodeca@intnet.cf; f. 1975 as the Société Nationale des Eaux; state-owned co responsible for supply, treatment and distribution of water; Dir-Gen. PAUL BELLET.

MAJOR COMPANIES

The following are among the largest companies in terms of either capital investment or employment.

Alpha Robusta Café: BP 320, Bangui; fax 21-61-44-49; purchase and distribution of coffee; Man. CHRISTELIN BANGANDOZOU.

Bata SA Centrafricaine: BP 364, Bangui; tel. 21-61-45-79; f. 1969; cap. 150m. francs CFA; footwear mfrs; Dir VICTOR DE RYCKE.

COLALU: rue Chavannes, BP 1326, Bangui; tel. 21-61-20-42; fax 21-61-55-29; e-mail sylvain_kobangue@yahoo.fr; f. 1969; cap. 69m. francs CFA; owned by Yeshi Group (Côte d'Ivoire); mfrs of household articles and sheet aluminium; Pres. CLAUDE MILLET; Dir-Gen. M. KAPPES.

Compagnie Industrielle d'Ouvrages en Textiles (CIOT): BP 190, Bangui; tel. 21-61-36-22; f. 1949; cap. 250m. francs CFA; mfrs of clothing and hosiery; Dir-Gen. MICHEL ROBERT.

Comptoir National du Diamant (CND): blvd B. Boganela, Bangui; tel. 21-61-07-02; f. 1964; 50% state-owned, 50% owned by Diamond Distributors (USA); mining and marketing of diamonds; Dir-Gen. M. VASSOS.

Entreprise Forestière des Bois Africains Centrafrique (EFBACA): BP 205, Bangui; tel. 21-61-25-33; f. 1969; 12% state-owned; exploitation of forests and wood-processing; Pres. VICTOR BALET; Dir JEAN QUENNOZ.

Huilerie Savonnerie Centrafricaine (HUSACA): BP 1020, Bangui; tel. 21-61-58-54; fax 21-61-68-11; mfrs of soap, edible oil and animal feed; Dir BASSAM ABDALLAH.

Industrie Centrafricaine du Textile (ICAT): BP 981, Bangui; tel. 21-61-40-00; f. 1965; cap. 586m. francs CFA; state-owned; textile complex; Man. Dir M. NGOUNDOUKOUA.

Industries Forestières de Batalimo (IFB): BP 517, Bangui; tel. 21-61-28-77; f. 1970; cap. 100m. francs CFA; Dir JACQUES GADEN.

Motte-Cordonnier-Afrique (MOCAF): BP 806, Bangui; tel. 21-61-18-13; f. 1951; cap. 1,123m. francs CFA; production of beer, soft drinks and ice; Pres. BERTRAND MOTTE; Dir-Gen. PHILIPPE MAGNAVAL.

Société Centrafricaine de Cigarette (SOCACI): BP 681, Bangui; Dir-Gen. PATRICK DE JEAN.

Société Centrafricaine de Déroulage (SCAD): BP 1607, Bangui; tel. 21-61-09-44; fax 21-61-56-60; f. 1972; cap. 700m. francs CFA; exploitation of forests, mfrs of plywood; also operates a sawmill; Dir-Gen. J. KAMACH; 392 employees.

Société Centrafricaine du Diamant (SODIAM): BP 1016, Bangui; tel. 21-61-03-79; cap. 100m. francs CFA; export of diamonds; Dir DIMITRI ANAGNOSTELLIS.

Société Centrafricaine d'Exploitation Forestière et Industrielle (SOCEFI): BP 3, M'Bata-Bangui; f. 1947; nationalized 1974; cap. 880m. francs CFA; operates a sawmill; also timber exporters and mfrs of prefabricated dwellings; Man. Dir PIERRE OPANZOYEN.

Société Centrafricaine des Gaz Industriels (SOCAGI): blvd Bouganda, BP 905, Bangui; tel. 21-61-16-42; fax 21-61-12-74; e-mail socagi@yahoo.fr; f. 1965; cap. 53m. francs CFA; manufacture and sale of industrial and medical gases; Pres. and Dir-Gen. PAUL LALAGUE.

Société Centrafricaine des Palmiers (CENTRAPALM): BP 1355, Bangui; tel. 21-61-49-40; fax 21-61-38-75; f. 1975; state-owned; production and marketing of palm oil; operates the Bossongo agro-industrial complex; Pres. MATHIEU-FRANCIS NGANAWARA; Gen. Man. Dr JOËL BEASSEM.

Société des Fibres Centrafricaines (SOFICA): BP 154, Bangui-Lakouanga; tel. 21-61-76-23; fax 21-61-06-17; f. 2007 to replace the Société Centrafricaine de Développement des Textiles (SOCADETEX); cotton producer.

Société Industrielle Centrafricaine (SICA): BP 1325, Bangui; tel. 21-61-44-99; f. 1967; cap. 200m. francs CFA; sawmill at M'baiki in the Lobaye area, annual capacity 18,000 cu m; Dir CHARLES SYLVAIN.

Société Industrielle Forestière en Afrique Centrale (SIFAC): BP 156, Bangui; f. 1970; cap. 95m. francs CFA; sawmill and joinery; Dir JACQUES GADEN.

Société de Plantations d'Hévéas et de Caféiers (SPHC): BP 1384, Bangui; f. 1974; cap. 160m. francs CFA; rubber and coffee plantations.

Sucrière en Afrique (SUCAF-RCA): ave Boganda, km 4, BP 1370, Bangui; tel. 21-61-32-88; fax 21-61-34-09; acquired in 2003 by the Castel group (France); sugar producer; factory at Ouaka; Dir-Gen. PHILLIPE BRAYE.

Sylvicole (SLOVENIA-BOIS): BP 183 Lakouanga, Bangui; tel. 21-61-13-30; f. 1970; cap. 250m. francs CFA; partly Slovenian-owned; sawmill; frmly the Société d'Exploitation et d'Industrialisation Forestière en RCA; Dir FRANC BENKOVIĆ.

Taillerie Centrafricaine de Diamant: 117 ave Boganda, Bangui; tel. 21-61-66-19; fax 21-61-62-28; diamond production; Dir-Gen. ATNIAL LEVI.

Total Centrafricaine de Gestion (TOCAGES): BP 724, Bangui; tel. 21-61-05-88; f. 1950; cap. 200m. francs CFA; 51% state-owned; storage, retailing and transport of petroleum products; Dir CHRISTIAN-DIMANCHE SONGUET.

TRADE UNIONS

Confédération Chrétienne des Travailleurs de Centrafrique (CCTC): BP 939, Bangui; tel. 21-61-05-71; fax 21-61-55-81; Pres. LOUIS SALVADOR.

Confédération Nationale de Travailleurs de Centrafrique: BP 2141, Bangui; tel. 75-50-94-36; fax 21-61-35-61; e-mail cnt@intnet.cf; Sec.-Gen. JEAN-RICHARD SANDOS-OULANGA.

Confédération Syndicale des Travailleurs de Centrafrique (CSTC): BP 386, km 5, Bangui; tel. 21-61-38-69; Sec.-Gen. SABIN KPOKOLO.

Organisation des Syndicats Libres du Secteur Public, Parapublic et Privé (OSLP): BP 1450, Bangui; tel. 21-61-20-00; Sec.-Gen. GABRIEL NGOUANDJI-TANGAS.

Union Générale des Travailleurs de Centrafrique (UGTC): BP 346, Bangui; tel. 21-61-05-86; fax 21-61-17-96; Pres. CÉCILE GUÉRÉ.

Union Syndicale des Travailleurs de Centrafrique (USTC): BP 1390, Bangui; tel. 21-61-60-15; e-mail vvesfon@yahoo.fr; Sec.-Gen. NOËL RAMADAN.

Transport

RAILWAYS

There are no railways at present. There are long-term plans to connect Bangui to the Transcameroon railway. A line linking Sudan's Darfur region with the CAR's Vakaga province has also been proposed.

ROADS

In 2000 there were an estimated 24,307 km of roads. Only about 3% of the total network is paved. Eight main routes serve Bangui, and those that are surfaced are toll roads. Both the total road length and the condition of the roads are inadequate for current requirements. In 1997 the European Union provided 32,500m. francs CFA to improve infrastructure in the CAR. In September a vast road improvement scheme was launched, concentrating initially on roads to the south and north-west of Bangui. The CAR is linked with Cameroon by the Transafrican Lagos–Mombasa highway. Roads are frequently impassable in the rainy season (July–October).

Bureau d'Affrètement Routier Centrafricain (BARC): Gare routière, BP 523, Bangui; tel. 21-61-20-55; fax 21-61-37-44; Dir-Gen. J. M. LAGUEREMA-YADINGUIN.

Compagnie Nationale des Transports Routiers (CNTR): Bangui; tel. 21-61-46-44; state-owned; Dir-Gen. GEORGES YABADA.

Fonds d'Entretien Routier (FER): BP 962, Bangui; tel. 21-61-62-95; fax 21-61-68-63; e-mail fondsroutier@admn.cf; f. 1981; Dir-Gen. MARIE-CLAIR BITOUANGA.

Projet Sectoriel de Transports (PST): BP 941, Bangui; tel. 21-61-62-94; fax 21-61-65-79.

TBC Cameroun SARL: BP 637, Bangui; tel. 21-61-20-16; fax 21-61-13-19; e-mail rca@tbclogistics.com; internet www.tbclogistics.com; f. 1963.

INLAND WATERWAYS

There are some 2,800 km of navigable waterways along two main water courses. The first, formed by the Congo river and its tributary the Oubangui, can accommodate convoys of barges (of up to 800 metric tons load) between Bangui and Brazzaville and Pointe-Noire in the Republic of the Congo, except during the dry season, when the route is impassable. The second is the river Sangha, also a tributary of the Congo, on which traffic is again seasonal. There are two ports, at Bangui and Salo, on the rivers Oubangui and Sangha, respectively. Bangui port has a handling capacity of 350,000 tons, with 350 m of wharfs and 24,000 sq m of warehousing. Efforts are being made to develop the Sangha upstream from Salo, to increase the transportation of timber from this area and to develop Nola as a timber port.

Agence Centrafricaine des Communications Fluviales (ACCF): BP 822, Bangui; tel. 21-61-09-67; fax 21-61-02-11; f. 1969; state-owned; supervises development of inland waterways transport system; Chair. GUY MAMADOU MARABENA.

Société Centrafricaine de Transports Fluviaux (SOCATRAF): rue Parent, BP 1445, Bangui; tel. and fax 21-61-43-15; e-mail socatraf@intnet.cf; f. 1980; 51% owned by ACCF; Man. Dir FRANÇOIS TOUSSAINT.

CIVIL AVIATION

The international airport is at Bangui-M'Poko. There are also 37 small airports for internal services.

Mondial Air Fret (MAF): BP 1883, Bangui; tel. 21-61-14-58; fax 21-61-62-62; f. 1998; Dir THÉOPHILE SONNY COLÉ.

Tourism

Although tourism remains relatively undeveloped, the CAR possesses considerable scenic attractions in its waterfalls, forests and wildlife. In 2010 some 54,000 tourists arrived. In that year receipts from tourism were estimated at US $6.0m.

Office National Centrafricain du Tourisme (OCATOUR): rue Roger Guérillot, BP 645, Bangui; tel. 21-61-45-66.

Defence

As assessed at November 2011, the armed forces numbered about 2,150 men (army 2,000 and air force 150). Military service is selective and lasts for two years. There was also a paramilitary gendarmerie with 1,000 members.

Defence Expenditure: Estimated at 25,500m. francs CFA in 2010.

Chief of Staff of the Armed Forces: Gen. FRANÇOIS MOBÉBOU.

Education

Education is officially compulsory for eight years between six and 14 years of age. Primary education begins at the age of six and lasts for six years. Secondary education begins at the age of 12 and lasts for up to seven years, comprising a first cycle of four years and a second of three years. In 2009/10 enrolment at primary schools included 71% of children in the relevant age-group (81% of boys; 60% of girls), according to UNESCO estimates; in 2008/09 secondary enrolment included only 11% (13% of boys; 8% of girls). In 2009/10 there were some 11,158 students enrolled in tertiary education. The provision of state-funded education was severely disrupted during the 1990s and early 2000s, owing to the inadequacy of financial resources.

Bibliography

Baxter, P. *France In Centrafrique: From Bokassa and Operation Barracude to the days of EUFOR.* Solihull, Helion and Company, 2011.

de Bayle des Hermens, R. *Recherches préhistoriques en République Centrafricaine.* Paris, Klincksieck, 2005.

Bevarrah, L. *Centrafrique: mon combat politique. Vers une nouvelle République.* Paris, L'Harmattan, 2010.

Bigo, D. *Pouvoir et obéissance en Centrafrique.* Paris, Editions Karthala, 1989.

Binoua, J. *Centrafrique: l'instabilité permanente.* Paris, L'Harmattan, 2005.

Brégeon, J.-N. *Administrateurs en Oubangui-Chari.* Paris, Editions Denoël, 1998.

Carter, G. M. (Ed.). *National Unity and Regionalism in Eight African States.* Ithaca, NY, Cornell University Press, 1966.

de Dreux Brezé, J. *Le Problème du regroupement en Afrique équatoriale.* Paris, Librairie Gale de Droit et de Jurisprudence, 1968.

Emerging Markets Investment Center. *Central African Republic Investment and Business Guide.* 2nd edn. USA, International Business Publications, 1998.

Central African Republic Business and Investment Yearbook. USA, International Business Publications, 2002.

Central African Republic Business Intelligence Report. USA, International Business Publications, 2003.

Germain, E. *Centrafrique et Bokassa 1965–1979: Force et déclin d'un pouvoir personnel.* Paris, L'Harmattan, 2001.

Goumba, A. *Les Mémories & les Réflexions politiques du Résistant anti-colonial, démocrate et militant Panafricaniste, Abel Goumba. De la Loi-Cadre à la mort de Barthélemy Boganda, Vol. 1.* Paris, Ccinia Communication, 2006.

Les Mémories & les Réflexions politiques du Résistant anti-colonial, démocrate et militant Panafricaniste, Abel Goumba. De la succession du Président B. Boganda au procès de la honte du Militant Abel Goumba, Vol. 2. Paris, Ccinia Communication, 2009.

Kalck, P. *Central African Republic (World Bibliographical Series).* Oxford, ABC-Clio, 1993.

Central African Republic, A Failure in Decolonization. New York, Praeger, 1971.

Historical Dictionary of the Central African Republic. 3rd edn. Lanham, MD, Scarecrow Press, 2005.

Mété-Nguemeu, Y. *Femmes de Centrafrique.* Editions Centrafrique Sans Frontières, Besançon, 2008.

N'Douba, P. *L'otage du général rebelle centrafricain François Bozizé: Journal d'un Captif des 'Libérateurs'.* Paris, L'Harmattan, 2006.

Ngoupandé, J.-P. *Chronique de la crise centrafricaine 1996–1997: le syndrome barracuda.* Paris, L'Harmattan, 1997.

O'Toole, T. *The Central African Republic. The Continent's Hidden Heart.* Boulder, CO, Westview Press, 1986.

Pigeon, P. *Les activités informelles en République Centrafricaine.* Paris, L'Harmattan, 2000.

Saulnier, P. *Le Centrafrique: Entre mythe et réalité.* Paris, L'Harmattan, 1998.

Bangui raconte: Contes de Centrafrique. Paris, L'Harmattan, 2000.

Serre, J. *David Dacko Premier Président de la République Centrafricaine 1930–2003.* Paris, L'Harmattan, 2007.

Titley, B. *Dark Age: The Political Odyssey of Emperor Bokassa.* Liverpool, Liverpool University Press, 1997.

Wagon, J.-B. *L'économie centrafricaine: pour rompre avec la logique de rente.* Paris, L'Harmattan, 1998.

Woodfork, J. *Culture and Customs of the Central African Republic.* Westport, CT, Greenwood Press, 2006.

Yele, R., and Doko, P. *Les Defis de la Centrafrique: Gouvernance et Stabilisation du Systeme Economique.* Dakar, CODESRIA, 2011.

Zoctizoum, Y. *Histoire de la République Centrafricaine*, 2 vols. Paris, L'Harmattan, 1984.

CHAD

Physical and Social Geography

DAVID HILLING

The Republic of Chad is bordered to the north by Libya, to the south by the Central African Republic, to the west by Niger and Cameroon and to the east by Sudan. The northernmost of the four independent states that emerged from French Equatorial Africa, Chad is, with an area of 1,284,000 sq km (495,800 sq miles), the largest in terms of size and population (11,175,915, according to the census of June 2009). Traditionally a focal point for equatorial and Saharan trade routes, the country's vast size, land-locked location and great distance from the coast create problems for economic development. The only large city is the capital, N'Djamena (known as Fort-Lamy during the colonial period), which had an estimated population of 1.1m. in 2011.

The relief is relatively simple. From 240 m in the Lake Chad depression in the south-west, the land rises northwards through the Guéra massif at 1,800 m to the mountainous Saharan region of Tibesti at 3,350 m. Eastwards, heights of 1,500 m are attained in the Ouaddaï massif. In the south the watershed area between the Chari and Congo rivers is of subdued relief and only slight elevation. The only rivers of importance, both for irrigation and seasonal navigation, are the Chari and Logone, which traverse the south-west of the country and join at N'Djamena, before flowing into Lake Chad.

Extending across more than 16° of latitude, Chad has three well-defined zones of climate, natural vegetation and associated economic activity. The southern third of the country has annual rainfall in excess of 744 mm (increasing to 1,200 mm in the extreme south), and has a savannah woodland vegetation. This is the country's principal agricultural zone, providing the two main cash crops, cotton and groundnuts, and a variety of local food crops (especially rice). Northwards, with rainfall of 250–500 mm per year, there is a more open grassland, where there is emphasis on pastoral activity, limited cultivation of groundnuts and local grains, and some collection of gum arabic. This marginal Sahel zone was adversely affected by drought during most of the 1970s and 1980s, and the cattle herds were greatly reduced in number. The northern third of the country has negligible rainfall and a sparse scrub vegetation, which grades north into pure desert with little apparent economic potential, although the 'Aozou strip', a region of 114,000 sq km in the extreme north, is believed to contain significant reserves of uranium and other minerals. The development of substantial petroleum reserves in the Doba Basin, in the south of the country, and also at Sedigi commenced in the late 1990s and continued in the 2000s, and production of petroleum at Doba commenced in 2003. There was also believed to be considerable potential for the commercial exploitation of gold, particularly at Mayo-Kebbi, in the south of the country.

Chad's total population is relatively small in relation to its large area, and is markedly concentrated in the southern half of the country. Religious and ethnic tensions between the people of the north and south have traditionally dominated the history of Chad. The population of the north is predominantly Islamic, of a nomadic or semi-nomadic character, and is largely engaged in farming and in breeding livestock. Rivalry between ethnic groups is strong. By contrast, the inhabitants of the south are settled farmers, who largely follow animist beliefs. The Sara tribes, some 10 ethnic groups with related languages and cultural links, comprise a large section of the population of the south. Since the end of the Second World War, the population of the south has inclined towards a more Westernized culture; the rate of literacy has increased rapidly, and Christianity has attracted a number of adherents. The population of the north, however, forms a traditional, Islamic society, and is largely unaffected by modern education. The state is secular and exercises neutrality in relation to religious affiliations. In 1995 the closely related Sara, Bongo and Baguirmi peoples represented the largest ethnic group, amounting to an estimated 20.1% of the population between them, followed by the Chadic (17.7%) and Arabs (14.3%). French and Arabic are the official languages. Karembou, Ouadi, Teda, Daza and Djonkor are the principal vernaculars.

Recent History

BHAIRAV RAJA

Based on an earlier article by EDWARD GEORGE

Formerly part of French Equatorial Africa, Chad became an autonomous republic within the French Community in November 1958. François Tombalbaye, a southerner and leader of the Parti Progressiste Tchadien (PPT), was elected Prime Minister in March 1959. Chad became independent on 11 August 1960, under Tombalbaye's presidency. However, the sparsely populated northern territory of Borkou-Ennedi-Tibesti (BET), accounting for some 47% of the area of Chad, remained under French military administration until 1964. In 1963 the PPT was declared the sole legal party. Discontent with the party's political monopoly, and with mismanagement and corruption by government officials, precipitated a serious rebellion, focused mainly in the north, in 1965. The Front de Libération Nationale du Tchad (FROLINAT), formed in Sudan in 1966, later assumed leadership of the revolt. In August 1968 French troops intervened in support of the Government.

As a result of the French military intervention, the rebellion was contained, and in 1972 the French reinforcements left Chad. Libya, which maintained a claim to sovereignty over the 'Aozou strip' in northern Chad, continued to provide support to FROLINAT. Following a deterioration in relations between Chad and France, in 1972 Tombalbaye signed a pact of friendship with Libya, which none the less annexed the 'Aozou strip' in 1973.

In April 1975 Tombalbaye was killed in a military coup, and Gen. Félix Malloum, former army Chief of Staff, assumed power. FROLINAT remained in opposition to the new Government. Following divisions within FROLINAT, its leader, Hissène Habré, an opponent of the Libyan annexation of the 'Aozou strip', was replaced by Goukouni Oueddei. (Habré continued, however, to lead a faction within FROLINAT.) The Government successfully sought French assistance to halt renewed advances by FROLINAT in 1978.

CIVIL CONFLICT AND LIBYAN INTERVENTION

In August 1978 Malloum appointed Habré as Prime Minister to lead a civilian Government. Relations between Malloum and Habré soon deteriorated, and in February 1979 fighting broke out in N'Djamena, the capital, between the Government's

Forces Armées Tchadiennes (FAT) and Habré's troops, the Forces Armées du Nord (FAN). With the tacit support of France, the FAN seized control of N'Djamena, while the rebel faction led by Goukouni (the Forces Armées Populaires, FAP) gained territory in the north. In March Malloum resigned and fled the country, after appointing Lt-Col (later Gen.) Wadal Abdelkader Kamougué as his successor.

In April 1979 a provisional Government was formed by FROLINAT, the FAN, the Mouvement Populaire pour la Libération du Tchad (MPLT) and the FAT. The leader of the MPLT, Lol Mahamat Choua, was appointed President; however, a committee, headed by Kamougué, which rejected the authority of the new Government, was established to govern the south. In August a parallel administration, known as the Gouvernement d'Union Nationale de Transition (GUNT), was established under the presidency of Goukouni, with Kamougué as Vice-President. In accordance with France's stated policy of neutrality, its troops were withdrawn from Chad in May. In June a treaty of friendship and co-operation was signed in the Libyan capital, Tripoli, between Libya and a representative of Goukouni. In October Libyan forces intervened in the hostilities, resulting in the defeat of Habré and the retreat of the FAN from N'Djamena, and a 15,000-strong Libyan contingent remained in the country. In November 1981 Libyan forces were withdrawn, and, at the behest of France, the Organization of African Unity (OAU, now the African Union—AU) sent a peace-keeping force to Chad. However, after Goukouni rejected an OAU plan for the organization of elections, hostilities intensified, and the FAN seized N'Djamena in June. Goukouni fled the country, and the coalition of factions that constituted the GUNT began to fragment.

HABRÉ IN POWER, 1982–90

In June 1982, following the capture of N'Djamena, the formation of a provisional Council of State, with Habré as Head of State, was announced. By the end of June the OAU force had withdrawn from Chad, and in October Habré was inaugurated as President. In January 1983 elements of the FAT joined the FAN to form the Forces Armées Nationales Tchadiennes (FANT). By July Goukouni's rebel troops, with assistance from Libya, had occupied the entire BET region. Following further advances by the FANT and Goukouni's forces (with Libyan support), France dispatched some 3,000 troops to Chad, and by September all fighting between the factions had ceased.

In September 1984 France and Libya agreed to the simultaneous withdrawal of their forces in Chad. The evacuation of French forces was completed in November, but Libyan troops remained, in contravention of the agreement. From October 1985 Libya began to reinforce its military presence in northern Chad. In February 1986 GUNT forces initiated Libyan-supported attacks on government positions to the south of the 16th parallel. The offensive was repelled by the FANT, and Habré appealed to France for increased military aid. Shortly afterwards, French military aircraft, operating from the Central African Republic (CAR), bombed a Libyan-built airstrip north-east of Faya-Largeau. A retaliatory air attack on N'Djamena airport caused minor damage. France subsequently established an air-strike force at N'Djamena to counteract any further Libyan attack (an intervention designated 'Opération Epervier'), while the USA provided supplementary military aid to Habré's forces.

In April 1989 the Minister of the Interior and Territorial Administration was arrested, following the discovery of an alleged coup plot. The Commander-in-Chief of the Armed Forces, Hassan Djamous, and his predecessor in that post, Idriss Deby, who were both implicated in the conspiracy, fled to Sudan with their supporters. FANT troops were dispatched to quell the mutiny, during which Djamous was killed. Deby escaped, with Sudanese assistance, to Libya.

In August 1989 Chad and Libya signed a draft agreement for the peaceful resolution of the dispute over the Aozou region: if a political settlement was not achieved within one year, the issue would be submitted to arbitration by the International Court of Justice (ICJ).

A new Constitution was approved by referendum on 10 December 1989, reportedly receiving the support of 99.9% of votes cast. The new Constitution confirmed Habré as President for a further seven-year term, upheld the principle of a single-party state and provided for the creation of an elected legislature, the Assemblée nationale.

In March 1990 Deby and his followers (subsequently known as the Mouvement Patriotique du Salut, MPS) attacked eastern Chad from bases in Sudan. France dispatched military equipment and personnel to reinforce 'Opération Epervier' at Abéché; although the French contingent did not participate in the military engagements, its presence undoubtedly induced the rebel forces to retreat. In August, shortly before the agreed deadline for a settlement, negotiations between Habré and the Libyan leader, Col Muammar al-Qaddafi, took place in Morocco. Both Governments subsequently agreed to refer the territorial dispute to the ICJ. Meanwhile, legislative elections to 123 seats in the new Assemblée nationale were held in July.

DEBY TAKES POWER

On 10 November 1990 forces led by Deby invaded Chad from Sudan, launching an attack on positions held by Chadian government forces north-east of Abéché. On 30 November Habré, together with his entourage, fled Chad, after the MPS had seized control of Abéché. Deby arrived in N'Djamena two days later, and declared his commitment to the creation of a democratic multi-party political system. The Assemblée nationale was dissolved, the Constitution was suspended and a provisional 33-member Council of State was formed, with Deby as interim Head of State. Following the publication of a report, compiled by the MPS, accusing Habré of violations of human rights and of corruption, Deby sought Habré's extradition from Senegal, where he had been granted political asylum. Later in December the Government announced that the FANT was to be restructured and designated the Armées Nationales Tchadiennes (ANT).

On 1 March 1991 a National Charter, drafted by the executive committee of the MPS, was adopted for a 30-month transitional period, at the end of which a constitutional referendum was to be held. The Charter confirmed Deby's appointment as President, Head of State and Chairman of the MPS, and required the Government to institute measures to prepare for the implementation of a multi-party system. Under the terms of the Charter, a new Council of Ministers and a 31-member legislative Conseil de la République were to replace the provisional Council of State. On 4 March Deby was formally inaugurated as President. The Council of State was dissolved, and the former President of the Assemblée nationale, Dr Jean Bawoyeu Alingué, was appointed Prime Minister of a new Government.

In May 1991 Deby announced that a national conference, scheduled for May 1992, would prepare a new constitution to provide for the introduction of a multi-party system and would be followed by legislative elections. Constitutional amendments permitting the registration of opposition movements would enter into force in January 1992. In October the Council of Ministers adopted regulations regarding the authorization of political parties. Under the new legislation, each party was required to have a minimum of 30 founder members, three each from 10 of Chad's 14 prefectures; the formation of parties on an ethnic or regional basis was prohibited. However, the MPS was exempted from the conditions of registration and opposition groups denounced the legislation as biased in its favour.

OPPOSITION TO THE DEBY GOVERNMENT

In September 1991 rebels attacked military garrisons in Tibesti, killing 50 people. Deby announced that the offensive had been instigated from Niger by Habré loyalists. In October disaffected troops attacked an arsenal at N'Djamena airport in an attempt to seize power; some 40 people were killed in the ensuing fighting. In December some 3,000 troops loyal to Habré attacked several towns in the region of Lake Chad. By early January 1992 the rebels, reported to be members of the Libya-based Mouvement pour la Démocratie et le Développement (MDD), were advancing towards N'Djamena, causing government forces to suffer heavy losses. France dispatched troops to reinforce the 'Epervier' force, ostensibly to protect French citizens. Shortly afterwards, the Government claimed that the rebels had been defeated. A number of prominent members of the opposition and former members of the Habré Government were subsequently arrested, and summary executions were reported. France condemned such violations of human rights, and warned that its continued support for Deby was dependent on the implementation of political reforms.

In April 1992 France announced that the role of 'Opération Epervier' as a defensive strike force was to cease, although French troops were to remain in Chad to assist in the restructuring of the ANT. In May the national conference was postponed and it was subsequently announced that it would take place in January 1993; later in May 1992 Joseph Yodoyman, a member of the Alliance Nationale pour la Démocratie et le Développement (ANDD), replaced Alingué as Prime Minister. Deby formed a new Council of Ministers, which included, for the first time, five members of the opposition.

CIVIL TENSION AND TRANSITION

The national conference was duly convened in January 1993, attended by some 800 delegates (representing, among others, the institutions of state, trade unions, professional associations and 30 political organizations). In April the conference adopted a Transitional Charter, elected Dr Fidel Moungar, hitherto Minister of National and Higher Education, as Prime Minister, and established a 57-member interim legislature, the Conseil Supérieur de la Transition (CST). Former President Choua, now leader of the Rassemblement pour la Démocratie et le Progrès (RDP), was elected Chairman of the CST. It was agreed that Deby was to remain in office as Head of State and Commander-in-Chief of the Armed Forces for one year (with provision for one extension), while a transitional Government, under the supervision of the CST, was to implement economic, political and social programmes drafted by the conference; multi-party elections were to take place at the end of this period. Moungar's Government retained only four members of the former Council of Ministers, and included representatives of a number of opposition parties.

Increasing disagreement between supporters of Deby and Moungar culminated, in October 1993, in the approval by the CST of a motion expressing no confidence in the Moungar administration. Moungar subsequently resigned and his Government was dissolved. In November the CST elected Nouradine Kassiré Delwa Coumakoye, hitherto Minister of Justice, as Prime Minister, and a new transitional Government, which retained 10 members of the former administration, was appointed. In December a committee was established to prepare a draft constitution, an electoral code and legislation governing the registration of political organizations.

In February 1994 the ICJ ruled in favour of Chad in the dispute over the sovereignty of the 'Aozou strip'. In April Libya agreed to commence the withdrawal of troops from the region, in an operation that was to be monitored by UN observers and officials from both countries. In May Libya and Chad issued a joint statement confirming that the withdrawal of Libyan troops had been completed as scheduled, and in June the two Governments signed a co-operation agreement.

CONSTITUTIONAL PROPOSALS AND TRANSITIONAL POLITICS

In March 1994 the constitutional committee presented its recommendations, including provisions for the election of a President for a term of five years, the installation of a bicameral legislature and a Constitutional Council, and the establishment of a decentralized administrative structure. In April the CST extended the transitional period for one year. The constitutional recommendations were to be submitted for approval at a national referendum in December, with legislative and presidential elections to be held by March 1995.

In September 1994 it was reported that the Minister of Mines and Energy, Lt-Col Mahamat Garfa (who had recently been dismissed as Chief of Army Staff), had fled N'Djamena with substantial government funds, and, together with some 600 members of the ANT, had joined Conseil National de Redressement du Tchad rebel forces in eastern Chad. Garfa subsequently established a grouping of eight rebel factions operative in eastern Chad, the Alliance Nationale de la Résistance (ANR), while remaining in exile himself. In October Choua was replaced as Chairman of the CST by a member of the MPS, Mahamat Bachar Ghadaia.

Deby officially announced in November 1994 that the process of democratic transition would be completed in April 1995, following presidential and legislative elections. In December 1994 Deby proclaimed a general amnesty for political prisoners and, excluding Habré, opposition members in exile. In January 1995 the CST adopted a new electoral code, and a Commission Électorale Nationale Indépendante (CENI) was established. Later in January the CST approved the draft of the Constitution, which had been amended in accordance with recommendations reached by a national conference in August 1994.

In March 1995 the CST extended the transitional period for a further year, and amended the National Charter to the effect that the incumbent Prime Minister was henceforth prohibited from contesting the forthcoming presidential election or from belonging to a political party. These measures attracted strong criticism from opposition parties, which subsequently sought a legal challenge to the validity of the extension of the transitional period. In April the CST elected Djimasta Koibla, a prominent member of Alingué's Union pour la Démocratie et la République (UDR), as Prime Minister. A new transitional Government was subsequently formed. A unilateral declaration by the Government, in July, of a national cease-fire was received with caution by the rebel movements.

In November 1995 the Government and the MDD signed a peace agreement providing for a cease-fire, an exchange of prisoners and the integration of a number of MDD troops into the ANT. Also in that month the CENI promulgated a new timetable whereby a constitutional referendum was to take place in March 1996, followed by a presidential election in June and legislative elections later that year. Reconciliation discussions were convened in Franceville, Gabon, in January 1996, with mediation by the Governments of Gabon, the CAR and Niger and in March, following protracted negotiations, the Government and 13 opposition parties signed an agreement providing for the imposition of a cease-fire and the establishment of a special security force to maintain order during the electoral period.

PRESIDENTIAL AND LEGISLATIVE ELECTIONS

The conclusion of the Franceville agreement allowed the electoral timetable to proceed as rescheduled. A number of opposition groups, particularly the southern-based federalist organizations, urged their members to reject the draft Constitution, which enshrined a unitary state, at the national referendum. None the less, the new Constitution was adopted by 63.5% of votes cast at the referendum on 31 March 1996.

By April 1996 15 presidential candidates, including Deby, had emerged. In the first round of voting, on 2 June, Deby secured 43.8% of votes cast, with Kamougué (contesting the election on behalf of the Union pour le Renouveau et la Démocratie—URD) taking 12.4% and Saleh Kebzaboh (of the Union Nationale pour le Développement et le Renouveau—UNDR) 8.5%. The second round of the election took place on 3 July 1996, contested by Deby and Kamougué with the majority of eliminated candidates urging a boycott. According to official results, Deby was elected with 69.1% of votes cast and was inaugurated as President on 8 August. Koibla was reappointed as premier.

Legislative voting eventually took place on 5 January and 23 February 1997, and in March the Court of Appeal announced the final results, according to which the MPS secured an absolute majority, with 63 of the 125 seats, while the URD won 29 seats, the UNDR 15 and the UDR four. The Assemblée nationale was installed on 4 April, and in early May Kamougué was elected its President, following an accord between his party, the URD, the MPS and the UNDR. Later that month Nassour Guélendouksia Ouaïdou (hitherto Secretary-General at the President's Office) was appointed Prime Minister. His Government included representatives of several parties, notably Kebzaboh, although the MPS retained the most senior ministerial portfolios.

INSURGENCY PROBLEMS

The restoration of peace, particularly in the south, was regarded as imperative, as efforts continued to secure external funding for the development of petroleum resources. In October 1997 the Government extended a general amnesty to members of the Front National du Tchad, the Front National du Tchad Renové (FNTR) and the Mouvement pour la Justice Sociale et la Démocratie, which were to be legalized as political parties. In May 1998 a peace accord was signed by the Government and the Forces Armées pour la République Fédérale/Victimes d'Agression (FARF/VA) providing for an immediate cease-fire in Logone Oriental and Logone Occidental prefectures, a general amnesty for FARF/VA rebels and the withdrawal of elements of the security services from the south; the accord renewed provisions included in a previous agreement of April 1997 for the transformation of the FARF/VA into a political party and the integration of its forces into the Chadian army.

From late 1998 reports emerged of a rebellion in the Tibesti region of northern Chad by the Mouvement pour la Démocratie et la Justice au Tchad (MDJT), led by Youssouf Togoimi, who had been dismissed as Minister of Defence in June 1997. By November 1999 the MDJT claimed to have defeated ANT forces in Aozou, killing some 80. In December it was announced that 13 'politico-military' groups, including FROLINAT and the FNTR, had formed a new alliance in opposition to the Deby regime, the Coordination des Mouvements Armés et Partis Politiques de l'Opposition (CMAP). In the same month another four 'politico-military' groups, led by Acheikh Ibn Oumar, formed the Comité Politique d'Action et de Liaison (CPAL). In February 2000 it was reported that the former armed wing of the MDD had reconstituted itself as the Mouvement pour l'Unité et la République (MUR), and that the MUR had subsequently allied itself with the MDJT and the Conseil Démocratique Révolutionnaire (CDR). In July the MDJT attacked a garrison in Bardaï and gained control of four towns in Tibesti.

PRESIDENTIAL ELECTION

Ouaïdou resigned as Prime Minister in December 1999. He was replaced by Nagoum Yamassoum, whose new Government included five UNDR members, among them Kebzaboh. In July 2000 the Assemblée nationale approved proposals for the creation of a new structure for the CENI, which was to plan a reorganization of constituencies in advance of presidential and legislative elections due to be held in 2001. An extensive reorganization of the Government at the end of August 2000 followed the dismissal of ministers belonging to the URD, owing to their party's rejection of the new electoral code. Furthermore, a number of members of the MPS resigned from the ruling party, reportedly in protest against violent acts committed by government forces.

In February 2001 it was announced that the presidential election would take place on 20 May and that elections to the Assemblée nationale, which had initially been scheduled for April 2001, were to be postponed until March 2002. In April 2001 Deby dismissed all UNDR ministers from the Government, following Kebzaboh's announcement that he was to contest the presidential election. Voting took place, as scheduled, on 20 May and Deby was re-elected as President, receiving 63.2% of the valid votes cast, according to the Constitutional Council, although opposition candidates complained of widespread fraud and malpractice.

EFFORTS TOWARDS NATIONAL RECONCILIATION

In August 2001 Deby announced that he was willing to engage in dialogue with both the CMAP and the CPAL. Although the CPAL rejected any negotiations, in late October the CMAP offered to send a delegation to N'Djamena to enter into discussions with Deby, if its security could be assured. Meanwhile, in September the CMAP accused FROLINAT-Conseil Provisoire de la Révolution, as the organization had been renamed, of having engaged in separate discussions with the Government and with unnamed foreign politicians; the grouping was consequently expelled from the CMAP. In December the CMAP presented the Government with proposals for a peace plan, and in January 2002 the Minister of Foreign Affairs, Mahamat Saleh Annadif, held discussions with CMAP members in France and with other opposition members in exile in Benin and Nigeria.

During December 2001 and January 2002 representatives of the Government and principal opposition leaders participated in negotiations intended to provide for opposition participation in the forthcoming legislative elections. Although opposition parties continued to demand a full reorganization of the voter registration procedures, in late January Deby announced that the elections would be held on 21 April; according to the revised electoral code, the new Assemblée nationale was to be enlarged to 155 members. In February the Fédération Action pour la République (FAR), the UNDR and the URD announced their intention to participate in the legislative elections.

Meanwhile, the involvement of Libya in the peace process was regarded as a major factor in the beneficial terms offered to the MDJT in a peace agreement, signed by the group's deputy leader, Adoum Togoi Abbo (a former Chadian ambassador to Libya), and the Chadian Government in early January 2002. According to the agreement, both sides would institute an immediate cease-fire and a general amnesty for prisoners. Moreover, the MDJT was to participate in the Chadian Government and other state institutions, while the rebel forces were to be regularized. Notably, the Libyan Government was to be responsible for monitoring the implementation of the agreement. However, Togoimi did not give his approval to the arrangements, and, as a split in the MDJT became evident, in early April the group issued a statement accusing the Government of inhibiting the peace process by its refusal to postpone legislative elections in order to allow the appointment of MDJT representatives to the Government.

LEGISLATIVE ELECTIONS

The elections to the Assemblée nationale were contested by some 40 parties on 21 April 2002. According to the final election results, which were issued on 19 May, the MPS won 110 seats in the Assemblée nationale, significantly increasing its representation. The RDP became the second largest party, with 12 seats, while the FAR became the largest opposition party, with nine seats. Coumakoye's VIVA—Rassemblement National pour la Démocratie et le Progrès (VIVA—RNDP) and the UNDR each won five seats, and the URD's representation was significantly reduced, to only three seats. In June Deby appointed his special counsellor, Haroun Kabadi, a senior official in the MPS, as Prime Minister, to head a 28-member Council of Ministers.

Meanwhile, in May 2002 it was reported that Togoi was being held in detention by forces loyal to Togoimi, who had confirmed his rejection of the peace agreement signed in January. Togoi was subsequently demoted to the position of Second Vice-Chairman of the MDJT, effectively leading his own faction within the organization. The death of Togoimi in Libya, in September, after he sustained injuries in a landmine explosion in northern Chad, raised hopes that peace talks between the Government and the MDJT would be reconvened, and Deby visited the north in order to encourage a resumption of negotiations. However, in October renewed fighting broke out in the north; following an attack by the MDJT on an airport at Faya N'Gourma, further clashes were reported near Fada and Ennedi.

In January 2003, following negotiations in Libreville, Gabon, hosted by the Gabonese President, Omar Bongo, the Government and the ANR signed a peace memorandum, in which members of the ANR were granted a general amnesty prior to their reintegration into the civilian sector. Moreover, Garfa, the leader of the ANR, returned to Chad for the first time since 1994. However, one of the constituent groups of the ANR, the Forces des Organisations Nationales pour l'Alternance et les Libertés au Tchad (FONALT), rejected the terms of the accord. A new Council of Ministers was appointed in late June: the new Prime Minister was Moussa Faki Mahamat, a close ally of Deby and a fellow northerner, while Yamassoum was appointed to the position of Minister of State, Minister of Foreign Affairs and African Integration; the dismissal of Kabadi as Prime Minister followed his removal, earlier in June, from the executive committee of the MPS, reportedly in response to dissatisfaction with his performance in this role.

Meanwhile, during the first half of 2003 reports emerged of the formation of a new umbrella grouping of 'politico-military' organizations opposed to the Deby regime, the Front Uni pour la Démocratie et la Paix (FUDP). By July, when Togoi was elected as the President of the FUDP, at a congress reportedly held in Nigeria, several 'politico-military' organizations had announced their affiliation to the grouping, including the MDD and the faction of the MDJT loyal to Togoi. The FUDP stated as its objective the establishment of a new constitution and of a transitional government, prior to the holding of free and transparent elections.

CONSTITUTIONAL AMENDMENTS

In March 2004 six 'politico-military' organizations, including a faction of the MDJT, the MDD, the CDR and the MUR, formed the Union des Forces pour le Changement (UFC). Oumar was named as Provisional National Co-ordinator of the new grouping, which declared itself committed to the development of national unity and the holding of fair and free elections. In April Ahmat Hassaballah Soubiane, a founder member of the MPS and the former Chadian ambassador to the USA and Canada (a post from which he was reportedly dismissed earlier in the year after criticizing Deby's rumoured plans to change the Constitution and seek a third term in office), announced in Washington, DC, USA, the formation of the Coalition pour la Défense de la Démocratie et des Droits Constitutionnels (CDDC). In May 25 opposition parties, including the URD, the UNDR and the RDP, announced that they had formed the Coordination des Partis Politiques pour la Défense de la Constitution (CPDC), which, like the CDDC, sought to resist Deby's proposed constitutional modifications.

Nevertheless, in May 2004 the Assemblée nationale approved eight constitutional amendments, most notably the removal of the restriction limiting the President to serving two terms of office and the establishment of a proposed upper legislative chamber, provided for by the 1996 Constitution but never formed; an Economic and Social Council, the members of which were to be appointed by the President, was to be formed, while the Head of State was to be granted additional powers to instigate further constitutional reform. The changes, which required endorsement in a national referendum, were vigorously criticized by opposition parties. In June 2004 the Constitutional Council rejected an opposition appeal to annul the constitutional revisions.

On 6 June 2005, according to official results, announced later in the month, some 66.8% of the votes cast in a referendum approved the proposed constitutional amendments, which thereby took effect. Some 67.8% of the registered electorate were reported to have participated in the plebiscite, as a further consequence of which Deby would be permitted to seek re-election in 2006. The CPDC denounced the results of the referendum as fraudulent and refused to meet with the Government to discuss the organization of the presidential poll, vowing to oppose Deby's re-election. In August 2005 President Deby carried out a major cabinet reorganization, increasing the number of posts from 29 to 35. Pascal Yoadimnadji remained as Prime Minister, the position he had held since February (prior to which he had been Minister for Agriculture), although many new appointments were of supporters and allies of Deby, as a reward for supporting his referendum campaign.

In October 2005 Deby announced that the Republican Guard was being dissolved, following the defection of 600–800 Chadian troops to a new rebel movement, Socle pour le Changement, l'Unité et la Démocratie (SCUD), operating in eastern Chad near the border with Sudan. The movement, led by Yahya Dillo, a former Chadian officer and a nephew of Deby, had been formed following the referendum and vowed to overthrow the Deby regime. Responding to this new threat, in November President Deby reorganized the senior military leadership, at national and at regional level. In late November SCUD forces carried out attacks on military camps near the capital, N'Djamena, seizing military supplies and extended their operations throughout eastern Chad. In early December another group of Chadian soldiers, including 82 senior officers, defected to SCUD.

On 15 March 2006 a coup plot within the army was discovered and suppressed, the coup's leaders fleeing to eastern Chad to join SCUD. In reprisal, one week later Chadian forces launched a series of attacks on rebel bases across the border in Sudan. On 9 April rebels from the Front Uni pour le Changement Démocratique (FUCD), under the command of Capt. Mahamat Nour Adbelkerim, launched an invasion of Chad from bases in Sudan, rapidly advancing towards N'Djamena. On 13 April the insurgents attacked the capital; government forces regained control of the city after fierce fighting, and subsequently drove the rebels back towards the border with Sudan. Government forces were assisted by French troops stationed in N'Djamena, which provided intelligence and logistical support.

DEBY RE-ELECTED TO A THIRD TERM

Despite the massive instability caused by the rebel incursion, the presidential election proceeded as scheduled on 3 May 2006, although a boycott was urged by the coalition of opposition parties. Three weeks later, the Constitutional Council released the final results: Deby (now renamed Deby Itno) was elected for a third successive five-year term as President, with 64.7% of the votes cast. Voter turn-out was low, however, at only 53.1%, and the four competing presidential candidates were known allies of Deby. The opposition denounced the results, demanding a national dialogue, and was supported in its requests by the international community. On 8 August Deby was inaugurated as President, and one week later he reappointed Yoadimnadji as Prime Minister. The 40-member Council of Ministers was largely unchanged, new appointments including that of former premier Coumakoye as Minister of State, Minister of Land Management, Town Planning and Housing.

In late July 2006 Deby began a five-day session of dialogue with 54 political parties in N'Djamena, which was, however, boycotted by the most influential opposition parties, including the CPDC and FAR. Nevertheless, the meeting adopted measures to reinforce democracy, including changes to the composition of the CENI, amendments to the electoral code and the introduction of subsidies for political parties.

Meanwhile, clashes with rebel forces continued. In early July 2006 rebels attacked Adré and Kalonge on the Chad–Sudan border, triggering an outbreak of inter-ethnic violence in Ouaddaï and Salamat, which reportedly caused hundreds of deaths. In response, in mid-November Prime Minister Yoadimnadji declared a state of emergency that covered all regions of Chad bordering Sudan and the CAR. Later in November the Assemblée nationale extended the state of emergency for six months after the army suffered heavy reverses.

Following bitter divisions within the FUCD after its failed attack on N'Djamena, in October 2006 a new rebel movement, the Union des Forces pour la Démocratie et le Développement (UFDD), was formed. This allied the CDR with the Union des Forces pour le Progrès et la Démocratie (UFPD), under Gen. Mahamat Nouri, a former defence minister and ambassador to Saudi Arabia. Another Zaghawa rebel movement, the Rassemblement Populaire pour la Justice, led by Abakar Tolli, also joined the UFDD. In late October UFDD forces briefly occupied Goz Beïda and Am Timan, before retreating to the border with Sudan. In response, the army attacked UFDD forces at Saraf Bogou, near the Sudanese border. According to the UFDD, 70 government troops were killed in the fighting, including army Chief of Staff Gen. Moussa Seugui, and 40 were taken prisoner. In late November UFDD forces occupied Abéché, seizing fuel, weapons, vehicles and food from UN World Food Programme (WFP) stores. The French Government dispatched a further 100 troops and two aircraft to bolster its forces in Chad. Three weeks of heavy fighting followed between rebel and government forces across Ouaddaï and Biltine provinces and the Sudanese border, with rebels belonging to the Rassemblement des Forces Démocratique (RAFD) seizing Guéréda and Koulbous.

In December 2006 the Chadian army launched a counter-offensive in the east of the country with thousands of troops, recapturing a 150-km strip along the border between Tiné and Adré. During these manoeuvres Chadian troops crossed into Sudan in pursuit of RAFD rebels. Later in December Deby signed a peace accord with the de facto head of the FUCD, Nour, in Tripoli. Under the terms of the agreement, Nour and those FUCD rebels loyal to him were granted an amnesty and were to be integrated into the national army, while Nour's aides were to receive government posts within three months. In accordance with the peace deal, on 15 February 2007 the army released 400 FUCD rebels who had been captured during the attack on N'Djamena the previous April.

In January 2007 the UN Security Council had agreed to send a mission to Chad and the CAR to assess whether a UN force should be deployed to protect the border with Sudan. Following the two-week mission, in late February the newly appointed UN Secretary-General, Ban Ki-Moon, proposed two options to the UN Security Council: a 6,000-strong force supported by helicopters; or a 10,900-strong ground-based force. However, in late February the Chadian Government rejected the proposed UN peace-keeping force, insisting that it would only allow an international civil police force to protect refugees.

On 23 February 2007 Prime Minister Pascal Yoadimnadji died suddenly from a brain haemorrhage in Paris, France. Three days later, Coumakoye was appointed as the new Prime Minister and on 4 March a new Council of Ministers was installed. Nine ministers were dismissed, and Nour was appointed Minister of National Defence, in accordance with the peace agreement signed in December 2006. In mid-March 2007 the legislature approved the Government's programme, which included commitments to peace and security, and promises to bolster social spending and engage in political dialogue.

Meanwhile, fighting continued in the east of the country. In April 2007 there were clashes near Amdjirema between the army and rebels from the Concorde Nationale Tchadienne (CNT), which was allied to the UFDD. Several days later, the Chadian army launched a cross-border raid on the Sudanese settlement of Forbaranga, killing 17 Sudanese citizens and provoking condemnation from the Sudanese and Egyptian Governments and the Arab League. In an attempt to defuse tensions between Chad and Sudan, on 3 May a peace accord was signed between President Deby and Sudan's President, Lt-Gen. Omar Hassan Ahmad al-Bashir, under the mediation of Saudi Arabia's King Abdallah. Under the agreement, both leaders pledged to cease training and funding rebel groups, and to stop all cross-border attacks.

DEPLOYMENT OF PEACE-KEEPERS

On 10 June 2007, following a meeting with France's new foreign minister Bernard Kouchner, Deby announced that his Government had agreed in principle to the deployment of a UN or European Union (EU) peace-keeping force along the Chadian border with Sudan. Two days later the Sudanese President agreed to a 26,000-strong UN-AU peace-keeping force in Darfur, following lengthy negotiations. Later in June Qaddafi mediated peace talks, held in Tripoli, between the Chadian Government and the four largest rebel groups: Nouri's UFDD, the Rassemblement des Forces pour le Changement (RFC), led by Timane Erdimi, the CNT, under Col Hassane Saleh al Gadam al Jinedi, and a UFDD splinter group, UFDD-Fondamentale (UFDD-F), under Abdelwahid Aboud Makaye. However, the talks ended without agreement, after the rebels insisted on the involvement of all of Chad's civilian opposition parties and human rights groups.

Following months of talks mediated and funded by the EU, France and the UN Development Programme, the Chadian Government signed an accord with the civilian opposition on 13 August 2007, under which legislative elections were to be organized before the end of 2009. The agreement included provisions for holding a new census, updating the voter register and redrawing electoral boundaries and reorganizing CENI. However, disagreements immediately broke out between the signatory parties, delaying progress with the accord's implementation.

In July 2007 EU foreign ministers announced plans for a military mission in Chad and the CAR which would monitor the border area and protect the refugee camps from attacks by bandits and militias. On 25 September the UN Security Council passed Resolution 1778, creating two peace-keeping forces: the UN Mission in the Central African Republic (MINURCAT) and the European Union Force Chad/CAR (EUFOR Tchad/RCA), which were due to be deployed before the end of the year. On 15 October the EU approved a 4,000-strong contingent for EUFOR, which was to establish six bases in eastern Chad and north-eastern CAR, and was to be supported by 1,100 French troops and the 26,000-strong hybrid peace-keeping force in Sudan, the UN-AU Mission in Darfur (UNAMID).

Meanwhile in mid-October 2007 the Government imposed a state of emergency in the eastern and northern provinces after violent clashes between the Tama and Zaghawa ethnic groups. The violence had erupted following attempts to forcibly disarm fighters from the Front Uni pour le Changement (FUC), under the leadership of the Minister of National Defence Nour. The Government immediately placed Nour under house arrest in N'Djamena, and on 1 December he was replaced by Gen. Mahamat Ali Abdallah Nassour, hitherto the Minister of State, Minister of Mines and Energy, whose portfolio was assumed by Boniface Sauguemi.

On 25 October 2007 the main Chadian rebel groups signed a cease-fire and peace accord with the Government in the Libyan town of Sirte, again under the mediation of Qaddafi. The accord provided for an immediate end to hostilities, a full amnesty for rebel fighters, and financial support for the rebels during the disarmament and reintegration of their forces. However, with the expiry of the cease-fire on 26 November, the rebels immediately resumed military operations, and began to amass their forces in preparation for a new attack on the capital. In December the leaders of three rebel groups, the UFDD, the RFC and the UFDD-F, announced the formation of a unified rebel military command, the Alliance Nationale (AN), which vowed to bring an end to Deby's regime.

ATTEMPT TO OVERTHROW DEBY ITNO

In late January 2008 some 2,000 members of the AN advanced on N'Djamena and on 2 February they seized control of the capital, besieging the presidential palace. After three days of fighting, in which at least 160 rebels, soldiers and civilians were killed and over 1,000 wounded, the rebels withdrew to the Sudanese border under constant aerial attack. The rebels appeared to have been severely weakened by their losses, and their activity in the border region calmed significantly in the wake of the fighting in N'Djamena. Although the French Government denied that it had assisted the Chadian authorities in defeating the rebel attack, reinforced French troops fought off a rebel attack at the airbase. In the wake of the attack the Government ordered the detention of key civilian opposition leaders, among them the CPDC spokesman, Ibn Oumar Mahamat Saleh, who subsequently disappeared. After intervention by French President Nicolas Sarkozy, the Government agreed to establish a commission of inquiry into the arrests, which was due to report its findings by July.

Deby accused the Sudanese Government of assisting the rebels with their preparations for the attack; however, in an attempt to reduce tensions, the Chadian and Sudanese Presidents signed a bilateral accord in the Senegalese capital, Dakar, in March 2008, agreeing to desist from aiding rebel forces in each other's countries. The agreement collapsed after combatants from the Sudanese Justice and Equality Movement (JEM), which was closely linked to Deby, launched an attack on the Sudanese capital, Khartoum, in May, prompting Sudan to suspend again diplomatic relations with Chad. Following mediation by Libya and Senegal, Sudan restored diplomatic relations with Chad in July, and although this was welcomed by the Chadian Government, the latter announced that the common border would remain closed to prevent the infiltration of armed groups into Chad.

In mid-April 2008 Deby dismissed Coumakoye as Prime Minister and appointed Youssouf Saleh Abbas, a former

Chadian special representative to the UN, in his place. Later that month Abbas appointed a new Government, in which four ministerial posts, including the defence and justice portfolios, were awarded to members of the CPDC.

Meanwhile, on 15 March 2008 EUFOR formally commenced its 12-month mission, with only around one-half of its 3,700-member force deployed. The same month MINURCAT was formally deployed in the country. By May EUFOR had increased in size to 2,380 EU troops garrisoned in two main camps, based on the outskirts of N'Djamena and in Abéché. EUFOR was expected to receive further support from the full deployment of MINURCAT, which had been reinforced to 592 police and security personnel by late 2008, providing protection for refugees and humanitarian workers in 12 UN refugee camps in the border area.

In June 2008 fighters from the AN launched attacks against government troops in the Dar Sila and Ouddaï regions, and briefly captured Goz Beïda, a key centre for humanitarian operations, as well as attacking four border posts. The attacks prompted the flight of civilians from N'Djamena to neighbouring Cameroon owing to fears of a further assault on the capital, but government forces intercepted the rebel forces at Am Timam, and successfully defeated them. During the fighting the rebels for the first time exchanged fire with EUFOR troops based in Goz Beïda, who were defending refugee camps located around the town, and near Abéché, but with no reported casualties. The UFDD claimed to have clashed with Zaghawa and Darfuri militias loyal to Deby in Birak, with heavy casualties on both sides. The failure of the June offensives greatly increased divisions between the rebel commanders, once more opening the schism within the UFDD and sparking bitter arguments over control of the AN. In August several senior commanders from Erdimi's RFC defected to the government army. Despite attempts by the rebels' Sudanese supporters to broker an agreement, fierce divisions prevented the rebels from launching a further offensive.

On 15 August 2008 N'Djamena's criminal court imposed death sentences *in absentia* on 12 current and former rebel leaders, and life sentences of forced labour on 32 other opponents of the Deby regime, for their involvement in the attack on the capital in February. Among those accused was former President Habré, who remained under house arrest in Senegal awaiting trial for separate charges of widespread human rights abuses under his regime (see below). Later in August the Minister of Finance and the Budget, Abakar Mallah Mourcha, was dismissed for his alleged involvement in embezzlement. He was replaced in late September by Gata Ngoulou, a former Secretary-General of the regional central bank, Banque des Etats de l'Afrique Centrale (BEAC).

In September 2008 the official Commission of Enquiry's report into the rebel attack on N'Djamena in February was released, following an investigation into allegations that Deby's regime had arrested several members of the opposition. The Commission confirmed that Mahamat Saleh had been arrested along with two others by Zaghawa militia men, and that he had subsequently died in custody, but it did not reveal the details of his death. The report also detailed human rights abuses and the deaths of almost 1,000 people during the fighting. The report was denounced by Mahamat Saleh's family for failing to name his killers, and although the EU welcomed the report, it urged the Government to commence judicial enquiries against those accused of the most serious crimes. In November the eight main rebel groups formed a new alliance, Union des Forces de la Résistance (UFR), headed by the RFC leader, Erdimi. However, the Front pour le Salut de la République, led by Ahmat Hassaballah Soubiane, rejected Erdimi's leadership and refused to join the UFR.

In January 2009 the UN Security Council authorized the creation of a 5,200-member UN force to replace EUFOR on 15 March. In addition, the Council authorized the expansion of MINURCAT, which was to incorporate EUFOR forces and have a total strength of 5,200 troops, 300 UN police and several military liaison officers, with a mandate to protect refugees and internally displaced persons. The reconstituted MINURCAT was expected to become fully operational by October. Two weeks later, the French Government announced that 1,000 French troops serving with EUFOR would withdraw, and that the remaining 650 would be incorporated into MINURCAT. However, the 1,000-strong French garrison in N'Djamena would remain for the foreseeable future. As envisaged, on 15 March EUFOR completed its mandate and transferred its peace-keeping responsibilities to MINURCAT, under the command of Senegalese Maj-Gen. Elhadji Mouhamedou Kandji, which began to redeploy its forces. MINURCAT was expected to be increased in strength to 4,700 troops by the end of 2009, 500 short of its authorized deployment level.

RENEWED FIGHTING IN EASTERN CHAD

Some 3,000–4,000 rebel fighters from the UFR launched a series of attacks in eastern Chad on 5 May 2009, provoking an intense aerial and ground counter-attack by government forces against rebel camps along and across the border in Sudan, which prompted condemnation from the Sudanese Government. Brief ground skirmishes were reported around Koukou Angarana and Kerfi, with concentrated fighting close to Am Dam. The rebel assault proved largely unsuccessful, and the Government claimed a decisive victory at Am Dam, announcing that it had killed 225 rebel soldiers and taken 210 prisoners. After the UFR made extensive counter-claims, the official media promptly relayed images of dead and captured rebel soldiers; Mahamat Hamouda Bechir, a senior commander of the UFR rebels, was among those captured. Following the attacks, President Deby replaced the army chief, Gen. Abderahim Bahar, with a former rebel commander, Gen. Hassane Saleh al Gadam al Jinedi.

The fighting had erupted only two days after Chad and Sudan had signed a reconciliation agreement, brokered by the Qatari Minister of State for Foreign Affairs and Libyan diplomats, in Doha, Qatar, and resulted in further hostility between the Chadian and Sudanese Governments. Chadian ministers swiftly denounced the Sudanese Government for their support of the rebels, while the French Government, the single largest contributor of international peace-keepers in Chad, lobbied within the UN Security Council, urging a formal condemnation of Sudan's role in supporting Chadian insurgents. The Security Council acknowledged that the attacks had been launched from 'outside of Chad'.

In mid-May 2009 it was reported that Chadian government forces had launched aerial and ground raids against rebel camps along the Sudanese border, striking up to 40 km inside Sudanese territory. The Chadian Government justified the incursion into Sudan with references to the 'right of pursuit' of those threatening state security and added that it would not hesitate to launch further raids wherever rebel groups were believed to be present, including in the CAR. Further air strikes on UFR positions near Um Dukhun, in western Darfur were reported in mid-July. These Chadian incursions prompted Sudan's ambassador to the UN to lodge a formal complaint with the UN Security Council; furthermore, the ambassador implied that France, which had a defence and intelligence co-operation agreement with Chad, was involved in the strikes. French aircraft were reported to have been conducting regular aerial reconnaissance flights over eastern Chad and Darfur. Later in July UN Secretary-General Ban Ki-Moon expressed concern over the air attacks and escalating cross-border violence, noting that, two days after the Chadian raids, there were reports of Sudanese government air raids on Darfurian rebel positions in the Jebel Moon area of western Darfur. Sudanese officials accused their Chadian counterparts of assisting the JEM.

The Chadian incursions into Sudan prompted hostile threats from officials of the latter country. The Sudanese Minister of State for Foreign Affairs, Al-Samani al-Wasila, claimed that his country's Government had no interest in undermining Chad's security and remained committed to the agreements that it had signed with the Chadian administration; however, al-Wasila added that Sudan would not exercise restraint should its interests and citizens come under threat, while the Chief of Staff of the Sudan Armed Forces, Lt-Gen. Abdel-Gadir Mohamed Nasr, declared that his forces were prepared to engage the Chadian army in combat. The Qatari Minister of State for Foreign Affairs, Ahmad bin Abdullah al-Mahmoud, stated that his country and Libya would continue to mediate between Chad and Sudan, despite their apparent disregard for the May 2009 agreement.

The rebels' defeat in May 2009 had served to accentuate divisions among the armed and political opposition to the Government. It prompted further dissent and realignments among rebels based in Sudan and eastern Chad, and fragmented Chadian opposition groups exiled in the Middle East and Europe. In late July three small rebel factions (collectively the Mouvement National—MN) signed a peace deal with representatives of Deby in Tripoli.

In April 2010 the Government claimed that the army had killed more than 100 rebels, and captured a further 80 injured rebel soldiers, in two clashes in eastern Chad. The rebels involved claimed to be members of the Front Populaire pour la Renaissance Nationale (FPRN), a splinter group of the UFR that had recently been established by Col Adam Yacoub. In December officials in Chad and the CAR announced that Chadian troops had repelled rebel attacks in Birao, a main town on the border between the two countries; several civilians had been killed in the fighting.

CONTROVERSY AND CORRUPTION

Meanwhile, in July 2009 Deby Itno announced the new composition of CENI, the reorganization of which had been provided for by the national agreement signed between the Government and the CPDC in August 2007 (see above). While nominally independent, one-half of the new election commission's 30 members belonged to the ruling MPS, while the remaining 15 were members of opposition parties. At the inaugural meeting of the restructured CENI, held in mid-June 2009, Ngarmadjal Garni, a former teachers' union leader, was elected as the commission's President. The lack of a credible electoral register had been a major source of contention at the time of the presidential poll in 2006; CENI was thus tasked with drawing up a new register based on data from Chad's second national census, which had been completed on 30 June 2009. However, the local press had questioned the reliability of the census data, thereby undermining the credibility of the new electoral register and leading to further controversy with regard to the legitimacy of polls. According to the election timetable announced by Garni in January 2010, the next legislative elections, which had originally been planned for 2006, were scheduled to be held in November 2010, with local and municipal polls to follow in December, and the presidential election to take place in April 2011.

Two major corruption scandals came to the fore in October 2009. The first case concerned allegedly fictitious contracts for school textbooks at the Ministry of National Education, worth a reported 2,500m. francs CFA (US $5.6m.). Those implicated included ministers and secretaries from the national education, finance and budget, and public health and agriculture ministries. In early November former Prime Minister Haroun Kabadi was arrested on corruption charges related to the case. The second scandal involved alleged corruption at the Paris branch of the BEAC. Most prominent among those implicated was the Minister of Finance and the Budget and former Secretary-General of BEAC, Gata Ngoulou, who denounced the allegations against him as a conspiracy.

As a consequence of the ongoing embezzlement allegations levelled at members of his government, Prime Minister Abbas tendered his resignation in March 2010. President Deby appointed Emmanuel Nadingar, hitherto Minister-delegate to the Prime Minister, responsible for Decentralization, as Abbas's replacement, and Nadingar subsequently announced the formation of a new Government, which included 18 new ministers.

THE 2011 PRESIDENTIAL AND LEGISLATIVE ELECTIONS

The legislative elections, which had been scheduled for 28 November 2010, were postponed following a meeting in September between the MPS and opposition leaders. According to CENI, this was due to timing constraints caused by complications encountered during electoral preparations. In October pro-presidential parties and the opposition agreed to the staging of legislative elections on 6 February 2011. The first parliamentary elections since 2002 finally took place on 13 February (following a further delay of one week, owing to the removal of the President of the CENI, who was alleged to have fraudulently tampered with the list of parliamentary candidates). International observers and even opposition leaders, including Kebzaboh of the UNDR, had acknowledged that another victory for the MPS was likely. Some 4.8m. people had registered to vote, and the EU and AU had dispatched observer missions to the country. The EU mission reported that it had found no evidence of fraud, despite observing a lack of materials and organization in some polling stations; Louis Michel, the head of the mission, endorsed the elections as fair, democratic and transparent, and also remarked on the relative stability in the country. A pro-presidential alliance, the Alliance pour la Renaissance du Tchad (ART), comprising the MPS, the RDP and VIVA—RNDP, secured 132 of the 188 seats in the enlarged Assemblée nationale, while the UNDR won 11. The new President of the CENI, Yaya Mahamat Liguita, confirmed that, despite some irregularities, the elections had been conducted peacefully, with a 56.6% participation rate.

The presidential election took place on 24–25 April 2011 (having been postponed from 3 April). However, opposition demands for electoral reform were not met and there was a consequent boycott of the poll by opposition candidates, including two of the most prominent opposition leaders, Ngarledjy Yorongar and Saleh Kebzaboh were. (In May a third prominent opposition leader and former Minister of Defence, Wadal Abdelkader Kamougué, died in hospital after a seizure.) The most serious of the opposition's electoral demands appeared to be the request to reprint voters cards, after Kebzaboh allegedly found a number of pre-dated cards on sale in N'Djamena's main market. A coalition of rebel groups had also urged the electorate not to vote. Of the remaining opposition candidates, Nadji Madou, a wealthy lawyer from the south of the country was considered to be a key candidate for young voters but was also considered to lack experience. Another candidate, Pahimi Padacke Albert, had more political experience, but mostly as a minister in Deby's Government.

On 10 May 2011 the CENI announced that Deby had won the presidential election with about 88.7% of votes cast, while Albert had received 6.0% of the votes and Madou 5.3%. Both opposition candidates rejected the electoral results. The CENI stated that 64.2% of voters had participated in the poll; however, Madou claimed that only between 19% and 24% of the electorate had voted.

NEW GOVERNMENT

Deby was sworn in for a fourth presidential term on 8 August 2011. On 13 August Deby reappointed eight ministers from the previous administration, including Nadingar to the office of Prime Minister, and Moussa Faki Mahamat as Minister of External Affairs and African Integration. The new, 40-member Government, which was formed on 17 August, included five representatives of the RDP and four of VIVA—RNDP, and four women. Among the new ministers, notably former presidential chief of staff Bénando Tatola was appointed as Minister-delegate at the Presidency of the Republic, responsible for National Defence and War Veterans, and Christian Georges Diguimbaye, hitherto the head of the Banque Agricole et Commerciale, became Minister of Finance and the Budget. In January 2012 President Deby replaced the Minister of Energy and Petroleum and the Minister of Planning, the Economy and International Co-operation, following the temporary closure of Djarmaya oil refinery (see Foreign Affairs).

INTERNALLY DISPLACED PERSONS IN CHAD

According the Office for the Coordination of Humanitarian Affairs (OCHA), at July 2010 about 170,000 people were internally displaced in eastern Chad and living in 38 camps, as a result of internal armed conflict, inter-ethnic violence over land and natural resources, and attacks by bandits against civilians. The majority of internally displaced persons (IDPs) had little or no means of sustaining themselves, making humanitarian assistance vital. According to OCHA, Chad also hosted 270,000 Sudanese refugees in 12 camps along the eastern border with Sudan, and 81,000 Central African refugees in 11 camps along the southern border with the CAR. The Internal Displacement Monitoring Centre (IDMC) suggests that the Government has taken measures to respond to the situation of IDPs, but that their impact has been limited. In 2007 the Government established the Comité National d'Assistance aux Personnes Deplacées, but it is considered to have limited resources and staff, and has delivered only sporadic assistance. In 2008 the Government also created the Coordination Nationale d'Appui à la Force Internationale à l'Est committee to co-ordinate humanitarian activities with MINURCAT, EUFOR and the humanitarian organizations operating in the country. The Government has yet to enact national legislation to protect IDPs. Of the 11.6m. IDPs in Africa, the IDMC estimates that 3m. live in the 'conflict triangle' of eastern Chad, Darfur and northern CAR. With the withdrawal of MINURCAT from Chad at the end of 2010 (see below), WFP and the IDMC feared that a worsening food crisis that had already affected 2m. people in Chad might be exacerbated. They cited concerns around severe limits to the access and capacity of humanitarian organizations and a government committed to military rather than social development spending as hampering conditions for the sustainable return, integration and resettlement of IDPs in the near future.

In May 2011 the Office of the UN High Commissioner for Refugees (UNHCR) announced that it had started assisting IDPs to return to their villages in eastern Chad, amid improved security in the region. The movements were taking place within the eastern Dar Sila and Assoungha regions (namely in the Koukou and Farchana areas) bordering the Western Darfur region of Sudan. UNHCR indicated that more than 14,000 of the 130,000 displaced Chadians in the two regions had registered for return. Some 50,000 unassisted returns by villagers had already taken place since 2010. The signing of a normalization agreement between Chad and Sudan in January and the subsequent deployment of the Chad-Sudan joint force two months later were considered to have significantly improved security along the Chad–Sudan border, where there were previously frequent rebel activities, acts of banditry and attacks against civilians.

CLIMATE-RELATED PROBLEMS

Lake Chad, shared by Chad, Nigeria, Cameroon and Niger is one of the world's great lakes. It is estimated to have lost 80% of its surface area between 1910 and 2010. The four countries combined to create the Lake Chad Basin Commission in 1964. They were joined by the CAR in 1994. The aims of the commission have been to regulate and control the use of water and other natural resources in the basin and to initiate, promote, and coordinate natural resource development projects and research. Analysts have deemed this project to be largely unsuccessful. The Chadian government has proposed policies and programmes to deal with the consequences of this calamity, but has few resources to implement them. Such climate-related hazards strongly affect food crops and livestock. There is no single cause for the disappearance of Lake Chad. Global warming is one factor blamed and local people maintain that rainfall has been steadily reducing by about five to 10mm a year. Other factors include irrigation and the damming of rivers feeding the lake for hydro-electric schemes, which have all combined to devastating effect, resulting in desertification.

WATER, FOOD INSECURITY AND HEALTH ISSUES

Chad has suffered acute cholera epidemics in recent years, which usually occur in the rainy seasons. In 2010 more than 6,800 people were infected and 209 died from the disease, while in August and September floods were the country's worst in 40 years. In 2011 cholera persisted throughout the dry season in Chad. With nearly 2,700 cases since the start of the year, aid groups were concerned that the disease might become a permanent epidemic in one of the world's poorest countries that has also suffered meningitis, measles and polio outbreaks. The Chadian health authorities deployed emergency teams and launched a campaign communicating basic rules of hygiene and sanitation; they also requested support from the international community to cope with the cholera epidemic. Aid groups such as Oxfam and Médecins Sans Frontières responded to the crisis by providing water, sanitation and health services at local hospitals where cholera treatment centres had been established, and in the parts of the country most affected by the disease. The Government in 2010 appealed for US $870m. from donors to fund a seven-year plan to address the country's water and sanitation problems.

In May 2012 at least 2.4m. people, mainly in Chad's central agro-pastoral zones of Guéra, Kanem, Bahr-el-Ghazal, Batha and Sila were classified by USAID as being in a 'stressed' food insecurity phase. The main reasons cited by WFP for food insecurity included rising food prices, as well as logistical challenges in moving food aid within a landlocked country. Concomitant reasons included the civil conflict in Libya and its aftermath in 2011–12, which had affected local trade with northern Chad, while radical Nigerian Islamist group Boko Haram activity in northern Nigeria had also slowed down trade in western Chad. The Chadian Government had announced the subsidized sale of cereals but aid officials suggested that more assistance was required. In May 2012 the British charity Oxfam suggested that in parts of Chad, Mali and Niger the malnutrition rates had exceeded 15%, with more than 1m. children at risk of starvation.

In May 2011 Chad was one of the 16 latest nations to join the Global Strategy for Women's and Children's Health, a US $40,000m. programme that UN Secretary-General Ban Ki-Moon had launched in 2010, increasing the country's budget for maternity and natal care, as well as committing to improve medical coverage for mothers and children. The commitments made by Chad would also focus on measures proven to be effective in preventing deaths, such as increased contraceptive use, attended childbirth, improved access to emergency obstetric care, prevention of mother-to-child transmission of HIV, and greater childhood immunization.

At the beginning of October 2011 President Deby, the UN Children's Fund (UNICEF), the World Health Organization (WHO), and the Bill & Melinda Gates Foundation launched a new polio immunization campaign, which was designed to immunize the country's 2.2m. children under the age of five against polio. The country has experienced a series of polio outbreaks. Approximately 41% of polio cases in Africa were reported in Chad during 2011, increasing the likelihood of the country becoming a reservoir for the spread of the virus to neighbouring countries.

FOREIGN AFFAIRS

Relations with Libya, Sudan and the CAR

During the late 1990s Chad forged increasingly close relations with its neighbours, particularly Libya. Chad was a founding member of the Community of Sahel-Saharan States, established in Tripoli in 1997. Following the conclusion of a peace agreement between the Chadian Government and the rebel MDJT in Tripoli in January 2002 (see above), Libya pledged aid for the development of Chad's Tibesti region. Since then, Qaddafi has been involved in numerous attempts to broker peace agreements between the Chadian Government and rebel forces, most recently in Sabratha, near Tripoli, in May 2009.

In December 1996 President Deby participated in efforts to mediate in the political crisis in the CAR, and in early 1997 Chadian troops joined the regional surveillance mission in that country. Chadian forces remained in the CAR as part of the UN peace-keeping mission (MINURCA) until its withdrawal in February 2000. In response to a coup attempt in the CAR in May 2001, Chad reportedly dispatched troops to defend the Government of President Ange-Félix Patassé. In November heightened unrest broke out in the CAR, following an attempt to arrest the recently dismissed Chief of Staff of the Armed Forces, Gen. François Bozizé, in connection with the May coup attempt. Bozizé crossed into southern Chad, with an estimated 300 armed supporters, and was granted refuge in Sarh. Meanwhile, as tension between the two countries remained high, repeated clashes were reported at the Chad–CAR border and, in January 2002, the Communauté Economique et Monétaire de l'Afrique Centrale (CEMAC) decided to send a mission of experts to the area.

In October 2002 a CEMAC summit in Libreville sought to defuse tensions between Chad and the CAR; in accordance with an agreement reached at the summit, Bozizé was subsequently granted asylum in France. In December a CEMAC force was deployed in Bangui, initially to protect Patassé and later to monitor joint patrols of the border by Chadian and CAR troops. Tensions subsequently abated somewhat, and in January 2003 the Governments of Chad, the CAR and Sudan announced their intention to establish a tripartite committee to oversee the security and stability of their joint borders. Following Bozizé's forcible assumption of power in the CAR in March, some 400 Chadian troops were reportedly dispatched to the CAR; around 120 Chadian troops were subsequently integrated into the CEMAC force that had been deployed in the CAR in late 2002. In June 2005 a further outbreak of fighting between rebel groups and government forces in the northern CAR caused large number of refugees to flee into southern Chad. By early 2006 the new arrivals had swelled the number of CAR refugees in Chad to an estimated 50,000. In November Bozizé and Deby issued a joint statement, accusing the Sudanese Government of trying to destabilize the region by supporting the rebels and allowing them to operate from bases in Sudan.

At the end of March 2004 indirect peace talks between the Government, the rebel Sudan Liberation Movement (SLM) and the JEM, attended by international observers, commenced in Chad, and on 8 April a 45-day humanitarian cease-fire was signed by representatives of the three parties. Further peace discussions ended in failure and the cease-fire subsequently collapsed. In June the Chadian Government announced that its troops had killed 69 *Janjaweed* (ethnic Arab militias that supported the Sudanese authorities), who had attacked the Chadian village of Birak, some 6 km from the Sudanese border. By August more than 170,000 Sudanese had fled to Chad, according to UNHCR, which had succeeded in relocating 118,000 of these refugees to camps away from the insecure border area, where raids by militias continued.

During early 2005 serious disagreements between the Governments of Chad and Sudan resulted in Chad suspending its role as the AU's official mediator in the Darfur conflict, although in June the Government was persuaded to resume participation in the talks. In December tensions with Sudan resurfaced, following alleged violations of Sudanese airspace by the Chadian air force and Sudan's continuing support for Chadian rebels from the Rassemblement pour la Démocratie et les Libertés (RDL) based in Darfur. Following the rebel attack on N'Djamena in April 2006 (see above), President Deby accused Sudan of supporting the invasion, formally severed diplomatic relations, and threatened to expel the 200,500 Sudanese refugees sheltering in eastern Chad. Chad formally withdrew from the AU-sponsored Darfur peace talks in protest, but a tentative peace deal was nevertheless signed on 5 May. The agreement was supported by the Sudanese Government and the leader of the Sudan Liberation Army (SLA), Minni Minnawi, but was rejected by a smaller faction of the SLA and by the JEM. On 8 August Chad formally re-established diplomatic relations with Sudan, following a meeting between the Chadian and Sudanese Presidents. This was followed in October by a meeting between Chadian and Sudanese military representatives in N'Djamena, which led to the signing of another security accord. However, in November Deby and Bozizé issued a joint statement condemning Sudan for supporting rebellions in both the CAR and Chad, and for instigating genocide in Darfur. Attacks by rebel forces on N'Djamena in February 2008 and Khartoum in May led to Sudan suspending diplomatic relations with Chad, although following Senegalese mediation the Sudanese Government restored ties in July. Violence continued in Darfur between Sudanese and rebel forces, with the Sudanese Government repeatedly accusing Chad of supporting JEM and SLA forces within its own borders, while the Chadian Government countered with claims that the Sudanese Government was assisting the Darfuri and Chadian rebel forces opposing Deby's regime.

In response to renewed pressure from foreign governments aimed at defusing bilateral tension and stabilizing the situation in Darfur following the failure of the March 2008 and May 2009 agreements (see above), diplomatic communication between Chad and Sudan resumed in October 2009. In January 2010 Chadian and Sudanese officials signed an accord in N'Djamena that provided for the normalization of bilateral relations. Each side pledged to desist from hosting or sponsoring rebel groups opposed to the other and to expel any remaining rebels from their respective territories by 21 February. In early February Deby visited Sudan for the first time since the outbreak of hostilities along the common border in 2005, and a supplementary agreement to establish joint border patrols was signed. The border force was to consist of 1,500 troops and 26 observers from each country; its headquarters would rotate on a six-monthly basis between El-Geneina, the capital of Western Darfur, and Abéché in Chad, with jointly manned observation posts to be established in 12 locations along the border. In mid-February Sudanese officials and JEM representatives, meeting in Doha, signed a framework agreement that was heralded as a significant step towards the achievement of a lasting peace deal. Deby was reported to have been crucial in brokering the accord with the leader of JEM, Khalil Ibrahim, with whom he was purported to have close family links. Following the conclusion of the Doha agreement, Sudanese President al-Bashir declared the war in Darfur to be over. However, certain factions of the SLM refused to participate in the preliminary peace talks, and heavy fighting was reported around the Darfuri town of Deribat just two days after the Doha agreement was signed. Furthermore, in early May JEM suspended its participation in the talks, accusing the Sudanese Government of bombing civilians, and subsequent clashes in Darfur further undermined the peace process. On 21 September Sudan transferred the command of the joint force to the Chadian army six months after its deployment on 24 March. The then Chadian Minister of Defence and former rebel leader, Wadal Abdelkader Kamougué, announced during the transference ceremony that the joint force represented 'a model for the standing co-operation between Khartoum and N'Djamena to secure the joint borders between them and provide security and stability for the two countries'. He also suggested that the joint forces had contributed to development projects, particularly in water provision to citizens.

Meanwhile, Deby urged Chadian rebels based in Sudan to repatriate and to participate in legislative elections scheduled to be held in November 2010, assuring them that he would guarantee their safety and facilitate their reintegration into civil society. It was reported that the UFR had left bases near El-Geneina in January. However, the UN noted the redeployment of Chadian armed opposition group elements from the border in western Darfur to areas around Saya and Mellit in northern Darfur, following claims issued by the UFR earlier that month that its positions near Tissi in Sudan had been bombed by the Chadian air force. In mid-February FPRN fighters reported clashes with government forces in the Chadian town of Hodjer Meram, near the border with Sudan. In May Chadian officials denied entry to JEM leader Ibrahim at N'Djamena airport; the Sudanese Government issued a statement praising the development, contending that it showed Deby's commitment to the agreement not to allow any armed rebel movement to use its territory to launch attacks on Sudan.

On 21 July 2010 Sudanese President al-Bashir arrived in Chad for his first visit to a full member state of the International Criminal Court (ICC), which had issued an international arrest warrant against him for war crimes committed in Darfur, including genocide. Reasons for the failure to arrest him included the AU's request to its members not to seize al-Bashir, as well as improved relations between Chad and Sudan after years of hostilities. However, New York-based Human Rights Watch urged Chad to arrest Deby, stating that 'Chad risks the shameful distinction of being the first ICC member state to harbour a suspected war criminal from the court'. Amnesty International also called on Chad not to shield al-Bashir and declared that the visit was an opportunity for justice. Sudan's expulsion of two of the most prominent Chadian rebel leaders, Mahamat Nouri and Timane Erdimi, on 20 July was considered to be a final concession in consolidating good relations ahead of that visit.

On 24 May 2011 the Sudanese Government transferred two leading members of the Chadian armed opposition to the Chadian authorities, two days before a tripartite summit in

Khartoum between President Deby, CAR President François Bozizé and Sudanese President al-Bashir. At the tripartite summit, it was agreed to establish a consultative mechanism of the three countries to address security issues, enhance the peaceful co-existence among joint tribes and encourage the voluntary return of refugees.

In December 2011 the UN Security Council's Panel of Experts imposed an arms embargo on both Chad and Sudan. They cited a porous border between Chad and Sudan as allowing arms to flow with no regulation or monitoring into Darfur. They indicated that this unregulated flow had continued to destabilize the region and deepen the crisis, with weapons belonging to Chadian forces ending up in Darfur.

In mid-2011 the Refugees Commissioner, Abdulla Suleiman, announced that UNHCR was implementing a plan to return Sudanese refugees from Chad and Egypt. The Commissioner issued statements affirming that considerable numbers of Sudanese nationals on the Sudan–Chad borders had begun to return to West Darfur, referring to a long-term plan that was expected to be implemented after the signing of an agreement between Sudan, Chad and UNHCR, aimed at securing the voluntary repatriation of Sudanese refugees resident in camps hosting 100,000 refugees in eastern Chad.

With the outbreak of civil war in Libya in February 2011, it was alleged that foreign mercenaries, including those from countries such as Chad and Zimbabwe, had been employed by the Libyan authorities to assist Libyan troops in suppressing the uprising against Qaddafi's rule. In April Chadian Minister of External Relations, African Integration and International Co-operation Moussa Faki Mahamat, rejected claims by Libyan rebels that Chadian officers were supporting Qaddafi's forces; he also announced that Chad had requested that France assist in monitoring its border with Libya, amid reports that thousands of Chadian combatants had crossed into Libya. Further allegations that Qaddafi had moved a large consignment of gold into Chad were also rejected by the Chadian Government. On 3 April the Government of Chad urged coalition forces to protect its citizens in rebel-held areas in Libya, declaring that a number had been executed for allegedly being mercenaries paid by Qaddafi; about 300,000 Chadian citizens were believed to have resided in Libya before the crisis. Owing to the political turmoil in Libya, in April WFP was forced to close the corridor through which it had previously transported food from the port in Benghazi (Libya) overland to Abéché and north-eastern Chad. In 2012 the flow of displaced people into Chad continued to be an instability concern for the Government.

Departure of MINURCAT

In January 2010 the Chadian Government requested that MINURCAT withdraw upon the expiry of its mandate on 15 March. (At that time MINURCAT had still not reached its authorized strength, with only approximately 3,500 soldiers deployed.) The Chadian President denounced the UN mission, which had been intended to provide security to the estimated 500,000 refugees in the east of the country, as a failure, arguing that not only had MINURCAT failed to do this but that it had also neglected to build promised infrastructure projects. MINURCAT's presence aroused nationalist resentment in both Chad and Sudan, and was regarded as an undermining force that threatened Deby's authority in particular. In response to the ongoing criticism of MINURCAT, the UN dispatched an assessment mission to N'Djamena later in January. The delegation reportedly offered a phased withdrawal, suggesting that MINURCAT consolidate civilian projects in the east before progressively transferring control of security to Chadian forces. This proposal was rejected by Chadian officials, who insisted that all UN military forces should leave by April. In an effort to overcome this impasse, in late February the UN Under-Secretary-General for Peacekeeping Operations, Alain Le Roy, visited Abéché, where MINURCAT troops were garrisoned, for talks with leaders of the UN mission and the Chadian Government. Following Le Roy's visit, in early March the Government agreed to extend MINURCAT's mandate by an additional two months, to 15 May, in order to facilitate an orderly transition of responsibility to local security forces.

On 12 May 2010 the UN Security Council extended MINURCAT's mandate for a further two weeks, until 26 May, and on 25 May the Security Council once again extended the mission's mandate, until 31 December. However, owing to the sustained pressure from the Deby administration for MINURCAT troops to leave the country, the nature of the UN mission's mandate was revised. In a statement on the unanimously approved Security Council resolution, UN Secretary-General Ban Ki-Moon announced that Chadian authorities would assume responsibility for the protection of civilians from 28 May. Under the terms of the resolution, MINURCAT's authorized strength was to be reduced in Chad to 1,900 troops by 15 July, and the mission was to begin a final withdrawal from 15 October. Both the UN and private aid agencies had expressed concerns that effecting a premature MINURCAT withdrawal would leave the refugees vulnerable to a potential 'security vacuum'. In accordance with the UN Security Council resolution of 25 May, the mandate of MINURCAT was officially ended on 31 December.

Senegal and the Habré issue

In 1998 it was reported that Chad was to seek the extradition from Senegal of former President Habré, with a view to his prosecution in relation to human rights abuses and in connection with the embezzlement of state funds. A committee of inquiry, established by the Deby regime, had held Habré's 'political police' responsible for the deaths of some 40,000 people and the torture of a further 200,000; the deposed President was also alleged to have taken some 7,000m. francs CFA in state funds when he fled Chad in 1990. In February 2000, following a ruling by a Senegalese court that he could be tried in that country for alleged crimes committed in Chad under his leadership, Habré was charged with complicity in acts of torture and barbarity, and placed under house arrest. The charges were rejected in July, however, on the basis that Senegal lacked the appropriate penal procedure to process such an international case; this ruling was upheld by Senegal's highest court of appeal in March 2001. None the less, in April President Abdoulaye Wade of Senegal stated that Habré's presence in the country was regarded as undesirable and gave him 30 days' notice to leave. Despite this, Habré remained in Senegal in 2006, while his alleged victims were seeking his extradition to stand trial in Belgium, under a law that (as amended in 2003) gave that country's courts universal jurisdiction in cases of human rights abuses and war crimes if Belgian citizens or long-term residents were among the plaintiffs. (Several of the alleged victims of abuses committed under Habré's regime had been granted Belgian citizenship.) In early 2006 the AU appointed a panel of seven legal experts to decide Habré's fate; in July Senegal agreed to a request by the AU to try Habré 'on behalf of Africa' in an international tribunal under the AU's auspices. In February 2007 the Senegalese Assemblée nationale approved legislation permitting the prosecution of cases of genocide, crimes against humanity, war crimes and torture, even if they were committed outside Senegal. In the mean time, legal proceedings continued in Chad, and on 15 August 2008 N'Djamena's criminal court imposed death sentences *in absentia* on 12 former and current rebel leaders, and life sentences of forced labour on 32 other opponents of the Deby regime, including Habré. In response, the Senegalese Minister of Justice expressed doubt that the trial in Senegal could proceed; however, the AU's African Court of Justice ruled that the sentence passed against Habré related to the February 2008 attack against the capital and did not cover human rights abuses committed under Habré's regime.

Faced with Senegal's inaction, in February 2009 Belgium requested that the ICJ order Senegal either to prosecute or extradite Habré. In May the Court accepted Senegal's formal pledge not to allow Habré to leave Senegal, pending its final judgment. A ruling by the Economic Community Of West African States (ECOWAS) Court of Justice in November 2010 requested that Senegal create a special jurisdiction to prosecute Habré. In the same month the AU and the EU intensified negotiations over a budget, and agreement was reached on a US $11.7m. (€8.59m.) budget for a 20-month investigation and a five-month trial. The negotiations culminated in donor funds being raised for a prosecution case to commence. Human Rights Watch Chadian victims' groups highlighted in June 2012 that a report from US Secretary of State Hillary Clinton criticized Senegal's continued failure to bring Habré to justice, vindicating demands that Senegal should swiftly extradite Habré to Belgium to face trial. At the end of June Senegal's President Macky Sall anounced that Habré would not be extradited to Belgium but tried in Senegal. In the same month the Senegalese Government established a working group to organize the trial of Habré, in line with the original commitments made in 2006.

Relations with France

It was generally believed that France regarded the maintenance of its military presence in Chad as a priority, given the country's proximity to several potential conflict zones. However, in March 2000 the Chadian Government demanded the recall of the French ambassador in N'Djamena; it was alleged that France's refusal to provide military support to government forces in the Tibesti region was a factor in the dispute. The French Minister of Defence, Michèle Alliot-Marie, visited Chad and met Deby in April 2003, when she expressed support for the actions of Chadian troops in the force deployed by CEMAC in the CAR (see above). Deby established a close relationship with the French President, Jacques Chirac, which ensured him diplomatic and military support when his regime was under attack from rebels. French troops and military advisers assisted in regaining control of N'Djamena for Deby's regime during the attack by FUCD forces in April 2006, and again in February 2008. The personal intervention of the new French President, Nicolas Sarkozy, in the arrest of six French aid workers from the humanitarian organization, Arche de Zoé, fostered a close relationship between the French and Chadian Presidents. Following the completion of EUFOR's mission in March 2009 (see above), the French Government announced it would withdraw 1,000 troops that it had contributed to the force, leaving 650 to be incorporated into MINURCAT, but also that it would keep in place the 1,000-member garrison in N'Djamena, which had protected the regime during previous assaults on the capital.

In mid-October 2009 Deby met Sarkozy to discuss regional and bilateral issues; among the issues reportedly discussed by the two Presidents was the future of France's military presence in Chad. Deby suggested to journalists that he would not oppose a withdrawal of French troops from Chad, which would be 'a sovereign decision of the French state'. Over 1,000 French troops had been based in Chad since 1986, technically on a temporary basis, under the so-called Opération Epervier, which had been launched to counter Libyan expansionist ambitions. Moreover, in October 2009 the French Ministry of Defence released a report detailing arms sales from France to sub-Saharan Africa in 2008. The report revealed that Chad was the second largest client for French weaponry, behind only South Africa, buying €13m. (US $20m.) of weaponry in 2008, representing an increase of about 50% compared with the previous year.

In June 2012 rebels attacked a uranium exploration site in Bakouma, in neighbouring CAR which was operated by French company Areva. French nationals were held hostage in the attack but were subsequently released. There was conflicting information about the origins of the rebels, with various reports suggesting that the attacks had been staged from Chad, by the Ugandan Lord's Resistance Army, or locally from the CAR.

Taiwan and China

From 1977 Chad maintained close diplomatic relations with the Republic of China (Taiwan), which lavished aid on the country in return for diplomatic recognition. As a result of ties with Taiwan, the People's Republic of China severed diplomatic relations with Chad in 1997. However, following intensive lobbying and financial inducements by the Chinese Government, on 6 August 2006 Chad formally established diplomatic ties with China, prompting Taiwan to suspend diplomatic relations. China has since greatly increased investment in Chad, particularly in the areas of energy and infrastructure, led by the China National Oil and Gas Exploration and Development Corporation, which has acquired extensive gas and oil concessions and was involved in the construction of Chad's first refinery at Djarmaya, north of N'Djamena. In January 2012 relations with China showed signs of becoming constrained. Six months after the inauguration of the Djarmaya oil refinery that had been constructed as a joint venture between the China National Petroleum Corporation (CNPC) and the Chadian Government, the Chadian authorities closed the refinery for about 10 days, owing to a dispute with the Chinese enterprise. The sources of the dispute originated in a lack of transparency on the part of the CNPC, the Chadian Government's determination to set pump prices for refined products without regard to cost, and fuel-smuggling from Nigeria.

Economy

VICTORIA HOLLIGAN

Chad is one of the least developed countries of Africa, and its geographical isolation, climate and meagre natural resources have resulted in an economy of narrow range. The United Nations Development Programme (UNDP) ranked Chad 183rd out of 187 countries in terms of human development (based on that organization's Human Development Index) in 2011. Since 2000 Chad's Human Development Index value has increased by 15%, or an average annual rate of about 1.3%. Specifically, life expectancy has increased by 1.6 years from 1980 to 2011 and the expected years of schooling increased by 4.7 years over the same period. Overall, according to UNDP, gross national income (GNI) per head has risen by 73% to US $1,105 in 2011, on a purchasing-parity basis (2005). The construction of a pipeline linking the oilfields in southern Chad to the port of Kribi in Cameroon, which commenced operations in July 2003, offered the prospect of considerably higher incomes. Nevertheless, by 2010 there was no material acceleration in poverty reduction as a result of petroleum development. Despite social indicators remaining below the sub-Saharan African average, a record 98.5% of primary school children were enrolled in school in 2010 and health infrastructure is currently being improved through the recruiting and training of new staff.

The country's economic construction task remained substantial and performance in the non-petroleum sector, where the bulk of the population makes a living, remained limited, because of great vulnerability to external shocks. During the late 2000s N'Djamena, the capital, suffered numerous major rebel assaults associated with the conflict with Sudan. The UN's Office for the Co-ordination of Humanitarian Affairs (OCHA) estimated that the crisis in the Darfur region of that country has driven about 280,000 Sudanese refugees into Chad, adding to some 75,000 refugees from the Central African Republic (CAR). Violence in Libya has also resulted in the return to Chad of over 100,000 migrant workers. The country also faces high environmental challenges, being one of the most climatically vulnerable countries in the world—the country experienced a cholera epidemic and severe flooding, in addition to food insecurity, in 2010.

The primary sector has traditionally dominated the economy. Hitherto, virtually all of the country's limited industrial and commercial production facilities have been located in or close to N'Djamena. Much economic activity is informal, and very few statistics are published. There are hardly any all-weather roads and no railways. The country is land-locked and its major economic centres are situated 1,400–2,800 km from the sea. Its structural problems of economic development, immense in any circumstances, have been rendered still more acute by civil conflict and by drought. Consequently, for most of the period since independence, the authorities have had to focus on 'crisis management' rather than on the pursuit of a longer-term economic strategy. In any event, policies formulated in N'Djamena have tended to have limited impact in the remote hinterland of the centre and north and also in large parts of the disaffected south. Despite an increase in public expenditure on basic services as part of the 50th anniversary of Chad's independence in 1960, the country is characterized by a poorly functioning legal system, unreliable water and electricity supplies, and weak infrastructure. In the absence of a dynamic private sector, the Government is Chad's largest employer. According to the national employment office, ONAPE, 22,068 new workers were engaged in 2009, with the majority of new jobs created in the extractive sector.

Petroleum development boosted economic growth in the early 2000s and production started in 2003, with gross domestic product (GDP) growth reaching 14.7% in that year (exports began in October), according to the IMF; in 2004 GDP growth of 33.6% was recorded. Growth in the non-petroleum sector remained slow, however, because of the impact of harsh climatic conditions on agriculture performance. In 2005 overall growth slowed to 8.6%, despite satisfactory harvests, as the rise in petroleum production levelled off and public investment in priority sectors failed to pick up. Growth is estimated to have further slowed in 2006, to 1.3%, according to the IMF, reflecting lower oil production than initially projected, rising instability in the east of the country and disruption to government expenditure following the dispute with the World Bank over the management of oil revenue. Real GDP growth decreased to 0.3% in 2007 as a result of a steep decline in oil production caused by technical issues in producing fields and weak agricultural growth. In 2008 non-oil GDP increased by 3.2%, while oil GDP declined by 11.7%, resulting in a net impact of a 0.5% decrease in real GDP; reduced petroleum production coupled with the detrimental impact on economic activity of the February rebel attack (see Recent History) were the main reasons for the GDP decline. In 2009 real GDP declined by 0.8%, owing to a reduction in agricultural activity and the effects of the global economic downturn on the domestic economy. Economic prospects improved substantially in 2010, with GDP growth estimated at some 13% by the IMF, supported by higher international oil prices and a good harvest. In 2011 the IMF estimated GDP growth at about 3%, with the start-up of new oilfields and a refinery operated by the China National Petroleum Corporation (CNPC) in the Bongor Basin offsetting a sharp decline in agricultural production. In 2012 the IMF forecast growth of more than 7%, based on the start-up of new oil and cement projects. Yet there is a risk that several major obstacles could hamper this projected rise in economic growth, including potential fluctuations in the international price of oil, the domestic security situation and low rainfall.

AGRICULTURE

Agriculture and livestock accounted for an estimated 20% of GDP in 2010, compared with 30% in 2002, and continued to employ the majority of the labour force. The main area of crop production is situated in the south of the country, with cattle production prevailing in the more arid northern zones. In the extreme north, camel- and sheep-rearing and date orchards are predominant. The principal food crops are sorghum and millet. Rice, maize, groundnuts and cassava are also grown for domestic consumption. According to the Division of Agricultural Statistics, the grain harvest of the 2008/09 season was 2.0m. tons, an increase of 1.9% compared with the previous season, owing to higher yields and favourable climatic conditions. Low rainfall in 2009/10 reduced cereal production in that season by 30%, to 1.4m. tons (including 442,000 tons of sorghum and 395,000 tons of pearl millet). Chad, together with the other Sahelian states, achieved a record harvest of 2.5m. tons of cereal in the 2010/11 season, owing to good rainfall. Cereal production fell by an estimated 49% to 1.6m. tons in the 2011/12 season, compared with the previous season, mainly due to erratic rains and prolonged dry spells that reduced grain yields and delayed harvest, according to FAO. Production of the main staple cereals, millet and sorghum is estimated to have halved over the same period. At the same time, food insecurity remains acute, especially in the Sahelian belt but also in parts of the border area with Sudan. Rural development schemes implemented in southern Chad, with assistance from France, the European Union (EU), Canada and the World Bank, aim to increase production of cereals and livestock. However, major problems remain in the area of distribution and marketing, which resulted in some localized scarcity. In addition, rising instability in the east of the country and in Darfur in recent years—causing the presence in eastern Chad of thousands of refugees that fled fighting in Darfur, as well as a rising number of internally displaced Chadians and people from the CAR—has caused severe localized food insecurity in some areas, as well as disruption to marketing activities and pricing mechanisms, raising the need for emergency food aid. According to FAO, an estimated 3.6m. people were in need of food assistance in Chad in December 2011. The ongoing unrest in Libya has resulted in many Chadians returning home, intensifying local food insecurity in some areas.

Some progress was made in the cultivation of rice by modern methods during the 1990s, with the area harvested appreciably increasing, from 36,854 ha in 1990 to 103,803 ha in 2002, although the area cultivated declined thereafter, to 91,000 ha in 2004, according to unofficial figures. Output has none the less varied markedly from year to year. In 2005 paddy rice production increased to an exceptional 141,000 metric tons, according to local sources, against a yearly average of 111,000 tons in 1999–2004, but fell back to 112,400 tons in 2006 and 106,400 tons in 2007, before increasing slightly, to 109,000 tons, in 2009, and nearly doubling to 200,000 tons in 2010. Sugar cane is another food crop of significance. According to local sources, production in 2006 totalled 366,000 tons, before falling to an estimated 355,600 tons in 2007 and remaining constant, at 380,000 tons, in 2008–09.

Cotton, which is Chad's main export crop, has encountered growing difficulties in recent years. In 2003 petroleum products replaced cotton and livestock as the main source of foreign exchange; consequently, cotton contributed an estimated 12.9% of total export revenue in 2003 and only 2.3% of total exports in 2009, compared with 41.1% in 2001. Cotton production has been widely encouraged since the 1920s, and seed cotton is grown on some 280,000 ha, in the south of the country. As a result of price incentives and satisfactory growing conditions in the south of the country, cotton production recovered from 102,200 tons in 2003 to 219,900 tons in 2004, according to official figures. However, a reduction in producer prices to 160 francs CFA per kg, reflecting falling world prices, contributed to a fall in cotton production, to an estimated 182,000 tons, in 2005. Cotton production fell dramatically to 98,100 tons in 2006 and 98,058 tons in 2007 owing to inadequate weather conditions and ongoing problems at the Société Cotonnière du Tchad (COTONTCHAD). In 2008 production increased by 3.1% to 101,085 tons, with exports of 41,000m. francs CFA (contributing some 2% of non-oil GDP). Output declined dramatically in 2009, to just 37,000 tons, as a result of ongoing problems in the sector. Despite a 45% increase in the international price of cotton in 2010, exports of cotton fibre fell by 18%, owing to the ongoing management issues at COTONTCHAD.

Gum arabic, which is harvested from traditional plantations of acacia trees in the north, is Chad's fourth largest export, after petroleum products, livestock and cotton. Despite a strong international demand, there has been little increase in levels of output in recent years, because of high transport costs and the lack of an organizational structure. According to local sources, in 2007 Chad produced an estimated 26,900 metric tons of gum arabic, up from 25,000 tons in 2006. Exports amounted to 15,000m. francs CFA in both 2007 and 2008. Chad is the world's second largest producer of gum arabic, after Sudan.

Livestock production has a significant role in the Chadian economy and alone contributed 8.3% of total GDP in 2005, according to the IMF. Livestock exports are the second most valuable source of foreign exchange, after petroleum (although, owing to the large informal economy and smuggling, reliable statistics can be difficult to acquire). In 2006 the value of exports was 267,000m. francs CFA, rising to 272,000m. francs CFA in 2008. The livestock sector generally yields more in terms of cash income than the cotton industry, but much of this is not officially registered. Cattle-raising is concentrated in the central and southern regions of the country. Livestock is often exported illicitly, without payment of taxes, mainly to Nigeria, where it is sold or bartered for consumer goods. In 2010, according to FAO, there were some 7.4m. head of cattle, 6.8m. goats and 3.0m. sheep. The production of meat fell by 7.4% in 2007 and by 5.6% in 2008 owing to frequent technical failures at abattoirs, according to the Banque des Etats de l'Afrique Centrale (BEAC). Efforts to rehabilitate the sector following the food crises of 2005 and 2008 resulted in a 3.6% increase in output in 2009. In the long term, there is considerable potential for livestock exports, subject to the upgrading of the herds and improvements in marketing arrangements.

Fishing is an important economic activity in the Lake Chad region; in 2010, according to data published by FAO, the annual catch amounted to around 40,000 metric tons. State supports for fish farmers contributed to the sector expanding by 3.0% in 2008 and by 4.4% in 2009.

MINING, POWER AND CONSTRUCTION

Industry, comprising mainly oil exportation and production activities, accounted for about one-third of GDP during 2000–08, and its contribution rose to in excess of 50% in 2009, falling to just under 40% in 2010. The exploitation of proven deposits of petroleum in Chad has long been inhibited by the high cost of importing plant and machinery long distances with poor or non-existent transport facilities. In response to the increase in world petroleum prices during the 1970s, petroleum extraction began in the Sédigui region, to the north of Lake Chad, in 1977. However, output was very modest—about 1,500 barrels per day (b/d) in 1979/80—and the operation was subsequently suspended because of the precarious security situation. In 1993 exploration in the Doba Basin (in southern Chad) revealed reserves of petroleum, which were subsequently estimated at more than 900m. barrels. Proposals for the development of 300 wells and a processing facility were announced, and an agreement was signed in 1995 by the Governments of Chad and Cameroon for the construction and operation of a 1,070-km pipeline to transport petroleum from Doba to the port of Kribi in Cameroon. In November 1999 the World Bank agreed to lend Chad and Cameroon US $93.0m. for the project, after overcoming environmental concerns and setting conditions for sound oil revenue management; this triggered fresh lending from commercial banks. The cost of the project was estimated to be $1,500m. for Chad and $3,700m. overall. Construction began in late 2000 by a consortium, Esso Chad, comprising ExxonMobil of the USA (40%), Petronas of Malaysia (35%) and the Chevron Corporation of the USA (25%). Objections by environmental and human rights organizations to the 25-year project were reinforced after it was reported that the Government had spent $3m. of a bonus received from petroleum companies on armaments. The Chad–Cameroon pipeline was completed one year ahead of schedule and production commenced in July 2003. Initial output amounted to an average 50,000 b/d in 2003. Production reached at times more than 200,000 b/d by late 2004, close to the full production capacity of 225,000 b/d. According to Esso Chad, petroleum production increased from an annual average of 24,000 b/d (an annual total of 8.6m. barrels) in 2003 to 168,000 b/d (61.4m. barrels) in 2004 and to 173,000 b/d (63.3m. barrels) in 2005, following the commencement of production at the Nya field. However, with production slowing at the three original Doba oil fields, despite the start of production at the Moundouli field, output fell to 153,000 b/d in 2006 (55.9m. barrels). Proven reserves in Lake Chad were estimated at 900m. barrels, but the country's total reserves are known to amount to at least 1,500m. barrels. The Government continued to issue exploration permits after the pipeline came on stream, and other companies are involved in oil exploration in Chad, in particular the CNPC, which is the majority shareholder in the H permit (437,000 sq km in three regions of Chad) following the acquisition of Canada's Encana 50% rights in February 2007 and previously Clivenden's rights in 2003 and 2005; and Taiwan's Overseas Petroleum and Investment Corporation, which was granted an exploration permit in early 2006. In order to increase its direct role in oil activities, in mid-2006 the Government created a national hydrocarbons company, the Société des Hydrocarbures du Tchad (SHT). President Deby has stated that in the future SHT will have a 60% stake in the country's oil sector. Concern has arisen over the fiscal risks of the state oil company; thus, the Council of Ministers was to exercise political oversight over all major SHT decisions with budgetary implications. Additionally, a new petroleum law was passed in May 2007, providing for the establishment of production-sharing agreements for new oilfields. In 2007 production fell by 7.6% to 52.4m. barrels, owing to technical problems and high water content, according to the BEAC. Nevertheless, oil production was expected to increase in the future, with the CNPC announcing the discovery of two oilfields in the Bongor Basin—Ronier and Mimisa—which were collectively estimated to contain at least 100m. metric tons of oil in 2007. Yet crude oil production declined by 10.6% in 2008, owing to poor reservoir performance and technical problems with high water cut wells, according to the BEAC. Oil production decreased again in 2009, to 46.6m. barrels, owing to a pressure drop in the reservoir as well the introduction of more high water cut wells. The following year persistent water in hydrocarbon deposits and lower pressure in the oil reservoir resulted in oil production falling slightly, to 44.7m. barrels. In 2011 the Exxon-operated Doha fields sustained a production plateau of around 120,000 b/d (43.8m. barrels per year), according to Exxon, owing to the implementation of a high-pressure water injection programme, well stimulations and additional wells. In the same year the CNPC-operated Bongor project commenced production at 20,000 b/d (3.7m. barrels per year), which was used in the new refinery. The CNPC, together with the state partner SHT, constructed a 20,000-b/d oil refinery and power plant in Djarmaya, which entered into operation in June 2011 to refine the crude oil from these new oilfields to satisfy local market demand. Phase I of the project has the annual processing capacity of 700,000 tons of gasoline and diesel, 20,000 tons of kerosene, 25,000 tons of polypropylene, 60,000 tons of liquefied petroleum gas and 40,000 tons of fuel oil, according to the CNPC. SHT funded its 40% share in the project through a loan from Libya.

Natron, found in pans on the northern edge of Lake Chad, is the only non-petroleum mineral of importance currently exploited in Chad. It is used as salt, for human and animal consumption, in the preservation of meats and hides and in soap production, and was exported to Nigeria via the Logone river from N'Djamena. Alluvial gold and materials for the construction industry are also extracted. There is believed to be considerable potential for the further exploitation of gold deposits and for the development of bauxite, titanium and uranium reserves. In 2001 the first gold mine in Chad, at Ganboké, in the south of the country, was opened by Afko Corea (Republic of Korea).

Electricity in Chad is generated by two main oil-powered plants operated by a public corporation, the Société Tchadienne d'Eau et d'Électricité (STEE); installed capacity is 45.8 MW. The annual output of electricity has stagnated since the mid-1970s, as a result of ageing equipment and the prohibitive costs of importing petroleum, and was put at 84m. kWh in 2004. The utility has also been severely affected by persistent non-payment of bills, notably by other public sector enterprises. In September 2000 the Government and Vivendi (of France—subsequently renamed Veolia Water) signed a management and operating contract for the STEE, with plans to repair existing generators and increase capacity. Construction work meanwhile commenced on the rehabilitation of the Sédigui oilfield and the construction of a pipeline linking Sédigui to a proposed refinery at Farcha, near N'Djamena. The project, which was expected to produce up to 5,000 b/d and cover the bulk of Chad's energy requirements, stalled in 2001. Work on the project was still suspended at mid-2010. In April 2004 Veolia renounced its contract to manage and potentially acquire the STEE, causing another reverse in the country's electricity sector. Generating capacity increased in the short term, following the installation of new donor-funded, oil-powered generators in 2004. In late 2006 generating capacity for the capital, N'Djamena, improved following the installation of a new generating station at Farcha. In 2008 STEE's finances suffered owing to a lack of effective management, persistent poor payment of bills, rising fuel costs, and technical problems. The Government declared its intention to break up the company into separate water and electricity entities to improve the ability of the company to deliver lower-cost energy to the population. After years of high energy prices and regular electricity shortages, the Government awarded a subsidy to STEE and strengthened the structures of the Farcha power station in 2009, as a result of which energy production increased by 18% in that year, with production expected to grow by 50% by 2011 upon completion of the rehabilitation of STEE's distribution networks. A further 20 MW of electricity is expected to be supplied from the CNPC-operated oil refinery.

The People's Republic of China has become an important economic partner of Chad through pursuing investment opportunities, as well as part of China's strategy to marginalize the involvement of the Republic of China (Taiwan) in Africa. In late 2011 China CAMC Engineering Co. (CAMC Engineering), finalized construction of a US $80m. cement factory in the town of Baoare, with expected annual output of 200,000 tons. In the same year CAMC Engineering secured a contract of about $1,060m. to construct a new international airport in Chad.

MANUFACTURING

Manufacturing (which contributed 5.8% of GDP in 2010) is centred in N'Djamena and Moundou, and is mainly devoted to the processing of agricultural products. After falling by 10.5% in 2010, manufacturing GDP was estimated by the IMF to have increased by 20% in 2011 and an increase of 33% was forecast for 2012, driven by the cotton industry. The processing of cotton is the principal industry, and the recovery in cotton production during the mid-1990s prompted COTONTCHAD to increase capacity at its eight mills in 1996–97. In 2011 only three of the mills were in operation, due to technical problems and issues related to financing the purchase of spare parts, according to local sources. Despite cotton's contribution to GDP increasing in 2011, COTONTCHAD has severe financial difficulties, and further restructuring is necessary to allow the company to benefit from favourable export cotton prices. The transfer to majority private ownership of the Société Nationale Sucrière du Tchad (as the Compagnie Sucrière du Tchad) was completed in April 2000. Although the company was forced temporarily to suspend its operations in 2004 because of illicit imports from Cameroon and Nigeria, sugar production recovered in 2008, to a record level of 380,000 metric tons. Other manufacturing activities in Chad include cigarette production and brewing; there is also a wide range of small-scale enterprises operating outside the recorded sector, including crafts and the production of agricultural implements. This unofficial sector makes a significant contribution to employment and overall production.

SERVICES

The services sector contributed over one-third to GDP in 2010—mainly comprising commerce (13% of GDP) and government services (11% of GDP)—and recorded a growth rate of 7.4%, owing to strong growth in the telecommunication and transportation sectors, according to the *African Economic Outlook*. After increasing by 8.8% in 2010, the services sector's contribution to GDP increased by an estimated 7%, driven by telecommunication and transport. Yet transportation within Chad is inadequate, and the already high cost of transport has been exacerbated by the crisis in Libya. Communications with the outside world are difficult, slow and costly because of the great distance from the sea, the character of the trade, and poor facilities in neighbouring countries. In 1999 the Government adopted a new road classification system, in accordance with which Chad was deemed to possess a year-round national road network of 2,600 km, a dry-season-only road network of 3,600 km and a regional rural road network of some 3,000 km. The total length of the road network was an estimated 40,000 km, of which only 412 km was paved. Transport limitations are a major obstacle to the country's economic development and efforts are being made to improve the internal transport system (with help from the World Bank, the European Development Fund and the USA), including the rehabilitation and construction of an ancillary road network as part of rural development in the south. A five-year investment plan covering 2006–10 aimed to repair 3,000 km of rural roads with national funding, while transport infrastructural improvements in adjacent countries, especially in Cameroon, were also expected to benefit Chad. Inland waterways are significant, with 2,000 km of the Chari and Logone rivers navigable in all seasons. In mid-2009 Chad received a grant from the African Development Fund of US $47.3m. to develop the Koumra–Sarh road, opening up the southern part of the country. This road was expected to improve transport links and the movement of goods and people in the southern Mandoul and Moyen-Chari regions, and also to reduce transport costs.

Plans to privatize the parastatal Société des Télécommunications du Tchad (SOTEL TCHAD), which has a monopoly on fixed and international telecommunications services, have been mooted. Three mobile telephone companies, Airltel (since 2004, formely Celtel), Millicom (since 2006) and Salam, operate in the country. Most mobile telephone services have been concentrated around the capital, N'Djamena, although both operating companies had plans to expand them to other areas.

PUBLIC FINANCE

Chad has historically faced severe public finance difficulties. Economic decline and civil strife have exacerbated the low level of tax revenue; burdened with deep and chronic budgetary deficits, before the substantial oil revenues, the Government had largely relied on foreign aid to maintain basic public services. In recent years oil revenues have resulted in the Government's fiscal balance materially improving, with a small overall fiscal surplus projected by the IMF in 2011. However, in the medium term Chad is vulnerable to oil price volatility and the forecast decline in oil production has negatively affected government financing.

Since the mid-1980s, as part of the IMF-sponsored structural adjustment programmes, the Government has attempted to increase revenue receipts and to reduce spending. The Government's economic programme, backed by an Enhanced Structural Adjustment Facility (ESAF) extended by the IMF in September 1995, again laid emphasis on improving revenue collection and also included the introduction of a single turnover tax, effective from the beginning of 1997. Spending was to be controlled through reform of the large state enterprises (in cotton, sugar and electricity) and of the civil service. Tax revenue consequently increased from 39,700m. francs CFA in 1995 (equivalent to 5.5% of GDP) to 68,000m. francs CFA in 1999 (equivalent to 7.2% of GDP), while recurrent expenditures were largely kept under control over the same period.

Under pressure from the World Bank, the Government adopted legislation on petroleum revenue management in 1999. Budgetary efforts have since continued to focus on strengthening revenue transparency and the monitoring of priority expenditures. Under the new legislation, 80% of direct revenue (royalties and dividends) from the petroleum sector was to be allotted to the development of education, health and infrastructure, while 10% was to be held in trust for future generations. In January 2000 the IMF approved a three-year programme for Chad under a Poverty Reduction and Growth Facility (PRGF)—the successor to the ESAF. The resources available under this arrangement were augmented in May 2001, in order to respond to food shortages, and again in January 2002, to address the decline in international prices of cotton.

Public finances were expected to take a new turn in 2003, although revenue from the petroleum sector did not actually accrue until late in the year. According to revised estimates, the overall budget deficit, on a commitment basis and including grants, reached 100,700m. francs CFA in 2003, equivalent to 6.3% of GDP. Delays in establishing the stabilization and sterilization mechanisms, as well as several of the organizations provided for under the legislation on petroleum revenue management, including the Petroleum Revenue Control and Monitoring Board and the Fund for Future Generations (FFG), explained the late receipt of petroleum revenue. However, in 2004 oil receipts rose to 57,700m. francs CFA. This surge in revenue helped to compensate for a shortfall in aid flows following the expiration of the PRGF in 2004. The budget deficit (on a commitment basis, including grants) was reduced to 69,400m. francs CFA, or 3% of GDP. Despite rising petroleum revenues, domestic payment arrears (including wages) continued to accumulate in that year.

In February 2005 the IMF approved a new three-year PRGF, worth US $38.2m. According to IMF estimates, revenues from the petroleum sector (largely royalties and dividends) increased to 130,400m. francs CFA in 2005. In December, however, the law on petroleum revenue management was revised to free up more resources for the treasury—money was taken from the FFG and the definition of priority sectors was widened to include public administration and security. This decision was caused by problems in revenue management and increasingly urgent needs as a result of growing instability in the region. In reaction, the World Bank suspended all funding to the country and froze the escrow account into which Chad's oil revenues were deposited. Meanwhile, the completion of the first review under the PRGF was postponed because of fiscal difficulties and the IMF suspended its disbursements. An agreement was eventually signed with the World Bank in July 2006 committing the Chadian Government to allocate 70% of all petroleum revenues (direct and indirect) to priority spending, while the FFG was officially suppressed. Total budget revenue increased by 27% to an estimated 1,040,900m. francs CFA in 2008, owing primarily to an increase of 16.4% from oil revenues because of higher oil prices. Over the same period, current expenditure grew by 34% to 602,200m. francs CFA owing mainly to an increase in military spending, transfers and subsidies, and of goods and materials. In fact, military spending has significantly increased since revenues from petroleum were first recorded, rising from 2.5% of non-oil GDP in 2003 to a projected 14.7% of non-oil GDP in 2008. An overall fiscal surplus of 5.2% of GDP in 2008 (including grants) turned into a deficit of 10.8% of GDP in 2009, financed by official reserves and statutory advances from the central bank. Oil revenue, which accounts for about 50% of state revenue, declined from 20.4% of GDP in 2008 to 11.6% of GDP, while state expenditure increased from 15.2% of GDP to 21.0% of GDP, mainly as a result of elevated military spending owing to the May 2009 rebel attack (see Recent History—5.8% of GDP) and government investment expenditure (7.5%). In 2010, despite an increase of almost 50% in budget revenue, the budget deficit rose to 11.5% of GDP, as a result of spending in excess of revenue and outwith the budget. Revenue from oil exports, at 655,200m. francs CFA, contributed 65.4% to total government revenue of 989,900m. francs CFA, with the non-oil sector contributing 24.5%, according to the African Economic Outlook. Expenditure rose by 19.2%, to 1,176,500m. francs CFA, mainly as a result of a doubling of transfers and subsidies, spending on independence anniversary projects, spending for the 2011 elections and spending on security due to the departure of the UN peace mission, MINURCAT. The deficit was funded through a combination of a drawdown of BEAC reserves and advances to the treasury by the central bank, and through an accumulation of domestic arrears. The deficit spending strategy of the Government and its dependence on oil revenue increases the vulnerability of Chad to internal and external shocks. Moreover, neither public development aid budget support nor formal programme with the IMF is available to Chad, owing to the level of deficit spending. In 2011 oil revenue increased to a projected 1,280,000m. francs CFA, accounting for a record 76% of total government revenue, according to the IMF. In the same year current expenditure was estimated to remain fairly constant to the level of the previous year, resulting in an estimated overall fiscal surplus (excluding grants and commitments) of 113m. francs CFA (3.9% of non-oil GDP).

FOREIGN TRADE, AID AND PAYMENTS

While exports and imports have fluctuated widely as a result of the civil war, weather and international oil prices, Chad's foreign trade has, almost without exception demonstrated a large deficit, owing to the low level of production in the economy and the high cost of transport, until revenue from oil exports resulted in a projected small balance-of-payments surplus in 2011. Before the development of the country's petroleum resources commenced in 2000, the principal imports had comprised food products (accounting for 19.1% of the cost of total imports in 1995). Total imports more than doubled in 2001, compared with the previous year, to reach 497,417m. francs CFA, before increasing more than two-fold again in 2002, to 1.1m. francs CFA, as a result of imports of machinery and other goods related to the Doba oil project. The trade deficit widened in 2002, to some 978,400m. francs CFA, as a result of import spending in the petroleum sector. There was a 35.9% decline in cotton export prices in 2002. This, combined with a 9.0% fall in the volume of cotton exports, and despite reasonably sound performances in other traditional sectors, caused total exports to decline in that year by 7.0%, to 128,900m. francs CFA.

Petroleum effectively became the primary source of foreign exchange earnings for Chad when the first barrel left Kribi in October 2003. As a result, total exports more than doubled to 350,400m. francs CFA in 2003, before reaching an unprecedented 1.1m. francs CFA in 2004 and 1.6m. francs CFA in 2005. Meanwhile, imports slowed following the completion of the oil pipeline, to 453,200m. francs CFA in 2003, and remained broadly stable at 462,300m. francs CFA in 2005 and 428,100m. francs CFA in 2006. Chad's trade balance thereby resulted in a surplus of 679,800m. francs CFA being recorded in 2004, and of 1.2m. francs CFA in 2005, according to the IMF. The trade surplus rose further in 2006, to 32.4% of GDP, helped by strong international petroleum prices. During 2007 the trade surplus declined slightly, to 30.3% of GDP, with exports falling by 78.5% for cigarettes, 28.8% for cotton, 7.5% for crude oil and 4.8% for consumer goods. Imports of oil, consumer goods and food, and building materials fell by 4.1%, 6.6% and 3.0%, respectively, while those of industrial equipment and transportation fell by some 47.8%, according to the BEAC. Terms of trade improved by some 45% between 2006 and 2008, with import cover nearly doubling from 5.3 months of imports of non-oil goods and services in 2006 to 10.5 months in 2008, according to the IMF. Although this represented a marked improvement compared with previous years, the balance of payment situation in the non-petroleum sector—where the majority of the population is employed—remained weak. In 2007 the trade deficit in the non-petroleum sector amounted to 224,400m. francs CFA and was projected by the IMF to increase to 318,800m. francs CFA in 2008. After declining by 44.9% in 2009, terms of trade increased by 41.6% in 2010 and 24.0% in 2011, representing an almost doubling of import cover of non-oil sector goods and services from 3.0 months in 2009 to 5.8 months in 2011, according to the IMF.

The current account of the balance of payments has been persistently in deficit, owing to the very high outflows on services, mostly transport costs. The external current account deficit (including external transfers) peaked at 1,390,500m. francs CFA in 2002, equivalent to 100.4% of GDP, the majority of which was financed through petroleum-related foreign direct investment (FDI); net FDI inflows totalled US $924m. in 2002, according to the UN Conference on Trade and Development. By 2005 the current account deficit was estimated to have declined to 26,500m. francs CFA, an equivalent of 0.9% of GDP, reflecting an improvement in the trade balance. The current account deficit widened to 11.2% of GDP in 2006 and to an estimated 13% of GDP in 2007. Sustained high oil prices in 2008 have significantly strengthened the external account and official reserves. The current account deficit expanded significantly from a 10.3% deficit in 2008 to a 31.8% deficit in 2009, largely owing to increased imports of goods and services related to new oil operations in the Bongor Basin. High oil prices in 2010 reduced the overall balance-of-payments deficit to 2.4% of GDP, according to the African Development Bank (AfDB). Goods exports represented 44.4% of GDP, of which 90% were derived from oil. Goods imports accounted for 12.8% of

GDP, benefiting from the depreciation of the euro, while services imports, mainly related to government-funded infrastructure projects, grew at a rate of 28.7%, compared with the previous year. In 2011 the current account was projected to record a small surplus equivalent to 3.9% of non-oil GDP, according to the IMF, driven by sustained high export oil prices and a decline in current and capital expenditure of an estimated 25% and 17% of GDP, respectively. In the same year export volume increased by 1% and import volume fell by 10%, associated with a decline in spending related to the CNPC-operated Bongor Basin oilfields and refinery, which entered into production in mid-2011.

FDI inflows, which declined significantly after the completion of the Chad–Cameroon pipeline from US $924m. in 2002 to $478m. in 2004, before recovering to $1,215m. in 2007, were expected to continue to take place predominantly in the oil sector, despite plans to liberalize the cotton sector. The oil sector is the main source of FDI, with inflows increasing by some 36.8% in 2010.

To offset the deficit, Chad relied heavily on foreign assistance, which was also needed to fund basic budgetary requirements and any development expenditure, as well as the episodes of military activity. France was the principal bilateral supplier of aid, including direct budgetary assistance (providing approximately 30% of all international financial assistance disbursed in 1990–98) until 2003. In 2004, however, France was overtaken by the USA. China, the EU and other multilateral agencies, and, more recently, Arab countries (particularly Kuwait) have also granted substantial assistance, principally for agricultural and infrastructure projects. Overseas development assistance (ODA) increased steadily from 2000, with net inflows totalling US $319m. ODA has significantly fallen since the advent of oil, demonstrated by total aid (including grants and loans) declining from 10% of GDP in 2004 to only 5% in 2007.

Most of Chad's borrowing was from government and other official sources, on highly concessionary terms. Consequently, while external debt increased significantly, from US $284m. in 1980 to $1,590m. at the end of 2005 (equivalent to 61.1% of GNI), debt-servicing remained relatively low. This was also attributable to the frequent failure to pay liabilities as they fell due (arrears on repayment were 1,100m. francs CFA at the end of 2003), as well as debt relief. In May 2001 Chad was declared eligible for debt-service relief under the Bretton Woods institutions' enhanced initiative for heavily indebted poor countries (HIPC), and in June the 'Paris Club' of official creditors provided a rescheduling of Chad's debt on 'Cologne terms'. Following the IMF's approval of a new PRGF in February 2005, the Government hoped to reach completion point (where full debt relief begins) rapidly, although this failed to materialize following the postponement of the conclusion of the PRGF's first review owing to the deterioration of the country's fiscal position. An IMF Staff Monitored Programme (SMP) was negotiated in July 2008, but failed management approval owing to cost over-runs. A new Poverty Reduction Strategy Paper, which was adopted in 2008, set out the Government's economic strategy to 2011, based on good governance, fiscal sustainability and effective spending of oil revenue to promote economic diversification and poverty reduction. Outstanding external debt increased from 21% of GDP at the end of 2008 to 24% at the end of 2009, according to the IMF. In 2010 external debt increased to 26%, yet the ratio of debt to goods and services improved to 2, compared with 3.1 in the previous year, as a result of strong oil export prices. Despite high oil prices, in 2011 external debt widened to 29.5% of GDP. As progress has not been realized on key areas, such as budgetary control and agreement on a medium-term fiscal framework, the IMF has not to date commenced a further SMP, which would allow the adoption of a new PRGF and an HIPC initiative, and potentially result in further debt relief under the Multilateral Debt Relief Initiative.

Statistical Survey

Source (unless otherwise stated): Institut national de la statistique, des études economiques et démographiques, BP 453, N'Djamena; tel. 22-52-31-64; fax 22-52-66-13; e-mail inseed@intnet.td; internet www.inseed-tchad.org.

Area and Population

AREA, POPULATION AND DENSITY

Area (sq km)	
Land	1,259,200
Inland waters	24,800
Total	1,284,000*
Population (census result)	
8 April 1993	6,279,931
20 May–30 June 2009†	
Males	5,509,522
Females	5,666,393
Total	11,175,915
Population (UN estimates at mid-year)‡	
2010	11,227,208
2011	11,525,497
2012	11,830,573
Density (per sq km) at mid-2012	9.2

* 495,800 sq miles.

† Figures are provisional.

‡ Source: UN, *World Population Prospects: The 2010 Revision*.

POPULATION BY AGE AND SEX

(UN estimates at mid-2012)

	Males	Females	Total
0–14	2,679,928	2,660,555	5,340,483
15–64	3,054,151	3,100,712	6,154,863
65 and over	150,168	185,059	335,227
Total	5,884,247	5,946,326	11,830,573

Source: UN, *World Population Prospects: The 2010 Revision*.

ETHNIC GROUPS

1995 (percentages): Sara, Bongo and Baguirmi 20.1; Chadic 17.7; Arab 14.3; M'Bourn 6.3; Masalit, Maba and Mimi 6.1; Tama 6.1; Adamawa 6.0; Sudanese 6.0; Mubi 4.1; Hausa 2.1; Kanori 2.1; Massa 2.1; Kotoko 2.0; Peul 0.5; Others 4.5 (Source: La Francophonie).

REGIONS

(2009 census, preliminary figures)

Barh El Gazel	260,865	Mayo-Kebbi Est	769,178
Batha	527,031	Mayo-Kebbi Ouest	565,087
Borkou	97,251	Moyen-Chari	598,284
Chari-Baguirmi	621,785	N'Djamena	993,492
Ennedi	173,606	Ouaddaï	731,679
Guéra	553,795	Salamat	308,605
Hadjer-Lamis	562,957	Sila	289,776
Kanem	354,603	Tandjilé	682,817
Lac	451,369	Tibesti	21,970
Logone Occidental	683,293	Wadi Fira	494,933
Logone Oriental	796,453	**Total**	11,175,915
Mandoul	637,086		

PRINCIPAL TOWNS
(population at 1993 census)

N'Djamena (capital)	530,965	Koumra	26,702
Moundou	99,530	Pala	26,115
Sarh	75,496	Am-Timan	21,269
Abéché	54,628	Bongor	20,448
Kelo	31,319	Mongo	20,443

Mid-2011 (incl. suburbs, UN estimate): N'Djamena 1,078,640 (Source: UN, *World Urbanization Prospects: The 2011 Revision*).

BIRTHS AND DEATHS
(annual averages, UN estimates)

	1995–2000	2000–05	2005–10
Birth rate (per 1,000)	47.6	47.6	45.9
Death rate (per 1,000)	17.3	17.8	17.1

2001 (preliminary): Live births 397,896; Deaths 138,025.

Sources: UN, *World Population Prospects: The 2010 Revision* and *Population and Vital Statistics Report*.

Life expectancy (years at birth): 49.2 (males 47.8; females 50.7) in 2010 (Source: World Bank, World Development Indicators database).

ECONOMICALLY ACTIVE POPULATION
('000 persons at mid-1990, ILO estimates)

	Males	Females	Total
Agriculture, hunting, forestry and fishing	1,179	1,102	2,281
Industry	105	9	115
Manufacturing	50	6	56
Services	245	100	344
Total labour force	1,529	1,211	2,740

Source: ILO.

1993 census (persons aged six years and over): Total employed 2,305,961; Unemployed 16,268; Total labour force 2,322,229.

Mid-2012 ('000, estimates): Agriculture, etc. 3,032; Total labour force 4,783 (Source: FAO).

Health and Welfare

KEY INDICATORS

Total fertility rate (children per woman, 2010)	6.0
Under-5 mortality rate (per 1,000 live births, 2010)	173
HIV/AIDS (% of persons aged 15–49, 2009)	3.4
Physicians (per 1,000 head, 2004)	0.04
Hospital beds (per 1,000 head, 2005)	0.40
Health expenditure (2009): US $ per head (PPP)	60
Health expenditure (2009): % of GDP	4.6
Health expenditure (2009): public (% of total)	19.7
Access to water (% of persons, 2010)	51
Access to sanitation (% of persons, 2010)	13
Total carbon dioxide emissions ('000 metric tons, 2008)	495.0
Carbon dioxide emissions per head (metric tons, 2008)	<0.1
Human Development Index (2011): ranking	183
Human Development Index (2011): value	0.328

For sources and definitions, see explanatory note on p. vi.

Agriculture

PRINCIPAL CROPS
('000 metric tons)

	2008	2009	2010
Rice, paddy	169.8	130.7	130.8*
Maize	226.0	209.0	208.9*
Millet	523.2	709.0*	620.9*
Sorghum	685.4	601.0	490.3*
Potatoes	42	50*	50*
Sweet potatoes*	75	90	88
Cassava (Manioc)	161	230*	231*
Taro (Coco yam)	26	33*	26*
Yams*	405	520	415
Sugar cane*	390	390	390
Beans, dry	63	80*	73*
Groundnuts, with shell	403	413*	394*
Sesame seed	39	35†	35†
Melonseed*	24	22	21
Onions, dry*	17	17	16
Dates*	19	19	19
Guavas, mangoes and mangosteens*	33	35	33

* FAO estimate(s).
† Unofficial figure.

Aggregate production ('000 metric tons, may include official, semi-official or estimated data): Total cereals 2,019 in 2008, 2,193 in 2009, 1,912 in 2010; Total pulses 109 in 2008, 125 in 2009, 122 in 2010; Total roots and tubers 709 in 2008, 922 in 2009, 810 in 2010; Total vegetables (incl. melons) 103 in 2008, 105 in 2009, 97 in 2010; Total fruits (excl. melons) 124 in 2008, 118 in 2009, 118 in 2010.

Source: FAO.

LIVESTOCK
('000 head, year ending September)

	2008	2009	2010*
Cattle	7,075	7,245	7,419
Goats	6,288	6,439	6,751
Sheep	2,886	2,956	3,027
Pigs	28*	29*	30
Horses	400	410	410
Asses	440	451	451
Camels	1,358	1,391	1,400
Chickens	5,450*	5,500*	5,550

* FAO estimate(s).

Source: FAO.

LIVESTOCK PRODUCTS
('000 metric tons, FAO estimates)

	2008	2009	2010
Cattle meat	88.7	91.1	94.8
Sheep meat	15.0	15.4	15.4
Goat meat	23.6	24.2	24.2
Cows' milk	188.1	192.6	195.6
Sheep's milk	12.4	12.7	13.1
Goats' milk	37.3	38.2	39.8
Hen eggs	3.9	4.0	4.0

Source: FAO.

Forestry

ROUNDWOOD REMOVALS
('000 cubic metres, excl. bark, FAO estimates)

	2008	2009	2010
Sawlogs, veneer logs and logs for sleepers*	14	14	14
Other industrial wood†	747	747	747
Fuel wood	6,830	6,949	7,070
Total	7,591	7,710	7,831

* Output assumed to be unchanged since 1993.
† Output assumed to be unchanged since 1999.

Source: FAO.

SAWNWOOD PRODUCTION
('000 cubic metres, incl. railway sleepers)

	1994	1995	1996
Total (all broadleaved)	2.4*	2.4	2.4

* FAO estimate.

1997–2010: Annual production as in 1996 (FAO estimates).

Source: FAO.

Fishing

('000 metric tons, live weight, FAO estimates)

	2007	2008	2009
Total catch (freshwater fishes)	45.0	40.0	40.0

2010: Catch assumed to be unchanged from 2009 (FAO estimates).

Source: FAO.

Mining

	2009	2010	2011
Crude petroleum ('000 metric tons)	6,187	6,403	5,971

Source: BP, *Statistical Review of World Energy*.

Industry

SELECTED PRODUCTS

	2002	2003	2004
Sugar (centrifugal, raw, '000 metric tons)	23.1	38.0	40.0
Beer ('000 metric tons)	12.4	11.0	8.4
Cigarettes (million packs)	36.0	37.0	40.0
Electric energy (million kWh)	106.6	86.0	84.0

Source: IMF, *Chad: Selected Issues and Statistical Appendix* (January 2007).

Oil of groundnuts ('000 metric tons): 32.0 in 2008–09; 31.5 in 2010 (Source: FAO).

Raw sugar ('000 metric tons): 35.0 in 2005–07.

Electric energy (million kWh): 102.0 in 2006; 105.0 in 2007; 103.0 in 2008 (Source: UN Industrial Commodities Statistics Database).

Finance

CURRENCY AND EXCHANGE RATES

Monetary Units

100 centimes = 1 franc de la Coopération Financière en Afrique Centrale (CFA).

Sterling, Dollar and Euro Equivalents (31 May 2012)

£1 sterling = 819.959 francs CFA;
US $1 = 528.870 francs CFA;
€1 = 655.957 francs CFA;
10,000 francs CFA = £12.20 = $18.91 = €15.24.

Average Exchange Rate (francs CFA per US $)

2009 472.186
2010 495.277
2011 471.866

Note: An exchange rate of 1 French franc = 50 francs CFA, established in 1948, remained in force until January 1994, when the CFA franc was devalued by 50%, with the exchange rate adjusted to 1 French franc = 100 francs CFA. This relationship to French currency remained in effect with the introduction of the euro on 1 January 1999. From that date, accordingly, a fixed exchange rate of €1 = 655.957 francs CFA has been in operation.

BUDGET
('000 million francs CFA)

Revenue	2009*	2010*	2011†
Petroleum revenue	284	676	611
Non-petroleum revenue	256	324	391
Tax revenue	239	313	371
Non-tax revenue	16	11	20
Total	540	1,000	1,001

Expenditure	2009*	2010*	2011†
Current expenditure	634	766	648
Wages and salaries	201	216	260
Goods and services	110	111	109
Transfers	302	411	259
Interest	21	29	20
External	16	16	10
Investment expenditure	353	522	499
Domestically financed	242	392	368
Foreign financed	111	130	132
Total	987	1,289	1,147

* Estimates.
† Budget figures.

Source: IMF, *Chad; Staff Report for the 2011 Article IV Consultation* (October 2011).

INTERNATIONAL RESERVES
(US $ million at 31 December)

	2009	2010	2011
Gold*	—	6.19	17.01
IMF special drawing rights	4.25	4.20	0.09
Reserve position in IMF	0.44	0.43	4.50
Foreign exchange	612.01	627.77	946.51
Total	616.70	638.59	968.11

* Valued at market-related prices.

Source: IMF, *International Financial Statistics*.

MONEY SUPPLY
('000 million francs CFA at 31 December)

	2009	2010	2011
Currency outside banks	280.10	333.94	356.21
Demand deposits at commercial and development banks	162.67	230.72	269.57
Total money (incl. others)	442.83	564.71	625.86

Source: IMF, *International Financial Statistics*.

COST OF LIVING
(Consumer Price Index for African households in N'Djamena; base: 2005 = 100)

	2007	2008	2009
All items	98.3	108.5	119.3

Source: IMF, *International Financial Statistics*.

NATIONAL ACCOUNTS
('000 million francs CFA)

Expenditure on the Gross Domestic Product

	2009	2010	2011
Government final consumption expenditure	1,125	1,193	1,128
Private final consumption expenditure	2,632	3,089	3,402
Gross fixed capital formation	1,015	1,373	1,527
Change in inventories	28	179	–141
Total domestic expenditure	4,800	5,834	5,916
Exports of goods and services	1,397	1,875	2,382
Less Imports of goods and services	1,933	2,447	2,424
GDP in purchasers' values	4,264	5,263	5,875

Gross Domestic Product by Economic Activity

	2009	2010	2011
Agriculture	828	999	929
Mining and quarrying	865	1,335	1,746
Electricity, gas and water	22	21	24
Manufacturing	292	304	320
Construction	302	361	398
Wholesale and retail trade, restaurants and hotels	810	982	1,053
Finance, insurance, real estate, etc.	600	677	725
Transport and communications	64	73	84
Public administration and defence	415	421	475
Less Imputed bank service charge.	22	25	28
GDP at factor cost	4,174	5,148	5,726
Indirect taxes	90	115	149
GDP in purchasers' values	4,264	5,263	5,875

Source: African Development Bank.

BALANCE OF PAYMENTS
('000 million francs CFA)

	2008	2009*	2010†
Exports of goods f.o.b.	1,894.9	1,279.1	1,565.0
Imports of goods f.o.b.	–884.9	–1,198.9	–1,456.0
Trade balance	1,010.0	80.2	109.1
Services (net)	–912.5	–984.5	–1,043.6
Balance on goods and services	97.5	–904.3	–934.5
Factor income (net)	–744.2	–337.4	–422.6
Balance on goods, services and income	–646.7	–1,241.7	–1,357.1
Private unrequited transfers (net)	47.4	65.9	54.8
Official unrequited transfers (net)	86.1	87.3	58.1
Current balance	–513.2	–1,088.5	–1,244.2
Capital transfers	56.4	80.6	87.3
Foreign direct investment	536.7	559.6	875.5
Other medium- and long-term investments	60.3	96.3	277.4
Short-term capital	–39.1	3.1	0.0
Errors and omissions	–54.2	0.0	0.0
Overall balance	209.5	–348.9	–4.0

* Estimates.
† Projections.

Source: IMF, *Chad: 2010 Article IV Consultation—Staff Report; Staff Supplements; Public Information Notice on the Executive Board Discussion; and Statement by the Executive Director for Chad* (June 2010).

External Trade

PRINCIPAL COMMODITIES

Imports c.i.f. (US $ '000)	1995
Food and live animals	41,182
Cereals and cereal preparations	16,028
Wheat and meslin (unmilled)	8,945
Sugar, sugar preparations and honey	17,078
Refined sugars, etc.	16,825
Beverages and tobacco	7,175
Mineral fuels, lubricants, etc.	38,592
Refined petroleum products	38,551
Motor spirit (gasoline) and other light oils	6,490
Kerosene and other medium oils	8,456
Gas oils	23,318
Chemicals and related products	15,507
Medicinal and pharmaceutical products	7,789
Basic manufactures	26,190
Non-metallic mineral manufactures	7,654
Metal manufactures	8,804
Machinery and transport equipment	51,246
General industrial machinery, equipment and parts	8,175
Road vehicles (incl. air-cushion vehicles) and parts*	17,873
Parts and accessories for cars, lorries, buses, etc.*	8,253
Miscellaneous manufactured articles	27,335
Printed matter	13,565
Postage stamps, banknotes, etc.	11,622
Total (incl. others)	215,171

* Excluding tyres, engines and electrical parts.

Source: UN, *International Trade Statistics Yearbook*.

Exports (US $ million)	2006	2007	2008
Petroleum and other oils (excl. crude)	97	27	136
Cotton	76	64	36
Total (incl. others)	3,410	3,677	4,275

Source: African Development Bank.

Total imports c.i.f. (million francs CFA): 850,830 in 2008; 1,086,028 in 2009; 1,238,193 in 2010 (Source: IMF, *International Financial Statistics*).

Total exports c.i.f. (million francs CFA): 1,938,997 in 2008; 1,251,294 in 2009; 1,683,942 in 2010 (Source: IMF, *International Financial Statistics*).

PRINCIPAL TRADING PARTNERS

Imports c.i.f. (US $ '000)	1995
Belgium-Luxembourg	4,771
Cameroon	33,911
Central African Repub.	3,010
China, People's Repub.	6,251
France	88,887
Germany	2,988
Italy	6,452
Japan	5,121
Malaysia	2,234
Netherlands	2,843
Nigeria	25,269
Spain	3,402
USA	13,966
Total (incl. others)	215,171

Source: UN, *International Trade Statistics Yearbook*.

2008 (US $ '000): *Exports:* China 41.6; Japan 195.8; Taiwan 102.5; United Kingdom 1.3; United States 3,470.8; Total (incl. others) 4,275 (Source: African Development Bank).

Transport

ROAD TRAFFIC
(motor vehicles in use at 31 December)

	1994	1995*	1996*
Passenger cars	8,720	9,700	10,560
Buses and coaches	708	760	820
Lorries and vans	12,650	13,720	14,550
Tractors	1,413	1,500	1,580
Motorcycles and mopeds	1,855	2,730	3,640

* Estimates.

Source: IRF, *World Road Statistics*.

2006: Passenger cars 18,867; Vans 24,874; Buses 3,278; Tractors 3,132; Motorcycles 63,036 (Source: Ministère de Travaux Publics et de Transport).

CIVIL AVIATION
(traffic on scheduled services*)

	1999	2000	2001
Kilometres flown (million)	3	3	1
Passengers carried ('000)	84	77	46
Passenger-km (million)	235	216	130
Total ton-km (million)	36	32	19

* Including an apportionment of the traffic of Air Afrique.

Source: UN, *Statistical Yearbook*.

Tourism

FOREIGN VISITORS BY NATIONALITY*

	2007	2008	2009
Belgium	326	491	335
Canada	420	42	512
Egypt	20	23	190
France	6,167	6,142	6,564
Germany	290	298	285
Italy	152	421	484
Libya	24	12	827
Saudi Arabia	8	1	—
Switzerland	178	216	36
United Kingdom	781	607	518
USA	2,760	1,699	2,579
Total (incl. others)	24,794	21,871	31,169

* Arrivals at hotels and similar establishments.

Total visitor arrivals: 71,000 in 2010 (preliminary).

Receipts from tourism (US $ million, incl. passenger transport): 14 in 2000; 23 in 2001; 25 in 2002.

Source: World Tourism Organization.

Communications Media

	2009	2010	2011
Telephones ('000 main lines in use)	58.3	51.2	31.2
Mobile cellular telephones ('000 subscribers)	2,281.3	2,875.3	3,665.7
Internet subscribers ('000)	4.6	n.a.	n.a.
Broadband subscribers	300	500	200

Television receivers ('000 in use): 10.9 in 2000.

Radio receivers ('000 in use): 1,670 in 1997.

Daily newspapers (national estimates): 2 in 1997 (average circulation 1,550 copies); 2 in 1998 (average circulation 1,560 copies).

Non-daily newspapers: 2 in 1995 (average circulation 10,000 copies); 14 in 1997; 10 in 1998.

Periodicals: 51 in 1997; 53 in 1998.

Personal computers: 16,000 (1.6 per 1,000 persons) in 2005.

Sources: International Telecommunication Union; UNESCO, *Statistical Yearbook*; UNESCO Institute for Statistics; UN, *Statistical Yearbook*.

Education

(2009/10 unless otherwise indicated)

	Institutions	Teachers	Students		
			Males	Females	Total
Pre-primary	24*	605	11,127	10,082	21,209
Primary	2,660†	30,227	973,325	706,336	1,679,661
Secondary	n.a.	14,057	318,002	130,752	448,754
Tertiary	n.a.	2,372‡	18,866	3,264	22,130

* 1994/95 figure; public institutions only.
† 1995/96.
‡ 2008/09.

Source: mainly UNESCO Institute for Statistics.

Pupil-teacher ratio (primary education, UNESCO estimate): 62.2 in 2009/10 (Source: UNESCO Institute for Statistics).

Adult literacy rate (UNESCO estimates): 34.5% (males 45.0%; females 24.2%) in 2010 (Source: UNESCO Institute for Statistics).

Directory

The Constitution

The Constitution of the Republic of Chad, which was adopted by national referendum on 31 March 1996, enshrines a unitary state. The President is elected for a term of five years by direct universal adult suffrage. The Prime Minister, who is appointed by the President, nominates the Council of Ministers. The legislature comprises a 188-member Assemblée nationale, which is elected by direct universal adult suffrage for a term of four years. The Constitution provides for an independent judicial system, with a High Court of Justice, and the establishment of a Constitutional Court and a High Council for Communication.

Constitutional amendments approved by the Assemblée nationale in May 2004 and confirmed by referendum in June 2005 provided for the abolition of the restriction on the number of terms that the President is permitted to serve (hitherto, the Head of State had been restricted to two terms in office), and for the abolition of an upper legislative chamber, the Sénat, provided for in the 1996 Constitution (which had not, however, been established). The amendments also provided for the establishment of a Conseil Économique, Social et Culturel, the members of which would be appointed by the President of the Republic.

The Government

HEAD OF STATE

President: Gen. IDRISS DEBY ITNO (assumed office 4 December 1990; elected President 3 July 1996; re-elected 20 May 2001, 3 May 2006 and 25 April 2011).

COUNCIL OF MINISTERS

(September 2012)

Prime Minister: EMMANUEL NADINGAR.

Minister of External Relations and African Integration: MOUSSA FAKI MAHAMAT.

Minister of Finance and the Budget: CHRISTIAN GEORGES DIGUIMBAYE.

Minister of Infrastructure and Equipment: ABBAS TOLLI.

Minister of Territorial Administration and Decentralization: BACHAR ALI SOULEYMANE.

Minister of Posts and New Information Technology: JEAN BAWOYEU ALINGUÉ.

Minister of Urban and Rural Water Supply: MAHAMAT ALI ABDALLAH.

Minister of Planning, the Economy and International Cooperation: BEDOUMRA KORDIÉ.

Minister of Justice, Keeper of the Seals: Dr ABDOULAYE SABRE FADOUL.

Minister of Public Health: Dr MAMOUTH NAHOR N'GAWARA.

Minister of Agriculture and Irrigation: Dr DJIMET ADOUM.

Minister of Pastoral Development and Animal Production: Dr MOCTAR MOUSSA MAHAMAT.

Minister of Public Sanitation and the Promotion of Good Governance: (vacant).

Minister of Public Security and Immigration: ABDELKÉRIM AHMADAYE BAKHIT.

Minister of Information and Communication, Government Spokesperson: HASSAN SILLA BAKARI.

Minister of the Environment and Fisheries: MAHAMAT OKORMI.

Minister of Social Action, Families and National Solidarity: FATIMÉ ISSA RAMADAN.

Minister of Higher Education: Dr AHMET DJIDDA MAHAMAT.

Minister of Secondary Education: OUMAR BEN MOUSSA.

Minister of Primary and Civic Education: FAÏTCHOU ETIENNE.

Minister of Professional Training of Arts and Crafts: DAYANG MENWA ENOCH.

Minister of Youth and Sports: HAÏKAL ZAKARIA BEN DJIBRINE.

Minister of Energy and Petroleum: BRAHIM ALKHALI.

Minister of Mines and Geology: NOJITOLBAYE KLADOUMADJI.

Minister of Land Settlement, Town Planning and Housing: ASSANE NGUÉADOUM.

Minister, in charge of Microfinance for the Promotion of Women and Youth: YAKOURA MALLOUM.

Minister of the Civil Service and Labour: MAHAMAT ABBA ALI SALAH.

Minister of Transport and Civil Aviation: ABDELKÉRIM SOULEYMANE TÉRIAO.

Minister of Trade and Industry: MAHAMAT ALLAHOU TAHER.

Minister of Land Affairs and State Property: JEAN BERNARD PADARÉ.

Minister of Small and Medium-sized Enterprises: HASSAN TÉRAP.

Minister of Human and Fundamental Rights: AMINA KODJIYANA.

Minister of Tourism and Handicrafts: ABDELRASSOUL ABOUBAKAR.

Minister of Culture: KHAYAR OUMAR DÉFALLAH.

Minister-delegate at the Presidency of the Republic, responsible for National Defence and War Veterans: BÉNANDO TATOLA.

Minister, Secretary-General of the Government, in charge of Relations with the National Assembly: SAMIR ADAM ANNOUR.

Secretary of State for External Relations and African Integration: TÉDÉBÉ RUTH.

Secretary of State for Territorial Administration and Decentralization: MAHAMAT MBODOU ABDOULAYE.

Secretary of State for Finance and the Budget: ROZZI MAMAÏ.

Secretary of State for Public Health: YOUSSOUF AHMAT.

Deputy Secretary-General of the Government, responsible for Relations with the National Assembly: GAOURANG BARAMA.

MINISTRIES

Office of the President: Palais rose, BP 74, N'Djamena; tel. 22-51-44-37; fax 22-52-45-01; e-mail Contact@presidencedutchad.org; internet www.presidencedutchad.org.

Office of the Prime Minister: BP 463, N'Djamena; tel. 22-52-63-39; fax 22-52-69-77; e-mail cpcprimt@intnet.td; internet www.primature-tchad.org.

Ministry of Agriculture and Irrigation: BP 441, N'Djamena; tel. 22-52-65-66; fax 22-52-51-19; e-mail conacils@intnet.td.

Ministry of the Civil Service and Labour: BP 637, N'Djamena; tel. and fax 22-52-21-98.

Ministry of Culture: BP 519, N'Djamena; tel. 22-52-26-58.

Ministry of Energy and Petroleum: BP 816, N'Djamena; tel. 22-52-56-03; fax 22-52-36-66; e-mail mme@intnet.td; internet www.ministere-petrole.td.

Ministry of the Environment and Fisheries: BP 905, N'Djamena; tel. 22-52-60-12; fax 22-52-38-39; e-mail facdrem@intnet.td.

Ministry of External Relations and African Integration: BP 746, N'Djamena; tel. 22-51-80-50; fax 22-51-45-85; e-mail tchaddiplomatie@gmail.com; internet www.tchad-diplomatie.org.

Ministry of Finance and the Budget: BP 816, N'Djamena; tel. 22-52-68-61; fax 22-52-49-08; e-mail d.dette@intnet.td.

Ministry of Higher Education: BP 743, N'Djamena; tel. 22-51-61-58; fax 22-51-92-31.

Ministry of Human and Fundamental Rights: N'Djamena.

Ministry of Information and Communication: BP 892, N'Djamena; tel. 22-52-40-97; fax 22-52-65-60.

Ministry of Infrastructure and Equipment: N'Djamena; internet infrastructures-tchad.org.

Ministry of Justice: BP 426, N'Djamena; tel. 22-52-21-72; fax 22-52-21-39; e-mail justice@intnet.td.

Ministry of Land Affairs and State Property: N'Djamena.

Ministry of Land Settlement, Town Planning and Housing: BP 436, N'Djamena; tel. 22-52-31-89; fax 22-52-39-35.

Ministry of Microfinance for the Promotion of Women and Youth: N'Djamena.

Ministry of Mines and Geology: BP 816, N'Djamena; tel. 22-51-83-06; fax 22-52-75-60; e-mail cons.mines@intnet.td.

Ministry of National Defence: BP 916, N'Djamena; tel. 22-52-35-13; fax 22-52-65-44.

Ministry of Pastoral Development and Animal Production: BP 750, N'Djamena; tel. 22-52-89-43.

Ministry of Planning, the Economy and International Cooperation: N'Djamena; tel. 22-51-45-87; fax 22-51-51-85; e-mail spee@intnet.td.

Ministry of Posts and New Information Technology: BP 154, N'Djamena; tel. 22-52-15-79; fax 22-52-15-30; e-mail ahmatgamar1@yahoo.fr.

Ministry of Primary and Civic Education: BP 743, N'Djamena; tel. 22-51-92-65; fax 22-51-45-12.

Ministry of Professional Training of Arts and Crafts: N'Djamena.

Ministry of Public Health: BP 440, N'Djamena; tel. 22-51-51-14; fax 22-51-58-00; internet www.sante-tchad.org.

Ministry of Public Sanitation and the Promotion of Good Governance: N'Djamena.

Ministry of Public Security and Immigration: BP 916, N'Djamena; tel. 22-52-05-76.

Ministry of Secondary Education: N'Djamena.

Ministry of Small and Medium-sized Enterprises: N'Djamena.

Ministry of Social Action, Families and National Solidarity: BP 80, N'Djamena; tel. 22-52-25-32; fax 22-52-48-88.

Ministry of Territorial Administration and Decentralization: Niamey.

Ministry of Tourism and Handicrafts: BP 86, N'Djamena; tel. 22-52-44-21; fax 22-52-51-19.

Ministry of Trade and Industry: Palais du Gouvernement, BP 424, N'Djamena; tel. 22-52-21-99; fax 22-52-27-33; e-mail mdjca-dg@intnet.td.

Ministry of Transport and Civil Aviation: N'Djamena.

Ministry of Urban and Rural Water Supply: N'Djamena.

Ministry of Youth and Sports: BP 519, N'Djamena; tel. 22-52-52-90; fax 22-52-55-38.

President and Legislature

PRESIDENT

Election, 24–25 April 2011, provisional results

Candidate	Votes	% of vote
Idriss Deby Itno (MPS)	2,503,813	88.66
Pahimi Padacke Albert (RNDT—le Réveil)	170,182	6.03
Nadji Madou (ASRI)	150,220	5.32
Total	2,824,215	100.00

LEGISLATURE

Assemblée nationale

Palais du 15 janvier, BP 01, N'Djamena; tel. 22-53-00-15; fax 22-31-45-90; internet www.primature-tchad.org/ass.php.

President: NASSOUR GUÉLENDOUKSIA OUAÏDOU.

General Election, 13 February 2011

Party	Seats
Alliance pour la Renaissance du Tchad (ART)*	132
Union Nationale pour le Développement et le Renouveau (UNDR)	11
Rassemblement National pour la Démocratie au Tchad—le Réveil	8
Union pour le Renouveau et la Démocratie-Parti pour la Liberté et le Développement (URD-PLD)	8
Fédération Action pour la République-Parti Fédération (FAR-PF)	4
Convention Tchadienne pour la Paix et le Développement (CTPD)	2
Parti Démocratique et Socialiste pour l'Alternance (PDSA)	2
Union pour la Démocratie et la République (UDR)	2
Others†	15
Total	184‡

* Comprising the Mouvement Patriotique du Salut, the Rassemblement pour la Démocratie et le Progrès and VIVA—Rassemblement National pour la Démocratie et le Progrès.

† A total of 15 other parties all secured one seat each.

‡ Results in the Mayo-Boneye constituency, which was to return four deputies, were not declared by the Commission Électorale Nationale Indépendante.

Election Commission

Commission Électorale Nationale Indépendante (CENI): N'Djamena; internet www.ceni-td.org; f. 2000; 31 mems; Pres. YAYA MAHAMAT LIGUITA.

Political Organizations

Legislation permitting the operation of political associations, subject to official registration, took effect in October 1991. A total of 101 political organizations contested the 2011 legislative elections, of which the following were among the most important:

Action Tchadienne pour l'Unité et le Socialisme (ACTUS): N'Djamena; e-mail actus@club-internet.fr; f. 1981; Marxist-Leninist; Sec.-Gen. Dr DJIMADOUM LEY-NGARDIGAL.

Alliance Nationale pour la Démocratie et le Développement (ANDD): BP 4066, N'Djamena; tel. 22-51-46-72; f. 1992; Leader SALIBOU GARBA.

Alliance Socialiste pour un Renouveau Intégral (ASRI): tel. 66-28-74-10; e-mail info@asritchad.org; internet www.asritchad.org; Pres. NADJI MADOU.

Alliance Tchadienne pour la Démocratie et le Développement (ATD): N'Djamena; e-mail info@atd-tchad.com; Leader ABDERAMAN DJASNABAILLE.

Concorde Nationale Tchadienne (CNT): Leader Col HASSANE SALEH AL GADAM AL JINEDI.

Convention pour la Démocratie et le Fédéralisme: N'Djamena; f. 2002; socialist; supports the establishment of a federal state; Leader ALI GOLHOR.

Convention Tchadienne pour la Paix et le Développement (CTPD).

Coordination des Partis Politiques pour la Défense de la Constitution (CPDC): f. 2004 to oppose President Deby's proposed constitutional modifications; mems include the URD and the UNDR.

Fédération Action pour la République-Parti Fédération (FAR-PF): BP 4197, N'Djamena; tel. 66-26-89-67 (mobile); fax 22-51-78-60; e-mail yorongar@gmail.com; internet www.yorongar.com; supports the establishment of a federal republic; Leader NGARLEDJY YORONGAR.

Front pour le Salut de la République (FSR): f. 2007 to unite opposition groups in attempt to oust President Deby Itno; member of the Mouvement National Coalition; Pres. Col AHMAT HASSABALLAH SOUBIANE.

Mouvement Patriotique du Salut (MPS): Assemblée nationale, Palais du 15 janvier, BP 01, N'Djamena; e-mail administrateur@tchad-gpmps.org; internet www.tchad-gpmps.org; f. 1990 as a coalition of several opposition movements; other opposition groups joined during the Nov. 1990 offensive against the regime of Hissène Habré, and following the movement's accession to power in Dec. 1990; Pres. D'IDRISS NDELE MOUSSA; Sec.-Gen. NEGOUM YAMASSOUM.

Parti Démocratique et Socialiste pour l'Alternance (PDSA).

Parti pour la Liberté et le Développement (PLD): N'Djamena; f. 1993; boycotted legislative elections in 2002; Sec.-Gen. IBN OUMAR MAHAMAT SALEH.

Rassemblement pour la Démocratie et le Progrès (RDP): N'Djamena; f. 1992; seeks to create a secure political environment by the establishment of a reformed national army; supported the re-election of Pres. Deby in 2001, but withdrew support from the Govt in Nov. 2003; Leader LOL MAHAMAT CHOUA.

Rassemblement National pour la Démocratie au Tchad—le Réveil: Leader ALBERT PAHIMI PADACKE.

Union pour la Démocratie et la République (UDR): N'Djamena; f. 1992; supports liberal economic policies and a secular, decentralized republic; boycotted legislative elections in 2002; Leader Dr JEAN BAWOYEU ALINGUÉ.

Union Nationale pour le Développement et le Renouveau (UNDR): N'Djamena; supports greater decentralization and increased limitations on the power of the state; Pres. SALEH KEBZABOH; Sec.-Gen. CÉLESTIN TOPONA.

Union pour le Renouveau et la Démocratie (URD): BP 92, N'Djamena; tel. 22-51-44-23; fax 22-51-41-87; f. 1992; Leader (vacant).

VIVA—Rassemblement National pour la Démocratie et le Progrès (VIVA—RNDP): N'Djamena; f. 1992; supports a unitary, democratic republic; Pres. KASSIRÉ DELWA COUMAKOYE.

A number of unregistered dissident groups (some based abroad) are also active. In 2010 these organizations, largely 'politico-military', included the following:

Alliance Nationale de la Résistance (ANR): f. 1996 as alliance of five movements; in early 2003 comprised eight rebel groups based in eastern Chad; signed peace agreement with Govt in Jan. 2003, although FONALT rejected this accord; Leader MAHAMAT ABBO SILECK.

Armée Nationale Tchadienne en Dissidence (ANTD): f. 1994; Leader Col MAHAMAT GARFA.

Forces des Organisations Nationales pour l'Alternance et les Libertés au Tchad (FONALT): rejected cease-fire signed by ANR with Govt in Jan. 2003; Leader Col ABDOULAYE ISSAKA SARWA.

Coordination des Mouvements Armés et Partis Politiques de l'Opposition (CMAP): internet www.maxpages.com/tchad/cmap2; f. 1999 by 13 'politico-military' orgs; a number of groups subsequently left, several of which later joined the FUDP (q.v.); Leader ANTOINE BANGUI.

Front Extérieur pour la Rénovation: Leader ANTOINE BANGUI.

Front de Libération Nationale du Tchad—Conseil Provisoire de la Révolution (FROLINAT—CPR): f. 1968 in Sudan; based in Algeria; Leader GOUKOUNI OUEDDEI.

Front Uni pour le Changement Démocratique (FUCD): f. 2005; signed a peace agreement with the Govt in Dec. 2006; Leader Capt. MAHAMAT NOUR ABDELKERIM.

Rassemblement pour la Démocratie et les Libertés (RDL): f. 2005 in Eastern Chad; Leader Capt. MAHAMAT NOUR ABDELKERIM.

Socle pour le Changement, l'Unité Nationale et la Démocratie (SCUD): f. 2005 in Eastern Chad; Leaders TOM ERDIMI, YAYA DILLO DJÉROU.

Front Uni pour la Démocratie et la Paix (FUDP): f. 2003 in Benin; seeks by all possible means to establish a new constitution and a transitional govt in advance of free and transparent elections; faction of MDJT (q.v.) led by Adoum Togoi Abbo claims membership, but this is rejected by principal faction of MDJT; Pres. Brig.-Gen. ADOUM TOGOI ABBO.

Conseil National de Redressement du Tchad (CNR): e-mail admin@cnrdutchad.com; internet www.cnrdutchad.com; leadership of group forced to leave Benin for Togo in mid-2003; Pres. Col ABBAS KOTY YACOUB.

Convention Populaire de Résistance (CPR): e-mail cpr60@voila.fr; f. 2001 by fmr mems of CNR (q.v.); Leader ABDEL-AZIZ ABDALLAH KODOK.

Front National du Tchad Renové (FNTR): Dabo, France; e-mail yasaid2001@yahoo.fr; internet www.maxpages.com/tchad/fntr; f. 1996; based in Dabo (France); publishes monthly bulletin, *Al-Widha*, in French and Arabic; Hon. Pres. MAHAMAT CHARFADINE; Sec.-Gen. SALAHADINE MAHADI.

Mouvement Nationale des Rénovateurs Tchadiens (MNRT): e-mail fpls@romandie.com; democratic opposition in exile; Sec.-Gen. ALI MUHAMMAD DIALLO.

Rassemblement des Forces pour le Changement (RFC): internet www.rfctchad.com; f. 2006 as Rassemblement des forces démocratiques; Pres. TIMANE ERDIMI.

Union des Forces pour le Changement (UFC): f. 2004; advocates suspension of the 1996 Constitution and the composition of a new Charter of the Republic to develop national unity, free, transparent elections and the rule of law; National Co-ordinator ACHEIKH IBN OUMAR.

Conseil Démocratique Révolutionnaire (CDR): Leader ACHEIKH IBN OUMAR.

Front Démocratique Populaire (FDP): Leader Dr MAHAMOUT NAHOR.

Front Populaire pour la Renaissance Nationale: Leader ADOUM YACOUB KOUKOU.

Mouvement pour la Démocratie et le Développement (MDD): e-mail mdd@mdd-tchad.com; internet membres.lycos.fr/mddtchad; comprises two factions, led by ISSA FAKI MAHAMAT and BRAHIM MALLAH.

Mouvement pour la Démocratie et la Justice au Tchad (MDJT): based in Tibesti, northern Chad; e-mail admin@mdjt.net; internet www.mdjt.net; fmr deputy leader, Brig.-Gen. ADOUM TOGOI ABBO, signed a peace agreement with Govt in Jan. 2002, although this was subsequently rejected by elements close to fmr leader, YOUSSOUF TOGOIMI (who died in Sept. 2002); split into two factions in 2003; the faction led by Togoi claimed membership of the FUDP (q.v.) and signed a peace agreement with the Govt in Dec. 2003, which was rejected by the faction led by Chair. Col HASSAN ABDALLAH MARDIGUÉ; announced a proposed merger with FROLINAT—CPR in December 2006.

Mouvement pour l'Unité et la République (MUR): f. 2000 by faction of the MDD (q.v.); Pres. HASSAN DADJOULA.

Union des Forces pour la Démocratie et le Développement (UFDD): f. 2006; Leader Gen. MAHAMAT NOURI.

Union des Forces pour la Démocratie et le Développement—Fondamentale (UFDD—F): Leader ABDELWAHID ABOUD MAKAYE.

Diplomatic Representation

EMBASSIES IN CHAD

Algeria: BP 178, rue de Paris, N'Djamena; tel. 22-52-38-15; fax 22-52-37-92; e-mail amb.algerie@intnet.td; Ambassador NADJIB MAHDI.

Cameroon: rue des Poids Lourds, BP 58, N'Djamena; tel. 22-52-28-94; Ambassador BAH OUMAROU SANDA.

Central African Republic: rue 1036, près du Rond-Point de la Garde, BP 115, N'Djamena; tel. 22-52-32-06; Ambassador DAVID NGUINDO.

China, People's Republic: BP 735, N'Djamena; tel. 22-52-29-49; fax 22-53-00-45; internet td.china-embassy.org; Ambassador YANG GUANGYU.

Congo, Democratic Republic: ave du 20 août, BP 910, N'Djamena; tel. 22-52-21-83.

Egypt: Quartier Clemat, ave Georges Pompidou, auprès rond-point de la SONASUT, BP 1094, N'Djamena; tel. 22-51-09-73; fax 22-51-09-72; e-mail am.egypte@intnet.td; Ambassador NABIH ABDELMADJID AL DAÏROUTI.

France: rue du Lt Franjoux, BP 431, N'Djamena; tel. 22-52-25-75; fax 22-52-28-55; e-mail amba.france@intnet.td; internet www.ambafrance-td.org; Ambassador BRUNO FOUCHER.

Holy See: rue de Béguinage, BP 490, N'Djamena; tel. 22-52-31-15; fax 22-52-38-27; e-mail nonceapo@intnet.td; Apostolic Nuncio Most Rev. JUDE THADDEUS OKOLO (Titular Archbishop of Novica).

Korea, Democratic People's Republic: N'Djamena; Ambassador KIM PYONG GI.

Libya: BP 1096, N'Djamena; tel. 22-51-92-89; e-mail alibya1@intnet.td; Ambassador GRÈNE SALEH GRÈNE.

Nigeria: 35 ave Charles de Gaulle, BP 752, N'Djamena; tel. 22-52-24-98; fax 22-52-30-92; e-mail nigndjam@intnet.td; Ambassador GARBA ABDU ZAKARI.

Russia: 2 rue Adjutant Collin, BP 891, N'Djamena; tel. 22-51-57-19; fax 22-51-31-72; e-mail amrus@intnet.td; Ambassador VLADIMIR N. MARTYNOV.

Saudi Arabia: Quartier Aéroport, rue Jander Miry, BP 974, N'Djamena; tel. 22-52-31-28; fax 22-52-33-28; e-mail najdiat.tchad@intnet.td; Ambassador ADIL DJAMIL ARIF.

Sudan: rue de la Gendarmerie, BP 45, N'Djamena; tel. 22-52-43-59; e-mail amb.soudan@intnet.td; Ambassador ABDALLAH AL-SHEIKH.

USA: ave Félix Eboué, BP 413, N'Djamena; tel. 22-51-70-09; fax 22-51-56-54; e-mail YingraD@state.gov; internet chad.usembassy.gov; Ambassador MARK M. BOULWARE, Jr.

Judicial System

The highest judicial authority is the Supreme Court, which comprises a Judicial Chamber, an Administrative Chamber and an Audit Chamber. There is also a Constitutional Council, with final jurisdiction in matters of state. The legal structure also comprises the Court of Appeal, and magistrate and criminal courts. A High Court of Justice, which is competent to try the President or members of the Government in cases of treason, embezzlement of public funds, and certain other crimes and offences, was inaugurated in June 2003.

Supreme Court: rue 0221, Quartier Résidentiel, 1er arrondissement, BP 5495, N'Djamena; tel. 22-52-01-99; fax 22-52-51-81; e-mail ccsrp@intnet.td; internet www.coursupreme-tchad.org; Pres. ABDEL-RAHIM BREMÉ HAMID; Pres. of the Judicial Chamber BELKOULAYE BEN COUMAREAUX; Pres. of the Administrative Chamber OUSMAME SALAH IDJEMI; Pres. of the Audit Chamber DOLOTAN NOUDJALBAYE; Prosecutor-Gen. AHMAT AGREY.

Constitutional Council: BP 5500, N'Djamena; tel. 22-52-03-41; e-mail conseil.sg@intnet.td; internet www.primature-tchad.org/cc.php; Pres. HOUDEÏNGAR DAVID NGARIMADEN; Sec.-Gen. DARKEM JOSEPH.

Court of Appeal: N'Djamena; tel. 22-51-24-26; Pres. MAKI ADAM ISSAKA.

High Court of Justice: BP 1407, N'Djamena; tel. 22-52-33-54; fax 22-52-35-35; e-mail dchcj@intnet.td; internet www.primature-tchad.org/hdj.php; f. 2003; comprises 15 deputies of the Assemblée nationale, of whom 10 are titular judges and five supplementaries, who serve in the absence of a titular judge. All 15 are elected for the term of four years by their peers; competent to try the President and members of the Government in cases of treason, embezzlement of public funds, and certain other crimes and offences; Pres. ADOUM GOUDJA.

Religion

It is estimated that some 50% of the population are Muslims and about 30% Christians. Most of the remainder follow animist beliefs.

ISLAM

Conseil Suprème des Affaires Islamiques: POB 1101, N'Djamena; tel. 22-51-81-80; fax 22-52-58-84; Pres. CHEIKH HISSEIN HASSAN ABAKAR.

CHRISTIANITY

The Roman Catholic Church

Chad comprises one archdiocese, six dioceses and one apostolic vicariate. Approximately 9% of the total population are Roman Catholics, most of whom reside in the south of the country and in N'Djamena.

Bishops' Conference

Conférence Episcopale du Tchad, BP 456, N'Djamena; tel. 22-51-74-44; fax 22-52-50-51; e-mail secreta.cet@intnet.td.

f. 1991; Pres. Most Rev. JEAN-CLAUDE BOUCHARD (Bishop of Pala).

Archbishop of N'Djamena: Most Rev. MATTHIAS N'GARTÉRI MAYADI, Archevêché, BP 456, N'Djamena; tel. 22-51-74-44; fax 22-52-50-51; e-mail archnja@intnet.td.

Protestant Churches

Entente des Eglises et Missions Evangéliques au Tchad (EEMET): BP 2006, N'Djamena; tel. 22-51-53-93; fax 22-51-87-20; e-mail eemet@intnet.td; f. 1964; asscn of churches and missions working in Chad; includes Assemblées Chrétiennes au Tchad (ACT), Assemblées de Dieu au Tchad (ADT), Eglise Evangélique des Frères au Tchad (EEFT), Eglise Evangélique au Tchad (EET), Eglise Fraternelle Luthérienne au Tchad (EFLT), Eglise Evangélique en Afrique Centrale au Tchad (EEACT), Eglise Evangélique Missionnaire au Tchad (EEMT); also five assoc. mems: Union des Jeunes Chrétiens (UJC), Groupe Biblique des Hôpitaux au Tchad (GBHT), Mission Evangélique contre la Lèpre (MECL), Croix Bleue du Tchad (CBT); Sec.-Gen. Mathias N'Gartéri Mayadi.

BAHÁ'Í FAITH

National Spiritual Assembly: BP 181, N'Djamena; tel. 22-51-47-05; e-mail ntirandaz@aol.com.

The Press

Al-Watan: N'Djamena; tel. 22-51-57-96; weekly; Editor-in-Chief Moussa Ndorkoï.

Audy Magazine: BP 780, N'Djamena; tel. 22-51-49-59; f. 2000; 2 a month; women's interest; Dir Tongrongou Agouna Grâce.

Bulletin Mensuel de Statistiques du Tchad: BP 453, N'Djamena; monthly.

Carrefour: Centre al-Mouna, BP 456, N'Djamena; tel. 22-51-42-54; e-mail almouna@intnet.td; f. 2000; every 2 months; Dir Sister Nadia Karaki; circ. 1,000 (2001).

Comnat: BP 731, N'Djamena; tel. 22-51-46-75; fax 22-51-46-71; quarterly; publ. by Commission Nationale Tchadienne for UNESCO.

Grenier: BP 1128, N'Djamena; tel. 22-53-30-14; e-mail cedesep@intnet.td; monthly; economics; finance; Dir Kohom Ngar-One David.

Info-Tchad: BP 670, N'Djamena; tel. 22-51-58-67; news bulletin issued by Agence-Info Tchad; daily; French.

La Lettre: BP 2037, N'Djamena; tel. and fax 22-51-91-09; e-mail ltdh@intnet.td; f. 1993; monthly; publ. by the Ligue Tchadienne des Droits de l'Homme; Dir Dobian Assingar.

N'Djamena Bi-Hebdo: BP 4498, N'Djamena; tel. 22-51-53-14; fax 22-52-14-98; e-mail ndjh@intnet.td; internet www.ndjh.org; f. 1989; 2 a week; Arabic and French; Dir Yaldet Bégoto Oulatar; Editor-in-Chief Dieudonné Djonabaye; circ. 3,000 (2010).

Notre Temps: BP 4352, N'Djamena; tel. and fax 22-51-46-50; e-mail ntemps.presse@yahoo.fr; f. 2000; weekly; opposed to the Govt of Pres. Deby Itno; Editorial Dir Nadjikimo Benoudjita; circ. 3,000 (2010).

L'Observateur: BP 2031, N'Djamena; tel. and fax 22-51-80-05; e-mail observer.presse@intnet.td; f. 1997; weekly; Dir Ngaradoumbe Sambory; circ. 4,000 (2010).

Le Progrès: 1976 ave Charles de Gaulle, BP 3055, N'Djamena; tel. 22-51-55-86; fax 22-51-02-56; e-mail progres@intnet.td; f. 1993; daily; Dir Mahamat Hissène; circ. 3,000 (2010).

Revue Juridique Tchadienne: BP 907, N'Djamena; internet www.cefod.org/Droit_au_Tchad/Revuejuridique/Sommaire_rjt.htm; f. 1999; Dir Mahamat Saleh Ben Biang.

Tchad et Culture: BP 907, N'Djamena; tel. 22-51-54-32; fax 22-51-91-50; e-mail cefod@intnet.td; internet www.cefod.org; f. 1961; monthly; Dir Ronelngué Toriaïra; Editor-in-Chief Naygotimti Bambé; circ. 4,500 (2002).

Le Temps: face Ecole Belle-vue, Moursal, BP 1333, N'Djamena; tel. 22-51-70-28; fax 22-51-99-24; e-mail temps.presse@intnet.td; f. 1995; weekly; Publishing Dir Michaël N. Didama; circ. 4,000 (2010).

La Voix: N'Djamena; weekly; circ. 5,000 (2010).

La Voix du Paysan: BP 1671, N'Djamena; tel. 22-51-82-66; monthly; Dir Djaldi Tabdi Gassissou Nasser.

NEWS AGENCY

Agence Tchadienne de Presse: BP 670, N'Djamena; tel. 22-52-58-67; fax 22-52-37-74; e-mail atp@infotchad.com; internet www.infotchad.com; f. 1966; Dir Hassan Abdelkerim Bouyebri.

Publishers

Grande Imprimerie du Tchad: route de Farcha, BP 691, N'Djamena; tel. 22-52-51-59.

Imprimerie AGB: ave Ornano, BP 2052, N'Djamena; tel. 22-51-21-67; e-mail agb@intnet.td.

Imprimerie du Tchad (IDT): BP 456, N'Djamena; tel. 22-52-44-40; fax 22-52-28-60; e-mail idt.tchad@intnet.td; Gen. Dir D. E. Maurin.

Broadcasting and Communications

TELECOMMUNICATIONS

In 2011 there was one fixed-line telephone and three mobile cellular telephone operators in Chad.

Office Tchadien de Regulation des Telecommunications: BP 5808, N'Djamena; tel. 52-15-13; fax 52-15-15; e-mail otrt@intnet.td; internet www.otrt.td; regulatory authority; Dir-Gen. Idriss Saleh Bachar.

Société des Télécommunications du Tchad (SOTEL TCHAD): BP 1132, N'Djamena; tel. 22-52-14-36; fax 22-52-14-42; e-mail sotel@intnet.td; internet www.sotel.td; f. 2000 by merger of telecommunications services of fmr Office National des Postes et des Télécommunications and the Société des Télécommunications Internationales du Tchad; Dir-Gen. Adam Abderamane Anou.

Salam: N'Djamena; wholly owned subsidiary of SOTEL TCHAD providing mobile cellular telephone services.

Airtel au Tchad: ave Charles de Gaulle, BP 5665, N'Djamena; tel. 22-52-04-18; fax 22-52-04-19; e-mail info.africa@airtel.com; internet africa.airtel.com/chad; f. 2000; acquired by Bharti Airtel (India) in 2010; fmrly Celtel-Tchad, subsequently Zain au Tchad, present name adopted in 2010; provides mobile cellular telecommunications in N'Djamena, Moundou and Abéché, with expansion to further regions proposed; Dir-Gen. Mbaye Sylla Khouma.

Millicom Tchad: N'Djamena; internet www.millicom.com; f. 2005; 87% owned by Millicom International Cellular (Luxembourg/Sweden); operates mobile cellular telecommunications network in N'Djamena (with expansion to other cities proposed) under the brand name 'Tigo'.

BROADCASTING

Regulatory Authorities

High Council of Communication (HCC): BP 1316, N'Djamena; tel. 22-52-36-00; fax 22-52-31-51; e-mail hcc@intnet.td; f. 1994; responsible for registration and regulation of radio and television stations, in addition to the printed press; funds independent radio stations; Sec.-Gen. Adoum Guemessou.

Office National de la Radiodiffusion et de la Télévision du Tchad (ONRTV): ave Mobotu, N'Djamena; tel. 22-52-15-13; fax 22-52-15-17; internet www.onrtv.org; Doubaï Kleptouin.

Radio

Private radio stations have been permitted to operate in Chad since 1994, although private broadcasts did not begin until 1997. By mid-2002 15 private and community stations had received licences, of which nine had commenced broadcasts. There was, additionally, a state-owned broadcaster, with four regional stations.

Radio Nationale Tchadienne (RNT): BP 4589, N'Djamena; tel. and fax 22-51-60-71; f. 1955; state-controlled; programmes in French, Arabic and 11 vernacular languages; four regional stations; Dir Hassan Silla Bakari.

Radio Abéché: BP 36, Abéché, Ouaddaï; tel. 269-81-49.

Radio Faya-Largeau: Faya-Largeau, Borkou.

Radio Moundou: BP 122, Moundou, Logone Occidental; tel. 269-13-22; programmes in French, Sara and Arabic; Dir Dimanangar Djaïnta.

Radio Sarh: BP 270, Sarh, Bahr Kôh; tel. 268-13-61; programmes in French, Sara and Arabic; Dir Biana Fouda Nactouandi.

Union des Radios Privées du Tchad (URPT): N'Djamena; f. 2002 as a federation of nine private and community radio stations; Pres. Zara Yacoub; Sec.-Gen. Djekourninga Kaoutar Lazar; includes the following:

DJA FM: BP 1312, N'Djamena; tel. 22-51-64-90; fax 22-52-14-52; e-mail myzara@intnet.td; f. 1999; music, cultural and informative programmes in French, Arabic and Sara; Dir Zara Yacoub.

Radio Brakoss (Radio de l'Agriculture): Moïssala, Mandoul; f. 1996; community radio station; operations suspended by the Govt in Feb. 2004, broadcasts resumed June 2004.

Radio Duji Lohar: BP 155, Moundou, Logone Occidental; tel. 22-69-17-14; fax 22-69-12-11; e-mail cdave@intnet.td; f. 2001.

Radio FM Liberté: BP 892, N'Djamena; tel. 22-51-42-53; f. 2000; financed by nine civil society orgs; broadcasts in French, Arabic and Sara; Dir Djekourninga Kaoutar Lazar.

Radio Lotiko: Diocese de Sarh, BP 87, Sarh; tel. 22-68-12-46; fax 22-68-14-79; e-mail lotiko@intnet.td; internet www.lotiko.org;

f. 2001; community radio station; Dir ABBÉ FIDÈLE ALLAHADOUM-BAYE.

La Voix du Paysan: BP 22, Doba, Logone Oriental; f. 1996; Roman Catholic; Dir DJALDI TABDI GASSISSOU NASSER.

Television

Télévision Nationale Tchadienne (Télé Tchad): BP 274, N'Djamena; tel. 22-52-26-79; fax 22-52-29-23; state-controlled; broadcasts c. 38 hours per week in French and Arabic; Dir HALIMÉ ASSADYA ALI.

Broadcasts from Africa 24, Canal France International, France 24, TV5, CNN and seven Arabic television stations are also received in Chad.

Finance

(cap. = capital; res = reserves; dep. = deposits; m. = million; br(s). = branch(es); amounts in francs CFA)

BANKING

In 2009 there were nine commercial banks in Chad.

Central Bank

Banque des Etats de l'Afrique Centrale (BEAC): ave Charles de Gaulle, BP 50, N'Djamena; tel. 22-52-21-65; fax 22-52-44-87; e-mail beacndj@beac.int; internet www.beac.int; HQ in Yaoundé, Cameroon; f. 1973; bank of issue for mem. states of the Communauté Economique et Monétaire de l'Afrique Centrale (CEMAC, fmrly Union Douanière et Economique de l'Afrique Centrale), comprising Cameroon, the Central African Repub., Chad, the Repub. of the Congo, Equatorial Guinea and Gabon; cap. 88,000m., res 227,843m., dep. 4,110,966m. (Dec. 2007); Gov. LUCAS ABAGA NCHAMA; Dir in Chad CHRISTIAN NGARDOUM MORNONDE; brs at Moundou and Sarh.

Other Banks

Banque Agricole et Commerciale (BAC): ave el-Niméry, BP 1727, N'Djamena; tel. 22-51-90-41; fax 22-51-90-40; e-mail bast@intnet.td; f. 1997; cap. 1,200m. (2002), total assets 1,845m. (Dec. 1999); Pres. MOUHAMED OUSMAN AWAD; Dir-Gen. ABDELKADER OUSMAN HASSAN; 1 br.

Banque Commerciale du Chari (BCC): ave Charles de Gaulle, BP 757, N'Djamena; tel. 22-51-89-58; fax 22-51-62-49; e-mail bcc@intnet.td; f. 1981 as Banque Tchad-Arabe Libyenne; present name adopted 1995; 50% state-owned, 50% owned by Libya Arab Foreign Bank (Libya); cap. and res 3,567m., total assets 20,931m. (Dec. 2001); Pres. BIDJERE BINDJAKI; Dir-Gen. HAMED EL MISTIRI.

Banque Sahélo-Saharienne pour l'Investissement et le Commerce (BSIC): ave Charles de Gaulle, BP 81, N'Djamena; tel. 22-52-26-92; fax 22-62-26-93; e-mail bsic@bsic-tchad.com; internet www.bsic-tchad.com; f. 2004; Pres. and Dir-Gen. ALHADJI MOHAMED ALWARFALLI.

Commercial Bank Tchad (CBT): rue du Capitaine Ohrel, BP 19, N'Djamena; tel. 22-52-28-29; fax 22-52-33-18; e-mail cbtbank@cbc-bank.com; internet www.cbc-bank.com; f. 1962; 50.7% owned by Groupe FOTSO (Cameroon), 17.5% state-owned; fmrly Banque de Développement du Tchad; cap. 4,020m., res 2,465m., dep. 38,624m. (Dec. 2005); Pres. YOUSSOUF ABBASALAH; Dir-Gen. GEORGES DJADJO; 1 br.

Orabank Tchad: ave Charles de Gaulle, BP 804, N'Djamena; tel. 22-52-26-60; fax 22-52-29-05; e-mail infitd@financial-bank.com; internet www.financial-bank.com; f. 1992; fmrly Financial Bank Tchad, name changed as above in 2012; 100% owned by Oragroup SA (Togo); cap. 4,350.0m., res 111.6m., dep. 40,191.0m. (Dec. 2009); Pres. PATRICK MESTRALLET; Dir-Gen. LOUKOUMANOU WAIDI.

Société Générale Tchadienne de Banque (SGTB): 2–6 rue Robert Lévy, BP 461, N'Djamena; tel. 22-52-28-01; fax 22-52-37-13; e-mail sgtb@intnet.td; internet www.sgtb.td; f. 1963; 30% owned by Société Générale (France), 15% by Société Générale de Banque au Cameroun; cap. and res 3,603m., total assets 36,579m. (Dec. 2003); Pres. and Dir-Gen. CHEMI KOGRIMI; 3 brs.

Bankers' Organizations

Association Professionnelle des Banques au Tchad: 2–6 rue Robert Lévy, BP 461, N'Djamena; tel. 22-52-41-90; fax 22-52-17-13; Pres. CHEMI KOGRIMI.

Conseil National de Crédit: N'Djamena; f. 1965 to formulate a national credit policy and to organize the banking profession.

INSURANCE

Assureurs Conseils Tchadiens Cecar et Jutheau: rue du Havre, BP 139, N'Djamena; tel. 22-52-21-15; fax 22-52-35-39; e-mail biliou.alikeke@intnet.td; f. 1966; Dir BILIOU ALIKEKE.

Gras Savoye Tchad: rue du Général Thillo, BP 5620, N'Djamena; tel. 22-52-00-72; fax 22-52-00-71; e-mail gras.savoye@intnet.td; affiliated to Gras Savoye (France); Man. DOMKRÉO DJAMON.

Société Mutuelle d'Assurances des Cadres des Professions Libérales et des Indépendants (SMAC): BP 644, N'Djamena; tel. 22-51-70-19; fax 22-51-70-61.

Société Tchadienne d'Assurances et de Réassurances (La STAR Nationale): ave Charles de Gaulle, BP 914, N'Djamena; tel. 22-52-56-77; fax 22-52-51-89; e-mail star@intnet.td; internet www.lastarnationale.com; f. 1977; privatized in 1996; brs in N'Djamena, Moundou and Abéché; cap. 500m.; Dir-Gen. RAKHIS MANNANY.

Trade and Industry

DEVELOPMENT ORGANIZATIONS

Agence Française de Développement (AFD): route de Farcha, BP 478, N'Djamena; tel. 22-52-70-71; fax 22-52-78-31; e-mail afdndjamena@groupe-afd.org; internet www.afd.fr; Country Dir JEAN-MARC PRADELLE.

Association Tchadienne pour le Développement: BP 470, Quartier Sabangali, N'Djamena; tel. 22-51-43-69; fax 22-51-89-23; e-mail darna.dnla@intnet.td; Dir DIGALI ZEUHINBA.

France Volontaires: BP 448, N'Djamena; tel. 22-52-20-53; fax 22-52-26-56; e-mail afvptchd@intnet.td; internet www.france-volontaires.org; f. 1965; name changed as above in 2009; Nat. Delegate ISMAÏLA DIAGNE.

Office National de Développement Rural (ONDR): BP 896, N'Djamena; tel. 22-52-23-20; fax 22-52-29-60; e-mail psapdn@intnet.td; f. 1968; Dir HASSAN GUIHINI DADI.

Service de Coopération et d'Action Culturelle: BP 898, N'Djamena; tel. 22-52-42-87; fax 22-52-44-38; administers bilateral aid from France; Dir PIERRE CATHALA.

Société de Développement du Lac (SODELAC): BP 782, N'Djamena; tel. 22-52-35-03; f. 1967 to develop the area of Lake Chad; cap. 179m. francs CFA; Pres. HASSANTY OUMAR CHAIB; Dir-Gen. ABBO YOUSSOUF.

CHAMBER OF COMMERCE

Chambre de Commerce, d'Industrie, d'Agriculture, des Mines et d'Artisanat: 13 rue du Col Moll, BP 458, N'Djamena; tel. 22-52-52-64; fax 22-52-52-63; e-mail cciama_tchad@yahoo.fr; f. 1935; brs at Sarh, Moundou, Bol and Abéché; Pres. Dr SOURADJ KOULAMALLAH; Dir-Gen. BEKOUTOU TAIGAM.

TRADE ASSOCIATIONS

Office National des Céréales (ONC): BP 21, N'Djamena; tel. 22-52-37-31; fax 22-52-20-18; e-mail onc1@intnet.td; f. 1978; production and marketing of cereals; Dir-Gen. MAHAMAT ALI HASSABALLAH; 11 regional offices.

Société Nationale de Commercialisation du Tchad (SONACOT): BP 630, N'Djamena; tel. 22-51-30-47; f. 1965; cap. 150m. francs CFA; 76% state-owned; nat. marketing, distribution and import-export co; Man. Dir MARBROUCK NATROUD.

EMPLOYERS' ORGANIZATIONS

Conseil National du Patronat Tchadien (CNPT): rue Bazelaire, angle ave Charles de Gaulle, BP 134, N'Djamena; tel. and fax 22-52-25-71; e-mail dgastat.tchad@intnet.td; Pres. MAHAMAT ADOUM ISMAEL; Sec.-Gen. MARC MADENGAR BEREMADJI; 67 mem. enterprises with total work-force of 8,000 (2002).

Union des Transporteurs Tchadiens: N'Djamena; tel. 22-51-45-27.

UTILITIES

Société Nationale d'Électricité (SNE): 11 rue du Col Largeau, BP 44, N'Djamena; tel. 22-51-28-81; fax 22-51-21-34; f. 1968; state-owned; created following the dissolution of the Société Tchadienne d'Eau et d'Electricité (STEE); production and distribution of electricity; Dir-Gen. MAHAMAT SÉNOUSSI CHÉRIF.

Société Tchadienne des Eaux (STE): N'Djamena; f. 2010; Dir-Gen. FÉLICIEN NGASNA MAÏNGAR.

MAJOR COMPANIES

The following are some of the largest private and state-owned companies in terms of capital investment or employment.

Boissons et Glacières du Tchad (BGT): Zone Industrielle de Farcha, BP 656, N'Djamena; tel. 22-51-31-71; fax 22-51-24-77; e-mail bgt@intnet.td; f. 1970; affiliate of Groupe Castel (France); cap. 110m.

francs CFA; production of mineral water, soft drinks and ice; Pres. MARCEL ILLE; Dir GASTON BONLEUX.

Compagnie Sucrière du Tchad (CST): BP 5763, N'Djamena; tel. 22-52-32-70; fax 22-52-28-12; e-mail cst@jlv.com; f. 1976; fmrly Société Nationale Sucrière du Tchad (SONASUT); affiliated to Groupe Somdiaa (France); cap. 6,460m. francs CFA (2001); refining of sugar; mfrs of lump sugar and confectionery; Dir-Gen. IBRAHIM BADJI MOLLIMI; 1,350 employees (2001).

Direction Huilerie Savonnerie (DHS): N'Djamena; f. 2001 by separation from Société Cotonnière du Tchad; production and marketing of cottonseed oil, soap and oilcake; transfer of state-held 75% stake to private ownership pending.

Esso Exploration & Production Chad: rue de Bordeaux, BP 694, N'Djamena; internet www.essochad.com; subsidiary of ExxonMobil Corpn (USA); prospecting for petroleum.

Grande Bijouterie du Tchad SA: BP 1233, N'Djamena; tel. 22-51-31-16; fax 22-51-58-84; sale of gold and diamond jewellery.

Manufacture de Cigarettes du Tchad (MCT): BP 572, N'Djamena; tel. 22-51-21-45; fax 22-51-20-40; f. 1968; cap. 340m. francs CFA; 15% state-owned; mfrs of cigarettes; Pres. PIERRE IMBERT; Man. Dir XAVIER LAMBERT.

Société Cotonnière du Tchad (COTONTCHAD): BP 151, Moundou, Logone Occidental; tel. 22-69-12-10; fax 22-69-13-32; f. 1971; 75% state-owned; restructured 2001; privatization proposed; buying, ginning and marketing of cotton; owns 11 cotton gins; Dir-Gen. DAVID HOUDEINGAR; 1,000 employees (2001).

Société d'Étude et d'Exploitation de la Raffinerie du Tchad (SEERAT): BP 467, N'Djamena; tel. 22-52-80-70; fax 22-52-71-08; f. 1991; construction of pipelines and petroleum refineries; Chair. YOUSSOUF MAINA.

Société des Hydrocarbures du Tchad (SHT): BP 6179, N'Djamena; f. 2006; state-owned petroleum company; Pres. ABDELKERIM HISSEIN MOUSSA; Man. Dir AHMAT KHAZALI ACYL.

Société Industrielle de Matériels Agricoles et d'Assemblage de Tracteurs (SIMATRACT): N'Djamena; Dir-Gen. YAMTEBAYE NADJITANGAR.

Société Moderne des Abattoirs—Abattoir Frigorifique de Farcha (AFF): Farcha; e-mail abattoir.farcha@intnet.td; privatized 1998; industrial slaughterhouse for meat industry; Dir-Gen. MAHAMAT AZIBERT.

Société Nationale de Ciment (SONACIM): N'Djamena; Pres. HASSAN ELI TIDEÏ.

Société Shell Tchad: route de Farcha, BP 110, N'Djamena; tel. 22-51-24-90; fax 22-51-22-67; f. 1971; cap. 205m. francs CFA; Pres. DAVID LAWSON LOUGHMAN; Dir-Gen. JEAN-RENÉ MBIANDJEU.

Société Tchadienne de Filature (SOTCHAFIL): BP 238, Sarh, Bahr Kôh; f. 1966; fmrly Société Textile du Tchad; textiles complex; Dir-Gen. IBRAHIM MALLOUM.

Tchad Oil Transport Co (TOTCO): BP 694, N'Djamena; fax 22-52-47-90; f. 1998, commenced active operations 2003; 95% owned by consortium of Chevron Corpn (USA), ExxonMobil (USA) and Petronas (Malaysia), 5% state-owned; controls transportation of petroleum through pipeline between Doba and Cameroonian border, and owns and operates three pumping stations.

Total Tchad: Zone Industrielle de Farcha, route de Mara, BP 75, N'Djamena; tel. 22-52-77-27; distribution of petroleum.

TRADE UNIONS

Confédération Libre des Travailleurs du Tchad (CLTT): ave Charles de Gaulle, BP 553, N'Djamena; tel. 22-51-76-11; fax 22-52-44-56; e-mail confederationlibre@yahoo.fr; Pres. BRAHIM BEN SAID; 22,500 mems (2001).

Union des Syndicats du Tchad (UST): BP 1143, N'Djamena; tel. 22-51-42-75; fax 22-52-14-52; e-mail ustchad@yahoo.fr; f. 1988; federation of trade unions; Pres. MICHEL BARKA; Sec.-Gen. FRANÇOIS DJONDANG.

Transport

RAILWAYS

There are no railways in Chad. In 1962 the Governments of Chad and Cameroon signed an agreement to extend the Transcameroon railway from Ngaoundere to Sarh, a distance of 500 km. Although the Transcameroon reached Ngaoundere in 1974, its proposed extension into Chad remains indefinitely postponed. In late 2011 construction was expected to commence of an 800-km railway from N'Djamena to Nyala in western Sudan, from where the existing line runs via Sudan's capital Khartoum to Port Sudan on the Red Sea. The project was to cost US $2,000m. and was partially funded by the Export Import Bank of China.

ROADS

The total length of the road network in 2006 was an estimated 40,000 km. There are also some 20,000 km of tracks suitable for motor traffic during the October–July dry season. The European Union is contributing to the construction of a highway connecting N'Djamena with Sarh and Léré, on the Cameroon border, and of a 400-km highway linking Moundou and Ngaoundere.

Coopérative des Transportateurs Tchadiens (CTT): BP 336, N'Djamena; tel. 22-51-43-55; road haulage; Pres. SALEH KHALIFA; brs at Sarh, Moundou, Bangui (CAR), Douala and Ngaoundere (Cameroon).

Fonds d'Entretien Routier: N'Djamena; internet fer-tchad.org; f. 2000; Dir AHMED DJAMALLADINE.

Société Tchadienne d'Affrètement et de Transit (STAT): 21 ave Félix Eboué, BP 100, N'Djamena; tel. 22-51-88-72; fax 22-51-74-24; e-mail stat.tchad@intnet.td; affiliated to Groupe Saga (France); road haulage.

INLAND WATERWAYS

The Chari and Logone rivers, which converge to the south of N'Djamena, are navigable. These waterways connect Sarh with N'Djamena on the Chari and Bongor and Moundou with N'Djamena on the Logone.

CIVIL AVIATION

The international airport is at N'Djamena. There are also more than 40 smaller airfields.

Autorité de l'Aviation Civile (ADAC): BP 96, N'Djamena; tel. 22-52-54-14; fax 22-52-29-09; Dir-Gen. GUELPINA CEUBAH.

Air Affaires Tchad: BP 256, N'Djamena; tel. 22-51-60-37; fax 22-51-06-20; e-mail airaffaires@yahoo.st; passenger and freight internal and charter flights.

Minair Tchad: ave Charles de Gaulle, BP 1239, N'Djamena; tel. 22-52-52-45; fax 22-51-07-80; e-mail abdel.ousman@intnet.td; passenger and freight air transport.

Toumaï Air Tchad (TAT): 66 ave Charles de Gaulle, 0036 rue 1020, Beck Ceccaldi, face à la Financial Bank, N'Djamena; tel. 22-52-41-07; fax 22-52-41-06; e-mail tatndj@toumaiair.com; internet www.toumaiair.com; f. 2004; scheduled passenger and cargo flights on domestic routes, and between N'Djamena and destinations in central and West Africa; Pres. and Dir-Gen. ZACHARIA DEBY ITNO.

Tourism

Chad's potential attractions for tourists include a variety of scenery from the dense forests of the south to the deserts of the north. Receipts from tourism in 2002 were estimated at US $25m. A total of 31,169 tourists visited Chad in 2009.

Office National Tchadien de Tourisme: BP 1649, N'Djamena; tel. 22-52-02-85; internet www.tchadtourisme.com; Dir Gen. MAHMOUD YOUNOUS.

Defence

As assessed at November 2011, the Armée Nationale Tchadienne (ANT) was estimated to number 25,350 (army approximately 20,000, air force 350, Republican Guard 5,000). In addition, there was a 9,500-strong gendarmerie. The army has been undergoing restructuring since 1996. Military service is by conscription. Under defence agreements with France, the army receives technical and other aid: in November 2010 there were 634 French troops deployed in Chad.

Defence Expenditure: Budgeted at 63,700m. francs CFA for 2010.

Chief of Staff of the Armed Forces: Gen. HASSANE SALEH AL GADAM AL JINEDI.

Chief of the Land Forces: Brig.-Gen. MASSOUD DRESSA.

Chief of Naval Staff: Lt MORNADJI MBAISSANEBE.

Chief of Air Force: Brig.-Gen. NADJITA BÉASSOUMAL.

Education

Education is officially compulsory for ten years between six and 16 years of age and is provided free of charge in public institutions. Primary education begins at the age of six and lasts for six years. Secondary education, from the age of 12, lasts for seven years, comprising a first cycle of four years and a second of three years. In 2009/10 enrolment in primary education was equivalent to 90% of students in the relevant age-group, while secondary enrolment in 2009/10 was equivalent to only 26% of children in the appropriate age-group (males 36%; females 15%). The Université de N'Djamena was opened in 1971. In addition, there are several technical colleges. Some 22,130 students were enrolled at higher education institutions in 2009/10. In 2005 spending on education represented 10.1% of total budgetary expenditure.

Bibliography

Abakar, M. *Chronique d'une enquête criminelle nationale. Le cas du régime de Hissein Habré, 1982–1990.* Paris, L'Harmattan, 2007.

Azevedo, M. J. *Roots of Violence: A History of War in Chad.* Amsterdam, Gordon and Breach, 1997.

Azevedo, M. J., and Naadozie, E. U. *Chad: A Nation in Search of its Future.* Boulder, CO, Westview Press, 1998.

Bangoura, M. T. *Violence politique et conflits en Afrique: le cas du Tchad.* Paris, L'Harmattan, 2005.

Bangui-Rombaye, A. *Tchad: élections sous contrôle, 1996–1997.* Paris, L'Harmattan, 1999.

Bouquet, C. *Tchad: Genèse d'un conflit.* Paris, L'Harmattan, 2000.

Britsch, J. *La mission Foureau-Lamy et l'arrivée des français au Tchad 1898–1990.* Paris, L'Harmattan, 1995.

Buijtenhuijs, R. *Le Frolinat et les révoltes populaires du Tchad (1965–1976).* The Hague, 1978.

Le Frolinat et les guerres civiles du Tchad (1977–1984). Paris, Editions Karthala, 1987.

Transition et élections au Tchad, 1993–1997: restauration autoritaire et recomposition politique. Paris, Editions Karthala, 1999.

Burr, M., and Collins, R. O. *Africa's Thirty Years' War: Libya, Chad and the Sudan 1963–1993.* Boulder, CO, Westview Press, 1999.

Chapelle, J. *Le peuple tchadien, ses racines et sa vie quotidienne.* Paris, L'Harmattan, 1986.

Cruise O'Brien, D. B., Dunn, J., and Rathbone, R. (Eds). *Contemporary West African States.* Cambridge, Cambridge University Press, 1989.

Decalo, S. *Historical Dictionary of Chad.* 3rd Edn. Metuchen, NJ, Scarecrow Press, 1997.

Dingammadji, A. *Ngarta Tombalbaye: Parcours et rôle dans la vie politique du Tchad.* Paris, L'Harmattan, 2007.

Les gouvernements du Tchad: De Gabriel Lisette à Idriss Déby Itno (1957-2010). Paris, L'Harmattan, 2011.

Djian, G. *Le Tchad et sa conquête (1900–1914).* Paris, L'Harmattan, 1996.

Kovana, V. *Précis des guerres et conflits au Tchad.* Paris, L'Harmattan, 2000.

Ladiba, G. *L'émergence des organisations islamiques au Tchad: Enjeux, acteurs et territoires.* Paris, L'Harmattan, 2012.

Lanne, B. *Tchad-Libye. La querelle des frontières.* Paris, Editions Karthala, 1982.

Répertoire de l'administration territoriale du Tchad (1900–1994). Paris, L'Harmattan, 1995.

Histoire politique du Tchad de 1945 à 1958. Paris, Editions Karthala, 1999.

Le Cornec, J. *Histoire politique du Tchad de 1900 à 1962.* Paris, Librairie générale de Droit et Jurisprudence, 1963.

Lemoine, T. *Tchad, 1960–1990: trente années d'indépendance.* Paris, Lettres du monde, 1997.

Lisette, Y. *Le RDA et le Tchad: Histoire d'une décolonisation.* Paris, Présence africaine, 2000.

Magnant, J.-P. (Ed.). *L'Islam au Tchad.* Talence, IEP, 1992.

Mays, T. M. *Africa's first peacekeeping operation: the OAU in Chad, 1981–1982.* Westport, CN, Praeger, 2002.

Nadji, O. *La guerre de N'Djamena. Tchad, 1979–2006. Un survivant raconte.* Paris, L'Harmattan, 2009.

Nebardoum, D. *Le labyrinthe de l'instabilité politique au Tchad.* Paris, L'Harmattan, 1998.

Contribution à une pensée politique de développement pour le Tchad. Paris, L'Harmattan, 2001.

Nolutshungu, S. C. *Limits of Anarchy: Intervention and State Formation in Chad.* Virginia, University Press of Virginia, 1996.

Petry, M., Bambe, N., and Liebermann, M. *Le pétrole du Tchad: Rêve ou cauchemar pour les populations?* Paris, Editions Karthala, 2005.

Samy, P. *Tchad: Déby vers una fin fatale.* Paris, Publibook, 2009.

Sikes, S. K. *Lake Chad versus the Sahara Desert: A Great African Lake in Crisis.* Newbury, Mirage, 2003.

Tétémadi Bangoura, M. *Violence politique et conflits en Afrique: le cas du Tchad.* Paris, L'Harmattan, 2006.

Toingar, E. *A Teenager in the Chad Civil War: A Memoir of Survival, 1982-1986.* Jefferson, NC, McFarland, 2006.

Triaud, J.-I. *Tchad 1900–1902: Une guerre franco-libyenne oubliée?—Une confrérie musulmane: La Sanusiyya face à la France.* Paris, L'Harmattan, 2001.

Tubiana, J., Arditi, C., and Pairault, C. (Eds). *L'identité tchadienne: L'héritage des peuples et les apports extérieurs.* Paris, L'Harmattan, 1994.

Wright, J. *Libya, Chad and the Central Sahara.* London, Hurst & Co., 1989.

Ye, M. N. *L'éducation de base au Tchad: Situation, enjeux et perspectives.* Paris, L'Harmattan, 1998.

Yorongar, N. *Tchad, le procès d'Idriss Déby: Témoignage à charge.* Paris, L'Harmattan, 2003.

THE COMOROS*

Physical and Social Geography

R. J. HARRISON CHURCH

The Comoro Islands, an archipelago of four small islands, together with numerous islets and coral reefs, lie between the east African coast and the north-western coast of Madagascar. The four islands cover a total land area of only 2,236 sq km (863 sq miles) and are scattered along a NW–SE axis, a distance of 300 km separating the towns of Moroni in the west and Dzaoudzi in the east. The French names for the islands, Grande-Comore (on which the capital, Moroni, is situated), Anjouan, Mohéli and Mayotte were changed in May 1977 to Ngazidja, Nzwani, Mwali and Mahoré, respectively, although the former names are still widely used. The islands are volcanic in structure, and Mt Karthala (rising to 2,440 m above sea-level) on Ngazidja is still active; it erupted in April 2005, causing an estimated 10,000 people to leave their homes, although no deaths were reported. Climate, rainfall and vegetation all vary greatly from island to island. There are similar divergences in soil characteristics, although in this instance natural causes have been reinforced by human actions, notably in deforestation and exhaustion of the soil.

The population was estimated at 773,346 in mid-2012, resulting in a population density of 415.3 per sq km. Moroni had an estimated population of 453,819 in 2011. The ethnic composition of the population is complex. The first settlers were probably Melano-Polynesian peoples who came to the islands from the Far East by the sixth century AD. Immigrants from the coast of Africa, Indonesia, Madagascar and Persia, as well as Arabs, had all arrived by about 1600, when the Comoros were becoming established as a port of call on European trade routes to India and the Indonesian archipelago. The Portuguese, the Dutch and the French further enriched the ethnic pattern, the latter introducing into the islands Chinese (who have since left) and Indians. In Mayotte and Mwali Arabic features are less evident, mainly because the two islands were settled by immigrants from the African coast and Madagascar. In fact, while Arab characteristics are strong in the islands generally, in particular in the coastal towns, the African is predominant in the territory as a whole. Islam is the prevalent religion of the islands. The official languages are Comorian (a mixture of Swahili and Arabic), French and Arabic. In Mayotte, Shimaoré (a Mahorian dialect of Comorian) and Shibushi are spoken; French is little used outside of the administration and education systems.

Recent History

Revised by the editorial staff

The Comoros, acquired as a French possession during 1841–1909, became a French Overseas Territory in 1947. Internal autonomy was granted in 1961, although substantial powers were retained by France. At a referendum held in December 1974, there was a 96% vote in favour of independence. This was strongly opposed, however, by the island of Mayotte (Mahoré), which sought the status of a French Overseas Department (Département d'outre mer). France sought to persuade the Comoran Government to draft a constitution for the islands that would allow a large measure of decentralization and thus satisfy the population of Mayotte, and proposed that any constitutional proposals should be ratified by referendum in each island separately before independence could be granted. These proposals were rejected by the Comoran Chambre des députés, and on 6 July 1975 the chamber approved a unilateral declaration of independence, and designated Ahmed Abdallah, the President of the Government Council, as President of the Republic. France retained control of Mayotte.

In August 1975 Abdallah was removed from office and replaced by Prince Saïd Mohammed Jaffar, who was in turn replaced as President in January 1976 by Ali Soilih. In February Mayotte voted overwhelmingly to retain its links with France. Preparations for the 1976 referendum in Mayotte were accompanied by a deterioration in relations between France and the Comoros. On 31 December 1975 France formally recognized the independence of Grande-Comore (Ngazidja), Anjouan (Nzwani) and Mohéli (Mwali), but all relations between the two Governments, together with aid and technical assistance programmes, were effectively suspended.

The Soilih regime initiated a revolutionary programme, blending Maoist and Islamic philosophies, aimed at creating an economically self-sufficient and ideologically progressive state. The excesses of Soilih's methods aroused widespread resentment among traditional elements of society, and his programme of reform seriously undermined the economy.

ABDALLAH IN POWER, 1978–89

In May 1978 Soilih was overthrown and subsequently killed in a coup, carried out by a small mercenary force led by a French national, Col Robert Denard, on behalf of the ex-President, Ahmed Abdallah. The new administration, headed by Abdallah, pledged to implement democratic reforms and to restore good relations with members of the League of Arab States (Arab League) and with France. French economic, cultural and military co-operation was duly resumed, and additional assistance was also forthcoming from Arab countries, the European Community (EC, now the European Union—EU) and the African Development Fund. A new Constitution approved by referendum in October was followed by presidential and legislative elections. Abdallah was elected President for a six-year term. Despite the constitutional guarantee of free activity for all political parties, the Assemblée fédérale established the Union Comorienne pour le Progrès (Udzima) as the sole legal party for a period of 12 years from 1982. Abdallah's regime pursued an increasingly authoritarian course: power was progressively centralized, reducing the role of the governors of the four islands, the federal Government became responsible for controlling the islands' economic resources and there were allegations of corruption and the ill-treatment of political detainees.

At a presidential election, which took place in September 1984, Abdallah, as sole candidate, was re-elected for a further six-year term by 99.4% of votes cast. Despite appeals by unofficial opposition groups for voters to boycott the election, some 98% of the electorate participated. In January 1985,

*Most of the information contained in this chapter relates to the whole Comoran archipelago, which the Comoros claims as its national territory and has styled 'The Union of the Comoros'. The island of Mayotte, however, is administered by France as an Overseas Department (Département d'outre-mer), and is treated separately at the end of this chapter.

following the adoption of constitutional amendments, the post of Prime Minister was abolished, and Abdallah assumed the powers of Head of Government. Elections to the Assemblée fédérale took place in March 1987. Although Abdallah had indicated that all political groups would be permitted to participate, opposition candidates were allowed to contest seats only on Ngazidja, where they obtained more than 35% of votes cast; Udzima retained full control of the legislature.

In November 1989 a constitutional amendment permitting Abdallah to serve a third six-year term as President was approved by 92.5% of votes cast in a popular referendum. However, this result was challenged by the President's opponents, and violent demonstrations ensued. On the night of 26–27 November Abdallah was assassinated by members of the presidential guard, under the command of Col Denard. As stipulated in the Constitution, the President of the Supreme Court, Saïd Mohamed Djohar, took office as interim Head of State, pending a presidential election. Denard and his supporters, however, staged a pre-emptive coup, in which 27 members of the security forces were reportedly killed. In mid-December Denard agreed to withdraw peacefully from the islands and, following the arrival of French paratroops in Moroni, was flown to South Africa with 25 other mercenaries. (In May 1999 Denard stood trial in France and was acquitted of Abdallah's assassination.)

THE DJOHAR PRESIDENCY, 1990–95

At the end of December 1989 the main political groups agreed to form a provisional Government of National Unity, and a general amnesty was extended to all political prisoners. The presidential election duly took place on 18 February 1990, but voting was abandoned, amid opposition allegations of widespread fraud. Balloting was held again on 4 and 11 March; after an inconclusive first round, Djohar, who was supported by Udzima, obtained 55.3% of the total votes cast, while Mohamed Taki, the leader of the Union Nationale pour la Démocratie aux Comores (UNDC), secured 44.7% of the vote. In late March Djohar appointed a new Government, which included two of his minor opponents in the presidential election: Prince Saïd Ali Kemal, a grandson of the last sultan of the Comoros and the founder of the opposition Islands' Fraternity and Unity Party (CHUMA), and Ali Mroudjae, a former Prime Minister and the leader of the Parti Comorien pour la Démocratie et le Progrès (PCDP). In April Djohar announced plans for the formal constitutional restoration of a multi-party political system, and indicated that extensive economic reforms were to be undertaken.

On 3 August 1991 the President of the Supreme Court, Ibrahim Ahmed Halidi, announced the dismissal of Djohar, on the grounds of negligence, and proclaimed himself interim President. Opposition leaders declared that the seizure of power was justified by the Constitution. Djohar responded by ordering the arrests of Halidi and several other members of the Supreme Court, and imposing a state of emergency. Later in August the Government banned all public demonstrations, following violent clashes between pro-Government demonstrators and members of the opposition. Djohar subsequently formed a new coalition Government, which included two members of the Front Démocratique (FD). In an attempt to appease increasing discontent on the island of Mwali, which had repeatedly demanded greater autonomy, two members of Mwalian opposition groups were appointed to the Government. However, the two dominant parties in the coalition, Udzima and the PCDP, objected to the ministerial changes, and accused Djohar of attempting to reduce their influence. Shortly afterwards the PCDP and Udzima left the Government.

In November 1991 Udzima denounced the proposed constitutional amendments and joined the opposition. Opposition leaders demanded the dissolution of the Assemblée fédérale, which they declared to be unlawfully constituted on the grounds that it had been elected under the former one-party system, and the formation of a government of national unity. Later in November, however, Djohar reached an agreement with the principal opposition leaders, including Taki, to initiate a process of national reconciliation, which would include the formation of a unity government and the convening of a new constitutional conference. The agreement also recognized the legitimacy of Djohar's election as President.

In January 1992 a transitional Government of National Unity was formed, under the leadership of Taki, who was designated as its 'Co-ordinator'. Djohar subsequently redesignated Taki as Prime Minister and formed a new interim cabinet. In June, despite concerted opposition by eight parties, led by Udzima and the FD, constitutional reform proposals which had been submitted in April were accepted by 74.3% of those voting in a referendum. The new constitutional provisions, which limited presidential tenure to a maximum of two five-year terms, also provided for a bicameral legislature, formed of an Assemblée fédérale, together with a 15-member Sénat, comprising five representatives from each island to be chosen by an electoral college. In early July Djohar dismissed Taki, on the grounds that he had allegedly appointed a former associate of Col Denard to a financial advisory post in the Government. Later that month a new Government was formed.

The first round of legislative elections, which took place on 22 November 1992, was marred by widespread violence and electoral irregularities, and a boycott was implemented by Udzima and the UNDC. Results in six constituencies were subsequently annulled, while the second round of voting, on 29 November, took place in only 34 of the 42 constituencies. Following partial elections on 13 and 30 December, reports indicated that candidates supporting the President, including seven members of the Union des Démocrates pour le Développement (UDD), had secured a narrow majority in the Assemblée fédérale. The leader of the UDD, Ibrahim Abdérémane Halidi, was appointed Prime Minister on 1 January 1993, and formed a new Council of Ministers.

In April 1993 nine people, including two sons of former President Abdallah and two prominent members of Udzima, were convicted on charges of complicity in the coup attempt in September 1992, and sentenced to death. After domestic and international pressure, the sentences were commuted.

Meanwhile, following the approval of a motion of censure by 23 of the 42 deputies in the Assemblée fédérale, Djohar replaced Halidi with Saïd Ali Mohamed. Mohamed subsequently formed a new Council of Ministers, which received the support of only 13 of the 42 members of the Assemblée. In mid-June 1993 19 deputies affiliated to Halidi proposed a motion of censure against the new Government, on the grounds that the Prime Minister had not been appointed from a party that commanded a majority in the Assemblée. However, Djohar declared the motion unconstitutional, dissolved the Assemblée and announced legislative elections. Shortly afterwards, he appointed a former presidential adviser, Ahmed Ben Cheikh Attoumane, as Prime Minister. A new Council of Ministers was subsequently formed.

In early September 1993 a number of opposition movements, led by Udzima and the UNDC, established an informal electoral alliance, known as the Union pour la République et le Progrès. The FD, the PCDP, CHUMA and the Mouvement pour la Démocratie et le Progrès (MDP) also announced that they would present joint candidates at the legislative elections, which had intitially been scheduled to take place in October. Later in September, however, Djohar postponed the legislative elections until November; in that month the legislative elections were rescheduled for December. Having failed to obtain party political support for an electoral alliance, Djohar announced in October the formation of a new party, the Rassemblement pour la Démocratie et le Renouveau (RDR), which included several prominent members of the Government. In November Djohar reorganized the Council of Ministers, and established a new National Electoral Commission (NEC), in compliance with the demands of the opposition.

In the first round of the legislative elections, which took place on 12 December 1993, four opposition candidates secured seats in the Assemblée fédérale, apparently provoking official concern. Following the second round of polling, it was reported that three people had been killed in violent incidents on Nzwani. The electoral commission subsequently invalidated results in eight constituencies. Partial elections later took place in these constituencies and in Moroni, where the second round of voting had been postponed at the demand of two government candidates; however, opposition candidates refused to participate on the grounds that voting was to be conducted under government supervision rather than that of the electoral commission. The RDR consequently secured all 10 contested seats in the partial elections, and 22 seats in total, thereby gaining a narrow majority in the Assemblée. In early January 1994 Djohar appointed the Secretary-General of the RDR, Mohamed Abdou Madi, as Prime Minister. Following the installation of a new Government, 12 prominent opposition parties adopted a joint resolution claiming that the RDR had obtained power illegally, and established a new alliance, known as the Forum pour le Redressement National (FRN), led by Abbas Djoussouf.

In October 1994 Djohar dismissed Abdou Madi as Prime Minister, and appointed Halifa Houmadi to the post. The resultant new Council of Ministers included only two members of the former administration. In April 1995 reports emerged of disagreements between Djohar and Houmadi. Djohar subsequently replaced Houmadi as Prime Minister with a former Minister of Finance, Mohamed Caabi El Yachroutu, who brought with him a reputation as a reformist, technocratic administrator, with good relations with the IMF and World Bank. A 13-member cabinet, including only five members of the previous administration, was formed.

INVASION, INTERVENTION AND INTERIM GOVERNMENT

In September 1995 about 30 European mercenaries, led by Denard, invaded Ngazidja, seized control of the miltary garrison at Kandani and captured Djohar. The mercenaries, who were joined by about 300 members of the Comoran armed forces, installed a former associate of Denard, Capt. Ayouba Combo, as leader of a transitional military committee. The French Government denounced the coup and suspended economic aid to the Comoros, but initially refused to intervene. In early October Combo announced that he had transferred authority to Mohamed Taki and the leader of CHUMA, Saïd Ali Kemal (both of whom had welcomed the coup), as joint civilian Presidents. The FRN, however, rejected the new leadership and entered into negotiations with El Yachroutu. Following an appeal for intervention from El Yachroutu, who invoked a defence co-operation agreement that had been negotiated in 1978, some 900 French military personnel landed on the Comoros. Shortly afterwards, Denard and his associates, together with the disaffected members of the Comoran armed forces, surrendered to the French troops. (In mid-2006 Denard was given a suspended sentence of five years by a French court for his involvement in the coup.)

Following the French military intervention, El Yachroutu declared himself interim President in accordance with the Constitution and announced the formation of a Government of National Unity, which included members of the constituent parties of the FRN. Djohar rejected El Yachroutu's assumption of power and announced the reappointment of Saïd Ali Mohamed as Prime Minister. Later in October 1995 a National Reconciliation Conference agreed that El Yachroutu would remain as interim President, pending the forthcoming election, which was provisionally scheduled for early 1996. The interim administration, which was supported by the armed forces, refused to recognize Djohar's appointments and announced that he would be prohibited from re-entering the country. At the end of October 1995 El Yachroutu granted an amnesty to all Comorans involved in the coup attempt and appointed representatives of the UNDC and Udzima (which had supported the coup) to the new Council of Ministers. Later in November, however, supporters of Djohar organized a political gathering to demand the resignation of El Yachroutu's administration. Meanwhile, political leaders on Mwali rejected the authority of both rival Governments, urged a campaign of civil disobedience and established a 'citizens' committee' to govern the island; discontent with the central administration also emerged on Nzwani.

THE TAKI PRESIDENCY, 1996–98

In the first round of the presidential election, held on 6 March 1996, Taki and the leader of the MDP, Abbas Djoussouf, secured the highest number of votes; it was subsequently reported that 12 of the 13 unsuccessful candidates had transferred their support to Taki in the second round of the election. Taki was duly elected to the presidency on 16 March, obtaining 64% of the vote, and was sworn in on 25 March. Taki appointed a new Council of Ministers, headed by Tadjidine Ben Saïd Massoundi, which included five of the presidential candidates who had given him their support in the second round of the election.

In early April 1996 Taki dissolved the Assemblée fédérale and announced that legislative elections would take place on 6 October. New governors, all belonging to the UNDC, were appointed to each of the three islands. In June, during a visit to France, discussions took place between Taki and the French President, Jacques Chirac. It was subsequently announced that Chirac had offered French assistance in the reorganization of public finance, education, public health and the judicial system. A consultative committee on the Constitution, established in September, considered requests from Taki for the reinforcement of presidential powers, including the President's right to choose governors for each island, and an end to the two-term limit on presidential office. The constitutional committee was boycotted by the FRN and other opposition parties. At the referendum on the constitutional reforms, held on 20 October, 85% voted in favour of the new Constitution. Legislative elections were postponed until 1 December. Meanwhile, Taki had succeeded in building a single-party ruling group to support his presidency. In October delegates from the UNDC, the RDR, Udzima and 20 other pro-Government parties merged, as the Rassemblement National pour le Développement (RND). This prompted Abbas Djoussouf and other anti-Taki politicians to form the Collectif de l'Opposition and announce, on 13 November, a boycott of the legislative elections. Results from the polls held on 1 December gave the RND 32 seats out of a total of 43 in the Assemblée fédérale. There were widespread reports of irregularities. The second round awarded a further four seats to the RND, giving it 36 seats, with the Islamist Front National pour la Justice (FNJ) obtaining three seats, and independent candidates four. Following the elections, the Prime Minister, Tadjidine Ben Saïd Massoundi, resigned. A new Government was appointed on 27 December, under Ahmed Abdou.

Separatist Problems

During July 1997 unrest rapidly escalated into a full-scale movement for secession on Nzwani and Mwali, which was aggravated by the Government's unsuccessful attempts to subdue separatists on Nzwani, who had declared their intention to seek a return to French sovereignty. The relative economic wealth of neighbouring Mayotte as a French Overseas Collectivité Territoriale was thought to have influenced popular feeling on Nzwani. Several separatist movements had emerged, notably the Mouvement populaire anjouanais, whose leader, Abdallah Ibrahim, was chosen to chair a 'political directorate' on Nzwani. On 3 August the 'political directorate' unilaterally declared Nzwani's secession from the Comoros; Ibrahim was subsequently elected as president of a 13-member 'politico-administrative co-ordination'. Meanwhile, separatist activity on Mwali intensified, and on 11 August secessionists declared the island's independence and appointed their own government.

President Taki, influenced by extremists in the Moroni administration, dispatched a force of at least 200 men to invade Nzwani on 2–3 September 1997. Barricades were erected in Mutsamudu and, after two days of heavy fighting, an unknown number of people, reportedly far more than 100, were killed as the invasion failed to suppress the insurrection. This failure prompted the dissolution of Ahmed Abdou's Government; Taki assumed absolute power for a three-week period, and then named a transitional commission, which excluded those who had advocated the invasion plan.

Underlying much of the unrest were attempts by Taki to centralize the administration of the archipelago; this was seen on Nzwani and Mwali as a bid for political and administrative supremacy on Ngazidja. At this stage the Organization of African Unity (OAU, now the African Union—AU) and the UN became increasingly involved with the unfolding crisis. A reconciliation conference was scheduled for the end of October 1997, at the OAU's headquarters in Addis Ababa, Ethiopia. Ibrahim held a referendum on Nzwani's secession on 26 October, despite the objections of the Moroni Government and the misgivings of some separatists, notably Abdou Madi; the reported result was 99.9% in favour of independence. France continued to reject absolutely demands for Nzwani to be reincorporated into the former colonial power.

Taki steadily lost his remaining support on Ngazidja; a separatist government was appointed by the secessionists on Nzwani in October, further inflaming inter-island relations. Opposition parties in Moroni demanded that Taki be removed, declared that they would participate in the formation of a government of national unity only if separatists from Nzwani and Mwali were involved, and insisted that the dispute had to be resolved under the aegis of the OAU. In early December Taki named a new Council of Ministers, under Nourdine Bourhane, although the transitional commission appointed in September remained in existence.

A referendum on a separatist constitution was carried by a reported 99.5% of votes cast on Nzwani in late February 1998. In March Ibrahim appointed a new Government. In an effort to establish dialogue with the opposition, Taki named a three-member committee of political veterans in mid-May to examine the problem. At the end of the month the Council of Ministers was reorganized in favour of moderates, and the President succeeded in bringing Abdou Madi back into government

In July 1998 a dispute over the future aims of the secessionist movement led to the dismissal of the island's Government, provoking violent clashes between islanders loyal to Ibrahim, who favoured independence within the framework of an association of the Comoran islands, and supporters of the outgoing Prime Minister, Chamassi Saïd Omar, who continued to advocate reattachment to France. It was subsequently reported that Ahmed Mohamed Hazi, a former Comoran army Chief of Staff and ally of Omar, had failed in an attempt to depose Ibrahim. At meetings later in the year with Djoussouf and the leadership of his own party, Taki proposed the establishment of a government of public salvation, an idea opposed by many members of the RND and several government ministers.

INTERIM GOVERNMENT AND ARMY COUP

On 6 November 1998 President Taki died unexpectedly. It was stated that he had suffered a heart attack, although several senior officials expressed serious doubts about the actual circumstances of the President's death. Tadjidine Ben Saïd Massoundi, the Nzwanian President of the High Council of the Republic and a former Prime Minister (March–December 1996), was designated acting President, in accordance with the Constitution, pending an election, which would be held after 30–90 days. Massoundi immediately revoked the ban on the movement of people and goods to Nzwani and, despite the continued opposition of several government ministers, proceeded with Taki's project for the formation of a government of public salvation. Djoussouf, the main opposition leader, was subsequently appointed Prime Minister, to head a Council of Ministers composed of members of the FRN and the RND. Divisions within the RND over its participation in the new Government led to a split in the party. In late January 1999 Massoundi extended his presidential mandate, which was soon to expire, pending a resolution of the crisis dividing the islands. In February an agreement was signed by the acting President and political parties opposed to the FRN-RND Government, which provided for the formation of a new government to be supported by up to three technical commissions. However, the FRN refused to participate in the agreement, declaring its intention to remain in power until a Comoran inter-island conference had been held.

Meanwhile, renewed tension within the separatist administration on Nzwani intensified in December 1998, provoking eight days of armed clashes between rival militias, which led to at least 60 deaths before a cease-fire agreement was signed. In January 1999 Ibrahim agreed to transfer some of his powers to a five-member 'politico-administrative directorate', as meetings commenced between the rival separatist factions. No consensus was achieved in the following months, however, and, when Ibrahim replaced the directorate with a 'committee of national security' in March, the new administration was immediately rejected by rival leaders. Resistance to the ruling administration in Moroni increased in March, when opposition leaders organized a protest meeting during which they strongly denounced Massoundi.

On 19–23 April 1999 an OAU-sponsored inter-island conference was held in Antananarivo, Madagascar. An accord was reached whereby the federal state would become a union within one year, with the presidency rotating among the three islands. However, the delegates from Nzwani failed to sign the agreement, insisting on the need for consultation prior to a full endorsement. Several days of rioting followed in Moroni, as demonstrators protested against Nzwani's refusal to ratify the accord, reportedly forcing more than 1,000 Nzwanians from their homes before order was restored.

On 30 April 1999 the Chief of Staff of the Comoran armed forces, Col Assoumani Azali, seized power in a bloodless coup, deposing Massoundi and dissolving the Government, the Assemblée fédérale and all other constitutional institutions. Having sought to justify his actions on the grounds that the authorities had failed to take the political measures necessary to control the security situation in the Comoros, Azali promulgated a new constitutional charter in which he proclaimed himself Head of State and of Government, and Commander-in-Chief of the armed forces. Full legislative functions were also vested in Azali, who undertook to relinquish power following the creation of the new institutions provided for in the Antananarivo accord. The appointment of a State Committee (composed of six members from Ngazidja, four from Mwali and two from Nzwani) was followed by that of a State Council, which was to supervise the activities of the State Committee and comprised eight civilians and 11 army officers. The OAU, which had not been represented at Azali's inauguration (although the UN had sent representatives), condemned the coup, withdrew its military observers from the Comoros and urged the international community not to recognize the new regime.

AZALI IN POWER

In June 1999 Azali created five technical commissions, which were to oversee various projects, including the drafting of new constitutions for the union and the islands, and the preparation of a donors' conference. However, despite an undertaking by Azali to transfer power to a civilian government within a year, domestic discontent with the new administration increased, as the main political parties boycotted a meeting at which they were to have nominated representatives to serve on the new commissions. Furthermore, France and the USA were reported to have suspended all military co-operation with the Republic.

In mid-June 1999 Lt-Col Abdérémane Saïd Abeid, who had previously occupied the role of national mediator on Nzwani, formed a Government of National Unity on the island, appointing himself as 'Co-ordinator'. Relations between Ngazidja and Nzwani appeared to be improving to some extent in early July, when Azali and Abeid met on Mwali. The meeting represented the most senior-level contact between the islands since the secessions of August 1997. In August 1999 elections to establish a 25-member national assembly on Nzwani were held. No official results were released, but reports indicated that the most staunch separatists won the majority of seats. In mid-September the Nzwani executive council announced its decision not to sign the Antananarivo peace agreement. In December the OAU threatened the imposition of sanctions on the island should its leaders not have signed the peace accord by 1 February 2000. In retaliation, Abeid announced that a referendum would be held on Nzwani on 23 January 2000 regarding the signature of the Antananarivo accord. According to the separatist authorities of Nzwani, the results of the referendum revealed an overwhelming majority (94.5%) in favour of full independence for the island; the OAU, however, announced that it did not recognize the outcome of the ballot, following allegations of intimidation and repression of those in favour of reconciliation. Following a series of meetings between Azali and a number of political parties from all three islands regarding the establishment of a more representative and decentralized government in Moroni, the State Committee underwent an extensive reorganization in early December, including the appointment of a new Prime Minister, Bianrifi Tarmidi (from Mwali). Although Mwali was well represented in the new executive, only one Nzwanian minister was appointed.

In May 2000 the OAU announced that the possibility of lifting sanctions against Nzwani separatists was also connected to the return to constitutional order on the Comoros; it advocated the restoration of the October 1996 constitution, the return of Tadjidine Ben Saïd Massoundi as head of state, as well as the appointment of an interim government and prime minister. The following month the OAU announced that a total maritime blockade of Nzwani would be established.

National Reconciliation

On 26 August 2000 an agreement, known as the Fomboni accord, was signed by Azali and Abeid. The accord provided for the drawing up of a new constitution, which would grant Nzwani, Ngazidja and Mwali considerable control over their own affairs. However, the central government would maintain jurisdiction over foreign affairs, external defence, currency, nationality and religion. There was to be a one-year transition period, following which the constitutional amendments were to be submitted to a referendum vote. However, the accord was severely criticized by the OAU on the grounds that it contravened the terms of the Antananarivo accord. Despite demonstrations organized by opposition members on Nzwani, a tripartite commission comprising delegates from each island was established in November to define the terms of the new constitution. In late November Tarmidi was replaced as Prime Minister by Hamada Madi 'Boléro', who formed a new Government. However, attempts to include opposition members in the new Government and the tripartite commission were unsuccessful.

On 17 February 2001 an agreement on national reconciliation was signed in Fomboni by representatives of the Comoran Government, the Nzwani administration, opposition parties and civil society. The OAU, the Organisation Internationale de la Francophonie (OIF) and the EU were to be guarantors of the peace accord, which provided for the establishment of a new Comoran entity. Under the provisions of the agreement an independent tripartite commission, comprising equal numbers of delegates from each of the islands and representing all of the signatory groups, was to draft a new constitution, which would be submitted to a national referendum for approval by June. However, in mid-March, following disagreements over the composition of a follow-up committee intended to monitor progress on implementation of the Fomboni agreement, the opposition withdrew from the reconciliation process. In mid-April the Nzwani administration also withdrew from the process. In July it was announced that the constitutional referendum had been postponed until September, ostensibly owing to lack of available funds to administer it.

On 8–9 August 2001 a military coup on Nzwani ended in the removal from power of Saïd Abeid Abdérémane. Abeid, who was arrested and subsequently fled Nzwani, was replaced by a collective presidency, consisting of Maj. Mohamed Bacar, Maj. Hassane Ali Toihili and Maj. Charif Halidi; a Government of eight civilian commissioners was appointed. The new leadership of Nzwani committed itself to the Fomboni agreement. However, on 24 September a further bloodless military coup was instigated by the deputy head of the Comoran army and close ally of Azali, Combo. Although Combo was initially declared leader of the army, and Ahmed Aboubakar Foundi was installed as leader of Nzwani, they were captured the following day, before subsequently escaping from the island. In November Abeid attempted unsuccessfully to regain control of Nzwani in a military coup; he was defeated by military forces loyal to Bacar and fled the island. Abeid, however, denied his involvement in the events, maintaining that the instigator had in fact been Allaoui Ahmed, who had reportedly allied himself with the Organisation pour l'Indépendance d'Anjouan, a political alliance that favoured a 'no' vote in the upcoming referendum on constitutional changes.

NEW CONSTITUTION AND PRESIDENTIAL ELECTIONS

At the constitutional referendum, which was held on 23 December 2001, some 76.4% of the electorate voted in favour of the proposed new Constitution. The country, which was to change its name to the Union of the Comoros, was to be led by the President of the Union, who was to head the Council of the Union, and governed by a legislative assembly, the Assemblée de l'Union. The position of President was to rotate between the islands, while the Vice-Presidents, who were also members of the Council of the Union, were to be inhabitants of the two remaining islands; the first President was to come from Ngazidja. Each of the three islands was to become financially autonomous and was to be ruled by its own local government and institutions. The Union was to be responsible for matters of religion, nationality, currency, foreign affairs and external defence, while shared responsibilities between the Union and the islands were to be determined at a later date. A transitional government was to be installed to monitor the implementation of the new institutions.

In early January 2002 Prime Minister Hamadi Madi 'Boléro' tendered his resignation. A transitional Government of National Unity was installed on 20 January, with 'Boléro' reappointed as Prime Minister, and included members of the former Government, opposition representatives and two of Nzwani's separatist leaders. However, on the following day the Government collapsed, following the withdrawal of the opposition representatives, as a result of a disagreement over the allocation of ministerial portfolios. Meanwhile, Azali resigned as Head of State and announced his intention to stand as an independent candidate in the forthcoming presidential election; 'Boléro' was to serve as President *ad interim*. In mid-February the Government of National Unity was re-established.

On 10 March 2002 voters on Nzwani and Mwali approved new local Constitutions; this was followed on 7 April by the approval of a new Constitution on Ngazidja (an earlier draft had been rejected). In a first round of voting in the federal presidential election on 17 March, contested by nine candidates, Azali secured 39.8% of the vote. Mahamoud Mradabi of the Shawiri party won 15.7% and Saïd Ali Kemal of CHUMA 10.7%; however, both Mradabi and Kemal boycotted the second round. Consequently, on 14 April Azali was elected unopposed as Federal President of the Union of the Comoros, reportedly securing more than 75% of the votes cast. However, the result was declared invalid by the NEC, on the grounds that the election had not been free and fair. Nevertheless, following the dissolution of the NEC, and the appointment of an independent electoral body, Azali was declared Federal President. Meanwhile, in late March and early April Maj. Mohamed Bacar and Mohamed Saïd Fazul were elected as regional Presidents of Nzwani and Mwali, respectively; on 19 May Abdou Soule Elbak was elected regional President of Ngazidja, defeating Azali's preferred candidate, Bakari Abdallah Boina. In early June Azali announced the formation of a new Government of the Union of the Comoros, which replaced the transitional Government of National Unity.

In June 2001 disagreement over the new political structure prompted the occupation of a number of government buildings by troops. In response, the Government of Ngazidja boycotted the inauguration of the new head of the armed forces, Col Soilihi Ali Mohammed, and warned the OAU that it suspected a coup was being planned, to be led by Soilihi. At the end of August street barricades were erected in Moroni, in protest at incomplete devolution on Ngazidja, which left Elbak with less authority than the other islands' Presidents.

In early March 2003 Elbak and Bacar denounced Azali's failure to implement measures to resolve the institutional crisis and accused the Federal President of repeated constitutional violations, requesting that the EU temporarily delay payment for fishing rights to the federal Government. Later in the month the federal Government announced the indefinite postponement of the legislative elections. In July an AU mission, led by the South African Minister of Foreign Affairs, Nkosazana Dlamini-Zuma, visited the Comoros. Talks brought together Azali and the regional Presidents with the aim of removing obstacles to legislative elections; the creation was proposed of a Constitutional Court, which would have jurisdiction over such power struggles in the future. In August, at a meeting in Pretoria, South Africa, representatives of the federal and island Governments signed a memorandum, according to which the federal Government would retain control of the army, but the administration of the police force would be devolved to the island Governments. Agreement was also reached that, during a transitional period leading to legislative elections, the customs services would be managed by a joint board, with taxes shared between the federal and island administrations. In December, following further mediation by the AU, the agreement reached in August was ratified by Azali and the three island Presidents in Moroni. A follow-up committee was appointed to monitor the implementation of the accord.

Elections to the three island assemblies were held on 14 and 21 March 2004 and were observed by an AU mission. Pro-Azali candidates won an overall total of only 12 seats in the assemblies, while candidates from 11 parties allied to Elbak secured 14 of the 20 seats in the Ngazidja assembly, supporters of Bacar won 18 of the 25 seats available on Nzwani (where the elections were to be re-run in two constituencies) and nine allies of Fazul were elected to the 10-member assembly on Mwali. The parliament of Ngazidja was installed in early April, and was followed by the swearing in of the Mwali and Nzwani parliaments on 15 and 16 May, respectively.

After several postponements, elections to the Assemblée de l'Union took place on 18 and 25 April 2004. According to final results, declared on 28 April, the Convention pour le Renouveau des Comores (CRC) won only six of the 18 directly elected seats, while a loose coalition supporting the three island Presidents secured 11 seats and CHUMA took one seat. The rate of voter participation in the second round was 68.5%. The 15 remaining seats in the 33-member federal assembly were taken by five nominees each from the island legislatures. Hamada Madi, the Minister of Defence and a close associate of President Azali, was defeated in Mwali and resigned his post on 30 April. In mid-July President Azali effected a cabinet reorganization, granting responsibility for co-ordinating Union affairs on their home islands to the two Vice-Presidents. The new Government comprised the two Vice-Presidents, seven ministers of state and two secretaries of state and included a representative each from Nzwani and Mwali, and one member of CHUMA.

In November 2004, in a follow-up to the 2001 agreement on national reconciliation signed in Fomboni, long-awaited legislation on the division of power between the national and island authorities was passed by the Assemblée de l'Union. The bill, which was supported by President Azali, had provoked much controversy as it sought to clarify authority over security forces and public assets. Authority over the gendarmerie was granted to the island Presidents, precipitating a demonstration by the armed forces. The island Presidents also expressed their dissatisfaction with the bill, which, they claimed, had been amended by the Assemblée without their consent. It was subsequently declared invalid by the Cour Constitutionelle (Constitutional Court) and returned to the Assemblée.

THE 2006 PRESIDENTIAL ELECTION

In October 2005 the Assemblée de l'Union approved legislation granting Comorans living abroad the right to vote. (It was estimated that some 200,000 Comorans were resident in France.) In early 2006 the Commission Nationale des Élections aux Comores announced that the presidential election would be held on 16 April and 14 May.

At the first round of the presidential election, duly held on 16 April 2006 on the island of Nzwani, in accordance with the constitutional requirements of the rotating presidency, 13 candidates participated, with three qualifying for the second, nation-wide, round. In the second round, held as scheduled on 14 May, Ahmed Abdallah Sambi, a respected businessman and Islamic theologian, won 99,112 votes, equivalent to 58.0% of the valid votes cast. Ibrahim Halidi, a former Prime Minister who was supported by outgoing President Azali, won 48,378 votes (28.3%), while Mohamed Djaanfari received 23,322 votes (13.7%). Voter turn-out was reported to have been 58.1%, and the election was praised by international observers as having been 'free and fair'. All three candidates came from the island of Nzwani, in accordance with the constitutional requirement that the presidency rotate between the three islands comprising the Union of the Comoros. On 26 May Sambi was sworn in as President, and on 29 May the composition of a new administration, comprising six ministers and two Vice-Presidents, was announced. Notably, the defence portfolio was transferred to the President's office.

ISLAND ELECTIONS

On 10 June 2007 the first round of presidential elections were held on two of the three islands, Ngazidja and Mwali. The election on Nzwani was postponed until 17 June, at the request of President Sambi and the AU, following outbreaks of violence and allegations of corruption and intimidation in the weeks leading to the elections. Nevertheless, Bacar proceeded to hold the election, claiming to have secured victory with 73.2% of the vote. He subsequently announced himself as President of Nzwani for a second term, despite both the AU and the Union Government declaring the results to be null and void. The political unrest continued on Nzwani while the second round of voting, largely agreed to have been free and fair, took place on Ngazidja and Mwali on 25 June. Mohamed Abdouloihabi was named as President of Ngazidja, while Mohamed Ali Said secured the presidency of Mwali. A delegation of officials from the AU met with President Sambi and the Nzwani authorities on 24 June to discuss the situation. A statement was subsequently issued in which demands were made for the authorities of Nzwani to hold free and fair elections, in compliance with an AU security plan.

In mid-February 2008, following the failure of further negotiations aimed at breaking the deadlock on Nzwani, the AU Peace and Security Council mandated the deployment of a Mission d'Assistance Électorale et Sécuritaire (MAES) to restore the authority of the Union on Nzwani by use of military force. (Sanctions imposed by the AU in October 2007 had had limited effect.) The 1,500-member MAES represented the first occasion that the AU had approved military intervention to enforce peace in a member country. On 25 March 2008 some 450 Sudanese, Tanzanian and Comoran troops landed on Nzwani and succeeded in regaining control of the island. The following day President Sambi announced that Union Vice-President Ikililou Dhoinine had been appointed interim President of Nzwani, pending the formation of a transitional government, and confirmed that the presidential election on the island would be reheld within two months. Bacar was reported to have fled Nzwani, initially taking refuge on Mayotte, where he requested political asylum. The Comoran authorities immediately sought his extradition from Mayotte; however, on 28 March Bacar was transported by the French military to Réunion, where he was, according to French officials, to be investigated for landing illegally on Mayotte in possession of weapons. That charge was dismissed, although Bacar and 22 of his supporters remained in custody on Réunion. On 31 March Laili Zamane Abdou, hitherto President of the Nzwani Court of Appeal, was sworn in as interim President. The following day he announced his new cabinet, the members of which were to be given the new title of Government Secretaries-General. In April a French court approved Bacar's release from prison, but he was to remain under house arrest on Réunion. On 15 June elections were held on Nzwani, with voter turn-out estimated to have been less than 50%. Moussa Toybou, the candidate supported by President Sambi, secured 42.5% of the vote, ahead of Mohammed Djaanfari, who was reported to have led opinion polls prior to the election. Both candidates contested a run-off ballot on 29 June, at which Toybou secured 52.4% of the vote; he was inaugurated in early July.

CONSTITUTIONAL REFERENDUM

In April 2009 it was announced that a referendum would be held the following month regarding proposed changes to the Constitution: these included the extension of Sambi's presidential mandate by one year and a general overhaul of the government structure to reduce expenditure (the complex system of governance was believed to cost the Comoros about 80% of its GDP); the three autonomous island Presidents would be named as governors and have their powers reduced, while the President would be granted the power to dissolve the legislature. According to official results released by the Constitutional Court, at the referendum held on 16 May 94.0% of voters approved the changes; voter turn-out was recorded at 51.8%. The reforms entered into effect on 23 May.

2009 LEGISLATIVE ELECTIONS

Delayed twice, the first round of the legislative elections eventually took place on 6 December 2009, with a second round held on 20 December. Of the 33 seats available in the Assemblée de l'Union, 24 were to be decided by direct universal suffrage, while the remaining nine were to be allocated by the island councillors at a rate of three per island. Results were announced on 13 December: the Mouvance Présidentielle secured three seats, although no seats were won by opposition parties. In the second round the presidential party took a further 134 seats, while three seats were won by allies of the President and four by opposition candidates. In Anjouan there were demonstrations against the results, with roads to the capital, Mutsamudu, being blocked.

In March 2010 legislation was approved postponing presidential elections, due to take place in May, until November 2011, thereby extending President Sambi's term of office by 18 months and denying Mwali the opportunity to assume the presidency for the next rotation. The decision prompted concern among several opposition leaders, who referred the issue to the AU. The OIF also denounced the decision, claiming that it was 'unilateral' and contrary to the 'spirit of dialogue and search for stability' that had been fostered during reconciliation talks. Delaying the election would harmonize the presidential and legislative election calendars, but this was a major reform that observers claimed should not be undertaken without prior consultation with the island governments.

Civil unrest over the decision to extend the presidential term resulted in the deployment of Libyan troops to the Comoros in April 2010 to ensure the President's security. Later that month Sambi stated that he would be willing to consider bringing forward the election date, following widespread violence on Mwali in opposition to the extension of the presidential term. However, in May Sambi appointed an interim administration, believed to be an attempt to consolidate his position. Of the 10 appointments made, nine were new to the Government, including Fahmi Said Ibrahim as Minister of External Relations and Co-operation, with responsibility for the Diaspora and Francophone and Arab Relations. Dhoinine retained his position as Vice-President but relinquished responsibility for the portfolios of finance, the budget and the promotion of female entrepreneurs. Dhoinine was assigned the land settlement, infrastructure, town planning and housing portfolios while Mohamed Bacar Dossar, dismissed as Minister of Defence in the previous month, was named as Minister of Finance, the Budget and Investments. On 22 June further minor governmental changes were implemented. In compliance with an agreement reached in the previous week, three new ministers were appointed by each of the Union's three islands, including Abdourahamane Ben Cheikh Achiraf as Minister of State, in charge of Elections.

THE 2010 PRESIDENTIAL AND GUBERNATORIAL ELECTIONS

A total of 10 candidates contested the first round of the presidential election, which was held as scheduled on 7 November 2010. According to results confirmed by the Constitutional Court on 13 November, Dhoinine, the Union Vice-President with responsibility for Land Settlement, Infrastructure, Town Planning and Housing, secured 28.2% of the votes cast, while Mohamed Saïd Fazul and Dr Abdou Djabir took 22.9% and 9.9% of the votes, respectively. The three candidates contested a run-off on 26 December at which Dhoinine was returned the victor having won 60.9% of the votes cast. The rate of voter participation was recorded by the Commission Électorale Nationale Indépendante at 52.8%. Gubernatorial polls held concurrently with the presidential ballots resulted in the re-election of Ali Said to the governorship of Mwali, while Anissi Chamsidine and Mouigni Baraka Saïd Soilih became Governors of Nzwani and Ngazidja, respectively. On 13 January 2011 the Constitutional Court confirmed the election of Dhoinine (and those of the island Governors), and later that month it was announced that Dhoinine was to be sworn in as President on 26 May. The three island Governors were to assume their positions three days prior to this date. Dhoinine was duly sworn in on 26 May, and on 30 May announced the formation of a new Government to which three Vice-Presidents were appointed: Dr Fouad Mohadji, who also assumed responsibility for Production, the Environment, Energy, Industry and Crafts; Mohamed Ali Soilihi, in charge of Finance, the Economy, the Budget and Investments and External Trading (Privatization); and Nourdine Bourhane, with responsibility for Land Settlement, Town Planning and Housing. In February 2012 plans to introduce a biometric electoral system were announced by the Government. No time scale for the implementation was immediately available.

FLOODING

In April 2012 torrential rain and storms caused severe flooding in the Comoros, affecting water and electricity supplies and telecommunications services. Some villages became inaccessible as roads were rendered impassable. On 26 April the President declared a state of emergency and reports suggested nearly 10,000 people had been moved into temporary shelters. The following day a humanitarian co-ordination meeting was convened with local donors. Supplies of clean drinking water and sewage services to Moroni were cut off completely for over a month, increasing the risk of cholera outbreaks; by late May supplies were slowly improving, although warnings were in place regarding the potability of the water. (Chlorine tablets were being provided as a priority in early June and water supplies had still not been fully restored by July.) As the flood waters receded the damage toll began to emerge: four people had been killed and an estimated 150 more had been injured; some 204 km of roads were in need of repair; assessments for long-term recovery and rehabilitation were under way. There were concerns that the loss of crop yields would affect food supplies but data was initially difficult to collect.

EXTERNAL RELATIONS

Diplomatic relations between the Comoros and France, suspended in 1975, were restored in 1978; in November of that year the two countries signed agreements on military and economic co-operation, apparently deferring any decision on the future of Mayotte. In subsequent years, however, member countries of the UN General Assembly repeatedly voted in favour of a resolution affirming the Comoros' sovereignty over Mayotte, with only France dissenting. Following Djohar's accession to power, diplomatic relations were established with the USA in June 1990. In September of that year the Comoros and South Africa signed a bilateral agreement providing for a series of South African loans towards the development of infrastructure in the Comoros. In September 1993 the Arab League accepted an application for membership from the Comoros. In November 1994 the Government signed an agreement with Israel that provided for the establishment of diplomatic relations between the two countries, prompting protests from the Arab League and from Islamic leaders in the Comoros. Djohar subsequently announced that the implementation of the agreement was to be postponed, pending a satisfactory resolution to the conflict in the Middle East. In mid-1999, following the military coup headed by Col Azali, France and the USA suspended all military co-operation with the Comoros; France re-established military co-operation in September 2002. In 2003 President Azali visited a number of countries, including the USA and the People's Republic of

China, in an effort to encourage foreign investment in the Comoros. In mid-2004 a joint commission with Sudan was created. President Azali visited France in early 2005, and the Franco-Comoran commission resumed, after a hiatus of 10 years. In November 2006 a framework partnership agreement was signed by the French Minister-Delegate for Co-operation, Development and La Francophonie, allocating a grant of €88m. to the Union for 2006–10. Following the accession of President Sambi, relations with and funding from Iran increased significantly, owing to his personal historical connections with that country. Relations with France were expected to deteriorate when, in March 2011, the French Assemblée nationale approved the decision for Mayotte to become an integrated French Overseas Department. In November 2010, at the Europe-Africa summit held in Tripoli, Libya, President Sambi expressed his concern over this process and urged the EU to put pressure on France to move towards a shared French-Comoran authority over Mayotte.

Economy

Revised by the editorial staff

INTRODUCTION

The Comoros, with few natural resources, a chronic shortage of cultivable land, a narrow base of agricultural crops and a high density of population, is among the poorest countries of sub-Saharan Africa, and is highly dependent on external trade and assistance. In 2010, according to estimates by the World Bank, the gross national income of the Comoros (excluding Mayotte), measured at average 2008–10 prices, was US $550m., equivalent to $750 per head (or $1,080 per head on an international purchasing-power parity basis). During 2001–10, it was estimated, the population increased at an average annual rate of 2.7%, while gross domestic product (GDP) per head increased, in real terms, by an average of 0.8% per year. Overall GDP increased, in real terms, at an average annual rate of 1.9% in 2001–10; it increased by 2.1% in 2010 and by 2.2% in 2011. At the census of September 1991, despite large-scale emigration to neighbouring countries, overall population density was 240 inhabitants per sq km (excluding Mayotte), with a density of 445.6 on the island of Nzwani (Anjouan). The problem of overpopulation on the three independent islands has worsened since the break with Mayotte, which has the largest area of unexploited cultivable land in the archipelago. Settlers from Nzwani and Ngazidja (Grande-Comore) have been compelled to leave Mayotte and return to their already overpopulated native islands, where the potential for agricultural development is extremely limited. Demographic pressure was considered to be one of the main causes of the attempted secession by Nzwani and Mwali (Mohéli) in 1997. However, by mid-2012, according to UN estimates, overall population density had declined to 415.3 inhabitants per sq km from 461.9 per sq km in mid-2008.

AGRICULTURE

Agriculture is the dominant economic activity in the Comoros (contributing 42.9% of GDP in 2010, according to the African Development Bank—AfDB—and employing 68.6% of the labour force in mid-2012, according to FAO). In 2004 the sector accounted for some 98% of export earnings. Local subsistence farming, using primitive implements and techniques, is inadequate to maintain the population. Despite a number of rural development projects financed by various international agencies, yields are very poor, storage facilities lacking, and much of the best land is reserved for export cash-crop production. Cassava, taro, rice, maize, pulses, coconuts and bananas are cultivated. Almost all meat and vegetables are imported. Torrential rains and flooding in April 2012 were expected to have a severe impact of agricultural production as the effects of crop damage and disease began to emerge. Vanilla producers on Grand-Comore reported in June that some 80%–90% of their crop had been destroyed.

In 2010 export earnings for vanilla totalled 309m. Comoros francs, a significant decline from 726m. Comoros francs in 2009. The main production of vanilla and the Comoros' other two main export crops—cloves and ylang ylang—comes from Nzwani. Political unrest has had a serious impact on both production and trade, and revenue from unofficial ('black market') sales has been used to pay for imports of staple foods and fuel for the island. The rise of this 'black market' trade was a major element in the imposition of economic sanctions by the Organization of African Unity (OAU, now the African Union—AU).

Prices for vanilla, of which the islands traditionally have been one of the world's larger producers (with average outputs of 140–200 metric tons per year), have been affected in recent years by competition from low-cost producers, notably Indonesia and Madagascar, and from synthetic substitutes. According to the Banque Centrale des Comores, production has since declined to an estimated 60 tons per year. In 2004 world vanilla prices fell dramatically, to around US $50 per kg, as a result of a good harvest in Madagascar. It fell even further in early 2007, to around $17 per kg, from a high of $600 per kg three years earlier. It remained at a stable (albeit low) level of $20–$30 per kg through to mid-2010. France accounts for about one-third of the Comoros' vanilla exports.

The Comoros is the world's main supplier of ylang ylang, producing an estimated 80% of the world's supply, for which prices have been generally favourable, although unit values declined somewhat in the late 1990s. However, ageing plantations and inadequate processing equipment have prevented this export from achieving its full potential, and output declined from 72 metric tons in 1989 to an estimated 45 tons in 2006. It was announced in mid-2007 that the Comoros could increase their production of ylang ylang by as much as 20,000 tons per year as a result of the 70,000 plants that have been planted since 2005.

Shortfalls in foreign-exchange revenue from these three commodities have been met by funds, under the Stabex (Stabilization of Export Earnings) scheme of the European Union (EU). According to the World Bank, agricultural GDP increased at an average annual rate of 1.7% in 2001–09; agricultural GDP grew by 4.5% in 2009.

Fishing is practised on a small scale, with a total catch of 52,300 metric tons in 2010. According to recent studies, the Comoros has a potential annual catch of 25,000–30,000 tons of tuna. In late 2005 an agreement on fishing rights in Comoran waters, which would extend until 2010, was reached with the European Union (EU). The agreement was renewed for a further three years in late 2010. (Moroni was selected to host a new Indian Ocean Commission Centre for Fishing Surveillance, largely funded by the EU.)

MANUFACTURING AND SERVICES

The manufacturing sector contributed 3.7% of GDP in 2010, according to the AfDB. The sector consists primarily of the processing of vanilla and essential oils on Nzwani, and a few factories supplying the domestic market. According to the World Bank, manufacturing GDP increased at an average annual rate of 1.8% in 2001–09; manufacturing GDP increased by 3.8% in 2009.

The Comoros has a fragile tourism industry, partly because of perceived political instability. Tourist arrivals increased from 7,627 in 1990 to 27,474 in 1998, but had decreased to 15,000 by 2010. In 2010 tourism receipts totalled US $35.0m. The majority of tourists are from France. The services sector contributed an estimated 46.6% of GDP in 2010, according to the AfDB. World Bank estimates showed that the sector's GDP increased at an average rate of 3.8% per year in 2000–06; it increased by 14.5% in 2006. In 2007 a new facility at Moroni airport was completed; the project was financed by the Government of the People's Republic of China and was expected to precipitate a three-fold increase in annual passenger turnover.

TRANSPORT AND UTILITIES

Economic development in the Comoros is impeded by poor infrastructure, an increasingly erratic power and water supply, a very limited road system and a lack of reliable transportation between the islands and with the outside world. At the end of 1995 it was announced that the country's air carrier, Air Comores, was to be liquidated. Charter operations have taken its place, providing long-haul air links with Dubai, Paris (France) and Johannesburg (South Africa), although there have been constant problems in maintaining a regular service. In the mid-1990s plans to privatize state-owned enterprises, such as the Société Nationale des Postes et des Télécommunications, were impeded by inter-government dissension. The flooding in early 2012 caused damage to infrastructure and left some 204 km roads in need of reconstruction. In August, at a press conference in Moroni, the Consumers' Association of Information Technology and Communications expressed its firm opposition to the process of privatizing Comores Telecom, insisting that a broad consultation procedure take place, incorporating all sectors of public, private and civil society. Of primary concern was the loss of jobs that would occur as a result of the privatization.

By mid-1997 it had been agreed that Electricité et Eau des Comores (to be renamed Comorienne de l'Eau et de l'Electricité, CEE) would pass into private management by the French company SOGEA, with finance provided by the Caisse Française de Développement (CFD, now the Agence Française de Développement). This project, involving 41m. French francs in CFD aid, was repeatedly delayed, and for much of 1997 there was no network electricity supply on the islands. In 2001 CEE was renationalized as the Service Public de l'Eau et de l'Electricité, only to be privatized for a second time in January 2002, as MA-MWE—Gestion de l'Eau et de l'Electricité aux Comores. In May 2003 an agreement was signed with Egypt, whereby the latter would provide some $2.2m. in electrical equipment and training to help upgrade services in the islands. In October a contract to provide the Comoros with a Global Standard for Mobiles telephone network was awarded to Alcatel. In early 2005 it was announced that France had provided €1.5m. to upgrade rural water distribution networks on Nzwani and Mwali. Water services were severely affected by flash flooding in April 2012 and clean drinking water supplies were slowly being returned to the public in June. Emergency provisions of chlorine tablets were prioritized by local donors.

DEVELOPMENT, TRADE AND FINANCE

France represents the main source of economic support (see below), while the other member states of the EU, Japan, Saudi Arabia, Kuwait and the United Arab Emirates (UAE) also provide financial assistance. Following the devaluation of the Comoros franc in January 1994, the French Government agreed to cancel outstanding debt arrears. At the end of that year, however, France suspended budgetary assistance (which had totalled 24m. French francs in 1994), in response to the Comoran Government's failure to agree a structural adjustment programme with the IMF and the World Bank, but later agreed to continue to provide aid for projects in the social sector and education. Finance in the latter area was also to be forthcoming from the UN Development Programme, the World Bank and the UN Children's Fund. Following a bilateral agreement concluded between France and the Comoros in early 2005, it was expected that France would increase its dispersal of aid to the Comoros. Under the 10th European Development Fund, the EU pledged financial support for increased development, with the improvement of transport infrastructure networks to be a priority for the period 2008–13; this is in addition to assistance provided by France, the UN Development Programme and the World Bank. The approval in 2011 of Mayotte's status as a French overseas départemement threatened relations between France and the Comoros, which sought shared authority over the island. Nevertheless, France responded to appeals by the Comoros in May 2012 for assistance following severe flooding, supplying water treatment products, medication and equipment.

The Comoros' foreign-trade accounts have shown a persistent deficit; imports have tended to increase, while export receipts have fluctuated widely, in response to trends in international prices for vanilla, cloves and ylang ylang. In 2008, according to the AfDB, the principal source of imports was the UAE (accounting for some 12.2% of the total); the other major sources were France, China and Pakistan. France was the principal market for exports (14.3%) in that year; the other major purchaser was Turkey. The leading exports in 2010 were cloves and vanilla. The principal imports in that year were petroleum products, rice, and meat and meat products.

The annual rate of inflation averaged 4.2% during 2000–09. In 2009 the rate was 4.6%. According to the IMF, an estimated 13.3% of the labour force were unemployed in 2005. As a whole, the islands tended to achieve lower deficits than did the Union administration, which had relatively high spending on infrastructures and salaries, partly to avoid strike action. In January 2005 the budget for that year was passed by the Assemblée de l'Union (Assembly of the Union), along with legislation governing the division of revenue between the central and island administrations. The Union administration was to receive 33.8% of revenue, while Ngazidja, Nzwani and Mwali were to receive 30.7%, 26.8% and 8.8%, respectively. The Comoran budget surplus was estimated at 8,701m. Comoros francs in 2010, however in 2011 the Union recorded a budget deficit of 24,042m. Comoros francs.

The Comoros' general government gross debt was 107,939m. Comoros francs in 2009, equivalent to 56.9% of GDP. The Comoros' external public debt at the end of 2009 totalled US $279m., of which $264m. was public and publicly guaranteed debt. According to the AfDB, the cost of debt-servicing in 2009 was equivalent to 10.2% of the value of exports of goods and services. In November 2009 discussions took place with the 'Paris Club' of international creditors during which it was agreed that debt-servicing costs would be reduced. The 'Paris Club' also reiterated its commitment to 'prudent debt management'. In June 2010 the IMF and the World Bank's International Development Association (IDA) announced that the Comoros had made sufficient progress in political and economic reforms to have reached the Decision Point under the initiative for heavily indebted poor countries and was eligible to receive debt relief on an interim basis. Debt relief from the IDA would total $45.1m. and the Comoros would receive $4.3m. from the IMF.

In January 1994 the devaluation of the Comoros franc led to a sharp increase in the price of imported goods, prompting strike action in the education and health sectors in support of higher salaries. In February 1997 an IMF-supervised six-month surveillance programme was agreed. The Government hoped that this would lead to the approval of an enhanced structural adjustment facility, but the programme was soon beset by problems. By July the IMF was warning that insufficient progress had been made, especially where privatization and salary payments were concerned. Following a six-month extension of the monitoring programme, in February 1998 the IMF again concluded that the Comoros had failed to meet its economic objectives. In August increasing arrears on loan repayments led the World Bank to suspend the disbursement of funds to the Comoros. In early 1999 the EU suspended all aid to the islands. The intensification of political instability, following the seizure of power by the military in April, had a particularly adverse effect on maritime trade and on tourism. In January 2000, following the required repayment of arrears by the Comoran authorities, the World Bank resumed the disbursement of funds to the Comoros. In early 2000 the Comoran authorities reduced customs duties by 80% on products from member countries of the Indian Ocean Commission (IOC), as part of moves to comply with the integrated regional programme for trade development. In July 2001 a group of 'Friends of the Comoros', co-ordinated by the World Bank, pledged aid of $11.5m. for the alleviation of poverty and to assist with constitutional developments towards the establishment of a new Comoran entity. The funds were granted by the

World Bank itself, the EU, the Organisation Internationale de la Francophonie, France, Mauritius and Morocco. Moreover, it was hoped that a number of agreements reached later that year, worth an estimated €5.9m., would encourage the further development of the production of vanilla, ylang ylang and cloves, and increase international demand for those crops.

In July 2002 the IMF proposed that a budget for the entire Union of the Comoros be drawn up, and also that the Government of the Union of the Comoros be responsible for the running of all state-owned companies. In November the federal Government and the EU signed a National Indicator Programme on co-operation during 2002–07; the Comoros was to receive €27.3m. under the Programme, mostly for education. Throughout late 2002 and early 2003 considerable economic disruption was caused on Ngazidja by the crisis over the distribution of political power on the island, following partial devolution, and many businesses were threatened by dual taxation by the local and federal Governments.

In 2005 the Government agreed a 12-month staff-monitored programme with the IMF, with a view to reaching agreement on a Poverty Reduction and Growth Facility (PRGF) programme. Among the proposals made by the IMF were the reform of the tax system and the privatization of the state-owned telecommunications and petroleum companies. In late 2005 an IMF mission visited the Comoros and, while maintaining that progress had been made in addressing the budget deficit, stated that more time would be required fully to assess the progress of reforms. Meanwhile, in December a donors' conference was held in Mauritius, at which some US $200m. was pledged to assist with the Comoros' four-year development and poverty reduction plan.

In December of 2006 an IMF team visited the Comoros in order to assess their Interim Poverty Reduction Strategy Paper. It was hoped that a positive evaluation would lead to a Fund-supported PRGF programme. However, plans to implement such a programme were postponed in mid-2007 as a result of the political crisis surrounding the island presidential elections. Following new elections in June 2008, it was hoped that a level of stability could be achieved. Rising food and petroleum prices in 2008, together with a sharp decline in the value of the country's exports, particularly vanilla, led the IMF, in December, to approve US $3.4m. under its Exogenous Shocks Facility to ease the Comoros' external debt burden. At the same time the IMF disbursed $1.7m. in funds to the country under its Emergency Post-Conflict Assistance programme in order to support structural reforms. In September 2009 the first full Poverty Reduction Strategy Paper was adopted and the IMF completed a review of the Comoros' progress on economic development. According to an IMF report published in March 2010, under the PGRF a three-year loan of $22.5m. was approved to assist the country in meeting its Millennium Development Goals. The main priority was to achieve average GDP growth of 4.3% for the period 2010–14. An increase in government expenditure on infrastructure, health and education was anticipated, along with the gradual privatization of a number of state-owned companies, including Comores Télécom.

Following a review of the Extended Credit Facility (ECF), which replaced the PRGF as the Fund's main tool for medium-term financial support to low-income countries, in January 2011 the IMF approved the disbursement of US $2.42m. In 2012 the IMF approved an extension to the ECF arrangement to December 2013. In June 2012, in its third review under the ECF, an immediate disbursement of the equivalent of $2.37m. was granted. The severe flooding in April (see Recent History) was a major setback to improvements in the economic stability of the Union. The AU offered financial support and a meeting of local donors was convened to help restore services and infrastructure.

Statistical Survey

Sources (unless otherwise stated): *Rapport Annuel*, Banque Centrale des Comores, place de France, BP 405, Moroni; tel. 7731814; fax 7730349; e-mail bancecom@comorestelecom.km; internet www.banque-comores.km.

Note: Unless otherwise indicated, figures in this Statistical Survey exclude data for Mayotte.

AREA AND POPULATION

Area: 1,862 sq km (719 sq miles). *By Island:* Ngazidja (Grande-Comore) 1,146 sq km, Nzwani (Anjouan) 424 sq km, Mwali (Mohéli) 290 sq km.

Population: 446,817, at census of 15 September 1991; 575,660, at census of 1 September 2003. *Mid-2012* (UN estimate): 773,346 (Source: UN, *World Population Prospects: The 2010 Revision*). *By Island* (1991 census): Ngazidja (Grande-Comore) 233,533; Nzwani (Anjouan) 188,953; Mwali (Mohéli) 24,331.

Density (at mid-2012): 415.3 per sq km.

Population by Age and Sex (UN estimates at mid-2012): *0–14:* 329,501 (males 167,797, females 161,704); *15–64:* 423,200 (males 212,546, females 210,654); *65 and over:* 20,645 (males 9,275, females 11,370); *Total* 773,346 (males 389,618, females 383,728) (Source: UN, *World Population Prospects: The 2010 Revision*).

Principal Town (incl. suburbs, mid-2011, UN estimate): Moroni (capital) 53,819. Source: UN, *World Urbanization Prospects: The 2011 Revision*.

Births and Deaths (incl. figures for Mayotte, UN estimates, 2005–10): Average annual birth rate 39.0 per 1,000; average annual death rate 9.4 per 1,000. Source: UN, *World Population Prospects: The 2010 Revision*.

Life Expectancy (years at birth, including Mayotte): 60.6 (males 59.3; females 62.0) in 2010. Source: World Bank, World Development Indicators database.

Economically Active Population (ILO estimates, '000 persons at mid-1980, including figures for Mayotte): Agriculture, forestry and fishing 150; Industry 10; Services 20; Total 181 (males 104, females 77) (Source: ILO, *Economically Active Population Estimates and Projections, 1950–2025*). *1991 Census* (persons aged 12 years and over, excluding Mayotte): Total labour force 126,510 (males 88,034, females 38,476) (Source: UN, *Demographic Yearbook*). *Mid-2012* (official estimates in '000): Agriculture, etc. 234; Total labour force 341 (Source: FAO).

HEALTH AND WELFARE

Key Indicators

Total Fertility Rate (children per woman, 2010): 4.9.

Under-5 Mortality Rate (per 1,000 live births, 2010): 86.

HIV/AIDS (% of persons aged 15–49, 2009): 0.1.

Physicians (per 1,000 head, 2004): 0.15.

Hospital Beds (per 1,000 head, 2006): 2.2.

Health Expenditure (2009): US $ per head (PPP): 34.

Health Expenditure (2009): % of GDP: 3.2.

Health Expenditure (2009): public (% of total): 53.2.

Access to Water (% of persons, 2010): 95.

Access to Sanitation (% of persons, 2010): 36.

Total Carbon Dioxide Emissions ('000 metric tons, 2008): 124.7.

Carbon Dioxide Emissions Per Head (metric tons, 2008): 0.2.

Human Development Index (2011): ranking: 163.

Human Development Index (2011): value: 0.433.

For sources and definitions, see explanatory note on p. vi.

AGRICULTURE, ETC.

Principal Crops ('000 metric tons, unless otherwise indicated, 2010, FAO estimates): Rice, paddy 19.4; Maize 6.4; Potatoes 0.8; Sweet potatoes 5.4; Cassava (Manioc) 57.0; Taro 10.6; Yams 4.2; Pulses 17.4; Groundnuts, with shell 1.0; Coconuts 88.2; Tomatoes 0.7; Bananas 44.4; Vanilla (dried, metric tons) 66; Cloves 2.8.

Aggregate Production ('000 metric tons, may include official, semi-official or estimated data): Total vegetables (incl. melons) 6.0; Total fruits (excl. melons) 47.8.

Livestock ('000 head, year ending September 2010, FAO estimates): Asses 5.0; Cattle 50.0; Sheep 23.0; Goats 118.0; Chickens 520.

Livestock Products (metric tons, 2010, FAO estimates): Cattle meat 1,243; Sheep and goat meat 469; Chicken meat 536; Cows' milk 5,200; Hen eggs 784.

Fishing ('000 metric tons, live weight of capture, 2010, FAO estimates unless otherwise indicated): Total catch 52.3 (Sardines 4.2—official figure; Sardinellas 5.5—official figure; Anchovies, etc. 5.2—official figure; Seerfishes 0.8; Skipjack tuna 4.5; Yellowfin tuna 8.0; Chub mackerel 2.6—official figure; Jack and horse mackerels 15.5—official figure; Carangids 0.7).

Source: FAO.

INDUSTRY

Electric Energy (million kWh): 51.0 in 2006; 53.0 in 2007; 54.0 in 2008 (Source: UN Industrial Commodity Statistics Database).

FINANCE

Currency and Exchange Rates: 100 centimes = 1 Comoros franc. *Sterling, Dollar and Euro Equivalents* (31 May 2012): £1 sterling = 614.970 Comoros francs; US $1 = 396.652 Comoros francs; €1 = 491.968 Comoros francs; 1,000 Comoros francs = £1.63 = $2.52 = €2.03. *Average Exchange Rate* (Comoros francs per US $): 354.140 in 2009; 371.458 in 2010; 353.900 in 2011. Note: The Comoros franc was introduced in 1981, replacing (at par) the CFA franc. The fixed link to French currency was retained, with the exchange rate set at 1 French franc = 50 Comoros francs. This remained in effect until January 1994, when the Comoros franc was devalued by 33.3%, with the exchange rate adjusted to 1 French franc = 75 Comoros francs. This relationship to French currency remained in effect with the introduction of the euro on 1 January 1999. From that date, accordingly, a fixed exchange rate of €1 = 491.968 Comoros francs has been in operation.

Budget (million Comoros francs, 2011): *Revenue:* Tax revenue 23,381; Non-tax revenue 4,946; Total 28,327 (excluding grants received 19,423). *Expenditure:* Current expenditure 33,569 (Wages and salaries 18,433); Capital expenditure 18,800; Total 52,369. Source: African Development Bank.

International Reserves (US $ million at 31 December 2011): Gold (national valuation) 0.92; Reserve position in IMF 0.83; Foreign exchange 139.32; Total 141.07. Source: IMF, *International Financial Statistics*.

Money Supply (million Comoros francs at 31 December 2011): Currency outside depository corporations 19,985; Transferable deposits 28,835; Other deposits 26,509; *Broad money* 75,329. Source: IMF, *International Financial Statistics*.

Cost of Living (Consumer Price Index; base: 2000 = 100): All items 144.8 in 2009; 150.3 in 2010; 153.2 in 2011. Source: African Development Bank.

Expenditure on the Gross Domestic Product (million Comoros francs at current prices, 2010, estimates): Government final consumption expenditure 22,597; Private final consumption expenditure 197,553; Gross fixed capital formation 23,485; Changes in inventories 3,380; *Total domestic expenditure* 247,015; Exports of goods and services 5,922; *Less* Imports of goods and services 58,609; *GDP in purchasers' values* 194,329. Source: African Development Bank.

Gross Domestic Product by Economic Activity (million Comoros francs at current prices, 2010, estimates): Agriculture, hunting, forestry and fishing 85,351; Manufacturing 7,398; Electricity, gas and water 2,774; Construction 10,782; Wholesale and retail trade, restaurants and hotels 50,740; Transport and communications 9,067; Finance, insurance, real estate and business services 8,366; Public administration and defence 23,686; Other services 996; *Sub-total* 199,160; Indirect taxes –4,832; *GDP in purchasers' values* 194,329. Source: African Development Bank.

Balance of Payments (million Comoros francs, 2010, provisional): Exports of goods f.o.b. 8,386; Imports of goods f.o.b. –67,015; *Trade balance* –58,629; Services (net) –10,233; *Balance on goods and services* –68,862; Income (net) –315; *Balance on goods, services and income* –69,177; Current transfers (net) 51,991; *Current balance* –17,186; Capital and financial account 23,453; Net errors and omissions –27; *Overall balance* 6,240.

EXTERNAL TRADE

Principal Commodities (million Comoros francs, 2010): *Imports c.i.f.:* Rice 7,254; Meat and meat products 5,184; Petroleum products 17,327; Iron and steel 2,919; Total (incl. others) 84,280. *Exports f.o.b.:* Vanilla 309; Cloves 5,410; Total (incl. others) 8,386. Source: African Development Bank.

Principal Trading Partners (million Comoros francs, 2008): *Imports:* China, People's Republic 8,562; France (incl. Monaco) 9,684; Pakistan 4,286; South Africa 2,226; United Arab Emirates 10,381; Total (incl. others) 85,406. *Exports:* France (incl. Monaco) 3,573; Germany 486; Singapore 931; Turkey 2,027; USA 327; Total (incl. others) 25,001. Source: African Development Bank.

TRANSPORT

Road Traffic (motor vehicles in use, 2007): Passenger cars 19,245; Vans and lorries 1,790; Motorcycles and mopeds 1,343; Total 22,378. Source: International Road Federation, *World Road Statistics*.

Shipping: *Merchant Fleet* (registered at 31 December 2009): Number of vessels 312; Total displacement (grt) 905,214 (Source: IHS Fairplay, *World Fleet Statistics*). *International Sea-borne Freight Traffic* (estimates, '000 metric tons, 1991): Goods loaded 12; Goods unloaded 107 (Source: UN Economic Commission for Africa, *African Statistical Yearbook*).

Civil Aviation (traffic at Prince Said Ibrahim international airport, 1999): Passengers carried ('000) 130.4; Freight handled 1,183 metric tons.

TOURISM

Tourist Arrivals (2007): France 8,975; Madagascar 818; Réunion 1,286; South Africa 409; Total (incl. others) 14,582. *2010:* 15,000.

Receipts from Tourism (US $ million, excl. passenger transport, unless otherwise indicated): 32.0 in 2009; 35.0 in 2010.

Source: World Tourism Organization.

COMMUNICATIONS MEDIA

Radio Receivers (1997): 90,000 in use. Source: UNESCO, *Statistical Yearbook*.

Television Receivers (1997): 1,000 in use. Source: UNESCO, *Statistical Yearbook*.

Telephones (2011): 23,600 main lines in use. Source: International Telecommunication Union.

Mobile Cellular Telephones (2011): 216,400 in use. Source: International Telecommunication Union.

Personal Computers: 5,400 (9.0 per 1,000 persons) in 2005. Source: International Telecommunication Union.

Internet Subscribers (2009): 1,600. Source: International Telecommunication Union.

EDUCATION

Pre-primary (2007/08, unless otherwise indicated): 483 teachers (2004/05); 14,058 pupils (males 7,280, females 6,778). Source: UNESCO Institute for Statistics.

Primary (2007/08, unless otherwise indicated): 348 schools (1998); 3,685 teachers (males 2,326, females 1,359); 111,115 pupils (males 58,775; females 52,340). Sources: UNESCO Institute for Statistics and IMF, *Comoros: Statistical Appendix* (August 2005).

Secondary (2004/05, unless otherwise indicated): Teachers: general education 2,812 (2006/07); teacher training 11 (1991/92); vocational 20. Pupils: 43,349 (males 24,921, females 18,428). Sources: UNESCO Institute for Statistics and IMF, *Comoros: Statistical Appendix* (August 2005).

Post-secondary Vocational (2004/05): 51 teachers (males 41, females 10); 734 pupils (males 399, females 335). Source: UNESCO Institute for Statistics.

Tertiary (2003/04): 130 teachers (males 111, females 19); 1,779 pupils (males 1,011, females 768). *2008/09:* 5,091 pupils. Source: UNESCO Institute for Statistics.

Pupil-teacher Ratio (primary education, UNESCO estimate): 30.2 in 2007/08. Source: UNESCO Institute for Statistics.

Adult Literacy Rate: 69.7% (males 80.2%; females 74.9%) in 2010. Source: UNESCO Institute for Statistics.

Directory

The Constitution

In accordance with an agreement on national reconciliation, signed on 17 February 2001 by representatives of the Government, the separatist administration on Nzwani, opposition parties and civil society, a new Constitution was presented in August and approved by referendum on 23 December. Under the terms of the new Constitution, the country was renamed the Union of the Comoros, and each of the three islands, Ngazidja, Nzwani and Mwali, was to be granted partial autonomy and was to be headed by a local government. The Union, governed by a central government, was to be headed by the President. The main provisions of the Constitution are summarized below.

PREAMBLE

The preamble affirms the will of the Comoran people to derive from the state religion, Islam, inspiration for the principles and laws that the State and its institutions govern; to guarantee the pursuit of a common future; to establish new institutions based on the rule of law, democracy and good governance, which guarantee an equal division of power between the Union and those islands that compose it; to adhere to the principles laid down by the Charters of the UN, the Organization of African Unity (now the African Union) and the Organization of the Islamic Conference and by the Treaty of the League of Arab States; and to guarantee the rights of all citizens, without discrimination, in accordance with the UN Declaration of Human Rights and the African Charter of Human Rights.

The preamble guarantees solidarity between the Union and the islands, as well as between the islands themselves; equality amongst the islands and their inhabitants, regardless of race, origin, or religion; the right to freedom of expression, education, health and justice; the freedom and security of individuals; the inviolability of an individual's home or property; and the right of children to be protected against abandonment, exploitation and violence.

THE UNION OF THE COMOROS

The Comoros archipelago constitutes a republic. Sovereignty belongs to the people, and is exercised through their elected representatives or by the process of referendum. There is universal secret suffrage, which can be direct or indirect, for all citizens who are over the age of 18 and in full possession of their civil and political rights. Political parties and groups operate freely, respecting national sovereignty, democracy and territorial integrity.

COMPETENCIES OF THE UNION AND THE ISLANDS

Each island freely administers its own affairs, while respecting the unity of the Union and its territorial integrity. Each island establishes its own fundamental laws, which must respect the Constitution. All Comorans within the Union have equal rights, freedoms and duties. All the islands are headed by an elected executive and assembly. The Union has ultimate authority over the individual islands and legislates on matters of religion, nationality, currency, foreign affairs, external defence and national identity. As regards those competencies shared by both the Union and the islands, the Union has ultimate jurisdiction only if the issue concerned affects more than one island, if the matter cannot be resolved by one island alone, or if the judicial, economic or social integrity of the Union may be compromised. The islands are responsible for those matters not covered by the Union, or by shared responsibility. The islands are financially autonomous.

THE UNION'S INSTITUTIONS

Executive Power

The President of the Union is the symbol of national unity. He is the guarantor of national independence, the unity of the Republic, the autonomy of the islands, territorial integrity and adherence to international agreements. He is the Head of State and is responsible for external defence and security, foreign affairs and negotiating and ratifying treaties.

The Council of the Union is composed of the President and two Vice-Presidents, selected from each island. The members of the Council are elected for a four-year term, and the position of President rotates between the islands, while the Vice-Presidents are inhabitants of the two remaining islands. The President appoints the members of the Government (ministers of the Union) and determines their respective portfolios. The composition of the Government must represent all of the islands equally.

Legislative Power

Legislative power is vested in the Assembly of the Union (Assemblée de l'Union), which is composed of 33 deputies, elected for a period of five years. Nine of the deputies are selected by the islands' local assemblies (three deputies per island) and 24 are directly elected by universal suffrage. The Assemblée de l'Union sits for two sessions each year and, if necessary, for extraordinary sessions.

Judicial Power

Judicial power is independent of executive and legislative power. The President of the Union is the guarantor of the independence of the judicial system and is assisted by the Higher Council of the Magistracy (Conseil Supérieur de la Magistrature). The Supreme Court (Cour Suprême) is the highest ruling authority in judicial, administrative and fiscal matters, and its rulings are final and binding. A Constitutional Court (Cour Constitutionelle) was created in 2004.

THE HIGH COUNCIL

The High Council considers constitutional matters, oversees the results of elections and referendums and guarantees basic human rights and civil liberties. Moreover, the High Council is responsible for ruling on any conflicts regarding the separate competencies of the Union and the islands. The President of the Union, the Vice-Presidents, the President of the Assemblée de l'Union, and the three island Governors each appoint one member to the High Council. Members are elected for a six-year mandate, renewable once; the President of the High Council is appointed by the members for a six-year term.

REVISION OF THE CONSTITUTION

The power to initiate constitutional revision is jointly vested in the President of the Union and the members of the Assemblée de l'Union. Constitutional revision must be approved by a majority of two-thirds of the deputies in the Assemblée de l'Union and by two-thirds of the members of the islands' local assemblies. However, the organizational structure of the Union cannot be revised, and any revision that may affect the unity and territorial boundaries of the Union is not permitted.

AMENDMENTS OF MAY 2009

At a referendum held on 16 May 2009 94.0% of voters approved changes to the Constitution, which took effect on 23 May. Most notably the presidential mandate was extended from four to five years, while the powers of the regional Governors (formerly Presidents) were significantly reduced.

The Government

HEAD OF STATE

Federal President: Dr Ikililou Dhoinine (elected 26 December 2010).

REGIONAL GOVERNORS

Mwali: Mohamed Ali Said.

Ngazidja: Mouigni Baraka Saïd Soilih.

Nzwani: Anissi Chamsidine.

GOVERNMENT OF THE UNION OF THE COMOROS
(September 2012)

Vice-President, with responsibility for Production, the Environment, Energy, Industry and Crafts: Dr Fouad Mohadji.

Vice-President, with responsibility for Finance, the Economy, the Budget and Investments and External Trading (Privatization): Mohamed Ali Soilihi.

Vice-President, with responsibility for Land Settlement, Town Planning and Housing: Nourdine Bourhane.

Minister of External Relations and Co-operation, with responsibility for the Diaspora, and for Francophone and Arab Relations: Mohamed Bakri Ben Abdoulfatah Charif.

Minister of Post and Telecommunications, Communication and the Promotion of New Information Technology, with responsibility for Transport and Tourism: Mouhidine Rastami.

Keeper of the Seals, Minister of Justice, the Civil Service, Administrative Reforms, Human Rights and Islamic Affairs: Dr Ahmed Anliane.

Minister of National Education, Research, Culture and the Arts, with responsibility for Youth and Sports: Mohamed Issimaila.

Minister of Health, Solidarity, Social Cohesion and Gender Empowerment: Dr Moinafouraha Ahmed.

Minister of Employment, Professional Training, Labour and Female Entrepreneurship, Government Spokesperson: SITI KASSIM.

Minister of the Interior, Information and Decentralization, with responsibility for Relations with the Institutions: ABDALLAH HAMADA.

MINISTRIES

Office of the Head of State: Palais de Beit Salam, BP 521, Moroni; tel. 7744808; fax 7744829; e-mail presidence@comorestelecom.km; internet www.beit-salam.km.

Ministry of Agriculture, Fisheries, the Environment, Energy, Industry and Crafts: Moroni.

Ministry of the Civil Service, Administrative and Institutional Reforms, Decentralization and Human Rights: Moroni.

Ministry of Defence, the Interior and Information: Moroni.

Ministry of External Relations and Co-operation: BP 428, Moroni; tel. 7732306; fax 7732108; e-mail mirex@snpt.km.

Ministry of Finance, the Budget and Investments: BP 324, Moroni; tel. 7744140; fax 7744141.

Ministry of Health, Solidarity and Gender Empowerment: Moroni.

Ministry of Industry, Labour, Employment, Female Entrepreneurship and External Trade: Moroni.

Ministry of Justice, Penitentiary Administration, Islamic Affairs and Relations with Parliament: BP 2028, Moroni; tel. 7744040; fax 7734045.

Ministry of Land Settlement, Infrastructure, Town Planning and Housing: BP 12, Moroni; tel. 7744500; fax 7732222.

Ministry of National Education, Research, Culture and the Arts: BP 73, Moroni; tel. 7744180; fax 7744181.

Ministry of Post and Telecommunications, Communication and the Promotion of New Information Technology: BP 1315, Moroni; tel. 7734266; fax 7732222.

Ministry of Transport and Tourism: Moroni; tel. 7732098.

President and Legislature

PRESIDENT

Presidential Election, First Round, 7 November 2010

Candidate	Votes	% of votes
Dr Ikililou Dhoinine	3,785	28.19
Mohamed Saïd Fazul	3,080	22.94
Dr Abdou Djabir	1,327	9.88
Bianrifi Tarmidi	1,250	9.31
Saïd Dhiuffur Bounou	1,154	8.59
Hamada Madi Boléro	1,060	7.89
Mohamed Larif Oukacha	977	7.28
Mohamed Hassanaly	523	3.90
Abdoulhakime Said Allaoui	208	1.55
Zahariat Said Ahmed	63	0.47
Total	13,427	100.00

Presidential Election, Second Round, 26 December 2010

Candidate	Votes	% of votes
Dr Ikililou Dhoinine	106,890	60.91
Mohamed Saïd Fazul	57,587	32.81
Dr Abdou Djabir	11,018	6.28
Total	175,495	100.00

LEGISLATURE

Assemblée de l'Union: BP 447, Moroni; tel. 7744000; fax 7744011.

President: BOURHANE HAMIDOU.

Elections, 6 and 20 December 2009

Party	Seats
Mouvance Présidentielle	17
Opposition Candidates	4
Allies of the Mouvance Présidentielle	3
Total	33*

* The remaining nine seats were filled by nominees from the islands' local assemblies, each of which selected three members.

Election Commission

Commission Électorale Nationale Indépendante aux Comores (CENI): Moroni; f. 2007 to succeed the Commission Nationale des Élections aux Comores; 10–13 mems; each island has a Commission Électorale Insulaire, consisting of 7 mems; Pres. MMADI LAGUERA.

Political Organizations

CHUMA (Islands' Fraternity and Unity Party): Moroni; e-mail chuma@pourlescomores.com; f. 1985; Leader SAÏD ALI KEMAL.

Convention pour le Renouveau des Comores (CRC): f. 2002; Leader Col ASSOUMANI AZALI; Sec.-Gen. HOUMED M'SAIDIE.

Djawabu: Leader YOUSSOUF SAÏD SOILIHI.

Forces pour l'Action Républicaine (FAR): Leader Col ABDOURAZAK ABDULHAMID.

Front de l'Action pour la Démocratie et le Développment (FADD): Nzwani; main opposition party on Nzwani.

Front Démocratique (FD): BP 758, Moroni; tel. 7733603; e-mail idriss@snpt.km; f. 1982; Chair. MOUSTOIFA SAÏD CHEIKH; Sec.-Gen. ABDALLAH HALIFA.

Front National pour la Justice (FNJ): Islamist fundamentalist orientation; Leader AHMED RACHID.

Mouvement des Citoyens pour la République (MCR): f. 1998; Leader MAHAMOUD MRADABI.

Mouvement Populaire Anjouanais (MPA): f. 1997 by merger of Organisation pour l'Indépendance d'Anjouan and Mouvement Séparatiste Anjouanais; principal separatist movement on Nzwani (Anjouan).

Mouvement pour la Démocratie et le Progrès (MDP—NGDC): Moroni; Leader ABBAS DJOUSSOUF.

Mouvement pour la République, l'Ouverture et l'Unité de l'Archipel des Comores (Mouroua) (Movement for the Republic, Openness and the Unity of the Comoran Archipelago): Moroni; f. 2005; advocates institutional reform; Pres. SAÏD ABBAS DAHALANI.

Mouvement pour le Socialisme et la Démocratie (MSD): Moroni; f. 2000 by splinter group of the FD; Leader ABDOU SOEFOU.

Parti Comorien pour la Démocratie et le Progrès (PCDP): route Djivani, BP 179, Moroni; tel. 7731733; fax 7730650; Leader ALI MROUDJAÉ.

Parti Républicain des Comores (PRC): BP 665, Moroni; tel. 7733489; fax 7733329; e-mail prc@online.fr; internet www.chez.com/prc; f. 1998; Leader MOHAMED SAÏD ABDALLAH M'CHANGAMA.

Parti Social Démocrate des Comores (PSDC-Dudja): Ngazidja; f. 2008; Leader ABDOU SOULÉ ELBAK; Sec.-Gen. Dr SOULE AHAMADA.

Parti Socialiste des Comores (Pasoco): tel. 7731328; Leader AHMED AFFANDI ALI.

Rassemblement pour une Initiative de Développement avec une Jeunesse Avertie (RIDJA): BP 1905, Moroni; tel. and fax 7733356; f. 1999; Leader SAÏD LARIFOU; Sec.-Gen. AHAMED ACHIRAFI.

Rassemblement National pour le Développement (RND): f. 1996; Chair. OMAR TAMOU; Sec. Gen. ABDOULHAMID AFFRAITANE.

Shawiri: Moroni; Leader Col MAHAMOUD MRADABI.

Shawiri—Unafasiya (SU): Moroni; f. 2003 following a split in Shawiri; Sec.-Gen. HADJI BEN SAÏD.

Union Nationale pour la Démocratie aux Comores (UNDC): Moroni; f. 1986; Pres. KAMAR EZZAMANE MOHAMED.

There are also a number of Islamist groups.

Diplomatic Representation

EMBASSIES IN THE COMOROS

China, People's Republic: Coulée de Lave, C109, BP 442, Moroni; tel. 7732521; fax 7732866; e-mail ambassadechine@snpt.km; Ambassador WANG LEYOU.

France: blvd de Strasbourg, BP 465, Moroni; tel. 7730615; fax 7730922; e-mail cad.moroni-ambassade@diplomatie.gouv.fr; internet www.ambafrance-km.org; Ambassador LUC HALLADE.

Libya: Moroni; Chargé d'affaires HUSSEIN ALI AL-MIZDAWI.

South Africa: BP 2589, Moroni; tel. 7734783; fax 7734786; e-mail moroni@foreign.gov.za; Ambassador MASILO MABETA.

Judicial System

Under the terms of the Constitution, the President is the guarantor of the independence of the judicial system, and is assisted by the Higher Council of the Magistracy (Conseil Supérieur de la Magistrature). The highest ruling authority in judicial, administrative and fiscal matters is the Supreme Court (Cour Suprême), which comprises a President, a Vice-President, an Attorney-General, at least nine councillors, at least one law commissioner, a general advocate, a chief clerk and other clerks. The High Council considers constitutional matters. A Constitutional Court (Cour Constitutionelle), comprising eight members—appointed by the President of the Union of the Comoros, the Vice-Presidents and the three regional Governors, was established in 2004.

Cour Constitutionelle (Constitutional Court): Moroni; e-mail mohamedyoussouf@hotmail.com; 8 mems.

Cour Suprême: Moroni; f. 2011.

Religion

The majority of the population are Muslims, mostly Sunni.

ISLAM

Organisation Islamique des Comores: BP 596, Coulée, Moroni; tel. 7732071.

CHRISTIANITY

The Roman Catholic Church

Adherents comprise just 1% of the total population.

Office of Vicariate Apostolic of the Comoros: Mission Catholique, BP 46, Moroni; tel. and fax 7631996; fax 7730503; e-mail mcatholique@comorestelecom.km; f. 1975; Vicar Apostolic Bishop CHARLES MAHUZA YAVA.

The Press

Albalad: Bacha ancien SOCOCOM, route Asgaraly, BP 7702, Moroni; tel. 7739471; e-mail amoindjie@albaladcomores.com; internet www.albaladcomores.com; daily; Dir of Publication ALI MOINDJIÉ.

Al Watwan: Nagoudjou, BP 984, Moroni-Coulée; tel. and fax 7734448; fax 7733340; e-mail contact@alwatwan.net; internet www.alwatwan.net; f. 1985; weekly; state-owned; Dir-Gen. HASSANE MOINDJIÉ (acting); Editor-in-Chief MOHAMED SOILIHI AHMED; circ. 1,500.

La Gazette des Comores: BP 2216, Moroni; tel. 7735234; e-mail la_gazette@snpt.km; weekly; Publication Dir ALLAOUI SAÏD OMAR.

Kashkazi: BP 5311, Moroni; internet www.kashkazi.com; f. 2005; weekly; French.

Le Matin des Comores: BP 1040, Moroni; tel. 7732995; fax 7732939; daily; Dir ALILOIAFA MOHAMED SAÏD.

NEWS AGENCY

Agence Comorienne de Presse (HZK-Presse): BP 2216, Moroni; tel. and fax 7632620; e-mail hzk_presse2@yahoo.fr; internet www.hzkpresse.com; f. 2004; Dir EL-HAD SAID OMAR.

PRESS ASSOCIATION

Organisation Comorienne de la Presse Écrite (OCPE): Moroni; f. 2004; Pres. ABOUBACAR MCHANGAMA.

Publisher

KomÉdit: BP 535, Moroni; e-mail edition@komedit.com; f. 2000; general.

Broadcasting and Communications

TELECOMMUNICATIONS

Autorité Nationale de Régulation des TIC (ANRTIC): Moroni; tel. 7634595; e-mail ibrahim.mzemohamed@gmail.com; f. 2009; Dir-Gen. MOHAMED HASSANE ALFEINE.

Comores Télécom (Comtel): BP 7000, Moroni; tel. 7631031; fax 7732222; e-mail marketing@comorestelecom.km; internet www.comorestelecom.km; formerly Société Nationale des Postes et des Télécommunications; post and telecommunications operations separated in 2004; scheduled for privatization; also operates mobile cellular telephone network (HURI); Dir-Gen. MAHAMOUDOU ABIAMRI.

BROADCASTING

Transmissions to the Comoros from Radio France Internationale commenced in early 1994. A number of privately owned radio and television stations also broadcast in the Comoros.

Office de la Radio Télévision des Comores (ORTC): Moroni; internet www.radiocomores.km; Comoran state broadcasting company; broadcasts Radio Comoros (f. 1960) and Télévision Nationale Comorienne (TNC, f. 2006); Dir-Gen. SOILIH MOHAMED SOILIH.

Radio-Télévision Anjouanaise (RTA): Mbouyoujou-Ouani, Nzwani; tel. 7710124; e-mail contact@rtanjouan.org; internet www.rtanjouan.org; f. 1997; television station f. 2003; owned by the Nzwani regional government; Dir (Radio) FAHARDINE ABDOULBAY; Dir (Television) AMIR ABDALLAH.

Radio

Radio-Comoro: BP 250, Moroni; tel. 7732531; fax 7730303; govt-controlled; domestic programmes in Comoran and French; international broadcasts in Swahili, Arabic and French; Dir-Gen. ISMAIL IBOUROI; Tech. Dir ABDULLAH RADJAB.

Radio Dzialandzé Mutsamudu (RDM): Mutsamudu, Nzwani; f. 1992; broadcasts on Nzwani; Co-ordinator SAÏD ALI DACAR MGAZI.

Radio KAZ: Mkazi, BP 1933; tel. 7735201.

Radio Ngazidja: Moroni; broadcasts on Ngazidja; also known as Radio Mdjidjengo; represents Ngazidja regional government; Man. MOHAMED ABDELKADER.

Television

Djabal TV: Iconi, BP 675, Moroni; tel. 7736767.

Mtsangani Television (MTV): Mtsangani, BP 845, Moroni; tel. 7733316; f. 1996; owned by Centre d'Animation Socio-culturelle de Matsangani; cultural and educational programmes.

TV—SHA: Shashagnogo; tel. 7733636.

Finance

In 2010 there were four banking institutions in the Comoros: one central bank, one commercial bank, one development bank and one savings bank.

BANKING

(cap. = capital; res = reserves; dep. = deposits; m. = million; brs = branches; amounts in Comoros francs)

Central Bank

Banque Centrale des Comores: pl. de France, BP 405, Moroni; tel. 7731814; fax 7730349; e-mail bancecom@comorestelecom.com; internet www.bancecom.com; f. 1981; bank of issue; cap. 1,100m., res 10,305m., dep. 17,606m. (Dec. 2006); Gov. MZÉ ABOUDOU MOHAMED CHANFIOU.

Commercial Bank

Banque pour l'Industrie et le Commerce—Comores (BIC): pl. de France, BP 175, Moroni; tel. 7730243; fax 7731229; e-mail bic@bnpparibas.com; f. 1990; 51% owned by BNP Paribas-BDDI Participations (France); 34% state-owned; cap. 300.0m., res 1,690.2m., dep. 16,263.3m. (Dec. 2009); Dir-Gen. CHRISTIAN GOULT; 6 brs.

Savings Bank

Société Nationale de la Poste et des Services Financiers (SNPSF): BP 5000, Moroni; tel. 734327; fax 730304; internet www.lapostecomores.com; f. 2005; Dir-Gen. IBRAHIM ABDALLAH.

Development Bank

Banque de Développement des Comores: pl. de France, BP 298, Moroni; tel. 7720818; fax 7730397; e-mail info@bdevcom.net; internet www.bdevcom.net; f. 1982; provides loans, guarantees and equity participation for small- and medium-scale projects; 50% state-owned; cap. and res 1,242.0m., total assets 3,470.5m. (Dec. 2002); Pres. MZE CHEI OUBEIDI; Gen. Man. SAÏD ABDILLAHI.

Trade and Industry

GOVERNMENT AGENCIES

Office National du Commerce: Moroni; state-operated agency for the promotion and development of domestic and external trade.

Office National d'Importation et de Commercialisation du Riz (ONICOR): BP 748, Itsambouni, Moroni; tel. 7735566; fax 7730144; e-mail onicor_moroni@snpt.km; Dir-Gen. ALADINE DAROUMI.

Société de Développement de la Pêche Artisanale des Comores (SODEPAC): Moroni; state-operated agency overseeing fisheries development programme.

DEVELOPMENT ORGANIZATION

Centre Fédéral d'Appui au Développement Rural (CEFADER): Moroni; rural development org. with branches on each island.

CHAMBERS OF COMMERCE

Union des Chambres de Commerce, d'Industrie et d'Agriculture des Comores: BP 763, Moroni; tel. 7730958; fax 7731983; e-mail secretariat@uccia.km; internet www.uccia-comores.com; privatized in 1995; Pres. AHMED ALI BAZI.

TRADE ASSOCIATIONS

Organisation Comorienne de la Vanille (OCOVA): BP 472, Moroni; tel. 7732709; fax 7732719.

There is a further association, the **Fédération du Secteur Privé Comorien** (FSPC).

EMPLOYERS' ORGANIZATIONS

Club d'Actions des Promoteurs Economiques: Moroni; f. 1999; Head SAÏD HASSANE DINI.

Organisation Patronale des Comores (OPACO): Oasis, BP 981, Moroni; tel. 7730848; internet www.opaco.km; f. 1991; Pres. MOHAMED ABDALLAH HALIFA.

UTILITIES

MA-MWE—Gestion de l'Eau et de l'Electricité aux Comores: BP 1762, Moroni; tel. 7733130; fax 7732359; e-mail cee@snpt.km; f. as Electricité et Eau des Comores; transferred to private management and renamed Comorienne de l'Eau et de l'Electricité in 1997; renationalized and renamed Service Public de l'Eau et de l'Electricité in 2001; reprivatized in Jan. 2002 and renamed as above; responsible for the production and distribution of electricity and water; Dir-Gen. HENRI MLANAO ALPHONSE.

Société d'Electricité d'Anjouan (EDA): Nzwani; Technical Dir YOUSSOUF ALI OICHEH.

STATE-OWNED ENTERPRISE

Societé Comorienne des Hydrocarbures (SCH): BP 28, Moroni; tel. 7730486; fax 7731883; imports petroleum products; Dir-Gen. HOUSSEINE CHEIKH SOILIH.

MAJOR COMPANIES

Agecom: BP 2242, Oasis, Moroni; tel. 7733677; importation of food products and construction material.

Exportations Salimamoud: BP 287, Magoudjou, Moroni; tel. 7732394; fax 7732395; import and export of meat products, vanilla.

TRADE UNION

Confédération des Travailleurs des Comores (CTC): BP 1199, Moroni; tel. and fax 7633439; e-mail syndicatctcomores@yahoo.fr; f. 1996; Sec.-Gen. IBOUROI ALI TABIBOU; 5,000 mems.

Transport

ROADS

In 2000 there were an estimated 880 km of classified roads. About 76.5% of the network was paved in that year.

SHIPPING

The port of Mutsamudu, on Nzwani, can accommodate vessels of up to 11 m draught. Goods from Europe are routed via Madagascar, and coastal vessels connect the Comoros with the east coast of Africa. The country's registered merchant fleet at 31 December 2009 numbered 312 vessels, totalling 905,214 grt.

Autorité Portuaire des Comores (APC): Moroni; f. 2001.

Société de Représentation et de Navigation (SORNAV): M.Z.I. Mavouna, BP 2493, Moroni; tel. 7730590; fax 7730377; e-mail sornav.moroni@comorestelecom.km; internet www.sornav.com; f. 1996; shipping agents; responsible for handling, unloading and shipping of goods; Dir-Gen. Capt. MANSOUR IBRAHIM.

CIVIL AVIATION

The international airport is at Moroni-Hahaya on Ngazidja. Work began on the upgrading of the airport in late 2004. Each of the other islands has a small airfield. International services are operated by Air Austral (Réunion), Air Mayotte, Air Tanzania, Sudan Airways, Precision Air (Tanzania) and Yemenia. Kenya Airways commenced flying to the Comoros and Mayotte in November 2006.

Agence Nationale de l'Aviation Civile et de la Météorologie (ANACM): Moroni; tel. 7730948; e-mail transport@anacm-comores.com; internet www.anacm-comores.com; f. 2008; Dir-Gen. MOHAMED ATTOUMANE (acting).

AB Aviation: Hadoudja, Moroni; tel. and fax 7732714; internet www.flyabaviation.com; f. 2010.

Air Service Comores (ASC): Moroni; tel. 7733366; internet www.airservicecomores.com; internal services and international flights to Madagascar.

Comores Aviation International: route Corniche, Moroni; tel. 7733400; fax 7733401; internet www.comoresaviation.com; f. 1999; twice-weekly charter flights between Moroni and Mayotte; Dir JEAN-MARC HEINTZ.

Tourism

The principal tourist attractions are the beaches, underwater fishing and mountain scenery. Increasing numbers of Comorans resident abroad are choosing to visit the archipelago; in 2004 it was estimated that 58.3% of visitors to the Comoros were former Comoran residents. In 2005 hotel capacity amounted to an estimated 836 beds. Tourist arrivals totalled some 15,000 in 2010. Receipts from tourism amounted to US $35m. in that year.

Defence

The national army, the Armée Nationale de Développement, comprised about 1,100 men in early 2009. In December 1996 an agreement was ratified with France, which provided for the permanent presence of a French military contingent in the Comoros. Following the military coup in April 1999, French military co-operation with the Comoros was suspended, but resumed in September 2002.

Defence Expenditure: Estimated at US $3m. in 1994.

Chief of General Staff of the Comoran Armed Forces: Lt-Col ABDALLAH GAMIL SOLIHI.

Education

Education is officially compulsory for 10 years between six and 16 years of age. Primary education begins at the age of six and lasts for six years. Secondary education, beginning at 12 years of age, lasts for seven years, comprising a first cycle of four years and a second of three years. According to UNESCO estimates, enrolment at primary schools in 2006/07 included 78% of children in the relevant age-group (males 81%; females 75%), while enrolment at secondary schools in 2004/05 was equivalent to 46% of children in the relevant age-group (males 52%; females 40%). In 2003/04 a total of 5,091 pupils were enrolled in tertiary education. Children may also receive a basic education through traditional Koranic schools, which are staffed by Comoran teachers. The Comoros' first university opened in December 2003, and in 2004/05 there were 2,187 students enrolled at that institution. In 2008 spending on education was equivalent to 7.6% of GDP.

Mayotte

Recent History

Recent History

Since the Comoros unilaterally declared independence in July 1975, Mayotte (Mahoré) has been administered separately by France. The independent Comoran state claims Mayotte as part of its territory and officially represents it in international organizations, including the UN. In December 1976, following a referendum in April (in which the population voted to renounce the status of an overseas territory), France introduced the special status of Territorial Collectivity (Collectivité territoriale) for the island. The French Government is represented on Mayotte by an appointed Prefect. There is a Conseil général (General Council) with 19 members, who are elected by universal adult suffrage. Mayotte has one representative in the Assemblée nationale (National Assembly) in Paris, France, and two in the Sénat (Senate).

Following the coup in the Comoros in May 1978, Mayotte rejected the new Government's proposal that it should rejoin the other islands under a federal system, and reaffirmed its intention of remaining linked to France. Until 1999 the main political party on Mayotte, the Mouvement Populaire Mahorais (MPM), sought full departmental status for the island, but France was reluctant to grant this in view of Mayotte's underdeveloped condition. The UN General Assembly has adopted several resolutions reaffirming the sovereignty of the Comoros over the island, and urging France to reach an agreement with the Comoran Government as soon as possible. The Organization of African Unity (OAU, now the African Union—AU) has endorsed this view.

Following elections to the Assemblée nationale in March 1986, Henry Jean-Baptiste, representing an alliance of the Centre des Démocrates Sociaux (CDS) and the Union pour la Démocratie Française (UDF), was elected as deputy for Mayotte. Relations between the MPM and the French Government rapidly deteriorated following the Franco-African summit in November 1987, when the French Prime Minister, Jacques Chirac, expressed his reservations to the Comoran President concerning the elevation of Mayotte to the status of a full overseas department (despite his announcement, in early 1986, that he endorsed the MPM's aim to upgrade the status of Mayotte).

In November 1989 the Conseil général demanded that the French Government introduce measures to curb immigration to Mayotte from neighbouring islands, particularly from the Comoros. In January 1990 pressure by a group from the town of Mamoudzou resulted in increasing tension over the presence of Comoran refugees on the island. A paramilitary organization, 'Caiman' (which demanded the expulsion of illegal immigrants), was subsequently formed. In May the Comoran President, Saïd Mohamed Djohar, undertook to pursue peaceful dialogue to resolve the question of Mayotte's sovereignty, and issued a formal appeal to France to review the island's status. Mayotte was used as a strategic military base in late 1990, in preparation for French participation in multinational operations during the 1991 Gulf War.

In June 1992 increasing tension resulted in further attacks against Comoran immigrants resident in Mayotte. In early September representatives of the MPM met the French Prime Minister, Pierre Bérégovoy, to request the reintroduction of entry visas in order to restrict immigration from the Comoros. Later that month the MPM organized a boycott of Mayotte's participation in the French referendum on the Treaty on European Union, in protest at the French Government's refusal to introduce entry visas. At the end of February 1993, following legal proceedings against him, Jean-Paul Costes was replaced as Prefect by Jean-Jacques Debacq.

At elections to the Assemblée nationale, which took place in March 1993, Jean-Baptiste was returned by 53.4% of votes cast, while Mansour Kamardine, the Secretary-General of the local branch of the right-wing French mainland party, the Rassemblement pour la République (RPR), obtained 44.3% of the vote. Kamardine subsequently accused Jean-Baptiste of illegally claiming the support of an electoral alliance of the RPR and the UDF, known as the Union pour la France, by forging the signatures of the Secretary-General of the RPR and his UDF counterpart on a document. However, Jean-Baptiste denied the allegations, and, in turn, began legal proceedings against Kamardine for alleged forgery and defamation. Elections to the Conseil général (which was enlarged from 17 to 19 members) took place in March 1994; the MPM secured 12 seats, the local branch of the RPR four seats and independent candidates three seats.

In July 1997 the relative prosperity of Mayotte was thought to have prompted separatist movements on the Comoran islands of Nzwani and Mwali to demand the restoration of French rule, and subsequently to declare their independence in August. Illegal immigration from the Comoros has continued to be a major concern for the authorities on Mayotte; during January–February 1997 some 6,000 Comorans were expelled from the island, with many more agreeing to leave voluntarily.

Meanwhile, uncertainty remained over the future status of Mayotte. In April 1998 a commission charged with examining the issue submitted its report, which concluded that the present status of Territorial Collectivity was no longer appropriate, but did not advocate an alternative. In May the MPM declared its support for an adapted form of departmental administration, and urged the French authorities to decide on a date for a referendum. Two rounds of preparatory talks on the island's constitutional future took place in December between local political organizations and senior French government officials; a project was drafted which addressed various options, although no consensus was reached. In August 1999, following negotiations between the French Secretary of State for Overseas Departments and Territories, Jean-Jack Queyranne, and island representatives, Mayotte members of the RPR and the PS, as well as the leader of the MPM, Bamana, signed a draft document providing for the transformation of Mayotte into a Departmental Collectivity (Collectivité départementale), if approved at a referendum. However, both Henry and Jean-Baptiste rejected the document. The two politicians subsequently announced their departure from the MPM and formed a new political party entitled the Mouvement Départementaliste Mahorais (MDM), while reiterating their demands that Mayotte be granted full overseas department status. Following the approval of Mayotte's proposed new status by the Conseil général (by 14 votes to five) and the municipal councils, an accord to this effect was signed by Queyranne and political representatives of Mayotte on 27 January 2000. On 2 July a referendum was held, in which the population of Mayotte voted overwhelmingly in favour of the January accord, granting Mayotte the status of Departmental Collectivity for a period of 10 years. In November the commission established to define the terms of Mayotte's new status published a report which envisaged the transfer of executive power from the Prefect to the Conseil général by 2004, the dissolution of the position of Prefect by 2007 and the concession of greater powers to the island Government, notably in the area of regional co-operation. The French Parliament approved Mayotte's status as a Departmental Collectivity in July 2001.

At elections to the Conseil général held in March 2001 no party established a majority. The MPM experienced significant losses, with only four of its candidates being elected, while the RPR won five seats, the Mouvement des citoyens (MDC) two, the MDM one, the PS one and various right-wing independent candidates six. Bamana was re-elected as President of the Conseil général. Philippe de Mester replaced Pierre Bayle as Prefect in September.

At the first round of the French presidential election, which was held on 21 April 2002, Chirac received the highest number of votes on Mayotte (and overall), winning 43% of votes cast on the island; the second round, held on 5 May, was also won by Chirac, who secured 88.3% of votes on the island, defeating the candidate of the Front national, Jean-Marie Le Pen. At elections to the Assemblée nationale, held in June, Kamardine, the candidate for the Union pour la Majorité Présidentielle (UMP, which incorporated the RPR, the Démocratie Libérale and significant elements of the UDF), defeated the MDM-UDF candidate, Siadi Vita. Jean-Jacques Brot replaced de Mester as Prefect in July.

At elections to the Conseil général held in March 2004, in an alliance with the MPM, the UMP (renamed Union pour un Mouvement Populaire in November 2003) won nine seats, the same number won by a centre-left list (Force de Rassemblement et d'Alliance pour le Progrès—FRAP) comprising the MDM, the MDC and two independent candidates. Saïd Omar Oili, also an independent candidate, tipped the balance in favour of FRAP and was elected President of a coalition Government. In January 2005 Jean-Paul Kihl replaced Jean-Jacques Brot as Prefect. In late January 2007 Vincent Bouvier was appointed to replace Kihl as Prefect and, although that position was scheduled to be abolished in 2007, in July 2008 Bouvier was replaced in that post by Denis Robin.

Meanwhile, Nicolas Sarkozy of the UMP secured 30.5% of the votes cast on Mayotte in the first round of the French presidential election, held on 22 April 2007. However, in the second round, which took place on 6 May, Ségolène Royal of the PS won 60.0% of the votes cast on Mayotte, although Sarkozy was elected to the presidency. At elections to the French Assemblée nationale, held on 10 and 17 June, Kamardine was defeated by Abdoulatifou Aly, who was affiliated to the Mouvement Démocrate (MoDem), which had been formed following the presidential election by François Bayrou, the leader of the UDF, to oppose Sarkozy's UMP.

In April 2008 the Conseil général adopted a resolution providing for the transfer of Mayotte's status from that of Overseas Collectivity to an Overseas Department (Département d'outre-mer). At the referendum, which was held on 29 March 2009, 95.2% of voters approved of Mayotte attaining the status of an Overseas Department within the French Republic (in contradiction to the recognition of the island by the AU and the Comoran Government as an inseparable part of the Comoran state). Some 61% of those eligible to vote participated in the ballot. Legislation amending Mayotte's status was presented to the French Parlement in mid-2009. In June 2010 it was announced that legislation banning polygamous marriages would come into effect when Mayotte attained the status of a Overseas Department in 2011; the minimum age for females to marry was also to be raised from 16 to 18. Meanwhile, in July 2009 Hubert Derache replaced Robin as Prefect.

In early December 2009 protests on the island of Pamandzi against the rise in the cost of living, and in particular in response to the increased cost of transport, resulted in some 15 people being injured during clashes with the security forces. In January 2010 President Sarkozy met with local officials on Mayotte to discuss the issue of immigration. It was estimated that as many as one-third of the residents of Mayotte had entered the territory illegally from the Comoros. In 2009 about 16,000 Comorans had been deported from Mayotte.

On 31 March 2011 Mayotte officially became the 101st Department of France and the fifth Overseas Department. On 3 April Daniel Zaïdani was elected President of the Conseil général. In July Thomas Degos was appointed Prefect following Derache's decision to resign in order to take up a post in the French Ministry of Defence and Veterans. In October the authorities of Mayotte made an official request to the EU (transferred in December to the European Commission) to recognize Mayotte as a Région ultrapériphérique (RUP) of France; a final decision on this petition was expected in mid-2012. Recognition as an RUP would allow Mayotte to draw upon EU funds to aid its economic development. In the short term, €2m. was to be released from January 2012 over two years. On 11 July the European Council published its decision that, effective from 1 January 2014, Mayotte would cease to be an overseas country or territory and would acquire the status of RUP. The formal decision stated that this should 'represent a step consistent with Mayotte's acquisition of a status close to that of the mainland'.

Meanwhile, in the first round of the French presidential election, held on 22 April 2012, President Sarkozy received 48.7% of the votes cast on Mayotte, while François Hollande secured 36.6%; both proceeded to a second ballot, held on 6 May. Sarkozy narrowly defeated Hollande in the second Mayotte vote, receiving 51.0% of the votes cast, compared with 49.1% for Hollande, although Hollande was ultimately elected to the presidency. Elections to the French Assemblée nationale were held on 10 and 17 June, at which Kamardine was again defeated, on this occasion by Ibrahim Aboubacar of the PS, who secured 55.0% of the votes in the second ballot.

Economy

Mayotte's gross domestic product per head was €6,575 in 2009, according to official figures. Total GDP in that year amounted to €1,396m. The official population of Mayotte was 186,452 at the census of 31 July 2007. The principal communes are Mamoudzou (population 53,022 at the 2007 census), Koungou (19,831) and Dzaoudzi (the capital, 15,339). The mid-2012 population estimate by the UN was recorded at 217,171. The 2002 census showed that there were some 55,000 foreign nationals living in Mayotte, of whom 53,000 were Comorans. In 2002 there were fewer than 10,000 valid residence permits and it was estimated that around 12% of the population were illegal immigrants. However, in November 2003 it was claimed that as many as one in four people in Mayotte were illegal immigrants; President Bamana went as far as to claim that some 70% of the prison population were foreigners. Studies that year suggested that, while the average number of immigrants between 1997 and 2002 had risen to 4,300, some 3,600 people were leaving Mayotte every year. According to official figures, more than two-thirds of the women who gave birth in Mayotte in 2004 were from the Comoros. The 2004 budget allocated €2m. towards the creation of an office for study of the immigration issue and purchase of a radar system.

The economy of Mayotte is based mainly on agriculture. In 2007 8.5% of the employed labour force were actively engaged in this sector. Vanilla, ylang ylang (an ingredient of perfume), coffee and copra are the main export products, but exports are limited by production costs and the local market is small. In 2005 no vanilla was exported, owing to global oversupply. Mayotte imports large quantities of foodstuffs, which comprised 23.9% of the value of total imports in 2011. Cassava, maize and pigeon peas are cultivated for domestic consumption; while rice is widely eaten there is little domestic production. More than 90% of farms grow bananas, often mixed with coconuts (grown for their milk and oil, both of which are used in cooking); together banana and coconut plantations occupy some 45% of agricultural land (approximately 20,000 ha in total, some 55% of the surface area of Mayotte). Mangoes are also widespread, and around one-third of mango trees grow wild. Livestock-rearing (of cattle, goats—for meat—and chickens) and fishing are also important activities. Aquaculture was first introduced in 1998 and in 2005 there were five producers catering mainly to the export market. Mayotte's total fishing catch totalled an estimated 20,992 metric tons in 2010. Industry (which is dominated by the construction sector) engaged 12.7% of the employed population in 2007. Imports of machinery and appliances comprised 16.4% of the value of total imports in 2011, chemical products 9.0%, transport equipment 8.1% and base metals and metal products comprised 5.8%. Total electricity production in 2010 was 171m. kWh. In 2005 electricity charges were reduced by more than one-fifth in line with new legislation that pegged local charges to those of metropolitan France until January 2007. Services engaged 78.8% of the employed population in 2007. The annual number of tourist arrivals (excluding cruise-ship passengers) totalled 48,200 in 2011; receipts from tourism in 2006 amounted to €16.3m.

In 2010 Mayotte's total budgetary revenue was €330m., while total expenditure was €307m. The consumer price index in Mayotte increased by 0.9% in the year to December 2009. As Mayotte's labour force has continued to increase, mostly owing to a high birth rate and continued illegal immigration, youth unemployment has caused particular concern. In 1997 41% of the population were unemployed, of whom some 37.8% were under 25 years of age; by 2007, however, the unemployment rate had declined to 26% The principal source of imports in 2009 was France (50.8%); the People's Republic of China was also a major supplier. France was also the principal market for exports (taking 40.0% of exports in that year); the other significant purchasers were the Comoros and Réunion. The principal export in 2009 was fish; exports of ylang ylang were also significant. In 2010 Mayotte recorded a trade deficit of €372.7m.

Development of transport infrastructure remains a priority and the French Government agreed a new, six-year development contract with Mayotte for 2008–14 valued at €551m., which would contribute further to a number of projects, including the expansion and modernization of the airport at Pamandzi, the construction of a second quay at the port of Longoni (which handled some 490,000 metric tons of goods in 2006) and work to improve rural roads. The contract also made provision for significant expenditure to increase access to clean drinking water and to improve sanitation, as well as the development of renewable energy sources. The long-term aim of the contract was to ensure Mayotte's economic and social autonomy. In January 2010 the French President, Nicolas Sarkozy, pledged additional state funding towards the construction of schools and of social housing for some 40,000 inhabitants by 2016. However, by April 2011 the construction industry was in serious decline and the Conseil général was obliged to freeze spending owing to high levels of public debt. With its new status as a French Department, measures were adopted in 2011 to align, by increments, Mayotte's minimum wage with that of France. Although there were plans to extend Dzaoudzi Pamandzi International Airport and the French Minister in charge of Overseas Territories announced a €50m. recovery plan for Mayotte based almost entirely on public sector construction, the trade unions remained sceptical about the island's imminent economic recovery. These concerns appeared to be justified by the fact that at the end of 2011 it was reported that some 89 companies had requested permission to place their staff on short-time employment contracts. Meanwhile, in late 2009 the Schéma Directeur d'Aménagement et de Gestion des Eaux was approved for the period 2010–15. The plan, aimed at improving the management of water resources on Mayotte, allocated €171m. in funds to provide, *inter alia*, equipment for the treatment of waste water and rainwater.

Statistical Survey

Source (unless otherwise indicated): Institut National de la Statistique et des Études Économiques (INSEE) de Mayotte; Z.I. Kawéni, BP 1362, 97600 Mamoudzou; tel. 269-61-36-35; fax 269-61-39-56; e-mail antenne-mayotte@insee.fr; internet www.insee.fr/fr/regions/mayotte/default.asp.

AREA AND POPULATION

Area: 374 sq km (144 sq miles).

Population: 160,265 at census of 30 July 2002; 186,452 at census of 31 July 2007. *Mid-2012* (UN estimate): 217,171 (Source: UN, *World Population Prospects: The 2010 Revision*).

Density (at mid-2012): 580.7 per sq km.

Population by Age and Sex (UN estimates at mid-2012): *0–14:* 100,505 (males 51,465, females 49,040); *15–64:* 112,526 (males 54,554, females 57,972); *65 and over:* 4,140 (males 2,146, females 1,994); *Total* 217,171 (males 108,165, females 109,006) (Source: UN, *World Population Prospects: The 2010 Revision*).

Population by Country of Origin (2002, before adjustment for double counting): Mayotte 103,705; France 6,323; Comoros 45,057; Madagascar-Mauritius-Seychelles 4,601; Total (incl. others) 160,301.

Principal Towns (population of communes at 2007 census): Mamoudzou 53,022; Koungou 19,831; Dzaoudzi (capital) 15,339; Dembeni 10,141.

Births and Deaths (2007): Registered live births 7,658 (birth rate 41.1 per 1,000); Registered deaths 587 (death rate 3.1 per 1,000). *2009:* Birth rate 39.0 per 1,000; Death rate 3.0 per 1,000.

Life expectancy (years at birth): 77.6 (males 74.0; females 81.3) in 2010 (Source: World Bank, World Development Indicators database).

Economically Active Population (persons aged 14 years and over, census of 31 July 2007): Agriculture and fishing 3,204; Construction 3,024; Other industry 1,805; Wholesale and retail trade 3,154; Hotels and restaurants 609; Transport, telecommunications and real estate 5,043; Public administration 6,535; Education, health and social care 7,247; Other services 7,289; *Total employed* 37,910 (males 24,157, females 13,753); Unemployed 13,614 (males 5,922, females 7,692); *Total labour force* 51,524 (males 30,079, females 21,445). *2009* (labour force survey March–June, persons aged 15 years and over): Total employed 35,600; Unemployed 7,600; Total labour force 43,200.

HEALTH AND WELFARE

Key Indicators

Total Fertility Rate (children per woman, 2004): 4.5.

Physicians (per 1,000 head, 1997): 0.4.

Hospital Beds (per 1,000 head, 1997): 1.4.

For definitions see explanatory note on p. vi.

AGRICULTURE, ETC.

Livestock (2003): Cattle 17,235; Goats 22,811; Chickens 80,565.

Fishing (metric tons, live weight, 2010): Capture 20,842 (Skipjack tuna 9,082; Yellowfin tuna 8,532); Aquaculture 150 (FAO estimate); *Total catch* 20,992 (FAO estimate). Source: FAO.

INDUSTRY

Electric Energy (million kWh, consumption): 171 in 2010.

FINANCE

Currency and Exchange Rates: 100 cent = 1 euro. *Sterling and Dollar Equivalents* (31 May 2012): £1 sterling = €1.250; US $1 = €0.806; €10 = £8.00 = US $12.40. *Average Exchange Rate* (euros per US dollar): 0.7198 in 2009; 0.7550 in 2010; 0.7194 in 2011. The French franc was used until the end of February 2002. Euro notes and coins were introduced on 1 January 2002, and the euro became the sole legal tender from 18 February. Some of the figures in this Survey are still in terms of French francs.

Budget of the Collectivity (€ million, 2011): Total revenue 278; Total expenditure 301.

French State Expenditure (€ million, 2011): Direct expenditure 410.1; Indirect expenditure 86.6; *Total expenditure* 496.7.

Money Supply (million French francs at 31 December 1997): Currency outside banks 789; Demand deposits 266; Total money 1,055.

Cost of Living (Consumer Price Index for December; base: December 2006 = 100): 109.5 in 2009; 112.4 in 2010; 113.8 in 2011.

Expenditure on the Gross Domestic Product (€ million, 2009, INSEE estimates): Government final consumption expenditure 726; Private final consumption expenditure 799; Gross fixed capital formation 372; *Total domestic expenditure* 1,897; Exports of goods and services 31; *Less* Imports of goods and services 532; *GDP in purchasers' values* 1,396.

EXTERNAL TRADE

Principal Commodities (€ million, 2011): *Imports c.i.f.* (excl. hydrocarbons): Foodstuffs 92.1; Mineral products 9.8; Chemical products 34.7; Plastic materials and rubber 10.5; Base metals and metal products 22.3; Machinery and appliances 62.8; Transport equipment 31.2; Total (incl. others) 384.0. *Exports f.o.b.:* Farmed fish 0.2; Ylang ylang 0.1; Re-exports 0.1; Total (incl. others) 5.0 (Source: Institut d'Émission des Départements d'Outre-mer, *Rapport Annuel 2011*).

Principal Trading Partners (€ million, 2009): *Imports:* Brazil 7.5; China, People's Republic 28.8; France (Metropolitan) 185.0; Mauritius 4.5; South Africa 5.8; United Arab Emirates 8.2; Total (incl. others) 364.3. *Exports* (incl. re-exports): Total 5.1. Note: The principal markets for exports are France (Metropolitan—some 40% of exports in 2009), Comoros (15% in 2009) and Réunion.

TRANSPORT

Road Traffic (2008): Motor vehicles in use 7,781.

Shipping (2006, unless otherwise indicated): *Maritime Traffic:* Vessel movements 530 (2005); Goods unloaded 390,954 metric tons; Goods loaded 66,278 metric tons; Passengers 23,437 (arrivals 7,697, departures 15,740). *Barges* (2002): Passengers 11,845; Light vehicles 532. *Cruise Ships* (2005): Vessel movements 36; Passengers 6,857.

Civil Aviation (2011): *Passengers Carried:* 317,528. *Freight Carried:* 2,202 metric tons. *Post Carried:* 606 metric tons.

TOURISM

Foreign Tourist Arrivals (excl. cruise-ship passengers): 49,500 in 2009; 52,800 in 2010; 48,200 in 2011.

Foreign Tourist Arrivals by Country of Residence (2011): France (metropolitan) 25,700; Réunion 19,000; Total (incl. others) 48,200.

Tourism Receipts (€ million): 13.7 in 2004; 14.5 in 2005; 16.3 in 2006.

COMMUNICATIONS MEDIA

Telephones ('000 main lines in use, 2010): 10.0.

Mobile Cellular Telephones ('000 subscribers, 2008): 48.1.

Internet Users ('000, 2000): 1.8.

Source: International Telecommunication Union.

EDUCATION

Pre-primary: 71 schools (2007); 15,673 pupils (2011).

Primary: 118 schools (2007); 33,644 pupils (2011).

General Secondary: 19 schools (2009); 20,536 pupils (2011).

Vocational and Technical: 9 institutions (2009); 7,198 students (2011).

Students Studying in France or Réunion (2009): Secondary 1,452; Higher 2,253; *Total* 3,705.

Teaching Staff (2008): Primary 2,354; Secondary 1,769.

Directory

The Government

(September 2012)

HEAD OF STATE

President: FRANÇOIS HOLLANDE.

Prefect: THOMAS DEGOS.

DEPARTMENTAL ADMINISTRATION

President of the General Council: DANIEL ZAÏDANI, 108 rue de l'Hôpital, BP 101, 97600 Mamoudzou; tel. 269-61-12-33; fax 269-61-10-18; internet www.cg976.fr.

REPRESENTATIVES TO THE FRENCH PARLIAMENT

Deputies to the French National Assembly: BOINALI SAÏD (Divers Gauche), IBRAHIM ABOUBACAR (PS).

Representatives to the French Senate: THANI MOHAMED SOILIHI (Divers Gauche), ABDOURAHAMANE SOILIHI (UMP).

GOVERNMENT DEPARTMENTS

Office of the Prefect: BP 676, Kawéni, 97600 Mamoudzou; tel. 269-63-50-00; fax 269-60-18-89; e-mail communication@mayotte.pref.gouv.fr; internet www.mayotte.pref.gouv.fr.

Department of Agriculture and Forestry: 15 rue Mariazé, BP 103, 97600 Mamoudzou; tel. 269-61-12-13; fax 269-61-10-31; e-mail daf976@agriculture.gouv.fr; internet www.hydro-mayotte.agriculture.gouv.fr.

Department of Education: rue Sarahangué, BP 76, 97600 Mamoudzou; tel. 269-61-10-24; fax 269-61-09-87; e-mail vice-rectorat@ac-mayotte.fr; internet www.ac-mayotte.fr.

Department of Health and Social Security: rue de l'Hôpital, BP 104, 97600 Mamoudzou; tel. 269-61-12-25; fax 269-61-19-56.

Department of Public Works: rue Mariazé, BP 109, 97600 Mamoudzou; tel. 269-61-12-54; fax 269-61-07-11; e-mail de-mayotte@equipement.gouv.fr.

Department of Work, Employment and Training: 3 bis, rue Mahabou, BP 174, 97600 Mamoudzou; tel. 269-61-16-57; fax 269-61-03-37; internet www.dtefp-mayotte.travail.gouv.fr.

Department of Youth and Sports: 14 rue Mariazé, BP 94, 97600 Mamoudzou; tel. 269-61-60-50; fax 269-61-82-10; e-mail dd976@jeunesse-sports.gouv.fr.

Political Organizations

Fédération du Front National (FN): route nationale 1, M'tsahara, 97630 M'tzamboro; BP 1331, 97600 Mamoudzou Cédex; tel. and fax 269-60-50-24; Regional Sec. HAMADA OUSSENI.

Fédération de Mayotte de l'Union pour un Mouvement Populaire (UMP): route nationale, Immeuble 'Jardin Créole', 97600 Mamoudzou; tel. 269-61-64-64; fax 269-60-87-89; e-mail alisouf@ump976.org; centre-right; local branch of the metropolitan party; Departmental Pres. ASSANI HAMISSI; Departmental Sec. ALI SOUF.

Fédération du Mouvement National Républicain (MNR) de Mayotte: 15 rue des Réfugiers, 97615 Pamandzi; tel. and fax 269-60-33-21; Departmental Sec. ABDOU MIHIDJAY.

Mouvement des Citoyens (MDC): Chirongui; Leader ALI HALIFA.

Mouvement Départementaliste Mahorais (MDM): 97610 Dzaoudzi; f. 2001 by fmr mems of the MPM; Pres. ZOUBERT ADINANI; Sec.-Gen. MOHAMED ALI BEN ALI.

Mouvement de la Gauche Ecologiste de Mayotte: 6 avenue Mamanne, Quartier Artisanal, Localité de Pamandzi, 97600 Pamandzi; tel. and fax 269-61-09-70; internet mayotte.lesverts.fr; fmrly Les Verts Mayotte; affiliated to Mouvement de la Gauche Réunionnaise; Gen. Sec. AHAMADA SALIME.

Mouvement Populaire Mahorais (MPM): route de Vahibé, Passamainti, 97600 Mamoudzou; Leader YOUNOUSSA BAMANA.

Parti Socialiste (PS): Dzaoudzi; local branch of the metropolitan party; Fed. Sec. IBRAHIM ABUBACAR.

Judicial System

Palais de Justice: Immeuble Espace, BP 106 (Kawéni), 97600 Mamoudzou; tel. 269-61-11-15; fax 269-61-19-63.

Tribunal de Grande Instance

16 rue de l'hôpital, BP 106, 97600 Mamoudzou; tel. 269-61-11-15; fax 269-61-19-63; Pres. JEAN-BAPTISTE FLORI; Prosecutor JEAN-LOUIS BEC.

Procureur de la République: JEAN-LOUIS BEC.

Tribunal d'Instance: Pres. ALAIN CHATEAUNEUF.

Religion

Muslims comprise about 98% of the population. Most of the remainder are Christians, mainly Roman Catholics.

CHRISTIANITY

The Roman Catholic Church

Mayotte is within the jurisdiction of the Apostolic Administrator of the Comoros.

Office of the Apostolic Administrator: 7 rue de l'hôpital, BP 1012, 97600 Mamoudzou; tel. and fax 269-61-11-53; fax 269-61-48-25; e-mail mcatholique@wanadoo.fr.

The Press

Albalad: Immeuble Mega, 97600 Kawéni, Mamoudzou; tel. 269-60-66-15; e-mail halda.halidi@awicompany.fr; internet www.albaladmayotte.com; f. 2010; owned by Al Waseet International; daily; French; Dir of Publication PASCAL ABLA; Editor-in-Chief HALDA HALIDI; circ. 1,000.

Flash Infos Mayotte: Société Mahoraise de Presse, 7 rue Salamani Cavani/M'Tsapéré, BP 60, 97600 Mamoudzou; tel. 269-61-20-04; fax 269-60-35-90; e-mail flash-infos@wanadoo.fr; internet www.mayottehebdo.com; f. 1999; owned by Somapresse; daily e-mail bulletin; Dir LAURENT CANAVATE.

Horizon Austral: Société Mahoraise de Presse, 7 rue Salamani Cavani/M'Tsapéré, BP 60, 97600 Mamoudzou; tel. 269-61-20-04; fax 269-60-35-90; e-mail contact@mayottehebdo.com; internet www.mayottehebdo.com; Dir of Publication LAURENT CANAVATE.

Le Mahorais: 11 centre commercial, Lukida, 97600 Mamoudzou; tel. 269-61-66-75; fax 269-61-66-72; e-mail lemahorais@wanadoo.fr; internet www.lemahorais.com; weekly; French; Publ. Dir SAMUEL BOSCHER; Editor-in-Chief LUCIE TOUZÉ.

Mayotte Hebdo: Société Mahoraise de Presse, 7 rue Salamani Cavani/M'Tsapéré, BP 60, 97600 Mamoudzou; tel. 269-61-20-04; fax 269-60-35-90; e-mail contact@mayottehebdo.com; internet www.mayottehebdo.com; f. 2000; weekly; French; incl. the economic supplement *Mayotte Eco* and cultural supplement *Tounda* (weekly); owned by Somapresse; Dir LAURENT CANAVATE; circ. 2,300.

Mayotte Magazine: BP 268, ZI Kawéni, 97600 Mamoudzou; tel. 06-39-09-03-29; e-mail contact@mayottemagazine.com; internet www.mayottemagazine.fr; f. 2007; 4 a year; Dir STÉPHANIE LÉGERON.

Zan'Goma: Impasse du Jardin Fleuri, Cavani, 97600 Mamoudzou; f. 2005; monthly; French; Publ. Dir MONCEF MOUHOUDHOIRE.

Broadcasting and Communications

TELECOMMUNICATIONS

Mayotte Télécom Mobile: 27, pl. Mariaźe, 97600 Mamoudzou; mobile cellular telephone operator; local operation of Société Réunionnaise du Radiotéléphone based in Réunion.

RADIO AND TELEVISION

Mayotte 1ère: BP 103, 97610 Dzaoudzi; tel. 269-60-10-17; fax 269-60-18-52; e-mail annick.henry@rfo.fr; internet mayotte.la1ere.fr; f. 1977; acquired by Groupe France Télévisions in 2004; fmrly Réseau France Outre-mer, name changed as above in 2010; radio broadcasts in French and more than 70% in Mahorian; television transmissions began in 1986; a satellite service was launched in 2000; Dir-Gen. GENEVIÈVE GIARD; Regional Dir GERALD PRUFER.

Finance

(br(s). = branch(es))

BANKS

In 2010 there were three commercial banks, two mutual banks and two other financial institutions in Mayotte.

Issuing Authority

Institut d'Émission des Départements d'Outre-mer: ave de la Préfecture, BP 500, 97600 Mamoudzou; tel. 269-61-05-05; fax 269-61-05-02; internet agence@iedom-mayotte.fr; internet www.iedom.fr; Dir VICTOR-ROBERT NUGENT.

Commercial Banks

Banque Française Commerciale Océan Indien: route de l'Agriculture, BP 222, 97600 Mamoudzou; tel. 269-61-10-91; fax 269-61-17-40; e-mail pleclerc@bfcoi.com; internet www.bfcoi.com; f. 1976; jtly owned by Société Générale and Mauritius Commercial Bank Ltd; Pres. GÉRALD LACAZE; brs at Dzaoudzi and Sada.

Banque de la Réunion: 30 pl. Mariage, 97600 Mamoudzou; tel. 269-61-20-30; fax 269-61-20-28; internet www.banquedelareunion.fr; owned by Groupe Banque Populaire et Caisse d'Epargne (France); 2 brs.

BRED Banque Populaire: Centre d'Affaires Mayotte, pl. Mariage, Z.I. 3, 97600 Mamoudzou; tel. 269-64-80-86; fax 269-60-51-10; internet www.bred.fr; owned by Groupe Banque Populaire et Caisse d'Epargne (France).

INSURANCE

AGF: pl. Mariage, BP 184, 97600 Mamoudzou; tel. 269-61-44-33; fax 269-61-14-89; e-mail jl.henry@wanadoo.fr; Gen. Man. JEAN-LUC HENRY.

Groupama: BP 665, Z.I. Nel, Lot 7, 97600 Mamoudzou; tel. 269-62-59-92; fax 269-60-76-08.

Prudence Créole: Centre Commercial et Médical de l'Ylang, BP 480, 97600 Mamoudzou; tel. 269-61-11-10; fax 269-61-11-21; e-mail prudencecreolemayotte@wanadoo.fr; 87% owned by Groupe Générali; 2 brs.

Vectra Paic Océan Indien: BP 65, 55 champs des Ylangs, 97680 Combani; tel. 269-62-44-54; fax 269-62-46-97; e-mail cfonteneau@wanadoo.fr.

Trade and Industry

DEVELOPMENT ORGANIZATION

Agence Française de Développement (AFD): Résidence Sarah, pl. du Marché, BP 610, Kawéni, 97600 Mamoudzou; tel. 269-61-05-05; fax 269-61-05-02; e-mail afdmamoudzou@groupe-afd.org; internet www.afd.fr; Dir PATRICK PEAUCELLIER.

EMPLOYERS' ORGANIZATIONS

Mouvement des Entreprises de France Mayotte (MEDEF): Z.I. Kawéni, Immeuble GMOI, BP 570, 97600 Mamoudzou; tel. 269-61-44-22; fax 269-61-46-10; e-mail contact@medef-mayotte.com; internet www.medef-mayotte.com; Pres. MICHEL TAILLEFER; Sec.-Gen. VINCENT SCHUBLIN.

Ordre National des Médecins: BP 675 Kawéni, 97600 Mamoudzou; tel. 269-61-02-47; fax 269-61-36-61.

UTILITIES

Electricity

Electricité de Mayotte (EDM): BP 333, Z.I. Kawéni, 97600 Kawéni; tel. 269-61-44-44; fax 269-60-10-92; e-mail edm.mayotte@wanadoo.fr; internet www.electricitedemayotte.com; f. 1997; subsidiary of SAUR; Dir-Gen. AUGUSTO SOARES DOS REIS.

Water

Syndicat Intercommunal de l'Eau et de l'Assainissement de Mayotte (SIEAM): BP 289, 97600 Mamoudzou; tel. 269-62-11-11; fax 269-61-55-00; e-mail sieam@sieam.fr; internet www.sieam.fr; Pres. MAOULIDA SOULA.

TRADE UNIONS

Confédération Inter-Syndicale de Mayotte (CISMA-CFDT): 18 rue Mahabou, BP 1038, 97600 Mamoudzou; tel. 269-61-12-38; fax 269-61-36-16; f. 1993; Gen. Sec. SAÏD BOINALI.

Affiliated unions incl.:

ScDEN-CGT: BP 793 Kawéni, 97600 Mamoudzou; tel. and fax 269-62-53-35; e-mail scdencgt.mayotte@free.fr; internet www.cgt-mayotte.info; represents teaching staff; Sec.-Gen. KHÉMAÏS SAIDANI.

SGEN-CFDT: c/o CISMA, 18 rue Mahabou, BP 1038, 97600 Mamoudzou; tel. 269-61-12-38; fax 269-61-18-09; e-mail mayotte@sgen.cfdt.fr; internet etranger.sgencfdt.free.fr/Mayotte/index.htm; represents teaching staff; Sec.-Gen. FRANÇOISE HOLZAPFEL.

Fédération Départementale des Syndicats d'Exploitants Agricoles de Mayotte (FDSEAM): 150 rue Mbalamanga-Mtsapéré, 97600 Mamoudzou; tel. and fax 269-61-34-83; e-mail fdsea.mayotte@wanadoo.fr; f. 1982; Pres. LAÏNA MOGNÉ-MALI; Dir ALI BACAR.

SNES Mayotte (SNES-FSU): 12 Résidence Bellecombe, 110 Lotissement Les Trois Vallées, Majicavo, 97600 Mamoudzou; tel. 269-62-50-58; fax 269-62-53-39; e-mail mayotte@snes.edu; internet www.mayotte.snes.edu; represents teaching staff in secondary education; Sec. FRÉDÉRIC LOUVIER.

Union Départementale Force Ouvrière de Mayotte (FO): Z. I. de Kaweni, Rond Point El-Farouk, BP 1109, 97600 Mamoudzou; tel. 269-61-18-39; fax 269-61-22-45; e-mail utfo.mayotte@wanadoo.fr; Sec.-Gen. HAMIDOU MADI MCOLO.

Transport

ROADS

In 2011 the road network totalled approximately 230 km, of which 90 km were main roads.

SHIPPING

Coastal shipping is provided by locally owned small craft. There is a deep-water port at Longoni. Construction of a second quay at Longoni was proposed under the 2006 budget; in December 2008 the Agence Française de Développement approved the allocation of a €10m. loan towards the extension of Longoni port.

Service des Affaires Maritimes: BP 37, 97615 Pamandzi; tel. 269-60-31-38; fax 269-60-31-39; e-mail c.mait.sam-mayotte@developpment-durable.gouv.fr; Head of Service OLIVIER BISSON.

Service des Transports Maritimes (STM): BP 186, 97600 Dzaoudzi; tel. 269-64-39-72; fax 269-60-80-25; e-mail denys.cormy@cg976.fr; internet www.mayotte-stm.com; Dir DENYS CORMY; 8 vessels.

CIVIL AVIATION

There is an airport at Dzaoudzi, serving daily commercial flights to the Comoros; four-times weekly flights to Réunion; twice-weekly services to Madagascar; and weekly services to Kenya and Mozambique. In January 2004 plans were approved for the construction of a new runway to allow the commencement of direct flights to Paris, France. The proposed establishment of Air Mayotte International was abandoned in September of that year. Plans for a new terminal at the airport in Dzaoudzi were announced in late 2010 as a result of which the number of visitors passing through the airport each year was to increase to 615,000 by 2025. Air Austral announced plans to commence a direct air service to Paris by late 2011; the scheduled launch date was subsequently delayed until March 2012.

Air Austral: pl. Mariage, BP 1429, 97600 Mamoudzou; tel. 269-60-90-90; fax 269-61-61-94; e-mail mayotte@air-austral.com; internet www.air-austral.com; Pres. GÉRARD ETHÈVE.

Tourism

Tropical scenery provides the main tourist attraction. Excluding cruise-ship passengers, Mayotte received 48,200 visitors in 2011; tourism receipts totalled €16.3m. in 2006. In 2007 there were nine hotels, with a total of some 366 rooms.

Comité Départemental du Tourisme de Mayotte (CDTM): rue Amiral Lacaze 5, 97400 Saint-Denis, Réunion; tel. 269-61-09-09; fax 269-61-03-46; e-mail mayottetourisme.lareunion@orange.fr; internet www.mayotte-tourisme.com; Dir GEORGE MECS.

Bibliography

Abdelaziz, M. R. *Comores: Les institutions d'un état mort-né*. Paris, L'Harmattan, 2001.

Caminade, P. *Comores-Mayotte, une histoire néocoloniale*. Marseille, Agone, 2004.

Chamoussidine, M. *Comores: L'enclos ou une existence en dérive*. Moroni, KomÉdit, 2002.

Cornu, H. *Paris et Bourbon, La politique française dans l'Océan indien*. Paris, Académie des Sciences d'Outre-mer, 1984.

Laroussi, F. *et al. Mayotte: une île plurilingue en mutation*. Mayotte, Editions du Baobab, 2009.

Mattoir, N. *Les Comores de 1975 à 1990: Une histoire politique mouvementée*. Paris, L'Harmattan, 2004.

Mmadi, A. *Pourquoi les Comores s'enfoncent-elles?* Grenoble, Thot, 2003.

Newitt, M. *The Comoros Islands: Struggle against Dependency in the Indian Ocean*. Aldershot, Gower, 1985.

Perri, P. *Les nouveaux mercenaires*. Paris, L'Harmattan, 1994.

Salesse, Y. *Mayotte: L'illusion de la France, propositions pour une décolonisation*. Paris, L'Harmattan, 1995.

Souef, M. *Les Comores en mouvement*. Levallois-Perret, De la lune, 2008.

Vérin, E., and P. *Histoire de la révolution comorienne: Décolonisation, idéologie et séisme social*. Paris, L'Harmattan, 1999.

Weinberg, S. *Last of the Pirates: The Search for Bob Denard*. London, Jonathan Cape, 1994.

THE DEMOCRATIC REPUBLIC OF THE CONGO

Physical and Social Geography

PIERRE GOUROU

PHYSICAL FEATURES

Covering an area of 2,344,885 sq km (905,365 sq miles), the Democratic Republic of the Congo (DRC, formerly Zaire) is bordered by the Republic of the Congo to the north-west, by the Central African Republic and South Sudan to the north, by Uganda, Rwanda, Burundi and Tanzania to the east, and by Zambia and Angola to the south. There is a short coastline at the outlet of the River Congo. The DRC is the largest country of sub-Saharan Africa. Despite its vast size, it lacks any particularly noteworthy points of relief, affording it a considerable natural advantage. Lying across the Equator, the DRC has an equatorial climate in the whole of the central region. Average temperatures range from 26°C in the coastal and basin areas to 18°C in the mountainous regions. Rainfall is plentiful in all seasons. In the north (Uele) the winter of the northern hemisphere is a dry season; in Katanga (formerly Shaba) in the south, the winter of the southern hemisphere is dry. The only arid region (less than 800 mm of rain per annum) is an extremely small area on the bank of the lower Congo.

The basin of the River Congo forms the country's dominant geographical feature. This basin had a deep tectonic origin; the continental shelf of Africa had given way to form an immense hollow, which drew towards it the waters from the north (Ubangi), from the east (Uele, Arruwimi), and from the south (Lualaba—that is the upper branch of the River Congo, Kasaï, Kwango). The crystalline continental shelf levels out at the periphery into plateaux in Katanga and the Congo-Nile ridge. The most broken-up parts of this periphery can be found in the west, in Bas-Congo, where the river cuts the folds of a Pre-Cambrian chain by a 'powerful breach', and above all in the east. Here, as a result of the volcanic overflow from the Virunga, they are varied by an upheaval of the rift valleys (where Lakes Tanganyika, Kivu, Edward and Albert are located).

The climate is generally conducive to agriculture and wood-forestry. Evergreen equatorial forest covers approximately 1m. sq km in the equatorial and sub-equatorial regions. In the north as in the south of this evergreen forest, tropical vegetation appears, with many trees that lose their leaves in the dry season. Vast stretches from the north to the south are, probably as a result of frequent fires, covered by sparse forest land, where trees grow alongside grasses (*biombo* from east Africa), and savannah dotted with shrubs.

The natural resources of the DRC are immense: its climate is favourable to profitable agriculture; the forests, if rationally exploited, could yield excellent results; the abundance of water should eventually be useful to industry and agriculture; and finally, there is considerable mineral wealth. The network of waterways is naturally navigable. The Congo carries the second largest volume of water of any river in the world. With the average flow to the mouth being 40,000 cu m per second, there are enormous possibilities for power generation, some of which are being realized at Inga. Indeed, the potential hydroelectric resources are considerable in the whole of the Congo basin.

The major exports of the DRC derive from the exploitation of its mineral resources. Copper is mined in upper Katanga, as are other metals—tin, silver, uranium, cobalt, manganese and tungsten. Diamonds are found in Kasaï, and tin, columbite, etc. in the east, around Maniema. In addition, many other mineral resources (such as iron ore and bauxite) await exploitation.

POPULATION

The DRC's population comprises numerous ethnic groups, which the external boundaries separate. The Kongo people are divided between the DRC, the Republic of the Congo and Angola; the Zande between the DRC and Sudan; the Chokwe between the DRC and Angola; the Bemba between the DRC and Zambia; and the Alur between the DRC and Uganda. Even within its frontiers, the ethnic and linguistic geography of the DRC is highly diverse. The most numerous people are: the Kongo; the people of Kwangu-Kwilu, who are related to them; the Mongo, with their many subdivisions, who inhabit the Great Forest; the Luba, with their related groups the Lulua and Songe; the Bwaka; and the Zande. The majority speak Bantu languages, of which there is a great diversity. However, the north of the DRC belongs linguistically to Sudan. The extreme linguistic variety of the DRC is maintained to some extent by the ability of the people to speak several languages, by the existence of 'intermediary' languages (a Kongo dialect, a Luba dialect, Swahili and Lingala) and by the use of French.

According to UN estimates, the country's population was 69,575,391 at mid-2012. The average density of population is low (estimated by the UN to be 29.7 per sq km at mid-2012), and the population is unevenly distributed. Certain parts of Mayombé (Bas-Congo) have 100 people per sq km, but the south of the republic is sparsely populated (at 1–3 people per sq km). The capital, Kinshasa, had 8,797,730 inhabitants in mid-2011, according to UN estimates, and is the principal urban centre. The second most important town, Lubumbashi, had an estimated 1,542,945 inhabitants in mid-2010, while other major centres of population were Mbuji-Mayi (1,488,468), Kanaga (878,263) and Kisangani (812,489).

Recent History

GREGORY MTHEMBU-SALTER

The European colonization of the area now comprising the Democratic Republic of the Congo (DRC, formerly Zaire) dates from 1879, when the Association Internationale du Congo (AIC), under the control of King Léopold II of Belgium, established a chain of trading stations along the River Congo. Economic exploitation of the surrounding territory expanded rapidly in response to rising international demand for wild rubber, following the invention of rubber tyres for motor vehicles. Rubber was collected by increasingly brutal methods, and by 1908 as much as one-third of the population was estimated to have died prematurely or been killed by the AIC. Following British and US diplomatic pressure, responsibility for the administration of the territory was transferred at this time from the King to the Belgian Government, and the Congo became a Belgian colony, known as the Belgian Congo.

Under Belgian rule, African political activity in the Congo was forbidden, and radical Congolese grouped instead in 'cultural associations'. The most prominent of the associations was the Alliance des Ba-Kongo (ABAKO), led by Joseph Kasavubu. After a violent demonstration organized by ABAKO in January 1959, the Belgian Government, alarmed at the prospect of a prolonged colonial war, greatly accelerated the independence process. Belgium favoured a unitary state based on the centralized colonial system, while ABAKO and most other Congolese political groups, except Patrice Lumumba's Mouvement National Congolais (MNC), demanded a federal structure. The constitutional arrangements that eventually emerged were a compromise, affirming the unitary character of the state, but allowing each province a government and legislature, and equal representation in a national senate.

THE FIRST REPUBLIC

The independence of the Republic of the Congo was proclaimed on 30 June 1960, with Kasavubu installed as President and Lumumba as Prime Minister. Just five days later, the armed forces mutinied. Their demands were partly satisfied by the replacement of the Belgian Chief of Staff Lt-Gen. Emile Janssens by Col (later Marshal) Joseph-Désiré Mobutu, who was aligned with Lumumba's MNC. Belgian troops intervened to protect their nationals, and at the same time, with the apparent connivance of Belgium, the USA and South Africa, the provinces of Katanga and South Kasaï resolved to secede. Lumumba requested UN assistance to prevent this, which Kasavubu opposed, and the disagreement culminated in Lumumba's dismissal by Kasavubu in September. Lumumba challenged his dismissal, and appealed to the legislature to remove Kasavubu. The deadlock was resolved later that month by the intervention of the armed forces, and Col Mobutu subsequently assumed control of the country, ruling with the assistance of a hastily assembled Collège des Commissaires Généraux (CCG). The CCG governed the Congo for one year, but failed to establish control of the north-eastern region, where some of Lumumba's former ministers had established a rival government in Stanleyville (later Kisangani).

Mobutu restored power to President Kasavubu in February 1961. A few days later Lumumba was murdered on Mobutu's orders, but outside involvement was suspected, and in 2002 the Belgian Government finally conceded a measure of responsibility. The furious reaction to Lumumba's death from African governments and the UN forced negotiations between Kasavubu and the MNC, and in August 1961 a new Government was formed, with Cyrille Adoula as Prime Minister. Most political groups supported the new administration, except Katanga separatists, led by Moïse Tshombe. A new Constitution entered into force on 1 August 1964, establishing a presidential system of government and a federalist structure.

Meanwhile, the Katanga secession bid collapsed in January 1963, and its leader, Tshombe, went into exile. During early 1964 rebellions broke out in the Kwilu region and in Sud-Kivu and northern Katanga provinces, and within a few months rebels had established their capital at Stanleyville. In July Kasavubu invited Tshombe to become interim Prime Minister, pending legislative elections, and in the following month the country was renamed the Democratic Republic of the Congo. In early 1965 the rebellion in the east was defeated by the army, assisted by Belgian troops and mercenaries.

In March and April 1965 the Tshombe Government organized legislative elections. The coalition led by Tshombe, the Convention Nationale Congolaise (CONACO), won a majority in the Chamber of Deputies, but was strongly challenged by an opposition bloc known as the Front démocratique congolais and political deadlock ensued. Led by Mobutu, the armed forces again intervened, and on 24 November Mobutu assumed full executive powers, declaring himself President of the 'Second Republic'.

'PRESIDENTIALISM' AND THE PARTY STATE

Mobutu immediately banned party politics and in 1966 established the Mouvement Populaire de la Révolution (MPR), while granting himself the sole right to legislate. Mobutu reduced the number of provinces from 21 to eight, and replaced provincial assemblies with governors appointed by and answerable to himself. In June of that year a new Constitution was approved by referendum, establishing a presidential regime, with a new legislature to be elected at a date to be determined by Mobutu. The Constitution provided for two legally authorized political parties, but the claims of existing political groups to official recognition were rejected. Later, the Constitution was amended so that the Government, the legislature and the judiciary all became institutions of the MPR, and all citizens automatically became party members. In October 1971 the country was renamed the Republic of Zaire. In 1972 the President took the name Mobutu Sese Seko Kuku Ngbendu Wa Za Banga, as part of a national policy of 'authenticity', which also resulted in the renaming of many towns and cities and the promotion of indigenous cultures.

From the 1960s onwards Mobutu gave shelter to one of the factions fighting for independence in neighbouring Angola, the Frente Nacional de Libertação de Angola (FNLA), which established guerrilla bases and refugee camps along the border in Bas-Zaïre province. However, in 1976, after a rival faction, the Movimento Popular de Libertação de Angola (MPLA), won power, Mobutu agreed with the new Angolan President, Augustino Neto, that Angolan refugees in Zaire would be repatriated and that Angola would return to Zaire several thousand former members of Tshombe's forces, who would then receive amnesty. In March 1977, however, some of the latter, distrusting the pledge of an amnesty, instead invaded Katanga (now renamed Shaba) from Angola, receiving support from many of its disaffected inhabitants. Mobutu secured military assistance from France and Morocco, whose troops defeated the Katangese forces, ending the 'First Shaba War'. The Zairean armed forces subsequently exacted retribution on Katangese who had supported the rebellion, helping to provoke the 'Second Shaba War'. In May 1978 several thousand Katangese based in Angola crossed the Zambian border and entered Shaba, occupying Kolwezi. French paratroops again intervened and recaptured the town, and in June a pan-African peace-keeping force arrived in Shaba, remaining there for more than a year.

ORGANIZATION OF OPPOSITION

During 1982 Zaire-based opponents of the country's one-party system formed a new party, the Union pour la Démocratie et le Progrès Social (UDPS), which was quickly banned by the Government, while Nguza Karl-I-Bond, formerly a close political associate of Mobutu, emerged as spokesman for a new coalition of opposition exile groups, the Front Congolais pour le Rétablissement de la Démocratie (FCD).

In May 1983 Mobutu offered an amnesty to all political exiles who returned to Zaire by 30 June. Some returned, but a substantial opposition movement remained in Belgium. Karl-I-Bond returned to Zaire in mid-1985 and was rewarded with the posting of US ambassador one year later, while Mobutu also ended restrictions on senior members of the banned UDPS.

In June 1987 several members of the UDPS, including Etienne Tshisekedi Wa Mulumba (its Secretary-General and a former Minister of the Interior), accepted Mobutu's offer of amnesty, and in October four other former UDPS leaders joined the MPR central committee. At the same time, Mobutu appointed other reconciled opponents of the Government to senior posts in state-owned enterprises. The improvement in relations was short-lived, and in April 1988 Tshisekedi was arrested after urging a boycott of legislative elections scheduled to take place that month in Kinshasa.

In April 1990 Mobutu declared the inauguration of the 'Third Republic' and announced his resignation as Chairman of the MPR. The National Executive Council was dissolved, and Prof. Lunda Bululu, the Secretary-General of the Communauté Economique des Etats de l'Afrique Centrale and formerly a legal adviser to Mobutu, replaced Kengo Wa Dondo as First State Commissioner. In May a new transitional Government was formed. Mobutu announced that a special commission would draft a new Constitution by the end of April 1991, and that a presidential election would be held before December of that year, with legislative elections to follow in 1992. He also promised the imminent 'depoliticization' of the armed forces, the gendarmerie, the civil guard, the security services and civil service.

NATIONAL CONFERENCE

The Government's announcement of a timetable for the restoration of multi-party politics prompted the emergence of a proliferation of political parties. Prominent among them was the Union des Fédéralistes et Républicains Indépendants (UFERI), led by Karl-I-Bond. A new and enlarged transitional Government, appointed in March 1991, included several representatives of minor parties, although more influential opposition parties refused to participate. In April Mobutu announced that a National Conference would convene at the end of the month, with the task of drafting a new constitution, but major opposition parties responded that they would not participate unless Mobutu relinquished power.

The Parti Démocrate et Social Chrétien (PDSC), the UDPS and the UFERI formed the Union Sacrée de l'Opposition Radicale (USOR), which urged a boycott of the National Conference. By the end of July 1991 USOR had expanded to include 130 parties, whereupon the coalition decided that its growing influence and Mobutu's increased weakness justified participation in the National Conference. The National Conference opened on 7 August 1991, with 2,850 delegates attending, including representatives of 900 opposition political parties. USOR delegates immediately threatened to withdraw unless all their political demands were met.

It rapidly became evident that the recently installed 'Government of Crisis' lacked credibility both domestically and internationally, and President Abdou Diouf of Senegal undertook a new initiative to break the impasse. Diouf's proposals committed both Mobutu and opposition supporters to the convening of a sovereign National Conference with legislative power, and to the appointment of a First State Commissioner from the opposition. A new Government was sworn in on 28 November 1991, with Nguza Karl-I-Bond as First State Commissioner. Serious divisions soon arose within the Conference after it resumed in December, and Karl-I-Bond suspended proceedings in January 1992.

Violence intensified during early 1992 as USOR and the Christian churches mobilized demonstrations against the suspension of the Conference. This further worsened Mobutu's international standing, leading to pressure from donor countries for the National Conference to be reinstated, and their continued suspension of aid. Isolated and under pressure, Mobutu, against the wishes of Karl-I-Bond, reconvened the Conference on 6 April. The Conference declared itself 'sovereign' on 17 April, with power to take binding legislative and executive decisions, and announced that it would draft a constitution and a timetable for legislative and presidential elections. By July Mobutu had apparently conceded to the Conference's demands, while insisting, however, on retaining control of the armed forces. On 15 August the Conference overwhelmingly elected Tshisekedi as the transitional Prime Minister with a two-year mandate, replacing Karl-I-Bond, who had not sought re-election. Tshisekedi then appointed a transitional 'Government of National Union', which included known opponents of Mobutu.

Tshisekedi and Mobutu clashed almost immediately, following an announcement by the President of his intention to promote the adoption of a 'semi-presidential constitution', in opposition to the parliamentary system favoured by the Conference. On 14 November the National Conference (without the participation of Mobutu's supporters) adopted a Constitution providing for the establishment of a 'Federal Republic of the Congo', the introduction of a bicameral legislature and the election, by universal suffrage, of a non-executive President to fulfil largely ceremonial functions. Executive and military power was to be exercised by the Prime Minister. The draft document was rejected by Mobutu.

HIGH COUNCIL OF THE REPUBLIC

On 6 December 1992 the National Conference dissolved itself and was succeeded by a 453-member High Council of the Republic (HCR), with the Roman Catholic Archbishop of Kisangani, Laurent Monsengwo Pasinya, as its President. Alarmed at the imminent seizure of his powers, Mobutu ordered the suspension of the HCR and the Government. Attempts by the presidential guard to obstruct the convening of the HCR were defeated by a public demonstration in Kinshasa organized by the HCR. The HCR's declaration of Tshisekedi as Head of Zaire's Government received the support of the USA, Belgium and France.

In mid-January 1993 the HCR declared Mobutu guilty of treason and threatened impeachment proceedings unless he recognized the legitimacy of the transitional Government. At the end of the month several Kinshasa-based units of the army rioted in protest against an attempt by the President to pay them with discredited banknotes. Order was eventually restored, but only after the deaths of some 65 people, and the intervention of French troops.

Rival Governments

In early March 1993, in an attempt to reassert his political authority, Mobutu convened a 'conclave' of political forces to debate the country's future, but the HCR and USOR declined to participate. In mid-March the 'conclave' appointed Faustin Birindwa, a former UDPS member and adviser to Tshisekedi, as Prime Minister, charged with the formation of a 'government of national salvation'. Mobutu also reconvened the dormant Assemblée nationale as a rival to the HCR. In April Birindwa appointed a Cabinet, which included Karl-I-Bond (as First Deputy Prime Minister in charge of Defence) and three members of USOR, who were immediately expelled from that organization. Meanwhile, six of Birindwa's ministers, all former activists in USOR, had announced the formation of the Union Sacrée Rénovée. Mobutu was widely recognized to be fostering such divisions in the opposition through the extensive use of his personal patronage, since, despite the reduction of his formal political powers, he retained access to much of the country's capital and assets.

In September 1993 Mobutu and the principal opposition groups agreed on the adoption of a single constitutional text for the transitional period, which was to be subject to approval by a national referendum. This would be followed by presidential and legislative elections, prior to the establishment of a new republic in January 1995.

EMERGENCE OF THE HCR—PT

A new agreement to form a transitional government was signed by the main political parties in January 1994. Encouraged by the level of political support for the initiative, Mobutu announced the dissolution of the HCR, the National Legislative Council and the Government, and a contest for the premiership between two candidates, Tshisekedi and Molumba

Lukoji, to be decided by a transitional legislature (the Haut Conseil de la République—Parlement de Transition, HCR—PT). Despite widespread protests, the HCR—PT was duly convened six days later, under the presidency of Archbishop Monsengwo.

On 8 April 1994 the HCR—PT endorsed a new transitional Constitution Act, according to which the Government would be accountable to the HCR—PT, and would assume some relinquished powers of the President, including the control of the central bank and the security forces and the nomination of candidates for senior posts in the civil service. In addition, a new Prime Minister was to be appointed from opposition candidates.

On 14 June 1994 the HCR—PT elected Léon Kengo Wa Dondo Prime Minister by a clear majority, but opposition leaders and the HCR—PT President rejected the election as invalid. A new transitional Government, announced on 6 July, was similarly rejected by the radical opposition. On 11 July, however, during a motion of confidence, the Government received overwhelming support from the HCR—PT, and the Prime Minister committed the new administration to the implementation of political reform and economic structural adjustment.

In July 1994, citing problems in the Kivu provinces caused by a mass influx of Rwandan refugees, the transitional Government extended its original 15-month tenure by two years. Meanwhile, opposition frustration at the absence of an electoral timetable escalated, and there were further violent demonstrations in the capital. In December the HCR—PT formalized the establishment of the National Electoral Commission (NEC), which was inaugurated in April 1996.

At the same time it was announced that a constitutional referendum in December 1996 would be followed by presidential, legislative, regional and municipal elections in 1997. A draft of the new Constitution, which provided for a federal state with a semi-presidential parliamentary system of government, was adopted in May 1996, and was approved by the HCR—PT in October.

THE FALL OF MOBUTU

In August 1996 Mobutu left for Switzerland to receive treatment for cancer. Rwandan Hutu militias and former soldiers of the Forces Armées Rwandais (ex-FAR) had by then, with the active assistance of the Zairean armed forces (Forces Armées de Zaïre—FAZ), converted Rwandan refugee camps into bases for rearmament and preparation for the future reconquest of Rwanda. By mid-1996 Rwandan Hutu militias, known as Interahamwe, with the support of Congolese Hutus and the FAZ, were killing and displacing Congolese Tutsis and other ethnic groups. The situation was complicated by long-term rivalries in the area, including widespread resentment of Sud-Kivu Tutsis (known as the Banyamulenge), and a decades-long dispute over their entitlement to Zairean nationality. In early October the Deputy Governor of Sud-Kivu ordered the Banyamulenge to leave the country within a week. The order was subsequently suspended, but none the less provoked a powerful reprisal from Banyamulenge militias, who, with the full support of the Rwandan and Ugandan Governments, made rapid advances against the combined forces of the ex-FAR, Interahamwe and the poorly trained FAZ. What had initially been a localized movement seeking to defend the Banyamulenge and combat extremist Hutus rapidly gathered momentum and became a national coalition fighting to overthrow the Mobutu regime. Banyamulenge rebels were joined by other dissidents to form the Alliance des Forces Démocratiques pour la Libération du Congo-Zaïre (AFDL). Soon to join the AFDL were the Katangese gendarmes, who had fought for the Angolan Government in its long-term civil conflict against the União Nacional para a Independência Total de Angola (UNITA), and who retained close contact with the Angolan Government. Laurent-Désiré Kabila, a ministerial aide under Lumumba, was rapidly promoted to the position of the AFDL's leader. By early November AFDL forces controlled a substantial area adjoining the border with Rwanda, Burundi and parts of Uganda, including the key towns of Goma, Bukavu and Uvira, and by the end of the month they had captured most of Nord- and Sud-Kivu. Mobutu's absence, and uncertainties as to the state of his health, weakened the Zairean Government's response to the AFDL, although the main reasons for the loss of territory were the strength of the foreign, particularly Rwandan, armed forces supporting (and in most cases leading) the AFDL, and the lack of commitment within the FAZ to defending the Government.

The AFDL's success in the east exacerbated anti-Tutsi sentiment in Kinshasa. In November 1996 the HCR—PT demanded the expulsion of all Tutsis from Zairean territory; following attacks on Tutsis and their property, many Tutsi residents of Kinshasa fled across the river to Brazzaville, in the Republic of the Congo. In the same month repeated public demonstrations demanded the resignation of Kengo Wa Dondo (himself part-Tutsi in origin) for having failed to respond effectively to the insurrection. Mobutu finally returned to Kinshasa on 17 December and while retaining Kengo Wa Dondo as Prime Minister ordered the formation of a crisis government, which included some opposition members, although it excluded the UDPS and was not approved by the HCR—PT. Before long, Tshisekedi's faction of the UDPS announced its support for the AFDL. In February 1997, following an effective general strike in Kinshasa, Mobutu banned all demonstrations and industrial action.

In March 1997, after brief hostilities, the AFDL took Kisangani, and in April captured Mbuji-Mayi and Lubumbashi. The HCR—PT, although technically inquorate, voted in March to dismiss Kengo Wa Dondo, who resigned at the end of that month, and was replaced by Tshisekedi. Tshisekedi dissolved the HCR—PT, which voted, in turn, to dismiss Tshisekedi. On 8 April Mobutu declared a national state of emergency, dismissing the Government and ordering the deployment of security forces throughout Kinshasa. Gen. Likulia Bolongo was appointed Prime Minister at the head of a new National Salvation Government, in which major opposition parties refused to participate. Following inconclusive peace talks between Mobutu and Kabila, mediated by the South African President, Nelson Mandela, in May, Kabila reiterated his intention to seize the capital by force.

KABILA ASSUMES POWER

On 16 May 1997 Mobutu fled Kinshasa and travelled to Togo, and then to Morocco, where he died on 7 September. On 17 May AFDL troops entered Kinshasa, encountering no resistance, and Kabila, from Lubumbashi, declared himself President of the Democratic Republic of the Congo (DRC, the name used in 1964–71). Kabila promised that presidential and legislative elections would take place within two years. On 23 May Kabila formed a provisional Government, dominated by members of the AFDL, but also including members of the UDPS and of the Front Patriotique. No Prime Minister was appointed, and Tshisekedi was not offered a cabinet post. On 26 May Kabila issued a decree banning all political parties and public demonstrations. A public gathering in Kinshasa on 28 May in support of Tshisekedi was dispersed by the army. On that day Kabila issued another decree, granting himself legislative and executive power and control over the armed forces and the treasury. Of the previously existing state institutions, only the judiciary was not dissolved. On the following day Kabila was sworn in as President of the DRC.

In January 1998 a cousin of Kabila, Gaëtan Kakudji, was appointed Minister of the Interior as part of a cabinet reorganization that effected a general shift in power towards Katanga politicians. Later that month two UDPS leaders were sentenced by a military tribunal to two years' imprisonment for 'agitating the public', and in February Tshisekedi was arrested and banished to his home village in Kasaï Oriental for six months.

In March 1998 a constitutional commission appointed earlier by Kabila submitted its draft constitution, which envisaged a five-year presidency, with the President enjoying extensive executive powers. On 26 May a transitional Constituent Assembly was established by presidential decree, excluding anyone who held public office during Mobutu's presidency. The Assemblée nationale, holding legislative powers, was to review the draft constitution and prepare it for approval by a national referendum.

REBELLION AND REGIONAL INTERVENTION

On 28 July 1998 Kabila ordered the expulsion of all remaining Rwandan army units from the country. Shortly afterwards, a rebellion assisted by the Rwandan armed forces was launched in Nord- and Sud-Kivu. Rebel forces, operating as the Rassemblement Congolais pour la Démocratie (RCD), swiftly captured Goma, Bukavu and Uvira, which was denounced by Kabila as a Rwandan invasion. In August the RCD and Rwandan troops swiftly captured Kitona and the nearby Banana naval installation, and within one week had captured Matadi and the Inga hydroelectric dam and cut off Kinshasa's electricity supply. Several government ministers defected to the rebels. On 19 August, at a meeting of Ministers of Defence of the Southern African Development Community (SADC, which the DRC had joined in September 1997), Zimbabwe and Namibia pledged to assist Kabila. Zimbabwean troops arrived in Kinshasa the following day and secured the international airport. Although the Rwandan Government believed that it had secured the agreement of the Angolan administration in its plan to overthrow Kabila, Angola also sent troops in late August, which recaptured Banana and Kitona, and by the end of August had defeated the RCD in the west of the country. The RCD, however, assisted by Rwandan and Ugandan troops, consolidated its control in the east, capturing Kisangani in late August and a series of smaller towns during September.

Diplomatic initiatives to end the war began on 7–8 September 1998, when regional heads of state met in Victoria Falls, Zimbabwe, under the chairmanship of the Zambian President, Frederick Chiluba. A cease-fire was agreed at the meeting, but was rejected by the RCD and by Kabila, who first demanded the withdrawal of Ugandan and Rwandan troops. On 15 September the annual SADC meeting in Mauritius endorsed the legitimacy of the intervention by Zimbabwe, Namibia and Angola and formally authorized Chiluba to continue his mediation efforts. Two weeks later, at a summit in Libreville, Gabon, the Governments of Gabon, Chad, the Republic of the Congo, the Central African Republic, Equatorial Guinea, Cameroon, Namibia and Angola recognized Kabila as the legitimate Head of State of the DRC and condemned the 'external aggression' against him.

Hundreds of Mai-Mai fighters (by then allied to Kabila) and Rwandan Interahamwe attacked Goma in September 1998, but were defeated by the RCD and Rwandan forces. Rwanda subsequently accused Kabila of rearming the Interahamwe (a claim later endorsed by the UN commission of inquiry into illicit trade in armaments in the Great Lakes region). Meanwhile, Kabila continued his efforts to enlist further support for his Government, which resulted in Chad temporarily deploying 2,000 troops in the DRC. The RCD continued its military offensive and on 14 October captured the strategic town of Kindu, which allowed RCD forces to advance into Kasaï and Katanga. Concerned at developments, the Presidents of Angola, Namibia and Zimbabwe increased their military deployment in the DRC. In November a new rebel group emerged called the Mouvement de Libération du Congo (MLC), led by Jean-Pierre Bemba Gombo (the son of a prominent Mobutuist, Bemba Saolona, who joined Kabila's Cabinet in 1999). The MLC soon developed close ties with the Ugandan Government, while Rwanda remained committed to the RCD. In November 1998, following talks with Mandela, the Rwandan Vice-President, Paul Kagame, finally admitted publicly that Rwandan troops were fighting alongside the RCD.

Divisions emerged in the RCD in 1999, with the Vice-Chairman, Arthur Z'ahidi Ngoma, resigning in February, alleging that the movement was under the control of the Rwandan and Ugandan Governments. In May the RCD, in an action supported by Rwanda, but condemned by Uganda, deposed Ernest Wamba dia Wamba as Chairman, and replaced him with Emile Ilunga. Wamba dia Wamba denounced this move as illegitimate and established a faction in Kisangani, the RCD—Mouvement de Libération (RCD—ML), while Goma became the headquarters of Ilunga's Rwanda-backed faction (RCD—Goma). Violence in Kisangani subsequently forced Wamba dia Wamba in October to relocate once more, to Bunia, where he remained under Ugandan army protection.

The Lusaka Accord

A peace summit was convened in Lusaka, Zambia, in late June 1999, and culminated in the signing of an accord on 10 July by the Presidents of the DRC, Zimbabwe, Angola, Rwanda and Uganda, but by none of the rebel leaderships. The accord provided for an immediate cease-fire, and for combatant forces inside the DRC to establish a Joint Military Commission (JMC), and to disarm identified militia groups, which included the Rwandan Interahamwe, Burundi's Force pour la défense de la démocratie, the Congolese Mai-Mai and Angola's UNITA. The accord also provided a timetable for the withdrawal of foreign forces, the deployment of UN peace-keepers and the organization of inter-Congolese political negotiations. Bemba signed the Lusaka Accord on 1 August, and on 6 August the UN Security Council authorized the dispatch of 80 UN military observers to Kinshasa and regional capitals as the first stage of the UN's deployment in the DRC, which commenced on 13 September. At the end of November the UN Security Council established the Mission de l'Organisation des Nations Unies en République Démocratique du Congo (MONUC). Signalling the final collapse of Rwanda and Uganda's increasingly precarious relationship in the DRC, and the heightened significance of control of the country's mineral and other natural resources in the schemes of the combatant factions, serious fighting erupted between Rwandan and Ugandan forces in Kisangani in mid-August and continued for four days. At the end of August all 51 founder members of the RCD signed the Lusaka Accord.

Internal Political Developments

In early 1999 Kabila announced the formation of village-level Comités du Pouvoir Populaire (CPP), and in April dissolved the AFDL, accusing many of its members of corruption. Efforts by the Organization of African Unity (OAU, now the African Union—AU) to initiate dialogue between the Government, opposition figures, rebel groups and civil society had failed by mid-2000.

Reaffirmation of the Lusaka Accord

In January 2000 the UN Secretary-General, Kofi Annan, recommended that MONUC be increased in size to 500 military observers, supported by some 5,000 combat troops with powers of enforcement, with the possibility of additional troops if the Lusaka Accord was respected by its signatories. Annan's proposal was approved by the Security Council on 24 February, and the mandate of the force was extended to the end of August. Recognizing that the 1999 cease-fire agreement had been widely ignored, participants at a meeting of the JMC in early April 2000 agreed to a new cease-fire, which came into effect on 14 April. Fighting subsequently subsided in most areas.

In May 2000 Kabila announced the formation of a 300-member transitional Parliament, the delegates of which were selected by a committee supervised by the Ministry of the Interior and subsequently approved by presidential decree. On 22 August Kabila inaugurated the new Parliament in Lubumbashi, and on the following day unilaterally declared the Lusaka Accord invalid. The Government authorized the deployment of MONUC troops in government-held territory on 24 August, but then refused permission for them to arrive.

DRC government forces captured the town of Pepa, which was held by RCD—Goma, in mid-October 2000, after launching an unexpected attack, at the same time as a regional summit on the DRC conflict convened in Maputo, Mozambique, where it was agreed that all combative forces should withdraw 15 km from their current positions. The 15-km withdrawal plan was taken up by another summit in Maputo later in the month, chaired by the South African President, Thabo Mbeki, who eventually secured agreement from all rebel forces. RCD—Goma reorganized its leadership in late October, with Ilunga being replaced as President by Adolphe Onusumba. Strongly assisted by Rwandan troops, RCD—Goma recaptured Pepa in November and secured control of Pweto on the Zambian border in December. At least 60,000 civilian refugees fled from Pweto to Zambia.

In December 2000 the Government transported 200 specially selected participants to a meeting in Libreville, Gabon, described as a 'preparatory national dialogue'. The dialogue was then abruptly postponed until January 2001, after which participants issued a statement urging the revision of the Lusaka Accord, in accordance with earlier government demands.

JOSEPH KABILA ASSUMES POWER

Kabila was assassinated, apparently by a member of his presidential guard, on 16 January 2001. Three days later the Presidents of Angola, Zimbabwe and Namibia met in Luanda, Angola, and agreed to leave their troops in the DRC. On 23 January Kabila's son, Joseph Kabila, was formally installed as the new President. During his first address, Kabila promised internal political liberalization and increased dialogue with the DRC's neighbours in order to end the war, and his inauguration as President immediately boosted the peace process. On 15 February the warring parties in the DRC revived their earlier agreement to withdraw 15 km from positions of military engagement, and on 15 March RCD—Goma and Rwandan army combatants retreated from Pweto. The first contingent of MONUC troops arrived in RCD-held Kalemie in mid-March, followed shortly afterwards by the deployment of MONUC troops in government-held Kananga. After some delay, MONUC forces were dispatched to RCD-held Kisangani in late April, closely followed by the dispatch of more UN troops to government-held Mbandaka, which completed the initial MONUC deployment.

Kabila appointed a new Government on 14 April 2001. Mwenze Kongolo, the former Minister of Justice, with associations to the Zimbabwean Government, was appointed Minister of National Security and Public Order, in a measure widely interpreted as indicating the consolidation of Zimbabwean influence on the new DRC Government. Opposition parties urged Kabila to allow political activity, and Tshisekedi returned to Kinshasa after a 16-month absence on 23 April. Kabila ended some restrictions on political activity in mid-May, and ordered the release of a number of detained human rights activists.

Wamba dia Wamba was ousted as the RCD—ML leader in August 2001 by Antipas Mbusa Nyamwisi. The Ugandan Government recognized Nyamwisi as the new RCD—ML leader, despite his open hostility to Bemba, Uganda's principal DRC ally. In October the UN Security Council voted to extend MONUC's mandate into a 'third phase', which was to involve the disarmament, demobilization, reintegration, repatriation and resettlement (DDRRR) of combatants identified as 'negative forces' by the Lusaka Accord, including the Interahamwe and the Mai-Mai.

In November 2001 a UN investigative committee accused Rwanda and Uganda of the illegal exploitation of the DRC's mineral resources, a charge that was angrily rejected by both Governments. MONUC's DDRRR campaign was launched in December, with the monitoring of nearly 2,000 Rwandan Hutu combatants, who had assembled in camps in Kamina, in DRC government territory, to present themselves for disarmament and demobilization.

In December 2001 representatives of RCD—Goma, the MLC and the DRC Government met in Abuja, Nigeria, for UN-mediated talks. The next round of the inter-Congolese dialogue commenced in Sun City, South Africa, in February 2002, with all the major parties and numerous minor ones in attendance. The discussions generated some significant agreements, but failed to find a formula to bring Kabila's Government, the MLC and RCD—Goma into a power-sharing partnership. Instead, Kabila, who in March formed a new political party, the Parti pour la Réconciliation et le Développement (PPRD), concluded a power-sharing agreement with the MLC and the RCD—ML on 17 April (the final day of the discussions). Despite the deal, mistrust persisted between the DRC Government and the MLC and the agreement was never implemented.

On 30 July 2002 a peace agreement, mediated by Mbeki, was signed by Kabila and Kagame in Pretoria, South Africa. Under the accord, Kabila pledged to arrest and disarm the Interahamwe militia in the DRC, while the Rwandan Government was to withdraw its troops from the country. President Robert Mugabe of Zimbabwe subsequently promised to withdraw remaining Zimbabwean troops, and in mid-August the DRC and Uganda reached an accord in the Angolan capital, Luanda, providing for the normalization of relations between the two countries and the full withdrawal of Ugandan troops in the DRC. Donors linked continued assistance to Rwanda to its troops leaving the DRC, and Rwandan troops were officially withdrawn in the first week of October. Zimbabwean troops left later that month. The troop withdrawals were verified by MONUC, but it lacked the resources to perform this task thoroughly, and it was widely alleged that both were incomplete.

The departure of Rwandan troops was swiftly followed by Mai-Mai attacks on areas controlled by RCD—Goma, apparently with assistance from the DRC Government. Uvira was seized by the Mai-Mai in mid-October 2002, but was reoccupied by RCD—Goma one week later. The DRC Government began to implement its part of the Pretoria Agreement by expelling 25 leaders of the Forces Démocratiques pour la Libération du Rwanda (FDLR). Controversially, eight of the leaders were repatriated to Rwanda, provoking a rebellion among Rwandan Hutu combatants encamped in Kamina. There were no further DDRRR campaigns by the DRC Government. The RCD—ML lost control of its stronghold, Bunia, in the Ituri region of Kasaï Oriental, in mid-August to a breakaway faction, headed by Thomas Lubanga, which subsequently became known as the Union des Patriotes Congolais (UPC). The RCD—ML relocated to the nearby town of Beni, from where it was reported to be receiving supplies from the DRC Government. During late 2002 the RCD—ML was engaged in fierce hostilities, in the region of Isiro, in Kasaï Oriental, with another breakaway faction of the RCD, the RCD—National (RCD—N), which was led by Roger Lumbala and supported by the MLC. In December the UN Secretary-General's special representative to the DRC, Amos Namanga Ngongi, mediated a cease-fire agreement between the RCD—ML, RCD—N and MLC, which lessened tensions for a short time, although skirmishes were again reported around Beni in early 2003. Meanwhile, in Bunia the UPC initially allied itself with Ugandan forces, but in December 2002 concluded an agreement with RCD—Goma, and subsequently received military supplies from the Rwandan Government.

In October 2002 the UN panel investigating the illegal exploitation of the DRC's resources published a new report, detailing the systematic exploitation of the DRC by 'élite networks' from Zimbabwe, Angola, Uganda, Rwanda, and the DRC itself. The report recommended that sanctions be imposed on all the individuals and companies named in the report, and reduced aid to countries accused of involvement in exploiting the DRC. The findings of the commission were rejected by every accused nation, and, although welcomed by the UN Security Council, no action was taken by the Council against those the report had accused.

TRANSITIONAL GOVERNMENT

Talks resumed in Pretoria in November 2002 between groups participating in the inter-Congolese national dialogue, which on 17 December signed a new agreement, providing for a transitional Government, to be headed by Kabila, with four Vice-Presidents. The Vice-Presidents were to be representatives of the incumbent DRC Government, the MLC, RCD—Goma and the political opposition. It was agreed that the new Government would be made up of representatives from all parties involved in the inter-Congolese national dialogue. To include all groups, most ministries were divided into several components (creating, for example, three education ministries and four finance and economy ministries). The new transitional Parliament was to comprise a 500-member Assemblée nationale and a 120-member Senate. In addition, new Congolese armed forces, composed of elements of the existing military, were to be established. On 2 April all parties officially signed a final accord providing for the adoption of the transitional organs of government (endorsing the Sun City and Pretoria Agreements).

On 29 June 2003 all former combatant groups finally signed an agreement on power-sharing in the future integrated transitional armed forces. This final stage in the peace process allowed Kabila on the following day to nominate a transitional Government, in which ministries were divided between rebel groups, the incumbent administration, political opposition and civil society organizations. The four Vice-Presidents were sworn in on 17 July, and the first session of the new power-sharing Government took place on 25 July. On 20 August Kabila announced the nominations to the military leadership of the new unified armed forces, which was to incorporate elements of all the former rebel groups and the Mai-Mai militia; former RCD—Goma and MLC commanders were appointed to senior posts, including services chiefs of staff. On 22 August the inaugural session of the new bicameral transitional Parliament was conducted at the People's Palace, in Kinshasa; seats in the Assemblée nationale and Senate were likewise divided between the former rebel groups, the Mai-Mai, the incumbent Government, political opposition and civil society. In September the French-led contingent officially transferred control of the Ituri region to MONUC reinforcements (after the UN Security Council at the end of July considerably increased MONUC's authorized maximum strength).

Tshisekedi returned to Kinshasa in late September 2003 for the first time since his alliance with the RCD—Goma in May 2002. Although Tshisekedi retained some support in the capital, he was widely criticized for boycotting talks with the unarmed opposition over the appointment of a Vice-President for the transitional Government, which resulted in the exclusion of the UDPS from the administration and its marginalization from mainstream politics.

The Government presented its DDRRR plan to donors in May 2004, and later that month the World Bank approved a US $100m. grant to fund it. The difficulties in implementing the programme were almost immediately emphasized, when, in late May, troops loyal to Kabila and the RCD—Goma clashed in Bukavu, resulting in several thousand Banyamulenge fleeing across the border into Rwanda. MONUC demanded that pro-RCD—Goma troops enter a cantonment camp established for integrating rebel forces, which most duly did by the end of the month. Two days later, however, several thousand troops loyal to Maj.-Gen. Laurent Nkunda, who supported the RCD—Goma, attacked the pro-Kabila forces, led by Col. Mbuza Mabe, and seized control of Bukavu on 2 June. The failure of MONUC troops to prevent this caused protest riots in Kinshasa, Lubumbashi and several other towns. Kabila accused Rwanda of redeploying troops on DRC territory, a charge that the Rwandan Government denied. As MONUC pressure on him increased, Nkunda later withdrew from Bukavu, allowing Mabe to reoccupy the city.

In mid-November 2004 the transitional Assemblée nationale adopted new legislation on the definition of Congolese nationality, specifying that anyone belonging to an ethnic group whose members or territory constituted the DRC at independence was Congolese. According to this definition, Banyamulenge and other Kinywarwanda-speakers from the Kivu provinces (except for those who crossed over in 1994) were Congolese, thereby meeting a key demand of the RCD—Goma and the Rwandan Government.

Following a parliamentary inquiry that accused a number of government members of corruption, in late November 2004 Kabila suspended six cabinet ministers and 12 heads of parastatals. Affected political parties protested, and the MLC suspended participation in the Government for a time (prompting a visit to Kinshasa by Mbeki to resolve the dispute), but in mid-January 2005 all except one of the ministers were replaced. Efforts by MONUC during 2004 to demobilize combatants in Ituri made little progress. In December 2004 Kabila appointed the chief commanders of the six main Ituri militia as generals in the armed forces, attracting strong criticism from human rights organizations that they were being rewarded for atrocities they had committed. There was further fighting in Ituri in January 2005, displacing thousands of people into Uganda; nevertheless, by the end of February an estimated 3,000 Ituri-based combatants had been demobilized.

DELAYS IN ELECTION TIMETABLE

In January 2005 Abbé Apollinaire Malu-Malu, the head of the Commission Electorale Indépendante (CEI), announced that elections would be delayed, leading to large public protests in Kinshasa and other towns, which were suppressed by the security forces. In late January a UN panel of experts monitoring an international armaments embargo on the eastern DRC produced a second report, alleging numerous embargo violations in Ituri and Nord- and Sud-Kivu. It documented a close link between mining interests and the conflict, with Ituri militia battling for control of gold exports, and rival factions of the armed forces and the Mai-Mai fighting over cassiterite and columbo-tantalite (coltan) deposits in the two Kivu provinces. The report alleged ongoing links between the Mai-Mai and the FDLR, contrary to the DRC Government's official position that it had ended all contacts with the Rwandan militia. The UN panel also concluded that the Rwandan, Burundian and Ugandan Governments were still supporting militia in eastern DRC, again contrary to their official undertakings. All three countries subsequently denied any involvement. In mid-February the Front des Nationalistes Intégrationnistes (FNI), one of the main Ituri militias, killed nine MONUC personnel. Several militia leaders were subsequently arrested, including the FNI's leader, Floribert Ndjabu Ngabu, and Thomas Lubanga of the UPC.

The FDLR announced in February 2005 that it would end its armed struggle, providing the Rwandan Government allowed it to return home and transform itself into a political party. The Rwandan Government replied that the FDLR could return but that its members would be investigated for possible involvement in the 1994 genocide. The offer was rejected by the FDLR. In January 2005 AU Heads of State, meeting in Abuja, Nigeria, had agreed to deploy an African force in eastern DRC to assist in the forcible disarmament of the FDLR, but, despite a promise of European Union (EU) funds, the plan was not implemented. The UN Security Council voted in April to adopt the recommendation of the UN panel of experts investigating implementation of the armaments embargo in eastern DRC, that the embargo be extended to the entire country. Later that month a number of military personnel and civilian politicians were arrested in the Katangan capital Lubumbashi, on suspicion of organizing a bid for the province's secession.

NEW CONSTITUTION APPROVED

On 13 May 2005 the transitional Assemblée nationale adopted a new Constitution, which was scheduled to be submitted to a popular referendum within six months. The Constitution provided for a President, who was to appoint the Prime Minister and his administration, which were then to formulate policy. The President, however, was to remain head of the Council of Ministers. Ministers, but not the President, were to be answerable to the Assemblée nationale. The Assemblée nationale was empowered to dismiss the Government, but not the President, while the President was to retain the right to dissolve the Assemblée nationale. The new Constitution also envisaged an increase in the number of provinces from 11 to 26, which were also to receive greater autonomy than previously. The transitional process was scheduled to end following elections on 29 March 2006. In June 2005 the CEI began registering voters, and by the end of the process in November had impressed many international observers by registering about 25m. people.

The demobilization and disarmament campaign in Ituri, meanwhile, made further progress during early 2005, and by June MONUC estimated that 15,000 combatants had been demobilized. However, a coalition of three militia groups, the Mouvement Révolutionnaire Congolais (MRC), formed in Uganda in June, determined to continue fighting, denouncing the demobilization campaign and demanding Iturian autonomy. Following the formation of the MRC, a Congolese government delegation travelled to Uganda to discuss the matter with President Yoweri Museveni, who promised not to allow MRC leaders to assemble in Kampala, the Ugandan capital. After a period of relative quiet, there was further violence in Ituri in October, prompting government troops to increase deployment in the area.

In July 2005 the Government announced a deadline of 30 September for all foreign troops to leave the country, and soon afterwards MONUC announced that it was ready to assist the armed forces in expelling an anti-Ugandan Government movement, the Lord's Resistance Army (LRA). Uganda had increasingly complained about the presence of anti-Ugandan Government militias in eastern DRC and warned that, if the DRC authorities failed to take action, the Ugandan armed forces might intervene. Meanwhile, in August Nkunda threatened from a secret location in Nord-Kivu to overthrow the Government. The Government formally stripped Nkunda of his rank, and during September arrested a number of those suspected of links with him. There were clashes between Nkunda's supporters and a joint force of government and MONUC troops near Rutshuru, in Nord-Kivu, in mid-January 2006, forcing over 50,000 civilians to flee from the region.

The long-awaited constitutional referendum was conducted on 18 December 2005. According to the official results, the new Constitution was approved by 84.3% of votes cast; 62% of the registered electorate participated in the ballot. Fewer than 10,000 copies of the Constitution had been circulated before the vote, and the pre-referendum campaign lasted only two weeks and was focused on major urban areas, meaning few people had an idea of what they were voting for. In January 2006 the CEI once again postponed elections, citing logistical difficulties.

Military reforms, meanwhile, which were to integrate previously warring factions into the armed forces, were proceeding more slowly than originally envisaged. By the end of 2005 only six of 18 planned integrated brigades had been established, trained and deployed. Nevertheless, at the same time as pursuing rebel militia in the east, in late 2005 the Government also launched military operations against Mai-Mai militia, under the command of Kyungu Mutanga (also known as Gédeon), in Haut-Katanga. The government initiative prompted mass population displacement, but managed to achieve the disarmament of some 2,000 Mai-Mai by the end of the year.

KABILA WINS DEMOCRATIC ELECTIONS

The new Constitution was formally promulgated by Kabila on 18 February 2006. On 21 February the Assemblée nationale approved electoral legislation allowing presidential and parliamentary candidates to register, which was enacted by Kabila on 9 March. The CEI announced at this time that elections would be rescheduled again, to 18 June. Within the two-week deadline 33 presidential candidates, including Kabila and Bemba (but not Tshisekedi), had emerged, while some 9,700 people had registered to contest the 500 seats in the Assemblée nationale. In March Lubanga was transferred from MONUC custody to the International Criminal Court (ICC) in The Hague, Netherlands, becoming the first person ever to be arrested by the Court, and in May government and MONUC troops intensified operations in Ituri, in an effort to ensure that elections were conducted peacefully. Following negotiations between the FNI, the Government and MONUC in mid-2006, the FNI pledged to stop fighting. In return, the Government announced in July that it would integrate FNI units into its forces. A few days later the MRC agreed also to end hostilities in return for integration into the armed forces. Meanwhile, in Haut-Katanga in May Gédeon and several hundred of his supporters surrendered to MONUC forces. In an attempt to ensure peaceful elections in the capital, in April the UN Security Council authorized the temporary deployment of an EU military force (EUFOR RD Congo), led by Germany, in Kinshasa and neighbouring Gabon. The European Council of Ministers gave its approval in mid-June and the troops began arriving shortly afterwards. The CEI announced on 1 May that the elections would be rescheduled one further time, to 30 July. This meant that the elections would take place after the official end of the transition agreed at Sun City, and the UDPS and many representatives of civil society argued that Malu-Malu lacked the authority to do this. However, Malu-Malu insisted that the new Constitution superseded the Sun City agreement, and allowed the transitional period to continue until elections were held.

The country's first democratic presidential and legislative elections in over 40 years took place on 30 July 2006. Despite reports of some procedural irregularities and violent incidents, most international observer missions announced that the elections had been conducted fairly. However, several presidential candidates subsequently accused the authorities of perpetrating mass falsification of the results, and in August six poll officials were arrested on suspicion of malpractice. According to the CEI, Kabila secured 44.8% and Bemba 20.0% of votes cast; about 70.5% of the electorate had voted. Most of Kabila's support came from Katanga and eastern provinces, while Bemba received the most votes in western provinces and Kinshasa. Kabila's failure to secure an absolute majority of votes cast necessitated a second round of the presidential election, scheduled for 29 October (when deputies were also to be elected to the provincial Assemblies), to be followed by elections to the Senate at the end of December. Hostilities between forces loyal to Kabila and Bemba's supporters continued in Kinshasa following the CEI's announcement of the first round results, and EUFOR reinforcements were dispatched to Kinshasa from Gabon, in an effort to restore peace in the capital. After three days of fighting, Kabila and Bemba reached an agreement to withdraw their forces from central Kinshasa.

In September 2006 the CEI released provisional results of the legislative elections, according to which the Parti du Peuple pour la Reconstruction et la Démocratie, as the PPRD had been restyled, secured 111 seats, while the MLC won 64. The other main winners in the legislative poll were the Parti Lumumbiste Unifié (PALU), which gained 34 seats, the Mouvement Social pour le Renouveau, which secured 27, the Forces du Renouveau (FR), which won 26, and the RCD, with 15. Some 63 other parties also secured parliamentary representation.

In mid-September 2006 PALU President Antoine Gizenga joined Kabila's Alliance pour la Majorité Présidentielle (AMP), giving the multi-party coalition 285 seats, and thus an absolute majority in the Assemblée nationale. In return, PALU was to be allowed to select the next Prime Minister. The second round of the presidential poll took place as scheduled, and on 15 November the CEI proclaimed Kabila the winner with 58.05% of the vote. Bemba officially contested the result before the Supreme Court, which rejected his petition on 27 November, upholding Kabila's victory. Bemba conceded defeat, while still alleging electoral fraud. Kabila was officially sworn in as President at a ceremony on 6 December.

Kabila appointed Gizenga as Prime Minister on 30 December 2006. Gizenga announced a new Government in February 2007: a total of 13 cabinet ministers were from the PPRD, five from PALU, and the remainder were members of the AMP. Despite international pressure, no ministerial seats were allocated to the MLC or its alliance partners. Francois Nzanga Mobutu, son of the former President, was appointed Minister of State, in charge of Agriculture, while Nyamwisi, now the leader of the FR, was appointed Minister of State, in charge of Foreign Affairs and International Co-operation.

Meanwhile, provincial election results were announced in December 2006, according to which the AMP won majorities in seven provincial Assemblies, while the Union pour la Nation won majorities in four. The provincial Assemblies voted in senatorial elections on 19 January 2007, in which the AMP won 48 seats and the MLC 14; 26 independent senators were elected. On 27 January the provincial Assemblies elected governors in nine provinces. Despite having majorities in four provincial Assemblies, Bemba's alliance secured only one governorship, allegedly owing to widespread bribery by the AMP.

UNREST CONTINUES IN EASTERN PROVINCES

Violent clashes broke out in Nord-Kivu in November 2006, after Nkunda relaunched military operations in its Rutshuru and Masisi districts. Nkunda and Congolese government representatives met for talks hosted by the Rwandan Government in Kigali in January 2007, at which it was agreed that Nkunda's forces would be integrated into the Congolese armed forces. Prior to this a process known as 'mixage' was agreed upon, according to which Nkunda's troops would fight alongside the Congolese armed forces, but as complete units rather than as individual soldiers. This ensured Nkunda's continued influence over his combatants, despite their integration into the Forces Armées de la République Démocratique du Congo (FARDC). However, by May the agreement had disintegrated, and Nkunda relaunched an aggressive campaign to capture territory in the province, resulting in the displacement of tens of thousands of people. Meanwhile, in Ituri an agreement was signed in November 2006 between the Government, the MRC, the FNI and the Forces de Résistance Patriotique en Ituri (FRPI), according to which their fighters would be granted amnesty in return for disarmament by the end of the year. The MRC and FRPI largely adhered to the agreement, but the FNI did not, and fighting resumed in Ituri between the FNI and the FARDC in February 2007. After several weeks of clashes, the FNI reversed its position, and its forces were formally integrated into the Congolese armed forces in April.

In February 2007 the Government established 15 March as the deadline for the disbanding of private militia. In place of his substantial private army, Bemba was offered 12 policemen as bodyguards, which he rejected as inadequate. The deadline passed, and on 22 March fighting erupted in central Kinshasa between the FARDC and Bemba's troops. The FARDC prevailed and Bemba fled to the South African embassy. Chief Prosecutor Tsaimanga Mukenda issued a warrant for his arrest, seeking to charge Bemba with high treason. Meanwhile, government troops broke into and looted the MLC headquarters in Kinshasa. International diplomatic efforts subsequently secured an agreement that Bemba could leave the country, ostensibly for medical treatment, and he flew to Portugal on 11 April. Kengo Wa Dondo was elected President of the Senate on 11 May.

Violence flared near Minembwe in Sud-Kivu in July 2007, when there were clashes between integrated units of the FARDC and non-integrated Banyamulenge troops under the command of Maj. Michel Rukunda. His men were eventually dislodged from their positions in the province's Haut Plateau region, while thousands of civilians were displaced from their homes. Meanwhile, in Ituri MONUC and the Congolese armed forces' disarmament and demobilization campaign appeared to be producing tangible results. In August over 3,500 militia fighters were demobilized, bringing the estimated total since the campaign began in 2006 to around 17,000. Also in August there was fighting between the FARDC and the Uganda People's Defence Forces (UPDF) in Lake Albert after Congolese armed forces attacked a barge prospecting for petroleum there, killing a British geologist. An emergency meeting between Ugandan and Congolese military chiefs was convened in Entebbe, Uganda, shortly afterwards, at which the two sides agreed to conduct a joint investigation into the matter. A few days later, however, FDLR fighters based in Nord-Kivu made an incursion into western Uganda, prompting a major UPDF deployment on the border. The Ugandan Minister of Foreign Affairs, Sam Kutesa, flew to Kinshasa shortly afterwards for talks with Kabila, who apologized for the incidents. However, there were renewed clashes between the Congolese armed forces and UPDF in September.

On 9 November 2007 an agreement was signed in Nairobi, Kenya, between the Congolese and Rwandan Governments. The agreement committed the former to evicting the FDLR from the DRC, while the latter agreed to prevent assistance to Nkunda's forces. Also that month, as part of the continuing military integration process, three Ituri leaders, Peter Karim of the FNI, Cobra Matata of the FRPI and Mathieu Ngoudjolo of the MRC, travelled to Kinshasa, where they were installed as officers in the Congolese armed forces. In February 2008, however, Ngoudjolo and another Ituri militia leader, Germain Katanga, were arrested and transferred to the ICC in The Hague, to be prosecuted for war crimes.

A government reorganization was effected in late November 2007, in which the number of ministers and deputy ministers was reduced from 60 to 45. Notable changes included the appointment of André Philippe Futa, a former Minister of Finance, as Minister of the National Economy; Futa was also awarded the trade portfolio.

The Congolese armed forces launched an offensive against Nkunda's forces in Nord-Kivu in December 2007. The offensive initially appeared successful, but Nkunda's forces soon counter-attacked, routing the DRC troops despite their substantial advantage in numbers, and recapturing all their positions. The Congolese armed forces' failure prompted the Government to reconsider its strategy in Nord-Kivu, and in early January 2008 a peace conference was launched in Goma, to which all the warring militia, including Nkunda's, though not the FDLR, were invited. The conference concluded on 23 January with all parties committing to a cease-fire. Fighting then subsided, although clashes between rival militia continued.

The Government began implementing its anti-FDLR strategy in early 2008. However, despite these efforts, the FDLR's position remained unchanged. The UN Security Council adopted a resolution in March demanding that the FDLR disarm and assemble in camps for repatriation, which was denounced by the FDLR and largely ignored by its combatants.

Bemba was arrested in Belgium in May 2008, at the instigation of the ICC, on charges of war crimes committed by his forces in the Central African Republic. In June the ICC charged Ngoudjolo and Katanga with war crimes, but the credibility of the Court's DRC prosecutions suffered a set-back in July, when the ICC ruled that Lubanga should be released because the prosecution had failed to disclose evidence to the defence. The ICC subsequently ruled that Lubanga should remain in detention pending an appeal by the prosecution. In March 2012, in the ICC's first conviction since its inception, the Court found Lubanga guilty of forcibly recruiting child soldiers; he was sentenced to 14 years' imprisonment in July.

Meanwhile, fierce fighting broke out in Nord-Kivu in August 2008 between the FARDC and Nkunda's forces, grouped in the Congrès National pour la Défense du Peuple (CNDP), and clashes were also increasingly reported between the CNDP and the FDLR, with the latter assisted by a new, predominantly Congolese, Hutu militia, the Patriotes Résistants du Congo (PARECO). The Government repeatedly alleged that the CNDP was receiving assistance from Rwanda, while the CNDP accused the FARDC of helping the FDLR. The revival of the conflict resulted in significant territorial gains for the CNDP.

Gizenga resigned as Prime Minister in September 2008, citing his age (83 years), and Kabila appointed Adolphe Muzito, also from PALU, in his place. A new Cabinet was announced in October, in which most of the principal ministers retained their posts.

The LRA began attacking villages in and around Dungu, in the Haut-Uele region of Kasaï Oriental province, in September 2008, and at the end of the month abducted at least 90 women and children. The fighting displaced tens of thousands of people, many of whom fled to southern Sudan. There were also renewed clashes in Ituri, between the FARDC and a new militia, the Front populaire pour la justice au Congo, which also attacked MONUC troops in the region.

A CNDP unit commanded by Bosco Ntaganda was reported in early November 2008 to have massacred at least 50 people in Kiwanja, in Nord-Kivu, despite the presence nearby of MONUC troops, who failed to intervene. MONUC later described the massacre as a war crime, while the CNDP alleged that the casualties had been PARECO combatants. Also in early November, an international summit was held in Nairobi to discuss the situation in eastern DRC, which was attended by Kabila, Rwandan President Kagame and other regional heads of state. After the meeting, the UN Secretary-General, Ban Ki-Moon, appointed former Nigerian President Olusegun Obasanjo as a special envoy to broker a settlement between the DRC Government and Nkunda. Reviving fears that the conflict might again become regional, SADC leaders met in Johannesburg, South Africa, on 9 November and agreed to dispatch a military reconnaissance team to Nord-Kivu, and also to provide military assistance to the FARDC if necessary. On 20 November the UN Security Council approved a MONUC request for 3,000 more troops. By the end of the month the CNDP had advanced to within just a few kilometres of the provincial capital of Goma, which MONUC promised to defend, with the fighting displacing hundreds of thousands of civilians. Nkunda then suspended the CNDP's military campaign at the request of Obasanjo, pending the results of negotiations between the CNDP and the Government.

RAPPROCHEMENT WITH RWANDA AND UGANDA

In a significant departure from his former stance, in November 2008 Kabila authorized the deployment of the UPDF to combat the LRA in Haut-Uele, and UPDF operations began in the province soon afterwards. Furthermore, in December the DRC and Rwanda agreed to launch joint FARDC-Rwandan Defence Force (RDF) operations in Nord-Kivu. Later in the month a UN panel of experts investigating the implementation of the arms embargo on the DRC reported extensive collusion between Rwanda and the CNDP on the one hand, and the FARDC and the FDLR on the other. The report's findings, although well documented, were angrily rejected by the DRC and Rwandan Governments. In early January 2009 Ntaganda announced Nkunda's suspension from the CNDP, claiming to have assumed command. Soon afterwards Ntaganda proclaimed the end of hostilities by the CNDP and its commitment to becoming a political party. Some 5,000 RDF troops entered Nord-Kivu on 20 January and Nkunda was detained in Rwanda. The FARDC and the RDF conducted operations, codenamed Operation Umoja Wetu, against the FDLR and its allies in Nord-Kivu until the end of February, when the RDF withdrew at Kabila's instruction.

The joint military campaign dispersed but did not defeat the FDLR, which launched vicious reprisals against Congolese citizens soon after the RDF had returned to Rwanda, killing hundreds and displacing hundreds of thousands of people. The Government and the CNDP signed a peace accord on 23 March 2009, and in May one of the key demands of the CNDP was met when the Assemblée nationale adopted legislation granting amnesty for 'acts of rebellion and acts of war' in Nord-Kivu.

The President of the Assemblée nationale, Vital Kamerhe, a prominent PPRD member from Sud-Kivu, had in January 2009 publicly dissociated himself from Kabila's invitation to the RDF, and called on the Government to explain itself. Kamerhe's intervention angered the PPRD leadership, which demanded he resign from his post in the legislature. Kamerhe resigned on 16 March, and was replaced by Evariste Boshab.

The UPDF left the DRC in March 2009, more than one month after its withdrawal had been requested by Kabila. The UPDF mission failed in its prime objective of capturing LRA leader Joseph Kony, but reported that it had killed a number of LRA combatants. Like the FDLR, however, the LRA retained its fighting capacity, and launched reprisals once the UPDF had retreated.

A new voter registration campaign was launched in June 2009, in preparation for local elections that were originally scheduled to have been held the previous year. However, in mid-2010 government spokespeople announced that local elections would not take place until 2012 or 2013, citing logistical challenges and a lack of funding.

In May 2009 the FARDC and MONUC launched a joint military operation, Operation Kimia II, against the FDLR and its allies. The offensive was initially concentrated in Sud-Kivu, but soon spread to Nord-Kivu, where there were major clashes in July, in Masisi, between the FARDC and a Mai-Mai group, the Alliance des patriots pour un Congo libre et souverain. As with Umoja Wetu earlier in the year, Kimia II had a major humanitarian impact, including extensive population displacement. There were widespread allegations that CNDP units within the FARDC were using the operation to effect 'ethnic cleansing' and to seize control of mining deposits formerly held by the FDLR. There were also increasing demands for MONUC to disassociate itself from Kimia II, but MONUC defended its involvement while simultaneously seeking to limit its support exclusively to FARDC units not accused of perpetrating atrocities.

Kabila and Kagame held their first bilateral summit in August 2009, in Goma, at which they discussed military operations against the FDLR and plans to develop Lake Kivu's methane gas reserves. The DRC and Rwanda subsequently restored full diplomatic relations, opening embassies in each other's capitals.

The Government announced in September 2009 that it wanted MONUC to leave the country by 2011. In May 2010 the UN Security Council voted to renew MONUC's mandate until 30 June 2011, although with a new name, the United Nations Organization Stabilization Mission in the Democratic Republic of the Congo (MONUSCO), and with reduced personnel levels. The Security Council subsequently agreed further to reduce MONUSCO's presence in the DRC.

Fighting erupted in October 2009 near Dongo in Équateur province, apparently owing to inter-ethnic disputes over land and fishing rights. By the end of that year at least 25,000 people had been displaced by the unrest, with many fleeing to the Republic of the Congo. The FARDC took control of Dongo in December, but the conflict continued, and the number of displaced increased, reaching 150,000 by February 2010. In April a local militia attacked Mbandaka, the capital of Équateur, briefly capturing the airport; however, the FARDC recaptured the airport two days later, aided by logistical support from MONUC.

A new report was released by the UN panel of experts in November 2009, alleging that Ntaganda was the deputy commander of Operation Kimia II, despite being wanted by the ICC for war crimes. (The ICC had issued an international warrant for Ntaganda, but the DRC Government refused to hand him over.) The report also claimed that Nyamwisi, now the Minister of Decentralization and Land Settlement, and Gen. Pacifique Masunzu, an FARDC commander, continued to extend logistical support to the FDLR. Nyamwisi and Masunzu denied the charges.

In January 2010 the FARDC launched a further operation in eastern DRC against the FDLR and its allies, dubbed Operation Amani Leo; MONUC again provided logistical support. The operation, combined with Umoja Wetu and Kimia II, appeared to weaken the FDLR, with an increasing number of combatants deserting the militia. In mid-February the Governments of the DRC and Rwanda signed a refugee repatriation agreement with the Office of the United Nations High Commissioner for Refugees, enabling the return of over 50,000 Congolese refugees from Rwanda, and also, potentially, the return of Rwandan refugees from the DRC. (Thousands of largely undocumented repatriations from Rwanda took place in subsequent months.) Later in February Kabila reorganized the Government. All the ministers responsible for economic-related portfolios were replaced, and 11 cabinet posts were abolished.

Human Rights Watch, an international non-governmental organization (NGO) based in the USA, reported in April 2010 that the LRA had perpetrated a deadly massacre in February in north-eastern DRC, killing over 300 civilians. In early May Sir John Holmes, the UN Under-Secretary-General for Humanitarian Affairs and Emergency Relief Co-ordinator, reported that the LRA had killed up to 100 people in another attack in north-eastern DRC, also in February. Holmes reported that FARDC and UPDF attacks had weakened the LRA, but that it had scattered throughout the region and remained highly dangerous.

In early June 2010 Floribert Chebeya, President of the human rights organization Voix des Sans Voix, was murdered in Kinshasa. Allegations of police involvement in Chebeya's death were widespread, and the Inspector-General of the police was suspended from his post a few days after the killing. In June 2011 a military court in Kinshasa sentenced the deputy head of police intelligence and three police officers to death, *in absentia*, for the murder. Another police officer was sentenced to life imprisonment.

THE 2011 ELECTIONS

The CEI announced in August 2010 that presidential and legislative elections would be held in November 2011. Local elections were postponed again, until 2013. The CEI's announcement prompted criticism from some quarters, since Kabila had signed a law in July 2010 to dissolve the commission and replace it with a new body, the Commission Electorale Nationale Indépendante (CENI). Consequently, many commentators maintained that the CEI lacked the power to announce an election schedule. Tshisekedi declared in August that he intended to contest the presidency. Numerous reports emerged subsequently of UDPS activists being arrested and beaten by the security forces in Kinshasa and other urban areas. In December Tshisekedi returned to Kinshasa (from Belgium), where he was welcomed by a large crowd. Shortly afterwards, Kamerhe, who had established a new political party—the Union pour la Nation Congolais, declared his intention to contest the presidential election.

Meanwhile, a draft of a UN report documenting violations of human rights and international humanitarian law in the DRC during 1993–2003 was leaked to the press in September 2010. The report gave details of numerous massacres and appealed for further judicial investigation to determine whether the killing of Rwandan refugees by the Rwandan armed forces during this period warranted prosecution as genocide. This prompted a furious response from the Rwandan authorities, although the Government of the DRC welcomed the report.

In September 2010 Kabila banned all mining activities in eastern DRC to enable the state authorities to tackle what the President called 'mafia' networks, including members of the FARDC involved in the illegal mining trade. In November a UN panel of experts report endorsed Kabila's analysis (though not the mining ban), detailing the deep involvement of criminal networks headed by senior FARDC commanders in illegal mining and trade in the Kivu provinces, and noting the regional insecurity resulting from these activities. The panel recommended a series of due diligence guidelines for companies trading in minerals from eastern DRC, which were endorsed in UN Security Council Resolution 1952 in December.

The Assemblée nationale and the Senate, in a rare joint sitting, approved eight significant amendments to the Constitution on 15 January 2011. The vote was held only a few days after the amendments were presented to Parlement, allowing little time for debate, and was boycotted by over 100 opposition members. The amendments included the restriction of the presidential election to just one round, and also granted the President the right to dissolve provincial assemblies and remove provincial governors. A further amendment deferred the enlargement of the number of provinces (from 11 to 26), while another transferred authority over judicial prosecutors from the judiciary to the Ministry of Justice and Human Rights. The constitutional amendments were widely denounced as a shift towards dictatorship, but were justified by the Government as being necessary in order to introduce greater certainty into politics and to reduce costs; they were signed into law by Kabila in June 2012.

On 27 February 2011 Kabila's Kinshasa residence was attacked by armed combatants, who were repelled by the Republican Guard. The Government subsequently accused Gen. Faustin Munene—a former FARDC chief of staff, who had resigned in 2010 and established a rebel movement, the Armée de Résistance Populaire—of involvement in the attack. Munene had been detained in Brazzaville in January, and, after the February attack, the Government of the DRC requested his extradition. The authorities in the Republic of the Congo, however, declined to extradite Munene.

Kabila removed Mobutu from the Cabinet in March 2011, apparently on the grounds of dereliction of his duties. Mobutu's party, the Union des Démocrates Mobutistes, subsequently withdrew from the AMP. In the same month Minister of Rural Development Philippe Undji was also dismissed, followed by the Minister of Transport and Communication Routes, Laure-Marie Kawanda Kayena, in May. The AMP was restructured (and renamed as the Majorité Présidentielle) in March, resulting in the PPRD becoming more powerful within the coalition.

In April 2011 the newly established CENI—headed by Rev. Daniel Ngoy Mulunda, a pastor with close ties to the presidency—announced that the presidential and legislative elections would be conducted on 28 November. Provincial elections were scheduled for March 2012. Over 32m. people were registered to vote, 7m. more than in 2006. However, there were allegations from civil society and opposition parties that the official voter registration tally was artificially high as a result of the fraudulent activities of pro-Government CENI officials.

Election campaigning, which officially commenced in late October 2011, was marred by numerous clashes between the security forces and Tshisekedi's supporters, particularly in the capital. Nevertheless, presidential and legislative elections took place peacefully in most parts of the country on 28–29 November, although there were disturbances in Kinshasa, Lubumbashi and the Kivu provinces. Provisional presidential results released by the CENI gave Kabila a clear victory, with 49.0% of the votes cast, but Tshisekedi, who secured 32.3% of the ballot, rejected the outcome of the election and proclaimed himself the winner. Tshisekedi declined to take his case to the Supreme Court, where Kabila had appointed 10 new judges shortly before the elections; Kamerhe, the third placed presidential candidate, and some other opposition party leaders did submit an appeal, but the Supreme Court upheld Kabila's election victory. Kabila was sworn in as President on 20 December. Tshisekedi attempted to hold his own inauguration ceremony in Kinshasa, but was prevented from leaving his house by the security forces.

The polls were strongly criticized by an EU observer mission and by many NGOs for a range of malpractices, but were endorsed by a South African government delegation acting on behalf of SADC. The EU mission published its report in March 2012, contending that the results of the elections were 'not credible' due to the high level of 'irregularities and fraud'. In February the CENI announced the provisional results of the legislative elections: Kabila's PPRD secured 62 seats in the Assemblée nationale, followed by the UDPS with 41. The parties in Kabila's coalition won a majority of legislative seats. Tshisekedi denounced the results as fraudulent and instructed all the UDPS deputies to boycott the Assemblée nationale, most of whom defied his order and were consequently expelled from the party.

Influential presidential adviser Katumba Mwanke was killed in a aeroplane crash near Bukavu in February 2012. Mwanke had played an important role in formulating the Government's economic policies and had helped to broker a number of large-scale industrial contracts with foreign investors. Kabila named Augustin Matata Ponyo, the Minister of Finance in the previous Government, as Prime Minister in April. Matata appointed a new Cabinet later that month, controversially excluding the leaders of the parties belonging to the presidential coalition. The PPRD dominated the new Government, and a member of Kabila's party was also appointed as President of the Assemblée nationale.

Violence erupted once more in the Kivu provinces in April 2012, primarily because of a mutiny by Congolese Tutsi troops, who later formed a new armed group called M23. By mid-2012 the FARDC, which vastly outnumbered M23, had been unsuccessful in its attempts to defeat the rebels militarily. Evidence emerged in May and June suggesting that M23 had received military assistance from Rwanda. The DRC Government accused the Rwandan authorities of aiding the mutiny and demanded the cessation of these activities. The Rwandan Government denied the allegations. There were also renewed attacks by the FDLR, particularly in Sud-Kivu, and other smaller militias, which were taking advantage of the FARDC's preoccupation with M23.

In June 2012 the CENI published a new electoral timetable, according to which provincial elections would take place in February 2013, with senatorial and gubernatorial elections in June 2013. Local elections, which had never been conducted since the fall of the Mobutu dictatorship, were postponed until 2014.

FOREIGN RELATIONS

Patrice Lumumba was removed in 1961, and Mobutu Sese Seko installed with the forceful assistance of Western powers, on the understanding that he would protect against communist expansion in Africa. Mobutu used this leverage skilfully, and extracted substantial aid from the West, particularly the USA, France and Belgium, until the late 1980s, when the collapse of first Eastern European and then Soviet communism reduced the concern of Western powers about the advance of communism in Africa, while at the same time increasing prominence was given in development assistance practices to issues of democracy and human rights, making it harder for donors to justify continued funds being made available to Mobutu's regime. French and Belgian troops took control of Kinshasa following riots in September 1991, and two months later the French Government formally withdrew support from Mobutu. In the following months Western powers became more interventionist, pressurizing Mobutu to cede power, while urging the opposition to accept Mobutu as titular Head of State, lest Mobutu's sudden removal lead to anarchy.

The war that began in 1998 resulted in the cancellation of virtually all of the previously pledged development assistance; all balance of payments support and debt-rescheduling was also suspended. During the war, international bodies, including the UN Security Council and the OAU, repeatedly stressed their support for the DRC's territorial integrity and their wish for foreign forces to withdraw. However, no influential donor nations took practical measures to support Kabila, and the USA and the United Kingdom continued to provide substantial financial assistance to Rwanda and Uganda, the two countries with troops in the DRC in conflict with government forces. The assassination of President Laurent-Désiré Kabila in January 2001 and the election of George W. Bush's Republican Administration in the USA in the previous year altered the situation. Donors had never had good relations with Kabila, but were more favourable towards his urbane son, Joseph Kabila, whose accommodating stance, particularly regarding economic policy, was in marked contrast to that of his father. In addition, Bush demonstrated less interest in Rwanda's grievances than did President Bill Clinton, his Democratic predecessor, and more concern for the DRC's development into a country safe to invest in. In June 2002 the IMF granted the DRC access to credit, under the first formal lending programme from a multilateral agency for a decade. In August the World Bank approved an assistance package, and preparations began for the DRC to gain access to debt relief under the initiative for heavily indebted poor countries. Despite the suspension of formal lending by the IMF from 2006–09, international donors remained strongly engaged in the country, not least to fund the 2006 elections, which cost more than US $460m. In late 2009 the IMF pledged the disbursement of a further $7,000m. in debt relief.

In an indication of improving relations with the People's Republic of China, in late 2007 the DRC Government signed a major agreement with Chinese parastatal companies, which envisaged a loan from the Export and Import Bank of China of US $9,000m. for the construction of infrastructure throughout the country. The agreement was criticized by the DRC's Western creditors, and by the IMF, for increasing the country's indebtedness and for its commercial, rather than concessional, interest rates.

The transitional Government maintained strong relations with Laurent Kabila's war allies, Zimbabwe, Angola and Namibia, but Zimbabwe's hard-won political and economic influence was overtaken by that of South Africa, owing to Mbeki's strong involvement in the peace process and preparation for elections, and the much stronger South African economy. Following the example of Mbeki, South African companies demonstrated strong interest in the DRC, particularly in the mining and construction sectors.

Joseph Kabila's decisions in late 2008 and early 2009, respectively, to invite the UPDF and the RDF into the country heralded a significant improvement in relations between the DRC Government and those of Rwanda and Uganda. Meanwhile, relations deteriorated between the Governments of the DRC and Angola, with the demarcation of their maritime borders being the main area of dispute. At stake were massive offshore petroleum reserves, currently being exploited by Angola but claimed by the DRC. In March the DRC Minister of Hydrocarbons, René Isekemanga Nkeka, accused Angola of 'illegally' pumping thousands of barrels of oil daily from the DRC's territorial waters. The charge was denied by Angola, and the two sides agreed in April to establish a joint commission to resolve the dispute. Another issue was the demarcation of the two countries' land borders, disagreements about which had resulted in occasional clashes between Angolan and Congolese troops in the border region. According to the UN Office for the Coordination of Humanitarian Affairs, between late August and mid-October some 16,000 DRC nationals had been expelled from Angola; similarly, some 14,000 Angolan refugees were expelled from the DRC in the same period. The repatriation of refugees prompted the Office of the UN High Commissioner for Refugees to intervene, terminating the repatriation process on the grounds that, given the volatile security situation, the refugees' personal safety and freedom would be compromised if they were to return home.

Relations with Rwanda deteriorated dramatically in June 2012, after the DRC Government accused the Rwandan authorities of aiding a mutiny in eastern DRC, led by the M23 militia group. Kagame strongly denied the allegations. A public report by Human Rights Watch and a leaked report from the UN both indicated Rwandan support for M23.

Economy

DUNCAN WOODSIDE

INTRODUCTION

The Democratic Republic of the Congo (DRC, formerly Zaire) is potentially one of the richest countries in the world, since it possesses an incredible volume and variety of mineral wealth. Many of its resources, particularly copper, cobalt, cassiterite (a tin ore) and columbo-tantalite (coltan), have become even more coveted in recent years, as the global economy's requirement for minerals has been increased by very strong GDP growth in hitherto marginal areas of the world. However, an unfortunate confluence of domestic and regional political circumstances left the DRC unable to secure its borders and protect its economic interests for over a decade, creating a huge unregulated market for its resources. A UN peace-keeping mission (the world's largest), a series of peace agreements and landmark elections in 2006, which gave President Joseph Kabila Kabange a widely accepted democratic mandate, finally provided a platform to encourage legitimate commercial activity in the country, particularly in the relatively secure copper and cobalt mining belt.

During Kabila's first full post-war administration (2006–11) the DRC attracted substantial and growing interest from foreign investors, who were keen to establish themselves as key commercial players in the country's lucrative natural resource sector. Apart from a severe (albeit temporary) correction during the 2008 global financial crisis, commodities have enjoyed an extended boom. The DRC's economy grew by 7.2% in 2010 and by 6.5% in 2011, in real terms, according to the IMF. Foreign direct investment (FDI) reached US $2,900m. in 2010, up from less than $300m. in 2006. Over the same period copper exports surged from 100,000 metric tons per year to 500,000 tons, according to the central bank. Much of the demand came from the People's Republic of China, which, by 2012, accounted for 40% of global copper consumption. In September 2011 it was reported that international brewing giant Heineken would invest $560m. over five years in expanding existing facilities in the country, under the auspices of local subsidiary Bralima.

However, foreign investors became increasingly cautious in the second half of 2011 and largely retained a 'wait-and-see' approach during early 2012, amid fresh political uncertainties generated by highly controversial elections. President Kabila retained power after the November 2011 presidential vote, although his nearest challenger, Etienne Tshisekedi Wa Mulumba, refused to accept the result, claiming widespread fraud. The European Union's (EU) monitoring mission surmised that the poll results 'were not credible in the light of numerous irregularities and fraud witnessed during the electoral process'. The Supreme Court officially confirmed the legitimacy of Kabila's new mandate in December. However, in the previous month Kabila had appointed 18 new (loyalist) judges to the Supreme Court. In the first quarter of 2012 Kabila was barely seen in public, adding to concerns within the international community and among foreign investors about an escalating governance crisis in the country.

The DRC's future economic success depends heavily on two key factors: bringing more of the mining sector (i.e., extractive industries other than copper) within the regulatory orbit of the State and tackling endemic corruption. Corruption became entrenched during the rule of the late dictator Mobutu Sese Seko, and the long period of chaotic civil conflict and political instability that followed his ousting and death in 1997 left the country's institutions in an even more ruinously dilapidated state than they were during his period in power. With regard to the mineral trade, while the Government has generated significant revenues from the oversight of the copper industry (mainly centred in the province of Katanga), it has largely been unable to control the trade in other minerals, most notably tin and gold, which are found in the eastern provinces. Not only has this affected state revenues (and hence the authorities' ability to fund post-war reconstruction), but it has also helped to sustain insurgent groups, thereby exacerbating insecurity.

In 2010–11 the Government undertook a number of initiatives to regulate the mineral trade in the east, including a temporary ban on mining exports from the provinces of Sud-Kivu, Nord-Kivu and Maniema (see Mineral Certification, below). However, the governance crisis engendered by the 2011 elections appeared likely to hinder further efforts to reform the mining sector. Furthermore, the Government's questionable new mandate, together with the regime's apparent disregard for the integrity of state institutions (including the independence of the judiciary) during the electoral cycle, raised concerns about corruption and adherence to the rule of law in the country.

With high levels of corruption, a lack of central government control over the extraction of mineral resources (excluding copper and cobalt) and huge internal displacement caused by past—and ongoing—insurgencies, the DRC's human development indicators are among the lowest in the world. The UN Development Programme (UNDP)'s 2011 *Human Development Report* ranked the DRC 187th out of a total of 187 countries in its Human Development Index, which takes account of life expectancy, access to education and national income.

A further factor that affects developmental prospects is the uncertain environment for corporate law. The Government has come into legal conflict with several international mining companies. Arguably, the most high-profile dispute involved Canada's First Quantum Minerals, a company with close ties to the World Bank. This disagreement damaged the relationship between the DRC Government and the multilateral lender. In its 2012 *Doing Business Report*, the World Bank placed the DRC 178th out of 183 ranked countries, while British investment bank Barclays Capital rated the country's copper and base metals sector as 'maximum risk' for international investors, largely due to this dispute. Foreign investors expressed further concern in March 2012, when Minister of Mines Martin Kabwelulu Labilo announced that the Government would be raising the minimum stake that it takes in mining ventures (upon the start of production) from 5% to 10%, while restrictions would be placed on the volume of unprocessed materials leaving the country. The capricious legal environment for foreign investors in the DRC, combined with the new politico-security risks in the aftermath of the 2011 elections (during which there was violence in copper-rich Katanga and diamond-rich Kasaï), threatened to undermine the long-term foreign investment outlook, even in the event of commodity prices remaining high.

MINING AND PETROLEUM

Recent Developments

International interest in mining in the DRC increased enormously after the democratic elections of 2006, which ushered in a legitimate government and created a semblance of stability in many key areas of the country after years of civil war. The country possesses an abundance of mineral resources, the most important being copper, diamonds, cobalt and zinc; there are also deposits of gold, cassiterite, manganese, cadmium, germanium, silver, wolframite and coltan, most of which have traditionally been exploited only on a small-scale industrial or artisanal basis. Copper, cobalt, zinc and germanium are found mainly in the south-eastern Katanga province, adjoining the Zambian Copperbelt. It is estimated that the DRC possesses up to 10% of the world's copper reserves. Diamonds are located mainly in the Kasaï provinces, although some mining activity is conducted in Orientale province. Cassiterite, wolframite, gold and coltan are exploited mainly in Nord-Kivu and Sud-Kivu provinces. According to the African Development Bank (AfDB), mining (including mineral processing) contributed an estimated 12.0% of GDP in 2011.

Until the second half of 2008 a further factor that enhanced foreign investor interest in the country was the surge in demand for—and consequent rise in the price of—major commodities, driven by strong growth in the global economy. The USA and the United Kingdom registered consistently solid productivity growth and emerging markets matured, particularly China and India (where double digit annual growth rates were recorded, involving the use of huge volumes of mineral resources). However, the financial crisis that crippled developed markets and economies in late 2008 caused a huge correction in most commodity prices, with the exception of precious metals. With the USA and much of Europe entering recession, demand for goods produced in China, India and other emerging markets—together with the raw minerals used in manufacturing such goods—dried up. In this context, the DRC's official mining sector suffered reverses from multiple sources. Most obviously, receipts from raw mineral exports reflected the adverse movement in the price of most commodities. The price of copper, for example, declined dramatically, from a high of US $9,000 per metric ton in July 2008 to less than $3,000 per ton in December. Unfortunately, this was not even partially offset by the rally in gold, which benefits from its status as a 'safe haven' asset during financial crises. Indeed, the Congolese authorities have had little control over the country's gold trade, as most mines remained in rebel-controlled areas. The DRC's official mining industry—and wider economy—also suffered because international mining companies were among the worst hit by the global financial crisis. Many mining firms saw their share values plunge, while they were unable to raise new debt, translating into a severe contraction in FDI in the DRC. However, the mining downturn proved to be temporary, as commodity prices recovered to elevated levels in subsequent years, bringing a renewed surge in FDI to the DRC's natural resources sector. In March 2012 copper was trading at around $8,500 per ton.

With the return of the rule of law exerted from Kinshasa came a comprehensive review of mining contracts, many of which had been awarded during the long period of civil war (1996–2002). This review, which commenced in June 2007, brought significant uncertainty for investors. The government-appointed commission revealed its findings in March 2008, recommending the renegotiation of 61 contracts across the key mineral sectors. The Congolese authorities further attempted to adjust the balance of power *vis-à-vis* international mining companies by imposing a ban on exports of unprocessed copper in May. This followed the imposition of a ban on unprocessed cobalt. Both bans were designed to incentivize foreign companies to establish refining facilities in the DRC, thereby creating more local employment. Expectations of this ban had already helped to increase the number of copper and cobalt furnaces in Katanga to 75 in the second quarter of 2008, compared to only 10 in March 2007.

However, the most important development during 2007 and 2008 was China's decision to invest some US $9,000m. in exchange for enhanced access to the mining sector. In May 2008 the Assemblée nationale gave preliminary approval to an agreement which provided for a $3,000m. loan to revive the mining industry and a $6,000m. facility to develop other infrastructure, among which would be 9,000 km of new roads and railway tracks, hospitals, housing, two dams and numerous schools. A further condition of the agreement was that 80% of the labour for the projects would be provided by Congolese nationals. In exchange, China would receive a 68% share in a venture between the DRC's state-owned mining corporation (the Générale des Carrières et des Mines—GÉCAMINES), the China Railway Engineering Company and Sinohydro Corporation. China would therefore gain access to the rights for more than 10m. metric tons of copper and 600,000 tons of cobalt. The Congolese Government would guarantee repayment of the infrastructure loan, which would be repaid from mining profits from the joint venture once the loan to the mining sector had been cleared. GÉCAMINES, with debts of $1,000m. at November 2006 and having reduced its workforce by several thousand, was thus provided with an opportunity for rehabilitation.

Although by early 2008 the terms of the US $3,000m. mining loan had yet to be confirmed, pending an evaluation by the GÉCAMINES-China Railway Engineering-Sinohydro Corpn joint venture, the contingent China-managed infrastructure projects were reported to have already begun. Both the DRC and China reiterated their commitment to the deal, despite pressure on the former from the IMF, which claimed to be concerned about the resultant increase in sovereign debt. Despite the apparent steadfast line of the two Governments over their agreement, it appeared that the IMF had indeed been successful in exerting some influence by late 2009, in part due to the Congolese Government's dependence on the largesse of the IMF against the backdrop of a deteriorating domestic economy. In October the DRC and China signed an amendment to the original agreement, which, according to the IMF, meant that the DRC's liability in terms of guaranteeing the projects would be significantly downscaled.

There were a number of smaller (but none the less significant) investments announced throughout 2007. In October Zhejiang Huayou Cobalt announced that it planned to build a copper and cobalt mining and refining project near Lubumbashi, in Katanga province. The envisaged investment would reach US $350m. by the end of 2015, according to the company. By 2015 the firm expected to be producing 200,000 metric tons of copper and 15,000 tons of cobalt. A further significant investment project in the DRC's mining sector announced in 2007 was the proposed construction of a $3,000m. aluminium smelter, in a joint venture between Australia's BHP Billiton and the Government. Initial estimates put the smelter's capacity at 800,000 tons of aluminium per year, making use of 2,000 MW of hydroelectric power from the proposed Inga-3 power station on the River Congo. In July China's Dalian Xinyang High Tech Development signed an agreement that granted cobalt prospecting and mining rights to a mine in Lubumbashi. Meanwhile, in April the Australian company Anvil Mining approved the construction of a 60,000-ton-per-year copper-making facility at its Kinsevere project, one of three major projects in the country. Anvil's facility was completed in August 2011, although in early 2012 the company experienced severe power problems (together with a lack of water), and it was expected that further upgrades would be necessary to bring capacity at the new plant up to 60,000 tons per year. Minmetals Resources, a Hong Kong-listed subsidiary of China's largest metals firm, acquired Anvil for $1,300m. in February 2012; China's share of global copper consumption had reached 40% by this time. GÉCAMINES confirmed that Anvil's lease on the Kinsevere facility (and its Mutoshi project) would remain valid.

MINERAL CERTIFICATION

Illegal armed groups have profited from mining and trading in a range of minerals, including gold, wolframite, coltan and cassiterite, particularly in the restive Nord-Kivu and Sud-Kivu provinces. This illegal trade began in earnest in 1996, initially when the armies of neighbouring Rwanda (and later Uganda) invaded. Although the Rwandan and Ugandan armies withdrew in 2002, their exit (in the context of a weakened Congolese national army) created a vacuum in terms of control over much of eastern DRC's mineral trade. This enabled a number of foreign and home-grown rebel groups to extend their own influence over mining activity. For many years illegal armed groups operating in the DRC benefited from an unregulated environment, whereby they were able to mine and sell their output to internationally connected intermediaries, who in turn had no fear of being punished. Not only has the central Government been deprived of revenues, but these illegal armed groups' control over mines has generated income that they have used to fund their rebellions.

It took many years before any significant action was taken to tackle this damaging status quo. Although the Kimberley Process Certification Scheme (KPCS—initiated by a UN General Assembly resolution in 2000, before a number of Southern African producing states began to enforce the scheme in 2003) represented an attempt to scrutinize and halt the trade in 'conflict diamonds', definitive progress in confronting the trade in other conflict-tarnished minerals was much slower. However, major international powers eventually agreed that substantive action was required to break the link between conflict and (non-diamond) mineral resources in eastern DRC. An initial key development was a UN Security Council resolution adopted in 2005, which made companies buying minerals sourced from illegal armed groups in the DRC liable to sanctions. A UN Panel of Experts, commissioned to report on the activity of armed groups in eastern DRC and the dynamics of the illicit mineral trade, in 2008 and 2009 presented evidence that European entities had been buying produce either mined or traded by one or more of the various armed groups. This resulted in two European companies withdrawing from activity in the DRC (see Cassiterite, below).

Another initiative emerged at the behest of the German Government, to accelerate scientific efforts to fingerprint minerals in order to trace their geological (and hence exact geographic) origin. The German Government set up bilateral assistance programmes with both the DRC and Rwandan Governments to begin this tracing initiative, with a view to expanding it to cover other minerals. The pilot programme began in Rwanda, and was expected to be extended to the DRC in 2010, with an analysis of output at two gold mines in Sud-Kivu.

However, owing to concerns that it would take several years before a formal certification scheme could hope to cover the whole of Nord-Kivu and Sud-Kivu provinces, the United Kingdom-based advocacy organization Global Witness lobbied in 2010 for companies buying minerals from the DRC to adopt voluntarily guidelines being drafted by the Organisation of Economic Co-operation and Development. These guidelines, which were expected to be ready by the end of 2010, would involve companies scrutinizing their own supply chains to ensure that they did not purchase minerals extracted from areas controlled by illegal armed groups or mined by children.

In December 2010 the USA's financial regulator, the Securities and Exchange Commission (SEC), voted unanimously to propose that companies listed in the USA must disclose whether they use 'conflict minerals' originating from the DRC or neighbouring countries. In July US President Barack Obama had signed the Dodd-Frank Wall Street Reform and Consumer Protection Act, which tasked the SEC with creating an audit framework for 'conflict minerals'. The proposals would require companies using cassiterite, coltan, gold or wolframite in their products to investigate their supply chains. In the event that a company verifiably concluded that a product did not contain 'conflict minerals', it would be permitted to label the relevant product 'DRC conflict free'. The SEC declared that a final draft of the rules would be confirmed between August and December 2011. There were concerns in the DRC that the new regulations would lead to an indiscriminate boycott of cassiterite, coltan, gold and wolframite, affecting legitimate exports originating from government-administered areas of the country as well as those from the regions controlled by illegal armed groups.

Exports had already been affected by a six-month ban on mineral shipments from Nord-Kivu, Sud-Kivu and Maniema provinces, imposed by President Joseph Kabila from early September 2010 until early March 2011, in an attempt to undermine local criminal networks. Elements of the national army's high command were also involved in the illegal exploitation of natural resources, according to a report by the UN Group of Experts on the DRC, published in November 2010. The report claimed that senior officers were using operations against illegal armed groups to extend their covert control over mineral assets in eastern DRC, enabling them to profit from the smuggling of cassiterite, timber and gold. However, the following year's report by the Group of Experts underlined that the Government's ban on mineral exports had given rise to undesired consequences, including militia groups illegally exploiting mines that legitimate owners were unable to access during the ban. Furthermore, the national army's withdrawal from the Bisie cassiterite mine in March 2011—in line with a lobbying campaign initiated by human rights organization Global Witness, which had highlighted abuses and embezzlement by local army commanders—resulted in the anti-Government militia Nduma Défense du Congo being able to expand its sphere of operations.

In February 2012 Minister of Mines Martin Kabwelulu Labilo announced details of a scheme requiring exporters of coltan, gold, tin and wolframite to prove that their output was 'conflict free'; the authorities planned to maintain a mapping programme, detailing 'conflict' and 'conflict-free' zones. However, quite how this scheme would work in practice had yet to be established. A key problem was that minerals extracted in government-controlled zones often had to pass through insurgent-controlled areas—where they were unofficially taxed—to reach the point of export. Moreover, some militias operated on a guerrilla basis, moving quickly in and out of areas, leading to the risk that the mapping exercise would prove largely arbitrary.

Meanwhile, the SEC planned to introduce its own 'conflict minerals' legislation, but the drafting process was hindered by repeated delays. Amid lobbying pressure from electronics companies, the 2011 deadline for imposing the disclosure requirement was missed. In March 2012 SEC Chairman Mary Schapiro acknowledged that her organization was still attempting to finalize the legislation, and further stated that there would be 'a phase-in period' of unspecified duration to allow 'sufficient time for some of the supply chain due diligence mechanisms to be developed and put in place'.

In a positive development, Rwanda (a long-standing conduit for the smuggling of minerals from the DRC) handed over to the Congolese authorities 82 metric tons of confiscated illicit output, including cassiterite and coltan. The move represented part of an extended rapprochement between the two countries. However, that rapprochement in itself had mixed implications for the drive to counteract militia-based exploitation of minerals in the DRC. The improvement in bilateral relations had been partly due to the DRC Government reaching out to the Rwanda-backed Congolese Tutsi militia, by integrating this group into the national army. This integration provoked huge resentment among other communities in eastern DRC, enabling commanders of rival militias to increase recruitment, and hence bolster their armed capacity not only to fight the Government, but also to control mining operations and mineral shipments themselves. In January 2012 four senior Rwandan army officers, including three generals, were dismissed due to alleged illegal business dealings in the DRC's mineral industry. Rwanda's head of military intelligence, Brig.-Gen. Richard Rutatina, was among those replaced.

Copper and Cobalt

Development in mining following the end of the civil war has evidently been substantial. Prior to this, however, the sector had been in a long period of stagnation and decline. Indeed, the kleptocracy of former dictator Mobutu Sese Seko had long since inhibited development of mining facilities in the country, where formal activity by the private sector was for long periods impossible. GÉCAMINES was the dominant producer in the 1980s, accounting for more than 90% of copper output, and all production of cobalt, zinc and coal. Production of copper ore declined from 1988 onwards as other world producers, such as Chile, established new opencast, lower-cost mines. Civil conflict then exacerbated the situation.

Since the withdrawal of foreign armies from the DRC in 2002, Chinese businesses have expressed strong interest in the Congolese market. Following President Kabila's visit to Beijing, China, in March 2005, the Chinese Cobec Corporation offered to rehabilitate the Kamatanda copper and cobalt mines and three copper-processing plants in Katanga for US $27.5m. In April Feza Mining, a joint venture between the Chinese Wambao Resources and the Congolaises des Mines et de Development (COMIDE), inaugurated a plant in Likasi with a production capacity of 4,000 tons of cobalt-copper alloys. Chinese expertise was also provided to equip the Congolese Société de Développement Industriel et Minière du Congo (SODIMICO) with a 14,600-ton capacity furnace to process cobalt and copper ore. These measures were part of a broader strategy from China to access essential inputs for its expanding economy. By 2004 China was purchasing about $100m. of Congolese cobalt.

Good governance in the mining sector increasingly became a major concern of both the donors and the Congolese legislature. In November 2004 the IMF announced that its financial assistance to the DRC would be conditional on an audit of the mining sector. Concern for good governance also arose from the many crises undergone by the official bodies in charge of the mining sector since July 2003, when the transitional Government was installed. In March 2005 the state mining organization the Cadastre Minier de la République Démocratique du Congo (CAMI) resumed its operations, after 10 months of interruptions. One of its first challenges was to recover the mining rights owed by the main companies, which amounted to over US $30m. In early 2006 a report by a parliamentary commission into the mining industry recommended that no further partnership agreements be signed between GÉCAMINES and foreign mining concerns, on the grounds that the joint ventures resulted in a reduction in profits for the loss-making parastatal.

However, this recommendation was ignored when the DRC and China reached an important preliminary agreement on joint mineral exploitation, designed to provide China with more than 10m. metric tons of copper and 600,000 tons of cobalt in exchange for modernizing infrastructure (see Recent Developments, above). The preliminary deal was approved by the Assemblée nationale in May 2008, shortly before copper prices peaked and a global financial crisis resulted in sharp falls of most commodity prices. Within months 300,000 miners in Katanga's copper and cobalt mining belt lost their jobs. The Central African Mining Exploration Company (CAMEC) closed its operations at Mukondo Mountain in Katanga during November. Other key operators, including Canada-listed Katanga Mining and Anvil Mining, also scaled down their activities. The cash price for copper fell from a peak of US $9,000 per ton in July 2008 to less than $3,000 per ton in December, although the price subsequently recovered to around $4,700 per ton by May 2009. By May 2010 the cash price for copper had recovered further, to around $6,770 per ton. While considerably below the speculative peak of July 2008, the extent of the recovery was clearly significant, with the price well above the long-term historical average. In March 2009 CAMEC announced that it was restarting copper and cobalt operations in the DRC, amid signs that global demand had demonstrated signs of recovery. However, private Western capital for investment in the DRC's mining sector was likely to take considerably longer to recover.

In October 2009 it emerged that Canada's First Quantum Minerals Ltd was required to pay US $6m. in damages over the failure of three lawsuits that it had filed against Congolese public bodies due to the cancellation of its $500m. Kingamyambo Musonoi Tailings (KMT) copper and cobalt project (also known as the Kolwezi project). As part of its review of 61 different mining projects (see Recent Developments, above), the DRC Government had withdrawn First Quantum's concession in August, after accusing the company of failing to generate output in line with agreed deadlines. This action had resulted in KMT and Congo Minerals Development (CMD—a 100%-owned subsidiary of First Quantum) filing three civil lawsuits (against GÉCAMINES, the central Government and Cami) in August and September. The dispute escalated significantly in 2010, to the detriment of the DRC's relationship with the World Bank, which—through its subsidiary, the International Finance Corpn—had obtained a minority stake in First Quantum's Kolwezi concession. In August Eurasian National Resources Corpn (ENRC), owned by the Kazakhstani Government, announced that it had acquired a controlling stake in Camrose Resources, the company with the rights to the Kolwezi concession. However, First Quantum argued that this transfer of ownership was invalid, due to a hearing at the International Court of Arbitration (ICA), which, the company claimed, had prohibited the sale of the Kolwezi assets while the case was under international review. In September the DRC's Minister of Mines, Martin Kabwelulu Labilo, prohibited World Bank officials from attending a number of mining meetings in the country, after the multilateral institution had criticized the cancellation of First Quantum's licence. However, an ICA tribunal refused First Quantum's request to prohibit transfer of the Kolwezi licence to third parties. Following this ruling, Kabwelulu claimed that the Government had 'won' the case, although First Quantum countered that the judgment was inconclusive. In January 2012 it appeared that the dispute had finally been resolved, when ENRC announced that it had reached a settlement with First Quantum, which involved the former paying the latter $750m., before a further payment of $500m. The DRC Government and First Quantum confirmed their satisfaction with the deal, while ENRC stated that the settlement would enable it to start exploiting the Kolwezi tailings facility. ENRC further stated that it would invest between $100m. and $200m. over a 12 to 18 month period, in order to bring the Kolwezi facility into production.

Another contract to be affected by the DRC Government's review was US mining company Freeport-McMoRan's concession for the Tenke Fungurume mine, which reportedly holds the world's largest reserve of unexploited copper and cobalt. The Congolese authorities pushed for an increase in the size of GÉCAMINES' 17.5% stake in the project. Agreement on a revised contract was finalized in April 2011, when President Kabila approved a deal that gave GÉCAMINES a 20% share in the project, while Freeport acquired 56% (down from 57.75%) and Canadian firm Lundin the remaining 24% (down from 24.75%). The Tenke project generated 120,271 metric tons of copper cathode in 2010, and a target of 130,000 tons was set for 2011. With the contract successfully renegotiated, expansion plans were able to proceed. It was anticipated that copper output would increase to between 175,000 tons and 225,000 tons per year, within three years, before a further expansion to 400,000 tons per year. In addition, Freeport was considering the construction of a cobalt refinery. In November 2011 Lundin reported that Freeport-McMoRan had agreed to a planned US $850m. expansion of the Tenke Fungurume facility, which would boost annual output by 50%, to 68,000 tons of copper cathode, upon completion in 2013. The expansion would be 70% funded by Freeport-McMoRan and 30% by Lundin.

The prospects were also good for exploitation of the Pumpi concession, adjacent to Tenke. In March 2011 Canada-based CuCo Resources raised C $45m. to develop Pumpi, after initial exploration results in 2010 indicated that the concession contained significant copper reserves. CuCo Resources also planned to develop a second area in the DRC, the Kisanfu concession.

Katanga Mining generated total sales of US $574.4m. in 2011, a rise of 7% compared with 2010. In September 2011 the IMF urged GÉCAMINES to publish details of revenues and contracts arising from the sale of stakes in two mining projects earlier that year. The Fund underlined that Congolese law obliged all state-run enterprises to publish such information and that revenues from asset sales should be transferred to the custody of the State.

Diamonds and Gold

Until 1986 Zaire was the world's leading producer of industrial diamonds. Although about 98% of the country's production, from Kasaï Oriental, is of industrial diamonds, gemstones are also found. Official production figures fluctuate and are inaccurate, as a result of extensive and elaborate smuggling networks. After the assassination of President Laurent-Désiré Kabila in January 2001, government policies in the sector changed radically. By April the diamond market was fully liberalized, while International Diamond Industries' monopoly on all Congolese diamond exports was abolished in May. In an attempt to prevent the illicit trade in diamonds by identifying the origin of the gems, the DRC Government signed an agreement with the Antwerp Diamond High Council in April, which provided for the establishment of a system of certification for all Congolese exports to Belgium.

In 2003 the DRC achieved record production of 27m. carats of diamonds, valued at US $642m. Artisanal production accounted for about 71% of the total in volume and 81.5% in value, with the rest provided by the Société Minière de Bakwanga (MIBA) and the Nouvelle Miniere de Senga Senga (SENGAMINES), a Congolese-Zimbabwean joint venture. The 23% increase in volume and 62.3% increase in value of total production were credited to stricter valuation controls performed by the Centre d'Expertise et d'Evaluation du Congo (CEEC) and to the implementation of the Kimberley Process at all stages.

Despite the increase in diamond production registered in 2003, illegal trade remained considerable. In May 2004 the KPCS discovered evidence of massive fraud in the trade of DRC diamonds, resulting in the expulsion of the Republic of the Congo from the system in July. Indeed, according to the DRC authorities, the Republic of the Congo authorities had been unable to prove that the diamonds exported from their country were produced locally.

In 2004 diamond exports (including parallel-market exports) were estimated at 33m. carats, valued at US $828m. According to CEEC sources, one of the main reasons for the good performance was the exclusion of the Republic of the Congo from the KPCS. The largest part of the exports was provided by artisanal production (22.1m. carats, valued at $617m.). Meanwhile, the production of SENGAMINES dropped sharply, and by June 2005 the company's activities had been completely suspended, although a new industrial company, the Kasaï Diamond Company, had commenced operating in April 2004. In December MIBA announced that it expected its output to rise substantially as a result of upgrading its installations.

Artisanal and small-scale miners extract gold in Nord-Kivu, Sud-Kivu and Ituri in the east of the country. Rehabilitation work commenced in 1989 at the main gold mine, in the north-eastern part of the country, owned by the Office des Mines d'Or de Kilo-Moto (OKIMO). By mid-2005 OKIMO had concluded a number of joint-venture agreements with foreign companies, including AngloGold Ashanti, Borgakim, Kibali-Gold, Amani Gold, Moto GoldMines (formerly Equs), Tangold, Goldfields, Blue Rose, Mwana Africa and Rambi Gold. OKIMO's purpose was to use the revenues from the leasing rights paid by these companies to finance its own mining operations and also to establish a new geological database on its concessions in order to negotiate new contracts.

However, gold exploitation in Ituri province has proved to be a difficult exercise. Indeed, the joint venture between OKIMO and AngloGold Ashanti, Ashanti Gold Kilo, which in April 2005 received authorization to exploit the Mongbwalu mine in a 8,000-sq km concession containing an estimated resource of 100 metric tons of gold ore, was accused by a UN report of having provided support and paid taxes to a local militia (charges that the company denied). The UN final report had important political consequences. In November 2002 President Joseph Kabila suspended seven senior officials named in the report, including three ministers and the managing directors of both GÉCAMINES and MIBA.

AngloGold and OKIMO reached a fresh joint-venture agreement in March 2010 to develop the Ashanti Goldfields Kilo (AGK) project, which includes the Mongbwalu concession. By that stage mineral resources of 3m. oz had been identified at Mongbwalu. Under the terms of the agreement, AngloGold would take an 86.2% majority share in the AGK venture, with OKIMO taking the remaining 13.8%. AGK would pay OKIMO US $10.5m. and the DRC Government a further $1.25m. It was expected that AngloGold would grant final approval to the project—together with a second development, at Kibali, in Orientale—during 2012. For the Kibali project, which had gold reserves of more than 10m. oz, AngloGold and Randgold Resources each took a 45% share, with OKIMO taking the remaining 10%. Randgold expected the Kibali mine to be operational in 2014, with a targeted production volume of 400,000 oz per year. A processing plant was also to be constructed, with a processing capacity of 4m.–6m. metric tons per year. Ahead of operations starting at Kibali, around 15,000 people from nearby villages needed to be relocated.

In the fourth quarter of 2011 Canada's Banro Corpn began exploiting the Twangiza mine in Sud-Kivu, in the first major commercial gold-mining initiative to commence operations in the DRC since independence. Banro was poised to increase production quickly, with output of 120,000 oz per year planned for 2012, before a rise to 400,000 oz in 2014. Twangiza represented only the first mine to be established by the company, out of a planned total of four, along a 200-km belt. To fund the three additional mines, Banro planned to generate initial revenues of US $120m. per year. If Banro's Twangiza project, AngloGold's Mongbwalu concession and the Randgold/AngloGold initiative were all generating output in line with current projections by 2014, then the DRC should, by that stage, be producing around 1m. oz of gold per year from these commercial operations.

In February 2009 to the south of Ituri, a joint DRC-Rwandan army offensive against exiled Rwandan Hutu extremists in Nord-Kivu diverted this militia away from some of its gold-mining interests, particularly in Lubero territory and Walikale territory. However, with the Rwandan army withdrawing after just over one month, the DRC's badly supplied army encountered difficulties in containing the militia (the Forces démocratiques pour la libération du Rwanda—FDLR), which quickly reclaimed much of the territory that it had lost. Much of the gold trade also remained beyond state control (and in the hands of the militia) in Sud-Kivu province. A report published by the DRC Sénat in September estimated that about 40 tons of gold—worth some US $1,240m. at that time—was being illegally exported from the country every year.

In March 2010 the DRC Government announced that it wanted the 19,884-strong Mission de l'organisation des nations unies en République démocratique du Congo (MONUC) to begin withdrawing its peace-keepers from the country during that year. Foreign investors in the mining sector expressed concern about this, amid ongoing insecurity in the mineral-rich east of the country. The British-based Mwana, owner of 80% of the Zani-Kodo gold prospect (with OKIMO holding the remaining 20%), raised particular concern about the implications for the security of its mining projects. In the previous month Mwana had announced that the defined indicated resource of the Zani-Kodo gold prospect had increased by 14%, to 217,277 oz of gold, while the inferred resource surged by 61%, to 421,013 oz.

Cassiterite

Cassiterite mining is a major industry in the DRC. The country accounts for around 6% of global output and is the largest exporter of cassiterite in Africa, according to the US Geological Survey. However, much of the cassiterite-mining industry has long been outside central government control, with various armed groups exploiting the mineral. Indeed, a UN Panel of Experts, reporting to the UN Security Council, presented significant evidence of links between illegal armed groups and the international sale of minerals sourced from the DRC in December 2008. The Panel's report alleged that the Belgium-based company Traxys purchased 1,631 metric tons of cassiterite and 226 tons of coltan in 2007 from four Congolese companies that had allegedly consistently bought from mines controlled by the FDLR militia. Traxys denied the Panel's allegations and in May 2009 announced that it was suspending its purchase of minerals from eastern DRC. This led to a decline in cassiterite exports from Nord-Kivu (the principal cassiterite-mining province), with the province's Association of Mineral Exporters reporting in May 2010 that shipments had declined by 40% in the first few months of the year. The suspension of purchases by Traxys had a further dramatic effect on the pattern of cassiterite exports from the DRC. In January and February 2010 Belgium's share of exports from Nord-Kivu fell to 21% of the total, down from 48% for the whole of 2009, according to figures from the DRC's Ministry of Mines. Malaysia and Rwanda instead became the leading export destinations, accounting for 61% of the total.

A peace agreement reached in March 2009 between the Congolese Government and another rebel group, the Congrès national pour la défense du peuple (CNDP), briefly raised the prospect of a significant extension of central government authority over cassiterite mining, helping to legitimize more of the trade in this mineral and to boost fiscal revenues. Like the FDLR (its main rival), the CNDP's key sphere of operations centred on the two Kivu provinces. In effect, however, the CNDP maintained parallel command structures after reaching the deal with Kinshasa, and actually extended its own influence over Nord-Kivu's mineral trade, taking effective control of the crucial Bisie mine, which accounts for about 70% of the province's cassiterite output. This meant that the CNDP hierarchy continued to benefit directly from the proceeds of cassiterite mining, with very little of the Bisie mine's revenues finding their way to the central Government in Kinshasa. It brought a fresh set of problems for the international drive to certify conflict minerals and extend the central Government's control over resources, since although the CNDP was officially recognized as having relinquished its status as a rebel group, it maintained an aggressive non-state militia structure that displayed little inclination toward transferring crucial economic assets to civilian government control.

Petroleum

Zaire became a producer of offshore petroleum in 1975, operating from fields on the Atlantic coast and at the mouth of the River Congo. Output was estimated at 10.0m. barrels in 2005 (and amounted to between 8.4m.–9.4m. barrels in 2008–10). In April 2008 the Government awarded the exploration rights for a 30-sq km onshore block in the east of the country, on the shores of Lake Albert at the Ugandan border, to a consortium led by South Africa's state-owned oil company PetroSA, maintaining that the earlier contracts with a Canadian company, Heritage Oil, were invalid. Lake Albert (and the surrounding area) is one of the most oil-rich areas in sub-Saharan Africa and it has been estimated that it may contain reserves of up to 1,000m. barrels. Tensions between Uganda and the DRC had increased in September and October 2007, when confrontations on the border at Lake Albert led to the death of a Heritage worker and several Congolese civilians. The countries held discussions aimed at resurveying and confirming their common border during several meetings in late 2007 and in 2008, although progress was slow and localized disputes continued.

The DRC's Assemblée nationale was in April 2010 considering legislation drafted by the Ministry of Energy that was designed to streamline the regulation of the petroleum sector and encourage greater foreign investment. The draft bill, which had already been adopted by the Sénat, proposed that the President approve or reject oil deals within 45 days of agreements being reached between companies and the Ministry of Energy. Oil-producing companies would typically be entitled to up to 60% of output under the proposals, with this figure rising to 70% in particularly challenging areas, including swamplands. From the perspective of international oil companies, this compared favourably with other countries' production-sharing agreements; for example, in Libya, the central Government takes a share of more than 90% of output in some contracts. In terms of oil companies' obligations, the proposals would commit firms to starting 'active field development' within 18 months of production-sharing terms having been agreed, compared to three years at present. The new legislation was designed to boost oil production in the DRC, where output was, at that stage, a paltry 25,000 barrels per day.

The Ministry of Energy announced in March 2010 that it would shortly open bidding for six oil blocks in Lake Kivu and 10 blocks on Lake Tanganyika. France's Total agreed in March 2011 to buy 60% of Block 3, located close to the border with Uganda. Total pledged to pay a fee of US $15m. and to fund the exploration costs, with the Government taking a 15% stake in the block and two South African companies, SacOil Holding and Divine Inspiration Group, retaining stakes of 12.5% each.

Minister of Hydrocarbons Celestin Mbuyu Kabango announced a long-term vision for the sector in February 2011, involving the creation of a national network to pipe oil and natural gas from the east to the Atlantic Ocean, a distance of up to 2,150 km. He also envisaged the construction of two refineries—one in the east of the country and one in the west. However, it was acknowledged that these plans could take 15 to 20 years to complete, given the vast distances involved and the country's poor infrastructure. The DRC, Uganda and Kenya had also discussed in October 2010 the construction of a pipeline to transport crude petroleum from Uganda's western border with the DRC through Kenya to the Indian Ocean. Over the medium term, this could prove to be of significant benefit to the DRC.

In January 2011 SOCO International, a hydrocarbons company based in the United Kingdom, announced that it had discovered oil and gas in its Bayingu-1 well, but that the reservoir location at the primary site (Lower Bucomazi) was 'poorly developed', while the oil flow at the secondary location (Chela) was 'residual'. SOCO's exploratory activity was negatively affected by the initiation of the Government's Strategic Environmental Assessment (SEA) in the Virunga National Park, in the east of the country. SOCO's Block 5 concession encompassed a section of the Park, which had been designated a World Heritage Site by UNESCO in 1979. The DRC's Minister of the Environment, Conservation of Nature and Tourism, José Endundu Bononge, declared in March 2011 that SOCO would be precluded from undertaking exploration in Block 5 until completion of the SEA (still pending in mid-2012). SOCO announced in the same month that it was to start drilling for petroleum at three locations in the Nganzi Block in the Congo Basin, in western DRC—the first onshore drilling in the country for four decades. However, the initial tests proved disappointing.

Another British firm, Tullow Oil, announced in March 2011 that it was withdrawing from the DRC and abandoning legal proceedings against the Government, which the company had initiated in an attempt to regain control over two oil blocks in the east of the country. Tullow had paid US $500,000 for the blocks in 2006, but in June 2010 two British Virgin Islands-registered firms, Caprikat and Foxwhelp, had taken control of the blocks, by virtue of a presidential decree issued by Kabila.

AGRICULTURE AND FORESTRY

The DRC's varying geography and climate produces a wide range of both food and cash crops. The principal food crops are cassava, plantains, maize, groundnuts and rice, grown mainly by small-scale subsistence farmers. Cash crops include coffee, palm oil and palm kernels, rubber, cotton, sugar, tea and cocoa, many of which are grown on large plantations. The DRC has the potential to be not only self-sufficient in food but also to be a net exporter. According to the AfDB, the agricultural sector (including forestry, livestock, hunting and fishing) contributed an estimated 38.9% of GDP in 2011.

Yet in 2005 (two years after the end of the civil war) nearly 42m. people out of an estimated population of 57m. were undernourished. About 48% of the deaths of children less than five years old were attributed to malnutrition by the Programme National de Nutrition. In May of that year FAO announced that US $200m. would be spent in relaunching agriculture programmes. The shortage of essential inputs (seeds, veterinary products) and the poor state of the road network were identified as obstacles to food production and distribution. New varieties of cassava yielding between 20 to 30 metric tons per ha were introduced in 2005, in order to increase food security, and during 2004 and 2005 the US Agency for International Development and Belgium assisted with various programmes, including the distribution of seeds to farmers. The EU financed the rehabilitation of 4,000 km of rural feeder roads in Kinshasa, Équateur, Bandundu, Nord-Kivu and Sud-Kivu, and contributed €12m. to agricultural development projects and food security. In some parts of the country, however, food production was hampered by insecurity and the lack of fertilizers and pesticides.

In December 2011 FAO launched an appeal for donations to fund its 2012 agenda in the DRC, having already spent US $10.5m. on its emergency and rehabilitation programme in the country during the first 11 months of 2011. FAO estimated at this stage that over 4m. people in the DRC were suffering from the effects of 'a severe food and livelihood crisis', largely due to declining productivity in the agricultural sector and fresh waves of internal displacement. In 2011 Kasaï Oriental, Kasaï Occidental and the northern reaches of Orientale all experienced a deterioration in food security. Disease also had a negative impact on food supplies, with banana wilt destroying 5,666 ha of banana crops during 2010, which led to the loss of 220,000 metric tons of the fruit, according to FAO. Cassava mosaic and Newcastle disease—the latter a virus that affects poultry—also caused serious problems in some parts of the country.

In a bid to combat banana wilt, cassava mosaic and Newcastle disease, the Governments of the DRC, Burundi and Rwanda agreed in March 2012 to re-establish the dormant Institut de Recherches Agronomique et Zootechnique. The organization, based in Lubumbashi, had not operated since 2009 due to a lack of finances, but, according to the DRC's Ministry of Agriculture and Rural Development, funding amounting to US $1.2m. every three years would henceforth be provided by each of the three countries.

In 2004 cotton output was estimated at 1,000 metric tons, less than 1% of the independence level of 180,000 tons. However, the Caisse de Stabilisation Cotonnière parastatal was making efforts to revive production by encouraging the development of the domestic textile industry, which was operating at only 20% of its installed annual capacity, and by promoting loans to farmers.

The River Congo basin and Lake Tanganyika offer considerable potential for the development of the fisheries sector. A government report, published in April 2000, estimated the potential catch at 220,000 metric tons of fish (almost twice as much as the country's requirements, estimated at 120,000 tons). In the early 2000s the fisheries sector was given a boost by the construction of cold storage facilities at the port of Matadi. In the first quarter of 2003 a new corporation, the Congolaise d'Industrie Agro-alimentaire, commenced production of dry fish at its new plant at Boma, on the Atlantic, with an initial modest target of 342 tons a year. In May a new company, the Société Congolaise de Pêche, landed 1,300 tons of fish for the domestic market at Ango-Ango port, and was actively pressurizing the DRC Government to obtain fishing rights in Angolan, Namibian and Mozambican waters. In 2010 the DRC's total recorded fishing catch amounted to an estimated 239,000 tons.

UN experts investigating the illegal exploitation of the country's resources criticized in their November 2001 report the terms of a huge logging agreement between the Congolese Government and the Société Congolaise pour l'Exploitation du Bois (SOCEBO), a subsidiary of COSLEG (the joint venture between the Zimbabwean military-controlled OSLEG corporation and COMIEX). Accordingly, SOCEBO obtained concession rights for the exploitation of 330,000 sq km of forests in Katanga, Bandundu, Kasaï and Bas-Congo provinces. However, the poor state of the roads and underestimation of the initial investment delayed implementation of the project. In 2002 SIFORCO's annual turnover was only US $2m., compared with $12m. before the war, as a result of the company's inability to supply timber from its concessions in the rebel territories. One concession, at Boliba, in Kasaï Occidental province, was completely looted, but another, at Buruba, resumed its activities in early 2003. During that year, however, SIFORCO produced 40,000 cu m at its Bumba concession in Équateur.

The DRC's crucial importance for global biodiversity has won increasing recognition internationally. The US Wildlife Conservation Society emphasized in early 2005 that the Congo basin hosted 415 species of mammals, 1,094 species of birds, 268 species of reptiles, 80 of amphibians, more than 1,000 of fish, over 1,300 of butterflies and 11,000 different plants. Beside this, the Congo forests provide vast carbon wells, which have a crucial role for the regulation of carbon dioxide and influence the regional climate in such a way that the Congo basin provides water to a large part of the African continent. Meanwhile, FAO pointed out that the sustainable management of DRC forest resources is essential, since the country hosts 45% of the continent's forest. At the same time FAO deplored the fact that the annual rate of deforestation in the DRC ranged between 0.4% and 0.6% and represented an ecological catastrophe.

ENERGY

The DRC's potential for producing hydroelectric power is matched on the African continent only by that of Cameroon. The country's most ambitious infrastructure project (which is estimated to account for a substantial proportion of the DRC's foreign indebtedness) is the Inga hydroelectric power project, based near the port of Matadi, at the mouth of the River Congo.

Despite the debt already incurred by the project, there have long been plans to expand the existing Inga hydropower facilities.

In April 2008 African politicians and financiers met in London, United Kingdom, under the auspices of the World Energy Council to discuss ways of funding the Grand Inga project, which was scheduled to begin supplying power to countries across the continent by 2025. The project, which would see power distributed to Saharan Africa, West Africa and South Africa, involved the creation of a continent-wide distribution network, a 15-km long reservoir and a 200-m dam. The new dam would be in addition to Inga's two existing hydroelectric dams and would produce an estimated 320m. kWh of electricity annually, with construction due to begin in 2014. The total cost of the project was estimated at US $80,000m.

The Inga plant supplies some power to the Republic of the Congo. The state electricity board, the Société Nationale d'Electricité (SNEL), is also linked to the grid of the Zambia Electricity Supply Corporation (ZESCO), and the South African Electricity Supply Commission (ESKOM) has carried out joint studies to optimize the connection with those companies and the Zimbabwe Electricity Supply Authority (ZESA). In 1996 ESKOM, SNEL, the Angolan power company, Empresa Nacional de Electricidade, and the Namibia Power Corporation initiated a study to interconnect their national electricity grids, in order to utilize the potential of the Inga dam.

In October 2002 SNEL signed a contract to supply 50 MW to Zambia with the Copperbelt Electricity Corporation (CEC) and the South African PB Power corporation. Under the contract, SNEL and CEC agreed to invest US $20m. each in the construction of a 147-km, 330-kv high-power line between Karavia (in the DRC) and Zambia. The target was to supply a total of 500 MW to southern Africa by 2004, of which 50 MW would be generated for Zambia and the remainder for Botswana, Zimbabwe and South Africa. In October 2003 the German consultant Fichtner was awarded a €6m. contract to determine the rehabilitation requirements of both Inga-1 and Inga-2 power stations. The rehabilitation was badly needed; by November only four of the five 58.5-MW turbines of Inga-1 and two of the eight 178-MW turbines of Inga-2 were operating. According to SNEL's management, the full rehabilitation of Inga-1 and Inga-2 would allow the export of 800 MW to Nigeria, which had already expressed the wish to build a high power line from Inga, with links to the Gabonese and Cameroonian grids. The Western Corridor (Westcor) project, linking Inga to Angola, Namibia and South Africa, with a further connection to Botswana, was proposed as the first expansion project to be implemented. It was to depend on the construction of the Inga-3 power station (4,300 MW) by a consortium grouping the companies of the five countries involved. In April 2004 a SDR-129.2m. loan was approved by the World Bank group, as a contribution to the first phase of the Southern African Power Market Project. The objective was to increase SNEL's export capacity to guarantee 500 MW of supply to its Southern African customers, through the strengthening and the expansion of the existing Inga–Katanga–Kasumbalesa corridor and the support to the rehabilitation of the Inga dam power stations.

In late 2011, as Kabila's first elected term in office came to an end, overall progress in developing the DRC's power sector remained slow. The authorities were still seeking a developer for Inga-3, while plans to construct the 39,000-MW Grand Inga project had stalled. It had been hoped that BHP Billiton would take a leading role in building Inga-3, as a result of its plan to construct an aluminium smelter, but the company confirmed in February 2012 that it had cancelled the latter proposal. In October 2011 Mbala Musanda, the head of SNEL, cautioned that the rapid expansion of the mining sector was placing a huge strain on power generation, with the country's power deficit on course to rise from 110 MW to 132 MW by 2015.

In 2011 US energy company ContourGlobal secured financing to initiate a large-scale project to harness reserves of methane gas at Lake Kivu. The project, which was to be overseen by the Rwandan company KivuWatt and was scheduled to commence initial operations in 2012, was to involve the construction of three onshore gas turbines with the capacity to generate 25 MW of electricity. In October 2009 US $168m. was provided by India to finance development works on the dam at Katende, and a further $45m. for work on the Kakobola dam; both projects, however, were under threat of termination owing to cash flow difficulties. Meanwhile, in June 2009 the World Bank approved a grant of $180.6m. through the International Development Association (IDA), aimed at establishing a regional power market in the Southern African Development Community. In April 2010 the DRC was seeking additional investment partners to provide funding assistance for continued work on electricity projects, including $361m. to renovate the Inga-1 and Inga-2 power stations, as well as $3.5m. for the construction of Inga-3, which was still at the planning stage.

WATER

By May 2003 the water distribution parastatal REGIDESO was planning to resume the production of drinking water in the rebel-occupied territories. REGIDESO's management estimated that a minimum of US $180m. would be necessary to guarantee the distribution of drinking water to the largest part of the Congolese population. By April 2004 REGIDESO envisaged the construction of a water treatment plant, with a daily 100,000 cu m capacity, near Kinshasa, which could increase domestic access to safe water by 16%. In February 2005 the Government estimated that it would be necessary to invest US $2,000m. in order to meet the UN's Millennium Development Goals on safe water distribution in the DRC. At that time the Government had only been able to commit $200m. for this objective. Three-quarters of the population consequently did not have access to safe drinking water. The improvement of the water distribution network was hampered by the magnitude of the fraud by customers who managed to access the water without paying for it. In January 2005 the EU pledged €24m. to improve water distribution and sanitation projects in Kinshasa and the provinces.

TRANSPORT AND COMMUNICATIONS

Poor transport and communications infrastructure has proved a major handicap to the DRC's economic development. With a small strip of coastline of just 40 km, the DRC depends on the port of Matadi, which is situated close to the mouth of the River Congo and is able to accommodate up to 10 deep-water vessels, for its maritime traffic. A study by the Ministry of Transport and Communication Routes in 2008 underlined the huge task required in rehabilitating the DRC's dilapidated rail infrastructure: it estimated that US $600m. in funds would be required. However, the vast amount of post-war investment in the country, particularly after the 2006 elections, indicated that the country's rail infrastructure would soon be modernized. A $9,000m. arrangement between the DRC and China, which offered the latter significant access to copper and cobalt (see Mining and Petroleum, above), was heavily tied to investment in Congolese infrastructure and an important part of the agreement involved Chinese modernization of the rail network. In the west rail links were to be upgraded between the capital Kinshasa, Matadi and also Muambe; in the east, between Kindu, Kalemie and Lubumbashi (in the south-east); and also from Lubumbashi to Ilebo and back to Kinshasa.

The World Bank became involved in China's planned modernization of the DRC's rail network, with the announcement of a joint US $600m. financing plan in May 2011. The deal involved $244m. from the World Bank, $200m. from China (as part of the minerals-for-infrastructure arrangement) and $156m. from the DRC Government. China would focus mainly on providing track and rolling stock, while part of the DRC Government's contribution would be comprised of tax breaks for Vecturis, a Belgian company that would operate the network. The programme would entail the rehabilitation of around 700 km of rail track in Kasaï and copper-rich Katanga. The World Bank pledged that it would also help to facilitate investment in the modernization programme from international mining companies, which have an interest in improving the country's rail infrastructure, since the transport of minerals by rail would allow the shipment of larger volumes than by road. The DRC's Minister of Mines (and interim Minister of Transport and Communication Routes), Martin

Kabwelulu, announced that the country had established contact with a total of 122 mining firms, in an attempt to secure assistance for the modernization programme and for the construction of new railways. One company to express interest in such investment was Freeport-McMoRan, holder of the licence for the $2,000m. Tenke Fungurume copper project. The World Bank was also considering the establishment of a risk insurance scheme for mining companies that committed funds to the programme.

Transport to the north and north-east is possible along the River Congo, and historically river traffic has probably been the single most important means of transport in the country. The Office National des Transports is responsible for almost 14,000 km of waterways. Traffic on the main waterways, the Rivers Congo and Ubangi, declined sharply, as a result of the advance of rebel forces along those rivers towards the capital of Équateur, Mbandaka. From June 2000 the situation worsened considerably, with a succession of offensives and counter-offensives opposing the government troops and the rebels on the Rivers Ubangi and Congo, upstream of Mbandaka. On several occasions vessels from the Republic of the Congo and the Central African Republic were searched both by the DRC government troops and by the rebels. Following the April 2002 Sun City agreement between the Kabila Government and the rebel MLC, traffic was resumed in May between Kinshasa and Bumba (Équateur). Later that month a convoy, escorted by UN peace-keepers, reached Kisangani, which was under the control of the Rwandan-supported Rassemblement Congolais pour la Démocratie. Yet despite the resumption of traffic on the River Congo, the lack of regular and systematic dredging of the river continued to cause many problems for the vessels operating between Kinshasa and Kisangani.

The road network is wholly inadequate for a country of the DRC's size: of the estimated 153,500 km of roads in 2004, only some 33,000 km were main roads, and most of the road network is in a very poor state of repair; indeed, only around 2,800 km is paved. Modernization of the road infrastructure was foreseen under the investment agreement with China, including the construction of a major roadway linking Katanga to the Kisangani river port. Additionally, 250 km of roads were to be rebuilt around Kinshasa, and a new ring road around the city was to be constructed.

As the civil war neared its end funds began to be pledged for road rehabilitation projects. The EU expressed its readiness in March 2001 to resume development co-operation, pending progress in the implementation of the Lusaka peace process and in the dialogue between all the DRC parties. The rehabilitation of main and subsidiary roads was considered both in the framework of emergency rehabilitation programmes and of a larger reconstruction programme, which was due to be presented to the European Council of Ministers in June. The €120m. programme was eventually signed in February 2002 and included rehabilitation work on the Kinshasa–Matadi road. In April a US $14.7m. programme, financed by the World Bank, to rehabilitate another main part of this road, was initiated. Furthermore, the EU also pledged in December 2001 €45m. for the rehabilitation of roads in Bandundu province, of which €20m. was to be allocated to the improvement of subsidiary roads. In total, the government projects identified by June 2001 in the public works, housing and urban architecture sectors amounted to $1,600m. Nevertheless, the Kinshasa authorities announced that they could only provide up to $200m. of this amount.

Domestic air services deteriorated rapidly from the 1980s and the national carrier was disbanded. In September 2000 a new private airline, Hewa Bora Airways (HBA), was allowed to operate on both domestic and international routes. The company benefited from this advantage over all its competitors to import duty-free aircraft and spare parts. In November 2001 HBA inaugurated its flights to Johannesburg, while South African Airways resumed its flights to Kinshasa after two years of interruption. Following the bankruptcy of the Belgian national carrier, Sabena, which was the main link between Kinshasa and Western Europe by late 2001, Air France also resumed its flights between Paris and Kinshasa in January 2002. In April a new Belgian company, SN Brussels Airlines, and HBA restored direct flights between the Belgian and Congolese capitals. Flights between Kinshasa and several cities under rebel control, such as Lisala, Basankusu and Bumba, in Équateur, and Beni, in Nord-Kivu, resumed in May. In April 2003 HBA announced plans to purchase two Boeing 737 aircraft, following its decision to open new connections between Kinshasa and other African capitals. At the same time, however, Trans Kasaï Air, which had been created in May 2000, requested the Government's financial support to resume its activities, after their interruption in February 2002. In May 2003 the Régie des Voies Aériennes parastatal airport authority estimated the total cost of the rehabilitation and improvement of the country's main airstrips at US $144.5m. Although significant improvements in infrastructures were made after the 2004–06 Multi-Sector Emergency Rehabilitation and Reconstruction programme allocated $256m. for rehabilitation, extension and increased security at 10 airports, as of mid-2008 all carriers from the DRC were subject to an EU ban, prohibiting them from entering EU airspace. In February 2012 Brussels Airlines received final approval from the DRC Government to establish a subsidiary in the country, to be called Korongo, which would serve destinations including Johannesburg.

A Global System for Mobile (GSM) Communications network was established in 1999, operated by Congolese Wireless Network (CWN), and during 2000 new wireless operators, such as Celtel, Sogetel, Afritel, Microcom and Libertés, emerged. In February the state telecommunications concern, the Office Congolais des Postes et des Télécommunications (OCPT), signed an agreement with a new operator, Millicom International, in order to offer fixed phone services, wireless connections and internet access to their clients. In July the Chinese company ZTE signed an agreement with the Congolese Government providing for the creation of the Congo Chine Télécom (CCT) corporation, which would benefit from a US $10m. loan from China's Export and Import Bank to develop several projects in the DRC's telecommunications sector. ZTE's plans were to establish 300,000 mobile telephone lines in Kinshasa. By May 2003 the South African corporation Vodacom had pledged to invest $475m. in several projects, which were to generate 3,000 jobs, and had emerged as the most important private investor in the DRC. In April 2004 Congo-Korea Telecoms announced a six-year plan to invest up to $8,000m. in the establishment of an optic-fibre cable telephone network and the installation of 2m. lines. In January 2005 Vodacom announced it had 1m. subscribers in the DRC and the management reiterated its commitment to invest $500m. during 2002–07 in order to cover 80% of the country's territory. Another important development in that year was the decision in March by the Tanzania-based company Lucent to invest $60m.–$100m. in the construction of two new telecommunications stations in Kinshasa and Lubumbashi, on behalf of OCPT. At the end of 2006 the DRC had five cellular telephone operators, with a total of 4.8m. subscribers. By the end of 2008 the number of cellular subscribers in the DRC had risen to 15% of the population (or 9.4m. people), according to figures quoted by Goldman Sachs in March 2009. Moreover, the company cited the DRC as offering one of the best potential growth rates in the region, given the still low level of market penetration. It predicted that subscribership would reach 47% of the population by the end of 2013. At the end of 2008 Vodacom was the market leader in the DRC in terms of subscribers, followed by Zain Congo (subsequently Airtel Congo) and CCT.

Vodacom announced in April 2010 that it was to seek arbitration over a dispute with local partner CWN (the latter holds a 49% stake in Vodacom Congo, while Vodacom holds the remaining 51%). The decision followed the failure of the two parties to agree on a capital restructuring exercise, according to the majority shareholder. In January Vodacom had described its relationship with CWN as 'dysfunctional', amid reports that the minority shareholder would launch legal action to force its partner to invest further in the joint venture. In a further set-back for the South African operator, a Kinshasa commercial court in March 2012 ordered the confiscation of its 51% shareholding in Vodacom Congo, for its failure to pay a US $21m. consultancy fee to Namemco Energy. An appeal against this verdict was pending, with Vodacom claiming that it had already settled all bills outstanding to Namemco, to a total value of $2.8m.

The sale of a 49% stake in mobile operator CCT to France Télécom was approved by the DRC Government in September 2011, according to the country's Ministry of Posts, Telecommunications and New Information and Communication Technologies. At that stage, CCT had 1.5m. subscribers and was the DRC's fourth largest cellular telecommunications company. In October France Télécom announced that it had completed the purchase of the remaining 51% stake in CCT, which was held by Chinese firm ZTE Corpn. The final deal would involve France Télécom paying ZTE US $10m. for its majority stake, the DRC Government $7m. for its minority stake, and then $71m. for a 10-year licence from the telecommunications ministry. The French company announced that it intended to fund its new subsidiary largely through a capital injection of $185m., which would be provided in tranches.

EXTERNAL TRADE

As the former colonial power, Belgium has traditionally been the DRC's main trading partner. In 2006 Belgium was the principal market for DRC exports (29.4%), followed by China (21.1%). Over subsequent years exports to China increased significantly, so that the People's Republic became easily the most significant destination for Congolese goods. In 2010 China received 46.9% of the DRC's exports, while Zambia took 23.3%, the USA 10.4% and Belgium 4.2%. In the same year 19.2% of the DRC's imports were sourced from South Africa, 12.5% from China, 9.2% from Belgium, 8.8% from Zambia, 6.9% from Zimbabwe and 5.8% from France.

Despite the increasing importance of China as an export destination—with the People's Republic establishing significant interests in the DRC's mineral industries (see Mining and Petroleum, above)—the African country has continued to struggle with a trade deficit in recent years. Although exports rose by an estimated 11.3% in US dollar terms in 2008, they failed to keep pace with the rise in imports, which surged by an estimated 27.6% during the course of the year, according to figures published by the IMF in March 2009. The trade deficit widened even further in 2009, with exports shrinking by 33.6% in US dollar terms (a much faster rate of contraction than the 26.3% decline in imports). Exports in 2009 registered US $4,370m., while imports totalled $4,949m., resulting in a trade deficit of $578m., according to IMF data. Mining exports in 2009 totalled $4,192m., accounting for 96% of the country's total exports. The current account deficit in that year reached $1,167m., including the afore-mentioned trade deficit, a $1,167m. deficit on the services account, a $779m. deficit on the income account and a $1,357m. surplus for current transfers (inclusive of $1,233m. of official aid). The global economic downturn meant that the trade deficit could no longer be financed by strong private capital inflows, as foreign mining companies retrenched their investments. This necessitated renewed assistance from multilateral lenders (see Balance of Payments and External Debt, below).

BALANCE OF PAYMENTS AND EXTERNAL DEBT

Following years of economic mismanagement, by the early 2000s the DRC's debt situation had become totally unsustainable. However, the installation of Joseph Kabila as President in early 2001 led to a resumption of dialogue with the Bretton Woods institutions. In February 2003 the World Bank expressed hopes that the DRC would qualify under the initiative for heavily indebted poor countries (HIPC) for a cancellation of 80% of total external debt by March of that year. However, the resignation in February of the Minister of Finance caused concern with the IMF/World Bank, after he explained publicly that his decision was motivated by his objection to a US $8m. increase in extra-budgetary military expenditure. Nevertheless, in March the IMF board approved the disbursement of $35m. from the Poverty Reduction and Growth Facility (PRGF), following a positive review of the Government's reforms. The criteria imposed by the Bretton Woods institutions included: the formation of the transitional Government, the effective restoration of peace in the country and amendments to the 2003 draft budget, in order to include expenditure and revenue from the rebel-held zones. In May the second review of the interim programme supported by the PRGF took place in Kinshasa. It assessed the progress made in several areas, including the liquidation of three commercial banks, the restructuring of GÉCAMINES and of OCPT, and the establishment of an ethical code of conduct for the public administration. Also in that month, the European Commission announced its decision to allocate €100m. to reimburse the DRC's arrears to the European Investment Bank, thereby allowing this financial institution to resume its loans to the DRC. In July the IMF and the World Bank announced that the DRC had qualified for debt reduction, amounting to about $10,000m. in total, under the enhanced HIPC initiative. The World Bank's IDA was to provide a total of $1,031m. in nominal debt-servicing relief, which was to be delivered in part through a 90% reduction in debt-servicing on IDA credit during 2003–26. The IMF pledged to provide assistance of $472m., which was to be delivered in part through an average annual reduction in debt-servicing of about 50% until 2012. Some bilateral debt rescheduling and cancellation had also taken place during the first half of 2003.

In March 2004 the IMF announced that it had successfully conducted its third review of the programme supported by the PRGF, providing for further rescheduling from other donors. In April Belgium and Japan rescheduled €62m. and US $700m. of bilateral debt, respectively. HIPC initiative assistance amounted to 6,505m. new Congolese francs in 2003 and an estimated 22,698m. new Congolese francs in 2004. At the end of 2004, according to the World Bank, total external debt was $11,841m. (of which $10,532m. was long-term debt), equivalent to 186.4% of gross national income.

The IMF's PRGF arrangement with the DRC expired in March 2006, before the completion of the final review, owing to fiscal slippages and delays in implementing structural measures. Overruns in expenditure, amounting to 2.5% of GDP, in the second half of 2005 were the result of spending by political institutions and the military, and increases in wages granted to ease social tensions. Higher than expected revenue from petroleum production had limited the underlying fiscal deficit to 0.2% of GDP, which was, nevertheless, significantly lower than the target surplus of 1.6% of GDP. The authorities requested a Staff Monitored Programme (SMP) for the period until the end of 2006, with the aim of maintaining macroeconomic stability during the elections, and policy implementation prior to the adoption of a successor PRGF arrangement.

According to IMF data released in late 2007 the DRC's total publicly guaranteed debt stood at an estimated US $11,500m., which included $4,600m. owed to multilateral lenders and more than $6,000m. to the 'Paris Club' of sovereign creditors. At that stage the country had yet to reach HIPC completion point (which would secure additional debt relief), in part owing to what the IMF termed 'mixed' macroeconomic performance. The Fund underlined that a new PRGF would be required in order to move to HIPC completion point, after the previous programme expired (and was not subsequently renewed) in March 2006. The DRC did not service its debt to bilateral creditors during the first quarter of 2007, but the Government did convey its intention to return to a medium-term IMF programme and to normalize relations with the 'Paris Club' of sovereign creditors.

However, the quest for debt forgiveness was subsequently complicated by the DRC agreeing a deal with China, which would see the People's Republic modernize much of the country's infrastructure in exchange for access to minerals. The bilateral deal was first mooted seriously in 2007, and although it had yet to be fully finalized two years later, both Governments reiterated their commitment to the agreement in the first half of 2009. The IMF consistently raised concerns about the accord, on the grounds that it could significantly increase the DRC's debt burden, in a context where it had failed to pay back existing debt. Although the infrastructure upgrades were to be funded by providing China with access to discounted copper and cobalt, the Fund was concerned about the DRC Government's status as the guarantor of the deal. China's ambassador to the DRC, Wu Zexian, described the IMF's stance as 'blackmail' in February 2009 and claimed that there would be no change to the key facets of the deal.

These concerns resulted not only in a stalemate between the DRC Government and the 'Paris Club', but also meant that the country remained without a formal IMF 'poverty reduction' programme, three years after the termination of the last PRGF in 2006. Yet, despite the absence of a formal programme and the friction over debt relief, the IMF approved an emergency loan of US $195.5m. in March 2009, as the global economic downturn contributed to the DRC facing a balance of payments crisis. A collapse in commodity prices and foreign investment in the mining sector meant that the DRC had a current account deficit (inclusive of transfers) of 23.9% of GDP in 2009, compared to 12.3% of GDP in 2008 and 1.5% of GDP in 2007, according to the IMF. Foreign exchange reserves, which had stood at $225m. in April 2008, were reported to be nearly exhausted, as the Congolese authorities attempted (largely in vain) to support the local currency. The Congolese franc was trading at around CF 825 = $1 in early May 2009, compared to CF 560 = $1 one year earlier (a depreciation of 47%).

Nevertheless, there were signs that the IMF and the DRC were heading for a wider rapprochement, as the multilateral lender congratulated the Government for taking its own stringency measures in response to the economic downturn and praised 'a fiscal stance that avoids recourse to central bank financing, and tight monetary policy'. As such, despite the ongoing controversy over the infrastructure agreement with China, it appeared that home-grown corrective macroeconomic policies would enable the country to secure a new programme involving direct budgetary support of around US $500m. This came to fruition with an announcement by the IMF in December 2009 that it had approved a three-year arrangement for the DRC, worth $551.5m., under a new PRGF. Additional assistance totalling $72.7m. was to be provided under the HIPC initiative, in order to reduce the cost of debt service payments made to the Fund. In securing this IMF programme, the country put itself back on a path that could result in debt forgiveness by the 'Paris Club'. The IMF stated at this stage that the minimum prerequisite for debt forgiveness was 12 months of satisfactory implementation of the new PRGF, although other factors—including improved provision of health care and education—would also be necessary to qualify for relief.

A deal with the 'Paris Club' was eventually confirmed in November 2010, when the coalition of sovereign creditors (together with Brazil) cancelled US $7,350m. of debt. This represented 54% of the DRC's external debt burden, according to figures for the end of 2009, and the Government expected to save around $520m. per year in (albeit suspended) debt-servicing costs as a result. However, the DRC was still hampered by significant unpaid obligations to commercial creditors, with a number of these considering legal action, according to the 'Paris Club'.

THE DOMESTIC ECONOMY

The country's economy underwent an acceleration in economic growth after the official end of the second civil war, which lasted from 1998 to 2002. Under the transitional Government (2003–06), the economy expanded at a steady and consistent rate: it grew by 6.6% in 2004, 6.5% in 2005 and 5.1% in 2006. The IMF estimated that the economy had expanded by 6.5% in 2007, with the acceleration owing to recoveries in the mining and manufacturing sectors, combined with increased investment in infrastructural projects.

However, the IMF expressed concern during late 2007 about a weakening of macroeconomic management that had taken place earlier in the year. The authorities had shown a reasonable degree of control over fiscal and monetary policy during the transitional period, but a fiscal loosening was experienced in early 2007. Indeed, the early months of 2007 were characterized by a political vacuum; despite Joseph Kabila being confirmed as the elected President in late 2006, it was not until late February 2007 that his new administration was approved by the Assemblée nationale. Public financial management was therefore jeopardized (budget reports indicated that the Government had been unable to complete its payments), while the Congolese franc depreciated by 12% in the first two months of the year and year-on-year inflation reached 21%. This deterioration in key macroeconomic variables was (at least temporarily) halted following the installation of the new Government. International reserves had recovered to US $160m. by April 2007, from a low of $100m. in February, while commitments were also made to rein in public spending. The 2007 budget, amounting to $2,170m., was announced in May of that year. Although it was eventually approved, there was criticism even within the ruling party that both revenue and expenditure targets were unrealistic. Expenditure increased by 67% compared with the previous budget, one-third of which was allocated to debt-servicing. There was renewed fiscal slippage in the last quarter of 2007 as the Government launched an offensive against rebels in the east of the country, which involved massing 20,000 troops with artillery support. The extra expenditure resulted in a renewed spike in inflation (to an annual rate of 16% by the end of 2007). However, the national currency was reasonably stable in late 2007 and the first half of 2008. Indeed, the Congolese franc was trading at around CF 551 = $1 in the second quarter of 2008, compared with around CF 555 = $1 in the first quarter of 2007, although the weakness of the US dollar on global currency markets did lend some support to the Congolese currency.

The economy grew by 8.0%, in real terms, during 2008 despite undergoing a severe reverse in the second half of the year, as global economic trends conspired heavily against the country. The global financial crisis provoked a huge decline in risk appetite among investors, hastening a dramatic reversal of the boom in commodity prices. This crippled the DRC's export earnings from the minerals trade, while also starving international mining companies of credit, so that foreign investment projects in the country were abruptly curtailed.

This dramatic negative reversal of investment flows, export receipts, real economic growth and tax revenues placed huge pressure on the DRC's financing position, both in terms of its domestic budget and the balance of payments. With regard to the budget, the Government initially resorted to direct borrowing from the central bank (i.e. forcing the central bank to print new money) late in 2008, as the earlier projected revenue flows failed to materialize (60% of government revenues had been expected to come from mining and oil). Further strain was placed on government finances by the need to respond to an offensive by a Congolese Tutsi-led rebel group in the country's mineral rich east. The Government was forced into an expensive mobilization of troops and equipment to prevent Goma, a provincial capital, falling to the rebels. The recourse to central bank funding of government spending resulted in inflation reaching 28% by the end of 2008, despite falling world food prices. Meanwhile, the value of the local currency declined dramatically, threatening to set in motion a vicious circle of domestically generated inflation, exchange rate depreciation and imported inflation.

These rapidly deteriorating macroeconomic fundamentals obliged the authorities to take remedial action, via both monetary policy and fiscal policy. With regard to monetary policy, the central bank raised its key interest rate in three stages from 28% to 65% in December 2008–January 2009, while the reserve requirement for banks was increased from 5% to 7%. This dramatic monetary squeeze was accompanied by equally significant fiscal retrenchment, as the Government abandoned its dangerous policy of relying on the central bank for funding. This reportedly entailed slashing the operational budgets of government institutions by 50%. The bold new fiscal strategy appeared to be bearing fruit by May 2009 when it was reported that the Government had registered a small fiscal surplus during the first four months of the calendar year (although an upward correction in the price of many key commodities also played a significant role in this performance turnaround).

The partial recovery in commodity prices brought a stabilization of the DRC's broad macroeconomic performance during the remainder of 2009. For the year as a whole the country managed to record positive economic growth, at a rate of 2.7%, according to the IMF. Meanwhile, the fiscal deficit (on a cash basis, and inclusive of grants) stood at 4.8% of GDP in 2009, according to the Fund. However, consumer price inflation remained stubbornly high, at 49% at the end of 2009, according to IMF estimates (up from 28% at the end of 2008).

The economy improved in 2010, as commodity prices continued to recover. Crucially, the price of copper—the commodity with the strongest bearing on the formal economy—surpassed its July 2008 peak in late 2010, reaching approximately US $9,500 per metric ton. As a result, economic growth in 2010 recovered to 7.2%, according to the IMF. Inflation in that year remained high, at 23.5%, although the IMF expected price growth to average 10% during 2011. In February 2011 the Fund released $77m. under the country's three-year, $541m. Extended Credit Facility (ECF), which had commenced in 2009.

In view of the rise in commodity prices, the DRC increased its 2011 budget by 20%, compared with 2010, to 6,750,000m. Congolese francs (US $7,300m.). The original budget projections were higher, but were reduced in order to limit the fiscal deficit to about 1.3% of GDP and avoid dependence on financing by the central bank, according to the IMF. The budget entailed higher spending on education and health services, as well as funding for the 2011 parliamentary and presidential elections. The Government expected to earn income equivalent to 0.5% of GDP from a privatization programme and efforts to ensure that state institutions pay tax obligations.

The IMF conducted its fourth in-country review of the DRC's ECF in August and September 2011. The Fund commended the DRC Government for achieving a strong performance with regard to several key indicators in the first half of the year, particularly in terms of real economic growth and revenue collection, with the latter supported by an increase in fuel price duty and the advance payment of some taxes. However, much of the strong economic performance was generated by the volatile natural resources sector, amid continued high global commodity prices; as such, the macroeconomic outlook remained vulnerable to a potential correction in these volatile and highly speculative markets. The IMF cautioned that the Government needed to maintain its policies ahead of the November elections, which provided a risk factor in terms of possible renewed fiscal slippage and higher inflation.

ECONOMIC DEVELOPMENT

The shift of policy towards a more market-orientated economy, which was advocated from 2001 by the new President, Joseph Kabila, contributed significantly to improve the climate between the DRC Government and the donor community. A raft of projects were launched by multilateral and bilateral donors over the next two years, before, in December 2003, at a World Bank Consultative Group meeting, US $3,980m. was pledged to finance the country's reunification and recovery during the 2004–06 period. According to the World Bank, new and confirmed financial contributions were to reach $1,080m. in 2004. This amount was to increase to $1,200m. in 2005 and continue in subsequent years, according to both political and economic progress. About 70% of the total was to be allocated to infrastructure projects and the remaining 30% to social sectors. The USA emerged as one of the most important bilateral donors, with a total of $330m., followed by the United Kingdom, which pledged $120m. over three years. Japan promised to finance the rehabilitation of the port of Matadi, at an estimated cost of $16m. Belgium committed to increase its bilateral aid from €18m. in 2003 to €25m. in 2004.

The list of projects included the rehabilitation of the river ports of Kisangani, Bumba and Lisala (US $12m.), the acquisition of new wagons and locomotives and railway rehabilitation works ($70.6m.), the rehabilitation of 10 airports ($35m.), and the acquisition of dredging and signalization materials for the RVF river transport authority ($4.5m.). During the Consultative Group meeting, the National Agency for the Promotion of Investments submitted a list of priorities, including the rehabilitation and the modernization of the Kinshasa Ndjili international airport, the construction of a railway between Kinshasa and Ilebo, housing projects in Kinshasa and the provincial capitals, the construction of two medium-sized hydroelectric power stations at Katende (Kasaï Occidental) and Tshiala (Kasaï Oriental), the rehabilitation of the Maluku steel plant, the revival of production of GÉCAMINES and of the export crops (cotton, coffee, tea, cocoa and rubber), the creation of logging companies, and of new urban transport companies in Kinshasa and the capitals of the provinces. Businesses were urged to invest in the DRC, with the authorities declaring that the country would offer increased legal security for investors by joining Organisation pour l'Harmonisation en Afrique du Droit des Affaires, an organization furthering the standardization of business legislation between the francophone countries, and that the services, water and electricity sectors would soon be liberalized. They also announced restructuring of the banking sector and reforms of tax legislation through the introduction of value-added tax before 2005 (which did not actually take place until early 2012). Participants of the meeting also indicated that funds would be conditional on the restoration of security in the country. For that reason, in May 2004 the World Bank board approved an IDA grant of $100m. to finance an Emergency Demobilization and Reintegration Project in the DRC, in order to support the DRC Government's efforts to demobilize an estimated 150,000 former combatants and to assist their reintegration into civilian life. Private companies also urged the authorities to simplify customs clearing formalities, particularly at the port of Matadi.

The adoption of a constitution, followed by local, legislative and presidential elections, was viewed as a priority by the donor community in order to provide a stable political framework to undertake the reconstruction and the development of the country. The cost of this operation, which was initially estimated at US $285m., was constantly revised upwards, partly owing to the extension of the transition period at least for another six months beyond the initial 30 June 2005 deadline. By mid-June, however, the EU Special Envoy in the Great Lakes expressed concern about the availability of funds to finance these operations. Accordingly, the total cost was increased to $467m., of which $103m. was for logistics and $43m. to guarantee the security of the electoral process. In principle, the DRC Government was to finance 10% of the total cost, but by mid-June only $197m. had been pledged by the donors, including $90m. by the EU. Another priority of the donor community was the reduction of poverty in a country which in 2003 ranked 168th of 174 countries, according to the UNDP's Human Development Index, and where revenue per caput and per day decreased from $1.31 in 1973 to $0.23 in 2000. In March 2005 the Bureau Central de Coordination, which channels the funds of various donors, announced that in 2004 it had approved projects valued at $974.26m., of which $847.8m. were pledged by the World Bank and $130.2m. by the AfDB. Institutional reforms absorbed 32% of the total, followed by water and electricity (22%), road and sanitation infrastructures (19%), agriculture (12%), rural development (6%), community development (5%), education (3%) and social protection (1%).

In April 2005 the World Bank considered that the implementation of US $1,700m. of aid focused on infrastructure, agriculture and social sectors and financed by the donor community was satisfactory and announced that it had already disbursed $440m. by the end by June 2007. However, the Congolese Minister of Public Works and Infrastructure announced in June 2005 that the implementation of the programme during the first three months of that year had suffered several delays. Disbursements accordingly amounted only to $95m., or 28.8% of the total commitments for the period ($329.2m.). In March 2005 the EU launched the second phase of its €80m. Public Administration Reform II Programme for rehabilitation support, of which 70% was to finance urban rehabilitation projects. During the previous month the EU Commission approved a €38m. programme for health, food security and support to internally displaced persons and rape victims. In June UNDP announced that $67m. would be available to finance anti-HIV/AIDS, tuberculosis and malaria programmes during the following two years. One of the main bilateral interventions was a $57m. loan from the Indian Government to finance energy, metallurgy and mining, railway, pharmaceutical and information technology projects throughout the country. In May Sweden announced that it would contribute €15m. to various projects, of which €10m. was for humanitarian aid, for the peace process and the organization of elections and the remaining €5m. for the education sector.

The provision of significant bilateral assistance was agreed by India in October 2009, when the DRC's Minister of Foreign Affairs, Alexis Thambwe Mwamba, met his Indian counterpart, S. M. Krishna, in the latter country. A credit line of US $263m. was made available by India, together with the promise to establish an IT centre of excellence in the DRC. The credit line would focus on three key projects: a 60 MW hydroelectric power plant in Katende (for which $168m. would be made available—see above); the rehabilitation of Kinshasa City Centre's Urban Railway System ($50m.); and the Kakabola hydroelectric power project ($45m.).

In January 2006 a report published in the medical journal *The Lancet* concluded that the humanitarian situation in the DRC was the most severe in the world, with some 38,000 people continuing to die every month, owing to insecurity, lack of a public health system and inadequate international aid. It was estimated that a total of 3.9m. people had died since 1998, mainly as a result of disease. At a donor conference, which was organized in Brussels in February, the UN secured pledges of US $681m. to alleviate the crisis and support long-term development in the DRC. The UN and European Commission subsequently initiated a humanitarian action plan, which allocated the funds to a number of sectors. The European Commission was to provide $45m. in humanitarian aid in 2006, following a total of $78m. in 2004 and 2005.

In late 2006 the IMF expressed concerns that the power-sharing Government was ignoring previously agreed resolutions and failing to implement IMF-sponsored projects. Under the SMP the fiscal deficit was to be tightened to 1.5% of GDP, down from the 9.5% recorded in 2005. This, however, did not happen, and instead spending had increased by 50% by mid-2006. At that time the World Bank was considering instigating a US $10,000m. programme of debt relief to the DRC. Meanwhile, Belgium resumed its co-operation with the DRC, donating €195m. to improve infrastructure in the health and education sectors. The World Bank also recognized the need to provide aid for reconstruction, granting an initial $180m. (part of funding measures worth $380m. for 2007). Nevertheless, IMF reports continued to reflect a deteriorating economy and in early 2007 the Fund warned the Government to curb spending. In May the United Kingdom granted $14m. to fund projects dedicated to improving education, health, the quality of drinking water and general governance. A more pressing concern, however, might be food shortages: an estimated 40m. people suffer from food insecurity.

In November 2007 the World Bank announced that donors had pledged US $4,000m. in funds for development in the DRC. The monies would be disbursed during 2008–10, with 75% of these funds representing new commitments. The World Bank stated that the money would be used for stabilization of the country, post-conflict reconstruction and governance reforms. This followed a meeting of donors from 15 countries in Paris, at which the DRC Government and the donors agreed that security sector reform was the 'key for lasting development'. In July 2012 the World Bank approved a grant of $75m. for the DRC's Health Sector Rehabilitation Support Project to help improve primary health care for 11m. people. The grant was to be used to provide basic services to ensure greater survival among women and children.

The USA has become an increasingly important bilateral donor to the DRC. Under the auspices of USAID, the US Government provided US $143.5m. to the central African nation in fiscal year 2006/07, $223.4m. in 2007/08 and $329.6m. in 2008/09. In the latter year the provision of aid by the US Government could be broken down as follows: $5.0m. for long-term development assistance, $33.0m. for disaster assistance, $69.4m. for health and 'child survival', $126.0m. for food aid, $52.8m. via an economic support fund, $1.5m. for narcotics control and law enforcement, $40.5m. for peace-keeping operations and $1.4m. for military-related funding and training.

Statistical Survey

Sources (unless otherwise stated): Département de l'Economie Nationale, Kinshasa; Institut National de la Statistique, Office Nationale de la Recherche et du Développement, BP 20, Kinshasa; tel. (12) 31401.

Area and Population

AREA, POPULATION AND DENSITY

Area (sq km)	2,344,885*
Population (census result)	
1 July 1984	
Males	14,543,800
Females	15,373,000
Total	29,916,800
Population (UN estimates at mid-year)†	
2010	65,965,795
2011	67,757,576
2012	69,575,391
Density (per sq km) at mid-2012	29.7

* 905,365 sq miles.

† Source: UN, *World Population Prospects: The 2010 Revision.*

POPULATION BY AGE AND SEX
(UN estimates at mid-2012)

	Males	Females	Total
0–14	15,943,014	15,850,142	31,793,156
15–64	17,850,149	18,073,590	35,923,739
65 and over	812,430	1,046,066	1,858,496
Total	34,605,593	34,969,798	69,575,391

Source: UN, *World Population Prospects: The 2010 Revision.*

REGIONS*

	Area (sq km)	Population (31 Dec. 1985)†
Bandundu	295,658	4,644,758
Bas-Zaïre	53,920	2,158,595
Équateur	403,293	3,960,187
Haut-Zaïre	503,239	5,119,750
Kasaï Occidental	156,967	3,465,756
Kasaï Oriental	168,216	2,859,220
Kivu	256,662	5,232,442
Shaba (formerly Katanga)	496,965	4,452,618
Kinshasa (city)‡	9,965	2,778,281
Total	2,344,885	34,671,607

* In October 1997 a statutory order redesignated the regions as provinces. Kivu was divided into three separate provinces, and several of the other provinces were renamed. The Constitution of February 2006 increased the existing 11 provinces to 26: Bas-Uele, Équateur, Haut-Lomami, Haut-Katanga, Haut-Uele, Ituri, Kasaï, Kasaï Oriental, Kongo Central, Kwango, Kwilu, Lomami, Lualaba, Lulua, Mai-Ndombe, Maniema, Mongala, Nord-Kivu, Nord-Ubangi, Sankuru, Sud-Kivu, Sud-Ubangi, Tanganyika, Tshopo, Tshuapa and Kinshasa (city).

† Provisional.

‡ Including the commune of Maluku.

Source: Département de l'Administration du Territoire.

PRINCIPAL TOWNS
(population at census of July 1984)

Kinshasa (capital)	2,664,309	Likasi	213,862
Lubumbashi	564,830	Boma	197,617
Mbuji-Mayi	486,235	Bukavu	167,950
Kolwezi	416,122	Kikwit	149,296
Kisangani	317,581	Matadi	138,798
Kananga	298,693	Mbandaka	137,291

Source: UN, *Demographic Yearbook*.

Mid-2011: (incl. suburbs, UN estimate) Kinshasa (capital) 8,797,730 (Source: UN, *World Urbanization Prospects: The 2011 Revision*).

BIRTHS AND DEATHS
(annual averages, UN estimates)

	1995–2000	2000–05	2005–10
Birth rate (per 1,000)	49.8	48.2	44.9
Death rate (per 1,000)	19.7	18.2	17.2

Source: UN, *World Population Prospects: The 2010 Revision*.

Life expectancy (years at birth): 48.1 (males 46.5; females 49.7) in 2010 (Source: World Bank, World Development Indicators database).

Economically Active Population (mid-2012, estimates in '000): Agriculture, etc. 14,684; Total labour force 26,115 (Source: FAO).

Health and Welfare

KEY INDICATORS

Total fertility rate (children per woman, 2010)	5.8
Under-5 mortality rate (per 1,000 live births, 2010)	170
HIV/AIDS (% of persons aged 15–49, 2005)	3.2
Physicians (per 1,000 head, 2004)	0.1
Hospital beds (per 1,000 head, 2006)	0.8
Health expenditure (2009): US $ per head (PPP)	31
Health expenditure (2009): % of GDP	9.6
Health expenditure (2009): public (% of total)	44.7
Access to water (% of persons, 2010)	45
Access to sanitation (% of persons, 2010)	24
Total carbon dioxide emissions ('000 metric tons, 2008)	2,816.3
Carbon dioxide emissions per head (metric tons, 2008)	<0.1
Human Development Index (2011): ranking	187
Human Development Index (2011): value	0.286

For sources and definitions, see explanatory note on p. vi.

Agriculture

PRINCIPAL CROPS
('000 metric tons)

	2008	2009	2010
Rice, paddy	317	317	317
Maize	1,156	1,156	1,156
Millet	38	38	38
Sorghum	6	6	6
Potatoes	94	94	95
Sweet potatoes	240	243	247
Cassava (Manioc)	15,014	15,034	15,050
Taro (Cocoyam)	66	66	67
Yams	88	89	90
Sugar cane	1,793*	1,827*	1,827†
Beans, dry	113	114	115
Peas, dry	1	1	1
Groundnuts, with shell	370	371	371
Oil palm fruit	1,135	1,150	1,164
Melonseed†	51	51	52
Cabbages and other brassicas†	25	25	26
Tomatoes	47*	49*	50†
Onions, dry†	55	56	60
Pumpkins, squash and gourds	31	30†	31†
Bananas	315	316	316
Plantains	1,207	1,200†	1,250†
Oranges	181	181	181
Avocados	65	66	67
Mangoes, mangosteens and guavas	208	210	212
Pineapples	198	199	201
Papayas	222	224	226
Coffee, green	32	32	32

* Unofficial figure.

† FAO estimate(s).

Aggregate production ('000 metric tons, may include official, semi-official or estimated data): Total cereals 1,526 in 2008, 1,527 in 2009, 1,528 in 2010; Total roots and tubers 15,572 in 2008, 15,618 in 2009, 15,643 in 2010; Total vegetables (incl. melons) 536 in 2008, 546 in 2009, 557 in 2010; Total fruits (excl. melons) 2,480 in 2008, 2,483 in 2009, 2,541 in 2010.

Source: FAO.

LIVESTOCK
('000 head, year ending September)

	2008	2009	2010*
Cattle	753	751†	755
Sheep	902	903†	905
Goats	4,046	4,100*	4,150
Pigs	965	967†	967
Chickens	19,948†	20,007†	20,500

* FAO estimate(s).

† Unofficial figure.

Source: FAO.

LIVESTOCK PRODUCTS
('000 metric tons)

	2008	2009*	2010*
Cattle meat	12.3	12.0	12.5
Goat meat	17.8	17.8	17.8
Pig meat	24.0	24.0	26.0
Chicken meat	10.7	10.8	10.9
Game meat	89.1	89.0	101.1
Sheep meat	2.8	2.8	2.8
Cows' milk*	6.8	6.9	8.0
Hen eggs*	8.7	8.7	8.9

* FAO estimates.

Source: FAO.

Forestry

ROUNDWOOD REMOVALS
('000 cubic metres, excl. bark, FAO estimates)

	2008	2009	2010
Sawlogs, veneer logs and logs for sleepers	310	310	310
Other industrial wood	4,282	4,282	4,282
Fuel wood	74,315	75,446	76,602
Total	78,907	80,038	81,194

Source: FAO.

SAWNWOOD PRODUCTION
('000 cubic metres, incl. railway sleepers)

	2008	2009	2010
Total (all broadleaved)	150	92	92

Source: FAO.

Fishing

('000 metric tons, live weight, FAO estimates)

	2005	2006	2007
Capture	236.6	236.6	236.0
Aquaculture	3.0	3.0	3.0
Total catch	239.6	239.6	239.0

2008–10: Catch assumed to be unchanged from 2007 (FAO estimates).

Source: FAO.

Mining

(metric tons unless otherwise indicated)

	2008	2009	2010
Hard coal	116,000	120,000*	120,000*
Crude petroleum ('000 barrels)	8,365	9,382	8,586
Copper ore*†	238,000	360,000	440,000
Tantalum and niobium (columbium) concentrates	527	468	350*
Cobalt concentrates*†	31,000	43,000	61,000
Gold (kg)*	3,300	3,500	3,500
Silver (kg)	34,083	n.a.	5,600*
Germanium (kg)*	2,500	2,500	2,500
Diamonds ('000 carats)‡	20,947	18,275	16,800*

* Estimated production.

† Figures refer to the metal content of mine output.

‡ An estimated 20% of the diamond output is gem quality; the majority of production is from artisanal mining.

Source: US Geological Survey.

Industry

SELECTED PRODUCTS
('000 metric tons, unless otherwise indicated)

	2006	2007	2008*
Maize flour	14	15	15
Wheat flour	186	179	184
Sugar	91	94	96
Cigarettes ('000 cartons)	3,048	3,433	3,536
Beer (million litres)	301	295	304
Soft drinks (million litres)	162	130	140
Soaps	24	8	25
Acetylene	10	7	19
Tyres ('000 units)	53	55	56
Cement	530	539	411
Steel	104	110	113
Explosives	26	27	—
Bottles ('000 units)	18	19	21
Cotton fabrics ('000 sq m)	852	267	—
Printed fabrics ('000 sq m)	6,411	5,616	—
Footwear ('000 pairs)	1,432	21,178	21,814
Blankets ('000 units)	12	12	13
Electric energy (million kWh)	7,633	7,543	7,495

* Estimates.

Source: IMF, *Democratic Republic of the Congo: Statistical Appendix* (January 2010).

Finance

CURRENCY AND EXCHANGE RATES

Monetary Units

100 centimes = 1 new Congolese franc.

Sterling, Dollar and Euro Equivalents (30 April 2012)

£1 sterling = 1,500.45 new Congolese francs;
US $1 = 922.73 new Congolese francs;
€1 = 1,219.29 new Congolese francs;
10,000 new Congolese francs = £6.66 = $10.84 = €8.20.

Average Exchange Rate (new Congolese francs per US $)

2009 809.786
2010 905.913
2011 919.491

Note: In June 1967 the zaire was introduced, replacing the Congolese franc (CF) at an exchange rate of 1 zaire = CF 1,000. In October 1993 the zaire was replaced by the new zaire (NZ), equivalent to 3m. old zaires. On 30 June 1998 a new Congolese franc, equivalent to NZ 100,000, was introduced. The NZ was withdrawn from circulation on 30 June 1999. Some of the figures in this survey are still given in terms of a previous currency.

BUDGET
('000 million new Congolese francs)*

Revenue†	2006	2007	2008‡
Taxes on income and profits	128,774	161,371	253,100
Corporations and enterprises	79,076	89,408	147,790
Individuals	40,756	58,107	85,601
Taxes on goods and services	146,301	192,774	282,866
Turnover taxes	110,056	150,917	221,628
Selective excises	35,543	40,406	59,431
Beer	13,804	16,911	26,771
Tobacco	11,040	11,985	20,146
Taxes on international trade	163,805	239,333	342,528
Import duties and taxes	154,045	230,596	326,240
Export duties and taxes	9,630	8,679	16,288
Others	129	58	0
Other revenue	89,818	167,509	326,795
Total	528,698	760,987	1,205,289

Expenditure	2006	2007	2008‡
Wages and salaries	218,898	300,984	452,220
Goods and services (incl. off-budget)	133,194	203,685	277,694
Interest on domestic debt	22,921	28,721	34,225
Interest on external debt	72,995	155,413	169,550
Transfers and subsidies	87,102	111,730	226,871
Exceptional expenditure	171,706	45,034	74,417
Investment	134,050	121,085	243,706
Total	840,866	966,653	1,478,682

* Figures refer to the consolidated accounts of the central Government.
† Excluding grants received ('000 million new Congolese francs): 328,507 in 2006; 76,014 in 2007; 121,484 in 2008 (estimate).
‡ Estimates.

Source: IMF, *Democratic Republic of the Congo: Statistical Appendix* (January 2010).

2009 ('000 million new Congolese francs, preliminary): *Revenue:* Customs and excise 560; Direct and indirect taxes 565; Petroleum royalties and taxes 132; Non-tax revenue 271; Total revenue 1,528 (excl. grants 679). *Expenditure:* Current expenditure 1,652; Capital expenditure 704; Exceptional expenditure 231; Total expenditure 2,586 (Source: IMF (see below)).

2010 ('000 million new Congolese francs, estimates): *Revenue:* Customs and excise 754; Direct and indirect taxes 778; Petroleum royalties and taxes 266; Non-tax revenues 455; Total revenue 2,253 (excl. grants 1,676). *Expenditure:* Current expenditure 1,724; Capital expenditure 1,678; Exceptional expenditure 245; Total expenditure 3,647 (Source: IMF (see below)).

2011 ('000 million new Congolese francs, projections): *Revenue:* Customs and excise 949; Direct and indirect taxes 1,048; Petroleum royalties and taxes 415; Non-tax revenues 594; Total revenue 3,006 (excl. grants 1,268). *Expenditure:* Current expenditure 2,525; Capital expenditure 2,421; Exceptional expenditure 322; Budget reserve 39; Total expenditure 5,308 (Source (2009–11): IMF, *Democratic Republic of the Congo: Third Review of the Three-Year Arrangement Under the Extended Credit Facility, Financing Assurances Review, and Request for Modification of Performance Criteria—Staff Report and Press Release on the Executive Board Discussion*—July 2011).

INTERNATIONAL RESERVES

(excluding gold, US $ million at 31 December)

	2009	2010	2011
IMF special drawing rights	612.58	543.93	541.20
Foreign exchange	422.80	755.72	726.30
Total	1,035.38	1,299.65	1,267.50

Source: IMF, *International Financial Statistics*.

MONEY SUPPLY

(million new Congolese francs at 31 December)

	2009	2010	2011
Currency outside banks	381,486	489,377	615,345
Demand deposits at deposit money banks	91,037	212,909	166,100
Total money (incl. others)	479,875	706,164	789,829

Source: IMF, *International Financial Statistics*.

COST OF LIVING

(Consumer Price Index for Kinshasa at 31 December; base: August 1995 = 100)

	2005	2006	2007
Food	546,165	697,790	762,946
Rent	622,109	736,670	817,241
Clothing	930,811	1,077,902	1,128,393
All items (incl. others)	644,137	798,297	877,842

Source: IMF, *Democratic Republic of the Congo: Statistical Appendix* (January 2010).

Cost of living (Consumer Price Index; base: 2005 = 100): 113.1 in 2006; 132.2 in 2007; 155.1 in 2008 (Source: IMF, *International Financial Statistics*).

NATIONAL ACCOUNTS

('000 million new Congolese francs at current prices)

Expenditure on the Gross Domestic Product

	2009	2010	2011*
Government final consumption expenditure	868	1,046	1,272
Private final consumption expenditure	6,993	9,183	11,196
Gross fixed capital formation	1,398	1,735	2,107
Change in inventories	73	71	98
Total domestic expenditure	9,332	12,035	14,673
Exports of goods and services	3,218	3,686	4,166
Less Imports of goods and services	3,517	3,770	4,025
GDP in purchasers' values	9,032	11,949	14,815

Gross Domestic Product by Economic Activity

	2009	2010	2011*
Agriculture, forestry, livestock, hunting, and fishing	3,715	5,027	5,525
Mining	801	1,254	1,697
Manufacturing	456	571	772
Construction and public works	454	632	855
Electricity and water	271	347	469
Wholesale and retail trade; restaurants and hotels	1,575	1,841	2,413
Finance, insurance, real estate, etc.	500	641	867
Transport and telecommunications	407	521	705
Public administration, defence and other services	511	653	886
Sub-total	8,690	11,487	14,189
Taxes, less subsidies, on imports	440	595	805
Less Imputed bank service charge	98	133	180
GDP at market prices	9,032	11,949	14,815

* Provisional figures.

Source: African Development Bank.

BALANCE OF PAYMENTS

(US $ million)

	2007	2008	2009
Exports of goods f.o.b.	6,143	6,585	4,370
Imports of goods f.o.b.	–5,257	–6,711	–4,949
Trade balance	886	–125	–578
Exports of services	392	522	651
Imports of services	–1,618	–2,146	–1,817
Balance on goods and services	–340	–1,749	–1,745
Other income received	26	27	26
Other income paid	–661	–1,348	–805
Balance on goods, services and income	–975	–3,070	–2,524
Current transfers (net)	821	1,231	1,357
Current balance	–153	–1,839	–1,166
Capital and financial account (net)	66	1,007	198
Net errors and omissions	–262	–115	81
Overall balance	–349	–946	–888

Source: IMF, *Democratic Republic of the Congo: Third Review of the Three-Year Arrangement Under the Extended Credit Facility, Financing Assurances Review, and Request for Modification of Performance Criteria—Staff Report and Press Release on the Executive Board Discussion* (July 2011).

External Trade

PRINCIPAL COMMODITIES
(US $ million)

Imports c.i.f.	2006	2007	2008*
Petroleum	486	571	778
Non-petroleum	2,405	4,686	5,933
Total	2,892	5,257	6,711

Exports f.o.b.†	2006	2007	2008*
Copper	869	2,040	2,333
Cobalt	373	2,310	2,523
Diamonds	884	836	702
Crude petroleum	579	612	783
Coffee	46	52	59
Total (incl. others)	2,931	6,143	6,585

* Estimates.

† Including 'parallel' exports (US $ million): 221 in 2006; 248 in 2007; 207 in 2008 (estimate).

Source: IMF, *Democratic Republic of the Congo: Statistical Appendix* (January 2010).

2009 (US $ million): Total imports 4,602; Total exports 4,277 (Source: African Development Bank).

SELECTED TRADING PARTNERS
(US $ million)

Imports c.i.f.	1995
Belgium-Luxembourg	147.2
Canada	9.8
China, People's Repub.	26.8
Côte d'Ivoire	35.5
Ecuador	65.1
Germany	48.2
India	9.9
Iran	10.3
Italy	26.5
Japan	11.8
Kenya	22.5
Morocco	9.2
Netherlands	36.5
Nigeria	72.5
South Africa	89.3
Togo	22.5
United Kingdom	50.2
Zambia	9.4
Total (incl. others)	889.2

Exports f.o.b.	1995
Angola	51.0
Belgium-Luxembourg	90.9
Canada	11.6
Germany	8.7
Israel	17.2
Italy	29.6
Philippines	30.2
Senegal	9.5
South Africa	219.7
Switzerland	29.7
United Kingdom	29.7
USA	107.6
Total (incl. others)	742.8

Source: UN, *International Trade Statistics Yearbook*.

2008 (US $ million): *Imports:* Belgium 286.7; China, People's Republic 892.0; France 183.6; USA 152.4; Zambia 301.2; Total (incl. others) 3,658. *Exports:* Belgium 220.0; France 103.5; South Africa 633.7; Zambia 161.7; Zimbabwe 8.4; Total (incl. others) 4,276.7 (Source: African Development Bank).

2009 (US $ million): Total imports 4,602; Total exports 4,277 (Source: African Development Bank).

Transport

RAILWAYS
(traffic)*

	1999	2000	2001†
Passenger-km (million)	145.2	187.9	222.1
Freight (million ton-km)	386.5	429.3	459.1

* Figures refer to Société Nationale des Chemins de Fer du Congo (SNCC) services only.

† Estimates.

Source: IMF, *Democratic Republic of the Congo: Selected Issues and Statistical Appendix* (June 2003).

ROAD TRAFFIC
(motor vehicles in use at 31 December)

	1994	1995*	1996*
Passenger cars	698,672	762,000	787,000
Buses and coaches	51,578	55,000	60,000
Lorries and vans	464,205	495,000	538,000
Total vehicles	1,214,455	1,312,000	1,384,000

* Estimates.

2007: Total vehicles 311,781.

Source: IRF, *World Road Statistics*.

1999: Passenger cars 172,600; Commercial vehicles 34,600 (Source: UN, *Statistical Yearbook*).

SHIPPING

Merchant Fleet
(registered at 31 December)

	2007	2008	2009
Number of vessels	21	21	21
Total displacement ('000 grt)	13.9	13.9	13.9

Source: IHS Fairplay, *World Fleet Statistics*.

International Sea-borne Freight Traffic
(estimates, '000 metric tons)

	1988	1989	1990
Goods loaded	2,500	2,440	2,395
Goods unloaded	1,400	1,483	1,453

Source: UN, *Monthly Bulletin of Statistics*.

CIVIL AVIATION
(traffic on scheduled services)

	1992	1993	1994
Kilometres flown (million)	4	4	6
Passengers carried ('000)	116	84	178
Passenger-km (million)	295	218	480
Total ton-km (million)	56	42	87

Source: UN, *Statistical Yearbook*.

2001: Passengers carried ('000) 95.2; Total ton-km (million) 7.4 (Source: World Bank, World Development Indicators database).

Tourism

FOREIGN TOURIST ARRIVALS BY ORIGIN

	2007	2008	2009
Africa	27,767	27,969	31,328
Congo, Republic	666	n.a.	1,916
East Asia	5,478	5,233	5,540
Europe	11,314	13,104	13,101
Belgium	3,033	4,159	4,087
France	2,992	2,793	2,654
Germany	843	1,266	1,424
Italy	609	1,102	1,182
Central America, North America, South America	2,933	3,665	3,433
Total	47,492	49,971	53,402

Total tourist arrivals: 81,000 in 2010.

Tourism receipts (US $ million): 2 in 1998.

Source: World Tourism Organization.

Communications Media

	2009	2010	2011
Telephones ('000 main lines in use)	42.3	42.0	42.0
Mobile cellular telephones ('000 subscribers)	9,458.6	11,820.3	15,673.1
Internet subscribers ('000)	73.4	75.7	n.a.
Broadband subscribers ('000)	6.8	8.7	14.9

Radio receivers ('000 in use): 18,030 in 1997.

Television receivers ('000 in use): 100 in 1998.

Personal computers: 500,000 in 1999.

Book production (titles published): 112 in 1996.

Daily newspapers: 12 in 2004 (estimated average circulation 129,000 in 1998).

Non-daily newspapers: 164 in 2004.

Sources: International Telecommunication Union; UNESCO Institute for Statistics.

Education

(2009/10 unless otherwise indicated)

	Teachers	Students		
		Males	Females	Total
Pre-primary	8,585	106,430	112,412	218,842
Primary	285,640	5,679,371	4,893,051	10,572,422
General secondary	218,320	1,757,143	1,040,186	2,797,329
Technical and vocational		458,954	228,176	687,130
Tertiary*	23,009	288,657	89,210	377,867

* 2008/09.

Institutions (1998/99): Primary 17,585; Secondary 6,007.

Source: UNESCO Institute for Statistics.

Pupil-teacher ratio (primary education, UNESCO estimate): 37.0 in 2009/10 (Source: UNESCO Institute for Statistics).

Adult literacy rate (UNESCO estimates): 66.8% (males 76.9%; females 57.0%) in 2010 (Source: UNESCO Institute for Statistics).

Directory

The Constitution

A new Constitution was approved by the transitional legislature in May 2005, and endorsed by a national referendum in December. The Constitution officially entered into effect on 18 February 2006 and was amended on 15 January 2011; its main provisions are summarized below:

GENERAL PROVISIONS

The state of the Democratic Republic of the Congo is divided for the purposes of administration into 25 provinces and the capital of Kinshasa (which has the status of a province). The provinces are granted autonomous powers for managing local resources, and also powers that are exercised in conjunction with the central Government, including control of between 40% and 60% of public funds. Each province has a Government and Assembly. The Constitution reaffirms the principle of democracy, guarantees political pluralism, and protects fundamental human rights and freedoms. The establishment of a one party system is prohibited and punishable by law as an act of treason.

PRESIDENT

The President is the Head of State and Commander-in-Chief of the armed forces. He is elected by direct universal suffrage for a term of five years, which is renewable once. Presidential candidates must be of Congolese nationality and a minimum of 30 years of age. The President nominates a Prime Minister from the political party that commands a majority in the legislature and other members of the Government on the proposal of the Prime Minister. He exercises executive powers in conjunction with the Government and subject to the approval of the legislature. The areas of defence, security and foreign affairs are conducted jointly by the President and the Government.

GOVERNMENT

The Government comprises the Prime Minister and a number of ministers and deputy ministers. The Government is responsible for conducting national politics, which it determines in conjunction with the President. The Government is accountable to the Assemblée nationale, which is empowered to adopt a motion of censure against it.

LEGISLATURE

Legislative power is vested in a bicameral Parlement, comprising a lower chamber, the Assemblée nationale, and an upper chamber, the Sénat. Members of the Assemblée nationale are elected by direct universal suffrage for a renewable term of five years. The number of deputies is determined by electoral law. Members of the Sénat are indirectly elected by the Assemblies of each of the country's provinces for a renewable term of five years. Both chambers have a President and two Vice-Presidents.

JUDICIARY

The Constitution guarantees the independence of the judicial system. Members of the judiciary are under the authority of the Conseil Supérieur de la Magistrature. The Cour de Cassation has jurisdiction over legal decisions and the Conseil d'État over administrative decisions. The Cour Constitutionnelle interprets the provisions of the Constitution and ensures the conformity of new legislation. The system also comprises a Haute Cour Militaire, and lower civil and military courts and tribunals. The Conseil Supérieur de la Magistrature has 18 members, including the Presidents and Chief Prosecutors of the main courts. The Cour Constitutionnelle comprises nine members, who are appointed by the President (including three nominated by Parlement and three by the Conseil Supérieur de la Magistrature) for a term of nine years. The Head of State appoints and dismisses magistrates, on the proposal of the Conseil Supérieur de la Magistrature.

The Government

HEAD OF STATE

President: Maj.-Gen. JOSEPH KABILA KABANGE (inaugurated 26 January 2001, re-appointed 7 April 2003, elected 6 December 2006, re-elected 28–29 November 2011).

CABINET

(September 2012)

Prime Minister: AUGUSTIN MATATA PONYO.

Deputy Prime Minister, Minister of the Budget: DANIEL MUKOKO SAMBA.

Deputy Prime Minister, Minister of National Defence and War Veterans: ALEXANDRE LUBA NTAMBO.

Minister of Foreign Affairs, International Co-operation and the Francophonie: RAYMOND TSHIBANDA N'TUNGAMULONGO.

Minister of the Interior, Security, Decentralization and Traditional Affairs: RICHARD MUYEJ MANGEZ.

Minister of Justice and Human Rights: WIVINE MUMBA MATIPA.

Minister of Media, in charge of Relations with Parliament and Initiation of New Citizenship: LAMBERT MENDE OMALANGA.

Minister of Planning, Implementation and Modernization: CÉLESTIN VUNABANDI KANYAMIHIGO.

Minister of Portfolio: LOUISE MUNGA MESOZI.

Minister of the Economy and Commerce: JEAN PAUL NEMOYATO BEGEPOLE.

Minister of Land Settlement, Town Planning, Housing, Infrastructure, Public Works and Reconstruction: FRIDOLIN KASWESHI MUSOKA.

Minister of Transport and Communication Routes: JUSTIN KALUMBA MWANA NGONGO.

Minister of the Environment, Conservation of Nature and Tourism: BAVON N'SA MPUTU ELIMA.

Minister of Mines: MARTIN KABWELULU LABILO.

Minister of Water Resources and Electricity: BRUNO KAPANJI KALALA.

Minister of Hydrocarbons: CRISPIN ATAMA TABE.

Minister of Industry and Small and Medium-sized Enterprises: REMY MUSUNGAYI BAMPALE.

Minister of Posts, Telecommunications and New Information and Communication Technologies: TRIPHON KIN KIEY MULUMBA.

Minister of Employment, Labour and Social Security: MODESTE BAHATI LUKWEBO.

Minister of Public Health: FÉLIX KABANGE NUMBI MUKWAMPA.

Minister of Higher and University Education and Scientific Research: CHELO LOTSIMA.

Minister of Primary and Secondary Education and Professional Training: MAKER MWANGU FAMBA.

Minister of Agriculture and Rural Development: JEAN CHRISOSTOME VAHAMWITI MUKESYAYIRA.

Minister of Land Affairs: ROBERT MBWINGA BILA.

Minister of Social Affairs, Humanitarian Action and National Solidarity: CHARLES NAWEJ MUNDELE.

Minister of Gender Equality, the Family and Children: GENEVIÈVE INAGOSI.

Minister of the Civil Service: JEAN CLAUDE KIBALA.

Minister of Youth, Sport, Culture and the Arts: BANZA MUKALAYI NSUNGU.

Minister-delegate to the Prime Minister, in charge of Finance: PATRICE KITEBI KIBOL MVUL.

There were also eight deputy ministers.

MINISTRIES

Office of the President: Hôtel du Conseil Exécutif, ave de Lemera, Kinshasa-Gombe; tel. (12) 30892; internet www.presidentrdc.cd.

Office of the Prime Minister: Kinshasa.

Ministry of Agriculture and Rural Development: Kinshasa.

Ministry of the Budget: blvd du 30 juin, Immeuble Alhadeff, Kinshasa; internet www.ministeredubudget.cd.

Ministry of the Civil Service: Kinshasa.

Ministry of Employment, Labour and Social Security: blvd du 30 juin, BP 3840, Kinshasa-Gombe.

Ministry of the Environment, Conservation of Nature and Tourism: 76 ave des Cliniques, Kinshasa-Gombe; tel. 8802401; internet www.minenv.itgo.com.

Ministry of Finance: blvd du 30 juin, BP 12998 KIN I, Kinshasa-Gombe; tel. (12) 33232; internet www.minfinrdc.cd.

Ministry of Foreign Affairs, International Co-operation and the Francophonie: Kinshasa.

Ministry of Gender Equality, the Family and Children: Kinshasa.

Ministry of Higher and University Education and Scientific Research: Kinshasa.

Ministry of Hydrocarbons: Kinshasa.

Ministry of Industry and Small and Medium-sized Enterprises: Kinshasa.

Ministry of the Interior, Security, Decentralization and Traditional Affairs: ave de Lemera, Kinshasa-Gombe; tel. (12) 23171.

Ministry of Justice and Human Rights: 228 ave de Lemera, BP 3137, Kinshasa-Gombe; tel. (12) 32432.

Ministry of Land Affairs: Kinshasa.

Ministry of Land Settlement, Town Planning, Housing, Infrastructure, Public Works and Reconstruction: Kinshasa.

Ministry of Media: Immeuble RATELESCO, 83 ave Tombalbaye, Kinshasa; tel. 818134753; e-mail mincomedia.rdc@gmail.com; internet www.comediardc.org.

Ministry of Mines: Kinshasa; internet www.miningcongo.cd.

Ministry of National Defence and War Veterans: BP 4111, Kinshasa-Gombe; tel. (12) 59375.

Ministry of Planning, Implementation and of Modernization: 4155 ave des Côteaux, BP 9378, Kinshasa-Gombe 1; tel. 810306644; e-mail miniplan@micronet.cd; internet www.ministereduplan.cd.

Ministry of Posts, Telecommunications and New Information and Communication Technologies: Immeuble Kilou, 4484 ave des Huiles, BP 800 KIN I, Kinshasa-Gombe; tel. (12) 24854.

Ministry of Primary and Secondary Education and Professional Training: Enceinte de l'Institut de la Gombe, BP 3163, Kinshasa-Gombe; tel. (12) 30098; internet www.eduquepsp.org.

Ministry of Public Health: blvd du 30 juin, BP 3088 KIN I, Kinshasa-Gombe; tel. (12) 31750.

Ministry of Social Affairs, Humanitarian Action and National Solidarity: Kinshasa.

Ministry of Transport and Communication Routes: Immeuble ONATRA, blvd du 30 juin, BP 3304, Kinshasa-Gombe; tel. (12) 23660.

Ministry of Water Resources and Electricity: Immeuble SNEL, 239 ave de la Justice, BP 5137 KIN I, Kinshasa-Gombe; tel. (12) 22570.

Ministry of Youth, Sport, Culture and the Arts: 77 ave de la Justice, BP 8541 KIN I, Kinshasa-Gombe.

President and Legislature

PRESIDENT

Presidential Election, 28–29 November 2011, provisional results

Candidate	Votes	% of votes
Joseph Kabila Kabange (Ind.)	8,880,944	48.95
Etienne Tshisekedi Wa Mulumba (Union pour la Démocratie et le Progrès Social)	5,864,775	32.33
Vital Kamerhe Lwa-Kanyiginyi (Union pour la Nation Congolaise)	1,403,372	7.74
Léon Kengo Wa Dondo (Union des Forces du Changement)	898,362	4.95
Antipas Mbusa Nyamwisi (Ind.)	311,787	1.72
François Joseph Mobutu Nzanga Ngbangawe (Union des Démocrates Mobutistes)	285,273	1.57
Jean Andeka Djamba (Alliance des Nationalistes Croyants Congolais)	128,820	0.71
Adam Bombole Intole (Ind.)	126,623	0.70
François Nicéphore Kakese Malela (Union pour le Réveil et le Développement du Congo)	92,737	0.51
Josué Alex Mukendi Kamama (Ind.)	78,151	0.43
Dr. Oscar Kashala Lukumuena (Union pour la Réconstruction du Congo)	72,260	0.40
Total	18,143,104*	100.00

* In addition, there were 768,468 blank or invalid votes.

LEGISLATURE

The bicameral Parlement of the Democratic Republic of the Congo comprises a lower chamber, or Assemblée nationale, and an upper chamber, or Sénat, members of which are elected by the deputies of the provincial Assemblées.

Assemblée nationale

President: AUBIN MINAKU.

General Election, 28–29 November 2011, provisional results

Party	Seats
Parti du Peuple pour la Reconstruction et la Démocratie (PPRD)	62
Union pour la Démocratie et le Progrès Social (UDPS/ Tshisekedi)	41
Parti du Peuple pour la Paix et la Démocratie (PPPD)	29
Mouvement Social pour le Renouveau (MSR)	27
Mouvement de Libération du Congo (MLC)	22
Parti Lumumbiste Unifié (PALU)	19
Union pour la Nation Congolaise (UNC)	17
Alliance pour le Renouveau au Congo (ARC)	16
Alliance des Forces Démocratiques du Congo (AFDC)	15
Eveil de la Conscience pour le Travail et le Développement (ECT)	11
Rassemblement pour la Reconstruction du Congo (RRC)	11
Mouvement pour l'Intégrité du Peuple (MIP)	10
Parti Démocrate Chrétien (PDC)	7
Union pour le Développement du Congo (UDCO)	7
Rassemblement Congolais pour la Démocratie—Kisangani Mouvement de Libération (RCD/K-ML)	6
Union Nationale des Démocrates Féderalistes (UNADEF)	6
Union des Nationalistes Féderalistes du Congo (UNAFEC)	6
Others*	147
Independents	16
Total	475†

* Comprising political parties that won fewer than six seats.
† The results in 25 constituencies had yet to be declared.

Sénat

President: LÉON KENGO WA DONDO.

Election, 19 January 2007

Party	Seats
Parti du Peuple pour la Reconstruction et la Démocratie	22
Mouvement de Libération du Congo	14
Forces du Renouveau	7
Rassemblement Congolais pour la Démocratie	7
Parti Démocrate Chrétien	6
Convention des Démocrates Chrétiens	3
Mouvement Social pour le Renouveau	3
Parti Lumumbiste Unifié	2
Others*	18
Independents	26
Total	108

* Comprising 18 political parties that each won one seat.

Election Commission

Commission Electorale Nationale Indépendante (CENI): 4471 blvd du 30 juin, Kinshasa; tel. 818110613; e-mail info@cei-rdc.org; internet www.ceni.gouv.cd; f. 2010 to replace the Commission Electorale Indépendante; 7 mems; Pres. Rev. DANIEL NGOY MULUNDA.

Political Organizations

In January 1999 a ban on the formation of political associations was officially ended, and in May 2001 remaining restrictions on the registration and operation of political parties were removed. At August 2011 some 417 political parties were registered with the Ministry of the Interior.

Alliance des Nationalistes Croyants Congolais (ANCC): Kinshasa; Pres. JEAN ANDEKA DJAMBA.

Alliance pour le Développement et la République (ADR): Kinshasa; f. 2011; Pres. FRANÇOIS MUAMBA TSHISHIMBI.

Camp de la Patrie: Kinshasa; Leader ARTHUR Z'AHIDI NGOMA.

Coalition des Démocrates Congolais (CODECO): f. 2006; Leader PIERRE WA SYAKASSIGHE PAY-PAY.

Congrès National pour la Défense du Peuple: Bukavu; tel. 993456427 (mobile); e-mail cndpadmin@cndp-congo.org; f. 2006; Pres. LAURENT NKUNDA MIHIGO; Sec. G. KAMBASU NGEVE.

Convention des Démocrates Chrétiens: Kinshasa; Leader FLORENTIN MOKONDA BONZA.

Démocratie Chrétienne Féderaliste—Convention des Féderalistes pour la Démocratie Chrétienne (DCF—COFEDEC): 2209 ave des Etoiles, Kinshasa-Gombe; Leader VENANT TSHIPASA VANGI.

Forces du Renouveau: Kinshasa; Leader ANTIPAS MBUSA NYAMWISI.

Alliance pour le Renouveau du Congo (ARC): 1165-1175 ave Tombalbaye, Kinshasa-Gombe; tel. 998911096 (mobile); fax 815947347 (mobile); e-mail arc_secgen@yahoo.fr; f. 2006; Leader OLIVIER KAMITATU ETSU.

Rassemblement Congolais pour la Démocratie—Mouvement de Libération (RCD—ML): 290 ave Libenge, Lingwala; broke away from main RCD in 1999; supported by Uganda; Pres. ANTIPAS MBUSA NYAMWISI.

Forces Novatrices pour l'Union et la Solidarité (FONUS): 13 ave de l'Enseignement, Kasa-Vubu, Kinshasa; f. 2004; advocates political pluralism; Pres. JOSEPH OLENGHANKOY; Sec.-Gen. JOHN KWET.

Front des Nationalistes Intégrationnistes (FNI): Bunia; f. 2003 in Uganda; ethnic Lendu rebel group, in conflict with Union des Patriotes Congolais in north-east; Leader FLORIBERT NDJABU NGABU.

Mouvement de Libération du Congo (MLC): 6 ave du Port, Kinshasa-Gombe; f. 1998; fmr Ugandan-supported rebel movement; incl. in Govt in July 2003; Leader JEAN-PIERRE BEMBA GOMBO; Sec.-Gen. THOMAS LUHAKA.

Mouvement Populaire de la Révolution (MPR): 5448 ave de la Justice, Immeuble Yoko, Kinshasa-Gombe; f. 1966 by Pres. Mobutu; sole legal political party until Nov. 1990; advocates national unity and opposes tribalism; Leader Prof. VUNDWAWE TE PEMAKO; Sec.-Gen. KITHIMA BIN RAMAZANI.

Mouvement Social pour le Renouveau (MSR): Kinshasa; f. 2006; Leader YVES MOBANDO YOGO.

Parti Démocrate Chrétien: Leader JOSÉ ENDUNDO BONONGE.

Parti Démocrate et Social Chrétien (PDSC): 3040 route de Matadi, C/Ngaliema, Kinshasa; tel. (12) 21211; f. 1990; centrist; Pres. ANDRÉ BOBOLIKO; Sec.-Gen. TUYABA LEWULA.

Parti Lumumbiste Unifié (PALU): 9 rue Cannas, C/Limete, Kinshasa; Leader ANTOINE GIZENGA.

Parti du Peuple pour la Reconstruction et la Démocratie (PPRD): Croisement des aves Pumbu et Batetela, Kinshasa-Gombe; f. March 2002 by Pres. Joseph Kabila; Sec.-Gen. EVARISTE BOSHAB.

Parti pour l'Unité et la Sauvegarde de l'Intégrité du Congo (PUSIC): Bunia; coalition of 4 tribal militia groups, led by Hema; Leader ROBERT PIMBU.

Rassemblement Congolais pour la Démocratie (RCD—Goma): 26 ave Lukusa, Kinshasa-Gombe; f. 1998; rebel movement until Dec. 2002 peace agreement; incl. in Govt July 2003; main Ilunga faction; supported by Rwanda; Leader AZARIAS RUBERWA; Sec.-Gen. FRANCIS BEDY MAKHUBU MABELE.

Rassemblement Congolais pour la Démocratie—National (RCD—N): blvd du 30 juin, S.V./64 Haut-Uélé (Isiro); broke away from RCD—ML in Oct. 2000; Leader ROGER LUMBALA.

Rassemblement des Forces Sociales et Fédéralistes (RSF): 98 rue Poto-poto, Kimbanseke; Leader VINCENT DE PAUL LUNDA BULULU.

Rassemblement pour une Nouvelle Société (RNS): 1 bis rue Lufu, C/Bandalungwa; e-mail info@congozaire.org; Leader Dr ALAFUELE M. KALALA.

Union des Démocrates Mobutistes (UDEMO): f. by son of fmr Pres. Mobutu; Leader FRANÇOIS JOSEPH MOBUTU NZANGA NGBANGAWE.

Union des Forces du Changement (UFC): Kinshasa; Pres. LÉON KENGO WA DONDO.

Union des Nationalistes Fédéralistes du Congo (UNAFEC): 5 ave Citronniers, Kinshasa-Gombe; Leader GABRIEL KYUNGA WA KUMWANZA.

Union des Patriotes Congolais (UPC): 25 blvd de la Libération, Bunia; rebel group of Hema ethnic group, fmrly in conflict with Lendu in north-east; registered as political org. 2004, after peace agreement with Govt; Leader THOMAS LUBANGA.

Union pour la Démocratie et le Progrès Social (UDPS): 546 ave Zinnia, Limete, Kinshasa; tel. 813140685 (mobile); e-mail udps@udps.net; internet www.udps.net; f. 1982; Leader Dr ETIENNE TSHISEKEDI WA MULUMBA; Sec.-Gen. RÉMY MASSAMBA.

Union pour la Nation Congolaise (UNC): ave Croix-Rouge 3, Commune de Barumbu, Kinshasa; tel. 999915385 (mobile); e-mail unc_sg@yahoo.fr; internet www.unc-rdc.com; Pres. VITAL KAMERHE LWA-KANYIGINYI.

Union pour la Reconstruction du Congo (UREC): Leader OSCAR LUKUMWENA KASHALA.

Union pour la République (UPR): 622 ave Monts des Arts, Kinshasa-Gombe; f. 1997; by fmr mems of the MPR; Leader BOBOY NYABAKA.

Union pour la République—Mouvement National (UNIR—MN): Immeuble VeVe center, 2 rue de Bongandanga, c/Kasa-Vubu, Kinshasa; tel. 812431078 (mobile); e-mail info@unir-mn.org; internet www.unir-mn.org; f. 2001; officially registered as a political party in 2005; Pres. FRÉDÉRIC BOYENGA-BOFALA; Sec.-Gen. OLIVIER MESKENS NTAMBU KUFUANGA.

Diplomatic Representation

EMBASSIES IN THE DEMOCRATIC REPUBLIC OF THE CONGO

Algeria: 50–52 ave Col Ebeya, Gombe, Kinshasa; tel. 818803717 (mobile); fax 813010577 (mobile); Ambassador ABDELDJALIL BELALA.

Angola: 4413–4429 blvd du 30 juin, BP 8625, Kinshasa; tel. (12) 32415; fax (13) 98971; e-mail consangolakatanga@voila.fr; Ambassador EMILIO DE CARVALHO GUERRA.

Belgium: Immeuble Le Cinquantenaire, pl. du 27 octobre, BP 899, Kinshasa; tel. (12) 20110; fax (12) 21058; e-mail kinshasa@diplobel.fed.be; internet www.diplobel.org/congo; Ambassador DOMINIQUE STRUYE DE SWIELANDE.

Benin: 3990 ave des Cliniques, BP 3265, Kinshasa-Gombe; tel. 98128659; e-mail abkin@raga.net; Ambassador OUSSOU-EDOUARDS AHO-GLELE.

Cameroon: 171 blvd du 30 juin, BP 10998, Kinshasa; tel. (12) 34787; Ambassador MARTIN CHUNGONG AYAFOR.

Canada: 17 ave Pumbu, Commune de la Gombe, BP 8341, Kinshasa 1; tel. 898950310 (mobile); fax 999975403 (mobile); e-mail knsha@international.gc.ca; internet www.dfait-maeci.gc.ca/world/embassies/drc; Ambassador JEAN-CAROL PELLETIER.

Central African Republic: 11 ave Pumbu, BP 7769, Kinshasa; tel. (12) 30417; Ambassador JOB ISIMA.

Chad: 67–69 ave du Cercle, BP 9097, Kinshasa; tel. (12) 22358; Ambassador (vacant).

Congo, Republic: 179 blvd du 30 juin, BP 9516, Kinshasa; tel. (12) 34028; Ambassador GUSTAVE ZOULA.

Côte d'Ivoire: 68 ave de la Justice, BP 9197, Kinshasa; tel. (12) 21208; Ambassador GUILLAUME AHIPEAU.

Cuba: 4660 ave Cateam, BP 10699, Kinshasa; tel. (12) 8803823; Ambassador LUIS CASTILLO.

Egypt: 519 ave de l'Ouganda, BP 8838, Kinshasa; tel. (51) 10137; fax (88) 03728; Ambassador MUHAMMAD EZZELDIN FODA.

Ethiopia: BP 8435, Kinshasa; tel. (12) 23327; Ambassador DIEUDONNE A. GANGA.

France: 97 ave de la République du Tchad, BP 3093, Kinshasa; tel. 815559999 (mobile); fax 815559937 (mobile); e-mail ambafrancerdc@gmail.com; internet www.ambafrance-cd.org; Ambassador PIERRE JACQUEMOT.

Gabon: ave du 24 novembre, BP 9592, Kinshasa; tel. (12) 68325; Ambassador CHRISTOPHE ELLA EKOGHA.

Germany: 82 ave Roi Baudouin, BP 8400, Kinshasa-Gombe; tel. 815561380 (mobile); e-mail amballemagne@ic.cd; internet www.kinshasa.diplo.de; Ambassador Dr AXEL WEISHAUPT.

Greece: Immeuble de la Communauté Hellénique, 3ème étage, blvd du 30 juin, BP 478, Kinshasa; tel. 815554941 (mobile); fax 815554945 (mobile); e-mail gremb.kin@mfa.gr; Ambassador KATRANIS ALEXANDROS.

Holy See: 81 ave Goma, BP 3091, Kinshasa; tel. (88) 08814; fax (88) 48483; e-mail nuntius@raga.net; Apostolic Nuncio Most Rev. ADOLFO TITO YLLANA (Titular Archbishop of Montecorvino).

India: 18B, ave Batetela, Commune de la Gombe, Kinshasa; tel. 815559770 (mobile); fax 815559774 (mobile); e-mail amb.indembkin@gbs.cd; Ambassador DEVENDRA NATH SRIVASTAVA.

Japan: Immeuble Citibank, 2ème étage, ave Colonel Lukusa, BP 1810, Kinshasa; tel. 818845305 (mobile); fax 870-7639-59668 (satellite); e-mail ambjaponrdc@yahoo.fr; internet www.rdc.emb-japan.go.jp; Ambassador TOMINAGA YOSHIMASA.

Kenya: 4002 ave de l'Ouganda, BP 9667, Kinshasa; tel. 815554797 (mobile); fax 815554805 (mobile); e-mail kinshasa@mfa.go.ke; Ambassador KARUCHU SYLVESTER GAKUMU.

Korea, Democratic People's Republic: 168 ave de l'Ouganda, BP 16597, Kinshasa; tel. 8801443 (mobile); fax 815300194 (mobile); e-mail kenem-drc@jobantech.cd; Ambassador RI MYONG-CHOL.

Korea, Republic: 65 blvd Tshatshi, BP 628, Kinshasa; tel. 819820302 (mobile); e-mail amb-rdc@mofat.go.kr; Ambassador LEE HO-SUNG.

Lebanon: 3 ave de l'Ouganda, Kinshasa; tel. (12) 82469; Ambassador SAAD ZAKHIA.

Liberia: 3 ave de l'Okapi, BP 8940, Kinshasa; tel. (12) 82289; Ambassador JALLA D. LANSANAH.

Mauritania: BP 16397, Kinshasa; tel. (12) 59575; Ambassador Lt-Col M'BARECK OULD BOUNA MOKHTAR.

Morocco: POB 912, ave Corteaux et Vallée No. 40, Kinshasa 1; tel. (12) 34794; Ambassador MOHAMED BEN KADDOUR.

Netherlands: 11 ave Zongontolo, 55 Immeuble Residence, BP 10299, Kinshasa; tel. 996050600 (mobile); fax 996050629 (mobile); e-mail kss@minbuza.nl; internet drcongo.nlambassade.org; Ambassador ROBERT VAN EMBDEN.

Nigeria: 141 blvd du 30 juin, BP 1700, Kinshasa; tel. 817005142 (mobile); fax 812616115 (mobile); e-mail nigemb@jobantech.cd; Ambassador GRANT EHIOBUCHE.

Portugal: 270 ave des Aviateurs, BP 7775, Kinshasa; tel. 815161277 (mobile); e-mail ambassadeportugal@micronet.net; Ambassador JOÃO PERESTRELLO.

Russia: 80 ave de la Justice, BP 1143, Kinshasa 1; tel. (12) 33157; fax (12) 45575; e-mail amrussie@ic.cd; Ambassador ANATOLII KLIMENKO.

Rwanda: Kinshasa; Ambassador AMANDIN RUGIRA.

South Africa: 77 ave Ngongo Lutete, BP 7829, Kinshasa-Gombe; tel. 814769100 (mobile); fax 815554322 (mobile); e-mail pearces@foreign.gov.za; Ambassador JOSEPH NTSHIKIWANE MASHIMBYE.

Spain: blvd du 30 juin, Bldg Communauté Hellénique, Commune de la Gombe, BP 8036, Kinshasa; tel. 818843195 (mobile); fax 813010396 (mobile); e-mail emb.kinshasa@mae.es; Ambassador Dr FÉLIX COSTALES ARTIEDA.

Sudan: 24 ave de l'Ouganda, Kinshasa; tel. 999937396 (mobile); Ambassador GAAFAR BABIKER EL-KHALIFA EL-TAYEB.

Sweden: 93 ave Roi Baudouin, Commune de la Gombe, BP 11096, Kinshasa; tel. 999301102 (mobile); fax 870-600-147849 (satellite);

e-mail ambassaden.kinshasa@foreign.ministry.se; internet www.swedenabroad.com/kinshasa; Ambassador METTE SUNNERGREN.

Switzerland: 654 blvd Col Tshatshi, BP 8724, Gombe, Kinshasa; tel. 898946800 (mobile); e-mail kin.vertretung@eda.admin.ch; internet www.eda.admin.ch/kinshasa; Ambassador JACQUES GREMAUD.

Tanzania: 142 blvd du 30 juin, BP 1612, Kinshasa; tel. 815565850 (mobile); fax 815565852 (mobile); e-mail tanzanrepkinshasa@yahoo.com; Ambassador GORDON LUHWANO NGILANGWA.

Togo: 3 ave de la Vallée, BP 10117, Kinshasa; tel. (12) 30666; Ambassador YAWO ADOMAYAKPOR.

Tunisia: 67–69 ave du Cercle, BP 1498, Kinshasa; tel. 818803901 (mobile); e-mail atkinshasa@yahoo.fr; Ambassador EZZEDDINE ZAYANI.

Uganda: ave des Cocotiers, Plot no. 15, pl. Wenge, Commune de la Gombe, BP 8804, Kinshasa; tel. 810507179 (mobile); e-mail ugambassy@simbatel.com; Ambassador Maj. JAMES KINOBE.

United Kingdom: 83 ave Roi Baudouin, BP 8049, Kinshasa; tel. 817150761 (mobile); fax 813464291 (mobile); e-mail ambrit@ic.cd; Ambassador NEIL WIGAN.

USA: 310 ave des Aviateurs, BP 397, Kinshasa; tel. 815560151 (mobile); fax 815560173 (mobile); e-mail AEKinshasaConsular@state.gov; internet kinshasa.usembassy.gov; Ambassador JAMES FREDERICK ENTWISTLE.

Zambia: 54–58 ave de l'Ecole, BP 1144, Kinshasa; tel. 819999437 (mobile); fax (88) 45106; e-mail ambazambia@ic.cd; Ambassador MAYBIN KAMBAMBA MUBANGA.

Judicial System

Under the Constitution that entered into effect in February 2006, the judicial system is independent. Members of the judiciary are under the authority of the Conseil Supérieur de la Magistrature. The Cour de Cassation has jurisdiction over legal decisions and the Conseil d'État over administrative decisions. The Cour Constitutionnelle interprets the provisions of the Constitution and ensures the conformity of new legislation. The judicial system also comprises a Haute Cour Militaire, and lower civil and military courts and tribunals. The Conseil Supérieur de la Magistrature has 18 members, including the Presidents and Chief Prosecutors of the main courts. The Cour Constitutionnelle comprises nine members, who are appointed by the President (including three nominated by the legislature and three by the Conseil Supérieur de la Magistrature) for a term of nine years. The Head of State appoints and dismisses magistrates, on the proposal of the Conseil Supérieur de la Magistrature.

Cour de Cassation

cnr ave de la Justice and ave de Lemera, BP 3382, Kinshasa-Gombe; tel. (12) 25104.

President of the Cour de Cassation: LWAMBA BINDU.

Procurator-General of the Republic: KABANGE NUMBI.

Cour Suprême de Justice: ave de la Justice 2, BP 13, Kinshasa-Gombe; Pres. BENOÎT LWAMBA BINDU.

Religion

Many of the country's inhabitants follow traditional beliefs, which are mostly animistic. A large proportion of the population is Christian, predominantly Roman Catholic, and there are small Muslim, Jewish and Greek Orthodox communities.

CHRISTIANITY

The Roman Catholic Church

The Democratic Republic of the Congo comprises six archdioceses and 41 dioceses. Some 51% of the population are Roman Catholics.

Bishops' Conference

Conférence Episcopale Nationale du Congo, BP 3258, Kinshasa-Gombe; tel. (12) 34528; fax (88) 44948; e-mail conf.episc.rdc@ic.cd; internet www.cenco.cd.

f. 1981; Pres. Most Rev. NICOLAS DJOMO LOLA (Bishop of Tshumbe).

Archbishop of Bukavu: FRANÇOIS-XAVIER MAROY RUSENGO, Archevêché, ave Mbaki 18, BP 3324, Bukavu; tel. 813180621 (mobile); e-mail archevechebk@yahoo.fr.

Archbishop of Kananga: Most Rev. MARCEL MADILA BASANGUKA, Archevêché, BP 70, Kananga; tel. 815013942 (mobile); e-mail archidiocesekananga@yahoo.fr.

Archbishop of Kinshasa: Cardinal LAURENT MONSENGWO PASINYA, Archevêché, ave de l'Université, BP 8431, Kinshasa 1; tel. (12) 3723546; e-mail archikin@ic.cd.

Archbishop of Kisangani: Most Rev. LAURENT MONSENGWO PASINYA, Archevêché, ave Mpolo 10B, BP 505, Kisangani; tel. 812006715 (mobile); fax (761) 608336.

Archbishop of Lubumbashi: Most Rev. JEAN-PIERRE TAFUNGA MBAYO, Archevêché, BP 72, Lubumbashi; tel. 997031991 (mobile); e-mail archidiolub@mwangaza.cd.

Archbishop of Mbandaka-Bikoro: Most Rev. JOSEPH KUMUONDALA MBIMBA, Archevêché, BP 1064, Mbandaka; tel. 817301027 (mobile); e-mail mbandakabikoro@yahoo.fr.

The Anglican Communion

The Church of the Province of the Congo comprises eight dioceses.

Archbishop of the Province of the Congo and Bishop of Kinshasa: Most Rev. Dr DIROKPA BALUFUGA FIDÈLE, 11 ave Basalakala, Quartier Immocongo, Commune de Kalamu, BP 16482, Kinshasa; tel. 998611180 (mobile); e-mail dirokpa1@hotmail.com.

Bishop of Arua: Rt Rev. Dr GEORGE TITRE ANDE, POB 226, Arua, Uganda; tel. 810393071 (mobile); e-mail revdande@yahoo.co.uk.

Bishop of Boga: Rt Rev. HENRY KAHWA ISINGOMA, CAC- Boga, Congo Liaison Office, POB 25586, Kampala, Uganda; e-mail peac_isingoma@yahoo.fr.

Bishop of Bukavu: Rt Rev. SYLVESTRE BALI-BUSANE BAHATI, CAC-Bukavu, POB 53435, Nairobi, Kenya.

Bishop of Katanga: Rt Rev. MUNO KASIMA, c/o UMM, POB 22037, Kitwe, Zambia; tel. 97047173 (mobile); fax (88) 46383; e-mail peac_isingoma@yahoo.fr.

Bishop of Kindu: Rt Rev. ZACHARIE MASIMANGO KATANDA, c/o ESCO Uganda, POB 7892, Kampala, Uganda; e-mail angkindu@yahoo.fr.

Bishop of Kisangani: Rt Rev. LAMBERT FUNGA BOTOLOME, c/o Congo Liaison Office, POB 25586, Kampala, Uganda; e-mail lambertfunga@hotmail.com.

Bishop of Nord Kivu: Rt Rev. METHUSELA MUSUBAHO MUNZENDA, CAZ-Butembo, POB 506, Bwera-Kasese, Uganda; fax 870-166-1121 (satellite); e-mail munzenda_eac@yahoo.fr.

Kimbanguist

Eglise de Jésus Christ sur la Terre par le Prophète Simon Kimbangu: BP 7069, Kinshasa; tel. (12) 68944; f. 1921; officially est. 1959; c. 5m. mems (1985); Spiritual Head HE SALOMON DIALUNGANA KIANGANI; Sec.-Gen. Rev. LUNTADILLA.

Protestant Churches

Eglise du Christ au Congo (ECC): ave de la Justice 75, BP 4938, Kinshasa-Gombe; internet congodisciples.org; f. 1902; a co-ordinating agency for all the Protestant churches, with the exception of the Kimbanguist Church; 62 mem. communities and a provincial org. in each province; Pres. Bishop MARINI BODHO; includes:

Communauté Baptiste du Congo-Ouest: BP 4728, Kinshasa 2; f. 1970; 450 parishes; Gen. Sec. Rev. LUSAKWENO-VANGU.

Communauté des Disciples du Christ: BP 178, Mbandaka; tel. 31062; f. 1964; 250 parishes; Gen. Sec. Rev. Dr ELONDA EFEFE.

Communauté Episcopale Baptiste en Afrique: 2 ave Jason Sendwe, BP 2809, Lubumbashi 1; tel. and fax (2) 348602; e-mail kitobokabwe@yahoo.fr; f. 1956; 1,300 episcopal communions and parishes; 150,000 mems (2001); Pres. Bishop KITOBO KABWEKA-LEZA.

Communauté Evangélique: BP 36, Luozi; f. 1961; 50 parishes; Pres. Rev. K. LUKOMBO NTONTOLO.

Communauté Lumière: BP 10498, Kinshasa 1; f. 1931; 150 parishes; Patriarch KAYUWA TSHIBUMBU WA KAHINGA.

Communauté Mennonite: BP 18, Tshikapa; f. 1960; Gen. Sec. Rev. KABANGY DJEKE SHAPASA.

Communauté Presbytérienne: BP 117, Kananga; f. 1959; Gen. Sec. Dr M. L. TSHIHAMBA.

Eglise Missionaire Apostolique: 375 ave Commerciale, BP 15859, Commune de N'Djili, Kinshasa 1; tel. 988165927; e-mail buzi4@hotmail.com; f. 1986; 5 parishes; 2,600 mems; Apostle for Africa Rev. LUFANGA-AYIMOU NANANDANA.

Evangelical Lutheran Church in Congo: 150 ave Kasaï, Lumbabashi; tel. (2) 22396; fax (2) 24098; e-mail bnationaleelco@yahoo.fr; 136,000 mems (2010); Pres. Bishop RENÉ MWAMBA SUMAILI.

The Press

DAILIES

L'Analyste: 129 ave du Bas-Congo, BP 91, Kinshasa-Gombe; tel. (12) 80987; Dir and Editor-in-Chief BONGOMA KONI BOTAHE.

L'Avenir: Immeuble Ruzizi, 873 ave Bas-Congo, Kinshasa-Gombe; tel. 999942485 (mobile); internet www.groupelavenir.cd; owned by Groupe de l'avenir; Chair. PIUS MUABILU.

Elima: 1 ave de la Révolution, BP 11498, Kinshasa; tel. (12) 77332; f. 1928; evening; Dir and Editor-in-Chief ESSOLOMWA NKOY EA LINGANGA.

Mjumbe: BP 2474, Lubumbashi; f. 1963; Dir and Editor TSHIMANGA KOYA KAKONA.

Le Phare: bldg du 29 juin, ave Col Lukusa 3392, BP 2481, Kinshasa; tel. 813330195 (mobile); e-mail info@le-phare.com; internet www.lepharerdc.com; f. 1983; Editor POLYDOR MUBOYAYI MUBANGA; circ. 5,000 (2012).

Le Potentiel: Immeuble Ruzizi, 873 ave du Bas-Congo, BP 11338, Kinshasa; tel. 98135483; e-mail lepotentiel@lepotentiel.com; internet www.lepotentiel.com; f. 1982; Editor MODESTE MUTINGA MUTUISHAYI; circ. 8,000.

La Prospérité: Kinshasa; tel. 818135157 (mobile); e-mail marcelngo@yahoo.fr; internet www.laprosperiteonline.net; f. 2001; Dir-Gen. MARCEL NGOYI.

Le Palmarès: Kinshasa.

La Référence Plus: BP 22520, Kinshasa; tel. (12) 45783; f. 1989; Dir ANDRÉ IPAKALA.

PERIODICALS

Afrique Editions: Kinshasa; tel. (88) 43202; e-mail bpongo@raga.net.

Allo Kinshasa: 3 rue Kayange, BP 20271, Kinshasa-Lemba; monthly; Editor MBUYU WA KABILA.

L'Aurore Protestante: Eglise du Christ au Congo, BP 4938, Kinshasa-Gombe; French; religion; monthly; circ. 10,000.

Cahiers Economiques et Sociaux: BP 257, Kinshasa XI, (National University of the Congo); sociological, political and economic review; quarterly; Dir Prof. NDONGALA TADI LEWA; circ. 2,000.

Cahiers des Religions Africaines: Faculté de Théologie Catholique de Kinshasa, BP 712, Kinshasa/Limete; tel. (12) 78476; f. 1967; English and French; religion; 2 a year; circ. 1,000.

Le Canard Libre: Kinshasa; f. 1991; Editor JOSEPH CASTRO MULEBE.

La Colombe: 32B ave Tombalbaye, Kinshasa-Gombe; tel. (12) 21211; organ of Parti démocrate et social chrétien; circ. 5,000.

Congo-Afrique: Centre d'Etudes pour l'Action Sociale, 9 ave Père Boka, BP 3375, Kinshasa-Gombe; tel. 898912981 (mobile); e-mail congoafrique@yahoo.fr; internet www.congo-afrique.org; f. 1961; economic, social and cultural; monthly; Editors FRANCIS KIKASSA MWANALESSA, RENÉ BEECKMANS; circ. 2,500.

Le Conseiller Comptable: 51 rue du Grand Séminaire, Quartier Nganda, BP 308, Kinshasa; tel. (88) 01216; fax (88) 00075; f. 1974; French; public finance and taxation; quarterly; Editor TOMENA FOKO; circ. 2,000.

Documentation et Information Protestante (DIP): Eglise du Christ au Congo, BP 4938, Kinshasa-Gombe; tel. and fax (88) 46387; e-mail eccm@ic.cd; French and English; religion.

Documentation et Informations Africaines (DIA): BP 2598, Kinshasa 1; tel. (12) 33197; fax (12) 33196; e-mail dia@ic.cd; internet www.peacelink.it/dia/index.html; Roman Catholic news agency reports; 3 a week; Dir Rev. Père VATA DIAMBANZA.

L'Entrepreneur Flash: Association Nationale des Entreprises du Congo, 10 ave des Aviateurs, BP 7247, Kinshasa 1; tel. (12) 22565; f. 1978; business news; monthly; circ. 1,000.

Etudes d'Histoire Africaine: National University of the Congo, BP 1825, Lubumbashi; f. 1970; French and English; history; annually; circ. 1,000.

KYA: 24 ave de l'Équateur, BP 7853, Kinshasa-Gombe; tel. (12) 27502; f. 1984; weekly for Bas-Congo; Editor (vacant).

Libération: Kinshasa; f. 1997; politics; supports the AFDL; weekly; Man. NGOYI KABUYA DIKATETA M'MIANA.

Mambenga 2000: BP 477, Mbandaka; Editor BOSANGE YEMA BOF.

Le Moniteur de l'Economie (Economic Monitor): Kinshasa; Man. Editor FÉLIX NZUZI.

Mutaani Magazine: Goma; tel. 995652115 (mobile); f. 2012.

Mwana Shaba: Générale des Carrières et des Mines, BP 450, Lubumbashi; monthly; circ. 25,000.

Njanja: Société Nationale des Chemins de Fer du Congo, 115 pl. de la Gare, BP 297, Lubumbashi; tel. (2) 23430; fax (2) 61321; railways and transportation; annually; circ. 10,000.

NUKTA: 14 chaussée de Kasenga, BP 3805, Lubumbashi; weekly; agriculture; Editor NGOY BUNDUKI.

Post: Immeuble Linzadi, 1538 ave de la Douane, Kinshasa-Gombe; e-mail thepostrdc@yahoo.com; internet www.congoonline.com/thepost; 2 a week; Editor-in-Chief MUKEBAYI NKOSO.

Problèmes Sociaux Zaïrois: Centre d'Exécution de Programmes Sociaux et Economiques, Université de Lubumbashi, 208 ave Kasavubu, BP 1873, Lubumbashi; f. 1946; quarterly; Editor N'KASHAMA KADIMA.

Promoteur Congolais: Centre du Commerce International du Congo, 119 ave Colonel Tshatshi, BP 13, Kinshasa; f. 1979; international trade news; 6 a year.

Sciences, Techniques, Informations: Centre de Recherches Industrielles en Afrique Centrale (CRIAC), BP 54, Lubumbashi.

Le Sport Africain: 13è niveau Tour adm., Cité de la Voix du Congo, BP 3356, Kinshasa-Gombe; monthly; Pres. TSHIMPUMPU WA TSHIMPUMPU.

Taifa: 536 ave Lubumba, BP 884, Lubumbashi; weekly; Editor LWAMBWA MILAMBU.

Telema: Faculté Canisius, Kimwenza, BP 3724, Kinshasa-Gombe; f. 1974; religious; quarterly; edited by the Central Africa Jesuits; circ. 1,200.

Vision: Kinshasa; 2 a week; independent; Man. Editor XAVIER BONANE YANGANZI.

La Voix des Sans-Voix: ave des Ecuries 3858, commune de Ngaliema, BP 11445, Kinshasa-Gombe; tel. (88) 40394; fax (88) 01826; e-mail vsv@ic.cd; internet www.congonline.com/vsv.

La Voix du Paysan Congolais: 1150 ave Tabora, C/Barumbu, BP 14582, Kinshasa; tel. 0999982097 (mobile); fax 0017754027683; e-mail lavoixdupaysan_rdc@yahoo.fr; internet lavoixdupaysancongolais.com; f. 2008; agricultural issues; 4 a year; Dir of Publication JEAN BAPTISTE LUBAMBA.

NEWS AGENCIES

Agence Congolaise de Presse (ACP): 44–48 ave Tombalbaye, BP 1595, Kinshasa 1; tel. 816573788 (mobile); e-mail info@acpcongo.cd; internet www.acpcongo.cd; f. 1957; state-controlled; Dir-Gen. JEAN-MARIE VIANNEY LONGONYA (acting).

Digital Congo: 21 ave Kabasele Tshiamala, Kinshasa-Gombe; tel. 8941010; e-mail lettres@digitalcongo.net; internet www.digitalcongo.net; news service owned by Multimedia Congo.

Documentation et Informations Africaines (DIA): BP 2598, Kinshasa 1; tel. (12) 34528; f. 1957; Roman Catholic news agency; Dir Rev. Père VATA DIAMBANZA.

Press Association

Union Nationale de la Presse du Congo (UNPC): BP 4941, Kinshasa 1; tel. (12) 24437.

Publishers

Aequatoria Centre: BP 276, Mbandaka; f. 1980; anthropology, biography, ethnicity, history, language and linguistics, social sciences; Dir HONORÉ VINCK.

CEEBA Publications: BP 246, Bandundu; f. 1965; humanities, languages, fiction; Man. Dir (Editorial) Dr HERMANN HOCHEGGER.

Centre de Documentation Agricole: BP 7537, Kinshasa 1; tel. (12) 32498; agriculture, science; Dir PIERTE MBAYAKABUYI; Chief Editor J. MARCELLIN KAPUKUNGESA.

Centre de Linguistique Théorique et Appliquée (CELTA): BP 4956, Kinshasa-Gombe; tel. 818129998 (mobile); e-mail anyembwe@yahoo.fr; f. 1971; language, arts and linguistics; Dir-Gen. ANDRÉ NYEMBWE NTITA.

Centre de Recherches Pédagogiques: BP 8815, Kinshasa 1; f. 1959; accounting, education, geography, language, science; Dir P. DETIENNE.

Centre de Vulgarisation Agricole: BP 4008, Kinshasa 2; tel. (12) 71165; fax (12) 21351; agriculture, environment, health; Dir-Gen. KIMPIANGA MAHANIAH.

Centre International de Sémiologie: 109 ave Pruniers, BP 1825, Lubumbashi.

Centre Protestant d'Editions et de Diffusion (CEDI): 209 ave Kalémie, BP 11398, Kinshasa 1; tel. (12) 22202; fax (12) 26730; f. 1935; fiction, poetry, biography, religious, juvenile; Christian tracts, works in French, Lingala, Kikongo, etc.; Dir-Gen. HENRY DIRKS.

Commission de l'Education Chrétienne: BP 3258, Kinshasa-Gombe; tel. (12) 30086; education, religion; Man. Dir Abbé MUGADJA LEHANI.

Connaissance et Pratique du Droit Congolais Editions (CDPC): BP 5502, Kinshasa-Gombe; f. 1987; law; Editor DIBUNDA KABUINJI.

Editions Lokole: BP 5085, Kinshasa 10; state org. for the promotion of literature; Dir BOKEME SHANE MOLOBAY.

Editions Paulines: BP 8505, Kinshasa; tel. 0998859777 (mobile); e-mail libanga.c@gmail.com; f. 1988; fiction, general non-fiction, poetry, religion, education; Dir CATTANEO PIERA; Sec. Sister M. ROSARIO ZAMBELLO.

Facultés Catholiques de Kinshasa: 2 ave de l'Université, Kinshasa-Limete; tel. and fax (12) 46965; e-mail facakin@ic.cd; f. 1957; anthropology, art, economics, history, politics, computer science; Rector Prof. Mgr HIPPOLYTE NGIMBI NSEKA.

Les Editions du Trottoir: BP 1800, Kinshasa; tel. (12) 9936043; e-mail smuyengo@yahoo.fr; f. 1989; communications, fiction, literature, drama; Pres. CHARLES DJUNJU-SIMBA.

Librairie les Volcans: 22 ave Pres. Mobutu, BP 400, Goma, Nord-Kivu; f. 1995; social sciences; Man. Dir RUHAMA MUKANDOLI.

Presses Universitaires du Congo (PUC): 290 rue d'Aketi, BP 1800, Kinshasa 1; tel. (12) 9936043; e-mail smuyengo@yahoo.fr; f. 1972; science, arts and communications; Dir Abbé SÉBASTIEN MUYENGO.

GOVERNMENT PUBLISHING HOUSE

Imprimerie du Gouvernement Central: BP 3021, Kinshasa-Kalina.

Broadcasting and Communications

REGULATORY AUTHORITY

Autorité de Régulation de la Poste et des Télécommunications du Congo (ARPTC): blvd du 30 juin, BP 3000, Kinshasa 1; tel. (13) 92491; e-mail info.arptc@arptc.cd; Pres. OSCAR MANIKUNDA.

Telecommunications

Airtel Congo: croisement des aves Tchad et Bas-Congo, Kinshasa; tel. 996000121 (mobile); e-mail info.airteldrc@cd.airtel.com; internet africa.airtel.com/drc; acquired by Bharti Airtel (India) in 2010; mobile cellular telephone network; fmrly Celtel Congo, subsequently Zain Congo, present name adopted in 2010; Dir-Gen. ANTOINE PAMBORO; 1.83m. subscribers (Dec. 2006).

Congo Chine Telecom (CCT): ave du Port, Kinshasa; tel. 8400085 (mobile); e-mail admin@cct.cd; internet www.cct.cd; mobile cellular telephone network; covers Kinshasa and Bas-Congo, Kasaï, Katanga and Orientale provinces; 100% owned by France Télécom; Dir-Gen. WANG XIANGGUO; 466,000 subscribers (Dec. 2006).

Oasis Telecom (Tigo): 372 ave Col Mondjiba, Kinshasa; tel. 898901000 (mobile); fax 898901001 (mobile); internet www.tigo.cd; 100% owned by Millicom; 50,000 subscribers (Dec. 2006).

Supercell: 99 ave des Tulipiers, BP 114, Goma; tel. 808313010 (mobile); e-mail rogern@supercell.cd; 69,000 subscribers.

Vodacom Congo: Immeuble Mobil–Oil, 2ème étage, 3157 blvd du 30 juin, BP 797, Kinshasa 1; tel. 813131000 (mobile); fax 813131351 (mobile); e-mail vodacom@vodacom.cd; internet www.vodacom.cd; 51% owned by Vodacom (South Africa); 2.33m. subscribers (Dec. 2006).

BROADCASTING

Radio-Télévision Nationale Congolaise (RTNC): ave Kabinda, Lingwala, Kinshasa; tel. 9999256200 (mobile); e-mail info@radiotele-rdc.net; internet www.radiotele-rdc.net; state radio, terrestrial and satellite television broadcasts; Dir-Gen. JOSE KAJANGUA.

Radio

Several private radio broadcasters operate in Kinshasa. Radio France Internationale broadcasts via FM in nine localities.

Radio Candip: Centre d'Animation et de Diffusion Pédagogique, BP 373, Bunia.

Mutaani FM: Goma; tel. 995652115 (mobile); internet mutaani.com/la_radio_en_direct; f. 2011.

Radio Okapi: 12 ave des Aviateurs, Gombe, Kinshasa; tel. 818906747 (mobile); e-mail contact@radiookapi.net; internet radiookapi.net; f. 2002; owned by the Fondation Hirondelle (Switzerland).

La Voix du Congo: Station Nationale, BP 3164, Kinshasa-Gombe; tel. (12) 23175; state-controlled; operated by RTNC; broadcasts in French, Swahili, Lingala, Tshiluba, Kikongo; regional stations at Kisangani, Lubumbashi, Bukavu, Bandundu, Kananga, Mbuji-Mayi, Matadi, Mbandaka and Bunia.

Television

Several private television broadcasters operate in Kinshasa.

Antenne A: Immeuble Forescom, 2ème étage, ave du Port 4, POB 2581, Kinshasa 1; tel. (12) 21736; private and commercial station; Dir-Gen. IGAL AVIVI NEIRSON.

Canal Z: ave du Port 6, POB 614, Kinshasa 1; tel. (12) 20239; commercial station; Dir-Gen. FRÉDÉRIC FLASSE.

Tele Kin Malebo (TKM): 32B route de Matadi, Ngaliema, Kinshasa; tel. (12) 2933338; e-mail malebokin@hotmail.com; private television station; nationalization announced 1997; Dir-Gen. NGONGO LUWOWO.

Télévision Congolaise: ave Kabinda, Lingwala, Kinshasa; tel. 9999256200 (mobile); e-mail info@radiotele-rdc.net; govt commercial station; operated by RTNC; broadcasts 2 channels.

Finance

(cap. = capital; res = reserves; dep. = deposits; m. = million; br(s). = branch(es); amounts in new Congolese francs unless otherwise indicated)

BANKING

The introduction as legal tender of a new currency unit, the new Congolese franc (CF), was completed on 30 June 1998. However, as a result of the civil conflict, its value immediately declined dramatically. In late 2003, following the restoration of relative peace and the installation of new transitional authorities, the central bank introduced new notes in an effort to revive the national currency and nation-wide operations were gradually restored. In 2010 there were 21 banks and 17 microfinance institutions.

Central Bank

Banque Centrale du Congo: 563 blvd Colonel Tshatshi au nord, BP 2697, Kinshasa; tel. 818105970 (mobile); fax (12) 8805152; e-mail webmaster@bcc.cd; internet www.bcc.cd; f. 1964; dep. 254,133m., total assets 2,174,871m. (Dec. 2009); Gov. JEAN-CLAUDE MASANGU MULONGO; 8 brs.

Commercial Banks

Advans Banque Congo: ave du Bas Congo 4, Commune de la Gombe, Kinshasa; tel. 995904466 (mobile); internet www.advansgroup.com; f. 2008; Dir-Gen. BRUNO DEGOY; 2 brs.

Afriland First Bank: 767 blvd du 30 juin, BP 10470, Kinshasa-Gombe; tel. 810775359 (mobile); e-mail jtoubi@afrilandfirstbank.com; internet www.afrilandfirstbank.com; f. 2004; 2 brs.

Bank of Africa: 22 ave des Aviateurs, Kinshasa-Gombe; tel. 993004600 (mobile); e-mail infos@boa-rdc.com; internet www.bank-of-africa.net; f. 2010; Pres. PAUL DERREUMAUX.

Banque Commerciale du Congo SARL (BCDC): blvd du 30 juin, BP 2798, Kinshasa 1; tel. 818845704 (mobile); fax 99631048 (mobile); e-mail dir@bcdc.cd; internet www.bcdc.cd; f. 1952 as Banque du Congo Belge; name changed as above 1997; cap. 4,975.8m., res 18,143.6m., dep. 207,535.8m. (Dec. 2009); Pres. GUY-ROBERT LUKAMA NKUNZI; Man. Dir YVES CUYPERS; 16 brs.

Banque Congolaise SARL: Immeuble Flavica 14/16, ave du Port, BP 9497, Kinshasa 1; tel. 996050000 (mobile); fax (13) 98298; e-mail bank@rayventures.com; internet www.congobank.com; f. 1988; cap. 14,363.0m., res –1,335.7m., dep. 170,284.4m. (Dec. 2008); Pres. ROGER ALFRED YAGHI; Dir-Gen. GEORGES ABILLAMA; 17 brs.

Banque Internationale de Crédit SARL (BIC): 191 ave de l'Equateur, BP 1299, Kinshasa 1; tel. 999921624 (mobile); fax 812616000 (mobile); e-mail bic@ic.cd; internet www.bic.cd; f. 1994; cap. and res 946.2m., dep. 12,352.7m. (Dec. 2003); Pres. PASCAL KINDUELO LUMBU; Dir-Gen. FREDERIC PULULU MANGONDA; 23 brs.

Banque Internationale pour l'Afrique au Congo (BIAC): 87 blvd du 30 juin, BP 8725, Kinshasa; tel. 815554000 (mobile); fax 8153010681 (mobile); e-mail contact@biac.cd; internet www.biac.cd; f. 1970; cap. 6,140.5m., res 5,539.4m., dep. 176,546.5m. (Dec. 2009); Pres. CHARLES SANLAVILLE; 30 brs.

Citigroup (Congo) SARL Congo: 657 Immeuble Citibank Congo, angle aves Col Lukusa et Ngongo Lutete, BP 9999, Kinshasa 1; tel. 815554808 (mobile); fax 813017070 (mobile); e-mail singa.boyenge@citicorp.com; f. 1971; res 1,111.5m., dep. 14,691.4m. (Dec. 2005); Man. Dir MICHAEL LOSEMBE; 1 br.

La Cruche Banque: 37 rue Kinshasa, Ville de Butembo, Nord-Kivu; tel. 815203045 (mobile); e-mail lacruchebank@yahoo.fr; internet www.lacruchebank.com; Pres. KATEMBO MBANGA.

Ecobank DRC: Immeuble Future Tower, 3642 blvd du 30 Juin, BP 7515, Kinshasa; tel. 996016000 (mobile); fax 996016070 (mobile); internet www.ecobank.com; Pres. JEAN-PIERRE KIWAKANA KIMAYALA; Dir Gen. SERGE ACKRE; 14 brs.

Rawbank Sarl: 3487 blvd du 30 juin, Immeuble Concorde, POB 2499, Kinshasa; tel. 998320000 (mobile); fax 89240224 (mobile); e-mail contact@rawbank.cd; internet www.rawbank.cd; f. 2002;

cap. 10,066.0m., res 12,982.6m., dep. 212,368.4m. (Dec. 2009); Pres. Mazhar Rawji; Dir-Gen. Thierry Taeymans; 19 brs.

Société Financière de Développement SARL (SOFIDE): Immeuble SOFIDE, 9–11 angle aves Ngabu et Kisangani, BP 1148, Kinshasa 1; tel. 816601531 (mobile); e-mail sofide2001@yahoo.fr; f. 1970; partly state-owned; provides tech. and financial aid, primarily for agricultural devt; cap. and res 285.3m., total assets 1,202.0m. (Dec. 2003); Pres. and Dir-Gen. Raphaël Senga Kitenge; 4 brs.

Standard Bank RDC: 12 ave de Mongala, BP 16297, Kinshasa 1; tel. 817006000 (mobile); fax 813013848 (mobile); e-mail stanbiccongoinfo@stanbic.com; internet www.standardbank.cd; f. 1973; subsidiary of Standard Bank Investment Corpn (South Africa); cap. 1,768.0m., res –1,163.6m., dep. 19,160.1m. (Dec. 2005); Chair. Clive Tasker; CEO Eric Mboma; 4 br.

Banking Association

Association Congolaise des Banques: 1 pl. du Marché, Kinshasa 1; tel. 817562771 (mobile); internet acb-asso.com; fax 999940863 (mobile); Pres. Michel Losembe; 20 mems.

INSURANCE

INTERAFF: Bldg Forescom, ave du Port 4, Kinshasa-Gombe; tel. (88) 01618; fax (320) 2091332; e-mail interaff@raga.net; internet www.ic.cd/interaff.

Société Nationale d'Assurances (SONAS): 3443 blvd du 30 juin, Kinshasa-Gombe; tel. (12) 5110503; e-mail sonask@hotmail.com; f. 1966; state-owned; cap. US $5m.; 9 brs.

Trade and Industry

GOVERNMENT AGENCY

Bureau Central de Coordination (BCECO): ave Colonel Mondjiba 372, Complexe Utex Africa, Kinshasa; tel. 815096430 (mobile); e-mail bceco@bceco.cd; internet www.bceco.cd; f. 2001; manages projects funded by the African Development Bank and the World Bank; Dir-Gen. Matondo Mbungu (acting).

DEVELOPMENT ORGANIZATIONS

Agence Congolaise des Grands Travaux: Kinshasa; tel. and fax 816909241 (mobile); e-mail contact@acgt.cd; internet acgt.cd; f. 2008; Dir-Gen. Charles Médard Ilunga Mwamba.

Bureau pour le Développement Rural et Urbain: Mont Ngafula, Kinshasa; e-mail bdru_kin@yahoo.fr.

Caisse de Stabilisation Cotonnière (CSCo): BP 3058, Kinshasa-Gombe; tel. (12) 31206; f. 1978 to replace Office National des Fibres Textiles; acts as an intermediary between the Govt, cotton ginners and textile factories, and co-ordinates international financing of cotton sector.

Centre National d'Appui au Développement et à la Participation Populaire (CENADEP): 1150 ave Tabora, Barumbu, BP 14582, Kinshasa; tel. 819982097; fax 17754027683; e-mail cenadep@yahoo.fr; internet www.cenadep.net; f. 1999.

La Générale des Carrières et des Mines (GÉCAMINES): 419 blvd Kamanyola, BP 450, Lubumbashi; tel. (2) 341105; fax (2) 341041; e-mail info@gecamines.cd; internet www.gecamines.cd; f. 1967 to acquire assets of Union Minière du Haut-Katanga; engaged in mining and marketing of copper, cobalt, zinc and coal; also has interests in agriculture; Dir-Gen. Ahmed Kalej Nkand.

Institut National pour l'Etude et la Recherche Agronomiques (INERA): BP 1513, Kisangani; internet www.inera-rdc.org; f. 1933; agricultural research.

Office National du Café: ave Général Bobozo 1082, BP 8931, Kinshasa 1; tel. (12) 77144; internet www.onc-rdc.cd; f. 1979; state agency for coffee and also cocoa, tea, quinquina and pyrethrum; Dir-Gen. Damas Emmanuel Kangwenye.

Pêcherie Maritime Congolaise: Kinshasa; DRC's only sea-fishing enterprise.

CHAMBER OF COMMERCE

Chambre de Commerce, d'Industrie et d'Agriculture du Congo: 10 ave des Aviateurs, BP 7247, Kinshasa 1; tel. (12) 22286; Pres. Ilunga Konya.

EMPLOYERS' ASSOCIATIONS

Fédération des Entreprises du Congo: 10 ave des Aviateurs, BP 7247, Kinshasa; tel. 812488890 (mobile); fax 812488909 (mobile); e-mail fec@ckt.cd; internet www.fec.cd; f. 1972 as the Association Nationale des Entreprises du Zaïre; name changed as above in 1997; represents business interests for both domestic and foreign institutions; Pres. Albert Yuma Mulimbi.

Confédération Nationale de Producteurs Agricoles du Congo (CONAPAC): 4746 ave de la Gombe, Kinshasa; tel. 998286456; e-mail conapacrdc@yahoo.fr; f. 2011; Pres. Paluku Mivimba.

UTILITIES

Electricity

Société Nationale d'Electricité (SNEL): 2831 ave de la Justice, BP 500, Kinshasa; tel. 815041639 (mobile); e-mail cco@snel.cd; internet www.snel.cd; f. 1970; state-owned; Pres. Makombo Monga Mawawi; Dir-Gen. Eric Mbala Musanda.

Water

Régie de Distribution d'Eau (REGIDESO): 59–63 blvd du 30 juin, BP 12599, Kinshasa; tel. (88) 45125; e-mail courrier@regidesordc.com; internet www.regidesordc.com; f. 1978; water supply admin; Pres. Rombeau Fumani Gibandi; Dir-Gen. Jacques Mukalay Mwema.

MAJOR COMPANIES

The following are some of the largest companies in terms either of capital investment or employment.

Manufacturing and Trading

BAT Congo SARL: 974 ave Gen. Bobozo, Kingabwa, BP 621, Kinshasa I; tel. 815559794; fax 815559790; f. 1950; wholly owned subsidiary of British American Tobacco Co Ltd, London; mfrs of tobacco products; Chair. and Man. Dir B. Mavambu Zoya.

Brasseries, Limonaderies et Malteries du Congo (BRALIMA): 1 ave du Flambeau, BP 7246, Kinshasa; tel. (12) 22141; f. 1923; production of beer, soft drinks and ice; Gen. Man. Hans van Memeren.

Cimenterie de Lukala: blvd du 30 juin, Immeuble CCCI, 3ème étage, BP 7598, Kinshasa 1; tel. 817005786 (mobile); fax 813010853 (mobile).

Compagnie des Margarines, Savons et Cosmétiques au Congo SARL (MARSAVCO CONGO): 1 ave Kalemie, BP 8914, Kinshasa; tel. (88) 00961; e-mail info@marsavco.com; internet www.marsavco.com; f. 1922; subsidiary of Unilever NV; mfrs of detergents, foods and cosmetics; Pres. C. Godde; 1,100 employees.

Compagnie Sucrière: blvd du 30 juin, bldg BCDC, BP 8816, Kinshasa, and BP 10, Kwilu Ngongo, Bas-Congo; tel. 818946387 (mobile); internet www.finasucre.com; f. 1925; mfrs of sugar, alcohol, acetylene, oxygen and carbon dioxide; Dir Eric van Eeckhout.

IBM World Trade Corporation (Congo): 6 ave du Port, BP 7563, Kinshasa 1; tel. (12) 23358; fax (12) 24029; f. 1954; sale and maintenance of computers and business machines and associated materials; Gen. Man. Mukadi Kabumbu.

Industries Congolaises des Bois (ICB): 23 ave de l'Ouganda, BP 10399, Kinshasa; state forestry and sawmilling enterprise.

Plantations Lever au Congo: 16 ave Colonel Lukusa, BP 8611, Kinshasa I; f. 1911; subsidiary of Unilever NV; plantations of oil palm, rubber, cocoa and tea; Man. Dir A. J. Ritchie.

Société BATA Congolaise: 33 ave Général Bobozo, BP 598, Kinshasa I; tel. (12) 27414; f. 1946; principal shoe mfr in the DRC; Man. Dir Yaya Désiré Tuluka; 100 employees.

Société Commerciale et Minière du Congo SA: BP 499, Kinshasa; subsidiary of Lonrho Ltd; engineering, motor trade, insurance, assembly and sale of earth-moving equipment.

Société Congo-Suisse de Produits Chimiques SARL: BP 14096, Kinshasa 1; tel. (12) 24707; sales agent for Ciba-Geigy pharmaceutical products.

Société Générale d'Alimentation (SGA): BP 15898, Kinshasa; state enterprise; import, processing and distribution of foodstuffs; largest chain of distributors in the DRC.

Minerals

Engen RDC: ave du Port 14/16, BP 2799, Kinshasa-Gombe; tel. 999923700 (mobile); fax (88) 01447; f. 1978; marketing of petroleum products; Dir-Gen. Charles Nikobasa; 74 employees.

Fina Recherche Exploitation Pétrolière (FINA REP SARL): 652 ave Lt Col. Lukusa, Gombe, BP 700, Kinshasa; tel. (12) 20103; fax (12) 20101; e-mail sofimmo@ic.cd; exploitation of petroleum; Pres. A. Nommer; Dir-Gen. Stéphane Lapauw.

Office des Mines d'Or de Kilo-Moto (OKIMO): BP 219–220, Bunia; internet www.okimo.org; state-owned; operates gold mines; Man. Dir Willy Bafoa Lifeta.

Perenco: 11ème étage, Immeuble BCDC, blvd du 30 Juin, BP 15596, Kinshasa; tel. 817008002 (mobile); internet www.perenco-drc.com; f. 2000; producer of petroleum; Dir-Gen. Eric Ivochevitch.

Société Aurifère du Kivu et Maniema (SAKIMA): f. 1997 as successor to Société Minière du Kivu; 93% owned by Banro Resources Corpn, 7% by DRC Government; exploitation of gold; Man. Dir Mario Flocchi.

Société Congo Gulf Oil: blvd du 30 juin, BP 7189, Kinshasa I; tel. (12) 23111; international mining consortium exploiting offshore petroleum at Muanda.

Société Congo—Italienne de Raffinage: BP 1478, Kinshasa I; tel. (12) 22683; fax (12) 25998; f. 1963; petroleum refinery; Pres. Lessedjina Ikwame Ipu'ozia; 600 employees.

Société de Développement Industriel et Minière du Congo (SODIMICO): 4219 ave de l'Ouganda, BP 7064, Kinshasa; tel. (12) 32511; subsidiary of GÉCAMINES; see Development Organizations; copper-mining consortium exploiting mines of Musoshi and Kinsenda in Katanga.

Société Minière de Bakwanga (MIBA): BP 377, Mbuji-Mayi, Kasaï Oriental; f. 1961; cap. 27m. zaires; 80% state-owned; industrial diamond mining; Dir Jeffrey Ovian.

Société Minière du Tenké-Fungurume: Immeuble UCB Centre, 5ème étage, BP 1279, Kinshasa; f. 1970 by international consortium comprising Charter Consolidated of London, Govt of Zaire, Mitsui (Japan), Bureau de Recherches Géologiques et Minières de France, Léon Tempelsman and Son (USA) and COGEMA (France); copper and cobalt mining; Dir B. L. Morgan.

Sonangol-Congo: 1513 blvd du 30 juin, BP 7617, Kinshasa 1; tel. (12) 25356; f. 1974; bought by the Sociedade Nacional de Combustíveis de Angola (SONANGOL) in 1998; petroleum refining, processing, stocking and transporting; Dir-Gen. Nkosi Pedro.

TRADE UNIONS

The Union Nationale des Travailleurs du Congo was founded in 1967 as the sole organization. In 1990 the establishment of independent trade unions was legalized, and by early 1991 there were 12 officially recognized organizations.

Confédération Démocratique du Travail: BP 10897, Quartier Industriel, C/Limete, Kinshasa 1; tel. (88) 0457311; e-mail cdtcongo@yahoo.fr; Pres. Liévin Kalubi.

Confédération Syndicale du Congo: 81 ave Tombalbaye, Kinshasa-Gombe; tel. 898922090 (mobile); fax (13) 98126; e-mail csc_congo@hotmail.com; internet www.csc.cd; f. 1991; Pres. Symphorien Dunia.

Syndicat des Enseignants du Congo (SYECO): Kinshasa; Sec.-Gen. Jean-Pierre Kimbuya.

Union Nationale des Travailleurs du Congo: Commune de la Gombe, BP 8814, 5 ave Mutombo Katshi, Kinshasa; tel. 998616193 (mobile); e-mail untcrdc@yahoo.fr; internet www.untc-congo.org; f. 1967; comprises 16 unions; Pres. Modeste Amédée Ndongala N'Sibu.

Transport

Compagnie des Transports du Congo: ave Muzu 52/75, Kinshasa; tel. (88) 46249; fax (322) 7065718; e-mail ros@ic.cd; road transport; Dir Roger Senger.

Office National des Transports (ONATRA): BP 98, Kinshasa 1; tel. (12) 21457; fax (12) 1398632; e-mail onatradf@ic.cd; f. 1935; operates 12,674 km of waterways, 366 km of railways and road and air transport; administers ports of Matadi, Boma and Banana; Man. Dir Raymond Georges.

RAILWAYS

In 2008 the rail network totalled 4,007 km, of which 858 km were electrified. The main line runs from Lubumbashi to Ilebo. International services run to Dar es Salaam (Tanzania) and Lobito (Angola), and also connect with the Zambian, Zimbabwean, Mozambican and South African systems. In May 1997 the railway system was nationalized. In late 2003, under a major government programme, the rehabilitation of 500 km of railway linking northern and southern regions of the country commenced. Work on the rehabilitation of railway lines in Kinshasa commenced in 2008 and was expected to be completed by 2012.

Kinshasa–Matadi Railway: BP 98, Kinshasa 1; 366 km operated by ONATRA; Pres. Jacques Mbelolo Bitwemi.

Société Nationale des Chemins de Fer du Congo (SNCC): 115 pl. de la Gare, BP 297, Lubumbashi; tel. (2) 346306; fax (2) 342254; e-mail sncc01@ic-libum.cd; f. 1974; 3,641 km (including 858 km electrified); administers all internal railway sections as well as river transport and transport on Lakes Tanganyika and Kivu; management contract concluded with a Belgian-South African corpn, Sizarail, in 1995 for the management of the Office des Chemins de Fer du Sud (OCS) and the Société des Chemins de Fer de l'Est (SFE) subsidiaries, with rail networks of 2,835 km and 1,286 km, respectively; assets of Sizarail nationalized and returned to SNCC control in May 1997; CEO Freddy Strumane.

ROADS

In 2004 there were an estimated 154,000 km of roads, of which some 42,000 km were highways. Following the installation of transitional authorities in July 2003, an extensive infrastructure rehabilitation programme, financed by external donors, including the World Bank, was initiated. Work on a principal road, connecting the south-western town of Moanda with Kinshasa and Lubumbashi, commenced late that year.

Office des Routes: Direction Générale, ave Ex-Descamp, BP 10899, Kinshasa-Gombe; tel. (12) 32036; construction and maintenance of roads; Man. Dir Mutima Batrimu Herman.

INLAND WATERWAYS

The River Congo is navigable for more than 1,600 km. Above the Stanley Falls the Congo becomes the Lualaba, and is navigable along a 965-km stretch from Ubundu to Kindu and Kongolo to Bukama. The River Kasaï, a tributary of the River Congo, is navigable by shipping as far as Ilebo, at which the line from Lubumbashi terminates. The total length of inland waterways is 14,935 km.

Régie des Voies Fluviales: 109 ave Lumpungu, Kinshasa-Gombe, BP 11697, Kinshasa 1; tel. (12) 26526; fax (12) 42580; f. 1971; administers river navigation; Pres. Benjamin Mukulungu; Gen. Man. Ruffin Ngomper Ilunga (acting).

Société Congolaise des Chemins de Fer des Grands Lacs: River Lualaba services: Bubundu–Kindu and Kongolo–Malemba N'kula; Lake Tanganyika services: Kamina–Kigoma–Kalundu–Moba–Mpulungu; Pres. and Gen. Man. Kibwe Mbuyu Kakudji.

SHIPPING

The principal seaports are Matadi, Boma and Banana on the lower Congo. The port of Matadi has more than 1.6 km of quays and can accommodate up to 10 deep-water vessels. Matadi is linked by rail with Kinshasa. The country's merchant fleet numbered 21 vessels and amounted to 13,922 gross registered tons at 31 December 2009.

Compagnie Maritime du Congo SARL: Immeuble AMICONGO-CMDC, 6ème étage, ave des Aviateurs 13, pl. de la Poste, Gombe, BP 9496, Kinshasa; tel. 898928782 (mobile); e-mail info@cmdc.cd; internet www.cmdc.cd; f. 1974; services: North Africa, Europe, North America and Asia to West Africa, East Africa to North Africa; Pres. Laure-Marie Kawanda Kayena; Dir-Gen. Caroline Mawandji Masala.

CIVIL AVIATION

International airports are located at Ndjili (for Kinshasa), Luano (for Lubumbashi), Bukavu, Goma and Kisangani. There are smaller airports and airstrips dispersed throughout the country.

Blue Airlines: BP 1115, Barumbu, Kinshasa 1; tel. (12) 20455; f. 1991; regional and domestic charter services for passengers and cargo; Man. T. Mayani.

Business Aviation: Aeroport Ndolo, Ndolo, Limete, Kinshasa; tel. 999942262 (mobile); fax 818142259 (mobile); e-mail businessaviation@gbs.cd; internet www.businessaviation.cd; regional services.

Compagnie Africaine d'Aviation: 6ème rue, Limete, Kinshasa; tel. (88) 43072; fax (88) 41048; e-mail ltadek@hotmail.com; f. 1992; Pres. David Blattner.

Congo Express: Kinshasa; f. 2010; operates from Kinshasa to Lubumbashi and Mbuji-Mayi; Man. Dir Didier Kindambu.

Fly Congo: 1928 ave Kabambare, BP 1284, Kinshasa; tel. 817005015 (mobile); f. 2012 to replace Hewa Bora Airways; international, regional and domestic scheduled services for passengers and cargo; Dir-Gen. Jean-Marc Pajot.

Korongo Airlines: Lubumbashi; internet www.flykorongo.com; f. 2010; expected to commence operations in April 2012; majority owned by Brussels Airlines; Dir-Gen. Christophe Allard.

Lignes Aériennes du Congo (LAC): 4 ave du Port, Kinshasa-Gombe, BP 8552, Kinshasa 1; tel. 819090001 (mobile); Pres. Louise L. Longange; Man. Dir Prosper Mazimpaka Faaty.

Malila Airlift: ave Basoko 188, BP 11526, Kinshasa-Gombe; tel. (88) 46428; fax 1-5304817707 (satellite); e-mail malila.airlift@ic.cd; internet malift.isuisse.com; f. 1996; regional services; Man. Véronique Malila.

Waltair Aviation: 9ème rue 206, Limete, Kinshasa; tel. (88) 48439; fax 1-3094162616 (satellite); e-mail waltair.rdc@ic.cd; regional services; Dir Vincent Gillet.

Tourism

The country offers extensive lake and mountain scenery, although tourism remains largely undeveloped. In 2009 tourist arrivals totalled 53,402. Receipts from tourism amounted to an estimated US $2m. in 1998.

Office National du Tourisme: 2A/2B ave des Orangers, BP 9502, Kinshasa-Gombe; tel. (12) 30070; f. 1959; Man. Dir BOTOLO MAGOZA.

Société Congolaise de l'Hôtellerie: Immeuble Memling, BP 1076, Kinshasa; tel. (12) 23260; Man. N'JOLI BALANGA.

Defence

The total strength of the armed forces of the Democratic Republic of the Congo, as assessed at November 2011, was estimated at between 144,000 and 159,000 (central staff 14,000; army 110,000–120,000; Republican Guard 6,000–8,000; navy 6,703; air force 2,548). The UN Organization Stabilization Mission in the Democratic Republic of Congo (MONUSCO) has a maximum authorized strength of about 22,000 personnel. MONUSCO has a mandate to remain in the country until the end of June 2013.

Defence Expenditure: Estimated at CF 213,000m. in 2012.

Commander-in-Chief: Maj.-Gen. JOSEPH KABILA KABANGE.

Chief of Staff of the Armed Forces: Lt-Gen. DIEUDONNE KAYEMBE MBANDAKULU.

Chief of Staff of the Army: Lt-Gen. DIDIER ETUMBA.

Chief of Staff of the Navy: Vice-Adm. DIDIER LONGILA.

Chief of Staff of the Air Force: Maj.-Gen. RIGOBERT MASAMBA MUSUNGUI.

Education

Primary education, beginning at six years of age and lasting for six years, is officially compulsory and is available free of charge in public institutions. Secondary education, which is not compulsory, begins at 12 years of age and lasts for up to six years, comprising a first cycle of two years and a second of four years. In 2008/09, according to UNESCO estimates, primary enrolment was equivalent to 93% of pupils (100% of boys; 86% of girls), while the comparable ratio for secondary enrolment was 38% (49% of boys; 27% of girls). There are four universities, located at Kinshasa, Kinshasa/Limete, Kisangani and Lubumbashi. In 2008/09 there were a total of 377,867 students (288,657 male, 89,210 female) enrolled in tertiary education. In 2010 spending on education represented 1.6% of total budgetary expenditure.

Bibliography

Abdulai, N. *Zaire: Background to the Civil War*. London, ARIB, 1997.

Adelman, H. (Ed.). *War and Peace in Zaire / Congo: Analysing and Evaluating Intervention, 1996–1997*. North Woodmere, NY, World Press, 2003.

Afoaku, O. G. *Explaining the Failure of Democracy in the Democratic Republic of the Congo: Autocracy and Dissent in an Ambivalent World*. New York, NY, Edwin Mellen Press, 2005.

Asch, S. *L'Eglise du Prophète Kimbangu*. Paris, Editions Karthala, 1983.

Ayoub, K. *L'ONU face à l'irrationnel en RDC*. Paris, L'Harmattan, 2011.

Brooke Simons, P. *Cullinan Diamonds: Dreams and Discoveries*. Constantia, Fernwood Press, 2004.

Camiller, P. *The African Dream: the Diaries of the Revolutionary War in the Congo*. New York, Grove Press, 2001.

Clark, J. *The African Stakes of the Congo War*. London, Palgrave, 2002.

Clement, J. A. P. (Ed.). *Postconflict Economics in Sub-Saharan Africa: Lessons from the Democratic Republic of the Congo*. Washington, DC, International Monetary Fund, 2004.

De Witte, L. *The Assassination of Lumumba*. New York, Verso Books, 2001.

Dunn, K. *Imagining the Congo: The International Relations of Identity*. New York, Palgrave Macmillan, 2003.

Edgerton, R. *The Troubled Heart of Africa: A History of the Congo*. New York, St Martin's Press, 2002.

Ekpebu, L. B. *Zaire and the African Revolution*. Ibadan, Ibadan University Press, 1989.

Ewans, M. *European Atrocity, African Catastrophe: Leopold II, the Congo Free State and its Aftermath*. London, Curzon Press, 2001.

Gondola, D. *The History of Congo*. Westport, CT, Greenwood Press, 2002.

Hayward, M. F. *Elections in Independent Africa*. Boulder, CO, Westview Press, 1987.

Hochschild, A. *King Leopold's Ghost*. London, Macmillan, 1999.

Hoyt, M. P. E., and Stearns, M. *Captive in the Congo: A Consul's Return to the Heart of Darkness*. Washington, DC, United States Naval Institute, 2000.

Huybrechts, A. *Transports et structures de développement au Congo. Etude de progrès économique de 1900 à 1970*. Paris and The Hague, Editions Mouton, 1970.

Institute for Global Dialogue. *The Transition in the Democratic Republic of the Congo: Problems and Prospects*. Midrand, 2006.

Jewsiewicki, B. (Ed.). *Etat indépendant du Congo, Congo belge, République démocratique du Congo, République du Zaïre?* Sainte-Foy, Québec, SAFI Press, 1984.

Kabamba, N. *Songye of the Democratic Republic of Congo*. Hallandale, FL, Aglob Publications, 2004.

Kadima, D., Kabemba, C., and Sharpe, K. *Whither Regional Peace and Security: The Democratic Republic of Congo After the War*. Pretoria, Africa Institute of South Africa, 2003.

Kelly, S. *America's Tyrant: The CIA (Central Intelligence Agency) and Mobutu of Zaire*. Lanham, MD, University of America Press, 1993.

Kitenge bin Kitoko, E. T., and Makosso, A.-C. *RDCongo, les élections et après: intellectuels et politiques posent les enjeux de l'après-transition*. Paris, L'Harmattan, 2006.

Leslie, W. J. *Zaire: Continuity and Political Change in an Oppressive State*. Boulder, CO, Westview Press, 1993.

MacGaffey, J. *The Real Economy of Zaire: An Anthropological Study*. London, James Currey, 1991.

MacGaffey, J., and Bazenguissa-Ganga, R. *Congo-Paris: Transnational Traders on the Margins of the Law* (African Issues Published in Association with International African Institute). Bloomington, IN, Indiana University Press, 2000.

MacGaffey, J., and Mukohya, V. *The Real Economy of Zaire: The Contribution of Smuggling and Other Unofficial Activities to National Wealth*. London, James Currey, 1991.

Makengo Nkutu, A. *Les institutions politiques de la RDC: de la République du Zaïre à la République Démocratique Du Congo (1990-à Nos Jours)*. Paris, L'Harmattan, 2010.

Marysse, S. *La libération du Congo dans le contexte de la mondialisation*. Antwerp, UFSIA, 1997.

Mbaya, K. (Ed.). *Zaire: What Destiny?* Dakar, CODESRIA, 1993.

Mealer, B. *All Things Must Fight To Live: Stories of War and Deliverance in Congo*. London, Bloomsbury, 2008.

Mokoli, M. M. *State Against Development: The Experience of Post-1965 Zaire*. Westport, CT, Greenwood Press, 1992.

Mukenge, T. *Culture and Customs of the Congo (Culture and Customs of Africa)*. Westport, CT, Greenwood Publishing Group, 2001.

Mungal, A. S. *Le consensus politique et la renaissance de la République démocratique du Congo*. Paris, Editions du Cerdaf, 2002.

Ndaywel è Nziem, I. *Nouvelle histoire du Congo: Des origines à la République Démocratique*. Brussels, Editions Le Cri, 2009.

Nest, M., Grignon, F., and Kisangani, E. F. (Eds.). *Democratic Republic of Congo: Economic Dimensions of War and Peace*. Boulder, CO, Lynne Rienner, 2006.

Nzongola-Ntalaja, G. *From Zaire to the Democratic Republic of the Congo*. Uppsala, Nordiske Afrikainstitutet, 1999.

The Congo from Leopold to Kabila: A People's History. London, Zed Books, 2002.

Pongo, M. K. *Transitions et Conflits au Congo-Kinshasa*. Paris, Éditions Karthala, 2001.

Prunier, G. *Africa's World War: Congo, the Rwandan Genocide, and the Making of a Continental Catastrophe*. USA, Oxford University Press, 2008.

Sanqmpam, S. N. *Pseudo-capitalism and the Overpolitical State: Reconciling Politics and Anthropology in Zaire*. Brookfield, VT, Ashgate Press, 1994.

Schatzberg, M. G. *The Dialectics of Oppression in Zaire*. Bloomington, IN, Indiana University Press, 1988.

Stearns, J. *Dancing in the Glory of Monsters: The Collapse of the Congo and the Great War of Africa*. New York, Public Affairs, 2011.

Trefon, T. (Ed.). *Reinventing Order in the Congo: How People Respond to State Failure in Kinshasa*. London, Zed Books, 2004.

Vellut, J.-L., Loriaux, F., and Morimont, F. *Bibliographies historiques du Zaïre à l'époque coloniale (1880–1960)*. Louvain-la-Neuve, Tervuren, 1996.

Weiss, H. *War and Peace in the Democratic Republic of the Congo* (Current African Issues, No. 22). Uppsala, Nordiske Afrikainstitutet, 2000.

Willame, J. C. *Eléments pour une lecture du contentieux Belgo-Zaïrois*. Les Cahiers du CEDAF, Vol. VI. Brussels, Centre d'etude et de documentation africaines, 1988.

Patrice Lumumba—La crise congolaise revisitée. Paris, Editions Karthala, 1990.

Wrong, M. *In the Footsteps of Mr. Kurtz: Living on the Brink of Disaster in Mobutu's Congo*. London, Harper Collins, 2001.

Wynaden, J., and Kushner, N. *Welcome to the Democratic Republic of the Congo (Welcome to my Country)*. Milwaukee, WI, Gareth Stevens, 2002.

Young, M. C. *Politics in the Congo: Decolonization and Independence*. Princeton, NJ, Princeton University Press, 1965.

Young, M. C., and Turner, T. *The Rise and Decline of the Zairean State*. Madison, WI, University of Wisconsin Press, 1985.

THE REPUBLIC OF THE CONGO

Physical and Social Geography

DAVID HILLING

POPULATION

The Congo river forms approximately 1,000 km of the eastern boundary of the Republic of the Congo, the remainder of which is provided by the Oubangui river from just south of the point at which the Equator bisects the country. Across these rivers lies the Democratic Republic of the Congo. To the north, the republic is bounded by the Central African Republic and Cameroon. Gabon lies to the west, and the Cabinda exclave of Angola to the south, adjoining the short Atlantic coastline. Covering an area of 342,000 sq km (132,047 sq miles) the country supported a population of 3,697,490 at the census of 28 April 2007. The population was estimated by the UN to have increased to 4,233,062 by mid-2012, giving an average density of 12.4 inhabitants per sq km. About one-third of the population is dependent on agriculture, primarily bush-fallowing, but this is supplemented where possible by fishing, hunting and gathering. The main ethnic groups are the Vili on the coast, the Kongo (centred on Brazzaville), and the Téké, Mbochi and Sanga of the plateaux in the centre and north of the country. The principal centres of urban population are the capital, Brazzaville (with an estimated population of 1,610,760 in mid-2011, according to the UN), and the main port of Pointe-Noire (715,334 at the 2007 census).

PHYSICAL FEATURES AND RESOURCES

The exploitation of substantial offshore petroleum deposits represents a major sector of the economy. The immediate coastal zone is sandy in the north, more swampy south of Kouilou, and in the vicinity of Pointe-Indienne yields small amounts of petroleum. A narrow coastal plain does not rise above 100 m, and the cool coastal waters modify the climate, giving low rainfall and a grassland vegetation. Rising abruptly from the coastal plain are the high-rainfall forested ridges of the Mayombé range, parallel to the coast and reaching a height of 800 m, in which gorges, incised by rivers such as the Kouilou, provide potential hydroelectric power sites. At Hollé, near the Congo-Océan railway and at the western foot of the range, there are considerable phosphate deposits. Mayombé also provides an important export commodity, timber, of which the main commercial species are okoumé, limba and sapele.

Inland, the south-western Niari valley has lower elevation, soils that are good by tropical African standards and a grassland vegetation, which facilitates agricultural development. A variety of agricultural products, such as groundnuts, maize, vegetables, palm oil, coffee, cocoa, sugar and tobacco, is obtained from large plantations, smaller commercial farms and also peasant holdings. These products provide the support for a more concentrated rural population and the basis for some industrial development.

A further forested mountainous region, the Chaillu massif, is the Congo basin's western watershed, and this gives way north-eastwards to a series of drier plateaux, the Batéké region and, east of the Likoula river, a zone of Congo riverine land. Here are numerous watercourses, with seasonal inundation, and dense forest vegetation, which supports some output of forest products, although the full potential has yet to be realized. The rivers Congo and Oubangui, with tributaries, provide more than 6,500 km of navigable waterway, which are particularly important, owing to the lack of a developed network of roads.

Recent History

KATHARINE MURISON

The Republic of the Congo became autonomous within the French Community in November 1958, with Abbé Fulbert Youlou as Prime Minister. Full independence followed on 15 August 1960; in March 1961 Youlou was elected President. In 1963 Youlou transferred power to a provisional Government led by Alphonse Massamba-Débat, who was elected President in December. In 1964 the Marxist-Leninist Mouvement National de la Révolution (MNR) was formed as the sole political party. In August 1968 Capt. (later Maj.) Marien Ngouabi deposed Massamba-Débat in a coup. A new Marxist-Leninist party, the Parti Congolais du Travail (PCT), replaced the MNR, and in January 1970 the country was renamed the People's Republic of the Congo.

In March 1977 Ngouabi was assassinated during an attempted coup by supporters of Massamba-Débat, who was subsequently executed. In April Col (later Brig.-Gen.) Jacques-Joachim Yhombi-Opango, a former Chief of Staff of the armed forces, was appointed Head of State. In February 1979 Yhombi-Opango surrendered his powers to a Provisional Committee appointed by the PCT. In March the President of the Committee, Col (later Gen.) Denis Sassou-Nguesso, was appointed President of the Republic and Chairman of the Central Committee of the PCT.

At the PCT congress in July 1989 Sassou-Nguesso was re-elected Chairman of the party and President of the Republic for a further five-year term. At legislative elections, held in September, the single list of 133 candidates, including, for the first time, candidates who were not members of the PCT, was approved by 99.2% of those who voted.

POLITICAL TRANSITION

In August 1990 Sassou-Nguesso announced the release of several political prisoners, including Yhombi-Opango, who had been imprisoned for alleged complicity in a coup plot in 1987. In December 1990 an extraordinary congress of the PCT abandoned Marxism-Leninism as its official ideology, and formulated constitutional amendments legalizing a multi-party system. The amendments were subsequently approved by the Assemblée nationale populaire (ANP), and took effect in January 1991. An interim Government, led by Gen. Louis Sylvain Goma as Prime Minister (a position he had previously held in 1975–84), was subsequently installed.

A national conference was convened in February 1991. Opposition movements were allocated seven of 11 seats on the conference's governing body. The conference voted itself a sovereign body whose decisions were to be binding. In April the conference announced that the Constitution was to be abrogated and that the ANP and other national and regional institutions were to be dissolved. In June a 153-member legislative Haut Conseil de la République (HCR) was established, in order to supervise the implementation of these measures, pending the adoption of a new constitution and the holding of elections. In the same month the Prime Minister replaced Sassou-Nguesso as Head of Government, and the country reverted to the name Republic of the Congo. André Milongo, a former World Bank official without formal political affiliation, succeeded Goma as Prime Minister. In December the HCR adopted a draft Constitution, which provided for legislative power to be vested in an elected Assemblée nationale and Sénat and for executive power to be held by an elected President.

Electoral Discord

The draft Constitution was approved by 96.3% of those who voted at a referendum in March 1992. At elections to the new Assemblée nationale in June and July, the Union Panafricaine pour la Démocratie Sociale (UPADS) became the largest party, winning 39 of the 125 contested seats, followed by the Mouvement Congolais pour la Démocratie et le Développement Intégral (MCDDI), with 29 seats, and the PCT (18). At elections to the Sénat, held in late July, the UPADS also became the largest party, with 23 of the 60 contested seats. At the presidential election, held in two rounds in August, Pascal Lissouba, the leader of the UPADS and a former Prime Minister, was victorious, winning 61.3% of the votes cast in the second round to defeat Bernard Kolélas, the leader of the MCDDI; Sassou-Nguesso and Milongo were among the other 14 candidates who unsuccessfully contested the first round. In September Lissouba appointed Maurice-Stéphane Bongho-Nouarra as Prime Minister. Shortly after a new Council of Ministers had been named, however, the PCT terminated a pact it had formed with the UPADS and instead formed an alliance with the Union pour le Renouveau Démocratique (URD), a new grouping of seven parties, including the MCDDI. The URD-PCT alliance, which now had a majority of seats in parliament, won a vote of no confidence in the Government in October, precipitating its resignation in November. Lissouba subsequently dissolved the Assemblée nationale, announcing that new legislative elections would be held. Claude Antoine Dacosta, a former FAO and World Bank official, was appointed Prime Minister of a transitional administration in December.

INTERNAL CONFRONTATION

At the first round of legislative elections, held in May 1993, the Mouvance Présidentielle (MP), comprising the UPADS and its allies, won 62 of the 125 seats in the Assemblée nationale, while the URD-PCT coalition, led by Kolélas, secured 49. Protesting that serious electoral irregularities had occurred, the URD-PCT refused to contest the second round of elections in early June (for seats where no candidate had received more than 50% of votes cast in the first round). After the second round, the MP held an absolute majority (69) of seats in the Assemblée nationale. In late June Lissouba appointed a new Council of Ministers, under Yhombi-Opango's premiership. Kolélas nominated a rival government and urged his supporters to instigate a campaign of civil disobedience. The political crisis soon precipitated violent conflict between armed militias, representing party political and ethnic interests, and the security forces. In late June the Supreme Court ruled that electoral irregularities had occurred at the first round of elections. In July the Government and the opposition negotiated a truce, and in August it was agreed that the disputed first-round results should be examined by a committee of impartial international arbitrators and that the second round of elections should be restaged. Following the repeated second round of elections, held in October, the MP retained its control of the Assemblée nationale, with 65 seats. The URD-PCT, with 57 seats, agreed to participate in the new Assemblée. In November, however, confrontations between armed militias and the security forces erupted again, with some 2,000 deaths reported during the second half of 1993. A cease-fire was agreed by the MP and the opposition in January 1994, although sporadic fighting continued.

In August 1996 Yhombi-Opango resigned as Prime Minister. In September the new Prime Minister, David Charles Ganao, the leader of the Union des Forces Démocratiques, appointed an expanded Council of Ministers, including representatives of the URD. Following partial elections to the Sénat, held in October, the MP remained the largest grouping in the upper chamber.

Factional Violence

In February 1997 19 opposition parties (including the PCT and the MCDDI) demanded a number of reforms, including the expedited establishment of republican institutions, the disarmament of civilians and the deployment of a multinational peace-keeping force. During May renewed unrest was reported, and in June an attempt by the Government to disarm the militia group associated with Sassou-Nguesso's Forces Démocratiques et Patriotiques (FDP) swiftly developed into a fierce conflict involving militia groups and opposing factions within the regular armed forces. Brazzaville was split effectively into three zones, controlled by supporters of Sassou-Nguesso, Lissouba and Kolélas, respectively. The conflict soon became polarized between troops loyal to the Lissouba administration and the 'Cobra' forces of Sassou-Nguesso. Despite efforts to mediate—led by Kolélas, President Omar Bongo of Gabon and the joint special representative of the UN and the Organization of African Unity (now the African Union—AU) to the Great Lakes region—none of the numerous cease-fires signed during mid-1997 endured. In June French troops assisted in the evacuation of foreign residents from Brazzaville; in mid-June they themselves departed, despite mediators' requests that they remain. Fighting intensified in August, spreading to the north. In September Lissouba appointed a Government of National Unity, under the premiership of Kolélas, thereby compromising the latter's role as a mediator. Sassou-Nguesso refused to accept the offer of five ministerial posts for his allies.

SASSOU-NGUESSO RESUMES POWER

In October 1997 Sassou-Nguesso's 'Cobra' forces, assisted by Angolan government troops, won control of Brazzaville and the strategically important port of Pointe-Noire. Lissouba and Kolélas fled the Congo. Sassou-Nguesso was inaugurated as President, and appointed a transitional Government. It was reported that some 10,000 people had been killed during the civil war and about 800,000 displaced. Sassou-Nguesso decreed that party militias would be disarmed and outlawed.

In January 1998 a Forum sur l'Unité et la Reconstruction was convened, comprising some 1,420 delegates. The Forum approved the immediate commencement of a three-year transitional period, pending the organization of presidential and legislative elections in 2001 and the approval by referendum of a new constitution. A 75-member Conseil National de Transition (CNT) was to act as a legislative body. The Forum also recommended that the leaders of the previous administration be charged with 'genocide and war crimes'; warrants for the arrest of Lissouba, Kolélas and Yhombi-Opango were issued in November.

Despite attempts to obtain an enduring peace settlement, clashes continued throughout 1998 in the Pool region, south of Brazzaville, a stronghold of the 'Ninja' militia loyal to Kolélas, causing thousands of refugees to flee the area. In December a full-scale battle for control of Brazzaville broke out between forces loyal to Kolélas (who remained in exile), allegedly supported by Angolan dissident groups, and Congolese government forces, augmented by Sassou-Nguesso's militia and Angolan government troops. More than 8,000 refugees were reported to have fled to the Democratic Republic of the Congo (DRC). In late December government forces launched offensives against Kolélas' forces in the south and west of the Congo.

In January 1999 sporadic fighting continued in Brazzaville and in the south-west, where the 'Cocoye' militia loyal to Lissouba was involved in skirmishes with government forces around the city of Loubomo (Dolisie), in the south-western Niari region. In late February the conflict in the area immediately south of Brazzaville intensified, and a further 10,000 people were estimated to have taken refuge in the DRC. By early March, however, the rebel militias had been forced to withdraw to the Pool region. In May the army secured the city of Kinkala, capital of the Pool region, and captured the main rebel base in the south-west of the Congo.

Peace Initiatives

In September 1999 it was reported that some 600 militiamen loyal to Kolélas had surrendered, and several prominent opposition members voluntarily returned from exile. In October the authorities announced that the armed forces had regained control of all towns in the Pool region. In November the Government declared that it had reached an agreement with the militias loyal to Lissouba and Kolélas, which included provision for a cease-fire and a general amnesty. The agreement was, however, rejected by Lissouba and Kolélas themselves. In December the CNT adopted legislation providing for an amnesty for those militiamen who surrendered their weapons before mid-January 2000.

In December 1999 President Bongo of Gabon was designated the official mediator between the Government and the militias. Following further discussions in Gabon, representatives of the armed forces and of the rebel militias signed a second peace agreement, which provided for the integration of militiamen into the armed forces and for measures to facilitate the return of displaced persons. Militia leaders continued, however, to demand the withdrawal of Angolan troops from the Congo. None the less, in late December a ceremony of reconciliation was held in Brazzaville between senior government figures and members of the previous Lissouba administration.

In February 2000 the committee in charge of observing the implementation of the peace process announced that the civil war was definitively over. It was estimated that around one-half of the estimated 810,000 people displaced by the conflict had returned to their homes. In May Kolélas was convicted, *in absentia*, of operating personal prisons in Brazzaville and of mistreating prisoners and causing their deaths during the 1997 civil war. Kolélas Bikinkita, in exile in the USA, was sentenced to death and ordered to pay compensation to their victims.

In November 2000 the Government adopted a draft Constitution, which included provisions for a presidential system of government, with a bicameral legislature and an independent judiciary. It was proposed that the Head of State be elected for a term of seven years, renewable once only. In December it was announced that some 12,000 militiamen had been disarmed during 2000, although observers reported that at least an equivalent number of militiamen remained at large in the Congo.

National Dialogue and Constitutional Reform

In February 2001 the Government established a commission to prepare for a period of national dialogue. However, internal and exiled opposition groups, displeased by their exclusion from this commission, and also citing security concerns, boycotted both the opening ceremony of the national dialogue in mid-March and regional debates that took place later in that month. None the less, some 2,200 delegates, representing public institutions, civil society associations, political parties loyal to the Government and independent parties, attended the debates, reportedly reaching a consensus on the draft Constitution. The national convention met in April, with the participation of several of those who had boycotted the first phase of national dialogue. The convention concluded with the adoption of an 'Agreement for Peace and Reconstruction'.

In July 2001 a new coalition of opposition parties sympathetic to Milongo, the Alliance pour la Démocratie et le Progrès (ADP), was formed, with the intention of fielding a single candidate in the presidential election due to be held in 2002. Meanwhile, the FDP reverted to its original name, the Forces Démocratiques Unies (FDU), and was expanded to consist of some 29 parties, with the purpose of uniting behind Sassou-Nguesso in the election (although the PCT was to contest the subsequent legislative elections independently of the FDU).

In September 2001 the CNT approved the text of the proposed Constitution, which was to be submitted to referendum following the compilation of an electoral census. Although the national convention had recommended that opposition parties participate in the electoral commission, only one opposition grouping, the ADP, was represented in the Commission Nationale d'Organisation des Élections (CONEL), which was, moreover, to be responsible to the Ministry of the Interior, Security and Territorial Administration. In mid-December Lissouba, Kolélas and Yhombi-Opango issued a joint statement from abroad condemning the electoral process as lacking impartiality. Several opposition parties subsequently threatened to boycott the elections in protest at the composition of the CONEL. In late December the Supreme Court sentenced Lissouba, *in absentia*, to 20 years' imprisonment with hard labour for the mismanagement of public funds in association with the state petroleum company.

SASSOU-NGUESSO AND THE PCT CONSOLIDATE POWER

In December 2001 the electoral schedule was announced: the constitutional referendum was to be held on 20 January 2002, followed by the presidential election on 10 March, elections to the Assemblée nationale on 12 May and 9 June, and indirect elections to the Sénat on 30 June. The new Constitution was approved on 20 January by some 84.5% of votes cast, with a participation rate of some 77.5% of the electorate.

Presidential Election, 2002

In February 2002 10 presidential candidates were approved by the Supreme Court, among them Sassou-Nguesso, Milongo, Martin Mberi and Joseph Kignoumbi Kia Mboungou, of the UPADS. It was reported that Sassou-Nguesso's candidacy had the support of more than 50 political organizations, including a faction of the MCDDI. Meanwhile, six political parties supportive of Milongo formed an opposition alliance, the Convention pour la Démocratie et le Salut (CODESA), which effectively supplanted the ADP. However, in early March Mberi, Milongo and an unaffiliated opposition candidate announced the withdrawal of their candidacies. Milongo, who had been widely regarded as the sole credible challenger to Sassou-Nguesso, urged his supporters to boycott the poll, stating his concerns about the transparency of electoral procedures and the impartiality of the CONEL.

With the principal opposition candidates thereby excluded, Sassou-Nguesso won an overwhelming victory in the presidential election contested by seven candidates on 10 March 2002, securing 89.4% of the votes cast. According to official figures, 69.4% of the electorate participated in the election. After the presidential election CODESA called for the postponement of the elections to the Assemblée nationale, so that amended electoral registers could be compiled. The Government subsequently delayed the elections until 26 May and 23 June.

Renewed Violence in the South

Meanwhile, in March 2002 renewed violence erupted in the Pool region, apparently instigated by members of a 'Ninja' militia group, led by Rev. Frédéric Bitsangou (also known as Ntumi). The conflict widened in early April, when two people were killed in an attack on a train on the Congo-Océan railway by members of the militia, although Ntumi denied his forces had initiated the attack. Following further insurgency in Mayama, some 80 km west of Brazzaville, government forces, reportedly assisted by Angolan troops, were dispatched to the region, and air attacks were launched against the rebels. By mid-April the unrest had spread to southern Brazzaville, and by late May some 50,000 people were reported to have been displaced. In late April government forces announced that they had regained control of the Congo-Océan railway, facilitating a normalization in the supply of fuel and food to the capital, although fighting continued in Pool. At the end of May government troops regained control of the rebel stronghold of Vindza.

Legislative Elections, 2002

The first round of elections to the 137-member Assemblée nationale, which was held on 26 May 2002, was contested by some 1,200 candidates from more than 100 parties. As a result of the unrest in the Pool region, voting was indefinitely postponed in eight constituencies, while disruption caused by protesters and administrative irregularities necessitated a re-run of polling in a further 12 constituencies on 28–29 May. Moreover, the CONEL subsequently disqualified 15 candidates. Turn-out in the first round, at which the PCT and its allies in the FDU won 38 of the 51 seats decided, was around 65%.

Prior to the second round of elections to the Assemblée, the security situation in Brazzaville deteriorated markedly. In mid-June 2002, while President Sassou-Nguesso was in Italy, a group of 'Ninja' militiamen attacked the capital's main military base, near to the international airport. In the subsequent fighting 72 rebels, three army officers and five civilians were killed, according to official reports, while some 100 rebel fighters were captured. In spite of requests by Milongo's party, the Union pour la Démocratie et la République—Mwinda (UDR—Mwinda), for a postponement of the elections in those areas of western Brazzaville where fighting had occurred, and which were largely deserted, the elections went ahead on 23 June, as scheduled, although the rate of participation, at an estimated 30% nation-wide, was appreciably lower than in the first round, and was as low as 10% in some constituencies in Brazzaville and in Pointe-Noire. Following the polls, supporters of Sassou-Nguesso held an absolute majority in the new Assemblée; the PCT emerged as the largest party, with 53 seats, while the FDU alliance held a total of 30 seats. Moreover, many of the 19 nominally independent deputies elected were believed to be loyal to Sassou-Nguesso. The UDR—Mwinda became the largest opposition party, with only six seats, while the UPADS held four seats. Although 17 deputies from smaller parties were elected, the MCDDI notably failed to secure representation in the Assemblée.

Local and municipal elections, held on 30 June 2002, were also marked by a low turn-out and further entrenched Sassou-Nguesso's power; the PCT itself gained 333 of the 828 elective seats, while the success of constituent parties of the FDU ensured that supporters of the President held more than two-thirds of the elective seats. As the councillors elected on 30 June were those who would, in turn, elect the members of the Sénat on 7 July, the victory of those loyal to Sassou-Nguesso in the upper parliamentary chamber was also to be expected. Following these elections, the 66-member Sénat comprised 56 supporters of the President (44 from the PCT and 12 from the FDU), two representatives of civil society organizations, one independent and only one member of a small opposition party. Thus, supporters of President Sassou-Nguesso had gained clear control of both executive and legislative power. In August Tchicaya was elected as President of the Assemblée nationale, and the Secretary-General of the PCT, Ambroise-Edouard Noumazalay, was elected as President of the Sénat. Sassou-Nguesso was inaugurated as elected President on 14 August; a few days later he announced the formation of a new Government, which included no representatives of the opposition.

Sporadic attacks by 'Ninja' militias in the Pool region, in particular against freight trains on the Congo-Océan railway, continued during the second half of 2002. In October unrest intensified, and several deaths of civilians were reported; up to 10,000 civilians were reported to have fled Pool between early October and mid-November. In early November an ad hoc presidential committee, comprising prominent citizens from the Pool region and politicians allied to Sassou-Nguesso or to Lissouba, proposed a cease-fire between government forces and the 'Ninja' forces allied to Ntumi, and the replacement of government army units in the region with gendarmerie patrols. In mid-November Sassou-Nguesso, rejecting the proposals of the committee, announced that a 'safe passage' would be provided from Pool to Brazzaville until mid-December for fighters who surrendered their arms, and reiterated that the terms of the peace agreement concluded in 1999 remained valid. However, fighting subsequently intensified and only 371 rebels were reported to have surrendered (estimates of the number of rebels at large varied from 3,000–10,000). Although Sassou-Nguesso announced an extension of the amnesty, as a result of which a further 90 rebels surrendered in early January 2003, some 15 civilians were killed in an attack in Pool at the beginning of that month, and in February the first outbreak of political violence in the neighbouring Bouenza region since 1999, in which a local police chief was killed, was reported.

PEACE AGREEMENT SIGNED

In March 2003 the Government and Ntumi's 'Ninja' militia group signed an agreement aimed at restoring peace to the Pool region. The rebels agreed to end hostilities and disarm, while the Government was to guarantee an amnesty for the rebels and integrate former combatants into the national armed forces. In August the Assemblée nationale formally approved an amnesty for former 'Ninja' fighters, to cover the period from January 2000. By September 2003 the situation in Pool had stabilized sufficiently to allow an electoral commission to be formed in the region. None the less, in October renewed clashes between 'Ninja' fighters and government forces near Mindouli resulted in at least 13 deaths. In December, following reports that Kolélas had unsuccessfully attempted to re-enter the Congo under an assumed identity from the DRC, clashes were reported in Brazzaville between 'Ninja' groupings allied to Ntumi and Kolélas, although peace was soon restored.

In January 2004 Ntumi announced a series of conditions for his return to Brazzaville from his base in Loukouo, in the Pool region, including the installation of a government of national unity, the return of exiled former leaders, the definition of his status and an agreement on the number of his fighters to be integrated into the army, police and gendarmerie. The Government largely rejected Ntumi's demands in March, insisting that the peace agreement signed one year earlier made no provision for the formation of a government of national unity or the return of exiles, and announced that working groups had recently been formed to monitor the demobilization, disarmament and reintegration of former rebels and to consider Ntumi's status. At least seven militiamen and two members of the armed forces were killed in clashes near Kinkala later that month, according to the Government.

In May 2004 the rail service linking Brazzaville to the Pool region resumed operations, and the Government announced that it had closed seven sites that had been established south of Brazzaville in October 2002 to shelter some 12,000 people who had fled fighting in Pool, following the completion of a programme to return them to their home villages. In August 2004 some 20 opposition parties and associations, including the MCDDI, formed a coalition, the Coordination de l'Opposition pour une Alternance Démocratique (CODE-A), with the stated aim of fostering non-violent political change in the Congo.

Instability persisted in the Pool region in late 2004. In mid-October the rail service between Brazzaville and Pointe-Noire was suspended following numerous attacks on trains in Pool. Ntumi denied claims that the attacks had been perpetrated by his 'Ninja' rebel group, also known as the Conseil National de la Résistance (CNR), and demanded an independent inquiry into the incidents. A combined force of former 'Ninja' militiamen and gendarmes had been responsible for escorting trains between the two cities until earlier that month, when the Government had decided to replace them with army troops owing to alleged looting by the 'Ninjas'. Meanwhile, displaced persons who had fled hostilities in Pool continued to return gradually during 2004 with government assistance, although the humanitarian situation in the region remained poor and it was reported that armed fighters were still intimidating civilians, despite the peace agreement signed in March 2003. (It was estimated that between 100,000 and 147,000 people had fled Pool between 1998 and 2002.)

President Sassou-Nguesso reorganized the Council of Ministers in January 2005, notably creating a new post of Prime Minister, which was allocated to Isidore Mvouba, hitherto Minister of State, Minister of Transport and Privatization, responsible for the Co-ordination of Government Action. CODE-A criticized the creation of the post of Prime Minister, accusing Sassou-Nguesso of violating the Constitution, which made no provision for the position.

DEMOBILIZATION EFFORTS

In March 2005 the Government initiated a new programme for the disarmament, demobilization and reintegration of 450 former combatants in the Pool region, for which it had allocated 201m. francs CFA. (More than 500 weapons were subsequently collected and destroyed under this programme.) Earlier demobilization efforts had reportedly reintegrated some 8,000 former militias into society. In May it was announced that the Government had commenced power-sharing talks with the CNR with the aim of bringing members of the movement into 'all national institutions'.

The PCT's representation in the 66-member Sénat was reduced to 39 seats as a result of partial elections held on 2 October 2005. The ruling party secured 23 of the 30 seats contested at the elections, which were boycotted by opposition parties from CODE-A and CODESA, partly in protest at the composition of a new CONEL recently appointed by presidential decree. Of the remaining seven contested seats, six were won by pro-presidential parties, while one independent was elected to the upper chamber.

Having obtained authorization from the Congolese authorities, Kolélas returned to the Congo in October 2005 to attend the burial of his wife, who had died in Paris, France. At least six people were subsequently killed in heavy fighting between 'Ninja' rebels and government troops in southern Brazzaville. In December, at the request of Sassou-Nguesso, the legislature granted amnesty to Kolélas, overturning his death sentence in the interests of national reconciliation. A few days later Kolélas apologized to the Congolese people for the harm he had caused during the 1997 civil war. Similarly, in March 2006 the acting President of the UPADS, Pascal Gamassa, requested forgiveness for his party's involvement in the civil war, on behalf of former President Lissouba.

In December 2005 the agreement of the European Union to disburse funds for the construction of a highway linking Kinkala with Brazzaville was attributed to improving security in Pool. It was hoped that the road (which was officially inaugurated in May 2009) would facilitate the provision of development aid to the region. The population of Pool had reportedly increased from 186,481 in 2000 to 362,358 in 2005 as people returned following the signing of the 2003 peace agreement. Nevertheless, the fragility of the security situation in Pool was evident in January 2006, when two international aid organizations, the International Committee of the Red Cross and Médecins sans Frontières, temporarily suspended their operations in the region after a number of their staff were threatened or attacked by armed bandits. Meanwhile, in the same month the World Bank granted the Congo US $17m. to disarm, demobilize and reintegrate 30,000 former fighters in eight regions. According to government figures, there were around 43,000 erstwhile combatants throughout the country. In March some 500 weapons, 800 grenades and 80,000 pieces of ammunition that had been collected from former militias since the beginning of the year were destroyed in a ceremony in Brazzaville attended by Sassou-Nguesso and the Secretary-General of the UN, Kofi Annan. Those who agreed to surrender their arms were provided with agricultural tools and development aid in return. However, an estimated 34,000 illegally held firearms remained in circulation, posing a serious threat to security, and Ntumi declared that his troops would not fully disarm until an agreement on 'political partnership' had been signed by the CNR and the Government. In August it was reported that the commission responsible for reintegrating former combatants into society had recovered and destroyed a total of 11,776 weapons and reintegrated 17,459 people.

Sassou-Nguesso resigned from the leadership of the PCT in early January 2007, on the grounds that the Constitution stated that the role of President of the Republic was incompatible with holding office within a political party. At the end of that month one of the constituent parties of the FDU, the Rassemblement pour la Démocratie et la République, announced its withdrawal from the pro-presidential majority, accusing the PCT of having reneged on an accord on collaboration signed in February 2002 by refusing to share power. The party, which had one representative in the Assemblée nationale, had never been allocated any government or other official posts. Meanwhile, Ntumi announced that the CNR was to be transformed into a legitimate political party, the Conseil National des Républicains (retaining the acronym CNR), and would participate in the forthcoming elections to the Assemblée nationale. In February the Government announced that the legislative elections would be held on 24 June and 22 July, under the supervision of a new, independent electoral commission, as demanded by the opposition. However, following the rejection of their demands for a review of electoral constituencies, in April opposition parties boycotted the vote at which the Assemblée nationale approved the creation of the new commission and the nomination of its members by presidential decree.

In April 2007 the PCT and the MCDDI agreed to form an electoral alliance to contest the next legislative, local and presidential elections. As a result of the negotiations that commenced in 2005, the Government and the CNR signed an agreement providing for the destruction of weapons held by members of the movement, the integration of 250 former combatants into the national armed forces and the appointment of Ntumi to the Government. In May 2007, in accordance with the agreement, Sassou-Nguesso designated Ntumi as Delegate-General to the President, in charge of promoting peace and reconciliation. On his return to Brazzaville, Ntumi was to be permitted to retain a 50-strong personal guard. A number of weapons collected from former combatants were destroyed in June in a ceremony held in Kinkala to mark the beginning of the process.

LEGISLATIVE ELECTIONS, 2007

The first round of the elections to the Assemblée nationale was held, as scheduled, on 24 June 2007, despite opposition complaints that the polls had been poorly organized. Some 40 smaller opposition parties staged a boycott, citing concerns over the independence of the electoral commission, although the UPADS, the UDR—Mwinda and the CNR opted to participate. Irregularities, mainly related to voter registration, marred the first round, leading to the repetition of polling in 19 constituencies on 8 and 15 July. The second round of the elections was subsequently postponed until 5 August in order to allow candidates sufficient time to campaign. Following the second round of voting, the PCT remained the largest party in the Assemblée nationale, with a total of 46 of the 137 seats, while its ally, the MCDDI, held 11 seats and parties belonging to the pro-presidential FDU 31. In addition, most of the 37 independent deputies were reported to be close to the President. Of the opposition parties, the UPADS increased its representation to 11 seats, but the UDR—Mwinda (which had suffered the death of its leader, Milongo, in July) secured only one seat and the CNR failed to win a seat. Observers from the AU noted continued problems with the conduct of the ballot and recommended the revision of the electoral register and the establishment of a single, independent body to organize future elections. In early September Justin Koumba, President of the CNT during 1998–2002 and hitherto President of the National Human Rights Commission, was elected as President of the Assemblée nationale.

Meanwhile, former Head of State and Prime Minister Yhombi-Opango returned to the Congo in August 2007 after 10 years in exile; he had been granted an amnesty in May, having been convicted *in absentia* of embezzlement and sentenced to 20 years' forced labour in 2001. Ntumi's scheduled return to Brazzaville in September 2007, to assume the government post to which he had been appointed in May, was aborted at the last minute, following disagreement between the CNR and the Government over security arrangements, particularly regarding the number of former militants permitted to accompany him.

André Obami Itou was elected President of the Sénat at the beginning of December 2007, following the death of the incumbent, Noumazalay, in the previous month. Later that month Sassou-Nguesso effected a minor government reshuffle; two ministers from the MCDDI notably joined the Council of Ministers. Also in December 58 political parties loyal to the President formed an alliance, the Rassemblement de la Majorité Présidentielle (RMP), led by the PCT, to contest the local and senatorial elections in 2008 and the presidential election in 2009.

In June 2008 a ceremony was held in Kinkala to initiate the World Bank-funded programme for the demobilization, disarmament and reintegration of 30,000 former combatants (comprising 5,000 followers of Ntumi, 6,000 government forces and 19,000 former militias who had already disbanded). Attending the event, Ntumi, who still remained based in Pool, proclaimed the dissolution of the armed 'Ninja' wing of the CNR. Meanwhile, Médecins sans Frontières announced its intention to withdraw from the Congo as a result of a significant improvement in security and humanitarian conditions in the region. Thousands of weapons and munitions collected from former combatants were destroyed in the following months.

At local and municipal elections held in June 2008, the RMP (now comprising around 100 political parties and associations) reportedly secured 364 of the 864 seats contested. In addition, more than 200 seats were won by parties or independent candidates considered close to the RMP, and a further 43 were taken by the MCDDI (still allied to the PCT). The UPADS was the most successful opposition party, obtaining 76 seats.

Partial elections to fill 42 seats in the 72-member Sénat, which had been expanded as a result of the creation of the department of Pointe-Noire, were held on 5 August 2008. The RMP secured 33 of the seats contested, while independent candidates took seven and the UPADS two (both in Niari). André Obami Itou was re-elected as President of the Sénat later that month.

SASSOU-NGUESSO RE-ELECTED, 2009

From late 2008 opposition parties repeatedly criticized the Government's decision to revise the existing voters' register ahead of the presidential election to be held in July 2009, rather than conducting a full electoral census of the population, and demanded the creation of a genuinely independent electoral commission. In November 2008 Ange Edouard Poungui, Prime Minister in 1984–89, was nominated to represent the UPADS in the presidential election, after Joseph Kignoumbi Kia Mboungou (the party's candidate in the 2002 poll) withdrew from the vote, citing a lack of transparency in the process. In January 2009 Mathias Dzon, the leader of the Union Patriotique pour le Renouveau National and Minister of Finance in 1997–2002, was officially designated the candidate of the Alliance pour la République et la Démocratie, a grouping of 14 minor opposition parties that had been formed in October 2007. At a meeting held in February 2009, 18 opposition parties, including the UPADS, UDR—Mwinda and members of the Alliance pour la République et la Démocratie (ARD), reiterated their demands for the creation of an independent electoral commission and the compilation of a new electoral register, and established the Front des Partis de l'Opposition Congolaise (FPOC) in an attempt at unity, although there seemed to be no suggestion that the new grouping would select a single candidate to challenge Sassou-Nguesso's anticipated bid for re-election. A four-day national dialogue arranged by the Government in April was boycotted by the FPOC; participants agreed that the CONEL would be in sole charge of organizing the presidential election and that there was insufficient time to conduct a full electoral census.

In early June 2009 Sassou-Nguesso finally confirmed his intention to contest the presidential election, which was to be held on 12 July. In mid-June the Constitutional Court declared four of the 17 prospective presidential candidates ineligible to stand, one for narrowly exceeding the age limit and three, including Poungui and another FPOC member, on the grounds that they did not fulfil residency requirements. The UPADS condemned the rejection of Poungui's candidacy, claiming that it was politically motivated. None the less, the FPOC was still to field three candidates: Dzon, Guy Romain Kimfoussia, the leader of UDR–Mwinda, and Clément Miérassa, the President of the Parti Social Démocrate Congolais. Later that month two candidates of the so-called 'moderate' opposition, which had participated in April's national dialogue, threatened to withdraw from the ballot in protest at the perceived inadequacy of preparations for the election, including the tardy publication of the electoral register. Six candidates, including those belonging to the FPOC and three independents, appealed to the Government for a postponement a few days before the poll, citing irregularities in the register, and later urged voters to boycott the election. A national human rights organization, the Observatoire Congolais des Droits Humains (OCDH), also disputed the validity of the register, claiming that the number of voters registered, some 2.1m., was far in excess of what could be expected.

The presidential election took place, as scheduled, on 12 July 2009. The six candidates who had appealed for a boycott immediately demanded a re-run of the vote, claiming that less than 10% of the electorate had participated, but the CONEL stated that the turn-out in the interior of the country had been 'massive', while the Government rejected opposition accusations of fraud and irregularities. On 15 July the Minister of Territorial Administration and Decentralization, Raymond Mboulou, announced provisional results, according to which Sassou-Nguesso had secured a decisive victory, with 78.6% of the votes cast. In second place, with 7.5% of the votes, was Joseph Kignoumbi Kia Mbougou (standing as an independent), followed by Nicéphore Fylla de Saint-Eudes of the Parti Républicain Libéral, with 7.0%, and Dzon, who had been widely considered to be Sassou-Nguesso's strongest rival, with only 2.3%. Contrary to opposition claims, an official turn-out of 66.4% was recorded. Observers from the AU and the Communauté Économique des États de l'Afrique Centrale (CEEAC) concluded that the poll had been conducted transparently, although the OCDH disagreed, alleging fraud and irregularities. The provisional results were confirmed later in July by the Constitutional Court, which rejected the appeals of five candidates for the annulment of the ballot, and Sassou-Nguesso was inaugurated on 14 August for a further seven-year term as President. Later that month it emerged that several opposition leaders had been barred from leaving the country pending the conclusion of an inquiry into their participation in an apparently unauthorized post-election protest march.

A new Government was appointed in September 2009. Most notably, Mvouba remained the most senior member of the administration, but was no longer afforded the title of Prime Minister. He assumed responsibility for one of four 'poles' (basic infrastructures, economy, sovereignty and socio-cultural issues), officially obtaining the title of Minister of State, Co-ordinator of Basic Infrastructures, and Minister of Civil Aviation and of Maritime Trade.

At Sassou-Nguesso's request and in the interests of national reconciliation, in December 2009 the legislature granted former President Lissouba, who was living in exile in France, amnesty from the prison sentence imposed on him eight years earlier. Lissouba's wife was permitted to return to the Congo in May 2010, meeting with Sassou-Nguesso during her visit. Meanwhile, Kolélas, who had been similarly pardoned in 2005, died in November 2009 in Paris, where he had been receiving medical treatment.

In late December 2009 Ntumi finally assumed the government post to which he had been appointed in May 2007 (see Demobilization Efforts, above). However, his return to Brazzaville followed reports of increased violence in the Pool region. Ntumi failed in his attempt to secure a seat in the Assemblée nationale in a by-election held in the Pool constituency of Minduli in July 2010. A military and police operation to restore full law and order to the Pool region commenced in October, partly with the aim of facilitating the implementation of much-needed infrastructural projects.

In September 2010 the UPADS and a breakaway faction, the UPADS—Historique, which had been formed following the expulsion from the UPADS of nine of its executive members in August 2008, signed an agreement on their reunification. At a PCT congress held in July 2011, Pierre Ngolo was elected Secretary-General of the party, replacing Mvouba, who had held the post in an interim capacity since the death of Ambroise-Edouard Noumazalay in 2007. President Sassou-Nguesso's son, Denis Christel Sassou-Nguesso, was also elected to the PCT's political bureau, prompting speculation that he was being prepared to succeed his father; he formally dissolved his own party, the Parti pour la Justice et la République, in early August. A minor government reorganization was carried out later that month, involving three ministries, while in December two ministers reversed roles, Henri Ossebi becoming Minister of Energy and Water Resources and Bruno Jean-Richard Itoua Minister of Scientific Research.

LEGISLATIVE ELECTIONS, 2011–12

Partial elections to the Sénat were held on 9 October 2011, having been postponed from 26 June at the request of the CONEL. The PCT, the RMP and allies secured a total of 33 of the 36 seats contested, the PCT winning 12 and the RMP 11. Notable new senators included Poungui, whose presidential candidacy for the UPADS had been rejected in the 2009 election, and Fylla de Saint-Eudes, who had achieved third place in that ballot. Obami Itou was re-elected as President of the Sénat later that month.

A series of major explosions caused by a fire in a munitions depot at an army barracks in Brazzaville in early March 2012 resulted in some 300 deaths, severe infrastructural damage and the displacement of some 14,000 people. Substantial international assistance was forthcoming, and the Government promised to pay compensation to those affected.

Legislation that provided for an increase in the number of deputies in the Assemblée nationale from 137 to 139 and specified that the chairpersons of local electoral commissions should be independent figures (rather than prefects or mayors) was adopted in mid-May 2012. The changes had been agreed at consultations conducted by the Government with political parties and civil society groups in late 2011.

Elections to the Assemblée nationale took place on 15 July and 5 August 2012, their organization having been delayed slightly following the explosions at the arms depot in March. The PCT consolidated its position as the largest party in the lower chamber, securing an absolute majority, with 89 of the 136 seats contested, followed by its ally, the MCDDI, and the opposition UPADS, which each won seven seats (both parties recording a poorer performance than in the 2007 polls); 12 independent candidates were elected. The PCT and its allies took a total of 117 seats in the Assemblée. The UPADS alleged that irregularities had occurred at both rounds of voting. Three seats remained vacant owing to the postponement of polling in three Brazzaville constituencies affected by the March explosions. In late September President Sassou-Nguesso effected a reorganization of the Government.

THE 'BEACH AFFAIR'

In July 2001 the families of some 353 missing Congolese citizens demanded a parliamentary inquiry into their disappearance from the Beach area of Brazzaville; it was reported that the missing people, former refugees from the civil war in the southern regions who had sought asylum in the DRC, had been arrested following their voluntary repatriation to the Congo in May 1999. In April 2004 the Congolese Government announced that six of the people believed to have disappeared in 1999 had been identified among a group of refugees being repatriated from the DRC, and claimed that more were still based in a camp in south-west DRC. Sassou-Nguesso subsequently ordered that a Congolese judicial inquiry be conducted into what had become known as the 'Beach affair', and in July 2004 four senior officers from the Congolese armed forces, including Gen. Norbert Dabira (also sought in France, see Foreign Relations, below), were indicted, having apparently volunteered to be tried in an attempt to clear their names. The trial of 15 senior army and police officers suspected of involvement in the 'Beach affair', on charges of murder, genocide, crimes against humanity and war crimes, commenced in Brazzaville in mid-July 2005. Many of the families of those missing and CODE-A had opposed the case being heard in the Congo, claiming that the judiciary was not truly independent of the executive. A month later all 15 defendants were acquitted of the charges against them. However, the court ordered the Government to pay compensation of 10m. francs CFA (one-10th of the amount sought) for each missing person to the families of 86 acknowledged victims, in recognition of the State's civil responsibility for the safety of its citizens. Following a nine-day visit to the Congo, conducted at the invitation of the Congolese Government in September and October 2011, a delegation of the UN Working Group on Enforced or Involuntary Disappearances noted that those responsible for enforced disappearances had been neither identified nor punished and that the fate of the disappeared remained unknown. Recommendations made by the Group included the continuation of investigations, the incorporation of enforced disappearance into the criminal code as an autonomous offence and the establishment of a truth and reconciliation commission.

FOREIGN RELATIONS

After the 1997 civil war the principal aim of Congolese foreign policy was to gain international recognition of the legitimacy of the Sassou-Nguesso Government, and to ensure the continued support of the Congo's bilateral and multilateral donors. These efforts were largely successful, particularly following Sassou-Nguesso's election to the presidency in March 2002.

France, the former colonial power, is the source of more than one-half of total assistance to the Republic of the Congo, the major supplier of imports and the primary business partner in the extraction of petroleum. During the 1997 civil war President Lissouba accused France of favouring the rebel forces of Sassou-Nguesso (who was reported to have allied himself with French petroleum interests) over the elected administration. In 1998 Lissouba and Kolélas attempted, unsuccessfully, to sue the French petroleum company Elf Aquitaine (now Total), claiming that it had provided support for Sassou-Nguesso. In May of that year France normalized relations with the Congo, resuming the supply of aid and instituting military co-operation, and Sassou-Nguesso made an official visit to France in September 2002, when he met President Jacques Chirac.

Relations between the Congo and France were, however, strained from mid-2002, as a result of an investigation by a French court into several Congolese officials, including President Sassou-Nguesso, in connection with the reported disappearance of 353 Congolese citizens, following their return from asylum in the DRC to the Congo in 1999 (see The 'Beach Affair', above). In December 2002 the Congo filed a case against France at the International Court of Justice (ICJ) at The Hague, Netherlands, claiming that the investigations represented a violation of Congolese sovereignty and disregarded Sassou-Nguesso's immunity as a Head of State. Hearings into the case at the ICJ commenced in April 2003, and in June the ICJ ruled that investigations into the Inspector-General of the Congolese armed forces, Gen. Norbert Dabira, could continue, while noting that no action that warranted the intervention of the ICJ had yet been undertaken against Sassou-Nguesso or other government ministers. However, the ICJ was not expected to issue an imminent ruling on the legitimacy of the jurisdiction of French courts over actions that were alleged to have occurred on Congolese territory. In November 2004 the Court of Appeal in Paris ruled that all French legal proceedings relating to the so-called 'Beach affair' should be halted, as the French judiciary did not have legitimate jurisdiction in the case. In January 2007 the French Court of Cassation overturned this ruling, raising the possibility of a resumption of French legal proceedings and prompting Sassou-Nguesso to accuse France of interfering in Congolese affairs. In June, however, the Court of Appeal in Versailles formally dismissed the case against the head of the Congo's national police force, Col Jean-François Ndenguet, in relation to the disappearances, a ruling that was upheld by the Court of Cassation in April 2008. In November 2010 the Congo withdrew its complaint against France at the ICJ, and proceedings at the Court were discontinued.

Sassou-Nguesso was again threatened with legal proceedings in France in December 2008, when the French wing of the anti-corruption non-governmental agency Transparency International, together with a Gabonese citizen, filed a lawsuit against the President and his Equato-Guinean and Gabonese counterparts, accusing them of using misappropriated public funds to purchase properties and other assets in France. A French judge ruled Transparency International's complaint to be 'admissible' in May 2009, but this decision was reversed in October by the Court of Appeal in Paris. In November 2010, however, the French Court of Cassation overturned the ruling of the Court of Appeal, thus allowing a judicial investigation to be opened into the case. Meanwhile, the French Government continued to provide considerable assistance to the Congo. France granted the Congolese Government €24m. in April 2005 to enable it to settle its arrears with the African Development Bank, and a framework agreement was signed providing for French assistance with the restructuring of the Congolese armed forces and national police force. A further €116m. was promised in March 2007, to be disbursed during 2007–11, principally for projects related to health, the environment and education.

In the 1997 conflict Angolan government troops provided support to Sassou-Nguesso, including the occupation of Pointe-Noire, the Congo's main seaport and focus of the petroleum industry. Angola had accused the Lissouba Government of providing assistance both to rebels of the União Nacional para a Independência Total de Angola (UNITA) and to Cabindan separatist guerrillas. In response to international criticism of his role, President José Eduardo dos Santos of Angola announced in early 1998 that the majority of his forces had departed the Congo. However, Angolan troops played an important role in the defeat of the rebel attack on Brazzaville in December 1998. In January 1999 the Heads of State of Angola, the Congo, and the DRC met to agree a common policy on the conflicts in their countries. In December the interior ministers of the three countries met in Luanda, Angola, and signed a co-operation accord. The accord created a tripartite commission to ensure border security, the free movement of people and goods, the training of personnel, and the provision of assistance to displaced persons. In late 2006 the office of the UN High Commissioner for Refugees (UNHCR) increased efforts to repatriate around 2,900 Angolan refugees who had fled to the Congo during the civil war in their own country, and at the end of 2011 the number of Angolan refugees in the Congo stood at 918. The refugee status of Angolans in the Congo expired at the end of June 2012.

Relations between the Republic of the Congo and the DRC steadily improved from the late 1990s. In December 1999 Sassou-Nguesso paid a brief visit to the DRC in order to discuss bilateral co-operation and the implementation of the tripartite Luanda accord, and further discussion on issues of common interest, including, notably, border security and the rehabilitation of refugees and displaced persons, regularly took place in subsequent years. In May 2001 some 19 DRC nationals suspected of involvement in the assassination of President Laurent-Désiré Kabila in January of that year were extradited from the Republic of the Congo to Kinshasa, DRC. In September 2002 Congolese authorities announced that, in accordance with a programme established in association with the International Organization for Migration, up to 4,000 soldiers from the DRC who had sought refuge in, or deserted to, the Congo were to be repatriated. Delegations from the Congo and the DRC, meeting in Brazzaville in May 2004, reached agreement on the urgent need to repatriate voluntarily and reintegrate former combatants who had taken refuge in their respective countries, and formed a joint technical committee charged with monitoring the implementation of national programmes of demobilization, disarmament and reintegration; the presence of these former soldiers and militiamen had often created tensions between the two countries. At least 400 Congolese refugees returned home from the DRC during 2004, and in April 2005 the repatriation of some 57,000 refugees from the Congo to the DRC's Équateur province commenced under an agreement signed in September 2004 by officials from the two countries and UNHCR. At the end of 2006 46,341 DRC refugees remained in the Congo. This number had been reduced to 27,605 by the end of 2007 and to 13,973 by the end of 2008, following the intensification of the voluntary repatriation programme. However, inter-ethnic violence in Équateur province led to a renewed influx of DRC refugees to north-eastern Congo from October 2009, with 103,213 registered with UNHCR by the end of the year. A tripartite agreement on the voluntary repatriation of the refugees was concluded by UNHCR and the two countries in June 2010, although 131,648 DRC refugees remained in the Congo at the end of 2011, according to UNHCR. A repatriation programme commenced in May 2012: UNHCR planned to assist 81,000 DRC refugees to return to Équateur province by July 2013.

The Congo, Rwanda and UNHCR signed an agreement in June 2003 providing for the voluntary repatriation of an estimated 5,000 Rwandan refugees believed to be resident in the Congo; the first group of refugees returned to Rwanda in June 2004. However, many of the refugees were reluctant to return to Rwanda, and at the end of 2011 the number of Rwandan refugees in the Congo totalled 8,674. However, the refugee status of Rwandans in the Congo expired at the end of June 2012.

At June 2011 there were some 9,500 Congolese refugees and asylum seekers in Gabon, where they had fled in 1997–98 as a result of the civil conflict. Following the expiry of the refugee status of Congolese nationals in Gabon in July, the Congolese Minister of Social Affairs, Humanitarian Action and Solidarity, Emilienne Raoul, announced that 300m. francs CFA had been allocated to facilitate the repatriation of those who did not seek to remain in Gabon as migrants; by the beginning of September 692 had returned to the Congo, with UNHCR assistance, while applications for residence permits for some 3,500 others had been lodged with the Gabonese authorities. According to UNHCR, 421 Congolese refugees remained in Gabon at the end of the year.

Economy

VICTORIA HOLLIGAN

According to the 2011 Human Development Index of the UN Development Programme (UNDP), the Republic of the Congo is one of the most developed countries on the African continent, with a ranking of 137 out of 187 countries, yet lack of diversification, high unemployment, food insecurity and the impact of the armed conflicts of the 1990s have hampered balanced economic growth. The income poverty rate is high, at more than 50% of the population. In terms of specific human development indicators, between 1980 and 2011 the Congo's life expectancy at birth increased by 1.1 years, and mean years of schooling grew by 3.4 years, according to the UN, while gross national income (GNI) per head rose by about 16%.

Since independence in 1960 economic policy in the Congo has moved from one end of the ideological spectrum to close to the other. For the first 15 years or so a systematic policy of state participation in productive enterprise was pursued, although the private sector was initially permitted to continue its activities, especially in mining, forestry and transport. Upon becoming Head of State in 1977, Jacques-Joachim Yhombi-Opango emphasized that the Congo would benefit from the expertise that private investment and a 'mixed' economy could provide. Under Gen. Denis Sassou-Nguesso, who ousted Yhombi-Opango two years later, foreign management consortia were introduced to restructure highly inefficient nationalized companies, while the petroleum sector was further opened to private foreign investment. However, full-scale economic restructuring was only undertaken following the devaluation of the franc CFA in January 1994, albeit with limited success.

In 1994 the Government of President Pascal Lissouba (1992–97) agreed, with reluctance, to an IMF-sponsored programme for the privatization of the major public sector industries and a substantial reduction in the number of civil servants. The Congo was accorded an Enhanced Structural Adjustment Facility (ESAF) by the IMF in 1996. However, progress was impeded by the civil war, which severely disrupted economic activity in Brazzaville, and by the sharp decline in the international price of petroleum, the mainstay of the economy. The IMF's structural adjustment policies have been widely criticized as being orientated toward providing fiscal and budgetary stability in a manner detrimental to the delivery of basic services, such as health care and education.

The new administration of Sassou-Nguesso, which took power in 1997, inheriting a devastated infrastructure, immediately confirmed its commitment to privatization. In 1998 the IMF agreed to a special post-conflict recovery credit, and in

2000 the Government announced a provisional three-year programme for the rehabilitation and development of the country's social and economic infrastructure. Measures were also to be implemented to improve the management of petroleum revenue. An IMF Staff Monitored Programme (SMP) was signed in 2001, and further post-conflict credits were approved by the World Bank in 2001 and 2002. Delays in implementing structural reforms and deteriorating fiscal performance meant that the IMF deemed progress unsatisfactory, but, following stronger progress in 2004, at the end of that year the IMF approved a three-year (2004–07) arrangement under its Poverty Reduction and Growth Facility (PRGF—the successor to the ESAF) valued at SDR 54.99m. However the programme faltered in the first half of 2006, owing to expenditure overrun and lack of progress in the implementation of structural reforms. With the PRGF suspended, an SMP was agreed (covering April–September 2007) in mid-2007, but fiscal slippages and partial or delayed implementation of some structural reforms meant that it was not successfully completed. A further SMP for January–June 2008 was subsequently implemented, upon satisfactory completion of which a new three-year PRGF, worth SDR 8.46m. and covering the period 2008–11, was approved by the IMF in December 2008. The PRGF, subsequently called the Extended Credit Facility (ECF), aimed to achieve balanced growth and fiscal sustainability, along with debt relief through the enhanced initiative for heavily indebted poor countries (HIPC). Despite the programme being implemented in the context of an international financial and economic crisis, the Government made good progress in applying reforms, especially related to oil governance, and through attempting to foster balanced economic growth. On the conclusion of Article IV consultations with the Congo in mid-2012, the IMF none the less emphasized the need to consolidate gains to the benefit of the population.

Partly as a result of Brazzaville's former status as the capital of French Equatorial Africa, and partly because the Congo and Oubangui rivers have long provided the main access to the Central African Republic (CAR) and Chad, services—transport and public administration in particular—traditionally played an unusually large role in the economy, and accounted for close to one-half of gross domestic product (GDP) in the early 1990s. The relative importance of services has since declined with the development of the petroleum sector, structural adjustment policies adopted by the Congolese Government in compliance with the IMF, and the impact of the civil war on transport activities.

Economic growth has fluctuated widely, reflecting a combination of periods of political instability and the development of the petroleum sector. A decline in petroleum production meant that overall GDP growth decelerated from a peak of 8.2% in 2000 to 3.6% in 2001, although it rose again, to 5.4%, in 2002. Meanwhile, the return to peace in 2000–02 boosted economic activity in the non-petroleum sector, with non-petroleum GDP growth averaging 16.6% in 2000, 12.1% in 2001 and 9.7% in 2002. Reflecting both a recovery in petroleum production and the robust contribution particularly of construction and manufacturing in the non-oil sector, real GDP increased by 7.8% in 2005 and by 6.1% in 2006. An overall decline in economic activity of 0.8% was reported in 2007, associated with a temporary reduction in oil production because of an accident on the main production platform, although the non-petroleum sector grew by 6.3%. In 2008 overall growth was lower than anticipated, recorded by the IMF at 5.6%, as a result of ongoing technical issues on the Nkossa platform related to the previous year's accident and a decline in exports particularly of timber. Petroleum GDP increased by 6.1%, and non-petroleum GDP by 5.4%. The telecommunications, construction and transport sectors drove the latter, according to the IMF.

The prominence of the oil sector has led to productive resources being diverted from traditional exports, such as coffee, cocoa and timber, towards oil-related activities. GDP grew by 7.5% in 2009, reflecting principally the contribution of petroleum (with 16.2% sectoral growth) and, to a lesser extent, that of the construction sector. Non-oil GDP grew by 3.9%. Measured by an estimated 9.1% increase in GDP, the economy was buoyant in 2010, as a result of strong performance in the oil sector, and non-oil activities such as construction and telecommunications. Oil GDP increased by 14.7%, and non-oil GDP by 6.5%. Economic growth remains fragile, however, as it is overly dependent on oil revenues, with the result that diversification is a key determinant of longer-term growth prospects. GDP increased by 5.3% in 2011, driven by expansion in the telecommunication, forestry and construction sectors. Petroleum GDP increased by less than 1%, as a result of ongoing technical issues with producing fields, while growth in the non-oil sector was strong, at 6.5%. GDP was expected to grow by 5.7% in 2012 and by 4.7% in 2013, contingent on new factories in the Brazzaville industrial zone achieving full production.

The Congo is lagging behind in the achievement of the Millennium Development Goals (MDG), and is likely to attain only two objectives—universal education and gender equality—by 2015. Despite education and health budgets remaining low, in 2010 the health budget rose by 28%, to 119,200m. francs CFA, compared with the previous year, and the education budget increased by 16%, to 79,300m. francs CFA, over the same period. Specifically in the education sector, the Government has committed to ensuring that all children receive primary education by means of abolishing school fees, distributing free school books and recruiting more teachers. The mortality rate for women in childbirth is one of the highest in Africa, at 624 deaths per 100,000 births. Yet there has been progress in treating HIV/AIDS, tuberculosis and malaria, with the proportion of persons with HIV/AIDS receiving retroviral treatment increasing by 55% between 2008 and 2011, according to *African Economic Outlook*. Malaria treatment for children under 15 years of age and for pregnant women is also available free of charge.

AGRICULTURE

Despite fertile soil and adequate rainfall, the agricultural sector remains small and mainly comprises subsistence farming. The sector currently only meets around 30% of the country's food demand, using around 5% of arable land. With the exception of palm products, sugar and tobacco, which are grown on modern plantations (particularly in the south-western Niari valley), most agricultural crops are produced by families on small farms. Although the Congo's food crop production has increased since the end of the civil war, the country remains far from self-sufficient; it was listed as one of the African countries faced with an exceptional food emergency in 2007. Food imports, mainly meat and fish products, cereals, flour and vegetables, cost about 130,000m. francs CFA per year, according to FAO, and account for 60% of cereal/meat needs and 50% of seafood needs. Agriculture contributed an average annual of 5.5% to GDP over the period 2000–07; its share amounted to 4.3% in 2008 and 5.4% in 2009, but fell to 3.4% in 2010 (a low level by sub-Saharan African standards), according to the African Development Bank (AfDB). In 2011, agriculture contributed 3.3% of GDP, according to *African Economic Outlook*.

Sugar cane and tobacco have traditionally been the most important cash crops. The state corporation that ran the sugar industry, the Sucrerie du Congo, was replaced in 1991 by a joint venture between the Government and a French company. The Société Agricole et de Raffinage de Sucre (SARIS-Congo) reorganized and re-equipped the plantations, allowing them to satisfy domestic demand. As a result, annual production of raw sugar reached a new record of 66,600 metric tons in 2006, just below its annual capacity of 70,000 tons. Exports were estimated at 30,500 tons in 2007 and were forecast to reach 33,500 tons in 2008, according to the Banque des Etats de l'Afrique Centrale (BEAC). However, poor infrastructure and insecurity in the region are a major hindrance to the sugar sector. In addition, the country is to lose preferential market access to the European Union (EU) under new trading arrangements for African, Caribbean and Pacific (ACP) countries.

Aware that the dominance of the oil sector has resulted in productive resources being diverted from agriculture, the Government is working to revive the agricultural sector and improve food security through investment and technology transfer with the World Bank, the EU and the governments of the People's Republic of China and South Africa. As part of the Agricultural Development Project launched by the World Bank in 2007, US $20m. was to be invested in agricultural and fishing developments in rural areas over the period 2008–13. The EU-funded Food and Nutritional Security Project, launched in February 2009, was to be implemented by FAO, the UN Children's Fund (UNICEF) and the World Food Programme over a six-year period. In 2011 an agreement was signed with FAO for watershed development in Brazzaville in order to increase food security. Further initiatives undertaken in that year included the construction of a second agricultural village and the purchase of a second batch of tractors and machinery for the opening of farming machines centres in the Niari, Kouilou and Cuvette ouest regions.

Agro-industrial projects have also been launched in the sector, including a project with a South African partner to produce alcohol from sugar cane and numerous biofuels projects. Three external partners requested use of 1.75m. ha of land to cultivate palm trees for the production of biofuels. The Italian renewable power specialist FRI-EL Green has entered into a 30-year agreement to cultivate palm oil on 10,000 ha of land owned by Sangha Palm and Régie Nationale des Palmeraies du Congo.

In 2010 the Congolese Government and Agri SA, the main South African farmers union, signed an agreement whereby 200,000 ha of farmland would be leased to South African farmers to grow maize and soya beans, and establish poultry and dairy farms. The land was to be leased initially for 30 years, with the possibility of renewal, and farmers were to benefit from a five-year 'tax holiday' and an import tax exemption for agricultural inputs. Although the scheme is intended to improve domestic food security by reducing food imports, both FAO and local farmers have been critical, on the grounds that it ignores the land rights of Congolese smallholders and shows little concern for whether benefits would be extended to the local population. Concern has also been expressed that the incoming farmers favour cultivation of profitable tropical fruit for export to Europe, as opposed to food for the local market.

Animal husbandry has developed slowly, owing to the prevalence of the tsetse fly and the importance of the forestry sector, which has restricted the availability of pasture. Although numbers of livestock are increasing, the country is not self-sufficient in meat and dairy products. While river-fishing remains artisanal, sea-fishing is carried out commercially on a small scale, especially for tuna.

Forestry

Forestry is a major economic activity. Forests cover about 55% of the Congo's total area and are a significant natural resource. Timber was the main export until it was superseded by petroleum in the mid-1970s. The principal woods exploited are okoumé, limba and sapele, and there are substantial plantations of eucalyptus in the south-west of the country. Until 1987 the purchase and sale of logs was a monopoly of the state-owned Office Congolais des Bois. By 2001 some 95% of timber production was carried out by the private sector, with foreign companies accounting for a majority share in production. The exploitation by foreign investors of forest resources, particularly in the north of the country, has been encouraged. The Government has also attempted to relieve pressure on virgin forest by requiring forestry companies to engage in reforestation and also by increasing production within managed plantations, partly to fulfil local demand for fuel wood. A 2002 revision to the forestry code, compelling companies to process at least 85% of their production locally or pay a supplementary tax on all log exports, had some limited success. The code was revised in 2007, replacing the supplementary tax with a fine. Government receipts from forestry declined from 29,749m. francs CFA in 2007 to 18,134m. francs CFA in 2008, as offending firms no longer paid the supplementary tax. In May 2011 the board of the Extractive Industries Transparency Initiative (EITI) stated that the Congo had made good progress in complying with regulations in the forestry sector, and the country is likely to be declared to be in compliance with the initiative in the near future.

The exploitation of fast-growing trees began in 1978 when the first eucalyptus plantations were introduced to produce paper pulp, and electricity and telephone poles for exports. There were major difficulties from 2001, when the majority shareholder, Shell Holding Bermuda, withdrew from Eucalyptus du Congo (ECO). Production subsequently declined dramatically, from 531,100 metric tons in 2000 to 61,200 tons in 2003. No production of eucalyptus was recorded in 2004 and 2005, but there was output of 130,500 tons in 2006 and 185,600 tons in 2007, according to BEAC, with the recovery largely relecting strong demand from China. Exports to China, mainly of logs, increased in value from US $3m. in 2000 to $130m. in 2007. According to statistics compiled by the IMF, timber production amounted to 1,880,500 cu m in 2007, of which 905,400 cu m were exported as logs. The global financial and economic crisis from late 2007 had a negative impact on the Congo's timber industry in terms of declining world prices and lower demand for timber products. Log production fell from 1,275,900 cu m in 2008 to 77,109 cu m in 2009. The sector continued to be adversely affected by the global economic recession in 2010, with timber production declining to 62,146 cu m. Yet, higher demand from Asian countries is set to benefit Congolese timber; China currently accounts for 70% of the Congo's timber exports, while Olam of Singapore is in the process of acquiring the Société Congolaise des Industrielle Bois (CIB), a subsidiary of Danish Group Dalhoff Larsen & Horneman (DLH Group). Meanwhile, the Canadian mining company MagIndustries Corpn, which acquired the newly formed Eucalyptus Fibre Congo (EFC) through its forestry division, MagForestry, in July 2005, recorded an increase in output of eucalyptus and pine chips from 162,301 tons in 2008 (half-year production from start-up) to 387,773 tons in 2009.

Statistics on forestry exports can be misleading, as they fail to account for illegal trade. In 2009 a legally binding Voluntary Partnership Agreement was reached with the EU to ensure that wood products exported from the Congo to the EU contained no illegally harvested timber, with the aim of protecting government revenues from taxes on the timber supply chain. From July 2011 all forestry exports entering the EU were obliged to have an authorization stamp confirming that the timber and wood products were of legal origin. This agreement was expected to help promote the sustainable development of the forestry sector, and provide new investment opportunities and jobs. In early 2011 the Congolese Government signed a contract with a British-based technology provider, Helveta, for a national traceability system to guarantee the legality of all wood products in the Congo and to enable Forest Law Enforcement, Governance and Trade (FLEGT) licences to be issued for wood exports. Currently, the country's Independent Forestry Observatory aims to oversee the application of forestry legislation, and the Congo is part of the UN Collaborative Programme on Reducing Emissions from Deforestation and Forest Degradation in Developing Countries (UN-REDD).

MINING AND ENERGY

The Congo is the fifth largest producer of crude petroleum in sub-Saharan Africa, after Nigeria, Angola, Sudan (including South Sudan and Equatorial Guinea). The country also holds significant reserves of natural gas. The petroleum sector's contribution to GDP declined in the first half of the 2000s, as a result of both the maturing of major oilfields and recovery in the non-petroleum sector. This trend was reversed in 2005, as petroleum production recovered, and in 2006 the petroleum sector accounted for 60.4% of GDP. Oil has maintained an overwhelming dominance in export earnings and government revenue. According to the IMF, petroleum revenue accounted for 84.0% of export earnings and 81.3% of total budget revenue in 2007. Actual earnings from crude petroleum exports totalled 1,284,000m. francs CFA in that year, according to the IMF, despite the continued depreciation of the US dollar (the currency in which international petroleum sales are denominated) and a decrease in petroleum production. Revenue from petroleum exports reached 3,386,000m. francs CFA in 2008, as a result of sustained high oil prices and new fields coming on stream. Owing to exceptionally strong production in conjunction with high oil prices, petroleum export revenue amounted to a record 4,110,000m. francs CFA in 2010, compared with 2,980,000m. francs CFA in 2009. This underlines the dependency of the economy on the petroleum sector, as the contribution of petroleum revenue increased from 10.6% of GDP in 2009 to 33.8% of GDP in 2010, and its share of government revenues correspondingly from 70% to 80%. The petroleum sector accounted for 67% of GDP and some 89% of exports in 2011, as high oil prices outpaced declining production.

At the end of 2011 the BP *Statistical Review of World Energy* estimated the Congo's proven petroleum reserves at some 1,900m. barrels, an increase of some 600m. barrels compared with estimates made in the 1990s. This rise in reserves is mostly explained by recent discoveries associated with the intensification of exploration activities in deep- and ultra-deep-water fields. Nkossa—the Congo's largest offshore field, with estimated reserves of 400m. barrels—came into production in 1996, and its development increased the Congo's annual output to 12.6m. metric tons by 1998. With Agip's Kitina field also entering production, output rose further in 1999, to 13.2m. tons. Petroleum production peaked at 13.3m. tons in 2000, before declining to 11.2m. tons in 2004, as a result of lower production in maturing fields (including Nkossa).

Production recovered to 12.5m. tons in 2005 and 13.5m. tons in 2006 as new fields, including Mboundi and Nsoko, came on stream. An accident on the Nkossa platform resulted in a temporary drop in production in 2007, to 11.5m. tons. Production recovered to 12.9m. tons (249,000 barrels per day—b/d) in 2008, with the deep-water Moho-Bilondo field coming on stream (reporting total reserves of 230m. barrels). Gas from the field was to be reinjected into the Nkossa field to improve recovery. The offshore development comprised 14 sub-sea wells tied back to a floating production unit, with oil being exported via the onshore Djeno terminal. The Azurite field within the Mer Profonde Sud licence, operated by Murphy (50%) with partners PA Resources (35%) and the state oil company Société Nationale des Pétroles du Congo (SNPC—15%), came on stream in 2009, using the industry's first floating, drilling, production, storage and offloading vessel (FDPSO), with reported reserves of 75m. barrels. With production from Moho-Bilondo nearly tripling in 2009, and the Azurite field coming on stream, overall output increased to 14.1m. tons (274,000 b/d) in that year. Further discoveries were made in the northern part of the Moho-Bilondo field, preliminary studies having been undertaken to develop resources of an estimated 300m. barrels of oil. Total Congo (formerly Elf Congo) is the operator of this field, with a 53.5% stake, while Chevron of the USA holds 31.5% and SNPC 15%. Output increased to a record 15.3m. tons (298,000 b/d) in 2010. Production was expected to decline after 2011 unless new discoveries are secured. Growth in the oil and gas sector fell below 1% in 2011, as technical issues impeded production at Nkossa. Despite the average production rate falling by 4% in 2011, continued high international prices offset the impact on the economy of reduced output.

Total Congo and Agip Congo, respectively wholly-owned subsidiaries of French-Belgian and Italian companies, together account for 98% of the Congo's petroleum production. France and China are the principal purchasers of the Djeno blend quality crude oil, whereas the USA is the main buyer of Nkossa blend.

In 1995 the Government announced that, henceforth, instead of demanding royalty payments from producers, it would enter into production-sharing agreements. Thus, it sold its 25% share in Elf Congo to the French company Elf Aquitaine (which previously held 75% of the share capital), and its 20% share in Agip Recherches Congo to the majority shareholder, Italy's Agip-ENI. The SNPC was established in 1998 to take over the downstream activities of the state-owned Société Nationale de Recherches et d'Exploitation Pétrolière (HYDRO-CONGO). In 2002 Total, the US ChevronTexaco (now Chevron) and the PEX consortium of the British company Puma Energy and X-Oil assumed the sale and distribution activities formerly conducted by HYDRO-CONGO. The Government has attempted to privatize the only petroleum refinery, La Congolaise de Raffinage (CORAF). Based in Pointe-Noire, the refinery resumed production in 2000 after a four-year hiatus. CORAF's output, which has remained well below its capacity of 1m. metric tons, only meets 70% of domestic requirements. An upgrade, to quadruple the capacity and modernize the facility, was scheduled for 2010 in an effort to attract private investors.

The Government has taken steps to increase transparency in managing petroleum sector revenue, for example by completing the audit of the 1999–2001 SNPC accounts in 2003 and by announcing, in 2004, its intention to join the EITI, although some irregularities continued to be recorded in 2005. The Congo was formally accepted as a candidate for the EITI in 2008, and is in the process of implementing the associated action plan providing for the certification of state oil revenue and the audit of state accounts from the SNPC and CORAF. National committees, including civil society representatives, are also involved to ensure the accountability of the state in meeting the EITI terms. As with the forestry sector, the EITI stated in May 2011 that the Congo is soon expected to be declared as being in compliance with the initiative. International firms also audited and certified the accounts of the SNPC and CORAF in 2011.

The Congo also possesses an estimated 3,200,000m. cu ft of proven natural gas, according to *Oil and Gas Journal*, which will be used for power generation at the Pointe-Noire gas-fired power plant, when constructed, and for industry (see below). Gas output increased by almost 50% in 2010, to 110,375 metric tons, as a result of high production rates from the Nkossa field.

Lead, zinc, gold and copper are produced in small quantities, and deposits of phosphate and bauxite are known. Foreign interest in the non-petroleum mining sector has increased. In 2008 MagMinerals Inc, a subsidiary of MagIndustries, was awarded a 25-year mining licence for a potash mine in the Kouilou concession. Construction of the US $730m. plant began in late 2009, and production of 600,000 metric tons was expected in 2011, doubling to 1.2m. tons in 2012. A multi-year gas purchase agreement was signed with Italy's ENI to provide energy for processing and power generation back-up from the offshore M'boundi field. All potash production was to be bought by Ameropa of Switzerland, and was expected to be exported to Brazil. MagMinerals decided to develop the potash mine ahead of magnesium deposits acquired in 1997 as the former was considered more profitable, cheaper and quicker to develop, given increasing demand for fertilizer from markets in South Asia, Europe and South America. The Congolese Government retained a 10% interest in the mine. In 2004 the Government granted diamond-exploration rights to an Israeli-owned company, Brazzaville Mining Resource, and in 2007 three diamond-exploration concessions were awarded to the Canadian-based Mexivada Mining. In 2008 Mexivada reported the discovery of gold in the Malambani concession, along with the discovery of a 0.5-mm white diamond in the Lepandza target, located near the Mayoko field. A further licence to prospect in the Malambani region has been granted. The Congo was disqualified from the Kimberley Process Certification Scheme in 2004, as a result of discrepancies between the country's diamond production and exports, but was readmitted in 2007. The US group Gerald Metals produced 16,000 tons of copper ore at Boko Songho and Yanga Koubanza in 2010, for export to Germany and China.

Production and distribution of electricity have been in the hands of the state-owned Société Nationale d'Electricité since 1967; proposals for its privatization have been repeatedly delayed since the late 1990s. Net generating capacity was 118 MW in 2003, of which about three-quarters were accounted for by the hydroelectric stations on the Bouenza and Djoué rivers. National electricity production totalled an estimated 1,947m. kWh in 2005, some 955m. kWh of which was hydroelectric. In 2010 there was a complete shutdown of the 35.5-MW thermal power station in Brazzaville; however, production of electricity increased at the Moukoukoulou hydroelectric plant and the Djeno gas-fired power station. An estimated 25% of the national requirement is imported from the neighbouring Democratic Republic of the Congo.

The Congo's enormous hydroelectric potential (as much as 3,000 MW, which could transform the country into a net exporter) remains underexploited, owing to the low level of domestic consumption and also because the infrastructure is lacking to export output to regional markets. The construction of a 120-MW hydroelectric power station at Imboulou on the Léfini river, by the Congolese Government and two Chinese companies, began in 2003 and was completed in May 2011. This new power station was expected to double the Congo's generating capacity. The Government also intends eventually to use the country's natural gas resources for electricity production. In December 2002 Agip and ChevronTexaco completed the country's first natural gas-fired power station near Pointe-Noire, with a capacity of 25 MW. A further plant, with a capacity of 300 MW, is being constructed at Pointe-Noire, along with 800 km of high-tension power lines linking the north and south.

MANUFACTURING

Administrative bottlenecks and ingrained corruption have continued to hinder private sector activities. Manufacturing mainly takes the form of the processing of agricultural and forest products, and most industry is based in Brazzaville, Pointe-Noire and Nkayi. The sector has been disadvantaged by the high value of the franc CFA, which has undermined its competitiveness, and by energy rationing. Nevertheless, brewing is a significant industry, followed by the processing of sugar cane and the supply from eucalyptus plantations to a telegraph pole and charcoal factory. These products also sell to export markets. Cement production started in 2004, with production estimated at 62,000 metric tons in 2005. The manufacturing sector grew at an average annual rate of more than 11% over the period 2000–07, and by 18.9% in 2008, yet only contributed 4.2% to GDP in that year. The brewing and sugar cane-processing sectors reported strong growth of 15.1% and 14.3%, respectively, in 2009, according to *African Economic Outlook*. Specifically, the SARIS sugar refinery produced 70,000 metric tons in 2009, 40% of which was designated for local consumption. The manufacturing sector's contribution to GDP fell to 2.8% in 2011, whereas that of the transport and communications sector increased, albeit marginally, from 4.2% in 2006 to 4.3% in 2011.

TRANSPORT AND TELECOMMUNICATIONS

The Republic of the Congo plays an important role in the trans-equatorial transport system that links Chad, the CAR and parts of Cameroon and Gabon with the Atlantic coast; all of the rail and much of the river portion of the system is located in the Congo. The deep-water port at Pointe-Noire is the terminus of this network, and is Central Africa's second most important gateway, after Douala in Cameroon. Annually, the port is estimated to handle 2.2m. metric tons of import freight and 640,000 tons of export freight. The river system (in all, more than 4,000 km is navigable) is also of great significance as a transport artery, reaching areas of the country that would otherwise be isolated (particularly in the north).

Some 60%–70% of the traffic on the 518-km Congo-Océan railway (which links Pointe-Noire and Brazzaville) is international. Operations were suspended as a result of fighting in the area in 1998–2000, and again in mid-2002. Improved security conditions have since permitted rail traffic to resume, but rehabilitation work has been slow, and the railway has continued to encounter frequent disruption. A 10-year investment programme, worth US $623m., was announced in 2007.

Other transport facilities, and especially the road network, are little developed, owing to the great distances and dense equatorial forest. Large areas in the north of the country have no road access, and proposals to build roads there have encountered opposition from environmental groups, as well as funding constraints. A substantial proportion of the road network became impassable as a result of the civil war, and some towns, particularly in the Pool region, became isolated without reliable access to major roads. Poor communications and a badly maintained transport infrastructure continued to constitute a major obstacle to economic development. As part of the Agricultural Development and Road Rehabilitation project launched by the World Bank in 2007, 1,300 km of roads (10.4% of the rural road network) was to be rehabilitated in 2008–13 to connect rural communities to key markets.

Spending on infrastructure has remained a priority of the Government's public investment programme. The major highways from Brazzaville to Kinkala, the capital of the Pool region, were being improved, with the support of the EU. Plans for a year-round river port to be constructed at Lékéti, from where an upgraded road would extend to Lékoni, in Gabon, were slow to materialize. However, the 183-km Route 1 from Pointe-Noire to Dolisie was resurfaced in 2009. There are international airports at Brazzaville (refurbishment of which was completed in the early 2000s) and Pointe-Noire, as well as five regional airports and 12 smaller airfields. Construction of a new international airport at Ollombo, approximately 500 km north of Brazzaville, began in early 2001; the airport, which opened in July 2008, was the subject of much controversy.

The telecommunications sector has expanded, with four private sector mobile phone companies, Azur Télécom, Zain (now Airtel Congo), MTN and Warid, operating in the country. The state-owned Société des Télécommunications du Congo (SOTELCO) was first mooted for privatization in 2002, following its separation from the Office National des Postes et Télécommunications. The installation of optical fibre as part of a submarine cable project in 2011 was expected to enhance the growth of the sector, which contributed 4.7% of GDP in 2010.

PUBLIC FINANCE

Following a significant contraction in petroleum revenues (as a result of a decline in world prices for petroleum products) from 1986, the Government turned to the IMF for support and adopted a structural adjustment programme with the aim of restoring balance in public finance through decreases in both current and capital spending. The reduction in the former was achieved by means of a wide range of measures, including a freeze on government salaries and the rationalization of several loss-making state-owned companies. There followed a substantial decrease in the deficit, as higher petroleum revenues from 1996 reflected the commencement of production at Nkossa and a rise in the share of revenues, from 17.5% to 31.0%, due to be paid to the Government in accordance with production-sharing agreements. However, the drastic fall in public expenditure failed to promote balanced growth and poverty reduction strategies. Current fiscal policy aims to improve the quality of public spending through efficient use of natural resource revenues to stimulate balanced economic growth.

In 2004 the Government took additional steps to increase transparency in the petroleum sector and centralize government revenues, and an estimated budget surplus (including grants and on a commitment basis) of 89,000m. francs CFA, equivalent to 3.9% GDP, was recorded. In that year alone the Government settled 1,613,000m. francs CFA in external payment arrears. Revenues from petroleum increased almost two-fold in 2005, reaching the equivalent of 32% of GDP. As a result, 170,000m. francs CFA, equivalent to 5.4% of GDP, was transferred to the central bank's newly created petroleum stabilization account. Non-petroleum revenues were lower than expected, owing to poor customs collections, but the Government continued to maintain tight control over both current and capital expenditure. As a result, the budget surplus increased to an estimated 500,300m. francs CFA in 2005, equivalent to 15.9% of GDP, and grew further, to 21.5% of GDP, in 2006. However, large expenditure overruns were recorded in that year, prompting the IMF to suspend the PRGF agreed in 2004. An SMP was pursued in 2007, although further fiscal slippages associated with higher subsidies to the petroleum sector and costs related to that year's legislative election meant that the programme was not successfully completed. The budget surplus narrowed to 13.9% of GDP in that year.

Upon satisfactory performance under a new SMP, for January–June 2008, a three-year PRGF, worth SDR 8.46m. and covering the period 2008–11, was approved by the IMF in December 2008. Spending discipline, along with relatively high oil prices, significantly improved the fiscal position in 2008, in the assessment of the IMF. Revenues from oil reached a record 2,118,000m. francs CFA in 2008, compared with

1,284,000m. francs CFA in 2007. Total revenues equivalent to 159.3% of non-petroleum GDP and total expenditures representing 79.5% of non-petroleum GDP resulted in an overall budget surplus on a commitment basis (including grants) of 79.8% of non-petroleum GDP (1,424,000m. francs CFA) in 2008. In the same year the basic non-petroleum primary deficit declined to the equivalent of 44.3% of non-petroleum GDP, compared with 55.7% in 2007. The overall budget surplus fell from 26% of GDP in 2008 to 5.4% of GDP in 2009, mainly reflecting lower oil revenues. However, a broadening of the tax base meant that non-petroleum revenues increased to the equivalent of 8.2% of GDP. In 2009 the Government attempted to stimulate economic growth and address poverty by increasing public investment to an estimated 30% of GDP, from 26% in the previous year. Revenue management was a key priority in 2010, with accompanying initiatives in the computerization of revenue recovery services, taxpayer registration, and an anti-fraud campaign. The budget surplus increased to 13.9% of GDP in 2010, with total revenue equivalent to 35.5% of GDP, mainly comprising oil revenues (which accounted for 25.7% of GDP). The overall budget surplus was estimated to increase to 22% of GDP in 2011. This reflected an increase in revenue to the equivalent of 44.2% of GDP, driven mainly by the oil sector, the contribution of which grew from 22.7% of GDP in 2010 to 30% in 2011. For 2012, a surplus of 20% was expected, as oil revenue again increased with the anticipated resolution of technical issues. Meanwhile, however, tax exemptions in the non-oil sector, fraud and tax evasion contributed to a decline in the tax revenues in the non-oil sector to the equivalent of 9% of GDP in 2011.

FOREIGN TRADE AND PAYMENTS

Having remained in deficit throughout the 1990s, rising international oil prices meant that the current account balance turned positive in 2000, at an equivalent of 7.9% of GDP. Strong petroleum prices continued to offset declining oil output and the weakness of the US dollar against the franc CFA in subsequent years. Tighter fiscal discipline from 2004, combined with rising petroleum production and prices in the following year, allowed the Government to clear much of the arrears on its external debt payments, while the current account surplus rose from 42,000m. francs CFA (equivalent to 2.2% of GDP) in 2004 to 344,000m. francs CFA (11.7%) in 2005. However, the current account returned to deficit, equivalent to 19.5% of GDP, in 2007, reflecting a decline in oil production, imports of equipment to repair the Nkossa platform, and service imports related to investment in the oil sector. Increased foreign investment in the oil, telecommunications and mining sectors partly financed this deficit. The current account deficit narrowed to 1.6% of GDP in 2008, driven by sustained high oil prices and heavy investment in the oil sector, resulting in an overall balance of payments surplus of 1,064,000m. francs CFA. Terms of trade deteriorated in 2009, with a renewed widening in the current account deficit, to 8.2% of GDP, reflecting a fall in the value of oil and timber exports, and increased imports of consumer and capital goods. In 2010 sustained high oil prices contributed to a surplus on the current account equivalent to 2.7% of GDP, according to the IMF. High value oil exports resulted in an increase in the current account surplus to 13.3% of GDP in 2011. The surplus was expected to widen further in 2012, to 14.6% of GDP, again driven by the oil sector. While development aid inflows remain low, at 4% of GDP, foreign direct investment, of which oil is the main beneficiary sector, grew by 26.4% in 2011, to US $2,800m.

While borrowing from official creditors expanded only slowly, borrowing from private creditors rose sharply in the early 1980s, and by the end of 1990 total external debt had risen to US $4,947m., or 212.9% of GNI, making the Congo the most heavily indebted African nation at the time, on a per-head basis. The debt-service ratio was equivalent to 35.3% of revenue from exports of goods and services, a dangerously high level in view of the Government's practice of borrowing against future petroleum earnings. A new programme of support by external donors, led by France, commenced in 1990, enabling the Congo to pay off some of its debt arrears, notably to the World Bank. Foreign indebtedness fluctuated slightly in the following years, before reaching a new high of $6,004m. in 1995, equivalent to 488.8% of GNI (at the new US dollar:CFA franc exchange rate). The situation eased thereafter, as a result of the rescheduling of $989m. in liabilities after the currency was devalued, and, more significantly, the new round of debt relief extended in 1996 following IMF approval of an ESAF. Bilateral official creditors granted 'Naples terms' (of repayment) on all liabilities incurred before 1986. The debt-service ratio thus fell markedly, from 35.3% in 1990 to 13.1% in 1995, and decreased further in the second half of the 1990s. The debt-service ratio fluctuated in the early 2000s, declining to just 1.0% in 2002 but increasing to 4.0% in the following year.

Interest and principal payment arrears again increased during the civil war, amounting to US $1,042m. and $2,649m., respectively, in 2003. By the end of that year the country's outstanding debt had risen to $5,527m., equivalent to 206.2% of GNI. While the country's total debt increased to $5,829m. in 2004, interest and principal payment arrears both declined, to $443m. and $1,778m. respectively. The Government made steady progress in regularizing its situation with external creditors in 2004 and 2005. In December 2004, following the IMF's approval of a three-year PRGF, the 'Paris Club' of official creditors agreed to cancel $1,680m. and reschedule $1,336m. of the Congo's debt. The country subsequently reached HIPC 'decision point' in 2006. However, 'completion point', which is when a country receives its full amount of debt relief, depended on significant progress being made in aspects of governance and transparency, including public finance management, regular auditing of the oil and forestry sectors, and satisfactory performance under the new PRGF agreed in 2008. The 'London Club' of private creditors meanwhile agreed to a restructuring of commercial debt in November 2007. The following year, the 'Paris Club' rescheduled the Congo's debt on 'Cologne terms' (of repayment). In early 2010 the Congo was deemed to have met the requirements of the IMF to reach 'completion point', thus becoming eligible for debt relief of $1,575m. A further $177.7m. of debt relief was available through the Multilateral Debt Relief Initiative, via debt stock reductions by the International Development Association, the AfDB and the IMF. As a result, external nominal debt fell from the equivalent of 199% of GDP in 2004 to 91% in 2007, and to an estimated 19% of GDP in 2011, according to the IMF. The Congo's bilateral external position also improved dramatically through its attainment of the HIPC 'completion point' in 2010. Debt relief of 74,000m. francs CFA was granted by Italy, 46,000m. francs CFA by Germany, 17,000m. francs CFA by the USA and 5,000m. francs CFA by Switzerland. The Caisse Congolaise d'Amortissement (CCA), the finance ministry department responsible for debt management, has made significant progress in the collection of reliable data, enabling more effective management of national debt. The debt-to-GDP ratio fell from almost 100% in 2007 to 55% in 2009, and to an estimated 20% in 2011, according to *African Economic Outlook*.

Statistical Survey

Source (unless otherwise stated): Direction Générale, Centre National de la Statistique et des Etudes Economiques, Immeuble du Plan, Rond point du Centre Culturel Français, BP 2031, Brazzaville; tel. and fax 22-281-59-09; e-mail cnsee@hotmail.com; internet www.cnsee.org.

Area and Population

AREA, POPULATION AND DENSITY

Area (sq km)	342,000*
Population (census results)	
30 July 1996	2,591,271
28 April 2007	
Males	1,821,357
Females	1,876,133
Total	3,697,490
Population (UN estimates at mid-year)†	
2010	4,042,899
2011	4,139,748
2012	4,233,062
Density (per sq km) at mid-2012	12.4

* 132,047 sq miles.

† Source: UN, *World Population Prospects: The 2010 Revision*.

POPULATION BY AGE AND SEX
(UN estimates at mid-2012)

	Males	Females	Total
0–14	862,464	848,902	1,711,366
15–64	1,185,630	1,180,647	2,366,277
65 and over	70,918	84,501	155,419
Total	2,119,012	2,114,050	4,233,062

Source: UN, *World Population Prospects: The 2010 Revision*.

ETHNIC GROUPS

1995 (percentages): Kongo 51.4; Téké 17.2; Mbochi 11.4; Mbédé 4.7; Punu 2.9; Sanga 2.5; Maka 1.8; Pygmy 1.4; Others 6.7 (Source: La Francophonie).

REGIONS AND MUNICIPALITIES
(population at 2007 census)

	Area (sq km)	Population	Capital
Bouenza	12,268	309,073	Madingou
Brazzaville	100	1,373,382	Brazzaville
Cuvette	74,850	156,044	Owando
Cuvette ouest		72,999	Ewo
Kouilou	13,695	807,289	Pointe-Noire
Lékoumou	20,950	96,393	Sibiti
Likouala	66,044	154,115	Impfondo
Niari	25,943	231,271	Loubomo (Dolisie)
Plateaux	38,400	174,591	Djambala
Pool	33,955	236,595	Kinkala
Sangha	55,795	85,738	Ouesso
Total	342,000	3,697,490	

PRINCIPAL TOWNS
(population at 2007 census)

Brazzaville (capital)	1,373,382	Loubomo (Dolisie)	83,798
Pointe-Noire	715,334	Nkayi	71,620

Mid-2011 (incl. suburbs, UN estimate): Brazzaville 1,610,760 (Source: UN, *World Urbanization Prospects: The 2011 Revision*).

BIRTHS AND DEATHS
(annual averages, UN estimates)

	1995–2000	2000–05	2005–10
Birth rate (per 1,000)	37.7	37.2	36.0
Death rate (per 1,000)	12.6	12.5	11.7

Source: UN, *World Population Prospects: The 2010 Revision*.

Life expectancy (years at birth): 57.0 (males 55.7; females 58.2) in 2010 (Source: World Bank, World Development Indicators database).

EMPLOYMENT
('000 persons at 1984 census)

	Males	Females	Total
Agriculture, etc.	105	186	291
Industry	61	8	69
Services	123	60	183
Total	289	254	543

Mid-2012 (estimates in '000): Agriculture, etc. 527; Total labour force 1,735 (Source: FAO).

Health and Welfare

KEY INDICATORS

Total fertility rate (children per woman, 2010)	4.5
Under-5 mortality rate (per 1,000 live births, 2010)	93
HIV/AIDS (% of persons aged 15–49, 2009)	3.4
Physicians (per 1,000 head, 2004)	0.2
Hospital beds (per 1,000 head, 2005)	1.6
Health expenditure (2009): US $ per head (PPP)	108
Health expenditure (2009): % of GDP	2.8
Health expenditure (2009): public (% of total)	47.5
Access to water (% of persons, 2010)	71
Access to sanitation (% of persons, 2010)	18
Total carbon dioxide emissions ('000 metric tons, 2008)	1,936.2
Carbon dioxide emissions per head (metric tons, 2008)	0.5
Human Development Index (2011): ranking	137
Human Development Index (2011): value	0.533

For sources and definitions, see explanatory note on p. vi.

Agriculture

PRINCIPAL CROPS
('000 metric tons)

	2008	2009	2010
Maize	9.9	10.2	10.5
Sweet potatoes*	6.0	7.2	7.7
Cassava (Manioc)	1,112.7	1,148.5	1,148.5
Yams*	12.0	15.4	16.5
Sugar cane*	565.0	600.0	650.0
Groundnuts, with shell	28.2	29.1	29.1
Oil palm fruit*	139.5	140.0	141.3
Bananas*	99.0	99.5	100.0
Plantains	78.6	80.4	81.1
Guavas, mangoes and mangosteens*	26.0	27.8	28.0
Avocados*	6.6	6.5	6.8

* FAO estimates.

Aggregate production ('000 metric tons, may include official, semi-official or estimated data): Total cereals 23.1 in 2008, 24.0 in 2009, 25.0 in 2010; Total roots and tubers 1,175.2 in 2008, 1,227.3 in 2009, 1,232.8 in 2010; Total vegetables (incl. melons) 118.8 in 2008, 125.4 in 2009, 114.4 in 2010; Total fruits (excl. melons) 254.6 in 2008, 260.7 in 2009, 263.8 in 2010.

Source: FAO.

LIVESTOCK
('000 head, year ending September)

	2008	2009	2010
Cattle*	325	310	330
Pigs	69	69*	70*
Sheep*	116	118	120
Goats*	295	315	320
Chickens*	2,450	2,500	2,600

* FAO estimate(s).

Source: FAO.

LIVESTOCK PRODUCTS
('000 metric tons)

	2008	2009	2010*
Cattle meat	6.1	5.6	6.2
Pig meat	1.7	1.8	1.9
Chicken meat	5.9*	6.0*	6.3
Game meat	30.0*	32.0*	39.6
Sheep and goat meat	1.3*	1.4*	1.5
Cows' milk	1.3*	1.3*	1.3
Hen eggs	1.5*	1.6*	1.6

* FAO estimate(s).

Source: FAO.

Forestry

ROUNDWOOD REMOVALS
('000 cubic metres, excluding bark, FAO estimates)

	2008	2009	2010
Sawlogs, veneer logs and logs for sleepers	1,700	1,262	1,695
Pulpwood	361	361	361
Other industrial wood	370	370	370
Fuel wood	1,295	1,315	1,336
Total	3,726	3,308	3,762

2011: Production assumed to be unchanged from 2010 (FAO estimates).

Source: FAO.

SAWNWOOD PRODUCTION
('000 cubic metres, including railway sleepers)

	2009	2010	2011
Total (all broadleaved)	199	179	165

Source: FAO.

Fishing

('000 metric tons, live weight)

	2008	2009	2010
Capture	54.1	61.2	65.2
Freshwater fishes	29.4	28.4	30.5
West African croakers	2.3	3.2	3.8
Sardinellas	9.6	12.2	9.3
Aquaculture	0.1	0.1*	0.1*
Total catch	54.2	61.3*	65.2*

* FAO estimate.

Source: FAO.

Mining

	2008	2009	2010
Crude petroleum ('000 barrels)	85,037	99,348	107,000
Gold (kg)*	100	100	150

* Estimated metal content of ore.

Source: US Geological Survey.

Industry

SELECTED PRODUCTS
('000 metric tons, unless otherwise indicated)

	2007	2008	2009
Raw sugar	56.0	67.0	n.a.
Veneer sheets ('000 cu metres)	14	14	n.a.
Jet fuels	55.0	31.0	34.0
Motor gasoline (petrol)	63.0	46.0	67.0
Kerosene	14	17	21
Distillate fuel oils	141	109	n.a.
Residual fuel oils	437	327	349
Electric energy (million kWh)	407	461	n.a.

Source: UN Industrial Commodity Statistics Database.

Finance

CURRENCY AND EXCHANGE RATES

Monetary Units
100 centimes = 1 franc de la Coopération Financière en Afrique Centrale (CFA).

Sterling, Dollar and Euro Equivalents (31 May 2012)
£1 sterling = 819.959 francs CFA;
US $1 = 528.870 francs CFA;
€1 = 655.957 francs CFA;
10,000 francs CFA = £12.20 = $18.91 = €15.24.

Average Exchange Rate (francs CFA per US $)

2009	472.186
2010	495.277
2011	471.866

Note: The exchange rate of 1 French franc = 50 francs CFA, established in 1948, remained in force until January 1994, when the CFA franc was devalued by 50%, with the exchange rate adjusted to 1 French franc = 100 francs CFA. The relationship to French currency remained in effect with the introduction of the euro on 1 January 1999. From that date, accordingly, a fixed exchange rate of €1 = 655.957 francs CFA has been in operation.

BUDGET
(central government operations, '000 million francs CFA)

Revenue*	2008	2009†	2010‡
Oil revenue	2,118	1,070	2,187
Non-oil revenue	324	372	422
Investment income	20	27	20
Total	2,462	1,469	2,629

Expenditure	2008	2009†	2010‡
Current expenditure	785	587	593
Wages and salaries	166	175	188
Materials and supplies	176	164	175
Transfers	228	172	153
Common charges	42	25	23
Budgetary reserves	—	15	10
Interest payments	150	10	8
External	140	3	2
Domestic	10	7	6
Local authorities	23	25	36
Capital expenditure	453	591	655
Externally financed	64	122	139
Domestically financed	390	469	516
Total	1,238	1,178	1,248

* Excluding grants received ('000 million francs CFA): 18 in 2008; 22 in 2009 (budgeted figure); 33 in 2010 (projection).
† Budgeted figures.
‡ Projections.

Source: IMF, *Republic of Congo: Second Review Under the Three-Year Arrangement Under the Poverty Reduction and Growth Facility—Staff Report; Press Release on the Executive Board Discussion; and Statement by the Executive Director for the Republic of Congo* (February 2010).

2011 ('000 million francs CFA, projections): *Revenue:* Oil revenue 2,627, Non-oil revenue 576, Investment income 36; Total 3,239 (excluding grants 35). *Expenditure:* Current expenditure 687, (Wages and salaries 225, Other current expenditure 411, Local authorities 40, Interest payments 11), Capital expenditure 981 (Externally financed 291, Domestically financed 690); Total 1,668 (Source: IMF, *Republic of Congo: Fifth and Sixth Reviews Under the Three-Year Arrangement Under the Extended Credit Facility and Financing Assurances Review—Staff Report; Staff Statement and Supplement; Press Release on the Executive Board Discussion; and Statement by the Executive Director for the Republic of Congo.*—August 2011).

INTERNATIONAL RESERVES
(US $ million at 31 December)

	2008	2009	2010
Gold (national valuation)	1.62	—	17.82
IMF special drawing rights	0.22	109.83	107.89
Reserve position in IMF	0.89	0.90	0.89
Foreign exchange	3,870.68	3,695.51	4,338.07
Total	3,873.41	3,806.25*	4,464.67

* Excluding gold.

Source: IMF, *International Financial Statistics*.

MONEY SUPPLY
('000 million francs CFA at 31 December)

	2009	2010	2011
Currency outside depository corporations	402.10	449.83	524.63
Transferable deposits	468.93	715.98	1,103.06
Other deposits	137.61	165.15	209.74
Broad money	1,008.64	1,330.96	1,837.42

Source: IMF, *International Financial Statistics*.

COST OF LIVING
(Consumer Price Index for Brazzaville; base: 2000 = 100)

	2007	2008	2009
Food	112.9	122.1	131.3
Clothing	96.0	97.3	100.0
Rent	130.9	137.3	144.7
Fuel and electricity	137.9	143.9	154.0
All items (incl. others)	119.9	128.7	135.1

2010: Food 143.3; All items (incl. others) 139.2.

2011: Food 145.5.

Source: ILO.

NATIONAL ACCOUNTS
('000 million francs CFA at current prices)

Expenditure on the Gross Domestic Product

	2008	2009*	2010*
Government final consumption expenditure	430	417	451
Private final consumption expenditure	1,726	1,605	1,646
Gross fixed capital formation	1,643	1,900	1,892
Changes in inventories	5	5	5
Total domestic expenditure	3,804	3,927	3,994
Exports of goods and services	3,864	3,139	4,858
Less Imports of goods and services	2,388	2,624	2,706
GDP at purchasers' values	5,279	4,443	6,145

Gross Domestic Product by Economic Activity

	2008	2009*	2010*
Agriculture, hunting, forestry and fishing	195	204	227
Mining and quarrying	3,723	2,738	4,243
Manufacturing	184	203	226
Electricity, gas and water	32	33	37
Construction	142	161	183
Trade, restaurants and hotels	274	307	343
Transport and communications	205	227	254
Public administration and defence	198	213	230
Other services	246	269	295
GDP at factor cost	5,197	4,353	6,040
Indirect taxes	82	89	105
GDP in purchasers' values	5,279	4,443	6,145

* Estimates.

Note: Deduction for imputed bank service charge assumed to be distributed at origin.

Source: African Development Bank.

BALANCE OF PAYMENTS
(US $ million)

	2005	2006	2007
Exports of goods f.o.b.	4,745.3	6,065.7	5,808.0
Imports of goods f.o.b.	−1,305.5	−2,003.5	−2,858.1
Trade balance	3,439.8	4,062.2	2,949.9
Exports of services	220.5	266.0	319.4
Imports of services	−1,417.1	−2,425.9	−3,527.7
Balance on goods and services	2,243.2	1,902.3	−258.3
Other income received	17.6	20.1	23.4
Other income paid	−1,595.5	−1,772.6	−1,908.1
Balance on goods, services and income	665.3	149.7	−2,143.1
Current transfers received	87.2	37.9	43.0
Current transfers paid	−56.9	−63.5	−81.0
Current balance	695.6	124.1	−2,181.0
Capital account (net)	11.2	9.6	31.7
Direct investment from abroad	513.6	1,487.7	2,638.4
Portfolio investment assets	−1.1	−1.3	−1.5
Other investment assets	−246.5	−228.9	266.2
Other investment liabilities	−492.7	−831.5	−356.4
Net errors and omissions	30.5	142.5	−201.1
Overall balance	510.5	702.1	196.4

Source: IMF, *International Financial Statistics*.

External Trade

PRINCIPAL COMMODITIES
(distribution by HS, US $ million)

Imports c.i.f.	2008	2009	2010
Machinery, nuclear reactors, boilers, etc.	210.3	291.9	329.5
Electrical, electronic equipment	128.4	138.0	134.1
Articles of iron or steel	155.4	72.3	83.9
Mineral fuels, oils, distillation products, etc.	193.2	109.9	248.6
Petroleum oils, not crude	189.9	98.1	221.9
Ships, boats and other floating structures	1,823.9	2,792.4	2,667.8
Cruise ship, cargo ship, barges	693.3	810.0	773.9
Light vessel, dredger; floating dock; floating/submersible drill platform	1,110.6	1,910.0	1,824.9
Total (incl. others)	3,539.6	4,447.1	4,369.4

Exports f.o.b.	2008	2009	2010
Mineral fuels, oils, distillation products, etc.	7,711.4	5,795.1	4,684.6
Crude petroleum oils	7,486.8	5,550.1	4,481.1
Ships, boats and other floating structures	1,030.5	1,955.1	1,851.2
Cruise ship, cargo ship, barges	478.5	717.9	679.7
Light vessel, dredger; floating dock; floating/submersible drill platform	541.4	1,169.4	1,107.3
Total (incl. others)	9,169.7	8,201.5	6,917.6

Source: Trade Map-Trade Competitiveness Map, International Trade Centre, www.intracen.org/marketanalysis.

PRINCIPAL TRADING PARTNERS
(US $ million)

Imports c.i.f.	2008	2009	2010
Angola	266.8	680.5	656.8
Belgium	158.2	181.7	163.7
Cameroon	199.2	55.3	63.9
China, People's Rep.	152.2	161.2	152.2
Côte d'Ivoire	36.1	99.1	135.4
Equatorial Guinea	62.5	281.9	269.3
France (incl. Monaco)	362.4	549.2	533.8
Gabon	646.0	209.6	206.6
Indonesia	50.5	24.4	24.3
Italy	228.9	112.0	124.5
Liberia	89.4	0.0	0.0
Malta	213.3	0.1	0.1
Namibia	6.9	64.0	60.5
Netherlands	62.3	166.6	168.2
Nigeria	50.7	117.9	123.4
Norway	48.4	28.9	18.7
Senegal	65.0	26.2	22.7
Singapore	71.4	457.5	441.0
South Africa	43.4	149.6	141.6
Spain	96.2	28.8	27.7
United Kingdom	181.2	301.6	289.3
USA	79.2	146.6	156.8
Total (incl. others)	3,539.6	4,447.1	4,369.4

Exports f.o.b.	2008	2009	2010
Angola	150.8	953.0	903.4
Brazil	20.1	200.1	163.3
China, People's Rep.	3,573.2	1,793.8	1,446.7
France (incl. Monaco)	875.5	1,073.5	867.7
Gabon	91.6	345.2	327.4
Iceland	0.0	85.8	69.3
India	265.2	86.8	70.2
Italy	151.3	82.6	53.4
Korea, Rep.	181.1	166.9	134.7
Netherlands	205.5	276.7	197.0
Nigeria	314.5	11.0	11.4
Portugal	222.8	215.3	159.4
Singapore	253.0	226.2	193.6
South Africa	105.9	38.4	36.4
Spain	144.8	102.2	73.2
Switzerland	9.4	40.4	105.4
Taiwan	582.6	636.5	513.9
USA	1,576.9	876.4	716.3
Total (incl. others)	9,169.7	8,201.5	6,917.6

Source: Trade Map-Trade Competitiveness Map, International Trade Centre, www.intracen.org/marketanalysis.

Transport

RAILWAYS
(traffic)

	1999	2000	2001
Passengers carried ('000)	56.5	546.0	742.0
Freight carried ('000 metric tons)	65.7	236.0	548.0

Passenger-km (million): 9 in 1999.

Freight ton-km (million): 21 in 1999.

Sources: UN, *Statistical Yearbook;* IMF, *Republic of Congo: Selected Issues and Statistical Appendix* (July 2004).

ROAD TRAFFIC
(estimates, '000 motor vehicles in use)

	1999	2000	2001
Passenger cars	26.2	29.7	29.7
Commercial vehicles	20.4	23.1	23.1

Source: UN, *Statistical Yearbook.*

2007 ('000 motor vehicles in use at 31 December): Passenger cars 56; Vans and lorries 36; Motorcycles and mopeds 3; Total (incl. others) 100 (Source: IRF, *World Road Statistics*).

SHIPPING

Merchant Fleet
(registered at 31 December)

	2007	2008	2009
Number of vessels	20	20	20
Total displacement ('000 grt)	3.8	3.8	3.8

Source: IHS Fairplay, *World Fleet Statistics.*

Freight Traffic at Pointe-Noire
(metric tons)

	1996	1997	1998
Goods loaded	670,150	708,203	n.a.
Goods unloaded	584,376	533,170	724,000*

* Rounded figure.

Source: mainly Banque des Etats de l'Afrique Centrale, *Etudes et Statistiques.*

CIVIL AVIATION
(traffic on scheduled services)*

	2001	2002	2003
Kilometres flown (million)	3	1	1
Passengers carried ('000)	95	47	52
Passenger-km (million)	157	27	31
Total ton-km (million)	22	3	3

* Including an apportionment of the traffic of Air Afrique.

Source: UN, *Statistical Yearbook.*

Tourism

FOREIGN VISITORS BY COUNTRY OF RESIDENCE*

	2007	2008	2009
Angola	2,837	2,134	2,558
Belgium	1,266	1,056	1,516
Cameroon	2,136	2,792	3,688
Congo, Democratic Rep.	4,154	5,224	4,489
France	14,466	22,473	23,017
Gabon	1,689	1,629	1,773
Italy	999	1,617	2,747
United Kingdom	743	819	3,094
USA	612	1,218	n.a.
Total (incl. others)	54,260	63,343	85,000

* Arrivals at hotels and similar establishments.

Total tourist arrivals ('000): 101 in 2010.

Receipts from tourism (US $ million, excl. passenger transport): 40 in 2005; 45 in 2006; 54 in 2007.

Source: World Tourism Organization.

Communications Media

	2009	2010	2011
Telephones ('000 main lines in use)	9.5	9.8	10.0
Mobile cellular telephones ('000 subscribers)	2,171.0	3,798.6	3,884.8
Internet users ('000)	245	n.a.	n.a.
Broadband subscribers	—	100	100

Source: International Telecommunication Union.

Non-daily newspapers (national estimates): 15 in 1995 (average circulation 38,000 copies) (Source: UNESCO, *Statistical Yearbook*).

Radio receivers ('000 in use): 341 in 1997 (Source: UNESCO Institute for Statistics).

Television receivers ('000 in use): 33 in 1997 (Source: UNESCO Institute for Statistics).

Daily newspapers (national estimates): 6 in 1997 (average circulation 20,500 copies) (Source: UNESCO, *Statistical Yearbook*).

Personal computers: 19,000 (5.6 per 1,000 persons) in 2005 (Source: UNESCO Institute for Statistics).

Education

(2009/10 except where otherwise indicated)

			Students		
	Institutions*	Teachers	Males	Females	Total
Pre-primary	95	1,868	21,169	22,303	43,472
Primary	1,168	14,347	364,335	340,758	705,093
Secondary	n.a.	9,915†	125,229‡	106,797‡	232,026‡
Tertiary	n.a.	1,170§	15,331	5,052	20,383

* 1998/99.
† 2004/05.
‡ 2003/04.
§ 2008/09.

Sources: mostly UNESCO Institute for Statistics.

Pupil-teacher ratio (primary education, UNESCO estimate): 49.1 in 2009/10 (Source: UNESCO Institute for Statistics).

Adult literacy rate (UNESCO estimates): 86.8% (males 92.1%; females 81.7%) in 2007 (Source: UNESCO Institute for Statistics).

Directory

The Constitution

The 1992 Constitution was suspended following the assumption of power by Gen. Denis Sassou-Nguesso on 15 October 1997. A new Constitution, which was approved by the Conseil National de Transition (interim legislative body) on 2 September 2001 and endorsed by a public referendum on 20 January 2002, took effect following presidential and legislative elections in March–July 2002. Its main provisions are summarized below:

PREAMBLE

The Congolese people, having chosen a pluralist democracy as the basis for the development of the country, condemn the tyrannical use of power and political violence and declare that the fundamental principles proclaimed and guaranteed by the UN Charter, the Universal Declaration of Human Rights and other international treaties form an integral part of the present Constitution.

I. THE STATE AND SOVEREIGNTY

Articles 1–6: The Republic of the Congo is a sovereign, secular, social and democratic State. The principle of the Republic is government of the people, by the people and for the people. National sovereignty belongs to the people, who exercise it through universal suffrage by their elected representatives or by referendum. The official language of the Republic is French. The national languages of communication are Lingala and Kituba.

II. FUNDAMENTAL RIGHTS AND LIBERTIES

Articles 7–42: All citizens are equal before the law. Arbitrary arrest and all degrading forms of punishment are prohibited, and all accused are presumed innocent until proven guilty. Incitement to ethnic hatred, violence or civil war and the use of religion to political ends are forbidden. Equal access to education, which is compulsory until the age of 16, is guaranteed to all. The State is obliged to create conditions that enable all citizens to enjoy the right to work. All citizens, excluding members of the police and military forces, may participate in trade union activity. Slavery is forbidden, and forced labour permitted only as a judicial punishment.

III. DUTIES

Articles 43–50: All citizens have duties towards their family, society, the State and other legally recognized authorities. All citizens are obliged to conform to the Constitution, the laws of the Republic and to fulfil their obligations towards the State and society.

IV. POLITICAL PARTIES

Articles 51–55: Political parties may not be identified with an ethnic group, a region, a religion or a sect. They must protect and promote fundamental human rights, the rule of law, democracy, individual and collective freedoms, national territorial integrity and sovereignty, proscribe intolerance, ethnically based extremism, and any recourse to violence, and respect the secular form of the State.

V. EXECUTIVE POWER

Articles 56–88: The President of the Republic is the Head of State, Head of the Executive and Head of Government. The President is directly elected by an absolute majority of votes cast, for a term of seven years, renewable once. Presidential candidates must be of Congolese nationality and origin, aged between 40 and 70 years, and have resided on national territory for at least 24 successive months prior to registering as a candidate. If required, a second round of voting takes place between the two highest-placed candidates in the first ballot. In the event of the death, resignation, or long-term incapacity of the President of the Republic, the President of the Sénat assumes limited executive functions for up to 90 days, pending an election, which he may not contest.

The President appoints ministers, senior civil servants, military staff and ambassadors. Ministers may not hold a parliamentary mandate or civic, public or military post, and their professional activity is restricted. The President of the Republic is the Supreme Head of the armed forces and the President of the Higher Council of Magistrates, and possesses the right of pardon. The President of the Republic chairs the Council of Ministers.

VI. LEGISLATIVE POWER

Articles 89–113: The Parliament is bicameral. Deputies are directly elected to the Assemblée nationale for a renewable term of five years. Senators are elected indirectly to the Sénat by local councils for a term of six years. One-half of the Sénat is elected every three years. Deputies and senators must be Congolese nationals, aged over 25 years in the case of deputies, or over 45 years in the case of senators, residing in national territory. A deputy or senator elected as a member of a political grouping may not resign from the grouping without simultaneously resigning his parliamentary position.

VII. RELATIONS BETWEEN THE LEGISLATIVE AND EXECUTIVE INSTITUTIONS

Articles 114–132: The President of the Republic may not dissolve the Assemblée nationale. The Assemblée nationale may not remove the President of the Republic. The legislative chambers consider proposed legislation in succession, with a view to adopting an identical text. If necessary, the President of the Republic may convene a joint commission to present a revised text to the two chambers. The President of the Republic may then call the Assemblée nationale to make a final decision. Special conditions apply to the passage of certain laws, including the national budget, and to a declaration of war or state of emergency.

VIII. JUDICIAL POWER

Articles 133–143: Judicial power is exercised by the Supreme Court, the Revenue and Budgetary Discipline Court, appeal courts and other national courts of law, which are independent of the legislature. The President of the Republic chairs a Higher Council of Magistrates, which guarantees the independence of the judiciary. The President of the Republic nominates judges to the Supreme Court and to the other courts of law, at the suggestion of the Higher Council of Magistrates. Judges of the Supreme Court may not be removed from office.

IX. CONSTITUTIONAL COURT

Articles 144–151: The Constitutional Court consists of nine members, each with a renewable mandate of nine years. One-third of the Court is renewed every three years. The President of the Republic nominates three members of the Constitutional Court independently, and the others at the suggestion of the President of each legislative chamber and of the Bureau of the Supreme Court. The President of the Republic nominates the President of the Constitutional Court. The Court ensures that laws, treaties and international agreements conform to the Constitution and oversees presidential elections.

X. HIGH COURT OF JUSTICE

Articles 152–156: The High Court of Justice is composed of an equal number of deputies and senators elected by their peers, and of members of the Supreme Court elected by their peers. It is chaired by the First President of the Supreme Court and is competent to try the President of the Republic in case of high treason. Members of the legislature, the Supreme Court and the Constitutional Court and government ministers are accountable to the High Court of Justice for crimes or offences committed in the execution of their duties, subject to a two-thirds' majority in a secret vote at a joint session of Parliament.

XI. ECONOMIC AND SOCIAL COUNCIL

Articles 157–160: The Economic and Social Council is a consultative assembly, which may become involved in any economic or social problem concerning the Republic, either of its own will or at the request of the President of the Republic or the President of either legislative chamber.

XII. HIGHER COUNCIL FOR THE FREEDOM OF COMMUNICATION

Articles 161–162: The Higher Council for the Freedom of Communication ensures freedom of information and communication, formulating recommendations on applicable issues.

XIII. MEDIATOR OF THE REPUBLIC

Articles 163–166: The Mediator of the Republic is an independent authority responsible for simplifying and humanizing relations between government and citizens, and may be addressed by any person dissatisfied with the workings of any public organization.

XIV. NATIONAL COMMISSION FOR HUMAN RIGHTS

Articles 167–169: The National Commission for Human Rights seeks to promote and protect human rights.

XV. POLICE AND MILITARY FORCES

Articles 170–173: The police and military bodies consist of the national police force, the national gendarmerie and the Congolese armed forces. These bodies are apolitical and subordinate to the civil authority. The creation of militia groups is prohibited.

XVI. LOCAL AUTHORITIES

Articles 174–177: The local administrative bodies of the Republic of the Congo are the department and the commune, and any others created by law.

XVII. INTERNATIONAL TREATIES AND AGREEMENTS

Articles 178–184: The President of the Republic negotiates, signs and, with the approval of Parliament, ratifies international treaties and agreements. Any proposed change to the territorial boundaries of the Republic must be submitted to popular referendum.

XVIII. ON REVISION

Articles 185–187: The Constitution may be revised at the initiative of the President of the Republic or members of Parliament. The territorial integrity of the Republic, the republican form of government, the secular nature of the State, the number of presidential terms of office permitted and the rights outlined in sections I and II (above) may not be the subject of any revision. Any constitutional amendments proposed by the President of the Republic are submitted directly to a referendum. Any constitutional changes proposed by Parliament must be approved by two-thirds of the members of both legislative chambers convened in congress, before being submitted to referendum. In both cases the Constitutional Court must have declared the acceptability of the proposals.

The Government

HEAD OF STATE

President: Gen. DENIS SASSOU-NGUESSO (assumed power 15 October 1997; inaugurated 25 October 1997; elected 10 March 2002; re-elected 12 July 2009).

COUNCIL OF MINISTERS

(September 2012)

Minister of State, Minister of Industrial Development and the Promotion of the Private Sector: ISIDORE MVOUBA.

Minister of State, Keeper of the Seals, Minister of Justice and Human Rights: AIMÉ EMMANUEL YOKA.

Minister of State, Minister of Transport, Civil Aviation and Maritime Trade: RODOLPHE ADADA.

Minister of State, Minister of Labour and Social Security: FLORENT NTSIBA.

Minister of State, Minister of the Economy, Finance, Planning, the Public Portfolio and Integration: GILBERT ONDONGO.

Minister of Foreign Affairs and Co-operation: BASILE IKOUÉBÉ.

Minister of the Interior and Decentralization: RAYMOND ZÉPHYRIN MBOULOU.

Minister of Mining and Geology: Gen. PIERRE OBA.

Minister of the Forest Economy and Sustainable Development: HENRI DJOMBO.

Minister of the Civil Service and State Reform: GUY BRICE PARFAIT KOLELAS.

Minister of Construction, Town Planning and Housing: CLAUDE ALPHONSE NSILOU.

Minister of Agriculture and Stockbreeding: RIGOBERT MABOUNDOU.

Minister of Energy and Water Resources: HENRI OSSEBI.

Minister of Equipment and Public Works: EMILE OUOSSO.

Minister of Health and Population: FRANÇOIS IBOVI.

Minister of Small and Medium-sized Enterprises and Crafts: ADÉLAÏDE YVONNE MOUGANY.

Minister at the Presidency, responsible for Territorial Management and Grand Projects: JEAN-JACQUES BOUYA.

Minister of Scientific Research and Technological Innovation: BRUNO JEAN-RICHARD ITOUA.

Minister at the Presidency, responsible for National Defence: CHARLES RICHARD MONDJO.

Minister of Hydrocarbons: ANDRÉ RAPHAËL LOEMBA.

Minister of Culture and the Arts: JEAN-CLAUDE GAKOSSO.

Minister of Trade and Supplies: CLAUDINE MOUNARI.

Minister of Posts and Telecommunications: THIERRY MOUNGALLA.

Minister of Social Affairs, Humanitarian Action and Solidarity: EMILIENNE RAOUL.

Minister of Higher Education: GEORGES MOYEN.

Minister of Primary and Secondary Education and Literacy: HELLOT MATSON MAMPOUYA.

Minister at the Presidency, responsible for the Special Economic Zones: ALAIN AKOUALA ATIPAULT.

Minister of Communication and Relations with Parliament: BIENVENUE OKIEMY.

Minister of Land Reform and the Preservation of the Public Domain: PIERRE MABIALA.

Minister of Sports and Physical Education: LÉON-ALFRED OPIMBAT.

Minister of Fisheries and Aquaculture: BERNARD TCHIBAMBELELA.

Minister of Technical Education, Vocational Training and Employment: SERGE BLAISE ZONIABA.

Minister of Tourism and the Environment: JOSUÉ RODRIGUE NGOUONIMBA.

Minister of Youth and Civic Education: ANATOLE COLLINET MAKOSSO.

Minister of the Promotion of Women and the Integration of Women into Development: CATHÉRINE EMBONDZA LIPITI.

Minister-delegate to the Minister of Transport, Civil Aviation and Maritime Trade, responsible for Maritime Trade: MARTIN PARFAIT AIMÉ COUSSOUD MAVOUNGOU.

Minister-delegate to the Minister of Transport, Civil Aviation and Maritime Trade, responsible for Navigable Paths and the River Economy: GILBERT MOKOKI.

Minister-delegate to the Minister of State, Minister of the Economy, Finance, Planning, the Public Portfolio and Integration: RAPHAËL MOKOKO.

MINISTRIES

Office of the President: Palais du Peuple, Brazzaville; tel. 22-281-17-11; internet www.presidence.cg.

Office of the Minister at the Presidency, responsible for National Defence: Brazzaville; tel. 22-281-22-31.

Office of the Minister at the Presidency, responsible for the Special Economic Zones: Brazzaville.

Ministry of Agriculture and Stockbreeding: BP 2453, Brazzaville; tel. 22-281-41-31; fax 22-281-19-29.

Ministry of the Civil Service and State Reform: BP 12151, Brazzaville; tel. 22-281-41-68; fax 22-281-41-49.

Ministry of Communication and Relations with Parliament: BP 114, Brazzaville; tel. 22-281-41-29; fax 22-281-41-28; e-mail depcompt@congonet.cg.

Ministry of Construction, Town Planning and Housing: BP 1580, Brazzaville; tel. 22-281-34-48; fax 22-281-12-97.

Ministry of Culture and the Arts: BP 20480, Brazzaville; tel. 22-281-02-35; fax 22-281-40-25.

Ministry of the Economy, Finance, Planning, the Public Portfolio and Integration: BP 64, Brazzaville; tel. 22-281-06-56; fax 22-281-58-08.

Ministry of Energy and Water Resources: Brazzaville.

Ministry of Equipment and Public Works: BP 2099, Brazzaville; tel. 22-281-59-41; fax 22-281-59-07.

Ministry of the Economy, Finance, Planning, the Public Portfolio and Integration: ave de l'Indépendance, croisement ave Foch, BP 2083, Brazzaville; tel. 22-281-45-24; fax 22-281-43-69; e-mail mefb-cg@mefb-cg.net; internet www.mefb-cg.org.

Ministry of Fisheries and Aquaculture: Brazzaville.

Ministry of Foreign Affairs and Co-operation: BP 2070, Brazzaville; tel. 22-281-10-89; fax 22-281-41-61.

Ministry of the Forest Economy and Sustainable Development: Immeuble de l'Agriculture, face à Blanche Gomez, BP 98, Brazzaville; tel. 22-281-41-37; fax 22-281-41-34; e-mail ajdbosseko@minifor.com.

Ministry of Health and Population: BP 20101, Brazzaville; tel. 22-281-30-75; fax 22-281-14-33.

Ministry of Higher Education: Ancien Immeuble de la Radio, BP 169, Brazzaville; tel. 22-281-08-15; fax 22-281-52-65.

Ministry of Hydrocarbons: BP 2120, Brazzaville; tel. 22-281-10-86; fax 22-281-10-85.

Ministry of Industrial Development and the Promotion of the Private Sector: Centre Administratif, Quartier Plateau, BP 2117, Brazzaville; tel. 22-281-30-09; fax 22-281-06-43.

Ministry of the Interior and Decentralization: BP 880, Brazzaville; tel. 22-281-40-60; fax 22-281-33-17.

Ministry of Justice and Human Rights: BP 2497, Brazzaville; tel. and fax 22-281-41-49.

Ministry of Labour and Social Security: Immeuble de la BCC, ave Foch, BP 2075, Brazzaville; tel. 22-281-41-43; fax 22-281-05-50.

Ministry of Land Reform and the Preservation of the Public Domain: Brazzaville; tel. 22-281-34-48.

Ministry of Mining and Geology: BP 2124, Brazzaville; tel. 22-281-02-64; fax 22-281-50-77.

Ministry of Posts, Telecommunications and ICT: BP 44, Brazzaville; tel. 22-281-41-18; fax 22-281-19-34.

Ministry of Primary and Secondary Education and Literacy: BP 5253, Brazzaville; tel. 22-281-24-52; fax 22-281-25-39.

Ministry of the Promotion of Women and the Integration of Women into Development: Brazzaville; tel. 22-281-19-29.

Ministry of Scientific Research and Technological Innovation: Ancien Immeuble de la Radio, Brazzaville; tel. 22-281-03-59.

Ministry of Security and Public Order: BP 2474, Brazzaville; tel. 22-281-41-73; fax 22-281-34-04.

Ministry of Small and Medium-sized Enterprises and Crafts: Brazzaville.

Ministry of Social Affairs, Humanitarian Action and Solidarity: Brazzaville.

Ministry of Sports and Physical Education: BP 2061, Brazzaville; tel. 06-660-89-24 (mobile).

Ministry of Technical Education, Vocational Training and Employment: BP 2076, Brazzaville; tel. 22-281-17-27; fax 22-281-56-82; e-mail metp_cab@yahoo.fr.

Ministry of Tourism and the Environment: Brazzaville.

Ministry of Trade and Supplies: BP 2965, Brazzaville; tel. 22-281-41-16; fax 22-281-41-57; e-mail mougany@yahoo.fr.

Ministry of Transport, Civil Aviation and Maritime Trade: Immeuble Mafoua Virgile, BP 2066, Brazzaville; tel. 22-281-53-39; fax 22-281-57-56.

Ministry of Youth and Civic Education: Brazzaville.

President and Legislature

PRESIDENT

Presidential Election, 12 July 2009

Candidate	Votes	% of votes
Denis Sassou-Nguesso	1,055,117	78.61
Joseph Kignoumbi Kia Mbougou	100,181	7.46
Nicéphore Fylla de Saint-Eudes	93,749	6.98
Mathias Dzon	30,861	2.30
Joseph Hodjuila Miokono	27,060	2.02
Guy-Romain Kinfoussia	11,678	0.87
Jean François Tchibinda Kouangou	5,475	0.41
Anguios Nganguia-Engambé	4,064	0.30
Bonaventure Mizidy Bavouéza	3,594	0.27
Clément Miérassa	3,305	0.25
Bertin Pandi-Ngouari	2,749	0.20
Marion Michel Madzimba Ehouango	2,612	0.19
Jean Ebina	1,797	0.13
Total	1,342,242	100.00

LEGISLATURE

The legislature, Parlement, comprises two chambers: a directly elected lower house, the Assemblée nationale; and an indirectly elected upper house, the Sénat.

Assemblée nationale

Palais du Parlement, BP 2106, Brazzaville; tel. 22-281-11-12; fax 22-281-41-28; e-mail dsancongo@yahoo.fr.

President: JUSTIN KOUMBA.

General Election, 15 July and 5 August 2012

Party	Seats
Parti Congolais du Travail (PCT)	89
Mouvement Congolais pour la Démocratie et le Développement Intégral (MCDDI)	7
Union Panafricaine pour la Démocratie Sociale (UPADS)	7
Rassemblement pour la Démocratie et le Progrès Social (RDPS)	5
Mouvement d'Action et pour le Renouveau (MAR)	4
Rassemblement Citoyen (RC)	3
Mouvement pour l'Unité, la Solidarité et le Travail (MUST)	2
Union Patriotique pour la Démocratie et le Progrès (UPDP)	2
Club 2002-Parti pour l'Unité et la République (Club 2002 PUR)	1
Club Perspectives et Réalités (CPR)	1
Parti Républicain et Libéral (PRL)	1
Union des Forces Démocratiques (UFD)	1
Union pour la République (UR)	1
Independents	12
Total	136*

* Voting in three constituencies did not take place.

Sénat

Palais du Parlement, Brazzaville; tel. and fax 22-281-18-34; internet www.senat.cg.

President: ANDRÉ OBAMI ITOU.

The upper chamber comprises 72 members, elected by representatives of local, regional and municipal authorities for a six-year term. After elections to the Sénat held on 9 October 2011 the strength of the parties was as follows:

Party	Seats
Rassemblement de la Majorité Présidentielle*	38
PCT	12
UPADS	4
Club 2002 PUR	2
MCDDI	2
Mouvement pour la Solidarité et la Démocratie	1
PRL	1
Independents	12
Total	72

* An alliance of parties and associations supporting Pres. Denis Sassou-Nguesso.

Elections to renew 36 seats were held on 9 October 2011, at which the PCT secured 12 seats, the RMP 11 seats, the UPADS two, the MCDDI two, the Club 2002 PUR two, the PRL and the MSD one seat each, and independent candidates won five seats.

Election Commission

Commission Nationale d'Organisation des Élections (CONEL): Brazzaville; f. 2001; reorganized in 2007; mems appointed by President of the Republic; Pres. HENRI BOUKA.

Advisory Council

Conseil Économique et Social (Economic and Social Council): Brazzaville; f. 2003; 75 mems, appointed by the President of the Republic; Pres. AUGUSTE-CÉLESTIN GONGARAD NKOUA.

Political Organizations

In early 2004 there were more than 100 political parties and organizations in the Republic of the Congo. The following were among the most important of those believed to be active in 2012:

Action pour le Congo (APC): Brazzaville.

Alliance pour la Démocratie et le Développement National (ADDN): Brazzaville; f. 2005; supports Govt of Pres. Sassou-Nguesso; Pres. BRUNO MAZONGA.

Alliance pour la République et la Démocratie (ARD): Brazzaville; internet www.alternance-congo.com; f. 2007.

Union Patriotique pour le Renouveau National (UPRN): Brazzaville; Leader MATHIAS DZON.

Club 2002-Parti pour l'Unité et la République (Club 2002 PUR): Brazzaville; f. 2002; Pres. WILFRID NGUESSO.

Conseil National de la Républicains (CNR): formed as political wing of 'Ninja' rebel group; Leader Rev. FRÉDÉRIC BITSANGOU (NTUMI).

Forces Démocratiques Nouvelles (FDN): Brazzaville.

Jeunesse en Mouvement (JEM): Brazzaville; f. 2002.

Mouvement d'Action pour le Renouveau (MAR): BP 1287, Pointe-Noire; Pres. ROLAND BOUITI VIAUDO.

Mouvement Congolais pour la Démocratie et le Développement Intégral (MCDDI): 744 route de Djoué, Brazzaville; e-mail info@mcddi.net; internet www.mcddi.org; f. 1990; Leader (vacant).

Mouvement pour la Démocratie et le Progrès (MDP): Brazzaville; f. 2007; Leader JEAN-CLAUDE IBOVI.

Mouvement pour la Solidarité et la Démocratie (MSD): Brazzaville; Leader RENÉ SERGE BLANCHARD OBA.

Parti Congolais du Travail (PCT): BP 80, Brazzaville; f. 1969; sole legal political party 1969–90; Pres. DENIS SASSOU-NGUESSO; Sec.-Gen. PIERRE NGOLO.

Parti Républicain et Libéral (PRL): Brazzaville; Pres. NICÉPHORE FYLLA DE SAINT-EUDES.

Parti Social Démocrate Congolais (PSDC): Brazzaville; Pres. CLÉMENT MIÉRASSA.

Parti pour l'Unité et la République (PUR): Brazzaville.

Parti la Vie: Brazzaville.

Rassemblement Citoyen (RC): route du Djoué, face Centre Sportif de Bacongo, Brazzaville; Pres. CLAUDE ALPHONSE NSILOU.

Rassemblement pour la Démocratie et le Progrès Social (RDPS): Pointe-Noire; f. 1990; Pres. BERNARD MBATCHI.

Rassemblement de la Majorité Présidentielle (RMP): Brazzaville; f. 2007; org. of some 100 political parties and associations supporting Pres. Sassou-Nguesso.

Union pour la Démocratie et la République—Mwinda (UDR—Mwinda): Brazzaville; e-mail journalmwinda@presse-ecrite.com; f. 1992; Leader GUY ROMAIN KIMFOUSSIA.

Union des Forces Démocratiques (UFD): Brazzaville; supports Govt; Pres. DAVID CHARLES GANOU.

Union Panafricaine pour la Démocratie Sociale (UPADS): BP 1370, Brazzaville; e-mail courrier@upads.org; internet www.upads.org; Pres. PASCAL LISSOUBA; Sec.-Gen. PASCAL TSATY MABIALA.

Union Patriotique pour la Démocratie et le Progrès (UPDP): 112 rue Lamothe, Brazzaville; Pres. GONGARA KOUA.

Union pour le Progrès (UP): 965 rue Sounda, pl. des 15 ans, Brazzaville; Pres. JEAN-MARTIN MBEMBA; Sec.-Gen. OMER DEFOUNDOUX.

Diplomatic Representation

EMBASSIES IN THE REPUBLIC OF THE CONGO

Algeria: rue Col Brisset, BP 2100, Brazzaville; tel. 22-281-17-37; fax 22-281-54-77; Ambassador AHMED ABDESSADOK.

Angola: ave Fourneau, BP 388, Brazzaville; tel. 22-281-47-21; fax 22-283-52-96; e-mail miranotom@yahoo.fr; Ambassador Dr PEDRO FERNANDO MAVUNZA.

Belgium: blvd Sassou Nguesso, BP 225, Brazzaville; tel. 22-281-07-65; e-mail brazzaville@diplobel.fed.be; internet www.diplomatie.be/brazzaville; Ambassador HERMAN MERCKX.

Cameroon: ave Bayardelles, Brazzaville; tel. 22-281-10-08; fax 22-281-56-75; Ambassador HAMIDOU KOMIDOR NJIMOLUH.

Central African Republic: BP 10, Brazzaville; tel. 05-526-75-55 (mobile); Ambassador MARIE-CHARLOTTE FAYANGA.

Chad: BP 386, Brazzaville; tel. 05-558-92-06 (mobile); Ambassador KALZEUBE KINGAR.

China, People's Republic: blvd du Marechal Lyauté, BP 213, Brazzaville; tel. 22-281-11-32; fax 22-281-11-35; e-mail amba_chine@yahoo.fr; internet cg.chineseembassy.org; Ambassador GUAN JIAN.

Congo, Democratic Republic: ave Nelson Mandela, Brazzaville; tel. 22-281-30-52; Ambassador CHRISTOPHE MUZUNGU.

Cuba: 28 rue Lacien Fourneaux, BP 80, Brazzaville; tel. 22-281-03-79; e-mail embacuba@congonet.cg; Ambassador MATIAS ELENO CHAPEUX SAN MIGUEL.

Egypt: 7 bis ave Bayardelle, BP 917, Brazzaville; tel. 22-281-07-94; fax 22-281-15-33; Ambassador KHALED EZZAT OMRAH.

Equatorial Guinea: Brazzaville; Ambassador ELA EBANG MBANG.

France: rue Alfassa, BP 2089, Brazzaville; tel. 22-281-55-41; e-mail webmestre@mail.com; internet www.ambafrance-cg.org; Ambassador JEAN-FRANÇOIS VALETTE.

Gabon: BP 20336, Brazzaville; tel. 22-281-56-20; Ambassador BARTHÉLEMY ONGAYE.

Holy See: rue Col Brisset, BP 1168, Brazzaville; tel. 06-950-56-66 (mobile); fax 22-281-55-81; e-mail nonapcg@yahoo.com; Apostolic Nuncio JAN ROMEO PAWLOWSKI.

Italy: 2 ave Auxence Ickonga, BP 2484, Brazzaville; tel. 22-281-58-41; fax 22-283-52-70; e-mail ambasciata.brazzaville@esteri.it; internet www.ambbrazzaville.esteri.it; Ambassador FRANCESCO PAOLO VENIER.

Libya: BP 920, Brazzaville; tel. 22-281-56-35; Chargé d'affaires a.i. IBRAHIM TAHAR EL-HAMALI.

Nigeria: 11 blvd Lyauté, BP 790, Brazzaville; tel. 22-281-10-22; fax 22-281-55-20; e-mail embnigbra@yahoo.co.uk; Ambassador VICTORIA JOLAADE BOSEDE ONIPEDE.

Russia: ave Félix Eboué, BP 2132, Brazzaville; tel. 22-281-19-23; fax 22-281-50-85; e-mail amrussie@ic.cd; internet www.congo.mid.ru; Ambassador YURII ALEKSANDROVICH.

Senegal: Brazzaville; Ambassador BATOURA KANE NIANG.

South Africa: 82 ave Marechal Lyautey, Brazzaville; tel. 22-281-08-49; e-mail brazzaville@foreign.gov.za; Ambassador Dr MANELISI GENGE.

USA: BP 1015, Brazzaville; tel. 22-281-33-68; e-mail BrazzavilleHR@state.gov; internet brazzaville.usembassy.gov; Ambassador CHRISTOPHER W. MURRAY.

Judicial System

The 2002 Constitution provides for the independence of the judiciary from the legislature. Judges are accountable to the Higher Council of Magistrates, under the chairmanship of the President of the Republic. The constituent bodies of the judiciary are the Supreme Court, the Revenue and Budgetary Discipline Court and the appeal courts. The High Court of Justice is chaired by the First President of the Supreme Court and is competent to try the President of the Republic in case of high treason, and to try members of the legislature, the Supreme Court, the Constitutional Court and government ministers for crimes or offences committed in the execution of their duties.

Cour Suprême (Supreme Court): BP 597, Brazzaville; tel. 22-283-01-32; First Pres. PLACIDE LENGA.

Haute Cour de Justice (High Court of Justice): Brazzaville; f. 2003; Pres. PLACIDE LENGA (First Pres. of the Supreme Court); Chief Prosecutor GEORGES AKIERA.

Cour Constitutionnelle (Constitutional Court): Brazzaville; Pres. AUGUSTE ILOKI; Vice-Pres. AUGUSTE ILOKI; Mems SIMON-PIERRE NGOUONIMBA NCZARY, THOMAS DHELLO, MARC MASSAMBA-NDILOU, JACQUES BOMBÈTE, JEAN-PIERRE BERRI, DELPHINE-EMMANUELLE ADOUKI, JEAN-BERNARD ANAËL SAMORY.

Religion

More than 40% of the population follow traditional animist beliefs. Most of the remainder are Christians (of whom a majority are Roman Catholics).

CHRISTIANITY

The Roman Catholic Church

The Congo comprises one archdiocese, five dioceses and an apostolic prefecture. An estimated 57% of the population are Roman Catholics.

Bishops' Conference

Conférence Episcopale du Congo, BP 200, Brazzaville; tel. 06-663-83-91 (mobile); fax 22-281-18-28; e-mail confepiscongo@yahoo.fr.

f. 1992; Pres. Most Rev. LOUIS PORTELLA MBUYU (Bishop of Kinkala).

Archbishop of Brazzaville: Most Rev. ANATOLE MILANDOU, Archevêché, BP 2301, Brazzaville; tel. 05-538-20-84 (mobile); fax 22-281-26-15; e-mail archibrazza@yahoo.fr.

Protestant Church

Eglise Evangélique du Congo: BP 3205, Bacongo-Brazzaville; tel. and fax 22-281-04-54; internet www.eecongo.org; f. 1909; Presbyterian; autonomous since 1961; 150,000 mems (2007); 120 parishes (2007); Pres. Rev. Dr PATRICE N'SOUAMI.

Eglise Evangélique Luthérienne du Congo: 137 rue Osséle-Mougali, BP 1456, 00242 Brazzaville; tel. 05-557-15-00 (mobile); e-mail evlcongo@yahoo.fr; Pres. Rev. JOSEPH TCHIBINDA MAVOUNGOU; 1,828 mems (2010).

ISLAM

In 1997 an estimated 2% of the population were Muslims.

Comité Islamique du Congo: 77 Makotipoko Moungali, BP 55, Brazzaville; tel. 22-282-87-45; f. 1988; Leaders HABIBOU SOUMARE, BACHIR GATSONGO, BOUILLA GUIBIDANESI.

BAHÁ'Í FAITH

Assemblée Spirituelle Nationale: BP 2094, Brazzaville; tel. 22-281-36-93; e-mail congolink1@aol.com.

The Press

In July 2000 legislation was adopted on the freedom of information and communication. The legislation, which confirmed the abolition of censorship and reduced the penalty for defamation from imprisonment to a fine, specified three types of punishable offence: the encouragement of social tension (including incitement to ethnic conflict), attacks on the authorities (including libels on the Head of State or on the judiciary) and libels against private individuals. The terms of the legislation are guaranteed by a regulatory body, the Higher Council for the Freedom of Communication.

DAILIES

ACI Actualité: BP 2144, Brazzaville; tel. and fax 22-281-01-98; publ. by Agence Congolaise d'Information; Dir-Gen. THÉODORE KIAMOSSI.

Les Dépêches de Brazzaville: 84 ave Denis Sassou N'Guesso, Immeuble Les Manguiers (Mpila), Brazzaville; tel. 05-532-01-09 (mobile); internet www.brazzaville-adiac.com; Dir of Publication JEAN-PAUL PIGASSE.

PERIODICALS

L'Arroseur: Immeuble Boulangerie ex-Léon, BP 15021, Brazzaville; tel. 05-558-65-51 (mobile); fax 05-558-37-60 (mobile); e-mail larroseur@yahoo.fr; f. 2000; weekly; satirical; Dir GERRY-GÉRARD MANGONDO; Editor-in-Chief JEAN-MARIE KANGA.

L'Autre Vision: 48 rue Assiéné-Mikalou, BP 5255, Brazzaville; tel. 05-551-57-06 (mobile); e-mail lautrevision@yahoo.fr; 2 a month; Dir JEAN PAULIN ITOUA.

Capital: 3 ave Charles de Gaulle, Plateau Centre Ville, BP 541, Brazzaville; tel. 05-558-95-10 (mobile); fax 05-551-37-48 (mobile); e-mail capital@hotmail.com; 2 a month; economics and business; Dir SERGE-DENIS MATONDO; Editor-in-Chief HERVÉ SAMPA.

Le Choc: BP 1314, Brazzaville; tel. 06-666-42-96 (mobile); fax 22-282-04-25; e-mail groupejustinfo@yahoo.fr; internet www.lechoc.info; weekly; Dir-Gen. and Publr ASIE DOMINIQUE DE MARSEILLE; Dir of Publication MARIEN NGAPILI.

Le Coq: Brazzaville; e-mail sosolecoq@yahoo.fr; f. 2000; weekly; Editor-in-Chief MALONGA BOUKA.

Le Défi Africain: Brazzaville; f. 2002; Dir of Publication JEAN ROMUALD MBEPA.

Les Echos du Congo: Immeubles Fédéraux 036, Centre-ville, Brazzaville; tel. 05-551-57-09 (mobile); e-mail wayiadrien@yahoo.fr; weekly; pro-govt; Dir-Gen. ADRIEN WAYI-LEWY; Editor-in-Chief INNOCENT OLIVIER TATY.

Epanza Makita: Brazzaville; f. 2004.

Le Flambeau: BP 1198, Brazzaville; tel. 06-666-35-23(mobile); e-mail congolink1@aol.com; weekly; independent; supports Govt of Pres. Sassou-Nguesso; Dir and Man. Editor PRINCE-RICHARD NSANA.

La Lettre de Brazzaville: Résidence Méridien, BP 15457, Brazzaville; tel. and fax 22-281-28-13; e-mail redaction@adiac.com; f. 2000; weekly; publ. by Agence d'Information d'Afrique Centrale; Man. Dir JEAN-PAUL PIGASSE; Editor-in-Chief BELINDA AYESSA.

Le Nouveau Stade: BP 2159, Brazzaville; tel. 06-668-45-52 (mobile); 2 a month; sports; Dir-Gen. LOUIS NGAMI; Editor-in-Chief S. F. KIMINA MAKUMBU.

La Nouvelle République: 3 ave des Ambassadeurs, BP 991, Brazzaville; tel. 22-281-00-20; state-owned; weekly; Dir-Gen. GASPARD NWAN; Editorial Dir HENRI BOUKOULOU.

L'Observateur: 165 ave de l'Amitié, BP 13370, Brazzaville; tel. 06-666-33-37 (mobile); fax 22-281-11-81; e-mail lobservateur_2001@yahoo.fr; f. 1999; weekly; independent; opposes Govt of Pres. Sassou-Nguesso; Dir GISLIN SIMPLICE ONGOUYA; circ. 2,000 (2004).

Le Pays: BP 782, Brazzaville; tel. 06-661-06-11 (mobile); fax 22-282-44-50; e-mail heblepays@yahoo.fr; f. 1991; weekly; Editorial Dir SYLVÈRE-ARSÈNE SAMBA.

La Référence: BP 13778, Brazzaville; tel. 05-556-11-37 (mobile); fax 06-662-80-13 (mobile); 2 a month; supports Govt of Pres. Sassou-Nguesso; Dir PHILIPPE RICHET; Editor-in-Chief R. ASSEBAKO AMAIDJORE.

La Rue Meurt (Bala-Bala): BP 1258, Brazzaville; tel. 06-666-39-80 (mobile); fax 22-281-02-30; e-mail laruemeurt@yahoo.fr; f. 1991; weekly; satirical; opposes Govt of Pres. Sassou-Nguesso; Publr MATTHIEU GAYELE; Editorial Dir JEAN-CLAUDE BONGOLO; circ. 2,000 (2004).

La Semaine Africaine: blvd Lyautey, face Chu, BP 2080, Brazzaville; tel. 06-678-76-94 (mobile); e-mail contact@lasemaineafricaine.com; internet www.lasemaineafricaine.com; f. 1952; 2 a week; Roman Catholic; general news and social comment; circulates widely in francophone equatorial Africa; Editor-in-Chief JOACHIM MBANZA; circ. 7,500.

Le Stade: BP 114, Brazzaville; tel. 22-281-47-18; f. 1985; weekly; sports; Dir HUBERT-TRÉSOR MADOUABA-NTOUALANI; Editor-in-Chief LELAS PAUL NZOLANI; circ. 6,500.

Tam-Tam d'Afrique: 97 rue Moussana, Ouenzé, BP 1675, Brazzaville; tel. 05-551-03-95 (mobile); e-mail gouala@yahoo.fr; weekly; economics, finance; circ. 1,500 (2004).

Le Temps: BP 2104, Brazzaville; e-mail kiala_matouba@yahoo.fr; weekly; owned by supporters of former Pres. Lissouba; Editor-in-Chief HENRI BOUKOULOU.

Vision pour Demain: 109 rue Bakongo Poto-Poto, BP 650, Brazzaville; tel. 04-441-14-22 (mobile); 6 a year; Dir SAINT EUDES MFUMU FYLLA.

NEWS AGENCIES

Agence Congolaise d'Information (ACI): ave E. P. Lumumba, BP 2144, Brazzaville; tel. and fax 22-281-01-98; e-mail agencecongoinfo@yahoo.fr; f. 1961; Gen. Man. AUGUSTE KINZONZI-KITOUMOU.

Agence d'Information d'Afrique Centrale (ADIAC): Les Manguiers, 76 ave Paul Doumer, Brazzaville; tel. 05-532-01-09 (mobile); fax 05-532-01-10 (mobile); e-mail belie@congonet.cg; internet www.brazzaville-adiac.com; f. 1997; Dirs JEAN-PAUL PIGASSE, BELINDA AYESSA; br. in Paris (France).

Publishers

Editions ADIAC—Agence d'Information d'Afrique Centrale: Hôtel Méridien, BP 15457, Brazzaville; tel. and fax 22-281-28-13; e-mail redaction@brazzaville-adiac.com; internet www.brazzaville-adiac.com; f. 1997; publishes chronicles of current affairs; Dirs JEAN-PAUL PIGASSE, BELINDA AYESSA.

Editions 'Héros dans l'Ombre': BP 1678, Brazzaville; e-mail leopold_mamo@yahoo.fr; f. 1980; literature, criticism, poetry, essays, politics, drama, research; Chair. LÉOPOLD PINDY MAMONSONO.

Editions Lemba: 20 ave des Emetteurs, Sangolo-OMS, Malèkélé, BP 2351, Brazzaville; tel. 06-667-65-58 (mobile); fax 22-281-00-17; e-mail editions_lemba@yahoo.fr; literature; Dir APOLLINAIRE SINGOU-BASSEHA.

Editions PAARI—Pan African Review of Innovation: BP 1622, Brazzaville; tel. 05-551-86-49 (mobile); e-mail edpaari@yahoo.fr; internet www.cafelitteraire.fr; f. 1991; social and human sciences, philosophy; Dir MÂWA-KIESE MAWAWA.

Imprimerie Centrale d'Afrique (ICA): ave du Gen. de Gaulle, BP 162, Pointe-Noire; f. 1949; Man. Dir M. SCHNEIDER.

Mokandart: BP 939, Brazzaville; tel. 06-668-46-69 (mobile); e-mail mokandart@yahoo.fr; adult and children's literature; Pres. ANNICK VEYRINAUD MAKONDA.

GOVERNMENT PUBLISHING HOUSE

Imprimerie Nationale du Congo (INC): BP 58, Brazzaville; Dir JULES ONDZEKI.

Broadcasting and Communications

REGULATORY AUTHORITIES

Agence de Régulation des Postes et des Communications Electroniques (ARPCE): Immeuble Socofran, ave du 5 juin, BP 2490, Mpila, Brazzaville; tel. 05-510-72-72 (mobile); e-mail contact@arpce.net; internet www.arpce.cg; f. 2009; regulatory authority; Dir-Gen. YVES CASTANOU.

Conseil Supérieur de la Liberté de la Communication (Higher Council for the Freedom of Communication): Brazzaville; f. 2003; 11 mems, nominated by the President of the Republic; Pres. JACQUES BANANGANZALA.

TELECOMMUNICATIONS

In 2011 there were five providers of mobile cellular telecommunications services in the country.

Airtel Congo: blvd Charles de Gaulle, angle allée Makimba, BP 1267, Pointe-Noire; tel. 05-520-00-00 (mobile); fax 22-294-88-75; e-mail info.africa@airtel.com; internet africa.airtel.com/congob; f. 1999 as Celtel Congo and fmrly Zain Congo; acquired by Bharti Airtel (India) in 2010; mobile cellular telephone operator; network covers Brazzaville, Pointe-Noire, Loubomo (Dolisie), Ouesso, Owando and other urban areas; Dir-Gen. BESTON TSHINSELÉ.

Équateur Telecom Congo: 35 William Guynet, Poto-Poto, Brazzaville; e-mail info@azur-congo.com; internet www.azur-congo.com; f. 2010; provides mobile cellular telephone services under the brand name Azur; Dir-Gen. STÉPHANE BEUVELET.

MTN Congo: ave Foch, face a la Mairie Centrale, Brazzaville; tel. 06-669-15-40 (mobile); e-mail yellonews@mtncongo.net; internet www.mtncongo.net; f. 2000; mobile cellular telephone operator; Dir-Gen. MATHIEU FREDDY TCHALA ABINA.

Société des Télécommunications du Congo (SOTELCO): BP 39, Brazzaville; tel. 22-281-00-00; fax 22-281-19-35; e-mail sotelco@congonet.cg; f. 2001 by division of postal and telecommunications services of the fmr Office National des Postes et Télécommunications; mobile cellular telephone system introduced in 1996; operates under the brand name Congo Telecom; majority govt-owned, part-owned by Atlantic TeleNetwork; further transfer to private ownership pending; Dir-Gen. CÉDRIC BEN CABINE AKOUALA.

Warid Congo SA: 4th Floor, Tour ARC, BP 238, Brazzaville; tel. 04-400-01-23 (mobile); internet waridtel.cg; mobile cellular telephone operator; Pres. Sheikh NAHAYAN MABARAK AL NAHAYAN; Dir-Gen. MICHEL OLIVIER ELAMÉ.

RADIO AND TELEVISION

Canal FM: BP 60, Brazzaville; tel. 22-283-03-09; f. 1977 as Radio Rurales du Congo; present name adopted 2002; community stations established by the Agence de Coopération Culturelle et Technique; transmitters in Brazzaville, Sembé, Nkayi, Etoumbi and Mossendjo; Dir ETIENNE EPAGNA-TOUA.

Digital Radio Télévision: BP 1974, Brazzaville; internet drtvcongo@drtvcongo.com; f. 2002; Dir-Gen. PAUL SONI-BENGA.

Radio Brazzaville: face Direction Générale, SOTELCO, Brazzaville; tel. 05-551-60-73 (mobile); f. 1999; official station; Man. JEAN-PASCAL MONGO SLYM.

Radio Liberté: BP 1660, Brazzaville; tel. 22-281-57-42; f. 1997; operated by supporters of Pres. Sassou-Nguesso.

Radio Magnificat: Centre Interdiocésain des Oeuvres (CIO), Brazzaville; tel. 05-531-12-60; e-mail radio.magnificat@yahoo.fr; f. 2006; Man. MAURICE MILANDOU.

Radiodiffusion-Télévision Congolaise (RTC): BP 2241, Brazzaville; tel. 22-281-24-73; state-owned; Pres. JEAN-GILBERT FOUTOU; Dir-Gen. GILBERT-DAVID MUTAKALA.

Radio Congo: BP 2241, Brazzaville; tel. 22-281-50-60; radio programmes in French, Lingala, Kikongo, Subia, English and Portuguese; transmitters at Brazzaville and Pointe-Noire; Gen. Man. ALPHONSE BOUYA DIMI; Dir of Broadcasting THÉOPHILE MIETE LIKIBI.

Télé Pointe-Noire: BP 769, Pointe-Noire; tel. 22-294-02-65; f. 1988.

Télé Congo: Brazzaville; f. 1960; operated by Radiodiffusion-Télévision Congolaise; Dir-Gen. JEAN OBAMBI.

Finance

(cap. = capital; res = reserves; dep. = deposits; m. = million; br(s). = branch(es); amounts in francs CFA)

BANKING

In 2008 there were seven commercial banks and one other financial institution in the Republic of the Congo.

Central Bank

Banque des Etats de l'Afrique Centrale (BEAC): BP 126, Brazzaville; tel. 22-281-10-73; fax 22-281-10-94; e-mail beacbzv@beac.int; internet www.beac.int; HQ in Yaoundé, Cameroon; f. 1973; bank of issue for mem. states of the Communauté Economique et Monétaire en Afrique Centrale (CEMAC, fmrly Union Douanière et Economique de l'Afrique Centrale) comprising Cameroon, the Central African Repub., Chad, the Repub. of the Congo, Equatorial Guinea and Gabon; cap. 88,000m., res 227,843m., dep. 4,110,966m. (Dec. 2007); Gov. LUCAS ABAGA NCHAMA; Dir in Repub. of the Congo CÉDRIC JOVIAL ONDAYE EBAUH; br. at Pointe-Noire.

Commercial Banks

Banque Commerciale Internationale: ave Amílcar Cabral, BP 147, Brazzaville; tel. 22-281-58-34; fax 22-281-03-73; internet www.bci.banquepopulaire.com; f. 2001 on privatization of Union Congolaise de Banques; renamed as above in 2006; cap. and res 2,868.2m., total assets 57,523.9m. (Dec. 2003); Pres. DOMINIQUE MARTINIE; Dir-Gen. ALAIN MERLOT; 16 brs.

Banque Congolaise de l'Habitat (BCH): ave Amílcar Cabral, BP 987, Brazzaville; tel. 22-281-25-88; fax 22-281-33-56; e-mail audriche.elenga@bch.cg; internet www.bch.cg; f. 2008; Dir-Gen. FADHEL GUIZANI.

BGFI Bank Congo: angle rue Reims, face à paierie de France, BP 14579, Brazzaville; tel. 22-281-40-50; fax 22-281-50-89; e-mail agence_brazzaville@bgfi.com; internet www.bgfi.com; subsidiary of BGFIBANK Group (Gabon); cap. 5,000m. (2007); Dir-Gen. NARCISSE OBIANG ONDO; 2 brs.

La Congolaise de Banque (LCB): ave Amílcar Cabral, BP 2889, Brazzaville; tel. 22-281-09-79; fax 22-281-09-77; internet lacongolaisedebanque.com; f. 2004 on privatization of Crédit pour l'Agriculture, l'Industrie et le Commerce (CAIC); cap. 4,000m. (2005); Dir-Gen. YOUNÈS EL MASLOUMI; 17 brs.

Crédit du Congo (CDCo): ave Emmanuel Daddet, BP 1312, Pointe-Noire; tel. 22-294-24-00; fax 22-294-16-65; e-mail svpinfos@creditducongo.com; internet www.creditducongo.com; f. 2002 to replace Banque Internationale du Congo; fmrly Crédit Lyonnais Congo; name changed as above in 2007; 91% owned by Attijariwafa bank (Morocco), 9% state-owned; cap. and res 2,868.2m., total assets 116,550.0m. (Dec. 2007); Pres. BOUBKER JAÏ; Dir-Gen. ABDELAHAD KETTANI; 4 brs.

Ecobank Congo: rond point de la Coupole, BP 2485, Brazzaville; tel. 05-547-00-35 (mobile); e-mail ecobankcg@ecobank.com; internet www.ecobank.com; Pres. GERVAIS BOUITI-VIAUDO; Dir-Gen. LAZARE KOMI NOULEKOU.

Société Congolaise de Financement (SOCOFIN): BP 899, Pointe-Noire; tel. 06-667-10-44 (mobile); fax 22-294-37-93; e-mail socofin.pnr@celtelplus.com; f. 2001; acquired by BGFI Bank in 2008; cap. 1,000m., res 109.5m., total assets 6,434.3m. (Dec. 2005); Pres. PHILIPPE DE LAPLAGNOLLE; Dir-Gen. BONGO MAVOUNGOU.

Co-operative Banking Institution

Mutuelle Congolaise d'Epargne et de Crédit (MUCODEC): ave Paul Doumer, BP 13237, Brazzaville; tel. 22-281-07-57; fax 22-281-01-68; e-mail contact@mucodec.com; internet www.mucodec.com; f. 1994; cap. and res 2,080m., total assets 29,000m. (Dec. 2003); Pres. BIENVENU MAZIÉZOULA; Dir-Gen. GÉRARD LEGIER; 45 brs.

Development Bank

Banque de Développement des Etats de l'Afrique Centrale: BP 1177, Brazzaville; tel. 22-281-18-85; fax 22-281-18-80; e-mail bdeac@bdeac.org; internet www.bdeac.org; cap. 34,811.2m., res –1,316.0m., dep. 44,021.0m. (Dec. 2009); Pres. MICHAËL ANDADÉ.

Financial Institution

Caisse Congolaise d'Amortissement (CCA): ave Foch, BP 2090, Brazzaville; tel. 22-281-57-35; fax 22-281-52-36; f. 1971; management of state funds; Dir-Gen. GEORGES NGUEKOUMOU.

INSURANCE

Assurances Générales du Congo: Brazzaville; tel. 22-918-93-00; fax 22-281-55-57; e-mail agccongo@yahoo.fr; f. 1999; Dir-Gen. RAYMOND IBATA.

Assurances et Réassurances du Congo (ARC): ave du Camp, BP 14524, Brazzaville; tel. 22-281-35-08; f. 1973; 50% state-owned; privatization pending; Dir-Gen. RAYMOND IBATA; brs at Brazzaville, Loubomo and Ouesso.

Gras Savoye Congo: 13 rue Germain Bikouma, angle route de la Radio, Immeuble Guenin, BP 1901, Pointe-Noire; tel. 22-294-79-72; fax 22-294-79-74; e-mail grassavoye.congo@cg.celtelplus.com; affiliated to Gras Savoye (France); insurance brokers and risk managers; Man. PHILIPPE BAILLÉ.

Nouvelle Société Interafricaine d'Assurances: 1 ave Foch, angle rue Sergent Malamine, face hôtel de ville, BP 1151, Brazzaville; tel. 22-281-13-34; fax 22-281-21-70; f. 2004; Dir-Gen. ANGÉLIQUE DIARRASSOUBA.

Société de Courtage d'Assurances et de Réassurances (SCDE): Immeuble Foch, ave Foch, BP 13177, Brazzaville; tel. 22-281-17-63.

Trade and Industry

GOVERNMENT AGENCY

Comité des Privatisations et de Renforcement des Capacités Locales: Immeuble ex-SCBO, 7ème étage, BP 1176, Brazzaville; tel. 22-281-46-21; fax 22-281-46-09; e-mail privat@aol.com; oversees and co-ordinates transfer of state-owned enterprises to the private sector.

DEVELOPMENT ORGANIZATIONS

Agence Française de Développement (AFD): rue Béhagle, BP 96, Brazzaville; tel. 22-281-53-30; fax 22-281-29-42; e-mail afdbrazzaville@afd.fr; internet www.afd.fr; French fund for economic co-operation; Country Dir PATRICK DAL BELLO.

Service de Coopération et d'Action Culturelle: BP 2175, Brazzaville; tel. 22-283-15-03; f. 1959; administers bilateral aid from France; Dir DOMINIQUE RICHARD.

Société Nationale d'Elevage (SONEL): BP 81, Loutété, Massangui; f. 1964; development of semi-intensive stock-rearing; exploitation of cattle by-products; Man. Dir THÉOPHILE BIKAWA.

CHAMBERS OF COMMERCE

Chambre de Commerce, d'Industrie, d'Agriculture et des Métiers de Brazzaville (CCIAMB): ave Amílcar Cabral, Centre Ville, BP 92, Brazzaville; tel. 05-521-70-04; tel. 22-281-16-08; internet cciambrazza.com; f. 1935; Pres. PAUL OBAMBI; Sec.-Gen. FIDÈLE BOSSA.

Chambre de Commerce, d'Industrie, d'Agriculture et des Métiers de Pointe-Noire: 3 blvd Général Charles de Gaulle, BP 665, Pointe-Noire; tel. 22-294-12-80; fax 22-294-07-13; e-mail infos@cciampnr.org; internet www.cciampnr.com; f. 1948; Chair. SYLVESTRE DIDIER MAVOUENZELA; Sec.-Gen. JEAN-BAPTISTE SOUMBOU.

Chambre Nationale d'Industrie et d'Agriculture du Congo: BP 1119, Brazzaville; tel. 22-283-29-56; fmrly Conférence Permanente des Chambres de Commerce du Congo; Pres. PAUL OBAMBI.

EMPLOYERS' ORGANIZATIONS

Confédération Générale du Patronat Congolais (COGEPACO): Brazzaville; Pres. JEAN GALESSAMY-IBOMBOT.

Forum des Jeunes Entreprises du Congo (FJEC): Quartier Milice, Villa 43B, ave de l'OUA, BP 13700, Makélékélé, Brazzaville; tel. 22-281-56-34; e-mail fjecbrazza@fjec.org; internet www.fjec.org; f. 1990; Sec.-Gen. PAUL KAMPAKOL.

Union Nationale des Opérateurs Economiques du Congo (UNOC): BP 5187, Brazzaville; tel. 22-281-54-32; e-mail unoc_patronat@yahoo.fr; f. 1985; operates a professional training centre; Pres. El Hadj DJIBRIL ABDOULAYE BOPAKA.

Union Patronale et Interprofessionnelle du Congo (UNICONGO): Immeuble CAPINFO, 1er étage, ave Paul Doumer, BP 42, Brazzaville; tel. 06-629-79-06 (mobile); fax 22-281-47-66; e-mail unicongobvz@unicongo.net; internet www.unicongo.org; f. 1958; Nat. Pres. CHRISTIAN BARROS; Sec.-Gen. JEAN-JACQUES SAMBA; membership of 20 feds (2008).

UTILITIES

Electricity

Agence Nationale d'Électrification Rurale du Congo (ANER): BP 2120, Brazzaville; tel. 05-570-19-52 (mobile); fax 22-281-50-77; e-mail aner_congo@yahoo.fr; f. 2003.

Société Nationale d'Electricité (SNE): 95 ave Paul Doumer, BP 95, Brazzaville; tel. 22-281-05-66; fax 22-281-05-69; e-mail snecongo@caramail.com; f. 1967; transfer to private management proposed; operates hydroelectric plants at Bouenza and Djoué; Dir-Gen. ALBERT CAMILLE PELLA.

Water

Société Nationale de Distribution d'Eau (SNDE): rue du Sergent Malamine, BP 229, Brazzaville; tel. 22-294-22-16; fax 22-294-28-60; internet www.sndecongo.com; f. 1967; transferred to private sector management by Bi-Water (United Kingdom) in 2002; water supply and sewerage; holds monopoly over wells and import of mineral water; Dir-Gen. EMILE MOKOKO.

MAJOR COMPANIES

The following are some of the largest companies in terms of either capital investment or employment.

Alucongo: POB 1105, Pointe-Noire; tel. 222940412; fax 222942010; e-mail commercialbernabe-cng.com; internet www.bernabeafrique.com; owned by Yeshi Group (Côte d'Ivoire); Dir ALUS TABOLA.

Boissons Africaines de Brazzaville (BAB): BP 2193, Brazzaville; tel. 22-283-20-06; f. 1964; subsidiary of Groupe Odzali; mfrs of carbonated drinks and syrups; Pres. and Dir-Gen. FRANÇOIS ODZALI.

Brasseries du Congo (BRASCO): POB 1147, Pointe-Noire; tel. 06-673-80-80 (mobile); fax 22-294-15-30; mfrs of beer, soft drinks, ice and carbon dioxide; 50% owned by CFAO (France), 50% by Heineken (Netherlands); Pres. J. N. FERRAND; Man. Dir C. M. VILLA; 570 employees.

Compagnie Bio Petro Chimie (CBPC): BP 242, Brazzaville; tel. 06-663-43-43.

Congo Mining Ltd: 3 ave de Loango, 2e étage, Ndjinji Arrondissement 1, EP Lumumba, Pointe-Noire; a subsidiary of Equatorial Resources Ltd; Dir-Gen. JOHN WELBORN.

La Congolaise des Bois Imprégnés (CBI): Pointe-Noire; f. 1986; production of electricity poles from eucalyptus trees; restructuring or privatization pending; 33 employees (2001).

Congolaise Industrielle des Bois (CIB): BP 41, Ouesso; tel. 06-900-14-30; e-mail rcongo@olamnet.com; f. 1968; acquired by Olam International (Singapore) in 2011; logs and timber production; sales 285m. francs CFA (2001); Pres. Dr HEINRICH LÜDER STOLL; Dir-Gen. CHRISTIAN SCHWARZ; 900 employees (2012).

La Congolaise de Raffinage (CORAF): BP 755, Pointe-Noire; tel. 06-654-06-62 (mobile); e-mail mazmofr@yahoo.fr; f. 1982; state-owned; subsidiary of SNPC; production of petroleum and petroleum products; Dir-Gen. DENIS AUGUSTE MARIE GOKANA.

ENI Congo: ave Charles de Gaulle, BP 706, Pointe-Noire; tel. 22-294-03-08; fax 22-294-11-54; f. 1968; cap. US $7m.; wholly owned by Eni (Italy); fmrly Agip Congo, present name adopted 2010; exploration and exploitation of petroleum resources; Chair. PIETRO CAVANNA; Man. Dir LUCA COSENTINO.

Eucalyptus Fibre Congo (EFC): BP 1227, Pointe-Noire; tel. 22-294-04-17; fax 22-294-40-54; f. 2005 to replace Eucalyptus du Congo (ECO); subsidiary of MagIndustries Corpn (Canada); production of wood pulp and other products for export from eucalyptus plantations; Dir-Gen. DAN ORLANDO.

Groupe Africa Oil and Gas Corpn—Congo: blvd Denis Sassous Nguesso, BP 15073, Brazzaville; tel. 22-282-61-78; internet aogc-congo.com; f. 2003; comprises Phenix SA, GPL SA and Afric; exploration, production and distribution of petroleum; Pres. DIEUDONNÉ BANTSIMBA; Dir-Gen. PIERRE NARCISSE LOUFOUA.

Industrie Forestière d'Ouesso (IFO): BP 300, Loubomo; tel. 22-291-02-04; fax 22-291-06-66; e-mail ifo1@inmarsat.francetelecom.fr; f. 1964; cap. 400m. francs CFA; timber mills; fmrly Société Congolaise des Bois; owned by Danzer Group (Germany); Dir JOSÉ QUARESMA.

Minoterie du Congo (MINOCO): BP 871, Pointe-Noire; tel. 22-294-37-07; fax 22-294-44-56; e-mail direction@minoco.cg; internet www.minoco.cg; f. 2000; affiliated with Seaboard Corpn (USA); fmrly Minoterie et Aliments du Bétail; production of flour and animal feed; cap. 3,200m. francs CFA; Dir-Gen. CHRISTOPH BARDY.

Perenco Congo: Concession Lillane, Quartier Ndjinji, Pointe-Noire; tel. 05-553-66-67 (mobile); fax 06-663-22-22 (mobile); f. 2001.

Régie Nationale des Palmeraies du Congo (RNPC): BP 8, Brazzaville; tel. 22-283-08-25; f. 1966; state-owned; transfer to private ownership proposed; production of palm oil; Man. Dir RENÉ MACOSSO.

Société Agricole et de Raffinage Industriel du Sucre (SARIS-Congo): Nkayi; sugar production; Dir-Gen. JACQUES COLLIGNON.

Société Commune de Logistique Petrolière (SCLOG): Pointe-Noire; f. 2002; 25% state-owned, privately managed; distribution of petroleum products; Dir-Gen. BOUBACAR BARRY.

Société des Huiles du Congo (HUILCA): Nkayi; tel. 22-292-11-60; f. 1988; 40% state-owned; production of oils and fats, vegetable oil refinery at Brazzaville; Pres. ANTOINE TABET; Dir-Gen. EMMANUEL PAMBOU.

Société Industrielle Agricole du Tabac Tropical (SIAT): BP 50, Brazzaville; tel. 22-283-16-15; fax 22-283-16-72; f. 1948; mfrs of cigarettes; Dir-Gen. BERNARD PUILLET; 70 employees (2001).

Société Industrielle de Déroulage et de Tranchage (SIDETRA): BP 1202, Pointe-Noire; tel. 22-294-20-07; f. 1966; 35% state-owned; forestry, production of sawn wood and veneers; 650 employees.

Société Libanaise de Bois de Placage: Likouala; f. 2000; factory producing logs and plywood from a region of forestry covering 199,000 hectares; 15-year licence granted in 2000.

Société Nationale de Construction (SONACO): Brazzaville; tel. 22-283-06-54; f. 1979; state-owned; building works; Man. Dir DENIS M'BOMO.

Société Nationale d'Exploitation des Bois (SNEB): Pointe-Noire; tel. 22-294-02-09; f. 1970; state-owned; production of timber; Chair. BRUNO ITOU.

Société Nationale des Pétroles du Congo (SNPC): BP 188, Brazzaville; tel. 22-281-09-64; fax 22-280-04-92; internet www.snpc-group.com; f. 1998; petroleum research and exploration; owns refinery at Pointe-Noire; cap. 900m. francs CFA; Pres. and Dir-Gen. JÉRÔME KOKO.

Société Nouvelle des Ciments du Congo (SONOCC): BP 72, Loutété; tel. 22-292-61-26; f. 2002 to replace Les Ciments du Congo; 56% owned by Chinese National Highway and Bridge Engineering Co (People's Republic of China), 44% state-owned; cap. 6,700m. francs CFA; Dir-Gen. LIANG QINGSHAN.

Société Nouvelle des Plastiques du Congo (SN PLASCO): route de l'Aéroport, BP Pointe-Noire; tel. 06-667-17-17; e-mail dg-pnr@sourcemayo.net; internet www.sourcemayo.net; f. 1974 as PLASCO; present name adopted 1990; mineral water; Dir-Gen. JEAN LUC LAISSY.

SOCOFRAN CDE: BP 1148, Pointe-Noire; tel. 22-294-00-18; fax 22-294-23-36; e-mail transit@cg.celtelplus.com; internet www.socofran.com; f. 1944; building, construction, public works; cap. 10,000m. francs CFA (2012); Pres. HUBERT PANDINO; Dir-Gen. FRÉDÉRIC PENIN; 2,000 employees.

Total Congo: rue de la Corniche, BP 1037, Brazzaville; tel. 22-281-11-12; fax 22-283-24-22; f. 1969; cap. US $17.2m.; fmrly Elf Congo, subsequently renamed TotalFinaElf Congo; present name adopted 2003; wholly owned by Total (France); exploration and exploitation of petroleum resources; Dir-Gen. JACQUES AZIBERT.

TRADE UNION FEDERATIONS

Independent trade unions were legalized in 1991.

Confédération Nationale des Syndicats Libres (CNASYL): Brazzaville; f. 1994; Sec.-Gen. MICHEL KABOUL MAOUTA.

Confédération Syndicale Congolaise (CSC): BP 2311, Brazzaville; tel. 22-283-19-23; f. 1964; 80,000 mems; Sec.-Gen. DANIEL MONGO.

Confédération Syndicale des Travailleurs du Congo (CSTC): BP 14743, Brazzaville; tel. 06-661-47-35 (mobile); f. 1993; fed. of 13 trade unions; Chair. ELAULT BELLO BELLARD; 40,000 mems.

Confédération des Syndicats Libres Autonomes du Congo (COSYLAC): BP 14861, Brazzaville; tel. 22-282-42-65; fax 22-283-42-70; e-mail b.oba@congonet.cg; Sec.-Gen. JEAN BERNARD.

Transport

RAILWAYS

In 2008 there were 795 km of railway track in the Congo. Rail traffic was severely disrupted by the 1997 civil war. The main line (of some 518 km) between Brazzaville and Pointe-Noire reopened briefly in November 1998 for freight traffic, but was subsequently closed following further unrest and sabotage. In early 2000 the Government signed two agreements with the Société Nationale des Chemins de Fer Français (France) relating to the repair of the line and associated infrastructure, and to the management of the network. Freight services resumed in August 2000, followed by passenger services in January 2001, although there was further disruption to the railways during unrest in mid-2002. In May 2004 the rail service linking Brazzaville to the Pool region resumed operations. In 2008 work started on a 1,000-km railway project to link Pointe-Noire with Ouesso, which was expected to be completed by 2013.

Chemin de Fer Congo-Océan (CFCO): ave Charles de Gaulle, BP 651, Pointe-Noire; tel. 05-559-91-24 (mobile); fax 22-294-04-47; internet www.cfco.cg; f. 1969; entered partnership with Rail Afrique International in June 1998; transfer to private management proposed; Dir-Gen. SAUVEUR JOSEPH EL BEZ.

ROADS

In 2004 there were an estimated 17,289 km of roads. Only about 5% of the total network was paved. The principal routes link Brazzaville with Pointe-Noire, in the south, and with Ouesso, in the north. A number of major construction projects initiated by President Sassou-Nguesso in 2000 and 2001 have involved the highways from Brazzaville to Kinkala, and from Brazzaville to the Pool region.

Régie Nationale des Transports et des Travaux Publics: BP 2073, Brazzaville; tel. 22-283-35-58; f. 1965; civil engineering, maintenance of roads and public works; Man. Dir HECTOR BIENVENU OUAMBA.

INLAND WATERWAYS

The Congo and Oubangui rivers form two axes of a highly developed inland waterway system. The Congo river and seven tributaries in the Congo basin provide 2,300 km of navigable river, and the Oubangui river, developed in co-operation with the Central African Republic, an additional 2,085 km.

Coordination Nationale des Transports Fluviaux: BP 2048, Brazzaville; tel. 22-283-06-27; Dir MÉDARD OKOUMOU.

Transcap—Congo: BP 1154, Pointe-Noire; tel. 22-294-01-46; f. 1962; Chair. J. DROUAULT.

SHIPPING

The deep-water Atlantic seaport at Pointe-Noire is the most important port in Central Africa, and Brazzaville is one of the principal ports on the Congo river. A major rehabilitation programme began in October 1999, with the aim of establishing Pointe-Noire as a regional centre for container traffic and as a logistics centre for offshore oil exploration.

La Congolaise de Transport Maritime (COTRAM): Pointe-Noire; f. 1984; national shipping co; state-owned.

Maersk Congo: 10 rue Massabi, Zone Portuaire, Pointe-Noire; tel. 22-294-21-41; fax 22-294-23-25; f. 1997; represents Maersk Sealand (Denmark).

Port Autonome de Brazzaville: BP 2048, Brazzaville; tel. 22-283-00-42; f. 2000; port authority; Dir JEAN-PAUL BOCKONDAS.

Port Autonome de Pointe-Noire (PAPN): BP 711, Pointe-Noire; tel. 22-294-00-52; fax 22-294-20-42; e-mail info@papn-cg.com; internet www.papn-cg.com; f. 2000; port authority; Dir-Gen. JEAN-MARIE ANIÉLÉ.

SAGA Congo: 18 rue du Prophète Lasse Zephirin, BP 674, Pointe-Noire; tel. 22-294-10-16; fax 22-294-34-04; e-mail emmanuelle.peillon@bollore.com.

Société Congolaise de Transports Maritimes (SOCOTRAM): BP 4922, Pointe-Noire; tel. 22-294-49-21; fax 22-294-49-22; e-mail info@socotram.com; internet www.socotram.fr; f. 1990; Dir JUSTE MONDELE.

CIVIL AVIATION

There are international airports at Brazzaville (Maya-Maya) and Pointe-Noire (Agostinho Neto). There are also five regional airports, at Loubomo (Dolisie, Ngot-Nzounzoungou), Nkayi, Owando, Ouesso and Impfondo, as well as 12 smaller airfields. In early 2001 the construction of a new international airport at Ollombo, some 500 km north of Brazzaville, began; the airport was inaugurated in late 2007.

Agence Nationale de l'Aviation Civile: rue de la Libération de Paris, Camp Clairon, BP 128, Brazzaville; e-mail courrier@anac-congo.org; internet anac-congo.org; Dir-Gen. MICHEL AMBENDÉ.

Aéro-Service: ave Charles de Gaulle, BP 1138, Pointe-Noire; tel. 05-556-41-41 (mobile); fax 22-294-14-41; e-mail info@aero-service.net; internet www.aero-service.net; f. 1967; scheduled and charter passenger and freight services; operates nationally and to regional destinations; Pres. and Dir-Gen. R. GRIESBAUM.

Équatorial Congo Airlines SA (ECAir): 1604 ave des Trois Martyrs, Quartier Batignolles, Brazzaville; tel. 06-509-05-09; e-mail info@flyecair.com; internet www.flyecair.com; f. 2011; operates flights between Brazzaville and Pointe-Noire; Dir-Gen. FATIMA BEYNA MOUSSA.

Trans Air Congo: Immeuble City Center, ave Amílcar Cabral, BP 2422, Brazzaville; tel. 22-281-10-46; fax 22-281-10-57; e-mail info@flytransaircongo.com; internet www.transaircongo.org; f. 1994; private airline operating internal scheduled and international charter flights; Pres. and Dir-Gen. BASSAM ELHAGE.

Tourism

Tourist visitors numbered 101,000 in 2010 (compared with tourist arrivals of 21,611 in 2002) and the industry has been identified as having considerable potential for growth by the Government. In 2007 earnings from tourism were estimated at US $54m.

Office National du Tourisme: BP 456, Brazzaville; tel. 22-283-09-53; f. 1980; Dir-Gen. ANTOINE KOUNKOU-KIBOUILOU.

Defence

As assessed at November 2011, the army numbered 8,000, the navy about 800 and the air force 1,200. In addition, there was a 2,000-strong gendarmerie. National service is voluntary for men and women, and lasts for two years.

Defence Expenditure: Estimated at 108,000m. francs CFA for 2010.

Supreme Commander of the Armed Forces: Gen. DENIS SASSOU-NGUESSO.

Chief of General Staff of the Congolese Armed Forces: Gen. NORBERT ROBERT MONDJO.

Chief of Staff of the Air Force: Col JEAN-BAPTISTE FÉLIX TCHIKAYA.

Chief of Staff of the Navy: Col FULGOR ONGOBE.

Commander of the Ground Forces: Gen. NOËL LEONARD ESSONGO.

Sec.-Gen. of the National Security Council: Col JEAN-DOMINIQUE OKEMBA.

Education

Education is officially compulsory for 10 years between six and 16 years of age and is provided free of charge in public institutions. Primary education begins at the age of six and lasts for six years. Secondary education, from 12 years of age, lasts for seven years, comprising a first cycle of four years and a second of three years. According to UNESCO estimates, in 2009/10 enrolment at primary schools included 91% of children in the relevant age-group (boys 92%; girls 89%). In 2003/04 enrolment at secondary schools was equivalent to 45% of children in the relevant age-group (boys 48%; girls 41%). In 2009/10 20,383 students were attending tertiary institutions. Some Congolese students also attend further education establishments abroad. In September 2004 the World Bank approved a grant of US $20m. to assist with the reconstruction of the country's educational sector, which had been severely damaged by years of civil conflict. In 2005 spending on education represented 8.1% of total budgetary expenditure.

Bibliography

Amin, S., and Coquery-Vidrovitch, C. *Histoire économique du Congo 1880–1968*. Paris, Anthropos, 1969.

Ayessa, B., and Pigasse, J. P. *Brazzaville: Chroniques 2001*. Brazzaville, Editions ADIAC, 2001.

Babu-Zale, R., *et al. Le Congo de Pascal Lissouba*. Paris, L'Harmattan, 1996.

Baniafouma, C. *Congo démocratie*. 5 vols. Paris, L'Harmattan, 1995–2003.

Clark, J. F. *The Failure of Democracy in the Republic of Congo*. Boulder, CO, Lynne Rienner Publishers, 2008.

Dabira, N. *Brazzaville à feu et à sang: 5 juin–15 octobre 1997*. Paris, L'Harmattan, 1998.

Dandou, W. *Un nouveau cadre constitutionnel pour le Congo-Brazzaville*. Paris, L'Harmattan, 2006.

Decalo, S., Thompson, V., and Adloff, R. *Historical Dictionary of Congo*. 3rd edn. Lanham, MD, Scarecrow Press, 1996.

Dzon, C. M. M. *Pour relancer le Congo : la politique du possible*. Paris, L'Harmattan, 2007.

Eliou, M. *La formation de la conscience nationale en République populaire du Congo*. Paris, Anthropos, 1977.

Gouemo, R. *Le Congo-Brazzaville: de l'état postcolonial à l'état multinational*. Paris, L'Harmattan, 2004.

Idourah, S. N. *Justice et pouvoir au Congo-Brazzaville 1958–92: La confusion des rôles*. Paris, L'Harmattan, 2002.

Ikiemi, S. *Le systeme bancaire du Congo-Brazzaville: organisation et perspectives*. Paris, L'Harmattan, 2006.

Kinata, C. *Les ethnochefferies dans le Bas-Congo français : collaboration et résistance: 1896-1960*. Paris, L'Harmattan, 2001.

Kouvibidila, G.-J. *Histoire du multipartisme au Congo-Brazzaville. Volume 1: La marche à rebours 1940–1991*. Paris, L'Harmattan, 2001.

Histoire du multipartisme au Congo-Brazzaville. Volume 2: Les débuts d'une crise attendue 1992–1993. Paris, L'Harmattan, 2001.

Histoire du multipartisme au Congo-Brazzaville. Volume 3: La République en otage mai–octobre 1993. Paris, L'Harmattan, 2003.

Lissouba, P. *Congo: Les fruits de la passion partagée*. Paris, Odilon, 1997.

Mabeko-Tali, J.-M. *Barbares et citoyens, l'identité nationale à l'épreuve des transitions africaines: Congo-Brazzaville, Angola*. Paris, L'Harmattan, 2005.

MacGaffrey, J., and Bazenguissa-Ganga, R. *Congo-Paris: Transnational Traders on the Margins of the Law*. Oxford, James Currey Publishers, 2000.

Makouta-Mboukou, J. P. *La destruction de Brazzaville ou la démocratie guillotinée*. Paris, L'Harmattan, 1999.

Mbéri, M. *Congo-Brazzaville: Regard sur 50 ans d'indépendance nationale 1960-2010*. Paris, L'Harmattan, 2011.

M'Kaloulou, B. *Dynamique paysanne et développement rural au Congo*. Paris, L'Harmattan, 1984.

M'paka, A. *Démocratie et vie politique au Congo-Brazzaville: Enjeux et recompositions politiques*. Paris, L'Harmattan, 2007.

Ndaki, G. *Crises, mutations et conflits politiques au Congo-Brazzaville*. Paris, L'Harmattan, 1998.

Ndinga Mbo, A. C. *Introduction a l'histoire des migrations au Congo-Brazzaville*. Paris, L'Harmattan, 2006.

Nkaya, M. (Ed.). *Le Congo-Brazzaville à l'aube du XXIe siècle: Plaidoyer pour l'avenir*. Paris, L'Harmattan, 2004.

Nsafou, G. *Congo: de la démocratie à la démocrature*. Paris, L'Harmattan, 1996.

Obenga, T. *L'Histoire sanglante du Congo-Brazzaville (1959–1997)*. Paris, Présence Africaine, 1998.

Pigasse, J.-P. *Congo: Chronique d'une guerre annoncée (5 juin–15 octobre 1997)*. Brazzaville, Editions ADIAC, 1998.

Rabut, E. *Brazza, commissaire général. Le Congo français (1886–1897)*. Paris, Editions de l'école des hautes études en sciences sociales, 1989.

Sassou-Nguesso, D. *Le Manguier, le fleuve et la souris*. France, Jean-Claude Lattes, 1997.

Soni-Benga, P. *La guerre inachevée du Congo-Brazzaville (15 octobre 1997–18 décembre 1998)*. Paris, L'Harmattan, 2001.

West, R. *Brazza of the Congo: European exploration and exploitation in French Equatorial Africa*. Newton Abbot, 1973.

Yengo, P. *La guerre civile du Congo-Brazzaville (1993-2002)*. Paris, Karthala, 2006.

Zika, J.-R. *Démocratisme et misère politique en afrique: Le cas du Congo-Brazzaville*. Paris, L'Harmattan, 2002.

CÔTE D'IVOIRE

Physical and Social Geography

R. J. HARRISON CHURCH

The Republic of Côte d'Ivoire is situated on the west coast of Africa, between Ghana to the east and Liberia to the west, with Guinea, Mali and Burkina Faso to the north. Côte d'Ivoire is economically the most important of the states of sub-Saharan francophone Africa. The country has an area of 322,462 sq km (124,503 sq miles), and at the 1998 census the population was 15,366,671, rising to 20,594,617 by mid-2012 (giving an average population density of 63.9 inhabitants per sq km), according to UN estimates. There is a diversity of peoples, with the Agni and Baoulé having cultural and other affinities with the Ashanti of Ghana. At the time of the 1998 census more than one-quarter of the population of the country were nationals of other states, with some 14.6% of the population nationals of Burkina Faso. The largest city is the former capital, Abidjan, which remains the principal commercial centre in Côte d'Ivoire, and which had an estimated population of 4,288,820 (including suburbs), according to UN estimates, in mid-2011. The official capital, the central city of Yamoussoukro, had an estimated population of 966,394 in that year. Bouaké, the largest city in the north, had a population of 573,700 in 2005.

From the border with Liberia eastwards to Fresco, the coast has cliffs, rocky promontories and sandy bays. East of Fresco, the rest of the coast is a straight sandbar, backed, as in Benin, by lagoons. None of the seaward river exits is navigable, and a canal was opened from the sea into the Ebrié lagoon at Abidjan only in 1950, after half a century's battle with nature.

Although Tertiary sands and clays fringe the northern edge of the lagoons, they give way almost immediately to Archaean and Pre-Cambrian rocks, which underlie the rest of the country. Diamonds are obtained from gravels south of Korhogo, and near Séguéla, while gold is mined at Ity, in the west. The Man mountains and the Guinea highlands on the border with Liberia and Guinea are the only areas of vigorous relief in the country. Substantial deposits of haematite iron ore may be developed near Man for export through the country's second deep-water port of San-Pédro. There is considerable commercial potential for large offshore deposits of petroleum and also of natural gas, exploitation of which began in 1995: Côte d'Ivoire aims to become self-sufficient in (and, in the medium term, a net exporter of) hydrocarbons. Plans for the development of nickel reserves are proceeding.

Except for the north-western fifth of Côte d'Ivoire, the country has an equatorial climate. This occurs most typically in the south, which receives annual rainfall of 1,250 mm–2,400 mm, with two maxima, and where the relative humidity is high. Much valuable rainforest survives in the south-west, but elsewhere it has been extensively planted with coffee, cocoa, bananas, pineapples, rubber and oil palm. Tropical climatic conditions prevail in the north-west, with a single rainy season of five to seven months, and 1,250 mm–1,500 mm of rain annually. Guinea savannah occurs here, as well as in the centre of the country, and projects southwards around Bouaké.

Recent History

BHAIRAV RAJA

Based on an earlier article by EDWARD GEORGE

THE HOUPHOUËT-BOIGNY ERA, 1960–93

From independence from French rule in August 1960 until his death in 1993, political life in Côte d'Ivoire was dominated by Dr Félix Houphouët-Boigny; he was the sole candidate for the presidency at every election until 1990, and his Parti Démocratique de la Côte d'Ivoire—Rassemblement Démocratique Africain (PDCI—RDA) the only legal political party. President Houphouët-Boigny guided the economic and political evolution of the country without any effective challenge to his rule. From the late 1960s efforts were made to 'Ivorianize' public administration and the economy. None the less, France remained influential in Côte d'Ivoire's political and economic life, and French financial backing, together with membership of the Franc Zone, were of major influence in Côte d'Ivoire's economic development.

Prior to the October 1985 presidential election, following a constitutional amendment abolishing the unfilled post of Vice-President, which effectively allowed only the President of the Assemblée nationale to succeed to the presidency on an interim basis, the question of an eventual successor to the ageing President was raised. Two potential contenders came to the fore: the Secretary-General of the PDCI—RDA, Philippe Yacé, and President of the Assemblée nationale Henri Konan Bédié. In October Houphouët-Boigny was re-elected unopposed, with a declared 100% of votes, although at legislative elections in the following month only 64 of the 147 incumbent deputies were returned. In January 1986 Bédié was re-elected President of the Assemblée nationale, and in February Yacé was elected President of the Economic and Social Council, the country's third most senior political office. (Yacé held this post until his death in November 1998.)

In 1990 there were demonstrations against government austerity policies introduced to comply with a precondition for assistance by international creditors. Persistent unrest led to the deployment of troops in Abidjan. In response, Houphouët-Boigny appointed Alassane Ouattara, the Governor of the Banque Centrale des États de l'Afrique de l'Ouest (BCEAO, the regional central bank), to head a commission to formulate alternative adjustment measures. In May, furthermore, Houphouët-Boigny agreed to the establishment of a plural political system. At the end of May a less stringent programme of austerity measures was announced, based on the recommendations of the Ouattara Commission.

Côte d'Ivoire's first contested presidential election took place on 28 October 1990, with Houphouët-Boigny challenged by Laurent Gbagbo, the candidate of the Front Populaire Ivoirien (FPI). The incumbent was elected for a seventh term of office by 81.7% of those who voted (69.2% of the electorate). In November the Assemblée nationale approved two constitutional amendments allowing, respectively, the President of the Assemblée to assume the functions of the President of the Republic, should this office become vacant, and the appointment of a Prime Minister, a post subsequently awarded to Ouattara.

According to the official results of the parliamentary elections held in November 1990, the PDCI—RDA secured 163 seats in the new legislature, while the FPI won nine (Gbagbo was among the successful FPI candidates). Francis Wodié, the leader of the Parti Ivoirien des Travailleurs (PIT), was also elected, as were two independent candidates. The incoming Assemblée nationale reconfirmed Bédié as its President.

The political and social climate deteriorated following the publication, in January 1992, of the findings of a commission of inquiry into the security forces' actions in the violent dispersal of a students' meeting at the University of Abidjan in May 1991. Although the commission found the Chief of the General Staff of the armed forces, Brig.-Gen. Robert Gueï, directly responsible for the acts of violence committed by his troops, Houphouët-Boigny emphasized that none of those incriminated by the report would be subject to disciplinary proceedings. In February 1992, after further violent demonstrations, 16 activists from the Fédération Estudiantine et Scolaire de Côte d'Ivoire (FESCI), including the union's Secretary-General, were arrested. A demonstration, organized by the FPI, degenerated into violence, and more than 100 protesters were arrested following clashes with security forces. In late February the FESCI leader was fined and sentenced to three years' imprisonment, convicted of reconstituting a banned organization. In March Gbagbo and eight others were fined and sentenced to two-year prison terms. President Houphouët-Boigny died on 7 December 1993. Later the same day Bédié announced his assumption of the duties of President of the Republic, with immediate effect, in accordance with the Constitution. Ouattara initially refused to recognize Bédié's right of succession, but resigned the premiership two days later, after France had acknowledged Bédié's legitimacy as President. Daniel Kablan Duncan, hitherto Minister-delegate, responsible for the Economy, Finance and Planning, was appointed Prime Minister.

THE BÉDIÉ PRESIDENCY

Several months of sporadic labour unrest were brought to an end by Houphouët-Boigny's death, and reactions to the 50% devaluation, in January 1994, of the CFA franc were generally more muted in Côte d'Ivoire than in other countries of the region. The new President and Prime Minister confirmed their commitment to adjustment measures initiated under Ouattara, including an accelerated programme of privatization. Meanwhile, Bédié conducted an effective purge of Ouattara sympathizers, appointing his own supporters to positions of influence in government agencies, the judiciary and in the state-owned media.

Bédié was elected Chairman of the PDCI—RDA in April 1994. His position as Head of State was further strengthened by Ouattara's departure for Washington, DC, USA, to take up the post of Deputy Managing Director of the IMF. In June a group of Ouattara loyalists left the PDCI—RDA to form what they termed a moderate, centrist organization, the Rassemblement des Républicains (RDR). By the end of the year the new party had supplanted the FPI as the principal parliamentary opposition. Ouattara officially announced his membership of the RDR in early 1995.

A new electoral code was adopted in December 1994, in preparation for the 1995 presidential and legislative elections. Opposition parties denounced clauses imposing restrictions on eligibility for public office, in particular requirements that candidates be of direct Ivorian descent and have been continuously resident in Côte d'Ivoire for five years prior to seeking election, both of which were interpreted as being directly aimed at preventing Ouattara from contesting the presidency. An FPI congress formally adopted Gbagbo as its candidate for the presidency, while the RDR invited Ouattara to stand; Ouattara, however, announced that he would not attempt to contest the presidency in violation of the law. The PDCI—RDA officially adopted Bédié as the party's presidential candidate. The FPI and the RDR subsequently stated that they would not be contesting the election as long as the conditions were not 'clear and open'; however, Wodié intended to contest the presidency as the candidate of the PIT.

The 1995 Elections

The presidential election took place on 22 October 1995, following a week of violent incidents in several towns. The opposition, grouped in a Front Républicain (FR), claimed that its appeal for an 'active boycott' of the poll had been largely successful, while the Government claimed that voters had participated both peacefully and in large numbers. Troops were deployed, ostensibly to prevent the disruption of voting by the opposition, although it was reported that polling had proceeded in only one of 60 designated centres in the FPI stronghold of Gagnoa. According to the official results of the presidential election, Bédié, with 95.2% of the valid votes cast, secured an overwhelming victory.

In early November 1995 it was announced that the FR had agreed to abandon its boycott of the legislative elections, scheduled for 26 November, in return for government concessions regarding the revision of voters' lists. The opposition suffered a reverse when the authorities announced that voting in three of Gagnoa's four constituencies, including the constituency that was to have been contested by Gbagbo, was to be postponed, owing to the disruption arising from the recent disturbances; moreover, the RDR candidate, party Secretary-General Djény Kobina was disqualified, on the grounds that he had been unable to prove direct Ivorian descent. Voting for the legislature was reported to have proceeded generally without incident. In December the Constitutional Council annulled the results of the elections in three constituencies. The PDCI—RDA thus held 146 seats, the RDR 14 and the FPI nine.

A government reorganization in August 1996 appeared to reflect Bédié's desire to remove from positions of influence figures connected with the insecurity prior to the 1995 elections (following reports of a military coup attempt at that time). Among those to leave the Government were Gueï, who was also dismissed from the army in January 1997. A commission of inquiry into the 1995 pre-election unrest was established in December 1996. By-elections for eight parliamentary seats (including those for which voting did not take place in 1995) took place in that month: the FPI won five seats and the PDCI—RDA three.

BRIG.-GEN. GUEÏ ASSUMES POWER

In August 1997 Bédié created a new National Security Council, directly responsible to the Head of State. Wide-ranging constitutional amendments were approved by the Assemblée nationale in June 1998. The RDR and the FPI objected to provisions conferring wider powers on the Head of State—specifically a clause allowing the President to delay elections or the proclamation of election results, on the grounds of 'events, serious troubles or *force majeure*'. The presidential mandate was, furthermore, to be extended to seven years, with no limit on the number of times an incumbent might seek re-election. Conditions of eligibility for public office were written into the Constitution: candidates would be required to be Ivorian by birth, of direct Ivorian descent and to have been continuously resident in Côte d'Ivoire for 10 years. In September Gbagbo and Kobina led a demonstration in Abidjan to denounce the amendments.

In August 1999 Ouattara was selected as the RDR's presidential candidate. However, Bédié regarded Ouattara as a Burkinabè citizen and warned that he would suppress any protests on his behalf. When Ouattara's claim to citizenship was subjected to a new inquiry by judicial police, clashes occurred in September between police and supporters of Ouattara in Abidjan. In October a court in Dimbokro, Ouattara's birthplace, cancelled his nationality certificate, prompting further violent demonstrations in Abidjan, during which a number of senior RDR leaders were arrested. The Secretary-General of the party since late 1998, Henriette Dagri-Diabaté, having been found guilty of inciting violence, was subsequently sentenced to two years' imprisonment. In December, while Ouattara was in Paris, France, publicly denouncing the Government's actions, a warrant was issued for his arrest.

With Bédié's authority and his personal popularity rapidly declining, a mutiny among soldiers, who converged on Abidjan on 23 December 1999, quickly escalated into a national crisis. The President initially sought to appease the soldiers, who seized most public buildings in the city, with the promise of improved pay and conditions; however, the troops subsequently altered their demands to include the reinstatement of Brig.-Gen. Gueï as Chief of Staff. On 24 December Gueï established a Comité National de Salut Publique (CNSP) to govern the country. Bédié fled to the French embassy, from where he moved to a French military base. The unexpected coup was apparently widely welcomed within Côte d'Ivoire, while both the RDR and FPI leaders speedily returned to the country from abroad. France also promptly accepted the coup and announced that it was to establish a dialogue with the new administration.

The new authorities rapidly succeeded in restoring order and calm, and an all-party Government was formed in January 2000. However, the publication of a draft Constitution in May provoked a renewed political crisis, as the articles restricting the eligibility of candidates for the presidency were retained. In reaction to the protests of the RDR about the clause, Gueï announced a government reorganization, in which all of the RDR ministers, with the exception of Dagri-Diabaté, were dismissed. Gueï also appointed a Prime Minister, Seydou Elimane Diarra, an experienced civil servant and diplomat, who was widely regarded as an impartial figure. In the same month the authorities in Côte d'Ivoire issued an international warrant for the arrest of Bédié, who was living in exile in France, on charges of embezzlement.

In a constitutional referendum conducted on 23 July 2000 86.5% of voters expressed their approval of the new Constitution, which had been supported by all the major parties, and which, *inter alia*, granted immunity from prosecution to members of the CNSP and to all those involved in the coup. Turn-out in the referendum was estimated at 56%.

GBAGBO BECOMES PRESIDENT

In July 2000 Ouattara, who asserted that he complied with all the restrictions on eligibility, announced his intention to contest the presidential election, scheduled for 17 September, as the RDR candidate. Former President Bédié also announced that he intended to seek the nomination of the PDCI—RDA, although Gueï was reported to have refused to grant permission for Bédié's return from France. In August Gueï announced that the country's four main political parties had agreed in advance to form a coalition government of national unity following the legislative elections. The Supreme Court upheld a ban on the participation of both Ouattara and Bédié in the presidential election, which had been postponed until 22 October, leaving the field clear for the two main contenders, Gueï and Gbagbo. Following a further minor government reorganization at the end of September, the FPI became the sole political party to be represented in the transitional Government.

After the election, as preliminary results indicated that Gbagbo was taking the lead, Gueï suspended the electoral commission and proclaimed himself as the winner. Gbagbo's supporters staged mass protests on the streets of Abidjan, and, on 25 October 2000, key units of the army and gendarmerie proclaimed their support for Gbagbo. Gueï promptly fled the country, while Gbagbo reinstated the electoral commission, which published official results showing that he had received 59.4% of the vote to Gueï's 32.7%. However, a low rate of participation (an estimated 33.2% overall, but markedly lower in the largely Muslim and RDR-supporting regions in the north, as well as in Yamoussoukro and other strongholds of the PDCI—RDA) cast doubt on the legitimacy of Gbagbo's victory. Gbagbo was sworn in on 26 October. On 27 October Pascal Affi N'Guessan, Minister of Industry and Tourism in the outgoing Government, was appointed as Prime Minister.

In continuing protest against Ouattara's exclusion, the RDR boycotted both the legislative elections held on 10 December 2000 and those held in January 2001 in a number of constituencies in the north, where unrest had led to the postponement of voting, with the result that the Assemblée nationale was now dominated by the FPI, with 96 seats, and the PDCI—RDA, with 94 seats. N'Guessan remained at the head of a new Government appointed in late January, which included, in addition to members of the FPI, ministers from the PDCI—RDA and the PIT, and two independents.

ATTEMPTS AT RECONCILIATION

An atmosphere of political uncertainty prevailed throughout 2001, amid rumours of attempted coups by disaffected army officers. In an attempt to secure his fragile authority, Gbagbo made new efforts at reconciliation between the principal political leaders; however, the issue of Ouattara's continued exclusion from the political process still proved divisive. In July N'Guessan was elected to replace Gbagbo as leader of the FPI. An official national reconciliation forum, chaired by Diarra and attended by representatives of political, religious and civil society organizations, opened in October; Bédié and Ouattara returned from exile to attend the forum. More substantial negotiations between Gbagbo, Bédié, Gueï and Ouattara took place in Yamoussoukro during January 2002. Thereafter, it appeared that Gueï had decided to support Ouattara's case for Ivorian nationality.

Ouattara was finally granted Ivorian citizenship in June 2002, although he remained barred from contesting the presidency, as a result of having held Burkinabè citizenship. A further attempt at reconciliation was evident in the appointment of four RDR ministers to a reorganized 'Government of National Unity' in August. However, discontent at the membership of the Government became evident almost immediately; in particular, opposition parties expressed their dissatisfaction at the overruling of their preferred candidates for ministerial appointments by Gbagbo. Consequently, the Union pour la Démocratie et pour la Paix de la Côte d'Ivoire (UDPCI), formed in early 2001 by followers of Gueï, withdrew its support from the Government; similar disputes also arose within the PIT and the PDCI—RDA.

MUTINY AND CIVIL CONFLICT

On 19 September 2002, while Gbagbo was on a state visit to Italy, groups of soldiers (who were mainly supporters of Gueï) defied orders to surrender their arms, precipitating a mutiny that quickly split the armed forces throughout the country. In Abidjan dissidents killed the Minister of State, Minister of the Interior and Decentralization, Emile Boga Doudou, a close ally of Gbagbo. Gueï was killed in Abidjan, apparently by soldiers loyal to Gbagbo; it was subsequently suggested that Gueï had been about to stage a coup. Gbagbo, returning on 20 September, implied that Burkina Faso was implicated in the insurgency. Amid renewed inter-ethnic tension and an upsurge in violence directed against northern Muslims and citizens of neighbouring states, and following an attack on his residence in Abidjan, Ouattara took up residence in the French embassy. (At the end of November he sought refuge in Gabon.) On 24 September the USA deployed some 200 special forces to Korhogo, to airlift foreigners from the rebel-held town. Moreover, an emergency summit of the Economic Community of West African States (ECOWAS), which was convened in Accra, Ghana, in late September, resolved to dispatch a peace-keeping force to act as a 'buffer' between government and rebel troops, and mandated the Presidents of Ghana, Guinea-Bissau, Niger, Nigeria and Togo, in addition to the South African President, Thabo Mbeki, in his capacity as Chairman of the African Union (AU), to form a 'contact group' to undertake negotiations between Gbagbo and the insurgents.

Master-Sgt Tuo Fozié, who had been sentenced *in absentia* to 20 years' imprisonment for his purported role in a coup attempt in January 2001, emerged as a spokesman for the rebels, who identified themselves as the Mouvement Patriotique de la Côte d'Ivoire (MPCI) and stated as their principal demand the removal of Gbagbo from the presidency and the holding of fresh presidential and legislative elections. Negotiations between the MPCI and ECOWAS mediators took place in early October 2002. Meanwhile, Gbagbo announced that the Government was prepared to enter into a cease-fire with the rebels. However, the signature of the accord by the Government, initially scheduled for 5 October, was delayed on two occasions, and subsequently cancelled, precipitating the departure of the ECOWAS contact group from Côte d'Ivoire. Thereafter, the Government's forces consistently failed to make any advances in rebel-held areas, especially around Bouaké, which had become the main rebel stronghold, but across the south, which remained under government control, the apparently systematic destruction of the homes of suspected rebel supporters (often ethnic Dioula in addition to people of Burkinabè, Malian or Guinean origin) occurred, resulting in both large-scale migration of foreign citizens away from the south and further loss of life. Although the Government swiftly invoked its 1961 defence treaty with France, the French role soon came to consist primarily of holding the line that now effectively divided the country between north and south.

In mid-October 2002 Gbagbo effectively assumed personal responsibility for defence. On 17 October Fozié unilaterally signed a cease-fire agreement on behalf of the MPCI, to take effect from the following day; Gbagbo announced his acceptance of the accord. At the end of October the Government and the MPCI entered into their first substantive negotiations in Lomé, Togo, under the aegis of ECOWAS. In early November the Government announced an amnesty for the rebels and the acceptance of their eventual reintegration into the national armed forces. However, the negotiations between the Government and the MPCI broke down following the apparently politically motivated assassination of the brother of a co-founder of the FPI, Louis Dakoury-Tabley, who had defected to join the MPCI negotiators. In protest, the leader of the rebel delegation, Guillaume Kigbafori Soro (the Secretary-General of the political wing of the MPCI), walked out of the talks, urging Gbagbo to stop the killings of foreigners and northerners.

Meanwhile, the rebellion had spread to western regions of Côte d'Ivoire, bordering Guinea and Liberia. In late October 2002 two new rebel groups, apparently comprising supporters of Gueï and also including mercenaries from Liberia, emerged. The Mouvement Populaire Ivoirien du Grand Ouest (MPIGO) and the Mouvement pour la Justice et la Paix (MJP) rapidly gained control of the western cities of Danane and Man. As clashes continued in the west, France steadily increased its overall presence to some 3,000 troops in January 2003, and the first contingent of ECOWAS forces, comprising 179 Senegalese troops, arrived in Côte d'Ivoire.

FORMATION OF A GOVERNMENT OF NATIONAL RECONCILIATION

In French-hosted talks at Marcoussis, near Paris, in January 2003, it was agreed by all parties that a government of national reconciliation would be formed under the premiership of Diarra; it would comprise a total of 41 representatives, including members of each of the main parties and several smaller parties, as well as of the rebel groups. The Marcoussis Accords were signed on 24 January, but immediately provoked a violent reaction among government supporters, who attacked the French embassy and other French-linked institutions in Abidjan, amid further assaults on immigrants. Gbagbo appeared to resist the terms agreed at Marcoussis, although he was coming under mounting international pressure, particularly from the UN Security Council, to honour the agreement.

Further rounds of negotiations and diplomacy took place throughout February 2003. Although the proposed government of national reconciliation remained in abeyance, Diarra was officially inaugurated as Prime Minister on 10 February. A new agreement was signed by the main parties and rebel movements in Accra on 8 March. The agreement provided for a six-month peace process, involving the deployment of more than 4,000 peace-keeping personnel, mainly provided by France, but also including ECOWAS troops. It was agreed that an international monitoring group would be provided by the UN, ECOWAS and the AU.

Several principal positions in the new Government were announced in mid-February 2003, but those appointed were mostly members of the FPI and the PDCI—RDA. The rebel movements and the RDR refused to attend the initial meetings of the Council of Ministers.

Meanwhile, the prevailing political and military difficulties in the country were beginning to create a humanitarian crisis. The continuing removal of people from their homes in the south was estimated to have forced 250,000 to flee to neighbouring countries, while a further 600,000 people were believed to be internally displaced. By April 2003 a 1,260-strong ECOWAS military mission in Côte d'Ivoire (ECOMICI) had been deployed to take over a section of the 'front line' near Yamoussoukro from French troops. On 1 May the Chief of Staff of the Ivorian armed forces, Gen. Mathias Doué, and the military leader of the MPCI, Col Michel Gueu, signed a cease-fire agreement, which was intended to apply to all rebel groups operating in Côte d'Ivoire. Later in May Soro confirmed that the MPCI's military activities had ceased. In mid-June the national army and rebel forces agreed to the eventual confinement of troops, and at the end of the month the Government announced that all former rebels would be disarmed by mid-September. Also in late June, the UN Mission in Côte d'Ivoire (MINUCI), authorized by the UN Security Council in May and charged with overseeing the implementation of the Marcoussis Accords, commenced operations in Abidjan. On 4 July, in a ceremony held at the presidential palace, MPCI leaders formally announced the end of the conflict. Although tensions continued, in August the Assemblée nationale approved legislation providing for an amnesty for those involved in political unrest between 17 September 2000 and 19 September 2002; however, those involved in abuses of human rights or violations of international humanitarian law were to be excluded from this amnesty. Meanwhile, the MPCI effectively absorbed the MPIGO and MJP, and announced that the organization was henceforth to be known as the Forces Nouvelles (FN).

Amid a long-running dispute over appointments to the defence and security portfolios, in September 2003 the FN suspended its participation in the Government, accusing Gbagbo of delaying the process of reconciliation. Moreover, the former rebels declared that they would not co-operate with the proposals for the disarmament and reintegration of former combatants. In late September, after an attack on a branch of the BCEAO and an outbreak of fighting in which at least 23 people were killed, French troops entered Bouaké and restored order, with the approval of the FN. In mid-October the Government prohibited demonstrations for a period of three months and also resolved to dissolve the Coordination des Jeunes Patriotes (CJP), a pro-Gbagbo militia; these measures followed several violent demonstrations in Abidjan, led by the CJP, which had demanded the expedited disarmament of the FN and had criticized the peace-keeping role of French troops in the conflict. In December the FN announced that its ministers were to resume participation in the Government. However, ongoing diplomatic efforts, under the aegis of ECOWAS, to advance the peace process appeared to have little success.

DELAYS TO THE PEACE PROCESS

In February 2004 the UN Security Council established the UN Operation in Côte d'Ivoire (UNOCI); with an authorized military strength of 6,240, the peace-keeping operation was to be deployed for an initial period of 12 months from 4 April, on which date authority was to be transferred from MINUCI and ECOMICI to UNOCI. Some 4,000 French troops were to remain in the country, with a mandate to act as a rapid deployment force if required by the UN mission. Nevertheless, the process of national reconciliation appeared to be stalling, with Soro's announcement, at the end of February, that former rebel fighters would not disarm prior to legislative and presidential elections scheduled for 2005. In March 2004 the PDCI—RDA announced that its ministers were to suspend their participation in the Government, in response to what it termed acts of humiliation and aggression against the party by supporters of Gbagbo; all parties represented in the Government, with the exception of Gbagbo's FPI and the PIT, expressed support for the action of the PDCI—RDA. A few days later the disarmament process was indefinitely postponed.

A protest march in Abidjan in March 2004, organized by seven of the 10 signatory parties of the Marcoussis Accords (known collectively as the G7), in defiance of a six-week ban on demonstrations announced by Gbagbo earlier that month, prompted clashes between protesters and members of the security forces. According to official figures, 37 were killed, although the G7, comprising the PDCI—RDA, the RDR, the UDPCI, the Mouvement des Forces d'Avenir (MFA) and the three former rebel movements now united in the FN, estimated the number of deaths at more than 300. An inquiry, conducted by the office of the UN High Commissioner for Human Rights, later reported that at least 120 civilians had been killed by the security forces in a 'carefully planned operation' organized by 'the highest authorities of the state'. Following the outbreak of violence, the RDR, the FN and the MFA announced that they were to suspend their participation in the Government and refused to negotiate with Gbagbo. The first contingent of UNOCI forces arrived in Côte d'Ivoire in early April.

THE ACCRA AGREEMENT

In mid-April 2004 President Gbagbo acceded to the opposition G7's principal demands in an attempt to restore stability, agreeing to respect the right to demonstrate, to ensure the security of the people and to allow equal access to the state media to all political organizations. The peace process remained stalled, however, and in mid-May Gbagbo dismissed three opposition ministers from the Government, including Soro. In June the CJP and other Gbagbo loyalists, who accused France of favouring the rebel movements, attacked the French embassy and erected a barricade near the French military headquarters.

In July 2004 all parties to the conflict, attending a meeting of West African heads of state that had been convened in Accra by the UN Secretary-General and the President of Ghana, signed an agreement on the implementation of the Marcoussis Accords. Under the agreement, which was to be monitored by UNOCI, ECOWAS and the AU, disarmament of the FN troops was to commence by 15 October, and progress on amending the Constitution with regard to presidential eligibility and other political reforms was to be made by the end of September. In mid-August, in accordance with the agreement, Gbagbo reinstated the three government ministers dismissed in May, and all ministers from opposition parties and the former rebel groups resumed participation in the Government. Shortly afterwards, the President signed a decree delegating some of his powers to the Prime Minister pending a presidential election. However, the 15 October 2004 disarmament deadline was not observed by the rebels, who declared that insufficient progress had been made towards the realization of the proposed political reforms.

RENEWED VIOLENCE

In early November 2004 the 18-month cease-fire was broken when the Ivorian air force launched bombing raids on Bouaké and other targets in the north of the country, reportedly resulting in the deaths of more than 80 civilians. On the third day of the offensive, nine French peace-keeping troops were killed when a French military base in Bouaké was bombed. In retaliation, French forces, acting on the direct orders of President Jacques Chirac, destroyed the entire fleet of the Ivorian air force on the ground. This precipitated several days of violence in Abidjan and elsewhere, with thousands of Ivorians, in particular members of the CJP, rioting, looting and attacking French and other foreign targets. French troops intervened to take control of Abidjan's airport and major thoroughfares, and to protect French and other foreign nationals, confronting rioters and protesters in the process; some 50 deaths were reported in the clashes. On 15 November the UN Security Council voted unanimously in favour of imposing an arms embargo, drafted by France, on Côte d'Ivoire. Meanwhile, Soro and eight other opposition ministers announced that they would not attend meetings of the Government, claiming that their security in Abidjan could not be guaranteed.

The South African President, Thabo Mbeki, designated as mediator by the AU, held talks with both the Ivorian Government and the FN in November and December 2004, with the aim of re-establishing the Marcoussis Accords. On 17 December the Assemblée nationale voted in favour of amending the Constitution to permit persons with only one, rather than two, Ivorian parents to contest the presidency (thus allowing Ouattara to contest the election scheduled for October 2005). Gbagbo, however, insisted that any constitutional change would require ratification by referendum. Unrest intensified and confrontations between police forces and a pro-Government militia in February resulted in at least two deaths. In April the mandate of UNOCI and French peace-keeping troops was extended until late June.

THE PRETORIA AGREEMENT

In early April 2005 President Mbeki hosted a summit in Pretoria, South Africa, attended by Bédié, Diarra, Gbagbo, Ouattara and Soro. An agreement was signed on 6 April committing all parties to the disbandment of militia groups and to the disarmament of the former rebel troops. On 14 April Mbeki issued a statement ruling that the Ivorian Constitutional Council should confirm the candidates of those parties that signed the Marcoussis Accords of 2003; this statement was thereby interpreted as permitting Ouattara's eventual candidacy. Following this statement, two of the FN ministers resumed participation in the Government. In the same month Gbagbo declared that he would accept Ouattara as a legitimate candidate at the presidential election, but implied that in so doing, normal constitutional provisions would be temporarily lifted.

Following a further round of discussions between the FN and the Ivorian armed forces in early May 2005, it was agreed that disarmament would commence at the end of June to be completed by 20 August, and that a new republican army would be established to incorporate both members of the existing armed forces and former rebel fighters. In June the UN Security Council agreed to extend the mandate of UNOCI and the French peace-keeping forces until January 2006, broadening the mandate granted to UNOCI to include an active role in disarmament, support for the organization of elections and the establishment of the rule of law. The UN Security Council also authorized an increase of 1,225 troops, enlarging UNOCI to 7,200, in addition to 4,000 French troops.

In July 2005 it was announced that some 40,000 former rebels and 15,000 pro-Government militia were to disarm by early October. The FN troops were to commence disarming on 1 August, although several prominent members of the FN stated that they would not disarm before the pro-Government militias had done so. Later in the month Gbagbo signed legislation on the establishment of an independent electoral commission and on nationality, using his exceptional constitutional powers to override the requirement for parliamentary approval.

On 1 August 2005 the FN declared that they were not ready to begin disarming, stating that the terms of the legislation recently decreed by Gbagbo differed from those that had been agreed in Pretoria in April. On 8 September UN Secretary-General Kofi Annan announced that the presidential election would be delayed indefinitely, owing to the failure of the country's political parties to implement the peace accords. On 27 September Gbagbo confirmed the postponement of the election, blaming the delay on the FN's refusal to disarm and the continuing division of the country between government-held and rebel-held zones. Following a meeting of the AU's Peace and Security Council in Addis Ababa, Ethiopia, on 6 October the AU announced proposals for the extension of Gbagbo's mandate as President by up to 12 months, for the appointment of a new Prime Minister acceptable to all parties and for the establishment of a working group to monitor the situation in the country, as well as a mediation group to advance the peace process. In mid-October the UN Security Council adopted Resolution 1633, endorsing the AU's recommendations and previous peace agreements. On 4 December the AU mediation team unexpectedly nominated Charles Konan Banny, Governor of the BCEAO, as the new Prime Minister. In mid-December the UN Security Council adopted a resolution to ban imports of diamonds from Côte d'Ivoire and to renew the arms embargo for a further year.

GOVERNMENT OF NATIONAL UNITY

On 28 December 2005 Prime Minister Banny announced his new Government of National Unity. The FPI was awarded seven ministries, the FN six, and the PDCI—RDA and the RDR five each. Banny also assumed the finance and communications portfolios, while the Secretary-General of the MPCI, Soro, was appointed to the new role of Minister of State for the Programme of Reconstruction and Reintegration. However, in January 2006 the new Government faced its first crisis, when the UN-mandated International Working Group (IWG) issued a statement rejecting the extension of the mandate of the Assemblée nationale, which had expired in December 2005. Interpreting the statement as a formal dissolution of the legislature, CJP militias loyal to President Gbagbo seized control of main roads and government buildings in Abidjan and the south-west of the country, and clashed with UN troops, who were forced to withdraw from their bases in Guiglo and Douékoué. On 27 January 2006 Banny defused tensions by issuing a decree that prolonged the mandate of the Assemblée nationale.

In late January 2006 the UN Security Council extended the mandate of UNOCI to 15 December, approving the transfer of an additional 200 peace-keepers from Liberia to Côte d'Ivoire. In February Banny called a meeting in Yamoussoukro of the leaders of the main political parties—Gbagbo, Ouattara, Bédié and Soro—to resolve outstanding political issues. However, the only significant agreement reached was the recognition by all parties of the legitimacy and composition of the electoral commission, the Commission Électorale Indépendante (CEI).

On 29 March 2006 Prime Minister Banny announced his intention to resume the identification campaign for the registration of voters. Although this was strongly contested by Gbagbo, who argued that the existing voter registers were adequate, the opposition supported Banny's initiative, arguing that up to 3m. Ivorians had no identification papers, preventing them from voting. Following AU mediation in early April, a compromise was reached that was termed *concomitance*, stipulating that the disarmament and identification processes would occur at the same time. Although the agreement was rejected by the FPI and the CJP, on 12 July the two-month identification process was officially launched. However, it was severely delayed by procedural challenges and claims of electoral fraud by both the FPI and the FN, while CJP militias erected barricades in Abidjan to disrupt the hearings.

In August 2006 Gbagbo pledged to issue a decree naming new magistrates to oversee the identification process. In protest, the FN withdrew from disarmament talks, claiming Gbagbo had tampered with the process. Given the political deadlock, at a meeting in early September the UN-mandated IWG agreed that the elections scheduled for October should be postponed.

In mid-August 2006 a fresh political crisis emerged when 525 metric tons of toxic waste were illegally unloaded at several locations around Abidjan, killing 17 people and causing more than 100,000 people to seek medical treatment (see below). After initial investigations implicated Ivorian business interests and authorities, Banny presented his Government's resignation to Gbagbo. The resignation was accepted but Gbagbo requested that Banny remain in office to form a new Council of Ministers. The FN denied Gbagbo's authority to accept the resignation, and refused to serve in a new administration. On 11 September a crisis meeting was held in Abidjan between Gbagbo, Banny, Ouattara, Bédié and Soro, under the mediation of the AU President Denis Sassou-Nguesso (President of the Republic of the Congo). However, no agreement was reached, and two days later Gbagbo reinstated the Government.

On 1 November 2006 the UN Security Council adopted Resolution 1721, which renewed the transitional period established by Resolution 1633 for a maximum of 12 months, and appealed for presidential and legislative elections to be held by 31 October 2007. The resolution extended the mandates of Gbagbo and Banny for the duration of the transitional period, and increased Banny's powers to enable him to issue decrees without the consent of the Assemblée nationale. The resolution also designated Sassou-Nguesso as official mediator. On 2 November 2006 Gbagbo made a televised address, accepting Resolution 1721 in principle, but implicitly rejecting Banny's authority over the armed forces. The following day Gbagbo received a public pledge of allegiance from the Chief of Staff of the Armed Forces, Gen. Philippe Mangou. The opposition parties, led by the FN, were also cautious in their acceptance of Resolution 1721, expressing doubts that it could be successfully implemented. In mid-December the UN Security Council extended the arms and diamonds sanctions in force against Côte d'Ivoire until October 2007; in January 2007 the mandate of UNOCI was extended until 30 June.

THE OUAGADOUGOU ACCORD

In February 2007 talks began in the Burkinabè capital, Ouagadougou, between representatives of the Government and the FN, under the mediation of President of Burkina Faso Blaise Compaoré. On 4 March Gbagbo and Soro signed the Ouagadougou Accord appealing for the resumption of the *audiences foraines* (localized courts to register citizens), which would be limited to issuing temporary birth certificates; the drawing up of a new electoral register under the supervision of the CEI, with a view to holding fresh national elections; the resumption of the demobilization process and the integration of the FN into the national army; and the dissolution of the 'buffer zone', to be followed by the deployment of joint army and FN patrols in the area and the extension of the Government's control across the whole country. The agreement also provided for the establishment of two new bodies: the Cadre Permanent de Concertation (CPC), comprising Gbagbo, Soro, Bédié, Ouattara and Compaoré; and the Comité d'Évaluation et d'Accompagnement (CEA), comprising representatives appointed by Gbagbo, Soro and Compaoré. A new government would be formed no later than 8 April, with national elections scheduled to be held by 4 January 2008.

In mid-March 2007 Gbagbo signed a decree setting up an integrated central command for the armed forces (the Centre de Commandement Integré—CCI), which would be jointly headed by army Chief of Staff Gen. Mangou and the FN Chief of Staff, Gen. Soumaïla Bakayoko. The CCI was tasked with completing the disarmament and demobilization process, and ensuring security during the identification campaign and elections. In further talks in Ouagadougou, Gbagbo nominated Soro as Prime Minister, and on 5 April Soro formally assumed office. Two days later, a new transitional Government was announced; it was dominated by FPI and FN figures but retained several members of the previous administration. The FPI was awarded the second most senior post in the Government, namely Minister of State for Planning and Development, as well as the justice and communication portfolios. The PDCI—RDA and RDR received the foreign affairs and agriculture portfolios, respectively. In mid-April Gbagbo issued an amnesty for crimes committed during the extended conflict, and the 'buffer zone' was officially abolished.

However, bitter infighting between FN and FPI ministers hindered progress with disarmament and electoral registration, and a deadline of 21 April 2007 for the relaunch of both processes was not met. In May the Government designated 60 teams for deployment around the country to restart the identification process. On 12 June the CPC held its first meeting in Yamoussoukro, agreeing to postpone the elections until the first quarter of 2008. On 26 June the last remaining government troops being held by the FN were freed at a ceremony in Bouaké.

THE DEMOBILIZATION PROCESS

Under the demobilization programme, 36,000 FN troops were to be demobilized in four stages by the end of October 2008. Around 5,000 would join the new Ivorian army, the Forces de Défense et de Sécurité, and 5,000 would enter the national police force and gendarmerie; the remaining 26,000 were expected to be reintegrated into civilian life under the national reintegration and rehabilitation programme. In addition, 12,000 militia troops loyal to Gbagbo were to be demobilized. However, the process caused renewed tensions within the FN, and in June 2008 FN troops staged a series of mutinies in Bouaké, partly in response to the Government's failure to pay demobilization allowances.

In July 2008 the CCI began demobilization talks with pro-Government militias in western Côte d'Ivoire, including the two largest forces, Front pour la Libération du Grand Ouest (FLGO) and Mouvement Ivoirien de Libération de l'Ouest de Côte d'Ivoire (MILOCI). Meanwhile, disquiet continued in the FN's ranks over the failure to pay allowances. In early August FN fighters and local gendarmes held protests in Bouaké over unpaid allowances, and later that month 300 FN troops marched through the city in protest, clashing with the police. In September the protests over unpaid allowances spread to the national army when troops mutinied at bases in

Yamoussoukro and Daoukro. After two days, the troops were persuaded to return to their barracks, although 104 soldiers were arrested and charged with insubordination. In December 86 of those charged were sentenced to prison terms of two to three years.

On 24 December 2008 Gbagbo and Soro signed a fourth complementary peace agreement to the Ouagadougou Accord, known as 'Ouaga IV', under Compaoré's mediation. The agreement created the framework for demobilizing 36,000 FN troops and an unspecified number of militia forces, integrating 9,000 of them into the national army and police force, and extending the central government administration into rebel-held areas. The agreement also proposed a timetable for disarming an estimated 70 militias, under which the process was to be concluded in April 2009.

Meanwhile, in January 2009 the UN Security Council extended UNOCI's mandate (which had been renewed at six-monthly intervals) to 31 July, agreeing to reduce its size from 8,115 to 7,450 troops; the following day France announced that it would also reduce the size of its military operation in Côte d'Ivoire, Opération Licorne, from 2,000 to 900 troops, by the end of May.

In April 2009 the CCI announced that a mixed force of 8,000 troops would redeploy into the north of the country as part of the process of reunification agreed under Ouaga IV. The force would comprise 2,000 troops from the national army, 2,000 gendarmes and 4,000 FN troops, with a mandate to re-establish the Government's authority across the national territory and provide security for the electoral process. The first contingents of this force were deployed to Bouaké in May and late that month a ceremony was held there to mark the transfer of power from the FN's 10 regional commanders to central government *préfets*, in accordance with Ouaga IV. However, the deployment of the CCI's security force was slow, with only 500 FN troops deploying to Bouaké by the end of May.

By September 2009, according to the Minister of Defence, Michel Amani N'Guessan, a total of 7,703 Forces Armées des Forces Nouvelles (FAFN—rebel forces) had demobilized, with 2,434 having returned to civilian life. However, at least a further 18,000 had failed to do so, in addition to an unspecified number of other militia forces, believed to total over 20,000. This contravened the October deadline set out in the Ouagadougou Accord.

THE IDENTIFICATION PROCESS

In September 2007 a trial phase of the *audiences foraines* in Ouragahio and Ferkéssédougou was gradually extended across the country. On 29 October the UN Security Council extended sanctions (including the arms embargo and ban on diamond imports) against Côte d'Ivoire for a further year, with the proviso that these would be lifted once free and fair elections had been held.

On 14 April 2008 Gbagbo issued a decree stating that the presidential election would take place on 30 November, to be followed by legislative elections at a later date. The CPC formally adopted the UN's five conditions for elections to proceed: the return of peace across the country; an inclusive political process; equal access to the state media; the completion of accurate voter lists; and the transparent publication of poll results. The Government subsequently signed an agreement with French company Sagem Sécurité to revise the electoral register and issue new voter identification cards, in collaboration with the CEI, the Office Nationale d'Identification and the Institut National de la Statistique.

On 15 May 2008 the *audiences foraines* formally ended, having held a total of 7,400 public hearings and issued 660,000 new birth certificates. The second phase of the revision of the national birth register commenced on 19 May. Once complete, this was to facilitate the compilation of a definitive electoral register, ahead of the presidential election. On 9 May Compaoré presided over the third meeting of the CPC in Yamoussoukro, discussing a significant deficit in funding for the election, the cost of which was estimated at 36,500m. francs CFA.

The CPC met for the fourth time in July 2008, once more under the mediation of Compaoré, who secured the renewed commitment of all parties to adhere to the 30 November election timetable. During the meeting Soro announced that funding for the electoral process had been secured from donors, with the European Union (EU) pledging 13,000m. francs CFA, the UN Development Programme 10,000m. francs CFA, and the Government funding the balance. Sagem Sécurité subsequently presented its operational plan for the registration process to Gbagbo and Soro, which was to involve 11,000 registration centres across the country staffed by 24,000 officials.

REPEATED ELECTORAL DELAYS

On 15 September 2008 the voter registration process finally began, with the opening of the first 1,000 of the 11,000 centres in seven cities in Côte d'Ivoire. However, industrial action disrupted voter registration in Abidjan and Bouaké in October, and late that month the CEI announced that only 300,000 out of an estimated 8m. voters had been registered. Soro admitted that the election would not be conducted as planned on 30 November, and the following day the CEA met to discuss a new deadline.

The CPC met for the fifth time on 10 November 2008 and unanimously agreed to postpone the holding of the election. It also requested that the CEI draw up a new timetable for completing voter registration and set a new election date. However, the registration process continued to be delayed by logistical problems, strikes over unpaid wages and allegations of fraud. In May 2009 Soro announced that the first round of the presidential election would take place on 29 November. The identification and registration of voters was finally completed on 30 June, following four extensions. According to UNOCI, a total of 6,362,842 Ivorians were registered. An additional 73,000 expatriate Ivorians were registered in Ivorian embassies abroad. However, the CEI estimated that at least 2m. eligible Ivorians had not registered. In July the UN Security Council renewed the mandate of UNOCI, which was tasked with supporting the organization of fair and transparent elections, for a further six months, to 31 January 2010. In August 2009 the CEI formally began the registration of candidates for the presidential election. The provisional electoral register was released in October. However, difficulties began when it was revealed that 2,752,181 voters had no previous official record, encouraging suspicions of electoral fraud. The opposition RDR warned that this could reopen the damaging debate on 'ivoirité' (see Foreign Relations and Regional Concerns).

When the final voter registrations were not released as scheduled on 1 November 2009, an emergency meeting was held between the Government and the main bodies involved in preparing the register. Personal details collected during the registration process were cross-referenced with existing data, resulting in 1.7m. voters having their identities confirmed, reducing the number of unregistered voters to 1,033,985, or 16.2% of the electorate. This was not considered to be a fraudulent situation, as the ineligible voters were shown to be evenly spread across the country; however, it was evident that the scheduled polling date of 29 November would not be met once again, and that the lengthy legal disputes required for this group of potential voters would delay the election timetable considerably. By 11 December the CEI had received more than 200,000 challenges to names on the register, and was unclear whether it had sufficient personnel to deal with such a high volume of complaints. The opposition leaders accused Gbagbo of lengthening the process in order to maintain his hold on power indefinitely.

As soon as the validation process ended, new controversy arose, with Gbagbo accusing Robert Beugré Mambé, President of the CEI, of fraudulently including 429,000 suspect voters on the electoral roll. The accusation was made after the discovery that the CEI had carried out the verification process independently of the Commission Nationale de Supervision de l'Identification and Sagem Sécurité. Gbagbo's supporters also suggested that Mambé favoured the registration of foreigners in order to increase the opposition vote, reopening the 'ivoirité' debate. Ouattara, however, expressed his support for Mambé, asserting that this was a further tactic by Gbagbo to delay the voting process. Mambé denounced the criticism of himself and the CEI and appealed for the UN mission to investigate the allegations of fraud. A criminal investigation was ordered by the Ministry of the Interior, which found evidence of misappropriation of electoral funds by Mambé and four senior CEI staff.

In response, Soro convened the electoral authorities for a series of meetings. The registration of some 429,000 suspect voters was subsequently annulled, and a new authenticating procedure was to be drawn up by 14 January 2010. There was growing concern among the country's citizens that efforts were being made to remove legitimate voters from the electoral register, most significantly in the north of the country, which had experienced high levels of immigration from neighbouring Mali and Burkina Faso. The opposition claimed that supporters of Gbagbo were trying to use the legal proceedings to remove northerners from the register, given that they would be unlikely to vote for Gbagbo.

POLITICAL IMPASSE

On 28 January 2010 the UN Security Council extended the mandate of UNOCI until the end of May, and authorized an increase in the maximum level of military personnel from 7,450 to 7,950. In the same month the UN Security Council renewed the arms embargo and ban on diamond imports in force, together with travel and financial restrictions against certain individuals, for another year.

In February 2010 tensions led to violent protests outside the court houses in the northern town of Katiola and the central-western town of Divo, in which one police officer was killed. In response to these protests, the outcome of an emergency meeting between Mambé, Gbagbo and Soro announced that the voter registration process would be extended once again until 14 February. However, on 10 February, shortly before that deadline, Gbagbo unilaterally suspended the CEI's activities, citing the need to prevent a further spread of violence in Vavouva.

On 12 February 2010 Gbagbo announced that he was dissolving the CEI and the Government with immediate effect, citing Article 48 of the Constitution that allowed the President to take 'exceptional measures' if confronted by a serious and immediate threat to national institutions. Gbagbo stated that the electoral process had broken down and that a free and fair election could no longer be guaranteed. Alphonse Djédjé Mady, leader of the Rassemblement des Houphouétistes pour la Démocratie et la Paix (RHDP, a coalition of four opposition parties founded in 2005), denounced the move as a coup and refused to recognize Gbagbo's authority, urging nation-wide protests. The peace process was stalled as opposition parties questioned the legality of President Gbagbo's move. Within one week of Gbagbo dissolving the Government, there were violent clashes with the police in Bouaké, Gagnoa, Korhogo and Daloa, and in opposition strongholds in Abidjan; at least 10 protesters were killed and a number of civilians and police officers injured.

Emergency talks were held, during which Soro attempted to broker a deal between the FPI and the RHDP and its allies. After further mediation by Compaoré, Soro announced the formation of a new Government on 22 February 2010. The administration was reduced from 33 to 27 members, with 11 portfolios awarded to the opposition and 16 to the FPI. A compromise was reached whereby the President and four Vice-Presidents of the CEI were to be replaced. The opposition ended the protests, and on 26 February a reconstituted CEI was formed with Youssouf Bakayoko, former Minister of Foreign Affairs and member of the PDCI—RDA, appointed as CEI President.

Meanwhile, in October 2009 a UN report warned that both sides were rearming in violation of the embargo. The report linked cocoa-smuggling with the systematic transfer of weapons and ammunition from neighbouring Burkina Faso to the northern territory controlled by the FN. The report accused the commanders of the FN's 10 zones (known as 'com-zones') with controlling and exploiting vast natural resources to sustain their control of northern Côte d'Ivoire. The report warned that in the government-controlled south of the country, security forces were being supplied with riot control equipment, which could be used to disguise illegal arms imports. The report also highlighted that the country's relatively porous borders had allowed the illegal trade in Ivorian conflict diamonds. On 31 March 2010 N'Guessan, an ally of Gbagbo, declared that the rebels must fully disarm before an election could take place. The rebels were accused of delaying disarmament in order to profit from the illegal taxation they continued to levy in the 'com-zones' they controlled.

On 11 March 2010, after three weeks of political deadlock, the new Government convened. The reconstituted CEI was tasked with resolving all disputes over the voter registration process by the end of March, after which voter cards were to be manufactured and distributed. The FPI demanded the removal of all 429,000 suspect voters from the list and threatened to conduct its own audit; opposition parties urged a reaudit of the 1,033,985 suspect voters identified in December 2009, while others called for a complete reaudit of all voters on the register.

On 21 April 2010 President Abdoulaye Wade of Senegal made an official visit to Côte d'Ivoire, at Gbagbo's invitation, to mediate in the political impasse. UN officials accused leaders on all sides of the political conflict of benefiting from the situation through an increase in illegal taxation, corruption and smuggling. On 27 May the UN Security Council temporarily extended the UNOCI mandate until 30 June, at which point it was extended again until the end of 2010. The resolution authorized the contingents to monitor armed groups in Côte d'Ivoire, protect civilians, supervise the arms embargo, promote the peace process, protect human rights, and support humanitarian assistance.

THE 2010 PRESIDENTIAL ELECTION

A revised provisional electoral list was published on 12 July 2010 and was confirmed on 2 August. Three days later, the Government announced a new date for the presidential election, of 31 October. After five years of delays, the first round of the presidential election accordingly took place on 31 October, following an official electoral campaign, which began on 15 October. The election, the first since 2000, was held under the terms of the 2007 Ouagadougou Political Agreement, the most recent in a series of partially implemented peace accords aimed at reunifying Côte d'Ivoire. More than 5.7m. Ivorians were registered to vote in 10,179 locations around the country. UNOCI provided assistance to the Government and the CEI, which included the transportation and distribution of equipment and other electoral materials, and security support. A total of 14 candidates contested the poll, the most prominent being Gbagbo (representing the FPI), Ouattara (the RDR) and Bédié (the PDCI—RDA).

The incumbent President Gbagbo took the highest number of votes cast in the first round of the presidential election, with 38.0%, while Ouattara was placed second, with 32.0% of the vote (followed by Bédié, who received 25.2%). Since no candidate won the election outright, a second round was conducted between Gbagbo and Ouattara on 28 November. On 1 December a spokesperson for the CEI was prevented from publicly announcing initial results of the second round by a supporter of Gbagbo, who destroyed the documents; the incident disrupted the procedures of the CEI and reportedly caused it to miss its legal deadline for announcing the results. On 2 December the CEI declared Ouattara as the victor, with 54.1% of the votes cast. On the following day, however, the President of the Conseil Constitutionnel, Paul Yao N'Dré (an ally of Gbagbo), announced that Gbagbo had won the election, after rejecting the second round results. The Conseil Constitutionnel ruled in favour of the annulment of votes that were cast in four prominent regions in the north of the country, where there was strong support for Ouattara, on grounds of malpractice. This prompted a post-election confrontation between the two sides that was to continue for four months. Citing voting irregularities, electoral violence, and a failure by the CEI formally to announce poll results within the legally mandated three-day period, the Conseil Constitutionnel annulled poll results in seven northern departments and proclaimed Gbagbo as President, ruling that he had received 51.5% of votes cast.

The Conseil Constitutionnel's decision awarded 2.05m. votes to Gbagbo (compared with about 1.8m. votes in the first round).

Both Gbagbo and Ouattara claimed to have won the second round of the election, were sworn in to the presidency in separate ceremonies, and appointed cabinets, forming parallel administrations. Both claimed to exercise national executive authority over state institutions and took steps to consolidate their control. Ouattara established his Government in the Golf Hotel in Abidjan, where he resided under the protection of a reported 800 UNOCI troops.

The Conseil Constitutionnel's decision was widely viewed with scepticism, since it resulted in the statistically highly unlikely invalidation of 597,010 votes, equivalent to 10.4% of the total registered electorate, or 13% of all votes cast during the second round. Furthermore, all the annulled districts were located in zones in the north of the country, which were considered an Ouattara electoral stronghold and largely controlled by the FN. In particular, the Special Representative of the UN Secretary-General for Côte d'Ivoire, Choi Young-Jin, endorsed Ouattara as the legitimate President, based on an independent tally process carried out entirely separately to that undertaken by the CEI. The UN, African regional organizations, including the AU and ECOWAS, as well as most international governments, rejected Gbagbo as the elected leader of the country. Gbagbo, however, asserted that the international community's rejection of the Conseil Constitutionnel's decision and its efforts to force him to concede the presidency infringed upon Ivorian national sovereignty and the constitutional rule of law, even though his former Government, among other signatories of the 2007 the Ouagadougou Accord and prior peace agreements, had agreed to the UN's electoral certification mandate.

POST-ELECTION VIOLENCE AND HUMAN RIGHTS ABUSES

On 2 December 2010 Gbagbo sealed the air, land and sea borders, without giving any reasons for the decision. The media regulator Conseil National de la Communication Audiovisuelle announced that it had suspended the transmissions of several foreign broadcasters. On 16 December pro-Ouattara demonstrators attempted to take control of the state-owned Radiodiffusion Télévision Ivorienne (RTI), which had been broadcasting pro-Gbagbo messages since the election. The action was violently suppressed by the security forces, which opened fire on the demonstrators, killing an estimated 20 and injuring many more. There were also security raids on numerous opposition-affiliated newspapers and printing presses, and at least nine foreign journalists were detained during the post-electoral period. Some of the Gbagbo Government's actions were later partially reversed, with opposition newspapers resuming publication, and some formerly banned radio stations broadcasting once again. However, harassment of, and threats against, journalists continued in early 2011, prompting nine independent or pro-Ouattara newspapers to suspend operations in March. Ouattara supporters were also accused by the Committee to Protect Journalists of exacting reprisals on their critics.

The contested election outcome heightened tension and precipitated further political violence, placing the Gbagbo administration in conflict with the UN Security Council, regional organizations, and key donor governments involved in monitoring, verifying or helping to administer the electoral process. As a result of concerns over the security situation, the UN temporarily relocated its non-essential staff to The Gambia on 6 December 2010. Limited armed clashes broke out between the security forces of the two sides, which reportedly included the greater part of the national military and police forces, in the case of Gbagbo, and the military wing of the FN in the case of Ouattara. There was also a spate of extrajudicial killings and other human rights abuses by state security forces during operations to suppress Ouattara's supporters. Furthermore, there were attacks on, and abductions of, Ouattara and Gbagbo partisans by groups of unidentified armed men, described as 'death squads'. In late January 2011 UNOCI comprised 9,024 troops and police. The mission had been temporarily supplemented by several hundred additional troops from the neighbouring UN Mission in Liberia (UNMIL).

As of late January 2011 the office of the UN High Commissioner for Human Rights (OHCHR), Navi Pillay, had substantiated nearly 300 post-electoral killings, and press reports stated that UN officials had increased their death toll estimate to 365 by early March. Most of the violence was related to post-election and related political tension, although there were communal clashes over issues that, while not directly related to the electoral outcome, were likely to have been aggravated by unresolved political issues, such as contended land or residency rights. For example, according to a UN report, on 3 January at least 35 people were killed in inter-ethnic violence between Dioula and Gueré militias, allegedly aided, in the case of the latter, by Liberian mercenaries.

An OHCHR report on the human rights situation in Côte d'Ivoire until 31 January 2011 also documented continuing reports of abductions, illegal detention and attacks against civilians. On 3 March state security forces killed seven unarmed female protesters, together with a baby of one of the women. Participants in a subsequent protest were fired on by state security forces, resulting in four fatalities, and a smaller rally was violently dispersed by pro-Gbagbo youth militants.

The total number of fatalities and abuses resulting from post-electoral violence was likely to be higher than the figure documented by the UN. Reporting by non-governmental human rights monitoring groups, such as Human Rights Watch (HRW) and Amnesty International, mirrored UN findings regarding a post-electoral rise in human rights abuses. HRW and Amnesty International, in particular, drew attention to the increase in the politically motivated use of rape as a means of intimidation. An Amnesty International report, issued in May, accused forces both loyal to Ouattara and Gbagbo of committing war crimes. In addition, UNOCI attempted to investigate reports of three mass graves, one in Abidjan, one in the south-central town of Gagnoa, and one in the town of Daloa, but was prevented from accessing the sites by state security forces, which Pillay condemned as a 'clear violation of international human rights and humanitarian law'. The rise in tension and violence prompted a number of international diplomatic missions to evacuate personnel and, in some cases, private citizens from Côte d'Ivoire.

There was also, reportedly, a sharp rise in militia recruitment by pro-Gbagbo and pro-FN elements, and a new pro-Gbagbo militia, the Force de Résistance et de Libération de la Côte d'Ivoire, was formed. In March 2011 Ouattara merged the military forces that had supported him into a new army under his control, the Forces Républicaines de Côte d'Ivoire (FRCI), with Guillaume Soro as its Commander. The UN also reported that a nominally demobilized pro-Gbagbo militia, the Compagnie des Scorpions Guetteurs (or the Front de Libération du Grand Centre), had been reactivated. Militant actions were alleged to be co-ordinated by high-ranking state officials together with pro-Gbagbo militia, youth groups and political party leaders. Police and other state security forces, in co-operation with youth groups, also reportedly looted the homes and property of a number of Ouattara government officials on 6 March. Reports indicated that pro-Ouattara youth groups were carrying out similar actions. Militant supporters of both presidential claimants in some cases perpetrated attacks on individuals and communities based on their presumed ethnicity and supposed political affiliation. According to Amnesty International, the FRCI supporters of Ouattara stepped up their violence in a campaign that started in late March, systematically killing hundreds in western Côte d'Ivoire.

OUATTARA SWORN IN AS PRESIDENT

On 11 April 2011 President Gbagbo was captured by forces loyal to Ouattara, which had launched intensive military assaults on his residence in Abidjan since late March. Ouattara's forces were assisted by UNOCI personnel, and by French armoured vehicles, helicopters and troops. UNOCI confirmed that Gbagbo had 'surrendered' to the forces loyal to Ouattara. Heavy fighting, in which between 1,500 and 3,000 people were believed to have been killed, had been waged in Abidjan for 11 days preceding Gbago's capture and arrest.

On 6 May 2011 Ouattara was officially sworn in as President. The President of the Conseil Constitutionnel, N'Dré, who had earlier refused to recognize Ouattara as President-elect, conducted the ceremony; Ouattara's speech emphasized national reconciliation. An inauguration ceremony attended by many heads of state, including French President Nicolas Sarkozy, followed on 21 May in Yamoussoukro. Ouattara subsequently requested that the International Criminal Court (ICC) investigate allegations of serious human rights crimes committed during the recent fighting, maintaining that atrocities perpetrated by supporters of both sides would be investigated. In June Ouattara appointed a new Government; Soro was retained as Prime Minister. It was subsequently announced that legislative elections would be held on 11 December.

In July 2011 Mamadou Coulibaly resigned as interim President of the FPI and created his own party, Liberté et Démocratie pour la République. Later that month the FPI appointed Sylvain Miaka Oureto as its new interim President and demanded that the Government release Gbagbo and his associates from detention as a condition for national reconciliation and for FPI participation in the legislative elections. (The former President and his son, Michel Gbagbo, had been held under house arrest since April.) Nevertheless, Laurent Gbagbo was transferred to the ICC in The Hague, Netherlands, in November to face four charges of crimes against humanity—murder, rape and other forms of sexual violence, persecution, and 'other inhuman acts'. In June 2012 the Gbagbo family challenged the detention of Michel Gbagbo, who held dual French-Ivorian nationality.

THE 2011 LEGISLATIVE ELECTIONS

Côte d'Ivoire held its first legislative elections in more than a decade on 11 December 2011. These polls ushered in the first democratically elected parliament since 2005, when the mandate of the previous Assemblée nationale had expired. To ensure the success of the elections, the authorities deployed 25,000 security personnel and also had the support of 7,000 UNOCI peace-keepers. Despite an initial agreement between the RDR and the PDCI—RDA to submit candidates under the umbrella of the RHDP, both parties registered candidates separately in most of the 205 electoral districts. The FN fielded the majority of its candidates, including Soro, under the RDR banner. The legislative vote was boycotted by the FPI.

On 16 December 2011 the CEI announced that the RDR had won 127 of the 255 parliamentary seats, while the PDCI—RDA secured 77, the UDPCI seven, the RHDP four, the MFA three and the Union pour la Côte d'Ivoire one; independent candidates gained control of 35 seats (although it was subsequently reported that several of them joined the RDR-led alliance), while voting was postponed in one constituency owing to the death of a candidate. According to the CEI, voter turn-out was higher than in the 2000 parliamentary elections, with 2.7m. people casting their votes out of a registered electorate of 5.6m. In early February 2012, however, the Conseil Constitutionnel upheld complaints of irregularities in 11 constituencies, in which the results were annulled; polls were repeated for those seats (and held in the constituency where the vote had been postponed due to the death of a candidate) on 26 February. Of the 13 seats contested on that date, the RDR won four, the UDPCI two and the PDCI—RDA one, while four independent candidates secured seats. The results in the remaining two constituencies remained undeclared. According to final results published by the CEI on 8 March, the RDR held 138 of the 253 declared seats, the PDCI—RDA held 86, independent candidates held 17 seats and the UDPCI held eight seats. Other party representations remained unchanged.

Also on 8 March 2012 Soro announced his resignation and that of his Government. Soro was elected President of the Assemblée nationale on 12 March and on the following day Jeannot Kouadio Ahoussou of the PDCI, and hitherto Minister of State, Keeper of the Seals, Minister of Justice, was appointed Prime Minister, while retaining the justice portfolio. All other members of the outgoing administration were reappointed to the posts that they had held in the Soro Government.

FOREIGN RELATIONS AND REGIONAL CONCERNS

Throughout his presidency Houphouët-Boigny tended to favour the maintenance of close links with the West. Relations with France were generally close, and remained cordial following Bédié's accession to the presidency. However, following the destruction of the Ivorian air force by the French military on 6 November 2004, in retaliation for an Ivorian bombing raid that had resulted in the deaths of nine French peace-keeping troops (see above), numerous French targets in Abidjan, including schools, businesses and homes, were attacked. French troops entered Abidjan to secure the international airport and to protect French citizens, airlifting many of them out of the city. Some 600 troops were dispatched to reinforce France's military presence in Côte d'Ivoire, while diplomatic relations between the two countries remained tense. The French Government subsequently admitted that its forces had killed some 20 Ivorian civilians during clashes with rioters in Abidjan; the Ivorian authorities claimed the number was significantly higher.

In 1999 the deterioration in the political situation in Côte d'Ivoire attracted considerable concern among the country's regional and international allies. In mid-November it was suggested that the Bédié administration's emphasis on the promotion of a sense of national identity or 'ivoirité' had helped to provoke outbreaks of violence against Burkinabè migrant workers, who were systematically expelled in November from areas bordering Burkina Faso by indigenous Krou militants. Despite international disapproval of many of the aspects of the Bédié regime, the coup in December, which brought Brig.-Gen. Robert Gueï to power, was, initially, widely condemned by France, the USA and the Organization of African Unity (OAU, now the African Union—AU), although intervention to restore Bédié was ruled out. In January 2000 the OAU ordered the military regime to announce a schedule for democratic elections or face exclusion from the July OAU summit. Gueï's subsequent announcement that he intended to stand as a presidential candidate was criticized by the international community, and the resumption of international support for Côte d'Ivoire was stated to be dependent upon the conduct of the forthcoming presidential and legislative elections.

Despite expressing disapproval at the exclusion of Alassane Ouattara from elections in 2000, France recommenced limited co-operation with Côte d'Ivoire in January 2001, with bilateral aid resuming from May. In the following month the EU agreed to resume its financial assistance, on the condition that substantive progress be made towards national reconciliation. From late 2002 France dispatched 3,500 additional troops to Côte d'Ivoire, under a mission codenamed Opération Licorne, to supplement the 550 already stationed in the country, and the French Government played an active role in the diplomatic efforts that led to the signature of the Marcoussis Accords in January 2003 (see above). However, France stated that it regarded the civil conflict as an internal Ivorian matter, disregarding Gbagbo's statements relating to the alleged involvement of external forces in the rebellion; such involvement would have resulted in the invocation of a clause in a defence treaty between the two countries, necessitating the active military support of France for the Ivorian authorities. None the less, there was widespread anti-French feeling, particularly in Abidjan, following the conclusion of the Marcoussis Accords, and several thousand French citizens resident in Côte d'Ivoire reportedly left the country. French businesses nevertheless remained dominant in Côte d'Ivoire. The election of French President Nicolas Sarkozy in May 2007 was expected to lead to major changes in French policy towards Africa, notably the scaling down of the French military contingent in Côte d'Ivoire. This was confirmed in January 2009 when the French Government announced that Opération Licorne would be reduced from 2,000 to 900 troops by mid-2009. The Sarkozy Government initially attempted to improve bilateral relations, largely by supporting Côte d'Ivoire in its negotiations with multilateral institutions to cancel a significant proportion of its debt arrears. However, France was believed to be losing patience with having to support an expensive peace-keeping operation while continuing to be the target of anti-colonial sentiment among Gbagbo's supporters. In February 2011, in response to the political impasse in Côte d'Ivoire, Opération

Licorne was strengthened to 1,100 troops (and subsequently to 1,600). French forces played an important role in the capture of Gbagbo in April, and French advisers supported the country's economic reconstruction following the installation of a new Government, headed by President Alassane Ouattara, in June. In January 2012 Ouattara made his first state visit to France, where he signed a new security agreement with President Sarkozy; by that time the French military contingency in Côte d'Ivoire had again been reduced, to just 450.

Although presented with considerable evidence to the contrary, Houphouët-Boigny consistently denied that his Government was supporting Charles Taylor's National Patriotic Front of Liberia (NPFL), which was instrumental in the overthrow of President Samuel Doe in mid-1990 (see Recent History of Liberia). In mid-1995 Côte d'Ivoire, which had hitherto tended to promote the full integration of refugees into Ivorian society (a process facilitated by the common ethnic origin of communities on both sides of the Côte d'Ivoire–Liberia border), announced that, henceforth, reception camps for Liberian refugees would be established. In early 1996 the Ivorian authorities announced that security measures were to be increased in the west (in an effort to prevent rebel incursions and the infiltration of refugee groups by Liberian fighters), and in July the Government proclaimed western Côte d'Ivoire to be a military 'operational zone', extending the powers of the armed forces to act in response to rebel activity. The installation of elected organs of state in Liberia in 1997 facilitated the return of refugees; the UN High Commissioner for Refugees (UNHCR) estimated the number of Liberian refugees in Côte d'Ivoire at 119,900 at the end of 1998, compared with 327,700 at the end of 1996. Although it had initially been intended that the full repatriation of Liberian refugees should be completed by the end of December 1999, the programme of repatriation proceeded more slowly than anticipated, and some 76,000 of a total of more than 100,000 Liberian refugees remaining in Côte d'Ivoire were still receiving limited support from UNHCR at the end of that year. Conversely, following improved conditions in Liberia, some 25,000 Ivorian nationals were believed by UNHCR to have fled to that country in 2002 to escape fighting in western Côte d'Ivoire; in 2004 some 10,000 Ivorians were reported to have sought refuge in Liberia, in response to the renewed outbreak of violence in Côte d'Ivoire in November. During the political crisis that followed the 2010 presidential election in Côte d'Ivoire, it was alleged that Gbagbo had enlisted Liberian mercenaries to abduct adversaries and carry out extrajudicial executions, while UNHCR estimated that around 180,000 Ivorians had crossed into Liberia. In August 2011 UNHCR signed an accord with the Governments of Côte d'Ivoire and Liberia to facilitate the voluntary repatriation of Ivorian refugees from Liberia. UNHCR estimated that some 24,690 Liberian refugees remained in Côte d'Ivoire at the beginning of 2012.

After the mutiny of 19 September 2002 and the effective division of Côte d'Ivoire into two parts, at least 1m. immigrants living and working in the south were forced out of their homes, losing their jobs and property. A massive migration of Burkinabè, Malian and Guinean workers followed the rampages of government gendarmes, militias and FPI youth organizations in immigrant areas of Abidjan and other southern towns. Many Burkinabè businesses were destroyed. Gbagbo and his ministers further heightened tension by accusing certain foreign countries, and by implication Burkina Faso, of providing military support to the rebel movements, although no evidence was produced to support such claims. As stability appeared to return to Côte d'Ivoire, the border with Burkina Faso, closed since the onset of the rebellion, was reopened in September 2003. In July 2004, at a meeting in Abidjan, representatives of the two countries pledged to combat 'destabilizing acts' against their respective countries and agreed to increase co-operation in security and defence matters; Burkina Faso had accused Côte d'Ivoire of violating its airspace earlier that month. Following the renewed outbreak of violence in Côte d'Ivoire in November, the Burkinabè President, Blaise Compaoré, commented in the French daily *Le Figaro* that it would be impossible to resolve the Ivorian conflict under the present regime in that country, reiterating previous statements. In late 2006 relations with the Burkinabè Government began to improve, after Compaoré offered to mediate in the crisis; he subsequently became involved in peace negotiations and presided over the signature of the Ouagadougou Accord (see above). In July 2008, on his first state visit to Burkina, Gbagbo signed a treaty of friendship and co-operation with President Compaoré. In early 2010 the Ivorian Minister of Economy and Finance pledged to pay an outstanding debt to the Burkinabè Post Office of 3,200m. francs CFA, non-payment of which had caused the suspension of transactions between the two countries since 2000 and had adversely affected the 3m. Burkinabè citizens working in the Ivorian cocoa plantations.

In August 2006 a Panamanian-registered ship, *Probo Koala*, illegally unloaded toxic waste, including petroleum residue, sulphur and caustic soda, at several locations around Abidjan. The ship had been in the custody of Trafigura, a Dutch company linked with Nigerian and Ivorian business interests. In November official inquiry findings blamed a wide range of authorities, including the port authority, the customs service, the municipal authorities and the transport and environment ministries, for negligence and fraud. In mid-February 2007 Gbagbo signed an agreement with Trafigura, under which the company agreed to pay €152m. towards a clean-up operation, the construction of a local waste-processing factory and in compensation to the victims, in return for immunity from prosecution. In 2008 a British law firm representing Ivorians affected by the toxic waste launched a class action against Trafigura in the British courts. In September 2009 the British High Court approved a GBP £30m. payout. Trafigura would pay 750,000 francs CFA to each of the 31,000 victims in the suit. The company continued to deny direct responsibility for the unloading, which was carried out by a subcontractor. It claimed that, despite an earlier draft suggesting the opposite, its own investigation report found no direct link between the waste and subsequent deaths, miscarriages, birth defects and chronic illnesses among the local population. This contradicted a report by a UN expert, Okechukwu Ibeanu, which found strong evidential links. Moreover, the environmental group Greenpeace claimed to have obtained e-mails from Trafigura employees revealing that the company knew that the ship contained hazardous waste and that it knowingly exported the waste in violation of EU law. On 10 March 2010 the Dutch Supreme Court ruled that the city of Amsterdam would face full responsibility for failing to supervise the ship that dumped toxic waste in Abidjan. In May Trafigura denied that it had paid witnesses in return for testimonies about toxic waste that was dumped in Cote d'Ivoire.

In April 2010 Côte d'Ivoire and Ghana held a two-day meeting on the demarcation of their shared maritime border, amid vigorous denials that the negotiations were connected with the discovery of large oil reserves by the Russian company Lukoil off the coast of Ghana in March. Both countries had submitted proposals on their maritime boundaries to the UN, which would be called upon to mediate if talks were to fail.

Foreign Response to the 2010 Disputed Presidential Election

The conflict over the results of the 2010 presidential election (see above) prompted wide-ranging political, financial, and threatened military, international pressure, which was aimed at forcing Gbagbo to concede the outcome and relinquish state power to Ouattara. Angola and Lebanon were the only countries to dispatch their ambassadors to attend Gbagbo's swearing-in ceremony. The AU, which, like the UN, formally recognized Ouattara as the legitimately elected President, warned that the conflicting results and subsequent political crisis could result in force against the Gbagbo regime. On 5 December 2010 former President of South Africa Thabo Mbeki attempted to mediate the issue on behalf of the AU, but with no success. The USA, the UN, the EU, ECOWAS, as well as former colonial power France, affirmed support for Ouattara. On 28 December Presidents Yayi Boni of Benin, Ernest Bai Koroma of Sierra Leone and Pedro Pires of Cape Verde were dispatched by ECOWAS to convince Gbagbo to resign and go into exile, while declaring it Gbagbo's last chance before the deployment of military force against him. On 25 January 2011 it was reported that Ugandan President Yoweri Museveni had declared his opposition to the UN's recognition of Ouattara as winner of the election and requested an AU investigation into the poll.

The role of France as intermediator in the post-election crisis also received considerable international attention. The former colonial power was keen to withdraw its troops from Côte d'Ivoire, after what was considered to be a delicate transition period. The French Opération Licorne force formed at the request of the UN, which totalled 1,600 troops in 2011, had attracted criticism of interference from international analysts. The complete withdrawal of French troops was considered by many to be essential in order not to taint President Ouattara's chances to achieve national reconciliation. Gbagbo had for a long time led a campaign to depict Ouattara as a 'colonial stooge' of the French.

Many regional newspapers across Africa urged President Ouattara to begin a process of reconciliation to win over Gbagbo supporters, stressing it as crucial for the sustainability of peace. There were mixed reports on France's involvement, with some newspapers citing its influence as necessary and timely, while others suggested that Ouattara was subservient to a 'neo-colonial' France. Among critics of the use of foreign military intervention in the capture of Gbagbo, Russia questioned the legality of the air-strikes, suggesting that the UN peace-keepers might have 'overstepped their mandate to be neutral'. The Chairman of the AU declared that foreign military intervention was unjustified.

Post-election Regional Concerns

In his first week of office, Ouattara voiced his concerns for the security of the West African region due to secondary effects involving mercenaries loyal to former President Gbagbo, who had fled to neighbouring countries. Another concern of Ouattara that was substantiated by the UN were reports that in the immediate post-electoral period, pro-Gbagbo troops had been assisted by mercenaries from Liberia, and possibly from other countries. Particular concern was raised due to Liberia's history of severe wartime human rights abuses, and because such irregular forces might be difficult to prosecute if they were accused of crimes. Ouattara warned that such mercenaries might begin to operate in other nations, such as Sierra Leone and Guinea. He cited it as a regional problem, particularly since many of the countries had suffered periods of fragility after emerging from long civil wars, as in the case of Liberia and Sierra Leone. Since December 2010, more than 100,000 people had fled Côte d'Ivoire, amid continued unrest in the west of the country, mainly to Liberia, Ghana, Guinea and Togo. A UNHCR spokesman accused mercenaries from neighbouring Liberia of taking advantage of the lawlessness to loot, rape and kill in the Guiglo region, further emphasizing that they were neither pro-Gbagbo nor pro-Ouattara forces, but merely profiting from the situation.

The issue of internally displaced persons (IDPs) was also pressing, with UNHCR estimating that up to 1m. people might have fled their homes due to the violence. It was also reported that most had taken refuge from the violence in Abidjan in March and April 2011, with many being former economic migrants from the country's poorer northern neighbours. In Côte d'Ivoire itself, more than 100,000 IDPs had been reported in the west, mainly in and around the cities of Danané, Duékoué and Man, while a further estimated 700,000 people had fled the conflict-stricken Abidjan neighbourhoods of Abobo, Anyama and Yopougon.

In June 2012 UNOCI raised concerns over the tens of thousands of combatants believed to have fought during the 2010–11 post-election conflict in Côte d'Ivoire. UNOCI stressed that they could still be armed and dangerous and appealed for a disarmament, demobilization and reintegration (DDR) programme to be implemented urgently. DDR measures were cited as having failed in 2004 and 2007, partly because of inadequate political support, a lack of expertise and recurrent violence.

In early June 2012 a militia group allegedly crossed from Liberia into western Côte d'Ivoire, where it ambushed and killed seven UN peace-keepers and 10 civilians near the Ivorian border town of Tai; the UN described the incident as the worst attack on peace-keepers in Côte d'Ivoire since 2004. The Danish Refugee Council estimated that 13,000 civilians in western Côte d'Ivoire had fled their homes following the violence. The Ivorian authorities laid the blame for the ambush on Liberian mercenaries and Ivorians loyal to former President Gbagbo. At least 48 people had been killed in cross-border attacks since the end of the conflict in 2011, and banditry and criminality in the region were rife. UNOCI estimated that 60,000–80,000 former fighters needed to be disarmed, while Côte d'Ivoire's Minister at the Presidency, in charge of Defence, Paul Koffi Koffi, placed the number at around 30,000. Furthermore, UNOCI suspected that some 3,000–4,000 pro-Gbagbo militants were sheltering in Liberia and Ghana.

Senior Ivorian officials held discussions with their Liberian counterparts and representatives of UNOCI and UNMIL in early June 2012. The talks ended with a joint communiqué pledging to stabilize territory on both sides of the border, improve information exchanges, tighten extradition procedures and increase consultation with community leaders. The Liberian Government agreed to address long-standing complaints that its nationals were party to military operations and serious human rights violations in the border region.

The FRCI had been strengthened by post-election recruitment drives and by Ouattara's efforts to integrate former rebels and government soldiers into a single force. In mid-2012 many police officers still lacked weapons, leaving the military to play a policing role in much of the country.

Economy

BHAIRAV RAJA

Based on an earlier article by EDWARD GEORGE

INTRODUCTION

For some 20 years following independence, Côte d'Ivoire was remarkable for its very high rate of economic growth. Gross domestic product (GDP) increased, in real terms, at an average annual rate of 11% in 1960–70 and 6%–7% in 1970–80, bringing it into the ranks of middle-income developing countries. During the 1980s the economy entered a period of overall decline. By late 1994, however, a marked recovery was in progress, with annual GDP growth reaching an average of 6.3% per year in 1995–98. A stimulus for this recovery was the 50% devaluation of the CFA franc in January 1994, which improved the competitiveness, in price terms, of Côte d'Ivoire's timber and non-traditional exports such as fish and rubber at a time when a boom in international prices for coffee was coming to an end. The economy's promising performance was interrupted by Henri Konan Bédié's Government's loss of policy control in 1998 and 1999, and the suspension of disbursements by the European Union (EU) and the IMF (see below). The military overthrow of the Bédié Government in December 1999, and the subsequent political instability that persisted after 2000 severely limited new foreign investment.

Following the outbreak of the civil conflict in November 2002, which severely disrupted cocoa and cotton output, real GDP contracted by 1.6% in 2003. During that year, with the country divided in two, there was a general decrease in economic activity, with a sharp decline in agro-processing and manufacturing. The country's crisis after 2002 posed the most serious economic problems in the north, which was forced to trade almost exclusively with neighbouring Mali and Burkina

Faso. A modest recovery followed, although economic growth has been erratic as a result of political uncertainty, which has restrained investment and periodically interrupted donor inflows. According to the IMF, real GDP grew by 1.8% in 2005, before declining to 0.7% in 2006, when growth in the extractive industries was offset by a sharper contraction in timber, textile and agro-industrial output. The Government estimated that real GDP grew by 1.6% in 2007 and by 2.3% in 2008. Real GDP growth strengthened to 4.2% in 2009, driven by rising oil and agricultural output and a recovery in global commodity prices, but slowed to 2.6% in 2010. Economic activity came to a practical halt during the fighting that followed the political impasse from November 2010 until the end of April 2011 (see Recent History). The Minister of the Economy and Finance, Charles Koffi Diby, stated that for the first time in Côte d'Ivoire's history the Government was unable to pay salaries in March 2011. As a result of the political crisis, real GDP contracted by 4.7% in 2011. Nevertheless, with an improvement in the security situation, the lifting of sanctions and a resumption of international co-operation, real GDP was projected to grow by 8.1% in 2012.

Inflation remained low in 2003–07, averaging an annual 2.9%. However, inflation rose sharply in 2008, averaging 6.3%, mostly as a result of increases in international oil and food prices, which forced the authorities to introduce emergency measures to alleviate high prices. Since the last quarter of 2008, however, inflationary pressures have moderated in line with declining international commodity prices. In 2010 inflation was recorded at 1.7%, a slight increase from 2009.

Population growth averaged about 3.6% per year in the late 1980s and early 1990s, one of the highest rates in the world, and, according to official sources, it grew at an average annual rate of 2.2% in 2000–11. The population was estimated by the UN at 20.6m. at mid-2012, with an average population growth rate of 3% per year for the 2005–10 period. Expanding employment opportunities attracted immigrants from less prosperous neighbouring countries, particularly Burkina Faso, Mali and Guinea, and at the time of the 1998 census foreign citizens constituted 26% of the population, providing vital manpower for plantations and urban services. Mounting political instability and inter-ethnic tensions in the early 2000s prompted a significant proportion of the immigrant population to leave Côte d'Ivoire. The rate of urban growth had been rapid (at around 150% of the overall rate of population growth), with some 44% of the population residing in urban areas in 1995—more than double the proportion recorded in 1960. By 2010 the population was evenly divided between rural and urban areas. Abidjan's population was measured at 2.9m. in the 1998 census, representing almost one-fifth of the country's population. This pressure on Abidjan was a significant factor in the designation of Yamoussoukro as the country's new political capital, from 1983, although Abidjan remains the principal centre for economic activity. However, the country's demographic patterns have been drastically altered by the upheavals that commenced in 2002, with over 1m. people estimated to have been internally displaced, declining to 519,100 by June 2010, according to the UN High Commissioner for Refugees. In mid-2011 the population of Abidjan was estimated at 4.3m. The country's second largest city, Bouaké, which became the effective capital of the northern half of the country after the 2002 civil conflict broke out, had an estimated population of 642,000 at mid-2010, while Yamoussoukro had an estimated population of 966,394 at mid-2011.

In terms of human development, Côte d'Ivoire is comparable to some of its neighbouring countries. The adult literacy rate for adults (15 years and above) was 55% in 2007, lower than Liberia (59%) and Ghana (67%), but considerably higher than Burkina Faso (29%). Life expectancy at birth for females in Côte d'Ivoire in 2010 was 55 years, which was similar to Liberia (57 years) and Burkina Faso (56 years), but lower than Ghana (65 years).

AGRICULTURE, FORESTRY AND FISHING

The Ivorian economy is strongly dependent on agriculture, which contributed 25% of GDP in 2008, declining to 23% of GDP in 2010. Agriculture employed 35.8% of the labour force in mid-2012, according to FAO estimates. Other estimates suggest that close to 70% of the population are heavily reliant upon agriculture and related activities. The sector provides about three-quarters of export earnings, and the sector's rapid growth was the basis for the economic expansion of the 1960s and 1970s. In 2001–10, according to World Bank estimates, agricultural GDP increased at an average annual rate of 1.8%. Agricultural GDP grew by 3.1% in 2008, 4.0% in 2009 and 4.7% in 2010.

From the beginning of the 1980s coffee was superseded as the leading cash crop by cocoa, production of which doubled between 1970 and 1979. The country became the world's largest cocoa producer after 1977, when its level of production overtook that of Ghana. Overall output continued to rise and in the main crop season of 1999/2000 (October–September) it reached 1.4m. metric tons. This increase owed much to a major replanting programme implemented by the Government in the 1980s, aimed at eliminating ageing cultivation in the traditional cocoa belt, in the south-east, and developing it in the west, where rainfall is abundant. However, the outbreak of the civil conflict in 2002 cut off cocoa-growing areas from the government-held coast and caused the flight of thousands of immigrant workers from the plantations, stifling growth. According to the Banque de France, cocoa production was 1.40m. tons in the 2003/04 season, but decreased to 1.37m. tons in 2004/05. In 2004 farmers protested against the very low price paid (300 francs CFA per kg, compared with 704 francs CFA per kg in 2002). Exports rose to 1.41m. tons in 2005/06, but declined to 1.23m. tons in 2006/07, as a result of an estimated 70,000 tons of Ivorian cocoa being smuggled out of the country, to Ghana, Burkina Faso and Togo, where prices paid were considerably higher. The Government estimated cocoa exports at 1.37m. tons in 2007/08, due to official efforts to prevent smuggling. In March 2008 the crop marketing organization Bourse du Café et du Cacao (BCC), set the official reference price at 500 francs CFA per kg, a 46% increase on the previous year. However, disputes with buyers over the official reference price and strikes by dock workers at Abidjan and San-Pédro ports caused severe disruption to cocoa exports. Unusually heavy rains in the 2008/09 season created ideal conditions for the spread of diseases. Without an increase in the planting of new trees and the provision of fertilizer, the Comité de Gestion de la Filière Café-Cacao (CGFCC), the management committee for the coffee and cocoa sector created in 2008, warned that exports could permanently drop to below 1m. tons per year; it estimated that exports of cocoa had declined from 1.27m. tons in 2008/09 to 1.22m. tons in 2009/10. Nevertheless, in 2010/11 the country delivered a record harvest of nearly 1.5m. tons, equivalent to 40% of the world's cocoa supply.

The change in government and the start of the presidency of Alassane Ouattara in May 2011 (see Recent History) signalled improved incomes for cocoa farmers, with producers set to receive 50%–60% of the international price for cocoa, compared with the 35% that they had received under the rule of former President Laurent Gbagbo (2000–11).

In June 2012 the Fair Labor Association, a USA-based civil society organization, suggested that there was widespread use of child labour in the supply chains for Nestlé, the world's largest food group. These findings were thought to be significant as Nestlé was estimated to purchase around 10% of Côte d'Ivoire's cocoa stock.

Output of coffee reached a record level of some 366,800 metric tons in 1981. It was in overall decline thereafter, and the surge in international coffee prices in 1993–94 and the leeway provided by the currency devaluation, which allowed increases in the price paid to producers, elicited a relatively modest response in terms of Ivorian output—the crop in 1995 was 194,968 tons. By 1998 the strength of prices had stimulated a sharp improvement in output, to 341,000 tons, the most substantial crop recorded since 1981. In subsequent years, further switching into cultivation of cocoa because of the narrowing in price differentials took place; there was a general decline in coffee production in the 2000s, with output recorded at a low of 95,600 tons in 2004/05, before recovering to 170,850 tons by 2007/08 and then falling again over the following two years.

In January 1999 the state marketing agency, Caisse de Stabilisation et de Soutien des Prix des Productions Agricoles

(Caistab), which traditionally had purchased all cocoa and coffee production, was privatized, and in August the market for cocoa and coffee was opened to competition. Following the discovery of large-scale embezzlement in the new body—Nouvelle Caistab (as the organization had been renamed)—its directors were dismissed in late 1999. The Nouvelle Caistab was dissolved and replaced, in March 2001, by the BCC, which was to be operated by farmers' representatives. Several other organizations competed for dominance in the cocoa and coffee markets, notably the Association Nationale des Producteurs de Café-Cacao de Côte d'Ivoire (ANAPROCI), a group of wealthier farmers with strong political connections; and the Syndicat Autonome des Producteurs de Café-Cacao de Côte d'Ivoire (SYNAPROCI), established in 2003. A report commissioned by the EU into the sector found that the new bodies had been mismanaged, had operated with no clear legal status and had received public funding from levies on cocoa exports without accountability. In 2006 EU auditors recommended the liquidation of ANAPROCI. Under Prime Minister Guillaume Soro, a new oversight committee was formed in May 2008. In October 2009 the Ministry of Agriculture completed an audit of cocoa co-operatives in the eastern part of the country. A large proportion of these co-operatives, collectively responsible for 25% of the country's output, were believed to have been fraudulently created by cocoa-marketing officials in order to embezzle state funds.

The high levels of taxation on cocoa exports—the Droit Unique de Sortie was set at 220 francs CFA per kg in October 2006—were blamed for the low prices paid to farmers and the emergence of new formal and informal trading networks with neighbouring countries. The levy was reduced to 210 francs CFA per kg for the 2008/09 season, and registration tax was reduced from 10% to 5% of the price of beans, inclusive of cost, insurance and freight. In response to farmers' protests, in December 2008 the Government promised to reduce taxes on cocoa from around 40%–60% in 2008 to 22% by 2011 (this pledge was honoured). In October 2009 the CGFCC launched the 2010/11 cocoa season with a series of measures to boost farmers' incomes and output. The reference price for cocoa beans was raised from 640 francs CFA per kg in the 2009/10 season to 950 francs CFA per kg in 2010/11. In addition, a programme was instigated in October 2009 by the CGFCC to replant 15,000 ha of cocoa trees with improved seed varieties.

The Government planned to develop cocoa processing and transformation, and pledged to increase the local processing of cocoa to 50% of output and coffee to 30% of output by 2011. In 2008 the country had three cocoa-grinding companies, owned by US, Swiss and French interests, producing 374,000 metric tons of ground cocoa per year. In December 2007 the country's first cocoa transformation plant, Société d'Usinage et de Conditionnement du Sud-Ouest (SUCSO), opened in the port of San-Pédro, and was expected to produce 15,000 tons of chocolate bars per year. In 2009 ANAPRO estimated that 40m. litres of cocoa liqueur could be produced, as well as biofuel and soap, from the 8,000 tons of cacao fruit harvested each year.

The political impasse of late 2010–mid 2011 (see Recent History) most severely affected the cocoa sector, where international sanctions had the greatest impact. In February 2011 Ouattara ordered a month-long suspension of the export of cocoa beans. The industry resumed trading in May. Export restrictions adversely affected port activities in San-Pédro, the leading shipment base for cocoa in Cote d'Ivoire.

Meanwhile, there were reports of a thriving black market, where opportunists were trying to buy up farmers' cocoa cheaply, for half the price it was worth in January 2011. Farmers had abundant cocoa and beans on the plantations in the bush, but many did not have the liquidity to be able to store them in warehouses. Experts suggested that traders would store the cocoa, waiting for the price to rise, or else smuggle the beans across the borders into Ghana, Guinea and Liberia.

From the 1960s Côte d'Ivoire became a major producer of palm oil, and local processing of palm products developed. A series of replanting programmes was supported by the World Bank, the European Community (now EU), France and the United Kingdom. Output of palm oil showed an overall increase in the 1990s, from an average of 208,885 metric tons per year in 1985–91 to 261,350 tons per year in 1995–2001. After collapsing during the civil war, palm oil output rose sharply to reach 390,000 tons in 2008, 394,300 tons in 2009 and 415,900 tons in 2010.

Cotton cultivation has become established in the north of the country. In the 1990s output of seed cotton averaged more than 300,000 metric tons per year, with a record crop of 399,933 tons achieved in the 1999 season. Most of the cotton was processed locally, both for export (some 80% of total production) and for the local textile industry. A new ginning plant, reportedly the largest in West Africa, was opened in M'bengue in May 2001, with planned output of more than 200,000 tons per year. The political upheavals since 2002 have directly affected national cotton production, with cotton output collapsing from 396,100 tons in 2002/03 to just 125,000 tons in 2007/08, as a result of low cotton prices that forced many farmers to switch to other cash crops, lack of fertilizers and political uncertainty. Cotton continued to perform poorly in subsequent years, due to the destruction of quality seeds in research centres in the former rebel zones, difficulties in financing the sector and low world market prices. According to the African Development Bank (AfDB), yields have contracted by an average of 14.5% per year since 2006. There are seven ginning companies in Côte d'Ivoire, with total capacity of 528,000 tons.

The rubber industry underwent strong growth from the mid-1980s, registering an average 70,825 metric tons per year in 1989–91, and an average of 115,874 tons in 1998–2000, as the Government pursued plans for Côte d'Ivoire to become Africa's leading rubber producer. Output was 178,300 tons in 2006, and 188,500 tons in both 2007 and 2008. Exports were estimated to be somewhat higher than local production, on account of the smuggling of rubber produced in Liberia. Côte d'Ivoire produced 227,000 tons of rubber in 2010, up by more than 10% from 2009. In 2011 a government strategy of privatization led to the sale of state holdings in the three major companies involved in rubber production—the Compagnie des Caoutchoucs du Pakidie, the Société Africaine de Plantations d'Hévéas and the Société des Caoutchoucs de Grand-Béréby. The 2010–11 political crisis precipitated a large refugee outflow from the country's southern rubber regions, thus restricting the sectoral labour market.

Côte d'Ivoire is also a significant producer of bananas and pineapples (historically the world's second largest producer after Costa Rica), with exports directed principally at the European market. Between 2004 and 2006 pineapple output declined from 216,000 metric tons to 176,700 tons. According to the organization representing the sector (Organisation Centrale des Producteurs-Exportateurs d'Ananas et de Bananes—OCAB), production for 2008 had contracted by 70% from 2004, to 60,000 tons. According to FAO figures, pineapple production amounted to 86,100 tons in 2008, before decreasing to 66,700 tons in 2009 and an estimated 65,000 tons in 2010. According to OCAB, banana output rose from 320,000 tons in 2004 to 360,000 tons in 2007, but subsequently declined to 230,000 tons in 2009, with a further 13% decrease estimated in 2010.

The country is normally self-sufficient in maize, cassava, yams and plantains, and the Government has encouraged the production of rice, large quantities of which are imported. Two of the country's sugar mills have been converted to rice-processing. By the mid-1980s the rice development programme was proving successful, and output of paddy rice averaged 1.21m. metric tons per year in 1996–2000 and 1.08m. tons per year in 2001–03. However, output had fallen to 606,300 tons by 2007, meeting less than 40% of domestic demand, which has increased rapidly as the population moving from rural areas to towns tended to switch its grain preference to rice. During 2008–10, according to FAO figures, the output of paddy rice averaged an annual 672,230 tons. Following a sugar development programme introduced by the Government, two complexes were in operation by 1980, but were producing sugar at twice the cost on the world market. This situation led to the cancellation of six more planned complexes and the reduction of sugar cane plantations, resulting in a decline in sugar cane production from the 1.82m. metric tons recorded in 1983 to an average of 1.17m. tons per year in 1997–2000. The industry has witnessed a gradual recovery since 2000, with production rising to 1.6m. tons in 2007, and remaining at around that level during 2008–10.

Forestry has always been a significant source of export earnings, from both logs and sawn timber. Most production is carried out by large integrated firms, many of which are foreign-owned. The area of exploitable timber had fallen to only about 1m. ha by 1987, compared with some 15.6m. ha at independence, because of inadequate reafforestation and the encroachment of agriculture on forest areas. In an attempt to conserve resources, the Government restricted commercial production to 3m. cu m per year. With domestic demand rising, the volume available for export declined, with exports falling from 3.1m. cu m (logs) in 1980 to only 29,000 cu m (and 521,000 cu m of sawn timber) in 1992. Export volumes subsequently recovered, to a total of 997,099 cu m in 1994, under the stimulus of much higher earnings in local currency terms. Meanwhile, the World Bank and other external agencies supported a reafforestation programme. Nevertheless, exports declined precipitously from the 1990s, and amounted to only an estimated 456,200 tons in 2007. According to UN figures, revenue from wood exports decreased from US $220.6m. in 2008 to $109.1m. in 2009, before recovering slightly to reach $118.5m. in 2010.

Livestock herds are small—in 2010 there were an estimated 1.6m. head of cattle, 1.7m. sheep, 1.3m. goats and 34.0m. chickens—and meat production satisfies only one-third of national demand. Fishing is a significant activity, with industrial fishing accounting for about two-thirds of the annual catch, which averaged 55,000–70,000 metric tons in the 1990s. Although production declined sharply in subsequent years, FAO estimated the total fish catch to have risen from 45,500 tons in 2009 to 73,500 tons in 2010. Ivorian participation in this sector is still low, and most traditional fishing is undertaken by non-Ivorians. Domestic production currently meets only about one-third of local demand, and in 2006 the country imported an estimated 250,000 tons of fish. In April 2007 the Government signed a six-year fishing accord with the EU, permitting EU-registered ships to fish 7,000 tons of tuna in Ivorian waters, at a cost of €35 per ton, in addition to an annual contribution of €595,000. There are three Ivorian canneries, which process an estimated 60,000 tons of tuna per year, and exported 37,000 cans of tuna in 2006.

MANUFACTURING AND MINING

The manufacturing sector, which, according to the World Bank, accounted for 19.2% of GDP in 2010, has been dominated by agro-industrial activities—such as the processing of cocoa, coffee, cotton, oil palm, pineapples and fish. It was stimulated, immediately after independence, by the need to replace goods traditionally imported from Senegal, the manufacturing centre for colonial French West Africa, and it formed one of the most dynamic areas of the economy during this period. The sector was boosted by the 1994 devaluation of the CFA franc, which greatly enhanced the competitiveness of the local product. Growth in the GDP of the industrial sector (including mining, construction and utilities, in addition to manufacturing) reached 13.1% in 1997 as output of petroleum and gas expanded (see below). However, industrial GDP declined by 9.5% in 2000 and by 2.4% in 2001 and declined further in the wake of the political crisis of 2002, contracting by 11.9% in that year, by 13.2% in 2003 and by 8.6% in 2004. The industrial sector had been developing new export capacities but many firms were now forced to curtail or suspend production, and further new investment was placed on hold. During 2001–10 industrial GDP declined at an average annual rate of 0.6%, according to World Bank estimates; industrial GDP rose by 3.7% in 2008, 5.2% in 2009 and 4.9% in 2010 (accounting for more than one-quarter of national GDP in that year).

The privatization of parastatal organizations in the mid-1990s included the state-owned telecommunications company, Côte d'Ivoire Télécom, as well as sugar, palm oil and cotton companies. Subsequent political uncertainties brought the privatization of other state enterprises to a halt.

The only significant activity in the mining sector (apart from hydrocarbons) is the extraction of diamonds and gold. Two diamond mines, at Tortiya and Séguéla, are in operation, but much larger quantities are produced in illicit operations. In December 2005 the UN Security Council imposed a ban on imports of rough diamonds from Côte d'Ivoire, which was subsequently extended. However, despite the UN ban, in June 2009 the Kimberley Process reported that diamond production was continuing to increase in Côte d'Ivoire. Most production of diamonds is by artisanal methods in the north of the country. According to the US Geological Survey, 210,000 carats were produced in 2008.

The exploitation of deposits of gold-bearing rock at Ity began in 1991, in a joint venture with the Compagnie Française des Mines. A second gold mine, at Angovia, which had ceased operations in 1993, resumed production in late 2009, when it was brought back into commission by British firm Cluff Gold. Production reached 3,672 kg in 2001, before declining to 3,570 kg in 2002. The heightened political tension from late 2002 had a detrimental impact on gold production, which declined sharply, to 1,313 kg in 2003, and had recovered only weakly, to 1,452 kg, by 2006. However, production increased substantially in the late 2000s, partly owing to the significant rise in the price of gold on the world market, reaching 6,947 kg in 2009, according to the US Geological Survey, before declining to 5,310 kg in 2010. In recent years an Australian company, Randgold, has been carrying out exploration on its Tongon licence, located 375 km north of Abidjan, which has estimated deposits of 3.2m. oz of gold. Following a US $280m. investment, production commenced in December 2010 and the Tongon mine was officially opened in October 2011. The mine was expected to produce 7.8 metric tons per year of gold, dwarfing output at the country's existing mines, and substantially boosting national output.

There is considerable potential for nickel mining. In 1996 Falconbridge of Canada signed an agreement with the Government to invest US $500m. in the development of reserves at Sipilou and Gounguessou in the north-west, where tests indicated over 250m. metric tons of nickel ore. However, no further progress with this project has been reported. In December 2007 an Indian company, Tata Steel, signed a joint-venture agreement with the parastatal Société pour le Développement Minier de la Côte d'Ivoire (SODEMI) to develop the iron ore deposit at Mont Nimba in the western region near the border with Guinea and Liberia. The Government was seeking investors to develop the large deposits of iron ore nearby at Mont Kalayo. In addition, there are substantial bauxite and manganese reserves.

ENERGY

Electricity generating capacity rose very rapidly in the early 1980s, as a result of the development of hydroelectric plants, which came to account for 90% of all power generated. However, the focus of development changed after the 1982–84 drought severely reduced the contribution of hydroelectric power, and policy switched to the development of thermal capacity. Long-discussed plans for a thermal plant in the Vridi port area of Abidjan, utilizing offshore reserves of natural gas, were finally realized in 1994. A consortium led by United Meridian of the USA developed the Panthère gas field to supply a 100-MW plant at Vridi, which began to supply the national grid in 1997. With gas output from Panthère more than doubling in 1997, to 139m. cu m, plans were developed to use these resources to expand Côte d'Ivoire's exports of electricity. The first 144-MW phase of a gas-fired complex at Azito, close to Abidjan, opened in January 1999; by 2008 output at the complex had increased to 300 MW. In April 2008 plans were announced to install a third 150-MW turbine in 2010, and in May 2008 plans were announced to increase output at Abidjan's main thermal power station from 210 MW to 320 MW by the end of 2009. In August 2008 the Government signed an agreement with Énergie Électrique Ivoirienne (EEI) to build a 120-MW gas-fired power station at Vridi, at an estimated cost of US $134m., to be financed by EEI's main shareholder, the Libyan African Investment Corporation. Meanwhile, natural gas output has increased, with the start of production in mid-1999 at the Foxtrot offshore gas field in Block CI-27, which is being developed by a US, French and Ivorian consortium. A new gas well was discovered in 2005. Applications for the development of other fields have been submitted to the Government. In addition to gas generation, the Compagnie Ivoirienne d'Électricité (CIE) has been developing plans to build a new hydroelectric power dam at Soubré on the Sassandra river, which could generate 270 MW of power by 2013.

In 2007 Côte d'Ivoire had installed electric generation capacity of 1,210 MW, although only 859 MW were available due to poor rainfall, decrepit equipment, chronic lack of investment, a poor distribution network, and illegal connections, thus falling short of the national demand of 876 MW. The majority of electricity is generated through thermal stations (58%), with the rest by hydroelectric stations (42%) at Ayame, Kossou, Taabo, Buyo and Grah. Côte d'Ivoire has the lowest cost in the region for industrial power, averaging just 58 francs CFA/kW in 2008. However, the availability of cheap industrial power and rapid urbanization have greatly increased demand, which grew by 7% per year in 2007 and 2008. As a result, power cuts have become more frequent. In an effort to improve the domestic grid, in June 2009 the World Bank made a grant of US $50m. to improve power distribution in Soubre, Gueyo, Abidjan and the capital, Yammoussoukro. As part of the West African Power Pool the country's power grid is connected to Ghana, Togo, Benin, Burkina Faso and Mali, which together imported 19% of the country's electricity output in 2006. In July 2009 the European Investment Bank (EIB) agreed to finance the construction of a new power line between Riviera (Côte d'Ivoire) and Prestea (Ghana), at an estimated cost of €1,750m., as part of a project to improve power supplies in West Africa. The CIE manages the state-owned generation facilities as well as electricity transmission and distribution, and it has a monopoly on electricity supply. During 2010 Côte d'Ivoire suffered from a power crisis, with severe shortages increasingly affecting large parts of the country. CIE, which supplies around 1m. customers, 60% of them in Abidjan, had failed to generate enough electricity; a series of power cuts provoked angry demonstrations and attacks on the CIE's offices in Abidjan.

There are plans to connect the Ivorian power grid to Liberia, Guinea and Sierra Leone. The Interconnection Côte d'Ivoire-Liberia-Sierra Leone-Guinea project aims to boost reconstruction efforts in those countries, which possess only limited transmission capabilities. Côte d'Ivoire's electricity exports peaked at 1,450m. kW in 2005, declining to 772m. kW in 2011 due to the power crisis.

Petroleum and Gas

According to SODEMI, Côte d'Ivoire has estimated reserves of 300m. barrels of oil and 1,700,000m. cu m of gas. Although offshore exploration for petroleum had virtually ceased by 1984, a new round of exploration undertaken in the early 1990s proved successful, with a major discovery of offshore petroleum, near Jacqueville and Grand-Lahou, in 1994. A joint venture by United Meridian of the USA and the state-owned Société Nationale d'Opérations Pétrolières de la Côte d'Ivoire (PETROCI) began production at the Lion field in April 1995. After production-sharing arrangements were renegotiated, Canadian Natural Resources (CNR) of Calgary, with Tullow Oil as a partner, developed the East Espoir field, and production resumed in 2002, averaging 35,000 barrels per day (b/d). CNR also operates the West Espoir field, which started production in mid-2006, and the Baobab field, which began operations from 11 wells in mid-2005 and is currently the largest single source of crude petroleum, with an estimated output potential of 65,000 b/d. CNR drilled four new wells on the Baobab field in early 2009, which were expected to further boost its output.

Total national petroleum production rose from just 2.1m. barrels in 2001 to 22.2m. barrels in 2006. However, production decreased to 17.5m. barrels in 2007, due to maturing fields, the silting of wells on the main oilfields, and technical delays in new fields starting production. According to SODEMI, production declined again in 2008, to 16.8m. barrels, but rose to 18.2m. barrels in 2009 as a result of investment to reduce silting and new discoveries on the Baobab fields. According to the Banque de France, the value of crude oil and petroleum products exports rose from 1,060,500m. francs CFA in 2005 to 1,569,600m. francs CFA in 2006, driven primarily by sharp rises in international oil prices, before falling back to 1,256,900m. francs CFA in 2007 and 955,000m. francs CFA in 2009 in line with falling output. Côte d'Ivoire became a candidate country for the international Extractive Industries Transparency Initiative (EITI) programme in 2008, a step seen by donor countries as important to winning debt relief. EITI projected state revenues from the oil sector to reach 130,000m. francs CFA in 2010, with EITI-reported government receipts, as an average percentage of total production value, estimated to be about 9% in 2007.

The principal oil refinery, owned by Société Ivoirienne de Raffinage (SIR), has a capacity of 71,000 b/d. It supplies fuel for domestic consumers, national industry and neighbouring countries. It receives oil directly by pipeline from the Lion field, and it also processes crude petroleum shipped from Nigeria. PETROCI owns a 48% stake in the company, and in December 2007 it signed an agreement with two US companies to build a second refinery in Abidjan, with a capacity of 60,000 b/d, at an estimated cost of US $1,400m. However, in 2009 the Government indicated that it was seeking finance for the project from China's Eximbank, which made it likely that Chinese companies would be awarded the contract to construct the new refinery. In March Angola's national oil company, SONANGOL, purchased a 22% stake in SIR from the Ivorian Government for $45m. In January 2010 SIR announced that it was forced to suspend operations owing to financial difficulties; declining profitability at the refinery had caused the margin on petroleum-refining to decrease from an average of $7.4 per barrel in 2008 to just $1.2 per barrel in 2009. The rise in international oil prices in recent years had not been matched by increases in domestic prices, owing to the Government's fuel-pricing regime. As a result, SIR estimated that it had made a loss of 50,000m. francs CFA in 2009. The Government owed SIR an estimated 150,000m. francs CFA in unpaid petrol taxes, further exacerbating the refinery's financial problems. SIR's management took the radical step of halting production until profit margins improved. The company was only able to guarantee supply of petroleum products until February 2010. In March the Government stepped in to secure a bank loan of 35,000,000m. francs CFA to ensure continued provision.

Natural gas has primarily been used to generate electricity. The largest source of natural gas is the Foxtrot field, producing around 80m. cu ft per day, followed by the Manta field, producing 32m. cu ft per day. Both of these are operated by Foxtrot International. Devon Energy has been operating the Panthère field, with production of around 70m. cu ft per day, and CNR announced the start of natural gas production from its West Espoir field in mid-2006. Total gas production declined from a peak of 1,742m. cu m in 2005 to an estimated 1,447m. cu m in 2008, but was forecast to rise in 2009 to 1,757m. cu m. Donors have insisted on improvements to transparency in the energy sector as a precondition for resuming full funding, and the Government has pledged to carry out audits of the oil, gas, refinery and electricity sectors, and to implement an automatic price adjustment system.

Côte d'Ivoire's hydrocarbons sector has continued to grow strongly, increasing its contribution to real GDP growth. According to PETROCI, oil and gas production brought in 955,000,000m. francs CFA in 2008. Crude petroleum represented 15% of total exports in 2008, while exports of refined petroleum products by SIR reached 21.5% of total exports. With demand for gas set to rise from a forecasted 150,000m. cu ft in 2009 to 230,000m. cu ft by 2014, mainly owing to the expansion of gas-fired power stations, PETROCI expected the sector's rapid growth to continue.

In March 2010 Russia's Lukoil discovered rich hydrocarbon reserves in Ghana's offshore area, most notably the prolific Jubilee Field, prompting a three-day meeting between Côte d'Ivoire and Ghana to discuss demarcation of their maritime border. It was agreed that if the two countries could not reach agreement the UN would be asked to mediate. In February US company Vanco discovered oil in the Dzata-1 field off Cape Three Points block, an area potentially in disputed territory.

TRANSPORT AND TELECOMMUNICATIONS

The most important transport facilities are the deep-water ports of Abidjan and San-Pédro, which handle freight not only for Côte d'Ivoire but also for its landlocked neighbours, Burkina Faso, Mali and Niger. The freight handled at the ports declined in 2002 and 2003, due to the outbreak of the civil conflict, decreasing to 14.5m. metric tons in the latter year, before recovering to 16.6m. tons in 2004 and 17.5m. tons in 2005. In 2006 there was significant growth in the volume of petroleum shipments through Abidjan, accounting for more than one-half of the port's traffic, increasing the volume of freight handled by both ports to 18.9m. tons in 2006, 21.4m. tons in 2007 and 22.0m. tons in 2008. Abidjan's port is operated by Société d'Exploitation du Terminal de Vridi, a subsidiary of France's Bolloré, which planned to invest 30,000m. francs CFA to boost the port's handling capacity from 600,000 containers in 2008 to 900,000 by 2012. San-Pédro is the main export point for cocoa beans. In mid-2012 the port authorities were seeking US $230m. to fund their expansion plans. More than 522,000 tons of cocoa beans, roughly one-half of export volumes, passed through San-Pédro in 2011, up from 435,000 tons in 2010. The port is also an exit point for natural resources such as rubber and timber. Both Ivorian ports have sought to increase container traffic. In 2012 the port of Abidjan announced plans to triple annual container capacity to 2.3m. TEU by 2016 to keep up with regional competitors following a decade of neglect.

Côte d'Ivoire has about 82,000 km of classified roads, only 8.1% of which are paved, according to the World Bank. Repair and extension of the road network has received funding from both multilateral agencies and donor governments (notably France, Germany and Japan). In July 2007 work started on completing a motorway between Abidjan and Yamoussoukro, with funding from four Middle Eastern development funds.

A railway line links Abidjan to Ouagadougou, Burkina Faso, with 660 km of line in Côte d'Ivoire. Management responsibility for the railway lies with SITARAIL, a consortium of French, Belgian, Ivorian and Burkinabè investors. SITARAIL's total freight traffic amounted to 830,000 metric tons in 2008. The number of passengers transported by the railway increased from 164,000 in 2004 to an estimated 500,000 in 2009. In July 2009 the company stated that it was seeking to raise 75,000m. francs CFA for infrastructure rehabilitation and 55,000m. francs CFA for new rolling stock. There are long-standing plans to extend the railway to Bamako (Mali) and Niamey (Niger). In October 2010 the Government announced plans to construct a 737-km railway line linking the port of San-Pédro with mines in the west of the country; work on the project was expected to commence in 2014.

Côte d'Ivoire has international airports at Abidjan, Bouaké and Yamoussoukro, and there are several regional airports. The management of Abidjan airport was ceded to a French consortium, Aeria, and its capacity now stands at 2m. passengers per year. Passenger movements declined from a level of 1.4m. in 2000 to only 700,000 in 2003, showing no significant growth in the following two years as many long-haul carriers suspended their services. Passenger numbers rose modestly to 822,000 in 2006. In April 2009 work was completed on a 26,000m. francs CFA project to expand Abidjan airport's passenger capacity, extend the runway and expand aircraft parking facilities. The Government also planned to build a new terminal, at a cost of 2,000m. francs CFA, for the exclusive use of charter flights and Muslim pilgrims, which will be financed by the Islamic Development Bank and the OPEC Fund for International Development.

The fixed-line telephone network is operated by the national telecoms company, Côte d'Ivoire-Télécom (CI-Télécom), which was sold to France Telecom in 1997, the Government retaining a 49% share. In 2007 CI-Télécom launched a programme to modernize and expand the national network, at a cost of 7,500m. francs CFA (US $16.7m.). This resulted in an increase in the number of fixed lines to 356,500 in 2008. None the less, the International Telecommunications Union (ITU) estimated that there were only 1.3 fixed line phone connections per 100 people in 2009, at a similar level to other sub-Saharan African nations that have bypassed hard telecommunications infrastructure technology. According to the ITU, the total number of fixed lines in Côte d'Ivoire decreased from 283,300 in 2010 to 268,200 in 2011.

Mobile telecommunications have developed significantly since 2002. Two mobile telephone companies, Orange Côte d'Ivoire (85% owned by France Télécom), and Télécel, dominated the market in 2006, each with 1.7m. subscribers. In July 2005 South Africa's Mobile Telephone Network International (MTN) purchased Télécel, relaunching its services as MTN Côte d'Ivoire. At the end of the year a new firm, Acell, was licensed; the latter was a joint venture between a local company, Atlantique Télécom, and Etisalat from the United Arab Emirates (UAE). After investment of US $100m., it started services under the name Moov Télécom in July 2006, capturing 500,000 new subscribers over the following three months. In June 2007 a fourth mobile telephone operator, consisting of Comium (owned by Etisalat) and KoZ (operated by the Lebanese Comium Group), was established. In January 2009 a fifth operator, Green Network (also referred to as GreenN), was launched by Libya's LAP GreenN, under the name of Oricel. There were seven licensed mobile telephone operators and five active operators by mid-2012. UAE-based Warid Telecom was expected to enter the market in the near future, and Nigeria's Globacom has also been awarded a licence.

In October 2011 Nigerian telecommunications operator Globacom announced that, in partnership with French operator Alcatel-Lucent, it planned to land its Glo-1 international submarine fibre optic cable in Côte d'Ivoire, which would help to lower the cost of international bandwidth. In addition, several other cables were scheduled to reach the country in the coming years. The Ivorian internet and broadband market has remained underdeveloped due to the high cost of international bandwidth, caused by a monopolization of access to the sole international connection currently serving the country. Despite these obstacles, Côte d'Ivoire has become West Africa's third largest internet market after Nigeria and Ghana, with services superior to those in many other African countries.

According to the ITU, by 2011 the number of mobile telephone subscribers had risen to 17.4m., up from just 1m. in 2002, meaning that the equivalent of more than 80% of the population had a mobile telephone subscription. There were an estimated 660,000 internet users in 2008. This had risen to 980,000 by 2009, resulting in an internet penetration of 4.6%. Only 1.4% of schools in the country had a computer by 2009.

ECONOMIC POLICY

Amid reports of massive embezzlement of public funds by individuals in the Government, the EU suspended all financial disbursements in 1998, while the IMF kept disbursements of its Enhanced Structural Adjustment Facility (ESAF) in abeyance during 1999. Uncertainty about Côte d'Ivoire's economic future subsequently intensified; the burden of its massive international debt could no longer attract negotiated relief, and there was inconsistency in the economic policies pursued by the successive leaderships of Brig.-Gen. Robert Gueï (1999–2000) and Laurent Gbagbo (2000–11). Corruption also became a major problem. The Government failed to adjust the prices of electricity and fuel in line with the costs of production, and a number of state-owned institutions, including banks, were close to collapse. Eventually, the Gbagbo Government appeared to acknowledge the severity of the crisis and recommenced the process of reform that had been aborted under Bédié's presidency (1993–99).

The IMF approved a new staff-monitored programme for the period July–December 2001, with a view to strengthening the management of public finances, relaunching the process of structural reform, improving financial relations with creditors and creating the conditions for sustained economic recovery. The Government also announced the resumption of a stalled privatization programme. In March 2002 formal agreement was reached with the IMF for the release of US $365m. under the Poverty Reduction and Growth Facility (PRGF—which had replaced the ESAF), but the major political crisis that commenced in September severely disrupted the Government's economic policy-making and the programme was suspended.

Prime Minister Charles Konan Banny, who was appointed in 2005, resumed dialogue with the IMF, and in May 2006 an IMF mission concluded that the fiscal position had improved on previous years and that control of expenditure had made some, albeit slight, headway. Following the visit to Abidjan of an IMF mission in late May 2007, in July the IMF awarded Côte d'Ivoire an emergency post-conflict assistance programme (EPCA), worth $62.2m. The EPCA was designed to support the Government's efforts to strengthen administrative capacity, and was considered a first step towards a PRGF, which would enable Côte d'Ivoire to work towards securing debt relief under the initiative for heavily indebted poor countries (HIPC) and the Multilateral Debt Relief Initiative (MDRI).

In April 2008 the IMF completed its first review of the EPCA, disbursing a second tranche worth US $66.2m. Although the budget deficit was reduced to 1.2% of GDP in 2007, the Fund noted above-target discretionary spending, which forced the Government to cut some priority sector projects. The IMF welcomed progress with structural reform, notably through improved collection of cocoa levies, which led to increased funding for rural projects. The main aim of the EPCA in 2008 was fiscal consolidation, through the re-establishment of the tax administration in rebel-held areas and the capping of public sector wages.

In May 2008 the total cost of post-conflict reconstruction, the demobilization of rebel forces and compensation for victims for 2009–13 was estimated at 2,500,000m. francs CFA. The same month donors led by Japan, France and the USA pledged a total of 115,000m. francs CFA in budget support and development funding. However, donors refrained from fully re-engaging in Côte d'Ivoire until there had been more progress with holding elections and re-establishing political stability.

In June 2008 the IMF carried out its second EPCA review, reporting further progress in economic recovery. Although the Government had met its spending and revenue targets, the Fund expressed concern over the rising level of subsidies to PETROCI, and it urged greater progress with reform of the cocoa and coffee sectors. In September the IMF, World Bank and AfDB carried out a joint mission to Abidjan to discuss a successor programme to the EPCA.

In January 2009 the Government presented its Poverty Reduction Strategy Paper (PRSP) to the IMF, which aimed to reduce the level of poverty from 49% in 2008 to 16.2% in 2015, with a focus on boosting rural development where poverty levels were twice as high as in urban areas. The cost of the PRSP, estimated at 17,650,000m. francs CFA in 2009–15, was expected to be funded by donors. In February 2009 the IMF, World Bank and AfDB carried out a joint mission to Abidjan to review progress made under the EPCA during 2008. The mission reported strong revenue growth, due to higher international commodity prices, and commended the Government for incorporating off-budget spending on presidential projects into the revised 2008 budget. Following the success of this mission, on 27 March 2009 the IMF awarded Côte d'Ivoire a new PRGF arrangement, worth US $566m. and covering the period 2009–11. The new PRGF was focused on expanding the tax revenue base, completing the unification of state finances and improving public expenditure management. In September 2009 a joint mission of the IMF, World Bank and AfDB visited Abidjan to carry out the first review of the PRGF. The November IMF report commended a satisfactory performance, a primary budget surplus and some normalization with external creditors. However, it also recommended major civil service reform and urged the Government to address deficits in the pension funds and electricity sector.

From late 2010 to May 2011 the country faced an expanding range of economic sanctions, as a consequence of the post-election impasse between President Gbagbo and Ouattara (see Recent History). Economic sanctions were used as part of a strategy to isolate Gbagbo and his Government financially. Bank employees and other ordinary citizens were most affected by the sanctions. In February 2011 there was a series of bank closures, and bank runs also proliferated in the main urban centres.

In June 2011 the UN removed the remaining sanctions against Ivorian enterprises. The IMF resumed aid to Côte d'Ivoire in October, and the USA announced that the country, excluded since 2005, was again eligible to benefit from the African Growth and Opportunity Act, which granted preferential access to the US market. The AfDB also resumed assistance from 2011, particularly in relation to strengthening social services, the capacity of the administration and infrastructure investment projects. In addition, the European Commission announced a US $260m. grant-based 'recovery package' to support basic social spending.

PUBLIC FINANCE

The political crises of 2000 and 2001 severely worsened the Government's overall financial position. By the end of 2001 there was an accumulated stock of domestic payment arrears of 361,000m. francs CFA, estimated at 4.7% of GDP. In an attempt to augment government revenues, new measures were announced in 2002, including a 5% tax on new project-related imports, an increase in the tax on cocoa exports, the reform of customs clearing procedures and the computerization of import management systems. In 2004 the Government announced a new tax on incomes to provide for its war effort and exerted pressure on businesses to contribute to a special reconstruction fund. The budget deficit was estimated at 1.0% of GDP in 2003, and it was assumed to have widened in subsequent years, although there was no formal reporting as the Government resorted to more ad hoc taxation measures to maintain an inflow of revenues. The authorities had difficulty in maintaining payments of public sector salaries and ceased servicing all debts to development banks due after 2004. The Government's domestic arrears were estimated at 3% of GDP, and there was an ongoing crisis in the banking sector, with the Caisse Autonome d'Amortissement unable to collect on 90% of its loans, and an estimated 24% of non-performing loans in the domestic banking system as a whole. The accumulation of arrears, both foreign and domestic, amounted to 26% of GDP at the end of 2005. The fiscal deficit (excluding grants) was estimated at 2.4% of GDP in 2006, financed largely by further domestic borrowing. Total external and domestic debt was estimated at 85.7% of GDP in 2006.

In December 2007 the Government adopted the 2008 budget, which envisaged augmenting both revenue and expenditure by 8.6%, to 2,130,000m. francs CFA, reflecting greater spending on priority social sectors and an 11.5% public sector wage increase, as well as improvements in tax revenue collection. Following violent street protests over the rising costs of food and fuel in March and July 2008, the Government was forced to introduce emergency measures, including the suspension or reduction of import taxes, duties and value-added tax (VAT) on basic foodstuffs, which cost an estimated 50,000m. francs CFA. In November the Government amended the 2008 budget, incorporating 186,000m. francs CFA of spending on presidential projects in Yamoussoukro and Abidjan, in accordance with the wishes of the IMF.

In January 2009 the Assemblée nationale approved the 2009 budget, which envisaged increasing spending by 6.4%, to 2,460,000m. francs CFA, including a 7.1% rise in public sector wages and the repayment of domestic arrears. The same month the Government started the process of unifying state finances by deploying tax and customs officials to the rebel-controlled north of the country; however, the process was expected to be slow given opposition by local interests. In April the Government revised the 2009 budget, incorporating the targets agreed in the new PRGF awarded the previous month. Spending was to rise to 2,525,000m. francs CFA, most of which related to new capital investments, increased poverty reduction expenditure and higher debt repayment. Revenue was to rise to 1,840,000m. francs CFA, reflecting higher customs revenue as a result of the unification of state finances, increased donor aid and the withdrawal of the emergency measures introduced in 2008. In June 2009 the Government paid arrears worth 128,900m. francs CFA to domestic suppliers, in an operation funded by the IMF and the World Bank. The measures introduced in 2008 to counter the high costs of food and energy were withdrawn; the import tax and the full rate of VAT (18%) were to be reintroduced for most products. Only rice, the national staple, would continue to benefit from the exemptions. According to the Minister of the Economy and Finance, these measures had cost an estimated 50,000m. francs CFA in terms of lost revenue.

In November 2009 the draft 2010 budget was presented. Fiscal spending was expected to increase by only 0.7%, compared with the revised 2009 budget, to 2,480,000m. francs CFA. Current expenditure was estimated at 1,490,000m. francs CFA, with health, education, water and sanitation receiving 39% of spending, compared with 15.6% in 2009 (in line with PRSP commitments). In contrast, domestic revenue was forecast to rise sharply, by 16.9%, to 2,150,600,000m. francs CFA, reflecting the ongoing recovery in tax revenues as the tax authorities extended their remit over the country's northern regions. Of this amount, 170,000m. francs CFA would be raised through domestic bonds and 330,400m. francs CFA through external financing. The restrained budget reflected the Government's PRGF commitments to increase social sector spending while continuing to consolidate fiscal accounts.

The banning of coffee and cocoa exports during the first four months of 2011, combined with the cessation of business activities, the waiving of the 2011 vehicle licence and the closure of commercial banks, all contributed to a decline in state revenues in that year. Preliminary revenue and expenditure estimates for 2011, as a percentage of GDP, were 11.7% and 16.9%, respectively, with a budget deficit of 2.3% of GDP.

The implementation of the National Health Development Plan 2009–13 was ongoing in mid-2012 but had not been fully applied owing to the additional emergencies that had been generated as a result of the 2010–11 political crisis. Despite this critical situation, the funding allocated to health was still considered very low, amounting to only 5% of the total budget in 2011 instead of the 15% required. Achieving the UN's health-related Millennium Development Goals, particularly those on reducing child and maternal mortality rates, and combating communicable diseases such as HIV/AIDS, malaria and tuberculosis, was considered barely feasible within this context.

FOREIGN TRADE AND PAYMENTS

Côte d'Ivoire's balance of trade has regularly been in surplus, owing to the level of export earnings from sales of coffee and cocoa. According to the Banque de France, trade surpluses of 1,625,700m. francs CFA and 1,219,400m. francs CFA were recorded in 2006 and 2007, respectively, driven by rising exports. Total exports of 4,062,200m. francs CFA were recorded in 2007, comprising petroleum products, cocoa beans, crude petroleum and cocoa products, and total imports of 2,842,800m. francs CFA, comprising crude petroleum (for refining), capital goods and food products. Nevertheless, there was a current account deficit on the balance of payments of $69,900m. francs CFA in 2007. Transfers and service earnings remained stable but imports showed a propensity to rise sharply in all branches of goods (including military equipment and armaments). However, the surge in the value of crude petroleum exports since 2005 was expected to boost both the trade payments surplus and foreign exchange reserves (estimated at US $2,252m. in 2008). The Direction Générale des Douanes reported that crude petroleum exports were worth 548,167m. francs CFA in 2007, up from 267,000m. francs CFA in 2005 (crude oil and petroleum products provided a combined value of 1,256,900m. francs CFA, compared to cocoa's value of 687,500m. francs CFA). According to UN figures, the trade surplus decreased by 26.7% from $3,320.2m. in 2009 to $2,434.2m. in 2010, owing to a 12.8% rise in imports and stagnant export revenue.

On the capital account, inflows of foreign direct investment had risen steadily since the end of the civil war, from just $283m. in 2004 to $427m. in 2007, although a slight decline, to $402m., was recorded in 2008, comparable to the highest levels of the late 1990s. This investment was channelled towards oil, gas and telecommunications.

With the suspension of an IMF credit facility and new uncertainties generated by the military coup of December 1999, the implementation of a HIPC debt relief programme was inevitably postponed. At the end of 2003 total debt stocks amounted to $12,187m. (equivalent to 93.8% of gross national income), including short-term arrears of $917m. In that year the debt-servicing ratio was 8.5%, significantly less than in previous years. Debt repayments to most international financial institutions ceased during the course of 2004. Arrears to the World Bank amounted to $64m. and, as a result, all new lending ceased. According to the World Bank, the external debt stock fell to $10,664m. at the end of 2005, mainly due to the depreciation of the US dollar against the euro, the currency in which most of the country's external debt is denominated. Total interest arrears rose to $683m., up from $483m. in 2004. In September 2009 the Government reached a preliminary agreement with the 'London Club' of commercial creditors to restructure 1,300,000,000m. francs CFA of debt, the equivalent of 18.6% of the country's external debt at the end of 2008. The debt comprised three euro-denominated and three US dollar-denominated bonds, due to mature in 2018 and 2028, respectively, which had previously been restructured in 1998. The London Club restructuring was seen as a further step towards regaining access to international capital markets. However, success in securing the agreement was once again dependent on progress with the political process. None the less, the restructuring arrangement was seen as consistent with the IMF and World Bank's HIPC initiative; repayments would be reduced during the implementation of the PRGF arrangement, which would lower debt service payments from 277,000,000m. to 55,400,000m. francs CFA during the programme, the funds being released to implement the Government's PRSP.

The country's arrears to the World Bank had increased to US $422m. by the time agreement was reached in April 2007 on a plan to repay part of them, as well as part of the $466m. in arrears owed to the AfDB. In February 2008 the Government settled arrears worth $184m. with the World Bank, which enabled the normalization of relations. Following this repayment, in April the World Bank made a grant of $308m. to clear the country's remaining debt arrears, in addition to $35m. in budget support.

In January 2009 the World Bank indicated that Côte d'Ivoire was eligible in principle for HIPC assistance, once a number of remedial measures had been taken. Following the award of the new PRGF, on 31 March Côte d'Ivoire officially reached the HIPC decision point, at which point US $3,000m. of the country's external debt was written off, out of an estimated total of $14,300m. at the end of 2007. Côte d'Ivoire reached completion point in June 2012, at which time the country became eligible for an additional $1,300m. of MDRI debt relief.

In a related development, in May 2009 the EIB agreed to defer Côte d'Ivoire's debt repayments and suspend interest charges on its outstanding debt until 2012. This would allow 18,600m. francs CFA to be used for social spending. The EIB was set to resume lending operations in the country, and was expected to be involved in financing infrastructure projects, notably the power interconnection between Côte d'Ivoire and Ghana, as well as microfinance operations.

In July 2009 the Government launched a five-year bond, hoping to raise 60,000m. francs CFA in regional markets. The funds would be used to reduce partly domestic arrears. Although the payment of domestic arrears had been accelerated—almost 130,000m. francs CFA had been cleared by June 2009—60,000,000m. francs CFA remained to be paid by the end of the year under the PRGF target. In addition, the country's sovereign risk had improved following the debt rescheduling arrangement signed with the 'Paris Club' of bilateral creditors in May 2009 (to write off $845m. of the country's debt and to defer repayment of $1,200m. arrears, $2,600m. of debt falling due and $179m. of moratorium interest until April 2012). This was expected to reduce Côte d'Ivoire's debt service payments to the Paris Club from $4,700m. to $391m. In May 2010 Côte d'Ivoire launched a three-and-a-half-year bond, again hoping to raise 60,000m. francs CFA.

In December 2009 France agreed to write off, reschedule or defer total external debt worth more than US $3,400m. As Côte d'Ivoire's main external creditor, France held an estimated 60% of the country's Paris Club debt, and the latest accord incorporated the Paris Club deal as well as further write-offs. This was expected to reduce debt-service repayments to France by 90% for the duration of the 2009–12 IMF programme. Furthermore, France pledged to write off a large part of the country's remaining $1,150m. debt once HIPC completion point was reached.

In April 2011 France agreed a US $400m. assistance package for the country, in reaction to the political and economic strife that had taken place from late 2010 (see Recent History).

However, in July 2011 Côte d'Ivoire sought a complete reassessment of $2,300m. of Eurobonds, after ruling out debt payments for that year due to the damage to the economy from post-election conflict. By that time the Government owed holders of its Eurobonds interest payments totalling $58m., after not paying coupons due in January and June. The Government indicated that it would resume contractual payments to its bondholders from 2012.

Statistical Survey

Source (unless otherwise stated): Institut National de la Statistique, BP V55, Abidjan; tel. 20-21-05-38; fax 20-21-44-01; e-mail site-ins@globeaccess.net; internet www.ins.ci.

Area and Population

AREA, POPULATION AND DENSITY

Area (sq km)	322,462*
Population (census results)	
1 March 1988	10,815,694
20 December 1998	
Males	7,844,621
Females	7,522,050
Total	15,366,671
Population (UN estimates at mid-year)†	
2010	19,737,800
2011	20,152,893
2012	20,594,617
Density (per sq km) at mid-2012	63.9

* 124,503 sq miles.

† Source: UN, *World Population Prospects: The 2010 Revision*.

ETHNIC GROUPS

1998 census (percentages, residents born in Côte d'Ivoire): Akan 42*; Voltaïque 18†; Mandé du nord 17‡; Krou 11; Mandé du sud 10§; Naturalized Ivorians 1; Others 1.

* Comprising the Baoulé, Agni, Abrou, Ebrié, Abouré, Adioukrou and Appollonien groupings.

† Comprising the Sénoufo, Lobi and Koulango groupings.

‡ Comprising the Malinké and Dioula groupings.

§ Comprising the Yacouba and Gouro groupings.

POPULATION BY AGE AND SEX

(UN estimates at mid-2012)

	Males	Females	Total
0–14	4,169,878	4,143,809	8,313,687
15–64	5,874,588	5,607,578	11,482,166
65 and over	428,633	370,131	798,764
Total	10,473,099	10,121,518	20,594,617

Source: UN, *World Population Prospects: The 2010 Revision*.

NATIONALITY OF POPULATION

(numbers resident in Côte d'Ivoire at 1998 census)

Country of citizenship	Population	%
Côte d'Ivoire	11,366,625	73.97
Burkina Faso	2,238,548	14.57
Mali	792,258	5.16
Guinea	230,387	1.50
Ghana	133,221	0.87
Liberia	78,258	0.51
Other	527,375	3.43
Total	15,366,672	100.00

POPULATION BY REGION

(1998 census)

Region	Population
Centre	1,001,264
Centre-Est	394,758
Centre-Nord	1,189,424
Centre-Ouest	2,169,826
Nord	929,686
Nord-Est	696,292
Nord-Ouest	740,175
Ouest	1,445,279
Sud	5,399,220
Sud-Ouest	1,400,748
Total	15,366,672

Note: In January 1997 the Government adopted legislation whereby Côte d'Ivoire's regions were to be reorganized. Further minor reorganizations were effected in April and July 2000. The new regions (with their regional capitals) are: Agnéby (Agboville), Bas-Sassandra (San-Pédro), Bafing (Touba), Denguélé (Odienné), 18 Montagnes (Man), Fromager (Gagnoa), Haut-Sassandra (Daloa), Lacs (Yamoussoukro), Lagunes (Abidjan), Marahoué (Bouaflé), Moyen-Cavally (Guiglo), Moyen-Comoé (Abengourou), N'zi-Comoé (Dimbokro), Savanes (Korhogo), Sud-Bandama (Divo), Sud-Comoé (Aboisso), Vallée du Bandama (Bouaké), Worodougou (Mankono) and Zanzan (Bondoukou).

PRINCIPAL TOWNS

(population at 1998 census)

Abidjan*	2,877,948	Korhogo	142,093
Bouaké	461,618	San-Pédro	131,800
Yamoussoukro*	299,243	Man	116,657
Daloa	173,107	Gagnoa	107,124

* The process of transferring the official capital from Abidjan to Yamoussoukro began in 1983.

2008 ('000 at December, official estimate): Abidjan 3,899.

Mid-2011 (incl. suburbs, UN estimates): Abidjan 4,288,820; Yamoussoukro 966,394 (Source: UN, *World Urbanization Prospects: The 2011 Revision*).

BIRTHS AND DEATHS

(annual averages, official estimates)

	2007	2008	2009
Birth rate (per 1,000)	37.5	37.1	36.7
Death rate (per 1,000)	13.8	13.6	13.3

Life expectancy (years at birth): 54.7 (males 53.7; females 55.9) in 2010 (Source: World Bank, World Development Indicators database).

ECONOMICALLY ACTIVE POPULATION*
(persons aged 6 years and over, 1988 census)

	Males	Females	Total
Agriculture, hunting, forestry and fishing	1,791,101	836,574	2,627,675
Mining and quarrying Manufacturing	78,768	6,283	85,051
Electricity, gas and water	13,573	1,092	14,665
Construction	82,203	2,313	84,516
Trade, restaurants and hotels	227,873	302,486	530,359
Transport, storage and communications	114,396	3,120	117,516
Other services	434,782	156,444	591,226
Sub-total	2,742,696	1,308,312	4,051,008
Activities not adequately defined	998	297	1,295
Total labour force	2,743,694	1,308,609	4,052,303

* Figures exclude persons seeking work for the first time, totalling 210,450 (males 142,688; females 67,762).

Source: UN, *Demographic Yearbook*.

2006 (official estimates): Total employed 7,787,952; Unemployed 216,158; Total labour force 8,004,110.

Mid-2012 ('000, estimates): Agriculture, etc. 2,811; Total labour force 7,846 (Source: FAO).

Health and Welfare

KEY INDICATORS

Total fertility rate (children per woman, 2010)	4.4
Under-5 mortality rate (per 1,000 live births, 2010)	123
HIV/AIDS (% of persons aged 15–49, 2009)	3.4
Physicians (per 1,000 head, 2008)	0.14
Hospital beds (per 1,000 head, 2006)	0.40
Health expenditure (2009): US $ per head (PPP)	95
Health expenditure (2009): % of GDP	5.2
Health expenditure (2009): public (% of total)	20.9
Access to water (% of persons, 2010)	80
Access to sanitation (% of persons, 2010)	24
Total carbon dioxide emissions ('000 metric tons, 2008)	7,015.0
Carbon dioxide emissions per head (metric tons, 2008)	0.4
Human Development Index (2011): ranking	170
Human Development Index (2011): value	0.400

For sources and definitions, see explanatory note on p. vi.

Agriculture

PRINCIPAL CROPS
('000 metric tons)

	2008	2009	2010
Rice, paddy	679.0	687.7	650.0*
Maize	630.2	637.4	700.0†
Millet	40.8	45.6	48.0*
Sorghum	40.8	41.3	43.0*
Sweet potatoes	51.0	45.6	52.0*
Cassava (Manioc)	2,531.0	2,262.0	2,450.0*
Taro (Cocoyam)	76.5	68.4	70.0*
Yams	5,945.4	5,313.4	5,700.0*
Sugar cane	1,660.1	1,578.6	1,650.0*
Cashew nuts, with shell	330.0	350.0	370.0*
Kolanuts	65.4	64.9	67.0*
Groundnuts, with shell	81.0	85.0	85.0*
Coconuts*	220.0	213.3	249.2
Oil palm fruit	1,424.0	1,748.8	1,500.0*
Cottonseed†	65.0	95.0	94.0
Tomatoes	28.8	30.2	33.2*
Aubergines (Eggplants)	77.7	81.5	82.0*
Chillies and peppers, green*	31.0	19.3	25.0
Maize, green*	202.5	161.0	185.0
Bananas	249.2	255.0	265.0*
Plantains	1,674.7	1,496.7	1,600.0*
Oranges*	36.0	40.0	40.0
Pineapples	86.1	66.7	65.0*
Guavas, mangoes and mangosteens	39.8	42.2	42.5*
Coffee, green	173.1	142.9	100.0†
Cocoa beans	1,382.0	1,223.0	1,242.0†
Natural rubber (dry weight)	203.0	209.5	215.0*

* FAO estimate(s).

† Unofficial figure(s).

Aggregate production ('000 metric tons, may include official, semi-official or estimated data): Total cereals 1,408.4 in 2008, 1,429.9 in 2009, 1,461.0 in 2010; Total roots and tubers 8,618.1 in 2008, 7,701.8 in 2009, 8,284.0 in 2010; Total vegetables (incl. melons) 628.6 in 2008, 561.4 in 2009, 619.4 in 2010; Total fruits (excl. melons) 2,241.0 in 2008, 2,072.7 in 2009, 2,187.0 in 2010.

Source: FAO.

LIVESTOCK
('000 head, year ending September)

	2008	2009	2010*
Cattle	1,538	1,573	1,550
Pigs	330	344	350
Sheep	1,631	1,670	1,700
Goats	1,282	1,307	1,325
Poultry	32,561	33,359	34,000

* FAO estimates.

Source: FAO.

LIVESTOCK PRODUCTS
('000 metric tons)

	2008	2009	2010*
Cattle meat	30.8	33.6	35.0
Sheep meat	8.2	8.2*	8.3
Goat meat	3.5	3.5*	3.7
Pig meat	6.9	7.1	7.3
Chicken meat	22.8	23.4	24.0
Game meat	135.0*	137.0*	140.4
Cows' milk	30.4	31.1	32.0
Hen eggs	30.4	30.0	32.0

* FAO estimate(s).

Source: FAO.

Forestry

ROUNDWOOD REMOVALS
('000 cubic metres, excluding bark, FAO estimates)

	2008	2009	2010
Sawlogs, veneer logs and logs for sleepers	1,469	1,469	1,469
Fuel wood	8,835	8,889	8,947
Total	10,304	10,358	10,416

Source: FAO.

SAWNWOOD PRODUCTION
('000 cubic metres, including railway sleepers, unofficial figures)

	2008	2009	2010
Total (all broadleaved)	600	600	700

Source: FAO.

Fishing

('000 metric tons, live weight)

	2008	2009	2010
Capture	50.0*	44.2	71.8
Freshwater fishes	4.4*	5.6	6.8
Bigeye grunt	2.0*	1.7	1.6
Round sardinella	6.0*	4.2*	10.0
Skipjack tuna	2.3	2.8	2.6
Aquaculture*	1.3	1.3	1.7
Total catch*	51.3	45.5	73.5

* FAO estimate(s).

Source: FAO.

Mining

(estimates)

	2008	2009	2010
Gold (kg)	4,205	6,947	5,310
Natural gas (million cu m)	1,600	1,600	1,600
Crude petroleum ('000 barrels)	22,000	21,500	16,400
Manganese ore (metric tons)	176,561	177,000	177,000

Source: US Geological Survey.

Industry

SELECTED PRODUCTS
('000 metric tons unless otherwise indicated)

	2007	2008	2009
Beer of barley*†	267	306	315
Palm oil—unrefined*	289	285	345
Raw sugar	145	150	n.a.
Plywood ('000 cu m)*	82	81‡	81‡
Jet fuel	47	53	49
Motor gasoline (petrol)	564	466	432
Kerosene	933	750	695
Gas-diesel (distillate fuel) oils	1,089	1,174	n.a.
Residual fuel oils	500	657	609
Cement§	469	360	283
Electric energy (million kWh)	5,631	5,800	5,894

Cotton yarn (pure and mixed, '000 metric tons): 24.7† in 1989.

Canned fish ('000 metric tons): 121.8 in 2002 (Source: FAO).

Beer of barley ('000 metric tons): 344† in 2010 (Source: FAO).

Palm oil—unrefined ('000 metric tons): 300.0‡ in 2010 (Source: FAO).

Plywood ('000 cu m): 82.1‡ in 2010 (Source: FAO).

Cement ('000 metric tons): 283 in 2010 (Source: US Geological Survey).

* Data from FAO.

† Estimated figure(s).

‡ Unofficial figure.

§ Data from the US Geological Survey.

Source: mainly UN Industrial Commodity Statistics Database.

Finance

CURRENCY AND EXCHANGE RATES

Monetary Units

100 centimes = 1 franc de la Communauté Financière Africaine (CFA).

Sterling, Dollar and Euro Equivalents (31 May 2012)

£1 sterling = 819.959 francs CFA;
US $1 = 528.870 francs CFA;
€1 = 655.957 francs CFA;
10,000 francs CFA = £12.20 = $18.91 = €15.24.

Average Exchange Rate (francs CFA per US $)

2009	472.19
2010	495.28
2011	471.87

Note: An exchange rate of 1 French franc = 50 francs CFA, established in 1948, remained in force until January 1994, when the CFA franc was devalued by 50%, with the exchange rate adjusted to 1 French franc = 100 francs CFA. This relationship to French currency remained in effect with the introduction of the euro on 1 January 1999. From that date, accordingly, a fixed exchange rate of €1 = 655.957 francs CFA has been in operation.

BUDGET
('000 million francs CFA)

Revenue*	2008	2009	2010†
Tax revenue	1,638.0	1,795.6	1,971.0
Direct taxes	541.7	542.9	598.1
Indirect taxes‡	1,096.3	1,252.7	1,372.9
Social security contributions	141.4	151.2	177.7
Oil and gas revenue	138.6	0.0	0.0
Other	58.8	110.9	97.8
Total	1,976.8	2,057.7	2,246.6

Expenditure§	2008	2009	2010†
Current expenditure	1,879.9	1,945.2	2,124.6
Wages and salaries	711.7	745.0	814.1
Social security benefits	188.6	203.4	217.1
Subsidies and other current transfers	164.7	216.1	281.5
Crisis-related expenditure	122.5	128.5	145.5
Other current expenditure	504.3	483.7	482.3
Interest due	188.1	168.5	184.2
Internal	64.5	42.0	52.5
External	123.6	126.5	131.7
Capital expenditure	319.6	334.3	355.4
Domestically funded	230.3	217.4	254.8
Funded from abroad	77.7	102.8	85.7
Total	2,199.5	2,279.5	2,480.0

* Excluding grants received ('000 million francs CFA): 179.5 in 2008; 63.1 in 2009; 35.8 in 2010 (programmed figure).

† Programmed figures.

‡ Excluding taxes on petroleum products.

§ Excluding net lending ('000 million francs CFA): 17.7 in 2008; 12.4 in 2009; 31.7 in 2010 (programmed figure).

Source: IMF, *Côte d'Ivoire: Second Review Under the Three-Year Arrangement Under the Extended Credit Facility, Request for Waivers of Non-observance of Performance Criteria, and Financing Assurances Review—Staff Report; Staff Statement; Press Release on the Executive Board Discussion; and Statement by the Executive Director for Côte d'Ivoire* (July 2010).

2010 ('000 million francs CFA): *Revenue:* Tax revenue 1,928.5 (Direct taxes 551.1, Indirect taxes 1,377.4); Social security contributions 162.8; Other revenue 84.9; Total 2,176.2 (excl. grants received 60.4). *Expenditure:* Current expenditure 2,115.8 (Wages and salaries 800.4, Social security benefits 212.6, Subsidies and other current transfers 272.5, Crisis-related expenditure 144.2, Other current expenditure 491.6, Interest due 194.5); Capital expenditure 348.6 (Domestically funded 259.2, Funded from abroad 89.4); Total 2,464.4 (excl. net lending 33.4) (Source: *Côte d'Ivoire—First Review Under the Three-Year Arrangement Under the Extended Credit Facility, Request for Modification of Performance Criteria, and Financing Assurances Review; Press Release* (May 2012)).

INTERNATIONAL RESERVES
(excluding gold, US $ million at 31 December)

	2009	2010	2011
IMF special drawing rights	427.5	420.5	418.9
Reserve position in IMF	1.3	1.3	1.4
Foreign exchange	2,838.1	3,202.6	3,895.6
Total	3,266.8	3,624.4	4,316.0

Source: IMF, *International Financial Statistics*.

MONEY SUPPLY
('000 million francs CFA at 31 December)

	2009	2010	2011
Currency outside banks	1,343.2	1,638.2	1,555.3
Demand deposits at deposit money banks*	967.6	1,091.1	1,555.6
Total money (incl. others)	2,341.7	2,736.6	3,142.0

* Excluding the deposits of public establishments of an administrative or social nature.

Source: IMF, *International Financial Statistics*.

COST OF LIVING
(Consumer Price Index for African households in Abidjan; base: 2000 = 100)

	2006	2007	2008
Food, beverages and tobacco	117.5	123.8	137.8
Clothing and footwear	101.4	100.9	100.2
Rent and utilities	128.3	127.7	133.5
All items (incl. others)	119.9	122.2	130.0

2009: Food, beverages and tobacco 142.3; All items (incl. others) 131.3.

2010: All items 132.9.

2011: All items 139.4.

Source: ILO.

NATIONAL ACCOUNTS
(million francs CFA at current prices)

Expenditure on the Gross Domestic Product

	2009	2010	2011
Government final consumption expenditure	1,531,143	1,610,006	1,569,166
Private final consumption expenditure	7,008,998	7,520,309	7,415,449
Change in inventories	131,752	144,927	−85,000
Gross fixed capital formation	973,178	1,025,493	916,721
Total domestic expenditure	9,645,071	10,300,735	9,816,336
Exports of goods and services	5,342,003	5,558,691	5,564,826
Less Imports of goods and services	4,106,327	4,507,244	4,231,162
GDP in purchasers' values	10,880,746	11,352,181	11,150,000

Gross Domestic Product by Economic Activity

	2009	2010	2011
Agriculture, forestry and fishing	2,812,587	3,003,878	3,241,441
Mining and quarrying	595,467	511,289	488,218
Manufacturing	1,339,401	1,377,779	1,327,640
Electricity, gas and water	264,653	272,438	285,242
Construction	433,265	556,430	460,724
Wholesale and retail trade, restaurants and hotels	1,484,458	1,550,787	1,468,680
Finance, insurance, real estate and business services	1,533,320	1,576,920	1,475,069
Transport and communications	422,679	428,761	408,865
Public administration and defence	845,187	863,726	924,758
Other services	586,648	599,515	641,878
Sub-total	10,317,665	10,741,523	10,722,515
Indirect taxes	910,491	967,944	761,695
Less Imputed bank service charge	347,408	357,287	334,210
GDP in purchasers' values	10,880,746	11,352,181	11,150,000

Source: African Development Bank.

BALANCE OF PAYMENTS
(US $ million)

	2007	2008	2009
Exports of goods f.o.b.	8,668.8	10,390.1	10,503.3
Imports of goods f.o.b.	−6,104.4	−7,068.6	−6,318.1
Trade balance	2,564.4	3,321.5	4,185.2
Exports of services	933.0	1,024.5	975.0
Imports of services	−2,483.7	−2,659.9	−2,485.0
Balance on goods and services	1,013.7	1,686.1	2,675.2
Other income received	218.1	236.6	223.9
Other income paid	−1,027.5	−1,138.7	−1,114.0
Balance on goods, services and income	204.3	784.0	1,785.1
Current transfers received	476.6	582.3	760.9
Current transfers paid	−819.9	−914.8	−875.8
Current balance	−139.0	451.6	1,670.2
Capital account (net)	92.9	89.3	103.8
Direct investment from abroad	426.8	446.1	380.9
Portfolio investment assets	−42.9	−28.6	−42.1
Portfolio investment liabilities	145.6	76.6	−8.8
Financial derivatives (net)	−7.0	−6.2	—
Other investment assets	−377.1	−369.9	−1,432.0
Other investment liabilities	181.6	−322.0	295.1
Net errors and omissions	39.9	−106.5	0.8
Overall balance	320.7	230.5	967.8

Source: IMF, *International Financial Statistics*.

External Trade

PRINCIPAL COMMODITIES
(distribution by SITC, US $ million)

Imports c.i.f.	2008	2009	2010
Food and live animals	1,376.8	1,442.3	1,273.8
Fish, crustaceans and molluscs, and preparations thereof	394.0	360.6	286.3
Fish, frozen, excl. fillets	385.9	353.5	278.3
Cereals and cereal preparations	657.8	787.0	648.8
Rice	468.3	597.3	460.2
Rice, semi-milled or wholly milled	468.3	597.3	460.1
Rice, semi-milled or wholly milled (unbroken)	332.0	458.7	348.7
Mineral fuels, lubricants, etc.	2,815.2	1,739.7	1,860.4
Petroleum, petroleum products, etc.	2,806.4	1,712.2	1,809.0
Crude petroleum and oils obtained from bituminous materials	2,669.0	1,622.9	1,689.7
Petroleum products, refined	119.1	76.5	106.0
Chemicals and related products	898.0	916.3	925.6
Medical and pharmaceutical products	228.5	251.2	238.5
Medicaments (incl. veterinary medicaments)	209.8	213.9	213.0
Basic manufactures	886.6	816.2	837.9
Iron and steel	259.3	207.0	205.1
Non-metallic mineral manufactures	191.1	162.2	174.4
Machinery and transport equipment	1,317.6	1,442.9	2,310.8
Road vehicles	404.4	341.3	407.7
Other transport equipment	25.4	55.3	864.4
Miscellaneous manufactured articles	261.9	277.8	267.8
Total (incl. others)*	7,883.7	6,959.9	7,849.3

Exports f.o.b.	2008	2009	2010
Food and live animals	3,715.2	4,646.5	4,759.6
Fish, crustaceans and molluscs, and preparations thereof	196.5	170.2	24.0
Fish, prepared or preserved	174.8	135.7	16.5
Vegetables and fruit	344.7	335.3	16.5
Fruit and nuts, fresh, dried	338.0	321.9	488.1
Coffee, tea, cocoa, spices and manufactures thereof	3,016.0	3,944.5	4,058.6
Coffee and coffee substitutes	204.5	217.3	230.3
Coffee, not roasted; coffee husks and skins	132.5	134.4	170.7
Cocoa	2,644.1	3,606.1	3,699.1
Cocoa beans, raw, roasted	1,754.1	2,596.1	2,492.5
Cocoa butter and paste	282.5	323.3	302.2
Crude materials (inedible) except fuels	910.9	609.2	1,014.9
Cork and wood	260.6	148.6	158.7
Wood, simply worked and railway sleepers of wood	220.6	109.1	118.5
Wood, non-coniferous species, sawn, planed, tongued, grooved, etc.	193.5	90.0	90.6
Textile fibres (not wool tops) and their wastes (not in yarn)	80.7	68.8	126.5
Raw cotton, excl. linters, not carded or combed	79.7	68.1	125.9
Mineral fuels, lubricants, etc.	3,627.9	3,019.2	2,432.7
Petroleum, petroleum products, etc.	3,625.4	3,016.7	2,430.0
Crude petroleum and oils obtained from bituminous materials	1,524.5	1,141.1	1,091.3
Petroleum products, refined	2,036.4	1,409.3	1,206.6
Chemicals and related products	369.7	405.2	320.5
Basic manufactures	376.3	346.8	287.1
Machinery and transport equipment	315.8	630.0	875.4
Road vehicles	41.4	86.5	26.6
Other transport equipment	194.4	423.3	744.7
Ships, boats and floating structures	96.8	338.8	726.4
Total (incl. others)†	9,778.8	10,280.1	10,283.5

* Including commodities and transactions not classified elsewhere in SITC (US $ million): 33.6 in 2008; 47.8 in 2009; 9.1 in 2010.

† Including commodities and transactions not classified elsewhere in SITC (US $ million): 94.9 in 2008; 220.7 in 2009; 185.5 in 2010.

Source: UN, *International Trade Statistics Yearbook*.

PRINCIPAL TRADING PARTNERS
(US $ million)

Imports c.i.f.	2008	2009	2010
Belgium	75.9	96.9	24.8
Brazil	86.4	67.7	59.5
China, People's Republic	542.1	501.0	545.7
Columbia	93.6	72.9	265.0
France (incl. Monaco)	999.6	991.5	931.4
Germany	224.5	205.2	216.4
India	131.5	127.7	—
Italy	160.9	152.7	169.4
Japan	204.6	146.7	176.1
Korea, Republic	108.9	99.3	97.7
Mauritania	114.7	117.2	163.4
Morocco	85.0	62.7	67.7
Netherlands	155.8	163.5	140.2
Nigeria	2,313.4	1,434.8	2,064.4
South Africa	89.3	98.9	135.6
Spain	193.9	182.3	153.9
Thailand	356.2	355.2	331.8
United Kingdom	158.8	103.1	119.2
USA	209.1	228.3	235.7
Venezuela	284.2	126.5	—
Viet Nam	82.0	144.6	105.9
Total (incl. others)	7,883.7	6,959.9	7,849.3

Exports f.o.b.	2008	2009	2010
Algeria	103.3	97.3	92.4
Belgium	204.6	238.6	5.1
Benin	104.2	96.9	110.6
Burkina Faso	412.0	381.4	360.4
Canada	36.6	144.8	242.9
Equatorial Guinea	148.4	112.6	249.4
Estonia	166.3	132.0	232.5
France (incl. Monaco)	1,357.8	1,123.1	715.9
Germany	694.6	738.0	521.7
Ghana	450.9	563.9	783.1
India	178.3	281.4	—
Italy	380.5	328.1	319.7
Malaysia	58.9	133.1	154.8
Mali	326.0	267.0	226.1
Netherlands	1,100.3	1,428.2	1,462.0
Nigeria	625.2	715.6	668.6
Poland	95.7	97.0	113.6
Senegal	163.8	146.3	113.0
Spain	223.6	191.1	253.2
Switzerland-Liechtenstein	74.3	218.1	170.3
Togo	138.5	70.4	66.8
United Kingdom	278.1	259.3	279.7
USA	945.1	800.3	1,060.1
Total (incl. others)	9,778.8	10,280.1	10,283.5

Source: UN, *International Trade Statistics Yearbook*.

Transport

RAILWAYS
(traffic)

	2001	2002	2003
Passengers ('000)	399.5	320.0	87.5
Freight carried ('000 metric tons)	1,016.3	900.7	149.7

Passenger-km (million): 93.1 in 1999 (Source: SITARAIL—Transport Ferroviaire de Personnel et de Marchandises, Abidjan).

Freight ton-km (million): 537.6 in 1999 (Source: SITARAIL—Transport Ferroviaire de Personnel et de Marchandises, Abidjan).

ROAD TRAFFIC
('000 motor vehicles in use)

	1998	1999	2000
Passenger cars	98.4	109.6	113.9
Commercial vehicles	45.4	54.1	54.9

2001–02 ('000 motor vehicles in use): Figures assumed to be unchanged from 2000.

Source: UN, *Statistical Yearbook*.

2007 (motor vehicles in use): Passenger cars 314,165; Buses and coaches 17,512; Vans and lorries 78,575; Motorcycles and mopeds 38,105 (Source: IRF, *World Road Statistics*).

SHIPPING

Merchant Fleet
(registered at 31 December)

	2007	2008	2009
Number of vessels	35	35	35
Total displacement ('000 grt)	9.2	9.2	9.2

Source: IHS Fairplay, *World Fleet Statistics*.

International Sea-borne Freight Traffic
(freight traffic at Abidjan, '000 metric tons)

	2001	2002	2003
Goods loaded	5,787	5,710	6,108
Goods unloaded	9,858	9,018	8,353

Source: Port Autonome d'Abidjan.

Freight traffic at San-Pédro ('000 metric tons, 2000): Goods loaded 1,102; Goods unloaded 251.

CIVIL AVIATION
(traffic on scheduled services)*

	1999	2000	2001
Kilometres flown (million)	6	3	1
Passengers carried ('000)	260	108	46
Passenger-km (million)	381	242	130
Total ton-km (million)	50	34	19

* Including an apportionment of the traffic of Air Afrique.

Source: UN, *Statistical Yearbook*.

Tourism

ARRIVALS BY COUNTRY OF RESIDENCE
('000)

	1996*	1997†	1998†
Belgium	4.3	4.2	4.5
Benin	12.5	11.1	14.3
Burkina Faso	11.0	11.9	17.1
Congo, Repub.	6.0	n.a.	7.6
France	66.7	69.0	73.2
Gabon	3.0	n.a.	5.4
Germany	3.2	3.8	3.9
Ghana	5.4	n.a.	6.7
Guinea	8.1	n.a.	12.5
Italy	5.0	14.0	7.6
Mali	10.7	n.a.	15.2
Niger	5.0	n.a.	5.4
Nigeria	7.9	n.a.	14.1
Senegal	13.0	12.1	16.6
Togo	8.7	8.2	10.8
United Kingdom	5.1	4.5	5.6
USA	15.3	17.0	18.8
Total (incl. others)	236.9	274.1	301.0

* Figures refer only to air arrivals at Abidjan—Félix Houphouët-Boigny airport.

† Figures refer to air arrivals at Abidjan—Félix Houphouët-Boigny airport and to arrivals at land frontiers.

Receipts from tourism (US $ million, excl. passenger transport): 317 in 1997; 331 in 1998; 337 in 1999; 291 in 2000; 289 in 2001; 490 in 2002.

Source: World Tourism Organization.

Communications Media

	2009	2010	2011
Telephones ('000 main lines in use)	282.1	283.3	268.2
Mobile cellular telephones ('000 subscribers)	13,184.3	15,599.0	17,416.4
Internet users ('000)	967.0	n.a.	n.a.
Broadband subscribers ('000)	10.0	7.9	15.4

Personal computers: 323,000 (16.8 per 1,000 persons) in 2005.

Source: International Telecommunication Union.

Non-daily Newspapers: 15 in 1996 (average circulation 251,000 copies) (Source: UNESCO, *Statistical Yearbook*).

Radio receivers ('000 in use): 2,260 in 1997 (Source: UNESCO, *Statistical Yearbook*).

Television receivers ('000 in use): 887 in 2000 (Source: UNESCO, *Statistical Yearbook*).

Daily Newspapers (national estimates): 12 (average circulation 235,000 copies) in 1997; 12 (average circulation 238,000 copies) in 1998; 21 in 2004 (Source: UNESCO Institute for Statistics).

Education

(2010/11 unless otherwise indicated)

		Students		
	Teachers	Males	Females	Total
Pre-primary	3,979	37,769	37,684	75,453
Primary	56,455	1,507,791	1,249,822	2,757,613
Secondary	29,565	474,203*	262,446*	736,649*
Tertiary†	n.a.	104,571	52,201	156,772

* 2001/02.

† 2006/07.

Institutions: 207 pre-primary in 1995/96; 7,599 primary in 1996/97.

Source: mostly UNESCO Institute for Statistics.

Pupil-teacher ratio (primary education, UNESCO estimate): 48.8 in 2010/11 (Source: UNESCO Institute for Statistics).

Adult literacy rate (UNESCO estimates): 56.2% (males 65.2%; females 46.6%) in 2010 (Source: UNESCO Institute for Statistics).

Directory

The Constitution

Following the *coup d'état* of 24 December 1999, the Constitution that had been in force, with amendments, since 1960 was suspended. A new Constitution was subsequently prepared by a consultative committee, and was approved by referendum in July 2000. The main provisions of the Constitution are summarized below:

PREAMBLE

The people of Côte d'Ivoire recognize their diverse ethnic, cultural and religious backgrounds, and desire to build a single, unified and prosperous nation based on constitutional legality and democratic institutions, the rights of the individual, cultural and spiritual values, transparency in public affairs, and the promotion of sub-regional, regional and African unity.

FREEDOMS, RIGHTS AND DUTIES

Articles 1–28: The State guarantees the implementation of the Constitution and guarantees to protect the rights of each citizen. The State guarantees its citizens equal access to health, education, culture, information, professional training, employment and justice. Freedom of thought and expression are guaranteed to all, although the encouragement of social, ethnic and religious discord is not permitted. Freedom of association and demonstration are guaranteed. Political parties may act freely within the law; however, parties must not be created solely on a regional, ethnic or religious basis. The rights of free enterprise, the right to join a trade union and the right to strike are guaranteed.

NATIONAL SOVEREIGNTY

Articles 29–33: Côte d'Ivoire is an independent and sovereign republic. The official language is French. Legislation regulates the promotion and development of national languages. The Republic of Côte d'Ivoire is indivisible, secular, democratic and social. All its citizens are equal. Sovereignty belongs to the people, and is exercised through referendums and the election of representatives. The right to vote freely and in secret is guaranteed to all citizens over 18 years of age.

HEAD OF STATE

Articles 34–57: The President of the Republic is the Head of State. The President is elected for a five-year mandate (renewable once only) by direct universal suffrage. Candidates must be aged between 40 and 65 years, and be Ivorian citizens holding no other nationality, and resident in the country, with Ivorian parents*. If one candidate does not receive a simple majority of votes cast, a second round of voting takes place between the two most successful candidates. The President holds executive power, and appoints a Prime Minister to co-ordinate government action. The President appoints the Government on the recommendation of the Prime Minister. The President presides over the Council of Ministers, is the head of the civil service and the supreme head of the armed forces. The President may initiate legislation and call referendums. The President may not hold any other office or be a leader of a political party.

* These stipulations were amended under the Marcoussis Accords of January 2003; candidates were required to be over 35 years of age and to have one Ivorian parent.

ASSEMBLÉE NATIONALE

Articles 58–83: The Assemblée nationale holds legislative power. The Assemblée nationale votes on the budget and scrutinizes the accounts of the nation. Deputies are elected for periods of five years by direct universal suffrage. Except in exceptional cases, deputies have legal immunity during the period of their mandate.

INTERNATIONAL AGREEMENTS

Articles 84–87: The President negotiates and ratifies treaties and international agreements. International agreements that modify internal legislation must be ratified by further legislation. The Constitution must be amended prior to the ratification of certain agreements if the Constitutional Council deems this necessary.

CONSTITUTIONAL COUNCIL

Articles 88–100: The Constitutional Council rules on the constitutionality of legislation. It also regulates the functioning of government. It is composed of a President, of the former Presidents of Côte d'Ivoire and of six councillors named by the President and by the President of the Assemblée nationale for mandates of six years. The Council supervises referendums and announces referendum and election results. It also examines the eligibility of candidates to the presidency and the legislature. There is no appeal against the Council's decisions.

JUDICIAL POWER

Articles 101–112: The judiciary is independent, and is composed of the High Court of Justice, the Court of Cassation*, the Council of State, the National Audit Court, and regional tribunals and appeals courts. The Higher Council of Magistrates examines questions relating to judicial independence and nominates and disciplines senior magistrates. The High Court of Justice judges members of the Government in cases relating to the execution of their duties. The High Court, which is composed of deputies elected by the Assemblée nationale, may only judge the President in cases of high treason.

* Although the Constitution of 2000 refers to the highest court of appeal as the Court of Cassation, at mid-2012 this court retained its previous designation, as the Supreme Court.

THE ECONOMIC AND SOCIAL COUNCIL

Articles 113–114: The Economic and Social Council gives its opinion on proposed legislation or decrees relating to its sphere of competence. The President may consult the Council on any economic or social matter.

THE MEDIATOR OF THE REPUBLIC

Articles 115–118: The Mediator is an independent mediating figure, appointed for a non-renewable six-year mandate by the President, in consultation with the President of the Assemblée nationale. The Mediator, who may not hold any other office or position, receives immunity from prosecution during the term of office.

OTHER ISSUES

Articles 119–133: Only the President or the Assemblée nationale, of whom a two-thirds' majority must be in favour, may propose amending the Constitution. Amendments relating to the nature of the presidency or the mechanism whereby the Constitution is amended must be approved by referendum; all other amendments may be enacted with the agreement of the President and of a four-fifths' majority of the Assemblée nationale. The form and the secular nature of the republic may not be amended. Immunity from prosecution is granted to members of the Comité National de Salut Public and to all those involved in the change of government of December 1999.

The Government

HEAD OF STATE

President of the Republic, Minister of Defence: ALASSANE DRAMANE OUATTARA (elected 28 November 2010; sworn in 6 May 2011).

COUNCIL OF MINISTERS
(September 2012)

Prime Minister and Keeper of the Seals, Minister of Justice: JEANNOT KOUADIO AHOUSSOU.

Minister of State, Minister of the Interior: HAMED BAKAYOKO.

Minister of State, Minister of Foreign Affairs: DANIEL KABLAN DUNCAN.

Minister of State, Minister of Employment, Social Affairs and Solidarity: GILBERT KAFANA KONÉ.

Minister of State, Minister of Planning and Development: ALBERT TOIKESSE MABRI.

Minister of State, Minister of Industry: MOUSSA DOSSO.

Minister of the Economy and Finance: CHARLES KOFFI DIBY.

Minister of Economic Infrastructure: PATRICK ACHI.

Minister of Mines, Petroleum and Energy: ADAMA TOUNGARA.

Minister of Health and the Fight Against AIDS: Prof. THÉRÈSE AYA N'DRI YOMAN.

Minister of National Education: KANDIA KAMISSOKO CAMARA.

Minister of the Civil Service and Administrative Reform: KONAN GNAMIEN.

Minister of Handicrafts and the Promotion of Small and Medium-sized Enterprises: SIDIKI KONATÉ.

Minister of Higher Education and Scientific Research: IBRAHIMA CISSÉ BACONGO.

Minister of Animal and Fishing Resources: KOBENA KOUASSI ADJOUMANI.

Minister of Agriculture: MAMADOU SANGAFOWA COULIBALY.

Minister of Trade: DAGOBERT BANZIO.

Minister of Technical Education and Professional Training: ALBERT FLINDÉ.

Minister in charge of Human Rights and Civil Liberties: GNÉNÉMA COULIBALY.

Minister of Culture and Francophone Affairs: MAURICE KOUAKOU BANDAMA.

Minister of the Family, Women and Children: RAYMONDE GOUDOU COFFIE.

Minister of Communication: SOULEYMANE COTY DIAKITÉ.

Minister of the Environment and Sustainable Development: RÉMI ALLAH KOUADIO.

Minister of Tourism: CHARLES AKÉ ATCHIMON.

Minister of Construction, Sanitation and Town Planning: MAMADOU SANOGO.

Minister of Sport and Leisure: PHILIPPE LÉGRÉ.

Minister of Posts and Information and Communication Technologies: BRUNO NABAGNÉ KONÉ.

Minister of Transport: GAOUSSOU TOURÉ.

Minister of Water and Forests: CLÉMENT BOUEKA NABO.

Minister in charge of African Integration: ALLY COULIBALY.

Minister of the Promotion of Youth and Social Services: ALAIN MICHEL LOBOGNON.

Minister of the Promotion of Housing: NIALÉ KABA.

Minister in charge of War Veterans and War Victims: MATHIEU BABAUD DARRET.

Minister of Urban Health: ANNE DÉSIRÉE OULOTO.

Minister-delegate to the Prime Minister, with responsibility for Justice: LOMA CISSÉ MATTO.

Minister of State, Secretary-General of the Presidency: AMADOU GON COULIBALY.

Minister, Director of the Presidential Cabinet: MARCEL AMON-TANOH.

Minister in charge of Presidential Affairs: TENÉ BIRAHIMA OUATTARA.

Minister at the Presidency, in charge of Defence: PAUL KOFFI KOFFI.

Minister at the Presidency, in charge of Relations with the Institutions: ALBERT AGGREY.

MINISTRIES

Office of the President: 01 BP 1354, Abidjan 01; tel. 20-22-02-22; fax 20-21-14-25; internet www.cotedivoirepr.ci.

Office of the Prime Minister: blvd Angoulvant, 01 BP 1533, Abidjan 01; tel. 20-31-50-00; fax 20-22-18-33; internet www.premierministre.ci.

Ministry of Agriculture: 25e étage, Immeuble Caisse de Stabilisation, BP V82, Abidjan; tel. 20-21-38-58; fax 20-21-46-18; e-mail minagra@cimail.net.

Ministry of Animal and Fishing Resources: 11e étage, Immeuble Caisse de Stabilisation, Plateau, Abidjan; tel. 20-21-33-94.

Ministry of the Civil Service and Administrative Reform: Immeuble Fonction Public, blvd Angoulvand, BP V93, Abidjan; tel. 20-21-42-90; fax 20-21-12-86; internet www.emploi.gouv.ci.

Ministry of Communication: 22e étage, Tour C, Tours Administratives, Plateau, Abidjan; tel. 20-21-07-84; internet www.communication.gouv.ci.

Ministry of Construction, Sanitation and Town Planning: 26e étage, Tour D, Tours Administratives, 20 BP 650, Abidjan; tel. 20-21-82-35; fax 20-21-35-68.

Ministry of Culture and Francophone Affairs: 22e étage, Tour E, Tours Administratives, BP V39, Abidjan; tel. 20-21-40-34; fax 20-21-33-59; e-mail culture.ci@ci.refer.org; internet www.mcf-culture.ci.

Ministry of Defence: Camp Galliéni, côté Bibliothèque Nationale, BP V241, Abidjan; tel. 20-21-02-88; fax 20-22-41-75.

Ministry of Economic Infrastructure: 23e étage, Immeuble Postel 2001, BP V6, Plateau, Abidjan; tel. 20-34-73-01; fax 20-21-20-43; e-mail minie@aviso.ci.

Ministry of the Economy and Finance: 16e étage, Immeuble SCIAM, ave Marchand, BP V163, Abidjan; tel. 20-20-08-42; fax 20-21-32-08; internet www.finances.gouv.ci.

Ministry of Employment, Social Affairs and Solidarity: Abidjan.

Ministry of the Environment and Sustainable Development: 10e étage, Tour D, Tours Administratives, BP V06, Abidjan; tel. 20-22-61-35; fax 20-22-20-50.

Ministry of the Family, Women and Children: Tour E, Tours Administratives, BP V200, Abidjan; tel. 20-21-76-26; fax 20-21-44-61.

Ministry of Foreign Affairs and African Integration: Bloc Ministériel, blvd Angoulvant, BP V109, Abidjan; tel. 20-22-71-50; fax 20-33-23-08; e-mail infos@mae.ci; internet www.mae.ci.

Ministry of Handicrafts and the Promotion of Small and Medium-sized Enterprises: Abidjan.

Ministry of Health and the Fight Against AIDS: 16e étage, Tour C, Tours Administratives, Plateau, Abidjan; tel. 20-21-52-40.

Ministry of Higher Education and Scientific Research: 20e étage, Tour C, Tours Administratives, BP V151, Abidjan; tel. 20-21-57-73; fax 20-21-22-25.

Ministry of Industry: 15e étage, Immeuble CCIA, rue Jean-Paul II, BP V65, Abidjan; tel. 20-21-64-73.

Ministry of Information and Communication Technology: 21e étage, Immeuble Postel 2001, BP V138, Abidjan; tel. 22-34-73-65; fax 22-44-78-47.

Ministry of the Interior: Immeuble SETU, en face de la préfecture, BP V241, Abidjan; tel. 20-22-38-16; fax 20-22-36-48.

Ministry of Justice and Human Rights: Bloc Ministériel, blvd Angoulvand A-17, BP V107, Plateau, Abidjan; tel. 20-21-17-27; fax 20-33-12-59; internet www.justice.gouv.ci.

Ministry of Mines, Petroleum and Energy: 15e étage, Immeuble SCIAM, ave Marchand, BP V40, Abidjan; tel. 20-21-66-17; fax 20-21-37-30.

Ministry of National Education: 28e étage, Tour D, Tours Administratives, BP V120, Abidjan; tel. 20-21-85-27; fax 20-22-93-22; e-mail menfb@ci.refer.org.

Ministry of Planning and Development: 16eme étage, Immeuble SCIAM, Plateau, Abidjan; tel. 20-20-08-42; fax 20-20-08-65; e-mail gvode@plan.gouv.ci.

Ministry of the Promotion of Housing: Abidjan.

Ministry of the Promotion of Youth and Social Services: 8e étage, Tour B, Tours Administratives, BP V136, Abidjan; tel. 20-21-92-64; fax 20-22-48-21.

Ministry of Sport and Leisure: Abidjan.

Ministry of the Struggle against AIDS: 7e étage, Immeuble Caisse de Stabilisation, Plateau, Abidjan; tel. 20-21-08-46.

Ministry of Technical Education and Professional Training: 10e étage, Tour C, Tours Administratives, Plateau, Abidjan; tel. 20-21-17-02.

Ministry of Tourism: 15e étage, Tour D, Tours Administratives, BP V184, Abidjan 01; tel. 20-34-79-13; fax 20-44-55-80; internet www.tourisme.gouv.ci.

Ministry of Trade: 26e étage, Immeuble CCIA, rue Jean-Paul II, BP V65, Abidjan; tel. 20-21-76-35; fax 20-21-64-74.

Ministry of Transport: 14e étage, Immeuble Postel 2001, BP V06, Abidjan; tel. 20-34-48-58; fax 20-34-48-54.

Ministry of Urban Health: Abidjan.

Ministry of Water and Forests: Abidjan.

President and Legislature

PRESIDENT

Presidential Election, First Round, 31 October 2010

Candidate	Votes	% of votes
Laurent Gbagbo (FPI)	1,756,504	38.04
Alassane Dramane Ouattara (RDR)	1,481,091	32.07
Henri Konan Bédié (PDCI—RDA)	1,165,532	25.24
Albert Toikesse Mabri (UDPCI)	118,671	2.57
Others*	96,023	2.08
Total†	4,617,821	100.00

* There were 10 other candidates.
† Excluding invalid votes (225,624).

Presidential Election, Second Round, 28 November 2010

Candidate	Votes	% of votes
Alassane Dramane Ouattara (RDR)	2,483,164	54.10
Laurent Gbagbo (FPI)	2,107,055	45.90
Total	4,590,219	100.00

The above results were released by the Commission Électorale Indépendant (CEI) on 2 December 2010. However, later on 2 December the President of the Conseil Constitutionnel, Paul Yao N'Dré, declared the CEI's announcement null and void and the following day released results indicating that Gbagbo had won the election, having received 51.45% of votes cast to Ouattara's 48.55%. The Special Representative of the UN Secretary-General for Côte d'Ivoire, Choi Young-Jin, described N'Dré's decision as 'having no factual basis'; furthermore, in his role as certifier of the Ivorian elections Choi declared Ouattara the winner. On 8 December the UN Security Council released a statement confirming its endorsement of Ouattara as the President-elect of Côte d'Ivoire.

LEGISLATURE

Assemblée nationale

01 BP 1381, Abidjan 01; tel. 20-20-82-00; fax 20-20-82-33; e-mail admin@anci.ci; internet www.anci.ci.

President: GUILLAUME SORO.

General Election, 11 December 2011*

Party	Seats
Rassemblement des Républicains (RDR)	127
Parti Démocratique de la Côte d'Ivoire—Rassemblement Démocratique Africain (PDCI—RDA)	77
Union pour la Démocratie et la Paix de la Côte d'Ivoire (UDPCI)	7
Rassemblement des Houphouëtistes pour la Démocratie et la Paix (RHDP)	4
Mouvement des Forces d'Avenir (MFA)	3
Union pour la Côte d'Ivoire (UPCI)	1
Independents	35
Total	254‡

* The election was boycotted by the Front Populaire Ivoirien (FPI).
‡ Voting in one constituency did not take place owing to the death of a candidate. On 31 January 2012 the Constitutional Council annulled the results of voting in 12 constituencies owing to irregularities. Subsequently, by-elections were held on 26 February in the 13 constituencies, at which the RDR won four seats, the UDPCI two seats, the PDCI—RDA one seat and independent candidates secured four seats. The results in the remaining two constituencies remained undeclared. According to final results published by the CEI on 8 March, the RDR held 138 of the 253 declared seats, the PDCI—RDA held 86 seats, independent candidates held 17 seats and the UDPCI held eight seats. Other party representations remained unchanged.

Election Commission

Commission Électorale Indépendant: 08 BP 2648, Abidjan; tel. 21-30-58-01; internet www.ceici.org; f. 2001; 30 mems; Pres. YOUSSOUF BAKAYOKO.

Advisory Councils

Constitutional Council (Conseil Constitutionnel): 22 blvd Carde, BP 4642, Abidjan 01; tel. 20-21-31-64; fax 20-21-21-68; internet www.gouv.ci/conconst.php; f. 2000; Pres. FRANCIS WODIÉ.

Economic and Social Council: blvd Carde, angle ave Terrasson de Fougère, 04 BP 304, Abidjan 04; tel. 20-21-14-54; internet ces-ci.org; f. 1961; Pres. MARCEL ZADI KESSY; 120 mems.

Political Organizations

In mid-2007 there were more than 100 registered political organizations.

Alliance pour la Nouvelle Côte d'Ivoire (ANCI): Cocody II Plateaux, 06 BP 677, Abidjan 06; tel. 22-41-56-45; fax 21-24-37-97; e-mail info@an-ci.org; internet www.an-ci.org; f. 2007 by fmr mems of Rassemblement des Républicains; Pres. ZEMOGO FOFANA; Sec.-Gen. JEAN-JACQUES BÉCHIO.

Alliance pour la Paix, le Progrès et la Souveraineté (APS): Abidjan; f. 2003 by fmr members of the UDPCI (q.v.); Pres. HILAIRE DIGBEU ANI.

Forces Nouvelles (FN): Bouaké; tel. 20-20-04-04; e-mail senacom@fnci.info; internet www.fnci.info; f. 2003 by the Mouvement Patriotique de Côte d'Ivoire (MPCI), following its absorption of the Mouvement Populaire Ivoirien du Grand Ouest (MPIGO) and the Mouvement pour la Justice et la Paix (MJP), both of which were based in Man, in the west of Côte d'Ivoire.

Front Populaire Ivoirien (FPI): Marcory Zone 4C, 22 BP 302, Abidjan 22; tel. 21-24-36-76; fax 21-35-35-50; internet www.fpi.ci; f. 1990; socialist; Pres. SYLVAIN MIAKA OURETO (acting).

Liberté et Démocratie pour la République (Lider): Abidjan; f. 2011; Leader MAMADOU COULIBALY.

Mouvement des Forces d'Avenir (MFA): 15 BP 794, Abidjan 15; tel. 21-24-42-02; e-mail contact@mfa-ci.com; internet www.mfa-ci.com; f. 1995; Pres. INNOCENT KOBENA ANAKY; Sec.-Gen. DAKPA PHILIPPE LEGRE.

Parti Africain pour la Renaissance Ivoirienne (PARI): Abidjan; f. 1991; Sec.-Gen. DANIEL ANIKPO.

Parti Démocratique de la Côte d'Ivoire—Rassemblement Démocratique Africain (PDCI—RDA): 05 BP 36, Abidjan 05; e-mail sg@pdcirda.org; internet www.pdcirda.org; f. 1946; Pres. HENRI KONAN BÉDIÉ; Sec.-Gen. ALPHONSE DJÉDJÉ MADY.

Parti Ivoirien des Travailleurs (PIT): Adjamé 220 logements, face Cinéma Liberté, Immeuble Mistral Appartement 602, 20 BP 43, Abidjan 20; tel. 20-37-79-42; fax 20-37-29-00; e-mail pit.ci@aviso.ci; internet www.pit-ci.org; social-democratic; f. 1990; First Nat. Sec. FRANCIS WODIÉ.

Rassemblement du Peuple de Côte d'Ivoire (RPCI): Abidjan; f. 2012; Pres. MORIFERÉ BAMBA.

Parti pour le Progrès et le Socialisme (PPS): Abidjan; f. 1993; Sec.-Gen. Prof. MORIFÉRÉ BAMBA.

Union des Sociaux-Démocrates (USD): 08 BP 1866, Abidjan 08; tel. 22-44-06-70; Pres. BERNARD ZADI ZAOUROU; Sec.-Gen. Me JÉRÔME CLIMANLO COULIBALY.

Rassemblement des Républicains (RDR): 8 rue Lepic, Cocody, 06 BP 111, Abidjan 06; tel. 22-44-33-51; fax 22-41-55-73; e-mail le-rdr@yahoo.fr; internet www.le-rdr.org; f. 1994 following split from PDCI—RDA; Pres. Dr ALASSANE DRAMANE OUATTARA; Sec.-Gen. HENRIETTE DAGRI-DIABATÉ.

Union Démocratique Citoyenne (UDCY): 37 bis rue de la Canebière—PISAM, 01 BP 1410, Abidjan 01; tel. 22-47-12-94; e-mail udcy_ci@hotmail.com; internet www.udcy.com; f. 2000 following split from PDCI—RDA (q.v.); Pres. THÉODORE MEL-EG.

Union pour la Démocratie et pour la Paix de la Côte d'Ivoire (UDPCI): 06 BP 1481, Abidjan 06; tel. 22-41-60-94; e-mail info@udpci.org; internet www.udpci.org; f. 2001 following split from PDCI—RDA by supporters of fmr Head of State Gen. Robert Gueï; mem. of alliance, Rassemblement des Houphouëtistes pour la Démocratie et la Paix, formed in advance of proposed (but subsequently postponed) presidential elections in 2005; Pres. ALBERT TOIKESSE MABRI; Sec.-Gen. ALASSANE SALIF N'DIAYE.

Diplomatic Representation

EMBASSIES IN CÔTE D'IVOIRE

Algeria: 53 blvd Clozel, 01 BP 1015, Abidjan 01; tel. 20-21-23-40; fax 20-22-37-12; Ambassador (vacant).

Angola: Lot 2461, rue des Jardins, Cocody-les-Deux-Plateaux, 01 BP 1734, Abidjan 01; tel. 22-44-45-91; fax 22-44-46-52; Ambassador GILBERTO BUTA LUTUKUTA.

Belgium: Cocody Ambassades, angle rue de Bélier et rue A56, 01 BP 1800, Abidjan 01; tel. 22-48-33-60; fax 22-44-16-40; e-mail abidjan@diplobel.fed.be; internet www.diplomatie.be/abidjan; Ambassador PETER HUYGHEBAERT.

Benin: rue des Jasmins, Lot 1610, Cocody-les-Deux-Plateaux, 09 BP 283, Abidjan 09; tel. 22-41-44-13; fax 22-41-27-89; e-mail ambabenin@aviso.ci; Ambassador ANTOINE DIMON AFOUDA.

Brazil: Immeuble Alpha 2000, 22ème étage, 01 BP 3820, Abidjan; tel. 20-22-74-83; fax 20-22-64-01; Ambassador ALFREDO JOSÉ CAVALCANTI JORDA DE CAMARGO.

Burkina Faso: Immeuble SIDAM, 5e étage, 34 ave Houdaille, 01 BP 908, Plateau, Abidjan 01; tel. 20-21-15-01; fax 20-21-66-41; e-mail amba.bf@africaonline.ci; Ambassador JUSTIN KOUTABA.

Cameroon: Immeuble le Général, blvd Botreau Roussel, 06 BP 326, Abidjan 06; tel. 20-21-33-31; fax 20-21-66-11; Ambassador (vacant).

Canada: Immeuble Trade Center, 23 ave Noguès, 01 BP 4104, Abidjan 01; tel. 20-30-07-00; fax 20-30-07-20; e-mail abdjn@international.gc.ca; internet www.canadainternational.gc.ca/cotedivoire; Ambassador CHANTAL DE VARENNES.

Central African Republic: 9 rue des Jasmins, Cocody Danga Nord, 01 BP 3387, Abidjan 01; tel. 20-21-36-46; fax 22-44-85-16; Ambassador YAGAO-N'GAMA LAZARE.

China, People's Republic: Lot 45, ave Jacques Aka, Cocody, 01 BP 3691, Abidjan 01; tel. 22-44-59-00; fax 22-44-67-81; e-mail ambchine@aviso.ci; Ambassador WEI WENHUA.

Congo, Democratic Republic: Carrefour France-Amérique, RAN Treichville, ave 21, 01 BP 541, Abidjan 01; tel. 21-24-69-06; Ambassador ISABELLE I. NGANGELLI.

Egypt: Immeuble El Nasr, 17e étage, rue du Commerce, 01 BP 2104, Abidjan 01; tel. 20-22-62-31; fax 20-22-30-53; e-mail amegypteci@afnet.net; Ambassador TAREQ IBRAHIM MAATY.

Ethiopia: Immeuble Nour Al-Hayat, 8e étage, 01 BP 3712, Abidjan 01; tel. 20-21-33-65; fax 20-21-37-09; e-mail ambethio@gmail.com; Ambassador ABDULAZIZ AHMED ADEM.

France: 17 rue Lecoeur, 17 BP 175, Abidjan 17; tel. 20-20-04-04; fax 20-20-04-47; e-mail scac.abidjan-amba@diplomatie.gouv.fr; internet www.ambafrance-ci.org; Ambassador GEORGE SERRE.

Gabon: Immeuble Les Heveas, blvd Carde, 01 BP 3765, Abidjan 01; tel. 22-44-51-54; fax 22-44-75-05; Ambassador FAUSTIN MOUNGUENGUI NZIGOU.

Germany: 39 blvd Hassan II, Cocody, 01 BP 1900, Abidjan 01; tel. and fax 22-44-20-30; fax 22-44-20-41; e-mail info@abidjan.diplo.de; internet www.abidjan.diplo.de; Ambassador KARL PRINZ.

Ghana: Lot 2393, rue J 95, Cocody-les-Deux-Plateaux, 01 BP 1871, Abidjan 01; tel. 20-33-11-24; fax 20-22-33-57; Ambassador Lt-Col (retd) ENOCH KWAME TWENEBOAH DONKOR.

Guinea: Immeuble Duplessis, 08 BP 2280, Abidjan 08; tel. 20-22-25-20; fax 20-32-82-45; Ambassador (vacant).

Holy See: Apostolic Nunciature, rue Mgr. René Kouassi 18, 08 BP 1347, Abidjan 08; tel. 22-40-17-70; fax 22-40-17-74; e-mail nuntius.ci@gmail.com; Apostolic Nuncio Most Rev. AMBROSE MADTHA.

India: Cocody Danga Nord, 06 BP 318, Abidjan 06; tel. 22-42-37-69; fax 22-42-66-49; e-mail amb.office@eoiabidjan.org; Ambassador ANIL SHARAN.

Iran: blvd de France, en Face de Campus Université de Cocody, rue Belier, Villa No. 1, Abidjan; tel. 22-48-75-48; fax 22-48-75-47; Ambassador NOBAKHTI SEYED REZA.

Israel: Immeuble Nour Al-Hayat, 9th Floor, ave Chardy, 01 BP 1877, Abidjan 01; tel. 20-21-31-78; fax 20-21-87-04; e-mail info@abidjan.mfa.gov.il; internet abidjan.mfa.gov.il; Ambassador DANIEL KEDEM.

Italy: 16 rue de la Canebière, Cocody, 01 BP 1905, Abidjan 01; tel. 22-44-61-70; fax 22-44-35-87; e-mail ambasciata.abidjan@esteri.it; internet www.ambabidjan.esteri.it; Ambassador GIANCARLO IZZO.

Japan: Immeuble Alpha 2000, ave Chardy, 01 BP 1329, Abidjan 01; tel. 20-21-28-63; fax 20-21-30-51; Ambassador SUSUMU INOUE.

Korea, Democratic People's Republic: Abidjan; Ambassador JONG HAKE.

Korea, Republic: Immeuble le Mans, 8e étage, 01 BP 3950, Abidjan 01; tel. 20-32-22-90; fax 20-22-22-74; e-mail ambcoabj@mofat.go.kr; Ambassador PARK YOON-JUNE.

Lebanon: Immeuble Trade Center, ave Noguès, 01 BP 2227, Abidjan 01; tel. 20-33-28-24; fax 20-32-11-37; e-mail ambliban@hotmail.com; Ambassador Dr ALI AJAMI.

Liberia: Immeuble La Symphonie, ave Général de Gaulle, 01 BP 2514, Abidjan 01; tel. 20-22-23-59; fax 22-44-14-75; Ambassador VIVIENNE TITI WREH.

Libya: Immeuble Shell, 01 BP 5725, Abidjan 01; tel. 20-22-01-27; fax 20-22-01-30; Chargé d'affaires TAHER A. S. BAKIR.

Mali: 46 blvd Lagunaire, 01 BP 2746, Abidjan 01; tel. 20-32-31-47; fax 20-21-55-14; Ambassador AMADOU OUSMANE TOURÉ.

Mauritania: rue Pierre et Marie Curie, 01 BP 2275, Abidjan 01; tel. 22-41-16-43; fax 22-41-05-77; Ambassador SIDI MOHAMED OULD SIDATY.

Morocco: 24 rue de la Canebière, 01 BP 146, Cocody, Abidjan 01; tel. 22-44-58-73; fax 22-44-60-58; e-mail sifmaabj@aviso.ci; Ambassador AHMED FAOUZI.

Niger: 23 ave Angoulvant, 01 BP 2743, Abidjan 01; tel. 21-26-28-14; fax 21-26-41-88; Ambassador MOUSSA ALOUA.

Nigeria: Immeuble Maison du Nigéria, 35 blvd de la République, 01 BP 1906, Abidjan 01; tel. 20-22-30-82; fax 20-21-30-83; e-mail info@nigeriaembassyci.org; internet www.nigeriaembassyci.org; Ambassador KAYODÉ OLAJULUWA.

Russia: BP 583, Riviera, Abidjan 01; tel. 22-43-09-59; fax 22-43-11-66; e-mail ambrus@globeaccess.net; Ambassador LEONID ROGOD.

Saudi Arabia: Plateau, Abidjan; Ambassador JAMAL BAKR ABDULLAH BALKHYOOR.

Senegal: Immeuble Nabil Choucair, 6 rue du Commerce, 08 BP 2165, Abidjan 08; tel. 20-33-28-76; fax 20-32-50-39; Ambassador SEYDOU KALOGA.

South Africa: Villa Marc André, rue Mgr René Kouassi, Cocody, 08 BP 1806, Abidjan 08; tel. 22-44-59-63; fax 22-44-74-50; e-mail ambafsudpol@aviso.ci; Ambassador (vacant).

Spain: impasse Abla Pokou, Cocody Danga Nord, 08 BP 876, Abidjan 08; tel. 22-44-48-50; fax 22-44-71-22; e-mail embespci@correo.mae.es; Ambassador FERNANDO MORAN CALVO-SOTELO.

Switzerland: Immeuble Botreau Roussel, 28 ave Delafosse, Plateau, 01 BP 1914, Abidjan 01; tel. 20-21-17-21; fax 20-21-27-70; e-mail abi.vertretung@eda.admin.ch; Ambassador (vacant).

Tunisia: Immeuble Shell, ave Lamblin, 01 BP 3906, Abidjan 01; tel. 20-22-61-23; fax 20-22-61-24; Ambassador NACEUR BOU ALI.

United Kingdom: Cocody Quartier Ambassades, rue l'Impasse du Belier, 01 BP 2581, Abidjan 01; tel. 22-44-26-69; fax 22-48-95-48; e-mail britemb@aviso.ci; Ambassador SIMON DAVID TONGE.

USA: Cocody Riviera Golf, 01 BP 1712, Abidjan 01; tel. 22-49-40-00; fax 22-49-43-23; e-mail abjpress@state.gov; internet abidjan.usembassy.gov; Ambassador PHILLIP CARTER, III.

Judicial System

Since 1964 all civil, criminal, commercial and administrative cases have come under the jurisdiction of the courts of first instance, the assize courts and the Courts of Appeal, with the Supreme Court (referred to in the Constitution of 2000 as the Court of Cassation) as the highest court of appeal.

Supreme Court: rue Gourgas, Cocody, BP V30, Abidjan; tel. 20-22-73-72; fax 20-21-63-04; internet www.gouv.ci/coursupreme.php; comprises three chambers: judicial, administrative and auditing; Pres. MAMADOU KONÉ; Pres. of the Judicial Chamber KAMA YAO; Pres. of the Administrative Chamber GEORGES AMANGOUA.

Courts of Appeal: Abidjan: First Pres. MARIE-FÉLICITÉ ARKHUST HOMA YAO; Bouaké: First Pres. CHRISTIAN ANIBIÉ KAKRÉ ZÉPHIRIN; Daloa: First Pres. GONHI SAHI.

Courts of First Instance: Abidjan: Pres. ANTOINETTE MARSOUIN; Bouaké: Pres. KABLAN AKA EDOUKOU; Daloa: Pres. WOUNE BLEKA; there are a further 25 courts in the principal centres.

High Court of Justice: composed of deputies elected from and by the Assemblée nationale; has jurisdiction to impeach the President or other mems of the Govt.

Constitutional Council: 22 blvd Carde, BP 4642, Abidjan 01; tel. 20-21-31-64; fax 20-21-21-68; internet www.gouv.ci/conconst.php; f. 2000 to replace certain functions of the fmr Constitutional Chamber of the Supreme Court; Pres. FRANCIS WODIÉ.

Religion

The Constitution guarantees religious freedom, and this right is generally respected. Religious groups are required to register with the authorities, although no penalties are imposed on a group that fails to register. At the 1998 census it was estimated that about 34% of the population were Christians (mainly Roman Catholics), 27% of the population were Muslims, 15% followed traditional indigenous beliefs, 3% practised other religions, while 21% had no religious affiliation. It is, however, estimated that the proportion of Muslims is in fact significantly higher, as the majority of unregistered foreign workers are Muslims. Muslims are found in greatest numbers in the north of the country, while Christians are found mostly in the southern, central, western and eastern regions. Traditional indigenous beliefs are generally prevalent in rural areas.

ISLAM

Conseil National Islamique (CNI): Mosquée d'Aghien les deux Plateaux, BP 174 Cédex 03, Abidjan 08; tel. and fax 22-42-67-79; e-mail infos@cnicosim.org; f. 1993; groups more than 5,000 local communities organized in 13 regional and 78 local organizations; Chair. Imam El Hadj IDRISS KOUDOUSS KONÉ.

Conseil Supérieur des Imams (COSIM): 05 BP 2092, Abidjan 08; tel. 21-35-87-51; fax 05-79-61-04; e-mail contact@cosim-ci.org; internet www.cosim-ci.org; Pres. CHEICK BOIKARY FOFANA.

Conseil Supérieur Islamique (CSI): 11 BP 71, Abidjan 11; tel. 21-25-24-70; fax 21-24-28-04; f. 1978; Pres. MOUSTAPHA SY FADIGA.

Other Islamic organizations include the Association des Musulmans Sunnites, Conseil des Imams Sunnites, Front de la Oummat Islamique and Haut Conseil des Imamats et Oulémas.

CHRISTIANITY

The Roman Catholic Church

Côte d'Ivoire comprises four archdioceses and 11 dioceses. An estimated 20% of the total population are Roman Catholics.

Bishops' Conference

Conférence Episcopale de la Côte d'Ivoire, BP 713 Cédex 03, Abidjan-Riviera; tel. 22-47-20-00; fax 22-47-60-65.

f. 1973; Pres. Most Rev. JOSEPH YAPO AKÉ (Archbishop of Gagnoa).

Archbishop of Abidjan: Most Rev. JEAN-PIERRE KUTWA, Archevêché, ave Jean-Paul II, 01 BP 1287, Abidjan 01; tel. 20-21-23-08; fax 20-21-40-22.

Archbishop of Bouaké: Most Rev. PAUL-SIMÉON AHOUANAN DJRO, Archevêché, 01 BP 649, Bouaké 01; tel. and fax 31-63-24-59; e-mail archebke@aviso.ci.

Archbishop of Gagnoa: Most Rev. JOSEPH YAPO AKÉ, Archevêché, BP 527, Gagnoa; tel. and fax 32-77-25-68; e-mail evechegagnoa@aviso.ci.

Archbishop of Korhogo: Most Rev. MARIE-DANIEL DADIET, BP 1581, Yamoussoukro; tel. 36-86-01-18; fax 36-86-08-31; e-mail dieulesauve@yahoo.fr.

Protestant Churches

Conseil National des Eglises Protestantes et Évangéliques de Côte d'Ivoire (CNEPECI): Abidjan; Pres. PAUL AYOH.

Eglise Evangélique des Assemblées de Dieu de Côte d'Ivoire: 26 BP 1396, Abidjan 26; tel. 21-35-55-48; fax 21-24-94-65; e-mail itpk2006@yahoo.fr; internet www.eeadci.org; f. 1960; Pres. BÉCHIÉ DÉSIRÉ GNANCHOU; Sec.-Gen. CHARLES ATTOUA GBANDA.

Eglise Harriste: 01 BP 3620, Abidjan 01; tel. 22-42-31-03; internet egliseharriste.org; f. 1913 by William Wadé Harris; affiliated to World Council of Churches 1998; allows polygamous new converts; 100,000 mems, 1,400 preachers, 7,000 apostles; Sec.-Gen. DOGBO JULES.

Eglise Méthodiste Unie de Côte d'Ivoire: 41 blvd de la République, 01 BP 1282, Abidjan 01; tel. 20-21-17-97; fax 20-22-52-03; e-mail emuciconf@yahoo.fr; internet www.emu-ci.org; f. 1924; publ. *Le Méthodiste* (monthly); f. autonomous since 1985; c. 800,000 mems; Pres. BENJAMIN BONI.

Eglise du Nazaréen (Church of the Nazarene): 22 BP 623, Abidjan 22; tel. 22-41-07-80; fax 22-41-07-81; e-mail awfcon@compuserve.com; internet www.nazarenemissions.org; f. 1987; active in evangelism, ministerial training and medical work; 4,429 mems; Dir JOHN SEAMAN.

Eglise Protestante Baptiste Oeuvres et Mission Internationale: 03 BP 1032, Abidjan 03; tel. 23-45-20-18; fax 23-45-56-41; e-mail epbomi@yahoo.com; internet www.epbomi.net; f. 1975; active in evangelism, teaching and social work; medical centre, 6,000 places of worship, 400 missionaries and 193,000 mems; Pres. Rev. Dr YAYE ROBERT DION.

Eglise Protestante Evangélique CMA de Côte d'Ivoire: BP 585, Bouaké 01; tel. 22-49-07-96; fax 31-63-54-12; e-mail contact@eglisecma-ci.org; internet www.eglisecma-ci.org; f. 1930; 300,000 mems; Nat. Pres. Rev. KOUAKOU CÉLESTIN KOFFI; Sec.-Gen AMANI N'GUESSAN.

Mission Evangélique de l'Afrique Occidentale (MEAO): 08 BP 1873, Abidjan 08; tel. and fax 22-47-59-95; e-mail hebohl@gmx.net; f. 1934; Team Leaders BRUCE PINKE, CAROLYN PINKE; affiliated church: Alliance des Eglises Evangéliques de Côte d'Ivoire (AEECI); 3 MEAO missionaries, 4 AEECI missionaries, 400 churches, 104 full-time pastors; Pres. ALAINGBRÉ PASCAL KOUASSI.

Mission Evangélique Luthérienne en Côte d'Ivoire (MELCI): BP 196, Touba; tel. 33-70-77-11; e-mail melci@aviso.ci; f. 1984; active in evangelism and social work; Dir GJERMUND VISTE.

Union des Eglises Evangéliques, Services et Œuvres de Côte d'Ivoire: 08 BP 20, Abidjan 08; tel. 40-22-75-00; e-mail ueesoci63@yahoo.fr; internet www.ueeso-ci.org; f. 1927; c. 250 places of worship; Pres. GILBERT GOUENTOUEU; Sec.-Gen. MICHEL LOH.

WorldVenture: BP 109, Korhogo; tel. 36-86-01-07; fax 36-86-11-50; internet www.worldventure.com; f. 1947; fmrly Conservative Baptist Foreign Mission Society, subsequently CB International; active in evangelism, medical work, translation, literacy and theological education in the northern area and in Abidjan.

The Press

Conseil National de la Presse (CNP): Cocody-les-Deux-Plateaux, 1ère tranche, Villa 224 bis, BP V 106, Abidjan; tel. 22-40-53-53; fax 22-41-27-90; e-mail info@lecnp.ci; internet www.lecnp.com; f. 1991; Pres. DÉBY DALLI GBALAWOULOU; Sec.-Gen. RENÉ BOURGOIN.

DAILIES

24 Heures: rue St Jean, duplex 65, Cocody–Val Doyen I, 10 BP 3302, Abidjan 10; tel. 22-41-29-53; fax 22-41-37-82; e-mail infos@24heures.net; internet www.24heuresci.com; f. 2002; Dir-Gen. ABDOULAYE SANGARÉ; Dir of Publication and Editor-in-Chief JOACHIM BEUGRÉ; circ. 21,000 (2005).

Côte d'Ivoire Economie: Cocody-les-Deux-Plateaux, rue K24, 28 BP 1473, Abidjan 28; tel. 22-41-77-50; fax 22-41-76-16; e-mail info@cotedivoire-economie.com; internet www.cotedivoire-economie.com; f. 2010; Dir-Gen. and Dir of Publication MARION N'GOUAN EZZEDINE; Editor-in-Chief JEAN-PIERRE PONT.

Le Courrier d'Abidjan: Riviera Bonoumin, 25 BP 1682, Abidjan 25; tel. 22-43-38-22; fax 22-43-30-46; internet www.lecourrierdabidjan.info; f. 2003.

Douze: rue Louis Lumière, Zone 4C, 10 BP 2462, Abidjan 10; tel. 21-25-54-00; fax 21-24-47-27; e-mail douze@afnet.net; publ. by Editions Olympe; f. 1994; sport; Dir MAZÉ SOUMAHORO; Editor-in-Chief FRANÇOIS BINI.

Fraternité Matin: blvd du Général de Gaulle, 01 BP 1807, Abidjan 01; tel. 20-37-06-66; fax 20-37-25-45; e-mail contact@fratmat.info; internet www.fratmat.info; f. 1964; official newspaper; state-owned; Dir-Gen. JEAN-BAPTISTE AKROU; Editorial Dir ALFRED DAN MOUSSA; circ. 26,000 (2011).

L'Intelligent d'Abidjan: Villa 12S, Bâtiment Star 4, 19 BP 1534, Abidjan 19; tel. 22-42-71-61; fax 22-42-11-70; e-mail Editeur@lintelligentdabidjan.org; internet www.lintelligentdabidjan.org; f. 2003; Dir-Gen. W. ALAFÉ ASSÉ.

L'Inter: 10 BP 2462, Abidjan 10; tel. 21-21-28-00; fax 21-21-28-05; e-mail linter@linter-ci.com; internet www.linter-ci.com; f. 1998; publ. by Editions Olympe; national and international politics and economics; Dir RAYMOND N'CHO NIMBA; Editor-in-Chief CHARLES A. D'ALMÉIDA; circ. 18,000 (2002).

Le JD (Jeune Démocrate): 23 BP 3842, Abidjan 23; tel. 23-51-62-45; fax 23-51-63-75; f. 1999; Dir IGNACE DASSOHIRI; Editor-in-Chief OCTAVE BOYOU.

Le Jour Plus: 26 Cocody-les-Deux-Plateau, 25 BP 1082, Abidjan 25; tel. 20-21-95-78; fax 20-21-95-80; f. 1994; publ. by Editions Le Nere; independent; Dir of Publication COULIBALY SEYDOU; Editor-in-Chief FRÉDÉRIC KOFFI; circ. 15,000 (2002).

Le Libéral: 01 BP 6938, Abidjan 01; tel. and fax 22-52-21-41; e-mail leliberal@aviso.ci; f. 1997; Dir YORO KONÉ; Editor-in-Chief BAKARY NIMAGA; circ. 15,000.

Le Matin d'Abidjan: 2 Plateaux Vallon 06, BP 2853, Abidjan 06; tel. 22-42-74-57; fax 22-42-59-06; e-mail info@lematindabidjan.com; internet www.lematindabidjan.com; Dir KOUAMENAN G. LAURENT.

Le National: Angré, Cocody, 16 BP 165, Abidjan 16; tel. 22-52-27-43; fax 22-52-27-42; f. 1999; nationalist; Publr LAURENT TAPÉ KOULOU; Editor-in-Chief (vacant); circ. 20,000 (2002).

Nord-Sud: Abidjan; internet nordsudquotidien.net; f. 2005; Dir TOURÉ MOUSSA; circ. 18,000 (2005).

Notr'Aurore: Immeuble SICOGI, Bâtiment K, Appt 124, Deux-Plateaux Aghien, blvd Latrille, Abidjan; tel. 22-42-08-21; fax 22-42-08-24; f. 2002; nationalist; Editor-in-Chief EMMANUEL GRIÉ.

Notre Voie: Cocody-les-Deux-Plateaux, 06 BP 2868, Abidjan 06; tel. 22-42-63-31; fax 22-42-63-32; e-mail gnh@africaonline.co.ci; internet www.notrevoie.com; f. 1978; organ of the FPI; Dir and Editor-in-Chief LAHOUA SOUANGA ETIENNE; circ. 20,000 (2002).

Le Nouveau Courrier: Abidjan; Editor-in-Chief SAINT-CLAVER OULA.

Le Nouveau Réveil: Adjamé Sud 80 Logements, Tours SICOGI, face Frat-Mat, Bâtiment A, 2e étage, porte 6, 01 BP 10684, Abidjan 01; tel. 20-38-42-00; fax 20-38-67-91; e-mail lenouveaureveil@yahoo.fr; internet www.lenouveaureveil.com; f. 2001 to replace weekly *Le Réveil-Hebdo* ; supports PDCI—RDA; Dir-Gen. DENIS KAH ZION; Dir of Publication PATRICE YAO; circ. 18,000 (2005).

Le Patriote: 23 rue Paul Langevin, Zone 4C, 22 BP 509, Abidjan 22; tel. 21-21-19-45; fax 21-35-11-83; e-mail info@lepatriote.net; internet www.lepatriote.net; organ of the RDR; Dir of Publication CHARLES SANGA; Editor-in-Chief KORÉ EMMANUEL; circ. 40,000 (2002).

Le Populaire: 19 blvd Angoulvant, résidence Neuilly, Plateau, 01 BP 5496, Abidjan 01; tel. 21-36-34-15; fax 21-36-43-28; Dir RAPHAËL ORE LAKPÉ.

Soir Info: 10 BP 2462, Abidjan 10; tel. 21-21-28-00; fax 21-21-28-06; e-mail quotidiensoirinfo@yahoo.fr; internet www.soirinfo.com; f. 1994; publ. by Editions Olympe; independent; Dir VAMARA COULIBALY; Editor-in-Chief NAZAIRE KIKIÉ; circ. 22,000 (2002).

Le Sport: Cocody Attoban, face au Groupe Scolaire Jules Ferry, 09 BP 3685, Abidjan 09; tel. 22-43-92-54; fax 22-43-01-90; internet www.lesport.ci; Dir of Publication ASSI ADON AMÉDÉE.

Supersport: Abidjan; internet www.supersport.ci; f. 2006; Dir-Gen. HAMIDOU FOMBA.

La Voie: face Institut Marie-Thérèse Houphouët-Boigny, 17 BP 656, Abidjan 17; tel. 20-37-68-23; fax 20-37-74-76; organ of the FPI; Dir ABOU DRAHAMANE SANGARÉ; Man. MAURICE LURIGNAN.

SELECTED BI-WEEKLIES AND WEEKLIES

L'Agora: Immeuble Nana Yamoussou, ave 13, rue 38, Treichville, 01 BP 5326, Abidjan 01; tel. 21-34-11-72; f. 1997; weekly; Dir FERNAND DÉDÉ; Editor-in-Chief BAMBA ALEX SOULEYMANE.

Le Démocrate: Maison du Congrès, ave 2, Treichville, 01 BP 1212, Abidjan 01; tel. 21-24-45-88; fax 21-24-25-61; f. 1991; weekly; organ of the PDCI—RDA; Dir NOËL YAO.

Le Front: Immeuble Mistral, 3e étage, 220 Logements, 11 BP 11 2678, Abidjan 11; tel. 20-38-13-24; fax 20-38-70-83; e-mail quotidienlefront@yahoo.fr; internet www.lefront.com; two a week; Editorial Dir FATOUMATA COULIBALY; Editor KPOKPA BLÉ.

Gbich!: 10 BP 399, Abidjan 10; tel. and fax 21-26-31-94; e-mail gbich@assistweb.net; internet www.gbichonline.com; weekly; satirical; Editor-in-Chief MATHIEU BLEDOU.

Le Nouvel Horizon: 220 Logements, blvd du Général de Gaulle, Adjamé, 17 BP 656, Abidjan 17; tel. 20-37-68-23; f. 1990; weekly; organ of the FPI; Dir ABOU DRAHAMANE SANGARÉ; circ. 15,000.

La Nouvelle Presse: rue des Jardins, Cocody-les-Deux-Plateaux, 01 BP 8534, Abidjan 01; tel. 22-41-04-76; fax 22-41-04-15; e-mail jvieyra@africaonline.co.ci; f. 1992; weekly; publ. by Centre Africain de Presse et d'Edition; current affairs; Editors JUSTIN VIEYRA, JÉRÔME CARLOS; circ. 10,000.

Le Repère: 220 Logements, Adjamé Sud-Tours SICOGI, face Frat-Mat, Bâtiment A, 2e étage P6, 04 BP 1947, Abidjan 04; tel. and fax 20-38-67-91; supports PDCI—RDA; two a week; Dir of Publication DENIS KAH ZION; circ. 10,000 (2004).

Sports Magazine: Yopougon-SOGEFIHA, 01 BP 4030, Abidjan 01; tel. 23-45-14-02; f. 1997; weekly; Dir JOSEPH ABLE.

Téré: 220 Logements, blvd du Général de Gaulle, Adjamé-Liberté, 20 BP 43, Abidjan 20; tel. and fax 20-37-79-42; weekly; organ of the PIT; Dir ANGÈLE GNONSOA.

Top-Visages: rue du Commerce, 23 BP 892, Abidjan 23; tel. 20-33-72-10; fax 20-32-81-05; e-mail contact@topvisages.net; internet www.topvisages.net; weekly; Editor-in-Chief E. TONGA BÉHI; circ. 40,000 (2004).

La Voie du Compatriote: Adjamé St-Michel, 09 BP 2008, Abidjan 09; tel. 20-37-50-13; f. 1998; weekly; Dir SINARI KAL.

SELECTED PERIODICALS

Côte d'Ivoire Magazine: Présidence de la République, 01 BP 1354, Abidjan 01; tel. 20-22-02-22; f. 1998; quarterly; Dir JEAN-NOËL LOUKO.

Juris-Social: Centre National de Documentation Juridique (CNDJ), Villa 381, ilôt 43, face Polyclinique Saint Jacques, blvd Latrille, Cocody-les-Deux-Plateaux, 01 BP 2757, Abidjan 01; tel. 20-22-74-85; fax 20-22-74-86; e-mail cndj@aviso.ci; internet www.cndj.ci; monthly; jurisprudence; CNDJ also publishes quarterly periodical *Juris OHADA*.

La Lettre de l'Afrique de l'Ouest: rue des Jardins, Cocody-les-Deux-Plateaux, 01 BP 8534, Abidjan 01; tel. 22-41-04-76; fax 22-41-04-15; f. 1995; publ. by Centre Africain de Presse et d'Edition; six a year; politics, economics, regional integration; Editors JUSTIN VIEYRA, JÉRÔME CARLOS.

Maisons et Matériaux: 08 BP 2150, Abidjan 08; tel. 22-42-92-17; monthly; Dir THIAM T. DJENEBOU.

News&Co: Cocody 2 Plateaux Vallons, 28 BP 580, Abidjan 28; tel. 22-51-04-72; fax 22-51-04-73; e-mail info@newseco-ci.com; internet www.newseco-ci.com; monthly; financial and economic affairs; publ. by Publi Services Editions; Dir of Publication MARION N'GOUAN EZZEDINE; Editor-in-Chief ELODIE VERMEIL; circ. 10,000.

Roots-Rock Magazine: Abidjan; tel. 22-42-84-74; f. 1998; monthly; music; Dir DIOMANDÉ DAVID.

RTI-Mag: 08 BP 663, Abidjan 08; tel. 20-33-14-46; fax 20-32-12-06; publ. by Radiodiffusion-Télévision Ivoirienne; listings magazine.

Sentiers: 26 ave Chardy, 01 BP 2432, Abidjan 01; tel. 20-21-95-68; fax 20-21-95-80; e-mail redaction@aviso.ci; Editor-in-Chief DIÉGOU BAILLY.

Stades d'Afrique: blvd du Général de Gaulle, 01 BP 1807, Abidjan 01; tel. 20-37-06-66; fax 20-37-25-45; f. 2000; sports; monthly; Dir-Gen. EMMANUEL KOUASSI KOKORÉ; Editor-in-Chief HÉGAUD OUATTARA.

Le Succès: 21 BP 3748, Abidjan 21; tel. 20-37-71-64; monthly; Dir AKPLA PLAKATOU.

Univers Jeunes: 01 BP 3713, Abidjan 01; tel. 20-21-20-00; fax 21-35-35-45; monthly; Editor-in-Chief MOUSSA SY SAVANÉ.

La Voix d'Afrique: rue des Jardins, Cocody-les-Deux-Plateaux, 01 BP 8534, Abidjan 01; tel. 22-41-04-76; fax 22-41-04-15; publ. by Centre Africain de Presse et d'Edition; monthly; Editor-in-Chief GAOUSSOU KAMISSOKO.

NEWS AGENCY

Agence Ivoirienne de Presse (AIP): ave Chardy, 04 BP 312, Abidjan 04; tel. 20-22-64-13; fax 20-21-35-99; e-mail aip@aip.ci; internet www.aip.ci; f. 1961; Dir DALLI DEBY.

PRESS ASSOCIATIONS

Association de la Presse Démocratique Ivoirienne (APDI): Abidjan; tel. 20-37-06-66; f. 1994; Chair. JEAN-BAPTISTE AKROU.

Union Nationale des Journalistes de Côte d'Ivoire (UNJCI): 06 BP 1675, Plateau, Abidjan 06; tel. 20-21-61-07; e-mail prunjci@unjci.org; f. 1991; Pres. MAMERY CAMARA.

Publishers

Centre Africain de Presse et d'Edition (CAPE): rue des Jardins, Cocody-les-Deux-Plateaux, 01 BP 8534, Abidjan 01; tel. 22-41-04-76; fax 22-41-04-15; Man. JUSTIN VIEYRA.

Centre d'Edition et de Diffusion Africaines (CEDA): 17 rue des Carrossiers, 04 BP 541, Abidjan 04; tel. 20-24-65-10; fax 21-25-05-67; e-mail infos@ceda-ci.com; internet www.ceda-ci.com; f. 1961; 20% state-owned; general non-fiction, school and children's books, literary fiction; Pres. and Dir-Gen. VENANCE KACOU.

Centre de Publications Evangéliques: 08 BP 900, Abidjan 08; tel. 22-44-48-05; fax 22-44-58-17; e-mail cpe@aviso.ci; internet www.editionscpe.com; f. 1967; evangelical Christian; Dir JULES OUOBA.

Editions Bognini: 06 BP 1254, Abidjan 06; tel. 20-41-16-86; social sciences, literary fiction.

Editions Eburnie: 01 BP 1984, 01 Abidjan; tel. 20-21-64-65; fax 20-21-45-46; e-mail eburnie@aviso.ci; f. 2001; illustrated books for children, social sciences, poetry.

Editions Neter: 01 BP 7370, Abidjan 01; tel. 22-52-52-68; f. 1992; politics, culture, history, literary fiction; Dir RICHARD TA BI SENIN.

Nouvelles Editions Ivoiriennes: 1 blvd de Marseille, 01 BP 1818, Abidjan 01; tel. 21-24-07-66; fax 21-24-24-56; e-mail edition@nei-ci.com; internet www.nei-ci.com; f. 1972; literature, criticism, essays, drama, social sciences, history, in French and English; Dir GUY LAMBIN.

Presses Universitaires et Scolaires d'Afrique (PUSAF—Editions Cissé): 08 BP 177, Abidjan 08; tel. 22-41-12-71; mathematics, economics, medicine.

Université Nationale de Côte d'Ivoire: 01 BP V34, Abidjan 01; tel. 22-44-08-59; f. 1964; academic and general non-fiction and periodicals; Publications Dir GILLES VILASCO.

GOVERNMENT PUBLISHING HOUSE

Imprimerie Nationale: BP V87, Abidjan; tel. 20-21-76-11; fax 20-21-68-68.

Broadcasting and Communications

TELECOMMUNICATIONS

In 2011 there were six operators in the Côte d'Ivoire telecommunications market. Four of these provided mobile cellular telephone services, one provided fixed-line services and one provided both mobile and fixed-line services. A new mobile company, Aircom, commenced operations in April 2012 under the brand name Café Mobile.

Regulatory Authorities

Agence des Télécommunications de Côte d'Ivoire (ATCI): Immeuble Postel 2001, 4e étage, rue Lecoeur, 18 BP 2203, Abidjan 18; tel. 20-34-43-74; fax 20-34-43-75; e-mail courrier@atci.ci; internet www.atci.ci; f. 1995; Pres. LASSINA KONÉ; Dir-Gen. ARTHUR ALLOCO KOUASSI.

Conseil des Télécommunications de Côte d'Ivoire (CTCI): 17 BP 110, Abidjan 17; tel. 20-34-43-04; f. 1995; deals with issues of arbitration; Pres. LEMASSOU FOFANA.

Service Providers

Atlantique Telecom—Moov (Moov): Immeuble Karrat, rue du Commerce, 01 BP 2347, Abidjan 01; tel. 20-25-01-01; fax 20-25-26-62; e-mail moovcontact@moov.com; internet www.moov.com; f. 2005 as jt venture by Atlantique Télécom (Côte d'Ivoire) and Etisalat (United Arab Emirates); 80% owned by Etisalat (United Arab Emirates); mobile cellular telecommunications; CEO NAGI ABBOUD; 3.8m. subscribers (April 2012).

Comium: Blvd VGE Marcory, cnr rue Lumière, 4106444W 11, BP 2591, Abidjan 11; tel. 21-35-90-41; internet www.koz.ci; f. 2009; Pres. NIZAR DALLOUL; Dir-Gen MICHEL HEBERT; 1.8m. subscribers (April 2012).

Côte d'Ivoire-Télécom (CI-Télécom): Immeuble Postel 2001, rue Lecoeur, 17 BP 275, Abidjan 17; tel. 20-34-40-00; fax 20-21-28-28; internet www.citelecom.ci; f. 1991; 51% owned by France Télécom, 49% state-owned; Pres. YAYA OUATTARA; Man. Dir MAMADOU BAMBA; 327,000 subscribers (June 2002).

Green Network (GreenN): Abidjan; tel. 60-00-60-60; internet www.greenn.ci; f. 2009; owned by Libya Africa Portfolio; Dir-Gen. ABDULGHANI RAMADAN; 2.9m. subscribers (April 2012).

MTN Côte d'Ivoire: Immeuble Loteny, 12 rue Crossons Duplessis, 01 BP 3685, Abidjan 01; tel. 20-31-63-16; fax 20-31-84-50; internet www.mtn.ci; f. 1996 as Loteny Télécom-Télécel; present name adopted 2005; mobile cellular telephone operator in more than 110 urban centres and on principal highway routes; 51% owned by Mobile Telephone Network International (South Africa); Chief Exec. WIM VAN HELLEPUTTE; 5.7m. subscribers (April 2012).

Orange Côte d'Ivoire: Immeuble Saha, blvd Valéry Giscard d'Estaing, Zone 4C, 11 BP 202, Abidjan 11; tel. 21-23-90-07; fax 21-23-90-11; internet www.orange.ci; f. 1996 as Ivoiris, present name adopted 2002; mobile cellular telephone operator in more than 60 urban centres; 85% owned by France Télécom; Man. Dir MAMADOU BAMBA; 6.2m. subscribers (April 2012).

BROADCASTING

Regulatory Authority

Haute Autorité de la Communication Audiovisuelle: Pl. de la République, 05 BP 56, Abidjan; tel. 20-31-15-80; internet www.haca.ci; f. 2011 to replace Conseil National de la Communication Audiovisuelle (CNCA); Pres. IBRAHIM SY SAVANÉ.

Radio

In 1993 the Government permitted the first commercial radio stations to broadcast in Côte d'Ivoire; of the five licences initially granted, four were to foreign stations. Between 1998 and early 2001, a further 52 licences were granted.

Radiodiffusion-Télévision Ivoirienne (RTI): blvd des Martyrs, Cocody, 08 BP883, Abidjan 08; tel. 22-48-61-62; fax 22-44-78-23; e-mail info.rti@rti.ci; internet www.rti.ci; f. 1962; state-owned; two national TV channels, La Première and TV2, and two national radio channels, La Nationale and Fréquence II; Pres. PASCAL BROU AKA; Dir-Gen. LAZARE AKA SAYÉ; Dir, La Première VICTOR DEBASS KPAN; Dir, TV2 ADÈLE DJEDJE; Dir, Radiodiffusion ELOI OULAÏ.

Abidjan 1: Deux Plateaux Hayat, au dessus de la pharcie des jardins, Abidjan; tel. 22-41-29-03; e-mail info@radioabidjan1.com; internet www.radioabidjan1.com; Dir JULIEN ADAYE.

City FM: Immeuble Alpha Cissé, avant la piscine d'Etat, Treichville, 01 BP 7207, Abidjan 01; tel. 21-25-10-28; f. 1999; Pres. and Man. Dir Me ALIOU SIBI.

Radio Espoir: 12 BP 27, Abidjan 12; tel. 21-75-68-01; fax 21-75-68-04; e-mail respoir@aviso.ci; internet www.radioespoir.ci; f. 1990;

Roman Catholic; broadcasts in French, local and sub-regional languages; Dir Fr BASILE DIANÉ KOGNAN.

Radio JAM: Abidjan; tel. 21-25-08-73; e-mail radiojamofficiel@yahoo.fr; internet www.radiojam.biz; Dir FRANÇOIS KONIAN.

Radio Nostalgie: Immeuble Le Paris, ave Chardy, 01 BP 157, Abidjan 01; tel. 20-21-10-52; fax 20-21-85-53; e-mail contact@nostalgie.ci; internet www.nostalgie.ci; f. 1993; Dir-Gen. HERVÉ CORNUEL.

Radio Notre Dame: BP 1555, Yamoussoukro; tel. 30-64-41-55; e-mail nfo@radionotredame-yakro.com; internet www.radionotredame-yakro.com; broadcasts religious programmes; Dir-Gen. JEAN-CLAUDE ATSAIN.

Radio Peleforo Gbon: route Ferké km 2, BP 841, Korhogo; tel. 21-86-22-62; fax 21-86-20-33.

Radio Soleil: 16 BP 1179, Abidjan 16; tel. 21-99-17-64; fax 21-79-12-48; e-mail badouel_jeannette@yahoo.fr; f. 2001; Dir JEANNETTE BADOUEL.

Côte d'Ivoire also receives broadcasts from the Gabon-based Africa No 1 radio station, from the French-language Africa service of the BBC (United Kingdom), and from Radio France Internationale.

Television

Radiodiffusion-Télévision Ivoirienne (RTI): see Radio section.

Canal+ Côte d'Ivoire: Immeuble Alpha 2000, 01 BP 1132, Abidjan 01; tel. 20-31-99-97; fax 20-22-72-22; e-mail abonne@canalhorizons.ci; internet www.canalplus-afrique.com; broadcasts commenced 1994; subsidiary of Canal Plus (France); Dir-Gen. SERGE AGNÉRO.

Finance

(cap. = capital; res = reserves; dep. = deposits; m. = million; br(s). = branch(es); amounts in francs CFA, unless otherwise indicated)

BANKING

In 2009 there were 20 commercial banks and three financial institutions in Côte d'Ivoire. Following the disputed presidential election of 28 November 2010, a number of commercial banking institutions announced the suspension of their operations. Of these, the Banque Internationale pour le Commerce et l'Industrie de la Côte d'Ivoire, Citibank, the Société Générale de Banques en Côte d'Ivoire and the Standard Chartered Bank Côte d'Ivoire were later forcibly nationalized by Laurent Gbagbo, who refused to relinquish the presidency. The Bourse Régionale des Valeurs Mobilières also suspended its operations, but subsequently resumed them from a new base in Bamako, Mali. Gbagbo was detained in April 2011, and in early May the legitimately elected President, Alassane Ouattara, confirmed that banking operations in the country would recommence.

Central Bank

Banque Centrale des États de l'Afrique de l'Ouest (BCEAO): blvd Botreau-Roussel, angle ave Delafosse, 01 BP 1769, Abidjan 01; tel. 20-20-85-00; fax 20-22-28-52; e-mail webmaster@bceao.int; internet www.bceao.int; f. 1962; HQ in Dakar, Senegal; bank of issue for the mem. states of the Union Économique et Monétaire Ouest-Africaine (UEMOA, comprising Benin, Burkina Faso, Côte d'Ivoire, Guinea-Bissau, Mali, Niger, Senegal and Togo); cap. 134,120m., res 1,474,195m., dep. 2,124,051m. (Dec. 2009); Gov. KONÉ TIÉMOKO MEYLIET; Dir in Côte d'Ivoire JEAN-BAPTISTE AMAN AYAYE; 7 brs in Côte d'Ivoire.

Commercial Banks

Access Bank Cote d'Ivoire: 6e étage, Immeuble Alliance, 17 ave Terrasson de Fougères, 01 BP 6928, Abidjan 01; tel. 20-31-58-30; fax 20-21-42-58; e-mail info.cotedivoire@accessbankplc.com; internet subs.accessbankplc.com; f. 1996; name changed as above in 2008; 88% owned by Access Bank (Nigeria); cap. 3,000m. (Dec. 2005); Pres. JACOB AWUKU AMEMATEKPO; Dir-Gen. AMADOU LY.

Bank of Africa—Côte d'Ivoire (BOA—CI): ave Terrasson de Fougères, angle Rue Gourgas, 01 BP 4132, Abidjan 01; tel. 20-30-34-00; fax 20-30-34-01; e-mail boaci@bkofafrica.com; internet www.boacoteivoire.com; f. 1996; 68.1% owned by BOA Group (Luxembourg); cap. 4,500m., res 3,343m., dep. 189,765m., total assets 208,647m. (Dec. 2008); Dir-Gen. LALA MOULAYE; 18 brs.

Banque Atlantique Côte d'Ivoire (BACI): Immeuble Atlantique, ave Noguès, Plateau, 04 BP 1036, Abidjan 04; tel. 20-31-59-50; fax 20-21-68-52; e-mail kone.dossongui@banqueatlantique.net; internet www.banqueatlantique.net; f. 1979; merged with Compagnie Bancaire de l'Atlantique Côte d'Ivoire in 2009; cap. and res 13,230m., dep. 224,832m. (Dec. 2007); Pres. KONE DOSSONGUI; Dir-Gen. SOULEYMANE DIARRASSOUBA; 3 brs.

Banque de l'Habitat de Côte d'Ivoire (BHCI): 22 ave Joseph Anoma, 01 BP 2325, Abidjan 01; tel. 20-25-39-39; fax 20-22-58-18; e-mail info@bhci.ci; internet www.bhci.ci; f. 1993; cap. and res 1,755m., total assets 16,834m. (Dec. 1999); Chair. DAVID AMUAH; Man. Dir SOULEYMANE DOGONI; 3 brs.

Banque pour le Financement de l'Agriculture (BFA): Immeuble Alliance B, 2e étage, rue Lecoeur, BP 103 Poste Entreprise, Cedex 1, Abidjan; tel. 20-25-61-61; fax 20-25-61-99; e-mail info@bfa.ci; internet www.bfa.ci; Dir-Gen. WENCESLAS APPIA; 4 brs.

Banque Internationale pour le Commerce et l'Industrie de la Côte d'Ivoire SA (BICI-CI): ave Franchet d'Espérey, 01 BP 1298, Abidjan 01; tel. 20-20-16-00; fax 20-20-17-00; e-mail michel.lafont@africa.bnpparibas.com; internet www.bicicinet.net; f. 1962; 67.5% owned by BNP Paribas (France); absorbed BICI Bail de Côte d'Ivoire in 2003 and Compagnie Financière de la Côte d'Ivoire in 2004; cap. and res 38,436.7m., total assets 276,432.1m. (Dec. 2004); Chair. ANGE KOFFY; 39 brs.

Banque Nationale d'Investissement (BNI): Immeuble SCIAM, ave Marchand, Plateau, 01 BP 670, Abidjan 01; tel. 20-31-51-00; fax 20-22-92-33; e-mail info@bni-ci.net; internet www.bni.ci; f. 1959 as Caisse Autonome d'Amortissement de Côte d'Ivoire (CAA); name and operations changed as above in 2004; cap. and res 28,408m., total assets 253,668m. (Dec. 2003); Dir-Gen. EUGÈNE NDA KASSI.

BIAO—Côte d'Ivoire (BIAO—CI): 8–10 ave Joseph Anoma, 01 BP 1274, Abidjan 01; tel. 20-20-07-20; fax 20-20-07-00; e-mail info@biao.co.ci; internet www.biao.co.ci; f. 1980; fmrly Banque Internationale pour l'Afrique de l'Ouest—Côte d'Ivoire; 20% state-owned; cap. 10,000.0m., res 173.0m., dep. 163,501.m. (Dec. 2005); Pres. SEYDOU ELIMANE DIARRA; Dir-Gen. MARTIN DJEDJES; 31 brs.

La Caisse d'Épargne de Côte d'Ivoire: 11 ave Joseph Anoma, 01 BP 6889, Abidjan 01; tel. 20-25-43-00; fax 20-25-53-11; e-mail info@caissepargne.ci; internet www.caissepargne.ci; f. 1998; Dir-Gen. MAMAH DIABAGATÉ.

Citibank Côte d'Ivoire: Immeuble Botreau-Roussel, 28 ave Delafosse, 01 BP 3698, Abidjan 01; tel. 20-20-90-00; fax 20-21-76-85; e-mail citibank@odaci.net; f. 1976; total assets US $198.7m. (2003); Dir-Gen. CHARLES KIE.

COFIPA Investment Bank CI: Immeuble Botreau Roussel, 5e étage, ave Delafosse, 04 BP 411, Abidjan 04; tel. 20-30-23-00; fax 20-30-23-01; e-mail Info@cofipa.ci; internet www.cofipa.ci; cap. and res 2,382.5m., total assets 19,171.2m. (Dec. 2002); Chair. MACAULEY OVIA; Man. Dir and CEO GUY KOIZAN; 49 brs.

Ecobank Côte d'Ivoire: Immeuble Alliance, 1 ave Terrasson de Fougères, 01 BP 4107, Abidjan 01; tel. 20-31-92-00; fax 20-21-88-16; e-mail ecobankci@ecobank.com; internet www.ecobank.com; f. 1989; 94% owned by Ecobank Transnational Inc (Togo); cap. 22,259m, dep. 296,326m, total assets 341,666m. (Dec. 2009); Chair. AKA AOUÉLÉ; Dir-Gen. CHARLES DABOIKO; 16 brs.

Société Générale de Banques en Côte d'Ivoire (SGBCI): 5–7 ave Joseph Anoma, 01 BP 1355, Abidjan 01; tel. 20-20-10-10; fax 20-20-14-92; e-mail info.sgbci@socgen.com; internet www.sgbci.ci; f. 1962; 66.8% owned by Société Générale (France); cap. 15,556m., res 25,298m., dep. 429,765m. (Dec. 2007); Pres. TIÉMOKO YADÉ COULIBALY; Dir-Gen. BERNARD LABADENS; 41 brs.

Société Ivoirienne de Banque (SIB): Immeuble Alpha 2000, 34 blvd de la République, 01 BP 1300, Abidjan 01; tel. 20-20-00-00; fax 20-20-01-19; e-mail info@sib.ci; internet www.sib.ci; f. 1962; 51% owned by Calyon, Paris La Défense (France), 49% state-owned; reduction of state holding to 19% proposed; cap. 4,000m., res 10,710m., total assets 148,340m. (Dec. 2006); Pres. LAMBERT FEH KESSE; Administrator and Dir-Gen. MOUNIR OUDGHIRI; 15 brs.

Standard Chartered Bank Côte d'Ivoire (SCBCI): 23 blvd de la République, face Commissariat du 1er arrondissement, 17 BP 1141, Abidjan 17; tel. 20-30-32-00; fax 20-30-32-01; e-mail info.CDI@sc.com; internet www.standardchartered.com/ci; f. 2001; subsidiary of Standard Chartered Bank (United Kingdom); cap. and res 9,218m., total assets 76,289m. (Dec. 2003); Pres. EBENEZER ESSOKA; CEO SERGES BAILLY; 4 brs.

United Bank for Africa Côte d'Ivoire: blvd Botreau-Roussel, Plateau, Abidjan; tel. 20-31-22-22; fax 20-31-22-26; e-mail ubacotedivoire@ubagroup.com; internet www.ubagroup.com/ubacotedivoire; f. 2008; Dir-Gen. GUILLAUME LIBY.

Versus Bank: Immeuble CRAAE-UMOA, blvd Botreau Roussel, angle ave Joseph Anoma, 01 BP 1874, Abidjan 01; tel. 20-25-60-60; fax 20-25-60-99; e-mail infos@versusbank.com; internet www.versusbank.com; f. 2004; cap. 3,000m.; Pres. DANO DJÉDJÉ; Dir-Gen. GUY KOIZAN.

Credit Institutions

Afribail—Côte d'Ivoire (Afribail—CI): 8–10 ave Joseph Anoma, 01 BP 1274, Abidjan 01; tel. 20-20-07-20; fax 20-20-07-00; 95% owned by BIAO—CI; cap. and res 334m., total assets 2,651m. (Dec. 2002); Chair. RENÉ AMANY; Pres. and Dir-Gen. ERNEST ALLOU TOGNAN.

Coopérative Ivoirienne d'Epargne et de Crédit Automobile (CIECA): 04 BP 2084, Abidjan 04; tel. 20-22-77-13; fax 20-22-77-35; cap. and res 805m. (Dec. 1998), total assets 1,169m. (Dec. 1999); Dir-Gen. DALLY ZABO.

Société Africaine de Crédit Automobilier (SAFCA): 1 rue des Carrossiers, Zone 3, 04 BP 27, Abidjan 04; tel. 21-21-07-07; fax 21-21-07-00; e-mail safca@afnet.net; f. 1956; cap. and res 5,681.8m., total assets 22,511.1m. (Dec. 2001); Pres. and Dir-Gen. THIERRY PAPILLION.

Société Africaine de Crédit-Bail (SAFBAIL): Immeuble SAFCA, 1 rue des Carrossiers, Zone 3, 04 BP 27, Abidjan 04; tel. 21-24-91-77; fax 21-35-77-90; e-mail safca@aviso.ci; f. 1971; cap. and res 2,922m., total assets 13,414m. (Dec. 1999); Chair. and Man. Dir DIACK DIAWAR.

SOGEFIBAIL—CI: 26 ave Delafosse, 01 BP 1355, Abidjan 01; tel. 20-32-85-15; fax 20-33-14-93; 35% owned by GENEFITEC, 35% by SOGEFINANCE, 25% by SGBCI; cap. and res 2,560.2m., total assets 4,452.3m. (Dec. 2003); Pres. JEAN-LOUIS MATTEI.

Bankers' Association

Association Professionnelle des Banques et Etablissements Financiers de Côte d'Ivoire (APBEFCI): Immeuble Aniaman, ave Lamblin, 01 BP 3810, Abidjan 01; tel. 20-32-20-08; fax 20-32-69-60; internet www.apbef-ci.org; affiliated to Confédération Générale des Entreprises de Côte d'Ivoire (q.v.); Pres. JACOB ANEMATEKPO.

STOCK EXCHANGE

Bourse Régionale des Valeurs Mobilières (BRVM): 18 ave Joseph Anoma, 01 BP 3802, Abidjan 01; tel. 20-32-66-85; fax 20-32-66-84; e-mail brvm@brvm.org; internet www.brvm.org; f. 1998 to succeed Bourse des Valeurs d'Abidjan; regional stock exchange serving mem. states of UEMOA; Dir-Gen. JEAN-PAUL GILLET.

INSURANCE

In 2006 there were 34 insurance companies in Côte d'Ivoire.

Abidjanaise d'Assurances: Immeuble Woodin Center, ave Noguès, 01 BP 2909, Abidjan 01; tel. 20-22-46-96; fax 20-22-64-81; Dir-Gen. MARC RICHMOND.

African American Insurance Co (AFRAM): Immeuble ex-Monopris, 2 ave Noguès, 01 BP 7124, Abidjan 01; tel. 20-31-30-44; fax 20-32-69-72; Dir-Gen. CHRISTIAN CASEL.

Alliance Africaine d'Assurances (3A): Immeuble Le Mans, 6e étage, ave Botreau Roussel, 01 BP 11944, Abidjan 01; tel. 20-33-85-07; fax 20-33-88-14; e-mail aaavie@aaavie.com; internet www.3a-vie.com; Dir-Gen. DRAMANE CISSE.

Atlantique Assurances Côte d'Ivoire: Immeuble MACI, 2e étage, 15 ave Joseph Anoma, Plateau, 01 BP 1841, Abidjan 01; tel. 20-31-78-00; fax 20-33-18-37; e-mail atlantiqueassurances@atlantiqueassurances.net; f. 1956; Dir-Gen. PIERRE MAGNE.

AXA Assurances Côte d'Ivoire: ave Delafosse Prolongée, 01 BP 378, Abidjan 01; tel. 20-31-88-88; fax 20-31-88-00; e-mail axarci@africaonline.co.ci; f. 1981; fmrly l'Union Africaine—IARD; insurance and reinsurance; Dir-Gen. ROGER BOA.

AXA Vie Côte d'Ivoire: 9 ave Houdaille, 01 BP 2016, Abidjan 01; tel. 20-22-25-15; fax 20-22-37-60; e-mail info@axa-vie.ci; f. 1985; fmrly Union Africaine Vie; life assurance and capitalization; Chair. JOACHIM RICHMOND; Dir PATRICE DESGRANGES.

Colina: Immeuble Colina, blvd Roume 3, 01 BP 3832, Abidjan 01; tel. 20-25-36-00; fax 20-22-59-05; e-mail colinaci@groupecolina.com; internet www.colina-sa.com; f. 1980; Chair. MICHEL PHARAON; Dir-Gen. M. J. ACKAH.

Compagnie Nationale d'Assurances (CNA): Immeuble Symphonie, 30 ave du Général de Gaulle, 01 BP 1333, Abidjan 01; tel. 20-21-49-19; fax 20-22-49-06; f. 1972; cap. 400m.; insurance and reinsurance; transfer to private ownership pending; Chair. SOUNKALO DJIBO; Man. Dir RICHARD COULIBALY.

Génération Nouvelle d'Assurances Côte d'Ivoire (GNA-CI): Ground Floor, Immeuble l'Ebrien, rue du commerce, Abidjan; tel. 20-25-98-00; fax 20-33-60-65; internet www.gnassurances.com; f. 2006; Pres. BARTHÉLEMY VIDJANNANGNI; Dir-Gen. FÉLIX KOUAME ZEGBE N'GUESSAN.

Gras Savoye Côte d'Ivoire: Immeuble Trade Center, ave Noguès, 01 BP 5675, Abidjan 01; tel. 20-25-25-00; fax 20-25-25-25; e-mail grassavoyeci@ci.grassavoye.com; affiliated to Gras Savoye (France); Man. JEAN-FRANÇOIS ALAUZE.

Mutuelle Centrale d'Assurances: 15 Immeuble Ebrien, 01 BP 12724, Abidjan 01; tel. 20-31-11-30; fax 20-31-11-32; e-mail mca@mca.ci; Administrator ANOKOI KODJO.

Nouvelle Société Africaine d'Assurances (NSIA AGCI): Immeuble Manci, rue A43, 01 BP 1571, Abidjan 01; tel. 20-31-75-00; fax 20-31-98-00; f. 1995; Pres. and Dir-Gen. JEAN KACOU DIAGOU.

NSIA-Vie: Immeuble Zandaman, ave Noguès, 01 BP 4092, Abidjan 01; tel. 20-31-98-00; fax 20-33-25-79; f. 1988; fmrly Assurances Générales de Côte d'Ivoire—Vie (AGCI-Vie); life; Pres. and Dir-Gen. JEAN KACOU DIAGOU.

Serenity: 41 blvd Général de Gaulle (face gare sud), Immeuble Ex-Monoprix, 01 BP 10244, Abidjan 01; tel. 20-32-16-52; fax 20-32-16-63; internet www.serenity-sa.com; f. 2009; Dir-Gen. MAURICE KIPRÉ DIGBEU.

Société Africaine d'Assurances et de Réassurances en République de Côte d'Ivoire (SAFARRIV): Immeuble SAFARRIV, 2, blvd Roume, 01 BP 1741, Abidjan 01; tel. 20-30-40-00; fax 20-30-40-01; e-mail groupe-safarriv@safarriv.ci; internet www.agf-ci.com; f. 1975; affiliated to AGF Afrique; Pres. TIÉMOKO YADÉ COULIBALY; Man. Dir CHRISTIAN ARRAULT.

Trade and Industry

GOVERNMENT AGENCIES

Autorité pour la Régulation du Café et du Cacao (ARCC): blvd Botreau Roussel, Immeuble Caistab 17ème–19ème étages, Plateau, 25 BP 1501, Abidjan 25; tel. 20-20-29-87; fax 20-20-27-05; e-mail courrier@arcc.ci; internet www.arcc.ci; f. 2000; implements regulatory framework for coffee and cocoa trade; Pres. GILBERT N'GUESSAN.

Bureau National d'Etudes Techniques et de Développement (BNETD): blvd Hassan II, Cocody, 04 BP 945, Abidjan 04; tel. 22-48-34-00; fax 22-44-56-66; e-mail info@bnetd.ci; internet www.bnetd.ci; f. 1978 as Direction et Contrôle des Grands Travaux; management and supervision of major public works projects; Dir-Gen. KRA KOFFI PASCAL.

Comité de Privatisation: 6 blvd de l'Indénié, 01 BP 1141, Abidjan 01; tel. 20-22-22-31; fax 20-22-22-35; f. 1990; state privatization authority; Pres. PAUL AGODIO; Dir-Gen. AHOUA DON MELLO.

Conseil du Régulation, de Stabilisation et de Développement de la Filière Café-Cacao (Conseil du Café-Cacao): 17 BP 797, Abidjan 17; tel. 20-25-69-69; fax 20-21-83-30; e-mail info@conseilcafecacao.ci; internet www.conseilcafecacao.ci; f. 2012 to replace the Comite de Gestion de la Filière Café-Cacao; comprises the Autorité pour la Régulation du Café et du Cacao (ARCC), the Bourse du Café et du Cacao (BCC), the Fonds de Régulation et de Contrôle du Café et du Cacao (FRCC) and the Fonds de Développement et de Promotion des Activités des Producteurs de Café et de Cacao (FDPCC); Pres. LAMBERT KOUASSI KONAN; Dir-Gen. MASSANDJÉ TOURÉ-LITSE.

Conseil Économique et Social: angle blvd Carde et ave Terrason de Fougère, 04 BP 304, Abidjan 04; tel. 20-21-14-54; internet ces-ci.org; f. 1961; Pres. MARCEL ZADI KESSY.

Fonds de Régulation et de Contrôle du Café et du Cacao (FRCC): Immeuble Caistab, 17 BP 797, Abidjan 17; tel. 20-20-27-11; fax 20-21-83-30; e-mail frc@frc.ci; internet www.frc.ci; f. 2002; assists small-scale producers and exporters of coffee and cocoa; administrative bd comprises five representatives of producers, two of exporters, three of banks and insurance cos, two of the state; Pres. ANGELINE KILI; Dir-Gen. FIRMIN KOUAKOU.

PETROCI: Immeuble les Hévéas, 14 blvd Carde, BP V194, Abidjan 01; tel. 20-20-25-00; fax 20-21-68-24; e-mail info@petroci.ci; internet www.petroci.ci; f. 1975 as Société Nationale d'Opérations Pétrolières de la Côte d'Ivoire (PETROCI); restructured 2000 to comprise three companies—Petroci Exploration Production, SA, Petroci Gaz and Petroci Industries Services; all aspects of hydrocarbons devt; Pres. PAUL GUI DIBO; Dir-Gen. DANIEL GNAGNI.

Société de Développement des Forêts (SODEFOR): blvd François Mitterrand, 01 BP 3770, Abidjan 01; tel. 22-48-30-00; fax 22-44-02-40; e-mail info@sodefor.ci; internet www.sodefor.ci; f. 1966; establishment and management of tree plantations, sustainable management of state forests, marketing of timber products; Dir-Gen. SANGARÉ MAMADOU.

Société pour le Développement Minier de la Côte d'Ivoire (SODEMI): 31 blvd des Martyrs, 01 BP 2816, Abidjan 01; tel. 22-44-29-94; fax 22-44-08-21; e-mail sodemidg@aviso.cg; f. 1962; geological and mineral research; Pres. NICOLAS KOUANDI ANGBA; Man. Dir KOUAMÉ KADIO.

Société pour le Développement des Productions Animales (SODEPRA): 01 BP 1249, Abidjan 01; tel. 20-21-13-10; f. 1970; rearing of livestock; Man. Dir (vacant).

DEVELOPMENT AGENCIES

Agence Française de Développement (AFD): blvd François Mitterrand, 01 BP 1814, Abidjan 01; tel. 22-40-70-40; fax 22-44-21-78; e-mail afdabidjan@afd.fr; internet www.afd.fr; Country Dir PHILIPPE-CYRILLE BERTON.

Association pour la Promotion des Exportations de Côte d'Ivoire (Apex-CI): 01 BP 3485, Abidjan 01; tel. 20-30-25-30; fax

20-21-75-76; e-mail marketing@apexci.org; internet www.apexci.org; Dir-Gen. GUY M'BENGUE.

Centre de Promotion des Investissements en Côte d'Ivoire (CEPICI): Quartier des Ambassades, angle rue Booker Washington et ave Jacques AKA, BP V152, Abidjan 01; tel. 22-44-45-35; fax 22-44-28-22; e-mail infos-cepici@cepici.ci; f. 1993; investment promotion authority; Dir-Gen. EMMANUEL ESSIS ESMEL.

France Volontaires: 01 BP 2532, Abidjan; tel. 20-22-85-09; fax 20-22-05-96; internet www.france-volontaires.org; f. 1965; name changed as above in 2009; Nat. Delegate JEAN-PIERRE JUIF.

Institut de Recherche pour le Développement: Quartier Marcory Zone 4C, rue Dr Alexander Fleming, 15 BP 917, Abidjan 15; tel. 21-35-96-03; fax 21-35-40-15; e-mail cote-ivoire@ird.fr; internet www.ird.ci; Admin. SÉKOU YEO.

CHAMBERS OF COMMERCE

Chambre d'Agriculture de la Côte d'Ivoire: 11 ave Lamblin, 01 BP 1291, Abidjan 01; tel. 20-32-92-13; fax 20-32-92-20; Sec.-Gen. GAUTHIER N'ZI.

Chambre de Commerce et d'Industrie de Côte d'Ivoire: 6 ave Joseph Anoma, 01 BP 1399, Abidjan 01; tel. 20-33-16-00; fax 20-30-97-35; e-mail info@chamco-ci.org; internet www.chamco-ci.org; f. 1992; Pres. JEAN-LOUIS BILLON; Dir-Gen. MAMADOU SARR.

TRADE ASSOCIATIONS

Association Nationale des Organisations Professionnelles Agricoles de Côte d'Ivoire (ANOPACI): Cocody Cité des Arts, Derrière la Cité BAD, rue C7, 20 BP 937, Abidjan 20; tel. 22-44-11-76; e-mail anopaci@yahoo.fr; internet www.anopaci.org; f. 1998; Pres. MATHIAS N'GOAN.

Bourse du Café et du Cacao (BCC): 04 BP 2576, Abidjan 04; tel. 20-20-27-20; fax 20-20-28-14; e-mail info@bcc.ci; internet www.bcc.ci; f. 2001 to replace marketing, purchasing and certain other functions of La Nouvelle Caistab (Caisse de Stabilisation et de Soutien des Prix des Productions Agricoles); Pres. LUCIEN TAPÉ DOH; Dir-Gen. TANO KASSI KADIO.

Fédération Ivoirienne des Producteurs de Café et de Cacao (FIPCC): Yamoussoukro; f. 1998; coffee and cocoa growers' asscn; Chair. CISSÉ LOCINÉ; c. 3,000 mems.

Organisation de Commercialisation de l'Ananas et de la Banane (OCAB): Abidjan; pineapple and banana growers' asscn; Pres. MICHEL GNUI; Exec. Sec. EMMANUEL DOLI.

EMPLOYERS' ORGANIZATIONS

Association Nationale des Paysans de Côte d'Ivoire (ANAPA-CI): Bouaké; Pres. KONÉ WAYARAGA.

Association Nationale des Producteurs de Café-Cacao de Côte d'Ivoire (ANAPROCI): BP 840, San-Pédro; tel. 34-71-20-98; fax 34-71-14-65; Pres. BOTI BI ZOUA; Sec.-Gen. THOMAS EYIMIN.

Confédération Générale des Entreprises de Côte d'Ivoire: 01 BP 8666, Abidjan 01; tel. 20-30-08-21; fax 20-22-28-25; e-mail cgeci@cgeci.org; internet www.cgeci.org; f. 1993 as Conseil National du Patronat Ivoirion; current name adopted 2005; Pres. JEAN KACOU DIAGOU; Dir-Gen. LAKOUN OUATTARA; nine affiliated federations, including the following:

Fédération Maritime de Côte d'Ivoire (FEDERMAR): Treichville, ave Christiani, 01 BP 4082, Abidjan 01; tel. 21-22-08-09; fax 21-22-07-90; e-mail issouf.fadika@ci.dti.bollore.com; f. 1958; Pres. ISSOUF FADIKA; Sec.-Gen. VACABA TOURÉ DE MOVALY.

Fédération Nationale des Industries et Services de Côte d'Ivoire (FNISCI): Immeuble Les Harmonies, Plateau, Abidjan 01; tel. 20-31-90-70; fax 20-21-53-52; e-mail infos@fnisci.net; internet siege.fnisci.net; f. 1993; Pres. JOSEPH-DESIRÉ BILEY; Dir-Gen. ADAMA COULIBALY; 180 mems.

Groupement Ivoirien du Bâtiment et des Travaux Publics (GIBTP): 25 rue des Carrossiers, Concession SIDELAF, zone 3, 01 BP 464, Abidjan 01; tel. 21-25-29-46; fax 21-25-29-57; f. 1934 as Syndicat des Entrepreneurs et des Industriels de la Côte d'Ivoire; present name adopted 1997; Pres. KONGO KOUADIO KOUASSI.

Syndicat des Commerçants Importateurs et Exportateurs (SCIMPEX): 01 BP 3792, Abidjan 01; tel. 20-21-54-27; fax 20-32-56-52; Pres. JACQUES ROSSIGNOL; Sec.-Gen. M. KOFFI.

Syndicat Autonome des Producteurs de Café-Cacao de Côte d'Ivoire (SYNAPROCI): Abidjan; f. 2003; Pres. BANNY KOFFI GERMAIN (acting).

Syndicat des Exportateurs et Négociants en Bois de Côte d'Ivoire: route du Lycée Technique, Cocody Danga, Villa No. 4, 01 BP 1979, Abidjan 01; tel. 22-44-44-80; fax 22-44-44-74; e-mail unemaf@africaonline.co.ci; f. 1960; Pres. SOULEYMANE COULIBALY.

Syndicat des Producteurs Industriels du Bois (SPIB): route du Lycée Technique, Cocody Danga, Villa No. 4, 01 BP 318, Abidjan; tel. 22-44-44-80; fax 22-44-44-74; e-mail unemaf@africaonline.co.ci; f. 1943; Pres. WILFRIED BIRKENMAIER.

Union des Entreprises Agricoles et Forestières: route du Lycée Technique, Cocody Danga, Villa No. 4, 01 BP 2300, Abidjan 01; tel. 22-44-44-80; fax 22-44-44-74; e-mail unemaf@africaonline.co.ci; f. 1952; Pres. YORO BI TRAZIÉ.

UTILITIES

Electricity

Compagnie Ivoirienne d'Electricité (CIE): 1 ave Christiani, 01 BP 6932, Abidjan 01; tel. 21-23-33-00; fax 21-23-63-22; e-mail info@cie.ci; internet www.groupecie.net; f. 1990; 71% controlled by Société Bouygues group (France); Pres. OUSMANE DIARRA; Dir-Gen. DOMINIQUE KACOU.

Compagnie Ivoirienne de Production d'Electricité (CIPREL): Tour Sidom, 12e étage, ave Houdaille, 01 BP 4039, Abidjan 01; tel. 20-22-60-97; independent power production; Dir-Gen. N'GUESSAN KOUASSI.

Gas

Gaz de Côte d'Ivoire (GDCI): 01 BP 1351, Abidjan; tel. 22-44-49-55; f. 1961; transfer to majority private ownership pending; gas distributor; Man. Dir LAMBERT KONAN.

Water

Société de Distribution d'Eau de la Côte d'Ivoire (SODECI): 1 ave Christiani, Treichville, 01 BP 1843, Abidjan 01; tel. 21-23-30-00; fax 21-24-30-06; e-mail sodeci@sodeci.ci; internet www.sodeci.com; f. 1959; production, treatment and distribution of drinking water; 46% owned by Groupe Bouygues (France), 51% owned by employees; Pres. FIRMIN AHOUNÉ; Dir-Gen. BASILE EBAH.

MAJOR COMPANIES

The following are among the largest companies in terms of either capital investment or employment.

Air Gaz Côte d'Ivoire: 15 BP 619, Abidjan 15; tel. 21-27-19-04; fax 21-27-17-64; internet www.airgazci.com; mfrs of industrial and medical gases; Gen. Man. MOUSSA KLEIT.

Air Liquide-Société Ivoirienne d'Oxygène et d'Acetylène (SIVOA): 131 blvd de Marseille, 01 BP 1753, Abidjan 01; tel. 21-21-04-57; fax 21-35-80-96; internet www.ci.airliquide.com; f. 1962; cap. 873m. francs CFA; 20% state-owned, 72% owned by Air Liquide (France); mfrs of industrial and medical gases; Pres. GÉRARD PRIET; Man. Dir KHADIM THIAM; 70 employees.

Bois Transformés d'Afrique (BTA): 01 BP 958, Abidjan 01; tel. 20-22-74-31; fax 20-22-74-69; f. 1972; cap. 233.5m. francs CFA; sawmills, plywood factory at Zagné; Dir-Gen. PHILIPPE DEKEULENEER.

Carnaud Metalbox SIEM: blvd Giscard d'Estaing, 01 BP 1242, Abidjan 01; tel. 21-35-89-74; fax 21-35-03-94; f. 1954; subsidiary of Carnaud Metalbox (France); cap. 1,889m. francs CFA; mfrs of cans; Man. Dir M. MOREAU.

Compagnie des Caoutchoucs du Pakidie (CCP): 01 BP 1191, Abidjan 01; tel. 20-37-15-38; fax 20-37-15-40; f. 1960; cap. 856m. francs CFA; rubber plantations and factory; Chair. FULGENCE KOFFI.

Compagnie Ivoirienne pour le Développement des Textiles Nouvelle (CIDT Nouvelle): route de Béoumi, 01 BP 622, Bouaké 01; tel. 31-63-30-13; fax 31-63-41-67; f. 1974; cap. 7,200m. francs CFA; transferred to majority private ownership in 1998; present name adopted 1999; development of cotton production, cotton ginning; Man. Dir SAMBA COULIBALY.

Cosmivoire: Zone Industrielle de Vridi, 01 BP 3576, Abidjan 01; tel. 21-75-77-57; fax 21-27-28-13; e-mail infocos@cosmivoire.ci; internet www.cosmivoire.ci; f. 1974; owned by SIFCA; cap. 702m. francs CFA; mfrs of soaps, cosmetics, oils, margarine, butter and alcohol; Pres. JEAN-BAPTISTE FOFANA; Man. Dir ANGORA TANO.

Ets R. Gonfreville (ERG): route de l'Aéroport, BP 584, Bouaké; tel. 31-63-32-13; fax 31-63-46-65; f. 1921; cap. 2,999m. francs CFA; spinning, weaving, dyeing and printing of cotton textiles; clothing mfrs; Man. Dir JACQUES RIVIÈRE; 2,500 employees (2001).

Filatures, Tissage, Sacs–Côte d'Ivoire (FILTISAC): Km 8, route d'Adzopé, 01 BP 3962, Abidjan 01; tel. 20-30-46-00; fax 20-30-46-11; e-mail info@filtisac.com; internet www.filtisac.com; f. 1965; cap. 4,407m. francs CFA (June 2002); sales US $44.9m. (2001); mfrs of jute bags and other packaging; Pres. YVES ROLAND; Man. Dir DÉSIRÉ GABALA; 2,000 employees (June 2002).

Globale Protection: Marcory Zone IV, blvd Valéry Giscard d'Estaing, 30 BP 561, Abidjan 30; tel. 21-25-91-75; fax 21-25-91-72; e-mail globale.protection@afnet.net; internet www.globaleprotection.com; f. 1996; mfrs of protection and surveillance systems; Dir-Gen. CHIRSTIAN LEJOSNE.

Grands Moulins d'Abidjan (GMA): Quai 1, Zone Portuaire, 01 BP 1743, Abidjan 01; tel. 20-21-28-33; fax 20-29-09-42; f. 1963; cap. 2,000m. francs CFA; flour milling and production of animal feed; Dir FÉLIX DIOUF; 331 employees (2001).

Groupe FIBAKO–IVOIREMBAL: Km 8, route d'Abobo Gare, 01 BP 3962, Abidjan 01; tel. 31-63-32-12; fax 31-63-18-92; f. 1946; fmrly Ficelleries de Bouaké–Société Industrielle Ivoirienne d'Emballage; cap. 950m. francs CFA; spinning, mfrs of sacking and plastic packaging; Man. Dir PHILIPPE GODIN.

Industrie de Transformation des Produits Agricoles (API): Zone Industrielle de Vridi, 15 BP 431, Abidjan 15; tel. 21-35-20-09; f. 1968; cap. 900m. francs CFA; wholly owned by Cacao Barry Group (France); marketing of cocoa products, processing of cocoa beans; Man. Dir HONORÉ AKPANGNI.

Mobil Oil Côte d'Ivoire: route de Petit Bassam, 15 BP 900, Abidjan 15; tel. 21-75-37-00; fax 21-75-38-00; f. 1974; cap. 2,000m. francs CFA; distribution of petroleum products; Chair. MICHEL BONNET; Dir J. LABAUNE.

National Electric-Côte d'Ivoire (NELCI): 16 BP 131, Abidjan 16; f. 1983; cap. 1,000m. francs CFA; assembly of radio and television receivers; Chair. TAMADA TAKASHI.

Nestlé Côte d'Ivoire: rue du Lycée Technique, 01 BP 1840, Abidjan 01; tel. 22-40-45-45; fax 22-44-43-43; e-mail annick.coulibaly@ci.nestle.com; f. 1959; cap. 5,518m. francs CFA (Dec. 1998); subsidiary of Nestlé (Switzerland); production of coffee and cocoa products, manufacture and sale of food products; sales US $117.6m. (2001); Chair. GEORGES N'DIA KOFFI; Man. Dir VLADIMIR WENDL; 710 employees (2001).

Palmindustrie: Pointe des Fumeurs, 01 BP V239, Abidjan 01; tel. 21-27-00-70; fax 21-25-47-00; f. 1969; cap. 34,000m. francs CFA; development of palm, coconut and copra products; Man. Dir BONIFACE NAMA BRITO; 10,700 employees (2001).

Plantations et Huileries de la Côte d'Ivoire (PHCI): 01 BP 715, Dabou; tel. and fax 23-57-27-15; f. 1954; production of palm oil; 82.64% owned by Blohorn HSL; Chair. PIERRE BONNEIL; Pres. and Dir-Gen. GEORGES BROU; 530 employees (2001).

Produits Ruraux de Négoce Côte d'Ivoire (PRN CI): rue de Textile, Zone Industrielle de Vridi, 01 BP 3836, Abidjan 01; tel. 21-27-00-60; fax 21-27-00-64; processing, storage and marketing of cocoa and coffee; Man. Dir THOMAS SEGUI.

Puma Energy Côte d'Ivoire SA: rue de Canal de Vridi 15, 15 BP 522, Abidjan 15; tel. 21-27-00-72; fax 21-27-02-41; petroleum; Dir-Gen. KABLAN N'ZI.

Shell Côte d'Ivoire: Zone Industrielle de Vridi, 15 BP 378, Abidjan 15; tel. 21-27-00-18; fax 21-27-24-99; internet www.shell.com/home/Framework?siteId=ci-en; f. 1974; cap. 3,150m. francs CFA, sales 62,618m. francs CFA (1999); 67% owned by Royal Dutch Shell (Netherlands); distribution of petroleum products; Pres. HONORÉ DAINHI.

SIFCA: rue des Thomiers, 01 BP 1289, Abidjan 01; tel. 21-75-75-75; fax 21-25-45-65; e-mail communication@sifca.ci; internet www.groupesifca.com; f. 1964; export of cocoa and coffee; sales US $677.9m. (2000); Pres. JEAN-LOUIS BILLON; Dir-Gen. YVES LAMBELIN; 17,000 employees.

Société Africaine de Cacao (SACO): Zone 4, site 6, rue Pierre et Marie Curie, 01 BP 1045, Abidjan 01; tel. 21-75-02-00; fax 21-35-94-96; f. 1956; cap. 1,733m. francs CFA; 65% owned by Groupe Barry Callebaut (France/Belgium), 35% state-owned; sale of state holding pending; mfrs of cocoa powder, chocolate products, cocoa butter and oil-cake; Dir-Gen. DIDIER BUECHER; 700 employees (2001).

Société Africaine de Plantations d'Hévéas (SAPH): 01 BP 1322, Abidjan 01; tel. 20-21-18-91; fax 20-22-18-67; e-mail saphci@globeaccess.net; f. 1956; cap. 14,593m. francs CFA (2009); 65.76% owned by Société Internationale des Plantations d'Hévéas (France); production of rubber on 18,324 ha of plantations; sales US $28.9m. (2000); Dir-Gen. BANGA AMOIKON; 2,763 employees (2008).

Société des Caoutchoucs de Grand-Béréby (SOGB): 17 BP 18, Abidjan 17; tel. 20-21-99-47; fax 20-33-25-80; f. 1979; 15% state-owned; rubber plantations and processing; cap. 21,602m. francs CFA; sales US $31.4m. (2001); Pres. FULGENCE KOFFI; Gen. Man. MARC MUTSAARS; 4,000 employees (2002).

Société de Conserves de Côte d'Ivoire (SCODI): Quai de Pêche, Zone Industrielle de Vridi, 01 BP 677, Abidjan 01; tel. 21-25-66-74; fax 21-25-07-52; f. 1960; cap. 908m. francs CFA; tuna canning; restructured 2006; Chair. PAUL ANTONIETTI; Gen. Man. FRANCIS AMBROISE.

Société de Construction et d'Exploitation d'Installations Frigorifiques (SOCEF): Port de Pêche, 04 BP 154, Abidjan 04; tel. 21-35-54-42; f. 1962; cap. 900m. francs CFA; mfrs of refrigeration units; Dir GÉRARD CLEMENT.

Société Cotonnière Ivoirienne (COTIVO): 01 BP 4037, Abidjan; tel. 23-51-70-01; fax 23-51-73-34; f. 1972; cap. 3,600m. francs CFA; textile complex; 27% state-owned; Pres. MICHEL HEMONNOT; Man. Dir NOËL BROU KOUAMÉ.

Société de Galvanisation de Tôles en Côte d'Ivoire (Tôles Ivoire): rue du Textile, 15 BP 144, Abidjan 15; tel. 21-21-42-00; fax 21-27-43-24; e-mail ivoiral@globeaccess.net; f. 1970; cap. 2,009m. francs CFA; mfrs of corrugated sheets for roofing; aluminium household articles; adhesives and industrial glues; paints and varnish; Pres. and Dir-Gen. MARC FLIS.

Société de Gestion des Stocks Pétroliers de Côte d'Ivoire (GESTOCI): blvd de Vridi, 15 BP 89, Abidjan 15; tel. 21-75-98-00; fax 21-27-17-82; f. 1983; management of petroleum stocks; cap. 240m. francs CFA (June 2002); Man. Dir ATSÉ BENJAMIN YAPO; 187 employees (June 2002).

Société Ivoirienne de Béton Manufacturé (SIBM): 12 rue Thomas Edison, 01 BP 902, Abidjan 01; tel. 21-35-52-71; fax 21-35-82-27; e-mail sibm@ivoireb.com; internet www.sibmci.com; f. 1978; cap. 800m. francs CFA; mem. of Société Africaine de Béton Manufacturé group; mfrs of concrete; Man. Dir DANIEL PAUL.

Société Ivoirienne de Câbles (SICABLE): Zone Industrielle de Vridi, 15 BP 35, Abidjan 15; tel. 21-27-57-35; fax 21-27-12-34; e-mail sicable@globeaccess.net; f. 1975; 51% owned by Pirelli SpA (Italy); mfrs of electricity cables; cap. 740m. francs CFA; sales 7,105m. francs CFA (2009); Chair. ANDRÉ BOURG; Man. Dir CLAUDE REAU; 89 employees (2002).

Société Ivoirienne de Ciments et Matériaux (SOCIMAT): blvd du Port, 01 BP 887, Abidjan 01; tel. 21-75-51-00; fax 21-75-51-18; e-mail marfil@cimbelier.ci; internet www.cimbelier.ci; f. 1952; cap. 707m. francs CFA; clinker-crushing plant; Man. Dir JOHANN PACHLER.

Société Ivoirienne de Raffinage (SIR): blvd de Petit-Bassam, Vridi, 01 BP 1269, Abidjan 01; tel. 21-27-01-60; fax 21-27-17-98; e-mail info@sir.ci; internet www.sir.ci; f. 1962; 48% owned by PETROCI; operates petroleum refinery at Abidjan; cap. 39m. francs CFA, sales 107,895m. francs CFA (2006); Pres. NOËL AKOSSI BENDJO; Dir-Gen. JOËL DERVAIN; 674 employees (2006).

Société Ivoirienne des Tabacs (SITAB): Zone Industrielle, 01 BP 607, Bouaké 01; tel. 20-20-23-12; fax 31-63-46-80; f. 1956; cap. 4,489m. francs CFA (Dec. 1998); mfrs of cigarettes; Chair. FRANÇOISE AIDARA; Man. Dir PIERRE MAGNE; 830 employees (2000).

Société de Limonaderies et Brasseries d'Afrique (SOLIBRA): 27 rue du Canal, 01 BP 1304, Abidjan; tel. 21-24-91-33; fax 21-35-97-91; f. 1955; mfrs of beer, lemonade and ice at Abidjan and Bouaflé; cap. 4,110m. francs CFA; sales US $96.5m. (2001); Pres. PIERRE CASTEL; Dir-Gen. JEAN-CLAUDE PALU; 600 employees (2001).

Société des Mines d'Ity (SMI): ave Joseph Blohorn, Impasse des Chevaliers de Malte, Cocody, 08 BP 872, Abidjan 08; tel. 22-44-63-63; fax 22-44-41-00; e-mail smiphp@aviso.ci; f. 1989; cap. 600m. francs CFA; 51% owned by COGEMA, 49% by SODEMI; mining of gold reserves (2.0 metric tons per year) at Ity; Pres. ABDOULAYE KONÉ; Man. Dir DANIEL YAÏ.

Société Multinationale de Bitumes (SMB): blvd de Petit-Bassam, Zone Industrielle de Vridi, 12 BP 622, Abidjan 12; tel. 21-23-70-70; fax 21-27-05-18; e-mail info.smb@siz.ci; internet www.smbci.ci; f. 1978; cap. 1,218m. francs CFA (Dec. 1998); 53% owned by SIR; Pres. YVES HYACINTHE DJERE BOHA; Dir-Gen. THOMAS POGABAHA CAMARA; 50 employees (2000).

Société Nationale Ivoirienne de Travaux (SONITRA): route d'Abobo, 01 BP 2609, Abidjan 01; tel. 20-30-58-58; fax 20-37-14-00; e-mail info@sonitra.ci; internet www.sonitra.ci; f. 1963; cap. 2,273m. francs CFA; 55% state-owned; building and construction; Gen. Man. SHAUL LAHAT; 1,393 employees.

Société Nouvelle Abidjanaise de Carton Ondulé (SONACO): Zone Industrielle de Yopougon, 01 BP 1119, Abidjan; tel. 23-51-52-00; fax 23-46-65-06; e-mail directiongenerale@sonaco.com.ci; internet www.rossmann.com/fr/implantations/international/sonaco.html; f. 1963; cap. 1,200m. francs CFA; mfrs of paper goods and corrugated cardboard; owned by Groupe Rossman (France); Dir-Gen. JEAN-MICHEL RUEDA; 188 employees (2007).

Société de Stockage de Côte d'Ivoire (STOCACI): rue des Thoniers, Zone Portuaire, 01 BP 1798, Abidjan 01; f. 1980; cap. 1,000m. francs CFA; treatment and storage of cocoa and other products; Chair. JEAN ABILE GAL; Vice-Chair. and Man. Dir MADELEINE TCHICAYA.

Société Sucrière de la Côte d'Ivoire (SUCRIVOIRE): 16 ave du Docteur Crozet, 01 BP 2164, Abidjan 01; tel. 20-21-04-79; fax 20-21-07-75; f. 1997 following majority privatization of Société pour le Développement des Cannes à Sucre, l'Industrialisation et la Commercialisation du Sucre (SODESUCRE); 45% state-owned; sugar production; Chair. and Man. Dir JOSEPH KOUAMÉ KRA.

Société de Tubes d'Acier et Aluminium en Côte d'Ivoire (SOTACI): Zone Industrielle de Yopougon, 01 BP 2747, Abidjan 01; tel. 23-51-54-54; fax 23-46-69-25; e-mail sotaci@sotaci.co.ci; internet www.sotaci.ci; f. 1977; cap. 3,461m. francs CFA; sales US

$66.8m. (2006); mfrs of steel and aluminium tubing and pipes; Pres. and Dir-Gen. ADHAM EL-KHALIL; Man. Dir DOMINIQUE MARCHAL; 800 employees.

Total Côte d'Ivoire: 01 BP 555, Abidjan 01; tel. 20-22-27-29; fax 20-21-82-52; f. 1967; petroleum marketing and distribution; fmrly Elf Oil-CI, subsequently renamed TotalFinaElf Côte d'Ivoire, present name adopted 2003; subsidiary of Total (France); cap. 3,148.1m. francs CFA; sales US $200.5m. (2001); Pres. FRANCIS JAN; Dir-Gen. CHRISTOPHE GIRARDOT; 93 employees (2002).

TRITURAF: 01 BP 1485, Bouaké 01; tel. 31-63-26-42; fax 31-63-17-91; f. 1973; fmrly Société Ivoirienne de Trituration de Graines Oléagineuses et de Raffinage d'Huiles Végétales; 60% owned by Unilever, Netherlands/United Kingdom; operations in Bouaké suspended following outbreak of civil conflict in 2002; processing of cotton; cap. 2,600m. francs CFA (Dec. 1999); Pres. RIK BOSMAN; 342 employees (2001).

Unilever Côte d'Ivoire (Blohorn HSL): 01 BP 1751, Abidjan 01; tel. 21-24-90-60; fax 21-24-68-14; f. 1932; cap. 6,040m. francs CFA; 90% owned by Unilever Group (Netherlands/United Kingdom); fmrly Blohorn Huilerie-Savonnerie-Lipochimie (Blohorn HSL); production and marketing of edible oils, incl. margarine, and of palm oil products, incl. soap; sales US $208m. (2006); Chair. MARC DESENFANS; 740 employees (2006).

Union Industrielle Textile de Côte d'Ivoire (UTEXI): Zone Industrielle de Vridi, 15 BP 414, Abidjan 15; tel. 21-27-44-81; fax 21-27-16-16; f. 1972; cap. 3,700m. francs CFA; 12.75% state-owned; spinning and weaving mill at Dimbokro; operations suspended from 2002; Chair. JACQUES ROSSIGNOL; Man. Dir NOBOYUKI YOSHIDA.

Union Ivoirienne de Traitement de Cacao (UNICAO): Zone Industrielle de Vridi, 15 BP 406, Abidjan 15; tel. 21-27-14-49; fax 21-27-56-82; e-mail unicao@globeaccess.net; f. 1989; cap. 6,000m. francs CFA; owned by Archer Daniels Midland Co (USA); processing of cocoa beans; Man. Dir H. KORNER; 263 employees (2001).

Uniwax: Zone Industrielle de Yopougon, 01 BP 3994, Abidjan 01; tel. 23-46-64-15; fax 23-46-69-42; e-mail uniwax@odaci.net; f. 1967; mfrs of batik fabrics; owned by Vlisco Group (Netherlands); cap. 1,750m. francs CFA; sales US $34.8m. (2001); Pres. and Dir-Gen. JEAN-LOUIS MENUDIER; 540 employees (2002).

TRADE UNIONS

Dignité: 03 BP 2031, Abidjan 03; tel. 21-37-74-89; fax 20-37-85-00; e-mail dignite@aviso.ci; Sec.-Gen. BASILE MAHAN-GAHE; 10,000 mems (2001).

Fédération des Syndicats Autonomes de la Côte d'Ivoire (FESACI): Abidjan; breakaway group from the Union Générale des Travailleurs de Côte d'Ivoire; Sec.-Gen. TRAORÉ DOHIA MAMADOU.

Union Générale des Travailleurs de Côte d'Ivoire (UGTCI): 05 BP 1203, Abidjan 05; tel. and fax 21-24-09-78; fax 20-24-08-83; e-mail ugtcisg@yahoo.fr; internet www.ugtci.org; f. 1962; Sec.-Gen. FRANÇOIS ADE MENSAH; 100,000 individual mems; 157 affiliated unions.

Transport

RAILWAYS

The rail network in Côte d'Ivoire totalled 1,316 km in 2000, including 660 km of track from Abidjan to Niangoloko, on the border with Burkina Faso; from there, the railway extends to Kaya, via the Burkinabè capital, Ouagadougou. Work on a 737-km railway project linking San-Pédro with the western parts of the country was expected to begin in 2014.

SITARAIL—Transport Ferroviaire de Personnel et de Marchandises: Résidence Memanou, blvd Clozel, Plateau, 16 BP 1216, Abidjan 16; tel. 20-20-80-00; fax 20-22-48-47; f. 1995 to operate services on Abidjan–Ouagadougou–Kaya (Burkina Faso) line; Man. Dir PIERRE MARTINEAU.

ROADS

In 2004 there were about 80,000 km of roads, of which some 6,500 km were paved. Some 68,000m. francs CFA was invested in the road network in 1994–98; projects included the upgrading of 3,000 km of roads and 30,000 km of tracks. Tolls were introduced on some roads in the mid-1990s, to assist in funding the maintenance of the network.

Fonds d'Entretien Routier (FER): 04 BP 3089, Abidjan 04; tel. 20-31-13-05; e-mail fer@aviso.ci; f. 2001; Dir-Gen. PHILIPPE GOTH.

Société des Transports Abidjanais (SOTRA): 01 BP 2009, Abidjan 01; tel. 21-24-90-80; fax 21-25-97-21; e-mail infos@sotra.ci; internet www.sotra.ci; f. 1960; 60% state-owned; urban transport; Dir-Gen. BOUAKÉ MÉITÉ.

SHIPPING

Côte d'Ivoire has two major ports, Abidjan and San-Pédro, both of which are industrial and commercial establishments with financial autonomy. Abidjan, which handled some 14.5m. metric tons of goods in 2003, is the largest container and trading port in West Africa. Access to the port is via the 2.7-km Vridi Canal. The port at San-Pédro, which handled 1.2m. tons of goods in 1999, remains the main gateway to the south-western region of Côte d'Ivoire. As a result of widespread civil unrest from September 2002, much international freight transport that formerly left or entered the West African region through ports in Côte d'Ivoire was transferred to neighbouring countries. At 31 December 2009 the country's merchant fleet comprised 35 vessels, with a total displacement of 9,200 grt.

Port Autonome d'Abidjan (PAA): BP V85, Abidjan; tel. 21-23-80-00; fax 21-23-80-80; e-mail info@paa-ci.org; internet www.paa-ci.org; f. 1992; transferred to private ownership in 1999; Pres. ANGE-FRANÇOIS BARRY-BATTESTI; Man. Dir HIEN SIÉ.

Port Autonome de San-Pédro (PASP): BP 339/340, San-Pédro; tel. 34-71-72-00; fax 34-71-72-15; e-mail pasp@pasp.ci; internet addns3@gmail.com; f. 1971; Pres. YÉBARTH LUCIEN; Man. Dir HILAIRE MARCEL LAMIZANA.

AMICI: Km 1, blvd de Marseille, 16 BP 643, Abidjan 16; tel. 21-35-28-50; fax 21-35-28-53; e-mail amici.abj@aviso.ci; f. 1998; 45% owned by Ivorian interests, 25% by Danish interests, 20% by German interests and 10% by French interests.

Compagnie Maritime Africaine—Côte d'Ivoire (COMAF—CI): rond-point du Nouveau Port, 08 BP 867, Abidjan 08; tel. 20-32-40-77; f. 1973; navigation and management of ships; Dir FRANCO BERNARDINI.

SAGA Côte d'Ivoire: rond-point du Nouveau Port, 01 BP 1727, Abidjan 01; tel. 21-23-23-23; fax 21-24-25-06; f. 1959; merchandise handling, transit and storage; privately owned; Pres. M. GEORGES; Dir-Gen. DAVID CHARRIER.

SDV—Côte d'Ivoire (SDV—CI): 01 BP 4082, Abidjan 01; tel. 20-20-20-20; fax 20-20-21-20; f. 1943; sea and air transport; storage and warehousing; affiliated to Groupe Bolloré (France); Pres. GILLES CUCHE.

Société Agence Maritime de l'Ouest Africain—Côte d'Ivoire (SAMOA—CI): rue des Gallions, 01 BP 1611, Abidjan 01; tel. 20-21-29-65; f. 1955; shipping agents; Man. Dir CLAUDE PERDRIAUD.

Société Ivoirienne de Navigation Maritime (SIVOMAR): 5 rue Charpentier, Zone 2B, Treichville, 01 BP 1395, Abidjan 01; tel. 20-21-73-23; fax 20-32-38-53; f. 1977; shipments to ports in Africa, the Mediterranean and the Far East; Dir SIMPLISSE DE MESSE ZINSOU.

Société Ouest-Africaine d'Entreprises Maritimes en Côte d'Ivoire (SOAEM—CI): 01 BP 1727, Abidjan 01; tel. 20-21-59-69; fax 20-32-24-67; f. 1978; merchandise handling, transit and storage; Chair. JACQUES PELTIER; Dir JACQUES COLOMBANI.

SOCOPAO–Côte d'Ivoire: Km 1, blvd de la République, 01 BP 1297, Abidjan 01; tel. 21-24-13-14; fax 21-24-21-30; shipping agents; Shipping Dir OLIVIER RANJARD.

CIVIL AVIATION

There are three international airports: Abidjan–Félix Houphouët-Boigny, Bouaké and Yamoussoukro. In addition, there are 25 domestic and regional airports, including those at Bouna, Korhogo, Man, Odienné and San-Pédro.

Autorité Nationale de l'Aviation Civile: 07 BP 148, Abidjan 07; tel. 21-27-74-24; fax 21-27-63-46; internet www.anac.ci; civil aviation authority; Dir JEAN KOUASSI ABONOUAN.

Air Côte d'Ivoire: Immeuble République, pl. de la République, 01 BP 7782, Abidjan 01; tel. 20-25-15-61; fax 20-32-04-90; f. 2012 to replace Air Ivoire (f. 1960); 50% state-owned; 20% owned by Air France, 23.58%.

Air Inter Ivoire: Aéroport de Port Bouët, 07 BP 62, Abidjan 07; tel. 21-27-84-65; internal flights.

Tourism

The game reserves, forests, lagoons, coastal resorts, rich ethnic folklore and the lively city of Abidjan are tourist attractions; Côte d'Ivoire also has well-developed facilities for business visitors, including golfing centres. Some 301,000 tourists visited Côte d'Ivoire in 1998; receipts from tourism in that year totalled US $331m. In 2002 receipts from tourism totalled $490m. Tourism was negatively affected by instability from the late 1990s, most recently as a result of the violence that followed the disputed presidential run-off election of November 2010.

Office Ivoirien du Tourisme et de l'Hôtellerie: Immeuble ex-EECI, pl. de la République, 01 BP 8538, Abidjan 01; tel. 20-25-16-00; fax 20-32-03-88; internet oith@tourismeci.org; internet tourismeci.org; f. 1992; Dir CAMILLE KOUASSI.

Defence

As assessed at November 2010, Côte d'Ivoire's active armed forces comprised an army of 6,500 men, a navy of about 900, an air force of 700, a paramilitary presidential guard of 1,350 and a gendarmerie of 7,600. There was also a 1,500-strong militia, and reserve forces numbered 10,000 men. Military service is by selective conscription and lasts for 18 months. In late February 2004 the UN Security Council established the UN Operation in Côte d'Ivoire (UNOCI) for an initial period of 12 months from early April, with an authorized military strength of 6,240. The mandate of the operation was periodically extended until July 2009, although in January that year the Security Council also agreed, in view of the improved security situation in Côte d'Ivoire, to reduce the authorized military strength of UNOCI from 8,115 to 7,450. However, following the disputed presidential election of November 2010 and a subsequent increase in violence in the country, the mandate of UNOCI was extended until 30 June 2011 and in January the Security Council approved the deployment of an additional 2,000 military personnel, bringing the total authorized strength of UNOCI to 10,650. In July 2012 the UN Security Council extended the mandate of the operation until 31 July 2013 and reduced its strength to 10,400.

Defence Expenditure: Estimated at 152,000m. francs CFA in 2011.

Chief of Staff of the Armed Forces: Gen. SOUMAILA BAKAYOKO.

Commander of Land-based Forces: Col SÉKOU TOURÉ.

Commander of the Navy: Frigate Capt. DJAKARIDJA KONATÉ.

Commander of the Air Force: Maj.-Col JEAN-JACQUES RÉNÉ OUEGNIN.

Education

Education at all levels is available free of charge. Primary education, which is officially compulsory for six years between the ages of seven and 13 years, begins at six years of age and lasts for six years. According to UNESCO estimates, enrolment at primary schools in 2008/09 included 61% of children in the relevant age-group (males 67%; females 56%). Secondary education, from the age of 12, lasts for up to seven years, comprising a first cycle of four years and a second cycle of three years. In 2001/02 total enrolment at secondary level was equivalent to 27% of children in the relevant age-group (males 35%; females 19%), according to UNESCO estimates. The Université de Cocody (formerly the Université Nationale de Côte d'Ivoire), in Abidjan, has six faculties, and there are two other universities, at Abodo-Adjamé (also in Abidjan) and at Bouaké. In 2006 there were 18 private universities and 120 private grande écoles in the country. The country's first Islamic university, Université Musulmane de Côte d'Ivoire (UMCI), was opened in 2009. Some 156,772 students were enrolled at tertiary-level institutions in 2006/07. In 2008 spending on education represented 24.6% of total budgetary expenditure.

Bibliography

Abo, F. K. *Pour un véritable réflexe patriotique en afrique: Le cas ivoirien.* Paris, L'Harmattan, 2002.

Akindès, F. *The Roots of the Military-political Crises in Cote D'Ivoire.* Uppsala, Nordic African Institute, 2004.

Côte d'Ivoire: la réinvention de soi dans la violence. Dakar, CODESRIA, 2011.

Bailly, D. *La restauration du multipartisme en Côte d'Ivoire: ou la double mort d'Houphouët-Boigny.* Paris, L'Harmattan, 1995.

Bassett, T. J. *The peasant cotton revolution in West Africa: Cote d'Ivoire, 1880-1995.* Cambridge, Cambridge University Press, 2001.

Baulin, J. *La succession d'Houphouët-Boigny.* Paris, Editions Karthala, 2000.

Bédié, H. Konan. *Les chemins de ma vie: Entretiens avec Eric Laurent.* Paris, Plon, 1999.

Boa-Thiémélé, R. L. *L'Ivoirité entre culture et politique.* Paris, L'Harmattan, 2003.

Boni, T. (Ed.). *Africulture 56: Côte d'Ivoire: le pari de la diversité.* Paris, L'Harmattan, 2003.

Charvin, R. *Côte d'Ivoire 2011: La bataille de la seconde indépendance.* Paris, L'Harmattan, 2011.

Contamin, B., and Fauré, Y.-A. *La bataille des entreprises publiques en Côte d'Ivoire: L'histoire d'un ajustement interne.* Paris, Editions Karthala, 1990.

Coulibaly, A. A. *Le système politique ivoirien de la colonie à la IIe République.* Paris, L'Harmattan, 2002.

Coulibaly, L. G. *Côte-d'Ivoire: Au coeur du bois sacré.* Paris, L'Harmattan, 2004.

Cruise O'Brien, D. B., Dunn, J., and Rathbone, R. (Eds). *Contemporary West African States.* Cambridge, Cambridge University Press, 1989.

Daniels, M. *Côte d'Ivoire.* Santa Barbara, CA, ABC Clio, 1996.

Diabaté, I., Dembele, O., and Akindes, F. (Eds). *Intellectuels ivoiriens face à la crise.* Paris, Editions Karthala, 2005.

Diarra, S. *Les faux complots d'Houphouët-Boigny.* Paris, Editions Karthala, 1997.

Doh-Djanhoundy, T. *Autopsie de la crise ivoirienne: la nation au coeur du conflit.* Paris, L'Harmattan, 2006.

Du Parge, A. *Parmi les rebelles: carnets de route en Côte d'Ivoire, 19 septembre 2002–19 septembre 2003.* Paris, L'Harmattan, 2003.

Dubresson, A. *Villes et industries en Côte d'Ivoire. Pour une géographie de l'accumulation urbaine.* Paris, Editions Karthala, 1989.

Ellenbogen, A. *Succession d'Houphouët-Boigny: Entre tribalisme et démocratie.* Paris, L'Harmattan, 2003.

Fauré, Y. A., and Médard, J.-F. *Etat et bourgeoisie en Côte d'Ivoire.* Paris, Editions Karthala, 1983.

Gbagbo, L. *Côte d'Ivoire: Fonder une nation africaine démocratique et socialiste en Côte d'Ivoire.* Paris, L'Harmattan, 1999.

Gombeaud, J.-L., Moutout, C., and Smith, S. *La Guerre du cacao, histoire secrète d'un embargo.* Paris, Calmann-Lévy, 1990.

Harrison Church, R. J. *West Africa.* 8th edn. London, Longman, 1979.

Hilaire, G. G. *Le rempart: attaque terroriste contre la Côte d'Ivoire.* Paris, L'Harmattan, 2004.

International Crisis Group. *Côte d'Ivoire: Can the Ouagadougou Agreement Bring Peace?* Brussels, ICG Publications, 2007.

Jarret, M. F., and Mahieu, F.-R. *La Côte d'Ivoire de la destabilisation à la refondation.* Paris, L'Harmattan, 2002.

Kokora, P. D. *Le Front populaire ivoirien: de la clandestinité à la légalité: le vécu d'un fondateur.* Paris, L'Harmattan, 1999.

Koné, A. *Houphouët Boigny et la Crise ivoirienne.* Paris, Editions Karthala, 2003.

Konseiga, A., Heidhues, F., and von Braun, J. *Regional Integration Beyond the Traditional Trade Benefits: Labor Mobility Contribution: The Case of Burkina Faso and Cote D'Ivoire (Development Economics & Policy).* Bern, Peter Lang, 2005.

Le Pape, M., and Vital, C. (Eds). *Côte d'Ivoire: l'année terrible, 1999–2000.* Paris, Editions Karthala, 2002.

Lisette, G. *Le Combat du Rassemblement Démocratique Africain.* Paris, Présence Africaine, 1983.

Lubeck, P. M. (Ed.). *The African Bourgeoisie: Capitalist Development in Nigeria, Kenya, and the Ivory Coast.* Boulder, CO, Lynne Rienner Publishers, 1987.

McGovern, M. *Making War in Côte D'Ivoire.* London, C. Hurst & Co, 2011.

Miran, M. *Islam, histoire et modernité en Côte d'Ivoire.* Paris, Editions Karthala, 2006.

Nandjui, P. *Houphouët-Boigny: l'homme de la France en Afrique.* Paris, L'Harmattan, 1995.

La prééminence constitutionnelle du Président de la République en Côte d'Ivoire. Paris, L'Harmattan, 2004.

Navarro, R. *Côte d'Ivoire: Le culte du blanc: Les territoires culturels et leurs frontières.* Paris, L'Harmattan, 2003.

Ouedraogo, J-B., and Sall, E. (Eds). *Frontieres de la Citoyennete et Violence Politique en Côte D'Ivoire.* Dakar, CODESRIA, 2008.

Rapley, J. *Ivorien Capitalism: African Entrepreneurs in Côte d'Ivoire.* London, Lynne Rienner Publishers, 1993.

World Bank. *Côte d'Ivoire Living Standards Survey: Design and Implementation.* Washington, DC, International Bank for Reconstruction and Development, 1986.

Zike, M. A. *Café / cacao: la rébellion ivoirienne contre les multinationales.* Abidjan, Edition Ami, 1990.

DJIBOUTI

Physical and Social Geography

I. M. LEWIS

The Republic of Djibouti is situated at the southern entrance to the Red Sea. It is bounded on the far north by Eritrea, on the west and south by Ethiopia, and on the south-east by Somalia. Djibouti covers an area of 23,200 sq km (8,958 sq miles), consisting mostly of volcanic rock-strewn desert wastes, with little arable land and spectacular salt lakes and pans. The climate is torrid, with high tropical temperatures and humidity during the monsoon season. The average annual rainfall is less than 125 mm. Only in the upper part of the basaltic range north of the Gulf of Tadjoura, where the altitude exceeds 1,200 m above sea-level, is there continuous annual vegetation.

At the census of May 2009 the population was officially estimated at 818,159. According to UN estimates, the population was 922,709 at mid-2012. In 1989 the capital town, Djibouti (whose port and railhead dominate the country's economy), had a population of about 329,337; by the 2009 census this was estimated to have risen to 475,322. The indigenous population is almost evenly divided between the Issa (who are of Somali origin) and the Afar, the former having a slight predominance. Both are Muslim Cushitic-speaking peoples with a traditionally nomadic economy and close cultural affinities, despite frequent local rivalry. The Afar inhabit the northern part of the country, the Issa the southern, and both groups span the artificial frontiers separating the Republic of Djibouti from Ethiopia, Eritrea and Somalia.

Since the development of the port of Djibouti in the early 1900s, the indigenous Issas have been joined by immigrants from the adjoining regions of Somalia. The Afar generally follow more restricted patterns of nomadic movement than the Issa, and a more hierarchical traditional political organization. While they formed a number of small polities, these were linked by the pervasive division running throughout the Afar population between the 'noble' Asaimara (or 'red') clans and the less prestigious Asdoimara (or 'white') clans. There is also a long-established Arab trading community. European expatriates are mainly French, mostly in government employment, commerce and the armed forces.

Recent History

WALTER S. CLARKE

INTRODUCTION

The Republic of Djibouti is a small country, which through its favourable location and pragmatic foreign policy has become a significant role-player in the troubled Horn of Africa. On the domestic front, there have been encouraging signs of political liberalization as a few candidates not associated with the pro-presidential Union pour la Majorité Présidentielle (UMP) won seats in municipal and regional elections held in January–February 2012. Djibouti's economy was, furthermore, expected to benefit from a rebuilt, standard-gauge railway to Dire Dawa and Addis Ababa (Ethiopia), and a new railway connecting Tigrai regional state in Ethiopia to a new port to be constructed at Tadjoura. There was also the prospect that Djibouti would soon also become an exporter of valuable minerals.

GEOGRAPHY AS ASSET

The Republic of Djibouti is a mini-state, but its leaders have worked creatively for years to stabilize the Horn of Africa. The two major ethnic groups in Djibouti, the Somali Issa sub-clan and the Afar, are minorities within much larger ethnic pools that stretch into Ethiopia, Kenya, Eritrea and Somalia. Other significant ethnic groups in Djibouti include the Somali sub-clans, the Gadabursi and Isaak, whose ethnic families originated in the former British Somaliland. The country has two official languages, French and Arabic, neither of which is native to the indigenous peoples of Djibouti. During its 35 years of independence Djibouti's two successive Somali leaders have been assiduous in naming members of other clans and ethnic groups to their Governments to demonstrate ethnic parity, while firmly discouraging anything that could be construed as formal opposition, dissent or disobedience.

Djibouti's leaders have been successful in securing foreign investment, owing to the attraction of the country's exclusive land and sea access to Ethiopia, and its strategic location at the southern end of the Red Sea and the north-western reaches of the Indian Ocean. The opening of the Suez Canal in 1869, and Britain's subsequent closure of facilities at Aden to French military vessels during France's Indo-Chinese conflicts, proved the utility of the French presence in the Horn of Africa. The coaling station established at Obock after 1862 served the French fleet during French campaigns in both Indo-China and Madagascar.

In 1884 Léonce Lagarde was appointed administrator of the territory of Obock. In 1888 the town of Djibouti was established on the southern coast of the Gulf of Tadjoura. It offered better anchorages and a more efficient location for caravans to begin the arduous trip to the highlands of southern Ethiopia. In 1892 the French administration was transferred from Obock to Djibouti, with Lagarde as Governor.

Governor Lagarde's energetic actions to expand the size of the French colony provided the foundations for the modern economy of Djibouti. In 1894 Emperor Menelik II of Ethiopia selected Djibouti to be his country's opening to the sea, and concluded a contract with the French to build a railway between Djibouti and Dire Dawa and on to the new Ethiopian capital, Addis Ababa. Lagarde secured Menelik's signature to a treaty on 20 March 1897, defining the border between the colony and Ethiopia, and stipulating that the port of Djibouti would handle Ethiopia's foreign trade. Work on the narrow-gauge railway began in 1897. In 1917 the railway reached Addis Ababa, building 781 km of track from sea level to 2,600 m in altitude. Only 97 km of track lie within the Republic of Djibouti.

MODERN POLITICS IN DJIBOUTI

British Somaliland became the first Somali dependency to achieve independence on 26 June 1960. The Italian UN Trust Territory of Somalia followed on 1 July 1960 and joined with the former British Somaliland that same day to form the Somali Republic, prompting French concerns over the expansion of pan-Somalism. As a result, the French authorities switched their political focus from the Somali Issas to the Afar population. A local Afar businessman, Ali Aref Bourhan, became President of the local government. When, in 1962, Hassan Gouled Aptidon, a senior Issa politician, returned from Paris, France (where he served as Djibouti's representative in the French Assemblée nationale), he found that his standing in Djibouti had eroded, and he was held responsible by many Issas for the decision of the French authorities to appoint an Afar to the most senior position in Djibouti.

In August 1966 a visit by French President Charles de Gaulle to Djibouti was marred by pro-independence protests, and de Gaulle declared that the Djibouti people would be given the opportunity to effect change if it was wanted. A referendum was held on 19 March 1967 to provide the inhabitants of French Somaliland with a choice of remaining within the French Republic or independence similar to that attained by Guinea in 1958. (After that country had chosen independence instead of membership of a proposed community of self-governing French overseas territories, the French had withdrawn abruptly and taken punitive economic reprisals.) There was heavy participation in the referendum, and those opposed to complete secession from the French Community won with 60% of the votes. On 5 July 1967 the French Government renamed French Somaliland the French Territory of the Afars and Issas. New elections to the local government were held on 29 July, and Ali Aref was again elected President.

Using money provided by the Somali Government, Gouled and his ally, a dissident leader of the Afar, Ahmed Dini Ahmed, participated in a number of visits to African countries and conferences to raise the profile of the Territory and to strengthen their campaign for independence. Within a year of its establishment, the Ligue Populaire Africaine pour l'Indépendance (LPAI) was recognized as the dominant political party by most potential voters and by the French Government. On 17 July 1976 Ali Aref resigned as Head of Government and was replaced by another Afar, Abdallah Mohamed Kamil, one of Djibouti's first university graduates and a notary.

Independence

In February 1977 the French Government sponsored a roundtable conference in Paris on the future of the Territory of the Afars and the Issas. Dates for a referendum on self-determination and eventual independence were set. At the roundtable sharp differences became apparent between Gouled and Ahmed Dini on the distribution of seats in the future legislature between Somalis, Afars and Arabs. Ahmed Dini and Abdallah Kamil wanted the distribution to be fixed in Paris, while Gouled wished to wait until after independence and make those decisions within Djibouti. Ahmed Dini's position prevailed, with 33 seats reserved for Somalis and 30 for Afars. Gouled subsequently developed a single list of candidates for the referendum and elections for the independent Assemblée nationale, scheduled to take place on 8 May. Gouled was elected as a representative of Djibouti town, and on 16 May he was selected by the new assembly as President of the government council; Gouled was sworn in at midnight on 26 June 1977, the eve of Djibouti's independence.

At independence there was still no document determining the responsibilities of the presidency or the roles of the members of the eventual government. It was unclear whether authority would be shared between the President and the Assemblée nationale or if the President would monopolize power. On 8 July 1977 President Gouled issued Ordinance Number One, which stated that the President would also serve as Head of Government. Gouled named Ahmed Dini as Prime Minister. Ahmed Dini accepted the nomination without enthusiasm, noting that the post of Prime Minister without power or responsibility was an empty gesture, and in December of the same year he, along with four other Afar ministers, resigned. The resignations were a bitter blow to President Gouled's hopes for meaningful Issa-Afar relations, and he did not make the departures publicly known until mid-January 1978. Abdallah Kamil was named as Prime Minister in February, also taking the foreign affairs and defence portfolios. President Gouled announced the dissolution of this Government in September, subsequently appointing Barkat Gourad Hamadou, an Afar from Dikhil, as Prime Minister. He was to remain in the post for 22 years until he resigned in February 2001 for health reasons. He was replaced in March by Dileita Mohamed Dileita, an Afar who had been a close associate of Ahmed Dini. More than a decade later, Dileita remains Prime Minister under Gouled's successor, Ismaïl Omar Guelleh.

THE AFAR INSURGENCY

During 1960–76 many Somali Issas found themselves systematically deprived of access to the territory's nationality and therefore unable to vote. The now flourishing township of Balbala, located just outside one of the former military gates to Djibouti town, owes its beginnings to those who could not prove that they were born in the former French Somaliland and thus were not permitted to live in Djibouti town. Although after independence President Gouled included Afars in his various governments, his fellow Issas quickly took charge of the administration and vastly increased their roles in commerce. Gouled had little patience with Afar complaints, but he maintained a paternalistic attitude towards potential opponents. He was re-elected President, unopposed, in June 1981 and April 1987.

Frustrations within the Afar community led to widespread affiliation with Ahmed Dini's Front pour la Restauration de l'Unité et de la Démocratie (FRUD) during the late 1980s and early 1990s. In late 1991 FRUD guerrillas overran a number of villages and military posts in the north and west of Djibouti. French forces in the country were strengthened, but their major role was in training the national army. The mutual defence treaty with France, signed at independence, could only be invoked in the event of a foreign invasion, and the French Government considered the Afar insurgency to be a domestic matter. The Djibouti Government claimed otherwise, but it considerably increased the size of its army, to more than 16,000, to respond to the civil war. By 1994 the war was consuming 35% of the national budget. In the early years of the conflict the FRUD occupied more than two-thirds of the national territory. The FRUD was permitted to register as a legal party in March 1996. Its radical wing, FRUD—Renaissance, led by Ahmed Dini, remained active and was subject to joint Djibouti-Ethiopian attacks in 1997 and in 1998. Some elements of the FRUD continue to recruit guerrillas and attack targets in northern Djibouti along the borders with Ethiopia and Eritrea.

President Gouled responded to the Afar-led civil war by cautiously initiating the establishment of a multi-party political system. He appointed a commission from his Rassemblement Populaire pour le Progrès (RPP), then the sole legal party, which proposed a new Constitution in March 1992. The draft Constitution, which permitted a maximum of four parties to contest the presidency and seats in the Assemblée nationale, and limited the President to two six-year terms of office, was submitted to a nation-wide referendum, reportedly receiving the approval of 97% of votes cast. The Afar opposition was somewhat appeased. By the 30 September deadline for party registration, however, only the RPP and one opposition group, the Parti du Renouveau Démocratique, were granted legal status. Elections to the Assemblée nationale were held on 18 December, and all 65 seats were won by the RPP. Five candidates contested the presidential election on 7 May 1993; Gouled received about 61% of the votes cast. Voter turn-out in both elections was only about 50%.

During 1995, while Gouled was hospitalized in France, a power struggle began between his nephew and principal adviser, Guelleh, and his long-time private secretary, Ismael Gedi Hared. In early 1999 Gouled announced that he would not contest the presidential election scheduled for April of that year. The RPP, which was then in alliance with a major faction within the FRUD, announced that Guelleh would represent the party. Guelleh secured a comfortable victory in the presidential election, taking 74.4% of the votes cast; he was opposed by Moussa Ahmed Idris, an independent candidate with support from two relatively minor parties.

THE GUELLEH PRESIDENCY

When Guelleh succeeded Gouled in April 1999, he inherited a political situation that remained highly regulated. As many observers expected, Guelleh established his new administration employing similar ethnic balances to those used by Gouled. In May Guelleh reappointed Gourad Hamadou as

Prime Minister; a new Council of Ministers was announced shortly afterwards. In September and October a number of charges were brought against a former senior military official, several former cabinet ministers, a number of defence lawyers and more than a dozen military personnel who had expressed an interest in a campaign of civil disobedience. French lawyers selected by defendants were unable to obtain visas to attend the proceedings.

The first significant political confrontation for the new President came in December 2000. Gen. Yacin Yabeh Gaab, commander of the Djibouti police force since independence, was informed that he was to be replaced the next day. A group of loyalists, including police officers, launched a coup against Guelleh and his Government, taking over the radio and television station and urging citizens to converge on the main military camp. However, few people turned out and, after a short confrontation, the military regained control. Yacin sought refuge in the French embassy, and after negotiations, in which Yacin was promised a fair trial, he was handed over to the local authorities.

In September 2002, to coincide with the 10th anniversary of the approval of the Constitution, the Government removed the constitutional limit on the number of permitted political parties. On 10 January 2003 nine parties, organized into two blocs, contested the legislative elections. According to official results, the UMP coalition, comprising the RPP, the legal FRUD, the Parti National Démocratique and the Parti Populaire Social Démocrate, secured 62.7% of the total votes cast, winning the majority of votes in each of the country's five constituencies, and took all 65 seats in the Assemblée nationale. Therefore, despite obtaining more than one-third of the votes cast, the opposition Union pour l'Alternance Démocratique (UAD) coalition, headed by Ahmed Dini, failed to secure any legislative representation. The UAD protested against the results, claiming that it should have won 22 seats, and demanded that the elections be annulled. In February, however, the Constitutional Council rejected the coalition's request. The UAD boycotted the presidential election in April 2005, in protest against Guelleh's rejection of a number of opposition demands. Consequently, Guelleh was the sole candidate in the election on 8 April, although he reportedly 'regretted' that he had no opponent; he was returned for a second term of office with 100% of votes cast, according to official figures. The UAD also boycotted legislative elections on 8 February 2008; these were thus contested solely by candidates from the UMP, which, according to official results, took 94.1% of the total votes cast and secured all 65 seats in the Assemblée nationale.

After the 2005 election President Guelleh stated that he had no intention of seeking a further term in office. In early 2008, however, he apparently reneged on this commitment, and a demonstration of his supporters, urging him to contest the next election, took place in Djibouti town. The further constitutional amendments that would be required for Guelleh to become eligible for re-election were met with widespread opposition, including from members of the governing RPP. As pressures grew on those objecting to the prospect of constitutional change, some public figures, among them a popular singer and a well-known poet, were arbitrarily imprisoned on charges of criticizing the Government. The director of Djibouti's state radio and television station, Abdi Atteyeh Abdi, was dismissed in July 2009, owing to his reported failure to support a third term for the President. In addition, Guelleh pre-emptively removed the President of the Constitutional Court, Mohamed Warsame Ragueh, and replaced him with a close relative and member of the Issa Mamassan sub-clan. Dissidents with resources outside the country, such as Abdourahman Boreh, a former close associate of the President, quickly fled into exile. Opposition groups in Europe and North America convened gatherings to condemn the President and Government of Djibouti. Boreh attempted to unify the opposition in Paris, but the exiled dissidents failed to agree on a programme or a joint candidate that could challenge the Djibouti domestic scene.

THE 2011 PRESIDENTIAL ELECTION

In April 2010 the Assemblée nationale adopted amendments to the Constitution that removed restrictions on the number of terms of office to be served by the President, imposed a 75-year age limit for prospective presidential candidates, reduced the presidential mandate from six years to five, provided for the creation of an upper legislative chamber, and abolished capital punishment. Plans to ensure that the presidential election, which was scheduled for 8 April 2011, proceeded smoothly appeared to be threatened when, on 5–6 February, hundreds of university and secondary school students protested in central Djibouti town and clashed with police attempting to restore order. The immediate cause of the rioting was serious disagreement over the grading of some law school examinations, but many observers believed that the recent successful protest movements in Tunisia and Egypt had encouraged the demonstrations. These disturbances were reportedly the largest such disorders in Djibouti since independence. A number of opposition activists were arrested in order to prevent a similar demonstration planned for 18 February, while the head of the Djibouti League of Human Rights, Jean-Paul Noël Abdi (who had reportedly attended the protest to oppose the use of live ammunition against the students), was detained on 8 February on charges of 'participating in an insurrection movement'.

Signs of anxiety within the Djibouti Government became even more clear with its evident exasperation at advice being given by Democracy International (DI), a non-governmental organization (NGO) funded by the US Agency for International Development (USAID), which produced a long list of recommendations following four preliminary visits to Djibouti in 2010. After returning to Djibouti in January 2011, DI advised the Government that public disinterest could affect voter participation. Its polling indicated that many Djiboutians had become disaffected with politics but that interest could be revived by having more than one candidate for election. DI recommended that some opposition participation in the national electoral commission would be a positive development, and that citizens be permitted to observe the elections, a practice that had never been adopted in Djibouti. DI also suggested that the Government should eliminate the custom of distributing money and other incentives to voters on the day of the election. In mid-March the Government abruptly cancelled the services of DI and ordered it to leave the country, claiming that the NGO was no longer neutral and that, in fact, its activities in Djibouti were illegal. After denouncing the accusations as 'preposterous', the US advisory team left the country.

Prior to the commencement of the official electoral campaign on 24 March 2011, all opposition party candidates withdrew from the poll, in protest against alleged state harassment and denial of access to media. After their withdrawal, all permits to hold public meetings were cancelled on the grounds that there was no necessity to hold rallies. Towards the end of the campaign former President of the Constitutional Court Ragueh emerged as an independent candidate for the presidency, in opposition to Guelleh.

The presidential election was held on 8 April 2011. According to the official results, published the following day, Guelleh was decisively re-elected, winning 80.6% of the votes. With just 152,000 registered voters, the turn-out was 69.7% of the eligible electorate. President Guelleh had stated shortly beforehand that he would not contest a further election. He was sworn in for his third term of office on 8 May, at a ceremony attended by many regional leaders and representatives.

President Guelleh announced his new Government on 12 May 2011. As in past administrations, there were some new appointees as well as eliminations and demotions—all of which were interpreted as clear signals about the changing mood of the President and his wife, Kadra Mahamoud Haïd, a Gadaboursi born in Djibouti. In total, 11 'heavyweights' were dropped from the cabinet, among them the ministers hitherto responsible for justice, education, housing, the interior, defence, energy, trade, communications and parliamentary relations. Their replacements tended to be younger, with the youngest being the Secretary of State for Youth and Sports, at 30 years of age. Three of the outgoing ministers were given ambassadorial appointments, and four others became technical advisers to either the President or Prime Minister Dileita.

SIGNS OF CHANGE?

As a means of building interest in electoral processes and to spark more development at local level, in 2008 the Government authorized regional and municipal elections. A second set of local elections was held in January 2012, and for the first time in Djibouti's history there were run-off elections when no clear winner emerged in two constituencies in Djibouti town. Neither of the winners in the second round was a member of a party affiliated with the governing UMP. One, Abdourahman Mohamed Guelleh 'TX', of the Rassemblement pour l'Action, le Développement et la Démocratie, was sworn in as the new mayor of Djibouti town on 18 March 2012. Immediately following the swearing-in ceremony the new young mayor visited the President, who congratulated him and exhorted him to serve the people well. (There was no indication in either the extensive favourable domestic or the uniformly negative foreign dissident press coverage that the President and mayor 'TX', who share the second patronymic of 'Guelleh', are related.)

FOREIGN AFFAIRS

Since taking office President Guelleh has been an active diplomat and peace-maker in the Horn of Africa. The breakdown of the Somali state in 1991 after the fall of Maj.-Gen. Mohammed Siad Barre, and the almost immediate effort by the former British Somaliland to regain its independence, remains the central issue of Djibouti's relations with Somalia. Djibouti generally maintains cordial relations with 'Somaliland', but these relations are periodically subject to strains due to Djibouti's reconciliation efforts in Somalia.

In September 1999 President Guelleh announced that Djibouti was ready to take on the issue of Somali reconciliation. He established a committee of 60 Somalis to represent themselves, rather than warlords, to act as advisers to the Government of Djibouti. They were asked to provide the foundation for a peace conference that began in Arta in May 2000. The first phase consisted of establishing an agenda and a participant list. The second phase began in June with 810 delegates, four delegations of 180 members each representing the major clan families, and a delegation of 90 members representing the smaller factions. The Arta talks ultimately failed as various Somali warlords refused to consider issues beyond their ethnic constituencies. President Guelleh has since made three additional attempts to foster Somali unity, most recently in November 2008.

Djibouti's relations with neighbouring Eritrea, which gained independence from Ethiopia in 1993, have always been strained. They reached a new low when Eritrea deployed troops onto Djibouti territory at Doumeira and Ras Doumeira, in the far north-east of the country, in April 2008. This was the third such incursion into Djibouti by Eritrean forces. In April 1996 there were clashes after Eritrean forces attacked Ras Doumeira, and in 1999 Eritrea accused Djibouti of supporting Ethiopia. The Eritreans first suggested that the 2008 actions were taken in response to movements of Ethiopian troops about 100 km away in the area of Mount Moussa Ali, where the borders of Ethiopia, Djibouti and Eritrea meet. For more than two years President Issaias Afewerki of Eritrea simply denied that his military was occupying Djibouti territory. According to observers, the Eritrean incursion was 7 km inside Djibouti's border and comprised as many as 4,000 Eritrean soldiers. Djibouti committed some 8,000 military personnel to the area, representing about two-thirds of its total armed forces. Fighting between the opposing forces broke out on 10 June 2008, when a number of Eritrean deserters reportedly escaped across the Djibouti border and Eritreans attempted to capture them. The aggressive Eritrean advances into Djibouti were strongly condemned by the UN Security Council, the League of Arab States, the African Union and the regional Intergovernmental Authority on Development (IGAD).

Following months of negotiations, mediation under the auspices of the Government of Qatar succeeded in securing the withdrawal of Eritrean forces from Djibouti territory in June 2010. Qatari troops subsequently monitored the border to ensure that no Eritrean troops returned. According to press reports, the agreement also contained undertakings from Eritrea to halt illegal arms shipments to Somalia, to cease inciting Afar tribesmen in northern Djibouti, and to pay compensation to Djibouti. Although Eritrea did remove its troops from Djibouti territory, President Afewerki has disregarded parts of the settlement.

Foreign Military Presence

France has maintained military forces in Djibouti for many years. At independence in 1977 there were approximately 4,000 French military personnel in the country: the 13th Demi-Brigade of the French Foreign Legion had been present since 1966. In addition to the Legionnaires, at independence there were 1,200 gendarmes, about 1,000 airforce personnel maintaining the last squadron of US-made F-100s still active in the world (subsequently replaced by more modern aircraft), and various naval personnel associated with the French Indian Ocean fleet. France subsequently withdrew the air wing and some of the ground forces; some 2,850 French military personnel were assigned to Djibouti under a mutual defence agreement signed at independence. This number declined with the transfer of the 13th Demi-Brigade of the French Foreign Legion from Djibouti to the United Arab Emirates in June 2011. France pays the Government of Djibouti €30m. annually for the right to maintain military facilities in the country.

Following the suicide attacks of 11 September 2001 on the mainland USA, there was a considerable broadening of counter-terrorism strategies world-wide. Among these actions, the US Administration stationed ships in the Indian Ocean and the Gulf of Aden to intercept terrorists who might attempt to escape Afghanistan to hide in ungoverned areas of Somalia. In November 2002 a joint task force was established as a seafaring command. In 2003 the Djibouti Government permitted the USA to establish a base at the former French Foreign Legion complex at Camp Lemonier. Designated the Combined Joint Task Force-Horn of Africa (CJTF-HOA), the new command was designed to foster improved defence, diplomacy and development, representing the Department of Defense, the Department of State and USAID. In 2012 there were some 2,000–2,500 US and allied personnel assigned to CJTF-HOA. In addition to its various military responsibilities, CJTF-HOA has been involved in dozens of civil action projects in Djibouti, Ethiopia and Kenya. The US base is also the headquarters for counter-terrorism efforts throughout East Africa.

Djibouti has become a major staging area for international air and naval forces that have joined efforts to oppose sea piracy in the Gulf of Aden and the Indian Ocean. Maritime reconnaissance aircraft from Germany, Spain, India, Japan and other nations now use the international airport to launch their anti-piracy operations. Djibouti port also supplies fuel and provisions to the many naval ships involved in anti-piracy patrols. In January 2009 Djibouti hosted a meeting of 17 countries from the Western Indian Ocean, the Gulf of Aden and the Red Sea. Convened by the International Maritime Organization, the states agreed on a document termed the Djibouti Code of Conduct, in which they declared themselves ready to co-operate to the fullest extent possible under international law to interdict, arrest and prosecute persons who have committed piracy. A regional meeting of the Djibouti Code of Conduct was held in the Yemeni capital, San'a, in July 2010. A Swedish helicopter wing began operations in April of that year. The Russian navy announced in May that it had no intention of building a base in Djibouti, but that its ships would continue to use the port of Djibouti.

In July 2011 the Japanese Maritime Self-Defense Force (MSDF) inaugurated in Djibouti its first overseas military base since the end of the Second World War. The MSDF had been present in the Horn of Africa since 2009, with two destroyers participating in maritime surveillance operations to counter sea piracy in the Gulf of Aden and the Indian Ocean. The base, constructed at a reported cost of €40m., is located on 12 ha of land just north of Djibouti's international airport, and includes an administrative building, a runway and hangars to service two PC-3 reconnaissance aircraft. Some 180 Japanese military personnel are assigned to the Djibouti base.

Economy

WALTER S. CLARKE

INTRODUCTION

The Republic of Djibouti is a small country, with a population of less than 1m. (the 2009 census recorded a population of 818,159, while the UN estimate for mid-2012 was 922,709), that has in recent years provided a fairly dependable surface outlet to the world for its very much larger neighbour, Ethiopia—sub-Saharan Africa's second largest country in terms of population. Substantial investments in port facilities and a much improved road system have benefited Ethiopia's trade links, as well as a number of Djibouti entrepreneurs and politicians. Several new projects are now planned that will considerably increase the importance of Djibouti as the commercial hub of the Horn of Africa. Nevertheless, a majority of its citizens remain poor and largely neglected by the state, to the concern of international humanitarian agencies and non-governmental organizations (NGOs).

Ethiopia aspires to become a middle-income country within the decade, and Djibouti is thus a vital component in Ethiopia's progress. The recent independence of South Sudan brought no agreement with its neighbour to the north on how to export its oil wealth, and the new country is now seeking alternative routes to the sea for its oil industry, thereby providing opportunities for Djibouti to play a key role. In the mean time, encouraging results for potential commercial exploitation of minerals with both Ethiopia and Djibouti bode well for greater co-operation in the Horn of Africa. As a small but critical player in the region, Djibouti has attracted the interest of the People's Republic of China, India, Turkey and other relative newcomers to trade and politics in the region.

According to the 2009 census, more than one-half of the population live in Djibouti town. The country's rural nomadic population make up a little more than one-third of the population. The remainder live in towns usually established along traditional trading routes and ports. Although Djibouti experienced an extraordinary boom in foreign investment in the late 2000s, primarily from the Arab Gulf states, more than one-half of Djibouti town's population lives below the internationally recognized poverty level of US $1.25 per day. Nomads are now mostly destitute, recovering slowly from the most severe drought in 60 years; they barely subsist on the lean benefits of their livestock, mostly camels and sheep, many of which would normally be exported to Saudi Arabia and Yemen to support the needs of the annual *Hajj* (pilgrimage to Mecca, Saudi Arabia). Virtually all of Djibouti's food supplies are imported, and, as in most poor countries, the rising costs of food in the world market place are creating enormous hardship. The Djibouti franc is pegged to the US dollar, and as the dollar has declined in value, import costs for Djibouti have increased proportionally.

Over most of its territory, the country physically presents either moon-like rocky desert or broad, dry plains with little vegetation. There are some forested areas in the north, most particularly the Forêt du Daï. There are no surface fresh water sources anywhere in Djibouti except during exceedingly rare rains, which may occur as infrequently as once in 18 months. The country endures very high daily temperatures, commonly exceeding 40°C, during at least 10 months of the year. Only in December and January are there periods of relatively mild, Mediterranean-like temperatures. The rugged climate fosters the toughness and resilience that characterizes the inhabitants of the country.

POLITICS AND BUSINESS

In Djibouti there appears to be no prohibition against politicians engaging in private business interests. The President, Ismaïl Omar Guelleh, his wife and their two daughters all have extensive roles in industry, especially in construction. Opportunities for profitable business are often made available to loyal supporters; the reverse is also true for those politician-entrepreneurs who fall out of favour. The most extreme case of the latter remains that of Abdourahman Boreh, a former long-term friend and business associate of President Guelleh. Boreh decided to test the political scene before running to succeed the President. He may have confided this interest to his old friend prematurely because, at that time, apparently in mid-2008, Guelleh was already planning to have the Constitution amended to permit him to run for a third term in 2011. Boreh, who was reviled by many Djiboutians because, as the wealthiest businessman in the country, he was thought to be a corrupting influence on the President and his extended family, was quickly forced out of the country, and his companies were all forfeited to the state. He was subsequently tried *in absentia* in Djibouti for alleged terrorism, found guilty and sentenced to 15 years' imprisonment.

According to an IMF report on a mission to Djibouti, conducted in October 2011, details of which were leaked to the press by the national human rights league, the Government of Djibouti was in the process of disposing systematically of all partnerships contracted with the emirate of Dubai through the offices of Boreh. These include the management contract for Djibouti's international airport, the customs service contract for the port and airport, and the special tax exemptions accorded to a luxury hotel built by Dubai's Nakheel Group. Only the new container port at Doraleh was left under the management of Dubai Ports World (DP World) because it was considered too large to hand over to another operator. Efforts were made to extradite Boreh from Dubai in 2010, although these were apparently ignored by the authorities there. In 2011 an extradition request was made to Spanish authorities while Boreh was in Tenerife. He was held in custody for four days in the Canary Islands, but, after several months of investigations, the Spanish authorities decided that there was a strong political component to the Djibouti case, and the request was denied.

In view of the situation in Djibouti, DP World was reported to be working to take over expansion and management of the port of Berbera in 'Somaliland', with the eventual aim of making it the major gateway port for Ethiopia.

ECONOMIC PERFORMANCE

The Government of Djibouti maintains a close and generally co-operative relationship with the IMF, the World Bank and other international financial institutions.

An IMF mission to Djibouti in March 2012 was devoted to a final review of the country's performance under an Extended Credit Facility (ECF) signed in September 2008. The results were favourable and were subsequently ratified by the IMF Executive Board in May 2012. The IMF observed that the primary goal of the programme—poverty reduction—was not achieved, but that overall growth was sustained by foreign direct capital intensive investment. Real GDP growth rose from 3.5% in 2010 to 4.5% in 2011; it was expected to increase to 4.8% in 2012. The relative stability of Djibouti's economy appears favourable when compared to double-digit inflation (13%–14%) in nearby Kenya and Tanzania.

The World Bank announced four new projects in June 2012 to help the country address current and future emergencies and to maintain stable development. These include: a Social Safety Net grant (US $5m.) to complement existing drought assistance programmes; a Power Access and Diversification project ($2m.) to strengthen and maintain the country's power supply; an Institutional Capacity and Management of the Education System project ($6m.) to assist ongoing reforms to augment the quality of the education system and its relevance to development; and a Rural Community Development and Water Mobilization grant ($3m.) to provide additional funding programmes to enable reliable water supplies to the country's nomads.

SOME NEW INVESTMENT PARTNERS

Djibouti's port authority announced in March 2012 that it expects to build five new ports in the next four years. These will require US $4,400m. in financing, some 85% percent of which had been secured at the time of the announcement. The new ports are needed to respond to Ethiopia's decision to invest in railways for exports, imports and intercity passenger traffic, South Sudan's need for alternative pipeline routes, and planned expansion of mineral exports (salt and potash). The Chairman of the Djibouti Ports and Free Zones Authority, Aboubaker Omar Hadi, claims to have commitments for loans from China, India, Turkey and Brazil, each of which is relatively new to investments in the Horn of Africa. Various international financial institutions, including the African Development Bank (AfDB), are also interested. Djibouti expects to finance as much as 35% of the cost from state revenues.

China and India have since 2010 both taken a strong interest in the Horn of Africa, seemingly as a means of promoting exports and securing large building projects. Renewal of the antiquated 781-km narrow-gauge railway from Djibouti town to Dire Dawa and Addis Ababa (Ethiopia) is the first project, in two phases, which will become a part of the approximately 5,000 km of railways planned for Ethiopia. The renewed Djibouti–Ethiopia rail link will be realigned, widened to standard gauge and converted to electrical power. The project is now underway, with a pledge of US $300m. from India and a loan of $100m. already secured from China's Export-Import Bank. From the announcement of the project in January 2012, feasibility studies were to begin immediately, to be completed in eight months. Actual construction is expected to take three-and-a-half years.

In June 2012 Ethiopia signed contracts with China (US $1,500m.) and Turkey ($1,700m.) to build a railway from Mekele through Ethiopian and Djibouti Afar country to a new port to be constructed at Tadjoura, on the north coast of the Gulf of Tadjoura. Its primary function will be the export of potash.

A fourth port is to be built at Goubet (Ghoubbet-el-Kharab), a collapsed volcanic cone (long believed by the indigenous Afars to harbour sea monsters) connected by an inlet to the Gulf of Tadjoura. The port is intended to facilitate the export of salt from Lake Assal, deposits of which are said to be the most extensive in the world. They have been exploited for centuries by the Afar.

A related capital project is the oil refinery built at the Doraleh port. The refinery originally belonged to Aramco in Saudi Arabia, with an original capacity of 20,000 barrels per day (b/d) of various petroleum products. It was dismantled and shipped to Djibouti by the Saudi Regional Petroleum Products Corporation. The total cost of the project was US $150m. The operation was quickly expanded to 40,000 b/d, with its operators looking to markets in East Africa. In November 2011 a 75% interest in the company was purchased by a financial company in Abu Dhabi (United Arab Emirates), with the intention of expanding daily capacity to 100,000 b/d. Output is expected to be extended beyond Djibouti, Sudan and Ethiopia to Kenya and Uganda.

Many decisions have yet to be taken regarding newly independent South Sudan. In February 2012, however, the governments of South Sudan, Ethiopia and Djibouti signed a memorandum of understanding to co-operate in developing infrastructural and road links, as well as power and telecommunications connections. The agreement also reportedly envisaged the possibility of constructing an oil pipeline.

HUMANITARIAN CRISIS

Life in Djibouti for its people and livestock remains precarious as the drought emergency has continued unabated for more than six years. According to the the UN Office for the Co-ordination of Humanitarian Affairs (OCHA), estimates made in June 2012 show that Djibouti's urban and rural areas were severely affected by food insecurity. There were some 42,400 refugees and 28,400 children under the age of five suffering from acute malnutrition. Furthermore, 18.5% of Djiboutians were living on less than US $1.25 per day. The under-five mortality rate at that time was estimated at 18.4%. Despite these dire estimates, the UN Consolidated Appeal for 2012 was funded at only 41%. The UN Food and Agriculture Organization (FAO) did not dispute the OCHA figures, but noted that some food prices had declined over the previous 12 months, especially that of Belem rice, preferred among the urban population, which had decreased by 13%. In the town of Djibouti, unemployment is estimated to average more than 60%. Since poverty in the capital is very high, the UN Children's Fund (UNICEF) has taken a special interest in its children. A report commissioned in 2009 by UNICEF and the Djibouti Ministry for the Promotion of Women, Family Wellbeing and Social Affairs found that almost 70% of children in Djibouti town were deprived of at least one of the basic children's rights to water and sanitation, information, nutrition, education and health. According to another study, the 2007–09 drought caused the country's nomadic pastoralists to reduce the quantity and quality of their daily diets. In terms of Global Acute Malnutrition (GAM) criteria, Djibouti's plight measured 17%, with a rate of 25% in the north-west. A GAM rate of 15% is considered the threshold for emergency conditions.

In addition to its own internally displaced population caused by drought and poverty, Djibouti also maintains a camp for Somali refugees at Ali Addeh, 130 km south of Djibouti town. When the camp was established in 1991, it was designed to accommodate about 7,000 refugees. In September 2011 the camp housed almost 20,700, many of whom had been in exile from Somalia for years. A new refugee camp is under construction at Holl-Holl for a further expected 10,000 refugees.

CONDUCTING BUSINESS IN DJIBOUTI

For a country that appears to be a favourite among the moneyed classes of the Gulf states, Djibouti does not rank very highly in comparison to the ease of doing business elsewhere. In 2012 edition of *Doing Business*, a publication of the World Bank, 183 economies were examined, including 46 in sub-Saharan Africa. Each country was studied using criteria that were measurable across the data set, as well as observations from previous years. Djibouti's rankings indicated little progress in recent years. According to the 2012 World Bank study, Djibouti ranked 170th of 183 overall, three places down from the previous year; 179th in starting a business (down four places); 142nd in dealing with licences (down 17); 148th in registering property (down eight); 177th in obtaining credit (down one); 179th in protecting investors (no change); 70th in paying taxes (down 10); 38th in trading across borders (down one); 160th in enforcing contracts (unchanged); and 141st in resolving insolvency (up two). In East Africa, only Eritrea ranked lower in all categories (Somalia was not included in the comparative study for logistical and security reasons). Ethiopia ranked much more highly than Djibouti in nearly all categories.

Meanwhile, the US Department of Commerce publication *Doing Business in Djibouti: 2010 Country Commercial Guide for US Companies*, used World Bank data but also observed that 'corruption exists in Djibouti and has sometimes been an obstacle to investment and business development in the past'. The report none the less stated that recent major foreign investors had noted that they had operated 'free of government interference and corruption'. The document reported that the transparency of Djibouti customs procedures had vastly improved since what is now DP World had taken over management of the ports in 2000, but that some businessmen still attempted to bribe customs officials to lower their import duties. The report advised US companies seeking to do business in Djibouti to exercise due caution and good business judgement in developing joint ventures with local firms.

Responding to continuing criticism of the difficulties in doing business in Djibouti, in April 2012 the Government held a forum in Djibouti town on improving the business environment. With the assistance of representatives of the European Commission and the Common Market for Eastern and Southern Africa, resource experts from a wide number of disciplines met with Djibouti government officials and the private sector. A National Committee on Doing Business in Djibouti was established, and a steering committee on business environment was formed to monitor future progress.

In support of the US military presence at Camp Lemonier (the former French air force and Foreign Legion facility adjacent to the international airport), the US Administration in July 2007 awarded a base operations cost contract to PAE Government Services, Inc, of Los Angeles, California, for US $26.4m. for one year, with four optional years, resulting in total expenditure of $140.7m. if all options were exercised. The base currently employs about 800 Djiboutian workers. Combined local contracts for services and products approached $50m. in 2009. There are about 2,500 US and allied military personnel resident at Camp Lemonier. The Japanese maritime force was also lodged at Camp Lemonier, but it opened its own facility in 2011—the first Japanese overseas military base since the Second World War.

PROSPECTS FOR 'GRAND PROJECTS' DIMINISH

The status of the proposed 30-km bridge linking the south-west tip of Yemen to Perim island, located in the Bab el-Mandeb about 6 km off shore, which would then cross the Red Sea and reach Djibouti at Ras Siyan, about 200 km north of Djibouti town, remains nebulous. There have been no new pronouncements about the project in 2011/12, other than an unsubstantiated rumour that the scheme is now projected for consideration in 2020. It is envisaged that the eventual bridge will carry six lanes of motor traffic, four light railway lines, and oil and water pipelines. A further key attraction of the bridge is spiritual, as it would provide opportunities for millions of African Muslims to reach Mecca by train and by bus. (The fact that the project was first projected publicly by the company founded by Muhammad bin Laden, father of the deceased al-Qa'ida leader, Osama bin Laden, no doubt cast the project in a negative light.)

Similarly, the Great Green Wall, an African Union project to plant heat-resistant trees and shrubs along a 7,100-km strip of land, 15 km wide, to halt the steady southern encroachment of the Sahara desert, is in abeyance. It may be necessary to wait until the outcome of North Africa's 'Arab Spring' becomes clearer before further progress can be made.

EDUCATION

UNICEF estimates that there are approximately 130,000 children in Djibouti who are of primary school age, yet only a relatively small percentage of them actually attend school. For those able to receive education, the overwhelming majority of schools and classrooms are in very poor condition. UNICEF and the NGO Dubai Cares have established a joint programme to improve schooling. Dubai Cares has contributed some US $2m. to improve classroom conditions and the quality of teaching, to promote greater access to schools and to increase the number of female students in the school system. New schools would improve the country's prospect of attaining the Millennium Development Goal of universal primary education by 2015. Dubai Cares planned to increase school enrolment from 66% to 75% by 2009. The construction and repair of schools appear to be among the preferred civil affairs projects for armed forces personnel assigned to the US-led Combined Joint Task Force-Horn of Africa at Camp Lemonier.

The University of Djibouti was founded by decree on in January 2006. Through an ambitious effort by the Government, with the assistance of donor states and some private funding, the aim was to establish a university with full capacities as soon as possible. The institution now has some 2,500 students in 54 disciplines, preparing for higher qualifications at all levels.

HEALTH INDICATORS

In principle, Djibouti provides universal health care to its population. However, there are significant disparities between health care in urban and rural areas, and there are clear signs that overall health services in the country are in decline. Expenditure on health care declined from 2.2% of the national budget in the early 1990s to 1.5% in 2002. Djibouti's population growth rate is estimated at 2% per year as a result of high fertility rates (4 children per woman) and immigration. Despite a fairly impressive per caput income by the standards of the region (the World Bank estimated gross national income of US $1,270 per head in 2009, or $2,440 at international purchasing-power parity), Djibouti has some of the poorest social indicators in the world. At birth, life expectancy is 60 years (at 2009). Between 1989 and 2002 infant mortality rates fell from 114 to 103.1 per 1,000 live births, while child mortality declined from 154 to 128.9 per 1,000. The under-five mortality rate at 2009 was 93 per 1,000 live births. Female genital mutilation remains a major public health scourge, with about 98% of married women between the ages of 15 and 49 subjected to this harmful practice.

According to the Poverty Reduction Strategy Paper compiled in 2004, about 15% of the total population are foreign nationals. The overall population suffers from rising incidence of tuberculosis (TB), malaria, cholera and HIV/AIDS. TB is historically the most common disease of poverty, and Djibouti recorded a rate of 588 cases of TB per 100,000 inhabitants. Only Swaziland had a higher rate of TB infection than Djibouti. Malaria became a problem in the 1980s after the independent Government facilitated urban housing and irrigation, and the Government has made efforts to control mosquitoes during the infrequent rainy seasons. Nearly all social diseases proliferated after the construction of truck routes linking Djibouti with the highlands of Ethiopia. Djibouti now records more than 4,000 cases of malaria each year. HIV/AIDS was first diagnosed in Djibouti in 1986, and it has vastly increased since that time. In 2002 a survey revealed that HIV/AIDS prevalence was 3% for the total population, a figure that many believed would be higher. However, it afflicted 5% of people between the ages of 20 and 35, generally assumed to be the most economically productive and sexually active. In 2009 UNAIDs put the rate at 2.5% of persons aged 15–49 years.

QAT

Many observers of Djibouti life and industry marvel at the precision and energy of the delivery system that follows the daily arrival on Ethiopian Airways of the 11–12 metric tons of qat (also known as chat or khat, a leaf used for its stimulant effects that is picked from a shrub— *catha edulis*—growing at altitudes above 3,000 ft in Ethiopia and Yemen) that are consumed nationally. Trucks stand by at Ambouli International Airport in Djibouti town; it takes no longer than about 15 minutes to empty the aircraft, before each distributor hastens to deliver orders to local suppliers. Some trucks proceed to the port to drop off the consignments that will be taken at high speed across the Gulf of Tadjoura to Obock and Tadjoura, where again the qat will be taken by road to delivery points across northern Djibouti. Speed is always of the essence because qat must be consumed within 48 hours of being harvested in order to be considered fresh. Qat is a habituating drug that is a part of the male social fabric of the Horn of Africa and Yemen. Normally chewed, or sometimes made into a tea, qat produces a mild hallucinogenic high that its users claim both facilitates conversation and eases hunger and thirst. Although qat sessions traditionally welcome only men, recent studies indicate that more women are now using qat, and that it is now being used at a younger age by both sexes. According to a recent World Bank study on qat usage in Yemen and Djibouti, qat consumption in Djibouti seems to rise with user income and may be a substitute for food consumption (in Yemen usage is uniform across all incomes). All authorities studying the qat phenomenon agree that it represents a significant problem, and many social benefits would accrue to countries that would cut or severely diminish the use of the drug.

In a recent investigatory visit to Djibouti on the status of women and children, the regional director for UNICEF found that extreme poverty affected 42% of the population and that 74% of the population were subject to relative poverty. UNICEF also found that 13% of children aged 15–19 chew qat. In discussions with government officials, it was agreed that UNICEF would work with the Government to develop programmes to respond to the use of the amphetamine-like stimulant by young people.

POWER GENERATION

A long-held ambition of sharing Ethiopia's massive hydroelectric potential with its high-cost energy-dependent neighbour

Djibouti was finally achieved on 27 May 2011, when a switch was thrown in Addis Ababa to open a power line adding an additional 20 MW to Djibouti's power grid. The 283-km transmission line between the two countries was 90% financed by loans and grants from the AfDB. Not only will Djibouti save 70% of the cost of diesel-powered generation, but the Ethiopian power, from hydroelectric sources, is 'clean and carbon free'. Ethiopian power experts were especially pleased that power peaks in the two countries are different, with Djibouti needing more power at night. The power station at the Djibouti end was officially inaugurated on 12 October 2011, with Ethiopia's Prime Minister Meles Zenawi and Djibouti's President Guelleh in attendance. Maximum power flow between the two countries using current facilities is estimated to peak at 35 MW, with the possibility of expansion to 50 MW. An AfDB feasibility study indicates that, with additional investment, capacity could rise to 100 MW, an amount that would consume only 0.05% of Ethiopia's present power potential.

Geologically, Djibouti lies at the junction of three tectonic plates. These spreading cleavages in the earth's mantle are forcing Africa away from Arabia, and thus generate often violent seismic activity in Djibouti. Examination of a geologic map of Djibouti reveals thousands of stress fractures; this explains why the earth frequently shudders in Djibouti. With huge amounts of energy so close to the surface, it has long been the aim of power experts to discover some economic means of harnessing Djibouti's volcanic foundation. Work began in 1986 on a major geothermal exploration project, funded by the World Bank and foreign aid, but the project was not completed. The arrival of cheaper power from Ethiopia has not diminished Djibouti's enthusiasm to develop its geothermal potential. On 19 July 2012 in Beijing, China, President Guelleh and the Chairman of the China Petroleum and Chemical Corporation (SINOPEC) witnessed the signing of an agreement for Chinese support to develop geothermal power from the Lake Assal rift. SINOPEC, one of the world's largest energy groups, has performed exploration and feasibility studies in China, but its experience in geothermal projects is narrow. This does not mean that Iceland's earlier collaboration with Djibouti is being abandoned: in fact, the Chinese signed an agreement with Iceland's Orka Energy in May 2012. Orka has already surveyed Djibouti's potential geothermal sites, and it is believed that SINOPEC intends to learn from Orka in its first overseas project in this sphere.

TOURISM

Djibouti has yet to make much of a mark in the area of tourism. In the last year for which statistics are available (1998), the total number of tourists visiting the country was estimated at 20,000. Income from tourism accounts for about 1% of GDP. There are many interesting places such as Lake Abbé, whose waters gather in Ethiopia but literally disappear into the sands along the frontier with Djibouti. Lake Assal, the second lowest depression on the earth's surface (after the Dead Sea) at 571 ft below sea level, is believed to have the highest salt content of any lake in the world. The Isles Sept Frères (Seven Brothers Islands), off the northern coast of Djibouti, are well known by snorkellers for the spectacular underwater life that can be seen around them. Fishing in the Gulf of Tadjoura is excellent, with skipjack tuna and sea bass in abundance.

Statistical Survey

Source (unless otherwise stated): Ministère de l'Economie, des Finances et de la Planification, chargé de la Privatisation, Cité Ministérielle, BP 13, Djibouti; tel. 21353331; fax 21356501; e-mail cabmefpp@intnet.dj; internet www.ministere-finances.dj.

AREA AND POPULATION

Area: 23,200 sq km (8,958 sq miles).

Population: 519,900 (including refugees and resident foreigners) at 31 December 1990 (official estimate); 818,159 at the census of 29 May 2009 (official figure). *2012* (UN estimate at mid-year): 922,709 (Sources: UN, *Population and Vital Statistics Report* and *World Population Prospects: The 2010 Revision*).

Density (mid-2012): 39.8 per sq km.

Population by Age and Sex (UN estimates at mid-2012): *0–14:* 323,712 (males 163,421, females 160,291); *15–64:* 567,122 (males 283,984, females 283,138); *65 and over:* 31,875 (males 14,229, females 17,646); *Total* 922,709 (males 461,634, females 461,075) (Source: UN, *World Population Prospects: The 2010 Revision*).

Regions (population at 2009 census): Ali-Sabieh 86,949; Arta 42,380; Dikhil 88,948; Djibouti (ville) 475,322; Obock 37,856; Tadjoura 86,704; *Total* 818,159.

Principal Town (population at 2009 census): Djibouti (capital) 475,322.

Births, Marriages and Deaths (2005–10, UN estimates): Average annual birth rate 29.4 per 1,000; Average annual death rate 10.5 per 1,000 (Source: UN, *World Population Prospects: The 2010 Revision*). *1999* (capital district only): Births 7,898; Marriages 3,808. *2011:* Crude birth rate 28.7 per 1,000; Crude death rate 10.0 per 1,000 (Source: African Development Bank).

Life Expectancy (years at birth): 57.5 (males 56.1; females 59.0) in 2010. Source: World Bank, World Development Indicators database.

Economically Active Population (estimates, '000 persons, 1991): Agriculture, etc. 212; Industries 31; Services 39; *Total* 282 (males 167, females 115) (Source: UN Economic Commission for Africa, *African Statistical Yearbook*). *Mid-2012* ('000 persons, estimates): Agriculture, etc. 297; Total labour force 407 (Source: FAO).

HEALTH AND WELFARE

Key Indicators

Total Fertility Rate (children per woman, 2010): 3.8.

Under-5 Mortality Rate (per 1,000 live births, 2010): 91.

HIV/AIDS (% of persons aged 15–49, 2009): 2.5.

Physicians (per 1,000 head, 2006): 0.2.

Hospital Beds (per 1,000 head, 2010): 1.4.

Health Expenditure (2009): US $ per head (PPP): 180.

Health Expenditure (2009): % of GDP: 7.8.

Health Expenditure (2009): public (% of total): 69.3.

Access to Water (% of persons, 2010): 88.

Access to Sanitation (% of persons, 2010): 50.

Total Carbon Dioxide Emissions ('000 metric tons, 2008): 524.4.

Carbon Dioxide Emissions Per Head (metric tons, 2008): 0.6.

Human Development Index (2011): ranking: 165.

Human Development Index (2011): value: 0.430.

For sources and definitions, see explanatory note on p. vi.

AGRICULTURE, ETC.

Principal Crops ('000 metric tons, 2010, FAO estimates): Beans, dry 1.5; Tomatoes 1.2; Lemons and limes 1.6. *Aggregate Production* ('000 metric tons, may include official, semi-official or estimated data): Vegetables (incl. melons) 32.2; Fruits (excl. melons) 3.2.

Livestock ('000 head, 2010, FAO estimates): Cattle 297; Sheep 466; Goats 512; Asses 8; Camels 70.

Livestock Products ('000 metric tons, 2010, FAO estimates): Cattle meat 6.1; Sheep meat 2.2; Goat meat 2.4; Camel meat 0.7; Cows' milk 9.2; Camels' milk 6.6.

Fishing (metric tons, live weight, 2010, FAO estimates): Groupers 133; Snappers and jobfishes 179; Barracudas 120; Carangids 204; Seerfishes 82; Other tuna-like fishes 100; Total catch (incl. others) 1,058.

Source: FAO.

INDUSTRY

Electric Energy (million kWh): 325.9 in 2008; 342.7 in 2009; 372.7 in 2010. Source: Banque Centrale de Djibouti, *Rapport Annuel 2010*.

FINANCE

Currency and Exchange Rates: 100 centimes = 1 Djibouti franc. *Sterling, Dollar and Euro Equivalents* (31 May 2012): £1 sterling = 275.539 Djibouti francs; US $1 = 177.721 Djibouti francs; €1 = 220.427 Djibouti francs; 1,000 Djibouti francs = £3.63 = $5.63 = €4.54. *Exchange Rate:* Fixed at US $1 = 177.721 Djibouti francs since February 1973.

Budget (million Djibouti francs, 2010): *Revenue:* Tax revenue 40,582 (Direct taxes 18,726, Indirect taxes 19,828, Other taxes 2,028); Other revenue (incl. property sales) 19,652; Total 60,234 (excl. official grants 10,705). *Expenditure:* Current expenditure 48,649 (Salaries and wages 22,911); Capital expenditure 23,491; Total 72,140. Source: Banque Centrale de Djibouti, *Rapport Annuel 2010*.

International Reserves (US $ million at 31 December 2011, excl. gold): IMF special drawing rights 14.14; Reserve position in IMF 1.69; Foreign exchange 228.28; Total 244.11. Source: IMF, *International Financial Statistics*.

Money Supply (million Djibouti francs at 31 December 2011): Currency outside banks 20,350; Demand deposits at commercial banks 102,746; *Total money* 123,096. Source: IMF, *International Financial Statistics*.

Cost of Living (Consumer Price Index; base: 2005 = 100): All items 123.6 in 2009; 128.5 in 2010; 134.2 in 2011. Source: IMF, *International Financial Statistics*.

Expenditure on the Gross Domestic Product (million Djibouti francs at current prices, 2010, provisional): Government final consumption expenditure 37,758; Private final consumption expenditure 170,960; Gross capital formation 34,994; *Total domestic expenditure* 243,712; Exports of goods and services 66,435; *Less* Imports of goods and services 109,470; *GDP in purchasers' values* 200,678. Source: African Development Bank.

Gross Domestic Product by Economic Activity (million Djibouti francs at current prices, 2010, provisional): Agriculture 6,864; Mining and quarrying 285; Manufacturing 4,376; Electricity, gas and water 9,215; Construction 22,998; Wholesale and retail trade, restaurants and hotels 33,584; Transport and communications 50,846; Finance, insurance and real estate 25,816; Public administration and defence 24,257; Other services 2,986; *GDP at factor cost* 181,227; Indirect taxes 19,451; *GDP in purchasers' values* 200,678. Note: Deduction for imputed bank service charge assumed to be distributed at origin. Source: African Development Bank.

Balance of Payments (US $ million, 2010): Exports of goods f.o.b. 85.1; Imports of goods f.o.b. −363.8; *Trade balance* −278.6; Exports of services 335.7; Imports of services −119.1; *Balance on goods and services* −62.0; Other income received 32.8; Other income paid −15.4; *Balance on goods, services and income* −44.7; Current transfers received 108.7; Current transfers paid −13.5; *Current balance* 50.5; Capital account (net) 55.3; Direct investment from abroad 36.5; Other investment assets −87.8; Other investment liabilities 55.5; Net errors and omissions −112.9; *Overall balance* −2.8. Source: IMF, *International Financial Statistics*.

EXTERNAL TRADE

Principal Commodities: *Imports c.i.f.* (US $ million, 2009): Food and beverages 173.0; Mineral fuels and lubricants 41.8; Chemical products 50.3; Basic manufactures 73.6; Telecommunications and sound equipment 57.9; Machinery and electrical appliances 211.2; Vehicles and transport equipment 66.6; Total (incl. others) 647.6. *Exports f.o.b.:* Food and live animals 69.9 (Milk products 29.4; Cereals 10.0); Basic manufactures 61.3; Machinery and transport equipment 177.2 (Road vehicles and parts 105.1); Commodities not classified according to kind 20.7; Total (incl. others) 363.7. Source: UN, *International Trade Statistics Yearbook*.

Principal Trading Partners (US $ million, 2009): *Imports c.i.f.:* Belgium 12.7; China, People's Republic 20.7; Egypt 10.5; Ethiopia 32.5; France 197.5; India 20.6; Italy 18.6; Japan 35.4; Netherlands 4.4; Pakistan 16.7; Saudi Arabia 38.7; Singapore 2.2; Ukraine 13.8; United Arab Emirates 119.7; United Kingdom 3.3; USA 25.6; Yemen 22.2; Total (incl. others) 647.6. *Exports f.o.b.:* Brazil 31.5; Ethiopia 128.6; France 73.0; Pakistan 15.2; Qatar 22.9; Somalia 43.2; Yemen 12.3; Total (incl. others) 363.7. Source: UN, *International Trade Statistics Yearbook*.

TRANSPORT

Railways (traffic, 2002): Passengers ('000) 570; Freight ton-km (million) 201. Source: IMF, *Djibouti: Statistical Appendix* (March 2004).

Road Traffic (motor vehicles in use, 1996, estimates): Passenger cars 9,200; Lorries and vans 2,040. Source: IRF, *World Road Statistics*.

Shipping: *Merchant Fleet* (registered at 31 December 2009): 12 vessels (displacement 3,018 grt) (Source: IHS Fairplay, *World Fleet Statistics*). *Freight Traffic* ('000 metric tons, 2010): Goods 3,451.9; Fuels 2,572.0 (Source: Banque Centrale de Djibouti, *Rapport Annuel 2010*).

Civil Aviation (international traffic, 2010): *Passengers:* 266,261; *Freight:* 10,369 metric tons. Source: Banque Centrale de Djibouti, *Rapport Annuel 2010*.

TOURISM

Tourist Arrivals ('000): 40 in 2006; 40 in 2007; 53 in 2008 (Source: African Development Bank).

Receipts from Tourism (excl. passenger transport, US $ million): 7.8 in 2008; 16.0 in 2009; 18 in 2010 (Source: World Tourism Organization).

COMMUNICATIONS MEDIA

Newspapers (1995): 1 non-daily (estimated circulation 1,000).

Periodicals (1989): 7 (estimated combined circulation 6,000).

Radio Receivers (1997): 52,000 in use.

Television Receivers (2000): 45,000 in use.

Telephones (2011): 18,400 main lines in use.

Mobile Cellular Telephones (2011): 193,000 subscribers.

Personal Computers: 32,000 (37.7 per 1,000 persons) in 2008.

Internet Subscribers (2010): 11,900.

Broadband Subscribers (2011): 11,300.

Sources: mainly UNESCO, *Statistical Yearbook;* UN, *Statistical Yearbook;* International Telecommunication Union.

EDUCATION

Pre-primary (2010/11 unless otherwise indicated): 2 schools (2004/05); 1,857 pupils (males 950, females 907); 75 teaching staff (2008/09).

Primary (2010/11 unless otherwise indicated): 82 schools (2004/05); 60,992 pupils (males 32,333, females 28,659); 1,731 teaching staff.

Secondary (2010/11): 50,965 pupils (males 28,564, females 22,401); 1,827 teaching staff.

Higher (2010/11): 4,705 students (males 2,828, females 1,877); 245 teaching staff.

Sources: UNESCO Institute for Statistics; Ministère de l'éducation nationale et de l'enseignement supérieur; Université de Djibouti.

Pupil-teacher Ratio (primary education, UNESCO estimate): 35.2 in 2010/11. Source: UNESCO Institute for Statistics.

Adult Literacy Rate (UNESCO estimate): 65.5% in 2003. Source: UN Development Programme, *Human Development Report*.

Directory

The Constitution

A new Constitution was approved by national referendum on 4 September 1992 and entered into force on 15 September. It was amended in February 2006, January 2008 and April 2010.

The Constitution of Djibouti guarantees the basic rights and freedoms of citizens; the functions of the principal organs of state are delineated therein.

The President of the Republic, who is Head of State and Head of Government, is directly elected, by universal adult suffrage, for a period of five years and must be between the ages of 40 and 75 at the time of the announcement of his or her candidature. The President nominates the Prime Minister and, following consultation with the latter, appoints the Council of Ministers. The legislature is the 65-member Assemblée nationale, which is elected, also by direct universal suffrage, for a period of five years.

The 1992 Constitution provided for the establishment of a maximum of four political parties. On 4 September 2002, however, this limit on the number of political parties was revoked.

The Government

HEAD OF STATE

President and Commander-in-Chief of the Armed Forces: ISMAÏL OMAR GUELLEH (inaugurated 7 May 1999, re-elected 8 April 2005 and 8 April 2011).

COUNCIL OF MINISTERS
(September 2012)

The Government is formed by the Rassemblement Populaire pour le Progrès.

Prime Minister: DILEITA MOHAMED DILEITA.

Minister of Justice and Penal Affairs, in charge of Human Rights: ALI FARAH ASSOWEH.

Minister of the Economy and Finance, in charge of Industry and Planning: ILYAS MOUSSA DAWALEH.

Minister of Defence: ABDOULKADER KAMIL MOHAMED.

Minister of Foreign Affairs and International Co-operation: MAHAMOUD ALI YOUSSOUF.

Minister of the Interior: HASSAN DARAR HOUFFANEH.

Minister of Health: ALI YACOUB MAHAMOUD.

Minister of National Education and Professional Training: MOUSSA AHMED HASSAN.

Minister of Higher Education and Research: DR NABIL MOHAMMED AHMED.

Minister of Agriculture, Fishing and Stockbreeding: MOHAMED AHMED AWALEH.

Minister of Equipment and Transport: MOHAMED MOUSSA IBRAHIM BALALA.

Minister of Muslim Affairs and Endowments: DR HAMOUD ADBI SULTAN.

Minister of Energy and Water, in charge of Natural Resources: DR FOUAD AHMED AYE.

Minister of Communication and Culture, in charge of Post and Telecommunications, and Government Spokesperson: ABDI HUSSAIN AHMED.

Minister of Labour, in charge of Administrative Reform: HASSAN ALI BAHDON.

Minister of Housing, Urban Planning and the Environment: HASSAN OMAR MOHAMED BOURHAN.

Minister of the Promotion of Women and Family Planning, in charge of Relations with Parliament: HASNA BARKAT DAOUD.

Minister-delegate to the Minister of Foreign Affairs, in charge of International Co-operation: AHMED ALI SILAY.

Minister-delegate to the Minister of the Economy and Finance, in charge of the Budget: AMAREH ALI SAID.

Minister-delegate to the Minister of the Economy and Finance, in charge of Trade, Small and Medium-sized Enterprises, Handicrafts and Tourism: ABDI ELMI ACHKIR.

Secretary of State in the Office of the Prime Minister, in charge of National Solidarity: ZAHRA YOUSSOUF KAYAD.

Secretary of State to the Minister of Housing, Urban Planning and the Environment, in charge of Accommodation: AMINA ABDI ADEN.

Secretary of State for Youth and Sports: DR DJAMA ELMI OKIEH.

MINISTRIES

Office of the President: Djibouti; e-mail sggpr@intnet.dj; internet www.presidence.dj.

Office of the Prime Minister: BP 2086, Djibouti; tel. 21351494; fax 21355049.

Ministry of Agriculture, Fishing and Stockbreeding: BP 453, Djibouti; tel. 21351297.

Ministry of Communication and Culture: BP 32, 1 rue de Moscou, Djibouti; tel. 21355672; fax 21353957; e-mail mccpt@intnet.dj; internet www.mccpt.dj.

Ministry of Defence: BP 42, Djibouti; tel. 21352034.

Ministry of the Economy, Finance and Planning: BP 13, Djibouti; tel. 21353331; fax 21356501; e-mail sg_mefpp@intnet.dj; internet www.ministere-finances.dj.

Ministry of Employment, Integration and Professional Training: Djibouti; tel. 21351838; fax 21357268; e-mail adetip@intnet.dj.

Ministry of Energy and Natural Resources: BP 175, Djibouti; tel. 21350340.

Ministry of Equipment and Transport: Palais du Peuple, BP 2501, Djibouti; tel. 21350990; fax 21355975.

Ministry of Foreign Affairs and International Co-operation: blvd Cheik Osman, BP 1863, Djibouti; tel. 21352471; fax 21353049; internet www.djibdiplomatie.dj.

Ministry of Health: BP 296, Djibouti; tel. 21353331; fax 21356300.

Ministry of Higher Education and Research: Djibouti.

Ministry of Housing, Urban Planning and the Environment: BP 11, Djibouti; tel. 21350006; fax 21351618.

Ministry of the Interior: BP 33, Djibouti; tel. 21352542; fax 21354862.

Ministry of Justice and Penal Affairs: BP 12, Djibouti; tel. 21351506; fax 21354012.

Ministry of Labour: Djibouti.

Ministry of Muslim Affairs and Endowments: Djibouti.

Ministry of National Education and Professional Training: BP 16, Cité Ministérielle, Djibouti; tel. 21350997; fax 21354234; e-mail education.gov@intnet.dj; internet www.education.gov.dj.

Ministry of the Promotion of Women and Family Planning: BP 458, Djibouti; tel. 21353409; fax 21350439; e-mail minfemme@intnet.dj; internet www.ministere-femme.dj.

Ministry of Trade and Industry: BP 1846, Djibouti; tel. 21351682.

Ministry of Youth, Sports, Leisure and Tourism: BP 2506, Djibouti; tel. 21355886; fax 21356830.

President and Legislature

PRESIDENT

Presidential Election, 8 April 2011

Candidate	% of votes
Ismaïl Omar Guelleh	80.63
Mohamed Warsama Ragueh	19.37
Total	100.00

ASSEMBLÉE NATIONALE

Assemblée nationale: BP 138, pl. Lagarde, Djibouti; tel. 21350172; internet www.assemblee-nationale.dj.

Speaker: IDRISS ARNAOUD ALI.

Elections to the Assemblée nationale were held on 8 February 2008. The 65 seats were contested solely by candidates from the Union pour la Majorité Présidentielle (UMP) after opposition parties boycotted the ballot. According to official results, the UMP received 103,463 (94.1%) of the 109,999 votes cast; the remaining 6,536 votes were invalid. Voter turn-out was estimated at 72.6%.

Election Commission

Commission Électorale Nationale Indépendante: Djibouti; f. 2002; President ADEN AHMED DOUALEH.

Political Organizations

On 4 September 2002, to coincide with the 10th anniversary of the approval of the Constitution, restrictions on the number of legally permitted political parties (hitherto four) were formally removed.

Union pour l'Alternance Démocratique (UAD): 2 rue de Pékin, Héron, Djibouti; tel. 21341822; fax 77829999 (mobile); e-mail realite_djibouti@yahoo.fr; coalition of major opposition parties; Pres. ISMAËL GUEDI HARED.

Alliance Républicaine pour le Développement (ARD): BP 1074, Marabout, Djibouti; tel. 21341822; e-mail realite_djibouti@yahoo.fr; internet www.ard-djibouti.org; f. 2002; Leader AHMAD YOUSSOUF HOUMED; Sec.-Gen. KASSIM ALI DINI.

Mouvement pour le Renouveau Démocratique et le Développement (MRD): BP 3570, ave Nasser, Djibouti; e-mail lerenouveau@mrd-djibouti.org; internet www.mrd-djibouti.org;

f. 1992 as the Parti du Renouveau Démocratique; renamed as above in 2002; Pres. DAHER AHMED FARAH; Sec.-Gen. SOULEIMAN HASSAN FAIDAL.

Parti Djiboutien pour le Développement (PDD): BP 892, Djibouti; tel. 77822860 (mobile); f. 2002; Pres. MOHAMED DAOUD CHEHEM; Sec.-Gen. ABDOULFATAH HASSAN IBRAHIM.

Union Djiboutienne pour la Démocratie et la Justice (UDJ): Djibouti; Chair. ISMAËL GUEDI HARED.

Union pour la Majorité Présidentielle (UMP): Djibouti; internet www.ump.dj; coalition of major parties in support of Pres. Guelleh; Pres. DILEITA MOHAMED DILEITA.

Front pour la Restauration de l'Unité et de la Démocratie (FRUD): Djibouti; tel. 21250279; f. 1991 by merger of 3 militant Afar groups; advocates fair representation in govt for all ethnic groups; commenced armed insurgency in Nov. 1991; split into 2 factions in March 1994; the dissident group, which negotiated a settlement with the Govt, obtained legal recognition in March 1996 and recognizes the following leaders; Pres. ALI MOHAMED DAOUD; Sec.-Gen. OUGOUREH KIFLEH AHMED; a dissident group, FRUD-Renaissance (led by IBRAHIM CHEHEM DAOUD), was formed in 1996.

Parti National Démocratique (PND): BP 10204, Djibouti; tel. 21342194; f. 1992; Pres. ADEN ROBLEH AWALLEH.

Parti Social Démocrate (PSD): BP 434, route Nelson Mandela, Djibouti; f. 2002; Pres. HASNA MOUMIN BAHDON; Sec.-Gen. HASSAN IDRISS AHMED.

Rassemblement Populaire pour le Progrès (RPP): Djibouti; e-mail rpp@intnet.dj; internet www.rpp.dj; f. 1979; sole legal party 1981–92; Pres. ISMAÏL OMAR GUELLEH; Sec.-Gen. IDRISS ARNAOUD ALI.

Union pour la Réforme (UPR): Djibouti; f. 2006; Pres. IBRAHIM CHEHEM DAOUD.

Diplomatic Representation

EMBASSIES IN DJIBOUTI

China, People's Republic: BP 2021, rue Addis Ababa, Lotissement Heron, Djibouti; tel. 21352247; fax 21354833; e-mail chinaemb_dj@mfa.gov.cn; internet dj.chineseembassy.org; Ambassador ZHANG GUOQING.

Egypt: BP 1989, Djibouti; tel. 21351231; fax 21356657; e-mail ambegypte2004@gawab.com; Ambassador FARGHALI ABDEL HALIM TAHA.

Eritrea: BP 1944, Djibouti; tel. 21354961; fax 21351831; Ambassador MOHAMED SAÏD MANTAY (recalled in June 2008).

Ethiopia: rue Clochette, BP 230, Djibouti; tel. 21350718; fax 21354803; e-mail ethemb@intnet.dj; Ambassador KHALED AHMED TAHA.

France: 45 blvd du Maréchal Foch, BP 2039, Djibouti; tel. 21350963; fax 21350272; e-mail ambfrdj@intnet.dj; internet www.ambafrance-dj.org; Ambassador RENÉ FORCEVILLE.

Libya: BP 2073, Djibouti; tel. 21350202; Chargé d'affaires HADI WAHECHI.

Qatar: Ambassador ALI BIN MUBARAK AL-MOHANNADI.

Russia: BP 1913, Plateau du Marabout, Djibouti; tel. 21350740; fax 21355990; e-mail russiaemb@intnet.dj; internet www.djibouti.mid.ru; Ambassador VALERII ORLOV.

Saudi Arabia: BP 1921, Djibouti; tel. 21351645; fax 21352284; Ambassador IBRAHIM ABD AL-AZIZ AN-NAOUFAL.

Somalia: BP 549, Djibouti; tel. 21353521; internet www.djibouti.somaligov.net; Chargé d'affaires a.i. ABDURRAHMAN ABDI HUSSEIN.

Sudan: BP 4259, Djibouti; tel. 21356404; fax 21356662; Ambassador HASSAN EL-TALIB.

United Arab Emirates: Djibouti; Ambassador SAÏD BEN HAMDAM BEN MUHAMMAD AN-NAGHI.

USA: Lot No. 350-B, Haramous, Djibouti; tel. 21353995; fax 21353940; e-mail amembadm@bow.intnet.dj; internet djibouti.usembassy.gov; Ambassador JAMES C. SWAN.

Yemen: BP 194, Djibouti; tel. 352975; Ambassador MOHAMMED ABDULLAH HAJAR.

Judicial System

The Supreme Court was established in 1979. There is a high court of appeal and a court of first instance in Djibouti; each of the six administrative districts has a 'tribunal coutumier'.

President of the Court of Appeal: KADIDJA ABEBA.

Conseil Constitutionnel: Plateau du Serpent, blvd Foch, BP 4081, Djibouti; tel. 21358662; fax 21358663; e-mail conseil@intnet.dj; f. 1992; Pres. AHMED IBRAHIM ABDI; six mems.

Religion

ISLAM

Almost the entire population are Muslims.

Qadi of Djibouti: MOGUE HASSAN DIRIR, BP 168, Djibouti; tel. 21352669.

Haut Conseil Islamique (High Islamic Council): Djibouti; f. 2004; 7 mems; Pres. Dr CHIKH BOUAMRANE; Sec.-Gen. ALI MOUSSA OKIEH.

CHRISTIANITY

The Roman Catholic Church

Djibouti comprises a single diocese, directly responsible to the Holy See. There were some 7,000 adherents in the country.

Bishop of Djibouti: GIORGIO BERTIN, Evêché, blvd de la République, BP 94, Djibouti; tel. and fax 21350140; e-mail evechcat@intnet.dj.

The Anglican Communion

Within the Episcopal Church in Jerusalem and the Middle East, Djibouti lies within the jurisdiction of the Bishop in Egypt.

Other Christian Churches

Eglise Protestante: blvd de la République, BP 416, Djibouti; tel. 21351820; fax 21350706; e-mail eped@intnet.dj; internet membres.lycos.fr/missiondjibouti; f. 1957; Pastor NATHALIE PAQUEREAU.

Greek Orthodox Church: blvd de la République, Djibouti; tel. 21351325; c. 350 adherents; Archimandrite STAVROS GEORGANAS.

The Ethiopian Orthodox Church is also active in Djibouti.

The Press

Al Qarn: angle rue de Moscou, blvd Cheick Osman, Djibouti; tel. 21355193; fax 21353310; e-mail alqarn@intnet.dj; internet www.alqarn.dj; biweekly; Arabic; Dir YASSIN ABDULLAH BOUH.

Djibouti Post: blvd Bonhoure, près de l'IGAD, BP 32, Djibouti; tel. 21352201; fax 21353937; internet www.lanation.dj/djibpost; fortnightly; English; circ. 500.

La Nation de Djibouti: blvd Bonhoure, près de l'IGAD, BP 32, Djibouti; tel. 21352201; fax 21353937; e-mail lanation@intnet.dj; internet www.lanation.dj; daily; Dir MOHAMED GASS BARKHADLEH; circ. 4,300.

Le Progrès: Djibouti; weekly; publ. by the RPP; Publr ALI MOHAMED HUMAD.

Le Renouveau: BP 3570, ave Nasser, Djibouti; tel. 21351474; weekly; independent; publ. by the MRD; Editor-in-Chief DAHER AHMED FARAH.

Revue de l'ISERT: BP 486, Djibouti; tel. 21352795; twice a year; publ. by the Institut Supérieur d'Etudes et de Recherches Scientifiques et Techniques (ISERT).

Le Temps: Djibouti; independent; fortnightly; Owners AMIN MOHAMED RABLEH, MOHAMED GOUMANEH GUIRREH, ABDOURAHMAN SOULEIMAN BACHIR.

NEWS AGENCY

Agence Djiboutienne d'Information (ADI): 1 rue de Moscou, BP 32, Djibouti; tel. 21354013; fax 21354037; e-mail adi@intent.dj; internet www.adi.dj; f. 1978; Dir YASSER HASSAN BOULLO.

Broadcasting and Communications

TELECOMMUNICATIONS

Djibouti Télécom: 3 blvd G. Pompidou, BP 2105, Djibouti; tel. 21352777; fax 21359200; e-mail adjib@intnet.dj; internet www.adjib.dj; f. 1999 to replace Société des Télécommunications Internationales; 100% state-owned; Dir-Gen. ABDIRAHMAN MOHAMED HASSAN.

BROADCASTING

Radio and Television

Djibnet: BP 1409, Djibouti; tel. 21354288; e-mail webmaster@djibnet.com; internet www.djibnet.com.

Radiodiffusion-Télévision de Djibouti (RTD): BP 97, 1 ave St Laurent du Var, Djibouti; tel. 21352294; fax 21356502; e-mail rtd@

intnet.dj; internet www.rtd.dj; f. 1967; state-controlled; programmes in French, Afar, Somali and Arabic; 17 hours radio and 5 hours television daily; Dir-Gen. Dr KADAR ALI DIRANEH.

Telesat Djibouti: route de l'Aéroport, BP 3760, Djibouti; tel. 21353457.

In the early 2010s a private television operator Djibsat provided a number of foreign channels, including Horn Cable Television (Somalia), TV5, TF1, M6, Canal+, Medsat and BBC.

Finance

(cap. = capital; res = reserves; dep. = deposits; m. = million; brs = branches; amounts in Djibouti francs)

BANKING

In 2010 there were 10 banks operating in Djibouti, of which four were Islamic banks.

Central Bank

Banque Centrale de Djibouti: BP 2118, ave St Laurent du Var, Djibouti; tel. 21352751; fax 21356288; e-mail bndj@intnet.dj; internet www.banque-centrale.dj; f. 1977 as Banque Nationale de Djibouti; present name adopted 2002; bank of issue; cap. and res 6,056m. (Feb. 2005); Gov. DJAMA MAHAMOUD HAID; Gen. Man. AHMED OSMAN.

Commercial Banks

Bank of Africa—Mer Rouge (BOA—MR): 10 pl. Lagarde, BP 88, Djibouti; tel. 21353016; fax 21351638; e-mail secretariat@bimr-banque.com; f. 1908 as Banque de l'Indochine; present name adopted 2010; cap. 1,500.0m., res 1,041.0m., dep. 60,594.3m. (Dec. 2009); Chair. and CEO PHILIPPE BOUYAUD; 3 brs.

Banque pour le Commerce et l'Industrie—Mer Rouge (BCI—MR): pl. Lagarde, BP 2122, Djibouti; tel. 21350857; fax 21354260; e-mail contact@bcimr.dj; f. 1977; 51% owned by BRED Banque Populaire (France); cap. 2,092.5m., res 209.3m., dep. 82,428.6m. (Dec. 2009); Pres. ERIC MONTAGNE; Dir-Gen. YAHYA OULD AMAR; 6 brs.

International Commercial Bank (Djibouti) SA: Immeuble 15, pl. du 27 juin, rue d'Ethiopie, Djibouti; tel. 21355006; fax 21355003; e-mail info@icbank-djibouti.com; f. 2007; 1 br.

Warka Bank: Djibouti; tel. 21311611; fax 21353693; f. 2010.

Development Bank

Fonds de Développement Economique de Djibouti (FDED): angle ave Georges Clemenceau et rue Pierre Curie, BP 520, Djibouti; tel. 21353391; fax 21355022; f. 2004; Dir-Gen. HIBA AHMED HIBA.

Islamic Banks

Dahabshil Bank International SA: pl. du 27 Juin, BP 2022, Djibouti; tel. 21352233; fax 21355322; e-mail info@dahabshilbank.com; internet www.dahabshilbank.com; f. 2009; Pres. MOHAMED SAID DUALEH.

Saba Islamic Bank (SIB): Immeuble Yassin Yabeh, pl. du 27 juin, BP 1972, Djibouti; tel. 21355777; fax 21357770; e-mail djSaba@SabaBank.com; f. 2006; Dir-Gen. JAMEEL M. ALANSY.

Salaam African Bank (SAB): ave Pierre Pascal, BP 2550, Djibouti; tel. 21351544; fax 21351534; e-mail info@banksalaam.com; internet www.banksalaam.com; f. 2008; Pres. OMAR ISMAÏL EGUEH; Dir-Gen. MOHAMED YUSUF AHMED.

Shoura Bank: Djibouti; tel. 21343892; fax 21343896; e-mail info@shoura-bank.com; f. 2010.

Banking Association

Association Professionnelle des Banques: c/o Banque pour le Commerce et l'Industrie—Mer Rouge, pl. Lagarde, BP 2122, Djibouti; tel. 21350857; fax 21354260; Pres. YAHYA OULD AMAR.

INSURANCE

In 2009 there were two insurance companies in Djibouti.

Les Assureurs de la Mer Rouge et du Golfe Arabe (AMERGA): 8 rue Marchand, BP 2653, Djibouti; tel. 21352510; fax 21355623; e-mail courrier@amerga.com; internet www.amerga.com; f. 2000; Dirs THIERRY MARILL, LUC MARILL, ABDOURAHMAN BARKAT ABDILLAHI, MOHAMED ADEN ABOUBAKER.

GXA Assurances: 3 rue Marchand, BP 200, Djibouti; tel. 21353636; fax 21353056; e-mail accueil@gxaonline.com; internet www.gxaonline.com; Country Man. CHRISTIAN BOUCHER.

Trade and Industry

CHAMBER OF COMMERCE

Chambre de Commerce de Djibouti: pl. Lagarde, BP 84, Djibouti; tel. 21351070; fax 21350096; e-mail ccd@intnet.dj; f. 1906; 44 mems, 22 assoc. mems; Pres. SAÏD OMAR MOUSSA; First Vice-Pres. MAGDA REMON COUBÈCHE.

UTILITIES

Electricity

Electricité de Djibouti (EdD): 47 blvd de la République, BP 175, Djibouti; tel. 21352851; fax 21354396; e-mail direction-edd@edd.dj; internet www.edd.dj; Dir-Gen. DJAMA ALI GUELLEH.

TRADE UNIONS

Union Djiboutienne pour les Droits Economiques Sociaux et Culturels et Civils et Politiques: rue Pierre Pascal, BP 2767, Djibouti; tel. 77823979 (mobile); e-mail uddesc@yahoo.fr; internet www.uddesc.org; f. 2005; confed. of 21 trade unions; Sec.-Gen. HASSAN CHER HARED.

Union Générale des Travailleurs Djiboutiens (UGTD): Sec.-Gen. ABDO SIKIEH.

Transport

RAILWAYS

In 2011 the Indian Government announced its intention to provide US $300m. towards the construction of a new railway line connecting Ethiopia and Djibouti.

Chemin de Fer Djibouti–Ethiopien (CDE): BP 2116, Djibouti; tel. 21350280; fax 21351256; e-mail adoches@hotmail.com; f. 1909; adopted present name in 1981; jtly owned by govts of Djibouti and Ethiopia; 781 km of track (121 km in Djibouti) linking Djibouti with Addis Ababa; Pres. ALI HASSAN BAHDON.

ROADS

In 2000 there were an estimated 3,065 km of roads; in 2009 it was estimated that 16% of Djibouti's roads were paved. About one-half of the roads are usable only by heavy vehicles. In 1981 the 40-km Grand Bara road was opened, linking the capital with the south. In 1986 the Djibouti–Tadjoura road, the construction of which was financed by Saudi Arabia, was opened, linking the capital with the north. In May 2004 the European Development Fund approved a US $38.4m. road construction project between Djibouti and Addis Ababa, and in October the Kuwait Fund for Arabic Economic Development approved a $20m. loan to build a road between Tadjoura and Obock.

SHIPPING

Djibouti, which was established as a free port in 1981, handled 11.3m. metric tons of freight in 2009.

Djibouti Maritime Management Investment Company (DMMI): BP 1812, Djibouti; f. 2004 to manage Djibouti's fishing port.

Djibouti Ports and Free Zones Authority (DPFZA): POB 198, Djibouti; tel. 359070; fax 359059; e-mail zfd@intnet.dj; internet www.djiboutifz.com; Chair. ABOUBAKER OMAR HADI.

Port Autonome International de Djibouti (PAID): BP 2107, Djibouti; tel. 21357372; fax 21355476; e-mail customer.care@port.dj; internet www.dpworld-djiboutiport.com; managed by DP World, UAE, since 2000; Gen. Man. JOHANNES DE JONG.

Principal Shipping Agents

Almis Shipping Line & Transport Co: BP 85, Djibouti; tel. 21356998; fax 21356996; Man. Dir MOHAMED NOOR.

Cie Maritime et de Manutention de Djibouti (COMAD): ave des Messageries Maritimes, BP 89, Djibouti; tel. 21351028; fax 21350466; e-mail hettam@intnet.dj; f. 1990; stevedoring; Man. Dir ALI A. HETTAM.

Global Logistics Services Djibouti: rue Clemenceau, POB 3239, Djibouti; tel. 77839000 (mobile); fax 21352283; e-mail gls.djibouti@gls-logistics.tk; shipping, clearing and freight-forwarding agent; Gen. Man. MOHAMED A. ELMI.

Inchcape Shipping Services & Co (Djibouti) SA: 9–11 rue de Genève, BP 81, Djibouti; tel. 21353844; fax 21353294; e-mail portagencydjibouti@iss-shipping.com; internet www.iss-shipping.com; f. 1942; Man. Dir AHMED OSMAN GELLEH.

International Transit Services: POB 1177, Djibouti; tel. 21251155; fax 21353258; e-mail its02@intnet.dj; Man. Dir ROBLEH MOHAMED.

J. J. Kothari & Co Ltd: rue d'Athens, BP 171, Djibouti; tel. 21350219; fax 21351778; e-mail ops@kothari.dj; internet www.kotharishipping.net; f. 1957; LLC; shipping agents; also ship managers, stevedores, freight forwarders, project cargo movers; Man. Dir NALIN KOTHARI; Dep. Man. Dir PIERRE VINCIGUERRA.

Smart Logistic Services: BP 1579, Djibouti; tel. 21343950; fax 21340523; e-mail sls@intnet.dj; internet www.smartforwarders.com; f. 2010; Man. Dir FAHMI A. HETTAM.

Société Djiboutienne de Trafic Maritime (SDTM): blvd Cheik Osman, BP 640, Djibouti; tel. 21352351; fax 21351103.

Société Maritime L. Savon et Ries: blvd Cheik Osman, BP 2125, Djibouti; tel. 21352352; fax 21351103; e-mail smsr@intnet.dj; Gen. Man. JEAN-PHILIPPE DELARUE.

CIVIL AVIATION

The international airport is at Ambouli, 6 km from Djibouti. There are six other airports providing domestic services. In late 2009 the European Union banned all Djibouti airlines from flying in its airspace.

Daallo Airlines: BP 2565, Djibouti; tel. 21353401; fax 21351765; e-mail daallo@intnet.dj; internet www.daallo.com; f. 1991; operates services to Somalia, Saudi Arabia, the United Arab Emirates, France, the United Kingdom, Kenya and Ethiopia; CEO MOHAMED IBRAHIM YASSIN.

Djibouti Airlines (Puntavia Airline de Djibouti): BP 2240, pl. Lagarde, Djibouti; tel. 21351006; fax 21352429; e-mail djibouti-airlines@intnet.dj; internet www.djiboutiairlines.com; f. 1996; scheduled and charter regional and domestic flights; Man. Dir Capt. MOUSSA RAYALEH WABERI.

Tourism

Djibouti offers desert scenery in its interior and watersport facilities on its coast. A casino operates in the capital. There were about 53,000 tourist arrivals in 2008. Receipts from tourism totalled US $18.0m. in 2010.

Office National du Tourisme de Djibouti (ONTD): pl. du 27 juin, BP 1938, Djibouti; tel. 21353790; fax 21356322; e-mail onta@intnet.dj; internet www.office-tourisme.dj; Dir MOHAMED ABDILLAHI WAIS.

Defence

Arrangements for military co-operation exist between Djibouti and France, and in November 2011 there were about 1,500 French military personnel stationed in Djibouti, while the US-led Combined Joint Task Force-Horn of Africa also had its headquarters in the country. Around 1,285 US military, naval and air force personnel were stationed there. In January 2010 Djibouti announced that it would contribute some 450 troops to the African Union Mission in Somalia. As assessed at November 2011, the total armed forces of Djibouti itself, in which all services form part of the army, numbered some 8,450 (including 200 naval and 250 air force personnel). There were also paramilitary forces numbering 2,000 gendarmes, as well as a 2,500-strong national security force. Conscription of all men between 18 and 25 years of age was introduced in 1992.

Defence Expenditure: Budgeted at 1,720m. Djibouti francs in 2010.

Commander-in-Chief of the Armed Forces: Pres. ISMAÏL OMAR GUELLEH.

Chief of Staff of the Army: Gen. ZAKARIA CHEIK IBRAHIM.

Education

The Government has overall responsibility for education. Primary education generally begins at six years of age and lasts for six years. Secondary education, usually starting at the age of 12, lasts for seven years, comprising a first cycle of four years and a second of three years. In 2008/09 primary enrolment included 44% of pupils in the relevant age-group (47% of boys; 42% of girls), and secondary enrolment was equivalent to 30% of pupils in the relevant age-group (35% of boys; 26% of girls). In 2007 spending on education represented 22.8% of total government expenditure. In 2010/11, according to UNESCO estimates, there were 60,992 primary school pupils and 50,965 pupils receiving general secondary and vocational education. Djibouti's sole university, the Université de Djibouti, was formed in January 2006 as a replacement for the Pôle Universitaire de Djibouti, which opened in 2000 and had 4,705 students in 2010/11.

Bibliography

Aden, M. *Ourrou-Djibouti 1991-1994: Du Maquis Afar à la Paix des Braves*. Paris, L'Harmattan, 2002.

Alwan, D. A., and Mibrathu, Y. *Historical Dictionary of Djibouti*. Lanham, MD, Scarecrow Press, 2001.

Coubba, A. *Djibouti: Une nation en otage*. Paris, L'Harmattan, 1993.

Dubois, C. *Djibouti 1888-1967: Héritage ou frustration?* Paris, L'Harmattan, 1997.

L'or blanc de Djibouti: Salines et sauniers (XIXe-XXe siècles). Paris, Editions Karthala, 2003.

Dubois, C., and Soumille, P. *Des chrétiens à Djibouti en terre d'Islam: XIXe-XXe siècles*. Paris, Editions Karthala, 2004.

Fontrier, M. *Abou-Bakr Ibrahim, Pacha de Zeyla–Marchand d'Esclaves: Commerce et Diplomatie dans le Golfe de Tadjoura 1840–1885*. Paris, L'Harmattan, 2003.

Imbert-Vier, S. *Tracer des frontières à Djibouti : Des territoires et des hommes aux XIXe et XXe siècles*. Paris, Editions Karthala, 2011.

Koburger, C. W. *Naval Strategy East of Suez: The Role of Djibouti*. New York, Praeger, 1992.

Labrousse, H. *Récits de la Mer Rouge et de l'Océan Indien*. Paris, Commission Française d'Histoire Maritime, 1992.

Laudouze, A. *Djibouti, Nation carrefour*. Paris, Editions Karthala, 1982.

Morin, D. *Dictionnaire historique afar (1288-1982)*. Paris, Editions Karthala, 2004.

Oberle, P., and Hugot, P. *Histoire de Djibouti: des origines à la république*. Paris, Editions Présence Africaine, 1985.

Schrader, P. J. *Djibouti*. Oxford, Clio Press, 1991.

'Ethnic Politics in Djibouti: From the "Eye of the Hurricane" to "Boiling Cauldron"', in *African Affairs*, Vol. 92, No. 367 (April 1993), pp. 203–221.

Tholomier, R. *Djibouti: Pawn of the Horn of Africa*. Metuchen, NJ, Scarecrow Press, 1981.

Thompson, V., and Adloff, R. *Djibouti and the Horn of Africa*. London, Oxford University Press, 1968.

Tramport, J. *Djibouti Hier: de 1887 à 1939*. Paris, Hatier, 1990.

Waberi, A., *Balbala*. Paris, Le Serpent à Lumes, 1997.

Weiss, E. *Djibouti: Évasion*. Paris, Editions du Fer à Marquer, 1990.

Woodward, P. *The Horn of Africa: State Politics and International Relations*. London, Tauris, 1996.

EQUATORIAL GUINEA

Physical and Social Geography

RENÉ PÉLISSIER

The Republic of Equatorial Guinea occupies an area of 28,051 sq km (10,831 sq miles). Geographically, the main components of the republic are the islands of Bioko (formerly known as Fernando Póo), covering 2,017 sq km, and Annobón (also known as Pagalu), 17 sq km; and, on the African mainland, bordered to the north by Cameroon, to the south and east by Gabon and westwards by the Gulf of Guinea, lies the province of Río Muni (also formerly known as Mbini), 26,017 sq km, including three coastal islets, Corisco (15 sq km) and the Great and Little Elobeys (2.5 sq km).

Bioko is a parallelogram-shaped island, 72 km by 35 km, formed from three extinct volcanoes. To the north lies the Pico de Basilé (rising to 3,007 m above sea level), with an easy access. In the centre of the island are the Moka Heights, while, further south, the Gran Caldera forms the remotest and least developed part of the island. The coast is steep to the south. Malabo is the only natural harbour. Crop fertility is high, owing to the combination of volcanic soils and plentiful rainfall. At the southern extremity of the Guinean archipelago lies the remote island of Annobón, south of the island of São Tomé.

Mainland Río Muni is a jungle enclave, from which a coastal plain rises steeply toward the Gabonese frontier. Its main orographic complexes are the spurs of the Monts de Cristal of Gabon. The highest peaks are Piedra de Nzas, Monte Mitra and Monte Chime, all rising to 1,200 m. The main river is the Mbini (formerly known as the Río Benito), non-navigable except for a 20-km stretch, which bisects the mainland province. On the Cameroon border is the Río Campo; its tributary, the Kye, is the de facto eastern border with Gabon. The coast is a long beach, with low cliffs towards Cogo. There is no natural harbour.

The country has an equatorial climate with heavy rainfall, especially in Bioko. The average temperature of Malabo is 25°C and the average rainfall is in excess of 2,000 mm. Humidity is high throughout the island, except on the Moka Heights. Río Muni has less debilitating climatic conditions.

The July 1994 census, recorded a total population of 406,151. The population was estimated by the UN to be 740,469 at mid-2012. The main city is Malabo (with 136,971 inhabitants, including suburbs, according to UN estimates in mid-2011), the capital of Bioko and of the republic, as well as the main economic, educational and religious centre. The other town of note is Luba. Bubi villages are scattered in the eastern and western parts of the island. On the mainland the only urban centre is the port of Bata, which had a population of 71,406 in 2001. Other ports are Mbini and Cogo. Inland, Mikomeseng, Nkumekie, Ebebiyín and Evinayong are small market and administrative centres. The country is divided into seven administrative provinces: Bioko Norte, Bioko Sur and Annobón for the two main islands; Centro-Sur, Kié-Ntem, Litoral and Wele-Nzas for the mainland and its adjacent islets.

The ethnic composition of Equatorial Guinea is unusually complex for so small a political unit. The Fang are the dominant group in Río Muni, where they are believed to comprise 80%–90% of the population. North of the Mbini river are the Ntumu Fang, and to the south of it the Okak Fang. Coastal tribes—notably the Kombe, Balengue and Bujeba—have been pushed towards the sea by Fang pressure. Both Fang and coastal peoples are of Bantu origin. Since independence in 1968, many inhabitants of Río Muni have emigrated to Bioko, where they have come to dominate the civil and military services. The Bubi, who are the original inhabitants of Bioko, may now number about 5,000. The Fernandino, of whom there are a few thousand, are the descendants of former slaves liberated by the British, mingled with long-settled immigrants from coastal west Africa. The working population of Annobón are mainly seafarers and fishermen.

The official languages are Spanish, French and, since October 2011, Portuguese. In Río Muni the Fang language is spoken, as well as those of coastal tribes. Bubi is the indigenous language on Bioko, although Fang is also widely used in Malabo, and Ibo is spoken by the resident Nigerian population.

Recent History

MARISÉ CASTRO

The Republic of Equatorial Guinea comprises the region of Río Muni, on the West African mainland, and the islands of Bioko, Annobón, Corisco and the Elobeys. It was granted independence on 12 October 1968, after 190 years of Spanish colonial rule. Following decolonization, Francisco Macías Nguema, a mainland Fang from the Esangui clan, took office as President of the new republic, after multi-party elections in which he had received the support of a moderate coalition grouping. Once in office, he moved swiftly to suppress opposition (outlawing all existing political parties) and to assert absolute power through a 'reign of terror', in which his nephew Lt-Col Obiang Nguema Mbasogo played a major role. The brutal nature of the regime, which killed tens of thousands of people, led to the flight of as many as one-third of the total population, including nearly all of the skilled and educated elements of Equato-Guinean society. Macías Nguema obtained much of his economic and military aid from Eastern bloc countries; relations with Spain deteriorated, and serious regional disputes arose with Gabon and Nigeria. The country's economy, centred on cocoa plantations on Bioko and relying on imported African labour, was devastated by the excesses of Macías Nguema's regime.

THE EARLY YEARS OF OBIANG NGUEMA'S PRESIDENCY

In August 1979 Macías Nguema was overthrown in a coup led byObiang Nguema Macías Nguema fled the capital but was captured, tried and executed in September. Obiang Nguema announced the restoration of the rule of law, but banned all political parties and ruled through a Supreme Military Council (SMC), which continued to be dominated by the Esangui clan.

In December 1981 the first civilians were appointed to the SMC, and in August 1982 a new Constitution was approved by 95% of voters in a referendum. Obiang Nguema was appointed to a seven-year term as President. As the sole candidate in the first presidential election since independence, he was elected in June 1989 with 99% of the votes cast. The election was not conducted by secret ballot. Similarly, the first legislative elections since 1968 were held in August 1983. All candidates were nominated by the President and were duly elected to serve a five-year term, albeit with no legislative powers. In October 1987 Obiang Nguema created a 'governmental party', the Partido Democrático de Guinea Ecuatorial (PDGE), which together with the higher ranks of the civil service and armed forces remained predominantly the preserve of the President's Esangui clan.

Although the atrocities of the Macías period abated, Obiang Nguema's pledge to restore democracy did not materialize, and the country remained a one-party state until 1991. He maintained his uncle's tradition of authoritarianism, and extended the family's control over the country's economic and political life, including the justice system, fuelling a culture of fear through military purges and the ruthless repression of any potential opposition. The international human rights organization Amnesty International has consistently denounced human rights violations and lack of freedoms in the country, and documented the Government's systematic harassment, detention and mistreatment of political opponents.

OPPOSITION PRESSURES

No political parties other than the ruling party were permitted until 1992, although some parties established by exiles abroad played an important role in bringing about what little political change has occurred.

During the Macías period the most influential exiled opposition party was the Alianza Nacional para la Restauración Democrática de Guinea Ecuatorial, based in Geneva, Switzerland. Following Obiang Nguema's accession to power, however, its influence declined and by 2000 it had ceased to exist. The exiled opposition split into numerous small and shifting groups, many of which were based in Spain. Political liberalization in Gabon led to the emergence in 1990 of Libreville as a new base for the Equato-Guinean opposition in exile. The most significant of these groups was the Unión para la Democracia y el Desarollo Social. Opposition groups and coalitions have continued to emerge outside the country, primarily in Spain, but, with the exception of the Partido del Progreso de Guinea-Ecuatorial (PPGE) led by Severo Moto Nsa, they have been short lived and have had little or no impact within Equatorial Guinea itself. These included the Coordinadora de la Oposición Conjunta (CODE) formed in Madrid, Spain, in 1999, which grouped Moto Nsa's faction of the PPGE, the Movimiento para la Autodeterminación de la Isla de Bioko (MAIB), the Frente Demócrata Republicano (FDR) and three other minor groupings. However, within one year the CODE had effectively ceased to exist.

Under growing internal and international pressure, Obiang Nguema eventually conceded the principle of political plurality in July 1991. A new Constitution containing such provisions was approved by referendum in mid-November; however, the few human rights safeguards contained in the 1982 Constitution were removed. Furthermore, provisions of the new Constitution exempted Obiang Nguema from any judicial procedures arising from his presidential tenure, while Equato-Guinean citizens who also held foreign passports and persons not continuously resident in Equatorial Guinea for 10 years (subsequently reduced to five) were barred from standing as election candidates, thus effectively excluding virtually all exiled political opponents from participation in national political life. In January 1992 a number of laws were promulgated, which included legislation on political parties and freedom of assembly and association. This was followed by the formation of a new transitional Government (comprising only PDGE members) and the implementation of a general amnesty that included all political exiles. Although some exiled opposition parties began slowly returning to seek legalization and prepare for the first multi-party legislative elections in 1993, Equato-Guinean exiles reacted cautiously to Obiang Nguema's efforts to encourage their return. His family's monopoly on power, persistent human rights abuses, corruption and economic factors, discouraged many émigrés from returning.

The first two opposition parties, the Unión Popular (UP) and the Partido Liberal, were legalized in June 1992, and in September an alliance of opposition parties, the Plataforma de Oposición Conjunta (POC) was formed. The legalization of the Convergencia para la Democracia Social (CPDS) in March 1993 brought the total number of legalized political parties to 14, which included a few still operating in exile. However, what little organized political opposition emerged found itself under constant threat, and few opposition parties survived beyond the mid-2000s, by which time most had either been co-opted by the Government and dissolved after their leaders joined the ruling PDGE, or had become too riddled with internal divisions to be effective.

The POC was dissolved in March 1996. In April 1997, following two months of negotiations, a new national pact was signed by representatives of the Government and of 13 opposition parties; the CPDS, which was instrumental in establishing the POC, was excluded from the talks. One month later the PPGE president, Moto Nsa, was arrested by the Angolan authorities on board a boat carrying a consignment of arms reportedly intended for use in a planned *coup d'état* in Equatorial Guinea. Moto Nsa was released in June and subsequently sought refuge in Spain, where he had resided continuously since 1983. The PPGE was banned and the party subsequently split, with one faction demanding Moto Nsa's expulsion from the party; other party members defected to the ruling PDGE. Only a small faction based in Spain, led by Moto Nsa, survived. In August Moto Nsa and 11 others were convicted *in absentia* of treason; Moto Nsa was sentenced to 101 years' imprisonment.

In September 2003 three political parties in Spain formed a 10-minister government-in-exile, with Moto Nsa as its President. In June 2005 the Equato-Guinean embassy in Madrid, Spain, was occupied and damaged by opposition activists who blamed the Obiang Nguema regime for the attempted murder that month of the brother of one of the FDR's leaders in Madrid. In April 2006 several people were found guilty of the attempted murder but the court failed to find evidence implicating the Equato-Guinean Government. Following the attack, the embassy was temporarily closed by the Equato-Guinean Government, which demanded that the Spanish Government guarantee its safety and deal firmly with Equato-Guinean opposition militants exiled in Spain. In December Spain revoked Moto Nsa's refugee status, which was restored on appeal in March 2008 by the Spanish Supreme Court; the ruling was confirmed by the Constitutional Court a year later. In January 2012 a group of PPGE members voted to suspend Moto Nsa from the party and the government-in-exile. Although Moto Nsa denied that he had lost control, such ructions within the rump party suggested that both organizations were in decline.

By the end of the first decade of the 21st century there was little meaningful or effective opposition left within Equatorial Guinea. The CPDS, the only truly independent legalized opposition party, had been systematically marginalized and undermined by routine harassment and the arrest of its members, and remained too small to have a significant impact on events.

Despite its evident weakness, fear of contagion from the political unrest in North Africa and the Middle East in early 2011 induced Obiang Nguema to view the opposition as a serious potential threat to his prestige and authority in the run-up to the African Union (AU) Summit in Malabo scheduled for June. In March Obiang Nguema banned all marches and demonstrations, and made use of his control of the media to impose a complete blackout on coverage of events in North Africa and the Middle East. Requests by the UP and CPDS to hold meetings and demonstrations in that month were rejected. Police and soldiers were deployed in the streets of the main cities to enforce the ban. As a pre-emptive measure to block any clandestine preparations for a May Day rally, at the end of April several leading members of the CPDS were arrested along with some 100 students, and released without charge a few days later.

In a meeting with all legalized political parties in March 2011 Obiang Nguema announced his intention to carry out political reforms, which would be submitted to referendum for approval, but he denied that this decision had been prompted by events in North Africa. He proposed the revision of the Constitution to limit the presidential mandate to two five-year terms, the creation of a Senate and the establishment of an Audit Court to counter corruption. One week later the CPDS and the UP issued a joint statement appealing for the urgent implementation of meaningful reforms leading to a true transition to democracy. They proposed the creation of a working group comprising all political parties to negotiate the reforms, and the revision of the electoral law, the law regulating local entities and the organic law of the Superior Judicial Council. They also demanded that legislative and municipal mandates be reduced to four years, and appealed for the adoption of urgent measures to guarantee the exercise of fundamental freedoms, a general amnesty for all political prisoners allowing for the return of political exiles, and the legalization of all political parties, trade unions and other civic associations.

In April 2011 the Comisión de Vigilancia y Seguimiento del Pacto Nacional (Commission for the Monitoring and Follow-up of the National Pact), established in 1997, met in Malabo for the first time since September 2008, to discuss the political reform proposals and the creation of a joint commission to liaise between the Government and political parties and to establish the modalities of the proposed legal reforms. In May 2011 Obiang Nguema announced a loose timetable for his reforms to be drafted, presented to parliament and finally submitted to a referendum in late 2011. The following day he issued a decree establishing the Comisión Nacional para el Estudio de la Reforma de la Ley Fundamental de Guinea Ecuatorial (National Commission for the Study of the Reform of the Equatorial Guinean Constitution), and appointed all its members, the majority of whom belonged to the PDGE, although other political party representatives were also included. However, the CPDS, the UP and the Acción Popular de Guinea Ecuatorial (APGE) objected to the President's unilateral appointment of their members, and declined the invitation to participate in the Commission on the grounds that none of their proposals had been included and that the timetable did not allow sufficient time for meaningful discussions. They expressed their suspicion that the reform was just another cosmetic exercise by the President that presented self-serving legislative reform as a concession to democratic opinion, in order to placate criticism and divert demands for substantive change. The APGE subsequently agreed to join the Commission (see below). The report of the reform commission was presented to parliament in July. Although a referendum date was not announced until late October, in August Obiang Nguema embarked on a tour of the country, the main focus of which was his campaign for a 'yes' vote in the referendum.

The referendum, eventually held on 13 November 2011, was plagued with numerous irregularities, and voters were subjected to harassment and intimidation by police and soldiers deployed in the polling stations, who also expelled opposition observers. Independent opposition political parties complained that they had only received the text of the proposals two weeks before the referendum, which had hindered their ability to campaign, while the electorate had not been provided with any information about the proposed reforms. As expected, the proposals were approved, with 97.7% of the votes recorded in favour, and the revised Constitution was promulgated on 16 February 2012. The new Constitution further increased Obiang Nguema's powers, effectively extending his term in office. Although it limited the President's tenure of office to two consecutive seven-year terms, the amended charter removed the upper age limit for presidential candidates, previously set at 75 years, and created the post of Vice-President, reserved exclusively for a PDGE party member. Further measures included the creation of a Senate, an Audit Court, a State Council, an Economic and Social Council, a Council for the Defence of the People, as well as the post of Ombudsman. The Constitution granted the President the power to appoint the Vice-President, the Ombudsman and the members of the Council for the Defence of the People. In mid-April a 28-member commission, 12 of whom represented opposition parties (including the CPDS), was created to draft the internal regulations of the newly created state bodies and to revise the existing laws so that they conformed to the new Constitution. The commission was also tasked with the revision of the country's electoral legislation.

ELECTIONS, 1968–2009

Elections continue to be overtly manipulated by the Government and the ruling PDGE, allowing Obiang Nguema and his supporters to maintain a democratic façade while consolidating power and forestalling any electoral gains by the opposition. Since 1968 there have been no free and fair elections. Before the advent of a formal multi-party political system, presidential and legislative elections were uncontested and duly won by Obiang Nguema, the sole presidential candidate, with almost 100% of the vote, and the PDGE, the members of which he appointed as the only candidates in legislative elections.

Since 1993 opposition political parties have contested both presidential and legislative elections to little effect, as Obiang Nguema and the PDGE have continued to win elections with unrealistically overwhelming majorities. Elections have been accompanied by the harassment of political opponents before and during polling, with numerous other irregularities and violations of the electoral law. Complaints by political opposition parties and their demands for fresh elections are consistently dismissed by the courts, which brand the complainants as dishonest and poor losers.

The first multi-party legislative elections took place in November 1993. They were, however, boycotted by most of the parties in the POC alliance, in protest against Obiang Nguema's refusal to review contentious clauses of the electoral law. Although representatives of the Organization of African Unity (now the AU) attended as observers, the UN declined a request by the Equato-Guinean authorities to monitor the elections, on grounds that correct procedures were evidently not being implemented. Following a turn-out variously estimated at 30%–50% of the electorate, the PDGE won 68 of the 80 seats in the legislative Cámara de Representantes del Pueblo (House of Representatives). In December the Government announced that henceforth all party political gatherings would be subject to prior official authorization.

Subsequent legislative elections in March 1999, April 2004 and May 2008 followed the same pattern of harassment and irregularities. At the 1999 elections, the PDGE claimed to have obtained more than 90% of the votes cast and took 75 of the 80 parliamentary seats. Two opposition parties, the UP and CPDS, gained four and one seats, respectively, but refused to take up the seats. Together with five other opposition parties they rejected the results and demanded the annulment of the elections on the grounds that the electoral law had been violated.

As expected, the PDGE won the 25 April 2004 elections, obtaining 68 of the 100 seats in the newly enlarged parliament. A coalition of eight parties allied to Obiang Nguema secured a further 30 seats, while the CPDS won the remaining two parliamentary seats. Although it contested the results of the poll, in June the CPDS took up its two seats, but refused to sit on any committees.

In the May 2008 elections, which were held concurrently with municipal elections, the PDGE obtained 90 of the 100 parliamentary seats. The coalition allied to the PDGE won nine seats, leaving the CPDS with just one seat in parliament.

Meanwhile, local elections scheduled for November 1994 were postponed until September 1995, after opposition parties boycotted the population census and numerous political opponents were arrested. In June 1994 the Government had agreed to modify the controversial electoral law and to conduct an electoral census prior to the election, but had instead begun to compile a general population census. Eventually, an electoral census was carried out with UN assistance and elections were held. Contested by 14 parties, they were the first truly representative multi-party elections to take place since independence and were monitored by international observers. The six member parties of the POC presented a united front, offering a single candidate in each constituency. The initial results indicated that opposition parties had won an overwhelming victory; however, the official results credited the ruling party with a majority of the votes cast in two-thirds of local administrations. Judicial appeals by the opposition against the outcome, supported by the team of international observers, were rejected. These were the freest elections held in the country since independence. Opposition hopes of most lasting change, however, were short lived as Obiang Nguema took measures to ensure that he retained tighter control of the electoral process in future polls. Threats, coercion, harassment and imprisonment of opposition party members all subsequently increased.

In the local elections held on 4 May 2008 the PDGE and its allies secured control of all councils, with 319 councillors elected out of a total of 332 (increased from 244), while the CPDS had 14 councillors elected.

The first presidential election under the multi-party political system was held in February 1996. Obiang Nguema was returned to office for a third term, securing more than 90% of the votes cast. The election was boycotted by the main opposition parties, in protest against alleged electoral irregularities and official intimidation. The electoral roll drawn up by the UN in 1995 was discarded in favour of an allegedly fraudulent list produced by the Government, and the conduct of the elections was severely criticized by foreign observers.

President Obiang Nguema was returned to office for a fourth term, having obtained 97.1% of the votes cast in elections held on 15 December 2002. The election process was condemned by the European Union (EU). Four opposition candidates withdrew on the day of the election in protest against alleged irregularities, including the presence of military personnel in some voting booths, intimidation of voters and threats to opposition parties' electoral monitors, some of whom were physically expelled from polling stations.

At the presidential election on 29 November 2009, contested by Obiang Nguema and four other candidates, the incumbent secured 95.8% of the vote.

OBIANG NGUEMA'S DOMINANCE OF THE POLITICAL SPHERE

With each new election and government enlargement, the Obiang Nguema family was able to consolidate further its position of power in the country with a fresh intake of family members and other close allies. President Obiang Nguema also made frequent use of government reorganizations to include more family members. It was not until 2003 that non-PDGE members were finally brought into government.

In February 2003 presidential candidates for the elections held in December 2002 were invited to join the newly enlarged parliament, but the CPDS declined the invitation, demanding as a precondition the release of political prisoners detained in June 2002 (including its Secretary-General, Plácido Micó Abogo). Micó Abogo was eventually granted a conditional presidential pardon in August 2003, along with 17 other political opponents sentenced the previous year.

The elections of 2004 resulted in the formation of a new Government led by Prime Minister Miguel Abia Biteo Borico, who was dismissed just two years later, in August 2006, along with his 51-member cabinet, accused of corruption and incompetence. Obiang Nguema then appointed a new Government led by Ricardo Mangue Obama Nfubea, a member of the Fang majority, thus breaking the tradition of appointing a Prime Minister drawn from the Bubi ethnic minority. The majority of the new Government had held portfolios in the previous administration, and all but two ministers were affiliated to the ruling PDGE.

In July 2008 Obama Nfubea was accused of corruption and mismanagement of the economy and dismissed along with his cabinet, most of whom were reinstated in the new administration led by Ignacio Milam Tang, hitherto the Equato-Guinean ambassador to Spain. In January 2010 Milam Tang was reappointed to lead a 68-member Government notable for its promotion of Obiang Nguema's eldest son, Teodoro (Teodorín) Nguema Obiang, from Minister Delegate of Agriculture and Forestry to Minister of State. In early March the President appointed his uncle, Manuel Nguema Mba, as his security adviser. Nguema Mba had been dismissed as Minister of National Security in February 2009 following the reported attack on the presidential palace in Malabo (see below).

The nepotistic trend was reaffirmed in further reorganizations in January and April 2011. The January reorganization included the appointment of Francisca Tatchoup Belope, of Bubi origin, as Minister of Economy, Commerce and Business Promotion, the first woman to hold such post, and Celestino Bacale, hitherto a leading member of the CPDS and a relative of a close ally of Obiang Nguema, as her Minister-delegate. A niece of the President, Monserrat Afang Ondo, was appointed Minister-delegate in charge of the Treasury, and four members of allied political parties were also appointed to the cabinet. A minor reorganization in April brought more family members into the Government, mainly at secretary of state level. At the same time, Mariola Bibang Obiang, a niece of the President, was appointed as the permanent representative to UNESCO; she was designated as ambassador to France in April 2012.

The grooming of the President's eldest son 'Teodorín' Nguema Obiang as future President of the country intensified in July 2010 with his election as leader of the youth movement of the PDGE. This move automatically promoted him to the post of vice-president of the party, thus enabling his appointment, not only as leader of the party, but also as supreme leader of the nation in the event of either illness or the death of his father. In September 2011 Teodorín Nguema was appointed as the country's deputy representative to UNESCO.

The main purpose of the constitutional reforms promulgated in February 2012 (see above) was to vouchsafe the continuity of Obiang Nguema and to secure his son's succession. They included the creation of the post of Vice-President, and it was widely expected that Teodorín Nguema would be appointed to this position, thus confirming his role as his father's replacement. The reforms reaffirmed the existing seven-year term, while conceding a limit of two terms in office, but removed the maximum age limit for presidential candidates. This would enable Obiang Nguema to stand in presidential elections beyond 2016 and for a second term after that. Crucially, the new Constitution increased Obiang Nguema's power as it granted him full legal control of the executive. In August 2011 Obiang Nguema announced his intention to lead the nation for as long as it continued to vote for him. In the event of his death occurring before completion of his term in office, he would be replaced by the Vice-President.

In April 2012 delegates to the Fifth Congress of the PDGE appointed Obiang Nguema as President for life and confirmed Teodorín Nguema as leader of the party's youth movement, while the President's wife, Constancia Mangue, was designated honorary President of the PDGE's women's organization. In accordance with the Constitution, in May Obiang Nguema dissolved the Government and appointed a new Council of Ministers. Surprisingly, former Prime Minister Ignacio Milam Tang was named as Vice-President, while Teodorín Nguema was appointed as Second Vice-President, in charge of Defence and State Security, a post not envisaged in the Constitution. The new Government was enlarged to 60 members and included an even greater number of Obiang Nguema's close relatives, a number that was expected to increase further once the Secretaries of State were appointed. The post of Prime Minister reverted to the Bubi ethnic group, with the premier now responsible for the co-ordination of the Government. Two Deputy Prime Ministers were also appointed, although the Constitution did not provide for those positions.

ATTEMPTED COUPS

Since the country's independence there have been numerous rumours of coup plots, which have rarely been substantiated. Obiang Nguema has long made systematic use of these rumours to justify the ruthless elimination of rivals and opponents. With the advent of regular elections, alleged coup plots would typically be announced in the run-up to polling and used to justify the repression of opposition parties.

In October 2003 reports circulated of a failed coup attempt. Dozens of military officers, including a close relative of Obiang Nguema, together with a number of civilians were arrested between November and December and tried secretly in February 2004. Details of the trial and sentences emerged later, with most of the defendants convicted and sentenced to between 20 and 30 years' imprisonment. The authorities claimed to have foiled at least three further coups in March, May and October 2004, one involving foreign nationals. In March 14 foreigners, South African and Armenian nationals resident in the country, were arrested following intelligence allegedly received from South Africa. Together with Moto Nsa and the members of his so-called government-in-exile, who were tried *in absentia*, 11 of the foreign nationals were convicted in November of an attempt to overthrow the

Government and kill President Obiang Nguema. They received gaol terms ranging from 14 to 63 years; Moto Nsa was sentenced to 63 years' imprisonment. The authorities accused some Western governments, businessmen and multinational companies of involvement in the alleged coup plot, which, they claimed, had been organized by Moto Nsa. He denied any involvement in the affair.

The arrest of the 14 foreign nationals in March 2004 followed that of 70 South Africans at Harare airport (Zimbabwe), where they had made a stop-over to pick up a consignment of arms. In late August they were convicted in a Zimbabwean court of contravening immigration laws; two were also convicted of contravening aviation laws, while Simon Mann, a British national and the suspected operational leader of the alleged coup attempt, was convicted of attempting to purchase weapons. The Equato-Guinean authorities relentlessly sought his extradition from Zimbabwe to face charges of plotting to overthrow the Government of Equatorial Guinea. In May 2007 the Harare Magistrates' Court granted the application requesting his extradition. Soon after, he was released from prison in Harare, having completed his sentence, but was arrested immediately and held in prison pending extradition procedures. After several appeals, Mann was secretly extradited to Equatorial Guinea in February 2008 where in July he was found guilty of attempting to overthrow Obiang Nguema and sentenced to 34 years' imprisonment. Mann was pardoned by President Obiang Nguema in early November 2009, together with the four South African nationals still in prison. According to some reports in May 2010, in exchange for a presidential pardon, Mann pledged not to take legal action or to make financial claims against any Equato-Guinean officials for his imprisonment. He also reportedly agreed to assist the authorities in any action they might take against others suspected of involvement in the coup plot.

In August 2004 Sir Mark Thatcher (a businessman and son of former British Prime Minister Baroness Margaret Thatcher) was arrested in South Africa on suspicion of having financed the alleged coup attempt. Although Thatcher initially denied involvement in the affair, in January 2005 he admitted contravening South African anti-mercenary legislation by agreeing to finance the use of a helicopter. He was fined R3m. (over US $500,000) and was given a four-year suspended sentence. In June the six Armenian nationals convicted of involvement in the coup attempt were pardoned by President Obiang Nguema and released from prison. In June 2006 one of the South African prisoners was pardoned on humanitarian grounds and released from prison, together with dozens of other political prisoners and detainees including those convicted in June 2002 and in September 2005 of involvement in attempted coups. A further 25 prisoners convicted in those trials were released following a presidential pardon in June 2008. Prior to this, in March, several former members of the proscribed PPGE were arrested in Malabo following the alleged discovery of weapons and ammunition in a vehicle that was being exported from Spain to Equatorial Guinea. The Equato-Guinean authorities claimed that they were to be used by Moto Nsa to stage a coup. Of the six that were tried, one was imprisoned for one year while the other five received gaol terms of six years for illegal possession of arms and ammunition. They were released by a presidential pardon in June 2011, together with the remaining prisoners convicted in February 2004. Moto Nsa was arrested in April 2008 in Spain and was charged with illegal arms-trafficking but was released on bail in August. In December the charges against him were dropped.

In February 2009 the Equato-Guinean authorities alleged that there had been an attack on the presidential palace in Malabo, for which they blamed the Nigerian armed group Movement for the Emancipation of the Niger Delta, which denied any involvement in the incident. The authorities subsequently accused Equato-Guineans of organizing, financing and participating in the attack, which, it was alleged, was carried out in order to kill the President. A number of foreign nationals were arrested in the aftermath of the alleged attack and subsequently expelled from the country. Ten members of the UP were arrested in February and March and subsequently charged with offences relating to the attack. In late September eight of them—including the wife of the former UP leader, Faustino Ondo Ebang—were conditionally released pending trial. The charges against them were dropped at the beginning of their trial in March 2010. However, Ondo Ebang (exiled in Spain since 2007 and tried *in absentia*) together with two other UP members and seven Nigerian nationals, believed to be fishermen and traders who were arrested at sea on the day of the alleged attack, were tried on charges of attempting to kill the President. While the Equato-Guineans were acquitted, but not released, the Nigerians were convicted as charged and received prison sentences of 12 years, although they were released by a presidential pardon in October. The two acquitted Equato-Guineans were tried again in August on the same charges, on this occasion by a military court, and sentenced to 12 years' imprisonment. They, too, were pardoned and released in October. On trial with them in the same military court were four Equato-Guineans exiled in Benin, who had been abducted in January 2010 and secretly transferred to Equatorial Guinea by members of the country's security personnel. The four were convicted of organizing and taking part in the alleged attack on the palace and were executed in August. The summary executions attracted international outrage.

POLITICS AFTER THE OIL BOOM

The discovery of significant oil and gas reserves in the mid-1990s transformed Equatorial Guinea from one of the poorest countries in Africa to one of its richest. The country became the third largest oil producer in sub-Saharan Africa. The vast majority of the population, however, derived minimal benefit from the discovery of these resources, and the country's infant mortality and life expectancy rates continued to rank among the world's worst.

With his rising world profile, from the early 2000s President Obiang Nguema came under increasing pressure from Western governments and international organizations to improve human rights, transparency, and to establish the rule of law and democracy. However, the President's pledges to implement democratic change were never translated into reality. Becoming more than just a useful façade, the Government provided the conduit through which the country's oil wealth could be most effectively tapped by the President and his immediate family. The incentive to encourage the emergence of civil society and political diversity diminished as control over government became increasingly lucrative.

Throughout the first decade of the new millennium Obiang Nguema strived to gain prestige, respectability, and a role on the world stage consistent with his status as one of the richest rulers in the world (with a personal fortune of US $600m. according to Forbes in 2006). He lavished considerable sums of money on advice from US consultancies aimed at shedding his regime's enduring reputation as corrupt and oppressive, not to mention his own image as one of Africa's harshest dictators. In June 2010, in what was seen as a perfect opportunity to adopt the mantle of a respectable senior statesman in a major world forum, Obiang Nguema attended the Fortune Global Forum in Cape Town, South Africa, where he outlined a carefully worded 10-year reform programme promising poverty alleviation, democracy, rule of law, transparency and human rights. His proposals were widely regarded with scepticism by the international community.

With Western oil companies operating in the country also under pressure to demonstrate good governance, the Government was persuaded in 2004 to seek participation in the Extractive Industry Transparency Initiative (EITI), an international voluntary scheme to increase transparency in the extractive industry sponsored by the Norwegian and British Governments and supported by the IMF and the World Bank. In February 2008 Equatorial Guinea was accepted as a candidate country. However, in April 2010 its candidacy was rejected by the EITI board on the grounds that it had not complied with the organization's rules. One of the EITI requirements for membership is genuine participation of civil society in the process, a requirement not met by Equatorial Guinea.

In October 2007 Obiang Nguema announced his intention to establish the UNESCO-Obiang Nguema Mbasogo International Prize for Research in the Life Sciences, endowed with US $3m. over five years, to be funded by the Government of Equatorial Guinea. In November 2008 UNESCO accepted the award. However, world-wide opposition from international non-governmental organizations (NGOs), academics and governments led to postponement of the awarding of the prize in March and June 2010, pending further consideration. South African Archbishop Desmond Tutu argued that the prize was an attempt to 'burnish the unsavoury reputation of a dictator'; others pointed to the country's poor human rights record, lack of freedoms, ongoing problems with corruption and the abject poverty endured by its citizens despite the country's considerable oil wealth. In October UNESCO finally suspended the award. In May 2011, and again in October, UNESCO's Executive Board reiterated this indefinite suspension when it declined to consider a petition by the Obiang Nguema administration to reinstate the prize. However, following intense international lobbying by the Equato-Guinean Government, support for the award grew, particularly among African nations. Despite the lack of consensus and a deeply divided vote, in March 2012 UNESCO's Executive Board approved the prize, albeit under a new name. All of the African countries represented on the Board supported this decision, while most Western nations strongly opposed it. However, it remained unclear whether the newly redesignated UNESCO-Equatorial Guinea prize would ever be implemented. Some members complained that procedures to change the name had not been followed, and there were concerns over financing the prize with funds from the Equato-Guinean public treasury, a violation of UNESCO's rules.

Despite these setbacks to Obiang Nguema's aspirations, the recent dramatic improvement in Equatorial Guinea's regional standing was well exemplified by his election as rotating president of the AU for 2011. Further confirmation of the trend came in November, when the third South America-Africa summit was held in Malabo instead of Tripoli, Libya, owing to the ongoing instability in that country. The Africa Cup of Nations football tournament was jointly hosted by Equatorial Guinea and Gabon in January 2012, representing the triumphal culmination of many years spent developing *quid pro quo* relationships with the country's regional neighbours.

CORRUPTION

Widespread corruption has been a persistent problem in Equatorial Guinea, but since the discovery and exploitation of oil in the mid-1990s its place at the heart of the regime has been highlighted by a series of serious accusations of corruption against President Obiang Nguema and his family. Allegations have included money-laundering and the squandering and misappropriation of state revenues for personal gain. The international NGO Transparency International has consistently ranked the Equato-Guinean Government as one of the most corrupt in the world. In 2011 it ranked it within the bottom 10 of the corruption index world-wide and among the four most corrupt in Africa.

Internally, President Obiang Nguema has often levelled charges of corruption against his ministers, and has adopted measures to combat this, including the creation by presidential decree of the Agencia Nacional de Investigación Financiera to fight money-laundering and the financing of terrorism in February 2007. However, the announcement of such measures appeared to have been geared more towards placating international criticism and diverting attention away from allegations of corruption involving his own family, and have had no lasting impact on the persistence of corrupt practices within the Government and state institutions. As part of those measures, hundreds of civil servants were dismissed during the short-lived premierships of Miguel Abia Biteo Borico and Ricardo Mangue Obama Nfubea. Both Prime Ministers were accused of corruption and dismissed after two years in office, in 2006 and 2008, respectively.

Obiang Nguema and his family have been the subject of two investigations by the US Senate's Permanent Subcommittee on Investigations. In 2004 the subcommittee, reporting on its investigation into alleged money-laundering practices by the former Riggs Banks, found that the bank held US $700m. in state funds deposited by US oil companies into personal accounts belonging to Obiang Nguema, his second son and Minister of Mines Gabriel Lima, and his nephew and Secretary of State for Treasury and Budget Melchor Esono Edjo, and revealed that between 2000 and 2003 they had unduly transferred large amounts of money from the Government Oil Revenue Account into shell corporations in bank secrecy jurisdictions and into bank accounts in other countries. The investigation had also uncovered several luxury housing purchases by the President and close relatives in the US state of Maryland.

The focus then turned to the President's eldest son, Teodorín Nguema, who had been the subject of intense investigation since 2007. In September of that year the US Department of Justice reported that between 2005 and 2007 Teodorín Nguema had funnelled some US $75m. through three European banks to several banks in the USA. The report also stated that the family's assets came largely from 'extortion and theft of public funds or other corrupt conduct'.

In February 2010 the same Senate subcommittee that investigated the Riggs Banks published a report on money-laundering, naming Teodorín Nguema as a prime suspect, who subsequently became the subject of a criminal investigation. By mid-2012, however, he had not been charged with any offence. The investigation revealed that he had circumvented money-laundering controls to transfer some US $110m. in suspected funds, which he used between 2004 and 2007 to finance expensive purchases in the USA. These included a mansion in Malibu, California, an aircraft and a fleet of luxury motorcycles and cars, together worth double the Equato-Guinean Government's 2005 budget for education. The Government denied the accusations levelled against Teodorín Nguema.

In October 2011 the US Department of Justice started legal proceedings to seize Teodorín Nguema's US assets, valued at US $71m., which it considered to have been obtained through corruption and money-laundering. The Equato-Guinean Government rejected the allegations and requested that the US courts dismiss the case, arguing that the Department of Justice had failed to prove the claims made against Teodorín Nguema. In April 2012 a US federal judge concluded that the complaint filed by the Department of Justice lacked sufficient evidence to support the allegations and hence dismissed the attempt to seize Teodorín Nguema's assets.

Meanwhile, in September 2008 a Spanish human rights group, Asociación Pro-Derechos Humanos de España, filed a case with Audiencia Nacional (the central investigation court) against 11 people, including President Obiang Nguema, several members of his family and members of the Government, whom they accused of misappropriating some US $26m. from the state oil company to buy property in several Spanish cities. The money had been allegedly transferred from the account held at the Riggs Bank in the USA and paid into branches of the Spanish bank, Santander. The case was referred to the Public Prosecutor for consideration. In March 2010 the anti-corruption department of the Public Prosecution Office in Las Palmas, Spain, authorized the investigating court to proceed with their investigation into the suspected money-laundering. The investigation was extended to properties owned by Obiang Nguema and his family in Las Palmas and other Spanish cities. After two years of investigating the matter, the Banco de España and the Unidad de Delitos Económicos y Fiscales de la Policía Judicial (Unit for Economic and Fiscal Crimes of the Judiciary Police) in Las Palmas concluded that there was evidence of money-laundering by Obiang Nguema's family and members of the Equato-Guinean Government. The police report, released in April 2012, stated that two Russians in Las Palmas had laundered misappropriated funds for the Obiang family and government ministers, using several 'offshore' companies registered in tax havens. Transactions included the transferral of $26.4m. from the Riggs Bank account to Santander between 2000 and 2003, as well as the purchase in 2006 of 25 apartments in Lanzarote, Spain, for €4.8m.

In 2007 French police also uncovered assets belonging to President Obiang Nguema's family, worth a combined US $6.3m. In late 2010 a French court ruled that a related corruption case brought by NGOs against the President's family could proceed. In June 2011, however, the French Public

Prosecutor blocked a petition by the investigating magistrates to extend the investigation to alleged irregularities with major purchases made in France by the Presidents of Equatorial Guinea, the Republic of the Congo and Gabon. It was alleged that in November 2009 Teodorín Nguema had bought 26 luxury cars and six motorcycles at a cost of some €12m., and that in March 2010 he bought works of art valued at €18m., which were paid for by a state forestry company presided over by him.

As part of the investigation, in September 2011 French police confiscated 11 luxury cars belonging to Teodorín Nguema, and in February 2012 they searched his mansion in central Paris, valued at €500m., and seized some 200 cu m of luxury goods and art objects worth an estimated €40m. The Equato-Guinean Government insisted that the mansion was for diplomatic use and was not a private residence, and accused France of violating diplomatic immunity laws. French magistrates contested the claim, arguing that the building housed a nightclub, a hairdressing salon and other rooms devoted to activities wholly unrelated to diplomacy. Reports subsequently emerged that Teodorín Nguema had bought the residence in 2004, but had sold it to his country in November 2011 after the police investigation began. Furthermore, to protect him from prosecution in France, in September Teodorín Nguema had been appointed as Equatorial Guinea's deputy representative to UNESCO, although the organization denied having received any notification of this development. Nevertheless, in April 2012 the French Public Prosecutor approved a request made by two magistrates for the issue of an international warrant for the arrest of Teodorín Nguema on suspicion of using public funds to buy property in France. The warrant had yet to be confirmed by the French Minister of Justice by mid-2012, although, following approval by the Public Prosecutor, the warrant came into immediate effect in countries within the EU. The Equato-Guinean Government accused France of attempting to destabilize the country and threatened to retaliate against French interests in Equatorial Guinea. The ruling PDGE marshalled demonstrations throughout the country in support of Teodorín Nguema, and in Malabo over 2,000 people demonstrated outside the French embassy. Following the police raid on his Paris mansion, Teodorín Nguema announced that he was taking legal action for libel against the President of the French chapter of Transparency International, who, in an article published in February, had accused Nguema of embezzling public money.

FOREIGN RELATIONS

Equatorial Guinea's relations with Spain, the former colonial power (which has traditionally provided substantial economic aid), have been consistently strained by reports of internal corruption, the misuse of aid funds and abuses of human rights, and the frequent detention and expulsion of Spanish citizens from Equatorial Guinea. This led to the temporary suspension of non-essential Spanish aid in the 1990s.

Spain's repeated refusals to extradite Moto Nsa, whom the Equato-Guinean authorities accused of involvement in an alleged coup attempt in March 2004, renewed tensions. The Equato-Guinean authorities also accused Spain of withholding information about the planning of the alleged coup, recalling its ambassador to Spain for one month. He was again recalled in July 2005 when the embassy was temporarily closed after an attack by opposition exiles (see above), not reopening until January 2006 when a new ambassador was appointed. High-level meetings between the two countries were held throughout 2006, culminating in a two-day visit to Spain by President Obiang Nguema in November amid much criticism from Equato-Guinean exiles and Spanish opposition parties. Since then, there has been a rapprochement between the two countries, with frequent visits by Spanish governmental and trade delegations to Equatorial Guinea, where important trade and co-operation agreements were signed.

From the early 1980s Obiang Nguema attempted to prise the country away from Spanish influence into France's economic sphere. In December 1983 Equatorial Guinea became a member of the Union Douanière et Economique de l'Afrique Centrale (which was replaced by the Communauté Economique et Monétaire en Afrique Éentrale—CEMAC—in 1999), and in August 1984 it joined the Banque des Etats de l'Afrique Centrale (BEAC). Full entry to the Franc Zone followed in January 1985, when the CFA franc replaced the epkwele as the national currency, and in February 1998 French became Equatorial Guinea's second official language. However, by 2011 legal procedures in France against President Obiang Nguema and his family had resulted in growing tension between the two countries. Relations deteriorated further in April 2012, when the French Public Prosecutor approved an international warrant for the arrest of Teodorín Nguema. The Equato-Guinean Government accused France of seeking to destabilize the country and threatened to retaliate against French interests in Equatorial Guinea unless it acted to halt the judicial process. The French Government insisted, however, that it had no powers to interfere with the judiciary.

Equatorial Guinea has also sought in recent years to establish relations with other European countries, particularly the United Kingdom, where it opened an embassy in May 2005. Relations with the Russian Federation have been strengthened, with Russia becoming a major supplier of arms and other military materiel by the late 2000s. In 2011 relations were re-established with Germany, and in July a German embassy was opened in Malabo.

Relations with the EU have long been fraught. The EU has repeatedly voiced its criticism of government policy, demanding the release of political prisoners and urging the Government to begin the process of democratization without delay, resorting on occasions to the suspension of aid and cancellation of agreements. Despite vociferous Equato-Guinean condemnation of the EU decision in June 2006 to prohibit the country's aircraft, including the presidential plane, from using EU airspace, co-operation projects on human rights and law and order were agreed in a straightforward manner in July. In March 2008 the Equato-Guinean Government signed the ninth European Development Fund (EDF), estimated at some €10.4m., most of which was intended to improve administrative capacity and to promote the rule of law, with €2.6m. allocated to enhancing the agricultural sector and strengthening regional integration and civil society. The signing of the EDF was conditional upon economic reforms and human rights improvements.

Since 2006 Equatorial Guinea has sought membership of the Comunidade de Países de Língua Oficial Portuguesa (CPLP), in which it had gained observer status. Throughout 2009 strong ties were formed with CPLP member states, particularly Brazil, which opened an embassy in Malabo and became a major investor in the country, and Portugal. In March 2010 a Portuguese delegation of government officials and businessmen visited Equatorial Guinea, where several trade agreements were signed. It was expected that, in exchange, Equatorial Guinea would be admitted to the CPLP as a full member later that year, in anticipation of which the Government announced a bill to adopt Portuguese as Equatorial Guinea's third official language. Following a major outcry against the country's admission, however, at its summit in July in Luanda, Angola, the CPLP opted to postpone the decision until 2012.

After a period of tense relations, the US embassy in Malabo was closed in 1996, apparently as part of a programme of cost-saving measures. Improving relations and pressure from US oil companies led to the reopening of the US embassy in Malabo in 2003, headed by a chargé d'affaires until 2006, when a resident ambassador was appointed. Since then, US investment in the country, estimated at US $5,000m. in 2002, has increased. In the wake of the terrorist attacks on the USA on 11 September 2001, the US Administration approved further military aid to train a coastguard service to protect petroleum installations in Equatorial Guinea. It was estimated that by 2015 Equatorial Guinea, together with Angola and Nigeria, would provide 25% of the USA's petroleum imports. Relations were slightly strained in February 2010 after the US Senate Subcommittee published its report on money-laundering naming Teodorín Nguema as a main suspect (see above).

Souring relations with Europe and the USA encouraged Obiang Nguema to diversify his alliances, and relations were established, or strengthened, with other countries, particularly with the People's Republic of China and the Democratic People's Republic of Korea (North Korea), which have become major economic partners. In September 1996 an agreement on economic co-operation was signed with China, which was renewed during President Obiang's visit to that country in November 2001. Agreements were signed on computing, infrastructure development and health care. China agreed to pardon part of Equatorial Guinea's debt and to provide interest-free loans. Since then co-operation between the two countries has expanded, aided by regular reciprocal visits by senior government officials of both countries. During his visit to China in October 2005, when further agreements on infrastructure and housing, natural resource exploitation, agriculture, silviculture and fishing were signed, President Obiang Nguema stated that thenceforth Equatorial Guinea's main development partner was to be China. In exchange for a share in Equatorial Guinea's petroleum exploitation, China then cancelled a reportedly large but undisclosed part of the debt owed by Equatorial Guinea. In August 2006 an agreement was signed in Malabo whereby some 15 Chinese companies were contracted to build thousands of social housing units, some 2,000 km of roads, a hydroelectric terminal to supply electricity to 23 mainland towns and another terminal on Bioko Island.

Strong links with Israel have developed since 2005, when a major programme for improving health care provision commenced. Israel has also become an important supplier of military equipment and provides military advisers and training to the Equato-Guinean armed forces and Presidential Guards.

Co-operation has also been promoted with Latin American countries, notably Cuba, with which a co-operation agreement in the areas of health, education and agriculture was signed in November 1999, renewed in May 2007 and expanded to include training in telecommunications and the media. In February 2008 a government delegation led by President Obiang Nguema embarked on a tour of several Latin American countries including Argentina, Brazil, Cuba, Venezuela and Uruguay. His visit to Argentina provoked demonstrations and protests against human rights abuses in Equatorial Guinea, a cause also taken up by parliamentarians and government officials, who boycotted a number of state ceremonies. The tour was eventually cut short and the visit to Uruguay was postponed indefinitely. Good relations with Venezuela were formalized with the opening in April 2010 of an Equato-Guinean embassy in Caracas.

REGIONAL STANDING

Since 2000 President Obiang Nguema has sought to play a more prominent role in regional African affairs, to reflect his country's new economic standing. He has established economic and diplomatic ties with most countries in Africa. Despite sporadic setbacks over territorial disputes, relations with neighbouring countries have gradually improved.

Already strong, relations with Morocco were further strengthened by the visit of King Muhammad VI of Morocco to Equatorial Guinea in April 2009. Morocco's military aid after 1979 had been crucial in maintaining Obiang Nguema's regime until 1994, when most troops were withdrawn except for a small number of guards overseeing the President's security. These guards were reportedly recalled in April 2012 and replaced with Equato-Guinean forces trained by Israel.

In mid-1994 Nigeria and Equatorial Guinea agreed to establish an international commission to demarcate maritime borders in the Gulf of Guinea, although negotiations were complicated by the presence of substantial petroleum reserves in the disputed offshore areas. Relations between the two countries improved with the signing of several agreements, including one on defence co-operation in 2000, and were further enhanced in 2002 when Equatorial Guinea supported Nigeria in its dispute with Cameroon over the Bakassi peninsula. Equato-Guinean opposition groups viewed the rapprochement between the two Governments with suspicion. These opposition groups have frequently accused Nigerian security personnel of connivance with Equato-Guinean security forces in the abduction and repatriation of Equato-Guinean exiles in Nigeria. In April 2008 the two countries held talks aimed at improving security in the Gulf of Guinea where pirates and smugglers were threatening offshore and coastal facilities. To counter increasing piracy, joint patrols by the two countries and Cameroon commenced in November 2009.

Relations with Cameroon became intermittently strained throughout the 2000s, on account of frequent repressive interventions by the Equato-Guinean authorities against illegal immigrants and the forcible expulsion of hundreds of Cameroonian nationals from the country. In the aftermath of a seaborne raid in December 2007 on a number of banks in Bata, and the alleged attack on the presidential palace in Malabo in February 2009 (see above), Equato-Guinean security forces again targeted Cameroonians, hundreds of whom were arrested and expelled in 2008 and 2009. In December 2006 the Equato-Guinean authorities unilaterally closed the country's border with Cameroon at Kye-Ossi following an assault on an Equato-Guinean nun by Cameroonian traders. Since August 2007 delegations from both countries have held meetings to draft a document to delineate and negotiate their maritime borders. Delegations met again in February 2010 in Malabo, but negotiations ended without agreement. Confrontations along the border at Kye-Ossi continued to be reported frequently. In March 2012, just two weeks after the Joint Cameroon-Equatorial Guinea Commission had met in Yaoundé to improve relations between the two countries, the Equato-Guinean authorities unilaterally closed the border for two days following an incident in which five Cameroonians were injured.

Unresolved territorial disputes with Gabon, revived by petroleum exploration activity in southern Río Muni have affected relations between the two countries. In March 2003 Gabonese forces occupied the small island of Mbañé, over which both countries have long claimed ownership. (Sovereignty over the islands of Cocoteros and Conga is also disputed.) In June Equatorial Guinea rejected a Gabonese proposal to share any petroleum revenues from the island, but a year later, in an attempt to settle the dispute amicably, Obiang Nguema proposed joint exploitation of the petroleum in the area. In January 2004 both countries agreed to seek UN mediation to settle the dispute, and a mediator was sent to the area in June. However, all subsequent meetings between the two countries under the auspices of the UN have failed to bear fruit and the dispute remains unresolved. A step towards an agreement was taken during a meeting between Obiang Nguema and Gabonese President Ali Bongo Ondimba in New York, USA, in February 2012, when the two leaders agreed to draft a legal document to be submitted to the International Court of Justice in The Hague, Netherlands, for consideration.

In May 1993 Equatorial Guinea and South Africa established diplomatic relations. Ties between the two countries improved dramatically after South Africa helped to foil an alleged coup plot in March 2004 (see above) and opened an embassy in Malabo. Since then, Equatorial Guinea and South Africa have signed numerous commercial and security agreements. In March 2011 the two countries signed an agreement in Malabo for the deployment of 28 South African soldiers to help guarantee security during the AU summit in June. Under the terms of the agreement, South Africa was also to equip and train the Equato-Guinean police.

Closer links were also forged with Zimbabwe following the arrest in March 2004 at Harare's International Airport of 70 alleged mercenaries accused of planning to overthrow the Government of Equatorial Guinea. In June the two Governments agreed to open diplomatic delegations in both countries, and in November President Robert Mugabe visited Equatorial Guinea, where he was acclaimed as the 'saviour of the nation' and Equatorial Guinea's 'favourite son' by the host country's authorities. President Obiang Nguema reciprocated the visit in April 2006 during which the two countries signed several trade agreements. Shortly after President Mugabe's visit in March 2007, Equatorial Guinea began to supply petroleum to Zimbabwe on favourable terms.

Strong relations were formed with Angola and in January 2006 an Equato-Guinean embassy opened in Luanda. A month later President Obiang Nguema and several of his ministers visited Angola and signed several co-operation agreements related to defence, internal and external security and public order, oil and transport. Angolan President José Eduardo dos Santos reciprocated the visit in February 2007.

In 2004, following a visit to Ghana by President Obiang Nguema, the two countries signed economic agreements, which included a study into refining Equato-Guinean oil in Ghana. In May 2010, during a three-day visit to Malabo by the Ghanaian President John Evans Atta Mills, an agreement was reached for the regular annual supply of 1m. barrels of Equato-Guinean crude petroleum to Ghana. The visit was reciprocated in September when Obiang Nguema visited Ghana, where he sought investment and assistance to develop the agricultural sector, particularly the cocoa industry.

In May 2009 Equatorial Guinea opened its first embassy in the Middle East, in Cairo, Egypt.

In recent years Equatorial Guinea has come to assume a prominent role within its region. In January 2010 Lucas Abaga Nchama, an Equato-Guinean, was appointed as governor of the BEAC. This was followed in February by the election of Equatorial Guinea to the AU's 15-member Peace and Security Council, to serve a three-year term. In April the CEMAC parliament was inaugurated in Malabo.

In January 2011 Obiang Nguema was formally elected as rotating chairman of the AU, Malabo having been chosen in July 2010 as the venue of the summit scheduled for June of the following year. The summit represented the culmination of years of intense lobbying by Obiang Nguema for prestigious regional roles commensurate with his growing economic influence. A new city, Sipopo, was purpose-built outside Malabo to accommodate the dignitaries attending the summit.

Economy

MARISÉ CASTRO

INTRODUCTION

The economy of Equatorial Guinea was traditionally based on agriculture and forestry, the principal products being timber, cocoa, coffee, palm oil, bananas and cassava. At independence in 1968, the country had a flourishing industrial sector based primarily on processing agricultural derivatives and timber, and the highest per head income in Africa. However, under Equatorial Guinea's first President, Francisco Macías Nguema, the economy was devastated, and both industrial and commercial agricultural production were eliminated. The cocoa sector, the main hard currency earner, never recovered from the 11 years of economic and political chaos. By the time Macías Nguema was deposed by his nephew, Lt-Col Obiang Nguema Mbasogo, in August 1979, Equatorial Guinea had become one of the poorest and most heavily indebted countries in Africa.

The discovery of significant petroleum and gas reserves in the mid-1990s transformed Equatorial Guinea, placing the country among the richest nations in Africa in terms of per head income and on a par with some of the most developed countries in the world. Equatorial Guinea became Africa's seventh largest oil producer (after Nigeria, Algeria, Libya, Angola, Egypt and Sudan). As the petroleum sector became increasingly important, bringing unprecedented levels of economic growth, the agricultural sector contracted sharply. By 2002 oil had become the country's most valuable asset, responsible for turning Equatorial Guinea into the fastest growing economy in the world. Massive foreign investments in the oil and gas sector, together with a sharp rise in oil exports and favourable terms of trade, contributed to the country's impressive gross domestic product (GDP) expansion, with average annual real growth reaching 26.2% between 2001 and 2005. During 2005–10 90% of the country's total revenue was generated from its non-renewable natural resources. Oil revenues increased dramatically in value from US $190m. in 2000 to an estimated $8,400m. in 2009 and $9,700m. in 2011, when it accounted for 90.4% of revenues according to the IMF.

In 2007 the World Bank reported that Equatorial Guinea had one of the 60 highest incomes in the world, at approximately US $20,000 per head per year, although government figures on the population count vacillate between 600,000 and 1m. In 2009 it estimated the country's gross national income (GNI) at $10,500m. One year later it reported that Equatorial Guinea's GNI, measured at average 2006–08 prices, was $9,875m., equivalent to $14,980 per head (or $21,700 per head on an international purchasing-power parity basis). GNI was estimated at $10,500m. in 2009. Overall GDP increased, in real terms, at an average annual rate of 20.9% between 2000 and 2008.

Only a small élite has benefited from the oil-derived wealth. It is estimated that 80% of the national revenue is still concentrated in the hands of the ruling oligarchy. The vast majority of the population, estimated at about 700,000 people in 2011, have derived minimal benefit and remain impoverished, surviving largely on subsistence agriculture and small family enterprises. The country as a whole remains underdeveloped, and government expenditure on social services has not increased in line with revenue growth. Infant mortality and life expectancy rates, together with other human development indicators, continue to rank among the world's worst. Nepotism, corruption, financial mismanagement, a lack of transparency and accountability, and weak state institutions are regularly cited as the most serious obstacles hindering the development of the country and a more equitable distribution of its wealth.

ECONOMIC POLICY

There is a paucity of reliable economic data on Equatorial Guinea. The authoritarian élites in power since independence have had little incentive to relinquish their secretive control over the country's finances, or to facilitate precise measurement of their performance as custodians of the nation's well-being. The basic statistics that have become available owe their existence largely to international bodies such as the World Bank and the IMF, and to the institutions of the six-nation Communauté Economique et Monétaire en Afrique Centrale (CEMAC), of which Equatorial Guinea was a founder member.

Following independence, Macías Nguema imposed a centralized economy, whereby private entrepreneurial activity was forbidden and all the significant economic sectors were taken over, and mismanaged, by the state, which became the main employer. Once Obiang Nguema seized power, the process of nationalization was reversed, and state enterprises, especially in agriculture and timber, were gradually privatized or granted as fixed term concessions, mostly to foreign companies. The state, however, continued to be the main employer in the country.

The private sector remains negligible to this day and is still largely monopolized by Obiang Nguema's family and associates. Limited financing for small and medium-sized businesses, insufficient skilled labour, and the prohibitive cost of imported goods also deter private sector development. The state continues to dominate domestic investment, concentrated predominantly in the hydrocarbons and construction sectors. The business environment remains difficult. According to the World Bank Doing Business index, the ease of doing business in Equatorial Guinea deteriorated between 2010 and 2011, when its ranking dropped from 161st out of 180 countries to 164th out of 183 countries. The same source cited the lack of regulatory quality and economic freedom, coupled with high perceived levels of corruption, as the major constraints on business activity. In the 2012 index the country's ranking rose to 155th, attributable mainly to a marked improvement in the availability of credit. Nevertheless, in that year the international anti-corruption organization Transparency International ranked Equatorial Guinea as one of the most corrupt countries in the world, placing it in 172th place out of 182 countries. Since 2004, 35% of the share capital of all foreign companies established in Equatorial Guinea must be held by Equato-Guinean citizens or companies belonging to Equato-Guineans. In addition, they are obliged to have at least three national partners, and one-third of the board must also be nationals.

The economy has become almost totally reliant on hydrocarbon revenues. The Government's expensive attempts to encourage diversification have failed to deliver significant results, despite repeated exhortations from the IMF and the World Bank, mindful of the country's evident symptoms of 'Dutch disease' (referring to the negative effects on the Netherlands' economy following the discovery of North Sea gas). Hydrocarbons production and timber accounted for nearly all of Equatorial Guinea's total exports in 2005, with oil and gas accounting for an estimated 93.2% of GDP. While non-oil revenue decreased from 3.8% of GDP in 2009 to 3.5% in 2010, in 2011 oil and oil derivatives accounted for 72% of GDP and 98.5% of exports.

The importance of the hydrocarbons sector has been formalized by a number of government measures. In February 2001 the Government created Petróleos de Guinea Ecuatorial (renamed Guinea Ecuatorial de Petróleo—GEPetrol—in October), a mixed venture with predominantly Equato-Guinean capital, to safeguard the country's interests against the foreign petroleum companies operating in the country. In July President Obiang Nguema announced plans to renegotiate hydrocarbons contracts to increase the country's participation in petroleum licences, which stood at around 5%. This increased to 15% with the granting of the first licence in 2001. In September 2002 a law was adopted that formalized state control of all oilfields. A new hydrocarbons law was approved in September 2006 aimed at increasing royalties due to the state, hitherto set at a minimum of 10% of production, and at extending state involvement in oil projects overall. In November 2008 this percentage stood at 25%. In January 2005 the Sociedad Nacional de Gas de Guinea (SONAGAS) was created to oversee gas exploration and development.

In 2008 Equatorial Guinea applied for membership of the Extractive Industries Transparency Initiative (EITI), partly to counter criticism of its lack of fiscal and oil revenue transparency and to comply with IMF recommendations. However, in April 2010 the EITI board rejected the country's request for an extension of the original validation deadline and withdrew its candidate status. In February 2012 the Government announced its intention to re-apply for EITI membership and revealed that it was receiving technical assistance from the World Bank in the elaboration of its application.

The oil revenue windfall provided the Equato-Guinean state with a perfect opportunity to improve the productive capacity and the economic and social conditions of its long-suffering population. However, the concentration of wealth and power in the hands of a tiny, self-serving family clique has meant that these oil revenues have not only been mismanaged, but much of them have also been systematically siphoned off and squandered by Obiang Nguema's family, the members of which occupy all the positions of real power within the Government.

Meanwhile, health and education remain underfunded, despite increased budget allocations to these sectors since 2006, when health accounted for 6.9% of total government expenditure and education for 4%. By 2010 the Government was reportedly spending 10% of the budget on health. Nevertheless, social sector spending remained low, at 14% of the total. The Government frequently acknowledges the problem and reiterates its intention to improve the situation, but to date few tangible changes have been effected.

The oil boom has also failed to improve human development outcomes, which remain poor, as evidenced by the country's low ranking on the UN Development Programme's (UNDP)Human Development Index (HDI). This provides a composite measure of three basic dimensions of human development: health, education and income. Despite the abundant petroleum revenues, the standard of living of the majority of the population has not been significantly affected and poverty remains widespread. A report published in October 2005 by UNDP showed that, in one year, Equatorial Guinea had fallen 12 places on the HDI, from 109th to 121st. By 2007 it had dropped further to 127th place, though it rose to 117th out of the 182 countries listed in 2010. The country was ranked 136th out of 187 countries in 2011, but its HDI value was higher than the average for sub-Saharan Africa. Life expectancy declined from 49.1 years in 2001 to 43.3 in 2005, before increasing to 53 in 2008, and then decreasing again to 51 in 2011. In January 2006 UNDP estimated that 60% of the population had no access to running water or electricity, and that 70% lived on less than US $2 per day. In the same year the IMF asserted that Equatorial Guinea had sufficient resources to be able to end poverty. Although no recent statistics have been made available, it is evident that little, if any, progress has been made in these areas, and there are serious doubts as to whether Equatorial Guinea will be able to achieve any of the UN's Millennium Development Goals by 2015.

In November 2007 the Government admitted to having the necessary resources to eradicate poverty and achieve full development by 2020, and announced a five-year plan to diversify the economy away from petroleum and gas by investing more than US $12,000m. in infrastructure, a petroleum refinery, motorways, a new airport, a new hydroelectric power plant, and a gas power plant, as well as new hospitals. According to the Government, expenditure in these areas in 2009 was above $10,000m. In February 2008 the Cámara de Representantes del Pueblo, the Equato-Guinean legislature, approved the Plan Nacional de Desarrollo Económico y Social: Horizonte 2020 (National Economic and Social Development Plan: Horizon 2020), ostensibly aimed at eradicating poverty within 12 years, but seen by many as a delaying tactic.

In June 2010 President Obiang Nguema attended the Fortune Global Forum in Cape Town, South Africa, and declared his commitment to poverty alleviation, economy diversification, accountability and transparency. He outlined five key policies, including reapplying for membership of the EITI and expanding the Social Development Fund, which is used for a full range of development objectives, from health and education to job creation and infrastructure building.

Economic policy in 2011–12 continued to be notionally subject to the Horizonte 2020 plan, which highlighted the objectives of economic diversification and poverty reduction. Progress in both areas remained slow, partly attributable to the difficult business environment, which constrained private sector investment. Despite the Government's declared commitment to economic diversification and investment in strategic sectors such as fisheries, agriculture and eco-tourism, investment in these areas remained limited, and diversification efforts were more likely to remain concentrated on infrastructural development and other capital projects.

Together with oil, construction has dominated economic activity since the mid-2000s, propelled by ambitious projects under the aegis of the Government's Programa de Inversiones Públicas (Public Investment Programme) to rebuild derelict infrastructure. However, some of the more grandiose prestige projects have failed to attract significant numbers of paying customers or to contribute in any tangible way to the socio-economic development of the country. One such example was the Malabo II project, which was carried out between 2006 and 2009 at an estimated cost of 70,000m. francs CFA and delivered new ministry buildings as well as a motorway linking Malabo airport to the Ela Nguema district. A similar project, Bata II, included the building of a marina and a ring-road in Bata, as well as numerous hotels and luxury housing. An even more ambitious project was the creation of the new city of Sipopo, a luxury tourism complex that cost the Government over €580m. Other prestige projects included the construction of the stadiums and related infrastructure that enabled Equatorial Guinea to co-host, together with Gabon, the Africa Cup of Nations football tournament in January–February 2012. Most ambitious of all was the founding of a new administrative capital, Oyala—to be modelled on Brazil's federal capital, Brasília—the construction of which was under way in Wele-Nzas province, in the centre of the continental region.

Some basic economic performance indicators have been made available by international agencies such as the World

Bank and the IMF. During 2000–08 GDP per head increased, in real terms, at an average annual rate of 17.6%, and was recorded at US $16,620 in 2007. Over the same period the population was estimated to have increased by an average of 2.8% per year. GDP per head was estimated at $17,958 in 2008, $18,600 in 2009 and $18,372 in 2010.

Overall GDP increased, in real terms, at an average annual rate of 20.9% in 2000–08, though a slowdown in hydrocarbon production brought overall GDP growth down to 9.7% between 2006 and 2009. According to the IMF, in 2009 GDP growth slowed to 5.7% owing to the impact of the global economic crisis, which had resulted in the price of a barrel of oil declining to US $70, from $100 earlier in the year. Nevertheless, this growth rate was higher than government projections, the boost attributable to exports of liquefied natural gas (LNG) and a surge in public spending, primarily in construction, utilities and housing, which expanded by an estimated 27.6%, while the petroleum sector contracted by approximately 6.6%. GDP contracted by 0.8% in 2010, the economy's worst performance since hydrocarbon exploitation began. According to the African Development Bank (AfDB) and the Organisation for Economic Co-operation and Development (OECD), the decrease in revenues during that year had been exacerbated by a decline in petroleum production as oilfields reached maturity. Economic growth of 7.1% was recorded in 2011. The IMF projected GDP growth of 4.0% and 6.8% in 2012 and 2013, respectively.

The rate of inflation has usually been higher in Equatorial Guinea than in other countries in the CEMAC. According to government figures, inflation was 4% in 2005, below the regional average of 4.8%, but rose to 8.5% in 2007, although the accuracy of these figures was disputed by the political opposition. According to the IMF, at the end of 2009 inflation stood at 7.2%, rising to 7.5% in 2010, before decreasing to 7.3% in 2011, with a rate of 7% expected in 2012.

MONETARY POLICY

In January 1985 Equatorial Guinea entered the central African Franc Zone, which became known as the CEMAC in 1994. This six-nation monetary union has its own central bank, the Banque des Etats de l'Afrique Centrale (BEAC), which determines monetary policy for all CEMAC members and prioritizes the control of inflation. Equatorial Guinea's own central bank and bank of issue, the Banco de Guinea Ecuatorial, ceased operations, and the epkwele, which had been linked to the Spanish peseta, was replaced by the franc CFA at a rate of 4 bipkwele = 1 franc CFA. By entering the monetary union, Equatorial Guinea accepted monetary and fiscal rules on the yearly inflation rate and total government debt. At the time it was hoped that Equatorial Guinea's entry into the Franc Zone would bring the country out of isolation by encouraging foreign trade and investment.

Submission to the BEAC was instrumental in keeping Equatorial Guinea's monetary and fiscal policy under control, and immediately brought exchange rate stability to the country. Since January 1999 the franc CFA has been pegged to the euro at a rate of €1 = 655,957 francs CFA, and its exchange rate vis-à-vis other currencies fluctuates through the euro. Other advantages accrued included the guaranteed issuing of money, access to a fully functional banking system and the establishment of a clear and consistent monetary policy. Equatorial Guinea's massive oil wealth has enabled it to play a major role in the affairs of the BEAC. As was to be expected of the richest country in the regional grouping, in 2009 Equatorial Guinea's deposits in the BEAC were greater than those of any other member nation. Since the mid-2000s the Government has been depositing some of its fiscal savings into a fund for future generations at the BEAC. Gross external reserves, mostly held by the BEAC, were estimated at US $3,000m. in 2007. The returns from these deposits account for a considerable proportion of the Equato-Guinean Government's non-oil revenues.

The high levels of fiscal spending that began in 2009 with the Government's ambitious public investment programme, combined with a decline in oil prices in the same year, led to the country's first fiscal deficit in a generation, equivalent to 3.5% of GDP. The deficit was reportedly funded by borrowing over US $500m. from the People's Republic of China, resulting in a three-fold total debt stock increase since 2008.

According to the IMF, total government expenditure was 35% of GDP in 2010, decreasing to 31.1% in 2011, and was projected to decline to 27.7% in 2012. The overall fiscal balance increased from a deficit of 8% of GDP in 2009 to a 3% deficit in 2011, resulting largely from the recovery of hydrocarbon revenues and a significant reduction in government spending.

Total revenue and grants were estimated at 47% of GDP in 2011, down from 51.2% in 2010. Collection of taxes has improved considerably since parliament approved a law regulating personal and corporation tax in October 2004.

Since the early 2000s Equatorial Guinea's levels of public and external debt have been among the lowest in the world, both in real terms and as a percentage of GDP. In 2004 total external debt was estimated at $115m., less than 3% of GDP, with external debt-servicing considered insignificant. Although external debt reached $700m. in 2009 (representing 5% of GDP), if viewed in comparison with annual exports of about $9,000m. and a GDP of about $13,000m., it remains low and sustainable. The IMF predicted that external debt would peak at 10.3% of GDP, before decreasing to below 5.5% of GDP by 2015. The Economist Intelligence Unit (EIU) estimated public and external debt at 4.4% and 4.5% of GDP, respectively, at the end of 2011, attributing this to a limited borrowing requirement after years of high oil revenues. The EIU further estimated that the country's external liabilities reached $1,000m. at the end of 2011, compared with exports of $15,000m. during that year and a GDP of about $23,000m.

AGRICULTURE, FORESTRY AND FISHING

Equatorial Guinea enjoys a fertile terrain capable of sustaining intensive cultivation of fruit and vegetables, which, in turn, could stimulate the development of a food-processing industry. However, the potential for a revival of an important economic role for agriculture has diminished owing to decades of neglect by successive Governments. Repeated government pledges to diversify the economy and promote agricultural development have come to little, as have programmes established to improve food security, and basic foodstuffs still have to be imported. Major obstacles continue to be the lack of material and financial support for farmers, and the poor road infrastructure outside the main cities.

Agriculture and timber, previously the main drivers of Equatorial Guinea's economy, became subsidiary components of the country's GDP once oil production started in 1997. Since 2000 the area of land devoted to agriculture and forestry has continued to shrink. Together with hunting and fishing, they contributed an estimated 2.9% of GDP in 2007, increasing to 3.1% in 2009, or 181,700m. francs CFA, (compared with 51.6% of GDP in 1995). Of this, agriculture contributed 2.2% of GDP in 2009, or 129,500m. francs CFA, rising to 3.4% in 2011. In 2005 agriculture employed an estimated 68.1% of the active population.

In May 2007 the Government announced plans to increase investment in the agricultural sector via a project worth US $3.5m., which was also to include the revamping of the Institute for Agricultural Promotion. However, little was done to compensate for the chronic underfunding of the sector, which remains largely subsistence-based. Cocoa was the main hard currency earner until the industry was destroyed under Macías Nguema. Nevertheless, it remains the primary export crop. Cocoa is the main crop of Bioko, where its cultivation still accounts for about 90% of the country's total output, and still employs the highest proportion of Equatorial Guinea's work-force. However, despite considerable pay increases in recent years, many workers are leaving cocoa plantations to work in the more lucrative petroleum industry.

Prior to independence, over 41,000 ha of land was under cocoa cultivation, underpinned by high guaranteed prices on the Spanish domestic market. More than 800 plantations belonged to Africans, but most of the land and production was controlled by Europeans. Nationalized by Macías Nguema, the cocoa plantations were offered back to their former owners after the coup of 1979. However, many plantations remained unclaimed and others were subsequently reconfiscated; most are now owned by members of the presidential entourage, and are managed by two Spanish companies. They are worked on a share-cropping basis by local small farmers. Only about one-third of the land that was cultivated before independence is now exploited, and most of the trees are old and poorly tended. The cocoa sector has also been undermined by the rising costs of inputs, the scarcity of skilled labour and, most damagingly, the instability of producer prices. After years of continuous decline, from 2006 cocoa production stabilized at around 3,000 metric tons per year. Also in 2006, the price of cocoa settled at 826 francs CFA per kg, which represented a 24% contraction over the previous three years. To rescue the 2007–08 harvest, in August 2007 the Government granted aid worth €300,000 to cocoa producers. In that year cocoa exports totalled €1.8m. However, earnings from cocoa, as well as from coffee, declined in 2009 as a result of the global financial crisis, and its share of total exports was 0.1%. As part of the Government's plan to diversify the economy in accordance with IMF recommendations made in April 2010, Equatorial Guinea has sought to revitalize the cocoa industry, and signed an agreement with Ghana in September.

Coffee was traditionally the second most important export crop after cocoa, and the sector began to recover slightly after 2006, owing to a relative increase in purchases from planters, though its contribution to GDP remained negligible. Like cocoa, earnings from coffee also declined in 2009 owing to the global financial crisis.

Cassava, coco yam, sweet potatoes, plantain, bananas, rice, maize, palm oil and eggs are all produced for the domestic market. In July 2002 the Instituto de Promoción Agraria began to grant credit to small farmers in Malabo as an incentive for them to grow food for the internal market, in an attempt to limit the country's dependence on imports, but little progress has been made on this front. As Obiageli Ezekwesili, the Vice-President for the World Bank, African Region, observed during his visit to Malabo in July 2011, the fact that fertile Equatorial Guinea was still obliged to import such basic foodstuffs as tomatoes from Cameroon showed it was suffering from a 'classic case of Dutch disease'. There are eventual prospects of substantial food exports to Gabon, which is persistently short of foodstuffs and already imports plantain from Río Muni. The Government is promoting the production of spices (vanilla, pepper and coriander) for export.

Timber, primarily from the mainland province of Río Muni, is the second largest revenue earner after petroleum and accounted for 25.8% of export revenue in 1996; however, by 2004 it accounted for only an estimated 1.2% of export revenue. By 2009 it had further decreased to 0.8%. In 2009 the value of timber exports was reported to be 129,500m. francs CFA. There are some 1.3m. ha of timber suitable for lumbering operations. The devaluation in 1994 of the CFA franc stimulated timber exploration and output to such an extent that its massive growth called into question its sustainability; the environmental impact on easily accessible areas close to the coast or to navigable waterways has already been devastating. It was estimated that during 1990–2000 Equatorial Guinea lost 0.6% of its forest annually. To preserve its forestry resources, the Government set limits on what land could be exploited and on the number of enterprises permitted to operate. This reduced the area of exploited forests from 1.2m. ha in 1994 to 400,000 ha in 2009 and the number of enterprises from 52 (mainly of European origin) to about 15. Since 1999 the sector has been dominated by Asian firms, and China became the main importer of Equato-Guinean timber. The principal exploited species of wood are okoumé (most of which is exported, with only 3% processed locally) and akoga. Output rose throughout the 1990s, reaching an estimated 811,000 cu m in 1996, although by 2001 this had declined to 514,800 cu m. In 2007 it was estimated that forest covered 80% of the country and that timber production had risen by 6.3%, owing to the increased capacities of timber-processing plants, although its contribution to GDP remained modest.

Fishing constitutes one of the most abundant resources of Equatorial Guinea, but has been seriously neglected. The country has an exclusive economic zone of 314,000 sq km and a potential minimum catch of 50,000 metric tons per year. Artisanal fishing predominates and cohabits with small-scale industrial fishing, which remain insufficient to satisfy local demand. In 2009 the sector contributed 0.1% to GDP and was valued at 4,500m. francs CFA. At independence, some 5,000 people worked in the fishing industry, and those of Annobón (Pagalu) were renowned as skilled fishermen. Tuna from the waters around Annobón and shellfish from Bioko were processed locally and exported. Under Macías Nguema, the fishing industry collapsed, and the USSR was granted a fishing monopoly. This was terminated in 1980, and replaced by agreements with Spain later that year, with Nigeria in 1982 (renewed in 1991), and with the European Community (EC, now the European Union—EU) in 1983, which has since been renewed at three-yearly intervals. In 2001 annual financial compensation for Equatorial Guinea was increased from €320,000 to €412,500, while the annual level of captures available to the 62 permitted European vessels was increased from 4,000 metric tons to 5,500 tons. The EU has also financed research and training schemes to improve Equatorial Guinea's own artisanal fishing operations. The total catch rose from 7,001 tons in 1999, to 7,719 tons by 2009. Given the importance of the primary sector, particularly with regard to employment, the Government had repeatedly pledged commitment to the diversification and development of agro-fisheries production. A processing plant was subsequently built in Mbini, Río Muni, and was expected to lead to an increase in total fish output. It was expected that by implementing the rural development programme Equatorial Guinea would eventually produce a surplus for the export market, particularly in the fishing industry, which remained underdeveloped.

INDUSTRY

Before independence, there was a diversified and flourishing light industrial sector, centred in Malabo and Bata; this infrastructure was effectively destroyed by Macías Nguema and has yet to be restored. The manufacturing sector contributed 13.0% of GDP in 2007. Two sawmills in Bata currently account for most of the country's industrial activity. Favourable market conditions led to an average annual increase of 11% in processed wood production between 2000 and 2006, and stimulated timber production, which increased by 6.3%. In 2007 gross wood production declined to 399,400 cu m, compared with 443,800 cu m in 2006 and 460,800 cu m in 2005. There is also a small cement works and a bleach factory. Food-processing and soap production are carried out on a small scale. Cocoa fermenting and drying is the only significant manufacturing industry on Bioko.

Industrial activity is concentrated almost entirely within the oil and gas sector. This has given rise to the development of a rapidly expanding construction sector, as revenue from the hydrocarbons industry was spent on large-scale public infrastructure projects, such as the rehabilitation of ports and airports, urban regeneration, and the development of the new districts of Malabo II, Bata II and Sipopo. Since 2005 the construction industry has been the second main contributor to economic growth, accounting for 7.4% of GDP in 2009, or €1,616m., according to the Instituto Español de Comercio Exterior (Spanish Institute for Foreign Trade), which also reported that between 2004 and 2009 the sector grew by 500%. As with the oil industry, the construction sector has had a negligible impact on the living standards of the population and has not contributed to sustainable diversification. Most, if not all, of the inputs needed by the industry have to be imported. Furthermore, although labour intensive, the industry, which is dominated by Chinese, French and North African companies, has not created employment opportunities for the Equato-Guinean population, as most companies import their own work-force. Although there are plans for industrial diversification, they are limited to the oil and gas industries. Some projects were already under way, including an oil refinery, which was being built in the town of Mbini, Río Muni, by the US firm KBR at a cost of US $422m. and was expected to be completed by 2013, with the capacity to refine 200,000 barrels per day (b/d). In August 2011 the Government signed an exclusive rights agreement with the US company Energy Allied International Corporation to develop the petrochemical industry, in which it was investing about $150m. The construction of a petrochemical plant in Malabo was also underway in mid-2012.

Oil and Gas

Oil production is dominated by US oil companies, though in the late 2000s facilities operated by other countries with emergent economies have come on stream. Oil and gas production remains the main source of revenue in the country. Oil is produced in three fields: Zafiro, Alba (off Bioko Island) and Ceiba-Okume (off Río Muni). Output increased steadily and reached its peak in 2008 at around 450,000 b/d, before declining in the following year. In May 2010 the Government announced that oil production stood at 295,000 b/d, and was expected to continue to decline in the period 2010–11, but insisted that it would maintain oil production at around 300,000 b/d throughout 2011 and increase it in 2012 as new wells came into production. Other estimates continued to place oil production for that period between 300,000 b/d and 400,000 b/d. Oil revenue increased from US $190m. in 2000 to an estimated $8,400m. in 2009, and was expected to rise in 2012 as oil prices were predicted to remain high. Hydrocarbons account for approximately 92% of government revenue. In 2010 the value of oil exports increased from francs CFA 3,150m. to francs CFA 3,916m., a 24% increase, the result of high oil prices in the international market. At the beginning of 2011 proven Equato-Guinean oil reserves totalled some 1,100m. barrels. The fact that this figure represented only 0.1% of the global total was attributed by a report to a lack of geological studies, the undertaking of which might confirm suspicions that the country's reserves account for as much as 10% of total reserves. However, according to OECD, oil reserves stood at 1,700m. barrels. Some forecasts suggested that Equatorial Guinea's oil reserves would be depleted by 2030, although other industry sources suggested that this estimate was overly pessimistic.

In 1984 the offshore Alba gas and condensate field was discovered by Spain's Repsol on behalf of Empresa Guineano-Española de Petróleos (Gepsa), a joint venture between the Government and Repsol. However, Gepsa was dissolved in 1990, and the concession was taken over, on a production-sharing basis, by a consortium of US independent operators, led by Walter International. Production began in late 1991, at a rate of 1,200 b/d. In 1995 the Northern Michigan Electric Co (NOMECO) took over the operation of the Alba wells. In January 2002 CMS Energy, the majority partner and operator of the Alba field and NOMECO's parent company, sold all its interests in Equatorial Guinea to the US company Marathon Oil for US $993m. Marathon Oil also acquired a majority interest in the Bioko Block and Atlantic Methanol Plant in Malabo, which began production in 2001. By 2006 Alba's production of condensate had reached 40,000 b/d.

Petroleum production has greatly increased since October 1995, when ExxonMobil's (known as Mobil Oil Corpn until 1999) Zafiro field came on stream; ExxonMobil, which has invested US $130m. in the country, began to produce 40,000 b/d from Zafiro in August 1996, rising to 280,000 b/d. by 2004. The Zafiro field is Equatorial Guinea's largest producer, producing about 70% of all Equatorial Guinea's oil, or about 300,000 b/d, with an estimated 600m. barrels in crude petroleum reserves.

Important oil discoveries off Río Muni led to conflict with neighbouring Gabon in 2003. In an attempt to settle the territorial dispute between the two countries regarding offshore fields in the vicinity of the islands of Corisco and the Great and Little Elobeys amicably, in May 2003 President Obiang Nguema proposed the joint Equato-Guinean-Gabonese exploitation of the oil in the area; the proposal was rejected by Gabon. In early 2001 the US company Triton Energy (now owned by Amerada Hess), in partnership with the South African oil and gas exploration group Energy Africa, began production at the Ceiba oilfield in the Río Muni basin off the Mbini coast, the second most important field after Zafiro and ahead of Alba. New discoveries increased the field's estimated proven reserves to 450,000m. barrels by 2008. Output from the field totalled an estimated 80,000 b/d in 2009. In March 2003 Energy Africa acquired a 20% stake in ChevronTexaco's production in block L, immediately north of Ceiba. Production in the Okume field, next to Ceiba, started in December 2006 and was expected to produce 60,000 b/d by 2008. However, a study by the BEAC in early 2006 indicated that, as with other oil-producing countries in the region, production in Equatorial Guinea would begin to decrease in 2007 after peaking in 2006 at 18.6m. metric tons and would only reach 16.2m. tons in 2009. Predictions that total oil production would reach some 580,000 b/d by 2008 proved to be over-optimistic, as by that time oil production had already begun to slow, owing to the decline in production at the Zafiro oilfield and to the fact that no new wells had begun production. An alternative estimate set production at just below 360,000 b/d. Original estimates of reserves in the Alba field stood at 69m. barrels of oil equivalent (boe). However, new discoveries have since increased the estimates to nearly 1,000m. boe. In November 2011 the Aseng field, operated by the US company Noble Energy, began production, seven months ahead of schedule. The field's initial output of 51,000 b/d was expected to double by 2013.

Although the oil industry is dominated by US companies, in recent years contracts have also been signed with companies from other countries. In July 2005 the Norwegian company Equity Resources signed a contract for the exploration with the Equato-Guinean state-owned GEPetrol of part of block E (south-east of Bioko). In January 2006 the Brazilian oil company PETROBRAS obtained 50% of exploration rights of block L, where the Ceiba oilfield is located, where it partnered with Chevron Equatorial Guinea Ltd (with a 22.5% stake); Amerada Hess (12.5%); Energy Africa (10%) and Sasol Petroleum International (5%). In February the Chinese hydrocarbons company China National Offshore Oil Company Ltd signed a five-year production-sharing contract with GEPetrol for an offshore block south of Bioko. Following the visit of President Obiang Nguema to Spain in November, Spanish oil company Repsol-YPF announced it would form part of the consortium contracted to undertake exploration of the Corisco Deep Block. Exclusive exploration rights were granted to US company Vanco Energy in 2003. With the formation of the consortium, Vanco Energy and Repsol-YPF each held 25% of the concession, while Mexxen Petroleum, the main operator, held 50%. Following the withdrawal from the project of ExxonMobil and SK Energy of the Republic of Korea, in May 2009 Repsol-YPF became the consortium's official operator for the exploration for gas in block C-1 until 2010, and was charged with assessing its profitability. Repsol, which held a 54% share in future production in the block (GEPetrol held the remaining 46%), announced in April 2010 that it was looking for a partner to carry out evaluation in the Langosta field of the block. Meanwhile, in May 2008 US-based Devon Energy sold its entire interests in the country, including the 22,000 b/d extracted off shore near Bioko, to GEPetrol for a reported US $2,200m.

In 2010 numerous agreements were signed between the Government of Equatorial Guinea and foreign companies for the exploration of several blocks. In January Gazprom Neft, a subsidiary of Russian company Gazprom, initialled a production-sharing agreement to develop two blocks, T and U, the reserves of which were estimated at 110m. metric tons of oil. This followed the signing of a memorandum of understanding (MOU) in November 2009, and the final contracts were concluded in June 2011 during President Obiang Nguema's visit to Russia. In May 2010 the independent oil explorer Afex Global signed an agreement with Equatorial Guinea to explore an undisclosed offshore block, which could result in the investment of US $7m.–$10m. in the country in the next three years. Drilling could start after three to five years should the exploration prove successful.

Other contracts agreed in 2011 included a new production-sharing agreement for offshore block D near Bioko signed in February between the Government of Equatorial Guinea, GEPetrol, Marathon Oil EG Production Ltd (a subsidiary of Marathon Oil) and SK Innovation Co Ltd. Marathon Oil was to hold 70.6% of the participating interest, while GEPetrol would hold 20% and SK Innovation Co Ltd the remaining interest. In August an agreement was reached with the Dutch firm Vopak to build a crude petroleum storage terminal in Malabo. This terminal would also enable the processing and distribution of oil on Bioko.

The Equato-Guinean oilfields also contain considerable reserves of natural gas. Gas is processed as condensate, liquefied petroleum gas, methanol and LNG. The Government regards gas as key to its programme of economic diversification and has announced plans to concentrate on the gas industry as oil production stagnates, with a goal of doubling gas exports by 2015. In May 2010 gas reserves were estimated at 127,426m. cu m, three times higher than previously estimated. The new reserve estimates could support a second LNG plant, which Equatorial Guinea plans to build by 2016, with a capacity of 2.8m.–3.7m. metric tons per year, as well as a second plant to produce methanol. A MOU was signed in May 2011 by the Government, SONAGAS and several companies operating on different blocks—including Noble Energy, Glencore and Atlas Petroleum (operating blocks I and O), the shareholders of the 3G Holding limited (Unión Fenosa Gas, Galp Energía and Ophir—operating block R), and the partners of EGLNG Holding Ltd—to develop LNG Train 2, construction of which started in 2012.

Since 2001 natural gas resources have been extracted by the US-based Atlantic Methanol Production Company. A US $400m. methanol plant, completed during the second half of 2001, was designated to process most of the natural gas that was previously being flared. In 2006 it was estimated that 70,000m. cu ft of gas was flared every year. The Government pledged to eliminate all gas flaring by 2008. The condensate output of the Alba fields, in particular, rose substantially and was generating as much as $300,000 per day within a few years. A new condensate plant, with an annual capacity of 3.4m. tons, constructed by Marathon Oil at a cost of $1,500m., was completed six months ahead of schedule and loaded its first cargo in May 2007. Equatorial Guinea thus became the 14th country in the world to export LNG. British Gas agreed to buy the total plant production, 3.4m. tons of LNG per year for 17 years at a cost of approximately $15,000m., with a view to exporting to the USA and other markets. However, in March 2009 the Deputy Minister for Energy announced that Equatorial Guinea would not sell any new gas to British Gas because the company was not shipping all the fuel to the USA. British Gas contended that the contract allowed for sales to other countries and that demand for gas from the USA had decreased as US gas production increased. Thus, in April 2010 British Gas and the Italian company Sinergie signed a 25-year agreement whereby Sinergie was to buy 145,000 cu m a year of LNG from Equatorial Guinea. The first shipment arrived in Italy in May 2010.

By 2008 estimated exports of natural gas were 15,170m. cu m. In May 2006 Nigeria and Equatorial Guinea signed an agreement whereby Nigeria would provide 600m.–800m. cu ft of gas per day to be processed in the LNG plant in Bioko. A co-operation agreement to establish a joint venture for gas infrastructure projects and the production of LNG was signed in October 2008 between Gazprom and the Equatorial Guinean LNG Holdings Ltd (EG LNG), in which Marathon Oil controls a 60% stake and SONAGAS holds 25%, with the remaining shares split between Japanese corporations Mitsui (8.5%) and Marubeni (6.5%). In February 2008 an agreement was signed with the Spanish company Unión Fenosa Gas, whereby the company, jointly with EON, formed a consortium with SONAGAS, Marathon Oil, Mitsui and Marubeni, to carry out the largest integrated energy project in the Gulf of Guinea. This included the construction of a second LNG train on Bioko Island, as well as three gas pipes, which would join Nigerian, Cameroonian and Equato-Guinean oilfields with the LNG plant in Punta Europa in Malabo. In April 2011 EON withdrew from the consortium and sold its holdings to Unión Fenosa Gas and Galp Energía.

Mining

Reserves of gold, iron ore, manganese, tantalum, uranium, bauxite and diamonds have also been discovered, but these have yet to be exploited. Nevertheless, in March 2009 the Government announced that it was cancelling all mining contracts signed before 27 February 2009, and gave exploration companies two months to renegotiate new agreements. The Government gave no details of the companies or minerals concerned, but stated that the decision formed part of a range of measures designed to safeguard the interests of the country's mining sector. In mid-2010 the Government signed a contract with the Canadian company Sillenger Exploration Corpn to carry out an aerial survey of an area of Río Muni to detect the presence of minerals. The survey began in January 2011, and also included an area of the Río Muni offshore shelf. The terms of the agreement granted Sillenger Exploration mining concessions, including oil and gas, of any discoveries made.

Power

Equatorial Guinea was estimated to have 2,600 MW of hydro-electric potential. The Government was making efforts to diversify its energy resources and improve electrification nation-wide. In mid-2011 Equatorial Guinea produced 27m. kWh and consumed 25.11m. kWh. Electricity is still provided only to the main towns on Bioko and Río Muni; supply remains erratic, and blackouts are common. In 1989 a 3.6-MW hydroelectric power station, built on the Riaba river (Bioko) at a cost of US $13.5m., was inaugurated, which provides most of the power on Bioko. During the dry season, the Malabo diesel plant supplements output from Riaba. In February 2000 a new thermal power station to supply Malabo came on stream. A further 3.6-MW thermal power station, constructed with aid from China, at Bikomo, near Bata, supplies 90% of Río Muni's energy requirements. Construction by a Chinese firm of the 120-MW Djibloho power station in Añisok, Río Muni, began in 2008. The first phase was due to be completed in 2012. When operational, it was expected to provide electricity to the whole of the continental region and to export its surplus to neighbouring countries. A 220-kilovolt substation was also being built in conjunction with the power station to supply electricity to the mainland region.

TRANSPORT AND COMMUNICATIONS

Following independence, the entire Equato-Guinean road network fell into disrepair. However, in the late 1990s Equatorial Guinea embarked on a programme of nation-wide road repair and the rehabilitation of buildings and infrastructure in the main cities. International donors provided assistance for the upgrading of road access from the town of Mbini in Río Muni to Cogo on the Gabonese frontier, much of which is impassable in the rainy season, hoping to stimulate exports of foodstuffs to Gabon, but by mid-2011 this had not occurred. China was financing a project to link Mongomo to Bata, and the EU was supporting an inter-state road project to link Equatorial Guinea to Gabon and Cameroon. 'Food for work' programmes are also being introduced, in order to maintain the network of feeder roads. Government-financed urban regeneration and infrastructure building intensified in the second half of the 2000s. In August 2006 an agreement was signed with China to build 2,000 km of roads throughout the country. According to the UNDP representative in Equatorial Guinea, by 2008 the country had one of the best road networks in Africa. Since 2010 a six-lane motorway has linked Malabo and the international airport to the new city of Sipopo, 16 km from Malabo. Sipopo was inaugurated in June 2011 in time to accommodate dignitaries attending the African Union (AU) Summit. There are no railways in the country.

Equatorial Guinea has two of the deepest seaports in the region at Bata and Malabo. Bata, which is used by the timber companies, handles by far the largest volume of exports. Malabo has an excellent natural harbour (formed by a sunken volcanic crater), which has been rehabilitated by a French company. There are regular shipping services to Europe, but maritime communications between Malabo, Bata and Annobón continue to be erratic, and there is little maritime traffic with neighbouring mainland states. Construction, by the Dutch firm Pils, of a new port in Malabo to service the oil industry was completed in 2008, and in March of that year a major new freetrade port at Luba, on the south-west coast of Bioko island, was inaugurated. The new port was to handle much of Equatorial Guinea's petroleum production in the future, and many of the petroleum companies operating in the country were expected to relocate to Luba. A new deep-water dock capable of simultaneously handling several large cargo ships was inaugurated in February 2009. One month later the Government announced its intention to double the capacity of its ports at Malabo and Bata. Work on the Malabo project was completed in 2011 at an estimated cost of US $2,000m.

The country has two international airports, one in Malabo and the other in Bata, both of which have been considerably expanded and improved in recent years, as part of the infrastructure-building programme. There are also five domestic airports. On the occasion of Equatorial Guinea's 42nd independence anniversary in October 2010, an airport and port were inaugurated on the island of Annobón. They were built by Moroccan company Somage, at a cost of about €100m. The new port allowed for larger cargo ships and passenger ferries, and it was hoped that it would open the island to trade.

Attempts to form a national airline have been beset by mismanagement and alleged corruption. Aerolíneas Guinea Ecuatorial, founded in 1982, had collapsed by 1985. Its successor, Ecuato Guineana de Aviación, established in 1986 as a partnership between the Government and Air Inter-Gabon, went into liquidation in 1990 after incurring heavy losses. However, the company has continued to operate limited regional and domestic services. In early 2006 there were 20 small airlines in the country, most operating domestically. Eighteen of them were temporarily grounded in May because they failed to meet the standards laid down by the International Civil Aviation Organization. In March, meanwhile, the EU banned Equato-Guinean aircraft from flying over EU territory. Air traffic has risen dramatically since the mid-1990s as a result of the growth in the petroleum industry, with an increasing number of international airlines flying to the country. Scheduled international services are provided four times a week by Iberia and Air Europe, between Malabo and Madrid, Spain, and Cameroon Airlines, between Malabo and Douala, Cameroon. Swiss International Airlines (formerly Crossair) operates flights between Zürich, Switzerland, and Malabo twice a week, while KLM and Air France operate flights three times a week between Malabo, and Amsterdam, Netherlands, and Paris, France, respectively. There is also a weekly flight to and from Houston, USA. In April 2008 Lufthansa commenced a thrice-weekly direct service between Malabo and Frankfurt, Germany.

Information and communications networks remain underdeveloped. Telephone lines, fixed and mobile, as well as internet services, are mostly provided by Guinea Ecuatorial de Telecomunicaciones, jointly with France Télécom. Mobile telephone usage has continued to expand, and in 2010 66% of the population subscribed to a mobile telephone service, while only 1.5% had access to fixed-line telephony. Rates of internet access were reportedly among the lowest in the world.

In 2010 Equatorial Guinea signed a construction and maintenance agreement with the submarine cable consortium Africa Coast to Europe for a 7,000-km fibre-optic cable extending from France to South Africa, which was expected to be operational in 2012. This would be the first international submarine cable to reach Equatorial Guinea and would greatly improve the connectivity of the country to global telecommunications networks, as well as between its major cities.

AID AND TRADE

Until the advent of oil, Equatorial Guinea's economy relied heavily on Spanish aid, which during the early 1990s totalled about 350m. pesetas annually. In January 1994 Spain suspended one-half of its aid following a diplomatic contretemps. Full assistance did not resume until 1998, when Spanish aid totalled just over 1.5m. pesetas. Of this, some two-thirds were allocated to health and education. In April 2004 Spain pardoned one-half of Equatorial Guinea's debt, estimated at €70m., and in December it waived a further US $17m. In February 2005 a Spanish aid package for Equatorial Guinea worth €24m. was announced. Since then, with the improvement of relations between the two countries, Spanish commercial interests in Equatorial Guinea have increased dramatically.

Because of the enormous wealth generated by oil revenues, Equatorial Guinea no longer receives large inflows of foreign aid, although Spain continues to be a major international donor, with annual funding of approximately €12m., primarily for education. France (the second main provider of aid until the end of the 1990s), China, Cuba and the EU continue to provide limited financial support, although they have become more significant as trade partners.

The IMF supported several programmes in Equatorial Guinea in the 1980s and 1990s. However, since 1996 there has been no formal agreement between the IMF and the Government of Equatorial Guinea, although there have been periodic consultations. In August 2001 the Government sought assistance from the IMF to restructure the economy, but negotiations broke down when the Government refused to comply with IMF demands for greater fiscal transparency, full disclosure of government bank accounts and external audits of the petroleum sector, claiming that the information was a state secret. In November 2003 the Government agreed to disclose the contents of Article IV, relating to consultations on the need for transparency regarding revenue from the oil sector and improvements in macroeconomic management. The IMF has repeatedly stressed the need for Equatorial Guinea to diversify its economy and establish greater fiscal discipline, accountability and transparency in the management of public sector resources, particularly regarding revenue from the energy sector.

Equatorial Guinea does not receive direct support from the World Bank. However, from July 2003 to June 2008 it received assistance via the Bank's Regional Integration Assistance Strategy for Central Africa, which included funding for several technical assistance and infrastructure programmes designed to improve trade links and enhance economic integration among the CEMAC countries. Technical assistance has also been provided since 2007 under a Service Agreement, including the creation of a Public Expenditure Review, support for the country's bid to join the EITI and statistical capacity-building to enable preparation of the national accounts. A second Service Agreement to help with the implementation of the Horizonte 2020 plan was signed at the end of the AU Summit in July 2011. This technical assistance was expected to include: continued statistical support to facilitate the preparation of the national accounts; a review of the country's debt management, incorporating a diagnostic and a reform plan; and an analysis of sources of growth, including an enterprise survey to assess the investment climate. The World Bank will also support the Government's plans to achieve EITI compliance.

The AfDB has also been a significant source of financial aid to Equatorial Guinea. In the 1990s it approved a donation of US $5m. for programmes aimed at alleviating the financial difficulties of small producers and agricultural diversification and production. In April 2009 it granted Equatorial Guinea €2.9m. worth of credit as a contribution to the implementation of the National Development Plan, which was to be used for health programmes—especially those related to maternal health, the eradication of contagious diseases and the development of health infrastructure—as well as for projects designed to eradicate poverty, fight corruption, and improve financial transparency and accountability. In late 2010 the AfDB granted financial assistance to the Equato-Guinean Ministry of the Economy, Trade and Business Development to improve governance, to strengthen technical assistance capacity and to train experts. These agreements were signed by both parties in May 2011. In mid-2012 the AfDB was funding a number of major projects with four outstanding loans. The most important of these was a €38.9m. loan in support of the education sector, aimed at training managerial staff and developing technical capacity in the diversification sectors. In May an AfDB delegation met with the new Equato-Guinean Minister of the Economy, Trade and Business Development and agreed that AfDB support during 2013–17 would focus on health, education, infrastructure maintenance and projects to facilitate integration of young people into the labour market.

In March 2008 the Equato-Guinean Government concluded a financial assistance agreement with the European Development Fund, estimated at some €10.4m., most of which was intended to improve administrative capacity and to promote the rule of law, with €2.6m. allocated to enhancing the agricultural sector and strengthening regional integration and civil society. The agreement was conditional upon the

Government implementing economic reforms and human rights improvements.

Oil production has changed the nature of Equatorial Guinea's trade relations, and in recent years the country has forged strong commercial links with emergent economies such as Brazil, Russia and South Africa. The Equato-Guinean authorities have also strengthened their connections with China, which is increasingly involved in the oil and construction industries. Nevertheless, Equatorial Guinea's greatest volume and value of trade continues to be with its traditional partners, the USA, Spain and France. Within Africa, trade links are particularly strong with Morocco and Egypt, which are very active in the construction sector, and with Ghana, with which an agreement was signed in May 2010 for Equatorial Guinea to provide 2m. barrels of crude petroleum every year to the newly built refinery in Accra. The first consignment was exported in July of that year. An agreement was also signed whereby Ghana would assist with revitalizing the Equato-Guinean cocoa industry.

Equatorial Guinea's exports consist mainly of oil and gas, together with small quantities of cocoa and timber. Hydrocarbons production and timber accounted for nearly all of the country's total exports in 2005, with oil and gas accounting for an estimated 93.2% of GDP and 98.9% of exports. In 2009 oil and oil derivatives accounted for 72% of GDP and some 90% of exports. Exports contracted in 2010 owing mainly to the decline in oil production. The main export markets remained the USA, Spain, the EU, China and Japan. The country is dependent upon imports, particularly of food, which constitutes about 10% of total imports, but also of agricultural inputs, machinery and other goods, which are imported from the USA, Spain and other EU countries.

Investing some US $7,000m. in 2008, the USA is the main source of investment in the petroleum industry of Equatorial Guinea, which is the fourth largest beneficiary of US foreign investment in sub-Saharan Africa. Some 65% of the petroleum produced is exported to the USA, which provides most of the inputs for the extractive industry.

In 2010 Spain imported over 1.5m. tons of crude petroleum from Equatorial Guinea, at a cost of €710m. At the same time, Equatorial Guinea has become Spain's fourth most important export market, purchasing mainly foodstuffs and machinery, which in 2010 were valued at €226m. A year later, the value of Equato-Guinean exports to Spain, mainly crude petroleum, reached €1,200m., while the value of imports from Spain rose to €250m.

The role of China as an economic partner and provider of development aid has increased significantly during the 21st century. In 2001 China agreed to waive some of Equatorial Guinea's debt and provide interest-free loans. Co-operation between the two countries expanded to the extent that in October 2005 the Equato-Guinean authorities declared China to be their main development partner; at the same time, China again cancelled a large part of the debt owed to it by Equatorial Guinea, in exchange for a share of Equatorial Guinea's oil and construction industries. China is very active in the construction industry, particularly in public works and infrastructure, and supplies most of the inputs and labour force required by the industry. It is also a major credit provider. The IMF reported that in 2006 China extended a US $2,000m. non-concessional credit line to Equatorial Guinea to fund electrification projects and improvements to Bata harbour. According to the IMF, the Chinese Government was reported to have extended an offer for a $380m. long-term concessional loan for the construction of housing. Although exports of oil to China have increased, in 2008 they still only accounted for 16% of total petroleum exports.

Statistical Survey

Source (unless otherwise stated): Dirección General de Estadística y Cuentas Nacionales, Ministerio de Planificacón, Desarrollo Económico e Inversiones Públicas, Malabo; tel. 333093352; internet www.dgecnstat-ge.org.

AREA AND POPULATION

Area: 28,051 sq km (10,831 sq miles): Río Muni 26,017 sq km, Bioko 2,017 sq km, Annobón 17 sq km.

Population: 300,000 (Río Muni 240,804, Bioko 57,190, Annobón 2,006), comprising 144,268 males and 155,732 females, at census of 4–17 July 1983 (Source: Ministerio de Asuntos Exteriores, Madrid); 406,151 at census of 4 July 1994 (provisional). *Mid-2012* (UN estimate): 740,469 (Source: UN, *World Population Prospects: The 2010 Revision*).

Density (mid-2012): 26.4 per sq km.

Population by Age and Sex (UN estimates at mid-2012): *0–14:* 288,125 (males 144,761, females 143,364); *15–64:* 431,650 (males 224,121, females 207,529); *65 and over:* 20,694 (males 10,470, females 10,224); *Total* 740,469 (males 379,352, females 361,117) (Source: UN, *World Population Prospects: The 2010 Revision*).

Provinces (population, census of July 1994): Annobón 2,820; Bioko Norte 75,137; Bioko Sur 12,569; Centro-Sur 60,341; Kié-Ntem 92,779; Litoral 100,047; Wele-Nzas 62,458.

Principal Town (incl. suburbs, UN estimate): Malabo 136,971 (Source: UN, *World Urbanization Prospects: The 2011 Revision*).

Births and Deaths (UN estimates, annual averages): Birth rate 37.3 per 1,000 in 2005–10; Death rate 15.1 per 1,000 in 2005–10. Source: UN, *World Population Prospects: The 2010 Revision*.

Life Expectancy (years at birth): 50.8 (males 49.6; females 52.2) in 2010. Source: World Bank, World Development Indicators database.

Economically Active Population (persons aged 6 years and over, 1983 census): Agriculture, hunting, forestry and fishing 59,390; Mining and quarrying 126; Manufacturing 1,490; Electricity, gas and water 224; Construction 1,929; Trade, restaurants and hotels 3,059; Transport, storage and communications 1,752; Financing, insurance, real estate and business services 409; Community, social and personal services 8,377; *Sub-total* 76,756; Activities not adequately defined 984; *Total employed* 77,740 (males 47,893, females 29,847); Unemployed 24,825 (males 18,040, females 6,785); *Total labour force* 102,565 (males 65,933, females 36,632). Note: Figures are based on unadjusted census data, indicating a total population of 261,779. The adjusted total is 300,000 (Source: ILO, *Yearbook of Labour Statistics*). *Mid-2012* ('000 persons, official estimates): Agriculture, etc. 184; Total labour force 291 (Source: FAO).

HEALTH AND WELFARE

Key Indicators

Total Fertility Rate (children per woman, 2010): 5.2.

Under-5 Mortality Rate (per 1,000 live births, 2010): 121.

HIV/AIDS (% of persons aged 15–49, 2009): 5.0.

Physicians (per 1,000 head, 2004): 0.3.

Hospital Beds (per 1,000 head, 2005): 2.2.

Health Expenditure (2009): US $ per head (PPP): 1,560.

Health Expenditure (2009): % of GDP: 4.5.

Health Expenditure (2009): public (% of total): 76.0.

Access to Water (% of persons, 2006): 43.

Access to Sanitation (% of persons, 2006): 51.

Total Carbon Dioxide Emissions ('000 metric tons, 2008): 4,814.8.

Carbon Dioxide Emissions Per Head (metric tons, 2008): 7.3.

Human Development Index (2011): ranking: 136.

Human Development Index (2011): value: 0.537.

For sources and definitions, see explanatory note on p. vi.

AGRICULTURE, ETC.

Principal Crops ('000 metric tons, 2010, FAO estimates): Sweet potatoes 90; Cassava 64; Coconuts 7; Oil palm fruit 35; Bananas 27; Plantains 42; Cocoa beans 1 (unofficial figure); Coffee, green 3.

Aggregate Production ('000 metric tons, may include official, semi-official or estimated data): Total roots and tubers 188; Total fruits (excl. melons) 69.

Livestock ('000 head, year ending September 2010, FAO estimates): Cattle 5; Pigs 6; Sheep 38; Goats 9; Chickens 340; Ducks 30.

Livestock Products (2010, FAO estimates): Meat 566 metric tons; Hen eggs 490 metric tons.

Forestry ('000 cubic metres, 2010, FAO estimates): *Roundwood Removals:* Fuel wood 447; Sawlogs, veneer logs and logs for sleepers 525; Total 972. *Sawnwood:* 4 (all broadleaved).

Fishing (metric tons, live weight, 2010): Freshwater fishes 1,000 (FAO estimate); Clupeoids 3,050; Sharks, rays, skates, etc. 3 (FAO estimate); Marine fishes 518 (FAO estimate); Total catch (incl. others) 7,391 (FAO estimate).

Source: FAO.

MINING

Production (2010): Crude petroleum 74m. barrels; Natural gas 6,500m. cu m (Source: US Geological Survey).

INDUSTRY

Palm Oil ('000 metric tons, FAO estimate): 3.7 in 2010. Source: FAO.

Veneer Sheets ('000 cubic metres, FAO estimate): 28.0 in 2010. Source: FAO.

Electric Energy (million kWh): 95 in 2006; 100 in 2007; 100 in 2008. Source: UN Industrial Commodity Statistics Database.

FINANCE

Currency and Exchange Rates: 100 centimes = 1 franc de la Coopération Financière en Afrique Centrale (CFA). *Sterling, Dollar and Euro Equivalents* (30 December 2011): £1 sterling = 783.813 francs CFA; US $1 = 506.961 francs CFA; €1 = 655.957 francs CFA; 10,000 francs CFA = £12.76 = $19.73 = €15.24. *Average Exchange Rate* (francs CFA per US dollar): 472.186 in 2009; 495.277 in 2010; 471.866 in 2011. *Note:* An exchange rate of 1 French franc = 50 francs CFA, established in 1948, remained in force until January 1994, when the CFA franc was devalued by 50%, with the exchange rate adjusted to 1 French franc = 100 francs CFA. This relationship to French currency remained in effect with the introduction of the euro on 1 January 1999. From that date, accordingly, a fixed exchange rate of €1 = 655.957 francs CFA has been in operation.

Budget ('000 million francs CFA, 2011): *Revenue:* Tax revenue 2,654.6; Non-tax revenue 65.1; Total revenue 2,719.8. *Expenditure:* Current expenditure 462.5 (Wages and salaries 73.0); Capital expenditure 1,802.8; Total expenditure 2,265.4. Source: African Development Bank.

International Reserves (excl. gold, US $ million at 31 December 2011): IMF special drawing rights 32.25; Reserve position in IMF 7.56; Foreign exchange 3,014.03; Total 3,053.84. Source: IMF, *International Financial Statistics.*

Money Supply ('000 million francs CFA at 31 December 2011): Currency outside deposit money banks 225.08; Demand deposits at deposit money banks 755.51; *Total money* (incl. others) 981.29. Source: IMF, *International Financial Statistics.*

Cost of Living (Consumer Price Index; base: 2000 = 100): All items 166.1 in 2009; 178.6 in 2010; 191.5 in 2011. Source: African Development Bank.

Expenditure on the Gross Domestic Product ('000 million francs CFA in current prices, 2011, provisional): Government final consumption expenditure 285.1; Private final consumption expenditure 549.7; Gross fixed capital formation 2,761.9; Change in inventories 0.2; *Total domestic expenditure* 3,596.9; Exports of goods and non-factor services 5,829.8; *Less* Imports of goods and services 3,034.4; *GDP at purchasers' values* 6,392.3. Source: African Development Bank.

Gross Domestic Product by Economic Activity ('000 million francs CFA in current prices, 2011, provisional): Agriculture, hunting, forestry and fishing 119.3; Mining and quarrying 5,547.6; Manufacturing 13.6; Electricity, gas and water 52.6; Construction 289.6; Trade, restaurants and hotels 57.2; Finance, insurance and real estate 51.3; Transport and communications 8.7; Public administration and defence 136.9; Other services 25.0; *GDP at factor cost* 6,301.8; Indirect taxes 90.5; *GDP at purchasers' values* 6,392.3. Note: Deduction for imputed bank service charge assumed to be distributed at origin. Source: African Development Bank.

Balance of Payments (US $ million, 2008): Exports of goods f.o.b. 14,465; Imports of goods c.i.f. –3,909; *Trade balance* 10,555; Services (net) –1,849; Net other income –6,953; *Balance on goods, services and income* 1,753; Current transfers (net) –81; *Current balance* 1,673; Direct investment (net) –570; Other investment (net) –693; Errors and omissions 424; *Overall balance* 834 (Source: IMF, *Republic of Equatorial Guinea: 2010 Article IV Consultation*—May 2010). *2011* ('000 million francs CFA): Trade balance 3,690.6; Services (net) –895.2; Other income (net) –3,076.7; Current transfers (net) –50.3; *Current balance* –331.7 (Source: African Development Bank).

EXTERNAL TRADE

Principal Commodities (distribution by SITC, US $ '000, 1990): *Imports c.i.f.:* Food and live animals 4,340; Beverages and tobacco 3,198 (Alcoholic beverages 2,393); Crude materials (inedible) except fuels 2,589 (Crude fertilizers and crude minerals 2,102); Petroleum and petroleum products 4,738; Chemicals and related products 2,378; Basic manufactures 3,931; Machinery and transport equipment 35,880 (Road vehicles and parts 3,764, Ships, boats and floating structures 24,715); Miscellaneous manufactured articles 2,725; Total (incl. others) 61,601. *Exports f.o.b.:* Food and live animals 6,742 (Cocoa 6,372); Beverages and tobacco 3,217 (Tobacco and tobacco manufactures 2,321); Crude materials (inedible) except fuels 20,017 (Sawlogs and veneer logs 12,839, Textile fibres and waste 7,078); Machinery and transport equipment 24,574 (Ships, boats and floating structures 23,852); Total (incl. others) 61,705 (Source: UN, *International Trade Statistics Yearbook*). *2008* (US $ million, estimates): Total imports f.o.b. 3,909.5 (Public sector equipment 2,485.9, Petroleum sector 733.4, Petroleum products 252.7, Other 437.4); Total exports f.o.b. 14,464.7 (Crude petroleum 11,929.0, Petroleum derivatives 2,436.6, Others 99.0) (Source: IMF, *Republic of Equatorial Guinea: Statistical Appendix*—April 2010).

Principal Trading Partners (US $ million, 2003): *Imports c.i.f.:* Belgium 14.6; France 87.0; Italy 58.0; Netherlands 20.4; United Kingdom 175.9; USA 336.3; Total (incl. others) 828.8. *Exports f.o.b.:* Canada 334.1; China, People's Repub. 411.9; Italy 182.6; Netherlands 43.6; Spain 739.3; Taiwan 53.4; USA 903.5; Total (incl. others) 2,721.8.

TRANSPORT

Road Traffic (estimates, motor vehicles in use at 31 December 2002): Passenger cars 1,811; Lorries and vans 727; Buses 302; Motorcycles 17.

Shipping: *Merchant Fleet* (at 31 December 2009): Vessels 39; Total displacement 27,194 grt (Source: IHS Fairplay, *World Fleet Statistics*). *International Sea-borne Freight Traffic* ('000 metric tons, 1990): Goods loaded 110; Goods unloaded 64 (Source: UN, *Monthly Bulletin of Statistics*).

Civil Aviation (traffic on scheduled services, 1998): Passengers carried ('000) 21; Passenger-km (million) 4 (Source: UN, *Statistical Yearbook*). *2004:* (traffic at Malabo and Bata airports): Total passengers movements 324,999 (arrivals 159,815, departures 165,184); Freight and mail carried 5,029.5 metric tons.

COMMUNICATIONS MEDIA

Radio Receivers: 180,000 in use in 1997.

Television Receivers: 4,000 in use in 1997.

Newspaper: 1 daily (estimated circulation 2,000) in 1996.

Book Production: 17 titles in 1998.

Telephones: 13,500 main lines in use in 2010.

Mobile Cellular Telephones: 399,300 subscribers in 2010.

Personal Computers: 9,000 (14.8 per 1,000 persons) in 2005.

Internet Users: 14,400 in 2009.

Broadband Subscribers: 1,200 in 2010.

Sources: UNESCO, *Statistical Yearbook;* UN, *Statistical Yearbook;* International Telecommunication Union.

EDUCATION

Pre-primary (2007/08, unless otherwise indicated): Schools 180*; Teachers 1,655 (males 208, females 1,447); Students 39,551 (males 17,065, females 22,486).

Primary (2009/10, unless otherwise indicated): Schools 483*; Teachers 3,131 (males 2,011, females 1,120); Students 85,061 (males 43,294, females 41,767).

Secondary (2001/02, estimates, unless otherwise indicated): Schools 59; Teachers 894 (males 855, females 39)†; Students 21,173 (males 13,463, females 7,710).

Higher (1999/2000, unless otherwise indicated): Teachers 206 (males 174, females 32)‡; Students 1,003 (males 699, females 304).

* 1998 figure.

† 1999/2000 figure.

‡ 1999/2000 figure.

Pupil-teacher Ratio (primary education, UNESCO estimate): 27.2 in 2009/10.

Adult Literacy Rate: 93.9% (males 97.1%; females 90.6%) in 2010.

Source: UNESCO Institute for Statistics.

Directory

The Constitution

The present Constitution was approved by a national referendum on 16 November 1991 and amended in January 1995. It provided for the introduction of a plural political system. Further amendments to the Constitution were endorsed at a national referendum held on 13 November 2011. These included the limitation of the President's tenure of office to two seven-year terms, but the upper age limit for presidential candidates, previously set at 75 years was withdrawn. The amendments also established the post of Vice-President, to be appointed by the President and who must be a member of the ruling Partido Democrático de Guinea Ecuatorial, and five other institutions—the Senate, the Audit Court, the State Council, the Economic and Social Council and the Council for the Defence of the People. The amended Constitution was promulgated on 16 February 2012. The President is immune from prosecution for offences committed before, during or after his tenure of the post. The Cámara de Representantes del Pueblo (legislature) serves for a term of five years. Both the President and the Cámara de Representantes del Pueblo are directly elected by universal adult suffrage. The President appoints a Council of Ministers, and leads the Government.

The Government

HEAD OF STATE

President and Supreme Commander of the Armed Forces: Gen. (retd) OBIANG NGUEMA MBASOGO (assumed office 25 August 1979; elected President 25 June 1989; re-elected 25 February 1996, 15 December 2002 and 29 November 2009).

COUNCIL OF MINISTERS

(September 2012)

The Government is formed predominantly by members of the Partido Democrático de Guinea Ecuatorial, with a small number of representatives from allied parties.

President: Gen. (retd) OBIANG NGUEMA MBASOGO.

Vice-President, in charge of Presidential Affairs: IGNACIO MILAM TANG.

Second Vice-President, in charge of Defence and State Security: TEODORO (TEODORÍN) NGUEMA OBIANG MANGUE.

Prime Minister, in charge of Administrative Co-ordination: VICENTE EHATE TOMI.

First Deputy Prime Minister, in charge of the Political Sector, Democracy, the Interior and Local Government: CLEMENTE ENGOGA NGUEMA ONGUENE.

Second Deputy Prime Minister, in charge of the Social Sector and Human Rights: ALFONSO NSUY MOKUY.

Minister of State at the Presidency of the Republic, in charge of Missions: ALEJANDRO EVUNA OWONO ASANGONO.

Minister of State at the Presidency of the Republic, in charge of Cabinet Affairs: BRAULIO NCOGO ABEGUE.

Minister of State at the Presidency of the Republic, in charge of Relations with Parliament and Legal Affairs: ANGEL MASIE MIBUY.

Minister of State at the Presidency of the Republic, in charge of Regional Integration: BALTASAR ENGOGA EDJO.

Minister of State of Justice, Religion and Penitentiary Institutions: FRANCISCO JAVIER NGOMO MBENONO.

Minister of State of National Defence: ANTONIO MBA NGUEMA.

Minister and Secretary-General of the Government: TOMÁS ESONO AVA.

Minister of Foreign Affairs and Co-operation: AGAPITO MBA MOKUY.

Minister of the Economy, Trade and Business Development: CELESTINO-BONIFACIO BAKALE OBIANG.

Minister of Finance and the Budget: MARCELINO OWONO EDU.

Minister of Planning, Economic Development and Investment: CONRADO OKENVE NDOHO.

Minister of Transport, Technology, Post and Telecommunications: FRANCISCO MBA OLO BAHAMONDE.

Minister of National Security: NICOLÁS OBAMA NCHAMA.

Minister of Education and Science: MARÍA DEL CARMEN EKORO.

Minister of Health and Social Welfare: TOMÁS MECHEBA FERNÁNDEZ.

Minister of Public Works and Infrastructure: JUAN NKO MBULA.

Minister of Mines, Industry and Energy: GABRIEL MBEGA OBIANG LIMA.

Minister of Labour and Social Security: MIGUEL ABIA BITEO BORICO.

Minister of Agriculture and Forestry: MIGUEL OYONO NDONG MIFUMU.

Minister of Information, the Press and Radio: AGUSTÍN NSE NFUMU.

Minister of Social Affairs and the Promotion of Women: MARÍA LEONOR EPAM BIRIBÉ.

Minister of Fisheries and the Environment: CRESCENCIO TAMARITE CASTAÑO.

Minister of the Civil Service and Administrative Reform: PURIFICACIÓN BUARI LASAQUERO.

Minister of Youth and Sport: FRANCISCO PASCUAL OBAMA ASUE.

Minister-delegate of Culture and Tourism: GUILLERMINA MOKUY MBA OBONO.

Minister-delegate of Foreign Affairs and Co-operation: PEDRO ELA NGUEMA BUNA.

Minister-delegate of Justice, Religion and Penitentiary Institutions: JUAN OLO MBA NSENG.

Minister-delegate of National Defence: VICENTE EYA OLOMO.

Minister-delegate of the Interior and Local Government: LEOCADIO NDONG MOÑUNG.

Minister-delegate of the Economy, Trade and Business Development: JOSE-ANGEL BORICO MOISES.

Minister-delegate of Finance and the Budget, in charge of Duties and Taxes: MONSERRAT AFANG ONDO.

Minister-delegate of Planning, Economic Development and Investment: FORTUNATO OFA MBO NCHAMA.

Minister-delegate, in charge of Civil Aviation: FAUSTO ABESO FUMA.

Minister-delegate of Education and Science: SANTIAGO ONDO ESONO.

Minister-delegate of Health and Social Welfare: DIOSDADO-VICENTE NSUE MILANG.

Minister-delegate of Mines, Industry and Energy, in charge of Energy: FIDEL-MARCOS MEÑE NCOGO.

Minister-delegate of Labour and Social Security: HERIBERTO MIKO MBENGONO.

Minister-delegate of Agriculture and Forestry: DIOSDADO-SERGIO OSA MONGOMO.

Minister-delegate of Information, the Press and Radio: TEOBALDO NCHASO MATOMBA.

In addition there were 16 Vice-Ministers.

MINISTRIES

Ministry of Agriculture and Forestry: Apdo 504, Malabo.

Ministry of the Economy, Trade and Business Development: Apdo 404, Malabo; tel. 333093105; fax 333092043.

Ministry of Forign Affairs and International Co-operation: Malabo; tel. 333093220; fax 333093132.

Ministry of Finance and the Budget: Malabo; internet www.ceiba-guinea-ecuatorial.org/guineees/indexbienv1.htm.

Ministry of the Interior and Local Corporations: Malabo; fax 333092683.

Ministry of Justice, Religion and Penitentiary Institutions: Apdo 459, Malabo; fax 333092115.

Ministry of Mines, Industry and Energy: Calle 12 de Octubre s/n, Malabo; tel. 333093567; fax 333093353; e-mail d.shaw@ecqc.com; internet www.equatorialoil.com.

Ministry of National Defence: Malabo; tel. 333092794.

Ministry of National Security: Malabo; tel. 333093469.

Ministry of Social Affairs and Women's Advancement: Malabo; tel. 333093469.

Ministry of Transport, Technology, Post and Telecommunications: Malabo; internet www.ceiba-guinea-ecuatorial.org/guineees/transport.htm.

President and Legislature

PRESIDENT

Presidential Election, 29 November 2009

Candidate	Votes	% of votes
Obiang Nguema Mbasogo (PDGE)	260,462	95.76
Plácido Micó Abogo (CPDS)	9,700	3.57
Archivaldo Montero (UP)	931	0.34
Bonaventura Monsuy Asumu (PCSD)	462	0.17
Carmelo Mba Bacale (APGE)	437	0.16
Total	271,992*	100.00

* The total number of votes officially attributed to candidates by the Constitutional Court amounted to 271,992. However, that body declared the total number of valid votes cast to be 271,964, and the percentage of votes awarded to Obiang Nguema Mbasogo to be 95.37%. According to the Constitutional Court, there were 1,167 invalid votes.

CÁMARA DE REPRESENTANTES DEL PUEBLO
(House of Representatives)

Speaker: Dr ÁNGEL SERAFÍN SERICHE.

General Election, 4 May 2008

Party	Seats
Partido Democrático de Guinea Ecuatorial (PDGE)	99*
Convergencia para la Democracia Social (CPDS)	1
Total	100

* Including nine seats won by members of the coalition allied to the PDGE.

Election Commission

Constitutional Court: Malabo; Pres. SALVADOR ONDO NKUMU.

Political Organizations

Alianza Democrática Progresista (ADP): pro-Govt party; Pres. FRANCISCO MBÁ OLÚ BAHAMONDE.

Acción Popular de Guinea Ecuatorial (APGE): pro-Govt party; Pres. CARMELO MBA BACALE; Sec.-Gen. MIGUEL ESONO.

Convención Liberal Democrática (CLD): pro-Govt party; Pres. ALFONSO NSUE MOKUY.

Convención Socialdemocrática Popular (CSDP): pro-Govt party; Leader SECUNDINO OYONO.

Convergencia para la Democracia Social (CPDS): Calle Tres de Agosto 72, 2°, 1 Malabo; tel. 333092013; e-mail cpds@intnet.gq; internet www.cpds-gq.org; Pres. SANTIAGO OBAMA NDONG; Sec.-Gen. PLÁCIDO MICÓ ABOGO.

Demócratas por el Cambio (DECAM): coalition based in Madrid, Spain; e-mail press@guinea-ecuatorial.org; internet www.guinea-ecuatorial.org; f. 2005; 16 mem. orgs; Gen. Co-ordinator DANIEL OYONO.

Fuerza Demócrata Republicana (FDR): f. 1995; Pres. FELIPE ONDO OBIANG; Sec.-Gen. GUILLERMO NGUEMA ELA.

Movimiento para la Autodeterminación de la Isla de Bioko (MAIB): e-mail info@maib.org; internet www.maib.org; f. 1993 by Bubi interests seeking independence of Bioko; clandestine; Gen. Co-ordinator WEJA CHICAMPO.

Partido de la Convergencia Social Demócrata (PCSD): pro-Govt party; Pres. BUENAVENTURA MONSUY ASUMU.

Partido Democrático de Guinea Ecuatorial (PDGE): Malabo; internet www.pdge-ge.org; f. 1987; sole legal party 1987–92; Chair. Gen. (TEODORO) OBIANG NGUEMA MBASOGO; Sec.-Gen. LUCAS NGUEMA ESONO.

Partido del Progreso de Guinea Ecuatorial (PPGE): Madrid, Spain; e-mail ppge@telepolis.com; internet www.guinea-ecuatorial.org; f. 1983; Christian Democrat faction led by SEVERO MOTO NSA.

Partido Socialista de Guinea Ecuatorial (PSGE): pro-Govt party; Sec.-Gen. TOMÁS MECHEBA FERNÁNDEZ-GALILEA.

Unión para la Democracia y el Desarrollo Social (UDDS): f. 1990; Sec.-Gen. AQUILINO NGUEMA ONA NCHAMA; in Cameroon.

Unión Democrática Independiente (UDI): Leader DANIEL M. OYONO (in Spain).

Unión Democrática Nacional (UDENA): Pres. JOSÉ MECHEBA.

Unión Democrática y Social de Guinea Ecuatorial (UDS): pro-Govt party; Pres. CARMELO MODÚ ACUSÉ BINDANG.

Unión Popular (UP): f. 1992; conservative; divided into two factions, one led by DANIEL DARÍO MARTÍNEZ AYACABA and another led by FAUSTINO ONDO in Madrid.

Diplomatic Representation

EMBASSIES IN EQUATORIAL GUINEA

Angola: Malabo; Ambassador ARMANDO MATEUS CADETE.

Brazil: Avda Parques de África, Carocolas, Apdo 119, Malabo; tel. 333099986; fax 333099987; Ambassador ELIANA DA COSTA Y SILVA.

Cameroon: 37 Calle Rey Boncoro, Apdo 292, Malabo; tel. and fax 333092263; Ambassador JOHN MPOUEL BALA LAZARE.

China, People's Republic: Carretera del Aeropuerto, Apdo 44, Malabo; tel. 333093505; fax 3330923-81; e-mail chinaemb_gq@mfa.gov.cn; Ambassador WANG SHIXIONG.

Congo, Republic: Malabo; Ambassador CÉLESTINE KOUAKOUA.

Cuba: Carretera de Luba y Cruce de Dragas s/n, Malabo; tel. and fax 333094793; e-mail embacubage@orange.gq; Ambassador VÍCTOR EMILIO DREKE CRUZ.

France: Carretera del Aeropuerto, Apdo 326, Malabo; tel. 333092005; fax 333092305; e-mail chancellerie.malabo-amba@diplomatie.gouv.fr; internet www.ambafrance-gq.org; Ambassador FRANÇOIS BARATEAU.

Gabon: Calle de Argelia, Apdo 18, Malabo; Ambassador JANVIER OBIANG ALLOGHO.

Germany: Edificio Venus, 4°.Piso, Carretera del Aeropuerto, Km 4, Malabo; e-mail embajada.alemana.malabo@diplo.de; Ambassador MICHAEL OTTO KLEPSCH.

Guinea: Malabo.

Korea, Democratic People's Republic: Malabo; tel. 333092047; Ambassador KWAK JI HWAN.

Morocco: Avda Enrique Nvo, Apdo 329, Malabo; tel. 333092650; fax 333092655; Ambassador JILALI HILAL.

Nigeria: 4 Paseo de los Cocoteros, Apdo 78, Malabo; tel. and fax 333093385; Ambassador SUNDAY BASSEY.

South Africa: Parque de las Avenidas de Africa s/n, Apdo 5, Malabo; tel. 333207737; fax 333092746; e-mail malabo@foreign.gov.za; Ambassador PAKAMISA AUGUSTINE SIFUBA.

Spain: Parque de las Avenidas de África s/n, Malabo; tel. 333092020; fax 333092611; e-mail emb.malabo@maec.es; Ambassador MANUEL GÓMEZ-ACEBO RODRIGUEZ.

USA: K-3, Carretera de Aeropuerto, Malabo; tel. 333098895; fax 333098894; e-mail usembassymalabo@yahoo.com; internet malabo.usembassy.gov; Ambassador MARK L. ASQUINO.

Judicial System

The Supreme Court of Justice and the Constitutional Court sit in Malabo. The Supreme Court has four chambers (Civil and Social, Penal, Administrative and Common) and consists of a President and 12 magistrates, from whom the President of each chamber is selected. Provincial courts have been created in all provinces to replace the former courts of appeal. At present they are only functional in Malabo and Bata. Courts of first instance sit in Malabo and Bata, and may be convened in the other provincial capitals. Local courts may be convened when necessary.

President of the Supreme Court of Justice: MARTIN NDONG NSUE.

President of the Constitutional Court: SALVADOR ONDO NKUMU.

Attorney-General: DAVID NGUEMA OBIANG.

Religion

More than 90% of the population are adherents of the Roman Catholic Church. Traditional forms of worship are also followed.

CHRISTIANITY

The Roman Catholic Church

Equatorial Guinea comprises one archdiocese and two dioceses.

Bishops' Conference

Arzobispado, Apdo 106, Malabo; tel. 333092909; fax 333092176; e-mail arzobispadomalabo@hotmail.com.

f. 1984; Pres. Most Rev. ILDEFONSO OBAMA OBONO (Archbishop of Malabo).

Archbishop of Malabo: Most Rev. ILDEFONSO OBAMA OBONO, Arzobispado, Apdo 106, Malabo; tel. 333092909; fax 333092176; e-mail arzobispadomalabo@hotmail.com.

Protestant Church

Iglesia Reformada Evangélica de Guinea Ecuatorial (Evangelical Reformed Church of Equatorial Guinea): Apdo 195, Malabo; f. 1960; c. 8,000 mems; Sec.-Gen. Pastor JUAN EBANG ELA.

The Press

Ebano: Malabo; f. 1940; weekly; govt-controlled.

El Árbol del Centro: Apdo 180, Malabo; tel. 333092186; fax 333093275; Spanish; cultural review; 6 a year; publ. by Centro Cultural Español de Malabo; Dir GLORIA NISTAL.

El Correo Deportivo: tel. 222259223 (mobile); e-mail lagacetademalabo@gmail.com; monthly; Dir ROBERTO MARTIN PRIETO.

La Gaceta: Malabo; tel. 222259223 (mobile); e-mail lagacetademalabo@gmail.com; f. 1996; monthly; Dir ROBERTO MARTÍN PRIETO; circ. 3,000.

El Lector: Malabo; f. 2011; fortnightly; Dir ANTONIO NSUE ADÁ.

La Verdad: Talleres Gráficos de Convergencia para la Democracia Social, Calle Tres de Agosto 72, Apdo 441, Malabo; publ. by the Convergencia para la Democracia Social; 5 annually; Editor PLÁCIDO MICÓ ABOGO.

Poto-poto: Bata; f. 1940; weekly; govt-controlled.

Voz del Pueblo: Malabo; publ. by the Partido Democrático de Guinea Ecuatorial.

PRESS ASSOCIATION

Asociación para la Libertad de Prensa y de Expresión en Guinea Ecuatorial (ASOLPEGE Libre): Calle Isla Cabrera 3, 5°, 46026 Valencia, Spain; tel. (660) 930629; e-mail asopge_ngo@hotmail.com; f. 2006 to replace ASOPGE (f. 1997); Pres. PEDRO NOLASCO NDONG OBAMA.

Asociación de Periodistas Profesionales de Guinea Ecuatorial: Malabo; f. 2007 by former Secretary of State for Information, Santiago Ngua.

Publisher

Centro Cultural Español de Malabo: Apdo 180, Malabo; tel. 333092186; fax 333092722; e-mail ccem@orange.gq.

Broadcasting and Communications

TELECOMMUNICATIONS

Dirección General de Correos y de Telecomunicaciones: Malabo; tel. 333092857; fax 333092515; Man. Dir M. DAUCHAT.

Guinea Ecuatorial de Telecomunicaciones, SA (GETESA): Calle Rey Boncoro 27, Apdo 494, Malabo; tel. 333092815; fax 333093313; e-mail info@getesa.gq; internet www.getesa.gq; f. 1987; 60% state-owned, 40% owned by France Telecom; Man. FRANCISCO NVE NSOGO.

RADIO

Radio Africa and Radio East Africa: Apdo 851, Malabo; e-mail pabcomain@aol.com; commercial station; owned by Pan American Broadcasting; music and religious programmes in English.

Radio Nacional de Guinea Ecuatorial: Apdo 749, Barrio Comandachina, Bata; Apdo 195, Avda 30 de Agosto 90, Malabo; tel. 333092260; fax 333092097; govt-controlled; commercial station; programmes in Spanish, French and vernacular languages; Dir (Bata) SEBASTIÁN ELÓ ASEKO; Dir (Malabo) JUAN EYENE OPKUA NGUEMA.

Radio Santa Isabel: Malabo; Spanish and French programmes.

Radio Televisión Asonga: Bata and Malabo; private; owned by Teodorín Ngumea Obiang.

TELEVISION

Televisión Nacional: Malabo; broadcasts in Spanish and French; Dir ERNESTO MFUMU MIKO.

Finance

(cap. = capital; res = reserves; dep. = deposits; m. = million; brs = branches; amounts in francs CFA)

BANKING

Central Bank

Banque des Etats de l'Afrique Centrale (BEAC): POB 501, Malabo; tel. 333092010; fax 333092006; e-mail beacmal@beac.int; internet www.beac.int; HQ in Yaoundé, Cameroon; agency also in Bata; f. 1973; bank of issue for mem. states of the Communauté Economique et Monétaire de l'Afrique Centrale (CEMAC, fmrly Union Douanière et Economique de l'Afrique Centrale), comprising Cameroon, the Central African Repub., Chad, the Repub. of the Congo, Equatorial Guinea and Gabon; cap. 88,000m., res 227,843m., dep. 4,110,966m. (Dec. 2009); Equatorial Guinea's deposits in 2010 totalled 776,000m; Gov. LUCAS ABAGA NCHAMA; Dir in Equatorial Guinea IVAN BACALE EBE MOLINA; 2 brs in Equatorial Guinea.

Commercial Banks

In 2008 there were four commercial banks in Equatorial Guinea.

Banco Nacional de Guinea Ecuatorial (BANGE): Bata; f. 2005; Dir-Gen. ROWELITO TANALIGA CAHILIG.

BGFIBANK Guinea Ecuatorial: Calle de Bata s/n, Apdo 749, Malabo; tel. 333096352; fax 333096373; e-mail agence_malabo@bgfi.com; internet www.bgfi.com/site/sp/bgfibank-guinea-ecuatorial.461.html; 55% owned by BGFIBANK, 35% owned by private shareholders, 10% state-owned; incorporated June 2001; cap. 5,000m., total assets 43,211m. (Dec. 2007); Chair. MELCHOR ESSONO EDJO; Dir-Gen. SERGE MICKOTO.

Caisse Commune d'Epargne et d'Investissement Guinea Ecuatorial (CCEI-GE): Calle del Presidente Nasser, Apdo 428, Malabo; tel. 333092203; fax 333093311; e-mail geccei@hotmail.com; 51% owned by Afriland First Bank (Cameroon); f. 1995; cap. and res 5,172m., total assets 81,191m. (Dec. 2003); Pres. BÁLTASAR ENGONGA EDJO'O; Dir-Gen. JOSEPH CÉLESTIN TINDJOU DJAMENI.

Commercial Bank Guinea Ecuatorial (CBGE): Carretera de Luba, Apdo 189, Malabo; e-mail cbgebank@cbc-bank.com; internet www.cbc-bank.com; f. 2003; cap. 1,500m. (Jan. 2003).

Société Générale des Banques en Guinée Equatoriale (SGBGE): Avda de la Independencia, Apdo 686, Malabo; tel. 333093337; fax 333093366; e-mail particuliers.sgbge@socgen.com; internet www.sgbge.gq; f. 1986; present name adopted 1998; 45.79% owned by Société Générale SA (France), 31.79% state-owned, 11.45% owned by Société Générale de Banques au Cameroun, 11.13% owned by local investors; cap. and res 2,780m., total assets 48,624m. (Dec. 2001); Chair. MARCELINO OWONO EDU; Man. Dir CHRISTIAN DELMAS; 5 brs in Bata, Ebebeyin, Luba and Malabo.

Development Banks

Banco de Fomento y Desarrollo (BFD): Malabo; f. 1998; 30% state-owned; cap. 50m.

Banque de Développement des Etats de l'Afrique Centrale: see Franc Zone.

Financial Institution

Caja Autónoma de Amortización de la Deuda Pública: Ministry of the Economy, Trade and Business Devt, Apdo 404, Malabo; tel. 333093105; fax 333092043; management of state funds; Dir-Gen. RAFAEL TUN.

INSURANCE

Equatorial Guinean Insurance Company, SA (EGICO): Avda de la Libertad, Malabo; state-owned.

Trade and Industry

GOVERNMENT AGENCIES

Cámaras Oficiales Agrícolas de Guinea: Bioko and Bata; purchase of cocoa and coffee from indigenous planters, who are partially grouped in co-operatives.

Empresa General de Industria y Comercio (EGISCA): Malabo; f. 1986; parastatal body jtly operated with the French Société pour l'Organisation, l'Aménagement et le Développement des Industries Alimentaires et Agricoles (SOMDIA); import-export agency.

Oficina para la Cooperación con Guinea Ecuatorial (OCGE): Malabo; f. 1981; administers bilateral aid from Spain.

DEVELOPMENT ORGANIZATIONS

Agencia Española de Cooperación Internacional para el Desarrollo (AECID): Parque de las Avenidas de Africa, Malabo; tel. 333091621; fax 333092932; e-mail ucemalabo@guineanet.net; internet www.aecid.es.

Asociación Bienestar Familiar de Guinea Ecuatorial: Apdo 984, Malabo; tel. and fax (09) 33-13; e-mail abifage1@hotmail.com; family welfare org.

Asociación Hijos de Lommbe (A Vonna va Lommbe): Malabo; e-mail avvl@bisa.com; internet www.bisala.com/avvl.html; f. 2000; agricultural devt org.

Camasa: Finca Sampaka, Km 7 Camino a Luba, Malabo; tel. 333098692; e-mail casamallo@hotmail.com; internet www.camasa.net; f. 1906; agricultural devt on Bioko island; operates projects for the cultivation and export of cocoa, pineapple, coffee, vanilla, nutmeg, peppers and tropical flowers.

Centro de Estudios e Iniciativas para el Desarrollo de Guinea Ecuatorial (CEIDIGE): Malabo; e-mail ceidbata@intnet.gq; internet www.eurosur.org/CEIDGE/portada.html; umbrella group of devt NGOs; Pres. José Antonio Nsang Andeme.

Family Care Guinea Ecuatorial (FGCE): Malabo; f. 2000; health and education devt; Dir Lauren Taylor Stevenson.

Instituto Nacional de Promoción Agropecuaria (INPAGE): Malabo; govt agricultural devt agency; reorg. 2000.

Sociedad Anónima de Desarrollo del Comercio (SOADECO-Guinée): Malabo; f. 1986; parastatal body jtly operated with the French Société pour l'Organisation, l'Aménagement et le Développement des Industries Alimentaires et Agricoles (SOMDIA); devt of commerce.

CHAMBERS OF COMMERCE

Cámara de Comercio Agrícola y Forestal de Malabo: Avda de la Independencia, Apdo 51, Malabo; tel. 333092343; fax 333094462; Dir Enrique Mercader Coasta.

Cámara de Comercio de Bioko: Avda de la Independencia 43, Apdo 51, Malabo; tel. and fax 333094576; e-mail camara@orange.gq; Pres. Gregorio Boho Camo.

INDUSTRIAL AND TRADE ASSOCIATIONS

INPROCAO: Malabo; production, marketing and distribution of cocoa.

Unión General de Empresas Privadas de la República de Guinea Ecuatorial (UGEPRIGE): Apdo 138, Malabo; tel. 222278326 (mobile); fax 333090559.

UTILITIES

Electricity

ENERGE: Malabo; state-owned electricity board.

Sociedad de Electricidad de Guinea Ecuatorial (SEGESA): Carretera de Luba, Apdo 139, Malabo; tel. 333093466; fax 333093329; e-mail segesa@internet.gq; state-owned electricity distributor; Man. Dir Benito Ondo.

Major Companies

Abayak: Malabo; owned by President Obiang's family.

Efusilia: Malabo; owned by Armengol Ondo, President Obiang's brother.

ExxonMobil: Complejo Residencial Abajak, Malabo.

Guinea Ecuatorial de Petróleo (GEPetrol): Calle Acacio Mane 39, BP 965, Malabo; tel. 333096769; fax 333096692; e-mail bonifacio.monsuy@ge-petrol.com; internet www.equatorialoil.com/pages/GEPetrol%20page.htm; f. 2001; state-owned petroleum company; National Dir Cándido Nsue Okomo.

Shimmer International: Bata; controls 90% of wood production in Rio Muni.

Sociedad Equatoguineana de Bebidas: Bata; production and bottling of various brands of beer, water and soft drinks; Dir-Gen. Cyril Brunel.

Sociedad Nacional de Gas de Guinea Ecuatorial (SONAGAS, G.E.): Malabo; e-mail j.ndong@sonagas-ge.com; internet www.sonagas-ge.com; f. 2005; oversees gas exploration and devt; Dir-Gen. Juan Antonio Ndong.

Sociedad Nacional de Vigilancia (SONAVI): Malabo; owned by Armengol Ondo.

Total Ecuatoguineana de Gestión (GE—Total): Malabo; f. 1984; 50% state-owned, 50% owned by Total (France); petroleum marketing and distribution.

TRADE UNIONS

A law permitting the establishment of trade unions was introduced in 1992. However, trade unions have not been granted authorization to operate.

Transport

RAILWAYS

There are no railways in Equatorial Guinea.

ROADS

In 2000 there were an estimated 2,880 km of roads and tracks. In 2006 a project commenced to build further 2,000 km of roads.

Bioko: a semi-circular tarred road serves the northern part of the island from Malabo down to Batete in the west and from Malabo to Basacato Grande in the east, with a feeder road from Luba to Moka and Bahía de la Concepción. Since 2010 a six-lane motorway has linked Malabo and the international airport to the new city of Sipopo, 16 km from the capital.

Río Muni: a tarred road links Bata with the nearby town of Mbini in the south; another tarred road links Bata with the frontier post of Ebebiyín in the east and then continues into Gabon; previously earth roads joining Acurenam, Mongomo and Anisok are now tarred. A new road links Bata to Mongomo.

SHIPPING

The main ports are Bata (general cargo and most of the country's export timber), Malabo (general), Luba (bananas, timber and petroleum), Mbini and Cogo (timber). There are regular shipping services to Europe from Bata and Malabo; however, communications between Bata and Malabo and Annobón remain erratic.

CIVIL AVIATION

There are two international airports, at Malabo and Bata, both of which have been expanded in recent years. Construction of a new runway at Bata began in 2011. There are also five domestic airports. All flights operated by carriers based in Equatorial Guinea are prohibited from flying in European Union airspace. SONAGESA, jointly operated by GEPetrol and SONAIR of Angola, offers direct connections between Malabo and Houston, TX, USA. Other international carriers regularly link Malabo to Madrid (Spain), Paris (France) Doula (Cameroon), Zürich (Switzerland), Amsterdam (Netherlands) and Frankfurt (Germany).

Air Consul: Apdo 77, Malabo; tel. and fax 333093291; e-mail airconsul@intnet.gq; Man. Fernandez Armesto.

EGA—Ecuato Guineana de Aviación: Apdo 665, Malabo; tel. 333092325; fax 333093313; internet www.ecuatoguineana.com/ega/ega.htm; regional and domestic passenger and cargo services; Pres. Melchor Esono Edjo.

Tourism

Tourism remains undeveloped. Future interest in this sector would be likely to focus on the unspoilt beaches of Río Muni and Bioko's scenic mountain terrain.

Defence

As assessed at November 2011, there were 1,100 men in the army, 120 in the navy and 100 in the air force. There was also a paramilitary force, referred to both as 'Antorchas' and 'Ninjas', which was trained by French military personnel. Military service is voluntary. Since 1979 Morocco has provided the bulk of the Presidential Guards, currently estimated at about 30 officers. It has also provided military advisers and training. Spain has also provided military advisers and training. Military aid has also been received from the USA. More recently, Israel has been providing military aid, advisers and training for special forces, including presidential security, and the aviation sector.

Defence Expenditure: Estimated at 3,800m. francs CFA in 2010.

Supreme Commander of the Armed Forces: Gen. (retd) OBIANG NGUEMA MBASOGO.

Inspector-Gen. of the Armed Forces and the Security Forces: Rear Adm. JOAQUÍN NDONG NVÉ.

Education

Education is officially compulsory and free for five years between the ages of six and 11 years. Primary education starts at six years of age and normally lasts for five years. Secondary education, beginning at the age of 12, spans a seven-year period, comprising a first cycle of four years and a second cycle of three years. In 2001/02 the total enrolment at primary and secondary schools was equivalent to 67% of the school-age population. According to UNESCO estimates, in 2002/03 total enrolment at primary schools included 66% of children in the relevant age-group (males 70%; females 63%), while secondary enrolment in 2000/01 included 24% of children in the relevant age-group (males 30%; females 18%). In 1999/2000 there were 1,003 pupils in higher education. Since 1979 assistance in the development of the educational system has been provided by Spain. Two higher education centres, at Bata and Malabo, are administered by the Spanish Universidad Nacional de Educación a Distancia. There is also a university, Universidad Nacional de Guinea Ecuatorial, founded in 1995, at Malabo and Bata, as well as the Escuela Nacional de Agricultura, a vocational college in Malabo. The French Government also provides considerable financial assistance. In September 2002 a new National Plan for Education was ratified. Its aims were to improve basic literacy and to introduce education on health-related topics. In 2003 spending on education represented 4.0% of total budgetary expenditure. According to UNESCO estimates, in 2010 the adult literacy rate was 93%, the highest in sub-Saharan Africa.

Bibliography

Agencia Española de Cooperación Internacional. *Segundo plano marco de cooperación entre el Reino de España y la República de Guinea Ecuatorial*. Madrid, AECI, 1990.

Boneke, J. B. *La transición de Guinea Ecuatorial: Historia de un fracaso*. Madrid, Labrys 54 Ediciones, 1998.

Castro, A., Mariano, and de la Calle Muñoz, M. L. *Geografía de Guinea Ecuatorial*. Madrid, Programa de Colaboración Educativa con Guinea Ecuatorial, 1985.

Castroviejo Bolívar, J., Juste Balleste, J., and Castelo Alvarez, R. *Investigación y conservación de la naturaleza en Guinea Ecuatorial*. Madrid, Oficina de Cooperación con Guinea Ecuatorial, 1986.

Cohen, R. (Ed.). *African Islands and Enclaves*. London, Sage Publications, 1983.

Cronj, S. *Equatorial Guinea: The Forgotten Dictatorship*. London, 1976.

Cusack, I. *Equatorial Guinea: The Inculcation and Maintenance of Hispanic Culture*. Bristol, University of Bristol, 1999.

Eman, A. *Equatorial Guinea during the Macías Nguema Régime*. Washington, DC, 1983.

Equatorial Guinea Research Group. *Executive Report On Strategies in Equatorial Guinea*. San Diego, CA, Icon Group International, annual.

Fegley, R. *Equatorial Guinea: An African Tragedy*. New York, Peter Lang, 1989.

González-Echegaray, C. *Estudios Guineos: Filología*. Madrid, IDEA, 1964.

Estudios Guineos: Etnología. Madrid, IDEA, 1964.

Jakobeit, C. 'Äquatorialguinea' in Hanisch, R., and Jakobeit, C. (Eds). *Der Kakaoweltmarkt*. Vol. 2. Hamburg, Deutsches Übersee-institut, 1991.

Klitgaard, R. *Tropical Gangsters*. London, I. B. Tauris, 1990.

Liniger-Goumaz, M. *Guinea Ecuatorial: Bibliografía General*. 5 vols. Bern and Geneva, 1976–85.

Equatorial Guinea: An African Historical Dictionary. Metuchen, NJ, Scarecrow Press, 2000.

De la Guinée équatoriale nguemiste. Eléments pour le dossier de l'afro-fascisme. Geneva, Editions du Temps, 1983.

Statistics of Nguemist Equatorial Guinea. Geneva, Editions du Temps, 1986.

Small is not always Beautiful: The Story of Equatorial Guinea. London, Hurst, 1988.

Mann, S. *Cry Havoc*. London, John Blake Publishing, 2011.

Martín de Molino, A. *Los Bubis, ritos y creencias*. Malabo, Centro Cultural Hispano-Guineano, 1989.

La ciudad de Clarence: Primeros años de la actual ciudad de Malabo, capital de Guinea Ecuatorial, 1827–1859. Malabo, Centro Cultural Hispano-Guineano, 1993.

Ndongo Bidyogo, D. *Historia y Tragedia de Guinea Ecuatorial*. Madrid, Cambio, 1977.

Nerín, G. *Guinea Ecuatorial: Historia en Blanco y Negro*. Barcelona, Atalaya Península, 1997.

Nfumu, A. N. *Macías: ¿Verdugo o Víctima?* Madrid, Herrero y asociados, Pool de Servicios Editoriales, S.L., 2004.

Nguema-Obam, P. *Aspects de la religion fang*. Paris, Editions Karthala, 1984.

Obiang Nguema, T. *Guinea Ecuatorial, País Joven: Testimonios Políticos*. Malabo, Ediciones Guinea, 1985.

Reeves, P. *Equatorial Guinea: 1996 Presidential Elections Observation Report*. Washington, DC, International Foundation for Election Systems, 1996.

Roberts, A. *The Wonga Coup*. London, Profile Books, 2006.

Sundiata, I. K. *Equatorial Guinea*. Boulder, CO, Westview Press, 1990.

From Slaving to Neoslavery. Madison, WI, University of Wisconsin, 1996.

Ugarte, M. *Africans in Europe: The Culture of Exile and Emigration from Equatorial Guinea to Spain*. Champaign, University of Illinois Press, 2010.

ERITREA

Physical and Social Geography

MILES SMITH-MORRIS

The State of Eritrea, which formally acceded to independence on 24 May 1993, covers an area of 121,144 sq km (46,774 sq miles). Its territory includes the Dahlak islands, a low-lying coralline archipelago offshore from Massawa. Eritrea, which has a coastline on the Red Sea extending for almost 1,000 km, is bounded to the north-west by Sudan, to the south and west by Ethiopia, and to the south-east by Djibouti. The terrain comprises the northern end of the Ethiopian plateau (rising to more than 2,000 m above sea-level), where most cultivation takes place, and a low-lying semi-desert coastal strip, much of which supports only pastoralism. Lowland areas have less than 500 mm of rainfall per year, compared with 1,000 mm in the highlands. Average annual temperatures range from 17°C in the highlands to 30°C in Massawa. The Danakil depression in the south-east descends to more than 130 m below sea-level and experiences some of the highest temperatures recorded on earth, frequently exceeding 50°C. Much of the coniferous forest that formerly covered the slopes of the highlands has been destroyed by settlement and cultivation; soil erosion is a severe problem.

The extent of Eritrea's natural resources awaits fuller exploration and evaluation. Copper ores and gold were mined from the Eritrean plateau in prehistoric times and there has been some extraction of iron ore. The Dallol depression, south of Massawa, is known to have valuable potash deposits. Some exploration for petroleum has taken place in Red Sea coastal areas; oil seepages and offshore natural gas discoveries have been reported.

The population of Eritrea was enumerated at just over 2.7m. in the Ethiopian census of 1984, but the war for independence resulted in large-scale population movements. Some 500,000 refugees fled to neighbouring Sudan and a significant, but unquantified, number of Eritreans has remained in Ethiopia. At mid-1991, according to official Ethiopian sources, the population of the Eritrean territory was estimated at 3,435,500. At mid-2012, according to UN estimates, Eritrea's population totalled 5,580,861. The population is fairly evenly divided between Tigrinya-speaking Christians, the traditional inhabitants of the highlands, and the Muslim communities of the western lowlands, northern highlands and east coast.

Recent History

WARKA SOLOMON KAHSAY

Revised for this edition by GREG CAMERON

Modern Eritrea dates from the establishment of an Italian colony in the late 19th century. From a small concession gained near Assab in 1869, the Italians extended their control to Massawa in 1885 and to most of Eritrea by 1889. In the same year the Ethiopian emperor, Menelik, and the Italian Government signed the Treaty of Ucciali, which effectively recognized Italian control over Eritrea (and from which Italy derived its subsequent claim to a protectorate over Ethiopia). The period of Italian rule (1889–1941) and the subsequent years under British military administration (1941–52) created a society, economy and polity more advanced than in the semi-feudal Ethiopian empire. Following the Second World War, Ethiopia, which historically regarded Eritrea as an integral part of its territory, intensified its claims to sovereignty. The strategic interests of the USA and its influence in the newly founded UN resulted in a compromise, in the form of a federation between Eritrea and Ethiopia. No federal institutions were established, and Eritrean autonomy was systematically stifled. In 1962 Eritrea was reconstituted as a province of Ethiopia.

THE LIBERATION STRUGGLE AND INDEPENDENCE

The dissolution of the federation brought forth a more militant Eritrean nationalism, whose political roots had been established during the process of consultation for the disposal of the Italian colony in the latter part of the period of British rule. The Eritrean Liberation Movement, founded in 1958, was succeeded by the Eritrean Liberation Front (ELF), which began an armed struggle in 1961. Organizational and ideological differences erupted into violence within the ELF in the mid-1960s, as a result of demands for reform from the increasing numbers of educated guerrilla fighters. Meanwhile, a reformist group separated from the ELF and formed the Popular Liberation Forces (renamed the Eritrean People's Liberation Front—EPLF—in 1977). A major consequence of the split was the civil war of 1972–74. The EPLF leadership consolidated a highly centralized and disciplined political and military organization, in contrast to the more loosely organized and factionalized ELF.

After a prolonged conflict, on 24 May 1991 the EPLF defeated the colonial regime, and immediately established an interim administration in Asmara. In April 1993 a UN-supervised referendum took place in an atmosphere of national celebration. Of the 1,102,410 Eritreans who voted, 99.8% endorsed national independence. Eritrea's long-awaited independence was officially confirmed on 24 May 1993, when the country attained international recognition.

Following Eritrea's accession to independence, a four-year transitional period was declared, during which preparations were to proceed for establishing a constitutional and pluralist political system. At the apex of the transitional Government were three state institutions: the Consultative Council, the National Assembly and the judiciary. In one of the National Assembly's first acts, Issaias Afewerki, the Secretary-General of the EPLF, was elected as head of state, by a margin of 99 votes to five.

President Afewerki appointed a new Consultative Council in June 1993, comprising 14 ministers (all members of the EPLF politburo) and 10 regional governors. The third congress of the EPLF was convened at Nakfa, in Sahel province, in February 1994. There the EPLF formally transformed itself from a military front into a national movement (the People's Front for Democracy and Justice—PFDJ), hoping to embrace all Eritreans (except those accused of collaboration during the liberation struggle). The party congress also confirmed its support for a plural political system, which was to be included in the final draft of a new constitution. Afewerki was elected Chairman of an 18-member Executive Committee (while remaining head of state, and leader of the PFDJ). A transitional National Assembly of 150 members was established, including 75 members of the PFDJ Central Committee and another 75 PFDJ members from the regions, selected by party leaders.

In March 1994 the National Assembly adopted a series of resolutions whereby the former executive body, the Consultative Council, was formally superseded by a State Council. Other measures included the creation of a 50-member Constitutional Commission, all but eight of whom were government appointees. International conferences on the draft constitution were held in the capital in July and in January 1995, presided over by Dr Bereket Habteselassie, the Chairman of the Constitutional Commission. However, although a new Constitution was ratified in May 1997, it has yet to be implemented. In May 1995 the National Assembly approved a law reducing the previous 10 administrative regions to six, each with regional, sub-regional and village administrations. In November the Assembly approved new names for the regions, unrelated to the ethnic groups that inhabited them, and finalized details of their exact boundaries and sub-divisions, based on catchment basins, to resolve historical land disputes behind ethnic conflict. In 2005 the President divided the country into five military command zones, which were to exist alongside the civilian administrative regions but were granted overriding powers.

CONFLICT WITH ETHIOPIA

Owing to strong relations between Eritrea and Ethiopia in the early 1990s, border contentions and ideological disputes raised during the struggle were not settled immediately after independence. However, relations deteriorated in late 1997 as disagreements arose following Eritrea's introduction of a new currency, the nakfa (see Economy). In May 1998 fighting erupted between Eritrean and Ethiopian troops after both laid claim to several border regions, including Badme, Zalambessa and Bure. Despite a series of peace initiatives by various regional and international parties, including the Organization of African Unity (OAU, now the African Union—AU), Rwanda and the USA, conflicts between the two countries continued intermittently over a period of two years.

The scale of the conflict was without parallel in Africa. Hundreds of thousands of troops were involved in the fighting; both sides were exceptionally well armed with modern weapons. In mid-May 2000 Ethiopia launched an offensive near the disputed towns of Badme and Zalambessa and succeeded in repulsing the Eritrean forces. Hostilities continued despite growing fears of a mounting humanitarian crisis. It was estimated that between 500,000 and 1m. Eritreans had fled as the conflict spread into Eritrea, with many seeking refuge in Sudan. The crisis was exacerbated by drought and food shortages, with about 850,000 Eritreans and an estimated 8m. Ethiopians in need of emergency assistance. The UN Security Council voted unanimously to impose a 12-month arms embargo on the two countries in an attempt to prevent any further intensification of hostilities; however, hours after this announcement Ethiopia declared that it had captured the key strategic town of Barentu, in south-western Eritrea, and had taken full control of the western front.

Ethiopia launched a massive new offensive, which led to the capture of Zalambessa, and on 25 May 2000 the Eritrean Government announced that it would withdraw troops from the disputed areas. Ethiopian forces continued to capture Eritrean towns over the following days, although both sides had by this stage agreed to attend peace talks under the auspices of the OAU, which began on 29 May in Algiers, Algeria. On 18 June a peace agreement was signed, which provided for an immediate cease-fire and the deployment of a UN peace-keeping force in a 25-km buffer zone until the disputed 966-km border had been demarcated.

In September 2000 the UN Security Council approved the deployment of a 4,200-strong UN Mission in Ethiopia and Eritrea (UNMEE) peace-keeping force. UNMEE, which was placed under the command of the Special Representative of the UN Secretary-General, Legwaila Joseph Legwaila, was charged with monitoring and ensuring that both Eritrea and Ethiopia complied with the agreement. A definitive peace agreement, formally bringing the war to an end, was signed in Algiers on 12 December. Both sides agreed to a permanent cessation of all hostilities and the release and repatriation of all prisoners of war. The UN pledged to establish two separate independent commissions to delineate the border, investigate the underlying causes of the conflict and assess compensation claims. The border commission was to demarcate the border in accordance with colonial maps. By late January 2001 the UNMEE force, drawn from more than 30 member countries, had been fully deployed and began making provisions for the establishment of a Temporary Security Zone (TSZ) in the 25-km area between the two countries' troops.

In April 2002 the five-member Boundary Commission at the International Court of Justice in The Hague, Netherlands, delivered its findings, which both countries had pledged to accept and respect. However, the Commission failed to locate Badme, the village where the war had begun, in either Eritrea or Ethiopia, and the village itself did not appear on any of the published maps. After the initial confusion, the Boundary Commission announced in March 2003 that Badme was indeed in Eritrean territory. Border demarcation was scheduled to begin that year, but Ethiopia's rejection of the border ruling put demarcation on indefinite hold.

The peace process suffered a further reversal in November 2003, when Eritrea withdrew its ambassador to the AU and accused the organization of neglecting its responsibilities over the dispute with Ethiopia. However, in the following month both countries agreed to establish three Sector Military Coordination Committees, under the chairmanship of UNMEE's Sector Commanders, in order to improve the mechanism for preventing any minor border incidents from escalating into wider conflict. Later in December Lloyd Axworthy, a former Canadian Minister of Foreign Affairs, was appointed as the UN's special envoy to the region, tasked with resolving the stalled peace process between Eritrea and Ethiopia. While Ethiopia welcomed the appointment, the Eritrean Government expressed its opposition, as it feared that it would result in amendments to the Boundary Commission's ruling. In November 2004 Ethiopia stated that it approved the ruling 'in principle' but called for dialogue over the implementation of the decision in sensitive areas. This was rejected by Eritrea, which insisted on 'full implementation' of the ruling. Eritrea continued to refuse to meet with Axworthy and the initiative collapsed shortly thereafter.

The Eritrean Government initiated a more assertive strategy, and sought to persuade the international community to put pressure on Ethiopia to accept the border ruling by banning UN helicopters from its airspace. Subsequently, UN Security Council Resolution 1640 threatened both nations with economic sanctions, demanding that Ethiopia pull back its troops from the border, demarcate the border without preconditions, and that Eritrea lift restrictions on UNMEE. Terming the threat of sanctions 'deplorable', Eritrea accused the Security Council of bias and in December ordered all UN personnel from the USA, Russia, Canada and European Union (EU) member states to leave the country. In response, UNMEE claimed that it had lost its ability to monitor much of the border.

Eritrea suffered a reversal when in December 2005 the Claims Commission, based in The Hague, set up to investigate war violations, ruled that Eritrea had triggered the border war with Ethiopia: since there was no armed attack against Eritrea, its attack on Ethiopia could not be justified as lawful self-defence under the UN charter. In its final ruling, delivered in August 2009, the Claims Commission awarded Ethiopia US $174m. and Eritrea $161.1m. in damages in respect of the 1998–2000 border war. The damages awarded to Eritrea included compensation for loss of property for people expelled from their land by Ethiopia, while the damages awarded to Ethiopia were to compensate for the human suffering and lost income of displaced persons. Eritrea, which was to pay Ethiopia $12.6m., stated that it would honour the ruling; however, Ethiopia rejected the ruling, declaring that the compensation awarded was insufficient.

On 31 March 2006, at the end of his term as Special Representative of the UN Secretary-General, Legwaila expressed profound disappointment that border demarcation was still pending. The Security Council extended UNMEE's mandate to 31 May and threatened sanctions against both countries should they continue to ignore Resolution 1640. The Eritrean Government, however, remained defiant, refusing to lift restrictions imposed on UNMEE's activities, and stated that the restrictions were by-products of the international community's failure to enforce Ethiopian compliance with the Boundary Commission's ruling. In May officials from the two countries met in London, United Kingdom, but no progress was made. Eritrea continued to demand demarcation, while Ethiopia insisted on dialogue. In late May the USA pressed the Security Council to scale back UNMEE's operations and UN Security Council Resolution 1681 extended UNMEE's mandate until 30 September, while reducing the number of troops from 3,300 to 2,300. The Security Council also demanded that both countries fully comply with Resolution 1640. Eritrean officials declared Resolution 1681 to be 'unjust' and demanded the full implementation of the Boundary Commission's ruling.

Eritrea moved some 1,500 troops and 14 tanks into the TSZ in October 2006. The UN Secretary-General, Kofi Annan, demanded that Eritrea withdraw its troops from the zone immediately. The eruption of war in Somalia in December expanded the battle ground beyond the borders of the two countries. Ethiopia supported the transitional Government while Eritrea backed the Somali Supreme Islamic Courts Council (SSICC). The conflict in Somalia rapidly became a proxy war between Eritrea and Ethiopia. With Ethiopian forces engaged in combat within Somalia, Eritrea's move into the TSZ was interpreted by the USA and the Ethiopian Government as part of a regional strategy to place military pressure on Ethiopia's northern front.

In November 2006 the Boundary Commission announced that it would demarcate the Ethiopian–Eritrean border on maps using high-resolution aerial photography to identify points where pillars should be placed to mark the boundary in the remaining disputed areas. The Commission also announced that it would allow the two countries to establish the physical boundary themselves, a move immediately rejected by both Governments. Eritrea demanded that the border be physically laid out on the ground, while Ethiopia, which rejected the boundary, stated that the Commission was acting outside its mandate. Owing to obstruction of its work on the ground by both parties, and despite UN Security Council Resolution 1710 of September 2006 urging full co-operation with the Boundary Commission, the Commission subsequently declared that both parties had to demarcate the border by the end of November 2007. Failing this, the boundary would stand as demarcated by the points the Commission had identified, following which the work would be completed and the Commission closed down.

In January 2007 the new UN Secretary-General, Ban Ki-Moon, warned that Ethiopia and Eritrea needed to do much more than settle their border issue if they were to establish peace, reconciliation and normalized relations. Subsequently, UN Security Council Resolution 1741 extended UNMEE's mandate to 31 July, while reducing the UN peace-keeping force from 2,300 to 1,700. The Security Council again demanded that Ethiopia accept fully and move to implement the border ruling. At the same time the Security Council requested that Eritrea immediately withdraw its forces from the TSZ and reverse its restrictions on UNMEE.

After providing remote demarcation by co-ordinates, the Boundary Commission was dissolved on 30 November 2007, thereby removing an important forum for dialogue between the two parties. In January 2008 Eritrea deployed its army in the TSZ and cut fuel supplies to UNMEE. It considered the virtual demarcation to be the end of the border dispute and argued that both the UNMEE and Ethiopian presence on its territory was a violation of its sovereignty. Ethiopia continued to refuse to recognize the virtual demarcation. The UN Security Council expressed concern over the ongoing stalemate, and on 30 January 2008 Resolution 1798 authorized the renewal of UNMEE's mandate until 31 July. Calling on both sides to avoid the use of force against the other, the Security Council also appealed to Eritrea to withdraw its forces from the TSZ, and to Ethiopia to decrease its military forces in the areas adjacent to the TSZ. The resolution further demanded that the Algiers process be completed, including the physical demarcation of the border. Ban warned in April that the withdrawal of the peace-keepers could spark renewed conflict on the 1,000-km border.

In July 2008 the UN Security Council voted unanimously to end the UN monitoring of the border dispute between Eritrea and Ethiopia, but urged the two countries to refrain from any use of force. Resolution 1827 stressed that the termination was 'without prejudice' to the two countries' obligations under the Algiers agreements of 2000. An Eritrean government spokesman stated that the UN mission had only been symbolic and diplomatic efforts to remove Ethiopia from Eritrean soil would continue, but the Eritrean Government continued to reject any initiative short of enforcing the border ruling.

Although both the Ethiopian and Eritrean authorities have played down the threat of renewed conflict, many areas along their border have seen periodic shooting incidents involving troops that remain in close proximity to one another. Meanwhile, both regimes support each other's opposition movements. Eritrean opposition groups hosted by Ethiopia and with active membership among the diaspora include the Eritrean Islamic Party for Justice and Development, remnants of the ELF, the Eritrean Islamic Congress, the Democratic Movement for the Liberation of Eritrean Kunama and the Red Sea Afar Democratic Organization (RSADO). Among others, these joined to form an umbrella organization—the Eritrean Democratic Alliance (EDA)—in May 2009. The EDA's 11 member organizations, together with other groups and civil society representatives, convened at the National Conference for Democratic Change, held in August 2010 in Addis Ababa, Ethiopia, and passed a resolution pledging to overthrow the Eritrean Government through military means and to unite the political and military wings of the various opposition groups. On the military front, the RSADO and the EDA reported staging co-ordinated military attacks against government troops inside Eritrea.

However, the claims were impossible to verify independently owing to travel restrictions in the country, and the Eritrean Government has maintained a stance of silence against such reports of attacks on its forces. The EDA has been criticized as being ineffectual and tied too closely to the Ethiopian regime, which, as a result, has lessened any support it might have in Eritrea. In May 2011 the EDA leadership publicly called for a Libya-style foreign intervention in Eritrea. More recently, Muhammad Ali Ibrahim, a member of the central council of the opposition Eritrean People's Democratic Party, part of the EDA, went missing in Kassala, in eastern Sudan, leading to fears that he might have been kidnapped by Eritrean security agents. There are reports of low-level insurgency by groups with an ethnic or Islamist affiliation. Meanwhile, Ethiopia accused Eritrea of sponsoring its opposition movements, most notably the Oromo Liberation Front. Ethiopia also alleged Eritrean involvement in bomb attacks on a café and on a bus in northern Ethiopia, near the Eritrean border, in April and May 2010, respectively, and accused its neighbour of attempting to disrupt the Ethiopian legislative elections in May. The Ethiopian Government of Meles Zenawi continued to demand preconditions to enforcing the binding border ruling.

In March 2012 Ethiopia made a 16-km incursion into south-eastern Eritrea, raiding rebel bases at Ramid, Gelahbe and Gimbi. It was the first attack by Ethiopian troops inside Eritrea since the end of the 1998–2000 border conflict. Moreoever, Addis Ababa accused the regime in Eritrea of training fighters who staged an attack in January 2012 that killed five Western tourists. The Eritrean authorities stated that the Ethiopian attack was provocative, but would not 'entrap' it. According to the Eritrean Minister of Foreign Affairs, Osman Salih Muhammad, 'The objective of the attack. . .is to divert attention from the central issue of the regime's flagrant violation of international law and illegal occupation of sovereign Eritrean territories', and he dismissed as 'ridiculous' the accusation that Eritrea was harbouring Ethiopian rebels.

The ongoing conflict in Somalia also continued to exacerbate the deadlock between Eritrea, Ethiopia and external powers. In 2007 the Eritrean Government vehemently opposed the UN authorization of a regional force comprising troops from the Intergovernmental Authority on Development (IGAD) and the AU to protect the Transitional Federal Government (TFG) in Somalia and to replace Ethiopian forces who were to be withdrawn. In April Eritrea suspended its membership of IGAD as a result of deteriorating relations with Somalia. In late May the

Alliance for the Re-liberation of Somalia was formed out of factions of the Islamic courts and anti-Ethiopian members of the TFG. Moderate elements of this alliance, led by Sheikh Sharif Sheikh Ahmed, the former leader of the SSICC and current President of the Somali Government, joined the peace process in Djibouti in 2008 to form a new transitional government in January 2009. However, 'extremist' factions of the courts remained in Eritrea and the Government in Asmara was accused of continuing to arm the Somali militant Islamist group, al-Shabaab, throughout 2009, while Ethiopia supported the unity Government.

In late 2009 Ethiopia, Uganda, IGAD and the USA urged the UN to impose sanctions on Eritrea for its continued support of radical Islamists in Somalia and for violating Security Council Resolution 751 (approved in 1992), which imposed an embargo on arms trade to Somali factions. After a series of accusations and denials, the UN Security Council, in December 2009, adopted Resolution 1907, which placed an arms embargo on Eritrea, imposed travel restrictions on political and military leaders, and additionally froze their overseas funds and financial assets. Thirteen members of the 15-member Council voted in favour of the resolution, while Libya voted against the motion and the People's Republic of China abstained. The resolution also extended the mandate of the UN monitoring group for the arms embargo in Somalia (established in 1992) to include monitoring and reporting on the implementation of the sanctions imposed on Eritrea. In a letter to the UN Security Council in January 2010, President Afewerki denied the accusations against Eritrea as wholly unfounded, and requested the formation of an independent international body to examine the allegations. The Council in return demanded that Eritrea co-operate with the UN monitoring group and recognize the Somali TFG, as well as settle its dispute with Djibouti. In April the monitoring group reported that Eritrea's support of Somali militant groups had either decreased or become less visible. Eritrea cited this as confirmation of a lack of evidence to support the sanctions. Eritrea also participated in the İstanbul Conference on Somalia in May, convened by the international community to promote the unity of Somali groups and support the TFG.

At mid-2011 the sanctions remained in force, which the Eritrean Government denounced as evidence of the West's pro-Ethiopian bias and conspiracy to undermine Eritrea. President Afewerki, on the occasion of the 20th Independence Day, 24 May 2011, claimed that all the accusations directed against the Eritrean Government, including over the issues of Somalia, terrorism, piracy, and acts of subversion and instability in the Horn region, served as an excuse to endorse the perceived aspiration of the USA and the UN Security Council to undermine the judicial process concerning the Eritrea–Ethiopia border issue. In 2011 the Council's Monitoring Group on Somalia and Eritrea reported that Eritrea was still funnelling funds through its embassies to al-Shabaab and other groups engaged in fighting the UN-recognized Somali Government. In August President Afewerki visited Uganda to discuss the Somali conflict with President Gen. (retd) Yoweri Kaguta Museveni; the visit was interpreted as a move by Eritrea to reduce its isolation in the region. Although Eritrea had withdrawn from Djibouti territory by 2011, it continues to hold 19 Djiboutian prisoners of war, to whom it has not permitted third-party access. President Afwerki addressed the 66th session of the UN in September 2011. In his speech he called for reform of the UN by strengthening the role and authority of the General Assembly, and for Ethiopia to end its occupation of sovereign Eritrean territory by December. The UN Security Council has tightened sanctions against Eritrea after its East African neighbours accused it of continuing to provide support to Islamist militants. The resolution required that foreign companies involved in Eritrea's mining industry ensure that funds from the sector are not used to destabilize the region. Thirteen council members voted for the resolution and two abstained. The Eritrean Government denied the accusations.

POST-WAR POLITICS

Eritrea, with its smaller population, fared worse in the conflict with Ethiopia, resulting in growing challenges to President Afewerki and a rift in the ruling front. While internal party conflicts had been experienced in the period before the war with Ethiopia, the war intensified these divisions. During the conflict a number of key military strategists of the liberation struggle and senior government officials were subjected to *mdskal* (work suspension with pay) and tension escalated in January 2000 with the banning of Gen. Ogbe Abraha, Chief of Staff of the Eritrean army during the war, from all official positions. Afewerki's overruling of the army hierarchy was blamed for the crisis within the army command structure and the collapse of Eritrean positions in the third round of fighting in May. Divisions between the President and senior PFDJ officials also emerged at a meeting of the party's Executive Committee in August, when Afewerki was criticized for failing to convene the Central Committee, the party's core leadership, and the National Assembly. While the unratified Constitution stipulated that the National Assembly should convene every six months and the Central Council every four months, the President refused to convene both houses in the period prior to and immediately after the outbreak of the conflict. In response to threats by senior party and government officials that they would call the National Assembly to session themselves, the President agreed to convene the Assembly in September and reluctantly accepted the decision to establish a commission to define rules for multi-party elections, scheduled for December 2001, which were subsequently rescinded.

In early 2001 Afewerki and the PFDJ Central Committee launched a political campaign among mid-level officials to discredit his opponents. The critics demanded an emergency meeting of the party's Central Committee and the National Assembly, reiterating their demands for the implementation of the Constitution. On 15 May senior party officials signed an open letter to party members accusing the President of working in an 'unconstitutional manner' and gave a series of press interviews demanding reform. This group comprised Central Committee members, including Minister of Local Government Jahmoud Ahmed Sherifo, who was increasingly coming into open conflict with President Afwerki. In mid-June the Minister of Foreign Affairs, Haile Woldetensae, and the Minister of Fisheries, Petros Solomon, both members of the Central Committee, were dismissed from their posts. In August the Minister of Justice was dismissed after delivering a paper critical of the Eritrean justice system during an international conference held in Asmara. Six of the G-15, as the signatories of the letter had become known, were detained in mid-September 2001, and the Government announced a temporary suspension of the independent press. Days later a further five members of the G-15 were arrested, as were nine journalists and two Eritreans employed at the US embassy. Three other G-15 members, who were outside Eritrea at the time of the dispute, had their passports revoked. Afewerki insisted that his former allies had become threats to national security and their questioning of his conduct during the war was portrayed as treasonous. Some, including Gen. Abraha, were reported to have died in detention as a result of poor conditions and the denial of medical treatment. According to Amnesty International's 2012 Report, the Eritrean Government has refused to confirm reports indicating that nine of the G-15 group had died in detention in recent years. Similarly, in October 2011 businessman Senay Kifleyesus was arrested, reportedly after he was cited criticizing President Afewerki in a confidential cable that had been released by the WikiLeaks organization.

In late January 2002 the National Assembly ratified the electoral law, which stipulated that 30% of the seats in the new legislative chamber would be reserved for women. The PFDJ announced in February that, following extensive consultations with local and regional representatives, the National Assembly had decided not to permit the formation of political parties, although it conceded that the principle of establishing political parties was 'acceptable'. However, in his annual interview with state media in 2010 President Afewerki contended that political parties were divisive and led to sub-national sentiments.

In 2003 non-partisan elections of local administrators and magistrates were held in villages throughout Eritrea, and in May 2004 elections took place for regional assemblies. Administrative regions continue to elect their legislative bodies, but administrative officials are appointed by central government and their powers continue to be overridden by military zonal commanders who have control over the implementation of development resources. The regime remained reluctant to implement a framework centred around a constitutional process of democratization and international human rights treaties. In May 2009 President Afewerki asserted that his regime ruled by consensus and that the PFDJ provided a forum for a broad-based popular participation. Membership of the PFDJ is required of all Eritreans who are employed in the civil service, the military and the PFDJ's companies. Special courts continue to bypass the regular judicial system.

POST-WAR STATE AND SOCIETY

The state's relations with churches, non-governmental organizations (NGOs) and other potential interest groups also came under scrutiny in the post-war period, although the roots of conflict can be found in the period before 1998. The EPLF's experiences in the liberation war had made it intensely committed to secularism, with strong control over societal groups, which were subsumed into the movement. The major faiths in Eritrea include the Orthodox Church, Islam, the Evangelical Lutheran Church and the Roman Catholic Church. The Eritrean Orthodox Church, which dominates highland culture, had been a notable casualty of the Ethiopian occupation of the country at the time of the liberation war. Several monasteries were occupied by Ethiopian soldiers and many of the monks and their students were killed. After independence, a movement promoting secession from the Ethiopian church gained widespread support. In June 1994 Eritrea sent five abbots from Eritrean monasteries to the headquarters of the Coptic church in Cairo, Egypt, where they were inducted as bishops by Shenouda III, the Coptic Orthodox pontiff. In September the first bishops of the Eritrean Orthodox Church were consecrated at a ceremony conducted in Cairo. These consecrations signified the formal separation of the Eritrean Orthodox Church from the Ethiopian Orthodox Church as an independent body. In May 1998 Abuna Philippos was consecrated as the first Eritrean Patriarch by Shenouda III in Alexandria. Following Philippos' death in 2002, Abuna Yakob was anointed as the second Patriarch. Yakob died in December 2003; Abune Antonios was elected as his successor in March 2004.

In January 2006 authorities reportedly placed Antonios under formal house arrest for protesting against the arrest of three Orthodox priests of the reformist Medhane Alem Church, and for refusing to co-operate with the Government in closing down that Church. Antonios argued that his dismissal was in direct violation of long-established Church canons, under which a Patriarch's election is a lifetime appointment that cannot be revoked. He was, however, stripped of his patriarchal vestments and holy artefacts in January 2007. Amnesty International reported that Antonios was transferred to an undisclosed location in May when a new pro-Government Patriarch was appointed, contrary to church regulations. The Government also formed the Commission of Religious Affairs of the Orthodox Church to oversee the appointments of priests. According to the US Department of State's *International Religious Freedom* report for 2011, published in September of that year, the deposed patriarch, Abune Antonios, remained under house arrest.

It is believed that one-half of Eritrea's population follows Islam; these populations are mainly found in lowland areas and pastoralist communities. The secular state respects Islamic holidays and traditions, and is vigilant against sectarianism. However, there is some concern among Muslim communities that language policies, which promote mother-tongue education, discriminate against Arabic (the mother tongue of less than 3% of the population), and in favour of Tigrinya. Officially, Arabic and Tigrinya are both recognized as state languages; in practice, it is Tigrinya that functions as the official language of government and the military. Eritrean Islamic Jihad (EIJ), which operates out of Sudan, has been held responsible for several bombs and landmines in the western lowlands and remains an ongoing threat into 2012, according to travel advisories.

Although Jehovah's Witnesses form only a small group, their post-independence history has been marked by conflicts with the state, as has been, to a lesser extent, the experience of Evangelical and Pentecostal churches. Other 'new' churches grew rapidly in the 1990s, as Eritreans returned from the diaspora, bringing new ways of worshipping with them or joining Evangelical churches that had been suppressed under the Ethiopian Dergue regime. A revival movement within the Orthodox Church also emerged at this time, demanding liturgical and institutional change, which was suppressed. In April 2002 all churches with less than 40 years' presence in Eritrea were ordered to close their branches outside Asmara, and churches in Asmara were similarly ordered to close in May. Church leaders were told that they could 'reapply' for licences to operate, but permits were not issued thereafter. The state currently recognizes only three Christian churches—the Roman Catholic Church, the Lutheran Church and the Orthodox Church—together with Islam. The others are recognized as unregistered religious groups and are not allowed to exercise their beliefs publicly. According to Amnesty International, members of banned faiths continued to be arrested, arbitrarily detained and ill-treated. More than 3,000 Christians from unregistered church groups, including 51 Jehovah's Witnesses, were believed to be arbitrarily detained. According to Human Rights Watch, sources who monitor religious persecutions reported continuing persecution of religious practitioners in 2011. Thirty members of an evangelical Christian church were arrested in Asmara in January. In May and June the Eritrean authorities reportedly arrested over 90 members of unrecognized Christian churches, including 26 college students.

The US Department of State's *International Religious Freedom* report for 2010, published in November of that year, included Eritrea among a group of eight countries in which 'violations of religious freedoms have been noteworthy'. The report claimed that 'more than 3,000 Christians from unregistered groups were detained in prison' and noted that the Government also 'retained substantial control over the four approved religious groups'. In its 2011 report, the State Department said that in May and June of that year the Government had rounded up approximately 3,000 religious workers from the government-approved Eritrean Orthodox, Evangelical (Lutheran) and Islamic faiths and sent them to the Wi'a military camp to take part in national service. There were reports that a lack of food and sanitary facilities at Wi'a had resulted in them contracting serious illnesses, while in previous years persons detained at Wi'a had died as a result of the poor conditions. Reports continued that persons detained in Wi'a were tortured. Previously, religious workers from government-approved faiths were often not required to perform military service.

Eritrean law criminalizes consensual same-sex sexual activity, and individuals continue to be detained for allegedly engaging in the practice. During 2011 there were unconfirmed reports that the Government had carried out periodic round-ups of individuals considered to be gay or lesbian. These minority groups faced severe societal discrimination, and there were reports that known gay men and lesbians in the armed forces had been subjected to severe abuse. There were no known lesbian, gay, bisexual or transgender organizations in the country.

According to human rights organizations, the law provides workers with the legal right to form and join unions to protect their interests; and allows unions to conduct their activities without interference. However, some government policies severely restrict free association or prevent the formation of some unions, including within the civil service, armed forces, police and other organizations providing essential services.

In May 2003 it was announced that 11th-grade students would be obliged to attend Sawa, the military camp, in their final year of high school, instead of taking the entrance exam for the University of Asmara. In September 2006 the University was closed. Students who pass the National Matriculation Exam (NME) have subsequently been sent to one of eight tertiary institutions: the Asmara Medical School, the College of Health Sciences, and six technical institutes established in 2006—the Mai Nefhi Institute of Science and Technology, Halhale College of Business and Economics, Adi-Keyih College of Social Sciences, Hamelmalo Agricultural College, the

Marine Training College of Dongolo and the Massawa Institute of Technology. (Students who fail the NME remain in Sawa, where they are enrolled on short technical and vocational training programmes.) The reform was officially intended to decentralize education to the regions and expand access to higher education, but the quality of service delivery has undoubtedly deteriorated as staff contend with large classroom sizes, poorly motivated students, transport bottlenecks and a less than satisfactory infrastructure. In order to address these challenges, the Government has allocated an investment of US $20m. for improving the quality of teaching, installing new laboratory equipment and expanding the country's educational facilities. According to the Executive Director of the board of institution of higher education, Dr Tadesse Mehari, in early 2011 more than 8,000 students had graduated over the past three years from the existing seven colleges in different parts of the country.

In light of efforts at food self-reliance, and a state media that is increasingly hostile to Western NGOs as the 'other face of colonialism', in March 2006 the Eritrean Government revoked the operating permits of three such NGOs. The Eritrean authorities claimed that the agencies had failed to meet the requirements for operational permits. In November 2006 the Eritrean Government ordered a further two international charities to leave the country. In 2011 the Government forced the closure of all remaining international NGO offices (Oxfam, the Lutheran World Federation, Irish Self-Help, Gruppo Missione Asmara of Italy, Refugee Trust International and Norwegian Church Aid), and seized NGO property that it claimed belonged to the Government.

In September 2001 all eight of Eritrea's independent newspapers (including those that were pro-Government) were forcibly closed and a number of journalists were arrested, accused of accepting foreign funding and for violating the 1996 press proclamation. Government sources insist that newspapers may re-apply for permission to operate, if they agree to abide by the law, but no permits have since been issued. The journalists arrested in 2001 remain in detention, while in March 2009 a group of a further 54 journalists from Radio Bana, an educational radio sponsored by the Ministry of Education, were imprisoned. Among 173 countries ranked for press freedom, Reporters sans Frontières (RSF, Reporters without Borders) named Eritrea as the worst violator of press freedom. According to RSF, around 30 journalists are currently held in prison camps and detention centres. Human Rights Watch and RSF have requested that the EU, which signed an agreement in 2009 to release €122m. to Eritrea, impose a travel ban on government officials in order to pressure the regime to improve its human rights record. In his annual interview with state media in 2010, President Afewerki claimed that a free press in actuality inculcates loyalty to—and safeguards the narrow agendas of—a few select interests, and thus had no place in Eritrea. In October 2011 Amnesty International reported that Dawit Isaak, one of 10 independent journalists also detained since 2001, might have died in detention, as he was no longer in the prison where he had previously been held. The Government did not confirm the reports.

Human rights organizations continue to report that thousands of prisoners of conscience and political prisoners are being held in arbitrary detention. Torture and other forms of ill-treatment are common, and the conditions for detainees are appalling. Large numbers of Eritreans continue to flee the country. According to RSF, four additional journalists were detained in 2011 and remained in custody: Neibel Edris, Ahmed Usman, Muhammad Osman and Tesfalidet Mebratu. Eritrea again finished last in the RSF's press freedom index for 2011–12, even below the Democratic People's Republic of Korea (North Korea).

The Military and National Service

The impact of the border dispute is visible in the militarization of Eritrean society. In the 2009 edition of *The Military Balance*, the International Institute for Strategic Studies stated that Eritrea's population was the world's second most militarized society. While population estimates of Eritrea widely vary from anywhere between 3m. and 5m., the country reportedly has an active conscripted army comprising some 200,000–300,000 personnel. The military and national service dominates the lives of most adult Eritreans and is compulsory for all able-bodied Eritreans between 18 and 40 years of age for an 18-month period, including six months of military training, although all are retained beyond this period without release (see below). Between 1994 and 2010 24 rounds of trainees completed national service at the Sawa Military Camp, with each round involving an average of 10,000–12,000 conscripts. The Eritrean Government reduced the country's military force to 47,000 prior to the outbreak of the conflict in 1998. Many veterans were integrated into the civil service and given selective access to higher education, government housing, state credits and tax exemptions on imported vehicles as compensation for their service. However, timely demobilization was disrupted with the border war and service personnel remain in the military.

In 1998 a National Development Campaign was briefly implemented, which called upon all of those who had participated in national service since 1994 to remobilize for one month and carry out development projects. The programme, designed to mobilize 50,000–60,000 Eritreans, was scheduled to start at the end of April 1998 and to continue throughout May. When the border conflict with Ethiopia started in mid-May, the development projects were abandoned, but the mobilized youth were transferred to the front, along with remobilized veterans. Youth and students mobilized willingly, indeed enthusiastically, throughout the war, but since its conclusion reports of youths evading national service have multiplied with the possibility of the indefinite postponement of demobilization and release from national service. *Gffas*, or 'round-ups' of those avoiding conscription have intensified, with soldiers stationed on street corners throughout urban areas, and on roads leading out of cities, checking identity and movement papers, and detaining those without service records. Even Eritreans not in active national service are required to carry identity cards. The Government does not issue travel documents or exit visas to Eritreans fit for mobilization. Those between the age of 14 and 50 are not permitted to leave the country. Citizens are also prevented from holding a passport unless they can prove that they have completed national service. Since married women with children are exempt from national service, they are unable to obtain a passport.

Those on national service—some have been in service for as long as 15 years—work mostly in development and civil service projects, mainly in construction. All are controlled by the Ministry of Defence, including university graduates teaching in high schools, and can be deployed at short notice. Mobility and change of location are not permitted, transfers are directed by the Ministry of Defence, and release from service is not permitted. Government officials cite the national service law of 1995, which stipulates that the age of eligibility for national service can be extended to 50 years under emergency or mobilization situations, and the 'no war and no peace' situation with Eritrea is used as a justification to indefinitely delay demobilization.

With national service likely to continue, dispirited youth seek to avoid conscription by evading the military police and fleeing across the border. Refugee agencies and the EU's *Price Monitoring and Analysis Country Brief* on Eritrea, published in May 2010, estimated that in 2008 there were 201,094 refugees and displaced persons outside the country. However, the Ethiopian Government reported in January 2009 that an average of 900 Eritreans were arriving each month at refugee camps in the country. In April 2010 Ethiopian authorities opened a new camp in the northern part of the country to accommodate the influx; more than 5,000 new arrivals from Eritrea were registered in the first four months of 2010, while the total number of Eritrean refugees in Ethiopia was estimated at 41,106.

In 2010 President Afewerki acknowledged that Eritrean youth were fleeing to neighbouring countries in significant numbers, but denied allegations that they were fleeing from political persecution, claiming instead that they were merely leaving in search of economic opportunities. Eritrean refugees have increasingly come to include women and children. Counter-measures employed by the Government in order to thwart the exodus of the young included the relocation of military training bases away from the Sudanese border and, since mid-2005, the detention of family members of illegal refugees, and political consciousness training for young civil servants and college students. Diplomats maintain that Eritreans are willing to pay several thousand US dollars for transportation to Sudan. If caught, they could spend months in gaol and be interrogated for days for information about the smugglers, according to human rights groups. Activists claim that even if they leave successfully, the families of illegal immigrants can be fined up to 50,000 nakfa. Those who succeed in reaching other countries are required to sign papers confessing to their treason and committing them to pay the 2% diaspora tax, in return for services that they might require from Eritrean embassies or for services their families back home in the form of licences, land and housing. The troubled situations in Libya and Egypt endangered the security of Eritrean refugees (in view of the fact that Libya is their main transit route to Europe). There were violent attacks against them in response to rumours that the Libyan Government had hired mercenaries from other African countries to assist the army in its 2011 conflict with Libyan opposition groups.

At present, nearly 2,000 Eritreans flee from the country every month. Those deserting are required to pay thousands of dollars to traffickers, before embarking on long and dangerous journeys. In March 2011 more than 100 Eritrean refugees from Libya seeking to travel to Italy on two boats drowned in the Mediterranean, while in May more than 750 Eritrean refugees in Tunisia, who had been displaced after political turmoil there, went missing at sea. In mid-2011 hundreds of refugees were being held hostage by human traffickers in the Sinai desert, in Egypt, for ransom. Despite these dangers, many Eritreans prefer to desert from the army, with the consequence that Eritrea now has one of the world's largest outflows of refugees. The UN High Commissioner for Refugees (UNHCR) estimated that 3,000 Eritreans fled the country every month, mostly to Ethiopia or Sudan, despite a 'shoot-to-kill' policy for anyone caught attempting to cross the border. UNHCR reported in early 2011 that 220,000 Eritreans, about 5% of the population, have fled. The new refugees included a significant number of unaccompanied children, some as young as six years-old. Among the most prominent defectors in 2011 were 13 members of a 25-member association football team who refused to return after a regional tournament in Tanzania. A UN Monitoring Group on Somalia and Eritrea found strong evidence that high-level Eritrean officials were facilitating escapes to earn hard currency, stating that: 'People-smuggling is so pervasive that it could not be possible without the complicity of Government and party officials, especially military officers'. Military officers charge about US $3,000 per person for a border crossing and up to $20,000 for smuggling escapees through Sudan and Egypt. According to the UN group, receipts are funnelled through Eritrean embassy staff into a Swiss bank account.

Eritrean refugees in Israel have found themselves facing race riots and a government policy that provides inadequate protection in line with international law concerning the treatment of refugees. There are some 60,000 illegal African immigrants in Israel, according to officials; most have arrived in the past few years. The majority, about 35,000, are from Eritrea and Sudan and have been given collective protection from expulsion by the Israeli Government. In the case of Eritreans, the UN has declared that they must not be returned to their native country as their lives will be endangered by the current dictatorial regime. According to press reports, most of these people have been given renewable permits to live in Israel, but have not been given the right to work nor the benefit of any social services other than schooling for their children. Some have been placed in holding tanks in the southern-most part of Israel, while the majority live in and around the tenements of southern Tel-Aviv and elsewhere.

REGIONAL AND INTERNATIONAL RELATIONS

Following its formal accession to independence in 1993, Eritrea gradually increased its international contacts, establishing diplomatic ties with Sudan, Ethiopia, Israel, Australia and Pakistan, and several international organizations. In September the first meeting of the Ethiopian-Eritrean joint ministerial commission was held in Asmara, during which agreement was reached on measures to allow the free movement of nationals between each country, and on co-operation regarding foreign affairs and economic policy.

In August 1994 Eritrea and Sudan signed an agreement concerning borders, security and the repatriation of refugees, and in November UNHCR initiated a repatriation programme for Eritrean refugees in Sudan. It was estimated that, as a result of the conflict between Ethiopia and Eritrea in 2000 (see above), a further 90,000 Eritreans had sought refuge in Sudan during May and June. In July, however, following the cessation of hostilities, UNHCR began operations to repatriate tens of thousands of Eritrean refugees. During 2001–02 Eritrea and Sudan co-operated closely with UNHCR on the repatriation of Eritrean refugees. In mid-2002 Eritrean officials stated that 52,000 of the estimated 174,000 Eritrean refugees had returned, mainly to the Gash-Barka region, and that another 16,000 were registered to leave. In May 2002 UNHCR announced that with effect from January 2003 it would cease to regard Eritreans in Sudan as refugees, as it maintained that Eritreans there should no longer fear persecution. Many of the refugees contested this ruling, however, and 27,000 heads of families, representing an estimated total of 100,000 individuals, re-applied for refugee status, the majority citing their religious beliefs and political affiliations as sources of conflict with the Afewerki regime. According to provisional UNHCR figures, 116,746 Eritrean refugees were in Sudan at the end of 2005.

In the mid-2000s bilateral relations appeared to improve, following several years of tension, despite accusations made by the Sudanese Government in July that Eritrea was supporting rebel factions from Darfur headquartered in Asmara. In September the Sudanese President, Lt-Gen. Omar Hassan Ahmad al-Bashir, urged Eritrea to expel the members of Darfur rebel groups from its territories, a request with which Eritrea complied. In November 2006 Eritrea and Sudan restored full cross-border links. Sudan is a key market for most of Eritrea's food imports, particularly sorghum, and is anticipated to be a source of cheaper petroleum in the future.

In 2008 Afewerki criticized the indictment of President al-Bashir by the International Criminal Court (ICC) for war crimes in Darfur, stating that it constituted interference in Sudan's internal affairs. In March 2009 President al-Bashir visited Eritrea at the invitation of Afewerki, both flouting the ICC's indictment. In February 2011 the Sudanese President conducted a one-day working visit to Eritrea, focusing on mutual strategic ties, the political developments in Sudan concerning the separation of South Sudan, as well as on the impact of the regional events in Tunisia and Egypt.

The long-standing relationship between the Government of Eritrea and southern Sudan began as far back as 1994, during a pan-African meeting in the Ugandan capital, Kampala, when Eritrea was the only participating state that advocated the exercise of southern Sudan's right to self-determination and national independence. A referendum on self determination in southern Sudan was held on 9–15 January 2011, with 98% of the population voting in favour of secession. A high-level Eritrean delegation, headed by the Minister of Foreign Affairs, Osman Salih Muhammad, subsequently visited Juba, southern Sudan, to congratulate the people, and to confirm Eritrea's willingness to recognize the official creation of the new state of South Sudan on 9 July. However, in May, in an interview with a pro-Government television station, Afewerki stated that Eritrea had supported Sudan's unity over the previous 20 years, emphasizing that dividing its territory might reverse its considerable advances in economic development.

In October 2011 the Afewerki Government lost a key political and financial supporter with the death of former Libyan leader Col Muammar al-Qaddafi. The Amir of Qatar, Maj.-Gen. Sheikh Hamad bin Khalifa Al Thani, and al-Bashir remain important supporters of the Eritrean regime.

In November 1995 Eritrea and Djibouti pledged to enhance bilateral co-operation. In November 1998 Djibouti suspended diplomatic relations with Eritrea, following allegations by the Eritrean authorities that it was supporting Ethiopia in the Eritrea–Ethiopia border conflict. In March 2000 Djibouti announced that it had resumed diplomatic relations with Eritrea. However, in February 2008 Eritrea accused Djibouti of allowing Ethiopia to deploy long-range artillery weapons on the strategic peak of Mount Musa Ali, where the borders of Djibouti, Eritrea and Ethiopia intersect. Djibouti accused Eritrea of deploying troops and military equipment to Ras Doumeira and Doumeira Island in March and reported military confrontations between the two countries on two separate occasions in June, following weeks of military build-up and mounting bilateral tensions; at least 35 people were killed. Eritrea denied claims of military aggression against Djibouti, and rejected the conclusions of a UN fact finding mission—which had contended that the dispute had the potential to destabilize the entire region—protesting that the UN Security Council had already censured Eritrea for attacking Djibouti without independently ascertaining facts on the ground. The UN Security Council adopted Resolution 1862 in January 2009, ordering Eritrea to withdraw to positions held before fighting broke out, and threatened economic and political sanctions in the event of non-compliance. Eritrea maintained its denial of any border problems and rejected all requests to begin talks with Djibouti to resolve the dispute peacefully. Throughout 2009 Djibouti accused Eritrea of arming and training militias to undermine its Government, but Eritrea categorically repudiated such claims, stating that armed opposition groups have been in existence in Djibouti since its independence in 1977.

On 8 June 2010 the Qatari Prime Minister and Minister of Foreign Affairs, Sheikh Hamad bin Jasim bin Jaber Al Thani, transmitted to the UN Secretary-General and the Security Council a copy of an agreement, signed on 6 June by President Afewerki and President Ismaïl Omar Guelleh of Djibouti, aimed at resolving the border conflict. The agreement entrusted Qatar with creating a mechanism to facilitate boundary demarcation, monitoring the border, facilitating the exchange of prisoners of war, and normalizing relations between the two countries.

Although President Afewerki repeatedly condemned the UN Security Council sanctions imposed in December 2009 (see above) as baseless and as having no effect on his regime's developmental goals, the steps that his regime took in recognizing the Transitional Federal Government of Somalia and in seeking mediation in the dispute with Djibouti suggested that the sanctions had been sufficient to compel the Government to take constructive measures to improve relations with its neighbours. In an extensive television interview in April 2011, the Eritrean President claimed that the Security Council had removed the diplomatic initiative from the negotiating parties and created a serious impediment to the advancement of the peaceful resolution of the Somali conflict.

In November 1995 there were reports that Eritrean troops had attempted to land on the Red Sea island of Greater Hanish, one of three islands (the others being Lesser Hanish and Zuqar) claimed by both Eritrea and Yemen. The invasion attempt had reportedly been prompted by Yemen's announced intention to develop Greater Hanish as a tourist resort, and its subsequent refusal to comply with an Eritrean demand that the island be evacuated. After a series of talks mediated by France, amid growing military tension between the two countries, in October 1996 Eritrea and Yemen confirmed that they would submit the dispute to an international tribunal, which subsequently ruled that the Hanish islands belonged to Yemen and had been illegally occupied by Eritrea. Both countries accepted the ruling, and shortly afterwards they agreed to establish a joint committee to strengthen bilateral co-operation. In March Eritrea and Yemen had exchanged ambassadors and sought ways to prevent future conflict over fisheries. In October 2010 an Eritrea-Yemen summit meeting was held in Asmara. Both countries' leaders discussed reactivating joint co-operation in political, and economic and security areas. However, as fighting and protest intensified in Yemen, particularly with the injury of President Ali Abdullah Saleh in an opposition attack on 3 June 2011, the future of the bilateral relationship seemed unclear. In April 2012 the Yemeni Government reported that three Yemeni sailors continued to be held in Eritrean prisons three years after their boat had inadvertently sailed into Eritrean waters. Yemen also reported at the end of March 2012 that Eritrean boats had attacked four Yemeni fishing boats in international territorial waters.

The USA has long had a military and security interest in Eritrea. In December 1997 the US Department of Defense financed two projects associated with Massawa port. There were also reports that the USA was considering transferring its military base from Saudi Arabia to Eritrea. An important US airbase and listening station had existed at Kagnew some 30 years earlier. Relations with the USA became complicated in 2001, with the arrest of Eritrean nationals working in the US embassy in Asmara (see above). None the less, at the same time Eritrea made great efforts to ingratiate itself with the USA, pledging its support for the 'war on terror'. Persistent rumours of the establishment of a US military base in the Dahlak islands were followed by Eritrean efforts to entice the USA to use Assab as an anti-terrorism base, instead of Djibouti, including a lobbying campaign in Washington, DC.

In July 2005 President Afewerki held talks with the Commander of US Central Command, Gen. John Abizaid, making clear his view that border demarcation was paramount over the 'war on terror'. Increasingly vitriolic in tone, by 2006, the Eritrean Government was repeatedly accusing the USA of favouring Ethiopia in the border dispute, and of interfering in the Somalia conflict on the pretext of fighting terrorism. In March 2007 Eritrea joined Belarus, China, Cuba, Iran, Myanmar, North Korea and Zimbabwe on the State Department's list of 'the world's most systematic human rights violators'. The USA accused Eritrea of aiding rebel groups trying to destabilize Ethiopia—the USA's main counter-terrorism ally in the region. In early 2007 visa services for Eritreans were suspended until diplomatic delegations were allowed unimpeded entry into Eritrea.

Relations worsened in 2007, when the Assistant Secretary of State for African Affairs, Jendayi Frazer, suggested that Eritrea might be added to the US list of State Sponsors of Terrorism. Frazer stated that the presence of exiled Somali Islamist leader Sheikh Hassan Dahir Aweys in Asmara was further evidence that Eritrea provided sanctuary for terrorists. The US Government has yet to officially add Eritrea to the list owing to the lack of evidence regarding the nature of Asmara's support for the al-Shabaab insurgency. Relations remained strained in 2009, despite the new US Administration, with Eritrea accused of supplying arms to the Somali Islamist insurgency, and the local US embassy staff detained in 2001 remaining in gaol. In 2009 the AU and IGAD requested that the UN Security Council impose sanctions in response to Eritrea's arming of insurgents in Somalia and for violating the UN arms embargo on Somalia. Following the imposition of such sanctions by the Council in December (see above), Eritrea reproached the USA and the United Kingdom for sponsoring the resolution.

In 2010 Eritrean media ran a sustained campaign of accusations against the USA. The Eritrean Government and its embassies in the West and the Middle East also organized a series of large demonstrations involving the Eritrean diaspora, denouncing the sanctions and US efforts to undermine Eritrea. In February the US embassy in Asmara suspended its consular services and issued a warning to US nationals against travel to Eritrea, citing a rise in anti-US sentiment. A message posted subsequently on the website of the US embassy accused the Eritrean Government of destabilizing the Horn region. In May the US Commission on International Religious Freedom, a US government-funded commission, cited widespread violations of religious freedom in Eritrea and urged US mining companies to desist from operating in Eritrea. Although this appeal went unobserved, it was cited by the Eritrean Government as further proof of the USA's intentions to obstruct the country's development. Eritrea accused the USA of hypocrisy in its 'war on terror' and concern for the stability of the Horn region, and claimed that Eritrean opposition groups, including the EIJ, were being funded and hosted by the USA and its ally Ethiopia. The relationship between the USA and Eritrea has become increasingly complex, as Afewerki has repeatedly denounced the perceived interference of the USA in the region and has even stated that the uprisings in North Africa and the Middle East are part of a US-promoted conspiracy.

Relations with European donor countries appeared to be improving. In early 2009 the EU signed an agreement with the Government to disburse a fund of €122m., intended to facilitate development activities for the period until 2013. Of this sum, €70m. was to be allocated to achieving food security, €34m. to expanding infrastructure, €10m. to promoting social services, and €8.3m. to preserving national heritage. In August 2006 the European Commission (EC) considered halting aid to Eritrea in protest at food aid being sold and the proceeds used for government work programmes, which violated the conditions under which the EC donated food. The EU continued to express concern over restrictions on international NGOs, the lack of private partners to implement projects involved and the use of national service conscripts in EU-funded development projects. However, despite calls by activists demanding an improved human rights record in return for donations, the EU is proceeding with the allocation of its funds. An accord for an additional €7.26m., to be used in emergency situations, was signed in late 2009. However, the European Parliament has been vocal in highlighting Eritrea's increasing human rights violations and has requested that a consideration of human rights records underpin fund allocations.

At the end of December 2010 four British employees of security firm Protection Vessels International, two of whom were former marines, were captured by the Eritrean navy and subsequently imprisoned. The Eritrean authorities reportedly refused demands by the British Government to be granted consular access to the detainees. As a result, diplomatic tensions increased and on 26 May 2011 the United Kingdom informed the Eritrean ambassador in London that Eritrean diplomats would be banned from undertaking their work outside of London without the written permission of the British Government, and further prohibited the Eritrean embassy from levying a 2% tax on Eritreans living in the United Kingdom, on the grounds that this was an illegal charge. In June the Eritrean Ministry of Foreign Affairs claimed that one of the arrested British citizens had been captured after entering Eritrea as a tourist from Djibouti and while trying to escape the country illegally. At the same time the British citizens were alleged to have stored caches of armaments, which had been discovered by Eritrean security forces on the island of Romia. The detainees were charged with espionage, terrorism and illegal entry of Eritrea. However, on 12 June the four British citizens were unexpectedly released, and the charges against them abandoned.

Since 2001 Eritrea has increasingly sought support beyond the West. China and Eritrea have developed their diplomatic and economic ties, including the signing of a US $1.8m. development agreement in June 2004. Eritrean-Chinese ties were strengthened in mid-2005, with further trade and aid agreements in place by July in the areas of infrastructure, trade and investment, and agriculture. However, beyond symbolic gestures, including the construction of the Orota Hospital in Asmara and official visits, Eritrea's efforts did not result in the anticipated Chinese investment and trade exchange. Moreover, according to Ministry of Trade and Industry reports in 2006, China's exports to Eritrea increased by 396% to $37.7m., while Eritrea's exports to China were worth just $720,000. Chinese investors have nevertheless shown interest in cotton cultivation and production. A $6m. loan agreement for food security was concluded at the end of December 2010. According to the US Department of State, Office of Foreign Assistance, Eritrea was the only African nation not to have requested US aid for the 2011 fiscal year. China remained the largest lender in 2010.

Although Eritrea has received modest amounts of foreign aid from China (in the form of soft loans), the United Arab Emirates, Iran, Libya and Qatar in recent years, no loans or grants were announced in 2011. Moreover, the bulk of the development and emergency assistance provided by the EU remains undisbursed because of ongoing concerns about transparency and accountability.

The state media in Eritrea initially failed to broadcast news of the popular uprisings in North Africa in February 2011. When they eventually did mention the events occuring in Tunisia, Egypt and Libya, it was to assert that Egyptian President Hosni Mubarak's Government deserved to fall for not adopting Afewerki's policy of self-reliance. On 2 March the Eritrean Government issued a statement that condemned a resolution suspending the right of membership of Libya in the UN Human Rights Council 'before conducting appropriate full and independent investigation on the matter'. President Afewerki explained that the North African and Middle Eastern uprisings were the result of popular displeasure with power and financial concentration in the hands of the élite, in conjunction with external intervention by the instigators of 'creative chaos'. The fact that many of the protests were directed at leaders who refused to leave office was not mentioned by the Eritrean President, but was, however, utilized by the Eritrean opposition in the diaspora. It was reported that the Government had taken precautions against a possible contagion effect by reorganizing the commanders and units of the Eritrean Defence Forces at around this time. Perhaps inspired by the popular protests in Arab states, a new opposition party, known as the Eritrean Youth Progressive Party, was established in mid-2011 in Manchester, United Kingdom, with one of its key demands being that Afewerki resign from office, although this party has yet clearly to state its manifesto and policies.

CONCLUSION

Eritrea in 2012 continued to be one of the most militarized countries in the world. With reports that thousands are incarcerated for suspected opposition to the Government, practising their religion as members of banned evangelical or other churches, evading military conscription or trying to flee the country, democracy and the rule of law remain elusive. The border dispute with Ethiopia remains at an impasse, with the Ethiopian Prime Minister still seeking preconditions to the implementation of a binding ruling and the Eritrean Government refusing to accept such a procedure. Nevertheless, Eritrea has begun to re-engage with other African countries, announcing, for example, that it would rejoin IGAD. It also reopened its mission to the AU, ending years of self-imposed exile from the continental organization and designating an ambassador, who is also accredited to all the regional economic organizations.

Economy

WARKA SOLOMON KAHSAY

Revised for this edition by GREG CAMERON

INTRODUCTION

The economic realities of Eritrea are dominated by the legacies of war, drought and the continued mobilization of its productive labour force. Unlike any other African countries, the economy is highly dependent on taxes paid by members of the diaspora and has few dynamic export sectors, although high hopes are placed on the mining sector, with the launch of commercial gold production in January 2011. Nevertheless, until relations with Ethiopia are resolved, domestic politics are normalized (see Recent History) and a peacetime economy is developed, economic recovery is expected to remain slow. While statistical reporting on the country's economy improved markedly from the late 1990s, the previously weak statistical base and economic dislocation mean that all figures should be regarded with caution. Since independence, the Government has never published a national budget, and restrictions on the activities of the UN and other international non-governmental organizations (NGOs) further complicate assessment of Eritrea's economic health. In 2010 President Issaias Afewerki dismissed international organizations' downbeat reports of Eritrea's economic indicators as fabricated statistics that were not to be taken seriously, highlighting that most such organizations did not have a presence in the country. He also stressed that his regime's focus was on improving the quality of life, reducing wealth inequalities and achieving food security. However, reports from the country indicate a steep decline in the quality and standard of living of its citizens, reflected in continuing scarcity of basic commodities, rationing in government stores, and the four-fold increase of food and fuel prices over the last six years.

In addition to its ambitious mining projects, the Government has been actively engaged in the agricultural sector, with the aim of improving water access and food security. Despite ongoing efforts, the FAO 2011 index reported a very high level of undernourishment among the population, estimated at 64%. Despite improved rainfall in 2009–10, the European Union (EU) forecast total domestic food production for 2010 at 272,000 metric tons, while total consumption was projected at 604,000 tons. According to World Bank estimates, gross national income (GNI) per head increased to US $340 in 2010 (or $540 on a purchasing-power parity basis), up from $300 in 2009. However, high consumer prices continue adversely to affect the purchasing power and gross domestic product (GDP) per head. Annual average inflation stood at 12.6% in 2007, before increasing to 19.9% in 2008 and further, to 20.0%, in 2009. At the end of 2010 it was 14.2% and the IMF projected a rate of 13.3% for 2011. The Government implemented measures intended to stabilize the rate of inflation, including the strict regulation of exchange rates, limitations on imports and the imposition of fixed prices. Advances have been made in social development, and hopes of further economic development centred on investment initiatives in the mining and free port sectors. According to the IMF, Eritrea's economy recovered from a 1.0% GDP contraction in 2006 to record positive growth of 1.4% in 2007, primarily owing to construction projects and an improved harvest. The Fund estimated that GDP had contracted by 9.8% in 2008, owing to severe drought and record high energy and food prices in the first half of the year. An IMF report published in December 2009 projected that, aided by a rebound in the agricultural sector, GDP growth would reach 3.6% in that year. The Fund forecast growth of 1.8% and 2.8% in 2010 and 2011, respectively, with growth in subsequent years expected to be bolstered by a projected increase in production in the mining sector. Eritrea's long-established diaspora, which helped fund the independence war and is found mainly in Europe, the USA and the Middle East, continues to provide up to one-third of the nation's GDP through remittances.

More recently, the IMF revised its growth forecasts for Eritrea's economy, projecting growth of 7.5% in 2012, mainly as a result of increases in agricultural production, mineral exports and the expansion of infrastructural projects. The achievement of such growth would make Eritrea the fastest-growing economy in East Africa in 2012. The Fund also predicted that the rate of inflation would decline from 13.3% in 2011 to 12.3% in 2012, in spite of continuing high fuel prices. The Government reportedly plans to achieve annual GDP growth of some 7% to 10% during the period 2012–15, after claiming a staggering figure of 17% growth in 2011. With output at the Zara and Koka gold mines scheduled to commence in late 2013, economists also predicted double-digit growth in the economy for that year. Nevertheless, it is important to bear in mind that statistical data are either not available or are unreliable; for instance, in 2009 the Economist Intelligence Unit estimated inflation to be at 15%, whereas the IMF placed it at 34.7%.

ECONOMIC ASPECTS OF WAR

The war with Ethiopia (1998–2000) has severely damaged the economy of Eritrea, generating deep and long-lasting impacts on agricultural production, labour, exports and governmental expenditure. The Government also had to cope with over 1m. displaced persons, US $600m. lost through property damage, losses of 55,000 homes, and of fertile land in the Debub and Gash-Barka regions, the substantial loss of $225m. in livestock, and some 65,000 Eritreans expelled from Ethiopia. In addition, trade with Ethiopia, which previously accounted for two-thirds of Eritrean exports and most of Eritrean imports, virtually ceased. Activity at the port of Assab declined sharply as most of Eritrea's war *matériel* was routed through Massawa.

Despite the signing of a peace accord in December 2000, levels of defence expenditure remained high. Total government expenditure on defence remained at 20.9% of GDP in 2009. In Eritrea landmines were laid in some of the most populated and fertile regions of the country. An estimated 12,000 ha in Debub Province, and most of the sub-region of Lalai Gash in Gash-Barka Province, including large tracts of fertile and pasture land, are completely unusable owing to the presence of unexploded landmines; an FAO report published in 2010 estimated that some 60,000 unexploded ordnances remained buried.

With one in 15 Eritreans enrolled in the armed forces, Eritrea maintains among the highest proportion of its population in the army of any country in the world. The army comprises around 320,000 active personnel and 250,000 reserve personnel. The need to demobilize an estimated 300,000 troops will undoubtedly place further strain on the country's already fragile economy. In 2004 the first phase of demobilization began, which was expected to process 65,000 soldiers. The National Commission for Demobilization and Reintegration Programme initially paid each soldier US $300 upon discharge, but later ceased paying money. The current 'no war, no peace' impasse continues, thereby delaying the demobilization programme indefinitely. Until full demobilization occurs, labour shortages will continue to have a negative effect on the financial viability of private enterprise and the ability of families to plough and to harvest crops. There has been no large-scale resettlement in rural areas during this post-border-war phase. Moreover, many soldiers have become urbanized in the army and face limited economic prospects in poorly developed rural villages.

In 2002 the Government launched the 'Warsai-Yikealo' initiative, which employs members of the national services in economic development projects in various sectors. In addition, the armed forces have been involved in farming, the digging of wells and the construction of dams for irrigation, and the building and renovating of road networks.

ECONOMIC POLICY AND AID

Eritrea's economic policy is to reject major loans and foreign food aid, in accordance with the aim for the state to become self-sufficient. This radical policy strategy to end dependency on foreign aid presents a great challenge, and in practice self-reliance entails continued economic activities with total government control. Import restrictions on private sector companies were imposed in 2003, and remained in place in 2012. Domestic entrepreneurs have complained that only firms closely affiliated to the ruling People's Front for Democracy and Justice (PFDJ) have been able to expand their operations or purchase privatized businesses. The PFDJ and, to a lesser extent, the National Union of Eritrean Youths and Students (NUEYS), are also increasingly active in the manufacturing, service and construction sectors. Relatively little is known about the wide range of ventures owned wholly or partially by the PFDJ, but they include businesses in the construction, information technology and tourism sectors, as well as a major cement factory that commenced production in late 2011. The NUEYS's most financially successful ventures have been in the distribution of liquid petroleum gas for home cooking and the distribution of filtered, bottled water for domestic consumption. Allegations are increasingly being made that businesses are owned by Eritrea's senior military officers, and that officers use military conscript labour to build their villas. Many private businessmen have migrated to neighbouring Sudan, Kenya and Uganda, and those who remain in Eritrea face stringent foreign currency regulations, harsh penalties for 'black market' exchanges, and a strong market disadvantage *vis-à-vis* the PFDJ enterprises. Private sector fixed capital formation was estimated at 5.3% of GDP in 2004, and declined to 4.7% of GDP in 2005.

In October 2008 the World Bank suspended payment of new credits to Eritrea for the first time owing to overdue debt repayment obligations. The total debt outstanding and disbursed owed to the International Development Association amounted to US $962m. in 2008, up from $860m. in 2007. In August 2009 the World Bank's portfolio of lending included five projects worth a combined total of $178.8m. in the areas of transport, energy, education and health. As of April 2011, there were two active World Bank projects, with a total commitment of $75.3m.; one of the projects is in the education sector and the other is for port rehabilitation.

General government net lending/borrowing was equivalent to 14.6% of GDP in 2010 and an estimated 12.9% of GDP in 2011. As a regulatory environment for doing business, the country was ranked 180th of 183 countries in 2010.

FOREIGN TRADE AND PAYMENTS

The outbreak of war between Eritrea and Ethiopia in May 1998 brought a sharp halt to trade between them, and discussions regarding future trading relations did not receive high priority during peace talks in December 2000.

With a significant number of Eritreans living outside the country, taxes paid directly to the Government by expatriates (accounting for 2% of their annual income) and remittances to families play a key role in the economy. The IMF stated that Eritrea's income from remittances declined to 23% of GDP in 2007 from 41% of GDP in 2005; this was offset to some extent by limiting imports. (Economic data should be treated with caution owing to the closed nature of the policy-making process.) Despite concerns that inflows might decline as a result of recent political turmoil and the global financial crisis, income from remittances (which was estimated at 11% of GDP in 2011) remained steady and continued to constitute a sizeable source of foreign exchange for the state, with government and party officials travelling abroad to rally support from the diaspora.

World Bank data for 2009 showed that exported goods were worth US $17m., while imports of goods cost the country $627m., resulting in a trade deficit of $610m. In 2011 the export volume of all goods and services amounted to 20.8% of GDP and the import volume of all items to 0.7% of GDP. Exported commodities included livestock, sorghum, textiles, salt, flowers, leather products and small manufactured goods, while the principal imports were petroleum products, food, and manufactured goods and machinery. In 2007 the principal markets for Eritrean exports were Italy (34.4%), the People's Republic of China (16.2%), Sudan (15.2%), France (9.4%) and Saudi Arabia (5.2%), while the principal sources of imports were Saudi Arabia (19.1%), Italy (15.1%), China (11.1%), Turkey (8.3%) and Germany (7.2%). Eritrea is a member of the Common Market for Eastern and Southern Africa (COMESA), but trade exchanges were virtually non-existent, in part owing to the closed or restricted border between Eritrea and Sudan in recent years. Relations with all regional neighbours, except for Sudan and Qatar, remained poor in the early 2010s, although recent protocol agreements between Eritrea and Sudan are expected to accelerate regional trade. In October the 26-km Arbatasher–Kassala asphalt road was officially inaugurated in Kassala by President Issaias Afewerki, the Amir of Qatar, Maj.-Gen. Sheikh Hamad bin Khalifa Al Thani, and the President of Sudan, Omar Hassan Ahmad al-Bashir. Sheikh Hamad is reported to have promised Qatari finance for a free trade economic zone straddling the Sudanese–Eritrean border. The Sudanese and Eritrean Presidents also agreed to the phasing out of visas in favour of identity cards to facilitate trade and travel between the two countries.

Foreign officials maintain that fiscal and debt sustainability remain the key challenges facing the Eritrean Government. By 2005, owing to unsustainable budget deficits, the Government increasingly reverted to a closely controlled economic model. Tight government monetary policy continues to accommodate the budget deficit, but reliance on monetary financing of the budget has hindered the private sector and prompted heavy government borrowing from the banking sector. The total public debt decreased from 175.2% of GDP in 2008 to 141.9% of GDP in 2009 and further declined to 134.7% of GDP in 2010, while external debt fell from 58% of GDP in 2008 to 47.8% of GDP in 2009. Despite these decreases, the IMF reports that Eritrea's domestic and external debt levels are unsustainable. The external debt service ratio in 2009 was 37.3% of GDP. Domestic debt service payments have been kept under control through high negative real interest rates on treasury bills.

The foreign exchange shortage has been addressed with foreign currency controls. In 2005 the Government unified the dual exchange rate system into a single official rate at 15 nakfa to every US $1, which represented a nominal appreciation of approximately 20%. Official exchange rates have remained much lower than those available on the 'black market'. In 2010 the 'black market' exchange rate stood at $1 = 40 nakfa. The use of foreign currency was declared illegal in April 2005, in an attempt to curb the growing 'black market' in foreign exchange. Persons involved in such transactions faced prison sentences of up to two years and fines of more than 2m. nakfa. Inflation was tackled through price controls imposed on 16 'declared goods', including basic foodstuffs, textiles, and building materials. In May 2005 the Government issued coupons, which could be obtained at state-owned 'fair-price' shops, for a limited number of 'priority goods' such as sugar, sorghum, wheat, teff (the staple indigenous grain), coffee, tea powder, lentils and cooking oil. In 2010 basic commodities were only available in government stores and were rationed according to the size of family, although their prices have increased dramatically in recent years. Permits for most private imports have been effectively denied to all but priority goods since February 2005. While the controls appear to have been relaxed recently, the impact on the private trader and retail sectors has been severe. Strict controls on the transfer of hard currencies remain in place, and the PFDJ-owned Red Sea Corporation controls import-export trade.

Savings have been made on the defence wage bill owing to the demobilization programme; civil service salaries have been frozen and cuts made in capital expenditure. However, there has been an increase in social spending, primarily in the pension and war victims' funds. The Government's current budgetary planning framework contains two key elements: the containment of domestic capital expenditure at 5.5% of GDP; and a projected decrease in expenditure on grants to follow an improvement in the food security situation (although multilateral agencies predict a long-term decline in agricultural production). The Government has also expressed an interest in pursuing Eritrea's eligibility for debt relief under the initiative for heavily indebted poor countries (HIPC). As of November

2011 only three potentially eligible countries—Eritrea, Somalia and Sudan—were yet to start the process of qualifying for debt relief under the HIPC initiative.

An IMF Consultative Group meeting concluded that the Eritrean economy is distressed by a heavy debt burden, shortages of foreign exchange and high inflation. The Group advised the Government to reduce its borrowing and engage with the donor community in search of grants and concessional loans; to liberalize the exchange and trade systems; and revitalize the private sector. The IMF also advised using mining revenues to reduce domestic debt. Mining, which began contributing to exports in 2011, was expected to increase growth to 2.8% in that year, while receipts from that sector would help bring the external account to near balance by 2012, with the result that gross international reserves would gradually rise to two months' worth of imports, according to the IMF. It was reported that the African Development Bank (AfDB) had pledged funds of US $12.9m. to the Government to support human resources development in the higher education sector in August 2011.

AGRICULTURE

Eritrea's arable land makes up only 12% of the country's total land area, while approximately 80% of the population subsists in the rural sector. The agricultural sector can support more than 60% of the population with a good harvest, but recurrent droughts in the past decade have caused a fall in average production to only 30% of cereal requirements. This, compounded by water shortages and limited grazing resources for livestock, left around 60%–80% of the population vulnerable to food insecurity.

World Bank data show that agriculture contributed 17.4% of GDP in 2008, down from 20.7% in 2005. Improved rainfall in 2009/10 was expected to translate into a recovery in the agricultural sector and according to the AfDB the sector accounted for 24.2% of GDP in 2009. Most sedentary agriculture is practised in the highlands, where good *azmera* (early season) and *kremti* (June to October) rainfall is sufficient to cultivate the main crops: teff, sorghum, millet, barley and wheat. According to the UN World Food Programme, up to 40% of households are headed by females and are especially vulnerable to food insecurity. In addition to smallholder agriculture, the Government also allocates land concessions to investors to enable crop production over relatively large areas. Concessions vary in size depending on location and water availability (rain-fed or irrigation) as well as on crops. Those near seasonal river beds normally measure between 10 and 30 ha and produce vegetables (onions, okra, carrots, etc.) and fruits such as bananas and oranges, while those in arid or semi-arid areas can be as large as 400 ha and are used primarily for cereals and oilseed crops. The contribution of concessions to the country's food economy remains mediocre. Pastoralists and livestock production predominate in the lowlands, with herding patterns, both within the lowlands and between the lowlands and highlands, in search of grazing areas. The main animals are sheep and goats, followed by cattle, camels, donkeys and horses. On average rural households possess between three and five sheep or goats; and apart from oxen, which are often put to graze in areas reserved for them, most livestock are reared on an extensive system that relies on natural pasture and crop residues. As a result, there is a marked annual fluctuation in stock condition, which reflects the availability of fodder and water. For pastoralists, the border war with Ethiopia largely halted the movement of livestock, both to traditional grazing lands across the border and to grazing areas within Eritrean territory that are still heavily mined; it has also closed important livestock trade routes. The years since independence have been marked by erratic production patterns, negatively affected by droughts, crop pests and war, despite government programmes to rehabilitate communications, transportation and irrigation. As a result, food aid and food imports have been required to supplement harvests.

Land reform legislation was promulgated in 1994, whereby the Government was to maintain ownership of all land, but farmers would be allowed a life-long lease on currently held land. In addition, every Eritrean citizen would automatically qualify for the right to use a specific plot throughout their life in their home village. The implications of this policy for pastoralist communities were unclear. There is also little evidence of land tenure change. Land tenure reform remains controversial *vis-à-vis* the traditional peasant communal form (*diessa*) and the merits of pro-market reforms in Eritrean agriculture will remain a moot point until substantial investment is made in human capital.

A government spokesman reported that 494,235 ha of land were cultivated in 2006. The major crops cultivated that year were sorghum, which covered almost 53% of the cultivated area, followed by barley at 9.1%. Other crops included pearl millet (8.5%), finger millet (5.8%), teff (5.2%), sesame (5.0%) and maize (4.3%). The Government has sought to integrate stocks of food aid into its long-term food security scheme. Travel restrictions placed on international NGOs and aid agencies have prevented an accurate assessment of the extent of humanitarian crisis in Eritrea. In October 2009 FAO estimated that as many as two in every three Eritreans were malnourished, the second highest percentage in the world after the Democratic Republic of the Congo (DRC). In June 2007 a UN spokesperson accepted that Eritrea would only receive food assistance as part of a government-run programme whereby donated food would be monitored and sold in markets, not distributed free, as part of its 'cash-for-work' programme. The 2007 output of the main cereal crops was estimated to be of average level, owing to better rains. However, at 400,000 metric tons, production barely covered one-half of consumption requirements and the Government had to import a total of 216,000 tons. In an effort to ensure supplies and stabilize prices, the Government ordered farmers to sell their produce to government stores at fixed prices. However, this strategy failed, and in early 2011 the Ministry of Agriculture took measures to stabilize the fruit and vegetable market, and to reduce the gap between the earnings of the farmers and the price paid by consumers in Asmara. The Ministry established a system for farmers to sell their products directly to consumers on two days a week, with close monitoring by ministry personnel. Consequently, farmers stated that the economy would benefit from this open market, since there were no intermediates between producers and consumers. However, the consumers complained that the farmers sold all their products at the market price, and demanded that the authorities intervene to control the farmers' price rises.

In 2008 the Ministry of Agriculture stated that around 598,000 ha of land were cultivated, but production was disappointing due to late and poorly distributed rains. In June 2009 the Lutheran World Federation, one of few aid agencies still operating in the country, estimated production at around 30%–35% of cereal requirement, while the annual requirement to feed 3.6m. people was around 659,000 metric tons. Although definite numbers are not available owing to restrictions on humanitarian agencies, the UN Children's Fund (UNICEF) in 2009 reported that more than 2m. Eritreans, more than one-half of the population, were affected by high food prices, and a projected 1.3m. people were already living below the poverty line. UNICEF, which assists with feeding centres for children, also reported that rates of malnutrition were significantly higher than the emergency threshold of 15% in most regions of the country in 2008.

Despite continued rationing of food supplies and high food prices, President Afewerki dismissed reports of food insecurity and humanitarian crises as attempts to smear his regime and the country's achievements. In 2009–10 the state media reported on the construction of infrastructure, including micro-dams, irrigation schemes, land-levelling and water reservoirs, intended to increase food production. In June 2009 the Ministry of Agriculture reported that more than 250 micro-dams and more than 350 water ponds had been constructed since independence. The Ministry also expanded its extension services to farmers, distributing a variety of seedlings and introducing new farming techniques and technology. The Government also reported that by March 2008 it had resettled all those displaced during the border war and anticipated an increase in production as a result. In 2009 a new scheme of relocating whole villages from the southern region's sub-zones of Senafe, Adi-Keyih, Areza, Mendefera, Adi-Quala, Dubarwa, and Emni-Haili began. Thousands of families had already been resettled in 'fertile' areas in the Gash-Barka Province sub-zones of Tessenei, Golij and Omhajer. Despite official justification of the project as a way to increase production, the scheme was viewed with suspicion, as villages were being relocated from the most fertile lands of the southern region. Most Eritrean analysts regarded it as a move to displace people from potential centres of dissent and opposition to the regime. It was also feared that this policy would feed into social tensions in the future as villages were resettled in the already hostile western lowlands.

Despite promising rains, the EU reported that the anticipated 2010 harvest of 272,000 metric tons would fall far short of the national requirement, and that Eritreans, like many people in the Horn of Africa, would continue to face food insecurity. According to official claims, livestock resources, including breeding beef dairy animals, boosted the output of milk to over 3m. litres by 2011. In this region cultivable land has been increased by 5,091 ha over the last four years, which has secured the supply of fruits and vegetables. Water dam projects were ongoing in 2012. For example, in Ashera administrative area, 85% of the new dam had been constructed. On completion, the dam was expected to hold enough water to allow 600 ha of land to be cultivated. Government reports from the Gash Barka region have noted that the improvements in farming and grazing of animals, coupled with the large Setit, Gash and Barka rivers, and in-conjunction with eight large dams, 32 reservoirs and 118 micro dams that support the agro-industries, are enhancing food security.

According to the 2010 Food Security Risk Index published by global risk consultancy firm Maplecroft, Eritrea would face extreme food insecurity in that year and was ranked the fourth least food-secure country globally, above only Afghanistan, the DRC and Burundi. Yet although the worst drought to affect the Horn of Africa countries caused millions of people to be at risk of starvation, and famine appeared imminent, Eritrea failed to be included on the humanitarian emergency list. As the result of another major drought in 2011, at least 10m. people required urgent humanitarian assistance, and many travelled from the countryside to Asmara to seek help. However, the Eritrean authorities denied the existence of food shortages and prevented UN and other international aid organizations from visiting the affected areas. They also announced that all EU development programmes were to be terminated.

Fisheries are a potential growth area for the Eritrean economy. Sardines, anchovies, tuna, shark and mackerel are fished in the Red Sea. UN fishery experts and the Government have estimated that Eritrea has the potential to achieve annual yields of around 80,000 metric tons, but state reports show that the catch for 2008/09 was only some 13,000 tons. The fishing industry is largely dominated by traditional small-scale fishermen. Fishermen complain of a lack of resources, including refrigeration facilities, power and food subsidies when fishing, and an underdeveloped transportation infrastructure. As a result, most local fishermen sell their catch at the bigger and closer market in Yemen. In 2009/10 the Government purchased 10 large shipping vessels, which, in conjunction with fish breeding programmes in various micro-dams and water reservoirs across the country, was expected to boost the annual fishing yield. The Government also outlined plans to build fish storage and processing facilities, and to provide cold transportation devices. The Government has yet to succeed in establishing the culture of fish consumption beyond the coastal parts of the country, and fish has yet to contribute to meeting food security plans. In January 2011 the Eritrean National Fish Corporation introduced a new modern technology to produce fish for the global market.

INDUSTRY

Eritrea's industrial base traditionally centred on the production of glass, cement, footwear and canned goods, and the sector's average annual growth rate in 1995–2004 was 6.2%, according to World Bank data. The Government and the United Nations Development Programme (UNDP) launched a three-year integrated programme in 2000 to rehabilitate the industrial sector; this has focused on the leather industry and agricultural machinery. A second phase of this programme was initiated in 2004. Since its inception in 1996, the Saving and Micro Credit Program (SMCP) has loaned 100m. nakfa, and in the first six months of 2006, the SMCP lent over 11.5m. nakfa to about 1,600 beneficiaries, mainly for business activities, although the scheme was recently extended to government employees.

The manufacturing sector provided an estimated 10.7% of GDP in 2004, rising to 23.2% in 2008, but declining to 20.4% in 2009, according to the IMF. All public enterprises in the sector were scheduled for divestment or liquidation, following the initiation of a programme of privatization in 1995. Since independence several small manufacturing companies have been established, including an innovative high-quality surgical intraocular lens factory that exports to countries in Europe, Africa and Asia. Until mid-1997 imported petroleum was processed at the Assab refinery, whose entire output of petroleum products was delivered to Ethiopia. However, the ageing and inefficient refinery at Assab was closed in late 1997, and the Government announced that it would import refined petroleum for the immediate future.

In April 2005 the Minister of Trade and Industry outlined steps being taken to assess the status of industrial plants, new investment ventures, the promotion of export activities and import-substitution industrialization, and the enhancing of the viability of public trading agencies. The ministerial meeting followed Eritrea's participation in a meeting of six African countries—Kenya, Uganda, Tanzania, Burundi, Ethiopia and Eritrea—in Zanzibar, Tanzania, in March on ways to improve the quality of their export-orientated products in line with the sixth World Trade Organization (WTO) ministerial conference held in December 2005 in Hong Kong. Eritrea is an observer, but not a full member of the WTO; this status allows it to pursue an export-orientated strategy without the reciprocal opening of its domestic economy, particularly in the service sector. Eritrean officials are hopeful that the Massawa Free Port Zone (FPZ) will attract significant investment. Eritrea's 29 Economic Processing Zones (EPZs), including Massawa EPZ, have been given preferential access to the markets of countries with a per caput GNI of less than US $1,000. This may give the Massawa EPZ a competitive advantage *vis-à-vis* countries with EPZs that have a per caput income in excess of $1,000. Production in the EPZs requires 40% local input.

The opening of Free Zones was officially announced at a meeting held with the Eritrean business community at the National Chamber of Commerce in November 2006. Investors in Free Zones are exempt from import or export taxes. In 2010 the Government reported that 12 foreign companies, from, among other countries, China, Israel, Italy, India, Djibouti, Sudan and the United Arab Emirates (UAE), had hitherto registered to use Massawa FPZ, mainly for small-scale plants involved in the production of, *inter alia*, construction materials, foodstuffs and batteries. It was hoped that Eritrea's location in one of the busiest shipping zones in the world would help to attract external investors. Nearly 20,000 vessels a year pass by Eritrea loaded with more than 9.9% of the estimated 7,700m. metric tons of cargo carried by global shipping. The Massawa FPZ encompasses around 5,000 ha. Once fully operational, the free zone was expected to create a significant number of new jobs for locals, as well as improved foreign trade links and an outlet for local products including fruits, livestock, fish and minerals. The Government also plans to renovate Assab, the second port, as a Free Zone, specializing in goods transshipments. In terms of overall business environment, the World Bank's *Doing Business 2010* report ranked Eritrea last out of 175 countries surveyed in terms of ease of doing business, and indicated that starting a business, obtaining construction permits, registering property and securing credit were all extremely difficult in Eritrea. The Bank estimated that foreign direct investment constituted 10.4% of GDP in 2009, with a slight decline, to 10.0% of GDP, in 2011. The World Bank downgraded Eritrea from 178th place in 2011 to 180th in 2012 for 'ease of doing business'. The risk of macroeconomic instability, and the use of price controls, regulations and rationing, particularly of foreign exchange, created an unfavourable business environment, according to the Bank.

MINING AND POWER

Eritrea's mineral resources are believed to be of significant potential value. Gold-bearing seams exist in many of the igneous rocks forming the highlands of Eritrea. There are at least 15 gold mines and a large number of prospects close to Asmara, and the potential for new discoveries in the area is considered good. There are two regions of widespread gold mineralization in the western lowlands, at Tokombia and Barentu. Other mineral resources include potash, zinc, magnesium, copper, iron ore and marble. In April 1995 a new mining law was promulgated, which declared all mineral resources to be state assets, but recognized an extensive role for private investors in their exploitation. Investor companies would enjoy a concessionary tax regime, pay royalties of 2%–5% and encounter no restriction on repatriating profits. The Government retained the right to acquire a 10% share in any mining undertaking, with an option to buy a further 30%. These terms are considered favourable relative to those in neighbouring countries such as Egypt (which mandates a 50% stake for the state) or Sudan (60%).

Canadian Nevsun Resources' Bisha mine, valued at US $250m., began commercial gold-silver production in February 2011 and is the first company to launch commercial production operations in Eritrea, commencing with gold, followed by zinc and copper. The mine was expected to produce in excess of 1.14m. oz of gold, 11.9m. oz of silver, 821m. lb of copper and over 1,000m. lb of zinc during its initially estimated 13-year life. In the first half of 2011 905,000 metric tons of gold were milled, with 89% of gold recovered. During the first and second quarter of 2011 the gold price realized per oz was $1,405 and $1,510, respectively. The rate of production during the second quarter was approximately 1,000 oz per day. Nevsun will receive payments for the Government's 30% purchased interest through the projected revenue from Bisha. In June, by which time the second phase of the copper plant had started, the company's operational cash flow increased to $186m. The operating highlights for the first quarter of 2012 were as follows: 358,000 tons of ore mined and 82,000 oz of gold produced. Nevsun remains the only company with a mining licence in Eritrea thus far, with the other companies noted below still being at the exploration stage.

Investments in Eritrea's potentially rich mining sector remain dominated by Western companies, despite efforts to reach out to Asian countries for trade contacts. Copper, zinc and lead sulphites are mined by the Canadian-based Lundin Mining Corpn, while many promising gold deposits have been secured by Australian, Canadian and South African firms. In 2009 the Government issued new licences to eight more international firms, bringing the total to 16 companies. In 2010 a new round of licences awarded earlier in the year had brought the total number of foreign companies exploring or about to explore in Eritrea to 14. A government spokesperson named the newcomers as the United Kingdom's Andiamo Exploration and London Africa; China's Land and Energy and Zhongchang Mining; the Eritrean-Libyan Mining Share; Australia's South Boulder and Gippsland; and India's Spice Minerals. In June 2011 Sunridge Gold Corpn resumed another phase of exploration around Asmara, with the possibility of expanding to the Debarwa deposit, in central Eritrea. The companies mining the Gupo Gold deposit produced 189,000 oz of gold at an average gold grade of 2.99 grams per metric ton. Another licence was granted to Canadian-based NGEx Resources Inc to explore potash mineralization around Bada, which covers 431 sq km. The exploration company has been operating in Eritrea since 1998 under the licence name of Sanu Resources. In 2009 the company's Hambok depot reported that its estimated resources contained 231.1m. lb of copper, 530.7m. lb of zinc, 2.3m. oz of silver, 68,800 oz of gold and an additional inferred resource at Kerkebet prospect. At an investment forum in London in May 2012 Eritrean government representatives sought to increase the profile of the mining sector and the streamlining of the mining code.

In view of Eritrea's acute energy shortage, the possibility of large reserves of petroleum and natural gas beneath the Red Sea is of particular importance. In early 1993 the Government made petroleum exploration regulations more stringent, and British Petroleum (BP), which had signed a contract for petroleum exploration with the former Ethiopian regime, had its exploration rights invalidated. A US petroleum company, Amoco (now BP), and the International Petroleum Corpn of Canada were the only two remaining companies with concessions. The latter had operating rights in the 31,000-sq-km Danakil block along the Eritrean coast, where there are believed to be good prospects for petroleum and gas discoveries. Following the cessation of hostilities with Ethiopia, the Eritrean Government signed a petroleum exploration agreement with CMS Oil and Gas of the USA in May 2001. According to the state media, a new petroleum jetty is under construction at the cost of US $31.6m., and is expected to accommodate large vessels and contribute to economic recovery. South Boulder Mines Ltd, exploiting the Colluli Area A potash deposit, on the edge of the Red Sea, reported its first resource result of 548m. tons of potash in January 2011. In July the company announced the extensive nature of the deposit, which was believed to be the largest in the world. A remarkable result was found from two mining holes: Hole-1 intersected a total thickness of 17.5m. of potash, with a combined grade of 17.3% potassium chloride (KCl), and Hole-2 intersected a total thickness of 22.0m. of potash, with a combined grade of 22.0% KCl. There were no significant developments as far as offshore energy was concerned in 2011. However, the Eritrean Government has expressed an interest in developing alternative and renewable energy sources, including geothermal, solar and wind power.

Eritrea's economic performance is also hampered by its lack of capacity to produce energy. Total production of electricity in 1998 was 186m. kWh, 74% of which was in Asmara. By 2007 production had increased to 271 kWh in 2007, and in 2009–10 state media reported the expansion of electricity lines to various parts of the country. Nevertheless, electrification relies on imported fuel, which costs the country at least US $100m. each year. In mid-1997 work commenced on the construction of the Hirgigo power station at Massawa. Financed by Arab and Italian donors, and World Bank loans, the completed station cost $172m., of which $22m. was dedicated to repairing damage caused by Ethiopian bombardment in 2000. The Hirgigo power station officially came on stream in March 2003. Alternative and renewable energy resources are anticipated to meet 30% of the country's energy requirements. A windmill plant was inaugurated in 2009 in Assab, and currently meets approximately 25% of the city's electricity requirement. Investments have also been made in solar energy, especially in the western lowlands. In the first conference of the International Organization of Alternative Energy, which was held in Abu Dhabi, UAE, in April 2011, Eritrea was elected a member of the Executive Committee of the organization.

CONSTRUCTION AND TRANSPORT

In 1993 the Government announced plans for the rehabilitation of the Asmara–Massawa railway line, which had been severely damaged during the war of independence. Construction work was completed in February 2003. At the beginning of 2011 the Government allocated US $30m. to the construction of about 50 km of modern railway lines over the next five years. The fund is planned to include a purchase of new trains and carriages. The new 26-km continental highway between Eritrea and Sudan funded by the Qatar Government was inaugurated in July. Comparatively speaking, Eritrea has a long road network for its land base, totalling 18,540 km. In 2010 the Ministry of Land, Water and the Environment reported that the construction of roads, water diversion schemes, water reservoirs, micro-dams, and renovation of existing roads expanded by 40% from the previous year.

Significant progress has also been made in rehabilitating the port of Massawa, which was heavily bombed by Ethiopia during the 1998–2000 war. Priority was given to the dredging of the harbour and the extension of the docks; in Assab the main objective was to accelerate the transfer of cargo through the purchase of cargo-handling equipment. Both ports were virtually closed to Ethiopian trade with the outbreak of hostilities between the two countries in May 1998. A US $48m. construction project, which is regarded as essential for tourism promotion, is underway for resorts on Eritrea's Dahlak islands and is nearing completion. Meanwhile, large apartment complexes are currently being constructed in the town of Gahtelay, using foam-core panels. Gedem cement factory, which is under construction in the Gedem region near the Eritrean port city of Massawa by the China New Era International Engineering Corpn, is close to production completion and the plant is expected to produce 10,000 quintals of cement per day.

In November 2010 and March 2011 the Eritrean transport sector purchased a total of 94 new buses in order to ease public transport problems. On 16 July Eritrean Airlines (EA) commenced direct international flights to six different countries. The arrival of a leased Airbus 320 in Asmara International Airport in July was welcomed by government officials, although it was rumoured that the US Administration had tried to put pressure on companies not to lease aircraft to Eritrea. The Chief Executive of EA, Shakil Aftab, expressed expectations that the airway would offer a fair price to passengers under a new commercial policy. In addition, it is announced that the EA planned to significantly expand operations with the acquisition of this new aircraft. However, it is difficult to estimate the approximate market potential at this stage.

TOURISM

Tourism in Eritrea remains undeveloped and has been further damaged by the war. Eritrea's vast diaspora, primarily in Organisation for Economic Co-operation and Development countries and the Middle East, form the bulk of arrivals; in terms of tourist arrivals, the country ranked 165th in the world. There are plans to promote architectural (Eritrea possesses a number of fine Italian modernist colonial-era buildings) and archaeological (pre-Axumite discoveries) tourism, to be financed in part by a World Bank loan for the Government's Cultural Assets Rehabilitation Project. Construction of Gash Setit Wildlife Reserve is ongoing. According to the World Tourism Organization (WTO), revenue from tourism in 2009 was US $26m., compared with $61m. in 2007. A UNDP-funded project, worth $300,000, assisted the Government in the establishment of regional offices for the Ministry of Tourism by providing the necessary equipment and furniture for proper planning, data collection and knowledge sharing. In addition, assistance was provided to develop and provide training programmes for hotel owners/managers and chefs in the areas of hotel management supervisory skills, food production and kitchen management, to render better services. The project ran from July 2006 to December 2008.

A regional conference on conserving biodiversity and expanding natural reserves in the Horn of Africa was conducted in August 2006 in Asmara by ecologists from Somalia, Djibouti and Eritrea. The authorities were confident that the construction of the Serejeca–Shebah road would enhance wildlife tourism in the Semenawi Keyih Bahri region. In addition, since the road passes through the agricultural centre of the eastern lowlands, it may play a leading role in transportation and marketing for the farmers and could also serve as a subsidiary to the Asmara–Massawa road. According to World Bank figures, 4.3% of the total Eritrean land area is nationally protected; travel and tourism accounted for less than 2% of the country's GDP in 2009. Domestic tourist visits increased by 5.5% in 2010, compared with 5.0% in 2005. International tourist arrivals reached 80,503 in 2007, falling to 69,897 in 2008 but rising to 79,334 in 2009, according to the WTO.

THE SOCIAL SECTOR

Reports indicated that in 2012, in spite of the Government's assertion that it had reached self-reliance in agricultural production, malnutrition and poverty were widespread in Eritrea, while basic consumer goods such as bread, milk, cooking oil and kerosene for cooking purposes remained scarce. People were therefore forced to use charcoal and wood to cook their meals, which led to the continuation of environmental degradation. In the longer term, sustained real economic growth of 7% or more will be required for Eritrea to reach the Millennium Development Goal (MDG) of halving the proportion of people living in extreme poverty by 2015.

The Government has sought to protect and build upon achievements in the social sphere, particularly health and education, while maintaining a modicum of state involvement in the economy. In terms of government spending, the education budget increased from 164m. nakfa in 2000 to 431m. nakfa in 2005. Education expenditure was 2.4% of GDP in 2006 and 4.1% of GDP in 2008. According to the Human Development Index, the adult literacy rate (for those aged 15 and above) stood at 64.2% in 2008/09; this increased to 67.2%, according to the UNDP's 2009 report, while the combined gross enrolment rate at primary, secondary, and tertiary levels was 33.3%, unchanged from the previous year. These low figures were despite the fact that elementary education is compulsory for all school-age children and education through all levels is free, although parents must provide school supplies. The Ministry of Education announced the opening of new schools and increased enrolment of students in 2009–10, but these reports were not corroborated by data published by international organizations. Meanwhile, in March 2007 legislation came into force making female genital mutilation punishable by fines and imprisonment. The National Union of Eritrean Women has reported that more than 90% of Eritrean women are circumcized.

The average life expectancy in Eritrea was estimated at 62.2 years in 2010. In 2008 the World Health Organization (WHO) recorded increased rates of child malnutrition and maternal mortality. The maternal mortality rate is reported to be among the highest in the world, while 15% of children under the age of five are said to suffer from acute malnutrition and an additional 44% are chronically malnourished. The Government has expanded immunization programmes and initiated community care services to reduce maternal and child mortality rates. WHO's 2008 report showed that national routine immunization covers 70% of the population, with some regional disparities. With respect to the major causes of morbidity in the country, government reports found a decreased prevalence of cases of tuberculosis (TB), diarrhoea and malaria. A Ministry of Health study conducted in 2009 indicated that malaria mortality had declined by 96.6% overall, and by 98.0% among children under the age of five. The Government actively distributes mosquito nets, provides malaria medication in most primary health stations, endeavours to raise public awareness of preventive mechanisms, and encourages regular check ups for people living in high-risk areas.

WHO's 2009–13 country co-operation strategy on Eritrea stated that the country had made considerable progress in the health infrastructure. There were 25 hospitals, 52 health centres, 180 health stations and 113 medical clinics, and the country was training medical doctors and health care professionals in two of its tertiary institutions. The report also noted that over 60 different medicine products are locally produced, key medicines are available in 95% of health facilities and there is no shortage of supplies and equipment. By November 2006 the Eritrean Government had paid over 709m. nakfa in a benefit scheme for families of fallen soldiers. World Bank figures for 2000–04 indicated that 57% of the population (72% urban and 54% rural) had sustainable access to improved water sources, increasing to 60% of the population in 2005 (74% urban and 57% rural). In late 2008 it was reported that potable water provisions had increased significantly from 7% to 71% in rural areas and from 30% to 90% in urban areas since independence. Only 9% of the population, however, had sustainable access to improved sanitation (34% urban and 3% rural), decreasing slightly to 32% in urban areas and remaining at 3% for rural areas. The HIV prevalence rate decreased from 2.4% in 2003 to 1.3% in 2007, according to WHO. In 2009 the number of people with HIV/AIDS was 25,000, reduced to nearly one-half, and with the growth rate slowing to 0.8%. A significant decline in HIV infection was apparent in 2010. Chronic diseases such as diabetes, hypertension and mental health conditions, as well as infectious diseases like TB, HIV/AIDS and other STDs, are treated free of charge. The WHO July 2011 health update reported that the Government had launched The Decade of Action for Road Safety for 2011–20 to address the human and economic loss from road traffic accidents. In addition, 39 medical doctors graduated for the first time in the country in December 2009; they were expected to strengthen the human resources development of the Ministry of Health.

The World Bank reports that many health outcome indicators in Eritrea compare favourably with its sub-Saharan African neighbours, and are improving faster, although it is frequently hard to find comprehensive, up-to-date data on outcomes. Based on recent MDG indicators, the infant mortality rate decreased from 55 deaths per 1,000 in 2000 to 40.8 deaths per 1,000 in 2008, the under-five mortality rate dropped from 83 deaths per 1,000 in 2000 to 68 deaths per 1,000 in 2007, and the total fertility rate decreased from 6.1 to 4.8 births per woman on average. Success in some disease control programmes, supported by the World Bank and other partners, is particularly impressive. While most other sub-Saharan African countries suffer from an increasing HIV epidemic, HIV prevalence in Eritrea is estimated to be low and under control at 1.3% of the adult population in 2009 compared to the sub-Saharan African average of 5%. Nevertheless, important challenges remain. Malnutrition is of particular concern among women and children. An estimated 46% of the population were estimated to be undernourished in 2002, and 40% of children were found to be underweight for their age. Around 37% of women have a low body mass index. Although it has declined very sharply in the past 10 years, the maternal mortality ratio in Eritrea is estimated at 752 per 100,000 live births. Crime rates are low, making Asmara one of the safest cities in the world, and state social service provision is generally efficient and honest. According to the Global Peace Index of 2011, Eritrea is ranked 104th of 149 countries worldwide based on its peacefulness. Underpinning this relative cohesiveness, and striking to all foreigners, is the sense of social and public purpose that makes Eritrea stand out in contemporary sub-Saharan Africa. Yet beyond the statistics and these notable achievements, life for the majority of Eritreans remains a burden of declining real wages, poorly paid jobs, rationed basic commodities, incredible hardship in the rural areas and indefinite national conscription. In the economic field, there are hopes for improvements with the start of gold-mining by foreign companies, mainly the Canadian firm Nevsun Resources, which began production in 2011. However, it is highly unlikely that gold revenues will help to initiate economic development or alleviate widespread poverty unless the severe structural deficiencies of Eritrea's economy are addressed. Moreover, the possibility of further regional conflict also weighs on the minds of many Eritreans. Many observers are doubtful that the leadership would accede to political pluralism even if the border stalemate with Ethiopia were resolved. The alienation between state and society is widening, perhaps irrevocably, and the current geopolitical matrix suggests little in the way of optimism.

Statistical Survey

Source (unless otherwise stated): Ministry of Trade and Industry, POB 1844, Asmara; tel. (1) 126155; fax (1) 120586.

Area and Population

AREA, POPULATION AND DENSITY*

Area (sq km)	121,144†
Population (census results)	
9 May 1984	
Males	1,374,452
Females	1,373,852
Total	2,748,304
Population (UN estimates at mid-year)‡	
2010	5,253,676
2011	5,415,280
2012	5,580,861
Density (per sq km) at mid-2012	46.1

* Including the Assab district.

† 46,774 sq miles.

‡ Source: UN, *World Population Prospects: The 2010 Revision*.

POPULATION BY AGE AND SEX
(UN estimates at mid-2012)

	Males	Females	Total
0–14	1,171,087	1,146,230	2,317,317
15–64	1,527,585	1,594,617	3,122,202
65 and over	53,576	87,766	141,342
Total	2,752,248	2,828,613	5,580,861

Source: UN, *World Population Prospects: The 2010 Revision*.

PRINCIPAL TOWNS
(estimated population at January 2012)

Asmara (capital)	1,376,318	Keren	82,198
Assab	101,284	Mitsiwa (Massawa)	53,090

Source: Stefan Helders, *World Gazetteer* (internet www.world-gazetteer.com).

BIRTHS AND DEATHS
(averages per year, UN estimates)

	1995–2000	2000–05	2005–10
Birth rate (per 1,000)	38.1	38.4	37.5
Death rate (per 1,000)	11.1	9.5	8.3

Source: UN, *World Population Prospects: The 2010 Revision*.

Life expectancy (years at birth): 61.0 (males 58.7; females 63.4) in 2010 (Source: World Bank, World Development Indicators database).

ECONOMICALLY ACTIVE POPULATION
('000, FAO estimates at mid-year)

	2010	2011	2012
Agriculture, etc.	1,547	1,590	1,634
Total labour force (incl. others)	2,098	2,165	2,236

Source: FAO.

Health and Welfare

KEY INDICATORS

Total fertility rate (children per woman, 2010)	4.5
Under-5 mortality rate (per 1,000 live births, 2010)	61
HIV/AIDS (% of persons aged 15–49, 2009)	0.8
Hospital beds (per 1,000 head, 2006)	1.2
Physicians (per 1,000 head, 2004)	0.05
Health expenditure (2009): US $ per head (PPP)	16
Health expenditure (2009): % of GDP	2.8
Health expenditure (2009): public (% of total)	47.7
Access to water (% of persons, 2008)	61
Access to sanitation (% of persons, 2008)	14
Total carbon dioxide emissions ('000 metric tons, 2008)	414.4
Carbon dioxide emissions per head (metric tons, 2008)	0.1
Human Development Index (2011): ranking	177
Human Development Index (2011): value	0.349

For sources and definitions, see explanatory note on p. vi.

Agriculture

PRINCIPAL CROPS
('000 metric tons)

	2008	2009	2010*
Wheat	5.4	26.1	27.3
Barley	6.4	65.1	67.0
Maize	4.1	16.7	20.5
Millet	12.2	17.2	17.0
Sorghum	68.0	59.2	66.7
Potatoes	0.2	0.1	0.1
Broad beans, horse beans, dry	1.8	0.1	0.1
Peas, dry	—	2.0	2.0
Chick-peas	—	6.6	6.5
Lentils	—	0.6	0.6
Vetches	—	2.3	2.3
Groundnuts, with shell	0.6	1.3	1.3
Sesame seed	0.5	0.2	0.1

* FAO estimates.

Aggregate production ('000 metric tons, may include official, semi-official or estimated data): Total cereals 105.8 in 2008, 226.9 in 2009, 247.4 in 2010; Total roots and tubers 76.8 in 2008, 71.6 in 2009, 37.5 in 2010; Total vegetables (incl. melons) 40.1 in 2008, 47.5 in 2009, 43.3 in 2010.

Source: FAO.

LIVESTOCK
('000 head, year ending September, FAO estimates)

	2008	2009	2010*
Cattle	2,036	2,046	2,057
Sheep	2,249	2,260	2,272
Goats*	1,730	1,740	1,750
Camels	337	339	345
Chickens	1,198	1,204	1,250

* FAO estimates.

Source: FAO.

LIVESTOCK PRODUCTS
('000 metric tons)

	2008	2009	2010*
Cattle meat	17.2	23.0	22.0
Sheep meat	3.8†	4.0	4.1
Goat meat*	5.8	5.8	5.9
Chicken meat*	1.6	1.6	1.6
Camels' milk*	5.3	5.3	5.4
Cows' milk*	103.0	103.6	131.2
Goats' milk*	8.7	8.7	9.1
Sheep's milk*	5.3	5.4	5.5
Hen eggs*	1.9	1.7	1.9
Wool, greasy*	0.6	0.6	0.9

* FAO estimates.
† Unofficial figure.

Source: FAO.

Fishing

(metric tons, live weight of capture)

	2008	2009	2010
Requiem sharks	115	165	307
Sea catfishes	15	42	128
Threadfin breams	n.a.	62	165
Snappers and jobfishes	37	75	58
Narrow-barred Spanish mackerel	496	573	414
Tuna-like fishes	589	640	423
Barracudas	58	78	69
Carangids	46	79	109
Queenfishes	53	185	176
Penaeus shrimps	38	219	323
Total catch (incl. others)	1,665	3,030	3,286

Source: FAO.

Mining

('000 metric tons, unless otherwise indicated, estimates)

	2008	2009	2010
Gold (kilograms)	30.0	30.0	35.0
Marble ('000 sq m)	35.0	32.0	36.0
Limestone	3.0	3.0	3.0
Salt	7.5	7.5	7.8
Granite	25.0	25.0	25.0

Source: US Geological Survey.

Industry

SELECTED PRODUCTS
('000 metric tons, unless otherwise indicated, estimates)

	2008	2009	2010
Cement	45.0	45.0	45.0
Basalt	50.0	45.0	50.0
Gravel	80.0	78.0	80.0
Coral	65.0	60.0	58.0

Electric energy (million kWh): 287 in 2008.

Sources: US Geological Survey; UN Industrial Commodity Statistics Database.

Finance

CURRENCY AND EXCHANGE RATES

Monetary Units
100 cents = 1 nakfa.

Sterling, Dollar and Euro Equivalents (31 May 2012)
£1 sterling = 23.837 nakfa;
US $1 = 15.375 nakfa;
€1 = 19.070 nakfa;
1,000 nakfa = £41.95 = $65.04 = €52.44.

Note: Following its secession from Ethiopia in May 1993, Eritrea retained the Ethiopian currency, the birr. An exchange rate of US $1 = 5.000 birr was introduced in October 1992 and remained in force until April 1994, when it was adjusted to $1 = 5.130 birr. Further adjustments were made subsequently. In November 1997 the Government introduced a separate national currency, the nakfa, replacing (and initially at par with) the Ethiopian birr. The exchange rate in relation to the US dollar was initially set at the prevailing unified rate, but from 1 May 1998 a mechanism to provide a market-related exchange rate was established.

Average Exchange Rate (nakfa per US $)
2009 15.3750
2010 15.3750
2011 15.3750

BUDGET
(million nakfa)

Revenue*	2007	2008†	2009‡
Tax revenue	2,405	2,459	2,374
Direct taxes	1,512	1,719	1,580
Indirect domestic taxes	487	395	435
Import duties and taxes	406	345	360
Non-tax revenue	1,888	1,393	1,401
Total	4,293	3,853	3,775

Expenditure§	2007	2008†	2009‡
Current expenditure	5,900	6,905	6,824
Wages, salaries and allowances	2,234	2,275	2,430
Materials and services	2,316	2,531	2,398
Subsidies and transfers	706	1,311	931
Interest	644	788	1,065
Domestic	571	648	853
External	73	140	212
Capital expenditure	2,224	2,331	2,134
Central treasury	1,012	704	681
Externally financed	1,203	1,627	1,453
Total	8,124	9,236	8,958

* Excluding grants received (million nakfa): 628 in 2007; 604 in 2008 (estimate); 737 in 2009 (projected).

† Estimates.

‡ Projections.

§ Excluding net lending (million nakfa): –95 in 2007; 608 in 2008 (estimate); 139 in 2009 (projected).

Source: African Development Bank, *Interim Country Strategy Paper for Eritrea* (2009–11).

INTERNATIONAL RESERVES
(US $ million at 31 December)

	1999	2000	2001
Gold (national valuation)	19.7	10.4	10.5
Reserve position in IMF	0.0	0.0	0.0
Foreign exchange	34.2	25.5	39.7
Total	53.9	35.9	50.3

Foreign exchange: 57.9 in 2008; 84.3 in 2009; 108.6 in 2010.

IMF special drawing rights: 5.7 in 2009, 5.6 in 2010, 5.5 in 2011.

Source: IMF, *International Financial Statistics*.

MONEY SUPPLY
(million nakfa at 31 December)

	2008	2009	2010
Currency outside depository corporations	5,153	6,637	8,155
Transferable deposits	10,166	10,655	11,554
Other deposits	14,656	17,397	20,388
Broad money	29,976	34,689	40,097

Source: IMF, *International Financial Statistics*.

COST OF LIVING
(Consumer Price Index; base: 2000 = 100)

	2009	2010	2011
All items	464.1	523.1	592.9

Source: African Development Bank.

NATIONAL ACCOUNTS
(million nakfa at current prices)

Expenditure on the Gross Domestic Product

	2008	2009	2010
Private final consumption expenditure	17,534	24,765	26,233
Government final consumption expenditure	5,594	5,760	7,034
Gross capital formation	2,698	2,628	4,005
Total domestic expenditure	25,826	33,153	37,272
Exports of goods and services	940	1,293	1,438
Less Imports of goods and services	5,545	5,898	6,161
GDP in purchasers' values	21,220	28,547	32,549

Gross Domestic Product by Economic Activity

	2008	2009	2010
Agriculture, forestry and fishing	2,971	4,032	5,563
Mining and quarrying	346	471	498
Manufacturing	1,155	1,568	1,750
Construction	3,087	4,190	4,442
Wholesale and retail trade	4,228	5,749	6,230
Transport and communications	2,708	3,682	3,990
Public administration and defence	6,107	8,060	9,003
Sub-total	20,603	27,752	31,476
Indirect taxes (net)	618	795	1,073
GDP in purchasers' values	21,220	28,547	32,549

Source: African Development Bank.

BALANCE OF PAYMENTS
(US $ million)

	2000	2001*	2002†
Exports of goods f.o.b.	36.7	19.9	51.8
Imports of goods c.i.f.	–470.3	–536.7	–533.4
Trade balance	–433.5	–516.7	–481.7
Exports of services	60.7	127.5	132.6
Imports of services	–28.3	–33.4	–30.3
Balance on goods and services	–401.1	–422.6	–379.4
Other income (net)	–1.4	–4.6	–6.1
Balance on goods, services and income	–402.5	–427.2	–385.5
Private unrequited transfers (net)	195.7	175.0	205.6
Official unrequited transfers (net)	102.4	120.8	80.3
Current balance	–104.5	–131.4	–99.6
Capital account (net)	—	7.3	3.6
Financial account	98.7	94.8	64.6
Short-term capital (net)	–14.7	18.7	15.9
Net errors and omissions	–9.5	36.5	–7.6
Overall balance	–15.2	7.2	–39.0

* Preliminary figures.

† Estimates.

Source: IMF, *Eritrea: Selected Issues and Statistical Appendix* (June 2003).

2010 (Nakfa million): Trade balance –5,366; Services (net) 321; Income (net) –306; Current transfers (net) 4,876; *Current account* –474 (Source: African Development Bank).

External Trade

PRINCIPAL COMMODITIES
(distribution by SITC, US $ '000)

Imports c.i.f. (excl. petroleum)	2001	2002	2003
Food and live animals	110.9	153.0	175.2
Animal and vegetable oils, fats and waxes	13.6	7.4	19.3
Chemicals and related products	45.5	36.4	26.2
Basic manufactures	101.5	115.6	63.3
Machinery and transport equipment	107.4	155.9	97.2
Miscellaneous manufactured articles	34.0	46.9	40.7
Total (incl. others)	422.9	537.9	432.8

Exports f.o.b.	2001	2002	2003
Food and live animals	8.8	37.7	2.4
Crude materials (inedible) except fuels	3.0	6.0	2.1
Chemicals and related products	0.7	0.6	0.1
Basic manufactures	5.6	4.8	1.1
Miscellaneous manufactured articles	0.5	1.5	0.7
Total (incl. others)	19.0	51.8	6.6

Source: UN, *International Trade Statistics Yearbook*.

PRINCIPAL TRADING PARTNERS
(US $ million)

Imports c.i.f.	2001	2002	2003
Belgium	11.9	13.7	8.6
Germany	11.8	16.4	6.7
Italy	79.0	70.4	50.1
Netherlands	13.9	17.4	10.4
Saudi Arabia	70.0	70.0	45.4
United Arab Emirates	64.6	90.7	52.9
United Kingdom	9.6	10.0	11.7
USA	20.4	38.5	68.9
Total (incl. others)	422.9	537.9	432.8

Exports f.o.b.	2001	2002	2003
Djibouti	—	0.8	—
Germany	0.7	0.5	0.1
India	3.2	0.5	0.5
Italy	2.1	1.8	0.8
Netherlands	0.4	0.3	0.7
Saudi Arabia	0.3	0.1	—
Sudan	9.7	43.4	1.3
Total (incl. others)	19.0	51.8	6.6

Source: UN, *International Trade Statistics Yearbook*.

Transport

ROAD TRAFFIC
(motor vehicles in use)

	1996	1997	1998
Number of registered vehicles	27,013	31,276	35,942

2007 (vehicles registered at 31 December): Passenger cars 31,033; Buses and coaches 1,825; Vans and lorries 22,514; Motorcycles and mopeds 3,042 (Source: IRF, *World Road Statistics*).

SHIPPING

Merchant Fleet
(registered at 31 December)

	2007	2008	2009
Number of vessels	14	13	13
Displacement (grt)	14,478	13,075	13,075

Source: IHS Fairplay, *World Fleet Statistics*.

CIVIL AVIATION

	1996	1997	1998
Passengers ('000)	168.1	173.8	105.2

Tourism

ARRIVALS BY COUNTRY OF ORIGIN

	2007	2008	2009
Germany	825	742	775
India	2,973	395	718
Italy	2,023	2,108	1,944
Japan	743	773	151
Kenya	610	312	234
Sudan	2,413	3,570	5,866
United Kingdom	731	680	843
USA	506	499	511
Total (incl. others)	80,503	69,897	79,334

Total tourist arrivals ('000): 84 in 2010.

Tourism receipts (US $ million, incl. passenger transport): 61 in 2007; 46 in 2008; 26 in 2009.

Source: World Tourism Organization.

Communications Media

	2008	2009	2010
Telephones ('000 main lines in use)	40.4	48.5	54.2
Mobile cellular telephones ('000 subscribers)	108.6	141.1	185.3
Internet subscribers ('000)	6.5	7.0	7.1
Broadband subscribers	n.a.	100	100

Personal computers: 50,000 (10.1 per 1,000 persons) in 2008.

Television receivers ('000 in use): 100 in 2000.

Book production (1993): 106 titles (including 23 pamphlets) and 420,000 copies (including 60,000 pamphlets). Figures for books, excluding pamphlets, refer only to school textbooks (64 titles; 323,000 copies) and government publications (19 titles; 37,000 copies).

Sources: mainly UNESCO, *Statistical Yearbook*; International Telecommunication Union.

Education

(2009/10 unless otherwise indicated)

	Institutions*	Teachers	Pupils
Pre-primary	95	1,143	40,506
Primary	695	7,535	286,021
Secondary: General	44	6,152	246,778
Secondary: Teacher-training	2	47*	922*
Secondary: Vocational	n.a.	261	1,304
University and equivalent level	n.a.	634	10,198

* 2001/02 figure(s).

Sources: UNESCO Institute for Statistics; Ministry of Education, Asmara.

Pupil-teacher ratio (primary education, UNESCO estimate): 38.0 in 2009/10 (Source: UNESCO Institute for Statistics).

Adult literacy rate (UNESCO estimates): 67.8% (males 78.7%; females 57.5%) in 2010 (Source: UNESCO Institute for Statistics).

Directory

The Constitution

On 23 May 1997 the Constituent Assembly unanimously adopted the Eritrean Constitution. A presidential regime was instituted, with the President to be elected for a maximum of two five-year terms. The President, as Head of State, has extensive powers and appoints, with the approval of the National Assembly (the legislature), the ministers, the commissioners, the Auditor-General, the President of the central bank and the judges of the Supreme Court. The President's mandate can be revoked if two-thirds of the members of the National Assembly so demand. 'Conditional' political pluralism is authorized. Pending the election of a new National Assembly, legislative power was to be held by a Transitional National Assembly, comprising the 75 members of the People's Front for Democracy and Justice (PFDJ) Central Committee, 60 members of the former Constituent Assembly and 15 representatives of Eritreans residing abroad.

The Government

HEAD OF STATE

President: ISSAIAS AFEWERKI (assumed power May 1991; elected President by the National Assembly 8 June 1993).

CABINET

(September 2012)

The Government is formed by the People's Front for Democracy and Justice.

President: ISSAIAS AFEWERKI.

Minister of Defence: Gen. SEBHAT EPHREM.

Minister of Justice: FAWZIA HASHIM.

Minister of Foreign Affairs: OSMAN SALIH MUHAMMAD.

Minister of Information: ALI ABDU.

Minister of Finance: BERHANE ABREHE.

Minister of Trade and Industry: Dr GIORGIS TEKLEMIKAEL.

Minister of Agriculture: AREFAINE BERHE.

Minister of Labour and Human Welfare: ASKALU MENKERIOS.

Minister of Fisheries: AHMED HAJI ALI.

Minister of Construction: ABRAHA ASFAHA.

Minister of Energy and Mines: TESFAI GEBRESELASSIE.

Minister of Education: SEMERE RUSOM.

Minister of Health: Dr SALIH MEKKI.

Minister of Transport and Communications: WOLDEMIKAEL ABRAHA.

Minister of Tourism: AMNA NUR HUSSEIN.

Minister of Land, Water and the Environment: WOLDEMICHAEL GEBREMARIAM.

Minister of Local Government: NAIZGHI KIFLU.

MINISTRIES

Office of the President: POB 257, Asmara; tel. (1) 122132; fax (1) 125123.

Ministry of Agriculture: POB 1048, Asmara; tel. (1) 181499; fax (1) 181415.

Ministry of Construction: POB 841, Asmara; tel. (1) 114588; fax (1) 120661.

Ministry of Defence: POB 629, Asmara; tel. (1) 165952; fax (1) 124990.

Ministry of Education: POB 5610, Asmara; tel. (1) 113044; fax (1) 113866; internet www.erimoe.gov.er.

Ministry of Energy and Mines: POB 5285, Asmara; tel. (1) 116872; fax (1) 127652.

Ministry of Finance: POB 896, Asmara; tel. (1) 118131; fax (1) 127947.

Ministry of Fisheries: POB 923, Asmara; tel. (1) 120400; fax (1) 122185; e-mail mofisha@eol.com.er; f. 1994.

Ministry of Foreign Affairs: POB 190, Asmara; tel. (1) 127838; fax (1) 123788; e-mail tesfai@wg.eol.

Ministry of Health: POB 212, Asmara; tel. (1) 117549; fax (1) 112899.

Ministry of Information: POB 872, Asmara; tel. (1) 120478; fax (1) 126747; internet www.shabait.com.

Ministry of Justice: POB 241, Asmara; tel. (1) 127739; fax (1) 126422.

Ministry of Labour and Human Welfare: POB 5252, Asmara; tel. (1) 181846; fax (1) 181760; e-mail mlhw@eol.com.er.

Ministry of Land, Water and the Environment: POB 976, Asmara; tel. (1) 118021; fax (1) 123285.

Ministry of Local Government: POB 225, Asmara; tel. (1) 114254; fax (1) 120014.

Ministry of Tourism: POB 1010, Warsay Ave, Dembe Sembel (Green Building), Asmara; tel. (1) 154100; fax (1) 154081; e-mail eritreantourism@tse.com.er.

Ministry of Trade and Industry: POB 1844, Asmara; tel. (1) 126155; fax (1) 120586; e-mail berhanem69@yahoo.co.uk.

Ministry of Transport and Communications: POB 1840, Asmara; tel. (1) 114222; fax (1) 127048; e-mail motc.rez@eol.com.er.

Provincial Administrators

There are six administrative regions in Eritrea, each with regional, sub-regional and village administrations.

Anseba Province: SALMA HASSAN.

Debub Province: MUSTAFA NUR HUSSEIN.

Debubawi Keyih Bahri Province: OSMAN MOHAMED OMAR.

Gash-Barka Province: MUSA RAB'A.

Maakel Province: KAHSAI GEBREHIWET.

Semenawi Keyih Bahri Province: TSIGEREDA WOLDEGERGISH.

Legislature

NATIONAL ASSEMBLY

In accordance with transitional arrangements formulated in Decree No. 37 of May 1993, the National Assembly consists of the Central Committee of the People's Front for Democracy and Justice (PFDJ) and 60 other members: 30 from the Provincial Assemblies and an additional 30 members, including a minimum of 10 women, to be nominated by the PFDJ Central Committee. The legislative body 'outlines the internal and external policies of the government, regulates their implementation, approves the budget and elects a president for the country'. The National Assembly is to hold regular sessions every six months under the chairmanship of the President. In his role as Head of the Government and Commander-in-Chief of the Army, the President nominates individuals to head the various government departments. These nominations are ratified by the legislative body. In March 1994 the National Assembly voted to alter its composition: it would henceforth comprise the 75 members of the Central Committee of the PFDJ and 75 directly elected members. In May 1997, following the adoption of the Constitution, the Constituent Assembly empowered a Transitional National Assembly (comprising the 75 members of the PFDJ, 60 members of the former Constituent Assembly and 15 representatives of Eritreans residing abroad) to act as the legislature until elections were held for a new National Assembly.

Chairman of the Transitional National Assembly: ISSAIAS AFEWERKI.

Election Commission

Electoral Commission: Asmara; f. 2002; five mems appointed by the President; Commissioner RAMADAN MOHAMMED NUR.

Political Organizations

Afar Federal Alliance: e-mail afa_f@hotmail.com; f. 2003.

Democratic Movement for the Liberation of Eritrean Kunama: Postfach 620 124, 50694, Köln, Germany; e-mail kcs@baden-kunama.com; internet www.baden-kunama.com; based in Germany; represents the Kunama minority ethnic group.

Eritrean Democratic Alliance (EDA): internet www.erit-alliance.com; f. 1999 as the Alliance of Eritrean National Forces, became Eritrean National Alliance in 2002, adopted present name in 2004; broad alliance of 13 parties opposed to PFDJ regime; Chair. BERHANE YEMANE 'HANJEMA'; Sec.-Gen. HUSAYN KHALIFA.

Eritrean Democratic Party (EDP): e-mail info@selfi-democracy.com; internet www.selfi-democracy.com; f. 2001 as the Eritrean People's Liberation Front—Democratic Party (EPLF—DP); breakaway group from the PFDJ; name changed to above in 2004; Chair. MESFIN HAGOS.

Eritrean Islamic Jihad (EIJ): radical opposition group; in Aug. 1993 split into a military wing and a political wing.

Eritrean Islamic Party for Justice and Development (EIPJD) (Al-Hizb Al-Islami Al-Eritree Liladalah Wetenmiya): internet www.alkhalas.org; f. 1988 as Eritrean Islamic Jihad Movement; changed name to al-Khalas in 1998; political wing of EIJ; Leader KHALIL MUHAMMAD AMER.

Eritrean Liberation Front (ELF): f. 1958; commenced armed struggle against Ethiopia in 1961; subsequently split into numerous factions (see below); mainly Muslim support; opposes the PFDJ; principal factions:

Eritrean Liberation Front—Central Command (ELF—CC): f. 1982; Chair. ABDALLAH IDRISS.

Eritrean Liberation Front—National Council (ELF—NC): Leader Dr BEYENE KIDANE.

Eritrean Liberation Front—Revolutionary Council (ELF—RC): Chair. AHMED WOLDEYESUS AMMAR.

Eritrean People's Democratic Front (EPDF): e-mail main-office@sagem-eritra.org; internet www.democrasia.org; f. 2004 by merger of People's Democratic Front for the Liberation of Eritrea and a faction of ERDF; Leader TEWOLDE GEBRESELASSIE.

Eritrean Popular Movement (EPM): f. 2004; Leader ABDALLAH ADEM.

Eritrean Revolutionary Democratic Front (ERDF): e-mail webmaster@eritreana.com; internet www.eritreana.com; f. 1997 following merger of Democratic Movement for the Liberation of Eritrea and a faction of People's Democratic Front for the Liberation of Eritrea; Leader BERHANE YEMANE 'HANJEMA'.

Gash Setit Organization: Leader ISMAIL NADA.

People's Front for Democracy and Justice (PFDJ): POB 1081, Asmara; tel. (1) 121399; fax (1) 120848; e-mail webmaster@shaebia.org; internet www.shaebia.org; f. 1970 as the Eritrean Popular Liberation Forces, following a split in the Eritrean Liberation Front; renamed the Eritrean People's Liberation Front in 1977; adopted present name in Feb. 1994; Christian and Muslim support; in May 1991 took control of Eritrea and formed provisional Govt; formed transitional Govt in May 1993; Chair. ISSAIAS AFEWERKI; Sec.-Gen. ALAMIN MOHAMED SAID.

Red Sea Afar Democratic Organization: Afar opposition group; Sec.-Gen. IBRAHIM HAROUN.

Diplomatic Representation

EMBASSIES IN ERITREA

China, People's Republic: 16 Ogaden St, POB 204, Asmara; tel. and fax (1) 185271; fax (1) 185275; e-mail chemb@eol.com.er; Ambassador LI LIANSHENG.

Djibouti: POB 5589, Asmara; tel. (1) 354961; fax (1) 351831; Ambassador AHMAD ISSA (recalled in June 2008).

Egypt: 5 Marsa Fatma St, POB 5570, Asmara; tel. and fax (1) 124935; fax (1) 123294; e-mail amb.egy.asmara@gmail.com; Ambassador MAHMOUD NAYEL.

France: POB 209, Asmara; tel. (1) 125196; fax (1) 123288; e-mail cad.asmara@diplomatie.gouv.fr; internet ambafrance-er.org; Ambassador ROGER AUQUE.

Germany: SABA Building, 8th Floor, Warsay St, POB 4974, Asmara; tel. (1) 186670; fax (1) 186900; e-mail info@asmara.diplo.de; internet www.asmara.diplo.de; Ambassador KLAUS PETER SCHICK.

Iran: Asmara; Ambassador REZA AMERI.

Israel: 32 Abo St, POB 5600, Asmara; tel. (1) 188521; fax (1) 188550; e-mail info@asmara.mfa.gov.il; Ambassador ODED BEN-HAIM.

Italy: POB 220, 11 171–1 St, Asmara; tel. (1) 120160; fax (1) 121115; e-mail ambasciata.asmara@esteri.it; internet www.ambasmara.esteri.it; Ambassador GAETANO MARTINEZ TAGLIAVIA.

Libya: Asmara.

Norway: 11 173–1 St, POB 5801, Asmara; tel. (1) 122138; fax (1) 122180; e-mail emb.asmara@mfa.no; internet www.norway-eritrea.org; Ambassador BÅRD HOPLAND.

Russia: 21 Zobel St, POB 5667, Asmara; tel. (1) 127162; fax (1) 127164; e-mail rusemb@eol.com.er; Ambassador IGOR NIKOLAVIC.

Saudi Arabia: POB 5599, Asmara; tel. (1) 120171; fax (1) 121027; Ambassador NASSER ALI AL-HOTI.

South Africa: 51–53 Hitseito St 245, Tiravalo, POB 11447, Asmara; tel. (1) 152521; fax (1) 152538; e-mail saemb_asma@yahoo.com; Ambassador MAHOMED IQBAL DAWOOD.

Sudan: Asmara; tel. (1) 202072; fax (1) 200760; e-mail sudanemb@eol.com.er; Ambassador SALAH MOHAMED AL-HASSAN.

United Kingdom: 66–68 Mariam Ghimbi St, POB 5584, Asmara; tel. (1) 120145; fax (1) 120104; e-mail asmara.enquiries@fco.gov.uk; internet www.ukineritrea.fco.gov.uk; Ambassador AMANDA SUSANNAH TANFIELD.

USA: POB 211, 179 Ala St, Asmara; tel. (1) 120004; fax (1) 127584; e-mail usembassyasmara@state.gov; internet eritrea.usembassy.gov; Chargé d'affaires a.i. JOEL REIFMAN.

Yemen: POB 5566, Asmara; tel. (1) 114434; fax (1) 117921; Ambassador Dr ABDELKADIR MOHAMMED HADI.

Judicial System

The judicial system operates on the basis of transitional laws, which incorporate pre-independence laws of the Eritrean People's Liberation Front, revised Ethiopian laws, customary laws and post-independence enacted laws. The independence of the judiciary in the discharge of its functions is unequivocally stated in Decree No. 37, which defines the powers and duties of the Government. It is subject only to the law and to no other authority. The court structure is composed of first instance sub-zonal courts, appellate and first instance zonal courts, appellate and first instance high courts, a panel of high court judges, presided over by the President of the High Court, and a Supreme Court presided over by the Chief Justice, as a court of last resort. The judges of the Supreme Court are appointed by the President of the State, subject to confirmation by the National Assembly.

Supreme Court: Asmara.

High Court: POB 241, Asmara; tel. (1) 127739; fax (1) 201828; e-mail prshict@eol.com.er.

Religion

Eritrea is almost equally divided between Muslims and Christians. Most Christians are adherents of the Orthodox Church, although there are Protestant and Roman Catholic communities. A small number of the population follow traditional beliefs.

CHRISTIANITY

The Eritrean Orthodox Church

In September 1993 the separation of the Eritrean Orthodox Church from the Ethiopian Orthodox Church was agreed by the respective church leaderships. The Eritrean Orthodox Church announced that it was to create a diocese of each of the country's then 10 provinces. The first five bishops of the Eritrean Orthodox Church were consecrated in Cairo, Egypt, in September 1994. In May 1998 Eritrea's first Patriarch (Abune) was consecrated in Alexandria, Egypt. In January 2006 Eritrea's third Patriarch, Abune Antonios I (who had been under house arrest since August 2005), was deposed by the Holy Synod.

Patriarch (Abune): DIOSKOROS.

The Roman Catholic Church

An estimated 3% of the total population are Roman Catholics.

Bishop of Asmara: Rt Rev. ABBA MENGHISTEAB TESFAMARIAM, 19 Gonder St, POB 244, Asmara; tel. (1) 120206; fax (1) 126519; e-mail kimehret@gemel.com.er.

Bishop of Barentu: Rt Rev. THOMAS OSMAN, POB 9, Barentu; tel. and fax (1) 127283.

Bishop of Keren: Rt Rev. KIDANE YEBIO, POB 460, Keren; tel. (1) 401907; fax (1) 401604; e-mail cek@tse.com.er.

The Anglican Communion

Within the Episcopal Church in Jerusalem and the Middle East, Eritrea lies within the jurisdiction of the Bishop in Egypt.

Leader: ASFAHA MAHARY.

ISLAM

Eritrea's main Muslim communities are concentrated in the western lowlands, the northern highlands and the eastern coastal region.

Leader: Sheikh AL-AMIN OSMAN AL-AMIN.

The Press

There is no independent press in Eritrea.

Chamber News: POB 856, Asmara; tel. (1) 120045; fax (1) 120138; monthly; Tigrinya, Arabic and English; publ. by Asmara Chamber of Commerce.

Eritrea Alhaditha: Asmara; tel. (1) 127099; e-mail alhadisa@zena.gov.er; Arabic; publ. by the Ministry of Information; Editor-in-Chief MOHAMMEDNUR YAHYA.

Eritrea Haddas: Asmara; tel. (1) 201820; Tigrinya; govt publ; Editor-in-Chief MOHAMMED IDRIS MOHAMMED.

Eritrea Profile: POB 247, Asmara; tel. (1) 114114; fax (1) 127749; e-mail eritreaprofile@yahoo.com; internet www.shabait.com; f. 1994; twice-weekly; English; publ. by the Ministry of Information; Man. Dir AZZAZI ZEREMARIAM; Editor AMANUEL MESFUN (acting).

Haddas Ertra (New Eritrea): Asmara; tel. (1) 116266; fax (1) 127749; f. 1991; six times a week; Tigrinya; govt publ; Editor SAMSOM HAILE; circ. 49,200.

Newsletter: POB 856, Asmara; tel. (1) 121589; fax (1) 120138; e-mail encc@aol.com.er; monthly; Tigrinya, Arabic and English; publ. by Eritrean National Chamber of Commerce; Editor MOHAMMED-SFAF HAMMED.

Broadcasting and Communications

Ministry of Transport and Communications (Communications Department): POB 4918, Asmara; tel. (1) 115847; fax (1)

126966; e-mail motc.rez@eol.com.er; Dir-Gen. MEKONNEN FISSEHAZION.

TELECOMMUNICATIONS

Eritrea Telecommunication Services Corpn (EriTel): 11 Semaetat St, POB 234, Asmara; tel. (1) 124655; fax (1) 120938; e-mail eritel@tse.com.er; internet www.tse.com.er; f. 1991; public enterprise; operates fixed-line and mobile cellular networks and internet services; Gen. Man. TESFASELASSIE BERHANE.

TFanus: 46 Daniel Comboni Street, POB 724, Asmara; tel. (1) 202590; fax (1) 126457; e-mail support@tfanus.com.er; internet www.tfanus.com.er; f. 1996; internet service provider.

BROADCASTING

Radio

Voice of the Broad Masses of Eritrea (Dimtsi Hafash): POB 242, Asmara; tel. (1) 120426; fax (1) 126747; govt-controlled; programmes in Arabic, Tigrinya, Tigre, Saho, Oromo, Amharic, Afar, Bilien, Nara, Hedareb and Kunama; Dir-Gen. GHIRMAY BERHE; Technical Dir BERHANE GEREZGIHER.

Voice of Liberty: Asmara; e-mail VoL@selfi-democracy.com; internet selfi-democracy.com; radio programme of the EDP; broadcasts for one hour twice a week.

Television

ERI-TV: Asmara; tel. (1) 116033; e-mail aslmelashe@yahoo.com; f. 1992; govt station providing educational, tech. and information service; broadcasting began in 1993; programming in Arabic, English, Tigre and Tigrinya; broadcasts for eight hours daily; Dir-Gen. ASMELASH ABRAHA.

Finance

(cap. = capital; res = reserves; dep. = deposits; m. = million; brs = branches; amounts in nakfa)

In November 1997 Eritrea adopted the nakfa as its unit of currency, replacing the Ethiopian birr, which had been Eritrea's monetary unit since independence.

BANKING

Central Bank

Bank of Eritrea: 21 Nakfa St 175, POB 849, Asmara; tel. (1) 123033; fax (1) 122091; e-mail kibreabw@boe.gov.er; f. 1993; bank of issue; Gov. KIBREAB W. MARIAM (acting).

Other Banks

Commercial Bank of Eritrea: 208 Liberty Ave, POB 219, Asmara; tel. (1) 121844; fax (1) 124887; e-mail gm.cber@gemel.com.er; f. 1991; cap. 400.0m., res 344.5m., dep. 13,791.6m. (Dec. 2004); Chair. BERHANE ABREHE; Gen. Man. YEMANE TESFAY; 15 brs.

Eritrean Development and Investment Bank: 29 Bedho St, POB 1266, Asmara; tel. (1) 126777; fax (1) 201976; e-mail edib@gemel.com.er; f. 1996; cap. 45m., total assets 194.2m. (Dec. 2003); provides medium- to long-term credit; Chair. HABTEAB TESFATSION; Gen. Man. Dr GOITOM W. MARIAM; 4 brs.

Housing and Commerce Bank of Eritrea: POB 235, Bahti Meskerem Sq., Asmara; tel. (1) 120350; fax (1) 202209; e-mail hcbgm@hcbe.com.er; internet erhcb.com; f. 1994; cap. 293m. (Dec. 2006); finances residential and commercial construction projects and commercial loans; Chair. HAGOS GHEBREHIWET; Gen. Man. BERHANE GHEBREHIWET; 10 brs.

INSURANCE

National Insurance Corporation of Eritrea Share Co (NICE): NICE Bldg, 171 Bidho Ave, POB 881, Asmara; tel. (1) 123000; fax (1) 123240; e-mail nice@nice-eritrea.com; internet www.nice-eritrea.com; f. 1992; partially privatized in 2004; 60% govt-owned; general and life; Gen. Man. ZERU WOLDEMICHAEL.

Trade and Industry

DEVELOPMENT ORGANIZATION

Eritrea Free Zones Authority: Asmara; f. 2001; CEO ARAIA TSEGGAI.

CHAMBER OF COMMERCE

Eritrean National Chamber of Commerce: POB 856, Asmara; tel. (1) 121589; fax (1) 120138; e-mail encc@gemel.com.er.

TRADE ASSOCIATION

Red Sea Trading Corporation: 29/31 Ras Alula St, POB 332, Asmara; tel. (1) 127846; fax (1) 124353; f. 1983; import and export services; operated by the PFDJ; Gen. Man. NEGASH AFWORKI.

UTILITIES

Electricity

Eritrean Electricity Corporation (EEC): POB 911, Asmara; fax (1) 121468; e-mail eeahrg@eol.com.er; Gen. Man. ABRAHAM WOLDEMICHAEL.

Water

Dept of Water Resources: POB 1488, Asmara; tel. (1) 119636; fax (1) 124625; e-mail wrdmlwe@eol.com.er; f. 1992; Dir-Gen. MEBRAHTU EYASSU.

MAJOR COMPANIES

Exploration activities have identified reserves of base and precious metals. About 20 mining companies were involved in mineral exploration in different areas in the early 2010s.

Assab Salt Works: Assab; salt.

Bisha Mining Co.: 1 Mariam Gimby, POB 4276, Asmara; tel. (1) 124941; internet www.bishamining.com; gold and silver; Gen. Man. KEVIN MOXHAM.

Gedem Cement Factory: Massawa; cement.

Margran PLC: POB 1105, Bahti Meskerem; tel. (1) 125004; fax (1) 122395; e-mail margran@eol.com.er; granite.

TRADE UNION

National Confederation of Eritrean Workers (NCEW): Asmara, Eritrea; f. 1979; Sec.-Gen. TEKESTE BAIRE.

Transport

Eritrea's transport infrastructure was severely damaged during the three decades of war prior to independence. International creditors have since provided loans for the repair and reconstruction of the road network and for the improvement of port facilities.

RAILWAYS

The 306-km railway connection between Agordat, Asmara and the port of Massawa was severely damaged during the war of independence and ceased operation in 1975. However, in 1999 an 81-km section of the Asmara–Massawa line (between Massawa and Embatkala) became operational, and in 2001 a further 18-km section, connecting Embatkala and Ghinda, was added. In February 2003 the reconstruction of the entire Asmara–Massawa line was completed. In 2007 work started on the reconstruction of the 124-km railway line west of Asmara to Akordat and Bisha, with the aim of eventually constructing a new international link from Bisha to Kassala, Sudan.

Eritrean Railway: POB 6081, Asmara; tel. (1) 123365; fax (1) 201785; Co-ordinator, Railways Rehabilitation Project AMANUEL GEBRESELLASIE.

ROADS

Eritrea has a long road network for its land base, totalling 18,540 km. Roads that are paved require considerable repair, as do many of the bridges across seasonal water courses destroyed in the war. The programme to rehabilitate the road between Asmara and the port of Massawa was completed in 2000.

SHIPPING

Eritrea has two major seaports: Massawa, which sustained heavy war damage in 1990, and Assab, which has principally served Addis Ababa, in Ethiopia. Under an accord signed between the Ethiopian and Eritrean Governments in 1993, the two countries agreed to share the facilities of both ports. Since independence, activity in Massawa has increased substantially; however, activity at Assab declined following the outbreak of hostilities with Ethiopia in May 1998. At 31 December 2009 Eritrea's registered merchant fleet numbered 13 vessels, with a total displacement of 13,075 grt.

Dept of Maritime Transport: POB 679, Asmara; tel. (1) 189156; fax (1) 186541; e-mail maritime@motc-gov.er; Dir-Gen. GHEBREMEDHIN HABTE KIDANE.

BC Marine Services: 189 Warsay St, POB 5638, Asmara; tel. (1) 202672; fax (1) 12747; e-mail info@bc-marine.com; internet www.bc-marine.com; f. 2000; services include marine consultancy, marine survey and ship management; brs in Assab and Massawa; Dir Capt. NAOD GEBREAMLAK HAILE.

Cargo Inspection Survey Services: St No. 171-5-171, POB 906, Asmara; tel. (1) 120369; fax (1) 121767; e-mail gellatly@eol.com.er.

Eritrean Shipping Lines: 80 Semaetat Ave, POB 1110, Asmara; tel. (1) 120359; fax (1) 120331; e-mail ersl@eol.com.er; f. 1992; provides shipping services in Red Sea and Persian (Arabian) Gulf areas and owns and operates four cargo ships; Gen. Man. TEWELDE TEKESTE.

Maritime Shipping Services Corpn (MASSCO): POB 99, Massawa; tel. (1) 552729; fax (1) 552438; e-mail mssegm@tse.com.er; f. 1991 as Maritime Ship Services Enterprise; est. as a corpn 2006; shipping agents, stevedoring and shorehandling; Gen. Man. SIMON GHEBREGZIABHIER.

CIVIL AVIATION

There are three international airports: at Asmara, Assab and Massawa. There are also eight domestic airports.

Civil Aviation Department: POB 252, Asmara; tel. (1) 124335; fax (1) 124334; e-mail motc.rez@eol.com.er; handles freight and passenger traffic for eight scheduled carriers which use Asmara airport; Dir-Gen. PAULOS KAHSAY.

Eritrean Airlines: 89 Harnet Ave, POB 222, Asmara; tel. (1) 125500; fax (1) 125465; e-mail customer-rel@eritreanairlines.com.er; internet www.flyeritrea.com; CEO KUBROM DAFLA.

Nasair Eritrea: POB 11915, Asmara; tel. (1) 200700; fax (1) 117622; e-mail nasreddin@nasaireritrea.com; internet www.nasaireritrea.com; f. 2006; CEO NASREDDIN IBRAHIM.

Tourism

The Ministry of Tourism is overseeing the development of this sector, although its advance since independence has been inhibited by the country's war-damaged transport infrastructure, and by subsequent conflicts with Ethiopia and other regional tensions. Eritrea possesses many areas of scenic and scientific interest, including the Dahlak Islands (a coralline archipelago rich in marine life), off shore from Massawa, and the massive escarpment rising up from the coastal plain and supporting a unique ecosystem. In 2009 79,334 tourists visited Eritrea. Tourist receipts in that year amounted to US $26m. Since May 2006 it has been necessary for foreign nationals to obtain a permit 10 days in advance in order to travel outside of the capital.

Eritrean Tourism Service Corpn: Asmara; operates govt-owned hotels.

Defence

As assessed at November 2011, Eritrea's active armed forces included an army of about 200,000, a navy of 1,400 and an air force of some 350; reserve forces numbered 120,000. National service is compulsory for all Eritreans between 18 and 40 years of age (with certain exceptions), for a 16-month period, including four months of military training. In September 2000 the UN Security Council approved the establishment of the UN Mission in Ethiopia and Eritrea (UNMEE, comprising 4,200 peace-keeping troops), which was subsequently deployed on the Eritrean side of the two countries' common border. UNMEE's mandate was periodically extended until the end of July 2008, when the UN Security Council adopted Resolution 1827, confirming the mission's termination.

Defence Expenditure: Budgeted at US $80m. in 2010.

Education

Education is provided free of charge in government schools and at the University of Asmara. There are also some fee-paying private schools. Education is officially compulsory for children between seven and 13 years of age. Primary education begins at the age of seven and lasts for five years. Secondary education, beginning at 12 years of age, lasts for as much as six years, comprising a first cycle of two years and a second of four years. According to UNESCO estimates, in 2009/10 primary enrolment included 34% of children in the relevant age-group (boys 36%; girls 31%), while the comparable ratio for secondary enrolment was only 29% (boys 32%; girls 25%). Total government expenditure on education and training in 2006 was estimated at the equivalent of 2.0% of GDP. In 2004/05 there were some 5,500 students enrolled on Bachelors degree courses at the University of Asmara; however, the University of Asmara was officially closed in September 2006. Higher education was henceforth to be provided by six newly established technical institutes, each associated with a relevant government ministry. The institutes provide education in the fields of science, technology, business and economics, social sciences, agriculture and marine training. In late 2010 two new schools were under construction in Gelalu sub-zone.

Bibliography

Abbay, A. *Identity Jilted or Re-imagining Identity? The Divergent Paths of the Eritrean and Tigrayan Nationalist Struggles.* Lawrenceville, NJ, Red Sea Press, 1998.

Bariagaber, A. *Conflict and the Refugee Experience: Flight, Exile, and Repatriation in the Horn of Africa*. Aldershot, Ashgate, 2006.

Bekoe, D. A. (Ed.). *East Africa and the Horn: Confronting Challenges to Good Governance*. Boulder, CO, Lynne Rienner Publishers, 2006.

Bereketeab, R. *Eritrea: The Making of a Nation.* Trenton, NJ, Red Sea Press, 2007.

Cliffe, L., and Davidson, B. (Eds). *The Long Struggle of Eritrea for Independence and Constructive Peace*. Nottingham, Spokesman, 1988.

Connell, D. *Against All Odds: A Chronicle of the Eritrean Revolution.* Trenton, NJ, Red Sea Press, 1993.

Building a New Nation: Collected Articles on the Eritrean Revolution (1983–2002), Vol. 2. Trenton, NJ, Red Sea Press, 2004.

Conversations with Eritrean Political Prisoners. Trenton, NJ, Red Sea Press, 2004.

Historical Dictionary of Eritrea. (2nd Edn). Lanham, MD, The Scarecrow Press, 2010.

Constitutional Commission of Eritrea. *Constitutional Proposals for Public Debate.* Asmara, Adulis Printing Press, 1995.

Denison, E., Ren Yu, G., and Begremedhin, N. *Asmara*. London, Merrell Publishers, 2003.

Doornbos, M., Cliffe, L., and Markakis, J. (Eds). *Beyond Conflict in the Horn: The Prospects of Peace and Development in Ethiopia, Somalia, Eritrea and Sudan*. Lawrenceville, NJ, Red Sea Press, 1992.

Doornbos, M., and Tesfai, A. (Eds). *Post-conflict Eritrea: Prospects for Reconstruction and Development.* Lawrenceville, NJ, Red Sea Press, 1999.

Duffield, M., and Prendergast, J. *Without Troops and Tanks: Humanitarian Intervention in Ethiopia and Eritrea.* Lawrenceville, NJ, Red Sea Press, 1995.

Ellingson, L. *The Emergence of Eritrea, 1958–1992.* London, James Currey Publishers, 1993.

Erlich, H. *The Struggle over Eritrea 1962–78*. Stanford, CA, Hoover Institution, 1983.

Fegley, R. *Eritrea.* Oxford, Clio Press, 1995.

Fukui, K., and Markakis, J. (Eds). *Ethnicity and Conflict in the Horn of Africa.* London, James Currey, 1994.

Gaim, K. *Critical Reflections on the Eritrean War of Independence: Social Capital, Associational Life, Religion, Ethnicity, and Sowing Seeds of Dictatorship.* Trenton, NJ, Red Sea Press, 2008.

Gebregergis, T. *Eritrea: An Account of an Eritrean Political Exile on his Visit to Liberated Eritrea: December 1991–March 1992.* Amsterdam, Liberation Books, 1993.

Habteselassie, B. *The Making of the Eritrean Constitution: the Dialectic of Process and Substance.* Trenton, NJ, Red Sea Press, 2003.

Wounded Nation: How a Once Promising Eritrea was Betrayed and its Future Compromised. Trenton, NJ, Red Sea Press, 2010.

Henze, P. B. *Eritrea's War: Confrontation, International Response, Outcome, Prospects.* Addis Ababa, Shama Books, 2001.

Iyob, R. *The Eritrean Struggle for Independence: Domination, Resistance, Nationalism 1941–93.* Cambridge, Cambridge University Press, 1995.

Jacquin-Berdal, D., and Plaut, M. (Eds). *Unfinished Business: Ethiopia and Eritrea at War*. Trenton, NJ, Red Sea Press, 2005.

Johan, K., and Ezra, G. *Kenisha: The Roots and Development of the Evangelical Church of Eritrea, 1866-1935*. Trenton, NJ, Red Sea, 2011.

Kibreab, G. *Ready and Willing...But Still Waiting: Eritrean Refugees in Sudan and the Dilemmas of Return*. Uppsala, Life and Peace Institute, 1996.

Critical Reflections on the Eritrean War of Independence: Social Capital, Associational Life, Religion, Ethnicity and Sowing Seeds of Dictatorship. Trenton, NJ, Red Sea Press, 2008.

Eritrea: A Dream Deferred. Woodbridge, James Currey, 2009.

Lewis, I. M. (Ed.). *Nationalism in the Horn of Africa*. London, Ithaca Press, 1983.

Maundi, M. O., Zartman, I. W., Khadiagala, G. M., and Nuamah, K. *Getting In: Mediators' Entry into the Settlement of African Conflicts* Washington, DC, United States Institute of Peace Press, 2006.

Mehreteab, A. *Wake Up, Hanna! Reintegration and Reconstruction Challenges for Post-War Eritrea*. Lawrenceville, NJ, Red Sea Press, 2004.

Mengisteab, K., and Yohannes, O. *Anatomy of an African Tragedy: Political, Economic and Foreign Policy Crisis in Post-Independence Eritrea*. Trenton, NJ, Red Sea Press, 2005.

Mesghenna, Y. *Italian Colonialism: A Case Study of Eritrea 1869–1934*. Lund, University of Lund, 1989.

Miran, J. *Red Sea Citizens: Cosmopolitan Society and Cultural Change in Massawa*. Bloomington, IN, Indiana University Press, 2009.

Müller, Tanya. *Making of Elite Women: Revolution and Nation Building in Eritrea*. Leiden, Brill Academic Publishers, 2005.

Murtaza, N. *The Pillage of Sustainability in Eritrea, 1600s–1900s Rural Communities and the Creeping Shadows of Hegemony*. Westport, CT, Greenwood Press, 1998.

O'Kane, D. *Biopolitics, Militarism, and Development: Eritrea in the Twenty-first Century (Dislocations)*. New York, Berghahn Books, 2009.

Negash, T. *Italian Colonialism in Eritrea, 1882–1941: Policies, Praxis and Impact*. Uppsala, Almqvist and Wiksell International, 1987.

No Medicine for the Bite of a White Snake: Notes on Nationalism and Resistance in Eritrea 1890–1940. Uppsala, University Press, 1987.

Eritrea and Ethiopia: The Federal Experience. New Brunswick, NJ, Transaction Publishers, 1997.

Negash, T., and Tronvoll, K. *Brothers at War*. Oxford, James Currey Publishers, 2000.

Eritrea: Revolution at Dusk. Lawrenceville, NJ, Red Sea Press, 2001.

Pateman, R. *Eritrea: Even the Stones are Burning*. Trenton, NJ, Red Sea Press, 1990.

Blood, Land, and Sex: Legal and Political Pluralism in Eritrea. Bloomington, IN, Indiana University Press, 2003.

Pool, D. *From Guerrillas to Government*. Oxford, James Currey Publishers, 2000.

Prouty, C., and Rosenfeld, E. *Historical Dictionary of Ethiopia and Eritrea*. 2nd edn. Lanham, MD, and London, Scarecrow Press, 1994.

Reid, R.(Ed.). *Eritrea's External Relations: Understanding its Regional Role and Foreign Policy*. London, Chatham House, 2009.

Rena, R. *A Handbook on the Eritrean Economy: Problems and Prospects for Development*. Dar es Salaam, New Africa Press, 2006.

Tekle, A. (Ed.). *Eritrea and Ethiopia: From Conflict to Co-operation*. Lawrenceville, NJ, Red Sea Press, 1994.

Tesfagiorgis, M. *Eritrea (Africa in Focus)*. Santa Barbara, CA, ABC-CLIO, 2010.

Tesfamichael, A., and Sebahtu, S. H. *Commercial Fish of the Eritrean Red Sea*. Clacton on Sea, Apex Publishing, 2006.

United Nations. *The United Nations and the Independence of Eritrea*. New York, United Nations Department of Public Information, 1996.

Wolde-Yesus, A. *Eritrea: Root Causes of War and Refugees*. Baghdad, Sinbad, 1992.

Wrong, M. *I Didn't Do It for You: How the World Betrayed a Small African Nation*. London, HarperCollins, 2005.

Yohannes, G. *Challenges of a Society in Transition: Legal Development in Eritrea*. Trenton, NJ, Red Sea Press, 2004.

ETHIOPIA

Physical and Social Geography

G. C. LAST

The Federal Democratic Republic of Ethiopia is a land-locked country in the Horn of Africa, covering an area of 1,133,380 sq km (437,600 sq miles). Ethiopia's western neighbours are Sudan and South Sudan; to the south it has a common border with Kenya; and to the east and south-east lie Djibouti and Somalia. To the north and north-east lies Eritrea.

PHYSICAL FEATURES

Elevations range from around 100 m below sea-level in the Dallol Depression (Kobar Sink), on the north-eastern border with Eritrea, to a number of mountain peaks in excess of 4,000 m above sea-level, which dominate the plateaux and of which the highest is Ras Dashen, rising to 4,620 m.

The southern half of Ethiopia is bisected by the Great Rift Valley, ranging between 40–60 km in width and containing a number of lakes. In the latitude of Addis Ababa, the western wall of the rift turns north and runs parallel to the west coast of Arabia, leaving a wide plain between the escarpment and the Red Sea coast of Eritrea. The eastern wall of the rift turns to the east in the latitude of Addis Ababa, forming an escarpment looking north over the Afar plains. The escarpments are nearly always abrupt, and are broken at only one point near Addis Ababa where the Awash river descends from the rim of the plateau.

The plateaux to the west of the rift system dip gently towards the west and are drained by right-bank tributaries of the Nile system, which have carved deep and spectacular gorges. The plateaux to the north of Lake Tana are drained by the Tekeze and Angareb rivers, headwaters of the Atbara. The central plateaux are drained by the Abbai (Blue Nile) river and its tributaries. The Abbai rises in Lake Tana and is known as the Blue Nile in Sudan. Much of the flood water in the Blue Nile system comes from the left-bank tributaries, which rise in the high rainfall region of south-west Ethiopia. This southern region is also drained by the Akobo, Gilo and Baro rivers, which form the headwaters of the Sobat river. The only river of significance to the west of the Rift Valley that is not part of the Nile system is the Omo, which drains southwards into Lake Turkana and is known in its upper course as the Gibie. The lower trough of the Omo has, in recent years, been the site of interesting archaeological discoveries of early human occupation, pre-dating the early remains at Olduvai in Tanzania. The Rift Valley itself contains a number of closed river basins, including the largest, the Awash, which flows north from the Rift Valley proper into the Afar plain and terminates in Lake Abe. It is in the middle and lower Awash regions of the Rift Valley that even earlier remains of man have been discovered, in the locality of Hadow, below the escarpment to the east of Dessie. The highlands to the east of the Rift are drained south-eastwards by the headstreams of the Webi-Shebelli and Juba river systems.

The location of Ethiopia across a series of major fault lines and its association with earth movements, particularly in the Afar plains, which are related to the continuing drift of the African continent away from the Asian blocks, makes it highly susceptible to minor earth tremors.

CLIMATE, VEGETATION AND NATURAL RESOURCES

Ethiopia lies within the tropics but the wide range of altitude produces considerable variations in temperature conditions, which are reflected in the traditional zones of the *dega* (the temperate plateaux), the *kolla* (hot lowlands) and the intermediate frost-free zone of the *woina dega*. The boundaries between these three zones lie at approximately 2,400 m and 1,700 m above sea-level. Average annual temperature in the *dega* is about 16°C, in the *woina dega* about 22°C and in the *kolla* at least 26°C. A main rainy season covers most of the country during June–August, when moist equatorial air is drawn in from the south and west.

Ethiopia is extremely vulnerable to drought conditions, particularly in the low-lying pastoral areas, and along the eastern escarpment where there is a widespread dependence upon the spring rains (*belg*). The development of cultivation in areas of marginal rainfall has accentuated this problem.

Despite the significant variations in local climates and in the distribution of rainfall, Ethiopia's climatic conditions can be described generally in terms of well-watered highlands and uplands, mostly receiving at least 1,000 mm of rain a year with the exception of the Tigraian plateau, and dry lowlands, generally having less than 500 mm of rain, with the significant exception of the Baro and Akobo river plains in the south-west, which lie in the path of summer rain-bearing winds.

The natural vegetation of the plateaux and highlands above 1,800 m is coniferous forest (notably *zigba* and *tid*), but these forests have now largely disappeared, existing only in the more inaccessible regions of the country. In the south-west higher rainfall, with lower elevations and higher temperatures, has produced extensive broad-leafed rain forests with a variety of species, including abundant *karraro*. Previously densely forested areas in the south-west have now, with the extension of all-weather road systems, been subject to extensive commercial exploitation and the activities of a growing population of traditional cultivators, with devastating impact on the natural vegetation.

Above the tree line on the plateaux are wide expanses of mountain grassland. The highlands are the site of settled agriculture in which some 4m. farmers produce a variety of grain crops. The growth of population and the depletion of resources in forest cover and soil have led to the practice of farming in areas that are very marginal and unreliable in rainfall, notably along the eastern escarpment. This has exacerbated drought and famine conditions. The most important traditional grain crop, teff, used in the highlands for the production of the staple food, injera, has been most seriously affected. This has had a notable impact, as the populations there do not adapt easily to replacement crops (and relief supplies) of maize and rice.

In the lowlands, dependent on rainfall conditions, there is a range of dry-zone vegetation. Extensive natural range-lands, particularly in the Borena and Ogaden plains in the south, are an important resource in Ethiopia and currently support some 30m. head of cattle.

Drought conditions, which began in 1972–73, in association with abnormal conditions affecting the whole Sahel region of Africa, have completely disrupted the pastoral economy in many areas, resulting in a high mortality rate both of humans and livestock and severely depleting vegetation cover.

To add to Ethiopia's problems is the frequent invasion by the so-called 'desert' locust. There are breeding grounds of this insect in the drier regions of the country, but much of the damage is done by large swarms of adults, which can contain more than 25m. locusts, each eating its own weight in vegetation daily, and which originate in the semi-desert areas of Sudan, South Sudan, Saudi Arabia, Somalia and Kenya.

Although the exploitation of gold and copper ores on the Eritrean plateau dates from prehistoric times, relatively little is known of the potential mineral resources of Ethiopia; by the mid-1990s only about one-quarter of the country had been geologically mapped. Probably the area with the highest mineral potential lies in the west and south-west (in the Wollega,

Illubabor and Kaffa regions). There are alluvial gold workings in the Adola area of the Sidamo region, and platinum deposits near Yubdo in the Wollega region. Potentially valuable deposits of potash have been located in the Dallol Depression; their exploitation awaits the development of other infrastructure and effective joint operations between Ethiopia and Eritrea.

Exploration for petroleum was carried out for some years in the Ogaden region without success. More recently, attention has been diverted to the southern borders of Ethiopia. In the Bale region between the rivers Web and Webi-Shebelli, it has been reported that petroleum reserves have been identified. The geothermal power potential of extensive sources in the Afar plain region is being evaluated.

Ethiopia commands excellent potential for the generation of hydroelectric power. A number of plants are in operation along the course of the Awash river, while numerous sites have been identified along the Blue Nile river basin, at which power production could be coupled with irrigation schemes.

POPULATION

According to a census conducted in May 2007, the total population was 73,750,932 (males 37,217,130; females 36,533,802). The population of the capital, Addis Ababa, had increased to 2,739,551, while a further eight towns each had more than 105,000 inhabitants. The growth rates in these larger urban settlements are high. At mid-2012 the UN estimated the population to be 86,538,535, with overall density of population of 76.4 inhabitants per sq km. However, this average conceals a very wide variation among the regions, as might be expected from the multiplicity of natural environments.

The distribution of population generally reflects the pattern of relief. The highlands, having a plentiful rainfall, are the home of settled agriculture and contain nearly all the major settlements. Land more than 2,000 m above sea-level was, in the past, free of the malarial mosquito, a factor contributing to the non-occupation of lowlands that are suitable for farming. However, recent evidence shows that this traditional limit is being breached as average temperatures rise and the mosquito adapts to higher elevations. It would not be unreasonable to assume that 10% of the population live below 1,000 m, 20% at 1,000 m–1,800 m and 70% above the 1,800 m contour line. The distribution of population has been affected by recurrent droughts, which have forced many people to leave their traditional areas in search of emergency aid, and by the erstwhile government policy of resettling famine victims from the former Tigrai and Wollo Administrative Regions in newly established villages in the lowlands of the south-west; additionally, the civil war, which intensified in 1989–91, caused the displacement of large numbers of the population.

The implementation of new administrative regions ('States'), which are based on ethnic distributions, has resulted in movement of minority groups, and the massive recruitment of young men for the war with Eritrea (1998–2000) was likely to have had long-term implications for population growth and distribution.

Recent History

MANICKAM VENKATARAMAN

Based on an earlier article by PATRICK GILKES

THE ETHIOPIAN EMPIRE

Ethiopia's history as an organized and independent polity dates back to the beginning of the second century AD during the Auximite rule in the northern regional state (*killil*) of Tigrai, which covered the present-day northern part of Ethiopia and included parts of Eritrea down to the coast around Massawa and Zula. Conversion to Christianity took place in the fourth century. In the fifth and sixth centuries it extended across the Red Sea, but its core lay in the northern Ethiopian highlands (present-day Tigrai and Eritrea). When Axum collapsed in the eighth century, power shifted south to Lasta, and later to Shoa. In the 16th century, 50 years of conflict with the Muslim sultanate of Adal exhausted both; they fell an easy prey to the Oromos, a pastoral people who expanded from the south.

Ethiopian political history has been marked by constant power struggles for supremacy between ambitious individuals such as Menelik of Shoa, Kassa Hailu of Gondar (named as Emperor Tewodros in 1855–68) and later Kassa Mircha of Tigrai (crowned as Emperor Yohannes IV in 1872–89) and Gobeze of Amhara regions. Internal and external invasions led to instability. While Yohannes IV was fighting the Egyptians, Italians and Sudanese Mahdists on the northern border, Menelik directed his energies to acquire modern armaments and continued Shoan expansion to the east, south and west of Shoa, conquering areas rich in coffee, gold, ivory and slaves. In 1896 he defeated the Italians at the battle of Adwa, but Italy retained control of the northern part of the country to create its colony Eritrea.

The first stage of Ethiopia's modernization was undertaken by Menelik II (1889–1913) and later by Haile Selassie (1930–1974). The creation of modern schools, a professional army, a written Constitution and an elected Parliament were the results of Haile Selassie's efforts. This process was interrupted by the Italian invasion and conquest of 1935–41, but after Ethiopia's liberation, Haile Selassie continued a largely successful policy of centralization. However, Ethiopia remained essentially feudal, with small Amhara-dominated modern sectors in the bureaucracy and in industry. In 1952, after protracted discussions, Eritrea, a UN-mandated territory after the Second World War, was federated with Ethiopia. Severe hardships, which were a result of frequent wars and periodic famine, particularly in Tigrai, were addressed neither adequately by Menelik nor by Haile Selassie and thus caused much resentment among non-Amhara nationalities. Haile Selassie himself preferred to concentrate on international affairs. The Ethiopian capital, Addis Ababa, became the headquarters of the Organization of African Unity (OAU, now the African Union—AU), and the UN Economic Commission for Africa. Selassie's most important ally was the USA: Ethiopia, the main recipient of US aid in Africa in the 1950s and 1960s, provided the USA with a major communications base at Kagnew, in Asmara, the capital of Eritrea.

The incorporation of Eritrea under Selassie's centralized control led to the dismantling of its institutions, including the press, trade unions, political parties and the elected Parliament. In 1962 Eritrea became a province of Ethiopia, igniting the Eritrean struggle for independence. Originally led by the Eritrean Liberation Front (ELF), supported mainly by Muslim pastoralists from lowland areas, by the early 1970s disaffected ELF members had founded the Popular Liberation Forces (renamed the Eritrean People's Liberation Front—EPLF—in 1977), which was more representative of the Tigraian Christian highland agriculturalists.

Long-term weaknesses of the regime included a growing agrarian crisis, inequitable distribution of land and lack of development. Furthermore, the Government forced ethnic nationalities to assimilate into the dominant Amhara nation. More immediately, the costs of the revolt in Eritrea after 1961, drought and famine in Wollo in 1972–74, and, by 1973, Haile Selassie's own near-senility and his failure to designate an heir, fuelled the grievances of the military, students and workers. A series of army mutinies, which commenced in January 1974, were paralleled by civilian strikes. Attempts at reform by a new Prime Minister made little progress, and from June a co-ordinating committee of the armed forces began to arrest leading officials. Haile Selassie was deposed in September, with little dissent, and was murdered the following year. The monarchy was formally abolished in March 1975.

MILITARY RULE

The imperial regime was replaced by the Provisional Military Administrative Council (PMAC), or *Dergue* (Committee), which adopted Marxism as its ideology and declared Ethiopia a socialist state in December 1974. As part of the Government's revolutionary reforms, known as *Ethiopia Tikdem* (Ethiopia First), more than 100 companies were nationalized or partly taken over by the State; trade unions were restructured; rural and urban land was nationalized; thousands of students were dispatched to the countryside as part of a national campaign for development; more than 30,000 local peasant associations were created with responsibility for tax collection, judicial affairs and administration; and similar associations, *kebeles*, were established in towns, with pyramids of higher-level organizations (district, regional and national). In April 1976 the theory of the revolution was outlined in the 'national democratic revolution programme', essentially the work of a Marxist-Leninist group, the All-Ethiopia Socialist Movement (MEISON), which wanted a Soviet-style communist party, but was prepared to accept the need for temporary military rule. Its rival, the Ethiopian People's Revolutionary Party (EPRP), another and more popular Marxist-Leninist grouping, argued for the immediate creation of a civilian government, and also supported the Eritrean struggle. The disputes between these two groups, over ideology and control of the new institutions, intensified into urban terrorism, and spilt over into the PMAC. In February 1977 the first Vice-Chairman of the *Dergue*, Lt-Col Mengistu Haile Mariam, seized power with MEISON support. Mengistu became Head of State and Chairman of the PMAC and launched, originally on behalf of MEISON, the 'red terror' campaign, aimed at eliminating the EPRP. Tens of thousands were killed or tortured, particularly in urban areas. In mid-1977 Mengistu turned against MEISON too and by late 1978 both organizations had been virtually eliminated.

The ideological and power struggles were intensified by a deteriorating military situation in Eritrea, where guerrillas had captured all but five towns, and in the south and south-east where Somalia attempted to take advantage of the weakness of the central administration and the army. In July 1977 Somalia, claiming the Somali-inhabited area of the Ogaden, invaded to support the Western Somali Liberation Front (WSLF) guerrillas, which it had been arming and training. Within five months Somali forces had overrun most of south and south-east Ethiopia, and the town of Harar was under attack. However, the overstretched Somali army ran out of supplies, just as Ethiopia, with Cuban help in training a 300,000-strong militia force, received a massive influx of Soviet military equipment. Somalia, previously a close ally of the USSR, expelled its Soviet military advisers and severed relations with Cuba; Ethiopia, in turn, suspended relations with the USA. In early 1978, with its new weaponry and the help of 16,000 Cuban troops, the Ethiopian army drove out the Somali army.

The Ethiopian army then moved to Eritrea. Within a few months it had retaken most of the towns, forcing the ELF to revert to guerrilla operations, and pushing the EPLF into the far north around the remote town of Nakfa. There the Ethiopian forces lost their momentum, and over several years accumulated serious losses in a series of unsuccessful attacks. Meanwhile, continuing religious, ethnic and ideological differences among the Eritrean movements erupted into civil war in 1981; the EPLF, in alliance with the Tigrai People's Liberation Front (TPLF), forced the ELF contingents into Sudan in 1982, where they were disarmed and later fragmented.

After the military successes of 1978, Mengistu turned his attention to organizing a political party. The Commission for Organizing the Party of the Working People of Ethiopia was established in 1979. Various revolutionary women's, youth, peasant and trade-union associations were founded, and the Workers' Party of Ethiopia was formally inaugurated in September 1984. However, it failed to attract either support or loyalty from the general population, which regarded it as a vehicle of the regime.

ETHNICITY ISSUES AND THE OVERTHROW OF MENGISTU

The rhetoric of the revolution raised expectations among various ethnic groups, particularly Oromos, Somalis, Afars and Tigraians, all of whom were vying for autonomy and/or independence. The Government had one partial success with the Afars when a 'progressive' Afar National Liberation Movement (ANLM) appeared, prepared to accept the PMAC's version of regional autonomy. ANLM members were appointed local administrators, but the speed of progress towards autonomy was unsatisfactory.

By the early 1980s the Oromo Liberation Front (OLF), advocating self-determination for the Oromo people and the use of Oromo culture and language, was gaining support from peasants critical of government efforts to establish co-operatives; originally, the *Dergue*'s principal support had been among Oromo peasantry who had benefited from the land reforms of 1975, aimed at restoring their lands from the Northerners. Most serious for the Government was the success of the TPLF. Although relations between the TPLF and the EPLF were strained for several years in the 1980s, after 1988, when the two groups were once more co-operating, the TPLF was able rapidly to take over the whole of Tigrai region.

The new Constitution of 1987 provided for an 835-seat elected legislature, the National Shengo, and for the creation of several autonomous regions based on ethnicity: Tigrai for the Tigraian people; Dire Dawa for Issa Somalis; the Ogaden region for other Somalis; and Assab for Afars in both Eritrea and Ethiopia. These allowed for elected assemblies with control over health, education, development, finance and taxation. In 1990, following an attempted coup the previous year, Mengistu made further concessions: Ethiopian socialism was abandoned; opposition groups were invited to participate in a unity party; free-market principles replaced economic planning; and peasants were allowed to bequeath land to their children. The peasantry was quick to abandon the highly unpopular enforced 'villagization' policy, and the area of land under cultivation increased significantly.

However, Mengistu's overtures failed to satisfy the TPLF and the EPLF; both were determined to oust him, regarding this as a prerequisite for achievement of their respective aims. Mengistu's military situation deteriorated steadily and Massawa was captured by the EPLF in February 1990, severing supply lines for the army in Eritrea. Disillusionment grew steadily within the army, which previously supported Mengistu owing to his determination to retain Eritrea and his commitment to a united Ethiopia; however, his apparent refusal to accept any political solution was ultimately seen as a liability. The economy was collapsing as fast as the military and political situation. The price of coffee, Ethiopia's sole foreign-exchange earner, was declining, and supplies of cheap Soviet petroleum ceased in mid-1989. The revolution in Eastern Europe precipitated a complete collapse of Ethiopia's overseas alliances, and the loss of critical arms supplies. Mengistu attempted to replace his Soviet allies with Israel, promising to allow the Ethiopian Jews (Falashas) to leave (13,000 had been flown from Sudan to Israel in a secret airlift in 1984); Israel initially provided cluster bombs and anti-guerrilla training, but, under strong US pressure, this support was stopped. However, in May 1991, as the regime collapsed, with government consent the Israelis took control of Addis Ababa airport for 36 hours to evacuate a further 14,000 of the remaining Falasha population.

Once in control of Tigrai region in 1989, the TPLF orchestrated a united front, the Ethiopian People's Revolutionary Democratic Front (EPRDF), with the Ethiopian People's Democratic Movement, a largely Amhara organization the development of which had allowed the TPLF to spread the struggle outside Tigrai region, and which was subsequently renamed the Amhara National Democratic Movement (ANDM). As the EPRDF advanced further south it supported or created other organizations: the Oromo People's Democratic Organization (OPDO), after the OLF refused to join the

EPRDF, and a short-lived officers' movement. The TPLF remained the major element in the front, but its own original demands for self-determination were replaced by its commitment to the removal of Mengistu and the establishment of a democratic government in Addis Ababa.

On 21 May 1991 Mengistu fled to Zimbabwe where he was granted political asylum. On 28 May the EPRDF entered the capital and subsequently established an interim Government. The EPLF attended the founding conference, but as an observer only, to mark Eritrea's de facto independence; it subsequently established a provisional Government in Eritrea pending the holding of a referendum in April 1993, when 99.8% of voters approved independence. *De jure* independence followed in May 1993. Relations with Ethiopia were formalized by a series of agreements covering defence, security, trade and the economy, and on the use of Assab, which was given free port status because of its particular importance to Ethiopia, rendered land-locked by the independence of Eritrea.

THE EPRDF AND FEDERAL POLITICS

In July 1991 the EPRDF convened a national conference attended by representatives of some 20 political organizations to discuss Ethiopia's political future and establish a transitional Government. The EPRDF drafted a national charter providing for an 87-seat Council of Representatives to govern during a two-year transition period. The EPRDF Chairman, Meles Zenawi, was elected Head of State, and the Vice-Chairman of the EPRDF, Tamirat Layne, was appointed Prime Minister. Some 32 political organizations were represented on the Council, with the EPRDF's component parts occupying 32 of the 87 seats. The next largest group on the Council was the OLF with 12 seats. Oromos were allocated a total of 27 seats, but they were divided between five different organizations. The portfolios of the Council of Ministers were similarly distributed, with 17 ministers from seven different organizations being appointed.

The EPRDF made it clear that it would support Eritrean independence, and emphasized self-determination for Ethiopia's various nationalities within a federal system as the answer to the political problem of a multi-ethnic state. The EPRDF originally established 12 self-governing regions with two chartered cities. Following a number of amendments, including the merger of four regions in the south-west, the new Constitution, which came into force in 1995, created nine regional states (*killil*) of Tigrai, Afar, Amhara, Oromia, Benishangul-Gumuz, Southern Peoples, Somali, Gambela and Harari, together with Addis Ababa and Dire Dawa as two administrative councils. The basis of the new states was ethnicity and language, although equally they reflected political power. In accordance with the decentralized governance provided by the charter, the regions were expected, in theory at least, to raise their own funding, but this proved difficult; by the late 2000s the bulk of revenue was still coming from central government sources.

Numerous political parties emerged in the period after 1991, most of which were ethnically based. However, their participation in elections was poor until the May 2005 legislative elections, which for the first time saw a significant increase in participation both by the people as well as by political parties. Notably, since 1992 the EPRDF has been victorious in all elections (regional, constituent assembly and national) and has retained power ever since the overthrow of the *Dergue* regime. As Tigraians constitute only about 5% of the population, the EPRDF fostered parallel political parties such as the Southern Ethiopian People's Democratic Front (SEPDF) with which it could form alliances to manoeuvre for political control. The existence of the EPRDF's OPDO was a major reason for the breakdown in relations with the OLF, despite the latter's position in government (from which it withdrew in 1992). In the months preceding the 1992 elections, there were numerous clashes as the two organizations manoeuvred for position in the Oromo regions. Both also sought to remove other nationalities from their areas.

In 1992–2001 the EPRDF and its supporting parties did extremely well in almost every region, and even in Addis Ababa it repeatedly won the vast majority of the regional seats. After its withdrawal from government in 1992, the OLF attempted to revive guerrilla activity. Most of its fighters were quickly apprehended but small groups continued to operate, and the OLF claimed responsibility for several bomb explosions along the Addis Ababa–Djibouti railway in 1996. Western diplomatic efforts to reconcile the OLF and the EPRDF made little progress, and an OLF congress in April 1998 adopted a firmer stance regarding the idea of an independent Oromo state. With relations between the People's Front for Democracy and Justice (PFDJ—formerly EPLF), the ruling regime in Asmara, and the EPRDF deteriorating as a consequence of the war of 1998–2000, Eritrea began supporting the Ethiopian opposition forces, notably offering the OLF an operating base in Asmara.

In 1999, with Eritrean support, the OLF infiltrated hundreds of Eritrean-trained fighters through Somalia into southern Ethiopia; most had been detained by the end of the year. In October 2000 a conference in Eritrea brought together six Oromo opposition parties, including the OLF and the Islamic Front for the Liberation of Oromia, as the United Liberation Forces of Oromia. The OLF National Congress held in Asmara in December 2004 consolidated relations between the OLF and the Eritrean Government, removing any chance that the OLF might participate in the May 2005 Ethiopian legislative elections.

In early March 2006 four people were injured in a bomb explosion in Addis Ababa. On 27 March one person was killed and at least 15 wounded in a series of bomb attacks in the capital. Explosions were also reported in the town of Jijiga in the east of the country and Gedo in the west, during April–May, killing 11 people. The police suspected the OLF of involvement in these incidents, despite a denial issued by the group in mid-May. In November the OLF indicated that it had approached Kenya, Nigeria and South Africa for help in mediating between itself and the Ethiopian Government to end decades of sporadic conflict in the remote but resource-rich Oromia region. At the same time fighting appeared to be continuing between the OLF and the Government. In March 2007 the Tigrai People's Democratic Movement (TPDM) and the Southern Ethiopian People's Front for Justice and Equality also claimed to have launched attacks against government forces. In April 2008 three people were killed and 18 others were injured in explosions in the capital; in May further blasts were reported, in which several people died. The Government blamed Eritrea and the OLF for the latter incidents. In January 2009 over 200 Ethiopian soldiers were reported to have been killed by the TPDM. Bomb blasts were also reported in April 2010 in the northern region of Adi Haro in which five people were killed and several injured; Eritrea was accused of carrying out the bombings. Furthermore, a series of explosions occurred in Addis Ababa in March 2011; the attacks were blamed on OLF rebels.

Armed opposition to the Government surfaced in several other regional states, including Afar and Gambela, as well as from the externally based Ogaden National Liberation Front (ONLF), formed as a breakaway group from the WSLF in the 1980s. The OLF and the ONLF signed a military co-operation agreement in July 1996, but have made little progress in their demands for greater autonomy and firm commitments for possible independence despite Eritrean support and training since 1998. They claim that the EPRDF has no intention of allowing secession, deliberately making the process lengthy and difficult—secession would require a two-thirds' majority in the regional legislature, a majority vote in a federally organized referendum, and an agreed transfer of power over a three-year period. The ONLF also received support from another Somali organization, the Islamic Union Party (al-Ittihad al-Islam), which has been fighting for an Islamic state in Somalia. Al-Ittihad claimed responsibility for bomb explosions in hotels in Addis Ababa and Dire Dawa in early 1996. The EPRDF responded from 1996 with a series of cross-border attacks into Somalia, aiming to disrupt al-Ittihad and its allies, occupying several towns and villages, and supplying arms to movements opposed to al-Ittihad in Somalia. These operations intensified in 1999 when Eritrea attempted to distract Ethiopia's attention from the war along the Ethio–Eritrean border by supplying weapons to the OLF and various Somali factions opposed to Ethiopia. Ethiopian troops again crossed the Somalia border in early 2001, following increased ONLF activity, and have subsequently been active in Somalia on numerous occasions (including the November 2011 intervention—see below), claiming legitimate security interests. Hostilities continued, and the town of Mustahil was reportedly occupied by the ONLF in June 2009, a claim refuted by the Ethiopian Government. In July the Ogaden National Liberation Army, the armed wing of the ONLF, claimed military successes against Ethiopian forces in several areas of the Ogaden region. Although the Government had signed peace agreements with some factions of the ONLF in 2010, sporadic fighting continued in Ogaden, with the ONLF claiming to have killed 50 Ethiopian soldiers in June 2012; the Ethiopian authorities denied such claims.

The situation in Gambela State deteriorated from late 2002, primarily as a result of the increasingly militant activities of Anywaa nationalist groups, concerned at what they saw as the growing influxes and regional influence of the Nuer. A series of clashes between Nuer and Anuak communities broke out in Itang in July 2002 and continued into 2003, with dozens of people killed. From mid-2003 attacks on regional civil servants, particularly highlanders, escalated. Tensions between Anywaa and the highlander community culminated in the massacre of hundreds of Anywaa men in Gambela town with the alleged participation of the Ethiopian army. In December eight officials from the office of the UN High Commissioner for Refugees and the Federal Agency for Refugee and Returnee Affairs were killed while surveying a new site for Nuer refugees 25 km from Gambela town, apparently by Anuak militants opposed to the relocation. Angered at the killings, Gambela townspeople targeted Anuak residents, and, according to government sources, 56 people were killed, 74 wounded and 410 houses were razed to the ground, before government forces intervened. (Opposition sources stated that the actual casualty figures were much higher.) The intervention of federal security forces in pursuit of suspected militants led to 37 arrests relating to the killings in Gambela town, and an estimated 10,000 Anuak fled to Pochalla in neighbouring Sudan in early January 2004. Intensive military and political efforts by the federal Government appeared to have calmed, if not resolved, the situation by mid-2004, and by June 7,900 of those who had fled Ethiopia in January were reported to have returned to the region. In late 2004 a Commission of Inquiry led by the President of the Federal Supreme Court placed a proportion of blame for some of the killings in late 2003 on the collusion and inappropriate action of the military and police. The situation improved with the disarming of Murle and Lou tribesmen. However, OLF incursions were reported, particularly near the Afar–Gambela border, supported by neighbouring Eritrea. The Government responded in October 2008 by initiating a crackdown on Oromo politicians, accusing some of being members of the OLF. In separate incidents, Anuak armed groups reportedly ambushed and killed 19 civilians in March 2012 and several more were killed allegedly over the issue of land grab and the Government's villigization policy.

ELECTIONS AND GOVERNMENT CONTROL

Elections for a Constituent Assembly in June 1994 demonstrated that the EPRDF had become a disciplined, tightly organized and highly centralized front using government resources to great effect. In December the Constituent Assembly ratified the draft Constitution (including controversial articles on the right to self-determination and secession, and state ownership of land) with little change from the approved draft, although recognition of *Shari'a* law for Muslims was included, following a major demonstration in Addis Ababa.

The final stage in the creation of the Federal Democratic Republic of Ethiopia came in May 1995 with elections to the lower house of the Federal Parliamentary Assembly (the House of People's Representatives) and to the regional State Councils, which elect representatives to the upper house of the Federal Parliamentary Assembly (the House of the Federation). Executive power lies with a Prime Minister, chosen by the majority party in the Federal Parliamentary Assembly. The EPRDF and its allies won an overwhelming victory, and Meles Zenawi, as Chairman of the EPRDF and of the TPLF, which remained the dominant element in the EPRDF, became Prime Minister in August 1995; Dr Negasso Gidada of the OPDO was elected President. In Tigrai region, the TPLF took all seats for both the federal and state assemblies; EPRDF parties were equally successful in the Amhara, Oromia and Southern regions. Despite Addis Ababa's reputation as a centre for opposition, the EPRDF won all 92 local assembly seats; independents secured only two of the city's 23 Federal Parliamentary Assembly seats. Overall, the election results were seriously undermined by the decision of most opposition parties to boycott, claiming insufficient access to media, extensive arrests and harassment of their officials and closure of party offices. International observers generally agreed with the criticisms; there was a consensus that, while the elections represented an advance on past experience, they were not entirely free or fair.

The EPRDF continued its dominance in the 2000 legislative elections. Opposition parties claimed numerous irregularities, including physical abuse, intimidation of monitors and vote-rigging. International observers largely accepted opposition complaints and, as in 1995, classified the elections as neither free nor fair. The OPDO won the largest number of seats in the House of People's Representatives, taking 178 of 546 seats available; the ANDM obtained 134 seats and the TPLF 38. In elections to the House of the Federation opposition parties enjoyed some success, although the EPRDF coalition parties won by huge margins in their respective regions. In other regional states, pro-EPRDF parties all secured majorities, although there were again claims of extensive voting irregularities. In February 2004 the Ethiopian Somali Democratic League won a majority of seats in local elections, which were finally held for the first time in 48 out of 51 districts of Somali State, with the opposition Western Somali Democratic Party taking seats in several districts.

Until mid-2005 EPRDF control of the political process and of political debate kept the opposition in disarray. The Council of Alternative Forces for Peace and Democracy in Ethiopia (CAFPDE), bringing together some 30 groups, was established in 1993, following a conference in Paris, France. CAFPDE finally achieved official registration in July 1996, and was a major critic of EPRDF policies on land, rents and leases, the economy and human rights. However, EPRDF pressure and its control of the media, coupled with CAFPDE's own divisions and weakness, limited its impact. An attempt to provide an alternative umbrella opposition grouping came when eight organizations met in Paris in September 1998 and formed the Coalition of Ethiopian Opposition Political Organizations (CEOPO). It included groups based both in Ethiopia and abroad, but the choice of prominent anti-EPRDF exiles for its leadership meant it did not participate in the May 2000 elections. A new opposition coalition, the United Ethiopian Democratic Forces (UEDF), emerged in March 2003. In February 2004 senior members of the UEDF held discussions with Prime Minister Meles on a range of issues relating to the May 2005 legislative elections. They requested changes to the National Electoral Board (NEB) and to the electoral law, the investigation and compensation of past abuses and access for international observers. In May 2004 the UEDF presented Meles with a detailed critique of existing 'first-past-the-post' electoral legislation, and by mid-year arrangements for observers from the AU had been agreed. By September a new party—Rainbow Ethiopia: Movement for Democracy and Social Justice—emerged, led by two prominent Ethiopian academics. By October Rainbow Ethiopia, together with the All Ethiopia Unity Party (previously the All Amhara People's Organization), the Ethiopian Democratic Unity Party (a merger of the Ethiopian Democratic Party and the Ethiopian Democratic Union), and the Ethiopian Democratic League, had jointly formed the Coalition for Unity and Democracy (CUD).

Alliance formation was thus a notable feature of the May 2005 legislative elections at which the CUD and the UEDF competed against the EPRDF. Although it brought about a dynamic change in Ethiopia, the two opposition alliances could not reach agreement on the fundamental political issues, namely the Ethiopian state and its institutions. Determined to open up the political process prior to the elections, the

Government sanctioned the conduct of live televised debates between the EPRDF and opposition parties on all aspects of governance and economic and social policy. While the pre-election scenario was largely peaceful, the aftermath was highly controversial. Notably, competing claims were made by the opposition and the ruling party on the vote-counting process where 299 constituencies were disputed. The final results, which were declared on 5 September by the NEB, suggested that the CUD had made significant inroads in rural areas of Amhara, winning strong support in much of Gojjam, Gondar and Simien Shoa, as well as some parts of the south. The UEDF, meanwhile, gained strongholds in Oromia and the Southern region. EPRDF-allied organizations dominated the vote in the smaller and border regions of Gambela, Benishangul-Gumuz, Harari and Afar. While the opposition took a combined total of 172 seats (the CUD 109, the UEDF 52 and the Oromo Federalist Democratic Movement—OFDM 11), an increase of 160 seats compared with the elections in 2000, the ruling EPRDF won 327 seats with 67.8% of the votes. The CUD refused to accept the final results, and in early October 100 CUD deputies boycotted the opening of the Federal Parliamentary Assembly and subsequently declined to take up their seats.

Post-election demonstrations deteriorated into violence in early June and November 2005, leading to the intervention of police and military personnel, whose forceful response resulted in several deaths, hundreds of injuries and the detention of thousands of CUD members in centres at Zwai and Sendafa. Several opposition leaders, including the head of the CUD, Hailu Shawel, were placed under house arrest and prevented from travelling overseas. In mid-December they, along with 114 others, were charged with treason and attempted genocide, a move condemned by the USA, the European Union (EU) and international human rights organizations. However, in mid-July 2006 38 of those arrested were pardoned and freed from prison, just days after being given life sentences over the election protests.

In October 2007 divisions within the Oromo National Congress (ONC, which was supported by the EPRDF) led to the creation of a breakaway party, the Oromo People's Congress. By March 2008 approximately 150 of the elected opposition members of parliament had assumed their seats. By-elections held in April resulted in an overwhelming victory for the ruling EPRDF, which secured 38 of the 39 contested parliamentary seats and 137 of the 138 council seats in Addis Ababa, while the CUD won the remaining seat in both cases. Concurrent local elections followed a similar pattern, with the EPRDF reportedly taking control of over 3.5m. of the 3.6m. elective seats. However, most of the opposition coalition parties boycotted the elections owing to alleged malpractice and intimidation by the Government. In June the CUD was renamed the Unity for Democracy and Justice Party (ANDENET) under the leadership of Birtukan Mideksa, hitherto Vice-President of the CUD, who, after being pardoned along with other opposition leaders for involvement in the post-election protests, was subsequently re-arrested in December on the same charges. (She was released in October 2010, following the May elections, after serving five years in jail.) In April 2009 the Government arrested 40 individuals, mostly Amhara with military backgrounds, who they claimed were secretly members of a new opposition party, the Movement for Justice, Freedom and Democracy (Ginbot 7), which had adopted a platform sanctioning any means, including violence, to effect political change. Ginbot 7 had been founded in May 2008 in the USA by Dr Berhanu Nega, one of the opposition leaders in the 2005 elections.

The EPRDF secured a resounding victory in the 23 May 2010 general election, winning 499 of the 547 elective seats, while parties allied to the EPRDF took control of a further 46 seats. A weak and divided opposition struggled to maintain a unified front against the ruling party and failed to attract support from the electorate. Notably, a UEDF-led opposition alliance, the Ethiopia Federal Democratic Unity Forum (FORUM), which included the ANDENET and the OFDM among others, only obtained a single seat in the legislature, compared with the 172 opposition seats won in 2005. The FORUM was hampered by internecine differences regarding ideological and organizational beliefs. Demonstrating the lack of unity within the opposition movement, the Somali Democratic Alliance Forces withdrew from the coalition before the election date, while the Ethiopian Democratic Unity Movement departed following the alliance's disastrous electoral performance. A total of 93.4% of the 32m. registered voters was reported to have participated in the poll, and, contrary to expectations, polling was overwhelmingly peaceful both in the run-up to and on the day of the election.

The EPRDF argued that its victory was due to the Government's record of strong economic growth; however, Human Rights Watch accused the Government of using threats and 'months of repression' to ensure its success. Observers noted that the election process was not as free and open as the 2005 campaign. The conduct of the 2010 elections was criticized by the EU and by opposition political parties, including those based outside of Ethiopia (notably Ginbot 7). AU observers endorsed the results, despite some irregularities. In May 2010 members of the Ethiopian diaspora established Ethiopian Satellite Television (ESAT), based in the USA, serving as a further platform to publicize opposition to the Government.

The much-awaited internal restructuring of the EPRDF took place at the 10th party congress in September 2010. Some senior members of the party resigned, while Hailemariam Desalegn, Chairman of the South Ethiopian People's Democratic Movement, was elected as Vice-Chairman of the EPRDF. A five-year Growth and Transformation Plan was conceived during the congress and was formally announced when the House of the Federation reconvened in October. Meles also reorganized the Council of Ministers in that month, notably appointing Desalegn as Deputy Prime Minister and Minister of Foreign Affairs. Furthermore, several ministries were restructured and a new Ministry of the Civil Service was created.

THE DEATH OF MELES ZENAWI

During mid-2012 rumours persisted that Prime Minister Meles was suffering from ill health, and his failure to attend the AU summit meeting in Addis Ababa in July compounded the suspicions of many observers. On 21 August it was announced that Meles had died the previous evening while receiving medical treatment in Belgium. Under the terms of the Constitution, Desalegn was immediately sworn in as Acting Prime Minister and in mid-September he was elected to replace Meles as Chairman of the EPRDF. On 20 September Desalegn was formally sworn in as Prime Minister.

HUMAN RIGHTS

Human rights continue to be a contentious issue, with international and local human rights organizations voicing serious criticisms, many of which were loudly reiterated following the Addis Ababa killings in early June 2005 and allegations of repression during the 2010 election campaign. Furthermore, the adoption of a new media law in July 2008 and the controversial Proclamation for the Registration and Regulation of Charities and Societies in January 2009 also drew criticism from several quarters. The media law, despite its positive aspects of the removal of censorship of private media and the detention of journalists suspected of infringement of the law, is viewed by critics and the opposition as a violation of the right to information. The proposed Charities and Societies Proclamation, aimed at promoting financial transparency and accountability to stakeholders, is seen by human rights groups as a controlling mechanism of civil society groups. Since 1992 reports by the Ethiopian Human Rights Council have detailed alleged extrajudicial killings, disappearances and numerous cases of arbitrary arrest and imprisonment. Amnesty International and Human Rights Watch have condemned detentions without trial, disappearances and the increasing use of torture. Journalists were among those arrested in November 2005 and all private newspapers that had criticized the Government in connection with the elections were suspended from operating, according to Amnesty International. Many released prisoners continue to suffer from intimidation and harassment, with some choosing to leave the country.

In March 2005 Human Rights Watch issued a report detailing alleged harassment and detentions in Oromia, in the run-up to the national elections. According to Amnesty International, hundreds of people detained in November 2005 were still incarcerated during 2006 without trial or charge, together with others accused of OLF membership. More recently, according to Amnesty International, Bekele Jirata, the General Secretary of the OFDM and dozens of others from the Oromo ethnic group were arrested in Addis Ababa and parts of the Oromo region; some of the detainees were accused of financially supporting the OLF.

In the wake of the Ethiopian offensive in Somalia, in 2006 international human rights groups pressed the Ethiopian Government to release details of detainees from 19 countries held at secret prisons, where US agents allegedly carried out interrogations of suspected terrorists. These foreign nationals were eventually released, although a Canadian of Ethiopian origin, Bashir Makhtal, remained rendered, accused of being a member of the ONLF (which the Ethiopian Government considers to be a terrorist organization). In August 2009 Makhtal was found guilty of charges related to terrorism and was sentenced to life imprisonment.

Meanwhile, in April 2007 the ONLF killed 65 Ethiopians and nine Chinese citizens in an attack on a petroleum exploration field operated by a Chinese company. The rebel group accused the Ethiopian army of moving nomads away from their grazing lands in order to prospect for oil. The Ethiopian Government suspected Eritrea of supporting the ONLF attack. In April 2008 it was reported that several ONLF members who had allegedly been involved in the attack had been arrested. Also in April 2007 another attack attributed to the ONLF occurred in Jijiga, which killed several people and injured the President of the Ogaden region and leader of the Somali People's Democratic Party, Abdullahi Hassan. In late July the International Committee of the Red Cross was ordered to leave the Ogaden region by the Ethiopian Government, which accused the humanitarian organization of 'collaborating with the enemy'. The ONLF alleged that the Government was imposing a food blockade on the region. In May 2010 the ONLF announced that it had killed 94 soldiers and seized an army base at Malqaqa, between Jijiga and Harar, claims that the Government refuted, instead reporting that 59 ONLF rebels had been killed in the attack. In a further raid two weeks later, the ONLF declared that it had captured the Hilala gas field in eastern Ogaden, a statement that was again denied by the Government. In September it was reported that Ethiopian troops had killed 123 ONLF rebels and that many more were surrounded. Meanwhile, in April the WSLF signed a peace agreement with the Ethiopian Government. Similarly, following a split within the ONLF, one faction, led by Salahadin Abdurahim Maow, signed a peace accord with the Government in October, agreeing to abide by the Constitution and thereby ending several decades of armed conflict. Conversely, the other faction of the ONLF, headed by Mohammed Omar Osman, appeared determined to continue its struggle. In the mean time, Ethiopian troops supporting the Somali Transitional National Government were accused of committing serious violations of international humanitarian law against civilians.

In March 2002 violence erupted in the Southern Nations, Nationalities and Peoples State between rival ethnic groups and the security forces. According to official figures, 128 people were killed in the disturbances at Tepi; according to Amnesty International up to 200 demonstrators, protesting against administrative changes, were shot dead by police. Opposition sources initially claimed that as many as 1,000 were killed. The EU subsequently demanded a 'transparent, public and open' inquiry into the incidents and expressed its concern that a large number of those believed to have been killed were the victims of 'revenge attacks' by local police officers. In August some 90 state employees, including 41 police-officers, were arrested for their roles in the violence. Meanwhile, in May, in Awasa, the capital of Sidama zone, hundreds of protesters were arrested after another demonstration over planned administrative changes was forcibly dispersed, with as many as 35 people killed by the police. In response to international disquiet, the Southern regional Government established an inquiry, which resulted in extensive changes and a planned restructuring of the regional police. In June 2012 disagreement over the issue of whether Awasa should be a regional or federal seat triggered violent confrontation between rival groups, resulting in an unknown number of deaths.

The continued delays over the trials of senior officials of the former regime raised comment, although few disagreed with the decision to charge them with crimes against humanity. In February 1994 Ethiopia requested the extradition of Mengistu, but the Zimbabwean Government consistently refused to grant this, and in March 2001 granted him permanent residence; in November 1999 South Africa refused an extradition request while Mengistu was receiving medical treatment on its territory. The trial of 69 former senior officials (23 *in absentia*, including Mengistu) on charges of crimes against humanity and war crimes began in December 1994, although proceedings were adjourned on numerous occasions. The trial finally concluded in December 2006 with the conviction of more than 50 individuals, including Mengistu, who continued to be protected from extradition by the Zimbabwean Government.

The 1995 Constitution provided for the establishment of a human rights commission and the post of ombudsman. Legislation approving both bodies was finally adopted in 2000, and a Human Rights Commissioner and Ombudsman were appointed in late 2004. In January 2009 the Proclamation for the Registration and Regulation of Charities and Societies was approved by Parliament. Its provisions included severe restrictions on the amount of foreign funding that Ethiopian civil society organizations working on human rights-related issues could receive from abroad (no more than 10% of total revenues). It would also lead to the establishment of a Civil Societies Agency with sweeping authority over organizations carrying out work on human rights and conflict resolution in Ethiopia. Another piece of draft legislation—an Anti-Terrorism Proclamation law—was submitted by the Council of Ministers and was adopted into law in July. According to Human Rights Watch, the proposed legislation, being premised on an extremely broad and ambiguous definition of terrorist activity, could permit the Government to repress a wide range of constitutionally and internationally protected rights. Human Rights Watch noted that, if implemented as currently drafted, the proposed law could provide the Ethiopian Government with a potent instrument with which to crack down on political dissent, including peaceful political demonstrations and public criticisms of government policy that were deemed supportive of armed opposition activity. It would permit long-term imprisonment and even the death penalty for 'crimes' bearing no resemblance to terrorism, as customarily defined. It would in certain cases deprive defendants of the right to be presumed innocent before being proved guilty, and of protections against use of evidence obtained through torture. The approval of this law would have serious implications within the wider context of political repression, suppression of free speech, an independent civil society, the impunity conferred on security forces, and the potential for consolidation of the ruling party's power following the 2010 elections. According to Human Rights Watch, more than 200 ethnic Oromos were detained without charge in March 2011. Government sources denied this allegation, claiming that those arrested were OLF members. In June, invoking the anti-terrorism law, the Government designated the OLF, the ONLF and the militant Islamist Somali organization al-Shabaab ('the Youth') as terrorist groups. In January 2012 the Federal High Court convicted five people, including three journalists, under the anti-terrorism law. The 2012 Amnesty International report criticized the arrests and detention of journalists as an attempt by the authorities to curb freedom of expression.

EPRDF DIVISIONS AND DOMESTIC POLITICAL ISSUES

In March 2001 major divisions emerged within the TPLF central committee and among senior members and politburo members of the EPRDF, of which the TPLF was the leading party. After the signing of a peace agreement with Eritrea in December 2000 (see below), the EPRDF commenced a comprehensive audit of its 10 years in power, preceded by a similar evaluation in its component parties. The extensive self-awareness (*gimgema*) sessions within the TPLF's central committee led to detailed criticisms of government policies. Critics, who included several of the leading ideologues in the TPLF, argued that the Government had subverted the Tigraian revolution, abandoning its Marxist principles and shifting from democratic centralism to bourgeois democracy; it accused Meles of 'selling out to capitalism and western powers'. Furthermore, Meles was criticized over political liberalization, devolution and federalism. The disagreements were fierce, and Meles survived a motion of no confidence in March 2001 by just five votes. His opponents, who included Siye Abraha, a former Minister of Defence, and Gebru Asrat, President of Tigrai State, were ousted from the TPLF central committee, as well as from their official government positions. The Government subsequently used claims of corruption to take action against Siye and other dissident government officials and business executives, many of whom remained in detention in mid-2005. The issue of corruption had initially been raised in September 2000 in President Gidada's New Year message, and a central anti-corruption office was established in November of that year as part of the civil service reform programme.

During 2001 Meles appealed to the other parties in the EPRDF—the ANDM, the OPDO and the SEPDF—for support. The OPDO and the SEPDF leaderships proved lukewarm, and later in the year both Kumsa Demksa, President of Oromia State and Secretary-General of the OPDO, and Abate Kisho, President of the Southern Nations, Nationalities and Peoples State, were removed from their posts after *gimgema* sessions, although the former was later rehabilitated.

Another of those dismissed from the OPDO was President Gidada, who was also expelled from the EPRDF, although he was allowed to complete his term of office. He was succeeded as President in October 2001 by Lt Girma Wolde Giorgis, a former President of the Parliament during the reign of Haile Selassie and a member of the House of People's Representatives since 1995. Prior to the expiry of his presidential term, Gidada accused the Government of embarking on a campaign of propaganda against him and complained of pressure from Meles. The OPDO lost 22 of the 27 members of its central committee, and several defected to the OLF. Among them was Almaz Meko, the Speaker of the House of the Federation, who was replaced in early 2004 by Mulatu Teshome, also an Oromo. The Minister of Defence, Gen. Abadula Gameda, was appointed Chairman of the OPDO, but difficulties persisted. After the student disturbances in Oromia State in March and April 2002 (see above), a considerable number of OPDO officials were detained and accused of links with the OLF.

The five-year Growth and Transformation Plan (GTP), which was launched in October 2010, placed great emphasis on the development of agriculture, industry and infrastructure. Increasing industrial investment from the People's Republic of China and India and generating higher levels of remittances were additional goals of the GTP. Also planned was a reorganization of the EPRDF, in order to establish it as a national party, rather than a regional front, with the aim of converting the ethnically based TPLF, ANDM, OPDO and SEPDF parties into regional branches of a central EPRDF. The informal influence of the political party *vis-à-vis* a bureaucratized and professionalized state sector, however, seemed to have declined markedly, with the bureau of capacity building taking over responsibilities for popular mobilization, both political and developmental.

In recent years, the suspected presence of radical elements of Islam and of an al-Qa'ida cell in the country has led to the Government's relations with Ethiopian Muslims becoming increasingly strained. There have been protests by Muslims regarding alleged government interference in their religious affairs in several parts of the country, including Addis Ababa. In March 2012 it was reported that more than 10 people had been killed in a violent incident in the Arsi zone of Oromia State following the arrest of an Islamic cleric.

EXTERNAL AFFAIRS

Internationally, the EPRDF has continued to maintain good relations with the USA and with European powers, despite difficulties associated in recent years with the Ethiopia-Eritrea Boundary Commission and the 2005 elections. Ethiopia remains one of the larger beneficiaries of EU infrastructure support and has been an important focus of the EU partnership programme, together with rural development programmes and projects to increase agricultural exports. Significant co-operation on food aid, poverty alleviation programmes and security also exists. Ethiopia and the EU signed a new country strategy paper in December 2007 for 2008–13, with a total budget of €644m. In July 2009 Prime Minister Meles, who attended the G8 summit in Italy, said the $20,000m. pledge by the summit would help African nations effectively to implement the New Partnership for Africa's Development. Human Rights Watch has noted that the Ethiopian Government is highly dependent on donor assistance, but donor governments—especially the USA and the United Kingdom—have largely refused to criticize repression in Ethiopia, viewing the Government therein as an ally in the US-led 'war on terror'. Trade relations with the United Kingdom improved in June 2011 with the signing of a double taxation agreement and subsequent visits to Ethiopia by British trade delegations in March 2012.

Relations with Sudan deteriorated sharply in 1995, following apparent Sudanese complicity in the attempted assassination of President Mubarak of Egypt in Addis Ababa in June. Relations have, however, steadily improved since 1998, following Ethiopia's conflict with Eritrea; Eritrea had been supporting Sudanese opposition movements since 1994. A series of development and security agreements between Sudan and Ethiopia were signed prior to the signing of the 2005 Comprehensive Peace Agreement that ended Sudan's civil war after more than 21 years, although implementation of these has been slow; road links have been upgraded to allow Ethiopian use of Port Sudan, and Ethiopia has become a substantial purchaser of Sudanese petroleum, easing pressure on the port of Djibouti. New agreements were also signed during the Ethiopia-South Sudan consultation forum, held in Addis Ababa in June 2008, aimed at strengthening existing co-operation in areas of trade, education, transport and capacity-building sectors; hydro-power and irrigation projects between Ethiopia, Sudan and Egypt, in conjunction with British and French companies, were being considered. In 2009 the first meeting of the Ethio-Sudan Joint Economic and Trade Committee was held with the purpose of discussing ways to strengthen further legal trade through free trade zone and border trade agreements. Sudan currently meets some 70% of Ethiopia's petroleum demand. The Committee meeting focused on the need to enhance bilateral co-operation in electricity, telecommunications and investment. In January 2010, during a meeting of the Ethiopia-Sudan border commission, both countries signed agreements to increase their co-operation in several areas, including security, trade, health and agriculture. The signing in May 2012 of an accord on the extradition of criminals symbolized a further strengthening of bilateral relations.

The outcome of the January 2011 referendum in South Sudan, in which secession from Sudan was overwhelmingly approved, was cautiously welcomed by Ethiopia. The Ethiopian Government was keen to maintain good relations with Sudan, owing to its dependence on Sudanese petroleum and fears of closer Sudan-Eritrea ties. Ethiopia's balanced approach to the secession was welcomed by both Sudan and South Sudan, and the Addis Ababa Agreement was signed in June in which Ethiopia agreed to deploy over 4,200 peace-keeping forces, supported by the UN Security Council, in the contested border region of Abyei. Ethiopian peace-keepers were already in operation in Sudan as part of the joint AU-UN hybrid peace-keeping operation in Darfur (UNAMID).

Regionally, Ethiopia has adopted an assertive role, heading efforts to foster a peace settlement in Somalia, and has supported efforts to give the Djibouti-based Intergovernmental Authority on Development (IGAD), which now includes Djibouti, Eritrea (membership suspended since 2007), Ethiopia, Kenya, Sudan, South Sudan, Somalia and Uganda, a more active political and security role, including mediation in the conflicts in Somalia and Sudan. Despite IGAD's effectiveness being severely limited, in view of its internal relationships, particularly the poor relations of Eritrea with Ethiopia and Sudan, it voiced serious concerns over Eritrea's role in the region and supported Ethiopia's efforts in Sudan. In April 2007

IGAD was accused of supporting Ethiopia's intervention in Somalia, which led to Eritrea's withdrawal from its membership. Meles has supported US proposals for an AU peace-keeping force, and backed both the US-led 'war on terror' and the war against Iraq. Meles also made a successful visit to the United Kingdom in February 2003, and was appointed a senior member of the British Prime Minister's Commission for Africa. Addis Ababa, previously the headquarters of the OAU, has continued in the same role for the AU, with an opening summit in 2003 followed by a meeting in July 2004 attended by the then UN Secretary-General, Kofi Annan. Ethiopia has established close relations with Israel, formed closer links with Saudi Arabia, and signed a security agreement with Yemen in October 1999.

Relations with Djibouti appeared to be consolidated when Djibouti replaced Assab as Ethiopia's main outlet to the sea, and with the election of Ethiopian-born Ismaïl Omar Guelleh as Djibouti's new President in May 1999. However, relations deteriorated after the Dubai Port Authority took over the management of Djibouti port in 2000. This increased capacity, but attempts to raise tariffs resulted in disagreements between the two countries. Djibouti's improved relations with Eritrea from 2000 were also of concern.

Differences also arose over Djibouti's organization of a Somali national reconciliation conference at Arta, Djibouti, in 2000, which led to the establishment of a Somali Transitional National Assembly (TNA) and a Transitional National Government (TNG). Ethiopia was unimpressed by the election of a President unwilling to engage with the self-proclaimed 'Republic of Somaliland', with which Ethiopia had close relations. The TNA made little effort to reach accommodation with the political elements excluded from the Djibouti conference, including 'Puntland'. With Ethiopian support, these elements subsequently established the Somali Reconciliation and Restoration Council (SRRC), which aimed to overthrow the TNG. While Ethiopia accepted the idea of a single Somali state excluding 'Somaliland', it wished for an alternative to the TNG and remained concerned by Islamist support for the Somali President, Abdulkassim Salad Hasan; the upsurge of guerrilla activity by the ONLF in Ethiopia's Somali State in 2002; and by Eritrea's decision to recognize the TNG and provide it with arms in early 2002. Ethiopia backed IGAD proposals for another reconciliation conference, which finally opened at Eldoret, Kenya, in October 2002. However, Ethiopian military involvement in Somalia in 2007 fuelled widespread criticism of Ethiopia among Djibouti's majority Somali-speaking population. Despite this, Djiboutian President Guelleh attended the 2007 AU summit held in Ethiopia and supported the African Union Mission to Somalia (AMISOM)—a peace-keeping operation established by the AU in January 2007. Bilateral relations improved following the commencement in June 2011 of electricity exports from Ethiopia to Djibouti and the signing of a memorandum of understanding in February 2012 to construct a new oil pipeline from South Sudan linking Ethiopia to Djibouti.

Relations with Kenya have remained cordial, with Ethiopia exploring the possibility of using Mombasa as a port; however, OLF activity along the border led to a number of cross-border operations and to several clashes between Ethiopian militia and Kenyan security forces in 2000 and 2001. Significant numbers of OLF fighters were reported to have been detained by Kenya in June 2004, with Ethiopian incursions into northern Kenya drawing protests in early 2005. In mid-2006 at least 50 people were reported to have been killed on both sides of the border in renewed clashes between the Ethiopian and Kenyan pastoralist tribes, exacerbated by prolonged drought in the region and the resulting decimation of livestock. Conflict resurfaced between communities living in the Lake Turkana border region in early June 2011, leading to the signing of a bilateral water-sharing framework agreement together with accords on agriculture and co-operative development. A jointly financed hydroelectric power project, Gibe III, was under construction in mid-2012, despite concerns over funding and protests by environmental organizations (including the UN Environment Programme). In March 2012 the large-scale Lamu transportation corridor project was launched as part of a move further to boost cross-border trade and transportation throughout the region. In June Ethiopia and Kenya agreed to establish five new joint security camps along their border to enhance peace in the area.

Conflict with Somalia

Ethiopia strongly supported the election of Col Abdullahi Yussuf Ahmed as Somali President in January 2005. As President of the autonomous region of 'Puntland', Yussuf had previously enjoyed Ethiopian support in his attempts to defeat armed Islamist militias operating in the region. The new Transitional Federal Government (TFG—the successor to the TNG) was relocated to Somalia from Kenya in mid-2005 but failed to gain a strong foothold outside of the towns of Baidoa and Jowhar. In March Meles joined with other IGAD leaders in an offer to send peace-keeping troops to Somalia; Meles' intervention was vehemently opposed by a large section of the Somali population, particularly in the capital, Mogadishu. The Ethiopian authorities grew increasingly concerned for the TFG's future in 2006. In January fighting erupted in Mogadishu between the Union of Islamic Courts (UIC) militia, accused by Ethiopia of having links with the al-Qa'ida (Base) organization of Saudi-born Islamist Osama bin Laden, and an alliance of former militia leaders and TFG ministers. The UIC subsequently gained control of the capital and much of southern Somalia and was thought to be planning an assault on Baidoa. Meles warned in late June that the Islamists threatened to destabilize the whole region, and stated that Ethiopia was prepared to use force to defend itself against any perceived threat. The claim of the UIC over the Ogaden, its support for the ONLF, the possible spread of radical Islam throughout Ethiopia's large Muslim population (see above), and access to the sea were the reasons for Ethiopia's strong opposition to the UIC coming to power in Somalia. Meles expressed his strong support for Yussuf, who had earlier appealed to Ethiopia to provide troops to defend the TFG from the Islamists' advance. In July reports suggested that around 500 Ethiopian troops and armoured vehicles had been covertly deployed in Baidoa and a neighbouring town. Ethiopia, however, denied the reports while reiterating its support for the TFG. Tensions increased later that month when the Somali Supreme Islamic Courts Council (SSICC, as the UIC had been restyled in June) leader, Sheikh Hassan Dahir Aweys, threatened to declare a *jihad* (holy war) to remove Ethiopian troops from Somali territory. The UN Secretary-General's Special Representative for Somalia urged Ethiopia and Eritrea, which had been suspected of arming the SSICC, not to intervene, amid fears that the two countries could begin a 'war-by-proxy' in Somalia.

The SSICC's success in capturing the port city of Kismayo and other areas surrounding Mogadishu in September 2006 further raised fears that Ethiopia would intervene directly to support the TFG. This external conflict helped to bolster government relations with Ethiopian opposition forces, and the Government's actions attracted support from the Ethiopian diaspora. When the Government sought parliamentary approval for military intervention in Somalia on 30 November, the opposition vote was split. Further inflaming the situation were reports that in March Eritrea had supplied the SSICC with arms. The defection of some prominent members of the TFG to Eritrea reinforced the perception that the latter was waging a 'war-by-proxy' against Ethiopia. (This viewpoint was strengthened following Eritrean resistance to IGAD's decision, in July 2010, to send an additional 2,000 AMISOM troops to Somalia.) The defeat of SSICC militias with the help of Ethiopian forces in December 2006 brought a semblance of peace, although periodic clashes occurred from January 2007. The US training of Ethiopian troops was viewed as tacit acknowledgement of US support for Ethiopian intervention in Somalia. On 9 June 2008 an agreement was signed in Djibouti between the TFG and the Alliance for the Reliberation of Somalia (ARS—a coalition of former members of the UIC formed in Asmara) providing for the withdrawal of Ethiopian troops within three months of the signing of the agreement. However, its credibility was undermined when fighting resumed, particularly in Mogadishu. Disagreements between AU and IGAD members over issues of funding, logistics and the duration of the force's mandate continued to delay the deployment of an AU mission to replace Ethiopian troops. In January 2009 the Ethiopian Government announced that it had completed the withdrawal of its troops from Somalia, claiming that the force had 'successfully completed its mission' to fend off Somali opposition fighters. Nevertheless, there were continued reports of Ethiopian incursions into Somalia throughout 2009 and in June the Ethiopian Government confirmed that 'reconnaissance missions' had been deployed in the country. The formation of a coalition government in Somalia in early 2009 under Sheikh Sharif Sheikh Ahmed, and the subsequent resignation of the Somali Prime Minister in September 2010 cast further doubts over the TFG's ability to hold the country together, thereby creating opposition among other Islamist groups, particularly the militant al-Shabaab, which remained a threat to neighbouring countries. A series of bomb attacks, allegedly perpetrated by al-Shabaab, were carried out in the Ugandan capital of Kampala in July, as well as in Kenya, claiming several lives, including those of Ethiopians. In response, the Ethiopian Government increased its troop contributions to the AU. In November 2011 Ethiopian and Kenyan troops entered southern Somalia in pursuit of al-Shabaab forces.

Conflict with Eritrea

Political and economic policies since May 1998 have been influenced, and occasionally dominated, by the war with Eritrea and its consequences. Relations between the two countries were cordial until 1997, with Eritrean independence generally, if sometimes reluctantly, accepted in Ethiopia. Eritrea was offended by Ethiopia's reaction to its new currency, the nakfa, introduced in 1997, and by Ethiopia's subsequent insistence on using 'hard' currencies in all transactions. Despite close links between Prime Minister Meles and President Issaias Afewerki of Eritrea, a minor border dispute in May 1998 escalated. Following the death of several Eritrean troops at Badme, Eritrea dispatched substantial reinforcements, seizing control of three areas previously under Ethiopian administration. When Eritrea refused to withdraw its forces, Ethiopia promptly declared war. The resulting conflict was calamitous for both countries with estimates of 70,000–100,000 killed and countless more wounded and displaced. The war lasted for nearly two years before Ethiopian forces gained the upper hand with significant inroads into Eritrean territory. Following the collapse of OAU-sponsored talks in Algiers, Algeria, in April 2000, Ethiopia launched a short, but highly successful, offensive in May–June. Ethiopian forces rapidly captured a number of towns, and threatened an advance on Asmara. On 25 May the Eritrean Government announced that it would withdraw its troops from all disputed areas. A cessation of hostilities was agreed in Algiers on 18 June. The terms were largely favourable to Ethiopia and included a return to the pre-May 1998 border positions, the establishment of a 25-km wide demilitarized security zone inside the Eritrean frontier, and the deployment of a UN peace-keeping force. A formal peace agreement, signed in Algiers on 12 December 2000, provided for a permanent cessation of all hostilities, the return of all prisoners of war, the demarcation of the common border by an independent commission, and the establishment of a commission to assess compensation claims. Both countries also pledged to co-operate with an independent investigation into the origins of the conflict.

In September 2000 the UN Security Council approved the deployment of a 4,200-strong UN Mission in Ethiopia and Eritrea (UNMEE), to police the Temporary Security Zone (TSZ). The Claims Commission completed the majority of its work by the end of 2004. In December 2005 it ruled that Eritrea was 'liable to compensate Ethiopia' for an attack in May 1998. The Boundary Commission held its first meeting in May 2001, and issued its decisions on delineation in April 2002. Both Ethiopia and Eritrea committed themselves to accepting these in advance, agreeing that they should be 'final and binding' and that there should be no appeal procedure. The Boundary Commission accepted the 1908 boundary line in the region of Badme, which it placed in Eritrea. While Eritrea quickly accepted the ruling, Ethiopia's concerns grew.

In September 2003 Meles formally rejected significant parts of the decision of the Boundary Commission, which he described as 'illegal', while insisting on Ethiopia's commitment to the framework of the peace agreement. UNMEE's mandate was extended for a further six months, to September 2004. While there had been only a few violent incidents on the border, the situation was considered increasingly fragile. Tension along the border escalated significantly towards the end of 2004. On 25 November Prime Minister Meles unexpectedly announced a five-point plan, pledging that his Government would accept the Boundary Commission's ruling 'in principle'; conduct dialogue on its implementation; normalize relations between the two countries; pay Ethiopian dues to the Commission; and resolve the dispute only by peaceful means. These overtures were abruptly rejected by Eritrea, and also drew widespread domestic criticism of what some interpreted as capitulation in agreeing to the demarcation.

Tensions along the disputed border escalated in early 2005. The UN Security Council extended UNMEE's mandate by six months in March, and again in September. In October Meles reaffirmed that Ethiopia was willing to accept the Boundary Commission's ruling 'in principle' and urged Eritrea to participate in talks regarding the delineation process. However, the Eritrean Government immediately rejected any further talks. The following month the Security Council approved Resolution 1640, which demanded that Ethiopia accept the Boundary Commission's ruling, and that troops be withdrawn from both sides of the border, threatening the imposition of economic sanctions should both countries refuse to comply. Eritrea increasingly continued to impose restrictions upon UNMEE activities, and by mid-2006 UNMEE staff remained in Ethiopia only. On 31 May 2006 the UN Security Council adopted Resolution 1681, which reduced the size of UNMEE's peace-keeping force by 1,000 to 2,300, citing the impasse in the delineation process; UNMEE's mandate was, however, extended to January 2007.

In November 2006 the Boundary Commission announced that it would demarcate the Ethiopian–Eritrean border on maps and leave the rival nations to establish the physical boundary themselves. The two nations subsequently boycotted a meeting of the Boundary Commission in The Hague, Netherlands. Eritrea accepted the resultant ruling, which awarded it Badme, but wanted it to be physically enforced on the ground, while Ethiopia, which rejected the boundary, contended that the Commission was acting outside its mandate. In the wake of the boycott by both countries, the Boundary Commission announced that it would give both parties one year to demarcate their border. As a result of obstruction of its work on the ground, the Commission stated that it had used modern techniques, including high-resolution aerial photography, to identify points at which pillars should be placed to mark the boundary in the disputed areas, and that it was now the responsibility of both countries to finish marking the boundary themselves. If they failed to do so by the end of November 2007, the boundary would stand as demarcated by the points identified by the Boundary Commission. The Commission was subsequently dissolved on 30 November 2007.

In January 2007 the UN Security Council, under the new Secretary-General, Ban Ki-Moon, extended UNMEE's mandate until 31 July 2007 and reduced the UN peace-keeping force in Ethiopia and Eritrea from 2,300 personnel to 1,700. The Council reiterated its demand that Ethiopia accept fully and without delay the final and binding decision of the Boundary Commission, and take immediate steps to enable, without preconditions, the complete demarcation of the border between the two countries. It requested that Eritrea withdraw its troops and equipment from the TSZ, and reiterated its demand that it reverse all restrictions on UNMEE's movement and operations, including those of the Secretary-General's acting Special Representative, and provide the Mission with the access, assistance, support and protection required for the performance of its duties. In mid-2007 Meles stated that the Ethiopian Government was strengthening the national army to defend against any potential attack by Eritrea.

While Ethiopia refused to recognize virtual demarcation of the border by the now disbanded Boundary Commission, Asmara unilaterally implemented it and pressured UNMEE peace-keepers to leave Eritrea by blocking fuel supplies, although the Eritrean Government denied having taken this action. In January 2008 Eritrea began to deploy its forces in the TSZ and argued that Ethiopia was now illegally occupying the territory awarded by the Boundary Commission. Ethiopia continued to insist on the need for dialogue on the normalization of relations ahead of physical demarcation. In May 2008 Eritrea appealed to the UN to terminate the mandate of UNMEE, and in July the UN Security Council voted unanimously to dissolve its peace-keeping force. In August 2009 the Claims Commission awarded Ethiopia a total of US $174m. in compensation for war damages, while Eritrea received $164m., resulting in a net payment to Ethiopia of $10m. Eritrea announced in January 2010 that an Ethiopian raid had been repelled in the Zalambessa border region and that 10 Ethiopian troops had been killed, although these claims were denied by the Ethiopian Government. In March 2011 Ethiopia warned that it would take all measures necessary against Eritrea, accusing it of planning attacks during the February AU Summit in Addis Ababa; furthermore, the Ethiopian Government openly declared its support for Eritrea's opposition groups and appealed for regime change. Ethiopia also maintained that al-Shabaab continued to receive weapons and assistance from Eritrea. In December 2011 the UN Security Council imposed additional sanctions on Eritrea for supporting armed groups in Somalia. Subsequent accusations (particularly by Kenya) that Eritrea was continuing to arm al-Shabaab militants were judged to be untrue by the UN monitoring group on Somalia and Eritrea. Relations continued to be tense following an incursion in March 2012 into Eritrean territory by Ethiopian troops to attack rebel camps allegedly belonging to a faction of the Afar Revolutionary Democratic Unity Front; at least 50 of the alleged rebels were killed in the assault. In June Eritrean forces retaliated by launching an attack on the disputed town of Badme, although no casualties were reported.

Economy

WARKA SOLOMON KAHSAY

Revised for this edition by MANICKAM VENKATARAMAN

INTRODUCTION

With a population of 86,538,535 at mid-2012, according to UN figures (although estimates do vary), Ethiopia is Africa's second most populous country, after Nigeria. It has the ninth largest land area on the continent, and has abundant agricultural, mineral and hydrological resources. Despite this, most Ethiopians suffer from acute rural impoverishment, their livelihoods critically dependent upon unstable, rain-fed agriculture. Ethiopians live some of the hardest, shortest lives in the world, with some of the lowest consumption levels per head and among the highest incidences of malnutrition and infant mortality. Although about 38m. Ethiopians were under 15 years of age, according to the 2007 census, poverty and minimal infrastructure meant that access to health and education services was chronically low. The lowest road density in Africa exacerbates the isolation and vulnerability of many rural communities, particularly in years of drought. The share of the rural population within 2 km of an all-season road is just under 20% and people live predominantly in rural areas. According to National Office of Population estimates, in 2007 61.9m. people lived in rural areas while 11.9m. lived in urban areas, or 83.9% and 16.1% of the population, respectively. According to the World Bank, Ethiopia's gross domestic product (GDP) per head on a purchasing-power parity basis stood at US $958 in 2009 and $1,041 in 2010.

Economic reforms since 1991 have brought significant improvements in both economic policy and performance, but the contribution of these policies to producing sustained economic growth and reducing poverty has been minimal due to drought, political resistance to government policy, war with Eritrea, and a legacy of decades of stagnation and daunting structural weaknesses. By 2002, however, the political environment had stabilized, and new strategies for public sector capacity-building and urban, rural, and pastoral development, begun in 2004, started to come to fruition in 2005. An impressive growth rate of 11.3% in 2007 (which was estimated to have slowed to 7.0% by 2010/11) contributed to poverty reduction efforts. However, food and petroleum price rises fuelled inflationary pressures that negatively impacted the urban poor. Moreover, food aid dependency in the rural areas remains as intractable as ever. Nevertheless, there has been growth in the manufacturing, construction and service sectors, particularly in real estate, trade and tourism, and banking and insurance, while infrastructure projects have improved the road network and rural telecommunications. Despite this macroeconomic progress, foreign exchange reserves totalled US $1,880m. at the end of 2010.

ECONOMIC STRUCTURES

Ethiopians' individual livelihoods and aggregate economic well-being depend almost entirely upon agriculture. National accounts, the accuracy of which, as with most official Ethiopian data, should be treated with considerable caution, suggested that in the financial year ending July 2010 42.9% of GDP stemmed from agriculture, declining to 41.1% in 2010/11. With the lowest level of urbanization in Africa, it was estimated that 46% of working women and 74% of working men were employed in the agricultural sector in 2011. Earnings from coffee rose by 20%–30% in the first quarter of 2010/11, compared with the previous year. Hides, skins and the stimulant qat constitute the other significant earners, with new sectors, including fruit and fresh flowers, beginning to emerge following the construction of chilled export facilities at Bole International Airport. Industry represented only some 11% of national income during the 1990s, rising to 15% in 2010/11, while services, including the state bureaucracy and the defence forces, accounted for 45.6% in 2010/11. Ethiopia has a diverse agricultural profile, with cropping patterns and livelihoods differing widely both between and within highland communities. Coffee and root crops are grown in the fertile central and southern areas, while the semi-arid eastern and southern lowlands are characterized largely by pastoral economies, notably of Somalis and Afars. Ethiopia contains the largest total livestock herds in Africa.

Despite such significant internal economic and geographical disparities, poverty is endemic throughout the country. The percentage of the population below minimum dietary energy consumption stood at 46% in 2004, according to World Bank data. This is despite the fact that the economically active population, as a proportion of the total population, stood at an aggregate of 78.4%, according to the 2005 National Labour Survey conducted by the Central Statistical Agency of Ethiopia, with the rate among males (86.1%) found to be higher than among females (71.2%). In 2009 the rate of unemployment at the national level stood at 21% of the total labour force. The International Food Policy Research Institute's 2010 Global Hunger Index ranked Ethiopia 29.8 on a 100 point scale, indicating an 'alarming' level of hunger in the country.

World Bank data estimated life expectancy at birth at 59 years in 2010. By 2010 total enrolment at primary school level had dramatically risen to the equivalent of 102.5% of those in the relevant age-group. In 2009/10 the adult literacy rate was 36% of the total population. According to the World Health Organization, the percentage of people in poverty decreased from 44% in 2000/01 to 29.6% in 2010/11, and the under-five mortality rate declined from 109 per 1,000 in 2009 to 106 per

1,000 in 2010. The budget allocation for poverty reduction and infrastructure development programmes for the 2010/11 fiscal year represented 70% of total spending, demonstrating the Government's commitment to lowering further the prevailing rate of poverty. In 2010 some 44% of the population had access to an improved water supply and 21% to improved sanitation.

Ethiopia's HIV/AIDS infection rates, estimated at 2.1% in 2007 (7.7% in urban areas and 0.9% in rural areas), slightly increased, to 2.3%, in 2009. There are currently some 1.5m. people living with the disease. Recent trends indicate an increasing prevalence in urban areas and stabilization in rural areas. The Government's approach to address this includes the integration of HIV/AIDS education in schools, new health facilities, the provision of counselling, mainstreaming HIV/AIDS programmes in all government branches and forming partnerships with international health organizations. These developments, together with more recent moves to strengthen malaria prevention programmes, represent significant progress. Nevertheless, meeting the Millennium Development Goals (MDGs) by 2015 remains a daunting challenge for the Ethiopian authorities. Ethiopia was ranked 174th out of the 187 countries listed in the UN Development Programme's 2011 Human Development Index. With 43.3 births per 1,000 population, the growth rate of the population was 2% in 2010. At current rates of growth, the population was expected to reach 100m. by 2015.

The largest single unexploited resource is rivers. The chronic instability of agricultural production could be partially alleviated by increased irrigation. At present, only an estimated 4% of cultivable land is even partially irrigated. Much of this is along the southern Awash valley. Similarly, Ethiopia's hydroelectric potential was largely untapped until recently, when generating capacity rose by one-third with the opening of the 420-MW Gilgel Gibe II facility in January 2010 at a cost of €490m. In late July 2006 construction work began on the 1,870-MW Gibe III hydroelectric power plant and dam in the Omo Gibe basin in the south-west of the country. When completed in 2013, Gibe III will be Africa's largest hydroelectric plant and will more than double Ethiopia's installed capacity. In April 2011 the construction of the Grand Renaissance Dam commenced following Egyptian consent. According to the Ethiopian Government, the dam was expected to produce 5,250 MW by 2017 and would be the largest in Africa when completed. Figures for 2009 indicated that, despite the increase in installed capacity, only 17% of Ethiopia's population had access to electricity.

With the partial exception of gold, which generated US $179.2m. of the $1,140m. of total export revenue in 2011, Ethiopia's mineral resources also remain largely unexploited, with mining representing only 0.7% of GDP in 2010, according to the African Development Bank (AfDB). However, this sector is expected to play a greater role in the economy over the coming years.

The country's considerable proven reserves of gold, estimated at about 500 metric tons according to government data, attracted investment of US $5m. from the International Finance Corporation in May 2010. Coal, potassium, tantalum and iron ore are other minerals yet to be exploited. Minerals used in construction, such as limestone and marble, are produced, the latter also being exported. In addition, since 1995 there has been limited exploration for semi-precious gemstones. In early 2004 the one-year contract signed in April 2003 between the Ethiopian Government and the Malaysian company Petronas for petroleum exploration in the Ogaden was renewed, and Petronas also signed a total of four contracts with the Government for petroleum exploration in the Gambela region. Petronas had plans to construct an $80m. gas refinery at Calub and eventually a $1,900m. pipeline to Djibouti for export. However, following the murder of a Petronas geologist in an ambush in April 2010, the company relinquished the four concessions in January 2011 and all the assets were returned to the Government. Meanwhile, in March 2006 licences were granted to the Malaysia-based company Pexco for exploration and development of petroleum reserves in the Ogaden and to Afar Exploration of the USA for exploratory work in the Afar region.

As of the early 2010s petroleum exploration was under way in the regions of Gambela, Southern Rift, Abay Basin and the Ogaden. The Ogaden is Ethiopia's most promising region for petroleum exploration. However, the ongoing conflict therein creates an insecure environment for companies such as Lundin Petroleum AB of Sweden, which, through its subsidiary Lundin East Africa, continues to carry out hydrocarbon exploration based on recently signed production contracts with the Ethiopian Government.

ECONOMIC STAGNATION AND REFORM

Given the country's structural constraints, sustained economic improvement is difficult, even with policies conducive to growth. The Government's emphasis on state farms, large-scale rural resettlement and collectivization schemes undermined agricultural production, while civil war in the provinces of Eritrea and Tigrai, recurrent drought, and environmental decay reinforced economic stagnation.

Initial land reforms resulted in limited increases in productivity. Social indicators did improve, notably in health and literacy, although rarely to the levels claimed by official sources. Despite nationalization and state control of banks, inbred fiscal and monetary conservatism helped to check inflation. However, the nationalization of industry, centralized control of distribution, and considerable investment in state farms and prestige industrial projects failed to produce sustained economic growth. Peasants' quotas, lack of agricultural incentives, poor access to credit and fertilizers, and tight political control via hierarchical peasants' associations were all inimical to rural investment and entrepreneurship. Poor agrarian production was further stunted by the famine of 1984–85. Modest economic recovery came with subsequent harvests, and from 1988 there was a loosening of economic controls. Successive military defeats in the north from 1989 weakened central government and further disrupted the highland economy.

REFORMS SINCE 1991

Economic dislocation owing to war, culminating in the overthrow of the Government in 1991, resulted in the collapse of tax collection and export earnings, while poor harvests further stunted growth in 1991–93. In addition to managing the economic consequences of the rapid demobilization of some 300,000 troops, the new Government had to disentangle the assets, liabilities, infrastructure and personnel of the Ethiopian and nascent Eritrean states. The Eritrean economy was, de facto, managed entirely independently from May 1991. Until late 1997 it continued to use the Ethiopian birr in what was in effect a currency union, buttressed by a series of bilateral agreements guaranteeing free movement of people and goods between the two countries. However, this arrangement ruptured in 1998 with the outbreak of hostilities (see below).

Despite limited experience and personnel, the Government has retained tight control of the content and timing of the reform programme. Relations with donors and allies have occasionally been strained; in 1997–98 a dispute with the IMF over the pace of financial sector reform resulted in a nine-month break in relations. However, the authorities won praise from donors for resolute 'ownership' of reform, and by 1998 had become one of the World Bank's favoured clients in sub-Saharan Africa.

The Government has implemented extensive economic reforms in four broad areas: the dismantling of direct controls and deregulation of both domestic and foreign trade; the overhaul of government taxation and expenditure, implemented in tandem with the restructuring of the civil service along federal lines; financial liberalization, including the devaluation of the birr and the fostering of private banking and insurance markets; and privatization.

In rural areas, market reforms have produced largely positive results, with increased output, prices and revenues for peasants, although marketing weaknesses have repeatedly undermined prices during good harvests. In towns, the benefits of liberalization have been less clear: wholesale and retail trade is now almost exclusively in private hands, but significant barriers to investment—including poor infrastructure, state bureaucracy and convoluted systems of urban land-leases—remain. The urban poor and middle classes have been adversely affected since 2003, as the cost of living has risen with the introduction of a range of new rental tariffs and municipal charges. The Government has formulated extensive sectoral investment programmes, notably for transport, health and education, to be implemented at federal and state level. The Government proposed a record 137,800m. birr budget for 2012/13, focusing on infrastructure development, education, health and power generation. The ruling Ethiopian People's Revolutionary Democratic Front has eschewed comprehensive planning, but it does have a loose, medium-term economic framework for federal and regional economic development. This 'agricultural development-led industrialization' strategy aims to promote medium-scale industries based on agricultural-processing in the larger regional capitals. It envisages the integration of such agro-processing plants with programmes to improve productivity in smallholder agriculture as well as larger-scale commercial farms. Despite deregulation and the ability of regional governments to grant licences for commercial farming, large-scale commercial agriculture remains beset with problems of infrastructure, land tenure and licensing.

Although several hundred small state-owned retail outlets were quickly sold, the privatization of larger companies has been piecemeal, slow and far from transparent. In an effort to address the country's economic problems, in 2010 the Government adopted a competition law, established a public-private partnership forum, attempted to strengthen the economic environment and introduced measures to control inflation. Overall private sector fixed capital formation amounted to 1.7% of GDP in 2000–05. Net foreign direct investment (FDI) totalled US $108.5m. in 2008, a decline of more than 50% compared with the previous year. However, FDI increased to around $2,000m. in 2010.

RECENT DEVELOPMENTS

Since 1991 government economic policy has been characterized by continuity, caution and slow but steady reform. Despite the shift from 'transitional' to federal government in 1995, a progressive restructuring and devolution of regional and local government since 1992, and the conflict with Eritrea during 1998–2000, there have been few changes to the broad orientation of economic policy as laid out in 1991–93. This coherence and consistency is largely due to the continuity of personnel. Changes to the ruling party leadership following the divisions in March 2001 (see Recent History) resulted in new emphasis on policy areas such as the urban and pastoral economies, along with a renewed vigour associated with capacity-building and continuities in economic reform. The gradual pace of reform and the secondary role accorded to foreign donors' advice have contributed to economic stability.

According to the World Bank, GDP increased, in real terms, by an average of 8.4% per year during 2001–10, although wide fluctuations were recorded. GDP growth of 11.3% in 2008/09 declined to 9.9% in 2009/10 and further, to 7.0%, in 2010/11, largely owing to the impact of the global economic crisis. Raising its earlier forecast of 5.5%, the IMF projected Ethiopia's GDP growth rate to remain at around 7.0% in 2012/13, owing to a deceleration in the rate of growth of inflation. With annual population growth averaging 2.6% during 2005–08, and, according to some estimates, as much as 3.0% in subsequent years, these increases in GDP, with intermittent contractions, represented only marginal per-caput improvements. Aggregate data mask erratic fluctuations, owing primarily to variations in rain-fed agriculture. Preliminary data suggested that real income per head declined significantly in the two fiscal years from July 1998–July 2000, and even more severely during 2002/03.

In early 2006 the Government imposed a ban on the export of teff, maize, sorghum and wheat in an effort to curb sharp rises in the prices of those commodities. According to the US Central Intelligence Agency (CIA), the rate of inflation increased to 44.4% in 2009, but decreased significantly, to 8.5%, in 2010 and to 7.0% in 2011. According to government data, inflation rose to 10.4% in the year to May 2012, partly as a result of an increase in food prices and construction materials. In an attempt to address inflation, the Government has set maximum retail prices for a number of staple products.

Even following good harvests, many millions of Ethiopians remain dependent on food aid, as they are simply too poor to purchase food. According to the Government, *belg* crop production in 2009/10 was some 4.7% below the record 2008/09 harvest, but approximately 7% above the average during the previous five years. Output in 2009 was estimated at 16.8m. metric tons. From October to December 2010 some areas experienced very poor *deyr* or *hageya* rains. Moreover, serious water and livestock feed supply shortages were reported in many lowland *woredas* (district authorities). The UN's World Food Programme (WFP) also announced that poor performance of *belg* crops and declining livestock conditions were contributing to deteriorating food security in most areas in East and West Hararghe zones (Oromia). The 2011 *gu* rains were delayed by more than six weeks and were characterized by poor distribution. Indeed, an April 2011 report from Addis Ababa stated that shortages of water and pasture, in particular, had become major problems in most areas of the country. Severe drought conditions, combined with low coffee plantation output, were expected to have an adverse impact on cash crop output in 2011.

The GDP deflator increased from 9.6% in 2004 to 25.9% in 2007/08. According to more recent government figures, overall federal government revenue (including grants) during 2010/11 stood at 85,611m. birr, while expenditure was 93,831m. birr. This represented a fiscal deficit of 8,220m. birr, a slight widening compared with the preceding years in nominal terms. The deficit is financed through foreign borrowing and domestic loans. Reserves of foreign exchange and gold at the end of 2011 were estimated at US $2,029m., with the country ranked 116th in the world in this respect.

The structures of the Ethiopia's expenditure and revenues have been reformed in conjunction with the elaboration of a federal state with nine regional states. Subsidies to the regions traditionally represented about one-third of the government budget. The country's two significant urban commercial centres, Addis Ababa and Dire Dawa, are administered separately. The formulae delineating tax-raising and expenditure prerogatives of central and regional governments remain somewhat convoluted, prompting accusations of poor transparency and accountability of regional authorities. The two small western regions bordering Sudan, as well as the mainly pastoral Afar and Somali regional administrations, have all experienced corruption and frequent changes in personnel. However, despite evidence of increasing dishonesty in recent years, large-scale graft and corruption remains much lower in Ethiopia than in other sub-Saharan states. Transparency International ranked Ethiopia 120th out of 183 countries in its 2010 report. Moreover, Ethiopia rated comparatively well with regard to the number of procedures required, totalling five, to start up a new business successfully, according to the World Bank in 2011; out of 183 economies, the country ranked 103rd in 2010 and 104th in 2011 in terms of 'ease of doing business'. As part of its five-year Growth and Transformation Plan, announced in 2010, the government budget for 2011/12 allocated 23,341m. birr to recurrent expenditure, 48,078m. birr to capital expenditure, 31,393m. birr to regional subsidies and 15,000m. birr to support for MDGs.

EXTERNAL TRADE

External tariffs have been simplified and reduced extensively since 1992. In 2011 exports of coffee, the principal cash crop, totalled US $846.9m. The value of qat exports, meanwhile, continued to increase exponentially, largely as a result of price rises, overtaking hides and skins (for which European prices had declined) in terms of export revenue. The Ethiopian Pulses, Oilseeds and Spices Processors Exporters' Association indicated that the annual profit from exports of oilseeds, pulses and spices reached $580m. in 2009, before declining to $435m. in 2010. Ethiopia runs a surplus of invisible earnings, largely owing to the performance of Ethiopian Airlines and Ethiopian Shipping Lines Corpn, the latter having prospered, in spite of the lack of a home port. In August 2010 Ethiopia announced that Ethiopian Airlines and the Export-Import Bank of the United States had signed an agreement worth over $1,600m. to support the financing of 15 new aircraft. In 2005 exports of goods and services represented 16.4% of GDP. Meanwhile, meetings between officials from Ethiopia and Sudan resulted in a new agreement in June 2010 on border trade zones. This agreement was to help Ethiopia to export products such as natural honey, leeks, horse beans, butter and sorghum, which have a combined estimated annual value of 1.9m. birr. In 2010, according to World Bank estimates, total exports amounted to $3,392m. (equivalent to 11% of GDP) and imports totalled $9,653m. (32% of GDP).

In February 2003 the General Council of the World Trade Organization (WTO) established a Working Party on the Accession of Ethiopia to examine the membership application of the African country. The Working Party held its first meeting in May 2008 to begin the examination of Ethiopia's foreign trade regime. Critics were concerned that Ethiopia would not meet WTO entry requirements and that further openings to the world economy, especially in the service sector, would worsen poverty in the country.

The Ethiopian birr has been devalued progressively since 1992, moving from US $1 = 2.07 birr to $1 = 17.81 birr in June 2012. Since mid-1993 the rate of the birr has been determined by auctions supervised by the central bank. In 1998 these became essentially wholesale auctions, supplying foreign exchange to an increasingly liberalized retail banking sector. The cautious pace of reform was successful, achieving a phased devaluation with minimal inflation and a steady narrowing of the parallel market premium.

PROBLEMS AND PROSPECTS

Acute, perennial food shortages remain the most immediate and protracted economic problem confronting the majority of Ethiopians. Since 1991 the Government, via the Disaster Prevention and Preparedness Commission, and donors have made significant improvements to the country's famine early-warning systems. An emergency food security reserve has been established, and food relief storage and distribution networks have been improved. Nevertheless, most rural communities remain highly vulnerable, owing to acute poverty and the vagaries of weather and pests. In times of shortage, aid efforts are hampered by the rural isolation of many highlanders. Recurrent droughts and the rise in global food prices have raised questions about the efficacy of current food aid policy. During the 2010 fiscal year the United States Agency for International Development (USAID) offered around $23m. for various development programmes in Ethiopia. In April 2010 the European Commission, through the Directorate-General for Humanitarian Aid, contributed $23m. to WFP's Ethiopian relief operation for vulnerable people. With 2m. Ethiopians still requiring emergency food aid in the southern and south-eastern lowlands, WFP pledged that it would provide assistance to 5.7m. people in 2011. Ethiopia has been the largest international aid recipient in the last decade or so.

Phase I of the World Bank-financed Pastoral Community Development Project (PCDP), with a total cost of US $60m., was approved in May 2003 and terminated at the end of December 2008. The PCDP sought to enable pastoralist communities to improve livelihoods, increase access to social services and engage in greater local development decision-making. The project, which was implemented in pastoral and agro-pastoral communities in the Afar, Oromia, Somali, and Southern Nations, Nationalities and Peoples regions, also sought to improve the pastoral early-warning system. About 600,000 rural households were targeted to benefit from the programme, which reflected the Government's policy of devolving power to regional states and district authorities. Initial World Bank reviews of the project deemed it to have been 'moderately successful'. The stated objectives of Phase II of the PCDP, which was approved in May 2008 and was to run until December 2013, were (i) increasing the resilience of Ethiopian pastoralists to external shocks; and (ii) improving the livelihoods of beneficiary communities, thereby contributing to overall poverty alleviation in Ethiopia. The projected cost of the second phase was more than double that of the first, at $133.25m. The International Development Association (IDA) provided $80m. in support of the PCDP II.

In the longer term, without significant improvements in agricultural productivity and the pastoral way of life, the Ethiopian economy will be unable to generate the agricultural surplus necessary both to fund economic diversification and to support the inevitable acceleration of urbanization. Growth in agricultural output in recent years has been primarily due to an expansion in cultivated land, rather than sustained increases in productivity. According to the IMF, yield growth between 1991/92 and 2004/05 remained at an average of around 0.2% per year. Only via sustained improvements in rural productivity, such as in irrigation, would living standards be improved. Although the Government is heavily promoting the use of fertilizer, many peasants resist, not least because of high-cost, unreliable returns and fears of exacerbating the acute soil erosion experienced in the highlands.

The Government's national poverty reduction strategy for 2006–10, the Plan for Accelerated and Sustained Development to End Poverty, acknowledged agriculture's significant and decisive role in the social and economic development of the country. Government policy seeks the transformation of subsistence agriculture to a market-orientated development, both in terms of food security and the commercialization of agriculture. The Government is advocating increased productivity (including reducing post-harvest losses), improving marketing systems and promoting high-value crops for export, while ensuring natural resource conservation for these areas. There is also provision in the strategy explicitly to link small enterprises with agriculture. To promote commercialization, the Ethiopia Commodity Exchange project aims to establish a commodity exchange to facilitate premium prices for quality produce, decrease transaction costs for market participation, and increase information and transparency for all market actors. As part of the Government's resettlement programme, plots in the Gambela region were reserved for the future relocation of more than 45,000 farmers and pastoralists.

The planned Canadian International Development Agency programme will aid agricultural colleges in Ethiopia through university linkages in order to support its private sector development initiatives. USAID's Ethiopia Agribusiness and Trade Expansion Activity aims to improve the competitiveness and productivity of farmers, traders and processors through the identification of export market opportunities. Meanwhile, the World Bank Rural Capacity Building project was approved in June 2006. One component of this project is the training of extension agents. The European Union (EU) is the principal development partner of Ethiopia, which receives the most European aid of all African, Caribbean and Pacific (ACP) countries. One focal sector of the 10th European Development Fund (EDF, 2008–13), for which approximately €650m. was allocated, was to be transport and regional integration, with a view to helping to boost economic progress, reduce poverty and improve the integration of many isolated communities. In addition, support to private sector growth and trade was to seek to increase the competitiveness of Ethiopia's private sector and assist the Government in its efforts to accelerate trade. Other priority areas of the 10th EDF included food security, rural development, agricultural and livestock markets, the management of natural resources, and the support of a macroeconomic environment conducive for economic growth and poverty reduction.

Another weakness in the Ethiopian economy is its dependence upon a single export crop, coffee. For around four decades coffee has routinely accounted for up to two-thirds of Ethiopia's foreign exchange earnings, and an estimated 260,000 metric tons of coffee are produced annually. Fluctuations in international coffee prices greatly accentuate the inherent instability of the Ethiopian economy (see above), although Ethiopia is unique among African coffee producers in consuming much of the crop at home. Since 1996 limited steps have been taken to improve the quality of Ethiopian coffee exports. Washing and processing facilities have been advanced, and the production of premium brands has been promoted. Most coffee is produced by smallholders. Since 1991 the marketing and export of coffee have increasingly been in private hands.

Attempts to diversify exports away from coffee have so far yielded few results. Flowers, fruit and vegetables for export are produced, but the quality of finishing, packaging and marketing lags behind that of neighbouring competitors such as Kenya. There are growing demands for policy debate to move beyond the donor-driven dichotomy of state ('inefficient') and market ('efficient') framework and instead critically take stock of what role the state can play in facilitating the required structural changes in the rural sector. More than 80 Indian companies have invested an estimated £1,500m. in buying huge plantations in Ethiopia. One of them, Kanan Devan Hills Plantations, is leasing 10,000 ha of land in the south-western Oromia region in order to grow tea. The land, which is given on a 90-year lease, will only command modest rent in order to encourage the project, and in return Indian tea workers will train Ethiopian labourers to work with the crop. By around 2020, the land is expected to produce 25m. kg of high-quality teas and to diversify the coffee-dominated cash crop sector. In Africa to date, more than 2.5 ha of land have been bought by foreign companies since 2004, and there are concerns that poor villagers might be ousted to make way for investments and that deals may be open to corruption.

Discussions regarding Ethiopia's eligibility for the IMF/World Bank debt-relief initiative for heavily indebted poor countries (HIPC) were delayed in 1999, owing to the ongoing hostilities between Ethiopia and Eritrea. Other important donors effectively suspended new project-lending in mid-1999. However, by 1998 actual disbursement was already lagging significantly behind pledges, largely owing to constraints in implementation capacity, which was further restricted by the war effort. In September 2000 the World Bank announced that it was to resume financial assistance to Ethiopia, which had been suspended for more than two years. Full HIPC debt reduction was agreed in principle in November 2001.

In late April 2004 it was announced that Ethiopia had reached its completion point under the HIPC initiative. In March 2006 the World Bank approved debt cancellation for 17 countries, including Ethiopia, under the HIPC initiative. Top-up funds were agreed to keep debt/export ratios down to 150%–175%, although they reached 216% in mid-2004 as a result of decreasing coffee export revenues, before declining to acceptable levels over the subsequent year. As a result, Ethiopia benefits from the following debt relief: US $1,300m. in net present value from multilateral donors; $700m. from bilateral donors; and $300m. from 'Paris Club' creditors. This is against a total external debt nominally valued at $7,151m. in 2003. Figures from 2009 showed that total outstanding and disbursed debt from official development assistance (ODA) and from IDA was $3,946m. and $1,069m., respectively. The net present value of external debt relative to GDP and to exports has, according to the World Bank, decreased to 7% and 50%, respectively. Domestic debt stood at 21% of GDP in 2007/08, and government gross debt totalled 41.4% of GDP in 2011. New external debts have been contracted mostly on concessional terms. According to the IMF, Ethiopia was among the 32 countries to have qualified to receive full HIPC initiative assistance from the Fund and the Multilateral Debt Relief Initiative after reaching completion point, as of December 2010.

Ethiopia's economy is, and will remain for the foreseeable future, highly dependent on external donor funding, which amounted to 17% of GDP in 2005. Ethiopia remains one of the largest beneficiaries of World Bank concessional lending through IDA, with a portfolio of 28 active projects as of March 2009 worth over US $2,750m., of which $1,800m. was provided as credit, with the remaining $950m. provided as grants. These projects focused on areas including governance and public sector development, agriculture and rural development, private sector development and water sector development. Aid assistance per caput in 2009 was $30.60. ODA has been increasing steadily since 2000 and Ethiopia is one of the world's biggest beneficiaries. According to the World Bank, a large number of donors are active in Ethiopia, with some 25 bilateral and multilateral donors. The World Bank provided up to $635m. in 2008/09 and agreed to continue financing several programmes under the EU's Cotonou Agreement until 2013.

An Ethio-Saudi entrepreneur, Muhammad Hussein al-Amoudi, has established extensive interests in real estate, hotels, beverages, banking, insurance, agriculture and mining. A second group of conglomerates is owned and managed by members or affiliates of the ruling EPRDF, particularly in the media and distribution sectors, prompting allegations that public contracts are awarded on the basis of party ties or ethnic favouritism. Critics of the Government claim that the economic influence and political connections of such consortia have squeezed smaller, genuinely independent entrepreneurs out of crucial markets, undermining private investor confidence. Such issues are not helped by the constrained nature of public debate on economic issues. The overall restructuring of Ethiopia's financial sector has long been a demand of external donors, with the Government insisting that the IMF should recognize the validity of its opposition to banking liberalization in the absence of a functioning money market. Value-added tax of 15% replaced sales tax on 1 January 2003.

THE ECONOMIC IMPACT OF WAR WITH ERITREA

Although the war led to markedly reduced investment in the economy, rapid deflation, rising public sector borrowing and a widening budget deficit, the initial, short-term, aggregate economic impact of the 1998–2000 conflict with Eritrea was surprisingly limited. Disruption to agricultural production was restricted largely to Tigrai, where 385,000 people were reportedly displaced. Disturbance to land-locked Ethiopia's foreign trade was also less than initially forecast. The decision to suspend use of the Eritrean ports of Assab and Massawa and to channel all foreign trade via Djibouti was taken unilaterally by Ethiopia. The flexibility of Djibouti's port facilities and the efficiency of road haulage from Djibouti to Addis Ababa and the highlands ensured a continuous flow of goods to and from Ethiopia. Currency and trade questions played a key role in the genesis of the conflict. The signing of a peace accord in December 2000, and the announcement of the Boundary Commission's decision regarding the demarcation of the Ethio-Eritrean border in April 2002 (see Recent History), resulted in a considerable reduction in levels of defence spending. In March 2003 a study by the Ethiopian Economic Policy Research Institute estimated that the total cost of the war to the Ethiopian Government amounted to US $29,000m. The war inevitably diminished the reporting and transparency of economic and fiscal data. During the war senior government officials stated that the cost of conflict had been met largely by deferring capital expenditure, implying severe reductions in sectoral investment programmes, and sharp decreases in health and education expenditure. These have been reversed since 2000, with rises in social sector spending central to Ethiopia's externally monitored poverty reduction strategy approved by donors in February 2005.

However, war further eroded domestic and international confidence in the economy. The expulsion of more than 50,000 largely urban Ethiopians with family ties to Eritrea undermined both the Government's legal commitment to property rights and general investor confidence. The apparently arbitrary criteria and rationale behind the expulsions exacerbated economic uncertainty, which was somewhat reduced when, in early 2004, the Government introduced legislation granting citizenship rights to long-term residents of Eritrean origin. Data presented by the Stockholm International Peace Research Institute indicated that defence expenditure declined slightly from approximately US $4,788m. in 2008/09 to $3,380m. in 2010.

The crisis of the war with Eritrea, and its possible resumption, added to the deeper pressures of rapid population growth and slow agrarian change. Political uncertainty, and low rates of economic growth and investment undermined already limited opportunities for employment and education, and inevitably fuelled an increase in migration, which amounted to a total of 662,444 people in 2000–04. Over the past 15 years or so large numbers of middle-class and urban youths have fled to the USA and the northern countries of the EU. Given the high level of poverty at home, such external migration, reaching 555,054 in 2005, according to the World Bank, is likely to intensify in the immediate future, thus heightening the role that remittances from abroad—which totalled US $387m. in 2010, a 9.6% increase from 2009, and accounted for 10% of GDP—will play in Ethiopia's economy. UN-sourced reports state that billions of dollars have been sent to Ethiopia through non-official channels. The net migration rate, according to the 2009 CIA *World Factbook*, stood at -0.02 migrants per 1,000 population. The recent economic downturn means that lower demand for Ethiopia's exports, and reduced remittances, aid and FDI may negatively impact the rebuilding of foreign exchange reserves, as well as economic growth in general, with deleterious consequences for reducing widespread poverty. The country's economic growth rate was projected to decrease from 7.5% in the 2011/12 fiscal year to 7.0% in the 2012/13 fiscal year.

Statistical Survey

Source (unless otherwise stated): Central Statistical Authority, POB 1143, Addis Ababa; tel. (11) 553010; fax (11) 550334; internet www.csa.gov.et.

Area and Population

AREA, POPULATION AND DENSITY

Area (sq km)	1,133,380*
Population (census results)	
11 October 1994	53,477,265
28 May 2007	
Males	37,217,130
Females	36,533,802
Total	73,750,932
Population (UN estimates at mid-year)†	
2010	82,949,541
2011	84,734,260
2012	86,538,535
Density (per sq km) at mid-2012	76.4

* 437,600 sq miles.

† Source: UN, *World Population Prospects: The 2010 Revision*.

POPULATION BY AGE AND SEX

(UN estimates at mid-2012)

	Males	Females	Total
0–14	17,468,438	17,253,747	34,722,185
15–64	24,234,436	24,602,767	48,837,203
65 and over	1,369,037	1,610,110	2,979,147
Total	43,071,911	43,466,624	86,538,535

Source: UN, *World Population Prospects: The 2010 Revision*.

ADMINISTRATIVE DIVISIONS

(population at 2007 census)

	Population		
	Males	Females	Total
Regional States			
1 Tigrai	2,126,465	2,190,523	4,316,988
2 Afar	775,117	615,156	1,390,273
3 Amhara	8,641,580	8,580,396	17,221,976
4 Oromia	13,595,006	13,398,927	26,993,933
5 Somali	2,472,490	1,972,729	4,445,219
6 Benishangul/Gumuz	398,655	385,690	784,345
7 Southern Nations, Nationalities and Peoples	7,425,918	7,503,630	14,929,548
8 Gambela	159,787	147,309	307,096
9 Harari	92,316	91,099	183,415
Chartered Cities			
1 Dire Dawa	171,461	170,373	341,834
2 Addis Ababa	1,305,387	1,434,164	2,739,551
Total*	37,217,130	36,533,802	73,750,932

* Including 96,754 persons, detailed as 'special enumeration', not allocated to administrative divisions.

Note: Totals may not be equal to the sum of components, owing to rounding.

PRINCIPAL TOWNS

(population at 2007 census)

Addis Ababa (capital)	2,739,551	Awasa	157,139
Dire Dawa	233,224	Bahir Dar	155,428
Nazret	220,212	Jimma	120,960
Mekele	215,914	Dessie	120,095
Gondar	207,044	Debre Zeit	99,928

Mid-2011 (incl. suburbs, UN estimate): Addis Ababa (capital) 2,979,100 (Source: UN, *World Urbanization Prospects: The 2011 Revision*).

BIRTHS AND DEATHS

(annual averages, UN estimates)

	1995–2000	2000–05	2005–10
Birth rate (per 1,000)	43.9	38.8	33.3
Death rate (per 1,000)	15.2	13.0	10.5

Source: UN, *World Population Prospects: The 2010 Revision*.

Life expectancy (years at birth): 58.7 (males 57.2; females 60.3) in 2010 (Source: World Bank, World Development Indicators database).

ECONOMICALLY ACTIVE POPULATION

('000 persons aged 10 years and over, March 2005)*

	Males	Females	Total
Agriculture, hunting, forestry and fishing	14,209.4	10,998.8	25,208.2
Mining and quarrying	51.4	30.6	82.1
Manufacturing	444.0	1,085.3	1,529.4
Electricity, gas and water	25.2	7.7	32.9
Construction	349.9	95.7	445.6
Wholesale and retail trade; repair of motor vehicles, motorcycles and personal and household goods	652.2	984.9	1,637.1
Hotels and restaurants	96.8	672.3	769.1
Transport, storage and communications	132.0	14.5	146.4
Financial intermediation	21.6	16.3	37.9
Real estate, renting and business services	36.1	16.2	52.3
Public administration and defence; compulsory social security	242.0	125.9	367.9
Education	178.2	104.5	282.7
Social work	45.6	32.5	78.1
Community, social and personal services	303.5	135.2	438.7
Households with employed persons	23.1	225.5	248.6
Extra-territorial organizations and bodies	42.7	25.1	67.9

—continued	Males	Females	Total
Sub-total	16,853.7	14,571.0	31,424.9
Not classifiable by economic activity	6.5	3.8	10.3
Total employed	16,860.3	14,574.8	31,435.1
Unemployed	427.9	1,225.8	1,653.7
Total labour force	17,288.2	15,800.6	33,088.8

* Excluding armed forces.

Source: ILO.

Mid-2012 (FAO estimates in '000): Agriculture, etc. 33,142; Total labour force 43,466 (Source: FAO).

Health and Welfare

KEY INDICATORS

Total fertility rate (children per woman, 2010)	4.2
Under-5 mortality rate (per 1,000 live births, 2010)	106
HIV/AIDS (% of persons aged 15–49, 2007)	2.1
Physicians (per 1,000 head, 2003)	0.03
Hospital beds (per 1,000 head, 2006)	0.20
Health expenditure (2009): US $ per head (PPP)	42
Health expenditure (2009): % of GDP	4.4
Health expenditure (2009): public (% of total)	53.6
Access to water (% of persons, 2010)	44
Access to sanitation (% of persons, 2010)	21
Total carbon dioxide emissions ('000 metric tons, 2008)	7,106.6
Carbon dioxide emissions per head (metric tons, 2008)	0.1
Human Development Index (2011): ranking	174
Human Development Index (2011): value	0.363

For sources and definitions, see explanatory note on p. vi.

Agriculture

PRINCIPAL CROPS

('000 metric tons)

	2008	2009	2010
Wheat	2,463	3,076*	3,000*
Barley	1,352	1,750*	1,400*
Maize	3,776	3,897*	4,400*
Oats	31	43	43†
Millet (Dagusa)	484	560	565†
Sorghum	2,316	2,971*	2,997†
Potatoes	403	572*	786†
Sweet potatoes	526	451*	402†
Yams	228*	406*	407†
Sugar cane†	2,300	2,200	2,400
Beans, dry	241	285*	263†
Broad beans, horse beans, dry	689	611*	607†
Peas, dry	232	236*	232†
Chick peas	287	312*	310†
Lentils	94	124*	123†
Vetches	185	204*	203†
Groundnuts, with shell	45	46*	56†
Castor beans	7*	7*	8†
Rapeseed	48	23*	40†
Safflower seed	8	6*	4†
Sesame seed	187	261*	314*
Linseed	170	151*	150†
Cabbages and other brassicas	250	277*	257†
Tomatoes	42*	40*	41†
Onions and shallots, green†	22	26	26
Onions, dry	175	169*	205†
Garlic	104	180*	180†
Bananas	261	209*	172†
Oranges	29	44	39†
Mangoes, mangosteens and guavas	80†	66*	77†

—continued	2008	2009	2010
Avocados	43	38*	34†
Papayas	250	260†	232†
Coffee, green	273	265*	270*

* Unofficial figure(s).

† FAO estimate(s).

Aggregate production ('000 metric tons, may include official, semi-official or estimated data): Total cereals 13,012 in 2008, 15,502 in 2009, 15,638 in 2010; Total roots and tubers 5,920 in 2008, 7,311 in 2009, 7,097 in 2010; Total vegetables (incl. melons) 1,391 in 2008, 1,640 in 2009, 1,679 in 2010; Total fruits (excl. melons) 866 in 2008, 792 in 2009, 684 in 2010.

Source: FAO.

LIVESTOCK

('000 head, year ending September)

	2008	2009	2010
Cattle	49,298	50,884*	50,884†
Sheep	26,117	25,017	25,980
Goats	21,799	21,961*	21,961†
Asses	5,422	5,715*	5,715†
Mules	374*	366*	366†
Horses	1,786	1,995*	1,995†
Camels	1009	760	808
Pigs†	29	29	29
Poultry	38,049	38,000†	38,000†

* Unofficial figure.

† FAO estimate(s).

Source: FAO.

LIVESTOCK PRODUCTS

('000 metric tons, FAO estimates)

	2008	2009	2010
Cattle meat	380.0	390.0	373.2
Sheep meat	81.5	85.0	86.5
Goat meat	67.9	65.5	66.3
Pig meat	1.7	2.0	1.6
Chicken meat	48.6	50.9	53.0
Game meat	83.0	89.6	84.7
Cows' milk	1,350	1,400	1774
Goats' milk	50.3	50.5	52.5
Sheep's milk	44.0	46.0	48.0
Hen eggs	34.0	30.9	35.1
Honey	42.0	40.7	45.3
Wool, greasy	7.3	7.6	14.4

Source: FAO.

Forestry

ROUNDWOOD REMOVALS

('000 cubic metres, excl. bark, FAO estimates)

	2008	2009	2010
Sawlogs, veneer logs and logs for sleepers	4	11	11
Pulpwood	7	7	7
Other industrial wood	2,917	2,917	2,917
Fuel wood	98,489	99,870	101,274
Total	101,417	102,805	104,209

Source: FAO.

SAWNWOOD PRODUCTION

('000 cubic metres, incl. railway sleepers)

	2001	2002	2003
Coniferous (softwood)	25*	1	1
Broadleaved (hardwood)	35*	13	17
Total	60	14	18

* FAO estimate.

2004–10: Figures assumed to be unchanged from 2003 (FAO estimates).

Source: FAO.

Fishing

(metric tons, live weight of capture)

	2008	2009	2010
Common carp	313	293	182
Other cyprinids	1,672	1,936	1,971
Tilapias	7,180	7,554	12,110
North African catfish	3,384	3,143	2,050
Nile perch	3,243	2,740	1,017
Total catch (incl. others)	16,770	17,047	18,058

Source: FAO.

Mining

('000 metric tons, unless otherwise indicated, year ending 7 July)

	2007/08	2008/09	2009/10
Gold (kilograms)	3,465	6,251	5,936
Limestone	1,900	2,000*	2,000*
Gypsum and anhydrite	33	36*	36*
Pumice	35	250*	350*
Sandstone*	1,400	1,500	1,500

* Estimate(s).

Source: US Geological Survey.

Industry

SELECTED PRODUCTS

('000 metric tons, year ending 7 July, unless otherwise indicated)

	2000/01	2001/02	2002/03
Wheat flour	165	143	137
Macaroni and pasta	26	23	30*
Raw sugar	251	248*	295*
Wine ('000 hectolitres)	25	27*	32*
Beer ('000 hectolitres)	1,605	1,812*	2,123*
Mineral waters ('000 hectolitres)	395	395*	433*
Soft drinks ('000 hectolitres)	677	995	845*
Cigarettes (million)	1,904	1,511*	1,511*
Cotton yarn	5.7	7.7*	5.5*
Woven cotton fabrics ('000 sq m)	45,000	45,000*	41,000*
Nylon fabrics ('000 sq m)	1,300	1,000*	1,400*
Footwear (including rubber, '000 pairs)	n.a.	6,677	7,138
Soap	14.8	19.2*	11.6*
Tyres ('000)*	209	198	191
Clay building bricks ('000)*	20	22	21
Quicklime*	11	8	11
Cement*	819	919	890

* Year ending 31 December of later year.

Cement ('000 metric tons): 1,300 in 2003/04.
Source: UN, *Industrial Commodity Statistics Yearbook*.

Raw sugar ('000 metric tons): 325.0 in 2004; 345.0 in 2005; 360.0 in 2006; 340.0 in 2007; 340 in 2008 (Source: UN Industrial Commodity Statistics Database).

Cement (hydraulic, '000 metric tons, year ending 7 July): 1,130.1 in 2003; 1,315.9 in 2004; 1,568.6 in 2005; 1,731 in 2006; 1,626 in 2007; 1,834 in 2008; 2,100 in 2009; 2,900 in 2010 (estimate) (Source: US Geological Survey).

Beer of millet ('000 metric tons): 220.7 in 2001; 208.0 in 2002; 244.1 in 2003 (Source: FAO).

Beer of barley ('000 metric tons, estimates): 502.6 in 2004; 545.1 in 2005; 618.9 in 2006; 634.5 in 2007; 635.0 in 2008; 734.9 in 2009; 670.4 in 2010 (Source: FAO).

Finance

CURRENCY AND EXCHANGE RATES

Monetary Units
100 cents = 1 birr.

Sterling, Dollar and Euro Equivalents (31 May 2012)
£1 sterling = 20.306 birr;
US $1 = 17.609 birr;
€1 = 18.066 birr;
100 birr = £4.92 = $5.68 = €5.54.

Average Exchange Rate (birr per US $)

2009	11.778
2010	14.410
2011	16.899

GENERAL BUDGET

(rounded figures, million birr, year ending 7 July)

Revenue	2004/05	2005/06	2006/07
Taxation	12,398	14,159	17,354
Taxes on income and profits	3,569	3,819	4,868
Personal income	1,132	1,414	1,828
Business profits	1,714	1,741	2,305
Domestic indirect taxes	2,721	3,111	3,997
Import duties	5,746	6,587	8,189
Other revenue	3,184	5,371	4,443
Reimbursements and property sales	193	310	168
Sales of goods and services	856	433	250
Total*	15,582	19,529	21,797

Expenditure	2004/05	2005/06	2006/07
Current expenditure	13,229	15,234	17,166
General services	5,816	6,522	7,073
Economic services	1,516	2,009	2,201
Social services	3,839	4,996	6,198
Interest and charges	1,011	1,054	1,207
External assistance (grants)†	721	586	411
Capital expenditure	11,343	14,041	18,398
Economic development	7,655	9,728	11,367
Social development	3,290	3,796	5,998
General services and compensation	397	517	1,033
External assistance (grants)†	1,513	2,196	3,081
Total	24,572	29,275	35,564

* Excluding grants received from abroad (million birr): 4,565 in 2004/05; 4,721 in 2005/06; 8,477 in 2006/07.

† Imputed value of goods and services provided, mainly aid in kind.

Source: IMF, *The Federal Democratic Republic of Ethiopia: Statistical Appendix* (July 2008).

2008/09 (million birr, year ending 7 July): *Revenue:* Taxation 28,998 (Direct taxes 9,858, Domestic indirect taxes 7,325, Import duties 11,814); Other revenue 11,176; Total 40,174 (excl. grants 14,454). *Expenditure:* Current expenditure 27,176 (Defence spending 4,000; Poverty-reducing expenditure 12,629; Interest and charges 1,286); Capital expenditure 30,599; Total 57,774 (Source: IMF, *Ethiopia: 2010 Article IV Consultation and First Review of the Arrangement under the Exogenous Shocks Facility—Staff Report; Staff Supplements; and Press Release on the Executive Board Discussion*—June 2010).

2009/10 (million birr, year ending 7 July, estimates): *Revenue:* Taxation 42,831 (Direct taxes 14,507, Domestic indirect taxes 10,640, Import duties 17,685); Other revenue 10,461; Total 53,292 (excl. grants 12,730). *Expenditure:* Current expenditure 32,994 (Defence spending 4,000; Poverty-reducing expenditure 16,361; Interest and charges 1,587); Capital expenditure 39,062; Total 72,056 (Source: IMF (see below)).

2010/11 (million birr, year ending 7 July, budget forecasts): *Revenue:* Taxation 53,735 (Direct taxes 17,969, Domestic indirect taxes 12,707, Import duties 23,059); Other revenue 9,575; Total 63,310 (excl. grants 18,744). *Expenditure:* Current expenditure 43,008 (Defence spending 4,581; Poverty-reducing expenditure 22,350; Interest and charges 3,013); Capital expenditure 50,974; Total 93,982 (Source (2009/10–2010/11): IMF, *The Federal Democratic Republic of Ethiopia: Second Review of the Arrangement under the Exogenous Shocks Facility—Staff Report; Press Release on the Executive Board Discussion; and Statement by the Executive Director for the Federal Democratic Republic of Ethiopia*—November 2010).

INTERNATIONAL RESERVES
(US $ million at 31 December, excluding gold)

	2007	2008	2009
IMF special drawing rights	0.1	—	27.4
Reserve position in IMF	11.6	11.5	11.8
Foreign exchange	1,278.1	859.0	1,741.7
Total	1,289.8	870.5	1,780.9

2010: IMF special drawing rights 150.0; Reserve position in IMF 11.6.

2011: IMF special drawing rights 149.3; Reserve position in IMF 11.5.

Source: IMF, *International Financial Statistics*.

MONEY SUPPLY
(million birr at 31 December)

	2006	2007	2008
Currency outside banks	11,606.4	14,445.8	17,432.9
Demand deposits at commercial banks	20,207.0	24,175.9	31,391.6
Total money (incl. others)	32,056.2	38,903.5	49,105.8

Source: IMF, *International Financial Statistics*.

COST OF LIVING
(Consumer Price Index; base: 2005 = 100)

	2008	2009	2010
All items	190.1	206.2	223.0

Source: IMF, *International Financial Statistics*.

NATIONAL ACCOUNTS
(million birr at current prices)

Expenditure on the Gross Domestic Product

	2009	2010	2011
Government final consumption expenditure	29,810	32,888	41,239
Private final consumption expenditure	290,448	329,705	415,988
Gross fixed capital formation	76,185	94,497	130,466
Total domestic expenditure	396,443	457,090	587,693
Exports of goods and services	35,233	52,168	85,955
Less Imports of goods and services	96,285	126,319	162,490
GDP in purchasers' values	335,392	382,939	511,157

Gross Domestic Product by Economic Activity

	2009	2010	2011
Agriculture, hunting, forestry and fishing	160,627	165,668	220,088
Mining and quarrying	1,270	2,475	7,852
Manufacturing	11,813	13,821	16,869
Electricity and water	3,717	4,393	5,233
Construction	16,074	15,882	20,051
Trade, hotels and restaurants	56,629	66,781	86,634
Finance, insurance and real estate	30,068	42,137	59,437
Transport and communications	12,766	15,982	24,739
Public administration and defence	10,320	12,199	15,890
Other services	15,513	18,001	21,366
Sub-total	318,797	357,339	478,159
Indirect taxes	19,139	28,412	36,692
Less imputed bank service charge	2,544	2,813	3,692
GDP in purchasers' values	335,392	382,939	511,157

Source: African Development Bank.

BALANCE OF PAYMENTS
(US $ million)

	2008	2009	2010
Exports of goods f.o.b.	1,554.7	1,538.1	2,400.0
Imports of goods f.o.b.	–7,206.3	–6,819.0	–7,364.5
Trade balance	–5,651.6	–5,280.9	–4,964.6
Exports of services	1,959.3	1,894.9	2,244.5
Imports of services	–2,410.3	–2,226.9	–2,546.5
Balance on goods and services	–6,102.6	–5,612.9	–5,266.6
Other income received	37.5	6.5	8.1
Other income paid	–35.9	–43.3	–71.7
Balance on goods, services and income	–6,101.0	–5,649.7	–5,330.1
Current transfers received	4,343.8	3,499.7	4,987.9
Current transfers paid	–48.5	–40.7	–83.2
Current balance	–1,805.7	–2,190.7	–425.4
Direct investment from abroad	108.5	221.5	288.3
Other investment assets	113.0	420.3	1,084.6
Investment liabilities	515.2	1,012.6	995.6
Net errors and omissions	1,450.7	–793.1	–2,929.9
Overall balance	381.6	–1,329.5	–986.8

Source: IMF, *International Financial Statistics*.

External Trade

PRINCIPAL COMMODITIES
(distribution by HS, US $ million)

Imports c.i.f.	2009	2010	2011
Cereals	368.2	374.4	471.4
Wheat and meslin	321.6	304.3	402.6
Animal, vegetable fats and oils, cleavage products, etc.	240.4	260.2	391.7
Palm oil and its fraction	204.8	222.7	330.9
Mineral fuels, oils, distillation products, etc.	1,305.7	1,642.1	1,632.0
Refined petroleum oils	1,222.5	1,544.4	1,484.3
Pharmaceutical products	323.2	250.4	120.7
Medicament mixtures (put in dosage)	256.5	204.2	110.5
Fertilizers	337.8	246.0	341.0
Mixtures of nitrogen, phosphorous and potassium fertilizers	250.3	169.0	250.2
Iron and steel	380.7	318.9	453.2
Articles of iron and steel	350.7	340.6	211.0
Nuclear reactors, boilers, machinery, etc.	1,025.8	1,115.7	1,150.3
Electrical and electronic equipment	1,175.1	1,129.2	626.3
Electric appliances for line telephony	414.0	529.3	107.0
Vehicles other than railway, tramway	520.4	836.3	893.8
Trucks, motor vehicles for the transport of goods	206.0	382.2	357.6
Total (incl. others)	7,973.9	8,601.8	8,896.3

Exports f.o.b.	2009	2010	2011
Live animals	62.0	132.4	190.4
Live bovine animals	36.7	77.6	137.8
Live trees, plants, bulbs, roots, cut flowers etc.	150.6	165.1	191.4
Cut flowers and flower buds for bouquets, fresh or dried	131.5	143.8	168.9
Edible vegetables and roots and tubers	294.0	408.8	416.7
Vegetables, fresh or chilled	168.5	245.1	238.1
Dried vegetables, shelled	104.1	136.5	139.3
Coffee, tea, mate and spices	382.9	727.6	887.1
Coffee	369.8	699.1	846.9
Oil seed, oleagic fruits, grain, seed, fruit, etc.	383.9	345.4	368.7
Oil seeds	380.3	338.8	363.8
Raw hides, skins (except furskins) and leather	42.8	67.2	122.7
Pearls, precious stones, metals, coins, etc.	93.0	183.9	132.5
Gold	92.5	182.3	124.6
Total (incl. others)	1,618.2	2,330.0	2,615.0

Source: Trade Map-Trade Competitiveness Map, International Trade Centre, www.intracen.org/marketanalysis.

PRINCIPAL TRADING PARTNERS
(US $ million)

Imports c.i.f.	2009	2010	2011
Belgium	56.5	89.0	52.6
Brazil	88.0	124.4	81.5
China, People's Republic	1,920.4	2,062.1	1,718.1
Egypt	70.6	99.5	82.9
France (incl. Monaco)	108.2	106.4	142.9
Germany	193.5	206.7	189.6
India	638.9	619.7	749.3
Indonesia	86.8	87.3	188.4
Italy	412.8	391.0	386.7
Japan	358.5	473.5	443.4
Jordan	36.1	100.1	129.2
Korea, Republic	136.9	94.5	134.9
Kuwait	3.2	3.1	222.1
Malaysia	215.4	229.1	274.1
Morocco	21.4	102.2	30.5
Netherlands	98.8	81.3	81.8
Pakistan	253.0	53.9	108.9
Russia	166.0	91.4	270.9
Saudi Arabia	933.8	1,023.3	896.8
South Africa	63.4	58.6	93.1
Spain	40.0	92.2	91.7
Sudan	71.5	109.3	145.6
Thailand	77.7	126.6	131.5
Turkey	260.9	238.7	359.7
Ukraine	96.7	85.0	140.8
United Arab Emirates	310.1	485.7	482.5
United Kingdom	102.9	89.1	109.8
USA	476.3	483.6	489.0
Total (incl. others)	7,973.9	8,601.8	8,896.3

Exports f.o.b.	2009	2010	2011
Belgium	35.6	56.6	69.5
China, People's Republic	243.1	241.8	283.4
Djibouti	51.6	67.1	75.6
Egypt	15.7	46.3	46.1
France (incl. Monaco)	18.0	37.8	50.2
Germany	128.9	265.3	318.8
India	19.4	29.9	33.8
Israel	46.5	51.9	67.2
Italy	67.6	69.2	111.2
Japan	9.9	38.7	35.9
Jordan	19.0	16.8	26.6
Netherlands	143.3	173.4	181.2
Pakistan	9.8	24.4	13.4
Saudi Arabia	114.1	146.5	167.3
Somalia	134.7	224.1	243.3
South Africa	4.2	73.7	6.5
Sudan	76.9	151.3	178.4
Sweden	10.8	23.7	39.0
Switzerland-Liechtenstein	105.3	126.9	129.4
Turkey	30.1	33.3	45.2
United Arab Emirates	72.7	111.3	82.5
United Kingdom	58.2	57.8	67.5
USA	73.5	102.3	98.0
Yemen	20.7	18.6	20.7
Total (incl. others)	1,618.2	2,330.0	2,615.0

Source: Trade Map-Trade Competitiveness Map, International Trade Centre, www.intracen.org/marketanalysis.

Transport

RAILWAYS
(traffic, year ending 7 July)*

	2002/03	2003/04	2004/05
Addis Ababa–Djibouti:			
Passenger-km (million)	253	40	34
Freight (million net ton-km)	—	81	56

* Including traffic on the section of the Djibouti–Addis Ababa line that runs through the Republic of Djibouti. Data pertaining to freight include service traffic.

ROAD TRAFFIC
(motor vehicles in use, year ending 7 July)

	2000	2001	2002
Passenger cars	59,048	59,737	67,614
Buses and coaches	9,334	11,387	18,067
Lorries and vans	34,355	43,375	34,102
Motorcycles and mopeds	n.a.	2,198	2,575
Road tractors	6,809	1,275	1,396
Total	109,546	117,972	123,754

2007: Passenger cars 70,893; Buses and coaches 17,098; Lorries and vans 148,997; Motorcycles and mopeds 7,328.

Source: IRF, *World Road Statistics*.

SHIPPING

Merchant Fleet
(registered at 31 December)

	2007	2008	2009
Number of vessels	10	9	10
Displacement (grt)	122,729	117,747	117,957

Source: IHS Fairplay, *World Fleet Statistics*.

International Sea-borne Shipping
(freight traffic, '000 metric tons, year ending 7 July)

	1996/97	1997/98	1998/99
Goods loaded	242	201	313
Goods unloaded	777	1,155	947

Source: former Ministry of Transport and Communications, Addis Ababa.

CIVIL AVIATION
(traffic on scheduled services)

	2007	2008	2009
Kilometres flown (million)	69	75	75
Passengers carried ('000)	2,290	2,715	2,914
Passenger-km (million)	7,947	9,303	9,746
Total ton-km (million)	1,041	1,399	1,478

Source: UN, *Statistical Yearbook*.

2010: Passengers carried ('000) 3,141 (Source: World Bank, World Development Indicators database).

Tourism

TOURIST ARRIVALS BY COUNTRY OF ORIGIN

	2006	2007	2008
Canada	7,349	8,391	8,574
Djibouti	4,650	4,562	5,038
France	6,649	7,338	8,965
Germany	7,428	11,691	12,643
India	7,975	8,895	10,560
Italy	8,386	9,882	11,235
Japan	2,402	1,905	2,012
Kenya	8,690	10,172	10,417
Netherlands	4,659	4,769	6,372
Saudi Arabia	8,463	8,330	7,160
Sudan	6,233	8,430	9,792
United Kingdom	16,076	17,094	18,283
USA	43,610	44,717	49,678
Yemen	4,724	4,269	5,641
Total (incl. others)*	290,458	311,947	330,157

* Including Ethiopian nationals residing abroad.

Total tourist arrivals ('000): 427 in 2009; 468 in 2010.

Receipts from tourism (US $ million, incl. passenger transport, unless otherwise indicated): 1,184 in 2008; 1,119 in 2009; 522 in 2010 (excl. passenger transport).

Source: World Tourism Organization.

Communications Media

	2009	2010	2011
Telephones ('000 main lines in use)	915.1	908.9	829.0
Mobile cellular telephones ('000 subscribers)	4,051.7	6,854.0	14,126.7
Internet subscribers ('000)	74.6	72.4	n.a.
Broadband subscribers ('000)	3.5	4.1	27.0

Book production: 444 titles in 1999.

Non-daily newspapers: 135 in 2004.

Daily newspapers: 3 in 2004 (average circulation 358,000 copies).

Radio receivers ('000 in use): 11,340 in 2000.

Television receivers ('000 in use): 1,260 in 2000.

Personal computers: 532,000 (6.8 per 1,000 persons) in 2007.

Sources: UNESCO, *Statistical Yearbook*; UN, *Statistical Yearbook*; International Telecommunication Union.

Education

(1999/2000 unless otherwise indicated)

	Institutions	Teachers	Students
Pre-primary	834	9,647*	341,315*
Primary	11,490	252,232*	13,635,289*
Secondary: general	410	85,944*	3,853,280*
Secondary: teacher training	12	294	4,813
Secondary: skill development centres	25	367	2,474
Secondary: technical and vocational	25	11,716*	353,420*
University level	6	8,355†	264,822†
Other higher:			
Government	11	578	18,412
Non-government	4	140	8,376

* 2009/10 figure.
† 2007/08 figure.

Sources: Ministry of Education, Addis Ababa; UNESCO Institute for Statistics.

Pupil-teacher ratio (primary education, UNESCO estimate): 54.1 in 2009/10 (Source: UNESCO Institute for Statistics).

Adult literacy rate (UNESCO estimates): 35.9% (males 50.0%; females 22.8%) in 2008 (Source: UNESCO Institute for Statistics).

Directory

The Constitution

The Constitution of the Federal Democratic Republic of Ethiopia was adopted by the transitional Government on 8 December 1994. The following is a summary of the main provisions of the Constitution, which came into force on 22 August 1995.

GENERAL PROVISIONS

The Constitution establishes a federal and democratic state structure and all sovereign power resides in the nations, nationalities and peoples of Ethiopia. The Constitution is the supreme law of the land. Human rights and freedoms, emanating from the nature of mankind, are inviolable and inalienable. State and religion are separate and there shall be no state religion. The State shall not interfere in religious matters and vice versa. All Ethiopian languages shall enjoy equal state recognition; Amharic shall be the working language of the Federal Government.

FUNDAMENTAL RIGHTS AND FREEDOMS

All persons are equal before the law and are guaranteed equal and effective protection, without discrimination on grounds of race, nation, nationality, or other social origin, colour, sex, language, religion, political or other opinion, property, birth or other status. Everyone has the right to freedom of thought, conscience and religion and the freedom, either individually or in community with others, and in public or private, to manifest his religion or belief in worship, observance, practice and teaching. Every person has the inviolable and inalienable right to life, privacy, and the security of person and liberty.

DEMOCRATIC RIGHTS

Every Ethiopian national, without discrimination based on colour, race, nation, nationality, sex, language, religion, political or other opinion, or other status, has the following rights: on the attainment of 18 years of age, to vote in accordance with the law; to be elected to any office at any level of government; to freely express oneself without interference; to hold opinions without interference; to engage in economic activity and to pursue a livelihood anywhere within the national territory; to choose his or her means of livelihood, occupation and profession; and to own private property.

Every nation, nationality and people in Ethiopia has the following rights: an unconditional right to self-determination, including the right to secession; the right to speak, to write and to develop its own language; the right to express, to develop and to promote its culture, and to preserve its history; the right to a full measure of self-government which includes the right to establish institutions of government in the territory that it inhabits. Women shall, in the enjoyment of rights and protections provided for by this Constitution, have equal rights with men.

STATE STRUCTURE

The Federal Democratic Republic of Ethiopia shall have a parliamentarian form of government. The Federal Democratic Republic shall comprise nine States. Addis Ababa shall be the capital city of the Federal State.

STRUCTURE AND DIVISION OF POWERS

The Federal Democratic Republic of Ethiopia comprises the Federal Government and the member States. The Federal Government and the States shall have legislative, executive and judicial powers. The House of People's Representatives is the highest authority of the Federal Government. The House is responsible to the people. The State Council is the highest organ of state authority. It is responsible to the people of the State. State government shall be established at state and other administrative levels deemed necessary. Adequate power shall be granted to the lowest units of government to enable the people to participate directly in the administration of such units. The State Council has legislative power on matters falling under state jurisdiction. Consistent with the provisions of this Constitution, the Council has the power to draft, adopt and amend the state constitution. The state administration constitutes the highest organ of executive power. State judicial power is vested in its courts. The States shall respect the powers of the Federal Government. The Federal Government shall likewise respect the powers of the States. The Federal Government may, when necessary, delegate to the States powers and functions granted to it by the Constitution.

THE FEDERAL HOUSES

There shall be two Federal Houses: the House of People's Representatives and the House of the Federation.

Members of the House of People's Representatives shall be elected by the people for a term of five years on the basis of universal suffrage and by direct, free and fair elections held by secret ballot. Members of the House, on the basis of population and special representation of minority nationalities and peoples, shall not exceed 550; of these, minority nationalities and peoples shall have at least 20 seats. The House of People's Representatives shall have legislative power in all matters assigned by this Constitution to federal jurisdiction. The political party or coalition of political parties that has the greatest number of seats in the House of People's Representatives shall form and lead the Executive. Elections for a new House shall be concluded one month prior to the expiry of the House's term.

The House of the Federation is composed of representatives of nations, nationalities and peoples. Each nation, nationality and people shall be represented in the House of the Federation by at least one member. Each nation or nationality shall be represented by one additional representative for each one million of its population. Members of the House of the Federation shall be elected by the State Councils. The State Councils may themselves elect representatives to the House of the Federation, or they may hold elections to have the representatives elected by the people directly. The House of the Federation shall hold at least two sessions annually. The term of mandate of the House of the Federation shall be five years. No one may be a member of the House of People's Representatives and of the House of the Federation simultaneously.

PRESIDENT OF THE REPUBLIC

The President of the Federal Democratic Republic of Ethiopia is the Head of State. The House of People's Representatives shall nominate the candidate for President. The nominee shall be elected President if a joint session of the House of People's Representatives and the House of the Federation approves his candidacy by a two-thirds' majority vote. The term of office of the President shall be six years. No person shall be elected President for more than two terms. The President's duties include the opening of the Federal Houses; appointing ambassadors and other envoys to represent the country abroad; granting, upon recommendation by the Prime Minister and in accordance with law, high military titles; and granting pardons.

THE EXECUTIVE

The highest executive powers of the Federal Government are vested in the Prime Minister and in the Council of Ministers. The Prime Minister and the Council of Ministers are responsible to the House of People's Representatives. In the exercise of state functions, members of the Council of Ministers are collectively responsible for all decisions they make as a body. Unless otherwise provided in this Constitution, the term of office of the Prime Minister is the duration of the mandate of the House of People's Representatives. The Prime Minister is the Chief Executive, the Chairman of the Council of Ministers, and the Commander-in-Chief of the national armed forces. The Prime Minister shall submit for approval to the House of People's Representatives nominees for ministerial posts from among members of the two Houses or from among persons who are not members of either House and possess the required qualifications. The Council of Ministers is responsible to the Prime Minister and, in all its decisions, is responsible to the House of People's Representatives. The Council of Ministers ensures the implementation of laws and decisions adopted by the House of People's Representatives.

STRUCTURE AND POWERS OF THE COURTS

Supreme Federal judicial authority is vested in the Federal Supreme Court. The House of People's Representatives may, by a two-thirds' majority vote, establish nation-wide, or in some parts of the country only, the Federal High Court and First-Instance Courts it deems necessary. Unless decided in this manner, the jurisdictions of the Federal High Court and of the First-Instance Courts are hereby delegated to the state courts. States shall establish State Supreme, High and First-Instance Courts. Judicial powers, both at federal and state levels, are vested in the courts. Courts of any level shall be free from any interference or influence of any governmental body, government official or from any other source. Judges shall exercise their functions in full independence and shall be directed solely by the law. The Federal Supreme Court shall have the highest and final judicial power over federal matters. State Supreme Courts shall have the highest and final judicial power over state matters. They shall also exercise the jurisdiction of the Federal High Court.

MISCELLANEOUS PROVISIONS

The Council of Ministers of the Federal Government shall have the power to decree a state of emergency in the event of an external invasion, a breakdown of law and order that endangers the constitutional order and cannot be controlled by the regular law enforcement agencies and personnel, a natural disaster or an epidemic. State executives can decree a state-wide state of emergency should a natural disaster or an epidemic occur.

A National Election Board independent of any influence shall be established, to conduct free and fair elections in federal and state constituencies in an impartial manner.

The Government

HEAD OF STATE

President: Lt GIRMA WOLDE GIORGIS (took office 8 October 2001; re-elected by vote of the House of People's Representatives 9 October 2007).

COUNCIL OF MINISTERS

(September 2012)

The Government is formed by members of the Amhara National Democratic Movement (ANDM), the South Ethiopian People's Democratic Movement (SEPDM), the Oromo People's Democratic Organization (OPDO), the Tigrai People's Liberation Front (TPLF), the Somali People's Democratic Party (SPDP) and one independent.

Prime Minister: HAILEMARIAM DESALEGN (SEPDM).

Minister of Defence: SIRAJ FERGESA (SEPDM).

Minister of Federal Affairs: Dr SHIFERAW TEKELEMARIAM (SEPDM).

Minister of Justice: BERHAN HAILU (ANDM).

Minister of the Civil Service: JUNIEDY SADO (OPDO).

Minister of Finance and Economic Development: SUFYAN AHMED (OPDO).

Minister of Agriculture: TEFERA DERIBEW (ANDM).

Minister of Industry: MEKONNEN MANYAZEWAL (Ind.).

Minister of Trade: KEBEDE CHANE (ANDM).

Minister of Science and Technology: DESSE DALKE (SEPDM).

Minister of Transport: DIRIBA KUMA (OPDO).

Minister of Cabinet Affairs and Head of the Office of the Prime Minister: MUKTAR KEDIR (OPDO).

Minister of Communication and Information Technology: DEBRETSION GEBREMIKAEL (TPLF).

Minister of Urban Development and Construction: MEKURIA HAILE (SEPDM).

Minister of Water and Energy: ALEMAYEHU TEGENU (OPDO).

Minister of Mines: SINKNESH EJIGU (OPDO).

Minister of Education: DEMEKE MEKONNEN (ANDM).

Minister of Health: Dr TEWEDROS ADHANOM (TPLF).

Minister of Labour and Social Affairs: ABDULFETAH ABDULAHI HASSEN (SPDP).

Minister of Culture and Tourism: AMIN ABDULKADIR (ANDM).

Minister of Women, Youth and Children's Affairs: ZENEBU TADESSE (ANDM).

Minister, Public Mobilization and Participation Adviser to the Prime Minister: REDWAN HUSSEIN (SEPDM).

Minister, Head of the Government Communication Office: BEREKET SIMON (ANDM).

Minister, Government Chief Whip: ASTER MAMO (OPDO).

Minister, Director-General of the Ethiopian Revenues and Customs Authority: MELAKU FANTA (ANDM).

MINISTRIES

Office of the President: POB 1031, Addis Ababa; tel. (11) 1551000; fax (11) 1552030.

Office of the Prime Minister: POB 1013, Addis Ababa; tel. (11) 1552044; fax (11) 1552020.

Office for Government Communication Affairs: Addis Ababa; tel. (11) 5540486; fax (11) 5540473; e-mail shekemal@yahoo.com.

Ministry of Agriculture: POB 62347, Addis Ababa; tel. (11) 5538134; fax (11) 5530776.

Ministry of the Civil Service: Addis Ababa.

Ministry of Communication and Information Technology: Addis Ababa.

Ministry of Culture and Tourism: POB 2183, Addis Ababa; tel. (11) 5512310; fax (11) 5512889; e-mail info@tourismethiopia.org; internet www.tourismethiopia.org.

Ministry of Defence: POB 1373, Addis Ababa; tel. (11) 5511777; fax (11) 5516053.

Ministry of Education: POB 1367, Addis Ababa; tel. (11) 1553133; fax (11) 1550877.

Ministry of Federal Affairs: POB 1031, Addis Ababa; tel. (11) 5512766; fax (11) 1552030.

Ministry of Finance and Economic Development: POB 1037, Addis Ababa; tel. (11) 1552800; fax (11) 1550118; internet www.mofaed.org.

Ministry of Foreign Affairs: POB 393, Addis Ababa; tel. (11) 5517345; fax (11) 5514300; e-mail mfa.addis@telecom.net.et; internet www.mfa.gov.et.

Ministry of Health: POB 1234, Addis Ababa; tel. (11) 5517011; fax (11) 5519366.

Ministry of Industry: Addis Ababa; tel. (11) 534942; fax (11) 5534932; internet www.moi.gov.et.

Ministry of Justice: POB 1370, Addis Ababa; tel. (11) 512288; fax (11) 517775; internet www.mojet.gov.et.

Ministry of Labour and Social Affairs: POB 2056, Addis Ababa; tel. (11) 5517080; fax (11) 5518396.

Ministry of Mines: POB 486, Addis Ababa; tel. (11) 5153689; fax (11) 5517874.

Ministry of Science and Technology: Addis Ababa.

Ministry of Trade: POB 704, Addis Ababa; tel. (11) 5518025; fax (11) 5514288; e-mail henok_fekadu@yahoo.com.

Ministry of Transport: Addis Ababa; tel. (11) 5516166; fax (11) 5515665; e-mail nigusmen@yahoo.com; internet www.motr.gov.et.

Ministry of Urban Development and Construction: POB 1238, Addis Ababa; tel. (11) 5518292; fax (11) 527969.

Ministry of Water and Energy: POB 486, Addis Ababa; tel. (11) 5153689; fax (11) 5517874.

Ministry of Women, Youth and Children's Affairs: POB 1364, Addis Ababa; tel. (11) 5517020.

Regional Governments

Ethiopia comprises nine regional governments, one chartered city (Addis Ababa) and one Administrative Council (Dire Dawa), which are vested with authority for self-administration. The executive bodies are respectively headed by Presidents (regional states) and Chairmen (Addis Ababa and Dire Dawa).

PRESIDENTS
(September 2012)

Tigrai: TSEGAYE BERHE.

Afar: ESMAEL ALISERO.

Amhara: AYALEW GOBEZE.

Oromia: Gen. ABADULA GEMEDA.

Somali: ABDULAHI HASAN MOHAMMED.

Benishangul/Gumuz: (vacant).

Southern Nations, Nationalities and Peoples: SHIFERAW SHIGUTTE.

Gambela: UMED UBONG.

Harari: MURAD ABDULHADIN.

CHAIRMEN
(September 2012)

Dire Dawa: ABDULAZIZ MOHAMMED.

Addis Ababa: KUMA DEMEKSA.

Legislature

FEDERAL PARLIAMENTARY ASSEMBLY

The legislature comprises an upper house, the House of the Federation (Yefedereshn Mekir Bet), with 108 seats (members are selected by state assemblies and are drawn one each from 22 minority nationalities and one from each professional sector of the remaining nationalities, and serve for a period of five years), and a lower house of no more than 550 directly elected members, the House of People's Representatives (Yehizbtewekayoch Mekir Bet), who are also elected for a five-year term.

Speaker of the House of the Federation: KASSA TEKLEBERHAN.

Deputy Speaker of the House of the Federation: MOHAMMED SIREE.

Yehizbtewekayoch Mekir Bet
(House of People's Representatives)

Speaker: ABADULA GEMEDA.

Deputy Speaker: SHITAYE MINALE.

General Election, 23 May 2010

Party	Seats
Ethiopian People's Revolutionary Democratic Front (EPRDF)	499
Somali People's Democratic Party (SPDP)	24
Benishangul Gumuz People's Democratic Party (BGPDP)	9
Afar National Democratic Party (ANDP)	8
Gambela People's Unity Democratic Movement (GPUDM)	3
Amhara National Democratic Movement (ANDM)	1
Ethiopia Federal Democratic Unity Forum (FORUM)	1
Harari National League (HNL)	1
Independent	1
Total	547

Election Commission

National Electoral Board of Ethiopia (NEB): POB 40812, Addis Ababa; tel. (11) 5153416; e-mail info@electionethiopia.org; internet www.electionethiopia.org; f. 1993; independent board of seven politically non-affiliated mems appointed, on the Prime Minister's recommendation, by the House of People's Representatives; Chair. KEMAL BEDRI KELO.

Political Organizations

A total of 79 political parties contested the 2010 legislative elections.

Afar National Democratic Party (ANDP): f. 1999; Chair. MOHAMED KEDIR.

Afar People's Democratic Organization (APDO): fmrly Afar Liberation Front (ALF); based in fmr Hararghe and Wollo Admin. Regions; Leader ISMAIL ALI SIRRO.

Benishangul Gumuz People's Democratic Party (BGPDP): f. 2009; Chair. HABTAMU HIKA.

Ethiopia Federal Democratic Unity Forum (FORUM): f. 2009; the Ethiopia Democratic Union Movement (EDUM) and the Somali Democratic Alliance Forces (SDAF) withdrew from the coalition in March 2010; Chair. MOGA FIRISA.

Ethiopian Social Democratic Party (ESDP): f. 1993 as the Council of Alternative Forces for Peace and Democracy in Ethiopia; opposes the EPRDF; Chair. Dr BEYENE PETROS.

Oromo Federalist Democratic Movement (OFDM): formed part of the Oromo Federalist Congress (OFC) for the 2010 elections; Chair. BULCHA DEMEKSA; Sec.-Gen. BEKELE JIRATA.

Oromo People's Congress (OPC): Addis Ababa; e-mail oromopeoplescongress@yahoo.com; internet www.oromopeoplescongress.org; f. 2007 by fmr mems of the ONC; formed part of the Oromo Federalist Congress (OFC) for the 2010 elections; Chair. Dr MERARA GUDINA.

Southern Ethiopia People's Democratic Union (SEPDU): f. 1994; Chair. TILAHUN EADESHAW.

Union of Tigrians For Democracy and Sovereignty (ARENA): f. 2007; Chair. GEBRU ASTRAT.

Unity For Democracy and Justice Party (ANDENET): f. 2008; Chair. Eng. GIZACHEW SHIFERAW.

Ethiopian Justice and Democratic Forces Front (EJDFF): f. 2008; Chair. GIRMAY HADERA.

Ethiopian Democratic Union (EDU): f. 2004; Chair. Dr KEBEDE HAILEMARIAM.

Ethiopian National Unity Party (ENUP): f. 2005; Chair. ZERIHUN GEBREGZIABER.

Oromia Liberation National Party (OLNP): Chair. Dr FARIS ISAYAS.

Unity of Southern Ethiopian Democratic Forces (USEDF): f. 2005; comprises Wolaita People's Democratic Front (WPDF), Gamo Democratic Union (GDU) and Gomogofa People's Democratic Union (GPDU); Chair. TEKLE BORENA.

Ethiopian National Democratic Party (ENDP): f. 1994 by merger of five pro-Govt orgs with mems in the Council of Representatives; comprises: the Ethiopian Democratic Organization, the Ethiopian Democratic Organization Coalition (EDC), the Gurage People's Democratic Front (GPDF), the Kembata People's Congress (KPC), and the Wolaita People's Democratic Front (WPDF); Chair. FEKADU GEDAMU.

Ethiopian People's Revolutionary Democratic Front (EPRDF): Addis Ababa; internet www.eprdf.org.et; f. 1989 by the TPLF as an alliance of insurgent groups seeking regional autonomy and engaged in armed struggle against the EDUP Govt; Chair. HAILEMARIAM DESALEGN; Vice-Chair. DEMEKE MEKONNEN; in May 1991, with other orgs, formed transitional Govt.

Amhara National Democratic Movement (ANDM): based in Tigrai; represents interests of the Amhara people; fmrly the Ethiopian People's Democratic Movement (EPDM); adopted present name in 1994; Chair. ADDISO LEGGESE.

Oromo People's Democratic Organization (OPDO): f. 1990 by the TPLF to promote its cause in Oromo areas; based among the Oromo people in the Shoa region; Leader Gen. ABADULA GEMEDA.

South Ethiopian People's Democratic Movement (SEPDM): f. 1992; Chair. HAILEMARIAM DESALEGN.

Tigrai People's Liberation Front (TPLF): f. 1975; the dominant org. within the EPRDF; Chair. (vacant); Vice-Chair. SEYOUM MESFIN.

Gambela People's Unity Democratic Movement (GPUDM): f. 2008; Chair. UMOD OBONG ALUM.

Harari National League (HNL): f. 1994; Chair. YASIN HUSEIN.

Movement for Justice, Freedom and Democracy (Ginbot 7): 8647 Richmond Highway, Alexandria, VA 22309, USA; e-mail org@ginbot7.org; internet www.ginbot7.org; f. 2008; Leader BERHANU NEGA.

Ogaden National Liberation Front (ONLF): e-mail foreign@onlf.org; internet www.onlf.org; f. 1984; seeks self-determination for the Ogaden region; Chair. MOHAMED OMAR OSMAN.

Oromo Liberation Front (OLF): POB 73247, Washington, DC 20056, USA; tel. (202) 462-5477; fax (202) 332-7011; e-mail info@oromoliberationfront.org; internet www.oromoliberationfront.org; f. 1973; seeks self-determination for the Oromo people; participated in the Ethiopian transitional Govt until June 1992; Chair. DAWUD IBSA AYANA; Vice-Chair. ABDULFATTAH A. MOUSSA BIYYO.

Sidama Liberation Front (SLF): e-mail info@sidamaliberation-front.org; internet www.sidamaliberation-front.org; campaigns for self-determination for Sidama people.

Somali Abo Liberation Front (SALF): operates in fmr Bale Admin. Region; has received Somali military assistance; Sec.-Gen. MASURAD SHU'ABI IBRAHIM.

Somali People's Democratic Party (SPDP): St Jijiga Somali Regional 365; internet www.spdp.org.et; f. 1998 by merger of Ogaden National Liberation Front (ONLF) and the Ethiopian Somali Democratic League (ESDL—an alliance comprising the Somali Democratic Union Party, the Issa and Gurgura Liberation Front, the Gurgura Independence Front, the Eastern Gabooye Democratic Organization, the Eastern Ethiopian Somali League, the Horyal Democratic Front, the Social Alliance Democratic Organization, the Somali Abo Democratic Union, the Shekhash People's Democratic Movement, the Ethiopian Somalis' Democratic Movement and the Per Barreh Party); Chair. ABDIFETAH SHECK ABDULAHI; Sec.-Gen. AHMED ARAB ADEN.

United Ethiopian Democratic Forces (UEDF): POB 73246, Washington, DC 20056-3246, USA; e-mail UEDFHIBRET@yahoo.com; internet www.hebret.org; f. 2003; US-based org.; Chair. Dr BEYENE PETROS.

Ethiopian National United Front (ENUF): POB 21387, Washington, DC 20009-21387, USA; tel. (202) 785-1618; e-mail admin@enufforethiopia.net; internet www.enufforethiopia.net; f. 2001; USA-based org.; Chair. BEKELE MOLLA.

United Ethiopian Democratic Party (UEDP): POB 101458, Addis Ababa; tel. (11) 5508727; fax (11) 5508730; e-mail uedpmedhinpr@gmail.com; internet www.uedpmedhin.org; f. 2003 by the merger of Ethiopian Democratic Unity Party and the Ethiopian Democratic Party; Sec.-Gen. Dr ADMASSU GEBREYEHU.

United Oromo Liberation Forces (UOLF): f. 2000 in Asmara, Eritrea, as a common Oromo Front seeking to overthrow the Ethiopian Govt; Sec.-Gen. GALASA DILBO; alliance comprises:

Islamic Front for the Liberation of Oromia: Leader ABDELKARIM IBRAHIM HAMID.

Oromo Liberation Council (OLC).

Oromo Liberation Front (OLF): see above.

United Oromo People's Liberation Front (UOPLF).

Unity of Ethiopians for Democratic Change (UEDC): f. 2007 as replacement for the Alliance for Freedom and Democracy; coalition of political parties and rebel groups opposed to the Govt.

Benishangul People's Movement (BPM): rebel group operating in western Ethiopia.

Ethiopian People Patriotic Front: CP 182, 1211 Geneva 13, Switzerland; tel. 223406025; e-mail info@eppf.net; internet www.eppf.net; armed anti-Govt group operating mainly in northwestern Ethiopia; Leader Prof. ALEBACHEW TEGEGNE.

Southern Ethiopia People's Front for Justice and Equality (SEPFJE): armed anti-Govt group operating in southern Ethiopia.

Tigrai People's Democratic Movement (TPDM): f. 1979; rebel group operating in northern Tigrai region of Ethiopia.

Diplomatic Representation

EMBASSIES IN ETHIOPIA

Algeria: Woreda 23, Kebele 13, House No. 1819, POB 5740, Addis Ababa; tel. (11) 3719666; fax (11) 3719669; Ambassador NOUREDDINE AOUAM.

Angola: Woreda 18, Kebele 26, House No. 6, POB 2962, Addis Ababa; tel. (11) 5510085; fax (11) 5514922; Ambassador ARCANJO MARIA DO NASCIMENTO.

Australia: Addis Ababa; Ambassador LISA FILIPETTO.

Austria: POB 1219, Addis Ababa; tel. (11) 3712144; fax (11) 3712140; e-mail addis-abeba-ob@bmeia.gv.at; internet www.bmeia.gv.at/botschaft/addis-abeba.html; Ambassador Prof. Dr RUDOLF AGSTNER.

Belgium: Comoros St, Kebele 8, POB 1239, Addis Ababa; tel. (11) 6611813; fax (11) 6613646; e-mail addisababa@diplobel.fed.be; internet www.diplomatie.be/addisababa; Ambassador GUNTHER SLEEUWAGEN.

Benin: Addis Ababa; Ambassador EDOUARD AHO-GELLE.

Botswana: POB 22282, Addis Ababa; tel. (11) 715422; fax (11) 714099; Ambassador MANYEPEDZA PATRICK LESETEDI.

Brazil: Bole Sub-City, Kebele 2, House No. 2830, POB 2458, Addis Ababa; tel. (11) 6620401; fax (11) 6620412; e-mail embradisadm@ethionet.et; Ambassador IZABEL CRISTINA DE AZEVEDO.

Bulgaria: Bole Kifle Ketema, Kebele 06, Haile Gabreselassie Rd, POB 987, Addis Ababa; tel. (11) 6610032; fax (11) 6613373; e-mail bulemba@ethionet.et; internet www.mfa.bg/addis-ababa/; Chargé d'affaires a.i. EMIL TRIFONOV.

Burkina Faso: Kebele 19, House No. 281, POB 19685, Addis Ababa; tel. (11) 6615863; fax (11) 6625857; e-mail ambfet@telecom.net.et; Ambassador BRUNO ZIDOUEMBA.

Burundi: POB 3641, Addis Ababa; tel. (11) 4651300; e-mail burundi.emb@telecom.net.et; Ambassador EPIPHANIE KABUSHEMEYE.

Cameroon: Bole Rd, Woreda 18, Kebele 26, House No. 168, POB 1026, Addis Ababa; tel. (11) 5504488; fax (11) 5518434; Ambassador MARTIN AYAFAR CHINGGONG.

Canada: Nefas Silk Lafto Kifle Ketema 3, Kebele 4, House No. 122, POB 1130, Addis Ababa; tel. (11) 3713022; fax (11) 3713033; e-mail addis@international.gc.ca; internet www.canadainternational.gc.ca/ethiopia-ethiopie/index.aspx; Ambassador DAVID USHER.

Cape Verde: Kebele 3, House No. 107, POB 200093, Addis Ababa; tel. (11) 6635466; Chargé d'affaires a.i. Custodia Lima.

Chad: Bole Rd, Woreda 17, Kebele 20, House No. 2583, POB 5119, Addis Ababa; tel. (11) 6613819; fax (11) 6612050; Ambassador Cherif Mahamat Zene.

China, People's Republic: Jimma Rd, Woreda 24, Kebele 13, House No. 792, POB 5643, Addis Ababa; tel. (11) 3711960; fax (11) 3712457; e-mail chinaemb_et@mfa.gov.cn; internet et.china-embassy.org; Ambassador Xie Xiaoyan.

Congo, Democratic Republic: Makanisa Rd, Woreda 23, Kebele 13, House No. 1779, POB 2723, Addis Ababa; tel. (11) 3710111; fax (11) 3713485; Ambassador Gérard Mapango Kemishanga.

Congo, Republic: Woreda 3, Kebele 51, House No. 378, POB 5639, Addis Ababa; tel. (11) 5514188; fax (11) 5514331; Ambassador Raymond Serge Bale.

Côte d'Ivoire: Woreda 23, Kebele 13, House No. 1308, POB 3668, Addis Ababa; tel. (11) 3711213; fax (11) 3712178; Ambassador Eugène Allou-Allou.

Cuba: Woreda 17, Kebele 19, House No. 197, POB 5623, Addis Ababa; tel. (11) 620459; fax (11) 620460; e-mail embacuba@ethiopia.cubaminrex.cu; Ambassador Clara Margarita Pulido.

Czech Republic: Kebele 15, House No. 289, POB 3108, Addis Ababa; tel. (11) 5516132; fax (11) 5513471; e-mail addisabeba@embassy.mzv.cz; internet www.mzv.cz/addisababa; Ambassador Zdeněk Dobiáš.

Denmark: Bole Kifle Ketema, Kebele 3, House No. 'New', POB 12955, Addis Ababa; tel. (11) 6187075; fax (11) 6187057; e-mail addamb@um.dk; internet www.etiopien.um.dk; Ambassador Stephan Schönemann.

Djibouti: POB 1022, Addis Ababa; tel. (11) 6613200; fax (11) 6612786; Ambassador Ismaïl Goulal Boudine.

Egypt: POB 1611, Addis Ababa; tel. (11) 1226422; fax (11) 1226432; Ambassador Tarek Ghoneim.

Equatorial Guinea: Bole Rd, Woreda 17, Kebele 23, House No. 162, POB 246, Addis Ababa; tel. (11) 6626278; Ambassador (vacant).

Eritrea: POB 2571, Addis Ababa; tel. (11) 5512844; fax (11) 5514911; Chargé d'affaires a.i. Sahih Omer.

Finland: Mauritania St, Kebele 12, House No. 1431, POB 1017, Addis Ababa; tel. (11) 3205920; fax (11) 3205923; e-mail sanomat.add@formin.fi; Ambassador Kirsti Aarnio.

France: Kabana, POB 1464, Addis Ababa; tel. (11) 1236022; fax (11) 1236029; e-mail scacamb@ethionet.et; internet www.ambafrance-ethiopie.org; Ambassador Jean-Christophe Belliard.

Gabon: Woreda 17, Kebele 18, House No. 1026, POB 1256, Addis Ababa; tel. (11) 6611075; fax (11) 6613700; Ambassador (vacant).

The Gambia: Kebele 3, House No. 79, POB 60083, Addis Ababa; tel. (11) 6624647; fax (11) 6627895; e-mail gambia@ethionet.et; Ambassador Dr Omar A. Touray.

Germany: Yeka Kifle Ketema (Khebena), Woreda 03, POB 660, Addis Ababa; tel. (11) 1235139; fax (11) 1235152; e-mail info@addis-abeba.diplo.de; internet www.addis-abeba.diplo.de; Ambassador Lieselore Cyrus.

Ghana: Jimma Rd, Woreda 24, Kebele 13, House No. 108, POB 3173, Addis Ababa; tel. (11) 3711402; fax (11) 3712511; Ambassador John Evonlah Aggrey.

Greece: off Debre Zeit Rd, POB 1168, Addis Ababa; tel. (11) 4654911; fax (11) 4654883; internet www.telecom.net.et/~greekemb; Ambassador Dionisios Kountoureas.

Guinea: Debre Zeit Rd, Woreda 18, Kebele 14, House No. 58, POB 1190, Addis Ababa; tel. 912200181 (mobile); internet guineaaddisembassy@gmail.com; Ambassador Cheick A. T. Camara.

Holy See: POB 588, Addis Ababa (Apostolic Nunciature); tel. (11) 3712100; fax (11) 3711499; Apostolic Nuncio Most Rev. George Panikulam (Titular Archbishop of Caudium).

India: Kabena, POB 528, Addis Ababa; tel. (11) 1552100; fax (11) 1552521; Ambassador Gurjit Singh.

Indonesia: Mekanisa Rd, Higher 23, Kebele 13, House No. 1816, POB 1004, Addis Ababa; tel. (11) 3712104; fax (11) 3710873; e-mail kbriadis@ethionet.et; internet www.indonesia-addis.org.et; Ambassador Ramli Sa'ud.

Iran: 317–318 Jimma Rd, POB 1144, Addis Ababa; tel. (11) 3710037; fax (11) 3712299; internet www.iranembassy-addis.net; Ambassador Mohammed Javad Zamanian Koopaie.

Ireland: Debre Zeit Rd, Woreda 20, Kebele 40, House No. 21, POB 9585, Addis Ababa; tel. (11) 4665050; fax (11) 4665020; e-mail addisababaembassy@dfa.ie; Ambassador Síle Maguire.

Israel: Woreda 16, Kebele 22, House No. 283, POB 1266, Addis Ababa; tel. (11) 6460999; fax (11) 64619619; e-mail embassy@addisababa.mfa.gov.il; internet addisababa.mfa.gov.il; Ambassador Belaynesh Zevadia.

Italy: Villa Italia, POB 1105, Addis Ababa; tel. (11) 1235717; fax (11) 1235689; e-mail ambasciata.addisabeba@esteri.it; internet www.ambaddisabeba.esteri.it; Ambassador Raffaele de Lutio.

Japan: Woreda 18, Kebele 7, House No. 653, POB 5650, Addis Ababa; tel. (11) 5511088; fax (11) 5511350; e-mail japan-embassy@telecom.net.et; internet www.et.emb-japan.go.jp; Ambassador Hiroyuki Kishino.

Kenya: Woreda 16, Kebele 1, POB 3301, Addis Ababa; tel. (11) 610033; fax (11) 611433; Ambassador (vacant).

Korea, Democratic People's Republic: Woreda 20, Kebele 40, House No. 892, POB 2378, Addis Ababa; tel. (11) 6182828; Ambassador Kim Hyok Chol.

Korea, Republic: Jimma Rd, Old Airport Area, POB 2047, Addis Ababa; tel. (11) 4655230; e-mail skorea.emb@telecom.net.et; Ambassador Chung Soonsuk.

Kuwait: Woreda 17, Kebele 20, House No. 128, POB 19898, Addis Ababa; tel. (11) 6615411; fax (11) 6612621; Ambassador Faez Moubel al-Mouteiri.

Lesotho: Bole Sub-City, Kebele 03, House No. 2118, Addis Ababa; tel. (11) 6614368; fax (11) 6612837; e-mail lesotho-addis@foreign.gov.ls; Ambassador Fine Maema.

Liberia: Roosevelt St, Woreda 21, Kebele 4, House No. 237, POB 3116, Addis Ababa; tel. (11) 5513655; Ambassador Dr Edward Gboloco Howard Clinton.

Libya: Ras Tessema Sefer, Woreda 3, Kebele 53, House No. 585, POB 5728, Addis Ababa; tel. (11) 5511077; fax (11) 5511383; Ambassador Ali Abdalla Awidan.

Madagascar: Woreda 17, Kebele 19, House No. 629, POB 60004, Addis Ababa; tel. (11) 612555; fax (11) 610127; Ambassador Jean Pierre Rakotoarivony.

Malawi: Bole Rd, Woreda 23, Kebele 13, House No. 1021, POB 2316, Addis Ababa; tel. (11) 3711280; fax (11) 3719742; e-mail malemb@telecom.net.et; Ambassador Dr Isaac Munlo.

Mali: Kebele 03, House No. 418, Addis Ababa; tel. (11) 168990; fax (11) 162838; e-mail keitamoone@maliembassy-addis.org; internet www.maliembassy-addis.org; Ambassador Amadou Ndiaye.

Mauritania: Lidete Kifle Ketema, Kebele 2, House No. 431a, POB 200015, Addis Ababa; tel. (11) 3729165; fax (11) 3729166; Ambassador Mohamed Abdellahi Ould Babana.

Mauritius: Kebele 03, House No. 750, POB 200222, Kifle Ketema, Addis Ababa; tel. (11) 6615997; fax (11) 6614704; e-mail addisemb@mail.gov.mu; internet www.addisababa.mail.gov.mu; Ambassador Mahendr Dosieah.

Morocco: 210 Bole Rd, POB 60033, Addis Ababa; tel. (11) 5508440; fax (11) 5511828; e-mail morocco.emb@ethionet.et; Ambassador Abdeljebbar Brahime.

Mozambique: Woreda 17, Kebele 23, House No. 2116, POB 5671, Addis Ababa; tel. (11) 3729199; fax (11) 3729197; e-mail embamoc.etiopia@minec.gov.mz; Ambassador Manuel Tomás Lubisse.

Namibia: Bole Sub-City, Kebele 19, House No. 575, POB 1443, Addis Ababa; tel. (11) 6611966; fax (11) 6612677; e-mail nam.emb@ethionet.et; Ambassador Kakena S. K. Nangula.

Netherlands: Old Airport Zone, Kifle Ketema, Lideta, Kebele 02/03, POB 1241, Addis Ababa; tel. (11) 3711100; fax (11) 3711577; e-mail add@minbuza.nl; internet ethiopia.nlembassy.org; Ambassador Hans Blankenberg.

Niger: Woreda 9, Kebele 23, POB 5791, Addis Ababa; tel. (11) 4651305; fax (11) 4651296; Ambassador Diallo Amina Djibo.

Nigeria: POB 1019, Addis Ababa; tel. (11) 1550644; Chargé d'affaires a.i. Chigozie Obi-Nnadozie.

Norway: POB 8383, Addis Ababa; tel. (11) 3710799; fax (11) 3711255; e-mail emb.addisabeba@mfa.no; internet www.norway.org.et; Ambassador Jens-Petter Kjemprud.

Poland: House No. 583, Dej Belay Zeleke Rd, Guelele Sub-City, Kebele 08, POB 27207/1000, Addis Ababa; tel. (11) 1574189; fax (11) 1574222; e-mail addisabeba.amb.sekretariat@msz.gov.pl; internet www.addisabeba.polemb.net; Ambassador Jarosław Roman Szczepankiewicz.

Portugal: Sheraton Addis, Taitu St, POB 6002, Addis Ababa; tel. (11) 171717; fax (11) 173403; e-mail embportadis@hotmail.com; Ambassador Dr Vera Maria Fernandes.

Romania: Houses No. 9–10, Bole Kifle Ketema, Kebele 03, POB 2478, Addis Ababa; tel. (11) 6610156; fax (11) 6611191; e-mail roembaddis@ethionet.et; Chargé d'affaires a.i. Gabriel Branzaru.

Russia: POB 1500, Addis Ababa; tel. (11) 6612060; fax (11) 6613795; e-mail russemb@ethionet.et; Ambassador Mikhail Y. Afanasiev.

Rwanda: POB 5618, Addis Ababa; tel. (11) 6610300; fax (11) 6610411; e-mail ambaddis@minaffet.gov.rw; internet www.ethiopia.embassy.gov.rw; High Commissioner Joseph Nsengimana.

Senegal: Africa Ave, POB 2581, Addis Ababa; tel. (11) 6611376; fax (11) 6610020; e-mail ambassene-addis@ethionet.et; Ambassador BASSIROU SÉNÉ.

Serbia: POB 1341, Addis Ababa; tel. (11) 5517804; fax (11) 5514192; e-mail serbembaddis@ethionet.et; Ambassador DRAGAN MOMCILOVIĆ.

Sierra Leone: Kefle Ketema-Nefas Silk Lafto, Kebele 05, House No. 2629, POB 5619, Addis Ababa; tel. (11) 3710033; fax (11) 3711911; e-mail salonembadd@yahoo.co.uk; Ambassador ANDREW GBEBAY BANGALI.

Slovakia: Bole Sub-City, Erer Ber Shola Residential Houses, Woreda 17, Kebele 14/15, House No. 123, POB 6627, Addis Ababa; tel. (11) 6450849; fax (11) 6474656; e-mail emb.addisababa@mzv.sk; internet www.mzv.sk/addisabeba.

Somalia: Bole Kifle Ketema, Kebele 20, House No. 588, POB 1643, Addis Ababa; tel. (11) 6180673; fax (11) 6180680; internet www.ethiopia.somaligov.net; Ambassador SAID AHMED NOOR.

South Africa: Alexander Pushkin St, Higher 23, Kebele 10, House No. 1885, Old Airport Area, POB 1091, Addis Ababa; tel. (11) 3713034; fax (11) 3711330; e-mail sa.embassy.addis@telecom.net.et; Ambassador CHRIS PEPANI.

Spain: Botswana St, POB 2312, Addis Ababa; tel. (11) 1222544; fax (11) 1222542; e-mail emb.addisabeba@maec.es; internet www.mae.es/embajadas/addisabeba/es/home; Ambassador MIGUEL ÁNGEL FERNÁNDEZ-PALACIOS MARTÍNEZ.

Sudan: Kirkos, Kebele, POB 1110, Addis Ababa; tel. (11) 5516477; fax (11) 5519989; e-mail sudan.embassy@telecom.net.et; Ambassador ABU ZAID AL-HASSAN.

Sweden: Lideta KK, Kebele 07/14, House No. 891, POB 1142, Addis Ababa; tel. (11) 5180000; fax (11) 5180030; e-mail ambassaden.addis-abeba@foreign.ministry.se; internet www.swedenabroad.se/addisabeba; Ambassador JENS ODLANDER.

Switzerland: Jimma Rd, Old Airport Area, POB 1106, Addis Ababa; tel. (11) 3711107; fax (11) 3712177; e-mail add.vertretung@eda.admin.ch; Ambassador DOMINIK LANGENBACHER.

Tanzania: POB 1077, Addis Ababa; tel. (11) 5511063; fax (11) 5517358; Ambassador (vacant).

Togo: Addis Ababa; Ambassador TILIOUFEI KOFFI ESAW.

Tunisia: Wereda 17, Kebele 19, Bole Rd, POB 100069, Addis Ababa; tel. (11) 6612063; fax (11) 6614568; Ambassador MOKHTAR CHAOUACHI.

Turkey: POB 1506, Addis Ababa; tel. (11) 6612321; fax (11) 6611688; e-mail turk.emb@ethionet.et; Ambassador ALI RIZA COLAK.

Uganda: Kirkos Kifle Ketema, Kebele 35, House No. 31, POB 5644, Addis Ababa; tel. (11) 5513088; fax (11) 5514355; e-mail uganda.emb@ethionet.et; Ambassador MULL KATENDE.

Ukraine: Woreda 17, Kebele 3, House No. 2116, POB 2358, Addis Ababa; tel. (11) 6611698; fax (11) 6621288; e-mail emb_et@mfa.gov.ua; Ambassador VLADYSLAV DEMYANENKO.

United Kingdom: POB 858, Addis Ababa; tel. (11) 6612354; fax (11) 6610588; e-mail britishembassy.addisababa@fco.gov.uk; internet www.ukinethiopia.gov.uk; Ambassador GREGORY DOREY.

USA: Entoto St, POB 1014, Addis Ababa; tel. (11) 5174000; fax (11) 5174001; e-mail pasaddis@state.gov; internet addisababa.usembassy.gov; Ambassador DONALD E. BOOTH.

Venezuela: Bole Kifle Ketema, Kebele 21, House No. 314–16, POB 1909, Addis Ababa; tel. (11) 6460601; fax (11) 5154162; Ambassador LUIS MARIANO JOUBERTT MATA.

Yemen: POB 664, Addis Ababa; Ambassador DARHAM NOMAN.

Zambia: Nifas Silk Kifle Ketema, Kebele 04, POB 1909, Addis Ababa; tel. (11) 3711302; fax (11) 3711566; e-mail zam.emb@ethionet.et; Ambassador FRANCIS SIMENDA.

Zimbabwe: POB 5624, Addis Ababa; tel. (11) 6613877; fax (11) 6613476; e-mail zimbabwe.embassy@telecom.net.et; Ambassador Dr ANDREW HAMA MTETWA.

Judicial System

The 1994 Constitution stipulates the establishment of an independent judiciary in Ethiopia. Judicial powers are vested in the courts, both at federal and state level. The supreme federal judicial authority is the Federal Supreme Court. This court has the highest and final power of jurisdiction over federal matters. The federal states of the Federal Democratic Republic of Ethiopia can establish Supreme, High and First-Instance Courts. The Supreme Courts of the federal states have the highest and the final power of jurisdiction over state matters. They also exercise the jurisdiction of the Federal High Court. According to the Constitution, courts of any level are free from any interference or influence from government bodies, government officials or any other source. In addition, judges exercise their duties independently and are directed solely by the law.

Federal Supreme Court: POB 6166, Addis Ababa; tel. (11) 1553400; fax (11) 1550278; e-mail webadmin@federalsupremecourt.gov.et; f. 1995; comprises civil, criminal and military sections; its jurisdiction extends to the supervision of all judicial proceedings throughout the country; the Supreme Court is also empowered to review cases upon which final rulings have been made by the courts (including the Supreme Court) where judicial errors have occurred; Pres. TEGNE GETANEH.

Federal High Court: POB 3483, Addis Ababa; tel. (11) 2751911; fax (11) 2755399; e-mail fedhc@telecom.net.et; hears appeals from the state courts; has original jurisdiction; Pres. WUBESHET SHIFERAW.

Awraja Courts: regional courts composed of three judges, criminal and civil.

Warada Courts: sub-regional; one judge sits alone with very limited jurisdiction, criminal only.

Religion

About 45% of the population are Muslims and about 40% belong to the Ethiopian Orthodox (Tewahido) Church. There are also significant Evangelical Protestant and Roman Catholic communities. The Pentecostal Church and the Society of International Missionaries carry out mission work in Ethiopia. There are also Hindu and Sikh religious institutions. It has been estimated that 5%–15% of the population follow animist rites and beliefs.

CHRISTIANITY

Ethiopian Orthodox (Tewahido) Church

The Ethiopian Orthodox (Tewahido) Church is one of the five oriental orthodox churches. It was founded in AD 328, and in 1989 had more than 22m. members, 20,000 parishes and 290,000 clergy. The Supreme Body is the Holy Synod and the National Council, under the chairmanship of the Patriarch (Abune). The Church comprises 25 archdioceses and dioceses (including those in Jerusalem, Sudan, Djibouti and the Western Hemisphere). There are 32 Archbishops and Bishops. The Church administers 1,139 schools and 12 relief and rehabilitation centres throughout Ethiopia.

Patriarchate Head Office: POB 1283, Addis Ababa; tel. (11) 1116507; internet webmaster@ethiopianorthodox.org; internet www.ethiopianorthodox.org; Patriarch (Abune) (vacant); Gen. Sec. L. M. DEMTSE GEBRE MEDHIN.

The Roman Catholic Church

At 31 December 2006 Ethiopia contained an estimated 68,138 adherents of the Alexandrian-Ethiopian Rite and 513,286 adherents of the Latin Rite.

Bishops' Conference: Ethiopian and Eritrean Episcopal Conference, POB 2454, Addis Ababa; tel. (11) 1550300; fax (11) 1553113; e-mail ecs@ethionet.et; internet www.ecs.org.et; f. 1966; Pres. Most Rev. BERHANEYESUS DEMEREW SOURAPHIEL (Metropolitan Archbishop of Addis Ababa).

Alexandrian-Ethiopian Rite

Adherents are served by one archdiocese (Addis Ababa) and two dioceses (Adigrat and Emdeber).

Archbishop of Addis Ababa: Most Rev. BERHANEYESUS DEMEREW SOURAPHIEL, Catholic Archbishop's House, POB 21903, Addis Ababa; tel. (11) 1111667; fax (11) 1551348; e-mail ecs@telecom.net.et.

Latin Rite

Adherents are served by the eight Apostolic Vicariates of Awasa, Gambela, Harar, Hosanna, Jimma-Bonga, Meki, Nekemte and Soddo.

Other Christian Churches

The Anglican Communion: Within the Episcopal Church in Jerusalem and the Middle East, the Bishop in Egypt has jurisdiction over seven African countries, including Ethiopia.

Armenian Orthodox Church: St George's Armenian Church, POB 116, Addis Ababa; f. 1923; Deacon VARTKES NALBANDIAN.

Ethiopian Evangelical Church (Mekane Yesus): POB 2087, Jomo Kenyatta Rd, Addis Ababa; tel. (11) 5533293; fax (11) 5534148; e-mail eecmyco@eecmy.org; internet www.eecmy.org; Pres. Rev. Dr WAKSEYOUM IDOSA; f. 1959; affiliated to Lutheran World Fed., All Africa Confed. of Churches and World Council of Churches; c. 5.57m. mems (2010).

Greek Orthodox Church: POB 571, Addis Ababa; tel. and fax (11) 1226459; Metropolitan of Axum Most Rev. PETROS YIAKOUMELOS.

Seventh-day Adventist Church: POB 145, Addis Ababa; tel. (11) 5511319; e-mail info@ecd.adventist.org; internet www.ecd.adventist.org; f. 1907; Pres. ALEMU HAILE; 130,000 mems.

ISLAM

Leader: Haji MOHAMMED AHMAD.

JUDAISM

A phased emigration to Israel of about 27,000 Falashas (Ethiopian Jews) took place during 1984–91. In February 2003 the Israeli Government ruled that the Falashmura (Ethiopian Christians whose forefathers had converted from Judaism) had been forced to convert to Christianity to avoid religious persecution and that they had the right to settle in Israel. In January 2004 Ethiopia and Israel agreed to allow the Falashmura to be flown to Israel; some 17,000 Falashmura and a further 3,000 Falashas arrived in Israel by May 2008. However, a further 8,700 Falashmura remained in a transit camp in Gondar in mid-2008 and the Israeli Government halted the transfer process in June. Israel resumed the transportation of Falashmura in January 2010, and in November 2010 the Israeli Government announced that the remaining Falashmura in Ethiopia—some 8,000 people—would be granted the right to immigrate to Israel. The process was expected to take place incrementally over the following four years.

The Press

DAILIES

Addis Zemen: POB 30145, Addis Ababa; internet www.addiszemen.com; f. 1941; Amharic; circ. 40,000.

The Daily Monitor: POB 22588, Addis Ababa; tel. (11) 1560788; e-mail themonitor@telecom.net.et; f. 1993; English; Editor-in-Chief NAMRUD BERHANE TSAHAY; circ. 6,000.

Ethiopian Herald: POB 30701, Addis Ababa; tel. (11) 5156690; f. 1943; English; Editor-in-Chief TSEGIE GEBRE-AMLAK; circ. 37,000.

PERIODICALS

Abyotawit Ethiopia: POB 2549, Addis Ababa; fortnightly; Amharic.

Addis Fortune: Tegene Bldg, 7th Floor, House No. 542, Ginbot Haya Ave, Kebele 03, POB 259, Addis Ababa; tel. (11) 4163020; fax (11) 4163039; internet www.addisfortune.com; weekly; English; Man. Editor TAMRAT G. GIORGIS.

Addis Tribune: Tambek International, POB 2395, Addis Ababa; tel. (11) 6615228; fax (11) 6615227; e-mail tambek@telecom.net.et; internet www.addistribune.com; f. 1992; weekly; English; Editor-in-Chief YOHANNES RUPHAEL; circ. 6,000.

Al-Alem: POB 30232, Addis Ababa; tel. (11) 6625936; fax (11) 6625777; f. 1941; publ. by the Ethiopian Press Agency; weekly; Arabic; Editor-in-Chief EYOB GIDEY; circ. 2,500.

Birritu: National Bank of Ethiopia, POB 5550, Addis Ababa; tel. (11) 5530040; fax (11) 5514588; e-mail mulget17@yahoo.com; internet www.nbe.gov.et; f. 1982; quarterly; Amharic and English; banking, insurance and macroeconomic news; owned by National Bank of Ethiopia; circ. 2,500; Editor-in-Chief (vacant); Dep. Editors-in-Chief MULUGETA AYALEW, BEKALU AYALEW.

Capital: POB 95, Addis Ababa; tel. (11) 5531759; fax (11) 5533323; e-mail syscom@telecom.net.et; internet www.capitalethiopia.com; f. 1998; weekly; Sunday; business and economics; Editor-in-Chief BEHAILU DESALEGN.

Ethiopian Reporter: Woreda 19, Kebele 56, House No. 221, POB 7023, Addis Ababa; tel. and fax (11) 4421517; e-mail mcc@telecom.net.et; internet www.ethiopianreporter.com; weekly; English and Amharic; Editor-in-Chief AMARE AREGAWI.

Maebel: Addis Ababa; weekly; Amharic; Editor-in-Chief ABERA WOGI.

Menilik: Editor-in-Chief ZELALEM GEBRE.

Negarit Gazeta: POB 1031, Addis Ababa; irreg.; Amharic and English; official gazette.

Nigdina Limat: POB 2458, Addis Ababa; tel. (11) 5513882; fax (11) 5511479; e-mail aachamber1@telecom.net.et; monthly; Amharic; publ. by the Addis Ababa (Ethiopia) Chamber of Commerce; circ. 6,000.

Press Digest: POB 12719, Addis Ababa; tel. (11) 5504200; fax (11) 5513523; e-mail phoenix.universal@telecom.net.et; f. 1993; weekly.

Satenaw: Editor-in-Chief TAMRAT SERBESA.

Tobia Magazine: POB 22373, Addis Ababa; tel. (11) 1556177; fax (11) 1552654; monthly; Amharic; Man. GOSHU MOGES; circ. 30,000.

Tobia Newspaper: POB 22373, Addis Ababa; tel. (11) 1556177; fax (11) 1552654; e-mail akpac@telecom.net.et; weekly; Amharic; Man. GOSHU MOGES; circ. 25,000.

Tomar: Benishangul; weekly; Amharic; Editor-in-Chief BEFEKADU MOREDA.

Yezareitu Ethiopia (Ethiopia Today): POB 30232, Addis Ababa; weekly; Amharic and English; Editor-in-Chief IMIRU WORKU; circ. 30,000.

NEWS AGENCY

Ethiopian News Agency (ENA): Patriot St, POB 530, Addis Ababa; tel. (11) 1550011; fax (11) 1551609; e-mail feedback@ena.gov.et; internet www.ena.gov.et; f. 1942; Chair. NETSANET ASFAW.

PRESS ASSOCIATIONS

Ethiopian Free Press Journalists' Association (EFJA): POB 31317, Addis Ababa; tel. and fax (11) 1555021; e-mail efja@telecom.net.et; f. 1993; granted legal recognition in 2000; activities suspended in late 2003; Pres. KIFLE MULAT.

Ethiopian Journalists' Association: POB 30288, Addis Ababa; tel. (11) 1117852; fax (11) 5513365; Pres. KEFALE MAMMO.

Publishers

Addis Ababa University Press: POB 1176, Addis Ababa; tel. (11) 1119148; fax (11) 1550655; f. 1968; educational and reference works in English, general books in English and Amharic; Editor MESSELECH HABTE.

Berhanena Selam Printing Enterprise: POB 980, Addis Ababa; tel. (11) 1553233; fax (11) 1553939; f. 1921; fmrly Govt Printing Press; publishes and prints newspapers, periodicals, books, security prints and other miscellaneous commercial prints; Gen. Man. MULUWORK G. HIWOT.

Educational Materials Production and Distribution Enterprise (EMPDE): POB 5549, Addis Ababa; tel. (11) 6463555; fax (11) 6461295; f. 1999; textbook publishers.

Ethiopia Book Centre: POB 1024, Addis Ababa; tel. (11) 1123336; f. 1977; privately owned; publr, importer, wholesaler and retailer of educational books.

Mega Publishing: POB 423, Addis Ababa; tel. (11) 1571714; fax (11) 1571715; general publishers.

Broadcasting and Communications

TELECOMMUNICATIONS

Ethiopian Telecommunication Agency (ETA): Bekelobet, Tegene Bldg, Kirkos District, Kebele 02/03, House No. 542, POB 9991, Addis Ababa; tel. (11) 4668282; fax (11) 4655763; e-mail tele.agency@ethionet.et; internet www.eta.gov.et; aims to promote the devt of high quality, efficient, reliable and affordable telecommunication services in Ethiopia; Dir-Gen. ESHETU ALEMU.

Ethio Telecom (ETC): POB 1047, Addis Ababa; tel. (11) 6632597; fax (11) 6632674; e-mail etcweb@ethionet.et; internet www.ethionet.et; f. 1894; under the management of France Telecom since December 2010; Chair. DEBRE TSION GEBRE MICHAEL; CEO JEAN-MICHEL LATUTE.

BROADCASTING

Radio

Radio Ethiopia: POB 654, Addis Ababa; tel. (11) 1551011; internet www.angelfire.com/biz/radioethiopia; f. 1941; Amharic, English, French, Arabic, Afar, Oromifa, Tigre, Tigrinya and Somali; Gen. Man. KASA MILOKO.

Radio Fana: POB 30702, Addis Ababa; internet www.radiofana.com; f. 1994; Amharic; operated by the EPRDF; Gen. Man. WOLDU YEMESSEL.

Radio Voice of One Free Ethiopia: broadcasts twice a week; Amharic; opposes current Govts of Ethiopia and Eritrea.

Voice of the Revolution of Tigrai: POB 450, Mekele; tel. (34) 4410545; fax (34) 4405485; e-mail vort@telecom.net.et; f. 1985; Tigrinya and Afargna; broadcasts 57 hours per week; supports Tigrai People's Liberation Front.

Television

Ethiopian Radio and Television Agency (ERTA): POB 5544, Addis Ababa; tel. (11) 5155326; fax (11) 5512685; e-mail gd1@erat.gov.et; internet www.erta.gov.et; f. 1964; semi-autonomous station;

accepts commercial advertising; programmes transmitted from Addis Ababa to 26 regional stations; Chair. BEREKET SIMON.

Finance

(cap. = capital; res = reserves; dep. = deposits; m. = million; br(s). = branch(es); amounts in birr)

BANKING

Central Bank

In 2010 there were 16 banks and 22 microfinance institutions in Ethiopia.

National Bank of Ethiopia: Sudan Ave, POB 5558, Addis Ababa; tel. (11) 5517438; fax (11) 5514588; e-mail nbe.gov@ethionet.et; internet www.nbe.gov.et; f. 1964; bank of issue; cap. 500.0m., res 1,814.8m., dep. 35,781.3m. (June 2009); Chair. NEWAYE-KIRSTOS GEBREAB; Gov. TEKLEWOLD ATNAFU; Vice-Gov. ALEMSEGED ASSEFA; 1 br.

Other Banks

Awash International Bank SC: Africa Ave, Bole Rd, POB 12638, Addis Ababa; tel. (11) 6614482; fax (11) 6639159; e-mail awash.bank@ethionet.et; internet www.awash-international-bank.com; f. 1994; cap. 540.0m., res 750.0m., dep. 5,700m. (Dec. 2009); Chair. ATO BEKELE NEDI; Pres. LEIKUN BERHANU; 64 brs.

Bank of Abyssinia SC: Red Cross Bldg, Ras Desta Damtew Ave, POB 12947, Addis Ababa; tel. (11) 5530663; fax (11) 5514130; e-mail info@bankofabyssinia.com; internet www.bankofabyssinia.com; f. 1905; closed 1935 and reopened 1996; commercial banking services; cap. 313.1m., res 132.6m., dep. 4,583.5m., total assets 5,476.6m. (June 2009); Chair. DAGNACHEW MEHARI; Pres. ADDISU HABBA; 61 brs.

Commercial Bank of Ethiopia: Gambia St, POB 255, Addis Ababa; tel. (11) 5511271; fax (11) 5514522; e-mail cbe_cc@combanketh.com; internet www.combanketh.com; f. 1943; reorg. 1996; state-owned; cap. 4,000.0m., res 1,037.5m., dep. 43,480.3m. (June 2009); Chair. BEREKET SEMON; Pres. BEKALU ZELEKE; 331 brs.

Construction and Business Bank: Higher 21, Kebele 04, POB 3480, Addis Ababa; tel. (11) 5512300; fax (11) 5515103; e-mail cbbsics@ethionet.et; internet www.cbb.com.et; f. 1975 as Housing and Savings Bank; provides credit for construction projects and a range of commercial banking services; state-owned; cap. and res 80.8m., total assets 1,019.1m. (June 2003); Chair. TADESSE HAILE; Gen. Man. ADDISU HABBA; 20 brs.

Dashen Bank: Beklobet, Garad Bldg, Debre Zeit Rd, POB 12752, Addis Ababa; tel. (11) 4671803; fax (11) 4653037; e-mail dashen.bank@ethionet.et; internet www.dashenbanksc.com; f. 1995; share company; cap. 591.8m., res 340.2m., dep. 10,375.9m. (June 2010); Pres. LULSEGED TEFERI; Chair. TEKLU HAILE; 58 brs.

Development Bank of Ethiopia: Zosip Broz Tito St, POB 1900, Addis Ababa; tel. (11) 5511188; fax (11) 5511606; e-mail dbe@ethionet.et; internet www.dbe.com.et; f. 1909; provides devt finance for industry and agriculture, technical advice and assistance in project evaluation; state-owned; cap. and res 418.8m., total assets 3,163.2m. (June 2002); Chair. MELAKU FANTA; Pres. ESAYAS BAHRE; 32 brs.

Lion International Bank SC (LIB): Addis Ababa; tel. (11) 6626000; fax (11) 6625999; e-mail lionbank@ethionet.et; internet www.anbesabank.com; f. 2006; Chair. BERHANU G. MEDHIN; Pres. MERESSA GEBREMARIAM; 24 brs.

NIB International Bank SC: Africa Avenue, Dembel City Centre, 6th Floor, POB 2439, Addis Ababa; tel. (11) 5503304; fax (11) 5527213; e-mail nibbank@ethionet.et; internet www.nibbank-et.com; f. 1999; cap. 487.1m., res 132.0m., dep. 3,497.0m. (June 2009); Chair. DEMBEL BALCHA; Pres. AMERGA KASSA; 45 brs.

Oromia International Bank SC: POB 27530, Addis Ababa; tel. 1579760; fax 578673; internet www.orointbank.com; f. 2008; cap. 197.2m., res 13.8m., dep. 820.9m. (June 2010); Pres. ABIE SANO; 30 brs.

United Bank SC: Beklobet, Mekwor Plaza Bldg, Debe Zeit Rd, Kirkos District, Kebele 06, POB 19963, Addis Ababa; tel. (11) 4655222; fax (11) 4655243; e-mail hibretbank@ethionet.et; internet www.unitedbank.com.et; f. 1998; commercial banking services; cap. 355.2m., res 93.9m., dep. 3,615.7m. (June 2009); Chair. GETACHEW AYELE; Pres. BERHANU GETANEH; 50 brs.

Wegagen Bank: Dembel Bldg, 6th–7th Floor, Africa Ave, POB 1018, Addis Ababa; tel. (11) 5523800; fax (11) 5523521; e-mail wegagen@ethionet.et; internet www.wegagenbank.com.et; f. 1997; commercial banking services; cap. 517.6m., res 183.3m., dep. 3,942.7m. (June 2009); Chair. WONDWOSSON KEBEDE; Pres. and CEO ARAYA GEBRE EGIZHABER; 49 brs.

Zemen Bank: Josef Tito St, POB 1212, Addis Ababa; tel. (11) 5501111; fax (11) 5539042; e-mail customerservice@zemenbank.com; internet www.zemenbank.com; f. 2008; Chair. ERMYAS TEKIL AMELGA; Pres. and CEO BRUTAWIT DAWIT ABDI.

Bankers' Association

Ethiopian Bankers' Association: POB 23850, Addis Ababa; tel. and fax (11) 5533874; e-mail ethbankers@ethionet.et; f. 2001; Sec.-Gen. DEREJE DEGEFU.

INSURANCE

In 2010 there were 12 insurance companies operating in Ethiopia.

Africa Insurance Co: Woreda 17, Kebele 19, House 093, POB 12941, Addis Ababa; tel. (11) 6637716; fax (11) 6638253; e-mail africains@ethionet.et; internet www.africainsurance.com.et; f. 1994; Man. Dir and CEO KIROS JIRANIE.

Awash Insurance Co: Tebaber Berta Bldg, 4th Floor, Wolo Sefer, Ethio-China Rd, POB 12637, Addis Ababa; tel. (11) 5526050; fax (11) 5526091; e-mail aic@ethionet.et; internet www.awashinsurance.com; f. 1994; cap. 32.7m.; Chair. KANAA DABA; Gen. Man. TSEGAYE KEMSI; 21 brs.

Ethiopian Insurance Corpn: POB 2545, Addis Ababa; tel. (11) 5512400; fax (11) 5517499; e-mail eic.md@ethionet.et; internet www.eic.com.et; f. 1976; life, property and legal liabilities insurance cover; Man. Dir YEWONDWOSEN ETEFA.

Global Insurance Co SC: Gobena Aba Tigu St, Somale Tera, POB 180112, Addis Ababa; tel. (11) 1567400; fax (11) 1566200; e-mail globalinsu@ethionet.et; f. 1997; cap. 26.3m.; Chair. AHMED ABUBAKER SHERIF; Man. Dir YAHYA MOHAMMED AFFAN (acting); 12 brs; 100 employees.

National Insurance Co of Ethiopia: POB 12645, Addis Ababa; tel. (11) 4661129; fax (11) 4650660; e-mail nice@telecom.net.et; Man. Dir and CEO HABTEMATIAM SHUMGIZAW.

Nile Insurance Co: POB 12836, Addis Ababa; tel. (11) 5537709; fax (11) 5514592; e-mail nileinsu@mail.telecom.net.et; f. 1995; Gen. Man. DAWIT G. AMANUEL.

Nyala Insurance SC: Mickey Leland St, POB 12753, Addis Ababa; tel. (11) 6626667; fax (11) 6626706; e-mail nisco@telecom.net.et; internet www.nyalainsurance.com; Chair. GETACHEW KIBRE SELASSIE; Man. Dir and CEO NAHU-SENAYE ARAYA.

Oromia Insurance Co SC (OIC): Biftu Bldg, 6th Floor, Ras Desta St, POB 10090, Addis Ababa; tel. (11) 8959580; fax (11) 5503192; e-mail oromiainsurance@ethionet.et; internet www.oromiainsurancecompany.com.et; f. 2009; Chair. ELIAS GENETI; CEO TESFAYE DESTA.

United Insurance Co SC: POB 1156, Addis Ababa; tel. (11) 5515656; fax (11) 5513258; e-mail united.insurance@telecom.net.et; Chair. GETAMESSAY DEGEFU; Man. Dir MESERET BEZABEH.

Trade and Industry

GOVERNMENT AGENCIES

Ethiopian Investment Agency: POB 2313, Addis Ababa; tel. (11) 5510033; fax (11) 5514396; e-mail ethiopian.invest@ethionet.et; internet www.ethioinvest.org; f. 1992; Dir-Gen. ABI WOLDEMESKEL.

Privatization and Public Enterprises Supervising Agency: POB 11835, Addis Ababa; tel. (11) 5530343; fax (11) 5513955; e-mail epa.etio@ethionet.et; internet www.ppesa.gov.et; Dir-Gen. BEYENE GEBREMESKEL.

DEVELOPMENT ORGANIZATION

Ethiopian Institute of Agricultural Research (EIAR): POB 2003, Addis Ababa; tel. (11) 6462633; fax (11) 6461294; internet www.eiar.gov.et; f. 1966; Dir-Gen. Dr SOLOMON ASSEFA.

CHAMBERS OF COMMERCE

Ethiopian Chamber of Commerce and Sectorial Associations: Mexico Sq., POB 517, Addis Ababa; tel. (11) 5514005; fax (11) 5517699; e-mail ethchamb@ethionet.et; internet www.ethiopianchamber.com; f. 1947; regional chambers in 11 localities; Pres. EYESSUSWORK ZAFU; Sec.-Gen. GASHAW DEBEBE.

Addis Ababa Chamber of Commerce: POB 2458, Addis Ababa; tel. (11) 5513882; fax (11) 5511479; e-mail AAchamber1@telecom.net.et; internet www.addischamber.com; Chair. MULU SOLOMON; Sec.-Gen. TESHOME BEYENE.

INDUSTRIAL AND TRADE ASSOCIATIONS

Arsi Agricultural Development Enterprise: Assela; f. 1980; privatization pending.

Bale Agricultural Development Enterprise: Robe.

Coffee Plantation Development Enterprise (CPDE): Deber Zeit Rd, POB 4363, Addis Ababa; tel. (11) 4670688; fax (11) 4168788; f. 1993; Dir-Gen. FESSEHA TEKELE.

Ethiopian Association of Basic Metal and Engineering Industries: Bole Sub-City, House Number 0377, Addis Ababa; tel. and fax (11) 6293429; e-mail eabmei@ethionet.et; internet www.eabmei.org; Pres. SISAY TESFAYE; Gen. Man. SOLOMON MULUGETA.

Ethiopian Cement Corpn: POB 5782, Addis Ababa; tel. (11) 1552222; fax (11) 1551572; Gen. Man. REDI GEMAL.

Ethiopian Chemical Corpn: POB 5747, Addis Ababa; tel. (11) 6184305; Gen. Man. ASNAKE SAHLU.

Ethiopian Coffee Export Enterprise: POB 2591, Addis Ababa; tel. (11) 5515330; fax (11) 5510762; f. 1977; Chair. SUFIAN AHMED; Gen. Man. DERGA GURMESSA.

Ethiopian Food Corpn: POB 2345, Addis Ababa; tel. (11) 5518522; fax (11) 5513173; f. 1975; produces and distributes food items, incl. edible oil, ghee substitute, pasta, bread, maize, wheat flour, etc.; Gen. Man. BEKELE HAILE.

Ethiopian Fruit and Vegetable Marketing Enterprise: POB 2374, Addis Ababa; tel. (11) 5519192; fax (11) 5516483; f. 1980; sole wholesale domestic distributor and exporter of fresh and processed fruit and vegetables, and floricultural products; Gen. Man. KAKNU PEWONDE.

Ethiopian Grain Trade Enterprise: POB 3321, Addis Ababa; tel. (11) 4652436; fax (11) 4652792; e-mail egte@ethionet.et; internet www.egtemis.com; Gen. Man. BERHANE HAILU.

Ethiopian Horticulture Producers and Exporters Association (EHPEA): Haile Selassie Ave, opp. WARYT Bldg, Gelila Bldg, 2nd Floor; POB 22241, Addis Ababa; tel. (11) 6636750; fax (11) 6636753; e-mail ehpea@ethionet.et; internet www.ehpea.org; f. 2002; 87 mems; Pres. TSEGAYE ABEBE.

Ethiopian Import and Export Corpn (ETIMEX): Addis Ababa; tel. (11) 5511112; fax (11) 5515411; f. 1975; state trading corpn; import of building materials, foodstuffs, stationery and office equipment, textiles, clothing, chemicals, general merchandise, capital goods; Gen. Man. ASCHENAKI G. HIWOT.

Ethiopian Metal and Engineering Corpn: Addis Ababa; Man. Dir Brig.-Gen. KINFE DAGNEW.

Ethiopia Peasants' Association (EPA): f. 1978 to promote improved agricultural techniques, home industries, education, public health and self-reliance; comprises 30,000 peasant asscns with c. 7m. mems; Chair. (vacant).

Ethiopian Petroleum Enterprise: POB 3375, Addis Ababa; tel. and fax (11) 5512938; f. 1976; Gen. Man. YIGZAW MEKONNEN.

Ethiopian Pulses, Oilseeds and Spice Processors Exporters' Association: POB 5719, Addis Ababa; tel. (11) 1550597; fax (11) 1553299; f. 1975; Gen. Man. ABDOURUHMAN MOHAMMED.

Ethiopian Sugar Corpn: POB 133, Addis Ababa; tel. (11) 5519700; fax (11) 5513488; Dir-Gen. ABAY TSEHAYE.

Green Star Food Co LLC: POB 5579, Addis Ababa; tel. (11) 5526588; fax (11) 5526599; e-mail greenstar@telecom.net.et; f. 1984; fmrly the Ethiopian Livestock and Meat Corpn; production and marketing of canned and frozen foods; Gen. Man. DAWIT BEKELE.

Natural Gum Processing and Marketing Enterprise: POB 62322, Addis Ababa; tel. (11) 5527082; fax (11) 5518110; e-mail natgum@ethionet.et; internet www.naturalgum.ebigchina.com; f. 1976; state-owned; Gen. Man. TEKLEHAIMANOT NIGATU BEYENE.

Pharmaceuticals Fund and Supply Agency (PFSA): POB 976, Addis Ababa; tel. (11) 2763266; fax (11) 2751770; e-mail pfsa@ethionet.et; Dir-Gen. HAILESELASSIE BIHON.

UTILITIES

Electricity

Ethiopian Electric Power Corpn (EEPCo): De Gaulle Sq., POB 1233, Addis Ababa; tel. (11) 1560042; fax (11) 1550822; e-mail eelpa@telecom.net.et; internet www.eepco.gov.et; Chair. GIRMA BIRRU; Gen. Man. ATO MIHRET DEBEBE.

Water

Addis Ababa Water and Sewerage Authority: POB 1505; Addis Ababa; tel. (11) 6623902; fax (11) 6623924; e-mail aawsa.ha@ethionet.et; f. 1971; Gen. Man. ASEGID GETACHEW.

Water Resources Development Authority: POB 1045, Addis Ababa; tel. (11) 6612999; fax (11) 6611245; Gen. Man. GETACHEW GIZAW.

MAJOR COMPANIES

Abyssinia Cements PLC: POB 122014, Addis Ababa; tel. (11) 6639755; fax (11) 6639756; f. 2007.

Ambo Mineral Water Factory: POB 1805, Addis Ababa; tel. (11) 5517333; fax (11) 5516252; e-mail info@ambowater.com; internet www.ambowater.com.

Bedele Brewery: POB 75, Addis Ababa; tel. 474450147 (mobile); fax 474451006 (mobile).

BGI Ethiopia PLC: POB 737, Addis Ababa; tel. (11) 5510677; fax (11) 5511711.

Dalol Oil Share Co.: Ambasel Bldg, 2nd Floor, Room 206, POB 11937, Addis Ababa; tel. (11) 4163838; fax (11) 4164002; e-mail info@daloloil.com; internet www.daloloil.com.

Ethiopian Minerals Development Share Co. (EMDSC): Addis Ababa; tel. (11) 6632290; fax (11) 6187143; e-mail eemindvt@ethionet.et; internet www.emdsc.org.et; f. 1995; name changed as above in 2000; Gen. Man. Dr ZERIHUN DESTA.

Ethiopian Steel PLC: Akaki Kaliti, POB 8692, Addis Ababa; tel. (11) 4342719; fax (11) 4341940.

The Ghions: Addis Ababa; tel. (11) 2793360; fax (11) 2794770; e-mail info@ghions.com; internet www.ghions.com; conglomerate comprising Ghion Industrial and Commercial PLC, Ghion Industrial and Chemical PLC, Ghion Gas PLC, Ghion Transport PLC, etc.

Habesha Brewery: Rahem Bldg, 4th Floor, Kebele 13/14, Yeka Sub-City, Addis Ababa; tel. (11) 6625655; fax (11) 6622175; e-mail info@habeshabreweries.com; internet www.habeshabreweries.com; f. 1960; Chair. MESFIN ABI.

Hagbes PLC: POB 1044, Addis Ababa; tel. (11) 6638654; fax (11) 6638653; importation and distribution of machinery.

MIDROC Ethiopia PLC: POB 8677, Addis Ababa; tel. (11) 5549969; e-mail mid.pr@ethionet.et; internet www.midroc-ethiopia.com.et; Chair. SHEIKH MOHAMMED HUSSEIN ALI AL-AMOUDI.

Derba MIDROC Cement PLC: Addis Ababa; f. 2012; mnfrs of cement.

Mugher Cement Enterprise: POB 30749, Addis Ababa; tel. (11) 425139; fax (11) 650685; internet www.mughercement.com.et; f. 1999, following amalgamation of the Mugher Cement Factory and the Addis Ababa Cement Factory; state-owned; Gen. Man. TEFERA ABEBE.

Total Ethiopia Share Co.: Addis Ababa; tel. (11) 4651125; fax (11) 4651039; Man. Dir MARC DE LATAILLADE.

TRADE UNION

Confederation of Ethiopian Trade Unions (CETU): POB 3653, Addis Ababa; tel. (11) 5155473; fax (11) 5514532; e-mail cetu@telecom.net.et; f. 1975; comprises nine industrial unions and 22 regional unions with a total membership of 320,000 (1987); Pres. KASSAHUN FOLLO; Sec.-Gen. MESFIN SILESHI.

Transport

RAILWAYS

In 2010 construction of a 5,000-km railway network to link Addis Ababa with various parts of the country was started. Phase one of the five-year project included the construction of a new 2,000-km line to the border with Djibouti. Under phase two, there were plans to set up a 30-km light railway network in Addis Ababa. In 2012 agreement was reached with Turkey's Yapi Merkezi and China Communications Construction Company regarding the construction of 715-km of track connecting Ethiopia to the port of Tadjoura in northern Djibouti. Railway construction is a central component of Ethiopia's five-year plan to boost economic growth, with plans to construct 1,200 km of railway between 2010 and 2015.

Chemin de Fer Djibouti-Ethiopien (CDE): POB 1051, Addis Ababa; tel. (11) 5517250; fax (11) 5513997; f. 1909; adopted present name in 1981; jtly owned by Govts of Ethiopia and Djibouti; 781 km of track (660 km in Ethiopia), linking Addis Ababa with Djibouti; Pres. ISMAIL IBRAHIM HOUMED.

Ethiopian Railways Corporation (ERC): POB 27558/1000, Addis Ababa 11 661 5833, +215 1 Fax.: +251; tel. (11) 6189060; fax (11) 6189065; internet www.erc.gov.et; f. 2007; CEO Dr GETACHEW BETRE.

ROADS

In 2007 the total road network comprised an estimated 44,359 km of primary, secondary and feeder roads, of which 13.67% were paved, the remainder being gravel roads. In addition, there are some 30,000 km of unclassified tracks and trails. A highway links Addis Ababa with Nairobi in Kenya, forming part of the Trans-East Africa Highway. In mid-2003 work commenced on the second phase of the Road Sector Development Programme, which upgraded 80% and 63% of paved and gravel roads, respectively, to an acceptable condition by 2007.

Comet Transport SC: POB 2402, Addis Ababa; tel. (11) 4423962; fax (11) 4426024; e-mail cometrans@telecom.net.et; f. 1994; Gen. Man. ALEMU ASHENGO.

Ethiopian Road Transport Authority: POB 2504, Addis Ababa; tel. (11) 5510244; fax (11) 5510715; e-mail kasahun_khmariam@yahoo.com; internet www.rta.gov.et; enforces road transport regulations, promotes road safety, registers vehicles and issues driving licences; Gen. Man. KASAHUN H. MARIAM.

Ethiopian Roads Authority: POB 1770, Addis Ababa; tel. (11) 5517170; fax (11) 5514866; e-mail era2@ethionet.et; internet www.era.gov.et; f. 1951; construction and maintenance of roads, bridges and airports; Dir-Gen. ZAID WOLDE GEBREAL.

Public Transport Corpn: POB 5780, Addis Ababa; tel. (11) 5153117; fax (11) 5510720; f. 1977; urban bus services in Addis Ababa and Jimma, and services between towns; restructured into three autonomous enterprises in 1994 and scheduled for privatization; Man. Dir AHMED NURU.

SHIPPING

The formerly Ethiopian-controlled ports of Massawa and Assab now lie within the boundaries of the State of Eritrea (q.v.). Although an agreement exists between the two Governments allowing Ethiopian access to the two ports, which can handle more than 1m. metric tons of merchandise annually, in mid-1998 Ethiopia ceased using the ports, owing to the outbreak of hostilities. Ethiopia's maritime trade currently passes through Djibouti (in the Republic of Djibouti), and also through the Kenyan port of Mombasa. An agreement was also signed in July 2003 to allow Ethiopia to use Port Sudan (in Sudan). At 31 December 2009 Ethiopia's registered merchant fleet numbered 10 vessels, with a total displacement of 117,957 grt.

Ethiopian Shipping Lines Corpn: POB 2572, Addis Ababa; tel. (11) 5518280; fax (11) 5519525; e-mail esl@ethionet.et; internet www.ethiopianshippinglines.com.et; f. 1964; serves Red Sea, Europe, Mediterranean, Gulf and Far East with its own fleet and chartered vessels; Chair. GETACHEW BELAY; Gen. Man. AMBACHEW ABRAHA.

Marine Transport Authority: POB 1238, Addis Ababa; tel. (11) 5158227; fax (11) 5515665; f. 1993; regulates maritime transport services; Dept Head ASKAL W. GEORGIS.

Maritime and Transit Services Enterprise: POB 1186, Addis Ababa; tel. (11) 5517564; fax (11) 5518197; e-mail mtse@telecom.net.et; internet www.telecom.net.et/~mtse; f. 1979; services include stevedoring, storehandling, bagging, forwarding and trucking; Chair. HAILEMARIAM DESSALEGN; Gen. Man. AHMED YASSIN.

CIVIL AVIATION

Ethiopia has two international airports (at Addis Ababa and Dire Dawa) and around 40 airfields. Bole International Airport in the capital handles 95% of international air traffic and 85% of domestic flights. A programme to modernize the airport, at an estimated cost of 819m. birr (US $130m.), was undertaken during 1997–2001. Construction of airports at Axum, Lalibela and Gondar was completed in April 2000.

Ethiopian Airlines: Bole International Airport, POB 1755, Addis Ababa; tel. (11) 6652222; fax (11) 6611474; e-mail publicrelations@ethiopianairlines.com; internet www.flyethiopian.com; f. 1945; operates regular domestic services and flights to 63 international destinations in Africa, Europe, Middle East, Asia and the USA; CEO TEWOLDE GEBREMARIAM.

Ethiopian Civil Aviation Authority (ECAA): POB 978, Addis Ababa; tel. (11) 6650200; fax (11) 6650281; e-mail civilaviation@ethionet.et; internet www.ecaa.gov.et; regulatory authority; provides air navigational facilities; Dir-Gen. Col WOSENYELEH HUNEGNAW.

Tourism

Ethiopia's tourist attractions include the early Christian monuments and churches, the ancient capitals of Gondar and Axum, the Blue Nile (or Tississat) Falls and the National Parks of the Simien and Bale Mountains. Tourist arrivals in 2010 totalled 468,000. In that year receipts from tourism (including passenger transport) amounted to US $522m.

Ministry of Culture and Tourism: POB 2183, Addis Ababa; tel. (11) 5512310; fax (11) 5512889; e-mail info@tourismethiopia.org; internet www.tourismethiopia.org.

Defence

Owing to hostilities with Eritrea in 1998–2000, there was a large increase in the size of the armed forces and in defence expenditure during this period. As assessed at November 2011, Ethiopia's active armed forces numbered an estimated 138,000, including an air force of some 3,000. In July 2000 the UN Security Council adopted a resolution (No. 1312) establishing the UN Mission in Ethiopia and Eritrea (UNMEE), which was to supervise the cease-fire and the implementation of a peace agreement between the two countries. UNMEE's mandate was periodically extended until the end of July 2008, when the UN Security Council confirmed its termination and all peace-keeping personnel were withdrawn. A total of 4,194 soldiers were stationed abroad, of which 159 were observers.

Defence Expenditure: Budgeted at 6,500m. birr in 2012.

Chief of Staff of the Armed Forces: Gen. SAMORA YUNIS.

Education

Education in Ethiopia is available free of charge, and, after a rapid growth in numbers of schools, it became compulsory between the ages of seven and 13 years. Since 1976 most primary and secondary schools have been controlled by local peasant associations and urban dwellers' associations. Primary education begins at seven years of age and lasts for eight years. Secondary education, beginning at 15 years of age, lasts for a further four years, comprising two cycles of two years, the second of which provides preparatory education for entry to the tertiary level. According to UNESCO estimates, in 2009/10 total enrolment at primary schools included 81% of children in the appropriate age-group (84% of boys; 79% of girls), while secondary enrolment was equivalent to 36% of children in the appropriate age-group (39% of boys; 32% of girls). There are 21 institutions of higher education in Ethiopia, including six universities (in Addis Ababa, Bahir Dar, Alemanya, Jimma, Awassa and Makele). A total of 291,610 students were enrolled in higher education in 2007/08, according to government statistics. In 2007 spending on education represented 23.3% of total government expenditure.

Bibliography

Abbink, J. *Ethiopian Society and History: A Bibliography of Ethiopian Studies 1957–1990.* Leiden, African Studies Centre, 1990.

Abegaz, B. (Ed.). *Essays on Ethiopian Economic Development*. Aldershot, Avebury, 1994.

Abir, M. *Ethiopia and the Red Sea: The Rise and Decline of the Solomonic Dynasty and Muslim–European Rivalry in the Region*. London, Frank Cass, 1980.

Abraham, K. *Ethiopia: from Bullets to the Ballot Box: The Bumpy Road to Democracy and the Political Economy of Transition*. Lawrenceville, NJ, Red Sea Press, 1994.

Ad-din Arabfaqih, S., Ad-din Ahmad Bin Abdul Qader, S. and Stenhouse, P. L. (trans.). *The Conquest of Abyssinia: Futuh Al Habasa*. Hollywood, CA, Tsehai Publishers, 2005.

Agyeman-Duah, B. *The United States and Ethiopia: Military Assistance and the Quest for Security 1953–1993.* Lanham, MD, University Press of America, 1994.

Attilo, A., Berhanu, K., and Ketsella, Y. *Ethiopia: Politics, Policy Making and Rural Development*. Addis Ababa, Addis Ababa University Press, 2006.

Bariagaber, A. *Conflict and the Refugee Experience: Flight, Exile, and Repatriation in the Horn of Africa*. Aldershot, Ashgate, 2006.

Bekele, S. (Ed.). *An Economic History of Ethiopia. Vol. I: The Imperial Era, 1941–1974.* Dakar, CODESRIA, 1995.

Bekoe, D. A. (Ed.). *East Africa and the Horn: Confronting Challenges to Good Governance*. Boulder, CO, Lynne Rienner Publishers, 2006.

Benti, G. *Addis Ababa: Migration and the Making of a Multiethnic Metropolis, 1941–1974.* Lawrenceville, NJ, Red Sea Press, 2007.

Berhanu, K., Olika, T., Kefale, A., and Erega, J. *Electoral Politics, Decentralized Governance and Constitutionalism in Ethiopia*. Addis Ababa, Addis Ababa University Press, 2007.

Berhe, A. *A Political History of the Tigray People's Liberation Front.* Tsehai Publishers, Los Angeles, CA, 2009.

Bruchhaus, E-M., and Sommer, M. (Eds). *Hot Spot Horn of Africa Revisited*. Muenster, LIT Verlag, 2008.

Clapham, C. *Transformation and Continuity in Revolutionary Ethiopia*. Cambridge, Cambridge University Press, 1988.

Doornbos, M., Cliffe, L., Ahmed, A. G. M., and Markakis, J. (Eds). *Beyond Conflict in the Horn: The Prospects of Peace and Development in Ethiopia, Somalia, Eritrea and Sudan*. Lawrenceville, NJ, Red Sea Press, 1992.

Erlich, H. *Ethiopia and the Middle East*. Boulder, CO, and London, Lynne Rienner Publishers, 1994.

Saudi Arabia and Ethiopia: Islam, Christianity and Politics Entwined. Boulder, CO, Lynne Rienner Publishers, 2007.

Freeman, D. and Pankhurst, A. *Peripheral People: The Excluded Minorities of Ethiopia*. Lawrenceville, NJ, Red Sea Press, 2003.

Fukui, K., and Markakis, J. (Eds). *Ethnicity and Conflict in the Horn of Africa*. London, James Currey, 1994.

Gebissa, E. (Ed.). *Contested Terrain: Essays on Oromo Studies, Ethiopianist Discourse and Politically Engaged Scholarship*. Lawrenceville, NJ, Red Sea Press, 2008.

Getachew, M. *Ethiopia and the United States: history, diplomacy and analysis*. New York, Algora Publishing, 2009.

Ghebre-Ab, H. (Ed.). *Ethiopia and Eritrea: A Documentary Study*. Trenton, NJ, Red Sea Press, 1993.

Gudina, M. *Ethiopia: From Autocracy to Revolutionary Democracy, 1960 – 2011*. Addis Ababa, Chamber Printing House, 2011.

Haile Selassie I. *The Autobiography of Emperor Haile Selassie I. 'My Life and Ethiopia's Progress'*. Oxford, Oxford University Press, 1976.

Haile-Selassie, T. *The Ethiopian Revolution, 1974–1991: From a Monarchical Autocracy to a Military Oligarchy*. London, Kegan Paul International, 1997.

Hameso, S.Y., and Hassen, M. (Eds). *Arrested Development in Ethiopia: Essays on Underdevelopment, Democracy, and Self-Determination*. Lawrenceville, NJ, Red Sea Press, 2006.

Hammond, J. *Fire from the Ashes: A Chronicle of the Revolution in Tigray, Ethiopia, 1975–1991*. Lawrenceville, NJ, Red Sea Press, 1999.

Hammond, Laura C. *This Place Will Become Home: Refugee Repatriation to Ethiopia*. Ithaca, NY, Cornell University Press, 2004.

Hansson, G. *The Ethiopian Economy 1974–94: Ethiopia, Tikdem and After*. London, Routledge, 1995.

Harbeson, J. W. *The Ethiopian Transformation*. Boulder, CO, Westview Press, 1988.

Henze, P. *Layers of Time: A History of Ethiopia*. London, Hurst, 2000.

Jacquin-Berdal, D. and Plaut, M. (Eds). *Unfinished Business: Ethiopia and Eritrea at War*. Lawrenceville, NJ, Red Sea Press, 2006.

Jalata, A. *Oromia and Ethiopia: State Formation and Ethnonational Conflict, 1868–2000*. Piscataway, NJ, Transaction Publishers, 2005.

Katsuyoski, F., and Markakis, J. (Eds). *Ethnicity and Conflict in the Horn of Africa*. London, James Currey, 1994.

Kefale, A. *Federalism and Ethnic Conflict in Ethiopia: A Comparative Regional Study*. Abingdon, Routledge, 2012.

Lockot, H. W. *Haile Selassie I: The Formative Years 1892–1936*. Berkeley, University of California Press, 1987.

The Mission: The Life, Reign and Character of Haile Selassie I. London, Hurst, 1992.

A History of Ethiopia. Berkeley, University of California Press, 2001.

Markakis, J. *National and Class Conflict in the Horn of Africa*. Cambridge, Cambridge University Press (African Studies Series, No. 55), 1988.

Ethiopia: Anatomy of a Traditional Polity. Addis Ababa, Shama Books, 2006.

Markakis, J. and Ayele, N. *Class and Revolution in Ethiopia*. Addis Ababa, Shama Publishers, 2006.

Maundi, M. O., Zartman, I. W., Khadiagala, G. M. and Nuamah, K. *Getting In: Mediators' Entry into the Settlement of African Conflicts* Washington, DC, United States Institute of Peace Press, 2006.

Negash, T. *Rethinking Education in Ethiopia*. New Brunswick, NJ, Transaction Publishers, 1996.

Eritrea and Ethiopia: The Federal Experience. Uppsala, Nordiska Africainstitutet, 1997.

Negash, T., and Tronvoll, K. *Brothers at War*. London, James Currey, 2000.

Ofcansky, T. P., and Shinn, D. H. (Eds). *Historical Dictionary of Ethiopia*. Lanham, MD, Scarecrow Press, 2004.

Ottaway, M. *Soviet and American Influence in the Horn of Africa*. New York, Praeger, 1982.

(Ed.). *The Political Economy of Ethiopia*. New York, Praeger, 1990.

Pankhurst, A. *Resettlement and Famine in Ethiopia: The Villagers' Experience*. Manchester, Manchester University Press, 1992.

Pankhurst, R. *Economic History of Ethiopia, 1880–1935*. Addis Ababa, 1968.

History of Ethiopian Towns: From Middle Ages to Early Nineteenth Century. Stuttgart, Steiner Verlag, 1982.

History of Ethiopian Towns: From Mid Nineteenth Century to 1935. Stuttgart, Steiner Verlag, 1985.

The Ethiopians. Oxford, Blackwell, 1999.

Pausewang, S., *et al.* (Eds). *Ethiopia: Rural Development Options*. London, Zed Books, 1990.

Ethiopia Since the Derg: A Decade of Democratic Pretension and Performance. London, Zed Books, 2003.

Phillipson, D. W. *Ancient Ethiopia*. London, British Museum Press, 1998.

Praeg, B. *Ethiopia and Political Renaissance in Africa*. New York, Nova Science Publishers, 2006.

Prouty, C., and Rosenfeld, E. *Historical Dictionary of Ethiopia and Eritrea*. 2nd edn. Lanham, MD, and London, Scarecrow Press, 1994.

Prunier, G., and Ficquet, E. *Understanding Contemporary Ethiopia*. London, C Hurst & Co, 2012.

Schwarz, Tanya. *Ethiopian Jewish Immigrants in Israel*. Curzon Press, 2000.

Sharomo, R., and Mesfin, B. *Regional Security in the Post Cold War Horn of Africa*. Pretoria, The Institute of Security Studies, 2011.

Sishagne, S. *Unionists and Separatists: The Vagaries of Ethio-Eritrean Relation, 1941-1991*. Tsehai Publishers, Los Angeles, CA, 2007.

Teferra, Daniel. *Economic Development and Nation Building in Ethiopia*. Lanham, MD, University Press of America, 2005.

Tronvoll, K. *War and the Politics of Identity in Ethiopia: Making Enemies and Allies in the Horn of Africa*. Woodbridge, James Curry, 2009.

Turton, D. *Ethnic Federalism: The Ethiopian Experience in Comparative Perspective*. Oxford, James Currey Ltd, 2006.

Woube, Mengistu. *Effects of Resettlement Schemes on the Biophysical and Human Environments: The Case of the Gambela Region, Ethiopia*. Boca Raton, FL, Universal Publishers, 2005.

Young, J. *Peasant Revolution in Ethiopia: The Tigray People's Liberation Front, 1975–91*. Cambridge, Cambridge University Press, 1997.

GABON

Physical and Social Geography

DAVID HILLING

Lying along the Equator, on the west coast of Africa, the Gabonese Republic covers an area of 267,667 sq km (103,347 sq miles) and comprises the entire drainage basin of the westward-flowing Ogooué river, together with the basins of several smaller coastal rivers such as the Nyanga and Como.

The low-lying coastal zone is narrow in the north and south but broader in the estuary regions of the Ogooué and of Gabon. South of the Ogooué numerous lagoons, such as the N'Dogo, M'Goze and M'Komi, back the coast, and the whole area is floored with cretaceous sedimentary rocks, which at shallow depth yield oil. The main producing oilfields are in a narrow zone stretching southwards from Port-Gentil, both on and off shore. The interior consists of Pre-Cambrian rocks, eroded into a series of plateau surfaces at heights of 450 m–600 m and dissected by the river system into a number of distinct blocks, such as the Crystal mountains, the Moabi uplands and the Chaillu massif. This area is one of Africa's most mineralized zones, with the large-scale exploitation of manganese and uranium contributing significantly to Gabon's economy. There are also deposits of high-grade iron ore, gold and diamonds.

Gabon has an equatorial climate, with uniformly high temperatures, high relative humidities and mean annual rainfalls of 1,500 mm–3,000 mm. More than 80% of the country's area is covered with rainforest, one of the highest national proportions in the world, and wood from the okoumé tree provided the basis for the country's economy until superseded by minerals in the 1960s. Grassland vegetation is restricted to the coastal sand zone south of Port-Gentil and parts of the valleys of the Nyanga, upper N'Gounié and upper Ogooué.

Agricultural development in the potentially rich forest zone has been limited by the small size of the country's population. At the December 2003 census the population was enumerated at 1,269,000, and in mid-2012, according to UN estimates, totalled 1,563,873, giving an average density of only 5.8 inhabitants per sq km. As the population is small in relation to national income, Gabon has one of the highest levels of income per head in mainland sub-Saharan Africa, although many of the country's enterprises depend on labour imported from neighbouring countries. The three main urban concentrations may now account for more than one-half of the population; in 1993 Libreville, the capital, had 419,596 inhabitants; Port-Gentil, the centre of the petroleum industry, 79,225; and Franceville and Moanda, the mining centres, had 31,183 and 21,882, respectively. By 2011 the population of Libreville was estimated to have increased to 686,356. The major rural concentrations are found in Woleu N'Tem, where coffee and cocoa are the main cash crops, and around Lambaréné, where palm oil and coffee are important. The country's principal ethnic groups are the Fang (30%) and the Eshira (25%).

Recent History

RALPH YOUNG

ONE-PARTY GOVERNMENT

Formerly part of French Equatorial Africa, Gabon gained internal autonomy in 1958 and full independence on 17 August 1960. Léon M'Ba, Gabon's first President, died in November 1967, and was succeeded by his Vice-President, Albert-Bernard (later El Hadj Omar) Bongo, who reconstituted the ruling party as the Parti Démocratique Gabonais (PDG), while imposing a one-party state in March 1968. Gabon experienced an economic boom during the 1970s driven by its petroleum sector. Economic problems in the early 1980s prompted the emergence of political opposition, led by the Mouvement de Redressement National (MORENA), formed by exiles in France in 1976. At a presidential election in November 1986 Bongo won a further seven-year term, with a reported 99.97% of the vote.

Following further economic deterioration, compulsory salary reductions for public sector employees in October 1988 provoked strikes, and MORENA resumed its campaign for democratic reform. In May 1989, however, Fr Paul M'Ba Abessole, its Chairman (and a Catholic priest), visited Gabon and met Bongo. M'Ba Abessole subsequently declared his support for the President and in early 1990, following his removal from MORENA's leadership, formed a separate organization, MORENA des Bûcherons.

CONSTITUTIONAL TRANSITION

Against a backdrop of rising public discontent a 'special commission for democracy', established by the PDG, submitted a report in February 1990 criticizing one-party rule. Bongo immediately promised change, proposing a five-year transition period before introducing multi-party politics. However, in late March a national conference of some 2,000 delegates demanded the formation of a transitional government before competitive elections. Bongo accepted these demands, and in April Casimir Oyé Mba, the Governor of the Banque des Etats de l'Afrique Centrale (BEAC), was appointed Prime Minister in a Government including opposition members.

In May 1990 the legislature approved constitutional amendments restoring multi-party politics. The current presidential mandate (effective until January 1994) would continue; thereafter, presidential elections would be contested, with the tenure of office reduced to five years, renewable only once. Following the suspicious death of Joseph Rendjambe, leader of the Parti Gabonais du Progrès (PGP), demonstrators attacked property belonging to Bongo and his associates, prompting a country-wide curfew. French troops intervened to protect the estimated 20,000 French residents. As the violence reached Port-Gentil, a state of emergency was imposed there. The national curfew was lifted in early July, although the state of emergency remained in Port-Gentil.

The first round of the legislative elections, held in mid-September 1990, was disrupted by violent protests. Following opposition complaints, the results in 32 constituencies were invalidated. The transitional Government subsequently admitted malpractice and the second electoral round was postponed until October. With a commission having both PDG and opposition members supervising the polling, the PDG won an overall majority.

A Government of National Unity was announced on 27 November 1990, with Oyé Mba reappointed as Prime Minister. The PDG received 16 portfolios; the remaining eight were distributed among five opposition parties. The new Constitution, promulgated on 22 December, endorsed reforms included in May's transitional Constitution. A constitutional council was to replace the Supreme Court's administrative chamber, while a national communications council would ensure impartiality by the state media.

The legislature's final composition was determined in March 1991 following further by-elections. The PDG held 66 seats, the PGP 19, the Rassemblement National des Bûcherons (RNB, formerly MORENA des Bûcherons) 17, MORENA-Originels seven, the Association pour le Socialisme au Gabon (APSG) six, the Union Socialiste Gabonaise (USG) three, and two smaller parties one seat each.

OPPOSITION REALIGNMENTS AND SOCIAL UNREST

In May 1991 six opposition parties formed the Coordination de l'Opposition Démocratique (COD). Withdrawing from the Assemblée nationale, it demanded the full implementation of the Constitution and access to the state-controlled media. Following a general strike organized by the COD, Bongo dissolved the Council of Ministers and announced the establishment of a Constitutional Court and a Communications Council. A new coalition Government was formed on 22 June.

At the presidential election on 5 December 1993, Bongo was re-elected with 51.2% of the votes; M'Ba Abessole secured 26.5%. The results provoked rioting, and a national curfew and state of alert were imposed. Rejecting the outcome, M'Ba Abessole established a Haut Conseil de la République (HCR), including a majority of the presidential candidates, as a 'parallel government', while Bongo invited opponents to join a government of national consensus. In January 1994 M'Ba Abessole redesignated the HCR as the Haut Conseil de la Résistance and urged his supporters to refuse to pay taxes and boycott the local elections. In mid-February the national curfew and the state of alert were lifted, only to be reimposed after a general strike over salary demands (to compensate for the substantial devaluation of the CFA franc in January) degenerated into violence. Negotiations between the Government and trade unions ended the strike after four days.

Following the opposition's refusal to join a government of national unity, in March 1994 a 38-member administration was formed with Oyé Mba reappointed as Prime Minister. In the same month the legislature approved a constitutional amendment establishing a Sénat. In September negotiations between the Government and the opposition took place in Paris, France, under the auspices of the Organization of African Unity (OAU, now the African Union—AU). These produced an agreement over a coalition government; legislative elections were to be held within 18 months under a revised electoral code and an independent electoral commission. In early October Oyé Mba dissolved the Government. Bongo replaced him with Dr Paulin Obame-Nguema, an experienced PDG figure and former Prime Minister, who included six opposition members in a 27member Council of Ministers.

In January 1995 the HCR refused to help draft the new electoral code until the Paris Accord was ratified, but opposition deputies ended their boycott following a Constitutional Court ruling that the Assemblée nationale could act as a parliamentary body pending the Sénat's formal installation, with the stipulation that the constitutional provisions adopted under the Accord would require endorsement by referendum. In April, in congruence with the Accord, the Council of Ministers approved legislation releasing prisoners detained on charges involving state security. At the national referendum in July, the constitutional amendments were approved by 96.5% of the votes cast.

LOCAL, PRESIDENTIAL AND LEGISLATIVE ELECTIONS

After renewed opposition complaints, Bongo agreed in May 1996 to establish a national electoral commission with opposition membership, and also accepted opposition access to state-controlled media and election funding. After the legislative elections in December, and several by-elections in August 1997, the PDG held 88 seats, the PGP nine and the RNB five; independents and the smaller parties took the rest. Obame-Nguema was reappointed Prime Minister, with a Council of Ministers dominated by PDG members. Elections to the new Sénat took place on 26 January and 9 February, with senators being elected by municipal councils and departmental assemblies. After subsequent by-elections the PDG emerged with 58 of the 91 seats, the RNB secured 20 and the PGP four.

On 18 April 1997 the legislature adopted constitutional amendments returning the presidential term to seven years, formally designating the Sénat as an upper chamber of a bicameral legislature, and creating a vice-presidency (though with no power of succession). In late May Bongo appointed Didjob Divungui-di-N'Dingue, a senior member of the Alliance Démocratique et Républicaine and a candidate in the 1993 presidential election, as Vice-President.

With a presidential election due in December 1998, the opposition parties withdrew from the national electoral commission in September, alleging irregularities in voter registration. At the election on 6 December, Bongo won 66.6% of the votes cast, while Pierre Mamboundou (representing the HCR) received 16.5% and M'Ba Abessole 13.4%. The turn-out was 53.8%. Opposition leaders claimed malpractice, demanding that the results be annulled before commencing the talks that Bongo offered. Bongo was inaugurated as President on 21 January 1999, and a new 42-member Council of Ministers, headed by Jean-François Ntoutoume Emane, was appointed.

Three opposition parties boycotted the legislative elections on 9 and 23 December 2001 over alleged inflation of voter registration lists, while others demanded that the first round be annulled. Abstention rates reportedly reached 56% nationally and 80% in Libreville and Port-Gentil. The PDG won 86 seats, with 19 others secured by 'allied' independents and affiliated parties. Opposition parties obtained just 14 seats, with M'Ba Abessole's renamed Rassemblement pour le Gabon (RPG) taking eight, Pierre Moussavou's Parti Social-démocrate (PSD) two and Mamboundou's Union du Peuple Gabonais (UPG) one. An enlarged Council of Ministers was announced in January 2002, with Ntoutoume Emane reappointed as Prime Minister. President Bongo included four opposition representatives, including Moussavou and M'Ba Abessole. At subsequent by-elections in May and June, the PDG increased its representation to 88 seats. The PDG consolidated its gains at local elections in December.

In January 2003 Vice-President Divungui-di-N'Dingue escaped an assassination attempt, with PSD activists blamed. Moussavou was dismissed from the Government. At Sénat elections in February, the PDG won more than 60 of the 91 seats, followed by the RPG with eight. The security of the Bongo regime was further assured in July, when a constitutional amendment was approved abolishing the two-term limit for serving presidents and reducing presidential elections from two rounds to one.

BONGO'S SEVENTH TERM

In September 2004 the President undertook a minor reshuffle of his Government, allowing Moussavou's return; his PSD had entered the 'presidential majority' the previous June. With M'Ba Abessole's RPG having joined in April 2004, this coalition embraced 29 of 35 registered parties. Of the remaining opposition politicians, only Pierre-Louis Agondjo Okawé (PGP) and Mamboundou (UPG) had well-established support bases (in the south-west and Port-Gentil, respectively). However, Agondjo Okawé died of a heart attack in August 2005, leaving his party badly divided.

With a weakened opposition, Bongo Ondimba, who had added his father's name to his own in November 2003, appeared unlikely to face a serious challenge at the presidential election scheduled for November 2005. In April, however, Zacharie Myboto, who had been part of the regime's core leadership before quitting the Government in early 2001, announced the formation of the Union Gabonaise pour la Démocratie et le Développement (UGDD).

At the presidential election on 27 November 2005 Bongo Ondimba secured 79.2% of the vote, with a 63.3% turn-out. Mamboundou took 13.6%, while Myboto, standing as an independent because his party was not yet officially recognized, received only 6.6%. In the new cabinet announced in January 2006, Ntoutoume Emane was replaced as Prime Minister by another economic reformer, Jean Eyéghé Ndong; however, key senior ministers kept their posts. With the opposition disputing the election results, police raided the UPG headquarters in mid-March, seizing files and computers. Fleeing to the South African embassy, Mamboundou emerged in mid-April for negotiations with Bongo Ondimba. These produced an agreement by the UPG to accept the election results in return for reforms to the electoral registration and voting process. Mamboundou subsequently admitted that the President had offered US $21.5m. for developments in his constituency.

In legislative elections held on 17 December 2006, the PDG retained power, securing 82 seats compared with 17 for the other parties in the 'presidential majority', including eight for the RPG. Mamboundou's UPG won eight seats and Myboto's UGDD four. The new Government, appointed in January 2007, comprised 44 ministers, including M'Ba Abessole. At by-elections in June, following the annulment of 20 results, the opposition's net gain was one seat.

In local and departmental elections on 27 April 2008, the PDG consolidated its position, gaining control of both Libreville and Port-Gentil with the help of allied parties; former Prime Minister Ntoutoume Emane became Libreville's new mayor. On 15 January 2009 a new and more broadly based Government took office. Expanded to 48 ministers, key regime figures, including Prime Minister Eyéghé Ndong, were retained. Three days later the PDG triumphed at elections for the Sénat, taking 75 of 102 seats; 19 were shared among six opposition parties, while independents took the rest.

Although the Government decided to abolish capital punishment in September 2007, civil liberties remained under pressure. The media's autonomy had been eroding since 2001 as Gabon's strict libel laws were used to suspend or proscribe at least 16 privately owned newspapers. With civil society increasingly vocal in February 2008 the Government suspended 20 civil society groups concerned with corruption, poverty and environmental issues, accusing them of engaging in political activities; they were told to clarify their mission statements with the Ministry of the Interior, Public Security and Immigration.

THE DEATH OF BONGO

In power for over 41 years, Bongo Ondimba had become the 'doyen' of African leaders and among the world's longest-surviving leaders. On 6 May 2009 he 'temporarily' stepped down from official duties, publicly to recover from the death, in mid-March, of his second wife, Edith Lucy (the daughter of the Republic of Congo's President, Denis Sassou-Nguesso). On 21 May Spanish authorities announced that Bongo Ondimba was 'gravely ill' at a Barcelona clinic. He died there on 8 June of a heart attack.

As constitutionally required, interim power was transferred on 10 June 2009 to the Sénat President, Rose Francine Rogombé, who was to be responsible for organizing an election within 40 days. Overriding opposition demands for a new electoral register, the Constitutional Court fixed 30 August as the election date. The PDG's selection of Ali Bongo Ondimba, the deceased President's eldest son, as its candidate proved divisive, with three regime 'notables' standing as independents: Jean Eyéghé Ndong (Prime Minister), Casimir Oyé Mba (Minister of Petroleum and Hydrocarbons and a former Prime Minister), and, most significantly, André Mba Obame (Minister of the Interior and a close associate of the Bongo family). Ultimately, 23 candidates took part in an open and spirited campaign, with five withdrawing on the eve of voting (including Eyéghé Ndong and Oyé Mba); by then Ali Bongo Ondimba and Mba Obame were front-runners. Bongo Ondimba secured 41.7% of the vote, while Mba Obame and the UPG's Pierre Mamboundou, took 25.9% and 25.2%, respectively; the turnout was just 44.2%. Ali Bongo Ondimba carried just three provinces in the east and south-east. Mba Obame captured the two northern provinces (including Libreville) dominated by the Fang community (with perhaps 40% of Gabon's population). Mamboundou's strength was concentrated in the centre and along the coast southward from Libreville, including Port-Gentil.

As opposition leaders contested the results, disturbances broke out in Libreville and Port-Gentil. Businesses linked to the Bongo family were attacked, as were the French consulate and facilities belonging to the French oil company Total. Following a recount the Constitutional Court declared on 12 October 2009 that Ali Bongo Ondimba had secured 141,665 valid votes (41.8%), while the number of votes attributed to Mamboundou and Mba Obame was amended to 86,875 (25.6%) and 85,814 (25.3%), respectively, thus reversing their placings. The court challenges delayed Ali Bongo Ondimba's inauguration until 16 October.

THE PRESIDENCY OF ALI BONGO ONDIMBA

The new President moved quickly to impose his authority. The Government appointed on 17 October 2009 was reduced from 44 to 30 members, of whom 19 were new. Paul Biyoghé Mba as Prime Minister and the outgoing ministers for foreign affairs and the interior—Paul Toungui and Jean-François Ndougou—were among a minority retaining their portfolios. To further slim down his Government, no vice-presidents or ministers of state were appointed by Ali Bongo Ondimba, and the size of ministerial cabinets was restricted. The members of the new Government were given one month to declare their assets to the official anti-corruption agency, while parliamentarians were forbidden to serve on the boards of either public or private organizations. The President's older sibling, Pascaline, was reassigned from her former post as presidential cabinet director to a position of senior status but little power.

While the ruling PDG had previously faced a divided opposition lacking leaders with national appeal, it now suffered significant defections of cadres in the two Fang-dominated provinces, Estuaire and Wolou Ntem. Several opposition parties met in November 2009 to negotiate an alliance. Although Mamboundou and M'Ba Abessole subsequently withdrew, in February 2010 the three Fang-based politicians formed the Union Nationale (UN), also recruiting Myboto's UGDD and two other small parties. The new formation appeared likely to experience problems in transcending its provincial base; but its leaders drew encouragement from the discontent among those affected by the post-electoral purge of the 'old guard'. By-elections were held in June 2010 for the seats automatically vacated by those quitting the PDG; Mba Obame and Eyéghé Ndong easily retained theirs, while the PDG captured the others, including Oyé Mba's.

A separate threat emerged in September 2009, when Gen. Jean-Philippe Ntumpa Lebani, head of the Conseil National de Sécurité and former commander of the élite Republican Guard, was arrested in connection with an alleged coup plot. He was sentenced, in February 2011, to seven years in prison.

In January 2011 a serious confrontation flared between the Government and Mba Obame. In December 2010 a French television documentary on Franco-African relations included a claim by a former French presidential adviser on Africa that Mba Obame had indeed won the 2009 elections. Mba Obame returned to Libreville in early 2011 after several months abroad and on 25 January used his own television channel to take the presidential oath of office; in evident reference to the UN's role in efforts to resolve the crisis in Côte d'Ivoire (where two rival leaders were contesting the presidency after a disputed election), he then moved his 19-member 'government' to the Libreville offices of the UN Development Programme (UNDP). The Government accused Mba Obame of 'high treason' and, on 26 January, banned his party. However, with unrest by Mba Obame's partisans localized, the Government chose to wait. After UN Secretary-General Ban Ki-Moon intervened, Mba Obame's team left the UNDP offices on 27 February.

Mba Obame's party, though formally prohibited, continued to function until August 2011, when its appeal against its ban was rejected. A vote in the Assemblée nationale to lift Mba Obame's parliamentary immunity—paving the way to a trial—occurred in early May; he then left for South Africa for medical treatment, before moving to exile in France.

Even before the crisis of January 2011, the Ali Bongo Ondimba regime sought links with the veteran opposition figure, Mamboundou. On returning to Gabon late in 2010 after medical treatment abroad, he publicly thanked the President for his financial support; Ali Bongo Ondimba attempted to persuade him to join the Government, though to no avail. The Government took other measures in anticipation of the legislative elections anticipated in late 2011. Among several constitutional changes approved in December 2010 was a measure bolstering the President's capacity to deal with situations of *force majeure*. In early January 2011 Ali Bongo Ondimba sought to re-energize his Government with a reorganization that brought in eight new ministers and removed six. On 10 May he reached an agreement with opposition leaders and civil society representatives to introduce biometric voting cards, a key opposition demand.

When the Constitutional Court rejected the Government's request to delay the legislative elections until 2012 to allow time for the new system's introduction, the Government and opposition were set on a collision course. Thirteen opposition parties suspended participation in the national electoral commission in July 2011. In August the Government toughened regulations concerning the registration of new parties, including a six-month waiting period for approval, while later that year, it manoeuvred discreetly to divide the opposition with offers of cabinet posts. The opposition suffered a more serious blow with the death on 15 October of Mamboundou, the UPG's founding leader who, although a mercurial politician, was none the less a key opposition figure. Eventually, on 4 November, after the closing of nominations of candidates, a coalition of 13 opposition parties announced a boycott of the elections. However, several parties refused to join and the UPG itself soon broke ranks.

The elections were held on 17 December 2011 and the ruling PDG, having chosen not to leave some constituencies uncontested to favour other parties in the 'presidential majority', was dominant, capturing 114 out of 120 seats. Three other seats went to small allied parties, leaving two opposition parties, the Union pour la Nouvelle République of Louis Gaston Mayila, and the Moussavou's PSD with one seat each. The turnout was officially declared as 34.3%, the boycott appearing to have been effective in the urban centres.

On 27 February 2012 Ali Bongo Ondimba appointed the former agricultural minister, Raymond Ndong Sima, as Prime Minister. An unexpected choice, Sima came from the opposition stronghold of Wolou Ntem Province, breaking the grip that Estuaire Province (and Libreville) had exercised on this office. Sima named a small Government of 16 ministers from which several senior figures—among them Paul Toungui, hitherto Minister of Foreign Affairs, International Co-operation and Francophone Affairs—were dropped.

With formal political opposition considerably weakened, political space emerged for an ever-growing network of increasingly partisan civil society organizations. When the French Prime Minister François Fillon visited Libreville in July 2011, some 13 groups (including two trade unions) presented a petition demanding an end to French support for Gabon's 'corrupt dictatorship'. Many civil society groups actively supported the electoral boycott and, during the French presidential election of May–June 2012, their representatives lobbied the campaign teams of all left-of-centre candidates while also developing links with French organizations promoting democracy and good governance.

EXTERNAL CONCERNS

Following the death in 1993 of Félix Houphouët-Boigny, the Côte d'Ivoire President who had been a highly influential figure in francophone African affairs, Bongo Ondimba increasingly assumed this role, and during the 1990s proved an important intermediary in internal conflicts both inside and outside central Africa, in addition to contributing Gabonese soldiers to regional peace-keeping missions. In February 2003, however, tension arose between Gabon and neighbouring Equatorial Guinea, following Gabon's occupation of Mbañé island, whose control, along with that of two other islets, had been disputed since 1972. Progress was made in July 2004, when both countries' Presidents pledged to explore jointly for petroleum in the affected offshore areas, pending UN mediation. They again committed themselves in February 2006 to a negotiated solution. Having appointed a Swiss legal expert as mediator in September 2008, UN Secretary-General Ban Ki-Moon invited the Presidents of both countries to New York, USA, in February 2011 for direct talks, but since then the issue has remained unresolved.

In the closing months of 2011, President Ali Bongo Ondimba received a baptism in the cross-currents of continental politics when it became clear that Jean Ping, Gabon's former foreign minister, faced a strong challenge to his bid for a second mandate as head of the AU's secretariat from the former South African foreign secretary, Nkosazana Dlamini-Zuma. A special January 2012 summit at the AU's headquarters in Addis Ababa, Ethiopia, produced deadlock. Ping remained in office until the AU's annual summit in mid-July, when the issue was settled in favour of Dlamini-Zuma.

Gabon's relations with France have always remained central. Gabon's petroleum, and formerly its uranium, have made it a strategic trading partner, and it was one of four African states still providing France with permanent military base facilities (in Gabon's case, for an 800-strong marine battalion at Libreville). Nevertheless, relations have periodically been strained, as notably over the state-owned petroleum company Elf-Aquitaine (now part of Total), which came under judicial scrutiny in 1997. During 2003 the prosecution of the head of Elf-Gabon and other Elf executives and business associates documented substantial off-ledger payments to foreign leaders, including President Bongo.

Though Franco-Gabonese relations experienced renewed intimacy under President Jacques Chirac, change emerged at the French presidential election of May 2007, when Chirac's successor, Nicholas Sarkozy, promised 'rupture' with 'Françafrique', the murky system of state and commercial interests that had long guided France's Africa policies. Yet during Sarkozy's first presidential trip to Africa that July, he described Gabon as a 'privileged partner'. Moreover, Jean-Marie Bockel, the French Secretary of State for Co-operation and Francophony, was dismissed in March 2008 after Bongo Ondimba protested at his public criticism of 'Françafrique'. However, Sarkozy had promised, in an address that February in Cape Town, South Africa, to withdraw most French forces stationed in Africa and reform France's defence accords with francophone African governments.

Tensions also developed in other spheres. In June 2007 a French judge found that Bongo Ondimba had demanded a substantial private payment to release from prison René Cardona, a French citizen and former business associate, and ordered that this be repaid. In the same month a judicial inquiry was opened after three French rights organizations complained that Bongo Ondimba and two other African presidents had used misappropriated public funds to purchase properties in France. Although a public prosecutor, answerable to the Ministry of Justice, successfully appealed against this action in November, it prompted a police inquiry revealing that the Bongo family possessed 39 properties, nine luxury cars and 70 bank accounts in France.

In November 2008 the anti-corruption NGO Transparency International France (TIF) and a Gabonese civil servant (who was subsequently arrested) submitted a fresh complaint concerning the French property holdings of the three presidents. In February 2009 a court ordered the seizure of nine of Bongo Ondimba's French bank accounts to enforce payment in the Cardona case. Although a sizeable French delegation attended Edith Bongo Ondimba's funeral on 19 March, the Council of Ministers had earlier issued an angry statement attacking the 'calumnies' in the French media against Gabon's President. On the day before Bongo Ondimba 'temporarily' suspended his official duties in May, a French judge ruled that the TIF complaint was 'admissible', opening the way to a formal judicial investigation. While the public prosecutor's department quickly appealed—blocking the case again the following October—President Bongo Ondimba's decision to go to Barcelona rather than Paris for medical treatment underlined the poor state of Gabon's relations with France. With the passing of Bongo Ondimba, francophone Africa lost an astute intermediary with impressive networks across the French political spectrum, while France lost a valuable, if sometimes difficult, African ally.

The post-Bongo transition in Gabon's foreign relations began even before the August elections, when it became evident that certain members of the Communauté Economique et Monétaire de l'Afrique Centrale (CEMAC), and notably Equatorial Guinea, were sympathetic to opposition candidates. The new Libreville regime did enjoy one initial success, at the UN in October, when two CEMAC members withdrew their candidacies to allow Gabon to take the UN Security Council seat being allocated to central Africa for 2010–11. However, large-scale embezzlement was uncovered in September 2009 at the Paris office of the BEAC, forcing Ali Bongo Ondimba to recall its Gabonese governor; in mid-January 2010 a CEMAC summit turned to Equatorial Guinea for a new BEAC governor, breaking a 1973 agreement which assigned this post to a Gabonese.

Although the French Government had proclaimed its neutrality during the 2009 election campaign, the warm congratulations that President Sarkozy conveyed to the victorious Ali Bongo Ondimba underlined expectations that the close relationship the French President had enjoyed with El Hadj Omar Bongo Ondimba would continue with his son. Ali Bongo Ondimba went to Paris in November 2009 for his first official trip outside Africa, while President Sarkozy reciprocated in February 2010, bringing a commitment to maintain the French military base at Libreville and a new defence agreement. However, the inquiry into the property holdings of African leaders continued to entangle this relationship. In November 2010 a new judicial hearing concluded that the case brought by TIF against the three Presidents was after all admissible, and a formal investigation commenced. When this uncovered evidence of continuing property acquisitions, the investigating judges applied unsuccessfully to the public prosecutor's department in April 2011 to extend the inquiry.

Diplomatic cables published by WikiLeaks revealed that the US Government viewed declining French engagement with Africa under Sarkozy as offering opportunities to extend US influence. During the January 2011 crisis the US Administration confirmed its recognition of Ali Bongo Ondimba as President. US President Barack Obama spoke with him by telephone to seek his advice over the situation in Côte d'Ivoire. In early June Ali Bongo Ondimba became the first francophone African President to be received in the White House, though a subsequent communiqué urged Gabon to increase its efforts to improve governance and control corruption. (Although Gabon was ranked 100th of 182 states on Transparency International's 2011 Corruption Perceptions Index, its placing was far superior to other CEMAC members, and had notably improved since Ali Bongo Ondimba took power).

A major scandal broke out in September 2011 that upset the French establishment while exposing Gabon's own involvement in the corrupt links that tied francophone African states to Paris. In interviews in the French media, Robert Bourgi, an unofficial Africa adviser to President Sarkozy and a long-time senior figure in the shadowy 'Françafrique' networks, claimed that between 1997 and 2005 he had transferred some US $20m. in donations from Bongo Ondimba and five other African presidents to senior French politicians, including Jacques Chirac and Dominique de Villepin (though not Sarkozy), to assist their election campaigns. The claim was firmly denied by Pascaline Bongo Ondimba, who had served her father as cabinet director over many years, while Ali Bongo insisted that he had no knowledge of such activities. However, Jean Eyéghé Ndong, the former Prime Minister who had quit the PDG to contest the presidency in the August 2009 elections, claimed that Omar Bongo Ondimba had himself told him of the payments.

If these revelations appeared to signal the final unravelling of the secretive 'Françafrique' circuits, the return to power of the French Parti Socialiste at the May 2012 presidential election posed new pressures for change. During the French election campaign the Socialist candidate François Hollande had sent the prospective foreign minister, Laurent Fabius, to several francophone capitals, including Libreville, to reassure African leaders that a socialist victory would not presage an abrupt shift in France's Africa priorities. Yet Hollande's choice as Africa advisor of a lawyer with experience of pursuing corruption and human rights cases against several African leaders would indicate an intention to place France's relations with its former colonies on a different footing.

Economy

RALPH YOUNG

INTRODUCTION

The combination of a small population (estimated at 1.6m. in mid-2012) and plentiful petroleum resources has given Gabon one of the highest incomes in sub-Saharan Africa. Gabon's gross national income (GNI) per head in 2010 was estimated by the World Bank at US $7,650. Although therefore an upper-middle-income country, it was only placed 106th of 187 countries in the UN Development Programme's 2011 Human Development Index. Gabon's ranking was considerably lower than countries with a similar GNI per head, but it was, even so, on course to meet five of the eight UN Millennium Development Goals by 2015. Given the dominant petroleum sector and its vulnerability to world price trends, the rate of economic growth has fluctuated widely. While growth in gross domestic product (GDP) averaged 9.5% per year in 1965–80, the annual average declined to 0.8% in 1985–90, after the collapse of petroleum prices in 1986. The development of the Rabi-Kounga oilfield boosted the average to 2.5% per year in 1990–2003. More recently, surging oil prices and strong demand for manganese and wood products saw real GDP grow by 5.6% in 2007. Though the onset of the global economic crisis in 2008 caused GDP growth to slow to 2.1% in 2008, and decline by 1.4% in 2009, the economy rebounded strongly with GDP growth of 5.7% in 2010, and of an estimated 5.6% in 2011.

The earlier period of rapid growth reflected the petroleum boom of the mid-1970s, when the surge in domestic production, prompted by favourable world prices, generated government investment spending and borrowing, which left the country heavily indebted and increased its vulnerability to adverse international conditions. Consequently, from the mid-1980s the Government undertook several economic adjustment programmes, though with limited success. Following the devaluation of the CFA franc in January 1994, the Government adopted a more extensive reform programme, again under IMF guidance; this included taxation reforms, a new investment code and several significant privatizations. Monetary and fiscal constraint offset the inflationary impact of the currency devaluation to reduce the rate from 36% in 1994 to 2.3% in 1998—well below the IMF's 5.0% target. However, slippage in expenditure preceding the December 1998 presidential election caused the Fund to abandon the 1995–98 programme. A new agreement was signed in October 2000, but collapsed in April 2002. The Government was forced to negotiate a 14-month stand-by arrangement in May 2004, with stricter conditions. This latter permitted, in June, a rescheduling of US $848m. of debt to official creditors. By early 2005 Gabon was on course to meet many of the terms set; however, increased government spending linked to the 2005 and 2006 elections and escalating costs of food and imported fuel saw inflation reach 5.9% in 2007 and 5.3% in 2008. Unlike in 1999, Gabon avoided sanctions; the privatization programme was well advanced, despite its political sensitivity, while the Government had responded to IMF criticism of its budgetary procedures and financial accountability arrangements.

In May 2007 the IMF approved Gabon's request for a US $117.3m. three-year stand-by agreement. However, public discontent over a 26% increase in fuel prices forced a year's suspension of the automatic fuel price adjustment mechanism agreed with the IMF; this was eventually inaugurated in

January 2009. In September 2007 it sought additional waivers from the IMF over the ceiling on its borrowings from local banks and price controls on palm oil, milk, cement and plywood. Although these were removed in December, in April 2008 the Government introduced a six-month suspension of all fees and taxes on key imported food products and capped profit margins on flour and rice.

Following the death of President Bongo Ondimba in June 2009, a new regime, led by his son, assumed power in mid-October 2009, and moved quickly in establishing its determination to relaunch the economy. President Ali Bongo Ondimba announced a Government reduced in size and imposed a ceiling on the salaries of public enterprise managers; the following month he ordered audits of all ministries. In late December the Government reorganized (and lengthened) the working week for both the public and private sectors. In mid-January 2010 the minimum monthly wage was nearly doubled, from 80,000 francs CFA to 150,000 francs CFA. In a separate measure to improve business confidence, the Government promised a significant reduction in company taxes by 2011. The new President pursued, with some success, a strategy of diversifying economic partners by seeking new investment sources in Asia. He also favoured a more interventionist strategy—not least concerning foreign companies exploiting Gabon's natural resources—and encouraged economic diversification centred on wood-processing, light metallurgy and ecotourism. That Gabon faced many challenges was underlined by a World Bank report in 2012 ranking Gabon's business environment 156th among 183 countries, the second worst performance among middle income countries.

In early 2010 the Government introduced a major investment plan entitled 'Gabon Emergent', for infrastructure improvements worth US $4,500m. until 2015; in October 2010 the Agence Nationale des Grands Travaux was established to manage these projects, with the US engineering corporation Bechtel providing technical expertise. The IMF was concerned that Gabon's administrative capabilities might be overstretched; in any case, the programme would depend on fluctuating commodity prices, and risked unleashing inflationary pressures.

AGRICULTURE

Owing to extensive tropical rainforests, only a small proportion of land area is suitable for agricultural activity, and only 2% is estimated to be under cultivation. With an estimated 86% of the population living in towns, and a poor road infrastructure, the contribution to GDP of the agriculture, forestry and fishing sector was estimated at only 5.2% in 2009.

In the 1980s the Government encouraged rubber as an export crop, and four plantations covering 11,000 ha were developed by the state-owned Société de Développement de l'Hévéaculture (HEVEGAB). By 2004 HEVEGAB was struggling to maintain its operations, and was privatized; since then production has recovered, reaching 13,700 metric tons in 2010. In 2009 rubber exports were worth US $23m. Olam, the Singapore agribusiness company, signed an agreement with the Government in March 2012 entailing an investment of $183m. for the development of a 28,000-ha rubber plantation at Bitam, in northern Gabon. A new factory to transform raw rubber into caoutchouc (a form of latex), with a potential annual capacity of 62,000 tons, was projected to begin operating in 2020. Palm oil is a second key cash crop. A parastatal organization, the Société de Développement de l'Agriculture au Gabon (AGROGABON), managed plantations covering 4,000 ha before its privatization in 2004. In 2009 these produced 5,870 tons of palm oil, but this declined to just 2,800 tons in 2010; the 1,680 tons that were exported in 2009 were worth $1.5m. Production and exports should increase substantially following Olam's commitment in November 2010 to invest $1,054m. in the palm oil sector's transformation, with an additional 200,000 ha being eventually brought into production (having an output potential of a million tons of palm kernels); the company is opening a new palm oil factory in December 2014.

To underpin its agro-industrial projects, Olam also signed a contract with the Government in November 2010 for the construction of a fertilizer factory in the special economic zone on Mandji Island, near Port-Gentil. Using natural gas (otherwise burned off during oil production), the plant would be capable of producing 2,200 metric tons of ammoniac and 3,800 tons of granulated urea per year. Due for completion in early 2012, the project cost an estimated US $1,300m., with Olam holding 62.9% of the shares, the Indian firm Tata 25.1%, and the state 12%.

Production of refined sugar increased from negligible levels to 21,000 metric tons in 1989, with the development of a large-scale complex at Franceville. It has since decreased, dropping to 9,500 tons by 2004. Sugar cane production stood at 240,000 tons in 2010. Cocoa and coffee were once relatively significant cash crops, but output has fallen, with annual cocoa crop production down from 1,500–2,000 tons to some 200 tons in recent years. Coffee production stood at 150 tons in 2010, down from around 1,000 tons annually in the early 1990s.

With Gabon currently importing some 85% of its foodstuffs, the Government announced an ambitious agricultural security programme in 2010, with a budget worth US $83m. A major contract was signed with an Israeli firm in April of that year to establish agro-industrial farms to boost production of fruit and vegetables.

The tsetse fly hindered animal husbandry before 1980, when the first tsetse-resistant cattle were imported. Livestock numbers in 2010 included 36,500 head of cattle, 215,000 pigs, and 288,000 sheep and goats. Poultry is mainly raised by smallholder farmers. Wild game provided 73% of the 34,000 metric tons of meat produced locally in 2010, while imports represented around 60% of total meat consumption.

The total fishing catch peaked at 45,000 metric tons in 2004, before declining to around 32,160 tons in 2010. Under an agreement signed with the European Union (EU) in 1998 and renewed in 2003, EU trawlers are allowed to fish up to 9,000 tons per year, in return for aid and a levy on the catch. Japanese aid financed both a fish-processing centre at Port-Gentil and freshwater fishing facilities at Lambaréné. The sector employs over 21,000 workers, but in 2009 contributed only 1.5% to GDP.

FORESTRY

Tropical forests cover over 80% of Gabon, and before independence the timber industry dominated the economy. Okoumé and ozigo have historically accounted for 75% of timber exports; however, Gabon's forests contain at least 20 other species of commercially exploitable trees. Gabon currently ranks as Africa's third largest producer of tropical wood, and the world's largest exporter of okoumé wood. The industry employs the largest workforce after government, and accounted for 5.9% of export earnings in 2009. A small number of European and, more recently, Chinese and Malaysian enterprises dominate the sector.

Timber exports averaged some 1.4m. cu m of industrial roundwood per year in 1990–92, but then increased steadily because of the unsettled political climate in several of Gabon's African competitors. Devaluation in 1994 gave an additional boost by doubling local currency earnings, though the Asian financial crisis in 1997 resulted in a one-third fall in earnings in 1998. Exports of wood products stood at 2.44m. cu m in 2008, earning Gabon US $995m., with an additional $857,000 earned from processed wood products. In 2009 the value of Gabon's wood exports plummeted to just $256m., though it recovered to $423.4m. in 2010. The total timber cut annually is higher than official production figures because of unregistered logging. In February 2010 the Government, in collaboration with the European Space Agency, established a satellite image station to monitor the rate of forest depletion.

A new Forestry Code was promulgated in 2001 requiring logging companies to produce plans for the sustainable management of their concessions. The Government also agreed to publish the lists of logging permit holders and to award new permits by public auction. The cumbersome tax system was reformed to reduce widespread tax evasion and in April 2007 the Government revoked 116 logging permits over non-payment of taxes. The much criticized Société Nationale des Bois du Gabon (SNBG) lost its monopoly over the export of okoumé and ozigo logs in January 2006. In 2009 the Government opened negotiations with the EU for participation in the latter's Action Plan for Forest Law Enforcement, Governance and Trade (introduced in 2003 to inhibit exports to EU member states of illegally produced logs or processed wood).

The Government had hoped to raise the share of locally processed wood from existing levels (of 10%–15%) to 75% by 2012; however, dissatisfied with progress, a ban was abruptly announced in November 2009 prohibiting the export of unprocessed wood with effect from January 2010. After logging firms protested, in early March President Ali Bongo Ondimba created a special fund (worth €30.5m.) to assist the industry's transition, and accepted a phased reduction of unprocessed wood exports to 40% of the total during 2010 and to 20% by 2012. The ban stimulated an immediate upsurge in plywood firms. Wood-processing capacity was further boosted in September 2011 by the opening of a 400-ha special economic zone at Nkok, 27 km from Libreville. Jointly owned by Olam and the Government (on a 60:40 basis), the zone is projected to expand to 1,126 ha and to cost an eventual US $200m. In December 2011 the Government announced the purchase, for €24m., of a 35%-stake in Rougier Afrique International, a major player in Gabon's forestry sector, with important forest concessions also in Cameroon and the Democratic Republic of the Congo.

In 2002, following the Summit on Sustainable Development in Johannesburg, South Africa, the Government created 13 new national parks, covering 3m. ha or 10.6% of the country's land area; With Gabon's forests containing an estimated 40% of the world's Western lowland gorilla population (*Gorilla gorilla*), this initiative received considerable donor support. Gabon's gorilla population has been seriously reduced by logging and hunting, and by periodic outbreaks of Ebola haemorrhagic fever. In May 2011 the Government dispatched 240 troops to aid park rangers in curbing the growing menace to elephant herds from professional poaching gangs. In June 2012 President Ali Bongo Ondimba presided over the burning of five metric tons of elephant tusks seized from poachers.

The national parks initiative provided an opportunity to refocus Gabon's modest tourism sector on ecotourism. The numbers of tourist arrivals has risen steadily from 155,000 in 2000 to 358,000 in 2008. A boost to tourist numbers (and the development of new hotel facilities) occurred with the 2012 African Cup of Nations soccer tournament—co-hosted in January and February by Gabon and neighbouring Equatorial Guinea, and requiring a €350m. investment in infrastructure by the Government. In January 2012 the Government signed a contract worth €47m. with the Singapore company Aman Resorts for the construction of two luxury hotels and a luxury park camp, with three other park lodges to follow.

MINING

The key to Gabon's economic growth since the 1970s has been its mineral wealth, principally in petroleum but also manganese and uranium. While the petroleum industry remained the economy's dominant sector, its contribution fluctuated with trends in world prices. Its share of GDP—totalling 40.4% in 1980—fell to a low of 16.5% in 1986. However, the development of the Rabi-Kounga field increased this to 46.2% by 2001 and, as oil prices surged, to around 50% between 2004 and 2008. With the global downturn, it dropped to 38% in 2009, and remained at a 40% share of GDP in 2010.

Petroleum exploitation began in 1956, but significant growth only commenced after 1967, with production remaining largely off shore. Output increased steadily until 1997, reaching a peak of 364,000 barrels per day (b/d)—and forcing Gabon's withdrawal from the Organization of the Petroleum Exporting Countries (OPEC) in 1996, as production exceeded OPEC's quota. Although once sub-Saharan Africa's third largest petroleum producer, by 2010 Gabon had slipped to fifth place. National output declined to 237,000 b/d in 2006, although supportive world petroleum prices since 2005 have allowed Gabon's smaller fields to bring production up to 250,000 b/d in 2010. Gabon's proven petroleum reserves, at 3,700m. barrels, are sufficient for another 41 years. The main producer was initially Elf-Gabon (a 25:75 joint venture between the Government and Elf-Aquitaine, now part of Total), but it was overtaken in 1993 by Shell-Gabon, which operates the Rabi-Kounga field with Total and Amerada-Hess. Some 25 oil companies are currently present in the sector, including AGIP, Petrobras, Conoco, Marathon, Amoco, Pioneer, and Vaalco.

Some 95% of petroleum production is exported as crude—with petroleum representing around 80% of export earnings; the USA, the People's Republic of China, France, Argentina and Brazil are Gabon's principal markets. Its own refining capacity is limited to a small plant at Port-Gentil, producing 17,000 b/d for local consumption. With the exception of 2009, buoyant oil prices in recent years have brought earnings of between US $6,781m. (2011) and $7,519m. (2008). Yielding income to the Government in the form of royalties, taxes on company profits, exploration permits, and returns from the 15 fields in which it has equity, petroleum provided around 60% of budget revenue in 2009 and 2010. As well as global markets, Gabon's petroleum earnings are sensitive to local factors. Following a costly 12-day strike in 2008, a government decree in February 2010 included petroleum, along with health and education, among sectors where the provision of a minimum service during future strikes would be obligatory. A four-day strike in April 2011 protesting against expatriate staff recruitment levels ended with the Government pledging further negotiations.

In March 2010 the Government announced that it would establish a new company to manage its commitments in the oil sector. The Gabon Oil Company, modelled on Angola's SONANGOL, would replace the former Petrogab, which had collapsed through mismanagement. A director was appointed in June 2011, but with many qualified Gabonese in the industry already working abroad, the recruitment of sufficient staff was not expected before late 2012. The Government became a participant in the Extractive Industries Transparency Initiative (EITI) in 2004, and in 2005 established a framework for strengthening transparency in the financial relations between the state and oil companies. A first report, in 2005, however, accounted for only 60% of oil revenues; subsequent reports in 2007 and 2008 were improvements, and also covered mining; but in June 2011, the EITI council warned that failure to complete the validation process by December 2012 would result in Gabon's exclusion from the scheme.

Since 1962 manganese ore has been mined at Moanda, near Franceville, by the Compagnie Minière de l'Ogooué (COMILOG). The world's fourth largest manganese producer, Gabon has estimated reserves of 52m. metric tons. Until the opening of a new port at Owendo near Libreville in 1988, most ore was exported through the neighbouring Republic of the Congo. Eramet of France held a 58% stake in COMILOG; other shareholders included the Gabonese state (25%) and Gencor of South Africa (15%). Production stood at 3.2m. metric tons in 2007 and 2008. Unfavourable world markets in 2009 saw production fall by 40%, to 1.9m. tons. A strong recovery in 2010 restored production to 3.2m. tons (around the carrying capacity of the Transgabonais railway, on which the mine depends). Early in 2010 the Government announced its intention to raise its holdings of Eramet's shares from 10% to 15% and its holdings in Comilog from 25.4% to 35.4% by 2015. Two additional manganese deposits were planned to come into operation by 2013—one, near Franceville, being developed by the Australian firm BHP Billiton, and the other, near Mbemlélé in central Gabon, by the Chinese company CICM Huangzhou Gabon. In 2010 Eramet began construction at Moanda of a plant to transform manganese with a production capacity of 85,000 tons per year. The Indian firm Abhijeet was also constructing a factory at the new Nkok special economic zone to produce ferromanganese for the steel industry. To oversee the quickening pace of development in this sector, the Government established the Compagnie Equatoriale des Mines, in March 2011.

Five non-governmental organizations and local inhabitants have brought a 'class action' against Eramet, currently before a Gabonese court, demanding €747m. in reparations over health problems and environmental damage caused by the manganese mine. A similar claim had been settled through negotiations with Areva, the French company which had produced around 35,000 tons of uranium metal from its mine at Moanda over four decades, until production ceased in 1999.

In April 2005 the Government signed an agreement with a Chinese consortium to exploit massive iron ore deposits at Belinga in north-east Gabon. The project included the construction of a 560-km railway, a new deep-water port at Cape Santa Clara and a hydroelectric dam. The US $4,000m. project attracted criticism over its environmental impact and terms which are seen as overly generous to China. Although some work commenced in late 2007, almost immediately the Gabonese Government demanded a renegotiation of terms. The new agreement, concluded in May 2008, substantially reduced the concession's area and raised the Gabonese stake in the Compagnie Minière de Belinga from 15% to 25%. With site tests having indicated larger deposits than initially thought, the Government informed the Chinese in 2010 that it would seek further contract negotiations. The Chinese partner appeared since 2008 to have put the Belinga project on hold, to mounting Government concern; in December 2011 the Gabonese Government suspended the contract, and in February 2012 announced that it had been awarded instead to BHP Billiton.

Alluvial deposits of gold in south-east Gabon have long been exploited by artisan miners, with annual output estimated at 300 kg. A Moroccan company, Mamagem International, and the Canadian firm SearchGold Resources were due to commence operations in 2011 at the Bakoudou-Magnima site in south-eastern Gabon to produce 1,300 kg of gold per year over an expected three- to four-year period. In January 2012 COMILOG agreed to a partnership arrangement with the state to exploit a deposit of rare minerals at Mabouié, not far from Lambaréné.

MANUFACTURING AND POWER

Gabon's manufacturing sector accounted for an estimated 3.5% of GDP in 2008, and was centred on oil refining, timber-processing and cement production. Other industries include agro-processing, industrial gas production, and the manufacture of soap, paint, cigarettes and textiles. The Government's efforts to develop natural resource-based industries have been boosted by its partnership with Olam for the establishment of the special economic zone at Nkok and the expansion of the existing zone at Mandji Island. However, since Gabon's domestic market is modest, the development of local industries must depend on regional markets, though existing trade with Gabon's neighbours is limited. A stock exchange, eventually expected to serve the entire region, opened in Libreville in January 2007.

Power and water supplies were formerly managed by the Société d'Energie et d'Eau du Gabon (SEEG), which was privatized in 1997, with 51% awarded to a consortium led by France's Compagnie Générale des Eaux (since renamed Veolia), and the balance sold to the Gabonese public. Though SEEG has expanded its services and supply capacity in both spheres, complaints by Libreville residents caused the Government in December 2009 to order an external audit to establish SEEG's compliance with the terms of the 20-year agreement; subsequently, the Government ordered SEEG to submit annual progress reports on renewing outworn facilities. In December 2011 the Government announced that the state would become the majority shareholder in a new agency covering the provision of basic services, the Société d'Electricité, de Téléphone, et d'Eau du Gabon.

TRANSPORT AND COMMUNICATIONS

Gabon's surface transportation system remains inadequate. Until 1979 there were no railways except for the cableway linking the Moanda manganese mine to the Republic of the Congo border, while the main rivers are navigable only for the last 80 km–160 km before reaching the Atlantic Ocean. The road network remains underdeveloped. In 2009 there were only 9,170 km of roads, with 11% being paved. A major road project was launched in August 2009 to link all nine provinces with paved roads.

The Transgabonais railway scheme was among the most prestigious achievements of President Bongo Ondimba, opening up the mineral-rich Franceville area. The 679-km single-track railway required an investment of 800,000m.–900,000m. francs CFA between 1974 and 1986, with external donors highly critical of the costs. The line became operational in 1989, although lack of finance prevented the completion of a 237-km link to the Belinga iron ore deposits (see above). The Office du Chemin de Fer Transgabonais (OCTRA) was sold in July 1999 to a consortium of timber interests headed by the state-owned timber concern, SNBG, which acquired the line on a 20-year concession; this was cancelled in 2003 over a failure to meet financial obligations. In August 2005 a new 30-year concession was awarded to the Société d'Exploitation du Transgabonais (SETRAG), an affiliate of the manganese mining firm COMILOG. In 2010 SETRAG's turnover of US $16.3m. represented a decrease of one-third from 2009, mainly due to the ban on the export of unprocessed timber exports.

Gabon's main port for petroleum exports is Port-Gentil, which also handles logs (floated down the Ogooué river), while Owendo is the principal port for mineral exports. A third deep-water port operates at Mayumba. In November 2010 the Singapore Port Authority was contracted to improve port capacity.

In the communications sector, Maroc Télécom, a subsidiary of the French telecommunications group Vivendi, acquired a 51% share of Gabon Télécom in February 2007. Mobile phone penetration has reached 90%, with four companies (Airtel Gabon, Moov Gabon, USAN Gabon and Libertis) now competing for market share. Also in early 2007 Gabon Post was liquidated and replaced by La Poste, a smaller agency with limited budgetary support.

Air transport plays a particularly important role. Although Libreville's Léon M'Ba International Airport has an annual capacity of 1.5m. passengers, a new international airport with capacity for 2m. is planned. As well as four other domestic airports (Port-Gentil, Franceville, Lambaréné and Moanda), there are various small airfields owned by private companies. In 1977, following its withdrawal from Air Afrique, Gabon established its own international carrier, Air Gabon, in which the state had an 80% interest. After drastic restructuring measures, the company was initially scheduled to be sold in 2002. With a lack of satisfactory bids, the Gabonese Government repurchased Air France's stake and recapitalized the company; however, in February 2006 the Government finally decided to liquidate Air Gabon. Plans to introduce a new national carrier were announced in October 2011.

FINANCE

Petroleum exploitation brought rapidly expanding government budgets, but the investment requirements of the Transgabonais railway were largely met by borrowing at non-concessionary rates; the budget was in deficit by 1983. The situation was gravely exacerbated by the collapse in petroleum prices in 1986, when the deficit reached 11.7% of GDP. Despite the completion of the Transgabonais and the surge in petroleum revenue in 1990 and 1991, the budget deficit remained. Modest budget surpluses were recorded in 1999 and 2000, with a more substantial surplus in 2001. In 2008 the budgetary surplus reached US $1,659.9m., but fell to $715.8m. in 2009, before a partial recovery to $1,245m. in 2011.

FOREIGN TRADE AND PAYMENTS

Gabon has maintained a considerable foreign trade surplus, even through periods of instability in petroleum prices. With Gabon's small population, exports have averaged some three times the value of imports. The trade surplus stood at US $7,171.0m. in 2008; it fell sharply, to $3,643.0m., in 2009, though recovered to $4,655m. in 2010 and $5,210m. in 2011. Yet the surplus on foreign trade has been exceeded by the deficit on services and transfers in nearly every year since 1985, given high outflows of interest payments on the external debt and of remittances of profits by foreign firms. The current account balance remains sensitive to petroleum price fluctuations. After successive deficits in 2001, 2002 and 2003, a recovery produced a surplus of $757m. in 2004 and $550m. in 2005. The surplus in 2008 reached 23.3% of GDP; in 2009, with disfavourable external conditions, it declined sharply, to 13.6% of GDP, while recovering slightly to an estimated 14.7% in 2010.

As the heavy foreign borrowing that characterized the late 1970s and early 1980s came to an end, the debt repayment burden has remained high, and arrears in payments mounted. That debt stood at US $4,223m. in 1991; of this, $539m. represented arrears. The currency devaluation of January 1994 changed the environment. After a stand-by agreement with the IMF, both the 'Paris Club' of official creditors and the 'London Club' of commercial creditors agreed to debt rescheduling. Yet by 1999 the total external debt had reached $4,425m. With a financing gap anticipated until 2014, the Government negotiated a new debt rescheduling agreement with the 'Paris Club' in June 2004 and another with the 'London Club' in mid-2005. Improved petroleum earnings meant that the external debt as a proportion of GDP decreased from 56% in 2003 to 50% in 2004, and to 32.5% in 2006.

However, in July 2007 Gabon proposed to the 'Paris Club' that it buy back the debt owed to official creditors (US $2,182,000m.). This was accepted in principle, with Gabon determining the exact scale of the buy-backs. After receiving favourable scores from two rating agencies, Gabon issued two bonds in early December—a 10-year bond for $1,600m. on the international capital market and a six-year bond for 815m. francs CFA on the regional money market. Both were successful, reducing Gabon's stock of external debt to $2,367m., or 15.6% of GDP, by late 2008. It stood at $1,999m. (15.7% of GDP) in late 2010, and $1,944m. (14.3% of GDP) at the end of 2011.

Despite Gabon's high income levels and the foreign investment its petroleum sector attracts, inflows of foreign aid remained relatively modest. In the period 1991–93 net aid disbursements averaged US $105m. per year, mostly representing official French support for the overvalued CFA franc. The devaluation of 1994, and the associated external support, brought a surge in aid inflows, to a net $182m. in that year and an average of $135m. per year in 1995–96. Net inflows of aid then fell back to $62m. in 2009, before rising again to $78m. in 2010, and to $104m. in 2011; France and the EU remain key sources (with 85% of the 2011 total). The vulnerabilities of Gabon's balance-of-payments situation—a feature frequently highlighted during the 1990s—has eased considerably in recent years, and foreign exchange reserves stood at $2,100m. in 2010 and $2,900m. in 2011 (sufficient to cover nine months' imports).

The solution of the problems of an unbalanced economy are becoming ever more urgent; in the absence of major new petroleum discoveries, Gabon's petroleum production—which currently generates around one-half of GDP—is forecast to fall significantly in coming years, having already decreased by one-third between 1996 and 2008. Shortly after the funeral of President Bongo Ondimba in June 2009, critical assessments of his legacy even surfaced in the official media acknowledging that attempts since 2003 to reduce the economy's dependency on petroleum had brought limited returns. The successor Government has sought to provide fresh impetus to these efforts, but the economy's fragility will continue while the country remains dependent on the export of a limited range of raw materials, and while economic diversification is hampered by infrastructural constraints.

Statistical Survey

Source (unless otherwise stated): Direction Générale de la Statistique et des Etudes Economiques, Ministère de la Planification et de la Programmation du Développement, BP 2119, Libreville; tel. 01-72-13-69; fax 01-72-04-57; e-mail plan@dgsee.yahoo.fr; internet www.stat-gabon.org.

Area and Population

AREA, POPULATION AND DENSITY

Area (sq km)	267,667*
Population (census results)	
31 July 1993	
Males	501,784
Females	513,192
Total	1,014,976
1 December 2003	1,269,000†
Population (UN estimates at mid-year)‡	
2010	1,505,463
2011	1,534,258
2012	1,563,873
Density (per sq km) at mid-2012	5.8

* 103,347 sq miles.

† Provisional (Source: UN, *Population and Vital Statistics Report*).

‡ Source: UN, *World Population Prospects: The 2010 Revision*.

POPULATION BY AGE AND SEX

(UN estimates at mid-2012)

	Males	Females	Total
0–14	273,325	268,206	541,531
15–64	479,641	474,637	954,278
65 and over	31,915	36,149	68,064
Total	784,881	778,992	1,563,873

Source: UN, *World Population Prospects: The 2010 Revision*.

REGIONS

(1993 census)

Region	Area (sq km)	Population	Density (per sq km)	Chief town
Estuaire	20,740	463,187	22.3	Libreville
Haut-Ogooué	36,547	104,301	2.9	Franceville
Moyen-Ogooué	18,535	42,316	2.3	Lambaréné
N'Gounié	37,750	77,781	2.1	Mouila
Nyanga	21,285	39,430	1.9	Tchibanga
Ogooué-Ivindo	46,075	48,862	1.1	Makokou
Ogooué-Lolo	25,380	43,915	1.7	Koulamoutou
Ogooué-Maritime	22,890	97,913	4.3	Port-Gentil
Woleu-N'Tem	38,465	97,271	2.5	Oyem
Total	267,667	1,014,976	3.8	

PRINCIPAL TOWNS

(population at 1993 census)

Libreville (capital)	419,596	Mouila	16,307
Port-Gentil	79,225	Lambaréné	15,033
Franceville	31,183	Tchibanga	14,054
Oyem	22,404	Koulamoutou	11,773
Moanda	21,882	Makokou	9,849

Mid-2011 (incl. suburbs, UN estimate): Libreville (capital) 686,356 (Source: UN, *World Urbanization Prospects: The 2011 Revision*).

BIRTHS AND DEATHS
(annual averages, UN estimates)

	1995–2000	2000–05	2005–10
Birth rate (per 1,000)	33.2	29.7	27.4
Death rate (per 1,000)	10.2	10.4	9.4

Source: UN, *World Population Prospects: The 2010 Revision*.

Life expectancy (years at birth): 62.3 (males 61.3; females 63.4) in 2010 (Source: World Bank, World Development Indicators database).

ECONOMICALLY ACTIVE POPULATION
('000 persons, 1991, estimates)

	Males	Females	Total
Agriculture, etc.	187	151	338
Industry	62	9	71
Services	69	26	95
Total labour force	318	186	504

Source: UN Economic Commission for Africa, *African Statistical Yearbook*.

2005 (persons aged 15 years and over): Total employed 639,180; Unemployed 115,499; Total labour force 664,117.

Mid-2012 (estimates in '000): Agriculture, etc. 185; Total 749 (Source: FAO).

Health and Welfare

KEY INDICATORS

Total fertility rate (children per woman, 2010)	3.3
Under-5 mortality rate (per 1,000 live births, 2010)	74
HIV/AIDS (% of persons aged 15–49, 2009)	5.2
Physicians (per 1,000 head, 2004)	0.3
Hospital beds (per 1,000 head, 2010)	6.3
Health expenditure (2009): US $ per head (PPP)	511
Health expenditure (2009): % of GDP	3.6
Health expenditure (2009): public (% of total)	47.9
Access to water (% of persons, 2010)	87
Access to sanitation (% of persons, 2010)	33
Total carbon dioxide emissions ('000 metric tons, 2008)	2,471.6
Carbon dioxide emissions per head (metric tons, 2008)	1.7
Human Development Index (2011): ranking	106
Human Development Index (2011): value	0.674

For sources and definitions, see explanatory note on p. vi.

Agriculture

PRINCIPAL CROPS
('000 metric tons, FAO estimates)

	2008	2009	2010
Maize	35	46	40
Cassava (Manioc)	243	307	270
Taro (Cocoyam)	55	70	55
Yams	164	210	168
Sugar cane	220	240	240
Groundnuts, with shell	20	18	18
Oil palm fruit	34	20	20
Bananas	14	12	14
Plantains	275	288	297
Natural rubber	14	13	14

Aggregate production ('000 metric tons, may include official, semi-official or estimated data): Total cereals 36 in 2008, 47 in 2009, 41 in 2010; Total roots and tubers 465 in 2008, 591 in 2009, 496 in 2010; Total vegetables (incl. melons) 38 in 2008, 39 in 2009, 36 in 2010; Total fruits (excl. melons) 302 in 2008, 311 in 2009, 325 in 2010.

Source: FAO.

LIVESTOCK
('000 head, year ending September, FAO estimates)

	2006	2007	2008
Cattle	35	36	37
Pigs	212	213	215
Sheep	195	196	196
Goats	90	91	92
Chickens	3,100	3,100	3,200

2009–10: Figures assumed to be unchanged from 2008 (FAO estimates).

Source: FAO.

LIVESTOCK PRODUCTS
('000 metric tons, FAO estimates)

	2008	2009	2010
Cattle meat	1.1	1.1	1.1
Pig meat	3.2	3.2	3.2
Chicken meat	3.8	3.8	3.8
Rabbit meat	1.9	1.9	1.9
Game meat	20.7	22.0	25.1
Cows' milk	1.8	1.8	1.9
Hen eggs	2.2	1.9	2.1

Source: FAO.

Forestry

ROUNDWOOD REMOVALS
('000 cubic metres)

	2005	2006	2007
Sawlogs, veneer logs and logs for sleepers	3,200	3,500	3,400
Fuel wood*	1,070	1,070	1,070
Total*	4,270	4,570	4,470

* FAO estimates.

2008–11: Production assumed to be unchanged from 2007 (FAO estimates).

Source: FAO.

SAWNWOOD PRODUCTION
('000 cubic metres, incl. railway sleepers)

	2007	2008	2009
Total	296	197	250

2010–11: Production assumed to be unchanged from 2009 (FAO estimates).

Source: FAO.

Fishing

('000 metric tons, live weight)

	2008	2009*	2010*
Capture	42.5*	32.0	32.0
Tilapias	4.7*	4.4	4.4
Other freshwater fishes	5.0*	5.0	5.0
Barracudas	0.4	0.3	0.3
Bobo croakers	1.4	1.0	1.0
West African croakers	1.1	0.8	0.8
Lesser African threadfin	0.8	5.0	5.0
Bonga shad	8.3	5.6	5.6
Penaeus shrimp	0.1	—	—
Aquaculture	0.1	0.1	0.2
Total catch	42.6*	32.1	32.2

* FAO estimate(s).

Source: FAO.

Mining

	2008	2009	2010
Crude petroleum ('000 barrels)	85,775	83,950	89,425
Natural gas (million cu m)	80	n.a.	n.a.
Diamonds (carats)	500	500	500
Manganese ore ('000 metric tons): gross weight*	3,150	1,950	3,200
Manganese ore ('000 metric tons): metal content†	100	50	100
Gold (kg)*‡	300	300	300

* Figures refer to the metal content of ore.

† Figures refer to the weight of chemical-grade pellets.

‡ Excluding production smuggled out of the country (estimated at more than 400 kg annually).

Source: US Geological Survey.

Industry

PETROLEUM PRODUCTS

('000 metric tons)

	2006	2007	2008
Motor spirit (petrol)	44	56	70
Kerosene	23	25	31
Distillate fuel oils	213	260	326
Residual fuel oils and asphalt	324	356	446
Butane	6.7	14.0	13.5

Source: mostly UN Industrial Commodity Statistics Database.

SELECTED OTHER PRODUCTS

	2003	2004	2005
Plywood ('000 cu mm)	37.8	52.8	68.1
Veneer sheets ('000 cu mm)	198.2	120.7	175.2
Alcoholic beverages ('000 hl)	755.9	750.1	852.1
Soft drinks ('000 hl)	568.4	537.9	587.0

Hydraulic cement ('000 metric tons, estimates): 230 in 2008; 250 in 2009; 200 in 2010 (Source: US Geological Survey).

Electric energy (million kWh): 1,610 in 2005; 1,723 in 2006; 1,844 in 2007; 2,040 in 2008 (Source: UN Industrial Commodity Statistics Database).

Finance

CURRENCY AND EXCHANGE RATES

Monetary Units

100 centimes = 1 franc de la Coopération Financière en Afrique Centrale (CFA).

Sterling, Dollar and Euro Equivalents (31 May 2012)

£1 sterling = 819.959 francs CFA;
US $1 = 528.870 francs CFA;
€1 = 655.957 francs CFA;
10,000 francs CFA = £12.20 = $18.91 = €15.24.

Average Exchange Rate (francs CFA per US $)

2009 472.19
2010 495.28
2011 471.87

Note: An exchange rate of 1 French franc = 50 francs CFA, established in 1948, remained in force until January 1994, when the CFA franc was devalued by 50%, with the exchange rate adjusted to 1 French franc = 100 francs CFA. This relationship to French currency remained in effect with the introduction of the euro on 1 January 1999. From that date, accordingly, a fixed exchange rate of €1 = 655.957 francs CFA has been in operation.

BUDGET

('000 million francs CFA)

Revenue*	2007	2008†	2009†
Petroleum revenue	958.5	1,296.7	632.4
Non-petroleum revenue	677.8	714.3	750.3
Direct taxes	193.5	232.7	256.0
Indirect taxes	130.3	133.4	145.7
Value-added tax	92.4	86.0	87.0
Taxes on international trade and transactions	281.9	275.5	271.2
Other revenue	72.1	72.7	77.4
Total	1,636.3	2,011.0	1,382.6

Expenditure‡	2007	2008†	2009†
Current expenditure	837.8	917.0	843.5
Wages and salaries	301.8	320.8	370.0
Goods and services	190.4	205.3	191.5
Transfers and subsidies	226.8	268.1	183.2
Interest payments	118.8	122.8	98.8
Domestic	26.6	22.8	12.3
External	92.2	100.0	86.6
Capital expenditure	246.8	295.0	306.1
Domestically financed investment	198.6	244.1	235.5
Externally financed investment	48.2	50.9	70.6
Capital grants	—	0.0	8.7
Capital transfers	—	38.7	55.7
Total	1,084.6	1,250.7	1,214.0

* Excluding grants received ('000 million francs CFA): 0.2 in 2007; 6.0 in 2008 (projection); 4.0 in 2009 (projection).

† Projections.

‡ Excluding net lending and road maintenance and other special funds ('000 million francs CFA): 39.3 in 2004 (funds only); 58.4 in 2005; 55.8 in 2006; 81.0 in 2007; 101.8 in 2008 (funds only, projection); 62.4 in 2009 (projection).

Source: IMF, *Gabon: Second and Third Reviews Under the Stand-By Arrangement and Requests for Waiver of Nonobservance of Performance Criteria and Modification of Performance Criterion—Staff Report; Press Release on the Executive Board Discussion; and Statement by the Executive Director for Gabon* (March 2009).

2009 ('000 million francs CFA, revised figures): Total revenue and grants 1,685; Total expenditure and net lending 1,348 (Source: IMF (see below)).

2010 ('000 million francs CFA, projections): Total revenue and grants 1,976; Total expenditure and net lending 1,664 (Source: IMF (see below)).

2011 ('000 million francs CFA, projections): Total revenue and grants 2,216; Total expenditure and net lending 1,860 (Source: IMF, *Gabon: 2010 Article IV Consultation—Staff Report; Staff Supplement; Public Information Notice on the Executive Board Discussion; and Statement by the Executive Director for Gabon* (May 2011)).

INTERNATIONAL RESERVES
(US $ million at 31 December)

	2009	2010	2011
Gold*	—	9.64	19.62
IMF special drawing rights	208.20	204.53	203.89
Reserve position in IMF	0.80	0.83	0.93
Foreign exchange	1,784.24	1,530.53	1,952.49
Total	1,993.24	1,745.53	2,176.93

* Valued at market-related prices.

Source: IMF, *International Financial Statistics*.

MONEY SUPPLY
('000 million francs CFA at 31 December)

	2009	2010	2011
Currency outside depository corporations	294.70	287.80	351.22
Transferable deposits	470.07	645.31	885.35
Other deposits	393.41	465.07	540.01
Securities other than shares	—	—	—
Total money (incl. others)	1,158.17	1,398.17	1,776.59

Source: IMF, *International Financial Statistics*.

COST OF LIVING
(Consumer Price Index; base: 2000 = 100)

	2007	2008	2009
Clothing	109.8	109.5	107.2
Rent, water, electricity, gas and other fuels	113.1	123.4	128.5
All items (incl. others)	112.7	118.5	120.8

2010: All items (incl. others) 122.6.

2011: All items (incl. others) 124.1.

Food (Consumer Price Index; base: 2007 = 100): 111.8 in 2009; 116.7 in 2010; 121.4 in 2011.

Source: ILO.

NATIONAL ACCOUNTS
('000 million francs CFA at current prices)

Expenditure on the Gross Domestic Product

	2008	2009	2010*
Government final consumption expenditure	709	791	853
Private final consumption expenditure	1,932	2,038	2,179
Gross fixed capital formation	1,331	1,250	1,664
Changes in inventories	32	27	58
Total domestic expenditure	4,004	4,106	4,754
Exports of goods and services	4,401	2,893	4,020
Less Imports of goods and services	1,951	1,868	2,209
GDP at purchasers' values	6,454	5,131	6,565

Gross Domestic Product by Economic Activity

	2008	2009	2010*
Agriculture, livestock, hunting, forestry and fishing	264	277	269
Mining and quarrying	3,684	2,282	3,438
Manufacturing	251	230	261
Electricity, gas and water	81	88	100
Construction	113	112	140
Trade, restaurants and hotels	333	350	374
Finance, insurance and real estate	668	687	711
Transport and communications	295	267	274
Public administration and defence	432	506	549
GDP at factor cost	6,121	4,799	6,117
Indirect taxes	333	332	449
GDP at purchasers' values	6,454	5,131	6,565

* Estimates.

Note: Deduction for imputed bank service charge assumed to be distributed at origin.

Source: African Development Bank.

BALANCE OF PAYMENTS
('000 million francs CFA)

	2009*	2010†	2011†
Exports of goods f.o.b.	5,950	7,469	8,071
Petroleum	5,192	6,531	6,781
Imports of goods f.o.b.	−2,307	−2,814	−2,861
Trade balance	3,643	4,655	5,210
Services and other income (net)	−2,597	−3,100	−3,400
Balance on goods, services and income	1,046	1,555	1,810
Current transfers (net)	−182	−219	−233
Current balance	864	1,336	1,577
Capital transfers (net)	3	0	0
Direct investment (net)	587	531	728
Other investment assets and liabilities (net)	−1,455	−1,487	−1,630
Overall balance	−1	380	675

* Estimates.

† Projections.

Source: IMF, *Gabon: 2010 Article IV Consultation—Staff Report; Staff Supplement; Public Information Notice on the Executive Board Discussion; and Statement by the Executive Director for Gabon* (May 2012).

External Trade

PRINCIPAL COMMODITIES
('000 million francs CFA)

Imports	2007	2008	2009
Food and live animals	308.8	359.3	352.9
Meat and meat preparations	98.8	117.8	104.6
Cereal and cereal preparations	89.6	105.0	111.1
Beverages and tobacco	49.8	54.4	54.1
Mineral fuels, lubricants, etc.	103.1	121.2	182.2
Petroleum, petroleum products and related materials	90.4	117.7	168.3
Chemicals and related products	192.8	332.7	243.7
Medicinal and pharmaceutical products	67.7	178.3	73.7
Basic manufactures	432.2	425.1	562.9
Iron and steel	190.3	150.3	217.5
Machinery and transport equipment	796.5	996.5	884.5

Imports—*continued*	2007	2008	2009
General industrial machinery and equipment	179.3	304.9	224.5
Electrical machinery, apparatus and appliances	93.4	109.0	119.6
Road vehicles	199.7	226.5	187.6
Miscellaneous manufactured articles	171.4	195.5	170.7
Total (incl. others)	2,110.2	2,563.1	2,500.9

Exports	2007	2008	2009
Crude materials (inedible), except fuels	754.3	744.1	637.9
Cork and wood	499.8	477.2	447.4
Metalliferous ore and metal scrap	226.4	211.3	161.5
Manganese ores and concentrates	223.0	206.9	157.5
Mineral fuels, lubricants, etc.	5,256.7	8,530.2	4,452.7
Basic manufactures	170.2	170.3	121.6
Cork and wood manufactures	164.8	156.4	111.0
Veneers, plywood, particle board and other wood	164.8	156.4	111.0
Total (incl. others)	6,302.0	9,565.9	5,356.0

Source: UN, *International Trade Statistics Yearbook*.

PRINCIPAL TRADING PARTNERS
(US $ million)

Imports c.i.f.	2007	2008	2009
Belgium	276.9	352.1	392.6
Brazil	43.7	58.9	45.3
Cameroon	65.4	60.3	52.1
China, People's Republic	82.7	101.0	122.2
Congo, Republic	15.3	56.4	19.5
France (incl. Monaco)	760.0	907.8	823.7
Germany	50.2	44.0	37.0
Greece	32.4	6.2	0.1
India	22.2	20.7	31.7
Italy	57.2	56.6	128.8
Japan	56.3	52.5	52.6
Netherlands	67.5	87.6	103.3
South Africa	44.8	42.1	44.8
Spain	58.2	48.0	46.0
Sweden	30.1	13.2	6.5
Thailand	43.6	72.7	42.5
Togo	11.0	29.8	3.5
United Arab Emirates	25.7	27.3	28.7
United Kingdom	33.7	64.1	72.1
USA	126.0	190.7	178.4
Total (incl. others)	2,110.2	2,563.1	2,500.9

Exports f.o.b.	2007	2008	2009
Bermuda	0.0	124.3	0.0
China, People's Republic	599.7	1,260.0	427.9
Congo, Republic	17.3	29.2	82.4
France (incl. Monaco)	711.7	574.3	244.9
India	57.6	613.1	43.3
Italy	75.4	266.7	36.2
Japan	349.0	66.1	5.4
Korea, Republic	8.2	2.1	86.1
Malaysia	155.1	133.0	215.3
Netherlands	31.3	346.9	159.3
South Africa	20.3	26.3	60.1
Spain	95.3	314.8	282.1
Thailand	198.4	0.3	1.1
Trinidad and Tobago	22.1	163.2	0.0
United Kingdom	97.2	2.0	112.4
USA	3,366.6	4,966.2	3,160.4
Total (incl. others)	6,302.0	9,565.9	5,356.0

Source: UN, *International Trade Statistics Yearbook*.

Transport

RAILWAYS
(traffic)

	2003	2004	2005
Passengers carried ('000)	206.8	214.4	218.5
Freight carried ('000 metric tons)	2,967.7	3,455.8	3,923.8

ROAD TRAFFIC
(estimates, motor vehicles in use)

	1994	1995	1996
Passenger cars	22,310	24,000	24,750
Lorries and vans	14,850	15,840	16,490

Source: IRF, *World Road Statistics*.

SHIPPING

Merchant Fleet
(registered at 31 December)

	2007	2008	2009
Number of vessels	49	49	50
Total displacement ('000 grt)	13.8	14.0	14.4

Source: IHS Fairplay, *World Fleet Statistics*.

International Sea-borne Freight Traffic
('000 metric tons, Port-Gentil and Owendo)

	2002	2003	2004
Goods loaded	15,429	16,005	17,144
Goods unloaded	763	739	776

Source: IMF, *Gabon: Statistical Appendix* (May 2005).

CIVIL AVIATION
(traffic on scheduled services)

	2007	2008	2009
Kilometres flown (million)	10	10	10
Passengers carried ('000)	535	546	525
Passenger-kilometres (million)	947	966	931
Total ton-kilometres (million)	161	157	148

Source: UN, *Statistical Yearbook*.

2010: Passengers carried ('000) 96.3 (Source: World Bank, World Development Indicators database).

Tourism

	2001	2002	2003
Tourist arrivals	169,191	208,348	222,257
Tourism receipts (US $ million, incl. passenger transport)	46	77	84

Receipts from tourism (US $ million, incl. passenger transport): 74 in 2004; 13 in 2005.
Source: World Tourism Organization.

Communications Media

	2009	2010	2011
Telephones ('000 main lines in use)	36.5	30.4	30.0
Mobile cellular telephones ('000 subscribers)	1,373.0	1,610.0	1,800.0
Internet subscribers ('000)	20.2	22.2	n.a.
Broadband subscribers ('000)	3.7	4.1	4.5

Radio receivers ('000 in use): 600 in 1999.

Television receivers ('000 in use): 400 in 2001.

Daily newspapers: 2 (estimated average circulation 34,800 copies) in 1998; 1 in 2004.

Personal computers: 47,000 (33.7 per 1,000 persons) in 2006.

Sources: UNESCO Institute for Statistics; UN, *Statistical Yearbook*; International Telecommunication Union.

Education

(2010/11 unless otherwise indicated, estimates)

			Pupils		
	Institutions	Teachers	Males	Females	Total
Pre-primary	9*	517†	22,416	22,809	45,225
Primary	1,175*	12,961	162,708	155,238	317,946
Secondary:					
General	88‡	5,062	70,623	75,457	146,080
Technical and vocational	11‡	394†	5,025‖	2,562‖	7,587‖
Tertiary	2*	585¶	4,806¶	2,667¶	7,473¶

* 1991/92 figure.
† 2000/01 figure.
‡ 1996 figure.
§ 1999/2000 figure.
‖ 2001/02 figure.
¶ 1998/99 figure.

Source: UNESCO Institute for Statistics.

Pupil-teacher ratio (primary education, UNESCO estimate): 24.5 in 2010/11 (Source: UNESCO Institute for Statistics).

Adult literacy rate (UNESCO estimates): 84.9% (males 91.9%; females 88.4%) in 2010 (Source: UNESCO Institute for Statistics).

Directory

Note: The telephone numbers listed in this Directory are those used when dialling from within Gabon. In order successfully to dial from abroad, it is necessary to omit the initial 0.

The Constitution

The Constitution of the Gabonese Republic was adopted on 14 March 1991 and amended in April 1997 and July 2003. The main provisions are summarized below.

PREAMBLE

Upholds the rights of the individual, liberty of conscience and of the person, religious freedom and freedom of education. Sovereignty is vested in the people, who exercise it through their representatives or by means of referendums. There is direct, universal and secret suffrage.

HEAD OF STATE

The President is elected by direct universal suffrage for a seven-year term. There is no limit on the number of terms that may be served. The President is Head of State and of the Armed Forces. The President may, after consultation with his ministers and leaders of the Assemblée nationale, order a referendum to be held. The President appoints the Prime Minister, who is Head of Government and who is accountable to the President. The President is the guarantor of national independence and territorial sovereignty.

EXECUTIVE POWER

Executive power is vested in the President and the Council of Ministers, who are appointed by the Prime Minister, in consultation with the President.

LEGISLATIVE POWER

The Assemblée nationale is elected by direct universal suffrage for a five-year term. It may be dissolved or prorogued for up to 18 months by the President, after consultation with the Council of Ministers and President of the Assemblée. The President may return a bill to the Assemblée for a second reading, when it must be passed by a majority of two-thirds of the members. If the President dissolves the Assemblée, elections must take place within 40 days.

The Constitution also provides for the establishment of an upper chamber (the Sénat), to control the balance and regulation of power.

POLITICAL ORGANIZATIONS

Article 2 of the Constitution states that 'Political parties and associations contribute to the expression of universal suffrage. They are formed and exercise their activities freely, within the limits delineated by the laws and regulations. They must respect the principles of democracy, national sovereignty, public order and national unity'.

JUDICIAL POWER

The President guarantees the independence of the judiciary and presides over the Conseil Supérieur de la Magistrature. Supreme judicial power is vested in the Supreme Court.

The Government

HEAD OF STATE

President: Ali Bongo Ondimba (inaugurated 16 October 2009).

Vice-President: Didjob Divungui-di-N'Dingue.

COUNCIL OF MINISTERS

(September 2012)

The Government is formed by members of the Parti Démocratique Gabonais.

Prime Minister and Head of Government: Raymond Ndong Sima.

Minister of Justice, Keeper of the Seals, Government Spokesperson: Ida Reteno Assonouet.

Minister of Foreign Affairs, International Co-operation and Francophone Affairs, responsible for the NEPAD and Regional Integration: Emmanuel Issozet Ngondet.

Minister of Health: Léon Nzouba.

Minister of Agriculture, Stockbreeding, Fisheries and Rural Development: Julien Nkoghé Békalé.

Minister of the Promotion of Investment, Public Works, Transport, Housing and Tourism, responsible for Territorial Management: Magloire Ngambia.

Minister of the Digital Economy, Communication and Posts: Blaise Louembé.

Minister of National Education, Higher and Technical Education and Professional Training, responsible for Culture, Youth and Sports: Séraphin Moundounga.

Minister of Water and Forests: Gabriel Ntchango.

Minister of Small and Medium-sized Enterprises, Handicrafts and Trade: Fidèle Mengue M'Engouang.

Minister of the Interior, Public Security, Immigration and Decentralization: Jean-François Ndongou.

Minister of National Defence: Pacôme Rufin Ondzounga.

Minister of the Family and Social Affairs: HONORINE NZET BITÉGUÉ.

Minister of Industry and Mines: RÉGIS IMMONGAULT TATAGANI.

Minister of the Economy, Employment and Sustainable Development: LUC OYOUBI.

Minister of the Budget, Public Accounts and the Civil Service: CHRISTIANE ROSE OSSOUKA RAPONDA.

Minister of Petroleum, Energy and Hydraulic Resources: ETIENNE NGOUBOU.

Minister-delegate to the Prime Minister, responsible for State Reform: CALIXTE ISIDORE NSIE EDANG.

Minister-delegate to the Minister of Foreign Affairs, responsible for the NEPAD and Regional Integration: DOMINIQUE NGUIENO.

Minister-delegate to the Minister of Agriculture, Stockbreeding, Fisheries and Rural Development: CÉLESTINE OGUEWA BA.

Minister-delegate to the Minister of Health: ALICE BIKISA NEMBE.

Minister-delegate to the Minister of the Interior, responsible for Security: AIMÉ-POPA NTZOUTSI MOUYAMA.

Minister-delegate to the Minister of the Digital Economy, Communication and Posts: FRANÇOISE ASSENGONE OBAME.

Minister-delegate to the Minister of National Education, Higher and Technical Education and Professional Training, responsible for Culture, Youth and Sports: ERNEST WALKER ONINWIN.

Minister-delegate to the Minister of the Budget, Public Accounts and the Civil Service, responsible for the Civil Service: RAPHAËL NGAZOUZET.

Ministers-delegate to the Minister of Promotion of Investment, Public Works, Transport, Housing and Tourism: JEAN EMMANUEL BIE (Transport), CHRISTIANE LECKAT (Housing).

Minister-delegate to the Minister of National Education, Higher and Technical Education and Professional Training, responsible for Technical Education and Professional Training: PAULETTE MOUNGUENGUI.

Minister-delegate to the Minister of the Economy, Employment and Sustainable Development: DÉSIRÉ GUEDON.

MINISTRIES

Office of the Prime Minister: BP 546, Libreville; tel. 01-74-70-90; fax 01-77-20-04.

Ministry of Agriculture, Stockbreeding, Fisheries and Rural Development: BP 3974 & 199, Libreville; tel. 01-76-13-78; fax 01-77-37-44.

Ministry of the Budget, Public Accounts and the Civil Service: BP 165, Libreville; tel. 01-79-50-00; fax 01-79-57-37; internet www.finances.gouv.ga.

Ministry of the Digital Economy, Communication and Posts: Libreville.

Ministry of the Economy, Employment and Sustainable Development: Libreville.

Ministry of the Family and Social Affairs: Libreville.

Ministry of Foreign Affairs, International Co-operation and Francophone Affairs: BP 2245, Libreville; tel. 01-72-95-21; fax 01-72-91-73.

Ministry of Health: BP 50, Libreville; tel. 01-76-36-11.

Ministry of Industry and Mines: Libreville.

Ministry of the Interior, Public Security, Immigration and Decentralization: BP 2110, Libreville; tel. 01-74-35-06; fax 01-72-13-89.

Ministry of Justice: BP 547, Libreville; tel. 01-74-66-28; fax 01-72-33-84.

Ministry of National Defence: BP 13493, Libreville; tel. and fax 01-77-86-96.

Ministry of National Education, Higher and Technical Education, Professional Training, Culture, Youth and Sports: BP 6, Libreville; tel. 01-72-44-61; fax 01-72-19-74.

Ministry of Petroleum, Energy and Hydraulic Resources: Libreville.

Ministry of the Promotion of Investment, Public Works, Transport, Housing and Tourism: Libreville.

Ministry of Small and Medium-sized Enterprises, Handicrafts and Trade: BP 3096, Libreville; tel. 01-74-59-21.

Ministry of Transport: BP 803, Libreville; tel. 01-74-71-96; fax 01-77-33-31.

Ministry of Water and Forests: Libreville.

President and Legislature

PRESIDENT

Presidential Election, 30 August 2009

Candidate	Valid votes	% of valid votes
Ali Bongo Ondimba (PDG)	141,952	41.73
André Mba Obame (Ind.)	88,028	25.88
Pierre Mamboundou (UPG)	85,797	25.22
Zacharie Myboto (UGDD)	13,418	3.94
Casimir Oyé Mba (Ind.)	3,118	0.92
Pierre-Claver Maganga Moussavou (PSD)	2,576	0.76
Bruno Ben Moubamba (Ind.)	963	0.28
Georges Bruno Ngoussi (Ind.)	915	0.27
Jules Artides Bourdès Ogouliguende (CDJ)	695	0.20
Albert Ondo Ossa (Ind.)	674	0.20
Others	2,028	0.60
Total	340,178*	100.00

* The total number of votes officially attributed to candidates by the Constitutional Court amounted to 340,164. However, that body declared the total number of valid votes cast to be 340,178. Additionally, there were 17,443 spoiled ballots. Several of the defeated candidates formally protested against the results and a recount of the votes was subsequently held. On 12 October the Constitutional Court announced that Bongo had secured 141,665 valid votes, equating to 41.79%, while the number of votes attributed to Mamboundou and Mba Obame was amended to 86,875 (25.64%) and 85,814 (25.33%), respectively, thus reversing their placings in the election. No figures for the remaining candidates or the total number of votes cast were made available.

ASSEMBLÉE NATIONALE

President: GUY NDZOUBA NDAMA.

Secretary-General: JEAN-BAPTISTE YAMA-LEGNONGO.

General Election, 17 December 2011

Party	Seats
Parti Démocratique Gabonais (PDG)	114*
Rassemblement pour le Gabon (RPG)	3
Cercle des Libéraux Réformateurs (CLR)	1
Parti Social-Démocrate (PSD)	1
Union pour la Nouvelle République (UPNR)	1
Total	120†

* One seat was won in alliance with the Parti Gabonais du Centre Indépendant (PGCI).

† The results of voting in six constituencies were subsequently annulled by the Cour constitutionnelle owing to irregularities. On 5 May 2012 by-elections were held for the six seats, all of which were won by the PDG, leaving party representations unchanged.

SÉNAT

President: ROSE FRANCINE ROGOMBÉ.

Secretary-General: FÉLIX OWANSANGO DEACKEU.

Election, 18 January 2009

Party	Seats
Parti Démocratique Gabonais (PDG)	75
Rassemblement pour le Gabon (RPG)	6
Parti Gabonais du Centre Indépendent (PGCI)	3
Union du Peuple Gabonais (UPG)	3
Cercle des Libéraux Réformateurs (CLR)	2
Parti Social-démocrate (PSD)	2
Union Gabonaise pour la Démocratie et le Développement (UGDD)	2
Alliance Démocratique et Républicaine (ADERE)	1
Independents	8
Total	102

Following the appointment of a PDG senator as ambassador to France, a by-election was held on 5 May 2012 for the vacated seat. This was won by the PDG.

Election Commission

Commission Electorale Nationale Autonome et Permanente (CENAP): Libreville; f. 2006 to replace the Commission Nationale Electorale; Pres. appointed by the Constitutional Court; Pres. RENÉ ABOGHÉ ELLA.

Political Organizations

Alliance Démocratique et Républicaine (ADERE): Pres. MBOUMBOU NGOMA; Sec.-Gen. DIDJOB DIVUNGUI-DI-N'DINGUE.

Cercle des Libéraux Réformateurs (CLR): f. 1993 by breakaway faction of the PDG; Leader JEAN-BONIFACE ASSELE.

Congrès pour la Démocratie et la Justice (CDJ): tel. 01-70-00-00; e-mail contact@bourdes-gabon.com; internet www.bourdes-gabon.com; Pres. JULES BOURDÈS OGOULIGUENDE.

Front National (FN): f. 1991; Leader MARTIN EFAYONG.

Mouvement d'Emancipation Socialiste du Peuple: Leader MOUANGA MBADINGA.

Parti Démocratique Gabonais (PDG): Immeuble PETROGAB, BP 75384, Libreville; tel. 01-70-31-21; fax 01-70-31-46; internet www.pdg-gabon.org; f. 1968; sole legal party 1968–90; Leader ALI BONGO ONDIMBA; Sec.-Gen. FAUSTIN BOUKOUBI.

Parti Gabonais du Centre Indépendant (PGCI): allied to the PDG; Leader JÉRÔME OKINDA.

Parti Gabonais du Progrès (PGP): f. 1990; Pres. (vacant); Vice-Pres. JOSEPH-BENOÎT MOUITY.

Parti Social-Démocrate (PSD): f. 1991; Leader PIERRE-CLAVER MAGANGA MOUSSAVOU.

Rassemblement des Démocrates Républicains (RDR): Leader MAX MEBALE M'OBAME.

Rassemblement pour la Démocratie et le Progrès (RDP): Pres. ALAIN CLAUDE BILIE BI NZE.

Rassemblement pour le Gabon (RPG): f. 1990 as MORENA des Bûcherons; renamed Rassemblement National des Bûcherons in 1991, name changed as above in 2000; allied to the PDG; Leader Fr PAUL M'BA ABESSOLE; Vice-Pres. Prof. VINCENT MOULENGUI BOUKOSSO.

Rassemblement National des Bûcherons—Démocratique (RNB): Libreville; f. 1991; Leader PIERRE ANDRÉ KOMBILA.

Union Démocratique et Sociale (UDS): f. 1996; Leader HERVÉ ASSAMANET.

Union Nationale (UN): f. 2010 through the merger of the Union Gabonaise pour la Démocratie et le Développement (UGDD), the Mouvement Africain de Développement (MAD) and the Rassemblement National des Républicains (RNR); forcibly dissolved by the Government in January 2011; Leader ZACHARIE MYBOTO.

Union pour la Nouvelle République: Immeuble Score, 657 ave du Col Parant, BP 4049, Libreville; tel. 01-77-40-13; fax 01-77-40-17; e-mail info@louisgastonmayila.com; internet www.louisgastonmayila.com; f. 2007 following the merger of the Front pour l'Unité Nationale (FUNDU) and the Rassemblement des Républicains Indépendants (RRI); Leader LOUIS-GASTON MAYILA.

Union du Peuple Gabonais (UPG): BP 6048, Awendjé, Libreville; tel. 07-14-61-61 (mobile); internet www.upg-gabon.org; f. 1989 in Paris, France; Leader (vacant); Sec.-Gen. DAVID BADINGA.

Union pour le Progrès National (UPN): Leader DANIEL TENGUE NZOUNDO.

Diplomatic Representation

EMBASSIES IN GABON

Algeria: Bord de mer, BP 4008, Libreville; tel. 01-44-38-02; fax 01-73-14-03; e-mail algerie@ambassade-lbv-algerie.com; Ambassador DJIHED-EDDINE BELKAS.

Angola: BP 4884, Libreville; tel. 01-73-04-26; fax 01-73-76-24; Chargé d'affaires EMÍLIO JOSÉ DE CARVAHLO GUERRA.

Benin: BP 3851, Akebe, Libreville; tel. 01-73-76-82; fax 01-73-77-75; e-mail ambassade.benin@inet.ga; internet www.maebenin.bj/Libreville.htm; Ambassador SYMPHORIEN CODJO ACHODÉ.

Brazil: blvd de l'Indépendance, BP 3899, Libreville; tel. 01-76-05-35; fax 01-74-03-43; e-mail emblibreville@inet.ga; internet libreville.itamaraty.gov.br; Ambassador BRUNO LUIZ DOS SANTOS COBUCCIO.

Cameroon: blvd Léon Mba, BP 14001, Libreville; tel. 01-73-28-00; Ambassador SAMUEL MVONDO AYOLO.

China, People's Republic: blvd Triomphale Omar Bongo, BP 3914, Libreville; tel. 01-74-32-07; fax 01-74-75-96; e-mail gzy@internetgabon.com; Ambassador SUN JIWEN.

Congo, Democratic Republic: BP 2257, Libreville; tel. 01-73-11-61; fax 01-73-81-41; Ambassador KABANGI KAUMBU BULA.

Congo, Republic: BP 269, Libreville; tel. 01-73-29-06; e-mail ambacobrazzalibreville@yahoo.fr; Ambassador EDOUARD ROGER OKOULA.

Côte d'Ivoire: Charbonnages, BP 3861, Libreville; tel. 01-73-82-70; fax 01-73-82-87; e-mail ambacigabon@yahoo.fr; Ambassador PHILIPPE MANGOU.

Egypt: Immeuble Floria, 1 blvd de la Mer, Quartier Batterie IV, BP 4240, Libreville; tel. 01-73-25-38; fax 01-73-25-19; Ambassador AHMED MUHAMMAD TAHA AWAD.

Equatorial Guinea: BP 1462, Libreville; tel. 01-73-25-23; fax 01-73-25-22; Ambassador JOSÉ ESONO BACALE.

France: 1 rue du pont Pirah, BP 2125, Libreville; tel. 01-79-70-00; fax 01-79-70-09; e-mail scac@ambafrance-ga.org; internet www.ambafrance-ga.org; Ambassador JEAN-DIDIER ROISIN.

Germany: blvd de l'Indépendance, Immeuble les Frangipaniers, BP 299, Libreville; tel. 01-76-01-88; fax 01-72-40-12; e-mail amb-allegmagne@inet.ga; internet www.libreville.diplo.de; Ambassador CHRISTIAN RUMPLECKER.

Guinea: BP 4046, Libreville; tel. 01-73-85-09; fax 01-73-85-11; Ambassador MOHAMED SAMPIL.

Italy: Immeuble Personnaz et Gardin, 321 rue de la Mairie, BP 2251, Libreville; tel. 01-74-28-92; fax 01-74-80-35; e-mail ambasciata.libreville@esteri.it; internet www.amblibreville.esteri.it; Ambassador RAFFAELE DE BENEDICTIS.

Japan: blvd du Bord de Mer, BP 2259, Libreville; tel. 01-73-22-97; fax 01-73-60-60; Ambassador MOTOI KATO.

Korea, Republic: BP 2620, Libreville; tel. 01-73-40-00; fax 01-73-99-05; e-mail gabon-ambcoree@mofat.go.kr; internet gab.mofat.go.kr; Ambassador KIM SEONG-JIN.

Lebanon: BP 3341, Libreville; tel. and fax 01-73-68-77; e-mail amb.lib.gab@inet.ga; Ambassador MICHELIN BAZ.

Mali: BP 4007, Quartier Batterie IV, Libreville; tel. 01-73-82-73; fax 01-73-82-80; e-mail ambamaga@yahoo.fr; Ambassador TRAORÉ ROKIATOU GUIKINE.

Mauritania: BP 3917, Libreville; tel. 01-74-31-65; fax 01-74-01-62; Ambassador El Hadj THIAM.

Morocco: blvd de l'Indépendance, Immeuble CK 2, BP 3983, Libreville; tel. 01-77-41-51; fax 01-77-41-50; e-mail sifamalbv@inet.ga; Ambassador ALI BOJI.

Nigeria: ave du Président Léon-M'Ba, Quartier blvd Léon-M'Ba, BP 1191, Libreville; tel. 01-73-22-03; fax 01-73-29-14; e-mail nigeriamission@internetgabon.com; Ambassador JOSEPH CHIBUZO EZEMA.

Russia: BP 3963, Libreville; tel. 01-72-48-68; fax 01-72-48-70; e-mail ambrusga@mail.ru; internet www.gabon.mid.ru; Ambassador VLADIMIR E. TARABRIN.

São Tomé and Príncipe: BP 489, Libreville; tel. 01-72-09-94; Ambassador URBINO JOSÉ GONHALVES BOTELÇO.

Senegal: Quartier Sobraga, BP 3856, Libreville; tel. 01-77-42-67; fax 01-77-42-68; e-mail ambasengab@yahoo.fr; Ambassador ABDOU MALAL DIOP.

South Africa: Immeuble les Arcades, 142 rue des Chavannes, BP 4063, Libreville; tel. 01-77-45-30; fax 01-77-45-36; e-mail libreville.consular@foreign.gov.za; Ambassador T. SHOPE-LINNEY.

Spain: Immeuble Diamant, 2ème étage, blvd de l'Indépendance, BP 1157, Libreville; tel. 01-72-12-64; fax 01-74-88-73; e-mail ambespga@mail.mae.es; Ambassador D. CÉSAR ALBA Y FÚSTER.

Togo: BP 14160, Libreville; tel. 01-73-29-04; fax 01-73-32-61; Ambassador ESSOHOHANAM ADEWI.

Tunisia: BP 3844, Libreville; tel. 01-73-28-41; Ambassador EZZEDINE KERKENI.

Ukraine: BP 23746, Libreville; tel. 01-44-51-03; e-mail emb_ga@mfa.gov.ua; Ambassador SERGIY MISHUSTIN.

USA: Avorbam, La Sablière, BP 4000, Libreville; tel. 01-45-71-00; fax 01-74-55-07; e-mail clolibreville@state.gov; internet libreville.usembassy.gov; Ambassador ERIC D. BENJAMINSON.

Judicial System

Justice is dispensed on behalf of the Gabonese people by the three autonomous chambers of the Supreme Court (judicial, administrative and accounting), the Constitutional Court, the Council of State, the Court of Accounts, the Courts of Appeal, the Provincial Courts, the High Court and the other special courts of law.

Supreme Court: BP 1043, Libreville; tel. 01-72-17-00; fax 01-76-66-18; three chambers: judicial, administrative and accounting; Pres. SIMON ALLOGHO EYA.

Constitutional Court: BP 547, Libreville; tel. 01-76-62-88; fax 01-76-10-17; has jurisdiction on: the control of the constitutionality of laws before promulgation; all electoral litigations; all matters concerning individual fundamental rights and public liberties; the interpretation of the Constitution; and arbitration of conflicts of jurisdiction arising among the state's institutions; Pres. MARIE MADELEINE MBORANTSUO.

Council of State: BP 547, Libreville; tel. 01-72-17-00.

Courts of Appeal: Libreville and Franceville.

Court of State Security: Libreville; 13 mems; Pres. FLORENTIN ANGO.

Conseil Supérieur de la Magistrature: Libreville; Pres. (vacant); Vice-Pres. BENJAMIN PAMBOU-KOMBILA (ex officio).

Audit Court (Cour des Comptes): BP 752, Libreville; tel. 01-70-54-15; fax 01-70-40-81; e-mail cour_des_comptes_gabon@yahoo.fr; Pres. GILBERT NGOULAKIA.

Religion

About 60% of Gabon's population are Christians, mainly adherents of the Roman Catholic Church. About 40% are animists and fewer than 1% are Muslims.

CHRISTIANITY

The Roman Catholic Church

Gabon comprises one archdiocese, four dioceses and one apostolic prefecture. Some 50% of the population are Roman Catholics.

Bishops' Conference

Conférence Episcopale du Gabon, BP 2146, Libreville; tel. 01-72-20-73.

f. 1989; Pres. Most Rev. TIMOTHÉE MODIBO-NZOCKENA (Bishop of Franceville).

Archbishop of Libreville: Most Rev. BASILE MVÉ ENGONE, Archevêché, Sainte-Marie, BP 2146, Libreville; tel. and fax 01-72-20-73; e-mail basilemve@yahoo.fr.

Protestant Churches

Christian and Missionary Alliance: BP 13021, Libreville; tel. 01-73-24-39; e-mail fdgabon@gmail.com; active in the south of the country; Dir Dr DAVID THOMPSON; 115 org. mem. churches, 11,226 baptized mems.

Eglise Evangélique du Gabon: BP 10080, Libreville; tel. 01-72-41-92; f. 1842; independent since 1961; 205,000 mems; Pres. Pastor GLIÇANT ASSOUMOU EDZANG ONDO; Sec. Rev. CLÉMENT AUBAME MEZUI.

The Evangelical Church of South Gabon and the Evangelical Pentecostal Church are also active in Gabon.

The Press

La Concorde: Libreville; f. 2005; owned by TV+ group; daily; Dir FRANÇOIS ONDO EDOU; circ. 10,000.

L'Economiste Gabonais: BP 3906, Libreville; quarterly; publ. by the Centre gabonais du commerce extérieur.

Gabon Libre: BP 6439, Libreville; tel. 01-72-42-22; weekly; Dir DZIME EKANG; Editor RENÉ NZOVI.

Gabon-Matin: BP 168, Libreville; daily; publ. by Agence Gabonaise de Presse; Man. HILARION VENDANY; circ. 18,000.

Gabon Show: Libreville; f. 2004; independent; satirical; printed in Cameroon; Man. Editor FULBERT WORA; weekly; circ. 3,000.

Gris-Gris International: Paris; f. 1990; weekly; independent; satirical; distribution forbidden in 2001; Editor-in-Chief RAPHAEL NTOUTOUME NKOGHE; Editor MICHEL ONGOUNDOU.

Journal Officiel de la République Gabonaise: BP 563, Libreville; f. 1959; fortnightly; Man. EMMANUEL OBAMÉ.

Ngondo: BP 168, Libreville; monthly; publ. by Agence Gabonaise de Presse.

Le Peuple: BP 2170, Libreville; tel. 06-03-09-94 (mobile); e-mail lepeuple@lepeuple.info; internet www.lepeuple.info; f. 2002; weekly; Dir of Publication and Editor-in-Chief AUGUSTIN MVEME OBIANG.

Le Progressiste: blvd Léon-M'Ba, BP 7000, Libreville; tel. 01-74-54-01; f. 1990; Dir BENOÎT MOUITY NZAMBA; Editor JACQUES MOURENDE-TSIOBA.

La Relance: BP 268, Libreville; tel. 01-72-93-08; weekly; publ. of the Parti démocratique gabonais; Pres. JACQUES ADIAHÉNOT; Dir RENÉ NDEMEZO'O OBIANG.

Le Réveil: BP 20386, Libreville; tel. and fax 01-73-17-21; weekly; Man. ALBERT YANGARI; Editor RENÉ NZOVI; circ. 8,000.

La Tribune des Affaires: BP 2234, Libreville; tel. 01-72-20-64; fax 01-74-12-20; monthly; publ. of the Chambre de Commerce, d'Agriculture, d'Industrie et des Mines du Gabon.

L'Union: Sonapresse, BP 3849, Libreville; tel. 01-73-58-61; fax 01-73-58-62; e-mail mpg@inet.ga; f. 1974; 75% state-owned; daily; official govt publ; Dir-Gen. ALBERT YANAGRI; circ. 20,000.

Zoom Hebdo: Carrefour London, BP 352, Libreville; tel. 01-76-44-54; fax 01-74-67-50; e-mail zoomhebdo@assala.net; internet www.zoomhebdo.com; Friday; f. 1991; Dir-Gen. HANS RAYMOND KWAAITAAL; circ. 12,000–20,000.

NEWS AGENCIES

Agence Gabonaise de Presse (AGP): BP 168, Libreville; tel. 01-44-35-07; fax 01-44-35-09; internet www.agpgabon.ga; f. 1960; Pres. LIN JOËL NDEMBET; Dir OLIVIER MOUKETOU.

Association Professionnelle de la Presse Ecrite Gabonaise (APPEG): BP 3849, Libreville; internet www.gabon-presse.org.

BERP International: BP 8483, Libreville; tel. 06-06-62-91 (mobile); fax 01-77-58-81; e-mail berp8483@hotmail.com; internet www.infosplusgabon.com/berp.php3; f. 1995; Dir ANTOINE LAWSON.

Publishers

Gabonaise d'Imprimerie (GABIMP): BP 154, Libreville; tel. 01-70-20-88; fax 01-70-31-85; e-mail gabimp@inet.ga; f. 1973; Dir CLAIRE VIAL.

Multipress Gabon: blvd Léon-M'Ba, BP 3875, Libreville; tel. 01-73-22-33; fax 01-73-63-72; e-mail mpg@inet.ga; internet multipress-gabon.com; monopoly distributors of magazines and newspapers; f. 1973; Chair. PAUL BORY; JEAN-LUC PHALEMPIN.

Société Imprimerie de Gabon: BP 9626, Libreville; f. 1977; Man. Dir AKWANG REX.

Société Nationale de Presse et d'Edition (SONAPRESSE): BP 3849, Libreville; tel. and fax 01-73-58-60; e-mail unionplus@intergabon.com; internet union.sonapresse.com; f. 1975; Man. Dir ALBERT YANGARI.

Broadcasting and Communications

TELECOMMUNICATIONS

At the end of 2011 there were four providers of mobile cellular telephone services in Gabon, while Gabon Télécom was the sole provider of fixed-line services.

Regulatory Authority

Agence de Régulation des Communications Électroniques et des Postes (ARCEP): Quartier Haut de Gué-Gué, face Bureau de la Francophonie, BP 50000, Libreville; tel. 01-44-68-11; fax 01-44-68-06; e-mail artel@inet.ga; internet www.artel.ga; f. 2012 following merger of the Agence de Régulation des Télécommunications (f. 2001) and the Agence de Régulation des Postes (f. 2001); regulatory authority; Pres. LIN MOMBO; Dir-Gen. SERGE ESSONGUÉ EWAMPONGO.

Infrastructure and Development

Agence Nationale des Infrastructures Numériques et des Fréquences: Cours Pasteur, Immeuble de la Solde, BP 798, Libreville; tel. 01-79-52-77; internet www.aninf.ga; f. 2011; Dir-Gen. ALEX BERNARD BONGO ONDIMBA.

Service Providers

Airtel Gabon SA: 124 ave Bouët, Montagne Sainte, BP 9259, Libreville; tel. 07-28-01-11 (mobile); e-mail info.africa@airtel.com; internet africa.airtel.com/gabon; f. 2000; fmrly Zain Gabon, present name adopted 2010; Dir-Gen. LOUIS LUBALA.

Gabon Télécom: Immeuble du Delta Postal, BP 20000, Libreville; tel. 01-78-70-00; fax 01-78-67-70; e-mail gabontelecom@gabontelecom.ga; f. 2001; provider of telecommunications, incl. satellite, internet and cellular systems; 51% owned by Maroc Telecom; Dir-Gen. OUSSALAH LHOUSSAINE.

Libertis: Immeuble du Delta Postal, BP 20000, Libreville; tel. 06-22-22-22 (mobile); e-mail contact@libertis.ga; internet www.libertis.ga; f. 1999; mobile cellular telephone operator; Dir-Gen. MOSTAPHA LAARABI; 250,000 subscribers in 2006.

Moov Gabon: Immeuble Rénovation, bvld du Bord de Mer, BP 12470, Libreville; tel. 01-76-83-83; fax 01-76-83-88; internet www.moov.ga; f. 2000; Dir-Gen. FRÉDÉRIC FERAILLE.

USAN Gabon: Libreville; e-mail info@azur-gabon.com; internet www.azur-gabon.com; f. 2009; provides mobile cellular services under Azur network; Dir-Gen. BRUNO VALAT.

BROADCASTING

Conseil National de la Communication: BP 6437, Libreville; tel. 01-72-82-60; fax 01-72-82-71; e-mail infos@cnc.ga; f. 1991; Pres. GUY BERTRAND MAPANGOU.

Radio

The national network, 'La Voix de la Rénovation', and a provincial network broadcast for 24 hours each day in French and local languages.

Africa No. 1: BP 1, Libreville; tel. 01-74-07-34; fax 01-74-21-33; e-mail africaradio1@yahoo.fr; internet www.africa1.com; f. 1981; 35% state-controlled; int. commercial radio station; daily programmes in French and English; Pres. ELMAHJOUR AMMAR GOMAA; Sec.-Gen. LOUIS BARTHÉLEMY MAPANGOU.

Radiodiffusion-Télévision Gabonaise (RTG): BP 150, Libreville; tel. 01-73-20-25; fax 01-73-21-53; internet www.rtg1.ga; f. 1959; state-controlled; broadcasts two channels RTG1 and RTG2; Dir-Gen. (RTG1) DAVID ELLA MINTSA; Dir-Gen. (RTG2) FLORENCE MBANI; Dir of Radio GILLES TERENCE NZOGHE.

Radio Fréquence 3: f. 1996.

Radio Génération Nouvelle: f. 1996; Dir JEAN-BONIFACE ASSELE.

Radio Mandarine: f. 1995.

Radio Soleil: f. 1995; affiliated to Rassemblement pour le Gabon.

Radio Unité: f. 1996.

Television

Radiodiffusion-Télévision Gabonaise (RTG): see Radio.

Radio Télévision Nazareth (RTN): BP 9563, Libreville; tel. 01-76-82-58; fax 01-72-20-44; e-mail rtntv@yahoo.fr; Pres. and Dir-Gen. GEORGES BRUNO NGOUSSI.

Télé-Africa: BP 4269, Libreville; tel. 01-72-49-22; fax 01-76-16-83; f. 1985; private channel; daily broadcasts in French.

Télédiffusion du Gabon: f. 1995.

TV Sat (Société de Télécommunications Audio-Visuelles): Immeuble TV SAT BP 184, Libreville; tel. 01-72-49-22; fax 01-76-16-83; f. 1994.

TV+: Immeuble Dumez, Bord de mer, BP 8344, Libreville; operation suspended in Jan. 2012; Owner ANDRÉ MBA OBAME.

Finance

(cap. = capital; res = reserves; dep. = deposits; m. = million; brs = branches; amounts in francs CFA)

BANKING

In 2008 there were five commercial banks and four other financial institutions in Gabon.

Central Bank

Banque des Etats de l'Afrique Centrale (BEAC): BP 112, Libreville; tel. 01-76-13-52; fax 01-74-45-63; e-mail beaclbv@beac.int; internet www.beac.int; HQ in Yaoundé, Cameroon; f. 1973; bank of issue for mem. states of the Communauté Economique et Monétaire de l'Afrique Centrale (CEMAC, fmrly Union Douanière et Economique de l'Afrique Centrale), comprising Cameroon, the Central African Repub., Chad, the Repub. of the Congo, Equatorial Guinea and Gabon; cap. 88,000m., res 227,843m., dep. 4,110,966m. (Dec. 2007); Gov. LUCAS ABAGA NCHAMA; Dir in Gabon DENIS MEPOREWA; 4 brs in Gabon.

Commercial Banks

Banque Internationale pour le Commerce et l'Industrie du Gabon, SA (BICIG): ave du Colonel Parant, BP 2241, Libreville; tel. 01-76-26-13; fax 01-74-40-34; e-mail bicigdoi@inet.ga; internet bicig-gabon.com; f. 1973; 26.30% state-owned, 46.67% owned by BNP Paribas SA; cap. 18,000m., res 8,495m., dep. 310,220m., (Dec. 2009); Pres. ETIENNE GUY MOUVAGHA TCHIOBA; Dir-Gen. CLAUDE AYO-IGUENDHA; 9 brs.

Banque Internationale pour le Gabon: Immeuble Concorde, blvd de l'Indépendance, BP 106, Libreville; tel. 01-76-26-26; fax 01-76-20-53.

BGFI Bank: blvd de l'Indépendence, BP 2253, Libreville; tel. 01-76-40-35; fax 01-74-08-94; e-mail agence_libreville@bgfi.com; internet www.bgfi.com; f. 1972 as Banque Gabonaise et Française Internationale (BGFI); name changed as above in March 2000; 8% state-owned; cap. 25,065.4m., res 32,117.8m., dep. 349,064.6m. (Dec. 2006); Chair. PATRICE OTHA; Gen. Man. HENRI-CLAUDE OYIMA; 3 brs.

Citibank: 810 blvd Quaben, rue Kringer, BP 3940, Libreville; tel. 01-73-19-16; fax 01-73-37-86; total assets 1,000m. (Dec. 2004); Dir-Gen. FUNMI ADE AJAYI; Dep. Dir-Gen. JULIETTE WEISTFLOG.

Financial Bank Gabon: Immeuble des Frangipaniers, blvd de l'Indépendance, BP 20333, Libreville; tel. 01-77-50-78; fax 01-72-41-97; e-mail financial.gabon@financial-bank.com; internet www.orabank.net; f. 2002; cap. 1,250m., res –394.3m., dep. 21,594.9m. (Dec. 2006); 85.47% owned by Oragroup SA (Togo); Pres. RENÉ-HILAIRE ADIAHENO; Dir-Gen. MAMOUDOU KANE.

Union Gabonaise de Banque, SA (UGB): ave du Colonel Parant, BP 315, Libreville; tel. 01-77-70-00; fax 01-76-46-16; e-mail ugbdio@internetgabon.com; internet ugb-interactif.com; f. 1962; 25% state-owned, 56.25% owned by Crédit Lyonnais (France); cap. 7,400.0m., res 10,281.5m., dep. 215,799.1m. (Dec. 2009); Chair. MARCEL DOUPAMBY-MATOKA; Man. Dir REDOUNE BENNIS; 4 brs.

Development Banks

Alios Finance Gabon (AFG): Immeuble SOGACA, BP 63, Libreville; tel. 01-76-08-46; fax 01-76-01-03; internet www.alios-finance.com; car finance; 43% owned by CFAO Gabon, 10% state-owned; cap. and res 2,828.0m., total assets 18,583.0m. (Dec. 2003); Dir-Gen. FAISSAL CHAHROUR.

Banque Gabonaise de Développement (BGD): rue Alfred Marche, BP 5, Libreville; tel. 01-76-24-29; fax 01-74-26-99; e-mail infos@bgd-gabon.com; internet www.bgd-gabon.com; f. 1960; 69.01% state-owned; cap. 25,200m., res 7,677m. (Dec. 2006); Dir-Gen. ROGER OWONO MBA.

Banque Nationale de Crédit Rural (BNCR): ave Bouet, BP 1120, Libreville; tel. 01-72-47-42; fax 01-74-05-07; f. 1986; 74% state-owned; under enforced administration since March 2002; total assets 5,601m. (Dec. 2000); Pres. GÉRARD MEYO M'EMANE; Man. JOSEPH KOYAGBELE.

Banque Populaire du Gabon: 413 blvd de l'Indépendance, BP 6663, Libreville; tel. 01-72-86-89; fax 01-72-86-91.

BICI-Bail Gabon: Immeuble BICIG, 5ème étage, ave du Colonel Parant, BP 2241, Libreville; tel. 01-77-75-52; fax 01-77-48-15; internet www.bicig.ga/bicibail.htm; BNP Paribas-owned.

Société Financière Transafricaine (FINATRA): blvd de l'Indépendance, BP 8645, Libreville; tel. and fax 01-77-40-87; e-mail finatra@bgfi.com; internet www.bgfi.com; f. 1997; 50% owned by BGFI Bank; cap. 2,000m., total assets 14,613m. (Dec. 2003); Dir-Gen. MARIE CÉLINE NTSAME-MEZUI.

Société Gabonaise de Crédit-Bail (SOGABAIL): Immeuble SOGACA, BP 63, Libreville; tel. 01-77-25-73; fax 01-76-01-03; e-mail sogaca@assala.net; 25% owned by CFAO Gabon, 14% state-owned; cap. and res 2,980.4m., total assets 4,123.2m.; Pres. M. LAPLAGNOLLE; Dir-Gen. THIERRY PAPILLON.

Société Nationale d'Investissement du Gabon (SONADIG): BP 479, Libreville; tel. 01-72-09-22; fax 01-74-81-70; f. 1968; state-owned; cap. 500m.; Pres. ANTOINE OYIEYE; Dir-Gen. NARCISSE MASSALA TSAMBA.

Financial Institution

Caisse Autonome d'Amortissement du Gabon: BP 912, Libreville; tel. 01-74-41-43; management of state funds; Dir-Gen. MAURICE EYAMBA TSIMAT.

INSURANCE

Agence Gabonaise d'Assurance et de Réassurance (AGAR): BP 1699, Libreville; tel. 01-74-02-22; fax 01-76-59-25; f. 1987; Dir-Gen. ANGE GOULOUMES.

Assinco: BP 7812, Libreville; tel. 01-72-19-25; fax 01-72-19-29; e-mail assinco@assinco-sa.com; internet assinco-sa.com; Dir EUGÉNIE DENDÉ.

Assureurs Conseils Franco-Africains du Gabon (ACFRA-GABON): BP 1116, Libreville; tel. 01-72-32-83; Chair. FRÉDÉRIC MARRON; Dir M. GARNIER.

Assureurs Conseils Gabonais (ACG): Immeuble Shell-Gabon, rue de la Mairie, BP 2138, Libreville; tel. 01-74-32-90; fax 01-76-04-39; e-mail acg@ascoma.com; represents foreign insurance cos; Dir MICHELLE VALETTE.

Axa Assurances Gabon: 1935 blvd de l'Indépendance, BP 4047, Libreville; tel. 79-80-80; fax 74-18-46; e-mail axa-assurances@axa-gabon.ga; internet www.axa-gabon.com; Dir JOËL MULLER.

Commercial Union: Libreville; tel. 76-43-00; Exec. Dir M. MILAN.

Fédération Gabonaise des Assureurs (FEGASA): BP 4005, Libreville; tel. 01-74-45-29; fax 01-77-58-23; Pres. JACQUES AMVAMÉ.

Gras Savoye Gabon: ave du Colonel Parant, BP 2148, Libreville; tel. 01-74-31-53; fax 01-74-68-38; e-mail contact@ga.grassavoye.com; internet www.ga.grassavoye.com; Dir CHRISTOPHE ROUDAUT.

Groupement Gabonais d'Assurances et de Réassurances (GGAR): Libreville; tel. 01-74-28-72; f. 1985; Chair. RASSAGUIZA AKEREY; Dir-Gen. DENISE OMBAGHO.

NSIA Gabon: Résidence les Frangipaniers, Blvd de l'Indépendance, BP 2221–2225, Libreville; tel. 01-72-13-90; fax 01-74-17-02; e-mail nsiagabon@groupensia.com; internet www.nsiagabon.com; f. 2000 by acquisition of Assurances Mutuelles du Gabon; name changed as above in 2006; owned by NSIA Participations S.A. Holding (Côte d'Ivoire); Dir-Gen. CÉSAR EKOMIE-AFENE.

Société Nationale Gabonaise d'Assurances et de Réassurances (SONAGAR): ave du Colonel Parant, BP 3082, Libreville; tel. 01-72-28-97; f. 1974; owned by l'Union des Assurances de Paris (France); Dir-Gen. JEAN-LOUIS MESSAN.

SOGERCO-Gabon: BP 2102, Libreville; tel. 01-76-09-34; f. 1975; general; Dir M. RABEAU.

Union des Assurances du Gabon-Vie (UAG-Vie): ave du Colonel Parant, BP 2137, Libreville; tel. 01-74-34-34; fax 01-72-48-57; e-mail uagvie@uagvie.com; internet www.sunu-group.com; life insurance; 80.65% owned by Groupe SUNU; Pres. ALBERT ALEWINA CHAVIHOT; Dir-Gen. APOLLINAIRE EVA ESSANGONE.

Trade and Industry

GOVERNMENT AGENCIES

Conseil Economique et Social du Gabon: BP 1075, Libreville; tel. 01-73-19-46; fax 01-73-19-44; comprises representatives from salaried workers, employers and Govt; commissions on economic, financial and social affairs, and forestry and agriculture; Pres. ANTOINE DE PADOUE MBOUMBOU MIYAKOU.

Agence de Promotion des Investissements Privés (APIP): BP 13740, Front de Mer, Libreville; tel. 01-76-87-65; fax 01-76-87-64; e-mail apip@netcourrier.com; internet www.invest-gabon.com; f. 2002; promotes private investment; Dir-Gen. LÉON PAUL NGOULAKIA.

Fonds Gabonais d'Investissement Stratégique: Libreville; f. 2010; Pres. CLAUDE AYO INGUENDA; SERGE THIERRY MICKOTO CHAVAGNE.

DEVELOPMENT ORGANIZATIONS

Agence Française de Développement (AFD): blvd de l'Indépendance, BP 64, Libreville; tel. 01-74-33-74; fax 01-74-51-25; e-mail afdlibreville@groupe-afd.org; internet www.afd.fr; fmrly Caisse Française de Développement; Dir FRANÇOIS PARMANTIER.

Agence Nationale des Grands Travaux (ANGT): Immeuble du bord de mer, 1er étage, à côté de l'ancien gouvernorat, BP 23765, Libreville; tel. 07-04-62-77 (mobile); e-mail info@angtmedia.com; internet www.angt-gabon.com; f. 2010; Dir-Gen. HENRI OHAYON.

Agence Nationale de Promotion de la Petite et Moyenne Entreprise (PromoGabon): BP 2111, Libreville; tel. 06-26-79-19 (mobile); fax 01-74-89-59; f. 1964; state-controlled; promotes and assists small and medium-sized industries; Pres. SIMON BOULAMATARI; Man. Dir GEORGETTE ONGALA.

Agence de Régulation du Marché des Produits Forestiers: Libreville; Dir-Gen. PIERRE NGAVOURA.

Centre Gabonais de Commerce Extérieur (CGCE): Immeuble Rénovation, 3ème étage, BP 3906, Libreville; tel. 01-72-11-67; fax 01-74-71-53; promotes foreign trade and investment in Gabon; Gen. Dir PIERRE SOCKAT.

Commerce et Développement (CODEV): BP 2142, Libreville; tel. 01-76-06-73; f. 1976; 95% state-owned; import and distribution of capital goods and food products; Chair. and Man. Dir JÉRÔME NGOUA-BEKALE.

Conservation et Utilisation Rationelle des Ecosystèmes Forestiers en Afrique Centrale (ECOFAC): BP 15115, Libreville; tel. 01-73-23-43; fax 01-73-23-45; e-mail coordination@ecofac.org; internet www.ecofac.org.

Fonds de Garantie pour le Logement (FGL): Libreville; f. 2011.

Groupes d'Etudes et de Recherches sur la Démocratie et le Développement Economique et Social au Gabon (GERDDES-Gabon): BP 13114, Libreville; tel. 06-25-14-38 (mobile); fax 07-38-04-20 (mobile); e-mail gerddesgabon@yahoo.fr; internet gerddes-gabon.asso-web.com; f. 1991; Pres. MARYVONNE C. NTSAME NDONG.

Institut Gabonais d'Appui au Développement (IGAD): BP 20423, Libreville; tel. and fax 01-74-52-47; e-mail igad@inet.ga; f. 1992; Dir-Gen. CHRISTIAN RENARDET.

Office Gabonais d'Amélioration et de Production de Viande (OGAPROV): BP 245, Moanda; tel. 01-66-12-67; f. 1971; devt of private cattle farming; manages ranch at Lekedi-Sud; Pres. PAUL KOUNDA KIKI; Dir-Gen. VEYRANT OMBÉ EPIGAT.

Palmiers et Hévéas du Gabon (PALMEVEAS): BP 75, Libreville; f. 1956; state-owned; palm-oil devt.

Programme Régionale de Gestion de l'Information Environnementale en Afrique Centrale (PRGIE): BP 4080, Libreville; tel. 01-76-30-19; fax 01-77-42-61; e-mail urge@adie-prgie.org; internet www.adie-prgie.org.

Société de Développement de l'Agriculture au Gabon (AGROGABON): BP 2248, Libreville; tel. 01-76-40-82; fax 01-76-44-72; f. 1976; 93% state-owned; acquired by the Société Industrielle Agricole du Tabac Tropical in April 2004; Man. Dir ANDRÉ PAUL-APANDINA.

Société de Développement de l'Hévéaculture (HEVEGAB): BP 316, Libreville; tel. 01-72-08-29; fax 01-72-08-30; f. 1981; acquired by the Société Industrielle Agricole du Tabac Tropical in April 2004; devt of rubber plantations in the Mitzic, Bitam and Kango regions; Chair. FRANÇOIS OWONO-NGUEMA; Man. Dir JANVIER ESSONO-ASSOUMOU.

Société Gabonaise de Recherches et d'Exploitations Minières (SOGAREM): Libreville; state-owned; research and devt of gold mining; Chair. ARSÈNE BOUNGUENZA; Man. Dir SERGE GASSITA.

Société Gabonaise de Recherches Pétrolières (GABOREP): BP 564, Libreville; tel. 01-75-06-40; fax 01-75-06-47; exploration and exploitation of hydrocarbons; Chair. HUBERT PERRODO; Man. Dir P. F. LECA.

Société Nationale de Développement des Cultures Industrielles (SONADECI): Libreville; tel. 01-76-33-97; f. 1978; state-owned; agricultural devt; Chair. PAUL KOUNDA KIKI; Man. Dir GEORGES BEKALÉ.

CHAMBER OF COMMERCE

Chambre de Commerce, d'Agriculture, d'Industrie et des Mines du Gabon: BP 2234, Libreville; tel. 01-72-20-64; fax 01-74-12-20; f. 1935; regional offices at Port-Gentil and Franceville; Pres. JEAN BAPTISTE BIKALOU; Sec.-Gen. LIN-FRANÇOIS MADJOUPAL.

EMPLOYERS' ORGANIZATIONS

Confédération Patronale Gabonaise: Immeuble les Frangipaniers, blvd de l'Indépendence, BP 410, Libreville; tel. 01-76-02-43; fax 01-74-86-52; e-mail infocpg@patronatgabonais.ga; internet www.confederation-patronale-gabonaise.org; f. 1959; represents industrial, mining, petroleum, public works, forestry, banking, insurance, commercial and shipping interests; Pres. HENRI-CLAUDE OYIMA; Sec.-Gen. CHRISTIANE QUINIO.

Syndicat des Industries du Gabon: BP 2175, Libreville; tel. 01-72-02-29; fax 01-74-52-13; e-mail sociga@ga.imptob.com; Pres. JACQUES-YVES LAUGE.

Union Nationale du Patronat Syndical des Transports Urbains, Routiers et Fluviaux du Gabon (UNAPASYTRUFGA): BP 1025, Libreville; f. 1977; represents manufacturers of vehicle and construction parts; Pres. LAURENT BELLAL BIBANG-BI-EDZO; Sec.-Gen. AUGUSTIN KASSA-NZIGOU.

Union des Représentations Automobiles et Industrielles (URAI): BP 1743, Libreville; Pres. M. MARTINENT; Sec. R. TYBERGHEIN.

UTILITIES

In 2011 the Government announced the formation of the state-owned Société d'Electricité, de Téléphone, et d'Eau du Gabon, which was to cover the provision of basic services.

Société d'Energie et d'Eau du Gabon (SEEG): BP 2187, Libreville; tel. 01-76-78-07; fax 01-76-11-34; e-mail laroche.lbv@inet.ga; internet www.seeg-gabon.com; f. 1950; 51% owned by Veolia (France); controls 35 electricity generation and distribution centres and 32 water production and distribution centres; Pres. and Dir-Gen. FRANÇOIS OMBANDA.

MAJOR COMPANIES

The following are some of the largest private and state-owned companies in terms of either capital investment or employment.

L'Auxiliaire du Bâtiment J.-F. Aveyra (ABA): BP 14382, Libreville; tel. 01-70-44-80; f. 1977; cap. 1,000m. francs CFA; production of construction materials, plastics; Chair. JEAN-FRANÇOIS AVEYRA; Man. Dir G. DUTILH.

CIMGABON: BP 477, Libreville; tel. 01-70-20-23; fax 01-70-27-05; e-mail dg.cimgabon@inet.ga; f. 1976; cap. 19,000m. francs CFA; privatized in Jan. 2001, 75% owned by Scancem International (Norway); clinker crushing works at N'Toum, Owendo (Libreville) and Franceville; Man. Dir DAVID JAMIESON.

Compagnie Minière de l'Ogooué (COMILOG): BP 27-28, Moanda; tel. 01-66-40-02; fax 01-66-11-57; e-mail dg@comilogsa.com; internet www.erachem-comilog.com; f. 1953; cap. 32,812.5m. francs CFA; owned by Eramet (France); manganese mining at Moanda; Pres. CLAUDE VILLAIN; Man. Dir MARCEL ABÉKÉ; 1,317 employees.

Corà Wood Gabon: BP 521, Port-Gentil; tel. 01-55-20-45; fax 01-55-36-43; e-mail info@corawood.com; internet www.corawood.com; f. 1945; fmrly Compagnie Forestière du Gabon; name changed as above in 2000; cap. 6,785m. francs CFA; 52% state-owned; scheduled to be privatized; production of okoumé plywood and veneered quality plywoods; Chair. MICHEL ESSONGHÉ; 1,975 employees.

Engen Gabon: 234 blvd Bessieux, BP 224, Libreville; tel. 01-74-01-01; fax 01-76-02-44; e-mail info@engen.ga; internet www.engen.ga; f. 1987; cap. 1,875m. francs CFA; fmrly PIZO Shell; 60% owned by Engen Petroleum Ltd (South Africa), 10% state-owned; Man. Dir ADAMA DOGATIENE SORO.

Foraid Gabon: BP 579, Port-Gentil; tel. 01-56-14-19; fax 01-56-54-72; e-mail foraidgabon@internetgabon.com; petrol logistics and construction; Dir MAX MERCIER.

Gabon Service Matériel Pétrolier (GSMP): BP 1067, Port-Gentil; tel. 01-55-53-21; e-mail gsm@inet.ga.

Gabonaise de Chimie (GCIAE): BP 20375, Z.I. d'Ouloumi, Libreville; tel. 01-72-06-56; fax 01-74-70-67; e-mail gciae@ymail.com; f. 1990; wholesalers of pharmaceuticals and agricultural chemicals; Pres. L. PHILIBERT; Admin.-Gen. DOMINIQUE GRIMALDI.

Marathon Petroleum: BP 1976, Port-Gentil; tel. 01-56-23-07; fax 01-56-23-06; oil exploration and works; Dir Gen. STEPHEN LUM.

Maurel & Prom: Zone portuaire de l'Oprag, BP 2862, Port-Gentil; tel. 01-56-46-91; fax 01-56-46-92; f. 2004.

Mobil Oil Gabon: Zone Industrielle Sud Owendo, BP 145, Libreville; tel. 01-70-05-48; fax 01-70-05-87; e-mail mobil@komo.tiggabon.com; f. 1972; cap. 547m. francs CFA; storage and distribution of petroleum products; Gen. Man. J. L. VINET.

PanOcean Energy Corporation, Ltd: Base DPS (face à la SBOM), BP 452, Port-Gentil; tel. 01-55-57-59; e-mail gabonoffice@paegabon.com; internet www.panafricanenergy.com; f. 1996; name changed as above in 2001; oil exploration and distribution; CEO PAUL L. KEYES.

Perenco Gabon: BP 780, Port-Gentil; tel. 01-55-06-41; fax 01-55-06-47; internet www.perenco-gabon.com; f. 1982; Dir-Gen. ERIC FAILLENET.

Petro Gabon: Centre ville, ave du Colonel Parant et Owendo, BP 20132, Libreville; tel. 01-76-56-94; fax 01-76-57-03; e-mail petrogabon@petrogabon.com; distributor of petroleum products; Dir-Gen. JEAN-BAPTISTE BIKALOU.

Rougier Océan Gabon SA (ROG): BP 130, Libreville; tel. 01-74-31-50; fax 01-74-31-48; e-mail gabon@groupe-rougier.com; cap. 1,200m. francs CFA; forestry and mfr of plywood; Chair. MAURICE ROUGIER; Dir HERVÉ BOZEC.

Shell-Gabon: BP 146, Port-Gentil; tel. 01-55-26-62; fax 01-55-45-29; f. 1960; cap. 15,000m. francs CFA; produced 69,000 barrels of oil in 2004; owned 75% by Royal Dutch-Shell group, 25% state-owned; exploration and production of hydrocarbons; Pres. and Man. Dir ADRIAN DREWETT.

Société Bernabé Gabon: BP 2084, Libreville; tel. 01-74-34-32; fax 01-76-05-21; cap. 1,000m. francs CFA; metallurgical products, construction materials, hardware; Man. Dir MARC BABUIN; Finance Dir SYLVIAN HAMOUD.

Société des Brasseries du Gabon (SOBRAGA): 20 blvd Léon M'Ba, BP 487, Libreville; tel. 01-70-19-69; fax 01-70-09-21; e-mail info@sobraga.com; internet www.sobraga.com; f. 1966; cap. 1,558m. francs CFA; mfrs of beer and soft drinks; Chair. and Dir Gen. FABRICE BONATTI.

Société de Cigarettes du Gabon (SOCIGA): BP 2175, Libreville; tel. 01-72-02-29; fax 01-74-52-13; e-mail sociga@ga.imptop.com; Dir-Gen. FRANCIS RABARIJOHN.

Société d'Exploitation des Produits Oléagineux du Gabon (SEPOGA): BP 1491, Libreville; tel. 01-76-01-92; fax 01-74-15-67; f. 1977; cap. 732m. francs CFA; 25% state-owned, 14% owned by Shell-Gabon; production and marketing of vegetable oils; Chair. PAUL KOUNDA-KIKI; Man. Dir EDMUND SCHEFFLER.

Société Gabonaise des Ferro-Alliages (SOGAFERRO): BP 2728, Moanda; f. 1974; cap. 1,000m. francs CFA; 10% state-owned; manganese processing; Chair. Dr HERVÉ MOUTSINGA; Man. Dir GILLES DE SEAUVE.

Société Gabonaise Industrielle (SOGI): BP 837, Libreville; tel. 01-76-15-37; fax 01-74-10-53; e-mail sogi@sogafric.ga; internet www.sogigabon.com; f. 1975; cap. 950m. francs CFA (2004); industrial construction, metal smelting; Dir-Gen. CHRISTIAN RENOUX.

Société Gabonaise d'Oxygène et Acétylène (GABOA): BP 545, Zone Industrielle d'Owendo, Libreville; tel. 01-70-07-46; fax 01-70-27-15; e-mail gaboa@internetgabon.com; Dir-Gen. KHADIM THIAM.

Société Gabonaise de Peintures et Laques (GPL): BP 4017, Libreville; tel. 01-72-02-34; fax 01-70-02-44; e-mail gpldir@internetgabon.com; f. 1975; 30% state-owned; mfrs of paints and varnishes; Dir CHARLES MARTIN.

Société Gabonaise de Raffinage (SOGARA): BP 530, Port-Gentil; tel. 01-56-30-00; fax 01-55-15-28; f. 1965; cap. 1,200m. francs CFA; 25% state-owned; refines locally produced crude petroleum; Chair. RENÉ RADEMBINO CONIQUET; Man. Dir PIERRE RETENO NDIAYE; 450 employees.

Société de la Haute Mondah (SHM): BP 69, Libreville; tel. 01-72-22-29; f. 1939; cap. 888m. francs CFA; forestry, plywood and saw-milling; Man. Dir M. DEJOIE.

Société Industrielle Textile du Gabon (SOTEGA): Libreville; tel. 01-72-19-29; f. 1968; cap. 260m. francs CFA; 15% state-owned; textile printing; Chair. RAPHAËL EBOBOCA; Man. Dir M. MARESCAUX.

Société Italo-Gabonaise des Marbres (SIGAMA): BP 3893, Libreville; tel. 01-72-25-83; f. 1974; cap. 542m. francs CFA; operates a marble quarry and factory at Doussé-Oussou; Man. Dir FRANCO MARCHIO.

Société Meunière et Avicole du Gabon (SMAG): BP 462, Z.I. d'Oloumi, Libreville; tel. 01-70-18-76; fax 01-70-28-12; e-mail smagb@internetgabon.com; f. 1968; cap. 1,341m. francs CFA; 30% state-owned; production of eggs, cattle feed, flour, bread; Pres. and Dir-Gen. JEAN PIERRE BÉKALÉ BE NZOGHE.

Société de Mise en Valeur du Bois (SOMIVAB): BP 3893, Libreville; tel. 01-78-18-27; cap. 1,550m. francs CFA; forestry, saw-mill, mfrs of sleepers for the Transgabonais railway; Chair. HERVÉ MOUTSINGA; Man. Dir FRANCO MARCHIO.

Société Nationale des Bois du Gabon (SNBG): BP 67, Libreville; tel. 01-79-98-71; fax 01-77-24-01; e-mail direction.commerciale@snbg-gabon.com; internet www.snbg-gabon.com; f. 1944; cap. 4,000m. francs CFA; 51% state-owned; has a monopoly of marketing all okoumé production; Pres. and Dir-Gen. SERGE RUFIN OKANA; 285 employees.

Société National Immobilière (SNI): BP 515, Libreville; tel. 01-76-05-81; fax 01-74-76-00; e-mail snigabon@internetgabon.com; internet www.snigabon.fr; f. 1976; cap. 1,250m. francs CFA; 77% state-owned; scheduled to be privatized; housing management and development; CEO JUSTE VALÈRE OKOLOGO W'OKAMBAT.

Société Pizo de Formulation de Lubrifiants (PIZOLUB): BP 699, Port-Gentil; tel. 01-55-28-40; fax 01-55-03-82; e-mail pizolub@internetgabon.com; f. 1978; cap. 860m. francs CFA; scheduled to be privatized; mfrs of lubricating materials; Chair. MARCEL SANDOUNG-OUT; Dir-Gen. LUCIEN OZOUAKI; 45 employees.

SOTRALGA: POB 3880, Libreville; tel. 01-70-32-69; e-mail dirsotralga@inet.ga; owned by Yeshi Group (Côte d'Ivoire).

Sucreries d'Afrique Gabon (SUCAF Gabon): BP 610, Franceville; tel. 01-67-03-61; fax 01-67-03-63; e-mail sdg_sucaf@sucafgabon.com; f. 1974; cap. 4,000m. francs CFA; 53% state-owned; sugar production and agro-industrial complex at Ouélé; Chair. SAMUEL MBAYE; Dir-Gen. GUILLAUME SORDET; 533 employees.

Total Gabon: bvld Hourcq, BP 525, Port-Gentil; tel. 01-77-62-10; fax 01-76-41-85; e-mail martin.amegasse-efoe@total.com; internet www.total-gabon.com; f. 1934; cap. 76,500m. francs CFA; 36.6m. barrels of petroleum produced in 2004; 25% state-owned, 57% owned by Total group (France); petroleum exploration and extraction; Pres. JACQUES MARRAUD DES GROTTES; Dir-Gen. JEAN-PHILIPPE MAGNAN.

Tullow Oil Gabon: rue Louise Charron Fortin, Batterie IV, Libreville; e-mail info@tullowoil.com; tel. 01-73-26-40; fax 01-73-26-41; exploration and exploitation of petroleum; Dir-Gen. DAVID ROUX.

TRADE UNIONS

Confédération Gabonaise des Syndicats Libres (CGSL): BP 8067, Libreville; tel. 06-03-97-73 (mobile); e-mail cgsl_2012@yahoo.fr; f. 1991; Sec.-Gen. JEAN CLAUDE BEKALÉ; 19,000 mems (2007).

Confédération Syndicale Gabonaise (COSYGA): BP 14017, Libreville; tel. 06-68-07-26 (mobile); fax 01-74-21-70; e-mail mintsacosyga@yahoo.fr; f. 1969 by the Govt, as a specialized organ of the PDG, to organize and educate workers, to contribute to social peace and economic devt, and to protect the rights of trade unions; Gen. Sec. MARTIN ALLINI; 14,610 mems (2007).

Organisation Nationale des Employés du Pétrole (ONEP): Libreville; Sec.-Gen. GUY ROGER AURAT RETENO.

Transport

RAILWAYS

The construction of the Transgabonais railway, which comprises a section running from Owendo (the port of Libreville) to Booué (340 km) and a second section from Booué to Franceville (357 km), was completed in 1986. By 1989 regular services were operating between Libreville and Franceville. Some 2.9m. metric tons of freight and 215,000 passengers were carried on the network in 1999, which in that year totalled 814 km. In 1998 the railways were transferred to private management.

Société d'Exploration du Chemin de Fer Transgabonais (SETRAG): BP 578, Libreville; tel. 01-70-24-78; fax 01-70-20-38; operates Transgabonais railway; 84% owned by COMILOG; Chair. MARCEL ABEKE.

ROADS

In 2004 there were an estimated 9,170 km of roads, including 2,793 km of main roads and 6,377 km of secondary roads; about 10.2% of the road network was paved.

AGS Frasers: BP 9161, Libreville; tel. 01-70-23-16; fax 01-70-41-56; e-mail direction-gabon@ags-demenagement.com; internet www.agsfrasers.com; Man. BERNARD DURET.

APRETRAC: BP 4542, Libreville; tel. 01-72-84-93; fax 01-74-40-45; e-mail apretrac@assala.net; Dir CHRISTOPHE DISSOU.

A.R.T.: BP 9391, Libreville; tel. 01-70-57-26; fax 01-70-57-28; freight; Dir-Gen. PHILIPPE BERGON.

Compagnie Internationale de Déménagement Transit (CIDT): BP 986, Libreville; tel. 01-76-44-44; fax 01-76-44-55; e-mail cidg@internetgabon.com; Dir THIERRY CARBONIE.

Fonds d'Entretien Routier–Deuxième Génération (FER 2): Galerie des Jardins d'Ambre, BP 16201, Libreville; tel. 01-76-93-90; fax 01-76-93-96; e-mail info@fer-gabon.org; internet www.fer-gabon.org; f. 1993; Pres. RAPHAËL MAMIAKA; Dir-Gen. LANDRY PATRICK OYAYA.

GETMA Gabon: BP 7510, Libreville; tel. 01-70-28-14; fax 01-70-40-20; e-mail claude.barone@assala.net; Dir CLAUDE BARONE.

Trans form: BP 7538, Libreville; tel. 01-70-43-95; fax 01-70-21-91; e-mail transformgab@yahoo.fr; f. 1995; Dir JEAN-PIERRE POULAIN.

Transitex: BP 20323, Libreville; tel. 01-77-84-26; fax 01-77-84-35; e-mail helenepedemonte@transitex.ga; freight; Man. FRÉDÉRIC GONZALEZ.

INLAND WATERWAYS

The principal river is the Ogooué, navigable from Port-Gentil to Ndjolé (310 km) and serving the towns of Lambaréné, Ndjolé and Sindara.

Compagnie de Navigation Intérieure (CNI): BP 3982, Libreville; tel. 01-72-39-28; fax 01-74-04-11; f. 1978; scheduled for privatization; responsible for inland waterway transport; agencies at Port-Gentil, Mayumba and Lambaréné; Chair. JEAN-PIERRE MENGWANG ME NGYEMA; Dir-Gen. FRANÇOIS OYABI.

SHIPPING

The principal deep-water ports are Port-Gentil, which handles mainly petroleum exports, Owendo, 15 km from Libreville, which services mainly barge traffic, and Mayumba. The main ports for timber are at Owendo, Mayumba and Nyanga, and there is a fishing port at Libreville. A new terminal for the export of minerals, at Owendo, was opened in 1988. In 2009 the merchant shipping fleet numbered 50 and had a total displacement of 14,400 grt.

Compagnie de Manutention et de Chalandage d'Owendo (COMACO): BP 2131, Libreville; tel. 01-70-26-35; f. 1974; Pres. GEORGES RAWIRI; Dir in Libreville M. RAYMOND.

Office des Ports et Rades du Gabon (OPRAG): Owendo, BP 1051, Libreville; tel. 01-70-00-48; fax 01-70-37-35; e-mail info@ports-gabon.com; internet ports-gabon.com; f. 1974; 25-year management concession acquired in April 2004 by the Spanish PIP group; national port authority; Pres. ALI BONGO; Dir-Gen. RIGOBERT IKAMBOUAYAT NDÉKA.

SAGA Gabon: Zone OPRAG, BP 518, Port-Gentil; tel. 01-55-58-19; fax 01-55-21-71; e-mail sagalbv@internetgabon.com; internet www.saga.fr; Chair. G. COGNON; Man. Dir DANIEL FERNÁNDEZ.

SDV Gabon: Zone Portuaire d'Owendo, BP 77, Libreville; tel. 01-70-26-36; fax 01-70-23-34; e-mail shipping.lbv@ga.dti.bollore.com; internet www.sdv.com; freight by land, sea and air.

Société Nationale d'Acconage et de Transit (SNAT): BP 3897, Libreville; tel. 01-70-04-04; fax 01-70-13-11; e-mail snat.direction@ga.dti.bollore.com; freight transport and stevedoring; Dir-Gen. MARC GÉRARD.

Société Nationale de Transports Maritimes (SONATRAM): BP 3841, Libreville; tel. 01-74-44-04; fax 01-74-59-87; f. 1976; relaunched 1995; 51% state-owned; river and ocean cargo transport; Man. Dir RAPHAEL MOARA WALLA.

SOCOPAO–Gabon: Immeuble Socapao, Zone Portuaire d'Owendo, BP 4, Libreville; tel. 01-70-21-40; fax 01-70-23-34; e-mail socopaolibreville@vpila.fr; f. 1983; freight transport and storage; Dir DANIEL BECQUERELLE.

CIVIL AVIATION

There are international airports at Libreville, Port-Gentil and Franceville, and 65 other public and 50 private airfields, linked mostly with the forestry and petroleum industries.

Agence Nationale de l'Aviation Civile (ANAC): BP 2212, Libreville; e-mail anac@anac-gabon.com; internet www.anac.ga; f. 2008; Pres. EMMANUEL NZÉ-BÉKALÉ; Dir-Gen. DOMINIQUE OYINAMONO.

Air Service Gabon (ASG): BP 2232, Libreville; tel. 01-73-24-08; fax 01-73-60-69; e-mail reservation@airservice.aero; internet www.airservice.aero; f. 1965; charter flights; Chair. JEAN-LUC CHEVRIER; Gen. Man. FRANÇOIS LASCOMBES.

Gabon Airlines SA: Aéroport International Léon M'ba, BP 12913, Libreville; tel. 01-72-02-02; internet www.gabonairlines.com; f. 2006; internal and international cargo and passenger services; Pres. and Dir-Gen. ANDRÉ GIACOMINI.

Gabon Fret: BP 20384, Libreville; tel. 01-73-20-69; fax 01-73-44-44; e-mail gabonfret.gf@gabonfret.com; internet www.gabonfret.com; f. 1995; air freight handlers; Dir DOMINIQUE OYINAMONO.

Nouvelle Air Affaires Gabon: BP 3962, Libreville; tel. 01-73-25-13; fax 01-73-49-98; e-mail online@sn2ag.com; internet www.sn2ag.com; f. 1975; domestic passenger chartered and scheduled flights, and medical evacuation; Chair. HERMINE BONGO ONDIMBA.

Société de Gestion de l'Aéroport de Libreville (ADL): BP 363, Libreville; tel. 01-73-62-44; fax 01-73-61-28; e-mail dg@adlgabon.com; internet www.adlgabon.com; f. 1988; 26.5% state-owned; management of airport at Libreville; Pres. CHANTAL LIDJI BADINGA; Dir-Gen. JEAN-MARC SANSOVINI.

Tourism

Tourist arrivals were estimated at 222,257 in 2003, and receipts from tourism totalled US $13m. in 2005. The tourism sector is being extensively developed, with new hotels and associated projects and the promotion of national parks.

Centre Gabonais de Promotion Touristique (GABONTOUR): 622 ave du Colonel Parant, BP 2085, Libreville; tel. 01-72-85-04; fax 01-72-85-03; e-mail accueil@gabontour.ga; internet www.gabontour.ga; f. 1988; Dir-Gen. ALBERT ENGONGA BIKORO.

Office National Gabonais du Tourisme: BP 161, Libreville; tel. 01-72-21-82.

Defence

As assessed at November 2011, the army consisted of 3,200 men, the air force of 1,000 men and the navy of an estimated 500 men. Paramilitary forces (gendarmerie) numbered 2,000. Military service is voluntary. France maintains a detachment of 762 troops in Gabon.

Defence Expenditure: Budgeted at an estimated 125,000m. francs CFA for 2011.

Commander-in-Chief of the Armed Forces: Gen. JEAN-CLAUDE ELLA EKOGHA.

Education

Education is officially compulsory and free of charge for 10 years between six and 16 years of age. According to UNESCO estimates, in 2000/01 80% of children in the relevant age-group (81% of boys; 80% of girls) attended primary schools, while in 2001/02 enrolment at secondary schools was equivalent to 53% of children in the relevant age-group. Primary and secondary education is provided by the State and mission schools. Primary education begins at the age of six and lasts for five years. Secondary education, beginning at 12 years of age, lasts for up to seven years, comprising a first cycle of four years and a second of three years. The Université Omar Bongo is based at Libreville and the Université des Sciences et des Techniques de Masuku at Franceville. In 1998 7,473 students were enrolled at institutions providing tertiary education. Many students go to France for university and technical training. In 2000 spending on education represented 3.8% of total budgetary expenditure.

Bibliography

Aicardi de Saint-Paul, M. *Le Gabon du roi Denis à Omar Bongo*. Paris, Editions Albatros, 1987. Trans. by Palmer, A. F., and Palmer, T., as *Gabon: The Development of a Nation*. New York and London, Routledge, 1989.

Ambouroué-Avaro, J. *Un peuple gabonais à l'aube de la colonisation*. Paris, Editions Karthala, 1983.

Barnes, J. F. *Gabon: Beyond the Colonial Legacy*. Boulder, CO, Westview Press, 1992.

Culture, Ecology and Politics in Gabon's Rainforest (African Studies). New York, Edwin Mellen Press, 2003.

Bongo, O. *El Hadj Omar Bongo par lui-même*. Libreville, Multipress Gabon, 1988.

Bory, P. *The New Gabon*. Monaco, 1978.

Bouquerel, J. *Le Gabon*. Paris, Presses universitaires de France, 1970.

Deschamps, H. *Traditions orales et archives du Gabon*. Paris, Berger-Levrault, 1962.

Fernandez, J. W. *Bwiti*. Princeton, NJ, Princeton University Press, 1982.

Garandeau, V. *La décentralisation au Gabon: Une réforme inachevée*. Paris, L'Harmattan, 2010.

Gardinier, D. E. *Historical Dictionary of Gabon*. Lanham, MD, Scarecrow Press, 1994.

Gaulme, F. *Le Pays de Cama Gabon*. Paris, Editions Karthala, 1983.

Le Gabon et son ombre. Paris, Editions Karthala, 1988.

Ghazvinian, J. *Untapped: The Scramble for Africa's Oil*. Orlando, FL, Harcourt, 2007.

Gray, C. *Colonial Rule and Crisis in Equatorial Africa: Southern Gabon, 1880–1940*. Rochester, NY, University of Rochester Press, 2002.

Institut de Recherche en Sciences Humaines (IRSH) *L'histoire de l'Assemblée Nationale*. Libreville, 2012.

Les Pouvoirs de l'Assemblée Nationale. Libreville, 2012.

Lexique du Parlementaire Gabonais. Libreville, 2012.

McKay, J. 'West Central Africa' in Mansell Prothero, R. (Ed.). *A Geography of Africa*. London, 1969.

Metegue N'Nah, N. *Histoire du Gabon : Des origines à l'aube du XXIe siècle*. Paris, L'Harmattan, 2006.

Mianzenza, A. D. *Gabon: l'agriculture dans une economie de rente*. Paris, L'Harmattan, 2001.

Nguema Minko, E. *Gabon: l'unité nationale ou la rancune comme mode de gouvernance*. Paris, L'Harmattan, 2010.

Obiang, J.-F. *France-Gabon: pratiques clientélaires et logiques d'état dans les relations franco-africaines*. Paris, Editions Karthala, 2007.

Pa, M. *Transition Politique et Enjeux Post Electoraux au Gabon*. Paris, L'Harmattan, 2011.

Péan, P. *Affaires africaines*. Paris, Fayard, 1983.

Raponda-Walker, A. *Notes d'histoire du Gabon*. Montpellier, Imprimerie Charité, 1960.

Rich, J. *A Workman is Worthy of His Meat: Food and Colonialism in the Gabon Estuary*. Lincoln, NE, University of Nebraska Press, 2007.

Shaxson, N. *Poisoned Wells: The Dirty Politics of African Oil*. Basingstoke, Palgrave Macmillan, 2007.

Vennetier, P. 'Problems of Port Development in Gabon and Congo' in Hoyle, B. S., and Hilling, D. (Eds). *Seaports and Development in Tropical Africa*. London, 1970.

Les Plans de Développement des Pays d'Afrique Noire. 4th edn. Paris, Ediafric, 1977.

Weinstein, B. *Gabon: Nation Building on the Ogooué*. Boston, MA, MIT Press, 1967.

L'Economie Gabonaise. Paris, Ediafric, 1977.

Yates, D. *The Rentier State in Africa: Oil Dependency and Neocolonialism in the Republic of Gabon*. Trenton, NJ, Africa World Press, 1996.

THE GAMBIA

Physical and Social Geography

R. J. HARRISON CHURCH

The Republic of The Gambia occupies an area of 11,295 sq km (4,361 sq miles). Apart from a very short coastline, The Gambia is a semi-enclave in Senegal, with which it shares some physical and social phenomena, but differs in history, colonial experience and certain economic affiliations. Its population (enumerated at 1,364,507 in April 2003, according to provisional census results) was one of the fastest growing of mainland Africa during the 1990s; however, this rate slowed during the 2000s. In mid-2012, according to UN estimates, the country's total population was 1,824,775, with a density of 161.6 inhabitants per sq km.

The Gambia essentially comprises the valley of the navigable Gambia river. Around the estuary (3 km wide at its narrowest point) and the lower river, the state is 50 km wide, and extends eastward either side of the navigable river for 470 km. In most places the country is only 24 km wide with but one or two villages within it on either bank, away from mangrove or marsh. The former extends about 150 km upstream, the limit of the tide in the rainy season, although in the dry season and in drought years the tide penetrates further upstream. Annual rainfall averages 1,150 mm. Coastal erosion has been increasing since 1980, and it is estimated that between 4 m and 5 m of coastal land was lost during the period 1990–94.

Small ocean-going vessels can reach Kaur, 190 km upstream, throughout the year; Georgetown, 283 km upstream, is accessible to some small craft. River vessels regularly call at Fatoto, 464 km upstream, the last of 33 wharf towns served by schooners or river boats. Unfortunately, this fine waterway is underutilized because it is separated from most of its natural hinterland by the nearby frontier with Senegal.

Some mangrove on the landward sides has been removed for swamp rice cultivation. Behind are seasonally flooded marshes with freshwater grasses, and then on the upper slopes of Tertiary sandstone there is woodland with fallow bush and areas cultivated mainly with groundnuts and millet.

The Gambia has no commercially exploitable mineral resources, although deposits of petroleum have been identified.

The principal ethnic groups are the Mandinka, Fula, Wolof, Jola, Serahule, Serere, Manjago and Bambara. There is also a small but influential Creole (Aku) community. Each ethnic group has its own vernacular language, although the official language is English.

Recent History

KATHARINE MURISON

Following the establishment of a coastal trading settlement at Bathurst (now Banjul) in 1816, the extension of British control over the territory now comprising the Republic of The Gambia was completed by the close of the 19th century. Political life during the colonial period developed slowly until the extension of the franchise to all adults after 1960. The People's Progressive Party (PPP), led by Dr (later Sir) Dawda Jawara, emerged as the dominant party in elections in 1962. On 18 February 1965 The Gambia became an independent state, within the Commonwealth, with Jawara as Prime Minister.

JAWARA AND THE PPP, 1965–94

From independence in 1965 until the military coup of July 1994, political life and government control were firmly concentrated in the hands of Jawara and the PPP, with Jawara becoming President when the country opted for republican status in 1970.

In July 1981 dissident members of the paramilitary field force (the country had no army at this time) allied with a number of small radical groupings to attempt a coup. Following a week of fierce fighting, in which at least 1,000 people were killed, the rebellion was crushed with support from Senegalese troops. There were two important ramifications of the coup attempt: the creation of an army and, in February 1982, the establishment of a confederation with Senegal. However, always more favoured by the Senegalese authorities than the Gambians, the Senegambian confederation was formally dissolved in September 1989.

Jawara was re-elected President in May 1982, with 72% of the votes, overwhelmingly defeating the leader of the National Convention Party (NCP), Sheriff Dibba, who conducted his campaign from detention, having been charged in connection with the abortive coup; he was subsequently acquitted and released. The PPP again emerged with a clear majority in parliament, winning 27 of the 35 seats. The NCP increased its representation to five elective seats at the May 1987 elections, but the remainder were won by the PPP. In the presidential election Jawara won 59% of the votes, defeating Dibba, with 27%, and Assan Musa Camara, the leader of the Gambia People's Party (GPP), with 14%. In the presidential election held in April 1992 Jawara secured 58% of the vote, defeating Dibba (with 22%), Camara and two others. In concurrent parliamentary elections the PPP retained a comfortable majority, although its representation was reduced to 25 members.

MILITARY GOVERNMENT

On 22 July 1994 Jawara and his Government were overthrown by a bloodless military coup. It was announced that government was now in the hands of an Armed Forces Provisional Ruling Council (AFPRC), led by Lt (later Col) Yahya Jammeh. The other members of the Council were Lts Sana Sabally, Sadibou Hydara, Edward Singhateh and Yankuba Touray (all of whom were subsequently promoted to the rank of captain). The AFPRC announced the suspension of the Constitution, a ban on all political parties and activity, the temporary closure of the country's borders and a dusk-to-dawn curfew, and gave warning that they would 'mercilessly crush' any opposition to the take-over. Jammeh formed a provisional Cabinet, comprising both soldiers and civilians. Almost immediately, however, two military members of the Cabinet were dismissed and arrested. The frequency of cabinet changes has been a continuous feature of the Jammeh regime.

International reaction to the military take-over, especially from major donors such as the USA, the European Union (EU), the United Kingdom and Japan, was generally unfavourable, and, when attempts to persuade the AFPRC to restore the elected regime failed, efforts were concentrated on a return to democratic rule. Arab donor states such as Saudi Arabia and Kuwait agreed to continue funding aid projects; relations with Libya improved significantly, and full diplomatic relations were restored in 1994. Diplomatic links were established with Taiwan in July 1995, whereupon the People's Republic of China suspended relations.

The AFPRC survived an attempted military counter-coup in November 1994. Several senior PPP figures were arrested but later released. A more serious attempt at a coup took place in January 1995, when two senior AFPRC members, Vice-Chairman Sabally and the Minister of the Interior, Hydara, reportedly attempted to assassinate Jammeh and seize power. The attempt was defeated, and Sabally and Hydara were removed from office and imprisoned. Hydara died in prison in June; Sabally subsequently received a nine-year prison sentence. Singhateh was promoted to the post of AFPRC Vice-Chairman. Persistent rumours in The Gambia suggested that Jammeh had fabricated allegations of a coup in order to eliminate those whom he regarded as potential rivals.

The frequency of arrests of politicians and journalists, as well as allegations of the harassment of civilians by the military, fuelled accusations of authoritarianism on the part of the Jammeh regime. In June 1995 the AFPRC established a new police organization, the National Intelligence Agency (NIA), which was given wide powers of surveillance and arrest, and in August the restoration of the death penalty (abolished in 1993) was attributed to an increase in the incidence of murder. A government decree issued in November 1995 accorded the Minister of the Interior unlimited powers of arrest and detention without charge.

Constitutional Debate

Much public debate in the mid-1990s focused on the timetable for, and manner of, a restoration of democratic civilian rule. In October 1994 the AFPRC announced what it termed a programme of rectification and transition to democratic constitutional rule, which provided for the restitution of elected civilian organs of state in 1998, four years after the seizure of power. The intended duration of military rule was denounced domestically and internationally. In November 1994 Jammeh announced the establishment of a 23-member National Consultative Committee (NCC) to examine the question of the transition. In January 1995 the NCC recommended that the transition period be reduced to two years from the time of the coup. Jammeh accepted the revised programme, but rejected a further NCC suggestion that an interim civilian government be established while he remained as Head of State. Although the reduction in the proposed duration of military rule was generally welcomed, prominent creditors, including the EU and the USA, continued to withhold assistance.

The AFPRC established a Constitutional Review Commission (CRC) in April 1995. The CRC submitted a draft constitutional document to the AFPRC in November, although its findings were not made public until March 1996, prompting suspicions that in the intervening period the AFPRC might have accepted, amended or rejected the Commission's recommendations without public consultation. In April the elections were postponed, on the grounds that there was insufficient time to complete preparations, and in May voting was set for September (presidential) and December (legislative); the ban on political parties was to remain in place until after the constitutional referendum, which was to be held in August. Many aspects of the proposed constitution and the new electoral arrangements provoked concern among opponents of the AFPRC. The stipulation that presidential candidates must be aged between 30 and 65 years ensured Jammeh's eligibility for office, while preventing many veteran politicians from participating; there was to be no restriction on the number of times a President might seek re-election. The revised demarcation of constituency boundaries, it was alleged, would unduly favour the incumbent regime, and significant financial obstacles to political organizations seeking elected public office had been presented by raising both the deposit required from candidates and the proportion of the vote necessary to secure the deposit's return.

The constitutional referendum took place on 8 August 1996. The rate of participation was more than 85%, and more than 70.4% of voters were reported to have endorsed the new document. A presidential decree reauthorizing party political activity was issued on 14 August. Shortly afterwards, however, it was announced that the PPP, the NCP and the GPP were to be prohibited from contesting the forthcoming elections, as were all holders of executive office in the 30 years prior to the 1994 military take-over; thus, the only pre-coup parties authorized to contest the elections were the People's Democratic Organization for Independence and Socialism (PDOIS) and the People's Democratic Party. The effective ban on participation in the restoration of elected institutions of all those associated with political life prior to July 1994 provoked strong criticism from the Commonwealth Ministerial Action Group on the Harare Declaration (CMAG), which had hitherto made a significant contribution to the transition process.

THE JAMMEH PRESIDENCY

As the ban on all political organizations remained in force until only weeks before the presidential election, the formation of parties was a rushed affair. The Alliance for Patriotic Reorientation and Construction (APRC) was established to support Jammeh's candidacy. Some of the elements associated with the pre-1994 parliamentary parties formed the United Democratic Party (UDP) under the leadership of a prominent human rights lawyer, Ousainou Darboe, who became the party's presidential candidate, while the PDOIS and the National Reconciliation Party (NRP) also selected candidates to contest the election. In September 1996 Jammeh and his AFPRC colleagues formally retired from the army: Jammeh was to contest the presidency as a civilian, as required by the Constitution.

The short presidential campaign was widely condemned as having been neither free nor fair, while international observers, including CMAG, expressed doubts as to the credibility of the election. The official results of voting, which took place on 26 September 1996, gave Jammeh 55.8% of the votes and Darboe, his nearest rival, 35.8%. The dissolution of the AFPRC was announced on 27 September; pending the legislative elections, the Cabinet was to be the sole provisional governing body. Jammeh was inaugurated as President on 18 October.

The legislative elections took place on 2 January 1997. Only the APRC had the resources to field candidates in all 45 constituencies (in five of these they were unopposed); the UDP contested 34 seats, the PDOIS 17 and the NRP five. The Gambian authorities, opposition groups and most international observers expressed broad satisfaction at the conduct of the poll. The official results of the elections gave the APRC a clear majority in the new National Assembly, with 33 seats. The UDP won seven seats, the NRP two seats and the PDOIS one seat; two independent candidates were also elected. As Head of State, Jammeh was empowered by the Constitution to nominate four additional members of parliament, from whom the Speaker (and Deputy Speaker) would be chosen. The opening session of the National Assembly accordingly elected Mustapha Wadda, previously Secretary-General of the APRC and Secretary at the Presidency, as Speaker. This session denoted the full entry into force of the Constitution and thus the inauguration of the Second Republic.

In February 1997 most remaining long-term political detainees were released. Later in the month, none the less, there were new arrests: among those detained was the Commander of the State Guard, Lt Landing Sanneh. The title of Secretary of State was now given to all members of the Cabinet. Most of the powers and duties hitherto associated with the vice-presidency were transferred to the Secretary of State for the Office of the President, a post now held by Singhateh (who, at 27, was too young to hold the office of Vice-President).

In July 1997 CMAG reiterated its previous concerns regarding the lack of a 'fully inclusive' political system in The Gambia, urging the immediate removal of the ban on political activities by certain parties and individuals and the investigation of allegations of the harassment of opposition members. In February 1998 the main independent radio station, Citizen FM, was ordered to cease broadcasts shortly after its director and a station journalist were arrested. (The station had recently broadcast information regarding the NIA, although the authorities attributed the closure to the station's failure to pay taxes.) In July 2000 the High Court reversed the original judgment, following an appeal by the director of Citizen FM, Baboucar Gaye. The state of the independent media again gave cause for concern in May 1999, when *The Daily Observer*, the only remaining newspaper that openly criticized the Government, was bought by a Gambian businessman closely associated with Jammeh; several journalists associated with criticisms of government policy were subsequently removed from their posts.

Meanwhile, opposition activists continued to allege harassment by the Government. In May 1998 nine people were arrested in a raid on the mosque at Brikama; among those detained was a prominent critic of Jammeh, Lamine Wa Juwara. A member of the UDP, Juwara had initiated a lawsuit seeking compensation for alleged wrongful imprisonment during the transition period. In July Juwara's claim for damages was rejected by the Supreme Court on the grounds that the Constitution granted immunity to the former AFPRC in connection with the transition period.

In December 1999 Jammeh called an extraordinary congress of the APRC in order to discuss the culture of embezzlement described in a report into official corruption by the Auditor-General. Further allegations of government corruption emerged in January 2000 after the disclosure, during legal proceedings in the United Kingdom, that significant sums generated by the sale of petroleum had been paid into an anonymous Swiss bank account. The crude petroleum had been granted to The Gambia for trading purposes by the Nigerian Government between August 1996 and June 1998, reportedly in recognition of Jammeh's opposition in 1995 to the imposition of sanctions by the Commonwealth against Nigeria. Darboe subsequently alleged that Jammeh had illegally diverted more than US $1.9m. of the proceeds of the sale of the petroleum, although Jammeh vigorously denied any involvement in the matter.

In January 2000 the security forces announced that they had forestalled an attempted military coup. It was reported that, during efforts to arrest the conspirators, a member of the State Guard had been killed, and the Commander of the State Guard, Lt Sanneh, who was the officer in charge of security at the presidential palace, had been wounded. Another member of the State Guard was killed on the following day while attempting to evade arrest. The Secretary of State for the Interior, Ousman Badjie, strenuously denied rumours that the authorities had invented the plot as a pretext to purge the State Guard and as a means of diverting press attention from the petroleum scandal. In June several army officers and civilians were arrested on suspicion of plotting to overthrow Jammeh's Government. Seven were subsequently charged with treason, but all had been acquitted by July 2004.

Meanwhile, in March 2000 it was announced that municipal and rural elections (last conducted in 1992) were to be held in November, while a presidential election was to be held in October 2001. In August 2000, however, the APRC suggested that it would not be possible to hold municipal elections as scheduled, since the National Assembly had yet to approve the local government bill.

In July 2001 Jammeh announced the abrogation of Decree 89 (which prohibited all holders of executive office in the 30 years prior to July 1994 from seeking public office), as demanded by the Commonwealth, although it emerged that prominent individuals who had participated in pre-1994 administrations, including Jawara and Sabally, were still prohibited from seeking public office under separate legislation. None the less, the PPP, the NCP and the GPP were subsequently re-established. In August the UDP, the PPP and the GPP formed a coalition to contest the forthcoming presidential election.

Jammeh and the APRC Retain Power

The presidential election was held on 18 October 2001. A turnout of some 90% was recorded. In addition to Darboe, the candidate of the UDP-PPP-GPP coalition, Jammeh was challenged by Dibba for the NCP, Hamat Bah for the NRP and Sidia Jatta for the PDOIS. Jammeh was re-elected to the presidency, with 52.8% of the votes cast, according to official results, ahead of Darboe, who won 32.6% of the votes. Members of the opposition subsequently disputed the legitimacy of the results, although international observers described the poll as being largely free and fair.

In December 2001 the UDP-PPP-GPP coalition announced that it would boycott legislative elections scheduled to be held in January 2002, as a result of the alleged addition of some 50,000 foreign citizens to electoral lists and the reputed transfer of voters between the electoral lists of different constituencies. Having denied these accusations, the Independent Election Commission (IEC) announced that the APRC had secured 33 of the 48 elective seats in the enlarged National Assembly, in constituencies where the party was unopposed owing to the boycott. At the elections, which took place on 17 January 2002, the APRC won 12 of the 15 contested seats, giving the party an overall total of 45 elective seats, the PDOIS obtained two seats and the NRP one. An additional five members of parliament were appointed by President Jammeh, in accordance with the Constitution. Dibba, whose NCP had formed an alliance with the APRC prior to the elections, was appointed Speaker of the new National Assembly.

The long-delayed municipal elections, which were finally held on 25 April 2002, were boycotted by the UDP and the PDOIS; consequently, the APRC was unopposed in some 85 of the 113 local seats and won a total of 99 seats, securing control of all seven regional authorities. The NRP was the only other political organization to gain representation in local government, winning five seats; the remaining nine seats were won by independent candidates.

In June 2002 former President Jawara returned to The Gambia from exile in the United Kingdom; at the end of the month he was officially received by Jammeh at the presidential residence, and later tendered his resignation as leader of the PPP. In August Juwara alleged that the UDP's campaign funds had been diverted prior to the April elections to pay for Darboe's outstanding income tax debts. The UDP expelled Juwara, who formed a new party, the National Democratic Action Movement (NDAM), in October. In November the opposition UDP-PPP-GPP coalition split, while President Jammeh dismissed a number of members of his Cabinet.

Press Freedom

In May 2002 the National Assembly approved legislation to impose stricter regulations on the print media, in accordance with which all journalists would be required to register with a National Media Commission. The law was condemned by The Gambia Press Union, which announced that it would not co-operate with the new Commission. In June 2003 the state-run National Media Commission was created and accorded far-reaching powers, including the authority to imprison journalists for terms of up to six months. All media organizations and independent journalists had to register with the Commission. In September 2003 the editor-in-chief of *The Independent*, Abdoulaye Sey, was reportedly detained for four days, soon after the newspaper published an article criticizing Jammeh. In October the offices of *The Independent* in Banjul were set on fire, and in April 2004 the printing press was set alight and destroyed.

In December 2004 the National Assembly repealed the controversial law that had created the National Media Commission, but approved legislation requiring newspapers and radio stations to re-register with the authorities within two weeks of the enactment of the law and abolishing the option of a fine for those convicted of libel or sedition, which would instead be punishable by prison terms of between six months and three years. The murder in Banjul a few days later of Deyda Hydara, the editor of the private newspaper *The Point*, who had criticized the new legislation, prompted a protest march in the capital, reportedly attended by some 300 journalists, and a one-week strike by workers in the independent media. The Gambia Press Union demanded an independent inquiry into the killing, amid suggestions that it had been politically motivated. The Government condemned Hydara's murder and pledged to find those responsible. In March 2005 it emerged that the legislation had been signed into law in late December 2004, although its promulgation had not been made public until two months later, in apparent contravention of the Constitution. Reporters sans frontières, an international organization concerned with press freedom, appealed to President Jammeh in May 2005 to accept external assistance in the investigation into Hydara's murder, owing to lack of progress in the case, and in the following years, on the anniversary of Hydara's death, repeatedly accused the Gambian authorities of making no attempt to identify and punish those responsible. Meanwhile, in March 2006 *The Independent* was closed down by the authorities and its general manager and editor-in-chief arrested, apparently in connection with an article naming people who had been arrested on suspicion of participating in an alleged coup attempt (see below). They were released without charge some three weeks later, although Lamin Fatty, a journalist for the newspaper, was arrested in April. In June 2007 Fatty was convicted of publishing false information and was ordered to pay a fine of some US $1,850 or serve one year's imprisonment.

In June 2008 the Community Court of Justice of the Economic Community of West African States (ECOWAS) ordered The Gambia to release and pay compensation to Ebrima Manneh, a journalist for *The Daily Observer*, who had disappeared in July 2006 after being allegedly detained by NIA officials; the Gambian authorities denied any knowledge of Manneh's whereabouts. In April 2009 organizations concerned with press freedom urged the Gambian Government to implement the Court's ruling on Manneh, whose whereabouts remained unknown; the Media Foundation for West Africa announced that it had referred the case to the working group on arbitrary detention of the Office of the UN High Commissioner for Human Rights, which, in November, stated that the continued detention of Manneh was a 'violation of international law' and demanded his immediate release. In mid-June Reporters sans frontières condemned the arrests of three senior officials of The Gambia Press Union and several journalists, which followed a statement by the Union, demanding a thorough investigation into the murder of Hydara, released in response to comments by the President denying any state involvement in the killing. Opposition leader Halifa Sallah, the publisher of the independent *Foroyaa* newspaper, was also briefly detained, after he demanded that the authorities either charge or release the journalists. Six of the journalists, including the editors-in-chief of *Foroyaa* and *The Point*, were sentenced to two years' imprisonment in August, having been convicted of sedition and defamation, prompting expressions of concern from press freedom groups and the EU. Jammeh pardoned all six journalists in September. Addressing journalists in March 2011, President Jammeh denied that his Government had been involved in the murder of Hydara and the disappearance of Manneh. In December two of Hydara's sons, in conjunction with the regional office of the International Federation of Journalists, submitted a case to the ECOWAS Community Court of Justice, seeking a full investigation into the editor's killing. Meanwhile, the Government continued to insist that Manneh was not in state custody, and in May 2012 the Inspector-General of the Police, Yankuba Sonko, suggested that the journalist was in the USA—a claim rejected by Manneh's family.

Anti-Corruption Campaign

In September 2003 President Jammeh dismissed Badjie and Famara Jatta, the Secretary of State for Finance and Economic Affairs. Bakary Njie, the Secretary of State for Communication, Information and Technology, was removed from his post in the following month. In October the President launched an anti-corruption drive, named 'Operation No Compromise', which led to a number of high-profile arrests. In November the leader of the APRC in the National Assembly, Baba Jobe, was charged with fraud and the Director-General of Customs and Excise was arrested. (Baba Jobe was sentenced to nine years' imprisonment in March 2004 and died while still serving his sentence in October 2011.) Moreover, in December 2003 Yankuba Touray, Njie's replacement as Secretary of State for Communication, Information and Technology, was dismissed. In May 2004 Sulayman Masanneh Ceesay was replaced as Secretary of State for the Interior and Religious Affairs by Samba Bah. In April Amadou Scattred Janneh was appointed Secretary of State for Communication, Information and Technology, while Sulayman Mboob became Secretary of State for Agriculture, thus bringing to 84 the number of secretarial changes since Jammeh was proclaimed Head of State in 1994.

A Presidential Anti-Corruption Commission of Inquiry commenced hearings in Banjul in July 2004. During the following months government secretaries of state and other current and former senior public officials were questioned regarding their financial affairs, but there was some criticism that the President and parliamentary deputies were exempt from appearing before the commission, which was to examine the period from 22 July 1994 to 22 July 2004. In October Blaise Baboucar Jagne was replaced as Secretary of State for Foreign Affairs by Sidi Moro Sanneh. In November the Chief of Staff of the Armed Forces, Col Baboucar Jatta, was unexpectedly dismissed and retired from the military, having led the armed forces since Jammeh seized power in 1994. His successor was also dismissed in the following month and replaced by Lt-Col Assan Sarr. There were further arrests of prominent figures in February 2005, including the head of the police force, Landing Badjie, and the head of the criminal investigation unit, Ousman Jatta. The Government dismissed Badjie from his post, accusing him of 'serious dereliction of duty'. Badjie and Jatta were reportedly released several days later without being charged.

Jammeh effected a cabinet reorganization in March 2005, dismissing Mousa Bala Gaye, the Secretary of State for Finance and Economic Affairs, Yankuba Kassama, the Secretary of State for Health and Social Welfare, and Mboob, the Secretary of State for Agriculture. The President assumed personal responsibility for agriculture. Jammeh defended the high rate of turnover in his Cabinet as being necessary to ensure transparency and accountability in government. Further cabinet changes followed later that month. Gaye, notably, made a swift return, as Secretary of State for Foreign Affairs, replacing Sanneh, who became Secretary of State for Trade, Industry and Employment. However, less than a week later Sanneh was replaced by Neneh Macdouall-Gaye. At the same time Col (retd) Baboucar Jatta joined the Government as Secretary of State for the Interior, succeeding Samba Bah. Meanwhile, Jammeh appointed Raymond Sock as Secretary of State for Justice and Attorney-General and Ismaila Sambou as Secretary of State for Local Government and Lands to replace Sheikh Tijan Hydara and Malafi Jarju, respectively, who were both dismissed in connection with the findings of the anti-corruption commission. Hydara was reappointed as Secretary of State for Justice and Attorney-General in October, while Lamin Kaba Bajo replaced Gaye as Secretary of State for Foreign Affairs. Gaye was initially appointed as Secretary of State for Trade, Industry and Employment, but in November returned to the position of Secretary of State for Finance and Economic Affairs.

In March 2005 the Presidential Anti-Corruption Commission of Inquiry submitted its report to Jammeh. A number of civil servants and government officials allegedly implicated in the report were dismissed, and more than 30 senior current and former officials accused of corruption were reportedly given a two-week deadline to reimburse the Government for assets that they had allegedly acquired illicitly. The Commission recommended the implementation of measures to ensure effective monitoring of tax payments, the adoption of new anti-corruption legislation and the creation of a permanent and independent commission to combat corruption. The Public Accountability and Anti-Corruption Unit was accordingly established in April. In June opposition leaders condemned the reappointment to the Cabinet, as Secretary of State for Agriculture, of Yankuba Touray, who had been ordered to repay some D2m. to the state following his appearance before the anti-corruption commission.

Opposition Realignments

In January 2005 the NDAM, the NRP, the PDOIS, the PPP and the UDP agreed to form a coalition, the National Alliance for Democracy and Development (NADD), to contest the presidential election due in 2006. In June 2005 four opposition deputies who had joined the NADD were expelled from the National Assembly, in accordance with the Constitution, which states that deputies choosing to change party must vacate their seats. The four deputies—Hamat Bah, the leader of the NRP, Sidia Jatta and Halifa Sallah, both leaders of the PDOIS, and Kemeseng Jammeh, of the UDP—subsequently lost an appeal against the decision at the Supreme Court, which declared their seats vacant as the NADD had been registered as a separate political party rather than an alliance of parties. Jatta, Sallah and Jammeh retained three of the four seats for the NADD at by-elections held in September, but Bah was defeated by the APRC candidate in the constituency of Upper Saloum.

In November 2005 Bah, Sallah and another senior member of the NADD, Omar Jallow, the Chairman of the PPP, were arrested. Sallah and Jallow were charged with sedition, while Bah was charged with the unauthorized possession of official documents. However, the state withdrew the charges against them in February 2006, following a meeting between President Jammeh, other representatives of the APRC and opposition leaders, mediated by the Nigerian President, Olusegun Obasanjo, under the auspices of the Commonwealth, at which participants signed an electoral code of conduct ahead of the elections due in 2007. Meanwhile, the NRP and the UDP withdrew from the NADD and formed a separate coalition. In March 2006 the NADD, now comprising the NDAM, the PDOIS and the PPP, announced that it had selected Sallah to be its presidential candidate. Darboe was to contest the election for the UDP-NRP coalition.

In March 2006 the Gambian Government announced that the security forces had thwarted a plan by a group of army officers to overthrow the Government while President Jammeh was visiting Mauritania. More than 40 people were reportedly arrested in connection with the alleged coup plot, although its purported leader, the Chief of Staff of the Armed Forces, Lt-Col Ndure Cham, was believed to have fled to Senegal. The Gambian Government requested Senegalese assistance in detaining Cham, who had only been appointed as head of the armed forces in November 2005, after his predecessor, Lt-Col Sarr, was dismissed for allegedly mistreating soldiers. In early April 2006 it was announced that five detainees, including the former Director-General of the NIA, had escaped from custody while being transferred to another prison, although there was speculation that they may have been executed. Later that month Sheriff Dibba was dismissed as Speaker of the National Assembly and detained for several days on suspicion of complicity in the foiled coup; he was replaced as Speaker by Belinda Bidwell. In April 2007 a court martial convicted 10 military officers of involvement in the plot, sentencing them to prison terms ranging from 10 years to life. Five others detained in connection with the coup attempt were granted a presidential pardon in July, but in the following month the High Court convicted three civilians of treason, sentencing them each to 20 years' imprisonment with hard labour; a fourth defendant was acquitted.

Jammeh's Third Term

Jammeh was re-elected to a third term of office at a presidential election held on 22 September 2006, winning 67.3% of the vote. Darboe secured 26.7% and Sallah 6.0%. The turn-out, at 58.6%, was considerably lower than that recorded in the 2001 election. None the less, Darboe alleged that unregistered voters had been allowed to cast ballots.

Elections to the National Assembly took place on 25 January 2007. The ruling APRC secured 42 seats (including five unopposed), while the UDP won four seats, the NADD one seat and an independent candidate the remaining seat. The polls were again marked by a low rate of participation, reported to be 41.7%. Fatoumata Jahumpa-Ceesay replaced Bidwell as Speaker of the National Assembly in the following month. In April the opposition became further divided when the NDAM withdrew from the NADD.

Jammeh reorganized his Cabinet in August and September 2007. Sheikh Omar Faye was appointed Secretary of State for Youth, Sports and Religious Affairs in August, but was replaced in the following month by Mass Axi Gye. (Responsibility for religious affairs was later transferred to the Secretary of State for Local Government and Lands, Ismaila Sambou.) Among other changes, Crispin Grey-Johnson, hitherto Secretary of State for Higher Education, Research, Science and Technology, was designated Secretary of State for Foreign Affairs and National Assembly Matters, and Ousman Jammeh was charged with heading the new Department of State for Petroleum, Energy and Mineral Resources. Edward Singhateh was notably dismissed as Secretary of State for Forestry and the Environment and as Secretary-General of the APRC, being replaced in the Cabinet by Momodou Kotu Cham. In November Dr Malick Njie was appointed as Secretary of State for Health and Social Welfare, succeeding Dr Tamsir Mbowe; both had been involved in developing a controversial HIV/AIDS treatment programme advocated by the President.

In November 2007 the National Assembly approved amendments to legislation on local government. Opposition parties disputed the constitutionality of the revisions, which empowered the President to remove mayors and other elected local representatives. None the less, Jammeh proceeded to dissolve the municipal councils, and local elections were held in January 2008. In an overwhelming victory, the APRC secured the mayoralties of both Banjul and Kanifing and 101 of the 114 council seats (including 54 unopposed). Jammeh reorganized the Cabinet again in March. Macdouall-Gaye was replaced as Secretary of State for Communication, Information and Information Technology by Fatim Badjie, while Grey-Johnson was appointed Secretary of State for Higher Education, Research, Science and Technology, Dr Omar Touray being allocated responsibility for foreign affairs. Njie was replaced as Secretary of State for Health and Social Welfare in November by Dr Mariatou Jallow. Jammeh dismissed Badjie and Grey-Johnson from the Government in February 2009, assuming personal responsibility for their portfolios, having already placed the religious affairs portfolio under his own remit in the previous month.

In May 2008 Juwara, the leader of the NDAM and hitherto a vocal opponent of Jammeh's administration, announced his defection to the APRC, further weakening the opposition.

A report published by Amnesty International in November 2008 contained serious allegations of human rights violations perpetrated by the Gambian army, police and NIA, including torture, extrajudicial executions and detentions without charge, and accused the Gambian Government of using the security forces to stifle opposition to Jammeh's regime. The report cited the alleged killings, in 2005, of 50 migrants (including 44 Ghanaians), who had apparently been detained by the Gambian security forces off the Gambian coast while attempting to reach Europe; a joint UN-ECOWAS investigative mission reportedly concluded in May 2009 that 'rogue elements' of the security forces were responsible for the deaths and disappearances of the migrants, but found no proof of the involvement of the Government in the incident, which had strained relations between The Gambia and Ghana. (Seeking to end bilateral tensions, the Governments of the two countries signed a memorandum of understanding in July, in which they pledged to pursue the arrest and prosecution of those involved in the migrants' disappearances and deaths. Although exonerated by the UN-ECOWAS mission, the Gambian Government also agreed to pay compensation to the families of the victims.)

A new political party, the Gambia Moral Congress (GMC), was registered in January 2009, bringing the total number of parties to 10.

Government Changes and Military and Police Arrests

In April 2009 the National Assembly adopted amendments to the Constitution, providing for a change in the title of members of the Government from Secretary of State to Minister, in line with general international practice, and the removal of the restriction on the number of cabinet ministers that may be appointed. In the following month, as part of a minor government reorganization, Yankuba Touray, a long-time ally of Jammeh, was dismissed as Minister of Fisheries, Water Resources and National Assembly Matters; he was later replaced by Antouman Saho, hitherto ambassador to the United Arab Emirates. Further dismissals of senior officials followed in June, with the removal from office of the Chief Justice, Abdou Karim Savage, the Speaker of the National Assembly, Jahumpa-Ceesay (whose nomination as a member of the legislature was also revoked), and the Minister of Finance and Economic Affairs, Mousa Bala Gaye. Emmanuel Agim, hitherto President of the Court of Appeal, was appointed as Chief Justice, while Elizabeth Renner was nominated by

Jammeh to fill the seat in the National Assembly vacated by Jahumpa-Ceesay, and was subsequently also elected Speaker. Abdou Kolley became Minister of Finance and Economic Affairs. In September Omar Touray was replaced as Minister of Foreign Affairs, International Co-operation and Gambians Abroad by Ousman Jammeh, hitherto Minister of Energy. Sira Ndow-Njie was appointed Minister of Energy in December. The Government was again reorganized in February 2010, with the departure of four ministers and the creation of a new Ministry of Economic Planning and Industrial Development. Among further government changes effected in March, Kolley was replaced as Minister of Finance and Economic Affairs by Momodou Foun but was later reappointed to the Cabinet as Minister of Trade, Employment and Regional Integration. In June Ousman Jammeh was reallocated the energy portfolio, following the dismissal of Ndow-Njie, while Dr Mamadou Tangara, hitherto Minister of Higher Education, Research, Science and Technology, was appointed as Minister of Foreign Affairs, International Co-operation and Gambians Abroad; Jammeh assumed personal responsibility for Tangara's former portfolio. Ousman Jammeh was dismissed from his post in late June; responsibility for the energy portfolio was moved to the Office of the President. Further changes were implemented in July, with Kolley being reinstated as Minister of Finance and Economic Affairs. Meanwhile, Yusupha A. Kah assumed the post of Minister of Trade, Employment and Regional Integration, and was replaced at the Ministry of Economic Planning and Industrial Development by Mambury Njie.

Meanwhile, there was a series of dismissals and arrests within the armed forces and the police force. The Chief of Defence Staff, Lt-Gen. Lang Tombong Tamba, and four other senior officers were removed from their posts in October 2009. In March 2010 Jammeh dismissed a further six senior military and police officials, most notably the Commander of the Navy, Sarjo Fofona, and the Inspector-General of the Police, Ensa Badjie, all of whom were subsequently arrested, while three officials of the National Drug Enforcement Agency were also dismissed and detained, as was Antouman Saho, who had been Minister of Fisheries, Water Resources and National Assembly Matters until February. (In August 2011 Badjie was convicted of various offences, including robbery and corruption, and sentenced to life imprisonment.) Also in March 2010 10 military officers and businessmen, including Tamba and Cham (the purported leader of the 2006 coup attempt), were charged with treason in connection with an alleged plot to overthrow the Government in 2009; Cham and another of those charged remained at large. In June 2010 Tamba and Fofona were charged with involvement in the 2006 coup plot. Tamba and seven others were sentenced to death in July 2010, having been found guilty of participation in the alleged 2009 conspiracy; they appealed against their convictions. The EU condemned the death sentences, while opposition groups expressed doubts regarding the coup plots, suggesting that they were a pretext to suppress dissent. In November 2010 a further 11 intelligence and security officials were arrested in connection with the 2009 plot. In May 2011 Tamba and Fofona were sentenced to 20 years' imprisonment in relation to the 2006 coup attempt.

In April 2010 the spokesman and campaign manager of the UDP, Femi Peters, received a one-year prison sentence and was fined D10,000 for organizing an unauthorized political rally; the EU and the British and US Governments expressed concern at his imprisonment.

President Jammeh revoked his nomination of Renner as a member of the National Assembly without explanation in November 2010, thus effectively removing her from the position of Speaker; Abdoulie Bojang, hitherto Deputy Speaker, was elected to succeed Renner later that month. Several cabinet changes were effected in late 2010 and early 2011. In December 2010 Dr Mariama Sarr-Ceesay was appointed as Minister of Higher Education, Research, Science and Technology, a post held by Jammeh since June, while in February 2011 former Secretary of State for Communication, Information and Information Technology Fatim Badjie returned to the Government as Minister of Health and Social Welfare. In late March Njogu Bah, hitherto Secretary-General and Head of the Civil Service, became Minister of Works, Construction and Infrastructure, replacing Yusupha Kah, who had been dismissed two weeks earlier. Ousman Jammeh was appointed as Secretary-General and Head of the Civil Service in May. However, he was dismissed and sentenced to three years' imprisonment in December for abuse of office and economic crimes related to the continued payment of the salary of a former government official. Njogu Bah was named as the new Secretary-General and Head of the Civil Service.

Meanwhile, a further alleged plot to overthrow the Government emerged in June 2011, with the arrest of four people, including Dr Amadou Scattred Janneh, Secretary of State for Communication, Information and Technology in 2004–05, who was charged with treason and sedition for allegedly distributing anti-Jammeh t-shirts. Ndey Tapha Sosseh, who had been President of The Gambia Press Union until her replacement in June, and journalist Mathew Jallow were similarly charged in the case in July, both *in absentia*. Janneh was sentenced to life imprisonment in January 2012, having been convicted of the charges against him, while the three others arrested with him received six-year sentences with hard labour; Sosseh and Jallow remained at large.

Presidential and Legislative Elections, 2011–12

In March 2011 the IEC announced that a presidential election would be held on 24 November, followed by elections to the National Assembly in the first quarter of 2012 and local polls in 2013. Prior to the presidential election opposition parties complained that the official campaign period had been reduced from four weeks to 11 days, thus severely restricting their access to state media. The opposition failed in efforts to unite behind a single presidential candidate to challenge Jammeh, fielding two candidates: Darboe, contesting the presidency for a fourth time for the UDP and also supported by the GMC, and Hamat Bah, representing the United Front, a coalition of the NRP, the NADD, the PDOIS and the Gambia People's Democratic Party. At the election, which was held, as scheduled, on 24 November 2011, Jammeh was re-elected, securing 71.5% of the valid votes cast, while Darboe won 17.4% and Bah 11.1%. A high turn-out, of 82.6%, was recorded. Darboe rejected the results, describing them as 'bogus, fraudulent and preposterous'. ECOWAS had refused to monitor the ballot on the grounds that the political environment in The Gambia was not conducive for free and fair elections to be held, citing repression and intimidation of both the opposition and the electorate and an unacceptable level of media control by the ruling party—allegations that the Government and the electoral commission refuted. However, observers from organizations including the African Union (AU), the Commonwealth and the EU generally deemed the conduct of the election to have been broadly transparent, but noted a significant imbalance in the media coverage and finances resources devoted to the campaigns of Jammeh and the two opposition candidates, with the APRC making full use of the state machinery to promote the incumbent.

Jammeh was sworn in to serve a fourth term of office on 19 January 2012, pledging to transform The Gambia into an 'economic superpower', to combat corruption and the illegal drugs trade and to create more jobs for the young. More controversially, he also threatened to 'wipe out' some 82% of those in the work-force, if they did not change their 'lazy' attitudes. A government reorganization was effected in the following month. Notable new appointees included Sheriff Gomez as Minister of the Interior, replacing Ousman Sonko, who was designated ambassador to Spain; High Court judge Lamin Jobarteh as Minister of Justice and Attorney-General; and NDAM leader Juwara, who had supported Jammeh's re-election bid, as Minister of Local Government and Lands.

Legislative elections were conducted on 29 March 2012, but were boycotted by six opposition parties, following the IEC's refusal to accede to their demands for a postponement of the polls in order to reform the electoral system. The APRC secured 43 of the 48 elective seats in the National Assembly (including 25 unopposed), while the only other participating party, the NRP, which contested eight seats, won only one (party leader Bah failing to secure election), with independents taking the remaining four. Some two weeks prior to polling, the ruling party had expelled 26 members who had registered to stand as independent candidates. ECOWAS again refused to monitor the elections, which were marked by a low turn-out, of 38.7%. Bojang was re-elected Speaker of the National Assembly in April.

A series of government changes took place in April and May 2012. Gomez was dismissed as Minister of the Interior in April, after only two months in office, being succeeded by Lamin Kaba Bajo, hitherto ambassador to Morocco, while Mambury Njie became Minister of Foreign Affairs, International Co-operation and Gambians Abroad, replacing Tangara, who was appointed initially as Minister of Fisheries, Water Resources and National Assembly Matters and subsequently as Minister of Higher Education, Research, Science and Technology, following the removal from office of Sarr-Ceesay. President Jammeh assumed personal responsibility for the fisheries portfolio. Meanwhile, Abdou Kolley was restored to the post of Minister of Finance and Economic Affairs, which he had relinquished to Njie in January 2011. The interior portfolio was reallocated again in May, to former incumbent Sonko, with Bajo returning to the diplomatic service.

In June 2012, following the submission of a report by a commission of inquiry into tax evasion, which revealed that more than D2,500m. public revenue had been lost as a result of such practices in 1999–2011, the Commissioner-General of The Gambia Revenue Authority, Bakary Sanyang, and 13 others were arrested and charged with offences including neglect of official duty, perjury and fraud.

In August 2012 President Jammeh announced that all prisoners (totalling 37) who had received death sentences would be executed. Despite international outrage nine citizens were put to death before Jammeh halted the programme.

FOREIGN RELATIONS

The Gambia maintains generally good relations with most countries in the region. Despite the presence in Senegal of prominent opponents of his regime, Jammeh has sought to improve relations with that country. In January 1998 the Senegalese Government welcomed an offer by Jammeh to mediate in the conflict in the southern province of Casamance (see Recent History of Senegal): the separatist Mouvement des forces démocratiques de la Casamance (MFDC) is chiefly composed of the Diola ethnic group, of which Jammeh is a member. The Gambian Government subsequently took part in further initiatives to promote reconciliation in the province. At the end of 2002 there were some 4,230 refugees from Casamance registered with the office of the UN High Commissioner for Refugees (UNHCR) in The Gambia, although this number had declined to 548 by the end of 2003. Although a peace agreement was signed by the MFDC and the Senegalese Government in December 2004, in August 2006 UNHCR reported that more than 4,500 people had fled to The Gambia from Senegal that month, following renewed fighting in Casamance between a faction of the MFDC and Senegalese government forces; some 1,600 Senegalese had crossed into The Gambia earlier that year. The total number of Senegalese refugees registered with UNHCR in The Gambia had risen to 6,946 by the end of 2006 and increased to 7,546 in 2007; the number remained at this level in 2008–09, decreasing slightly in 2010, to 7,359, before rising to 8,359 in 2011.

Meanwhile, tensions arose between The Gambia and Senegal in August 2005 when The Gambia Ports Authority doubled the cost of using the ferry across the Gambia river. With the support of their Government, many Senegalese lorry drivers blockaded the main border crossings between the two countries, adversely affecting regional trade. In October Jammeh agreed to reverse the price increase pending further consultations, while the Senegalese President, Abdoulaye Wade, pledged to end the blockade of the border. Agreement was also reached on the construction of a bridge over the Gambia river. In December the Gambian and Senegalese Governments decided that the bridge project should be a regional initiative, to be undertaken by the Gambia River Basin Development Organization. Plans for the establishment of a permanent secretariat for bilateral co-operation were also announced. Relations were again strained in March 2006, however, following allegations of Senegalese complicity in an abortive coup in The Gambia (see above). The Senegalese Government denied any involvement in the plot and recalled its ambassador to The Gambia for consultations; a new ambassador was appointed in June. A visit to The Gambia by President Wade in January 2010 followed claims made by Jammeh in the previous month that the Senegalese Government aided and hosted Gambian dissidents and allegations by *The Daily Observer* that Senegal was seeking to destabilize The Gambia. Wade dismissed the accusations and signed a joint communiqué with Jammeh, in which they pledged to enhance peace and security and reaffirmed their commitment to implement the earlier agreements to construct a bridge over the Gambia river and to establish a permanent secretariat for bilateral co-operation. (In December 2011 the African Development Bank approved funding of US $107.4m. to finance the construction of the bridge.)

In November 2010 The Gambia severed diplomatic relations with Iran, which had been close during Jammeh's presidency. Although no official explanation was forthcoming for this move, it was believed to be connected to the discovery in October of weapons at the Nigerian port of Lagos that were allegedly being transported from Iran to The Gambia (in apparent contravention of UN sanctions forbidding the sale of arms to and from Iran). The incident also provoked tensions between The Gambia and Senegal, following speculation that the arms were ultimately to have been smuggled to MFDC rebels in Casamance. Gambian-Senegalese relations had improved by February 2011, however, when The Gambia acknowledged having received weapons from Iran, but claimed that they were to be used to ensure Gambian national security. At the same time the Gambian and Senegalese Governments agreed to create the long-awaited permanent secretariat later that year and to organize joint military manoeuvres and border patrols. Nevertheless, a renewed dispute regarding the fees charged to Senegalese lorry drivers seeking to cross Gambian territory disrupted cross-border trade and movement for some three months from March. Wade's successor as Senegalese President, Macky Sall, visited The Gambia in April 2012, some three weeks after his election. Sall requested Jammeh's assistance in restoring peace to Casamance, while the Gambian President expressed his willingness to work with the new Government in Senegal. The permanent secretariat had yet to become operational, however.

In September 2011 the Gambian Government strongly rejected allegations made by the President of Guinea, Alpha Condé, that it had been complicit in a failed attempt to assassinate him in July.

The Gambia maintains particularly cordial relations with Taiwan. During a visit to Taiwan in December 2007, President Jammeh expressed The Gambia's continued support for Taiwan's efforts to gain membership of the UN. Bilateral relations were further strengthened in April 2009, during another state visit by Jammeh to Taiwan, and in April 2012, when Taiwanese President Ma Ying-jeou spent four days in The Gambia.

President Jammeh also fostered strong relations with the Libyan regime of Col Muammar al-Qaddafi after he seized power in 1994. Nevertheless, in a strongly worded and unexpected statement released in February 2011, in response to the use of violence against anti-Government protesters in Libya, Jammeh urged Qaddafi to stand down as Libyan leader immediately and criticized the AU for its 'unacceptable silence' on the matter. Jammeh's reaction to events in Libya was met with scepticism, however, with observers suggesting that he was seeking to dissociate himself from Qaddafi in an attempt to prevent any such popular uprising occurring in The Gambia. The Gambian Government proceeded to expel Libyan diplomats from The Gambia in April and assumed control of Libyan-owned assets and enterprises in May, pending the formation of a UN-recognized government in Libya. In March 2012 the Gambian Supreme Court upheld a request by the Government to transfer control of assets belonging to the Libyan African Investment Company to the ruling National Transitional Council in Libya.

Relations with the United Kingdom were strained in 2001, following the expulsion of the British Deputy High Commissioner, Bharat Joshi, from The Gambia in August. The Gambian authorities alleged that the diplomat had interfered in the country's internal affairs, following his attendance at an opposition meeting, but emphasized that the action had been taken against Joshi, and not the United Kingdom. However, in September the Gambian Deputy High Commissioner in London was expelled from the United Kingdom, and further retaliatory measures were implemented against The Gambia. In January 2002 the EU representative, George Marc-André, was declared *persona non grata* by the Gambian authorities and requested to leave the country. The UN Development Programme's representative in Banjul was expelled from The Gambia in February 2007 after criticizing controversial claims made by Jammeh that he had developed a cure for HIV/AIDS. In February 2010 a second UN official, the representative of the UN Children's Fund (UNICEF), was expelled from The Gambia.

In September 2003 The Gambia contributed 150 troops to the ECOWAS Mission in Liberia (ECOMIL). In October the Gambian troops were transferred to a longer-term UN stabilization force, the UN Mission in Liberia (UNMIL), which replaced ECOMIL, with a mandate to support the implementation of a comprehensive peace agreement in that country. At mid-2012 military personnel from The Gambia were also participating in UN peace-keeping operations in Côte d'Ivoire, as well as Liberia, and in the joint UN-AU mission in Darfur, Sudan. In addition, in June 2012 the National Assembly approved the deployment of Gambian troops to Guinea-Bissau and Mali, to participate in ECOWAS missions aimed at supporting a swift restoration of constitutional order in both countries, where coups had taken place earlier that year.

Economy

RALPH YOUNG

INTRODUCTION

Apart from the development of its tourism industry, the principal features of the Gambian economy have shown only modest change since independence. The country has remained poor, underdeveloped and dependent. With a small population (of about 1.8m. in mid-2012), illiteracy at around 54%, a relatively undiversified economy, and an erratic, arid climate, the prospects for dramatic economic development are slight. The Gambia was ranked 168th out of 187 countries in the UN Development Programme's 2011 Human Development Index; its gross national income (GNI) per head in 2010 was US $450, less than one-half of that of neighbouring Senegal. Yet there has been an improvement in recent years in the provision of health and education, and access to safe drinking water has widened, while life expectancy has increased to 58 years and the proportion of The Gambia's population officially living in poverty declined to 48% in 2010, from 58% in 2003. HIV/AIDS prevalence remains low, at 2.0% of the population over 15 in 2009. Furthermore, The Gambia has survived three years of challenging external economic conditions in relatively sound shape, with positive levels of gross domestic product (GDP) growth since 2008.

AGRICULTURE AND FISHING

Agriculture's contribution to GDP declined steadily between 2000 and 2011, from 36% to 27%. However, agriculture still accounted for about three-quarters of the labour force. Agricultural production remains predominantly organized through small-scale peasant units; traditional patterns of shifting cultivation are widely used, and the bulk of production is subsistence-based. The most crucial factor affecting agricultural production is the level of rainfall. Since the mid-1960s the country has experienced recurrent drought, which has adversely affected production levels and led to significant environmental degradation. Plentiful rainfall during 2009 and 2010 ensured that the agricultural sector proved the key driver of growth at a time when tourist receipts and remittances from Gambians working abroad were in sharp decline. However, poor rainfall during the 2011/12 season was expected to reduce production considerably.

The predominant cash crop in The Gambia is groundnuts, first introduced from Brazil in the 18th century. Groundnuts accounted for 28.7% of the value added by agriculture in 2005 and an estimated 43% in 2008 (a year of good rainfall). Although the proportion of cultivated land devoted to groundnuts declined slowly for most of the 1990s, it began to increase again from 1997, and the area used to grow groundnuts in 2003, at 138,900 ha, was the largest recorded since independence; this figure stood at 135,500 ha in 2010. Recorded production in the early 1990s had slumped to only about one-third of annual crops during the boom years of the 1970s, due to poor seed varieties, low rainfall, shortage of fertilizers, bureaucratic inefficiency and labour shortages caused by migration to urban areas. Additionally, the relative levels of official producer prices in The Gambia and neighbouring Senegal has encouraged the smuggling of the Gambian crop to Senegal in years when the latter's prices were more favourable. From the late 1990s Gambian production recovered, although it remained highly variable. The 2001 crop, at 151,100 metric tons, was the highest recorded since 1982, although this figure declined by more than 50% in 2002, to just 71,500 tons. Recovering to 135,700 tons in 2004, it subsequently contracted to 100,000 tons in 2006 and 2007; following higher rainfall, production reached 121,950 tons in 2009 and 137,631 tons in 2010. While the country produces less than 1% of the world's exported groundnuts, the national significance of the crop is immense. Some 20% of groundnut production is for domestic consumption by growers, the rest being cultivated for export, particularly in processed forms (groundnut-processing constitutes the major industrial activity). In 2009 The Gambia exported 18,000 tons of shelled groundnuts (worth US $9.2m.) and 5,927 tons of groundnut oil ($6.6m.); groundnut cake exports amounted to 5,548 tons ($1.2m.), a drop from the 7,182 tons (worth $1.5m.) exported in 2007. Exports of groundnuts and groundnut products have accounted for varying levels of export earnings, though in recent years they have represented over 60% of agricultural exports (and in 2009 almost 75%). The Gambia's ongoing dependence on the groundnut sector remains an obstacle to sustained growth, lagging as it has behind other sectors with development potential in terms of modernization and productivity.

For subsistence purposes, rice is a more important crop than groundnuts. Most of the crop is consumed by producers and their families, although some is sold locally; the country remains a net importer of rice. Traditionally, rice has been grown in the swamplands along the edge of the Gambia river, but since independence there have been efforts to expand pump-irrigated rice production. While increased rice production would provide the best route to self-sufficiency in basic foodstuffs, the rate of population growth has generally exceeded increases in output. Production of paddy rice in 2000, at 34,100 metric tons, was the largest crop recorded since 1982; low rainfall in 2002 led to an output of only 20,452 tons. Although production rebounded in 2004, to 32,600 tons, it fell to 17,934 tons in 2005, then increasing steadily to attain record crops of 79,000 tons in 2009 and 99,890 tons in 2010. The Gambia was, none the less, forced to import 30,505 tons of rice in 2009 to meet local demand. Other important subsistence crops include millet (with an output of 158,018 tons in 2010), sorghum (39,000 tons) and cassava (7,600 tons). In recent years there has been some expansion of fruit cultivation (bananas, mangoes, papayas and oranges) and horticulture, although little of this production is exported.

Livestock-rearing makes a significant contribution to the rural economy, and the country's livestock resources in 2010 included a substantial cattle herd (with 425,000 head), goats (352,000), sheep (251,000) and pigs (28,500). Fishing, largely using traditional methods, is an important source of local food, while contributing around 2% to The Gambia's GDP. The total freshwater and marine catch was 50,985 metric tons in 2009 and 46,449 tons in 2010. The Government received aid of US $13m. from Norway in 2009 to improve its fisheries management and development, and in 2010 the African Development Bank (AfDB) and the International Fund for Agricultural Development provided $60m. to support the development of the livestock industry.

TOURISM

The Gambia's post-independence development of tourism represents its most important and successful attempt at economic diversification and expansion. Already by the 1994 coup tourism had become the country's largest source of foreign exchange. The industry began in 1965, but it was not until 1972 that its development received significant government support, with the creation of 'tourism development areas'. The Gambian Tourist Authority was established in 2001, and a Tourism Development Master Plan was introduced in 2003, partly funded by the AfDB. Despite some diversification, the vast majority of tourists still arrive from the United Kingdom, Germany and Scandinavia, with around one-half being British. Tourism in The Gambia is mostly available in the form of 'packages' organized by Western European (especially British) tour operators, whose decisions on whether or not to expand the promotion of tourism to The Gambia are vital to the industry's development. Largely for climatic reasons, the tourism season runs from October to April, when The Gambia has the considerable advantage of warm, dry conditions. Attempts to promote off-season tourism have been generally unsuccessful, and most employees in the sector are thus laid off during these months; those in the informal sector trades like woodcarving and weaving that are dependent on tourism likewise suffer a loss of income. The Gambia is still mainly regarded by Western visitors as a 'beach' destination; hotel development has therefore taken place mainly in the coastal areas. Attempts to attract tourists up-river for at least part of their stay have met with little success, apart from short day-trips organized by hotels and tour companies. However, by 2003 some 10 ecotourism camps had been established, and in July of that year the former James Island slaving fortress was declared a UNESCO World Heritage Site.

The aftermath of the 1994 coup posed serious problems for The Gambia's tourism sector. European tour operators had emphasized the country's democratic stability for many years, but this image was negated by the military's seizure of power. Following another attempted coup that November, the British Government advised travellers that The Gambia was an 'unsafe' destination, with most major British tour operators then withdrawing from the country; the Swedish and Danish Governments offered similar warnings. Although the official advice was changed by March 1995, tourist numbers for 1994/95, at some 43,000, were less than one-half of the level in 1993/94, causing the closure of many hotels and extensive unemployment in the sector. To compensate for the decline in European tourist numbers, the Government inaugurated an annual 'Roots Festival' in May 1996 to attract African-American visitors. In 1997 the volume of tourists began to return to pre-coup levels, reaching some 96,126 arrivals in 1998/99 and rising to 110,815 in 2004/05 and 143,000 in 2006/07; they remained at around this level during 2008/09. However, with the onset of the global economic crisis from late 2008, the number of tourist arrivals plummeted to 91,000 in 2009/10, making only a modest recovery in 2010/11. Underlining its status as The Gambia's most significant foreign exchange earner, tourism contributed 14.8% of GDP in 2006 and around 20% of GDP in 2008, although its share declined to 12.6% of GDP in 2011.

TRADE AND AID

The Gambia's economy in most years maintains an unfavourable trade balance, but rising food and fuel prices increased the gap between exports and imports from US $138.1m. in 2006 to $221.3m. in 2008; the gap narrowed to $202.5m. in 2009, before rising to $215.0m. in 2010 and an estimated $215.9m. in 2011. Moreover, of its exports, some 90% or more were previously accounted for by the re-export of goods imported into The Gambia under low import tariffs and then re-exported (not always in a legal manner) to neighbouring countries—principally to Senegal, but also Guinea, Guinea-Bissau and Mali. Potentially politically sensitive, this trade periodically led to border problems with Senegal (see below). The profitability of the re-export trade has been eroded by the harmonization of import and sales taxes among members of the Economic Community of West African States (ECOWAS) and improvements in ports and customs operations in Senegal. Although re-export earnings had reached one-third of GDP in past years, they declined to 9.8% in 2008. India and the People's Republic of China have been displacing the European Union (EU) as the most important destinations for The Gambia's exports, and now account for nearly 45% of the total, though they provide little more than one-quarter of its imports. The Gambia's main exports in 2009 were groundnut products, fish and fish preparations, and cashew nuts.

Evidence that Latin American drugs cartels, which in recent years have sought to use West African bases for the transshipment of drugs to Europe, had penetrated the re-export networks of The Gambia emerged in 2010, when two significant drugs caches were seized by police, including one containing two metric tons of cocaine.

Since independence The Gambia has remained heavily dependent on external funding. Development assistance has frequently exceeded one-half of GNI. Until the 1994 coup the major foreign donors were the EU, the USA, the United Kingdom, Canada, the Nordic countries, Japan, Saudi Arabia and China. Opposition from within the donor community to the imposition of military rule in 1994 resulted in significant reductions in development assistance. Most bilateral aid programmes were either scaled down or abandoned. In response, the regime of Yahya A. J. J. Jammeh tried to foster new sources of foreign assistance. Taiwan, notably, agreed in July 1995 to lend some US $35m. following the restoration of diplomatic relations (severed in 1994); by 1998 Taiwan had become the country's biggest unilateral aid donor, though its presence has recently diminished. The Gambia also received significant financial assistant from Libya after the restoration of diplomatic relations in November 1994, and co-operation accords were likewise signed with Cuba and Iran. In March 2002, following the Government's lifting of a ban on electoral participation by the main opposition parties, the USA removed its own sanctions. Later that year The Gambia's eligibility to benefit from favourable trading terms under the US African Growth and Opportunity Act (AGOA) was confirmed; in April 2008 The Gambia was granted a textile visa under AGOA, permitting the export of textile goods to the USA free of duties and quotas. Official development assistance—mainly targeted at projects designed to help the rural poor—roughly doubled between 2005 and 2010, rising from $60m. to $121m.; the bilateral share of this accounted for 28% of the total in 2010. In that year the five principal donors were the EU, the Global Fund, Japan, the World Bank's International Development Association, and the Islamic Development Bank (IDB). Overall, however, the levels of official aid have remained below those received by neighbouring states due to ongoing donor concerns over the regime's record on human rights and press freedom. The Gambia's continuing aid dependence leaves it vulnerable to external pressures; for example, the six journalists sentenced to two-year prison terms in August 2009 for sedition were released the following month after the EU and other governments voiced 'displeasure'.

Significant levels of direct foreign investment were also maintained, reaching US $52m. in 2005, $82m. in 2006, some $73m. in 2007–09 and $86m. in 2010; a spurt of investment in the banking sector since 2007 was believed to have partially compensated for a decline in external investment in other areas. A further and important source of external finance has been the remittances of the estimated 500,000 Gambians working abroad, mainly in the United Kingdom, other parts of Western Europe and the USA. In 2007 and 2008 these amounted to $52.5m. and $53.8m., respectively (or 8.1% and 6.6% of GDP). Remittance levels fell sharply in 2009, to $43m., but recovered gradually, to $45.2m. in 2010 and an estimated

$47.9m. in 2011 (4.7% of GDP in both years). Such remittance levels had adverse effects on the local house-building industry.

ECONOMIC RESTRUCTURING

Having performed relatively strongly in the decade after independence, the Gambian economy then entered a decline, which reached crisis proportions in the mid-1980s. The balance of payments was in increasing deficit, leading to an accumulation of external payments' arrears and increased external borrowing. Government expenditure continued to expand, unsupported by a parallel expansion of state revenue. Increased government intervention in the economy through loan-guarantee schemes, extended parastatal activity, subsidized interest rates and exchange and price controls had the effect of distorting the economy. By 1984 The Gambia was unable to meet its obligations to the IMF, causing the latter to warn of a ban on further drawings by the country. In August 1985 the Government adopted an Economic Recovery Programme (ERP), drawn up in consultation with, and with support from, the Bretton Woods institutions. Although the implementation of the ERP was to be limited partly by capacity constraints, this did represent a significant attempt at economic liberalization. One of the first measures of the ERP was the flotation, in January 1986, of the dalasi, introduced in July 1971 to replace the Gambian pound. The creation of an interbank market for foreign exchange resulted in a devaluation of the dalasi of 120% over six months, with further falls thereafter, until a stabilization was achieved in the early 1990s. This policy resulted in the rechannelling of significant amounts of foreign exchange from the informal sector into the official sector. The ERP also entailed considerable retrenchment in the civil service, with the loss of about 20% of public sector jobs. Meanwhile, producer prices for groundnuts were increased, which, with the devaluation, went some way towards correcting the economy's urban bias. The Central Bank first raised, then decontrolled, interest rates. Parastatal organizations were either privatized or subjected to strict financial discipline through performance contracts. Efforts to combat customs fraud increased customs revenue by one-third. The positive medium-term effects of the ERP included fiscal stabilization, significant reductions in inflation and higher rates of GDP growth. The Programme for Sustained Development (PSD), inaugurated in 1990, was essentially a continuation of this strategy.

The Gambia Utilities Corpn (GUC), the Gambia Commercial and Development Bank and the Gambia Produce Marketing Board (GPMB), which had a monopoly over the purchase and export marketing of groundnuts from 1973 until 1990, were privatized under the PSD in 1992 and 1993. The first of these privatizations proved unsuccessful, with the GUC returning to state control in February 1996 as the National Water and Electricity Co (NAWEC). The GPMB divestiture in turn was reversed in 1999 with the expropriation of its successor, The Gambia Groundnut Corpn (GGC), from the Swiss company Alimenta; although damaging the divestiture programme's credibility, a settlement was eventually reached with Alimenta in 2001.

Although the Gambian economy had been damaged by reductions in foreign aid and the sharp contraction of the tourism industry following the military take-over, the Jammeh regime did not pursue any significant reversals of macroeconomic policy (apart from slowing down the divestiture programme), and pledged its commitment to free market capitalism. Following a decline of 4.0% in 1994/95, GDP increased by 3.1% in 1995/96 as tourist numbers began to recover, and by 2.1% in 1996/97. Currency exchange rates remained relatively stable following the coup. Despite the apparent stabilization of the economy, the new regime's enforced dependence on borrowing from the domestic banking system and its enthusiasm for ambitious infrastructural and other 'prestige' projects (financed mainly by international loans) caused The Gambia's outstanding debt to reach US $503.6m. by 2002. The Government's long-term aim, outlined in its Vision 2020 document published in September 1996, setting targets for all sectors of the economy, was to achieve the status of a middle-income economy by 2020.

Crucial support for the Gambian economy came from the IMF, which in mid-1998 approved funding under its Enhanced Structural Adjustment Facility (ESAF) for 1998–2000. The programme, subsequently operating under the terms of the Poverty Reduction and Growth Facility (PRGF), aimed to restrict average annual inflation to 3%, and to achieve real GDP growth averaging 4.5% annually, particularly by encouraging private sector development; to this end, the Government had undertaken in the 1998 budget to sign binding agreements with several parastatals, notably the port authority, public transport corporation, social security and housing fund, and the telecommunications and utilities operators, to reduce the state's role on condition of the attainment of certain performance criteria. The formation of The Gambia Divestiture Agency in 2001 was intended to give the privatization programme a firmer institutional basis. By this stage NAWEC had already been reorganized as a joint venture with ESKOM, the South African state electricity company, and the telecommunications operation of The Gambia Telecommunications Co (GAMTEL) had been separated from its radio and television activities to prepare it for divestiture. Also in 2001 the Gambia Investment Promotion and Free Zones Agency was established to encourage private investment, especially in manufacturing, while in 2002 the Government was granted a US $16m. loan by the World Bank to develop a Free Zone at Banjul International Airport as part of The Gambia Trade Gateway Project. However, the IMF opposed the Government's decision to take over the struggling GGC. Indeed, the increased budgetary expenditure associated with repayments resulting from the seizure of the company's property contributed to the failure to reach the PRGF's fiscal deficit targets in 2001; although the fiscal deficit declined to the equivalent of 3.6% of GDP in 2000, the GGC payments, combined with substantial tax arrears owed by state enterprises, increased it to 8.7% in 2001. Nevertheless, in December 2000 it was announced that The Gambia had become eligible for debt relief under the IMF's initiative for heavily indebted poor countries (HIPC), provided that certain reform conditions were met.

In June 2002 the Government presented a Poverty Reduction Strategy Paper, and a further PRGF, for the period 2002–05, equivalent to US $27m., was agreed with the IMF in the following month. The principal objectives of the PRGF were to maintain real GDP growth of some 6% annually, to limit inflation to below 4% and to reduce the overall deficit (excluding grants) to some 2% of GDP by 2005. However, in December 2003 the IMF suspended PRGF assistance to The Gambia over concerns about concealed government spending. In December 2004 the Government repaid two non-complying disbursements worth $10.1m., as requested by the IMF. Moreover, with the reprivatization of the groundnut-marketing enterprise identified as a criterion for the 'floating' completion point for debt relief under the IMF's HIPC programme, the attempt during 2005–06 to privatize the state-owned groundnut-processing plants proved unsuccessful. Nevertheless, a staff-monitored programme, designed to improve growth and reduce poverty, was successfully completed in March 2006, and a new three-year poverty strategy, PRGF II, was approved in February 2007. During the year the Government produced a 'roadmap' affirming its commitment to divestiture in the groundnut sector. In December 2007 the World Bank and the IMF announced that The Gambia had finally reached completion point under the HIPC initiative and had also become eligible for debt cancellation under the Multilateral Debt Relief Initiative (MDRI) agreed by the Group of Eight industrialized nations at a summit in Gleneagles, United Kingdom, in mid-2005. At mid-2012 the GGC remained in public ownership, despite World Bank concern at the absence of progress over its privatization, as did GAMTEL, which had been partially privatized in 2007 to the Lebanese firm Spectrum, only for this arrangement to be terminated in 2008 after Spectrum drastically increased its phone tariffs.

Whereas real GDP growth had averaged 3.6% annually during 2004–06, it reached an average annual rate of 6.5% in 2008–10, despite challenging international conditions. Sustained by a buoyant performance in the agricultural sector in 2010, the economy resisted the effects of a depressed tourism sector and falling remittances from abroad to achieve a creditable 5.5% growth rate in 2011. After reaching 17% in 2003, when the IMF suspended the PRGF, inflation had been reduced substantially to 5.0% in 2005 and to 2.1% in 2006. Inflation increased to 6.8% in 2007, due to rising global fuel and food prices, before decreasing to 5.0% in 2008 and 2.1% in early 2009; it rose to 6.1% in mid-2011 before declining again to achieve an average rate of an estimated 5% for the year as a whole. The deficit on the current account of the balance of payments was US $169.2m. in 2010 and an estimated $146.3m. in 2011. The Gambia maintained sufficient international reserves to cover five months of imports by late 2010.

The Gambia's external debt, which had totalled US $676.7m. (or 133.1% of GDP) at the beginning of 2007, was, through the HIPC and MDRI programmes, reduced to $165m. Moreover, in February 2008 it was announced that the 'Paris Club' of creditor countries would write off outstanding debts owed by The Gambia equivalent to $13.0m. However, two new external shocks had emerged with considerable short-term implications: the impact of the surge in fuel and food prices during 2007 and the first half of 2008 and a global financial crisis that indicated the likelihood of a prolonged recession in the Western economies, to which The Gambia's prospects were, at various levels, linked. By late 2010 external debt had risen to $377m., with the IDB the largest creditor. The debt-to-GDP ratio is currently around 28%. As of mid-2012 the Government's response to these adverse circumstances was judged satisfactory by the IMF, although significant budgetary slippage had occurred in 2009 and again in late 2010; a strict cash-budget programme (with no expenditures permitted without revenues being available) was required in 2011 to restore fiscal discipline. The IMF warned that external shocks of this nature underlined the fact that The Gambia's external debt remained problematically high given the country's narrow export base, and that the Jammeh regime had also accustomed itself to unsustainable levels of domestic borrowing (equivalent to 29.2% of GDP by the end of 2011). Such a level of borrowing was 'crowding out' local businesses from access to credit, and was generating interest charges that represented a heavy burden (of around 18%) on the annual government budget. With public resources also under pressure from a steady erosion in tax revenue—from 17.2% of GDP in 2007 to 12.2% in 2011—the Government committed itself to introducing a value-added tax system in January 2013 and acknowledged the need for major reforms to The Gambia's cumbersome tax arrangements.

In May 2012 the IMF approved a new extended Credit Facility worth US $28.3m. to help meet balance of payments needs (due to an anticipated decline in agricultural production) and to assist government efforts to attract donor support for The Gambia's new poverty reduction strategy, the Programme for Accelerated Growth and Employment 2012–15; this had been published in December 2011 against a background of IMF warnings that mobilizing the necessary financial resources would be a 'major challenge'.

Statistical Survey

Sources (unless otherwise stated): Department of Information Services, 14 Daniel Goddard St, Banjul; tel. 4225060; fax 4227230; Central Statistics Department, Central Bank Building, 1/2 Ecowas Ave, Banjul; tel. 4228364; fax 4228903; e-mail director@csd.gm; internet www.gambia.gm/Statistics/statistics.html.

Area and Population

AREA, POPULATION AND DENSITY

Area (sq km)	11,295*
Population (census results)	
15 April 1993	1,038,145
15 April 2003†	
Males	676,726
Females	687,781
Total	1,364,507
Population (UN estimates at mid-year)‡	
2010	1,728,394
2011	1,776,103
2012	1,824,775
Density (per sq km) at mid-2012	161.6

* 4,361 sq miles.

† Provisional.

‡ Source: UN, *World Population Prospects: The 2010 Revision*.

ETHNIC GROUPS

1993 census (percentages): Mandinka 39.60; Fula 18.83; Wolof 14.61; Jola 10.66; Serahule 8.92; Serere 2.77; Manjago 1.85; Bambara 0.84; Creole/Aku 0.69; Others 1.23.

POPULATION BY AGE AND SEX
(UN estimates at mid-2012)

	Males	Females	Total
0–14	398,746	392,881	791,627
15–64	481,596	512,417	994,013
65 and over	20,372	18,763	39,135
Total	900,714	924,061	1,824,775

Source: UN, *World Population Prospects: The 2010 Revision*.

ADMINISTRATIVE DIVISIONS
(population at 2003 census, provisional results)

Banjul	34,828	Kanifing	322,410
Basse	183,033	Kerewan	172,806
Brikama	392,987	Kuntaur	79,098
Georgetown	106,799	Mansakonko	72,546

PRINCIPAL TOWNS
(population at 1993 census)

Serrekunda	151,450	Lamin	10,668
Brikama	42,480	Gunjur	9,983
Banjul (capital)	42,407	Basse	9,265
Bakau	38,062	Soma	7,925
Farafenni	21,142	Bansang	5,405
Sukuta	16,667		

Mid-2011 (incl. suburbs, UN estimate): Banjul 506,277 (Source: UN, *World Urbanization Prospects: The 2011 Revision*).

BIRTHS AND DEATHS
(annual averages, UN estimates)

	1995–2000	2000–05	2005–10
Birth rate (per 1,000)	44.7	42.4	39.3
Death rate (per 1,000)	12.2	10.9	9.8

Source: UN, *World Population Prospects: The 2010 Revision*.

Life expectancy (years at birth): 58.2 (males 57.0; females 59.4) in 2010 (Source: World Bank, World Development Indicators database).

ECONOMICALLY ACTIVE POPULATION*
(persons aged 10 years and over, 1993 census)

	Males	Females	Total
Agriculture, hunting and forestry	82,886	92,806	175,692
Fishing	5,610	450	6,060
Mining and quarrying	354	44	398
Manufacturing	18,729	2,953	21,682
Electricity, gas and water supply	1,774	84	1,858
Construction	9,530	149	9,679
Wholesale and retail trade; repair of motor vehicles, motorcycles and personal and household goods	33,281	15,460	48,741
Hotels and restaurants	3,814	2,173	5,987
Transport, storage and communications	13,421	782	14,203
Financial intermediation	1,843	572	2,415
Other community, social and personal service activities	25,647	15,607	41,254
Sub-total	196,889	131,080	327,969
Activities not adequately defined	10,421	6,991	17,412
Total labour force	207,310	138,071	345,381

* Figures exclude persons seeking work for the first time, but include other unemployed persons.

Mid-2012 (estimates in '000): Agriculture, etc. 640; Total labour force 849 (Source: FAO).

Health and Welfare

KEY INDICATORS

Total fertility rate (children per woman, 2010)	4.9
Under-5 mortality rate (per 1,000 live births, 2010)	98
HIV/AIDS (% of persons aged 15–49, 2009)	2.0
Physicians (per 1,000 head, 2003)	0.1
Hospital beds (per 1,000 head, 2009)	1.1
Health expenditure (2009): US $ per head (PPP)	83
Health expenditure (2009): % of GDP	6.1
Health expenditure (2009): public (% of total)	53.4
Access to water (% of persons, 2010)	89
Access to sanitation (% of persons, 2010)	68
Total carbon dioxide emissions ('000 metric tons, 2008)	410.7
Carbon dioxide emissions per head (metric tons, 2008)	0.3
Human Development Index (2011): ranking	168
Human Development Index (2011): value	0.420

For sources and definitions, see explanatory note on p. vi.

Agriculture

PRINCIPAL CROPS
('000 metric tons)

	2008	2009	2010
Rice, paddy	38.3	79.0	99.9
Maize	44.9	54.6	66.0
Millet	125.6	144.9	158.0
Sorghum	25.6	31.9	39.0
Cassava (Manioc)*	8.4	7.4	7.6
Groundnuts, with shell	109.6	122.0	137.6
Oil palm fruit*	35.0	35.0	35.0
Guavas, mangoes and mangosteens*	1.2	1.3	1.2

* FAO estimates.

Aggregate production ('000 metric tons, may include official, semi-official or estimated data): Total cereals 235.2 in 2008, 311.0 in 2009, 363.5 in 2010; Total pulses 3.3 in 2008, 2.7 in 2009, 2.9 in 2010; Total vegetables (incl. melons) 11.7 in 2008, 9.3 in 2009, 12.2 in 2010; Total fruits (excl. melons) 8.1 in 2008, 8.9 in 2009, 8.6 in 2010.

Source: FAO.

LIVESTOCK
('000 head, year ending September)

	2008	2009	2010
Cattle	420	432	425
Goats	374	380	352
Sheep	200	215	251
Pigs	25	27	29
Asses	42	43	42
Horses	41	37	38
Chickens	720	800	850

Source: FAO.

LIVESTOCK PRODUCTS
('000 metric tons, FAO estimates)

	2008	2009	2010
Cattle meat	4.0	4.1	4.1
Goat meat	1.0	1.0	1.0
Sheep meat	0.6	0.6	0.6
Chicken meat	1.1	1.2	1.2
Game meat	1.2	1.2	1.2
Cows' milk	8.8	9.1	9.3
Hen eggs	0.9	0.9	0.9

Source: FAO.

Forestry

ROUNDWOOD REMOVALS
('000 cubic metres, excluding bark, FAO estimates)

	2008	2009	2010
Sawlogs, veneer logs and logs for sleepers*	106	106	106
Other industrial wood†	7	7	7
Fuel wood	675	684	694
Total	788	797	807

* Assumed to be unchanged since 1994.
† Assumed to be unchanged since 1993.

Source: FAO.

Fishing

('000 metric tons, live weight of capture)

	2008	2009	2010
Tilapias	1.1	1.2	1.2
Sea catfishes	3.5	3.8	3.8
Bonga shad	11.7	12.6	12.6
Sardinellas	7.1	7.6	7.6
Sharks, rays, skates	0.5	0.5	0.5
Total catch (incl. others)	42.6	45.9	46.4*

* FAO estimate.

Source: FAO.

Mining

	2008	2009	2010
Laterites ('000 metric tons)	115	103	174
Silica sand ('000 metric tons)	1,065	1,062	1,121

2007 (metric tons): Clay 6,713; Zircon 355.

Source: US Geological Survey.

Industry

SELECTED PRODUCTS

('000 metric tons unless otherwise stated)

	2008	2009	2010
Beer of barley*	2.6	3.5	3.5
Palm oil—unrefined*	2.5	2.1	3.0
Groundnut oil†	16.0	18.8	19.2
Electric energy (million kWh)‡	242.0	n.a.	n.a.

* FAO estimates.
† Unofficial figures.
‡ Source: UN Industrial Commodity Statistics Database.

Beer of millet ('000 metric tons, FAO estimates): 50.4 in 2003, 55.4 in 2004–05.

Source: mainly FAO.

Finance

CURRENCY AND EXCHANGE RATES

Monetary Units
100 butut = 1 dalasi (D).

Sterling, Dollar and Euro Equivalents (30 April 2012)
£1 sterling = 49.2058 dalasi;
US $1 = 30.2600 dalasi;
€1 = 39.9856 dalasi;
1,000 dalasi = £20.32 = $33.05 = €25.01.

Average Exchange Rate (dalasi per US $)
2009 26.644
2010 28.012
2011 29.462

BUDGET

(million dalasi)

Revenue*	2010	2011	2012†
Tax revenue	3,528	3,780	4,111
Direct taxes	1,109	1,225	1,284
Domestic taxes on goods and services	1,500	1,683	1,827
Taxes on international trade	867	830	952
Other taxes	53	42	47
Non-tax revenue	433	484	540
Total	3,961	4,264	4,651

Expenditure‡	2010	2011	2012†
Current expenditure	4,059	4,579	5,342
Wages and salaries	1,516	1,693	1,725
Other goods and services	1,216	1,273	1,896
Interest payments	766	967	1,098
Internal	629	785	947
External	137	183	151
Subsidies	561	646	623
Capital expenditure	2,407	2,292	2,834
Gambia Local Fund	599	307	329
Foreign financed	1,808	1,985	2,505
Total	6,466	6,871	8,175

* Excluding grants received (million dalasi): 1,065 in 2010; 1,355 in 2011; 1,982 in 2012 (budget projection).
† Budget projections.
‡ Excluding lending minus repayments (million dalasi): –1,440 in 2010; –1,252 in 2011; –1,542 in 2012 (budget projection).

Source: IMF, *The Gambia: Request for a Three-Year Arrangement Under the Extended Credit Facility—Staff Report; Staff Supplement; Staff Statement; Press Release on the Executive Board Discussion; and Statement by the Executive Director for The Gambia* (June 2012).

INTERNATIONAL RESERVES

(US $ million at 31 December)

	2009	2010	2011
IMF special drawing rights	38.58	37.88	37.73
Reserve position in IMF	2.33	2.37	2.37
Foreign exchange	183.26	161.37	183.15
Total	224.18	201.63	223.24

Source: IMF, *International Financial Statistics*.

MONEY SUPPLY

(million dalasi at 31 December)

	2009	2010	2011
Currency outside banks	2,004.81	2,064.62	2,376.33
Demand deposits at commercial banks	3,594.96	3,957.34	4,290.49
Total money	5,599.77	6,021.96	6,666.82

Source: IMF, *International Financial Statistics*.

COST OF LIVING

(Consumer Price Index for Banjul and Kombo St Mary's; base: 1974 = 100)

	1997	1998	1999
Food	1,511.8	1,565.8	1,628.8
Fuel and light	2,145.8	1,854.9	2,076.0
Clothing*	937.5	981.8	999.9
Rent	1,409.6	1,431.3	1,428.6
All items (incl. others)	1,441.5	1,457.3	1,512.8

* Including household linen.

All items (Consumer Price Index for Banjul and Kombo St Mary's; base: 2005 = 100): 117.4 in 2009; 123.4 in 2010; 129.3 in 2011 (Source: IMF, International Financial Statistics).

NATIONAL ACCOUNTS

(million dalasi at current prices)

Expenditure on the Gross Domestic Product

	2009	2010	2011*
Government final consumption expenditure	1,949	2,175	2,427
Private final consumption expenditure	19,813	21,911	23,822
Gross fixed capital formation	6,647	7,418	8,279
Increase in stocks	698	779	870
Total domestic expenditure	29,107	32,283	35,398
Exports of goods and services	1,635	1,824	2,036
Less Imports of goods and services	6,802	7,590	8,471
GDP in purchasers' values	23,941	26,518	28,963

Gross Domestic Product by Economic Activity

	2009	2010	2011*
Agriculture, hunting, forestry and fishing	6,833	8,069	8,538
Mining and quarrying	603	705	716
Manufacturing	1,201	1,231	1,308
Electricity, gas and water	299	331	349
Construction	910	1,004	957
Wholesale and retail trade; restaurants and hotels	6,114	6,127	7,409
Finance, insurance and real estate	3,034	3,376	3,688
Transport and communications	2,545	2,724	3,109
Public administration and defence	870	1,115	1,232
Other services	453	490	528
Sub-total	22,862	25,172	27,834
Less Imputed bank service charge	1,018	851	1,147
GDP at factor cost	21,842	24,321	26,688
Indirect taxes, *less* subsidies	2,099	2,197	2,275
GDP in market prices	23,941	26,518	28,963

* Estimates.

Source: African Development Bank.

BALANCE OF PAYMENTS
(US $ million, year ending 30 June)

	2008	2009	2010
Exports of goods f.o.b.	205.50	174.17	167.38
Imports of goods f.o.b.	–274.55	–259.96	–236.31
Trade balance	–69.05	–85.79	–68.93
Exports of services	117.58	104.19	88.26
Imports of services	–85.65	–82.57	–71.60
Balance on goods and services	–37.12	–64.16	–52.27
Other income received	12.72	11.68	14.35
Other income paid	–47.15	–19.78	–22.40
Balance on goods, services and income	–71.56	–72.26	–60.31
Current transfers received	96.48	160.21	212.75
Current transfers paid	–21.99	–58.79	–135.28
Current balance	2.93	29.16	17.16
Direct investment from abroad	70.79	39.45	37.14
Other investment assets	1.30	20.06	20.30
Investment liabilities	–67.99	–40.58	–73.40
Net errors and omissions	–29.71	–27.82	–94.48
Overall balance	–22.68	20.26	–93.28

Source: IMF, *International Financial Statistics*.

External Trade

PRINCIPAL COMMODITIES
(US $ million)

Imports c.i.f.	2007	2008	2009
Food and live animals	74.5	73.4	77.1
Cereal and cereal preparations	31.6	34.5	39.4
Beverages and tobacco	6.6	5.9	5.1
Crude materials, inedible (excluding fuels)	7.6	7.4	4.2
Mineral fuels, lubricants, etc.	54.1	64.1	47.3
Petroleum, petroleum products and related materials	53.5	63.3	47.2
Animal and vegetable oils	18.5	16.9	21.9
Chemicals and related products	16.1	23.1	22.8
Medicinal and pharmaceutical products	8.9	8.6	13.3
Basic manufactures	39.4	43.2	42.9

Imports c.i.f.—*continued*	2007	2008	2009
Textile yarn, fabrics, made-up articles and related products	15.0	14.0	11.7
Non-metallic mineral manufactures	10.6	13.7	18.3
Machinery and transport equipment	80.2	65.7	61.6
Machinery specialized for particular industries	9.5	4.1	8.3
Telecommunications, sound recording and reproducing equipment	9.3	6.0	5.9
Road vehicles	41.9	38.3	30.8
Miscellaneous manufactured articles	23.9	22.6	20.9
Total (incl. others)	320.9	322.2	303.9

Exports f.o.b.	2007	2008	2009
Food and live animals	6.1	6.7	24.4
Fish, crustaceans, molluscs and preparations thereof	3.2	3.4	5.2
Vegetables and fruit	1.5	2.9	9.1
Beverages and tobacco	—	0.4	0.1
Crude materials, inedible (excluding fuels)	1.9	3.5	8.2
Animal and vegetable oils, fats and waxes	3.0	0.1	7.4
Machinery and transport equipment	0.8	0.9	5.2
Road vehicles	0.6	0.4	2.0
Total (incl. others)	12.5	13.7	66.0

Source: UN, *International Trade Statistics Yearbook*.

PRINCIPAL TRADING PARTNERS
(US $ million)

Imports c.i.f.	2007	2008	2009
Belgium	12.4	9.8	11.4
Brazil	11.4	13.8	17.3
China, People's Repub.	34.0	34.7	34.9
Côte d'Ivoire	21.5	28.8	43.5
Denmark	46.2	23.7	4.9
France (incl. Monaco)	9.5	8.8	10.2
Germany	26.3	35.1	17.2
Hong Kong	6.5	6.2	3.9
India	6.5	5.6	10.7
Japan	8.8	6.1	4.5
Netherlands	18.0	22.7	17.2
Senegal	8.8	9.7	5.6
Singapore	4.7	4.5	5.6
Spain	7.4	3.7	6.5
Thailand	0.5	4.3	10.8
Turkey	1.7	4.3	8.5
United Arab Emirates	6.7	11.7	8.6
United Kingdom	24.7	26.1	23.7
USA	41.8	35.2	7.1
Total (incl. others)	320.9	322.2	303.9

Exports f.o.b.	2007	2008	2009
France (incl. Monaco)	1.7	0.3	4.9
Netherlands	0.8	1.6	0.9
Senegal	3.2	2.4	17.7
United Kingdom	2.5	1.4	4.9
Total (incl. others)	12.5	13.7	66.0

Source: UN, *International Trade Statistics Yearbook*.

Transport

ROAD TRAFFIC
(motor vehicles in use, estimates)

	2002	2003	2004
Passenger cars	7,919	8,168	8,109
Buses	2,261	1,300	1,200
Lorries and vans	1,531	1,862	1,761

2007: Passenger cars 8,815; Buses and coaches 1,012; Vans and lorries 2,601.

Source: IRF, *World Road Statistics*.

SHIPPING

Merchant Fleet
(registered at 31 December)

	2007	2008	2009
Number of vessels	15	15	15
Total displacement (grt)	34,635	34,635	34,635

Source: IHS Fairplay, *World Fleet Statistics*.

International Sea-borne Freight Traffic
('000 metric tons)

	1996	1997	1998
Goods loaded	55.9	38.1	47.0
Goods unloaded	482.7	503.7	493.2

CIVIL AVIATION
(traffic on scheduled services)

	1992	1993	1994
Kilometres flown (million)	1	1	1
Passengers carried ('000)	19	19	19
Passenger-km (million)	50	50	50
Total ton-km (million)	5	5	5

Source: UN, *Statistical Yearbook*.

Tourism

FOREIGN VISITORS BY COUNTRY OF ORIGIN*

	2007	2008	2009
Belgium	2,746	3,192	3,118
Denmark	4,372	4,540	4,547
Germany	6,418	5,289	3,539
Netherlands	15,921	18,920	14,246
Norway	3,212	5,324	4,123
Sweden	7,458	8,370	8,302
United Kingdom	66,042	62,108	63,937
USA	1,297	1,394	1,930
Total (incl. others)	142,626	146,759	141,569

* Air charter tourist arrivals.

Total tourist arrivals ('000): 91 in 2010.

Receipts from tourism (US $ million, incl. passenger transport, unless otherwise indicated): 81 in 2008; 64 in 2009; 32 in 2010 (excl. passenger transport).

Source: World Tourism Organization.

Communications Media

	2009	2010	2011
Telephones ('000 main lines in use)	48.5	48.8	49.1
Mobile cellular telephones ('000 subscribers)	1,312.9	1,478.3	1,581.0
Internet users ('000)	130.1	n.a.	n.a.
Broadband subscribers	300	400	400

Personal computers (number in use): 57,000 (35.3 per 1,000 persons) in 2005.

Television receivers (number in use): 4,000 in 2000.

Radio receivers ('000 in use): 196 in 1997.

Daily newspapers: 2 in 2004 (average circulation 2,100 copies in 1998).

Non-daily newspapers: 4 in 1996 (estimated average circulation 6,000 copies).

Book production: 10 titles in 1998 (10,000 copies).

Sources: UNESCO Institute for Statistics; UNESCO, *Statistical Yearbook*; UN, *Statistical Yearbook*; International Telecommunication Union.

Education

(2006/07)

	Institutions	Teachers	Students		
			Males	Females	Total
Primary	491	4,428	108,540	111,883	220,423
Junior secondary	186	2,385	34,432	32,047	66,479
Senior secondary	66	845	19,024	14,697	33,721

Source: Department of State for Education, Banjul.

2009/10 (UNESCO estimates): *Pupils:* Pre-primary 64,677; Primary 229,013; Secondary 124,397 (Source: UNESCO Institute for Statistics).

Pupil-teacher ratio (primary education, UNESCO estimate): 36.6 in 2008/09 (Source: UNESCO Institute for Statistics).

Adult literacy rate (UNESCO estimates): 50.0% (males 60.0%; females 40.4%) in 2010 (Source: UNESCO Institute for Statistics).

Directory

The Constitution

Following the coup of July 1994, the 1970 Constitution was suspended and the presidency and legislature, as defined therein, dissolved. A Constitutional Review Commission was inaugurated in April 1995; the amended document was approved in a national referendum on 8 August 1996. The Constitution of the Second Republic of The Gambia entered into full effect on 16 January 1997.

Decrees issued during the transition period (1994–96) are deemed to have been approved by the National Assembly and remain in force so long as they do not contravene the provisions of the Constitution of the Second Republic.

The Constitution provides for the separation of the powers of the executive, legislative and judicial organs of state. The Head of State is the President of the Republic, who is directly elected by universal adult suffrage. No restriction is placed on the number of times a President may seek re-election. Legislative authority is vested in the National Assembly, comprising 48 members elected by direct universal suffrage and five members nominated by the President of the Republic. The Speaker and Deputy Speaker of the Assembly are elected, by the members of the legislature, from among the President's nominees. The Constitution upholds the principle of executive accountability to parliament. Thus, the Head of State appoints government members, but these are responsible both to the President and to the National Assembly. Committees of the Assembly have powers to inquire into the activities of ministers and of government departments, and into all matters of public importance.

In judicial affairs, the final court of appeal is the Supreme Court. Provision is made for a special criminal court to hear and determine all cases relating to the theft and misappropriation of public funds.

The Constitution provides for an Independent Electoral Commission, an Independent National Audit Office, an Office of the Ombudsman, a Lands Commission and a Public Service Commission, all of which are intended to ensure transparency, accountability and probity in public affairs.

The Constitution guarantees the rights of women, of children and of the disabled. Tribalism and other forms of sectarianism in politics are forbidden. Political activity may be suspended in the event of a state of national insecurity.

The Government

HEAD OF STATE

President: Col (retd) Alhaji YAHYA A. J. J. JAMMEH (proclaimed Head of State 26 July 1994; elected President 26 September 1996, re-elected 18 October 2001, 22 September 2006 and 24 November 2011).

Vice-President: ISATOU NJIE-SAIDY.

THE CABINET
(September 2012)

President and Minister of Defence, Fisheries, Water Resources and National Assembly Matters: Col (retd) Alhaji YAHYA A. J. J. JAMMEH.

Vice-President and Minister of Women's Affairs: Dr ISATOU NJIE-SAIDY.

Minister of Finance and Economic Affairs: ABDOU KOLLEY.

Minister of Tourism and Culture: FATOU MASS JOBE-NJIE.

Minister of Foreign Affairs, International Co-operation and Gambians Abroad: Dr MAMADOU TANGARA.

Minister of Higher Education, Research, Science and Technology: (vacant).

Minister of Health and Social Welfare: FATIM BADJI.

Minister of Trade, Regional Integration and Employment: KEBBA S. TOURAY.

Minister of Basic and Secondary Education: FATOU LAMIN FAYE.

Minister of Forestry and the Environment: FATOU GAYE.

Minister of Petroleum: TENENG MBA JAITEH.

Minister of Local Government and Lands: LAMIN WAA JUWARA.

Minister of Justice and Attorney-General: LAMIN JOBARTEH.

Minister of the Interior: OUSMAN SONKO.

Minister of Youth and Sports: ALIEU K. JANNEH.

Minister of Agriculture: SOLOMON OWENS.

Minister of Works, Construction and Infrastructure: FRANCIS LITI MBOGE.

MINISTRIES

Office of the President: PMB, State House, Banjul; tel. 4223811; e-mail info@statehouse.gm; internet www.statehouse.gm.

Office of the Vice-President: State House, Banjul; tel. 4227605; fax 4224401; e-mail info@ovp.gov.gm; internet www.ovp.gov.gm.

Ministry of Agriculture: The Quadrangle, Banjul; tel. 4228270; fax 4229325; e-mail info@moa.gov.gm; internet www.moa.gov.gm.

Ministry of Basic and Secondary Education: Willy Thorpe Bldg, Banjul; tel. 4228232; fax 4224180; e-mail info@mobse.gov.gm; internet www.mobse.gov.gm.

Ministry of Finance and Economic Affairs: The Quadrangle, POB 9686, Banjul; tel. 4227221; fax 4227954; e-mail info@mof.gov.gm; internet www.mof.gov.gm.

Ministry of Fisheries, Water Resources and National Assembly Matters: Marina Parade, Banjul; tel. 4227773; fax 4225009; e-mail info@mofwrnam.gov.gm; internet www.mofwrnam.gov.gm.

Ministry of Foreign Affairs, International Co-operation and Gambians Abroad: 4 Marina Parade, Banjul; tel. 4223577; fax 4227917; e-mail info@mofa.gov.gm; internet www.mofa.gov.gm.

Ministry of Forestry and the Environment: Kairaba Ave, Serekunda; tel. 4399447; fax 4399518; e-mail info@mofen.gov.gm; internet www.mofen.gov.gm.

Ministry of Health and Social Welfare: The Quadrangle, Banjul; tel. 4228624; fax 4229325; e-mail info@moh.gov.gm; internet www.moh.gov.gm.

Ministry of Higher Education, Research, Science and Technology: Bertil Harding Highway, Kotu, Banjul; tel. 4466752; fax 4465408; e-mail info@moherst.gov.gm; internet www.moherst.gov.gm.

Ministry of Information and Communication Infrastructure: GRTS Bldg, MDI Rd, Kanifing, Banjul; tel. 4378028; fax 4378029; e-mail info@moici.gov.gm; internet www.moici.gov.gm.

Ministry of the Interior: 5 J. R. Forster St, Banjul; tel. 4223277; fax 4201320; e-mail info@moi.gov.gm; internet www.moi.gov.gm.

Ministry of Justice and Attorney-General's Chambers: Marina Parade, Banjul; tel. 4225352; fax 4229908; e-mail info@moj.gov.gm; internet www.moj.gov.gm.

Ministry of Local Government and Lands: The Quadrangle, Banjul; tel. 4222022; fax 4225261; e-mail info@molgl.gov.gm; internet www.molgl.gov.gm.

Ministry of Petroleum: Bertil Harding Highway, Kotu, Banjul; tel. 8806317; fax 8200896; e-mail info@mop.gov.gm; internet www.mop.gov.gm.

Ministry of Tourism and Culture: New Administrative Bldg, The Quadrangle, Banjul; tel. 4229844; fax 4227753; e-mail info@motc.gov.gm; internet www.motc.gov.gm.

Ministry of Trade, Regional Integration and Employment: Central Bank Bldg, Independence Dr., Banjul; tel. 4228868; fax 4227756; e-mail info@motie.gov.gm; internet www.motie.gov.gm.

Ministry of Works, Construction and Infrastructure: MDI Rd, Kanifing, Banjul; tel. 4375761; fax 4375765; e-mail info@mowci.gov.gm; internet www.mowci.gov.gm.

Ministry of Youth and Sports: The Quadrangle, Banjul; tel. 4225264; fax 4225267; e-mail info@moys.gov.gm; internet www.moys.gov.gm.

President and Legislature

PRESIDENT

Presidential Election, 24 November 2011

Candidate	Valid votes	% of valid votes
Yahya A. J. J. Jammeh (APRC)	470,550	71.54
Ousainou N. Darboe (UDP)	114,177	17.36
Hamat Bah (Independent)	73,060	11.11
Total*	657,787	100.00

* In addition, there were 264 invalid votes.

NATIONAL ASSEMBLY

Speaker: ABDOULIE BOJANG.

National Assembly: Parliament Buildings, Independence Dr., Banjul; tel. 4227241; fax 4225123; e-mail assemblyclerk@yahoo.com; internet www.nationalassembly.gm.

General Election, 29 March 2012*

Party	Votes	% of votes	Seats
Alliance for Patriotic Reorientation and Construction (APRC)	80,289	51.82	43
National Reconciliation Party (NRP)	14,606	9.43	1
Independents	60,055	38.76	4
Total	154,950	100.00	48†

* The election was boycotted by six of the seven main opposition parties, including the United Democratic Party and the National Alliance for Democracy and Development.

† The President of the Republic is empowered by the Constitution to nominate five additional members of parliament. The total number of members of parliament is thus 53.

Election Commission

Independent Electoral Commission (IEC): Election House, Bertil Harding Highway, Kanifing East Layout, POB 793 Banjul; tel. 4373804; fax 4373803; e-mail info@iec.gm; internet www.iec.gm; f. 1997; Chair. Alhaji MUSTAPHA CARAYOL.

Political Organizations

Alliance for Patriotic Reorientation and Construction (APRC): Sankung Sillah Bldg, Kairaba Ave, Banjul; tel. 9745687; f. 1996; governing party; Chair. President YAHYA A. J. J. JAMMEH.

Gambia Moral Congress (GMC): 78 Bertil Harding Highway, Kotu, Banjul; e-mail info@Gambia-Congress.org; internet www.gambia-congress.org; f. 2008; Exec. Chair. MAI N. K. FATTY.

The Gambia Party for Democracy and Progress (GPDP): POB 4014, Kombo St Mary, Serrekunda; tel. 9955226; f. 2004; Sec.-Gen. HENRY GOMEZ.

National Alliance for Democracy and Development (NADD): 30 Papa Sarr St, Churchill, Serrekunda; f. Jan. 2005 to contest 2006 elections; Co-ordinator HALIFA SALLAH; comprises parties listed below.

People's Democratic Organization for Independence and Socialism (PDOIS): POB 2306, 1 Sambou St, Churchill, Serrekunda; tel. and fax 4393177; e-mail foroyaa@qanet.gm; f. 1986; socialist; Leaders HALIFA SALLAH, SAM SARR, SIDIA JATTA.

People's Progressive Party (PPP): c/o Omar Jallow, Ninth St East, Fajara M Section, Banjul; tel. and fax 4392674; f. 1959; fmr ruling party in 1962–94; centrist; Chair. OMAR JALLOW.

National Convention Party (NCP): 38 Sayerr Jobe Ave, Banjul; tel. 6408128 (mobile); f. 1977; left-wing; Leader EBRIMA JANKO SANYANG.

National Democratic Action Movement (NDAM): 1 Box Bar Rd, Nema, Brikama Town, Western Division, Banjul; tel. 7788882; e-mail ndam_gambia@hotmail.com; f. 2002; reformist; Leader and Sec.-Gen. LAMIN WAA JUWARA.

National Reconciliation Party (NRP): 69 Daniel Goddard St, Banjul; tel. 4201371; fax 4201732; f. 1996; formed an alliance with the UDP in 2006; Leader HAMAT N. K. BAH.

United Democratic Party (UDP): 1 Rene Blain St, Banjul; tel. 4221730; fax 4224601; e-mail info@udpgambia.com; internet www.udpgambia.com; f. 1996; formed an alliance with the NRP in 2006 and with the GMC in 2011; reformist; Sec.-Gen. and Leader OUSAINU N. DARBOE; Nat. Pres. DEMBO BOJANG.

Diplomatic Representation

EMBASSIES AND HIGH COMMISSIONS IN THE GAMBIA

Cuba: C/801, POB 4627, Banjul; tel. and fax 4495382; e-mail embacuba@ganet.gm; Ambassador MARIA INES FERNANDEZ.

Guinea-Bissau: 78 Atlantic Rd, Fajara (Bakau), Banjul; tel. 4226862; Ambassador FRANCISCA MARIA MONTEIRA SILVA VAZ TURPIN.

Libya: Independence Dr., Banjul; tel. 4223213; fax 4223214; Ambassador Dr ALI MUHAMMAD DUKALY.

Nigeria: 52 Garba Jalumpa Ave, Bakau, POB 630, Banjul; tel. 4495803; fax 4496456; e-mail nighcgambia@yahoo.com; High Commissioner ESTHER JOHN AUDU.

Senegal: 159 Kairaba Ave, POB 385, Banjul; tel. 4373752; fax 4373750; Ambassador DIAMÉ SIGNATÉ.

Sierra Leone: 67 Daniel Goddard St, Banjul; tel. 4228206; fax 4229819; e-mail mfodayyumkella@yahoo.co.uk; High Commissioner Alhaji KEMOH FADIKA.

Taiwan (Republic of China): 26 Radio Gambia Rd, Kanifing South, POB 916, Banjul; tel. 4374046; fax 4374055; e-mail rocemb@gamtel.gm; Ambassador SAMUEL CHEN.

United Kingdom: 48 Atlantic Rd, Fajara, POB 507, Banjul; tel. 4495133; fax 4496134; e-mail bhcbanjul@fco.gov.uk; internet ukingambia.fco.gov.uk/en; High Commissioner DAVID MORELY.

USA: The White House, Kairaba Ave, Fajara, PMB 19, Banjul; tel. 4392856; fax 4392475; e-mail consularbanjul@state.gov; internet banjul.usembassy.gov; Ambassador PAMELA ANN WHITE.

Judicial System

The judicial system of The Gambia is based on English Common Law and legislative enactments of the Republic's parliament, which include an Islamic Law Recognition Ordinance whereby an Islamic Court exercises jurisdiction in certain cases between, or exclusively affecting, Muslims.

The Constitution of the Second Republic guarantees the independence of the judiciary. The Supreme Court is defined as the final court of appeal. Provision is made for a special criminal court to hear and determine all cases relating to theft and misappropriation of public funds.

Supreme Court of The Gambia

Law Courts, Independence Dr., Banjul; tel. 4227383; fax 4228380.

Consists of the Chief Justice and up to six other judges.

Chief Justice: EMMANUEL A. AGIM.

The **Banjul Magistrates Court**, the **Kanifing Magistrates Court** and the **Divisional Courts** are courts of summary jurisdiction presided over by a magistrate or in his absence by two or more lay justices of the peace. There are resident magistrates in all divisions. The magistrates have limited civil and criminal jurisdiction, and appeal from these courts lies with the Supreme Court. **Islamic Courts** have jurisdiction in matters between, or exclusively affecting, Muslim Gambians and relating to civil status, marriage, succession, donations, testaments and guardianship. The Courts administer Islamic *Shari'a* law. A cadi, or a cadi and two assessors, preside over and constitute an Islamic Court. Assessors of the Islamic Courts are Justices of the Peace of Islamic faith. **District Tribunals** have appellate jurisdiction in cases involving customs and traditions. Each court consists of three district tribunal members, one of whom is selected as president, and other court members from the area over which it has jurisdiction.

Attorney-General: LAMIN JOBARTEH.

Solicitor-General: PA HARRY JAMMEH.

Religion

About 85% of the population are Muslims. The remainder are mainly Christians, and there are small numbers of animists, mostly of the Diola and Karoninka ethnic groups.

ISLAM

Banjul Central Mosque: King Fahd Bin Abdul Aziz Mosque, Box Bar Rd, POB 562, Banjul; tel. 4228094; Imam Ratib Alhaji TAFSIR GAYE.

Supreme Islamic Council: Banjul; Chair. Alhaji BANDING DRAMMEH; Vice-Chair. Alhaji OUSMAN JAH.

CHRISTIANITY

Christian Council of The Gambia: MDI Rd, Kanifing, POB 27, Banjul; tel. 4392092; f. 1966; seven mems (churches and other Christian bodies); Chair. Rt Rev. ROBERT P. ELLISON (Roman Catholic Bishop of Banjul); Sec.-Gen. Rev. EDU GOMEZ.

The Anglican Communion

The diocese of The Gambia, which includes Senegal and Cape Verde, forms part of the Church of the Province of West Africa. The Archbishop of the Province is the Bishop of Koforidua, Ghana. There are about 1,500 adherents in The Gambia.

Bishop of The Gambia: Rt Rev. Dr SOLOMON TILEWA JOHNSON, Bishopscourt, POB 51, Banjul; tel. 4228405; fax 4229495; e-mail anglican@qanet.gm.

The Roman Catholic Church

The Gambia comprises a single diocese (Banjul), directly responsible to the Holy See. Some 3% of the population are Roman Catholics. The diocese administers a development organization (Caritas, The Gambia), and runs 63 schools and training centres. The Gambia participates in the Inter-territorial Catholic Bishops' Conference of The Gambia and Sierra Leone (based in Freetown, Sierra Leone).

Bishop of Banjul: Rt Rev. ROBERT PATRICK ELLISON, Bishop's House, POB 165, Banjul; tel. 4391957; fax 4390998; e-mail rpel202@yahoo.co.uk.

Protestant Churches

Abiding Word Ministries (AWM): 156 Mosque Rd, PMB 207, Serrekunda Post Office, Serrekunda; tel. 7640126; fax 4374069; e-mail info@awmgambia.com; internet www.awmgambia.com; f. 1988; Senior Pastor Rev. FRANCIS FORBES.

Evangelical Lutheran Church in The Gambia: POB 5275, Brikama West Coast Region; tel. 9083755; fax 7043336; e-mail leadership@elctg.org; internet www.elctg.org.

Methodist Church: 1 Macoumba Jallow St, POB 288, Banjul; tel. 4227506; fax 4228510; f. 1821; Chair. and Gen. Supt Rev. NORMAN A. GRIGG.

BAHÁ'Í FAITH

National Spiritual Assembly: POB 2532, Serrekunda; tel. 4229015; e-mail nsagambia@gamtel.gm; internet bci.org/bahaigambia.

The Press

All independent publications are required to register annually with the Government and to pay a registration fee.

The Daily News: 65 Kombo Sillah Dr., Churchill's Town, POB 2849, Serrekunda; tel. 8905629; e-mail dailynews34@yahoo.com; internet dailynews.gm; f. 2009; 3 a week; Dir MADI M. K. CEESAY; Editor-in-Chief SAIKOU JAMMEH.

The Daily Observer: Gacem Rd, Kanifing Industrial Area, Bakau, POB 131, Banjul; tel. 4399801; fax 4496878; e-mail webmaster@observer.gm; internet www.observer.gm; f. 1992; daily; pro-Govt; Editor-in-Chief ALHAGIE JOBE; circ. 5,000.

Foroyaa (Freedom): 1 Sambou St, Churchill's Town, POB 2306, Serrekunda; tel. and fax 4393177; e-mail online@foroyaa.gm; internet www.foroyaa.gm; f. 1987; daily; publ. by the PDOIS; Editors HALIFA SALLAH, SAM SARR, SIDIA JATTA.

The Gambia Daily: Dept of Information, 14 Daniel Goddard St, Banjul; tel. 4225060; fax 4227230; e-mail gamna@gamtel.gm; f. 1994; govt organ; Dir of Information EBRUMA COLE; circ. 500.

The Point: 2 Garba Jahumpa Rd, Fajara, POB 66, Bakau, New Town, Banjul; tel. 4497441; fax 4497442; e-mail thepoint13@yahoo.com; internet www.thepoint.gm; f. 1991; 3 a week; Man. Dir PAP SAINE; Editor-in-Chief BABOUCARR SENGHORE (acting); circ. 3,000.

The Standard: Sait Matty Rd, POB 4566, Bakau; tel. 4496466; fax 4496481; e-mail info@standard.gm; internet www.standard.gm; f. 2010; daily; Publr SHERIFF BOJANG.

NEWS AGENCY

The Gambia News Agency (GAMNA): Dept of Information, 14 Daniel Goddard St, Banjul; tel. 4225060; fax 4227230; e-mail gamna@gamtel.gm; Dir EBRIMA COLE.

PRESS ASSOCIATION

The Gambia Press Union (GPU): 78 Mosque Rd, Serrekunda, POB 1440, Banjul; tel. and fax 4377020; e-mail gpu@qanet.gm; internet www.gambiapressunion.org; f. 1978; affiliated to West African Journalists' Association; Pres. EMIL TOURAY; Sec.-Gen. GIBAIRU JANNEH.

Publishers

National Printing and Stationery Corpn: Sankung Sillah St, Kanifing; tel. 4374403; fax 4395759; f. 1998; state-owned.

Baroueli: 73 Mosque Rd, Serrekunda, POB 976, Banjul; tel. 4392480; e-mail baroueli@qanet.gm; f. 1986; educational.

Observer Company: Bakau New Town Rd, Kanifing, PMB 131, Banjul; tel. 4496087; fax 4496878; e-mail webmaster@observer.gm; internet www.observer.gm; f. 1995; indigenous languages and non-fiction.

Sunrise Publishers: POB 955, Banjul; tel. 4393538; e-mail sunrise@qanet.gm; internet www.sunrisepublishers.net; f. 1985; regional history, politics and culture; Man. PATIENCE SONKO-GODWIN.

Broadcasting and Communications

TELECOMMUNICATIONS

In 2011 the Gambia telecommunications sector comprised three mobile cellular telephone operators and one fixed-line operator. A fifth licence was issued to Nigeria-owned Globacom in 2010

Africell (Gambia): 43 Kairaba Ave, POB 2140, Banjul; tel. 4376022; fax 4376066; e-mail mmakkaoui@africell.gm; internet www.africell.gm; f. 2001; provider of mobile cellular telecommunications; CEO ALIEU BADARA MBYE.

Comium Gambia: 27 Kairaba Ave, Pipeline, KSMD, Banjul; tel. 6601601; fax 6601602; e-mail info@comium.gm; internet www.comium.gm; f. 2007; operates mobile cellular telephone network under the Nakam brand; Man. Dir AMER ATWI.

The Gambia Telecommunications Co Ltd (GAMTEL): Gamtel House, 3 Nelson Mandela St, POB 387, Banjul; tel. 4229999; fax 4228004; e-mail gen-info@gamtel.gm; internet www.gamtel.gm; f. 1984; state-owned; Man. Dir BABOUCAR SANYANG (acting).

Gamcel: 59 Mamadi Maniyang Highway, Kanifing; tel. 4398169; fax 4372932; internet www.gamcel.gm; f. 2000; wholly owned subsidiary of GAMTEL providing mobile cellular telephone services.

QCell Gambia: QCell House, Kairaba Ave, Serrekunda; tel. 3333111 (mobile); fax 4376311; internet www.qcell.gm; f. 2008; mobile cellular services; CEO MUHAMMED JAH.

BROADCASTING

Radio

The Gambia Radio and Television Services (GRTS): GRTV Headquarters, MDI Rd, Kanifing, POB 158, Banjul; tel. 4373913; fax 4374242; e-mail bora@gamtel.gm; internet www.grts.gm; f. 1962; state-funded, non-commercial broadcaster; radio broadcasts in English, Mandinka, Wolof, Fula, Diola, Serer and Serahuli; Dir-Gen. Alhaji MODOU SANYANG.

Citizen FM: Banjul; independent commercial broadcaster; broadcasts news and information in English, Wolof and Mandinka; rebroadcasts selected programmes from the British Broadcasting Corpn; operations suspended in Oct. 2001; Propr BABOUCAR GAYE; News Editor EBRIMA SILLAH.

Farafenni Community Radio: Farafenni; tel. 9931964; Gen. Man. SAINEY DIBBA.

FM B Community Radio Station: Brikama; tel. 4483000; fax 4484100; e-mail brikamacommunityradio@yahoo.co.uk; f. 1998; FM broadcaster; Admin. Man. BAKARY K. TOURAY.

Radio 1 FM: 44 Kairaba Ave, POB 2700, Serrekunda; tel. 4396076; fax 4394911; e-mail george.radio1@qanet.gm; f. 1990; private station broadcasting FM music programmes to the Greater Banjul area; Dir GEORGE CHRISTENSEN.

Radio Gambia: Mile 7, Banjul; tel. 4495101; fax 4495923; e-mail semafye@hotmail.com.

Sud FM: Buckle St, POB 64, Banjul; tel. 4222359; fax 4222394; e-mail sudfm@gamtel.gm; licence revoked in 2005; Man. MAMADOU HOUSSABA BA.

Teranga FM: Sinchu Alhagie Village, Kombo North, West Coast Region; f. 2009; Man. ISMAILA SISAY.

West Coast Radio: Manjai Kunda, POB 2687, Serrekunda; tel. 4460911; fax 4461193; e-mail info@westcoast.gm; internet www.westcoast.gm; FM broadcaster; Man. Dir PETER GOMEZ.

Unique FM: Garba Jahumpa Rd, Bakau; tel. 7555777; internet www.uniquefm.gm; f. 2007; Man. LAMIN MANGA.

The Gambia also receives broadcasts from Radio Democracy for Africa (f. 1998), a division of the Voice of America, and the British Broadcasting Corpn.

Television

The Gambia Radio and Television Services (GRTS): see Radio; television broadcasts commenced 1995.

There is also a private satellite channel, Premium TV.

Finance

(cap. = capital; res = reserves; dep. = deposits; m. = million; br(s). = branch(es); amounts in dalasi)

BANKING

At the end of 2010 there were 14 banks operating in the country, of which one was an Islamic bank and 13 were conventional commercial banks.

Central Bank

Central Bank of The Gambia: 1–2 ECOWAS Ave, Banjul; tel. 4228103; fax 4226969; e-mail info@cbg.gm; internet www.cbg.gm; f. 1971; bank of issue; monetary authority; cap. 81.0m., res 4.3m., dep. 1,702.7m. (Dec. 2009); Gov. MODOU BAMBA SAHO.

Other Banks

Access Bank (Gambia) Ltd: 47 Kairaba Ave, Fajara, KSMD; tel. 4396679; fax 4396640; e-mail jammehm@accessbankgambia.com; internet www.accessbankplc.com/gm; f. 2007; Man. Dir LEAK OJIOGO.

Arab-Gambian Islamic Bank: 7 ECOWAS Ave, POB 1415, Banjul; tel. 4222222; fax 4223770; e-mail info@agib.gm; internet www.agib.gm; f. 1996; 21.1% owned by The Gambia National Insurance Co Ltd, 20.0% owned by Islamic Development Bank (Saudi Arabia); cap. and res 9.0m., total assets 116.9m. (Dec. 2001); Chair. SUZANNE IROCHE; Man. Dir SALISU SIRAJO; 1 br.

Bank PHB: 11A Liberation Ave, POB 211, Banjul; tel. 4227944; fax 4229312; e-mail mgcisse@ibc.gm; internet gambia.bankphb.com; f. 1968; fmrly International Bank for Commerce (Gambia) Ltd, name changed as above August 2008 following acquisition by Bank PHB Nigeria; cap. 60m., res 59.9m., dep. 434.6m. (Dec. 2006); Man. Dir CHUKS CHIBUNDU; 2 brs.

Banque Sahelo-Saherienne pour l'Investissement et Commerce Gambie Ltd: 52 Kairaba Ave, PMB 204, KMC; tel. 4498078; fax 4498080; e-mail bsic@bsicgambia.gm; f. 2008; Gen. Man. YOUSEF SGHAYER AHMED TURKMAN.

Ecobank Gambia Ltd: 42 Kairaba Ave, POB 3466, Serrekunda; tel. 4399030; fax 4399034; e-mail egacustomercare@ecobank.com; cap. 79.5m., dep. 629m. (Dec. 2009); Man. Dir FITZGERALD ODONKOR.

First International Bank Ltd: 2 Kairaba Ave, Serrekunda; tel. and fax 4396580; e-mail info@fibgm.com; internet www.fibankgm.com; f. 1999; 61.9% owned by Slok Ltd (Nigeria); cap. 150.7m., res 6.8m., dep. 570.3m. (Dec. 2010); Chair. EDRISSA JOBE; Man. Dir YASSIN BAYO; 8 brs.

Guaranty Trust Bank (Gambia): 56 Kairaba Ave, Fajara, POB 1958, Banjul; tel. 4376371; fax 4376398; e-mail webmaster@gambia.gtbplc.com; internet www.gambia.gtbplc.com; f. 2002; subsidiary of Guaranty Trust Bank PLC (Nigeria); Chair. AMADOU SAMBA; Man. Dir LEKAN SANUSI.

International Commercial Bank (Gambia) Ltd: GIPFZA House, Ground Floor, 48 Kairaba Ave, Serrekunda, KMC, POB 1600, Banjul; tel. 4377878; fax 4377880; e-mail icbank@icbank-gambia.com; internet www.icbank-gambia.com; f. 2005; CEO LALIT MOHAN TEWARI; 3 brs.

Oceanic Bank Gambia: Adam's Shopping Center, Bertil Hardling Highway, Kololi, POB 1884, Banjul; tel. 4466711; fax 4466710; e-mail Info@oceanicbankgambia.com; internet www.oceanicbankgambia.com; a subsidiary of Oceanic Bank International PLC (Nigeria); Man. Dir KINGSLEY KEINDE ADEBISI.

Prime Bank Gambia Ltd: 42 Kairaba Ave, KSMD, Banjul; tel. 4399283; fax 4399044; e-mail info@primebankgambia.com; internet www.primebankgambia.gm; f. 2009; Chair. G. W. HAIKAL; Exec. Dir FADI A. MENDY.

Skye Bank Gambia: 70 Kairaba Ave, Fajara, KSM; tel. 4414370; e-mail info@skyebankgm.com; subsidiary of Skye Bank PLC (Nigeria); Man. Dir AKIM YUSUF.

Standard Chartered Bank (Gambia) Ltd: 8/10 ECOWAS Ave, POB 259, Banjul; tel. 4202929; fax 4202692; e-mail Humphrey.Mukwereza@gm.standardchartered.com; internet www.standardchartered.com/gm; f. 1894; 75% owned by Standard Chartered Holdings BV, The Netherlands; cap. 60m., res 157.6m., dep. 2,183.7m. (Dec. 2009); Chair. MOMODOU B. A. SENGHORE; CEO HUMPHREY MUKWEREZA; 5 brs.

Trust Bank Ltd (TBL): 3–4 ECOWAS Ave, POB 1018, Banjul; tel. 4225777; fax 4225781; e-mail info@trustbank.gm; internet www.tblgambia.com; f. 1997; fmrly Meridien BIAO Bank Gambia Ltd; 22.12% owned by Data Bank, 36.97% by Social Security and Housing Finance Corpn; cap. 200.0m., res 121.1m., dep. 3,477.4m. (Dec. 2011); Chair. KEN OFORI ATTA; Man. Dir PA MACOUMBA NJIE; 17 brs.

Zenith Bank (Gambia) Ltd: 49 Kairaba Ave, Fajara, POB 2823, Serrekunda; tel. 4399471; f. 2008; subsidiary of Zenith Bank PLC; Man. Dir EMEKA ANYAEGBUNA.

INSURANCE

In 2010 there were 11 insurance companies operating in the country.

Capital Express Assurance (Gambia) Ltd: 22 Anglesea St, POB 268, Banjul; tel. 4227480; fax 4229219; e-mail capinsur@gamtel.gm; f. 1985; subsidiary of Capital Express Assurance Limited (Nigeria); CEO KUNLE ADEGBOYE.

The Gambia National Insurance Co Ltd (GNIC): 19 Kairaba Ave, Fajara, KSMD, POB 750, Banjul; tel. 4395725; fax 4395716; e-mail info@gnic.gm; internet www.gnic.gm; f. 1974; privately owned; Chair. MATARR O. DRAMMEH; Man. Dir FYE K. CEESAY; 3 brs.

Global Security Insurance Co Ltd: 73A Independence Dr., POB 1400, Banjul; tel. 4223716; fax 4223715; e-mail global@gamtel.gm; f. 1996; Man. Dir KWASU DARBOE.

Great Alliance Insurance Co: 10 Nelson Mandela St, POB 1160, Banjul; tel. 4227839; fax 4229444; f. 1989; Pres. BAI MATARR DRAMMEH; Man. Dir DEBORAH H. FORSTER.

IGI Gamstar Insurance Co Ltd: 79 Daniel Goddard St, POB 1276, Banjul; tel. 4228610; fax 4229755; e-mail gamstarinsurance@hotmail.com; f. 1991; Man. Dir FRANK UCHE.

International Insurance Co. Ltd: Duwa Jabbi Bldg, 5 OAU Blvd, POB 1254, Banjul; tel. 4202761; fax 4202763; e-mail iic@gamtel.gm; Man. Dir SENOR THOMAS.

Londongate (Gambia) Insurance Co: 1–3 Liberation Ave, POB 602, Banjul; tel. 4201740; fax 4201742; e-mail izadi@londongate.gm; internet www.londongate.co.uk/gambia_profile.htm; f. 1999; owned by Boule & Co Ltd; Man. Dir SHAHROKH IZADI.

New Vision Insurance Co Ltd: 3–4 ECOWAS Ave, POB 239, Banjul; tel. 4223045; fax 4223040; Dir BIRAN BAH.

Prime Insurance Co Ltd: 10C Nelson Mandela St, POB 277, Banjul; tel. 4222476; e-mail prime@qanet.gm; f. 1997; Gen. Man. JARREH F. M. TOURAY.

Sunshine Insurance Company Ltd: 7/8 Nelson Mandela St, Banjul; tel. 4202645; fax 4202648; e-mail sunshine.insurance@qanet.gm; Man. Dir ALMAMY B. JOBARTEH.

Takaful Gambia Ltd: 22 Serign Modou Sillah St, Banjul; tel. 4227480; fax 4229219; e-mail info@takaful.gm; Man. Dir MAMODOU M. JOOF.

Insurance Association

Insurance Association of The Gambia (IAG): Banjul; tel. 4229952; fax 4201637; e-mail info@iag.gm; internet www.iag.gm; f. 1987; Pres. DAWDA SARGE; Sec.-Gen. HENRY M. JAWO.

Trade and Industry

GOVERNMENT AGENCIES

The Gambia Investment and Export Promotion Agency (GIEPA): GIEPA House, 48A Kairaba Ave, Serrekunda, KMC, POB 757, Banjul; tel. 4377377; fax 4377379; e-mail info.gipfza@qanet.gm; internet www.gipfza.gm; f. 2001; fmrly The Gambia Investment Promotion and Free Zones Agency (f. 2001), the implementing agency of the Gateway Project, funded by the World Bank and the Gambian Government, responsible for fostering local and foreign direct investment; name changed as above in 2010; Chair. FATOU SINYAN MERGAN; CEO FATOU M. JALLOW.

Indigenous Business Advisory Services (IBAS): POB 2502, Bakau; tel. 4496098; e-mail payibas@gamtel.gm; Man. Dir MANGA SANYANG.

DEVELOPMENT AGENCY

The Gambia Rural Development Agency (GARDA): Soma Village, Jarra West, PMB 452, Serrekunda; tel. 4496676; fax 4390095; f. 1990; Exec. Dir KEBBA BAH.

CHAMBER OF COMMERCE

The Gambia Chamber of Commerce and Industry (GCCI): 55 Kairaba Ave, KSMD, POB 3382, Serrekunda; tel. 4378929; fax 4378936; e-mail gcci@gambiachamber.com; internet www.gambiachamber.com; f. 1967; Pres. BAI MATARR DRAMMEH; CEO EDRISSA MASS JOBE.

INDUSTRIAL AND TRADE ASSOCIATIONS

Association of Gambian Entrepreneurs (AGE): POB 200, Banjul; tel. 4393494.

The Gambia Cotton Growers Association: Banjul; Pres. ALPHA BAH; Sec.-Gen. OMAR SUMPO CEESAY.

UTILITIES

Public Utilities Regulatory Authority (PURA): 94 Kairaba Ave, Bakau; tel. 4399601; fax 4399905; e-mail info@pura.gm; internet www.pura.gm; f. 2001; monitors and enforces standards of performance by public utilities; Chair. ABDOULIE TOURAY; Dir-Gen. ALAGI B. GAYE.

National Water and Electricity Co Ltd (NAWEC): 53 Mamady Manjang Highway, Kanifing, POB 609, Banjul; tel. 4376607; fax 4375990; e-mail nawecmd@qanet.gm; internet www.nawec.gm; f. 1996; in 1999 control was transferred to the Bassau Development Corpn, Côte d'Ivoire, under a 15-year contract; electricity and water supply, sewerage services; Chair. MUSTAPHA COLLEY; Man. Dir MOMODOU JALLOW.

MAJOR COMPANIES

Banjul Breweries Ltd: Kanifing Industrial Estate, Kombo St Mary Division, POB 830, Banjul; tel. 4391863; fax 4392266; e-mail banbrew@gamtel.gm; internet www.julbrew.gm; f. 1975; Gen. Man. A. F. HUBERTS; 112 employees (2005).

Boule & Co Ltd: NTC Complex, 3/4 Liberation Ave, POB 602, Banjul; tel. 4228818; fax 4226694; e-mail info@bouleco.com; internet www.bouleco.com; f. 1976; general merchants; Chair. and Man. Dir CHARBEL N. ELHAJJ.

CFAO Gambia: POB 297, Mamadi Maniyang Hwy, 14 Liberation Ave, Banjul, Gambia; tel. 396906; internet www.cfaogroup.com; f. 1887; fmrly Compagnie Française de l'Afrique Occidental; general merchants; Man. Dir G. DURAND; 100 employees (2001).

K. Chellaram & Sons (Gambia) Ltd: Kanifing Industrial Estate, POB 275, Banjul; tel. 4392912; fax 4392910; e-mail nchellaram@aol.com; internet www.chellaramsgambia.com; f. 1958; importers and general merchants; Man. Dir NITIN R. CHELLARAM.

Elton Oil Gambia: 78 Atlantic Rd, Fajara, POB 4043, Bakau; tel. 4496690; fax 4496405; e-mail info@elton.gm; internet www.elton.gm; Chair. CHEIKH SADIBOU DIOP; Man. Dir EDRISSA MASS JOBE.

GALP Gambia Ltd: Independence Dr., POB 263, Banjul; tel. 4228028; fax 4227992; marketing and sale of petroleum products; Man. Dir JULIUS FREEMAN.

The Gambia Cotton Company (GAMCOT): Banjul; state-owned; scheduled for privatization; Gen. Man. WOPPA BALDEH.

The Gambia Groundnut Corpn (GGC): Banjul; distribution and marketing of groundnuts; subject to a take-over by the Government in Jan. 1999; 528 employees; Man. Dir ANTHONY CARVALHO.

Gamsen Construction: 50 Garba Jahumpa Rd, Bakau, POB 2844, Serrekunda; tel. 4497448; fax 4394766; construction and civil engineering; jtly owned by ALFRON and ATEPA Technologies, Senegal; Man. Dir AMADOU SAMBA.

Gamwater: 1 Gacem Rd, Kanifing Industrial Estate, POB 1880, Banjul; tel. 4378947; fax 4378374; Man. Dir AMADOU SAMBA.

Maurel and Prom: 22 Buckle St, Banjul; fax 4228942; general merchants; Man. J. ESCHENLOHR.

Moukhtara Holding Co Ltd (MHC): 10 Moukhtara St, Kanifing Industrial Estate, POB 447, Banjul; tel. 4392574; fax 4393085; e-mail moukhtara.gambia@gamtel.gm; internet www.moukhtara.com; f. 1975; holding co with interests in confectionery, educational books and stationery, timber, bricks, plastics, cosmetics and tissue paper; Man. Dir SAYED MOUKHTARA.

New Gambia Industrialists: 3 Essa Joof Rd, Kombo St, Kanifing, POB 954, Banjul; tel. 4373185; fax 4373185; e-mail ngi@qanet.gm; f. 1991; civil, mechanical and electrical design and construction; 20 employees.

Shyben A. Madi & Sons Ltd: 3 Liberation Ave, POB 184, Banjul; tel. 4226666; fax 4227377; e-mail sam.madi@gamtel.gm; internet www.sam.gm; general merchants; Man. Dir GEORGE S. MADI.

TAF Holding Co Ltd: Cemetery Rd, Kanifing Industrial Estate, POB 121, Banjul; tel. 4392333; fax 4390033; e-mail information.services@tafgambia.com; internet www.tafgambia.com; f. 1990; has subsidiaries in construction, real estate and tourism; Dir MUSTAPHA NJIE; 500 employees.

Zingli Manufacturing Co Ltd: Kanifing Industrial Estate, POB 2402, Serrekunda; tel. 4392282; mfrs of corrugated iron and wire.

TRADE UNIONS

Association of Gambian Sailors (AGS): c/o 31 OAU Blvd, POB 698, Banjul; tel. 4223080; fax 4227214; Sec.-Gen. ABDOU SANYANG.

The Gambia Dock and Maritime Workers' Union: Albert Market, POB 852, Banjul; tel. 4229448; fax 4225049; Sec.-Gen. LANDING SANYANG.

The Gambia National Trades Union Congress (GNTUC): Trade Union House, 31 OAU Blvd, POB 698, Banjul; Pres. MUSTAPHA WADA; Sec.-Gen. EBRIMA GARBA CHAM.

Gambia Teachers' Union (GTU): POB 133, Banjul; tel. and fax 4392075; e-mail gtu@gamtel.gm; f. 1937; Pres. LAMIN DARBOE (acting); Sec.-Gen. ANTOINETTE CORR-JACK.

The Gambia Workers' Confederation: Trade Union House, 72 OAU Blvd, POB 698, Banjul; tel. and fax 4222754; e-mail gambiawc@hotmail.com; f. 1958 as The Gambia Workers' Union; present name adopted in 1985; Sec.-Gen. PA MOMODOU FAAL; 52,000 mems (2007).

Transport

The Gambia Public Transport Corpn: Factory St, Kanifing Housing Estate, POB 801, Kanifing; tel. 4392230; fax 4392454; f. 1975; operates road transport and ferry services; Man. Dir BAKARY HUMA.

RAILWAYS

There are no railways in The Gambia.

ROADS

In 2004 there were an estimated 3,742 km of roads in The Gambia, of which 1,652 km were main roads, and 1,300 km were secondary roads. In that year only 19.3% of the road network was paved. Some roads are impassable in the rainy season. The expansion and upgrading of the road network is planned, as part of the Jammeh administration's programme to improve The Gambia's transport infrastructure. Among intended schemes is the construction of a motorway along the coast, with the aid of a loan of US $8.5m. from Kuwait. In early 1999 Taiwan agreed to provide $6m. for road construction programmes, and in early 2000 work began on the construction of a dual carriageway between Serrekunda, Mandina and Ba, supported by funds from the Islamic Development Fund and the Organization of the Petroleum Exporting Counties. In 2006 the European Union provided a grant of €44m. to rehabilitate five roads.

SHIPPING

The River Gambia is well suited to navigation. A weekly river service is maintained between Banjul and Basse, 390 km above Banjul, and a ferry connects Banjul with Barra. Small ocean-going vessels can reach Kaur, 190 km above Banjul, throughout the year. Facilities at the port of Banjul were modernized and expanded during the mid-1990s, with the aim of enhancing The Gambia's potential as a transit point for regional trade. In 1999 three advanced storage warehouses were commissioned with total storage space of 8,550 sq m. The Gambia's merchant fleet consisted of 15 vessels, totalling 34,635 grt, at 31 December 2009.

The Gambia Ports Authority: 34 Liberation Ave, POB 617, Banjul; tel. 4227269; fax 4227268; e-mail info@gamport.gm; internet www.gambiaports.com; f. 1972; Man. Dir MOHAMMED LAMIN GIBBA.

The Gambia Shipping Agency Ltd: 1A Cotton St, POB 257, Banjul; tel. 4227518; fax 4227929; e-mail Thomas.nielsen@bollore.com; f. 1984; shipping agents and forwarders; Gen. Man. THOMAS NIELSEN; 30 employees.

Interstate Shipping Co (Gambia) Ltd: 43 Buckle St, POB 220, Banjul; tel. 4229388; fax 4229347; e-mail interstate@gamtel.gm; transport and storage; Man. Dir B. F. SAGNIA.

Maersk Gambia Ltd: 80 OAU Blvd, POB 1399, Banjul; tel. 4224450; fax 4224025; e-mail gamsalimp@maersk.com; f. 1993; owned by Maersk Line.

CIVIL AVIATION

Banjul International Airport is situated at Yundum, 27 km from the capital. Construction of a new terminal, at a cost of some US $10m., was completed in late 1996. Facilities at Yundum have been upgraded by the US National Aeronautics and Space Administration, to enable the airport to serve as an emergency landing site for space shuttle vehicles.

The Gambia Civil Aviation Authority (GCAA): Banjul International Airport, Yundum; tel. 4472831; fax 4472190; e-mail dggcaa@qanet.gm; internet www.gambia.gm/gcaa; f. 1991; Man. Dir MALICK CHAM (acting).

The Gambia International Airlines: PMB 353, Banjul; tel. 4472770; fax 4223700; internet www.gia.gm; f. 1996; state-owned; sole handling agent at Banjul, sales agent; Chair. ISATOU HYDARA; Man. Dir BAKARY NYASSI (acting).

Slok Air International (Gambia) Ltd: 55 Kairaba Ave, POB 2697, Banjul; e-mail info@slok-air.com; internet www.slok-air.com; commenced operations in The Gambia in 2004; CEO ABDULKAREEM IDRIS.

Tourism

Tourists are attracted by The Gambia's beaches and also by its abundant birdlife. A major expansion of tourism facilities was carried out in the early 1990s. Although there was a dramatic decline in tourist arrivals in the mid-1990s (owing to the political instability), the tourism sector recovered well. In 2009 some 141,569 tourists visited The Gambia and in that year estimated earnings from tourism were US $64m. While visitor numbers remained constant in the late 2000s, the global financial crisis was reported to have impacted negatively on The Gambia's tourism industry, with earnings falling by some 35% between 2007 and 2009. An annual 'Roots Festival' was inaugurated in 1996, with the aim of attracting African-American visitors to The Gambia.

The Gambia Hotel Association: c/o Golden Beach Hotel, Coastal Rd, POB 2345, Bijilo; tel. 4465111; fax 4463722; e-mail gambiahotels@gamtel.gm; internet www.gambiahotels.gm; Chair. ALIEU SECKA.

The Gambia Tourist Authority: Kololi, POB 4085, Bakau; tel. 4462491; fax 4462487; e-mail info@gta.gm; internet www.visitthegambia.gm; f. 2001; Chair. and Dir-Gen. ALIEU MBOGE.

Defence

As assessed at November 2011, the Gambian National Army comprised 800 men (including a marine unit of about 70 and the National Guards) in active service. The Armed Forces comprise the Army, the Navy and the National Guards. Military service has been mainly voluntary; however, the Constitution of the Second Republic, which entered into full effect in January 1997, makes provision for conscription.

Defence Expenditure: Estimated at D189m. in 2010.

Chief of Defence Staff: Maj.-Gen. OUSMAN BADJIE.

Commander of the Gambian National Army: Brig.-Gen. SERIGN MODOU NJIE.

Commander of the Navy: Commodore SILLAH KUJABBIE (acting).

Education

Primary education, beginning at seven years of age, is free but not compulsory and lasts for nine years. It is divided into two cycles of six and three years. Secondary education, from 16 years of age, lasts for a further three years. According to UNESCO estimates, in 2009/10 total enrolment at primary schools included 66% of children in the relevant age-group (boys 64%; girls 67%), while secondary enrolment was equivalent to 54% of the appropriate age-group (boys 56%; girls 53%). The Jammeh administration has, since 1994, embarked on an ambitious project to improve educational facilities and levels of attendance and attainment. A particular aim has been to improve access to schools for pupils in rural areas. Post-secondary education is available in teacher training, agriculture, health and technical subjects. Some 1,591 students were enrolled at tertiary establishments in 1994/95. In 1977 The Gambia introduced Koranic studies at all stages of education, and many children attend Koranic schools (*daara*). The University of The Gambia, at Banjul, was officially opened in 2000. Some 2,842 students were enrolled at the university in 2009/10. In 2004 current expenditure by the central Government on education was an estimated D224.3m., equivalent to 17.5% of non-interest current expenditure.

Bibliography

Cooke, D., and Hughes, A. 'The Politics of Economic Recovery: The Gambia's Experience of Structural Adjustment, 1985–94', in *The Journal of Commonwealth and Comparative Politics,* Vol. 35, No. 1. London, Frank Cass, 1997.

Gray, J. M. *A History of the Gambia.* New York, Barnes & Noble, and London, Frank Cass, 1966.

Harrison Church, R. J. *West Africa.* 8th edn. London, Longman, 1979.

Hughes, A. 'From Colonialism to Confederation: The Gambian Experience of Independence 1965–1982', in Cohen, R. (Ed.), *African Islands and Enclaves.* London, Sage Publications, 1983.

'The Senegambian Confederation', in *Contemporary Review*, February 1984.

'The Collapse of the Senegambian Confederation', in *The Journal of Commonwealth and Comparative Politics,* Vol. 30, No. 2. London, Frank Cass, 1992.

Hughes, A. (Ed.). *The Gambia: Studies in Society and Politics.* Birmingham, University of Birmingham, Centre of West African Studies, 1991.

Hughes, A., and Gailey, A. *Historical Dictionary of The Gambia.* Metuchen, NJ, Scarecrow Press, 2000.

Hughes, A., and Perfect, D. *Political History of The Gambia, 1816–1994.* Woodbridge, James Currey, 2008.

Kanyongolo, E., and Norris, C. *The Gambia: Freedom of Expression Still Under Threat: The Case of Citizen FM.* London, Article 19, 1999.

Luom, M. *An Analysis of the Gambian Coup of 1994.* Ottawa, ON, Carleton University Press, 2001.

People's Progressive Party Special Editorial Commission. *The Voice of the People, the Story of the PPP, 1959–1989.* Banjul, The Gambia Communications Agency and Barou-Ueli Enterprises, 1992.

Radelet, S. 'Reform without Revolt: The Political Economy of Economic Reform in The Gambia', in *World Development*, Vol. 28, No. 8. Oxford, Pergamon Press, 1992.

Rice, B. *Enter Gambia: The Birth of an Improbable Nation.* London, Angus & Robertson, 1968.

Saine, A. S. *The Paradox of Third-wave Democratization in Africa: The Gambia Under AFPRC-APRC Rule, 1994-2008.* Lanham, MD, Lexington Books,2010.

Schroeder, R. A. *Shady Practices: Agroforestry and Gender Politics in The Gambia.* Berkeley, CA, University of California Press, 1999.

Sweeney, P. (Ed.). *The Gambia and Senegal.* London, APA, 1996.

Tomkinson, M. *Gambia.* 2nd edn. London, Michael Tomkinson Publishing, 2001.

Touray, O. *The Gambia and the World: A History of the Foreign Policy of Africa's Smallest State, 1965–1995.* Hamburg, Hamburg Institute of African Affairs, 2000.

Wiseman, J. A. *Democracy in Black Africa: Survival and Revival.* New York, Paragon House, 1990.

'Military Rule in The Gambia: An Interim Assessment', in *Third World Quarterly,* Vol. 17, No. 5. London, 1996.

'The Gambia: From Coup to Elections', in *Journal of Democracy,* Vol. 9, No. 2. Washington, DC, 1998.

Wiseman, J. A., and Chongan, E. I. *Military Rule and the Abuse of Human Rights in The Gambia: The View from Mile 2 Prison.* Trenton, NJ, Africa World Press, 2000.

Wiseman, J. A., and Vidler, E. 'The July 1994 Coup d'Etat in The Gambia: The End of an Era', in *The Round Table,* No. 333. Abingdon, Carfax, 1995.

Wright, D. R. *The World and A Very Small Place in Africa.* Armonk, NY, M. E. Sharpe, 1997.

GHANA

Physical and Social Geography

E. A. BOATENG

PHYSICAL FEATURES

Structurally and geologically, the Republic of Ghana exhibits many of the characteristics of sub-Saharan Africa, with its ancient rocks and extensive plateau surfaces marked by prolonged sub-aerial erosion. About one-half of the surface area is composed of Pre-Cambrian metamorphic and igneous rocks, most of the remainder consisting of a platform of Palaeozoic sediments believed to be resting on the older rocks. These sediments occupy a substantial area in the north-central part of the country and form the Voltaic basin. Surrounding this basin on all sides, except along the east, is a highly dissected peneplain of Pre-Cambrian rocks at an average of 150 m–300 m above sea-level but containing several distinct ranges of up to 600 m. Along the eastern edge of the Voltaic basin and extending right down to the sea near Accra is a narrow zone of highly folded Pre-Cambrian rocks forming the Akwapim-Togo ranges. These ranges rise to 300 m–900 m above sea-level, and contain the highest points in Ghana. Continuing northwards across Togo and Benin, they form one of west Africa's major relief features, the Togo-Atakora range.

The south-east corner of the country is occupied by the Accra-Ho-Keta plains, which are underlain by the oldest of the Pre-Cambrian series (known as the Dahomeyan) and contain extensive areas of gneiss, of which the basic varieties weather to form agriculturally useful soils. Extensive areas of young rocks, formed between the Tertiary and Recent ages, are found only in the broad delta of the Volta in the eastern part of the Accra plains, and in the extreme south-west corner of the country along the Axim coast; while in the intervening littoral zone patches of Devonian sediments combine with the rocks of the Pre-Cambrian peneplain to produce a coastline of sandy bays and rocky promontories.

Most of the country's considerable mineral wealth, consisting mainly of gold, diamonds, manganese and bauxite, is associated with the older Pre-Cambrian rocks, although petroleum has been discovered in commercial quantities in some of the younger sedimentaries.

The drainage is dominated by the Volta system, which occupies the Voltaic basin and includes the vast artificial lake of 8,502 sq km formed behind the hydroelectric dam at Akosombo. A second dam is sited at Kpong, 8 km downstream from Akosombo. Most of the other rivers in Ghana, such as the Pra, Birim, Densu, Ayensu and Ankobra, flow between the southern Voltaic or Kwahu plateau and the sea.

CLIMATE AND VEGETATION

Climatic conditions are determined by the interaction of two principal airstreams: the hot, dry, tropical, continental air mass or harmattan from the north-east, and the moist, relatively cool, maritime air mass or monsoon from the south-west across the Atlantic. In the southern part of the country, where the highest average annual rainfall (of 1,270 mm–2,100 mm) occurs, there are two rainy seasons (April–July and September–November), while in the north, with averages per year of 1,100 mm–1,270 mm, rainfall occurs in only a single season between April and September, followed by a long dry season dominated by the harmattan. There is much greater uniformity as regards mean temperatures, which average 26°C–29°C. These temperatures, coupled with the equally high relative humidities, which fall significantly only during the harmattan, tend to produce oppressive conditions, relieved only by the relative drop in temperature at night, especially in the north, and the local incidence of land and sea breezes near the coast.

Vegetation in Ghana is determined mainly by climate and soil conditions. The area of heavy annual rainfall broken by one or two relatively short dry seasons, to be found in the south-west portion of the country and along the Akwapim-Togo ranges, is covered with evergreen forest in the wetter portions and semi-deciduous forest in the drier portions, while the area of rather lower rainfall, occurring in a single peak in the northern two-thirds of the country and the anomalously dry area around Accra, is covered with savannah and scrub. Prolonged farming activities and timber exploitation have reduced the original closed forest vegetation, while in the savannah areas extensive cultivation and bush burning have also caused serious degradation of the vegetation.

POPULATION

Ghana covers an area of 238,533 sq km (92,098 sq miles). The September 2010 census recorded a population of 24,658,823, giving an approximate density of 103.4 inhabitants per sq km. At mid-2012, according to UN estimates, the population was 25,545,937 with a density of 107.1 inhabitants per sq km. The highest densities occur in the urban and cocoa-farming areas in the southern part of the country, and also in the extreme north-eastern corner, where intensive compound farming is practised.

There are no fewer than 75 spoken languages and dialects in Ghana, each more or less associated with a distinct ethnic group. The largest of these groups are the Akan (comprising about one-half of Ghana's population), Mossi, Ewe and the Ga-Adangme. Any divisive tendencies that might have arisen from this situation have been absent, largely as a result of government policies; however, a distinction can be made between the southern peoples, who have come most directly and longest under the recent influence of European life and the Christian religion, and the northern peoples, whose traditional modes of life and religion have undergone relatively little change, owing mainly to their remoteness from the coast. One of the most potent unifying forces has been the adoption of English as the official language, although it is augmented by eight major national languages.

Recent History

RICHARD SYNGE

Following the Second World War, a sustained political campaign to secure independence for the Gold Coast from British colonial rule led to the emergence in 1949 of the Convention People's Party. Its leader, Dr Kwame Nkrumah, became Prime Minister of an indigenous ministerial Government popularly elected in 1951. Subsequent progress towards full independence followed a UN-supervised plebiscite in May 1956, when the British-administered section of Togoland, a UN Trust Territory, voted to join the Gold Coast in an independent state. On 6 March 1957 the new state of Ghana was granted independence within the Commonwealth, becoming the first British dependency in sub-Saharan Africa to attain independence under majority rule. Ghana became a republic on 1 July 1960, with Nkrumah as executive President.

Under Nkrumah's leadership, Ghana established close relations with the USSR and its allies, while remaining economically dependent on Western countries. Following widespread discontent at the country's worsening economic problems, and at widespread political corruption, Nkrumah was deposed by a military coup in February 1966, led by Gen. Joseph Ankrah. In October 1969 power was returned to an elected civilian Government led by Dr Kofi Busia, a prominent opposition activist from the Nkrumah period. In January 1972 the armed forces again took power, under the leadership of Lt-Col (later Gen.) Ignatius Kutu Acheampong. In 1977 his military junta announced its intention to relinquish power to a new government following a general election, to take place in June 1979. These arrangements, however, were forestalled in July 1978 by Lt-Gen. (later Gen.) Frederick Akuffo, the Chief of the Defence Staff, who assumed power in a bloodless coup.

THE RAWLINGS COUPS

Tensions within the armed forces became evident in May 1979 when a group of junior military officers led by Flt-Lt Jerry Rawlings staged an unsuccessful coup attempt. Following a brief period in detention, Rawlings and his associates successfully seized power, amid great popular acclaim. In June Rawlings formed an Armed Forces Revolutionary Council (AFRC), and Acheampong, Akuffo and other senior officers were swiftly tried, convicted of corruption and executed.

The AFRC indicated that its assumption of power was temporary, and the general election took place in June 1979, as scheduled. The People's National Party (PNP), led by Dr Hilla Limann, emerged with the largest number of parliamentary seats and formed a coalition Government with support from the smaller United National Convention. Dr Limann took office as President in September. However, dissatisfaction with measures taken by the Government to improve the economy provoked renewed discontent within the armed forces. On 31 December 1981 Rawlings seized power for the second time, assuming the chairmanship of a Provisional National Defence Council (PNDC). On this occasion, Rawlings expressed no intention of restoring power to civilian politicians; instead, the PNDC adopted measures to 'democratize' political decision-making and to decentralize power. City and district councils were replaced by People's Defence Committees, in an attempt to create mass participation at local level, and to encourage public vigilance.

The 'democratization' of the army led to the creation of factions, and to increasing divisions between military personnel along ethnic lines. Unsuccessful attempts to overthrow Rawlings were reported in November 1982 and in early 1983. Although Rawlings and the PNDC remained under challenge from exiled opponents, there was some improvement in economic conditions during 1984. During 1985, however, the PNDC detected a further attempt from within the army to overthrow the regime.

CONSTITUTIONAL TRANSITION

In 1990 there were increasing demands for an end to the ban on political activities and associations, and for the abolition of a number of laws, particularly those concerning the detention of suspects. In July of that year, in response to pressure from Western donors to increase democracy in return for a continuation in aid, the PNDC announced that a National Commission for Democracy (NCD), under the chairmanship of Justice Daniel Annan, a member of the PNDC, would organize a series of regional debates, which would review the decentralization process and consider Ghana's political and economic future.

In late March 1991 the NCD presented its report, which recommended the election of an executive President for a fixed term, the establishment of a legislature and the creation of the post of Prime Minister. In May the PNDC endorsed the restoration of a plural political system, and accepted the NCD's recommendations. A 260-member Consultative Assembly was established, which was to review recommendations by a government-appointed committee of constitutional experts. A new constitution was subsequently to be submitted for endorsement by a national referendum.

In March 1992 Rawlings announced a programme for constitutional transition and the Consultative Assembly endorsed the majority of the constitutional recommendations, which were subsequently presented for approval by the PNDC. However, the proposed creation of the post of Prime Minister was rejected by the Assembly; executive power was to be vested solely in the President, who would appoint a Vice-President. In addition, the draft constitution included a provision that members of the Government be exempt from prosecution for acts committed during the PNDC's rule. At a national referendum held on 28 April, however, the adoption of the draft constitution was approved by 92% of votes cast, with 43.7% of the electorate voting. In May the Government introduced legislation that ended the ban on the formation of political associations; political parties were required to apply to the Interim National Electoral Commission (INEC) for legal recognition. Under the terms of the legislation, however, 21 former political organizations remained proscribed, while emergent parties were not permitted to use the names or slogans of these organizations.

In June 1992 a number of political organizations emerged, many of which were established by supporters of former politicians; six opposition groups subsequently obtained legal status. In the same month a coalition of pro-Government organizations, the National Democratic Congress (NDC), was formed to contest the elections on behalf of the PNDC. However, an existing alliance of supporters of Rawlings, the Eagle Club, refused to join the NDC, and formed the Eagle Party of Ghana, subsequently known as the EGLE (Every Ghanaian Living Everywhere) Party.

In September 1992, in accordance with the new Constitution, Rawlings retired from the armed forces (although he retained the title of Commander-in-Chief of the Armed Forces in his capacity as Head of State), and was subsequently chosen as the presidential candidate of the NDC. (The NDC later formed an electoral coalition with the EGLE Party and the National Convention Party—NCP.) A member of the NCP, Kow Nkensen Arkaah, became Rawlings' vice-presidential candidate. Four other political groups nominated presidential candidates: the People's Heritage Party (PHP); the National Independence Party (NIP); the People's National Convention (PNC, which nominated ex-President Limann); and the New Patriotic Party (NPP). Although the establishment of a united opposition to Rawlings was discussed, the parties failed to achieve agreement, owing, in part, to the apparent conviction of the NPP (which was recognized as the strongest of the movements) that its presidential candidate could defeat Rawlings.

Less than 48.3% of the registered electorate voted in the presidential election, which took place on 3 November 1992.

Rawlings secured 58.3% of the vote, defeating the NPP candidate, Prof. A. A. Boahen, who won 30.4%. The Commonwealth observers declared that the election had been free and fair. However, the opposition parties, led by the NPP, claimed that widespread electoral irregularities had taken place. Incidents of violence and rioting by opposition supporters ensued, in which an NDC ward chairman was killed; in addition, a series of explosive devices were detonated in Accra and Tema. A prominent member of the PHP was later detained, together with other opposition supporters, accused of complicity in the bombings. The Government rescheduled the legislative elections for 22 December.

In early December 1992 Boahen announced that the opposition had direct evidence of electoral fraud perpetrated by the Government. The opposition parties declared, however, that they would not legally challenge the result of the presidential election, but that they would boycott the forthcoming general election. Accordingly, these elections (which had been again postponed until 29 December) were contested only by the NDC and its allies, the EGLE Party and the NCP. On this basis, the NDC obtained 189 of the 200 seats in the Parliament, while the NCP secured eight seats, the EGLE Party one seat and independent candidates two seats. On 7 January 1993 Rawlings was sworn in as President of the Fourth Republic, the PNDC was dissolved and the new Parliament was inaugurated.

THE FOURTH REPUBLIC

In early January 1993 a number of severe economic austerity measures were introduced under the 1993 budget. The NPP, the PNC, the NIP and the PHP subsequently formed an alliance, the Inter-Party Co-ordinating Committee (ICC), which strongly criticized the budget (widely believed to have been formulated under terms approved by the World Bank and the IMF), and announced that it was to act as an official opposition to the Government, despite its lack of representation in Parliament. In mid-April elections were held for the 10 regional seats in the consultative Council of State, and in May a new Council of Ministers (which included several members of the former PNDC administration) was sworn in. However, the member parties of the ICC continued to dispute the results of the presidential election. In August the NPP announced that it was prepared to recognize the legitimacy of the election results, thereby undermining the solidarity of the ICC. In December the PHP, the NIP and a faction of the PNC (all of which represented supporters of ex-President Nkrumah) merged to form the People's Convention Party (PCP).

Ethnic Tensions

In February 1994 long-standing hostility between the Konkomba ethnic group, which originated in former Togoland, and the landowning Nanumba escalated, following demands by the Konkomba for traditional status that would entitle them to own land; some 500 people were killed in ethnic clashes in the Northern Region. Government troops were dispatched to restore order and imposed a state of emergency in seven districts for a period of three months; however, skirmishes between a number of ethnic factions continued, and it was reported that some 6,000 Konkomba had fled to Togo.

In June 1994 the seven ethnic factions involved in the fighting signed a peace agreement that provided for the imposition of an immediate cease-fire and renounced violence as a means of settling disputes over land ownership. The Government subsequently announced that troops were to be permanently stationed in the Northern Region in order to pre-empt further conflict, and appointed a negotiating team, which was to attempt to resolve the inter-ethnic differences. In August the state of emergency was finally ended. In March 1995 the Government again imposed a curfew in the Northern Region, in response to renewed ethnic violence, in which about 100 people were killed. In April a joint committee, comprising prominent members of the Konkomba and Nanumba ethnic groups, was established in an effort to resolve the conflict.

There was a further upsurge in ethnic tensions in the Northern Region in the early 2000s, when competition between the two ruling Dagomba clans, the Andani and the Abudu, culminated in the abduction and murder of the king of the Dagomba, Ya Na Yakubu Andani, in Yendi in March 2002. The event provoked further severe clashes, in which more than 30 people were killed, and most subsequent government attempts to resolve the crisis in the region proved politically contentious.

Elected Government

Presidential and legislative elections took place, as scheduled, on 7 December 1996. Rawlings was re-elected President by 57.2% of the votes cast, while John Kufuor of the NPP secured 39.8% of the votes. In the parliamentary poll the NDC's representation was reduced to 133 seats, while the NPP won 60 seats (and a further one in June 1997, owing to a postponed contest), the PCP five and the PNC one seat. Despite opposition claims of malpractice, international observers declared that the elections had been conducted fairly, and an electoral turnout of 76.8% was reported. On 7 January 1997 Rawlings was again sworn in as President.

In August 1998 the NCP and the PCP merged to form a new movement, the Convention Party (CP, later renamed the Convention People's Party—CPP, in honour of Nkrumah's party of the same name). In October the NPP again nominated Kufuor as its presidential candidate, to contest the election scheduled to take place in 2000. Under the terms of the Constitution, Rawlings was prohibited from seeking re-election to a third term in office, and had announced that the incumbent Vice-President, Prof. John Evans Atta Mills, was to contest the election on behalf of the NDC. At an NDC congress, which took place in December, the party constitution was amended to create the position for Rawlings of 'Life Chairman' of the party. Following dissatisfaction within the NDC at the changes carried out at the party congress, in June 1999 a disaffected group of party members formed a new political group, the National Reform Party (NRP).

Rawlings Replaced by Kufuor

Despite instances of pre-election violence, voting took place relatively peacefully on 7 December 2000. One of the principal concerns of voters in the preceding months was the deteriorating state of the economy (during 2000 alone there was a surge in inflation and a collapse in the value of the cedi), but there was also a strong movement in favour of political change, particularly in the more prosperous southern and western parts of the country. In the first round of the presidential election, which was contested by seven candidates, Kufuor secured 48.2% of the votes, compared to 44.5% for Atta Mills (representing the NDC), a result that necessitated a second round of voting later in the month. In the legislative elections, the NPP won 100 of the 200 seats; the NDC lost its majority in Parliament and returned 92 seats. In the second round of the presidential election, Kufuor, benefiting from declarations of support from all the minor parties, defeated Atta Mills, with 56.9% of the votes.

The incoming Government indicated that it would undertake investigations into cases of suspected corruption by members of the former NDC administration. The Kufuor Government's primary concern was, however, to restore stability and growth to the economy, and, controversially, it opted to seek full debt relief under the initiative for heavily indebted poor countries of the World Bank and the IMF. The Government also moved to establish a 'truth and reconciliation' process to examine human rights abuses committed in Ghana since independence. An important example of this new political emphasis was the exhumation of the remains of the military officers executed in 1979 and the return of these remains to their families in December 2001. The establishment of the National Reconciliation Commission (NRC) in May 2002 opened up a channel for complaints about human rights abuses and torture committed by previous Governments. By the end of that year the NRC had received nearly 3,000 complaints, mostly relating to events that took place under previous military regimes, and it commenced a series of public hearings in January 2003. One of the first to testify was a member of Nkrumah's presidential guard, who was held after the 1966 coup for 22 months. Other witnesses recounted torture suffered under the Rawlings regime. The NDC accused the Government of conducting a political witch-hunt against members of the former regime, but Rawlings himself appeared before the NRC in February 2004, when he denied direct knowledge of extra-judicial killings.

'Fast-track' court procedures were established to accelerate the delivery of justice in general, as well as specifically to deal with the cases that involved former office-holders. In December 2001 a former Deputy Minister of Finance in the Rawlings administration, Victor Selormey, was found guilty of diverting US $1.3m. of public money and was sentenced to eight years' imprisonment. In April 2003 a 'fast-track' court gaoled three former officials of the NDC for their involvement in securing a $20m. loan for a rice-growing project that never materialized.

Among the first signs of economic improvement was a decline in the rate of depreciation of the cedi during 2001. There was also an increase in remittances by private individuals and companies abroad. However, despite an overall increase in business confidence, the new Government encountered significant political difficulties in pushing forward its liberalization policies and in persuading public opinion of the need for more comprehensive privatization of state-owned enterprises, in part because of the fear of further inflation. Although occasionally challenged by Rawlings and by reports of potentially inappropriate financial dealings, the Kufuor administration's authority appeared to be enhanced by its commitment to reconciliation and accountability. At an NPP delegates' conference in January 2003, Kufuor was selected unopposed as the party's presidential candidate for the election due in 2004. Atta Mills successfully defeated his challengers and was again nominated as the NDC's candidate.

Presidential and legislative elections were held concurrently on 7 December 2004, and were notable for their high rate of voter participation, officially recorded at 85.1%. The elections were conducted without violence and were widely judged to be free and fair. Kufuor was re-elected President, with 52.5% of the vote, while Atta Mills secured 44.6%. Of the 230 parliamentary seats, the NPP won 128, the NDC 94, the PNC four, the CPP three and an independent candidate one. The new Parliament was inaugurated on 7 January 2005. Kufuor and Aliu Mahama were sworn in as President and Vice-President, respectively.

At the national congresses of the NPP and the NDC in December 2005 there were significant changes among party office holders. The NPP Chairman, Haruna Esseku, was replaced by Pete Mac Manu following allegations of financial abuse, prompting an inquiry by the Serious Fraud Office, while several senior NDC office holders, known to be opposed to the continued dominance of Rawlings, were voted out of office, prompting others in the party to resign. Dr Kwabena Adjei was elected Chairman of the NDC. Observers noted considerable jockeying for senior positions in both parties; none the less, in 2006 the NDC once again chose Atta Mills as its presidential candidate for 2008.

In May 2007 the Electoral Commission convened a meeting to discuss a proposal that would allow Ghanaians living abroad to vote in national elections. The controversial proposed amendment to the Representation of the People Act resulted in public protests and the NDC boycotting Parliament; the opposition party also threatened to reject the results of the forthcoming legislative and presidential elections, scheduled for December 2008, should the law be promulgated. In July 2007 Kufuor effected substantial changes to the Government, following the resignations of a number of ministers who intended to contest the 2008 presidential election. The number of ministers and deputy ministers was reportedly increased to 82; most notably Albert Kan Dapaah, hitherto Minister of the Interior, was appointed Minister of Defence, while the former Minister for Information and National Orientation, Kwamena Bartels, assumed the interior portfolio. In December 2007 nominations for candidates to the presidency were announced; Nana Akufo-Addo, who had held the foreign affairs portfolio until July, was to represent the NPP, while Mahama was to contest the election on behalf of the PNC. Dr Kwesi Ndoum of the CPP also presented his candidacy.

Early 2008 saw several cabinet changes; in January President Kufuor dismissed Minister of National Security Francis Poku following disagreements between the minister and the Inspector-General of Police, Patrick Kwateng Acheampong. Poku reportedly refused to accept Acheampong's authority. In March the Minister of Energy, Joseph Kofi Adda, was dismissed amid claims of poor performance, although no official reason was cited. Felix Owusu-Adjepong, formerly Minister of Parliamentary Affairs, was named as Adda's replacement.

Further ministerial changes were implemented in May 2008, including the dismissal of Bartels from the Ministry of the Interior. Former Minister of Defence Dr Kwame Addo-Kufuor was appointed to replace him. In March two people were killed when ethnic violence broke out in the Upper East Region of the country shortly after Bartels had announced a review of a curfew on the Bawku Township. Two further deaths were reported in late May at a time when clashes over land ownership in the Northern Region were reported. The volatile situation was understood to be a factor leading to Bartels' dismissal.

The 2008 Elections

The December 2008 elections were largely seen as a decisive moment for Ghana. President Kufuor's neutrality in the NPP primaries was questioned in some sections of the media following speculation that he preferred Alan Kyeremanteng's candidature to that of Akufo-Addo. This perceived bias of Kufuor against Akufo-Addo, to some extent, accounted for the polarization of the party hierarchy along ethnic lines, especially between the Ashanti and the Akyem caucuses in the party. Akufo-Addo subsequently selected Dr Alhaji Mahamudu Bawumiah, then Deputy Governor of the Bank of Ghana, as his running mate in the elections after a series of consultations with the party hierarchy, but his selection was strategically linked to the co-ordination of the campaign in the northern part of the country and the expected votes for the party from that region. The NDC party congress meanwhile selected Atta Mills as its presidential candidate for the third consecutive occasion, but Atta Mills's choice of John Dramani Mahama as a running mate was met with stiff opposition from Rawlings (opening a new rift within the NDC). However, the choice of Mahama was considered to be a master-stroke by many political analysts in Ghana. Significantly, in the immediate aftermath of the NDC and NPP congresses to select presidential candidates, two new political parties emerged to contest the elections. The Democratic Freedom Party emerged from the NDC, while the Patriotic Freedom Party defected from the NPP.

The campaign process was excessively characterized by violence and personal attacks, and the issue of ethnicity was used by both the NDC and the NPP. The Elections Security Task Force (ESTF), a joint collaboration between the various security agencies and some key civilian agencies, was formed as a national institution to provide security before, during and after the elections. The national ESTF was headed by the Inspector-General of the police force, with the same structures replicated at the regional and district levels.

In the presidential election, held on 7 December 2008, Akufo-Addo received the highest number of votes cast, gaining 49.1% of the vote, but failed to win the outright 50% plus one vote required by the Constitution. Consequently, a run-off ballot was held on 28 December between Akufo-Addo and the second placed candidate, Atta Mills, who received 47.9% of the votes cast in the first round. The run-off ballot resulted in a narrow victory for Atta Mills of the NDC, with 50.2% of the vote, but he also failed to obtain the required number of votes for him to emerge as the winner in the second round. A rerun poll at Tain on 2 January 2009, which Atta Mills won, became the deciding constituency, and he was subsequently declared President-elect by the Chairman of the Electoral Commission. In addition, the NDC won the majority of the parliamentary seats in the legislative elections, which were also held on 7 December 2008, securing 113 seats in Parliament. The NPP received 109 seats, the PNC two, and the CPP one, while independents obtained four seats, with the result in one constituency undeclared.

Transition from Kufuor to Atta Mills

In accordance with the Constitution, Atta Mills was sworn into office on 7 January 2009. Upon assumption of office, President Mills promised to ensure accountability and the rule of law. He also put in place a transitional team, made up of members of both the incoming and outgoing parties, but was hindered by the public outcry relating to the *ex-gratia* claims in the

Chinery-Hesse report, which had been commissioned by President Kufuor to determine the end of service benefits for former Presidents and other public officials. Despite tension between the presidency and members of Parliament, most of the President's ministerial nominees were approved by Parliament in March 2009.

The 'Better Ghana' agenda promised by the NDC was criticized by the opposition NPP when the 'one hundred days in office' targets, as outlined in the NDC manifesto, were assessed. The NPP censured the Government for failing to fulfil its promises. The President, on the other hand, stated that the Government had achieved 80% of its mandate under the 100-day pledges. However, shortages in the supply of pre-mix fuel for fishing activities in August 2009 attracted much criticism from the media and the opposition. This prompted the Government to institute a number of measures, including changing the colour of the pre-mix products in order to prevent adulteration by unscrupulous operators in the supply market.

Shortly after assumption of office in January 2009, the key indicators of the national economy started to show signs of decline as the effects of the global financial crisis began to be felt. The cedi depreciated against the major international trading currencies, interest rates increased, and inflation rose with marginal national reserve cover. While the Government claimed that the economy it inherited had been mismanaged, the opposing NPP argued that it had left the economy in a robust state. However, the negative trends in the macroeconomic indicators subsequently reversed, and, owing to a combination of factors such as the provision of an IMF loan facility of US $602.6m. and prudent fiscal management, the economy began to show signs of stability in the second quarter of 2009.

The Rule of Law and Public Accountability

Shortly after assuming office, the new NDC Government instituted a commission of inquiry to investigate the 'Ghana @ 50' celebrations held under the erstwhile NPP administration in 2007. A three-member committee was established, chaired by Justice Isaac Duose, an Appeals Court Judge, to examine allegations of financial misappropriation and corruption during the celebrations at national, regional and district levels. The central figure in the investigation was former Chief of Staff Dr Wreko Brobbey, who had been the Chief Executive of the 'Ghana @ 50' Secretariat. Charges were brought against him, and against Asamoah Boateng, the former Minister of Information in the Kufuor administration, his wife and six others for their alleged involvement in a contract deal to undertake renovation work at the Ministry of Information without following due process. The former head of the National Investment Bank, Daniel Charles Gyimah, also stood trial on a count of wilfully causing financial losses of US $60m. to the State. These and other cases were still in court in 2011—a situation that prompted former President Rawlings to accuse the Atta Mills Government of being in league with the NPP to overlook corrupt practices on both sides of the political divide.

The Minister of Health, Dr George Sepa Yankey, and the Minister of State at the Presidency, Seidu Amadu, resigned in early October 2009 following allegations that they had accepted bribes from a British construction company, which had the previous month been ordered by a British court to pay fines of more than US $7m. for offering illegal payments to officials in Ghana in the 1990s. President Mills subsequently appointed Benjamin Kunbour and Joseph Nii Laryea Afotey Agbo as Minister of Health and Minister of State at the Presidency, respectively. An investigation into the conduct of the two former ministers was promised.

Security Agencies and Human Rights

The security agencies, mainly the police and Bureau of National Investigations (BNI), have been involved in the pursuit of public accountability and combating crime in the country. After the establishment of the Atta Mills administration, the BNI initiated the arrest and interrogation of former government functionaries such as former Chief of Staff Kwadwo Mpiani, and Asamoah Boateng, who attempted to travel out of the country on two occasions while under investigation. These arrests were described by the NPP as 'witch hunting' of party functionaries by the Atta Mills administration. The NPP also questioned why the arrests were carried out by the BNI and not the police. Moreover, human rights issues were raised due to the way the BNI conducted its operations, using methods including the interrogation of suspects without their lawyers, and the seizure of passports. The courts decided that the confiscation of travel documents, such as passports, and interrogation of suspects without their legal counsels were acts that violated the human rights of persons under investigation and interrogation. The declaration by the courts had far-reaching implications on the limits of the powers of the security agencies and how these powers can be used. It was unclear how such declarations by the courts might impact on the campaign for public accountability and crime prevention. Renewed efforts by the police to counter armed robbery, for instance, involved a 'shoot and kill' policy, which was widely criticized by some security and human rights analysts. The Commission on Human Rights and Administrative Justice hinted that the police were justified in the 'shoot and kill' policy, but only if the circumstances demanded that such a method be applied for self-defence. The police, however, have been cautioned against abuses of such powers.

Another significant factor regarding the operations of the BNI and former government officials was the mobilization of party supporters to besiege the premises of investigative agencies, as happened in the case of Asamoah Boateng during his detention by the BNI in August 2009. A similar event occurred during the 2008 elections when party supporters belonging to the NDC and the NPP took turns to besiege the premises of the Electoral Commission, demanding that the results be called in their favour. It took the timely intervention of the security services to prevent violent confrontations between the two parties. The violence that characterized such actions appeared to reflect a growing culture of lawlessness and impunity in Ghanaian politics. In August 2008, at the Ghana Journalists' Association Best Journalist Awards ceremony, Vice-President Mahama cautioned the security agencies to respect the human rights of people under investigation while appealing to the public to desist from acts preventing the security agencies from conducting their legitimate duties.

Proposed Constitutional Revision and the Death of Atta Mills

In January 2010 President Mills inaugurated a nine-member Constitution Review Commission (CRC), chaired by Prof. Albert K. Fiadjoe, which was charged with recommending changes to the 1992 Constitution for approval (or rejection) at a referendum. Among changes believed to be under consideration were the abolition of the death penalty, a redistribution and separation of power between the presidential executive and the legislature, and the placing of a limit on the number of ministers the President was allowed to appoint. Later in January 2010 Mills carried out a reorganization of the Government. Most notably, Martin Amidu, a former Deputy Attorney-General, became Minister of the Interior, while changes were also made to the information, tourism and employment and social welfare portfolios. Community and district constitutional review consultations, with the aim of providing all citizens with the opportunity to contribute to the work of the CRC, began in five regions in April 2010 and continued into 2011. In December 2011 Atta Mills received the CRC's final report, which recommended, *inter alia*, restricting the President's power of appointment, strengthening Parliament and the independence of the judiciary, and greater decentralization to local government. The report also advocated the creation of a National Development Planning Commission, the abrogation of the death penalty and, controversially, the preservation of the constitutional clauses granting former PNDC members immunity from prosecution.

A further government reorganization was effected in January 2011 when the Attorney-General and Minister of Justice, Betty Mould-Iddrisu, was moved to the Ministry of Education, in an apparent rebuke for the lack of progress of several government cases in court. Her replacement was Amidu, who was himself replaced as Minister of the Interior by the former Minister of Health, Dr Benjamin Kunbour. The Minister of Youth and Sports, Akua Sena Dansua, was moved to the Ministry of Tourism after being heavily criticized for alleged interference in football administration.

Persistent and widely broadcast criticism by former President Rawlings of the performance of Atta Mills and his administration, starting from the time of his inauguration in 2009, eventually led to an open split within the NDC in 2011. Rawlings' wife, Nana Konadu Agyeman Rawlings, resigned her vice-chairmanship of the party in April and announced her intention to bid to be selected as the presidential candidate at the party's convention in July. Significant campaigning around the country, involving fierce denunciations by each side of the other, reached a climax in June. The principal accusation regularly made by Rawlings himself was that the Atta Mills Government was as guilty of corruption as he claimed that the NPP had been during its eight years in office. In the event, Atta Mills secured the NDC presidential nomination after winning 97% of the votes cast, reinforcing his control over the party. (Akufo Addo had again been elected as the NPP's presidential candidate in August 2010.)

Another highly divisive issue underlying the open rift in the NDC was Rawlings' demand that the killers of the Dagomba king, Ya Na Yakubu Andani, in March 2002 be brought to justice. Following new investigations, a murder trial of 14 accused persons opened at the 'fast-track' High Court in Accra in September 2010, prompting violent clashes between the rival Andani and Abudu clans outside the courthouse. In March 2011, after the court acquitted and discharged the 14 defendants, owing to a lack of prosecution evidence, the Government filed a notice of appeal against the court ruling. However, Rawlings and his wife renewed their allegations of a conspiracy to protect the king's killers and accused Atta Mills of failing to keep one of his main election promises.

In late January 2012, following the dismissal of Amidu from his posts as Attorney-General and Minister of Justice (he had earlier accused a number of cabinet ministers of having been involved in a corruption scandal) and the resignation of Mould-Iddrisu as Minister of Education, President Atta Mills carried out a government reorganization. Among the new appointments, William Kwasi Aboah became the new Minister of the Interior, Kunbour assumed responsibility for the justice portfolio and Lee Ocran was appointed as the new Minister of Education.

On 24 July 2012 President Atta Mills, who had reportedly been ill for some time, died in a military hospital in Accra. In accordance with the Constitution, Vice-President Mahama assumed the presidency on the same day and was to remain in office pending the holding of a presidential election in December. Tens of thousands of people attended Atta Mills' state funeral, which was held in Accra on 10 August, and three days of national mourning were declared.

FOREIGN RELATIONS

Relations with Togo have frequently been strained, in particular as a result of the presence in Ghana of opponents of the Togolese President, Gnassingbé Eyadéma (see the chapter on Togo). By late 1992 more than 100,000 Togolese had taken refuge in Ghana, following the deterioration in the political situation in Togo. In January 1993 Ghana announced that its armed forces were to be mobilized, in reaction to concern at the increasing civil unrest in Togo. In March the Government of Togo accused Ghana of supporting an armed attack on the military camp at Lomé, the Togolese capital, where Eyadéma resided. In January 1994 a further attack on Eyadéma's residence was attributed by the Togolese authorities to armed dissidents based in Ghana, again contributing to a deterioration in relations between the neighbouring states. The Ghanaian chargé d'affaires in Togo was subsequently arrested, while Togolese forces killed 12 Ghanaians and bombarded a customs post at Aflao and several villages near the two countries' common border. Ghana, however, denied the accusations of involvement in the coup attempt and threatened to retaliate against further acts of aggression. In May allegations by the Togolese Government that Ghana had been responsible (owing to lack of border security) for bomb attacks in Togo further heightened tensions. Later that year, however, relations between the two countries improved, and in November full diplomatic links were formally restored, with the appointment of a Ghanaian ambassador in Togo. In February 1996 both parliaments established friendship groups to examine ways of easing tensions. By the end of 1996 some 48,000 Togolese refugees were estimated to have received payment for voluntary repatriation. Against this background of strained relations with Togo, the election of Kufuor in December 2000 quickly resulted in an improvement. There was a resumption of normal movements across the common border and a restoration of regular business dealings. Subsequently, Kufuor's Government played a conciliatory role after the death of Eyadéma in February 2005, at a time when other countries were expressing outrage at the unconstitutional seizure of power on behalf of the late Togolese President's son, Faure Gnassingbé. Following the presidential election held in Togo in April 2005, at which Gnassingbé secured a decisive victory, bilateral relations were expected further to improve. However, following Gnassingbé's election, by July some 15,000 Togolese refugees had registered in Ghana. In August 2009 President Gnassingbé visited Ghana for meetings with President Atta Mills and senior security officials to discuss improved border security and the control of cross-border crime and drugs- and people-trafficking. In May 2010 it was reported that some 3,500 refugees had fled from Ghana into northern Togo, as a result of renewed ethnic conflict and land disputes in the north of the country.

Ghana participated in the Economic Community of West African States (ECOWAS) Cease-fire Monitoring Group (ECOMOG) peace-keeping force, which was dispatched to Liberia in August 1990 following the outbreak of conflict between government and rebel forces in that country (see the chapter on Liberia). The Ghanaian contingent remained in ECOMOG while Rawlings (in his role as Chairman of the Conference of Heads of State and Government of ECOWAS) mediated continuing negotiations between the warring Liberian factions. Financial assistance was received from the Government of Canada for the care of the Liberian refugees, whose numbers had risen to 42,000 by late 2004, by which time many were beginning to be repatriated. In 2003 Ghana also hosted peace negotiations concerning Liberia, and from September contributed troops to the ECOWAS Mission in Liberia (ECOMIL). In October the Ghanaian troops were transferred to a longer-term UN stabilization force, the UN Mission in Liberia (UNMIL), which replaced ECOMIL, with a mandate to support the implementation of a comprehensive peace agreement in that country. By the end of 2010 the number of Liberian refugees remaining in Ghana had fallen to 11,585. Due to the improving security climate in Liberia, in June 2012 the Ghanaian Government revoked the refugee status that had been granted to Liberians who had fled the conflict in their country. Henceforth, former refugees would be required to return to Liberia or apply for residency in Ghana. In February 2010 the Liberian President, Ellen Johnson-Sirleaf, made a two-day visit to Ghana following which it was agreed to reactivate the Ghana-Liberia Permanent Joint Commission for Co-operation. Ghana contributed 736 personnel to UNMIL at December 2011.

In June 1997 the Ghanaian Government announced the establishment of a task force to monitor the situation in Sierra Leone, following a military coup in the previous month (see the chapter on Sierra Leone); troops were dispatched to participate in a peace-keeping force. Following the reinstatement of the democratically elected Government in March, ECOMOG units remained in the country and continued to launch attacks against rebel forces, which still retained control of a number of areas. In December 2005 the Ghanaian troops participating in the UN Mission in Sierra Leone (UNAMSIL) returned to Ghana on the termination of the peace-keeping mission.

As ECOWAS Chairman for 2002/03, President Kufuor played an active role in searching for solutions to the severe ethnic and political divisions that emerged in Côte d'Ivoire from September 2002. In a series of meetings staged in Accra, he was able to keep lines of communication open between the Ivorian President, Laurent Gbagbo, and the opposition parties and rebel movements within Côte d'Ivoire. As negotiations progressed towards the implementation of a peace process from March 2003, Ghanaian troops were despatched to participate in an ECOWAS peace-keeping mission in Côte d'Ivoire, the only troops from an English-speaking country to do so. A conference held in Accra in August 2004 led to the signing of a peace accord between rival Ivorian factions. During 2005 there were several reports of infiltration by armed groups across the border from northern Côte d'Ivoire into northern Ghana, although Ghana's armed forces succeeded in preventing any continued occupation by such groups. At December 2011 546 Ghanaian personnel were deployed in Côte d'Ivoire as part of UN Operation in Côte d'Ivoire (UNOCI). Political instability and factional violence in Côte d'Ivoire following a disputed presidential election in late 2010 precipitated the inflow of large numbers of Ivorian refugees into Ghana (estimated to total 18,000 by October 2011). Alassane Ouattara, who had been sworn in as the new Ivorian President in May 2011 after months of fighting, visited Ghana in October and pressured Atta Mills to extradite Ivorian refugees accused of committing human rights abuses during the post-election turmoil. A repatriation accord was also signed by Ghana, Côte d'Ivoire and the office of the UN High Commissioner for Refugees, to facilitate the voluntary return of Ivorian refugees, while former fighters were to be resettled in other countries.

As a member of ECOWAS, the new NDC Government vigorously pursued the good neighbourliness policy embarked upon by NPP President Kufuor in the West African sub-region. However, the new Government preferred to add value to foreign relations by pursuing economic diplomacy, an agenda that led to an agreement with the Nigerian Government to supply Ghana with 60,000 barrels of crude petroleum on concessionary terms, to boost its energy requirement. The West Africa Gas Pipeline and the West Africa Power Pool projects are both strategic investments in the sub-region, at multilateral level, that were pursued by Ghana under the administration of Atta Mills. President Atta Mills continued to engage the Gambian authorities for the peaceful resolution of the dispute over the killing and disappearance in 2005 of 44 Ghanaians living in The Gambia. This led to the two countries signing a memorandum of understanding to ease their strained relations and to renew friendly ties following a joint UN/ECOWAS report that ruled out the complicity of the Gambian authorities in the deaths and disappearance of the Ghanaian nationals.

Bilateral relations between Ghana and the USA have strengthened since 1992, and two incumbent US Presidents, Bill Clinton and George W. Bush, have both separately visited Ghana during Rawlings' and Kufuor's terms, respectively, to solidify the relations between the two countries and also to commend Ghana for the positive steps it has made regarding democratic development and good governance in Africa. Through such commitments, Ghana currently benefits from the African Growth and Opportunity Act and the Millennium Challenge Account. US President Barack Obama's visit to Ghana in July 2009, during which he made his first African policy statement, provided a further endorsement of Ghana as a champion of democracy in Africa.

Economy

LINDA VAN BUREN

Revised for this edition by CHARLIE TARR

Amid great fanfare, Ghana's offshore Jubilee oilfield began to pump its first commercial gas in December 2010, marking the country's debut as one of the world's petroleum-exporting nations. Production averaged 55,000 barrels per day (b/d) at mid-2011, rose to 70,000 b/d by May 2012 and was expected to increase further to 90,000 b/d by the end of 2012. Earlier projections of 120,000 b/d by 2012 proved to have been over ambitious. However, Tullow Ghana Ltd, a subsidiary of Tullow Oil, which operates the Jubilee Field, gave assurances that this target would be met by 2013. Prospects for Ghana's oil industry remain significant as oil and gas discoveries continued to be made both along a large part of the country's coastline as well as in the Volta Basin. In March 2011 oil was also discovered at the Enyenra deepwater offshore well.

Ghana's earnings from oil exports in 2011 were projected at US $400m. According to the World Bank, real gross domestic product (GDP) grew an impressive 14.4% in 2011, boosted by a surge in oil production. GDP was expected to decelerate to 7.5% in 2012 and to remain at around 7% until 2015. The strong positive economic growth recorded in 2011, spurred by agriculture (notably cocoa) and the gold sector, was Ghana's eighth consecutive year of positive growth, despite the global economic recession and the inability of many of the world's economies to return to a sustained period of growth. Good rains gave a general boost to Ghanaian agricultural production. Meanwhile, the number of those in poverty declined from about 52.0% of the population in 1991/92 to 28.5% in 2005/06. At the current pace, Ghana was likely to achieve the Millennium Development Goal of halving its poverty rate well before the target date of 2015.

At independence in 1957 Ghana possessed one of the strongest economies in Africa. However, the economy weakened sharply over the following 25 years. During that period real per caput income declined by more than one-third, and the government tax base was diminished. The resulting large deficits led to rising inflation and a burgeoning external debt burden. They also resulted in lower expenditure on, and a general neglect of, the country's infrastructure, as well as its education and health services. By 1981 annual average inflation was running at 142%. The Government of President Jerry Rawlings (1993–2001) introduced two Economic Recovery Programmes (ERPs), developed in close collaboration with the World Bank and the IMF. The first ERP (ERP I), launched in 1983, represented the stabilization phase of the economy's recovery, while ERP II, covering the period 1987–90, constituted the structural adjustment and development stage of that recovery.

The Government of President John Agyekum Kufuor (2001–09) succeeded in reducing the rate of inflation to 10.7% by 2007, but thereafter progress on containing inflation stalled. In 2008 the inflation target of 7% was missed by a wide margin in the run-up to the general election; inflation as of 31 December of that year stood at 18.2%. During the first year in power of the Government of President John Evans Atta Mills (2009–12), inflation rose to a peak of 20.7% in June 2009, but then fell back to 12.8% in 2010. It stood at 9.2% in the first quarter of 2011.

In May 2007 the Kufuor Government demonetized and 'redenominated'. New cedi notes were introduced on 3 July 2007 and old notes ceased to be legal tender in January 2008. In 2008 the new cedi depreciated by 20.1% against the US dollar and by 16.3% against the euro, but it appreciated by 8.1% against the pound sterling. In the year to 18 May 2009, the cedi lost 32.8% of its value against the US dollar, which is the currency in which global cocoa, gold and oil sales are denominated. Thereafter, the Ghanaian currency stabilized significantly, although it weakened from 1.40 new cedis = US $1 at 22 May 2010 to 1.50 new cedis = $1 at 22 May 2011, a depreciation of 6.2%. The cedi depreciated further in 2012, a result of an increase in the fiscal deficit and the persistent global economic slowdown. It was estimated that the cedi might decrease by a further 15% in 2012, to 1.78 new cedis = $1 owing to uncertainty surrounding the 2012 elections.

The Ghanaian economy is based primarily on the country's lucrative gold and cocoa sectors; in 2003 gold and cocoa together contributed 58% of export revenue. The proportion rose to 68% in 2007 and to 78% in 2010, before decreasing to 54% in 2011. The IMF forecast that in 2012 oil revenues would reach US $3,374m., exceeding predicted gold earnings of $3,251m. and projected cocoa revenues of $1,827m.

Ghana, the pre-independence name of which was the Gold Coast, is the ninth largest gold producer in the world and the second largest in Africa, after South Africa. Ghana has been known as a source of gold for many centuries. Large-scale extraction commenced in the 1880s, and the sector underwent a major revival in the 1990s, which subsequently proved to be sustainable, despite a weakness in the international price of gold at the time. Export revenue from gold rose steeply in 2006, as a result of both a 13.2% rise in export volume and a 26% increase in the global price. This upward trend continued, rising steadily every year thereafter. Ghana's mines produced 90.2 metric tons of gold in 2009. The price of gold increased from US $1,179.75 per troy oz at 20 May 2010 to $1,490.75 per oz at 20 May 2011, a rise of 26.3% in a single year. Prices were expected to stabilize slightly, to $1,247.5 per oz, in 2012.

The production of cocoa was established in Ghana mainly as an African smallholder crop, in the latter part of the 19th century. In the late 1950s, at the time of its political independence, Ghana was the world's leading exporter of cocoa, and this crop continued to account for 45%–70% of commodity exports in most years from the early 1970s until the 1990s, when increased mineral revenues led to a decline in cocoa's share of exports, to some 18% in 2000. Severe political instability in neighbouring Côte d'Ivoire from September 2002 coincided with bad weather in other cocoa-growing areas of the world to create a 'mini-boom' for Ghana's cocoa growers. The price paid to cocoa farmers in the 2009/10 season was first set at 2,208 new cedis per metric ton, an increase of 35% from the 1,632 new cedis per ton of the 2008/09 season. However, with prices slightly higher in Ghana's neighbours to the east and west—Togo and Côte d'Ivoire, respectively—the smuggling of cocoa out of Ghana and into these adjacent countries became a problem, so much so that in January 2010 the Atta Mills Government raised the producer price to 2,400 new cedis per ton. This 2009/10 payment was equivalent to 72% of the net free-on-board (f.o.b.) value of cocoa exports, thereby exceeding the target (see below). However, this price rise proved insufficient to halt the smuggling. In October 2011 cocoa farmers received an extra 80 new cedis for each ton of cocoa, a 76% increase on the f.o.b. price. Cocoa produced during the 2011/12 cocoa season was valued at 3,280 new cedis per ton, an increase on the 2010/11 season price of 3,200 new cedis. Exports of timber from Ghana's forests also began in the 1880s. Exports of timber and timber products amounted to 320,660 cu m in 2009. According to Ghana's Forestry Commission, the volume of exports fell by 5.4% in 2010, although revenues increased marginally. The European Union is the largest importer of Ghanaian timber, buying 33% of the total by volume and 43% by value.

ECONOMIC PERFORMANCE

Real GDP increased at an average annual rate of 4.4% in 1990–2003 and of 5.5% in 2000–08. The Atta Mills Government set a target for 2010 of real GDP growth of 6%. According to the IMF, GDP grew by 8% in 2010 and by an estimated 14.4% in 2011; it projected that the rate of growth would decelerate to 8.2% in 2012.

Estimates for 2010 indicated that total visible exports on a f.o.b. basis amounted to US $6,551m., of which gold contributed $3,017m. and cocoa accounted for $2,102m. Total visible imports on a f.o.b. basis cost an estimated $10,297m. in 2010, of which oil imports totalled $2,117m. and all non-oil imports accounted for $8,181m. The trade balance, thus, carried a $3,747m. deficit, and export revenue covered less than two-thirds of import costs. The current account of the balance of payments (including grants) is perennially in deficit, with the shortfall for 2010 calculated by the IMF at $2,164m. This increased to $3,715m in 2011 and was forecast at $2,914m. in 2012.

The World Investment Report 2011 stated that foreign direct investment (FDI) inflows into Ghana rose from US $1.700m. in 2009 to US$2.500m. in 2010, whereas FDI inflows across Africa as a whole declined by 6.8%. According to the Government, FDI in 2011 rose to $7,000m., compared with $2,000m. in 2009. Figures from the Ghana Investment Promotion Centre (GIPC), which exclude the oil sector, suggested FDI levels at $904m. in January to June 2011.

AGRICULTURE

In 2011 the agricultural sector (including forestry and fishing) accounted for 28.3% of GDP and employed about 50% of the working population. Cocoa, which is native not to Africa but to South America, is traditionally Ghana's most important cash crop, occupying more than one-half of all the country's cultivated land. Ghana is the world's second largest producer of cocoa, after neighbouring Côte d'Ivoire. Ghana produced 17.0% of the total global output of cocoa in 2009/10; this increased to 20.7% in 2011 as other countries continued to fill the void left by a decrease in production in Côte d'Ivoire (see above). Worldwide cocoa production fell by 8.1% in 2011. As of July 2011, cocoa prices had declined to US $234.98 per kg, a fall of 25.8% from the previous year ($316.7 per kg).

In 1985 the Cocoa Marketing Board was reorganized as the Ghana Cocoa Board (COCOBOD). In 1993 COCOBOD was formally divested of its monopoly over the internal marketing of cocoa. The Kufuor Government began the licensing of private cocoa-exporting companies in 2001. From 2004 the Ghanaian cocoa grower received a statutory minimum of 70% of the net f.o.b. price that cocoa achieves on world markets; the proportion actually received rose to a record high of 75.2% in October 2010. Estimates by the International Cocoa Organization (ICCO) indicated that Ghana produced 740,000 metric tons of cocoa beans in the 2009/10 season (the cocoa year runs from 1 October to 30 September), rising to a record 960,000 tons in 2010/11. By way of comparison, Côte d'Ivoire officially produced over 1.3m. tons in 2010/11.

Ghana has also achieved some diversity in cash crop production since the 1990s. On a small scale, both for local consumption and for export, Ghanaian farmers have begun to grow such crops as cashew nuts, brazil nuts, oranges, lemons, limes, apples, melons, papayas (pawpaws), mangoes, avocados, tomatoes, cucumbers, onions, green beans, aubergines (eggplants, or, as they are called in Ghana, 'garden eggs'), chillies, okra, peppercorns, ginger and raspberries. In 2010 the Atta Mills Government launched a cotton support programme, which was to assist 3,000 cotton growers in three northern regions with a view to boosting cotton exports.

Food production is based principally on the farming of cassava, yams, cocoyams (taro), plantains and maize. Of all the sub-sectors in agriculture, by far the largest share of GDP is contributed by non-cocoa agriculture and livestock, at an estimated 27.3% in 2010, compared with cocoa's contribution of 6.4%.

Cattle-farming is restricted to the Northern Region and the Accra plains; the national herd stood at 1.45m. head in 2010. Production of meat is insufficient to meet local annual demand of about 200,000 metric tons. Imports of livestock from adjacent countries have been considerable, though declining in recent years, owing to shortages of foreign exchange. In 2010 Ghana had 4.86m. goats, 3.76m. sheep, 536,000 pigs and 44m. chickens. Consumers ate more chicken than any other meat, mainly because the price of imported chicken had been relatively low. Domestic fisheries (marine and Lake Volta) supply only between one-half and two-thirds of the country's total annual demand of 600,000 tons. In 2007 the Kufuor Government introduced a steel vessel on Lake Volta to patrol the lake and curtail the use of illegal fishing equipment. An estimated 80,000 Ghanaians fish in Lake Volta, netting some 82,000 tons of fish per year.

Ghana has extensive forests, mostly in the south-west. Efforts are proceeding to promote timber exports, which are projected eventually to reach 700,000 cu m per year; by comparison, timber exports in 2009 amounted to 320,660 cu m. Successive governments have undertaken to phase out exports of raw logs and to encourage local processing of timber products. Ghana, however, possesses enough timber to meet its foreseeable domestic and export requirements until 2030. The forestry sector accounted for an estimated 3.2% of GDP in 2010. Forestry and logging grew by 3.5% in 2008, exceeding the government target of 3% growth. More than 95% of all roundwood removals in Ghana are for locally consumed fuel wood.

Despite the success of cocoa production in 2010/11, the agriculture sector generally underperformed in this period. The sector achieved 2.8% growth in 2011, short of its 5.3% target. This was attributed partly to a sluggish performance by the forestry and logging sector. The crops sector only missed its target of 5.5% growth by 0.1%, yet this increase was modest in comparison to the 14% rise posted by the cocoa sector.

MANUFACTURING

Apart from traditional industries such as food-processing, Ghana has a number of long-established large and medium-sized enterprises, including a petroleum refinery and plants producing textiles, vehicles, cement, paper, chemicals and footwear, and a number of export-based industries, such as cocoa-processing and wood-processing plants.

The manufacturing industries have traditionally been under-used, high-cost and strongly dependent on imported equipment and materials. Expansion was deterred by low levels of investment, by transport congestion and by persistent shortages of imported materials and spares. Moreover, the consistent overvaluation of the cedi and the irregularity of supply of raw materials increased the attractiveness of imports relative to home-produced goods.

The Kufuor Government placed heavy upward pressure on companies' costs by raising the minimum wage by 31% to 5,500 cedis per day (about US $0.76), fuel prices by an average of 64%, water tariffs by 96% and electricity tariffs by 103% in the run-up to the 2008 elections. Higher global prices for oil also had an effect on companies' outgoings.

Among the largest capital-intensive industries in Ghana is an aluminium smelter at Tema, operated by the Volta Aluminium Co (Valco). Construction of the Valco plant began in 1964 and commercial production of aluminium commenced in March 1967. Formerly owned by the multinational Kaiser Aluminium and Chemical Corpn (90%) and Alcoa (10%), the Tema plant had a potential output capacity of 200,000 metric tons of primary aluminium per year; however, annual production was less than 50,000 tons in the mid-1980s, owing to lower world demand and reduced energy supplies from the drought-stricken Akosombo hydroelectricity plant. In 1997 the 30-year agreement that fixed the electricity price paid by Valco to the state-owned Volta River Authority expired and no new agreement was reached despite US mediation and arbitration by the International Chamber of Commerce. Even in the absence of an agreement, power continued to be supplied until 2003, effectively subsidized by the Ghanaian taxpayer. In November 2004 Kaiser Aluminium completed the sale of its remaining interest in Valco to the Ghanaian Government, and despite an initial agreement with Alcoa to revitalize the company, Alcoa subsequently sold its stake in June 2008 to the Ghanaian Government, leaving Valco entirely under government ownership. Throughout this period operations at Valco had been sporadic and at times the company had completely shut down. In January 2011 smelting operations resumed at the plant and by May the company was operating one of the five cell lines (20% capacity) employing over 500 employees.

Meanwhile, the Divestiture Implementation Committee (DIC) undertook to sell the Government's shares in no fewer than 300 enterprises. Other state-owned entities were later added to the list, and by 2009 the DIC had divested 335 such entities. In 2011 plans were at an early stage to invite private participation in existing electricity generation, water supply and railway operations. The Atta Mills Government decided in 2009 to outsource the privatization process itself, with the DIC maintaining a register of prequalified private sector firms subcontracted to undertake such tasks as financial valuation and asset valuation of enterprises still in state hands and to prepare information memoranda for them. Companies that export from Ghana are allowed to retain 100% of their export proceeds in foreign exchange accounts at Ghanaian banks under the Export Proceeds Retention Scheme.

The Ghana Free Zones Board, which was established in 1995 under the Rawlings Government, invited companies to invest in export-processing activities in Ghana, to be concentrated in export-processing zones (EPZs) which were largely exempt from duties, taxes or income taxes for at least 10 years. In addition, companies were allowed to sell up to 30% of their output into the Ghanaian market. Although criticized by both the Rawlings and Kufuor governments for disadvantaging the domestic markets, by 2010 over 200 companies were operating under free zone licences in four EPZs at Tema, in Ghana's principal port city, Ashanti, Sekondi and Shama.

Evidence of increasing foreign investor confidence is apparent in the repurchase by multinationals, such as Unilever and Guinness, of shares in their Ghanaian operations that had been government-held. Dividends, profits and the original investment capital could be repatriated freely in convertible currency, and tax incentives and benefits were improved. FDI into the manufacturing sector continued in 2011, despite a slow sectoral growth of 1.7%. Total FDI investment for 2011 reached US $322m.

MINING

Gold has been overwhelmingly the largest component of Ghana's mineral production. Non-gold mining output was sluggish in 2008, but gold production grew by 30.2%. Gold exports increased by 29.6% in the same year, earning US $2,246.3m. Estimates indicated that gold was likely narrowly to maintain its leading position in the Ghanaian economy in 2011, the first year of oil production: gold was projected to contribute 32.0% to GDP in that year, compared with 31.5% from oil. In terms of export revenue, however, the IMF forecast that oil would contribute 31.9% of total export revenue, compared with 31.6% accounted for by gold. However, according to Ghana's Chamber of Mines, gold production decreased by 2%–3% in 2011. The first half of 2011 had indicated a promising year for the Ghanaian gold sector, with revenues accelerating by 33% to $2,200 m., aided by high world market gold prices. Total production reached 1,497,023 oz in the first six months of 2011, an increase of 3% from the same period in 2010. Despite this upward trend at the beginning of the year, mining firms switched to either maintenance or expansion rather than maximizing existing production. A significant rebound in both output and revenue was witnessed in 2012. In the first quarter of that year gold production rose by 64%, compared with the same period in 2011, primarily as a result of mining companies increasing output in line with higher prices. New companies also entered the fray, encouraged by a reinvigorated domestic market. Low-grade ore has become a viable option for extractors while prices remain high.

In the 1990s South African investors bought Tarkwa Goldfields (which had estimated gold reserves of 13m. oz) from the State Gold Mining Corpn of Ghana. In 2003 South African company Gold Fields announced further investment in Tarkwa of R1,100m. In December the US company Newmont Mining Corpn of Denver, Colorado, announced a US $350m. investment in the Ahafo gold-mining project, in the Brong Ahafo Region of western Ghana. The 269.5 sq m Ahafo project had 12 ore bodies, and a feasibility study found that the project had the capacity to produce 500,000 equity oz per year and that 'proven and probable' reserves amounted to 108.6m. metric tons. Ahafo produced its first gold in July 2006 and went on to produce 202,000 oz of gold in that year. Some 1,700 households were resettled to accommodate the mining operations. Newmont also owns a 1,468 sq m open-pit gold mine at Akyem, in Birim North district in Eastern Region. Akyem has 80m. tons of 'proven and probable' reserves. First discovered in 1902 and long closed, the old Bibiani gold mine in western Ghana's Sefwi–Bibiani greenstone belt was acquired in 2008 by Noble Mineral Resources Ltd of Australia and has reported reserves of 2m. oz. Red Back Mining Inc of Canada owns 100% of the Chirano gold mine, through a wholly owned Ghanaian subsidiary, Chirano Gold Mines Ltd (CGML). The Vancouver-based company acquired a 15-year concession over the 11 ore bodies at Chirano in 2004. Total reserves are reported to be 23m. oz. Ghana also has some 25,000–50,000 artisanal gold miners, known as *galamsey*, who mine shallow workings such as pits, sluices and tunnels. Illegal mining continues to be a problem for the Government; in 2011 more than 300 illegal miners were trapped and died in sites throughout the country, according to figures published by the Chamber of Mines.

The principal gold mine situated at Obuasi is the ninth largest in the world. In 2004 the merger of Ashanti Goldfields of Ghana with AngloGold Ltd of South Africa took effect, and the company, renamed AngloGold Ashanti, became the world's largest gold-mining company. AngloGold Ashanti continues to operate the Obuasi, Siguiri, Iduapriem and Geita mines in Ghana while also maintaining mining activities in Argentina, Australia, Brazil, Namibia, South Africa and Tanzania. There were plans to open further mines, notably a project by PMI Gold Corpn at Obatan which was on target for full production in 2014 with inferred resources of 1.4m. oz.

The petroleum sector became the focus of much attention following discoveries announced in 2007 and 2008. The 2010 budget called for the establishment of an Oil and Gas Industrialization Plan during that year and envisaged 'additional refineries' and 'the development of petrochemical products such as PVC and plastics'. Ghana first entered petroleum production in 1978, when a US company began extracting petroleum from the continental shelf near Saltpond. Reserves at Saltpond were estimated at 7m. barrels, but average output during the early 1980s was only 1,250 barrels per day (b/d). In 1983 the Rawlings Government established the Ghana National Petroleum Corpn (GNPC) to develop offshore areas under production-sharing contracts. Exploration and production rights were set out under the 1984 Petroleum Exploration Law, which allowed the Government to take an initial 10% share in any venture, with the option of buying 50% of production and holding a 50% royalty on output. The 2006/07 budget promised a review of the Petroleum Exploration Law in order to make Ghana more attractive to oil prospectors. In 2006 the Kufuor Government ratified four oil exploration contracts. The first was with GASOP Oil Ghana Limited (GOGL), for a concession offshore between Saltpond and West Cape Three Points, in which two wells, Takoradi 11-1 and Shama 9-1, were dug; according to GOGL, seismic studies found a 'significant amount of oil and gas'. The second was with the US company Amerada Hess of New York, for a concession at Deepwater Tano Cape Three Points. The third was with Tullow Oil Ghana Ltd (TOGL) and Sabre Oil and Gas Limited (SOGL), for a concession at Shallow Water Tano. The fourth was with TOGL, SOGL, Anadarko Petroleum and Kosmos Energy Ghana Limited, for a concession at Deepwater Tano. The US company Kosmos Energy, based in Dallas, Texas, announced two petroleum discoveries in its explorations in Ghana in 2007 and 2008. The first, in June 2007, was the Mahogany-1 well, 63 km off shore in what was renamed in December 2007 as the Jubilee Field; production commenced in December 2010. The second, in February 2008, was the Odum-1 well, 13 km east of Mahogany-1. In addition, Tullow Oil plc of the United Kingdom, which also has an interest in Mahogany-1, announced in August 2007 the discovery of a 'significant' presence of light oil in the Hyedua-1 well in the offshore Deepwater Tano concession. Tullow followed this by announcing in May 2008 that drilling in the Mahogany-2 well, also in the Jubilee Field, had 'intersected a significant column of light oil'. Tullow indicated in 2009 that Deepwater Tano held 'further high-impact prospects' and drilled two more wells, Tweneboa and Teak, in that year; these, according to Tullow, have 'upside potential in excess of half a million barrels each'. Further exploration continued in the Jubilee Field in 2012, where Kosmos Energy invested US $37m. in production and exploration activities during the second quarter of the year. The Ghanaian Government, in partnership with Tullow Oil, Anadarko Petroleum Corpn and others, announced a $20,000m. investment over the next 10 years towards the discovery of new oil fields. New discoveries continue in the Deepwater Tano Block. There have been additional recent discoveries at Mahogany, Teak, Akasa and Banda.

In September 1995 Ghana joined Nigeria, Togo and Benin in signing an agreement to proceed with the construction of a West African Gas Pipeline (WAGP) from Nigeria. In May 2003 Ghana and other partners signed a further agreement for the creation of the West African Pipeline Company (WAPC) to operate the pipeline. The Ghanaian Government reported that it had paid its 16.3% share of WAPC in full during 2004. The pipeline had been expected to deliver its first methane gas by the end of 2006, but this was subsequently delayed until June 2008. The WAGP from Itoki in Nigeria to Takoradi in Ghana was completed in 2008, as was a pipeline from Takoradi to the Volta River Authority (VRA) power plant (see below) at Aboadze. Gas was delivered through the WAGP to Takoradi, and nearly two years later, gas finally flowed from Takoradi to Aboadze.

Ghana's sole refinery, the 45,000-b/d Tema oil refinery (TOR), is operated by the Ghanaian-Italian Petroleum Co and is owned by GNPC. In 2004 TOR's activities were restricted to the refining of crude petroleum only; the procurement and importation of finished petroleum products was opened to private sector oil-marketing companies (OMCs), but only by tender, and limited to the incremental amount between TOR's supply and the national demand. The first such tender was held in 2004. Ghana's Petroleum Deregulation Policy came into effect in 2005 with the announcement that new prices for petroleum products would be set by the OMCs under the supervision of an independent National Petroleum Authority (NPA). Legislation to support the regulatory functions of the NPA was enacted in 2005. Perhaps unexpectedly, the 2011 budget, announced in November 2010, was silent on the subject of new oil-refining capacity in the country's first year of oil production. The 2011 budget raised the debt recovery levy from 0.02 new cedis to 0.08 new cedis per litre of petrol and diesel; the purpose of the levy was to help lower the debt burden of TOR, which the budget stated 'remains high and threatens the financial viability of the country's banking system'.

Ghana possesses substantial reserves of bauxite, although only a small proportion, at Awaso in the Western Region, is currently mined. Exploitation of these deposits was carried out by Canada's Rio Tinto Alcan on behalf of the Ghana Bauxite Co, in which the Government holds a 20% interest. Bauxite output, which at present is all exported, declined from more than 300,000 metric tons per year during the 1950s to less than 30,000 tons by the mid-1980s, owing to the rapid deterioration of the Western railway line linking Awaso with port facilities at Takoradi. Repairs on the railway line enabled bauxite exports to recover from 1985, and Awaso produced 700,000 tons of bauxite in 2001. However, by 2006 the line had again fallen into disrepair, and the ore had to be transported by road instead. In 2009 production amounted to 490,367 tons, and large quantities of bauxite were reported to be building up at Awaso awaiting evacuation. In 2010 Bosai Minerals of the People's Republic of China acquired Rio Tinto Alcan's 80% stake in the Awaso bauxite operation. In 2012 bauxite output increased significantly, by 82%, with shipments of ore up by 71% (from 173,601 tons in the first half of 2011 to 295,993 tons for the same period in 2012.)

Manganese ore is mined at Nsuta, in the Western Region, by the Ghana Manganese Co (a subsidiary of Consolidated Minerals). Production peaked at 1.6m. metric tons in 2004 before falling back to an estimated 1.0m. tons in 2009 and recovering somewhat, to 1.2m. tons, in 2010. As with Awaso's bauxite, Nsuta's manganese ore suffers when the Western railway line falls into disrepair, and during 2006 manganese ore was also transported to port by road, with detrimental effects to the region's roads. Ghana ranks as one of the world's largest producers of manganese, and Nsuta is the world's third largest manganese mine. As of 2012 only 3% of its capacity had been mined.

Diamonds are mined from alluvial deposits; no kimberlite pipe has yet been discovered. The diamonds are 85% industrial; of the 15% classified as gemstones, the size is small, rarely comprising fewer than four stones per carat. Diamonds are mined both by Ghana Consolidated Diamonds (formerly Consolidated Africa Selection Trust) at Akwatia and by local diamond 'winners'. Total recorded production dwindled from 3.2m. carats in 1960 to 300,000 carats in 1988; output recovered to about 1m. carats in 2006, but subsequently declined to 643,000 carats in 2008, 376,000 carats in 2009 and 334,000 carats in 2010. The Precious Minerals Marketing Co (PMMC) attempted to achieve a clean bill of health with regard to the sale of 'conflict diamonds' in 2003, but these efforts received a reverse when it was alleged that it had sold some stones to an Israeli company for less than US $3 per carat. The PMMC denied that the stones were 'conflict diamonds'.

Despite a decrease in revenue from both diamonds and manganese, Ghana's mineral revenues in the first half of 2012 rose by 19%, compared with the same period of the previous year, to US $2,757.5m.

ELECTRICITY

In 2010 Ghana's installed operational electricity-generating capacity was 1,810 MW, of which the flagship Akosombo hydroelectricity plant provided 1,020 MW, the Takoradi thermal power plant contributed 550 MW, and the veteran Kpong plant supplied 160 MW. Until the opening of the Akosombo plant on Lake Volta in 1966, electricity production came solely from diesel generators operated by the Electricity Co of Ghana or by the mines. In 1986 the Akosombo plant, with an installed generating capacity of 912 MW at the time, and later the 160-MW Kpong plant, together provided virtually all of Ghana's electricity requirements and allowed electricity to be exported to Togo and Benin when rain was sufficient. In the drought-affected early 1980s the VRA, which operates electricity supply from Lake Volta, was forced to restrict output, and major commercial consumers, such as Valco (which takes, on average, more than 60% of the power supply from Akosombo), were compelled to reduce production levels. To lessen Valco's dependence on the Akosombo facility, which, as a hydroelectric facility, is vulnerable to drought, Valco opted to invest in thermal-generating capacity. It contributed US $1,000m. to a new 1,000-MW thermal complex at Tema, to make use of Nigerian gas to be delivered by the WAGP (see above). This facility comprises the 126-MW Tema Thermal 1 plant, commissioned in 2008, and the 49.5-MW Tema Thermal 2 plant. Following considerable delay, the 230-MW Kpone Thermal 1 power plant, also at Tema, was projected to be commissioned by 2015. Takoradi's 550-MW capacity was upgraded to 650 MW in 2009. In 2000 the Rawlings Government proposed the building of a 400-MW, $622m. hydroelectric facility at Bui, on the Black Volta River in western Ghana. An environmental group, Ghana Energy Foundation, opposed the scheme, suggesting in April 2001 that a series of micro-hydro projects, along small rivers in the country, would be both better for the ecosystem and more cost-effective, as the large scheme would flood a wide area, including the Bole Game Reserve, and would necessitate a huge outlay in compensation and resettlement costs. In 2008 the Kufuor Government was pressing ahead with the Bui scheme and secured a $562m. loan from China to help fund it; the remaining $60m. was to come from the Ghanaian Government. In March 2009 the Atta Mills Government reiterated its intention to move forward with the Bui scheme. In December the Chinese construction company Sino Hydro commenced building the Bui hydroelectric dam; the project was scheduled to be completed in the second quarter of 2013. By July 2012 concrete works at the main dam were 95% completed and the third turbine shaft of the third unit had been installed. A hydrology design report indicated that the reservoir required two further rainy seasons to attain the minimum level required to start power generation. China's Eximbank also backed a $90m. rural electrification programme, which started up in August 2007 with the aim of connecting 550 communities to the national grid.

TRANSPORT

The country's two major ports are both artificial: Takoradi, built in the 1920s, and Tema, which was opened in 1961 to replace the Accra roadstead and which became an industrial centre. According to the Ghana Ports and Harbour Authority, Ghana's ports handled about 9m. metric tons of cargo in the peak year of 2005 and about 8m. tons in 2007. The decline was attributable in part to difficulties in transporting bauxite and manganese ore to Takoradi (see above). Of total traffic, about 850,000 tons was transit traffic, bound for landlocked Sahelian countries such as Burkina Faso. Approximately 86% of all cargo throughput was imports. In total, 1,652 vessels called at Tema and Takoradi in 2010. Turnaround time was about 3.5 days in 2010, compared with about 3.6 days in 2009.

There are 1,300 km of railway, forming a triangle between Takoradi, Kumasi and Accra-Tema. Exports traditionally accounted for the greater part of railway freight tonnage, but cocoa, timber, bauxite and manganese ore were all diverted to the roads as rail facilities deteriorated, and the railways have required a regular government subsidy since 1976. According to a Government consultative group meeting in June 2012 only the Western line (Kumasi–Takoradi) was partially operational.

In 2005 Ghana had a total road network of approximately 57,614 km, of which just 15% was paved. The road system is good by tropical African standards, but its maintenance has been a constant problem. The overwhelming focus of construction in the transport sector in the late 1990s was on roads. A key road improvement project in 2008 was to upgrade the Accra–Kumasi road to a dual carriageway. By 2012 the roads network comprised 66,200 km with 41% considered in 'good condition'. In 2003 the Kufuor Government established Metro Mass Transit Ltd (MMT) with the aim of creating a mass transit public bus company in the country. By the end of 2008 MMT operated bus services in Accra, Cape Coast, Koforidua, Kumasi, Sunyani, Agona Swedru, Takoradi, Tamale, Ho, Bogatanga, Wa and Akim Oda. In April 2011 a new route serving Kpando was launched.

The creation of Lake Volta, stretching some 400 km inland from the Akosombo dam, opened up new possibilities for internal lake transportation, but lake transport is still relatively modest. Kotoka International Airport, near Accra, is Ghana's gateway airport; it underwent refurbishment work in 2009 and 2010. Following upgrading, Tamale Airport gained international status in December 2008. Other airports, at Kumasi, Sunyani, Takoradi and Wa, serve inland traffic. The 2011 budget proposed to increase the airport tax for intercontinental travellers from US $75 to $100 for economy passengers, to $150 for business-class passengers and to $200 for first-class passengers. Ghana International Airlines (GIA) replaced Ghana Airways as the nation's flag-carrying airline after the latter went into liquidation in June 2005. GIA operated the Accra–London route in 2008 and 2009. In May 2010 a GIA-liveried aircraft was seized by British Transport Police moments after touching down at Gatwick Airport, London, in connection with an alleged breach of its leasing contract; subsequent flights were cancelled, and the Ghanaian Government in that month suspended GIA's operations. Antrak Air, wholly Ghanaian-owned, in May 2011 operated domestic services between Accra and Kumasi, Sunyani, Takoradi and Tamale. Fastjet, a new pan-African low-cost airline (rebranded from the Lonrho-owned Fly540), planned to launch in Ghana by the end of 2012, with additional hubs in Kenya, Tanzania and Angola.

PUBLIC FINANCE

It was announced in the 2010 budget that four revenue agencies—the VAT Service, the Customs, Excise and Preventive Service, the Internal Revenue Service and the Large Taxpayer Unit—were to be merged into a more efficient one-stop tax agency, the Ghana Revenue Authority. A nine-member board was duly appointed in September of that year.

Debt is a significant drain on Ghana's fiscal resources. Ghana's heavy use of IMF facilities during the two administrations of President Rawlings contributed significantly to the country's foreign debt. Total external debt stood at US $6,347.9m. at 31 December 2005, of which 64% was multilateral debt denominated in Special Drawing Rights. During 2006 the provisions of the IMF's initiative for heavily indebted poor countries and the Multilateral Debt Relief Initiative reduced Ghana's total external debt by 66.2%, to $2,143.8m. at 30 September. Not affected, however, was Ghana's domestic debt, which stood at 17,061,200m. old cedis (equivalent to $1,900m.) at that date. After this debt relief, however, Ghana continued to engage in imprudent borrowing. Domestic debt was boosted by an issuance of Golden Jubilee savings bonds in 2007, the year that marked the 50th anniversary of Ghana's independence. The 2009 budget statement attributed this expanding debt level to 'renewed borrowing on non-concessional terms. . .mostly for economically unproductive projects'.

The Kufuor Government had contracted 46 new loans during 2008, totalling $2,630.9m., of which more than one-half—58%—was borrowed from export-credit sources (on commercial, not concessional, terms). Shortly before the Kufuor Government left office Ghana's total foreign debt stood at $5,055m. at 31 December 2008. By 31 December 2010, under the Atta Mills Government, Ghana's total public debt stock had risen again, to 66.6% of GDP, with external debt accounting for 41.7% and domestic debt accounting for 24.9%; total external debt was estimated at $6,483m., even higher than it had been five years earlier, prior to the introduction of debt relief measures. This trend continued in 2011 and into 2012, as the Ghanaian current account deficit continued to widen. The deficit was projected to increase from an estimated 7.4% of GDP in 2012 to 9.9% of GDP in 2014. It was anticipated that an improvement in the trade account would temper this trend, with a forecast deficit of 8.6% by 2016. The situation was exacerbated by an 8.3% weakening of the new cedi against the US dollar in the first quarter of 2012, compared with only a 2% fall during the same period in 2011.

It was anticipated that spending would increase by 22% in the pre-election period to December 2012, with the Government accelerating infrastructure projects throughout the country. Part of this expenditure was to be driven by borrowing secured against future oil revenues (up to 70%). Although tax revenues were expected to rise as the oil sector inevitably expanded, it was predicted that the Government's current account would widen further in the short to medium term.

Statistical Survey

Source (except where otherwise stated): Ghana Statistical Service, POB GP1098, Accra; tel. (30) 2671732; fax (30) 2671731; internet www.statsghana.gov.gh.

Area and Population

AREA, POPULATION AND DENSITY

Area (sq km)	238,533*
Population (census results)	
26 March 2000	18,912,079
26 September 2010	
Males	12,024,845
Females	12,633,978
Total	24,658,823
Population (UN estimates at mid-year)†	
2011	24,965,819
2012	25,545,937
Density (per sq km) at mid-2012	107.1

* 92,098 sq miles.

† Source: UN, *World Population Prospects: The 2010 Revision*; estimates not adjusted to take account of the results of the 2010 census.

POPULATION BY AGE AND SEX

(UN estimates at mid-2012)

	Males	Females	Total
0–14	4,999,349	4,761,804	9,761,153
15–64	7,514,243	7,262,965	14,777,208
65 and over	483,288	524,288	1,007,576
Total	12,996,880	12,549,057	25,545,937

Source: UN, *World Population Prospects: The 2010 Revision*.

REGIONS

(population at 2010 census)

Region	Area (sq km)	Population	Density (per sq km)	Capital
Ashanti	24,389	4,780,380	196.0	Kumasi
Brong Ahafo	39,557	2,310,983	58.4	Sunyani
Central	9,826	2,201,863	224.1	Cape Coast
Eastern	19,323	2,633,154	136.3	Koforidua
Greater Accra	3,245	4,010,054	1,235.8	Accra
Northern	70,384	2,479,461	35.2	Tamale
Upper East	8,842	1,046,545	118.4	Bolgatanga
Upper West	18,476	702,110	38.0	Wa
Volta	20,570	2,118,252	103.0	Ho
Western	23,921	2,376,021	99.3	Takoradi
Total	238,533	24,658,823	103.4	

PRINCIPAL TOWNS

(population at 2010 census)

Kumasi	2,035,064	Tema	402,637
Accra (capital)	1,848,614	Tamale	371,351
Sekondi-Takoradi	559,548	Cape Coast	169,894

Mid-2011 (incl. suburbs, UN estimate): Accra 2,573,220 (Source: UN, *World Urbanization Prospects: The 2011 Revision*).

BIRTHS AND DEATHS

(annual averages, UN estimates)

	1995–2000	2000–05	2005–10
Birth rate (per 1,000)	35.0	33.8	32.6
Death rate (per 1,000)	10.4	9.6	8.3

Source: UN, *World Population Prospects: The 2010 Revision*.

Life expectancy (years at birth): 63.8 (males 62.9; females 64.8) in 2010 (Source: World Bank, World Development Indicators database).

ECONOMICALLY ACTIVE POPULATION

(persons aged 15 years and over at 2010 census)

	Males	Females	Total
Agriculture, hunting, forestry and fishing	2,303,140	2,008,595	4,311,735
Mining and quarrying	92,353	21,852	114,205
Manufacturing	449,826	670,296	1,120,122
Electricity, gas and water	27,690	13,141	40,831
Construction	308,527	8,998	317,525
Trade, restaurants and hotels	687,439	1,836,662	2,524,101
Transport, storage and communications	380,946	29,672	410,618
Financing, insurance, real estate and business services	158,493	81,175	239,668
Public administration and defence	111,618	42,012	153,630
Education	228,400	177,800	406,200
Health and social services	54,835	69,556	124,391
Household activities	33,626	44,307	77,933
Activities of extra-territorial organizations	2,015	917	2,932
Other services	217,940	311,847	529,787
Total employed	5,056,848	5,316,830	10,373,678
Unemployed	283,346	349,648	632,994
Total labour force	5,340,194	5,666,478	11,006,672

Health and Welfare

KEY INDICATORS

Total fertility rate (children per woman, 2010)	4.2
Under-5 mortality rate (per 1,000 live births, 2010)	74
HIV/AIDS (% of persons aged 15–49, 2009)	1.8
Physicians (per 1,000 head, 2009)	0.1
Hospital beds (per 1,000 head, 2009)	0.9
Health expenditure (2009): US $ per head (PPP)	77
Health expenditure (2009): % of GDP	5.0
Health expenditure (2009): public (% of total)	56.7
Access to water (% of persons, 2010)	86
Access to sanitation (% of persons, 2010)	14
Total carbon dioxide emissions ('000 metric tons, 2008)	8,591.8
Carbon dioxide emissions per head (metric tons, 2008)	0.4
Human Development Index (2011): ranking	135
Human Development Index (2011): value	0.541

For sources and definitions, see explanatory note on p. vi.

Agriculture

PRINCIPAL CROPS
('000 metric tons)

	2008	2009	2010
Rice, paddy	301.9	391.4	491.6
Maize	1,470.0	1,619.5	1,871.7
Millet	193.8	245.5	219.0
Sorghum	330.9	350.5	324.4
Sweet potatoes*	112.3	122.1	130.3
Cassava (Manioc)	11,351.1	12,230.6	13,504.1
Taro (Cocoyam)	1,688.3	1,504.0	1,354.8
Yams	4,894.8	5,777.9	5,960.5
Sugar cane*	145.0	145.0	145.0
Groundnuts, with shell	470.1	485.1	530.9
Coconuts	316.3†	273.8†	297.9*
Oil palm fruit	1,896.8	2,103.6	2,004.3
Tomatoes	284.0*	317.5	350.0*
Chillies and peppers, green*	282.2	176.2	294.1
Onions, dry*	44.4	49.1	50.0
Beans, green*	29.3	23.3	27.6
Okra*	89.7	71.4	82.5
Bananas	63.0	65.0	64.5*
Plantains	3,337.6	3,562.5	3,537.7
Oranges	550.0	560.0	556.1*
Lemons and limes*	43.7	46.7	46.0
Pineapples*	70.0	74.7	73.7
Cocoa beans	680.8	710.6	632.0
Natural rubber	16.6	19.1	15.0†

* FAO estimate(s).

† Unofficial figure.

Aggregate production ('000 metric tons, may include official, semi-official or estimated data): Total cereals 2,297 in 2008, 2,607 in 2009, 2,907 in 2010; Total roots and tubers 18,046 in 2008, 19,635 in 2009, 20,950 in 2010; Total vegetables (incl. melons) 744 in 2008, 649 in 2009, 819 in 2010; Total fruits (excl. melons) 4,146 in 2008, 4,396 in 2009, 4,364 in 2010.

Source: FAO.

LIVESTOCK
('000 head, year ending September)

	2008	2009	2010
Horses	2.6	2.6	2.7
Asses*	14.0	14.0	14.0
Cattle	1,422	1,438	1,454
Pigs	506	521	536
Sheep	3,529	3,642	3,759
Goats	4,405	4,625	4,855
Chickens	39,816	43,320	44,000*

* FAO estimate(s).

Source: FAO.

LIVESTOCK PRODUCTS
('000 metric tons, FAO estimates)

	2008	2009	2010
Cattle meat	25.4	25.5	25.5
Sheep meat	15.9	16.4	16.9
Goat meat	13.7	14.3	14.3
Pig meat	17.0	17.5	17.5
Chicken meat	44.5	48.0	48.7
Game meat	64.9	69.3	74.1
Cows' milk	37.2	37.7	38.7
Hen eggs	33.7	36.7	36.7

Source: FAO.

Forestry

ROUNDWOOD REMOVALS
('000 cubic metres, excl. bark)

	2008	2009	2010
Sawlogs, veneer logs and logs for sleepers	1,392	1,300	1,250
Fuel wood*	35,363	36,564	37,791
Total	36,755	37,864	39,041

* FAO estimates.

2011: Production assumed to be unchanged from 2010 (FAO estimates).

Source: FAO.

SAWNWOOD PRODUCTION
('000 cubic metres, incl. railway sleepers)

	2009	2010	2011
Total (all broadleaved)	532	513	533*

* Unofficial figure.

Source: FAO.

Fishing

('000 metric tons, live weight)

	2008	2009	2010
Capture	359.8	321.8*	351.2*
Freshwater fishes	85.0	88.7*	90.0*
Bigeye grunt	17.7	17.4	13.7
Red pandora	6.4	3.9	4.8
Round sardinella	24.9	19.5	36.7
Madeiran sardinella	15.8	6.3	11.3
European anchovy	40.6	54.4	45.1
Skipjack tuna	37.4	36.1	53.8
Yellowfin tuna	14.3	18.4	12.5
Bigeye tuna	9.3	10.6	6.8
Atlantic bumper	9.9	2.6	7.5
Aquaculture*	5.6	7.2	10.2
Total catch*	365.4	329.0	361.4

* FAO estimate(s).

Source: FAO.

Mining

('000 metric tons unless otherwise indicated)

	2008	2009	2010
Bauxite	796	490	512
Manganese ore: gross weight	1,261	1,013	1,194
Manganese ore: metal content*	440	350	420
Silver (kg)†	3,200*	3,928	4,000*
Gold (kg)‡	72,980	79,883	76,332
Salt (unrefined)*	239	250	250
Diamonds ('000 carats)	643	376	334

* Estimated figure(s).

† Silver content of exported doré.

‡ Gold content of ores and concentrates, excluding smuggled or undocumented output.

Crude petroleum: 400,000 barrels in 2004.

Source: US Geological Survey.

Industry

SELECTED PRODUCTS

('000 metric tons unless otherwise indicated)

	2002	2003	2004
Groundnut oil*	98.9	76.4	61.5
Coconut oil	6.5*	7.0†	7.0†
Palm oil†	108.0	108.4	114.0
Palm kernel oil*	15.0	17.5	20.7
Butter of karité nuts (shea butter)*	8.4	9.8	18.3
Beer of barley*	100.0	100.0	100.0
Beer of millet*	66.6	73.8	60.2
Beer of sorghum*	234.6	258.3	340.7
Gasoline (petrol)	5,850	5,580	5,580†
Jet fuel	625	625	625†
Kerosene	1,950	1,950	1,950†
Distillate fuel oil	4,450	4,450	4,450†
Residual fuel oil	1,250	1,250	1,250†
Cement†	1,900	1,900	1,900
Aluminium (unwrought)‡	117	16	—
Electric energy (million kWh)	7,273	5,882	6,039

* FAO estimate(s).

† Provisional or estimated figure(s).

‡ Primary metal only.

2009: Groundnut oil 65.5 (FAO estimate); Coconut oil 7.0 (unofficial figure); Palm oil 130.0 (unofficial figure); Palm kernel oil 16.0 (unofficial figure); Beer of barley 142.0 (FAO estimate); Cement 1,800 (estimated figure); Electric energy (million kWh) 8,958.

2010: Groundnut oil 72.2 (FAO estimate); Coconut oil 7.0 (FAO estimate); Palm oil 120.0 (unofficial figure); Palm kernel oil 16.0 (unofficial figure); Beer of barley 155.2 (FAO estimate); Electric energy (million kWh) 10,167.

2011: Electric energy (million kWh) 11,200.

Sources: FAO; US Geological Survey; Energy Commission of Ghana.

Finance

CURRENCY AND EXCHANGE RATES

Monetary Units

100 Ghana pesewas = 1 Ghana cedi.

Sterling, Dollar and Euro Equivalents (30 April 2012)

£1 sterling = 2.7692 Ghana cedis;
US $1 = 1.7030 Ghana cedis;
€1 = 2.2503 Ghana cedis;
10 Ghana cedis = £3.61 = $5.87 = €4.44.

Average Exchange Rate (Ghana cedis per US $)

2009	1.4088
2010	1.4310
2011	1.5119

Note: A new currency, the Ghana cedi, equivalent to 10,000 new cedis (the former legal tender), was introduced over a six-month period beginning in July 2007. Some statistical data in this survey are still presented in terms of the former currency, the new cedi.

GENERAL BUDGET

(million Ghana cedis)

Revenue*	2009	2010	2011
Tax revenue	4,803.6	6,504.5	9,854.6
Income and property	1,716.9	2,454.0	4,036.6
Personal (PAYE)	773.5	1,014.6	1,360.9
Company tax	661.9	987.7	1,568.0
Domestic goods and services	330.2	374.4	606.2
Petroleum tax	278.7	256.5	438.5
International trade	762.7	1,146.2	1,516.0
Import duties	745.9	1,136.2	1,511.0
Value added tax	1,268.4	1,618.3	2,376.1
Import exceptions	318.5	386.4	634.6
National health insurance levy	319.0	388.0	550.2
Other	88.0	137.3	135.0
Non-tax revenue	870.3	1,226.1	1,822.0
Total	5,674.0	7,730.6	11,676.6

Expenditure	2009	2010	2011
Recurrent expenditure	5,631.8	8,045.9	9,705.0
Wages and salaries	2,478.7	3,182.5	4,534.9
Goods and services	621.2	961.8	723.9
Transfers	1,331.3	1,991.4	2,504.6
National Health Fund (NHF)	153.5	351.3	377.0
Reserve fund	168.3	470.8	330.5
Interest payments	1,032.3	1,439.4	1,611.2
Domestic (accrual)	773.5	1,124.3	1,307.9
External (accrual)	258.8	315.0	303.3
Capital expenditure	2,425.7	3,168.6	3,675.0
Domestic	799.1	1,136.0	1,962.8
External	1,626.6	2,032.6	1,712.2
Total	8,057.5	11,214.5	13,380.0

* Excluding grants received (million Ghana cedis): 1,101.2 in 2009; 1,080.2 in 2010; 1,175.0 in 2011.

Source: Bank of Ghana, Accra.

INTERNATIONAL RESERVES

(US $ million at 31 December)

	2009	2010	2011
Gold (national valuation)	237.4	303.4	321.7
IMF special drawing rights	455.4	448.6	430.6
Foreign exchange	2,930.8	4,314.6	5,052.8
Total	3,623.6	5,066.6	5,805.1

Source: IMF, *International Financial Statistics*.

MONEY SUPPLY
(million Ghana cedis at 31 December)

	2009	2010	2011
Currency outside depository corporations	2,083.5	2,929.2	3,767.3
Transferable deposits	4,299.6	5,709.8	8,296.7
Other deposits	3,954.7	4,998.3	6,216.1
Broad money	10,337.7	13,637.3	18,280.0

Source: IMF, *International Financial Statistics*.

COST OF LIVING
(Consumer Price Index; annual averages; base: 2002 = 100)

	2009	2010	2011
Food and non-alcoholic beverages	275.0	291.8	303.6
Clothing and footwear	226.1	262.3	296.2
Housing, water, electricity and other fuels	385.2	424.7	469.7
Health	502.2	553.7	596.8
Transport	450.6	494.1	603.9
Communications	273.2	273.0	273.5
Recreation and culture	430.3	519.7	563.7
Education	277.9	281.0	288.1
All items (incl. others)	303.9	336.5	365.8

NATIONAL ACCOUNTS
(million Ghana cedis at current prices)

Expenditure on the Gross Domestic Product

	2009	2010	2011
Government final consumption expenditure	4,294	4,768	7,430
Private final consumption expenditure	28,349	35,860	46,091
Increase in stocks	349	480	440
Gross fixed capital formation	7,216	11,354	14,069
Total domestic expenditure	40,208	52,462	68,031
Exports of goods and services	10,720	13,572	22,094
Less Imports of goods and services	15,482	21,134	29,727
Statistical discrepancy	1,151	1,143	–1,133
GDP in purchasers' values	36,598	46,042	59,264
GDP in constant 2006 prices	22,454	24,252	27,743

Gross Domestic Product by Economic Activity

	2009	2010	2011
Agriculture and livestock	9,154	10,295	11,654
Forestry and logging	1,314	1,614	1,549
Fishing	874	1,001	952
Mining and quarrying	740	1,013	4,690
Manufacturing	2,478	2,941	3,711
Electricity and water	413	634	792
Construction	3,144	3,706	5,114
Transport, storage and communications	4,415	5,409	6,570
Wholesale and retail trade, restaurants and hotels	4,305	5,294	6,477
Finance, insurance, real estate and business services	3,009	4,185	5,057
Public administration and defence	2,479	3,024	3,540
Education	1,506	1,877	2,307
Health and social work	513	674	728
Other community, social and personal services	1,318	1,722	2,159
Sub-total	35,662	43,388	55,300
Indirect taxes, less subsidies	936	2,654	3,964
GDP at market prices	36,598	46,042	59,264

BALANCE OF PAYMENTS
(US $ million)

	2008	2009	2010
Exports of goods f.o.b.	5,269.7	5,839.7	7,960.1
Imports of goods f.o.b.	–10,268.5	–8,046.3	–10,922.1
Trade balance	–4,998.8	–2,206.6	–2,962.0
Exports of services	1,800.9	1,769.7	1,477.3
Imports of services	–2,298.2	–2,943.1	–3,003.2
Balance on goods and services	–5,496.0	–3,380.0	–4,488.0
Other income received	85.6	101.1	52.9
Other income paid	–344.2	–397.6	–587.9
Balance on goods, services and income	–5,754.6	–3,676.5	–5,022.9
Current transfers (net)	2,211.5	2,078.0	2,322.4
Current balance	–3,543.1	–1,598.5	–2,700.5
Capital account (net)	463.3	563.9	337.5
Direct investment abroad	–8.8	–6.9	—
Direct investment from abroad	1,220.4	1,684.7	2,527.4
Portfolio investment assets		41.3	723.0
Portfolio investment liabilities	–49.0	–84.9	–102.5
Other investment liabilities	643.5	1,452.0	822.7
Net errors and omissions	515.3	–1,022.3	–163.0
Overall balance	–758.5	1,029.4	1,444.6

Source: IMF, *International Financial Statistics*.

External Trade

PRINCIPAL COMMODITIES
(distribution by SITC, US $ million)

Imports c.i.f.	2008	2009	2010
Food and live animals	1,097.7	947.3	1,111.5
Fish, crustaceans and molluscs, and preparations thereof	120.5	116.3	141.6
Fish, fresh, chilled or frozen	97.1	97.9	128.4
Cereals and cereal preparations	502.4	416.5	374.9
Rice	214.4	224.6	201.4
Sugar and honey	92.0	117.9	185.7
Crude materials (inedible), except fuels	126.3	116.8	116.9
Mineral fuels, lubricants, etc.	1,180.4	196.7	78.1
Crude petroleum and oils obtained from bituminous materials	1,084.0	171.2	78.0
Petroleum products, refined	69.0	56.6	61.9
Chemicals and related products	951.7	871.7	1,084.5
Basic manufactures	1,504.0	1,261.5	1,827.2
Non-metallic mineral manufactures	362.7	277.9	335.6
Iron and steel	343.6	255.6	462.2
Machinery and transport equipment	3,106.3	2,392.3	3,276.8
Power-generating machinery and equipment	212.4	143.7	134.4
Machinery specialized for particular industries	435.6	276.6	478.5
General industrial machinery and equipment, and parts thereof	361.5	298.2	380.6
Telecommunications, sound recording and reproducing equipment	405.0	211.9	401.3
Other electric machinery, apparatus and appliances, and parts thereof	367.0	376.5	399.6
Road vehicles and parts*	1,188.0	967.6	1,042.3
Passenger motor vehicles (excluding buses)	544.4	497.6	524.1
Motor vehicles for the transport of goods or materials	399.3	286.0	334.0
Miscellaneous manufactured articles	409.2	373.9	426.8
Total (incl. others)	8,536.1	6,464.8	8,057.1

* Data on parts exclude tyres, engines and electrical parts.

Exports f.o.b.	2008	2009	2010
Food and live animals	1,266.8	1,259.6	1,075.3
Fish, crustaceans and molluscs, and preparations thereof	43.9	13.9	14.5
Vegetables and fruit	143.5	48.0	36.4
Fruit and nuts, fresh, dried	122.3	31.2	22.4
Fruit, fresh or dried	112.9	19.5	15.5
Coffee, tea, cocoa, spices and manufactures thereof	1,048.3	1,162.3	979.7
Cocoa	1,039.8	1,154.3	970.2
Cocoa beans, raw, roasted	974.1	1,088.8	847.4
Cocoa butter and paste	15.1	11.5	33.0
Cocoa butter (fat or oil)	44.9	49.9	86.5
Crude materials (inedible) except fuels	349.1	207.9	244.7
Cork and wood	147.3	90.1	92.8
Wood, non-coniferous species, sawn, planed, tongued, grooved, etc.	138.2	78.8	76.4
Wood, non-coniferous species, sawn lengthwise, sliced or peeled	123.8	64.8	60.9
Mineral fuels, lubricants, etc.	50.6	88.9	6.0
Basic manufactures	236.3	276.4	295.1
Cork and wood manufactures (excl. furniture)	138.3	126.4	103.6
Veneers, plywood, 'improved' wood and other wood, worked	130.7	123.3	99.3
Wood sawn lengthwise, veneer sheets, etc., up to 6 mm in thickness	55.4	44.8	58.6
Aluminium and aluminium alloys, unwrought	23.9	23.4	113.2
Machinery and transport equipment	97.4	80.8	66.8
Gold, non-monetary, unwrought or semi-manufactured	1,716.7	2,950.5	3,369.2
Total (incl. others)	3,809.9	5,070.5	5,233.4

Source: UN, *International Trade Statistics Yearbook*.

PRINCIPAL TRADING PARTNERS
(US $ million)

Imports c.i.f.	2008	2009	2010
Australia	127.7	92.8	109.1
Belgium	428.9	341.9	445.6
Brazil	182.1	144.4	213.3
Canada	234.9	163.7	184.9
China, People's Republic	999.6	835.8	1,060.9
Congo, Republic	253.8	3.0	8.7
France (incl. Monaco)	235.0	294.8	498.4
Germany	328.0	232.9	272.4
India	369.9	267.8	320.0
Indonesia	156.0	77.6	83.8
Italy (incl. San Marino)	171.5	193.1	190.9
Japan	188.8	116.5	148.9
Korea, Republic	243.7	166.4	344.2
Netherlands	285.6	233.9	278.8
Nigeria	745.0	135.1	34.6
South Africa	365.9	273.4	333.2
Spain	115.2	79.1	114.5
Sweden	264.9	197.2	126.3
Thailand	224.3	155.4	158.2
United Arab Emirates	103.9	84.7	143.7
United Kingdom	370.7	323.1	387.5
USA	653.5	522.9	1,101.3
Total (incl. others)	8,536.1	6,464.8	8,057.1

Exports f.o.b.	2008	2009	2010
Belgium	43.3	48.4	110.1
Benin	5.4	125.4	37.6
Burkina Faso	81.7	207.6	72.9
China, People's Republic	71.6	46.0	51.3
Côte d'Ivoire	28.9	62.7	26.5
Estonia	50.3	35.3	79.0
France (incl. Monaco)	91.2	68.6	65.0
Germany	56.6	57.5	67.4
India	203.0	59.2	48.6
Italy (incl. San Marino)	62.6	49.3	38.6
Japan	19.6	97.2	41.4
Malaysia	120.5	71.7	30.9
Mali	5.6	9.9	126.7
Netherlands	447.5	439.0	291.8
Nigeria	86.0	79.3	101.1
South Africa	1,676.2	2,363.7	2,798.7
Spain	59.8	50.1	66.8
Switzerland-Liechtenstein	100.7	515.5	215.5
Togo	12.6	50.2	70.1
Turkey	54.9	41.1	29.8
United Arab Emirates	16.2	57.2	353.4
United Kingdom	140.5	162.3	175.8
USA	108.1	100.8	102.8
Total (incl. others)	3,809.9	5,070.5	5,233.4

Source: UN, *International Trade Statistics Yearbook*.

Transport

RAILWAYS
(traffic)

	2002	2003	2004
Passenger-km (million)	61	86	80
Net ton-km (million)	244	242	216

Source: UN, *Statistical Yearbook*.

ROAD TRAFFIC
(motor vehicles in use at 31 December)

	2006	2007	2009*
Passenger cars	275,424	493,770	439,527
Buses and coaches	43,665	121,113	145,144
Lorries and vans	92,154	158,379	124,512
Motorcycles and mopeds	100,636	149,063	203,756

* Data for 2008 were not available.

Source: IRF, *World Road Statistics*.

SHIPPING

Merchant Fleet
(registered at 31 December)

	2007	2008	2009
Number of vessels	235	239	236
Total displacement ('000 grt)	118.2	116.9	116.0

Source: IHS Fairplay, *World Fleet Statistics*.

International Sea-borne Freight Traffic
(estimates, '000 metric tons)

	1991	1992	1993
Goods loaded	2,083	2,279	2,424
Goods unloaded	2,866	2,876	2,904

Source: UN Economic Commission for Africa, *African Statistical Yearbook*.

CIVIL AVIATION
(traffic on scheduled services)

	2002	2003	2004
Kilometres flown (million)	12	12	5
Passengers carried ('000)	256	241	96
Passenger-km (million)	912	906	363
Total ton-km (million)	107	101	41

Source: UN, *Statistical Yearbook*.

Tourism

ARRIVALS BY NATIONALITY

	2004	2005	2006
Côte d'Ivoire	28,069	25,155	25,921
France	21,096	10,089	11,915
Germany	28,168	14,094	17,132
Liberia	15,310	14,472	16,938
Netherlands	14,133	13,663	14,673
Nigeria	80,131	47,983	56,278
Togo	17,472	11,888	13,859
United Kingdom	50,547	36,747	36,795
USA	38,508	50,475	62,795
Total (incl. others)*	583,819	428,533	497,129

* Includes Ghanaian nationals resident abroad: 158,917 in 2004; 159,821 in 2005; 155,826 in 2006.

Total tourist arrivals ('000): 698 in 2008; 803 in 2009; 931 in 2010.

Receipts from tourism (US $ million, excl. passenger transport): 919 in 2008; 768 in 2009; 620 in 2010.

Source: World Tourism Organization.

Communications Media

	2009	2010	2011
Telephones ('000 main lines in use)	267.4	277.9	284.7
Mobile cellular telephones ('000 subscribers)	15,108.9	17,436.9	21,165.8
Internet subscribers ('000)	92.7	53.1	n.a.
Broadband subscribers ('000)	28.9	50.1	62.6

Personal computers: 250,000 (10.7 per 1,000 persons) in 2008.

Source: International Telecommunication Union.

Radio receivers ('000 in use): 4,400 in 1997.

Television receivers ('000 in use): 2,390 in 2000.

Daily newspapers: 4 titles in 1998 (average circulation 260,000).

Book production (titles, 1998): 7.

Sources: UNESCO Institute for Statistics; UNESCO, *Statistical Yearbook*; UN, *Statistical Yearbook*.

Education

(2010/11, unless otherwise indicated)

			Students ('000)		
	Institutions	Teachers	Males	Females	Total
Pre-primary*	n.a.	37,789	671.9	666.6	1,338.5
Primary	13,115†	124,359	1,979.2	1,881.2	3,860.4
Junior secondary	6,394†	83,339	715.7	632.6	1,348.3
Senior secondary	512†	31,747	437.6	362.3	799.9
Tertiary	n.a.	7,924	179.6	106.3	285.9

* 2008/09 figures.
† 1998/99 figure.

1998/99: *Teacher training* 38 institutions; *Technical institutes* 61 institutions; *Polytechnics* 8 institutions; *Universities* 7 institutions.

Source: UNESCO and former Ministry of Education, Accra.

Pupil-teacher ratio (primary education, UNESCO estimate): 31.0 in 2010/11 (Source: UNESCO Institute for Statistics).

Adult literacy rate (UNESCO estimates): 67.3% (males 73.2%; females 61.2%) in 2010 (Source: UNESCO Institute for Statistics).

Directory

The Constitution

Under the terms of the Constitution of the Fourth Republic, which was approved by national referendum on 28 April 1992, Ghana has a multi-party political system. Executive power is vested in the President, who is Head of State and Commander-in-Chief of the Armed Forces. The President is elected by universal adult suffrage for a term of four years, and designates a Vice-President (prior to election). The duration of the President's tenure of office is limited to two four-year terms. It is also stipulated that, in the event that no presidential candidate receives more than 50% of votes cast, a new election between the two candidates with the highest number of votes is to take place within 21 days. Legislative power is vested in a 230-member unicameral Parliament, which is elected by direct adult suffrage for a four-year term. (This number was increased from 200 at the general election of December 2004.) The Council of Ministers is appointed by the President, subject to approval by the Parliament. The Constitution also provides for a 25-member Council of State, principally comprising presidential nominees and regional representatives, and a 20-member National Security Council (chaired by the Vice-President), both of which act as advisory bodies to the President.

The Government

HEAD OF STATE

President and Commander-in-Chief of the Armed Forces: JOHN DRAMANI MAHAMA (took office 24 July 2012).

Vice-President: KWESI BEKOE AMISSAH-ARTHUR.

CABINET
(September 2012)

Minister of Finance and Economic Planning: Dr KWABENA DUFFUOR.

Minister of Defence: Lt-Gen. (retd) JOSEPH HENRY SMITH.

Minister of the Interior: WILLIAM KWASI ABOAH.

Minister of Foreign Affairs and Regional Integration: Alhaji MUHAMMED MUMUNI.

Attorney-General, Minister of Justice: Dr BENJAMIN KUNBUOR.

Minister of Roads and Highways: JOE GIDISU.

Minister of Local Government and Rural Development: SAMUEL OFUSO-AMPOFO.

Minister of Health: ALBAN BAGBIN.

Minister of Food and Agriculture: KWESI AWHOI.

Minister of Education: LEE OCRAN.

Minister of Trade and Industry: HANNAH TETTEH.

Minister of Communications: HARUNA IDDRISU.

Minister of Water Resources, Works and Housing: ENOCH TEYE MENSAH.

Minister of the Environment, Science and Technology: HANI SHERRY AYITEY.

Minister of Energy: Dr JOE OTENG ADJEI.

Minister of Lands and Natural Resources: MIKE ALLEN HAMMAH.

Minister of Transport: Alhaji COLLINS DAUDA.

Minister of Employment and Social Welfare: MOSES ASAGA.

Minister of Women's and Children's Affairs: JULIANA JOCELYN AZUMAH MENSAH.

Minister of Tourism: AKUA SENA DANSUA.

Minister of Information: FRITZ BAFFOUR.

Minister of Youth and Sports: CLEMENT KOFI HUMADO.

Minister of Culture and Chieftaincy: ALEXANDER ASUM-AHENSAH.

Ministers of State at the Presidency: RAFATU HALUTIE DUBIE, STEPHEN AMOANOR KWAO, JOHN GYETUAH, DOMINIC AZIMBE AZUMAH.

In addition there were 28 Deputy Ministers.

REGIONAL MINISTERS
(September 2012)

Ashanti: KWAKU AGYEMANG-MENSAH.

Brong Ahafo: KWADWO NYAMEKYE-MARFO.

Central: AMA BENYIWA-DOE.

Eastern: VICTOR EMMANUEL SMITH.

Greater Accra: NII ARMAH ASHITEY.

Northern: MOSES MAGBENBA.

Upper East: MARK WAYONGO.

Upper West: AMIN AMIDU SULEMANI.

Volta: HENRY KAMEL FORD.

Western: PAUL EVANS AIDOO.

MINISTRIES

Office of the President: POB 1627, Osu, Accra; tel. (30) 2666997; internet www.oop.gov.gh.

Ministry of Communications: POB M38, Accra; tel. (30) 2666465; fax (30) 2667114; e-mail info@moc.gov.gh; internet www.moc.gov.gh.

Ministry of Culture and Chieftaincy: POB 1627, State House, Accra; tel. (30) 2685012; fax (30) 2678361; e-mail chieftancycultur@yahoo.com.

Ministry of Defence: Burma Camp, Accra; tel. (30) 2775665; fax (30) 2772241; e-mail kaddok@internetghana.com.

Ministry of Education: POB M45, Accra; tel. (30) 2666070; fax (30) 2664067.

Ministry of Employment and Social Welfare: POB 1627, State House, Accra; tel. (30) 2684532; fax (30) 2663615.

Ministry of Energy: FREMA House, Spintex Rd, POB T40 (Stadium Post Office), Stadium, Accra; tel. (30) 2683961; fax (30) 2668262; e-mail moen@energymin.gov.gh; internet www.energymin.gov.gh.

Ministry of the Environment, Science and Technology: POB M232, Accra; tel. (30) 2660005.

Ministry of Finance and Economic Planning: POB M40, Accra; tel. (30) 2665587; fax (30) 2666079; e-mail minister2009@mofep.gov.gh; internet www.mofep.gov.gh.

Ministry of Food and Agriculture: POB M37, Accra; tel. (30) 2663036; fax (30) 2668245; e-mail info@mofa.gov.gh; internet www.mofa.gov.gh.

Ministry of Foreign Affairs and Regional Integration: Treasury Rd, POB M53, Accra; tel. (30) 2664952; fax (30) 2665363; e-mail ghmaf00@ghana.com.

Ministry of Health: POB M44, Accra; tel. (30) 2684208; fax (30) 2663810; e-mail info@moh-ghana.org; internet www.moh-ghana.org.

Ministry of Information: POB M41, Accra; tel. and fax (30) 2229870; e-mail webmaster@mino.gov.gh; internet www.ghana.gov.gh.

Ministry of the Interior: POB M42, Accra; tel. (30) 2684400; fax (30) 2684408; e-mail mint@mint.gov.gh; internet www.mint.gov.gh.

Ministry of Justice and Attorney-General's Department: POB M60, Accra; tel. (30) 2665051; fax (30) 2667609; e-mail info@mjag.gov.gh.

Ministry of Lands and Natural Resources: POB M212, Accra; tel. (30) 2687314; fax (30) 2666801; e-mail motgov@hotmail.com; internet www.ghana-mining.org/ghweb/en/ma.html.

Ministry of Local Government and Rural Development: POB M50, Accra; tel. (30) 2682018; fax (30) 2682003.

Ministry of Roads and Highways: Accra; tel. (30) 2618668; fax (30) 2672676; internet www.mrt.gov.gh.

Ministry of Tourism: POB 4386, Accra; tel. (30) 2666314; fax (30) 2666182; e-mail humphrey.kuma@tourism.gov.gh; internet www.touringghana.com.

Ministry of Trade and Industry: POB M47, Accra; tel. (30) 2663327; fax (30) 2662428; e-mail info@moti.gov.gh; internet www.moti.gov.gh.

Ministry of Transport: POB M57, Accra; tel. (30) 2681780; fax (30) 2681781; e-mail info@mot.gov.gh; internet mot.gov.gh.

Ministry of Water Resources, Works and Housing: POB M43, Accra; tel. (30) 2665940; fax (30) 2685503; e-mail mwh@ighmail.com.

Ministry of Women's and Children's Affairs: POB M186, Accra; tel. (30) 2688187; fax (30) 2688182; e-mail info@mowacgov.com; internet www.mowacghana.net.

Ministry of Youth and Sports: Accra.

President and Legislature

PRESIDENT

Presidential Election, First Round, 7 December 2008

Candidate	Valid votes	% of valid votes
Nana Akufo-Addo (NPP)	4,159,439	49.13
John Evans Atta Mills (NDC)	4,056,634	47.92
Paa Kwesi Nduom (CPP)	113,494	1.34
Edward Nasigre Mahama (PNC)	73,494	0.87
Emmanuel Ansah Antwi (DFP)	27,889	0.33
Kwesi Amoafo Yeboah (Ind.)	19,342	0.23
Thomas Ward-Brew (DPP)	8,653	0.10
Kwabena Adjei (RPD)	6,889	0.08
Total	8,465,834*	100.00

* Excluding 205,438 spoiled papers.

Presidential Election, Second Round, 28 December 2008

Candidate	Valid votes	% of valid votes
John Evans Atta Mills (NDC)	4,521,032	50.23
Nana Akufo-Addo (NPP)	4,480,446	49.77
Total	9,001,478*	100.00

* Excluding 92,886 spoiled papers.

PARLIAMENT

Parliament: Parliament House, Accra; tel. (30) 2664042; fax (30) 2665957; e-mail clerk@parliament.gh; internet www.parliament.gh.

Speaker: JOYCE BAMFORD-ADDO.

General Election, 7 December 2008

Party	Seats
National Democratic Congress (NDC)	113
New Patriotic Party (NPP)	109
People's National Convention (PNC)	2
Convention People's Party (CPP)	1
Independents	4
Total	229*

* The result in the remaining constituency was not immediately made available.

COUNCIL OF STATE

Chairman: Prof. DANIEL ADZEI BEKOE.

Election Commission

Electoral Commission (EC): POB M214, Accra; tel. (30) 2228421; internet www.ec.gov.gh; f. 1993; appointed by the President; Chair. Dr KWADWO AFARI-GYAN.

Political Organizations

Convention People's Party (CPP): 64 Mango Tree Ave, Asylum Down, POB 10939, Accra-North; tel. (30) 2227763; e-mail info@conventionpeoplesparty.org; internet conventionpeoplesparty.org; f. 1998 as Convention Party by merger of the National Convention

Party (f. 1992) and the People's Convention Party (f. 1993); present name adopted in 2000; Nkrumahist; Chair. LADI NYLANDER; Gen. Sec. IVOR KOBBINA GREENSTREET.

Democratic Freedom Party (DFP): POB 1040, Accra; tel. (30) 2237590; internet votedfp.org; f. 2006; Leader Dr OBED YAO ASAMOAH.

Democratic People's Party (DPP): 698/4 Star Ave, Kokomlemle, Accra; tel. (30) 2221671; f. 1992; Chair. THOMAS WARD-BREW; Gen. Sec. G. M. TETTEY.

EGLE (Every Ghanaian Living Everywhere) Party: POB TN 16132, Teshie Nungua, Accra; tel. (30) 2713994; fax (30) 2776894; f. 1992 as the Eagle Party.

Great Consolidated People's Party (GCPP): Citadel House, POB 3077, Accra; tel. (30) 2311498; f. 1996; Nkrumahist; Chair. Dr HENRY HERBERT LARTEY; Sec.-Gen. NICHOLAS MENSAH.

National Democratic Congress (NDC): 641/4 Ringway Close, POB 5825, Kokomlemle, Accra-North; tel. (30) 2223195; fax (30) 2220743; e-mail info@ndc.org.gh; internet www.ndc2008.com; f. 1992; party of fmr Pres. Jerry Rawlings; Chair. Dr KWABENA ADJEI; Gen. Sec. JOHNSON ASIEDU NKETIAH.

National Democratic Party (NDP): Accra; f. 2012 by breakaway faction of NDC; Chair. Dr NII ARMAH JOSIAH ARYEH; Gen. Sec. Dr JOSPEH MAMBOA ROCKSON.

National Reform Party (NRP): 31 Mango Tree Ave, Asylum Down, POB 19403, Accra-North; tel. (30) 2228578; fax (30) 2227820; f. 1999 by a breakaway group from the NDC; Sec.-Gen. OPOKU KYERETWIE.

New Patriotic Party (NPP): C912/2 Duade St, Kokomlemle, POB 3456, Accra-North; tel. (30) 2227951; fax (30) 2224418; f. 1992; Gen. Sec. NANA OHENE NTOW.

People's National Convention (PNC): POB AC 120, Arts Centre, Accra; tel. (30) 2236389; f. 1992; Nkrumahist; Chair. Alhaji AHMED RAMADAN; Gen. Sec. BERNARD MORNAH.

Reformed Patriotic Democrats (RPD): POB 13274, Kumasi; tel. 243616660 (mobile); f. 2007 by former mems of the NPP; Founding Leader KWABENA AGYEI.

United Ghana Movement (UGM): 1 North Ridge Cres., POB C2611, Cantonments, Accra; tel. (30) 2225581; fax (30) 2223506; e-mail info@ugmghana.org; f. 1996 by a breakaway group from the NPP; Chair. WEREKO BROBBY.

United Renaissance Party (URP): Nima Hwy, POB 104, Accra-North; tel. (30) 28914411; f. 2006; Chair. KOFI WAYO.

Diplomatic Representation

EMBASSIES AND HIGH COMMISSIONS IN GHANA

Algeria: 22 Josif Broz Tito Ave, POB 2747, Cantonments, Accra; tel. (30) 2776719; fax (30) 2776828; Ambassador LARBI KATTI.

Angola: Accra; Ambassador ANA MARIA TELES CARREIRA.

Benin: 19 Volta St, Second Close, Airport Residential Area, POB 7871, Accra; tel. (30) 2774860; fax (30) 2774889; Ambassador PIERRE SADELER.

Brazil: Millennium Heights Bldg 2A, 14 Liberation Link, Airport Commercial Area, POB CT3859, Accra; tel. (30) 2774908; fax (30) 2778566; e-mail brasemb@africaonline.com.gh; internet www.embrazil.com.gh; Ambassador LUIS IRENE GALA.

Bulgaria: 3 Kakramadu Rd, POB 3193, East Cantonments, Accra; tel. (30) 2772404; fax (30) 2774231; e-mail bulemb2003@yahoo.com; internet www.mfa.bg/accra; Chargé d'affaires a.i. GEORGE MITEV.

Burkina Faso: 772 Asylum Down, off Farrar Ave, POB 65, Accra; tel. (30) 2221988; fax (30) 2221936; e-mail ambafaso@ghana.com; Ambassador PIERRE SEM SANOU.

Canada: 42 Independence Ave, Sankara Interchange, POB 1639, Accra; tel. (30) 2211521; fax (30) 2211523; e-mail accra@international.gc.ca; internet www.canadainternational.gc.ca/ghana; High Commissioner TRUDY KERNIGHAN.

China, People's Republic: 6 Agostino Neto Rd, Airport Residential Area, POB 3356, Accra; tel. (30) 2777073; fax (30) 2774527; e-mail chinaemb_gh@mfa.gov.cn; internet gh.chineseembassy.org; Ambassador GONG JIANZHONG.

Côte d'Ivoire: 9 18th Lane, off Cantonments Rd, POB 3445, Christiansborg, Accra; tel. (30) 2774611; fax (30) 2773516; e-mail acigh@ambaci-ghana.org; Ambassador BERNARD HUI KOUTOUA.

Cuba: 20 Amilcar Cabral Rd, Airport Residential Area, POB 9163 Airport, Accra; tel. (30) 2775868; fax (30) 2774998; e-mail embghana@africaonline.com.gh; Ambassador (vacant).

Czech Republic: C260/5, 2 Kanda High Rd, POB 5226, Accra-North; tel. (30) 2223540; fax (30) 2225337; e-mail accra@embassy.mzv.cz; internet www.mzv.cz/accra; Ambassador MILOSLAV MACHÁLEK.

Denmark: 67 Dr Isert Rd, North Ridge, POB CT596, Accra; tel. (30) 2253473; fax (30) 2228061; e-mail accamb@um.dk; internet www.ambaccra.um.dk; Ambassador CARSTEN NILAUS PEDERSEN.

Egypt: 38 Senchi St, Airport Residential Area, Accra; tel. (30) 2776795; fax (30) 2777579; e-mail boustaneaccra@hotmail.com; Ambassador IBRAHIM SAEED.

Ethiopia: 2 Milne Close, Airport Residential Area, POB 1646, Accra; tel. (30) 2775928; fax (30) 2776807; e-mail ethioemb@ghana.com; Ambassador GIFTY ABASIGA ABABULGU.

France: 12th Rd, off Liberation Ave, POB 187, Accra; tel. (30) 2214550; fax (30) 2214589; e-mail info@ambafrance-gh.org; internet www.ambafrance-gh.org; Ambassador FRANCIS HURTUT.

Germany: 6 Ridge St, North Ridge, POB 1757, Accra; tel. (30) 2211000; fax (30) 2221347; e-mail info@accra.diplo.de; internet www.accra.diplo.de; Ambassador Dr MARIUS HAAS.

Guinea: 11 Osu Badu St, Dzorwulu, POB 5497, Accra-North; tel. (30) 2777921; fax (30) 2760961; e-mail embagui@ghana.com; Ambassador MAMADOU FALILOU BAH.

Holy See: 8 Drake Ave, Airport Residential Area, POB 9675, Accra; tel. (30) 2777759; fax (30) 2774019; e-mail nuncio@ghana.com; Apostolic Nuncio Most Rev. LÉON KALENGA BADIKEBELE (Titular Archbishop of Magnetum).

India: 9 Ridge Rd, Roman Ridge, POB CT 5708, Cantonments, Accra; tel. (30) 2775601; fax (30) 2772176; e-mail indiahc@ncs.com.gh; internet www.indiahc-ghana.com; High Commissioner RAJINDER BHAGAT.

Iran: 12 Arkusah St, Airport Residential Area, POB 12673, Accra-North; tel. (30) 2774474; fax (30) 2777043; Ambassador MOHAMMED SULEYMANI.

Israel: Accra; Ambassador SHARON BAR-LI.

Italy: Jawaharlal Nehru Rd, POB 140, Accra; tel. (30) 2775621; fax (30) 2777301; e-mail ambasciata.accra@esteri.it; internet www.ambaccra.esteri.it; Ambassador LUCA FRATINI.

Japan: Fifth Ave, POB 1637, West Cantonments, Accra; tel. (30) 2765060; fax (30) 2762553; Ambassador KEIICHI KATAKAMI.

Korea, Democratic People's Republic: 139 Nortei Ababio Loop, Ambassadorial Estate, Roman Ridge, POB 13874, Accra; tel. (30) 2777825; Ambassador KIM PYONG GI.

Korea, Republic: 3 Abokobi Rd, POB GP13700, East Cantonments, Accra-North; tel. (30) 2776157; fax (30) 2772313; e-mail ghana@mofat.go.kr; internet gha.mofat.go.kr; Ambassador LEE SANG-HAK.

Lebanon: F864/1, off Cantonments Rd, Osu, POB 562, Accra; tel. (30) 2776727; fax (30) 2764290; e-mail lebanon@its.com.gh; Ambassador JAWDAT EL-HAJJAR.

Liberia: 10 Odoi Kwao St, Airport Residential Area, POB 895, Accra; tel. (30) 2775641; fax (30) 2775987; Ambassador RUDOLPH P. VON BALLMOOS.

Libya: 14 Sixth St, Airport Residential Area, POB 9665, Accra; tel. (30) 2774819; fax (30) 2774953; Ambassador Dr ALI AHMED GHUDBAN.

Malaysia: 18 Templesi Lane, Airport Residential Area, POB 16033, Accra; tel. (30) 2763691; fax (30) 2764910; e-mail mwaccra@africaonline.com.gh; High Commissioner Dato' HAJJAH RAZINAH GHAZALI.

Mali: 1st Bungalow, Liberia Rd, Airport Residential Area, POB 1121, Accra; tel. and fax (30) 2666942; e-mail ambamali@ighmail.com; Ambassador Gen. TOUMANY SISSOKO.

Netherlands: 89 Liberation Rd, Ako Adjei Interchange, POB CT1647, Accra; tel. (30) 2214350; fax (30) 2773655; e-mail acc@minbuza.nl; internet www.ambaccra.nl; Ambassador (vacant).

Niger: E104/3 Independence Ave, POB 2685, Accra; tel. (30) 2224962; fax (30) 2229011; Ambassador ABDOULMOUMINE HADJIO.

Nigeria: 20/21 Onyasia Cres., Roman Ridge Residential Area, Accra; tel. (30) 2776158; fax (30) 2774395; e-mail nighicomgh@yahoo.com; High Commissioner ADEMOLA OLUSEYI ONAFOWOKAN.

Russia: Jawaharlal Nehru Rd, Switchback Lane, POB 1634, Accra; tel. (30) 2775611; fax (30) 2772699; e-mail russia@4u.com.gh; internet www.ghana.mid.ru; Ambassador VLADIMIR V. BARBIN.

Senegal: 8F Odoi Kwao St, Airport Residential Area, PMB CT 342, Cantonments, Accra; tel. (30) 2770285; fax (30) 2770286; e-mail senegalaccra@hotmail.fr; Ambassador CHÉRIF OUMAR DIAGNÉ.

Sierra Leone: 83A Senchi St, Airport Residential Area, POB 55, Cantonments, Accra; tel. (30) 2769190; fax (30) 2769189; e-mail slhc@ighmail.com; High Commissioner MOKOWA ADU- GYAMFI.

South Africa: Speed House 1, 3rd Soula St, Labone North POB 298, Accra; tel. (30) 2740450; fax (30) 2762381; e-mail sahcgh@africaonline.com.gh; High Commissioner (vacant).

Spain: Drake Ave Extension, Airport Residential Area, PMB KA44, Accra; tel. (30) 2774004; fax (30) 2776217; e-mail emb.accra@mae.es; Ambassador JULIA ALICIA OLMO Y ROMERO.

Switzerland: Kanda Highway, North Ridge, POB 359, Accra; tel. (30) 2228125; fax (30) 2223583; e-mail acc.vertretung@eda.admin.ch; internet www.eda.admin.ch/accra; Ambassador ANDREA SEMADENI.

Togo: Togo House, near Cantonments Circle, POB C120, Accra; tel. (30) 2777950; fax (30) 2765659; e-mail togamba@ighmail.com; Ambassador JEAN-PIERRE GBIKPI-BENISSAN.

United Kingdom: Osu Link, off Gamel Abdul Nasser Ave, POB 296, Accra; tel. and fax (30) 2221665; fax (30) 2213274; e-mail high.commission.accra@fco.gov.uk; internet ukinghana.fco.gov.uk; High Commissioner Dr PETER EDWARD JONES.

USA: 24 Fourth Circular Rd, POB 194, Cantonments, Accra; tel. (30) 2741150; fax (30) 2741692; e-mail pressaccra@state.gov; internet ghana.usembassy.gov; Ambassador DONALD GENE TEITELBAUM.

Judicial System

The civil law in force in Ghana is based on the Common Law, doctrines of equity and general statutes which were in force in England in 1874, as modified by subsequent Ordinances. Ghanaian customary law is, however, the basis of most personal, domestic and contractual relationships. Criminal Law is based on the Criminal Procedure Code, 1960, derived from English Criminal Law, and since amended. The Superior Court of Judicature comprises a Supreme Court, a Court of Appeal, a High Court and a Regional Tribunal; Inferior Courts include Circuit Courts, Circuit Tribunals, Community Tribunals and such other Courts as may be designated by law. In 2001 'fast-track' court procedures were established to accelerate the delivery of justice.

Supreme Court

Consists of the Chief Justice and not fewer than nine other Justices. It is the final court of appeal in Ghana and has jurisdiction in matters relating to the enforcement or interpretation of the Constitution.

Chief Justice: GEORGINA THEODORA WOOD.

Court of Appeal: Consists of the Chief Justice and not fewer than five Judges of the Court of Appeal. It has jurisdiction to hear and determine appeals from any judgment, decree or order of the High Court.

High Court: Comprises the Chief Justice and not fewer than 12 Justices of the High Court. It exercises original jurisdiction in all matters, civil and criminal, other than those for offences involving treason. Trial by jury is practised in criminal cases in Ghana and the Criminal Procedure Code, 1960, provides that all trials on indictment shall be by a jury or with the aid of Assessors.

Circuit Courts: Exercise original jurisdiction in civil matters where the amount involved does not exceed 100,000 new cedis. They also have jurisdiction with regard to the guardianship and custody of infants, and original jurisdiction in all criminal cases, except offences where the maximum punishment is death or the offence of treason. They have appellate jurisdiction from decisions of any District Court situated within their respective circuits.

District Courts: To each magisterial district is assigned at least one District Magistrate who has original jurisdiction to try civil suits in which the amount involved does not exceed 50,000 new cedis. District Magistrates also have jurisdiction to deal with all criminal cases, except first-degree felonies, and commit cases of a more serious nature to either the Circuit Court or the High Court. A Grade I District Court can impose a fine not exceeding 1,000 cedis and sentences of imprisonment of up to two years and a Grade II District Court may impose a fine not exceeding 500 new cedis and a sentence of imprisonment of up to 12 months. A District Court has no appellate jurisdiction, except in rent matters under the Rent Act.

Juvenile Courts: Jurisdiction in cases involving persons under 17 years of age, except where the juvenile is charged jointly with an adult. The Courts comprise a Chairman, who must be either the District Magistrate or a lawyer, and not fewer than two other members appointed by the Chief Justice in consultation with the Judicial Council. The Juvenile Courts can make orders as to the protection and supervision of a neglected child and can negotiate with parents to secure the good behaviour of a child.

National Public Tribunal: Considers appeals from the Regional Public Tribunals. Its decisions are final and are not subject to any further appeal. The Tribunal consists of at least three members and not more than five, one of whom acts as Chairman.

Regional Public Tribunals: Hears criminal cases relating to prices, rent or exchange control, theft, fraud, forgery, corruption or any offence which may be referred to them by the Provisional National Defence Council.

Special Military Tribunal: Hears criminal cases involving members of the armed forces. It consists of between five and seven members.

Attorney-General: Dr BENJAMIN KUNBUOR.

Religion

According to the 2000 census, 69% of the population were Christians and 16% Muslims, while 7% followed indigenous beliefs.

CHRISTIANITY

Christian Council of Ghana: POB GP919, Accra; tel. (30) 2776678; fax (30) 2776725; e-mail info@christiancouncilofghana.org; internet www.christiancouncilofghana.org; f. 1929; advisory body comprising 16 mem. churches and 2 affiliate Christian orgs (2005); Chair. Most Rev. Prof. EMMANUEL ASANTE; Gen. Sec. Rev. Dr FRED DEEGBE.

The Anglican Communion

Anglicans in Ghana are adherents of the Church of the Province of West Africa, comprising 14 dioceses and a missionary region, of which nine are in Ghana.

Archbishop of the Province of West Africa and Bishop of Accra: Most Rev. JUSTICE OFEI AKROFI, Bishopscourt, POB 8, Accra; tel. (30) 2662292; fax (30) 2668822; e-mail adaccra@ghana.com.

Bishop of Cape Coast: Rt Rev. DANIEL ALLOTEY, Bishopscourt, POB A233, Adisadel Estates, Cape Coast; tel. (33) 2132502; fax (33) 2132637; e-mail danallotey@priest.com.

Bishop of Ho: Rt Rev. MATTHIAS MEDADUES-BADOHU, Bishopslodge, POB MA 300, Ho; e-mail matthiaskwab@googlemail.com.

Bishop of Koforidua: Rt Rev. FRANCIS QUASHIE, POB 980, Koforidua; tel. (34) 2022329; fax (34) 2022060; e-mail cpwa_gh@yahoo.com; internet koforidua.org.

Bishop of Kumasi: Rt Rev. DANIEL YINKAH SAFO, Bishop's Office, St Cyprian's Ave, POB 144, Kumasi; tel. and fax (32) 2024117; e-mail anglicandioceseofkumasi@yahoo.com.

Bishop of Sekondi: Rt Rev. JOHN KWAMINA OTOO, POB 85, Sekondi; tel. (31) 20669125; e-mail angdiosek@yahoo.co.uk.

Bishop of Sunyani: Rt Rev. THOMAS AMPAH BRIENT, Bishop's House, POB 23, Sunyani, BA; tel. (35) 2027205; fax (35) 2027203; e-mail anglicandiocesesyi@yahoo.com.

Bishop of Tamale: Rt Rev. EMMANUEL ANYINDANA ARONGO, POB 110, Tamale NR; tel. (37) 2022639; fax (37) 2022906; e-mail bishopea2000@yahoo.com.

Bishop of Wiawso: Rt Rev. ABRAHAM KOBINA ACKAH, POB 4, Sefwi, Wiawso; e-mail bishopackah@yahoo.com.

The Roman Catholic Church

Ghana comprises four archdioceses, 15 dioceses and one apostolic vicariate. Some 13% of the total population are Roman Catholics.

Ghana Bishops' Conference

National Catholic Secretariat, POB 9712, Airport, Accra; tel. (30) 2500491; fax (30) 2500493; e-mail dscncs@africaonline.com.gh; internet www.ghanacbc.org.

f. 1960; Pres. Rt Rev. LUCAS ABADAMLOORA (Bishop of Navrongo-Bolgatanga).

Archbishop of Accra: Most Rev. GABRIEL CHARLES PALMER-BUCKLE, Chancery Office, POB 247, Accra; tel. (30) 2222728; fax (30) 2231619; e-mail cpalmerbuckle@yahoo.com; internet www.accracatholic.org.

Archbishop of Cape Coast: Most Rev. MATTHIAS KOBENA NKETSIAH, Archbishop's House, POB 112, Cape Coast; tel. (33) 2133471; fax (33) 2133473; e-mail archcape@ghanacbc.com.

Archbishop of Kumasi: Most Rev. GABRIEL JUSTICE YAW ANOKYE, POB 99, Kumasi; tel. (32) 2024012; fax (32) 2029395; e-mail cadiokum@ghana.com.

Archbishop of Tamale: Most Rev. PHILIP NAAMEH, Archbishop's House, Gumbehini Rd, POB 42, Tamale; tel. and fax (37) 2022425; e-mail tamdio2@yahoo.co.uk.

Other Christian Churches

African Methodist Episcopal Zion Church: POB MP522, Mamprobi, Accra; tel. (30) 2669200; f. 1898; Pres. Rt Rev. WARREN M. BROWN.

Christian Methodist Episcopal Church: POB AN 7639, Accra; tel. 244630267 (mobile); internet www.cmetenth.org/Ghana%20Regional%20Conference.htm; Pres. KENNETH W. CARTER; Mission Supervisor Rev. ADJEI K. LAWSON.

Church of Pentecost: POB 2194 Accra; tel. (30) 2777611; fax (30) 2774721; e-mail cophq@thechurchofpentecost.com; internet www.thecophq.org; Chair. Apostle Dr OPOKU ONYINAH; Gen. Sec. Apostle ALFRED KODUAH; 1,503,057 mems.

Evangelical-Lutheran Church of Ghana: POB KN197, Kaneshie, Accra; tel. (30) 2223487; fax (30) 2220947; e-mail elcga@africaonline.com.gh; Pres. Rt Rev. Dr PAUL KOFI FYNN; 27,521 mems (2010).

Evangelical-Presbyterian Church of Ghana: 19 Main St, Tesano, PMB, Accra-North; tel. (30) 2220381; fax (30) 2233173; e-mail epchurch@ghana.com; f. 1847; Moderator Rev. FRANCIS AMENU; 295,000 mems.

Ghana Baptist Convention: PMB, Kumasi; tel. (30) 225215; fax (30) 228592; e-mail mail@gbconvention.org; internet www.gbconvention.org; f. 1963; Pres. Rev. Dr KOJO OSEI-WUSUH; Sec. Rev. KOJO AMO; 65,000 mems.

Ghana Mennonite Church: POB 5485, Accra; fax (30) 2220589; f. 1957; Moderator Rev. THEOPHILUS TETTEH; Sec. JOHN ADETA; 5,000 mems.

Ghana Union Conference of Seventh-day Adventists: POB GP1016, Accra; tel. (30) 2223720; fax (30) 2227024; e-mail guc@adventistsghana.org; internet www.adventistgh.org; f. 1943; Pres. Pastor SAMUEL A. LARMIE; Sec. Pastor KWAME KWANIN-BOAKYE; 268,171 mems.

Methodist Church of Ghana: Wesley House, E252/2, Liberia Rd, POB 403, Accra; tel. (30) 2670355; fax (30) 2679223; e-mail mcghqs@ucomgh.com; internet www.methodistchurch-gh.org; Presiding Bishop Most Rev. Dr ROBERT ABOAGYE-MENSAH; 584,969 mems (2007).

Presbyterian Church of Ghana: POB 106, Accra; tel. (30) 2662511; fax (30) 2665594; e-mail pcghg@yahoo.com; internet www.pc-ghana.org; f. 1828; Moderator Rt Rev. YAW FRIMPONG-MANSON; Clerk Rev. Dr CHARLES GYANG DUAH; 422,500 mems.

The African Methodist Episcopal Church, the Christ Reformed Church, the F'Eden Church, the Gospel Revival Church of God and the Religious Society of Friends (Quakers) are also active in Ghana.

ISLAM

In 2000 some 16% of the population of Ghana were Muslims, with a particularly large concentration in the Northern Region. The majority are Malikees.

Coalition of Muslim Organizations (COMOG): Accra; Pres. Alhaji Maj. MOHAMMED EASAH.

Ghana Muslim Representative Council: Accra.

Chief Imam: Sheikh USMAN NUHU SHARABUTU.

BAHÁ'Í FAITH

National Spiritual Assembly: POB 7098, Accra-North; tel. (30) 2222127; e-mail bahaighana@yahoo.com; Sec. GLADYS QUARTEY-PAPAFIO.

The Press

DAILY NEWSPAPERS

The Daily Dispatch: 1 Dade Walk, North Labone, POB C1945, Cantonments, Accra; tel. (30) 2763339; e-mail ephson@usa.net; Editor BEN EPHSON.

Daily Graphic: Graphic Communications Group Ltd, 3 Graphic Rd, POB 742, Accra; tel. (30) 2684001; fax (30) 2234754; e-mail gpack@graphic.com.gh; internet www.graphic.com.gh; f. 1950; state-owned; Editor RANSFORD TETTEH; circ. 100,000.

Daily Guide: Accra; internet dailyguideghana.com; owned by Western Publications Ltd; Editor GINA BLAY.

Ghanaian Chronicle: 37 Bobo St, Tesano, PMB, Accra-North; tel. (30) 2232713; fax (30) 2232608; e-mail chronicl@africaonline.com.gh; internet www.ghanaian-chronicle.com; Editor EMMANUEL AKLI; circ. 60,000.

The Ghanaian Times: New Times Corpn, Ring Rd West, POB 2638, Accra; tel. (30) 228282; fax (30) 220733; e-mail info@newtimes.com.gh; internet www.newtimes.com.gh; f. 1958; state-owned; Editor ENIMIL ASHON; circ. 45,000.

The Mail: POB CT4910, Cantonments, Accra; e-mail mike@accra-mail.com; internet www.accra-mail.com; Editor Alhaji ABDUL RAHMAN HARUNA ATTAH.

The Statesman: DTD 10 Sapele Loop, Kokomlemle, Accra; tel. and fax (30) 2220057; fax (30) 2220043; e-mail statesman_gh@yahoo.com; internet www.thestatesmanonline.com; f. 1949; official publ. of the New Patriotic Party; Editor-in-Chief ASARE OTCHERE-DARKO; Editor FRANK AGYEI-TWUM.

The Telescope: Takoradi; f. 2005; Editor LOUIS HENRY DANSO.

PERIODICALS

Thrice-weekly

The Independent: Clear Type Press Bldg Complex, off Graphic Rd, POB 4031, Accra; tel. and fax (30) 2661091; f. 1989; Editor ANDREW ARTHUR.

Network Herald: 34 Crescent Rd, Labone, Accra; tel. (30) 2701184; fax (30) 2762173; e-mail support@ghana.com; internet www.networkherald.gh; f. 2001; Editor ELVIS QUARSHIE.

Bi-weekly

Ghana Palaver: Palaver Publications, POB WJ317, Wejia, Accra; tel. (30) 2850495; e-mail editor@ghana-palaver.com; internet www.ghana-palaver.com; f. 1994; Editor JOJO BRUCE QUANSAH.

The Ghanaian Lens: Accra; Editor KOBBY FIAGBE.

The Ghanaian Voice: Newstop Publications, POB 514, Mamprobi, Accra; tel. (30) 2324644; fax (30) 2314939; Editor CHRISTIANA ANSAH; circ. 100,000.

Weekly

Business and Financial Times: POB CT16, Cantonments, Accra; tel. and fax (30) 2785366; fax (30) 2775449; e-mail info@thebftonline.com; internet www.thebftonline.com; f. 1989; 3 a week; Editor WILLIAM SELASSY ADJADOGO; circ. 40,000.

The Crusading Guide: POB 8523, Accra-North; tel. (30) 2763339; fax (30) 2761541; internet www.ghanaweb.com/CrusadingGuide; Editor KWEKU BAAKO, Jr.

Free Press: Tommy Thompson Books Ltd, POB 6492, Accra; tel. (30) 2225994; independent; Editor FRANK BOAHENE.

Ghana Life: Ghana Life Publications, POB 11337, Accra; tel. (30) 2229835; Editor NIKKI BOA-AMPONSEM.

Ghana Market Watch: Accra; internet www.ghanamarketwatch.com; f. 2006; financial; CEO AMOS DOTSE.

Graphic Showbiz: Graphic Communications Group Ltd, POB 742, Accra; tel. (30) 2684001; fax (30) 2684025; e-mail graphicshowbiz@gmail.com; internet www.graphicghana.info; f. 2000; state-owned; Editor NANABANYIN DADSON.

Graphic Sports: Graphic Communications Group Ltd, POB 742, Accra; tel. (30) 2228911; fax (30) 2234754; e-mail info@graphicghana.com; state-owned; Editor FELIX ABAYATEYE; circ. 60,000.

Gye Nyame Concord: Accra; e-mail gnconcord@yahoo.com; internet www.ghanaweb.com/concord.

The Heritage: POB AD676, Arts Center, Accra; tel. (30) 2236051; fax (30) 2237156; e-mail heritagenewspaper@yahoo.co.uk; internet www.theheritagenews.com; Chair. STEPHEN OWUSU; Editor A. C. OHENE.

The Mirror: Graphic Communications Group Ltd, POB 742, Accra; tel. (30) 2228911; fax (30) 2234754; e-mail info@graphicghana.com; internet www.graphicghana.info; f. 1953; state-owned; Sat.; Editor E. N. O. PROVENCAL; circ. 90,000.

The National Democrat: Democrat Publications, POB 13605, Accra; Editor ELLIOT FELIX OHENE.

Public Agenda: Box MP2989, Accra-North; tel. (21) 2238820; e-mail pagenda@4u.com.gh; f. 1994; Editor AMOS SAFO; circ. 12,000.

The Standard: Standard Newspapers & Magazines Ltd, POB KA 9712, Accra; tel. (30) 2513537; fax (30) 2500493; e-mail snam.ncs@ghanacbc.org; internet www.ghanacbc.org; Roman Catholic; Editor ISAAC FRITZ ANDOH; circ. 10,000.

The Vanguard: Accra; Editor OSBERT LARTEY.

The Weekend: Newstop Publications, POB 514, Mamprobi, Accra; tel. (30) 2324644; fax (30) 2314939; Editor EMMANUEL YARTEY; circ. 40,000.

Weekly Spectator: New Times Corpn, Ring Rd West, POB 2638, Accra; tel. (30) 2228282; fax (30) 2229398; internet spectator.newtimesonline.com/spectator; state-owned; f. 1963; Sun.; Editor ENIMIL ASHON; circ. 165,000.

Other

The African Woman Magazine: Ring Rd West, POB AN 15064, Accra; tel. and fax (30) 2241636; e-mail mail@theafricanwoman.com; internet www.theafricanwoman.com; f. 1957; monthly; Editor NII ADUMUAH ORGLE.

AGI Newsletter: c/o Assn of Ghana Industries, POB 8624, Accra-North; tel. (30) 2779023; e-mail agi@agighana.org; internet www.agighana.org; f. 1974; monthly; Editor CARLO HEY; circ. 1,500.

AGOO: Newstop Publications, POB 514, Mamprobi, Accra; tel. (30) 2324644; fax (30) 2314939; monthly; lifestyle magazine; Publr KOJO BONSU.

Armed Forces News: General Headquarters, Directorate of Public Relations, Burma Camp, Accra; tel. (30) 2776111; f. 1966; quarterly; Editor ADOTEY ANKRAH-HOFFMAN; circ. 4,000.

Business Watch: Sulton Bridge Co Ltd, POB C3447, Cantonments, Accra; tel. (30) 2233293; monthly.

Christian Messenger: Presbyterian Book Depot Bldg, POB 3075, Accra; tel. and fax (30) 2663124; e-mail danbentil@yahoo.com; f. 1883; English-language; fortnightly; Editor GEORGE MARTINSON; circ. 40,000.

Ghana Journal of Science: National Science and Technology Press, Council for Scientific and Industrial Research, POB M32, Accra; tel. (30) 2500253; monthly; Editor Dr A. K. AHAFIA.

Ghana Review International (GRi): POB GP14307, Accra; tel. (30) 2677437; fax (30) 2677438; e-mail accra@ghanareview.com; internet www.ghanareview.com; publishes in Accra, London and New York; CEO NANA OTUO ACHEAMPONG; print circ. 100,000.

Ghana Today: Information Services Dept, POB 745, Accra; tel. (30) 2228011; fax (30) 2228089; e-mail isd@mino.gov.gh; English; political, economic, investment and cultural affairs; Dir ELVIS ADANYINA.

Ideal Woman (Obaa Sima): POB 5737, Accra; tel. (30) 2221399; f. 1971; monthly; Editor KATE ABBAM.

New Legon Observer: POB LG 490, Accra, Ghana; tel. (30) 2512503; fax (30) 2512504; e-mail newlegonobserver@ug.edu.gh; internet www.egnghana.org/publications/newLegonObserver.php; f. 2007; publ. by Ghana Society for Development Dialogue; fortnightly; Acting Editor ERNEST ARYEETEY.

The Post: Ghana Information Services, POB 745, Accra; tel. (30) 2228011; fax (30) 2228089; e-mail isd@mino.gov.gh; f. 1980; monthly; current affairs and analysis; Dir ALPHONSE KOBLAVIE (acting); circ. 25,000.

Radio and TV Times: Ghana Broadcasting Corpn, Broadcasting House, POB 18167, Accra; tel. (30) 2508927; fax (30) 2773612; f. 1960; quarterly; Editor SAM THOMPSON; circ. 5,000.

Students World: POB M18, Accra; tel. (30) 2774248; fax (30) 2778715; e-mail afram@wwwplus.co.za; f. 1974; monthly; educational; Man. Editor ERIC OFEI; circ. 10,000.

Uneek: POB 230, Achimota, Accra; tel. (30) 2543853; fax (30) 2231355; e-mail info@uneekmagazine.com; internet www.uneekmagazine.com; f. 1998; monthly; leisure, culture; CEO and Editor FRANCIS ADAMS.

The Watchman: Watchman Gospel Ministry, POB GP4521, Accra; tel. and fax (30) 2500631; e-mail watchmannewspaper@yahoo.com; f. 1986; Christian news; fortnightly; Pres. and CEO DIVINE P. KUMAH; Chair. Dr E. K. OPUNI; circ. 5,000.

Other newspapers include **The Catalyst**, **The Crystal Clear Lens**, **The Enquirer** and **Searchlight**. There are also internet-based news sites, including **Ghana Today**, at www.ghanatoday.com, and **ThisWeekGhana**, at www.thisweekghana.com.

NEWS AGENCY

Ghana News Agency: POB 2118, Accra; tel. (30) 2662381; fax (30) 2669841; e-mail ghnews@ghana.com; internet www.ghananewsagency.org; f. 1957; Gen. Man. NANA APPAU DUAH; 10 regional offices and 110 district offices.

PRESS ASSOCIATION

Ghana Journalists' Association: POB 4636, Accra; tel. and fax (30) 2234694; e-mail info@gjaghana.org; internet gjaghana.org; Pres. RANSFORD TETTEH.

Publishers

Advent Press: Osu La Rd, POB 0102, Osu, Accra; tel. (30) 2777861; fax (30) 2775327; e-mail eaokpoti@ghana.com; f. 1937; publishing arm of the Ghana Union Conference of Seventh-day Adventists; Gen. Man. EMMANUEL C. TETTEH.

Adwinsa Publications (Ghana) Ltd: 17 Suncity Rd, Agbogba North Legon, POB 92, Legon, Accra; tel. and fax (24) 2366537; e-mail adwinsa@yahoo.com; internet www.adwinsa.com; f. 1977; general, educational; Man. Dir KWAKU OPPONG AMPONSAH.

Afram Publications: C 184/22 Midway Lane, Abofu-Achimota, POB M18, Accra; tel. (30) 2412561; e-mail aframpub@pubchgh.com; internet www.aframpublications.com.gh; f. 1973; textbooks and general; Man. Dir ERIC OFEI.

Africa Christian Press: POB 30, Achimota, Accra; tel. (30) 2244147; fax (30) 2220271; e-mail acpbooks@ghana.com; f. 1964; religious, fiction, theology, children's, leadership; Gen. Man. RICHARD A. B. CRABBE.

Allgoodbooks Ltd: POB AN10416, Accra-North; tel. (30) 2664294; fax (30) 2665629; e-mail allgoodbooks@hotmail.com; f. 1968; children's; Man. Dir MARY ASIRIFI.

Asempa Publishers: POB GP919, Accra; tel. 289672514; e-mail asempa@iburstgh.com; f. 1970; religion, social issues, African music, fiction, children's; Gen. Man. SARAH O. APRONTI.

Catholic Book Centre: North Liberia Rd, POB 3285, Accra; tel. (30) 2226651; fax (30) 2237727.

Educational Press and Manufacturers Ltd: POB 9184, Airport-Accra; tel. (30) 2220395; f. 1975; textbooks, children's; Man. G. K. KODUA.

Encyclopaedia Africana Project: POB 2797, Accra; tel. (30) 2776939; fax (30) 2779228; e-mail eap@africaonline.com.gh; internet encyclopaediaafricana.org; f. 1962; reference; Dir GRACE BANSA.

Frank Publishing Ltd: POB MB414, Accra; tel. (30) 2240711; f. 1976; secondary school textbooks; Man. Dir FRANCIS K. DZOKOTO.

Ghana Publishing Co Ltd (Assembly Press): POB 124, Accra; tel. (30) 2664338; fax (30) 2664330; e-mail info@ghanapublishingcompany.com; internet www.ghanapublishingcompany.com; f. 1965; state-owned; textbooks and general fiction and non-fiction; Chair. Rev. HELENA OPOKU-SARKODIE; Man. Dir DAVID K. DZREKE.

Ghana Universities Press: POB GP4219, Accra; tel. (30) 2513401; fax (30) 2513402; f. 1962; scholarly, academic and general and textbooks; CEO Dr K. M. GANU.

Sam-Woode Ltd: A.979/15 Dansoman High St, POB 12719, Accra-North; tel. (30) 2305287; fax (30) 2310482; e-mail samwoode@ghana.com; internet samwoode.com; f. 1984; educational and children's; Chair. KWESI SAM-WOODE.

Sedco Publishing Ltd: Sedco House, 5 Tabon St, North Ridge, POB 2051, Accra; tel. (30) 2221332; fax (30) 2220107; e-mail info@sedcopublishing.com; internet www.sedcopublishing.com; f. 1975; educational; Chair. COURAGE K. SEGBAWU; Man. Dir FRANK SEGBAWU.

Sub-Saharan Publishers: PO Box 358, Legon, Accra; tel. and fax (30) 2233371; e-mail sub-saharan@ighmail.com; Man. Dir AKOSS OFORI-MENSAH.

Unimax Macmillan Ltd: 42 Ring Rd South Industrial Area, POB 10722, Accra-North; tel. (30) 2227443; fax (30) 2225215; e-mail info@unimacmillan.com; internet www.unimacmillan.com; representative of Macmillan UK; atlases, educational and children's; Man. Dir EDWARD ADDO.

Waterville Publishing House: 101 Miamona Cl., South Industrial Area, POB 195, Accra; tel. (30) 2689973; fax (30) 2689974; e-mail e.amoh@a-riiscompany; internet a-riiscompany.com; f. 1963; general fiction and non-fiction, textbooks, paperbacks, Africana; Man. Dir EMMANUEL AMOH.

Woeli Publishing Services: POB NT601, Accra New Town; tel. and fax (30) 289535570; e-mail woeli@woelipublishing.com; f. 1984; children's, fiction, academic; Dir WOELI A. DEKUTSEY.

PUBLISHERS' ASSOCIATIONS

Ghana Book Development Council: POB M430, Accra; tel. (30) 2229178; f. 1975; govt-financed agency; promotes and co-ordinates writing, production and distribution of books; Exec. Dir D. A. NIMAKO.

Ghana Book Publishers' Association (GBPA): POB LT471, Laterbiokorshie, Accra; tel. (30) 2912764; fax (30) 2810641; e-mail ghanabookpubs@yahoo.co.uk; internet www.ghanabookpublishers.org; f. 1976; Pres. ASARE KONADU YAMOAH.

Private Newspaper Publishers' Association of Ghana (PRINPAG): POB 125, Darkuman, Accra; Exec. Sec. KENTEMAN NII LARYEA SOWAH.

Broadcasting and Communications

TELECOMMUNICATIONS

In 2011 there were five companies operating in the telecommunications sector in Ghana. Airtel Ghana and Vodafone Ghana provided both mobile cellular and fixed-line telephone services, whereas the three other operators provided solely mobile cellular telephone services. In that year there were 284,721 subscribers to fixed-line services and 21.2m. subscribers to mobile services.

Regulatory Authority

National Communication Authority (NCA): 1 Rangoon Close, POB 1568, Cantonments, Accra; tel. (30) 2776621; fax (30) 2763449; e-mail info@nca.org.gh; internet www.nca.org.gh; f. 1996; regulatory body; Chair. KOFI TOTOBI QUAKYI; Dir-Gen. PAAROCK ASSUMAN VANPERCY.

Major Telecommunications Companies

Airtel Ghana: PMB, Accra; e-mail customercare.gh@gh.airtel.com; internet www.gh.zain.com; f. 2008; name changed as above in 2010; provides both mobile cellular and fixed-line telephone services; Man. PHILIP SOWAH; 2.63m. subscribers (Dec. 2011).

Expresso Telecoms Ghana: POB 10208, Accra; tel. 28282100 (mobile); fax 28210103 (mobile); internet www.expressotelecom.com; frmly Kasapa Telecom Ltd; present name adopted 2010; owned by Expresso Telecom Group (UAE); Man. Dir EL AMIR AHMED EL AMIR YOUSIF; 186,751 subscribers (Dec. 2011).

Millicom Ghana Ltd: Millicom Place, Barnes Rd, PMB 100, Accra; tel. 277551000 (mobile); fax 277503999 (mobile); e-mail info@tigo.com.gh; internet www.tigo.com.gh; f. 1990; mobile cellular telephone services through the network Tigo; Man. Dir CARLOS CACERES; 3.92m. subscribers (Dec. 2011).

MTN Ghana: Auto Parts Bldg, 41A Graphic Rd, South Industrial Area, POB 281, International Trade Fair Lane, Accra; tel. 244300000 (mobile); fax (30) 2231974; e-mail customercare@mtn.com.gh; internet www.mtn.com.gh; f. 1994; Ghana's largest mobile cellular telephone provider, through the network MTN (formerly Areeba); 100% owned by MTN (South Africa); CEO MICHAEL IKPOKI; 10.15m. subscribers (Dec. 2011).

Vodafone Ghana: Telecom House, nr Kwame Nkrumah Circle, PMB 221, Accra-North; tel. (30) 2200200; fax (30) 2221002; e-mail info.gh@vodafone.com; internet www.vodafone.com.gh; f. 1995; name changed as above in 2008, following acquisition of 70% shares in Ghana Telecommunications Company (GT) by Vodafone Group PLC (United Kingdom), 30% govt-owned; operates mobile cellular, fixed-line networks and data services; Chair. KOBINA QUANSAH; CEO KYLE WHITEHALL; 4.55m. subscribers (Dec. 2011).

BROADCASTING

There are internal radio broadcasts in English, Akan, Dagbani, Ewe, Ga, Hausa and Nzema, and an external service in English and French. There are three transmitting stations, with a number of relay stations. The Ghana Broadcasting Corporation operates two national networks, Radio 1 and Radio 2, which broadcast from Accra, and four regional FM stations. In January 2010 the Minister for Communications announced that the Government intended to switch off the analogue television signal in all regional capitals by the end of 2012 and that digital broadcasting would commence earlier in that year.

Ghana Broadcasting Corpn (GBC): Broadcasting House, Ring Rd Central, Kanda, POB 1633, Accra; tel. and fax (30) 2227779; e-mail radioghana@yahoo.com; internet www.gbcghana.com; f. 1935; Dir-Gen. BERIFI AFARI APENTENG; Dir of TV CHARLES KOFI BUCKNOR; Dir of Radio YAW OWUSU ADDO.

CitiFM: 11 Tettey Loop, Adabraka, Accra; tel. (30) 2226171; fax (30) 2224043; e-mail info@citifmonline.com; internet www.citifmonline.com; f. 2004; Man. Dir SAMUEL ATTA MENSAH.

Joy FM: 355 Faanofa St, Kokomlemle, POB 17202, Accra; tel. (30) 2701199; fax (30) 2224405; e-mail info@myjoyonline.com; internet www.myjoyonline.com; f. 1995; news, information and music broadcasts; Dir KWESI TWUM.

Metro TV: POB C1609, Cantonments, Accra; tel. (30) 2765701; fax (30) 2765703; e-mail admin@metroworld.tv; internet www.metrotv.com.gh; Chair. KWADWO DABO FRIMPONG; CEO TALAL FATTAL.

Radio Ada: POB KA9482, Accra; tel. (30) 2500907; fax (30) 2516442; e-mail radioada@kalssinn.net; f. 1998; community broadcasts in Dangme; Dirs ALEX QUARMYNE, WILNA QUARMYNE.

Radio Gold FM: POB 17298, Accra; tel. (30) 3300281; fax (30) 3300284; e-mail radiogold@ucomgh.com; internet www.myradiogoldlive.com; Man. Dir BAFFOE BONNIE.

Sky Broadcasting Co Ltd: 45 Water Rd, Kanda Overpass, North Ridge, POB CT3850, Cantonments, Accra; tel. (30) 2225716; fax (30) 2221983; e-mail vayiku@yahoo.com; internet www.spirit.fm; f. 2000; Gen. Man. STEVE ESHUN.

TV3: 12th Rd, Kanda (opposite French embassy), Accra; tel. (30) 2763458; fax (30) 2763450; e-mail info@tv3.com.gh; internet www.tv3.com.gh; f. 1997; private television station; progamming in English and local languages; CEO SANTOKH SINGH.

Vibe FM: Pyramid House, 3rd Floor, Ring Rd Central, Accra; internet www.vibefm.com.gh; educational; CEO MIKE COOKE.

Finance

(cap. = capital; res = reserves; dep. = deposits; m. = million; br(s). = branch(es); amounts in new cedis, unless otherwise indicated)

BANKING

The commercial banking sector comprised 26 commercial banks, three development banks, five merchant banks and five foreign banks in 2008. There were also 134 rural and community banks and 44 non-banking financial institutions.

Central Bank

Bank of Ghana: 1 Thorpe Rd, POB 2674, Accra; tel. (30) 2666902; fax (30) 2662996; e-mail bogsecretary@bog.gov.gh; internet www.bog.gov.gh; f. 1957; bank of issue; cap. 10.0m., res 741.1m., dep. 3,685.9m. (Dec. 2009); Gov. Dr HENRY KOFI WAMPAH (acting).

Commercial Banks

Amalgamated Bank Ltd: 131–3 Farrar Ave, Cantonments, POB CT1541, Accra; tel. (30) 2249690; fax (30) 2249697; e-mail enquiries@amalbank.com.gh; internet www.amalbank.com.gh; f. 1997; cap. 7.2m., res 19.6m., dep. 300.9m. (Dec. 2009); Chair. STEPHAN ATA; Man. Dir MENSON TORKORNOO.

Fidelity Bank: Ridge Towers, PMB 43, Cantonments, Accra; tel. (30) 2214490; fax (30) 2678868; e-mail info@myfidelitybank.net; internet www.fidelitybank.com.gh; f. 2006; cap. 25.9m., res 4.9m., dep. 315.1m. (Dec. 2009); Chair. WILLIAM PANFORD BRAY; CEO and Man. Dir EDWARD EFFAH; 8 brs.

Ghana Commercial Bank Ltd: Thorpe Rd, POB 134, Accra; tel. (30) 2664914; fax (30) 2662168; e-mail gcbmail@gcb.com.gh; internet www.gcb.com.gh; f. 1953; 21.4% state-owned; cap. 72.0m., res 80.3m., dep. 1,259.4m. (Dec. 2009); Chair. PRYCE KOJO THOMPSON; Man. Dir SIMON DORNOO; 136 brs.

NTHC Ltd: Martco House, Okai Mensah Link, off Kwame Nkrumah Ave, POB 9563, Adabraka, Accra; tel. (30) 2238492; fax (30) 2229975; e-mail nthc@ghana.com; internet www.nthcghana.com; fmrly National Trust Holding Co Ltd; f. 1976 to provide stockbrokerage services, asset management and financial advisory services; cap. 9,000m. (2001); Chair. KWADWO OWUSU-TWENEBOA; Man. Dir Dr A. W. Q. BARNOR.

Prudential Bank Ltd: 8 Nima Ave, Ring Rd Central, PMB GPO, Accra; tel. (30) 2781201; fax (30) 2781210; e-mail headoffice@prudentialbank.com.gh; internet www.prudentialbank.com.gh; f. 1996; Exec. Chair. JOHN SACKAH ADDO; Man. Dir STEPHEN SEKYERE ABANKWA; 16 brs.

uniBank (Ghana) Ltd: Royal Castle Rd, POB AN15367, Kokomlemle, Accra; tel. (30) 2233328; fax (30) 2253695; e-mail info@unibankghana.com; internet www.unibankghana.com; f. 2001; total assets 69.2m. (Dec. 2007); Chair. OPOKU-GYAMFI BOATENG; Man. Dir AMMISHADDAI ADU OWUSU-AMOAH.

Development Banks

Agricultural Development Bank (ADB): ADB House, 37 Independence Ave, POB 4191, Accra; tel. (30) 2770403; fax (30) 2784893; e-mail info@agricbank.com; internet www.agricbank.com; f. 1965; 51.8% state-owned, 48.2% owned by Bank of Ghana; credit facilities for farmers and commercial banking; cap. and res 390,064.5m., dep. 968,713.0m. (Dec. 2002); Chair. Alhaji IBRAHIM ADAM; Man. Dir STEPHEN KPORDZIH; 50 brs.

National Investment Bank Ltd (NIB): 37 Kwame Nkrumah Ave, POB 3726, Accra; tel. (30) 2661701; fax (30) 2661730; e-mail info@nib-ghana.com; internet www.nib-ghana.com; f. 1963; 86.4% state-owned; provides long-term investment capital, jt venture promotion, consortium finance man. and commercial banking services; cap. 70.0m., res –9.6m., dep. 336.7m. (Dec. 2009); Chair. EMMANUEL ABLO; Man. Dir Dr P. A. KURANCHIE; 27 brs.

Merchant Banks

CAL Bank Ltd: 23 Independence Ave, POB 14596, Accra; tel. (30) 2680068; fax (30) 2680081; e-mail info@calbank.net; internet www.calbank.net; f. 1990; cap. 25.0m., res 32.0m., dep. 276.9m. (Dec. 2009); Chair. PAAROCK VANPERCY; Man. Dir FRANK BRAKO ADU, Jr.

Databank: 61 Barnes Rd, Adabraka, PMB, Ministries Post Office, Accra; tel. (30) 2610610; fax (30) 2681443; e-mail info@databankgroup.com; internet www.databankgroup.com; f. 1990; Exec. Chair. KEN OFORI-ATTA; Exec. Dir R. YOFI GRANT; 3 brs.

Ecobank Ghana Ltd (EBG): 19 7th Ave, Ridge West, POB 16746, Accra; tel. (30) 2681166; fax (30) 2680428; e-mail ecobankgh@ecobank.com; internet www.ecobank.com; f. 1989; 92.2% owned by Ecobank Transnational Inc (Togo, operating under the auspices of the Economic Community of West African States); merged with The Trust Bank Ltd June 2012; cap. 100.0m., res 106.9m., dep. 1,012.2m.

(Dec. 2009); Chair. LIONEL VAN LARE DOSOO; Man. Dir SAMUEL ASHITEY ADJEI; 7 brs.

First Atlantic Merchant Bank Ltd: Atlantic Pl., 1 Seventh Ave, Ridge West, POB C1620, Cantonments, Accra; tel. (30) 2682203; fax (30) 2479245; e-mail info@firstatlanticbank.com.gh; internet www.firstatlanticbank.com.gh; f. 1994; cap. 7.0m., res 9.2m., dep. 261.2m. (Dec. 2009); Chair. PHILIP OWUSU; Man. Dir JUDE ARTHUR.

Merchant Bank (Ghana) Ltd: Merban House, 44 Kwame Nkrumah Ave, POB 401, Accra; tel. (30) 2666331; fax (30) 2667305; e-mail info@merchantbank.com.gh; internet www.merchantbank.com.gh; f. 1972; cap. 25.0m., res 23.3m., dep. 611.6m. (Dec. 2009); Chair. MARIAN ROSAMOND BARNOR; Man. Dir JOSEPH TETTEH; 15 brs.

Foreign Banks

Barclays Bank of Ghana Ltd (UK): Barclays House, High St, POB 2949, Accra; tel. (30) 2664901; fax (30) 2669254; e-mail barclays.ghana@barclays.com; internet www.barclays.com/africa/ghana; f. 1971; 90% owned by Barclays Bank Plc; 10% owned by Govt of Ghana; total assets 1,196m. (Dec. 2007); Man. Dir BENJAMIN DABRAH; 62 brs.

Guaranty Trust Bank (Ghana) Ltd: 25A Castle Rd, Ambassadorial Area Ridge, PMB CT416, Accra; tel. (30) 2676474; fax (30) 2662727; e-mail gh.corporateaffairs@gtbank.com; internet www.gtbghana.com; f. 2004; 70% owned by Guaranty Trust Bank Plc, 15% owned by Netherlands Development Finance Co (FMO), 15% owned by Alhaji Yusif Ibrahim; Man. Dir. DOLAPO OGUNDIMU.

International Commercial Bank (Ghana) Ltd (Taiwan): Meridian House, Ring Rd Central, PMB 16, Accra; tel. (30) 2236136; fax (30) 2238228; e-mail icb@icbank-gh.com; internet www.icbank-gh.com; f. 1996; cap. and res 31,205m., total assets 218,318m. (Dec. 2003); CEO LALGUDI KRISHNAMURTHY GANAPATHIRAMAN; 11 brs.

SG-SSB Bank Ltd: Ring Rd Central, POB 13119, Accra; tel. (30) 2202001; fax (30) 2248920; internet www.sg-ssb.com.gh; f. 1976 as Social Security Bank; 51.0% owned by Société Générale, France; cap. 62.3m., res 28.4m., dep. 420.9m. (Dec. 2009); Chair. GÉRALD LACAZE; Man. Dir ALAIN BELLISSARD; 37 brs.

Stanbic Bank Ghana: Valco Trust House, Castle Rd Ridge, POB CT2344, Cantonments, Accra; tel. (30) 2687670; fax (30) 2687669; e-mail stanbicghana@stanbic.com.gh; internet www.stanbic.com.gh; f. 1999; subsidiary of the Standard Bank of South Africa Ltd; cap. and res 14,981m., total assets 97,253m. (Dec. 2001); Chair. DENNIS W. KENNEDY; Man. Dir ANDANI ALHASSAN; 2 brs.

Standard Chartered Bank Ghana Ltd (UK): High St, POB 768, Accra; tel. (30) 2664591; fax (30) 2667751; internet www.standardchartered.com/gh; f. 1896 as Bank of British West Africa; cap. 61.1m., res 41.1m., dep. 844.5m. (Dec. 2009); Chair. PETER SULLIVAN; Country CEO KWEKU BEDU ADDO; 19 brs.

Zenith Bank Ghana (Nigeria): Premier Towers, Liberia Rd, PMB CT393, Accra; tel. (30) 2660075; fax (30) 2660087; e-mail info@zenithbank.com.gh; internet www.zenithbank.com; Chair. MARY CHINERY-HESSE; CEO DANIEL ASIEDU.

Banking Association

Ghana Association of Bankers (GAB): Accra; tel. (30) 2670629; internet ghanaassociationofbankers.com; f. 1980; CEO DANIEL ATO KWAMINA MENSAH.

STOCK EXCHANGE

Ghana Stock Exchange (GSE): Cedi House, 5th Floor, Liberia Rd, POB 1849, Accra; tel. (30) 2669908; fax (30) 2669913; e-mail info@gse.com.gh; internet www.gse.com.gh; f. 1990; 35 listed cos in early 2009; Chair. NORBERT KUDJAWU; Man. Dir KOFI YAMOAH.

INSURANCE

In 2004 there were 19 insurance companies.

Donewell Insurance Co Ltd: Fihankra House, POB 2136, Osu, Accra; tel. (30) 2760483; fax (30) 2760484; e-mail info@donewellinsurance.com; internet www.donewellinsurance.com; f. 1992; Chair. JOHN S. ADDO; Man. Dir PERRY ATAWORA ADAMBA.

Enterprise Insurance Co Ltd: Enterprise House, 11 High St, POB GP50, Accra; tel. (30) 2666847; fax (30) 2666186; e-mail enquiries@eicghana.com; internet www.eicghana.net; f. 1972; Chair. TREVOR TREFGARNE; Man. Dir GEORGE OTOO.

Ghana Union Assurance Co Ltd: F828/1 Ring Rd East, POB 1322, Accra; tel. (30) 2780627; fax (30) 2780647; e-mail gua@ghanaunionassurancecompany.com; f. 1973; insurance underwriting; Man. Dir NANA AGYEI DUKU.

Metropolitan Insurance Co Ltd: Caledonian House, Kojo Thompson Rd, POB GP20084, Accra; tel. (30) 2220966; fax (30) 2237872; e-mail met@metinsurance.com; internet www.metinsurance.com; f. 1991; Chair. SAM E. JONAH; CEO KWAME-GAZO AGBENYADZIE.

SIC Insurance Co Ltd: 28/29 Ring Road East, Osu, POB 2363, Accra; tel. (30) 2780600; fax (30) 2662205; e-mail sicinfo@sic-gh.com; internet www.sic-gh.com; f. 1962; 60% state-owned; all classes of insurance; Chair. MAX COBBINA; Man. Dir BENJAMIN K. ACOLATSE.

Social Security and National Insurance Trust (SSNIT): Pension House, POB MB 149, Accra; tel. (30) 266773; fax (30) 2686373; e-mail public@ssnit.org.gh; internet www.ssnit.org.gh; f. 1972; covers over 974,666 contributors (Feb. 2012); Dir-Gen. FRANK ODOOM.

Starlife Assurance Co Ltd: C653/3 5th Cres., Asylum Down, POB AN 5783, Accra; tel. (30) 2258946; fax (30) 2258947; e-mail info@starlifegh.com; internet www.starlife.com.gh; f. 2005; Chair. OPOKU GYAMFI BOATENG; Exec. Vice-Chair. FRANK OPPONG-YEBOAH.

Vanguard Assurance Co Ltd: 21 Independence Ave, POB 1868, Accra; tel. (30) 2666485; fax (30) 2782921; e-mail vacmails@vanguardassurance.com; internet www.vanguardassurance.com; f. 1974; foreign travel, general accident, marine, motor and life insurance; Chair. KWADWO OBUAOBISA KETEKU; CEO GIDEON AMENYEDOR; 13 brs.

Trade and Industry

GOVERNMENT AGENCIES

Divestiture Implementation Committee: F35, 5 Ring Rd East, North Labone, POB CT102, Cantonments, Accra; tel. (30) 2772049; fax (30) 2773126; e-mail info@dic.com.gh; internet www.dic.com.gh; f. 1988; Exec. Sec. BENSON POKU-ADJEI.

Environmental Protection Agency (EPA): 91 Starlets Rd, POB M326, Accra; tel. (30) 2664697; fax (30) 2662690; e-mail epaed@africaonline.com.gh; internet www.epa.gov.gh; f. 1974; Chair. EMMANUEL F. SIISI-WILSON; Exec. Dir JONATHAN A. ALLOTEY.

Export Development and Investment Fund (EDIF): Ridge Tower, 13th Floor, Ridge, POB M493, Accra; tel. (30) 2671567; fax (30) 2671573; e-mail info@edifghana.org; f. 2000; Chief Exec. (vacant); Chair. Prof. FRANCIS DODOO.

Forestry Commission of Ghana (FC): 4 3rd Ave Ridge, PMB 434, Accra; tel. (30) 2401210; fax (30) 2401197; e-mail info@hq.fcghana.com; internet www.fcghana.com; CEO SAMUEL AFARI-DARTEY.

Ghana Export Promotion Authority (GEPA): Republic House, Tudu Rd, POB M146, Accra; tel. (30) 2683153; fax (30) 2677256; internet www.gepaghana.com; f. 1974; Chair. KOBINA ADE COKER; CEO AGYEMAN KWADWO OWUSU.

Ghana Free Zones Board: POB M626, Accra; tel. (30) 2780535; fax (30) 2785036; e-mail info@gfzb.com; internet www.gfzb.com; f. 1995; approves establishment of cos in export-processing zones; Exec.-Sec. KWADWO TWUM BOAFO.

Ghana Heavy Equipment Ltd (GHEL): Old Warehouse under the Bridge, Airport West, POB 1524, Accra; tel. (30) 2680118; fax (30) 2660276; e-mail info@ghelghana.com; internet ghelghana.com; fmrly subsidiary of Ghana National Trading Corpn; organizes exports, imports and production of heavy equipment; CEO YIDANA MAHAMI.

Ghana Investment Promotion Centre (GIPC): Public Services Commission Bldg, Ministries, POB M193, Accra; tel. (30) 2665125; fax (30) 2663801; e-mail info@gipcghana.com; internet www.gipc.org.gh; f. 1994; negotiates new investments, approves projects, registers foreign capital and decides extent of govt participation; Chair. Dr ISHMAIL YAMSON; CEO GEORGE ABOAGYE.

Ghana Minerals Commission (MINCOM): 12 Switchback Rd Residential Area, POB M248, Cantonments, Accra; tel. (30) 2771318; fax (30) 2773324; e-mail mincom@mc.ghanamining.org; internet www.ghanamining.org; f. 1986 to regulate and promote Ghana's mineral industry; CEO BENJAMIN NII AYI ARYEE.

Ghana National Petroleum Authority (NPA): Centurion Bldg No. 11, 5 Circular Rd, PMB CT, Accra; tel. (30) 2766196; fax (30) 2766193; e-mail info@npa.gov.gh; internet www.npa.gov.gh; f. 2005; oversees petroleum sector; Chair. KOJO FYNN; Chief Exec. ALEX MOULD.

Ghana Standards Board: POB MB245, Accra; tel. (30) 2500065; fax (30) 2500092; e-mail info@gsb.gov.gh; internet www.gsb.gov.gh; f. 1967; establishes and promulgates standards; promotes standardization, industrial efficiency and devt and industrial welfare, health and safety; operates certification mark scheme; 402 mems; Chair. WILLIAM ABOAH; Exec. Dir GEORGE BEN CRENTSIL (acting).

Ghana Trade Fair Co Ltd: Trade Fair Centre, POB 111, Accra; tel. (30) 2776611; fax (30) 2772012; e-mail gftc@ghana.com; internet www.gitf-europe.de; f. 1989; CEO EBENEZER ERASMUS OKPOTI KONEY (acting).

Ghana Trade and Investment Gateway Project (GHATIG): POB M47, Accra; tel. (30) 2663439; fax (30) 2773134; e-mail gateway1@ghana.com; promotes private investment and trade, infrastructural devt of free-trade zones and export-processing zones.

GNPA Ltd: POB 15331, Accra; tel. (30) 2228321; fax (30) 2221049; e-mail info@gnpa-ghana.com; internet www.gnpa-ghana.com; f. 1976 as Ghana National Procurement Agency; state-owned; part of Ministry of Trade and Industry; procures and markets a wide range of goods and services locally and abroad.

National Board for Small-scale Industries (NBSSI): POB M85, Accra; tel. (30) 2668641; fax (30) 2661394; e-mail nbssided@ghana.com; f. 1985; part of Ministry of Trade and Industry; promotes small and medium-scale industrial and commercial enterprises by providing credit, advisory services and training; Exec. Dir LUKMAN ABDUL-RAHIM.

DEVELOPMENT ORGANIZATIONS

Agence Française de Développement (AFD): 8th Rangoon Close, Ring Rd Central, POB 9592, Airport, Accra; tel. (30) 2778755; fax (30) 2778757; e-mail afdaccra@afd.fr; internet www.afd.fr; f. 1985; fmrly Caisse Française de Développement; Resident Man. BRUNO LECLERC.

Private Enterprise Foundation (PEF): POB CT1671, Cantonments, Accra; tel. (30) 2515603; fax (30) 2515600; e-mail info@pefghana.org; internet www.pefghana.org; f. 1994; promotes development of private sector; Pres. ASARE AKUFFO.

Social Investment Fund: Accra; tel. (21)778921; fax (21) 778404; internet sifinghana.org; f. 1998; Chair. JACOB BENJAMIN QUARTEY-PAPAFIO; Exec. Dir JOSEPH ACHEAMPONG (acting).

CHAMBER OF COMMERCE

Ghana National Chamber of Commerce and Industry (GNCCI): Adabla Plaza, 2nd Floor, 3 Oroko St, Kokomlemle, POB 2325, Accra; tel. (30) 27012780; fax (30) 2255202; e-mail info@ghanachamber.org; internet www.ghanachamber.org; f. 1961; promotes and protects industry and commerce, organizes trade fairs; 2,500 individual mems and 10 mem. chambers; Pres. SETH ADJEI BAAH; CEO EMMANUEL DONI-KWAME.

INDUSTRIAL AND TRADE ORGANIZATIONS

Federation of Associations of Ghanaian Exporters (FAGE): POB M124, Accra; tel. (30) 2766176; fax (30) 2766253; e-mail fage-ghana@gmx.net; internet www.fageplus.com; non-governmental, not-for-profit org. for exporters of non-traditional exports; over 2,500 mems.

Forestry Commission of Ghana, Timber Industry Development Division (TIDD): 4 Third Ave, Ridge, POB MB434, Accra; tel. (30) 2221315; fax (30) 2220818; e-mail info@hq.fcghana.com; internet www.ghanatimber.org; f. 1985; promotes the development of the timber industry and the sale and export of timber.

Ghana Cocoa Board (COCOBOD): Cocoa House, 41 Kwame Nkrumah Ave, POB 933, Accra; tel. (30) 2661872; fax (30) 2665893; e-mail cocobod@cocobod.gh; internet www.cocobod.gh; f. 1947; monopoly purchaser of cocoa until 1993; responsible for purchase, grading and export of cocoa, coffee and shea nuts; also encourages production and scientific research aimed at improving quality and yield of these crops; controls all exports of cocoa; subsidiaries include the Cocoa Marketing Co (Ghana) Ltd and the Cocoa Research Institute of Ghana; Chair. Dr PERCIVAL YAW KURANCHIE; CEO ANTHONY FOFEI.

Grains and Legumes Development Board: POB 4000, Kumasi; tel. (32) 2024231; fax (32) 2024778; e-mail gldb@africaonline.com.gh; f. 1970; subsidiary of Ministry of Food and Agriculture; produces, processes and stores seeds and seedlings, and manages national seed security stocks; Chair. Dr GODFRIED ADJEI DIXON; Exec. Dir Dr ROBERT AGYEIBI ASUBOAH.

EMPLOYERS' ORGANIZATION

Ghana Employers' Association (GEA): State Enterprises Commission Bldg, POB GP2616, Accra; tel. (30) 2678455; fax (30) 2678405; e-mail gea@ghanaemployers.com; internet www.ghanaemployers.com; f. 1959; 600 mems (2006); Pres. TERENCE RONALD DARKO; Vice-Pres. SAMER CHEDID.

Affiliated Bodies

Association of Ghana Industries (AGI): Addison House, 2nd Floor, Trade Fair Centre, POB AN8624, Accra-North; tel. (30) 2779023; fax (30) 2763383; e-mail agi@agighana.org; internet www.agighana.org; f. 1957; Pres. NANA OWUSU AFARI; Exec. Dir ANDREW LAWSON; c. 500 mems.

Ghana Booksellers' Association: POB 10367, Accra-North; tel. (30) 2773002; fax (30) 2773242; e-mail minerva@ghana.com; Pres. FRED J. REIMMER; Gen. Sec. ADAMS AHIMAH.

Ghana Chamber of Mines: 22 Sir Arku Korsah Rd, Airport Residential Area, POB 991, Accra; tel. (30) 2760652; fax (30) 2760653; e-mail chamber@ghanachamberofmines.org; internet www.ghanachamberofmines.org; f. 1928; Pres. DANIEL OWIREDU; CEO Dr TONI AUBYNN.

Ghana Timber Association (GTA): POB 1020, Kumasi; tel. and fax (32) 2025153; f. 1952; promotes, protects and develops timber industry; Pres. BOATENG OPOKU.

UTILITIES

Regulatory Bodies

Energy Commission (EC): FREMA House, Plot 40, Spintex Rd, PMB Ministries, Accra; tel. (30) 2813756; fax (30) 2813764; e-mail info@energycom.gov.gh; internet www.energycom.gov.gh; f. 2001; Chair. Prof. ABEEKU BREW-HAMMOND; Exec. Sec. Dr ALFRED OFOSU AHENKORAH.

Public Utilities Regulatory Commission (PURC): 51 Liberation Rd, African Liberation Circle, POB CT3095, Cantonments, Accra; tel. (30) 2244181; fax (30) 2244188; e-mail purcsec@purc.com.gh; internet www.purc.com.gh; f. 1997; Chair. EMMANUEL ANNAN.

Electricity

Electricity Co of Ghana (ECG): Electro-Volta House, POB 521, Accra; tel. (30) 2676727; fax (30) 2666262; e-mail ecgho@ghana.com; internet www.ecgonline.info; Chair. Dr KWEKU OSAFO; Man. Dir CEPHAS GAKPO.

Ghana Grid Company Ltd (GRIDCo): POB CS 7979, Tema; tel. (30) 27011185; fax (30) 2676180; e-mail gridco@gridcogh.com; internet www.gridcogh.com; f. 2006; CEO CHARLES A. DARKU.

Volta River Authority (VRA): Electro-Volta House, 28th February Rd, POB MB77, Accra; tel. (30) 2664941; fax (30) 2662610; e-mail prunit@vra.com; internet www.vra.com; f. 1961; govt owned; controls the generation and distribution of electricity; Northern Electricity Department of VRA f. 1987 to distribute electricity in northern Ghana; CEO KWEKU ANDOH AWORTWI.

Water

In mid-2006 the Volta Basin Authority (VBA) was created by Ghana, Benin, Burkina Faso, Côte d'Ivoire, Mali and Togo to manage the resources of the Volta River basin.

Ghana Water Co Ltd (GWCL): POB MB194, Accra; tel. (30) 2666781; fax (30) 2663552; e-mail info@gwcl.com.gh; internet www.gwcl.com.gh; f. 1965 to provide, distribute and conserve water supplies for public, domestic and industrial use, and to establish, operate and control sewerage systems; jointly managed by Aqua Vitens (the Netherlands) and Rand Water (South Africa); Chair. ARNOLD H. K. SESHIE; Man. Dir KWEKU BOTWE.

MAJOR COMPANIES

The following are among the largest companies in terms of capital investment or of employment.

AngloGold Ashanti: Gold House, Patrice Lumumba Rd, Roman Ridge, POB 2665, Accra; tel. (30) 2722190; fax (30) 2775947; e-mail investors@anglogold.com; internet www.anglogoldashanti.com; f. 1897 as Ashanti Goldfields; merged 2004 with AngloGold; gold-mining at the Obuasi and Iduapriem mines; leases mining and timber concessions from the Govt, which holds a 17% interest; Pres. RUSSELL EDEY; CEO MARK CUTIFINI; 8,924 employees (2004).

Chase Petroleum: Heritage Tower, 13th Floor, Ridge Ambassadorial Enclave, West Ridge, Accra; tel. (30) 2670191; fax (30) 2670194; e-mail info@chaseghana.com; internet www.chaseghana.com; f. 1999; trading and distribution of petroleum products; CEO KWAKU BEDIAKO.

Cocoa Processing Co Ltd: PMB, Tema; tel. and fax (30) 3212153; fax (30) 3206657; e-mail info@goldentreeghana.com; internet www.goldentreeghana.com; f. 1981; produces high-grade cocoa products for export and domestic consumption; wholly-owned subsidiary of COCOBOD; two factories divested to WAMCO Ltd in 1992 and 1993; Man. Dir RICHARD AMARH TETTEH; 600 employees (2005).

Equatorial Coca-Cola Bottling Co (ECCBC) (Coca-Cola Bottling Co of Ghana Ltd): Accra–Tema Motorway, Industrial Area, Spintex Rd, POB C1607, Accra; internet www.ghana.coca-cola.com; bottling plants in Accra and Kumasi.

Ghana Bauxite Co Ltd: 10 Sixth St, Airport Residential Area, PMB, Accra; tel. (30) 2765830; fax (30) 2760732; e-mail bauxite@ghana.com; f. 1940; 20% state-owned, 80% owned by Bosai Minerals Group (People's Republic of China); fmrly British Aluminium Co Ltd; mining of bauxite at Awaso with loading facilities at Takoradi; Man. Dir BEN ADOO.

Ghana Consolidated Diamonds Ltd: 10 3rd Roman Close, off North Roman Road, POB GP2978, Accra; tel. (30) 2664577; fax (30) 2664635; f. 1986; grades, values and processes diamonds, buys all locally won, produced or processed diamonds; engages in purchasing, grading, valuing, export and sale of local diamonds; owned by Sappers and Associates (UK); privatized in 2003; Chair. KOFI AGYEMAN; Man. Dir MAXWELL KUSI MANSAH.

Ghana Cotton Co Ltd (GCCL): POB 371, Tamale; tel. (37) 2022241; fax (37) 2023096; production, processing and marketing of cotton and its by-products; Man. Dir GEORGE OSEIKU.

Ghana Manganese Co Ltd (GMC): POB 2, Nsuta-Wassaw, Western Region; tel. (31) 2320225; fax (31) 2320443; e-mail headoffice@ghaman.com; internet www.ghamang.net; transferred to private ownership in 1995; Chair. B. WINKLER; Man. Dir JURGEN EIJGENDAAL.

Ghana National Petroleum Corpn (GNPC): Harbour Rd, PMB, Tema, Accra; tel. (30) 3206020; fax (30) 3206592; e-mail info@gnpcghana.com; internet www.gnpcghana.com; f. 1983; exploration, development, production and disposal of petroleum; Chair. ATO AHWOI; Man. Dir NANA BOAKYE ASAFU-ADJAYE.

Ghana Oil Company Limited: Kojo Thompson/Adjabeng Rd, POB GP 3183, Accra; tel. (30) 2688214; fax (30) 2688164; e-mail hq@goilonline.com; internet goilonline.com; marketing and distribution of petroleum products; Chair. Prof. WILLIAM AFIAKWA ASOMANING; Man. Dir YAW AGYEMANG-DUAH.

Goldfields Ghana Ltd: Plot 53, North Ridge, POB 16160, Accra; tel. (30) 2225812; fax (30) 2228448; f. 1995; operates a gold mine, Tarkwa, and one at Damang, through its subsidiary Abosso Goldfields Ltd; 70% owned by Gold Fields Ltd, South Africa; Man. Dir RICHARD ROBINSON.

Guinness Ghana Breweries Ltd (GGBL): PO Box 114, Achimota, Accra; tel. (30) 2400649; fax (30) 2400673; e-mail gblacc@ghana.com; f. 1955; Chair. ISHMAEL YAMSON; Man. Dir EKWUNIFE OKOLI; 600 employees.

Nestlé Ghana Ltd: Plot 33, South Legon Commercial Area, Motorway Extension, PMB KIA, Accra; tel. (30) 2517020; fax (30) 2401195; e-mail consumerservices@gh.nestle.com; f. 1957; Man. Dir SAMER CHADID; 556 employees.

Phyto-Riker (GIHOC) Pharmaceuticals Ltd: Mile 7, off Nsawam Rd, POB AN5266, Dome, Accra-North; tel. (30) 2400482; fax (30) 2400998; e-mail info@phyto-riker.com; internet www.phyto-riker.com.gh; fmrly Ghana Industrial Holding Corpn Pharmaceuticals Ltd (f. 1962); Chair. KEN OFORI-ATTA; CEO JERVIS DANQUAH (acting); 200 employees.

Precious Minerals Marketing Co Ltd (PMMC): Diamond House, POB M108, Accra; tel. (30) 2664931; fax (30) 2662586; e-mail pmmc@pmmcghana.com; internet www.pmmcghana.com; f. 1963; govt-owned; Chair. STEPHEN ADUBOFOUR; Man. Dir ARISTOTLE KOTEY (acting).

rLG Communications: Osu Oxford St, close to Photo Club, Accra; tel. (30) 2768258; fax (30) 2778272; internet www.rlgcommunications.org; f. 2001; manufacturer of mobile phones; CEO ROLAND AGAMBIRE.

Tema Oil Refinery Ltd (TOR): POB 599, Tema; tel. (30) 3302881; fax (30) 3302884; e-mail tor@tor.com.gh; internet www.torghana.com; f. 1963; sole oil refinery in Ghana; state-controlled since 1977; Chair. Dr JOHN KOBINA RICHARDSON; Man. Dir ATO AMPIAH; 350 employees (2001).

Total Petroleum Ghana Ltd: 95 Kojo Thompson Rd, Adabraka, POB 553, Accra; tel. (30) 2221445; e-mail totalgha@ghana.com; f. 2006 by merger of Total Petroleum Ghana Ltd and Total Ghana Ltd (f. 1960); 60% owned by Total Outre Mer SA; distribution of petroleum products, incl. liquefied petroleum gas; Man. Dir JONATHAN MOLAPO.

Unilever Ghana Ltd: POB 721, Tema; tel. (30) 3218100; fax (30) 3210352; e-mail vicky.wireko@unilever.com; internet www.unileverghana.com; f. 1955 as United Africa Co of Ghana Ltd; comprises 6 divisions and assoc. cos; subsidiary of Unilever plc (United Kingdom); agricultural, industrial, specialized merchandising, distributive and service enterprises; cap. 9.9m. cedi (Dec. 1999); Chair. ISHMAEL YAMSON; 900 employees (2001).

Volta Aluminium Co Ltd (Valco): POB 625, Tema; tel. (30) 3204203; fax (30) 3231423; 100% govt-owned; operates an aluminium smelter at Tema (annual capacity 200,000 metric tons); CEO Dr CHARLES MENSA; 1,265 employees (2002).

West Africa Mills Co Ltd (WAMCO): Wamco Rd, Takoradi; cocoa processing for export; Gen. Man. ANTHONY K. N. CLEMENT; c. 800 employees (2003).

CO-OPERATIVES

Department of Co-operatives: POB M150, Accra; tel. (30) 2666212; fax (30) 2772789; f. 1944; govt-supervised body, responsible for registration, auditing and supervision of co-operative socs; Registrar R. BUACHIE-APHRAM.

Ghana Co-operatives Council Ltd (GACOCO): POB 4034, Accra; tel. 244267014 (mobile); fax (30) 2672014; e-mail gacopco@yahoo.com; f. 1951; co-ordinates activities of all co-operative socs and plays advocacy role for co-operative movement; comprises 11 active nat. asscns and 2 central orgs; Sec.-Gen. ALBERT AGYEMAN PREMPEH.

The national associations and central organizations include the Ghana Co-operative Marketing Asscn Ltd, the Ghana Co-operative Credit Unions Asscn Ltd, the Ghana Co-operative Distillers and Retailers Asscn Ltd, and the Ghana Co-operative Poultry Farmers Asscn Ltd.

TRADE UNIONS

Ghana Federation of Labour: POB Trade Fair 509, Accra; tel. (30) 2252105; fax (30) 2307394; e-mail gflgh@hotmail.com; Sec.-Gen. ABRAHAM KOOMSON; 10,540 mems.

Ghana National Association of Teachers (GNAT): POB 209, Accra; tel. (30) 2221576; fax (30) 2226286; e-mail info@ghanateachers.org; internet www.ghanateachers.org; f. 1931; Pres. PAUL APANGA; Gen. Sec. IRENE DUNCAN ADANUSA; 178,000 mems (2003).

Ghana Trades Union Congress (GTUC): Hall of Trade Unions, Liberia Rd, POB 701, Accra; tel. (30) 2662568; fax (30) 2667161; e-mail info@ghanatuc.org; internet www.ghanatuc.org; f. 1945; 17 affiliated unions; Chair. ALEX K. BONNEY; Sec.-Gen. KOFI ASAMOAH.

General Agricultural Workers' Union (GAWU): Hall of Trade Unions, 5th Floor, Liberia Rd, POB 701, Accra; tel. (30) 2665514; fax (30) 2672468; e-mail gawughanatuc@yahoo.com; f. 1959; Gen. Sec. KINGSLEY OFEI-NKANSAH.

Ghana Mineworkers' Union (GMWU): Hall of Trade Unions Bldg, off Barnes and Liberia Roads, Tudu, POB 701, Accra; tel. (21) 665563; e-mail admin@gmwu.org; internet www.gmwu.org; f. 1944; Chair. JOHN KOJO BRIMPONG; Gen. Sec. PRINCE WILLIAM ANKRAH.

Teachers' and Educational Workers' Union (TEWU): Hall of Trade Unions, Liberia Road, POB 701, Accra; tel. (30) 2663050; fax (30) 2671544; e-mail tewu@vodafone.com.gh; internet www.tewu.panafrica.ws; f. 1958; Chair. Alhaji PETER K. LUMOR; Sec.-Gen. MAHAMMADU SEIDU BOGOBIRI.

Transport

RAILWAYS

Ghana has a railway network of 977 km, which connects Accra, Kumasi and Takoradi. In 2010 a concessionary loan of US $4,000m. was secured from the Export-Import Bank of China to extend the Takoradi-Kumasi railway to Paga on the border with Burkina Faso.

Ghana Railway Co Ltd (GRC): POB 251, Takoradi; f. 1901; responsible for the operation and maintenance of all railways; to be run under private concession from April 2004; 947 km of track in use in 2003; Chair Dr CLEMENT HAMMAH; Man. Dir K. B. AMOFA (acting).

Ghana Railway Development Authority (GRDA): Ministry of Transport, PMB, Accra; tel. (21) 681780; fax (21) 681781; internet grda.gov.gh; f. 2005; regulatory and devt authority; Chair. DAN MARKIN; Man. Dir EMMANUEL OPOKU.

ROADS

In 2012 Ghana had a total road network of approximately 66,200 km, of which 41% was considered to be in 'good condition'. Construction work on 36 bridges nation-wide, funded by the Japanese Government, commenced in 2003. In 2005 €11m. was pledged by the European Union for upgrading the road network in key cocoa-producing areas.

Ghana Highway Authority: POB 1641, Accra; tel. (30) 2666591; fax (30) 2665571; e-mail eokonadu@highways.mrt.gov.gh; internet www.highways.gov.gh; f. 1974 to plan, develop, administer and maintain trunk roads and related facilities; Chair. JOE GIDISU (acting); Chief Dir TESCHMAKER ANTHONY ESSILFIE.

Intercity State Transport Company (STC) Coaches Ltd: POB 7384, 1 Adjuma Cres., Ring Rd West Industrial Area, Accra; tel. (30) 2221912; fax (30) 2221945; e-mail stc@ghana.com; f. 1965; fmrly State Transport Co; transferred to private sector ownership in 2000 and renamed Vanef STC; above name adopted in 2003; regional and international coach services; Man. Dir EDWARD LORD ATTIVOR.

SHIPPING

The two main ports are Tema (near Accra) and Takoradi, both of which are linked with Kumasi by rail. There are also important inland ports on the Volta, Ankobra and Tano rivers. At 31 December 2009 the merchant fleet comprised 236 vessels, totalling 116,000 grt.

Ghana Maritime Authority (GMA): E354/3 Third Ave, East Ridge, PMB 34, Ministries, Accra; tel. (30) 2662122; fax (30) 2677702; e-mail info@ghanamaritime.org; internet www

.ghanamaritime.org; f. 2002; policy-making body; part of Ministry of Transport; regulates maritime industry; Dir-Gen. ISSAKA PETER AZUMA.

Ghana Ports and Harbour Authority (GPHA): POB 150, Tema; tel. (30) 3202631; fax (30) 3202812; e-mail headquarters@ghanaports.net; internet www.ghanaports.gov.gh; f. 1986; holding co for the ports of Tema and Takoradi; Dir-Gen. NESTER PERCY GALLEY.

Alpha (West Africa) Line Ltd: POB 451, Tema; operates regular cargo services to West Africa, the United Kingom, the USA, the Far East and northern Europe; shipping agents; Man. Dir AHMED EDGAR COLLINGWOOD WILLIAMS.

Liner Agencies and Trading (Ghana) Ltd: POB 214, Tema; tel. (30) 3202987; fax (30) 3202989; e-mail enquiries@liner-agencies.com; international freight services; shipping agents; Dir J. OSSEI-YAW.

Maersk Ghana Ltd: Obourwe Bldg, Torman Rd, Fishing Harbour Area, POB 8800, Community 7, Tema; tel. (30) 3218700; fax (30) 3202048; e-mail gnamkt@maersk.com; internet www.maerskline.com/ghana; f. 2001; owned by Maersk Line (Denmark); offices in Tema, Takoradi and Kumasi; Man. Dir JEFF GOSCINIAK.

Scanship (Ghana) Ltd: Mensah Utreh Rd, Commercial Warehouse Area, POB 64, Tema; tel. (30) 3202561; fax (30) 3202571; e-mail scanship.ghana@gh.dti.bollore.com; shipping agents.

Shipping Association

Ghana Shippers' Council: Enterprise House, 5th Floor, High St, POB 1321, Accra; tel. (30) 2555915; fax (30) 2668768; e-mail scouncil@shippers-gh.com; internet www.ghanashipperscouncil.org; f. 1974; represents interests of 28,000 registered Ghanaian shippers; also provides cargo-handling and allied services; Chief Exec. KOFI MBIAH.

CIVIL AVIATION

The main international airport is at Kotoka (Accra). There are also airports at Kumasi, Takoradi, Sunyani, Tamale and Wa. The construction of a dedicated freight terminal at Kotoka Airport was completed in 1994. In 2001 622,525 passengers and 44,779 metric tons of freight passed through Kotoka Airport. The rehabilitation of Kumasi Airport began in 2006, and, following upgrade work, Tamale Airport became the country's second international airport in December 2008.

Ghana Civil Aviation Authority (GCAA): PMB, Kotoka International Airport, Accra; tel. (30) 2776171; fax (30) 2773293; e-mail info@gcaa.com.gh; internet www.gcaa.com.gh; f. 1986; Chair. ALBAN SUMANA BAGBIN; Dir-Gen. KWAME MAMPHEY.

Afra Airlines Ltd: 7 Nortei St, Airport Residential Area, Accra; tel. 244932488 (mobile); e-mail lukebutler@afraairlines.com; f. 2005; CEO LUKE BUTLER.

Antrak Air: 50 Senchi St, Airport Residential Area, Accra; tel. (30) 2782814; fax (30) 2782816; e-mail info@antrakair.com; internet www.antrakair.com; f. 2003; passenger and cargo services for domestic and international routes; Chair. ASOMA BANDA.

Gemini Airlines Ltd (Aero Gem Cargo): America House, POB 7238, Accra-North; tel. (30) 2771921; fax (30) 2761939; e-mail aerogemcargo@hotmail.com; f. 1974; operates weekly cargo flight between Accra and London; Gen. Man. ENOCH ANAN-TABURY.

Tourism

Ghana's attractions include fine beaches, game reserves, traditional festivals, and old trading forts and castles. In 2010 some 931,000 tourists visited Ghana; revenue from tourism totalled US $620m. in that year (excluding passenger transport).

Ghana Tourist Board: POB GP3106, Accra-North; tel. (30) 2222153; fax (30) 2244611; e-mail gtb@africaonline.com.gh; internet www.touringghana.com; f. 1968; Exec. Dir JULIUS DEBRAH.

Ghana Association of Tourist and Travel Agencies (GATTA): Swamp Grove, Asylum Down, POB 7140, Accra-North; tel. (30) 2222398; fax (30) 2231102; e-mail info@gattagh.com; internet www.gattagh.com; Pres. HILLARIUS MCCASH AKPAH; Exec. Sec. TINA OSEI.

Ghana Tourist Development Co Ltd: POB 8710, Accra-North; tel. (30) 2770720; fax (30) 2770694; e-mail info@ghanatouristdevelopment.com; internet www.ghanatouristdevelopment.com; f. 1974; develops tourist infrastructure, incl. hotels, restaurants and casinos; operates duty-free shops; Man. Dir ALFRED KOMLADZEI.

Defence

As assessed at November 2011, Ghana's total armed forces numbered 15,500 (army 11,500, navy 2,000 and air force 2,000). In March 2000 the Government restructured the armed forces; the army was subsequently organized into north and south commands, and the navy into western and eastern commands. In January 2004 a peacekeeping training centre, which was primarily to be used by ECOWAS, was established in Accra. In 2011 a total of 2,598 Ghanaian troops were stationed abroad, of whom 25 were observers.

Defence Expenditure: Estimated at 198,000m. new cedis in 2011.

Commander-in-Chief of the Armed Forces: Pres. JOHN DRAMANI MAHAMA.

Chief of Defence Staff and Commander of the Navy: Maj.-Gen. PETER AUGUSTINE BLAY.

Chief of Air Staff: Air Vice-Marshall MICHAEL SAMSON-OJE.

Chief of Army Staff: Maj.-Gen. JOSEPH NARH ADINKRAH.

Chief of Naval Staff: Rear Adm. MATTHEW QUARSHIE.

Education

Education is officially compulsory and free of charge for eight years, between the ages of six and 14. Primary education begins at the age of six and lasts for six years, comprising two cycles of three years each. Secondary education begins at the age of 12 and lasts for a further seven years, comprising a first cycle of three years and a second of four years. Following three years of junior secondary education, pupils are examined to determine admission to senior secondary school courses, or to technical and vocational courses. In 2008/09, according to UNESCO, primary enrolment included 77% of children in the relevant age-group (boys 76%; girls 77%), while the comparable ratio for secondary enrolment in that year was estimated at 47% (boys 49%; girls 45%). Some 285,900 students were enrolled in tertiary education in 2010/11. There were seven universities in Ghana in 1998/99. Tertiary institutions also included 38 teacher-training colleges, eight polytechnics and 61 technical colleges.

Bibliography

Agbodeka, F. *An Economic History of Ghana from the Earliest Times.* Accra, Ghana Universities Press, 1992.

Amenumey, D. E. K. *The Ewe Unification Movement: A Political History.* Accra, Ghana Universities Press, 1989.

Amoah, M. *Reconstructing the Nation in Africa: The Politics of Nationalism in Ghana.* London, I. B. Tauris, 2007.

Ankama, S. K. *The Westminster Model in Africa and a Search for African Democracy.* London, Silkan Books, 1996.

Aryeetey, E., Harrigan, J., and Nissanke, M. (Eds). *Economic Reforms in Ghana: The Miracle and the Mirage.* Oxford, James Currey, 1999.

Ayensu, K. B., and Darkwa, S. N. *The Evolution of Parliament in Ghana.* Accra, Sub-Saharan Publishers, 2006.

Babatope, E. *The Ghana Revolution from Nkrumah to Jerry Rawlings.* Enugu, Fourth Dimension Publishers, 1984.

Baynham, S. *The Military and Politics in Nkrumah's Ghana.* Boulder, CO, Westview Press, 1988.

English, P. *Recovery is Not Enough: The Case of Ghana.* New York, World Bank, 1999.

Frimpong, J. H. *The Vampire State in Africa: The Political Economy of Decline in Ghana.* London, James Currey, 1991.

Gocking, R. S. *The History of Ghana.* Westport, CT, Greenwood Press, 2005.

Goodall, H. B. *Beloved Imperialist: Sir Gordon Guggisberg, Governor of the Gold Coast.* Durham, Pentland Press, 1998.

Greenhalgh, P. *West African Diamonds: An Economic History 1919–83.* Manchester, Manchester University Press, 1985.

Gyimah-Boardi, E. (Ed.). *Ghana under PNDC Rule.* Dakar, CODESRIA, 1993.

Hansen, E. *Ghana under Rawlings: Early Years.* Oxford, ABC and Malthouse Press, 1991.

Hasty, J. *The Press and Political Culture in Ghana.* Bloomington, IN, Indiana University Press, 2005.

Herbst, J. *The Politics of Reform in Ghana, 1982–1991.* Berkeley, CA, University of California Press, 1993.

Huq, M. M. *The Economy of Ghana: The First 25 Years since Independence.* London, Macmillan, 1988.

Hutchful, E. *Ghana's Adjustment Experience: The Paradox of Reform.* Oxford, James Currey, 2002.

Jackson, K. A. *When Gun Rules: A Soldier's Testimony of the Events Leading to June 4 Uprising in Ghana and its Aftermath.* Accra, Woeli Publishing Services, 1999.

Kanbur, R., and Aryeetey, E. (Eds). *Economy of Ghana: Analytical Perspectives on Stability, Growth and Poverty.* Oxford, James Currey, 2008.

Mahama, J. D. *My First Coup d'Etat: Memories from the Lost Decades of Africa.* London, Bloomsbury Publishing, 2012.

Manuh, T. (Ed.). *At Home in the World? International Migration and Development in Contemporary Ghana and West Africa.* Accra, Sub-Saharan Publishers, 2006.

Milne, J. *Kwame Nkrumah—A Biography.* London, Panaf Books, 2000.

Ninsin, K. A. (Ed.). *Ghana: Transition to Democracy.* Dakar, CODESRIA, 1998.

Ninsin, K. A., and Drah, F. K. (Eds). *The Search for Democracy in Ghana: A Case Study in Political Instability in Africa.* Accra, Asempa Publishers, 1987.

Ghana's Transition to Constitutional Rule. Accra, Ghana University Press, and Oxford, ABC, 1991.

Political Parties and Democracy in Ghana's Fourth Republic. Accra, Woeli Publishing Services, 1993.

Nugent, P. *Big Men, Small Boys and Politics in Ghana: Power, Ideology and the Burden of History, 1982–1994.* London, Pinter, 1995.

The Flight-Lieutenant Rides (To Power) Again: National Delusions, Local Fixations and the 1996 Ghanaian Elections. Edinburgh, Centre of African Studies, Edinburgh University (Occasional Papers, no. 76), 1998.

Okafor, G. M. *Christianity and Islam in West Africa; the Ghana Experience: A Study of the Forces and Influence of Christianity and Islam in Modern Ghana.* Würzburg, Oros, 1997.

Okeke, B. E. *4 June: A Revolution Betrayed.* Enugu, Ikenga Publishers, 1982.

Osei, A. P. *Ghana: Recurrence and Change in a Post-Independence African State.* New York, P. Lang, 1999.

Owusu-Ansah, D., and McFarland, M. D. *Historical Dictionary of Ghana.* 2nd edn. Lanham, MD, Scarecrow Press, 1995.

Perbi, A. A. *A History of Indigenous Slavery in Ghana, From the 15th to the 19th Century.* Accra, Sub-Saharan Publishers, 2004.

Pinkney, R. *Ghana under Military Rule 1966–1969.* London, Methuen, 1972.

Democracy and Dictatorship in Ghana and Tanzania. New York, St. Martin's Press, 1997.

Quay, R. *Underdevelopment and Health Care in Africa: The Ghanaian Experience.* Lewiston, Edwin Mellen Press, 1996.

Rathbone, R. J. A. R. *Nkrumah and the Chiefs: The Politics of Chieftaincy in Ghana, 1951–60.* Oxford, James Currey, 2000.

Rimmer, D. *Staying Poor: Ghana's Political Economy, 1950–1990.* Oxford, Pergamon, 1992.

Stockwell, S. E. *The Business of Decolonization: British Business Strategies in the Gold Coast.* Oxford, Clarendon Press, 2000.

Tsikata, D. *Living in the Shadow of the Large Dams: Long Term Responses of Downstream and Lakeside Communities of Ghana's Volta River Project.* Leiden, Brill Academic Publishers, 2006.

Yeebo, Z. *Ghana: The Struggle for Popular Power—Rawlings: Saviour or Demagogue?* Accra, New Beacon Books, 1992.

GUINEA

Physical and Social Geography

R. J. HARRISON CHURCH

The Republic of Guinea covers an area of 245,857 sq km (94,926 sq miles), containing exceptionally varied landscapes, peoples and economic conditions. The census of 31 December 1996 recorded a population of 7,156,406, which had increased to 10,480,709 by mid-2012, according to UN estimates (giving an average density of 42.6 inhabitants per sq km). The population is concentrated in the plateau area of central Guinea: about one-quarter of the population is estimated to be living in Conakry and its environs; Conakry itself had a population of 1,092,936 in 1996. It was estimated by the UN to have increased to some 1,786,300 by mid-2011.

Guinea's coast is part of the extremely wet south-western sector of West Africa, which has a monsoonal climate. Thus Conakry, the capital, has five to six months with almost no rain, while 4,300 mm fall in the remaining months. The coastline has shallow drowned rivers and estuaries with much mangrove growing on alluvium eroded from the nearby Fouta Djallon mountains. Much of the mangrove has been removed, and the land bunded for rice cultivation. Only at two places, Cape Verga and Conakry, do ancient hard rocks reach the sea. At the latter they have facilitated the development of the port, while the weathering of these rocks has produced exploitable deposits of bauxite on the offshore Los Islands.

Behind the swamps a gravelly coastal plain, some 65 km wide, is backed by the steep, often sheer, edges of the Fouta Djallon, which occupies the west-centre of Guinea. Much is over 900 m high, and consists of level Primary sandstones (possibly of Devonian age) which cover Pre-Cambrian rocks to a depth of 750 m. The level plateaux, with many bare lateritic surfaces, are the realm of Fulani (Peul) herders. Rivers are deeply incised in the sandstone. These more fertile valleys were earlier cultivated with food crops by slaves of the Fulani, and then with bananas, coffee, citrus fruits and pineapples on plantations under the French. Falls and gorges of the incised rivers have great hydroelectric potential. This is significant in view of huge deposits of high-grade bauxite located at Fria and Boké. The climate is still monsoonal but, although the total rainfall is lower—about 1,800 mm annually—it is more evenly distributed than on the coasts, as the rainy season is longer. In such a mountainous area there are sharp variations in climatic conditions over a short distance, and from year to year.

On the Liberian border the Guinea highlands rise to 1,752 m at Mt Nimba, where substantial deposits of haematite iron ore are eventually to be developed. These rounded mountains contrast greatly with the level plateaux and deep narrow valleys of the Fouta Djallon. Rainfall is heavier than in the latter, but is again more evenly distributed, so that only two or three months are without significant rain. Coffee, kola and other crops are grown in the forest of this remote area. Diamonds are mined north of Macenta and west of Beyla, and gold at Siguiri and Léro.

Recent History

MARIE GIBERT

Based on an earlier article by RICHARD SYNGE with subsequent revisions by EDWARD GEORGE

THE SÉKOU TOURÉ PERIOD

On 2 October 1958, having rejected membership of a proposed community of self-governing French overseas territories, French Guinea became the independent Republic of Guinea. Ahmed Sékou Touré, the Secretary-General of the Parti Démocratique de Guinée—Rassemblement Démocratique Africain (PDG—RDA), which had led the campaign for independence, became the Republic's first President, and the PDG—RDA the sole political party. Punitive economic reprisals were taken by the departing French authorities, and French aid and investment were suspended. Sékou Touré's Government initially obtained assistance from the USSR and withdrew from the Franc Zone in 1960, but after 1961 the USA became a more significant source of aid.

Radical socialist policies were applied to Guinea's internal economy. In 1975 all private trading was forbidden, and financial transactions were supervised by an 'economic police', which was widely suspected of extortion and smuggling. Resentment against their activities culminated in August 1977 in widespread demonstrations and rioting, as a so-called 'women's revolt' in Conakry quickly extended to other towns. In response, Sékou Touré disbanded the 'economic police' and permitted the resumption (from July 1979) of small-scale private trading. In 1978 it was decided to merge the PDG—RDA and the State, and in January 1979 the country was renamed the People's Revolutionary Republic of Guinea.

CONTÉ AND THE MILITARY COMMITTEE

Sékou Touré died suddenly in March 1984. Before a successor could be chosen, the army staged a coup in April, and a Comité Militaire de Redressement National (CMRN) seized power. Its principal leaders Col (later Gen.) Lansana Conté and Col Diarra Traoré, who became President and Prime Minister, respectively, had both held senior positions for some years. A semi-civilian Government was appointed, and efforts were furthered to improve regional relations and links with potential sources of economic aid (most notably France). In May the country resumed the designation of Republic of Guinea. The PDG—RDA and organs of Sékou Touré's 'party state' were dismantled under this Second Republic, which was initially greeted with great enthusiasm. State surveillance and control were ended, and many political detainees were freed. In the first months of his presidency Conté adopted an open style of government, inviting constructive advice and criticism from all sectors of society.

Undercurrents of Opposition

In December 1984 Conté abolished the office of Prime Minister, demoting Traoré to a lesser ministerial post. In July 1985, while Conté was attending a regional summit meeting in Togo, Traoré attempted a coup, supported mainly by members of the police force. Troops loyal to Conté swiftly regained control, and the President returned two days later. Traoré and many of his family were among more than 200 people arrested, and the armed forces conducted a purge of his suspected sympathizers.

Traoré and a half-brother of Sékou Touré were executed in the immediate aftermath of the coup attempt and about 60 other military officers were later sentenced to death.

The coup attempt effectively strengthened Conté's position, allowing him to pursue the extensive economic reforms demanded by the World Bank and the IMF as a prerequisite for the disbursement of new funds. In December 1985 Conté reorganized the Council of Ministers, introducing a majority of civilians for the first time since he took power and creating resident 'regional' ministries.

In October 1988, commemorating the 30th anniversary of the country's independence, Conté announced the establishment of a committee to draft a new constitution, which would be submitted for approval in a national referendum. In October 1989 Conté revealed plans whereby a Comité Transitoire de Redressement National (CTRN) would succeed the CMRN and oversee a five-year transitional period, prior to the establishment of a two-party political system under an elected president and legislature.

Conté appealed in November 1990 for the return to Guinea of political exiles. However, three members of an illegal opposition movement, the Rassemblement Populaire Guinéen (RPG), were imprisoned later in the month. Rejecting widespread demands for an accelerated programme of political reform, the Government proceeded with its plan for a gradual transition to a two-party political system. The draft Constitution was submitted to a national referendum in December, and was declared to have been approved by 98.7% of those who voted (some 97.4% of the registered electorate). In February 1991 the 36-member CTRN was inaugurated, under the chairmanship of Conté. In October Conté announced that the registration of an unlimited number of political parties would come into effect on 3 April 1992, and that legislative elections would take place before the end of 1992 in the context of a full multi-party political system.

CONTÉ AND THE THIRD REPUBLIC

The Constitution of the Third Republic was promulgated on 23 December 1991. In January 1992 Conté ceded the presidency of the CTRN, in accordance with constitutional provision for the separation of the powers of the executive and legislature. In the following month most military officers and all *Guinéens de l'extérieur* (former dissidents who had returned from exile after the 1984 coup) were removed from the Government: it later became apparent that some of these long-serving ministers had left public office in order to establish a pro-Conté political party, the Parti de l'Unité et du Progrès (PUP).

The RPG was among the first opposition parties to be legalized in April 1992. The most prominent other challengers to the PUP were the Parti pour le Renouveau et le Progrès (PRP), led by a well-known journalist, Siradiou Diallo, and the Union pour la Nouvelle République (UNR), led by Mamadou Boye Bâ. However, the fragmented nature of the opposition undermined attempts to persuade the Government to convene a national political conference. The opposition alleged that the PUP was benefiting from state funds, and that the Government was coercing civil servants into joining the party. Clashes between pro- and anti-Conté activists (seemingly fuelled by ethnic rivalries) occurred frequently from mid-1992, and in October the Government again banned all unauthorized public gatherings.

In December 1992 the Government announced the indefinite postponement of the legislative elections, which had been scheduled for the end of the month, citing technical and financial difficulties. It was later indicated that the elections would be organized in late 1993, and that they would be preceded by a presidential election, the date of which was eventually established as 19 December. Despite confused reports of opposition appeals for a boycott of the presidential election on (and the absence of voters' lists in some polling centres), the rate of participation was, officially, 78.5% of the registered electorate. Conté was elected at the first round of voting, having secured an absolute majority (51.7%) of the votes cast. The leader of the RPG, Alpha Condé, his nearest rival, took 19.6% of the votes; however, the Supreme Court's invalidation (having found evidence of malpractice) of the results of voting in the Kankan and Siguiri prefectures, in both of which Condé had won more than 90% of the votes, fuelled opposition claims that the poll had been manipulated in favour of Conté. Conté (who had, as required by the Constitution, resigned from the armed forces in order to contest the presidency) was inaugurated as President on 29 January 1994.

In March 1995 it was announced that elections to the new Assemblée nationale would take place on 11 June. Parties of the so-called 'radical' opposition (principally the RPG, the PRP and the UNR) frequently alleged harassment of their activists by the security forces, claiming that efforts were being made to prevent campaigning in areas where support for the opposition was likely to be strong. As preliminary results indicated that the PUP had won an overwhelming majority in the 114-seat legislature, the radical opposition protested that voting had been conducted fraudulently, stating that they would take no further part in the electoral process and that they would boycott the Assemblée nationale. According to the official results, the PUP won 71 seats—having taken 30 of the country's 38 single-member constituencies, together with 41 of the 76 seats allocated by proportional representation. Eight other parties won representation, among them the RPG, which took 19 seats, the PRP and the UNR, both of which won nine seats. Some 63% of the electorate were reported to have voted. The results were confirmed by the Supreme Court in July, whereupon the new legislature formally superseded the CTRN.

The three radical opposition parties joined forces with nine other organizations in July 1995, creating a new opposition front, the Coordination de l'Opposition Démocratique (Codem), which indicated its willingness to enter into a dialogue with the authorities.

Military Unrest

In early February 1996 Conté was reportedly seized as he attempted to flee the presidential palace during a mutiny by disaffected elements of the military. He was released after making concessions, including a doubling of salaries and immunity from prosecution for those involved in the uprising. About 50 people were killed and 100 injured as rebels clashed with forces loyal to the Conté regime. In all, as many as 2,000 soldiers, including members of the presidential guard, were believed to have joined the rebellion. By June some 42 members of the armed forces had reportedly been charged in connection with the coup plot.

The replacement, in April 1996, of two close associates of Conté, the armed forces Chief of Staff and the governor of Conakry (also a military officer), was regarded as an indication of the President's commitment to a restructuring of both the civilian and military administration. In July Conté announced (for the first time under the Third Republic) the appointment of a Prime Minister. The premiership was assigned to a non-partisan economist, Sidya Touré, who also assumed responsibility for the economy. A comprehensive reorganization of the Government included the division of the Ministry of the Interior into two separate departments (one responsible for territorial administration and decentralization, the other for security). Touré stated that his Government's priorities were to be economic recovery and the combating of institutionalized corruption, with the aim of securing renewed assistance from the international donor community, and of attracting increased foreign investment. In February 1997, following the conclusion of a new financing arrangement with the IMF, Touré relinquished control of the economy portfolio to two ministers-delegate, including Ibrahima Kassory Fofana, who became Minister of the Economy and Finance.

Trials and Tensions

A total of 96 defendants were brought before the newly established State Security Court in mid-February 1998, to answer charges related to the attempted coup two years earlier; hearings commenced in March, but defence lawyers refused to represent their clients on the grounds that their rights were being infringed by the State Security Court. The Court did not reconvene until mid-September. At the end of the month 38 of the accused received custodial sentences ranging from seven months to 15 years, some with hard labour; 51 defendants were acquitted.

Codem was critical of the Government's preparations for the forthcoming presidential election, notably proposals for the establishment of a new body, the Haut Conseil aux Affaires Électorales (HCE), to act in conjunction with the Ministry of the Interior and Decentralization in preparing and supervising the poll. The 68-member HCE was to be composed of representatives of the presidential majority, together with opposition delegates, ministerial representatives and members of civil society. Conté was challenged by four candidates, including Bâ, representing the Union pour le Progrès et le Renouveau (UPR—formed in September by a merger of the UNR and the PRP) and Alpha Condé (who had been resident abroad since early 1997, owing to fears for his personal safety) for the RPG. Voting proceeded on 14 December 1998, despite several violent incidents during the election campaign. Further violence followed the arrest, two days after the poll, of Condé, who was accused of attempting to leave the country illegally (Guinea's borders had been sealed prior to the election) and of seeking to recruit troops to destabilize Guinea. By the end of December at least 12 people were reported to have been killed as a result of violence in Conakry, Kankan, Siguiri and Baro. Condé was formally charged in late December with having recruited mercenaries with the aim of overthrowing the Conté regime. Some 100 other opposition activists remained in detention. Meanwhile, the opposition withdrew its representatives from the HCE, denouncing the conduct of the election as fraudulent. The official results, issued by the HCE on 17 December and confirmed by the Supreme Court two weeks later, showed a decisive victory for Conté, with 56.1% of the valid votes cast. Bâ took 24.6% and Condé 16.6%. The electoral turn-out was recorded at 71.4% of the registered electorate.

At his inauguration, on 30 January 1999, President Conté proclaimed that all abuses, including those committed by the security forces, would be severely punished. In March Sidya Touré was dismissed as premier and replaced by Lamine Sidimé, hitherto the Chief Justice of the Supreme Court and of no party-political affiliation. Fofana, widely credited with Guinea's recent economic successes, was reappointed Minister of the Economy and Finance, while Dorank Assifat Diasséhy, redesignated Minister at the Presidency, retained the national defence portfolio.

From 1999 opposition groups and human rights organizations urged the release from detention of Alpha Condé and other activists arrested at the time of the presidential election. In February 2000 members of the Assemblée nationale, including members of the PUP, urged the President to release Condé, pointing out that the latter possessed parliamentary immunity from prosecution, and suggesting that his release would encourage democracy in Guinea. Nevertheless, in April, some 16 months after the initial arrests, the trial began of Condé and his 47 co-defendants on charges that included plotting to kill Conté, hiring mercenaries and threatening state security. Following several delays and interruptions to the trial, in mid-September Condé was sentenced to five years' imprisonment, while six other defendants also received prison terms.

Regional Upheavals

In September 2000 an armed rebellion in south-east Guinea reportedly resulted in at least 40 deaths. Instability subsequently intensified in regions near the borders with Sierra Leone and Liberia, with incidences of cross-border attacks on Guinean civilians and the military. Fighting between armed groups and Guinean soldiers was reported to have led to some 360 deaths between early September and mid-October. The Government attributed the upsurge in violence to forces supported by the Governments of Liberia and Burkina Faso, and to members of the Sierra Leonean rebel group, the Revolutionary United Front (RUF, see the Recent History of Sierra Leone), who, the Government alleged, were acting in alliance with Guinean dissidents. In October a previously unknown organization, the Rassemblement des Forces Démocratiques de Guinée (RFDG), claimed responsibility for the armed attacks, which, it stated, were intended to overthrow President Conté. In the same month, in a speech that was widely regarded as inflammatory, Conté accused refugees from Sierra Leone and Liberia of forming alliances with rebel groups seeking to destabilize Guinea. In November a number of cross-border attacks were attributed to forces associated with the RUF, and to former members of a faction of a dissolved Liberian dissident group, the United Liberation Movement of Liberia for Democracy (ULIMO), ULIMO—K (see the Recent History of Liberia), which President Conté had previously supported. The President cited the state of insecurity in the country as the reason for further postponement of Guinea's legislative elections.

In January 2001 Conté dismissed Diasséhy from his defence portfolio, which henceforth became the direct responsibility of the President. In late January and early February a series of attacks around Macenta were reported to have resulted in more than 130 deaths. Allegations persisted that an unofficial alliance between former ULIMO—K rebels and Guinean government forces had broken down, with the result that ULIMO—K forces were now attacking Guinean military and civilian targets. Renewed clashes around Guéckédou delayed the proposed deployment by the Economic Community of West African States (ECOWAS) of an ECOMOG (ECOWAS Ceasefire Monitoring Group) force, which had been intended to monitor stability and border security in the region from mid-February, and in the event no such force was deployed.

During 2001 the dynamics of the cross-border conflict changed dramatically as a result of the success of the UN-assisted peace process in Sierra Leone, and the growth of an armed rebellion in Liberia against the regime of President Charles Taylor, which was co-ordinated by a new group, Liberians United for Reconciliation and Democracy (LURD). Sierra Leonean RUF fighters, who were associated with Guinean rebels and supplied much of their weaponry, were defeated by Kamajor militias loyal to the Sierra Leonean Government; under forceful pressure from the Guinean military, they subsequently retreated across the border to participate in Sierra Leone's demobilization process. The Guinean rebels thereby lost their means of challenging their own government forces and began to disperse, although one group, the Union des Forces pour une Guinée Nouvelle, led by Dr N'Faly Kaba, claimed in several statements that its armed wing, supported by Taylor, was planning a nation-wide armed uprising to remove Conté from power. Despite such threats, made from neighbouring capital cities, there was a reduction in rebel activity, and government forces were able to reinforce their authority in the border regions, often with scant regard for the needs of refugees in these areas. In June 2001 Human Rights Watch alleged that security forces and vigilante groups in Guinea had frequently detained, tortured and assaulted Sierra Leonean and Liberian refugees, notably at roadside checkpoints. The organization also stated that RUF- and Liberian-backed forces had repeatedly attacked and set fire to refugee camps in border regions. Taylor, meanwhile, persistently accused Guinea of providing military support to the LURD rebellion in Liberia.

Conté Extends his Rule

In mid-May 2001 Alpha Condé and two of his co-defendants were released from prison, following the granting of a presidential pardon. Condé, none the less, was prohibited from participating in political activities for a period of unspecified duration. In mid-June President Conté announced his intention to hold a national referendum on a proposed constitutional amendment that would permit the President of the Republic to seek longer and limitless terms of office, justifying it by reference to the ongoing instability in border regions. In late June gendarmes enforced the closure of the headquarters of the Union des Forces Républicaines (UFR), the party led by former Prime Minister Sidya Touré, who had announced the formation of a group to oppose Conté's proposed constitutional amendment.

The referendum was held on 11 November 2001. According to official results, 98.4% of voters endorsed the constitutional revisions, with a turn-out of 87.2% of the registered electorate recorded, although opposition and media sources claimed that participation was lower than 20%. The presidential term of office was thus extended from five years to seven, with effect from the presidential election due in 2003, and the constitutional provision restricting the President to two terms of office was rescinded. Moreover, the President was to be permitted to appoint local government officials, who had hitherto been elected. Despite the overwhelming official result in favour of the amendments, opposition to the referendum was expressed very strongly, in particular by Boubacar Biro Diallo (who remained Speaker of the reconvened Assemblée nationale, the mandate of which had, officially, expired in July 2000), who deplored the lack of involvement of the legislature in deciding such a major constitutional change. Meanwhile, Bâ urged the international community to assist the opposition in removing Conté.

In mid-April 2002 President Conté issued a decree scheduling the repeatedly postponed elections to the Assemblée nationale for 30 June. However, concern was expressed that transparency in the conduct of the polls would not be guaranteed, and in late May four opposition parties, which had announced their intention to boycott the legislative elections, including the RPG and the UFR, announced the formation of a political alliance, the Front de l'Alternance Démocratique (FRAD). In early June Conté appointed François Lonsény Fall, previously the representative of Guinea to the UN, as Minister at the Presidency, responsible for Foreign Affairs.

At the legislative election on 30 June 2002 a turn-out of 71.6% of the registered electorate was recorded; the PUP increased its majority in the legislature, winning all 38 single-member constituency seats and 47 of the 76 seats allocated by proportional representation, giving it a total of 85 seats. The UPR became the second largest party in the Assemblée, securing 20 seats, while four other parties shared the remaining nine seats. In late September the Secretary-General of the PUP, Aboubacar Somparé, was chosen as Speaker of the Assemblée nationale. In mid-October 2002 Bâ was elected as President of a new party, the Union des Forces Démocratiques de Guinée (UFDG), which largely comprised a faction of the UPR that had boycotted the elections to the Assemblée nationale. The UFDG was affiliated to the FRAD, which announced its intention of nominating a common opposition candidate at the presidential election scheduled to be held in December 2003.

The absence of an obvious successor to Conté, who was known to be suffering ill health, caused widespread concern from 2002–03, with fears that a destabilizing 'power vacuum' could arise in the event of his death. The FRAD opposition alliance boycotted the December 2003 presidential election, owing to a perceived lack of independence on the part of the electoral commission and the alliance's lack of access to the state-controlled media. The only rival to Conté was the leader of a minor political party, Mamadou Bhoye Barry, and Conté was declared the winner with 95.3% of the vote. The Government claimed that voter turn-out was 82%. The European Union (EU) declined to send observers on the grounds that the conditions under which the vote was conducted were neither free nor fair.

Following the election, President Conté was rarely seen in public, prompting renewed concerns about his apparent ill health. In February 2004 Conté dismissed Sidimé as Prime Minister, and appointed Fall in his place. In March a new Minister of the Economy and Finance, Mady Kaba Camara, was appointed; the Governor of the central bank, Ibrahim Chérif Bah, was also dismissed, amid increasing concern at the country's economic performance. In April it was announced that Fall had resigned as Prime Minister and had fled the country; Fall claimed that he had been obstructed in trying to implement economic reforms. During 2004 public protests took place in Conakry against increases in the cost of living. The post of Prime Minister remained vacant until early December, when Cellou Dalein Diallo, hitherto Minister of Fishing and Aquaculture, was appointed to that position.

Following an alleged assassination attempt against the President on 19 January 2005, when shots were fired on a presidential convoy, thousands of suspects were rounded up for questioning. An elderly Muslim cleric, Mohamed Touré, died in prison, and other supporters of the opposition were still being held in detention several months later. In an atmosphere of increasing anarchy, the opposition parties in the FRAD alliance demanded Conté's resignation, and in July Alpha Condé returned from exile. In a further extension of ongoing social unrest sparked by high inflation, the principal trade unions staged a week-long strike in February 2006 to support their call for wage increases.

The political crisis deepened in March 2006 following the President's return from medical treatment in Switzerland. On 4 April it appeared that Prime Minister Diallo had won the President's support for increased powers and an extensive government reshuffle, including the appointment of deputy prime ministers in charge of the economy and foreign aid, was approved. However, before the radio announcement of the presidential decree authorizing these changes was completed, troops invaded the radio and television headquarters to stop the broadcast. On the following day another presidential decree was issued, cancelling the previous decree (thereby restoring the previous members of the Government to office) and dismissing Diallo for having committed a 'grave error'. Those perceived to have been responsible for the Prime Minister's sudden removal were the Chief of Staff of the Armed Forces, Gen. Kerfalla Camara, and the hitherto Minister, Secretary-General to the Presidency, Fodé Bangoura, who, following the dismissal of Diallo, was promoted to the position of Minister of State for Presidential Affairs, in which capacity he held effective control of defence, security and economic and financial affairs, and was the most senior member of the Government other than the President.

Mounting Political Crisis

The sudden dismissal of Diallo, who had won widespread respect for his commitment to reform, was largely perceived to be linked to his efforts to expose corrupt dealings between the central bank and Conté's close business associate Mamadou Sylla, who was alleged to have withdrawn US $22m. in cash from the bank in recompense for arms he had delivered to the Government in 2000–01. With Conté undergoing frequent medical examination and treatment, the vacuum at the head of the administration was filled by Bangoura, who was elevated to Minister-Secretary General to the Presidency while also remaining Minister of State for Parliamentary Affairs. The country's trade unions planned a round of protests demanding better economic management and lower prices of essential goods; strikes continued throughout much of June, and the trade unions only suspended their action after prices were nominally cut by up to 30%. Investigations were launched into the case against Sylla, who was eventually detained later in the year along with a former Deputy Governor of the central bank, Fodé Soumah. There were clear signs of tensions in the barracks as Conté continued to remove some officers and promote others.

On 27 December 2006 Conté, whose declining health prevented him from managing government affairs in any detail, again increased the powers of Bangoura, without naming a premier. Shortly afterwards Conté ordered the release from detention of both Sylla and Soumah, precipitating a larger wave of protests, which were led most visibly by the Confédération Nationale des Travailleurs de Guinée (CNTG) and the Union Syndicale des Travailleurs de Guinée. They called for a general strike to commence on 10 January 2007. As protesters marched in Conakry and other major towns, they demanded the return to jail of Sylla and Soumah, but the unions were quick to add more far-reaching demands such as the appointment of a new premier, lower fuel prices and the enforcement of heavier taxation on foreign mining companies. The unions' demands successfully won the support of the political opposition parties, whose previous inability to forge a common front was attributed to their largely parochial and ethnic appeal.

The new round of nation-wide protests quickly led to the suspension of activity at mining operations, railways and ports and the closure of many businesses. The security forces often reacted violently, even to minor provocations, and at times singled out the Peul ethnic minority for especially harsh treatment. Over the last three weeks of January 2007 some 60 people lost their lives. Many foreign companies and organizations suspended operations and began to evacuate staff. After the Chairman of the African Union (AU) Commission, Alpha Oumar Konaré, urged a spirit of co-operation and dialogue, on 19 January Conté raised expectations that he was considering appointing a Prime Minister when he removed

Bangoura from the position of Minister of State. The unions declared their support for premiership candidates such as Cellou Diallo, Kabiné Komara (a businessman and senior banking official) and Aboubacar Sylla, but another potential nominee appeared in the person of former ECOWAS Executive Secretary Lansana Kouyaté, who visited the country to offer his services. A negotiation process was also initiated by the Speaker of the Assemblée nationale, Aboubacar Somparé, focusing on the powers that might be granted to a new premier. On 22 January demonstrators staged a large march through Conakry to demand change; the march was suppressed by the presidential guard and many union organizers were detained.

Somparé's negotiations resulted in an agreement on the prime ministerial role that was signed on 27 January 2007 by the Minister of State for the Economy, Madikaba Camara, as well as by representatives of employers and unions. It declared that the Prime Minister should head and appoint the Council of Ministers and senior officials and hold responsibility for public finance and economic policy. Following this, the trade unions ordered the suspension of the general strike and urged Guineans to return to work. However, on 9 February, when Conté named his close associate Eugène Camara (a former planning minister) as his choice for Prime Minister, the protests erupted again and a number of demonstrators were shot in the following days. On 12 February Conté declared a state of emergency.

A resolution to the crisis was by this stage urgently sought both by ECOWAS and by individual West African Governments. An ECOWAS delegation led by the former Nigerian Head of State, Gen. Ibrahim Babangida, and ECOWAS Executive Secretary Mohamed Ibn Chambas arrived in Conakry in mid-February 2007. In their discussions with the trade unions they found support for the candidacy of Kouyaté, who also had significant experience in the attempts to resolve the Liberia and Sierra Leone crises, and whose candidacy was strongly supported by Côte d'Ivoire's President, Laurent Gbagbo.

On 26 February 2007 Conté agreed to the appointment of Kouyaté as Prime Minister, and negotiations began regarding the appointment of a new administration, which was announced on 28 March and comprised mostly pro-Kouyaté technocrats with no previous experience in government. The new Prime Minister outlined a reform agenda, including re-establishing peace, security and macroeconomic stability, strengthening government institutions, creating an independent judiciary and boosting youth employment.

However, instability continued and on 4 May 2007 soldiers held violent street protests in Conakry, demanding the payment of salary arrears. The mutiny resulted in widespread property damage, the destruction of several houses belonging to government ministers, and at least six deaths. After refusing to meet with Kouyaté, on 15 May the mutinous soldiers held talks with Conté, agreeing to suspend their protests in return for the dismissal of five senior officers, as well as the appointments of Gen. Bailo Diallo as defence minister and Gen. Diarra Camara as Chief of Staff of the Army. Conté also promised that each soldier would be paid 1m. Guinean francs (US $240) as partial compensation for unpaid salary arrears.

In early May 2007 the Government announced that the legislative elections would be postponed until December. The delay was due to logistical obstacles, a lack of resources, and the need to set up an independent electoral commission—the Commission Électorale Nationale Indépendante (CENI)—and to update the voter register. In June the election was again postponed (to March 2008) with the support of the main opposition parties, in order to allow more time for pre-electoral preparations to be completed.

On 1 January 2008 Conté indicated his growing unease with the reforms being pursued by Kouyaté's Government, describing Kouyaté as a 'disappointment' in his New Year address to the nation. On 20 May the President dismissed Kouyaté, appointing the former education minister and his close ally, Ahmed Tidiane Souaré, as the new Prime Minister. The reason for Kouyaté's removal appeared to be Conté's anger at the publication in a French magazine, *Jeune Afrique*, of details of an independent audit of government ministries, which revealed widespread embezzlement and mismanagement, including the misappropriation of €500m. at the customs administration.

Souaré's first challenge was to put an end to the army mutiny that began on 25 May 2008 at the Alpha Yaya Diallo camp outside Conakry and rapidly spread across the capital. In spite of the new Prime Minister's reassurances that the soldiers' demands for payment of salary arrears and improved housing would be met, looting continued in the capital, prompting clashes with the presidential guard. The rebellion only came to an end after Conté agreed to meet the soldiers and the Government promised to disburse arrears amounting to US $1,100 per person. The police's attempt to stage a similar mutiny in June was swiftly quashed by the army.

On 19 June 2008 Souaré announced the appointment of a broad-based Council of Ministers comprising 34 ministers and two secretaries of state, with all principal portfolios allocated to close allies of the President or politically neutral technocrats. Only two key ministers from the previous Government retained their positions: Ousmane Doré, the Minister of the Economy and Finance, and Ahmed Kanté, the Minister of Mines and Geology. Kanté was dismissed in August, however, reportedly in connection with controversy surrounding a letter sent by the Office of the President to Rio Tinto questioning the multinational company's rights over the Simandou mining concession (although no official reason was given). Doré was, in turn, dismissed in September, along with the Minister of Security and Civil Protection: both were replaced with officials professing greater loyalty to the President.

Guinea celebrated 50 years of independence on 2 October 2008, amid renewed fears over the poor health of Conté, who was unable to attend most of the public festivities. In the same month the CENI announced the further postponement of the legislative elections until March 2009 at the earliest because of continued difficulties in completing voter registration and insufficient financial and other resources. During the last months of 2008 protests took place in various parts of the country, against the lack of basic services, the high cost of many goods and poor pay, and amid growing concerns, supported by record drugs seizures, that Guinea was becoming a major hub for international drugs-trafficking.

CAMARA AND THE CONSEIL NATIONAL POUR LA DÉMOCRATIE ET LE DÉVELOPPEMENT

Conté died on 22 December 2008. Although his death had long been expected, in the ensuing days the Constitution, which provided for the appointment as interim President of the Speaker of the Assemblée nationale and the organization of elections within 60 days, was not respected. A few hours after Conté's death was announced, a group of young mid-ranking army officers seized key positions in Conakry. On 23 December the national radio station proclaimed the military takeover. Protests by Prime Minister Soaré and Speaker Somparé were to no avail and both men eventually recognized the military junta, the Conseil National pour la Démocratie et le Développement (CNDD).

On 24 December 2008 the national television station broadcast an address by the new self-proclaimed Head of State, Capt. Moussa Dadis Camara. Camara, a member of the Guerza ethnic group from the south-eastern Guinée Forestière region, was in charge of the army's fuel supply prior to the coup and had played a decisive mediating role in the military mutinies that erupted in 2007–08. The newly formed CNDD encompassed various parts of the army, including the presidential guard, as well as a large number of mid-ranking officers from the country's main ethnic groups, thus apparently constituting a consensual base for Camara's rule. Some initial clashes underlined the fragility of the junta, however, and Col Aboubacar Sidiki Camara, who had been allocated a cabinet position, was dismissed after rejecting Moussa Dadis Camara's decision to prolong the detention of several army officers who were accused of plotting a counter-coup.

The junta swiftly began to dismantle Conté's patronage networks with the dismissal and retirement of 22 generals only a few days after the coup. In early January 2009 the CNDD appointed Kabiné Komara, a technocrat with experience both in public administration and in the country's private sector, as the new Prime Minister. The composition of the new Council of Ministers, announced in mid-January, confirmed the junta's determination to keep politics under military control, as 10 ministries, including the most important portfolios (national defence, security and civil protection, and economy and finance), were allocated to members of the military. This was further underlined by Camara's much publicized decisions to review all contracts with mining companies, to initiate a vast anti-corruption campaign, and to prosecute people allegedly involved in drugs-trafficking activities. The CNDD followed these decisions with dramatic actions, notably the arrest of four former mining ministers suspected of embezzlement and fraud (and their release in April with the expectation that they would pay back US $5.3m.), and the arrest and public confession in February of the late President's son, Ousmane Conté, who was accused of involvement in the cocaine trade. Similar public confessions or acts of contrition obtained from Conté allies or representatives of major mining companies were broadcast on national television, during which Camara gave way to vehement outbursts of anger.

In spite of widespread support for the coup among the population, opposition parties and trade unions, the CNDD maintained the suspension of all forms of political and trade union activity until late February 2009 to avoid unrest. Under pressure from the opposition, civil society and the international community, Camara was obliged to revise his initial promise that the military transition to democratic rule would take less than two years, and announced in February that elections would be held by the end of 2009. In March it was announced that the legislative polls would take place on 11 October, followed by the first round of the presidential election on 13 December, with a second round to be conducted two weeks later if required. In late April Camara cancelled a trip to Libya at the last minute, following rumours that soldiers were preparing to attempt a coup during his absence. Roadblocks were established throughout the capital and more than 30 officers were arrested, casting doubt upon the CNDD's unity and capacity to maintain control over the army. Although he had threatened, in April, to contest the presidential election, Camara announced in mid-May that he would not stand and that neither the Prime Minister nor any of the members of the CNDD would be permitted to present their candidacies either.

In June 2009 the former Prime Minister and leader of the opposition UFDG, Cellou Diallo, was forbidden to hold a political meeting in Kérouané, in Haute-Guinée. The interdiction provoked renewed debate over the CNDD's willingness to hold democratic elections by the end of the year as promised. In reaction to further delays in the electoral process, Guinea's main political forces and civil society organizations regrouped within a coalition called the Forces Vives(FV); this group proposed a new electoral timetable under which the first round of voting in the presidential election would take place on 31 January 2010, with legislative elections following on 26 March. Camara, who had made public his displeasure with the initial electoral timetable, readily accepted the suggestion from the FV. In late August 2009, however, members of the FVs stopped attending election preparation meetings with the CNDD as they feared Camara would soon announce his candidacy.

Tensions increased throughout September 2009, as a series of protests demanded that Camara keep his promise not to stand in the presidential election, and increasing harassment of opposition members and journalists was reported. The opposition, civil society organizations and the trade unions reacted to Camara's refusal to commit to a clear transitional timetable by calling for a major demonstration on 28 September, which marked the anniversary of Guinea's independence referendum. Although the CNDD tried to prevent the gathering by declaring it illegal, tens of thousands of Guineans marched to a stadium in Conakry and entered the site in spite of the security forces' attempts to block the entrances. Before the opposition leaders could deliver their speeches, army units, mainly belonging to the presidential guard, started to shoot directly into the crowd. Soldiers also publicly raped women and beat and arrested opposition leaders, who were later released. Independent observers claimed that 150 demonstrators were killed and more than 1,000 were wounded. The CNDD, however, declared that there had been 58 deaths, four from gunshot wounds and the rest in the stampede that followed. Camara later declared that he could not accept responsibility for the violence because he was not in full control of the army.

The international community overwhelmingly condemned the events of 28 September 2009 and broke off all co-operation with Guinea. ECOWAS suspended Guinea from the group, imposed an international arms embargo and appointed the President of Burkina Faso, Blaise Compaoré, as mediator between the CNDD and opposition forces. Compaoré's mediation made little progress, however, as the opposition rejected his proposals in November, claiming that the proposals favoured Camara—in particular his plan to stay in power until the presidential election. The opposition demanded Camara's immediate resignation and replacement by a transitional, civilian administration.

In early December 2009 Camara was shot in the head and neck by his *aide-de-camp*, Lt Aboubacar 'Toumba' Diakité. The incident was rumoured to have been linked to the events of 28 September; Diakité, who had been observed giving orders to troops and threatening demonstrators on that day, apparently feared that he would be made the 'scapegoat' for Camara and the CNDD leadership. Camara survived the incident and was flown to Morocco where he spent the following weeks recovering; it was agreed that he would remain outside the country on leave of absence to continue his convalescence. Meanwhile, the Minister at the Presidency, in charge of National Defence, Gen. Sékouba Konaté, assumed control of the junta and declared himself Interim President. In mid-December a UN commission of inquiry formed after the 28 September massacre published its findings. It ruled that Camara, Diakité and Moussa Tiegboro Camara, a member of Camara's presidential cabinet, could be subjected to international criminal proceedings, while other junta leaders could also be held liable. The CNDD's own internal inquiry, published in February 2010, blamed Diakité alone.

TRANSITION UNDER KONATÉ

Camara's disappearance from the Guinean political scene effectively eased the mediation process with the opposition. Konaté gave a national address on 6 January 2010 in which he explained that he would opt for a transitional ruling body led by a Prime Minister from the opposition and that elections, in which the junta would not participate, would be promptly organized. On 15 January Konaté and Camara signed the Ouagadougou Accord in the capital of Burkina Faso, by which both leaders agreed that Guinea would return to civilian rule within six months. Although Camara's supporters voiced their displeasure through violent demonstrations, Konaté was able to maintain control over the armed forces. Camara appeared in a televised press conference on 8 January and confirmed the agreement and his intention to stay in self-imposed exile.

The junta selected as the new Prime Minister Jean-Marie Doré, the leader of the Union pour le Progrès de la Guinée (UPG) and the spokesman for the opposition, while Rabiatou Serah Diallo, President of the CNTG, was appointed at the head of the Conseil National de la Transition (CNT), which was to have legislative responsibilities during the transition. Doré's new 34-member Government was announced on 15 February 2010; the positions were evenly allocated between the Forces vives, the CNDD, and academics, civil servants and professionals, under the clear assumption that no minister would be allowed to participate in the presidential election.

The preparation of the presidential election was the main political focus over the following months. On 6 May 2010 Konaté broadcast a decree confirming that the presidential election would take place on 27 June. On 7 May he signed a decree adopting a new Constitution, drafted by the CNT, and on 10 May the CENI released the final voter register, which contained 4.29m. voters. Campaigning officially began on 17 May, after the Supreme Court approved a total of 24 candidates, including the long-standing opposition figure, Alpha Condé, and four former prime ministers under Conté—Cellou Diallo, Sidya Touré, François Lonsény Fall and Kouyaté. Konaté, meanwhile, disbanded personal militias, warned the soldiers of severe consequences should they attempt to derail the transition process and set up a 16,000-

strong special military force to oversee the election, the Force Spéciale de la Sécurisation du Processus Électoral (Fossepel).

In early June 2010 the head of the CENI informed Konaté that the 27 June election date was untenable. Konaté, however, resolved to go ahead with plans, and the election proceeded calmly on 27 June. On the following day the CENI acknowledged widespread technical failings, but ECOWAS observers confirmed that no deliberate, systematic fraud had been carried out. The announcement of the results, which had been scheduled for three days after the election, was repeatedly delayed, giving the leading candidates and their supporters ample opportunity to question the transparency of the electoral process. On 2 July the CENI announced that Cellou Diallo and Alpha Condé would contest the second round. Protests at the results, in particular from Touré and his supporters, continued until 7 July, when Konaté threatened to resign but was persuaded to remain in his post after foreign diplomats intervened and politicians, including Touré, apologized.

After considering the complaints filed by 20 presidential candidates, the Supreme Court confirmed on 20 July 2010 that Diallo, who had received 43.7% of the votes, and Condé, with 18.3%, would contest the presidency in the second round. Although the Supreme Court did not confirm the date of the second round, the leading candidates rapidly began negotiations. Touré who had been placed third in the first round with 13.0% of the votes, urged his supporters to vote for Diallo, while Kouyaté, who had come fourth in the first round, declared his support for Condé, who was eventually able to bring together 16 political parties into his Alliance Arc-en-ciel (Rainbow Coalition). Konaté, meanwhile, announced major promotions within the army, in recognition of the soldiers' support for the electoral process.

Following a meeting with the Minister for Territorial Administration and Political Affairs, Nawa Damey, the CNT, the CENI and the two remaining candidates, Diallo and Condé, Konaté announced on 9 August 2010 that the second round of the presidential election would take place on 19 September. Later that month, Prime Minister Doré announced his intention to change the Constitution in order to involve Damey in the preparation and organization of the election, thereby calling into question the CENI's independence. Doré's plan was severely criticized by most leading political figures, however, and the Prime Minister retracted his proposals, stating that he was only seeking a clearer definition of the role that the CENI and various ministries would play in the election.

During the following weeks the second round of the presidential election was repeatedly postponed. There were, first, disagreements over the composition of the CENI and the impartiality of its members. In early September 2010 the President of the CENI, Ben Sékou Sylla, and its Director of Planning, Boubacar Diallo, were found guilty of fraudulent activity during the first round of the election, and sentenced to one year's imprisonment. Sylla died on 14 September from a pre-existing medical condition. His proposed replacement proved unacceptable to Cellou Diallo's faction, and this precipitated violent clashes between supporters of the two presidential candidates, in which one person was killed and at least 50 others were injured. Konaté eventually resolved the situation on 19 October when he appointed a Malian general, Siaka Toumani Sangaré, an experienced election supervisor, at the head of the CENI. Logistical and security issues also delayed the conducting of the second round.

The second round of the presidential election finally took place peacefully on 7 November 2010. International observers concluded that the conduct of the poll had vastly improved compared with the first round, in terms of technical safeguards and preparation, and that the result could be regarded as credible. On 14 November, as the announcement of the provisional results appeared imminent, Condé and Diallo both claimed victory. Diallo started questioning the fairness of the vote as it appeared that the contest might be close, and withdrew his UFDG party officials from the vote count, citing electoral fraud and pre-election intimidation. The CENI none the less announced on 15 November that Condé was the provisional winner, with 52.5% of the vote: 67.9% of the electorate had participated (15% more than in the first round, according to official figures). After the announcement there was an outbreak of violence in the capital and throughout the country, essentially between members of Fossepel and pro-Diallo activists. On 17 November the head of Fossepel and Chief of Staff of the Armed Forces, Gen. Nouhou Thiam, declared an eight-day state of emergency.

The Supreme Court confirmed Condé's victory on 3 December 2010. Diallo immediately conceded defeat and urged his supporters to remain calm. Analysis of the regional results showed that the main battlegrounds had been Conakry and the coastal region, and that Condé had been able to secure the decisive votes in the latter, most probably by convincing the electorate that his 'rainbow coalition' was the most representative political force in Guinea and by exploiting fears of domination by the Peul community, widely believed to be already in control of much of the country's business and economic activities.

CONDÉ AND GUINEA'S FIRST DEMOCRATIC GOVERNMENT

Condé was officially sworn into office on 21 December 2010. Diallo did not attend the inauguration and later rejected the idea of a national unity government, which both candidates had seemed to favour between the two rounds of the presidential election. Diallo, instead, insisted that he would seek to influence legislation from the opposition benches of the Assemblée nationale, and that the legislative elections should take place, in accordance with the Constitution, within the next six months.

While Diallo's decision freed Condé from the constraints of forming a national unity government, the new President was none the less obliged to bear in mind the multiple alliances established within his 'rainbow' coalition. The number of ministers, deputy ministers and ministers of state—more than 40—in the Council of Ministers appointed on 5 January 2011 reflected this. Condé, however, favoured two technocrats, Mohamed Saïd Fofana and Kerfalla Yansané, for the key positions of Prime Minister and Minister of the Economy and Finance, respectively. Condé himself assumed the position of Minister of National Defence, underlining the importance he placed on army reform, while Alassane Condé, a former minister and member of the CENI, generally believed to be a close associate of the new President, was appointed Minister of Territorial Administration and Political Affairs. Lonsény Fall, the former Prime Minister and presidential candidate in the first round of voting, and the spokesman for Condé's Alliance Arc-en-Ciel, was given the potentially powerful position of Secretary-General to the Presidency. Condé was also careful to appoint three members of the Peul community in order to counter further accusations of an anti-Peul stance: Christian Sow, a well-respected lawyer, was appointed Minister of Justice, Ousmane Bah, a former opposition politician, Minister of State in charge of Public Works and Transport, and Yéro Baldé First Deputy Governor of the central bank. Controversial appointments included those of three generals from the transitional government, and that of Papa Koly Kourouma, an ally of the deposed junta leader, Camara, as Minister of State in charge of Energy and the Environment. Also in January Condé confirmed as the official in charge of combating drugs-trafficking Col Moussa Tiegboro Camara, formerly designated by the UN commission of inquiry as one of those responsible for the September 2009 massacre.

Among the Government's first announcements in January 2011 were a suspension of rice exports, intended to limit food price inflation, an immediate reduction in the price of a 50-kg sack of rice from US $35 to $20, and free maternal health-care services. A two-day seminar gathering the entire Council of Ministers and representatives from the public service, civil society and the international community also helped to draw up a 100-day plan, the Plan d'Actions Prioritaires, which included measures to stabilize the currency and reduce opportunities for corruption, and a biometric census among state employees to eliminate 'ghost workers' from the payroll. These first measures, while popular, were not sufficient to distract the opposition and civil society from the legislative elections, for which a date remained to be set. On 6 February the national civil society platform, the Conseil National des Organisations de la Société Civile Guinéenne (CNOSCG), accused Condé of violating the Constitution by failing to define a schedule for the legislative and local elections. In response, the Minister of Territorial Administration, Alassane Condé, proposed in March to hold the legislative elections at the end of 2011, citing irregularities in the electoral register to account for the delay. While the Government professed its eagerness to create a modern voter registry system, the opposition insisted that the same electoral register used for the presidential poll should be adequate for the legislative elections. The delay in announcing a definitive date for the elections was also due to new disagreements over the composition of the CENI.

Tensions arose in March 2011 when the Government ordered the armed forces to enforce stricter controls on money-changers and bureaux de change to curtail unofficial trading in the Guinean franc. The troops, commanded by Tiegboro Camara, were perceived to have acted in a heavy-handed and disorganized manner. This measure, and the previous suspension of rice exports, were interpreted by many as a direct attack on Peul traders, once again raising fears that Condé might be tempted to exploit ethnic differences.

On 1 June 2011 a coalition of opposition parties denounced the Government's plans to initiate a new electoral census from mid-June, accusing Condé's party, the RPG, of seeking to establish a partisan voters' registry. The opposition also expressed its concern at the dissolution of four of Conakry's five municipal councils, to be replaced by special delegations suspected of being pro-Condé. In the same month, during a press conference, the CNOSCG expressed the Guinean civil society's disappointment with the new regime, describing political tensions and attempts by the police to intimidate the private media and student activists. It also urged the Government to establish a truth and reconciliation commission, as promised by Condé just after his election. The CNOSCG none the less praised the Government's efforts at combating corruption and embezzlement. On 11 June the CENI announced that legislative elections would take place in November, and evaluated their cost at US $30m. A three-day consultation process on the election took place later in June, convening members of the Government and other representatives of the administration, opposition parties, civil society and the international community.

President Condé's residence came under attack in two separate incidents on 19 July 2011. A number of suspects were subsequently arrested in connection with the assassination attempts, including 25 military personnel, the most significant of whom was the former Chief of Staff of the Armed Forces, Gen. Nouhou Thiam. On 25 July Guinea's media regulation body, the Conseil National de Communication, temporarily suspended all broadcasts and publication of material related to the attack, with the apparent intention of ending the circulation of rumours on the incident. Two days after the suspension, all representatives of the independent media issued a statement that deplored the move, declaring that it violated the Constitution.

In September 2011 the CENI confirmed that the legislative elections would be held on 29 December, although it was later stated that the decision had been taken by the CENI's President, Lounceny Camara alone. On 28 September an opposition rally, calling for transparent parliamentary elections, was violently dispersed by police, resulting in at least two people being killed, several injured and hundreds arrested. Although the Government had initially refused permission for the rally to take place, it had withdrawn the ban and authorized it on 26 September.

In October 2011 the CENI's director of operations, Pathé Dieng, was dismissed. Dieng was one of the co-signatories of an open letter that denounced the lack of transparency and unilateralism of the CENI's President. Dieng's dismissal was quickly followed by the resignation of the directors of information and logistics of the CENI, which once again cast doubt on the commission's capacity to organize the elections by December.

On 5 December 2011 there were skirmishes between the police and the supporters of former presidential candidate, Kouyaté, as he made a triumphant entry into his hometown of Kankan, also known to be a secure support base for the President. Kouyaté, who was a member of the President's Alliance Arc-en-Ciel, expressed doubts about the results that had given Condé the presidency, in a further sign of the progressive disintegration of the presidential coalition. On 19 December the CENI once again postponed the legislative elections, this time without giving any new date. The revision of the voters' register, which the opposition believed to be unnecessary, and the composition of the CENI were once again believed to be the main reasons for the new postponement. In December the Government also announced that 4,006 military personnel, too old for active service, would leave the army at the end of the year, in the first move to downsize Guinea's bloated military force.

On 1 February 2012 the Attorney-General of the Conakry appeals court instructed three investigating judges to establish the individual responsibility of Tiegboro Camara in the violent repression of the opposition rally of 28 September 2009. This was the Guinean judiciary's first attempt at addressing the issue of the impunity of those accused by the UN commission of inquiry of having taken an active part in the repression.

In April and May 2012, following an announcement by President Condé that the legislative elections were postponed indefinitely for technical reasons, the opposition organized a series of street protests and other mass actions against the postponement and the unresolved issue of the composition of the CENI. The largest of these protests, attended by 50,000 people according to the opposition, was violently repressed by riot police, and 19 participants were hospitalized.

EXTERNAL AFFAIRS

Guinea's relations with its neighbours were generally good in the early post-independence period. In 1980 Guinea joined the Mano River Union (MRU), originally founded by Liberia and Sierra Leone, which aimed to promote economic and political co-operation between its members. However, the outbreak of civil conflicts in Liberia and Sierra Leone in the early 1990s prevented the MRU from operating effectively, as its members supported rival rebel factions in each other's territories.

Although Guinea remained remarkably stable throughout the 1990s and early 2000s, it played an essential role in Sierra Leone's and Liberia's civil wars. The Guinean army was involved in the neighbouring civil wars through its repeated deployment to those countries' borders and through its participation in regional peace-keeping missions in Sierra Leone. Guinea also welcomed Sierra Leone's ousted leaders: Joseph Saidu Momoh in 1992, Valentine Strasser in 1996, and Ahmed Tejan Kabbah, who established a government-in-exile in Conakry a year later. Conté was repeatedly accused of providing protection and support to rebel movements, including ULIMO and LURD, which were fighting against Charles Taylor's National Patriotic Front of Liberia (NPFL).

Guinean territory, and especially its Forestière region, were the object of numerous rebel attacks, most notably in late 1993 and 2000. The conflicts in both Sierra Leone and Liberia also led to a large influx of refugees, who in the late 1990s were estimated to number some 5%–10% of the total population of Guinea. Conté was, to a certain extent, able to use these external threats in order to legitimize his rule and gather popular support within Guinea as well as international assistance for his regime and army.

Guinea sought to play a more positive role in the region, however, and became a member of the ECOWAS 'committee of four' (with Côte d'Ivoire, Ghana and Nigeria) charged with ensuring the implementation of decisions and recommendations pertaining to the situation in Sierra Leone in 1997. In the early 2000s relations between the Guinean authorities and their Sierra Leonean counterparts eased. In June 2001 President Kabbah of Sierra Leone and Conté met in Kambia, in northern Sierra Leone, to discuss regional tensions; following the discussions, it was announced that the commercial highway between Conakry and Freetown, closed since 1998, was to reopen. After the return of relative peace to Sierra Leone from 2002, Guinea maintained military control of the strategic Sierra Leonean border town of Yenga, which was believed to have significant diamond deposits, provoking strong criticism from Sierra Leonean opposition politicians. In late 2007 the new President of Sierra Leone, Ernest Bai Koroma, flew to Conakry to hold talks with Kouyaté and Conté in an attempt to resolve the dispute. Following the exiling of Liberia's former President, Charles Taylor, in 2003, relations with subsequent administrations in Liberia improved.

In May 2004 the MRU, which had hitherto been inactive, was reactivated by a summit of the leaders of Guinea, Sierra Leone and Liberia. Effective co-operation between the three countries has remained very limited, but an ongoing dialogue has been taking place. Sierra Leone's Koroma and Liberian President Ellen Johnson-Sirleaf closely followed the transition that followed Conté's death and visited Guinea on several occasions, expressing their concern for their neighbour's political stability. While the Guinean army continued to occupy the Sierra Leonean territory of Yenga, and was accused of forays into Liberia in 2010, its democratic transition in that year raised hopes that relations with its neighbours would soon be normalized. President Condé invited his Sierra Leonean counterpart, Ernest Bai Koroma for an official state visit on 13–14 October 2011, during which the two Presidents promised to proceed with plans to allow the free movement of goods, services and people between their two countries. They also resolved to find a diplomatic solution to the problem of Yenga and announced joint security operations. In March 2012 Guinea and Sierra Leone agreed to a demarcation of the boundaries of their continental shelves in order to prevent future disagreements, predominantly over fishing rights, but also over proceeds from possible deep-sea oil deposits.

Guinea's political situation and the repeated postponement of its legislative election, however, remained a primary concern for the region and its organization, ECOWAS. In November 2011 the ECOWAS Commission sent a widely respected Togolese diplomat, Edem Kodjo, to Conakry to discuss the political situation with President Condé and the opposition. The following month the new President of Côte d'Ivoire, Alassane Ouattara, also visited the country to urge reconciliation. And in January 2012 former Senegalese President and head of the Organisation Internationale de la Francophonie (OIF) visited Conakry to act as a mediator. However, the coups in neighbouring Mali and Guinea-Bissau (where President Condé had led ECOWAS mediation efforts during the presidential election in March) seemed to take the regional focus away from Guinea over the following months.

After the suspension of co-operation that immediately followed Guinea's declaration of independence, diplomatic relations with France were resumed in 1976, and in the following year the two countries reached an agreement on economic co-operation. In general, the Conté administration maintained good relations with the French Government, which is Guinea's primary source of financial and technical assistance. However, the progress of the trial of opposition leader Alpha Condé remained a source of concern to the French authorities, and during his visit to Guinea in July 1999 President Jacques Chirac of France sought assurances from the Government that the trial would be 'transparent'. A meeting of the joint commission for Franco-Guinean co-operation took place in Conakry in November. However, in mid-2000 a meeting of francophone parliamentarians called on Guinea's donor countries to suspend assistance in protest at the conduct of the Condé trial. In May 2006 France agreed to release some €100m. of budgetary support for the Guinean Government for the period 2006–10 that had hitherto been suspended. France, like the rest of the international community, condemned the coup that followed Conté's death, but maintained its co-operation with the army.

Following the attack on the opposition gathering on 28 September 2009, France immediately announced that it was indefinitely suspending its military and institutional co-operation and urged Camara to agree to a transition to civilian rule. One of the newly elected President Condé's first visits abroad was to France, in March 2011, where he was accompanied by several ministers and business leaders. Following this visit, the former colonial power promised its support for military reform as well as in the electricity and agricultural sectors. Condé, who spent decades in France as a student and in political exile, was known to be closely acquainted with a number of French politicians, including former Minister of Foreign Affairs Bernard Kouchner. President Condé was accordingly one of the first African Presidents to welcome the election of the French socialist party's candidate, François Hollande, to the presidency in May 2012. He made an official state visit to meet the new French President in Paris, France, at the end of June.

Guinea, a member of the Organization of the Islamic Conference (OIC), has forged links with the governments of other predominantly Islamic countries, notably signing several co-operation agreements with Iran in the mid-1990s. Guinea has also received significant material assistance from Libya and from the People's Republic of China, which has become Guinea's principal trading partner. In July 2008 a Chinese delegation, which included representatives from the China Development Bank, visited Guinea to discuss investments. Although political developments from late 2008 prevented further commitments, including finance for a much-needed US $1m. hydroelectric dam, Chinese companies sought to benefit from the declared intention of the CNDD administration to renegotiate major contracts and its obvious need for new investments and tax income. China Sonangol, a joint venture between the Chinese Dayuan International Development and the Angolan national oil company, Sonangol, was thus able to acquire offshore oil exploration acreage in October 2009.

The coup that followed the death of President Conté in December 2008 was generally condemned by the international community. Both the USA and the EU strongly criticized the CNDD's assumption of power, with the USA suspending all but humanitarian aid to Guinea. Neighbouring countries, especially Liberia, Sierra Leone and Côte d'Ivoire, were particularly cautious in their reactions, taking account of the fact that instability in Guinea could quickly extend to their territories. West African states in general agreed to frame their responses within ECOWAS, which issued a strong condemnation of the coup, suspended Guinea from all ECOWAS activities pending a restoration of constitutional order, and demanded that elections take place before the end of 2009. ECOWAS, however, also pledged support for the ensuing democratic transition. The AU also denounced the December 2008 coup and suspended Guinea from participating in the activities of the organization. Senegal was the only neighbouring country openly to endorse the coup, when the Senegalese President, Abdoulaye Wade, stated that the CNDD merited support as it was attempting to establish a truly democratic regime. The Libyan leader, Muammar al-Qaddafi, also endorsed the coup just before becoming the AU Assembly's new Chairperson. An international contact group on Guinea, composed of representatives of the African and international communities, was formed at the end of January 2009 to monitor and support the country's democratic transition, and met for the first time in mid-February in Conakry.

Reactions to the violent suppression of the Guinean opposition in September 2009 were equally severe. The international community immediately called for an international inquiry into the events, while the AU and the EU imposed targeted sanctions on members of the CNDD. The EU published a list of 42 names in October 2009; this was subsequently expanded to 71 names in late December. ECOWAS, meanwhile, took the lead in the mediation process, appointing the President of Burkina Faso, Blaise Compaoré, as chief mediator in the ensuing negotiations between the ruling junta and the civilian opposition. Following the signing of the Ouagadougou Accord in January 2010, the international community agreed to provide funds in support of the electoral preparation and organization; all other forms of international assistance, however, remained suspended.

The international community welcomed the election of Alpha Condé to the presidency in November 2010, and expressed its willingness to resume its support to Guinea and assist in the country's political and economic reforms. Condé travelled to Angola, Burkina Faso, Libya and Senegal during his first few weeks in power, indicating his desire to establish strong ties with the African community. Following the lifting of sanctions against Guinea on 9 December, the President attended the 16th AU summit in Ethiopia at the end of January 2011. The Chinese Minister of Foreign Affairs,

Yang Jiechi, visited Guinea in February and announced that China would make available a total of US $27m. in aid. In May the European Commissioner responsible for Development, Andris Piebalgs, visited Guinea and announced that the Government would now have access to suspended funds from the ninth European Development Fund, and would be able to clear Guinea's arrears with the Fund. He insisted, however, that the full resumption of aid would be contingent on the successful conducting of legislative elections. President Condé was also one among four African Presidents—along with Boni Yayi of Benin, Mahamadou Issoufou of Niger and Alassane Ouattara of Côte d'Ivoire—to visit US President Barack Obama in July 2011, in an open attempt by both sides to promote Africa's successful democratic transitions. In spite of the full resumption of relations with the IMF and the Government's implementation of wide-ranging economic reforms, Guinea's main donors expressed a growing frustration, in the course of 2012, with the indefinite postponement of the legislative elections and the lack of progress towards a full-fledged democracy.

Economy

MARIE GIBERT

INTRODUCTION

With successful management of its substantial mineral deposits and excellent agricultural potential, Guinea could eventually be one of the richest countries in West Africa. However, the country's economic record since independence has been significantly below expectations. The country's gross domestic product (GDP) expanded, in real terms, at an average rate of 3.0% per year in 1970–80, reflecting the rapid development of the bauxite sector during that decade, but declined by an average of 1.4% per year in 1980–85. The causes of Guinea's relatively poor performance during this period were largely political. First, there was the abrupt severance of the country's links with France in 1958, which was followed by the withdrawal of French officials and the discontinuation of aid, as well as the loss of the leading traditional market for Guinea's exports. Second, the newly independent Guinea immediately sought to set up a socialist economy, with direct state control of production and consumption in virtually every sector—an objective demanding managerial input that Guinea lacked, and which resulted in great inefficiency and waste. Mining, the one economic sector where state control was diluted, developed as an enclave, with admittedly major benefits for Guinea's export earnings but little linkage and feedback into the rest of the economy, which remained essentially based on agriculture and which suffered from Ahmed Sékou Touré's system of highly centralized management. The economy consequently became highly dualistic, with the development of a large informal sector in response to the near monopoly of the State over formal economic activity.

During the 1990s, in an attempt to remove at least the domestic constraints on growth, the Lansana Conté regime introduced a series of policy reforms, agreed with the IMF and the World Bank. These included the transfer to private interests, or elimination, of parastatal organizations, the liberalization of foreign trade and the abolition of price controls, together with monetary and banking reforms and a reduction in the number of civil service personnel. The recovery programme initially received substantial international support, in the form of debt relief and new funds from bilateral and multilateral sources. However, the reform process collapsed in 2002 as the country began to build up budget deficits in an inflationary environment. Most financial assistance from the international community was suspended until more rational economic management could be imposed. In 2004 the economic situation began to deteriorate seriously, without effective political management, even as mineral revenues began to increase in response to escalating world prices and demand. Rising inflation provoked widespread social unrest, and there was an expanding differential between the official and unofficial exchange rates of the Guinean franc.

The lack of a clear economic direction after 2003 brought about not only high inflation but a deterioration in living standards, as the number of people living below the poverty line rose to 53% in 2007/08. Average annual inflation surged from 3.0% in 2002 to 34.7% in 2006, coinciding with the collapse of economic reform during a long round of political upheavals. Inflation then fell to an average of 23.4% at the end of 2007 as a result of tighter monetary policy by the central bank and the depreciation of the Guinean franc. The inflation rate continued to fall in 2008, to 18.4%, and in 2009, to an estimated 9%, as commodity prices declined with the onset of the global financial crisis. Inflation rose again sharply in 2010, however, to 20.8%, essentially due to nominal exchange-rate depreciation and increasing global commodity prices, before receding slightly to an estimated 19% in 2011, as a result of the new Government's stabilization policies. Continuing growth in real GDP, at 2.7% in 2004, 3.3% in 2005 and an estimated 2.4% in 2006, was attributed principally to an expansion in mineral exports and some modest investment in infrastructure projects. According to the IMF, real GDP growth declined to 1.5% in 2007, mainly as a result of national strikes during the first two months of the year. It then increased sharply to 4.5% in 2008, owing to increased activity in the mining and construction sectors. The death of President Conté in December 2008 precipitated the assumption of power by the Conseil National pour la Démocratie et le Développement. The leaders of the military coup proclaimed that economic recovery and the eradication of corruption were their main priorities; however, their actions were condemned by the international community and a period of great economic uncertainty followed as donors froze their development assistance and the military junta began to reassess and renegotiate some major mining contracts. Amid the political crisis following the massacre of protesters in Conakry in September 2009, several controversial contracts were signed with Chinese and other new investors attracted by the prospects of shares in substantial new production of minerals—including bauxite, iron ore, gold and diamonds. Unsurprisingly, given the political uncertainty and the suspension of donor assistance, Guinea's real GDP contracted by 0.3% in 2009.

In 2010 further rounds of mineral-rights negotiation and renegotiation continued at the same time as the military regime set about disengaging itself from power through the national elections of mid-2010. Real GDP growth was estimated at 1.9% for that year. Following the election of Alpha Condé to the presidency in November, the new Government appointed in January 2011 set about preparing plans for ambitious economic reforms, which included stabilizing the currency, reducing inflation and opportunities for corruption, encouraging investment in the country's agricultural and mining sectors, and introducing a biometric census among state employees to eliminate 'ghost workers' from the payroll. As a result of these policies and increased mining output, Guinea's real GDP increased to 3.6% in 2011. The democratic transition and new Government's policies also enabled the progressive resumption of relations with donors as well, as with the IMF, which could lead to significant debt relief under the enhanced heavily indebted poor countries (HIPC) initiative.

POPULATION AND EMPLOYMENT

Guinea experienced a high level of emigration during the Sékou Touré regime; according to the 1983 census, almost 2m. Guineans (some of whom returned following the 1984 coup) were estimated to be living abroad. The census conducted in December 1996 enumerated a population of 7,156,406, including an estimated 640,000 refugees from Sierra Leone, Liberia and Guinea-Bissau. The urban population numbered 2.1m. Most of the refugees have since returned to their home countries. The UN estimated the population at 10,480,709 in 2012.

The active labour force in 2010 was estimated at 4,090,000. Although agriculture remained the principal sector of employment in the mid-2000s, an increasing proportion of the population has been engaged in industrial and service activities since the 1980s. The reduction in job opportunities in the public sector, previously guaranteed to all university graduates, has caused a rise in urban unemployment and fuelled student unrest.

AGRICULTURE, FORESTRY AND FISHING

Despite the rapid development and potential of the mining sector, agriculture remains an important economic activity in terms of employment (engaging some 79.3% of the labour force in mid-2011), even if the value of its output is gradually decreasing (13% of GDP in 2010). Under the Sékou Touré regime, agricultural production was depressed by the demands and inefficiencies of the collectivist regime and, in consequence, smuggling of produce by peasant farmers was widespread. On taking power, the Conté Government immediately abolished collectives, raised producer prices and ended the production tax. Improvements to the infrastructure (notably to the road network) and the easier availability of farm credits began to stimulate an increase in production by small-scale farmers.

Production of foods has thus recovered in recent years, with annual production in the late 1990s and early 2000s some 20% more than the average output recorded in 1979–81. In 2010 output of paddy rice (cultivated mainly in the south-eastern Guinée Forestière region) was estimated by FAO at 1.6m. metric tons, while production of cassava was 1m. tons, maize 580,100 tons and sweet potatoes 174,600 tons. The rise in output has, in the long term, failed to keep pace with population growth, so that Guinea—a net exporter of food in the past—now imports large quantities, representing about double the value of its agricultural exports. The staple crops are supplemented by the substantial livestock herd (raised by traditional methods), which FAO estimated at 4.9m. cattle, 1.6m. sheep and 1.9m. goats in 2010.

The major commercial crops are bananas, coffee, pineapples, oil palm, groundnuts and citrus fruit. The banana plantations, which suffered in the late 1950s from disease and, with independence, from the withdrawal of European planters and the closing of the protected French market, have shown a good recovery, with estimated output averaging about 150,000 metric tons per year since the late 1990s (and an estimated 201,500 tons in 2010, according to FAO figures). Coffee production averaged 20,000 tons per year in the late 1990s and early 2000s and an totalled an estimated 27,000 tons in 2010 (unofficial figure). Pineapple production, which measured approximately 16,000 tons per year in the late 1970s, increased to more than 70,000 tons per year by the late 1990s. FAO estimated output of 107,500 tons in 2010. An export trade in fruit and vegetables for the European market has been developed, as quality control and transportation links have improved. In 1986 a nine-year project was launched to plant 13,000 ha with rubber and oil palm in Guinée Forestière, with the aim of re-establishing, in a modified form, the plantation agriculture that was characteristic of the colonial period, and of attracting foreign investment to this sector. Meanwhile, a cotton development scheme in Kankan, aided by France, was inaugurated in 1985, aiming to produce a total of 43,000–50,000 tons from plantations in Haute-Guinée (where it is the largest single development project) and Moyenne-Guinée. In March 2012 the Government announced, in its new poverty reduction strategy paper, its intention to urgently address the country's low production rates in the agricultural, livestock and fisheries sectors and to draw up a national agricultural investment plan. This plan includes measures to encourage agricultural entrepreneurship, notably through subsidies, improve market access, stimulate scientific research, diversify agricultural activities, develop crops for export and combat illegal fishing.

There is considerable potential for timber production, with forests covering more than two-thirds of the land area. Timber resources are currently used mainly for fuel, with production of roundwood totalling an estimated 12.6m. cu m in 2010. In early 2008 the Government signed agreements with two companies, International Ingermas and Agro-énergie-développement, worth an estimated US $200m., to develop the cultivation of crops for biofuel production.

The fishing sector remains relatively undeveloped. Only around one-third of the total catch from Guinean waters—estimated at 109,900 metric tons in 2010—is accounted for by indigenous fleets, the rest being taken by factory ships and industrial trawlers. Since 1983 the Guinean Government has concluded a series of fishing accords with the European Community (EC, now European Union—EU). It has since been agreed to award foreign licences exclusively to EU fleets, in an effort to preserve the viability of fish stocks on the continental shelf. A Fisheries Partnership Agreement was concluded between the EU and Guinea in May 2009, but the European Commission subsequently decided to suspend the payment of the financial compensation (€1.1m.) for the first year of application, following the repression of the Guinean opposition in September 2009, and the suspension has been maintained since. The African Development Bank (AfDB) has helped to finance the establishment of onshore facilities and the supply of equipment for small-scale fishermen. In addition, the rehabilitation of the port of Conakry, implemented in the mid-1990s, included the installation of deep-freeze equipment to serve the fishing industry, while further improvements to facilities were expected to include an enlargement of the port, which had been one of several regional ports to receive increased trade following the onset of civil rebellion in Côte d'Ivoire in late 2002.

MINING AND POWER

Mining has long been Guinea's most dynamic sector and the country's most important source of foreign exchange, providing more than 90% of recorded export revenues for much of the 1980s and around 80% in the 1990s. It has been contributing around one-fifth of GDP each year from the late 1980s to the late 2000s, but, owing to recent growth in the mining sector, its share increased to 26% of GDP in 2010.

Minerals accounted for 90% of export earnings in 2006, when the value of bauxite exports was US $405m., gold $319m., alumina $142m. and diamonds $43m. In 1995 the Government introduced revisions to the mining code, which were intended to encourage foreign investment and to define the State's new non-participatory role in the mining sector. The Government also announced the foundation of the Centre de Promotion et de Développement Miniers (CPDM), which was to act as the advisory and regulatory body for the mining sector. Currently bauxite, diamonds and gold are commercially exploited, with the exploitation of iron ore at Simandou expected to start in 2015, but it is also anticipated that deposits of nickel and titanium may prove viable. A number of oil companies are expected to conduct exploration works in Guinea's offshore area. A first deepwater oil well was drilled in October 2011 by the US-based company Hyperdynamics. Further exploration, and exploitation plans, will no doubt depend on this well's first results. The further development of the mining sector is dependent on improvements in infrastructure and power supply and more extensive geological surveying.

In April 2007 the Government created a committee to review all mining contracts, with the aim of renegotiating contracts that had allowed unduly favourable terms for the mining companies; introducing new conditions for skills transfer, local content and environmental protection; and increasing the sector's contribution to tax revenue. Following the military coup in December 2008 it was announced that all mining contracts would be reviewed again in order to eradicate corruption, and the mining rights of some international companies were subsequently cancelled and awarded elsewhere, while others were able to negotiate new contracts. In October

2009 the Government signed contracts worth US $7,000m. with two Chinese institutions with links to mining interests: the China International Fund (CIF), a Hong Kong investment company, and China Sonangol promised to build substantial electric power generating capacity, railways, roads and bridges, and to launch a new airline. The then Minister of Mining and Geology, Mamoudou Thiam, led extensive rounds of negotiations with powerful corporate interests hoping to acquire rights to bauxite, iron ore, nickel, gold and diamonds. Although the new President, Alpha Condé, had pledged, during his electoral campaign, to revise mining concessions, he announced in January 2011 that the existing mining contracts would not be altered, but that the Government would be seeking to increase its stake to at least 35% from its existing 15% share. In August the transitional parliament, the Conseil National de la Transition (CNT), adopted a law establishing a new state mining company, Société Guinéenne du Patrimoine Minier (SOGUIPAMI). SOGUIPAMI was set up to manage funds for geological exploration and the state's interest in foreign mining operations. Ahmed Kanté, a former Minister of Mines and Geology and the President's personal mining advisor, was appointed as SOGUIPAMI's director. Less than one month later, in September, the CNT adopted a new mining code, which replaced the 1995 code. The new code sought to improve the management of the country's mineral resources, notably through the creation of SOGUIPAMI and a Commission Nationale des Mines (CNM), which was charged with managing licences. The new code also provided for greater transparency, in line with Guinea's reinstatement in March as a candidate to the extractive industries transparency initiative (EITI). In line with the President's initial declarations, the new code granted the state an automatic 15% stake in mining projects and retained the right to increase this stake to 35%, purchased at market value. Customs duties were also raised from 5.6% to 8%, while tax holidays were abolished, except in the case of value-added tax. The code also included clear guidelines to limit environmental damage in mining areas and to charge a levy of between 0.5% and 1% on mining companies' turnover for the purposes of local development in these areas. Following mixed reactions from the mining community, the Minister of Mines and Geology, Mohamed Lamine Fofana, assured that the Government was ready to make amendments to the new code if these improved the country's competitiveness. In line with the new mining code, in March 2012 a presidential decree created the CNM, in which government officials and members of civil society, including trade union leaders, were represented. The CNM was tasked with ensuring that the provisions of the new mining code were followed and its first task was to review the existing mining and exploration licences and to formulate recommendations as to their acceptance, rejection or modification.

Bauxite and Alumina

The country possesses nearly one-half of the world's known bauxite reserves, estimated at 12,000m. metric tons, with a very high-grade ore. Guinea ranks second only to Australia in terms of ore production, and is the world's largest exporter of bauxite. From the mid-1980s, however, bauxite revenues were affected by a weakening in world demand for aluminium and the considerable surplus in world production capacity. Annual output has been running at around the 12m.–17m. metric tons level since the early 1980s, reaching a high of 18.4m. tons in 1996. Output was 16.4m. tons in 2004, remained at close to the same level in 2006–08, and decreased to 13.6m. tons in 2009, owing to the temporary closure of all bauxite mining operations serving the Friguia aluminium smelter, as a result of civil unrest. Ongoing expansion and rehabilitation programmes at the country's mines were projected to increase annual output to 20m. tons, and it was expected that a restructuring of the sector, through the reduction in the state interest to 15% of equity, would enhance both investment and efficiency. Nevertheless, in 2006–09, despite some advances in negotiations with foreign investors, the deteriorating political situation brought many mining operations to a halt. The progressive stabilization of the political situation in 2010 had a positive effect on bauxite production, which increased to 17.4m. tons.

The exploitation of bauxite reserves at Fria, by the Cie Internationale pour la Production de l'Alumine Fria (an international consortium that included Pechiney of France—now Alcan), began in the 1930s. Processing into alumina began in 1960 at what remains the country's only refinery, located near Kindia. Following independence, the Government took a 49% share in the company, which was renamed Friguia. The refinery's output eased from a peak of 692,000 metric tons (recorded in 1980, and close to the plant's total capacity of 700,000 tons annually) to some 550,000 tons (calcined equivalent) in 2000. In October 1998 the international consortium ceded its 51% stake in Friguia to the Guinean Government. In late 1999 the Government formed a controlling company, the Alumina Company of Guinea Ltd (ACG), and concluded a management and technical assistance agreement with the Reynolds Metal Company of the USA (which subsequently merged with Alcoa Inc, also of the USA), by which it was hoped to achieve significant improvements in production efficiency. However, in 2002 Russian Aluminium (RUSAL) took a majority stake in ACG as part of a US $350m. plan to increase Friguia's production capacity to 1.4m. tons per year; subsequently in 2006 RUSAL increased its stake in ACG to 100% at the same time as it developed plans for the expansion of the Kindia mine (see below). The military junta that took power in December 2008 ordered an independent audit on the privatization of the Friguia refinery, and in September 2009 a local court declared that the sale of Friguia to RUSAL should be declared null and void as it had been bought for one-tenth of its actual value. Guinea's transitional Government, which was appointed in February 2010, then announced the formation of a joint body with RUSAL to find a solution to their dispute and determine appropriate compensation and taxation. In the absence of a new agreement, RUSAL's licence for Friguia's exploitation was expected to come under review, together with all other existing mining and exploration licences, by the new Commission Nationale des Mines created in March 2012. In the meantime, the Russian company faced prolonged strike action in April, with workers demanding a minimum wage of $400 per month plus medical costs. In spite of the personal intervention of President Condé, and the official suspension of the strike, production had not resumed by July.

The country's principal bauxite mine is at Boké-Sangarédi, in the north-west, which was commissioned in 1973 by the Cie des Bauxites de Guinée (CBG), a joint venture between the Government and the Halco group (an international consortium of Canadian, US, French, German and Australian aluminium companies). Output increased from around 900,000 metric tons per year to the complex's full capacity (at that time) of 10m. tons in 1981, eased subsequently, and then rose to 13.6m. tons in 1999. Plans were advanced during the early 2000s for the construction of an alumina refinery, with an annual capacity of 2.8m. tons and at a cost estimated at US $2,500m. The investors were initially grouped in Guinea Aluminium Products Corporation (GAPCO), a combination of Japanese and US interests. Following international trends of increasing demand for aluminium (and consequent higher prices), the investors took a growing interest in the development of the proposed refinery and in November 2005 Halco and the Guinean Government signed an agreement to provide the Canadian-based Global Alumina Corporation (GAC) with access to CBG resources for the new refinery. Global Alumina announced in 2006 that it would commence mining in 2008 and that it would bring its refinery into production in 2009 with a capacity of 3.0m. tons a year. In return for sharing and managing GAC access to its infrastructure, CBG was due to receive additional mining titles for a further 2,000m. tons of bauxite. However, after delays caused by rising costs and lack of funding, in May 2007 GAC formed a joint venture with the Australian mining company BHP-Billiton to restart development of the project, now estimated to cost US $4,800m., with the aim of commencing production by 2011 with capacity of 1.5m. tons per year. The companies planned to develop two further refineries with similar capacity. In January 2009, however, the consortium's board of directors decided to defer consideration of the development plan for the refinery.

Production of bauxite by the Office des Bauxites de Kindia began in 1974 and averaged about 3m. metric tons per year, compared with design capacity of 5m. tons, in the late 1980s. The company suffered severe financial difficulties, and output fluctuated around the 1m.–2m. tons level from 1992 when the company was reorganized as the Société des Bauxites de Kindia (SBK); production was 1.3m. tons in 1999. A majority stake was subsequently acquired by RUSAL, which in May 2001 announced a US $40m. investment programme to modernize equipment in order to ensure the continued productivity of SBK. Further agreement was reached with RUSAL in 2006 that bauxite production would soon double from the now-renamed Cie des Bauxites de Kindia's scheduled rate of 2.8m. tons. In early 2008 RUSAL signed an agreement with China Power Investment (CPI) to build a bauxite and alumina refinery complex in Guinea and an aluminium smelter in China, with production at both complexes expected to start in late 2009. These investment decisions were subject to considerable uncertainty in 2009 and 2010, although CPI was reported to have started exploration and to have prepared plans for a railway, a new deepwater port and a new electric power plant. In August 2011 the China Power Investment Corporation announced that it would invest $6,000m. in a bauxite mine and an alumina refinery near the town of Boffa.

Diamonds

Production of diamonds reached 80,000 carats per year in the early 1970s: the official figure did not include substantial illicit production, and mining was suspended in the late 1970s to prevent smuggling and theft. In 1980 the Government allowed the resumption of diamond mining by private companies, and AREDOR-Guinée was founded in 1981 with Australian, Swiss and British participation, and also—for the first time in Guinea—participation by the International Finance Corporation (IFC), the private sector lending arm of the World Bank. The Government had a 50% holding and was to take 65% of net profits. AREDOR-Guinée began production in 1984, and output reached a peak of 204,000 carats in 1986. However, mining was suspended in 1994. AREDOR has since been restructured, with Canada's Trivalence Mining taking a majority stake with a view to developing new kimberlite resources within the concession. In 2006 South Africa's De Beers negotiated a resumption of activities and was awarded permits for exploration in the Macenta area. In July 2008 the Ministry of Mines and Energy recommended that the Government cancel the diamond mining licence granted for the AREDOR mine, owing to inactivity over the preceding three years. The rights to the mine were eventually granted to the Batax Bouna International Mining Corporation, a company owned by Guinean interests. In 2009 West African Diamonds plc (WAD) began producing small amounts of diamonds at its Bomboko and Mandala mine, where two plants were constructed and commissioned to process alluvial diamonds. WAD, which changed its name to Stellar Diamond plc in February 2010, also continued its exploration activities on the Droujba and Bouro North properties. According to the US Geological Survey (USGS), Guinea's diamond production totalled 374,000 carats in 2010.

Gold

Gold is mined both industrially and by individuals (the latter smuggle much of their output abroad). A joint venture with Belgian interests, the Société Aurifère de Guinée (SAG), was established in 1985 to develop gold mining in the Siguiri and Mandiana districts. Alluvial production began in 1988 and reached 2,000 kg in the following year; however, extraction ceased in 1992, owing to financial and technical difficulties and conflicts with artisanal miners. Golden Shamrock of Australia took a 70% interest in the project, which was in turn taken over by Ghana's Ashanti Goldfields in 1996; production by SAG (renamed Société Ashanti Goldfields de Guinée—now AngloGold Ashanti Guinea) resumed in early 1998, with output in its first year estimated at 160,000 troy oz. Production peaked at 283,000 oz in 2001 before falling to 250,000 oz in 2003 and just 100,000 oz in 2004 as a result of a dispute with the Government, which placed an embargo on exports from the mine. Following the lifting of the ban, production recovered to 290,000 oz in 2005, 301,000 oz in 2006, 330,000 oz in 2007 and 392,000 oz in 2008. Production decreased to 372,000 oz in 2009 and 352,000 oz in 2010, owing to the mining of lower-grade areas following the depletion of the high-grade Bidini and Santchoro pits. AngloGold Ashanti continued oil-sampling and -drilling exploration around the Siguiri mine during 2010.

The Société minière de Dinguiraye (a joint venture with Norwegian, Australian and French interests) began production at the Léro site in 1995; output in 2004 was estimated at 70,000 oz. The Norwegian-based Kenor developed an extension of the mine east of the Karta river, at Fayalala, which increased overall production at the mine to an estimated 400,000 oz in 2006. The Léro site changed management several times in the 2000s. The current owner, OAO Severstal Resources of Russia, planned the revision of potential targets by 2011. A Canadian company, Semafo, has developed a mine at Kiniero, which produced an estimated 33,000 oz in 2010. Several other foreign enterprises are also actively prospecting for gold. In 2010, according to USGS, 15,217 kg of gold were mined in Guinea (excluding artisanal mining).

Iron Ore and Uranium

Working of the iron ore deposits on the Kaloum peninsula (near Conakry) was begun in 1953 by an Anglo-French group, and provided a stable output of about 700,000 metric tons per year in 1960–69, after which operations were abandoned. An ambitious project for the exploitation of the far superior deposits at Mt Nimba has been discussed for many years. In May 2008 Rio Tinto revealed that it was seeking a Chinese partner to develop the world's largest unexploited iron reserves, estimated at 2,250m. tons, at Simandou in south-eastern Guinea, at a cost of US $6,000m. However, in June the Government indicated that it would review Rio Tinto's contract to ensure that it complied with the proposed new mining code, and in December the Government withdrew Rio Tinto's rights to the northern half of the concession. It was confirmed in February 2009 that the northern sector had been awarded to BSG Resources, an Israeli company owned by the Beny Steinmetz Group, and in July Rio Tinto was ordered to remove its equipment from the northern half of the concession. In March 2010 the Aluminium Corporation of China (Chinalco) and Rio Tinto signed a memorandum of understanding to develop jointly Rio Tinto's Simandou concession, whereby Chinalco agreed to pay $1,350m. for roughly 45% of Rio Tinto's concession, while Rio Tinto retained just over 50% and 5% remained with the IFC. Although the Government expressed its opposition to the deal, Rio Tinto emphasized that it did not need its approval. In April 2010 Vale of Brazil, the world's largest iron ore producer, announced that it had acquired a majority 51% stake in BSG Resources' Guinean concession. Vale announced that it expected annual output to start at 10m. tons in 2012 and to reach 50m. tons by 2015. In April 2011 the new Government formally approved the acquisition by Rio Tinto and Chinalco of two blocks of the Simandou concession. Under the terms of the agreement, Rio Tinto agreed to pay $700m. immediately to the Guinean treasury in exchange for an eight-year tax 'holiday'. The agreement also established that the Guinea state's share in the project would increase to 35% after a period of 20 years. Rio Tinto announced in October that it had brought forward the date of its first iron ore shipment to mid-2015. With regards to the two other Simandou blocks, the Government announced in January 2012 that it would review BSG Resources' permit, which could be subject to cancellation.

In May 2010 Bellzone Mining, an Australian company, acquired a 25-year concession to develop the Kalia iron ore mine, located near the town of Faranah. Shortly after securing the concession, Bellzone announced that it would establish a joint venture with the CIF, a Hong Kong investment company, which agreed to spend US $2,700m. on infrastructure to facilitate the production and export of iron ore.

In August 2007 the Government announced that a uranium deposit in Firawa and Bohoduo, in the southern Guinée Forestière region, had been discovered by an Australian company, Murchison International, which planned to develop the deposits. Murchison International, now Forte Energy NL, has conducted mineralogical and metallurgical studies at the Firawa deposit, which indicated the presence of rare earth elements, as well as that of uranium. Forte Energy expected to begin field activities at the deposit site in 2011.

Petroleum

Since 2002 Hyperdynamics, a US company, has acquired 80,000 sq km of Guinea's offshore territory in order to explore its oil reserves. However, the company faced difficulties in funding the agreed exploration work and in September 2009 it concluded an agreement with the Government to relinquish some of the offshore blocks in return for more relaxed reception of the ongoing delays. In October the majority of the acreage relinquished by Hyperdynamics was acquired by China Sonangol, a joint venture between the Angolan national oil company, Sonangol, and Dayuan International Development, the main shareholder of the CIF. This followed the announcement of the discovery of a significant oil deposit in neighbouring Sierra Leone in September 2009. In October 2011 Hyperdynamics drilled Guinea's first deepwater oil well, Sabu-1, situated 57 km from the Société Guinéenne des Pétroles (SOGUIP) 2B-1 well, the only offshore area where oil reserves were previously identified in 1977. Positive results were expected to allow Hyperdynamics, which had suffered increasing losses in 2011, to raise further funds for exploration and exploitation.

Energy

Installed electricity generation capacity was estimated at 320 MW in 2006, of which one-half was privately operated, notably by mining companies. Supplies of energy outside the mining and industrial sector are vastly inadequate. The national electricity utility, Electricité de Guinée, supplies power to only 18% of the population from the national grid; even Conakry is subject to frequent and prolonged power cuts during dry periods. None the less, the country has a very large, as yet unexploited, hydroelectric potential, estimated at some 1,000 MW. In 1999 a 75-MW plant was commissioned on the Konkouré river at Garafiri. This, together with a planned station at Kaléta, 100 km downstream, was expected to increase total generating capacity by 155 MW. In August 2011 the Government signed an agreement with China International Water and Electric for the construction of the Kaléta dam, which was expected to cost US $526m., with the Government co-financing 25% of the project. Work on the dam officially began in April 2012. Guinea's rural electrification rate was estimated at only 3% in 2011. In January of that year the AfDB approved a loan of US $23m. to increase this rate to 15%.

MANUFACTURING

The principal aim of Guinea's small manufacturing sector, which accounted for 7.1% of GDP in 2009, has been import-substitution, but the experience of the state-run projects that were established under Sékou Touré was disappointing. Lack of foreign exchange for raw materials, of skilled workers and of technical expertise, combined with poor management and low domestic purchasing power, meant that most of the plants were operating substantially below capacity. The sector was rationalized under the Conté administration, with the former state-run textile and fruit-processing companies closed and no new factories established. Manufacturing is now largely limited to food, drinks and cigarettes, and basic inputs such as cement, metal manufactures and fuel products, all geared to the domestic market.

TRANSPORT AND INFRASTRUCTURE

The inadequacy of Guinea's transport infrastructure has been cited by the World Bank as the 'single most severe impediment to output recovery'. None the less, some improvements have been made since the mid-1980s. The road network is being almost entirely reconstructed, to restore links between Conakry and the country's interior, while road tracks have been built to open up rural areas. The network comprised 44,348 km of roads (of which 4,342 km were paved) in 2003. By 2009 an estimated 35% of all roads were paved. In 2001 work commenced on an EU-financed road link from Kankan to the Malian capital, Bamako. In May 2011 a new bridge, built with the support of the EU, was inaugurated in Forécariah, on the road linking Conakry to neighbouring Sierra Leone.

The rail network is better developed, but is entirely geared to serving the bauxite sector: a 135-km heavy-gauge railway links the Boké bauxite deposits with the deep-water port at Kamsar, which handles around 9m. metric tons per year and is thus the country's major export outlet in tonnage terms. The repeated attempts, by successive governments, to convince mining companies with concessions in the country to invest in its railway system have so far remained unsuccessful. Although BSG Resources and Vale, which own an iron ore concession in the Simandou area, had begun the rehabilitation of the 662-km railway linking Conakry to Kankan, President Condé announced in April 2011 that the project had been cancelled, as he disapproved of Vale's choice of another Brazilian firm, Zagope, to undertake the work. In January 2012 the Government invited Rio Tinto to conduct a feasibility study for the railway, which would enable the delivery to a port in the Forecariah area (yet to be constructed) of the iron ore extracted at the Simandou blocks from 2015.

The port of Conakry, which handled 3.9m. tons of foreign trade in 1999, has been extended and modernized as part of a programme that envisages the construction of naval-repair and deep-water port facilities. In March 2011 the French conglomerate Bolloré became the new manager of the port of Conakry, although the contract to handle the port had been awarded three years previously to Necotrans, another French shipping network. The Bolloré group had allegedly supported the new President's electoral campaign in 2010.

The international airport at Conakry-Gbessia handled some 300,000 passengers in 1999; there are several smaller airfields in the interior. In 2010 plans were under way for the construction of a new international airport, at Matakango. Several major donors, including the World Bank, have made funds available for both rural and urban water-supply networks; in 2001 the Government invited bids for private sector management of water-supply companies. According to the International Telecommunication Union, there were only 18,000 fixed telephone lines in 2010. The privatization of the national telecommunications company, Société des Télécommunications de Guinée, was reversed in 2006 after the main stakeholder, Telekom Malaysia, handed operation of the company back to the Government and announced its intention to sell its 60% stake. The mobile telephone network has expanded dramatically in recent years, and by 2010 the sector's four operators had an estimated combined total of 4m. subscribers (40% of the population)—Guinea experienced the third highest mobile cellular growth rate (88%) in Africa in 2003–08. There were an estimated 100,000 internet users in 2010.

FINANCE

Government revenue remains heavily reliant on income from the mining sector and the Government has struggled to improve fiscal management and reduce the budget deficit. The deficit (including grants) rose to 6.2% of GDP in 2003 (compared with 4.4% in 2002), but owing to sharply increasing mining revenue the deficit was estimated to have narrowed to 4.9% of GDP in 2004 and 1.5% of GDP in 2005. However, as a result of poor public-expenditure management, low domestic revenue and the suspension of donor budgetary support, the budget deficit subsequently increased to 3.2% of GDP in 2006. After achieving an overall budget surplus of 0.3% of GDP in 2007, the budget was once more in deficit in 2008, at 1.3% of GDP. This reflected the dismissal of Prime Minister Lansana Kouyaté's Government, which had been able to impose greater budgetary discipline in 2007, and the fall, over the second half of 2008, of international aluminium prices reduced revenue from the mining sector. The poor quality of fiscal reporting meant that no figure was available for 2009, but in early 2011 Guinea's Prime Minister, Mohamed Saïd Fofana, noted that the budget deficit was estimated to have reached 14.4% of GDP in 2010, reflecting the fact that previous governments had engaged in ad hoc revenue-generation measures and lacked appropriate financial controls. The Government that took office in January 2011 confirmed that the military junta had printed an unprecedented quantity of money to finance expenditure and that 35% of this spending was directed to the armed forces. The new Government immediately set about completing the audits of state finances, which had been initiated by the preceding transitional administration, and announced new audits for each ministry. The new IMF staff-monitored programme also encouraged the Government to implement tighter fiscal controls on spending, which along with a windfall revenue received from the mining sector in May, led to a sharp decline in the budget deficit to an estimated 2.5% of GDP at the end of 2011.

Relations with the IMF have been difficult owing to the Government's unwillingness or inability to adhere to the reform agenda. In May 2001 the IMF approved an arrangement for Guinea, worth a total of US $82m. over three years, under the Poverty Reduction and Growth Facility (PRGF); the programme aimed, initially, to generate annual GDP growth of 6.5% in 2004. However, non-compliance with agreed fiscal targets led to the IMF's suspension of disbursements under the PRGF in late 2002 and prevented the adoption of a staff-monitored programme (SMP) in early 2003; as a result, budgetary assistance from donors also virtually ceased. Furthermore, a second SMP, covering the period April 2005 to March 2006, collapsed owing to the Government's lack of commitment to reform. However, relations with the Fund improved under Prime Minister Kouyaté, whose administration improved fiscal management and demonstrated its commitment to structural reform. In January 2008 the IMF approved a new PRGF, running retroactively from July 2007 until June 2010. The PRGF was worth $75m., in addition to budgetary support valued at €45m. from France and the EU. The PRGF's main aims were to strengthen fiscal and monetary policy, improve tax collection, increase poverty-reducing expenditure, and carry out urgent reform of the water and electricity utilities to improve service delivery. The PRGF's macroeconomic targets included increasing real GDP growth to 4.9% in 2008 and 5.2% in 2009, and reducing inflation to less than 10% by 2009. The PRGF, however, was abruptly suspended following the military coup in December 2008. The first sign of an IMF re-engagement came one month after the appointment of a transitional Government, in March 2010, when a joint delegation from the IMF, the World Bank and the AfDB held talks with Guinea's transitional legislative body, the Conseil National de la Transition (National Transitional Council). The new Government appointed in early 2011 immediately expressed its wish to resume relations with the international financial institutions and further contacts were established with the IMF. In June the agreement of a staff-monitored programme for the remainder of the year marked a full restoration of relations, and the IMF mission which visited the country in November noted that good progress had been made under the programme through improved fiscal revenue and tight spending control. In February 2012 the executive board of the IMF approved a three-year arrangement for Guinea under the extended credit facility (ECF). An initial disbursement of US $28.4m., of the total $198.9m., was immediately extended.

An important element of the economic liberalization initiated in the final years of the Sékou Touré regime and pursued with vigour by the Conté administration was the reform of the banking sector, ending the state monopoly by allowing the establishment of private commercial banks and then closing down the six state-controlled institutions. Government plans fully to privatize the Banque Internationale pour le Commerce et l'Industrie de la Guinée (BICIGUI) have not materialized; however, by 2005 the Government had reduced its shareholding in the bank from 51% of the total to 38% (and subsequently to 15.1%). BICIGUI accounts for 45% of the country's banking resources and for about one-third of credits to the private sector.

FOREIGN TRADE AND PAYMENTS

With the development of bauxite resources from the early 1970s, the country's external trade position greatly improved. The sharp rise in bauxite exports resulted in strong growth in export earnings after 1975, and sales of bauxite and alumina contributed more than 90% of recorded earnings in the early 1980s. Export earnings were subsequently increased by sales of diamonds and gold. The sustained growth in exports allowed a similarly strong rise in spending on imports, in large part reflecting capital investment in the mining sector. However, as earnings from bauxite and alumina declined from 1991 onwards, and spending on imports was relatively little changed, the trade account moved into deficit, reaching a peak of US $169.7m. in 1994. By 1996, with bauxite and alumina earnings recovering from their trough of 1994, the trade account had moved back into surplus and remained so until 1998. The trade account fluctuated throughout the late 1990s and early 2000s. Since 2004, although the rise in international commodity prices has considerably increased the value of Guinea's exports, the total value of its imports has risen at a faster rate and in 2009 a trade deficit of $10.4m. was recorded. Chile and Spain were Guinea's most important export markets in 2011, accounting for 34.1% and 12.8% of total exports, respectively, mostly consisting of bauxite and alumina, followed by India (5.6%). The main source of imports in 2011 was China (38.2%), followed by the Netherlands (23.3%), the USA (15.5%) and France (11.5%). The current account is, on average, in deficit because of high outflows on services (including interest payments and profit remittances), reaching an estimated $329.2m. in 2010, equivalent to 7% of GDP. Foreign exchange reserves, which had remained uncomfortably low throughout the 2000s, increased from $124m. at the end of 2010 to an estimated $754.3m. at the end of 2011.

Inflows of foreign direct investment (FDI), primarily into the mining sector, have grown strongly in recent years. According to the UN Conference on Trade and Development, FDI inflows rose from an average of US $21m. per year during 1990–2000 to $386m. in 2007 and $382m. in 2008. In 2009, essentially owing to the political situation in the country, inflows fell to $141m., before rising again to $303m. in 2010. This very sharp rise reflects the growing interest that international investors have shown in Guinea's mineral riches.

Guinea's foreign debt totalled US $1,387m. at the end of 1981—equivalent to 86% of the country's gross national income (GNI) in that year—a level that was broadly maintained in the following four years. Although the burden of servicing the debt was alleviated by concessionary interest rates on most of the borrowing and by the buoyancy of Guinean exports, it remained at a high level throughout this period, fluctuating within the range of 14%–24% of exports of goods and services, and obligations were not discharged in full. Arrears on both repayment and interest had apparently reached $300m. at the time of the 1984 coup. In early 1986, following final agreement between the IMF and the Conté administration on the terms of the economic stabilization programme (which included a 93% devaluation of the currency), the country's Western creditors agreed to a rescheduling of debt, covering arrears and debt-service due up to early 1987. However, with the external debt and debt-service continuing to rise, the 'Paris Club' of official creditors rescheduled debt in every year from 1990 to 1992. With a rising share of concessionary loans, this meant that, while total foreign debt remained close to 100% of GNI (at $3,110m. at the end of 1994, it was equivalent to 94% in that year), the debt-service ratio was kept at a manageable 11%–14% in 1992–94. Another round of rescheduling, in January 1995, was under the highly concessionary 'Naples terms', and included the cancellation of one-half of debt-servicing liabilities due in 1994 and 1995 to France, Germany, Norway and the USA. The award of the new ESAF in 1997 generated another round of 'Paris Club' restructuring, again under 'Naples terms', and Guinea was also permitted to convert up to 20% of its outstanding debt (double the usual limit) into local-currency equity in the form of investment in development projects. Further debt relief under the HIPC initiative was not granted, as a consequence of the collapse of the IMF's PRGF programme in 2002.

The country reached HIPC 'decision point' in December 2000, but by mid-2007 the country had failed to reach 'completion point' when it would become eligible for further bilateral debt relief under the Multilateral Debt Relief Initiative (MDRI). The award of a new PRGF programme in January 2008 increased the likelihood of the country reaching HIPC completion within the next two to three years. In January 2008 the 'Paris Club' wrote off US $180m. of debt and agreed to restructure a further $120m.; in May France agreed to cancel $86m. of debt, rescheduled a further $14m. and pledged $93m. of development funding from 2010 onwards. Total external debt was estimated at $3,092m. at the end of 2008 (equivalent to 59.5% of GDP). The military coup in December 2008, however, once again suspended co-operation between the IMF and the Guinean Government and progress towards HIPC completion. The new Government appointed following Condé's election announced in early 2011 that it would seek to reconnect with the HIPC initiative, and contacts were re-established with the IMF. Prime Minister Fofana claimed in January that Guinea's debt stock was $2,300m., equivalent to 69% of GDP. In March 2012 the IMF announced that it had revised the time in which Guinea could reach completion point under the HIPC initiative to the second half of 2012. In April the 'Paris Club' group of creditors, to which Guinea owed $750m., announced that it would provide $344m. of debt relief to Guinea over eight years. The agreement was expected to reduce the country's debt-servicing costs by 84%.

Statistical Survey

Source (unless otherwise stated): Direction Nationale de la Statistique, BP 221, Conakry; tel. 21-33-12; e-mail dnstat@biasy.net; internet www.stat-guinee.org/.

Area and Population

AREA, POPULATION AND DENSITY

Area (sq km)	245,857*
Population (census results)	
4–17 February 1983	4,533,240†
31 December 1996‡	
Males	3,497,551
Females	3,658,855
Total	7,156,406
Population (UN estimates at mid-year)§	
2010	9,981,590
2011	10,221,804
2012	10,480,709
Density (per sq km) at mid-2012	42.6

* 94,926 sq miles.
† Excluding adjustment for underenumeration.
‡ Including refugees from Liberia and Sierra Leone (estimated at 640,000).
§ Source: UN, *World Population Prospects: The 2010 Revision*.

POPULATION BY AGE AND SEX
(UN estimates at mid-2012)

	Males	Females	Total
0–14	2,272,860	2,187,288	4,460,148
15–64	2,868,360	2,806,848	5,675,208
65 and over	155,644	189,709	345,353
Total	5,296,864	5,183,845	10,480,709

Source: UN, *World Population Prospects: The 2010 Revision*.

ETHNIC GROUPS

1995 (percentages): Peul 38.7; Malinké 23.3; Soussou 11.1; Kissi 5.9; Kpellé 4.5; Others 16.5 (Source: La Francophonie).

ADMINISTRATIVE DIVISIONS
(1996 census)

Region	Area (sq km)	Population	Density (per sq km)	Principal city
Conakry	450	1,092,936	2,428.7	Conakry
Basse-Guinée	47,063	1,460,577	31.0	Kindia
Moyenne-Guinée	52,939	1,639,617	31.0	Labé
Haute-Guinée	99,437	1,407,734	14.2	Kankan
Guinée Forestière	45,968	1,555,542	33.8	N'Zérékoré
Total	245,857	7,156,406	29.1	

Note: The regions were subsequently reorganized. The new regions (which in each case share their name with the regional capital) are: Boké; Conakry; Faranah; Kankan; Kindia; Labé; Mamou; and N'Zérékoré.

PRINCIPAL TOWNS
(population at 1996 census)

Conakry (capital)	1,092,936	Kindia	96,074
N'Zérékoré	107,329	Guéckédou	79,140
Kankan	100,192	Kamsar	61,526

Mid-2011 (incl. suburbs, UN estimate): Conakry 1,786,300 (Source: UN, *World Urbanization Prospects: The 2011 Revision*).

BIRTHS AND DEATHS
(annual averages, UN estimates)

	1995–2000	2000–05	2005–10
Birth rate (per 1,000)	43.4	41.5	39.9
Death rate (per 1,000)	18.1	15.7	13.9

Source: UN, *World Population Prospects: The 2010 Revision*.

Life expectancy (years at birth): 53.6 (males 52.1; females 55.3) in 2010 (Source: World Bank, World Development Indicators database).

ECONOMICALLY ACTIVE POPULATION
('000 persons at 1996 census)

	Males	Females	Total
Agriculture, hunting and forestry	1,140,775	1,281,847	2,422,622
Fishing	9,969	889	10,858
Mining and quarrying	26,599	8,376	34,975
Manufacturing	84,974	5,911	90,885
Electricity, gas and water supply	4,366	324	4,690
Construction	59,802	724	60,526
Wholesale and retail trade; repair of motor vehicles and motorcycles and personal and household goods	176,527	191,230	367,757
Restaurants and hotels	3,162	2,790	5,952
Transport, storage and communications	75,374	1,696	77,070
Financial intermediation	1,728	626	2,354
Real estate, renting and business activities	877	209	1,086
Public administration and defence; compulsory social security	50,401	12,791	63,192
Education	15,044	3,773	18,817
Health and social work	4,762	3,522	8,284
Other community, social and personal service activities	44,897	48,292	93,189
Private households with employed persons	5,553	6,202	11,755
Extra-territorial organizations and bodies	3,723	1,099	4,822
Total employed	1,708,533	1,570,301	3,278,834

Mid-2012 ('000 persons): Agriculture, etc. 3,999; Total labour force 5,070 (Source: FAO).

Health and Welfare

KEY INDICATORS

Total fertility rate (children per woman, 2010)	5.2
Under-5 mortality rate (per 1,000 live births, 2010)	130
HIV/AIDS (% of persons aged 15–49, 2009)	1.3
Physicians (per 1,000 head, 2005)	0.1
Hospital beds (per 1,000 head, 2005)	0.3
Health expenditure (2009): US $ per head (PPP)	60
Health expenditure (2009): % of GDP	5.3
Health expenditure (2009): public (% of total)	8.2
Access to water (% of persons, 2010)	74
Access to sanitation (% of persons, 2010)	18
Total carbon dioxide emissions ('000 metric tons, 2008)	1,393.5
Carbon dioxide emissions per head (metric tons, 2008)	0.1
Human Development Index (2011): ranking	178
Human Development Index (2011): value	0.344

For sources and definitions, see explanatory note on p. vi.

Agriculture

PRINCIPAL CROPS

('000 metric tons)

	2008	2009	2010
Rice, paddy	1,534.1	1,499.0*	1,614.9*
Maize	952.2	565.7*	580.1*
Fonio	341.2	329.9*	388.6*
Sweet potatoes	204.6	194.5*	174.6*
Cassava (Manioc)	1,122.2	989.3*	1,030.8*
Taro (Cocoyam)*	31.2	27.8	17.5
Yams	27.4	24.0*	24.4*
Sugar cane*	283	283	283
Pulses*	63	50	56
Groundnuts, with shell	315.1	277.0†	291.7†
Coconuts	48.4†	37.3†	39.0*
Oil palm fruit*	830.0	830.0	830.0
Bananas*	162.0	179.6	201.5
Plantains*	449.7	479.9	461.7
Guavas, mangoes and mangosteens*	166.0	165.0	163.9
Pineapples*	109.0	108.0	107.5
Seed cotton*	42	39	40
Coffee, green†	30.2	34.0	27.0

* FAO estimate(s).

† Unofficial figure(s).

Aggregate production ('000 metric tons, may include official, semi-official or estimated data): Total cereals 3,187.1 in 2008, 2,659.5 in 2009, 2,858.9 in 2010; Total roots and tubers 1,397.5 in 2008, 1,246.4 in 2009, 1,258.1 in 2010; Total vegetables (incl. melons) 515.5 in 2008, 410.5 in 2009, 536.9 in 2010; Total fruits (excl. melons) 1,153.2 in 2008, 1,228.1 in 2009, 1,218.7 in 2010.

Source: FAO.

LIVESTOCK

('000 head, year ending September)

	2008	2009*	2010*
Cattle	4,409	4,652	4,907
Sheep	1,419	1,500	1,586
Goats	1,696	1,800	1,910
Pigs	86.4	90.7	95.2
Chickens*	18,900	20,050	22,500

* FAO estimates.

Source: FAO.

LIVESTOCK PRODUCTS

('000 metric tons)

	2008	2009*	2010*
Cattle meat	49.4	52.0	55.0
Chicken meat*	6.8	7.2	8.1
Sheep meat	5.6	6.0	6.3
Goat meat	8.4	8.9	9.0
Game meat*	4.7	5.0	5.4
Cows' milk*	106.0	111.9	115.0
Goats' milk*	11.5	12.2	12.7
Hen eggs*	22.2	23.5	23.5

* FAO estimates.

Source: FAO.

Forestry

ROUNDWOOD REMOVALS

('000 cubic metres, excl. bark, FAO estimates)

	2008	2009	2010
Sawlogs, veneer logs and logs for sleepers	138	138	138
Other industrial wood	513	513	513
Fuel wood	11,846	11,901	11,959
Total	12,496	12,552	12,610

Source: FAO.

SAWNWOOD PRODUCTION

('000 cubic metres, incl. railway sleepers, FAO estimates)

	2007	2008	2009
Total (all broadleaved)	30.0	30.0	30.0

2010: Production assumed to be unchanged from 2009 (FAO estimate).

Source: FAO.

Fishing

('000 metric tons, live weight)

	2008	2009	2010
Freshwater fishes*	12.0	14.0	16.0
Sea catfishes	8.9	8.8*	8.8*
Bobo croaker	7.7	7.6*	7.6*
West African croakers	3.9	3.9*	3.9*
Sardinellas	1.7	1.7*	4.9*
Bonga shad	32.9	32.9*	32.9*
Marine fishes	21.7	20.7	20.2
Total catch (incl. others)*	94.5	96.1	109.9

* FAO estimate(s).

Source: FAO.

Mining

('000 metric tons unless otherwise indicated)

	2008	2009	2010
Bauxite (dry basis)*	16,000	13,600	15,100
Gold (kilograms)	19,945	18,091	15,217
Salt (unrefined)	15	15	15†
Diamonds ('000 carats)‡	3,098	697	374

* Estimated to be 7% water.
† Estimate.
‡ Including artisanal production.

Source: US Geological Survey.

Industry

SELECTED PRODUCTS

('000 metric tons unless otherwise indicated)

	2008	2009	2010
Palm oil (unrefined)*†	50	50	50
Beer of barley*‡	16.7	16.7	16.7
Raw sugar§	20	n.a.	n.a.
Alumina (calcined equivalent)‖	593	530	597
Electric energy (million kWh)§	1,000	n.a.	n.a.

* Data from FAO.
† Unofficial figures.
‡ FAO estimates.
§ Data from UN Industrial Commodity Statistics Database.
‖ Data from the US Geological Survey.

Salted, dried or smoked fish ('000 metric tons, FAO estimates): 11.0 in 2000–02 (Source: FAO).

Finance

CURRENCY AND EXCHANGE RATES

Monetary Units

100 centimes = 1 franc guinéen (FG or Guinean franc).

Sterling, Dollar and Euro Equivalents (30 December 2011)

£1 sterling = 10,961.116 Guinean francs;
US $1 = 7,089.526 Guinean francs;
€1 = 9,173.137 Guinean francs;
100,000 Guinean francs = £9.12 = $14.11 = €10.90.

Average Exchange Rate (Guinean francs per US $)

2009	4,801.1
2010	5,726.1
2011	6,658.0

BUDGET

('000 million Guinean francs)

Revenue*	2010	2011†	2012‡
Mining-sector revenue	1,032	1,518	1,489
Other revenue	3,124	4,495	6,037
Tax revenue	2,944	3,821	5,744
Taxes on domestic production and trade	1,526	1,943	3,022
Taxes on international trade	685	902	1,554
Non-tax revenue	180	674	293
Total	4,155	6,012	7,526

Expenditure§	2010	2011†	2012‡
Current expenditure	5,570	5,434	6,696
Wages and salaries	1,551	1,824	2,124
Other goods and services	2,546	1,891	2,182
Subsidies and transfers	926	1,122	1,655
Interest due on external debt	191	293	383
Interest due on domestic debt	356	304	352
Capital expenditure	2,479	2,737	4,759
Domestically financed	2,187	1,715	2,704
Externally financed	279	1,006	2,039
Capital transfer	13	17	16
Total	8,049	8,171	11,454

* Excluding grants received ('000 million Guinean francs): 103 in 2010; 1,161 in 2011 (estimate); 1,272 in 2012 (projection).
† Estimates.
‡ Projections.
§ Excluding lending minus repayments ('000 million Guinean francs): 0 in 2010; 4 in 2011 (estimate); 11 in 2012 (projection).

Source: IMF, *Guinea: 2011 Article IV Consultation and Requests for a Three-Year Arrangement Under the Extended Credit Facility, and for Additional Interim Assistance Under the Enhanced Initiative for Heavily Indebted Poor Countries—Staff Report; Public Information Notice and Press Release on the Executive Board Discussion; and Statement by the Executive Director for Guinea* (March 2012).

INTERNATIONAL RESERVES

(US $ million at 31 December)

	2004	2005
Gold (national valuation)	1.29	1.27
IMF special drawing rights	—	0.02
Reserve position in IMF	0.12	0.11
Foreign exchange	110.37	94.93
Total	111.78	96.33

IMF special drawing rights: 128.88 in 2009; 116.16 in 2010; 94.34 in 2011.

Reserve position in IMF: 0.12 in 2009–11.

Source: IMF, *International Financial Statistics*.

MONEY SUPPLY

(million Guinean francs at 31 December)

	2003	2004	2005
Currency outside banks	478,133	536,169	786,587
Demand deposits at commercial banks	386,359	518,469	590,420
Total (incl. others)	893,055	1,143,312	1,394,203

Source: IMF, *International Financial Statistics*.

COST OF LIVING

(Consumer Price Index for Conakry; base: 2002 = 100)

	2004	2005	2006
Foodstuffs, beverages and tobacco	147.1	201.6	287.3
Clothing and shoes	109.8	121.9	151.6
Housing, water, electricity and gas	114.0	142.7	174.7
All items (incl. others)	130.1	170.9	230.2

Source: IMF, *Guinea: Selected Issues and Statistical Appendix* (January 2008).

Cost of Living (Consumer Price Index; base: 2000 = 100): 388.0 in 2009; 448.2 in 2010; 543.2 in 2011 (Source: African Development Bank).

NATIONAL ACCOUNTS

('000 million Guinean francs at current prices)

Expenditure on the Gross Domestic Product

	2009	2010	2011
Government final consumption expenditure	1,889.1	3,550.8	4,061.1
Private final consumption expenditure	17,896.4	20,416.7	23,303.5
Gross fixed capital formation	3,631.8	4,634.4	7,926.5
Changes in inventories	−8.5	4.8	11.1
Total domestic expenditure	23,408.8	28,606.7	35,302.2
Exports of goods and services	5,357.0	9,182.8	12,461.5
Less Imports of goods and services	6,640.7	10,780.7	14,405.9
GDP at market prices	22,125.0	27,008.5	33,357.7

Gross Domestic Product by Economic Activity

	2009	2010	2011
Agriculture, livestock, forestry and fishing	5,232.1	5,490.6	6,337.1
Mining and quarrying	4,258.2	6,359.7	8,084.7
Manufacturing	1,492.4	1,715.8	2,066.9
Electricity, gas and water	90.7	104.2	126.5
Construction	2,304.9	2,695.3	3,422.9
Trade, restaurants and hotels	3,579.8	4,179.7	5,466.8
Transport and communications	1,193.7	1,388.3	1,710.5
Public administration and defence	1,511.5	1,839.2	2,295.6
Other services	559.4	673.8	889.0
GDP at factor cost	20,222.7	24,446.6	30,399.9
Indirect taxes	1,902.0	2,562.0	2,957.8
GDP at purchasers' values	22,125.0	27,008.5	33,357.7

Note: Deduction for imputed bank service charge assumed to be distributed at origin.

Source: African Development Bank.

BALANCE OF PAYMENTS

(US $ million)

	2008	2009	2010
Exports of goods f.o.b.	1,342.0	1,049.7	1,471.2
Imports of goods f.o.b.	−1,366.1	−1,060.1	−1,404.9
Trade balance	−24.1	−10.4	66.3
Exports of services	102.9	72.2	62.4
Imports of services	−444.3	−330.7	−395.5
Balance on goods and services	−365.5	−268.8	−266.9
Other income received	9.9	22.2	14.9
Other income paid	−101.1	−190.4	−92.0
Balance on goods, services and income	−456.7	−437.1	−344.0
Current transfers received	102.6	61.9	81.5
Current transfers paid	−86.0	−51.5	−66.8
Current balance	−440.1	−426.7	−329.2
Capital account (net)	34.8	16.4	16.9
Direct investment abroad	−63.6	—	—
Direct investment from abroad	381.9	49.8	101.4
Portfolio investment assets	—	—	0.1
Other investment assets	−44.1	56.1	−77.4
Other investment liabilities	162.4	409.9	289.5
Net errors and omissions	−16.2	48.6	38.7
Overall balance	15.0	154.1	39.8

Source: IMF, *International Financial Statistics*.

External Trade

PRINCIPAL COMMODITIES

(distribution by HS, '000 million Guinean francs)

Imports c.i.f.	2008	2009	2010
Live animals and animal products	32.8	27.1	55.2
Vegetable products	673.2	1,425.7	917.1
Prepared foodstuffs, beverages, alcohol and tobacco	542.2	515.2	784.6
Mineral products	3,066.6	1,909.1	4,309.8
Chemicals and related products	573.8	501.6	841.5
Plastics, rubbers, and articles thereof	183.1	167.2	290.7
Paper and paper articles	81.4	73.2	124.7
Textiles and textile articles	126.3	211.1	204.1
Base metals and articles thereof	446.0	326.8	416.8
Articles of stone, plaster and cement	45.3	62.6	88.4
Machinery and mechanical appliances	1,587.0	1,468.4	1,348.7
Transport equipment	393.6	343.0	672.3
Miscellaneous manufactured articles	82.8	36.0	73.4
Total (incl. others)	7,724.9	6,685.0	9,538.3

Exports f.o.b.	2008	2009	2010
Vegetable products	71.9	152.1	139.6
Mineral products	2,710.7	1,621.9	2,271.9
Chemicals and related products	773.1	641.9	930.6
Wood and wood articles	124.0	21.7	309.7
Base metals and articles thereof	25.1	66.3	704.1
Articles of stone, plaster and cement	2,246.7	1,820.4	4,605.6
Total (incl. others)	6,181.6	4,497.8	9,252.0

2011 (US $ million): *Imports:* Food 213; Other consumer goods 269; Petroleum products 393; Intermediate goods 316; Equipment goods 650; Total (incl. others) 1,841. *Exports:* Bauxite 436; Aluminium 189; Diamonds 57; Gold 890; Total (incl. others) 1,601 (Source: African Development Bank).

PRINCIPAL TRADING PARTNERS

(US $ million)

Imports c.i.f.	2006	2007	2008
Australia	12.0	19.4	71.7
Belgium	78.1	197.4	95.6
Brazil	16.4	20.8	53.8
China, People's Republic	80.1	74.7	123.4
Côte d'Ivoire	169.3	55.2	31.1
France (incl. Monaco)	110.7	109.0	185.4
Gabon	7.3	2.9	37.6
Germany	13.4	14.9	21.7
India	83.1	63.7	48.4
Indonesia	19.9	12.2	11.5
Italy	8.2	8.7	27.8
Japan	34.4	58.4	47.4
Morocco	14.5	9.0	14.9

Imports c.i.f.—*continued*	2006	2007	2008
Netherlands	59.4	174.8	377.6
South Africa	28.5	31.0	45.2
Spain	12.5	58.7	41.0
Thailand	21.0	14.2	28.1
Turkey	7.4	19.5	15.4
Ukraine	15.0	7.7	11.4
United Arab Emirates	9.9	22.8	39.4
United Kingdom	34.2	36.0	144.3
USA	57.6	78.5	95.1
Total (incl. others)	1,063.9	1,281.5	1,835.5

Exports f.o.b.	2006	2007	2008
Belgium	8.7	0.4	6.9
Canada	24.3	50.9	57.7
China, People's Republic	13.6	1.3	19.9
France (incl. Monaco)	51.2	187.0	349.8
Germany	61.9	84.4	83.9
Ireland	69.7	196.1	106.3
Morocco	2.3	0.8	2.7
Netherlands	1.6	7.4	2.4
Romania	12.0	14.7	0.0
Russia	0.0	98.7	151.3
Spain	88.7	163.8	141.5
Switzerland-Liechtenstein	11.5	34.3	278.4
Ukraine	18.8	14.6	40.7
United Kingdom	0.2	6.5	0.3
USA	79.6	145.5	96.1
Total (incl. others)	770.5	1,059.0	1,430.5

Source: UN, *International Trade Statistics Yearbook*.

2009 ('000 million Guinean francs): *Imports c.i.f.:* China, People's Republic 530.5; USA 289.0; Total (incl. others) 6,685.0. *Exports f.o.b.:* China, People's Republic 16.5; USA 201.6; Total (incl. others) 4,492.9.

2010 ('000 million Guinean francs): *Imports c.i.f.:* China, People's Republic 780.0; USA 272.8; Total (incl. others) 9,538.3. *Exports f.o.b.:* China, People's Republic 264.3; USA 362.5; Total (incl. others) 9,252.0.

Transport

RAILWAYS
(estimated traffic)

	1991	1992	1993
Freight ton-km (million)	660	680	710

Source: UN Economic Commission for Africa, *African Statistical Yearbook*.

ROAD TRAFFIC
('000, motor vehicles in use, estimates)

	2001	2002	2003
Passenger cars	41.6	43.1	47.5
Buses and coaches	24.8	20.5	20.9
Lorries and vans	11.1	10.5	15.7

SHIPPING

Merchant Fleet
(registered at 31 December)

	2007	2008	2009
Number of vessels	42	42	44
Total displacement ('000 grt)	19.5	19.5	23.3

Source: IHS Fairplay, *World Fleet Statistics*.

International Sea-borne Freight Traffic
(Port of Conakry, '000 metric tons)

	2008	2009	2010
Goods loaded	4,173	3,409	3,759
Goods unloaded	2,740	2,539	3,118

CIVIL AVIATION
(traffic on scheduled services)

	1997	1998	1999
Kilometres flown (million)	1	1	1
Passengers carried ('000)	36	36	59
Passenger-km (million)	55	55	94
Total ton-km (million)	6	6	10

Source: UN, *Statistical Yearbook*.

Passengers carried (Conakry-Gbèssia airport, '000): 258 in 2007; 301 in 2008; 248 in 2009.

Freight carried (Conakry-Gbèssia airport, metric tons): 4,954 in 2007; 4,437 in 2008; 3,020 in 2009.

Tourism

FOREIGN VISITOR ARRIVALS*

Country of origin	2005	2006	2007
Belgium	1,126	970	685
Canada	1,135	1,023	798
China, People's Repub.	1,575	1,696	1,874
Côte d'Ivoire	2,453	1,261	1,103
France	7,984	7,376	4,488
Germany	1,029	1,114	603
Mali	1,295	818	870
Senegal	4,523	3,406	2,171
Sierra Leone	1,328	1,620	802
USA	3,237	380	911
Total (incl. others)†	45,330	46,096	30,194

* Arrivals of non-resident tourists at national borders, by nationality.
† Air arrivals at Conakry-Gbèssia airport.

Receipts from tourism (US $ million, incl. passenger transport, unless otherwise indicated): 4.0 in 2008; 4.9 in 2009; 2.0 in 2010 (excluding passenger transport).

Source: World Tourism Organization.

Communications Media

	2009	2010	2011
Telephones ('000 main lines in use)	22	18	18
Mobile cellular telephones ('000 subscribers)	3,489	4,000	4,500
Internet users ('000)	95	n.a.	n.a.
Broadband subscribers ('000)	n.a.	0.5	0.6

Personal computers: 45,000 (4.9 per 1,000 persons) in 2005.

Source: International Telecommunication Union.

Television receivers ('000 in use): 351 in 2000 (Source: UNESCO, *Statistical Yearbook*).

Radio receivers ('000 in use): 380 in 1999 (Source: UNESCO, *Statistical Yearbook*).

Daily newspapers: 2 titles in 2004 (Source: UNESCO, *Statistical Yearbook*).

Non-daily newspapers: 1 title in 1996 (average circulation 20,000) (Source: UNESCO, *Statistical Yearbook*).

Education

(2009/10 unless otherwise indicated)

	Institutions*	Teachers	Students ('000) Males	Females	Total
Pre-primary	202	3,599	61.7	59.0	120.7
Primary	5,765	34,451	802.9	650.5	1,453.4
Secondary†	557	17,564	357.1	203.4	560.5
General	n.a.	16,988	361.1	212.0	573.1
Tertiary‡	7	2,163	60.6	19.6	80.2

* 1996/97.

† 2008/09.

‡ 2007/08.

Source: mainly UNESCO Institute for Statistics.

Pupil-teacher ratio (primary education, UNESCO estimate): 42.2 in 2009/10 (Source: UNESCO Institute for Statistics).

Adult literacy rate (UNESCO estimates): 41.0% (males 52.0%; females 30.0%) in 2010 (Source: UNESCO Institute for Statistics).

Directory

The Constitution

Following the death of President Gen. Lansana Conté in December 2008 and the assumption of power by the Conseil National pour la Démocratie et le Développement, the Constitution of the Third Republic of Guinea was suspended. On 7 May 2010 Interim President Gen. Sékouba Konaté approved the adoption of a new Constitution, the main provisions of which are summarized below.

The Constitution defines the clear separation of the powers of the executive, the legislature and the judiciary. The President of the Republic, who is Head of State, must be elected by an absolute majority of the votes cast, and a second round of voting is held should no candidate obtain such a majority at a first round. The duration of the presidential mandate is five years, renewable only once, and elections are by universal adult suffrage. A President may not serve more than two terms. Any candidate for the presidency must be more than 35 years old. The President appoints a Prime Minister, who is Head of Government, and proposes the structure and composition of the Government for approval by the President. Legislative power is vested in the Assemblée nationale. The legislature is elected, by universal suffrage, with a five-year mandate.

The Government

HEAD OF STATE

President and Minister of National Defence: ALPHA CONDÉ (inaugurated 21 December 2010).

COUNCIL OF MINISTERS

(September 2012)

Prime Minister: MOHAMED SAÏD FOFANA.

Minister of State, in charge of Public Works and Transport: OUSMANE BAH.

Minister of State, in charge of Energy and the Environment: PAPA KOLY KOUROUMA.

Minister of State, in charge of Security and Civil Protection: Gen. MAMADOUBA TOTO CAMARA.

Minister of the Economy and Finance: KERFALA YANSANÉ.

Minister of Foreign Affairs and Guineans Abroad: EDOUARD GNAKOÏ LAMAHET.

Minister of Justice and Keeper of the Seals: CHRISTIAN SOW.

Minister of Information: DIRIS DIANÉ DORÉ.

Minister of Mines and Geology: MOHAMED LAMINE FOFANA.

Minister of Telecommunications and ICT: HOYÉ GUILAVOGUI.

Minister of the Promotion of Women and Children: NANTÉNIN CHÉRIF KONATÉ.

Minister of Urban Development, Housing and Construction: Gen. MATHURIN BANGO.

Minister of Youth and Youth Employment: SANOUSSI BANTAMA SOW.

Minister of Sport: ABOUBACAR TITI CAMARA.

Minister of Literacy and the Promotion of National Languages: BAMBA CAMARA.

Minister of Industry and Small and Medium-sized Enterprises: RAMATOULAYE BAH.

Minister of Tourism, Hotels and Handicrafts: MARIAMA BALDÉ.

Minister of Stockbreeding: Gen. MAMADOU KORKA DIALLO.

Minister of Employment, Technical Education and Vocational Training: DAMANTANG ALBERT CAMARA.

Minister of Labour and the Civil Service: FATOUMATA TOUNKARA.

Minister of Territorial Decentralization and Political Affairs: ALASSANE CONDÉ.

Minister of Agriculture: JEAN-MARC TELLIANO.

Minister of Commerce: MOHAMED DORVAL DOUMBOUYA.

Minister of Higher Education and Scientific Research: MORIKÉ DAMARO CAMARA.

Minister of Culture and Heritage: AHMED TIDIANE CISSÉ.

Minister of Health and Public Hygiene: Dr NAMAN KÉITA.

Minister of Planning: (vacant).

Minister of International Co-operation: KOUTOUBOU MOUSTAPHA SANOH.

Minister of Auditing and Economic and Financial Control: (vacant).

Minister of Pre-university Education: IBRAHIMA KOUROUMA.

Minister of Fisheries and Aquaculture: MOUSSA CONDÉ.

Minister-delegate, in charge of Transport: TIDIANE TRAORÉ.

Minister-delegate, in charge of the Environment: SARAMADY TOURÉ.

Minister-delegate for the Budget: MOHAMED DIARÉ.

Minister-delegate for the Promotion of Women and Children and Social Affairs: DIAKA DIAKITÉ.

Minister-delegate, in charge of Guineans Abroad: ROUGUI BARRY.

Minister-delegate for National Defence: Commdr ABDOUL KABÈLÈ CAMARA.

Minister-delegate to the Minister of Security and Civil Protection, in charge of the Reform of Security Services: MOURAMANI CISSÉ.

MINISTRIES

Office of the President: BP 1000, Boulbinet, Conakry; tel. 30-41-10-16; fax 30-41-16-73.

Office of the Prime Minister: BP 5141, Conakry; tel. 30-41-51-19; fax 30-41-52-82.

Office of the Secretary-General at the Presidency: Conakry.

Ministry of Agriculture: face à la Cité du Port, BP 576, Conakry; tel. 30-41-11-81; fax 30-41-11-69; e-mail dourasano@hotmail.com.

Ministry of Auditing and Economic and Financial Control: Conakry.

Ministry of Commerce: Conakry.

Ministry of Culture and Heritage: Conakry.

Ministry of Decentralization and Local Development: Conakry.

Ministry of the Economy and Finance: Boulbinet, BP 221, Conakry; tel. 30-45-17-95; fax 30-41-30-59.

Ministry of Employment, Technical Education and Vocational Training: Conakry.

Ministry of Energy and the Environment: route du Niger, Coléah, Conakry; tel. 60-22-50-54 (mobile).

Ministry of Fisheries and Aquaculture: face à la Cité du Port, BP 307, Conakry; tel. 30-41-12-58; fax 30-41-43-10; e-mail minipaq.jpl@eti-bull.net; internet www.fis.com/guinea.

Ministry of Foreign Affairs and Guineans Abroad: face au Port, ex-Primature, BP 2519, Conakry; tel. 30-45-12-70; fax 30-41-16-21; internet www.mae.gov.gn.

Ministry of Health and Public Hygiene: blvd du Commerce, BP 585, Conakry; tel. 30-41-20-32; fax 30-41-41-38.

Ministry of Higher Education and Scientific Research: face à la Cathédrale Sainte-Marie, BP 964, Conakry; tel. 30-45-12-17; fax 30-41-20-12.

Ministry of Industry and Small and Medium-sized Enterprises: Conakry.

Ministry of Information: Conakry.

Ministry of International Co-operation: Conakry.

Ministry of Justice: face à l'Immeuble 'La Paternelle', Almamya, Conakry; tel. 30-41-29-60.

Ministry of Labour and the Civil Service: Boulbinet, Conakry; tel. 30-45-20-01.

Ministry of Literacy and the Promotion of National Languages: Conakry.

Ministry of Mines and Geology: BP 295, Conakry; tel. 30-41-38-33; fax 30-41-49-13.

Ministry of National Defence: Camp Samory-Touré, Conakry; tel. 30-41-11-54.

Ministry of Planning: BP 221, Conakry; tel. 30-44-37-15; fax 30-41-43-50.

Ministry of Pre-university Education: Boulbinet, BP 2201, Conakry; tel. 30-45-19-17.

Ministry of the Promotion of Women and Children: Corniche-Ouest, face au Terminal Conteneurs du Port de Conakry, BP 527, Conakry; tel. 30-45-45-39; fax 30-41-46-60.

Ministry of Public Works and Transport: BP 715, Conakry; tel. 30-41-36-39; fax 30-41-35-77.

Ministry of Security and Civil Protection: Coléah-Domino, Conakry; tel. 30-41-45-50.

Ministry of Sport: Conakry.

Ministry of Stockbreeding: Conakry.

Ministry of Telecommunications and ICT: BP 3000, Conakry; tel. 30-43-17-81; fax 30-45-18-96.

Ministry of Territorial Decentralization and Political Affairs: face aux Jardins du 2 Octobre, Tombo, BP 2201, Conakry; tel. 30-41-15-10; fax 30-45-45-07.

Ministry of Tourism, Hotels and Handicrafts: BP 1304, Conakry; tel. 30-44-26-06; fax 30-44-49-90.

Ministry of Urban Development, Housing and Construction: Conakry.

Ministry of Youth and Youth Employment: ave du Port Secrétariat, BP 262, Conakry; tel. 30-41-19-59; fax 30-41-19-26.

President and Legislature

PRESIDENT

Presidential Election, First Round, 27 June 2010

Candidate	% of votes
Cellou Dalein Diallo (UFDG)	43.69
Alpha Condé (RPG)	18.25
Sidya Touré (UFR)	13.02
Lansana Kouyaté (PEDN)	7.04
Papa Koly Kouroumah (RDR)	5.74
Ibrahima Abe Sylla (NGR)	3.23
Jean-Marc Telliano (RDIG)	2.33
Others*	6.70
Total	100.00

* There were 17 other candidates.

Presidential Election, Second Round, 7 November 2010

Candidate	Votes	% of votes
Alpha Condé (RPG)	1,474,973	52.52
Cellou Dalein Diallo (UFDG)	1,333,666	47.48
Total	2,808,639	100.00

LEGISLATURE

Assemblée nationale

Palais du Peuple, BP 414, Conakry; tel. 30-41-28-04; fax 30-45-17-00; e-mail s.general@assemblee.gov.gn; internet www.assemblee.gov.gn.

Speaker: ABOUBACAR SOMPARÉ.

General Election, 30 June 2002

Party	% of votes	Seats
Parti de l'Unité et du Progrès (PUP)	61.57	85
Union pour le Progrès et le Renouveau (UPR)	26.63	20
Union pour le Progrès de la Guinée (UPG)	4.11	3
Parti Démocratique de Guinée—Rassemblement Démocratique Africain (PDG—RDA)	3.40	3
Alliance Nationale pour le Progrès (ANP)	1.98	2
Union pour le Progrès National—Parti pour l'Unité et le Développement (UPN—PUD)	0.69	1
Others	1.61	—
Total	100.00	114*

* Comprising 76 seats allocated by proportional representation from national party lists and 38 seats filled by voting in single-member constituencies, all of which were won by the PUP.

Election Commission

Commission Électorale Nationale Indépendante (CENI): Villa 17, Cité des Nations, Conakry; tel. 64-24-22-06; e-mail bensekou@ceniguinee.org; internet www.ceniguinee.org; f. 2005; comprises seven representatives of the parliamentary majority, seven representatives of the parliamentary opposition, five representatives of the state administration and three representatives of civil society; Pres. (vacant).

Advisory Council

Conseil Économique et Social: Immeuble FAWAZ, Corniche Sud, Coléaah, Matam, BP 2947, Conakry; tel. 30-45-31-23; fax 30-45-31-24; e-mail ces@sotelgui.net.gn; f. 1997; 45 mems; Pres. MICHEL KAMANO; Sec.-Gen. MAMADOU BOBO CAMARA.

Political Organizations

There were 65 officially registered parties in mid-2010.

Alliance Nationale pour le Progrès (ANP): Conakry; Leader Dr SAGNO MOUSSA.

Front Uni pour la Démocratie et le Changement (FUDEC): Ratoma, Conakry; tel. 60-22-76-71 (mobile); fax 66-87-28-62 (mobile); internet www.fudec.org; f. 2009; Pres. FRANÇOIS LONSÉNY FALL.

Nouvelle Génération pour la République (NGR): Kissosso; tel. 64-29-05-72; Leader IBRAHIMA ABE SYLLA.

Parti Démocratique de Guinée—Rassemblement Démocratique Africain (PDG—RDA): Conakry; f. 1946; revived 1992; Sec.-Gen. El Hadj ISMAËL MOHAMED GASSIM GHUSSEIN.

Parti Dyama: Conakry; e-mail mansourkaba@yahoo.fr; internet www.guinea-dyama.com; moderate Islamist party; Pres. MOHAMED MANSOUR KABA.

Parti Écologiste de Guinée (PEG—Les Verts): BP 3018, Quartier Boulbinet, 5e blvd, angle 2e ave, Commune de Kaloum, Conakry; tel. 30-44-37-01; Leader OUMAR SYLLA.

Parti de l'Éspoir pour le Développement National (PEDN): Commune Ratoma, BP 1403, Conakry; tel. 65-55-00-00; e-mail info@pednespoirl.org; internet pednespoirl.org; Pres. LANSANA KOUYATÉ.

Parti du Peuple de Guinée (PPG): BP 1147, Conakry; socialist; boycotted presidential election in 2003, following the Supreme Court's rejection of its nominated candidate; Leader CHARLES-PASCAL TOLNO.

Parti de l'Unité et du Progrès (PUP): Camayenne, Conakry; internet www.pupguinee.org; Pres. (vacant); Sec.-Gen. El Hadj Dr SÉKOU KONATÉ.

Rassemblement pour la Défense de la République (RDR): Leader PAPA KOLY KOUROUMA.

Rassemblement pour le Développement Intégré de la Guinée (RDIG): Leader JEAN-MARC TELLIANO.

Rassemblement du Peuple de Guinée (RPG): Conakry; e-mail admin@rpgguinee.org; internet www.rpgguinee.org; f. 1980 as the Rassemblement des Patriotes Guinéens; socialist; Pres. ALPHA CONDÉ.

Union Démocratique de Guinée (UDG): Dixinn Centre, Conakry; tel. 60-52-40-26; f. 2009; Leader El Hadj MAMADOU SYLLA.

Union des Forces Démocratiques (UFD): BP 3050, Conakry; tel. 30-34-50-20; e-mail ufdconakry@yahoo.fr; internet www.ufd-conakry.com; Pres. MAMADOU BAADIKKO BAH.

Union des Forces Démocratiques de Guinée (UFDG): BP 3036, Conakry; e-mail baggelmalal@yahoo.fr; internet www.ufdg.org; f. 2002 by faction of UPR in protest at that party's participation in elections to Assemblée nationale; Pres. CELLOU DALEIN DIALLO.

Union des Forces Républicaines (UFR): Immeuble 'Le Golfe', 4e étage, BP 6080, Conakry; tel. 64-30-47-50 (mobile); fax 30-45-42-31; e-mail ufrguinee@yahoo.fr; internet www.ufrguinee.org; f. 1992; liberal-conservative; Pres. SIDYA TOURÉ; Sec.-Gen. BAKARY G. ZOUMANIGUI.

Union pour le Progrès de la Guinée (UPG): Conakry; Leader JEAN-MARIE DORÉ.

Union pour le Progrès et le Renouveau (UPR): BP 690, Conakry; tel. 30-25-26-01; e-mail basusmane@mirinet.net.gn; internet www.uprguinee.org; f. 1998 by merger of the Parti pour le Renouveau et le Progrès and the Union pour la Nouvelle République; Pres. OUSMANE BAH.

Union pour le Progrès National—Parti pour l'Unité et le Développement (UPN—PUD): Conakry; Leader MAMADOU BHOYE BARRY.

Diplomatic Representation

EMBASSIES IN GUINEA

Algeria: Cité des Nations, Quartiers Kaloum, BP 1004, Conakry; tel. 30-45-15-05; fax 30-41-15-35; Ambassador RABAH FASSIH.

Angola: Conakry; Ambassador EDUARDO RUAS DE JESUS MANUEL.

China, People's Republic: Quartier Donka, Cité Ministérielle, Commune de Dixinn, BP 714, Conakry; tel. 60-25-32-94 (mobile); fax 30-46-95-83; e-mail chinaemb_gn@mfa.gov.cn; internet gn.chineseembassy.org; Ambassador ZHAO LIXING.

Congo, Democratic Republic: Quartier Almamya, ave de la Gare, Commune du Kaloum, BP 880, Conakry; tel. 30-45-15-01.

Côte d'Ivoire: blvd du Commerce, BP 5228, Conakry; tel. 30-45-10-82; fax 30-45-10-79; e-mail acign@ambaci-guinee.org; Ambassador DIARRASSOUBA M. YOUSSOUF.

Cuba: Cité Ministérielle, Quartier Donka, Commune de Dixinn, Conakry; tel. 30-46-95-25; fax 30-46-95-28; e-mail embagcon@sotelgui.net.gn; Ambassador CARLOS GUTIÉRREZ CORRALES.

Egypt: Corniche Sud 2, BP 389, Conakry; tel. 30-46-85-08; fax 30-46-85-07; e-mail ambconakry@hotmail.com; Ambassador BAHAA ELDIN MOHATAR WAHAFI.

France: ave du Commerce, BP 373, Conakry; tel. 30-47-10-00; fax 30-47-10-15; e-mail ambafrance.conakry@diplomatie.gouv.fr; internet www.ambafrance-gn.org; Ambassador BERTRAND COCHERY.

Germany: 2e blvd, Kaloum, BP 540, Conakry; tel. 30-41-15-06; fax 30-45-22-17; e-mail amball@sotelgui.net.gn; internet www.conakry.diplo.de; Ambassador HARTMUT KRAUSSER.

Ghana: Immeuble Ex-Urbaine et la Seine, BP 732, Conakry; tel. 30-44-15-10; Ambassador DOMINIC ABOAGYE.

Guinea-Bissau: Quartier Bellevue, Commune de Dixinn, BP 298, Conakry; Ambassador MALAM CAMARA.

Holy See: c/o Archevêché de Conakry, BP 2016, Conakry; tel. 64-58-49-59; e-mail nunziaturaguinea@gmail.com; Apostolic Nuncio Most Rev. MARTIN KREBS (Titular Archbishop of Taborenta).

Iran: Donka, Cité Ministérielle, Commune de Dixinn, BP 310, Conakry; tel. 30-01-03-19; fax 30-47-81-84; e-mail ambiran@yahoo.com; Ambassador BAKHTIAR ASADZADEH SHEIKHJANI.

Japan: Lanseboundji, Corniche Sud, Commune de Matam, BP 895, Conakry; tel. 30-46-85-10; fax 30-46-85-09; Ambassador NAOTSUGU NAKANO.

Korea, Democratic People's Republic: BP 723, Conakry; Ambassador RI KYONG SON.

Liberia: Cité Ministérielle, Donka, Commune de Dixinn, BP 18, Conakry; tel. 30-42-26-71; Chargé d'affaires a.i. SIAKA FAHNBULLEH.

Libya: Commune de Kaloum, BP 1183, Conakry; tel. 30-41-41-72; Ambassador B. AHMED.

Malaysia: Quartier Mafanco, Corniche Sud, BP 5460, Conakry; tel. 30-22-17-54; e-mail malconakry@kln.gov.my; Ambassador (vacant).

Mali: rue D1–15, Camayenne, Corniche Nord, BP 299, Conakry; tel. 30-46-14-18; fax 30-46-37-03; e-mail ambamaliguinee@yahoo.fr; Ambassador HASSANE BARRY.

Morocco: Cité des Nations, Villa 12, Commune du Kaloum, BP 193, Conakry; tel. 30-41-36-86; fax 30-41-38-16; e-mail sifamgui@biasy.net; Ambassador MAJID HALIM.

Nigeria: Corniche Sud, Quartier de Matam, BP 54, Conakry; tel. 30-46-13-41; fax 30-46-27-75; Ambassador Dr AISHA LARABA ABDULLAHI.

Russia: Matam-Port, km 9, BP 329, Conakry; tel. 30-40-52-22; fax 30-47-84-43; e-mail ambrus@biasy.net; internet www.guinee.mid.ru; Ambassador DMITRII V. MALEV.

Saudi Arabia: Quartier Camayenne, Commune de Dixinn, BP 611, Conakry; tel. 30-46-24-87; fax 30-46-58-84; e-mail gnemb@mofa.gov.sa; Ambassador AMJAD BIN HOSAIN BIN ABDUL HAMEED BDAIWI.

Senegal: bâtiment 142, Coleah, Corniche Che Sud, BP 842, Conakry; tel. 30-44-61-32; fax 30-46-28-34; Ambassador YAKHAM DIOP.

Sierra Leone: Quartier Bellevue, face aux cases présidentielles, Commune de Dixinn, BP 625, Conakry; tel. 30-46-40-84; fax 30-41-23-64; Ambassador ADIKALIE FODAY SUMAH.

South Africa: Coleah, Mossoudougou, Conakry; tel. 30-49-08-75; fax 30-49-08-79; e-mail conakrys@foreign.gov.za; Ambassador (vacant).

Ukraine: Commune de Dixinn, Corniche Nord, Cité Ministérielle, Rue DI 256, BP 1350, Conakry; tel. 62-35-38-01 (mobile); fax 62-35-38-03 (mobile); e-mail ambukra@gmail.com; internet www.mfa.gov.ua/guinea; Ambassador ANDRIY ZAYATS.

United Kingdom: BP 6729, Conakry; tel. 63-35-53-29 (mobile); fax 63-35-90-59 (mobile); e-mail britembconakry@hotmail.com; Ambassador GRAHAM CHARLES TRAYTON STYLES.

USA: Koloma, Ratoma, BP 603, Conakry; tel. 65-10-40-00 (mobile); fax 65-10-42-74 (mobile); e-mail Consularconkr@state.gov; internet conakry.usembassy.gov; Ambassador PATRICIA NEWTON MOLLER.

Judicial System

The Constitution of 7 May 2010 embodies the principle of the independence of the judiciary, and delineates the competencies of each component of the judicial system, including the Supreme Court and the Revenue Court.

Supreme Court

Corniche-Sud, Camayenne, Conakry; tel. 30-41-29-28; Pres. MAMADOU SYLLA

Director of Public Prosecutions: ANTOINE IBRAHIM DIALLO.

Religion

It is estimated that 85% of the population are Muslims and 8% Christians, while 7% follow animist beliefs.

ISLAM

National Islamic League: BP 386, Conakry; tel. 30-41-23-38; f. 1988; Sec.-Gen. (vacant).

CHRISTIANITY

The Roman Catholic Church

Guinea comprises one archdiocese and two dioceses. About 3% of the population are Roman Catholics.

Bishops' Conference

Conférence Episcopale de la Guinée, BP 1006 bis, Conakry; tel. and fax 30-41-32-70; e-mail dhewara@eti.met.gn; Pres. Most Rev. VINCENT COULIBALY (Archbishop of Conakry).

Archbishop of Conakry: Most Rev. VINCENT COULIBALY, Archevêché, BP 2016, Conakry; tel. and fax 30-43-47-04; e-mail conakriensis@yahoo.fr.

The Anglican Communion

Anglicans in Guinea are adherents of the Church of the Province of West Africa, comprising 12 dioceses. The diocese of Guinea was established in 1985 as the first French-speaking diocese in the Province. The Archbishop and Primate of the Province is the Bishop of Koforidua, Ghana.

Bishop of Guinea: Rt Rev. ALBERT D. GÓMEZ, Cathédrale Toussaint, BP 1187, Conakry; tel. 30-45-13-23; e-mail agomezd@yahoo.fr.

BAHÁ'Í FAITH

Assemblée Spirituelle Nationale: BP 2010, Conakry 1; e-mail asngunee@yahoo.fr; Sec. MAMMA TRAORE.

The Press

REGULATORY AUTHORITY

Haute Autorité de la Communication (HAC): en face Primature, BP 2955, Conakry; tel. 30-45-54-82; fax 30-41-23-85; f. 2010; regulates the operations of the press, and of radio and television; regulates political access to the media; nine mems; Pres. MARTINE CONDÉ.

NEWSPAPERS AND PERIODICALS

Le Démocrate: Quartier Ratoma Centre, Commune de Ratoma, BP 2427, Conakry; tel. 60-20-01-01; e-mail mamadoudianb@yahoo.fr; weekly; Dir HASSANE KABA; Editor-in-Chief MAMADOU DIAN BALDÉ.

Le Diplomate: BP 2427, Conakry; tel. and fax 30-41-23-85; f. 2002; weekly; Dir SANOU KERFALLAH CISSÉ.

L'Enquêteur: Conakry; e-mail habib@boubah.com; internet enqueteur.boubah.com; f. 2001; weekly; Editor HABIB YAMBERING DIALLO.

Fonike: BP 341, Conakry; daily; sport and general; state-owned; Dir IBRAHIMA KALIL DIARE.

Horoya (Liberty): BP 191, Conakry; tel. 30-47-71-17; fax 30-45-10-16; e-mail info@horoyaguinee.net; govt daily; Dir OUSMANE CAMARA.

L'Indépendant: Quartier Ratoma Centre, Commune de Ratoma, BP 2427, Conakry; tel. 60-20-01-01; e-mail lindependant@afribone.net.gn; weekly; also *L'Indépendant Plus*; Publr ABOUBACAR SYLLA; Dir HASSANE KABA; Editor-in-Chief MAMADOU DIAN BALDÉ.

Journal Officiel de Guinée: BP 156, Conakry; fortnightly; organ of the Govt.

La Lance: Immeuble Baldé Zaïre, BP 4968, Conakry; tel. and fax 30-41-23-85; weekly; general information; Dir SOULEYMANE E. DIALLO.

Le Lynx: Immeuble Baldé Zaïre Sandervalia, BP 4968, Conakry; tel. 30-41-23-85; fax 30-45-36-96; e-mail le-lynx@afribone.net.gn; internet www.afribone.net.gn/lynx; f. 1992; weekly; satirical; Editor SOULEYMANE DIALLO.

La Nouvelle Tribune: blvd Diallo Tally, entre 5e et 6e ave, BP 35, Conakry; tel. 30-22-33-02; e-mail abdcond@yahoo.fr; internet www.nouvelle-tribune.com; weekly, Tuesdays; independent; general information and analysis; Dir of Publ. and Editing ABDOULAYE CONDÉ.

L'Observateur: Immeuble Baldé, Conakry; tel. 30-40-05-24; e-mail ibrahimanouhou@yahoo.fr; internet www.observateur-guinee.com; weekly; independent; Dir NOUHOU BALDÉ.

L'Oeil du Peuple: BP 3064, Conakry; tel. 30-67-23-78; weekly; independent; Dir of Publishing ISMAËL BANGOURA.

Sanakou: Labé, Foutah Djallon, Moyenne-Guinée; tel. 30-51-13-19; e-mail sanakoulabe@yahoo.fr; f. 2000; monthly; general news; Publr IDRISSA SAMPIRING DIALLO; Editor-in-Chief YAMOUSSA SOUMAH; circ. 1,000.

Le Standard: Conakry; Dir of Publication HASSANE KABA.

3-P Plus (Parole-Plume-Papier) Magazine: 7e ave Bis Almamyah, BP 5122, Conakry; tel. 30-45-22-32; fax 30-45-29-31; e-mail 3p-plus@mirinet.net.gn; internet www.mirinet.net.gn/3p_plus; f. 1995; journal of arts and letters; supplements *Le Cahier de l'Economie* and *Mag-Plus: Le Magazine de la Culture*; monthly; Pres. MOHAMED SALIFOU KEÏTA; Editor-in-Chief SAMBA TOURÉ.

NEWS AGENCY

Agence Guinéenne de Presse: BP 1535, Conakry; tel. 30-41-14-34; e-mail info@agpguinee.net; f. 1960; Man. Dir NÈTÈ SOVOGUI.

PRESS ASSOCIATION

Association Guinéenne des Editeurs de la Presse Indépendante (AGEPI): Conakry; f. 1991; an assn of independent newspaper publishers; Chair. HASSANE KABA.

Publishers

Les Classiques Guinéens (SEDIS sarl): 545 rue KA020, Mauquepas, BP 3697, Conakry; tel. 11-21-18-57; fax 13-40-92-62; e-mail cheick.sedis@mirinet.net.gn; f. 1999; art, history, youth literature; Dir CHEICK ABDOUL KABA.

Editions du Ministère de l'Education Nationale: Direction nationale de la recherche scientifique et technique, BP 561, Conakry; tel. 30-43-02-66; e-mail dnrst@mirinet.net.gn; f. 1959; general and educational; Deputy Dir Dr TAMBA TAGBINO.

Editions Ganndal (Knowledge): BP 542, Conakry; tel. and fax 30-46-35-07; e-mail ganndal@mirinet.net.gn; f. 1992; educational, youth and children, general literature and books in Pular; Dir MAMADOU ALIOU SOW.

Société Africaine d'Edition et de Communication (SAEC): Belle-Vue, Commune de Dixinn, BP 6826, Conakry; tel. 30-29-71-41; e-mail dtniane@yahoo.fr; social sciences, reference, literary fiction; Editorial Assistant OUMAR TALL.

Broadcasting and Communications

TELECOMMUNICATIONS

In 2011 there were five providers of mobile cellular telephone services and one provider of fixed-line telephone services in Guinea.

Regulatory Authority

Autorité de Régulation des Postes et des Télécommunications (ARPT): BP 1500, Conakry; e-mail contact@arptguinee.org; internet www.arptguinee.org; f. 2008; Dir-Gen. DIABY MOUSTAPHA MAMY.

Service Providers

Areeba Guinée: Quartier Almamya, Commune de Kaloum, BP 3237, Conakry; tel. 64-22-22-22 (mobile); fax 64-33-33-33 (mobile); internet www.areeba.com.gn; f. 2005; mobile cellular telephone provider; 75% owned by MTN (South Africa); Dir-Gen. P. J. PHIKE.

Cellcom Guinée: Immeuble WAQF-BID, Almamya, C/Kaloum, BP 6567, Conakry; tel. 65-10-01-00 (mobile); fax 65-10-01-01 (mobile); e-mail info@gn.cellcomgsm.com; internet www.gn.cellcomgsm.com; f. 2008; Dir-Gen. HANOCH DOMBEK.

Intercel: Quartier Coleah Larseboundji, près du pont du 8 novembre, Immeuble le Golfe, BP 965, Conakry; tel. 30-45-57-44; fax 30-40-92-92; e-mail info@gn.intercel.net; mobile cellular telephone operator; fmrly Telecel Guinée; acquired by Sudatel (Sudan) in 2011; Dir-Gen. DJIBRIL TOBE.

Orange Guinée: Conakry; tel. 62-77-00-00 (mobile); internet www.orange-guinee.com; f. 2007; 85% owned by the Groupe Sonatel (Senegal); Dir-Gen. ALASSANE DIÈNE.

Société des Télécommunications de Guinée (SOTELGUI): 4e blvd, BP 2066, Conakry; tel. 30-45-27-50; fax 30-45-03-06; e-mail vickycu@sotelgui.net.gn; internet www.sotelgui.net; f. 1992; state-owned; provides fixed-line services; 12,000 landline subscribers and 549,713 subscribers (2010); Dir-Gen. MOUSSA KEITA.

Lagui: Conakry; wholly owned subsidiary of SOTELGUI providing mobile telephone services.

BROADCASTING

Regulatory Authority

Haute Autorité de la Communication (HAC): see The Press.

Radio

Espace FM: Quartier Matoto, Immeuble Mouna, BP 256, Conakry; tel. 64-20-20-92; e-mail services@espacefmguinee.info; internet espacefmguinee.info.

Milo FM: BP 215, Kankan; tel. 30-72-00-82; e-mail info@milo-fm.com; internet www.milo-fm.com; Dir-Gen. LANCINÉ KABA.

Radiodiffusion-Télévision Guinéenne (RTG): BP 391, Conakry; tel. 30-44-22-01; fax 30-41-50-01; broadcasts in French, English, Créole-English, Portuguese, Arabic and local languages; Dir-Gen. IBRAHIMA AHMED BARRY; Dir of Radio ISSA CONDÉ.

Radio Rurale de Guinée: BP 391, Conakry; tel. 30-42-11-09; fax 30-41-47-97; e-mail ruralgui@mirinet.net.gn; network of rural radio stations.

Television

Radiodiffusion-Télévision Guinéenne (RTG): see Radio; transmissions in French and local languages; one channel; f. 1977.

Finance

(cap. = capital; res = reserves; dep. = deposits; m. = million; brs = branches; amounts in Guinean francs)

BANKING

Central Bank

Banque Centrale de la République de Guinée (BCRG): 12 blvd du Commerce, BP 692, Kaloum, Conakry; tel. 30-41-26-51; fax 30-41-48-98; e-mail gouv.bcrg@eti-bull.net; internet www.bcrg-guinee.org; f. 1960; bank of issue; cap. 50,000m., res 20,881m., dep. 7,171,432m. (Dec. 2009); Gov. LOUCENY NABÉ; First Deputy Gov. YÉRO BALDÉ BALDÉ.

Commercial Banks

Banque Internationale pour le Commerce et l'Industrie de la Guinée (BICIGUI): ave de la République, BP 1484, Conakry; tel. 30-41-45-15; fax 30-41-39-62; e-mail dg.bicigui@africa.bnpparibas.com; internet www.bicigui.com; f. 1985; 30.8% owned by BNP Paribas BDDI Participations (France), 15.1% state-owned; cap. and res 37,989.3m., total assets 315,689.5m. (Dec. 2003); Pres. IBRAHIMA SOUMAH; Dir-Gen. MANGA FODÉ TOURÉ; 20 brs.

Banque Populaire Maroco-Guinéenne (BPMG): Immeuble BPMG, blvd du Commerce, Kaloum, BP 4400, Conakry 01; tel. 30-41-36-93; fax 30-41-32-61; e-mail bpmg@sotelgui.net.gn; f. 1991; 55% owned by Crédit Populaire du Maroc, 42% state-owned; cap. and res 9,936m., total assets 65,549m. (Dec. 2004); Pres. EMMANUEL GNAN; Dir-Gen. AHMED IRAQUI HOUSSAINI; 3 brs.

Ecobank Guinée: Immeuble Al Iman, ave de la République, BP 5687, Conakry; tel. 30-45-57-77; fax 30-45-42-41; e-mail ecobankgn@ecobank.com; internet www.ecobank.com; f. 1999; wholly owned by Ecobank Transnational Inc. (Togo); cap. 25,000.0m., res 27,667.3m., dep. 975,266.4m. (Dec. 2009); Pres. SAIKOU BARRY; Man. Dir MAMADOU MOUSTAPHA FALL; 9 brs.

First American Bank of Guinea: blvd du Commerce, angle 9e ave, BP 4540, Conakry; tel. 30-41-34-32; fax 30-41-35-29; f. 1994; jtly owned by Mitan Capital Ltd (Grand Cayman) and El Hadj Haidara Abdourahmane Chérif (Mali).

International Commercial Bank SA: Ex-cité Chemin de Fer, Immeuble Mamou, BP 3547, Conakry; tel. 30-41-25-90; fax 30-41-54-50; e-mail enquiry@icbank-guinea.com; internet www.icbank-guinea.com; f. 1997; total assets 19.6m. (Dec. 1999); Pres. JOSÉPHINE PREMLA; Man. Dir HAMZA BIN ALIAS; 3 brs.

Société Générale de Banques en Guinée (SGBG): Immeuble Boffa, Cité du Chemin de Fer, BP 1514, Conakry; tel. 30-45-60-00; fax 30-41-25-65; e-mail contact@sgbg.net.gn; internet www.sgbg.net; f. 1985; 53% owned by Société Générale (France); cap. and res 13,074m., total assets 228,196m. (Dec. 2003); Pres. GÉRALD LACAZE; Dir-Gen. JEAN-PHILIPPE EQUILBECQ; 8 brs.

Union Internationale de Banques en Guinée (UIBG): 6e ave de la République, angle 5e blvd, BP 324, Conakry; tel. 62-35-90-90 (mobile); fax 30-97-26-30; e-mail info-gn@orabank.net; f. 1988; fmrly the Union Internationale de Banques en Guinée, present name adopted in 2011; 54.0% owned by Oragroup SA (Togo), 14.3% owned by Orabank Tchad; cap. 25,000m., res –1,139.1m., dep. 259,713.9m. (Dec. 2009); Pres. ALPHA AMADOU DIALLO; Dir-Gen. MAMADOU SENE.

Islamic Bank

Banque Islamique de Guinée: Immeuble Nafaya, 6 ave de la République, BP 1247, Conakry; tel. 30-41-21-08; fax 30-41-50-71; e-mail info@big-banque.com; internet www.big-banque.com; f. 1983; 50.01% owned by Dar al-Maal al-Islami Trust (Switzerland), 49.99% owned by Islamic Development Bank (Saudi Arabia); cap. and res 2,368.5m., total assets 26,932.1m. (Dec. 2003); Pres. ADERRAOUF BENESSAIAH; Dir-Gen. LYAGOUBI ABDOUILAH.

INSURANCE

Gras Savoye Guinée: 4e ave, angle 4e blvd, Quartier Boulbinet, Commune de Kaloum, BP 6441, Conakry; tel. 30-45-58-43; fax 30-45-58-42; e-mail gsguinee@sotelgui.net.gn; affiliated to Gras Savoye (France); Man. CHÉRIF BAH.

International Insurance Co: Conakry; tel. 62-03-81-05; f. 2007; Dir-Gen. KABINET KONDÉ.

Société Guinéenne d'Assurance Mutuelle (SOGAM): Immeuble Sonia, BP 434, Conakry; tel. 30-44-50-58; fax 30-41-25-57; f. 1990; Chair. Dr M. K. BAH; Man. Dir P. I. NDAO.

Union Guinéenne d'Assurances et de Réassurances (UGAR): pl. des Martyrs, BP 179, Conakry; tel. 30-41-48-41; fax 30-41-17-11; e-mail ugar@ugar.com.gn; f. 1989; 40% owned by AXA (France), 35% state-owned; cap. 2,000m.; Man. Dir RAPHAËL Y. TOURÉ.

Trade and Industry

GOVERNMENT AGENCIES

Agence de Promotion des Investissements Privés-Guichet Unique (APIP–GUINEE): BP 2024, Conakry; tel. 30-41-49-85; fax 30-41-39-90; e-mail dg@apiguinee.org; internet www.apiguinee.org; f. 1992; promotes private investment; Dir-Gen. MOHAMED LAMINE BAYO.

Centre de Promotion et de Développement Miniers (CPDM): BP 295, Conakry; tel. 30-41-15-44; fax 30-41-49-13; e-mail cpdm@mirinet.net.gn; f. 1995; promotes investment and co-ordinates devt strategy in mining sector; Dir MOCIRÉ SYLLA.

Entreprise Nationale Import-Export (IMPORTEX): BP 152, Conakry; tel. 30-44-28-13; state-owned import and export agency; Dir MAMADOU BOBO DIENG.

Office de Développement de la Pêche Artisanale et de l'Aquaculture en Guinée (ODEPAG): 6 ave de la République, BP 1581, Conakry; tel. 30-44-19-48; devt of fisheries and fish-processing.

DEVELOPMENT ORGANIZATIONS

Agence Française de Développement (AFD): 5e ave, KA022, BP 283, Conakry; tel. 30-41-25-69; fax 30-41-28-74; e-mail afdconakry@groupe-afd.org; internet www.afd.fr; Country Dir PHILIPPE MICHAUD.

France Volontaires: BP 570, Conakry; tel. 30-35-08-60; internet www.france-volontaires.org; f. 1987; name changed as above in 2009; devt and research projects; Nat. Delegate FRANCK DAGOIS.

Service de Coopération et d'Action Culturelle: BP 373, Conakry; tel. 30-41-23-45; fax 30-41-43-56; administers bilateral aid; Dir in Guinea TOBIE NATHAN.

CHAMBERS OF COMMERCE

Chambre de Commerce, d'Industrie et de l'Artisanat de la Guinée (CCIAG): Quartier Tombo, Commune de Kaloum, BP 545, Conakry; tel. 60-26-02-31; fax 30-47-70-58; e-mail cciag@sotelgui.net.gn; internet www.cciag.org; f. 1985; Pres. MORLAYE DIALLO.

Chambre Economique de Guinée: BP 609, Conakry.

TRADE AND EMPLOYERS' ASSOCIATIONS

Association des Commerçants de Guinée: BP 2468, Conakry; tel. 64-21-92-42; fax 30-45-31-66; e-mail thouca_acic@yahoo.fr; f. 1976; Pres. THIERNO OUMAR CAMARA.

Association des Femmes Entrepreneurs de Guinée (AFEG): BP 104, Kaloum, Conakry; tel. 67-28-02-95; e-mail afeguine@yahoo.fr; f. 1987; Pres. HADJA RAMATOULAYE SOW.

Conseil National du Patronat Guinéen (CNPG): Dixinn Bora, BP 6403, Conakry; tel. and fax 30-41-24-70; e-mail msylla@leland-gn.org; f. 1992; Pres. El Hadj MAMADOU SYLLA.

Fédération Patronale de l'Agriculture et de l'Elevage (FEPAE): BP 5684, Conakry; tel. 30-22-95-56; fax 30-41-54-36; Pres. El Hadj MAMADOU SYLLA; Sec.-Gen. MAMADY CAMARA.

UTILITIES

Electricity

Electricité de Guinée (EDG): BP 1463, Conakry; tel. 30-45-18-56; fax 30-45-18-53; e-mail di.sogel@biasy.net; f. 2001 to replace Société Guinéenne d'Electricité; majority state-owned; production, transport and distribution of electricity; Dir-Gen. SÉKOU SANFINA DIAKITÉ.

Water

Service National d'Aménagement des Points d'Eau (SNAPE): BP 2064, Conakry; tel. 30-41-18-93; fax 30-41-50-58; e-mail snape@mirinet.net.gn; supplies water in rural areas; Dir-Gen. IBRAHIMA SORY SANKON.

Société Nationale des Eaux de Guinée (SONEG): Belle-vue, BP 150, Conakry; tel. 30-45-44-77; e-mail oaubot@seg.org.gn; f. 1988; national water co; Dir-Gen. Dr OUSMANE ARIBOT; Sec.-Gen. MAMADOU DIOP.

MAJOR COMPANIES

The following are among the largest companies in terms either of capital investment or employment.

Alumina Company of Guinea (Friguia/ACG): BP 554, Conakry; f. 1999 to control Friguia (f. 1957); majority owned by Russian Aluminium (RUSAL), 15% state-owned; mining of bauxite and production of alumina; technical and management agreement with Alcoa (USA); Dir-Gen. ANATOLII PANCHENKO.

AngloGold Ashanti Guinea (SAG): BP 1006, Conakry; tel. 30-41-58-09; fax 30-41-15-80; e-mail ashanti@sotelgui.net.gn; f. 1985 as Société Aurifère de Guinée; name changed 1997; cap. US $20m.; sales US $67.3m. (1999); 85% owned by AngloGold Ashanti Goldfields (Ghana/South Africa); gold prospecting and exploitation at Siguiri; Man. Dir TERRY MULPETER; 1,978 employees (2005).

AREDOR: BP 1218, Conakry; tel. 30-44-31-12; f. 1981 as Association pour la recherche et l'exploitation de diamants et de l'or; cap. US $8m.; 85% owned by Trivalence Mining Corpn (Canada); diamond mining.

Ciments de Guinée: BP 3621, Conakry; tel. 30-41-45-12; fax 30-41-45-13; e-mail webmaster-trading@holcim.com; one cement plant (Sinfonia); annual production 400,000 metric tons (2000); 58.7% owned by Holcim (Switzerland), 38.7% state owned; cap. 6,393m. FG; sales US $25m. (2000); Man. Dir MOHAMED ALI BENSAID.

Compagnie des Bauxites de Guinée: BP 523, Conakry; tel. 30-44-18-01; fax 30-42-11-91; internet www.cbg-guinee.com; f. 1964; cap. US $2m.; 51% owned by Halco (Mining) Inc (a consortium of interests from USA, Canada, France, Germany and Australia), 49% state-owned; bauxite mining at Boké; Pres. JOHN L. PERVOLA; Dir-Gen. KÉMOKO TOURÉ; 3,000 employees (2001).

Compagnie des Bauxites de Kindia (CBK): BP 613, Conakry; tel. 30-41-38-28; fax 30-41-38-29; e-mail sbk@mirinet.net.gn; internet www.rusal.com/business/geography/alumina/kindii; f. 1969 as Office des Bauxites de Kindia, a jt venture with the USSR; production began 1974; name changed 1992; managed by Russian Aluminium (RUSAL) for 25-year (2001–26) contract; bauxite mining at Debélé; Man. Dir ANATOLII PANCHENKO; 1,750 employees (2001).

Compagnie des Eaux Minérales de Guinée (CEG): BP 3023 Conakry; tel. 30-46-16-19; fax 30-41-28-66; e-mail cegcoyah@leland-gn.org; f. 1987; mineral water bottling plant.

Compagnie Shell de Guinée: BP 312, Conakry; tel. 30-46-37-37; fax 30-46-49-12; e-mail corporate@csgcky.simis.com; distribution of petroleum products; owned by Royal Dutch/Shell (Netherlands/United Kingdom); Dir-Gen. SAMBA SEYE.

Guinea Alumina Corpn: Immeuble Mamou, 2ème étage, BP 5090, Conakry; tel. 63-33-33-93; internet www.guineaalumina.com; Pres. KARIM KARJIAN; Dir-Gen. EDDY KENTER (acting).

Mobil Oil Guinea: autoroute Fidel Castro, Commune de Matam, BP 305, Conakry; tel. 30-46-52-74; fax 30-40-92-06; petroleum and gas exploration and distribution; owned by ExxonMobil Corpn (USA); Gen. Man. AYITE AMOUZOU KODJO.

La Nouvelle Soguipêche: Port de pêche, BP 1414, Conakry; tel. 30-44-35-85; f. 1999 to replace Société Guinéenne de Pêche; fishing and processing of fish products.

Société d'Aquaculture de Koba (SAKOBA): BP 4834, Conakry; tel. 30-44-24-75; fax 30-41-46-43; f. 1991; 49% state-owned, 51% owned by private Guinean and French interests; prawn-farming venture; 700 employees.

Société Arabe Libyo-Guinéenne pour le Développement Agricole et Agro-industrielle (SALGUIDIA): BP 622, Conakry; tel. 30-44-46-54; fax 30-41-13-09; e-mail salgdia@sotelgui.net.gn; cap. 15m. FG; f. 1997; fmrly Société Industrielle des Fruits Africains; fruit growing (pineapples, grapefruit, oranges and mangoes); fruit canning and juice extracting; marketing; Pres. FALILOU BARRY; Man. Dir SHARIF TELLISSY.

Société des Bauxites de Dabola-Tougué (SBDT): BP 2859, Conakry; tel. and fax 30-41-47-21; f. 1992; owned jtly by Govts of Guinea and Iran; bauxite mining at Dabola and Tougué; Dir-Gen. FOFANA FATOUMATA THYIWTO DIALLO.

Société Guinéenne des Hydrocarbures (SGH): BP 892, Conakry; tel. 30-46-12-56; f. 1980; 50% state-owned; research into and exploitation of offshore petroleum reserves; Gen. Man. F. WALSH.

Société Guinéenne de Lubrifiants et d'Emballages (SOGUILUBE): BP 4340, Conakry; tel. 30-44-50-58; fax 30-44-49-92; blends lubricants; 50% owned by Royal Dutch/Shell (Netherlands/United Kingdom), 50% by Govt of Guinea.

Société Minière de Dinguiraye (SMD): BP 2162, Conakry; tel. 30-46-36-81; fax 30-46-35-73; e-mail smd.gui@eti-bull.net; 85% owned by Crew Gold Corpn (Canada), 15% state-owned; exploitation of gold deposits in the Lefa corridor and devt of other areas of Dinguiraye concession; Man. Dir PETER CONNERY.

Société de Pêche de Kamsar (SOPEKAM): Kamsar Free Zone; f. 1984; 40% state-owned, 40% Universal Marine & Shark Products (USA); fishing and processing of fish products; fleet of 18 fishing vessels.

TGH Plus: BP 1562, Conakry; tel. 30-46-40-01; fax 30-46-19-83; e-mail tgh.plus@eti-bull.net; f. 1993; natural gas distribution; private co; Pres. and Man. Dir BAH ALIMOU YALI; 54 employees (2001).

Total Guinée: route du Niger, Coleah Km 4, BP 306, Conakry; tel. 30-35-29-50; f. 1988; storage of petroleum products; Dir-Gen. PHILIPPE CHAUVIN.

TRADE UNIONS

Confédération Nationale des Travailleurs de Guinée (CNTG): Bourse du Travail, Corniche Sud 004, BP 237, Conakry; tel. 30-41-50-44; fax 11-45-49-96; e-mail cntg60@yahoo.fr; f. 1984; Sec.-Gen. AMADOU DIALLO.

Organisation Nationale des Syndicats Libres de Guinée (ONSLG): BP 559, Conakry; tel. 30-41-52-17; fax 30-43-02-83; e-mail onslguinee@yahoo.fr; 27,000 mems (1996); Sec.-Gen. YAMOUDOU TOURÉ.

Union Syndicale des Travailleurs de Guinée (USTG): BP 1514, Conakry; tel. 30-41-25-65; fax 30-41-25-58; e-mail fofi1952@yahoo.fr; independent; 64,000 mems (2001); Sec.-Gen. IBRAHIMA FOFANA.

Transport

RAILWAYS

There are 1,086 km of railways in Guinea, including 662 km of 1-m gauge track from Conakry to Kankan in the east of the country, crossing the Niger at Kouroussa. The contract for the first phase of the upgrading of this line was awarded to a Slovak company in early 1997. Three lines for the transport of bauxite link Sangaredi with the port of Kamsar in the west, via Boké, and Conakry with Kindia and Fria, a total of 383 km. In 2011 plans were under way for the reconstruction of the 662-km Conakry-Kankan line, which has not been in operation since 1983.

Office National des Chemins de Fer de Guinée (ONCFG): BP 589, Conakry; tel. 30-44-46-13; fax 30-41-35-77; f. 1905; Man. Dir MOREL MARGUERITE CAMARA.

Chemin de Fer de Boké: BP 523, Boké; operations commenced 1973.

Chemin de Fer Conakry–Fria: BP 334, Conakry; operations commenced 1960; Gen. Man. A. CAMARA.

Chemin de Fer de la Société des Bauxites de Kindia: BP 613, Conakry; tel. 30-41-38-28; operations commenced 1974; Gen. Man. K. KEITA.

ROADS

The road network comprised 44,348 km of roads (of which 4,342 km were paved) in 2003. In 2009 an estimated 35% of all roads were paved. An 895-km cross-country road links Conakry to Bamako, in Mali, and the main highway connecting Dakar (Senegal) to Abidjan (Côte d'Ivoire) also crosses Guinea. The road linking Conakry to Freetown (Sierra Leone) forms part of the Trans West African Highway, extending from Morocco to Nigeria.

La Guinéenne-Marocaine des Transports (GUIMAT): Conakry; f. 1989; owned jtly by Govt of Guinea and Hakkam (Morocco); operates nat. and regional transport services.

Société Générale des Transports de Guinée (SOGETRAG): Conakry; f. 1985; 63% state-owned; bus operator.

SHIPPING

Conakry and Kamsar are the international seaports. Guinea handled 5.3m. metric tons of foreign trade in 2003. The country's registered merchant fleet at 31 December 2009 numbered 44 vessels, totalling 23,300 grt.

Getma Guinée: Immeuble KASSA, Cité des Chemins de Fer, BP 1648, Conakry; tel. 30-41-26-66; fax 30-41-42-73; e-mail info@getmaguinee.com.gn; internet www.getma.com; f. 1979; fmrly Société Guinéenne d'Entreprises de Transports Maritimes et

Aeriens; marine transportation; cap. 1,100m. FG; Chair. and CEO JEAN-JACQUES GRENIER; 135 employees.

Port Autonome de Conakry (PAC): BP 805, Conakry; tel. 30-41-27-28; fax 30-41-26-04; e-mail pac@eti-bull.net; internet www.biasy.net/~pac; haulage, porterage; Gen. Man. MAMADOUBA SAKHON.

Société Navale Guinéenne (SNG): BP 522, Conakry; tel. 30-44-29-55; fax 30-41-39-70; f. 1968; state-owned; shipping agents; Dir-Gen. MAMADI TOURÉ.

Transmar: 33 blvd du Commerce, Kaloum, BP 3917, Conakry; tel. 30-43-05-41; fax 30-43-05-42; e-mail elitegn@gmail.com; shipping, stevedoring, inland transport.

CIVIL AVIATION

There is an international airport at Conakry-Gbessia, and smaller airfields at Labé, Kankan and Faranah. Facilities at Conakry have been upgraded, at a cost of US $42.6m.; the airport handled some 300,000 passengers in 1999. In 2010 plans were under way for the construction of a new international airport at Matakang.

Air Guinée International: Conakry; f. 2010 to replace Air Guinée (f. 1960); regional and internal services; Dir-Gen. MOHAMED EL-BORAÏ.

Guinée Air Service: Aéroport Conakry-Gbessia; tel. 30-41-27-61.

Guinée Inter Air: Aéroport Conakry-Gbessia; tel. 30-41-37-08.

Société de Gestion et d'Exploitation de l'Aéroport de Conakry (SOGEAC): BP 3126, Conakry; tel. 30-46-48-03; f. 1987; manages Conakry-Gbessia int. airport; 51% state-owned.

Union des Transports Aériens de Guinée (UTA): scheduled and charter flights to regional and int. destinations.

Tourism

Some 30,194 tourists visited Guinea in 2007; receipts from tourism in 2010 totalled US $2.0m.

Office National du Tourisme: Immeuble al-Iman, 6e ave de la République, BP 1275, Conakry; tel. 30-45-51-63; fax 30-45-51-64; e-mail ibrahimabakaley@yahoo.fr; internet www.ontguinee.com; f. 1997; Dir-Gen. IBRAHIM A. DIALLO.

Defence

As assessed at November 2011, Guinea's active armed forces numbered 12,300, comprising an army of 8,500, a navy of 400 and an air force of 800. Paramilitary forces comprised a republican guard of 1,600 and a 1,000-strong gendarmerie, as well as a reserve 'people's militia' of 7,000. Military service is compulsory (conscripts were estimated at some 7,500 in 2001) and lasts for two years.

Defence Expenditure: Estimated at 275,000m. Guinean francs in 2010.

Chief of Staff of the Armed Forces: Gen. KÈLÈFA DIALLO.

Chief of Staff of the Army: Commdr MORIBA ABEL MARA.

Chief of Staff of the Air Force: Maj. MAMADY MARA.

Chief of Staff of the Navy: Capt. MOHAMED CAMARA.

Chief of Staff of the National Gendarmerie: Maj. IBRAHIMA BALDE.

Education

Education is provided free of charge at every level in state institutions. Primary education, which begins at seven years of age and lasts for six years, is officially compulsory. According to UNESCO estimates, in 2009/10 enrolment in primary education included 77% of children in the relevant age-group (males 83%; females 70%), while in 2008/09 enrolment at secondary schools included 29% of children in the appropriate age-group (boys 36%; girls 22%). Secondary education, from the age of 13, lasts for seven years, comprising a first cycle (collège) of four years and a second (lycée) of three years. There are universities at Conakry and Kankan, and other tertiary institutions at Manéyah, Boké and Faranah; some 80,200 students were enrolled at these institutions in 2007/08. In 2008 spending on education represented 19.2% of total budgetary expenditure.

Bibliography

Adamolekun, L. *Sékou Touré's Guinea: An Experiment in Nation Building*. London, Methuen, 1976.

Bangoura, D. (Ed.). *Guinée: L'alternance politique à l'issue des élections présidentielles de décembre 2003; actes des colloques des 21 novembre 2003 et 17 mars 2004*. Paris, L'Harmattan, 2004.

Quelle transition politique pour la Guinée? Paris, L'Harmattan, 2006.

Barry, A. O. *Parole futée, peuple dupé: discours et révolution chez Seékou Touré*. Paris, L'Harmattan, 2003.

Les racines du mal guinéen. Paris, Editions Karthala, 2004.

Binns, M. *Guinea*. Oxford, Clio Press, 1996.

Camara, D. K. *La diaspora Guinéenne*. Paris, L'Harmattan, 2003.

Camara, M. S. *Le pouvoir politique en Guinée sous Sékou Touré*. Paris, L'Harmattan, 2007.

Camara, S. S. *La Guinée sans la France*. Paris, Presses de la Fondation Nationale des Sciences Politiques, 1976.

Condé, A. *La décentralisation en Guinée: une expérience réussie*. Paris, L'Harmattan, 2003.

Devey, M. *La Guinée*. Paris, Editions Karthala, 1997.

Diallo, B. Y. *La Guinée, un demi-siècle de politique (1945-2008): Trois hommes, trois destins*. Paris, L'Harmattan, 2011.

Diallo, El Hadj M. *Histoire du Fouta Djallon*. Paris, L'Harmattan, 2002.

Dicko, A. A. *Journal d'une défaite: autour du référendum du 28 septembre 1958 en Afrique noire*. Paris, L'Harmattan, 1992.

Faye, O. T. *Guinée: Chronique d'une démocratie annoncée*. Trafford Publishing, Victoria, BC, 2007.

Jeanjean, M. *Sékou Touré: un totalitarisme africain*. Paris, L'Harmattan, 2004.

Kaba, L. *Le "non" de la Guinée à de Gaulle*. Paris, Chaka, 1990.

Kake, I. B. *Sékou Touré, le héros et le tyran*. Paris, Jeune Afrique Livres, 1987.

Keita, S. K. *Ahmed Sékou Touré, l'homme et son combat anticolonial (1922–58)*. Conakry, Editions SKK, 1998.

Des complots contre la Guinée de Sékou Touré 1958–84. Boulbinet, Les Classiques Guinéens—SOGUIDIP, 2002.

Larrue, J. *Fria en Guinée: première usine d'alumine en terre d'Afrique*. Paris, Editions Karthala, 1997.

Lewin, A. *Ahmed Sékou Touré (1922–1984), president de la Guinée*. (7 vols). Paris, L'Harmattan, 2009.

Mcgovern, M. *Unmasking the State: Making Guinea Modern*. Chicago, IL, University of Chicago Press, 2012.

O'Toole, T. E. *Historical Dictionary of Guinea*. Metuchen, NJ, Scarecrow Press, 1988.

Rivière, C. *Guinea: The Mobilization of a People* (trans. by Thompson, V., and Adloff, R.). Ithaca, NY, Cornell University Press, 1977.

Ruë, O. *L'aménagement du littoral de Guinée (1945–1995): mémoires de mangroves: des mémoires de développement pour de nouvelles initiatives*. Paris, L'Harmattan, 1998.

Said, M. B. *La Guinée en marche, mémoires inédits d'un changement*. Paris, L'Harmattan, 2008.

Soumah, I. *L'avenir de l'industrie minière en Guinée*. Paris, L'Harmattan, 2009.

Soumah, M. *Guinée: de Sékou Touré à Lansana Conté*. Paris, L'Harmattan, 2004.

Guinée: la démocratie sans le peuple. Paris, L'Harmattan, 2006.

Touré, S. *L'expérience guinéenne et l'unité africaine*. Paris, Présence africaine, 1959.

Vieira, G. *L'Eglise catholique en Guinée à l'épreuve de Sékou Touré (1958–1984)*. Paris, Editions Karthala, 2005.

Yansané, A. Y. *Decolonization in West African States, with French Colonial Legacy: Comparison and Contrast: Development in Guinea, the Ivory Coast, and Senegal, 1945–1980*. Cambridge, MA, Schenkman Publishing Co, 1984.

GUINEA-BISSAU

Physical and Social Geography

RENÉ PÉLISSIER

The Republic of Guinea-Bissau is bounded on the north by Senegal and on the east and south by the Republic of Guinea. Its territory includes a number of coastal islets, together with the offshore Bissagos or Bijagós archipelago, which comprises 18 main islands. The capital is Bissau.

The country covers an area of 36,125 sq km (13,948 sq miles), including some low-lying ground that is periodically submerged at high tide. Except for some higher terrain (rising to about 300 m above sea-level), close to the border with Guinea, the relief consists of a coastal plain deeply indented by *rias*, which facilitate internal communications, and a transition plateau, forming the Planalto de Bafatá in the centre, and the Planalto de Gabú, which abuts on the Fouta Djallon.

The country's main physical features are its meandering rivers and wide estuaries, where it is difficult to distinguish mud, mangrove and water from solid land. The principal rivers are the Cacheu, also known as Farim on part of its course, the Mansôa, the Geba and Corubal complex, the Rio Grande and, close to the Guinean southern border, the Cacine. Ocean-going vessels of shallow draught can reach most of the main population centres, and there is access by flat-bottomed vessels to nearly all significant outposts except in the north-eastern sector.

The climate is tropical, hot and wet with two seasons. The rainy season lasts from mid-May to November and the dry season from December to April. April and May are the hottest months, with temperatures ranging from 20°C to 38°C, and December and January are the coldest, with temperatures ranging from 15°C to 33°C. Rainfall is abundant (1,000 mm–2,000 mm per year in the north), and excessive on the coast. The interior is savannah or light savannah woodland, while coastal reaches are covered with mangrove swamps, rain forest and tangled forest.

At the census of March 2009 the population was enumerated at 1,520,830, giving a population density of 42.1 inhabitants per sq km. In mid-2012 the UN estimated that the population had increased to 1,579,631. The main population centre is Bissau, which had an estimated 365,097 inhabitants at the 2009 census. Bafatá, Bolama, Farim, Cantchungo, Mansôa, Gabú, Catió and Bissorã are the other important towns. Prior to the war of independence, the main indigenous groups were the Balante (about 32% of the population), the Fulani or Fula (22%), the Mandyako or Mandjak (14.5%), the Malinké, Mandingo or Mandinka (13%) and the Papel (7%). The non-Africans were mainly Portuguese civil servants and traders, and Syrian and Lebanese traders. Although Portuguese is the official language, a Guinean *crioulo* is the lingua franca. In 2009, according to the World Health Organization, the average life expectancy at birth was 53 years.

Recent History

ALEXANDRE ABREU

The campaign for independence in Portuguese Guinea (now the Republic of Guinea-Bissau) began in the 1950s with the formation of the Partido Africano da Independência da Guiné e Cabo Verde (PAIGC), under the leadership of Amílcar Cabral. After a few years of preparation and covert action, an armed conflict that would last for 11 years began in 1963. In January 1973 Cabral was assassinated by PAIGC dissidents, but by that time the pro-independence movement already controlled a large share of the territory. Guinea-Bissau unilaterally declared its independence from Portugal on 24 September 1973, under the presidency of Luís Cabral, the brother of Amílcar Cabral. Portugal withdrew its forces from Guinea-Bissau in August 1974, in the wake of its own democratizing revolution, and on 10 September it officially recognized the independence of its former colony. Guinea-Bissau became a single-party state governed by the PAIGC. While introducing measures to lay the foundations for a socialist state, the Government adopted a non-aligned stance in its foreign relations, receiving military aid from the Eastern bloc, as well as economic assistance from Western countries and Arab states. At the same time, friendly relations with Portugal were renewed.

Until 1980 the PAIGC supervised both Cape Verde and Guinea-Bissau, which maintained two separate Constitutions, but with a view to eventual unification. These arrangements were abruptly terminated in November 1980, when Cabral was overthrown by the Prime Minister, João Bernardo Vieira. A military-dominated revolutionary council took control of government and the coup led to the ousting of numerous cadres of Capeverdian origin from positions of power within the PAIGC and the administration.

VIEIRA AND THE PAIGC

The period following the 1980 coup was one of considerable political ferment, but President Vieira remained the dominant force throughout. In May 1982 Vieira postponed forthcoming elections and Vítor Saúde Maria, the Vice-Chairman of the ruling Council of the Revolution, was appointed Prime Minister. A struggle for primacy ensued between Vieira and Saúde Maria, the issue eventually being decided in Vieira's favour. A new Constitution was introduced in 1984, following elections to a new legislative assembly, which consolidated the position of Vieira as Head of State, Chief of Government, Commander-in-Chief of the Armed Forces and head of the PAIGC.

In October 1985 Vieira attempted further to consolidate his grip on power with the arrest and subsequent trial of around 40 military and government officials, most of whom were members of the Balante ethnic group, for allegedly plotting a coup against the President. Despite numerous international appeals for clemency, six of these, including Attorney-General Viriato Pã and Vice-Chairman of the Council Paulo Correia, were executed. This process would prove to have lasting consequences: resentment on the part of the Balante, who constitute a majority in Guinea-Bissau's military to the present day, is widely believed to have played an important role in events that were to occur much later, including the 1998 army rebellion and Vieira's assassination in 2009 (see below).

In the mid-1980s measures aimed at economic liberalization were introduced, in reaction to rising inflation and mounting public and foreign debt. In 1986 the Government abolished trading restrictions, and further proposals were introduced with a view to reducing state controls over trade and the economy, and increasing foreign investment. In 1987 the Government and the World Bank agreed on a structural adjustment programme that included further liberalization measures. Concerns surrounding the Government's new economic policies led to an increase in political tension. Vieira was confirmed as President for a further five-year term in 1989, but the pressures for political liberalization to follow economic liberalization were inescapable. Following the establishment of a constitutional revision commission, regional elections were held in 1989. A more comprehensive reform of Guinea-Bissau's political system would soon follow.

Constitutional Transition and Build-up to the 1998–99 Conflict

In April 1990, from its base in Lisbon, Portugal, an émigré opposition group, the Resistência da Guiné-Bissau—Movimento Bafatá (RGB—MB), proposed political negotiations with the PAIGC, with the implied threat that civil war might ensue should its demands for reform not be met. Shortly afterwards, faced with mounting international pressure for political democratization, Vieira gave approval in principle to the introduction of a multi-party political system. In June another external opposition movement, the Frente para a Libertação e Independência da Guiné (FLING), demanded an immediate conference of all political parties. In August Vieira informed a meeting of the PAIGC Central Committee that members of the legislature, the Assembleia Nacional Popular (ANP), would in future be elected by universal adult suffrage, and in January 1991, at an extraordinary conference of the PAIGC, Vieira confirmed that the transition to a multi-party system would be completed by 1993, when a presidential election would be held.

Constitutional amendments, formally terminating single-party rule, were approved unanimously by the ANP in May 1991. The reforms terminated the PAIGC's role as the sole political force, severed the link between the party and the armed forces, and guaranteed the operation of a free-market economy. A number of opposition parties were subsequently created. In November the Frente Democrática (FD) became the first party to be legalized by the Supreme Court, formally ending 17 years of one-party politics. The post of Prime Minister, which had been abolished in May 1984, was revived with the appointment of Carlos Correia to the position.

Throughout late 1991 and 1992 several other opposition parties were formed and registered, including the RGB—MB and the Partido para a Renovação Social (PRS), led by Kumba Yalá. In January four of these opposition parties, the RGB—MB, the Frente Democrática Social (FDS), the Partido Unido Social Democrático (PUSD) and the Partido da Convergência Democrática (PCD), agreed to set up a 'democratic forum' for consultations, and demanded that the Government dissolve the political police and cease using state facilities for political purposes. They also urged a revision of press law, free access to the media, the creation of an electoral commission and the declaration of election dates in consultation with all the opposition parties. In July 1994 Vieira announced that simultaneous presidential and legislative multi-party elections would be held in March 1994, but these were subsequently postponed until July 1994 due to financial and technical difficulties.

The elections finally took place on 3 July 1994. The PAIGC secured a clear majority in the ANP, winning 62 seats, but the results of the presidential election were inconclusive, with Vieira winning 46.3% of the votes, while his nearest rival, Yalá of the PRS, secured 21.9% of the votes. As no candidate had obtained an absolute majority, a second round of the presidential election between the two leading candidates was conducted on 7 August. Despite receiving the combined support of all the opposition parties, Yalá was narrowly defeated, securing 48.0% of the votes to Vieira's 52.0%. International observers later declared the elections to have been free and fair. Vieira was inaugurated as President on 29 September, and he appointed Manuel Saturnino da Costa as Prime Minister in late October. The Council of Ministers, comprising solely members of the PAIGC, was appointed in November. In November 1996 government plans to join the Union Economique et Monétaire Ouest-africaine (UEMOA) were rejected by the ANP. Later that month, however, on receiving a plea from Vieira, the legislature approved a constitutional amendment authorizing the Government to seek membership of UEMOA, which it duly attained in March 1997. Guinea-Bissau subsequently entered the Franc Zone on 17 April. The national currency—the peso—was replaced by the CFA franc, and the Banque Centrale des Etats de l'Afrique de l'Ouest (BCEAO) took over central banking functions.

The Political-Military Conflict of 1998–99

In June 1998 a group of dissident troops, led by Brig. Ansumane Mané, who had recently been dismissed as Chief of Staff of the Armed Forces by President Vieira over his alleged involvement in the trafficking of armaments to the Senegalese region of Casamance, seized control of the international airport and the Bra military barracks in the capital. Mané subsequently formed a 'military junta for the consolidation of democracy, peace and justice' and demanded the resignation of Vieira and his administration, as well as the holding of democratic elections in July. With the support of Senegalese and Guinean soldiers, who had been dispatched upon Vieira's request to his neighbours for assistance, troops loyal to the Government attempted unsuccessfully to regain control of rebel-held areas of the city, and heavy fighting ensued. In the following days an estimated 200,000 residents of Bissau fled the city, prompting fears of a humanitarian disaster.

On 26 July 1998, following mediation by a delegation from the lusophone commonwealth body, the Comunidade dos Países de Língua Portuguesa (CPLP), the Government and the rebels agreed to implement a truce. In August representatives of the Government and the rebels met, under the auspices of the CPLP and the Economic Community of West African States (ECOWAS), on Sal island, Cape Verde, where agreement was reached to transform the existing truce into a cease-fire. The accord provided for the reopening of the international airport and for the deployment of international forces to maintain and supervise the cease-fire.

In September 1998 talks between the Government and the rebels resumed in Abidjan, Côte d'Ivoire. In October the rebels agreed to a government proposal for the creation of a demilitarized zone separating the opposing forces in the capital. However, before the proposal could be formally endorsed, the cease-fire collapsed as fighting erupted in the capital and several other towns. On 20 October the Government imposed a nation-wide curfew, and on the following day Vieira declared a unilateral cease-fire. By that time most government troops had defected to the rebel forces, which were believed to control most of the country. On 23 October Mané agreed to observe a 48-hour truce to allow Vieira time to clarify his proposals for a negotiated peace settlement, and agreement was subsequently reached for direct talks to be held in Banjul, The Gambia. At the talks the rebels confirmed that they would not seek Vieira's resignation. Further negotiations, under the aegis of ECOWAS, in Abuja, Nigeria, resulted in the signing of a peace accord on 1 November. Under its terms, the two sides reaffirmed the August cease-fire, and resolved that the withdrawal of Senegalese and Guinean troops from Guinea-Bissau be conducted simultaneously with the deployment of an ECOMOG (ECOWAS Cease-fire Monitoring Group) interposition force. It was also agreed that a government of national unity would be established, to include representatives of the rebel junta, and that presidential and legislative elections would be held no later than March 1999. In early November 1998 agreement was reached on the composition of a Joint Executive Commission to implement the peace accord. On 3 December Francisco José Fadul was appointed Prime Minister, and later that month Vieira and Mané reached agreement on the allocation of portfolios.

In January 1999 Fadul announced that presidential and legislative elections would not take place in March as envisaged in the Abuja accord, but would be conducted at the end of the year. In the same month agreement was reached between the Government, the rebel military junta and ECOWAS on the strength of the ECOMOG interposition force, which was to comprise some 700 troops, and on a timetable for the withdrawal of Senegalese and Guinean troops from the country. However, at the end of January hostilities resumed in the capital, resulting in numerous fatalities and the displacement of some 250,000 residents. On 9 February talks between the Government and the rebels produced agreement on a cease-fire and provided for the immediate withdrawal of Senegalese and Guinean troops, and on 20 February the new Government of National Unity was announced. The disarmament of rebel troops and those loyal to the President, as provided for under the Abuja accord, began in early March, and the withdrawal of Senegalese and Guinean troops was completed that month.

TRANSITIONAL GOVERNMENT

In early May 1999 Vieira announced that legislative and presidential elections would take place on 28 December. On 7 May, however, to widespread condemnation by the international community, Vieira was overthrown by the rebel military junta. Fighting had erupted in Bissau the previous day when rebel troops seized stockpiles of weapons that had been held at Bissau airport since the disarmament of the rival forces in March. The rebels, who claimed that their actions had been prompted by Vieira's refusal to allow his presidential guard to be disarmed, surrounded the presidential palace and forced its capitulation. Vieira subsequently took refuge at the Portuguese embassy, where on 10 May he signed an unconditional surrender. The President of the ANP, Malam Bacai Sanhá, was appointed acting head of state pending a presidential election. The Government of National Unity, including the ministers appointed by Vieira, remained in office. The PAIGC subsequently appointed Manuel Saturnino da Costa to replace Vieira as party President.

At a meeting conducted in late May 1999 by representatives of the Government, the military junta and the political parties, agreement was reached that Vieira should stand trial for his own involvement in the trafficking of arms to separatists from Casamance and for political and economic crimes relating to his terms in office. Vieira subsequently agreed to stand trial, but only after receiving medical treatment abroad, after which, he pledged, he would return to Guinea-Bissau. ECOWAS foreign ministers, meeting in Togo, condemned Vieira's overthrow, and demanded that he be allowed to leave Guinea-Bissau. It was also decided that ECOMOG forces would be withdrawn from the country; the last ECOMOG troops left in early June. In that month Vieira was permitted to leave Guinea-Bissau to seek medical treatment in France. Sanhá cited humanitarian reasons for allowing Vieira's departure, but emphasized that he would return to stand trial.

Also in June 1999 interim President Sanhá asserted that presidential and legislative elections would take place by 28 November. In July constitutional amendments were introduced, limiting the tenure of presidential office to two terms and abolishing the death penalty. In September an extraordinary congress of the PAIGC voted to expel Vieira from the party. The incumbent Minister of Defence and Freedom Fighters, Francisco Benante, was appointed leader of the party. Later in October the Attorney-General announced that he had sufficient evidence to prosecute Vieira for crimes against humanity, expressing his intention to seek Vieira's extradition from Portugal.

POST-CONFLICT POLITICAL DEVELOPMENTS, 2000–11

The Yalá Presidency

Presidential and legislative elections were conducted on 28 November 1999, with voting extended for a further day owing to logistical problems. As no candidate received the necessary 50% of the votes to win the presidential election outright, Yalá of the PRS and Sanhá of the PAIGC contested a second round of voting on 16 January 2000, which Yalá won with 72% of the votes cast. The PRS secured the most seats in the legislature (38 of 102) and Caetano N'Tchama, a member of that party, was appointed Prime Minister in February, heading a Council of Ministers that included members of several former opposition parties. In May it was reported that tensions were increasing between Yalá and certain elements in the army, who viewed the head of the military junta, Gen. Ansumane Mané, as the rightful leader of the country, on the grounds that it was he who had ousted Vieira from power.

Poor relations between civilians and the military remained a major obstacle to political stability, despite the approval by the ANP, in August 2000, of a measure formally making the Head of State the Supreme Commander of the Armed Forces. The conflict between the Government and the military junta worsened in November, following the promotion by Yalá of a number of high-ranking officers. Gen. Mané rejected the promotions and appointed himself Commander-in-Chief of the Armed Forces. The dissent came to a head on 23 November, when forces loyal to the Government defeated a rebellion led by Mané, who was killed a few days later by the security forces.

Following the November 2000 insurgency, the PAIGC divided into various factions, the two most significant of which incorporated hard-liners and young moderate reformers, respectively. Another outcome of the crisis was the increasing dominance of the Balante ethnic group over state institutions. In December a thorough overhaul of the military leadership and command structure brought Balante into most positions of authority. The dissolution of the junta did not lead to political and social stability, and the main liability of the new Government continued to be the unpopularity of the Prime Minister. As friction increased between Yalá and his own party, the PRS, the President dismissed N'Tchama in March 2001. Faustino Fudut Imbali, who was appointed to replace him, formed a broadly based Council of Ministers, including a substantial number of members of opposition parties.

On 3 December 2001, following months of rumours, a group comprising mainly officers from the Mandinka ethnic group, led by Lt-Col Almani Camara, attempted a military coup. (The Government released only vague information about the incident, leading some observers to question whether it had in fact taken place.) A few days later, Imbali, having been accused of abuse of power by the President, was replaced as Prime Minister by the Minister of Internal Administration, Almara Nhassé, and a new Council of Ministers was appointed, in which the PRS held 20 of the 24 posts.

In January 2002 the armed forces revealed that 29 of those suspected of involvement in the December coup attempt had been detained, and that evidence had been gathered against them and presented to the judicial system. The governing PRS held its congress in that month, and elected the Prime Minister as its new party President, further reinforcing his standing. At the end of January the fourth extraordinary congress of the PAIGC elected Carlos Gomes Júnior as its new leader. The PAIGC congress also took the controversial measure of pardoning and reintegrating former members who had either abandoned or been expelled from the party. The inclusion in this pardon of former President Vieira provoked an angry reaction from Yalá.

Political instability intensified again in November 2002, when President Yalá dissolved the ANP and dismissed the Council of Ministers, accusing both bodies of creating a political stalemate and economic crisis. Yalá appointed Mário Pires, a founding member of the PRS, at the head of a transitional Government. The announcement that elections were due to take place on 20 April 2003 precipitated a profound realignment of political forces, including the creation of several new political parties and the formation of two coalitions. March 2003 marked the return from exile in Portugal of former Prime Minister Fadul, who became leader of the PUSD. Fadul and his party immediately became the targets of harassment by the authorities. Also in March 2003 Yalá postponed the legislative elections to 6 July. Further government changes were effected in April, and later that month and in early May the Ministers of Defence and of the Presidency of the Council of Ministers, respectively Marcelino Cabral and José de Pina, were dismissed and arrested shortly afterwards without explanation. The two men were not freed until June, and their detention created serious friction between the Government and the military. The cabinet was then reorganized again by the President in June and July, and in late June Yalá announced that legislative elections would be held on 12 October.

Military Intervention and Elections

Following a further postponement of the elections, on 14 September 2003 Yalá was detained by soldiers acting on the orders of the Chief of Staff of the Armed Forces, Gen. Veríssimo Seabra, who declared himself interim President and Emílio Costa his second-in-command. Both belonged to the army faction that had led the 1998–99 rebellion, under the late Gen. Ansumane Mané, which had ousted Vieira. Seabra and a newly appointed Military Committee for the Restoration of Constitutional Order and Democracy held talks with representatives of civil society and political organizations, apparently aimed at forming a transitional, civilian-led government. A 16-member commission was charged with appointing the transitional government and preparing for new elections. Meanwhile, the UN, the African Union and several African countries condemned the coup, and ECOWAS dispatched a mission to Bissau to mediate between the military authorities and Yalá. However, the ECOWAS mission withdrew its demand that Yalá be reinstated once the scale of his unpopularity became clear. National support for the new Government was strong, and all political parties (including Yalá's PRS) signed a declaration supporting the coup. Yalá formally resigned on 17 September, after it emerged that he had approached army officers from his own Balante ethnic group and offered them posts in a future government if they helped him to launch a counter-coup.

On 22 September 2003 the military announced the appointment of Henrique Rosa, a businessman and former head of the national electoral commission, as President. The appointment as Prime Minister of Artur Sanhá, the Secretary-General of the PRS, aroused controversy, however, after 15 of the 17 parties consulted about the new Government protested that they had been promised a new premier without political affiliations. Their objections were nevertheless overruled by the coup leaders, apparently in an attempt to ensure that the Balante ethnic group was fully represented in the Government.

In October 2003 a 56-member National Transition Commission (CNT) was formed, comprising military officials, politicians and representatives of civil society, to oversee the preparations for legislative elections, which were set for 28 March 2004. Rosa pledged to continue in his post until the presidential election in March 2005 completed the democratization process. Responding positively to the CNT's rapid moves towards elections, the international community granted the transitional Government recognition and agreed to help fund the cost of the polls. Although banned from further political activity, Yalá continued to increase political tensions with inflammatory public statements in the months following his ousting, and, as a result, he was placed under house arrest.

In early 2004 divisions began to appear in the transitional Government as campaigning for the elections commenced. Seeking to distance itself from the ousted President, the PRS replaced Yalá with Alberto Nambeia as party leader, although Prime Minister Sanhá continued to be the public face of the party. Legislative elections were held on 28 March 2004, and were declared free, fair and transparent by a team of more than 100 international observers. According to the Comissão Nacional de Eleições (CNE—National Election Commission), some 75% of Guinea-Bissau's 603,000 registered voters cast ballots. The PAIGC secured 45 of the 100 seats in the ANP, narrowly failing to attain an overall majority. The PRS obtained 35 seats and the PUSD 17. Pledging to form a broadly based coalition Government, Gomes Júnior attempted to form an alliance with the PUSD. However, negotiations between the two parties proved unsuccessful, and the PAIGC signed a formal agreement with the PRS whereby the latter pledged to support the Government's legislative plan in return for several important posts in the ANP and in government departments and parastatal organizations.

A new Government, led by Gomes Júnior, was appointed in May 2004 following the completion of the six-month term of the CNT. The new Government faced a crisis in October, when soldiers from an army contingent recently returned from a UN peace-keeping mission in Liberia mutinied, seemingly over the payment of overdue salaries. The mutiny resulted in the deaths of the Chief of Staff, Gen. Seabra, and the army's information officer, Lt-Col Domingos de Barros. The new Chief of Staff, Maj.-Gen. Baptista Tagmé Na Wai, appointed following the mutiny, vowed to work to unify the army and respect the authority of the future head of state, regardless of his political affiliation.

In March 2005 the Government announced that a presidential election would take place on 19 June. The PRS nominated Yalá as its candidate, and former President Vieira subsequently returned to Guinea-Bissau, from exile in Portugal, with the intention of contesting the presidency as an independent candidate. The participation of both men in the election contravened the terms of the transitional agreement, which barred them from political activity for five years, and raised concerns that they could reignite tensions. Statements by Yalá in early 2005 that he would seize the presidency by force if he were barred from running, and that he still considered himself legally to be President, also raised fears of a fresh coup attempt. In April the Supreme Court overturned legal obstacles to the candidacies of Vieira and Yalá on grounds that were not made clear. Meanwhile, the PAIGC nominated Malam Bacai Sanhá as its presidential candidate, and Rosa confirmed that he would not stand in the election.

The presidential election proceeded as scheduled on 19 June 2005. It was monitored by 200 international observers, and was subsequently declared to have been free and fair. Sanhá secured 35.5% of the votes cast, while Vieira won 28.9% and Yalá 25.0%. The rate of voter participation was recorded at 87.6%. As none of the candidates achieved an outright majority, a second round of voting was scheduled for 24 July, to be contested by the two leading candidates. Yalá subsequently announced his support for Vieira in the second ballot. Final results of the second round revealed that Vieira had won 52.4% of the votes. Voter turn-out was 78.6%. Sanhá, who alleged widespread electoral fraud, declared that he would contest the legitimacy of the election; however, the result was upheld by the Supreme Court in August.

Vieira Returns to Power

On 1 October 2005 Vieira was sworn in as President of the Republic, ending months of political uncertainty. In his inauguration speech to the ANP, Vieira promised to respect the constitutional separation of powers and to work with the Government of Prime Minister Gomes Júnior. However, less than two weeks later 14 of the PAIGC's 45 members of parliament defected to join the two largest opposition parties, the PRS and PUSD, in a new coalition—the Fórum de Convergência para o Desenvolvimento (FCD)—with the aim of removing the Prime Minister from power. Gomes Júnior responded by requesting a vote of confidence, but before the ANP could be convened he and his Government were dismissed by Vieira. Gomes Júnior protested against his dismissal, insisting that the PAIGC, which had won the largest number of seats in the legislative election, had the right to form the Government. Nevertheless, on 2 November 2005 Vieira appointed his ally, former PAIGC Vice-President Aristides Gomes, as the new Prime Minister.

In January 2007 political tensions flared after the former Navy Chief of Staff, Mohamed Lamine Sanhá, was shot dead in Bissau. Sanhá was a member of the junta formed following the 1998 army rebellion, and was the third of its members to be killed—after the deaths of Gen. Mané in November 2000 and Gen. Seabra in October 2004. Sanhá's death sparked violent protests by angry youths who erected barricades in central Bissau and burned down several houses, leaving one person dead and many injured. In response to the Government's denials of involvement in the assassination, the leader of the PAIGC, Gomes Júnior, claimed in an interview with a Portuguese news agency that Vieira had masterminded the murders of former members of the junta that overthrew him. Angered by the allegation, Vieira's Government issued an arrest warrant against Gomes Júnior, who took refuge within a building of the UN Peace-building Support Office in Guinea-Bissau (UNOGBIS), where he remained under UN protection for 17 days. Eventually, the UN brokered an agreement whereby the Government withdrew the arrest warrant and guaranteed the safety of Gomes Júnior and his family.

In March 2007 a new political crisis erupted when the PRS and the PUSD withdrew from the FCD governing coalition and signed a political stability pact with the PAIGC, pledging to form a government of national unity. Shortly afterwards, on 19 March, the Government lost a vote of no confidence in the ANP by 54 votes to 28. Vieira initially refused to make a public statement concerning the vote, but public protests intensified in Bissau, and on 28 March Aristides Gomes tendered his resignation as Prime Minister, forcing Vieira to respond.

Eventually, after three weeks of political uncertainty, Vieira acquiesced, and on 10 April he appointed Martinho N'Dafa Cabi as Prime Minister. The new Government was heavily weighted in favour of the PAIGC and the PRS, with those parties holding nine and six cabinet posts, respectively. However, at Vieira's insistence, the key posts of the interior, finance and foreign affairs were awarded to his supporters. Notably, Vieira's former security adviser, Baciro Dabó, took the interior portfolio, and Issufo Sanhá that of finance.

Cabi's Government immediately implemented measures to address the acute fiscal crisis and regain the confidence of donors, including a moratorium on unauthorized government spending, and a pledge to settle outstanding public sector salary arrears and to provide assistance to the struggling cashew nut sector. During its first months in office the Government was judged to have performed competently, prompting donors, led by the World Bank and the IMF, to re-engage fully in Guinea-Bissau and release large inflows of aid. However, despite Cabi's reportedly good relationship with the President, deep-seated animosity between Vieira and the PAIGC's old guard threatened to revive political deadlock.

In mid-2007 concerns surfaced over the use of Guinea-Bissau as a conduit for drugs shipments from South America to countries of the European Union (EU). The country's extensive mangrove deltas and network of offshore islands are ideal for smuggling operations, and with seizures of drugs spiralling and the suspected involvement of the country's military and political leadership with the drugs-traffickers, concerns began to be voiced that Guinea-Bissau could become Africa's first 'narco-state'. In June the Minister of Internal Administration, Baciro Dabó, set up an inter-ministerial commission to investigate the involvement of politicians in drugs-trafficking. Several ministers and high-ranking officials were questioned, but the Government subsequently seemed to undermine the process, first by refusing to publish the commission's findings, and then by dismissing the Chief of the Police. Reports of death threats and attacks on journalists investigating the Government's alleged links to drugs cartels rose sharply, forcing a number of journalists to flee the country.

On 29 February 2008 the President of the PAIGC, Gomes Júnior, announced that his party was withdrawing its support for the Government, accusing the Prime Minister of 'disrespect and indiscipline'. A few days later, however, the PAIGC's executive committee disagreed with the announcement, confirming the party's support for the Government and casting doubt on Gomes Júnior's authority as party leader. On 26 March, following a meeting with donors over the forthcoming elections, Vieira issued a presidential decree confirming the date of the legislative election for 16 November.

In June 2008 Aristides Gomes founded a new party, the Partido Republicano para a Independência e o Desenvolvimento (PRID), which pledged its support for Vieira, threatening to draw support away from the PAIGC. Later in that month the PAIGC held its long-delayed seventh party congress in Gabú and re-elected Gomes Júnior as party President, thus ending months of intra-party competition. In July the PAIGC withdrew from the Government, in response to a decision by Cabi to dismiss four high-ranking officials without informing the other coalition members. In the following month Vieira issued a decree dissolving the ANP and formally ending the tenure of the coalition Government, and on 6 August he reappointed Carlos Correia as Prime Minister. Correia subsequently announced the formation of a new Government, in which the majority of ministerial posts were awarded to members of the PAIGC. There was further upheaval in August, when it was reported that the Navy Chief of Staff, Rear-Adm. José Americo Bubo Na Tchuto, had been dismissed and placed under house arrest following his involvement in an alleged coup plot. It was later reported that he had fled to The Gambia.

The 2008 Elections

Legislative elections took place without incident on 16 November 2008, after the Chief of Staff of the Armed Forces, Na Wai, and the 19 contesting parties pledged to ensure peaceful elections and respect the results. The PAIGC increased its representation in the 100-member ANP to 67 seats, thus achieving a parliamentary majority for the first time since 1999, while the PRS suffered a fall in its representation to just 28 seats. The PRID, led by Aristides Gomes, won just three seats, ending its hopes of challenging the PAIGC's electoral base. Two other parties, the Partido para a Nova Democracia (PND) and the Aliança Democrática (AD), each won one seat. The PUSD, which had been the third political force in the previous ANP, with 17 seats, and a member of the government coalition created at the end of 2005, unexpectedly failed to secure representation in the new ANP.

On 23 November 2008, just two days after the CNE had announced the provisional election results, the presidential residence was attacked by a group of soldiers. President Vieira and his wife emerged unhurt following the three-hour armed conflict between the assailants and the presidential guard. Later that day the army identified the suspected architect of the attack as Alexandre Tchama Yalá, a navy sergeant and nephew of former President Kumba Yalá. Sgt Yalá, who was subsequently arrested in Senegal, was believed to have close links to Rear-Adm. Bubo Na Tchuto, who had been accused of organizing a coup attempt in August. However, despite Yalá's arrest and that of seven other members of the armed forces suspected of helping him, doubts remained over the instigators and motives of the attack, and Vieira demanded the protection of the 400-strong Aguentas militia, which had protected him during the 1998–99 military rebellion.

In December 2008 the Supreme Court confirmed the election results previously announced by the CNE, despite complaints filed by both the PRS and an opposition coalition, the Aliança de Forças Patrióticas (AFP). On 25 December Vieira appointed PAIGC President Gomes Júnior as the new Prime Minister, and two days later Gomes Júnior announced his new Government, the 31 members of which all hailed from the PAIGC.

Assassination of Vieira

Tensions arose between Chief of Staff Na Wai and President Vieira in early January 2009, when militiamen from the Aguentas opened fire on Gen. Na Wai's car. Although the Aguentas claimed that the shooting had been accidental, Na Wai accused them of trying to assassinate him and declared the militia illegal, thus forcing Vieira to disband them.

On the evening of 1 March 2009 Na Wai became the third Chief of Staff of the Armed Forces since the 1998–99 conflict to be assassinated, when a bomb exploded in the army headquarters. In the early hours of 2 March a group of soldiers entered the presidential residence, meeting with little resistance, and murdered Vieira, after which they proceeded to loot the President's house. There was widespread speculation regarding the motives and the culprits behind the two attacks, but little concrete evidence. The version that was most circulated in the international media at the time suggested that Vieira had himself ordered Na Wai's murder, and that the President was killed in retaliation by soldiers and officers loyal to the general. However, other rumours have suggested the involvement of Rear-Adm. Bubo Na Tchuto or of senior government figures. Despite the arrest of five soldiers and the establishment of a civilian commission of inquiry into both assassinations, and of a military commission of inquiry into the assassination of Na Wai, little substantiated information has since emerged on the two murders. Requests by the international community and by Guinea-Bissau's civil society for an independent international commission of inquiry to be set up were rejected, and the progress of subsequent investigations appeared to have been thwarted by a lack of political will.

The army swiftly denounced the killings as the work of isolated elements, and confirmed its support for a constitutional transition. On 3 March 2009 the President of the ANP, Raimundo Pereira, was appointed interim President, and he promised that a presidential election would be held within the constitutionally decreed 60 days. In mid-March the deputy navy chief, Commdr José Zamora Induta, was appointed interim Chief of Staff of the Armed Forces, and in April the Government announced that a presidential election would take place on 28 June. Yet another violent incident involving the military occurred on 30 March, when former Prime Minister Francisco José Fadul, now President of the Audit Court, who had declared his intention to stand for President, was allegedly assaulted by military personnel at his home in Bissau following critical statements during a radio broadcast. In early May 2009 the Supreme Court validated 13 presidential candidacies, including those of PAIGC candidate Sanhá, PRS leader and former President Kumba Yalá (who converted to Islam in 2008 and was thenceforth known as Mohamed Yalá Embaló), and independent candidate Henrique Rosa. The election campaign was marred by further violence, when on 5 June 2009 one of the presidential candidates, former Minister of Territorial Administration, Baciro Dabó (a close ally of Vieira), was shot dead in his home by armed men. A few hours later, a former Minister of Defence, Helder Proença, was also shot dead, along with a bodyguard and a driver, when travelling to Bissau. Other senior members of the PAIGC were arrested at the same time. The killings were justified by the Ministry of the Interior, which stated that Dabó and Proença had resisted arrest in the context of a thwarted coup plot and alleged that the two men had been conspiring to overthrow the Government. However, the circumstances of the killings were very unclear, and long-standing antagonism between the two men and senior government and military figures prompted speculation that the killings had been premeditated.

Despite these assassinations, the first round of the presidential election proceeded without incident on 28 June 2009, and voting was deemed to be free and transparent by international election observers. According to results released by the CNE, Sanhá took 39.6% of the votes, followed by Yalá with 29.4% and Henrique Rosa with 24.2%. At the second round, which took place on 26 July between the first- and second-placed candidates, Sanhá secured 63.3% of the votes and was declared President. In keeping with a memorandum of understanding signed with Sanhá the previous week, Yalá immediately accepted the outcome and congratulated his rival.

The Sanhá Presidency

Sanhá was sworn in on 8 September 2009, and he appointed a new Council of Ministers, again headed by Gomes Júnior, in late October. In his inauguration speech, the President promised to lead the country into a new era of peace and stability and to cast light on the murders of Vieira and Na Wai. In spite of the recent political violence and unrest, the international community largely regarded the new political climate as conducive to greater stability and economic development, and expressed support for Gomes Júnior, Sanhá and Commdr Induta (who was confirmed as Chief of Staff of the Armed Forces).

On 28 December 2009, Rear-Adm. Bubo Na Tchuto, who had been in exile in The Gambia since August 2008, entered the country surreptitiously by boat. Once news of this emerged, the Government reacted promptly by seeking to arrest and prosecute him. Claiming to fear for his life, Na Tchuto requested, and was given, refuge in the UNOGBIS headquarters. On 8 January 2010, after lengthy negotiations between UN officials, the Government and the Attorney-General, an agreement was reached whereby Na Tchuto would be handed over to the authorities in return for guarantees regarding his physical security and his right to fair trial. However, the agreement was not implemented, and Na Tchuto remained at UNOGBIS (which upon completion of its mandate on 31 December 2009 was formally replaced by the UN Integrated Peace-Building Office in Guinea-Bissau—UNIOGBIS).

On 1 April 2010 the Deputy Chief of Staff of the Armed Forces, António Indjai, led an attempted coup that involved the arrest and overthrow of Induta and the brief detention of Prime Minister Gomes Júnior. Soldiers loyal to Indjai went to the UNIOGBIS headquarters and requested that Na Tchuto be handed over to them. The latter left of his own free will, and appeared alongside Indjai throughout the day, prompting speculation that he may have been involved in the planning of the coup from inside UNIOGBIS's facilities. Induta was arrested along with the head of military intelligence, Samba Djaló, and a number of other officers, after which he was transferred to a military compound outside Bissau.

After detaining Induta and assuming control over the armed forces, Indjai and his entourage arrested Prime Minister Gomes Júnior at the government headquarters. Upon news of his detention, hundreds of civilians gathered outside the building to express their rejection of the attempted coup. Indjai responded by announcing over the radio that he would murder Gomes Júnior and 'commit atrocities' against the population unless the demonstrators dispersed. He also moved Gomes Júnior to the army headquarters. A few hours later, however, the Prime Minister was released and returned to his office. According to media reports, Indjai may have been expecting President Sanhá to support the ousting of Gomes Júnior, given the rivalry between the two, in which case Indjai would have been surprised to learn of the President's refusal to endorse what would have been a major disruption of the constitutional order. The coup thus subsided, its immediate consequences being the overthrow of Induta as Chief of Staff, his de facto replacement with Indjai, and Na Tchuto's return to the forefront of the political-military arena.

The international community swiftly condemned the attempted coup and called for the Constitution to be respected. On 2 April 2010 Indjai made a public statement in which he apologized for threatening to kill the Prime Minister and to retaliate against the population. Both the President and the Prime Minister also issued statements in the following days in which they sought to play down the events of 1 April and to ensure that the situation had returned to normal. On 8 April the US Department of State issued a statement accusing Na Tchuto and Ibraima Papá Camara, the Chief of Staff of the Air Force, of involvement in drugs-trafficking, and announced the freezing of the two men's assets on US territory. For its part, the EU announced that in view of the events of 1 April it would not extend its Security Sector Reform (SSR) mission beyond 30 September, and indeed terminated it on that date.

Throughout April 2010 there were rumours of fresh attempts to arrest the Prime Minister. After reportedly seeking refuge in foreign embassies on more than one occasion, Gomes Júnior fled the country and remained abroad for more than a month, allegedly for health reasons, returning to Bissau in mid-June. The lengthy impasse that arose over the formal nomination of the new Chief of Staff of the Armed Forces (the post had been left formally vacant after the ousting and arrest of Induta) was eventually resolved in Indjai's favour by a presidential decree dated 25 June, which legitimized his authority. On 7 October Na Tchuto, who had on 1 June been formally acquitted of the charges pending against him since 2008, was in turn formally reinstated as Navy Chief of Staff by President Sanhá.

Tension remained high in the following months, with signs of precarious and shifting alliances involving Sanhá, Gomes Júnior, Indjai and Na Tchuto. In May 2010, while on a trip to France, President Sanhá informed foreign media that senior government figures had been involved in the assassination of Vieira and Na Wai, but refrained from elaborating further. Further strains between the offices of the President and Prime Minister emerged over the latter's dismissal, in late October, of the Minister of the Interior, Hadja Satu Camará Pinto, who was considered to be close to the President. Since the formal process of dismissal required confirmation by presidential decree, and the President was receiving medical treatment abroad at the time, Camará Pinto could not be officially removed and she initially refused to relinquish her post. Then, in early November widespread rumours suggested that the President, who remained abroad, was in a critical condition, causing agitation and concern among the population. Although the rumours were subsequently denied, the uncertainty over both Sanhá's condition and Camará Pinto's dismissal was only fully ended a few weeks later, when President Sanhá returned to the country, made several public appearances, and issued a decree removing Camará Pinto and installing a new minister in her place.

The resolution of this episode signalled the attainment of a situation of relative stability, which enabled the release from custody of former Chief of Staff Induta on 22 December, after eight months in detention. Former head of military intelligence Samba Djaló was also released, as were several figures suspected of involvement in the murder of Vieira and Na Wai. All of these events appeared to indicate the willingness of the various sides in dispute to make a number of concessions and work towards greater stability. As a consequence, the apparent risk of a new coup began to subside in the following months, even though the balance that was reached implied the legitimization of Indjai's and Na Tchuto's dominance over the armed forces and the continuing impunity of the perpetrators of the 2009 assassinations.

The succession of events following the 1 April 2010 rebellion marked a shift in the relative pre-eminence of Guinea-Bissau's Northern and Southern partners, as the former remained adamant in their demand that Indjai and Na Tchuto not be rewarded for taking control of the armed forces, while Southern partners such as Angola and ECOWAS exhibited more pragmatism and, as a consequence, were able to take on more central roles. ECOWAS, subsequently joined by the lusophone CPLP, began in August to design a new security sector support and reform initiative. Once this framework was adopted in November, Angola took the lead at bilateral level, signing a technical and military co-operation agreement with the Government of Guinea-Bissau, under which a two-year Angolan Armed Forces Security Mission in Guinea-Bissau (MISSANG) was established in January 2011. The Angolan contingent comprised around 200 members, who arrived in Bissau in March with the stated aim of assisting in the reduction of the number of national servicemen, helping to renovate the army barracks, and generally assisting in the improvement and reform of the country's military and police forces.

July and August 2011 saw a renewed increase in political tension, as hundreds of people took to the streets of Bissau on four occasions, accusing Gomes Júnior of plotting Vieira's assassination in 2009 and demanding the Prime Minister's resignation. Meanwhile, on 2 August the Attorney-General, Amine Saad, resigned, claiming to being subject to unspecified pressures in respect of the Vieira and Na Wai murder cases.

President Sanhá's medical condition deteriorated throughout 2011, causing him to be evacuated for treatment in Europe on several occasions. On 26 December, during one of these absences, a new military rebellion took place—or was alleged to have taken place, since its circumstances were especially unclear and controversial. According to statements made by Indjai, a group of armed men attacked the Army headquarters and two other military facilities in Bissau in a thwarted attempt to seize weapons and take them to the Navy headquarters. There was sporadic shooting around Bissau; checkpoints were set up; and several dozen people were arrested, most notably Navy Chief of Staff Na Tchuto for allegedly masterminding the incident. At least one person was killed, and several others were wounded. According to reports at the time, the rebellion also aimed at ousting the Prime Minister, but Gomes Júnior was apparently rescued by Angolan soldiers and granted refuge at the Angolan embassy.

On 27 December 2011 Iaia Dabó—the brother of Baciro Dabó, who had been murdered in June 2009—was assassinated at a police station after turning himself in. A few days later, on 30 December, the Prime Minister declared that the rebellion had constituted an attempt on his life, but 15 opposition parties responded by issuing a joint statement in which they claimed that the alleged coup had in fact been 'a parody', contrived by the Government and the armed forces high command in order to give a pretext for a 'purge'. Even though the incident was very unclear, with contradictory statements by opposing actors and limited substantiated information, its eventual outcome, in terms of those arrested or killed, did amount to a strengthening of Gomes Júnior's and Indjai's positions. Somewhat unexpectedly after the events of April 2010 (see above), this seemed to signal a rapprochement between the Prime Minister and the Chief of Staff, as well as increasing rivalry between the latter and Na Tchuto—apparently resolved in Indjai's favour.

DEATH OF SANHÁ AND THE 2012 COUP

On 9 January 2012, after several years of ill health, President Sanhá died in Paris, France, of undisclosed causes. Under the terms of the Constitution, Raimundo Pereira, President of the ANP and an associate of Gomes Júnior, became interim President of the Republic, and preparations began with a view to holding a presidential election within the constitutionally prescribed 60 days. Sanhá's death occurred at a time of considerable political instability, and the loss of his balancing influence added decisively to that instability. In late January Prime Minister Gomes Júnior stated publicly that he should be the PAIGC's 'natural candidate' for the presidency. The central committee of the PAIGC convened on 4 February to appoint the party's presidential candidate, but, to the surprise of many, its members were presented with a fait accompli, Gomes Júnior having already been selected by the party's political bureau. Moreover, the confirmation of his nomination by the central committee was conducted by a show of hands, rather than by secret ballot, which further ensured that Gomes Júnior was able to circumvent opposition within the party. Two of the most prominent faces of that opposition, Manuel Serifo Nhamadjo and Baciro Djá, who wished to dispute the nomination, eventually decided to run as independent candidates, thus openly challenging the party leadership.

Nine candidates stood in the first round of the election, which took place on 18 March 2012 and was deemed free and fair by 80 international observers. Voter turn-out was 55%, the lowest ever recorded in Guinea-Bissau. The official results were not released until 21 March. Gomes Júnior, with 49.0% of the vote, narrowly failed to win the election outright at this first round. He was followed by Yalá, with 23.4%, Serifo Nhamadjo, with 15.8%, and Henrique Rosa, with 5.4%. Before the results had been made public, however, another violent incident shook Guinea-Bissau's political-military landscape: the night after the election Col. Samba Djaló, erstwhile head of military intelligence and a close associate of former Chief of Staff Induta, was murdered outside his home. There was speculation regarding possible links between the election and Djaló's death, but the following day an armed forces spokesman dismissed such rumours and sought to disassociate the two events. Two days later, claiming to fear for his own life, Induta, himself long deemed a close associate of Gomes Júnior, sought and was given refuge at the EU delegation in Bissau. (He would subsequently flee to The Gambia in late May.) Also before the official results of the election had been announced, five candidates, including Yalá, Nhamadjo and Rosa, issued a joint statement asserting that the election had been beset with irregularities and demanding a re-run. Yalá, who, having come second in the first round, would ordinarily have proceeded with Gomes Júnior to the run-off, also announced that he was withdrawing his candidacy. On 28 March, however, the CNE ruled against the defeated candidates' case, maintaining that the alleged irregularities had not decisively altered the ranking of the candidates in the ballot. The second round of the presidential election was subsequently set for 29 April.

On 9 April 2012 one of the first-round candidates, Henrique Rosa, accused the Angolan security presence MISSANG of functioning as Gomes Júnior's 'Praetorian Guard'. The same day, after weeks of mounting tension between Guinea-Bissau's military leadership and MISSANG, Chief of Staff Indjai ordered the Angolan contingent to withdraw from the country, maintaining that the Government of Angola had been covertly sending heavy weapons to Guinea-Bissau without duly informing the Guinea-Bissau armed forces, thereby contravening the terms of MISSANG's presence in the country. Gomes Júnior countered that MISSANG's presence was legitimized by an official agreement between the two states, and that it was not in the Chief of Staff's power to order its withdrawal. The Angolan Minister of Foreign Affairs, George Rebelo Chicoty, swiftly travelled to Bissau and announced that MISSANG would indeed be withdrawn in response to 'hostility on the part of some Bissau-Guineans'. It would, however, be replaced by a multinational force, to be co-ordinated by the CPLP, of which the Angolan contingent would form a part—the implication thus being that the Angolans would in fact remain in the country.

This gradual escalation in political tension reached its apex on 12 April 2012, when a self-styled Military Command staged a coup by arresting Gomes Júnior and interim President Raimundo Pereira after attacking the former's home with rocket-propelled grenades. In a statement released the same day the Command justified the coup as a reaction of self-defence on the part of the Guinea-Bissau armed forces, in the supposed face of an 'imminent aggression'. Alleged evidence of this was produced a few days later, in the form of a letter purportedly written by Gomes Júnior to UN Secretary-General Ban Ki-Moon, in which the former requested that a UN peace-keeping force, 'with ample powers', be sent to the country to control the Guinea-Bissau military. The relation between the Military Command and the formal leadership of the Guinea-Bissau armed forces was not disclosed for some days. As it turned out, the two were virtually indistinguishable: although there were rumours at first that Indjai had himself been overthrown, it soon became clear that the Chief of Staff was in fact the mastermind of the coup and the leader of the Military Command. Meanwhile, the international community vehemently and unanimously condemned the coup, urged that constitutional order be re-established, and demanded the immediate release of Gomes Júnior and Pereira. However, the situation deteriorated further on the night of 12 April, as the pillaging of the homes of several ministers and holders of high political office by elements of the armed forces prompted fears of a descent into chaos. As a result, tens of thousands left the capital for the countryside in the days that followed.

Meanwhile, on the afternoon of 12 April 2012 the Military Command convened a meeting with representatives of the opposition parties with the aim of preparing a transfer of power. As it quickly became clear, the goal of the coup had been to oust Gomes Júnior before the second round of the presidential election—thus ensuring that he would not be able to control the PAIGC, the Government and the presidency all at once—not for the military to assume direct power. The transitional arrangement negotiated between the Military Command and the political opposition thus involved the appointment as interim President of Serifo Nhamadjo, the PAIGC dissident who had come third in the first round of the presidential election. At first, few believed that this outcome would be deemed acceptable, as the international community remained steadfast in its refusal to endorse any unconstitutional solution. On 18 April, however, Nigeria's stated willingness to accept the negotiated arrangement (according to some analysts, such a solution suited its own aims given its own rivalry with Angola) breached the international community's unanimous resolve. That breach was then exploited by ECOWAS, which in a series of meetings with Guinea-Bissau's military leaders brokered a settlement that ended up legitimizing the coup and consolidating its outcome. Included in the agreement were the release of Gomes Júnior and Pereira (who were indeed released on 27 April, subsequently heading to Côte d'Ivoire and then to Portugal); a one-year transitional period, to be followed by presidential and parliamentary elections; the confirmation of Nhamadjo as interim President; and the replacement of MISSANG with a 600-strong ECOWAS contingent.

The following weeks were characterized by considerable dispute regarding this issue at the international level, with ECOWAS, Senegal and Nigeria throwing their weight behind the negotiated settlement, while the CPLP, Portugal and Angola remained adamant in their refusal to acknowledge the post-coup leadership. This gave rise to conflicting interpretations regarding who should have the lawful right to represent Guinea-Bissau in international forums: Nhamadjo attended an ECOWAS leaders' summit in Abuja, Nigeria, in late June 2012 as President of Guinea-Bissau (and returned with promises of financial help), but it was Pereira who represented the country at the CPLP summit held in Maputo, Mozambique, in mid-July. The UN, where the Security Council had imposed individual sanctions on the perpetrators shortly after the coup, urged ECOWAS and the CPLP to work together in order to achieve a unified position, but little subsequent progress was made in this respect. For its part, the USA appeared to tend towards legitimizing the post-coup situation, having issued a number of statements that signalled its willingness to work alongside Guinea-Bissau's de facto leaders.

Meanwhile, on 16 May 2012 Serifo Nhamadjo appointed Rui Duarte de Barros, who had been Minister of Finance during Yalá's presidency in the early 2000s, to lead the transitional Government. Rui de Barros was sworn in as interim Prime Minister the following day, and his 28-member cabinet, comprising elements of various parties and factions opposed to Gomes Júnior, took office on 23 May. MISSANG completed its withdrawal on 9 June, two weeks after the first 70 members of what was to become the 600-strong ECOWAS force arrived in the country. It would therefore seem that the leaders of the armed forces, by aligning themselves with elements of the political opposition (namely the PRS and the PAIGC factions opposed to Gomes Júnior), as well as with certain sub-regional interests (i.e. ECOWAS, Nigeria and Senegal), had succeeded in forging the legitimization and de facto acceptance of the coup. Certainly, time was running in favour of the consolidation of the post-coup situation, even though it remained to be seen how Guinea-Bissau's population and civil society would react if and when their constitutional right to assemble and demonstrate, which had been suspended by the Military Command after the coup, were re-established. The extent to which the post-Gomes Júnior regime would be a stable one was a different matter yet again—especially after Na Tchuto's release from custody on 20 June, with, according to some, the potential to challenge Indjai's supremacy within the military.

FOREIGN AFFAIRS

In its foreign relations, Guinea-Bissau is motivated primarily by the need to secure aid and, in this context, the country has actively promoted co-operation with both Northern and Southern donors. Until recently, Guinea-Bissau's main development partners consisted of European bilateral donors, especially Portugal, and multilateral partners like the EU, the UN and ECOWAS. In recent years, however, South-South co-operation, especially with Angola, the People's Republic of China and Brazil, has taken an increasingly central role.

Angola has latterly emerged as a key partner by virtue of its investments in mineral resource extraction and infrastructure, and its leadership of the ECOWAS-CPLP SSR process which involved the deployment of the 270-strong MISSANG. However, meaningful economic and political links between the two countries are long-standing. In 1996 Guinea-Bissau was among the five lusophone African nations that, together with Brazil and Portugal, formally established the CPLP, a lusophone commonwealth intended to benefit each member state by means of joint co-operation in technical, cultural and social matters. Relations with Angola were strengthened following a visit by President Vieira to the Angolan capital, Luanda, in February 2007, during which a number of economic and technical co-operation agreements were signed; Angola subsequently opened an embassy in Guinea-Bissau in May of that year. In July 2008 Angolan public-private partnership Angola Bauxite announced that it was carrying out feasibility studies for the exploration and exploitation of Guinea-Bissau's bauxite, reserves of which are estimated to total approximately 113m. metric tons. The project was due to entail a direct investment of more than US $300m., and would additionally involve the construction of a deep-water port at Buba and a railway line linking the mines with the port—in turn requiring investment of a further $500m.–$700m. However, the April 2012 coup has compromised all of these plans, both because it was explicitly motivated by, *inter alia*, animosity on the part of the Guinea-Bissau armed forces towards MISSANG, and because ousted Prime Minister Gomes Júnior played a pivotal role in the partnership between the two countries. Thus, along with the withdrawal of MISSANG in early May 2012 (see above), the Angolan Government also decided to freeze its investments in Guinea-Bissau pending the restoration of constitutional order.

China has also become a very important bilateral partner over the course of the last decade. In May 1990 China had ceased diplomatic relations with Guinea-Bissau, following the latter's establishment of relations with Taiwan. However, relations with the People's Republic were restored in April 1998, after Guinea-Bissau's Government gave its support to the 'one China' policy, and have continued to improve as China gradually seeks to step up its presence as a major player in Africa. Chinese co-operation activities in Guinea-Bissau have been especially prominent in the infrastructural domain: following a visit by President Vieira to China in November 2006, the Chinese Government financed and undertook several large-scale construction projects in Guinea-Bissau, including the new parliamentary building and government palace, a new military hospital, and several schools. Additionally, China provided funds for emergency budget support in 2008 and has on several occasions sent medical and agricultural development teams on technical assistance missions. In the aftermath of the April 2012 coup China has shown evidence of its customary pragmatism—at first condemning the coup and demanding the re-establishment of constitutional order, but eventually agreeing to work with the country's de facto leaders.

Brazil completes Guinea-Bissau's trio of emerging bilateral partners, even though its co-operation initiatives have not enjoyed the same level of public prominence as those of Angola and China. Nevertheless, over the past 10 years Brazil has built up a steady presence in Guinea-Bissau through co-operation initiatives in such domains as agricultural development, education and police training. Additionally, under a Student Graduation Agreement signed between the two countries, almost 1,200 students from Guinea-Bissau have graduated from Brazilian universities over the course of the last decade. Guinea-Bissau has also become one of the first few countries to benefit from joint development projects aimed at poverty and hunger alleviation in the context of the IBSA Trust Fund, which was established in 2003 by India, Brazil and South Africa with a view to enhancing South-South co-operation. However, all these activities were frozen following the 2012 coup: Brazil has strenuously opposed the coup both at the bilateral level and in the context of the UN and CPLP, and has suspended its co-operation activities in Guinea-Bissau.

Among Guinea-Bissau's Northern bilateral partners, the former colonial power, Portugal, has traditionally played the foremost role. Indeed, relations with Portugal have generally been very cordial ever since the independence of Guinea-Bissau and the change to a democratic regime in Portugal in 1974. In the early 2000s, during the Yalá presidency, there were some minor disputes, but relations improved again following his overthrow, leading to the implementation in subsequent years of several substantial bilateral co-operation programmes in such areas as military co-operation, justice, public administration and education. Additionally, a significant number of Portuguese non-governmental organizations are actively involved in development projects throughout Guinea-Bissau, and play an especially important role in the education, health and rural development domains. Following the 2012 coup, Portugal remained steadfast in its support of Gomes Júnior and in its refusal to accept the transitional arrangement negotiated between the Military Command, the opposition parties and ECOWAS. In addition to suspending a large share of its co-operation activities in Guinea-Bissau, Portugal announced that it would decrease the scale of its diplomatic representation in the country pending the restoration of constitutional order.

Guinea-Bissau's foreign relations are also heavily influenced by a sense of vulnerability to the interests of its larger francophone neighbours, Senegal and Guinea. Relationships with Senegal, in particular, have been characterized by various vicissitudes, including a number of acute crises over the demarcation of maritime borders, the common land border and the conflict between the Senegalese armed forces and separatists of the Mouvement des Forces Démocratiques de la Casamance (MFDC). The issue of Casamance in fact constituted a triggering factor in the 1998–99 political-military conflict (see above), during the course of which President Vieira requested and obtained the support of military forces from both Senegal and Guinea. Military intervention by both these neighbours, albeit in response to a request for assistance by Vieira, was regarded by the vast majority of the population of Guinea-Bissau as an invasion, and was a low point in relations between the countries in question. After the military junta's victory, incidents continued in the border area between Guinea-Bissau and Senegal for some time, despite diplomatic efforts to resolve the crisis.

In the years after the 1998–99 conflict relations between Guinea-Bissau and Senegal gradually improved, as the Government of Guinea-Bissau showed its willingness to collaborate with the Senegalese Government's efforts to bring stability to the Casamance region. On 30 December 2004 a general peace accord was finally signed between the Senegalese Government and the MFDC. However, in June 2005 a dissident faction of the MFDC, which was opposed to the peace deal, launched a series of attacks in Casamance, prompting fears that the cease-fire might collapse. Responding to the growing instability in the border region, in March 2006 the Guinea-Bissau army launched a large-scale operation, involving more than 2,500 soldiers and heavy weaponry, targeting the dissident rebels' bases in the area around São Domingos, in northern Guinea-Bissau. By the time military operations ended on 27 April, more than 100 soldiers and an unknown number of rebels had been killed, with many more injured, and the remaining rebels had been expelled from northern Guinea-Bissau. As a result of the fighting, the UN estimated that 10,000 refugees fled the area around São Domingos to nearby villages and towns, while a further 2,500 fled across the border into Senegal.

The UN has played a central role in the efforts of the international community to contribute to the political stabilization of Guinea-Bissau. On 30 April 1999 the UN Secretary-General established UNOGBIS, with a mandate to aid peace-building efforts, support the consolidation of democracy and the rule of law, encourage friendly relations with its neighbours and assist in the electoral process. In October 2002 the UN deepened its commitment to assisting Guinea-Bissau through its political, economic and social crises when the UN Economic and Social Council (ECOSOC) created an ad hoc advisory group to study the country's needs in these areas. UN long-term actions were, however, once more suspended after the 2003 coup. After 2006 the UN again increased its support to Guinea-Bissau, as it became clear that the country's security and political situation remained fragile in spite of the holding of democratic elections. In December 2007 Guinea-Bissau was added to the agenda of the new UN Peace-building Commission: a specific Guinea-Bissau configuration of the Commission, headed by Brazil, was charged with co-ordinating the international community's conflict prevention efforts in Guinea-Bissau and identifying key programmes to prevent the country from sliding back into conflict. In 2008, in response to the numerous signs indicating that Guinea-Bissau had become a hub for drugs-trafficking between Latin America and Europe, the UN Office on Drugs and Crime (UNODC) established a project office in Bissau in order to support the Government's counter-trafficking efforts, as well as the training of a special judicial police task force.

In January 2010 UNOGBIS was succeeded by UNIOGBIS, which has a similar mandate to the mission that preceded it and is headed by Special Representative Joseph Mutaboba. UNIOGBIS's first few months in operation involved considerable controversy over Rear-Adm. Bubo Na Tchuto, who was granted refuge at the UNIOGBIS headquarters for a period of three months, immediately after which he was involved in the attempted coup of 1 April 2010 (see above). The controversy revolved around, initially, whether it was appropriate for UNIOGBIS to provide refuge to Na Tchuto and, later, whether he had actively participated in the planning of the coup from inside the UNIOGBIS compound.

In May 2012, in the aftermath of the 12 April coup, the UN Security Council adopted Resolution 2048, which called for the Military Command to return power to civilian hands and allow the electoral process to continue, and imposed a travel ban on five leaders of the coup, including Chief of Staff António Indjai. The position of the UN was subsequently one of encouraging ECOWAS and the CPLP to forge a unified strategy to enable a return to constitutional order.

In addition to the more politically focused activity of UNIOGBIS, the majority of agencies belonging to the UN system, including the Office of the UN High Commissioner for Refugees, the World Food Programme, the UN Development Programme, the UN Children's Fund (UNICEF) and the World Health Organization, are also present in Guinea-Bissau and are actively implementing a variety of projects and programmes.

A number of other international and regional organizations have played an important role in assisting Guinea-Bissau in overcoming its problems. Among them are regional organizations such as the EU, ECOWAS and the CPLP. The EU, a major donor in Guinea-Bissau, has provided support to state and rule of law reform programmes through the European Development Fund. In 2008 Guinea-Bissau joined the European Agency for the Management of Operational Co-operation at the External Borders (Frontex), extending European naval patrols into Guinea-Bissau's territorial waters. Also in 2008 the EU approved the deployment of the EU Security Sector Reform in Guinea-Bissau (EU SSR Guinea-Bissau). However, the pursuit of the mission's objectives was repeatedly hampered by resistance from within elements of the armed forces, and in the wake of the events of 1 April 2010 the EU announced that the mission would be suspended and that its mandate would not be extended beyond 30 September. In January 2011 the EU opened Article 96 consultations with the Guinea-Bissau Government, in view of the perceived risk of gross disrespect for the rule of law. These were concluded in March, with agreement between the two parties on a list of necessary reforms. A follow-up mission in January 2012 considered that insufficient progress had been made regarding these commitments, and EU co-operation programmes thus remained suspended. Following the April 2012 coup, the EU decided not only to extend that suspension for a further year, until July 2013, but also to impose a travel ban and asset freeze on six coup leaders, including Indjai.

ECOWAS played a prominent role in the resolution of the 1998–99 political-military conflict, and has continued to engage actively in the country's post-conflict transition. During the 1998–99 conflict, ECOWAS mediated between the warring parties on several occasions, and dispatched a 700-member ECOMOG interposition force over the course of several months in 1999. In 2003, following the overthrow of President Yalá, ECOWAS once again dispatched a special mission to act as mediator. After the attempted coup in Bissau on 1 April 2010, ECOWAS vehemently condemned the disruption to the constitutional order and called for urgent military reform. In this context, ECOWAS began in the following months to draft a new SSR initiative, which was eventually adopted in November and became the ECOWAS-CPLP SSR roadmap under which MISSANG was deployed to Guinea-Bissau in March 2011. In April 2012, in the aftermath of the latest coup, ECOWAS distanced itself significantly from the CPLP and took on an entirely new role as it became the key international partner that negotiated the transitional arrangement with the Military Command, thereby effectively legitimizing the de facto situation. In subsequent months it invited the post-coup authorities of Guinea-Bissau to attend its regional summits, and pledged financial support for the transition.

Economy

ALEXANDRE ABREU

INTRODUCTION

Guinea-Bissau is one of the poorest countries in the world. According to the World Bank, its gross domestic product (GDP, measured at current prices) totalled US $973m. in 2011, equivalent to $629 per head. On the basis of this indicator, Guinea-Bissau ranked 155th of 175 countries for which figures were available. Not surprisingly, the country's social and human development indicators are also among the lowest in the world: the UN Development Programme (UNDP) ranked Guinea-Bissau 176th of 187 countries in its 2011 Human Development Index, reflecting the country's low levels of productivity and economic diversification, as well as the serious difficulties that it faces in the health and education domains.

The majority of the country's population (70% in 2009) lives in rural areas, for the most part subsisting on a combination, in varying proportions, of smallholder agriculture, fishing, forestry and cattle-breeding. Among those activities that take on a monetized form, the harvesting and sale of cashew nuts, typically undertaken on an independent smallholder basis, play a paramount role: not only does this crop constitute the single main source of income for most rural households, it also accounts for 70%–95% of the country's total exports in any given year. As a whole, primary sector activity accounts for nearly 50% of GDP. Extractive and manufacturing industries remain at a very early stage of development, although some recent developments in the area of natural resource extraction (particularly bauxite and petroleum) suggest the possibility of a resource-driven boost to GDP in the future. The contribution of the service sector to domestic output (around 40% in 2010) is largely accounted for by public administration and commerce, with incipient foreign investment in telecommunications, banking, hotels and restaurants, and petrol distribution. The structure of budget receipts is dominated by foreign aid and the sale of fishing licences to international partners.

After the considerable economic upheaval caused by the 1998–99 conflict, including a drop in GDP by an estimated 28.1% in 1998, economic growth briefly resumed around the turn of the millennium, but experienced further declines in 2002 (of 7.1%) and 2003 (of 2.9%), due to a fall in both prices and production of cashews, a reduction in foreign aid, and renewed political instability. From 2004 onwards, however, economic growth recovered again and it has stayed on a relatively steady course, averaging an annual 2.9% in 2004–09. However, if population growth over the same period is taken into account, average annual GDP per caput growth was a much more modest 0.5% during 2004–09. After stagnant GDP growth in 2010, the record-breaking 2011 cashew harvesting season enabled a GDP growth rate of a remarkable 16% (according to World Bank data), but political instability in 2012 is certain to curb this newly acquired momentum, not least in so far as it has already compromised the year's cashew exports.

Inflationary pressures have been kept more or less in check since Guinea-Bissau joined the Franc Zone in 1997 (its currency being pegged to the euro at a fixed rate of €1 = 655.957 francs CFA), but have nevertheless fluctuated according to the evolution of the international prices of the country's main imports, particularly foodstuffs and oil. This was especially apparent in 2008, when the consumer price index increased by 10.5%, but, after a brief interlude in 2009 (when it fell by 1.7%), consumer prices rose again throughout 2010 and 2011.

The roots of the country's economic difficulties originate far in the past. Portugal, the colonial power until 1973–74, was itself relatively undeveloped, and until a very late stage was never willing or able to develop its colony. Instead, it opted for the maintenance of traditional economic structures with a view to ensuring political control, alongside the extraction of mercantile profits from a small number of crops like groundnuts and cotton. Following independence in 1974, the Government established a centrally planned economy, and an ambitious investment programme—financed mainly by foreign borrowing—was initiated, with emphasis on the industrial sector. However, the economy, which had been adversely affected by the campaign for independence, continued to deteriorate, and by the early 1980s Guinea-Bissau had an underdeveloped agricultural sector, a growing external debt, dwindling exports and escalating inflation. Additionally, the production of many goods had been halted, as the depletion of the country's reserves of foreign exchange made it difficult to import fuel or spare parts.

In response to the deteriorating economic situation, the Government initiated a process of economic liberalization in 1984. A Structural Adjustment Programme (SAP) was adopted for 1987–90, which aimed to correct macroeconomic and foreign imbalances, increase producer prices and strengthen the role of the private sector. In 1990 the Government began the reform of the country's public enterprises, and initiated the first phase of its programme of privatization. By mid-1995 the process of removing subsidies from public enterprises, which had begun in 1991, had been virtually completed. Overall, Guinea-Bissau's process of economic liberalization was relatively successful in addressing macroeconomic and foreign imbalances, but it also brought about a deterioration in human development indicators and hardly succeeded in boosting a dynamic private sector. The privatization of public enterprises, in particular, was often undertaken to the benefit of the ruling élite and a small group around it, and eventually led to the dismantling of several of those companies. Then, towards the end of the decade, the political-military conflict of 1998–99 plunged the country into a cycle of political instability, with economic consequences that only truly began to be reversed after 2004. Current economic prospects seem more promising, especially as the exploration of the country's rich mineral wealth by foreign investors is likely to increase domestic income significantly. However, as always in Guinea-Bissau, any progress will depend on future developments in the political and security domains.

AGRICULTURE AND FISHING

Agriculture is the principal economic activity. The primary sector (including forestry, fishing and cattle-breeding) engaged an estimated 82% of the working population in 2006 and accounted for some 44% of GDP in 2010. The main cash crop is cashew nuts, of which, according to government sources, a record 200,000 metric tons were produced in the 2011 season, 174,000 tons of which were exported. In the past few years, the export of cashew nuts has consistently contributed between 70% and 95% of the total value of the country's exports. In addition to cashew nuts, rice, roots and tubers, maize, beans, millet, sorghum, cassava, sweet potatoes, fruits, sugar cane, cotton, coconuts and groundnuts are also produced in considerable amounts. Livestock and timber production are also significant. Fishing is important on two different levels: artisanal fishing provides a key source of protein, especially for island, coastal and riverside communities, while the sale of industrial fishing licences to other countries constitutes a major source of government revenue.

Among food crops, rice is the staple fare of the population. The southern region of Tombali has historically been the 'rice basket' of Guinea-Bissau, accounting for more than one-half of the country's total production. According to FAO, production of paddy rice increased significantly from a low point during the 1998–99 conflict (80,300 metric tons in 1999) to 127,300 tons in 2007 and to 177,000 tons in 2010. However, this has not been enough to offset the significant increase in rice imports over the last two decades, which has been the result of population growth, rice field deterioration, lack of seeds and fertilizers, and a shift to cashew cultivation and its barter for imported rice. Thus, in the 2009/10 season, the country was estimated to have imported around 20% of its total rice consumption.

Food insecurity is a major concern for Guinea-Bissau, especially because of low agricultural productivity, dependence on imported cereals, high world food prices in recent years, and high volatility and a long-term downward trend of the world price for cashew nuts. In 2007 the combination of late rains, low cashew nut prices and high prices for imported rice led to severe food shortages for 43% of the population during the 'lean season', running from July to October, ahead of the first rice harvest. Rising international food prices added to the crisis in the first half of 2008, and the Government decided to abolish a significant part of the taxes collected on imported rice in order to relieve domestic prices. Food prices decreased somewhat in 2009, but renewed world food price rises in 2010–11 once again put food insecurity firmly on the agenda. A Food Security and Vulnerability Analysis undertaken by the World Food Programme (WFP) in 2011 found that 20% of the country's rural households could be considered food insecure at that time, and that 8% were in a situation of severe food insecurity. In order to address and mitigate this problem, WFP has effected a number of projects, including food for work, school feeding, and nutritional assistance for mothers and children, which currently benefit around 155,000 people. Similar projects are being implemented by several development non-governmental organizations.

Among Guinea-Bissau's traditional exports during the colonial period were groundnuts (grown in the interior as an extension of the Senegalese cultivation), cotton, oil-palm products on the islands and the coast, and coconuts. In 1977 groundnut exports, totalling 16,335 metric tons, accounted for 60% of total export earnings. However, according to the IMF, exports of groundnuts had ceased altogether by 1993, and they have not subsequently resumed. According to FAO data, production of groundnuts (in shell) totalled 69,651 tons in 2010, although this output catered exclusively to the domestic market.

By contrast, cashew nuts have become by far the country's principal cash crop over the past two decades. Although cashews were being harvested as far back as the colonial period, this crop only truly began to dominate from the late 1980s onwards. As more of the country's land area was allocated to cashew groves and as the trees gradually matured, production kept increasing steadily, offsetting the long-term downward trend in the world price for cashew nuts. By 2002 total production had risen to 68,000 metric tons; according to Government sources, it reached a record 200,000 tons in the 2011 season, of which 174,000 tons were exported. However, the country's trade in cashew nuts has been hampered on a number of occasions by disputes between producers, buyers and the Government over prices and export taxes. In 2006, for example, a buyers' dispute over government-fixed prices led to a sharp decline in the cashew nut trade, reducing annual production and export revenue. In 2011 conflict between buyers and the Government broke out again when, halfway through the cashew harvesting season, the Ministry of Commerce announced the imposition of a new tax on the export of cashew nuts amounting to 50 francs CFA per kg (about US $100 per ton). In response, the Association of Cashew Exporters urged its members to suspend their activities, but the dispute was eventually settled without compromising the record-breaking 2011 season.

The majority of Guinea-Bissau's cashew nuts are purchased by India for processing. However, by the early 2000s Indian processors were increasingly using domestic producers, and it was hoped that the establishment of processing firms in Guinea-Bissau would open new markets for direct sales to Europe (with a higher potential revenue from processed nuts). In 2006, after the Government seized 6,000 metric tons of cashews from the Singaporean trading group Olam International's warehouse in Bissau for alleged tax evasion, the company suspended its operations in the country, severely disrupting that year's marketing season. In 2008 the Government signed a co-operation agreement with Mozambique's Instituto de Fomento do Caju (Institute for the Promotion of Cashews—INCAJU) to exchange expertise on developing the cashew-processing sector. So far, however, the existing processing units have limited capacity, and the vast majority of the country's cashew nut output continues to be exported unprocessed.

The Constitution of Guinea-Bissau establishes that the land is the common property of all the people. However, the Government does grant private concessions to work it and has maintained the rights of those tilling their fields. The post-independence regime confiscated some properties and introduced state control over foreign trade and domestic retail trade through 'People's Stores', the inefficiency and corruption of which led to serious shortages of consumer goods and contributed to the downfall of the regime of Luís Cabral in 1980. In 1983/84 the Government partially privatized the state-controlled trading companies, and raised producer prices by about 70%, in an attempt to accelerate agricultural output. Despite the introduction of these measures, Guinea-Bissau continued to operate a 'war economy', superimposed on a rudimentary peasant economy where most products were bought and sold by the state. From 1987 onwards, however, plans were accelerated for the removal of price controls on most agricultural products, except essential goods, and for the liberalization of internal marketing systems. A new Land Law was adopted in 1998 but never implemented, and further efforts at reform were subsequently stalled by the outbreak of civil war. At present, a combination of customary tenure and government concessions is in practice, which has given rise to localized conflicts between commercial farmers and local communities.

The fishing industry has expanded rapidly since the late 1970s, and it has been estimated that the potential annual catch in Guinea-Bissau's waters could total some 300,000 metric tons. However, the total local catch has fluctuated around just 6,000–7,000 tons in the last decade. The local fishing sector is principally artisanal, while industrial fishing is conducted largely by foreign vessels operating under licence, depriving Guinea-Bissau of a potential revenue source in processing. Fishing agreements have been signed between the Government and the European Union (EU) since 1980. Under the terms of the most recent agreement, concluded in February 2012, the EU is to pay €9.2m. annually for the use of Guinea-Bissau's waters, €3.0m. of which is to be allocated to supporting Guinea-Bissau's fisheries policy. Securing access to West Africa's rich stocks of fish is a priority for the EU, which, in recent years, has been forced to reduce quotas in its own waters to counter the effects of overfishing. Other agreements have been negotiated by the Government of Guinea-Bissau with the People's Republic of China, Senegal, Côte d'Ivoire and the West Africa Fisheries Sub-Regional Commission. Altogether, fisheries contribute more than 40% of government budget receipts. However, the high level of illegal fishing—estimated in one study at 23% of the total catch—continues to deprive Guinea-Bissau of an important source of revenue, while also contributing to stock depletion. In recent years several dozen foreign vessels have been impounded, having been caught fishing illegally in Guinea-Bissau's waters, but many go undetected. If illegal fishing is effectively prevented, fishing may become one of Guinea-Bissau's main sources of revenue, as the country's maritime zone is potentially among the richest in West Africa.

Cattle-breeding is a very important activity among the Balante as well as the Muslim ethnic groups of the interior. Members of some communities practise transhumance, moving with their herds to riverside areas during the dry season. In 2010 there were 642,000 head of cattle, 419,000 pigs, 441,000 goats and 454,000 sheep, according to FAO estimates. Meat consumption is significant in some parts of the territory, and some hides and skins are exported.

INDUSTRY, MINING, TRANSPORT AND TELECOMMUNICATIONS

There is little industrial activity other than food-processing, brewing and wood-processing. Industry (including mining, manufacturing, construction and energy) employed an estimated 5.1% of the economically active population in 2002 and provided about 14% of GDP in 2010. According to the World Bank, industrial value-added declined by 40% in 1998 due to the conflict, but it subsequently recovered, with a record annual growth rate of 14.2% in 2002 and an average annual growth rate of 3.9% during 2004–08. More recent comparable figures are not available.

Energy is derived principally from thermal and hydroelectric power. According to UNDP, electricity consumption per caput in 2004 was a meagre 44 kWh, only 4.8% more than in 1990. The state electricity company, Empresa de Electricidade e Águas da Guiné-Bissau (EAGB), performs poorly, but attempts by the Government to restructure the company and attract private sector investment have so far proved unsuccessful. In April 2011, however, the Government announced a five-year plan aimed at restructuring the energy and water supply sector, which includes an intention to liquidate the EAGB and divide it into several smaller companies, in order to encourage the participation of private capital, the opening up of these two sectors to private competition, and new investments in infrastructure and in public lighting based on the use of renewable energy sources. Fewer than 10% of households in Guinea-Bissau are estimated to have regular access to electricity. Energy production since 1999 has been insufficient to meet demand in Bissau, the centre of non-agricultural economic activity, which suffers frequent blackouts in various parts of the city. The current generating capacity is just 5 MW, compared to a total estimated demand of 30 MW in Bissau alone. As a result, most energy is currently supplied by private generators. The supply deficit is due mainly to fuel shortages and equipment failures resulting from poor maintenance. In 2006 the Chinese Government agreed to finance the construction of the 18-MW Saltinho Rapids dam on the Corubal river, 100 km south-east of Bissau, at an estimated cost of US $87m. By 2012, however, construction of the dam had not begun. Guinea-Bissau is part of the Gambia River Basin Development Organization (Organisation pour la Mise en Valeur du Fleuve Gambie—OMVG), which oversees development projects in the three river basins of The Gambia, Guinea-Bissau, Guinea and Senegal. The OMVG plans to build two new dams on the Gambia and Konkoure rivers, which will supply Guinea-Bissau with 42% of its power needs, and to construct 15 transformers across the country to facilitate the transport and distribution of electricity. In June 2011 a project to provide street lighting in Bissau using solar power was jointly announced by the UN Integrated Peace-Building Office in Guinea-Bissau (UNIOGBIS) and the Bissau municipal authorities. A year later, however, public lighting had been installed on only one-half of one of the avenues designated by the project.

Mining is at an incipient stage but has seen important developments over the past few years. Prospecting for bauxite, petroleum, phosphates and gold has made significant progress, and commercial exploration of some of these is due to begin in the near future—albeit dependent on developments in the political and security spheres. In 2006 a Swiss-led international consortium, GB Phosphates, signed a contract with the Government with a view to developing phosphate reserves at Farim, with mining due to start in late 2008. Following serious disagreements with the consortium, the Government decided to terminate the mining contract in September of that year and the licence was suspended. In May 2009, however, an agreement was reached between the consortium and the new Government, allowing preparatory activities to resume. The project was publicly announced in April 2011, with production due to begin in 2014. Total phosphate reserves of 166m. tons are estimated, which will entail exploration over a period of 35–40 years, creating some 600 jobs and involving investment of some US $300m.

The exploration of the country's bauxite reserves, located in the south-eastern region of Boé, close to the border with Guinea, has also been negotiated with the Government and is currently under preparation. In September 2007 Guinea-Bissau and Angola signed an agreement to explore jointly for bauxite in the region. A private Angolan company, Bauxite Angola, took a 70% share in the project (with the Governments of Angola and Guinea-Bissau holding the remaining 20% and 10% shares, respectively), paying the Government US $13m. for an exploration licence. In July 2008 the Government announced that Bauxite Angola would invest some $300m. for the development of the bauxite reserves, including the construction of a mine that was expected to produce 2m. tons of bauxite per year over 56 years, a new deep-water port at Buba and a railway linking the two. Depending on the results of feasibility studies, the project was also expected to include an alumina plant using bauxite from the mine and powered by a hydroelectric dam on the Geba river. Following the April 2012 coup, however, Angola froze its investments in Guinea-Bissau pending the restoration of constitutional order, so future developments in this sphere will depend on Guinea-Bissau's political trajectory and the character of its future relationship with Angola.

The exploratory mining of other minerals has been under way: West Africa Mining AG of Switzerland announced in April 2010 that prospecting for gold ore deposits in 46 areas of Guinea-Bissau had yielded systematically positive results; and negotiations between the Government and two Russian and Chinese corporations have been recently conducted around the possibility of commercial exploitation of the ilmenite and zircon deposits in the north of Guinea-Bissau.

There have also been important developments in offshore petroleum exploration, as the increase in international oil prices over the past few years has improved the commercial viability of Guinea-Bissau's reserves. In October 1993 an agreement was signed with Senegal, providing for the joint management of the countries' maritime zones. The agreement, which was to operate for an initial 20-year period, provided for an 85%:15% division of petroleum resources between Senegal and Guinea-Bissau, respectively, altered to 80%:20% in August 2000. Guinea-Bissau formally ratified the agreement in December 1995, and the Agence de Gestion et Coopération was created to administer petroleum and fishing activity in the

100,000 sq km joint area. The southern section of the joint exploration area, on the border with Guinea, which may contain significant deposits, was contested until 1985, when a joint commission was formed with Guinea to facilitate exploration in the two countries' maritime border area. Since 2004 a number of international petroleum companies, including France's Maurel & Prom, Sweden's Svenska Petroleum Exploration, Dutch company Super Nova, Larsen Oil and Gas (an international consortium) and Angola's Sociedade de Hidrocarbonetos de Angola, have been granted licences to undertake offshore exploratory drilling and stakes in the country's offshore petroleum blocks. Guinea-Bissau's public petroleum company, PetroGuin, announced in late 2009 that prospecting for oil was progressing steadily in nine of the country's 14 offshore blocks. The country's total offshore reserves are estimated to exceed 1,000m. barrels of heavy crude oil.

Although Guinea-Bissau is a small country, road access to many areas is problematic: there are some 4,380 km of roads, of which only around 500 km are paved. Many areas, especially in the south of the country, are cut off during the rainy season. Road rehabilitation projects in the 2000s have been funded by, *inter alia*, the EU, the African Development Bank (AfDB), the Economic Community of West African States (ECOWAS), Portugal, France and the People's Republic of China. In December 2003 Guinea-Bissau's largest civil engineering project, the 750-m Ponte Amílcar Cabral over the Mansôa river at João Landim, was completed. The bridge, which links the north and south of the country, was financed by the EU. In 2006 work began on a new bridge over the Cacheu river, at São Domingos, with funding from the EU and the Union Economique et Monétaire Ouest-africaine (UEMOA). The bridge was opened in June 2009, providing a transport link between Bissau and the border with Senegal. Water transport could be greatly developed, as 85% of the population live within 20 km of a navigable waterway. The country's main commercial port is Bissau, which handles about 90% of the country's foreign trade. In November 2007 the Angolan Government announced that a consortium of private Angolan companies would fund a US $500m. project to build a deepwater port at Buba, which could provide an outlet for future bauxite exports from the Boé deposits, and also serve as an alternative point of access to the continental hinterland. Like the mining venture in Boé, however, these plans were frozen following the April 2012 coup. In September 2011, meanwhile, a new, €10m. fishing harbour was inaugurated in Bissau, with the capacity to hold four large vessels.

There is one international airport—Osvaldo Vieira Bissau International—in Bissau, and there are smaller airstrips in other parts of the country, including on the island of Bubaque. In November 2010 the Spanish companies Petromiralles and Saicus Air were granted a 30-year licence to rehabilitate and operate the Osvaldo Vieira International Airport. Guinea-Bissau's national airline, Transportes Aéreos da Guiné-Bissau, was liquidated in 1997 following an unsuccessful privatization. The Portuguese national airline, TAP, currently has a monopoly on flights to Europe via its three-weekly flights to Lisbon, Portugal. Flights to Dakar, Senegal—from where there are daily connections to other African destinations, Europe and elsewhere—are provided by Senegal Airlines and Cape Verde's Transportes Aéreos de Cabo Verde (TACV), while Royal Air Maroc flies between Bissau and Casablanca twice a week.

Guinea-Bissau's telecommunications infrastructure has deteriorated sharply as the prolonged political instability has stifled investment. By 2009 the fixed-line telephone network had fallen to just 4,400 functioning lines, down from 9,800 in 2004. However, this was partly related to, and certainly offset by, the astonishingly rapid increase in the number of mobile phone users. In 2003 the Government opened bids for licences to operate cellular services and established a national mobile telecommunications company, Guinetel. Three other companies submitted bids: Canelux (Portugal), Dataport Enterprises (Morocco), and Investcom Holdings (a Lebanese-Luxembourg venture). However, only two mobile phone companies subsequently started operating in Guinea-Bissau: Guinetel and MTN (South Africa). In March 2007 the Government awarded a third mobile phone licence to Orange Senegal. The new operator, Orange Bissau, started operations in November of the same year. The current level of network coverage across the entire country is high, with the exception of a few remote rural and island areas. According to the International Telecommunication Union, there were 594,100 mobile-phone users in Guinea-Bissau in 2010, compared with just 39,500 in 2004. The number of internet users in 2010 was estimated at 2.45 per 100 inhabitants.

EXTERNAL TRADE AND FINANCE

The total value of Guinea-Bissau's exports of goods and services, according to the World Bank, increased consistently after the turn of the millennium, from US $67.4m. in 2001 to an estimated $142m. in 2011. World Trade Organization data show that India, a major importer of cashew nuts, was the largest market for merchandise exports in 2011 (41.5%), followed by Nigeria (33.9%). Cashew nuts are Guinea-Bissau's most important export commodity.

Before the adoption of the franc CFA to replace the peso in 1997, demand for manufactured goods, machinery, fuel and food had ensured a high level of imports, the value of which on average exceeded 40% of annual GDP throughout the 1980s. However, foreign exchange controls and the closure of some state enterprises caused a large decline in imports of industrial raw materials in the subsequent decade, which was compounded by the upheaval caused by the 1998–99 conflict. According to the World Bank, imports then experienced a very considerable expansion from 2002 onwards, from US $86.0m. in 2002 to an estimated $284.0m. in 2008. The largest categories in 2009, according to the International Trade Centre, were mineral fuels, oils and distillation products ($75.7m.), cereals ($30.5m.) and electrical and electronic equipment ($18.4m.). In 2011 the principal sources of imports were Portugal (28.3%), Senegal (15.6%) and the People's Republic of China (4.7%).

The 2012 budget considered total (domestic and external) revenue in the order of 116,100m. francs CFA, of which 61,800m. francs CFA was domestic revenue. Total planned expenditure also corresponded to 116,100m. francs CFA, including current expenditure of 61,800m. francs CFA and investment expenditure of 51,600m. francs CFA. The Government thus projected a balanced budget in the 2012 fiscal year, although this is likely to have been compromised by the impact of the political crisis from April.

An extensive reorganization of Guinea-Bissau's banking system took place after 1989, involving the replacement of the Banco Nacional da Guiné-Bissau by three institutions: a central bank, a commercial bank (Banco Internacional da Guiné-Bissau, which began operations in March 1990), and a national credit bank, established in September 1990, to channel investment. A fourth financial institution was responsible for managing aid receipts. IThe banking sector was severely weakened by the 1998–99 military conflict, which forced all banks to close temporarily. Major changes to the country's financial sector took place in the 2000s, with the closure of both the Banco Internacional da Guiné-Bissau and the Banco Totta e Açores, and the emergence of several new private banks and a multitude of microfinance institutions. By 2012 four commercial banks—Ecobank, Banco Regional de Solidariedade, Banco da União and Banco da África Ocidental—together operated around 20 branches across the country, and more than 100 microfinance institutions were estimated to be functioning. Nevertheless, bank usage remains extremely low: only about 2.5% of the population is estimated to use formal banking services.

Guinea-Bissau applied to join the Franc Zone in November 1987, but withdrew its application in January 1990 following the formulation of an exchange rate agreement with Portugal linking the Guinea peso rate to that of the Portuguese escudo. This accord was considered to form the initial stage in the creation of an 'escudo zone'. However, Guinea-Bissau renewed its application to join the Franc Zone in 1993, joined the UEMOA in March 1997, and was admitted to the Franc Zone in April of the same year. The Guinea peso and the franc CFA co-existed for a period of three months to allow for the gradual replacement, at foreign exchange offices, of the national currency at a rate of 1 franc CFA = 65 Guinea pesos. With the entry of Guinea-Bissau into the Franc Zone, the Banco Central da Guiné-Bissau ceased to operate as the country's central bank; its functions were assumed by the Banque Centrale des Etats de l'Afrique de l'Ouest (BCEAO), which has its headquarters in Senegal. Since the replacement of the French franc with the euro in 1999, the franc CFA, which is backed by the French Treasury, has had a fixed parity against the euro of €1 = 655.957 francs CFA.

DEVELOPMENT AND AID

Multilateral aid forms the major source of international assistance. In 2010 it accounted for 82% of net official development assistance totalling US $141m., according to the Organisation for Economic Co-operation and Development. The largest individual donors in 2009/10 were the African Development Fund (the AfDB's lending arm for poverty reduction), at $86m., EU institutions, at $38m., and the International Development Association (the World Bank's concessionary lending arm), at $19m. Portugal, at $15m., was the single most important bilateral donor, although Japan and Spain each also donated more than $10m. In addition, Angola has emerged as a key development partner, including through the disbursement of grants and other forms of financial and technical assistance. Guinea-Bissau has been a signatory to the Lomé Conventions and to their successor, the Cotonou Agreement—signed in Cotonou, Benin, in 2000 and ratified by Guinea-Bissau in April 2003—and has been a regular recipient of European Development Fund assistance. Following the April 2010 attempted coup in Guinea-Bissau, the EU suspended a part of its co-operation programmes pending Article 96 consultations, and that suspension was extended in response to the April 2012 coup.

Guinea-Bissau's external debt rose dramatically throughout the post-independence period, from US $7.9m. in 1975 to $319m. in 1985 and $895m. in 1995, according to the World Bank. Before the military conflict of 1998–99, faced with a stock of external debt of $921m. by 1997, equivalent to 362% of gross national income, the Government undertook efforts to renegotiate the country's external debt with the assistance of UNDP. In March 1998 the IMF announced its approval of the Government's execution of its SAP for 1995–98, thus improving Guinea-Bissau's eligibility for debt relief under the initiative for heavily indebted poor countries (HIPC).

After preparing and submitting its first Poverty Reduction Strategy Paper (PRSP) in 2004, Guinea-Bissau was awarded two Staff-Monitored Programmes (SMP), two Emergency Post-Conflict Assistance (EPCA) programmes and one Extended Credit Facility (ECF) by the IMF between 2005 and 2010. Then, in December 2010 the IMF and World Bank announced that the country had undertaken the requisite policy actions and, accordingly, had reached HIPC completion point. Debt relief amounting to about US $700m. of the estimated $1,200m. external debt was thus granted direct under the HIPC initiative, while the country also became eligible for additional assistance of $370m. under a Multilateral Debt Relief Initiative. This announcement was followed by a number of similar decisions by bilateral partners, including Brazil and Angola in May 2011. In June of that year the 'Paris Club' of official creditors announced that a collective decision had been made to cancel $256m. of the country's $285m. bilateral debt.

A second PRSP, for 2011–15, was finalized in 2011, its main objectives consisting of reducing poverty, increasing income and employment opportunities, improving access to basic public services, and strengthening the rule of law. The new PRSP was announced against the background of the results of the second poverty assessment survey, undertaken by the authorities in 2010, which showed a deterioration in the poverty situation: the poverty rate at the line of US $2 per day was estimated at 69% in 2010 (compared with 65% in 2002), whereas the extreme poverty rate at the line of $1 increased from 21% in 2002 to 33% in 2010. Nevertheless, other large-scale surveys have shown an improvement in some key human development indicators: school enrolment rates increased from 45% in 2006 to 65% in 2010, while child mortality decreased from 223 to 155 deaths per 1,000 live births.

INDUSTRIAL ACTION

Due to the characteristics of its largely rural and informal economy, Guinea-Bissau's formal employment spectrum is relatively small, and to a large extent accounted for by the public sector. For this reason, industrial negotiations and labour unrest in the country have typically been centred on various branches of the public administration. A single state-controlled trade union confederation was created after the country's independence. Only much later, in the context of economic and political liberalization, were independent trade unions made legal and a new trade union confederation, Confederação Geral dos Sindicatos Independentes da Guiné-Bissau, established.

There was a period of almost constant labour unrest in the early 2000s, as a result of the Government's financial problems and its difficulties in paying civil servants' wages on time. Strikes took place in 2002–03, as by August 2003 many civil servants had not been paid for nine months. Following the overthrow of President Yalá, the interim administration had some success in clearing the wage arrears inherited from the previous administration (which in some cases dated back a year). However, the lack of resources and the huge accumulation of wage arrears led to further strikes in early 2004. In April 2008 the World Bank granted an additional US $20m. in budget support to pay the salary arrears of primary schoolteachers, who had been on strike since January. In spite of donor support, however, teachers began a further month-long strike in June, and in October the entire public sector observed a three-day strike, demanding three months of salary arrears and the payment of transport and overtime allowances. The new Government that was appointed in January 2009 immediately began paying salary arrears, with financial support from various sources, particularly the IMF, which tended to decrease the frequency and intensity of strikes. However, industrial action was not solely motivated by unpaid salaries: for example, magistrates and court officials staged strike action on a number of occasions in 2010–12 in support of their demands for better pay and work conditions. Following the April 2012 coup, the entire public administration went on strike, both to demand the restoration of constitutional order and to protest against the lack of payment of public sector salaries. This strike was called off at the end of May, after the new transitional Government settled the arrears.

Statistical Survey

Source (unless otherwise stated): Instituto Nacional de Estatística Guiné-Bissau, Av. Amílcar Cabral, CP 6, Bissau; tel. 3225457; e-mail inec@mail.gtelecom.gw; internet www.stat-guinebissau.com.

Area and Population

AREA, POPULATION AND DENSITY

Area (sq km)	36,125*
Population (census results)	
1 December 1991	983,367
15–29 March 2009	
Males	737,634
Females	783,196
Total	1,520,830
Population (UN estimates at mid- year)†	
2010	1,515,224
2011	1,547,049
2012	1,579,631
Density (per sq km) at mid-2012	43.7

* 13,948 sq miles.

† Source: UN, *World Population Prospects: The 2010 revision*.

POPULATION BY AGE AND SEX
(UN estimates at mid-2012)

	Males	Females	Total
0–14	323,784	322,423	646,207
15–64	435,401	445,501	880,902
65 and over	23,779	28,743	52,522
Total	782,964	796,667	1,579,631

Source: UN, *World Population Prospects: The 2010 Revision*.

ETHNIC GROUPS

1996 (percentages): Balante 30; Fulani 20; Mandjak 14; Mandinka 12; Papel 7; Other 16 (Source: Comunidade dos Países de Língua Portuguesa).

POPULATION BY REGION
(2009 census)

Bafatá	210,007	Quinará	63,610
Biombo	97,120	Sector Autónomo Bissau (SAB)	387,909
Bolama/Bijagós	34,563	Tombali	94,939
Cacheu	192,508	**Total**	1,520,830
Gabú	215,530		
Oio	224,644		

PRINCIPAL TOWNS
(population at 2009 census)

Bissau (capital)	365,097*	Bigene	51,412
Gabú†	81,495	Farim	48,264
Bafatá	68,956	Mansôa	46,046
Bissorã	56,585	Pitche	45,594

* Figure for Sector Autónomo Bissau (SAB) administrative division.

† Formerly Nova Lamego.

BIRTHS AND DEATHS

	2009	2010	2011
Birth rate (per 1,000)	38.7	38.7	37.9
Death rate (per 1,000)	17.0	16.7	16.4

Source: African Development Bank.

Life expectancy (years at birth): 47.7 (males 46.2; females 49.2) in 2010 (Source: World Bank, World Development Indicators database).

ECONOMICALLY ACTIVE POPULATION
('000 persons at mid-1994)

	Males	Females	Total
Agriculture, etc.	195	175	370
Industry	15	5	20
Services	80	14	94
Total	290	194	484

Source: UN Economic Commission for Africa, *African Statistical Yearbook*.

Mid-2012 (estimates in '000): Agriculture, etc. 463; Total labour force 588 (Source: FAO).

Health and Welfare

KEY INDICATORS

Total fertility rate (children per woman, 2010)	5.1
Under-5 mortality rate (per 1,000 live births, 2010)	150
HIV/AIDS (% of persons aged 15–49, 2009)	2.5
Physicians (per 1,000 head, 2008)	0.5
Hospital beds (per 1,000 head, 2009)	1.0
Health expenditure (2009): US $ per head (PPP)	91
Health expenditure (2009): % of GDP	8.6
Health expenditure (2009): public (% of total)	10.6
Access to water (% of persons, 2010)	64
Access to sanitation (% of persons, 2010)	20
Total carbon dioxide emissions ('000 metric tons, 2008)	282.4
Carbon dioxide emissions per head (metric tons, 2008)	0.2
Human Development Index (2011): ranking	176
Human Development Index (2011): value	0.353

For sources and definitions, see explanatory note on p. vi.

Agriculture

PRINCIPAL CROPS
('000 metric tons)

	2008	2009	2010
Rice, paddy	148.8	181.9	177.0*
Maize	16.7	6.6	12.3*
Millet	31.4	12.3	28.1*
Sorghum	18.3	14.6	17.6
Cassava	47.7	27.7	88.8*
Sugar cane†	6.0	6.0	6.0
Cashew nuts†	81.0	64.7	91.1
Groundnuts, with shell	46.5	30.7	69.7
Coconuts	45.5*	39.5*	40.1†
Oil palm fruit†	80.0	80.0	80.0
Plantains†	41.3	44.0	42.4
Oranges†	6.1	6.7	6.5

* Unofficial figure.

† FAO estimate(s).

Aggregate production ('000 metric tons, may include official, semi-official or estimated data): Total cereals 217.0 in 2008, 217.2 in 2009, 237.0 in 2010; Total roots and tubers 130.2 in 2008, 100.4 in 2009, 161.9 in 2010; Total vegetables (incl. melons) 32.9 in 2008, 26.1 in 2009, 34.2 in 2010; Total fruits (excl. melons) 82.4 in 2008, 89.6 in 2009, 87.1 in 2010.

Source: FAO.

LIVESTOCK

('000 head, year ending September, FAO estimates)

	2008	2009	2010
Cattle	599	620	642
Pigs	401	410	419
Sheep	389	420	454
Goats	393	416	441
Chickens	1,750	1,925	2,000

Source: FAO.

LIVESTOCK PRODUCTS

('000 metric tons, FAO estimates)

	2008	2009	2010
Cattle meat	6.7	6.1	6.4
Pig meat	12.5	12.8	12.8
Cows' milk	16.3	16.9	17.3
Goats' milk	3.6	3.8	4.0

Source: FAO.

Forestry

ROUNDWOOD REMOVALS

('000 cubic metres, excluding bark)

	2008	2009	2010
Sawlogs, veneer logs and logs for sleepers	1.9	1.9*	1.9*
Other industrial wood*	130.0	130.0	130.0
Fuel wood*	2,523.1	2,561.3	2,600.0
Total*	2,655.0	2,693.2	2,731.9

* FAO estimate(s).

2011: Production assumed to be unchanged from 2010 (FAO estimates).

Source: FAO.

SAWNWOOD PRODUCTION

('000 cubic metres, including railway sleepers, FAO estimates)

	1970	1971	1972
Total	10	16	16

1973–2011: Production assumed to be unchanged from 1972 (FAO estimates).

Source: FAO.

Fishing

(metric tons, live weight, FAO estimates)

	2007	2008	2009
Freshwater fishes	150	150	150
Marine fishes	2,650	2,866	2,862
Sea catfishes	340	385	385
Meagre	240	240	240
Mullets	1,500	1,500	1,500
Sompat grunt	200	230	230
Lesser African threadfin	370	420	420
Total catch (incl. others)	6,500	6,804	6,800

2010: Catch assumed to be unchanged from 2009 (FAO estimates).

Source: FAO.

Industry

SELECTED PRODUCTS

('000 metric tons unless otherwise indicated)

	2001	2002	2003
Hulled rice	69.1	68.4	67.7
Groundnuts (processed)	6.8	6.7	6.6
Bakery products	7.6	7.7	7.9
Frozen fish	1.7	1.7	1.7
Dry and smoked fish	3.6	3.7	3.8
Vegetable oils (million litres)	3.6	3.6	3.7
Beverages (million litres)	3.5	0.0	0.0
Dairy products (million litres)	1.1	0.9	0.9
Wood products	4.7	4.5	4.4
Soap	2.6	2.5	2.4
Electric energy (million kWh)	18.9	19.4	15.8

Source: IMF, *Guinea-Bissau: Selected Issues and Statistical Appendix* (March 2005).

Electric energy (million kWh, estimates): 70 in 2007; 70 in 2008; 72 in 2009 (Source: UN Industrial Commodity Statistics Database).

Finance

CURRENCY AND EXCHANGE RATES

Monetary Units

100 centimes = 1 franc de la Communauté Financière Africaine (CFA).

Sterling, Dollar and Euro Equivalents (31 May 2012)

£1 sterling = 819.959 francs CFA;
US $1 = 528.870 francs CFA;
€1 = 655.957 francs CFA;
10,000 francs CFA = £12.20 = $18.91 = €15.24.

Average Exchange Rate (francs CFA per US $)

2009 472.186
2010 495.277
2011 471.866

Note: An exchange rate of 1 French franc = 50 francs CFA, established in 1948, remained in force until January 1994, when the CFA franc was devalued by 50%, with the exchange rate adjusted to 1 French franc = 100 francs CFA. This relationship to French currency remained in effect with the introduction of the euro on 1 January 1999. From that date, accordingly, a fixed exchange rate of €1 = 655.957 francs CFA has been in operation. Following Guinea-Bissau's admission in March 1997 to the Union Economique et Monétaire Ouest-africaine, the country entered the Franc Zone on 17 April. As a result, the Guinea peso was replaced by the CFA franc, although the peso remained legal tender until 31 July. The new currency was introduced at an exchange rate of 1 franc CFA = 65 Guinea pesos. At 31 March 1997 the exchange rate in relation to US currency was $1 = 36,793.3 Guinea pesos.

BUDGET

Revenue ('000 million francs CFA)*	2010	2011†	2012‡
Tax revenue	33.1	37.9	46.7
Non-tax revenue	11.5	11.9	15.1
Fishing licences	5.2	5.0	8.3
Total	44.6	49.9	61.8

Expenditure ('000 million francs CFA)	2010	2011†	2012‡
Current expenditure	49.3	55.3	61.8
Wages and salaries	20.7	23.8	26.3
Goods and services	8.6	9.1	11.0
Transfers	10.7	12.6	12.5
Other current expenditures	8.6	9.0	11.8
Scheduled interest payments	0.7	0.8	0.3
Capital expenditure and net lending	36.2	42.5	44.6
Total	85.5	97.9	106.4

* Excluding budget grants received ('000 million francs CFA): 40.0 in 2010; 38.9 in 2011 (programmed figure); 39.8 in 2012 (projection).

† Programmed figures.

‡ Projections.

Source: IMF, *Guinea-Bissau: Third Review Under the Three-Year Arrangement Under the Extended Credit Facility and Financing Assurances Review—Staff Report; Joint IMF / World Bank Debt Sustainability Analysis; Informational Annex; Press Release on the Executive Board Discussion; and Statement by the Executive Director for Guinea-Bissau* (December 2011).

CENTRAL BANK RESERVES

(US $ million at 31 December)

	2009	2010	2011
IMF special drawing rights	18.64	19.09	19.02
Reserve position in IMF	0.15	0.20	0.32
Foreign exchange	149.80	137.15	200.66
Total	168.59	156.43	220.00

Source: IMF, *International Financial Statistics*.

MONEY SUPPLY

(million francs CFA at 31 December)

	2009	2010	2011
Currency outside banks	56,318	64,086	85,912
Demand deposits at deposit money banks	30,850	40,400	69,032
Total money (incl. others)	87,483	104,871	156,519

Source: IMF, *International Financial Statistics*.

COST OF LIVING

(Consumer Price Index; base: 2003 = 100)

	2006	2007	2008
Food, beverages and tobacco	105.2	111.3	129.1
Clothing	108.0	112.0	104.0
Rent, water, electricity, gas and other fuels	105.8	111.6	121.5
All items (incl. others)	106.4	111.2	122.9

2009: Food, beverages and tobacco 128.3; All items (incl. others) 120.8.

2010: Food, beverages and tobacco 99.4; All items (incl. others) 122.2.

2011: Food, beverages and tobacco 106.7.

Source: ILO.

NATIONAL ACCOUNTS

Expenditure on the Gross Domestic Product

(US $ million at current prices)

	2009	2010*	2011†
Government final consumption expenditure	53,297	55,196	58,544
Private final consumption expenditure	364,196	368,527	378,429
Gross capital formation	31,212	39,818	51,424
Change in inventories	400	422	953
Total domestic expenditure	449,105	463,963	489,350
Exports of goods and services	60,502	73,360	82,396
Less Imports of goods and services	114,523	118,523	125,651
GDP in purchasers' values	395,084	418,800	446,097

Gross Domestic Product by Economic Activity

(million francs CFA at current prices)

	2009	2010*	2011†
Agriculture, hunting, forestry and fishing	165,500	166,792	168,352
Mining and quarrying	110	116	116
Manufacturing	44,142	44,877	44,877
Electricity, gas and water	1,636	1,670	1,770
Construction	5,154	5,739	5,838
Trade, restaurants and hotels	79,184	80,173	80,584
Finance, insurance and real estate	1,491	1,495	1,495
Transport, storage and communications	20,028	21,142	21,842
Public administration and defence	41,712	41,724	41,924
Other services	17,487	17,500	17,600
Sub-total	376,444	381,228	384,398
Indirect taxes	24,422	26,376	27,939
Less Imputed bank service charge	5,782	–11,197	–33,760
GDP at purchasers' values	395,084	418,800	446,097

* Estimates.

† Projections.

Source: African Development Bank.

BALANCE OF PAYMENTS

('000 million francs CFA)

	2008	2009	2010
Exports of goods f.o.b.	54.5	55.5	59.5
Imports of goods f.o.b.	–89.0	–95.5	–97.3
Trade balance	–34.5	–40.0	–37.8
Exports of services	5.4	5.4	5.7
Imports of services	–23.9	–30.8	–25.2
Balance on goods and services	–53.0	–65.3	–57.3
Other income (net)	–6.0	–4.8	–0.5
Balance on goods, services and income	–59.0	–70.1	–57.8
Official current transfers	24.3	31.5	14.5
Private current transfers	16.4	13.7	15.5
Current balance	–18.3	–25.0	–27.7
Capital account (net)	38.4	34.6	30.8
Financial account (net)	–39.0	–11.4	–457.9
Statistical discrepancy	11.4	6.0	–3.3
Overall balance	–7.5	4.2	–458.1

Source: IMF, *Guinea-Bissau: Third Review Under the Three-Year Arrangement Under the Extended Credit Facility and Financing Assurances Review—Staff Report; Joint IMF / World Bank Debt Sustainability Analysis; Informational Annex; Press Release on the Executive Board Discussion; and Statement by the Executive Director for Guinea-Bissau* (December 2011).

External Trade

PRINCIPAL COMMODITIES
(million francs CFA)

Imports c.i.f.	2008	2009	2010
Rice	9,769	9,876	8,963
Wheat flour	2,251	2,376	1,731
Beverages	4,451	4,546	3,731
Petroleum and petroleum products	20,000	18,531	20,000
Construction materials	3,400	3,516	4,013
Total (incl. others)	89,010	93,916	96,121

Exports f.o.b.	2008	2009	2010
Cashew nuts	46,213	45,863	46,812
Total (incl. others)	57,421	56,418	57,021

Source: African Development Bank.

PRINCIPAL TRADING PARTNERS
(million francs CFA)

Imports	2008	2009	2010
China, People's Republic	1,278	1,233	900
India	70	1,426	1,236
Portugal	3,251	2,132	3,031
Senegal	11,351	9,321	11,821
Total (incl. others)	89,010	93,916	96,121

Exports	2008	2009	2010
India	35,351	34,213	33,512
Singapore	1,123	—	1,216
Total (incl. others)	57,421	56,418	57,021

Source: African Development Bank.

Transport

ROAD TRAFFIC
(motor vehicles in use, estimates)

	1994	1995	1996
Passenger cars	5,940	6,300	7,120
Commercial vehicles	4,650	4,900	5,640

2008 (motor vehicles in use): Passenger cars 42,222; Buses and coaches 289; Vans and lorries 9,323; Motorcycles and mopeds 4,936.

Source: International Road Federation, *World Road Statistics*.

SHIPPING

Merchant Fleet
(registered at 31 December)

	2007	2008	2009
Number of vessels	25	25	24
Total displacement (grt)	6,627	6,627	6,141

Source: IHS Fairplay, *World Fleet Statistics*.

International Sea-Borne Freight Traffic
(UN estimates, '000 metric tons)

	1991	1992	1993
Goods loaded	40	45	46
Goods unloaded	272	277	283

Source: UN Economic Commission for Africa, *African Statistical Yearbook*.

CIVIL AVIATION
(traffic on scheduled services)

	1996	1997	1998
Kilometres flown (million)	1	0	0
Passengers carried ('000)	21	21	20
Passenger-km (million)	10	10	10
Total ton-km (million)	1	1	1

Source: UN, *Statistical Yearbook*.

Tourism

TOURIST ARRIVALS BY NATIONALITY

	2005	2006	2007
Cape Verde	159	401	1,498
China, People's Republic	46	659	1,488
Cuba	29	329	309
France	599	834	2,984
Italy	213	343	1,871
Korea, Republic	36	523	1,289
Portugal	1,552	2,599	2,245
Senegal	235	921	2,798
Spain	324	231	1,458
USA	57	320	265
Total (incl. others)	4,978	11,617	30,092

Receipts from tourism (US $ million, excl. passenger transport): 2.8 in 2006; 28.4 in 2007; 38.2 in 2008.

Source: World Tourism Organization.

Communications Media

	2008	2009	2010
Telephones ('000 main lines in use)	4.6	4.8	5.0
Mobile cellular telephones ('000 subscribers)	500.2	560.3	594.1
Internet subscribers ('000)	0.7	0.7	n.a.

2011 ('000 subscribers): Mobile cellular telephones 401.9.

Personal computers: 3,000 (2.0 per 1,000 persons) in 2005.

Radio receivers ('000 in use): 49 in 1997.

Daily newspapers: 1 (average circulation 6,200 copies) in 1998.

Sources: UNESCO Institute for Statistics; UNESCO, *Statistical Yearbook*; UN, *Statistical Yearbook*; International Telecommunication Union.

Education

(2009/10 unless otherwise indicated, UNESCO estimates)

	Teachers	Students		
		Males	Females	Total
Pre-primary	309	4,360	4,590	8,950
Primary	5,371	144,075	134,815	278,890
Secondary: general	1,913*	46,445	31,581	78,026
Secondary: technical and vocational		656†	239†	895†
Tertiary†	32	399	74	473

* 1999.

† 2000/01.

Institutions (1999): Pre-primary 54; Primary 759.

Students (2005/06): Primary 269,287; Secondary 55,176; Tertiary 3,689.

Teachers (2005/06): Primary 4,327; Secondary 1,480; Tertiary 25.

Pupil-teacher ratio (primary education, UNESCO estimate): 51.9 in 2009/10 (Source: UNESCO Institute for Statistics).

Adult literacy rate (UNESCO estimates): 54.2% (males 68.2%; females 40.6%) in 2010.

Source: UNESCO Institute for Statistics.

Directory

The Constitution

A new Constitution for the Republic of Guinea-Bissau was approved by the Assembleia Nacional Popular (ANP) on 16 May 1984 and amended in May 1991, November 1996 and July 1999 (see below). The main provisions of the 1984 Constitution were:

Guinea-Bissau is an anti-colonialist and anti-imperialist Republic and a State of revolutionary national democracy, based on the people's participation in undertaking, controlling and directing public activities. The Partido Africano da Independência da Guiné e Cabo Verde (PAIGC) shall be the leading political force in society and in the State. The PAIGC shall define the general bases for policy in all fields.

The economy of Guinea-Bissau shall be organized on the principles of state direction and planning. The State shall control the country's foreign trade.

The representative bodies in the country are the ANP and the regional councils. Other state bodies draw their powers from these. The members of the regional councils shall be directly elected. Members of the councils must be more than 18 years of age. The ANP shall have 150 members, who are to be elected by the regional councils from among their own members. All members of the ANP must be over 21 years of age.

The ANP shall elect a 15-member Council of State (Conselho de Estado), to which its powers are delegated between sessions of the Assembleia. The ANP also elects the President of the Conselho de Estado, who is also automatically Head of the Government and Commander-in-Chief of the Armed Forces. The Conselho de Estado will later elect two Vice-Presidents and a Secretary. The President and Vice-Presidents of the Conselho de Estado form part of the Government, as do Ministers, Secretaries of State and the Governor of the National Bank.

The Constitution can be revised at any time by the ANP on the initiative of the deputies themselves, or of the Conselho de Estado or the Government.

Note: Constitutional amendments providing for the operation of a multi-party political system were approved unanimously by the ANP in May 1991. The amendments stipulated that new parties seeking registration must obtain a minimum of 2,000 signatures, with at least 100 signatures from each of the nine provinces. (These provisions were adjusted in August to 1,000 and 50 signatures, respectively.) In addition, the amendments provided for the ANP (reduced to 100 members) to be elected by universal adult suffrage, for the termination of official links between the PAIGC and the armed forces, and for the operation of a free-market economy. Multi-party elections took place in July 1994.

In November 1996 the legislature approved a constitutional amendment providing for Guinea-Bissau to seek membership of the Union Economique et Monétaire Ouest-africaine and of the Franc Zone.

In July 1999 constitutional amendments were introduced limiting the tenure of presidential office to two terms and abolishing the death penalty. It was also stipulated that the country's principal offices of state could only be held by Guinea-Bissau nationals born of Guinea-Bissau parents.

The Government

HEAD OF STATE

Interim President: MANUEL SERIFO NHAMADJO.

COUNCIL OF MINISTERS
(September 2012)

Prime Minister: RUI DUARTE DE BARROS.

Minister of the Presidency of the Council of Ministers, Social Communication and Parliamentary Affairs: FERNANDO VAZ.

Minister of Foreign Affairs, International Co-operation and Communities: Dr FAUSTINO FUDUT IMBALI.

Minister of National Defence and Fighters for the Country's Freedom: CELESTINO DE CARVALHO.

Minister of the Interior: Eng. ANTÓNIO SUKA NTCHAMA.

Minister of National Education, Youth, Culture and Sport: Dr VICENT PUNGURA.

Minister of Public Health and Social Solidarity: Dr AGOSTINHO CÁ.

Minister of Justice: Dr MAMADÚ SAIDO BALDÉ.

Minister of Natural Resources and Energy: DANIEL GOMES.

Minister of Finance: Dr ABUBACAR DEMBA DAHABA.

Minister of the Economy and Regional Integration: Dr DEGOL MENDES.

Minister of Infrastructure: Dr FERNANDO GOMES.

Minister of Trade, Industry and the Promotion of Local Products: Dr ABUBACAR BALDÉ.

Minister of Agriculture and Fisheries: Dr MALAM MANÉ.

Minister of Territorial Administration and Local Government: Dr BAPTISTA TÉ.

Minister of the Civil Service, Labour and State Reform: Dr CARLOS JOAQUIM VAMAIN.

In addition there were 13 Secretaries of State.

MINISTRIES

Office of the President: Bissau; internet www.presidencia-gw.org.

Office of the Prime Minister: Av. dos Combatentes da Liberdade da Pátria, CP 137, Bissau; tel. 3211308; fax 3201671.

Ministry of Agriculture and Rural Development: Av. dos Combatentes da Liberdade da Pátria, CP 102, Bissau; tel. 3221200; fax 3222483.

Ministry of the Civil Service, Employment and Modernization: Bissau.

Ministry of the Economy, Planning and Regional Integration: Av. dos Combatentes da Liberdade da Pátria, CP 67, Bissau; tel. 3203670; fax 3203496; e-mail info@mail.guine-bissau.org; internet www.guine-bissau.org.

Ministry of Energy, Industry and Natural Resources: CP 311, Bissau; tel. 3215659; fax 3223149.

Ministry of Finance: Rua Justino Lopes 74A, CP 67, Bissau; tel. 3203670; fax 3203496; e-mail info@mail.guine-bissau.org.

Ministry of Fisheries: Av. Amílcar Cabral, CP 102, Bissau; tel. 3201699; fax 3202580.

Ministry of Foreign Affairs and Communities: Av. dos Combatentes da Liberdade da Pátria, Bissau; tel. 3204301; fax 3202378.

Ministry of Infrastructure: Av. dos Combatentes da Liberdade da Pátria, CP 14, Bissau; internet www.minisinfraestruturas-gov.com; tel. 3206575; fax 3203611.

Ministry of the Interior: Av. Unidade Africana, Bissau; tel. 3203781.

Ministry of Justice: Av. Amílcar Cabral, CP 17, Bissau; tel. 3202185; internet mj-gb.org.

Ministry of National Defence: Amura, Bissau; tel. 3223646.

Ministry of National Education, Culture and Science: Rua Areolino Cruz, Bissau; tel. 3202244.

Ministry of the Presidency of the Council of Ministers: Bissau.

Ministry of Public Health: CP 50, Bissau; tel. 3204438; fax 3201701.

Ministry of Social Communication and Parliamentary Affairs: Bissau.

Ministry of Territorial Administration: Bissau.

Ministry of Trade, Tourism and Crafts: 34A Av. Pansau na Isna, Bissau; tel. and fax 3206062; e-mail turismom@yahoo.com; internet www.minturgb-gov.com.

Ministry of War Veterans: Bissau.

Ministry of Women, Families, Social Cohesion and the Fight against Poverty: Av. dos Combatentes da Liberdade da Pátria, Bissau; tel. 3204785.

Ministry of Youth and Sports: Bissau.

President and Legislature

PRESIDENT

Presidential Election, First Round, 18 March 2012*

Candidate	Votes	% of votes
Carlos Gomes Júnior	154,797	48.97
Mohamed Yalá Embaló (PRS)	73,842	23.36
Manuel Serifo Nhamadjo	49,767	15.74
Henrique Rosa	17,070	5.40
Others†	20,631	6.53
Total	316,107	100.00

* Under the terms of the Constitution, a second round of the presidential election was scheduled to take place on 29 April in order to determine which of the two leading candidates from the first round would be elected. However, on 12 April members of the military seized power and announced the dissolution of the organs of state and their intention to form a National Transitional Council (Conselho Nacional de Transição).

† There were five other candidates.

LEGISLATURE

Assembleia Nacional Popular: Palácio Colinas de Boé, Bissau; tel. 3201991; fax 3206725.

President: MANUEL SERIFO NHAMADJO.

General Election, 16 November 2008

Party	Votes	% of votes	Seats
Partido Africano da Independência da Guiné e Cabo Verde (PAIGC)	227,036	49.75	67
Partido para a Renovação Social (PRS)	115,409	25.29	28
Partido Republicano para a Independência e o Desenvolvimento (PRID)	34,305	7.52	3
Partido para a Nova Democracia (PND)	10,721	2.35	1
Partido dos Trabalhadores (PT)	10,503	2.30	—
Partido Unido Social Democrático (PUSD)	7,695	1.69	—
Partido para Democracia, Desenvolvimento e Cidadania (PADEC)	7,073	1.55	—
Aliança Democrática (AD)	6,321	1.39	1
Partido Social Democrata (PSD)	6,315	1.38	—
Total (incl. others)	456,312	100.00	100

Election Commission

Comissão Nacional de Eleições (CNE): Av. 3 de Agosto 44, CP 359, Bissau; tel. 3203600; fax 3203601; e-mail cne-info@guinetel.com; internet www.cne-guinebissau.org; Pres. DESEJADO LIMA DA COSTA.

Political Organizations

The legislative elections of November 2008 were contested by the 19 parties and two coalitions listed below:

Aliança Democrática (AD): c/o Assembleia Nacional Popular, Bissau; f. 2008; Leader VÍTOR FERNANDO MANDINGA.

Frente Democrática (FD): Bissau; f. 1991; officially registered in Nov. 1991; Pres. JORGE FERNANDO MANDINGA.

Partido da Convergência Democrática (PCD): Bissau; Leader VÍTOR FERNANDO MANDINGA.

Aliança de Forças Patrióticas (AFP): Bissau; f. 2008; Pres. AMINE MICHEL SAAD.

Forum Cívico Guinéense-Social Democracia (FCG-SD): Bissau; Pres. ANTONIETA ROSA GOMES; Sec.-Gen. CARLOS VAIMAN.

Frente Democrática Social (FDS): c/o Assembleia Nacional Popular, Bissau; f. 1991; Pres. LUCAS DA SILVA.

Partido de Solidariedade e Trabalho (PST): Bissau; f. 2002; Leader IANCUBA INDJAI; Sec.-Gen. ZACARIAS BALDÉ.

União para a Mudança (UM): Bissau; f. 1994; Leader AMINE MICHEL SAAD.

Centro Democrático (CD): Bissau; tel. and fax 452517; e-mail empossaie@centrodemocratico.com; internet www.cd.empossaie.com; f. 2006; Sec.-Gen. VICTOR DJELOMBO.

Liga Guinéense de Protecção Ecológica (LIPE): Bairro Missirá 102, CP 1290, Bissau; tel. and fax 3252309; f. 1991; ecology party; Interim Pres. MAMADU MUSTAFA BALDÉ.

Movimento Democrático Guinéense (MDG): Bissau; f. 2003; Pres. SILVESTRE CLAUDINHO ALVES.

Partido Africano da Independência da Guiné e Cabo Verde (PAIGC): CP 106, Bissau; internet www.paigc.org; f. 1956; fmrly the ruling party in both Guinea-Bissau and Cape Verde; although Cape Verde withdrew from the PAIGC following the coup in Guinea-Bissau in Nov. 1980, Guinea-Bissau has retained the party name and initials; Pres. CARLOS DOMINGOS GOMES JÚNIOR; Sec. AUGUSTO OLIVAIS.

Partido para Democracia, Desenvolvimento e Cidadania (PADEC): Bissau; f. 2005; Leaders FRANCISCO JOSÉ FADUL.

Partido Democrático Guinéense (PDG): f. 2007; Pres. EUSEBIO SEBASTIAO DA SILVA.

Partido Democrático Socialista (PDS): Bissau; f. 2006; Pres. JOÃO SECO MAMADÚ MANÉ.

Partido para a Nova Democracia (PND): Bissau; f. 2007; Pres. IBRAIMA DJALÓ.

Partido Popular Democrático (PPD): Bissau; f. 2006; Pres. BRAIMA CORCA EMBALÓ.

Partido de Progresso (PP): Bissau; f. 2004; Pres. IBRAHIMA SOW.

Partido da Reconciliação Nacional (PRN): Bissau; f. 2004; Leader ALMARA NHASSÉ; Sec.-Gen. OLUNDO MENDES.

Partido para a Renovação Social (PRS): c/o Assembleia Nacional Popular, Bissau; f. 1992; Pres. MOHAMED YALÁ EMBALÓ.

Partido Republicano para a Independência e o Desenvolvimento (PRID): Bissau; f. 2008; Pres. ARISTIDES GOMES.

Partido Social Democrata (PSD): c/o Assembleia Nacional Popular, Bissau; f. 1995 by breakaway faction of the RGB—MB; Pres. ANTONIO SAMBA BALDÉ.

Partido Socialista-Guiné Bissau (PS-GB): Bissau; f. 1994; Pres. CIRILO OLIVEIRA RODRIGUES.

Partido dos Trabalhadores (PT): Bissau; e-mail contact@nodjuntamon.org; internet www.nodjuntamon.org; f. 2002; left-wing; Pres. ARREGADO MANTENQUE TÉ.

Partido Unido Social Democrático (PUSD): Bissau; f. 1991; officially registered in Jan. 1992; Pres. AUGUSTO BARAI MANGO.

União Nacional para Democracia e Progresso (UNDP): Bissau; f. 1998; Pres. ABUBACAR BALDÉ.

União Patriótica Guinéense (UPG): Bissau; f. 2004 by dissident members of the RGB; Pres. FRANCISCA VAZ TURPIN.

Diplomatic Representation

EMBASSIES IN GUINEA-BISSAU

Angola: Bissau; Ambassador FELICIANO DOS SANTOS.

Brazil: Rua São Tomé, Esquina Rua Moçambique, CP 29, Bissau; tel. 3212549; fax 3201317; e-mail emb_brasil_bxo@hotmail.com; Ambassador JORGE GERALDO KADRI.

China, People's Republic: Av. Francisco João Mendes, Bissau; tel. 3203637; fax 3203590; e-mail chinaemb_gw@mail.mfa.gov.cn; Ambassador LI BAOJUN.

Cuba: Rua Joaquim N'Com 1, y Victorino Costa, CP 258, Bissau; tel. 3213579; fax 3201301; e-mail embcuba@sol.gtelecom.gw; Ambassador PEDRO FÉLIZ DOÑA SANTANA.

France: Bairro de Penha, Av. dos Combatentes da Liberdade da Pátria, Bissau; tel. 3257400; fax 3257421; e-mail cad.bissao-amba@diplomatie.gouv.fr; internet www.ambafrance-gw.org; Ambassador MICHEL FLESCH.

The Gambia: 47 Victorino Costa, Chao de Papel, CP 529, 1037 Bissau; tel. 3205085; fax 3251099; e-mail gambiaembbissau@hotmail.com; Ambassador CHERNO B. TOURAY.

Guinea: Rua 14, no. 9, CP 396, Bissau; tel. 3212681; Ambassador TAMBA TIENDO MILLIMONO.

Korea, Democratic People's Republic: Bissau; Ambassador KIM KYONG SIN.

Nigeria: Bissau; Ambassador AHMED ADAMS.

Libya: Rua 16, CP 362, Bissau; tel. 3212006; Representative DOKALI ALI MUSTAFA.

Portugal: Av. Cidade de Lisboa, CP 76, 1021 Bissau; tel. 3201261; fax 3201269; e-mail embaixada@bissau.dgaccp.pt; Ambassador Dr ANTÓNIO MANUEL RICOCA FREIRE.

Russia: Av. 14 de Novembro, CP 308, Bissau; tel. 3251036; fax 3251028; e-mail russiagb@eguitel.com; Chargé d'affaires a.i. VIACHELAV ROZHNOV.

Senegal: Rua Omar Torrijos 43A, Bissau; tel. 3212944; fax 3201748; Ambassador Gen. ABDOULAYE DIENG.

South Africa: c/o Bissau Palace Hotel, Rm No. 9, Av. 14 de Novembro, CP 1334, Bissau; tel. 6678910; e-mail bissau@foreign.gov.za; Ambassador LOUIS MNGUNI.

Spain: Praza Dos Hèroes Naçionais; tel. 6722246; fax 3207656; e-mail emb.bissau@maec.es; Ambassador D. ANGEL BALLESTEROS GARCÍA.

Judicial System

The Supreme Court is the final court of appeal in criminal and civil cases and consists of nine judges. Nine Regional Courts serve as the final court of appeal for the 24 Sectoral Courts, and deal with felony cases and major civil cases. The Sectoral Courts hear minor civil cases.

President of the Supreme Court: MARIA DO CÉU SILVA MONTEIRO.

Religion

According to the 1991 census, 45.9% of the population were Muslims, 39.7% were animists and 14.4% were Christians, mainly Roman Catholics.

ISLAM

Associação Islâmica Nacional: Bissau; Sec.-Gen. Alhaji ABDÚ BAIO.

Conselho Superior dos Assuntos Islâmicos da Guiné-Bissau (CSAI-GB): Bissau; Exec. Sec. MUSTAFA RACHID DJALÓ.

CHRISTIANITY

The Roman Catholic Church

Guinea-Bissau comprises two dioceses, directly responsible to the Holy See. The Bishops participate in the Episcopal Conference of Senegal, Mauritania, Cape Verde and Guinea-Bissau, currently based in Senegal. Approximately 10% of the total population are adherents of the Roman Catholic Church.

Bishop of Bafatá: Rev. CARLOS PEDRO ZILLI, CP 17, Bafatá; tel. 3411507; e-mail domzilli@yahoo.com.br.

Bishop of Bissau: JOSÉ CÂMNATE NA BISSIGN, Av. 14 de Novembro, CP 20, 1001 Bissau; tel. 3251057; fax 3251058; e-mail diocesebissau@yahoo.it.

The Press

REGULATORY AUTHORITY

Conselho Nacional de Comunicação Social (CNCS): Bissau; f. 1994; dissolved in 2003, recreated in November 2004; Pres. AUGUSTO MENDES.

NEWSPAPERS AND PERIODICALS

Banobero: Rua José Carlos Schwarz, CP 760, Bissau; tel. 3230702; fax 3230705; e-mail banobero@netscape.net; weekly; Dir FERNANDO JORGE PEREIRA.

Comdev Negócios (Community Development Business): Av. Domingos Ramos 21, 1° andar, Bissau; tel. 3215596; f. 2006; independent; business; Editor FRANCELINO CUNHA.

Correio-Bissau: Bissau; weekly; f. 1992; Editor-in-Chief JOÃO DE BARROS; circ. 9,000.

Diário de Bissau: Rua Vitorino Costa 29, Bissau; tel. 3203049; daily; Owner JOÃO DE BARROS.

Expresso de Bissau: : Rua Vitorino Costa 30, Bissau; tel. 6666647; e-mail expressobissau@hotmail.com.

Fraskera: Bairro da Ajuda, 1ª fase, CP 698, Bissau; tel. 3253060; fax 3253070; weekly.

Gazeta de Notícias: Av. Caetano Semeao, CP 1433, Bissau; tel. 3254733; e-mail gn@eguitel.com; internet www.gaznot.com; f. 1997; weekly; Dir HUMBERTO MONTEIRO; circ. 1,000.

Journal Nô Pintcha: Av. do Brasil, CP 154, Bissau; tel. 3213713; internet www.jornalnopintcha.com; Dir SRA CABRAL; circ. 6,000.

Kansaré: Edifico Sitec, Rua José Carlos Schwarz, Bissau; e-mail kansare@eguitel.com; internet www.kansare.com; f. 2003; Editor FAFALI KOUDAWO.

Última Hora: Av. Combatentes da Liberdade da Pátria (Prédio Suna Ker), Bissau; tel. 5932236; e-mail damil@portugalmail.com; Dir ATHIZAR PEREIRA; circ: 500.

Voz de Bissau: Rua Eduardo Mondlane, Apdo 155, Bissau; tel. 3202546; twice weekly.

Wandan: Rua António M'Bana 6, CP 760, Bissau; tel. 3201789.

NEWS AGENCIES

Agência de Notícias da Guiné-Bissau (ANG): Av. Domingos Ramos, CP 248, Bissau; tel. 2605200; fax 2605256; e-mail informacao@anguinebissau.com; internet www.anguinebissau.com.

Publisher

Ku Si Mon: Bairro d'Ajuda, Rua José Carlos Schwarz, CP 268, Bissau; tel. 6605565; e-mail kusimon@eguitel.com; internet www.guine-bissau.net/kusimon; f. 1994; privately owned; Portuguese language; Dir ABDULAI SILA.

Broadcasting and Communications

TELECOMMUNICATIONS

Regulatory Authority

Autoridade Reguladora Nacional das Tecnologias de Informação (ARN): Av. Domingos Ramos 53, Praça Cheguevara, CP 1372, Bissau; tel. 3204874; fax 3204876; e-mail geral@arn-gb.com; internet arn-gb.com; f. 2010 to replace Instituto das Comunicações da Guiné-Bissau; also manages radio spectrum; Pres. GIBRIL MANÉ.

Service Providers

Guiné Telecom (GT): Bissau; tel. 3202427; internet www.gtelecom.gw; f. 2003 to replace the Companhia de Telecomunicações da Guiné-Bissau (Guiné Telecom—f. 1989); state-owned; privatization pending.

Guinetel: Bissau; f. 2003; mobile operator; CEO JOÃO FREDERICO DE BARROS.

MTN Guinea Bissau: 7 Av. Unidade Africana, CP 672, Bissau; tel. 3207000; fax 6600111; e-mail contact@mtn-bissau.com; internet www.mtn-bissau.com; f. 2007; CEO ANTHONY MASOZERA; 110 employees.

Orange Bissau: Praça dos Herois Nacionais, BP 1087, Bissau; tel. 5603030; e-mail abdul.dapiedadeTMP@orange-sonatel.com; internet orange-bissau.com; f. 2007; provides fixed-line and mobile telecommunications services.

RADIO AND TELEVISION

An experimental television service began transmissions in 1989. Regional radio stations were to be established at Bafatá, Cantchungo and Catió in 1990. In 1990 Radio Freedom, which broadcast on behalf of the PAIGC during Portuguese rule and had ceased operations in 1974, resumed transmissions. Other radio stations included Radio Televisão Portuguesa Africa (RTP/Africa), which broadcast from Bissau, and Rádio Sintchã Oco.

Radiodifusão Nacional da República da Guiné-Bissau (RDN): Av. Domingos Ramos, Praça dos Martires de Pindjiguiti, CP 191, Bissau; tel. 3212426; fax 3253070; e-mail rdn@eguitel.com; f. 1974; govt-owned; broadcasts in Portuguese on short-wave, MW and FM; Dir-Gen. LAMINE DJATA.

Rádio Bafatá: CP 57, Bafatá; tel. 3411185.

Rádio Bombolom: Bairro Cupelon, CP 877, Bissau; tel. 3201095; f. 1996; independent; Dir AGNELO REGALA.

Rádio Mavegro: Rua Eduardo Mondlane, CP 100, Bissau; tel. 3201216; fax 3201265.

Rádio Pindjiguiti: Bairro da Ajuda, 1ª fase, CP 698, Bissau; tel. 3253070; f. 1995; independent.

Televisão da Guiné-Bissau (TGB): Bairro de Luanda, CP 178, Bissau; tel. 3221920; fax 3221941; internet www.televisao-gb.net; f. 1997; Dir-Gen. LUÍS DOMINGOS CAMARÁ DE BARROS.

Finance

(cap. = capital; res = reserves; m. = million; amounts in francs CFA)

BANKING

Central Bank

Banque Centrale des Etats de l'Afrique de l'Ouest (BCEAO): Av. dos Combatentes da Liberdade da Pátria, Brá, CP 38, Bissau; tel. 3256325; fax 3256300; internet www.bceao.int; HQ in Dakar, Senegal; f. 1955; bank of issue for the mem. states of the Union Economique et Monétaire Ouest-africaine (UEMOA, comprising Benin, Burkina Faso, Côte d'Ivoire, Guinea-Bissau, Mali, Niger, Senegal and Togo); cap. 134,120m., res 1,474,195m., dep. 2,124,051m. (Dec. 2009); Gov. KONÉ TIÉMOKO MEYLIET; Dir in Guinea-Bissau JOÃO ALAGE MAMADU FADIA.

Other Banks

Banco da África Ocidental, SARL: Rua Guerra Mendes 18, CP 1360, Bissau; tel. 3203418; fax 3203412; e-mail bao-info@eguitel.com; internet bancodaafricaocidental.com; f. 2000; International Finance Corporation 15%, Grupo Montepio Geral (Portugal) 15%, Carlos Gomes Júnior 15%; cap. and res 1,883m. (Dec. 2003); Chair. ABDOOL VAKIL; Man. Dir RÓMULO PIRES.

Banco Regional de Solidariedade: Rua Justino Lopes, Bissau; tel. 3207112.

Banco da União (BDU): Av. Domingos Ramos 3, CP 874, Bissau; tel. 3207160; fax 3207161; internet www.bdu-sa.com; f. 2005; 30% owned by Banque de Développement du Mali; CEO HUGO DOS REIS BORGES.

Caixa de Crédito da Guiné: Bissau; govt savings and loan institution.

Caixa Económica Postal: Av. Amílcar Cabral, Bissau; tel. 3212999; postal savings institution.

Ecobank Guinea-Bissau: Av. Amílcar Cabral, BP 126, Bissau; tel. 3207360; fax 3207363; e-mail info@ecobankgw.com; Chair. João José Silva Monteiro; Man. Dir Gilles Guerard.

STOCK EXCHANGE

In 1998 a regional stock exchange, the Bourse Régionale des Valeurs Mobilières, was established in Abidjan, Côte d'Ivoire, to serve the member states of the UEMOA.

INSURANCE

GUINEBIS—Guiné-Bissau Seguros: Rua Dr Severino Gomes de Pina 36, Bissau; tel. 211458; fax 201197.

Instituto Nacional de Previdência Social: Av. Domingos Ramos 12, CP 62, Bissau; tel. and fax 3211331; fax 3204396; e-mail inps_informatica@hotmail.com; internet www.inps-gb.com; state-owned; Dir-Gen. Mamadu Iaia Djaló.

Trade and Industry

DEVELOPMENT ORGANIZATION

Ajuda de Desenvolvimento de Povo para Povo ná Guiné Bissau (ADPP): CP 420, Bissau; tel. 6853323; e-mail adppartemisa@eguitel.com.

CHAMBER OF COMMERCE

Câmara de Comércio, Indústria, Agricultura e Serviços da Guiné-Bissau (CCIAS): Av. Amílcar Cabral 7, CP 361, Bissau; tel. 3212844; fax 3201602; f. 1987; Pres. Braima Camará; Sec.-Gen. Saliu Ba.

INDUSTRIAL AND TRADE ASSOCIATIONS

Associação Comercial, Industrial e Agricola (ACIA): CP 88, Bissau; tel. 3222276.

Direcção de Promoção do Investimento Privado (DPIP): Rua 12 de Setembro, Bissau Velho, CP 1276, Bissau; tel. 3205156; fax 3203181; e-mail dpip@mail.bissau.net.

Fundaçao Guineense para o Desenvolvimento Empresarial Industrial (FUNDEI): Rua Gen. Omar Torrijos 49, Bissau; tel. 3202470; fax 3202209; e-mail fundei@fundei.bissau.net; internet www.fundei.net; f. 1994; industrial devt org.; Pres. Macária Barai.

Procajú: Bissau; private sector association of cashew producers.

UTILITIES

Gas

Empresa Nacional de Importação e Distribuição de Gás Butano: CP 269, Bissau; state gas distributor.

MAJOR COMPANIES

Grupo Carlos Gomes Júnior (GRUCAR): CP 329, Bissau; tel. 213709; fax 201474; owned by Carlos Gomes Júnior.

Internegoce: CP 429, Bissau; tel. 203701; e-mail canjurai@hotmail.com.

PetroGuin: Rua Eduardo Mondlane 20, CP 387, Bissau; tel. and fax 3221155; e-mail dg.petroguin@yahoo.com.br; internet www.petroguin.com; state-owned; fmrly Empresa Nacional de Pesquisas e Exploração Petrolíferas e Mineiras (PETROMINAS); exploration for and production of petroleum and natural gas; Dir-Gen. Leonardo Cardoso.

Petromar—Sociedade de Abastecimentos Petrolíferos Lda: Rua 7, CP 838, Bissau; tel. 3214281; fax 3201557; e-mail castro@sol.gtelecom.gw; f. 1990; 65% owned by Petrogal GB and 35% by Grucar; import and distribution of petroleum, gas and lubricants; Pres. Carlos Bayan Ferreira; CEO Eng. José Castro.

TRADE UNIONS

Confederação Geral dos Sindicatos Independentes da Guiné-Bissau (CGSI-GB): Rua nº10, Bissau Apartado 693, Bissau; tel. 204110; fax 204114; e-mail cgsi-gb@hotmail.com; internet http://www.lgdh.org/CONFEDERACAOGERALDOSSINDICATOSINDEPENDENTES.htm; Sec.-Gen. Filomeno Cabral.

Sindicato Nacional dos Marinheiros (SINAMAR): Bissau.

Sindicato Nacional dos Professores (SINAPROF): CP 765, Bissau; tel. and fax 3204070; e-mail ict@mail.bissau.net; Pres. Luís Nancassa.

União Nacional dos Trabalhadores da Guiné (UNTG): 13 Av. Ovai di Vievra, CP 98, Bissau; tel. and fax 3207138; e-mail untgcs.gb@hotmail.com; Pres. Desejado Lima da Costa; Sec.-Gen. Estêvão Gomes Có.

Transport

RAILWAYS

There are no railways in Guinea-Bissau. However, the proposed construction of a railway line by Bauxite Angola, linking the bauxite extraction site in Boé with the future deep-water port at Buba, has been announced.

ROADS

According to the Minister of Infrastructure, there are 2,755 km of 'classified' roads in Guinea-Bissau, of which 770 km are paved. There are plans in place for a further 300 km to be paved by 2020.

SHIPPING

Plans have been announced to build a major deep-water port at Buba, the capacity of which will make it one of the largest in West Africa. At 31 December 2009 the merchant fleet comprised 24 vessels, totalling 6,141 grt. In mid-2004 plans were announced to improve links with the Bijagós islands, by providing a regular ferry service.

Empresa Nacional de Agências e Transportes Marítimos: Rua Guerva Mendes 4–4a, CP 244, Bissau; tel. 3212675; fax 3213023; state shipping agency; Dir-Gen. M. Lopes.

CIVIL AVIATION

There is an international airport at Bissau, which there are plans to expand, and 10 smaller airports serving the interior. TAP Portugal and Transportes Aéreos de Cabo Verde (TACV) fly to Bissau.

Tourism

There were 30,092 tourist arrivals in 2007. Receipts from tourism totalled US $38.2m. in 2008.

Central de Informação e Turismo: CP 294, Bissau; tel. 213905; state tourism and information service.

Direcção Geral do Turismo: CP 1024, Bissau; tel. 202195; fax 204441.

Defence

As assessed at November 2011, the armed forces officially totalled an estimated 6,458 men (army 4,000, navy 350, air force 100 and paramilitary gendarmerie 2,000). Military service was made compulsory from 2007, as part of a programme of reform for the armed forces. Following the military uprising of April 2010, the EU decided to suspend, and then not to renew, the mandate of its Security Sector Reform (SSR) mission in Guinea-Bissau, which ended on 30 September 2010. Subsequently, a new joint SSR roadmap was approved by ECOWAS and the Lusophone Community CPLP in November 2010 and is currently under way. In this context, a two-year Angolan Armed Forces Security Mission in Guinea-Bissau (MISSANG) was launched in January 2011, one of the aims of which was to reduce the number of army troops to 2,500.

Defence Expenditure: Budgeted at 9,520m. francs CFA in 2011.

Chief of Staff of the Armed Forces: Gen. António Indjai.

Army Chief of Staff: Brig.-Gen. Armando Gomes.

Acting Navy Chief of Staff: Sanha Clussé.

Chief of Staff of the Air Force: Ibraima Papá Camara.

Education

Education is officially compulsory only for the period of primary schooling, which begins at six years of age and lasts for seven years. Secondary education, beginning at the age of 13, lasts for up to five years (a first cycle of three years and a second of two years). According to UNESCO estimates, in 2009/10 enrolment at primary schools included 74% of children in the relevant age-group (males 75%; females 72%), while enrolment at secondary schools in 2005/06 was equivalent to only 36% of children in the relevant age-group. In 2000/01 473 students were enrolled in tertiary education. There are three tertiary level institutions in Guinea-Bissau: the Universidade Amílcar Cabral (public); the Universidade Colinas do Boé (private); and the Faculdade de Direito de Bissau (a law school funded and run within the ambit of Portuguese co-operation). According to the 2005 budget, expenditure on education was forecast at 15.0% of total spending.

Bibliography

Bigman, L. *History and Hunger in West Africa: Food Production and Entitlement in Guinea-Bissau and Cape Verde.* Westport, CT, Greenwood Press, 1993.

Bock, A. J. *Segurança Alimentar: Potencialidade dos Recursos na Guiné-Bissau e Política Alimentar.* Lisbon, Instituto Superior de Agronomia, 2009.

Boubacar-Sid, B., Creppy, E., and Gacitua-Mario, E. (Eds). *Conflict, Livelihoods, and Poverty in Guinea-Bissau.* Washington, DC, World Bank Publications, 2007.

Cabral, A. *Unity and Struggle* (collected writings) (trans. by M. Wolfers). London, Heinemann Educational, 1979.

Documentário. Lisbon, Cotovia, 2008.

Cabral, L. *Crónica da Libertação.* Lisbon, O Jornal, 1984.

Cann, J. P. *Counter-insurgency in Africa: The Portuguese Way of War 1961–1974.* Westport, CT, Greenwood Press, 1997.

Chabal, P. *Amílcar Cabral: Revolutionary Leadership and People's War.* 2nd edn. London, C. Hurst & Co (Publishers) Ltd, 2001.

Chabal, P. (Ed.). *A History of Postcolonial Lusophone Africa.* London, Hurst and Company, 2002.

Chilcote, R. *Amílcar Cabral's Revolutionary Theory and Practice: a Critical Guide.* Boulder, CO, Lynne Rienner, 1991.

Davidson, B. *No Fist is Big Enough to Hide the Sky: The Liberation of Guinea-Bissau and Cape Verde.* 2nd edn. London, Zed Press, 1984.

Einarsdóttir, J. *Tired of Weeping: Mother Love, Child Death and Poverty in Guinea-Bissau.* 2nd edn. Madison, WI, University of Wisconsin Press, 2004.

Fisas Armengol, V. *Amílcar Cabral y la Independencia de Guinea-Bissau.* Barcelona, Nova Terra, 1974.

Forrest, J. B. *Guinea-Bissau: Power, Conflict and Renewal in a West African Nation.* Boulder, San Francisco, CA, and Oxford, Westview Press, 1992.

Lineages of State Fragility: Rural Civil Society in Guinea-Bissau. Athens, OH, University of Ohio Press, 2003.

Galli, R., and Jones, D. *Guinea-Bissau: Politics, Economics and Society.* New York, and London, Pinter Publishers, 1987.

Hawthorne, W. *Planting Rice and Harvesting Slaves: Tranformations along the Guinea-Bissau Coast, 1400-1900.* Portsmouth, NH, Heinemann, 2003.

Lobban, R. A., and Mendy, P. K. *Historical Dictionary of Guinea-Bissau.* 2nd edn. Lanham, MD, Scarecrow Press, 1997.

Lopes, C. *Guinea-Bissau: From Liberation Struggle to Independent Statehood.* Boulder, CO, Westview Press, 1987.

Monteiro, A. I. *O Programa de Ajustamento Estrutural na Guiné-Bissau: Análise dos Efeitos Socioeconómicos.* Bissau, INEP, 1996.

da Mota Teixeira, A. *Guiné Portuguesa.* 2 vols. Lisbon, 1964.

Nóbrega, A. *A luta pelo poder na Guiné Bissau.* Lisbon, Instituto Superior de Ciências Sociais e Políticas, 2003.

Núñez, B. *Dictionary of Portuguese-African Civilization.* Vol. I. London, Hans Zell, 1995.

Paulini, T. *Guinea-Bissau, Nachkoloniale Entwicklung eines Agrarstaates.* Göttingen, 1984.

Pereira, L. T., and Moita, L. *Guiné-Bissau: Três Anos de Independência.* Lisbon, CIDAC, 1976.

Proença, C. S. *Os efeitos da política de estabilização e ajustamento estrutural no bem-estar das famílias urbanas: o caso de Bissau 1986–93.* Lisbon, ISEG, 1998.

Rimmer, D. *The Economies of West Africa.* London, Weidenfeld and Nicolson, 1984.

Silva, A. *A Independência da Guiné-Bissau e a Descolonização Portuguesa.* Porto, Afrontamento, 1997.

Sousa, J. S. *Amílcar Cabral (1924–1973) vida e morte de um revolucionário africano.* Lisboa, Nova Vega, 2011.

Vigh, H. E. *Navigating Terrains of War: Youth and Soldiering in Guinea-Bissau.* Oxford, Berghahn Books, 2006.

World Bank. *Guinea-Bissau: A Prescription for Comprehensive Adjustment.* Washington, DC, 1988.

Guinea-Bissau Integrated Poverty and Social Assessment (IPSA) – Transitions from Post Conflict to Long-Term Development: Policy Considerations for Reducing Poverty. 2 Vols. Washington, DC, 2006.

Zeverino, G. *O Conflito Político-Militar na Guiné-Bissau (1998-1999).* Lisbon, Instituto Português de Apoio ao Desenvolvimento, 2005.

KENYA

Physical and Social Geography

W. T. W. MORGAN

PHYSICAL FEATURES

The total area of the Republic of Kenya is 582,646 sq km (224,961 sq miles) or 571,416 sq km (220,625 sq miles) excluding inland waters (mostly Lake Turkana and part of Lake Victoria). Kenya is bisected by the Equator and extends from approximately 4°N to 4°S and 34°E to 41°E.

The physical basis of the country is composed of extensive erosional plains, cut across ancient crystalline rocks of Pre-Cambrian age. These are very gently warped—giving an imperceptible rise from sea level towards the highlands of the interior, which have their base at about 1,500 m above sea-level. The highlands are dominated by isolated extinct volcanoes, including Mt Kenya (5,200 m) and Mt Elgon (4,321 m), while outpourings of Tertiary lavas have created plateaux at 2,500 m–3,000 m. The Great Rift Valley bisects the country from north to south and is at its most spectacular in the highlands, where it is some 65 km across and bounded by escarpments 600 m–900 m high. The trough is dotted with lakes and volcanoes which are inactive but generally associated with steam vents and hot springs. Westwards the plains incline beneath the waters of Lake Victoria, and eastwards they have been down-warped beneath a sediment-filled basin.

CLIMATE AND NATURAL RESOURCES

Although Kenya lies on the Equator, its range of altitude results in temperate conditions in the highlands above 1,500 m, with temperatures that become limiting to cultivation at about 2,750 m, while Mt Kenya supports small glaciers. Average temperatures may be roughly calculated by taking a sea-level mean of 26°C and deducting 1.7°C for each 300 m of altitude. For most of the country, however, rainfall is more critical than temperature. Only 15% of the area of Kenya can be expected to receive a reliable rainfall adequate for cultivation (750 mm in four years out of five). Rainfall is greatest at the coast and in the west of the country, near Lake Victoria and in the highlands, but the extensive plains below 1,200 m are arid or semi-arid. In the region of Lake Victoria and in the highlands west of the Rift Valley, rain falls in one long rainy season. East of the Rift Valley there are two distinct seasons: the long rains (March–May) and the short rains (September–October).

The high rainfall areas tend to be intensively cultivated on a small-scale, semi-subsistence basis with varying amounts of cash cropping. Food crops are in great variety, but most important and widespread are maize, sorghum, cassava and bananas. The principal cash crops, which provide the majority of exports, are tea, coffee (mainly *Coffea arabica*), pyrethrum and sisal. The first three are particularly suited to the highlands and their introduction was associated with the large-scale farming on the alienated lands of the former 'White Highlands'. Horticultural produce (in particular, cut flowers) is an increasingly significant export. The dairy industry is important both for domestic consumption and for export. The herds of cattle, goats, sheep and camels of the dry plains support a low density of mainly subsistence farmers.

Fisheries are of local importance around Lake Victoria and are of great potential at Lake Turkana.

Soda ash is mined at Lake Magadi in the Rift Valley. Deposits of fluorspar, rubies, gold, salt, vermiculite, iron ore and limestone are also exploited. However, mineral resources make a negligible contribution to Kenya's economy.

POPULATION AND CULTURE

A total population of 38,610,097, excluding adjustment for underenumeration, was recorded at the census of August 2009. At mid-2011 the population was officially estimated at 42,749,417. The resultant overall density of 74.8 inhabitants per sq km is extremely unevenly distributed, with a large proportion of the population contained in only 10% of the area; densities approach 400 per sq km on the small proportion of the land that is cultivable. None the less, by 2001 about 33% of the population resided in urban areas, principally in Nairobi (population estimated to be 3.4m. in 2011) and Mombasa (1m. in 2010). The towns also contain the majority of the non-African minorities of some 81,791 Asians, 40,760 Arabs and 32,338 Europeans (2009 census).

Kenya has been a point of convergence of major population movements in the past, and, on a linguistic and cultural basis, the people have been divided into Bantu, Nilotic, Nilo-Hamitic (Paranilotic) and Cushitic groups. Persian and Arab influence at the coast is reflected in the Islamic culture. Kiswahili is the official language, although English, Kikuyu and Luo are widely understood.

Recent History

MICHAEL JENNINGS

COLONIAL RULE TO THE KENYATTA ERA

Kenya, formerly known as British East Africa, was declared a British protectorate in 1895. Subsequent white settlement met with significant African armed resistance by 1914, and by the early 1920s some African political activity had begun to be organized. In 1944 the Kenya African Union (KAU), an African nationalist organization, was formed. Leadership of the movement, which drew its main support from the Kikuyu, passed in 1947 to Jomo Kenyatta, himself a Kikuyu. During 1952–56 a campaign of violence was conducted by the Mau Mau, a predominantly Kikuyu secret society. A state of emergency was declared by the British authorities, Kenyatta was detained and a ban on all political activity remained in force until 1955. During this period, two Luo political activists, Tom Mboya and Oginga Odinga, came to prominence. Following the removal of the state of emergency in January 1960, a transitional Constitution was introduced, legalizing political parties and according Africans a large majority in the legislative council. The KAU was reorganized as the Kenya African National Union (KANU), and Mboya and Odinga were elected to the party's leadership. Following his release in August 1961, Kenyatta assumed the presidency of KANU, which won a decisive victory at the general election of May 1963. Kenyatta became Prime Minister in June, and independence followed on 12 December. The country was declared a republic (with Kenyatta as President) exactly one year later.

By 1965 KANU had divided into a 'conservative' wing, led by Mboya, and a 'radical' group, led by Odinga, who left KANU to form the Kenya People's Union (KPU). Kenyatta moved swiftly to curtail the activities of the KPU, introducing legislation giving the Government powers of censorship and the right to hold suspects in detention without trial. Following the assassination of Mboya in July 1969, the KPU was banned and Odinga was placed in detention, where he remained for 15 months. During the early 1970s President Kenyatta became increasingly reclusive and autocratic. He was elected, unopposed, for a third five-year term in September 1974, but died in August 1978.

THE MOI PRESIDENCY

Daniel arap Moi succeeded to the presidency in October 1978. Despite initial signals of greater openness, Moi became increasingly intolerant of criticism, and in June 1982 Kenya's Constitution was amended to create a one-party state. Amid growing concern over his human rights record, Moi was returned unopposed for a third term in March 1988. Following his re-election, Moi moved to further entrench the power of the presidency. In July the National Assembly approved constitutional amendments that allowed the President to dismiss judges at will.

In May 1990 a broad alliance of intellectuals, lawyers and church leaders was established (under the leadership of former cabinet minister Kenneth Matiba), seeking to legalize political opposition. The Government responded by arresting several leaders of the movement. In August 1991 six opposition leaders, including Odinga, established the Forum for the Restoration of Democracy (FORD). The party was immediately outlawed, but continued to operate clandestinely.

POLITICAL PLURALISM AND ETHNIC TENSIONS

As a result of international and domestic pressure, Moi instituted a programme of reform and introduced a multi-party political system. By early 1992 several new parties were registered, including the Democratic Party (DP), established by Mwai Kibaki who had resigned as Minister of Health. Following a split in FORD in August 1992, FORD—Asili, led by Matiba, and FORD—Kenya, led by Odinga, were registered as separate parties in October. With the opposition divided, Moi won a fourth term as President in December 1992.

By the end of 1995 11 opposition National Assembly delegates had defected to KANU, and leadership struggles paralysed FORD—Kenya and FORD—Asili. In December 1996 Raila Odinga, the son of Oginga Odinga, was reportedly expelled from FORD—Kenya and joined the National Development Party (NDP), subsequently becoming its leader in 1997.

In May 1996 the opposition-dominated public accounts committee accused a number of senior members of the Government of withholding information vital to its investigation into the collapse of a number of Kenyan banks. This was linked to the loss of an estimated US $430m. in public funds from fraudulent claims for export tax rebates (the affair was to become known as the Goldenberg scandal).

During this period, the Government was accused of inciting ethnic tensions and violence to undermine the opposition. Clashes between 1992 and 1995 left at least 3,500 people dead and more than 320,000 homeless. Government-sponsored clashes were particularly fierce in the Rift Valley, and between Kikuyu and Kalenjin. Tensions continued to grow throughout the next decade.

Elections and Internal Concerns

In August 1998 a car bomb exploded at the US embassy in Nairobi (concurrently with a similar attack on the US mission to Dar es Salaam, Tanzania). Some 254 people were killed in Nairobi and more than 5,000 suffered injuries. The attacks were believed to have been co-ordinated by international Islamist fundamentalist terrorists, led by Saudi-born dissident Osama bin Laden.

Meanwhile, presidential and legislative elections on 29 December 1997 returned Moi and KANU to Government, amid allegations of electoral fraud and political violence. Furthermore, international concern over corruption began to shape Kenya's relationship with international donors. Despite being implicated in the Goldenberg scandal, Prof. George Saitoti was appointed Vice-President in April 1999. Efforts to combat corruption were largely superficial, and in December 2000 the Kenya Anti-Corruption Authority (KACA—established in 1987), was effectively dismantled after the Constitutional Court ruled that its powers of prosecution were illegal. In January 2001 the IMF and the World Bank expressed concern over the setbacks in the reforms and suspended aid to Kenya until the situation could be resolved. The National Assembly blocked legislation to establish a new anti-corruption authority in August 2001. The IMF confirmed the continuation of its suspension of aid to Kenya. On the following day Moi announced the creation of a new police unit to tackle corruption, which would investigate all 132 cases that the KACA had been handling.

Electoral Campaigning

Following an agreement with the NDP in January 2001, in June Moi created Kenya's first coalition government, with the appointment of Raila Odinga as Minister of Energy. In mid-March 2002 the NDP was dissolved and absorbed into KANU. In August 2002 Odinga established the Rainbow Alliance faction within KANU in an attempt to pressure Moi into accepting the will of the party in selecting a presidential candidate, following divisions over Moi's support for Uhuru Kenyatta (son of late President Jomo Kenyatta). In September the NAPK announced that Kibaki, leader of the DP, was to be its candidate in the forthcoming election, and in October Kenyatta was confirmed as the official KANU candidate. In response, six government ministers, including Odinga, and 30 KANU deputies resigned from the party and joined the opposition. In mid-October negotiations between the ex-KANU politicians (who had formed the Liberal Democratic Party—LDP) and the NAPK culminated in the establishment of the National Rainbow Coalition (NARC), an alliance of 14 opposition parties, headed by Kibaki. FORD—People (formed in 1997 by former members of Ford—Asili) and the Social Democratic Party of Kenya (SDP) refused to join the alliance, with both parties nominating their own presidential candidates in early November.

THE KIBAKI ADMINISTRATION

Presidential and legislative elections took place on 27 December 2002. The opposition secured an emphatic victory, with Kibaki taking 62.3% of the votes cast in the presidential election and NARC securing 125 of the 210 elected seats in the National Assembly. Kenyatta received 31.2% of votes and KANU won 64 seats. In his first Cabinet, Kibaki appointed Michael Wamalwa as Vice-President and Odinga as Minister of Roads, Public Works and Housing. However, the LDP, led by Odinga, accused Kibaki of breaking a power-sharing agreement and demanded a reshuffle. In August Vice-President Wamalwa died while undergoing hospital treatment in the United Kingdom. Following a month of bitter infighting over who should succeed him, Moody Awori was appointed as Vice-President. In December Kibaki offered four cabinet positions to KANU politicians in order to increase support for his faction. A cabinet reorganization in June 2004 included KANU and FORD—People members in a further effort to shift the balance of power and undermine the LDP in particular.

Moi resigned as Chairman of KANU in September 2003, leaving Uhuru Kenyatta as acting Chairman. In September 2004 Kenyatta appealed to the party to apologize for its abuses of power in a bid to undermine the popularity of NARC. Kenyatta was elected as Chairman of KANU in February 2005.

Political Fragmentation and Crisis

Constitutional reform, a central element of the opposition campaign before the December 2002 elections, became a touchstone for rivalries within NARC. In mid-2005 a draft constitution, which included provisions for a weak prime ministerial post, was adopted by the National Assembly and submitted to a national referendum. The 'Yes' campaign, led by Kibaki, was represented by a banana, and the 'No' campaign, led by Odinga, by an orange. At the referendum on 21 November, the draft was rejected by some 57% of voters. In response, Kibaki dismissed the entire Cabinet and banned opposition rallies and demonstrations. In December a new Cabinet was announced, predominantly comprising Kibaki's allies (although 16 ministers and deputy ministers refused to take up their positions).

In mid-2006 the ruling NARC coalition collapsed as the political fall-out from the constitutional crisis continued. In June, after a succession of attempts to secure control over NARC, Kibaki established a new governing party, NARC—Kenya, in an effort to reimpose his authority. Meanwhile, the LDP, led by Odinga, had left NARC to establish the Orange Democratic Movement (ODM).

In mid-2006 Kenyatta sought to enter into an alliance with the ODM, and was expelled from the party. Within the ODM, he contested for the leadership in an attempt to secure the ODM nomination for the presidential elections, challenging Odinga and Kalonzo Musyoka. However, the following year, Kenyatta returned to KANU, allying himself with Kibaki. In August Musyoka left the ODM, and initiated a legal challenge for the title of the party. Odinga won, and Musyoka established ODM—Kenya, standing as that party's presidential candidate. The divisions within the ODM seemed to favour Kibaki's campaign, leading the newly established Party of National Unity (PNU). Nevertheless, the ODM retained its lead in the opinion polls.

Crime and Violence

In November 2006 clashes between rival gangs in Nairobi's Kibera slum left at least eight people dead and caused thousands to flee their homes. Police imposed a night-time curfew and increased patrols of the area. In the following month, when a former leader of the Mungiki gang attempted to hold a rally, police and demonstrators clashed; four people died as a result. In May 2007 Mungiki members were accused of killing and beheading six people as part of a campaign to establish control over transport operators. Two police officers were murdered by suspected Mungiki attackers, and police and paramilitaries responded by launching a security operation in June. John Kamunya, a former leader of Mungiki, was gaoled for possession of weapons and narcotics, prompting further violence in and around Nairobi that, according to reports, led to the deaths of 11 people. Police tactics came under review in October when the Kenya National Commission on Human Rights alleged that the police had executed around 500 suspected Mungiki members during the previous five months. In April 2008 the murder of Mungiki leader Maina Nyaiko's wife led to further violence, which resulted in 14 deaths. Later that month the Chairman of the Kenya National Youth Alliance—the political wing of Mungiki—was shot dead.

The 2007 Elections and their Aftermath

The presidential and legislative elections and their aftermath were seen by some observers as evidence of the continued use of ethnic identity as a mobilizing force in Kenyan politics. However, other social cleavages were also of importance in shaping both the election results and the ensuing crisis—notably religious and generational differences, with opinion polls showing a clear divide between those under 35 (a majority of whom supported Odinga), and those over 50 (who were mostly Kibaki supporters), and on issues over land-ownership and access. Nevertheless, the efforts by KANU under Moi, in particular, in the 1990s to politicize ethnic identities, and subsequent political manipulation of ethnic groups by politicians from all parties, provided a foundation for the violence in Kenya in January and February 2008.

The presidential and legislative elections took place concurrently on 27 December 2007 amid high turn-outs (especially in western Kenya). After delays to the count, precipitating violent protests in which at least 13 people were killed, President Kibaki was declared the victor on 30 December by the Electoral Commission of Kenya (ECK) with 4,584,721 votes. Odinga, who unofficial results suggested was leading in the poll, officially received 4,352,993 votes. Musyoka, standing for ODM—Kenya, received 879,903 votes. The ODM claimed a parliamentary majority, securing 99 elected and six nominated seats. Kibaki's PNU won 43 seats; ODM—Kenya won 16, and KANU 14. The European Union (EU) Election Observation Mission to Kenya condemned the vote, suggesting that the polls had been manipulated in favour of Kibaki. Odinga refused to accept the result, claiming victory in the presidential poll, a position supported by independent observers. Nevertheless, Kibaki was sworn in as President on 30 December.

The announcement of Kibaki's victory prompted an upsurge in violence, and by 31 December 2007 some 120 people had been killed in clashes between rival supporters and police. Protests in Nairobi were met with violence by police, whom Odinga accused of deliberately targeting ODM supporters, also alleging that they had adopted a shoot-to-kill policy following the killing of seven protesters. The Government accused opposition politicians of fomenting violence against Kibaki's supporters, following attacks by Kalenjin militia on Kikuyu; Odinga denied the allegations. Nevertheless, violence and killings escalated rapidly, particularly in the Rift Valley, where violence between Kalenjin, Luo and Kikuyu ethnic groups sparked repeated revenge attacks.

The violence occurred in two main waves: the first took place between 30 December 2007 and 10 January 2008, focused on the Rift Valley, and especially around Eldoret; the second occurred on 24–28 January in Nakuru and Naivasha, involving clashes between Luo, Kalenjin and Kikuyu communities. In the north, the violence centred on long-standing tensions between the Kalenjin and Kikuyu communities, with Kalenjin armed gangs turning on Kikuyu soon after the results were announced. In mid-January the UN estimated that 500 people had been killed since the elections, with a further 250,000 displaced. Armed militia set up road blocks, targeting rival ethnic groups and property. Widespread instances of rape, maiming and killing were reported, and in several attacks large numbers of people were killed. On 3 January 35 people, mostly women and children who had sought refuge inside the Kiambaa Pentecostal church in Eldoret, were killed when the church was set alight. At the end of January Mugabe Were, an ODM parliamentarian, was murdered, precipitating further violence in Kibera.

Meanwhile, negotiations to end the political impasse and violence continued slowly and fitfully. Former UN Secretary-General Kofi Annan succeeded in persuading Kibaki and Odinga to meet in January 2008. Kibaki's team insisted that the talks were simply about restoring peace; however, Annan, with the support of the EU, was intent on establishing a government of national reconciliation. Kibaki had in mid-January announced the partial composition of his new Cabinet; despite the ODM having secured the largest number of seats in the legislature, no representatives from that party were included in the new Government. In mid-February 2008 talks resumed under the mediation of Annan. On 28 February, with over 1,000 people dead and at least 500,000 people having fled their homes, the two sides signed a power-sharing agreement, under the terms of which the post of executive Prime Minister would be created; two Deputy Prime Ministers would be appointed, one nominated by the ODM and one by the PNU, and ministerial posts would be divided between the two parties.

The Coalition Government

The settlement resulted in an end to the violence in Kenya, although serious tensions remained, and continued deadlock in the negotiations for the allocation of cabinet positions led to renewed violence in the ODM strongholds of Kibera and Kisumu. International pressure forced the renewal of negotiations, and on 12 April 2008 Kibaki and Odinga announced an agreement. The Cabinet would consist of 40 members, and 52 assistant ministers, with the PNU retaining the strategically important finance, foreign affairs, internal security, roads and energy portfolios. On 17 April Odinga was sworn in as Prime Minister, Kenyatta was named Deputy Prime Minister and Minister of Trade, and Wycliffe Musalia Mudavadi was appointed Deputy Prime Minister and Minister of Local Government. Musyoka, who had been appointed Vice-President and Minister of Home Affairs in January, remained in that position. In late April Kibaki and Odinga toured the Rift Valley together, appealing for reconciliation.

Following the parliamentary elections, results in three constituencies were not immediately made available and a further two seats became vacant following the deaths of members of the National Assembly. As a result, by-elections were held in five constituencies on 11 June 2008, following which the ODM held 102 seats and the PNU 45. After the nomination of the ODM's Kenneth Otiato Marende as Speaker of the National Assembly, the ODM won a further by-election, taking its total to 103 seats.

In August 2008 the Kenya National Commission on Human Rights (KNCHR) issued a report on the post-election violence. Six ministers were implicated in the report: Kenyatta of the PNU; and Sally Kosgei, Henry Kosgey, William Ruto, Najib Balala and Kipkalya Kones of the ODM. The report also named 20 parliamentary deputies, a bishop and several Christian and Muslim preachers, and alleged that violence had been planned before the elections and that state security forces had adopted a shoot-to-kill policy. The Independent Review Commission (IREC), which investigated the workings of the elections noted major problems with the working of the ECK, suggesting that around one-third of eligible voters had been excluded from the electoral roll, and that it contained the names of 1.2m. dead people.

The Commission of Inquiry into the Post-Election Violence (CIPEV, chaired by Justice Philip Waki) issued its report in October 2008. Concluding that some of the violence had been planned and organized by prominent politicians and business people, it demanded the establishment of a tribunal to prosecute those implicated. Waki handed a sealed envelope containing the names of the 10 key individuals most directly linked to organizing and funding the violence to former UN Secretary-General Annan. The report claimed that the National Security Intelligence Service had predicted the violence, but that the police and provincial administrations had failed to act on the information. Police were also accused of using extreme force against protesters, shooting innocent people in Nairobi, Nyanza and Western provinces. The ODM was accused of organizing violence in the North Rift, with Minister of Agriculture Ruto, although not explicitly named in the report, rumoured to have been included on the secret list handed to Annan. The CIPEV report also suggested that meetings had taken place in State House to organize the violence in Naivasha.

Odinga announced that he favoured accepting the recommendations of both the IREC and CIPEV reports without reservation, against the wishes of Ruto and other Kalenjin deputies who resisted demands for the establishment of tribunals. As a result, Odinga appeared to be further distanced from the Kalenjin block of the ODM.

In December 2008 two key recommendations from the IREC and CIPEV reports were implemented: the ECK was dissolved, and an agreement was reached between Odinga and Kibaki to establish a tribunal to prosecute those suspected of planning the violence. The National Assembly was given 45 days in which to set up the tribunal, which was to commence its activities in March 2009; were this deadline not met, the sealed list of names was to be handed to the International Criminal Court (ICC). A bill was put before the National Assembly in February, but was rejected amid fears that it would not be sufficiently independent. In July it was announced that the Government would not establish a tribunal, but that the matter would instead be dealt with by local courts, which would first be reformed, according to Odinga.

The relationship between Odinga and Kibaki appeared to deteriorate from late 2008. In April 2009 both Kibaki and Odinga claimed the right to nominate the Leader of Government Business in the National Assembly, with Kibaki nominating Vice-President Stephen Kalonzo Musyoka, and Odinga nominating himself. Speaker Kenneth Otiato Marende appointed himself as interim leader of the group in a move to overcome the political stalemate, and appealed to the Government to reach a compromise. A meeting between Odinga and Kibaki to restore unity failed, and, in a sign of worsening tensions within the Government, Minister of Justice, National Cohesion and Constitutional Affairs Martha Karua—an ally of Kibaki—resigned, citing concerns over the slow pace of reform and government interference in the appointment of judges. In mid-April Odinga wrote a letter to Kibaki threatening to boycott cabinet meetings over fears that the ODM was being sidelined by the President. Subsequent crisis talks failed to heal the rift, and in late April Odinga demanded a new election if differences could not be resolved through negotiation. Kibaki accused Odinga of attempting a coup.

In November 2009 ICC Prosecutor Luis Moreno-Ocampo arrived in Kenya to begin preliminary investigations into the 2007–08 election violence. A list of suspects (now numbering 20) composed by the CIPEV was handed over to the ICC, and in late November Moreno-Ocampo made his first submission to the ICC Pre-Trial Chamber. Meanwhile, a number of Kalenjin witnesses who had given evidence to the KNCHR claimed that they had been threatened. Senior members of the KNCHR were alleged to have passed on their details to local officials. A former deputy commandant in the administration police, Oku Kaunya, who had given evidence about election violence and voting irregularities to the CIPEV, fled into exile in Germany in the same month, following allegations of a contract on his life. At the end of March 2010 the ICC formally approved an investigation into the violence. In an important precedent, the decision was taken to commence the inquiry despite the lack of a formal request from the Kenyan Government. ICC investigators arrived in Kenya in April, followed by Prosecutor Moreno-Ocampo in May.

In late 2009 divisions within ODM emerged over the draft constitution, exacerbating tensions between Odinga and Ruto (who led the opposition campaign to the draft constitution). In February 2010 Odinga sought to suspend Ruto and Minister of Education Samson Ongeri over allegations of fraud. However, Kibaki reversed the suspensions, and Odinga called on his allies to boycott cabinet meetings in response. The constitutional referendum campaign provoked significant violence between competing groups. In mid-June two grenades were thrown into the crowd at a rally campaigning against the proposed new constitution. Six people were killed and many more wounded. Organizers blamed government security forces, accusing them of seeking to undermine opposition to the draft constitution, allegations that the Government denied. Meanwhile, three deputies who supported the 'No' campaign (against the draft constitution) were detained on charges of 'hate speech', and Ruto was summoned before the National Cohesion and Integration Commission.

At the national referendum, which took place on 4 August 2010, the draft constitution was approved by a clear majority of about 67% of votes cast. The new Constitution officially entered into force on 27 August. Under the Constitution, power was devolved to some 47 new counties, which were to be represented by a new parliamentary chamber, the Senate.

Relations between Odinga and Ruto continued to be strained. Following his acquittal in a corruption case in April 2011, Ruto renewed his anti-Odinga alliance with Vice-President Kalonzo Musyoka and Kenyatta (the so-called KKK Alliance, reflecting their ethnic origins of Kalenjin, Kamba and Kikuyu, respectively, but formally named in March as the G7 Alliance), in an effort to undermine the prospect of Odinga succeeding Kibaki in 2012.

On 15 December 2010 Moreno-Ocampo named six Kenyans, alleging that they had organized the post-election violence; these were Kenyatta, Ruto, Cabinet Secretary Francis Muthaura, former head of police Mohammed Hussein Ali, the Chairman of the ODM and Minister of Industrialization Henry Kosgey, and radio executive Joshua arap Sang. Ruto, Sang and Kosgey were allies of Odinga, while Kenyatta, Muthuara and Ali (who were accused of organizing attacks on supporters of Odinga following the elections) were widely viewed as allies of Kibaki. The six, all of whom denied complicity in the attacks, were ordered to submit voluntarily to the jurisdiction of the ICC, or international arrest warrants would be issued against them. In response, the National Assembly voted the following week for Kenya to withdraw from the treaty that set up the ICC. While the vote had no power to effect any such change, it signalled to the Government the solidarity of opposition against international attempts to bring those responsible for the violence to account. Police were also warned to be prepared in case the naming of the suspects led to renewed violence.

Despite significant popular support for the prosecution of those involved in the post-election violence, the Government called on the ICC to halt its investigations, arguing that the new Constitution allowed the Government powers to undertake its own investigation and the prosecution of anyone implicated in organizing the violence (a position supported by the African Union—AU in February 2011). In March the ICC issued its formal summons for the six suspects, and the following month they appeared before the ICC in The Hague to face criminal charges related to their roles in organizing the violence. In May the ICC formally replied to the Kenyan Government's request to halt proceedings, refusing to do so on the grounds that the Government had shown insufficient willingness to undertake its own investigations. At the end of August, an appeal from the Kenyan Government to abandon the trial of those suspected of organizing the post-election violence was rejected by the ICC, leaving the prospect of two candidates for the 2012 presidential elections being brought before the court. Ruto was dismissed from his position as higher education minister in late August 2011.

At the end of January 2012 the ICC announced that Kenyatta, Muthaura, Ruto and arap Sang would all stand trial. Kenyatta resigned as finance minister (although he retained the post of Deputy Prime Minister) and Muthaura stepped down as Cabinet Secretary, as Kibaki called for calm.

Protests against high food and fuel prices, and strikes against low wages continued throughout 2011 and 2012. Hundreds of farmers marched through Nairobi in May 2011 in protest at the government decision to allow imports of genetically modified maize to ease high prices. In early July large protests were staged in Nairobi at the continued high food and fuel prices, and were violently suppressed by the police. In early March 2012 the Government dismissed around 25,000 nurses for failing to return to work after a four-day strike, stating that anyone seeking to return to work would have to reapply for their position. After two weeks of strikes, the Government and unions reached an agreement reversing the dismissals.

In June 2011 the Kenya Revenue Authority antagonized parliamentary deputies, when it announced that under the new Constitution they should pay tax on both salary and benefits, and that such taxes should be backdated to the adoption of the Constitution in August the previous year. Deputies had continued to resist pressure throughout the year to pay higher taxes (citing their heavy workload), despite pressure from the Revenue Authority, claiming they had reached an agreement with Kibaki on tax levels for deputies during the tenure of the current National Assembly.

An explosion in September 2011 caused by a leaking petroleum pipeline killed an estimated 100 people and injured many more in the Sinai slum area of Nairobi. The state-owned Kenya Pipeline Company, who operated the structure, was the focus of angry accusations that its poor maintenance of the pipeline had allowed the tragedy to occur.

A committee established to investigate the impartiality of Kenya's judges in the aftermath of the 2007 post-election violence declared four senior judges to be unfit for office in April 2012. Included amongst the named judges was President of the Appeal Court, Justice Riaga Omollo, who was subsequently dismissed.

In June 2012 internal security minister George Saitoti was killed, together with his deputy, in a helicopter crash. Saitoti, who had been implicated in the Goldenberg scandal, had been planning to run for the presidency in the forthcoming elections. Saitoti had been seen as an important challenger to Odinga's presidential ambitions should Kenyatta be forced to withdraw as a result of the ICC trial. However, Kenyatta (as well as Ruto) made clear their determination to stand in the elections.

Corruption

Corruption issues continued to dominate Kenyan politics and its relationship with donors throughout Kibaki's tenure, despite an initial show of commitment to addressing graft. John Githongo was appointed as Permanent Secretary for Governance and Ethics to head the anti-corruption campaign; civil servants were obliged from May 2003 to account for their income and assets; and an inquiry was launched into the Goldenberg financial scandal (which emerged in 1996—see above). However, it soon became apparent that the Government was doing little to address the problem. In 2004 the EU withheld aid in response to fraud allegations against contracts issued by four ministries. Githongo resigned in February 2005, fleeing to the United Kingdom in early 2006 and alleging that threats had been made against his life. Following the leaking of Githongo's report on the Anglo-Leasing scandal (involving contracts for replacing Kenya's passport system in 2002) in January 2006, the Minister of Energy, Kiraitu Murungi, and Minister of Finance, Daudi Mwiraria, resigned, and demands were made for Vice-President Awori, named in the report, to be dismissed. In the following month a report into the Goldenberg affair implicated Minister of Education, Science and Technology (and former Vice-President) Saitoti, who resigned. He could not be prosecuted, however, owing to a previous court order, and in November Saitoti and Murungi were reappointed to the Cabinet.

The adoption in September 2007 of legislation banning the investigation of corruption cases prior to May 2003, further undermined Kenya's reputation for tackling corruption. The immediate beneficiaries were family members and key associates of former President Moi, who had been accused in a report leaked two weeks earlier of stealing more than £2,000m.

In July 2008 the Minister of Finance, Amos Kimunya, resigned, following a National Assembly vote of no confidence in him, following accusations of corruption over the sale of a luxury hotel. Nevertheless, he was reappointed to the Government in January 2009. Meanwhile, Minister of Agriculture Ruto was implicated in a maize-purchasing scandal, as serious food shortages in Kenya led to the declaration of a state of emergency in January. Ruto denied any involvement and dismissed the directors of the National Cereals and Produce Board of Kenya. Minister of Energy Murungi removed the Kenya Pipeline Company Managing Director, after it emerged that 126m. litres of petroleum worth an estimated US $95m. had been misappropriated in December 2008. Murungi's Permanent Secretary was implicated in the scandal, according to a report into the affair, but denied any knowledge of the matter.

In October 2010 Ruto was suspended over allegations of corruption over the sale of forest land in the early 2000s, although he was cleared of the charges by the chief magistrate's court in April 2011. A week after Ruto was suspended, the Minister of Foreign Affairs, Moses Wetangula, resigned in the face of a parliamentary vote on his suspension, following allegations of his involvement in corrupt land deals in the establishment of new embassies in Japan, Egypt, Nigeria, Pakistan and Belgium. In the same week the mayor of Nairobi faced charges of corruption over land sales in the city. In January 2011 Minister of Industrialization Kosgey, who was one of the six suspects named by the ICC for his involvement in the post-election violence, resigned following allegations of corruption against him. Ruto was dismissed in a government reorganization in August in which Wetangula was reinstated as Minister of Foreign Affairs.

In May 2011 the Government of the British Crown Dependency island of Jersey issued arrest warrants for a former head of Kenya Power and Lighting, Samuel Gichuru, and a former Minister of Energy, Chris Okemo, for corruption. The Jersey Government alleged they had both received bribes from European engineering companies and a US communications company. However, the Kenyan Government refused to extradite either suspect. The following month the Anti-Corruption Commission announced that it would screen 1,600 police officers to establish whether any were implicated in corruption, with a view to removing officers found to have been involved in graft. However the Central Organisation of Trade Unions called for the investigation to be suspended, claiming that it was being used as an excuse by the Government to reduce numbers of senior police officers, and demanded union involvement in the process to ensure impartiality.

In May 2012 the National Assembly approved the appointment of Mumo Matemu as head of the Ethics and Anti-Corruption Commission, a post which had not been filled since the establishment of the commission the previous September.

EXTERNAL RELATIONS

The East African Community (EAC), encompassing Kenya, Tanzania and Uganda, collapsed amid acrimony in 1977. Efforts in the mid-1990s sought to revive the body, reflecting warmer relations between the three countries. The new EAC was officially inaugurated in Arusha, Tanzania, in January 2001. In March 2004 a protocol was signed to establish a customs union, coming into effect on 1 January 2005 and creating a common market within the EAC. In December 2006 Rwanda and Burundi were accepted as members of the EAC, expanding the block to include around 90m. people.

Relations between Kenya and Ethiopia declined in the mid-1990s, following increased incidence of cross-border cattle raids and attacks on Kenyan security forces by bandits. Despite commitments on both sides to tighten border security, in November 1998 some 189 people (mainly Somalis) were murdered, a massacre believed to have been carried out by the Ethiopian guerrilla force, the Oromo Liberation Front (OLF). The following year the Kenyan Government protested to Ethiopia over an incursion by Ethiopian forces in pursuit of OLF fighters. Further incursions were reported despite renewed pledges to tighten security. In April 2006 Kenya deployed troops following raids in which 10 people died and 10,000 fled their homes.

Relations with Somalia have similarly centred on the porous nature of the border between the two countries, and tensions between ethnic Somali and Kenyan communities in north-eastern Kenya. In 1999 Somali militia overwhelmed the Ammuma border post in June and seized arms, a number of Kenyan army trucks and other military equipment. Violent clashes along the border between Kenya and Somalia recurred in February 2000, and again throughout 2004 and 2005.

Moi agreed in 2000 to mediate between the interim Government and opposing rebel factions in Somalia, and in November 2002 hosted US-supported peace talks between rival factions. In July 2003 President Kibaki appointed Mohammed Affey as Kenya's first ambassador to Somalia for 13 years. In August 2004 the members of Somalia's new National Assembly, based in Kenya, were sworn in. The transitional parliament held its inaugural session in Nairobi in September.

In September 2006 Kenya, Ethiopia and Somalia's Transitional National Government agreed to plans for an international peace force to be based in Somalia. In January 2007, as the US-backed action by Ethiopia against the Union of Islamic Courts in Somalia continued, Kenya closed its border with Somalia. Tanks and helicopters were deployed to the border area to enforce the closure and assist with the capture of Islamist forces trying to escape into Kenya. In March 2009 the EU, the USA and the Kenyan Government established a system for the trial of suspected Somali pirates, taking them out of the jurisdiction of the Kenyan domestic courts. The first trials under this system began in Mombasa in October. However, in October 2010 the Government ended an agreement with the EU to hold trials for suspected Somali pirates, arguing that its prisons were already too overcrowded, and accusing the EU of failing to provide the resources it had promised.

In March 2011 Kenyan forces were reported to have crossed into Somalia to engage with Somali al-Shabaab insurgents (reports that were subsequently denied by the Kenyan Government). By mid-2011 heavy influxes of Somali refugees, following prolonged severe drought and food shortages across the Horn of Africa region, added significantly to the crowding problems of the main refugee camp at Dadaab, in northern Kenya. Around 370,000 people were housed in a camp intended for 90,000, and the Government came under international pressure to open new camps for the continuing influx of refugees. However, citing concerns that this would encourage further numbers of Somali civilians to cross the border, the Government maintained that it could not offer further assistance to the refugees.

Relations between Kenya and Sudan deteriorated in June 1988, as they exchanged mutual accusations of aiding rebel factions. From the late 1990s Kenya hosted a series of peace talks between the Sudanese Government and opposition leaders, under the auspices of the Intergovernmental Authority on Development (IGAD), in an attempt to resolve the conflict in southern Sudan. In January 2005 the Sudanese Government and southern rebels signed a peace accord in Nairobi at a ceremony that officially ended the 21-year civil war.

The departure of Moi from political prominence in December 2002 led to an initial warming of relations between the Government and donors. Aid flows resumed, and donor nations welcomed the commitment of the Government to tackling corruption and improving governance. However, by mid-2004 relations had once again soured. The resignation of Githongo in February 2005, and concerns that the Government was blocking reforms and prosecutions, renewed the impression that too little was being done. In March 2007 the World Bank announced that it was renewing lending to Kenya after an 18-month break, approving US $154.5m. for livelihood protection and natural resource management programmes. The decision reflected revised anti-corruption measures for World Bank-funded projects introduced in an effort to circumvent high-level corruption.

During the political crisis of January–February 2008 international donors sought to apply pressure on Kenyan politicians, particularly Kibaki and his allies, to negotiate a resolution. The EU adopted a firm stance early on in the crisis, demanding a government of national unity. While the USA initially congratulated Kibaki on victory by early January it supported demands for a negotiated settlement. African leaders were also drawn into efforts to mediate, notably Tanzania's President Jakaya Kikwete and Uganda's Yoweri Museveni.

Frustrated with slow progress in establishing a tribunal to prosecute those accused of organizing the post-election violence, the EU in November 2008 threatened to withhold aid unless the CIPEV's recommendations were implemented, while the British Government warned of the imposition of a travel ban on those implicated. US demands for the dismissal of Chief Justice Evans Gicheru, Police Commissioner Maj.-Gen. Hussein Ali, Attorney-General Amos Wako, and the head of the Kenya Anti-Corruption Commission Aaron Ringera were rejected by Kibaki and Odinga as foreign interference in domestic affairs.

In September 2010 relations between the EU and Kenya became tense over the failure of the Kenyan authorities to arrest Sudanese President Omar al-Bashir, who had been indicted by the ICC, during a visit that he made to the country. Kenyan ambassadors in EU states were summoned by governments to explain, and Kenya was reported to the UN Security Council by the ICC for its failure to comply with the international arrest warrant that the Court had issued against al-Bashir. In November 2011 the Sudanese Government expelled the Kenyan ambassador and recalled its own from Nairobi after a Kenyan judge issued an arrest warrant for al-Bashir, following a case brought after al-Bashir visited the country in August.

In April 2012 the British Government released secret files from the colonial period, which covered the Mau Mau uprising. The existence of the files had been long suspected by some British academics and Kenyan campaigners. The papers were to be used in a case brought against the British Government by Kenyans detained during the Mau Mau emergency.

Security Concerns

On 28 November 2002 three suicide bombers attacked the Paradise Hotel, just outside Mombasa, killing 16 people, including 12 Kenyans and three Israeli tourists, and injuring 80 people. Two missiles were simultaneously fired at an Israeli charter aircraft as it took off from Mombasa airport. Both missiles narrowly missed their target. US and Israeli officials, assisting in the investigations into the attacks, suspected that a Somali militant Islamist group—al-Ittihad al-Islam—had carried out the attacks with support from the militant Islamist al-Qa'ida (Base) organization. In June 2003 four Kenyans were charged with murder in connection with the attacks, and their trial began in Nairobi in February 2004. A further three Kenyans were tried separately for their alleged involvement in the Mombasa attacks, the 1998 bombing of the US embassy and an alleged plot to target the new US embassy between November 2002 and June 2003.

In response to criticism of Kenya's weak security infrastructure, the Suppression of Terrorism Bill was approved in 2004; a new Anti-Terrorism Unit was established within the police force; and a National Counter-Terrorism Centre run by Kenya's National Security and Intelligence Services was created. The Government worked closely with IGAD countries to tackle regional terrorist activities, and travel restrictions on Somalia were periodically imposed. A substantial number of arrests were made between 2002 and 2004.

In July 2006 five Pakistani nationals were arrested in Mombasa on suspicion of activities linked to terrorism. Officers from the USA were sent to the country to participate in their interrogation. In June 2007 an explosion in central Nairobi, near the former location of the US embassy, killed one person and injured 30 others. Police made arrests but refused to comment on whether this incident was linked to international terrorism. In August 2008 Fazul Abdullah Mohamed, alleged to be the organizer of the embassy bombings, and the Paradise Hotel attack in 2002, escaped from Kenyan anti-terrorist police.

In September 2011 the high-profile kidnapping of a British tourist, and the murder of her husband, by suspected al-Shabaab militia led to an increase in instability in northern Kenya. Further kidnappings occurred and violence in the border areas increased. In October Kenyan troops entered Somalia, initially in pursuit of al-Shabaab soldiers accused of a series of kidnappings in Kenya. However, the military strategy soon widened from establishing a buffer zone in the border areas to a more concerted effort to defeat al-Shabaab in conjunction with the joint AU mission (known as Amisom). The Kenyan airforce launched attacks on al-Shabaab positions, although they were accused in late October of bombing a refugee camp in southern Somalia which killed five people. The Kenyan authorities denied responsibility for the bombing, blaming al-Shabaab for the attack.

In November 2011 Israel offered support to Kenya to help secure its borders. In response to Kenya's advance into Somalia, al-Shabaab militia launched attacks within Kenya in late 2011 in Garissa, Mandera, and the refugee camp of Dadaab, which left many dead and injured. In mid-January 2012 six people were killed and three abducted (including two local officials) in an attack on a police post in Wajir district. International humanitarian staff were also targeted, with several abductions over the period, as well as the high-profile kidnapping of tourists from northern Kenya.

Despite initial slow progress, Kenyan forces gradually began to push back the al-Shabaab militia, and by February 2012 had captured the strategic town of Badhadhe, south of Kismayo. However, Kenyan soldiers were accused by human rights organizations of arbitrary detention and violence against Somali refugees and others in the border areas. In May Kenyan military forces in Somalia officially joined Amisom's command. The USA had refused to fund Kenya's military engagement until it placed itself under the AU mission, and the move was seen as part of a deal to secure US support. Prime Minister Odinga pointedly asked for EU and US military, strategic and financial support in June, although the EU rejected such calls as falling outside its mandate in the region.

Security in Kenya outside the border areas also worsened following the decision to send troops into Somalia. In October 2011 a bar and a bus station in Mombasa were attacked by suspected militants linked or sympathetic to al-Shabaab using grenades. Over the following months a succession of similar attacks took place in Mombasa and Nairobi. In March 2012 six people were killed and many more injured when grenades were thrown into crowds at a Nairobi bus station. Attacks on Christian churches in Mombasa and Nairobi in March and April also resulted in at least two deaths and many injuries. The attacks continued in May when more than 30 people were injured in a bombing on a shopping centre in Nairobi. The explosion was initially blamed on an electrical fault, although, security forces soon announced that al-Shabaab was responsible.

In June 2012 two Iranians were arrested on suspicion of planning an attack in Mombasa, and later that month the US embassy warned of an imminent threat of a terrorist attack in the area. The following day a grenade exploded in a Mombasa bar killing three people and injuring others. In the same month raids on two churches in Garissa, close to the Somali border, left 15 people dead. Muslim leaders in Garissa announced they would help form self-defence groups to protect churches as a sign of solidarity against the violence.

Economy

DUNCAN WOODSIDE

Based on an earlier article by LINDA VAN BUREN

INTRODUCTION

Kenya's economic performance was disappointing in 2011. The country's gross domestic product (GDP) expanded by just 4.4% in real terms, according to figures released by the National Bureau of Statistics and the Ministry of Planning in May 2012. This increase did little to boost per capita income, given rapid continued population growth. Moreover, the 2011 growth figure was a significant deceleration from the 5.8% recorded in 2010. In part, this deterioration was due to renewed constraints on demand for Kenya's exports in key European markets, owing to an intensification of the euro zone debt crisis. However, domestic factors also contributed to the lower rate of growth. A drought undermined agricultural output, which grew by just 1.5%, in real terms, during 2011, compared with 6.4% in the previous year. Farmers were also negatively affected by high input costs, including for imported fertilizer, owing largely to a weakening of the shilling. Currency depreciation also adversely affected the import-dependent manufacturing sector, where output growth slowed to 3.3%, in real terms, in 2011, from 4.4% in 2010.

Overall economic growth would have been worse in 2011, had it not been for a continued strong performance by the banking and construction sectors. The financial sector expanded by 7.8%, in real terms, owing partly to an extended retail property boom, which saw prices of high-end residential real estate in Nairobi surge by 25% in 2011, according to one international property agent. The country's capital city, therefore, saw the biggest increase in property prices anywhere in the world in 2011, followed closely by the Kenyan coast, where prices increased by 20% in that year (the city of Miami, USA, was ranked third for price growth, with an increase of 19.1%). Tourism also continued to grow, despite a spate of kidnappings of foreigners in northern Kenya, including at the coastal resort of Lamu/Shela, in September and October 2011. Overall, tourism earnings reached Ks. 97,000m. (US $1,200m.) in 2011, a substantial increase from Ks. 73,000m. ($887m.) in the previous year. Tourist arrivals rose by some 15%, to 1,265,136 people in 2011, according to the Kenya Tourism Board.

However, the tourism sector was likely to perform less well in 2012. The full effect of the kidnappings, which coincided with the murder of a British tourist, did not feed through to the 2011 data as these incidents had happened relatively late in the year. In addition, the United Kingdom's Foreign and Commonwealth Office (FCO) in January 2012 advised British citizens to take extra care in public places and at events, including in locations where foreign travellers gather, amid intelligence about an imminent terror attack in Nairobi. Previously, the FCO had urged British citizens to avoid travel to within 150 km of Kenya's border with Somalia (which included Lamu), but the updated advice was likely also to have a negative impact on inland safari tourism, since the majority of such expeditions begin in Nairobi. Several bombs and grenades exploded in Kenya in late 2011 and the first half of 2012, as the al-Shabaab Islamist group repeatedly vowed to take revenge for the Kenyan army invading southern Somalia in October 2011. Although the various attacks targeted areas frequented by locals (rather than foreign nationals), tourist arrivals in Kenya fell by 3.2% year-on-year in January 2012. There was a particularly sharp drop in international tourists passing through Moi Airport, Mombasa, where arrivals dropped by 21.8% in the first quarter of 2012, to 72,753 people. Overall, Kenya's Ministry of Planning was even more cautious about the country's economic growth prospects for 2012, than it had been in 2011. In May 2012 it predicted that real economic output would expand by between 3.5% and 4.5% in that year, amid concerns about inflation and a consequent tightening of monetary policy. Inflation stood at an annual average rate of 16.7% in February 2012, despite the central bank raising the key lending rate by 11 percentage points in the last quarter of 2011, to 18%. The lagged effect of monetary tightening would have a clear impact on domestic credit, particularly in the overheated real estate sector, auguring badly for the construction market. Finally, the Ministry of Planning was also concerned about Kenya's presidential elections, which were due to take place by March 2013. These polls posed considerable risks to the confidence of both foreign and domestic investors, especially given that two leading contenders—Deputy Prime Minister Uhuru Kenyatta and former Minister of Higher Education William Ruto—were facing trial at the International Criminal Court for alleged crimes against humanity perpetrated during the 2007–08 election crisis (see Recent History).

Good levels of rainfall in Kenya in 2010 had boosted agricultural output, lowered domestic food prices and improved the supply of hydroelectrically generated power. These were the main factors responsible for the more than doubling of real GDP growth from 2.6% in 2009 to the 5.8% recorded in 2010. Thus, by the mid-point of its five-year term, the coalition Government that was formed after violence swept through much of the country following the disputed 27 December 2007 elections had succeeded in restoring a degree of economic stability to Kenya, and its economy had proved to be more resilient than expected. The World Bank, in a report released in June 2010, stated that Kenya had 'high hopes for a strong economic performance during this new decade'. The post-election violence initially had devastating political and economic effects on a country that, for the most part, had known peace for more than 40 years, and, even after calm returned, much remained to be rectified.

The economic sectors most affected by the post-election violence in 2008 were agriculture, as many farmers had been displaced from their fields, and tourism, after international press coverage of the violence led potential tourists to choose alternative destinations. In a microeconomic sense, those personally involved were most occupied in 2008 by the issue of compensation for their losses. This took the form of insurance payments, for those fortunate enough to have insurance cover, and demands for compensation from the Government. President Mwai Kibaki claimed in June 2008 that, of an estimated 350,000 Kenyans who had been internally displaced, 172,000 had been resettled in May alone. The UN World Food Programme (WFP) estimated that 186,000 displaced people had received food aid in the first four weeks of the Emergency Operation (EMOP), which commenced at the start of July 2008 and ran until the following May.

In a macroeconomic sense, the Kenyan authorities were occupied during much of 2008 with quantifying the damage that the post-election violence had caused to the country's reputation abroad: its saleability as an upmarket tourism destination (tourism is the most important source of foreign exchange in most years), its attractiveness to foreign investors, and its ability to secure the backing of multilateral and bilateral lenders and donors. The violence coincided with other negative factors, some of them completely unrelated: soaring fuel prices, power black-outs, water rationing in Nairobi, backlogs at the port of Mombasa, fertilizer shortages, high inflation, and even the brief closure of Mombasa airport as a result of the failure of the landing lights. In the first quarter of 2008 Kenya's GDP contracted by 1.3%, not least because of a sudden 90% drop in tourist arrivals. The second quarter saw a rebound to 3.4% GDP growth, with real growth for the whole of 2008 amounting to 1.8%, before the above-mentioned rebound in 2009 and 2010.

The coalition Government continued to win the approval of the IMF. In June 2009 the IMF extended a US $200m. concessional loan to Kenya under the Rapid Access Component of its Exogenous Shocks Facility. This was followed by a further $350m. from the Fund to help Kenya build up its foreign reserves from 3.4 months' worth of import cover to the statutory minimum of four months' worth. That target still eluded the Kenyan authorities; forward import cover was estimated at 3.3 months' worth in May 2011 and was forecast to climb steadily, but slowly, towards the target, not breaking through the 4 months' threshold until reaching 4.4 month's worth in 2013/14. The IMF in January 2011 agreed a three-year, $508.7m. Extended Credit Facility in support of Kenya's balance of payments, noting that 'the ratification of the new constitution by the August 2010 referendum has spurred confidence'. Of the total, $101.7m. was disbursed immediately.

A number of high-level corruption scandals has been uncovered in recent years, but the installation of the new coalition Government in April 2008 had by mid-2012 demonstrated little or no improvement with regard to this problem. Kenya's citizens and donors have expressed a desire for significant and tangible action to deal with the problem of corruption. An estimated 46% of Kenyans were still living below the official poverty line in 2011. The Government's strategy for development and poverty reduction was set out in its Vision 2030 programme, unveiled in 2007 and launched in January 2008. With an investment of US $7,500m., the programme sought to transform Kenya into a globally competitive and prosperous nation with a high quality of life by 2030.

In the United Nations Human Development Programme's 2011 report, Kenya was ranked 143rd out of a total of 169 countries. Although gross national income was a relatively encouraging US $1,492 per capita, inequality remained high and poverty continued to blight outlying areas, particularly Turkana, in the north-west of the country. Average life expectancy in that year was just 57.1 years.

AGRICULTURE

At independence in 1963, formal sector agriculture in Kenya was export-orientated and was based upon large-scale commercial agriculture in the settled 'White Highlands' and on European- and Asian-owned plantations. Much of the Kenyatta Government's agricultural effort in the early years of independence was devoted to a land reform programme designed to transfer land from the European settlers and to resettle Africans upon it. Later, the Kenyatta Government turned its attention to the 'Kenyanization' of commerce, which at that time was dominated by non-African and frequently non-citizen businesses. Although the agricultural sector's direct contribution to GDP declined slightly from the 1990s onwards as the share contributed by tourism rose, it remains significant, accounting (together with forestry and fishing) for 25% of GDP in 2010. The sector's indirect contribution to GDP is also very important: the World Bank estimates that agriculture-based sub-sectors of the manufacturing and services sectors provide about 30% of GDP annually. The principal cash crops are tea, horticultural produce and coffee. In 2010 some 80% of the working population made their living on the land, the same percentage as in 1980. More than one-half of total agricultural output is subsistence production. According to the World Bank, agricultural GDP increased at an average annual rate of 1.0% in 2001–10; according to official figures it grew by 6.3% in 2010.

Agricultural output is greatly dependent upon the weather, since only about 20% of Kenya's irrigation potential has been harnessed. The 'short rains' of October–December 2008 failed, reducing the 2008/09 maize harvest to 24.5m. metric tons—well below the national demand of 3m. tons per year. The coalition Government responded by introducing a range of subsidies on inputs such as fertilizers and seeds and on tractor hire. Much depended on the 'long rains' of March–May 2009, yet these too were disappointing. Favourable weather returned thereafter, with good 'short rains' in October–December 2009, good 'long rains' in March–May 2010 and good 'short rains' in October–December 2010. The strategic maize reserve grew to 1.1m. tons as of May 2010, and the Government predicted that Kenya would become a net exporter of food by 2012.

Kenya has some 1.7m. smallholders in the monetary sector and 3,200 large farms, ranches and plantations. There is an acute shortage of arable land, and only 7% of the country is classified as first-class land. The majority of smallholders have plots of less than 2 ha, and successive subdivision of plots among farmers' heirs impels large numbers of people to travel to towns in search of employment.

Kenya's leading visible earner of foreign exchange in the 21st century has been tea, and in 2007 the country became the world's largest exporter of the commodity. High-quality tea has been grown in Kenya since 1903. Kenya is the biggest supplier of tea to the United Kingdom, accounting for about 40% of all British tea imports. According to the Tea Board of Kenya, Kenya's output of processed tea rose from 314.1m. kg in 2009 to 398.5m. kg in 2010, and exports increased from 343m. kg to 441m. kg over the same period. The share of small farms in the total area under tea expanded rapidly under the high-density settlement schemes of the Kenya Tea Development Authority, later Agency (KTDA), which distinguished itself as one of the most successful parastatals in Africa. About 500,000 smallholders sell their tea to the 60 tea factories of the KTDA. Each tea factory is an independent company, while the KTDA in 1998 became a management company. Elections are held annually in which the smallholder tea growers choose the directors of the tea factories. The country's large tea estates, grouped in the Kenya Tea Growers' Association, cover about 31,017 ha. Smallholders produce about 60% of the total tea crop, while the large factories account for about 40%. All in all, the tea sector provides a livelihood for more than 3m. Kenyans. Kenyan tea consistently commands high prices in world markets, but this quality comes at a cost. The KTDA imported 62,284 metric tons of fertilizer in 2007, at a cost of about US $18.2m. In 2008 the cost of fertilizer had soared to more than $55m., owing to high prices of petroleum, an important component of fertilizer. Anticipating that most of the growers would find the higher costs intolerable and therefore would not buy the fertilizer, the KTDA suspended fertilizer imports and instead advised growers to source their own fertilizer, for example, manure from inside Kenya.

Kenya's high elevation favours the cultivation of a variety of fruits and vegetables, and by March 2003 horticulture earnings had eclipsed coffee revenue. Kenya is the second largest horticultural exporter in sub-Saharan Africa, after South Africa. Fresh flowers, fruits and vegetables are air-freighted to Europe and the Middle East. Kenya's horticultural produce ranges from French beans, mangetout and sugar snap peas to lettuce, cucumbers, tomatoes, onions, garlic, leeks, carrots, turnips, potatoes, sweet potatoes, yams, cabbages, broad beans, peas, pimentos, asparagus, artichokes, cauliflower, broccoli, spinach and peppercorns. The range of fruits includes mangoes, avocados, passion fruits, papayas, guavas, watermelons, bananas, apples, pears, peaches, nectarines, apricots, plums, grapefruits, oranges, tangerines, lemons, limes, coconuts, pineapples, currants and strawberries. In floriculture, Kenya has more than 100 farms raising flowers for export, directly employing some 50,000–60,000 people. According to the Kenya Flower Council, Kenya accounts for 60% of African cut-flower exports, in terms of value, and is the largest exporter of cut flowers to the European Union (EU). The horticultural sector coped admirably with the formidable challenges posed by the post-election violence of early 2008. Where necessary, flower companies even housed their employees within the plantation confines to assure their safety and their continued availability for work. The result was that in the troubled first quarter of 2008, the horticultural sector achieved a 30% rise in volume and a 50% rise in the value of exports. The export of cut flowers amounted to 93,000 metric tons in 2008, earning Ks. 40,000m. in foreign currency. In 2011 Kenya exported more than 40 varieties of flowers, especially roses, carnations and statice, and 98% of these flowers were supplied to the European market.

The rise of the tea and horticultural sectors coincided with a decline in coffee production; in recent years, however, a reversal of this trend has been observed. Although Kenya's premium Arabica coffee has long commanded a high price, the instability of the global coffee market has acted as a disincentive to Kenyan producers, many of whom decided to abandon coffee in favour of more profitable crops. That all coffee produced in Kenya still has to be sold at auction at Waikulima House in Nairobi remains contentious. Coffee growers, who still produce some of the best Arabica coffee in the world, argue that they are regularly offered higher prices than they can obtain at the Nairobi coffee auction, and they have lobbied the Government to allow them to sell independently, on the open market. In 2008 a total of 43 coffee co-operatives in Thika, Murang'a North and Murang'a South combined to purchase a Ks. 60m., four-metric-ton-per-hour coffee mill to enable them to mill their own coffee, and brand and market it, without going through auctioneers. The International Coffee Organization (ICO) agreed a new International Coffee Agreement in 2007, ratified by Kenya in 2008. According to the ICO, Kenya harvested a record 51,000 tons of coffee in the year ending 31 March 2011, an increase of 35% compared with the previous year. Exports amounted to 33,406 tons in 2010/11 (1 April 2010 to 31 March 2011), up by 14.8% from 29,088 tons one year earlier.

Production of sugar cane increased from 5.1m. tons in 2009 to 5.6m. tons in 2010. Pressing for development in the industry is the Sugar Campaign for Change (SUCAM), formed in 2001. SUCAM has listed the industry's main problems as outdated technology, low-yielding cane varieties, ineffective and unco-ordinated institutions, poor roads, a weak regulatory regime and lack of credit for small-scale farmers. All these factors increase the cost of growing sugar in Kenya; to produce an equal amount of sugar costs Malawi US $120, compared with $300 in Kenya. SUCAM estimates that the industry needs Ks. 20,000m. just to clear the sugar factories' debts and that a further Ks. 30,000m. is needed for 'co-generation', ethanol production and sugar-refining. Kenya is more exposed to global sugar price fluctuations than it need be, according to SUCAM; it could cushion itself by offering a variety of sugar products and not just raw sugar alone. Cane is sold to the sugar companies by smallholders and co-operatives; it has been argued that the sugar companies' need to compensate these growers prevents them from achieving the profitability that overseas competitors can attain by growing all their cane on huge estates. Of the eight sugar companies, the largest by far is Mumias, which is listed on the Nairobi Stock Exchange. Kenya has agreed an Interim Economic Partnership Agreement (EPA) with the EU over sugar exports to that bloc. From 1 October 2009 to 30 September 2015, free EU market access is to be granted to 'least developed countries' (LDCs) under the Everything But Arms protocol; this is a positive development for the other four countries of the East African Community (EAC), which are all classed as LDCs, but not for Kenya, which does not have this classification. Instead, non-LDC African, Caribbean and Pacific countries, including Kenya, were extended 'safeguard periods' from 1 October 2009, to give them time to reform their sugar sectors and make them sufficiently competitive to compete in the European market once the safeguard period expires. The Kenyan Government has formulated a National Sugar Adaptation Strategy to prepare the country's sugar industry for the post-protectionism era. The sugar sector provides an income for 35,000 direct employees and for about 100,000 outgrowers; the outgrowers contribute 88% of the cane, a much higher proportion than in many other sugar-producing countries.

Kenya's principal food crop is maize. Output levels depend heavily on weather conditions and tend to follow a boom-and-bust cycle, although the sector experienced steady growth for three years and reached a record 3.3m. metric tons in 2006. In that year Kenya grew enough maize to satisfy domestic demand. This is not always the case; in most years Kenya has to import between 60,000 and 75,000 tons of maize. The maize crop amounted to 2.4m. tons in 2009, but increased to 3.2m. in 2010. Kenya has a high consumer demand for wheat, yet normally provides less than 50% of its requirements. However, in 2010 total wheat production reached a record 512,000 tons.

Livestock and dairy production are important both for domestic consumption and for export. The country had an estimated 17.8m. head of cattle in 2010. A substantial proportion of dairy cattle are in small herds of up to 10 animals. Kenya has traditionally exported butter, cheese and skimmed milk powder and maintains strategic stocks of these products. In 2010 FAO reported that Kenya had an estimated 30.3m. chickens, 13.3m. goats, 9.9m. sheep, 1.0m. camels and 347,400 pigs. Kenya, which has a reputation for high-quality honey, also had 2.5m. beehives in 2009, producing about 25,000 metric tons of natural honey.

INDUSTRY

Kenya is the most industrially developed country in East Africa, with a relatively good infrastructure, extensive transport facilities and considerable private sector activity. The manufacturing sector contributed 11.3% of GDP in 2010 and employed about 200,000 people in that year. In June 2007 the Government proposed the elimination of 205 of the 1,325 licences required by businesses. A total of 110 had already been removed, and some 400 licences were also to be simplified. The Government's Regulatory Reform Strategy stated the intention of reducing government bureaucracy in priority areas by 25% by the 2010/11 budget (see below). Industry as a whole grew by 7.5% in 2010, according to official figures.

Manufacturing is, in practice, based on import substitution, although the Moi Government in its last few years placed great emphasis on developing export-orientated industries. The World Bank, in its June 2010 report, noted that Kenya was one of the few developing countries in the world whose export sector shrank, rather than grew, over the past five decades. Exports as a share of GDP fell from 40% in 1960 to 26% in 2009.

Kenya's vehicle assembly plants produce trucks, commercial vehicles, pick-ups, buses, minibuses, four-wheel-drive vehicles and passenger cars from kits supplied from abroad. About 30% of components are produced locally. The Government has announced plans to reduce its 35% interest in Kenya Vehicle Manufacturers Ltd (formerly Leyland Kenya) in Thika and its 51% interest in the other two assembly firms. Tyres are manufactured by Firestone East Africa, with the capacity to produce 700,000 tyres per year.

Kenya Petroleum Refineries Limited (KPRL) is a joint venture that owns the Mombasa oil refinery. KPRL is owned 50% by the Kenyan Government and 50% by Essar Energy Overseas Limited of India, which purchased its share in July 2009 from Shell (17.1%), BP (17.1%) and Chevron (15.8%). The first refinery entered production in 1963, followed by a second in 1974. The refineries convert imported crude oil into petrol (gasoline), kerosene (jet fuel), liquid petroleum gas, gas oil and fuel oil, both for the Kenyan market and for re-export to other countries such as Uganda. KPRL's refinery is capable of handling 4.2m. metric tons of crude petroleum annually, although in June 2008 it was operating at only about 38% of its capacity. Refined petroleum products were, until relatively recently, Kenya's largest source of foreign exchange, but the refinery has been in need of modernizing. Essar planned to spend US $400m. on upgrading the refinery by adding secondary units. An oil pipeline operated by Kenya Pipeline Co (KPC) conveys petroleum products from Mombasa to Nairobi ('Line I') and from Nairobi to Eldoret to Kisumu. Line I, completed in 1978, is 450 km long, has a diameter of 14 inches and can move 440 cu m per hour. At the time of its construction, provision was made to enable the capacity to be increased to 800 cu m per hour. Beyond Nairobi, Line II, with a diameter of eight inches, and Line III, with a diameter of six inches, can transport 160 cu m per hour. In October 2009 KPC signed a contract with China Petroleum Pipeline Engineering Corpn for the construction of a 325-km-long 'Line IV' pipeline from Nairobi to Eldoret. The 14-inch diameter pipeline runs parallel to the existing multi-product KPC pipeline. As of April 2011 the Chinese company had completed all 28 of the pipeline's river crossings, and full completion was scheduled for the end of the year.

MINERALS

Mining activity in Kenya is as yet limited, but prospecting is continuing. Magadi Soda Company (MSC) is the largest soda ash producer in Africa. It extracts soda ash, Kenya's principal mineral product, for export, at Lake Magadi, in the Rift Valley. In 1997 a Canadian company announced the discovery of mineral sands at Kwale, 105 km south of Mombasa, containing reserves of 200m. metric tons of titanium- and zirconium-bearing sands. These discoveries followed earlier discoveries at Kwale of rutile, zircon and ilmenite. Base Resources Ltd, headquartered in Perth, Australia, and formerly known as Base Iron Ltd, acquired the Kwale project in February 2010 and announced that Kwale should begin producing in 2013.

Kenya's other principal mineral products are fluorspar, gold, salt, vermiculite and limestone. An exploration drilling programme in March–October 2009 found 22.15m. metric tons of indicated mineral resources as well as 5.02m. tons of implied mineral resources. The extraction of extensive deposits of rubies began in 1974; gems of up to 30 carats have been reported. Deposits of tsavorite, a green grossularite garnet discovered at Tsavo in the 1970s, have received high valuations and have been exploited at the Lualani mine in the Taita Hills since 1981. Other minerals identified in Kenya include apatite, graphite, kaolin, kyanite, topazes and green tourmalines. Kansai Mining Corporation of Canada, through the wholly owned Mid-Migori Mining Co Ltd, holds an annually renewable gold-mining concession covering 310.5 sq km of the Migori Greenstone Belt in Nyanza, western Kenya.

British oil exploration company Tullow announced in March 2012 that it had discovered a potentially significant source of petroleum in Kenya's Turkana district. The company stated that it, together with partner Africa Oil Corp, had encountered a net oil pay of over 20 m after drilling to a depth of 1,041 m at the Ngamia-1 well on Block 10BB. The company revealed, two months later, that it had encountered a total net oil pay of over 100 m, having increased the depth of drilling at the deposit to 1,515 m. Tullow added that it would extend its exploration further, partly through activity at nearby Block 10A, where it planned to locate another rig. It also intended to begin drilling at its Twiga-1 well, situated in Block 13T.

POWER

Kenya has 1,500 MW of installed generating capacity, the majority of which is hydroelectric. The country supplies about 80% of its national requirement domestically. Electricity, apart from small local stations, is supplied by hydroelectric plants in the Tana river basin and in the Turkwel Gorge, by the geothermal station at Olkaria, and by the diesel-fired Kipevu plant on the south coast. The five Seven Forks hydrostations lie on the Tana river and have a combined installed capacity of 543.2 MW: Gitaru (225 MW), Kiambere (144 MW), Kamburu (94.2 MW), Kindaruma (40 MW) and Masinga (40 MW). Another station, with a capacity of 106 MW, operates at Turkwel Gorge in Turkana district. In 2007 France extended a €40m. credit to upgrade Kipevu 1 from 60 MW to 90 MW. The 74-MW Kipevu 2 was formally inaugurated in 2002, at a cost of US $86m. Kenya was the first African country to harness geothermal potential for electricity generation, in the form of the Olkaria scheme in the Rift Valley. Olkaria I has three 15-MW generators, Olkaria II has two 32-MW generators, and Olkaria III has one 12-MW binary generator; construction of the 70-MW Olkaria IV began in June 2007. In April 2010 the People's Republic of China extended a $98m. concessional loan to Kenya to fund the drilling of 26 steam production wells at Olkaria IV. Construction of the 60-MW $263.6m. Japanese-funded and Japanese-built Sondu-Miriu hydropower project began in 1999; Phase 1 was commissioned in 2005, but the inauguration of Phase 2 was delayed. Sondu-Miriu is to deliver an annual energy output of 331 GWh. Construction of the $60m. Sangoro hydropower station, near Sondu-Miriu, will add 20 MW to the national grid.

Power demand exceeds power supply, and electricity tariffs are high. Lack of adequate electricity supply is often cited as a deterrent to manufacturing development in Kenya. In a bid to address this problem, the Kibaki Government sought in 2005 to 'fast-track' projects such as Sondu-Miriu and Olkaria IV. Two further 'fast-track' units, to be situated at Kakuru and Eldoret, were also planned. The Kenya Power Co (now the Kenya Electricity Generating Co Ltd—KenGen) was established in 1997 to deal exclusively with the generation of electricity; the Kenya Power and Lighting Co (KPLC) continued to be responsible for electricity transmission and distribution. A 30% stake of the Government's equity in KenGen was privatized in 2005 in a share flotation that was significantly oversubscribed. In 2009 the KPLC announced plans to import 200 MW of power from neighbouring Ethiopia by 2012.

In August 2011 Kenya began working with the International Development Association (IDA), a division of the World Bank, on the Lake Turkana Wind Power Project (LTWPP), a €582m. venture designed to provide 300 MW of inexpensive power to Kenya's national grid. At that time 300 MW was equivalent to 20% of installed generating capacity. Harnessing wind power would help to reduce over-dependence on hydroelectric generation, an energy source that is vulnerable to drought. Plans for LTWPP entailed building 365 turbines on 40,000 acres of territory in Loiyangalani district, at altitudes ranging from 450 m to 2,300 m above sea level. However, the project would likely take time to complete, not least due to the poor condition of roads in the area. For example, it was estimated that 12,000 truck journeys would be required, in order to bring all the necessary materials to the site. In May 2012 a delay to the project was announced, just one month before construction was due to begin, amid concerns among funders about Kenya Power's commitment to the project. In particular, the international funders, including the African Development Bank, were reportedly seeking assurances that Kenya Power would guarantee the purchase of electricity generated by the project, and that it would complete a 400-km line to transmit output to the national grid.

FINANCIAL SECTOR

Kenya's financial sector has expanded significantly in recent years, stoked by rising middle-class incomes and an extended property boom. There were a total of 112 foreign exchange bureaux, 43 commercial banks, six deposit-taking microfinance institutions, two credit reference bureaux and one mortgage finance company operating in Kenya by February 2012, according to the country's central bank. At that time, the banking sector's aggregate balance sheet totalled Ks. 2,076,200m., up 16.4% from Ks. 1,783,600m. in February 2011. Government debt, loans to individuals and loans to businesses accounted for the bulk of the financial sector's assets, with government securities representing 20%, and loans to the private sector 57% of the total asset base. The deposit base stood at Ks. 1,542,400m. at that time

The largest three banks in Kenya as of January 2011 were Barclays Bank Kenya, Standard Chartered Kenya and Kenya Commercial Bank. In the first three months of 2012 the latter experienced a 35% year-on-year increase in pre-tax profit, which reached Ks. 3,400m. This followed an increase of some 30% in operating income to Ks. 10,300m., from Ks. 7,900m. in the first quarter of 2011. In May 2012 Standard Chartered Kenya, which is a subsidiary of London-listed Standard Chartered, announced that it would offer equity totalling Ks. 3,200m. in shares, after revealing earlier in the year that it planned to begin banking operations in a number of neighbouring markets. This news followed a 41% year-on-year increase in the local unit's pre-tax profit to Ks. 3,300m. in the first quarter of 2012.

The central bank's tightening of monetary policy, which resulted in an increase in the lending rate to 18% in December 2011, up from 7% at the end of the third quarter of 2011, dampened fears that Kenya's banking sector might overheat. The strong growth of Kenya's banking sector in recent years, which has been driven by a substantial increase in commercial activity in major urban centres and the increasing disposable incomes of the middle class, has not resulted in a proliferation of non-performing loans (NPLs), at least in terms of such loans' share of the overall capital base. Indeed, NPLs accounted for a relatively modest 4.5% of total loans within the banking sector in January 2012, down from 10.6% in December 2007, according to central bank statistics published in early 2012. Later in 2012 it was clear that the monetary tightening was feeding through to consumer prices, as inflation slowed to an annual average of 12.2% in May 2012, from 19.7% in November 2011.

COMMUNICATIONSAND TRANSPORT INFRASTRUCTURE

This sector experienced phenomenal growth in the 2000s, owing to the proliferation of mobile cellular telephones. The number of mobile telephone subscribers in Kenya increased from 24,000 in 1999 to 19.4m. in 2009. (By comparison Kenya had just 664,000 fixed telephone lines in use in 2009, compared with 106,000 in 1984.) This growth may have been rapid, but it was largely unstructured, leading to wide variations in airtime costs across international borders, which operators sought to exploit. In 1999 Kenya Posts and Telecommunications Corpn was divided, pending privatization, into three entities: Telkom Kenya, the Postal Corpn of Kenya and the Communications Commission of Kenya (a regulatory body). In 2007 a 51% share in Telkom Kenya was awarded to a consortium of France Telecom and Alcazar Capital Ltd of the United Arab Emirates for €270m. The consortium was charged with preparing Telkom Kenya for an initial public offering on the Nairobi Stock Exchange by 2013. Telkom Kenya was offered a licence to operate mobile telephone services as part of the deal.

Kenya's extensive transport system includes road, rail, air, and coastal and inland waterways. The chief port is Mombasa, whose history predates the colonial era and which is now the largest port on the East African coast. It is operated by the Kenya Ports Authority (KPA). Mombasa handled a total cargo throughput of 19m. metric tons in 2010, of which 5.4m. tons was transit cargo, to be transported across Kenya to and from Uganda, Burundi, Rwanda and the eastern part of the Democratic Republic of the Congo. At times the port of Mombasa also serves Sudan, South Sudan, the now-landlocked Ethiopia, parts of Somalia and even north-western Tanzania. About 70% of all cargo handled today is container traffic, which is growing at a rate of 12% per year. Some 1,900 ships from 20 shipping lines called at Mombasa in 2010. Mombasa's container port handled 696,000 20-ft (6-m) equivalent units (TEUs) in 2010, 12.4% more than in 2009. In June 2010 the Japan International Cooperation Agency extended US $201.8m. in concessional loans to Kenya to build a second Mombasa container port, west of Kipevu. Phase 1 of the project was to add 450,000 TEU upon completion in 2013, thereby doubling Mombasa's container-handling capacity. When all the phases have been completed, the project should add 1.2m. TEU of capacity. The total cost is projected at Ks. 16,000m.

KPA also operates the country's three inland container depots: Embakasi, serving Nairobi; Eldoret; and Kibos, serving Kisumu. KPA has the capacity to tranship significantly more cargo than can be evacuated inland, placing Kenya's rail and road systems in the critical path inhibiting further port expansion. In 2007 KPA engaged two companies to decongest the port by removing 6,000 containers per month to other locations; the port had been offloading some 15,000 containers per month, more than double its rated capacity of 7,000. The limiting factor was not an inability to handle 15,000 containers but instead a lack of space to store them. The second container port was expected to improve the situation significantly.

Kenya boasts one of the few profitable airlines in Africa. Kenya Airways (KQ) has operated its own international services since the break-up of East African Airways in 1977. In 1989 the airline inaugurated a freighter service to Europe, fresh flowers and vegetables being the main outward cargo, with the result that the service was able to operate full in both directions. Privatization took place in 1995, when KLM Royal Dutch Airlines paid US $24m. for a 26% stake. The airline's initial public offer on the Nairobi Stock Exchange was in 1996 and was well subscribed. In 2003 the carrier acquired a 49% shareholding in Tanzania's Precision Air. KQ's profit for the year to 31 March 2008 was Ks. 5,500m. before tax or Ks. 3,869m. after tax; this was 5.6% lower than its profit in 2006/07, but the 2007/08 profit was achieved in a year of exorbitant fuel prices, a global economic slowdown and the post-election violence. The carrier made a loss in 2008/09 but returned to profitability in the following year, registering a before-tax profit of Ks. 2,671m. ($33.3m.) in the year ending 31 March 2010. KQ carried more than 3m. passengers in 2010/11, and its route network has expanded rapidly, especially across the whole of Africa. It flies to 28 African countries, from

Senegal to Seychelles and from Egypt to South Africa. Its long-haul destinations extend as far as London, Paris and Amsterdam in Europe and as far as Guangzhou, Hong Kong and Bangkok in the Far East. In the domestic and regional markets, KQ faces competition from Fly 540. Five Forty Aviation Ltd of Nairobi began operating low-cost services as Fly 540 in 2006, and Lonrho acquired a 49% share for $1.5m. in 2007. The carrier served 10 Kenyan destinations and operated regional services to airports in Tanzania, Uganda and Burundi as of May 2011. Kenya Airways raised Ks. 14,500m. through the sale of fresh stock to existing shareholders in June 2012. However, the offering did not meet its target, since only 70% of the shares on offer were bought. The carrier had hoped to raise Ks. 20,700m. from the sale.

A 590-km road between Kitale and Juba, in South Sudan, provides an all-weather road link between that country and Kenya. The 2009/10 national budget allocated Ks. 10,000m. to road construction, including Ks. 1,200m. for a road linking Modagashe to Garrisa and Wajir, in the north-east.

The railway in Kenya was built between 1896 and 1901 and has a 1-m gauge. It runs from the coast at Mombasa, through Nairobi, to western Kenya, and on to points in Tanzania and Uganda. In 2008 it was announced that Toll Holdings of Australia, through its subsidiary PDL Toll, would take over management of the railway. Meanwhile, EAC authorities unveiled development plans for the railway in May 2008 under the title Kenya Railways Vision 2050; this called for a 16-year, US $1,500m. overhaul that would involve laying 2,156 km of new railway line in standard (1.435-m) gauge. Assessments of the total cost varied; tenders in November 2009 found that the cost would significantly exceed the budget, and the project was terminated without a contract being awarded. The World Bank, in its June 2010 report, was highly critical of the Grand Coalition Government's handling of the proposed upgrading of the railway and port. It pointed out that in the time it took Kenya to revise its Railway Master Plan, Djibouti had fully completed the construction of its new port. Kenya would benefit greatly from an integrated modernization of both its railway and port.

The construction of a new port at the historic town of Lamu formally began in March 2012 at an inauguration ceremony attended by Kenya's President Mwai Kibaki, South Sudan's President Salva Kiir and Ethiopia's Prime Minister Meles Zenawi. The port forms the core of the Lamu Port South Sudan Ethiopia Transport Corridor (Lapsset), which also includes rail links, highways, oil pipelines and a refinery. The project was officially launched after Kenya and South Sudan signed a memorandum of understanding in January 2012, although, at that time, the respective countries' responsibilities for financing the project had yet to be finalized. There were also uncertainties about the financial viability of the entire project, as risk aversion increased in global capital markets during 2012, owing to an intensification of the sovereign debt crisis in the euro zone. The project, if completed, would involve the construction of a 20-berth deepwater port at Lamu on Kenya's coast, a 120,000 barrel per day oil refinery, 1,260 km of oil pipelines between South Sudan and the port (together with 980 km between Ethiopia and Kenya), 1,710 km of standard gauge railway, 880 km of highway and an international airport.

TOURISM

Kenya's tourism sector has generally exhibited steady and strong growth in most years since independence, and by the 1990s the sector had become the country's largest source of foreign exchange. Kenya's post-election violence of early 2008 dealt a heavy blow to the tourism industry, which, more than any other sector, is based on overseas markets' perceptions of the situation in Kenya rather than on the actual situation. Aware of the need for damage control, Kenya's tourism leaders instigated the US $200m. 'Kenya is open for business' campaign. This comprised marketing initiatives in the countries that send the most tourists to Kenya and also a familiarization trip to the Maasai Mara for 250 overseas travel executives to demonstrate that normality had resumed. The majority of tourists come from the United Kingdom, Germany, Tanzania, Uganda and the USA. Kenya's tourism sector has shown itself to be resilient. The sector contributed 12% of GDP in 2007, earning $1,000m., when tourist arrivals exceeded 1.8m. The post-election violence reduced tourist arrivals to 729,000 in 2008, but 2009 saw a recovery to 952,481, and in 2010 arrivals rose to a record 1.1m., excluding cross-border tourist arrivals.

BALANCE OF PAYMENTS, FOREIGN TRADE AND DEBT

Kenya's total external debt at 31 December 2010 stood at $7,930m., equivalent to 24% of GDP. The World Bank in June 2010 lauded Kenya for having reduced its total public debt from 60% of GDP in 2000 to 40% of GDP in 2008, 'despite never having received substantial debt relief'.

Regional trade is important to Kenya, which has consistently had a favourable trade balance with its neighbours, to which it exports petroleum products, food and basic manufactures in particular. A treaty for the re-establishment of the EAC providing for the promotion of free trade between the member states (envisaging the eventual introduction of a single currency), and for the development of infrastructure, tourism and agriculture within the Community, was finally ratified by the Kenyan, Tanzanian and Ugandan heads of state in June 2000. The new EAC was officially inaugurated in January 2001. In March 2004 the Presidents of Kenya, Tanzania and Uganda signed a protocol on the creation of a customs union. In 2007 Burundi and Rwanda joined the EAC.

Kenya's visible trade balance and its current account balance are perennially in deficit, but the invisible trade balance, boosted by the tourism sector, is perennially in surplus. In most years the overall balance of payments is in surplus. In 2009/10 visible exports on a free-on-board (f.o.b.) basis earned US $4,885.5m., to which the largest contributor was tea, which earned $1,127.2m. (23% of the total), followed by horticulture, which contributed $714.8m. (15%), and coffee, which earned $194.2m. (4%). These top three earners together contributed 42% of the total, while a variety of non-traditional exports contributed the remainder. In the same year imports on a f.o.b. basis cost $10,480.1m., of which oil accounted for $2,835.6m. Export revenue, thus, covered just 46.6% of total import costs. The visible trade balance carried a deficit of $5,594.6m. The balance on services carried a $1,815.4m. surplus, a marked recovery from the $1,185.0m. recorded in 2008/09. The 2009/10 current account carried a deficit of $1,680.6m. including official transfers, and $1.661.3m., excluding official transfers, demonstrating the relatively unimportant role that net transfers play in Kenya's balance of payments.

The trade deficit in 2011/12 increased dramatically to US $8,504.3m., according to the IMF, as imports of goods and services reached $14,216.3m. and exports totalled $5,712.0m. The surge in imports was partly accounted for by a continued rise in oil prices, which took hydrocarbon imports to $4,463.4m., up from $3,299.2m. in 2010/11. Meanwhile, the current account deficit in 2011/12 rose to $4,313.6m., up from $3,062.9m. in 2010/11. The main recipient of Kenya's exports in calendar year 2010 was Uganda, which purchased 10.1% of its shipments, followed by Tanzania (9.8%), the United Kingdom (8.8%), Holland (8.2%), the USA (5.8%), Egypt (4.7%) and the Democratic Republic of the Congo (4.3%). The principal sources of imports were China (13.6%), India (13.4%), the United Arab Emirates (9.7%), South Africa (8.4%), Saudi Arabia (6.8%) and Japan (4.7%).

Aid and Development

Since independence, Kenya has received substantial amounts of development aid. The World Bank-sponsored Consultative Group of aid donors to Kenya meets regularly to pledge financing for the country's development strategy. The sources of aid have diversified considerably in recent years. The share provided by the United Kingdom has fallen, while multilateral agencies, particularly the World Bank and the European Development Fund, have increased their share. In April 2011 the World Bank had 22 active projects in Kenya and had committed more than US $2,000m. in the country, plus five regional projects that included Kenya. Most of the projects involved transport infrastructure. The IMF in January 2011 agreed a three-year, $508.7m. Extended Credit Facility (ECF) intended to support the balance of payments. Of the total, $101.7m. was disbursed immediately. In April 2012 the IMF completed its third review under the ECF, paving the way for the release of a further $110.9m., which would take total disbursements under the three-year programme thus far to $420.7m. In December 2011 the overall value of the three-year facility had been increased further, to an aggregate $753.6m., meaning that an additional $332.9m. had still to be disbursed before the end of the programme. In its April 2012 assessment the IMF stated that 'performance under the program was favorable', due in part to strong control of spending, which ensured that fiscal targets were achieved. Indeed, the central government budget deficit (excluding grants) was 5.2% of GDP in 2010/11, in line with the IMF programme, after a shortfall of 7.2% in 2009/10. However, the ECF provided some leeway in 2011/12, in the shape of a target deficit (again excluding grants) of 6.3% of GDP, before a gradual improvement to 4.8% of GDP by 2014/15. However, including grants, an increase in aid was expected to result in a moderate improvement in the fiscal performance, with the deficit on this measure projected by the IMF to fall from 4.8% of GDP in 2011/12, to 3.3% in 2014/15.

Statistical Survey

Source (unless otherwise stated): Kenya National Bureau of Statistics, POB 30266, Nairobi; tel. (20) 317583; fax (20) 315977; e-mail director@knbs.go.ke; internet www.knbs.or.ke.

Area and Population

AREA, POPULATION AND DENSITY

Area (sq km)	
Land area	571,416
Inland water	11,230
Total	582,646*
Population (census results)†	
24 August 1999	28,686,607
24 August 2009	
Males	19,192,378
Females	19,417,719
Total	38,610,097
Population (UN estimates at mid-year)‡	
2010	40,512,682
2011	41,609,729
2012	42,749,417
Density (per sq km) at mid-2012§	74.8

* 224,961 sq miles.
† Excluding adjustment for underenumeration.
‡ Source: UN, *World Population Prospects: The 2010 Revision*.
§ Land area only.

POPULATION BY AGE AND SEX

(UN estimates at mid-2012)

	Males	Females	Total
0–14	9,121,005	9,013,377	18,134,382
15–64	11,713,202	11,759,771	23,472,973
65 and over	520,074	621,988	1,142,062
Total	21,354,281	21,395,136	42,749,417

Source: UN, *World Population Prospects: The 2010 Revision*.

PRINCIPAL ETHNIC GROUPS

(population at 2009 census)

African	38,445,941	European	32,338
Arab	40,760	Other	9,267
Asian	81,791	**Total**	38,610,097

POPULATION BY PROVINCE

(2010, projected estimates)

Nairobi	3,240,155	Nyanza	5,201,996
Central	3,908,907	Rift Valley	9,101,524
Coast	3,205,175	Western	4,552,522
Eastern	5,587,781	**Total**	36,287,423
North-Eastern	1,489,363		

Note: Projections not adjusted to take account of 2009 census results.

PRINCIPAL TOWNS

(estimated population at census of August 1999)

Nairobi (capital)	2,143,020	Meru	78,100
Mombasa	660,800	Kitale	63,245
Nakuru	219,366	Malindi*	53,805
Kisumu*	194,390	Nyeri*	46,969
Eldoret*	167,016	Kericho	30,023
Thika	82,665	Kisii	29,634

* Boundaries extended between 1979 and 1989.

Mid-2011 (incl. suburbs, UN estimate): Nairobi (capital) 3,363,130 (Source: UN, *World Urbanization Prospects: The 2011 Revision*).

BIRTHS AND DEATHS

(annual averages, UN estimates)

	1995–2000	2000–05	2005–10
Birth rate (per 1,000)	38.0	38.7	38.0
Death rate (per 1,000)	11.8	12.8	11.3

Source: UN, *World Population Prospects: The 2010 Revision*.

Life expectancy (years at birth): 56.5 (males 55.4; females 57.6) in 2010 (Source: World Bank, World Development Indicators database).

EMPLOYMENT

(labour force survey, selected urban and rural settlements, '000s)*

	2009	2010	2011
Agriculture and forestry	340.3	343.8	345.9
Mining and quarrying	6.5	6.6	8.8
Manufacturing	266.4	268.1	275.7
Electricity and water	19.6	19.6	20.7
Construction	93.4	101.3	109.0
Wholesale and retail trade	215.4	226.9	238.6
Transport and communications	143.5	151.3	157.4
Finance, insurance, real estate and business services	97.2	99.3	107.3
Community, social and personal services	817.7	843.7	835.7
Total	2,000.0	2,060.6	2,099.1

* Data are for salaried employees in the formal sector only, and therefore exclude self-employed and unpaid family workers and a vast number of workers in the informal sector (8,388.9 in 2009; 8,826.2 in 2010; 9,272.1 in 2011, according to official estimates). According to ILO, the 1999 census recorded an employed population of 14,474,200.

Health and Welfare

KEY INDICATORS

Total fertility rate (children per woman, 2010)	4.7
Under-5 mortality rate (per 1,000 live births, 2010)	85
HIV/AIDS (% of persons aged 15–49, 2009)	6.3
Physicians (per 1,000 head, 2002)	0.1
Hospital beds (per 1,000 head, 2010)	1.4
Health expenditure (2009): US $ per head (PPP)	75
Health expenditure (2009): % of GDP	4.8
Health expenditure (2009): public (% of total)	43.3
Access to water (% of persons, 2010)	59
Access to sanitation (% of persons, 2010)	32
Total carbon dioxide emissions ('000 metric tons, 2008)	10,392.3
Carbon dioxide emissions per head (metric tons, 2008)	0.3
Human Development Index (2011): ranking	143
Human Development Index (2011): value	0.509

For sources and definitions, see explanatory note on p. vi.

Agriculture

PRINCIPAL CROPS
('000 metric tons)

	2008	2009	2010
Wheat	336.7	219.3	512.0
Barley	44.6	42.1	64.2
Maize	2,367.2	2,439.0	3,222.0
Millet	38.5	54.0	53.9
Sorghum	54.3	99.0	164.1
Potatoes	600.0*	400.0	450.0*
Sweet potatoes	894.8	930.8	383.6
Cassava (Manioc)	751.0	820.0	323.4
Sugar cane	5,112.0	5,610.7	5,709.6
Beans, dry	265.0	465.4	390.6
Cow peas, dry	48.0	60.2	72.3
Pigeon peas	84.2	46.5	103.3
Cashew nuts*	10.5	8.4	8.6
Coconuts	59.7	60.1	72.6
Seed cotton*	23.0	22.5	18.0
Cottonseed	15.1	14.9	11.8
Cabbages and other brassicas	461.1	627.8	583.1
Tomatoes	402.1	526.9	539.2
Onions, dry	123.3	88.9	89.0*
Carrots and turnips	89.1	82.3	90.1
Bananas†	843.5	843.5	791.6
Plantains†	843.5	843.5	791.6
Guavas, mangoes and mangosteens	448.6	474.6	553.7
Avocados	103.5	70.8	113.2
Pineapples	339.9	257.6	272.2
Papayas*	88.0	84.6	85.7
Coffee, green	42.0	57.0	42.0
Tea (made)	345.8	314.1	399.0
Tobacco, unmanufactured	8.5	10.3	14.2
Sisal	22.1	19.0	23.9

* FAO estimate(s).

† Unofficial figure.

Aggregate production ('000 metric tons, may include official, semi-official or estimated data): Total cereals 2,866.4 in 2008, 2,898.8 in 2009, 4,099.9 in 2010; Total roots and tubers 2,273.7 in 2008, 2,177.9 in 2009, 1,186.4 in 2010; Total vegetables (incl. melons) 1,757.3 in 2008, 2,096.8 in 2009, 2,114.2 in 2010; Total fruits (excl. melons) 3,010.4 in 2008, 2,894.0 in 2009, 2,933.3 in 2010.

Source: FAO.

LIVESTOCK
('000 head, year ending September)

	2008	2009	2010
Cattle	18,383.2	17,468.0	17,862.9
Sheep	9,907.3	9,903.3	9,899.3*
Goats	14,478.3	13,872.3	13,291.7*
Pigs	346.8	344.0	347.4
Camels	1,132.5	947.2	1,000.0*
Chickens	32,987	31,827	30,398

* FAO estimate.

Source: FAO.

LIVESTOCK PRODUCTS
('000 metric tons)

	2008	2009	2010
Cattle meat	458.0	483.0	462.0
Sheep meat	39.2	40.8	41.5
Goats' meat	44.7	46.3	46.9
Pig meat	16.2	18.1	15.3
Chicken meat	24.3	25.2	27.1
Game meat*	19.9	21.4	25.1
Camel meat*	27.0	22.8	21.9
Cows' milk	3,990.0	4,070.0	5,157.0
Sheep's milk*	29.7	29.7	30.8
Goats' milk*	134.6	128.9	115.2
Camels' milk*	28.1	29.2	30.0
Hen eggs	76.6	81.0	80.6
Honey*	27.2	25.1	24.0

* FAO estimates.

Source: FAO.

Forestry

ROUNDWOOD REMOVALS
('000 cubic metres, excluding bark, FAO estimates)

	2007	2008	2009
Sawlogs, veneer logs and logs for sleepers	607.0	607.0	607.0
Pulpwood	450.0	450.0	450.0
Other industrial wood	189.0	189.0	189.0
Fuel wood	26,400.0	26,400.0	26,400.0
Total	27,646.0	27,646.0	27,646.0

2010: Production assumed to be unchanged from 2009 (FAO estimates).

Source: FAO.

SAWNWOOD PRODUCTION
('000 cubic metres, including railway sleepers)

	2004	2005	2006
Coniferous (softwood)	70	116	121
Broadleaved (hardwood)	8	20	21
Total	78	136	142

2007–10: Production assumed to be unchanged from 2006 (FAO estimates).

Source: FAO.

Fishing

('000 metric tons, live weight)

	2008	2009	2010
Capture	135.4	133.6	143.1
Silver cyprinid	47.0	49.3	47.7
Nile tilapia	12.7	17.3	26.1
Nile perch	45.0	43.7	39.4
Aquaculture	4.5	4.9	12.2
Total catch	139.9	138.5	155.3

Note: Figures exclude crocodiles, recorded by number rather than by weight. The number of Nile crocodiles caught was: 4,504 in 2008; 6,906 in 2009; 5,259 in 2010.

Source: FAO.

Mining

('000 metric tons)

	2008	2009	2010
Soda ash	513.4	404.9	473.7
Fluorspar	98.2	15.7	44.5
Salt	24.3	24.1	25.0*
Limestone flux*	42.0	38.0	40.0

* Estimated production.

Source: US Geological Survey.

Industry

SELECTED PRODUCTS

('000 metric tons unless otherwise indicated)

	2006	2007	2008
Wheat flour	392.8	370.3	310.7
Raw sugar	417.1	520.4	511.9
Beer ('000 hectolitres)	3,115.6	3,934.2	4,248.6
Cigarettes (million)	10,261.6	12,203.7	12,169.0
Cement	2,405.9	2,615.0	2,829.6
Jet fuel	240	236	221
Motor gasoline (petrol)	179	207	182
Gas-diesel oils	368	397	374
Residual fuel oils	596	534	515
Electric energy (million kWh)	7,322	6,772	7,055

2009 ('000 metric tons): Jet fuel 217; Motor gasoline (petrol) 157; Residual fuel oils 498.

Source: UN Industrial Commodity Statistics Database.

Finance

CURRENCY AND EXCHANGE RATES

Monetary Units

100 cents = 1 Kenya shilling (Ks.).
Ks. 20 = 1 Kenya pound (K£).

Sterling, Dollar and Euro Equivalents (31 May 2012)

£1 sterling = Ks. 134.61;
US $1 = Ks. 88.83;
€1 = Ks. 107.69;
Ks. 1,000 = £7.43 sterling = $11.52 = €9.29.

Average Exchange Rate (Ks. per US $)

2009 77.352
2010 79.233
2011 88.811

Note: The foregoing information refers to the Central Bank's mid-point exchange rate. However, with the introduction of a foreign exchange bearer certificate (FEBC) scheme in October 1991, a dual exchange rate system is in effect. In May 1994 foreign exchange transactions were liberalized and the Kenya shilling became fully convertible against other currencies.

BUDGET

(Ks. '000 million, year ending 30 June)

Revenue*	2009/10†	2010/11‡	2011/12§
Tax revenue	466.5	557.2	640.6
Taxes on income and profits	209.1	258.7	308.4
Taxes on goods and services	216.1	252.5	275.6
Value-added tax	142.0	171.9	193.8
Excise duties	74.1	80.6	81.8
Taxes on international trade	41.3	46.1	56.6
Import duties	41.3	46.1	56.6
Non-tax revenue	81.6	110.4	159.2
Total (incl. others)	548.1	667.5	799.8

Expenditure‖	2009/10†	2010/11‡	2011/12§
Recurrent expenditure	504.3	578.5	678.1
Wages and benefits	172.6	198.5	229.4
Defence	56.9	60.6	75.9
Interest payments	63.5	76.2	85.2
Internal	57.4	69.2	77.7
External	6.1	7.0	7.5
Development expenditure	213.5	216.9	309.6
Domestically financed	151.9	149.9	195.8
Foreign financed	61.6	67.0	113.8
Drought expenditure	6.2	8.3	8.3
Constitutional reform	—	5.6	8.0
Total	724.0	809.3	1,004.0

* Excluding grants received (Ks. '000 million): 20.7 in 2009/10 (estimate); 18.8 in 2010/11 (preliminary figure); 48.1 in 2011/12 (programmed figure).

† Estimates.

‡ Preliminary figures.

§ Programmed figures.

‖ Excluding net lending (Ks. '000 million): 1.2 in 2009/10 (estimate); 2.5 in 2010/11 (preliminary figure); 2.6 in 2011/12 (programmed figure).

Source: IMF, *Kenya: Third Review Under the Three-Year Arrangement Under the Extended Credit Facility and Request for Modification of Performance Criteria - Staff Report; Press Release* (April 2012).

INTERNATIONAL RESERVES

(excl. gold, US $ million at 31 December)

	2009	2010	2011
IMF special drawing rights	350.6	318.5	16.9
Reserve position in IMF	20.2	20.0	20.0
Foreign exchange	3,478.1	3,981.7	4,227.5
Total	3,849.0	4,320.2	4,264.4

Source: IMF, *International Financial Statistics*.

MONEY SUPPLY
(Ks. million at 31 December)

	2009	2010	2011
Currency depository corporations	100,850	122,925	136,983
Transferable deposits	427,532	557,124	621,196
Other deposits	515,682	597,485	764,029
Broad money	1,044,064	1,277,534	1,522,208

Source: IMF, *International Financial Statistics*.

COST OF LIVING
(Consumer Price Index at December; base: October 1997 = 100)

	2001	2002	2003
Food and non-alcoholic beverages	135	142	162
Alcohol and tobacco	138	139	147
Clothing and footwear	110	111	112
Housing	128	132	134
Fuel and power	156	169	170
Household goods and services	119	120	123
Medical goods and services	153	160	169
Transport and communications	128	131	139
Recreation and education	130	133	137
Personal goods and services	121	123	124
All items (incl. others)	131	137	148

Source: IMF, *Kenya: Statistical Appendix* (June 2009).

All items (Consumer Price Index, annual averages; base 2005 = 100): 173.2 in 2009; 180.1 in 2010; 205.3 in 2011 (Source: IMF, *International Financial Statistics*).

NATIONAL ACCOUNTS
(Ks. million at current prices)

Expenditure on the Gross Domestic Product

	2008	2009	2010*
Government final consumption expenditure	348,076	372,797	424,698
Private final consumption expenditure	1,583,651	1,850,699	1,985,066
Changes in inventories	−4,120	6,365	−16,131
Gross fixed capital formation	409,597	452,549	508,453
Total domestic expenditure	2,337,204	2,682,410	2,902,085
Exports of goods and services	581,806	571,305	702,103
Less Imports of goods and services	879,821	865,997	966,002
Statistical discrepancy	71,984	−22,265	−87,025
GDP at market prices	2,111,173	2,365,453	2,551,161

Gross Domestic Product by Economic Activity

	2008	2009	2010*
Agriculture, forestry and fishing	480,203	565,274	562,167
Mining and quarrying	14,930	12,083	17,650
Manufacturing	228,304	234,423	254,461
Electricity, gas and water	43,767	55,738	61,213
Construction	80,407	97,118	109,148
Wholesale and retail trade, restaurants and hotels	237,767	272,371	304,680
Transport, storage and communications	216,053	232,945	249,560
Finance, insurance, real estate and business services	205,129	246,551	266,747
Public administration and defence	106,914	104,757	119,152
Other services	263,614	286,974	308,011
Sub-total	1,877,088	2,108,234	2,252,789
Less Financial intermediation services indirectly measured	18,231	28,232	20,112
Indirect taxes, less subsidies	252,317	285,450	318,485
GDP in market prices	2,111,173	2,365,453	2,551,161

* Provisional figures.

BALANCE OF PAYMENTS
(US $ million)

	2008	2009	2010
Exports of goods f.o.b.	5,039.8	4,502.3	5,224.7
Imports of goods f.o.b.	−10,689.0	−9,489.8	−11,527.7
Trade balance	−5,649.2	−4,987.6	−6,303.0
Exports of services	3,250.8	2,882.8	3,675.5
Imports of services	−1,870.2	−1,811.8	−2,015.7
Balance on goods and services	−4,268.6	−3,916.5	−4,643.2
Other income received	176.2	181.9	136.4
Other income paid	−221.4	−212.4	−291.8
Balance on goods, services and income	−4,313.8	−3,947.0	−4,798.6
Current transfers received	2,419.3	2,341.3	2,368.4
Current transfers paid	−88.1	−82.8	−82.0
Current balance	−1,982.6	−1,688.5	−2,512.2
Capital account	94.5	260.9	240.2
Direct investment abroad	−43.8	−46.0	−1.6
Direct investment from abroad	95.6	116.3	185.8
Portfolio investment assets	−35.9	−23.7	−51.2
Portfolio investment liabilities	9.8	2.8	33.5
Other investment assets	−631.6	544.6	97.2
Other investment liabilities	1,701.3	1,871.9	1,882.1
Net errors and omissions	297.4	79.8	267.7
Overall balance	−495.3	1,118.0	141.6

Source: IMF, *International Financial Statistics*.

External Trade

PRINCIPAL COMMODITIES
(distribution by SITC, US $ million)

Imports c.i.f.	2008	2009	2010
Food and live animals	688.9	1,117.0	846.2
Cereals and cereal preparations	421.7	811.4	437.3
Crude materials (inedible) except fuels	225.3	224.2	262.9
Mineral fuels, lubricants, etc.	3,029.4	2,187.1	2,670.2
Petroleum, petroleum products, etc.	2,976.7	2,138.7	2,596.1
Crude petroleum oils	1,176.5	705.8	915.2
Refined petroleum products	1,769.6	1,399.2	1,646.3
Animal and vegetable oils, fats and waxes	496.8	356.9	490.8
Chemicals and related products	1,454.0	1,325.7	1,602.7
Medicinal and pharmaceutical products	301.6	297.8	351.4
Plastics in primary forms	341.0	288.4	378.6
Basic manufactures	1,602.3	1,408.8	1,774.6
Iron and steel	512.9	437.3	548.7
Machinery and transport equipment	3,110.1	3,097.3	3,841.1
Power-generating machinery and equipment	350.8	317.2	306.5
Machinery specialized for particular industries	365.5	339.3	369.5
General industrial machinery, equipment and parts	329.6	272.0	356.4
Electrical machinery, apparatus, etc.	185.1	196.5	233.8
Road vehicles and parts	817.7	785.2	869.6
Passenger motor cars (excl. buses)	311.9	296.0	345.5
Motor vehicles for goods transport and special purposes	190.8	165.3	212.8
Aircraft, associated equipment and parts	235.5	349.5	517.6
Miscellaneous manufactured articles	431.5	417.2	504.0
Total (incl. others)	11,127.8	10,202.0	12,092.9

Exports f.o.b.	2008	2009	2010
Food and live animals	1,827.7	1,681.1	2,095.9
Vegetables and fruit	451.6	358.9	451.6
Fresh or simply preserved vegetables	274.1	224.7	270.4
Coffee, tea, cocoa and spices	1,098.8	1,110.4	1,388.9
Tea	931.8	894.1	1,163.8
Crude materials (inedible) except fuels	763.1	638.3	612.8
Cut flowers and foliage	527.4	422.5	397.4
Mineral fuels, lubricants, etc.	197.7	187.5	216.9
Petroleum, petroleum products, etc.	192.3	183.9	211.4
Refined petroleum products	173.3	177.9	205.2
Chemicals and related products	574.0	457.2	466.5
Basic manufactures	654.1	547.8	625.6
Iron and steel	158.4	118.1	153.5
Miscellaneous manufactured articles	510.6	429.5	449.2
Total (incl. others)	5,000.9	4,463.4	5,169.1

Source: UN, *International Trade Statistics Yearbook*.

PRINCIPAL TRADING PARTNERS
(US $ million)

Imports c.i.f.	2008	2009	2010
Bahrain	198.8	97.9	57.9
Belgium	119.7	91.2	96.3
China, People's Repub.	932.2	965.2	1,522.5
Egypt	157.4	124.3	232.1
Finland	77.2	55.7	178.6
France (incl. Monaco)	237.6	206.8	235.8
Germany	389.7	294.4	332.6
India	1,309.5	1,078.1	1,301.6
Indonesia	335.7	243.1	339.8
Italy	181.7	179.9	151.1
Japan	649.3	632.7	734.6
Korea, Repub.	119.3	138.6	248.7
Netherlands	192.1	225.9	232.7
Russia	166.2	63.3	122.1
Saudi Arabia	373.1	356.4	406.8
Singapore	360.7	342.2	400.1
South Africa	678.2	913.8	754.2
Switzerland-Liechtenstein	80.4	69.8	143.0
Tanzania	105.5	101.1	133.0
Thailand	131.4	91.6	107.3
Ukraine	82.7	131.9	110.4
United Arab Emirates	1,655.7	1,161.8	1,462.9
United Kingdom	402.6	473.2	626.3
USA	402.3	649.1	496.0
Total (incl. others)	11,127.8	10,202.0	12,092.9

Exports f.o.b.	2008	2009	2010
Afghanistan	62.6	98.9	150.5
Belgium	40.9	43.9	52.5
Burundi	50.5	59.5	68.8
Congo, Democratic Repub.	143.6	146.5	161.4
Egypt	224.7	153.8	228.5
Ethiopia	63.9	55.9	55.3
France (incl. Monaco)	72.1	56.1	65.5
Germany	89.3	95.1	97.3
India	98.2	66.5	106.9
Malawi	58.2	40.7	53.8
Netherlands	380.1	340.7	338.9
Pakistan	202.3	196.3	227.9
Russia	49.5	46.8	57.0
Rwanda	130.4	123.4	132.9
Somalia	186.7	145.1	164.7
South Africa	52.9	46.3	30.8
Sudan	204.6	165.1	237.5
Tanzania	424.9	389.3	420.2
Uganda	614.7	598.3	657.3
United Arab Emirates	109.8	138.7	237.8
United Kingdom	550.6	498.1	507.2
USA	299.6	226.1	284.9
Yemen	40.7	42.9	57.0
Zambia	79.9	62.5	59.1
Total (incl. others)	5,000.9	4,463.4	5,169.1

Source: UN, *International Trade Statistics Yearbook*.

2011 (Ks. million): Total imports 1,315.7; Total exports 511.0.

Transport

RAILWAYS
(traffic)

	2000	2001	2002*
Passenger-km (million)	302	216	288
Freight ton-km (million)	1,557	1,603	1,538

* Provisional figures.

Freight carried ('000 metric tons): 1,532 in 2009; 1,572 in 2010; 1,596 in 2011 (provisional).

ROAD TRAFFIC
(motor vehicles in use)

	2007	2008	2009*
Motor cars	410,812	450,137	499,679
Light vans	202,671	209,628	219,901
Lorries, trucks and heavy vans	75,347	81,285	91,431
Buses and mini-buses	55,997	61,886	84,844
Motorcycles and autocycles	78,981	130,307	252,960
Other motor vehicles	30,961	32,710	45,229

* Provisional figures.

SHIPPING

Merchant Fleet
(registered at 31 December)

	2007	2008	2009
Number of vessels	36	36	32
Total displacement ('000 grt)	15.1	15.1	14.4

Source: IHS Fairplay, *World Fleet Statistics*.

International Sea-borne Freight Traffic
('000 metric tons)

	1999	2000	2001*
Goods loaded	1,845	1,722	1,998
Goods unloaded	6,200	7,209	8,299

* Provisional figures.

Freight handled ('000 metric tons at Kenyan ports): 19,062 in 2009; 18,977 in 2010; 19,953 in 2011 (provisional).

CIVIL AVIATION
(traffic on scheduled services)

	2007	2008	2009
Kilometres flown (million)	57	61	64
Passengers carried ('000)	2,858	2,881	2,949
Passenger-km (million)	7,952	8,047	7,925
Total ton-km (million)	1,023	1,022	987

Source: UN, *Statistical Yearbook*.

Passengers carried ('000, all services): 7,516 in 2010; 8,722 in 2011 (provisional).

Tourism

FOREIGN TOURIST ARRIVALS
(overnight stays at accommodation establishments)

	2007	2008	2009
France	304,300	63,800	231,800
Germany	926,100	339,500	685,600
India	60,500	51,200	83,300
Italy	536,500	158,200	383,200
Switzerland	174,200	66,800	127,500
Tanzania	54,700	43,100	71,100
Uganda	52,200	43,200	103,000
United Kingdom	1,223,100	486,600	909,700
USA	270,900	148,100	233,800
Total (incl. others)	5,044,400	2,080,100	4,062,400

Tourism receipts (US $ million, excl. passenger transport): 800 in 2010; 884 in 2011 (provisional).

Source: World Tourism Organization.

Total tourist arrivals ('000): 1,490 in 2009; 1,609 in 2010; 1,823 in 2011 (provisional).

Communications Media

	2009	2010	2011
Telephones ('000 main lines in use)	664	381	284
Mobile cellular telephones ('000 subscribers)	19,365	24,969	26,981
Internet subscribers ('000)	8.3	12.2	n.a.
Broadband subscribers ('000)	8.3	4.2	49.0

Personal computers: 492,000 (13.7 per 1,000 persons) in 2005.

Source: International Telecommunication Union.

Television receivers ('000 in use, 2000): 768.

Radio receivers ('000 in use, 1999): 6,383.

Daily newspapers (2004): 5 titles (average circulation 310,000 copies in 2000).

Book production (titles, 1994): 300 first editions (excl. pamphlets).

Sources: UNESCO, *Statistical Yearbook*; UN, *Statistical Yearbook*.

Education

(2008/09 unless otherwise indicated)

	Institutions	Teachers	Pupils
Pre-primary	23,977[1]	92,555	1,914,222
Primary	17,611[1]	152,848	7,150,259
Secondary:			
general secondary	3,057[1]	106,033	3,188,707
technical	36[2]	1,937	15,672
teacher training	26[3]	808[4]	18,992[5]
Higher	n.a.[6]	n.a.[6]	167,983

[1] 1998/99 figures.
[2] 1988 figure.
[3] 1995 figure.
[4] 1985 figure.
[5] 1992 figure.
[6] In 1990 there were four universities, with 4,392 teachers.

2009/10 (provisional figures) *Institutions:* Primary 27,489; Secondary 7,308; Higher 32. *Pupils:* Primary 9,381,211; Secondary 1,701,501; Higher 21,106.

Sources: Ministry of Education, Nairobi; UNESCO Institute for Statistics.

Pupil-teacher ratio (primary education, UNESCO estimate): 46.8 in 2008/09 (Source: UNESCO Institute for Statistics).

Adult literacy rate (UNESCO estimates): 87.4% (males 90.6%; females 84.2%) in 2010 (Source: UNESCO Institute for Statistics).

Directory

The Constitution

A new Constitution replacing the Constitution introduced at independence on 12 December 1963 (and as subsequently amended) was approved at a national referendum on 4 August 2010 and entered into force on 27 August.

The territory of Kenya is divided into 47 counties. There shall be a County Government for each county, consisting of a County Assembly and a County Executive. The latter is headed by a County Governor elected directly by the people.

Legislative authority is vested in and exercised by Parliament, which consists of the National Assembly and the Senate. Members of Parliament serve concurrent five-year terms. The National Assembly consists of 290 members, each elected by the registered voters of single member constituencies; 47 women, each elected by the registered voters of the counties, each county constituting a single member constituency; 12 members nominated by parliamentary political parties according to their proportion of members of the National Assembly to represent special interests including the youth, persons with disabilities and workers; and the Speaker, who is an ex officio member. The Senate consists of 47 members each elected by the registered voters of the counties, each county constituting a single member constituency; 16 women members who shall be nominated by political parties according to their proportion of members of the Senate; two members, being one man and one woman, representing the youth; two members, being one man and one woman, representing persons with disabilities; and the Speaker, who shall be an ex officio member.

The President is the Head of State and Government and exercises the executive authority of the Republic, with the assistance of the Deputy President and Cabinet Secretaries. The President is also Commander-in-Chief of the Kenya Defence Forces and is the Chairperson of the National Security Council. An election of the President shall be held on the same day as a general election of Members of Parliament. A candidate shall be declared elected as President if the candidate receives more than one-half of all the votes cast in the election and at least 25% of the votes cast in each of more than one-half of the counties. If no candidate is elected, a fresh election shall be held within 30 days after the previous election and in that fresh election the only candidates shall be the candidate, or the candidates, who received the greatest number of votes and the candidate, or the candidates, who received the second greatest number of votes. When a vacancy occurs in the office of President the Deputy President shall assume office as President for the remainder of the term of the President. If the office of Deputy President is vacant, or the Deputy President is unable to assume the office of President, the Speaker of the National Assembly shall act as President and an election to the office of President shall be held within 60 days after the vacancy arose in the office of President.

The Deputy President shall be the principal assistant of the President and shall deputise for the President in the execution of the President's functions.

The Cabinet consists of the President, the Deputy President, the Attorney-General and not fewer than 14 or more than 22 Cabinet Secretaries. The President shall nominate and, with the approval of the National Assembly, appoint Cabinet Secretaries. A Cabinet Secretary shall not be a Member of Parliament.

The Constitution can be amended either by a simple majority of the citizens voting in a referendum, or by the adoption of a Bill by not less than two-thirds of the members of both Houses of Parliament.

The Government

HEAD OF STATE

President: MWAI KIBAKI (took office 30 December 2002; re-elected 27 December 2007).

CABINET

(September 2012)

The Government is formed by a coalition of the Party of National Unity, the Orange Democratic Movement, and the Orange Democratic Movement—Kenya.

Prime Minister: RAILA AMOLLO ODINGA.

Vice-President and Minister of Home Affairs: STEPHEN KALONZO MUSYOKA.

Deputy Prime Minister: UHURU KENYATTA.

Deputy Prime Minister: WYCLIFFE MUSALIA MUDAVADI.

Minister of Finance: ROBINSON NJERU GITHAE.

Minister of the East African Community: MUSA SIRMA.

Minister of Foreign Affairs: Prof. SAMSON KEGEO ONGERI.

Minister of Justice, National Cohesion and Constitutional Affairs: EUGINE WAMALWA.

Minister of Nairobi Metropolitan Development: JAMLECK KAMAU.

Minister of Public Works: CHRISTOPHER MOGERE OBURE.

Minister of Trade: MOSES WETANGULA.

Minister of Water and Irrigation: CHARITY KALUKI NGULI.

Minister of Regional Development Authorities: FREDRICK OMULO GUMO.

Minister of Information and Communications: SAMUEL LESRON POGHISIO.

Minister of Energy: KIRAITU MURUNGI.

Minister of Lands: AGGREY JAMES ORENGO.

Minister of the Environment and Mineral Resources: CHIRAU ALI MWAKWERE.

Minister of Forestry and Wildlife: NOAH WEKESA.

Minister of Tourism: DANSON MWANZO.

Minister of Agriculture: Dr SALLY JEPNGETICH KOSGEY.

Minister of Livestock Development: MOHAMED ABDI KUTI.

Minister of Fisheries Development: AMASON JEFFAH KINGI.

Minister of the Development of Northern Kenya and Other Arid Lands: IBRAHIM ELMI MOHAMED.

Minister of Co-operative Development: JOSEPH NYAGAH.

Minister of Industrialization: (vacant).

Minister of Housing: PETER SOITA SHITANDA.

Minister of State for Special Programmes: ESTHER MURUGI MATHENGE.

Minister of Gender, Children and Social Development: Dr NAOMI NAMSI SHABAN.

Minister of Public Health and Sanitation: BETH WAMBUI MUGO.

Minister of Medical Services: Prof. PETER ANYANG' NYONG'O.

Minister of Labour: JOHN KIONGA MUNYES.

Minister of Youth and Sports: ABABU NAMWAMBA.

Minister of Higher Education, Science and Technology: Prof. MARGARET KAMAR.

Minister of Education: MUTULA KILONZO.

Minister of Roads: FRANKLIN BETT.

Minister of Transport: AMOS KIMUNYA.

Minister of Provincial Administration and Internal Security: KATOO OLE METITO.

Minister of Local Government: Dr PAUL NYONGESA OTUOMA.

Minister of State in the Office of the President, responsible for Defence: YUSUF MOHAMED HAJI.

Ministers of State in the Office of the Vice-President: GERALD OTIENO KAJWANG' (Immigration and Registration of Persons), WILLIAM OLE NTIMAMA (National Heritage and Culture).

Ministers of State in the Office of the Prime Minister: WYCLIFFE AMBETSA OPARANYA (Planning, National Development and Vision 2030), DALMAS ANYANGO OTIENO (Public Service).

Attorney-General: GITHU MUIGAI.

MINISTRIES

Office of the President: Harambee House, Harambee Ave, POB 62345, 00200 Nairobi; tel. (20) 2227411; e-mail president@statehousekenya.go.ke; internet www.cabinetoffice.go.ke.

Office of the Vice-President and Ministry of Home Affairs: Jogoo House 'A', Taifa Rd, POB 30478, 00100 Nairobi; tel. (20) 228411; fax (20) 243620; internet www.homeaffairs.go.ke.

Office of the Prime Minister: Treasury Bldg, 14th Floor, Harambee Ave, POB 74434, 00200 Nairobi; tel. (20) 252299; e-mail info@primeminister.go.ke; internet www.primeminister.go.ke.

Office of the Deputy Prime Minister and Ministry of Local Government: Jogoo House 'A', Taifa Rd, POB 30004, Nairobi; tel. (20) 2217475; fax (20) 217869; internet www.localgovernment.go.ke.

Ministry of Agriculture: Kilimo House, Cathedral Rd, POB 30028, Nairobi; tel. (20) 2718870; internet www.kilimo.go.ke.

Ministry of Co-operative Development and Marketing: NSSF Bldg, Block 'A', Eastern Wing, Bishop Rd, POB 30547, 00100, Nairobi; tel. (20) 2731531; fax (20) 2731511; internet www.cooperative.go.ke.

Ministry of the Development of Northern Kenya and Other Arid Lands: Kenya Int. Conference Centre, 13th Floor, Harambee Ave, POB 53547, 00200 Nairobi; tel. (20) 2227223; fax (20) 2227982.

Ministry of the East African Community: Co-operative House, 16th Floor, Haile Selassie Ave, POB 8846, 00200 Nairobi; tel. (20) 2245741; fax (20) 2229650; e-mail ps@meac.go.ke; internet www.meac.go.ke.

Ministry of Education: Jogoo House 'B', Harambee Ave, POB 30040, 00100 Nairobi; tel. (20) 318581; fax (20) 214287; e-mail info@education.go.ke; internet www.education.go.ke.

Ministry of Energy: Nyayo House, 23rd Floor, Kenyatta Ave, POB 30582, 00100 Nairobi; tel. (20) 310112; fax (20) 228314; e-mail info@energy.go.ke; internet www.energy.go.ke.

Ministry of the Environment and Mineral Resources: NHIF Bldg, Ragati Rd, POB 30126, 00100 Nairobi; tel. (20) 2730808; fax (20) 2725707; internet www.environment.go.ke.

Ministry of Finance: Treasury Bldg, Harambee Ave, POB 30007, Nairobi; tel. (20) 228411; internet www.treasury.go.ke.

Ministry of Fisheries Development: Maji House, Ngong Rd, POB 58187, 00200 Nairobi; tel. (20) 2716103; fax (20) 316731; e-mail fisheries@kenya.go.ke; internet www.fisheries.go.ke.

Ministry of Foreign Affairs: Old Treasury Bldg, Harambee Ave, POB 30551, 00100 Nairobi; tel. (20) 318888; fax (20) 240066; e-mail press@mfa.go.ke; internet www.mfa.go.ke.

Ministry of Forestry and Wildlife: NHIF Bldg, Ragati Rd, POB 30126, Nairobi; tel. (20) 2730808; internet www.forestryandwildlife.go.ke.

Ministry of Gender, Children and Social Development: NSSF Bldg, Block 'A', Eastern Wing, 6th Floor, Bishop Rd, POB 16936, 00100 Nairobi; tel. (20) 2727980; fax (20) 2734417; e-mail information@gender.go.ke; internet www.gender.go.ke.

Ministry of Higher Education, Science and Technology: Jogoo House 'B', Harambee Ave, POB 9583, 00200 Nairobi; tel. (20) 318581; e-mail info@scienceandtechnology.go.ke; internet www.scienceandtechnology.go.ke.

Ministry of Housing: Ardhi House, Ngong Rd, POB 30119, 00100 Nairobi; tel. (20) 2718050; fax (20) 2713833; e-mail ps@housing.go.ke; internet www.housing.go.ke.

Ministry of Industrialization: Teleposta Towers, GPO 11th Floor, POB 30418, 00100 Nairobi; tel. (20) 315001; e-mail info@industrialization.go.ke; internet www.tradeandindustry.go.ke.

Ministry of Information and Communications: Teleposta Towers, Kenyatta Ave, POB 30025, 00100 Nairobi; tel. (20) 2251152; fax (20) 315147; internet www.information.go.ke.

Ministry of Justice, National Cohesion and Constitutional Affairs: Cooperative Bank House, Haile Selassie Ave, POB 56057, 00200 Nairobi; tel. (20) 224029; e-mail info@justice.go.ke; internet www.justice.go.ke.

Ministry of Labour: Social NSSF Bldg, Block 'C', Bishop Rd, POB 40326, 00100 Nairobi; tel. (20) 2729800; fax (20) 2726497; e-mail info@labour.go.ke; internet www.labour.go.ke.

Ministry of Lands: Ardhi House, Ngong Rd, POB 30450, 00100 Nairobi; tel. (20) 2718050; fax (20) 2721248; internet www.ardhi.go.ke.

Ministry of Livestock Development: Kilimo House, Cathedral Rd, POB 34188, 00100 Nairobi; tel. (20) 2718870; fax (20) 2711149; e-mail info@livestock.go.ke; internet www.livestock.go.ke.

Ministry of Medical Services: Afya House, Cathedral Rd, POB 30016, 00100 Nairobi; tel. (20) 2717077; fax (20) 2713234; e-mail enquiries@health.go.ke; internet www.medical.go.ke.

Ministry of Nairobi Metropolitan Development: Kenya Int. Conference Centre, 25th Floor, Harambee Ave, POB 30130, 00100

Nairobi; tel. (20) 317224; fax (20) 317226; e-mail info@nairobimetro.go.ke; internet www.nairobimetro.go.ke.

Ministry of Public Health and Sanitation: Medical HQ, Afya House, Cathedral Rd, POB 30016, 00100 Nairobi; tel. (20) 2717077; fax (20) 2713234; e-mail psph@health.go.ke; internet www.publichealth.go.ke.

Ministry of Public Works: Ministry of Works Bldg, Ngong Rd, POB 30260, Nairobi; tel. (20) 2723101; e-mail info@publiworks.go.ke; internet www.works.go.ke.

Ministry of Regional Development Authorities: NSSF Bldg, Block 'A', Eastern Wing, 21st Floor, Bishop Rd, POB 10280, 00100 Nairobi; tel. (20) 2724646; fax 2737693; e-mail psmrd@regional-dev.go.ke; internet www.regional-dev.go.ke.

Ministry of Roads: Ministry of Works Bldg, Ngong Rd, POB 30260, Nairobi; tel. (20) 2723101; fax (20) 720044; internet www.publicworks.go.ke.

Ministry of Special Programmes: Comcraft House, 5th Floor, Haile Selassie Ave, POB 40213, 00100 Nairobi; tel. (20) 247880; fax (20) 227622; e-mail info@sprogrammes.go.ke; internet www.sprogrammes.go.ke.

Ministry of Tourism: Utalii House, off Uhuru Hwy, POB 30027, Nairobi; tel. (20) 313010; fax (20) 318045; e-mail info@tourism.go.ke; internet www.tourism.go.ke.

Ministry of Trade: Teleposta Towers, Kenyatta Ave, POB 30430, 00100 Nairobi; tel. (20) 315001; fax (20) 252896; e-mail info@trade.go.ke; internet www.trade.go.ke.

Ministry of Transport: Transcom House, Ngong Rd, POB 52692, 00200 Nairobi; tel. (20) 2729200; fax (20) 2730330; e-mail ps@transport.go.ke; internet www.transport.go.ke.

Ministry of Water and Irrigation: Maji House, Ngong Rd, POB 49720, 00100 Nairobi; tel. (20) 2716103; fax (20) 2727622; e-mail pro@water.go.ke; internet www.water.go.ke.

Ministry of Youth and Sports: Kencom House, 3rd Floor, Moi Ave, POB 34303, 00100 Nairobi; tel. (20) 240068; fax (20) 312351; e-mail infor@youthaffairs.go.ke; internet www.youthaffairs.go.ke.

President and Legislature

PRESIDENT

Election, 27 December 2007*

Candidate	Votes
Mwai Kibaki (PNU)	4,584,721
Raila Odinga (ODM)	4,352,993
Stephen Kalonzo Musyoka (ODM—Kenya)	879,903
Others	59,411†

* Results released by the Office of the Government Spokesperson. The figure for the total number of votes cast at the election was not immediately made available.

† There were six other candidates.

NATIONAL ASSEMBLY

Speaker: Kenneth Otiato Marende.

General Election, 27 December 2007

Party	Seats
ODM	99
PNU	43
ODM—Kenya	16
KANU	14
Safina	5
NARC—Kenya	4
FORD—People	3
NARC	3
New FORD—Kenya	2
CCU	2
PICK	2
DP	2
SKS	2
Others	10
Vacant	3*
Total	210†

* Results in three constituencies were not immediately made available and a further two seats were made vacant with the deaths of members of the National Assembly. Following by-elections in five constituencies held on 11 June 2008, the ODM held 102 seats, while the PNU held 45. All other part representations remained unchanged.

† In addition to the 210 directly elected seats, 12 are held by nominees. The Attorney-General and the Speaker are, ex officio, members of the National Assembly.

Election Commission

Independent Electoral and Boundaries Commission (IEBC): Loita St, Anniversary Towers, 6th Floor, POB 45371, 00100 Nairobi; tel. (20) 2769000; e-mail info@iebc.or.ke; internet www.iebc.or.ke; f. 2011 to replace Electoral Commission of Kenya, which was disbanded following disputed elections in 2007; Chair. Ahmed Issack Hassan.

Political Organizations

Chama Cha Uma (CCU): Nairobi; Founder Dr Patrick Lumumba.

Dawa Ya Wakenya (Remedy for Kenya): f. 2007 by politicians from the North-Eastern region and the north of the Rift Valley to defend the rights of the inhabitants of those areas and to campaign for improved infrastructure, social services and security; Chair. Hassan Haji; Gen. Sec. Moru Shambaru.

Democratic Party of Kenya (DP): Gitanga Rd, POB 53695, 00200 Nairobi; tel. 722794736 (mobile); f. 1991; Leader Joseph Munyao; rival faction led by Ngengi Muigai.

Forum for the Restoration of Democracy—Asili (FORD—Asili): 58 Duplex Apt, Upper Hill, POB 69564, 00400 Nairobi; e-mail fordasili@gmail.com; tel. (20) 2712214; f. 1992; Chair. Jane Elizabeth Ogwapit.

Forum for the Restoration of Democracy—Kenya (FORD—Kenya): Odinga House, Argwings Kodhek Rd, POB 43591, 00100 Nairobi; tel. (20) 3869338; e-mail fordkenya@yahoo.com; f. 1992; predominantly Luo support; Chair. Musikari Kombo.

Forum for the Restoration of Democracy for the People (FORD—People): Muchai Dr., off Ngong Rd, POB 5938, 00200 Nairobi; tel. (20) 2737015; f. 1997 by fmr mems of FORD—Asili; Nat. Chair. Reuben Oyondi.

Kenya African National Union (KANU): Yaya Center, Chania Rd, POB 72394, 00200 Nairobi; tel. (20) 6751284; fax (20) 3573115; internet www.kanuonline.com; f. 1960; sole legal party 1982–91; absorbed the National Development Party (f. 1994) in 2002; Chair. Uhuru Kenyatta.

Kenya National Congress (KNC): Gatundu Rd. Kileleshwa, POB 61215, 00200 Nairobi; tel. 722754814 (mobile); f. 1992; Chair. Nancy Mungai.

Kenya National Democratic Alliance (KENDA): Int. Casino Complex, Museum Hill, Westlands, POB 10135, 00400 Nairobi; tel. 720841184 (mobile); f. 1991; Chair. Kamlesh Pattni; Sec.-Gen. Bernard Kalove.

Liberal Democratic Party (LDP): Nairobi; f. 2002 by fmr mems of KANU; Chair. David Musha; Sec.-Gen. J. J. Kamotho.

Liberal Party: Chair. Wangari Maathai.

Mazingira Green Party of Kenya (MPK): POB 14832, Nairobi; tel. 737444901 (mobile); f. 2007; campaigns for the equitable sharing of wealth, sustainable use of natural resources, women's rights and the defence of Kenyan cultural values; Leader Wangari Maathai.

National Party of Kenya (NPK): Nairobi; internet nationalpartyofkenya.org; f. 1992; Chair. Charity Kaluki Ngilu; Sec.-Gen. Fidelis Mweke.

National Rainbow Coalition (NARC): Mwenge House, Ole Odume Rd, off Gitanga Rd and near Methodist Guest House, Nairobi; tel. (20) 571506; f. 2002; Chair. Charity Kaluki Ngilu.

National Rainbow Coalition—Kenya (NARC—Kenya): Woodlands Rd, off Lenana Rd, Kilimani, POB 34200, 00100 Nairobi; tel. (20) 2726783; fax (20) 2726784; e-mail narckenya06@yahoo.com; internet www.narckenya.org; f. 2006 by former mems of NARC; Chair. Martha Karua.

New FORD—Kenya: Kikombe House, Joseph Kangethe Rd, Woodley, POB 67404, 00200 Nairobi; tel. 721399626 (mobile); f. 2007; Chair. Soita Shitanda.

New Kenya African National Union (New—KANU): Nairobi; f. 2006 by former members of KANU; Pres. Nicholas Biwott.

Orange Democratic Movement (ODM): Orange House, Menelik Rd, Kilimani Area, POB 2478, 00202 Nairobi; tel. (20) 2053481; f. 2005; split in August 2007; Leader Raila Amolo Odinga.

Orange Democratic Movement—Kenya (ODM—Kenya): Chungwa House, Othaya Rd, POB 403, 00100 Nairobi; tel. (20) 2726385; fax (20) 2726391; f. 2007 following split in the ODM; Leader Stephen Kalonzo Musyoka.

Party of Independent Candidates of Kenya (PICK): Uganda House, 2nd Floor, Kenyatta Ave, POB 21821, 00400 Nairobi; tel. (20) 3513899; e-mail pickenya@yahoo.com; Chair. G. N. Musyimi.

Party of National Unity (PNU): Lenana Rd, opp. CVS Plaza, POB 5751, 00100 Nairobi; tel. 722510733 (mobile); f. 2007; coalition of 14 parties including: KANU, the SPK, the SKS, Safina, NARC—Kenya, the DP, New FORD—Kenya, FORD—People, FORD—Asili, FORD—Kenya and the MPK; Chair. MWAI KIBAKI.

Safina ('Noah's Ark'): Safina Place, Jamhuri Cres., off Ngong Rd, POB 14746, 00100 Nairobi; tel. (20) 3864242; fax (20) 3864242; f. 1995; aims to combat corruption and human rights abuses and to introduce proportional representation; Chair. PAUL MUITE.

Shirikisho Party of Kenya (SPK): Githere Plaza, Haile Selassie Ave, POB 84648, 80100 Mombasa; f. 1997; Sec.-Gen. YUSUF MAHMOUD ABOUBAKAR.

Sisi Kwa Sisi (SKS): Nairobi; f. 2001; Sec.-Gen. JULIUS MWANGI.

Social Democratic Party of Kenya (SDP): 404 Summit House, Moi Ave, Monrovia Lane, POB 4403, 00100 Nairobi; tel. 722620953 (mobile); f. 1992; Chair. MWANDAWIRO MGHANGA.

United Agri Party of Kenya: f. 2001; Chair. GEORGE KINYUA; Sec.-Gen. SIMON MITOBIO.

United Democratic Movement: Mararo Ave, APA Insurance Arcade, POB 60064, 00200 Nairobi; tel. (20) 3862337; e-mail udmafya@gmail.com; Chair. Rev. PAUL CHEBOI; Sec.-Gen. MARTIN OLE KAMWARO.

The following organizations are banned:

February Eighteen Resistance Army: believed to operate from Uganda; Leader Brig. JOHN ODONGO (also known as Stephen Amoke).

Islamic Party of Kenya (IPK): Mombasa; f. 1992; Islamist fundamentalist; Chair. Sheikh KHALIFA MUHAMMAD; Sec.-Gen. ABDULRAHMAN WANDATI.

Diplomatic Representation

EMBASSIES AND HIGH COMMISSIONS IN KENYA

Algeria: Mobil Plaza, POB 64140, 00620 Nairobi; tel. (20) 3755559; fax (20) 3755560; e-mail algerianembassy@wananchi.com; Ambassador ALI BENZERGA.

Argentina: Kitisuru Rd, POB 30283, 00100 Nairobi; tel. (20) 4183119; fax (20) 4183054; e-mail ekeny@bidii.com; Ambassador DANIEL CHUBURU.

Australia: ICIPE House, Riverside Dr., off Chiromo Rd, POB 39341, 00623 Nairobi; tel. (20) 4277100; fax (20) 4277139; e-mail australian.hc.kenya@dfat.gov.au; internet www.kenya.embassy.gov.au; High Commissioner GEOFFREY PETER TOOTH.

Austria: 536 Limuru Rd, Muthaiga, POB 30560, 00100 Nairobi; tel. (20) 4060022; fax (20) 4060025; e-mail nairobi-ob@bmeia.gv.at; internet www.bmeia.gv.at/botschaft/nairobi; Ambassador CHRISTIAN HASENBICHLER.

Bangladesh: Lenana Rd, POB 41645, Nairobi; tel. (20) 8562816; fax (20) 8562817; e-mail bdhc@bdootnairobi.com; High Commissioner A. K. M. SHAMSUDDIN.

Belgium: Muthaiga, Limuru Rd, POB 30461, 00100 Nairobi; tel. (20) 7122011; fax (20) 7123050; e-mail nairobi@diplobel.fed.be; internet www.diplomatie.be/nairobi; Ambassador BART OUVRY.

Brazil: Tanar Center, UN Crescent Rd, UN Close, Gigiri, POB 30754, 00100 Nairobi; tel. (20) 7125765; fax (20) 7125767; e-mail geral@kenbrem.co.ke; Ambassador (vacant).

Burundi: Coop Trust Plaza, Upper Hill, off Bunyala Rd, POB 61165, 00200 Nairobi; tel. (20) 2719200; fax (20) 2719211; e-mail embunai@yahoo.fr; Ambassador EZECHIEL NIBIGIRA.

Canada: Limuru Rd, Gigiri, POB 1013, 00621 Nairobi; tel. (20) 3663000; fax (20) 3663900; e-mail nrobi@international.gc.ca; internet www.canadainternational.gc.ca/kenya; High Commissioner DAVID COLLINS.

Chile: Riverside Dr. 66, Riverside, POB 45554, 00100 Nairobi; tel. (20) 4452950; fax (20) 4443209; e-mail echile@echile.co.ke; Ambassador KONRAD PAULSEN.

China, People's Republic: Woodlands Rd, Kilimani District, POB 30508, Nairobi; tel. (20) 2722559; fax (20) 2726402; e-mail chinaemb_ke@mfa.gov.cn; internet ke.china-embassy.org; Ambassador LIU GUANGYUAN.

Colombia: UN Cresent House No 91/244, POB 48494, 00100 Nairobi; tel. (20) 7120850; fax (20) 7120304; e-mail enairobi@cancilleria.gov.co; Ambassador (vacant).

Congo, Democratic Republic: Electricity House, 12th Floor, Harambee Ave, POB 48106, 00100 Nairobi; tel. (20) 2229772; fax (20) 3754253; e-mail ambardckenyal@yahoo.com; Ambassador TADUMI ON'OKOKO.

Cuba: International House, Mama Ngina St, 13th Floor, POB 41931, 00606 Nairobi; tel. (20) 2241003; fax (20) 2241023; e-mail embacuba@swiftkenya.com; internet emba.cubaminrex.cu/kenyaing; Ambassador JULIO CÉSAR GONZÁLEZ MARCHANTE.

Cyprus: Eagle House, 5th Floor, Kimathi St, POB 30739, 00100 Nairobi; tel. (20) 2220881; fax (20) 312202; e-mail cyphc@nbnet.co.ke; High Commissioner AGIS LOIZOU.

Czech Republic: Jumia Pl., Lenana Rd, POB 48785, 00100 Nairobi; tel. (20) 2731010; fax (20) 2731013; e-mail nairobi@embassy.mzv.cz; internet www.mzv.cz/nairobi; Ambassador MARGITA FUCHSOVÁ.

Denmark: 13 Runda Dr., Runda, POB 40412, 00100 Nairobi; tel. (20) 7122848; fax (20) 7120638; e-mail nboamb@um.dk; internet www.ambnairobi.um.dk; Ambassador BO JENSEN.

Djibouti: Comcraft House, 2nd Floor, Haile Selassie Ave, POB 59528, Nairobi; tel. (20) 339640; Ambassador ADEN MARIAM AHMED GOUMEH.

Egypt: Othaya Rd, Kileleshwa, POB 30285, 00100 Nairobi; tel. (20) 3870360; fax (20) 3870383; Ambassador SAHER HASANEEN TAWFEEK HAMZA.

Eritrea: New Rehema House, 2nd Floor, Westlands, POB 38651, Nairobi; tel. (20) 4443164; fax (20) 4443165; Ambassador BEYENE RUSSOM.

Ethiopia: State House Ave, POB 45198, 00100 Nairobi; tel. (20) 2732052; fax (20) 2732054; e-mail ethiopian22embassy@yahoo.com; Ambassador DISSASA DIRBISSA WINSA.

Finland: Eden Sq., Blk 3, 6th Floor, Greenway Rd, off Westlands Rd, POB 30379, 00100 Nairobi; tel. (20) 3750721; fax (20) 3750714; e-mail sanomat.nai@formin.fi; internet www.finland.or.ke; Ambassador HELI SIRVE.

France: Barclays Plaza, 9th Floor, Loita St, POB 41784, 00100 Nairobi; tel. (20) 2778000; fax (20) 2778180; e-mail ambafrance.nairobi@diplomatie.gouv.fr; internet www.ambafrance-ke.org; Ambassador ETIENNE DE PONCINS.

Germany: Ludwig Krapf House, Riverside Dr. 113, POB 30180, Nairobi; tel. (20) 4262100; fax (20) 4262129; e-mail info@nairobi.diplo.de; internet www.nairobi.diplo.de; Ambassador MARGIT HELLWIG-BÖTTE.

Greece: Nation Centre, 13th Floor, Kimathi St, POB 30543, 00100 Nairobi; tel. (20) 340722; fax (20) 2216044; e-mail gremb.nai@mfa.gr; Ambassador ELEFTHERIOS KOVARITAKIS.

Holy See: 151 Manyani Rd West, Waiyaki Way, POB 14326, 00800 Nairobi; tel. (20) 5030152; fax (20) 4446789; e-mail nunciokenya@nunciokenya.org; Apostolic Nuncio Most Rev. ALAIN PAUL CHARLES LEBEAUPIN (Titular Archbishop of Vico Equense).

Hungary: Kabarsiran Ave, off James Gichuru Rd, Lavington, POB 61146, Nairobi; tel. (20) 4442612; fax (20) 4442101; e-mail mission.nai@kum.hu; internet www.mfa.gov.hu/kulkepviselet/ke; Ambassador SÁNDOR JUHÁSZ.

India: Jeevan Bharati Bldg, 2nd Floor, Harambee Ave, POB 30074, Nairobi; tel. (20) 2225104; fax (20) 316242; e-mail hcindia@kenyaweb.com; internet www.hcinairobi.co.ke; High Commissioner SIBABRATA TRIPATHI.

Indonesia: Menengai Rd, Upper Hill, POB 48868, Nairobi; tel. (20) 2714196; fax (20) 2713475; e-mail indonbi@indonesia.or.ke; internet www.indonesia.or.ke; Ambassador BUDI BOWOLEKSONO.

Iran: Dennis Pritt Rd, POB 49170, Nairobi; tel. (20) 711257; fax (20) 339936; Ambassador Dr SEYED ALI SHARIFI SADATI.

Israel: Bishop's Rd, POB 30354, 00100 Nairobi; tel. (20) 2722182; fax (20) 2715966; e-mail info@nairobi.mfa.gov.il; internet nairobi.mfa.gov.il; Ambassador GIL HASKELL.

Italy: Int. House, 9th Floor, Mama Ngina St, POB 30107, 00100 Nairobi; tel. (20) 2247750; fax (20) 2247086; e-mail ambasciata.nairobi@esteri.it; internet www.ambnairobi.esteri.it; Ambassador PAOLA IMPERIALE.

Japan: Mara Rd, Upper Hill, POB 60202, 00200 Nairobi; tel. (20) 2898000; fax (20) 2898531; e-mail jinfocul@eojkenya.org; internet www.ke.emb-japan.go.jp; Ambassador TOSHIHISA TOKATA.

Korea, Republic: Anniversary Towers, 15th Floor, University Way, POB 30455, 00100 Nairobi; tel. (20) 2220000; fax (20) 2217772; e-mail emb-ke@mofat.go.kr; internet ken.mofat.go.kr; Ambassador KIM CHAN-WOO.

Kuwait: Muthaiga Rd, POB 42353, Nairobi; tel. (20) 761614; fax (20) 762837; Ambassador YAQOUB YOUSEF EID AL-SANAD.

Libya: Jamahiriya House, Loita St, POB 47190, Nairobi; tel. (20) 250380; fax (20) 243730; e-mail jamahiriyanbi@wananchi.com; Chargé d'affaires HESHAM ALI SHARIF.

Malaysia: 58 Red Hill Rd, Gigiri, POB 42286, 00200 Nairobi; tel. (20) 7123373; fax (20) 7123371; e-mail malnairobi@kln.gov.my; High Commissioner ZAINOL RAHIM ZAINUDDIN.

Mexico: Kibagare Way, off Loresho Ridge, POB 14145, 00800 Nairobi; tel. (20) 4182593; fax (20) 4181500; e-mail mexico@embamex.co.ke; internet www.sre.gob.mx/kenia; Ambassador LUIS JAVIER CAMPUZANO PINA.

Morocco: UN Ave, Gigiri, POB 617, 00621 Nairobi; tel. (20) 7120765; fax (20) 7120817; e-mail sifmanbi@clubinternetk.com; Ambassador ABDELILAH BENRYANE.

Mozambique: Bruce House, 3rd Floor, Standard St, POB 66923, Nairobi; tel. (20) 221979; fax (20) 222446; e-mail embamoc.quenia@minec.gov.mz; High Commissioner MANUEL JOSÉ GONCALVES.

Netherlands: Riverside Lane, off Riverside Dr., POB 41537, 00100 Nairobi; tel. (20) 4288000; fax (20) 4288264; e-mail nlgovnai@africaonline.co.ke; internet kenia.nlembassy.org; Ambassador JOOST REINTJES.

Nigeria: Lenana Rd, Hurlingham, POB 30516, Nairobi; tel. (20) 3864116; fax (20) 3874309; e-mail ng@nigeriahighcom.org; High Commissioner SOLOMON OYATERU.

Norway: Lion Pl., 1st Floor, Wayiaki Way, POB 46363, 00100 Nairobi; tel. (20) 4251000; fax (20) 4451517; e-mail emb.nairobi@mfa.no; internet www.norway.or.ke; Ambassador PER LUDVIG MAGNUS.

Pakistan: St Michel Rd, Westlands Ave, POB 30045, 00100 Nairobi; tel. (20) 4443911; fax (20) 4446507; e-mail parepnairobi@iwayafrica.com; internet www.mofa.gov.pk/kenya; High Commissioner RAFUZZAMAN SIDDIQUI.

Poland: 58 Red Hill Rd, POB 30086, 00100 Nairobi; tel. (20) 7120019; fax (20) 7120106; e-mail ambnairo@kenyaweb.com; internet www.nairobi.polemb.net; Ambassador MAREK ZIÓŁKOWSKI.

Portugal: Reinsurance Plaza, 10th Floor, Aga Khan Walk, POB 34020, 00100 Nairobi; tel. (20) 313203; fax (20) 214711; e-mail portugalnb@jambo.co.ke; Ambassador LUIS LORUÁO.

Romania: Eliud Mathu St, Runda, POB 63240, 00619 Nairobi; tel. (20) 721214073; e-mail secretariat@romanianembassy.co.ke; Ambassador LULIA PATAKI.

Russia: Lenana Rd, POB 30049, Nairobi; tel. (20) 2728700; fax (20) 2721888; e-mail russembkenya@mail.ru; Ambassador ALEXANDER MAKARENKO.

Rwanda: International House, 12th Floor, Mama Ngina St, POB 48579, Nairobi; tel. (20) 560178; fax (20) 561932; internet kenya.embassy.gov.rw; High Commissioner YAMINA KARITANYI.

Saudi Arabia: Muthaiga Rd, POB 58297, Nairobi; tel. (20) 762781; fax (20) 760939; Ambassador NBEEL KHALAF A. ASHOUR.

Serbia: State House Ave, POB 30504, 00100 Nairobi; tel. (20) 2710076; fax (20) 2714126; e-mail nairobi@embassyofserbia.or.ke; internet www.embassyofserbia.or.ke; Ambassador ZDRAVKO BISIĆ.

Slovakia: Milimani Rd, POB 30204, Nairobi; tel. (20) 2721896; fax (20) 2717291; e-mail slovakembassy@jambo.co.ke; Ambassador MICHAEL MLYNAIR.

Somalia: POB 30769, Nairobi; tel. (20) 580165; fax (20) 581683; internet www.kenya.somaligov.net; Ambassador MOHAMMED ALI NUR.

South Africa: Roshanmaer Place, Lenana Rd, POB 42441, 00100 Nairobi; tel. (20) 2827100; fax (20) 2827236; e-mail nairobi@foreign.gov.za; High Commissioner NDUMISO NDIMA NTSHINGA.

South Sudan: Bishops Gate, 6th Floor, 5 Ngong Ave, cnr Bishop Rd, POB 73699, 00200 Nairobi; tel. (20) 4349107; fax (20) 4349109; Ambassador MICHAEL MAJOK AYOM DOR.

Spain: CBA Bldg, Mara and Ragati Rds, Upper Hill, POB 45503, 00100 Nairobi; tel. (20) 2720222; fax (20) 2720226; e-mail emb.nairobi@maec.es; Ambassador NICOLÁS MARTÍN CINTO.

Sri Lanka: Lenana Rd, POB 48145, Nairobi; tel. (20) 3872627; fax (20) 3872141; e-mail slhckeny@africaonline.co.ke; High Commissioner JAYANTHA DISSANAYAKE.

Sudan: Kabarnet Rd, off Ngong Rd, POB 48784, 00100 Nairobi; tel. (20) 3875159; fax (20) 3878187; e-mail embassy@sudanebassyke.org; internet www.sudanembassyke.org; Ambassador KAMAL ISMAIL SAEED (recalled Nov. 2011).

Sweden: Lion Pl., 3rd Floor, Waiyaki Way, Westlands, POB 30600, 00100 Nairobi; tel. (20) 4234000; fax (20) 4452008; e-mail ambassaden.nairobi@foreign.ministry.se; internet www.swedenabroad.com/nairobi; Ambassador ANN DISMORR.

Switzerland: General Mathenge Dr. 89, POB 30752, 00100 Nairobi; tel. (20) 2673282; fax (20) 2673535; e-mail nai.vertretung@eda.admin.ch; Ambassador JACQUES PITTELOUD.

Tanzania: Re-Insurance Plaza, 9th Floor, Taifa Rd, POB 47790, 0100 Nairobi; tel. (20) 312027; fax (20) 2218269; e-mail highcom@tanzaniahc.or.ke; High Commissioner Dr BATILDA BURIAN.

Thailand: Rose Ave, off Denis Pritt Rd, POB 58349, 00200 Nairobi; tel. (20) 2715243; fax (20) 2715801; e-mail thainbi@thainbi.or.ke; internet www.thaiembassy.org/nairobi; Ambassador ITTIPORN BOONPRACONG.

Turkey: Gigiri Rd, off Limuru Rd, POB 64748, 00620 Nairobi; tel. and fax (20) 7126929; e-mail tcbenair@accesskenya.co.ke; internet www.nairobi.emb.mfa.gov.tr; Ambassador HUSEYIN AVNI AKSOY.

Uganda: Uganda House, 1st Floor, Kenyatta Ave, POB 60853, 00200 Nairobi; tel. (20) 4449096; fax (20) 4443772; e-mail info@ugandahighcommission.co.ke; High Commissioner Brig. (retd) MATAYO KYALIGONZA.

Ukraine: POB 63566, 00619 Nairobi; tel. (20) 3748922; fax (20) 3756028; e-mail emb_ke@mfa.gov.ua; Ambassador VOLODYMIR BUTYAGA.

United Kingdom: Upper Hill Rd, POB 30465, 00100 Nairobi; tel. (20) 2844000; fax (20) 2844088; e-mail bhcinfo@jambo.co.ke; internet ukinkenya.fco.gov.uk; High Commissioner Dr PETER TIBBER (acting).

USA: UN Ave, Village Market, POB 606, 00621 Nairobi; tel. (20) 3636000; fax (20) 3633410; internet nairobi.usembassy.gov; Chargé d'affaires a.i. ROBERT F. GODEC.

Venezuela: Int. House, 3rd Floor, Mama Ngina St, POB 34477, 00100 Nairobi; tel. (20) 340134; fax (20) 248105; e-mail embavene@swiftkenya.com; Ambassador (vacant).

Yemen: cnr Ngong and Kabarnet Rds, POB 44642, Nairobi; tel. (20) 564379; fax (20) 564394; Ambassador AHMAD MAYSARI.

Zambia: Nyerere Rd, POB 48741, Nairobi; tel. (20) 7224850; fax (20) 2718494; e-mail zambiacom@swiftkenya.com; High Commissioner MARY MIDRED ZAMBEZI.

Zimbabwe: 2 Westlands Close, Westlands, POB 30806, 00100 Nairobi; tel. (20) 3744052; fax (20) 3748079; e-mail zimna@africaonline.co.ke; Ambassador KELEBERT NKOMANI.

Judicial System

The superior courts are the Supreme Court, the Court of Appeal and the High Court.

Chief Justice: Dr WILLY MUNYWOKI MUTUNGA.

Supreme Court: Nairobi; comprises the Chief Justice, who shall be the president of the court, the Deputy Chief Justice and five other judges; has jurisdiction to hear and determine disputes relating to the elections to the office of President and appellate jurisdiction to hear and determine appeals from the Court of Appeal and any other court or tribunal as prescribed by national legislation.

Court of Appeal: POB 30187, Nairobi; comprises not fewer than 12 judges; the final court of appeal for Kenya in civil and criminal process; sits at Nairobi, Mombasa, Kisumu, Nakuru and Nyeri.

High Court: Between Taifa Rd and City Hall Way, POB 30041, Nairobi; tel. (20) 221221; e-mail hck-lib@nbnet.co.ke; has unlimited criminal and civil jurisdiction at first instance; jurisdiction to determine the question whether a right or fundamental freedom in the Bill of Rights has been denied, violated, infringed or threatened; jurisdiction to hear an appeal from a decision of a tribunal appointed under the Constitution to consider the removal of a person from office; and jurisdiction to hear any question respecting the interpretation of this Constitution.

The subordinate courts are the Magistrates' courts, the Kadhis' courts, the Courts Martial and any other court or local tribunal as may be established by an Act of Parliament.

Resident Magistrates' Courts: have country-wide jurisdiction, with powers of punishment by imprisonment for up to five years or by fines of up to K£500. If presided over by a chief magistrate or senior resident magistrate, the court is empowered to pass any sentence authorized by law. For certain offences, a resident magistrate may pass minimum sentences authorized by law.

District Magistrates' Courts: of first, second and third class; have jurisdiction within districts and powers of punishment by imprisonment for up to five years, or by fines of up to K£500.

Kadhis' Courts: have jurisdiction within districts, to determine questions of Islamic law; comprise a Chief Kadhi and no fewer than three other Kadhis.

Religion

According to the 2009 census, Protestants, the largest religious group, represent approximately 48% of the population. Approximately 24% of the population is Roman Catholic, 11% of the population practises Islam, 0.1% practises Hinduism and the remainder follow various traditional indigenous religions or offshoots of Christian religions. There are very few atheists. Muslim groups dispute government estimates; most often they claim to represent 15% to 20% of the population, sometimes higher. Members of most religious groups are active throughout the country, although certain religions dominate particular regions. Muslims dominate North-Eastern Province, where the population is chiefly Somali. Muslims also dominate Coast Province, except for the western areas of the Province, which are predominantly Christian. Eastern Province is approximately 50% Muslim (mostly in the north) and 50% Christian (mostly in the south). The rest of the country is largely Christian. Many foreign missionary groups operate in the country, the largest of which are the African Inland Mission (Evangelical Protestant), the Southern Baptist Church, the Pentecostal Assembly of Kenya, and the Church Missionary Society of Britain (Anglican). The Government generally has permitted these missionary groups to assist the poor and to operate schools and hospitals. The missionaries openly promote their religious beliefs and have encountered little resistance.

CHRISTIANITY

National Council of Churches of Kenya: Jumuia Pl., POB 45009, 00100 Nairobi; tel. (20) 2711862; fax (20) 2724183; e-mail gsoffice@ ncck.org; internet www.ncck.org; f. 1943 as Christian Council of Kenya; 24 mem. churches and 18 Christian orgs; Chair. Rev. JOSEPH WAITHONGA; Sec.-Gen. Rev. Canon PETER KARANJA MWANGI.

The Anglican Communion

Anglicans are adherents of the Church of the Province of Kenya, which was established in 1970. It comprises 28 dioceses, and has about 2.5m. members.

Archbishop of Kenya and Bishop of Nairobi: Most Rev. Dr DAVID M. GITARI, POB 40502, Nairobi; tel. (20) 2714755; fax (20) 2718442; e-mail davidgitari@insightkenya.com.

Greek Orthodox Church

Archbishop of East Africa: NICADEMUS OF IRINOUPOULIS, Nairobi; jurisdiction covers Kenya, Tanzania and Uganda.

The Roman Catholic Church

Kenya comprises four archdioceses, 20 dioceses and one Apostolic Vicariate. Some 24% of the total population are adherents of the Roman Catholic Church.

Kenya Episcopal Conference

Kenya Catholic Secretariat, Waumini House, 4th Floor Westlands, POB 13475, Nairobi; tel. (20) 443133; fax (20) 442910; e-mail csk@ users.africaonline.co.ke; internet www.catholicchurch.or.ke.

f. 1976; Pres. Cardinal JOHN NJUE (Archbishop of Nairobi); Sec.-Gen. Rev. Fr VINCENT WAMBUGU.

Archbishop of Kisumu: Most Rev. ZACCHAEUS OKOTH, POB 1728, 40100 Kisumu; tel. (57) 2020725; fax (57) 2022203; e-mail archdiocese-kisumu@africaonline.co.ke.

Archbishop of Mombasa: Most Rev. BONIFACE LELE, Catholic Secretariat, Nyerere Ave, POB 84425, Mombasa; tel. (41) 2311801; fax (41) 2228217; e-mail catholicsecretariat@msarchdiocese.org.

Archbishop of Nairobi: Cardinal JOHN NJUE, Archbishop's House, POB 14231, 00800 Nairobi; tel. (20) 241391; fax (20) 4447027; e-mail arch-nbo@wananchi.com.

Archbishop of Nyeri: Most Rev. PETER J. CAIRO, POB 288, 10100 Nyeri; tel. (61) 2030446; fax (61) 2030435; e-mail adn@wananchi .com.

Other Christian Churches

Africa Gospel Church: POB 458, Kericho 20200; tel. (52) 20123; e-mail agc@agckenya.org; internet www.agckenya.org; Admin. Sec. JOSEPH TONUI.

African Christian Church and Schools: POB 1365, Thika; e-mail accsheadoffice@yahoo.com; f. 1948; Moderator Rt Rev. JOHN NJUNGUNA; Gen. Sec. Rev. SAMUEL MWANGI; 50,000 mems.

African Israel Nineveh Church: Nineveh HQ, POB 701, Kisumu; f. 1942; High Priest Rt Rev. JOHN KIVULI, II; Gen. Sec. Rev. JOHN ARAP TONUI; 350,000 mems.

Baptist Convention of Kenya: POB 14907, Nairobi; internet bcok .org; f. 1972; Pres. Rev. Bishop Dr JULIUS A. MBAGAYA; Gen. Sec. GIDEON MAKUTHI.

Church of God in East Africa: Pres. Rev. Dr BYRUM MAKOKHA.

Evangelical Alliance of Kenya (EAK): Valley Rd, POB 20571, 00100 Nairobi; tel. (20) 2721269; e-mail secretariat@eakenya.org; internet eakenya.org; Co-ordinator Rt Rev. Bishop Dr BONIFES ADOYO; Sec.-Gen. Rev. Dr WELLINGTON MUTISO.

Evangelical Lutheran Church in Kenya (ELCK): POB 44685, 00100 Nairobi; tel. and fax 38131231; e-mail bishopobarewa@yahoo .com; internet elckenya.com; f. 1948; Presiding Bishop Most Rev. WALTER OBARE OMWANZA; Gen. Sec. Rev. JOHN HALAKHE; 100,000 mems (2010).

Kenya African Church of the Holy Spirit: POB 183, Kakamega; internet kenyaafricanchurchoftheholyspirit.org; f. 1927; 20,000 mems.

Kenya Evangelical Lutheran Church: POB 54128, 00200 City Sq., Jogoo Rd, off Nile Rd, Nairobi; tel. and fax (20) 78-04-54; e-mail info@kelc.or.ke; internet www.kelc.or.ke; Bishop ZACHARIAH W. KAHUTHU; 44,000 mems (2010).

Methodist Church in Kenya: POB 47633, 00100 Nairobi; tel. (20) 2724828; fax (20) 2729790; e-mail mckconf@insightkenya.com; internet www.methodistchurchkenya.org; f. 1862; autonomous since 1967; Presiding Bishop Rev. Dr STEPHEN KANYARU M'IMPWII; 900,000 mems (2005).

Presbyterian Church of East Africa: Jitegemea House, Muhoho Ave, South C, POB 27573, 00506 Nairobi; tel. (20) 6008848; fax (20) 6009102; e-mail info@pcea.or.ke; internet www.pceaheadoffice.or .ke; f. 1891; Moderator Rt Rev. Dr DAVID RIITHO GATHANJU; Sec.-Gen. Rev. FESTUS KABURU GITONGA.

Other denominations active in Kenya include the African Brotherhood Church, the African Independent Pentecostal Church, Africa Inland Church in Kenya, the African Interior Church, the Episcopal Church of Kenya, the Free Pentecostal Fellowship of Kenya, the Full Gospel Churches of Kenya, the National Independent Church of Africa, the Pentecostal Assemblies of God, the Pentecostal Evangelistic Fellowship of God and the Reformed Church of East Africa.

BAHÁ'Í FAITH

National Spiritual Assembly: POB 47562, Nairobi; tel. (20) 725447; e-mail nsakenya@yahoo.com; mems resident in 9,654 localities.

ISLAM

Supreme Council of Kenyan Muslims (SUPKEM)

Islamia House, 2nd and 3rd Floors, Njugu Lane, POB 415163, Nairobi 00100; tel. and fax (20) 243109; e-mail admin@supkem .com; internet supkem.com; Nat. Chair. Prof. ABD AL-GHAFUR AL-BUSAIDY; Sec.-Gen. ADAN WACHU.

Chief Kadhi: SHEIKH AHMED MUHDHAR.

The Press

PRINCIPAL DAILIES

Business Daily: Nation Center, 2nd Floor, Kimathi St, POB 49010, 00100 Nairobi; tel. (20) 3288104; fax (20) 211130; e-mail bdfeedback@ ke.nationmedia.com; internet www.businessdailyafrica.com; Editorial Dir JOSEPH ODINDO; Man. Editor OCHIENG RAPURO.

Daily Nation: Nation Centre, Kimathi St, POB 49010, 00100 Nairobi; tel. (20) 3288000; fax (20) 2337710; e-mail newsdesk@ nation.co.ke; internet www.nation.co.ke; f. 1960; English; owned by Nation Media Group; Man. Editor MUTUMA MATHIU; Editorial Dir JOSEPH ODINDO; circ. 195,000.

The People: POB 10296, 00100 Nairobi; tel. (20) 2249686; fax (20) 2228503; e-mail info@people.co.ke; internet www.people.co.ke; f. 1993; Man. Editor MUGO THEURI; circ. 40,000.

The Standard: Mombasa Rd, POB 30080, 00100 Nairobi; tel. (20) 3222111; fax (20) 214467; e-mail ads@standardmedia.co.ke; internet www.standardmedia.co.ke; f. 1902 as African Standard; renamed East African Standard before adopting present name in 2004; Editor OKETCH KENDO; circ. 59,000.

The Star: Lion Place, Waiyaki Way, POB 74497-0200, Nairobi; tel. (20) 4244000; fax (20) 4447410; e-mail webmaster@the-star.co.ke; internet www.the-star.co.ke; Editor CATHERINE GICHERU.

Taifa Leo: POB 49010, Nairobi 00100; tel. (20) 3288419; e-mail taifa@ke.nationmedia.com; Kiswahili; f. 1960; daily and weekly edns; Kiswahili; owned by Nation Media Group; Man. Editor NICHOLAS MUEMA; circ. 15,000.

Kenya also has a thriving vernacular press, but titles are often short-lived. Newspapers in African languages include:

SELECTED PERIODICALS

Weeklies and Fortnightlies

The Business Chronicle: POB 53328, Nairobi; tel. (20) 544283; fax (20) 532736; f. 1994; weekly; Man. Editor MUSYOKA KYENDO.

Coastweek: Oriental Bldg, 2nd Floor, Nkrumah Rd, POB 87270, Mombasa; tel. (41) 2230125; fax (41) 2225003; e-mail coastwk@ africaonline.co.ke; internet www.coastweek.com; f. 1978; English, with German section; Friday; Editor ADRIAN GRIMWOOD; Man. Dir SHIRAZ D. ALIBHAI; circ. 54,000.

Diplomat East Africa: Vision Plaza, Ground Floor, Suite 37, Mombasa Rd, POB 23399, Nairobi; tel. (20) 2525253; e-mail editor@diplomateastafrica.com; internet www.diplomateastafrica .com.

The East African: POB 49010, 00506 Nairobi; tel. (20) 3288000; fax (20) 2213946; e-mail newsdesk@nation.co.ke; internet www .theeastafrican.co.ke; f. 1994; weekly; English; owned by Nation

Media Group; Editor-in-Chief JOE ODINDO; Man. Editor MBATAU WA NGAI.

Kenya Gazette: POB 30746, Nairobi; tel. (20) 334075; internet www.kenyalaw.org/KenyaGazette; f. 1898; official notices; weekly; circ. 8,000.

Kenya Today: c/o Office of Public Communications, KICC Bldg, 3rd Floor, POB 45617, 00100 Nairobi; e-mail comms@comms.go.ke; f. 2009; govt-owned; weekly; Dir JERRY OKUNGU.

Sunday Nation: POB 49010, Nairobi; f. 1960; English; owned by Nation Media Group; Man. Editor BERNARD NDERITU; circ. 170,000.

Sunday Standard: POB 30080, Nairobi; tel. (20) 552510; fax (20) 553939; English; Man. Editor DAVID MAKALI; circ. 90,000.

Taifa Jumapili: POB 49010, Nairobi; tel. (20) 3288419; e-mail taifa@ke.nationmedia.com; f. 1987; Kiswahili; owned by Nation Media Group; Man. Editor NICHOLAS MUEMA; circ. 15,000.

Monthlies

Africa Law Review: Tumaini House, 4th Floor, Nkrumah Ave, POB 53234, Nairobi; tel. (20) 330480; fax (20) 230173; e-mail alr@africalaw.org; f. 1987; English; Editor-in-Chief GITOBU IMANYARA.

East African Medical Journal: POB 41632, 00100 Nairobi; tel. (20) 2679322; fax (20) 0710521831; e-mail eamj@wananchi.com; English; f. 1923; Editor-in-Chief Prof. WILLIAM LORE; circ. 4,500.

Executive: POB 47186, Nairobi; tel. (20) 530598; fax (20) 557815; e-mail spacesellers@wananchi.com; f. 1980; business; Publr SYLVIA KING; circ. 25,000.

Kenya Farmer (Journal of the Agricultural Society of Kenya): c/o English Press, POB 30127, Nairobi; tel. (20) 20377; f. 1954; English and Kiswahili; Editor ROBERT IRUNGU; circ. 20,000.

Kenya Yetu: POB 8053, Nairobi; tel. (20) 250083; fax (20) 340659; f. 1965; Kiswahili; publ. by Ministry of Information and Communications; Editor M. NDAVI; circ. 10,000.

News from Kenya: POB 8053, Nairobi; tel. (20) 253083; fax (20) 340659; publ. by Ministry of Information and Communications.

PC World (East Africa): Gilgil House, Monrovia St, Nairobi; tel. (20) 246808; fax (20) 215643; f. 1996; Editor ANDREW KARANJA.

Presence: POB 10988, 00400 Nairobi; tel. (20) 577708; fax (20) 4948840; f. 1984; economics, law, women's issues, fiction.

Sparkle: POB 47186, Nairobi; tel. (20) 530598; fax (20) 557815; e-mail spacesellers@wananchi.com; f. 1990; children's; Editor ANNA NDILA NDUTO.

Other Periodicals

African Ecclesiastical Review: POB 4002, 30100 Eldoret; tel. (53) 2061218; fax (53) 2062570; e-mail gabapubs@africaonline.co.ke; internet www.gabapublications.org; f. 1969; scripture, religion and devt; 4 a year; Editor and Dir Sister JUSTIN C. NABUSHAWO; circ. 2,500.

Afya: POB 30125, Nairobi; tel. (20) 501301; fax (20) 506112; e-mail amrefkco@africaonline.co.ke; journal for medical and health workers; quarterly.

Azania: POB 30710, 00100 Nairobi; tel. (20) 4343190; fax (20) 4343365; f. 1966; annual (Dec.); English and French; history, archaeology, ethnography and linguistics of East African region; circ. 650.

Defender: AMREF, POB 30125, Nairobi; tel. (20) 201301; f. 1968; quarterly; English; health and fitness; Editor WILLIAM OKEDI; circ. 100,000.

East African Agricultural and Forestry Journal: POB 30148, Nairobi; f. 1935; English; quarterly; Editor J. O. MUGAH; circ. 1,000.

Inside Kenya Today: POB 8053, Nairobi; tel. (20) 340010; fax (20) 340659; English; publ. by Ministry of Tourism; quarterly; Editor M. NDAVI; circ. 10,000.

Kenya Statistical Digest: POB 30007, Nairobi; tel. (20) 338111; fax (20) 330426; publ. by Ministry of Finance; quarterly.

Safari: Norwich Bldg, 4th Floor, Mama Ngina St, POB 30339, Nairobi; tel. (20) 2246612; fax (20) 2215127; 6 a year; English.

Target: POB 72839, Nairobi; f. 1964; English; 6 a year; religious; Editor FRANCIS MWANIKI; circ. 17,000.

NEWS AGENCY

Kenya News Agency (KNA): Information House, POB 8053, Nairobi; tel. (20) 223201; internet www.kenyanewsagency.go.ke; f. 1963; Dir S. MUSANDU.

Publishers

Academy Science Publishers: POB 24916, Nairobi; tel. (20) 884401; fax (20) 884406; e-mail asp@africaonline.co.ke; f. 1989; part of the African Academy of Sciences; Editor-in-Chief Prof. KETO E. MSHIGENI.

AMECEA Gaba Publications: Amecea Pastoral Institute, POB 4002, 30100 Eldoret; tel. (53) 2061218; fax (53) 2062570; e-mail gabapubs@africaonline.co.ke; internet www.gabapublications.org; f. 1958; anthropology, religious; owned by AMECEA Bishops; Editor and Dir Sister JUSTINE C. NABUSHAWO.

Camerapix Publishers International: POB 45048, GPO 00100, Nairobi; tel. (20) 4448923; fax (20) 4448818; e-mail rukhsana@camerapix.co.ke; internet www.camerapix.com; f. 1960; travel, topography, natural history; Man. Dir RUKHSANA HAQ.

East African Educational Publishers: cnr Mpaka Rd and Woodvale Grove, Westlands, POB 45314, 00100 Nairobi; tel. (20) 4444700; fax (20) 2324761; e-mail eaep@eastafricanpublishers.com; internet www.eastafricanpublishers.com; f. 1965 as Heinemann Kenya Ltd; present name adopted 1992; academic, educational, creative writing; some books in Kenyan languages; Chair. Dr HENRY CHAKAVA; Gen. Man. KIARIE KAMAU.

Evangel Publishing House: Lumumba Drive, off Kamiti Rd, Thika Rd, Private Bag 28963, 00200 Nairobi; tel. (20) 8560839; fax (20) 8562050; e-mail info@evangelpublishing.org; internet www.evangelpublishing.org; f. 1952; Christian literature; current backlist of over 300 titles; marriage and family, leadership, Theological Education by Extension (TEE); Gen. Man. LUCY NDUTA (acting).

Jomo Kenyatta Foundation: Industrial Area, Enterprise Rd, POB 30533, 00100 Nairobi; tel. (20) 557222; fax (20) 531966; e-mail publish@jomokenyattaf.com; internet www.jkf.co.ke; f. 1966; primary, secondary, university textbooks; Man. Dir NANCY W. KARIMI.

East African Publishers Ltd: POB 45314, Nairobi; tel. (20) 2324761; fax (20) 4451532; e-mail info@eastafricanpublishers.com; internet www.eastafricanpublishers.com; f. 1964; school, university and general; Man. Dir SIMON NGIGI.

Kenya Literature Bureau: Bellevue Area, Popo Rd, off Mombasa Rd, POB 30022, 00100 Nairobi; tel. (20) 600839; fax (20) 601474; e-mail customer@kenyaliteraturebureau.com; f. 1947 as East African Literature Bureau; name changed as above in 1980; educational and general books; CEO E. A. OBARA.

Longman Kenya Ltd: Banda School, Magadi Rd, POB 24722, Nairobi; tel. (20) 8891220; fax (20) 8890004; e-mail bandaschool@swiftkenya.com; internet www.bandaschool.com; f. 1966.

Moran (EA) Publishers Ltd: Judda Complex, Forest Rd, POB 30797, 00100 Nairobi; tel. (20) 2013580; fax (20) 2013583; e-mail info@moranpublishers.co.ke; internet www.moranpublishers.co.ke; f. 1970; as Macmillan Kenya Publishers Ltd; renamed as above in 2010; atlases, children's educational, guide books, literature; Man. Dir DAVID MUITA.

Newspread International: POB 46854, Nairobi; tel. (20) 331402; fax (20) 607252; f. 1971; reference, economic devt; Exec. Editor KUL BHUSHAN.

Oxford University Press (Eastern Africa): Elgon Rd, Upper Hill, The Oxford Place, POB 72532, Nairobi; tel. (20) 2732047; fax (20) 2732011; e-mail enq@oxford.co.ke; internet www.oxford.co.ke; f. 1954; children's, educational and general; Regional Man. MURIUKI NJERU.

Paulines Publications Africa: POB 49026, 00100 Nairobi; tel. (20) 447202; fax (20) 442097; e-mail publications@paulinesafrica.org; internet www.paulinesafrica.org; f. 1985; African bible, theology, children's, educational, religious, psychology, audio CDs, tapes, videos; Pres. Sister MARIA KIMANI; Dir Sister TERESA MARCAZZAN.

Storymoja Publishers: Njamba House, Shanzu Rd, off Lower Kabete Rd, Westlands, POB 264, 00606 Nairobi; tel. (20) 208959; e-mail info@storymojaafrica.co.ke; internet www.storymojaafrica.co.ke; Gen. Man. MARTIN NJAGA.

GOVERNMENT PUBLISHING HOUSE

Government Printing Press: POB 30128, Nairobi; tel. (20) 317840.

PUBLISHERS' ORGANIZATION

Kenya Publishers' Association: POB 42767, 00100 Nairobi; tel. (20) 3752344; fax (20) 3754076; internet www.kenyapublishers.org; f. 1971; organizes Nairobi International Book Fair each Sept; Chair. DAVID MUITA.

Broadcasting and Communications

TELECOMMUNICATIONS

In 2011 there were four providers of mobile telephone services in Kenya, one of which, Telkom Kenya Ltd, was also the sole provider of fixed-line services. At September 2011 there were 355,493 subscribers to fixed-line telephone services and 26,493,940 subscribers to mobile telephone services.

Airtel Kenya: Parkside Towers, Mombasa Rd, Nairobi; tel. (20) 6910000; e-mail info.africa@airtel.com; internet africa.airtel.com/kenya; f. 2004; mobile cellular telephone network provider; fmrly Celtel; name changed as above in 2010; Man. Dir SHIVAN BHARGAVA.

Essar Telecom Kenya Ltd: Brookside Grove, Muguga Green Lane, Westlands, POB 45742, 00100 Nairobi; tel. (20) 750049003; e-mail communications@yu.co.ke; internet www.yu.co.ke; f. 2008; owner of yuMobile brand; Country Man. MADHUR TANEJA.

Telkom Kenya Ltd: Telkom Plaza, Ralph Bunche Rd, POB 30301, Nairobi; tel. (20) 2221000; e-mail customercare@orange-tkl.co.ke; internet www.telkom.co.ke; f. 1999; 51% owned by France Telecom; provides both fixed-line and mobile telephone services; Chair. EDDY NJOROGE; Man. Dir MICKAËL GHOSSEIN.

Safaricom Ltd: Safaricom House, Waiyaki Way, Westlands, POB 66827, 00800 Nairobi; tel. (20) 4273272; e-mail info@safaricom.co.ke; internet www.safaricom.co.ke; f. 1999; owned by Telkom Kenya Ltd and Vodafone Airtouch (UK); operates a national mobile cellular telephone network; Chair. NICHOLAS NG'ANG'A; CEO ROBERT WILLIAM COLLYMORE.

Regulatory Authority

Communications Commission of Kenya (CCK): Waiyaki Way, POB 14448, 00800 Westlands, Nairobi; tel. (20) 4242000; fax (20) 4451866; e-mail info@cck.go.ke; internet www.cck.go.ke; f. 1999; Chair. Eng. PHILIP O. OKUNDI; Dir-Gen. CHARLES J. K. NJOROGE.

BROADCASTING

Radio

Kenya Broadcasting Corpn (KBC): Broadcasting House, Harry Thuku Rd, POB 30456, Nairobi; tel. (20) 223757; fax (20) 220675; e-mail md@kbc.co.ke; internet www.kbc.co.ke; f. 1989; state corpn responsible for radio and television services; Chair. CHARLES MUSYOKI MUOKI; Man. Dir WAITHAKA WAIHENYA.

Radio: National service (Kiswahili); General service (English); Vernacular services (Borana, Burji, Hindustani, Kalenjin, Kikamba, Kikuyu, Kimasai, Kimeru, Kisii, Kuria, Luo, Luhya, Rendile, Somali, Suba, Teso and Turkana).

Capital FM: Lonrho House, 19th Floor, City Sq., POB 74933, Nairobi; tel. (20) 2210020; fax (20) 340621; e-mail info@capitalfm.co.ke; internet www.capitalfm.co.ke; f. 1999; commercial station broadcasting to Nairobi and environs.

Easy FM: Nation Centre, Kimathi St, POB 49010, Nairobi; tel. (20) 32088801; fax (20) 241892; e-mail info@nation.co.ke; internet www.nationmedia.com; f. 1999; commercial radio station broadcasting in English and Kiwahili; fmrly Nation FM; owned by Nation Media Group; Man. Dir IAN FERNANDES.

IQRA Broadcasting Network: Kilimani Rd, off Elgeyo Marakwet Rd, POB 21186, 00505 Nairobi; tel. (20) 3861542; fax (20) 4443978; e-mail iqrafm@swiftkenya.com; Islamic radio station broadcasting religious programmes in Nairobi; Man. Dir SHARIF HUSSEIN OMAR.

Kameme FM: Longonot Pl., Kijabe St, POB 49640, 00100 Nairobi; tel. (20) 2217963; fax (20) 2249781; e-mail info@kamemefm.com; internet www.kameme.co.ke; commercial radio station broadcasting in Kikuyu in Nairobi and its environs; Man. Dir ROSE KIMOTHO.

Kitambo Communications Ltd: Bishop's Tower, 4th Floor, Bishop's Rd, POB 56155, Nairobi; tel. (20) 4244000; commercial radio and television station broadcasting Christian programmes in Mombasa and Nairobi; Man. Dir Dr R. AYAH.

Radio Africa Ltd (KISS FM): 2nd Floor, Lion Pl., Waiyaki Way, POB 74497, 00200 Nairobi; tel. (20) 4244000; Man. Dir KIPRONO KITTONY.

Radio Citizen: Communication Centre, Maalim Juma Rd, off Dennis Pritt Rd, POB 7468, Nairobi; tel. (20) 2721415; fax (20) 2724220; e-mail citizen@royalmedia.co.ke; internet radiocitizen.co.ke; commercial radio station broadcasting in Nairobi and its environs; owned by Royal Media Services Ltd; Chair. SAMUEL KAMAU MACHARIA.

Sauti ya Rehema RTV Network: Gulab Lochab Bldg, Oginga Oginga St, POB 4139, Eldoret; tel. (20) 2045239; e-mail elirop2003@gmail.com; f. 1999; Christian, broadcasts in Eldoret and its environs; Man. Dir Rev. ELI ROP.

Television

Kenya Broadcasting Corpn (KBC): see Radio

Television: KBC–TV; services in Kiswahili and English; operates three channels—KBC1, KBC2 and Metro TV.

Citizen TV: Communication Centre, Maalim Juma Rd, off Dennis Pritt Rd, POB 7468, Nairobi; tel. (20) 2721415; fax (20) 2724220; e-mail citizen@royalmedia.co.ke; internet www.citizentv.co.ke; f. 1999, relaunced 2006; commercial station broadcasting in Nairobi and its environs; Chair. SAMUEL KAMAU MACHARIA.

Family Media: Dik Dik Gardens, off Gatundu Rd, Kileleshwa, POB 2330, Nairobi; tel. (20) 4200000; fax (20) 4200100; e-mail info@familykenya.com; internet www.familykenya.com; f. 1999; Gen. Man. PAUL COOGAN.

Kenya Television Network (KTN–TV): Nyayo House, 22nd Floor, POB 56985, Nairobi; tel. (20) 3222111; fax (20) 215400; e-mail news@ktnkenya.com; internet www.ktnkenya.tv; f. 1990; commercial station operating in Nairobi and Mombasa; Man. Dir D. J. DAVIES.

NTV: POB 49010, Nairobi; e-mail ntv@nation.co.ke; internet www.nationmedia.com/ntv; f. 1999 as Nation TV; commercial station; owned by Nation Media Group; Man. Dir IAN FERNANDES.

Stellagraphics TV (STV): NSSF Bldg, 22nd Floor, POB 42271, Nairobi; tel. (20) 218043; fax (20) 222555; f. 1998; commercial station broadcasting in Nairobi; Gen. Man. KANJA WARURU.

Finance

(cap. = capital; res = reserves; dep. = deposits; m. = million; brs = branches; amounts in Kenya shillings)

BANKING

At the end of 2010 there were 43 licensed commercial banks and one mortgage finance company operating in Kenya, of which 31 were locally owned and 13 were foreign owned.

Central Bank

Central Bank of Kenya (Banki Kuu Ya Kenya): City Sq., Haile Selassie Ave, POB 60000, 00200 Nairobi; tel. (20) 22863000; fax (20) 2250783; e-mail info@centralbank.go.ke; internet www.centralbank.go.ke; f. 1966; bank of issue; cap. 5,000m., res 34,005m., dep. 125,637m. (June 2009); Gov. Prof. NJUGUNA NDUNG'U.

Commercial Banks

African Banking Corpn Ltd: ABC-Bank House, Mezzanine Floor, Koinange St, POB 46452, Nairobi; tel. (20) 2223922; fax (20) 2222437; e-mail headoffice@abcthebank.com; internet www.abcthebank.com; f. 1984 as Consolidated Finance Co; converted to commercial bank and adopted present name 1995; cap. 525.0m., res 5.5m., dep. 7,505.3m. (Dec. 2009); Chair. ASHRAF SAVANI; CEO SHAMAZ SAVANI; 7 brs.

Bank of Africa—Kenya: Re-Insurance Plaza, Taifa Rd, POB 69562, 00400 Nairobi; tel. (20) 3275000; fax (20) 2214166; e-mail bkofkenya@boakenya.com; internet www.boakenya.com; f. 2004; cap. 2,000.0m., res 364.3m., dep. 20,829.1m. (Dec. 2009); Chair. PAUL DERREUMAUX; Man. Dir KWAME AHADZI.

Barclays Bank of Kenya Ltd: 8th Barclays Plaza, Loita St, POB 30120, 00100 Nairobi; tel. (20) 2214270; fax (20) 2213915; e-mail barclays.kenya@barclays.com; internet www.barclays.com/africa/kenya; f. 1978; cap. 2,716m., res 4,612m., dep. 131,654m. (Dec. 2009); Chair. SAMUEL O. J. AMBUNDO; Man. Dir ADAN MOHAMMED; 87 brs.

CFC Stanbic Bank Ltd: CFC Centre, Chiromo Rd, Westlands, POB 30550, 00100 Nairobi; tel. (20) 3268000; fax (20) 3752905; e-mail customercare@stanbic.com; internet www.cfcstanbicbank.co.ke; formed by merger of CFC Bank Ltd and Stanbic Bank Kenya Ltd in June 2008; 100% owned by CFC Stanbic Holdings Ltd; cap. 2,441.3m., res 1,177.8m., dep. 82,799.7m. (Dec. 2009); Man. Dir GREG BRACKENRIDGE.

Chase Bank (Kenya) Ltd: Riverside Mews, Ring Rd Riverside and Riverside Westlane, POB 66015, 00800 Nairobi; tel. (20) 2774000; fax (20) 4454816; e-mail info@chasebank.co.ke; internet www.chasebankkenya.co.ke; cap. 1,000.0m., res 85.4m., dep. 10,863.7m. (Dec. 2009); Chair. OSMAN MURGIAN; Man. Dir and Pres. MOHAMED ZAFRULLAH KHAN.

Commercial Bank of Africa Ltd: Commercial Bank Bldg, Upper Hill, cnr Mara and Ragati Rds, POB 30437, Nairobi; tel. (20) 2884000; fax (20) 335827; e-mail cba@cba.co.ke; internet www.cba.co.ke; f. 1962; owned by Kenyan shareholders; cap. 4,515.4m., res 2,334.9m., dep. 57,492.7m. (Dec. 2009); Chair. MIRABEAU H. DA GAMA-ROSE; Pres. and Man. Dir ISAAC O. AWUONDO; 12 brs.

Consolidated Bank of Kenya Ltd: Consolidated Bank House, Koinange St, POB 51133, 00200 Nairobi; tel. (20) 340551; fax (20) 340213; e-mail headoffice@consolidated-bank.com; internet www.consolidated-bank.com; f. 1989; state-owned; cap. 1,119.5m., res 186.8m., dep. 5,678.3m. (Dec. 2009); Chair. EUNICE W. KAGANE; Man. Dir DAVID NDEGWA WACHIRA.

Dubai Bank Kenya Ltd: ICEA Bldg, Kenyatta Ave, POB 11129-00400, Nairobi; tel. (20) 311109; fax (20) 2245242; e-mail info@dubaibank.co.ke; internet www.dubaibank.co.ke; 20% owned by World of Marble and Granite, Dubai (United Arab Emirates), 22.4% owned by Abdul Hassan Ahmed, 16% owned by Hassan Bin Hassan

Trading Co LLC, Dubai (United Arab Emirates), 17.6% owned by Ahmed Mohamed; cap. 411.4m., res 12.0m., dep. 986.2m. (Dec. 2009); Chair. HASSAN AHMED ZUBEIDI; Man. Dir MAYANK SHARMA.

Ecobank Kenya Ltd: Ecobank Towers, 5th Floor, Muindi Mbingu St, POB 49584, 00100 Nairobi; tel. (20) 22883000; fax (20) 22883304; e-mail eke-fedhamgr@ecobank.com; internet www.ecobank.com; f. 1972 as Akiba Bank Ltd, present name adopted 2008; cap. 2,519.3m., res 161.7m., dep. 11,308.5m. (Dec. 2009); Chair. N. P. G. WARREN; Man. Dir TONY OKPANACHI; 3 brs.

Equatorial Commercial Bank Ltd: Nyerere Rd, POB 52467, Nairobi; tel. (20) 2710455; fax (20) 2710700; e-mail Customerservice@ecb.co.ke; internet www.equatorialbank.co.ke; cap. 600m., res 41.1m., dep. 3,702.0m. (Dec. 2009); Chair. DAN AMEYO; Man. Dir PETER HARRIS.

Equity Bank: 14th Floor, NHIF Bldg, Ragati Rd, POB 75104, 00200 Nairobi; tel. (20) 2262000; fax (20) 2737276; e-mail info@equitybank.co.ke; internet www.equitybank.co.ke; f. 1984; Chair. PETER MUNGA; CEO JAMES MWANGI.

Family Bank: Fourways Tower, Muindi Mbingu St, POB 74145, 00200 Nairobi; tel. (20) 318173; fax (20) 318174; e-mail info@familybank.co.ke; internet www.familybank.co.ke; f. 1984; Chair. TITUS K. MUYA; CEO PETER MUNYIRI.

Fidelity Commercial Bank Ltd: IPS Bldg, 7th Floor, Kimathi St, POB 34886, Nairobi; tel. (20) 2242348; fax (20) 2243389; e-mail customerservice@fidelitybankkenya.com; internet www.fidelitybank.co.ke; f. 1993 as Fidelity Finance; present name adopted 1996; cap. 323.5m., res 101.9m., dep. 3,820.1m. (Dec. 2008); Exec. Dir SULTAN KHIMJI; Man. Dir RANA SENGUPTA.

Fina Bank Ltd: Fina House, Kimathi St, POB 20613, 00200 Nairobi; tel. (20) 2246943; fax (20) 2247164; e-mail banking@finabank.com; internet www.finabank.com; f. 1986 as The Finance Institute of Africa Ltd; converted to commercial bank as above in 1996; cap. 528.3m., res 239.8m., dep. 15,932.4m. (Dec. 2009); Chair. DHANJI HANSRAJ CHANDARIA; Man. Dir TIM MARSHALL.

Giro Commercial Bank Ltd: POB 46739, Giro House, Kimathi St, 00100 Nairobi; tel. (20) 22217776; fax (20) 22230600; e-mail info@girobankltd.com; f. 1992 as Giro Bank Ltd; name changed as above in 1999 after merging with Commerce Bank Ltd; 21.76% owned by Blandford Investments Ltd, Nairobi; cap. 309.5m., res 218.0m., dep. 4,959.3m. (Dec. 2007); Chair. CHANDAN JETHANAND GIDOOMAL; Man. Dir T. K. KRISHNAN.

Gulf African Bank (GAB): Geminia Insurance Plaza, Kilimanjaro Ave, Upper Hill, POB 43683, Nairobi; tel. (20) 2740000; fax (20) 2729031; e-mail info@gulfafricanbank.com; internet www.gulfafricanbank.com; f. 2007; 20% owned by Bank Muscat International (BMI), 10% owned by the International Finance Corpn (IFC); cap. 250m., res 1,547m., dep. 6,425m. (Dec. 2009); Chair. SULEIMAN SAID SHAHBAL; CEO NAJMUL HASSAN.

Imperial Bank Ltd: Bunyala Rd, Upper Hill, POB 44905, 00100 Nairobi; tel. (20) 22719612; fax (20) 22719498; e-mail info@imperialbank.co.ke; internet www.imperialbank.co.ke; f. 1992 as Imperial Finance and Securities Company; converted to a bank and name changed as above in 1995; 100% owned by Kenyan shareholders; cap. 1,085.0m., res 205.2m., dep. 12,862.2m. (Dec. 2009); Chair. ALNASHIR POPAT; Man. Dir ABDULMALEK JANMOHAMED.

Kenya Commercial Bank Ltd: Kencom House, Moi Ave, POB 48400, 00100 Nairobi; tel. (20) 3270000; fax (20) 2216405; e-mail kcbhq@kcb.co.ke; internet www.kcb.co.ke; f. 1970; 23.1% state-owned; cap. 2,217.8m., res 18,368.3m., dep. 169,212.9m. (Dec. 2009); Chair. PETER W. MUTHOKA; CEO MARTIN ODUOR-OTIENO; 123 brs and sub-brs.

Middle East Bank Kenya Ltd: Mebank Tower, Milimani Rd, POB 47387, 00100 Nairobi; tel. (20) 2723120; fax (20) 343776; e-mail ho@mebkenya.com; internet www.mebkenya.com; f. 1981; 25% owned by Banque Belgolaise SA (Belgium), 75% owned by Kenyan shareholders; cap. 506.8m., res 31.0m., dep. 2,199.4m. (Dec. 2009); Chair. A. A. K. ESMAIL; Man. Dir PHILIP B. ILAKO; 2 brs.

National Bank of Kenya Ltd (Banki ya Taifa La Kenya Ltd): National Bank Bldg, Harambee Ave, POB 72866, Nairobi; tel. (20) 2226471; fax (20) 311444; e-mail info@nationalbank.co.ke; internet www.nationalbank.co.ke; f. 1968; 42% owned by National Social Security Fund, 22.5% state-owned; cap. 6,675.0m., res 906.9m., dep. 34,347.0m. (Dec. 2008); Chair. M. E. G. MUHINDI; Man. Dir REUBEN M. MARAMBII; 23 brs.

Oriental Commercial Bank Ltd: POB 14357, Apollo Centre, Ring Rd, 00800 Nairobi; tel. (20) 3743289; fax (20) 3743270; e-mail info@orientalbank.co.ke; internet www.orientalbank.co.ke; f. 1991; name changed as above in 2003; cap. 1,643.8m., res 10.4m., dep. 822.9m. (Dec. 2007); Chair. SHANTI SHAH; Man. Dir and CEO R. B. SINGH; 4 brs.

Paramount Universal Bank Ltd: Sound Plaza, 4th Floor, Woodvale Grove, Westlands, POB 14001, 00800 Nairobi; tel. (20) 44492668; fax (20) 4449265; e-mail info@paramountbank.co.ke; internet www.paramountbank.co.ke; f. 1993 as Combined Finance Ltd; name changed as above in 2000; 25% owned by Tormount Holdings Ltd, St Helier, 25% owned by Anwarali Merali, 25% owned by Tasneem Padamshi; Chair. ANWARALI MERALI; Man. Dir AYAZ MERALI.

Standard Chartered Bank Kenya Ltd: Stanbank House, Moi Ave, POB 30003, Nairobi; tel. (20) 32093000; fax (20) 2214086; e-mail mds.office@ke.standardchartered.com; internet www.standardchartered.com/ke; f. 1987; 74.5% owned by Standard Chartered Holdings (Africa) BV (Netherlands); cap. 1,639.8m., res 4,191.7m., dep. 67,750.5m. (Dec. 2006); Chair. HARRINGTON AWORI; CEO RICHARD M. ETEMESI; 29 brs.

Trans-National Bank Ltd: Transnational Plaza, 2nd Floor, Mama Ngina St, POB 34353, 00100 Nairobi; tel. (20) 2224235; fax (20) 339227; e-mail info@tnbl.co.ke; internet www.tnbl.co.ke; f. 1985; cap. 583.7m., res 19.5m., dep. 1,907.1m. (Dec. 2008); Chair. MICHAEL CHERWON; CEO DHIRENDRA RANA; 9 brs.

Merchant Banks

Diamond Trust Bank Ltd: Nation Centre, 8th Floor, Kimathi St, POB 61711, 00200 Nairobi; tel. (20) 2849000; fax (20) 2245495; e-mail info@dtbkenya.co.ke; internet www.dtbafrica.com; f. 1945; cap. 652.1m., res 2,670.8m., dep. 45,853.3m. (Dec. 2008); Chair. MAHMOOD MANJI; Man. Dir NASIM MOHAMED DEVJI.

National Industrial Credit Bank Ltd (NIC): NIC House, Masaba Rd, POB 44599, 00100 Nairobi; tel. (20) 718200; fax (20) 718232; e-mail info@nic-bank.com; internet www.nic-bank.com; Chair. J. P. M. NDEGWA; Man. Dir JAMES MACHARIA.

Co-operative Bank

Co-operative Bank of Kenya Ltd: Co-operative Bank House, Haile Selassie Ave, POB 48231, Nairobi; tel. (20) 3276100; fax (20) 2219831; e-mail md@co-opbank.co.ke; internet www.co-opbank.co.ke; f. 1968; cap. 2,856.5m., res 1,596.9m., dep. 56,198.0m., total assets 65,708.9m. (Dec. 2007); Chair. STANLEY C. MUCHIRI; Man. Dir GIDEON MURIUKI; 29 brs.

Development Banks

Development Bank of Kenya Ltd: Finance House, 16th Floor, Loita St, POB 30483, 00100 Nairobi; tel. (20) 340426; fax (20) 2250399; e-mail dbk@devbank.com; internet www.devbank.com; f. 1963 as Development Finance Co of Kenya; current name adopted 1996; owned by Industrial and Commercial Devt Corpn (89.3%), the Commonwealth Development Corpn (10.7%); cap. 347.5m., res 884.7m., dep. 3,774.0m. (Dec. 2008); Chair. Prof. HAROUN NGENY KIPKEMBOI MENGECH; CEO VICTOR J. O. KIDIWA.

East African Development Bank: Rahimtulla Tower, 2nd Floor, Upper Hill Rd, POB 47685, Nairobi; tel. (20) 340642; fax (20) 2731590; e-mail cok@eadb.org; internet www.eadb.org; Dirs J. KINYUA, F. KARUIRU.

IDB Capital Ltd: National Bank Bldg, 18th Floor, Harambee Ave, POB 44036, Nairobi; tel. (20) 247142; fax (20) 334594; e-mail idbkenya@swiftkenya.com; internet www.idbkenya.com; f. 1973 as Industrial Development Bank Ltd; adopted present name in 2005; 49% state-owned; cap. 272m., res 83m., dep. 190m. (Dec. 2002); Chair. DAVID LANGAT; Man. Dir JAMES B. OCHAMI.

STOCK EXCHANGE

Nairobi Securities Exchange (NSE): Nation Centre, 1st Floor, Kimathi St, POB 43633, 00100 Nairobi; tel. (20) 2831000; fax (20) 2224200; e-mail info@nse.co.ke; internet www.nse.co.ke; f. 1954; Chair. EDWARD NJOROGE; CEO PETER MWANGI.

INSURANCE

In 2009 there were 52 insurance companies operating in Kenya

Insurance Regulatory Authority: Zep-Re Place, off Mara Road, Upper Hill, POB 43505, 00100 Nairobi; tel. 20-4996000; fax (20) 2710126; internet www.ira.go.ke; f. 2006; Chair. STEVE O. MAINDA; CEO SAMMY MUTUA MAKOVE.

Africa Merchant Assurance Co Ltd: Transnational Plaza, 2nd Floor, Mama Ngina St, POB 61599, 00200 Nairobi; tel. (20) 312121; fax (20) 340022; e-mail marketing@amaco.co.ke; internet www.amaco.co.ke; f. 2000; Gen. Man. KENNEDY ABINCHA.

APA Insurance Ltd: Ring Rd Parklands, Westlands, POB 30065, 00100 Nairobi; tel. (20) 2862000; e-mail info@apainsurance.org; internet www.apainsurance.org; f. 2003; Chair. JOHN P. N. SIMBA; Man. Dir ASHOK K. M. SHAH.

Apollo Life Assurance Ltd: Apollo Centre, 3rd Floor, Vale Close, off Ring Rd, Westlands, POB 30389, 00100 Nairobi; tel. (20) 223562; fax (20) 339260; e-mail insurance@apollo.co.ke; internet www.apollo.co.ke; f. 1977; life and general; Chair. BUDHICHAND M. SHAH; CEO PIYUSH SHAH.

Blue Shield Insurance Co Ltd: Blue Shield Towers, Upper Hill, Hospital Rd, off Mara Rd, POB 49610, 00100 Nairobi; tel. (20) 2712600; fax (20) 2712625; e-mail info@blueshield.co.ke; internet www.blueshield.co.ke; f. 1983; life and general; Chair. BETH MUIGAI; Man. Dir KULOVA WANJALA.

British-American Insurance Co: Mara and Ragati Rds Junction, Upper Hill, POB 30375, 00100 Nairobi; tel. (20) 2710927; e-mail insurance@british-american.co.ke; internet www.british-american.co.ke; f. 1965; Man. Dir STEPHEN WANDERA.

Cannon Assurance (Kenya) Ltd: Gateway Business Park, Mombasa Rd, Block D, POB 30216, Nairobi; tel. (20) 3966000; fax (20) 829075; e-mail info@cannonassurance.com; internet www.cannonassurance.com; f. 1964; life and general; Man. Dir MAINA MUKOMA.

CfC Life Assurance Co Ltd: CfC House, Mamlaka Rd, POB 30364, 00100 Nairobi; tel. (20) 2866000; fax (20) 2718365; e-mail cfclife@cfclife.co.ke; internet www.cfclife-kenya.com; f. 1964; life and general; Man. Dir ABEL MUNDA.

Chartis Kenya Insurance Co Ltd: Eden Sq. Complex, Chiromo Rd, POB 49460, 00100 Nairobi; tel. (20) 3676000; fax (20) 3676001; e-mail chartiskenya@chartisinsurance.com; internet www.chartisinsurance.com; Man. Dir JAPH OLENDE.

The Co-operative Insurance Co of Kenya Ltd: Mara Rd, Upper Hill, POB 59485, 00200 Nairobi; tel. (20) 2823000; fax (20) 2823333; e-mail cic@cic.co.ke; internet www.cic.co.ke; Chair. JAPHETH ANAVILA MAGOMERE; Man. Dir NELSON C. KURIA.

East Africa Reinsurance Co Ltd: EARe House, 98 Riverside Dr., POB 20196, 00200 Nairobi; tel. (20) 4443588; fax (20) 4455391; e-mail info@eastafricare.com; internet www.eastafricare.com; Chair. J. P. M. NDEGWA; Man. Dir HAROON MOTARA.

Fidelity Shield Insurance Ltd: 4th Floor, Rank Xerox House, Parklands Rd, Westlands, POB 47435, 00100 Nairobi; tel. (20) 4443063; fax (20) 4445699; e-mail info@fidelityshield.com; internet www.fidelityshield.com; Man. Dir SHEHNAZ SUMAR.

First Assurance Co Ltd: Gitanga Rd, Lavington, POB 30064, 00100, Nairobi; tel. (20) 3867374; fax (20) 3872204; f. 1979 as Prudential Assurance Co. of Kenya Ltd; present name adopted 1991; life and general; Chair. M. H. DA GAMA ROSE; Man. Dir STEPHEN GITHIGA.

GA Insurance Ltd: GA Insurance House, 4th Floor, Ralph Bunche Rd, POB 42166, 00100 Nairobi; tel. (20) 2711633; fax (20) 2714542; e-mail insure@gakenya.com; internet www.gakenya.com; general; Chair. SURESH B. R. SHAH; CEO VIJAY SRIVASTAVA.

Heritage Insurance Co Ltd: CFC House, Mamlaka Rd, POB 30390, 00100 Nairobi; tel. (20) 2783000; fax (20) 2727800; e-mail info@heriaii.com; internet www.heritageinsurance.co.ke; f. 1976; general; Chair. J. G. KIEREINI; Man. Dir JOHN H. D. MILNE.

Insurance Co of East Africa Ltd (ICEA): ICEA Bldg, Kenyatta Ave, POB 46143, Nairobi; tel. (20) 221652; fax (20) 338089; e-mail hof@icea.co.ke; internet www.icea.co.ke; life and general; Man. Dir J. K. NDUNGU.

Jubilee Insurance Co Ltd: Jubilee Insurance House, 5th Floor, Wabera St, POB 30376, 00100 Nairobi; tel. (20) 3281000; fax (20) 3281150; e-mail jic@jubileekenya.com; internet www.jubileeafrica.com; f. 1937; long term (life and pensions) and short term (general and medical) insurance; Chair. NIZAR JUMA; Gen. Man. PATRICK TUMBO NYAMEMBA.

Kenindia Assurance Co Ltd: Kenindia House, 11th Floor, Loita St, POB 40512, Nairobi; tel. (20) 316099; fax (20) 218380; e-mail kenindia@kenindia.com; internet www.kenindia.com; f. 1978; life and general; Chair. M. N. MEHTA; Man. Dir M. N. SARMA.

Kenya Reinsurance Corpn Ltd (KenyaRe): Reinsurance Plaza, Taifa Rd, POB 30271, Nairobi; tel. (20) 2240188; fax (20) 2252106; e-mail kenyare@kenyare.co.ke; internet www.kenyare.co.ke; f. 1970; Chair. NELIUS KARIUKI; Man. Dir JADIAH MWARANIA.

Lion of Kenya Insurance Co Ltd: Williamson House, Jubilee Insurance Bldg, Kirem Arcade, 4 Ngong Ave, POB 30190, 00100 Nairobi; tel. (20) 710400; fax (20) 711177; e-mail insurance@lionofkenya.com; internet www.lionofkenya.com; f. 1978; general; Chair. C. W. OBURA; CEO JOHN K. KIMEU.

Madison Insurance Co Kenya Ltd: Upper Hill Rd, POB 47382, 00100 Nairobi; tel. (20) 2721970; e-mail madison@madison.co.ke; internet www.madison.co.ke; life and general; Chair. SAMUEL G. NGARUIYA; Man. Dir F. MUCHIRI; 14 brs.

Mercantile Insurance Co Ltd: Fedha Towers, 16th Floor, Muindi Mbingu St, Nairobi; tel. (20) 2219486; fax (20) 215528; e-mail mercantile@mercantile.co.ke; internet www.mercantile.co.ke; Chair. N. P. G. WARREN; Man. Dir SUPRIYO SEN.

Monarch Insurance Co Ltd: Prudential Assurance Bldg, 4th Floor, Wabera St, POB 44003, Nairobi; tel. (20) 310032; fax (20) 340691; e-mail info@themonarchinsco.com; internet www.themonarchinsco.com; f. 1975; life and general; Man. Dir CHARLES MAKONE.

Pan Africa Life Assurance Ltd: Pan Africa House, Kenyatta Ave, POB 44041, 00100 Nairobi; tel. (20) 247600; fax (20) 217675; e-mail insure@pan-africa.com; internet www.panafrica.co.ke; f. 1946; life and general; Chair. JOHN SIMBA; CEO TOM GITOGO.

Phoenix of East Africa Assurance Co Ltd: Ambank House, 17th and 18th Floors, University Way, POB 30129, 00100 Nairobi; tel. (20) 2251350; fax (20) 2211848; e-mail general@phoenix.co.ke; general; Gen. Man. KAUSHAL KUMAR.

PTA Reinsurance Co (ZEP-RE): Zep-Re Pl., Longonot Rd, Upper Hill, POB 42769, Nairobi; tel. (20) 212792; fax (20) 224102; e-mail mail@zep-re.com; internet www.zep-re.com; f. 1992; Chair. MICHAEL GONDWE; Man. Dir RAJNI VARIA.

REAL Insurance Co: Royal Ngao House, Hospital Rd, POB 40001, 00100 Nairobi; e-mail general@realinsurance.co.ke; tel. (20) 717888; fax (20) 712620; internet www.realinsurance.co.ke; f. 1979; general; Chair. S. K. KAMAU; CEO JOSEPH W. KIUNA.

Standard Assurance (Kenya) Ltd: POB 42996, Nairobi; tel. (20) 224721; fax (20) 224862; Man. Dir WILSON K. KAPKOTI.

UAP Provincial Insurance Co of East Africa Ltd: Bishop Garden Towers, Bishops Rd, POB 43013, 00100 Nairobi; tel. (20) 850000; fax (20) 719030; e-mail uapinsurance@uapkenya.com; f. 1980; general; Chair. FRANCIS OGUTU; CEO JAMES WAMBUGU.

Insurance Association

Association of Kenya Insurers (AKI): Victoria Towers, 3rd Floor, Kilimanjaro Ave, Upper Hill, POB 45338, 00100 Nairobi; tel. (20) 2731330; fax (20) 2731339; e-mail info@akinsure.com; internet www.akinsure.or.ke; Chair. STEPHEN WANDERA.

Trade and Industry

GOVERNMENT AGENCIES

Export Processing Zones Authority: Administration Bldg, Viwanda Rd, Athi River Export Processing Zone, off Nairobi-Namanga Highway, Athi River, POB 50563, Nairobi; tel. (45) 26421; fax (45) 26427; e-mail info@epzakenya.com; internet www.epzakenya.com; established by the Govt to promote investment in Export Processing Zones; Chief Exec. J. O. B. AKARA.

Export Promotion Council: Anniversary Towers, 1st and 16th Floors, University Way, POB 40247, Nairobi; tel. (20) 228534; fax (20) 218013; e-mail chiefexe@epc.or.ke; internet www.epckenya.org; f. 1992; Chair. Prof. PETER NJERU NDWIGA; CEO RUTH MWANIKI.

Kenya Investment Authority: Railways HQ, Block D, 3rd Floor, Workshops Rd, POB 55704, 00200 Nairobi; tel. (20) 2221401; fax (20) 2243862; e-mail info@investmentkenya.com; internet www.investmentkenya.com; f. 1986; promotes and facilitates local and foreign investment; Man. Dir SUSAN KIKWAI.

Kenya National Trading Corpn Ltd: Yarrow Rd, off Nanyuki Rd, POB 30587, Nairobi; tel. (20) 2430861; fax (20) 556331; e-mail customercare@kntcl.com; internet www.kntcl.com/; f. 1965; promotes wholesale and retail trade; Chair. MOHAMMED HASSAN; Man. Dir GLADYS MAINA.

DEVELOPMENT ORGANIZATIONS

Agricultural Development Corpn: Development House, 10th Floor, POB 47101, Nairobi; tel. (20) 250695; fax (20) 243571; e-mail info@adc.co.ke; internet www.adc.co.ke; f. 1965 to promote agricultural devt and reconstruction; Chair. L. W. WARUINGI; CEO WILLIAM K. KIRWA.

Agricultural Finance Corpn: POB 30367, Nairobi; tel. (20) 317199; fax (20) 219390; e-mail info@agrifinance.org; internet www.agrifinance.org; a statutory organization providing agricultural loans; Man. Dir OMUREMBE IYADI.

Horticultural Crops Development Authority: POB 42601, Nairobi; tel. (20) 8272601; fax (20) 827264; e-mail md@hcda.or.ke; internet www.hcda.or.ke; f. 1968; invests in production, dehydration, processing and freezing of fruit and vegetables; exports of fresh fruit and vegetables; Chair. JOSEPH G. KIBE; Man. Dir ALFRED SEREM.

Housing Finance Co of Kenya Ltd: Rehani House, cnr Kenyatta Ave and Koinange St, POB 30088, 00100 Nairobi; tel. (20) 317474; fax (20) 340299; e-mail housing@housing.co.ke; internet www.housing.co.ke; f. 1965; Chair. STEVE MAINDA; Man. Dir FRANK M. IRERI.

Industrial and Commercial Development Corpn: Uchumi House, 17th Floor, Aga Khan Walk, POB 45519, Nairobi; tel. (20) 229213; fax (20) 317456; e-mail info@icdc.co.ke; internet www.icdc.co.ke; f. 1954; govt-financed; assists industrial and commercial devt; Chair. MARTIN KARIUKI MURAGU; Exec. Dir PETER KIMURWA.

Kenya Industrial Estates Ltd: Nairobi Industrial Estate, Likoni Rd, POB 78029, Nairobi; tel. (20) 651348; fax (20) 651355; e-mail admin@kie.co.ke; internet www.kie.co.ke; f. 1967 to finance and develop small-scale industries; Chair. AHMED MOHAMMED; Man. Dir JULIUS OBARE MOKOGI.

Kenya Industrial Research and Development Institute: POB 30650, Nairobi; tel. (20) 6003842; fax (20) 6007023; e-mail info@kirdi.go.ke; internet www.kirdi.go.ke; f. 1942; reorg. 1979; restructured 1995; research and devt in industrial and allied technologies including engineering, agro-industrial, mining and environmental technologies; Chair. Eng. Dr SIPHILA MUMENYA; Dir Dr CHARLES M. Z. MOTURI.

Kenya Tea Development Agency: Moi Ave, POB 30213, Nairobi; tel. and fax (20) 3227000; e-mail info@ktdateas.com; internet www.ktdateas.com; f. 1964 as Kenya Tea Development Authority to develop tea growing, manufacturing and marketing among African smallholders; operates 65 tea factories and six subsidiaries; privatized in 2000; Chair. PETER KANYAGO; CEO LERIONKA TIAMPATI.

CHAMBER OF COMMERCE

Kenya National Chamber of Commerce and Industry: Ufanisi House, Haile Selassie Ave, POB 47024, Nairobi; tel. (20) 220867; fax (20) 334293; internet www.kncci.org; f. 1965; 69 brs; Nat. Chair. DAVID M. GITHERE; Chief Exec. TITUS G. RUHIU.

INDUSTRIAL AND TRADE ASSOCIATIONS

Coffee Board of Kenya: Coffee Plaza, 10th Floor, Exchange Lane, off Haile Selassie Ave, POB 30566, Nairobi; tel. and fax (20) 315754; fax (20) 311079; e-mail info@coffeeboard.co.ke; internet www.coffeeboard.co.ke; f. 1947; Chair. RICHARD MORRIS GITONGA; Man. Dir LOISE W. NJERU.

East African Tea Trade Association (EATTA): Tea Trade Centre, Nyerere Ave, POB 85174, 80100 Mombasa; tel. (41) 2220093; fax (41) 2225823; e-mail info@eatta.co.ke; internet www.eatta.com; f. 1957; organizes Mombasa weekly tea auctions; Chair. PETER KIMANGA; Man. Dir EDWARD MUDIBO; 178 mems in 9 countries.

Fresh Produce Exporters' Association of Kenya (FPEAK): New Rehema House, 4th Floor, Rhapta Rd, Westlands, POB 40312, 00100 Nairobi; tel. (20) 4451488; fax (20) 445189; e-mail info@fpeak.org; internet www.fpeak.org; Chair. RICHARD COLLINS; CEO Dr STEPHEN MBITHI MWIKYA.

Kenya Association of Manufacturers (KAM): Mwanzi Rd, off Peponi Rd, Westlands, POB 30225, Nairobi; tel. (20) 3746005; fax (20) 3746028; e-mail kam@users.africaonline.co.ke; internet www.kam.co.ke; Chair. JASWINDER BEDI; Exec. Sec. LUCY MICHENI; 200 mems.

Kenya Dairy Board: NSSF Bldg, 10th and 11th Floors, Bishops Rd, POB 30406, Nairobi; tel. (20) 310559; fax (20) 244064; e-mail info@kdb.co.ke; internet www.kdb.co.ke; f. 1958; Chair. MARTHA MULWA; Man. Dir MACHIRA GICHOHI.

Kenya Fish Processors' and Exporters' Association: 5th Floor, New Rehema House, Raphta Rd, Westlands, POB 345, 00606 Nairobi; tel. and fax (20) 4440858; e-mail info@afipek.org; internet www.afipek.org; f. 2000; Chair. NADIR JESSA; CEO BETH WAGUDE.

Kenya Flower Council: Muthangari Gardens, off Gitanga Rd, POB 56325, 00200 Nairobi; tel. and fax (20) 3876597; e-mail info@kenyaflowercouncil.org; internet www.kenyaflowercouncil.org; regulates production of cut flowers; CEO JANE NGIGE.

Kenya Meat Commission: POB 30414, Nairobi; tel. (45) 6626041; fax (45) 6626520; e-mail info@kenyameat.co.ke; internet www.kenyameat.co.ke; state-owned; f. 1953; purchasing, processing and marketing of beef livestock; Man. Commr ALI HASSAN MOHAMMED.

Kenya Planters' Co-operative Union Ltd: Nairobi; e-mail gm@kpcu.co.ke; coffee processing and marketing; Chair. J. M. MACHARIA; Gen. Man. RUTH MWANIKI.

Kenya Sisal Board: Mutual Bldg, Kimathi St, POB 41179, Nairobi; tel. (20) 248919; fax (20) 240091; e-mail kensisal@sisalboardkenya.go.ke; internet www.sisalboardkenya.go.ke; f. 1946; Man. Dir CHARLES K. KAGWIMI.

Kenya Sugar Board: Sukari Plaza, off Waiyaki Way, POB 51500, Nairobi; tel. (20) 2023316; fax (20) 593273; e-mail info@kenyasugar.co.ke; internet www.kenyasugar.co.ke; f. 2002 to succeed the Kenya Sugar Authority; Chair. OKOTH OBADO; CEO ROSEMARY MKOK.

Mild Coffee Trade Association of Eastern Africa (MCTA): Nairobi; Chair. F. J. MWANGI.

National Cereals and Produce Board (NCPB): POB 30586, Nairobi; tel. (20) 536028; fax (20) 542024; e-mail info@ncpb.co.ke; internet www.ncpb.co.ke; f. 1995; grain marketing and handling, provides drying, weighing, storage and fumigation services to farmers and traders, stores and manages strategic national food reserves, distributes famine relief; Chair. JIMNAH MBARU; Man. Dir ALFRED BUSOLO.

Pyrethrum Board of Kenya (PBK): POB 420, Nakuru; tel. (51) 2211567; fax (51) 2210466; e-mail pbk@pyrethrum.co.ke; internet www.kenya-pyrethrum.com; f. 1935; 14 mems; Chair. SOLOMON BOIT; Man. Dir ISAAC MULAGOLI.

Tea Board of Kenya: Naivasha Rd, off Ngong Rd, POB 20064, 00200 Nairobi; tel. (20) 3874446; fax (20) 3862120; e-mail info@teaboard.or.ke; internet www.teaboard.or.ke; f. 1950; regulates tea industry on all matters of policy, licenses tea processing, carries out research on tea through **Tea Research Foundation of Kenya**, monitors tea planting and trade through registration, promotes Kenyan tea internationally; Chair. TITUS G. KIPYAB; Man. Dir SICILY K. KARIUKI.

EMPLOYERS' ORGANIZATIONS

Federation of Kenya Employers (FKE): Waajiri House, Argwings Kodhek Rd, POB 48311, Nairobi; tel. (20) 2721929; fax (20) 2721990; e-mail fkehq@fke-kenya.org; internet fke-kenya.org; Chair. PATRICK OBATH; Exec. Dir JACQUELINE MUGO.

Association of Local Government Employers (ALGAE): POB 52, Muranga; Chair. SAMUEL NYANGESO.

Kenya Association of Hotelkeepers and Caterers: Heidelberg House, 2nd Floor, Mombasa Rd, POB 9977, 00100 Nairobi; tel. (20) 6004419; fax (20) 6002539; e-mail info@kahc.co.ke; internet www.kahc.co.ke; f. 1944; CEO MIKE MACHARIA.

Kenya Bankers' Association: POB 73100, Nairobi; tel. (20) 2221704; fax (20) 2219520; e-mail info@kba.co.ke; internet www.kba.co.ke; f. 1962; Chair. RICHARD ETEMESI; CEO HABIL O. OLAKA; 43 mem orgs.

Kenya Coffee Producers' Association (KCPA): Wakulima House, 4th Floor, Room 408, Haile Selassie Ave, Ronald Ngala, POB 8100, 00300 Nairobi; tel. (20) 311235; e-mail info@kcpa.or.ke; internet www.kcpa.or.ke; f. 2009; Chair. JAMES K. GITAO.

Kenya Vehicle Manufacturers' Association: POB 1436, Thika; tel. (20) 350309; fax (67) 31434; e-mail kvm@kvm.co.ke; internet www.kvm.co.ke; f. 1974; name changed as above in 1989; Chair. KENNETH KEBAARA.

UTILITIES

Electricity

Energy Regulatory Commission (ERC): Integrity Centre, 1st Floor, cnr Valley and Milimani Rds, POB 42681, 00100 Nairobi; tel. (20) 2717627; fax (20) 2717603; e-mail info@erc.go.ke; internet www.erc.go.ke; f. 1997 as Energy Regulatory Board; present name assumed in 2007; govt-owned; regulates the generation, distribution, supply and use of electric power; Chair. HINDPAL SINGH JABBAL; Dir-Gen. Eng. KABURU MWIRICHIA.

Kenya Electricity Generating Co Ltd (KenGen): Stima Plaza, Phase 3, Kolobot Rd, Parklands, POB 47936, Nairobi; tel. (20) 3666000; fax (20) 248848; e-mail comms@kengen.co.ke; internet www.kengen.co.ke; f. 1997 as Kenya Power Co; present name adopted 1998; generates 82% of Kenya's electricity requirements; partially privatized in 2006; Chair. TITUS KITILI MBATHI; Man. Dir and CEO EDWARD NJOROGE.

Kenya Power and Lighting Co (KPLC): Electricity House, Harambee Ave, POB 301779, Nairobi; tel. (20) 221251; fax (20) 337351; e-mail custcare@kplc.co.ke; internet www.kplc.co.ke; partially privatized in 2006; 4% owned by Transcentury Group; co-ordinates electricity transmission and distribution; Man. Dir JOSEPH K. NJOROGE.

WATER

Nairobi City Water and Sewerage Co (NWSC): Kampala Rd, off Enterprise Rd, POB 30656, 00100 Nairobi; tel. (20) 3988000; internet www.nairobiwater.co.ke; f. 2002; Chair. PETER KUGURU; Man. Dir PATRICK OMUTIA.

MAJOR COMPANIES

The following are among the largest companies in terms either of capital investment or employment.

Athi River Mining (Kenya) Ltd (ARM): Rhino House, Chiromo Rd, Westlands, POB 41908, 00100 Nairobi; tel. (20) 2667675; fax (20) 2667677; e-mail info@armafrica.com; internet www.armafrica.com; f. 1974; mines and processes industrial minerals and chemicals; ISO certified manufacturer of cement and lime; manufactures cement, quick and hydrated lime, sodium silicate, industrial minerals, special cements and building products and fertilizers; sales Ks. 1,240m. (2003); Chair. RICK ASHLEY; Man. Dir PRADEEP H. PAUNRANA; 700 employees.

Bamburi Cement Ltd: Kenya-Re Towers, 6th and 9th Floors, Upper Hill, off Ragati Rd, Upper Hill, POB 10921, 00100 Nairobi; tel. (20) 2710487; fax (20) 2710581; e-mail corp.info@bamburi.lafarge.com; internet www.lafarge.co.ke; f. 1951; 29.3% owned by Fincem

Holdings Ltd, 29.3% owned by Kencem Holdings Ltd; produces portland cement; turnover Ks. 22,111m. (2007); Chair. RICHARD KEMOLI; Man. Dir HUSSEIN MANSI; 850 employees.

BAT (Kenya) Ltd: Likoni Rd, Industrial Area, POB 30000, Nairobi; tel. (20) 533555; fax (20) 531616; e-mail batkenya@bat.com; internet www.bat.com; f. 1956; subsidiary of British American Tobacco Co Ltd, UK; mfrs of tobacco products; Chair. E. MWANIKI; 700 employees.

Bata Shoe Co (Kenya) Ltd: POB 23, Limuru 00217; tel. (20) 2013352; fax (20) 2010621; e-mail info@batakenya.com; internet www.batakenya.com; f. 1943; mfrs of footwear; Man. Dir NASIR RAFIQUE.

Bedi Investments Ltd: Lower Factory Rd, Industrial Area, POB 230, Nakuru; tel. (51) 2212320; fax (51) 2216214; e-mail info@bedi.com; internet www.bedi.com; f. 1972; manufactures finished fabrics, yarns and garments; Chair. JARNAIL BEDI; CEO JASWINDER S. BEDI; 745 employees.

BOC Kenya Ltd: Kitui Rd, Industrial Area, POB 18010, 00500 Nairobi; tel. (20) 6944000; e-mail bocinfo@boc.co.ke; internet www.boc.co.ke; supplier of industrial and medical gasses and accessories; Chair. JOSEPH KIBE; Man. Dir MARIA MSISKA.

Brollo Kenya Ltd: Miritini, POB 90651, 80100 Mombasa; tel. (41) 2312123; fax (41) 2314553; e-mail info@brollokenya.com; internet brollokenya.com; manufactures value added steel and tubular products; Chair. L. P. DOSHI.

Brookside Dairy Ltd: POB 236, 00232 Ruiru; tel. (20) 2506210; fax (20) 2015203; e-mail maziwa@brookside.co.ke; internet www.brookside.co.ke; manufacture of dairy products; sales US $4.5m. (2004); Gen. Man. JOHN GETHI; 1,000 employees.

Chemelil Sugar Co Ltd: POB 177, Muhoroni 40107; tel. (20) 2031883; fax (20) 2031886; e-mail csc@chemsugar.co.ke; internet www.chemsugar.co.ke; f. 1965; production and processing of sugar; Chair. MARGARET K. CHEMENGICH; Man. Dir CHARLES A. OWELLE; 1,244 employees.

CMC Holdings Ltd: Lusaka Rd, POB 30060, 00100 Nairobi; tel. (20) 554211; fax (20) 543793; e-mail info@cmcmotors.com; internet www.cmcmotors.com; f. 1948; investment co, with interests in motor, aviation, engineering, and agricultural machinery and equipment; Man. Dir WILLIAM LAY; 1,100 employees.

East African Breweries Ltd (EABL): Thika Rd, Ruaraka, POB 30161, Nairobi; tel. (20) 8644000; fax (20) 8561090; e-mail eabl.info@eabl.com; internet www.eabl.com; f. 1922; brews Tusker, Pilsner, Whitecap, Allsopps, Bell Lager and Kibo Gold; Chair. CHARLES MUCHENE; Group Man. Dir DEVLIN HAINSWORTH.

East African Cables Ltd: Addis Ababa Rd, Industrial Area, POB 18243, 00500 Nairobi; tel. (20) 6607000; fax (20) 559310; e-mail info@eacables.com; internet www.eacables.com; manufacture and sale of electrical cables and conductors; Chair. ZEPHANIAH G. MBUGUA; CEO GEORGE MWANGI.

East African Packing Industries Ltd (EAPI): Kitui Rd, off Kampala Rd, POB 30146, Nairobi; tel. (20) 3955000; fax (20) 3955500; e-mail sales@eapi.co.ke; internet www.eapi.co.ke; f. 1959; produces multiwall paper bags, corrugated cardboard containers and toilet tissue; Chair. A. P. HAMILTON; Man. Dir RON FASOL; 400 employees.

East African Portland Cement Co Ltd: Namanga Rd, off Mombasa Rd, Athi River, POB 20, Nairobi; tel. (45) 6622777; fax (45) 6620406; e-mail info@eapcc.co.ke; internet www.eastafricanportland.com; f. 1932; cement mfrs; Chair. MARK K. OLE KARBOLO; Man. Dir KEPHAR TANDE.

Eveready East Africa Ltd: Standard Building, 5th Floor, Wabera St, POB 44765, 00100 Nairobi; tel. (20) 2216139; fax (20) 343213; e-mail info@eveready.co.ke; internet www.eveready.co.ke; manufactures batteries, lights and personal care products; Man. Dir JACKSON MUTUA; c. 250 employees.

Insteel Ltd: Ol Kalou Rd, Industrial Area, POB 78161, 00507 Nairobi; tel. (20) 555099; fax (20) 533944; e-mail insteel@insteellimited.com; internet www.insteellimited.com; f. 1983; manufactures steel water pipes and hollow sections; sales Ks. 1,345m. (2004); COO and Dir H. P. MODI; 300 employees.

Kakuzi Ltd: Punda Milia Rd, Makuyu, POB 24, Thika; tel. (15) 64620; fax (15) 64240; e-mail mail@kakuzi.co.ke; internet www.kakuzi.co.ke; f. 1927; 26.1% owned by Bordure Ltd, 24.6% by Lintak Investments Ltd, 5.0% by Kenya Reinsurance Corpn; tea and coffee growing, livestock farming, horticulture, forestry development; Chair. KENNETH TARPLEE; Man. Dir GRAHAM MCLEAN.

Kaluworks Ltd: POB 90421, Mombasa; tel. (41) 2491401; fax (41) 2492752; e-mail corporate@kaluworks.com; f. 1929; mfr of aluminium kitchenware and catering equipment for export, mfrs of aluminium sheets, coils and circles; sales US $28.7m. (2003); COO V. NAIR; Man. Dir R. R. TEWARY; Exec. Dir R. C. SHARMA; 800 employees.

Kapa Oil Refineries Ltd (KAPA): Main Mombasa Rd, POB 18492, 00500 Nairobi; tel. (20) 6420000; fax (20) 6420642; e-mail info@kapa-oil.com; internet www.kapa-oil.com; f. 1975; mfrs of cooking fats and edible oils, margarines, baking powder, detergents, laundry soaps and glycerine; Man. Dir NIRAL SHAH; 1,000 employees.

Kenya Oil Co Ltd: POB 44202, Nairobi; tel. (20) 249333; fax (20) 230967; e-mail info@kenolkobil.com; internet www.kenolkobil.com; f. 1959; import of crude petroleum; marketing of fuel and lubricants; Chair. JACOB I. SEGMAN; Country Man. DAVID OHANA; 190 employees.

Kenya Petroleum Refineries Ltd: Refinery Rd, Changamwe, POB 90401, 80100 Mombasa; tel. (41) 3433511; fax (41) 3432603; e-mail refinery@kprl.co.ke; internet www.kprl.co.ke; f. 1960 as East African Oil Refineries Ltd; Chair. SULEIMAN R. SHAKOMBO; CEO RAJ K. VARMA.

Kenya Pipeline Co: Kenpipe Plaza, Sekondi Rd, off Nanyuki Rd,Industrial Area, POB 73442, 00200 Nairobi; tel. (20) 2606500; fax (20) 3540032; e-mail info@kpc.co.ke; internet www.kpc.co.ke; f. 1973; state-owned; Chair. SAMUEL M. MALUKI; Man. Dir SELEST N. KILINDA.

Kenya Seed Co Ltd: Teachers Plaza, 2nd Floor, POB 553, Kitale; tel. (54) 31909; fax (54) 30385; e-mail info@kenyaseed.co.ke; internet www.kenyaseed.com; f. 1956; 52.88% owned by Agricultural Development Corpn; seed growers and merchants; Chair. ANDREW MULLEI; Man. Dir WILLIE KIPKORIR BETT; 392 employees.

Kenya Shell Ltd: Laiboni Centre, Lenana Rd, Kilimani, POB 43561, 00100 Nairobi; tel. (20) 3205555; fax (20) 2714575; e-mail shellkenya@ksl.shell.com.

Kenya Tea Packers Ltd (KETEPA): POB 413, 20200 Kericho; tel. (52) 20530; fax (52) 20536; e-mail ketepa@ketepa.com; internet www.ketepa.com; f. 1977; 70% owned by Kenya Tea Development Agency Ltd; production of packed tea; Man. Dir TIMOTHY CHEGE; 500 employees.

Kwale International Sugar Co. Ltd (KISCOL): Ramisi, Kwale; tel. (20) 2106021; fax (20) 8560979; e-mail info@kwale-group.com; internet www.kwale-group.com; f. 2007; Dir (Projects) HARSHIL KOTECHA.

Libya Oil Kenya Ltd (Oilibya): Oilibya Plaza, Muthaiga Rd, POB 64900, 0620 Nairobi; tel. (20) 3622000; fax (20) 3622345; e-mail info@oilibya.co.ke; internet www.oilibya.co.ke; f. 2006; Man. Dir RIDA ELAMIR.

Mabati Rolling Mills Ltd: Athi River, POB 271, 00204 Nairobi; tel. (20) 6247000; fax (20) 6427501; internet www.mabati.com; CEO KAUSHIK SHAH.

Mumias Sugar Co Ltd: Private Bag, Mumias; tel. (56) 641620; fax (56) 641234; e-mail msc@mumias-sugar.com; internet www.mumias-sugar.com; f. 1971; privatized in 2001; sugar production; Chair. JOHN BOSSE; Man. Dir Dr PETER KEBATI; 3,000 employees.

National Oil Corporation of Kenya Ltd (NOCK): AON Minet House, 5th and 7th Floors, off Nyerere Rd, POB 58567, Nairobi; tel. (20) 6952000; fax (20) 6952400; e-mail mdnock@nockenya.co.ke; internet www.nockenya.co.ke; f. 1981; 100% owned by Govt of Kenya; Chair. PETER K. MUNGA; Man. Dir SUMAYYA HASSAN-ATHMANI.

New KCC Ltd: Creamery House, Dakar Rd, POB 30131, Nairobi; tel. (20) 552952; fax (20) 558705; e-mail info@newkcc.co.ke; internet www.newkcc.co.ke; f. 1925 as Kenya Co-operative Creameries Ltd; name changed as above in 2009; processes and markets the bulk of dairy produce; Chair. MATU WAMAE; Man. Dir Dr DANIEL LANGAT; 5,000 employees.

Njoro Canning Factory (Kenya) Ltd: POB 7076, Nakuru; tel. (51) 211736; fax (51) 2217754; e-mail info@njorocanning.com; internet www.njorocanning.co.ke; f. 1978; produces canned, dried and frozen vegetables; Chair. and Man. Dir T. K. PATEL; 1,000 employees.

Numerical Machining Complex Ltd (NMC): Workshops Rd, POB 70660, 00400 Nairobi; tel. (20) 2241701; fax (20) 2244759; e-mail enquiries@nmc.co.ke; internet www.nmc.co.ke; f. 1994; manufacturer of machinery and components; Man. Dir Eng. GEORGE S. ONYANGO.

Orbit Chemical Industries Ltd (OCIL): POB 48870, Nairobi; tel. (20) 2338200; fax (20) 3540021; e-mail orbit@orbitchem.com; internet www.orbitchem.com; f. 1972; manufacture of chemicals, soaps and detergents; Chair. V. D. CHANDARIA; 500 employees.

Sameer Africa Ltd: cnr Mombasa and Enterprise Rds, POB 30429, 00100 Nairobi; tel. (20) 3962000; fax (20) 3962888; e-mail info@sameerafrica.co.ke; internet www.sameerafrica.com; f. 1969; formerly Firestone East Africa (1969) Ltd; corporate identity changed to Sameer Africa Ltd in 2005; tyre and tube mfrs; sales Ks. 3,400m. (2004); Chair. ERASTUS K. MWONGERA; Man. Dir M. KARANJA; 686 employees.

Sasini Ltd: POB 30151, 00100 Nairobi; tel. (20) 342166; fax (20) 316573; e-mail info@sasini.co.ke; internet www.sasini.co.ke; f. 1952; owned by Sameer Investments Ltd; tea and coffee farming and production; turnover Ks. 1.3m. (2006); Chair. JAMES B. MCFIE; Man. Dir CAESAR M.J. MWANGI; 5,000 employees.

SpinKnit Dairy Ltd: POB 78377, Viwandani 00507, Nairobi; tel. (20) 3540478; fax (20) 558370; e-mail customerservice@spinknit.com; internet www.spinknitdairy.com; f. 1996; manufacture of hand-knitted clothing, yarn, blankets, towels; Man. Dir SHASHI SHAH; 750 employees.

Steelmakers Ltd: POB 44574, 00100 Nairobi; tel. (20) 821790; fax (20) 821796; e-mail msa@steelmakers.com; f. 1986; production of foundry products and hot rolled steel profiles and sections; Chair. RASIK PATEL; Man. Dir KALPESH PATEL; 1,200 employees.

Tata Chemicals Magadi: POB 1, 00205 Magadi; tel. (20) 6999000; fax (20) 6999360; e-mail info-magadi@tatachemicals.com; internet www.tatachemicals.com/magadi; f. 1911; fmrly Magadi Soda Co., name changed as above in 2005; mfr of soda ash sodium carbonate and salt; Man. Dir MIKE ODERA.

Total Kenya Ltd: Regal Plaza, Limuru Rd, POB 30736, Nairobi; tel. (20) 2897000; fax (20) 3668396; e-mail administrator@total.co.ke; internet www.total.co.ke; f. 1963; name changed as above in 1991; distribution of petroleum products; Man. Dir ALEXIS VOVK.

Trans-Century Ltd: Longonot Place, 7th Floor, Kijabe St, POB 42334-00100 GPO, Nairobi; tel. (20) 2245350; fax (20) 2245253; e-mail contacts@transcentury.co.ke; internet www.transcentury.co.ke; f. 1997; Chair. ZEPHANIAH MBUGUA; CEO and Man. Dir GACHAO KIUNA.

Civicon Ltd: POB 99491-80107, Mombasa; tel. 736605560 (mobile); e-mail info@civiconkenya.com; internet www.civiconkenya.com; f. 1975; engineering and construction; Exec. Dirs DAVID HORSEY HORSEY, HORACE HORSEY; Gen. Man. MIKE HUTH.

Unga Group Ltd: Ngano House, Commercial St, POB 30096, Nairobi; tel. (20) 532471; fax (20) 545448; e-mail information@unga.com; f. 1928; 51% owned by Victus Ltd; mfrs of flour, maize meal, porridges, animal feed and animal minerals; sales Ks. 7,306m. (2006); Chair. RICHARD KEMOLI; Man. Dir NICHOLAS HUTCHINSON; 400 employees.

Unilever Tea Kenya Ltd (UTKL): POB 42011, Nairobi; tel. (20) 532520; fax (20) 532521; e-mail richard.fairburn@unilever.com; internet www.unilever-esa.com; f. 1825 as Brooke Bond Kenya Ltd; name changed as above in 2004; growth, production and sale of tea; sales Ks. 4,2595m. (2002); Man. Dir RICHARD ARTHUR FAIRBURN; 18,000 employees.

Williamson Tea Kenya Ltd: Williamson House, 4th Ngong Ave, POB 42281, Nairobi; tel. (20) 2710740; fax (20) 271873; e-mail gwkenya@Williamson.co.ke; internet www.williamsontea.com; f. 1952; fmrly George Williamson Kenya Ltd; 50.41% owned by Williamson Tea Holdings PLC (United Kingdom); tea cultivation and production; Chair. and Man. Dir N. G. SANDYS-LUMSDAINE; 5,910 employees.

TRADE UNIONS

Central Organization of Trade Unions (Kenya) (COTU): Solidarity Bldg, Digo Rd, POB 13000, Nairobi; tel. (20) 6761375; fax (20) 6762695; e-mail info@cotu-kenya.org; internet www.cotu-kenya.org; f. 1965 as the sole trade union fed.; Chair. RAJABU W. MWONDI; Sec.-Gen. FRANCIS ATWOLI.

Amalgamated Union of Kenya Metalworkers: Avon House, Mfangano St, POB 73651, Nairobi; tel. (20) 211060; e-mail aukmw@clubinternetk.com; Gen. Sec. MAERO TINDI.

Bakers', Confectionery Manufacturing and Allied Workers' Union (Kenya): Lengo House, 3rd Floor, Room 20, Tom Mboya St, opposite Gill House, POB 57751, 00200 Nairobi; tel. (20) 330275; fax (20) 222735; e-mail bakers@form-net.com.

Communication Workers' Union of Kenya: Hermes House, Tom Mboya St, POB 48155, Nairobi; tel. (20) 219345; e-mail cowuk@clubinternet.com.

Dockworkers' Union (DWU): Dockers House, Kenyatta Ave, POB 98207, Mombasa; tel. (41) 2491974; f. 1954; Gen. Sec. SIMON SANG.

Kenya Airline Pilots' Association: KALPA House, off Airport North Rd, POB 57505, 00200 Nairobi; tel. (20) 820354; fax (20) 820410; internet www.kalpa.co.ke.

Kenya Building, Construction, Timber, Furniture and Allied Industries Employees' Union: Munshiram Bldg, POB 49628, 00100 Nairobi; tel. (20) 2223434; fax (20) 2691296; e-mail kbtfaie@yahoo.com; Gen. Sec. FRANCIS KARIMI MURAGE.

Kenya Chemical and Allied Workers' Union: Hermes House, Tom Mboya St, POB 73820, Nairobi; tel. (20) 249101; Gen. Sec. WERE DIBI OGUTO.

Kenya Electrical Trades Allied Workers' Union: Aqua Plaza, Murang'a Rd, POB 47060, Nairobi; tel. (20) 3752087; e-mail ketawuhq@todays.co.ke.

Kenya Engineering Workers' Union: Simla House, Tom Mboya St, POB 73987, Nairobi; tel. (20) 311168; Gen. Sec. JUSTUS MULEI.

Kenya Game Hunting and Safari Workers' Union: Comfood Bldg, Kilome Rd, POB 47509, Nairobi; tel. (20) 25049; Gen. Sec. J. M. NDOLO.

Kenya Jockey and Betting Workers' Union: Kirim and Sons Bldg, 3rd Floor, POB 55094, Nairobi; tel. (20) 332120.

Kenya Local Government Workers' Union: Dundee House, Country Rd, POB 55827, Nairobi; tel. (20) 217213; Gen. Sec. WASIKE NDOMBI.

Kenya Petroleum Oil Workers' Union (KPOWU): KCB Bldg, 4th Floor, Jogoo Rd, POB 10376, Nairobi; tel. (20) 55549; Gen. Sec. JACOB OCHINO.

Kenya Plantation and Agricultural Workers' Union: Co-operative House, Kenyatta St, POB 1161, 20100 Nakuru; tel. and fax (51) 2212310; e-mail kpawu@africaonline.co.ke; Gen. Sec. FRANCIS ATWOLI.

Kenya Quarry and Mine Workers' Union: Coffee Plaza, Exchange Line Off Hailesellasie Ave, POB 48125, Nairobi; tel. (20) 229774; f. 1961; Gen. Sec. WAFULA WA MUSAMIA.

Kenya Railway Workers' Union (KRWU): RAHU House, Mfangano St, POB 72029, Nairobi; tel. (20) 340302; f. 1952; Nat. Chair. FRANCIS O'LORE; Sec.-Gen. JOHN T. CHUMO.

Kenya Scientific Research, International Technical and Allied Institutions Workers' Union: Ngumba House, Tom Mboya St, POB 55094, Nairobi; tel. (20) 215713; Sec.-Gen. FRANCIS D. KIRUBI.

Kenya Shipping, Clearing and Warehouse Workers' Union: Yusuf Ali Bldg, 4th Floor, POB 84067, Mombasa; tel. (11) 312000.

Kenya Shoe and Leather Workers' Union: NACICO Plaza, 3rd Floor, POB 49629, Nairobi; tel. (20) 252788; Gen. Sec. JAMES AWICH.

Kenya Union of Commercial, Food and Allied Workers: Comfood Bldg, POB 2628, 00100 Nairobi; tel. (20) 245054; fax (20) 313118; e-mail info@kucfaw.org; Sec.-Gen. HANNINGTON OKOTH KOROMBO.

Kenya Union of Domestic, Hotel, Educational Institutions, Hospitals and Allied Workers (KUDHEIHA): Sonalux House, 4th Floor, POB 41763, 00100 Nairobi; tel. (20) 241509; fax (20) 243806; e-mail kudheihaworkers@hotmail.com; f. 1952; workers; Sec.-Gen. ALBERT NJERU.

Kenyan Union of Entertainment and Music Industry Employees: Coffee Plaza, 4th Floor, POB 8305, Nairobi; tel. (20) 243249.

Kenya Union of Journalists: POB 47035, 00100 Nairobi; tel. (20) 250888; fax (20) 250880; e-mail info@kujkenya.org; f. 1962; Gen. Sec. and CEO ERIC ORINA; Chair. TERVIL OKOKO.

Kenya Union of Printing, Publishing, Paper Manufacturers and Allied Workers: Meru South House, 5th Floor, Tom Mboya St, POB 72358, Nairobi; tel. (20) 215981; e-mail kupripupa04@yahoo.com; Gen. Sec. JOHN BOSCO.

Kenya Union of Sugar Plantation Workers: POB 19019, Kisumu; tel. (57) 2021595; e-mail kuspw@swiftkisumu.com; Gen. Sec. FRANCIS BUSHURU WANGARA.

National Seamen's Union of Kenya: Mombasa; tel. (11) 312106; Gen. Sec. I. S. ABDALLAH MWARUA.

Transport and Allied Workers' Union: NACICO Plaza, 3rd Floor, POB 45171, Nairobi; tel. (20) 545317; Gen. Sec. JULIAS MALII.

Independent Union

Kenya National Union of Teachers: POB 30407, 00100 Nairobi; tel. (20) 2220387; fax (20) 2222701; e-mail knut@nbnet.co.ke; internet www.knut.or.ke; f. 1957; Sec.-Gen. DAVID OKUTAH OSIANY.

Transport

RAILWAYS

In 2004 there were some 1,920 km of track open for traffic. In 2006 the Rift Valley Railways consortium assumed management of the Kenya Railways Corpn. In 2009 plans were announced to construct a railway line connecting Mombasa with Malaba, with a possible extension to Kampala, Uganda. The project was expected to start in late 2011 and be completed in 2016. In 2010 a new railway project was under way to connect Jomo Kenyatta International Airport (JKIA) with Embakasi and the Nairobi city centre to relieve congestion on the road system. In 2011 plans were announced to construct a railway line linking the proposed port of Lamu with oil fields in South Sudan and eventually with Ethiopia. Construction work on the project began in 2012.

Kenya Railways Corpn: POB 30121, Nairobi; tel. (20) 221211; fax (20) 224156; internet www.krc.co.ke; f. 1977; management of operations assumed by Rift Valley Railways consortium in Nov. 2006; Chair. Gen. (retd) JEREMIAH KIANGA; Man. Dir NDUVA MULI.

ROADS

At the end of 2004 there were an estimated 63,265 km of classified roads, of which 6,527 km were main roads and 18,885 km were secondary roads. Only an estimated 14.1% of road surfaces were paved. An all-weather road links Nairobi to Addis Ababa, in Ethiopia, and there is a 590-km road link between Kitale (Kenya) and Juba (South Sudan). The rehabilitation of the important internal road link between Nairobi and Mombasa (funded by a US $165m. loan from the World Bank) was undertaken during the late 1990s.

Akamba Public Road Services: Industrial Area, POB 40322, Nairobi; tel. (20) 556062; fax (20) 559885; e-mail info@akambabus.com; internet www.akambabus.com; operates bus services from Nairobi to all major towns in Kenya and to some major towns in Uganda and Tanzania.

East African Road Services Ltd: Nairobi; tel. (20) 764622; f. 1947; operates bus services from Nairobi to all major towns in Kenya; Chair. S. H. NATHOO.

Kenya Bus Service Management Ltd: Utali Lane, View Park Towers, 10th Floor, Rm 1010, POB 41001, 00100 Nairobi; tel. (20) 2223235; fax (20) 2223110; e-mail info@kenyabus.net; internet kenyabus.net; promotes and develops transport enterprises; Man. Dir EDWINS MUKABANAH.

Kenya Roads Board: Kenya Re Towers, 3rd Floor, Ragati Rd, Upper Hill, POB 73718, Nairobi; tel. (20) 722865; internet www.krb.go.ke; f. 2000 to co-ordinate maintenance, rehabilitation and devt of the road network; Chair. ALFRED JUMA.

Kenya National Highways Authority (KeNHA): Blue Shield Towers, Hospital Rd, Upper Hill, POB 49712, 00100 Nairobi; tel. (20) 8013842; e-mail info@kenha.co.ke; internet www.kenha.co.ke; Chair. HANNAH W. MURIITHI; Dir-Gen. Eng. M.O. KIDENDA.

Kenya Rural Roads Authority: Blue Shield Towers, 6th Floor, Hospital Rd, Upperhill, POB 48151, 00100 Nairobi; tel. (20) 2710464; e-mail kerra@roadsnet.go.ke; internet www.kerra.go.ke; Dir-Gen. Eng. MWANGI MAINGI.

Kenya Urban Roads Authority: 2nd Floor, IKM Place, 5th Ngong Ave, POB 41727, 00100 Nairobi; tel. (20) 8013844; e-mail info@kura.go.ke; internet www.kura.go.ke; Chair. Prof. Eng. SIXTUS K. MWEA; Dir-Gen. Eng. JOSEPH NKADAYO.

SHIPPING

The major international seaport of Mombasa has 16 deep-water berths, with a total length of 3,044 m, and facilities for the off-loading of bulk carriers, tankers and container vessels. Kenyan ports handled some 16.4m. metric tons of cargo in 2008. In December 2009 the Kenyan merchant fleet comprised 106 vessels with a total displacement of 32,800 grt. In 2011 there were plans for the construction of a second international port at Lamu.

Kenya Maritime Authority: White House, Moi Ave, Mombasa; tel. (41) 2318398; fax (41) 2318397; e-mail info@maritimeauthority.co.ke; internet www.maritimeauthority.co.ke; f. 2004; regulates, co-ordinates and oversees maritime affairs; Chair. Col. JOSEPH NGURU; Dir-Gen. NANCY W. KARIGITH.

Kenya Ports Authority: POB 95009, Mombasa; tel. (41) 2112999; fax (41) 311867; internet www.kpa.co.ke; f. 1978; sole operator of coastal port facilities; also operates two inland container depots at Nairobi and Kisumu; Chair. SHUKRI BARAMADI; Man. Dir JAMES MLEWA.

Inchcape Shipping Services Kenya Ltd: Inchcape House, Archbishop Makarios Cl., off Moi Ave, POB 90194, 80100 Mombasa; tel. (41) 2314245; fax (41) 2314662; e-mail mail@iss-shipping.com; internet www.iss-shipping.com; covers all ports in Kenya and Tanzania; Man. Dir DAVID MACKAY.

Mackenzie Maritime Ltd: Maritime Centre, Archbishop Makarios Close, POB 90120, Mombasa; tel. (11) 221273; fax (11) 316260; e-mail mml@africaonline.co.ke; shipping agents; Man. Dir M. M. BROWN.

Marship Ltd: Mombasa; tel. (11) 314705; fax (11) 316654; f. 1986; shipbrokers, ship management and chartering agents; Man. Dir MICHELE ESPOSITO.

Mitchell Cotts Kenya Ltd: Voi St, Shimanzi, POB 42485, 80100 Mombasa; tel. (20) 2315780; fax (20) 2226181; e-mail sales@mitchellcotts.co.ke; internet www.mitchellcottskenya.com; f. 1926; transport and shipping agents; freight handling and distribution; warehousing; Man. Dir DANIEL TANUI.

Motaku Shipping Agencies Ltd: Motaku House, Tangana Rd, POB 80419, 80100 Mombasa; tel. (41) 2229065; fax (41) 2220777; e-mail motaku@motakushipping.com; f. 1977; ship managers and shipping agents, freight broker and charter; Man. Dir KARIM KUDRATI.

PIL (Kenya) Ltd: Liberty Plaza, Mombasa Rd, POB 40109, Nairobi; tel. (20) 825082; fax (20) 821086; e-mail admin@nbo.pilship.com; internet www.pilship.com.

Shipmarc Ltd: POB 99553, Mombasa; tel. (41) 229241; fax (41) 221390; e-mail info@shipmarckenya.com.

Southern Line Ltd: POB 90102, 80107 Mombasa; tel. (11) 229241; fax (11) 221390; e-mail shipmarc@africaonline.co.ke; operating dry cargo and tanker vessels between East African ports, Red Sea ports, the Persian (Arabian) Gulf and Indian Ocean islands.

Spanfreight Shipping Ltd: Cannon Towers, Moi Ave, POB 99760, Mombasa; tel. (11) 315623; fax (11) 312092; e-mail a23ke464@gncomtext.com; Exec. Dir DILIPKUMAR AMRITLAL SHAH.

CIVIL AVIATION

Kenya has four major international airports: Jomo Kenyatta International Airport (JKIA), in south-eastern Nairobi, Moi International Airport, at Mombasa, Eldoret International Airport, in Eldoret, and Kisumu International Airport, at Kisumu. Wilson Airport, in south-western Nairobi, and the airport at Malindi handle internal flights. Kenya also has about 250 smaller airfields.

Kenya Airports Authority: Jomo Kenyatta International Airport, POB 19001, Nairobi; tel. (20) 825400; fax (20) 822300; e-mail info@kenyaairports.co.ke; internet www.kenyaairports.co.ke; f. 1991; state-owned; responsible for the provision, management and operation of all airports and private airstrips; Man. Dir GEORGE MUHOHO.

Aero Kenya: Shelter Afrique House, Mamlaka Rd, Nairobi; tel. (20) 2719091; fax (20) 2719264; e-mail info@aerokenya.com; f. 1997; operates domestic charter and schedule services; Man. Dir Capt. CHARLES K. MUTHAMA.

African Express Airways: Airport North Rd, Jomo Kenyatta International Airport, POB 19202, 00501 Nairobi; tel. (20) 2014746; fax (20) 2049888; e-mail afex@africanexpress.co.ke; internet www.africanexpress.co.ke.

Airkenya Express Ltd: Wilson Airport, POB 30357, 00100 Nairobi; tel. (20) 605745; fax (20) 602951; e-mail info@airkenya.com; internet www.airkenya.com; f. 1985; operates internal scheduled and charter passenger services; Gen. Man. DINO BISLETI.

Astral Aviation: 1st Floor, Mechanised Freight Terminal, Specialised Freight Rd, 1st Ave, Jomo Kenyatta International Airport, POB 594, 00606 Nairobi; tel. (20) 827222; fax (20) 827243; e-mail info@astral-aviation.com; internet www.astral-aviation.com; f. 2001; cargo services; CEO SANJEEV S. GADHIA.

Blue Bird Aviation Ltd: Wilson Airport, Langata Rd, POB 52382, Nairobi; tel. (20) 602338; fax (20) 602337.

Eagle Aviation (African Eagle): POB 93926, Mombasa; tel. (11) 434502; fax (11) 434249; e-mail eaglemsa@africaonline.co.ke; f. 1986; scheduled regional and domestic passenger and cargo services; Chair. RAJA TANUJ; CEO Capt. KIRAN PATEL.

Five Forty Aviation Ltd (fly540.com): ABC Pl. Westlands, POB 10293, Nairobi; tel. (20) 4453252; fax (20) 4453257; e-mail info@fly540.com; internet www.fly540.com; f. 2006; low-cost airline operating domestic and regional flights; COO NEIL STEFFEN.

Jetlink Express: Unit 3, Jomo Kenyatta International Airport, Nairobi; tel. (20) 827915; e-mail customercare@jetlink.co.ke; internet www.jetlink.co.ke; f. 2006; provides internal services and also operates flights to Juba (South Sudan), Goma (DRC) and Kigali (Rwanda); Man. Dir and CEO Capt. ELLY ALUVALE.

Kenya Airways Ltd (KQ): Airport North Road, Jomo Kenyatta International Airport, POB 19142, Nairobi; tel. (20) 6422000; fax (20) 823488; e-mail contact@kenya-airways.com; internet www.kenya-airways.com; f. 1977; in private sector ownership since 1996; passenger services to Africa, Asia, Europe and Middle East; freight services to Europe; internal services from Nairobi to Kisumu, Mombasa and Malindi; also operates a freight subsidiary; Chair. EVANSON MWANIKI; Man. Dir and CEO TITUS NAIKUNI.

OneJetOne Airways Kenya Ltd: Mombasa Rd, POB 47969, Nairobi; internet www.onejetone.com; f. 2010; expected to commence operations in late 2011, but at March 2012 the company had still not commenced operating; CEO ARJUN RUZAIK.

CIVIL AVIATION AUTHORITY

Kenya Civil Aviation Authority: Jomo Kenyatta International Airport, POB 30163, 00100 Nairobi; tel. (20) 827470; fax (20) 822300; e-mail info@kcaa.or.ke; internet www.kcaa.or.ke; f. 2002; regulatory and advisory services for air navigation; Chair. KEVIN KARIUKI; Dir-Gen. HILARY KIOKO.

Tourism

Kenya's main attractions for visitors are its wildlife, with 25 National Parks and 23 game reserves, the Indian Ocean coast and an equable year-round climate. In 2011 there were an estimated 1.8m. foreign visitors. Earnings from the sector totalled an estimated US $844m. (excluding passenger transport) in that year.

Kenya Tourism Board: Kenya-Re Towers, Ragati Rd, POB 30630, 00100 Nairobi; tel. (20) 271126; fax (20) 2719925; e-mail info@kenyatourism.org; internet www.magicalkenya.com; f. 1997; promotes Kenya as a tourist destination, monitors the standard of tourist facilities.

Kenya Tourist Development Corpn: Utalii House, 11th Floor, Uhuru Highway, POB 42013, Nairobi; tel. (20) 2229751; fax (20) 2227817; e-mail info@ktdc.co.ke; internet www.ktdc.co.ke; f. 1965; Chair. CHARLES WACHIRA NGUNDO; Man. Dir OBONDO KAJUMBI.

Defence

As assessed at November 2011, Kenya's armed forces numbered 24,120, comprising an army of 20,000, an air force of 2,500 and a navy of 1,620. Military service is voluntary. The paramilitary police general service unit was 5,000 strong. In 2011 a total of 2,416 troops were stationed abroad, of which 34 were observers.

Defence Expenditure: Budgeted at Ks. 58,400m. for 2012.

Commander-in-Chief of the Armed Forces: Pres. MWAI KIBAKI.

Chief of General Staff: Gen. JULIUS WAWERU KARANGI.

Army Commander: Lt-Gen. JOHN KASAON.

Air Force Commander: Maj.-Gen. JOFF OTIENO.

Navy Commander: Brig.-Gen. NGEWA MUKALA.

Education

The Government provides, or assists in the provision of, schools. In 2007/08 enrolment at pre-primary level was 26% (26% of boys; 26% of girls). Primary education, which is compulsory, is provided free of charge. The education system involves eight years of primary education (beginning at six years of age), four years at secondary school and four years of university education. According to UNESCO estimates, in 2008/09 enrolment at primary schools included 83% of pupils in the relevant age-group (males 82%; females 83%), while enrolment at secondary schools included 50% of children in the relevant age-group (males 52%; females 49%). Tertiary enrolment in 2001/02 included just 3% of those in the relevant age-group (4% males; 2% females), according to UNESCO estimates. There are six state universities and seven private universities. In 2008/09 a total of 167,983 students were enrolled in higher education. In 2004 spending on education represented 29.2% of total budgetary expenditure.

Bibliography

Anguka, J. *Absolute Power: The Ouko Murder Mystery*. London, Pen Press Publishers Ltd, 1998.

arap Moi, D. T. *Kenya African Nationalism: Nyayo Philosophy and Principles*. London, Macmillan, 1986.

Azam, J.-P., and Daubrée, C. *Bypassing the State: Economic Growth in Kenya, 1964–1990*. Paris, OECD, 1997.

Bailey, J. *Kenya: The National Epic*. Nairobi, East African Education Publishers, 1993.

Bates, R. H. *Beyond the Miracle of the Market: The Political Economy of Agrarian Development in Kenya*. (2nd edn) Cambridge, Cambridge University Press, 2005.

Booth, K. M. *Local Women, Global Science: Fighting AIDS in Kenya*. Bloomington, IN, Indiana University Press, 2003.

Branch, D. *Kenya: Between Hope and Despair, 1963-2011*. New Haven, CT, Yale University Press, 2011

Central Bank of Kenya. *Kenya: Land of Opportunity*. Nairobi, Central Bank of Kenya, 1991.

Clough, M. S. *Mau Mau Memoirs: History, Memory and Politics*. Boulder, CO, Lynne Rienner Publishers, 1998.

Cohen, D. W., and Odhiambo, E. S. A. *Burying SM: The Politics of Knowledge and the Sociology of Power in Africa*. London, James Currey, 1992.

Coughlin, P., and Gerrishon, K. I. (Eds). *Kenya's Industrialization Dilemma*. (Contains industrial studies carried out under the Industrial Research Project.) Nairobi, Kenyan Heinemann, 1991.

Eshiwani, G. S. *Education in Kenya since Independence*. Nairobi, East African Educational Publishers, 1993.

Faulkner, C. *A Two Year Wonder: The Kenya Police 1953–1955*. Elgin, Librario Publishing Ltd, 2005.

Fogken, D., and Tellegen, W. *Tied to the Land: Living Conditions of Labourers on Large Farms in Trans-Nzoia District, Kenya*. Leiden, African Studies Centre, 1995.

Gibbon, P. (Ed.). *Markets, Civil Society and Democracy in Kenya*. Uppsala, Nordic Africa Institute, 1995.

Govt of Kenya. *Economic Reforms for 1996–1998: The Policy Framework Paper*. Nairobi, Govt Printing Press, 1996.

Haugerud, A. *The Culture of Politics in Modern Kenya*. Cambridge, Cambridge University Press, 1995.

Himbara, D. *Kenyan Capitalists, the State and Development*. Boulder, CO, Lynne Rienner Publishers, 1993.

Hoorweg, J., Fogken, D., and Klaver, W. *Seasons and Nutrition at the Kenya Coast*. Brookfield, VT, Ashgate Publishing, 1996.

Hornsby, C. *Kenya: A History Since Independence*. London, I.B. Tauris, 2011.

Hughes, L. *Moving the Maasai: A Colonial Misadventure*. Basingstoke, Palgrave Macmillan, 2006.

Karp, I. *Fields of Change Among the Iteso of Kenya* (Routledge Library Editions: Anthropology and Ethnography). London, Routledge, 2004.

Kenyatta, J. *Facing Mount Kenya*. London, Heinemann, 1979.

Kimenyi, M. S. (Ed.), *et al. Restarting and Sustaining Economic Growth and Development in Africa: The Case of Kenya* (Contemporary Perspectives on Developing Societies). Brookfield, VT, Ashgate Publishing, 2003.

King, K. *Jua Kali Kenya: Change and Development in an Informal Economy, 1970–1995*. Athens, OH, Ohio University Press, 1996.

Knighton, B. *Religion and Politics in Kenya*. Basingstoke, Palgrave Macmillan, 2009.

Kyle, K. *The Politics of the Independence of Kenya*. London and Basingstoke, Palgrave, 1999.

Leakey, L. *Defeating Mau Mau* (Routledge Library Editions: Anthropology & Ethnography). London, Routledge, 2004.

Lewis, J. *Empire State-Building: War and Welfare in Kenya, 1925–52*. Athens, OH, Ohio University Press, 2001.

Little, P. D. *The Elusive Granary: Herder, Farmer and State in Northern Kenya*. Cambridge, Cambridge University Press, 1992.

Lovatt Smith, D. *Kenya, the Kikuyu and Mau Mau*. Mawenzi Books, 2005.

Lynch, G. *I Say to You: Ethnic Politics and the Kalenjin in Kenya*. Chicago, IL, University of Chicago Press, 2011.

Malobe, W. O. *Mau Mau and Kenya: An Analysis of a Peasant Revolt*. Bloomington, IN, Indiana University Press, 1993.

Miller, N., and Yeager, R. *Kenya: The Quest for Prosperity*. Boulder, CO, Westview Press, 1994.

Morton, A. *Moi: The Making of an African Statesman*. London, Michael O'Mara Books, 1998.

Murunga, G. R., and Nasong'o, S. W. (Eds). *Kenya: The Struggle for Democracy*. London, Zed Books, 2007.

Mwau, G., and Handa, J. *Rational Economic Decisions and the Current Account in Kenya*. Aldershot, Avebury, 1995.

Ndegwa, P. *Development and Employment in Kenya: A Strategy for the Transformation of the Economy; Report of the Presidential Committee on Employment*. Southwell, Leishman and Taussig, 1991.

Nowrojee, B. *Divide and Rule: State-Sponsored Ethnic Violence in Kenya*. Washington, DC, Human Rights Watch and Africa Watch, 1993.

Ochieng, W. R., and Maxon, R. M. *An Economic History of Kenya*. Nairobi, East African Educational Publishers, 1992.

Odhiambo, E. S. *Mau Mau and Nationhood*. Athens, OH, Ohio University Press, 2003.

Ogot, B. A., and Ochieng, W. R. (Eds). *Decolonization and Independence in Kenya, 1940–1993*. London, James Currey, 1995.

Okanja, O. *Kenya at Forty-five: 1963-2008 (Economic Performance, Problems and Prospects)*. Twickenham, Athena Press, 2010.

Otiende, J. E., Wamahiu, S. P., and Karugu, A. M. *Education and Development in Kenya: An Historical Perspective*. Nairobi, Oxford University Press, 1992.

Owino, J. *Kenya into the 21st Century*. London, Minerva Press, 2001.

Paarlberg, R. L. *The Politics of Precaution*. Baltimore, MD, Johns Hopkins University Press, 2001.

Pearson, S., *et al. Agricultural Policy in Kenya*. Ithaca, NY, Cornell University Press, 1995.

Presley, C. A. *Kikuyu Women and Social Change in Kenya*. Boulder, CO, Westview Press, 1992.

Rotberg, R. I. (Ed.). *Kenya (Africa: Continent in the Balance Series)*. Broomall, PA, Mason Crest Publishers, 2005.

Sabar, G. *Church, State and Society in Kenya*. London, Frank Cass Publishers, 2001.

Somjee, S. *Material Culture of Kenya*. Nairobi, East African Educational Publications, 1993.

Spencer, P. *The Maasai of Matapato: A Study of Rituals of Rebellion*. London, Routledge, 2003.

The Samburu: A Study in Geocentracy. London, Routledge, 2003.

Thomas-Slayter, B., and Rocheleau, D. *Gender, Environment and Development in Kenya: A Grassroots Perspective*. Boulder, CO, Lynne Rienner, 1995.

Trench, C. C. *Men Who Ruled Kenya: The Kenya Administration 1892–1963*. London, Radcliffe Press, 1993.

wa Wamwere, K. *The People's Representative and the Tyrants: or, Kenya, Independence without Freedom*. Nairobi, New Concept Typesetters, 1993.

I Refuse to Die. New York, Seven Stories Press, 2004.

Widner, J. A. *The Rise of a Party State in Kenya: From 'Harambee' to 'Nyayo'*. Berkeley, CA, University of California Press, 1992.

Willis, J. *Mombasa, the Swahili and the Making of the Mijikenda*. New York, Oxford University Press, 1993.

LESOTHO

Physical and Social Geography

A. MacGREGOR HUTCHESON

PHYSICAL FEATURES

The Kingdom of Lesotho, a small, land-locked country of 30,355 sq km (11,720 sq miles), is enclosed on all sides by South Africa. It is situated at the highest part of the Drakensberg escarpment on the eastern rim of the South African plateau. About two-thirds of Lesotho is very mountainous. Elevations in the eastern half of the country are generally more than 2,440 m above sea-level, and in the north-east and along the eastern border they exceed 3,350 m. This is a region of very rugged relief, bleak climate and heavy annual rainfall (averaging 1,905 mm), where the headstreams of the Orange river have incised deep valleys. Westwards the land descends through a foothill zone of rolling country, at an altitude of 1,830 m–2,135 m, to Lesotho's main lowland area. This strip of land along the western border, part of the Highveld, averages 40 km in width and lies at an altitude of about 1,525 m. Annual rainfall averages in this region are 650 mm–750 mm, and climatic conditions are generally more pleasant. However, frost may occur throughout the country in winter, and hail is a summer hazard in all regions. The light, sandy soils that have developed on the Karoo sedimentaries of the western lowland compare unfavourably with the fertile black soils of the Stormberg basalt in the uplands. The temperate grasslands of the west also tend to be less fertile than the montane grasslands of the east.

POPULATION AND NATURAL RESOURCES

At the census of April 2006 the population was 1,872,721 (excluding absentee workers in South Africa), giving an average density of 61.7 inhabitants per sq km. The noticeable physical contrasts between east and west Lesotho are reflected in the distribution and density of the population. While large parts of the mountainous east (except for valleys) are sparsely populated, most of the fertile western strip, which carries some 70% of the population, has densities in excess of 200 inhabitants per sq km. Such population pressure, further aggravated by steady population growth, has resulted in: (i) the permanent settlement being pushed to higher levels (in places to 2,440 m) formerly used for summer grazing, and on to steep slopes, thus adding to the already serious national problem of soil erosion; (ii) an acute shortage of cultivable land and increased soil exhaustion, particularly in the west; (iii) land holdings that are too small to maintain the rural population; and (iv) the country's inability, in its current stage of development, to support all of its population, thus necessitating the migration of large numbers of workers to seek paid employment in South Africa. It was estimated in 1995 that some 25% of the adult male labour force were employed in South Africa, mainly in the mines. The number of Basotho employed in South Africa declined greatly in the late 1990s and 2000s. Lesotho's economy depends heavily on their remitted earnings, which had fallen considerably in the late 2000s, and a migratory labour system on this scale has grave social, economic and political implications for the country.

Lesotho's long-term development prospects largely rely upon the achievement of optimum use of its soil and water resources. About 11% of the country is cultivable and, since virtually all of this is already cultivated, only more productive use of the land can make Lesotho self-sufficient in food (20% of domestic needs are currently imported from South Africa). The high relief produces natural grasslands, well suited for a viable livestock industry, but this has been hindered through inadequate pasture management, excessive numbers of low-quality animals and disease. Lesotho and South Africa are jointly implementing the Lesotho Highlands Water Project (see Economy), which will provide employment for thousands of Basotho and greatly improve Lesotho's infrastructure. Reserves of diamonds have been identified in the mountainous north-east, and there are small surface workings at Lemphane, Liquobong and Kao. Uranium deposits have been located near Teyateyaneng in the north-west, but their exploitation must await a sustained improvement in world prices. The search for other minerals continues.

Recent History

CHRISTOPHER SAUNDERS

Lesotho, formerly known as Basutoland, became a British protectorate in 1868 at the request of the Basotho paramount chief, Moshoeshoe I, in the face of Boer expansionism. Basutoland was annexed to Cape Colony (now part of South Africa) in 1871, but became a separate British colony in 1884, and was administered as one of the High Commission territories in southern Africa. Unlike the other territories—Bechuanaland (now Botswana) and the protectorate of Swaziland—Basutoland was entirely surrounded by South African territory.

Modern party politics began in 1952 with the founding of the Basutoland Congress Party (BCP, renamed the Basotho Congress Party in 1966) by Dr Ntsu Mokhehle. Basutoland's first general election, held on the basis of universal adult suffrage, took place in April 1965. The majority of seats in the new Legislative Assembly were won by the Basutoland National Party (BNP, renamed the Basotho National Party at independence), a conservative group that had the support of the South African Government. The BNP's leader, Chief Leabua Jonathan, became Prime Minister, and Moshoeshoe II, the paramount chief, was recognized as King. Basutoland gained its independence, as the Kingdom of Lesotho, on 4 October 1966.

When in the first post-independence general election, held in January 1970, the BCP appeared to have won a majority of seats in the National Assembly, Chief Jonathan declared a state of emergency, suspended the Constitution and arrested Mokhehle and other leaders of the BCP. The election was annulled, and the country effectively passed under the Prime Minister's control. King Moshoeshoe went briefly into exile, but returned in December after agreeing to take no part in politics. The BCP split into an 'internal' faction, whose members were acquiescent in the political status quo, and an 'external' faction, whose members were prepared to take up arms to overthrow Jonathan: the latter group was led by Mokhehle after he fled the country in 1974, following a coup attempt.

The Jonathan regime was initially supported by South Africa, but as Jonathan's support among the Basotho, most of whom disliked his pro-South African policies, declined, he became increasingly critical of the South African Government, winning international credit for opposing its policy of apartheid. In November 1974 he revived Lesotho's claim to 'conquered territory' in South Africa's Orange Free State (OFS—now the Free State Province). The vigorous anti-South African stance that Lesotho took at the UN and the Organization of African Unity (OAU, now the African Union) in the first half of 1975 increased tensions between the two countries, as did Lesotho's refusal to recognize South Africa's proclamation of an 'independent' Transkei in October 1976. Jonathan did meet the South African Prime Minister, P. W. Botha, in August 1980, the first meeting of the leaders of the two countries since 1967, and accepted a preliminary agreement on the Lesotho Highlands Water Project (LHWP—see Economy), providing for Lesotho to supply water to South Africa, but he openly criticized apartheid, and declared his support for the prohibited African National Congress of South Africa (ANC). Lesotho's reluctance to sign a joint non-aggression pact with South Africa caused further friction between the two countries. In April 1983 Jonathan announced that Lesotho was effectively in a state of war with South Africa. South Africa responded by applying strict border controls on its main frontier with Lesotho, resulting in food shortages. The border controls were eased in June, after a meeting between both countries in which they agreed to curb cross-border guerrilla infiltration, but were reimposed in July. Further talks with South Africa followed and, soon afterwards, Lesotho declared that it had received an ultimatum from the republic, either to expel some 3,000 refugees or to face the economic consequences. In September two groups of refugees left the country. Relations with South Africa remained at a low ebb for most of 1984. However, after talks between the two countries in April 1985, and an announcement by Lesotho that the ANC had agreed to withdraw completely from its territory, relations improved slightly. On 1 January 1986, however, South Africa blockaded its border with Lesotho, impeding access to vital supplies of food and fuel. Two weeks later troops of the Lesotho paramilitary force, led by Maj.-Gen. Justin Lekhanya, surrounded government buildings. On 20 January, having returned from 'security consultations' in South Africa, Lekhanya, together with Maj.-Gen. S. K. Molapo, the commander of the security forces, and S. R. Matela, the chief of police, deposed the Jonathan Government.

MILITARY RULE, 1986–93

The new regime established a Military Council, headed by Lekhanya and including senior officers of the paramilitary force (which subsequently became the Royal Lesotho Defence Force—RLDF). The National Assembly was dissolved, and all executive and legislative powers were vested in the King, who acted on the advice of the Military Council. One week after the coup some 60 members of the ANC were deported from Lesotho, and the South African blockade was lifted. The main opposition groups initially welcomed the military takeover, although Mokhehle's wing of the BCP demanded the immediate restoration of the 1966 Constitution and the holding of free elections within six months. All formal political activity was, however, suspended by the Military Council in March 1986.

In April 1988 the five main opposition parties appealed to the OAU, the Commonwealth and the South African Government to restore civilian rule. In the following month, after 14 years of exile, Mokhehle was allowed to return to Lesotho for peace talks, together with other members of the BCP. It was widely believed that the South African Government had played a part in promoting this reconciliation. In 1989 the BCP's armed wing was reported to have been disbanded, and by 1990 the two factions of the BCP had reunited under the leadership of Mokhehle.

In early 1990 conflict developed between Lekhanya and King Moshoeshoe. Following the King's refusal to approve changes made by Lekhanya to the Military Council, Lekhanya suspended his executive and legislative powers. Lekhanya promised that a return to civilian government would take place in 1992 and, to reassure business interests, a programme for privatizing state enterprises was announced. In March 1990 the Military Council assumed the executive and legislative powers that had been vested in the King, and Moshoeshoe (who remained head of state) went into exile in the United Kingdom.

Lekhanya invited King Moshoeshoe to return from exile in October 1990, but the King stated that he would only do so if military rule was ended and an interim government formed by representatives of all political parties, pending the restoration of the 1966 Constitution and the holding of an internationally supervised general election. On 6 November Lekhanya promulgated an order deposing the King with immediate effect, and Lesotho's 22 principal chiefs elected Moshoeshoe's eldest son, Prince Bereng Seeisa, as the new King. He succeeded to the throne on 12 November, as King Letsie III, having undertaken not to involve himself in the political life of the country.

On 30 April 1991 Lekhanya was removed as Chairman of the Military Council in a coup led by Col (later Maj.-Gen.) Elias Phitsoane Ramaema, a member of the Military Council. Ramaema soon announced the repeal of the law that had banned party political activity in 1986, and by July ta new Constitution had been drafted. Following talks in the United Kingdom with Ramaema, under the auspices of the Secretary-General of the Commonwealth, former King Moshoeshoe returned to Lesotho in July 1992. A general election, returning Lesotho to democracy, finally took place on 27 March 1993.

THE MOKHEHLE GOVERNMENT AND THE 'ROYAL COUP'

The BCP swept to power in that election, winning all 65 seats in the new National Assembly. On 2 April 1993 Mokhehle was sworn in as Prime Minister, and King Letsie swore allegiance to the new Constitution. Although independent local and international observers pronounced the election to be broadly free and fair, the BNP, which had the support of members of the former military regime, alleged widespread irregularities and refused to accept the results.

In July 1994 Mokhehle appointed a commission of inquiry into the circumstances surrounding the dethronement of former King Moshoeshoe II in 1990. After petitioning the High Court to abolish the commission on the grounds of bias on the part of its members, King Letsie dissolved Parliament, dismissed the Mokhehle Government and suspended sections of the Constitution, citing 'popular dissatisfaction' with the BCP administration. A provisional government was to be established, pending a general election, which was to be organized by an independent commission. A prominent human rights lawyer, Hae Phoofolo, was appointed Chairman of the transitional Council of Ministers, and announced that his primary concern was to amend the Constitution to enable the restoration of Moshoeshoe as monarch. In the mean time, Letsie acted as legislative and executive head of state.

The suspension of constitutional government was widely condemned outside Lesotho. Several countries threatened economic sanctions, and the USA withdrew financial assistance. At negotiations between King Letsie and Mokhehle held in Pretoria, South Africa, in August 1994, Letsie was urged to reinstate all elected institutions. In September Letsie and Mokhehle signed an agreement, guaranteed by Botswana, South Africa and Zimbabwe, providing for the restoration of Moshoeshoe as reigning monarch, and for the immediate restitution of the elected organs of government; the commission of inquiry into Moshoeshoe's dethronement was to be abandoned; persons involved in the 'royal coup' were to be immune from prosecution; the political neutrality of the armed forces and public service was to be guaranteed; and consultations were to be undertaken with the expressed aim of broadening the democratic process.

On 25 January 1995 Moshoeshoe II was restored to the throne, following the voluntary abdication of Letsie III, who took the title of Crown Prince. When Moshoeshoe was killed in a motor accident in January 1996, the Crown Prince was formally elected by the College of Chiefs to succeed his father and returned to the throne, resuming the title King Letsie III, in February. Like his father, Letsie undertook not to involve the monarchy in any aspect of political life. His coronation took place on 31 October 1997 at a ceremony in the capital, Maseru.

In June 1997, following a protracted struggle between rival factions for control of the party, Mokhehle resigned from the

BCP and, with the support of a majority of BCP members in the National Assembly, formed a new political party, the Lesotho Congress for Democracy (LCD), to which he transferred executive power. At the LCD's annual conference, held in January 1998, Mokhehle resigned as leader, and was made honorary Life President of the party. (He died in January 1999.) In February 1998 Bethuel Pakalitha Mosisili, the Deputy Prime Minister, was elected to replace him as party leader.

THE 1998 GENERAL ELECTION AND SUBSEQUENT UNREST

Elections to an expanded National Assembly took place on 23 May 1998. The LCD secured 78 of the 80 seats, while the BNP won only one seat. Voting in the remaining constituency was postponed, owing to the death of a candidate. Despite the pronouncement of regional and international observers that the election had been fair, demonstrators in Maseru protested against the results and accused both the LCD and the Independent Electoral Commission (IEC) of irregularities. Although Mosisili was elected Prime Minister by the National Assembly, and a new Cabinet was appointed at the beginning of June, at the end of that month more than 200 defeated opposition candidates filed petitions in the High Court calling for the annulment of the election results and a re-examination of the ballot papers. In July, after the Court granted the complainants access to the relevant documentation, and evidence of irregularities began to emerge, anti-Government protests broke out in the capital. In August crowds besieged the royal palace and demanded that the King exercise his power to annul the elections and appoint a government of national unity. Letsie, however, declined to act.

As protests escalated in Maseru, the Southern African Development Community (SADC), under South African leadership, intervened. A commission was appointed under Pius Langa, the Deputy President of South Africa's Constitutional Court, to investigate the allegations of electoral fraud. When the report was eventually released, in September 1998, it stated that, while voting irregularities had occurred, they were insufficient to invalidate the results of the election. Meanwhile, influential elements within the Lesotho Defence Force (LDF, as the RLDF had been redesignated) openly declared their support for the opposition. Prime Minister Mosisili, fearing a possible collapse of law and order and an imminent military coup, sought assistance from SADC. South African troops arrived in late September, followed by a contingent from Botswana. 'Operation Boleas', as the military intervention was named, was poorly conducted and met considerable resistance from the LDF. There were 68 deaths, and extensive looting spread rapidly from Maseru to other towns, causing serious damage to the economy. Thousands of people fled into the countryside and to South Africa.

With the gradual restoration of calm and with South African mediation, an Interim Political Authority (IPA), representing the various parties, was formed to prepare for a new general election, which was to be held within 18 months. The remaining SADC troops were withdrawn in May 1999. The multi-party IPA, which was inaugurated in December 1998, rapidly became embroiled in controversy over arrangements for the proposed elections. The Government wished the existing voting system to remain, but the BNP (under the leadership of Lekhanya) demanded a system of full proportional representation, on the South African model. Following protracted negotiations, the issue was eventually referred to arbitration. In October 1999 a tribunal proposed a system combining both simple majority voting (for 80 seats) and proportional representation (for 50 new seats). This was accepted by the IPA and Government in December. However, when the draft legislation on the new electoral system was introduced to Parliament in February 2000, the LCD-dominated National Assembly rejected it, prompting the IPA to accuse the Government of reneging on its undertaking to abide by the tribunal's decision and the December accord.

The LCD subsequently proposed to the legislature that the country should retain the existing simple majority system, which had led to the 1998 violence, and which the opposition had rejected. The LCD-sponsored legislation was endorsed by the National Assembly, but rejected by the Senate, on the grounds that it differed from the electoral model approved by the IPA. Opposition parties urged the IPA to demand the dissolution of Parliament and the replacement of the LCD Government with one of national unity. The opposition accepted that a postponement of the elections was inevitable, but blamed the LCD and the National Assembly for stalling the process. Following international mediation, the opposition parties agreed to the LCD remaining in office, in return for assurances that the electoral system would be changed as soon as possible.

In May 2000 the IPA and the Government adopted a provisional electoral timetable; Mosisili announced that a general election would be held between March and May 2001, on the grounds that there was insufficient time to prepare for a poll in 2000. The IPA was to remain in existence until the results of the election were announced. In July 2000 the election date was provisionally set for 26 May 2001, although legislation pertaining to a new voting system had still to be finalized and approved by Parliament. Political leaders remained divided over the proposed expansion of the National Assembly and the number of seats to be decided by simple majority voting and by proportional representation. The LCD now favoured 40 seats elected by proportional representation, and 80 by constituencies; this arrangement for the new 120-seat National Assembly was finally agreed by all parties and approved by Parliament in January 2002. Meanwhile, in September 2001 internal strife within the LCD prompted a group of deputies, led by Kelebone Maope, hitherto Deputy Prime Minister, to split from the party and establish a new organization, the Lesotho People's Congress (LPC), which was subsequently declared the main opposition party.

THE 2002 GENERAL ELECTION

The general election that took place on 25 May 2002 was contested by 19 parties. Voting was conducted peacefully, although there were a number of logistical problems, and polling had to be extended to a second day in a number of constituencies. The voting process was generally accepted as being free and fair by observers and a turn-out of some 68% was recorded. The ruling LCD won 54.9% of the valid votes cast and 77 of the 78 contested constituency seats (voting was postponed in two constituencies). The LPC gained the remaining contested seat and four of the 40 seats allocated by proportional representation. The BNP won 22.4% of the vote and secured 21 of the seats allocated by proportional representation.

The BNP leader, Lekhanya, demanded a forensic audit of the results, claiming that they had been manipulated. He refused to attend the ceremony at which Mosisili was sworn in as Prime Minister for another five-year term, and threatened to boycott the new National Assembly. However, there was no widespread support for his legal challenge to the election results, and he was persuaded that the BNP should participate in Parliament. Although the Government now enjoyed greater legitimacy than its predecessor, many weaknesses remained in the democratic process. Parliament sat for brief periods only, and with few effective deputies, and no portfolio committee system in place, opposition parties found it difficult to play a constructive political role. Mosisili himself was criticized for appointing relatives to his new Cabinet.

Mosisili identified three main challenges facing his new Government when it took office in June 2002. First, almost one-third of the adult population of Lesotho was estimated to be living with HIV/AIDS. Second, over 50% of the population was unemployed. Finally, there was a major food crisis, precipitated in part by the failure to keep sufficient reserves of grain. In response to a poor harvest and the high cost of importing maize, the Government declared a state of famine in April, hoping to attract foreign aid. By June the World Food Programme and FAO estimated that some 500,000 people, almost one-quarter of the kingdom's population, needed emergency food aid. All three crises intensified in the following years.

In March 2004 Mosisili and the Roman Catholic Archbishop of Lesotho took public HIV tests to try to increase awareness of the disease and encourage others to be tested. On World AIDS Day in 2005 the King launched a 'Know Your Status' campaign.

It offered confidential and voluntary HIV testing and counselling, and aimed to reach all households by the end of 2007. With an adult prevalence rate of 23.2% in a total population of 1.8m., an estimated 265,000 people were living with HIV, 50,000 of whom needed antiretroviral treatment. Although free testing and treatment was available at hospitals, by mid-2006 only 80,000 people had been tested, and fewer than 10,000 were receiving antiretrovirals. Nurses and doctors were in very short supply, and efforts to import medical staff were largely unsuccessful. By 2006 the country had about 100,000 AIDS orphans, and a growing number of street children were to be seen in urban areas. The impact of HIV/AIDS, combined with severe flooding in late 2011, forced many agricultural workers off the land. Unemployment, especially among the young, was very high, and over 40% of the population lived in extreme poverty. Lesotho ranked 160th out of 187 countries in the UN Development Programme's 2011 Human Development Index.

Meanwhile, the Prime Minister reorganized his Cabinet in November 2004, demoting the hitherto Minister of Home Affairs Thomas Thabane, regarded as a potential successor to Mosisili, to the position of Minister of Communications, Science and Technology. However, in October 2006 Thabane resigned from the Cabinet and the LCD, accusing the party of rampant corruption. Along with 17 other dissident LCD deputies, he formed a new party, the All Basotho Convention (ABC), which began attracting large crowds of supporters, particularly among younger people, at rallies in the urban areas. In response to this challenge, the Government announced that the parliamentary elections would be brought forward by three months, giving the electoral authorities little time to register new voters and preventing the ABC from organizing effectively. Fewer than 1m. people were registered in time for the elections. Wary of its now fragile legislative majority, and in response to the ABC allying itself with the Lesotho Workers' Party, the LCD proposed an electoral alliance with the smaller National Independent Party (NIP). The NIP leader, Anthony Manyeli, strongly opposed the idea, but the LCD made an agreement with his deputy, Tsibiso Motikoe and Manyeli was removed from the party. The alliances had the effect of subverting the spirit of the mixed electoral system, for it was supposed to ensure that votes cast for the ruling party via proportional representation would be discounted to ensure overall proportionality. Constituency members were allowed to cross the floor, but not those elected by proportional representation. If the LCD allied with another party, its majority would be less likely to be endangered by floor-crossing.

LEGISLATIVE ELECTIONS, 2007

In the legislative elections that took place on 17 February 2007, fewer than one-half of the registered voters cast their ballots. The LCD was re-elected for a third term, winning 61 of the 80 contested constituency seats, mainly in rural areas and the south. The ABC won 17 constituency seats, primarily in Maseru and other urban centres. Of the 40 seats allocated by proportional representation, the NIP was awarded 21, giving the LCD-NIP alliance control of 82 seats in the 120-member assembly. Meanwhile, Manyeli had obtained an order from the High Court overturning his ousting and the formation of the LCD-NIP alliance, although the Court of Appeal subsequently upheld the alliance. Following this judgment and with increasing discontent at the allocation of proportional representation seats, a coalition of opposition parties, including the ABC, called a national strike in March, which paralysed much of the country. The Government reacted by emphasizing that SADC and other observers had agreed that the election had been free and fair and that the courts had upheld the LCD-NIP alliance. After a series of armed attacks on ministers and their bodyguards, Mosisili imposed a curfew within the capital in June 2007, and met President Thabo Mbeki of South Africa to obtain promises of security assistance if required. Tensions continued, however, and in April 2009 armed men attacked Mosisili's residence in a failed assassination attempt. Government officials blamed the ABC for the attack, but did not produce any firm evidence to support their allegations. In May 2011 seven people were extradited from South Africa and charged with plotting to assassinate Mosisili.

Meanwhile, a mediation process set in motion after the 2007 legislative elections and led by the Christian Council of Lesotho and facilitators from SADC was concluded in early 2011. As part of an agreement on electoral reforms ahead of the May 2012 elections, new legislation was adopted enabling political parties to petition the High Court regarding the allocation of proportional representation seats, and according additional powers to the IEC. In April 2011 SADC announced that the Government, the opposition and the IEC had agreed that 'all the issues to the dialogue had been dealt with, thus paving the way for the next elections'.

Challenged by elements within the LCD opposed to his leadership, in February 2012 Mosisili, along with 43 other deputies, formed a new party, the Democratic Congress (DC). With the support of 44 members of the 120-member National Assembly, including the Speaker, Mosisili was able to survive a no confidence vote and remain as Prime Minister. The rump of the LCD became the main opposition party, led by former Minister of Communications, Science and Technology Mothejoa Metsing. The LCD sought support from the ABC, with limited success. Although the DC appealed to anti-Chinese sentiment and blamed Mosisili's former Assistant Minister of Trade, Industry, Co-operatives and Marketing, who remained in the LCD, for authorizing the establishment of so many Chinese retail and manufacturing businesses in Lesotho, the issue did not become a major source of contention, in part because Chinese companies had built a new parliament building and other public infrastructure.

THE DC REMOVED FROM GOVERNMENT

On 15 March 2012 King Letsie dissolved Parliament, in preparation for the upcoming legislative elections. The most significant challenge to Mosisili was believed to be from the ABC, but that party had been weakened by internal disputes. Although the election campaign proceeded peacefully, the country's single television channel, controlled by the Government, was accused of demonstrating bias towards the DC. Former Malawian President (Elson) Bakili Muluzi, who headed the Commonwealth election observer team, reported that he had obtained assurances that Mosisili would step down if he did not win, and that the army would not seek to influence the outcome. In the event, the elections, which took place on 26 May, were the closest in Lesotho's history, with the DC winning 48 of the 120 seats, but not an overall majority. This allowed Thabane's ABC (which secured 30 seats) and the smaller parties to form a coalition to oust Mosisili from power. The LCD, with 26 seats, and the BNP, with five, were the junior partners in the coalition. Thabane was sworn in as Prime Minister on 8 June and later that month King Letsie approved the nominations of the members of the Cabinet. Metsing was appointed Deputy Prime Minister and Minister of Local Government and Chieftainship Affairs and the LCD secured the stewardship of nine other ministerial portfolios including those of finance and foreign affairs and international relations.

RELATIONS WITH SOUTH AFRICA

Being entirely surrounded by South Africa, relations with that country remain a central issue for Lesotho. Only a few voices have appealed for the country to be incorporated into South Africa, however, in spite of the potential economic advantages of such a union, with most Basotho in favour of retaining their country's sovereignty.

Following the military coup of January 1986, Lesotho and South Africa agreed that neither country would allow its territory to be used for attacks on the other. In October of that year the treaty for the LHWP was signed by the two countries to generate hydroelectric power and to increase the supply of the Vaal river, which provided water to South Africa's industrial heartland. The Mohale and Katse dams, the first phase of the LHWP, were then built at a cost of US $4,000m. As South Africa moved towards democratic governance, it agreed to establish diplomatic relations with Lesotho at ambassadorial level in May 1992. Following the election of the ANC-dominated Government in 1994, relations became more cordial.

Following the SADC intervention of September 1998, South African influence in Lesotho increased. Many South African officials were sent to the mountain kingdom, and an intergovernmental liaison committee was established. In April 2001, during a state visit by President Mbeki, it was agreed to replace this committee with a joint bi-national commission at ministerial level, and in May 2002 the foreign ministers of the two countries signed an agreement on economic development and co-operation. This envisaged a number of joint projects, including the establishment of a Maloti-Drakensberg Trans-Frontier Conservation and Development programme. Prevention of cross-border crime remained an issue for the joint commission, but after the 2004 South African election the two countries agreed that those travelling across the border would no longer need a visa, only a passport.

The LHWP was by far the largest joint project between Lesotho and South Africa. Sections of Phase 1B become operational in 1998, with the transfer of water from a network of reservoirs at Mohale's Hoek, Katse and Mulela in the Lesotho Highlands. The project was extended in 2003 to include the construction of another tunnel from the Katse reservoir. In March 2004 South African President Thabo Mbeki and King Letsie III held a ceremony to mark the completion of Phase 1B of what had become the world's largest water transfer operation. The annual royalties that Lesotho received from South Africa for the LHWP constituted the country's largest source of foreign exchange and amounted to as much as 75% of its budget. In April 2009 the South African Government announced, at a meeting of the joint bilateral commission, that it had approved the allocation of R7,400m. for Phase 2 of the LHWP, which was to include the construction of a new dam in the Maloti Mountains. Work began in early 2011 on the Metolong dam, after the securing of funding from South Africa and a range of other foreign donors and lenders, including the World Bank and the European Union (EU); upon completion, the dam would supply water to Maseru and neighbouring areas. In August Lesotho and South Africa signed an agreement to implement the second phase of the LHWP. Construction was expected to begin in 2012 on the Polihali dam on the Senqu River, which would then be connected by tunnel with the Katse dam, although some 2,500 people would have to relocated.

The kingdom gained international credit for the way it addressed the corruption that had taken place in the building of the LHWP. Masupha Sole, the former Chief Executive of the LHWP, was found guilty in May 2002 of accepting bribes totalling some US $2m. over a 10-year period, and sentenced to a 15-year prison term. The severity of his sentence seemed designed to demonstrate that Lesotho was determined to prosecute individuals and companies involved in corrupt practices. In September of that year a Canadian construction company was found guilty of paying bribes to Sole in return for a contract to work on the LHWP and was fined $2.5m., while Germany's largest engineering consultancy, Lahmeyer International, was fined $1.9m. in early 2004. The Transformation Resource Centre, a local non-governmental organization representing the communities displaced by the LHWP, appealed for an audit of all the tenders allocated in the LHWP before Phase 2 was approved and pointed out that compensation had yet to be paid to some of those displaced by construction of the dams. In 2011 the South African authorities submitted a complaint to the Lesotho Government after Sole, who had been released from gaol after serving one-half of his sentence, was hired as a technical adviser on Phase 2 of the project. In response to this pressure, he was removed from the project.

Despite opposition from South Africa, which sought a common SADC approach to the EU, Lesotho signed an interim Economic Partnership Agreement (EPA) with the EU in November 2007. This ensured that trade preferences would not be lost following the termination of the Cotonou preferences at the end of 2007. Under the new agreement, the EU would liberalize 100% of its imports from Lesotho from 1 January 2008, while Lesotho would liberalize 86% by value of its imports from the EU. Lesotho was, however, highly dependent on the revenue that it obtained from the Southern African Customs Union (SACU); that revenue declined sharply from 2009 owing to the global recession and to a change in the revenue-sharing formula that disadvantaged Lesotho. Already one of the poorest countries on the continent, Lesotho suffered a further setback when South Africa effectively removed benefits to clothing imports from Lesotho in December 2008. In that year almost 40,000 people were employed in some 20 clothing factories in Lesotho, which had been established to take advantage of preferences granted under the USA's African Growth and Opportunity Act, and clothing manufacturing contributed almost 20% of gross domestic product. However, demand subsequently declined as a result of the global recession, while Lesotho-made garment exports to the USA were exposed to more competition from cheap imports from the People's Republic of China, precipitating a rapid sectoral contraction. The EPA issue was on the agenda when President Jacob Zuma of South Africa made a brief state visit to Lesotho in August 2010, and when Mosisili met his counterparts from South Africa, Swaziland, Botswana and Namibia at a SACU summit in Pretoria in March 2011 it was agreed that SACU countries would in future present a unified approach to trade negotiations with the EU and other trading partners. The EU negotiations proceeded slowly, however, and by mid-2012 their outcome still remained unclear.

Economy

LINDA VAN BUREN

Revised for this edition by OBI IHEME

INTRODUCTION

The global economic recession of 2008 and 2009 had a severe effect on the Lesotho economy. With the customs revenues on which Lesotho heavily depends having plunged, with no prospect of a return to pre-recession levels for several years, the medium-term outlook for the mountain kingdom was pessimistic. Global demand for Lesotho's exports of textiles and diamonds declined, while demand for Basotho labour in South African mines continued its downward trend. Most directly, consumers in the USA were buying less clothing, with the result that demand for Lesotho's clothing exports to that country decreased sharply. As a result, more than 40,000 jobs were put at risk in the kingdom. Lesotho's textile companies were also no longer able to obtain export-import financing and letters of credit from the Far Eastern banks that formerly provided these services. Furthermore, the recession meant that the world's affluent consumers were cutting back on spending, including buying fewer luxury items such as gold, platinum and diamonds. As a result, the South African mines that produce these precious metals and gemstones were drastically reducing expenditure and shedding labour, causing the Basotho workers in these mines to lose their jobs and the Lesotho Government to lose the statutory remittances that these workers generated. (By treaty, a share of their earnings has automatically accrued to the Lesotho Government, in the form of the compulsory Lesotho Deferred Payment Scheme, established in 1974.) All this means that the Southern African Customs Union (SACU) Common Revenue Pool has been shrinking rapidly. Lesotho's share of SACU revenues has accounted for as much as 60% of its total tax revenue in previous years; however, by 2010 this had declined to about

33%. There is a time delay in the readjustments of the Pool, posing the frightening prospect that the mountain kingdom may have to pay back some of the revenue that it has already received. The Government estimated that Lesotho may have to reimburse the Pool M600m.–M900m. 'in the coming years'. The IMF forecast that Lesotho's income from SACU revenues would decline by 23% in 2010. Yet the future of these revenues is uncertain, and the entire role of SACU is vulnerable, in light of moves by the Southern African Development Community (SADC) towards a free trade area, a full customs union, a common market, a monetary union, a shared central bank and a regional currency, all to be phased in gradually by 2018. Also under threat are the remittances that Basotho migrants working in South Africa send back to Lesotho.

Fundamental structural modifications to the economy will have to take place in order to compensate for these impending changes, which are largely beyond Lesotho's control. Although the Lesotho Government has expressed its intention to make the necessary reductions in public expenditure, the IMF has found the implementation of these structural reforms to have been 'slow'. Nevertheless, in early June 2010 the Fund announced a US $61.4m. three-year Extended Credit Facility to support these reforms and the balance of payments.

As a small, landlocked country that is completely surrounded by South Africa, Lesotho is even more vulnerable to external factors than most African states, and its economic and political fortunes are inextricably linked to those of its much larger neighbour. In common with most non-oil-producing African nations, Lesotho suffered from the high global prices of fuel and food in 2007–08; in Lesotho's case, these coincided with strenuous efforts to revive the textile industry and with drought, which reduced the country's domestic agricultural output. However, other, more positive factors compensated, which enabled Lesotho's gross domestic product (GDP) to grow by an estimated 5.1% in 2007. This growth rate was, nevertheless, lower than the 7.2% achieved in 2006. The target for 2008 was 7.0%, but this proved to be unrealistic, and GDP grew by just 2.9% in that recession-hit year. Inflation, which for the most part rises and falls with inflation in South Africa, ballooned to 10.6% by the end of 2008, mainly as a result of high prices of imported fuel and food. Inflation was contained thereafter, easing to 3.8% in 2010, before rising to 4.1% in April 2011 and 6.6% in April 2012, driven mainly by higher alcohol and tobacco prices.

The full effects on the Lesotho economy of the ending of the World Trade Organization (WTO)'s Multi-fibre Arrangement (MFA—also known as the Agreement on Textiles and Clothing) in January 2005 became apparent in the 2005/06 fiscal year. During much of 2004 the textile sector had been aided by favourable access to the US market under the provisions of two US initiatives, the African Growth and Opportunity Act (AGOA—see below) and the MFA. Under the MFA, access to the US market by the People's Republic of China and India had been strictly limited by export quotas. These countries could reach the US market only by setting up operations in eligible third-party countries, such as Lesotho. China was especially active in Lesotho during the MFA years, and 80% of Lesotho's textile operations were foreign-owned. However, after the MFA ended, China and India were free to sell direct to the USA. China, in particular, was able to flood the US market with inexpensive textile goods that cost 30%–40% less to produce than those made in Lesotho. Furthermore, the earnings from Lesotho's textile exports to the USA were denominated in US dollars, which meant that the loti (plural: maloti—M) equivalent of these proceeds was lower, as the loti is tied to the South African rand (R) at par, and during 2004 the dollar endured a period of weakness against the rand. At the same time, the costs of production, paid in maloti, remained static, making Lesotho's exports less competitive than they previously had been. Some textile producers found themselves in a cash-flow crisis.

The population of Lesotho was an estimated 2.2m. in June 2011, with an annual growth rate of 1.0% during 2001–10. The pressure on productive land is reflected in the wide disparity of population density. In the lowlands of the west, where virtually all arable land and 57% of the population are concentrated, the population density reaches 160 inhabitants per sq km, compared with a national average density of an estimated 73.0 per sq km at mid-2012.

AGRICULTURE

Although only about 11% of the total land area of 30,355 sq km can support arable cultivation, a further 66% is suitable for pasture. Subsistence agriculture is the primary occupation for the great majority of Basotho (an estimated 84% of the internal labour force in May 2011) and accounts for about one-fifth of export earnings. The sector's contribution to GDP fluctuates with changes in yields caused by soil erosion, the prevalence of poor agricultural practices and the impact of drought and other adverse weather conditions, but the overall trend is downward. Agriculture accounted for 47% of GDP in 1970 but for only about 8.6% in 2011. Apart from increases in the use of fertilizers and tractors since 1970, the sector remains largely unmodernized. Most crops continue to be produced using traditional methods, by peasant farmers who have little security of tenure under existing laws. Most of the sector's decline is accounted for by the crop sector; the livestock sector's downturn has been less pronounced. Drought is a recurring problem. Even in relatively good years, Lesotho grows less than one-half of its annual requirement of about 330,000 metric tons of cereals. For example, in 2010 Lesotho produced 128,000 tons of maize and 23,800 tons of sorghum. Wheat, barley and oats are also grown. The UN's World Food Programme attributed the country's lower cereal production to the fact that farmers left more land fallow in 2009 because of the high cost of inputs such as fertilizers and seeds. Other factors contributing to the agricultural sector's decline were soil erosion and the effect of HIV/AIDS on farming households.

The cereal deficit is covered through commercial imports (accounting for about 87% of the total shortfall) and through food aid for the remainder. The Government has for some time been preaching the merits of developing irrigation potential and planting high-value cash crops; however, the decline in the area planted is attributed not to a change of use but to a lack of use. Fields have been left uncultivated owing to a lack of cash for inputs and for paying farm labourers. Despite the Government's claim that the planting of high-value export cash crops is the answer to Lesotho's agricultural woes, summer wheat is so far the only crop to have been exported in significant quantities, with most exports sold to South Africa. Other crops include beans, peas, melons and potatoes. The considerable potential of the livestock sector has been little exploited, although cattle exports have traditionally accounted for about one-third of agricultural exports, with wool and mohair providing a further 30% each. In 2010 FAO assessed Lesotho's national herd at 1.2m. sheep, 875,000 goats and 626,000 cattle. An export-orientated abattoir in Maseru, along with associated fattening pens, sought to satisfy domestic demand and to export to regional and European Union (EU) markets. Milk production is also being promoted.

Heavy flooding in early 2011 caused many deaths and serious damage to infrastructure across the country. The floods also severely affected the agricultural sector, resulting in great loss of livestock and crops, which created the need for the emergency importation of food. By mid-2012 the sector's prospects for a full recovery were still unclear.

MANUFACTURING AND MINING

Confronted by the chronic problems of agriculture and by the need to create jobs for a rapidly expanding resident population, Lesotho has promoted development in other sectors, with varying degrees of success. Its main assets are proximity and duty-free access to the South African market. An additional asset has been the abundance of labour. Lesotho also enjoys an adult literacy rate that is one of the highest in Africa (89.7% in 2009, according to UNESCO estimates), and immigrant Basotho workers command an excellent reputation among employers in South Africa. Lesotho's manufacturing sector, composed mainly of light manufacturing, grew by an average of 4.9% per year in 2000–07 and by 11.0% in 2007, before the global economic recession took its toll on the country's textile exports to the USA; it was estimated that manufacturing GDP contracted by some 4.5% in 2008 and by a similar level in 2009.

To help boost the manufacturing sector, the Lesotho Government removed many of the stifling regulations that had impeded sectoral performance. Nevertheless, Lesotho will need to assure the competitiveness of its products if it is to extend the success of the textiles export sub-sector into the longer term. These textile exports are of vital importance to Lesotho, yet of minimal importance to their market. Of total worldwide textile exports in 2007, sub-Saharan Africa accounted for less than 0.4%, and of the African total, Lesotho accounted for just 2%. Looking to the future, a further negative factor will be the impending introduction, in 2012, of AGOA's new rules of origin required for countries to export textiles to the US market. The expiration of WTO concessions on textile exports to the USA was also expected to affect negatively economic growth in the medium term. At present, Lesotho imports nearly all its textile raw material, with a large portion of it coming from China. From 2012 the raw material will need to be sourced from an AGOA-eligible country. Lesotho grows no cotton and thus will have to import cotton from neighbouring states, most of which are likely to want to use their cotton crop to feed their own textile factories for AGOA purposes. Lesotho does produce wool and mohair, but wool accounts for just 5% of the global fibre industry, and the primary textile demand in the USA is not for wool. Wool and mohair exhibited a marked decline after 2000, brought on by diminishing global demand.

In manufacturing in general, the Lesotho National Development Corporation, founded in 1967, and the Basotho Enterprises Development Corporation (BEDCO), which provides finance to local entrepreneurs, have been the main bodies stimulating development, promoting a wide variety of small industries, including tyre retreading, tapestry weaving, shoemaking and the production of clothing (particularly denim jeans), food-processing and beverages, candles, ceramics, explosives, fertilizers, furniture, electric lamp assembly, television sets, diamond-cutting and -polishing, and jewellery. Inducements to foreign companies have included a low corporate income tax rate and free repatriation of profits; and there is no withholding tax on dividends paid by manufacturing companies to shareholders, domestic or foreign. Corporate income tax was cut in 2006/07 from 35% to 25%, but special reductions were introduced for manufacturing for export: from 15% to 10% for companies exporting within SACU, and from 15% to 0% for companies exporting to countries outside SACU. Government statistics demonstrated that these tax reductions resulted in an increase, not a decrease, in corporate tax revenue. In addition, there are generous allowances and tax 'holidays', duty-free access to EU and SACU markets, the provision of industrial infrastructure (although more is needed in this respect), and the construction of industrial estates in Maseru and Maputsoa, with further estates planned elsewhere in the country. The Government in 2007 pledged to boost manufacturing by providing a Minimum Infrastructure Platform (MIP) for production and exports, comprising the removal of 'investment impediments', the provision of skilled labour, and investment in infrastructure and support services. Tangible components of the MIP strategy included the commencement of the construction phase of the Metolong water supply project, a US $30m. Chinese-backed expansion of Telecom Lesotho, the expansion of electricity supply, and improvements to cross-border immigration and customs facilities, to urban water and sewerage systems and to urban roads. The Government created a US $10m. fund in the 2012 budget for improving the manufacturing sector and expanding markets for goods.

Diamond mining was limited to small artisanal diggings, exploited by primitive methods until production began at a small modern mine at Letšeng-la-Terae, in the Maloti Mountains of northern Lesotho, in 1977, developed and administered by De Beers Consolidated Mines of South Africa. Most of the diamonds from the two kimberlite pipes were of industrial quality, although a few unusually large gemstones were also reportedly found. Recovery rates, at only 2.8 carats per 100 metric tons, proved to be the lowest of any mine in the De Beers group, and operations ceased in 1982. In the late 1990s, however, the Government explored the feasibility of reopening the mine, forming Letšeng Diamonds (Pty) Ltd, a joint venture with a South African company; the Lesotho Government retained a 24% share in the mine. A mining licence was issued in 1999, and small-scale production began in 2003 with a workforce of some 291 people. In 2006 Gem Diamonds Ltd of the United Kingdom acquired 70% of Letšeng Diamonds for US $118.5m.; the Lesotho Government retained the remaining 30%. The mine produced three major diamonds in three years, including a 603-carat white diamond recovered in 2006; this stone, the 14th largest diamond ever found, was named the 'Lesotho Promise' and was sold at auction in Antwerp, Belgium, for $12.36m. The average per carat value of Lesotho's diamonds was the highest in the world. A new treatment plant to double the mine's capacity treated its first ore in March 2008, and full production commenced in the second quarter of 2008. The forecast had been for Letšeng to produce an average of 65,000 carats per year over an 18-year period, although this forecast was exceeded in 2007 when Letšeng produced 76,875 carats. In addition to the Letšeng-la-Terae site, in 2001 the Lesotho Government awarded a 25-year licence for the exploration of a 390-ha site containing five kimberlite pipes (only two of which have been exploited to date) to the Liqhobong Mining Development Company (LMDC), a joint venture now owned 75% by Kopane Diamond Developments of the United Kingdom and 25% by the Lesotho Government. Production began in early 2006 with output forecast at 250,000–290,000 carats per year from the satellite pipe, with a stone value estimated at $40 per carat. A positive pre-scoping study of the main pipe found that a 4m. ton per year operation over a life of 10 or more years would yield up to 700,000 carats each year. According to Kopane, independent valuations in 2008 estimated the average stone value to be 12,514 carats at $86 per carat. However, production at the smaller satellite pipe was suspended in December of that year owing to falling world diamond prices; production continued at the main pipe. Lesotho's newest diamond mine is Kao, 30 km from Letšeng. Kao, a joint venture owned 93% by Global Diamond Resources of the United Kingdom, began producing in November 2007 and was forecast to have a life of 23 years, producing 740,000 carats per year. The Mothae diamond mine, whose principal investor is Lucara Diamond Corpn of Canada, was due to enter production in 2012. Garnets and other semi-precious gemstones have been discovered at Letšeng-la-Terae, but the potential for commercial exploitation has not been confirmed.

Diamond production has become increasingly important to Lesotho's economy. While accounting for only 0.5% of GDP at the turn of the millennium, the sector's share had risen to 7.9% by 2010/11, and given the expansion of existing mines, with additional facilities coming on stream, the IMF forecast that the diamond industry would generate 20% of GDP from 2016/17. Diamond prices were recovering, prompting efforts to reopen the Liqhobong and Kao mines, which had been closed during the global financial crisis, and inaugurate the new Mothae and Lemphane mines. Given the dominance of South African and other foreign companies in Lesotho's mining sector, coupled with the vulnerabilities faced by many of the sector's local employees, the Government highlighted the importance of mining firms upholding their social responsibility obligations.

TOURISM

Tourism has seen significant development since independence. In 2002 the Government identified the development of the tourism sector as a priority, aimed at reducing the deficit on the current account of the balance of payments. Tourism receipts in 2008 were US $34m., while tourist arrivals totalled an estimated 310,000 in 2010. Eco-tourism is seen as a niche market offering potential for Lesotho. A ski resort on a 500-ha site in the Mahlasela Valley in the Lesotho Highlands, which lies at an altitude of 3,222m above sea level and boasts the highest annual snowfall in Southern Africa, opened in 2007. The country has two hotel/casino complexes and 12 other hotels in and around Maseru, in addition to a number of smaller hotels, guesthouses and lodges in all 10 districts.

Tourism also has great potential for employing a large number of workers, but, for this to be realized, in the medium term the sector must contribute much more than its present share of GDP, estimated at around 1.5%. As the country is surrounded by South Africa, plans were being developed to create a joint tourist route between the two countries, in which there would be an anticipated investment of US $23m.

POWER AND WATER

Lesotho's major exploitable natural resource is running water. The Governments of Lesotho and South Africa signed a treaty in 1986 to create the Lesotho Highlands Water Project (LHWP). The agreement for this huge and controversial scheme was reconfirmed in the mid-1990s, after the change of government in South Africa. Parastatal bodies in each country were assigned responsibility for the implementation of the project; in Lesotho this fell to the Lesotho Highlands Development Authority (LHDA). A massive undertaking for any country (particularly for one as small as Lesotho), with costs originally estimated at US $3,770m., the LHWP proposed the diversion of water from Lesotho's rivers for export to South Africa, with self-sufficiency in hydro-generated electricity as the major by-product. About 75% of the cost of the $2,500m. Phase 1A was raised in Southern Africa (including some 57% from banks), with diversified external sources providing the balance, including $110m. from the World Bank in 1989. The commercial segment of the debt was to be met from royalty payments received on water sales to South Africa. Phase 1B, the total cost of which was projected to be $1,100m., was also to be funded largely from South African capital and money markets and from the water users themselves.

Construction of Phase 1A was completed in 1998. Phase 1B involved the construction of the 145-m-high Mohale dam on the Senqunyane river, a 15-m weir on the Matsoku river, and water tunnels from both these sites to the Katse dam, linking up with the facilities built there in Phase 1A to transfer the water to South Africa. Water spilled over Mohale dam for the first time in February 2006, signalling that its reservoir had reached capacity.

With the completion of Phase 1B, the whole of Phase 1 was officially inaugurated at Mohale in 2004. A feasibility study to help South Africa and Lesotho decide whether to implement Phase 2 was completed in 2008. It identified a 'special project' to construct the Polihali dam in Mokhotlong and a tunnel to transfer water to South Africa. South Africa approved the project in 2009, and construction was expected to begin in 2012–13. The construction of a further dam and power station, generating 1,000 MW and costing US $993m., also comprised part of Phase 2.

As of 2009 fewer than one Basotho in 10 was connected to the national electricity grid. The World Bank estimated that the cost of bringing mains electricity to the remaining 90% of the population was about US $1,000 per household, in a country where GNI per head was $950.

The demand for water in Lesotho exceeds supply. The Government in 2004 fast-tracked the Lesotho Lowlands Water Supply Scheme, centred on the Metolong dam on the Phuthiatsana river to the south-east of Maseru, which, it was envisaged, could be on stream by 2012. The dam would also supply water to Maseru and to the communities of Roma, Morija and Mazenod and would potentially provide year-round irrigation in the valley of the Phuthiatsana river. The March 2007 budget speech established the commencement of construction of the Metolong scheme during the 2007/08 fiscal year as a priority, and financing was secured, primarily from Arab sources. The Kuwait Fund for Arab Economic Development extended a concessional loan of US $13.36m. in March 2007, Arab Bank for Economic Development in Africa (BADEA) pledged $9.78m. in July 2007, and the Organization of the Petroleum Exporting Countries (OPEC) Fund for International Development committed $5.7m. in September 2007. The Government of Lesotho earmarked M200m. (about $19.6m.) towards the scheme in the 2009/10 budget. In May 2009 the World Bank extended an IDA credit of $16.5m. over 40 years with 10 years' grace and an IDA grant of $8.5m. towards the Metolong project.

Additionally, in October 2011 Lesotho signed a US $15,000m. agreement with South African company Harrison and White Investments to develop the Lesotho Highlands Power Project, which will produce 6,000 MW and 4,000 MW of wind power and hydropower, respectively, mainly for export to South Africa. The Minister of Natural Resources, Monyane Moleleki, claimed that the project would create approximately 25,000 jobs over 15 years and would become a significant source of revenue. The first phase of the scheme will involve the construction of a wind farm, producing 150 MW of power.

TRANSPORT AND COMMUNICATIONS

Owing to its mountainous terrain, much of Lesotho was previously virtually inaccessible except by horse or light aircraft. However, a substantial network of nearly 6,000 km of tracks, passable by four-wheel-drive vehicles, has now been built up, largely by 'food for work' road builders in the mountain areas. Lesotho's economic development has relied heavily on South African road and rail outlets. A greater degree of independence in international communications was reached after the Maseru international airport became operational in 1986. In 2009 Lesotho had three airports with paved runways and 25 with unpaved runways. Lesotho has 2.6 km of railway line, which is operated as part of South Africa's railway system.

The Lesotho Telecommunications Corporation was privatized in 2000 as Telecom Lesotho. It is 70% owned by Econet Wireless Group and 30% by the Lesotho Government. Telecom Lesotho and Econet Ezi—Cel Lesotho merged in April 2008 to form Econet Telecom Lesotho. The Lesotho Communications Authority (LCA) in early 2012 approved the Communications Act of 2012, which came into force in April and replaced the LCA Act of 2000.

EMPLOYMENT, WAGES AND MIGRANT LABOUR

Industrial diversity has continued to elude Lesotho, and the country remains overly dependent on fragile sources for job creation. The exodus of Basotho workers to the South African mines was caused by land shortage, by the depressed state of agriculture, by the lack of employment opportunities inside the kingdom, and by low wages in the formal sectors. In the mid-1990s an average of 110,686 Basotho worked in South African mines; by 2007 this number had halved, to 53,467. Unemployment in Lesotho was officially estimated at 45% in 2011, when more than one-half of the population were thought to be either unemployed or underemployed. Manufacturing, especially the textile sector, created the most new jobs, but this sub-sector's ability to create jobs is vulnerable to external factors. A memorandum of understanding (MOU) signed between the USA and China in November 2005 provided African textile exporters a return to a protected status. Lesotho's textile sector recovered and showed strong growth in 2006 and 2007. However, the global economic recession that began to manifest itself in early 2008 led to a drying up of US demand for Lesotho's textile and apparel exports. At a time when more and more Basotho were losing their jobs in South African mines and heading home, textile companies were also laying off workers. The sector has struggled to create jobs because it is capital intensive and requires expensive equipment. Nevertheless, the IMF estimated that about 2,000 people worked in the textiles industry, and, with new plants being activated, another 1,000 were expected to be employed by 2016.

The Government responded with a two-pronged strategy to help alleviate the escalating unemployment problem. First, the 2009/10 budget allocated M112m. to the Integrated Watershed Management Project, which uses the services of unemployed Basotho in all 10 districts to rehabilitate severely eroded land. Second, M50m. was allocated to the Development Fund for Councils. Under this scheme, communities identify suitable local infrastructural projects, such as developing irrigation systems or building roads, and unemployed Basotho in that community are engaged on a rotation basis.

The Lesotho economy's dependence on receipts from services and transfers, in the form of migrants' remittances (see above), has traditionally been reflected in the fact that the country's GNI is generally more than twice the value of its GDP. (In most other African states the net outflow of remittances means that GDP is greater than GNI.) Apart from their obvious role in financing the large trade gap, the remittances are central to the income of up to 60% of families and are also used by the Government to finance development.

SACU AND OTHER AGREEMENTS

Together with Botswana, Namibia, South Africa and Swaziland, Lesotho is a member of SACU, which dates formally from 1910, when the Union (now the Republic) of South Africa was established. The 1969 SACU agreement provided for payments to Botswana, Lesotho and Swaziland (the BLS countries, later BLNS after Namibia gained independence in 1990 and joined) to be made on the basis of their share of goods imported by SACU countries, multiplied by an 'enhancement' factor of 1.42 as a form of compensation for the BLS countries' loss of freedom to conduct a completely independent economic policy, and for the costs that this restriction involved in trade diversion and loss of investment. SACU revenue was paid two years in arrears and earned no interest, but even so, for Lesotho it formed up to 70% of government recurrent revenues in some years.

Although Lesotho's statutory share of these revenues is the smallest of any member state, Lesotho is the most heavily dependent on this income as a source of government revenue. Indeed, SACU tariff revenue comprises the largest share of Lesotho's GDP, accounting for more than 60% of the national budget in 2008/09, according to the Bertelsmann Foundation. A new SACU agreement was signed in October 2002, under which the BLNS countries were to receive a share of the SACU revenue pool in inverse proportion to their level of economic development. From May 2004 Lesotho was to receive 13% of the total customs pool. Receipts from this source peaked at M4,917.7m. in 2009/10. The out-turn of the 2010/11 budget indicated that Lesotho's total domestic revenue declined by 30%, precipitated by a 56% reduction in SACU receipts to M2,161.9m. Lesotho's SACU receipts were forecast to recover gradually, increasing to M2,752.6m. in 2011/12, to M4,287.0m. in 2012/13 and to M4,480.1m. in 2013/14. The Lesotho Government has recognized the necessity of linking its recurrent expenditure not to SACU receipts but rather to domestic revenue sources, relying on SACU receipts only for the funding of development projects. To strengthen other revenue sources, the Government established the new Lesotho Revenue Authority (LRA) in 2003. The LRA was immediately charged with the task of introducing value-added tax (VAT) on 1 July 2003, levied initially at 14% (the same level as in South Africa), and replacing the old Sales Tax, which had been levied at 10%. Imported goods valued at more than M150 were subject to the tax. Most imported goods come from South Africa. VAT revenue amounted to M1,244m. in 2010/11.

In 1980 Lesotho followed Botswana and Swaziland in their moves towards monetary independence by introducing the loti, replacing the South African rand at par. This measure was designed to give Lesotho greater control over factors influencing its development and over cash outflows by Basotho visiting South Africa. In 1986 the Tripartite Monetary Area (TMA, now the Common Monetary Area—CMA), comprising Lesotho, Swaziland and South Africa (and later including Namibia, which became independent from South Africa in 1990), was formed.

EXTERNAL TRADE AND PAYMENTS

Until the 1980s Lesotho was largely able to ignore its balance of payments; owing to its membership of the erstwhile South African-dominated Rand Monetary Agreement (RMA), situations that in other countries would have shown up as a balance of payments problem would, in Lesotho, have appeared as a general credit shortage. In fact, this happened only rarely until the 1980s, as Lesotho's chronic trade deficit, resulting from a limited export base and large requirements of food imports, was more than offset by current transfers, migrant remittances and surpluses on the capital account of the balance of payments. In 2010 Lesotho's total merchandise export revenue on a free-on-board (f.o.b.) basis was US $860.3m., of which income from the export of garments was $374.5m. Total imports on a f.o.b. basis cost $1,884.8m., of which $180.6m. was for inputs for the garment industry, primarily from China. The resultant trade deficit was $1,024.5m., and export revenue covered less than 28% of import costs. The deficit on the current account, including official transfers, in 2010 was estimated at $342.8m. Gross international reserves at 31 December 2010 stood at $970m., enough to cover 4.7 months' worth of imports of goods and services.

GDP increased, in real terms, at an average annual rate of 3.7% in 2000–09 and by 6.9% in 2010, according to the World Bank. In 2011 the African Economic Outlook estimated GDP growth at 3.1%. In 2010 GDP amounted to M15,590m. while gross national product (GNP) totalled M19,257m. Given the importance of trade with South Africa to the economic and social welfare of communities near the border, it will be imperative for the Government to continue implementing trade reforms such as introducing open border policies and recruiting and training staff for the customs and other border control agencies.

PUBLIC FINANCE

Lesotho's gross government debt was equivalent to 37.8% of GDP and to 30.6% of GNP in 2010, and, according to the African Economic Outlook, 99.6% of this debt was owed to the World Bank and the African Development Bank. In the same year the debt service ratio as a percentage of exports of goods and services was 4.1%. The 2011/12 budget, announced in February 2011, envisaged total revenue of M7,367.16m., while total expenditure was set at M12,919.4m., of which M8,210.3m. was recurrent and M4,709.1m. was capital spending. The resultant budgetary deficit was projected at M5,552.24m. As most Basotho remain without access to proper banking facilities, they became vulnerable to a proliferation in 2007 of 'unlicensed deposit-taking entities'. The February 2008 budget speech lamented that these entities posed 'a significant risk to the financial system'. These entities promised huge returns on the deposits that they took and then disappeared. To stop this practice, the Government promised to review regulation and supervision laws.

CONCLUSION

Lesotho continues to face formidable economic challenges. The acute shortage of fertile land, the problem of soil erosion and the backward state of agriculture make it highly unlikely that this sector can absorb the increase in population that is now resulting from returning migrants. Much will depend on the attitudes of the Government in South Africa and on the Lesotho Government's ability to find alternative sources of revenue to the Lesotho Deferred Payment Scheme (see above), SACU receipts and the LHWP. The Government did find one such source, in its again-burgeoning textile sector, but this industry's future is uncertain. Without vertical integration and without the ability to source its raw material locally, it is vulnerable to fluctuating conditions overseas, far beyond Lesotho's control. The Government is aware that if the gains made in this sector are to be sustained, it will have to work with the private sector to make textile production in Lesotho more cost effective, despite the necessity of importing the raw material from a qualifying source under the terms of the third-country fabric provisions of AGOA from 2012. Protective schemes like AGOA can help in the short term, but they do not provide long-term solutions. The Government also recognized that agricultural problems were only partly the result of natural phenomena such as drought and climate change and that some of the difficulties had been man-made. The 2007 budget speech cited a World Bank ranking of 175 countries in the world in terms of ease of doing business, in which Lesotho occupied 114th position. This compared unfavourably with Swaziland (76th), Botswana (48th), Namibia (42nd) and South Africa (28th). However, the Government subsequently took steps to improve the enabling business environment, such as reviewing the Companies Act 25 of 1967, which aimed to reduce the length of the bureaucratic process for registering and starting a business. While much work remains to be done, some improvements have been made.

There is concern that foreign inward investment has been concentrated on the textile industry—a narrow, low-technology base—and that there has been little development beyond this sector; the Government acknowledges that diversification is an important priority, but the challenge will be to translate these good intentions into actions. The fact also remains that 40,000 new jobs need to be created every year to keep up with demand, and Lesotho's work-force is, like those of its neighbours, seriously affected by the HIV/AIDS pandemic: an estimated 23.2% of all Basotho adults of working age were living with HIV/AIDS in December 2008, one of the highest incidences of HIV in the world. In 2006 Lesotho became the first nation in Africa—and the second nation in the world, after Brazil—to embark on an ambitious Universal Voluntary Counselling and Testing plan, which involves carrying out door-to-door on-the-spot HIV tests for the entire population.

The Lesotho economy is coming under severe negative pressure from a combination of unemployed Basuto mine workers returning to the kingdom, the ever decreasing remittances as a source of government revenue, the loss of jobs in the textile industry, and the declining reliability of SACU receipts. However, while the diamond industry will not create the thousands of jobs that are needed or provide raw materials for the textile companies, the income from the sale of diamonds could indeed, if husbanded well, be the revenue source that Lesotho needs to fund more sustainable job creation solutions in other sectors of the economy.

The African Economic Outlook reported that in 2011 the main driver of economic growth was the private sector, and this trend was forecast to continue over the medium term. The public sector's 1.7% share of growth in that year was expected to decrease by 0.4% in the medium term. In 2011 the share of exports in growth was 5.9%, which was likely decrease to approximately 1.7% per annum, largely due to the foreseen negative impact on the textile sector of the expiry of WTO textile industry concessions. Another negative impact on GDP will be the expected increase in imports for domestic construction. High international commodity prices and ongoing uncertainties surrounding the global economic outlook were further concerns for Lesotho's policy-makers.

Statistical Survey

Sources (unless otherwise stated): Bureau of Statistics, POB 455, Maseru 100; tel. 22323852; fax 22310177; internet www.bos.gov.ls; Central Bank of Lesotho, POB 1184, Maseru 100; tel. 22314281; fax 22310051; e-mail cbl@centralbank.org.ls; internet www.centralbank.org.ls.

Area and Population

AREA, POPULATION AND DENSITY

Area (sq km)	30,355*
Population (*de jure* census results)	
14 April 1996	1,862,275
9 April 2006	
Males	912,798
Females	963,835
Total	1,876,633
Population (UN estimates at mid-year)†	
2010	2,171,318
2011	2,193,842
2012	2,216,850
Density (per sq km) at mid-2012	73.0

* 11,720 sq miles.

† Source: UN, *World Population Prospects: The 2010 Revision*.

POPULATION BY AGE AND SEX
(UN estimates at mid-2012)

	Males	Females	Total
0–14	407,772	402,301	810,073
15–64	647,725	664,247	1,311,972
65 and over	38,379	56,426	94,805
Total	1,093,876	1,122,974	2,216,850

Source: UN, *World Population Prospects: The 2010 Revision*.

DISTRICTS
(population at 2006 census)

District	Population
Berea	250,006
Butha-Buthe	110,320
Leribe	293,369
Mafeteng	192,621
Maseru	431,998
Mohale's Hoek	176,928
Mokhotlong	97,713
Qacha's Nek	69,749
Quthing	124,048
Thaba-Tseka	129,881
Total	1,876,633

PRINCIPAL TOWNS
(population at 1986 census)

Maseru (capital)	109,400	Hlotse	9,600
Maputsoa	20,000	Mohale's Hoek	8,500
Teyateyaneng	14,300	Quthing	6,000
Mafeteng	12,700		

Source: Stefan Helders, *World Gazetteer* (www.world-gazetteer.com).

Mid-2011 (including suburbs, UN estimate): Maseru 238,553 (Source: UN, *World Urbanization Prospects: The 2011 Revision*).

BIRTHS AND DEATHS
(annual averages, UN estimates)

	1995–2000	2000–05	2005–10
Birth rate (per 1,000)	33.7	30.7	28.5
Death rate (per 1,000)	13.5	17.9	16.7

Source: UN, *World Population Prospects: The 2010 Revision*.

Life expectancy (years at birth): 47.4 (males 48.1; females 46.6) in 2010 (Source: World Bank, World Development Indicators database).

ECONOMICALLY ACTIVE POPULATION
(household survey, persons aged 10 years and over, 1999)

	Males	Females	Total
Agriculture	270,919	175,760	446,679
Fishing	125	—	125
Mining and quarrying	2,392	611	3,003
Manufacturing	7,957	13,839	21,795
Electricity, gas and water supply	1,722	1,541	3,263
Construction	18,947	10,548	29,495
Wholesale and retail trade; repair of motor vehicles, motorcycles and household goods	11,099	17,915	29,014
Hotels and restaurants	918	3,529	4,447
Transport, storage and communications	9,307	1,363	10,670
Financial intermediation	1,041	810	1,851

—continued	Males	Females	Total
Real estate, renting and business activities	3,405	2,032	5,437
Public administration and defence; compulsory social security	5,181	2,395	7,576
Education	5,125	8,099	13,224
Health and social work	2,070	2,895	4,965
Other community, social and personal service activities	1,765	7,686	9,451
Households with employed persons	4,474	21,970	26,444
Extra-territorial organizations and bodies	126	—	126
Total employed	346,573	270,993	617,566
Unemployed	90,964	140,778	231,742
Total labour force	437,537	411,771	849,308

Source: ILO.

2008 (labour force survey, persons aged 15 years and over): Subsistence agriculture 247,258; Government and parastatals 43,762; Private sector 182,868; Private households 135,263; *Total employed* 609,152; Unemployed 179,390; *Total labour force* 788,541.

Mid-2012 (estimates in '000): Agriculture, etc. 368; Total labour force 961 (Source: FAO).

Health and Welfare

KEY INDICATORS

Total fertility rate (children per woman, 2010)	3.2
Under-5 mortality rate (per 1,000 live births, 2010)	85
HIV/AIDS (% of persons aged 15–49, 2009)	23.6
Physicians (per 1,000 head, 2003)	0.05
Hospital beds (per 1,000 head, 2006)	1.30
Health expenditure (2009): US $ per head (PPP)	139
Health expenditure (2009): % of GDP	9.4
Health expenditure (2009): public (% of total)	74.3
Access to water (% of persons, 2010)	78
Access to sanitation (% of persons, 2010)	26
Human Development Index (2011): ranking	160
Human Development Index (2011): value	0.450

For sources and definitions, see explanatory note on p. vi.

Agriculture

PRINCIPAL CROPS
('000 metric tons)

	2008	2009	2010
Wheat	3.7	7.4	20.1
Maize	59.7	57.1	128.2
Sorghum	10.2	10.2	23.8
Potatoes*	96.5	83.9	98.2
Beans, dry	3.2	3.5	2.7*
Peas, dry	1.0	1.4	1.1*
Vegetables*	35	28	31

* FAO estimate(s).

Source: FAO.

LIVESTOCK
('000 head, year ending September)

	2008	2009	2010
Cattle	616	617	626
Sheep	1,276	1,242	1,229
Goats	917	953	875
Pigs	95	92	84
Horses	78	74	70
Asses	136	160	136
Chickens	605	771	502

Source: FAO.

LIVESTOCK PRODUCTS
('000 metric tons, FAO estimates)

	2008	2009	2010
Cattle meat	10.4	10.4	10.4
Cows' milk	32.5	33.8	33.7
Pig meat	4.0	3.5	3.5
Chicken meat	2.3	2.3	2.3
Game meat	4.5	4.7	5.1
Hen eggs	1.6	1.7	1.7
Wool, greasy	4.5	3.9	3.7

Source: FAO.

Forestry

ROUNDWOOD REMOVALS
('000 cubic metres, excluding bark, FAO estimates)

	2008	2009	2010
Total (all fuel wood)	2,076.1	2,084.0	2,091.9

Source: FAO.

Fishing

(metric tons, live weight)

	2008	2009	2010
Capture	50	45	45
Common carp	16	15	15
North African catfish	2	5	5
Other freshwater fishes	32	25	25
Aquaculture	91	108	300
Common carp	1	1	—
Rainbow trout	90	107	300
Total catch	141	153	345

Source: FAO.

Mining

(cubic metres unless otherwise indicated)

	2008	2009	2010
Fire clay*	15,000	15,000	15,000
Diamond (carats)	253,053	91,815	100,000
Gravel and crushed rock*	300,000	300,000	300,000

* Estimated production.

Source: US Geological Survey.

Finance

CURRENCY AND EXCHANGE RATES

Monetary Units
100 lisente (singular: sente) = 1 loti (plural: maloti).

Sterling, Dollar and Euro Equivalents (31 May 2012)
£1 sterling = 13.228 maloti;
US $1 = 8.532 maloti;
€1 = 10.582 maloti;
100 maloti = £7.56 = $11.72 = €9.45.

Average Exchange Rate (maloti per US $)

2009	8.4737
2010	7.3212
2011	7.2611

Note: The loti is fixed at par with the South African rand.

BUDGET
(million maloti, year ending 31 March)

Revenue*	2006/07	2007/08	2008/09
Tax revenue	1,907.4	2,346.4	2,858.0
Taxes on net income and profits.	970.7	1,216.4	1,538.5
Company tax	199.6	293.7	383.3
Individual income tax	629.5	785.4	850.7
Other income and profit taxes	141.7	137.4	304.5
Taxes on property	66.5	74.6	74.6
Taxes on goods and services	856.3	1,003.1	1,230.8
Value-added tax	714.6	847.9	987.7
Excise taxes	65.6	118.1	98.9
Other taxes	13.8	12.7	14.0
Non-tax revenue	519.8	621.8	838.8
Sales of goods and services	412.9	446.9	420.0
Water royalties	286.7	292.4	324.1
Property income	78.2	107.5	376.9
Fines and forfeits	17.1	0.8	1.4
Miscellaneous revenue	11.6	66.7	40.5
SACU	3,945.0	4,097.7	4,900.6
Total	6,372.1	7,065.8	8,597.3

Expenditure and net lending	2006/07	2007/08	2008/09
Compensation of employees	1,584.4	1,898.0	2,326.3
Wages and salaries	1,457.9	1,730.8	2,140.5
Goods and services	1,597.1	1,776.5	2,286.6
Subsidies	—	—	204.0
Interest payments	308.1	296.1	118.4
Grants	670.7	797.1	766.0
Social benefits	170.9	223.0	226.9
Other expenditures	355.2	375.5	534.1
Total	4,686.3	5,366.3	6,462.2

* Excluding grants received (million maloti): 92.4 in 2006/07; 191.7 in 2007/08; 220.8 in 2008/09.

2009/10 (million maloti): *Revenue:* Tax revenue 8,169; Non-tax revenue 692; Grants 693; Total 9,554. *Expenditure:* Current expenditure 6,947 (Wages and salaries 2,525); Capital expenditure 3,035; Total 9,982 (Source: African Development Bank).

2010/11 (million maloti): *Revenue:* Tax revenue 6,097; Non-tax revenue 1,311; Grants 1,498; Total 8,906. *Expenditure:* Current expenditure 6,818 (Wages and salaries 2,571); Capital expenditure 3,352; Total 10,170 (excl. net lending –7). (Source: African Development Bank).

INTERNATIONAL RESERVES
(excl. gold, US $ million at 31 December)

	2004	2005	2006
IMF special drawing rights	0.62	0.44	0.22
Reserve position in IMF	5.53	5.15	5.45
Foreign exchange	495.35	513.52	652.74
Total	501.50	519.11	658.41

2009: IMF special drawing rights 49.00; Reserve position in IMF 5.66.

2010: IMF special drawing rights 52.61; Reserve position in IMF 5.56.

2011: IMF special drawing rights 54.22; Reserve position in IMF 5.55.

Source: IMF, *International Financial Statistics*.

MONEY SUPPLY
(million maloti at 31 December)

	2009	2010	2011
Currency outside depository corporations	487.18	538.96	688.70
Transferable deposits	3,692.06	4,450.05	2,132.83
Other deposits	1,567.63	1,588.82	3,858.58
Broad money	5,746.87	6,577.83	6,680.10

Source: IMF, *International Financial Statistics*.

COST OF LIVING
(Consumer Price Index; base: March 2010 = 100)

	2009	2010	2011
Food (incl. non-alcoholic beverages)	97.7	101.1	108.1
Alcoholic beverages and tobacco	93.1	101.7	108.3
Housing, water, electricity, and other fuels	99.2	102.5	114.3
Clothing (incl. footwear)	97.2	100.4	101.8
Health	98.5	100.8	102.2
Transport	96.3	100.2	103.2
Communication	99.2	100.6	101.7
Education	94.1	100.0	101.0
All items (incl. others)	97.4	100.9	105.9

NATIONAL ACCOUNTS
(million maloti at current prices)

Expenditure on the Gross Domestic Product

	2008	2009	2010
Government final consumption expenditure	4,959	5,776	5,941
Private final consumption expenditure	13,427	14,779	16,724
Changes in inventories	–46	5	–77
Gross fixed capital formation	3,787	4,057	4,547
Total domestic expenditure	22,127	24,617	27,135
Exports of goods and services	7,560	6,644	6,990
Less Imports of goods and services	16,255	16,760	18,171
GDP in purchasers' values	13,433	14,502	15,956

Gross Domestic Product by Economic Activity

	2008	2009	2010
Agriculture	992	1,025	1,222
Mining and quarrying	1,145	926	1,121
Manufacturing	2,343	2,105	1,816
Electricity, gas and water	510	532	662
Construction	614	790	915
Wholesale and retail trade, restaurants and hotels	1,171	1,157	1,282
Transport and communication	756	848	956
Finance, insurance, real estate and business services	2,417	2,655	2,799
Public administration and defence	1,354	1,753	1,764
Other services	1,345	1,756	1,927
Sub-total	12,647	13,547	14,464
Less Imputed bank service charge.	270	304	297
Indirect taxes, less subsidies	1,056	1,258	1,788
GDP in purchasers' prices	13,433	14,502	15,956

Source: African Development Bank.

BALANCE OF PAYMENTS
(US $ million)

	2008	2009	2010
Exports of goods f.o.b.	884.0	734.1	851.8
Imports of goods f.o.b.	−1,531.7	−1,587.2	−1,998.3
Trade balance	−647.6	−853.0	−1,146.5
Exports of services	43.0	43.8	48.0
Imports of services	−371.3	−384.6	−516.2
Balance on goods and services	−975.9	−1,193.9	−1,614.8
Other income received	768.7	772.3	878.3
Other income paid	−341.8	−304.6	−346.3
Balance on goods, services and income	−549.0	−726.2	−1,082.7
Current transfers received	716.8	748.7	688.0
Current transfers paid	−24.1	−24.8	−26.8
Current balance	143.7	−2.4	−421.4
Capital account (net)	18.6	74.6	123.3
Direct investment abroad	1.8	1.9	2.3
Direct investment from abroad	110.0	100.9	117.0
Other investment assets	−218.4	−174.7	−245.2
Other investment liabilities	29.6	74.9	−9.6
Net errors and omissions	188.2	−102.8	219.9
Overall balance	273.4	−27.5	−213.8

Source: IMF, *International Financial Statistics*.

External Trade

PRINCIPAL COMMODITIES
(million maloti)

Imports	2005	2006	2007
Food and beverages	1,135	1,198	1,549
Industrial supplies	2,015	1,917	2,803
Fuel and lubricants	415	474	684
Machinery and other capital equipment	275	288	553
Parts and accessories	182	298	326
Transport equipment	129	206	418
Parts and accessories for transport equipment	169	191	254
Consumer goods	1,175	1,294	1,488
Goods not specified elsewhere	2	0	2
Unspecified imports	2,932	3,564	2,828
Total	8,429	9,430	10,905

Exports	2006	2007	2008
Food and live animals	126	196	326
Crude materials, inedible except fuels	45	74	74
Mineral fuels and electricity	1	1	—
Chemicals and related products	24	4	6
Manufactured goods	668	1,213	1,663
Machinery and transport equipment	394	545	1,014
Miscellaneous manufactured articles	3,364	3,506	3,738
Other commodities	16	6	49
Total	4,638	5,543	6,870

PRINCIPAL TRADING PARTNERS
(million maloti)

Imports c.i.f.*	2005	2006	2007
Africa	7,709.9	8,574.3	10,473.7
SACU†	7,665.2	8,524.6	10,613.0
Asia	1,315.3	1,462.8	1,786.8
China, People's Repub.	238.9	265.7	324.5
Hong Kong	386.3	429.6	524.8
Taiwan	448.4	498.7	609.2
European Union	61.5	68.4	83.6
North America	38.1	42.3	51.7
USA	31.8	35.4	43.2
Total (incl. others)	9,135.7	10,160.0	12,420.7

Exports f.o.b.	2005	2006	2007
Africa	813.3	930.9	1,113.1
SACU†	714.2	817.5	1,077.5
European Union	711.0	813.8	973.1
North America	2,600.0	2,976.1	3,558.6
Canada	56.1	64.3	76.8
USA	2,543.8	2,911.8	3,381.7
Total (incl. others)	4,138.1	4,736.7	5,663.8

* Valuation exclusive of import duties. Figures also exclude donated food.
† Southern African Customs Union, of which Lesotho is a member; also including Botswana, Namibia, South Africa and Swaziland.

Source: IMF, *Kingdom of Lesotho: Statistical Appendix* (January 2010).

2008 (US $ million): *Imports:* Germany 14.6; Japan 19.4; South Africa 1,015.2; Total (incl. others) 1,066.2. *Exports:* Canada 1.1; South Africa 202.4; USA 35.8; Total (incl. others) 244.7 (Source: UN, *International Trade Statistics Yearbook*).

Transport

ROAD TRAFFIC
(motor vehicles in use at 31 December, estimates)

	1994	1995	1996
Passenger cars	9,900	11,160	12,610
Lorries and vans	20,790	22,310	25,000

Source: International Road Federation, *World Road Statistics*.

CIVIL AVIATION
(traffic on scheduled services)

	1997	1998	1999
Kilometres flown (million)	0	1	0
Passengers carried ('000)	10	28	1
Passenger-km (million)	3	9	0
Total ton-km (million)	0	1	0

Source: UN, *Statistical Yearbook*.

Tourism

FOREIGN TOURIST ARRIVALS BY COUNTRY OF RESIDENCE

	2007	2008	2009
Botswana	1,679	1,796	2,060
Germany	5,778	3,349	5,015
South Africa	261,099	246,014	302,655
Swaziland	1,246	1,233	1,406
United Kingdom	4,168	2,245	4,619
USA	621	1,311	3,212
Zimbabwe	3,457	4,149	4,513
Total (incl. others)	300,350	293,073	343,743

Total tourist arrivals ('000): 414 in 2010.

Tourism receipts (US $ million, excl. passenger transport, unless otherwise indicated): 24 in 2008; 40 in 2009; 34 in 2010.

Source: World Tourism Organization.

Communications Media

	2009	2010	2011
Telephones ('000 main lines in use)	40.0	38.6	35.6
Mobile cellular telephones ('000 subscribers)	661.0	987.4	1,051.0
Internet users ('000)	76.8	n.a.	n.a.
Broadband subscribers	400	400	n.a.

Personal computers: 5,000 (2.5 per 1,000 persons) in 2005.

Radio receivers ('000 in use): 104 in 1997.

Television receivers ('000 in use): 70 in 2001.

Non-daily newspapers (1996): 7 (average circulation 74,000 copies).

Sources: UNESCO Institute for Statistics; International Telecommunication Union.

Education

(2009/10 unless otherwise indicated)

	Institutions	Teachers	Students		
			Males	Females	Total
Pre-primary	n.a.	2,159	n.a.	n.a.	52,646
Primary	1,455*	11,508	197,909	190,769	388,678
Secondary:					
general	240*	5,837†	51,622	69,169	120,791
technical and vocational	8‡	200†	526	1,990	2,516*
teacher training	1‡	108§	n.a.	n.a.	2,335‖
University	1‡	638*	3,810*	4,690*	8,500*

* 2005/06.

† 2006/07.

‡ 2002/03.

§ 2001/02.

‖ 2004/05.

Source: partly UNESCO Institute for Statistics.

Pupil-teacher ratio (primary education, UNESCO estimate): 33.8 in 2009/10 (Source: UNESCO Institute for Statistics).

Adult literacy rate (UNESCO estimates): 89.6% (males 83.3%; females 95.6%) in 2010 (Source: UNESCO Institute for Statistics).

Directory

The Constitution

The Constitution of the Kingdom of Lesotho, which took effect at independence in October 1966, was suspended in January 1970. A new Constitution was promulgated following the March 1993 general election. Its main provisions, with subsequent amendments, are summarized below:

Lesotho is an hereditary monarchy. The King, who is Head of State, has no executive or legislative powers. Executive authority is vested in the Cabinet, which is headed by the Prime Minister, while legislative power is exercised by the 120-member National Assembly, which comprises 80 members elected on a single-member constituency basis and 40 selected by a system of proportional representation. The National Assembly is elected, at intervals of no more than five years, by universal adult suffrage in the context of a multi-party political system. There is also a Senate, comprising 22 traditional chiefs and 11 nominated members. The Prime Minister is the official head of the armed forces.

The Government

HEAD OF STATE

King: HM King LETSIE III (acceded to the throne 7 February 1996).

CABINET
(September 2012)

The Cabinet is a coalition formed by the All Basotho Convention (ABC), the Basotho National Party (BNP) and the Lesotho Congress for Democracy (LCD).

Prime Minister and Minister of Defence, Police and National Security: THOMAS MOTSOAHAE THABANE (ABC).

Deputy Prime Minister and Minister of Local Government and Chieftainship Affairs: MOTHETJOA METSING (LCD).

Minister of Gender, Youth, Sports and Recreation: THESELE 'MASERIBANE (BNP).

Minister of Development Planning: Prof. MABOEE MOLETSANE (ABC).

Minister of Public Service: Dr MOTLOHELOA PHOOKO (LCD).

Minister of Energy, Meteorology and Water Affairs: THAHANE TIMOTHY THAHANE (LCD).

Minister of Finance: Dr LEKETEKETE VICTOR KETSO (LCD).

Minister of Foreign Affairs and International Relations: MOHLABI TSEKOA (LCD).

Minister of Home Affairs and Public Safety and Parliamentary Affairs: JOANG MOLAPO (BNP).

Minister of Tourism, the Environment and Culture: 'MAMAHELE RADEBE (ABC).

Minister of Public Works and Transport: KEKETSO RANTŠO (LCD).

Minister of Justice, Human Rights, Correctional Service, Law and Constitutional Affairs: HAAE EDWARD PHOOFOLO (ABC).

Minister of Communications, Science and Technology: TŠELISO MOKHOSI (LCD).

Minister of Health and Social Welfare: Dr PINKIE MANAMOLELA (ABC).

Minister of Forestry and Land Reclamation: KHOTSO MATLA (LCD).

Minister of Trade, Industry, Co-operatives and Marketing: TEMEKI PHOENIX TŠOLO (ABC).

Minister of Mining: TLALI KHASU (ABC).

Minister of Agriculture and Food Security: LITŠOANE SIMON LITŠOANE (ABC).

Minister of Education and Training: 'MAKABELO PRISCILLA MOSOTHOANE (LCD).

Minister of Social Development: 'MATEBATSO DOTI (ABC).

Minister of Employment and Labour: LEBESA MALOI (LCD).

Ministers in the Prime Minister's Office: MOLOBELI SOULU (ABC), MOPHATO MOSHOETE MONYAKE (ABC).

In addition there were seven deputy ministers.

MINISTRIES

Office of the Prime Minister: POB 527, Maseru 100; tel. 22311000; fax 22320662; internet www.gov.ls/pm.

Ministry of Agriculture and Food Security: POB 24, Maseru 100; tel. 22316407; fax 22310186; e-mail minagric@leo.co.ls; internet www.gov.ls/agric.

Ministry of Communications, Science and Technology: Moposo House, 3rd Floor, POB 36, Maseru 100; tel. 22324715; fax 22325682; e-mail m.makhorole@mcst.gov.ls; internet www.gov.ls/comms.

Ministry of Defence, Police and National Security: POB 527, Maseru 100; tel. 22311000; fax 22310518; e-mail nmokatsa@yahoo.co.uk; internet www.gov.ls/defence.

Ministry of Development Planning: Maseru 100.

Ministry of Education and Training: POB 47, Maseru 100; tel. 22317900; fax 22326119; e-mail letsoelam@education.gov.ls; internet www.education.gov.ls.

Ministry of Energy, Meteorology and Water Affairs: Maseru 100.

Ministry of Employment and Labour: Private Bag A1164, Maseru 100; tel. 22322602; fax 22325163; e-mail infolabour@leo.co.ls; internet www.labour.gov.ls.

Ministry of Finance: POB 395, Maseru 100; tel. 22311101; e-mail hmf@finance.gov.ls; internet www.finance.gov.ls.

Ministry of Foreign Affairs and International Relations: POB 1387, Maseru 100; tel. 22311150; fax 22310178; e-mail information@foreign.gov.ls; internet www.foreign.gov.ls.

Ministry of Forestry and Land Reclamation: POB 92, Maseru 100; tel. 22313057; fax 22310515; e-mail lincmox@ilesotho.com.

Ministry of Gender, Youth, Sports and Recreation: POB 729, Maseru 100; tel. and fax 22311006; e-mail honsec@mgysr.gov.ls; internet www.gov.ls/gender.

Ministry of Health and Social Welfare: POB 514, Maseru 100; tel. 22317707; fax 22321014; e-mail lesenyehom@health.gov.ls; internet www.health.gov.ls.

Ministry of Home Affairs and Public Safety and Parliamentary Affairs: POB 174, Maseru 100; tel. 22320017; fax 22310013; e-mail mohonoel@homeaffairs.gov.ls; internet www.gov.ls/safety.

Ministry of Justice, Human Rights, Correctional Services, Law and Constitutional Affairs: POB 402, Maseru 100; tel. 22322683; fax 22311092; e-mail dps@justice.gov.ls; internet www.justice.gov.ls.

Ministry of Local Government and Chieftainship Affairs: POB 686, Maseru 100; tel. 22323415; fax 22327782; e-mail minmolg@leo.co.ls; internet www.localgovt.gov.ls.

Ministry of Mining: POB 772, Maseru 100; tel. 22323163; fax 22310527; internet www.gov.ls/natural.

Ministry of Public Service: POB 228, Maseru 100; tel. 22315946; fax 22310883; e-mail minister@mps.gov.ls; internet www.gov.ls/service.

Ministry of Public Works and Transport: POB 20, Maseru 100; tel. 22324697; fax 22310658; e-mail cio@mopwt.gov.ls; internet www.gov.ls/works.

Ministry of Social Development: Maseru 100.

Ministry of Tourism, the Environment and Culture: POB 52, Maseru 100; tel. 22313034; fax 22310194; e-mail pmasita.mohale@mtec.gov.ls; internet www.mtec.gov.ls.

Ministry of Trade, Industry, Co-operatives and Marketing: POB 747, Maseru 100; tel. 22312938; fax 22310644; e-mail mafura@mticm.gov.ls; internet www.trade.gov.ls.

Legislature

PARLIAMENT

National Assembly

POB 190, Maseru; tel. 22323035; fax 22310023; internet www.parliament.ls/TheNationalAssembly/About.aspx.

Speaker: SEPHIRI MOTANYANE.

General Election, 26 May 2012

Party	Constituency seats	Compensatory seats*	Total seats
Democratic Congress (DC)	41	7	48
All Basotho Convention (ABC)	26	4	30
Lesotho Congress for Democracy (LCD)	12	14	26
Basotho National Party (BNP)	—	5	5
Popular Front for Democracy (PFD)	1	2	3
National Independent Party (NIP)	—	2	2
Basotho Batho Democratic Party (BBDP)	—	1	1
Basutoland Congress Party (BCP)	—	1	1
Basotho Democratic National Party (BDNP)	—	1	1
Lesotho People's Congress (LPC)	—	1	1
Lesotho Workers' Party (LWP)	—	1	1
Marematlou Freedom Party (MFP)	—	1	1
Total	80	40	120

* Allocated by proportional representation.

Senate

POB 553, Maseru 100; tel. 22315338; fax 22310023; internet www.parliament.ls/Senate/AboutSenate.aspx.

President: Chief LETAPATA MAKHAOLA.

The Senate is an advisory chamber, comprising 22 traditional chiefs and 11 members appointed by the monarch.

Election Commission

Independent Electoral Commission (IEC): Moposo House, 7th Floor, Kingsway, POB 12698, Maseru 100; tel. 22314991; fax 22310398; internet www.iec.org.ls; f. 1997 as successor to the Constituency Delimitation Commission; Chair. LIMAKATSO MOKHOTHU.

Political Organizations

In March 2012 a total of 15 parties were registered by the Independent Electoral Commission. At least a further 10 parties had applied to be registered to participate in the May legislative elections.

All Basotho Convention (ABC): Maseru; f. 2006 by fmr mems of the Lesotho Congress for Democracy; Pres. THOMAS MOTSOAHAE THABANE.

Basotho Batho Democratic Party (BBDP): f. 2006; Leader JEREMANE RAMATHEBANE.

Basotho Democratic National Party (BDNP): e-mail joangmolapo@hotmail.com; internet bdnp.blogspot.com; f. 2006; Leader THABANG NYEOE; Sec.-Gen. PELELE LETSOALA.

Basotho National Party (BNP): POB 124, Maseru 100; f. 1958; Leader THESELE MASERIBANE; Sec.-Gen. RANTHOMENG MATETE; 280,000 mems.

Basutoland Congress Party (BCP): POB 111, Maseru 100; tel. 8737076; f. 1952; Leader THULO MAHLAKENG.

Democratic Congress: Maseru; f. 2012; formed by Prime Minister Mosisili who broke away from the ruling LCD; Leader BETHUEL PAKALITHA MOSISILI.

Lesotho Congress for Democracy (LCD): POB 7, Mohole's Hoek; tel. 785207; f. 1997 as a result of divisions within the BCP; Chair. MOEKETSI MOLETSANE; Sec.-Gen. MOTHETJOA METSING; 200,000 mems.

Lesotho People's Congress (LPC): f. 2001 following split in the LCD; Leader KELEBONE ALBERT MAOPE; Sec.-Gen. SHAKHANE MOKHEHLE.

Lesotho Workers' Party (LWP): Maseru; f. 2001; Leader MACAEFA BILLY.

Marematlou Freedom Party (MFP): POB 0443, Maseru 105; tel. 315804; f. 1962 following merger between the Marema Tlou Party and Basutoland Freedom Party; Leader MOEKETSE MALEBO; Dep. Leader THABO LEANYA.

National Independent Party (NIP): Maseru; f. 1984; Pres. ANTHONY CLOVIS MANYELI.

Popular Front for Democracy (PFD): Maseru; f. 1991; left-wing; Leader LEKHETHO RAKUOANE.

Diplomatic Representation

EMBASSIES AND HIGH COMMISSIONS IN LESOTHO

China, People's Republic: POB 380, Maseru 100; tel. 22316521; fax 22310489; e-mail chinaemb_ls@mfa.gov.cn; internet ls.china-embassy.org; Ambassador HU DINGXIAN.

Ireland: Tona-Kholo Rd, Private Bag A67, Maseru 100; tel. 22314068; fax 22310028; e-mail maseruembassy@dfa.ie; internet www.embassyofireland.org.ls; Ambassador GERRY GERVIN.

Libya: 173 Tona-Kholo Rd, Maseru West, POB 432, Maseru 100; tel. 22320148; fax 22327750; Chargé d'affaires a.i. ABDUL-MOEINE GARGOUM.

South Africa: Lesotho Bank Tower, 10th Floor, Kingsway, Private Bag A266, Maseru 100; tel. 22315758; fax 22310128; e-mail sahcmas@lesoff.co.ls; High Commissioner HAPPY MAHLANGU.

USA: 254 Kingsway, POB 333, Maseru 100; tel. 22312666; fax 22310116; e-mail infomaseru@state.gov; internet maseru.usembassy.gov; Ambassador MICHELE THOREN BOND.

Judicial System

HIGH COURT

The High Court is a superior court of record, and in addition to any other jurisdiction conferred by statute it is vested with unlimited original jurisdiction to determine any civil or criminal matter. It also has appellate jurisdiction to hear appeals and reviews from the subordinate courts. Appeals may be made to the Court of Appeal.

POB 90, Maseru; tel. 22312188; internet www.justice.gov.ls/judiciary/high_court.html.

Chief Justice: MAHAPELA LEHOHLA.

COURT OF APPEAL

POB 90, Maseru; tel. 22312188; internet www.justice.gov.ls/judiciary/appeal.html.

President: MATHEALIRA RAMODIBEDI.

SUBORDINATE COURTS

Each of the 10 districts possesses subordinate courts, presided over by magistrates.

Chief Magistrate: MOLEFI MAKARA.

JUDICIAL COMMISSIONERS' COURTS

These courts hear civil and criminal appeals from central and local courts. Further appeal may be made to the High Court and finally to the Court of Appeal.

CENTRAL AND LOCAL COURTS

There are 71 such courts, of which 58 are local courts and 13 are central courts which also serve as courts of appeal from the local courts. They have limited civil and criminal jurisdiction.

Religion

About 90% of the population profess Christianity.

CHRISTIANITY

African Federal Church Council (AFCC): POB 70, Peka 340; f. 1927; co-ordinating org. for 48 African independent churches.

Christian Council of Lesotho (CCL): POB 547, Maseru 100; tel. 22313639; fax 22310310; f. 1833; 112 congregations; 261,350 mems (2003); Chair. Rev. PHILLIP MOKUKU; Sec. CATHERINE RAMOKHELE.

The Anglican Communion

Anglicans in Lesotho are adherents of the Anglican Church of Southern Africa (formerly the Church of the Province of Southern Africa). The Metropolitan of the Province is the Archbishop of Cape Town, South Africa. Lesotho forms a single diocese, with an estimated 200,000 members.

Bishop of Lesotho: MALLANE ADAM TAASO, Bishop's House, POB 87, Maseru 100; tel. 22311974; fax 22310161; e-mail diocese@ilesotho.com.

The Roman Catholic Church

Lesotho comprises one archdiocese and three dioceses. Some 52% of the total population are Roman Catholics.

Lesotho Catholic Bishops' Conference

Catholic Secretariat, POB 200, Maseru 100; tel. 22312525; fax 22310294.

f. 1972; Pres. (vacant).

Archbishop of Maseru: Most Rev. GERARD TLALI LEROTHOLI, Archbishop's House, 19 Orpen Rd, POB 267, Maseru 100; tel. 22312565; fax 22310425; e-mail archmase@lesoff.co.za.

Other Christian Churches

At mid-2000 there were an estimated 279,000 Protestants and 257,000 adherents professing other forms of Christianity.

African Methodist Episcopal Church: POB 223, Maseru 100; tel. 22311801; fax 22310548; e-mail bishopsarah@leo.co.ls; f. 1903; Presiding Prelate Rt Rev. SARAH F. DAVIS; 15,000 mems.

Lesotho Evangelical Church: POB 260, Maseru 100; tel. 22323942; f. 1833; independent since 1964; Pres. Rev. TSELISO MASEMENE; Exec. Sec. Rev. GILBERT RAMATLAPENG; 230,000 mems (2003).

Other denominations active in Lesotho include the Apostolic Faith Mission, the Assemblies of God, the Dutch Reformed Church in Africa, the Full Gospel Church of God, Methodist Church of Southern Africa and the Seventh-day Adventists. There are also numerous African independent churches.

BAHÁ'Í FAITH

National Spiritual Assembly of the Bahá'ís of Lesotho: POB 508, Maseru 100; tel. 22312346; e-mail bahailesotho@leo.co.ls.

The Press

Lesotho does not have a daily newspaper.

Leseli ka Sepolesa (The Police Witness): Press Dept, Police Headquarters, Maseru CBD, POB 13, Maseru 100; tel. 22317262; fax 22310045; fortnightly; Sesotho; publ. by the Lesotho Mounted Police Services; Editor-in-Chief CLIFFORD MOLEFE.

Leselinyana la Lesotho (Light of Lesotho): Morija Printing Works, POB 7, Morija 190; tel. 22360244; fax 22360005; e-mail mpw@lesoff.co.ls; f. 1863; fortnightly; Sesotho, with occasional articles in English; publ. by the Lesotho Evangelical Church; Editor MABATSOENENG EMELY SIBOLLA; circ. 12,000.

Lesotho Times: Maseru; tel. 22315335; fax 22315352; e-mail editor@lestimes.co.ls; internet www.lestimes.com.

Lesotho Today/Lentsoe la Basotho (Voice of the Lesotho Nation): POB 353, Maseru 100; tel. 22323561; fax 22322764; internet www.lesothotoday.co.ls; f. 1974; weekly; Sesotho; publ. by Ministry of Communications, Science and Technology; Editor KAHLISO LESENYANE; circ. 14,000.

Makatolle: POB 111, Maseru 100; tel. 22850990; f. 1963; weekly; Sesotho; Editor M. RAMANGOEI; circ. 2,000.

MoAfrika: MoAfrika Broadcasting and Publishing Services, Carlton Centre Bldg, 1st Floor, POB 7234, Maseru 100; tel. 22321854; fax 22321956; f. 1990 as *The African*; weekly; Sesotho and English; Editor-in-Chief Prof. SEBONONOLA R. K. RAMAINOANE; circ. 5,000.

Moeletsi oa Basotho: Mazenod Institute, POB 18, Mazenod 160; tel. 22350465; fax 22350010; e-mail mzpwrks@lesoff.co.za; f. 1933; weekly; Sesotho; publ. by the Roman Catholic Church; Editor FRANCIS KHOARIPE; circ. 20,000.

Mohahlaula: Allied Bldg, 1st Floor, Manonyane Centre, POB 14430, Maseru 100; tel. 22312777; fax 22320941; weekly; Sesotho; publ. by Makaung Printers and Publrs; Editor WILLY MOLLUNGOA.

Mololi: Cooperatives Bldg, Main North 1 Rd, POB 9933, Maseru 100; tel. 22312287; fax 22327912; f. 1997; Sesotho; organ of the Lesotho Congress for Democracy; Editor (vacant).

Mopheme (The Survivor): Allied Bldg, 1st Floor, Manonyane Centre, POB 14184, Maseru; tel. and fax 22311670; e-mail mopheme@lesoff.co.za; weekly; English and Sesotho; publ. by Newsshare Foundation; Owner and Editor LAWRENCE KEKETSO; circ. 2,500.

Public Eye/Mosotho: House No. 14A3, Princess Margaret Rd, POB 14129, Old Europa, Maseru 100; tel. 22321414; fax 22310614; e-mail editor@publiceye.co.ls; internet www.publiceye.co.ls; f. 1997; weekly; 80% English, 20% Sesotho; publ. by Voice Multimedia; also publ. *Eye on Tourism* and *Family Mirror* magazines; Editor-in-Chief BETHUEL THAI; circ. 20,000 (Lesotho and South Africa).

PERIODICALS

Justice and Peace: Catholic Bishops' Conference, Our Lady of Victories Cathedral Catholic Centre, POB 200, Maseru 100; tel. 22312750; fax 22312751; quarterly; publ. by the Roman Catholic Church.

Moqolotsi (The Journalist): House No. 1B, Happy Villa, POB 14139, Maseru 100; tel. and fax 22320941; e-mail medinles@lesoff.co.za; monthly newsletter; English; publ. by the Media Institute of Lesotho (MILES).

NGO Web: 544 Hoohlo Extension, Florida, Maseru 100; tel. 22325798; fax 22317205; e-mail lecongo@lecongo.org.ls; quarterly; English and Sesotho; publ. of the Lesotho Council of NGOs; circ. 2,000.

Shoeshoe: POB 36, Maseru 100; tel. 22323561; fax 22310003; quarterly; women's interest; publ. by Ministry of Communications, Science and Technology.

Other publications include *Mara LDF Airwing/Airsquadron* and *The Sun/Thebe*.

NEWS AGENCY

Lesotho News Agency (LENA): Lesotho News Agency Complex, Lerotholi St, opp. Royal Palace, POB 36, Maseru 100; tel. 22325317; fax 22324608; e-mail l_lenanews@hotmail.com; internet www.lena.gov.ls; f. 1985; Dir MOTHEPANE KOTELE; Editors MOROA MOPELI, LITEBOHO MAHULA.

Publishers

Longman Lesotho (Pty) Ltd: 104 Christie House, 1st Floor, Orpen Rd, Old Europa, POB 1174, Maseru 100; tel. 22314254; fax 22310118; e-mail connie.burford@pearsoned.com; Man. Dir SEYMOUR R. KIKINE.

Macmillan Boleswa Publishers Lesotho (Pty) Ltd: 523 Sun Cabanas Hotel, POB 7545, Maseru 100; tel. 22317340; fax 22310047; e-mail macmillan@lesoff.co.ls; Man. Dir PAUL MOROLONG.

Mazenod Institute: POB 39, Mazenod 160; tel. 22350224; f. 1933; Roman Catholic; Man. Fr B. MOHLALISI.

Morija Sesuto Book Depot: POB 4, Morija 190; tel. and fax 22360204; f. 1862; owned by the Lesotho Evangelical Church; religious, educational and Sesotho language and literature.

St Michael's Mission: The Social Centre, POB 25, Roma; tel. 22316234; f. 1968; religious and educational; Man. Dir Fr M. FERRANGE.

GOVERNMENT PUBLISHING HOUSE

Government Printer: POB 268, Maseru; tel. 22313023.

Broadcasting and Communications

TELECOMMUNICATIONS

In 2011 there were two providers of mobile cellular telephone services and one provider of fixed-line telephone services.

Lesotho Communications Authority (LCA): Moposo House, 6th Floor, Kingsway Rd, POB 15896, Maseru 100; tel. 22224300; fax 22310984; e-mail lca@lca.org.ls; internet www.lca.org.ls; f. 2000; regulates telecommunications and broadcasting; Chief Exec. MONEHELA POSHOLI.

Econet Telecom Lesotho (ETL): POB 1037, Maseru 100; tel. 22211000; fax 22310600; e-mail enquiries@telecom.co.ls; internet www.telecom.co.ls; 70% holding acquired by the Econet Wireless Group in 2007; 30% state-owned; Chair. PAKO PETLANE; CEO NICO HEYNS.

Vodacom Lesotho (Pty) Ltd: Block B, 7th Floor, Development House, Kingsway Rd, POB 7387, Maseru 100; tel. 52212201; fax 22311079; internet www.vodacom.co.za; f. 1996; jt venture between Telecom Lesotho and Vodacom (Pty) Ltd; fmrly VCL Communications; mobile cellular telecommunications provider; CEO PIETER UYS.

BROADCASTING

RADIO

The first licences for private radio stations were issued in 1998. Licences are issued by the Lesotho Telecommunications Authority. Radio Lesotho is the only station to broadcast nationwide; all the other stations are restricted to urban areas and their peripheries.

Catholic Radio FM: Our Lady of Victories Cathedral, Catholic Centre POB 200, Maseru 100; tel. 22323247; fax 22310294; f. 1999.

Harvest FM: Carlton Centre, 3rd Floor, Room No. 312, POB 442, Maseru 100; tel. 22313168; fax 22313858; e-mail mlekhoaba@harvestfm.co.ls; internet www.harvestfm.co.ls; operated by Harvest FM Trust; affiliated to United Christian Broadcasters Africa, South Africa; evangelical religious programming; Station Man. MARY MOSHOESHOE.

Joy FM: Lesotho Sun Hotel, Suites 2204–2206, Private Bag A457, Maseru 100; tel. 22310920; fax 22310104; internet www.joyfm.co.ls; f. 2001; Sesotho and English; relays Voice of America broadcasts.

Khotso FM: Institute of Extramural Studies, National University of Lesotho POB 180, Roma; Private Bag A47, Maseru 100; tel. 22322038; fax 22340000; community radio station; sister station of DOPE FM (f. 2004).

MoAfrika FM: Carlton Centre, 2nd Floor, Kingsway, POB 7234, Maseru 100; tel. and fax 22321956; e-mail info@moafrika.co.ls; internet www.moafrika.co.ls; affiliated to the *MoAfrika* newspaper; Sesotho, Xhosa and Mandarin; news and entertainment; Man. and Editor-in-Chief Prof. SEBONONOLA R. K. RAMAINOANE.

People's Choice Radio (PCFM): LNDC Centre, Development House, Level 9, Block D, POB 8800, Maseru 100; tel. 22322122; fax 22310888; internet www.pcfm.co.ls; f. 1998; news and entertainment; Man. Dir MOTLATSI MAJARA.

Radio Lesotho: Lesotho News Agency Complex, Lerotholi St, opp. Royal Palace, POB 36, Maseru 100; tel. and fax 22322714; e-mail enquiries@africanextension.com; internet www.radiolesotho.co.ls; f. 1964; state-owned; part of Lesotho Nat. Broadcasting Services; Sesotho and English; Dir of Broadcasting LEBOHANG DADA MOQASA.

TELEVISION

Lesotho Television (LTV): Lesotho News Agency Complex, Lerotholi St, opp. Royal Palace, POB 36, Maseru 100; tel. 22324735; fax 22310149; e-mail mfalatsa@yahoo.com; f. 1988 in association with M-Net, South Africa; state-owned; part of Lesotho Nat. Broadcasting Services; Sesotho and English.

Finance

(cap. = capital; res = reserves; dep. = deposits; m. = million; brs = branches; amounts in maloti)

BANKING

In 2008 there were four commercial banks in Lesotho.

Central Bank

Central Bank of Lesotho: cnr Airport and Moshoeshoe Rds, POB 1184, Maseru 100; tel. 22314281; fax 22310051; e-mail cbl@centralbank.org.ls; internet www.centralbank.org.ls; f. 1978 as the Lesotho Monetary Authority; present name adopted in 1982; bank of issue; cap. 25.0m., res 1,479.1m., dep. 5,093.2m. (Dec. 2009); Gov. and Chair. Dr M. SENAOANA.

Commercial Banks

First National Bank Lesotho: POB 11902, Maseru 100; tel. 22222200; f. 2004; CEO J. JORDAAN; 1 br.

Lesotho PostBank (LPB): Oblate House, Kingsway Rd, Private Bag A121, Maseru 100; tel. 22317842; fax 22313170; e-mail info@lpb.co.ls; internet www.lpb.co.ls; f. 2004; state-owned; Chair. TŠELISO MOKELA; CEO MPHO VUMBUKANI; 12 brs.

Nedbank (Lesotho) Ltd: 115–117 Griffith Hill, Kingsway St, POB 1001, Maseru 100; tel. 22312696; fax 22310025; e-mail georgego@nedcor.co.za; internet www.nedbank.co.ls; f. 1997; fmrly Standard Chartered Bank Lesotho Ltd; 100% owned by Nedbank Ltd (South Africa); cap. 20m., res 205m., dep. 1,969m. (Dec. 2009); Chair. SOPHIA MOHAPI; Man. Dir LAZARUS MURAHWA; 3 brs and 7 agencies.

Standard Lesotho Bank: Banking Bldg, 1st Floor, Kingsway Rd, Kingsway Town Centre, POB 1053, Maseru 100; tel. 22315737; fax 22317321; internet www.standardbank.co.ls; f. 2006 following merger between Lesotho Bank (1999) Ltd (f. 1972) and Standard Bank Lesotho Ltd (fmrly Stanbic Bank Lesotho Ltd); Chair. THABO MAKEBA; Man. Dir COLIN ADDIS; 11 brs.

INSURANCE

In 2008 there were five insurance companies in Lesotho.

Alliance Insurance Co Ltd: Alliance House, 4 Bowker Rd, POB 01118, Maseru West 105; tel. 22312357; fax 22310313; e-mail alliance@alliance.co.ls; internet www.alliance.co.ls; f. 1993; life and short-term insurance; Man. Dir ROB DUNCAN; Gen. Mans MOK'HAPHEK'HA LAZARO, THABISO MADIBA.

Lesotho National General Insurance Co Ltd (LNIG): Lesotho Insurance House, Kingsway, Private Bag A65, Maseru 100; tel. 22313031; fax 22310007; e-mail manager@lngic.com; f. 1977 as Lesotho National Insurance Group; 60% owned by Regent Insurance Co Ltd (South Africa), 20% state-owned, 20% owned by Molepe Investment Holdings (Pty) Ltd; part-privatized in 1995; incorporating subsidiaries specializing in life and short-term insurance; Chair. Dr TIMOTHY THAHANE; Man. Dir R. J. LETSOELA.

Metropolitan Lesotho Ltd: Metropolitan Bldg, Kingsway St, POB 645, Maseru; tel. 22222300; fax 22317278; internet www.metropolitan.co.ls; f. 2003; subsidiary of Metropolitan Holdings Ltd, South Africa; Man. Dir NKAU MATETE.

Trade and Industry

GOVERNMENT AGENCIES

Privatisation Unit: Privatisation Project, Lesotho Utilities Sector Reform Project, Ministry of Finance and Development Planning, Lesotho Bank Mortgage Division Bldg, 2nd Floor, Kingsway St, Private Bag A249, Maseru 100; tel. 22317902; fax 22317551; e-mail mntsasa@privatisation.gov.ls; internet www.privatisation.gov.ls; CEO MOSITO KHETHISA.

Trade Promotion Unit: c/o Ministry of Trade, Industry, Co-operatives and Marketing, POB 747, Maseru 100; tel. 322138; fax 310121; e-mail tradepu@lesoff.co.za.

DEVELOPMENT ORGANIZATIONS

Basotho Enterprises Development Corpn (BEDCO): Sebaboleng Trade and Industrial Centre, POB 1216, Maseru 100; tel. 22312094; fax 22310455; e-mail info@bedco.org.ls; internet www.bedco.org.ls; f. 1980; promotes and assists in the establishment and devt of Basotho-owned enterprises, with emphasis on small- and medium-scale; Chair. MOHLOMI D. RANTEKOA; CEO TS'ELISO MOKHOSI.

Lesotho Co-operative Handicrafts: Basotho Hat Bldg, Kingsway, PO Box 148, Maseru; tel. 22322523; e-mail lch@ilesotho.com; internet www.basothohat.co.ls; f. 1978; marketing and distribution of handicrafts; Gen. Man. KHOTSO MATLA.

Lesotho Council of Non-Governmental Organizations: House 544, Hoohlo Extension, Private Bag A445, Maseru 100; tel. 22317205; fax 22310412; e-mail lecongo@lecongo.org.ls; internet www.lecongo.org.ls; f. 1990; promotes sustainable management of natural resources, socio-economic devt and social justice; Exec. Dir MABULARA TS'UENE (acting).

Lesotho National Dairy Board: Maseru; f. 1991; prescribes standards of production, storage, packaging, processing and distribution of dairy products.

Lesotho Highlands Development Authority (LHDA): Lesotho Bank Tower, 3rd Floor, Kingsway, POB 7332, Maseru 100; tel. 22311280; fax 22310665; e-mail lhwp@lhda.org.ls; internet www.lhda.org.ls; f. 1986 to implement the Lesotho Highlands Water Project, being undertaken jtly with South Africa; Chair. J. EAGAR; CEO PETER MAKUTA (acting).

Lesotho National Development Corpn (LNDC): Development House, Block A, Kingsway, Private Bag A96, Maseru 100; tel. 22312012; fax 22310038; e-mail info@lndc.org.ls; internet www.lndc.org.ls; f. 1967; state-owned; total assets M477.5m. (March 2006); interests in manufacturing, mining, food-processing and leisure; Chair. MOHLOMI RANTEKOA; CEO JOSHUA SETIPA.

CHAMBER OF COMMERCE

Lesotho Chamber of Commerce and Industry: Kingsway Ave, POB 79, Maseru 100; tel. 22316937; fax 22322794; Pres. SIMON KUENA PHAFANE.

INDUSTRIAL AND TRADE ASSOCIATIONS

Livestock Marketing Corpn: POB 800, Maseru 100; tel. 22322444; f. 1973; sole org. for marketing livestock and livestock products; liaises with marketing boards in South Africa; projects incl. an abattoir, tannery, poultry and wool and mohair scouring plants; Gen. Man. S. R. MATLANYANE.

EMPLOYERS' ORGANIZATION

Association of Lesotho Employers: 18 Bowker Rd, POB 1509, Maseru 100; tel. 22315736; fax 22325384; e-mail makeka@leo.co.ls; f. 1961; represents mems in industrial relations and on govt bodies, and advises the Govt on employers' concerns; Pres. RADITAPOLE LETSOELA; Exec. Dir THABO MAKEKA.

UTILITIES

Lesotho Electricity Authority (LEA): Moposo House, 6th Floor, Kingsway, Private Bag A315, Maseru; tel. 22312479; fax 22315094; e-mail secretary@lea.org.ls; internet www.lea.org.ls; f. 2004; Chair. FRANCINA LIAKO MOLOI; Chief Exec. NTOI PAUL RAPAPA.

Lesotho Electricity Co (LEC): 53 Moshoeshoe Rd, POB 423, Maseru 100; tel. 22312236; fax 22310093; e-mail info@lec.co.ls; internet www.lec.co.ls; f. 1969; 100% state-owned; Chair. Dr K. LESOETSA; Man. Dir F. M. HLOAELE.

Lesotho Water and Sewerage Authority (WASA): POB 426, Maseru 100; tel. 22312449; fax 22312006; internet www.wasa.co.ls; Chair. REFILOE TLALI.

MAJOR COMPANIES

Kingsway Construction (Pty) Ltd: Private Bag A53, Maseru 100; tel. 22313181; fax 22310137; f. 1986; Chair. T. HENDRY; 220 employees.

Lesaco Sandstone Cc (LESACO): POB 43522, Heuwelsig 9332; tel. 826513229; fax 514474400; e-mail lesaco@xsinet.co.za; f. 1989; import, export and mfrs of natural sandstone products; CEO R. FACTA; 90 employees.

Lesotho Brewing Co (Pty) Ltd: Maseru; tel. 22311111; fax 22310020; e-mail njmatete@lbc.co.ls; f. 1981; 39% owned by SABMiller Africa BV, Netherlands; beer and carbonated soft drinks; Chair. PEETE MOLAPO; Man. Dir GREG UYS; 315 employees.

Lesotho Dairy Products Pty Ltd: Old Thaba-Bosiu Rd, Botsabelo Botsabelo, Maseru 100; tel. 22313875; fax 22310397; f. 1987.

Lesotho Flour Mills: Private Bag A62, Maseru 100; tel. 22313498; fax 22310037; f. 1979; 51% owned by Seaboard USA; mfrs of maize and wheat products and animal feed; incorporates Lesotho Maize Mills, Lesotho Farm Feed Mills, and Lesotho Sugar Packers; privatized in 1998; Man. Dir JAN H. VAN DER MOLEN; 334 employees.

Lesotho Milling Co Pty Ltd: POB 39, Maputsoe; tel. 22430622; fax 22430010; e-mail lesco@yebo.co.za; f. 1980; milling and export of maize; Man. Dir GRAHAM GATCKE; 140 employees (2009).

Lesotho Pharmaceutical Corpn (LPC): POB 256, Mafeteng 900; tel. 22700326; fax 22700002; e-mail gertie@lpc.co.ls; pharmaceutical products; CEO GERTRUDE MOTHIBE; 110 employees.

TRADE UNIONS

Congress of Lesotho Trade Unions (COLETU): POB 13282, Maseru 100; tel. 22320958; fax 22310081; f. 1998; Sec.-Gen. VUYANI TYHALI; 15,587 mems.

Construction and Allied Workers' Union of Lesotho (CAWULE): Manonyana Centre, 2nd Floor, Room 24, POB 132282, Maseru 100; tel. 63023484; fax 22321951; f. 1967; Pres. L. PUTSOANE; Sec. T. TLALE.

Factory Workers' Union (FAWU): Maseru; f. 2003 following split from the Lesotho Clothing and Allied Workers' Union; Pres. KHABILE TSILO; Sec.-Gen. BILLY MACAEFA.

Lesotho Association of Teachers (LAT): POB 12528, Maseru 100; tel. and fax 22317463; Exec. Sec. PAUL P. SEMATLANE.

Lesotho Clothing and Allied Workers' Union (LECAWU): LNDC Centre, 2nd Floor, Rm 12–14, Kingsway Rd, POB 11767, Maseru 100; tel. 22324296; fax 22320958; e-mail lecawu@lesoff.co.ls; Sec.-Gen. MATŠEPO LEHLOKOANA; 6,000 mems.

Lesotho Congress of Democratic Unions (LECODU): POB 15851, Maseru 100; tel. and fax 22323559; f. 2004; Sec.-Gen. DANIEL MARAISANE; 15,279 mems (2005).

Lesotho General Workers' Union: POB 322, Maseru 100; f. 1954; Chair. J. M. RAMAROTHOLE; Sec. T. MOTLOHI.

Lesotho Teachers' Trade Union (LTTU): POB 0509, Maseru West 105; tel. 22322774; fax 22311673; e-mail lttu@leo.co.ls; Gen. Sec. MALIMABE JOAKIM MOTOPELA.

Lesotho Transport and Allied Workers' Union: Maseru 100; f. 1959; Pres. M. BERENG; Gen. Sec. TSEKO KAPA.

Transport

RAILWAYS

Lesotho is linked with the South African railway system by a short line (2.6 km in length) from Maseru to Marseilles, on the Bloemfontein–Natal main line.

ROADS

In 2000 Lesotho's road network totalled 5,940 km, of which 1,084 km were main roads and 1,950 km were secondary roads. About 18.3% of roads were paved. In 1996 the International Development Association granted US $40m. towards the Government's rolling five-year road programme. From 1996/97 an extra-budgetary Road Fund was to finance road maintenance. In March 2000 a major road network was opened, linking Maseru with the Mohale Dam.

CIVIL AVIATION

King Moshoeshoe I International Airport is at Thota-Moli, some 20 km from Maseru; in January 2002 the Government announced plans for its expansion. International services between Maseru and Johannesburg are operated by South African Airlink. The national airline company, Lesotho Airways, was sold to a South African company in 1997 as part of the Government's ongoing privatization programme; however, after two years of losses the company was liquidated in 1999.

Tourism

Spectacular mountain scenery is the principal tourist attraction, and a new ski resort was opened in 2003. Tourist arrivals totalled 343,743 in 2009. In 2010 receipts from tourism amounted to an estimated US $34m.

Lesotho Tourism Development Corpn (LTDC): cnr Linare and Parliament Rds, POB 1378, Maseru 100; tel. 22312238; fax 22310189; e-mail ltdc@ltdc.org.ls; internet www.ltdc.org.ls; f. 2000; successor to the Lesotho Tourist Board; Chair. MAMORUTI MALIE.

Defence

Military service is voluntary. As assessed at November 2011, the Lesotho Defence Force (LDF, formerly the Royal Lesotho Defence Force) comprised 2,000 men, including an air wing of 110 men. The creation of a new commando force unit, the first professional unit in the LDF, was announced in October 2001, as part of ongoing efforts to restructure the armed forces.

Defence Expenditure: Estimated at M374m. for 2012.

Commander of the Lesotho Defence Force: Lt-Gen. THUSO MOTANYANE.

Education

All primary education is available free of charge, and is provided mainly by the three main Christian missions (Lesotho Evangelical, Roman Catholic and Anglican), under the direction of the Ministry of Education. Education at primary schools is officially compulsory for seven years between six and 13 years of age. Secondary education, beginning at the age of 13, lasts for up to five years, comprising a first cycle of three years and a second of two years. According to UNESCO estimates, in 2008/09 total enrolment at primary schools included 73% of children in the appropriate age-group (72% of boys; 75% of girls); in that year enrolment at secondary schools included 29% of children in the relevant age-group (22% of boys; 36% of girls). Some 8,500 students were enrolled at the National University of Lesotho, at Roma, in 2005/06. Proposed expenditure on education in 2008 represented 23.7% of total government expenditure. In January 2006 17 new schools, constructed with the assistance of the Government of Japan, were opened; they were expected to accommodate some 14,000 pupils.

Bibliography

Akindele, F., and Senyane, R. (Eds). *The Irony of the 'White Gold'.* Morija, Transformation Resource Centre, 2004.

Chaka-Makhooane, L., *et al. Sexual Violence in Lesotho: The Realities of Justice for Women.* Morija, Women and Law in Southern Africa Research and Education Trust, 2002.

Chigara, B. *Southern African Development Community Land Issues Volume I: Towards a New Sustainable Land Relations Policy.* Abingdon, Routledge, 2011.

Eldredge, E. A. *Power in Colonial Africa: Conflict and Discourse in Lesotho.* Madison, WI, University of Wisconsin Press, 2007.

Ferguson, J. (Ed.). *The Anti-Politics Machine: Development, Depoliticization and Bureaucratic State Power in Lesotho.* Cambridge, Cambridge University Press; Cape Town, David Philip, 1990.

Gary, J., *et al* (Eds). *Lesotho's Long Journey: Hard Choices at the Crossroads: A Comprehensive Overview of Lesotho's Historical, Social, Economic and Political Development With a View to the Future.* (Commissioned and funded by Irish Aid.) Maseru, Sechaba Consultants, 1995.

Gill, S. J. *A Short History of Lesotho, From the Late Stone Age Until the 1993 Elections.* Morija, Morija Museum and Archives, 1993.

Hinks, C. W. *Quest for Peace. An Ecumenical History of the Church in Lesotho.* Morija, Christian Council of Lesotho, 2009.

Kabemba, C. (Ed.), *et al. From Military Rule to Multiparty Democracy: Political Reforms and Challenges in Lesotho.* Johannesburg, Electoral Institute of Southern Africa (EISA), 2003.

Kimyaro, S. S. (Ed.), *et al. Turning a Crisis into an Opportunity: Strategies for Scaling up the National Response to the HIV/AIDS Pandemic in Lesotho.* New York, New Rochelle, 2004.

Leduka, R. C. *Informal Land Delivery Processes and Access to Land for the Poor in Maseru, Lesotho.* Birmingham, International Development Department, School of Public Policy, University of Birmingham, 2004.

Letuka, P., Mapetla, M., and Matashane-Marite, K. *Gender and Elections in Lesotho: Perspectives on the 2002 Elections.* Johannesburg, Electoral Institute of Southern Africa (EISA), 2004.

Lundahl, M., McCarthy, C., and Petersson, L. *In the Shadow of South Africa: Lesotho's Economic Future.* Aldershot, Ashgate, 2003.

Lundahl, M., and Petersson, L. *The Dependent Economy: Lesotho and the Southern Africa Customs Union.* Boulder, CO, Westview Press, 1991.

Machobane, L. B. B. J. *Government and Change in Lesotho, 1800–1966: A Study of Political Institutions.* Maseru, Macmillan Lesotho, 1990.

The King's Knights: Military Governance in the Kingdom of Lesotho, 1986–1993. Roma, Institute of Southern African Studies, National University of Lesotho, 2001.

Machobane, L. B. B. J., and Manyeli, T. L. *Essays on Religion and Culture among Basotho, 1800–1900.* Mazenod, Mazenod Publrs, 2001.

Makoa, F. K. *Elections, Election Outcomes and Electoral Politics in Lesotho.* Pretoria, Africa Institute of South Africa, 2002.

Maloka, E. T. *Basotho and the Mines: A Social History of Labour Migrancy in Lesotho and South Africa, c. 1890–1940.* Dakar, Council for the Development of Social Science Research in Africa, 2004.

Mapetla, M., *et al. State of Good Governance in Lesotho, 1993-2003.* Roma, National Univeristy of Lesotho, 2007.

Maqutu, W. C. M. *Contemporary Constitutional History of Lesotho.* Mazenod, Mazenod Institute, 1990.

Maro, P. *Environmental Change in Lesotho: An Analysis of the Causes and Consequences of Land-Use Change in the Lowland Region.* New York, Springer, 2011.

McCall Theal, G. *Basutoland Records: Vols 4–6, 1868–1872.* Roma, Institute of Southern African Studies, National University of Lesotho, 2002.

Mochebelele, M. T., *et al. Agricultural Marketing in Lesotho.* Ottawa, International Development Research Centre, 1992.

Mohapeloa, J. M. *Tentative British Imperialism in Lesotho, 1884–1910: a Study in Basotho-colonial Office Interaction, and South Africa's Influence on it.* Morija, Morija Museum and Archives, 2002.

Moremoholo, E. *Lesotho's Economy Beyond Independence: The Role and Impact of Chinese Investment on Quality of Life.* Lambert Academic Publishing, 2012.

Mphanya, N. *A Brief History of the Basutoland Congress Party: Lekhotla la Mahatammoho, 1952–2002.* Morija, 2004.

Murray, C. *Families Divided: The Impact of Migrant Labour in Lesotho.* Cambridge, Cambridge University Press, 2009.

Olaleye, W. *Democratic Consolidation and Political Parties in Lesotho.* Johannesburg, Electoral Institute of Southern Africa (EISA), 2004.

Pherudi, M. L. *Storm in the Mountain.* Maluti, Hochland Printers, 2004.

Pule, N. W., and Thabane, M. (Eds). *Essays on Aspects of the Political Economy of Lesotho, 1500–2000.* Roma, Department of History, National University of Lesotho, 2002.

Rosenberg, S., Weisfelder, R. F., and Frisbie-Fulton, M. *Historical Dictionary of Lesotho.* Lanham, MD, Scarecrow Press, 2004.

Rwelamira, M. *Refugees in a Chess Game: Reflections on Botswana, Lesotho and Swaziland Refugee Policies.* Trenton, NJ, Red Sea Press, 1990.

Southall, R., and Petlane, T. (Eds). *Democratisation and Demilitarisation in Lesotho: The General Election of 1993 and its Aftermath.* Pretoria, Africa Institution of South Africa, 1996.

LIBERIA

Physical and Social Geography

CHRISTOPHER CLAPHAM

The Republic of Liberia was founded in 1847 by freed black slaves from the USA who were resettled from 1821 onwards along the western Guinea coast between Cape Mount (11° 20' W) and Cape Palmas (7° 40' W). Liberia extends from 4° 20' N to 8° 30' N, with a maximum breadth of 280 km between Buchanan and Nimba. The country occupies an area of 97,754 sq km (37,743 sq miles) between Sierra Leone to the west, the Republic of Guinea to the north and Côte d'Ivoire to the east.

PHYSICAL FEATURES AND POPULATION

An even coastline of 570 km, characterized by powerful surf, rocky cliffs and lagoons, makes access from the Atlantic Ocean difficult, except at the modern ports. The flat coastal plain, which is 15 km–55 km wide, consists of forest and savannah. The interior hills and mountain ranges, with altitudes of 180 m–360 m, form part of an extended peneplain, covered by evergreen (in the south) or semi-deciduous (in the north) rainforests. The northern highlands contain Liberia's greatest elevations, which include the Nimba mountains, reaching 1,752 m above sea-level, and the Wologisi range, reaching 1,381 m. The descent from the higher to the lower belts of the highlands is characterized by rapids and waterfalls.

Liberia has two rainy seasons near Harper, in the south, and one rainy season (from May to October) in the rest of the country. From Monrovia, on the coast in north-west Liberia, with an average of 4,650 mm per year, rainfall decreases towards the south-east and the hinterland, reaching 2,240 mm per year at Ganta. Average temperatures are more extreme in the interior than at the coast. Monrovia has an annual average of 26°C, with absolute limits at 33°C and 14°C, respectively. At Tappita temperatures may rise to 44°C in March and fall to 9°C during cool harmattan nights in December or January. Mean water temperature on the coast is 27°C.

The drainage system consists of 15 principal river basins, of which those of the Cavalla river, with an area of 30,225 sq km (including 13,730 sq km in Liberia), and of the St Paul river, with an area of 21,910 sq km (11,325 sq km in Liberia), are the largest. The water flow varies considerably and may reach over 100,000 cubic feet per second (cfs) at the Mt Coffee gauge of the St Paul river in August or decrease to 2,000 cfs during the dry season in March.

The first Liberian census enumerated a population of 1,016,443 in April 1962. The fourth Liberian census, conducted on 21 March 2008, enumerated a population of 3,476,608, an increase of 66% compared with the total population at the 1984 census. The population was estimated by the UN to have increased to 4,244,683 by mid-2012.

The demographic pattern of Liberia is characterized by a number of features typical of developing countries: a high birth rate (estimated at 40.5 per 1,000 in 2005–10); a high proportion of children under 15 years of age (estimated at 43.4% of the total population in 2012); and a low expectation of life at birth (estimated at 56 years in 2010). The average population density is low (43.4 inhabitants per sq km at mid-2012), but urbanization has been rapid, resulting in an estimated 45.6% of the population living in urban areas in 1996. The population of Monrovia increased from 80,992 in 1962 to 208,629 in 1978, and to 421,058 in 1984; influxes of people displaced by the fighting may have taken the population above 1.3m. during the 1989–96 war. In 2011 the population of Monrovia was estimated at 750,376.

The war of 1989–96 caused massive displacements of population: at many times during the conflict one-third of the population fled to neighbouring countries, and a further one-third were internally displaced. The mass repatriation of Liberian refugees commenced in 1997. Following further rebel activity in Liberia from early 2001, some 119,293 Liberian refugees were in Guinea and about 43,000 in Côte d'Ivoire at 1 January 2003, according to the office of the UN High Commissioner for Refugees (UNHCR). The advance of hostilities to Monrovia in mid-2003 precipitated a further humanitarian crisis. Following the signing of a comprehensive peace agreement in August, the security situation improved significantly, with the deployment of UN peace-keeping troops and the initiation of a disarmament programme for former combatants. During 2004 more than 50,000 refugees returned to Liberia, while UNHCR completed the voluntary repatriation programme for some 13,000 Sierra Leonean refugees. At the end of 2011 an estimated 23,650 Liberian refugees remained in Côte d'Ivoire and 11,295 in Ghana. At that time 128,067 refugees from Côte d'Ivoire were in Liberia; some 100,000 of these had entered the country following the conflict that broke out in Côte d'Ivoire after the disputed presidential election of November 2010.

Recent History

QUENTIN OUTRAM

Liberia traces its origins to liberated US slaves who were resettled along the western Guinean coast by US philanthropic organizations from 1821 onwards. The country declared itself an independent sovereign state in 1847 and has remained an independent republic ever since. The new state adopted a Constitution modelled on that of the USA, although citizenship was confined to the settlers, 'Americo-Liberians' or 'Americos', who were then, and have always remained, a small proportion of the Liberian population, never exceeding a few tens of thousands. In 1878 the True Whig Party (TWP) regained the presidency and remained in continuous control of the polity from that year until 1980. During the 19th century a number of serious armed conflicts between the 'Americo' settlers and the indigenous peoples of Liberia occurred; the final revolt of the indigenous population was not suppressed until the early 1930s. By this time Liberia was taking the first steps towards establishing a modern economy. In 1926 agreements were made with the Firestone Tire and Rubber Co of the USA, under which the company leased land for the development of rubber plantations and constructed the necessary infrastructure for their operation. In 1929, however, the USA accused Liberia of running a system of forced labour within the country and supplying labour to the island of Fernando Póo in Spanish Guinea (now Equatorial Guinea) and the French colony of Gabon, in a system considered to be barely distinguishable from an organized slave trade. The resulting League of Nations inquiry substantially confirmed these charges. The subsequent reforms, together with the Firestone agreement, represented a transition from pre-modern to modern labour practices in Liberia. However, the issue of Fernando Póo has been mainly remembered in Liberia as a humiliation by the international community, and continues to be deployed with this meaning in Liberian political rhetoric.

The modernization of Liberia progressed significantly with the election of President William V. S. Tubman in 1943. Tubman's 1944 inaugural address initiated two policies ('unification' and 'open door') which were to guide Liberian politics until 1980. The 'unification' policy sought to assimilate indigenous Liberians to the established 'Americo' society and polity. The indigenous population gained the right to vote in 1946, although this was limited by a property qualification. The 'open door' policy reaffirmed Liberia's openness to foreign investment and its commitment to a capitalist economy. Less publicized by the Government was a conservative foreign policy, and during the Cold War Liberia maintained its traditionally close relations with the USA. Liberia took a significant role in the establishment of the Organization of African Unity (OAU, now the African Union—AU) in 1961, and in ensuring that it remained only an association of independent states. Liberia's relations with its immediate neighbours followed a similarly conservative stance. In 1973 Liberia and Sierra Leone established the Mano River Union (MRU), originally conceived as a customs union, and in 1975 Liberia signed the Treaty of Lagos establishing the Economic Community of West African States (ECOWAS).

In the early 1970s Liberia presented a picture of remarkable political stability, emphasized by the peaceful succession of Tubman's Vice-President, William Tolbert, to the presidency in 1971 and symbolized by the continuing power of the TWP, the oldest political party in Africa. However, the country was effectively a one-party state, which showed little respect for freedom of speech and where the judiciary and the legislature demonstrated little independence of the executive. Despite the US-style Constitution, the 'Americo' élite maintained a political culture based on a presidency with largely unrestricted powers, secured by practices of co-option, incorporation and an extensive, centralized network of patronage. In the 1970s internal discontent and dissent emerged rapidly, generated by the failure of the 'unification' policy to eliminate substantial economic, social and political disparities between the 'Americo' élite and indigenous Liberians, increasing economic difficulties, and encouraged by Tolbert's experiments with liberalism and the rising expectations of an increasingly educated class of technocrats and functionaries. In 1973 Togba-Nah Roberts (later Togba-Nah Tipoteh), a US-educated professor of economics at the University of Liberia, formed the Movement for Justice in Africa (MOJA), dedicated to radical change in Liberia and throughout Africa. Among its leading members was the US-educated Amos Sawyer, an assistant professor of political science (later to be President of the Interim Government of National Unity). In 1975 the Progressive Alliance of Liberia (PAL) was established among the Liberian diaspora in the USA, with an openly revolutionary programme. Its Chairman was Gabriel Baccus Matthews, a Liberian educated in the USA. Liberia's economic difficulties culminated in 1979, when PAL and a number of other groups organized a demonstration against a proposed 36% increase in the government-controlled price of rice, the staple food. The demonstration was suppressed by the armed forces, resulting in a number of deaths. Although an amnesty was soon granted to those arrested, the episode exposed the weakness of Tolbert's administration. In January 1980 PAL was reconstituted as a registered political party, the Progressive People's Party (PPP), and in March the PPP urged a national strike to force Tolbert's resignation. Tolbert ordered the arrest of Matthews and the rest of the PPP leadership on treason charges, and the PPP was prohibited. The political atmosphere became increasingly tense, and in April 17 non-commissioned officers and soldiers of the Armed Forces of Liberia (AFL) seized power and assassinated Tolbert.

THE DOE REGIME, 1980–90

All of the 17 who seized power were indigenous Liberians. They declared a junta, the People's Redemption Council (PRC), and elected Master Sgt (later Gen.) Samuel Doe, a Krahn, as Chairman. Thomas Quiwonkpa, a Gio, became Commanding General of the AFL. Individuals associated with the Tolbert regime and other members of the former 'Americo' élite gradually became prominent in Doe's Government; among these were Charles Taylor, who became de facto director of the state General Services Agency. At lower levels, the regime became increasingly staffed by Krahn and Gio, as both Doe and Quiwonkpa sought to gain support within their own ethnic groups. In late 1983 military supporters of Quiwonkpa launched an unsuccessful raid on Nimba County from Côte d'Ivoire. Quiwonkpa fled to the USA and a number of his supporters, including Charles Taylor, left the country at about the same time. After Taylor took refuge in the USA, Doe demanded his extradition, accusing him of embezzlement; he was arrested in May 1984 in Massachusetts and imprisoned. He escaped in September 1985.

A presidential election was held in October 1985. According to the official results, now universally acknowledged as fraudulent, Samuel Doe won 50.9% of the vote; most observers consider that Jackson F. Doe (a former Minister of Education under Tolbert, later an adviser to Doe, but no relation of the President) was the rightful victor. Jackson Doe's defeat increased the resentment towards Samuel Doe's regime, especially in Nimba County, from where Jackson Doe, a Gio, originated. A nominally civilian administration, with Samuel Doe as President, was installed in January 1986. In November 1985 Quiwonkpa launched another unsuccessful coup attempt, this time prompting Doe to conduct a bloody and, in part, ethnically targeted purge. The human rights abuses perpetrated in 1985–86 brought considerable international attention to Liberia and a previously unknown salience to ethnic identity for Krahn, for Mandingo (a group popularly associated with the Doe regime), for Gio, and for a group closely associated with the latter, the Mano.

In 1987 a group of Liberian exiles, including Prince Yormie Johnson, a former aide to Quiwonkpa and later the leader of one of the warring factions in the 1989–96 Liberian civil war, assisted Capt. Blaise Compaoré's successful coup in Burkina Faso. Another group gradually came under the leadership of Taylor. Compaoré introduced him to Col Muammar al-Qaddafi of Libya and Taylor gained Qaddafi's support. Dissidents under various leaderships, including that of Taylor, undertook military training in Libya and Burkina Faso in the late 1980s. At some point (which remains obscure), probably in 1988 or 1989, certainly by 1991, Taylor formed an alliance or reached an understanding with another group of Libyan-trained dissidents, the Revolutionary United Front of Sierra Leone (RUF), led by a former corporal, Foday Sankoh. On 24 December 1989 some 100 armed members of Taylor's group, the National Patriotic Front of Liberia (NPFL), launched an attack on Liberia, entering the country near Butuo, in Nimba County, from Côte d'Ivoire.

THE 1989–96 CIVIL WAR

The civil war initiated by the NPFL incursion followed a highly complex course. Starting as an insurrection against the Doe regime in late 1989, the hostilities degenerated rapidly into a predominantly inter-ethnic conflict, and then gradually transformed into a war between powerful rebel leaders. In this last stage several factions fought not only for control over the state, but also for control over easily exploitable resources. The war became notable for the exceptionally brutal maltreatment of civilians, with numerous incidents of looting, forced labour, arbitrary arrest and detention, torture, rape and murder. In response, civilians often fled, and displacements of refugees were often extraordinarily large in relation to the size of the population; it has been estimated that 'nearly all' Liberians fled their homes at least once during the wars of 1989–96 and 1999–2003. While there is no reliable estimate of the numbers killed during the conflict, the figure of 200,000 is the one most frequently quoted.

Four phases of heavy fighting can be distinguished: December 1989–December 1990; October 1992–July 1993; September 1994–August 1995; and April–June 1996. The first phase began with the NPFL's initial offensive in December 1989. The human rights advocacy group Africa Watch described this phase of the civil war as 'near-genocidal', with Krahn and, to a lesser extent, Mandingo on the one side and Gio and Mano on the other. Africa Watch also reported the use of child combatants by the NPFL at this time, a practice which continued to be reported until the end of the civil war and one with which all the factions, except the AFL, were associated. The NPFL, supplied with arms by Côte d'Ivoire, made rapid progress and in July 1990 it launched its attack on Monrovia. Prince Johnson broke away from the NPFL, forming the Independent National Patriotic Front of Liberia (INPFL), and occupied the Monrovia Freeport and some of the outlying areas of the capital.

In August 1990 forces provided by the ECOWAS Cease-Fire Monitoring Group (ECOMOG) arrived in Monrovia. A few weeks later ECOMOG, in alliance with the INPFL, began an offensive against the NPFL and rapidly gained control of the port area of Monrovia. The joint action with the INPFL compromised ECOMOG's neutrality and established a pattern of ECOMOG collaboration with anti-NPFL factions which continued for the rest of the war. In September 1990, with the aid (witting or unwitting) of ECOMOG, Samuel Doe was captured by the INPFL, tortured and finally murdered. ECOMOG advanced to create a neutral zone, separating the forces of the AFL (already considered to be little more than another faction), the INPFL and the NPFL, and in November 1990 a cease-fire was signed in Bamako, Mali. An Interim Government of National Unity (IGNU) was installed by ECOWAS, with Amos Sawyer as its President. The IGNU excluded the heads of the warring factions and their representatives, and was wholly dependent on ECOMOG for its survival. The Bamako cease-fire continued uneasily for nearly two years. Peace negotiations conducted at Yamoussoukro, Côte d'Ivoire, in 1991 achieved little progress. The peace agreements of this period gave no incentive to the NPFL to demobilize, and its disarmament was perfunctorily performed and continually delayed.

During 1991 Mandingo Liberian refugees in Sierra Leone joined with another exile group, the Liberian United Defense Force, comprising both Mandingo and Krahn, and including former members of the AFL, to form the United Liberation Movement of Liberia for Democracy (ULIMO). Alhaji G. V. Kromah, a Mandingo who had served in the Tolbert and Doe administrations, presented himself as ULIMO's leader with increasing success. ULIMO, which received the support of President Joseph Saidu Momoh's Government in Sierra Leone, opposed Taylor's attempts to destabilize Sierra Leone through the RUF, and joined counter-attacks by the Sierra Leonean army against the RUF soon after its formation. ULIMO also gained support from Guinea, and ULIMO incursions into NPFL territory in north-west and south-west Liberia from late 1991 escalated into serious inter-factional armed conflict in August 1992, with ULIMO gaining control of large areas of Lofa and Grand Cape Mount counties, including their diamond fields.

In October 1992 the NPFL launched an unexpected attack on Monrovia, which initiated the second phase of heavy fighting. In November the UN Security Council responded to the upsurge in fighting by imposing a mandatory armaments embargo against the factions under Resolution 788. In late 1992 Prince Johnson's INPFL collapsed, and he took no further part in the war. In January 1993 ULIMO launched attacks against the NPFL and the RUF from the Sierra Leonean border. ULIMO consolidated its hold on Lofa and Grand Cape Mount counties and expelled the NPFL from Bomi County. ULIMO's position prevented the NPFL from receiving RUF support and gave it sole control over the land routes between Liberia and Sierra Leone. In early 1993 ECOMOG regained control of the outskirts of Monrovia and advanced south-eastwards along the coast, eventually capturing the port of Buchanan, the capital of Grand Bassa County. In June at least 547 displaced persons were massacred at Harbel, the headquarters of the Firestone rubber plantation in Margibi County. In September a UN panel of inquiry chaired by S. Amos Wako, the Kenyan Attorney-General, found the AFL to have been responsible; in 2008 witnesses before the Liberian Truth and Reconciliation Commission stated that the NPFL committed the massacre.

Following its military successes, ULIMO was included in the peace negotiations, and in July 1993 Kromah, together with representatives of the UN Secretary-General, the OAU, ECOWAS, the IGNU and the NPFL, signed a cease-fire agreement at Cotonou, Benin. The aim of the Cotonou Agreement was to secure peace by yielding a share in a still supposedly civilian interim government to those warring factions sufficiently powerful to insist on representation at the negotiations. The accord provided for the establishment of the Liberia National Transitional Government (LNTG), headed by a five-person Council of State, or collective presidency. The ECOWAS Chairman requested greater support from the UN, and from late 1993 the UN Military Observer Group in Liberia (UNOMIL) was deployed in the country. In November a new faction, the self-styled Liberian Peace Council (LPC), led by George Saigbe Boley, attacked resource-rich areas under NPFL control in the south-east. The LPC's attacks provided Taylor with an excuse to halt NPFL participation in the disarmament process; other factions followed suit, and the peace process was suspended. Nevertheless, Sawyer, in accordance with the Cotonou Agreement, transferred power to David Kpomakpor, the Chairman of the Council of State, in March 1994.

After more than a year of violent dissension among its leadership, ULIMO had divided at the end of 1993, resulting in repeated armed clashes in and around Tubmanburg, Bomi County, between the rival groups within the faction. The two groups became known as ULIMO—K, under Kromah, which operated from Guinea in the north, and ULIMO—J, under Roosevelt Johnson, with headquarters at Tubmanburg. A new faction, the Lofa Defence Force (LDF), led by François Massaquoi, emerged in early 1994 and attacked ULIMO—K positions. In August the UN Secretary-General admitted that the disarmament process had 'largely come to a halt'.

In the same month a coalition of the LPC, the AFL, ULIMO—J and the LDF began assembling forces for an attack on Gbarnga, the NPFL stronghold. In September, however, the coalition offensive was pre-empted by ULIMO—K forces, which succeeded in taking Gbarnga. Coalition forces immediately launched attacks against NPFL fighters in the north and east of Liberia. This marked the beginning of the third phase of heavy fighting in the civil war. At the end of 1994 forces loyal to Taylor regained control of Gbarnga. Meanwhile, in Monrovia, a coup attempt was staged by elements in the AFL loyal to Doe, led by Gen. Charles Julu. Julu's coup was defeated by ECOMOG, which proceeded to a partial disarming of the AFL; reportedly some AFL elements then joined the LPC and ULIMO—J. Julu was captured and, in 1995, sentenced to seven years' imprisonment, but was later pardoned and released.

On the diplomatic front, a further series of peace negotiations began, under ECOWAS auspices, in September 1994. The new Chairman of ECOWAS, Flt-Lt Jerry Rawlings of Ghana, appeared to have added a new pragmatism to ECOWAS deliberations. The principle of a civilian transitional government was abandoned, and the NPFL and the other principal factions were allowed representation in the Council of State. The first agreement in this new round of diplomacy was signed in Akosombo, Ghana, in September. A cease-fire was implemented in December. However, armed clashes between the factions continued. In August 1995 a further peace agreement, signed at Abuja, Nigeria, provided for the establishment of a new LNTG, headed by a six-member Council of State, in which Charles Taylor of the NPFL, Alhaji Kromah of ULIMO—K, and George Boley of the LPC all secured representation.

Despite the cease-fire provisions of the Abuja Agreement, intermittent fighting between ULIMO—J and ULIMO—K continued. In November 1995 a further cease-fire agreement was signed (but not consistently implemented) by the leaders of the NPFL and ULIMO—K. The return of refugees and displaced persons remained slow, and some 768,000 refugees remained in neighbouring countries. In December 1995 and January 1996 ULIMO-J forces, possibly assisted by the LDF, attacked ECOMOG positions in Tubmanburg, causing significant ECOMOG and civilian casualties. The fighting was brought to a halt, but the situation remained tense, and, after this, the peace process never recovered.

In April 1996 Taylor and Kromah launched a military assault on Johnson and his supporters in the capital, and, for the first time since 1990, hostilities spread to central Monrovia. This marked the beginning of the fourth phase of heavy fighting in the civil war. In May 1996 a cease-fire was agreed. ECOMOG was redeployed throughout Monrovia, and armed combatants withdrew from the capital. However, fighting continued in the south-east and the west, especially between the ULIMO factions. By mid-1996 ECOMOG had regained control of the outskirts of Monrovia and a zone extending from the Po river in the west, to Kakata, in Margibi County, in the north, and to Buchanan in the east. In August a revised form of the Abuja Agreement was signed. ECOWAS threatened that violators of the Agreement would face charges at a war crimes tribunal, and that other sanctions targeted specifically at the factional leaderships would be imposed. In September a local cease-fire was finally agreed between the ULIMO—J and ULIMO—K factions which had been engaged in hostilities around Tubmanburg. The agreement allowed aid agencies access to the area for the first time in seven months; the levels of starvation discovered among the estimated 25,000 civilians there were among the worst to have been reliably reported at any time and at any place.

Progress towards demobilization, in accordance with the second Abuja Agreement, was achieved in early 1997. At the end of February the three faction leaders on the Council of State, Taylor, Kromah and Boley, resigned from their posts in order to contest the presidential election stipulated by the Abuja Agreement. Each formed a political party as a vehicle for their candidacy: Taylor established the National Patriotic Party (NPP), Kromah the All Liberian Coalition Party (ALCOP), and Boley re-formed Samuel Doe's National Democratic Party of Liberia (NDPL). Several political parties that had become inactive during the civil conflict re-emerged to present candidates. Ellen Johnson-Sirleaf represented the Unity Party (UP), Gabriel Baccus Matthews the United People's Party (UPP), while Togba-Nah Tipoteh, rather than Amos Sawyer, became the candidate of the Liberian People's Party (LPP). Voting took place on 19 July 1997. International observers declared that no serious irregularities occurred. Taylor secured an outright victory in the presidential poll, with 75% of the votes cast. Johnson-Sirleaf obtained 10%; no other candidate secured more than 5% of the votes cast. In the legislative elections the NPP won 49 of the 64 seats in the House of Representatives and 21 of the 26 seats in the Senate. Taylor was duly inaugurated as President on 2 August. The UN armaments embargo remained in force but UNOMIL was dissolved following the expiry of its final mandate at the end of September. Refugees began to return to Liberia in significant numbers; by January 1998 the numbers remaining in neighbouring countries had declined to 480,000. In January 1999 it was announced that most of the remaining ECOMOG troops in Liberia were to be relocated to Sierra Leone, and they finally withdrew from Liberia in October of that year.

THE TAYLOR REGIME, 1997–2003

The new legislature confirmed the Constitution that had been revised under Doe in 1984. Under this Constitution, the state was highly centralized and the counties had no independent revenue-raising powers and were governed by superintendents appointed by the President; these features remain in the present day. Two new counties were created in 2000: River Gee, formed from lower Grand Gedeh County, with its capital at Fish Town, and Gbarpolu, created from southern Lofa County, with its capital at Bopolu. The legislature was largely inactive under Taylor's administration. The judiciary remained weakened by inadequate funding and shortages of qualified personnel and subject to political, social and financial pressures limiting its independence.

Shortly after his election Taylor appointed a number of opposition politicians and the former faction leaders Johnson and Kromah to the Government, allegedly as a gesture of reconciliation. Within a year, however, prominent opposition politicians came under attack from Taylor's regime. Johnson was removed from the Cabinet and Kromah from his post as head of the Reconciliation Commission; both went into exile. In August Johnson unexpectedly returned and in September Taylor's security forces attempted to capture Johnson and close down his base in Monrovia. After the ensuing fighting, an agreement was reached under which Johnson was allowed to leave the country for Sierra Leone. Some 18,000 Krahn fled to Côte d'Ivoire following the attack.

In October 1998 32 civilians (several, including Johnson, Kromah, Boley and Johnson-Sirleaf, *in absentia*) were charged with treason; of these, 18 were arrested. Nine AFL officers, all Krahn, were also arrested and charged with sedition. In April 1999 12 of the civilians, all of them Krahn, were convicted and each sentenced to 10 years' imprisonment. Four of the nine AFL officers were convicted in February 2000, and each was sentenced to 10 years' imprisonment with hard labour. Despite Taylor's declaration of a general amnesty for all treason suspects living abroad in March 2002, both Kromah and Johnson refused to return to Liberia at that point. Johnson was reported to have died of natural causes in Nigeria in October 2004, while Kromah eventually assumed a position at the University of Liberia. Boley, who had returned to the USA in 1997, was deported in 2012 for contravention of the US Child Soldiers Accountability Act of 2008 and for extrajudicial killings; however, he was not arrested on his arrival in Monrovia.

Party political activity was limited under Taylor's regime and the strongest civil political opposition to Taylor's policies came from within the NPP itself. More active opposition may have been discouraged by the deaths of two prominent former associates of Taylor. Samuel Dokie and members of his family were killed following an order for their arrest issued by the director of the Special Security Service, Benjamin Yeaten, in November 1997. Dokie was a former supporter of Taylor during the war, but had joined a group of NPFL dissidents in 1994. (In January 2009 Yeaten was indicted for Dokie's murder and the murder of two others in June 2003. Yeaten remains at large at mid-2012.)

Security agencies proliferated under Taylor's administration; their identities, command structures and financing were often unclear. Two élite paramilitary security forces, the Anti-Terrorist Unit (ATU) or Anti-Terrorist Brigade and the Special Security Service (SSS), were created in 1997. Both reported directly to the President; the ATU was headed by the President's son, Charles McArthur Emmanuel Taylor, Jr, also known as Roy Belfast, Jr, but most commonly known as 'Chuckie' Taylor. During 2000 a paramilitary police unit, the Special Operations Division (SOD) emerged. In addition to these security forces, almost every large organization, including government ministries, parastatals and private businesses, and some prominent individuals, employed private security forces. Those hired by logging companies became well-known after the international scrutiny of the industry began in 2001. Reports of harassment by security forces, often unidentified, were frequent during Taylor's administration, and serious abuses of human rights—usually perpetrated by members of the state apparatus—became common.

Liberia's international relations during Taylor's regime were dominated by Taylor's role in fomenting regional instability, particularly in Sierra Leone. The international community made increasingly strong accusations during 1998 and 1999 that Taylor was covertly continuing his support for the RUF. The collapse of the Lomé Agreement in 2000 raised the issue of Taylor's involvement in the Sierra Leone conflict to a new prominence. Press reports suggested that Taylor was training RUF combatants under the control of Sam Bockarie, who had left Sierra Leone for Liberia on Taylor's instructions in December 1999. In August 2000 the UN Security Council resolved to establish a Special Court to prosecute war crimes perpetrated in the Sierra Leonean civil war, and it became evident that Taylor could face trial for war crimes committed by the RUF in Sierra Leone.

From late 1999 the issue of 'conflict diamonds' (diamonds illicitly mined and exported by rebel forces) had become increasingly prominent. In June 2000 the British Government once more referred to links between the RUF and 'supporters in Liberia' and urged a UN boycott of unlicensed diamonds from Sierra Leone. In July the UN Security Council adopted Resolution 1306, prohibiting the international sale of diamonds originating with the RUF, and demanded that the Liberian

Government comply with the ban. A Panel of Experts established by the UN reported in December that there was substantial evidence that the Government of Liberia was supporting the RUF in providing training, armaments and logistical support, and in allowing its territory to be used as a base for attacks and as a refuge. UN Security Council Resolution 1343 of March 2001 demanded that the Liberian Government immediately cease its support for the RUF and other armed rebels in the region. The Resolution replaced the 1992 armaments embargo on Liberia, which had never been rescinded, with a revised embargo with immediate effect. The Security Council further threatened to impose an embargo on the direct or indirect import of all rough diamonds from Liberia, whatever their origin, and to place an international travel ban on senior members of the Liberian Government and the armed forces if Liberia did not demonstrably cease its support of the RUF within two months. In May 2001 the UN determined that Liberia had failed to take sufficient measures to comply with its demands and, in particular, expressed dissatisfaction with Liberia's inability to provide evidence of Bockarie's departure from the country. Accordingly, the diamond embargo and the travel ban were imposed. The list of those affected by the travel ban included not only senior government figures and their immediate families, as expected, but also businessmen, arms dealers and figures from the logging industry.

The armament and diamond embargoes and the travel ban were reviewed in early 2002. By this time, as the Liberian Government emphasized repeatedly, the war in Sierra Leone had officially ended. However, the UN again concluded that Liberia had failed to comply fully with the Security Council's demands, the crucial evidence being that Liberian armed forces were in possession of new armaments and ammunition, indicating a breach of the arms embargo. The Security Council reimposed the armaments and diamond embargoes and the travel ban for a further 12 months, from May 2002, under Resolution 1408. The Resolution also indicated that, should preparation of an effective certificate-of-origin scheme be completed, Liberian diamonds proven to be legally mined would be exempted from the embargo, and it urged Liberia to establish transparent and internationally verifiable audit regimes to ensure that revenue derived from the maritime registry and the timber industry were used only for legitimate purposes.

In October 2002 the UN Panel of Experts reported that some 1,250–1,500 former RUF combatants continued to operate in élite Liberian military units, under the command of Gen. Yeaten, but with continuing loyalty to Bockarie. In March 2003 the Liberian Minister of Foreign Affairs confirmed that Liberia had breached the armaments embargo, citing Liberia's right to self-defence as justification. Also in March the Sierra Leone Special Court issued indictments against seven former leaders of armed factions in Sierra Leone, including Sankoh, Bockarie and Johnny Paul Koroma, the former leader of the Armed Forces Revolutionary Council (AFRC). The indictments alleged that Sankoh, Bockarie and Koroma had acted in co-operation with Taylor, and the possibility that Taylor himself might be indicted for war crimes began to be taken more seriously. The Special Court further claimed that Bockarie was supported by the Liberian Government and threatened to indict Taylor if he did not transfer him to the Sierra Leonean authorities, later also demanding the arrest of Koroma, who was reported to have fled to Liberia. In May 2003 the UN Security Council adopted Resolution 1478, renewing sanctions for a further 12 months, and also imposed a 10-month ban on imports of round logs and timber products from Liberia, effective from July.

In May 2003 came the announcement of the death of Bockarie, who, together with a group of supporters, had left Liberia for Côte d'Ivoire in 2001 and fought with Ivorian rebels. Bockarie's group included Koroma, Yeaten, 'Chuckie' Taylor and Robert Gaye (or Gueï) Jr, the son of the former Ivorian leader Robert Gueï. Bockarie was killed by Liberian troops as he and his followers attempted to enter Liberia from Côte d'Ivoire. On 4 June, while Taylor was in Accra, Ghana, the Special Court unsealed its indictment of Taylor for war crimes, crimes against humanity and serious violations of international law, and issued an international warrant for his arrest. However, the Ghanaian authorities failed to take any action to arrest Taylor and he returned to Monrovia on the following day.

RESURGENCE OF CIVIL CONFLICT, 1999–2003

By this time Liberia was in the midst of a renewed civil war. The conflict first re-emerged in April 1999, when an unidentified armed militia, led by an insurgent known as 'Mosquito Spray', attacked the town of Voinjama, in Lofa County. In August an unidentified group captured five towns in the Foya and Kolahun districts of Lofa County. In both cases AFL troops, operating in conjunction with RUF/AFRC forces under Bockarie, rapidly regained control.

There was a renewed outbreak of fighting in upper Lofa County in July and August 2000. Armed rebels took control of several towns, causing the displacement of an initial 30,000 civilians. The dissidents identified themselves as Liberians United for Reconciliation and Democracy (LURD), a previously unknown grouping. Its political programme was limited to the removal of President Taylor. (In 2003 it was reported that approximately 90% of the LURD command and 60% of its combatants were former ULIMO supporters, although the movement also included former members of the NPFL, INPFL, AFL, Sierra Leonean Kamajors and RUF, and a few remnants of the Sierra Leonean 'West Side Boys'.) Taylor at various times accused both Alhaji Kromah and Roosevelt Johnson of involvement with the rebels, but LURD appears to have remained distant from the faction leaders of the 1989–96 conflict. With greater credibility, Charles Julu, the Doe loyalist, was also accused of involvement. In September 2000 Taylor, who had charged Guinea with responsibility for the August 1999 attack, staged an offensive, with the RUF supporting Liberian government troops, on Guinean towns near the border with northern Liberia. Guinea retaliated by bombarding the Liberian town of Zorzor with long-range artillery. From this time it became widely accepted that LURD was receiving support and assistance from Guinea.

Renewed attacks near Zorzor in October 2000 prompted the flight of a further 15,000 civilians. In late November and early December fighting erupted in northern Nimba County. At the end of April 2001 the fighting was reported to have advanced in Lofa County, reaching Salayea district. Some 80,000 persons were reported to have been internally displaced by the conflict and another 162,000 had become refugees in neighbouring countries. At the end of May UN intelligence sources considered that Lofa was under LURD control.

In late 2001 fighting advanced increasingly near to Monrovia. By March 2002 Bopolu, in Gbarpolu County, was increasingly referred to as a LURD base area. In April there were reports of a split in the leadership of LURD between its military spokesman, 'Gen.' Joe Wylie, and Sekou Damate Conneh, the national Chairman. Conneh was reported to head a Mandingo faction within LURD, while Wylie led a predominantly Krahn faction. LURD occupied Tubmanburg in May 2002, and claimed to be in control of Lofa, Gbarpolu and Bomi Counties and significant regions in central Liberia at the end of that month. Government forces regained control of Tubmanburg and the surrounding towns in July. In August the Government announced that it had recaptured Voinjama, the capital of Lofa County and, in September, Bopolu, but admitted that Voinjama and Zorzor remained under LURD control.

During the first half of 2003 hostilities spread into Côte d'Ivoire, LURD regained the initiative and a new armed faction emerged in south-eastern Liberia. In early January Côte d'Ivoire accused Liberian mercenaries of attacking the village of Neka and later that month Côte d'Ivoire announced that Liberian government troops had participated in Ivorian rebel attacks on Toulépleu, close to the Liberian border. Also in January, unidentified forces crossed into Liberia from Côte d'Ivoire and captured the town of Beam, in Grand Gedeh County. In the west, LURD regained control of Bopolu, Sawmill and Tubmanburg. In late March reports began to emerge of a new armed group, the Movement for Democracy in Liberia (MODEL), which attacked and held Zwedru in Grand Geddeh County. MODEL was reported to comprise principally Krahn former members of the AFL and Doe loyalists who were predominantly based in Côte d'Ivoire. Some observers alleged that the Ivorian Government provided it with armaments and financial assistance, while financial support from the US Krahn diaspora was also suspected. Members of the Ivorian Mouvement pour la Justice et la Paix (MJP) and the Mouvement Populaire Ivoirien du Grand Ouest (MPIGO) clashed with Liberian rebels and RUF members formerly allied with them. In the course of this conflict, Felix Doh, the leader of MPIGO, was killed in late April, possibly by Bockarie, who had been leading former RUF elements. The death of Bockarie himself was announced only a few days later, on 7 May (see above). At this point, according to a report by the UN Secretary-General, about 60% of Liberian territory was under rebel control. On 19 May MODEL captured Harper and Pleebo, both timber-exporting harbour towns near the Ivorian border, and later that month began to advance towards Buchanan, Liberia's second largest city. By this time only Margibi and Grand Bassa Counties were unaffected by the fighting.

In mid-May 2003 Taylor announced his intention to attend peace discussions, which were convened for early June in Accra. In response to demands from the USA, LURD and MODEL halted their advances on Monrovia and Buchanan on 29 May and pledged to observe a cease-fire. The peace discussions began on 4 June 2003, but were thrown into chaos by the announcement of Taylor's indictment for war crimes by the Sierra Leone Special Court (see above). Taylor returned to Monrovia on 5 June, where he immediately announced that he had suppressed an attempted coup involving some of his senior officials and an unnamed foreign embassy. On the same day LURD launched a major attack on Monrovia, rapidly reaching Monrovia's western suburbs, and causing an exodus from refugee camps on the outskirts of Monrovia towards the city centre and the eastern suburbs. The US embassy urged Taylor to resign from office. On 7 June a government counter-offensive forced the rebels to withdraw over the St Paul's Bridge which connected the western suburbs and the city centre. On 11 June the Ghanaian Minister of Foreign Affairs and the ECOWAS Executive Secretary arrived in Monrovia to mediate a truce, and there was a lull in the fighting as LURD withdrew to the Po River, 20 km west of Monrovia. The Liberian authorities estimated at that time that about 400 civilians and military personnel had been killed in the fighting around Monrovia. About 50,000 internally displaced civilians were living in temporary conditions in the national sports stadium and other buildings in central and eastern Monrovia, and the humanitarian situation was causing grave concern. Peace talks resumed on 12 June and a new cease-fire agreement was signed on 17 June. The accord required the deployment of a multinational stabilization force and a 30-day period of consultation prior to the adoption of a comprehensive peace agreement, the main provision of which would be the departure of Taylor from the presidency.

Less than one week after the cease-fire was signed, LURD attacked Monrovia again, seizing Bushrod Island and the Freeport. About 300 civilians were killed before LURD withdrew once more, in early July 2003. At the end of June the UN Secretary-General had recommended to the Security Council that a multinational intervention force be deployed in Liberia. On 6 July Taylor announced that he had accepted, in principle, an offer of asylum from the Nigerian President, Olusegun Obasanjo, but stipulated that he would not leave the country until a peace-keeping force arrived. On 17 July a third attack on Monrovia by LURD forces prompted the USA to order a naval task force to Liberia. On 23 July a summit meeting of ECOWAS Heads of State in the Senegalese capital, Dakar, agreed to dispatch an initial 1,300 Nigerian peace-keeping troops to Liberia. On 1 August the UN Security Council adopted Resolution 1497, authorizing the establishment of a multinational force in Liberia. The deployment of the ECOWAS Mission in Liberia (ECOMIL) began on 4 August, when an advanced party of troops arrived in Monrovia. The fighting in Monrovia came to an end on their arrival without ECOMIL having to engage in combat.

On 11 August 2003, following continued pressure from West African governments and the international community, Taylor relinquished power to his Vice-President, Moses Zeh Blah, before leaving Liberia for exile in Calabar, south-eastern Nigeria. Blah was inaugurated as interim Head of State, pending the installation of a government of national unity. Taylor's departure fulfilled the main demand of the rebel leadership, and was received with jubilant celebration in Monrovia. On the following day the US naval task force reached the Liberian coast. The Government and LURD rebels withdrew their forces from the Monrovia Freeport and the city centre, ceding control of the area to ECOMIL, which was assisted by about 200 US marines. On 18 August the Government of Liberia signed a comprehensive peace agreement (CPA) with leaders of the LURD and MODEL factions in Accra. The CPA provided for an immediate cease-fire, a disarmament, demobilization, rehabilitation and reintegration (DDRR) programme, a restructuring of the national army to include former rebel combatants, the disbanding of all irregular forces, Blah's departure from office by 14 October—by which time he was to transfer power to a transitional power-sharing administration which was to govern Liberia until January 2006—and elections, to be held not later than October 2005. On 21 August 2003 the delegations elected Charles Gyude Bryant, a businessman and founder member of the Liberian Action Party (LAP), as Chairman of the transitional administration, later known as the National Transitional Government of Liberia (NTGL). In mid-September the strength of the ECOMIL contingent reached 3,500 personnel. At this time LURD was estimated to number some 5,000 combatants, MODEL some 1,500–3,000 and government forces some 20,000–30,000. There were an estimated 500,000 internally displaced Liberians, about 300,000 Liberian refugees in neighbouring countries and about 50,000 refugees from Sierra Leone and Côte d'Ivoire in Liberia at this time. On 19 September the UN Security Council adopted Resolution 1509, establishing the UN Mission in Liberia (UNMIL), designed to take over the functions of ECOMIL, and with an authorized strength of 15,000 military personnel and 1,115 civilian police officers in a component known as CIVPOL. At the end of September the US Department of Defense announced the withdrawal of the naval task force. On 1 October ECOMIL transferred its troops, role and authority to UNMIL. On 14 October, in accordance with the peace agreement, President Blah transferred power to Bryant and the NTGL was formally installed.

THE NATIONAL TRANSITIONAL GOVERNMENT, 2003–06

Despite Taylor's departure, fears continued to be expressed that his influence on Liberian politics persisted. In December 2003 the UN Security Council reaffirmed the travel ban on Taylor and his associates, and in March 2004, under Resolution 1532, the Security Council imposed a freeze on the assets of Taylor, his family and his associates. In March 2005 the UN Secretary-General reported continuing concerns that some of Taylor's former commanders and business associates were planning to undermine the peace process. Also in March, Taylor's associate, Guus van Kouwenhoven (see Economy), was arrested by Dutch police and charged with war crimes and violating UN sanctions. (He was convicted of the latter charge in June 2006 and sentenced to eight years' imprisonment, but won an appeal against the conviction in March 2008; this judgment was itself overturned by the Dutch Supreme Court in April 2010. A retrial began in December and remained in progress at mid-2012.) Demands for the Nigerian Government to extradite Taylor to the Special Court in Sierra Leone gathered strength in 2005. However, Nigeria indicated that it would hand over Taylor only at the request of the new administration in Liberia, to be elected in October.

UNMIL first reached a figure approximating its authorized strength in late July 2004 and completed its deployment. Cease-fire violations became less frequent as UNMIL troops were deployed; none were reported after September. Despite incidents of violent unrest, there was a notable improvement in the observance of human rights in Liberia after the inauguration of the NTGL and the disarmament of the factions. However, high levels of violent crime, especially rape and other sexual violence, continued to cause concern. Incidents of 'mob justice' and the formation of vigilante groups were frequently reported. The incapacity of the judicial and prison systems became the focus of continuing concerns.

The formal disarmament programme began in December 2003, but was immediately suspended after violent disturbances and was not relaunched until mid-April 2004. Apart from a riot of former government forces in Monrovia in May, during which one protester was killed, the programme then proceeded smoothly and was formally terminated on 31 October. The armed factions were formally dissolved in early November. Between December 2003 and March 2005 101,000 combatants had been disarmed and demobilized and some 28,000 weapons had been collected. The disparity between the number of combatants and the number of weapons caused widespread concern and suspicions that armaments had been concealed within Liberia or removed to areas just beyond Liberia's borders. Illegal and lengthy occupations of the Guthrie rubber plantation by ex-combatants, apparently still armed and with commanding officers still present, and of the Sapo National Park by former MODEL combatants, again apparently in possession of weapons, also raised doubts about the effectiveness of the disarmament programme.

UN sanctions continued and at the end of December 2003 the UN Security Council adopted Resolution 1521, which authorized the renewal of the armaments, diamond and logging embargoes imposed on Liberia while revising the basis for these sanctions. Although the previous concern over Taylor's support for the RUF was no longer relevant, the UN Security Council noted that the cease-fire and peace agreement were not being universally implemented, particularly in areas to which UNMIL troops had not yet been deployed; that the NTGL had yet to extend its authority to much of the country; and that illicit trade in diamonds and logs remained a potential threat to peace and stability. The sanctions were renewed once again in December 2004 under Resolution 1579, which extended the armaments, logging and travel embargoes for 12 months and the diamond embargo for a further six months. In June 2005 the diamond embargo was extended for a further six months under Resolution 1607.

Elections to the presidency, Senate and House of Representatives were scheduled for October 2005. Of the 22 presidential candidates approved by the National Elections Commission (NEC), by far the best known was George Manneh Weah, a Liberian footballer, who had become internationally famous in the 1990s. Other leading contenders included Winston A. Tubman, a former UN envoy to Somalia and nephew of the former President, and Harry Varney Gboto-Nambi Sherman, an adviser to Chairman Bryant, as well as candidates from the 1997 election, notably Ellen Johnson-Sirleaf and Togba-Nah Tipoteh. Taylor's party, the NPP, was represented by his former Minister of Agriculture, Roland Chris Yarkpah Massaquoi; Alhaji G. V. Kromah was the only faction leader from the 1989–96 conflict and Sekou Damate Conneh the only rebel leader from the 1999–2003 conflict to contest the presidency. Bryant and other members of the NTGL were not eligible to participate under the terms of the CPA.

Legislative and presidential elections were held, as scheduled, on 11 October 2005, and international and local observers agreed that the elections were generally free and fair. In the presidential ballot no candidate secured more than one-half of the votes cast. Weah, representing the Congress for Democratic Change (CDC), came first with 28.3% of the votes, followed by Johnson-Sirleaf of the UP with 19.8% and Charles Brumskine (Liberty Party—LP) with 13.9%. No other candidate secured more than 10% of votes cast. In the concurrently held elections for the 30-seat Senate, 10 parties secured at least one seat. The largest parties were the Coalition for the Transformation of Liberia (COTOL), which won seven seats, and the UP, which won three. In elections to the 64-seat House of Representatives, 11 parties secured at least one seat. The CDC became the largest single party in the lower house, with 15 seats; the LP secured nine seats while the UP won eight seats. The legislature consequently became politically fragmented and neither of the two leading presidential candidates could command a majority of supporters in either house. Associates or former associates of Taylor to secure legislative seats included Jewel Howard-Taylor, Taylor's then recently divorced wife, and Adolphus Dolo and Saah Richard Gbollie, both former Taylor commanders. All three were on the UN's travel ban list. Prince Johnson, the former leader of the INFPL, who returned to Liberia in 2004 as a self-proclaimed evangelical Christian after an 11-year period of exile, won a Senate seat in his native Nimba County.

In accordance with the Constitution, a second-round ballot between the two leading presidential candidates was held on 8 November 2005. Observers again declared the election to have been free and fair. Johnson-Sirleaf won 59.4% of the votes cast, compared with 40.6% secured by Weah, who strongly contested the results, alleging 'massive and systematic' fraud. Nevertheless, on 21 December, following considerable pressure from regional leaders, Weah announced that he would not persist in his challenge to the results and Johnson-Sirleaf was sworn into office on 16 January 2006.

THE FIRST JOHNSON-SIRLEAF ADMINISTRATION, 2006–12

Johnson-Sirleaf's inaugural address stressed national reconciliation, political inclusion, sustainable development and economic governance reform. Despite her emphasis on inclusion, her nominations for government appointments failed to provide a position for Weah and the only opposition politicians to receive posts (Joseph Korto, Walter Gwenigale and Jeremiah Sulunteh) were those who had transferred their support to her in the second round of the presidential elections. The majority of nominees were 'technocrats', most importantly Antoinette Monsio Sayeh, a former World Bank official, who was nominated as Minister of Finance, an appointment widely welcomed by the international community. (Sayeh left the Ministry to become Director of the African Department at the IMF in July 2008; she was replaced by Augustine Kpehe Ngafuan, formerly her Budget Director, and no policy changes ensued.) The nominations of Samuel Kofi Woods, a human rights activist who had fled Liberia in 1999 citing threats to his life, and Tiawon Gongloe, a prominent human rights activist imprisoned by Taylor, as Minister of Labour and Solicitor-General, respectively, indicated a welcome commitment to human rights. (Gongloe became Minister of Labour in 2009 and left the Cabinet in 2010.) Amos Sawyer, the former President of the IGNU, was nominated to head the Governance Reform Commission (GRC). (In October 2007 the GRC was transformed into a statutory body, the Governance Commission.) However, some nominations caused controversy. Morris (or Mohammed) Dukuly, who organized Johnson-Sirleaf's campaign and who was proposed as Chief of Staff to the presidency, had been a ULIMO—K parliamentary deputy in the mid-1990s, and had been dismissed as Liberia's representative at the International Maritime Organization in 2005, allegedly in connection with the misappropriation of funds. (Dukuly resigned his post in 2006.) The nomination of Kabineh Ja'neh, formerly of LURD, as an Associate Justice of the Supreme Court also provoked opposition from a number of local human rights organizations which alleged his participation in human rights abuses. However, only the nominations of Ja'neh and of Jonathan Sagbe as Deputy Minister of Youth and Sports were vetoed by the Senate. Subsequent reorganizations, including a major restructuring in December 2010, did not alter the character of Johnson-Sirleaf's administration.

The first political problem confronting Johnson-Sirleaf was what decision to take regarding former President Taylor. Although the new President initially described Taylor's fate as a 'secondary issue', she rapidly ceded to pressure from a number of governments, intergovernmental organizations and human rights groups demanding the transfer of Taylor from Nigeria to the Special Court in Sierra Leone. Liberia formally requested Taylor's extradition on 17 March 2006. Two days later Taylor disappeared from his residence in Calabar; he was recaptured shortly afterwards attempting to cross the Nigeria–Cameroon border. Taylor was immediately flown to Monrovia, from where he was transferred to Sierra Leone. At his first appearance before the Special Court on 3 April he pleaded not guilty to five charges of war crimes, five charges of crimes against humanity, and a charge of conscripting children, a serious violation of international humanitarian law. On 30 April the Court requested that the Netherlands allow

Taylor's trial be heard at the International Criminal Court (ICC) in The Hague. In June the United Kingdom agreed that Taylor could serve any custodial term in a British prison and Taylor was transferred to the custody of the ICC with the assent of the UN Security Council in the same month. In December 'Chuckie' Taylor, the former head of the ATU, was charged in the USA with committing torture in Liberia. (He was found guilty in October 2008 and in February 2009 sentenced to 97 years' imprisonment; both conviction and sentence were upheld by a federal appeals court in July 2010. Taylor is now serving his sentence at a federal prison in Kentucky.) The trial of former President Taylor began in The Hague in June 2007 and entered its substantive phase in January 2008.

Meanwhile, in January 2006 President Johnson-Sirleaf began to address state corruption. In her inaugural address, she emphasized acceptance of the Governance and Economic Management Assistance Programme (GEMAP—a range of anti-corruption measures forced on the NTGL by the UN, ECOWAS and major donors in 2005), and shortly afterwards she initiated a review of all concessions and contracts signed by the NTGL; all existing forestry concessions were rescinded. In December the former Minister of Finance in the NTGL, Lusine Kamara, his deputy, Tugbeh Doe, and the former Minister of Commerce, Samuel Wlue, were arrested and charged with misappropriating over US $9m. In February 2007 Gyude Bryant was charged with misappropriating $1.3m. during his period as Chairman of the NTGL. In May 2008 Bryant, Edwin Snowe, the former head of the Liberia Petroleum Refining Company (LPRC) and three others were charged with embezzling funds from the LPRC during Bryant's presidency. Bryant, Snowe and the three others were acquitted of all charges alleging corruption while holding public office in April 2009; the remaining charges against Bryant were dropped in September 2010. Proceedings against Kamara, Doe and Wlue appeared to have been abandoned. The continuing failure of the authorities to prosecute and convict those accused of corruption led to a public perception that the Johnson-Sirleaf administration was 'weak on corruption', according to the UN Secretary-General.

Programmes to address human rights issues, initiated under the NTGL, progressed slowly. The Truth and Reconciliation Commission (TRC) was formally relaunched in February 2006 under the chairmanship of Jerome Verdier, a human rights activist, and its hearings began in February 2008. The Commission presented its final report in July 2009 and an updated final report in December. It recommended that a number of persons, including the leaders of the warring factions during both the 1989–96 and 1999–2003 wars, should be prosecuted for human rights violations, including war crimes, by an Extraordinary Criminal Tribunal for Liberia. The Tribunal would have to be established by a new statute. The TRC also recommended that those who had associated with or financed the warring factions should be barred from public office; it explicitly included Johnson-Sirleaf in this category in the light of her February admission that she had donated US $10,000 to Taylor's NPFL in 1990. Johnson-Sirleaf subsequently announced that she would not resign from office and the TRC's recommendations concerning her were not expected to make progress. In August the legislature agreed that it would postpone any action on the TRC's final report until January 2010 and no action had been taken by the legislature by mid-2012. Commissioners for the Independent National Commission on Human Rights (INHCR), also originally constituted under the NTGL, were finally approved by the Senate in September 2010. The TRC, the mandate of which expired after presenting its final report, described the INCHR as the 'inheritors of the TRC process'. In October 2011 it was announced that the Nobel Peace Prize had been awarded to Tawakkol Karman of Yemen, President Johnson-Sirleaf of Liberia, and Leymah Gbowee, a Liberian peace activist. In November a committee termed the National Peace and Reconciliation Initiative, headed by Leymah Gbowee, was established by the President with a role that appeared to replicate that of the TRC.

UN sanctions continued in the early stages of Johnson-Sirleaf's first administration. The logging ban was allowed to expire in June 2006 and the diamond ban was rescinded by Resolution 1753 of April 2007. The arms embargo has remained in place, renewed most recently by Resolution 2025 of December 2011, which extended the ban for a further 12 months. However, in December 2006 Resolution 1731 excluded non-lethal military equipment intended for the use of Liberian police and security forces from the ambit of the ban, and Resolution 1903 of 2009 excluded the Liberian Government from the scope of the ban entirely. The travel bans and assets freezes have also remained in place, although in 2008 and 2009 the UN Sanctions Committee removed a number of individuals from the list, including van Kouwenhoven. The GEMAP formally ended in September 2009, although the IMF and the World Bank retained advisers with co-signatory powers at the Ministry of Finance and the Central Bank of Liberia.

In 2006 Johnson-Sirleaf inherited an incomplete DDRR programme and incomplete restructuring programmes for the Liberian National Police and the AFL; reform of the justice and prison systems had barely begun. In December 2007 a final group of some 8,800 former combatants were placed in a rehabilitation and reintegration programme funded by the Government of Norway. However, violent demonstrations by former combatants continued into 2008 and 2009; some incidents suggested that groups of ex-combatants had significant organizational capacity and retained military command structures. The Government's DDRR programmes ended officially in April 2009. However, in the same month a joint mission to western Côte d'Ivoire by UNMIL, the UN Operation in Côte d'Ivoire (UNOCI) and the UN Development Programme (UNDP) to investigate reports that some 1,500 or 2,000 Liberian combatants or ex-combatants had joined Côte d'Ivoire militias found evidence consistent with those reports, although some of the Liberian combatants had claimed Ivorian nationality. In December 2010 Johnson-Sirleaf publicly warned Liberian ex-combatants and their commanders not to get involved in the Ivorian crisis. Despite this, Liberian fighters, as well as Ivorian combatants, were discovered returning from Côte d'Ivoire with Ivorian refugees in 2011. Some, including notorious Liberian mercenary fighters Isaac Chegbo and Augustine Vleyee, better known by their respective *noms de guerre* 'Bob Marley' and 'Bush Dog', were arrested by the Liberian authorities. All were either released absolutely, or on bail, during 2011 and 2012.

The security situation during Johnson-Sirleaf's first administration remained generally calm, though fragile, with the major threats to stability arising from unemployed ex-combatants and land disputes internally and, externally, from the unstable situations in Côte d'Ivoire and Guinea. In July 2007 Charles Julu, the former AFL general, Doe loyalist, and leader of the 1994 coup attempt (see above) was arrested on a charge of treason, along with George Koukou, formerly an NPP Senator during the Taylor administration and Speaker of the National Transitional Assembly under the NTGL, Andrew Dorbor, a former colonel in the AFL, and two others. Koukou was pardoned by Johnson-Sirleaf in January 2008; Julu and Dorbor were found not guilty in May and released. Tensions along the border with Guinea eased, following the installation of new Guinean President Alpha Condé after democratic elections in 2010. In November 2010 Ivorian refugees, fleeing from the violent unrest following the disputed presidential election held earlier that month, began arriving in Nimba, Grand Gedeh and Maryland Counties. Escalating violence in Côte d'Ivoire in March and April resulted in a dramatic increase in the number of refugees, with an estimated 180,000 crossing the border into Liberia in 2011. In June Liberian security personnel located and destroyed a substantial cache of weapons in River Gee County which was believed to have been left by fighters from Côte d'Ivoire. In July, in the first of a series of onslaughts on western Côte d'Ivoire launched from bases in Liberia, work camps near the village of Ponan were attacked and at least eight people were killed. In September the villages of Zriglo and Nigré, about 25 km south of the town of Taï, were attacked and some 23 people killed. In December the UN Panel of Experts reported that it had received information that Ibrahim Bah, who formerly liaised between Taylor and the RUF, and Benjamin Yeaten, both of whom were on the travel ban list imposed by UN Resolution 1521, had travelled to Sierra Leone and Côte d'Ivoire, respectively, during late 2010 and early 2011 to recruit mercenaries for the Ivorian conflict. The Panel also noted that the unregulated artisanal gold-mining industry formed a pool of potential recruits and a source of income for mercenary groups in eastern Liberia.

Following the demobilization of the AFL in December 2005, recruitment and training of soldiers for the new national army began in January 2006. The new force was originally intended to have a strength of 4,000, but funding shortfalls reduced this target to 2,000. The new AFL reached its planned strength in August 2008, but command and control structures remain underdeveloped and the AFL was not expected to be capable of independent operations before at least 2014. The Africa Command of the US armed forces took over the training of the AFL and the Liberia Defence Sector Reform Programme in 2010, and a small number of US trainers remained in place in 2012.

The UN began planning for a gradual withdrawal of UNMIL in 2006. The first reductions in troop strengths were completed in September 2008, followed by second and third stages completed in 2009 and 2010, respectively, at which point UNMIL's authorized strength stood at 7,952. Consideration of further reductions was deferred until after the 2011 elections. UNMIL's mandate has been repeatedly extended, most recently by Resolution 2008 of 2011 until 30 September 2012.

Concerns regarding high levels of violent crime, including rape, had been voiced since 2005. In April 2006 a detailed report by the International Crisis Group drew attention to major defects in the justice system, including illiteracy among Justices of the Peace, dysfunctional circuit courts, a widespread lack of confidence in the system among the public resulting in incidents of 'mob justice', corruption, impunity and illegal practices by chiefs applying traditional law. In September the Ministry of Justice issued a statement admitting that the Liberian National Police, despite the assistance of the CIVPOL unit of UNMIL, were unable to cope with the rising levels of crime in Monrovia and its environs, and requested that citizens form vigilante groups to protect themselves. An additional UN police unit arrived in January 2007, bringing CIVPOL's strength up to 1,201 officers, but progress in this area has been slow and public confidence in the police and justice systems remains low. Johnson-Sirleaf described the justice system as 'a cancer' in her 2008 annual address. In August 2008 the UN Secretary-General recommended an increase in the size of the CIVPOL unit from five to seven formed police units, despite the planned reduction in the size of the military component of UNMIL, a proposal endorsed by Security Council Resolution 1836 of 2008. A Jordanian police unit arrived accordingly in January 2009; a further Indian unit arrived later in the year. CIVPOL was exempted from the third stage of the UNMIL drawdown of 2009–10 and its strength stood at 1,330 out of an authorized 1,375 at 1 August 2011.

The election of Johnson-Sirleaf to the presidency in 2005 was widely welcomed by the international community, and Liberia's relations with the USA and other major aid donors improved dramatically. US President George W. Bush awarded Johnson-Sirleaf the Presidential Medal of Freedom in November 2007 and paid a visit to Liberia in February 2008, the first by a US President in 30 years. US Secretary of State Hillary Clinton visited Liberia in August 2009. In June 2010 Liberia won the support of the IMF and the World Bank for a major package of debt relief measures (see Economy).

In her annual address of January 2010, Johnson-Sirleaf announced that she would seek re-election in the polls scheduled for October 2011. This announcement ended some uncertainty over her intentions; she had pledged to serve only a single term in the 2005 election campaign, and, further, the TRC had determined that a number of leading figures, including Johnson-Sirleaf, should not run again for public office for 30 years. That this decision of the TRC could be ignored was suggested by the precedent set by Alhaji Kromah, the former leader of ULIMO—K, who was covered by the same ruling as Johnson-Sirleaf, but contested a Senate seat in a by-election in November 2009 without objection from the NEC. On 23 August 2011 a referendum was held to ratify a number of amendments to the Constitution adopted by the legislature the previous year. The most important of these were, first, a provision to reduce the 10-year residency requirement for presidential candidates to five years and, second, a provision to replace the two-round system for legislative elections with a single-round, first-past-the-post system. The first was rejected; the second, after a Supreme Court ruling in September, was found to have been approved. The candidacy of Johnson-Sirleaf and five other candidates for the presidency was jeopardized by the failure to reduce the 10-year requirement. In the event, the NEC allowed the candidates to proceed.

The elections precipitated a flurry of party-political activity. New parties were formed, increasing the number listed by the NEC to 22 by mid-2011. Efforts by the parties to reduce the consequent fragmentation of the vote by forming coalitions and negotiating mergers continued. The main party-political cleavage in Liberia was between the UP of Johnson-Sirleaf and the CDC. In October 2010 the UP merged with the LAP and the Liberian Unification Party, all of which obtained their core support from the business and governmental élite. The CDC eventually abandoned its attempts to form a four-party coalition and sought a merger with the LP instead, eventually planning to present Charles Brumskine of the LP, a presidential candidate in 2005 and formerly an NPFL senator, as presidential candidate, and George Weah, the defeated candidate in the presidential run-off elections of 2005, as vice-presidential candidate. However this agreement collapsed and the LP eventually stood alone. The New Deal Movement and six other parties, including the LPP, NDPL, NPP and the UPP, formed a National Democratic Coalition, although the NDPL and the NPP withdrew from the alliance in July. Eventually, 16 candidates for the presidency were accepted by the NEC. They included Ellen Johnson-Sirleaf representing the UP, Brumskine of the LP, Chea Cheapoo of the PPP, former leader of the INPFL armed faction Prince Yormie Johnson of the new National Union for Democratic Progress, Dew Mayson of the NDC, Togba-Nah Tipoteh of the Freedom Alliance Party of Liberia, and Winston Tubman, a nephew of the former President, representing the CDC, with George Weah standing for Vice-President.

At the first round of the presidential election on 11 October 2011 (in which some 72% of the electorate participated), Johnson-Sirleaf was placed first, with 43.9% of the votes cast, Tubman second with 32.7% of the vote, Johnson third with 11.6% and Brumskine fourth with 5.5%. No other candidate gained more than 2% of the valid votes. Johnson-Sirleaf led in 10 of the 15 counties, Tubman in three, Johnson only in his native Nimba County and Brumskine only in his native Grand Bassa County. Only one-half of the seats in the Senate were contested, one in each county. The NPP gained three seats and the CDC one. Former Taylor commanders Adolphus Dolo and Saah Richard Gbollie both chose not to seek re-election to the Senate. The term of Jewel Howard-Taylor, the senior Senator for Bong County, does not expire until 2014. In the House of Representatives, which comprised 73 seats after the creation of nine additional seats carried out under the 2010 Threshold Act, the National Union for Democratic Progress for the first time secured six seats and the LP increased its representation by two seats. Both chambers remained highly fragmented. In the Senate, nine parties and six independents shared 30 seats; the UP remained the largest party, with nine seats, followed by the NPP with four and the CDC with three. In the House of Representatives, 11 parties and nine independents shared the 73 seats, with the largest parties remaining the UP with 24 seats, the CDC with 11, and the LP with seven. International observers pronounced themselves broadly satisfied with the conduct of the election.

In the interval between the first and second rounds of the presidential election, Johnson and other candidates, including Brumskine and Tipoteh, endorsed Johnson-Sirleaf. However, Tubman alleged that the first round had been unfairly conducted and the CDC announced it would boycott the second round of voting unless the National Elections Commissioners were replaced, an intervention condemned by ECOWAS, the AU and the US Department of State. In an unauthorized demonstration, which was staged by approximately 1,000 unarmed CDC supporters on 7 November 2011, at least one person was killed and several injured as Liberian security services attempted to disperse the crowd. Johnson-Sirleaf won the second round on 8 November, with 90.7% of the votes cast and 39% of the electorate participating. Threats of violence from CDC supporters may have been partly responsible for the much reduced voter turnout.

THE SECOND JOHNSON-SIRLEAF ADMINISTRATION

At her inauguration to a second presidential term in January 2012, President Jonson-Sirleaf called for national reconciliation after the conflicts of the election period. The ceremony was attended by US Secretary of State Clinton and, in a retreat from open confrontation, by Tubman, who had previously vowed not to co-operate with the new administration. (Tubman was expelled from the CDC in March, leaving Weah as its most powerful figure.)

Johnson-Sirleaf's new Cabinet was marked by some continuity, rewards for loyalty, and by some controversial changes. Her stated aim was to balance appointments in terms of county, gender and ethnicity. Augustine Ngafuan, hitherto Minister of Finance, was nominated as Minister of Foreign Affairs in place of Toga Gaywea McIntosh, who became a Vice-President of ECOWAS; hitherto Planning and Economic Affairs Minister Amara Konneh was appointed as Minister of Finance; Brownie Samukai was returned to the post of Minister of Defence; former Senator Blamoh Nelson received the internal affairs portfolio in place of Harrison Karnwea, who wished to retire; Samuel Kofi Woods was reappointed as Minister of Public Works. Controversy was provoked by Tubman, who complained in late January 2012 that promises to award government posts to the CDC had not been fulfilled. Instead, Johnson-Sirleaf nominated Lenn Eugene Nagbe, formerly the Secretary-General of the CDC, who had joined the UP as Deputy National Campaign Manager in June 2011, as Minister of Transport. In February 2012 the media voiced criticisms over the appointment of various family members: her sons Charles Sirleaf and Robert Sirleaf as a Deputy Governor of the Central Bank and as Chairman of the National Oil Co. of Liberia, respectively; Fomba Sirleaf, her step-son, as head of the National Security Agency; and Varney Sirleaf, a nephew, as a Deputy Minister of Administration in the Ministry of Internal Affairs.

The first six months of Johnson-Sirleaf's second term were marked by echoes of one long-finished war and sounds of another from over the border in Côte d'Ivoire. In April 2012 former President Taylor was convicted of all 11 counts under the indictment against him at The Hague, and in May he was sentenced to 50 years' imprisonment. The ICC's ruling was received quietly in Monrovia. In June Taylor's lawyers gave formal notice that he would appeal against his conviction.

Cross-border raids on western Côte d'Ivoire became larger in scale in 2012. In February a camp called Konankro, 8 km from Zriglo, was attacked and looted; six people were killed. In April the village of Sakré was attacked and eight people were killed, precipitating the flight of a reported 3,000 people. In June a patrol of UNOCI peace-keepers between the villages of Taï and Para was ambushed. Seven peace-keepers from Niger were killed and, according to press reports, there were also casualties amongst Ivorian troops and civilians. This attack led to further displacement of civilians. The Liberian Government responded by closing the border (a largely symbolic act in a region where the borders are highly porous), and dispatched troops to the area.

The impending withdrawal of UNMIL may pose the greatest security challenge for Liberia in the next few years. A UN Technical Assessment Mission visited Liberia in February and March 2012. It concluded that the country faced no imminent military threat, either internal or external, despite the recent cross-border raids between Côte d'Ivoire and Liberia, but that the threat from civil unrest remained substantial. It recognized that groups of former combatants with command and control structures intact remained in some parts of the country. Violent crime, particularly sexual violence, continued to be a particular concern. Progress towards national reconciliation was regarded as limited. Advances in establishing an effective and professional police force remained disappointing. The UN Secretary-General therefore recommended that the reduction in UNMIL's strength should be gradual, with a repatriation of some 4,200 troops between August 2012 and July 2015, leaving a force of approximately 3,750 at the end of that period. The Secretary-General recommended no reduction in the UNMIL civilian police component, instead advising the authorization of an increase in its strength by three police units to be added, as and when needed, over the course of 2012–15.

In her years of office Johnson-Sirleaf has resolved the problem posed by former President Taylor's exile, secured the lifting of the UN embargoes on timber and diamond exports, achieved all but complete relief from Liberia's external debts, begun to revitalize the economy, initiated the resumption of basic service delivery by the Government, and, above all, maintained peace. These are remarkable achievements. Nevertheless, the challenges confronting her administration remain immense.

Economy

QUENTIN OUTRAM

INTRODUCTION

Before the 1989–96 civil conflict, the Liberian economy was divided between a largely foreign-owned, export-orientated sector producing plantation crops, minerals and timber, and a traditional, subsistence agricultural sector. Revenues derived from exports supported the state, and allowed its leaders and functionaries to enjoy relatively high standards of living. In contrast, the agricultural sector, which employed a high proportion of the population, was of low productivity and here poverty was endemic. In the late 1970s and 1980s crises in the world economy caused economic decline; the 1989–96 civil war and the renewed conflict during 1999–2003 devastated the economy.

During the 1989–96 war real gross domestic product (GDP) may have declined to as low as 10% of its 1987 level. After the end of that conflict, the economy initially recovered rapidly but then faltered and real GDP in 2002 was still less than one-half of the level achieved before the 1989–96 war. The 1999–2003 conflict and the UN sanctions in force against Liberia between 2001 and 2007 (see Recent History), had a significant impact on the economy, and real GDP contracted by more than 30% in 2003. Following the end of the conflict and a slow initial recovery, growth has been rapid; real GDP has grown by over 6% per annum on average since 2004. The IMF expected growth to continue at between 5% and 9% per year in 2012–14.

In 2012 agricultural activity continued to provide a subsistence living for the majority of the population, although many recently returned refugees and others were reliant on international humanitarian aid. Unemployment was believed to be widespread in urban areas, but frequently reiterated estimates—derived from a 1991 government report—that 80%–85% of Liberians are unemployed, if still valid at all, apply only to the small formal sector, not to the economy as a whole. Liberia's 2010 gross national income (GNI) per head was estimated at US $340 at purchasing-power parity exchange rates and has become one of the lowest in the world. According to a major survey conducted in 2007, 64% of the population lived below the poverty line, apparently unable to fulfil their basic needs, and 48% of the population lived in extreme poverty, and were unable to afford the cost of the food necessary to feed themselves and their families. The health and educational status of many Liberians remains extremely poor.

The Liberian state has often had a baleful impact on the economy. Charles Taylor's regime of 1997–2003 was marked by large-scale economic misappropriation by Taylor and his associates. In May 2005 the US-based advocacy group Coalition for International Justice published a detailed report that concluded that Taylor had obtained an annual income of at least US $105m. during his presidency. State corruption continued under the National Transitional Government of Liberia (NTGL), in power until 2006, and has remained a problem during the administrations of Ellen Johnson-Sirleaf.

AGRICULTURE

Agriculture employed 61% of the economically active population in 2012, according to FAO estimates, and the agricultural sector (including forestry and fishing) accounted for an estimated 57% of GDP. The main cash crop is rubber. The principal food crops are rice and cassava (manioc), and these crops, together with palm oil and some fish or meat, form the basis of the national diet.

Paddy rice production averaged more than 290,000 metric tons per year in the late 1980s; there were also substantial imports of rice, averaging 96,000 tons annually during the same period, largely to satisfy urban markets. Production of paddy rice was estimated to have declined to only 50,000 tons in 1994 during the civil conflict and much of the population became dependent on emergency relief grain. Renewed warfare in 1999–2003 resulted in another collapse in production, which reached only an estimated 100,000 tons in 2003. Production is believed to have increased substantially since 2004, reaching an estimated 296,000 tons in 2010. Imports of milled rice rose to well over 100,000 tons annually between 2003 and 2008, but fell to 93,000 tons in 2009, according to FAO estimates. Global increases in staple food prices have adversely affected Liberia, with rice prices increasing by more than 60% between May 2007 and December 2008; they remain well above previous levels. In February 2008 a survey of 800 children under five years old living in Monrovia found 17.6% of them to be suffering from acute undernutrition, a figure indicative of a nutritional crisis. The UN World Food Programme, the major provider of food aid in Liberia, planned to assist some 650,000 people in Liberia in 2012.

Production of cassava, which increased from 280,000 metric tons in 1985 to 380,000 tons in 1989, was not as badly disrupted by the 1989–96 or 1999–2003 conflicts as rice-growing, possibly because cassava requires less consistent attention than rice. Production declined to a low of 175,000 tons in 1995, according to FAO estimates. By 2000 cassava was reported to be a much more significant component of the national diet than before the civil war and the area under cultivation was increasing rapidly. Production rose from an estimated 282,200 tons in 1997 to an estimated 493,000 tons in 2010.

Before the 1989–96 war the rubber industry was divided about equally in terms of land area between a domestically owned sector, comprising both smallholders and commercially operated plantations, and a small number of large, foreign-owned concessions. Rubber plantations covered an estimated 110,000 ha in 1990. The concessions produced about 70% of total annual production, which amounted to about 100,000 metric tons in the late 1980s. The recovery of the rubber sector after the 1989–96 war was fairly rapid and the sector was little affected by the 1999–2003 conflict. Output reached 120,800 tons in 2007 according to FAO estimates, before declining to 84,800 tons in 2008 and 59,500 tons in 2009 due to the impact of the global economic downturn. Since then, output has recovered a little, to 62,000 tons, in 2010. Export revenues rose rapidly after 2003, buoyed by rising international rubber prices, to an estimated US $225m. in 2008, but decreased dramatically, to US $93m., in 2009. A recovery, to US $156m., followed in 2010, and continued in 2011, to an estimated US $250m.

There are now six foreign-owned plantations: Firestone, the Liberian Agricultural Co (LAC) plantation, and the Salala, Kumpulan Guthrie, Cavalla and Cocopa plantations. There is also one major Liberian-owned plantation, the Sinoe Rubber Plantation. By far the largest of these is the Firestone concession, based at Harbel, 56 km east of Monrovia. Although the original concession covered a reputed 1m. acres (405,000 ha), the plantation extends over only 53,000 ha of this area. The US Firestone sold its Liberian interests to the Japanese tyre company Bridgestone in 1988, and the plantation is now owned by Bridgestone Americas through its subsidiary Firestone Natural Rubber, which owns the operating company Firestone Liberia Inc. The Firestone plantation was seriously affected by the 1989–96 war but during the 1999–2003 conflict was able to continue production almost without interruption. In February 2005 Firestone signed an agreement with the NTGL, which extended its lease, due to expire in 2025, until 2091. The lease was renegotiated by the Johnson-Sirleaf administration in 2007–08 and provided improved terms for Liberia in the areas of taxation, transfer pricing, rental payments, the regulation of employment, and the provision of education and health services. The term was also shortened to 36 years, expiring in 2041. The President stated in 2008 that the Firestone agreement would be the model for the renegotiation of leases elsewhere in the rubber sector and in the oil palm industry. Later that year the Firestone Agricultural Workers' Union of Liberia with the assistance of the United Steel Workers' Union of the USA negotiated a new labour agreement with Firestone under which the union gained substantial increases in pay, conditions and benefits. In 2010 a further landmark agreement was reached under which the transport of heavy loads of latex on the backs of tappers was replaced by a motorized system. These agreements also banned child labour at the plantation. In 2011 a judgment in the US Seventh Circuit Court of Appeals dismissed a suit against Firestone Natural Rubber for employing children but confirmed the right of the plaintiff, the International Labor Rights Fund, to sue Firestone under the US Alien Tort Statute of 1789. Firestone has long been Liberia's largest private sector employer and in 2012 the plantation was reported to employ about 6,500 workers, about the same as before the 1989–96 war.

The LAC plantation comprises 14,000 ha of a 121,000-ha concession 45 km north-west of Buchanan, in Grand Bassa County, and employed 3,000 people before the 1989–96 war. Owned by the US rubber company Uniroyal between 1961 and 1980, LAC is now wholly owned by the Compagnie Internationale de Cultures (SOCFINAF), a subsidiary of the Luxembourg-registered but Belgium-based Société Financière des Caoutchoucs Luxembourg (SOCFIN). In 2011 LAC produced 14,200 metric tons of rubber from its own plantation and smallholder plantations under its supervision. Yields from the plantation were low, owing to the increasing age of the trees. It now directly employs some 1,600 workers.

LAC's owner, SOCFINAF, is also a majority shareholder of the Weala Rubber Co, now known as the Salala Rubber Corporation after Weala's merger with the company of that name in 2007. Both facilities are located in Margibi County. In 2008 Salala obtained a US $10m. loan from the International Finance Corporation to rehabilitate and expand its operations. The concession area is 8,500 ha, of which 3,800 ha are planted with rubber. It employed 900 workers at the end of 2011 and produced 10,300 metric tons of rubber during the year.

The Kumpulan Guthrie concession comprised 120,000 ha located north of Monrovia in Bomi and Cape Mount counties; 8,000 ha were planted with rubber. Its new Malaysian owners completed the rehabilitation of the plantation in 2001, but almost immediately announced that they were ceasing operations in view of the continuing instability in the country. The plantation appears to have been under the control of rebels of the Liberians United for Reconciliation and Democracy (LURD) from early 2003 until August 2006, when the plantation was repossessed. The Government then granted a temporary management permit to the Rubber Planters' Association of Liberia (RPAL). In 2007 Kumpulan Guthrie merged with Sime Darby Bhd, a Malaysian plantations-based conglomerate which is now the world's largest listed plantation company. In May 2009 it was announced that Johnson-Sirleaf had signed a new 63-year concession agreement with Sime Darby to rehabilitate, operate and expand the plantation. Sime Darby agreed to invest a reported US $800m. over a 20-year period and will plant oil palm as well as rubber; it has agreed to construct a vegetable oil refinery and provide housing and medical facilities for an expected 22,000 employees. Liberia provided a further 100,000 ha of land. The concession area now extends across Grand Cape Mount, Gbarpolu, Bomi and Bong counties. Sime Darby took control of the plantation in January 2010 and the first palm oil seeds were planted in May. In February 2011 the plantation employed 2,500 workers. In 2012 Sime Darby was accused of devastating sacred sites, and of causing the destruction of livelihoods and forced displacement, through its land clearance operations. The company denied the allegations.

Part of the original Firestone concession area became the Cavalla Rubber Corporation (CRC) plantation in Maryland County. The concession area is approximately 8,000 ha, of which 3,910 ha are developed. Control of the plantation was ceded to Samuel Doe's Government in 1981. In 1983 Doe's Government granted 50% ownership to the Société Internationale de Plantations et de Finance (SIPEF), a Belgian company, in exchange for its management of the whole. The plantation ceased operations between 1992 and 1998, owing to the civil conflict, and in 2003 it was occupied by forces of the Movement for Democracy in Liberia (MODEL). The plantation was put under the management of the RPAL in 2006 at which point it was believed to employ 1,350 workers. The same year SIPEF sold its interests to Salala Rubber Investments (SRI). RPAL handed over the plantation to SRI in 2007. SRI then sold 60% of its stake to the Société Internationale de Plantations d'Hévéas (SIPH) in April 2008; SRI retains the other 40%. SIPH is 56% owned by the Ivorian agribusiness SIFCA Group; Michelin, the French tyre company, owns another 20%. SIFCA also owns the Maryland Oil Palm Plantation (MOPP). Construction of a rubber-processing factory began in March 2009. Protests against SIFCA by workers in Pleebo, Maryland County, culminated in the fatal shooting of a demonstrator in May 2011. The disputes between the CRC, the MOPP and local residents were reported to remain 'heated' in April 2012.

The Cocopa Rubber Plantation in Nimba County was originally owned by the Liberian Company (LIBCO), the corporation organized in 1947 by former US Secretary of State Edward R. Stettinius to promote investment in Liberia. After Stettinius's death in 1948, his holdings in LIBCO were transferred to a US company called the Liberian Development Corporation. Stettinius's brother-in-law, Juan T. Trippe, the founder of Pan American Airways, acquired a substantial shareholding in this corporation. The plantation had some 2,400 ha under cultivation in the 1970s. In 1996 LIBCO contracted the management of the plantation to a Liberian company owned by Taylor's Minister of Agriculture, Roland Massaquoi. The plantation was reported to have been occupied by ex-combatants in 2006. It was taken over by the Johnson-Sirleaf Government in January 2007 and was returned to representatives of LIBCO in April. LIBCO, which was believed to be under the control of Charles W. Trippe Jr, a US national and Juan Trippe's grandson, was reported to be planting 3,200 ha of land with rubber in 2009.

The Sinoe Rubber Plantation, originally owned by a German company, was acquired by the family of President William Tolbert in 1973. The concession area, which is located in Sinoe County, is 240,000 ha, of which 20,000 ha are developed. After the Tolberts fled the country in the 1980s, the plantation was controlled by a variety of management companies. It was seized by MODEL forces in March 2003 and then fell under the control of an ex-LURD general, Paulson Garteh (also known as 'General Satan'), and a group of ex-combatants. The plantation was then taken over by an ex-combatant named Leon Worjlah, usually known as 'White Flower', operating through a local association called the Citizen's Welfare Committee, until his arrest in November 2008. In May 2009 President Johnson-Sirleaf announced that the Government intended to take over the plantation and then lease it out to private investors. The County Superintendent, J. Milton Teahjay, claimed to have eliminated the 'atmosphere of gangsterism' on the plantation in May 2010.

Palm oil, despite its importance in Guinea, Côte d'Ivoire and Ghana, has been produced on only a small scale in Liberia. FAO estimated the area harvested in Liberia in 2010 to be only 17,000 ha, compared with Guinea's 310,000 ha, and production to be 174,000 metric tons of oil palm fruit yielding 42,000 tons of palm oil. However, in 2007 Liberia signed two concession agreements intended to develop the palm oil sector. One was with LIBINCO Oil Palm Inc, which obtained a 34,500-ha concession in Palm Bay, Grand Bassa County, of which 8,500 ha had been previously planted and required rehabilitation, and the remainder clearing and planting. The company also obtained the rights to a further 80,000 ha in River Cess County. The other concession agreement was with Equatorial Biofuels (EBF), which obtained the Butaw Oil Plantation concession of 55,000 ha in Sinoe County. LIBINCO was acquired by EBF in February 2008. The latter company was restructured in 2009 as a subsidiary of Equatorial Palm Oil Inc, under which name the company is now known in Liberia. Its operating subsidiary in Liberia took delivery of a Malaysian-built processing mill in August, which was at that time the only palm oil-processing mill in Liberia. It began production in May 2011 and was expected to reach full capacity in July, with an output of about 15 tons of crude palm oil per day. In December 2009 plans were announced to provide 240,000 ha of land for palm oil production in Grand Kru, Sinoe and Maryland counties to Golden Veroleum, a subsidiary of the Golden Agri Resources Co, itself a subsidiary of the Sinar Mas Group of Indonesia. The plans raised environmental concerns. Allegations of deforestation and wildlife habitat destruction by Sinar Mas in Indonesia led to the cancellation of supply contracts by Unilever, Nestlé and Carrefour, and a divestment of shares by British banking group HSBC in 2009 and 2010. A US $1,600m. concession agreement with Golden Veroleum was signed in August 2010. The company employed about 500 people in Liberia at the end of 2011 and expected eventually to engage 35,000.

Other agricultural products include sugar cane (with an output of 265,000 metric tons in 2010, according to FAO), bananas (145,000 tons), plantains (46,000 tons), yams (18,000 tons), sweet potatoes (18,000 tons) and taro or cocoyams (17,000 tons). None of these is exported in significant quantities. Small quantities of cocoa beans, coconuts, coffee, oranges and pineapples are also produced.

Little information is available on livestock. FAO estimates indicated that there were some 338,000 goats, 264,000 sheep, 265,000 pigs and 40,000 head of cattle in Liberia in 2010. In the same year FAO estimated that the country produced some 31,000 metric tons of meat, of which about one-quarter was game meat ('bushmeat'), a significant food source in rural areas.

Marine and freshwater fishing provided a livelihood and a source of nutrition in some areas. In 2010, according to FAO estimates, the total catch, most of which was comprised of marine species, amounted to about 8,000 metric tons.

FORESTRY

Liberia possesses substantial forest reserves: forest covers 4.4m. ha, or 45.6% of the total land area of Liberia. The forests are almost entirely lowland tropical moist forests, but savannah woodlands occur on the coast and in the north-west. Some 240 different timber species occur in Liberia, of which about 40 are traded commercially. The most valuable species are mahoganies and African walnut. The Sapo National Park, in Sinoe County, designated in 1983, is the one major protected area of rainforest. In October 2003 the Sapo National Park Act extended the park from 130,845 ha to 180,500 ha, and the Nimba Nature Reserve Act created a forest nature reserve contiguous to similar reserves in Guinea and Côte d'Ivoire. Groups of illicit miners and hunters, including ex-combatants, have periodically occupied Sapo Park since 2004.

Historically, smallholder agriculture, where land clearing by slash and burn is common, has been responsible for 95% of all deforestation, and the use of trees for domestic fuel has dwarfed the activities of commercial timber producers. Before the 1989–96 war commercial logging practices were selective, focusing on the extraction of high-value species, and the rate of deforestation resulting directly from logging was slow. The mass population displacements during the 1989–96 war slowed the rate of deforestation arising from agricultural activities and the insecurity of that time inhibited large-scale logging operations. After 1996 commercial logging greatly increased deforestation before UN timber sanctions resulted in the suspension of the commercial industry in 2003–04. FAO estimated that, despite very low rates of deforestation in the early 1990s, Liberian forestland was lost at an average annual rate of 0.6% during 1990–2000. Deforestation accelerated slightly, to 0.7% annually, in 2000–10.

Of the estimated 7.5m. cu m of roundwood production in 2010, 7.0m. cu m was used as fuel. Additionally, about 0.2m. metric tons of charcoal was produced. Charcoal dominates the urban household energy market and is a major item in retail trade. Recent reports suggest that a significant export trade with neighbouring countries is emerging. Wood is the usual domestic fuel in rural areas and remains an important energy source for small-scale industry.

Forest exploitation is based on leased concessions supervised by the Forestry Development Authority (FDA). Virtually all significant national forestland was under concessionary arrangements with commercial logging companies by the late 1980s. The recovery of the industry after the 1989–96 war was initially slow, but accelerated rapidly in 1999, with output rising to 336,000 cu m in that year. This was followed by a dramatic increase to 934,000 cu m in 2000 and 982,000 cu m in 2001, and another surge, to 1.4m. cu m, in 2002. The IMF estimated that about 80% of the output of the industrial roundwood production was exported, yielding some US $85m. in 2002. By 2002 output from the forestry sector overall had increased to almost 290% of the pre-war (1987) level in real value terms, and forestry represented an estimated 23.9% of total GDP.

By the mid-point of Taylor's regime the industry was dominated by 11 companies. Of these, the Oriental Timber Co (OTC) was the largest, with an output, according to the FDA, of 385,000 cu m, or 57% of total production in 2000. In December 2000 a UN report concluded that the Chairman of the OTC since 1999, Guus or 'Gus' van Kouwenhoven, a Dutch national, was responsible for the logistics of arms transfers through Liberia into Sierra Leone, utilizing the position and resources of the OTC. In view of this and evidence of other connections between the Liberian timber trade and regional instability, the advocacy group Global Witness urged the UN Security Council to impose a total embargo on Liberian timber exports in January 2001. The October report of the UN Panel of Experts on Liberia noted a payment for armaments made directly from the Singapore accounts of one of the OTC holding companies. Other logging companies, including the Exotic Tropical Timber Enterprise, once managed by Leonid Minin, described by UN officials as an 'arms dealer', were believed to be involved in similar activities. The UN Security Council imposed a 10-month ban on exports of round logs and timber products from Liberia, which took effect in July 2003. Successive renewals kept timber sanctions in place until 2006 (see Recent History). The sanctions caused commercial companies, including the OTC, to suspend operations, repatriate staff and withdraw equipment. The UN Panel of Experts found no evidence of industrial logging or timber exports in investigations during 2004–06 and concluded that industrial logging had come to a halt.

In February 2006 the newly elected President, Johnson-Sirleaf, decreed that all existing forestry concessions were null and void. She also established a Forest Reform Monitoring Committee (FRMC) to develop forestry policy. In June the UN Panel of Experts reported a 'dramatic' improvement in FDA operations, particularly in revenue collection. In view of these developments, in the same month the UN Security Council suspended the timber sanctions under Resolution 1689 for a period of 90 days. Permanent removal of the sanctions was made dependent on the adoption of forestry legislation in accordance with FRMC proposals. A reformed Forestry Law was duly brought into effect in October 2006 and the sanctions were terminated. The Law required the FDA to formulate a regulatory system for the commercial logging industry before renewed commercial forestry was permitted. Progress towards this was slow, impeded by irregularities in the award of forest resource licences by the FDA among other factors, and commercial logging remained at a standstill in 2007 and 2008. Nevertheless, the FDA estimated that there were some 6,000 unlicensed pit sawyers operating in 2008; fees charged to pit sawyers by the FDA generated US $430,000 in 2007–08.

In February 2009 Tarpeh Timber, a Liberian-owned company, felled the first legally harvested tree of the post-sanctions regime. Production of sawlogs and veneer logs amounted to 240,000 cu m in that year, rising to 300,000 cu m in 2010. Other industrial roundwood contributed a further 180,000 cu m in 2009 and 2010. However, roundwood exports remained very low, at only 3,623 cu m, valued at just over US $1m., in 2009. (FAO estimates were unchanged for 2010.) By 2010 there were 20 companies operating in the sector, of which the largest was Buchanan Renewable Energy (BRE). This company produces wood chips from redundant rubber trees. The chips are exported to Europe for use as biomass fuel for electricity generation. In 2009 44,000 metric tons of chips were exported. BRE was formed and majority owned by Pamoja Capital SA, the investment management branch of the Canadian McCall MacBain Foundation. In June 2010 20% of BRE was acquired by Vattenfall, the Swedish state-owned power company, which had a sourcing agreement with BRE and a further 10% was acquired by another Swedish government entity, Swedfund, a provider of development finance.

MINING AND PETROLEUM EXPLORATION

The mining sector was once a major sector of the economy, accounting for 10.9% of GDP in 1989; in 2010 it accounted for just 0.2%. Iron ore was the principal product. In the 1980s, however, the reduction in international demand severely depressed production and during the 1989–96 civil war the iron ore industry closed down completely. The most well-known extraction site was the Mount Nimba site, near the Guinean border. The mine was formerly worked by the Liberian-American Minerals Company (LAMCO), which constructed the 267-km Buchanan–Yekepa railway line to enable the export of the ore. A contract to reopen the mine and rehabilitate the railway was signed with Mittal Steel, now ArcelorMittal, in September 2005. The contract was renegotiated by the Johnson-Sirleaf administration during 2006. This concession agreement left the railway and the port of Buchanan under government ownership and contained provisions concerning taxation and royalties revised in Liberia's favour. Construction work began in October 2007, but the global recession led ArcelorMittal to scale back its activities in 2009. A first test shipment of iron ore took place in September 2011. ArcelorMittal aims to ship 4m. metric tons annually from 2012.

In February 2005 it was reported that BHP Billiton of Australia had acquired exploration licences in various regions of western Liberia. In June Mano River Resources, a Canadian company previously active in the gold and diamond sector, announced that it had been awarded a three-year mineral exploration agreement for iron ore in the Putu range in Grand Gedeh County; the Russian company Severstal agreed to provide finance for this project in May 2008. Mano River Resources merged with African Aura Resources in October 2009 to form African Aura Mining Inc, which was awarded a 25-year Mineral Development Agreement in 2010, although production from the Putu concession was not expected to start before 2016. African Aura was divided into Afferro Mining (iron) and Aureus Mining (gold) in April 2011. The Putu project will require the construction of a new 130-km rail line to the coast and a new deep-water port.

In July 2007 it was reported that 13 companies, including ArcelorMittal and Tata Steel, had expressed an interest in the 'western cluster' of iron ore deposits at the Mano River and Bomi Hills, both previously mined, and at the Bea Mountains, not previously exploited. The successful bidder was Delta Mining Consolidated Ltd of South Africa, an unknown company. In September 2008 it was reported that Delta Mining was insolvent and had generated no revenues since it began operations in 2006. Liberia then reopened the bidding. However, Tata Steel withdrew and only four bids were received in the second round: they were from Global Steel Holdings Ltd of India, Fomento of Goa, India, the little known Capital Steel Group of the People's Republic of China, and Elenilto Minerals and Mining of Israel. Elenilto, an affiliate of the Engelinvest Group controlled by Jacob Engel, an Israeli businessman primarily known as a real estate developer, was awarded a 25-year licence. However, the Liberia Anti-Corruption Commission (LACC) agreed to investigate the award of the licence in May 2011. Elenilto formed a subsidiary, Western Cluster Ltd (WCL), to hold its interests. In early August 2011, before the LACC had completed its investigation, Elenilto announced it had sold a 51% stake in WCL to Bloom Fountain Ltd, a wholly-owned subsidiary of Sesa Goa Ltd (a majority-owned subsidiary of Vedanta Resources plc), for US $90m. Vedanta Resources has been the subject of a divestment campaign since February 2010, when the Church of England (United Kingdom) sold its shareholding, citing concerns over human rights violations by the company. In late August 2011 President Johnson-Sirleaf announced that she had signed a Mining Development Agreement with WCL. In the 2011/12 financial year Elenilto appears to have paid Liberia a 'social contribution' of US $3.5m. In May 2012 Elenilto sold its remaining 49% of WCL to Sesa Goa, receiving a reported US $150m. on the two sales. Elenilto thus gained a large profit on purely paper transactions in Liberian assets and Vedanta gained exploitation rights to Liberian iron ore without participation in a public-bidding process.

In June 2008 it was announced that four bids to rehabilitate and operate the iron ore site at Bong Mines had been received; the contract was awarded to the China-Union Investment Company in January 2009. In November the Chinese ambassador to Liberia, Zhou Yuxiao, admitted that China-Union had been delaying payment of the US $45m. signature fee and starting operations because of the global economic crisis. At the end of 2009 China-Union sold 85% of the project to the state-owned China-Africa Development Fund, which in turn sold a 60% stake to the state-owned Wuhan Iron and Steel Group (WISCO) in March 2010. The Ministry of Lands, Mines and Energy admitted in its 2009 annual report that China-Union had been granted preferential fiscal terms and that other mining companies were seeking parity of treatment. In mid-2012 operations were yet to begin.

In June 2010 Liberia signed a Mineral Development Agreement with BHP Billiton for the exploration and mining of iron ore deposits at areas known as Goe Fantro, Kintoma, St John River South and the Tolo Range in Nimba, Bong, Margibi and Grand Bassa counties, all within reach of the Yekepa-Buchanan railway being rehabilitated by ArcelorMittal. The mines were expected eventually to generate 3,500 jobs.

Diamond deposits were first discovered in the lower Lofa river area in 1957, and continue westwards to the border with Sierra Leone at the Mano River. These deposits consist of both alluvial deposits and kimberlite dykes, and yield both industrial and gem diamonds. Alluvial diamond occurrences have also been located in the Cavalia and Ya Creek drainage systems in Nimba County, in Grand Bassa and Montserrado counties, and there have been reports of discoveries near Greenville. Alluvial deposits have often been worked by 'artisanal' miners using traditional methods. Reserves are estimated at about 10m. carats. Historical data on production and exports are believed to be distorted by illicit production and smuggling. However, according to the US Geological Survey (USGS), 263,000 carats of industrial diamonds and 67,000 carats of gem diamonds were produced in 1988. The warring factions became heavily involved in diamond production during the 1989–96 civil conflict, and may have produced 40,000–60,000 carats of gem diamonds and 60,000–90,000 carats of industrial diamonds annually in the later years of the war.

The export of rough diamonds from Liberia was banned under UN resolutions in May 2001 (see Recent History). By September 2004 the UN Panel of Experts reported that it was convinced that diamond production and export levels were negligible, with activity discouraged not only by the sanctions but also by the insecurity in the main diamond-producing areas and shortages of equipment. With the improving security situation towards the end of 2004, the Panel noted a steady increase in mining activity and indications that diamonds were once again being smuggled onto international markets. In 2006 an artisanal diamond rush to an area near the site of the Butaw Oil Palm Corporation's plantation occurred. This and other artisanal mining along the Lofa River and in parts of Nimba produced diamonds at a rate of between 130,000 and 150,000 carats per annum according to the Panel.

Progress towards achieving Kimberley Process compliancy and the removal of UN diamond sanctions was slow under the Taylor regime and the NTGL, but accelerated under the Johnson-Sirleaf administration. The diamond sanctions were removed in April 2007 by UN Security Council Resolution 1753, and Liberia was formally admitted to the Kimberley Process Certification Scheme in May. Legal exports of rough diamonds resumed in September. The UN Panel of Experts, which remained seized of matters concerning the Liberian diamond trade until December 2011, reported that authorized exports of rough diamonds reached 47,000 carats valued at US $9.9m. in 2008, the first full year of operation under the Kimberley Process, generating US $297,000 in export taxes. This was followed by 28,000 carats, valued at US $9.1m., yielding US $274,000 in export taxes, in 2009; 23,000 carats valued at US $15.6m. in 2010; and 34,000 carats valued at US $13.8m. in the first 9 months of 2011. The high value per carat in 2010 was partly due to the export of a 194.09-carat diamond with an estimated value of US $6.7m., and a small number of high-value stones, achieving prices per carat of US $10,000 and more, continue to be found. However, recent experience suggests that diamond-mining will remain a useful, but not spectacular, contributor to public revenues. Global Witness, central to the campaign over conflict diamonds (see Recent History), left the Kimberley Process in December 2011, stating that it had failed to become a conflict prevention mechanism and was now only a 'cynical corporate accreditation scheme'.

Recent formal diamond exploration activity in Liberia has been limited. African Aura Mining Inc, active in the country since 2000, terminated its Liberian diamond exploration activities in 2008 after concluding that they were unlikely to yield a return. The Trans Hex Group of South Africa also terminated its diamond exploration project in 2009, as did Fundy Minerals Ltd of Canada in 2010.

Alluvial gold has been exploited since the 1940s in an area near Zwedru in Grand Gedeh County, and exploration for primary (lode) gold in the 1970s rapidly focused on this area. Reserves of alluvial gold are distributed throughout the country, but the most significant occurrences are in western Liberia between the Lofa and Mano rivers, in Bong and Nimba counties along the St John river and Ya Creek, and in the south-east of the country. Liberia's total reserves of gold are estimated at 3m. troy oz. Prior to the 1989–96 civil conflict, production was small-scale, with some 6,000–14,000 diggings for gold and diamonds believed to exist. The prevalence of illicit production renders output estimates highly uncertain, but the industry was undoubtedly on a small scale by world standards. Production continued throughout the 1989–96 war, organized by the various rebel factions. USGS estimated that post-war production fluctuated around low levels until rising to 311 kg in 2007 and 624 kg in 2008 and has since fluctuated around 570 kg per annum. According to a report by the UN Panel of Experts in December 2011, Liberian officials believed that perhaps 65% of Liberia's gold output was being exported illicitly, primarily through Guinea.

Although a number of companies have been granted gold exploration licences, few have been active in recent years. Exploration by Aureus Mining has advanced furthest at its Bea Mountains concession. Resources at the Weaju and New Liberty properties in the Bea Mountains have been estimated to be capable of yielding 233,000 oz and 751,000 oz of gold, respectively. The company obtained a Mineral Development Agreement from Liberia to cover the Bea Mountains properties, but the worsening civil conflict halted activities in January 2003. Exploration work resumed in 2005 and a class 'A' mining licence authorizing a hard rock (underground) mine was granted in 2009. Exploration and feasibility studies continued in 2012. Hummingbird Resources plc of the United Kingdom, listed on the British Alternative Investment Market (AIM) since the end of 2010, has secured exploration licences in south-eastern Liberia covering 7,000 sq km. It claimed discoveries at several sites, together capable of yielding 3.8m. oz of gold in February 2012.

Offshore deposits of hydrocarbons were first discovered during explorations carried out in 1968–73, but remained unexploited. The Government established the National Oil Co of Liberia (NOCAL) in 1999 to develop Liberia's petroleum resources. The renewed civil conflict prevented progress until

February 2004, when NOCAL announced a bidding round for 17 exploration blocks, covering 55,000 sq km, of which six blocks would be awarded. The blocks extend from the Liberian coast for about 120 km and are approximately 30 km wide on average. They are numbered in sequence, from LB-01 bordering the territorial waters of Côte d'Ivoire to LB-17 bordering those of Sierra Leone. In addition, 13 'ultra-deep' blocks have been defined on the seaward side of blocks LB-01 to LB-17. The 2004 bidding round was regarded as unsuccessful, attracting applications from only six companies.

In June 2005 it was announced that NOCAL had signed three production-sharing contracts: one with Oranto Petroleum (covering LB-11), one with a US company, Broadway Consolidated (LB-13), and one with a consortium comprising Regal Liberia of the United Kingdom and European Hydrocarbons (LB-08 and LB-09). Of these three, only Oranto was an established oil producer. The agreements provided for an exploration phase prior to production, and the three companies were not expected to commence production in the short term. In 2007 production-sharing agreements between Liberia and the Broadway and Oranto companies were ratified by the legislature. Ratification of production-sharing agreements with Regal/European Hydrocarbons, Woodside Petroleum of Australia and Repsol of Spain followed in March 2008. Further exploration contracts were awarded to Anadarko Petroleum of Houston, Texas, USA (LB-10) and Tongtai Petroleum of Hong Kong in September 2008 (LB-06 and LB-07); the contract with Anadarko was ratified by the legislature in June 2009. In the same month Oranto secured rights to LB-14 and consequently all the blocks, except LB-01 to LB-05 in the south-east, were allocated.

In September 2009 Anadarko announced that oil had been discovered in its Venus well in deep water off shore from Sierra Leone about 60 km from Liberian waters. This, in conjunction with the same company's discovery of the Jubilee field off shore from Ghana, enhanced the prospects for oil discoveries off shore from Liberia. A bidding round for exploration licences for the five remaining blocks (LB-01 to LB-05) was held in 2009–10, but no contract was awarded.

The ownership of Liberia's oil exploration contracts have been affected by subsequent sales. In March 2012 the situation was as follows: Tongtai Petroleum (LB-06 and LB-07) had been joined by the China National Offshore Oil Corporation; LB-08 and LB-09 were owned by African Petroleum Ltd, an Australian company; LB-10 was 80% owned by Anadarko, 10% owned by Mitsubishi of Japan and 10% by Repsol; LB-11, LB-12 and LB-14 were 70% owned by Chevron of the USA and 30% by Oranto; LB-13 was owned by the former Broadway Consolidated now renamed Peppercoast Petroleum Ltd and re-registered in British Crown Dependency the Isle of Man; LB-15, LB-16 and LB-17 were owned by Anadarko (47.5%), Repsol (27.5%) and Tullow Oil of the United Kingdom. African Petroleum, headed by Frank Timis, was fined £600,000 by the AIM Disciplinary Committee in 2009 for making misleading statements concerning a Greek oil well, a transgression described by AIM as 'unprecedented in the seriousness of the rule breaches involved'. Peppercoast's holding was subject to a mandatory sale by NOCAL in 2011; at mid-2012 negotiations with ExxonMobil concerning a 70% stake and Canadian Overseas Petroleum of Canada (30%) were in progress.

From 2010 onwards, as the prospects of finding commercially viable oil deposits improved, disquiet among civil society organizations at the contract-awarding practices of NOCAL increased. In September 2011 Global Witness published substantial research documenting the bribery of legislators by NOCAL, financial mismanagement, a lack of transparency and the award of contracts to companies without financial capacity or with links to persons of questionable repute. Randolph A. K. W. McClain, the newly appointed President and CEO of NOCAL, announced a programme of reform in February 2012, a move welcomed by Global Witness, which described itself as 'optimistic'. The same month African Petroleum announced the discovery of a 'potentially large accumulation of oil deposits' in block LB-09.

MANUFACTURING

The significance of the manufacturing sector to the Liberian economy has always been limited. The sector accounted for about 10% of GDP in 2011. The Liberia Labour Force Survey of 2010 estimated manufacturing employment at 70,000 people, or about 7% of the total labour force. The largest sub-sectors by value of output are beverages and beer, followed by cement. The remainder of the sector consists of paint and domestic chemical manufacturing and the production of candles and mattresses. There are few companies of any size and many firms are owned and operated by only one person. A 2001 report indicated that the 11 largest manufacturing firms together employed no more than 500 people. Large-scale industry is limited to a 125,000-ton capacity cement factory, which commenced operations in 1968, and is now owned by Heidelberg Cement of Germany. It employed 63 persons in 2012. The company was constructing a new 500,000-ton mill in 2012.

THE TERTIARY SECTOR

The tertiary sector (transport, utilities, construction, commerce, private services and public administration) produced an estimated 45% of GDP in 1989. The sector collapsed during the 1989–96 war, with the value of output declining from an estimated US $504m. in 1989 to about US $9m. in 1996. Output recovered to an estimated 30% of GDP in 2011. Construction, commerce, road transport and private services are dominated by informal employment, while public administration is the major sector of formal employment in the Liberian economy. There were an apparent 58,500 public sector employees in 2006. In March 2007 President Johnson-Sirleaf stated that 17,000 ghost workers had been removed from government employment records, and estimated that public sector employment had dropped to 31,900 during that year. It recovered to an estimated 38,000 in 2010.

Transport and Telecommunications

Liberia's road network is inadequate and mostly in very poor repair. A main road between Monrovia and Freetown, Sierra Leone, completed in 1988, reduced the distance between the two capitals from 1,014 km to 544 km. Travel by road to Guinea in the north and Côte d'Ivoire in the east remains difficult. Many neighbouring villages remain connected only by footpaths. Analysis of satellite images indicated that the road network grew substantially after 1999, largely owing to the opening of forest roads by logging companies, and totalled 13,585 km in 2005. Of the officially recognized network of primary, secondary and feeder roads of 9,915 km, only 734 km of road, all in the primary class, were paved in 2008. Reconstruction and rehabilitation work began in 2007 and was marked by the official reopening of the bridge over the River Mano, at the Liberia–Sierra Leone border on the Monrovia–Freetown route. A grant from the World Bank of US $23.4m. was provided for the reconditioning of Monrovia's major roads and the Monrovia–Buchanan highway in 2007. In March 2010 the World Bank promised additional funding to complete this project, and in October, shortly after announcing support for a 10-year road development programme, it pledged US $31m. for the rehabilitation of the Monrovia–Ganta road.

The railways from Monrovia to Mano River via Bomi Hills (145 route-km), from Monrovia to Bong Mines (78 route-km) and from Buchanan to Yekepa (267 route-km) were constructed for the transport of iron ore. The closure of Liberia's iron ore industry during the 1989–96 conflict resulted in the cessation of all traffic on these lines. ArcelorMittal's investment programme included the restoration of the Buchanan–Yekepa line and work started on this project in October 2007 and has now been completed. China-Union's concession agreement included the rehabilitation and modernization of the Bong Mines to Monrovia line, and the agreement with African Aura Mining, now Afferro Mining, specified that it would build a railway to a new port in Sinoe County.

In early 2012 the Liberian-registered merchant fleet comprised 3,030 vessels of 1,000 or more dead weight tons (dwt), with a total displacement of 189.9m. dwt. None of this fleet is owned by Liberian nationals. The fleet remained the second largest open-registry fleet in the world in terms of tonnage in

2012, after Panama. The Liberian registry is regarded as one of the more reputable open registries, with below average casualty and detention rates, and the registry has grown significantly since 2006. Although the political responsibility of the Bureau of Maritime Affairs in Liberia, the management of the Liberian registry was, from its inception in 1949, conducted by the International Trust Co, an associate company of International Registries Incorporated (IRI) of New York, USA. Since the registry was, for all intents and purposes, managed from the USA it was little affected by the 1989–96 civil conflict. The management of the registry was transferred to the newly created Liberia International Ship and Corporate Registry (LISCR), controlled by Taylor associates and based in Virginia, USA, from January 2000. In 2004 the registry contributed some US $13.5m. of revenue, equivalent to about 20% of all official government revenue in that year, according to IMF sources. Contributions were considerably less in 2005 and were less again in 2006, prompting President Johnson-Sirleaf to announce a review of the agreement with LISCR in her 2007 annual address. A revised 10-year contract with LISCR to manage the registry was approved by the legislature in August 2009. Despite this, maritime revenue was only US $16.3m., or 5.7% of total government revenue, in 2009–10, and US $18.4m., or 5.1% of total revenue, in 2010–11, figures that were far below initial expectations.

Liberia's principal ports are the Monrovia Freeport, Buchanan, Greenville and Harper. Before the 1989–96 war these ports handled about 200,000 metric tons of general cargo and about 400,000 tons of petroleum products per year. The 1989–96 war resulted in extensive damage to dock and warehouse facilities; siltation and uncleared wrecks also impeded a quick return to normal operations. In 2011 all oil imports and nearly all the dry-bulk and container traffic were handled by the Freeport. The Freeport has four piers and one main wharf. China-Union's Bong Mines concession agreement requires it to contribute to the reconditioning of the port. In 2010 APM Terminals, part of A.P. Moller-Maersk of Denmark, obtained a 25-year concession for the Freeport, under which it would operate marine services and develop the port's facilities, spending an estimated US $120m. over the duration of the contract. The port at Buchanan was managed by the OTC until the company's withdrawal from Liberia in 2003; ArcelorMittal's planned investment programme includes its restoration. Greenville and Harper are shallow-water ports which have been used mainly for the export of logs.

Liberia's principal airports are Roberts (or Robertsfield) International Airport (RIA), at Harbel, 56 km east of Monrovia, and the smaller James Spriggs Payne Airport, at Monrovia. The UN Security Council grounded all Liberian-registered aircraft by Resolution 1343 of 2001. A new aviation registry was subsequently established in conformity with international procedures, and the UN grounding order lapsed in May 2002. The new registry has remained inactive, however. Any airline that might be established subject to Liberian regulatory oversight was subjected to a pre-emptive ban from European Union (EU) airspace promulgated by the European Commission in March 2006 and since repeatedly reiterated, most recently in April 2012.

Delta Airlines of the USA inaugurated the first direct service from the USA to Liberia for over 20 years in September 2010. In 2012 services into RIA were also operated by SN Brussels Airlines, with flights from Brussels; by Royal Air Maroc with a service from Casablanca, Morocco; by Kenya Airways with a service from Nairobi, Kenya; and by regional airlines, including Virgin Nigeria, operating services from Abidjan, Accra, and Lagos. The Spriggs Payne Airport was used primarily by UNMIL and UN agencies.

Almost all of the installations of the parastatal Liberia Telecommunications Corpn, now Libtelco, were damaged during the 1989–96 war, and the fighting in Monrovia in 2003 resulted in further damage. The Johnson-Sirleaf administration suspended all activities of the Corporation in 2006, leaving its assets in the care of a skeleton staff while the administration prepared plans to reactivate and privatize it. No firm privatization plan had been prepared by mid-2012, however. The Africa Coast to Europe (ACE) project to bring a sub-marine telecommunications cable from Europe to the west coastal states of Africa was announced in 2010. The cable arrived in Monrovia in November 2011, amidst general excitement. The management of traffic onto and off the cable is to be undertaken by the Cable Consortium of Liberia, 60% owned by the Government of Liberia, 20% by Libtelco; 10% by the Lonestar Communications Corpn and 10% by Cellcom. Both the latter two are Liberian mobile phone operators. The project will bring secure broadband connectivity to Liberia and eliminate its dependence on satellite connections. Growth in mobile cellular telephone ownership and use has been rapid since 2001, and it was estimated that there were nearly 1.6m. mobile phone subscribers in Liberia in 2010, or about 393 per 1,000 people; however, this was still one of the lower figures in Africa. There were four licensed Global System for Mobile Communications (GSM) mobile operators in 2011: Lonestar Communications, operating since 2000 and a subsidiary of MTN Communications of South Africa; LiberCell (Atlantic Wireless) and Cellcom, both operating since 2004; and Comium, a Lebanese company, which acquired a GSM licence in December 2004. Lonestar and Cellcom were by far the largest companies in 2010, with 762,000 and 640,000 mobile subscribers, respectively. Cellcom, LiberCell and Comium provide internet services. Domestic postal services resumed in 2006 after a 14-year absence.

Power and Utilities

Liberia imports all of the petroleum products that it consumes. The Taylor Government resisted pressure from the IMF to liberalize the market in petroleum products, but the NTGL granted import franchises to a number of companies in April 2004; President Johnson-Sirleaf stated that these companies' share of the market had risen from 11% in 2005 to 40% in 2007. Nevertheless, petrol prices remain state controlled. Consumption of petroleum declined from about 8,000 b/d in 1988 to an estimated 4,500 b/d in 2010. In 2008 Johnson-Sirleaf announced that her policy was to prepare the Liberia Petroleum Refining Corpn (LPRC) for privatization, although little progress towards this had been made by mid-2012. Harry Greaves, the LPRC Managing Director appointed by Johnson-Sirleaf in 2006 and, like her, a minister under Tolbert, was dismissed in September 2009, after the discovery of multi-million dollar procurement irregularities. In May 2011 the General Auditing Commission carried out an investigation into LPRC's activities during 2006/07, the first year of Greaves's control, and numerous further irregularities were discovered. Johnson-Sirleaf reacted by dissolving the whole board of LPRC in July 2011. Further controversy over the disposal of oil provided as a development grant-in-kind by the Government of Japan surrounded the reconstructed LPRC board in 2011–12.

The government-owned Liberia Electricity Corpn (LEC) produced about one-half of the total output of electricity in the mid-1980s, most of the rest being produced by the iron ore mining companies then operating in the country. The LEC operated two systems, the Monrovia Grid and the Rural Electrification Network which served the remainder of the country through 11 isolated grids supplied by diesel generators. Total net electricity production declined to an estimated 301m. kWh in 1990. During the 1989–96 conflict all the power generating plant was looted or destroyed, including the Mt Coffee hydroelectric dam, which was wrecked in December 1990. Since then businesses and other organizations have depended largely on privately owned generators for electricity. The LEC installed a diesel generating set rated at 7 MW in 2000 and this was the only functioning public generating plant in Liberia until 2006. Total net electricity production, almost all from privately owned diesel generators, rose from an estimated 310m. kWh in 1998 to 340m. kWh in 2009. In her inaugural address in January 2006, President Johnson-Sirleaf reiterated campaign promises to restore electric light to Monrovia within six months. To this end, in March it was announced that the LEC had leased four generators with a combined power rating of 2,665 kVA. At a keenly awaited event, electric light was restored to parts of Monrovia on 26 July, Independence Day, an event described by the President as symbolizing Liberia's journey from darkness to illumination.

Since then, however, progress has been slow. The Chairman and members of the LEC board of directors were dismissed in 2008 by Johnson-Sirleaf for mismanagement of funds. In January 2009 the President announced that the China-Union mining company had agreed to rebuild the Mt Coffee facility as part of its concession to work the Bong Mines iron ore deposits. In the same year a contract was signed with Buchanan Renewables for a US $150m. concession to generate energy from retired rubber trees, with the project then expected to be in operation by 2010. The project was still in its preliminary phases at mid-2012. In April 2010 the International Finance Corporation, part of the World Bank Group, announced that Manitoba Hydro International of Canada, later joined by the Kenya Power and Lighting Co, had been awarded a US $53m., five-year management contract to improve electricity services in Monrovia. The contract was to begin in July. The World Bank envisaged Liberia's eventual connection to the West African Power Pool (WAPP), which would allow it to import electricity from neighbouring countries. A US $145m. interest-free loan and a US $32m. grant was facilitated by the World Bank to advance the WAPP project in 2012. A transmission line from Côte d'Ivoire to Liberia, Sierra Leone and Guinea will be constructed to enable the export of cheap Ivorian electricity.

The provision of piped water was limited to urban areas before the 1989–96 war, and rural areas are still often dependent on supplies collected from wells, bore holes, ponds and streams. It was estimated that 73% of the population had access to improved drinking water sources in 2010 (88% in urban areas, 60% in rural) and 18% of the population had access to improved sanitation facilities (26% urban, 7% rural). In Monrovia, the parastatal Liberia Water and Sewer Corpn (LWSC) provided 273m.–365m. litres of water per day before the war. The central water supply and sewage disposal system in Monrovia was damaged and looted during and after the 1992 offensive on the capital; the resulting shortage of safe water was alleviated by donor-operated distribution systems and the partial restoration of piped water supplies in July 2006. Output of water increased from about 3.4m. litres per day in 2009 to 17.5m. in 2010 and 22.6m. in 2011. Outbreaks of disease linked to unsafe water supplies remain a major public health problem.

THE MACROECONOMY

The rapid expansion of the Liberian economy in the 1950s and 1960s was largely generated by exports of rubber, iron ore and timber, and by infrastructural projects financed by foreign aid. After the first major decline in international prices in 1974, rubber and iron ore exports stagnated. It is from this period that Liberia's later macroeconomic difficulties originated. Public sector deficits increased from negligible levels in 1975 to 13% of GDP in 1979; external debt nearly quadrupled. The Doe regime borrowed massively, almost entirely from abroad and mainly at commercial rates, and used the funds obtained to finance unproductive public investments and maintain domestic consumption. By 1988 external public debt had risen to US $1,800m., equivalent to 164% of GDP, while scheduled debt-servicing payments would have taken 40% of export earnings.

Currency, Banking, Exchange Rates and Consumer Prices

Before 1981 the US dollar was the principal currency in Liberia; it remained legal tender in mid-2012 alongside the Liberian dollar, and was the main currency for trade and financial transactions and for larger cash payments. In 2010 US dollars accounted for 74% of Liberian 'broad money' (M2), a proportion which has been rising strongly in recent years, giving rise to speculation that the economy will eventually become fully dollarized.

In November 1999 a new central bank, the Central Bank of Liberia (CBL), was established. The CBL introduced measures to supervise the commercial banking sector effectively, and the inter-bank clearing system was also restored during 2000. However, the commercial banking system has remained fragile. Although bank lending has increased rapidly, processing fees continue to be the main source of banking income. Loans to businesses have been focused on commerce and construction, with few loans made to agriculture or manufacturing. The number of microfinance institutions has increased from two in 2006 to eight in 2011, with the number of clients rising from 8,200 to 51,683 during the same period.

From 1940 the Liberian dollar was maintained nominally at par with the US dollar. The official 1:1 exchange rate became increasingly unrealistic during the 1989–96 war and the rate was allowed to float from the end of August 1998. The exchange rate remained stable until the end of 2000, at about 41 Liberian dollars to the US dollar. In December 2000, however, in response to an upsurge in government spending financed by a recourse to the banking system, to the deteriorating security situation and to fears of UN sanctions, the Liberian dollar started to weaken and reached L $70 = US $1 in mid-2002. Following the end of the 1999–2003 conflict, there was an immediate strengthening to about L $43 = US $1, but since then the rate has gradually deteriorated, reaching L $72.50 = US $1 at the end of December 2011.

A new Consumer Price Index (CPI) was compiled in May 1998, replaced by a Harmonized CPI (HCPI) from January 2007. The main threat to price stability in Monrovia is presented by government monetary policy, import prices, and currency depreciation. The CPI remained fairly stable in the first few years after 1996, but currency depreciations after 2001 led to rapidly rising prices, with the CPI increasing by 10%–14% annually during 2001–03. Price stability was restored in early 2004 and inflation stood below 10% per year until 2007, when global increases in fuel and food prices pushed the HCPI annual inflation rate to a peak of 26.5% in August 2008. Although inflationary pressures have since generally moderated, annual inflation climbed back to 11.4% in the 12 months to December 2011.

INTERNATIONAL TRADE AND DEBT

International trade has generated Liberia's growth. Merchandise exports increased from negligible levels before the Second World War to US $400.2m. in 1974, stimulated by strong demand in the world economy for iron ore and supported by continuing exports of rubber and other primary commodities. In 1974 exports were equivalent in value to 87% of GDP. Exports stagnated, in volume terms, in the late 1970s as a result of international recession. In the 1980s the volume of exports broadly declined, and stagnating (or contracting) export unit values exacerbated the effects on the economy. Nevertheless, the dominance of the export sector continued: exports were equivalent to 58% of GDP in 1980 and 50% in 1989.

After the 1989–96 civil conflict, identified exports, according to IMF estimates, recovered to US $166.5m. in 2002. The impact of the war with LURD and MODEL was severe in 2003, with total exports declining to US $108.9m. Timber exports collapsed to a negligible level in 2004 as UN sanctions took effect. Since then, the trade balance has demonstrated continued weakness arising from the narrow commodity composition of exports, the instability of export demand, and Liberia's vulnerability to global increases in the prices of rice and petroleum, two of its main imports. In 2011 exports of goods rose to an estimated US $371m. and imports to an estimated US $982m. Combined with a net deficit on trade in services of US $836m., these figures produced a deficit on trade in goods and services of US $1,448m., financed largely by donor assistance and foreign direct investment. Net private remittances from abroad have become a significant element in the balance of payments in recent years, amounting to an estimated US $86m. in 2011.

Liberia first fell into arrears to the IMF in 1984. In March 1990 the IMF declared Liberia a 'non-co-operating' country and threatened Liberia with expulsion from the Fund owing to the Government's failure to pay outstanding arrears. By this time Liberia's total external debt had risen to US $1,849m. The 1989–96 conflict resulted in the suspension of debt-servicing payments and the arrears accumulated at a rapid rate. By 1997 accumulated arrears and penalties had increased Liberia's total external debt to some US $2,012m. (equivalent to almost US $700 per head), of which most was in arrears.

The Taylor administration offered only minimal co-operation with the IMF, and in March 2003 the IMF finally suspended Liberia's voting rights at the IMF. The NTGL expressed its commitment to normalizing relations with the Fund and resumed token repayments in January 2004, but in 2005 the IMF voiced renewed concerns over the lack of transparency in government transactions and inadequate budgetary control. Progress towards the normalization of relations came to a halt until the election of President Johnson-Sirleaf. In May 2006 the IMF pronounced itself 'encouraged' by developments in economic management in Liberia, and in October the IMF lifted the declaration of non-co-operation that had been in force since 1990. In November the IMF announced that it had secured funding pledges of US $842m. from its members, enabling it to write off Liberia's debt to the Fund. In February 2008 it deemed Liberia eligible for debt relief assistance under the initiative for heavily indebted poor countries (HIPC). In March the Fund restored Liberia's voting and related rights at the Fund, a decision which allowed the Fund to provide US $952m. of financing to the country. In April the 'Paris Club' of creditors agreed to cancel US $254m. of debt and to reschedule US $789m. The USA immediately announced its intention of going beyond the 'Paris Club' agreement and cancelling all its debts owed by Liberia. China announced its intention to forgive all outstanding claims in 2008, and debt reliefs were also granted by the International Fund for Agricultural Development, the Saudi Fund and others. In April 2009 private creditors agreed to discount the value of their loans by 97%; the remainder was paid off by the World Bank and other donors. In June 2010 the IMF and the World Bank announced that they had decided to support a US $4,600m. package of debt relief for Liberia, including US $2,700m. under the HIPC initiative. This announcement brought to an end an external debt problem which had hung over Liberia for 30 years. Antoinette Sayeh, the Director of the IMF's African Department and a former Liberian Minister of Finance, stated that this represented 'a tremendous achievement'.

PUBLIC FINANCE AND AID

A new tax code, developed in accordance with IMF advice, was introduced in July 2001, based on a personal income tax, a business income tax and a new flat-rate general sales tax. A new tariff structure, bringing Liberian tariffs into closer accordance with Economic Community of West African States (ECOWAS) rates, was also announced in 2000. Taxes on international trade and transactions yielded US $105.4m. in the 2010/11 financial year (from July to June in Liberia), or 28% of total government revenue of US $374.9m.; taxes on income yielded US $111.2m., or 30% of the total; taxes on goods and services generated US $48.4m. (13%); and non-tax revenues accounted for most of the remainder.

Johnson-Sirleaf's first budget, submitted to the legislature at the end of June 2006, was for US $120m., an expenditure to be covered by taxation receipts without recourse to borrowing. Expenditure allocations were shifted towards education and health, and away from defence, which received only 1% of the total. Since then the administration has succeeded in increasing the budget totals substantially, to US $282.2m. for 2009/10, US $382.9m. for 2010/11 and US $472.9m. for 2011/12. Of the total 2012/13 budget of US $649.7m., some US $212.1m. (33%) was allocated to public administration, reflecting the high cost of the state apparatus; US $86.0m. (13%) was allocated to health and social services; US $76.9m. (12%) was allocated to education; and US $71.0m. (11%) was allocated to security and the rule of law.

Liberia's alignment with Western countries during the Cold War was undoubtedly encouraged by the willingness of the USA to provide substantial quantities of aid. While developmental and budgetary aid largely ceased in 1990, the USA and others provided emergency assistance to counteract the effects of the civil conflict. Post-conflict reconstruction and development aid was inhibited by concerns over mismanagement and corruption, especially before the departure of Taylor in 2003. In February 2004 an International Reconstruction Conference for Liberia, held under UN auspices, received offers of funds totalling US $520m. Disbursements of this aid were slow, however, totalling only US $189m. in 2004 and US $270m. in 2005, with donors citing continuing concerns about Liberian financial management practices as the cause of the delays. Very little of this aid was channelled through the NTGL and virtually no aid was provided for general support of the government budget. In the first year of the Johnson-Sirleaf administration in 2006, net ODA receipts remained steady at an estimated US $260m., but rose substantially to US $701m. in 2007 and to US $1,251m. in 2008, before decreasing to US $513m. in 2009. A substantial recovery, to US $1,419m., took place in 2010. Some aid donors, including the World Bank, the AfDB, Germany, the United Kingdom and Ireland, have donated funds directly to the Johnson-Sirleaf Government, but the UN system, the USA, Norway and the EU remained reluctant to do so. Of the projected US $361m. aid receipts in 2012/13, 87% are expected to be for project aid, bypassing the state budget.

GROWTH AND ECONOMIC PROSPECTS

Reconstruction of the country's economy, especially its infrastructure, was far from complete before the conflict of 1999–2003 wrought further damage. Slow progress under the NTGL has been superseded by renewed hope and advances under the Johnson-Sirleaf administrations. The removal of timber and diamond sanctions, the restoration of electricity and piped water to parts of Monrovia, the start of road rehabilitation and the beginning of a new phase in iron-ore mining have been significant achievements. Relations with international financial institutions have improved dramatically, and the debt relief secured in 2010 was an historic achievement. However, poverty remains widespread and severe, and has been exacerbated by rising fuel and food prices. The interest in offshore oil exploration has yet to yield substantial results. The recovery of the timber and diamond sectors awaits foreign investment which, in these as in other sectors, remains restricted by the devastated infrastructure. Progress against corruption has been slow and faltering. Even sustained and rapid growth will not return the economy to the position it achieved in the 1980s for many years to come.

Statistical Survey

Sources (unless otherwise stated): Liberia Institute of Statistics and Geo-Information Services, POB 629, Tubman Blvd, Sinkor, Monrovia; internet www.tlcafrica.com/lisgis/lisgis.htm; Central Bank of Liberia, POB 2048, cnr of Warren and Carey Sts, Monrovia; tel. 6225685 (mobile); fax 6226114 (mobile); internet www.cbl.org.lr.

Area and Population

AREA, POPULATION AND DENSITY

Area (sq km)	97,754*
Population (census results)	
1 February 1984	2,101,628
21 March 2008	
Males	1,739,945
Females	1,736,663
Total	3,476,608
Population (UN estimates at mid-year)†	
2010	3,994,122
2011	4,128,572
2012	4,244,683
Density (per sq km) at mid-2012	43.4

* 37,743 sq miles.
† Source: UN, *World Population Prospects: The 2010 Revision*.

POPULATION BY AGE AND SEX

(UN estimates at mid-2012)

	Males	Females	Total
0–14	937,970	903,339	1,841,309
15–64	1,144,038	1,140,868	2,284,906
65 and over	52,800	65,668	118,468
Total	2,134,808	2,109,875	4,244,683

Source: UN, *World Population Prospects: The 2010 Revision*.

COUNTIES

(population at 2008 census)

Bomi	84,119	Margibi	209,923
Bong	333,481	Maryland	135,938
Gbarpolu	83,388	Montserrado	1,118,241
Grand Bassa	221,693	Nimba	462,026
Grand Cape Mount	127,076	Rivercess	71,509
Grand Gedeh	125,258	River Gee	66,789
Grand Kru	57,913	Sinoe	102,391
Lofa	276,863	**Total**	3,476,608

PRINCIPAL TOWNS

(2003)

Monrovia (capital)	550,200	Harbel	17,700
Zwedru	35,300	Tubmanburg	16,700
Buchanan	27,300	Gbarnga	14,200
Yekepa	22,900	Greenville	13,500
Harper	20,000	Ganta	11,200
Bensonville	19,600		

Source: Stefan Helders, *World Gazetteer* (internet www.world-gazetteer.com).

Mid-2011 (incl. suburbs, UN estimate): Monrovia 750,376 (Source: UN, *World Urbanization Prospects: The 2011 Revision*).

BIRTHS AND DEATHS

(annual averages, UN estimates)

	1995–2000	2000–05	2005–10
Birth rate (per 1,000)	44.0	42.4	40.5
Death rate (per 1,000)	19.8	15.4	12.0

Source: UN, *World Population Prospects: The 2010 Revision*.

Life expectancy (years at birth): 56.1 (males 55.2; females 57.2) in 2010 (Source: World Bank, World Development Indicators database).

ECONOMICALLY ACTIVE POPULATION

(formal sector only)

	2008	2009	2010*
Agriculture and forestry	22,616	34,882	38,615
Mining	1,421	1,907	1,691
Manufacturing	2,215	2,075	1,367
Construction	390	1,659	3,856
Wholesale and retail trade	10,028	10,998	7,536
Transport and communications	4,984	5,563	9,423
Banking and insurance	2,189	4,044	6,426
Business services	6,231	9,467	10,179
Social and community services	9,213	20,160	28,020
Government	47,681	34,000	37,532
Total	106,968	124,755	144,647

* Estimates.

Total employed in informal sector: 487,000 in 2008; 569,790 in 2009; 672,352 (estimate) in 2010.

Health and Welfare

KEY INDICATORS

Total fertility rate (children per woman, 2010)	5.2
Under-5 mortality rate (per 1,000 live births, 2010)	103
HIV/AIDS (% of persons aged 15–49, 2009)	1.5
Physicians (per 1,000 head, 2004)	0.03
Hospital beds (per 1,000 head, 2009)	0.7
Health expenditure (2009): US $ per head (PPP)	50
Health expenditure (2009): % of GDP	12.2
Health expenditure (2009): public (% of total)	34.5
Access to water (% of persons, 2010)	73
Access to sanitation (% of persons, 2010)	18
Total carbon dioxide emissions ('000 metric tons, 2008)	608.7
Carbon dioxide emissions per head (metric tons, 2008)	0.2
Human Development Index (2011): ranking	182
Human Development Index (2011): value	0.329

For sources and definitions, see explanatory note on p. vi.

Agriculture

PRINCIPAL CROPS

('000 metric tons)

	2008	2009	2010
Rice, paddy*	295	293	296
Cassava (Manioc)	560†	495*	493*
Taro (Cocoyam)†	30	27	17
Yams†	21	18	18
Sweet potatoes†	21	20	18
Sugar cane†	265	265	265
Oil palm fruit	174	174	174
Bananas†	120	123	145
Plantains†	44	47	46
Natural rubber*	85	60	62

* Unofficial figure(s).
† FAO estimate(s).

Aggregate production ('000 metric tons, may include official, semi-official or estimated data): Total cereals 295 in 2008, 293 in 2009, 296 in 2010; Total roots and tubers 632 in 2008, 560 in 2009; 546 in 2010; Total vegetables (incl. melons) 104 in 2008, 83 in 2009, 107 in 2010; Total fruits (excl. melons) 183 in 2008, 190 in 2009, 209 in 2010.

Source: FAO.

LIVESTOCK
('000 head, year ending September, FAO estimates)

	2008	2009	2010
Cattle	39	39	40
Pigs	200	230	265
Sheep	241	252	264
Goats	285	311	338
Chickens	6,250	6,500	6,800
Ducks	270	290	300

Source: FAO.

LIVESTOCK PRODUCTS
(metric tons, FAO estimates)

	2008	2009	2010
Pig meat	6,783	7,822	9,020
Chicken meat	10,000	10,400	10,880
Game meat	6,700	7,146	7,700
Cows' milk	754	799	819
Hen eggs	5,775	4,950	5,200

Source: FAO.

Forestry

ROUNDWOOD REMOVALS
('000 cubic metres, excluding bark)

	2008	2009	2010
Sawlogs, veneer logs and logs for sleepers	240	240	300
Other industrial wood*	180	180	180
Fuel wood*	6,503	6,751	7,008
Total	6,923	7,171	7,488

* FAO estimates.

Source: FAO.

SAWNWOOD PRODUCTION
('000 cubic metres, including railway sleepers)

	2006	2007	2008
Total (all broadleaved)	60	60	80

2009–10: Figure assumed to unchanged from 2008 (FAO estimate).

Source: FAO.

Fishing

(metric tons, live weight of capture)

	2007	2008	2009*
Freshwater fishes	1,743	763	750
African sicklefish	150	185	180
Barracudas	356	126	130
Blue butterfish	n.a.	n.a.	n.a.
Bobo croaker	201	260	260
Cassava croaker	381	229	220
Clupeoids	n.a.	1	1
Hammerhead sharks	332	n.a.	100
Marlins, sailfishes, etc.	459	180	180
Sardinellas	1,599	626	630
Sharks, rays, skates, etc.	504	108	100
Snappers	243	251	250
Total catch (incl. others)	14,488	7,890	8,000

* FAO estimates.

2010: Figures assumed to be unchanged from 2009 (FAO estimates).

Source: FAO.

Mining

	2008	2009	2010*
Diamonds ('000 carats)	47	28	25
Gold (kilograms)	624	524	800

* Preliminary.

Note: In addition to the commodities listed, Liberia produced significant quantities of a variety of industrial minerals and construction materials (clays, gypsum, sand and gravel, and stone), but insufficient information is available to make reliable estimates of output levels.

Source: US Geological Survey.

Industry

SELECTED PRODUCTS
(litres, unless otherwise indicated)

	2009	2010	2011*
Beverages	19,979,814	25,457,394	30,986,250
Cement (metric tons)	70,584	71,733	60,764
Paint	211,694	270,217	284,072
Candles (kilograms)	323,200	578,844	473,383
Bleach	529,396	662,285	816,152
Rubbing alcohol	231,060	743,960	309,767
Mattresses (number)	47,278	122,029	142,066
Treated (finished) water (million gallons)	299.7	1,408.4	1,821.1

* Estimates.

Electric energy (million kWh): 351 in 2006; 353 in 2007; 353 in 2008 (Source: UN Industrial Commodity Statistics Database).

Finance

CURRENCY AND EXCHANGE RATES

Monetary Units

100 cents = 1 Liberian dollar (L $).

Sterling, Dollar and Euro Equivalents (30 April 2012)

£1 sterling = L $120.331;
US $1 = L $74.000;
€1 = L $97.784;
L $1,000 = £8.31 = US $13.51 = €10.23.

Average Exchange Rate (L $ per US $)

2009 68.2867
2010 71.4033
2011 72.2267

Note: The aforementioned data are based on market-determined rates of exchange. Prior to January 1998 the exchange rate was a fixed parity with the US dollar (L $1 = US $1).

BUDGET
(US $ million)

Revenue*	2010/11	2011/12†	2012/13†
Tax revenue	269.2	338.9	349.3
Taxes on income, profits and capital gains	111.2	120.0	112.6
Taxes on goods and services	48.4	72.0	75.1
Taxes on international trade and transactions	105.4	141.3	155.7
Other taxes	4.3	5.7	5.8
Non-tax revenue	65.3	98.3	97.9
Total	334.6	437.3	447.2

Expenditure‡	2010/11	2011/12†	2012/13†
Current expenditure	309.4	418.8	414.4
Wages and salaries	138.6	186.0	198.8
Other goods and services	86.3	116.1	119.0
Subsidies and transfers	80.5	112.0	91.5
Interest on debt	4.0	4.7	5.1
Capital expenditure	73.5	54.1	112.0
Total	382.9	472.9	526.4

* Excluding grants received (US $ million): 40.3 in 2010/11; 33.5 in 2011/12 (budget projection); 52.8 in 2012/13 (budget projection).

† Budget projections.

‡ Includes net lending.

Source: IMF, *Liberia: Eighth Review Under the Three-Year Arrangement Under the Extended Credit Facility—Staff Report; Press Release on the Executive Board Discussion; and Statement by the Executive Director for Liberia.* (May 2012).

INTERNATIONAL RESERVES

(US $ million at 31 December)

	2009	2010	2011
IMF special drawing rights	201.43	210.49	223.56
Reserve position in IMF	0.05	0.05	0.05
Foreign exchange	170.97	—	—
Total	372.46	210.54	223.61

Source: IMF, *International Financial Statistics.*

MONEY SUPPLY

(L $ million at 31 December)

	2009	2010	2011
Currency outside banks*	4,161.8	5,007.9	6,704.3
Demand deposits at commercial banks	12,686.0	18,204.7	23,364.7
Total money (incl. others)	17,610.5	24,170.1	31,295.3

* Figures refer only to amounts of Liberian coin in circulation. US notes and coin also circulate, but the amount of these in private holdings is unknown. The amount of Liberian coin in circulation is small in comparison to US currency.

Source: IMF, *International Financial Statistics.*

COST OF LIVING

(Consumer Price Index; base: May 1998 = 100)

	2003	2004	2005
Food	140.9	153.8	167.0
Fuel and light	154.4	217.6	342.1
Clothing	121.2	128.7	137.3
Rent	131.8	156.1	180.9
All items (incl. others)	157.0	169.3	187.6

Source: IMF, *Liberia: Selected Issues and Statistical Appendix* (May 2006).

All items (Consumer Price Index; base 2000 = 100): 167.6 in 2006; 186.7 in 2007; 219.4 in 2008; 235.7 in 2009; 253.3 in 2010; 274.8 in 2011 (Source: African Development Bank).

NATIONAL ACCOUNTS

Expenditure on the Gross Domestic Product

(US $ million at current prices)

	2008	2009	2010
Government final consumption expenditure	145	125	142
Private final consumption expenditure	1,519	1,535	1,789
Gross capital formation	150	166	175
Total domestic expenditure	1,814	1,826	2,106
Exports of goods and services	234	244	258
Less Imports of goods and services	1,296	1,238	1,491
GDP in purchasers' values	751	832	873
GDP at constant 2005 prices	730	764	803

Source: UN Statistics Division, National Accounts Main Aggregates Database.

Gross Domestic Product by Economic Activity

(L $ million at current prices)

	2009	2010	2011
Agriculture	663	696	745
Mining and quarrying	22	23	25
Manufacturing	54	57	61
Electricity, gas and water	6	6	7
Construction	25	26	28
Trade, restaurants and hotels	23	24	25
Transport and communications	53	54	58
Finance, insurance and real estate, etc.	17	18	19
Public administration and defence	33	35	37
Other services	19	20	21
Sub-total	915	959	1,025
Less Imputed bank service charge	8	9	9
GDP at factor cost	906	950	1,015
Indirect taxes, less subsidies	85	89	95
GDP in market prices	991	1,039	1,110

Source: African Development Bank.

BALANCE OF PAYMENTS

(US $ million)

	2008	2009	2010
Exports of goods f.o.b.	249.0	180.0	241.2
Imports of goods c.i.f.	–728.8	–559.0	–719.1
Trade balance	–479.8	–379.0	–477.9
Exports of services	509.6	274.1	158.0
Imports of services	–1,411.1	–1,145.2	–1,078.6
Balance on goods and services	–1,381.4	–1,250.1	–1,398.5
Other income received	22.4	18.1	31.2
Other income paid	–170.7	–145.9	–7.0
Balance on goods, services and income	–1,529.7	–1,377.9	–1,374.2
Current transfers (net)	911.5	836.8	637.3
Current balance	–618.2	–541.1	–736.9
Capital account (net)	1,197.0	1,526.0	1,594.3
Direct investment from abroad	394.5	217.8	452.3
Other investment assets	–33.2	200.4	1.4
Other investment liabilities	–13.4	158.5	–6.8
Net errors and omissions	–465.1	10.8	847.1
Overall balance	461.6	1,572.4	2,151.4

Source: IMF, *International Financial Statistics.*

External Trade

PRINCIPAL COMMODITIES
(US $ million)

Imports c.i.f.	2008	2009	2010
Food and live animals	206.8	161.8	185.4
Rice	105.6	65.7	47.3
Beverages and tobacco	13.9	18.6	17.6
Mineral fuels and lubricants	13.2	10.5	64.5
Petroleum	147.2	68.5	150.8
Chemicals and related products	36.5	29.6	31.8
Basic manufactures	104.7	84.0	70.7
Machinery and transport equipment	215.2	125.1	126.7
Miscellaneous manufactured articles	60.1	27.0	44.8
Total (incl. others)	813.5	551.6	709.8

Exports f.o.b.	2008	2009	2010
Rubber	206.8	93.1	157.0
Cocoa beans and coffee	3.4	3.7	5.3
Diamonds	10.0	6.9	15.3
Gold	13.3	11.9	19.8
Iron ore	1.5	0.9	3.1
Total (incl. others)	242.4	148.8	222.0

PRINCIPAL TRADING PARTNERS
(US $ million)

Imports c.i.f.	1986	1987	1988
Belgium-Luxembourg	8.5	11.2	15.0
China, People's Repub.	7.1	14.7	4.8
Denmark	10.6	7.6	5.9
France (incl. Monaco)	6.5	6.4	4.7
Germany, Fed. Repub.	32.7	52.3	39.5
Italy	2.5	2.2	7.3
Japan	20.1	15.0	12.0
Netherlands	20.6	26.8	14.4
Spain	2.5	6.6	3.1
Sweden	2.4	0.6	4.6
United Kingdom	24.2	18.4	12.7
USA	42.5	58.0	57.7
Total (incl. others)	259.0	307.6	272.3

Source: UN, *International Trade Statistics Yearbook*.

Exports f.o.b.	2004	2005	2006*
Belgium	30.6	28.5	39.2
China, People's Repub.	5.5	1.2	n.a.
France	1.7	n.a.	n.a.
USA	63.7	96.8	133.3
Total (incl. others)	103.8	131.8	180.8

* Estimates.

Imports (US $ million): 813.5 in 2008; 551.6 in 2009; 709.8 in 2010.

Exports (US $ million): 242.4 in 2008; 148.8 in 2009; 222.0 in 2010.

Transport

RAILWAYS
(estimated traffic)

	1991	1992	1993
Passenger-km (million)	406	417	421
Freight ton-km (million)	200	200	200

Source: UN Economic Commission for Africa, *African Statistical Yearbook*.

ROAD TRAFFIC
(estimates, '000 vehicles in use at 31 December)

	1999	2000	2001
Passenger cars	15.3	17.1	17.1
Commercial vehicles	11.9	12.8	12.8

2002: Figures assumed to be unchanged from 2001.

Source: UN, *Statistical Yearbook*.

2007 (motor vehicles in use at 31 December): Passenger cars 7,428; Buses and coaches 554; Lorries and vans 2,772; Motorcycles and mopeds 333 (Source: IRF, *World Road Statistics*).

SHIPPING

Merchant Fleet
(registered at 31 December)

	2007	2008	2009
Number of vessels	2,171	2,306	2,456
Displacement ('000 gross registered tons)	76,572.6	82,389.4	91,695.8

Source: IHS Fairplay, *World Fleet Statistics*.

International Sea-borne Freight Traffic
(estimates, '000 metric tons)

	1991	1992	1993
Goods loaded	16,706	17,338	21,653
Goods unloaded	1,570	1,597	1,608

Source: UN Economic Commission for Africa, *African Statistical Yearbook*.

CIVIL AVIATION
(traffic on scheduled services)

	1990	1991	1992
Passengers carried ('000)	32	32	32
Passenger-km (million)	7	7	7
Total ton-km (million)	1	1	1

Source: UN, *Statistical Yearbook*.

Communications Media

	2009	2010	2011
Telephones ('000 main lines in use)	2.2	5.9*	3.1*
Mobile cellular telephones ('000 subscribers)	1,085.1	1,571.3	2,029.9
Internet users ('000)	20	n.a.	n.a.
Broadband subscribers	200	200	100

* Includes fixed wireless telephones.

Source: International Telecommunication Union.

Radio receivers ('000 in use): 790 in 1997 (Source: UNESCO, *Statistical Yearbook*).

Television receivers ('000 in use): 70 in 1997 (Source: UNESCO, *Statistical Yearbook*).

Daily newspapers: 6 in 1998 (estimated average circulation 36,600); 3 in 2004 (Source: UNESCO Institute for Statistics).

Education

(2007/08 unless otherwise indicated)

		Students		
	Teachers	Males	Females	Total
Pre-primary	11,778	251,049	240,515	491,564
Primary	22,253	286,584	253,303	539,887
Secondary	11,880	90,383	67,859	158,242
Secondary technical and vocational*	603	26,988	18,079	45,067
Post-secondary technical and vocational*	430	8,842	6,789	15,631
University	772†	25,236*	18,871*	44,107*

* 1999/2000.

† 2000/01.

Source: UNESCO Institute for Statistics.

Pupil-teacher ratio (primary education, UNESCO estimate): 24.3 in 2007/08 (Source: UNESCO Institute for Statistics).

Adult literacy rate (UNESCO estimates): 60.8% (males 64.8%; females 56.8%) in 2010 (Source: UNESCO Institute for Statistics).

Directory

The Constitution

The Constitution of the Republic of Liberia entered into effect on 6 January 1986, following its approval by national referendum in July 1984. Its main provisions are summarized below:

PREAMBLE

The Republic of Liberia is a unitary sovereign state, which is divided into counties for administrative purposes. There are three separate branches of government: the legislative, the executive and the judiciary. No person is permitted to hold office or executive power in more than one branch of government. The fundamental human rights of the individual are guaranteed.

LEGISLATURE

Legislative power is vested in the bicameral National Assembly, comprising a Senate and a House of Representatives. Deputies of both chambers are elected by universal adult suffrage. Each county elects two members of the Senate (one for a term of nine years and one for six years), while members of the House of Representatives are elected by legislative constituency for a term of six years. Legislation requires the approval of two-thirds of the members of both chambers, and is subsequently submitted to the President for endorsement. The Constitution may be amended by two-thirds of the members of both chambers.

EXECUTIVE

Executive power is vested in the President, who is Head of State and Commander-in-Chief of the armed forces. The President is elected by universal adult suffrage for a term of six years, and is restricted to a maximum of two terms in office. A Vice-President is elected at the same time as the President. The President appoints a Cabinet, and members of the judiciary and armed forces, with the approval of the Senate. The President is empowered to declare a state of emergency.

JUDICIARY

Judicial power is vested in the Supreme Court and any subordinate courts, which apply both statutory and customary laws in accordance with standards enacted by the legislature. The judgments of the Supreme Court are final and not subject to appeal or review by any other branch of government. The Supreme Court comprises one Chief Justice and five Associate Justices. Justices are appointed by the President, with the approval of the Senate.

POLITICAL PARTIES AND ELECTIONS

Political associations are obliged to comply with the minimum registration requirements imposed by the Elections Commission. Organizations that endanger free democratic society, or that organize, train or equip groups of supporters, are to be denied registration. Prior to elections, each political party and independent candidate is required to submit statements of assets and liabilities to the Elections Commission. All elections of public officials are determined by an absolute majority of the votes cast. If no candidate obtains an absolute majority in the first ballot, a second ballot is conducted between the two candidates with the highest number of votes. Complaints by parties or candidates must be submitted to the Elections Commission within seven days of the announcement of election results. The Supreme Court has final jurisdiction over challenges to election results.

The Government

HEAD OF STATE

President: Ellen Johnson-Sirleaf (inaugurated 16 January 2006; re-elected 8 November 2011).

Vice-President: Joseph Nyumah Boakai.

THE CABINET

(September 2012)

Minister of Agriculture: Dr Florence Chenoweth.

Minister of Commerce and Industry: Miatta Beysolow.

Minister of Defence: Brownie Samukai.

Minister of Education: Othello Gongar.

Minister of Finance: Amara Konneh.

Minister of Foreign Affairs: Augustine Ngafuan.

Minister of Gender and Development: Varbah Gayflor.

Minister of Health and Social Welfare: Dr Walter Gwenigale.

Minister of Information, Culture and Tourism: Lewis G. Brown, II.

Minister of Internal Affairs: Blamoh Nelson.

Minister of Justice: Christiana Tah.

Minister of Labour: Jeremiah Sulunteh.

Minister of Lands, Mines and Energy: Roosevelt Jayjay.

Minister of National Security: Victor Helb.

Minister of Planning and Economic Affairs: (vacant).

Minister of Posts and Telecommunications: Frederick Norkeh.

Minister of Public Works: Samuel Kofi Woods.

Minister of Transport: Lenn Eugene Nagbe.

Minister of Youth and Sports: Etmonia Tarpeh.

MINISTRIES

Office of the President: Executive Mansion, POB 10-9001, Capitol Hill, 1000 Monrovia 10; e-mail gmoore@emansion.gov.lr; internet www.emansion.gov.lr.

Ministry of Agriculture: 19th St, Sinkor, POB 10-9010, 1000 Monrovia 10; tel. 226399; internet www.moa.gov.lr.

Ministry of Commerce and Industry: Ashmun St, POB 10-9014, 1000 Monrovia 10; tel. 226283; internet www.moci.gov.lr.

Ministry of Defence: Benson St, POB 10-9007, 1000 Monrovia 10; tel. 226077; internet www.mod.gov.lr.

Ministry of Education: E. G. N. King Plaza, Broad St, POB 10-1545, 1000 Monrovia 10; tel. and fax 226216; internet www.moe.gov.lr.

Ministry of Finance: Broad St, POB 10-9013, 1000 Monrovia 10; tel. 47510680 (mobile); internet www.mof.gov.lr.

Ministry of Foreign Affairs: Mamba Point, POB 10-9002, 1000 Monrovia 10; tel. 226763; internet www.mofa.gov.lr.

Ministry of Gender and Development: Monrovia; internet www.mogd.gov.lr.

Ministry of Health and Social Welfare: Sinkor, POB 10-9004, 1000 Monrovia 10; tel. 226317; internet www.moh.gov.lr.

Ministry of Information, Culture and Tourism: Capitol Hill, POB 10-9021, 1000 Monrovia 10; tel. and fax 226269; internet www.micat.gov.lr.

Ministry of Internal Affairs: cnr Warren and Benson Sts, POB 10-9008, 1000 Monrovia 10; tel. 226346; internet www.moia.gov.lr.

Ministry of Justice: Ashmun St, POB 10-9006, 1000 Monrovia 10; tel. 227872; internet www.moia.gov.lr.

Ministry of Labour: Mechlin St, POB 10-9040, 1000 Monrovia 10; tel. 226291; internet www.mol.gov.lr.

Ministry of Lands, Mines and Energy: Capitol Hill, POB 10-9024, 1000 Monrovia 10; tel. 226281; internet www.molme.gov.lr.

Ministry of National Security: Monrovia.

Ministry of Planning and Economic Affairs: Broad St, POB 10-9016, 1000 Monrovia 10; tel. 226962; internet www.mopea.gov.lr.

Ministry of Posts and Telecommunications: Carey St, 1000 Monrovia 10; tel. 886552947 (mobile); e-mail internationalbureaurl@yahoo.com.

Ministry of Presidential Affairs: Executive Mansion, Capitol Hill, 1000 Monrovia 10; tel. 228026; internet www.emansion.gov.lr.

Ministry of Public Works: Lynch St, POB 10-9011, 1000 Monrovia 10; tel. 227972; internet www.mopw.gov.lr.

Ministry of Transport: 1000 Monrovia 10; internet www.mopt.gov.lr.

Ministry of Youth and Sports: Monrovia; internet www.lys.gov.lr.

President and Legislature

PRESIDENT

Presidential Election, First Round, 11 October 2011

Candidate	Votes	% of votes
Ellen Johnson-Sirleaf (Unity Party)	530,020	43.93
Winston A. Tubman (Congress for Democratic Change)	394,370	32.68
Prince Yormie Johnson (National Union for Democratic Progress)	139,786	11.58
Charles Walker Brumskine (Liberty Party)	65,800	5.45
Kennedy Gbleyah Sandy (Liberia Transformation Party)	13,612	1.13
Gladys G. Y. Beyan (Grassroots Democratic Party of Liberia)	12,740	1.06
Others	50,314	4.17
Total	1,206,642	100.00

Presidential Election, Second Round, 8 November 2011

Candidate	Votes	% of votes
Ellen Johnson-Sirleaf (Unity Party)	607,618	90.71
Winston A. Tubman (Congress for Democratic Change)	62,207	9.29
Total	669,825	100.00

LEGISLATURE

House of Representatives

Speaker: ALEX JANEKAI TYLER.

General Election, 11 October 2011

Party	Seats
Unity Party	24
Congress for Democratic Change	11
Independents	9
Liberty Party	7
National Union for Democratic Progress	6
National Democratic Coalition	5
Alliance for Peace and Democracy	3
National Patriotic Party	3
Movement for Progressive Change	2
Liberia Destiny Party	1
Liberia Transformation Party	1
National Reformation Party	1
Total	73

Senate

President: JOSEPH NYUMAH BOAKAI.

General Election, 11 October 2011

Party	Seats
Unity Party	9
Independents	6
National Patriotic Party	4
Congress for Democratic Change	3
Alliance for Peace and Democracy	2
Liberty Party	2
Liberia Destiny Party	1
Liberia Transformation Party	1
National Democratic Coalition	1
National Union for Democratic Progress	1
Total	30

Election Commission

National Elections Commission: Tubman Blvd, 16th St, Sinkor, Monrovia; internet www.necliberia.org; independent; Chair. ELIZABETH J. NELSON (acting).

Political Organizations

Some 23 political parties were listed by the National Elections Commission in mid-2011 and a further five parties were granted accreditation in June. The most significant of these parties are listed below:

Alliance for Peace and Democracy (APD): Benson St, Monrovia; tel. 6918196 (mobile); e-mail karwease@go.metrostate.edu; internet www.members.tripod.com/tipoteh12/index.html; f. 2005; Chair. MARCUS S. G. DAHN.

All Liberian Coalition Party (ALCOP): Broad St, Monrovia; tel. 6524735; f. 1997 from elements of fmr armed faction the United Liberation Movement of Liberia for Democracy; Leader Alhaji G. V. KROMAH; Chair. ANSU DOLLEY.

Congress for Democratic Change (CDC): Tubman Blvd, POB 2799, Monrovia; tel. 6513469 (mobile); internet www.cdcforliberia.org; f. 2004; Leader GEORGE MANNEH WEAH; Chair. GERALDINE DOE-SHERIFF.

Free Democratic Party (FDP): Center St, Monrovia; tel. 6582291 (mobile); Leader DAVID M. FARHAT; Chair. S. CIAPHA GBOLLIE.

Liberia Destiny Party (LDP): Congo Town Back Rd, Monrovia; tel. 6511531 (mobile); f. 2005; Chair. BOIMAH TAYLOR; Sec.-Gen. BORBOR B. KROMAH.

Liberia National Union (LINU): 16th St, Sinkor Monrovia; tel. 77059282; Chair. AARON S. M. WESSEH.

Liberty Party (LP): Old Rd, Sinkor Opposite Haywood Mission, POB 1340, Monrovia; tel. 6547921 (mobile); f. 2005; Leader CHARLES WALKER BRUMSKINE; Chair. ISRAEL AKINSANYA.

Nation Democratic Party of Liberia (NDPL): Capitol By-Pass, Monrovia; f. 1997 from the fmr armed faction the Liberia Peace Council; Chair. D. NYANDEH SIEH, Sr.

National Patriotic Party (NPP): Sinkor, Tubman Bldg, Monrovia; tel. 6515312 (mobile); f. 1997 from the fmr armed faction the National Patriotic Front of Liberia; won the majority of seats in legislative elections in July 1997; Leader ROLAND CHRIS YARKPAH MASSAQUOI; Chair. THEOPHILUS C. GOULD.

National Reformation Party (NRP): Duala Market, Monrovia; tel. 6511531 (mobile); Chair. Rev. MAXIMILLIAN T. W. DIABE.

National Union for Democratic Progress (NUDP): VP Rd, Old Rd, Monrovia; tel. 6645421 (mobile); Chair. GBAWOU KOWOU.

New Deal Movement (NDM): Randall St, Monrovia; tel. 6567470 (mobile); e-mail info@newdealmovement.com; internet newdealmovement.com; f. 2002; Leader Prof. GEORGE KLAY KIEH, Jr; Chair. HENRY W. YALLAH.

Progressive Democratic Party (PRODEM): McDonald St, Monrovia; tel. 6521091 (mobile); f. early 2005 by mems of fmr rebel movement, Liberians United for Reconciliation and Democracy (emerged 1999); Chair. GARBLA WILLIAMS.

Unity Party (UP): 86 Broad St, Monrovia; tel. 6512528 (mobile); e-mail info@theunityparty.org; f. 1984; Leader ELLEN JOHNSON-SIRLEAF; Chair. HARRY VARNEY GBOTO-NAMBI SHERMAN.

Diplomatic Representation

EMBASSIES IN LIBERIA

Algeria: Capitol By-Pass, POB 2032, Monrovia; tel. 224311; Chargé d'affaires a.i. MUHAMMAD AZZEDINE AZZOUZ.

Cameroon: 18th St and Payne Ave, Sinkor, POB 414, Monrovia; tel. 261374; Ambassador BENG'YELA AUGUSTINE GANG.

China, People's Republic: Tubman Blvd, Congotown, POB 5970, Monrovia; tel. 228024; fax 226740; e-mail Chinaemb_lr@mfa.gov.cn; internet lr.china-embassy.org; Ambassador ZHAO JIANHUA.

Congo, Democratic Republic: Spriggs Payne Airport, Sinkor, POB 1038, Monrovia; tel. 261326; Ambassador (vacant).

Côte d'Ivoire: Tubman Blvd, Sinkor, POB 126, Monrovia; tel. 261123; Ambassador SORO KAPÉLÉTIEN.

Cuba: 17 Kennedy Ave, Congotown, POB 3579, Monrovia; tel. 262600; Ambassador Dr MIGUEL GUSTAVO PÉREZ CRUZ.

Egypt: Coconut Plantation, Randal St, Mamba Point, POB 462, Monrovia; tel. 226226; fax 226122; Ambassador SAMEH LOTFI.

France: German Compound, Congo Town, Monrovia; tel. 6579373 (mobile); e-mail ambafrance.liberia@yahoo.fr; Ambassador GÉRARD LARÔME.

Germany: Tubman Blvd, Monrovia; tel. 6438365 (mobile); e-mail info@monrovia.diplo.de; Ambassador Dr BODO SCHAFF.

Ghana: cnr 11th St and Gardiner Ave, Sinkor, POB 471, Monrovia; tel. 261477; Ambassador Maj.-Gen. FRANCIS ADU-AMANFOH.

Guinea: Monrovia; Ambassador ABDOULAYE DORÉ.

Lebanon: 12th St, Monrovia; tel. 262537; Ambassador MANSOUR ABDALLAH.

Libya: Monrovia; Ambassador MUHAMMAD UMARAT-TABI.

Morocco: Tubman Blvd, Congotown, Monrovia; tel. 262767; Ambassador MOHAMED LASFAR.

Nigeria: Tubman Blvd, Congotown, POB 366, Monrovia; tel. 6823638 (mobile); fax 226135; e-mail nigerianmonrovia@yahoo.com; Ambassador CHIGOZIE OBI-NNADOZIE.

Russia: Payne Ave, Sinkor, POB 2010, Monrovia; tel. 261304; Ambassador ANDREY V. POKROVSKII.

Senegal: Monrovia; Ambassador MOCTAR TRAORÉ.

Sierra Leone: Tubman Blvd, POB 575, Monrovia; tel. 261301; Ambassador Rev. MARIE J. BARNETT.

South Africa: Monrovia; Ambassador MASILO ESAU MEBETA.

USA: POB 98, 502 Benson St, Monrovia; tel. 776777000 (mobile); fax 77010370 (mobile); e-mail ConsularMonrovia@state.gov; internet monrovia.usembassy.gov; Ambassador (vacant).

Judicial System

In February 1982 the People's Supreme Tribunal (which had been established following the April 1980 coup) was renamed the People's Supreme Court, and its Chairman and members became the Chief Justice and Associate Justices of the People's Supreme Court. The judicial system also comprised People's Circuit and Magistrate Courts. The five-member Supreme Court was established in January 1992 to adjudicate in electoral disputes.

Chief Justice of the Supreme Court of Liberia: JOHNNIE N. LEWIS.

Justices: FRANCIS S. KORPKPOR, Sr, GLADYS K. JOHNSON, KABINEH M. JA'NEH, JAMESETTA H. WOLOKOLLIE.

Religion

Liberia is officially a Christian state, although complete religious freedom is guaranteed. Christianity and Islam are the two main religions. There are numerous religious sects, and many Liberians hold traditional beliefs.

CHRISTIANITY

Liberian Council of Churches: 15th St, Sinkor, POB 10-2191, 1000 Monrovia; tel. 6517879 (mobile); e-mail liberiancouncil@yahoo.com; internet www.liberiancouncilofchurches.org; f. 1982; 11 mems, two assoc. mems, one fraternal mem.; Pres. Rev. Dr DAVID R. DANIELS, Jr.

The Anglican Communion

The diocese of Liberia forms part of the Church of the Province of West Africa, incorporating the local Episcopal Church. Anglicanism was established in Liberia in 1836, and the diocese of Liberia was admitted into full membership of the Province in 1982. The Metropolitan of the Province is the Bishop of Koforidua, Ghana.

Bishop of Liberia: Rt Rev. JONATHAN BAU-BAU BONAPARTE HART, POB 10-0277, 1000 Monrovia 10; tel. 224760; fax 227519; e-mail bishop@liberia.net.

The Roman Catholic Church

Liberia comprises the archdiocese of Monrovia and the dioceses of Cape Palmas and Gbarnga. An estimated 9% of the total population were Roman Catholics.

Catholic Bishops' Conference of Liberia

POB 10-2078, 1000 Monrovia 10; tel. 227245; fax 226175.

f. 1998; Pres. Rt Rev. LEWIS ZEIGLER (Archbishop of Monrovia).

Archbishop of Monrovia: Most Rev. LEWIS ZEIGLER, Archbishop's Office, POB 10-2078, 1000 Monrovia 10; tel. 6519766 (mobile); fax 77003719 (mobile); e-mail apostolic_adm@yahoo.com.

Other Christian Churches

Assemblies of God in Liberia: POB 1297, Monrovia; f. 1908; 14,578 adherents, 287 churches; Gen. Supt JIMMY KUOH.

Lutheran Church in Liberia (LCL): POB 10-1046, 13th St, Payne Ave, Sinkor, 1000 Monrovia 10; tel. 226323; fax 380637; e-mail lutheranchurchinliberia@yahoo.com; f. 1947 as Evangelical Lutheran Church, reorg. in 1965 under indigenous leadership as LCL; Pres. Bishop SUMOWARD E. HARRIS; 71,196 mems (2010).

Providence Baptist Church: cnr Broad and Center Sts, Monrovia; tel. 77534172 (mobile); e-mail admin@providencebc.net; internet www.providencebc.net; f. 1821; 2,500 adherents, 300 congregations, 6 ministers, 8 schools; Senior Pastor Rev. Dr SAMUEL BROOMFIELD REEVES, Jr.

Liberia Baptist Missionary and Educational Convention, Inc: POB 390, Monrovia; tel. 222661; f. 1880; 72,000 adherents, 270 churches (2007); Pres. Rev. J. K. LEVEE MOULTON; Nat. Vice-Pres. Rev. J. GBANA HALL; Gen. Sec. CHARLES W. BLAKE.

United Methodist Church in Liberia: cnr 12th St and Tubman Blvd, POB 1010, 1000 Monrovia 10; tel. 223343; e-mail bishop.jinnis@liberiaumc.org; internet www.umcliberia.org; f. 1833; c. 168,300 adherents, 600 congregations, 700 ministers, 394 lay pastors; Resident Bishop Rev. Dr JOHN G. INNIS.

Other active denominations include the National Baptist Mission, the Pentecostal Church, the Presbyterian Church in Liberia, the Prayer Band and the Church of the Lord Aladura.

ISLAM

The total community numbers about 670,000.

National Muslim Council of Liberia: Monrovia; Leader Shaykh KAFUMBA KONNAH.

The Press

NEWSPAPERS

Daily Observer: POB 1858, Monrovia; tel. 6513788 (mobile); e-mail editor@liberianobserver.com; internet www.liberianobserver.com; f. 1981; independent; daily; Dir KENNETH Y. BEST.

Heritage: cnr Broad and Nelson Sts, Monrovia; e-mail info@heritageliberia.net; internet www.news.heritageliberia.net; Man. Editor MOHAMMED M. KANNEH.

Informer: Monrovia; tel. 886519515 (mobile); e-mail editoratinformer@yahoo.com; internet www.informerliberia.net; Man. Dir DARKOLLIE SUMO.

The Inquirer: POB 3600, Monrovia; tel. 6538573 (mobile); fax 227036; e-mail theinquirernews@yahoo.com; internet www.theinquirer.com.lr; daily; Man. Editor PHILIP WESSEH.

National Chronicle: Monrovia; Editor EDWARD MORTEE.

New Dawn: Monrovia; tel. 6484201; e-mail mail@thenewdawnliberia.com; internet www.thenewdawnliberia.com; Editor-in-Chief OTHELLO B. GARBLAH.

New Republic: Monrovia; tel. 6568024 (mobile); e-mail etogba2005us@yahoo.com; internet tnrliberia.net; Publr ALPHONSO TOWEH; Editor-in-Chief ELLIS TOGBA.

News: ACDB Bldg, POB 10-3137, Carey Warren St, Monrovia; tel. 227820; independent; weekly; Chair. WILSON TARPEH; Editor-in-Chief JEROME DALIEH.

PERIODICALS

Business Liberia: Monrovia; internet businessliberiamagazine.com; f. 2009; publ. by Baker Pearson Communications, Inc; Editor-in-Chief SEANAN DENIZOT.

The Kpelle Messenger: Kpelle Literacy Center, Lutheran Church, POB 1046, Monrovia; Kpelle-English; monthly; Editor Rev. JOHN J. MANAWU.

Liberia Orbit: Voinjama; e-mail orbit@tekmail.com; internet www.liberiaorbit.org; national current affairs; Editor LLOYD SCOTT.

Liberian Post: e-mail info@liberian.org; internet www.liberian.org; f. 1998; independent internet magazine; tourist information; Publr WILLEM TIJSSEN.

Liberia Travel & Life: Monrovia; e-mail editorial@liberiatravellifemagazine.com; internet www.liberiatravellifemagazine.com; 4 a year; publ. by Baker Pearson Communications, Inc; Editor-in-Chief HESTA BAKER PEARSON.

New Democrat: Clay St, Central Town, Monrovia; tel. 5548626 (mobile); fax 77249415 (mobile); e-mail newdemnews@yahoo.com; internet www.newdemocratnews.com; national news and current affairs; Editor TOM KAMARA.

Patriot: Congo Town 1000, Monrovia; internet www.allaboutliberia.com/patriot.htm.

The People Magazine: Bank of Liberia Bldg, Suite 214, Carey and Warren Sts, POB 3501, Monrovia; tel. 222743; f. 1985; monthly; Editor and Publr CHARLES A. SNETTER.

PRESS ORGANIZATIONS

Liberia Institute of Journalism: Kashour Bldg, 2nd Floor, cnr Broad and Johnson Sts, POB 2314, Monrovia; tel. 227327; Dir VINICIUS HODGES.

Liberia Media Center: LMC Box 1153, 1st St, Sinkor, Jallah Town, Monrovia; tel. 6400206 (mobile); e-mail info@lmcliberia.com; internet www.lmcliberia.com; f. 2005; Pres. PETER QUAQUA.

Press Union of Liberia: Benson St, POB 20-4209, Monrovia; tel. and fax 227105; internet www.pressunionlib.net; f. 1985; Pres. PETER QUAQUA.

NEWS AGENCY

Liberian News Agency (LINA): POB 9021, Capitol Hill, Monrovia; tel. 222229; Dir-Gen. ERNEST KIAZOLY (acting).

Broadcasting and Communications

TELECOMMUNICATIONS

Much of the fixed-line infrastructure in Liberia was destroyed during the civil conflict that ended in 2003. The Liberia Telecommunications Corpn, non-operational since 1990, was restructured as Libtelco in 2007 and began providing fixed wireless services in 2008. In 2011 it was still the sole operator licensed to provide fixed-line services, although its fixed-line network remained non-operational. In that year there were four providers of mobile cellular telephone services in the country.

REGULATORY AUTHORITY

Liberia Telecommunications Authority: 12th St, Sinkor, Tubman Blvd, Monrovia; tel. 27302012; e-mail info@lta.gov.lr; internet www.lta.gov.lr; f. 2007; Chair. ANGELIQUE E. WEEKS.

SERVICE PROVIDERS

Cellcom: Haile Selassie Ave, Capitol By-Pass, Monrovia; tel. 77777008 (mobile); fax 77000101 (mobile); e-mail info@cellcomgsm.com; internet www.lr.cellcomgsm.com; mobile cellular telephone provider; CEO AVISHAI MARZIAMNO; 640,526 subscribers (2010).

Comium: Comium Bldg, Congo Town, Monrovia; tel. 5600600 (mobile); fax 5600611 (mobile); e-mail info@comium.com.lr; internet www.comium.com.lr; mobile cellular telephone provider; CEO MICHAEL CARROLL; 137,848 subscribers (2010).

LiberCell: Monrovia; e-mail info@awli.net; internet www.libercell.info; f. 2004; mobile cellular telephone provider; Chair. AZZAM SBAITY; CEO BACHAR SAGHIR; 29,405 subscribers (2010).

Libtelco: 18th St and Tubman Blvd, Sinkor, Monrovia; tel. 25551000; fax 25551099; e-mail info@libtelco.com.lr; internet www.libtelco.com.lr; f. 1973 as the Liberia Telecommunications Corporation; Chair. MUSA DEAN; Man. Dir BEN WOLO; 4,463 prepaid subscribers (2010).

Lonestar Cell: LBDI Bldg, Congo Town, Monrovia; tel. 6500000 (mobile); fax 6501101 (mobile); internet www.lonestarcell.com; f. 2001; mobile cellular telephone provider; subsidiary of Mobile Telephone Networks (Pty) Ltd, South Africa; CEO MAZEN MROUE; 762,159 subscribers (2010).

BROADCASTING

Radio

Liberia Communications Network: Congo Town 1000, Monrovia; govt-operated; broadcasts information, education and entertainment 24 hours daily in English, French and several African languages; short-wave service.

Liberia Rural Communications Network: POB 10-02176, 1000 Monrovia 10; tel. 271368; f. 1981; govt-operated; rural devt and entertainment programmes; Dir J. RUFUS KAINE (acting).

Radio Truth FM: Monrovia.

Radio Veritas: POB 3569, Monrovia; tel. 4712834 (mobile); e-mail radioveritas@hotmail.com; internet radioveritas.org; f. 1981; Catholic; independent; nation-wide shortwave broadcasts; Dirs Fr ANTHONY BOWAH, LEDGERHOOD RENNIE.

Star Radio: 12 Broad St, Snapper Hill, Monrovia; tel. 77104411 (mobile); e-mail star@liberia.net; internet www.starradio.org.lr; independent news and information station; f. July 1997 by Fondation Hirondelle, Switzerland, with funds from the US Agency for International Development; broadcasts in English, French and 14 African languages; Man. JAMES K. MORLU.

Television

Liberia Broadcasting System: POB 594, Monrovia; tel. 224984; internet www.liberiabroadcastingsystem.com; govt-owned; Chair. CLETUS SIEH; Dir-Gen. ALHAJI G. V. KROMAH (acting).

Finance

(cap. = capital; res = reserves; dep. = deposits; m. = million; br. = branch; amounts in Liberian dollars, unless otherwise indicated)

BANKING

In 2010 there were eight commercial banks in Liberia.

Central Bank

Central Bank of Liberia: cnr Warren and Carey Sts, POB 2048, 1000 Monrovia; tel. 6225685 (mobile); fax 6226114 (mobile); e-mail webmaster@cbl.org.lr; internet www.cbl.org.lr; f. 1974 as National Bank of Liberia; name changed March 1999; bank of issue; cap. 7,598.5m., res 3,817.4m., dep. 9,226.7m. (Dec. 2009); Gov. JOSEPH MILLS JONES.

Other Banks

AccessBank Liberia Ltd: Johnson St, Monrovia; tel. 77006688 (mobile); f. 2008; CEO MARY CLARE ODONG.

Ecobank Liberia Ltd: Ashmun and Randall Sts, POB 4825, Monrovia; tel. 6553919 (mobile); fax 227029; e-mail ecobanklr@ecobank.com; internet www.ecobank.com; commenced operations Aug. 1999; cap. and res US $2.1m., total assets US $10.2m. (Dec. 2001); Chair. G. PEWU SUBAH; Man. Dir KOLA ADELEKE.

First International Bank (Liberia) Ltd: Luke Bldg, Broad St, Monrovia; tel. 77026241 (mobile); e-mail info@fib-lib.com; internet www.fib-lib.com; f. April 2005; Chair. FRANCIS L. M. HORTON; Exec. Dir ARISA AWA.

Global Bank Liberia Ltd (GBLL): Ashmun and Mechlin Sts, POB 2053, Monrovia; tel. 6425760 (mobile); e-mail mail@globalbankliberia.com; internet www.globalbankliberia.com; f. 2005; Italian-owned; Pres. Dr RICCARDO SEMBIANTE.

Guaranty Trust Bank (Liberia) Ltd (GTBLL): United Nations Dr., Clara Town, Bushrod Island, POB 0382, Monrovia; tel. 77499992 (mobile); fax 77499995 (mobile); internet www.gtbanklr.com; f. 2007; Chair. TAYO ADERINOKUN; CEO DAN OROGUN.

International Bank (Liberia) Ltd: 64 Broad St, POB 10292, 1000 Monrovia; tel. 6557473 (mobile); fax 4074245 (mobile); e-mail customercare@ibliberia.com; internet www.ibliberia.com; f. 1948 as International Trust Co of Liberia; name changed April 2000; 75.5% owned by Liberian Financial Holdings; 19.1% Trust Bank Ltd (The Gambia); cap. 2m. (1989), dep. 96.4m. (Dec. 1996); CEO PATRICK ANUMEL (acting); Gen. Man. HENRY SAAMOI; 3 brs.

Liberian Bank for Development and Investment (LBDI): Ashmun and Randall Sts, POB 547, Monrovia; tel. 227140; fax 226359; e-mail lbdi@lbdi.net; internet www.lbdi.net; f. 1961; 18.7% govt-owned; cap. and res US $12.5m., total assets US $26.8m. (Dec. 2001); Chair. AUGUSTINE K. NGAFUAN; Pres. FRANCIS A. DENNIS, Jr.

United Bank for Africa Liberia Ltd: POB 4523, Monrovia; tel. 6569375 (mobile); e-mail ubaliberia@ubagroup.com; internet www.ubagroup.com/ubaliberia; f. 2006; CEO EBELE E. OGBUE.

Banking Association

Liberia Bankers' Association: POB 292, Monrovia; mems include commercial and devt banks; Pres. FRANCIS A. DENNIS, Jr.

INSURANCE

American National Underwriters, Inc: Carter Bldg, 39 Broad St, POB 180, Monrovia; tel. 114921; general; Gen. Man. S. B. MENSAH.

Insurance Co of Africa: 2nd Floor, International Bank Building, 64 Broad St, Monrovia; tel. 6513281 (mobile); internet icaliberia.com; f. 1969; life and general; Pres. SAMUEL OWAREE MINTAH.

National Insurance Corpn of Liberia (NICOL): LBDI Bldg Complex, POB 1528, Sinkor, Monrovia; tel. 262429; f. 1983; state-owned; sole insurer for Govt and parastatal bodies; also provides insurance for the Liberian-registered merchant shipping fleet; Man. Dir MIATTA EDITH SHERMAN.

United Security Insurance Agencies Inc: Randall St, POB 2071, Monrovia; life, personal accident and medical; Dir EPHRAIM O. OKORO.

Trade and Industry

GOVERNMENT AGENCIES

Budget Bureau: Capitol Hill, POB 1518, Monrovia; tel. 226340; Dir-Gen. MATHEW DINGIE.

General Services Agency (GSA): Old USTC Compound, UN Dr., POB 10-9027, Monrovia; tel. 6901333 (mobile); e-mail info@gsa.gov.lr; internet www.gsa.gov.lr; Dir-Gen. ALPHONSO GAYE.

DEVELOPMENT ORGANIZATIONS

Forestry Development Authority: POB 10-3010, Kappa House, Eli Saleby Compound, Monrovia; tel. 224940; fax 226000; e-mail john.woods@fda.gov.lr; internet www.fda.gov.lr; f. 1976; responsible for forest management and conservation; Chair. EDWIN ZELEE; Man. Dir MOSES WOGBEH.

Liberia Industrial Free Zone Authority (LIFZA): One Free Zone, Monrovia; tel. 533671; e-mail mskromah@lifza.com; internet www.lifza.com; f. 1975; 98 mems; Man. Dir MOHAMMED S. KROMAH.

National Investment Commission (NIC): Fmr Executive Mansion Bldg, POB 9043, Monrovia; tel. 7873001 (mobile); internet www.nic.gov.lr; f. 1979; autonomous body negotiating investment incentives agreements on behalf of Govt; promotes agro-based and industrial devt; Chair. O'NATTY B. DAVIS; Exec. Dir CIATA BISHOP.

CHAMBER OF COMMERCE

Liberia Chamber of Commerce: Capitol Hill, POB 92, Monrovia; tel. 77857805 (mobile); e-mail secgen@chamberofcommerce.org.lr; internet www.chamberofcommerce.org.lr; f. 1951; Pres. MONIE RALPH CAPTAN; Sec.-Gen. DAVID G. FROMAYAN.

INDUSTRIAL AND TRADE ASSOCIATIONS

Liberian Produce Marketing Corpn: POB 662, Monrovia; tel. 222447; f. 1961; govt-owned; exports Liberian produce, provides industrial facilities for processing of agricultural products and participates in agricultural devt programmes; Man. Dir NYAH MARTEIN.

Liberian Resources Corpn (LIBRESCO): controls Liberia's mineral resources; 60% govt-owned; 40% owned by South African co, Amalia Gold.

EMPLOYERS' ASSOCIATION

National Enterprises Corpn: POB 518, Monrovia; tel. 261370; importer, wholesaler and distributor of foodstuffs, and wire and metal products for local industries; Pres. EMMANUEL SHAW, Sr.

UTILITIES

Electricity

Liberia Electricity Corpn (LEC): Waterside, UN Dr., Monrovia; tel. 6653650 (mobile); e-mail mlackay@libelcorp.com; internet www.libelcorp.com; Chair. DUNSTAN L. D. MACAULEY; Man. Dir JOSEPH MAYAH.

National Oil Co of Liberia (NOCAL): Episcopal Church Plaza, 3rd and 4th Floors, Ashmun and Randall Sts, 1000 Monrovia; tel. 77023859 (mobile); e-mail info@nocal.com.lr; internet www.nocal.lr.com; f. 2000; Chair. ROBERT SIRLEAF; Pres. and CEO CHRISTOPHER NEYOR.

MAJOR COMPANIES

The following are among the largest companies in terms either of capital investment or employment.

Bong Mining Co Ltd: POB 538, Monrovia; tel. 225222; fax 225770; f. 1958; iron ore mining, upgrading of crude ore and transportation of concentrate and pellets to Monrovia Freeport for shipment abroad; capacity: 4.5m. tons of concentrate and 3m. tons of pellets annually; Pres. HANSJOERG RIETZSCH; Gen. Man. HANS-GEORG SCHNEIDER; 2,200 employees.

Bridgestone Firestone Co: POB 140, Harbel; f. 1926 by Firestone Rubber Co (USA); acquired by Japanese co, Bridgestone, in 1988, although Firestone retained control of local management; Man. Dir CLYDE TABOR; c. 3,000 employees.

Equatorial Palm Oil PLC (EPO): POB 1432, 1000 Monrovia; tel. 77026767 (mobile); fax 77555550 (mobile); internet www.epoil.co.uk; Chair. MICHAEL FRAYNE; Man. Dir PETER BAYLISS.

Liberia Cement Corpn (CEMENCO): POB 150, Monrovia; tel. 222650; fax 226219; mfrs of Portland cement; Gen. Man. HORST WALLWITZ.

Liberia Petroleum Refining Co (LPRC): POB 90, Monrovia; tel. 222600; sole producer of domestically produced fuels, with designed capacity of 15,000 b/d; products include diesel fuel, fuel oils, liquid petroleum gas; supplies domestic market and has limited export facilities for surplus products; Chair. Prof WILSON TARPEH; Man. Dir T. NELSON WILLIAMS II.

National Iron Ore Co Ltd: POB 548, Monrovia; f. 1958; 85% govt-owned co mining iron ore at Mano river; Gen. Man. S. K. DATTA RAY.

Shell Liberia Ltd: Bushrod Island, POB 360, Monrovia; tel. 221238; f. 1920; distributors of petroleum products; Man. M. Y. KUENYEDZI; 15 employees.

TRADE UNION

Liberian Labor Congress: J. B. McGill Labor Center, Gardnersville Freeway, POB 415, Monrovia; f. 2008 following merger of Liberian Federation of Labor Unions and Congress of National Trade Unions; Pres. ELITHA T. MANNING, Jr; Sec.-Gen. MARCUS S. BLAMAH.

Transport

RAILWAYS

Bong Mine Railway: POB 538, Monrovia; tel. 225222; fax 225770; f. 1958; Gen. Man. HANS-GEORG SCHNEIDER.

ROADS

In 2000 the road network in Liberia totalled an estimated 10,600 km, of which about 657 km were paved. The main trunk road is the Monrovia–Sanniquellie motor road, extending north-east from the capital to the border with Guinea, near Ganta, and eastward through the hinterland to the border with Côte d'Ivoire. Trunk roads run through Tapita, in Nimba County, to Grand Gedeh County and from Monrovia to Buchanan. A bridge over the Mano river connects with the Sierra Leone road network, while a main road links Monrovia and Freetown (Sierra Leone). In 2003 the Liberian authorities announced plans for the extensive rehabilitation of the road network (which had been extensively damaged during the 1989–96 armed conflict), including a highway linking Monrovia with Harper, which was to be funded by the People's Republic of China.

SHIPPING

In December 2009 Liberia's open-registry fleet (2,456 vessels), the second largest in the world (after Panama) in terms of gross tonnage, had a total displacement of 91.7m. grt.

Bureau of Maritime Affairs: Tubman Blvd, Sinkor, POB 10-9042, 1000 Monrovia 10; tel. and fax 77206108 (mobile); e-mail info@bma-liberia.com; internet www.bma-liberia.com; Commissioner BINYAH C. KESSELLY.

Liberia National Shipping Line (LNSL): Monrovia; f. 1987; jt venture by the Liberian Govt and private German interests; routes to Europe, incl. the United Kingdom and Scandinavia.

National Port Authority: Freeport of Monrovia, Bushrod Island, Monrovia; tel. 6402906 (mobile); fax 77861997 (mobile); e-mail natportliberia@yahoo.com; internet www.nationalportauthorityliberia.org; f. 1967; administers Monrovia Freeport and the ports of Buchanan, Greenville and Harper; Chair. Dr C. WILLIAM ALLEN; Man. Dir MATILDA PARKER.

CIVIL AVIATION

Liberia's principal airports are Robertsfield International Airport, at Harbel, 56 km east of Monrovia, and James Spriggs Payne Airport, at Monrovia.

Liberia Civil Aviation Authority: Monrovia; Dir-Gen. RICHELIEU A. WILLIAMS.

ADC Liberia Inc: Monrovia; f. 1993; services to the United Kingdom, the USA and destinations in West Africa.

Air Liberia: POB 2076, Monrovia; f. 1974; state-owned; scheduled passenger and cargo services; Man. Dir JAMES K. KOFA.

Tourism

Liberia's natural assets, especially its beaches and the Sapo National Park and other areas of primary tropical rainforest, have the potential to support both a beach-based and an eco-tourism industry. However, no such industry has ever been developed in Liberia and tourism has been entirely in abeyance since 1990 because of the almost continuous civil conflict since that time. The development of the country's tourist potential will be limited by high levels of violent crime and a tourism infrastructure that remains meagre or absent.

Defence

Following a major rebel offensive against the capital in June 2003, the UN Security Council on 1 August authorized the establishment of an Economic Community of West African States (ECOWAS) peacekeeping contingent, the ECOWAS Mission in Liberia (ECOMIL), which was to restore security and prepare for the deployment of a longer-term UN stabilization force. The UN Mission in Liberia (UNMIL), which was officially established on 19 September and replaced ECOMIL on 1 October, had a total authorized strength of up to 15,000, and was mandated to support the implementation of a comprehensive peace agreement and a two-year transitional administration. Following the completion of the disarmament programme, in January 2005 a US military commission arrived in Liberia to assist in the restructuring of the armed forces, which was ongoing in the early 2010s. In June 2006 the armed forces began recruiting women as part of the reform process. As assessed at November 2011, the total strength of the Liberian armed forces was 2,050.

Defence Expenditure: Estimated at US $8m. in 2010.

Chief of Staff of the Armed Forces of Liberia: Maj.-Gen. SURAJ ALAO ABDURRAHMAN.

Education

Education is provided by a mixture of government, private, church and mosque schools. The civil conflicts of 1989–1996 and 1999–2003 devastated the education system as buildings and equipment were damaged and looted, and teachers, parents and children became refugees or internally displaced. By September 2005 3,817 of the country's 4,500 schools were reported to be functioning again. Education in Liberia is officially compulsory for 10 years, between six and 16 years of age. Primary education begins theoretically at six years of age and lasts for six years (grades 1–6). Secondary education, beginning theoretically at 12 years of age, lasts for a further six years, and is divided into two three-year cycles, known in Liberia as 'junior high school' (grades 7–9) and 'senior high school' (grades 10-12). Pre-primary education is undertaken from the age of five or younger and is important for those students whose mother language is not English, since English is the language of instruction throughout the school system. School attendance is not enforced and in 2006 an estimated 61% of primary school age children were out of school (60% of boys and 61% of girls). Although the 1984 Liberian Constitution includes the aspiration to provide universal free education, and fees in public primary schools have been officially abolished, school attendance is discouraged by the poor quality of education offered, by the remaining school fees, by charges and by the cost of uniforms and travel. The higher education sector consists of the University of Liberia in Monrovia, Cuttington University College in Bong County, the Booker Washington Institute in Kakata, Margibi County, and the William V. S. Tubman College in Maryland County. According to UNESCO, a total of 44,107 students were enrolled in tertiary education in 1999–2000.

Bibliography

Aboagye, F. B., and Bah, Alhaji M. S. *A Tortuous Road to Peace: The Dynamics of Regional, UN and International Humanitarian Interventions in Liberia*. Pretoria, Institute for Security Studies, 2005.

Adebajo, A. *Liberia's Civil War: Nigeria, Ecomog and Regional Security in West Africa*. Boulder, CO, Lynne Rienner Publishers, 2002.

Alao, A. *The Burden of Collective Goodwill: The International Involvement in the Liberian Civil War*. Aldershot, Ashgate, 1998.

Alao, A., Mackinlay, J., and Olonisakin, F. *Peacekeepers, Politicians and Warlords: The Liberian Peace Process (Foundations of Peace Series)*. Tokyo, United Nations University Press, 2000.

Berkeley, B. *The Graves Are Not Yet Full: Race, Tribe and Power in the Heart of Africa*. New York, Basic Books, 2001.

Clegg, C. A. *The Price of Liberty: African Americans and the Making of Liberia*. Chapel Hill, NC, University of North Carolina Press, 2004.

Deme, M. *Law, Morality, and International Armed Intervention: The United Nations and Ecowas (African Studies: History, Politics, Economics and Culture)*. Abingdon, Routledge, 2005.

Dolo, E. *Democracy versus Dictatorship: The Quest for Freedom and Justice in Africa's Oldest Republic, Liberia*. Lanham, MD, University Press of America, 1996.

Dunn, D. E., Bevan, A. J., and Burrowes, C. P. *Historical Dictionary of Liberia*. 2nd edn. Metuchen, NJ, Scarecrow Press, 2001.

Dunn, D. E., and Tarr, S. B. *Liberia: A National Polity in Transition*. Metuchen, NJ, Scarecrow Press, 1988.

Ellis, S. *The Mask of Anarchy: The Destruction of Liberia and the Religious Dimension of an African Civil War*. New York, New York University Press, 2006.

Gershoni, Y. *Black Colonialism: The Americo-Liberian Scramble for the Hinterland*. Boulder, CO, Westview Press, 1985.

Gifford, P. *Christianity and Politics in Doe's Liberia*. Cambridge, Cambridge University Press, 2003.

Givens, W. *Liberia: The Road to Democracy under the Leadership of Samuel Kanyon Doe*. London, Kensal Press, 1986.

Hall, R. *On Africa's Shore: A History of Maryland in Liberia, 1834–1857*. Baltimore, MD, Maryland Historical Society, 2003.

Harris, J. *Mother Liberia*. New York, Vantage Press, 2004.

Hoffman, D. *The War Machines: Young Men and Violence in Sierra Leone and Liberia*. Durham, NC, Duke University Press, 2011.

Horton A. P., *Liberia's Underdevelopment*. Lanham, MD, University Press of America, 1994.

Huband, M. *The Liberian Civil War*. London, Frank Cass, 1998.

Huffman, A. *Mississippi in Africa: The Saga of the Slaves of Prospect Hill Plantation and their Legacy in Liberia Today*. New York, Gotham Books, 2004.

Hyman, L. S. *United States Policy Towards Liberia, 1822 to 2003: Unintended Consequences*. New Jersey, NJ, Africana Homestead Legacy Publications, 2003.

Jaye, T. *Issues of Sovereignty, Strategy and Security in the Economic Community of West African States (Ecowas) Intervention in the Liberian Civil War*. Lewiston, NY, Edwin Mellen Press, 2003.

Johnson-Sirleaf, E. *This Child Will Be Great: Memoir of a Remarkable Life by Africa's First Woman President*. New York, HarperCollins, 2010.

Kastfelt, N. *Religion and African Civil Wars*. London, Palgrave Macmillan, 2005.

Keih, G. K., Jr. *Dependency and the Foreign Policy of a Small Power*. Lewiston, NY, Edwin Mellen Press, 1992.

The First Liberian Civil War. New York, Peter Lang, 2008.

Levitt, J. *The Evolution of Deadly Conflict in Liberia: From 'Paternaltarianism' to State Collapse.* Durham, NC, Carolina Academic Press, 2005.

Illegal Peace in Africa: An Inquiry into the Legality of Power Sharing with Warlords, Rebels, and Junta. Cambridge, Cambridge University Press, 2012.

Liebenow, J. G. *Liberia: The Quest for Democracy.* Bloomington, IN, Indiana University Press, 1987.

Lyons, T. *Voting for Peace: Postconflict Elections in Liberia* (Studies in Foreign Policy). Washington, DC, Brookings Institution Press, 1999.

Magyar, K. P., and Conteh-Morgan, E. (Eds). *Peace-keeping in Africa: ECOMOG in Liberia.* Basingstoke, Macmillan, 1998.

McDaniel, A. *Swing Low, Sweet Chariot: The Mortality Cost of Colonizing Liberia in the Nineteenth Century* (Population and Development). Chicago, IL, University of Chicago Press, 1995.

Mgbeoji, I. *Collective Insecurity: The Liberian Crisis, Unilateralism and Global Order.* Vancouver, BC, University of British Columbia Press, 2003.

Moran, M. H. *Liberia: The Violence of Democracy (Ethnography of Political Violence).* Philadelphia, PA, University of Pennsylvania Press, 2005.

Morse, K., and Sawyer, A. *Beyond Plunder: Toward Democratic Governance in Liberia.* Boulder, CO, Lynne Rienner Publishers, 2005.

Moses, W. J. (Ed.), *Liberian Dreams: Back-to-Africa Narratives from the 1850s.* Philadelphia, PA, University of Pennsylvania Press, 1998.

Nass, I. A. *A Study in Internal Conflicts: The Liberian Crisis and the West African Peace Initiative.* Enugu, Fourth Dimension Publishing, 2001.

Olukoju, A. *Culture and Customs of Liberia.* Westport, CT, Greenwood Press, 2006.

Pham, J.-P. *Liberia: Portrait of a Failed State.* New York, Reed Press, 2004.

Reno, W. *Warlord Politics and African States.* Boulder, CO, Lynne Rienner Publishers, 1998.

Rimmer, D. *The Economies of West Africa.* London, Weidenfeld and Nicolson, 1984.

Saha, S. C. *Culture in Liberia: An Afrocentric View of the Cultural Interaction between the Indigenous Liberians and the Americo-Liberians.* Lewiston, NY, Edwin Mellen Press, 1998.

Sawyer, A. *The Emergence of Autocracy in Liberia: Tragedy and Challenge.* San Francisco, CA, ICS Press, 1992.

Beyond Plunder: Toward Democratic Governance in Liberia. Boulder, CO, Lynne Rienner Publishers, 2005.

Sirleaf, A. M. *The Role of the Economic Community of the West African States: Ecowas—Conflict Management in Liberia.* New York, 1stBooks Library, 2003.

Stryker, R. L. *Forged from Chaos: Stories and Reflections from Liberia at War.* New York, 1stBooks Library, 2003.

Sundiata, I. *Brothers and Strangers: Black Zionism, Black Slavery, 1914–1940.* Durham, NC, Duke University Press, 2004.

Tellewoyan, J. *The Years the Locusts have Eaten: Liberia 1816–2004.* Philadelphia, PA, Xlibris Corporation, 2005.

Tyler-McGraw, M. *An African Republic: Black and White Virginians in the Making of Liberia.* Chapel Hill, NC, University of North Carolina Press, 2007.

US Library of Congress. *Liberia during the Tolbert Era: A Guide.* Washington, DC, 1984.

Vogt, M. A. (Ed.). *Liberian Crisis and ECOMOG: A Bold Attempt at Regional Peace-keeping.* Lagos, Gabumo Publishing Co, 1992.

Waugh, C. M. *Charles Taylor and Liberia: Ambition and Atrocity in Africa's Lone Star State.* London, Zed Books, 2011.

Weller, M. (Ed.). *Regional Peace-Keeping and International Enforcement: The Liberian Crisis.* Cambridge, Grotius Publications, Cambridge University Press, 1994.

Williams, G. I. H. *Liberia: The Heart of Darkness.* New Bern, NC, Trafford, 2002.

Yoder, J. C. *Popular Political Culture, Civil Society, and State Crisis in Liberia.* Lewiston, NY, Edwin Mellen Press, 2003.

MADAGASCAR

Physical and Social Geography

VIRGINIA THOMPSON

PHYSICAL FEATURES

The Democratic Republic of Madagascar comprises the island of Madagascar, the fourth largest island in the world, and several much smaller offshore islands. Madagascar lies 390 km from the east African mainland across the Mozambique Channel. It extends 1,600 km from north to south and is up to 570 km wide. The whole territory covers an area of 587,295 sq km (226,756 sq miles). Geologically, the main island is basically composed of crystalline rock, which forms the central highlands that rise abruptly from the narrow eastern coastal strip and descend gradually to the wide plains of the west coast.

Topographically, Madagascar can be divided into six fairly distinct regions. Antsiranana province, in the north, is virtually isolated by the island's highest peak, Mt Tsaratanana, rising to 2,800 m above sea level. Tropical crops can be grown in its fertile valleys, and the natural harbour of Antsiranana is an important naval base. Another rich agricultural region lies in the north-west, where a series of valleys converge on the port of Mahajanga. To the south-west along the coastal plains lies a well-watered region where there are large animal herds and crops of rice, cotton, tobacco and manioc. The southernmost province, Toliary (Tuléar), contains most of Madagascar's known mineral deposits, as well as extensive cattle herds, despite the almost total lack of rainfall. In contrast, the hot and humid climate of the east coast favours the cultivation of the island's most valuable tropical crops—coffee, vanilla, cloves, and sugar cane. Although this coast lacks sheltered anchorages, it is the site of Madagascar's most important commercial port, Toamasina. Behind its coral beaches a continuous chain of lagoons, some of which are connected by the Pangalanes Canal, provides a partially navigable internal waterway. The island's mountainous hinterland is a densely populated region of extensive rice culture and stock raising. Despite its relative inaccessibility, this region is Madagascar's administrative and cultural centre, the focal point being the capital city of Antananarivo.

Climatic conditions vary from tropical conditions on the east and north-west coasts to the hotness and dryness of the west coast, the extreme aridity of the south and the temperate zone in the central highlands. Forests have survived only in some areas of abundant rainfall, and elsewhere the land has been eroded by over-grazing and slash-and-burn farming methods. Most of the island is savannah-steppe, and much of the interior is covered with laterite. Except in the drought-ridden south, rivers are numerous and flow generally westward, but many are interspersed by rapids and waterfalls, and few are navigable except for short distances.

POPULATION AND CULTURE

Geography and history account for the diversity and distribution of the population, which was enumerated at 12,092,157 at the census of August 1993. By mid-2012 the population had increased to 21,928,516, according to UN estimates. At the 1993 census the average density was 20.6 inhabitants per sq km. Population density had increased to 37.3 inhabitants per sq km by mid-2012, according to UN estimates. The island's 18 principal ethnic groups are the descendants of successive waves of immigrants from such diverse areas as South-East Asia, continental Africa and Arab countries. The dominant ethnic groups, the Merina and the Betsileo, who inhabit the most densely populated central provinces of Antananarivo and Fianarantsoa, are of Asian-Pacific origin. In the peripheral areas live the tribes collectively known as *côtiers*, of whom the most numerous are the Betsimisaraka on the east coast, the Tsimihety in the north, and the Antandroy in the south. Although continuous migrations, improved means of communication and a marked cultural unity have, to some extent, broken down geographical and tribal barriers, traditional ethnic antagonisms—notably between the Merina and the *côtiers*—remain close to the surface.

Increasing at an average annual rate of 3.0% during 2001–10, the Malagasy are fast exceeding the island's capacity to feed and employ them. The UN estimated that 42.4% of the population was under 15 years of age in 2012, and that the urban component was steadily growing, thus aggravating urban socio-economic problems. Antananarivo, the capital, is by far the largest city (with a population of 1,986,710 in mid-2011) and continues to expand, as do all the six provincial capitals.

Recent History

JULIAN COOKE

Based on an earlier article by MERVYN BROWN

Madagascar was annexed by France in 1896 but the imposition of colonial rule did not resolve the long-established ethnic conflict that existed between the dominant Merina tribe, based on the central plateau, and the coastal peoples (*côtiers*). The introduction in 1946 of elected deputies from Madagascar to the French parliament brought two opposing parties to the fore: the Mouvement Démocratique pour la Rénovation Malgache, a predominantly Merina group that favoured immediate independence, and the Parti des Déshérités de Madagascar (PADESM), a *côtier* party opposed to rapid constitutional change. Violent ethnic and partisan confrontations during 1947, in which about 80,000 people were killed, led the French authorities to suspend all political activity in Madagascar.

INDEPENDENCE

In 1956 France introduced new constitutional arrangements that opened the way to a resumption of political activity. The predominantly *côtier*-supported Parti Social Démocrate (PSD), formed from progressive elements of PADESM and led by Philibert Tsiranana, emerged as the principal party. In October 1958 Madagascar became a self-governing republic within the French Community, and in 1959 Tsiranana was elected President. Full independence as the Malagasy Republic followed on 26 June 1960.

The PSD, which practised a moderate socialism, was joined by nearly all of its rivals. The only significant opposition was the left-wing Parti du Congrès de l'Indépendance de Madagascar (AKFM), led by Richard Andriamanjato, a Merina Protestant pastor and Mayor of Antananarivo.

Following a period of economic decline in the late 1960s, a serious agrarian uprising and student unrest occurred in 1971. A new radical opposition group, the Mouvement National pour l'Indépendance de Madagascar (MONIMA), led by Monja Jaona and based in the agricultural south-west of the island, became a significant opposition movement. In January 1972, as the sole candidate, Tsiranana was re-elected as President with 99.9% of the votes cast, but the result bore little relation to the true state of political opinion. There was a resurgence of violent protest, and in May Tsiranana relinquished power to Gen. Gabriel Ramanantsoa, the Merina Chief of Staff of Madagascar's armed forces.

MILITARY GOVERNMENT

Ramanantsoa moved swiftly to restore public order and thus gained popularity. In a referendum in October 1972 he obtained the endorsement of 96% of those voting to govern for a transitional period of five years, while a new constitutional structure was established.

The promotion of Malagasy as the official language and the 'Malagasization' of education was welcomed by student and nationalist opinion, but also revived fears among *côtiers* of Merina domination. Nationalists and radicals, including the extreme left-wing Mouvement pour le Pouvoir Prolétarien (MFM) led by Manandafy Rakotonirina, supported major changes in foreign policy involving the establishment of diplomatic relations with the People's Republic of China, the Soviet bloc countries and Arab nations; the withdrawal from the Franc Zone and the Organisation Commune Africaine et Mauricienne; and, in particular, the renegotiation of the co-operation agreements with France, which resulted in the evacuation of French air and naval bases.

However, Ramanantsoa's authority was undermined by the country's worsening financial position, by disunity in the armed forces and the Government, and by continuing discord between *côtiers* and Merina. In the Council of Ministers a radical faction led by Col Richard Ratsimandrava demanded administrative and political reform, based on a revival of the traditional communities, known as *fokonolona*. In February 1975 Ramanantsoa transferred power to Ratsimandrava, but he was assassinated six days later. Gen. Gilles Andriamahazo immediately assumed power, imposing martial law and suspending political parties. In June Andriamahazo was succeeded as head of state by Lt-Commdr Didier Ratsiraka, a *côtier* and former Minister of Foreign Affairs. Ratsiraka established a Supreme Revolutionary Council (CSR), and the country was re-named the Democratic Republic of Madagascar. Ratsiraka declared his intention to carry out administrative and agrarian reforms based on the *fokonolona*, to reorganize the armed forces as an 'army of development' and to pursue a non-aligned foreign policy. At a referendum held in December, Ratsiraka's proposals were endorsed by 94.7% of voters and Ratsiraka assumed the presidency in January 1976 for a seven-year term.

THE SECOND REPUBLIC

Ratsiraka espoused socialism. He moved quickly to nationalize a number of industries and to formally establish a non-aligned foreign policy. However, in reality, close ties to the Soviet Union remained. Unable to establish a single-party state, Ratsiraka instead formed the Avant-garde de la Révolution Malgache (AREMA) as the nucleus of the Front National pour la Défense de la Révolution Socialiste Malgache (FNDR), a coalition of parties that would include the MFM, the AKFM and the PSD-derived Elan Populaire pour l'Unité Nationale (known as Vonjy), the latter the only political organization permitted by the Constitution.

At the presidential election held in November 1982, Ratsiraka was re-elected with 80% of the vote, while his opponent Jaona won only 20%. Jaona denounced the result as fraudulent and appealed for a general strike in support of demands for a new poll. Following rioting in December, Jaona was imprisoned and expelled from the CSR. He was later released, however, and in August 1983 he took the Antananarivo seat in legislative elections; AREMA won a reduced majority of 65% of the votes, but secured 117 of the 137 seats.

Political Reform

Ratsiraka's regime declined in popularity, owing in part to continued economic hardship, with a 25% decrease in per caput income in 1982–87 and with heavy migration caused by famines in the south. The country's churches were open in their criticism and by 1987 opposition within the FNDR to Ratsiraka had increased. Nevertheless, at the presidential election, held in March 1989, Ratsiraka received 62% of the total votes cast, while Manandafy of the MFM took 20%, Dr Jérôme Razanabahiny of Vonjy 15% and Jaona just 3%. In the legislative elections in May AREMA increased its already substantial parliamentary majority by a further three seats, winning 120 of the 137 seats, although the abstention rate was high, at 25%.

Despite his electoral success, Ratsiraka remained under pressure and in August 1989 reorganized both the CSR and the Government, appointing several members of the opposition, including Jaona. In March Andriamanjato formed the AKFM/Fanavaozana, a breakaway faction of the AKFM, while the press (now free from censorship) and the Christian Council of Churches in Madagascar (FFKM) demanded reforms including the termination of the FNDR's monopoly on political activity.

In the local government elections of September 1989, AREMA once more gained the majority of votes, except in Antananarivo, although the average abstention rate was 30%. AREMA's electoral strength and a divided opposition enabled Ratsiraka to limit constitutional changes, agreeing only to abolish the requirement for political parties to be members of the FNDR. With the resumption of multi-party politics in 1990 a number of new parties were formed, including the centre-right Mouvement des Démocrates Chrétiens Malgaches (MDCM), the PSD reformed by leading members of Vonjy, and the Union Nationale pour le Développement et la Démocratie (UNDD), led by a medical professor, Albert Zafy. The withdrawal of Soviet support compelled Ratsiraka to look to Western countries, particularly France, for economic aid. A state visit by President François Mitterrand in June 1990 demonstrated improved relations, as France cancelled Madagascar's US $750m. debt and resumed use of facilities at the naval base of Antsiranana.

The FFKM invited all the parties to attend conferences in August and December 1990 to discuss a programme of reform, and at the latter conference 16 opposition factions together with trade unions and other groups established an informal alliance, under the name Forces Vives (FV), to co-ordinate proposals for constitutional reform.

Confrontation and General Strike

During the session of the National Assembly in May 1991, FV supporters submitted their alliance's proposals for amending the Constitution, including the elimination of references to socialism, a reduction in the powers of the President and a limit on the number of terms he could serve. However, the only amendments considered were those presented by the Government, which, while numerous, did not meet the FV's basic demands. In early June the FV leadership demanded a constitutional conference and, when the Government failed to respond, appealed for a general strike from 10 June, which was to last six months. The opposition began a series of peaceful demonstrations in support of their demands, staged mainly in Antananarivo but also in the provincial capitals. The strike was widely supported and paralysed economic activity in the capital.

In July 1991 negotiations between the FV and Ratsiraka's party failed owing to the FV's insistence on the resignation of the President: Ratsiraka refused on the grounds that he had been democratically elected, while the FV maintained that the 1989 elections were not democratic since only political parties adhering to the FNDR were allowed to operate. The FV also denounced abuses of human rights and widespread corruption in the Government and in the President's family. In mid-July the FV appointed its own 'transitional Government', with a retired general, Jean Rakotoharison, as President and with Zafy as Prime Minister. On 28 July 1991 Ratsiraka dissolved his Government and pledged to organize a referendum on a new constitution by the end of the year. On 8 August Ratsiraka nominated a new Prime Minister, Guy Razanamasy, the

Mayor of Antananarivo, who invited the FV to join the Government. The FV rejected the offer and on 10 August organized a large but peaceful protest march on the President's residence to demand his resignation. The President's bodyguard fired into the crowd, killing 100 and wounding many more. On the same day a further 20 people were killed in the suppression of a demonstration in Mahajanga. The French Government subsequently suspended military aid and advised Ratsiraka to resign, offering him asylum in France. Ratsiraka used his support from leaders of the five provinces other than the capital to be declared President of Madagascar as a federation of six states. On 26 August Razanamasy formed a Government, which contained some defectors from the FV. The FV denounced the new Government as 'puppets' of Ratsiraka and continued their protests.

Interim Settlement

The stalemate continued until an interim agreement on 31 October 1991 provided for the creation of a transitional Government to hold office for a maximum period of 18 months pending the adoption of a new constitution and the holding of elections. Under the agreement, Ratsiraka would relinquish all executive powers but remain as President with the ceremonial duties of head of state and titular Head of the Armed Forces. Zafy would become President of a 31-member Haute Autorité de l'État, while Andriamanjato and Manandafy became joint Presidents of the advisory Conseil de Redressement Économique et Social, comprising 130 members. Zafy initially objected to the retention of Ratsiraka, and the general strike continued until December when the new Government was expanded to include more FV members.

Ratsiraka reasserted his intention to stand for re-election and demanded that a federalist draft constitution be submitted to a referendum as an alternative to the unitary draft being considered by a national forum. After much debate, a clause was included in the electoral code excluding the candidature of anyone who had been elected President twice under the Second Republic, while the Constitution adopted by the forum was of a parliamentary type, with a largely ceremonial President and executive power vested in a Prime Minister elected by the National Assembly. A referendum on the constitution was eventually held on 19 August when, despite various attempts at disruption by federalist supporters of Ratsiraka, the new Constitution was approved by 72% of the valid votes, with a turn-out of some two-thirds of the electorate.

The federalists intensified pressure for Ratsiraka's right to stand for re-election. A number of violent incidents led the transitional authorities to allow Ratsiraka to contest the presidential election, which took place peacefully on 25 November 1992. Of the eight candidates, Zafy received 45% of votes cast, while Ratsiraka took 29% and Manandafy 10%. A second round contested by the two leading candidates took place on 10 February 1993, when Zafy obtained 67% of the vote, against only 33% for Ratsiraka. Zafy was formally invested as President in late March, amid violent clashes between security forces and federalists in the north of the country.

On 16 June 1993 the elections to the National Assembly were held under a system of proportional representation. Although several elements of the FV coalition presented separate lists of candidates, the remaining parties in the alliance, known as the Cartel HVR, proved the most successful group, securing 45 of the 138 seats; Manandafy's MFM obtained 16 seats, while a new pro-Ratsiraka movement, FAMIMA, won 11. At the prime ministerial election on 9 August, Manandafy obtained 32 votes, Roger Ralison (the candidate of the Cartel) took 45 votes and Francisque Ravony won, securing 55 votes. Ravony, a respected lawyer and son-in-law of former President Tsiranana, was the favoured candidate both of Zafy and of the business community and had served as a Deputy Prime Minister in the transitional Government.

THE THIRD REPUBLIC

At the end of August 1993 Ravony formed a new Council of Ministers. Effective action on the economy proved difficult, in part owing to the fragmented nature of the National Assembly, which comprised some 25 separate parties in two largely informal coalitions of equal size, known as the HVR group and the G6. Neither was specifically a government or opposition organization, and ministers were appointed from both alliances and also from independent members. A number of deputies opposed the acceptance of structural adjustment measures, required by the World Bank and IMF as a precondition to the approval of financial credit, owing to the additional widespread hardship that would ensue.

Ravony's position was also undermined by public opposition from Zafy and Andriamanjato, who rejected the IMF and World Bank demands as an affront to national sovereignty and favoured financial arrangements with private enterprises, known as 'parallel financing'. In January 1995, at the insistence of the Bretton Woods institutions, Ravony dismissed the Governor of the central bank while, in a balancing move to appease the HVR group, the Minister of Finance resigned and Ravony assumed the portfolio himself. The Government subsequently pledged to undertake further austerity measures, while the IMF and World Bank approved the doubling of the minimum wage and additional expenditure on health and education to counteract the effect of the structural adjustment reforms.

In June 1995 members of the G6 group staged a demonstration demanding the impeachment of Zafy, on the grounds that he had exceeded his constitutional powers and supported Andriamanjato's demands for 'parallel financing'. At the same time Ravony strengthened his parliamentary position by recruiting additional deputies to his hitherto single-member party, the Committee for the Support of Democracy and Development in Madagascar (CSDDM). The CSDDM then joined the G6, which became the G7 and had a clear majority in the National Assembly.

After a failed motion of censure against the Prime Minister, Zafy announced that he could not co-operate with Ravony and called a referendum for 17 September 1995 to endorse a constitutional amendment, whereby the President, rather than the National Assembly, would select the Prime Minister. Ravony declined to campaign against the referendum and announced that he would resign when the result was formally announced in October. At the referendum, in which many of Ravony's supporters abstained, the constitutional amendment was approved by 64% of the valid votes. Ravony and his Government duly resigned, and President Zafy appointed as Prime Minister Emmanuel Rakotovahiny, the leader of his own party, the UNDD. The new Government contained no members of the G7 majority group and was heavily weighted in favour of the UNDD at the expense of other groups from the former HVR.

The Government was weakened by public disagreement between the Prime Minister and the Minister of Finance over the 1996 budget, and could make no progress in negotiations with the IMF and the World Bank. There were strikes by university students and railway workers and an unprecedented strike by officials of the finance ministry, joined by customs officials at the ports. Under increasing pressure, Zafy offered a reorganization of the Government but insisted on retaining Rakotovahiny as Prime Minister. In April most of the parties that had previously supported Zafy joined in a new group, the Rassemblement pour la Troisième République (RP3R), to oppose him. The IMF stressed that it could negotiate only with a cohesive government united in favour of agreements with the Bretton Woods institutions.

When Zafy failed to reorganize the Government, the G7 and RP3R joined in May 1996 in a motion of censure against it, which was carried by 109 votes to 15. Rakotovahiny resigned and Zafy appointed a non-political Prime Minister, Norbert Ratsirahonana, the President of the Haute Cour Constitutionelle (HCC). Ratsirahonana won general approval for his programme of economic reform in the context of agreements with the IMF and World Bank, together with action on poverty, corruption and crime. He proposed a government that included several members of the G7 majority group and only one UNDD member, but Zafy vetoed all but one G7 minister and insisted on the retention of five UNDD members. Most G7 and RP3R deputies walked out when Ratsirahonana presented his Government and programme to the National Assembly on 10 June. However, in July Ratsirahonana obtained a vote of confidence by linking it with legislation necessary for reaching agreements with the IMF and World Bank.

On 26 July 1996 the National Assembly voted by 99 votes to 34 to impeach President Zafy for various violations of the Constitution. After granting Zafy one month to contest the charges, the HCC endorsed the impeachment and removed him from office; on the same day Zafy resigned. The Court appointed the Prime Minister, Ratsirahonana, as interim President pending the outcome of a new presidential election, to be held within two months. He formed a new Government that excluded those ministers whom Zafy had forced him to accept. Despite the impeachment, Zafy immediately declared himself a candidate for the presidential election, as did ex-President Ratsiraka and acting President Ratsirahonana.

The Return of Ratsiraka

In the first round of the presidential election on 3 November 1996, which was marked by a high abstention rate, Ratsiraka came first with 37% of the valid votes, followed by Zafy with 23%. In the second round on 29 December Ratsiraka won narrowly with 51% of the valid votes to Zafy's 49%, but abstentions and spoiled votes comprised 52% of the electorate. In February 1997 Ratsiraka appointed as Prime Minister Pascal Rakotomavo, who formed a Government consisting largely of technocrats. During the election campaign Ratsirahonana had successfully completed negotiations with the IMF, which led in due course to a resumption of international aid and debt relief arrangements. Ratsiraka announced his intention to fulfil an electoral promise to hold a national referendum on two alternative new constitutions. The legislative elections due in August 1997 were consequently postponed for 10 months.

The Government then decided that the referendum on 15 March 1998 would concern amendments to the existing Constitution rather than two alternative new constitutions, although these revisions were so extensive that they amounted to an almost completely new Constitution, greatly increasing the President's powers at the expense of the legislature and weakening the independence of the judiciary while also providing for a considerable degree of decentralization of government to the provinces. Although most opposition parties decided not to campaign actively for a 'No' vote in the referendum, the amendments were only narrowly adopted, by 51% of the valid votes, cast by 66% of the electorate. The amended Constitution allowed the President to complete his term of office and to be re-elected twice.

Elections to an enlarged 150-member National Assembly took place on 17 May 1998. A new electoral law favoured the larger parties as the previous system of proportional representation using party lists was replaced by 82 single-member constituencies and a form of proportional representation for 34 two-member constituencies. Ratsiraka's party, AREMA, received only 25% of the votes but won 63 of the 150 seats, while its coalition partners, LEADER/Fanilo and AKFM/Fanavaozana, won 19 seats, thus forming a majority in the Assembly. In July Ratsiraka appointed as Prime Minister Tantely Andrianarivo, who formed a coalition Government that was dominated by AREMA.

Although the Government was later strengthened by the support of the Rassemblement pour le Socialisme et la Démocratie (RPSD) and 24 independent deputies, it lost support over its economic performance, notably the long delay in obtaining the release of additional structural adjustment funds from the World Bank and the IMF. The opposition divided into two groups: the radicals, including Zafy's Asa, Fahamarinana, Fampandrosoana, Arinda (AFFA) and Manandafy's MFM, which demanded the overthrow of the Government and a new constitution; and the moderates, led by Ratsirahonana's Ny Asa Vita No Ifampitsara (AVI), which engaged in more constructive opposition. Elections for provincial councillors in the new Constitution's autonomous provinces took place on 3 December 2000. With the opposition vote split among a number of parties, AREMA received the most votes in all six provinces, with an absolute majority in all except Antananarivo. All the governors, now elected by provincial councillors rather than being appointed by the central Government, were members of AREMA. On 18 March 2001 the provincial councillors joined with the mayors of the communes to elect two-thirds of the Senate, with the remaining one-third to be nominated by the President. AREMA was again victorious, winning 49 of the 60 seats, thus completing the presidential party's domination at all levels of both government and legislature. Despite this, opposition to the Ratsiraka regime remained strong.

Disputed Presidential Election

The country was plunged into a crisis after the presidential election held on 16 December 2001. The results for the first round issued by the Government, and confirmed by a newly appointed HCC, gave Marc Ravalomanana, Mayor of Antananarivo, 46% of the votes cast and Ratsiraka 40%, necessitating a second round of voting. However, Ravalomanana, supported by a consortium of observers, claimed that he had won 52% of the vote and therefore should be proclaimed President. Massive demonstrations by his supporters failed to persuade the HCC, but Ravalomanana declared himself President and appointed a Government, headed by Jacques Sylla, which subsequently took over government offices in the capital. Ratsiraka withdrew his Government to the port of Toamasina, while his supporters erected road blocks and destroyed bridges on all roads leading to the capital, creating in effect a blockade of the plateau area.

At a meeting in Dakar, Senegal, called by the Organization of African Unity (OAU), the two contenders agreed in mid-April 2002 to a recount (followed by a second round if necessary) and a cessation of the blockade and the violence. Meanwhile, the Supreme Court in Madagascar ruled that the recent appointment of the HCC had been irregular and accordingly reinstated the former HCC, the members of which carried out the recount and declared Ravalomanana the winner, with 51.5% of the votes cast to Ratsiraka's 35.9%. Ravalomanana was duly inaugurated as President on 6 May. However, Ratsiraka refused to accept the recount. He persisted in demanding a second round of voting, and the blockade and the violence in coastal towns continued.

The OAU and France supported Ratsiraka by continuing to demand the establishment of a government of national reconciliation and the holding of new elections. Other Western countries followed the French lead in withholding recognition from Ravalomanana. Both 'Presidents' appointed new ministers of defence as well as army and gendarmerie chiefs of staff. Following the formal transfer of power to Ravalomanana's appointees, the majority of the armed forces accepted Ravalomanana as Commander-in-Chief.

There were further OAU attempts at mediation and reconciliation, which became more urgent when Ravalomanana's troops successfully occupied the area around Sambava in the north-east. In June 2002 Ravalomanana agreed to bring forward the legislative elections and made a gesture towards a government of national reconciliation by reorganizing his Government to include two former supporters of Ratsiraka, although this did not satisfy France and the OAU, which declared the Malagasy seat at the OAU vacant until new elections were held. The exclusion of Madagascar was maintained in July at the OAU summit in Durban, South Africa, at which the Organization was transformed into the African Union (AU).

On 26 June 2002, Madagascar's Independence Day, the USA recognized Ravalomanana as President and released Malagasy assets in the USA. Recognition quickly followed from Australia, Germany and Japan. France continued to appeal for reconciliation, but limited its demands to the inclusion of two more AREMA members in the Government. When Ravalomanana complied in early July, the French immediately released Malagasy assets in France and signed new aid agreements with Ravalomanana. French recognition, followed by that of the other European Union (EU) Governments, effectively ended Ratsiraka's resistance. On 5 July he flew with most of his ministers into exile in France.

Peace and Reconciliation

President Ravalomanana proclaimed a policy of national reconciliation, but it proved difficult to resist the widespread demand for the punishment of those responsible for the suffering and damage caused by the blockade and for the brutal behaviour of the pro-Ratsiraka militia. Over 200 leading supporters of Ratsiraka, both civilian and military, were arrested and imprisoned for sometimes lengthy periods before being either condemned to heavy fines and imprisonment or released for lack of evidence. Ravalomanana also set up a National Council to tackle the corruption in government that had become endemic during the Second and Third Republics.

Ravalomanana brought forward the legislative elections due in May 2003 to 15 December 2002, having amended the electoral rules to abolish the limited element of proportional representation. The President's party, Tiako i Madagasikara (TIM—I Love Madagascar), won 104 of the 160 seats, while allies from AVI and elements of the RPSD joined in a Front Patriotique (FP) that gained a further 22 seats. AREMA, which had been split by a demand to boycott the elections, came second in many constituencies, but the new 'first-past-the-post' system limited its seats to three. There were also 23 independent deputies.

The new Government formed by Prime Minister Sylla in January 2003 was reduced from 30 to 20 ministers and was dominated by TIM. Several smaller parties that had supported Ravalomanana in the presidential election as members of the Committee for Support of Marc Ravalomanana (KMMR), but had not been rewarded with ministerial posts, set up an opposition group, KMMR Nouveau. Nevertheless, there was little threat to the dominance of TIM and the popularity of the President. In August 2003 Ratsiraka was sentenced *in absentia* to 10 years' hard labour for embezzling public funds, and in December former Prime Minister Andrianarivo was sentenced to 12 years' hard labour and fined heavily for embezzling public funds and endangering state security, although he was later granted permission to go overseas to seek medical treatment. Following expressions of international concern, President Ravalomanana granted pardons to former Ratsiraka loyalists who had been sentenced to less than three years' imprisonment.

The blockade of the capital had inflicted severe damage on the economy. In August the President suspended all taxes on a wide range of imported goods in the hope of stimulating the economy, but while the President retained much of his popularity, support for his party declined. In communal and municipal elections in November 2003 TIM candidates received little more than 50% of the national vote. In January 2004 Ravalomanana restructured the Council of Ministers, further reducing its size and appointing several former supporters of Ratsiraka in order to diversify its ethnic composition. From that month army reservists who had supported Ravalomanana in 2002 staged various demonstrations, expressing their discontent with the Government for failing to pay their demobilization bonuses as promised, while other public protests took place over the strong increase in prices of consumer goods.

Unrest continued as the price of rice increased by 150% between March and November 2004; an increase of 50% in one week of November brought hundreds of people onto the streets of the capital in protest. Declining purchasing power was a factor in a series of strikes in early 2005 by magistrates, university lecturers and students, and there were violent clashes between police and students in Antananarivo. In March there was a reorganization of the Government involving the abolition of the post of Deputy Prime Minister. In December Gen. Charles Rabemananjara was appointed Minister of the Interior and Administrative Reform, following an alleged attempt on the President's life.

The steep increase in the price of petroleum in 2005 was a set-back to the Government's hopes of reducing inflation and improving living standards. Its position was further weakened by dissent within TIM, manifested in the dismissal by the National Assembly of its President, Jean Lahiniriko, in May 2006. In accordance with UN recommendations, the Government organized a national dialogue in May, but it was boycotted by most of the opposition as the Government was not prepared to accept their main proposals, especially a revision of the electoral law. Nevertheless, further consultative talks were held in August. In the same month former Prime Minister Pierrot Rajaonarivelo was sentenced *in absentia* to 15 years' imprisonment after being convicted of the embezzlement of public funds.

Ravalomanana Re-elected

The Government brought forward the date of the presidential election to 3 December 2006. This appeared to be contrary to the Constitution but was approved by the HCC, which barred four of the possible 18 candidates, including Rajaonarivelo, whose attempts to return from exile in France in October were thwarted. The final results announced by the HCC awarded Ravalomanana 54.8% of the vote, well ahead of Lahiniriko, who took 11.7%, Roland Ratsiraka (nephew of the former President) with 10.1% and Herizo Razafimahaleo with 9.0%, and sufficient to avoid a second round of voting. Voter turn-out was 62% and international observers commented favourably on the way the election was held. During the election campaign there was an attempted coup by Gen. Randrianafidisoa, commonly known as 'Fidy'. The attempt was suppressed and Gen. Fidy was later sentenced to four years' imprisonment. In January 2007 the President appointed Rabemananjara, who retained the interior portfolio, as the new Prime Minister.

Although turn-out was low, at a referendum held on 4 March 2007, 75% of voters approved a number of amendments to the Constitution that generally increased the power of the President, granting him, for example, greater powers in times of emergency and the right to terminate his appointments to the Senate, which had its term reduced from seven to five years. The six autonomous provinces were to be suppressed by 2009 and instead the 22 regions were given more powers, while the communities or *fokonolona* were introduced as the base of the country's development. A further change was the introduction of English as a third official language alongside French and Malagasy, the national language, in an effort to boost links with English-speaking trading partners such as the Southern African Development Community (SADC).

Political rivalries intensified following the President's decision in July 2007 to dissolve the National Assembly and to set 23 September as the date for legislative elections. The campaign was subdued, and the eventual turn-out some 46%. TIM won 105 of the reduced number of 127 seats contested, compared with 112 of 160 in 2003. The opposition was still divided in spite of an effort to form a united front and still inclined to boycott elections in search of reforms to the electoral law. Only two other smaller parties won seats, while the remaining seats were awarded to independent candidates, a number of whom subsequently allied themselves to the Government.

Rabemananjara retained his position as Prime Minister in the new Government, but there were several changes in the cabinet, the most notable of which was the appointment of Cécile Manorohanta as Minister of National Defence, the first time a woman or a civilian had held the post.

The Rise of Andry Rajoelina

In municipal and communal elections held in December 2007 a large number of opposition parties boycotted the vote, including LEADER/Fanilo and the RPSD, which had both won a sizeable number of mayoral positions in 2003. Turn-out was low, at around 40%. The most striking result was in Antananarivo, where a young businessman, Andry Rajoelina, secured victory over the TIM candidate with 63% of the vote.

In April 2008 the regional councillors joined an electoral college together with the country's deputies and mayors to elect a senator for each region; TIM took all 22 senatorial positions, although it had been in a minority in three regions. The President used his right to nominate one-third of the new total of 33 senators to appoint people from outside TIM. A new Government was announced in June, when a still-divided opposition demanded improved media access and open debates.

Unrest in the capital and other cities was evident in protests that took place in August and September 2008, while a dispute between the Government and Rajoelina intensified on issues such as the debt position of the capital. The President proposed a meeting to discuss changes to the law on political parties, not all of which attended the conference, held in December. The conference also served to stimulate a revival of various opposition groups, which increasingly backed Rajoelina and his party Tanora malaGasy Vonona (TGV—Determined Malagasy Youth). Economic hardship and an increasing sense of the autocratic nature of the President's regime were compounded by disquiet at two particular decisions—the purchase of a new presidential jet at a cost of US $60m., and plans to lease substantial tracts of land to Daewoo Logistics of the Republic of Korea (South Korea).

Tensions were exacerbated by the Government's decision on 17 December 2008 to close the broadcasting station Télévision Viva, which was owned by Rajoelina and had broadcast an interview with former President Ratsiraka. Rajoelina orchestrated protest marches that led to clashes with security forces, with two people shot dead on 24 January 2009 and at least 25 killed in a fire at a looted building the following day. Rajoelina claimed executive power for himself on 31 January, although the Government responded by replacing him as Mayor of Antananarivo with a special delegation. Rajoelina in turn appointed his own successor and named Monja Roindefo, the son of the late Monja Jaona, as the prime minister of his rival government, the Haute Autorité de Transition (HAT—High Transitional Authority).

The crisis deepened considerably on 7 February 2009 when guards opened fire on protesters marching towards the presidential palace at Ambohitsorohitra, killing at least 28 people. Two days later Manorohanta resigned from her post as Minister of National Defence. Following mediation efforts notably from the UN and the AU, a meeting was held between Ravalomanana and Rajoelina on 21 February, during which they agreed to halt the street protests and political arrests but could not agree on how to end the unrest. The army, which had traditionally remained neutral in political disputes, became increasingly involved, with a mutiny on 8 March at the Capsat division, the resignation on 10 March of the new Minister of Defence after army pressure, and the presence of forces on the streets of the capital from 12 March. Army units occupied the Ambohitsorohitra palace and the central bank on 16 March, while Ravalomanana, who appealed for a referendum to be held to determine whether or not he should remain in power, took refuge at the presidential palace of Iavoloha, in southern Antananarivo. On 17 March Ravalomanana dissolved the Government and resigned the presidency. Before heading into exile with his family, he handed power to a three-man military executive committee led by the most senior figure in the armed forces, Vice-Adm. Hyppolite Ramaroson, which in turn transferred executive powers to Rajoelina. While there was some dispute over the actual events, the army's role in the changes pointed to the first successful coup in Madagascar's history. Rajoelina was inaugurated as President of the HAT on 21 March. As the Constitution stipulated that the minimum age for the President of Madagascar was 40, the 34-year old Rajoelina announced that a new constitution was to be drawn up. Rajoelina's appointment was approved by the HCC but drew strong criticism from overseas; most aid was halted, and Madagascar was suspended from both the AU and SADC.

In late March 2009 Rajoelina appointed a 22-member Government, retaining those ministers named in February. The Government immediately cancelled the Daewoo contract and the National Assembly was suspended on 19 March. The HAT announced a number of populist measures and also a draft timetable for the transition of power, which drew criticism for the proposed length of time before the staging of a presidential election (reduced subsequently from two years to 19 months, and set for October 2010) and which quickly fell behind schedule. The HAT also faced criticism for its intolerance of opposition in the media and for its sometimes arbitrary treatment of opponents. In April 2009 soldiers arrested Pety Rakotonirina, the 'prime minister' recently appointed by Ravalomanana, who himself was sentenced on 3 June *in absentia* to four years in prison and fined US $70m. for the misuse of public funds relating to the presidential jet. The HAT announced other investigations into land and tax deals that allegedly favoured companies within Ravalomanana's Tiko group.

Ravalomanana's supporters replaced those of Rajoelina in organizing street protests, which were later banned by the HAT; clashes were frequent and a number of people died. In exile, primarily in South Africa, Ravalomanana attempted to secure international support for his position and for his return to Madagascar, while Rajoelina in turn sought backing for his regime, but to little effect.

Negotiations to find a solution to the crisis continued intermittently from April 2009 under the aegis of various bodies, but with limited progress. The parties involved were Rajoelina's HAT, Ravalomanana's TIM, the Comité pour la Réconciliation Nationale led by Albert Zafy, and representatives of former President Ratsiraka and his AREMA party. One of the key issues was the possible return from exile and the eligibility to stand in the forthcoming presidential election of Ravalomanana and Ratsiraka. Following a summit held in Maputo, Mozambique, on 5–9 August, with mediation by the Groupe International de Contact (GIC—comprising representatives from the UN, the AU, SADC and the Organisation Internationale de la Francophonie), the four parties agreed upon a Transitional Charter that was to remain in place for a maximum duration of 15 months, after which presidential and legislative elections would be held. The Charter also provided for the establishment of a bicameral transitional legislature and a National Union Government of Transition, comprising a Prime Minister, three Deputy Prime Ministers and 28 ministers. The Prime Minister was to be selected by consensus and officially appointed by Rajoelina, who, in his capacity as President of the Transition, would exercise the functions of head of state. A new constitution was to be drafted for a Fourth Republic, and an amnesty was to cover events from January 2002 up to the signing of the Charter. A number of political prisoners were released after the accords. However, a second meeting in Maputo, on 27–29 August 2009, to confirm the sharing of posts, failed to reach agreement on the roles of President and Prime Minister.

On 5 September 2009 Rajoelina officially appointed as Prime Minister Monja Roindefo, who on 8 September announced a new Government with 31 ministers. However, these moves were rejected by the three former Presidents as unilateral and not in accordance with the Maputo agreement, a view endorsed by the AU and SADC. The opposition held a series of protest meetings that were dispersed by the authorities, which also arrested a number of Ravalomanana's supporters; on 21 September Rakotonirina was given a two-year suspended sentence. On 24 September Rajoelina was prevented from addressing the General Assembly of the UN, as members of SADC argued that he was not the legitimate head of government.

The GIC managed to reach an agreement with the parties on 6 October 2009 whereby Rajoelina would remain President of the Transition, with Rakotovahiny as Vice-President and Eugène Mangalaza, a professor of anthropology, as Prime Minister. However, Roindefo refused to stand down, and Manorohanta was appointed as interim Prime Minister while the issue was reviewed by the Conseil d'État and the HCC. The supporters of the HAT were divided over the accords, and a 'fifth movement' was established.

A further round of talks commenced in the Ethiopian capital, Addis Ababa, on 3 November 2009, under the threat of economic sanctions from the EU. An agreement was reached on 6 November whereby Rajoelina would remain as President, but would share power with two Vice-Presidents—Rakotovahiny representing Zafy, and Fetison Andrianirina representing Ravalomanana—while Mangalaza, an ally of Ratsiraka, would continue as Prime Minister, alongside three Deputy Prime Ministers. There would be a further 31 ministers, with six from each of the four main movements and seven from other political groupings, but there was no agreement on the allocation of portfolios. Following pressure from the army, the three opposition leaders met again in Maputo, without Rajoelina, and announced on 7 December a timetable for the installation of the new institutions and the division of ministerial posts. Rajoelina denounced the declaration as treason, and the HAT banned flights from Mozambique and South Africa, leaving many senior opponents stranded until the restrictions were retracted following international criticism.

Rajoelina pursued his unilateral approach by announcing that legislative elections would be held in March 2010. On 20 December 2009 he appointed a new Prime Minister, Albert Camille Vital, a retired army colonel, and declared a new constitutional law that returned the country largely to the position in which it had been when he assumed power in March. The opposition held further protest meetings and attempted to re-establish the Congress on 28 December, the same day as an attempted mutiny in the army reflected divisions over the accords. The GIC held a further meeting in Addis Ababa on 6 January 2010 that rejected Rajoelina's unilateral moves, while SADC also echoed this criticism. Amid continuing tension, Jean Ping, the AU representative, visited Madagascar and recommended the deferral of elections, to which Rajoelina agreed on 26 January. Rajoelina proposed the creation of a new election commission, the Commission Électorale Nationale Indépendante (CENI), although the opposition parties refused to join. The AU summit in early February criticized the 'illegal regime' in Madagascar, while the European Parliament also condemned the HAT's coup and abuse of human rights. The pressure on Rajoelina mounted in mid-February when the AU imposed a deadline of one month to enact the accords and to remove Ny Hasina Andriamanjato from the post of Minister of Foreign Affairs. His replacement with the hardline Ramaroson was viewed as a sign of defiance, while the HAT refused to attend a GIC meeting in early March. On 17 March the AU duly imposed sanctions on Rajoelina and 108 other members of the HAT.

In mid-March 2010 the army exerted increased pressure on the HAT to find a political solution, and Rajoelina announced that he would attend a meeting in South Africa with Ravalomanana to discuss a new proposal. Sporadic violence continued, including several bomb attacks, and there were clear divisions within the army, while the churches took a more active role in seeking a solution. Three days of talks in Pretoria, chaired by South African President Jacob Zuma, saw no agreement on the timing of elections and an amnesty. Rajoelina declined to attend a second round of talks and instead held discussions with the military on their potential involvement in government. He proposed holding a referendum on a new constitution in August, followed by legislative elections in September and a presidential election in December, in which he would not stand. However, Rajoelina's continued unilateralism, the arrest of opposition politicians and the closure of a church radio station resulted in an intensification of international criticism.

An SADC delegation visited Madagascar in July 2010, while an EU-sponsored agreement between various civic societies led to the creation of a new body, the Co-ordination Nationale des Organisations de la Société Nationale (CNOSC). On 27 July a national dialogue started, which involved a debate on the transition, the constitution and the electoral code. In August Rajoelina at first rejected, then embraced, proposals by a new pro-HAT grouping that appealed for a referendum in November and elections in 2011. Although the group included some individuals from the opposition parties, their leaders rejected this development. Meanwhile, Prof. Raymond Ranjeva, a former international judge, sought to establish a non-partisan movement, the Vonjy Aina. In a meeting in August 2010 SADC maintained its exclusion of Madagascar but proposed the establishment of a liaison office. On 24 August the trial started of 19 people implicated in the killings of 7 February 2009, in which the defence lawyers resigned and Ravalomanana, who rejected what he called a 'mock trial', was sentenced to life imprisonment with hard labour for his part in the affair.

Since a planned national conference was postponed, the CNOSC arranged instead a preliminary meeting. In a rare sign of conciliation, the Apostolic Nuncio hosted a meeting between Rajoelina and the opposition leaders, but the latter boycotted the conference, which was held in September 2010. At the meeting, it was decided that Rajoelina would remain as President of the Transition alongside a *côtier* Prime Minister, while a referendum on a new constitution was approved and appeals were made for the country's mayors to be replaced by special delegates, although the HAT decided instead to hold mayoral elections in December.

The official campaign for the constitutional referendum started in October 2010, but was boycotted by the opposition. The draft constitution included provisions allowing the HAT to remain in power until new elections were held; reducing the minimum age for the President from 40 to 35 years, thus allowing Rajoelina legitimately to assume the presidency; removing English as an official language; prohibiting foreigners from owning or leasing land for more than 30 years; replacing 'fahafahana' (liberty) with 'fitiavana' (love) in the country's motto; and establishing a Parlement de la Transition comprised of a Congrès de la Transition and a Conseil Supérieur de la Transition. The referendum on 17 November was overshadowed by a mutiny by troops at the Base Aéro-Navale d'Ivato, near the capital, which was stormed by forces loyal to the regime on 20 November. The new Constitution of the Fourth Republic was approved by 74.2% of voters, according to the HCC. Turn-out was 53%. The CENI highlighted a number of problems with the vote, but, while the result was not accepted by the international community, it strengthened the position of Rajoelina, who later received some de facto recognition at the UN. He officially inaugurated the Fourth Republic on 12 December, while Leonardo Simão, the envoy of SADC and a former Mozambican Minister of Foreign Affairs and Co-operation, returned to Madagascar to renew his consultations with the various parties.

THE FOURTH REPUBLIC

The HAT's planned March 2011 elections were postponed in January. There were further attempts at conciliation, and negotiations took place between members of the TIM and the TGV but foundered on the issues of the choice of Prime Minister and Ravalomanana's return from exile. In January SADC began to emphasize reaching a consensus rather than uniformity. In February Simão presented to representatives of the various parties new proposals for a 'road map' towards a solution to the crisis. The details were largely based on the Ivato accords of 2010 and were favourable to the HAT. Rajoelina would be confirmed as President and head of state, with the right to designate a Prime Minister from a list proposed by the different parties. He would also have the final decision on any additions to the transitional parliament and to the CENI, which was not to be reformed. A broad amnesty covering 2002–09 was proposed, and Ravalomanana was to be prevented from returning from exile until the situation was judged to be stable after elections, which Rajoelina and other members of the HAT would be to contest provided that they stood down from their positions beforehand. Simão advised Rajoelina to end the various legal prosecutions under way and also urged Ravalomanana to avoid any destabilizing actions. The HAT blocked attempts by both Ravalomanana and Ratsiraka to return to Madagascar.

Zafy appealed for a new transition, but the HAT instead declared that elections would be held in September 2011. Tension increased after an apparent attempt on the life of Rajoelina on 4 March, when a home-made bomb exploded by the road as his convoy passed, although to little effect. On 9 March eight political movements, excluding the three opposition organizations, met to initial the accord on the new road map. As agreed, Vital resigned as Prime Minister but was quickly reappointed. A new Government, supposedly of national unity, was announced on 26 March. In April the US State Department published its 2010 report on human rights, in which it criticized, *inter alia*, Rajoelina's illegal assumption of power, his decision to remain as President until new elections were held and a number of human rights abuses.

While protest marches were being staged in Antananarivo, the SADC security troika met to discuss the Madagascar crisis. An SADC extraordinary summit took place in Namibia in May 2011, but made only very limited progress. The summit appealed for a political process open to all and for an urgent meeting of the relevant Malagasy parties, to be held at SADC headquarters in Botswana. The meeting took place on 6–7 June, but no agreement was reached between the parties. The final communiqué noted the points of convergence, including the holding of free, fair and credible elections.

SADC endorsed the road map, urged the opposition parties to sign it and called on the HAT to allow political exiles to return unconditionally; however, the regime stated that it would still imprison Ravalomanana should he return. Rajoelina gave SADC a deadline of the end of August to agree a timetable for signing the road map, but held back from pushing for immediate elections. The road map was finally signed on 17 September during a visit by an SADC delegation, and was widely welcomed by the international community, including the UN, with Rajoelina attending that month's session in New York.

A further SADC visit enabled an agreement to be reached on 14 October 2011 regarding a timetable of events, including the appointment of a new prime minister and a government by mid-November. Vital duly resigned as Prime Minister and was replaced by Jean Omer Beriziky, a former ambassador to the EU and a nominee of the Zafy movement; however, he was rejected by the Ravalomanana movement as being too close to Rajoelina. The Zafy and Ravalomanana movements formed a new front with Monja Roindefo's MONIMA, and laid claim to one-half of the new ministerial seats. Intense negotiations on the composition of the new Government led to the deadline being missed, but the new ministers were finally announced on 21 November, a development that was welcomed by France and other EU members.

Ratsiraka returned from nine years in exile on 24 November 2011, proposing a summit of the four presidents but refusing to join a Government that he viewed as being non-consensual. Thus, the new Parlement de la Transition formed on 1 December had fewer members than had been stipulated in the road map. Rajoelina met President Nicolas Sarkozy on 7 December during a visit to France, which was seen as further recognition of the HAT. The AU, however, announced the next day that it would not lift its suspension of Madagascar until there had been further progress on the return of exiles and the holding of elections. In January 2012 the HAT declared that it would now establish the remaining institutions required under the road map.

Ravalomanana attempted to return to Madagascar on 21 January 2012, but his flight was turned back to South Africa. There were violent clashes between his supporters and the security forces, while the US Administration was particularly critical of the regime. The opposition boycotted the opening of the new parliamentary session on 23 January. Ravalomanana's wife was also prevented from an attempt to return from exile, while the HAT missed SADC's deadline of the end of February to agree an amnesty law. A new independent electoral commission was sworn in on 12 March. After an eventful trial Ranjeva and his daughter were acquitted on 21 March of complicity in the demand by members of the armed forces to dissolve the HAT on the day of the referendum in November 2010, while several senior officers were given prison sentences. The amnesty law was finally passed on 12 April 2012, but was controversial as it excluded those who had been found guilty of human rights abuses including those sentenced for murder, thus excluding Ravalomanana.

There were a series of strikes, court cases and disputes in the country while the Government was in apparent deadlock, compounded by the decision of the Ravalomanana movement to suspend its participation in the Parlement de la Transition. A meeting in early May 2012 between the signatories of the road map was inconclusive and on 11 May SADC's security troika expressed its deep concern over the impasse, as did the EU. A further deadline for a timetable to be agreed was missed at the end of May, but on 8 June a UN mission proposed that elections to the presidency and legislature should take place in May and June 2013. Efforts were also made to arrange a meeting between Rajoelina and Ravalomanana, which finally took place in late July in Seychelles, although no agreement could be reached on the issue of Ravalomanana's return to Madagascar. Further talks between the two men took place in August. The discussions were reported to be cordial but appeared to agree on little more than a confirmation of the proposed dates for the elections in 2013.

FOREIGN AFFAIRS

Despite close relations with the Soviet Union, President Ratsiraka adopted a foreign policy that was nominally non-aligned. In the early 1990s Ravony's Government reversed this approach and established relations with Israel, South Africa, South Korea and the Repubic of China (Taiwan). These arrangements were not altered after Ratsiraka's return as President in 1997, but by 2000, under pressure from the People's Republic of China, the Taiwan office had been closed. However, relations with China were somewhat strained by popular resentment at a large influx of Chinese small traders undercutting Malagasy shopkeepers. Successive foreign ministers made the promotion of the economy the main focus of foreign policy and moved to strengthen relations with South Africa, the newly industrialized countries of South-East Asia and the Far East. France remained the principal trading partner and supplier of bilateral aid. Political relations with France became even closer after the settlement, in 1998, of the long-standing dispute over compensation for nationalized French assets. Disagreement remained over the sovereignty of the Iles Glorieuses and three other uninhabited islets in the Mozambique Channel, which are claimed by France, but in 2000 it was agreed that the islands would be co-administered by France, Madagascar and Mauritius, without prejudice to the question of sovereignty. In 2002 the new Malagasy Government's relations with France were soured by French support for Ratsiraka, but France declared its intention of remaining the leading donor of aid, and relations soon recovered their traditional closeness.

Relations with African countries were also adversely affected by the support of the OAU (now the AU) for the outgoing President and Madagascar's exclusion from that organization. It was not until July 2003 that Madagascar was formally readmitted. In 2004 Madagascar and Mauritius signed political and economic agreements, and in that year Madagascar also joined SADC.

In November 2005 a visit by a delegation from the People's Republic of China, headed by the Deputy Prime Minister, highlighted the extent of Chinese involvement and investment in many areas of the Malagasy economy. The closer links were confirmed in further visits to Madagascar in 2006 and Ravalomanana's visit to Beijing in April 2007 to attend the Forum on China-Africa Co-operation. In that month the President also visited Germany, then the holder of the EU Presidency, securing financial support for his Madagascar Action Plan.

The political crisis that began in late 2008 and Rajoelina's subsequent assumption of power have isolated Madagascar from the international community, although there have been substantial efforts to find a solution. The country was quickly suspended from SADC and the AU, losing the right to host the AU summit in July 2009. Ravalomanana has been active in seeking support for his position, while Rajoelina himself launched a form of diplomatic initiative in May with visits to Libya, the Chair of the AU at that time, and to Senegal, where former President Abdoulaye Wade was active in discussions to resolve the crisis. In December the USA excluded Madagascar from the benefits due under its African Growth and Opportunity Act, and in March 2010 the AU imposed sanctions on Rajoelina and 108 other members of the HAT. The USA has not replaced its retiring ambassador as a form of sanction, although a new Apostolic Nuncio arrived in June 2010, as well as new ambassadors from Pakistan and Turkey. The HAT announced in December that it would open embassies in Turkey, Morocco and Singapore. It declared that it would recall its ambassadors in France, Germany, Italy, Belgium, South Africa, the USA and India, all of whom had been appointed by Ravalomanana, and replace them with chargé d'affaires, as there was no international recognition of the regime; the embassy in the United Kingdom was also closed.

The HAT has received more support from France and the Organisation Internationale de la Francophonie, and Mauritius in particular, while the USA has remained critical of the regime, particularly on the issue of human rights. The EU position has been somewhere between the two, although it has been ready to reopen aid donations once it sees further progress on the political road map. Madagascar remains suspended from the AU and SADC, but the role of the HAT in representing the country at the UN is less contested.

Economy

JULIAN COOKE

INTRODUCTION

In 2010 Madagascar's gross national income (GNI) at current prices was, according to estimates by the World Bank, US $430 per caput for the population of some 22m., ranking the country among the world's poorest; on a purchasing-power parity basis, GNI stood at $960 per caput. During 2003–11 it was estimated that the population increased at an average annual rate of nearly 3%. Over the same period Madagascar's gross domestic product (GDP) per head increased in real terms by an average of 0.8% per year, even though overall GDP increased at an average annual rate of over 3.0%. The economy had previously grown at improved rates, with growth of 4.9% in 2006, 6.2% in 2007 and 7.3% in 2008. However, with the global economic crisis and Madagascar's own political crisis (see Recent History), the economy was estimated to have contracted by 3.7% in 2009 and by a further 1.0% in 2010; only limited growth, of 0.7%, was achieved in 2011. In that year, according to the UN, the incidence of poverty was 76.5%, compared with 68% in 2008. Madagascar was ranked 151st out of 169 countries on the UN Human Development Index in 2011, compared with 135th in 2010.

AGRICULTURE, FORESTRY AND FISHING

The agricultural sector (including forestry and fishing) accounted for an estimated 28.8% of GDP in 2011 and engaged some 80% of the country's active labour force. Although agriculture has accounted for about 80% of Madagascar's export revenues, growth in mining production will reduce this proportion.

The island's agricultural sector has suffered from adverse climatic conditions, from a lack of insecticides, spare parts and fertilizers, and from the poor maintenance of rural roads. The introduction of higher producer prices during the 1980s aimed to increase the output of food crops, in particular to achieve self-sufficiency in food, but Madagascar continues to import rice for consumption. A further major policy objective was to improve the quality of export crops, while limiting the expansion in output. Continued pressures meant that agricultural GDP only increased at an average annual rate of 2.6% in 2001–09, according to the World Bank, although the rate reached 8.5% in 2009. There has been increased emphasis on microfinance to stimulate development, but the country's recent political crisis has heavily curtailed development aid and government reforms.

Madagascar is affected by cyclones, which vary in intensity and frequency each year. In February 2011 Cyclone Bingiza affected 10 regions, destroying large areas of cropland. The cyclone caused 34 deaths, left 77,000 people homeless, and injured or affected a further 200,000. In early 2012 first Cyclone Giovanna then the tropical storm Irina caused extensive damage and over 100 deaths between them. Another issue confronting the agricultural industry is the increased threat from locusts: by mid-April 2011 they had infested 207,000 ha, compared with 126,000 ha in 2010. By April 2011 the state had treated 112,000 ha with insecticide and planned to treat 150,000 ha by June, with the US $8m. cost funded by FAO. A shortage of funds limited preventative measures in the first half of 2012.

Paddy rice is the main crop, grown by 70% of the population, whose basic food is rice—the average annual consumption per head is about 135 kg, one of the highest rates in the world—and it occupies about 1.2m. ha, or between one-third and one-half of the total area under cultivation. In June 2008 the Government officially launched a 38,000m.-ariary programme that had started earlier in the year to grow rice in the off-season, using faster-yielding seeds. In 2009, in spite of some further cyclone damage and poor rains in the south, the total rice harvest was calculated by FAO to have increased by 2.4% to 2.8m. tons (milled), although other figures suggested an overall increase of 40% in 2007–09. In 2010, despite a reduction in cyclone damage, a prolonged period of dry weather affected the production of crops in the centre and south of the island. There was limited cyclone damage in 2011 and 2012, and rainfall alleviated the drought in the south of the country, where the staple crops are maize and cassava. However, the region still suffers from chronic food insecurity, and Madagascar as a whole has the highest levels of malnutrition in Southern Africa, according to FAO; figures from the UN Children's Fund (UNICEF) indicated that 50.5% of the population suffer from malnutrition, rising to 70% in southern regions such as Androy and Anosy.

Madagascar is the world's largest producer of natural vanilla, produced from approximately 25,000 ha of plants grown in the north-east of the country. The USA and France are the main purchasers. Output has fluctuated widely in recent years, between 600 metric tons and 4,400 tons per year, and is very sensitive to damage from cyclones and tropical storms, as experienced in 2007, when an estimated 20% of the crop was lost, and again in 2008 and 2009. Prices rose to a record level of US $400 per kg in 2003, when production almost halved to 2,650 tons. The price rise stimulated competition from cheap synthetic substitutes, which contributed to a collapse in prices, to $20 per kg, by 2006, from which they have since recovered slightly to $30 per kg. The Government and producer confederations follow a policy of limited exports and managed prices. Exports for 2009 were estimated to have declined to 1,500 tons from 1,800 tons in 2008, and the harvest in 2010 was estimated to be under 1,000 tons; exports were only 668 tons, worth $19m., less than one-half of the value in the previous year. The combination of the fusarium fungus, prices as low as $15 per kg and the impact of political instability on the main producing region affected output in 2011, and although prices were forecast to rise given the shortfall in production, they were in the end little changed.

A second important cash crop is cloves, production of which rose from the late 1980s as farmers responded to the liberalization of controls. Production stabilized at around 11,750 metric tons in 2000–02, and then rose sharply to 18,950 tons in 2003. However, in 2005 output nearly halved to 9,873 tons and has not moved higher than 10,000 tons since, with production in 2009 estimated at 7,594 tons. Output in 2010 declined further, in part due to the productive cycle of the tree and in part due to cyclone damage and the felling of trees to extract essential oils for use in the perfume industry. Much of Madagascar's production is sent to Singapore for re-export.

Coffee was also an important agricultural export, but declining international prices led to lower production and in 2004 coffee represented only an estimated 0.5% of the value of total exports. In 2000 a relaunch of the sector financed by the European Union (EU) aimed to encourage a shift from Robusta beans to the higher-value Arabica beans, but was only a partial success and the EU support has ended. Annual coffee production decreased from an average of 1.1m. bags during the 1980s to fewer than 400,000 bags in 2000, before recovering to 725,000 bags in 2008. However, the total declined again in 2009 to 625,000 bags. According to the International Coffee Organization, exports of 60-kg bags more than halved to 52,097 in the 12 months to May 2010 but recovered to 72,847 bags in the year to May 2011 and 122,338 bags in the same period of 2012.

Among other products, litchis (or lychees), ylang-ylang and geranium flowers (for essential oils) are exported. In 2009–10 a focus on quality led to anticipated litchis exports of 19,000 metric tons, after a record 26,000 tons in the previous year, with a concomitant higher price; in 2011 the harvest was 120,000 tons, of which 20% was exported to Europe. Madagascar has a dominant share of 70% of the European market at Christmas and New Year. From 2000 production of cinnamon (canella) and pepper decreased, and production of seed cotton also declined from a peak of around 50,000 tons in 1986 to 12,500 tons in 2004. Sisal is a minor export crop, which was adversely affected for a number of years by synthetic substitutes; it is particularly vulnerable to drought in the south.

Annual production has ranged widely and was 18,000 tons in 2010. There are five sugar factories, four of which were rehabilitated in the late 1980s with French aid, and the fifth, built with Chinese assistance, began operating in 1987. The state-owned company Société Siramamy Malagasy managed all the factories, but the sugar estates have suffered from under-investment. The EU agreed in early 2008 to finance a €1.5m. project to rehabilitate the industry, to which it committed a further €8.4m. under its current development programme, although it subsequently suspended funding following the March 2009 coup. While two new factories were due to have opened in early 2009, with production expected to reach the extra 25,000 tons allowed under a revised EU export quota, the existing factories suspended production and had substantial salary payments outstanding until December 2009; further progress in the sector may depend on a possible privatization. There is also some potential in biofuels, with two British companies involved in the planting of jatropha, an oil-producing plant; one company, Jason World Energy, built a US $19m. plant in 2008–09, and production commenced in 2010, although demand has diminished considerably and output was limited. One of the British companies in 2012 also reported disappointing results from its jatropha project. Groundnuts, bananas, pineapples, coconuts, butter beans and tobacco are also grown on a small scale. In late 2009 Madagascar resumed exports of tobacco after a hiatus of 30 years.

There is little in the way of a forestry sector, even though FAO estimated that in 2005 the country's 28.9m. ha of forest and other wooded land made up just over one-half of the total area of the country. The majority of forest products are the wood and charcoal that generate over 80% of domestic fuel consumption, and contribute heavily to deforestation. Only about 20% of the land area is covered by primary forests, which remain under threat despite an increase in reforestation and despite recent research that suggests a stabilization; deforestation increased by 86% in 2000–05 compared with the previous five-year period, the highest rate of any tropical country. Debt conversion schemes for environmental projects have helped, as did President Marc Ravalomanana's commitment in 2003 to triple the country's total protected territory to 6m. ha by 2008. By 2006 good progress had already been made, with 1.1m. ha added to protected schemes in that year, following a similar total in 2005. The development of the country's national parks was also closely associated with potential for the eco-tourism sector, and was assisted by the inclusion in June 2007 of some of Madagascar's eastern forests on UNESCO's World Heritage list. The illegal shipping of wood is a serious problem, which has been exacerbated since the 2009 political crisis by a spate of illegal logging—of rosewood in particular—in the Masoala and Manjegy parks in the north-east of the country, and which has continued in spite of a government ban, prompting concerns about the viability of some species. The World Bank committed in June 2011 to provide US $52m. of funding for Madagascar's national parks.

Madagascar has sizeable potential in its coastal resources, with FAO indicating that the country's fishing production rose from under 20,000 tons in 1950 to 159,100 tons in 2007. However, this figure declined to 131,300 tons in 2008 although it was a little higher in 2011, at 135,700 tons. Sea fishing by coastal fishermen was industrialized with assistance from Japan and France. Shrimp-fishing expanded considerably in the 1990s to become an important source of export revenue, valued at US $155m. in 2003. However, concerns regarding over-fishing and environmental damage intensified as the sector reached a maximum sustainable level, and there was a major decline in shrimp catches in 2005; by 2008 the total shrimp catch was under 4,000 tons. However, fish-farming is a rapidly growing industry, with some 50,000 ha of suitable territory in swamps along the western coast; production was 6,886 tons in 2011. Vessels from EU countries, Japan and Russia fish by agreement for tuna and prawns in Madagascar's exclusive maritime zone, which extends 370 km (200 nautical miles) off the coast. Illegal fishing in Malagasy waters is increasingly problematic and was estimated in 2008 to cost the country $900m. a year, but the country lacks sufficient resources to police the area. An $18m. tuna-canning complex was established as a joint venture with a French company at Antsiranana, financed predominantly by France and the European Investment Bank (EIB). The International Finance Corporation, the EIB and France also provided funds for Pêcheries de Nosy Bé to replace three trawlers and to modernize the shrimp-processing plant at Hellville in the north-west. In late 2008 a government programme, which received French financial support, was launched to boost the €100m. prawn industry by controlling over-fishing and reducing fuel costs. A report in January 2012 indicated that fish catches in 1950–2008 had in fact been double the size officially recorded, helping to explain the decline in stocks.

Madagascar had an estimated 9.9m. head of cattle in 2010, according to FAO, but they are generally regarded as an indication of wealth rather than as a source of income, making the development of a commercial beef sector difficult. The price of zebu cattle was estimated to have declined by one-half in the two years to 2010 owing to the economic pressures in the south of the country. There is some ranching, and an estimated 150,500 metric tons of beef and veal were produced commercially in 2010, according to FAO. Some beef is exported, but volumes have declined in recent years to about 800 tons per year, despite an EU quota of 11,000 tons. There is a pressing need to revive veterinary services, to improve marketing and to rehabilitate abattoirs, partly to meet EU import standards. Live animals and some canned corned beef are exported to African countries, the Gulf states and Indian Ocean islands. There are increasing numbers of dairy cattle, estimated at some 500,000 in 2004. FAO also estimated that in 2010 there were 1.3m. goats, 730,000 sheep, and 1.4m. pigs, with about 55,000 tons of pig meat produced, equivalent to just under one-quarter of total meat production.

INDUSTRY

Industry accounted for an estimated 16.6% of Madagascar's GDP in 2011 and employed about 3.4% of the engaged labour force in 2005. Industrial GDP increased at an average annual rate of 2.7% in 2001–09. The sector's GDP grew by 19.2% in 2008, but declined by 8.5% in 2009. The island's major industrial centres, other than mines, are located in the High Plateaux or near the port of Toamasina. Food-processing accounts for a significant portion of all industrial value added, while brewing, paper and soap are also important sectors. Textile production declined by one-half between 1990 and 2000, largely owing to illegal imports, but then expanded due to the success of the export-processing zones (EPZs) under the preferential terms of the USA's African Growth and Opportunity Act (AGOA), before decreasing again following Madagascar's exclusion from the Act in 2010 owing to US disapproval of the regime change in 2009. Textile exports to the USA amounted to US $279m. in 2008, one-half of the country's total, but declined substantially in 2009 and 2010, when only five of the 30 firms that previously exported under AGOA continued to do so. The textile industry increased exports by 20% in 2011, although the prospects for 2012 were lower given the weakness in key European markets.

There are cement plants at Mahajanga and Toamasina, and production of cement has grown massively, from only 50,000 metric tons in 2001 to approximately 410,000 tons in 2010. The cement plant owned by Madagascar Long Cimenterie (Maloci) of China has a capacity of 360,000 tons; the company was producing cement at the rate of 300,000 tons per year in 2010. Domestic cement demand was estimated to be about 500,000 tons with the mining industry an important customer. Government plans for a series of construction projects from 2010 may provide a stimulus to demand for cement. A fertilizer plant at Toamasina, which began operations in 1985, produces some 90,000 tons per year of urea- and ammonia-based fertilizers. Other industries include the manufacture of wood products and furniture, agricultural machinery, and the processing of agricultural products, especially tobacco.

A number of EPZs were established in the 1980s and attracted foreign investors, particularly from South-East Asia, Mauritius and France. In 2004 1,276 companies employed an estimated 115,000 people in the EPZs, although textile companies were a significant part and their number of employees was initially reduced by an estimated 10,000 in 2005. Development of the manufacturing sector overall has been hampered by poor infrastructure and high transportation costs. The political crisis in 2009 and 2010 discouraged investors and led to a number of businesses closing, although major projects in the mining sector were more affected by cost overruns and weaker commodity prices. Nevertheless, Sipromad planned a US $10m. investment in the tobacco industry during 2011–14, in partnership with British American Tobacco; in the mobile telephony sector, Zain (owned by Bharti Airtel of India) planned to spend $50m. to increase its market share to 50%; and Phoenix Breweries of Mauritius, the 40% shareholder in Nouvelles Brasseries de Madagascar, set a target of taking a 25% share of the Malagasy beer market after finally launching its Skol brand.

Madagascar was ranked 137th out of 183 countries in the World Bank's *Doing Business 2012* report, and rose to 100th out of 182 nations in Transparency International's 2011 corruption index.

MINING

Madagascar has sizeable deposits of a wide range of minerals, and their exploitation had been on the increase, with higher commodity prices helping to offset the expense of reaching their remote location, until the recent political crisis deterred investors.

Chromite, graphite and mica are all exported, as are small quantities of semi-precious stones such as topaz, garnet and amethyst. The main deposits of chromium ore at Andriamena produced over 100,000 metric tons in 2005, while the reopened Bemanevika pit (with its reserves of 2.2m. tons) was expected to underpin production in future years; severe destocking by the main consumers of the product in the People's Republic of China and Japan reduced demand in 2009, but output almost doubled, to 90,000 tons in 2010. Graphite output declined from 15,000 tons in 2004 to an average of 5,000 tons per year between 2005 and 2010 as a result of the increasing costs of petroleum products used for drying. Processing costs also increased because of declining grades at local graphite deposits as higher-grade materials were depleted. Production of mica, which had reached 1,138 tons in 1997, had declined to 358 tons in 2009, but increased dramatically, to 2,069 tons, in 2010.

One major project is Rio Tinto's ilmenite (titanium ore) mine near to Fort Dauphin (Tolagnaro) in the south-east, operated through its subsidiary QIT Madagascar Minerals Ltd. Construction of the mining facilities together with a deep-sea, multi-purpose port facility at Ehoala commenced in 2006, but ran well over budget, costing an estimated US $1,100m., almost twice the amount initially expected. The company made its first shipment from the new facility in May 2009 and exported 160,000 metric tons in that year, followed by 287,000 tons in 2010. The production forecast for 2011 was 473,000 tons, and its potential annual capacity of 750,000 metric tons, due to be reached in 2013, would equate to 10% of global output per year. The project should bring substantial revenues to the Malagasy Government, which has a 20% holding, and stimulate economic development in the south-east of the country. However, there have been considerable concerns over the social impact of the development, and over its environmental impact on such a fragile landscape. A separate $150m. ilmenite project near Toliara was being studied by Madagascar Resources, which merged in mid-2010 with the Australian company Malagasy Minerals, while a Chinese state company, Mainland Mining Ltd, started production in 2007 at a site near Toamasina that was expected to produce 100,000 tons in 2008.

The other major current project is the exploitation of nickel and cobalt deposits at Ambatovy in the Moramanga area. The operator, Sherritt International of Canada, announced in April 2011 that it expected to be in partial production within a few months, although the start of production was later postponed to 2012. The mine is projected to reach full production (60,000 metric tons of nickel and 5,600 tons of cobalt per year) after 2013, with operating costs expected to be among the lowest in the world. A consortium led by Korea Resources Corpn took a 27.5% stake in the mine through the provision of US $1,200m. of finance and will receive one-half of the planned output of the mine for the first 15 years (South Korea is the world's fourth largest consumer of nickel). Sumitomo also has a 27.5% stake, while Sherritt (which acquired in 2007 the initiator of the mine, another Canadian company, Dynatec) holds 40%. The cost of the project has been frequently revised upwards, now reaching a figure of $5,500m. Upon completion, it was expected to contribute some $85m. per year to Madagascar's gross national product, and to have a life of 28 years.

Other mineral projects include the eventual exploitation of an estimated 100m. metric tons of bauxite at Manantenina in the south-east of the country, in which Alcan has been involved since 2006 and which involves an Australian company, Aziana, which had a stock market listing in November 2011 and is also developing a gold mine at Alakamisy. The mining of substantial coal deposits missed initial production targets in 2010, although Pan African Mining (acquired by Asia Thai Mining in 2008) has forecast annual production of 3m.–5m. tons. Lemur Resources, another company that had a stock market listing in the second half of 2011, reported that its Imaloto project in south-west Madagascar had deposits of thermal coal greater than the 175m. tons previously estimated. A Thai company, PTT, bought for $50m the two-thirds' share of Red Island Minerals in its Sakoa coal project, from which it plans to double production to 22m. tons by 2020.

A number of companies are developing platinum projects, including Jubilee Platinum, which has 100,000 ha of concessions in a deferred joint venture with Impala Platinum in north-central and south-eastern Madagascar and which was due to start a drill test programme in April 2010. There is also potential in copper, in uranium and in gold, for which minimal official production has been recorded, but which unofficially provided an estimated 2 tons–3 tons annually. There are deposits of iron ore at Bekisopa in the south, being developed by Cline Mining Corpn, and at Soalala, near Mahajanga in the west, where a Chinese joint venture led by Wuhan Iron & Steel paid US $100m. in May 2010 for the right to mine reserves estimated at up to 800m. tons. There are further deposits of heavy minerals and Tantalus Rare Earths of Germnay has a project in the north-west, which it estimated contained 46,000 tons of oxides potentially worth over $8,000m. Energizer Resources of Canada also has a joint venture with Malagasy Minerals in rare earths.

There was a discovery of sapphires north of Fort-Dauphin in the early 1990s, and again in early 1997 in the north of the island, where the arrival of thousands of unofficial miners caused serious damage to the Ankarana nature reserve. A further discovery at Ilakaka in the south in 1998 prompted another influx and aroused the interest of foreign investors. Sapphires worth some US $100m. were reported to have been mined by early 1999, although little tax income came to the country, and the Government ordered the suspension of sapphire-mining, pending the results of studies into the effects of exploitation on the environment. However, unauthorized mining continued and one-half of the world's sapphires are now estimated to come from Madagascar. Unauthorized exports of gems led the Government to ban all exports in early 2008. There are plans for commercial exploitation of sapphires. Rubies are mined at Vatomandry on the east coast, and emeralds at Manajary and elsewhere, while there is potential in diamond-mining.

In early 2000 a new mining code came into force, setting out the legal and environmental framework for the sector. Most mining companies signed up to the Extractive Industries Transparency Initiative in 2012. Investment in the mining sector has been substantial and has strengthened the country's economy and currency. Royalties and fees are still at a low level, but as production increases they should rise and could reach the Government's target of US $15m. and $45m., respectively, in 2012, if mineral exports rise to $300m. A degree of uncertainty over a review of mining contracts by the new regime has deterred investors, although the major investment into Soalala is one indication of continued Chinese interest.

ENERGY

Madagascar's prospects for reducing fuel imports were improved by the development of hydroelectric power. The Andekaleka hydroelectric scheme, which began operations in 1982, supplies the regions of Antananarivo and Antsirabé, as well as the Andriamena chromite mine. There are seven hydroelectric stations, which provided an estimated 70% of electricity production in 2009, while the remainder came from thermal installations. The EIB has provided €25m. to cover one-half of the cost of an expansion to the hydroelectric scheme, and in late 2011 the Bank of Africa was involved in the proposed financing of a US $200m. project due to start production in 2015. However, fuel wood and charcoal are estimated still to provide 84% of the country's total energy needs. Petroleum products account for 11% of energy consumption and the remaining 5% is provided by electricity. Fuel imports accounted for between 13.8% and 18.7% of total merchandise imports during 2003–07, after a peak of 34.2% in 2002 during the political crisis; fuel accounted for 15.2% of imports in 2010. Madagascar has sizeable potential onshore and offshore petroleum reserves, which should vastly improve the country's economic position. In February 2012 the Government also announced a project to generate 50 MW of electricity from wind turbines, at a cost of some $80m.

In the 1980s several foreign companies signed concession agreements with the Government to prospect in a number of areas, particularly in the Morandava basin in western Madagascar. The war in the Persian (Arabian) Gulf in 1990–91 stimulated interest among Western petroleum companies in locating deposits of petroleum outside the Gulf region, although only deposits of oil and natural gas regarded as non-commercial were found. Contracts for further exploration were granted in 1997, in 1999 and in mid-2004, while work continued on deposits of heavy petroleum at Tsimororo and on the Bemolanga oil sands. Madagascar Oil initially developed the Bemolanga project, but in September 2008 Total announced that it was to acquire a 60% stake by funding the US $30m. initial appraisal stages and additional drilling; there are reserves of an estimated 10,000m. barrels of oil but production was not expected to commence before 2019. High international petroleum prices in 2006 and advances in deep-sea technology improved the potential profitability of reserves, which helped the Government's auction for drilling rights. Official estimates of offshore basin reserves were 500m. barrels, although exact amounts remain unknown. By July 2006 the Government had awarded nine prospecting licences to companies from the People's Republic of China, France, Norway, South Korea, the United Kingdom and the USA; a further auction in November was less successful, yet still brought new entrants. In 2008 a Chinese consortium announced plans to develop a $300m. onshore block, while Niko Resources of Canada announced that it was to obtain a 75% stake in EnerMad's offshore block by funding a $125m. seismic programme. Exxon Mobil and Sterling Energy (both of the USA) planned to start drilling at the end of 2010 at their deep-water Sifaka prospect at Ampasindava, where estimated reserves totalled 1,200m. barrels. Initial projections estimated that Madagascar could produce 60,000 barrels per day by 2010, but the recent political crisis has affected investment into the sector. In October 2010 the Government postponed an auction for a further 90 exploration blocks, and in December Madagascar Oil was involved in a dispute relating to unpaid tax, amid moves by the Government to buy back four of the company's exploration blocks, with no indication of a possible price. The dispute was resolved in the second half of 2011 and the company raised $26m. in February 2012 to help fund development of its Tsimiroro field.

In 2005 the Government awarded a two-year contract for the management of the national electricity and water utility Jiro sy Rano Malagasy (JIRAMA) to the German company Lahmeyer International. However, the management company experienced extensive financial problems, exacerbated by high rates of inflation and petroleum prices and by the depreciation of the Malagasy currency. The World Bank offered emergency funding of US $5m. for JIRAMA to maintain operations and a further $10m. in 2006, to help restore a minimum level of operational and financial performance, and to reflect support for the Government's decision to increase prices ahead of the presidential election. In 2005 two tariff increases were implemented, raising electricity prices by 76%. This was consolidated in 2006 with a further increase of 15%, and an increase of 20% in water charges. The Lahmeyer contract was not extended after its two-year term. JIRAMA's problems continued in 2007 when power shortages and cuts disrupted industrial production and contributed to unrest in several cities. Reforms are still needed to meet growing demand (the number of subscribers increased on average by 8% per year between 1996 and 2005) and to widen access to electricity, limited to only 24% of the population in 2005 and to barely 5% of those living outside the major cities, as well as to supply the growing energy-intensive mining sector, although the Sherritt nickel project has financed its own 25-MW plant. Electricity and water prices were increased by 15% in October 2008. Despite these increases, JIRAMA made a substantial loss, equivalent to 0.3% of GDP, in 2008. The new Government, which assumed power in March 2009, introduced a 10% reduction in electricity prices in May. JIRAMA lost 127,000m. ariary (£36m.) in 2011 and again raised its prices in early 2012.

TRANSPORT

Madagascar's mountainous topography has hindered the development of adequate communications, and the limited infrastructure is prone to cyclone damage, making even major routes impassable in bad weather. In June 2000 the Government started a motorway and road development programme funded by the World Bank and the EU. In 2002 the EU pledged US $10m. for the reconstruction of bridges destroyed during the political crisis, and in 2003 Japan committed to assist the building of several bridges and a bypass road in the capital, which was opened in early 2007. Improving and integrating the transport infrastructure was a major feature of the Ravalomanana Government's Madagascar Action Plan (MAP), which aimed to increase regularly maintained national roads from 5,700 km out of nearly 50,000 km in 2005 to 12,000 km by 2012, and to boost rural roads from 1,300 km to 13,000 km over the same period, giving two-thirds of communes permanent access to all-weather roads. Road projects have been particularly affected by the suspension of international aid that resulted from the regime change in 2009.

In 2009 there were 854 km of railways. Three lines totalling 673 km in the north of the country ran from Antananarivo to the port of Toamasina and to Antsirabé, and from Moramanga to the rice-growing region of Lake Alaotra, while a fourth line in the south was 163 km in length and ran between Fianarantsoa and the east coast port of Manakara. Comazar of South Africa was awarded the operating concession for the Madarail Ltd northern railway network in 2001, including access to the port at Toamasina. Comazar committed to invest 150m. French francs over five years to upgrade the network, and in 2003 the EIB granted a €11m. loan towards its rehabilitation, completing the privatization process. Tonnage doubled in the five years to 2008 and was expected to increase further with the delivery of five new engines that year. The southern railway suffered heavy cyclone damage in 2000 and did not attract a sufficient bid at the end of 2005 for the concession to operate it, and instead Madarail was awarded a two-year management contract.

Domestic air services are important to Madagascar, on account of its size, difficult terrain and the poor quality of road and rail networks. There are 54 airports, of which 32 have scheduled commercial services. The main international airport is at Antananarivo. The Government now owns 94% of the national airline, Air Madagascar, which lost its monopoly on domestic services in 1995; few competitors subsequently emerged, although Air Transport et Transit Régional started a regional operation, which was suspended in 2008. On international routes, Air Madagascar in effect operates a duopoly with Air France; it has improved its finances, despite the high level of fuel prices, and has introduced new flights on international routes while also reducing its domestic network. The possible privatization of Air Madagascar was delayed owing to outstanding debts, and the company was rumoured to be close to bankruptcy in early 2009 as a result of the global economic slowdown and the impact on tourism of the country's own political crisis. A project to double capacity at the main international airport at an estimated cost of US $132m. was started in 2008 but was later suspended. In April 2011 the EU announced in a review of airlines that it would ban two Air Madagascar Boeing 767-300 aircraft from EU airspace due to serious safety shortcomings, which forced the company to adjust its schedule; it subsequently leased replacement aircraft and appointed a new chief executive. The airline remains on the EU's blacklist, but will benefit from leasing two Airbus A-340s from Air France.

Toamasina and Mahajanga, the principal seaports, have suffered from a lack of storage space and equipment, but are receiving new investment in part financed by a tax on the importing of containers that was introduced in 2000. Toamasina port handles about 70% of Madagascar's foreign trade and was in the process of being enlarged when it was destroyed by a cyclone in 1986; it suffered further serious damage from cyclones in 1994, in 2003 and in 2007, which also damaged Mahajanga. Toamasina port is independently managed by the Philippine company International Container Terminal Services, Inc, which in July 2007 completed the US $30m. first phase of its modernization programme. Other ports are operated by the Malagasy Ports Authority, which in 2006 upgraded three of the country's other significant ports (Mahajanga, Toliary and Antsiranana/Nosy-Bé) to prepare them for similar private concessions and investment. Coastal shipping is conducted mainly by private companies. The Government announced plans in 2007 to rehabilitate the Pangalanes canal, which runs for 600 km near the east coast from Toamasina to Farafangana.

TOURISM

Tourist arrivals reached 160,071 in 2000, when tourism receipts totalled US $116m. and made the sector the country's second most important source of foreign currency earnings. Activity in the sector was seriously affected in 2002 by the political and economic turmoil following the disputed presidential election of December 2001, although it recovered well in 2003 with 139,000 arrivals and improved again in 2004 with 228,785 arrivals. Revenue from tourism totalled $232m. in 2006, when the number of tourists was 312,000, an increase of 14% on the 277,000 arrivals in 2005, helped by marketing efforts in France and Italy, the leading sources of visitors. The number of tourists increased again in 2007, by 11% to 344,348. Even though cyclone damage affected business in early 2008, the number of arrivals in that year rose to 375,010. With its unique biodiversity and strikingly varied scenery, Madagascar has considerable potential for the development of eco-tourism, which should be helped by the Government's commitment to expand the country's protected areas and the improving infrastructure. New hotels have opened, although foreign investors have had difficulty in acquiring full ownership of land. The political crisis has had a huge impact on tourist arrivals, which declined by 57%, to 162,687, in 2009. Hotel occupancy levels decreased to as low as 10% in the first half of the year, and many establishments were forced to close temporarily or to lay off staff. With a degree of stability and with less stringent advice from foreign governments to their citizens regarding travel to Madagascar, there was an improvement from the second half of 2009. The Ministry of Tourism and Crafts set a target of 255,000 visitors for 2011; the total for the first half of the year was a little over 100,000, which was an increase of 16% on 2010, as was the nine-month figure of 165,000. The government target for 2012 was 245,000 visitors.

EXTERNAL TRADE AND BALANCE OF PAYMENTS

Imports increased at an unhealthy rate for the economy in the 1980s, owing to the official policy of industrialization and an overriding emphasis on investment. As the balance of payments became increasingly unfavourable, the Government was obliged to yield to pressure from the IMF, the World Bank, and Western aid donors and creditors to liberalize trade and to adjust the Malagasy franc exchange rate. The reforms succeeded in reducing the external current account deficit, as a result of improved export earnings. However, the deficit continued to fluctuate and by 2005 it had increased to $592m.

In 2000 there was a deficit of US $283m. on the current account of the balance of payments, which increased to $626m. in 2005 and an estimated $890m. in 2007. Madagascar has, since 2004, been a member of the Southern African Development Community (SADC), which has plans for the establishment of a customs union and of a common market in 2015; Madagascar currently runs a sizeable trade deficit, with its exports to other members of SADC only one-eighth of the value of its imports from them. In 2010 Madagascar's total imports—swelled as in 2009 by the importation of equipment for mining projects—were estimated at $1,958m., while the country's exports totalled around $1,412m. The principal sources of imports in that year were China (13%), Thailand (12%), Bahrain (7%) and France (7%); the main products were capital goods, consumer goods and petroleum. The dominant markets for exports were France (29%), the USA (20%), Germany (6%) and China (4%); the main products included vanilla, shellfish, cotton goods and chromite.

ECONOMIC POLICY, PLANNING AND AID

In November 2000 Madagascar participated in the formation of a free trade area between nine (subsequently increased to 11) of the 20 countries of the Common Market for Eastern and Southern Africa (COMESA), which eliminated all tariff barriers, and in December the International Development Association (IDA) and the IMF agreed to support a comprehensive debt reduction package under the enhanced initiative for heavily indebted poor countries (HIPC), amounting to US $1,500m., or 40% of total debt outstanding.

In March 2001 the IMF approved a new three-year loan of US $103m. under the Poverty Reduction and Growth Facility (PRGF), with $15m. available immediately, following the successful completion of the first three-year programme in December 2000. The 'Paris Club' of official creditors consequently agreed an interim settlement that directly cancelled $161m. of debt and rescheduled $93m. over a period of 23 years, with a six-year period of grace. Textile exports, particularly to the USA, had increased substantially during the period of an IMF-supported programme, and Madagascar's eligibility for the textile provisions of AGOA, also approved in March 2001, allowed duty-free access to the US market until 2004, leading to further rises. The establishment within the EPZs of information technology firms (processing archives and data for large foreign firms) was also a positive development.

However, in response to the political and economic disruption that followed the disputed presidential election in December 2001 (see Recent History), international financial organizations froze the nation's assets and the central bank was closed, rendering the country unable to service its debts. The six months of economic blockades, destruction of infrastructure and general strikes meant that the economy had largely ceased to function. It was estimated that between 150,000 and 500,000 jobs were lost in the economic crisis, and the loss of foreign investment was sizeable, if hard to quantify.

In July 2002 donors pledged some US $2,300m. of aid over four years; the IMF and World Bank accounted for one-half of this figure while France and the USA granted aid of $150m. and $100m., respectively. In its economic programme, the new Government emphasized its commitment to good governance and its plans for private sector development, including long-awaited legislation on foreign investment in mining. The international aid allowed the country to repay the arrears that had accumulated on its external payments during the crisis, and from August the foreign exchange markets reopened, with the currency settling to a relatively stable level following an initial depreciation. The IMF disbursed a $100m. Structural Adjustment Recovery Credit in October and a $50m. Emergency Economic Recovery Credit in November, as well as loans towards reforming public sector management and developing the private sector. Following legislative elections in December 2002 (in which year real GDP declined by 12.7%), the Fund approved the disbursement of $15m. under the PRGF, extending the arrangement until November 2004, and granted a further $4m. in interim assistance under the HIPC initiative.

In early 2003, despite comparative political stability, the social and economic situation in Madagascar declined further, owing to a long drought and some cyclone damage. However, France, Germany and the United Kingdom cancelled further significant amounts of Malagasy debt, and in June the IMF granted an additional US $15.9m. under the PRGF. From the end of July the country replaced the Malagasy franc with its former currency, the ariary; the two currencies were initially intended to circulate simultaneously until November 2004, but this was subsequently extended to 2006; accounts were changed on 1 January 2005, at a rate of 1 ariary to 5 francs.

A depreciation of the currency in 2004, together with further severe cyclone damage and high international petroleum prices, had an inflationary effect on the economy, leading to national discontent and international concern. However, the performance of the EPZs, the busy construction sector and the improving agricultural industry all supported the rate of real GDP growth. In response to the severe cyclones in March, the IMF immediately released US $35m. in funds and extended the PRGF until March 2005. In July 2004 the World Bank granted a Poverty Reduction Support Credit of $88m. and a credit of $37m. under the Poverty Reduction Strategy Paper (PRSP) programme. In August the EU approved two grants to the country amounting to €165m. for development programmes in the southern provinces in 2005–11. In mid-2004 President Jacques Chirac of France announced, during an informal visit to Madagascar, that France would forgive the remaining public debt owed to it by the African country, which amounted to some €70m., once the country had met the conditions of the IMF's HIPC initiative. Madagascar was admitted as a member of SADC in August. Meanwhile, as a member of COMESA, Madagascar started to participate in a customs union operational from December. In November 2004, following the successful fulfilment of the criteria of the HIPC initiative in the preceding month, the 'Paris Club' of creditors once more restructured the country's debt, with many participants joining France in cancelling the whole amount owed to them. The overall debt was scheduled to decrease by some $836m., and the ratio of debt service to exports of goods and services was estimated to have decreased to 6% in 2004, compared with 32% in 1990. Subsequently, Madagascar also successfully completed the PRGF. The economy had withstood challenging factors in 2004 and grown at a rate of 5.3%, compared with 9.8% in 2003.

In April 2005 Madagascar was the first country to negotiate an agreement with the USA under its Millennium Challenge Account programme, whereby some US $110m. was to be disbursed over five years. In July, following a summit of the Group of Eight leading industrialized countries (G8) held in Gleneagles, United Kingdom, Madagascar qualified as a primary candidate for debt cancellation, owing to its success in the HIPC schedule, and received a second Poverty Reduction Support Credit, of $80m., from the World Bank; a grant of $129m. under an IDA 'integrated growth poles' project, to stimulate economic growth in the three EPZs; and a further IDA credit of $30m. for health sector projects to combat HIV/AIDS (which remains at a low level of incidence). In 2005 the economic growth rate was 4.6%, which was lower than forecast owing to substantial fuel price increases exacerbated by inconsistencies in power supply from JIRAMA. The ending of the textile industry's international Multi-fibre Arrangement in January 2005, which led to a surge of Chinese goods entering the US market, had a negative impact on the industrial sector, particularly the EPZs. However, agriculture performed better than in preceding years as the country escaped severe cyclones, with the primary sector accounting for 27.9% of GDP. Foreign direct investment doubled in 2005 from the previous year.

In 2006 the Government formulated the MAP for 2007–12, to succeed the PRSP and to pursue the World Bank's Millennium Development Goals of halving poverty by 2015. In mid-2006 the World Bank approved a new PRGF arrangement of US $81m. over three years, in support of the Government's own economic programme for 2006–08. Also in mid-2006 the French telecommunications company Alcatel was awarded the tender to construct the $205m. East African Submarine Cable System, linking countries including Madagascar via 9,900 km of high-performance fibre-optic cable along the seabed between South Africa and Sudan. This project was completed in early 2010 and should greatly reduce communication costs in the region.

Madagascar has had one of the lowest tax revenue-to-GDP ratios in the world, at around 10%, although there was an increase, to 11.5%, in 2006 and a further improvement, to 12.5%, in 2008. The combination of higher duties in some areas (such as on petroleum and diesel in 2006), measures to improve the administration of value-added tax (VAT) and a simplified tax structure should help to raise the figure to nearer 15%. GDP increased by an estimated 4.9% in 2006, but this was still not sufficient to significantly reduce poverty in the country, particularly if the rate of population growth continued at around 3%. Necessary reductions in expenditure were in part offset by the benefits of the Multilateral Debt Relief Initiative, which amounted to 0.6% of GDP. The EU's approval of the Malagasy Government's policies prompted an increased allocation of funds under the ninth programme of the Fonds Européens de Développement (FED) and a commitment of €462m. under the 10th FED. The budget deficit remained at around 5% of GDP.

In 2007 the World Bank and the IMF confirmed their support for the country and its prudent macroeconomic policies, agreeing a further US $140m. per year for 2007–11 under the Strategic Country Assistance programme and $69m. of finance for investment in health, mines, transport, telecommunications and governance. A number of UN agencies agreed in July 2007 to provide $310m. to support the MAP in 2008–11, while France continued to be the largest bilateral donor, promising €250m. in 2007–10 for major infrastructure projects and micro-finance. The EU increased its allocation under the 10th FED to €588m., of which 40% was scheduled for improving the road network. Continued problems of power supply in cities such as Antsiranana and Toliary affected industry and prompted civil unrest. The Government's constitutional reforms included plans to increase the role of the communes in economic development, with a target of trebling local tax collection and giving the communes 10% of the total budget by 2012, compared with 1.5% in 2005. The severe cyclone season during late 2006 and early 2007 caused extensive damage to infrastructure and crops. There were further damaging cyclones in early 2008, the worst of which was Ivan in February, which affected over one-half of the country's regions, killed more than 100 people, and damaged rice and other crops; the combined cost of cyclones in the 2008 season was estimated at $333m.

The economy was calculated to have grown at a rate of 6.2% in 2007, during which year the Government simplified the country's tax system while again emphasizing revenue collection. In 2008 the rate of economic growth was estimated at 7.3%. The increase in public expenditure from 17.8% to 22% of GDP in 2008 contributed to a public deficit of 4.5%, compared with 2.6% in 2007. Despite increased energy prices and the devastating effect of cyclones, the rate of inflation remained relatively modest, at about 7.5% at the end of 2007, although the Government revised its expectation for 2008 to 10%. In the second half of the year local fuel prices only declined by 7%, despite a 69% decrease on world markets, and in mid-2009 the rate of inflation stood at 10%, with the depreciation of the ariary by about one-quarter against the US dollar adding to inflationary pressures. Increased investment in the mining sector contributed to a strong currency, but the ariary then weakened in 2009 as a result of the political crisis and the resultant reduction in investment and tourism. The country's success in improving its image under the Ravalomanana administration was reflected in an improvement from 151st to 144th position in the World Bank's 2009 *Doing Business* report.

In early 2008 the IMF completed further reviews of Madagascar's economic performance and allowed the country to draw down a further US $25m. of low-interest loans, while in June the World Bank approved its $50m. Poverty Reduction Support Credit. The USA allocated €22m. to Madagascar for 2008 through the United States Agency for International Development (USAID) and the Millennium Challenge Corporation (MCC), of which €17m. was for rural development and

€5m. for the environment. The World Bank agreed in October to provide $30m. of additional funding for rural development, while the UN approved $19m. to boost agricultural production.

The Government increased its focus on the key issue of water supply in 2008, creating a new Ministry of Water and allocating, with the support of the African Development Bank, 140,000m. ariary to a variety of regional projects, while the country was also one of three beneficiaries of a new US $60m. Global Sanitation Fund. In the second half of 2008 President Ravalomanana appealed for an extra €3,000m. from donors, or twice the then level, to enable the Government to fulfil its targets under the MAP. However, restrictions on aid started with the suspension of some $35m. of payments at the end of 2008 while the IMF reviewed some issues in the Government's finances, and continued with the early suspension of aid by countries such as Norway in protest against the regime change in March 2009, while the evacuation of expatriate staff disrupted aid programmes. The EU announced that it would not commence any new projects in Madagascar, affecting $180m. worth of road rehabilitation works; the World Bank suspended payments to its projects in March; and the MCC terminated in May its $110m. grant, although it had already run for four of its five years, during which it had disbursed $85m. In April the UN announced a 'flash appeal' to raise $36m. to help feed some 2.6m. urban dwellers and 400,000 affected by food insecurity in the south, where low levels of rainfall had again affected crop yields; however, in July the UN reduced the appeal to $22m., one-half of which it had already received.

The Malagasy economy remained surprisingly resilient during the first year of the political crisis, due to both the financial stability engendered by strict economic policies and the increased level of food production. GDP declined in 2009, however, by an estimated 3.7%. There were reductions in income from tourism, textiles and shrimp-fishing, while the construction industry, which had accounted for about one-fifth of the economic growth in 2003–08, contracted by 40%. Government finances remained under pressure throughout 2009, despite improved revenue collection and a lower level of debt interest. Tax receipts for the year were 85% of a reduced target, and customs revenues were only 65% of their target; there was a sharp decline in tourism-related revenue and in trade, compounded by strikes at the main port of Toamasina. Populist moves to reduce prices, such as a 10% decrease in electricity costs as of May and subsidizing rice to 500 ariary per kg, were costly. Job losses in 2009 reached 280,000 in October and strike action increased, while the ending of the AGOA incentives for the textile industry from December led to the closure of many factories. Most aid remained suspended, although humanitarian aid continued; the Government received 2,000m. ariary in 2009, just one-sixth of the projected amount, and in 2010 the USA agreed to provide some US $150m. of aid for food and health. The Government sought finance and investment from new sources, such as Saudi Arabia, while the $100m. Chinese purchase of rights to the Soalala iron ore prospect in May 2010 provided a crucial injection of money. Declining revenues have affected the country, and the World Bank estimated that government expenditure was only 12% of GDP in 2010, one-third lower than in 2008 and one-half of the perceived optimal level. The economy was estimated to have contracted by a further 1% in 2010.

The Government's economic forecast for 2011 was for growth of 2.8%, which was unlikely to be reached even with the Ambatovy project, a state-funded construction programme (including £30m. planned on social housing) and the resumption of tourism. Indeed, revised data indicated that growth had in fact been 0.7%. Forbes judged Madagascar to be the world's worst economy in 2011, based on a survey of 177 countries with adequate three-year data. The government forecast in December 2011 was for growth in 2012 of 2%, this figure already having been downgraded from a previous level of 2.8% and liable to further adjustment. Nevertheless, the reduction in government spending of 25% since 2009 has at least enabled a balanced budget. Inflation has also been relatively stable, at around 9%.

There has been a sizeable reduction in foreign aid in recent years, with the UN estimating in mid-2011 that sanctions during the political crisis had cost the country US $600m. The total amount of aid declined from $626m. in 2008 to $401m. in 2009 and $447m. in 2010 (although the data excluded aid from China and most Arab countries). There were marked reductions in funding for budgetary support ($97m. to $6m. over the same period), infrastructure ($169m. to $80m.), the environment ($50m. to $16m.) and commerce ($43m. to $11m.). Nevertheless, aid for agriculture increased slightly, to $51m., while that for the social sectors rose significantly, from $180m. to $256m.: educational funding remained relatively stable, at around $60m., while the figures for health increased from $92m. to $160m. and for social protection from $26m. to $38m., with an inflow of funds from new donors. Humanitarian aid has continued, and a proportion of aid has been reclassified as such. USAID agreed in late 2011 to provide $35m. for healthcare projects primarily in the north and west of the island; the World Bank announced in February 2012 that it would resume funding for its 14 projects, which would entail $220m. by mid-2013; and the UN stated in March that it would provide $151m. for a range of programmes. The EU has indicated that it is prepared to give €100m. of aid from the second half of 2012.

The levels of poverty in Madagascar have deteriorated in recent years, reaching 76.5% in 2011 compared with 68% in 2008. There have been increased incidences of pneumonic plague, of which 310 cases that claimed 49 lives were reported in March 2011; the Government undertook a programme of mass disinfection in April that covered 28,000 families in the capital. Lack of funding has affected social conditions. The Ministries of National Education and Public Health saw their capital and non-wage expenditure contract by 70% and 20%, respectively, between 2008 and 2010, and there was a decline in net enrolment in primary schools from 83% in 2005 to 73% in 2010.

There has been an increase in the informal sector, which accounts for an estimated 67% of jobs, compared with 9% for the state and 24% for the private sector. The growth in micro-finance has aided the informal sector, and an estimated 14% of the population had access to funds in 2011, compared with 8% 2008.

Statistical Survey

Source (unless otherwise stated): Institut National de la Statistique de Madagascar, BP 485, Anosy Tana, 101 Antananarivo; tel. (20) 2227418; e-mail dridnstat@wanadoo.mg; internet www.instat.mg; Ministry of the Economy and Industry, Bâtiment Commerce, Ambohidahy, 101 Antananarivo; internet www.mepspc.gov.mg.

Area and Population

AREA, POPULATION AND DENSITY

Area (sq km)	587,295*
Population (census results)	
1974–75†	7,603,790
1–19 August 1993	
Males	6,088,116
Females	6,150,798
Total	12,238,914
Population (UN estimates at mid-year)‡	
2010	20,713,819
2011	21,315,136
2012	21,928,516
Density (per sq km) at mid-2012	37.3

* 226,756 sq miles.

† The census took place in three stages: in provincial capitals on 1 December 1974; in Antananarivo and remaining urban areas on 17 February 1975; and in rural areas on 1 June 1975.

‡ Source: UN, *World Population Prospects: The 2010 Revision*.

POPULATION BY AGE AND SEX

(UN estimates at mid-2012)

	Males	Females	Total
0–14	4,675,760	4,618,122	9,293,882
15–64	5,936,570	6,010,239	11,946,809
65 and over	320,340	367,485	687,825
Total	10,932,670	10,995,846	21,928,516

Source: UN, *World Population Prospects: The 2010 Revision*.

PRINCIPAL ETHNIC GROUPS

(estimated population, 1974)

Merina (Hova)	1,993,000	Sakalava	470,156*
Betsimisaraka	1,134,000	Antandroy	412,500
Betsileo	920,600	Antaisaka	406,468*
Tsimihety	558,100		

* 1972 figure.

PRINCIPAL TOWNS

(population at 1993 census)

Antananarivo (capital)	1,103,304	Mahajanga (Majunga)	106,780
Toamasina (Tamatave)	137,782	Toliary (Tuléar)	80,826
Antsirabé	126,062	Antsiranana (Diégo-Suarez)	59,040
Fianarantsoa	109,248		

2001 (estimated population, incl. Renivohitra and Avaradrano): Antananarivo 1,111,392.

Mid-2011 (incl. suburbs, UN estimate): Antananarivo 1,986,710 (Source: UN, *World Urbanization prospects: The 2011 Revision*).

BIRTHS AND DEATHS

	2009	2010	2011
Birth rate (per 1,000)	35.6	35.3	35.0
Death rate (per 1,000)	6.6	6.5	6.4

Source: African Development Bank.

Life expectancy (years at birth): 66.5 (males 64.9; females 68.1) in 2010 (Source: World Bank, World Development Indicators database).

ECONOMICALLY ACTIVE POPULATION

(labour force survey, '000 persons)

	2005
Agriculture, hunting and forestry	7,745.3
Fishing	99.0
Mining and quarrying	18.8
Manufacturing	267.5
Electricity, gas and water	27.5
Construction	13.0
Wholesale and retail trade; repair of motor vehicles, motor cycles and personal and household goods	470.5
Hotels and restaurants	63.9
Transport, storage and communications	86.3
Financial intermediation	4.1
Public administration and defence; compulsory social security	202.4
Education	44.5
Health and social work	9.9
Other community, social and personal service activities	517.7
Total employed	9,570.4
Unemployed	274.3
Total labour force	9,844.7
Males	4,942.2
Females	4,902.4

Source: ILO.

Mid-2012 (estimates in '000): Agriculture, etc. 7,731; Total labour force 11,188 (Source: FAO).

Health and Welfare

KEY INDICATORS

Total fertility rate (children per woman, 2010)	4.7
Under-5 mortality rate (per 1,000 live births, 2010)	62
HIV/AIDS (% of persons aged 15–49, 2009)	0.2
Physicians (per 1,000 head, 2007)	0.2
Hospital beds (per 1,000 head, 2005)	0.3
Health expenditure (2009): US $ per head (PPP)	41
Health expenditure (2009): % of GDP	4.2
Health expenditure (2009): public (% of total)	64.5
Access to water (% of persons, 2009)	46
Access to sanitation (% of persons, 2009)	15
Total carbon dioxide emissions ('000 metric tons, 2008)	1,910.5
Carbon dioxide emissions per head (metric tons, 2008)	0.1
Human Development Index (2011): ranking	151
Human Development Index (2011): value	0.480

For sources and definitions, see explanatory note on p. vi.

Agriculture

PRINCIPAL CROPS

('000 metric tons)

	2008	2009	2010
Rice, paddy	3,914	4,540	4,738
Maize	430	425	412
Potatoes	221	225	225
Sweet potatoes	903	911	919
Cassava (Manioc)	3,021	3,020	3,009
Taro (Cocoyam)*	250	240	270
Sugar cane*	2,600	3,000	3,000
Beans, dry	81	82	82
Groundnuts, in shell†	47	36	42
Coconuts	84†	73†	82*
Oil palm fruit*	21	21	21
Tomatoes*	37	44	41
Bananas*	306	282	232

—continued	2008	2009	2010
Oranges*	90	90	55
Guavas, mangoes and mangosteens	210	221*	258*
Avocados	24	18*	16*
Pineapples*	60	72	70
Cashewapple*	70	70	63
Coffee, green*	60	65	81
Vanilla*	3	3	2
Cinnamon (Canella)*	1	1	2
Cloves*	8	8	8
Sisal*	18	13	18
Tobacco, unmanufactured*	2	2	2

* FAO estimate(s).
† Unofficial figure(s).

Aggregate production ('000 metric tons, may include official, semi-official or estimated data): Total cereals 4,356 in 2008, 4,979 in 2009, 5,164 in 2010; Total roots and tubers 4,394 in 2008, 4,395 in 2009, 4,423 in 2010; Total vegetables (incl. melons) 278 in 2008, 358 in 2009, 352 in 2010; Total fruits (excl. melons) 1,035 in 2008, 1,029 in 2009, 941 in 2010.

Source: FAO.

LIVESTOCK
('000 head, year ending September, FAO estimates)

	2008	2009	2010
Cattle	9,700	9,800	9,900
Pigs	1,360	1,370	1,380
Sheep	720	725	730
Goats	1,260	1,270	1,280
Chickens	25,500	26,000	26,500
Ducks	4,000	4,100	4,200
Geese and guinea fowls	3,000	3,000	3,000
Turkeys	2,100	2,150	2,200

Source: FAO.

LIVESTOCK PRODUCTS
('000 metric tons, FAO estimates)

	2008	2009	2010
Cattle meat	150.5	150.5	150.5
Sheep meat	2.8	2.8	2.8
Goat meat	9.5	10.0	10.0
Pig meat	54.6	55.0	55.0
Chicken meat	36.8	37.5	37.5
Duck meat	11.4	11.6	11.6
Goose meat	12.6	12.6	12.6
Turkey meat	8.8	9.0	9.0
Cows' milk	549	555	703
Hen eggs	15.8	16.2	16.1
Other eggs	4.5	4.5	4.5
Honey	4.0	4.1	4.4

Source: FAO.

Forestry

ROUNDWOOD REMOVALS
('000 cubic metres, excl. bark)

	2008	2009	2010
Sawlogs, veneer logs and logs for sleepers	267*	235	271*
Pulpwood*	10	10	10
Fuel wood*	13,100	13,100	13,100
Total*	13,377	13,345	13,381

* FAO estimate(s).

Source: FAO.

SAWNWOOD PRODUCTION
('000 cubic metres, incl. railway sleepers)

	2008	2009*	2010
Coniferous (softwood)	42	42	42*
Broadleaved (hardwood)	50	50	62
Total	92	92	104*

* FAO estimate(s).

Source: FAO.

Fishing

('000 metric tons, live weight)

	2008	2009	2010
Capture*	120.5	131.3	128.8
Cichlids*	23.4	23.6	25.5
Other freshwater fishes*	4.9	4.9	5.3
Narrow-barred Spanish mackerel	6.6	6.6	6.6
Other marine fishes	44.1	52.8	49.2
Shrimps and prawns	6.7	7.3	6.5
Aquaculture*	10.8	6.1	6.9
Giant tiger prawn	8.0	3.3	4.0
Total catch*	131.3	137.4	135.7

* FAO estimates.

Note: Figures exclude aquatic plants ('000 metric tons, capture only): 0.8 in 2008–10. Also excluded are crocodiles, recorded by number rather than weight, and shells. The number of Nile crocodiles caught was: 2,640 in 2008; 2,450 in 2009; n.a. in 2010.

Source: FAO.

Mining

(metric tons)

	2008	2009	2010
Chromite*	84,000	60,000	90,000†
Salt (marine)†	75,000	75,000	75,000
Graphite (natural)‡	4,967	3,437	3,783
Mica‡	1,233	358	2,069

* Figures refer to gross weight. The estimated chromium content is 27%.
† Estimates.
‡ Figures refer to exports.

Source: US Geological Survey.

Industry

SELECTED PRODUCTS

(metric tons unless otherwise indicated)

	1999	2000	2001
Raw sugar	61,370	62,487	67,917
Beer ('000 hectolitres)	610.1	645.5	691.7
Cigarettes	3,839	4,139	4,441
Woven cotton fabrics (million sq metres)	20.4	23.3	29.6
Leather footwear ('000 pairs)	460	570	568
Plastic footwear ('000 pairs)	375	303	291
Paints	1,918	1,487	1,554
Soap	15,884	15,385	15,915
Motor spirit—petrol ('000 cu metres)	98.0	122.6	128.3
Kerosene ('000 cu metres)	65.0	65.2	75.1
Gas-diesel (distillate fuel) oil ('000 cu metres)	119.0	150.4	150.2
Residual fuel oils ('000 cu metres)	198.8	225.7	247.2
Cement	45,701	50,938	51,882
Electric energy (million kWh)*	721.3	779.8	833.9

* Production by the state-owned utility only, excluding electricity generated by industries for their own use.

2006: Raw sugar 20,000 metric tons; Electric energy 1,173m. kWh (estimate) (Source: UN Industrial Commodity Statistics Database).

2007: Raw sugar 20,000 metric tons; Electric energy 1,221m. kWh (estimate) (Source: UN Industrial Commodity Statistics Database).

2008: Raw sugar 16,000 metric tons; Electric energy 1,291m. kWh (estimate) (Source: UN Industrial Commodity Statistics Database).

Cement ('000 metric tons, estimates): 460 in 2008; 370 in 2009; 410 in 2010 (Source: US Geological Survey).

Finance

CURRENCY AND EXCHANGE RATES

Monetary Units

5 iraimbilanja = 1 ariary.

Sterling, Dollar and Euro Equivalents (31 May 2012)

£1 sterling = 3,307.96 ariary;
US $1 = 2,133.62 ariary;
€1 = 2,646.33 ariary;
10,000 ariary = £3.02 = $4.69 = €3.78.

Average Exchange Rate (ariary per US $)

2009 1,956.2
2010 2,090.0
2011 2,025.1

Note: A new currency, the ariary, was introduced on 31 July 2003 to replace the franc malgache (franc MG). The old currency was to remain legal tender until 30 November. Some figures in this survey are still given in terms of francs MG.

BUDGET

('000 million ariary, central government operations)

Revenue and grants	2008	2009*	2010†
Tax revenue	2,087.2	1,782.0	1,980.2
Non-tax revenue	49.7	80.2	268.3
Grants	548.3	192.3	173.8
Total	2,685.2	2,054.5	2,422.3

Expenditure	2008	2009*	2010†
Current expenditure	1,753.9	1,797.2	1,838.5
Budgetary expenditure	1,631.7	1,443.7	1,560.0
Wages and salaries	758.9	802.0	934.2
Other non-interest expenditure	745.5	513.2	477.9
Interest payments	127.3	128.5	147.9
Treasury operations (net)	120.0	353.2	278.5
Counterpart funds-financed operations	2.2	0.3	—
Capital expenditure	1,244.8	725.6	740.5
Total	2,998.7	2,522.8	2,579.0

* Provisional.
† Estimates.

INTERNATIONAL RESERVES

(excl. gold, US $ million at 31 December)

	2009	2010	2011
IMF special drawing rights	153.2	148.6	144.5
Foreign exchange	982.3	1,022.9	1,134.5
Total	1,135.5	1,171.6	1,279.1

Source: IMF, *International Financial Statistics*.

MONEY SUPPLY

('000 million ariary at 31 December)

	2009	2010	2011
Currency outside banks	1,010.72	1,174.61	1,477.52
Demand deposits at deposit money banks	1,392.18	1,444.17	1,768.94
Total money	2,402.91	2,618.79	3,246.47

Source: IMF, *International Financial Statistics*.

COST OF LIVING

(Consumer Price Index for Malagasy in Antananarivo; base: 2000 = 100)

	2008	2009	2010
Food	223.2	241.6	257.2
Electricity, gas and other fuels	234.7	n.a.	n.a
Clothing*	157.5	178.2	205.3
Rent	315.2	277.0	311.4
All items (incl. others)	221.4	241.2	263.5

* Including household linen.

2011: Food 292.0; All items (incl. others) 288.5.

Source: ILO.

NATIONAL ACCOUNTS

('000 million ariary at current prices)

Expenditure on the Gross Domestic Product

	2008	2009	2010
Government final consumption expenditure	1,492	1,581	1,717
Private final consumption expenditure	12,989	14,288	15,767
Increase in stocks Gross fixed capital formation	6,483	5,309	3,436
Total domestic expenditure	20,964	21,178	20,920
Exports of goods and services	4,268	4,186	4,836
Less Imports of goods and services	9,151	8,635	7,491
GDP in purchasers' values	16,081	16,729	18,264

Gross Domestic Product by Economic Activity

	2008	2009	2010
Agriculture, hunting, forestry and fishing	3,589	4,490	4,700
Mining and quarrying	17	27	41
Manufacturing	2,131	2,250	2,431
Electricity, gas and water	192	191	215
Construction	709	647	654
Wholesale and retail trade, restaurants and hotels	1,909	2,085	2,250
Transport and communications	3,100	3,063	3,523
Finance, insurance, real estate and business services	203	208	288
Public administration and defence	650	664	777
Other services	2,136	1,967	2,161
Sub-total	14,636	15,592	17,040
Less Imputed bank service charges	187	182	267
Indirect taxes, less subsidies	1,630	1,319	1,491
GDP in purchasers' values	16,081	16,729	18,264

Source: African Development Bank.

BALANCE OF PAYMENTS
(US $ million)

	2003	2004	2005
Exports of goods f.o.b.	854	990	834
Imports of goods f.o.b.	–1,111	–1,427	–1,427
Trade balance	–258	–437	–592
Exports of services	322	425	498
Imports of services	–619	–637	–615
Balance on goods and services	–555	–649	–710
Other income received	16	15	24
Other income paid	–94	–89	–104
Balance on goods, services and income	–632	–723	–790
Current transfers received	357	245	208
Current transfers paid	–183	–62	–45
Current balance	–458	–541	–626
Capital account (net)	143	182	192
Direct investment from abroad	13	53	85
Other investment assets	–29	295	11
Other investment liabilities	–110	–97	–102
Net errors and omissions	67	–35	91
Overall balance	–374	–143	–349

Source: IMF, *International Financial Statistics*.

External Trade

PRINCIPAL COMMODITIES
(US $ million)

Imports c.i.f.	2008	2009	2010
Food and live animals	300.3	243.5	274.9
Cereals and cereal preparations	148.3	105.7	121.7
Rice	74.0	47.2	53.5
Mineral fuels, lubricants and related materials	510.1	327.4	386.0
Petroleum, petroleum products and related materials	501.3	319.4	374.3
Petroleum and oils obtained from bituminous materials (not crude)	490.8	315.0	368.8
Residual petroleum products	10.5	4.4	5.5
Chemicals and related products	272.5	192.9	221.0
Medicinal and pharmaceutical products	66.9	61.2	67.2
Basic manufactures	1,197.8	1,139.6	634.2

Imports c.i.f.—*continued*	2008	2009	2010
Textile yarn and related products	536.2	299.0	255.0
Woven cotton fabrics	145.4	56.3	42.1
Machinery and transport equipment	1,214.8	881.1	751.8
Power generating machinery and equipment	147.8	62.3	40.4
Electric machinery, apparatus and appliances	125.6	96.1	128.8
Road vehicles	232.1	133.4	120.6
Miscellaneous manufactures	207.0	249.8	171.4
Total (incl. others)	3,850.6	3,159.3	2,545.8

Exports f.o.b.	2008	2009	2010
Food and live animals	323.8	285.1	248.4
Fish, crustaceans and molluscs and preparations thereof	159.6	115.5	114.1
Crustaceans and molluscs	122.0	87.9	71.2
Vegetables and fruit	36.2	32.9	36.7
Coffee, tea, cocoa, spices	117.3	116.4	80.6
Spices	85.5	98.2	56.7
Vanilla	50.1	44.2	17.6
Cloves	30.1	48.4	31.7
Crude materials, inedible, except fuels	94.3	82.0	120.1
Basic manufactures	71.8	96.2	72.8
Miscellaneous manufactures	948.7	474.4	363.4
Articles of apparel and clothing accessories	885.8	431.4	302.7
Men's and boys' outerwear	315.2	65.2	47.1
Women's, girls' and infants' outerwear	250.2	104.7	42.2
Knitted or crocheted outerwear	19.8	14.6	5.7
Total (incl. others)	1,667.4	1,095.9	1,082.2

Source: UN, *International Trade Statistics Yearbook*.

PRINCIPAL TRADING PARTNERS
(US $ million)

Imports	2008	2009	2010
Argentina	58.5	11.3	n.a
Bahrain	306.0	109.9	139.7
Belgium	60.0	198.7	96.6
Canada	17.2	63.0	110.8
China, People's Repub.	810.1	355.4	310.1
France	343.7	331.0	367.5
Germany	161.6	68.7	57.3
Hong Kong	11.7	91.3	62.8
India	182.1	124.7	60.1
Indonesia	72.1	32.9	20.2
Italy	49.6	36.1	26.4
Japan	122.1	22.9	18.0
Korea, Republic	80.3	76.4	56.5
Kuwait	—	85.9	82.0
Malaysia	36.3	43.1	32.5
Mauritius	85.5	146.5	133.3
Pakistan	54.7	42.6	65.1
Saudi Arabia	54.2	15.6	42.8
Singapore	20.6	81.9	96.7
South Africa	234.1	142.0	197.1
Thailand	71.9	578.9	45.8
United Arab Emirates	78.4	55.1	73.0
United Kingdom	39.4	n.a.	n.a.
USA	192.5	108.0	146.9
Total (incl. others)	3,850.6	3,159.3	2,545.8

Exports	2008	2009	2010
Belgium	20.0	18.3	16.4
Canada	13.1	11.9	42.3
China, People's Republic	52.3	52.3	56.7
Côte d'Ivoire	0.2	0.1	49.2
France	751.1	362.6	358.6
Germany	108.3	69.9	78.9
Hong Kong	9.5	16.1	9.5
India	10.6	20.8	46.1
Italy	40.4	27.9	30.9
Mauritius	18.1	19.2	22.6
Netherlands	26.7	17.2	17.5
Singapore	22.8	24.0	18.5
South Africa	24.9	15.7	26.2
Spain	30.5	23.5	31.1
United Arab Emirates	4.7	13.1	34.9
United Kingdom	31.3	35.1	35.3
USA	364.7	196.0	44.5
Total (incl. others)	1,667.4	1,095.9	1,082.2

Source: UN, *International Trade Statistics Yearbook*.

Transport

RAILWAYS
(traffic)

	1997	1998	1999
Passengers carried ('000)	359	293	273
Passenger-km (million)	37	35	31
Freight carried ('000 metric tons)	227	213	141
Ton-km (million)	81	71	46

Source: Réseau National des Chemins de Fer Malagasy.

2000: Passenger-km (million) 19; Ton-km (million) 26 (Source: UN, *Statistical Yearbook*).

ROAD TRAFFIC
(vehicles in use)

	1994	1995	1996*
Passenger cars	54,821	58,097	60,480
Buses and coaches	3,797	4,332	4,850
Lorries and vans	35,931	37,232	37,972
Road tractors	488	560	619

* Estimates.

2008: Passenger cars 146,273; Buses and coaches 280,835; Lorries and vans 83,788.

2009: Passenger cars 141,236; Buses and coaches 280,835; Lorries and vans 88,815.

Source: IRF, *World Road Statistics*.

SHIPPING

Merchant Fleet
(registered at 31 December)

	2007	2008	2009
Number of vessels	106	105	106
Displacement ('000 gross registered tons)	35.4	32.6	32.8

Source: IHS Fairplay, *World Fleet Statistics*.

International Sea-borne Freight Traffic
('000 metric tons)

	1987	1988	1989
Goods loaded:			
Mahajanga	17	18	29
Toamasina	252	350	361
other ports	79	100	137
Total	348	468	527
Goods unloaded:			
Mahajanga	37	32	31
Toamasina	748	778	709
other ports	48	53	52
Total	833	863	792

1990 ('000 metric tons): Goods loaded 540; Goods unloaded 984 (Source: UN, *Monthly Bulletin of Statistics*).

CIVIL AVIATION
(traffic on scheduled services)

	2007	2008	2009
Kilometres flown (million)	16	10	9
Passengers carried ('000)	616	559	500
Passenger-km (million)	1,248	1,041	819
Total ton-km (million)	136	106	88

Source: UN, *Statistical Yearbook*.

Tourism

TOURIST ARRIVALS BY NATIONALITY

	2007	2008	2009
Canada and USA	13,671	11,250	4,881
France	181,130	210,000	95,985
Germany	10,330	11,250	3,253
Italy	28,692	15,000	4,881
Japan	7,397	7,500	1,627
Mauritius	12,309	15,000	6,507
Réunion	37,878	52,501	21,149
Switzerland	6,887	7,500	2,278
United Kingdom	10,687	15,000	3,253
Total (incl. others)	344,348	375,010	162,687

Note: Most data for 2008 are rounded.

2010 ('000): Total tourist arrivals 196.

2011: ('000, provisional): Total tourist arrivals 225.

Tourism receipts (US $ million, incl. passenger transport, unless otherwise indicated): 620 in 2008; 518 in 2009; 321 in 2010 (excl. passenger transport).

Source: World Tourism Organization.

Communications Media

	2009	2010	2011
Telephones ('000 main lines in use)	186.2	142.1	138.1
Mobile cellular telephones ('000 subscribers)	6,283.8	7,711.7	8,159.6
Internet subscribers ('000)	8.3	8.8	n.a.
Broadband subscribers ('000)	4.6	5.4	6.8

Personal computers: 102,000 (5.8 per 1,000 persons) in 2005.

Source: International Telecommunication Union.

1996: Book production (incl. pamphlets): titles 119, copies ('000) 296; Daily newspapers: number 5, circulation ('000 copies) 66 (Source: UNESCO, *Statistical Yearbook*).

1997: Radio receivers ('000 in use) 3,050 (Source: UNESCO, *Statistical Yearbook*).

2000: Television receivers ('000 in use) 375.

Education

(2009/10, unless otherwise indicated, UNESCO estimates, public and private schools)

		Pupils ('000)		
	Teachers	Males	Females	Total
Pre-primary (all programmes)	7,075	81.3	82.4	163.7
Primary (all programmes)	105,673	2,145.3	2,096.7	4,242.0
Secondary*	43,539	526.5	496.0	1,022.5
General	39,912	582.8	558.6	1,141.4
Vocational†	2,058	21.2	11.9	33.1
Tertiary	4,494	38.8	35.6	74.4

* 2008/09.

† 2007/08.

Source: UNESCO Institute for Statistics.

2005/06: 6 universities; 14 private institutes of higher education.

Pupil-teacher ratio (primary education, UNESCO estimate): 40.1 in 2009/10 (Source: UNESCO Institute for Statistics).

Adult literacy rate (UNESCO estimates): 64.5% (males 67.4%; females 61.6%) in 2009 (Source: UNESCO Institute for Statistics).

Directory

The Constitution

On 17 November 2010 the Constitution of the Fourth Republic of Madagascar was approved at a national referendum by some 74% of the participating electorate. The President of the Republic is the Head of State and is elected by direct universal suffrage for a five-year mandate, renewable only once. Candidates for the presidency must be at least 35 years of age and have resided in Madagascar for at least six months prior to the date of the submission of candidacies. The President nominates a Prime Minister from the party or group of parties which secures the largest number of seats in the National Assembly (Assemblée nationale). The President also nominates members of the Government, upon the advice of the Prime Minister. Members of the National Assembly are elected by direct universal suffrage for five-year terms. The Constitution also provides for the election of members to the Sénat, each of whom serves a five-year mandate.

The Government

HEAD OF STATE

President of the Haute Autorité de la Transition: ANDRY RAJOELINA (inaugurated 21 March 2009).

GOVERNMENT OF NATIONAL UNITY

(September 2012)

Prime Minister and Acting Minister of the Environment and Forests: JEAN OMER BERIZIKY.

Deputy Prime Minister, in charge of Development and Land Settlement: HAJO HERIVELONA RANDRIANIAINARIVELO.

Deputy Prime Minister, in charge of the Economy and Industry: PIERROT BOTOZAZA (suspended in mid-July 2012).

Minister of Foreign Affairs: PIERROT RAJAONARIVELO.

Minister of Agriculture: ROLAND RAVATOMANGA (suspended in mid-July 2012).

Minister of Trade: OLGA RAMALASON (suspended in mid-July 2012).

Minister of Communication: HARRY LAURENT RAHAJASON.

Minister of Culture and Heritage: ELIA RAVELOMANANTSOA.

Minister of Decentralization: RUFFINE TSIRANANA (suspended in mid-July 2012).

Minister of Water: JULIEN REBOZA.

Minister of National Education: RÉGIS MANORO.

Minister of Stockbreeding: IHANTA RANDRIAMANDRATO (suspended in mid-July 2012).

Minister of Energy: NESTOR RAZAFINDROARIAKA.

Minister of Higher Education: ETIENNE HILAIRE RAZAFINDEHIBE.

Minister of Technical Education and Professional Training: JEAN ANDRÉ NDREMANJARY.

Minister of Finance and the Budget: HERY RAJAONARIMAMPIANINA.

Minister of the Civil Service, Labour and Social Legislation: TABERA RANDRIAMANANTSOA.

Minister of the Armed Forces: Gen. ANDRÉ LUCIEN RAKOTOARIMASY.

Minister of Hydrocarbons: BERNARD MARCEL.

Minister of the Interior: FLORENT RAKOTOARISOA.

Minister of Youth and Leisure: JACQUES ULRICH RANDRIANTIANA.

Minister of Justice and Keeper of the Seals: CHRISTINE RAZANAMAHASOA.

Minister of Mining: DANIELLA RANDRIANFENO TOLOTRANDRY RAJO.

Minister of Fisheries and Fishing Resources: SYLVAIN MANORIKY.

Minister of Population and Social Affairs: OLGA VAOMALALA.

Minister of Posts, Telecommunications and New Technologies: NY HASINA ANDRIAMANJATO.

Minister of Handicrafts: ELISA ZAFITOMBO ALIBENA.

Minister of Relations with the Institutions: VICTOR MANANTSOA.

Minister of Public Health: JOHANITA NDAHIMANANJARA.

Minister of Internal Security: ARSÈNE RAKOTONDRAZAKA.

Minister of Sport: GÉRARD BOTRALAHY.

Minister of Tourism: JEAN MAX RAKOTOMAMONJY.

Minister of Transport: BENJAMINA RAMARCEL RAMANANTSOA.

Minister of Public Works and Meteorology: Col. BOTO MANOVATSARA.

Secretary of State responsible for the National Gendarmerie: Gen. RANDRIANAZARY.

MINISTRIES

Office of the President: BP 955, 101 Antananarivo; tel. (20) 2254703; fax (20) 2256252; e-mail communication@presidence.gov.mg; internet www.presidence.gov.mg.

Office of the Prime Minister: BP 248, Palais d'Etat Mahazoarivo, 101 Antananarivo; tel. (20) 2264498; fax (20) 2233116; e-mail stp-ca@primature.gov.mg; internet www.primature.gov.mg.

Ministry of Agriculture: BP 301, Anosy, 101 Antananarivo; tel. (20) 2261002; fax (20) 2264308; e-mail info@agriculture.gov.mg; internet www.agriculture.gov.mg.

Ministry of the Armed Forces: BP 08, Ampahibe, 101 Antananarivo; tel. (20) 2222211; fax (20) 2235420; e-mail mdn@wanadoo.fr; internet www.defense.gov.mg.

Ministry of the Civil Service, Labour and Social Legislation: BP 207, Cité des 67 Hectares, 101 Antananarivo; tel. (20) 2224209; fax (20) 2233856; e-mail ministre@mfptls.gov.mg; internet www.mfptls.gov.mg.

Ministry of Communication: BP 305, 101 Antananarivo.

Ministry of Culture and Heritage: 101 Antananarivo; e-mail ministre@mcp.gov.mg; internet www.mcp.gov.mg.

Ministry of Decentralization: Antananarivo.

Ministry of Development and Land Settlement: Antananarivo; internet www.matd.gov.mg.

Ministry of the Economy and Industry: Bâtiment Commerce, Ambohidahy, 101 Antananarivo; tel. (20) 2264681; fax (20) 2234530; e-mail sg@mepspc.gov.mg; internet www.mei.gov.mg.

Ministry of Energy: BP 280, rue Farafaty Ampandrianomby, 101 Antananarivo; tel. (20) 2257193; fax (20) 2241776; e-mail bsg_mem@yahoo.fr; internet www.mem.gov.mg.

Ministry of the Environment and Forests: BP 610, rue Fernand Kasanga, Tsimbazaza, 101 Antananarivo; tel. (20) 2266805; fax (20) 2235410; e-mail sp@meeft.gov.mg; internet www.meeft.gov.mg.

Ministry of Finance and the Budget: BP 61, Antaninarenina, Antananarivo; tel. (20) 2230173; fax (20) 2264680; e-mail mrazanajato@mefb.gov.mg; internet www.mefb.gov.mg.

Ministry of Fisheries and Fishing Resources: 101 Antananarivo.

Ministry of Foreign Affairs: BP 836, Anosy, 101 Antananarivo; tel. (20) 2221198; fax (20) 2234484; e-mail contact@madagascar-diplomatie.net; internet www.madagascar-diplomatie.net.

Ministry of Higher Education and Scientific Research: 101 Antananarivo; internet www.mesupres.gov.mg.

Ministry of the Interior: BP 833, Anosy, 101 Antananarivo; tel. (20) 2223084; fax (20) 2235579; internet www.mid.gov.mg.

Ministry of Internal Security: BP 23 bis, 101 Antananarivo; tel. (20) 2221029; fax (20) 2231861; internet www.policenationale.gov.mg.

Ministry of Justice: rue Joel Rakotomalala, BP 231, Faravohitra, 101 Antananarivo; tel. (20) 2237684; fax (20) 2264458; e-mail presse.justice@justice.gov.mg; internet www.justice.gov.mg.

Ministry of Mining and Hydrocarbons: BP 280, rue Farafaty Ampandrianomby, 101 Antananarivo; tel. (20) 2257193; fax (20) 2241776; e-mail bsg_mem@yahoo.fr; internet www.mem.gov.mg.

Ministry of National Education: BP 247, Anosy, 101 Antananarivo; tel. (20) 2224308; fax (20) 2223897; e-mail mlraharimalala@yahoo.fr; internet www.education.gov.mg.

Ministry of Population and Social Affairs: 2 rue Razanakombana, Ambohijatovo, 101 Antananarivo; tel. 330968906 (mobile); e-mail hndev@gmail.com; internet www.population.gov.mg.

Ministry of Posts, Telecommunications and New Technologies: pl. de l'Indépendance, Antaninarenina, 101 Antananarivo; tel. (20) 2222902; fax (20) 2234115; internet www.mtpc.gov.mg.

Ministry of Public Health: BP 88, Ambohidahy, 101 Antananarivo; tel. (20) 2263121; fax (20) 2264228; e-mail ministre@sante.gov.mg; internet www.sante.gov.mg.

Ministry of Public Works and Meteorology: BP 295, 101 Antananarivo; tel. (20) 2228715; fax (20) 2220890; e-mail secreab@mtpm.gov.mg; internet www.mtpm.gov.mg.

Ministry of Relations with the Institutions: 101 Antananarivo.

Ministry of Sport: BP 681, Ambohijatovo, pl. Goulette, 101 Antananarivo; tel. (20) 2227780; fax (20) 2234275; e-mail mjs_101@yahoo.fr; internet www.mscl.gov.mg.

Ministry of Stockbreeding: 101 Antananarivo.

Ministry of Technical Education and Professional Training: BP 793, 101 Antananarivo.

Ministry of Tourism and Handicrafts: 101 Antananarivo; e-mail mintour@dts.mg; internet www.mtoura.gov.mg.

Ministry of Trade: 101 Antananarivo; internet www.commerce.gov.mg.

Ministry of Transport: BP 610, rue Fernand Kasanga, Tsimbazaza, 101 Antananarivo; tel. (20) 2262816; fax (20) 2235410; internet www.transport.gov.mg.

Ministry of Water: Antananarivo; e-mail dircab@mineau.gov.mg; internet www.mineau.gov.mg.

Ministry of Youth and Leisure: 101 Antananarivo; internet www.mjl.gov.mg.

President and Legislature

PRESIDENT

Presidential Election, 3 December 2006

Candidate	Votes	% of votes
Marc Ravalomanana	2,435,199	54.79
Jean Lahiniriko	517,994	11.65
Iarovana Roland Ratsiraka	450,717	10.14
Herizo J. Razafimahaleo	401,473	9.03
Norbert Lala Ratsirahonana	187,552	4.22
Ny Hasina Andriamanjato	185,624	4.18
Others	266,191	5.99
Total	4,444,750*	100.00

* Excluding 87,196 invalid votes.

LEGISLATURE

On 7 October 2010 the High Constitutional Court approved a decree by President Rajoelina establishing a Parlement de la Transition. Accordingly, on 11 October a 256-member lower parliamentary chamber, the Congrès de la Transition, was installed, with representation assigned according to the arrangement established in an accord reached in August: notably, a gathering of all the political parties and associations that participated in the drafting of the agreement, known as l'Espace de Concertation des Partis Politiques (ESCOPOL), was allocated 62 seats, Tiako i Madagasikara (TIM) 52, Tanora malaGasy Vonona (TGV) 52 and a grouping of parties supporting Rajoelina, the Union des Démocrates et Républicains—Fanovana (UDR—Fanovana) 29. On 12 October a 90-member upper chamber, the Conseil Supérieur de la Transition, took office; the deputies included 25 representatives of the UDR—Fanovana, 21 of the TIM, 18 of ESCOPOL and 10 of the TGV. The Parlement de la Transition was restructured on 1 December 2011, with the Congrès de la Transition comprising 365 members and the Conseil Supérieur de la Transition comprising 163 members. In the Congrès de la Transition, the ESCOPOL was allocated 62 seats; the Mouvance Ravalomanana (MR) 57 seats; the TGV and the Union des Démocrates et des Républicains pour le Changement (UDR-C) 52 seats each; the President of the HAT, the Monima-Uamad, Hery Politika Mitambatra (HPM), the Mouvement pour la Démocratie de Madagascar (MDM), AREMA and the Autres Sensibilités (AS) 20 seats each; and 22 seats were allocated to eminent persons. In the Conseil Supérieur de la Transition, the MR was allocated 30 seats; the UDR-C and the TGV 25 seats each; the ESCOPOL 18 seats; the President of the HAT, the Monima-Uamad, the MDM, AREMA, the AS and the HPM 10 seats each; and five seats were allocated to eminent persons.

President of the Congrès de la Transition: MAMY RAKOTOARIVELO.

President of the Conseil Supérieur de la Transition: Gen. DOLIN RASOLOSOA.

Election Commission

Commission Électorale Nationale Indépendante pour la Transition (CENIT): Immeuble Microréalisation, 4 étage, 67 ha, 101 Antananarivo; tel. (20) 2225179; fax (20) 2225881; e-mail ceni@ceni-madagascar.mg; internet www.ceni-madagascar.mg; 21 mems; Pres. BÉATRICE JEANINE ATALLAH.

Political Organizations

In August 2011 there were some 285 political organizations registered in Madagascar.

Association pour la Renaissance de Madagascar (Andry sy Riana Enti-manavotra an'i Madigasikara) (AREMA): f. 1975 as Avant-garde de la Révolution Malgache; adopted present name 1997; party of fmr Pres. Adm. (retd) Ratsiraka (now in exile); control disputed between two factions, headed by Gen. Sec. PIERROT RAJAONARIVELO (in exile), and Asst Gen. Sec. PIERRE RAHARIJAONA.

Comité pour la Réconciliation Nationale (CRN): Villa la Franchise, Lot II-I 160 A, Alarobia, Antananarivo; tel. (20) 2242022; f. 2002 by fmr President Zafy; radical opposition; formed part of the 3FN (Trois Forces Nationales) group of opposition parties, established in Sept. 2005; Leader ALBERT ZAFY.

FAFI-V: f. 2009; Pres. NAIVO NAIVO RAHOLDINA.

Hasin'i Madagasikara: Lot K 7-97 bis IIA Mamory Ivato, BP 682, 101 Antananarivo; tel. 340220665 (mobile); e-mail madahasin@

gmail.com; internet hasinimadagasikara.mg; f. 2009; Pres. SARAHA GEORGET RABEHARISOA.

Herim-Bahoaka Mitambatra (HBM) (Union of Popular Forces): formed part of the coalition supporting Marc Ravalomanana prior to the 2006 presidential election; Leader TOVONANAHARY RABETSITONTA.

Libéralisme Économique et Action Démocratique pour la Reconstruction Nationale (LEADER/Fanilo) (Torch): f. 1993 by Herizo Razafimahaleo; Sec. Gen. MANASSÉ ESOAVELOMANDROSO.

Malagasy Tonga Saina (MTS): Antananarivo; Pres. ROLAND RATSIRAKA.

Mouvement pour la Démocratie à Madagascar (MDM): Villa Khannet, Maibahoaka, Ambohidratrimo; tel. (34) 3118672; internet www.mdm-iarivo.mg; Pres. PIERROT RAJAONARIVELO.

Mouvement pour le Progrès de Madagascar (Mpitolona ho Amin'ny Fandrosoan'ny Madagasikara) (MFM): 42 & 44 Cité Ampefiloha Bldg, 101 Antananarivo; tel. (20) 2437560; e-mail contact@mfm-madagascar.com; internet www.mfm-madagascar.com; f. 1972 as Mouvement pour le Pouvoir Prolétarien (MFM); adopted present name in 1990; advocates liberal and market-orientated policies; Leader MANANDAFY RAKOTONIRINA; Sec.-Gen. OLIVIER RAKOTOVAZAHA.

Ny Asa Vita no Ifampitsara (AVI) (People are judged by the work they do): f. 1997 to promote human rights, hard work and devt; Leader NORBERT RATSIRAHONANA.

Parti Socialiste et Démocratique pour l'Union de Madagascar (PSDUM): f. 2006; Pres. JEAN LAHINIRIKO.

Rassemblement des Forces Nationales (RFN): f. 2005; a coalition of parties comprising the AKFM, LEADER/Fanilo and Fihavanantsika (led by Pasteur Daniel Rajakoba); formed part of the 3FN (Trois Forces Nationales) group of opposition parties, established in Sept. 2005; Leader Pasteur EDMOND RAZAFIMAHEFA.

Rassemblement pour le Socialisme et la Démocratie (RPSD): f. 1993 by fmr mems of PSD; also known as Renaissance du Parti Social-démocratique; Jean-Eugène Voninahitsy formed a breakaway party known as the RPSD Nouveau in 2003; Leader EVARISTE MARSON.

TAMBATRA: Antananarivo; Pres. PETY RAKOTONIAINA.

Tanora malaGasy Vonona (TGV) (Determined Malagasy Youth): Antananarivo; internet www.tgvonona.org; f. 2007; Leader ANDRY RAJOELINA.

Tiako i Madagasikara (TIM) (I Love Madagascar): internet www.tim-madagascar.org; f. 2002; supports former Pres. Ravalomanana; Pres. YVAN RANDRIASANDRATRINIONY.

Diplomatic Representation

EMBASSIES IN MADAGASCAR

China, People's Republic: Ancien Hôtel Panorama, BP 1658, 101 Antananarivo; tel. (20) 2240129; fax (20) 2240215; e-mail chinaemb_mg@mfa.gov.cn; internet mg.china-embassy.org; Ambassador WO RUIDI.

Comoros: Antananarivo; tel. (20) 2265819; Ambassador (vacant).

Egypt: Lot MD 378 Ambalatokana Mandrosoa Ivato, BP 4082, 101 Antananarivo; tel. (20) 2245497; fax (20) 2245379; Ambassador MAGID FOAD SALEH FOAD.

France: 3 rue Jean Jaurès, BP 204, 101 Antananarivo; tel. (20) 2239898; fax (20) 2239927; e-mail ambatana@moov.mg; internet www.ambafrance-mada.org; Ambassador JEAN CHRISTOPHE BEILLARD.

Germany: 101 rue du Pasteur Rabeony Hans, BP 516, Ambodirotra, 101 Antananarivo; tel. (20) 2223802; fax (20) 2226627; e-mail info@antananarivo.diplo.de; internet www.antananarivo.diplo.de; Ambassador HANS-DIETER STELL.

Holy See: Amboniloha Ivandry, BP 650, 101 Antananarivo; tel. (20) 2242376; fax (20) 2242384; e-mail nuntiusantana@wanadoo.mg; Apostolic Nuncio Most Rev. EUGENE MARTIN NUGENT (Titular Archbishop of Domnach Sechnaill).

India: 4 Làlana Emile Rajaonson, Tsaralalana, BP 1787, 101 Antananarivo; tel. (20) 2223334; fax (20) 2233790; e-mail indembmd@blueline.mg; Ambassador AZAD SINGH TOOR.

Indonesia: 26–28 rue Patrice Lumumba, BP 3969, 101 Antananarivo; tel. (20) 2224915; fax (20) 2232857; Chargé d'affaires a.i. SLAMET SUYATA SASTRAMIHARDZA.

Iran: route Circulaire, Lot II L43 ter, Ankadivato, 101 Antananarivo; tel. (20) 2228639; fax (20) 2222298; Ambassador ABDOL RAHIM HOMATASH.

Japan: 8 rue du Dr Villette, BP 3863, Isoraka, 101 Antananarivo; tel. (20) 2226102; fax (20) 2221769; Ambassador TETSURO KAWAGUCHI.

Korea, Democratic People's Republic: 101 Antananarivo; tel. (20) 2244442; Ambassador RI YONG HAK.

Libya: Lot IIB, 37A route Circulaire Ampandrana-Ouest, 101 Antananarivo; tel. (20) 2221892; Chargé d'affaires a.i. Dr MOHAMED ALI SHARFEDIN AL-FITURI.

Mauritius: Villa David IV, Manakambahiny, 101 Antananarivo; tel. (20) 2221864; fax (20) 2221939; e-mail memad@moov.mg; Ambassador ERNEST GÉRARD LEMAIRE.

Morocco: Bâtiment D1, Rez-de-chaussée, Ankorondrano, BP 12, 104 Antananarivo; tel. (20) 2221347; fax (20) 2221124; e-mail amar_med@hotmail.com; Ambassador MUHAMMAD AMAR.

Norway: Explorer Business Park, Bâtiment 2D, Antananarivo; tel. (20) 2230507; fax (20) 2237799; e-mail emb.antananarivo@mfa.no; internet www.amb-norvege.mg; Ambassador DAG NISSEN.

Russia: BP 4006, Ivandry-Ambohijatovo, 101 Antananarivo; tel. (20) 2242827; fax (20) 2242642; e-mail ambrusmad@blueline.mg; internet www.madagascar.mid.ru; Ambassador VLADIMIR B. GONCHARENKO.

South Africa: Lot IVO 68 bis, rue Ravoninahitriniarivo, Ankorondrano, BP 12101-05, 101 Antananarivo; tel. (20) 2243350; fax (20) 2249514; e-mail antananarivo@foreign.gov.za; Ambassador MOKGETHI SAMUEL MONAISA.

Switzerland: Immeuble ARO, Solombavambahoaka, Frantsay 77, BP 118, 101 Antananarivo; tel. (20) 2262997; fax (20) 2228940; e-mail ant.vertretung@eda.admin.ch; internet www.eda.admin.ch/antananarivo; Ambassador ERIC MAYORAZ.

Turkey: Hotel Carlton, Chambre no. 1410, rue Pierre Stibbe, BP 959 Antananarivo 101; tel. (20) 2226060; fax (20) 2267609; Ambassador AHMET ENÇ ERCEMUND.

USA: 14–16 rue Rainitovo, Antsahavola, BP 620, 101 Antananarivo; tel. (20) 2221257; fax (20) 2234539; internet www.antananarivo.usembassy.gov; Chargé d'affaires a.i. ERIC M. WONG.

Judicial System

According to the Constitution of the Fourth Republic of Madagascar, endorsed by national referendum on 17 November 2010, justice is administered by the Supreme Court, the High Constitutional Court, the High Court of Justice and any courts of appeal that may be established.

HIGH CONSTITUTIONAL COURT

Haute Cour Constitutionnelle: BP 835, Ambohidahy, 101 Antananarivo; tel. (20) 2266061; e-mail hcc@hcc.gov.mg; internet www.hcc.gov.mg; interprets the Constitution and rules on constitutional issues; nine mems; Pres. JEAN-MICHEL RAJAONARIVONY.

HIGH COURT OF JUSTICE

Haute Cour de Justice: 101 Antananarivo; 9 mems.

SUPREME COURT

Cour Suprême: Palais de Justice, Anosy, 101 Antananarivo; 9 mems; Pres. CLÉMENTINE CÉCILE RAJAONERA DELMOTTE; Attorney-General COLOMBE RAMANANTSOA (acting); Chamber Pres YOLANDE RAMANGASOAVINA, FRANÇOIS RAMANANDRAIBE.

OTHER COURTS

Tribunaux de Première Instance: at Antananarivo, Toamasina, Antsiranana, Mahajanga, Fianarantsoa, Toliary, Antsirabé, Ambatondrazaka, Antalaha, Farafangana and Maintirano; for civil, commercial and social matters, and for registration.

Cours Criminelles Ordinaires: tries crimes of common law; attached to the Cour d'Appel in Antananarivo but may sit in any other large town. There are also 31 Cours Criminelles Spéciales dealing with cases concerning cattle.

Tribunaux Spéciaux Economiques: at Antananarivo, Toamasina, Mahajanga, Fianarantsoa, Antsiranana and Toliary; tries crimes specifically relating to economic matters.

Tribunaux Criminels Spéciaux: judges cases of banditry and looting; 31 courts.

Religion

It is estimated that more than 50% of the population follow traditional animist beliefs, some 41% are Christians (about two—thirds of whom are Roman Catholics) and some 7% are Muslims.

CHRISTIANITY

Fiombonan'ny Fiangonana Kristiana eto Madagasikara (FFKM)/Conseil Chrétien des Eglises de Madagascar (Christian Council of Churches in Madagascar): Vohipiraisana, Ambohijatovo-Atsimo, BP 798, 101 Antananarivo; tel. (20) 2623433; e-mail ffkmfoibe@gmail.com; f. 1980; four mems and two assoc. mems; Pres. Pastor Dr ENDOR MODESTE RAKOTO; Gen. Sec. Rev. GILBERT RANDRIANIRINA.

Fiombonan'ny Fiangonana Protestanta eto Madagasikara (FFPM)/Fédération des Eglises Protestantes à Madagascar (Federation of the Protestant Churches in Madagascar): VK 3 Vohipiraisana, Ambohijatovo-Atsimo, BP 4226, 101 Antananarivo; tel. (20) 2415888; e-mail edmrazafi@fuller.edu; f. 1958; two mem. churches; Pres Rev. Dr LALA RASENDRAHASINA; Gen. Sec. Rev. Dr EDMOND RAZAFIMANANTSOA.

The Anglican Communion

Anglicans are adherents of the Church of the Province of the Indian Ocean, comprising seven dioceses (five in Madagascar, one in Mauritius and one in Seychelles). The Archbishop of the Province is the Bishop of Antananarivo. The Church has about 160,000 adherents in Madagascar, including the membership of the Eklesia Episkopaly Malagasy (Malagasy Episcopal Church), founded in 1874.

Bishop of Antananarivo: Rt Rev. SAMOELA JAONA RANARIVELO, Evêché anglican, Lot VK57 ter, Ambohimanoro, 101 Antananarivo; tel. (20) 2220827; fax (20) 2261331; e-mail eemdanta@yahoo.com.

Bishop of Antsiranana: Rt Rev. ROGER CHUNG PO CHEN, Evêché anglican, 4 rue Grandidier, BP 278, 201 Antsiranana; tel. (20) 8222650; e-mail mgrchungpo@blueline.mg; internet www.antsirananadiocese.org.

Bishop of Fianarantsoa: Rt Rev. GILBERT RATELOSON RAKOTONDRAVELO, Evêché anglican, BP 1418, 531 Fianarantsoa.

Bishop of Mahajanga: Rt Rev. JEAN-CLAUDE ANDRIANJAFIMANANA, Evêché anglican, BP 169, 401 Mahajanga; e-mail eemdmaha@dts.mg.

Bishop of Toamasina: Rt Rev. JEAN PAUL SOLO, Evêché anglican, rue James Seth, BP 531, 501 Toamasina; tel. (20) 5332163; fax (20) 5331689.

The Roman Catholic Church

Madagascar comprises five archdioceses and 16 dioceses. About 26% of the total population were Roman Catholics.

Bishops' Conference

Conférence Episcopale de Madagascar, 102 bis, rue Cardinal Jerôme Rakotomalala, BP 667, 101 Antananarivo; tel. (20) 2220478; fax (20) 2224854; e-mail ecar@vitelcom.mg.

f. 1969; Pres. Most Rev. FULGENCE RABEMAHAFALY (Archbishop of Fianarantsoa).

Archbishop of Antananarivo: ODON MARIE ARSÈNE RAZANAKOLONA, Archevêché, Andohalo, BP 3030, 101 Antananarivo; tel. (20) 2220726; fax (20) 2264181; e-mail didih@simicro.org.

Archbishop of Antsiranana: Most Rev. MICHEL MALO, Archevêché, 5 blvd le Myre de Villers, BP 415, 201 Antsiranana; tel. and fax (82) 21605; e-mail archevediego@blueline.mg.

Archbishop of Fianarantsoa: Most Rev. FULGENCE RABEMAHAFALY, Archevêché, pl. Mgr Givelet, BP 1440, Ecar Ambozontany, 301 Fianarantsoa; tel. (20) 7550027; fax (20) 7551436; e-mail ecardiofianar@mel.moov.mg.

Archbishop of Toamasina: Most Rev. DÉSIRÉ TSARAHAZANA, 11 rue du Commerce, BP 98, 501 Toamasina; tel. (20) 5332128.

Archbishop of Toliary: Most Rev. FULGENCE RABEONY, Archevêché, Maison Saint Jean, BP 30, 601 Toliary; tel. (20) 9442416; e-mail diocese_tulcar@wanadoo.mg.

Other Christian Churches

Fiangonan'i Jesoa Kristy eto Madagasikara/Eglise de Jésus-Christ à Madagascar (FJKM): Lot 11 B18, Tohatohabato Ranavalona 1, Trano 'Ifanomezantsoa', BP 623, 101 Antananarivo; tel. (20) 2228237; fax (20) 2227033; e-mail fjkm@wanadoo.mg; internet foibefjkm.mg; f. 1968; Pres. LALA HAJA RASENDRAHASINA; Gen. Sec. Rev. RÉMY RALIBERA; 2m. mems.

Fiangonana Loterana Malagasy (Malagasy Lutheran Church): BP 1741, 19, rue Jules Pochard, 101 Antananarivo; tel. (20) 2422703; e-mail drmodeste@yahoo.fr; internet www.flm-mada.org; f. 1867; Pres. Rev. Dr ENDOR MODESTE RAKOTO; 3m. mems (2009).

The Press

In December 1990 legislation was adopted guaranteeing the freedom of the press and the right of newspapers to be established without prior authorization.

PRINCIPAL DAILIES

Bulletin de l'Agence Nationale d'Information 'TARATRA' (ANTA): 8/10 Làlana Rainizanabololona, Antanimena, BP 194, 101 Antananarivo; tel. (20) 2234308; e-mail administration@taratramada.com; internet www.taratramada.com; f. 1977; Malagasy; Editor-in-Chief HANITRA RABETOKOTANY.

Le Courier de Madagascar: Antananarivo; Dir of Publication FRANCK RAMAROSON; circ. 12,000.

L'Express de Madagascar: BP 3893, 101 Antananarivo; tel. (20) 2221934; fax (20) 2262894; e-mail lexpress@malagasy.com; internet www.lexpressmada.com; f. 1995; French and Malagasy; Editor-in-Chief SYLVAIN RANJALAHY; circ. 10,000.

Gazetiko: rue Ravoninahitriniarivo, BP 1414 Ankorondrano, 101 Antananarivo; tel. (20) 2269779; fax (20) 2227351; e-mail gazetiko@midi-madagasikara.mg; internet www.gazetiko.mg; Malagasy; circ. 50,000.

La Gazette de la Grande Ile: Lot II, W 23 L Ankorahotra, route de l'Université, BP 8678, Antananarivo; tel. 340561396 (mobile); e-mail administration@lagazette-dgi.com; internet www.lagazette-dgi.com; French; 24 pages; Pres. LOLA RASOAMAHARO; Editor-in-Chief CHRISTIAN ANDRIANARISOA; circ. 15,000–30,000.

Imongo Vaovao: 11K 4 bis Andravoahangy, BP 7014, 101 Antananarivo; tel. (20) 2233110; f. 1955; Malagasy; Dir ANDRÉ RATSIFEHERA; circ. 15,000.

Madagascar Matin: Antananarivo; Editor-in-Chef LAHINIRIKO DENIS ALEXANDRE; circ. 18,000.

Madagascar Tribune: Immeuble SME, rue Ravoninahitriniarivo, BP 659, Ankorondrano, 101 Antananarivo; tel. (20) 2222635; fax (20) 2222254; e-mail contact@madagascar-tribune.com; internet www.madagascar-tribune.com; f. 1988; independent; French and Malagasy; Editor RAHAGA RAMAHOLIMIHASO; circ. 12,000.

Maresaka: Cité Logt. 288, Analamahitsy, 101 Antananarivo; tel. (20) 2431665; f. 1953; independent; Malagasy; Editor R. RABEFANANINA; circ. 5,000.

Midi Madagasikara: Làlana Ravoninahitriniarivo, BP 1414, Ankorondrano, 101 Antananarivo; tel. (20) 2269779; fax (20) 2227351; e-mail contact@midi-madagasikara.mg; internet www.midi-madagasikara.mg; f. 1983; French and Malagasy; Dir-Gen. JULIANA ANDRIAMBELO RAKOTOARIVELO; circ. 21,000 (Mon.–Fri.), 35,000 (Sat.).

Les Nouvelles: 8/10, rue Rainizanabololona, BP 194, 101 Antananarivo; tel. (20) 2235433; fax (20) 2229993; e-mail administration@les-nouvelles.com; internet www.les-nouvelles.com; in French and Taratra; f. 2003; Dir-Gen. NAINA ANDRIANTSITOHAINA.

Ny Vaovaontsika: BP 11137, MBS Anosipatrana; tel. (20) 2227717; e-mail nyvaovaontsika@mbs.mg; f. 2004; re-est. as a daily; Malagasy; owned by the Malagasy Broadcasting System; Editor-in-Chief ROLAND ANDRIAMAHENINA; circ. 10,000.

Le Quotidien: BP 11 097, 101 Antananarivo; tel. (20) 2227717; fax (20) 2265447; e-mail lequotidien@mbs.mg; internet www.lequotidien.mg; f. 2003; owned by the Tiko Group plc; French.

La Vérité: Immeuble SODIAT, Mandrosoa Ivato, BP 5068, Antananarivo 105; tel. (20) 2629521; fax (20) 2244953; e-mail laverite@blueline.com.

PRINCIPAL PERIODICALS

Basy Vava: Lot III E 96, Mahamasina Atsimo, 101 Antananarivo; tel. (20) 2220448; f. 1959; daily; Malagasy; Dir GABRIEL RAMANANJATO; circ. 3,000.

Dans les Médias Demain (DMD): 51 rue Tsiombikibo, BP 1734, Ambatovinaky, 101 Antananarivo; tel. (20) 2241664; fax (20) 2241665; e-mail admin@dmd.mg; f. 1986; independent; economic information and analysis; weekly; Editorial Dir JEAN ERIC RAKOTOARISOA; circ. 4,000.

Gazetinao: Lot IPA 37, BP 1758, Anosimasina, 101 Antananarivo; tel. (33) 1198161; e-mail mitantanasymitarika@yahoo.fr; f. 1976; French and Malagasy; monthly; religion and culture; Editor-in-Chief DAVID ALDEN EINSTEN RAKOTOMAHANINA; circ. 3,000.

L'Hebdo: BP 3893, 101 Antananarivo; tel. (20) 2221934; e-mail courrier@hebdomada.com; f. 2005; French and Malagasy; weekly; Editor-in-Chief NASOLO VALIAVO ANDRIAMIHAJA.

Isika Mianakavy: Ambatomena, 301 Fianarantsoa; f. 1958; Roman Catholic; Malagasy; monthly; Dir J. RANAIVOMANANA; circ. 21,000.

Journal Officiel de la République de Madagascar/Gazetim-Panjakan' Ny Repoblika Malagasy: BP 248, 101 Antananarivo;

tel. (20) 2265010; fax (20) 2225319; f. 1883; official announcements; Malagasy and French; weekly; Dir HONORÉE ELIANNE RALALAHARISON; circ. 1,545.

Jureco: BP 6318, Lot IVD 48 bis, rue Razanamaniraka, Behoririka, 101 Antananarivo; tel. (20) 2255271; e-mail jureco@malagasy.com; law and economics; monthly; French; Dir MBOARA ANDRIANARIMANANA.

Lakroan'i Madagasikara/La Croix de Madagascar: BP 7524, CNPC Antanimena, 101 Antananarivo; tel. (20) 2266128; fax (20) 2224020; e-mail lakroa@moov.mg; internet www.lakroa.mg; f. 1927; Roman Catholic; French and Malagasy; weekly; Dir Fr VINCENT RABEMAHAFALY; circ. 25,000.

La Lettre de Madagascar (LLM): Antananarivo; f. 2003; 2 a month; in French and English; economic; Editor-in-Chief DANIEL LAMY.

Mpanolotsaina: BP 623, 101 Antananarivo; tel. (20) 2226845; fax (20) 2226372; e-mail fjkm@wanadoo.mg; religious, educational; Malagasy; quarterly; Dir RAYMOND RAJOELISOL.

New Magazine: BP 7581, Newprint, route des Hydrocarbures, 101 Antananarivo; tel. (20) 2233335; fax (20) 2236471; e-mail newmag@wanadoo.mg; internet www.newmagazine.mg; monthly; in French; Dir CLARA RAVOAVAHY.

Ny Mpamangy-FLM: 9 rue Général Gabriel Ramanantsoa Isoraka, 101 Antananarivo; tel. (20) 2228943; f. 1882; monthly; Dir LUCIE NOROSOANOMENJANAHARY; circ. 3,000.

Ny Sakaizan'ny Tanora: BP 538, Antsahaminitra, 101 Antananarivo; tel. (20) 2228943; f. 1878; monthly; Editor-in-Chief ELISABETH RAHELINORO; circ. 5,000.

Revue de l'Océan Indien: Communication et Médias Océan Indien, rue H. Rabesahala, BP 46, Antsakaviro, 101 Antananarivo; tel. (20) 2222536; fax (20) 2234534; e-mail roi@dts.mg; internet www.madatours.com/roi; f. 1980; monthly; French; Dir-Gen. HERY M. A. RANAIVOSOA; circ. 5,000.

Sahy: Lot VD 42, Ambanidia, 101 Antananarivo; tel. (20) 2222715; f. 1957; political; Malagasy; weekly; Editor ALINE RAKOTO; circ. 9,000.

Sosialisma Mpiasa: BP 1128, 101 Antananarivo; tel. (20) 2221989; f. 1979; trade union affairs; Malagasy; monthly; Dir PAUL RABEMANANJARA; circ. 5,000.

Vaovao: BP 271, 101 Antananarivo; tel. (20) 2221193; f. 1985; French and Malagasy; weekly; Dir MARC RAKOTONOELY; circ. 5,000.

NEWS AGENCIES

Agence Nationale d'Information 'TARATRA' (ANTA): 7 rue Jean Ralaimongo, Ambohiday, BP 386, 101 Antananarivo; tel. and fax (20) 2236047; e-mail taratra.mtpc@mtpc.gov.mg; f. 1977; Man. Dir JOÉ ANACLET RAKOTOARISON.

Mada: Villa Joëlle, Lot II J 161 R, Ivandry, 101 Antananarivo; tel. (20) 2242428; e-mail courrier@mada.mg; internet www.mada.mg; f. 2003; independent information agency; Dir RICHARD CLAUDE RATOVONARIVO.

Publishers

Edisiona Salohy: BP 4226, 101 Antananarivo; Dir MIRANA VOLOLOARISOA RANDRIANARISON.

Editions Ambozontany Analamalintsy: BP 7553, 101 Antananarivo; tel. and fax (20) 2243111; e-mail editionsj@moov.mg; f. 1952; religious, educational, historical, cultural and technical textbooks; Dir Fr GUILLAUME DE SAINT PIERRE RAKOTONANDRATONIARIVO.

Imprimerie Nouvelle: PK 2, Andranomahery, route de Majunga, BP 4330, 101 Antananarivo; tel. (20) 2221036; fax (20) 2269225; e-mail nouvelle@wanadoo.mg; Dir EUGÈNE RAHARIFIDY.

Imprimerie Takariva: 4 rue Radley, BP 1029, Antanimena, 101 Antananarivo; tel. (20) 2222128; f. 1933; fiction, languages, school textbooks; Man. Dir PAUL RAPATSALAHY.

Madagascar Print and Press Co (MADPRINT): rue Rabesahala, Antsakaviro, BP 953, 101 Antananarivo; tel. (20) 2222536; fax (20) 2234534; f. 1969; literary, technical and historical; Dir GEORGES RANAIVOSOA.

Maison d'Edition Protestante Antso: 19 rue Venance Manifatra, Imarivolanitra, BP 660, 101 Antananarivo; tel. (20) 2220886; fax (20) 2226372; e-mail fjkm@dts.mg; f. 1972; religious, school, social, political and general; Dir HANS ANDRIAMAMPIANINA.

Office du Livre Malgache: Lot 111 H29, Andrefan' Ambohijanahary, BP 617, 101 Antananarivo; tel. (20) 2224449; f. 1970; children's and general; Sec.-Gen. JULIETTE RATSIMANDRAVA.

Société Malgache d'Edition (SME): BP 659, Ankorondrano, 101 Antananarivo; tel. (20) 2222635; fax (20) 2222254; e-mail tribune@wanadoo.mg; f. 1943; general fiction, university and secondary textbooks; Man. Dir RAHAGA RAMAHOLIMIHASO.

Société Nouvelle de l'Imprimerie Centrale (SNIC): Route des Hydrocarbures, BP 1414, 101 Antananarivo; tel. (20) 2221118; fax (20) 2234421; e-mail contact@snic.mg; internet www.snic.mg; f. 1961; books, newspapers and magazines; CEO JEREMY RABESAHALA.

Société de Presse et d'Edition de Madagascar: Antananarivo; non-fiction, reference, science, university textbooks; Man. Dir RAJAOFERA ANDRIAMBELO.

Trano Printy Fiangonana Loterana Malagasy (TPFLM): BP 538, 9 rue Général Gabriel Ramanantsoa, 101 Antananarivo; tel. (20) 2224569; fax (20) 2262643; e-mail impluth@yahoo.fr; f. 1877; religious, educational and fiction; Man. RAYMOND RANDRIANATOANDRO.

GOVERNMENT PUBLISHING HOUSE

Imprimerie Nationale: BP 38, 101 Antananarivo; tel. (20) 2223675; e-mail dinm@wanadoo.mg; all official publs; Dir JEAN DENIS RANDRIANIRINA.

Broadcasting and Communications

In 2011 there were four providers of mobile telephone services in the country, one of which, TELMA, also provided fixed-line services.

TELECOMMUNICATIONS

Regulatory Authority

Office Malagasy d'Etudes et de Régulation des Télécommunications (OMERT): BP 99991, route des Hydrocarbures-Alarobia, 101 Antananarivo; tel. (20) 2242119; fax (20) 2321516; e-mail omert@moov.mg; internet www.omert.org; f. 1997; Gen. Man. AUGUSTIN ANDRIAMANANORO.

SERVICE PROVIDERS

Airtel Madagascar: Explorer Business Park, Ankorondrano, Antananarivo 101; tel. (33) 1100100; e-mail info.africa@airtel.com; internet africa.airtel.com/madagascar; f. 1997 as Madacom; fmrly Celtel and subsequently Zain Madagascar; name changed as above in 2010; Dir-Gen. HEIKO SCHLITTKE.

Madamobil SA: Immeuble ARO Ampefiloha, 3ème étage, Porte A32, 101 Antananarivo; tel. (20) 2631886; e-mail contact@life.mg; internet www.life.mg; f. 1997; provides mobile telephone services under the brand name 'Life'; Pres. and Dir PATRICK PERTEGNAZZA.

Orange Madagascar: Antananarivo; internet www.orange.mg; f. 1998; fmrly Antaris, la Société Malgache de Mobiles; name changed as above 2003; mobile telecommunication GSM network provider; market leader; Dir-Gen. MICHEL BARRÉ.

Télécom Malagasy SA (TELMA): BP 763, 101 Antananarivo; tel. (20) 2532705; fax (20) 2253871; e-mail telmacorporate@telma.mg; internet www.telma.mg; 68% owned by Distacom (Hong Kong); owns DTS Wanadoo internet service provider; Chair. DAVID WHITE; Dir-Gen. PATRICK PISAL-HAMIDA.

BROADCASTING

In 2010, in addition to the state-owned Radio Nationale Malgache and Télévision Nationale Malagache, there were some 197 private FM radio stations and 21 private television stations in Madagascar.

Radio

Le Messager Radio Evangélique: BP 1374, 101 Antananarivo; tel. (20) 2234495; internet mreradio.com; broadcasts in French, English and Malagasy; Dir JOCELYN RANJARISON.

Radio MBS (Malagasy Broadcasting System): BP 11137, Anosipatrana, Antananarivo; tel. (20) 2266702; fax (20) 2268941; e-mail marketing@mbs.mg; internet www.mbs.mg; broadcasts by satellite; Man. SARAH RAVALOMANANA.

Radio Nationale Malagasy: BP 442, Anosy, 101 Antananarivo; tel. (20) 2221745; fax (20) 2232715; e-mail rnmdir@dts.mg; internet www.rnm.mg; state-controlled; part of the Office de Radiodiffusion et de Télévision de Madagascar (ORTM); broadcasts in French and Malagasy; Dir JOHARY RAVOAJANAHARY.

Radio Antsiva: BP 632, Enceinte STEDIC, Village des Jeux, Zone Industrielle Nord, route des Hydrocarbures, 101 Antananarivo; tel. (20) 2254849; e-mail antsiva@freenet.mg; internet www.antsiva.mg; f. 1994; broadcasts in French and Malagasy.

Radio Don Bosco: Maison Don Bosco, BP 60, 105 Ivato; tel. (20) 2244387; fax (20) 2244511; e-mail rdb@radiodonbosco.org; internet www.radiodonbosco.org; f. 1996; Catholic, educational and cultural; Dir LUCA TREGLIA.

Radio Lazan'iarivo (RLI): Lot V A49, Andafiavaratra, 101 Antananarivo; tel. (20) 2229016; fax (20) 2267559; e-mail rli@simicro.mg;

broadcasts in French, English and Malagasy; privately owned; specializes in jazz music; Dir IHOBY RABARIJOHN.

Radio Viva: Antananarivo; Owner ANDRY RAJOELINA.

Television

MA TV: BP 1414 Ankorondrano, 101 Antananarivo; tel. (20) 2220897; fax (20) 2234421; f. 1995; Pres. FREDY ANDRIAMBELO; Dir-Gen. WILLY FREDY ANDRIAMBELO.

MBS Television (Malagasy Broadcasting System): BP 11137, Anosipatrana, Antananarivo; tel. (20) 2266702; fax (20) 2268941; e-mail journaltv@mbs.mg; internet www.mbs.mg; broadcasts in French and Malagasy.

Radio Télévision Analamanga (RTA): Immeuble Fiaro, 101 Antananarivo; tel. (20) 2224503; e-mail rta@rta.mg; internet www.rta.mg; incl. four provincial radio stations; Dir-Gen. SELVEN NAIDU.

Télévision Nasionale Malagache: BP 1202, Anosy, 101 Antananarivo; tel. (20) 2222381; state-controlled; part of the Office de Radiodiffusion et de Télévision de Madagascar (ORTM); broadcasts in French and Malagasy; Gen. Man. JPHARY RAVAOJANAHARY.

Télévision Viva: Antananarivo; Owner ANDRY RAJOELINA.

Finance

(cap. = capital; res = reserves; dep. = deposits; m. = million; brs = branches; amounts in ariary)

BANKING

Central Bank

Banque Centrale de Madagascar: rue de la Révolution Socialiste Malgache, BP 550, 101 Antananarivo; tel. (20) 2221751; fax (20) 2234532; e-mail sbu@bfm.mg; internet www.banque-centrale.mg; f. 1973; bank of issue; cap. 111,000m., res 32,420m., dep. 1,305,852m. (Dec. 2008); Gov. GUY RATOVONDRAHONA (acting).

Other Banks

Bank of Africa (BOA)—Madagascar: 2 pl. de l'Indépendance, BP 183, 101 Antananarivo; tel. (20) 2239100; fax (20) 2266125; e-mail boa@boa.mg; internet www.boa.mg; f. 1976 as Bankin'ny Tantsaha Mpamokatra; name changed as above 1999; 38.86% owned by Bank of Africa Group (Luxembourg), 10% state-owned; commercial bank, specializes in micro-finance; cap. 33,000.0m., res 36,511.4m., dep. 1,048,790.9m. (Dec. 2008); Chair. and Pres. PAUL DERREUMAUX; Gen. Man. JACQUES DILET; 55 brs.

Banque Industrielle et Commerciale de Madagascar (BICM): 2 rue du Dr Raseta Andraharo, BP 889, 101 Antananarivo; tel. (20) 2356568; fax (20) 2356656; e-mail bicm@bicm.mg; internet www.bicm.mg; f. 2002; successor of the Banque Internationale Chine Madagascar, fmrly Compagnie Malgache de Banque; cap. 5,779.2m., dep. 3,680.4m. (Dec. 2007) res –1,804.6m.(Dec. 2005); Pres. CHI MING HUI; Dir-Gen. Dr HUANG WEI GUANG.

Banque Malgache de l'Océan Indien (BMOI) (Indian Ocean Malagasy Bank): pl. de l'Indépendance, BP 25 bis, Antaninarenina, 101 Antananarivo; tel. (20) 2238251; fax (20) 2238544; e-mail bmoi.st@bnpparibas.com; internet www.bmoi.mg; f. 1989; 75% owned by BNP Paribas SA (France); cap. and res 40,200.0m., dep. 377,700.0m. (Dec. 2006); Pres. GASTON RAMENASON; Dir ALAIN RIPERT; 8 brs.

Banque SBM Madagascar: rue Andrianary Ratianarivo Antsahavola 1, 101 Antananarivo; tel. (20) 2266607; fax (20) 2266608; e-mail bsbmmtana@sbm.intnet.mu; f. 1998; 79.99% owned by SBM Global Investments Ltd (Mauritius), 20.01% owned by Nedbank Africa Investments Ltd (South Africa); cap. 7,404.1m., res 2,363.5m., dep. 92,221.2m. (Dec. 2007); Chair. CHAITLALL GUNNESS; Gen. Man. KRISHNADUTT RAMBOJUN.

BFV—Société Générale: 14 rue Général Rabehevitra, BP 196, Antananarivo 101; tel. (20) 2220691; fax (20) 2237140; e-mail relation.client@socgen.com; internet www.bfvsg.mg; f. 1977 as Banky Fampandrosoana ny Varotra; changed name in 1998; 70% owned by Société Générale (France), 28.5% state-owned; cap. 14,000.0m., res 48,833.0m., dep. 583,398.8m. (Dec. 2008); Pres. PHILIPPE LAMÉ; 40 brs.

BNI Madagascar: 74 rue du 26 Juin 1960, BP 174, 101 Antananarivo; tel. (20) 2222800; fax (20) 2233749; e-mail info@bni.mg; internet www.bni.mg; f. 1976 as Bankin 'ny Indostria; 51% owned by IUB Holding (France), 32.58% state-owned; cap. 10,800.0m., res 43,496.2m., dep. 693,056.1m. (Dec. 2007); Pres. and Chair. EVARISTE MARSON; Man. Dir PASCAL FALL; 25 brs.

Mauritius Commercial Bank (Madagascar) SA (MCB): 77 rue Solombavambahoaka Frantsay, Antsahavola, BP 197, 101 Antananarivo; tel. (20) 2227262; fax (20) 2228740; e-mail mcb.int@mcbmadagascar.com; internet www.mcbmadagascar.com; f. 1992 as Union Commercial Bank; name changed as above in 2007; 70% owned by Mauritius Commercial Bank Ltd; cap. 17,913.9m., res 6,753.6m., dep. 134,956.2m. (Dec. 2008); Chair. JEAN FRANÇOIS DESVAUX DE MARIGNY; Gen. Man. MARC MARIE JOSEPH DE BOLLIVIER; 3 brs.

INSURANCE

ARO (Assurances Réassurances Omnibranches): Antsahavola, BP 42, 101 Antananarivo; tel. (20) 2220154; fax (20) 2234464; e-mail aro1@moov.mg; internet www.aro.mg; state-owned; Dir-Gen. PATRICK ANDRIAMBAHINY.

ASCOMA Madagascar: 13 rue Patrice Lumumba, BP 673, 101 Antananarivo; tel. (20) 2223162; fax (20) 2222785; e-mail madagascar@ascoma.com; internet www.ascoma.com; f. 1952; Dir VIVIANE RAMANITRA.

Compagnie Malgache d'Assurances et de Réassurances 'Ny Havana': Immeuble 'Ny Havana', Zone des 67 Ha, BP 3881, 101 Antananarivo; tel. (20) 2226760; fax (20) 2224303; e-mail nyhavana@nyhavana.mg; internet www.nyhavana.mg; f. 1968; state-owned; cap. 7,704m. (2010); Dir-Gen. ROGER EMILE RANAIVOSON.

Mutuelle d'Assurances Malagasy (MAMA): Lot 1F, 12 bis Ambalavao-Isotry, BP 185, 101 Antananarivo; tel. (20) 2261882; fax (20) 2261883; e-mail assurancemama@moov.mg; f. 1968; Dir SETH AIMÉ RANDRIANARIJAONA.

Trade and Industry

DEVELOPMENT ORGANIZATIONS

Bureau d'Information pour les Entreprises (BIPE): Nouvel Immeuble ARO, Ampefiloha, 101 Antananarivo; tel. (20) 2230512; internet www.bipe.mg; part of the Ministry of the Economy and Industry.

Economic Development Board of Madagascar (EDBM): ave Gabriel Ramanantsoa, Antaninarenina, Antananarivo 101; tel. (20) 2268121; fax (20) 2266105; e-mail edbm@edbm.mg; internet www.edbm.gov.mg; f. 2006; service for the facilitation and promotion of investment in Madagascar; advisory service for starting a business, obtaining visas and land acquisition; CEO ERIC RAKOTO ANDRIANTSILAVO.

La Maison de l'Entreprise: rue Samuel Ramahefy Ambatonakanga, BP 74, 101 Antananarivo; tel. (20) 2225386; fax (20) 2233669; e-mail cite@cite.mg; internet www.cite.mg; f. 1967; supports and promotes Malagasy businesses; Dir-Gen. ISABELLE GACHIE.

Office des Mines Nationales et des Industries Stratégiques (OMNIS): 21 Làlana Razanakombana, BP 1 bis, 101 Antananarivo; tel. (20) 2224283; fax (20) 2222985; e-mail secdg@omnis.mg; internet www.omnis-madagascar.mg; f. 1976; promotes the exploration and exploitation of mining resources, in particular oil resources; Dir-Gen. BONAVENTURE RASOANAIVO.

Société d'Etude et de Réalisation pour le Développement Industriel (SERDI): BP 3180, 101 Antananarivo; tel. (20) 2225204; fax (20) 2229669; f. 1966; Dir-Gen. RAOILISON RAJAONARY.

CHAMBERS OF COMMERCE

Fédération des Chambres de Commerce et d'Industrie de Madagascar (FCCIM): BP 166, 20 rue Henri Razanatseheno, Antaninarenina, Antananarivo 101; tel. (20) 2221322; fax (20) 2220213; e-mail cciaa@tana-cciaa.org; internet www.cci-madagascar.org; 20 mem. chambers; Pres. CHABANI NOURDINE; Dir-Gen. JOSIELLE RAFIDY (acting).

Chambre de Commerce et d'Industrie d'Antananarivo (CCIA): BP 166, 20 rue Henri Razanatseheno, Antaninarenina, 101 Antananarivo; tel. (20) 2220211; fax (20) 202220211; e-mail communication.tnr@cci.mg; internet www.cci.mg; f. 1993; Pres. JEAN MARTIN RAKOTOZAFY.

TRADE ASSOCIATION

Société d'Intérêt National des Produits Agricoles (SINPA): BP 754, rue Fernand-Kasanga, Tsimbazaza, Antananarivo; tel. (20) 2220558; fax (20) 2220665; f. 1973; monopoly purchaser and distributor of agricultural produce; Chair. GUALBERT RAZANAJATOVO; Gen. Man. JEAN CLOVIS RALIJESY.

EMPLOYERS' ORGANIZATIONS

Groupement des Entreprises de Madagascar (GEM): Kianja MDRM sy Tia Tanindrazana, Ambohijatovo, BP 1338, 101 Antananarivo; tel. (20) 2223841; fax (20) 2221965; e-mail gem@iris.mg; internet www.gem-madagascar.com; f. 1975; 16 nat. syndicates and five regional syndicates comprising 1,000 cos and 59 directly affiliated cos; Pres. JOSÉPHINE NORO ANDRIAMAMONJIARISON; Sec.-Gen. ZINAH RASAMUEL RAVALOSON.

Groupement National des Exportateurs de Vanille de Madagascar (GNEV): BP 21, Antalaha; tel. (13) 20714532; fax (13) 20816017; e-mail rama.anta@sat.blueline.mg; 18 mems; Pres. JEAN GEORGES RANDRIAMIHARISOA.

Malagasy Entrepreneurs' Association (FIV.MPA.MA): Lot II, 2e étage, Immeuble Santa, Antanimena, Antananarivo; tel. (20) 2229292; fax (20) 2229290; e-mail fivmpama@moov.mg; comprises 10 trade assocs, representing 200 mems, and 250 direct business mems; Chair. HERINTSALAMA RAJAONARIVELO.

Syndicat des Industries de Madagascar (SIM): Immeuble Holcim, Lot 1 bis, Tsaralalàna; BP 1695, 101 Antananarivo; tel. (20) 2224007; fax (20) 2222518; e-mail syndusmad@moov.mg; internet www.sim.mg; f. 1958; Pres. HERY STÉPHANE RAVELOSON; 96 mems (2010).

Syndicat des Planteurs de Café: 37 Làlana Razafimahandry, BP 173, 101 Antananarivo.

Syndicat Professionel des Producteurs d'Extraits Aromatiques, Alimentaires et Medicinaux de Madagascar (SYPEAM): 7 rue Rakotoson Toto Radona, Antsahavola, BP 5038, Antananarivo 101; tel. (20) 2235363; e-mail itd.madagascar@moov.mg; f. 1994; Pres. CHARLES RANDRIAMBOLOLONA.

UTILITIES

Electricity and Water

Office de Regulation de l'Electricité (ORE): rue Tsimanindry, Ambatoroka, Antananarivo; tel. (20) 2264813; fax (20) 2264191; e-mail ore@ore.mg; internet www.ore.mg; f. 2004; Pres. AIMÉE ANDRIANASOLO.

Jiro sy Rano Malagasy (JIRAMA): BP 200, 149 rue Rainandriamampandry, Faravohitra, 101 Antananarivo; tel. (20) 2220031; fax (20) 2233806; e-mail dgjirama@jirama.mg; internet www.jirama.mg; f. 1975; controls production and distribution of electricity and water; managed by local manager; Pres. HAJA RESAMPA; Dir-Gen. RASIDY DÉSIRÉ.

MAJOR COMPANIES

The following are some of the largest in terms either of capital investment or employment.

Brasseries STAR Madagascar: rue Dr Raseta, Andranomahery, BP 3806, 101 Antananarivo; tel. (20) 2227711; fax (20) 2234692; f. 1953; cap. 10,090.9m. FMG; mfrs of beer and carbonated drinks; Pres. H. FRAISE; Gen. Man. YVAN COUDERC.

Compagnie Salinière de Madagascar: 4 rue Béniowsky, BP 29, 201 Antsiranana; tel. (20) 8221373; fax (20) 8229394; e-mail consalmag@wanadoo.mg; internet www.salines-diego.com; f. 1895; cap. 1,312m. FMG; exploitation of salt marshes (60,000 tons a year); Pres. PANAYOTIS TALOUMIS; Dir-Gen. DIMITRI CHARALAMBAKIS; 200 employees (2007).

COTONA: route d'Ambositra, BP 45, Antsirabé; tel. (20) 4449422; fax (20) 4449222; e-mail sag@cotona.com; f. 1952; owned by Socota Textile Mills Ltd; cap. 8,000m. FMG; spinning, weaving, printing and dyeing of textiles; Chair. SALIM ISMAIL; Dir-Gen. HAKIM FAKIRA; 959 employees.

DINIKA International SA (Entreprise d'Etudes Pluridisciplinaires): BP 3359, 101 Antananarivo; tel. (20) 2222233; fax (20) 2221324; f. 1979; civil engineering, architecture.

Dynatec Madagascar SARL: BP 4254, Bâtiment C2, Explorer Business Park, Ankorondrano, 101 Antananarivo; tel. (20) 2254030; fax (20) 2254412; f. 2003; nickel and cobalt mining at Ambatovy.

Etablissements Gallois: 15 rue Béniowsky, BP 159, 101 Antananarivo; tel. (20) 2222951; fax (20) 2234452; internet www.ets-gallois.com; leading producer of graphite and sisal; Pres. ROBERT FÉLIX; Man. Dir JEAN-CLAUDE FÉLIX-GALLOIS.

Galana Distribution Petrolière SA: Immeuble Ikopa Centre, BP 60, 118 Antananarivo; tel. (20) 2246803; fax (20) 2246797; e-mail info@galana.com; internet www.galana.com; subsidiary of Galana, Kenya; owns the national petroleum refinery at Toamasina: Galana Raffinerie Terminale SA; Dir-Gen. PHILIPPE GULDEMONT.

Groupe SODIAT: Borosy Talatamaty, Route d'Ambohidratrimo, BP 5068, Antananrivo 105; tel. (20) 2244027; fax (20) 2242564; e-mail sodiat@blueline.mg; internet www.sodiatgroupe.com; f. 1990; Dir-Gen. MAMINIAINA RAVATOMANGA.

Hasy Malagasy SA (HASYMA): BP 692, Antananarivo; tel. (20) 2264239; fax (20) 2234958; e-mail hasyma@wanadoo.mg; f. 1973; 51.98% owned by Développement des Agro-industries du Sud—Dagris (France); accounts for 75% of national cotton production; Gen. Dir YANNICK DAVENEL.

Holcim (Madagascar) SA: BP 332, 1 bis, rue Patrice Lumumba, Tsaralalana; tel. (20) 2232908; fax (20) 2233277; part of Holcim Overseas Group companies (Holcim (Outre-Mer)); fmrly Matériaux de Constructions Malgaches—MACOMA, renamed as above 2002; annual production capacity is 0.4m. metric tons; operates a cement plant in Antsirabe and three concrete plants; Chief Exec. ANDREAS ROGENMOSER; Dir-Gen PASCAL NAUD.

Jovenna: Complexe Kube, Bâtiment A, Zone Galaxy Andraharo, BP 12087, Antananarivo; tel. (20) 2369470; fax (20) 2369453; e-mail bureau@jovenna.mg; internet www.jovenna.mg; 80% owned by Jovenna International Holding Madagascar, 20% owned by Govt of Madagascar; one of three petroleum distributors to purchase the assets of the state company Solitany Malagasy; Man. Dir BENJAMIN MEMMI.

Kraomita Malagasy SA (KRAOMA): rue Andrianaivoravelona Zanany, BP 936, Ampefihola, 101 Antananarivo; tel. (20) 2224304; fax (20) 2224654; e-mail kraoma@moov.mg; internet www.kraoma.mg; f. 1966 as Cie Minière d'Andriamena (COMINA); cap. 3,231.6m. ariary; 100% state-owned; chrome mining and concentration; Pres. JEANNE DAVIDSON RAOLIMALALA; Gen. Man. MEJAMIRADO RAZAFIMIHARY; 380 employees.

Madagascar Oil: Immeuble Trano Fitaratra, 9th Floor, Antananarivo; internet www.madagascaroil.com; f. 2004; Chair. and CEO JOHN LAURIE HUNTER.

Marbres et Granits de Madagascar (MAGRAMA): 8 rue de la Réunion, 101 Antananarivo; tel. (20) 2230042; fax (20) 2228578; mines labradorite from Ambatofinandrahana and Bekily.

Les Moulins de Madagascar: Antananarivo; f. 2007; reopened 2011; Man. JONATHAN REED.

La Nouvelle Brasserie de Madagascar (NBM): Antananarivo; internet www.skol.mg; Dir-Gen. GUY LECLOUX.

Omnium Industriel de Madagascar (OIM JB): BP 207, 24 rue Radama, 101 Antananarivo; tel. (20) 2222373; fax (20) 2228064; e-mail oim@oimjb.com; f. 1929; cap. 1,300m. FMG; mfrs of shoes and luggage; operates a tannery; Pres. and Dir-Gen. A. BARDAY; 174 employees (2004).

Pan-African Mining Madagascar Sarl (PAM): Lot II N 174 PA Analamahitsy, 101 Antananarivo; tel. (20) 2201961; fax (20) 2201960; e-mail pammsarl@wanadoo.mg; internet www.panafrican.com; f. 2003; mining exploration, particularly for gold, nickel, precious stones and uranium; a subsidiary of Pan-African Mining Corpn (Canada); Assoc. Man. OLIVIER RAKOTMALALA.

Papeteries de Madagascar SA (PAPMAD): BP 1756, 101 Antananarivo; Ambohimanambola 103; tel. and fax (20) 220635; fax 224394; e-mail papmad@malagasy.com; f. 1963; cap. 6,364m. FMG (2000); paper-making; Chair. PATRICK RAJAONARY; 472 employees (2003).

QIT Madagascar Minerals (QMM): BP 4003, Villa 3H, Lot II J-169 Ivandry, 101 Antananarivo; tel. (20) 2242559; fax (20) 2242506; e-mail media.enquiries@riotinto.com; internet www.riotintomadagascar.com; f. 2001; 80% owned by Rio Tinto plc (United Kingdom/Australia), 20% state-owned; construction of an ilmenite mine and deep-sea port in the Fort Dauphin region; CEO GARY O'BRIEN.

Société Alubat/NACM Service: 352 route Circulaire Anjahana, BP 1073, 101 Antananarivo; tel. (20) 2223126; fax (20) 2233744; e-mail alubat@simicro.mg; f. 1960; mfrs of cutlery, tools, implements and metal parts; Dir-Gen. PATRICIA KWAN HUA; 40 employees (2004).

Société Bonnetière Malagasy (SOBOMA): BP 3789, 101 Antananarivo; tel. (20) 2244354; fax (20) 2244891; f. 1968; produces knitwear; Pres. RÉNÉ TARDY; Dir-Gen. JEAN-PIERRE TARDY; 300 employees.

Société des Cigarettes Melia de Madagascar (SACIMEM): route d'Ambositra, BP 128, Antsirabé 110; tel. (20) 4448241; f. 1956; cap. 881m. FMG; mfrs of cigarettes; Pres. and Dir-Gen. PHILIPPE DE VESINNE LARUE; Dir LAURENT TABELLION.

Société d'Etudes de Constructions et Réparations Navales SA (SECREN): 201 Diego Suarez, POB 135, Antsiranana; tel. (20) 29321; fax (20) 29326; e-mail secren@wanadoo.mg; 37.5% state-owned; f. 1975; transfer to the private sector pending; cap. 400m. ariary; ship-building and repairs; Gen. Man. ABEL NTSAY; 1,000 employees (2007).

Société d'Exploitation des Sources d'Eaux Minérales Naturelles d'Andranovelona SA (Sema Eau Vive): BP 22, 101 Antananarivo; tel. (20) 2227711; fax (20) 2234692; produces mineral water.

Société de Filature et de Tissage de Madagascar (FITIM): BP 127, Mahajanga; tel. (20) 6222127; fax (20) 6229345; e-mail fitim@malagasy.com; f. 1930; cap. 1,444m. FMG; spinning and weaving of jute; Pres. C. A. WILLIAM RAVONINJATOVO; Dir-Gen. AZIZ HOUSSEN; 113 employees.

Société Malgache de Cosmetiques et de Parfumerie (SOMALCO): Tanjombato, BP 852, 101 Antananarivo; tel. (20) 2246537; fax (20) 2247079; e-mail somalco@sicob.mg; perfumery, cosmetics and toothpaste; Pres. GOULSENBANOU BARDAY; Dir-Gen. NIGAR BARDAY.

Société Malgache de Pêcherie (SOMAPECHE): BP 324, Mahanga; 33% state-owned; cap. 200m. FMG; sea fishing; Pres. J. RABEMANANJARA; Dir-Gen. J. BRUNOT.

Société des Produits Chimiques de Madagascar SA (PROCHIMAD): Mandrosoa Ivato, BP 3145, 101 Antananarivo; tel. (20) 2244140; fax (20) 2244726; e-mail prochimad@blueline.mg; manufactures chemicals and fertilizers; Pres. and Dir-Gen. CHARLES ANDRIANTSITOHAINA.

Société Siramamy Malagasy SA (SIRAMA): BP 1633, Impasse, rue de Belgique Isoraka, 101 Antananarivo; tel. (20) 2225235; fax (20) 2227231; f. 1949; 74.4% state-owned; cap. 2,500m. FMG; sugar refinery at St Louis; accounts for 85% of national sugar production; cap. 1,874.8m. FMG; Pres. and Dir-Gen. ZAKA HARISON RAKOTONIRAINY; 4,691 employees (2005).

Société Verrerie Malagasy (SOVEMA): BP 84, Toamasina; f. 1970; 31.2% state-owned; cap. 235.6m. FMG; bottles and glass articles; Pres. and Dir-Gen. A. SIBILLE.

Total: Immeuble Titaratra, Ankolondrano, 101 Antananarivo; tel. (20) 2239040; fax (20) 2237545; internet www.total.mg; subsidiary of Total, France; one of four petroleum distributors to purchase the assets of the state company Solitany Malagasy; Chair. JEAN JACQUES PAPÉE; Gen. Man. THIERRY GAUTIER.

TRADE UNIONS

Cartel National des Organisations Syndicales de Madagascar (CARNOSYMA): BP 1035, 101 Antananarivo.

Confédération des Travailleurs Malagasy Révolutionnaires (FISEMARE): Lot IV N 76-A, Ankadifotsy, BP 1128, Befelatanana-Antananarivo 101; tel. (20) 2221989; fax (20) 2267712; f. 1985; Pres. PAUL RABEMANANJARA.

Confédération des Travailleurs Malgaches (Fivomdronamben'ny Mpiasa Malagasy—FMM): Lot IVM 133 A Antetezanafovoany I, BP 846, 101 Antananarivo; tel. (20) 2224565; e-mail rjeannot2002@yahoo.fr; f. 1957; Sec.-Gen. JEANNOT RAMANARIVO; 30,000 mems.

Fédération des Syndicats des Travailleurs de Madagascar (Firaisan'ny Sendika eran'i Madagaskara—FISEMA): Lot III, rue Pasteur Isotry, BP 172, 101 Antananarivo; tel. (33) 1187414; e-mail fisema@gmail.co; internet fisema.org; f. 1956; Sec.-Gen. JOSÉ RANDRIANASOLO; 8 affiliated unions representing 60,000 mems.

Sendika Kristianina Malagasy (SEKRIMA) (Christian Confederation of Malagasy Trade Unions): Soarano, route de Mahajanga, BP 1035, 101 Antananarivo; tel. (20) 2223174; f. 1937; Pres. MARIE RAKOTOANOSY; Gen. Sec. JEANNE CLAIRETTE RAZANARIMANANA; 158 affiliated unions representing 40,000 mems.

Union des Syndicats Autonomes de Madagascar (USAM): Lot III M 33 BC, Andrefan'Ambohijanahary, BP 1038, 101 Antananarivo; tel. and fax (20) 2227485; e-mail usam@moov.mg; f. 1954; Pres. THÉOPHILE JOËL RUFIN RAZAKARIASY; Sec.-Gen. SAMUEL RABEMANANTSOA; 49 affiliated unions representing 30,000 mems.

Transport

RAILWAYS

In 2009 there were 854 km of railway, including four railway lines, all 1-m gauge track. The northern system, which comprised 673 km of track, links the east coast with Antsirabé, in the interior, via Moramanga and Antananarivo, with a branch line from Moramanga to Lake Alaotra, and was privatized in 2001. The southern system, which comprised 163 km of track, links Manakara, on the east coast, with Fianarantsoa.

Fianarantsoa-Côte Est (FCE): FCE Gare, 301 Fianarantsoa; tel. (20) 7551354; e-mail fce@blueline.mg; internet www.fce-fianarantsoa-madagascar.com; f. 1936; southern network, 163 km.

Madarail: Gare de Soarano, 1 ave de l'Indépendance, BP 1175, 101 Antananarivo; tel. (20) 2234599; fax (20) 2221883; e-mail madarail@wanadoo.mg; internet www.comazar.com/madarail.htm; f. 2001; jt venture, operated by Comazar, South Africa; 45% of Comazar is owned by Sheltam Locomotive and Rail Services, South Africa; 31.6% is owned by Transnet Freight Rail, South Africa; operates the northern network of the Malagasy railway (650 km); Chair. ERIC PEIFFER; Gen. Dir PATRICK CLAES; 878 employees.

ROADS

In 2001 there were an estimated 49,837 km of classified roads; about 11.6% of the road network was paved. In 1987 there were 39,500 km of unclassified roads, used only in favourable weather. A road and motorway redevelopment programme, funded by the World Bank (€300m.) and the European Union (EU) (€61m.), began in June 2000. In August 2002 the EU undertook to disburse US $10m. for the reconstruction of 11 bridges destroyed during the political crisis in that year. In 2003 Japan pledged $28m. to build several bridges and a 15-km bypass. The Government planned to have restored and upgraded 14,000 km of highways and 8,000 km of rural roads to an operational status by 2015. In 2005, according to the IMF, 8,982 km of roads had been maintained or rehabilitated.

INLAND WATERWAYS

The Pangalanes canal runs for 600 km near the east coast from Toamasina to Farafangana. In 1990 432 km of the canal between Toamasina and Mananjary were navigable.

SHIPPING

There are 18 ports, the largest being at Toamasina, which handles about 70% of total traffic, and Mahajanga; several of the smaller ports are prone to silting problems. A new deep-sea port was to be constructed at Ehoala, near Fort Dauphin, in order to accommodate the activity of an ilmenite mining development by 2008. At 31 December 2009 the country's merchant fleet numbered 106 vessels and amounted to 32,800 gross registered tons.

CMA—CGM Madagascar: Village des jeux, Bat. C1 Ankorondrano, BP 12042, 101 Antananarivo; tel. (20) 2235949; fax (20) 2266120; e-mail tnr@cma-cgm.mg; internet www.cma-cgm.com; maritime transport; Gen. Man. JOËL LE JULIEN.

Compagnie Générale Maritime Sud (CGM): BP 1185, Lot II U 31 bis, Ampahibe, 101 Antananarivo; tel. (20) 2220113; fax (20) 2226530.

Compagnie Malgache de Navigation (CMN): rue Rabearivelo, BP 1621, 101 Antananarivo; tel. (20) 2225516; fax (20) 2230358; f. 1960; coasters; 13,784 grt; 97.5% state-owned; privatization pending; Pres. ELINAH BAKOLY RAJAONSON; Dir-Gen. ARISTIDE EMMANUEL.

SCAC-SDV Shipping Madagascar: rue Rabearivelo Antsahavola, BP 514, 102 Antananarivo; tel. (20) 2220631; fax (20) 2247862; operates the harbour in Antananarivo Port.

Société Malgache des Transports Maritimes (SMTM): 6 rue Indira Gandhi, BP 4077, 101 Antananarivo; tel. (20) 2227342; fax (20) 2233327; f. 1963; 59% state-owned; privatization pending; services to Europe; Chair. ALEXIS RAZAFINDRATSIRA; Dir-Gen. JEAN RANJEVA.

CIVIL AVIATION

The Ivato international airport is at Antananarivo, while the airports at Mahajanga, Toamasina and Nossi-Bé can also accommodate large jet aircraft. There are 211 airfields, two-thirds of which are privately owned. In 1996 the Government authorized private French airlines to operate scheduled and charter flights between Madagascar and Western Europe.

Aeromarine: Zone Industrielle FORELLO, Tanjombato, BP 3844, 102 Antananarivo; tel. (20) 2248286; fax (20) 2258026; e-mail aeromarine@blueline.mg; internet www.aeromarine.mg; f. 1991; Dir-Gen. RIAZ BARDAY.

Air Madagascar (Société Nationale Malgache des Transports Aériens): 31 ave de l'Indépendance, Analakely, BP 437, 101 Antananarivo; tel. (20) 2222222; fax (20) 2233760; e-mail commercial@airmadagascar.com; internet www.airmadagascar.com; f. 1962; 90.60% state-owned; 3.17% owned by Air France (France); transfer to the private sector pending; restructured and managed by Lufthansa Consulting since 2002; extensive internal routes connecting all the principal towns; external services to France, Italy, the Comoros, Kenya, Mauritius, Réunion, South Africa and Thailand; Chair. HERY RAJAONARIMAMPIANINA; Dir-Gen. HUGHES RATSIFERANA.

Air Transport et Transit Régional (ATTR): tel. (32) 0518811; fax (32) 3205218; e-mail attr.reservation@blueline.mg; internet www.attrmada.com; f. 2006; private; regular local and regional services; services suspended in 2008; Dir Gen. FRÉDÉRIC RABESAHALA.

Aviation Civile de Madagascar (ACM): 13 rue Fernand Kasanga, BP 4414, 101 Tsimbazaza-Antananarivo; tel. (20) 2222438; fax (20) 2224726; e-mail acm@acm.mg; internet www.acm.mg; f. 2000; Chair. RANTO RABARISOA; Dir-Gen. JEAN RAZAFY ROBERT.

Transports et Travaux Aériens de Madagascar (TAM): 17 ave de l'Indépendance, Analakely, Antananarivo; tel. (20) 2222222; fax (20) 2224340; e-mail tamdg@wanadoo.mg; f. 1951; provides airline services; Administrators LALA RAZAFINDRAKOTO, FRANÇOIS DANE.

Tourism

Madagascar's attractions include unspoiled scenery, many unusual varieties of flora and fauna, and the rich cultural diversity of Malagasy life. In 2008 some 375,010 tourists visited Madagascar, the majority were from France (56.0%). There was a dramatic fall in the number of tourists visiting Madagascar in 2009, to 162,687; however, tourist numbers recovered somewhat in 2010 and 2011 rising to 196,000 and 225,000, respectively. Revenue from tourism in 2008 was estimated at US $620m. In 2009 this declined to $518m. and to 321m. in 2010.

Direction d'Appui aux Investissements Publiques: BP 610, rue Fernand Kasanga Tsimbazaza, 101 Antananarivo; tel. (20) 2262816; fax (20) 2235410; e-mail mintourdati@wandaoo.mg; internet www.tourisme.gov.mg.

Office National du Tourisme de Madagascar: 3 rue Elysée Ravelontsalama, Ambatomena, 101 Antananarivo; tel. (20) 2266115; fax (20) 2266098; e-mail ontm@moov.mg; internet www.madagascar-tourisme.com; Pres. JOEL RANDRIAMANDRANTO.

Defence

As assessed at November 2011, total armed forces numbered 13,500 men: army 12,500, navy 500 and air force 500. There is a paramilitary gendarmerie of 8,100.

Defence Expenditure: Budgeted at an estimated 146,000m. ariary in 2011.

Chief of Staff of the Armed Forces: Col ANDRÉ ANDRIARIJAONA.

Education

Education is officially compulsory between six and 13 years of age. Madagascar has both public and private schools, although legislation that was enacted in 1978 envisaged the progressive elimination of private education. Primary education generally begins at the age of six and lasts for five years. Secondary education, beginning at 11 years of age, lasts for a further seven years, comprising a first cycle of four years and a second of three years. A new educational system, comprising 10 years of basic education and two years of secondary education, was intended for gradual introduction from the academic year 2008/09. However, the process of implementation was suspended in March 2009. According to UNESCO estimates, in 2006/07 primary enrolment included 98% of children in the relevant age-group (male 98%; females 99%), while in 2008/09 secondary enrolment included 26% of children in the relevant age-group (males 26%; females 25%). In 2009/10 74,400 students attended institutions providing tertiary education; there are six universities in Madagascar. In 2008 spending on education represented 13.4% of total budgetary expenditure.

Bibliography

Allen, P. *Madagascar: Conflicts of Authority in the Great Island.* Boulder, CO, Westview Press, 1995.

Allen, P., and Covell M. *Historical Dictionary of Madagascar.* Lanham, MD, Scarecrow, 2005.

Archer, R. *Madagascar depuis 1972, la marche d'une révolution.* Paris, L'Harmattan, 1976.

Astuti, R. *People of the Sea: Identity and Descent among the Vezo of Madagascar.* Cambridge, Cambridge University Press, 1995.

Bastian, G. *Madagascar, étude géographique et économique.* Nathan, 1967.

Bloch, M. *From Blessing to Violence.* Cambridge, Cambridge University Press, 1996.

Bradt, H., and Brown, M. *Madagascar.* Oxford, Clio Press, 1993.

Brown, M. *Madagascar Rediscovered.* London, Damien Tunnacliffe, 1978.

A History of Madagascar. London, Damien Tunnacliffe, 1995.

Cadoux, C. *La République malgache.* Paris, Berger-Levrault, 1970.

Chaigneau, P. *Rivalités politiques et socialisme à Madagascar.* Paris, Centre des Hautes Etudes sur lAfrique et lAsie Modernes, 1985.

Covell, M. *Madagascar. Politics, Economics and Society.* London, Frances Pinter, 1987.

Deleris, F. *Ratsiraka: socialisme et misère à Madagascar.* Paris, L'Harmattan, 1986.

Deschamps, H. *Histoire de Madagascar.* 4th edn. Paris, Berger-Levrault, 1972.

Duruflé, G. *L'Ajustement structurel en Afrique (Sénégal, Côte d'Ivoire, Madagascar).* Paris, Editions Karthala, 1987.

Feeley-Harnick, G. *A Green Estate: Restoring Independence in Madagascar.* Washington, DC, Smithsonian Institution Press, 1991.

de Gaudusson, J. *L'Administration malgache.* Paris, Berger-Levrault, 1976.

Goodman, S., and Benstead, J. *The Natural History of Madagascar.* Chicago, IL, Chicago University Press, 2004.

Grehan, J. *The Forgotten Invasion: Madagascar 1942.* Pulborough, Historic Military Press, 2007.

Heseltine, N. *Madagascar.* London, Pall Mall, 1971.

Hugon, P. *Economie et enseignement à Madagascar.* Paris, Institut International de Planification de l'Education, 1976.

Litalien, R. *Madagascar 1956–1960. Etape vers la décolonisation.* Paris, Ecole Pratique des Hautes Etudes, 1975.

Massiot, M. *L'organisation politique, administrative, financière et judiciaire de la République malgache.* Antananarivo, Librairie de Madagascar, 1970.

Mutibwa, P. *The Malagasy and the Europeans: Madagascar's Foreign Relations 1861–95.* London, Longman, 1974.

Pascal, R. *La République malgache: Pacifique indépendance.* Paris, Berger-Levrault, 1965.

Pezzotta, F. *Madagascar, a Mineral and Gemstone Paradise.* East Hampton, CT, Lapis International LLC, 2001.

Pryor, F. L. *Malawi and Madagascar: The Political Economy of Poverty, Equity and Growth.* New York, Oxford University Press, 1991.

Rabemananjara, J. *Nationalisme et problèmes malgaches.* Paris, 1958.

Rabenoro, C. *Les relations extérieures de Madagascar, de 1960 à 1972.* Paris, L'Harmattan, 1986.

Radrianja, S., and Ellis, S. *Madagascar: A Short History.* Chicago, IL, Chicago University Press, 2009.

Raison-Jourde, F. *Les souverains de Madagascar.* Paris, Editions Karthala, 1983.

Rajoelina, P. *Quarante années de la vie politique de Madagascar, 1947–1987.* Paris, LHarmattan, 1988.

Rajoelina, P., and Ramelet, A. *Madagascar, la grande île.* Paris, L'Harmattan, 1989.

Ralaimihoatra, E. *Histoire de Madagascar*. 2 vols. Antananarivo, Société Malgache d'Editions, 1966–67.

Ramahatra, O. *Madagascar: une économie en phase d'ajustement.* Paris, L'Harmattan, 1989.

Roubaud, F. *Identités et transition démocratique: l'exception malgache.* Paris, L'Harmattan, 2001.

Schuurman, D., and Ravelojoana, N. *Madagascar.* London, New Holland, 1997.

Spacensky, A. *Madagascar: cinquante ans de vie politique (de Ralaimongo à Tsiranana).* Paris, Nouvelles Editions Latines, 1970.

Tronchon, J. *L'insurrection malgache de 1947.* Paris, Editions Karthala, 1986.

Tyson, P. *The Eighth Continent: Life, Death and Discovery in the Lost World of Madagascar.* New York, William Morrow & Co, 2000.

Vérin, P. *Madagascar.* Paris, Editions Karthala, 1990.

Vindard, G. R., and Battistini, R. *Bio-geography and Ecology of Madagascar.* The Hague, 1972.

MALAWI

Physical and Social Geography

A. MacGREGOR HUTCHESON

The land-locked Republic of Malawi extends some 840 km from north to south, varying in width from 80 to 160 km. It has a total area of 118,484 sq km (45,747 sq miles), including 24,208 sq km (9,347 sq miles) of inland water, and is aligned along the southern continuation of the east African Rift Valley system. There are land borders with Tanzania to the north, with Zambia to the west, and with Mozambique to the south and east. Frontiers with Mozambique and Tanzania continue to the east, along the shores of Lake Malawi.

Malawi occupies a plateau of varying height, bordering the deep Rift Valley trench, which averages 80 km in width. The northern two-thirds of the Rift Valley floor are almost entirely occupied by Lake Malawi, which is 568 km in length and varies in width from 16 km to 80 km. The lake covers an area of 23,310 sq km, and has a mean surface of 472 m above sea-level. The southern third of the Rift Valley is traversed by the Shire river, draining Lake Malawi, via the shallow Lake Malombe, to the Zambezi river. The plateau surfaces on either side of the Rift Valley lie mainly at 760 m–1,370 m, but elevations up to 3,002 m are attained; above the highlands west of Lake Malawi are the Nyika and Viphya plateaux (at 2,606 m and 1,954 m, respectively) and the Dedza mountains and Kirk Range, which rise to between 1,524 m and 2,440 m in places. South of Lake Malawi are the Shire highlands and the Zomba and Mulanje mountain ranges; the Zomba plateau rises to 2,087 m, and Mt Mulanje, the highest mountain in central Africa, to 3,050 m above sea-level.

The great variations in altitude and latitudinal extent are responsible for a wide range of climatic, soil and vegetational conditions within Malawi. There are three climatic seasons. During the cool season, from May to August, there is very little cloud, and mean temperatures in the plateau areas are 15.5°C–18°C, and in the Rift Valley 20°C–24.5°C. The coldest month is July, when the maximum temperature is 22.2°C and the minimum 11.7°C. In September and October, before the rains, a short hot season occurs when humidity increases: mean temperatures range from 27°C–30°C in the Rift Valley, and from 22°C–24.5°C on the plateaux at this time. During October–November temperatures exceeding 37°C may be registered in the low-lying areas. The rainy season lasts from November to April, and over 90% of the total annual rainfall occurs during this period. Most of Malawi receives an annual rainfall of 760 mm–1,015 mm, but some areas in the higher plateaux experience over 1,525 mm.

Malawi possesses some of the most fertile soils in south-central Africa. Of particular importance are those in the lake-shore plains, the Lake Chilwa-Palombe plain and the upper and lower Shire valley. Good plateau soils occur in the Lilongwe-Kasungu high plains and in the tea-producing areas of Thyolo, Mulanje and Nkhata Bay districts. Although just over one-half of the land area of Malawi is considered suitable for cultivation, rather less than 50% of this area is cultivated at present; this is an indication of the agricultural potential yet to be realized. The lakes and rivers have been exploited for their considerable hydroelectric and irrigation potential.

Malawi is one of the more densely populated countries of Africa, with 13,077,160 inhabitants (an average density of 138.7 per sq km) at the 2008 census. The UN estimated the population at 14,844,822 in mid-2012 (giving an average density of 157.5 per sq km). Population patterns are affected by the high rate of incidence of HIV/AIDS, which is particularly prevalent in urban areas. Labour has been a Malawian resource for many years, and thousands of migratory workers seek employment in neighbouring countries, particularly in South Africa.

As a result of physical, historical and economic factors, Malawi's population is unevenly distributed. At the 2008 census the Southern Region, the most developed of the three regions, contained 45% of the population, while the Central Region had 42% and the Northern Region only 13%.

Recent History

CHRISTOPHER SAUNDERS

On 6 July 1964 the British colony of Nyasaland became the independent state of Malawi. For almost three decades thereafter the country was dominated by Dr Hastings Kamuzu Banda, who had led the struggle against British rule. He ruled dictatorially from 1971 as President-for-life. His Malawi Congress Party (MCP) was the only legal political organization, and no political opposition was tolerated. Human rights organizations repeatedly criticized the treatment of political detainees. Banda was prepared to work with colonial Portugal and he established diplomatic relations with apartheid South Africa in 1967. For a long time Malawi's relations with its independent neighbours were strained, but it became a member of the Southern African Development Co-ordination Conference (later to become the Southern African Development Community—SADC) in 1980. During the 1980s Mozambique alleged that members of the Resistência Nacional Moçambicana operated from bases in Malawi, and it was not until the mid-1990s that the bulk of a large refugee population from Mozambique was repatriated.

In the early 1990s, in the era following the end of the Cold War, the Banda regime increasingly came under pressure to reform. In March 1992 the bishops of the influential Roman Catholic Church published an open letter condemning the state's abuses of human rights. Political exiles from Malawi began to organize in Lusaka, Zambia, and in May industrial unrest in the southern city of Blantyre escalated into violent anti-Government riots, which spread to the capital, Lilongwe. Shortly afterwards international donors suspended non-humanitarian aid pending reform, and in September both the Alliance for Democracy (AFORD), a pressure group for political reform, and the United Democratic Front (UDF), a political party to challenge Banda, were formed. In the following month Banda reluctantly conceded to demands for a national referendum by secret ballot on the introduction of multi-party democracy.

Despite efforts by the Government to disrupt the opposition, 63.2% of those who voted in the referendum, held in mid-June 1993, supported the reintroduction of multi-party politics. Banda agreed to establish a National Executive Council, to oversee the transition to a multi-party system, and a National Consultative Council to draft a new constitution. Both councils were to comprise members of both the Government and the opposition. He also announced a general amnesty for political exiles, and stated that a general election would be held, on a multi-party basis, within a year. In late June the Constitution was amended to allow the registration of political parties other than the MCP; AFORD and the UDF were among the organizations subsequently accorded legal status.

Banda became seriously ill in October 1993 and underwent neurological surgery in South Africa. A three-member Presidential Council assumed executive power in his absence. In mid-November the National Assembly adopted a number of constitutional amendments that, inter alia, included the repeal of the institution of a life presidency and of the requirement that election candidates be members of the MCP. After making an unexpected recovery, Banda resumed full presidential powers on 7 December and the Presidential Council was dissolved. Shortly afterwards, in response to increasing pressure from the opposition, the Government amended the Constitution to provide for the appointment of an acting President in the event of the incumbent being incapacitated. Banda stood as the MCP's presidential candidate in the May 1994 election, but Bakili Muluzi, the leader of the UDF, obtained 47.3% of the votes, Banda only 33.6% and Chakufwa Chihana, the leader of AFORD, 18.6%. The UDF won 84 of the 177 seats in the National Assembly, the MCP 55 and AFORD 36.

THE MULUZI PRESIDENCY, 1994–2004

Although President Muluzi included members of smaller parties in his Cabinet, AFORD signed a 'memorandum of understanding' with the MCP to work together in opposition, and for a time this deprived the Government of a majority in the National Assembly. In June 1994 Muluzi established an independent commission of inquiry to investigate the deaths in 1983 of Dick Matenje, then the Secretary-General of the MCP, and three other senior politicians in what had been claimed to be a road accident. In January 1995 Banda, now a chief suspect for the deaths, was placed under house arrest, and John Tembo, who had been Governor of the Reserve Bank of Malawi (the central bank) and a rival of Matenje at the time of his death, and two former police officers were arrested and charged with murder and conspiracy to murder. A former inspector-general of the police, who was alleged to have destroyed evidence relating to the deaths, was later also charged with conspiracy to murder. In December, however, Banda and the other defendants were acquitted, and although the Director of Public Prosecutions subsequently appealed against this decision, it was upheld by the Supreme Court in July 1997. In the same month Banda resigned as President of the MCP, and in November he died in South Africa after undergoing emergency medical treatment.

After two postponements, presidential and legislative elections were held on 15 June 1999. Muluzi was re-elected to the presidency, securing 51.4% of the votes cast, while Gwanda-guluwe Chakuamba, the President of the MCP, obtained 43.3%. In the election to an expanded National Assembly, 658 candidates and 11 parties contested 193 seats. The ruling UDF won 93 of these, the MCP 66 and AFORD 29. Despite declarations from international observers that the elections were largely free and fair, the MCP-AFORD alliance challenged Muluzi's victory and the results in 16 districts. The opposition alleged irregularities in the voter registration process and claimed that Muluzi's win was unconstitutional, as he had failed to gain the support of 50% of all registered voters. None the less, he was inaugurated for a second term in late June and a new Cabinet was appointed. In August the UDF regained a parliamentary majority when four independent deputies who had broken with the party prior to the elections realigned themselves with it, and in October the UDF won three by-elections, increasing its number of deputies to 100.

In December 1999 a report published by the electoral commissions forum of the SADC criticized the country's electoral commission and recommended that it should consist solely of members with no party political affiliation. A recount of votes cast in the presidential election began, and later in December lawyers representing the MCP-AFORD alliance claimed to have discovered evidence of electoral fraud carried out to the benefit of the UDF. However, in May 2000 the High Court dismissed the opposition's case and declared Muluzi's election to the presidency lawful. Meanwhile, the MCP suffered as the result of a power struggle between Chakuamba and Tembo, its Vice-President. From early 2001 the possibility that Muluzi might seek a third five-year term as President dominated Malawian politics. Senior members of the UDF campaigned for the Constitution to be amended to make this possible. Following the rejection of the idea of a third term by opposition parties and leaders of both the Protestant and Roman Catholic churches, Muluzi banned assemblies or demonstrations that either supported or condemned the proposal, on the grounds of security. Militant young members of the UDF attacked opposition supporters.

Drought exacerbated a food crisis in 2002, as many began to starve in what remained one of the poorest countries in the world. In February the President declared a state of famine, in the hope of securing large amounts of aid, but donor countries held the Government partly responsible for failing to manage the crisis properly and initially aid was not forthcoming. It was revealed that emergency stores of maize, amounting to more than 160,000 metric tons, had been sold during the previous two years, primarily to Kenya. The authorities claimed that this sale had taken place on the advice of the IMF, but the IMF denied this, stating that it had recommended that only a fraction of the reserves be sold. In August the Minister of Poverty Alleviation, Leonard Mangulama, was dismissed from the Government and charged with abuse of office for selling off the grain stores during his term in office as Minister of Agriculture. By mid-2002 an estimated 3m. people were in need of food aid, which began to arrive in large quantities from the USA, the European Union and the United Kingdom. The situation was compounded by the effects of an outbreak of cholera and the AIDS crisis. By the end of 2003 an estimated 14% of the adult population (aged between 15 and 49 years) was living with HIV/AIDS and, despite measures taken to deal with the pandemic, the rate of infection continued to increase. From December 2002 the food situation began to improve, as rain, together with millions of seed and fertilizer packs, supplied mainly by the British Government, enabled new crops to be planted.

Amid continuing criticism, the UDF abandoned its efforts to secure a third term for Muluzi. In April 2003 Muluzi dissolved the Cabinet and named Bingu wa Mutharika, who had recently been appointed Minister of Economic Planning and Development, as the party's candidate in the presidential election, which duly took place on 20 May 2004. The Malawi Electoral Commission (MEC) initially claimed that it had registered 6.6m. voters, but after complaints from opposition parties, the voters' roll was revised and almost 1m. people removed from it. While the election body blamed incorrect information given to its officials by those registering, opposition parties held the MEC responsible for failing properly to manage the process. Under the Constitution, voters had 21 days to scrutinize the roll, and the opposition coalition argued that the MEC had not allotted sufficient time for this to occur, and that vote-rigging was possible. The Supreme Court nevertheless ordered the election to proceed, stating that it was impractical to recall all the surplus ballot papers, which the coalition feared might be misused by the UDF.

Polling itself proceeded peacefully, although upon the release of the results opposition parties alleged electoral malpractice and threatened legal challenges. Mutharika was declared the winner of the presidential election, with 35.9% of the vote. Tembo received 27.1% and Chakuamba, his former MCP rival, who now led the newly formed Republican Party (RP), 25.7%. In the concurrent parliamentary election, the UDF won only 49 seats in the 193-seat legislature, which necessitated the forging of alliances with other parties in order to govern. The MCP won the largest number of seats, taking 56, while the RP secured 15, the National Democratic Alliance eight and AFORD only six. Most election observer groups stated that while the poll had been free, it had not been fair, owing to the inadequacies in the registration process and the bias of the public media in favour of the UDF. The MEC was blamed for failing to ensure fair media coverage for all parties and candidates, and for failing to update the voters' roll satisfactorily. Both the MCP and the Mgwirizano (Unity) Coalition of smaller parties, headed by Chakuamba, sought the nullification of the presidential election. There were widespread calls for the MEC to be disbanded owing to its chaotic handling of the election, and fears that the international community might again decide to suspend aid to the impoverished country if indeed the election was deemed not to have been free or fair.

THE MUTHARIKA PRESIDENCY, 2004–12

Mutharika was sworn in as the country's new President on 24 May 2004. The UDF quickly secured a working majority in Parliament, as Muluzi, who remained as National Chairman of the party, was able to attract opposition support for the new Government. For a time it appeared that Muluzi would retain influence over his successor, but as Mutharika commenced investigations into associates of Muluzi on suspicion of corruption, relations between the two men became increasingly strained. In February 2005 Mutharika resigned from the leadership of the UDF, beginning a long battle between the President and his former party. After announcing his resignation at a meeting in Lilongwe, organized by the Anti-Corruption Bureau, he dismissed three members of the Government loyal to Muluzi, announced his intention to form a new political party and began to create a parliamentary support base from small parties, independents and disaffected UDF members. Mutharika formally launched his Democratic Progressive Party (DPP) in May 2005 and by July 18 UDF deputies had joined the new party. He pledged that it would promote good governance and transparency, and make improvements to the country's economy. One of his first acts as President was to introduce an Agricultural Input Subsidy Programme to provide subsidized fertilizer and seed to farmers. This took time to take effect. In 2005 1.7m. of the country's 11m. people required food aid after the recurrence of drought in the early months of that year, but within a few years the distribution of subsidized seed and fertilizer had produced a remarkable transformation of the agricultural sector and Malawi had become a net maize exporter.

During 2005 the infighting among the political élite grew more intense. In May the Minister of Education and Human Resources, Yusuf Mwawa, was arrested on charges of corruption and misuse of public funds. When the opposition accused Mutharika of acting dictatorially, he in turn accused the UDF of seeking to slow the pace of his clampdown on corruption and of undermining his moves to modernize the economy. After the UDF and Tembo agreed to co-operate, the National Assembly voted in October to begin proceedings to impeach the President. Envoys from key donor countries, including the United Kingdom, the USA and South Africa, signed a letter to the opposition parties requesting that they reconsider their decision in the interests of the country generally, but Mutharika was summoned to face an indictment before the National Assembly. The impeachment process was, however, halted by the High Court on constitutional grounds, and the impeachment motion was eventually withdrawn in late January 2006. Further UDF members subsequently crossed the floor to join the DPP. Following a judgment of the Constitutional Court in November that placed restrictions on deputies who changed party allegiance, Mutharika's political opponents requested a court ruling on whether the Speaker of Parliament should declare a seat vacant when a parliamentarian crossed the floor. This would have a potentially serious impact on the DPP: most of the 80 deputies who stood to be affected were from the President's party.

Mutharika's dismissal of Cassim Chilumpha, Vice-President and a close ally of Muluzi, in February 2006 for neglecting his duties, was the subject of an appeal in the High Court, which ordered his reinstatement in March. However, in April he was arrested and charged with treason and conspiring with South African mercenaries to assassinate the President. Lawyers for Chilumpha argued that he was immune from prosecution while in office, but for a time he remained in custody, before being placed under house arrest, and then released. He continued to deny the charges against him, and claimed that his treatment was a result of his refusal to join the DPP. Muluzi was arrested in July on charges of corruption on his return from the United Kingdom, where he had been recuperating from a spinal cord operation, but was soon released. In March 2007 he announced at a rally that he would stand as the UDF candidate in the 2009 presidential election. In the following month, however, a set of constitutional revisions were approved at a constitutional review conference held in Lilongwe. These limited a President to two terms and laid down a minimum requirement of a first degree in order to stand for President. Muluzi, who did not have a university degree, claimed that the two-term rule applied to consecutive terms only.

The opposition parties welcomed the High Court ruling in June 2007 that the Speaker of Parliament had the power to declare a seat vacant in the event of a deputy crossing the floor, subsequently refusing to approve the national budget for 2007/08 in an attempt to force the Speaker to deal with the issue. Civil society groups complained that the opposition was placing the floor-crossing issue before development, as the budget provided funds to help farmers buy subsidized fertilizers, and until the budget was approved some donor funds could not be disbursed. In September the UDF finally succumbed to pressure and agreed to adopt the 2007/08 budget. Mutharika then prorogued the National Assembly, stating that it was wasting taxpayers' money by debating issues that had no bearing on the lives of ordinary Malawians. From September 2007 to April 2008 the National Assembly did not meet, as the President wished to prevent the Speaker, who was a member of the MCP, from invoking the section of the Constitution that prohibited members of parliament from switching party allegiance. Had he done so, the DPP would have lost most of its deputies and the opposition might again have attempted to impeach the President. When the legislature eventually did meet, the opposition initially boycotted the Assembly, and again threatened to block the passage of the budget unless the Speaker removed those deputies who had crossed the floor. In August an agreement was reached between the Government and the opposition parties, which had a majority in Parliament, whereby they would approve the 2008/09 budget in return for an assurance from the Government that a special parliamentary session would be held to resolve the floor-crossing issue.

Meanwhile, Mutharika warned his predecessor, who was again in the United Kingdom, that he could face charges of treason for plotting to overthrow the Government, and when Muluzi did return he was duly placed under house arrest. He was later granted permission to leave his residence, subject to certain conditions. In May 2008 senior army officers and several UDF members were arrested on the grounds of alleged involvement in a plot against the President.

In early 2009 Muluzi, the UDF's candidate in the forthcoming presidential election, was arrested and charged with redirecting donor funds into his private bank account while President. This, together with confirmation by the Constitutional Court that he was ineligible to contest the election having already served two terms, ended Muluzi's bid for the presidency and left Tembo as Mutharika's main opponent. After a long and bitter campaign, in which the DPP used the media to good effect and Mutharika accused the opposition of being anti-development, the country's fourth multi-party election took place peacefully on 19 May. Mutharika won an overwhelming victory, being returned for a second term as President by 64.4% of the votes cast. The DPP and its allies, representing all regions of the country, secured control of the National Assembly in the concurrent legislative poll, with the party winning 112 of the 192 seats: the MCP, which had its support base mainly in the central region and which had been the largest party in the previous legislature, took only 27 seats (compared with 56 in the 2004 election) and the UDF, predominantly a southern party, 18 seats (compared with 49). Tembo, who took 29.9% of the votes in the presidential election, claimed that the vote was rigged, and the Commonwealth observer mission pointed to bias in the state media, but Muluzi quickly accepted the result. The size of Mutharika's win was clearly in large part a consequence of his record in economic affairs, having turned Malawi into a food exporter and achieved three years of high growth. By the time of the election, however, the international financial crisis was beginning to affect Malawi. The country obtained 40% of its state revenues from the sale of tobacco, earnings from which fell in 2010. In 2008 Malawi severed ties with the Republic of China (Taiwan), and subsequently established diplomatic relations with the People's Republic of China, which became a new market for Malawi's tobacco exports and agreed to fund the construction of a new parliamentary building. However, hopes for economic recovery have come to rely primarily on large uranium deposits located in the north of the country; it was hoped that Malawi would soon become one of the largest producers of uranium in Africa.

Although Malawi was one of very few sub-Saharan African countries in which the US-based Freedom House noted an improvement in civil liberties in its report for 2009, a homosexual couple who had held a public engagement ceremony were arrested in December of that year. It was subsequently alleged that the couple had been beaten in custody and forced to undergo medical examinations. Amnesty International and other human rights organizations protested against their detention, but the two men went on trial in April 2010 on charges of 'gross indecency' and were found guilty. However, some claimed that the laws under which the men had been prosecuted violated the country's Constitution. It was feared that the verdict would encourage homophobic sentiment and impede the fight against HIV/AIDS, as homosexuals were less likely to seek counselling and treatment. None the less, the adverse publicity that this case brought the country did not seem to concern the ruling élite. The couple were sentenced to 14 years' imprisonment; although they were pardoned by President Mutharika in May and subsequently released, Mutharika reiterated that homosexuality remained illegal in Malawi.

In 2010 Mutharika held the honorary position of Chair of the African Union, but in his second term as President he displayed increasingly authoritarian tendencies. He threatened journalists, and stated that he would dissolve newspapers that tarnished his Government's image. Local government elections were to have been held by May, but were postponed first because the Government said that it wanted to reform the local government system, and then in May 2011 ostensibly so that they could take place concurrently with legislative and presidential elections in 2014.

In mid-December 2010 Joyce Banda, the country's first female Vice-President, was expelled from the DPP after she refused to endorse Mutharika's brother, the Minister of Education, Science and Technology, Prof. Arthur Peter Mutharika, for the ruling party's 2014 presidential nomination. Banda's expulsion came as members of the DPP sought to undermine the Vice-President, suspecting that she planned to run for the presidency herself. The Protestant, Catholic and Muslim faith groups criticized the way in which she had been treated as well as the DPP's plans for a dynastic succession. (Banda formed a new political party, the People's Party in March 2011.) Meanwhile, in February a lecturer at the country's principal university, Chancellor College, spoke of the popular uprisings in North Africa and the Middle East. Spies in his class informed the police, who subsequently interrogated him. Other lecturers then abandoned classes in protest at his detention, but the President refused to apologize and accused the lecturers of promoting 'academic anarchy'.

Following the online release by WikiLeaks, an organization publishing leaked private and classified content, of a diplomatic cable in which the British High Commissioner had referred to Mutharika as 'ever more autocratic and intolerant of criticism', the High Commissioner was expelled from Lilongwe in mid-April 2011. The United Kingdom responded by expelling Malawi's acting High Commissioner from London at the end of the month.

The donor community, which accounted for about 40% of Malawi's development budget, had by this time become increasingly uneasy about the country's apparent trend towards authoritarianism. The USA's Millennium Challenge Corporation (MCC) had delayed approving a US $350m. grant for Malawi's collapsing electricity network in response to the Government's opposition to homosexual marriages and threats to media freedom, but the grant was finally approved in April 2011. After the expulsion of the British High Commissioner, however, the United Kingdom—Malawi's single largest bilateral donor—announced in May that it had frozen new aid to Malawi, pending a review of its ties with the country. Mutharika was reported to have told Malawi's donors to 'go to hell'. When the British Secretary of State for International Development wrote to him to express his Government's concerns about corruption and a lack of government accountability in Malawi, Malawi's Minister of Finance declared that while the British decision to withhold new aid would necessitate austerity measures, Malawi was ready to make difficult decisions.

Peaceful protests were then organized by a variety of civil society groups on the theme 'Uniting for Peaceful Resistance Against Poor Economic and Democratic Governance—A Better Malawi Is Possible' for 20 July. The protests, influenced by similar activity in the Arab world, were met by live fire from the police and at least 19 people were killed. In response the USA froze the MCC aid agreement signed in April. Further protests against the President were planned, but were postponed when he agreed to mediation with civil society groups, including trade unions and religious organizations, under the auspices of the UN. The talks began in mid August, but produced no satisfactory outcome.

Mutharika announced the formation of a new Government on 6 September 2011, which was reduced in size to 31 members but included his wife, Callista Mutharika, who was named as National Co-ordinator of Maternal, Infant and Child Health and HIV/Nutrition/Malaria and Tuberculosis. In his last months in office, President Mutharika continued to ignore calls by the Catholic Church and other civil society groups, as well as by Malawi's donors, to engage with his critics and introduce reforms. As the economy deteriorated, poverty increased and there arose the threat of widespread social unrest. Urban protests took place over fuel and electricity shortages, the lack of political freedom and extensive corruption in the Government. On 5 April 2012 the 78-year-old President suddenly died of a heart attack. At first his death was kept quiet by the authorities, his body was sent to South Africa, and his son and the DPP leader, Peter Mutharika, tried to organize his own succession. With civil society insisting on a constitutional successor, however, the plotters of what would have been in effect a coup were outwitted when Joyce Banda confirmed with the head of the army that he would support her. On 7 April the Vice-President became Southern Africa's first female President. This ushered in a new era for Malawi.

PRESIDENT BANDA TAKES OVER

Once in office, Joyce Banda moved quickly to break with the policies of her autocratic predecessor. She removed from her Cabinet the late President's brother and widow, and replaced the chief of police, who had been blamed for the July 2011 shootings, with a human rights advocate. She also dismissed the Governor of the Reserve Bank of Malawi, and made other key changes at the central bank, the Treasury, the Ministry of Information and Civic Education, and elsewhere. President Banda made clear that she would work to restore good relations with Malawi's donors, and pressed the US Secretary of State, Hillary Clinton, to release US $350m. from the MCC, informing her that Malawi was 'committed to restoring the rule of law, respect for human rights and freedoms and demonstrating good economic governance'. To boost the economy and mend relations with donors, Banda then agreed to abandon the peg between the kwacha and the US dollar. This meant that the over-valued currency was devalued by one-third, something that the IMF, which had suspended its aid facility for Malawi, had long sought in order to alleviate foreign exchange and fuel shortages, and to assist Malawian businesses and facilitate people's return to work.

In her first state of the nation address in May 2012, Banda announced that she would ask Parliament, in which her party now had a majority, to legalize homosexuality as a matter of urgency. In that month the National Assembly approved changing the design of the country's flag back to the independence design showing black, red and green stripes with a red rising sun, thereby replacing the new flag introduced by Mutharika in 2010. In June Banda also told the nation that she was selling the presidential jet that Mutharika had bought in 2009 and the Government's fleet of 60 luxury cars. In response to Banda's moves, the United Kingdom, Malawi's biggest aid donor, dispatched a new High Commissioner to Lilongwe, and pledged £23m. to help stabilize the Malawian economy and £10m. for the country's health system. The British Government suggested that the proceeds from the sale of the jet and cars be used to provide basic services to Malawi's poor.

Economy

LINDA VAN BUREN

Revised for this edition by OBI IHEME

INTRODUCTION

Malawi is undergoing significant changes after the recent accession to power of President Joyce Banda. Following the sudden fatal heart attack suffered by former President Bingu wa Mutharika in April 2012, Malawi's political stability and international relations were expected to improve greatly as a result of the accession to the presidency of former Vice-President Banda. The previous administration's popularity within Malawi had been steadily eroding because of increasing unemployment, worsening fuel and power shortages, and an intensifying crackdown on freedom of speech and politics. President Banda consolidated her power through political manoeuvering that resulted in her People's Party—which included previous members of Mutharika's Democratic Progressive Party, to which she also previously belonged—securing a parliamentary majority. She also replaced several of the former President's key loyalists, including the chief of police, who was implicated in the poor handling of civil unrest in 2011 that killed at least 19 people. Banda began reversing many of the late President's policies, and also pledged to reverse the country's criminalization of homosexuality, which, while showing her progressive leanings, could severely antagonize the very conservative electorate and turn voters against her, especially if her economic reforms do not soon deliver much-needed relief to Malawians. Furthermore, if Banda proceeds with an official investigation into whether the late President's allies sought to prevent her from assuming power, it could be seen to demonstrate that she is focusing too much on removing any remaining challenges to her power.

Externally, Malawi had been suffering from increasingly strained relations with its donors, given its internal political situation and inability to meet its targets under the Extended Credit Facility (ECF) from the IMF. Particularly noteworthy in this regard was the expulsion by President Mutharika of the British High Commissioner in April 2011, after a diplomatic cable was leaked in which the envoy claimed that the then President could not accept criticism. The United Kingdom, Malawi's largest donor, responded by expelling Malawian diplomats, and suspended all aid programmes to Malawi. Furthermore, donors have found especially disagreeable Malawi's criminalization of homosexuality. Besides offering to reverse this law, President Banda endeared herself to donors by respecting the International Criminal Court's warrant for the arrest of Sudanese President Omar al-Bashir. In July 2012 Malawi was to have hosted the African Union Commission's (AUC) annual summit, but eventually refused to do so when the AUC refused her request to block al-Bashir's attendance.

ECONOMIC OVERVIEW

The Malawi economy was cushioned from the worst effects of the 2008–09 global economic recession by favourable weather, a bumper tobacco crop and the entry into production in 2009 of its uranium resources, which boosted both gross domestic product (GDP) and the current account balance. According to the Economist Intelligence Unit (EIU), real GDP grew by 4.5% in 2011 and growth was expected to rise to 6.4% by 2016. Nevertheless, foreign exchange shortages in Malawi reached an acute level in 2009 and 2010, with large numbers of people attempting to obtain foreign exchange at officially sanctioned sources and with parallel markets in foreign exchange rapidly emerging. Malawi's foreign reserves dipped to a level capable of covering less than 25 days' worth of imports in January 2010. With insufficient foreign reserves to pay the cost of its fuel imports, fuel supplies in the country became scarce, and foreign exchange became unavailable legally for all but the highest priorities. However, in May 2012 the Government liberalized the exchange rate regime by removing the kwacha's peg to the US dollar, causing the Malawian kwacha to fall in value by 50% overnight, beginning a downward trend that was expected to continue for the rest of the year. The EIU estimated a continued weakening of the kwacha from 2014 onwards.

Despite the robust rate of growth during 2005–10, Malawi remained among the 10 poorest countries in the world in 2010, according to the IMF. According to the *UN Human Development Report 2009*, 73.9% of all Malawians lived below the extreme poverty line of US $1.25 per day, and 90.4% lived on less than $2.00 a day. The administration of President Mutharika also experienced difficulties in its relations with the IMF prior to elections in 2009. According to the IMF, 'a loosening of fiscal and monetary policies during the run-up to elections in May 2009 led to high government domestic borrowing in fiscal year 2008/09 (ending in June 2009) and to rapid money and credit growth.' These factors, the Fund added, 'contributed to low international reserves'. As a result, when external factors became adverse during the global recession and while fuel prices were high, Malawi had no foreign reserves to protect it from the full effect of these external shocks. Additionally, the country's growth was profoundly affected by its inability to meet the financial and budgetary targets of the IMF's ECF. This, combined with disagreements over Malawi's internal policies, led to the Fund and other donors suspending support, foreign exchange shortages and scarcities of critical commodities such as fuel and other manufacturing inputs. The situation was further worsened by poor tobacco sales.

In general, the country's economic advancement has been impeded by problems of subsistence agriculture and its over-dependence on one principal export crop, tobacco. The development of uranium-mining provided a new, alternative revenue source (see below). Low educational levels and the effects of HIV/AIDS have resulted in a shortage of skilled personnel; indeed, the country is not expected to meet its Millennium Development Goal of ensuring universal primary education by 2015. The country has few other exploitable mineral resources, and industry is dependent on imports and hampered by inadequate infrastructure; the problem is compounded by the limitations of the country's landlocked position and its small domestic market.

The previous Government drew up a national development plan called the Malawi Growth and Development Strategy (MGDS II, 2011–16), which identified nine key priority areas: Agriculture and Food Security; Energy, Industrial Development, Mining and Tourism; Transport Infrastructure and the Nsanje World Inland Port; Public Health, Sanitation, Malaria and HIV and AIDS Management; Integrated Rural Development; Education, Science and Technology; Green Belt Irrigation and Water Development; Child and Youth Development and Empowerment; Climate Change, Natural Resources and Environment Management. The current budget is based on this plan and allocates funds to most of these areas.

AGRICULTURE

Agriculture is the most important sector of the economy; including forestry and fishing, it accounted for 34.1% of GDP and 83.7% of export revenue in 2010. The sector engaged some

78.1% of the working population in mid-2012, according to FAO. The vast majority of these people work in the smallholder sector, which accounts for nearly 80% of the cultivated area and close to 86% of agricultural output, which is mostly on a subsistence basis. About two-thirds of the raw materials for Malawi's manufacturing industry are agricultural products grown locally. Agricultural GDP grew at an average annual rate of 3.9% in 2001–10, according to the World Bank, although the sector is at the mercy of unreliable weather patterns and exhibits pronounced swings between crop failure in some years and crop excess in others. The 2009 season produced exceptionally good harvests in several crops, following favourable weather. However, lack of availability of credit to small-scale farmers remains a significant hindrance to agricultural growth. Furthermore, the expected removal in 2012 of fuel subsidies under the Farm Input Subsidy Programme was expected adversely to affect farmers even more, reducing coverage from 1.6m. to 1.4m. families, according to an African Economic Outlook (AEO) forecast. Malawi's staple food crop is maize.

Under IMF pressure, in 2000 the Government agreed to a range of agricultural reforms, which included an end to wholesale subsidization by the Agricultural Development and Marketing Corporation and instead targeted specific food subsidies towards the poorest citizens. To carry out the latter plan, the National Food Reserve Agency was established in 1999; its objective was to administer disaster relief by managing a Strategic Grain Reserve.

The World Bank chose Malawi as the first country in which to roll out its new weather-derivative (WD) financial product. This initiative is based on a model that estimates maize production using rainfall data. If, based on specific triggers, severe drought should recur in Malawi, the WD scheme would pay out compensation swiftly, without the need to wait for on-the-ground, and often protracted, damage assessments to quantify losses. Initially, the maximum compensation that could be paid out in this pilot case would be US $3m. Countries participating in the scheme would do so on a premium basis, often with the premiums paid by donors; in Malawi's case, its premiums were being paid by the United Kingdom's Department for International Development (DfID), although in mid-2011 DfID suspended all budgetary support to Malawi.

Diversification away from maize and towards other food crops has been recommended. One such alternative crop is sorghum, which was grown in Malawi for centuries before the British planted maize. The sorghum harvest fluctuates, from 18,175 metric tons in poor years such as 2005 to 63,700 tons in good years such as 2010. The Government is also trying to encourage cultivation of cassava, which is more drought-resistant than maize. Cassava production rose steadily from 2005 onwards, reaching a peak of 3.8m. tons in 2009. However, cassava is not as nutritious as maize, and supplies are erratic: the crop is harvested as it is needed, and there are poor transfer rates of surplus stocks to areas where they are required. Potatoes, pulses and plantains are also important food crops.

In cash crops, there was a marked improvement in Malawi's groundnut sector as output rose steadily from 2003 onwards, reaching an estimated 275,200 metric tons in 2009, before declining to around 222,000 tons in 2010, according to FAO estimates. The output of green coffee beans, mostly Arabica grown on steep slopes, also fluctuates; 2008 was a poor year, with a harvest of just 1,122 tons, whereas 2009 was a bumper year, with a crop of some 4,200 tons. Production was an estimated 1,800 tons in 2010, according to FAO estimates. The Smallholder Coffee Farmers Trust (SCFT) was set up in 1999 as a transitional organization, aimed at capacity-building and the training of 4,000 smallholder growers in five co-operatives in northern Malawi to run their own businesses. These coffee growers elect the leadership of the SCFT, rendering the trust far more responsive to the growers' needs than parastatals and their appointed leadership tend to be. The SCFT pays the growers at least 60% of the export price of their coffee.

Tobacco is grown on about 150,000 ha in most years; however, during periods of low earnings, this area falls. Malawi is the only significant African producer of burley, which is the most important of the six types of tobacco cultivated in Malawi. Output of this variety achieved record levels in several consecutive years after 1991, the first year in which its cultivation on smallholdings was permitted (the production of burley had previously been confined to estates) and in which quotas for burley production on smallholdings were eliminated. Output of flue-cured tobacco, which traditionally has been grown only on estates, and of the four types of tobacco traditionally cultivated by smallholders (dark-fire-cured, southern-dark-fired, sun- or air-cured and oriental) is declining. With millions of people in the developed world trying to give up smoking, the long-term prospects for the global crop, as well as for Malawi's tobacco industry, are not good. During his administration President Mutharika openly encouraged Malawi's tobacco growers to turn to other crops instead. According to Malawi's Tobacco Control Commission, in 2000 there were 61,834 registered tobacco estates, but by 2007 the number had dwindled to 11,314. There were also 51,389 clubs in 2004 that largely produced burley, but in 2007 this had fallen to 15,901. Nevertheless, Malawi's production of unmanufactured tobacco increased from 160,238 metric tons in 2008 to 208,155 tons in 2009, and increased further, to an estimated 215,000 tons, in 2010, according to FAO estimates. Tobacco exports earned US $512.8m. and contributed 46% of total export revenue in 2010. The 2010/11 budget introduced a 3% withholding tax on tobacco sold at auction or sold directly to buyers. However, the kwacha's depreciation in mid-2012 was expected to make the price of Malawian tobacco more competitive internationally.

Livestock improvements have made the country self-sufficient in meat and liquid milk. In 2010, according to FAO estimates, the national herd comprised 4.05m. goats, 2.15m. pigs, 1.12m. cattle, 195,000 sheep and 16.0m. chickens. Traditionally, almost all livestock has been kept by smallholders.

In this landlocked country nestled around one of Africa's largest lakes, fish provides about 70% of animal protein consumption, and the fisheries sector is thought to employ about 250,000 people. The annual catch fluctuates; it recorded a low of 54,194 metric tons in 2003, but reached a record 101,400 tons, according to FAO estimates, in 2010. Much of the commercial fishing activity centres on Nkhotakota, on the western shore of Lake Malawi. The lake has more than 500 species of fish, including several species of tilapia; the tilapia catch in 2010 amounted to 11,200 tons, according to FAO estimates. Fish stocks in some of Malawi's lakes have been almost obliterated by a combination of overfishing (as drought reduces crops and impels more people to fish in order to survive), declining water levels and pollution.

Timber and pulpwood plantations have been developed since the early 1970s, with the area under state plantations totalling 20,800 ha in 1985. In 1964 54,000 ha of pine and eucalyptus were planted on the Viphya plateau, in the north, to supply a proposed pulp and paper project that was not completed. These fast-growing species soon reached maturity and were ready for harvesting, yet less than 15% of this sustainable resource's potential is being exploited. Acacia, conifers and baobab trees grow in the highlands. Malawi holds the responsibility for the Southern African Development Community (SADC) Forestry Sector Co-ordinating Unit and has the highest rate of deforestation of all the SADC states, at 1.6% per year. Malawi annually produces about 520,000 cu m of industrial roundwood. Of the 6.81m. cu m of roundwood felled in 2010, 5.41m. cu m, or 79.4%, was burned as wood fuel.

MAJOR EXPORTS

The EIU projected tobacco export growth during 2013–16 to average 6% per year, as a result of the kwacha's depreciation. Tobacco alone contributed about 60% of export revenue until uranium exports began in 2009. Estimates for 2010 indicated that tobacco export revenue totalled US $512.8m. (45.8% of total export revenue). In 2003 Malawi became the largest exporter of tobacco in Africa, overtaking Zimbabwe, exports from which fell dramatically from 2001 onwards owing to the severe disruption of the Zimbabwean economy. In Malawi tobacco is sold at auction from March to October each year. It reportedly costs a Malawian grower an average of $1.00 to produce 1 kg of leaf, and since a substantial proportion of that cost is for imported fertilizers, there is a significant foreign exchange component in the cost of growing tobacco in Malawi. In the 2010 auction season the Mutharika Government set a trading price of $2.00 per kg. However, with an abundant crop being offered for sale, early prices were 19% below the trading price, at $1.62 per kg. Between 15 March and 7 April Malawi growers sold 16.5m. kg of leaf, earning $26.7m. The 2011 auction season got off to its usual faltering start, and the Lilongwe and Limbe auctions were temporarily suspended because bidding fell well below the gazetted floor prices. Minimum prices had been set at $1.80 per kg of burley and at $2.83 per kg of flue-cured. According to the Bloomberg news service, by late June 2012 prices had fallen to an average of $2.13 per kg in that season, and Malawi had sold 56.3m. kg, earning $120.1m.

Much of Malawi's sugar production is consumed locally. The principal foreign customer is the European Union (EU), followed by the USA. Illovo Sugar (Malawi) Ltd (formerly the Sugar Corporation of Malawi—SUCOMA) is the sole sugar producer in Malawi; the company has two sugar mills, at Dwangwa and Nchalo. The Dwangwa sugar project covers some 5,250 ha of the Central Region. Illovo reported a record sugar cane harvest in 2007 in Malawi, of 2.5m. metric tons, and similar amounts were recorded in 2008–10. The Limphasa Sugar Corporation plans to invest US $40m. in sugar cane production in the northern lakeshore district of Nkhata Bay in 2013. Set to become Malawi's second largest sugar producer, it owns a 600 ha plantation in the area, which it intends to expand to 1,500 ha in the short term, then up to 5,000 ha by 2013. The company plans to produce 90,000 tons per year.

Malawi is, after Kenya, Africa's second largest producer and exporter of tea More than four-fifths of the land under tea cultivation is controlled by large estates, and around 5,200 smallholders work the remainder. The United Kingdom is by far the most important foreign purchaser. In 2010, according to FAO estimates, Malawi produced a record 66,600 metric tons of tea; however, in 2011 this declined to an estimated 47,000 tons.

Cassava, rice, sunflower seed and medium-staple cotton are also exported. Malawi produced an exceptionally good crop of 76,761 metric tons of seed cotton in 2008, followed by a 73,000-ton harvest in 2009, yielding 27,000 tons of cotton lint and 46,000 tons of cottonseed. A growing horticultural sector is expanding to include a variety of export crops, from the more traditional cabbages, tomatoes and onions to such items as nutmeg, fennel and vanilla. Malawi produces about 4,000 tons of tung nuts per year, the oil from which is used in paints and varnishes as a drying agent and to provide a water-resistant finish. Bird's eye chillies and macadamia nuts are also exported; the latter has been identified as a sub-sector with high potential for value to be added locally.

INDUSTRY

According to World Bank figures, the industrial sector contributed 16.1% of GDP in 2009. Malawi, like other African countries, came under pressure to privatize loss-making government-owned companies, and the Privatisation Commission of Malawi was established in 1996. Between 1996 and 2004 about one-half of the country's parastatals were privatized; they employed some 500,000 people and generated around 20% of GDP. The pace of privatization has been slow; by June 2010, 47 entities had been wholly or partially privatized. In several cases, entities offered for privatization failed to attract buyers.

Malawi has provided a range of incentives for potential investors, including low-cost estate sites, tariff protection, exclusive licensing where justified, generous investment allowances and unrestricted repatriation of capital, profits and dividends. However, the rate of new investment has been inhibited both by the small size of the local market and by the limited possibilities for exports. The Government's package of investment incentives seeks to attract foreign investment in such sectors as manufacturing, agriculture, agribusiness, tourism and mining. These incentives include tax allowances of 40% on new buildings and machinery, of 15% on investments in certain designated areas, of 50% on training expenditure and of 20% on used buildings and machinery. In addition, Export Processing Zone (EPZ) status was established in 1995; in Malawi, EPZ is not a geographical entity but a status conferred on qualifying companies regardless of location. Companies granted this status can operate free from withholding tax on dividends, duties on the import of capital equipment and raw materials, and value-added tax. They are also, in theory, allowed free access to foreign exchange in Malawi and full repatriation of profits, dividends, investment capital and interest, and principal payments for international loans. By 2000 21 companies had received approval for EPZ status, but by 2010 seven of them had ceased trading.

In an important development for the industrial sector, in January 2012 Vale of Brazil announced that it had signed a US $1,000m. contract with the Government to construct a railway line across southern regions of Malawi, although it is not yet clear when work will commence. The AEO estimates that growth rates in manufacturing and construction will increase from their respective levels of 2.1% and 7.5% in 2011, to 5.9% and 9.0% in 2012.

Mining

Deposits of a number of minerals have been discovered, including bauxite, asbestos, coal, phosphates, gemstones, uranium, vermiculite, granite, glass sands, graphite and several types of construction stone—but only a few industrial minerals have so far been exploited to any extent. The most controversial mining project in the country is the US $200m. Kayelekera uranium project near Karonga, which, after much negotiation and legal wrangling, finally received approval from the Mutharika Government in 2007. A joint venture between the Malawi Government (15%) and Paladin Energy Ltd of Australia (85%), Kayelekere was officially commissioned by President Mutharika in April 2009. The mine was forecast to produce 1,000 metric tons of uranium oxide per year, earning $100m. This sum would be equivalent to around 5% of Malawi's GDP and to some 20% of export earnings. The first yellowcake was exported in August 2009. However, this venture experienced problems when, in May 2012, about 1,000 workers conducted a five-day strike that crippled production. The employees were demanding a 66% pay increase, presumably to cope with the expected rise in inflation. Several days later the Paladin management agreed to review its workers' wages by November. Uranium exports earned $24m. in 2009 and an estimated $182 m. in 2010, the first full year of operation. Further uranium deposits have also been found at Kanyika, in northern Kasungu. They are, together with tantalum and a similar element, niobium (also known as columbium), in a concession held by Globe Metals and Mining of Australia. The project is expected to have reserves of 56m. metric tons and a life of 20 years. A 'bankable feasibility study' was due for completion in the second half of 2011. Niobium is used mostly in alloys, in particular in the special steel alloy that is used for gas pipelines.

There has been some exploitation of Malawi's coal reserves; the country's only producing coal mine is Mchenga, in the Livingstonia coalfield. Mchenga was privatized in 1999, when it was sold to Coal Products Ltd for K42m. Mchenga is estimated to contain some 2.3m. metric tons of bituminous coal, and the Livingstonia coalfield contains a further 5m. tons of probable reserves and 20m. tons of 'possible' reserves, according to the Government. At full capacity, Mchenga can produce 8,000 tons per month, supplying a regional demand of about 12,500 tons per month; its target is to achieve 5,000 tons per month. Further coal deposits, as yet unexploited, have been identified at the Ngana coalfield (15m. tons proven, plus another 5m. tons probable), the Nthalire coalfield (15m. tons 'possible', according to the Government), the Lengwe coalfield (10m. tons probable), the Mwabvi coalfield (5m. tons proven, 50m. tons 'possible'), the Lufira coalfield (600,000 tons proven, 50m. tons probable) and the North Rukuru coalfield (500,000 tons proven, 5m. tons probable and as much as 165m. tons 'possible'). North Rukuru's proven reserves lie at the Musisi Forest Reserve, near Kayelekera. Clays suitable for use in the production of ceramics have also been identified. Surveys have also found deposits of marble and granite, while reserves of vermiculite exist at Fereme. Semi-precious stones are mined, mostly on an artisanal basis. Natural (as opposed to heat-treated) gem-quality corundum is mined at Chimwadzulu Hill and is marketed as Nyala rubies and sapphires. Finds of up to seven carats have been recorded. Aquamarines and blue agates have also been found. Other gemstones, found in small quantities, include amethysts, garnets and yellow tourmaline.

In 1997 the Geological Survey Department reported that deposits of gold had been found at Mwanza and on the outskirts of Lilongwe and that there were indications of diamond reserves at Livingstonia, in the north. Cost factors have prevented the exploitation of Malawi's bauxite reserves in the Mulanje area, which have been assessed at almost 29m. metric tons of ore, containing an average of 43.9% alumina. Their development would involve heavy transport costs, owing to the remote location of the area, supplemented by further transport costs to the coast, making their exploitation uneconomic in present world market conditions. The feasibility of the project could improve if development of Malawi's hydroelectric capacity were to result in sufficient low-cost power to meet the substantial requirements of alumina smelting. Indeed, a major restraint on the entire mining sector's expansion is that current levels of electricity generation are insufficient for most heavy industrial mining.

The mining sector has also suffered from other problems that hinder Malawi's efforts to diversify its economy. Lynas Corporation, a rare earths miner, is currently re-evaluating its proposed A$600m. investment in the Kangankunde rare earths resource (KGK) in light of a legal conflict over the project's ownership.

Power

The Electricity Supply Corporation of Malawi (ESCOM) was earmarked for privatization in 1998, but 14 years later it remained government-owned. ESCOM announced in December 2008 that it was to build a new 100-MW hydroelectric facility on the Rukuru River in northern Malawi. A shortage of reliable electricity supply is often cited as a factor hindering growth in the manufacturing and mining sectors. Blackouts are a continual occurrence, with load-shedding scheduled daily in mid-2011. ESCOM operates both thermal and hydroelectric power stations in its grid; the latter supply 98% of the central grid generating capacity. In theory, Malawi has an installed generating capacity of 285 MW, but only about 240 MW was operational at mid-2011. Three hydroelectric plants on the Middle Shire River together have the capacity to supply 280.7 MW. The three are Nkula, the oldest and the farthest upstream; Tedzani; and Kapichira, the farthest downstream. Nkula A, built in 1966 and 1967, was the first hydroelectric power station in Malawi. It has three turbines each of 8 MW, for a total installed capacity of 24 MW. Nkula B comprises five turbines each of 20 MW, for a total of 100 MW. The two Nkula stations together have an installed capacity of 124 MW. The main problem at Nkula is old age and outdated technology. Furthermore, Nkula B was damaged by flooding and was closed for rehabilitation in 2008; it reopened in August of that year. Nkula A suffered from accumulation of debris in February 2009. Downstream from Nkula are Tedzani's three stations. They comprise Tedzani I, built in 1973 with a capacity of 20 MW; Tedzani II, built in 1977 also with a capacity of 20 MW; and Tedzani III, completed in 1995 with a capacity of 52.7 MW. Siltation is a problem at Tedzani, necessitating dredging. Tedzani was also damaged by flooding and also was closed for rehabilitation until August 2008. Downstream from Tedzani on the Shire River is Kapichira, on Kapichira Falls. Kapichira I was completed in 2000. It was designed for four turbines each of 32 MW, but only two were ever installed; therefore, Kapichira I's total installed capacity is 64 MW. Problems at Kapichira include siltation and a 'vibration fault', necessitating nine weeks of repair work in 2007. In 2008 the Mutharika Government was involved in discussions with potential donors, including the World Bank, over funding for the Rukuru project and also for another proposed hydroelectric power plant on the Ruo River.

Outside the grid, ESCOM operates four small diesel sets in remote areas in the north. Some companies, for example sugar estates, generate their own electricity supply. Although the central grid is currently operating at below capacity, ESCOM has invested in new capacity in an attempt to satisfy projected future demand, as well as to reinforce the existing grid. At present, fewer than 5% of the population have access to electricity, most of whom live in urban areas. Under pressure from the IMF for ESCOM to operate without subsidization, the Mutharika Government raised electricity tariffs by 36% on 1 December 2009 and by a further 20% on 1 January 2011, with further increases expected in the second half of 2011 and 2012. The majority of Malawi's domestic energy requirements are supplied by fuel wood, which accounted for more than 90% of energy needs (compared with 3% for hydropower, 4% for petroleum products and 1% for coal) in the 2000s.

Petroleum and diesel fuel constitute Malawi's principal imports. In the 1980s a factory producing ethyl alcohol (ethanol) from molasses commenced operations, and in its first five years of service it produced 6.8m. litres of ethanol annually, for 20% blending with petroleum, equivalent to 10% of Malawi's petroleum needs. In 2006 Energem of Canada built and commissioned two bulk refined-product storage and distribution depots, one at Chirimba, in Blantyre, and the other in Lilongwe. The two depots together cost US $2.5m. and can handle 1,724 metric tons of refined fuel products per month. In 2009 Malawi had insufficient foreign exchange reserves to pay the cost of its fuel imports, resulting in a shortage of all types of fuel products that extended into 2010 and 2011.

The power sector was expected to benefit from a decision by the USA's Millennium Challenge Corporation's (MCC) to reinstate the Malawi Compact in June 2012 after a three-month suspension following the Government of Malawi's non-compliance with the MCC's criteria. The Compact is a US $350.7m. programme designed to improve the lives of 5m. Malawians over a 20-year period by reducing poverty through improving the availability, quality and reliability of the power supply; it will also focus on hydropower generation. It is anticipated to reduce the price of corporate and household energy, and thus increase both company profits and personal income.

Transport and Tourism

Malawi Railways developed an internal rail network covering 797 km, extending to Mchinji on the Zambian border. It also operated 465 km of the 830-km single-line rail link from Salima, on the central lake shore, to Mozambique's Indian Ocean port of Beira. Another rail link provided access to the Mozambican port of Nacala, north of Beira. The railway was privatized in 1999, when it was transferred to CFM/SDCN, a consortium owned by Mozambique's Empresa Nacional dos Portos e Caminhos de Ferro de Moçambique (CFM) and the USA's Railroad Development Corpn (RDC), and also including Portugal's Tertir and South Africa's Rennies. The railway was subsequently renamed the Central East African Railways Co Ltd (CEAR). At the time of transfer, only about 10% of the rolling stock was operational, but by June 2000 the consortium reported that it had returned nearly 90% to active service. The Government continued to own the land and essential buildings. RDC was to operate CEAR under a 20-year contract agreed in 2000. In January 2005 the same consortium that owned CEAR purchased Mozambique's Nacala port and railway. In 2008 RDC sold its interest in CEAR to INSITEC of Mozambique. In 2008 CEAR carried 220,000 metric tons of freight along the 797-km corridor with 19 locomotives and 403 wagons; the main cargo being maize, containers, fuel, fertilizers, cement, tobacco and sugar.

Malawi's road network is being gradually upgraded, with construction gathering pace in the late 2000s. The 2010/11 budget allocated K37,000m. to road rehabilitation. Three of the largest projects were the K4,300m. Jenda–Edingeni road, the K3,500m. Zomba–Blantyre road and the K2,700m. Zomba–Jali–Kamwendo road.

Malawi has two international airports: Lilongwe International Airport (also known as Kamuzu International) and Chileka International Airport at Blantyre. There are also domestic airports serving Mzuzu, in the north, and Club Makokola, in the south. Lilongwe is regularly served by a number of international and regional airlines, as well as by the national carrier, Air Malawi. Lilongwe International Airport, Chileka International Airport and Air Malawi Limited have all been long earmarked for privatization, but progress has been slow. The privatization of the state-owned Air Malawi Ltd was postponed in 2005 pending an improvement in market conditions within the depressed global airline industry. The airline has expressed a preference for seeking a 'strategic partner' as opposed to a change of equity ownership.

In tourism, Malawi markets itself as the 'warm heart of Africa'. The Government is currently aiming to expand the tourism sector, which has grown substantially since Malawi began to develop its considerable tourism potential in the mid-1970s. Malawi, like other tourism destinations in the region, has been affected by the destabilization in Zimbabwe. In 2010 tourism receipts totalled US $47m., while the number of visitors reached 746,000, increasing from 228,100 in 2000. Government holdings in Blantyre Rest House, Government Hostel (now Hotel Masongola), Kasungu Inn, Likhubula Lodge, Chigumukire Lodge, Kachere Lodge, Dzalanyama Lodge, Ntchisi Lodge, Limbe Rest House and Mangochi Lodge were all privatized by 2003. Malawi also promotes its five national parks, including Nyika National Park, with its high escarpment providing views of the north shore of Lake Malawi; Kasungu National Park, with its rolling woodlands, grassy river channels and elephant herds; and Liwonde National Park, with its reed swamps, floodplains and tropical birds. A tourism development plan identified potential areas for eco-tourism at Likhubula Falls, Manchewe Falls, Likoma Island, the three Maleri Islands and the Nkhotakota Wildlife Reserve.

EXTERNAL TRADE AND PAYMENTS

Malawi's prospects for sustained development depend upon the achievement of improved export performance. Although private investment in industry is encouraged, it is agriculture that the IMF has traditionally identified as the 'engine of the Government's growth strategy'. In mining, the Kayelekera uranium project has boosted the value of exports by around 20%. According to UN figures, exports, on a free-on-board (f.o.b.) basis, earned US $1,066.2m. in 2010, a decrease of 10.2% compared with the $1,187.9m. registered in 2009; tobacco exports accounted for 55% of the total in 2010. Meanwhile, imports on an f.o.b. basis increased by 7.5%, from $2,021.7m. in 2009 to $2,173.0m. in 2010; petroleum imports accounted for 9.9% of the 2010 total. The resulting visible trade deficit increased from $833.8m. in 2009 to $1,106.8m. in 2010, with visible exports covering 49% of visible imports in the latter year.

Malawi has sustained a deficit on the current account of its balance of payments in every year since 1966, and the IMF forecasts annual shortfalls to continue until 2014. The deficit on the current account, excluding grants, improved from $1,091.9m. in 2009 to $978.4m. in 2010, while the current account deficit, including grants, narrowed from $426.9m. in 2009 to an estimated $95.6m. in 2010. The overall balance of payments showed a marked improvement, from a deficit of $88.9m. in 2009 to a surplus of $230.1m. in 2010.

PUBLIC FINANCE

Prior to elections in May 2009, the Mutharika Government indulged in what the IMF termed 'a loosening of fiscal and monetary policies', which led to high government domestic borrowing, rapid money growth, rapid credit growth and low international reserves. The targets for net domestic repayment by the central Government and for net international reserves, in particular, were 'missed by wide margins', according to the IMF. However, the Fund has shown renewed confidence in Malawi's Government following the accession to power of President Banda in April 2012. In June the IMF renewed the suspended ECF (see below), thereby doubling its assistance to the country forthe period up to 2015.

The 2010/11 budget, presented in May 2010 by Minister of Finance Ken Kandodo, forecast total revenue from domestic sources at K201,000m. and envisaged total expenditure of K297,000m., an 11% increase compared with the 2009/10 out-turn figure. Of the total, K217,000m. was recurrent, an increase of 11.3% compared with the 2009/10 out-turn figure, and K78,000m. was for development, an increase of 16.4% compared with the 2009/10 out-turn figure. The resultant deficit was K96,000m. excluding grants, but Kandodo factored in K85,000m. in grants expected from donors to achieve a total revenue including grants of K287,000m. It is this figure that he used to calculate the budgetary deficit of K9,900m., which he described as 1.2% of GDP. The actual deficit excluding grants, K96,000m., was equivalent to 11.6% of GDP.

FOREIGN AND GOVERNMENT DEBT

Prior to its significant debt relief package in August 2006, Malawi had the highest debt-to-GDP ratio in the world. Malawi's total public sector external debt was US $2,900m. in February 2006. Under the initiative for heavily indebted poor countries (HIPC) in August 2006, HIPC debt relief brought this figure down from 143% of GDP in 2005 to 50.6% in 2006. The debt service ratio as a percentage of export revenue was 22.1% in 2005 and 30.7% in 2006. This had declined to 6.7% in 2008, and fell further to 1.3% in 2009, before increasing slightly, to 1.8%, in 2010, with a further modest increase, to 2.2%, projected for 2011. The IMF stressed the 'critical' importance of channelling the benefits of debt relief into a sustainable poverty reduction strategy. Also of great concern to the IMF is Malawi's 'domestic debt spiral'. To help achieve the goal of keeping total public debt below 10% of GDP, the IMF agreed that debt relief under the Multilateral Debt Relief Initiative could be used to reduce domestic debt. As a result, the Government's net consolidated domestic debt declined from 14.8% of GDP in 2007 to 9.5% in 2008. However, at the end of June 2011 the AEO estimated the country's external debt at $912.4m., or 15% of GDP, and domestic debt at 16.5% of GDP.

The United Kingdom was Malawi's major aid donor in the years after independence and has remained an important source of funding. However, comments made by the British High Commissioner to the country regarding Mutharika's intolerance of criticism provoked a diplomatic disagreement and resulted in the suspension of the United Kingdom's provision of aid. The apartheid Government of South Africa was also a significant source of donor aid, particularly in providing finance for the purpose-built capital, Lilongwe, where construction of government buildings began in 1968. Other major donors are the EU (currently the main donor overall), France, Canada, the USA, Germany, Denmark, Japan, the African Development Bank and the World Bank's International Development Association. The IMF in February 2010 approved a US $79.4m. three-year ECF for Malawi, which was suspended in 2011 following the Government's inability to meet its targets. However, in June 2012 the IMF doubled its assistance to a total of $157m. over the next three years.

PROSPECTS AND PROBLEMS

In the longer term, President Banda's Government faces the challenge of reducing Malawi's very heavy dependence on a single cash crop, especially since that crop is tobacco. Signs that tobacco's fortunes are on the wane have been evident for many years now, and the low prices that characterize each year's opening auctions have become painfully predictable. The negative repercussions are felt across the spectrum, from the worsening national balance of payments to the declining incomes of smallholder tobacco-growing families. These factors undoubtedly weighed on the Mutharika Government's decision in 2007 to proceed with the Kayelekera uranium-mining project, which, although controversial, provides a long-sought alternative revenue source to tobacco.

A Poverty and Vulnerability Assessment, compiled by the Malawi Government and the World Bank, was released in June 2006. It compared figures from the Integrated Household Surveys of 1998 and 2005, and concluded that there had been little or no progress in reducing poverty and inequality over that period. The assessment found that more than one-half of the country's population continued to live well below the poverty line on some US $0.32 per day. Over one-fifth of Malawians, mostly in rural areas in the south and north of the country, lived on $0.20 per day and were not able to meet the daily recommended food requirements. According to the assessment, with 63% of Malawi's 14.7m. people under the age of 20 years, more than one-half of the poor were children, and the growth of an estimated 44% of pre-school children was 'stunted' because of malnutrition. Despite the abundant maize harvests of the late 2000s, aid agencies warned that communities of vulnerable people remained, especially in the north. In 2010 the IMF itemized six major obstacles to the Malawi Government's efforts towards poverty reduction: lack of a market-based exchange rate; changes in the international environment for tobacco consumption; over-reliance on rain-dependent agriculture; business policies that discourage investment and production; vulnerability to uncertainties in the external environment; and poor infrastructure.

None the less, Malawi's political future looks much brighter than it has done in recent years, after the accession to power of President Joyce Banda in April 2012. During her short time in office, Banda has consolidated her power by replacing members of the former administration that were hostile to her assuming the presidency as is constitutionally mandated. She has also initiated an ambitious economic reform programme, and allowed political freedoms denied under her predecessor. While the new President's economic reforms show the promise of bringing medium- to long-term macroeconomic stability to Malawi and improving its citizens' welfare, there could be large-scale popular protests if the reforms do not soon begin to soften the impact of anticipated price rises in basic commodities and the withdrawal of subsidies.

President Banda also faces high youth unemployment in both the formal and informal sectors. Although the AEO estimates that only 2.7% of those aged 15–24 years are currently without work, the official statistics do not accurately portray the true situation since anyone working one hour per week is classified as employed. The unemployment problem is made worse by poor data, the absence of any youth policies, and a lack of coherent action and weak institutional capacity for skills development.

In the short to medium term, Malawi's new Government planned to remove fuel and electricity subsidies, and undertake a currency adjustment that was expected to increase inflation in 2012. On the other hand, large disbursements of foreign aid and the incomes of tobacco farmers were predicted to rise, as was a popular subsidy for fertilizer. President Banda must deftly handle her economic reform programme in order to retain political support before the next presidential and legislative elections, which are due to be held in May 2014.

Statistical Survey

Sources (unless otherwise indicated): National Statistical Office of Malawi, POB 333, Zomba; tel. 1524377; fax 1525130; e-mail enquiries@statistics.gov.mw; internet www.nso.malawi.net; Reserve Bank of Malawi, POB 30063, Capital City, Lilongwe 3; tel. 1770600; fax 1772752; e-mail webmaster@rbm.mw; internet www.rbm.mw.

Area and Population

AREA, POPULATION AND DENSITY

Area (sq km)	
Land	94,276
Inland water	24,208
Total	118,484*
Population (census results)	
1–21 September 1998	9,933,868
8–28 June 2008	
Males	6,358,933
Females	6,718,227
Total	13,077,160
Population (official projections at mid-year)	
2010	13,947,952
2011	14,388,550
2012	14,844,822
Density (per sq km) at mid-2012	157.5†

* 45,747 sq miles.

† Land area only.

POPULATION BY AGE AND SEX

(official projections at mid-2012)

	Males	Females	Total
0–14	3,425,361	3,456,742	6,882,103
15–64	3,615,406	3,850,321	7,465,727
65 and over	220,732	276,260	496,992
Total	7,261,499	7,583,323	14,844,822

REGIONS

(population at census of June 2008)

Region	Area (sq km)*	Population	Density (per sq km)	Regional capital
Southern	31,753	5,858,035	184.5	Blantyre
Central	35,592	5,510,195	154.8	Lilongwe
Northern	26,931	1,708,930	63.5	Mzuzu
Total	94,276	13,077,160	138.7	

* Excluding inland waters, totalling 24,208 sq km.

PRINCIPAL TOWNS

(population at census of June 2008)

Lilongwe (capital)	674,448	Karonga	40,334
Blantyre	661,256	Kasungu	39,640
Mzuzu	133,968	Mangochi	39,575
Zomba	88,314	Salima	27,852

BIRTHS AND DEATHS

(annual averages, UN estimates)

	1995–2000	2000–05	2005–10
Birth rate (per 1,000)	45.4	43.4	44.0
Death rate (per 1,000)	17.9	16.6	13.7

Source: UN, *World Population Prospects: The 2010 Revision*.

2008 (official estimates): Live births 609,487 (birth rate 46.5 per 1,000); deaths 195,014 (death rate 14.9 per 1,000).

Life expectancy (years at birth): 53.5 (males 53.4; females 53.5) in 2010 (Source: World Bank, World Development Indicators database).

ECONOMICALLY ACTIVE POPULATION*

(persons aged 10 years and over, 1998 census)

	Males	Females	Total
Agriculture, hunting, forestry and fishing	1,683,006	2,082,821	3,765,827
Mining and quarrying	2,206	293	2,499
Manufacturing	94,545	23,938	118,483
Electricity, gas and water	6,656	663	7,319
Construction	70,196	3,206	73,402
Trade, restaurants and hotels	176,466	80,923	257,389
Transport, storage and communications	29,438	3,185	32,623
Financing, insurance, real estate and business services	10,473	3,484	13,957
Public administration	82,973	18,460	101,433
Community, social and personal services	52,980	33,016	85,996
Total employed	2,208,940	2,249,989	4,458,929
Unemployed	34,697	15,664	50,361
Total labour force	2,243,637	2,265,653	4,509,290

* Excluding armed forces.

Mid-2012 (estimates in '000): Agriculture, etc. 5,221; Total labour force 6,684 (Source: FAO).

Health and Welfare

KEY INDICATORS

Total fertility rate (children per woman, 2010)	6.0
Under-5 mortality rate (per 1,000 live births, 2010)	92
HIV/AIDS (% of persons aged 15–49, 2009)	11.0
Physicians (per 1,000 head, 2008)	0.02
Hospital beds (per 1,000 head, 2007)	1.1
Health expenditure (2009): US $ per head (PPP)	65
Health expenditure (2009): % of GDP	6.7
Health expenditure (2009): public (% of total)	65.2
Access to water (% of persons, 2010)	83
Access to sanitation (% of persons, 2010)	51
Total carbon dioxide emissions ('000 metric tons, 2008)	1,228.4
Carbon dioxide emissions per head (metric tons, 2008)	0.1
Human Development Index (2011): ranking	171
Human Development Index (2011): value	0.400

For sources and definitions, see explanatory note on p. vi.

Agriculture

PRINCIPAL CROPS

('000 metric tons)

	2008	2009	2010
Rice, paddy	114.9	136.0	144.2*
Maize	2,634.7	3,582.5	3,800.0†
Millet	31.9	26.9	28.5*
Sorghum	62.0	60.0	63.7*
Potatoes	2,993.8	3,427.8	4,706.4*
Cassava (Manioc)	3,491.2	3,823.2	3,420.1*
Beans, dry	124.7	164.7	152.3*
Chickpeas*	38.1	52.4	48.1
Cow peas, dry*	52.4	72.1	80.1
Pigeon peas	149.9	184.2	182.9*
Groundnuts, with shell	243.2	275.2	222.0†
Cabbages and other brassicas*	54.8	69.7	64.7
Tomatoes*	30.4	38.4	39.2
Onions, dry*	56.1	48.6	58.8
Guavas, mangoes and mangosteens*	78.4	82.7	96.4
Bananas*	394.0	400.0	418.0
Plantains*	338.1	351.8	324.9
Sugar cane*	2,500	2,500	2,500
Coffee, green	1.1	4.2	1.8†
Tea	41.6	52.6	66.6*
Tobacco, unmanufactured	160.2	208.2	215.0*

* FAO estimate(s).

† Unofficial figure.

Aggregate production ('000 metric tons, may include official, semi-official or estimated data): Total cereals 2,845.8 in 2008, 3,808.0 in 2009, 4,039.1 in 2010; Total roots and tubers 6,485.4 in 2008, 7,251.3 in 2009, 8,127.1 in 2010; Total vegetables (incl. melons) 264.4 in 2008, 320.0 in 2009, 326.7 in 2010; Total fruits (excl. melons) 1,027.7 in 2008, 1,051.6 in 2009, 1,032.6 in 2010.

Source: FAO.

LIVESTOCK

('000 head, year ending September)

	2008	2009	2010*
Cattle	947	983	1,122
Pigs	1,229	1,444	2,148
Sheep	189	200	195
Goats	3,106	3,480	4,051
Chickens*	15,500	15,700	16,000

* FAO estimates.

Source: FAO.

LIVESTOCK PRODUCTS

('000 metric tons)

	2008	2009	2010*
Cattle meat	28.8	30.1	34.2
Goat meat	19.6	21.4	21.6
Pig meat	34.0	44.7*	44.7
Chicken meat	19.1	21.3	21.6
Cows' milk	35.5	40.4	51.2
Hen eggs*	20.0	20.3	20.2

* FAO estimate(s).

Source: FAO.

Forestry

ROUNDWOOD REMOVALS

('000 cu m, excluding bark, FAO estimates)

	2008	2009	2010
Sawlogs, veneer logs and logs for sleepers	200	200	200
Other industrial wood	1,200	1,200	1,200
Fuel wood	5,293	5,348	5,405
Total	6,693	6,748	6,805

Source: FAO.

SAWNWOOD PRODUCTION

('000 cu m, including railway sleepers)

	1991*	1992†	1993
Coniferous (softwood)	28	28	30
Broadleaved (hardwood)	15	15	15†
Total	43	43	45

* Unofficial figures.

† FAO estimate(s).

1994–2010: Production assumed to be unchanged from 1993 (FAO estimates).

Source: FAO.

Fishing

('000 metric tons, live weight)

	2008	2009	2010
Capture	70.0	69.3	98.2
Cyprinids	27.2	26.8	44.8
Tilapias	11.1	12.4	11.2
Cichlids	22.0	20.2	33.3
Torpedo-shaped catfishes	5.3	5.0	4.3
Other freshwater fishes	4.4	4.9	4.6
Aquaculture	1.7	1.6	3.2
Total catch	71.7	70.9	101.4

Note: Figures exclude aquatic mammals, recorded by number rather than weight. The number of Nile crocodiles caught was: 3,370 in 2008; 3,105 in 2009; 3,250 in 2010.

Source: FAO.

Mining

('000 metric tons unless otherwise indicated)

	2008	2009	2010
Bituminous coal	57.5	59.2	79.2
Lime	23.5	25.9	31.8
Gemstones (kg)	11,946	306,700	206,900
Stone (crushed for aggregate)	522.1	970.6	989.8
Limestone	46.0	47.2	57.3

Source: US Geological Survey.

Industry

SELECTED PRODUCTS

('000 metric tons, unless otherwise indicated)

	2000	2001	2002
Raw sugar	96	107	260*
Beer ('000 hectolitres)	739	1,033	n.a.
Blankets ('000)	574	281	n.a.
Cement	198	111	174

* Natural sodium carbonate (Na_2Co_3).

2003 ('000 metric tons): Raw sugar (Na_2Co_3) 257; Cement 161 (Source: US Geological Survey).

Electric energy (million kWh): 1,580 in 2006; 1,637 in 2007; 1,801 in 2008.

Raw sugar ('000 metric tons): 230 in 2006; 280 in 2007; 310 in 2008.

Source (unless otherwise indicated): UN Industrial Commodity Statistics Database.

Cement ('000 metric tons, hydraulic): 240.0 in 2008–09; 250.0 in 2010 (estimates) (Source: US Geological Survey).

Finance

CURRENCY AND EXCHANGE RATES

Monetary Units

100 tambala = 1 Malawi kwacha (K).

Sterling, Dollar and Euro Equivalents (30 December 2011)

£1 sterling = 253.176 kwacha;
US $1 = 163.752 kwacha;
€1 = 211.878 kwacha;
1,000 Malawi kwacha = £3.95 = $6.11 = €4.72.

Average Exchange Rate (kwacha per US $)

2009	141.167
2010	150.487
2011	156.515

BUDGET

(K million, year ending 30 June)

Revenue	2003/04	2004/05	2005/06*
Tax revenue	27,793.2	43,635.0	55,797.8
Taxes on income and profits	12,706.6	19,854.0	23,973.0
Companies	4,796.6	5,386.0	6,710.3
Individuals	7,910.0	14,468.0	17,263.5
Taxes on goods and services	12,160.4	18,830.0	25,909.8
Surtax	8,630.0	13,739.0	17,796.6
Excise duties	3,530.4	5,091.0	8,113.2
Taxes on international trade	3,766.1	5,952.0	7,374.4
Less Tax refunds	840.0	1,001.0	1,460.2
Non-tax revenue	4,874.0	4,461.0	8,127.0
Departmental receipts	1,173.2	2,447.0	4,595.3
Total	32,667.2	48,096.0	63,924.8

Expenditure	2003/04	2004/05	2005/06*
General public services	21,889.6	22,719.7	35,519.5
General administration	19,445.9	17,581.0	26,997.5
Defence	1,139.1	2,552.6	4,157.3
Public order and safety	1,304.6	2,586.1	4,364.7
Social and community services	12,606.7	17,509.0	24,363.2
Education	6,310.1	8,631.9	9,500.8
Health	3,692.4	5,247.6	11,057.9
Social security and welfare	2,105.7	2,706.4	2,221.3
Housing and community amenities	356.7	395.8	1,325.6
Recreational, cultural and other social services	75.4	76.8	106.2
Broadcasting and publishing	66.4	450.5	151.3
Economic affairs and services	4,799.0	8,721.1	6,927.3
Energy and mining	108.9	105.2	115.4
Agriculture and natural resources	2,482.4	4,345.5	2,837.2
Tourism	150.0	—	—
Physical planning and development	101.6	1,144.3	527.9
Transport and communications	1,496.3	2,048.5	2,299.1
Industry and commerce	210.7	390.0	599.6
Labour relations and employment	231.2	346.5	404.2
Scientific and technological services	—	314.4	144.0
Other economic services	17.9	26.7	—
Unallocable expenditure	1,505.2	677.3	—
Total recurrent expenditure	40,800.5	49,627.0	66,810.0
Debt amortization	18,736.5	18,752.0	17,328.0
Total	59,537.0	68,379.0	84,138.0

* Estimates.

2009/10 (K million, year ending 30 June, budgeted figures): *Revenue:* Tax revenue 139,900; Non-tax revenue 23,200; Total 163,100 (excl. grants 81,093). *Expenditure:* Current expenditure 188,182 (Wages and salaries 43,539, Interest payments 19,794, Other 124,849); Development expenditure 66,587; Total 256,769 (incl. net lending 2,000) (Source: IMF (see below)).

2010/11 (K million, year ending 30 June, projected figures): *Revenue:* Tax revenue 169,942; Non-tax revenue 29,384; Total 199,326 (excl. grants 93,520). *Expenditure:* Current expenditure 213,361 (Wages and salaries 51,423, Interest payments 20,705, Other 141,233); Development expenditure 99,421; Total 312,781 (Source: IMF (see below)).

2011/12 (K million, year ending 30 June, projected figures): *Revenue:* Tax revenue 198,307; Non-tax revenue 33,770; Total 232,077 (excl. grants 85,954). *Expenditure:* Current expenditure 228,228 (Wages and salaries 59,598, Interest payments 18,673, Other 149,957); Development expenditure 105,465; Total 333,694 (Source (2009/10–2011/12): IMF, *Malawi: Staff Report for 2009 Article IV Consultation and Request for a Three-Year Arrangement Under the Extended Credit Facility*—March 2010).

INTERNATIONAL RESERVES

(US $ million at 31 December)

	2009	2010	2011
Gold (national valuation)	14.03	15.68	15.68
IMF special drawing rights	1.93	1.62	0.43
Reserve position in IMF	3.80	3.73	3.72
Foreign exchange	143.63	302.01	193.29
Total	163.39	323.04	213.12

Source: IMF, *International Financial Statistics*.

MONEY SUPPLY

(K million at 31 December)

	2009	2010	2011
Currency outside banks	27,493.1	31,848.3	43,491.2
Demand deposits at commercial banks	54,407.1	70,263.9	90,512.3
Total money (incl. others)	81,900.3	102,112.2	134,003.5

Source: IMF, *International Financial Statistics*.

COST OF LIVING
(Consumer Price Index; base: 2000 = 100)

	2008	2009	2010
Food (incl. beverages)	240.3	258.0	271.2
Clothing (incl. footwear)	237.6	259.1	279.5
Rent	319.1	328.3	350.2
All items (incl. others)	265.4	287.7	309.0

2011: Food 279.8; All items (incl. others) 332.6.

Source: ILO.

NATIONAL ACCOUNTS
(K million at current prices)

Expenditure on the Gross Domestic Product

	2007	2008	2009
Government final consumption expenditure	163,227	108,524	126,526
Private final consumption expenditure	317,938	458,284	534,304
Gross fixed capital formation	70,285	134,027	156,262
Changes in inventories	14,735	15,933	18,576
Total domestic expenditure	566,185	716,768	835,668
Exports of goods and services	132,707	133,320	155,435
Less Imports of goods and services	201,800	277,665	323,724
GDP in purchasers' values	497,092	572,423	667,379

Gross Domestic Product by Economic Activity

	2007	2008	2009
Agriculture, forestry and fishing	153,063	176,258	202,969
Mining and quarrying	19,384	22,321	25,704
Manufacturing	23,691	27,281	31,415
Electricity, gas and water	12,868	14,818	17,063
Construction	16,229	18,688	21,520
Wholesale and retail trade, restaurants and hotels	44,967	51,782	59,629
Transport and communications	26,087	30,041	34,593
Finance, insurance and real estate	47,767	55,005	63,341
Public administration and defence	48,843	56,244	64,768
Other services	28,385	32,687	45,849
GDP at factor cost	421,283	485,125	566,852
Taxes on products	75,809	87,298	100,527
GDP at purchasers' values	497,092	572,423	667,379

Note: Deduction for imputed bank service charge assumed to be distributed at source.

Source: African Development Bank.

BALANCE OF PAYMENTS
(K million, preliminary)

	2008	2009	2010
Exports of goods f.o.b.	120,705.2	131,004.3	171,797.7
Imports of goods f.o.b.	−188,021.1	−205,518.2	−236,757.0
Trade balance	−67,315.9	−74,513.9	−64,959.3
Net services	−33,579.3	−38,996.5	−45,219.2
Balance on goods and services	−100,895.2	−113,510.4	−110,178.5
Net other income	−2,945.0	−5,407.2	−8,874.9
Balance on goods, services and income	−103,840.2	−118,917.6	−119,053.4
Net transfers	11,226.0	10,738.0	12,948.5
Current balance	−92,614.2	−108,179.6	−106,104.9
Government transfers (net)	43,069.1	71,160.2	87,903.6
Government drawings on loans	14,487.5	14,197.0	34,614.8
Public enterprises (net)	1,746.2	1,704.7	1,749.9
Private sector (net)	518.0	554.2	572.2
Short-term capital (net)	85.9	91.9	98.4
Errors and omissions	24,503.6	−906.8	—
Statistical discrepancy	17,264.8	14,100.0	−32,880.0
Overall balance	9,060.9	−7,278.4	−14,046.0

External Trade

PRINCIPAL COMMODITIES
(distribution by SITC, US $ million)

Imports c.i.f.	2008	2009	2010
Food and live animals	136.7	158.7	148.5
Cereals and cereal preparations	94.1	102.0	99.6
Beverages and tobacco	75.2	62.8	97.8
Tobacco and tobacco products	74.0	58.4	95.5
Mineral fuels, lubricants, etc.	214.8	210.6	217.1
Petroleum, petroleum products, etc.	211.7	208.9	214.7
Refined petroleum products	202.0	198.3	198.6
Chemicals and related products	603.5	464.1	532.4
Medicinal and pharmaceutical products	95.4	114.2	133.9
Manufactured fertilizers	367.1	176.8	206.2
Basic manufactures	271.4	328.9	346.6
Paper, paperboard, etc.	38.4	53.8	49.6
Textile yarn, fabrics, etc.	44.2	46.9	41.6
Iron and steel	66.9	63.2	73.7
Machinery and transport equipment	593.8	529.4	515.2
Machinery specialized for particular industries	238.1	96.6	102.3
General industrial machinery, equipment and parts	41.7	53.1	54.4
Office machinery and automatic data-processing equipment	23.3	32.1	33.7
Telecommunications, sound recording and reproducing equipment	45.8	74.7	75.5
Road vehicles	181.7	191.7	159.3
Goods vehicles (lorries and trucks)	59.6	61.3	46.9
Miscellaneous manufactured articles	228.3	191.0	222.0
Total (incl. others)	2,203.7	2,021.7	2,173.0

Exports f.o.b.	2008	2009	2010
Food and live animals	139.2	213.6	209.8
Sugar and honey	53.0	70.3	69.4
Raw cane sugars	50.7	70.2	69.0
Coffee, tea, cocoa and spices	42.5	84.4	87.8
Tea	36.9	78.3	80.8
Beverages and tobacco	593.2	760.5	587.1
Tobacco and tobacco products	590.0	759.5	585.2
Unstripped tobacco	428.2	472.4	241.6
Stripped or partly stripped tobacco	161.7	268.6	331.1
Crude materials (inedible) except fuels	57.2	109.3	170.2
Textile fibres	23.4	30.1	17.0
Basic manufactures	30.9	12.1	16.0
Machinery and transport equipment	15.5	28.1	27.1
Miscellaneous manufactured articles	35.1	53.2	38.1
Total (incl. others)	879.0	1,187.9	1,066.2

Source: UN, *International Trade Statistics Yearbook*.

PRINCIPAL TRADING PARTNERS
(US $ million)

Imports	2008	2009	2010
Belgium	8.6	6.0	—
China, People's Repub.	72.4	119.7	198.4
Denmark	40.8	35.0	22.4
France (incl. Monaco)	16.7	52.2	62.8
Germany	22.4	34.2	25.2
Hong Kong	15.1	23.7	23.3
India	106.8	95.8	165.0
Indonesia	15.1	18.5	22.9
Italy	7.6	10.3	8.6
Japan	32.7	18.0	62.5
Kenya	54.9	39.8	49.4
Korea, Repub.	18.0	18.2	19.8
Mozambique	447.1	259.5	31.3
Netherlands	46.3	18.9	37.3
South Africa	585.2	691.5	654.2
Tanzania	128.6	79.4	36.9
United Arab Emirates	111.0	80.3	108.0
United Kingdom	74.8	85.3	83.0
USA	45.0	52.7	62.3
Zambia	68.5	72.7	120.5
Zimbabwe	38.5	38.2	32.9
Total (incl. others)	2,203.7	2,021.7	2,173.0

Exports	2008	2009	2010
Belgium	114.7	208.3	132.5
Denmark	2.1	5.3	7.8
Egypt	25.3	73.2	98.3
France (incl. Monaco)	8.1	5.3	—
Germany	36.7	38.5	65.7
India	2.8	27.4	12.4
Kenya	6.9	13.7	19.3
Korea, Repub.	28.2	10.7	14.2
Mozambique	23.9	64.1	36.2
Netherlands	51.8	52.2	49.8
Philippines	8.4	26.8	14.1
Poland	30.6	15.8	17.2
Portugal	34.0	28.7	18.5
Russia	25.0	36.1	11.2
South Africa	88.7	121.6	61.6
Spain	6.3	7.6	8.6
Switzerland (incl. Liechtenstein)	36.0	52.6	14.1
Turkey	17.3	17.7	6.1
United Kingdom	78.4	50.4	49.1
USA	50.3	48.6	63.7
Zambia	15.4	23.0	35.5
Zimbabwe	22.6	35.8	57.9
Total (incl. others)	879.0	1,187.9	1,066.2

Source: UN, *International Trade Statistics Yearbook*.

Transport

RAILWAYS
(traffic)

	2009	2010	2011
Passengers carried ('000)	572	561	271
Passenger-km ('000)	38,336	35,950	17,360
Net freight ton-km ('000)	46,673	43,990	39,168

ROAD TRAFFIC
(estimates, motor vehicles in use at 31 December)

	1994	1995	1996
Passenger cars	23,520	25,480	27,000
Lorries and vans	26,000	29,000	29,700

2007: Passenger cars 53,300; Lorries and vans 59,800; Buses 6,500; Motor-cycles 10,400.

Source: International Road Federation, *World Road Statistics*.

SHIPPING

Inland Waterways
(lake transport)

	2009	2010	2011
Passengers carried ('000)	39	57	57
Passenger-km ('000)	3,300	4,889	4,047
Net freight-ton km	3,110	2,871	1,367

CIVIL AVIATION
(traffic on scheduled services)

	2007	2008	2009
Kilometres flown (million)	3	5	5
Passengers carried ('000)	116	160	157
Passenger-km (million)	83	209	200
Total ton-km (million)	8	24	23

Source: UN, *Statistical Yearbook*.

Tourism

FOREIGN TOURIST ARRIVALS BY COUNTRY OF RESIDENCE

	2007	2008	2009
Mozambique	111,924	139,296	188,694
North America	45,630	43,085	43,766
Southern Africa*	104,226	106,724	100,958
United Kingdom and Ireland	48,627	50,786	54,476
Zambia	63,581	76,408	102,956
Zimbabwe	171,684	143,363	77,281
Total (incl. others)	734,598	742,457	755,031

* Comprising South Africa, Botswana, Lesotho and Swaziland.

2010 ('000) Total tourist arrivals 746.

Tourism receipts (US $ million, excl. passenger transport): 43 in 2008; 44 in 2009; 47 in 2010.

Source: World Tourism Organization.

Communications Media

	2009	2010	2011
Telephones ('000 main lines in use)	111.3	160.1	173.5
Mobile cellular telephones ('000 subscribers)	2,374.1	3,037.5	3,855.8
Internet subscribers ('000)	150.0	305.0	n.a.
Broadband subscribers ('000)	3.9	5.1	9.8

Personal computers: 25,000 (1.8 per 1,000 persons) in 2005.

Radio receivers ('000 in use): 4,929 in 1998.

Television receivers ('000 in use): 40 in 2001.

Book production (first editions only): 120 titles in 1996.

Daily newspapers: 5 in 1998 (estimated average circulation 26,000 copies).

Non-daily newspapers: 4 in 1996 (estimated average circulation 120,000 copies).

Sources: UNESCO Institute for Statistics; UN, *Statistical Yearbook*; International Telecommunication Union.

Education

(2009/10 unless otherwise indicated)

	Institutions	Teachers	Students
Primary	5,461*	43,110	3,417,404
Secondary	n.a.	22,878*	692,157
Tertiary	6†	861‡	10,296

* 2007/08.

† 2003 figure.

‡ 2006/07 figure.

Source: partly UNESCO Institute for Statistics.

Pupil-teacher ratio (primary education, UNESCO estimate): 79.3 in 2009/10 (Source: UNESCO Institute for Statistics).

Adult literacy rate (UNESCO estimates): 74.8% (males 81.1%; females 68.5%) in 2010 (Source: UNESCO Institute for Statistics).

Directory

The Constitution

A new Constitution, replacing the (amended) 1966 Constitution, was approved by the National Assembly on 16 May 1994, and took provisional effect for one year from 18 May. During this time the Constitution was to be subject to review, and the final document was promulgated on 18 May 1995. The main provisions (with subsequent amendments) are summarized below:

THE PRESIDENT

The President is both Head of State and Head of Government. The President is elected for five years, by universal adult suffrage, in the context of a multi-party political system. The Constitution provides for up to two Vice-Presidents.

PARLIAMENT

Parliament comprises the President, the Vice-President(s) and the National Assembly. The National Assembly has 193 elective seats, elections being by universal adult suffrage, in the context of a multi-party system. Cabinet ministers who are not elected members of parliament also sit in the National Assembly. The Speaker is appointed from among the ordinary members of the Assembly. The parliamentary term is normally five years. The President has power to prorogue or dissolve Parliament.

In 1995 the National Assembly approved proposals for the establishment of a second chamber, the Senate, to be implemented in 1999. The chamber was not established by that date, however, and in January 2001 the National Assembly approved a proposal to abandon plans for its creation.

EXECUTIVE POWER

Executive power is exercised by the President, who appoints members of the Cabinet.

The Government

HEAD OF STATE

President: JOYCE BANDA (took office 7 April 2012).

Vice-President: KHUMBO KACHALI.

CABINET

(September 2012)

President, Commander-in-Chief of the Malawi Defence Force and Police Service and Minister of Public Service, Statutory Corporations, Civil Service Administration, National Relief and Disaster Management, Nutrition and HIV/AIDS: JOYCE BANDA.

Vice-President, Minister of Health: KHUMBO KACHALI.

Minister of Finance: Dr KEN LIPENGA.

Minister of Foreign Affairs and International Co-operation: EPHRAIM MGANDA CHIUME.

Minister of Education, Science and Technology: EUNICE KAZEMBE.

Minister of Energy and Mining: Dr CASSIM CHILUMPHA.

Minister of Gender, Children and Social Welfare: ANITA KALINDE.

Minister of Economic Planning and Development: ATUPELE AUSTIN MULUZI.

Minister of Justice and Attorney-General: RALPH KASAMBALA.

Minister of Agriculture and Food Security: Prof. PETER NELSON MWANZA.

Minister of Water Development and Irrigation: RICHIE BIZWICK MUHEYA.

Minister of Transport and Public Works: MOHAMMED SIDIK MIA.

Minister of Local Government and Rural Development: GRACE ZINENANI MASEKO.

Minister of Information: MOSES KUNKUYU.

Minister of Industry and Trade: JOHN BANDE.

Minister of Lands and Housing: HENRY DAMA PHOYA.

Minister of Home Affairs: ULADI MUSSA.

Minister of National Defence: KEN KANDODO.

Minister of Tourism, Wildlife and Culture: DANIEL SYMPHORIANA LIWIMBI.

Minister of Labour: EUNICE MAKANGALA.

Minister of the Environment and Climate Change: CATHERINE GOTANI HARA.

Minister of Youth and Sport: ENOCK CHAKUFWA CHIHANA.

Minister of Disability and the Elderly: REEN KACHERE.

There were also nine Deputy Ministers.

MINISTRIES

Office of the President and Cabinet: Private Bag 301, Capital City, Lilongwe 3; tel. 1789311; fax 1788456; internet www.malawi.gov.mw/opc/opc.htm.

Office of the Vice President: POB 30399, Capital City, Lilongwe; tel. 1788444; fax 1788218; e-mail vicepres@malawi.gov.mw.

Ministry of Agriculture, Irrigation and Water Development: POB 30134, Capital City, Lilongwe 3; tel. 1789033; fax 1789218; e-mail agriculture@agriculture.gov.mw; internet www.moafsmw.org.

Ministry of Education, Science and Technology: Private Bag 328, Lilongwe 3; tel. 1789422; fax 1788064; e-mail education@malawi.gov.mw; internet www.malawi.gov.mw/Education/Home%20%20Education.htm.

Ministry of Finance: Capital Hill, POB 30049, Lilongwe 3; tel. 1789355; fax 1789173; internet wwww.finance.gov.mw.

Ministry of Foreign Affairs and International Co-operation: POB 30315, Lilongwe 3; tel. 1789323; fax 1788482; e-mail foreign@malawi.net; internet www.foreignaffairs.gov.mw.

Ministry of Gender, Child Development and Community Development: Private Bag 330, Capital City, Lilongwe 3; tel. 1770411; fax 1770826.

Ministry of Health: POB 30377, Capital City, Lilongwe 3; tel. 1789400; fax 1789431; e-mail doccentre@malawi.net; internet www.malawi.gov.mw/Health/Home%20Health.htm.

Ministry of Industry and Trade: POB 30366, Capital City, Lilongwe 3; tel. 1770244; fax 1770680; e-mail minci@malawi.net; internet www.trade.gov.mw.

Ministry of Information and Civic Education: Private Bag 326, Capital City, Lilongwe 3; tel. 1775499; fax 1770650; e-mail psinfo@sdnp.org.mw; internet www.malawi.gov.mw/Information/Home%20Information.htm.

Ministry of Justice and Constitutional Affairs: Private Bag 333, Capital City, Lilongwe 3; tel. 1788411; fax 1788332; e-mail justice@malawi.gov.mw; internet www.justice.gov.mw; also comprises the Attorney-General's Chambers and the Directorate of Public Prosecutions.

Ministry of Labour: Private Bag 344, Capital City, Lilongwe 3; tel. 1773277; fax 1773803; e-mail labour@malawi.net; internet www.malawi.gov.mw/Labour/Home%20%20Labour.htm.

Ministry of Lands, Housing and Urban Development: POB 30548, Lilongwe 3; tel. 1774766; fax 1773990; e-mail commissioner@lands.gov.mw; internet www.lands.gov.mw.

Ministry of Local Government and Rural Development: POB 30312, Lilongwe 3; tel. 1789388; fax 1788083; e-mail mlgrd@localgovt.mw; internet www.mlgrd.gov.mw.

Ministry of National Defence: Private Bag 339, Lilongwe 3; tel. 1789600; fax 1789176; e-mail defence@defence.gov.mw.

Ministry of Natural Resources, Energy and the Environment: Private Bag 350, Lilongwe 3; tel. 1789488; fax 1773379; internet www.malawi.gov.mw/natres/natres.htm.

Ministry of Tourism, Wildlife and Culture: Lilongwe 3; tel. 1772702; fax 1770650; e-mail tourism@malawi.net.

Ministry of Transport and Public Infrastructure: Private Bag 322, Capital City, Lilongwe 3; tel. 1789377; fax 1789328; e-mail c.k.kumangirana@gmail.com; internet www.malawi.gov.mw/Transport/Home%20Transport.htm.

Ministry of Youth Development and Welfare: Lingadzi House, Private Bag 384, Lilongwe 3; tel. 1774999; fax 1771018; e-mail sports@malawi.gov.mw; internet www.malawi.gov.mw/Youth/Home%20%20Youth.htm.

President and Legislature

PRESIDENT

Presidential Election, 19 May 2009

Candidate	Votes	% of votes
Bingu wa Mutharika (DPP)	2,961,099	64.36
John Tembo (MCP)	1,373,459	29.85
Walter Chibambo (PETRA)	35,296	0.77
Others	230,903	5.02
Total	4,600,757	100.00

NATIONAL ASSEMBLY

National Assembly: Parliament Bldg, Private Bag B362, Lilongwe 3; tel. 1773566; fax 1774196; internet www.parliament.gov.mw.

Speaker: HENRY CHIMUNTHU BANDA.

General Election, 19 May 2009

Party	Seats
Democratic Progressive Party (DPP)	112
Malawi Congress Party (MCP)	27
United Democratic Front (UDF)	18
Alliance for Democracy (AFORD)	1
Malawi Forum for Unity and Development (MAFUNDE)	1
Maravi People's Party (MPP)	1
Independents	32
Total	192*

* Voting in one constituency did not take place owing to the death of a candidate. A by-election held on 14 August 2009 was won by an independent candidate. In 2010 by-elections were held in four constituencies (two in January and two in October) owing to the deaths of three incumbent members and the ineligibility of one member. The DPP won three seats, while the UDF took one. In September 2011 a by-election was held for a vacant seat, which was won by AFORD.

Election Commission

Malawi Electoral Commission (MEC): Old Controller of Stores Bldg, Private Bag 113, Blantyre; tel. 1822033; fax 1821846; e-mail ceo@mec.org.mw; internet www.mec.org.mw; f. 1998; Chair. ANASTAZIA MSOSA; Chief Elections Officer WILLIE KALONGA.

Political Organizations

Alliance for Democracy (AFORD): Private Bag 28, Lilongwe; f. 1992; in March 1993 absorbed membership of fmr Malawi Freedom Movement; Pres. DINDI GOWA NYASULU.

Congress of Democrats (CODE): Mzuzu; Pres. RALPH KASAMBARA.

Congress for National Unity (CONU): Lilongwe; f. 1999; Pres. Bishop DANIEL KAMFOSI NKHUMBWA.

Democratic Progressive Party (DPP): Lilongwe 3; internet dppmw.org; f. 2005 following Bingu wa Mutharika's resignation from the UDF; Pres. Prof. ARTHUR PETER MUTHARIKA; Sec.-Gen. WAKUDA KAMANGA.

Malawi Congress Party (MCP): Private Bag 388, Lilongwe 3; tel. 999223228; internet www.malawicongressparty.org; f. 1959; sole legal party 1966–93; Pres. JOHN TEMBO.

Malawi Democratic Party (MDP): Lilongwe; Pres. KAMLEPO KALUA.

Malawi Forum for Unity and Development (MAFUNDE): f. 2002; aims to combat corruption and food shortages; Pres. GEORGE MNESA.

Maravi People's Party (MPP): Lilongwe; Pres. ULADI MUSSA; Sec.-Gen. Dr YUSUF HAUDI.

Movement for Genuine Democratic Change (MGODE): Plot No. 52, Kanjedza Drive, Mzuzu; f. 2003 by fmr mems of AFORD; Chair. SAM KANDODO BANDA; Dir GREENE LULILO MWAMONDWE; Sec.-Gen. RODGER NKWAZI.

National Democratic Alliance (NDA): Blantyre; tel. 1842593; f. 2001 by fmr mems of the UDF; officially merged with the UDF in June 2004 but maintained independent structure; Pres. BROWN JAMES MPINGANJIRA; Nat. Chair. JAMES MAKHUMULA NKHOMA.

National Rainbow Coalition (NARC): POB 40508, Kanengo, Lilongwe 4; tel. 1774007; internet www.narcparty.com; f. 2008; Pres. LOVENESS GONDWE.

National Solidarity Movement: Leader NGWAZI KAZUNI KUMWENDA.

National Unity Party (NUP): Blantyre; Pres. HARRY CHIUME; Sec.-Gen. HARRY MUYENZA.

New Dawn for Africa (NDA): Legends Compound, Blantyre, POB 76, Liwonde; f. 2003; associated with the UDF; Pres. THOM CHIUMIA; Sec.-Gen. CHIKUMBUTSO MTUMODZI.

New Republican Party (NRP): f. 2005; Pres. GWANDAGULUWE CHAKUAMBA; Vice-Pres. KEN ZIKHALE NG'OMA.

People's Party: Lilongwe; f. 2011 by Joyce Banda following her expulsion from the DPP; Pres. JOYCE BANDA; Sec.-Gen. HENRY CHIBWANA.

People's Progressive Movement (PPM): f. 2003 by fmr mems of the UDF; Pres. MARK KATSONGA; Sec.-Gen. KNOX VARELA.

People's Transformation Party (PETRA): POB 31964, Chichiri, Blantyre 3; tel. 1871577; fax 1871573; e-mail umunthu@sdnp.org.mw; internet www.petra.mw; f. 2002; Pres. KAMUZU CHIBAMBO; Sec.-Gen. DEREK LAKUDZALA.

Republican Party (RP): Lilongwe; Pres. STANLEY MASAULI.

United Democratic Front (UDF): POB 5446, Limbe; internet www.udf.malawi.net; f. 1992; officially merged with the NDA in June 2004 but maintained independent structure; rival faction led by Cassim Chilumpha and Friday Jumbe; Chair. Dr GEORGE NGA NTAFU; Sec.-Gen. KENNEDY MAKWANGWALA.

The Movement for the Restoration of Democracy in Malawi (f. 1996) is based in Mozambique and consists of fmr Malawi Young Pioneers; it conducts occasional acts of insurgency.

Diplomatic Representation

EMBASSIES AND HIGH COMMISSIONS IN MALAWI

China, People's Republic: No. 342, Area 43, POB 31799, Lilongwe; tel. 1794751; fax 1794752; e-mail chinaemb_mw@mfa.gov.cn; internet mw.chineseembassy.org/eng; Ambassador PAN HEJUN.

Egypt: 10/247 Tsoka Rd, POB 30451, Lilongwe 3; tel. 1780668; fax 1794660; Ambassador AKRAM MOHSEN HAMDY.

Germany: Convention Dr., POB 30046, Lilongwe 3; tel. 1772555; fax 1770250; e-mail info@lilongwe.diplo.de; internet www.lilongwe.diplo.de; Ambassador Dr PETER WOESTE.

Holy See: Lilongwe; Apostolic Nuncio JULIO MURAT.

Ireland: Arwa House, 3rd Floor, Capital City, Lilongwe; tel. 1776405; e-mail lilongweemdiplomats@dfa.ie; Ambassador LIAM MACGABHANN.

Japan: Plot No. 14/191, Petroda Glass House, POB 30780, Lilongwe 3; tel. 1770284; fax 1773528; Ambassador FUJIO SAMUKAWA.

Mozambique: Area 40/14A, POB 30579, Lilongwe 3; tel. 1774100; fax 1771342; e-mail embamoc.malawi@minec.gov.mz; High Commissioner PEDRO JOÃO DE AZEVEDO DAVANE.

Nigeria: Lilongwe; Ambassador MOHAMMED LAWAN GANA.

South Africa: Kang'ombe House, 3rd Floor, City Centre, POB 30043, Lilongwe 3; tel. 1773722; fax 1772571; e-mail sahc@malawi.net; High Commissioner N. I. MABUDE.

Tanzania: POB 922, Capital City, Lilongwe 3; tel. 1770150; fax 1770148; e-mail tanzanianhighcomm@tz.lilongwe.mw; High Commissioner Maj.-Gen. (retd) MAKAME RASHID.

United Kingdom: British High Commission Bldg, Capital Hill, POB 30042, Lilongwe 3; tel. 1772400; fax 1772657; e-mail bhclilongwe@fco.gov.uk; internet ukinmalawi.fco.gov.uk; High Commissioner MICHAEL NEVIN.

USA: Area 40, Plot No. 18, 16 Jomo Kenyatta Rd, POB 30016, Lilongwe 3; tel. 1773166; fax 1770471; e-mail consularlilong@state.gov; internet lilongwe.usembassy.gov; Ambassador JEANINE E. JACKSON.

Zambia: Area 40/2, City Centre, POB 30138, Lilongwe 3; tel. 1772100; fax 1774349; High Commissioner RICHARD KACHINGWE.

Zimbabwe: POB 30187, Lilongwe 3; tel. 1774988; fax 1772382; e-mail zimhighcomllw@malawi.net; Ambassador THANDIWE S. DUMBUTSHENA.

Judicial System

The courts administering justice are the Supreme Court of Appeal, High Court and Magistrates' Courts.

The High Court, which has unlimited jurisdiction in civil and criminal matters, consists of the Chief Justice and five puisne judges. Traditional Courts were abolished under the 1994 Constitution. Appeals from the High Court are heard by the Supreme Court of Appeal in Blantyre.

High Court of Malawi

POB 30244, Chichiri, Blantyre 3; tel. 1670255; fax 1670213; e-mail highcourt@sdnp.org.mw; internet www.judiciary.mw; Registrar H. S. POTANI.

Chief Justice: LOVEMORE MUNLO.

Religion

According to the census of 2008, 82.7% of the population profess Christianity. Islam is practised by about 13.0% of the population.

CHRISTIANITY

Malawi Council of Churches (MCC): POB 30068, Capital City, Lilongwe 3; tel. 1783499; fax 1783106; f. 1939; Chair. Rev. JOSEPH P. BVUMBWE; Gen. Sec. Rev. Dr OSBORNE JODA-MBEWE; 24 mem. churches.

The Anglican Communion

Anglicans are adherents of the Church of the Province of Central Africa, covering Botswana, Malawi, Zambia and Zimbabwe. The Church comprises 15 dioceses, including four in Malawi. The current Archbishop of the Province is the Bishop of Northern Zambia. There were about 230,000 adherents in Malawi at mid-2000.

Bishop of Lake Malawi: FRANCIS KAULANDA, POB 30349, Capital City, Lilongwe 3; tel. 1797858; fax 1797548; e-mail anglama@eomw.net.

Bishop of Northern Malawi: Rt Rev. FANUEL EMMANUEL CHIOKO MAGANGANI, POB 120, Mzuzu; tel. 1331486; fax 1333805; e-mail angdioofnm@sdnp.org.mw.

Bishop of Southern Malawi: Rt Rev. JAMES TENGATENGA, POB 30220, Chichiri, Blantyre 3; tel. 1641218; fax 1641235; e-mail angsoma@sdnp.org.mw; internet www.angsoma.org.mw.

Bishop of Upper Shire: BRIGHTON MALASA, Private Bag 1, Chilema, Zomba; tel. and fax 1539203; e-mail dionorth@zamnet.zm.

Protestant Churches

At mid-2001 there were an estimated 2.1m. Protestants in Malawi.

Assemblies of God in Malawi: POB 1220, Lilongwe; tel. 1761057; fax 1762056; Pres. LAZARUS CHAKWERA; 639,088 mems in 3,114 churches (2005).

Baptist Convention of Malawi (BACOMA): Lali Lubani Rd, POB 30212, Chichiri, Blantyre 3; tel. 1671170; e-mail bacoma@sdnp.org.mw; 175,000 adherents, 1,375 churches (2007); Gen. Sec. Rev. FLETCHER KAIYA.

Church of Central Africa Presbyterian (CCAP): Blantyre Synod, POB 413, Blantyre; tel. and fax 1633942; e-mail btsynod@malawi.net; internet www.blantyresynod.org; comprises 3 synods in Malawi (Blantyre, Livingstonia and Nkhoma); Co-ordinator Rev. J. J. MPHATSE; Gen. Sec. DANIEL GUNYA; Exec. Dir ROBSON CHITENGO; more than 1m. adherents in Malawi.

Evangelical Association of Malawi: POB 2120, Blantyre; tel. and fax 999936681 (mobile); Chair. Rev. Dr LAZARUS CHAKWERA; Gen. Sec. FRANCIS MKANDAWIRE.

Evangelical Lutheran Church in Malawi: POB 650, Lutheran Church Centre, Plot 22, Chidzanja Rd, Lilongwe; tel. and fax 1726288; fax 1725910; e-mail elcmwi@elcmw.org; Bishop. Dr JOSEPH P. BVUMBWE; 80,000 mems (2010).

Seventh-day Adventist Church: Robins Rd, Kabula Hill, POB 951, Blantyre; tel. 1820264; fax 1820528; e-mail musda@malawi.net; Pres. FRACKSON KUYAMA; Exec. Sec. BAXTER D. CHILUNGA; 360,000 mems.

The African Methodist Episcopal Church, the Churches of Christ, the Free Methodist Church, the New Apostolic Church and the United Evangelical Church in Malawi are also active. At mid-2000 there were an estimated 2m. adherents professing other forms of Christianity.

The Roman Catholic Church

Malawi comprises two archdioceses and five dioceses. There are some 3.9m. adherents of the Roman Catholic Church (equivalent to approximately 23% of the total population).

Episcopal Conference of Malawi

Catholic Secretariat of Malawi, Chimutu Rd, POB 30384, Capital City, Lilongwe 3; tel. 1782066; fax 1782019; e-mail ecm@malawi.net; internet episcopalconferenceofmalawi.org.

f. 1969; Sec.-Gen. Rev. GEORGE BULEYA.

Archbishop of Blantyre: Most Rev. TARCISIUS GERVAZIO ZIYAYE, Archbishop House, POB 385, Blantyre; tel. and fax 1637905; e-mail archdblantyre@africa-online.net.

Archbishop of Lilongwe: Most Rev. RÉMI JOSEPH GUSTAVE SAINTE-MARIE, POB 33, Lilongwe; tel. 1754667; fax 1752767.

ISLAM

Muslim Association of Malawi (MAM): POB 497, Blantyre; tel. 1622060; fax 1623581; f. 1946 as the Nyasaland Muslim Assn; umbrella body for Muslim orgs; provides secular and Islamic education; Chair. SHEIKH IDRISA; Sec.-Gen. Dr SALMIN OMAR IDRUS.

BAHÁ'Í FAITH

National Spiritual Assembly: POB 30922, Lilongwe 3; tel. 1771177; fax 1771713; e-mail bahaimalawi@africa-online.net; f. 1970; mems resident in over 1,200 localities.

The Press

The Chronicle: Private Bag 77, Lilongwe; tel. 999913457; e-mail thechronicle@africa-online.net; f. 1993; publ. by Jamieson Promotions Ltd; weekly; English and Chichewa; Owner and Editor-in-Chief ROBERT JAMIESON; circ. c. 5,000 (2006).

The Daily Times: Scott Rd, Private Bag 39, Blantyre; tel. 1871663; fax 1871233; e-mail dailytimes@bnltimes.com; internet www.bnltimes.com/index.php/daily-times; f. 1895; fmrly the *Nyasaland Times*; Mon.–Fri., Sun.; English; publ. by Blantyre Newspapers Ltd (Chayamba Trust); affiliated to the MCP; Editor BRIAN LIGOMEKA; circ. Mon.–Fri. c. 20,000, Sun. c. 40,000 (2006).

The Democratus: Aquarius House, Convention Dr., City Centre, Box 1100, Lilongwe 3; tel. 1770033; internet democratusmalawi.blogspot.com; f. 2004; publ. by Democratus Ltd; Wed. and Sun.; Chair. ZIKHALE NG'OMA.

The Dispatch: The Dispatch Publications Ltd, POB 30353, Capital City, Lilongwe 3; tel. 1751639; fax 9510120; e-mail thedispatchmw@sdnp.org.mw; Thur. and Sun; Publr and Man. Editor MARTINES NAMINGAH; circ. Thur. 5,000, Sun. 7,000.

The Enquirer: POB 1745, Blantyre; tel. 1670022; e-mail pillycolette@yahoo.co.uk; English and Nyanja; affiliated to the UDF; Owner LUCIOUS CHIKUNI.

The Guardian: Capital City, Private Bag B341, Lilongwe; tel. 1761996; fax 1761996; Man. Editor DUWA MUTHARIKA-MUBAIRA; circ. c. 5,000 (2006).

The Lamp: Montfort Media, POB 280, Balaka, Zomba; tel. 1545267; e-mail montfortmedia@malawi.net; f. 1995; fortnightly; Roman Catholic and ecumenical; Editor Fr GAMBA PIERGIORGIO; circ. 5,500.

Malawi Government Gazette: Government Printer, POB 37, Zomba; tel. 1523155; fax 1522301; f. 1894; weekly.

Malawi News: Scott Rd, Private Bag 39, Blantyre; tel. 1871679; fax 1871233; internet www.malawinews.bppmw.com; f. 1959; weekly; English and Chichewa; publ. by Blantyre Newspapers Ltd (Chayamba Trust); Man. Editor EDWARD CHISAMBO; Editor STEVEN NHLANE, Jr; circ. c. 40,000 (2006).

The Malawi Standard: POB 31781, Blantyre 3; tel. 1674013; e-mail bligomeka@yahoo.co.uk; fortnightly; Editor BRIAN LIGOMEKA.

The Mirror: POB 30721, Blantyre; tel. 1675043; f. 1994; weekly; English and Nyanja; affiliated to the UDF; Owner and Publr BROWN MPINGANJIRA; circ. 10,000.

The Nation: POB 30408, Chichiri, Blantyre 3; tel. 1673611; fax 1674343; e-mail nation@nationmalawi.com; internet www.nationmw.net; f. 1993; daily; publ. by Nation Publs Ltd; weekly edn of *The Weekend Nation* (circ. 30,000); English and Nyanja; Owner ALEKE BANDA; Editor EDWARD CHITSULO; circ. 15,000.

Odini: POB 133, Lilongwe; tel. 1721135; fax 1721141; f. 1949; fortnightly; Chichewa and English; Roman Catholic; Dir P. I. AKOMENJI; circ. 12,000.

UDF News: POB 3052, Blantyre; tel. 1645314; fax 1645725; e-mail echapusa@yahoo.co.uk; organ of the UDF; fortnightly; English and Nyanja.

Weekly Courier: Lilongwe 3; affiliated to the Democratic Progressive Party; Man. Editor DENIS MZEMBE; circ. c. 3,000 (2006).

The Weekly News: Dept of Information, POB 494, Blantyre; tel. 1642600; fax 1642364; f. 1996; English and Nyanja; publ. by the Ministry of Information and Civic Education; Editor-in-Chief GEORGE TUKHUWA.

There is also an online newspaper, the **Nyasa Times** (internet www.nyasatimes.com).

PERIODICALS

Boma Lathu: POB 494, Blantyre; tel. 1620266; fax 1620039; f. 1973; quarterly; Chichewa; publ. by the Ministry of Information and Civic Education; circ. 100,000.

Business Monthly: POB 906646, Blantyre 9; tel. 16301114; fax 1620039; f. 1995; English; economic, financial and business news; Editor ANTHONY LIVUZA; circ. 10,000.

Fairlane Magazine: POB 1745, Blantyre; tel. 1880205; e-mail fairlane@sndp.org.mw; internet www.fairlanemagazine.com; f. 2006; 6 a year; lifestyle magazine; English and Chichewa; Man. Dir MARIE FRANCE CHIKUNI.

Kuunika (The Light): POB 17, Nkhoma, Lilongwe; tel. 1722807; e-mail nkhomasynod@globemw.net; f. 1909; monthly; Chichewa; publ. by the Church of Central Africa (Presbyterian) Nkhoma Synod; Presbyterian; Editor Rev. M. C. NKHALAMBAYAUSI; circ. 6,000.

Malawi Medical Journal: College of Medicine and Medical Assn of Malawi, Private Bag 360, Blantyre 3; tel. and fax 1878254; e-mail mmj@medcol.mw; internet www.mmj.medcol.mw; f. 1980; replaced *Medical Quarterly*; quarterly; Chair. Prof. ERIC BORGSTEIN; Editor-in-Chief Prof. MALCOLM E. MOLYNEUX.

Moni Magazine: POB 5592, Limbe; tel. 1651833; fax 1651171; f. 1964; monthly; Chichewa and English; circ. 40,000.

Moyo Magazine: Health Education Unit, POB 30377, Lilongwe 3; 6 a year; English; publ. by the Ministry of Health; Editor-in-Chief JONATHAN NKHOMA.

Pride: POB 51668, Limbe; tel. 1640569; f. 1999; quarterly; Publr JOHN SAINI.

This is Malawi: POB 494, Blantyre; tel. 1620266; fax 1620807; f. 1964; monthly; English and Chichewa edns; publ. by the Dept of Information; Editor ANTHONY LIVUZA; circ. 12,000.

Together: Montfort Media, POB 280, Balaka, Zomba; tel. 1545267; e-mail together@sdnp.org.mw; f. 1995; quarterly; Roman Catholic and ecumenical, youth; Editor LUIGI GRITTI; circ. 6,000.

Other publications include *Dzukani*, *Inspiration* and *Msilikali*.

NEWS AGENCY

Malawi News Agency (MANA): POB 28, Blantyre; tel. 1622122; fax 1634867; f. 1966; Exec. Dir GEORGE THINDWA.

Publishers

Christian Literature Association in Malawi (CLAIM): POB 503, Blantyre; tel. 1620839; f. 1968; Chichewa and English; general and religious; Gen. Man. J. T. MATENJE.

Likuni Press and Publishing House: POB 133, Lilongwe; tel. 1721388; fax 1721141; f. 1949; English and Chichewa; general and religious.

Macmillan Malawi Ltd: Private Bag 140, Kenyatta Dr., Chitawira, Blantyre; tel. 1676449; fax 1675751; e-mail mayeso@macmillanmw.net; Gen. Man. HASTINGS MATEWERE.

Montfort Press and Popular Publications: POB 5592, Limbe; tel. 1651833; fax 1641126; f. 1961; general and religious; Gen. Man. VALES MACHILA.

GOVERNMENT PUBLISHING HOUSE

Government Press: Government Printer, POB 37, Zomba; tel. 1525515; fax 1525175.

Broadcasting and Communications

TELECOMMUNICATIONS

In early 2012 there were two mobile cellular telephone operators, one fixed-line telephone operator and one fixed wireless operator in Malawi. In March 2011 a mobile telephone service licence was issued to Celcom Ltd, which was expected to commence operations by October 2012. Later in 2011 dual licences were awarded to all telecommunications operators, permitting them to provide both fixed-line and mobile services.

Regulatory Authority

Malawi Communications Regulatory Authority (MACRA): Salmon Amour Rd, Private Bag 261, Blantyre; tel. 1883611; fax 1883890; e-mail info@macra.org.mw; internet www.macra.org.mw; f. 1998; Chair. EMMANUEL TED NANDOLO; Dir-Gen. CHARLES NSALIWA.

Service Providers

Access Communications Ltd: Accord Centre, Masauko Chipembere Highway, Limbe, POB 343, Blantyre; tel. 212200200; fax 1871887; e-mail switch@access.mw; internet www.access.mw; f. 2010; fixed wireless.

Airtel Malawi: Mwai House, City Centre, POB 57, Lilongwe; tel. 1774800; fax 1774802; e-mail info.africa@airtel.com; internet africa.airtel.com/malawi; f. 1999; fmrly Zain Malawi, present name adopted in 2010; Man. Dir SAULOS CHILIMA.

Malawi Telecommunications Ltd (MTL): Lamya House, Masauko Chipembere Highway, POB 537, Blantyre; tel. 1870278; fax 1846445; e-mail mtlceo@malawi.net; internet www.mtl.mw; f. 2000 following division of Malawi Posts and Telecommunications Corpn into two separate entities; privatized in 2006; 80% owned by Telecom Holdings Ltd, 20% state-owned; CEO PIUS MULIPA (acting).

Telekom Networks Malawi (TNM): Livingstone Towers, 5th Floor, POB 3039, Blantyre; tel. 888800800 (mobile); fax 1830077; e-mail customercare@tnm.co.mw; internet www.tnm.co.mw; f. 1995; owned by Malawi Telecommunications Ltd; operates mobile cellular telephone network; CEO WILLEM SWART.

BROADCASTING

In early 2011 there were 26 licensed broadcasters in Malawi. In November of that year the Malawi Communications Regulatory Authority awarded licences to four television stations (Galaxy, CAN, ABC and Getway) and four radio stations (Galaxy, Mulakho, Maziko and Usisya).

Radio

Malawi Broadcasting Corpn: POB 30133, Chichiri, Blantyre 3; tel. 1671222; fax 1671257; e-mail dgmbc@malawi.net; internet www.mbcradios.com; f. 1964; merged with Television Malawi in July 2010; state-run; 2 channels: MBC 1 and Radio 2 (MBC 2); programmes in English, Chichewa, Chitonga, Chitumbuka, Kyangonde, Lomwe, Sena and Yao; Chair. INKOSI YA MAKOSI MBELWA IV; Dir.-Gen. BENSON TEMBO.

Private commercial and religious radio stations include:

African Bible College Radio (Radio ABC): POB 1028, Lilongwe; tel. 1761965; fax 1761602; e-mail radioabc@malawi.net; internet africanbiblecolleges.org; f. 1995; regional Christian religious programming; Station Man. MACLEOD MUNTHALI.

Calvary Family Radio: POB 30239, Blantyre 3; tel. 1671627; fax 1671642; e-mail calvaryministries@hotmail.com; operated by the Calvary Family Church; religious community radio station.

Capital Radio 102.5 FM: Umoyo House, 2nd Floor, Victoria Ave, Blantyre; Private Bag 437, Chichiri, Blantyre 3; tel. 1820858; fax 1823382; e-mail stationmanager@capitalradiomalawi.com; internet www.capitalradiomalawi.com; f. 1999; commercial radio station; music, news and entertainment; Man. Dir and Editor-in-Chief ALAUDIN OSMAN.

Channel for All Nations (CAN): POB 1220, Lilongwe; tel. 1761763; fax 1762056; e-mail kawembale@yahoo.com; f. 2004; operated by the Assemblies of God Church; regional Christian religious programming.

Dzimwe Community Radio (DCR): POB 425, Chichiri, Blantyre; tel. 1672288; fax 1624330; e-mail mamwa@yahoo.com; f. 1997; operated by the Malawi Media Women's Asscn; focus on rural women's issues; Station Man. JANET KARIM.

Joy FM: Private Bag 17, Limbe, Blantyre; tel. 1638330; fax 1638329; e-mail joyradio@globemalawi.net; commercial radio station; Owner BAKILI MULUZI.

MIJ FM: POB 30165, Chichiri, Blantyre 3; tel. 1675087; fax 1675649; e-mail mij@clcom.net; internet www.mij.mw/aboutradio.html; f. 1996; operated by students of the Malawi Institute of Journalism; community radio station; closed by the Govt during May 2004.

Nkhota Kota Community Radio: Nkhota Kota; f. 2003 with assistance from UNESCO; focus on social and devt issues.

Power 101 FM: POB 761, Blantyre; tel. 1844101; fax 1841387; e-mail fm101@malawi.net; f. 1998; commercial radio station; music and entertainment; Dir and Station Man. OSCAR THOMSON.

Radio Alinafe: Maula Cathedral, POB 631, Lilongwe; tel. 1759971; fax 1752767; e-mail radioalinafe@sdnp.org.mw; f. 2002; Chichewa and English; operated by the Archdiocese of Lilongwe; regional Roman Catholic religious programming; Dir GABRIEL JANA; Editor MOSES KAUFA.

Radio Islam: Agason Bldg, Milward Rd, PO Box 5400, Limbe; tel. 1841408; fax 1845728; e-mail info@radioislam.org.mw; internet radioislam.org.mw; f. 2001; operated by the Islamic Zakaat Fund; religious programming; Dir MUHAMMAD MUHAMMAD AHMED.

Radio Maria Malawi: POB 408, Mangochi; tel. 1599626; fax 1599691; e-mail radiomaria@malawi.net; internet www.radiomaria.mw; f. 2003; operated by Asscn of Radio Maria Malawi as part of the World Family of Radio Maria, Italy; Roman Catholic religious programming; Chichewa, Chiyao and English; Gen. Man. JOSEPH KIMU; Dir of Programmes HENRY SAINDI.

Radio Tigawane: Bishop's House, POB 252, Mzuzu; tel. 1332271; e-mail tigawane@sndp.org.mw; f. 2005; operated by the Diocese of Mzuzu; regional Roman Catholic religious programming; Tumbuka, Chichewa and English; Project Co-ordinator EUGENE NGOMA.

Star Radio: Plantation House, 4th Floor, 11 Victoria Ave, Blantyre; tel. and fax 1832787; e-mail info@starradiomw.com; internet www.starradiomw.com; f. 2006; commercial radio station; Station Man. KAJOWOLA PHIRI.

Trans World Radio Malawi (TWR): POB 52, Lilongwe; tel. and fax 1751870; e-mail twr@malawi.net; f. 2000; part of Trans World Radio-Africa, South Africa; Christian religious programming; Chair. ISAAC MTAMBO; Nat. Dir VICTOR KAONGA.

Zodiak Broadcasting Station (ZBS): Private Bag 312, Lilongwe 3; tel. 1762557; fax 1762751; internet www.zodiakmalawi.com; f. 2005; operated by Zodiak Broadcasting Services; programmes in Chichewa and English; Man. Dir GOSPEL KAZAKO.

Television

MBC: (see Radio).

Luntha Television: Andiamo Loop, POB 45, Balaka; tel. 1553009; fax 1553492; e-mail info@lunthatv.com; internet luntha.project4.webfactional.com; f. 2007; religious broadcaster.

Finance

(cap. = capital; res = reserves; dep. = deposits; m. = million; br(s). = branch(es); amounts in kwacha)

BANKING

In 2010 there were 11 commercial banks and three other financial institutions in Malawi.

Central Bank

Reserve Bank of Malawi: Convention Dr., POB 30063, Capital City, Lilongwe 3; tel. 1770600; fax 1772752; e-mail webmaster@rbm.mw; internet www.rbm.mw; f. 1965; bank of issue; cap. 19,484m., res 12,191m., dep. 48,715m. (Dec. 2009); Gov. CHARLES CHUKA; br. in Blantyre.

Commercial Banks

INDEBank Ltd: INDEBank House, Kaohsiong Rd, Top Mandala, POB 358, Blantyre; tel. 1820055; fax 1823353; e-mail enquiriesho@indebank.com; internet www.indebank.com; f. 1972 as Investment and Devt Bank of Malawi Ltd; total assets 2,162.6m. (Dec. 2003); 41.38% owned by Trans-Africa Holdings Ltd, 30% owned by Press Trust, 25.67% owned by ADMARC Investments Holding, 2.95% owned by Employee Ownership Scheme; commercial and devt banking; provides loans to statutory corpns and to private enterprises in the agricultural, industrial, tourism, transport and commercial sectors; Chair. FRANKLIN KENNEDY; Man. Dir and CEO WILLIAM CHATSALA; 6 brs.

Loita Bank Ltd: c/o Fintech (Malawi) Ltd, Peoples Bldg, 1st Floor, Victoria Ave, Private Bag 264, Blantyre; tel. 1822099; fax 1822683; e-mail lib@mw.loita.com; internet www.loita.com; total assets 3,100.3m. (Dec. 2003); 100% owned by Loita Capital Partners Int.; Chair. and CEO N. JUSTIN CHIMYANTA; 2 brs.

National Bank of Malawi: 19 Victoria Ave, POB 945, Blantyre; tel. 1820622; fax 1820321; e-mail chiefexec@natbankmw.com; internet www.natbank.co.mw; f. 1971; 52% owned by Press Corpn Ltd, 25% owned by Old Mutual Group; cap. 466m., res 2,592m., dep. 55,338m. (Dec. 2009); Chair. Dr MATHEWS CHIKAONDA; CEO GEORGE B. PARTRIDGE; 25 service centres.

NBS Bank Ltd: Ginnery Cnr, Chipembere Highway, off Masajico, POB 32251, Chichiri, Blantyre; tel. 1876222; fax 1875041; e-mail nbs@nbsmw.com; internet www.nbsmw.com; f. 2003; 60% owned by NICO, 8% owned by the Nat. Investment Trust; fmrly New Building Society; cap. 246.7m., res 733.7m., dep. 24,317m. (Dec. 2009); Chair. FELIX L. MLUSU; CEO JOHN S. BIZIWICK.

Nedbank (Malawi) Ltd: Development House, cnr Henderson St and Victoria Ave, POB 750, Blantyre; tel. 1620477; fax 1620102; e-mail office@mw.nedcor.com; f. 1999; fmrly Fincom Bank of Malawi Ltd; 68.8% owned by Nedbank Africa Investments Ltd, 28.4% owned by SBM Nedcor Holdings Ltd; total assets 1,426.9m. (Dec. 2003); Chair. C. DREW; Man. Dir PAUL TUBB.

Standard Bank Ltd: Kaomba Centre, cnr Glyn Jones Rd and Victoria Ave, POB 1111, Blantyre; tel. 1820144; fax 1820117; e-mail stanbicmw@standardbank.co.mw; internet www.standardbank.co.mw; f. 1970 as Commercial Bank of Malawi; present name adopted June 2003; 60.18% owned by Stanbic Africa Holdings Ltd, 20.00% owned by Nat. Insurance Co; cap. 213m., res 2,392m., dep. 38,147m. (Dec. 2009); Chair. ALEX CHITSIME; Man. Dir CHARLES MUDIWA; 8 brs.

Development Bank

Opportunity International Bank of Malawi Ltd (OIBM): Opportunity Bank Bldg, POB 1794, Lilongwe; tel. 1758403; fax 1758400; e-mail lilongwe@oibm.mw; internet www.oibm.mw; f. 2003; 63.7% owned by Opportunity Transformation Investments, USA, 25.3% owned by Opportunity Micro Investments (UK) Ltd, United Kingdom, 11% owned by Trust for Transformation; total assets 967.4m. (Dec. 2005); Chair. FRANCIS PELEKAMOYO; CEO RODGER VOORHIES.

Discount Houses

CDH Investment Bank: Unit House, 5th Floor, Victoria Ave, POB 1444, Blantyre; tel. 1821300; fax 1822826; e-mail info@cdh-malawi.com; internet www.cdh-malawi.com; f. 1998; 84% owned by Trans-Africa Holdings; total assets 6,728.8m. (Dec. 2005); Chair. ROBERT SEKOH ABBEY; Man. Dir and CEO MISHECK ESAU.

First Discount House Ltd: Umoyo House, 1st Floor, 8 Victoria Ave North, POB 512, Blantyre; tel. 1820219; fax 1523044; e-mail fdh@fdh.co.mw; internet www.fdh.co.mw; f. 2000; 40.16% owned by Kingdom Financial Holdings Ltd, 39.84% owned by Thomson F. Mpinganjira Trust, 20% owned by Old Mutual Life Assurance Co (Malawi) Ltd; total assets 5,960.7m. (Dec. 2004); CEO THOMSON F. MPINGANJIRA; Chair. NIGEL M. K. CHAKANIRA.

Merchant Banks

First Merchant Bank Ltd: Livingstone Towers, Glyn Jones Rd, Private Bag 122, Blantyre; tel. 1821955; fax 1821978; e-mail fmb.headoffice@fmbmalawi.com; internet www.fmbmalawi.com; f. 1994; cap. 111.3m., res 2,281.5m., dep. 11,539.5m. (Dec. 2008); 44.9% owned by Zambezi Investments Ltd, 22.5% owned by Simsbury Holdings Ltd, 11.2% owned each by Prime Capital and Credit Ltd, Kenya, and Prime Bank Ltd, Kenya; Chair. RASIKBHAI C. KANTARIA; Man. Dir KASHINATH N. CHATURVEDI; 7 brs.

Leasing and Finance Co of Malawi Ltd: Livingstone Towers, Glyn Jones Rd, POB 1963, Blantyre; tel. 1820233; fax 1820275; f. 1986; subsidiary of First Merchant Bank Ltd since June 2002; total assets 2,087.4m. (Dec. 2006); Chair. HITESH ANADKAT; Gen. Man. MBACHAZWA LUNGU.

Savings Bank

Malawi Savings Bank: Umoyo House, Victoria Ave, POB 521, Blantyre; tel. 1625111; fax 1621929; internet www.msb.mw; f. 1994; 99.9% state-owned; total assets 1,191.7m. (Dec. 2003); Sec.-Treas. P. E. CHILAMBE; Gen. Man. IAN C. BONONGWE.

STOCK EXCHANGE

Malawi Stock Exchange: Old Reserve Bank Bldg, 14 Victoria Ave, Private Bag 270, Blantyre; tel. 1824233; fax 1823636; e-mail mse@mse-mw.com; internet www.mse.co.mw; f. 1996; owned by the Reserve Bank of Malawi; 14 cos listed in 2011; Chair. AUGUSTINE CHITHENGA; CEO SYMON MSEFULA.

INSURANCE

In 2010 the insurance sector comprised 12 insurance companies and one reinsurance company. Of these, eight companies dealt in non-life insurance.

NICO Holdings Ltd: CHIBISA House, 19 Glyn Jones Rd, POB 501, Blantyre; tel. 1831902; fax 1822364; e-mail info@nicomw.com; internet www.nicomw.com; f. 1970; fmrly National Insurance Co Ltd; transferred to private sector in 1996; incorporates NICO Gen. Insurance Co Ltd, NICO Life Insurance Co Ltd and NICO Technologies Ltd; offices at Blantyre, Lilongwe, Mzuzu and Zomba; agencies country-wide; Chair. GEORGE A. JAFFU; CEO and Man. Dir FELIX L. MLUSU.

Old Mutual Malawi: 30 Glyn Jones Rd, Old Mutual Building, POB 393, Blantyre; tel. 1820677; fax 1822649; e-mail info@oldmutual.co.mw; internet www.oldmutualmalawi.com; f. 1845; subsidiary of Old Mutual PLC, United Kingdom; Chair. SIMON ITAYE; Man. Dir CHRIS KAPANGA.

REAL Insurance Co of Malawi Ltd: Delamere House, Victoria Ave, POB 442, Blantyre; tel. 1824044; fax 1823862; e-mail blantyre@realinsurance.co.mw; internet www.realinsurance.co.mw; associate of RSA PLC, United Kingdom; Chair. THOMAS O. B. KANYUKA; CEO ELLECTION MLAVIWA (acting).

United General Insurance Co Ltd (UGI): Michiru House, Victoria Ave, POB 383, Blantyre; tel. 1821770; fax 1821980; e-mail ugi@ugimalawi.com; internet www.ugimalawi.com; f. 1986 as Pearl Assurance Co Ltd; latterly Property and Gen. Insurance Co Ltd; present name adopted following merger with Fide Insurance Co Ltd in July 1998; 74% owned by ZimRE Holdings, Zimbabwe; Chair. ALBERT NDUNA; Man. Dir IAN K. KUMWENDA.

Vanguard Life Assurance Co (Pvt) Ltd: MDC House, 2nd Floor, Glyn Jones Rd, POB 1625, Blantyre; tel. 1823326; fax 1823056; e-mail vanguard@vanguardlifemw.com; internet www.vanguardlifemw.com; f. 1999; 90% owned by Fidelity Life Assurance Ltd, Zimbabwe; Chair. S. TEMBO; Man. Dir GEORGE MAZHUDE.

Trade and Industry

GOVERNMENT AGENCIES

Agricultural Development and Marketing Corpn (ADMARC): POB 5052, Limbe; tel. 1840044; fax 1840486; e-mail admce@admarc.co.mw; internet www.admarc.co.mw; f. 1971; involved in cultivation, processing, marketing and export of grain and other crops; Chair. ERNEST MALENGA; CEO Dr CHARLES J. MATABWA.

Malawi Export Promotion Council (MEPC): Kanabar House, 2nd Floor, Victoria Ave, POB 1299, Blantyre; tel. 1820499; fax 1820995; e-mail mepco@malawi.net; internet www.malawiepc.com; f. 1971; promotes and facilitates export and investment, and provides technical assistance and training to exporters; Gen. Man. LAWRENCE M. CHALULUKA.

Malawi Housing Corpn: POB 414, Blantyre; tel. 1876822.

Malawi Investment Promotion Agency (MIPA): Aquarius House, Private Bag 302, Lilongwe 3; tel. 1770800; fax 1771781; e-mail mipa@mipamw.org; internet www.malawi-invest.net; f. 1993; promotes and facilitates local and foreign investment; CEO JAMES R. KAPHWELEZA BANDA.

Petroleum Control Commission: POB 2827, Blantyre; e-mail sichioko@pccmalawi.com; state-owned; held monopoly on fuel imports until 2000; also serves regulatory role; Chair. Rev. Dr LAZARUS CHAKWERA; Gen. Man. ISHMAEL CHIOKO.

Privatisation Commission of Malawi: Livingstone Towers, 2nd Floor, Glyn Jones Rd, POB 937, Blantyre; tel. 1823655; fax 1821248; e-mail info@pcmalawi.org; internet www.pcmalawi.org; f. 1996; has sole authority to oversee divestiture of govt interests in public enterprises; Chair. ALEX CHITSIME; CEO JIMMY LIPUNGA; 75 privatizations completed by January 2008.

Tobacco Control Commission: POB 40045, Kanengo, Lilongwe 4; tel. 1712777; fax 1712632; e-mail tcclib@tccmw.com; internet www.tccmw.com; f. 1939; regulates tobacco production and marketing; advises Govt on sale and export of tobacco; Chair. GAMALIEL BANDAWE; CEO Dr BRUCE MUNTHALI; regional offices in Mzuzu and Limbe.

DEVELOPMENT ORGANIZATIONS

Council for Non-Governmental Organizations in Malawi (CONGOMA): Nyambadwe, Feed the Children Complex, along Chileka-Magalasi Rd, POB 480, Blantyre; tel. 111917800; e-mail congoma@gmail.com; f. 1992; promotes social and economic devt; Chair. VOICE MHONE; Exec. Dir RONALD MTONGA; 86 mem. orgs (2004).

Small Enterprise Development Organization of Malawi (SEDOM): POB 525, Blantyre; tel. 1622555; fax 1622781; e-mail sedom@sdnp.org.mw; f. 1982; financial services and accommodation for indigenous small- and medium-scale businesses; Chair. STELLA NDAU.

CHAMBER OF COMMERCE

Malawi Confederation of Chambers of Commerce and Industry (MCCCI): Masauko Chipembere Highway, Chichiri Trade Fair Grounds, POB 258, Blantyre; tel. 1871988; fax 1871147; e-mail mccci@mccci.org; internet www.mccci.org; f. 1892; promotes trade and encourages competition in the economy; Chair. MATTHEWS J. CHIKANKHENI; CEO CHANCELLOR L. KAFERAPANJIRA; 400 mems.

INDUSTRIAL AND TRADE ASSOCIATIONS

Dwangwa Cane Growers Trust (DCGT): POB 156, Dwangwa; tel. 1295111; fax 1295164; e-mail dcgt@malawi.net; f. 1999; fmrly Smallholder Sugar Authority; CEO WILFRED CHAKANIKA.

National Hawkers and Informal Business Association (NAHIBA): Chichiri Trade Fair, POB 60544, Ndirande, Blantyre; tel. 1945315; fax 1624558; e-mail nazulug@yahoo.com; f. 1995; Exec. Dir EVA JOACHIM.

Smallholder Coffee Farmers Trust: POB 20133, Luwinga, Mzuzu 2; tel. 1332899; fax 1333902; e-mail mzuzucoffee@malawi.net; f. 1971; successor to the Smallholder Coffee Authority, disbanded in 1999; producers and exporters of Arabica coffee; Gen. Man. HARRISON KALUA; 4,000 mems.

Smallholder Tea Co (STECO): POB 135, Mulanje; f. 2002 by merger of Smallholder Tea Authority and Malawi Tea Factory Co Ltd.

Tea Association of Malawi Ltd (TAML): Kidney Crescent Rd, POB 930, Blantyre; tel. 1671182; fax 1671427; e-mail taml@malawi.net; internet www.taml.co.mw; f. 1934; CEO CLEMENT C. THINDWA; 10 mems.

Tobacco Association of Malawi (TAMA): 13/64 Independence Dr., TAMA House, POB 31360, Lilongwe 3; tel. 1773099; fax 1773493; e-mail tama@tamalawi.com; internet www.tamalawi.com; f. 1929; Pres. RUEBEN JEFRED MAIGWA; Chief Exec. FELIX MKUMBA; brs in Mzuzu, Limbe and Chinkhoma; 75,000 mems.

Tobacco Exporters' Association of Malawi Ltd (TEAM): Private Bag 403, Kanengo, Lilongwe 4; tel. 1775839; fax 1774069; f. 1930; Chair. CHARLES A. M. GRAHAM; Gen. Man. H. M. MBALE; 9 mems.

EMPLOYERS' ORGANIZATIONS

Employers' Consultative Association of Malawi (ECAM): Ndola Cres., House No 498A, POB 2134, Blantyre; tel. and fax 1830075; fax 1830075; e-mail ecam@ecammw.com; internet www.ecammw.com; f. 1963; Pres. BUXTON M. KAYUNI; Dep. Exec. Dir ODRIDGE J. KHUNGA; 250 mem. asscns and 6 affiliates representing 80,000 employees.

Master Printers' Association of Malawi: POB 2460, Blantyre; tel. 1632948; fax 1632220; f. 1963; Chair. PAUL FREDERICK; 21 mems.

Motor Traders' Association: POB 311, Blantyre; tel. and fax 1833312; f. 1954; Chair. JOLLY NKHOJERA; 13 mems (2008).

UTILITY

Electricity

Electricity Supply Corpn of Malawi (ESCOM): ESCOM House, 9 Haile Selassie Rd, POB 2047, Blantyre; tel. and fax 1822000; fax 1822008; e-mail info@escommw.com; internet www.escommw.com; f. 1966; controls electricity generation and distribution; Chair. KAYISI M. SADALA; CEO PETER MTONDA (acting).

Malawi Energy Regulatory Authority (MERA): Development House, 2nd Floor, City Centre, Private Bag B496, Lilongwe3; tel. 1775810; fax 1772666; e-mail mera@meramalawi.mw; internet www.meramalawi.mw; f. 2004; regulatory autority; Chair. JOHN D. K. SAKA.

Water

Blantyre Water Board: POB 30369, Chichiri, Blantyre 3; tel. 18720000; e-mail bwb@bwb.mw; internet www.bwb.mw; f. 1995; supplies potable water to Blantyre City and its environs; Chair. W. R. G. MANDOWA; Chief Exec. ANDREW THAWE.

Lilongwe Water Board: Madzi House, off Likuni Rd, POB 96, Lilongwe; tel. 1750366; fax 1752294; e-mail madzi@lwb.mw; internet www.lwb.mw; f. 1947; Chair. SENIOR CHIEF KAOMBA.

There are also three regional water boards—Central Region Water Board, Northern Region Water Board, Southern Region Water Board—serving the population in small towns and rural areas.

MAJOR COMPANIES

The following are among the largest companies in terms of capital investment or employment.

Agrimal Malawi Ltd: POB 143, Blantyre; tel. 1870933; fax 1870651; e-mail miscor@africa-online.net; f. 2001, fmrly Chillington Agrimal (Malawi) Ltd; 44% owned by Plantation and Gen. Investments PLC; mfrs of agricultural hand tools, hoes and implements; Gen. Man. PRAKASH PAI.

Alliance One Tobacco (Malawi) Ltd: POB 30522, Lilongwe 3; tel. 1710044; fax 1710312; f. 2005 through merger of Standard Commercial Tobacco (Malawi) Ltd and Dimon (Malawi) Ltd; tobacco merchants; Man. Dir COLIN ARMSTRONG.

Auction Holdings Ltd: POB 40035, Kanengo, Lilongwe 4; tel. 1710377; fax 1710384; e-mail ahll@globemw.net; f. 1962; privatized 1997; cap. K914.0m. (2004); tobacco and tobacco products; auction floor operators; 88% state-owned, 5% owned by the Nat. Investment Trust Ltd; Chair. Dr C. J. MATABA; Group Gen. Man. G. C. MSONTHI; 3,000 employees.

Bakhresa Grain Milling (Malawi) Ltd: Charterland Rd, POB 5847, Limbe; tel. 1643272; fax 1643342; e-mail mahesh@bakhresagroup.com; fmrly Grain and Milling Co Ltd (GRAMIL), acquired by Said Salim Bakhresa Co Ltd, Tanzania, in 2003; 100% owned by Bakhresa Family; grain millers; Gen. Man. MAHESH JOSYABHATLA; 150 employees.

BATA Shoe Company (Malawi) Ltd: POB 936, Blantyre; tel. 1670511; fax 1670519; e-mail bata@africa-online.net; mfrs of shoes; Man. Dir A. T. MUZONDIWA.

Blantyre Netting Co Ltd (Blanet): POB 30575, Chichiri, Blantyre 3; tel. 1677398; fax 1671227; polypropylene woven sacks, ropes, bristles, strapping tapes, nylon twines, nets; Admin. Man. DIVERSON LIVATA; 400 employees.

British American Tobacco Malawi Ltd: Chipembere Highway, POB 428, Blantyre; tel. 1670033; fax 1670808; f. 1942; mfrs and distributors of cigarettes; Chair. and Man. Dir KEITH GRETTON; 185 employees.

Illovo Sugar (Malawi) Ltd: Private Bag 580, Limbe; tel. 1843988; fax 1840135; e-mail illovomalawi@illovo.co.za; internet www.illovosugar.com; f. 1965; fmrly Sugar Corpn of Malawi Ltd (SUCOMA); present name adopted 2004; 76% owned by Illovo Sugar Group, South Africa, 10% owned by Old Mutual Life Assurance Co; sugar mills at Dwangwa and Nchalo; sugar production and processing; Group Chair. ROBBIE WILLIAMS; Man. Dir IAN PARROTT; 8,000 permanent employees, 5,000 seasonal employees.

Lafarge Cement Malawi: POB 523, Heavy Industrial Area, Blantyre; tel. 1671933; fax 1871264; e-mail lafarge@lafarge.com; internet www.lafarge.mw; f. 1974 as Portland Cement Co; mfrs and distributors of cement; projected annual capacity: 140,000 metric tons; Man. Dir TIMOTHY KALOKI; 650 employees.

Malawi Cotton Co: Blantyre; Chinese-owned; Man. Dir JU WENBIN.

Nyasa Tobacco Manufacturing Co.: Lilongwe; Man. Dir KONRAD BUCKLE.

Packaging Industries (Malawi) Ltd: POB 30533, Chichiri, Blantyre 3; tel. 1870533; fax 1871283; e-mail pim@malawi.net; f. 1969; 60% owned by Transmar; cap. K13.5m. (2006); mfrs of cardboard boxes, paper sacks and liquid packaging containers; Man. Dir SIMON A. ITAYE; 163 employees (Sept. 2006).

Paladin Africa Ltd: Level 2, Section B, Samala House, City Centre, Private Bag 32, Lilongwe 3; tel. 1774894; fax 1774896; e-mail contact@paladinafrica.com; internet www.paladinenergy.com.au; operates Kayelekera uranium mine in Karonga; Dir and Chair. JOHN BORSHOFF; Gen. Man. JOHN CHANDLER.

Petroleum Importers Ltd (PIL): Unit House, 6th Floor, Victoria Ave, Private Bag 200, Blantyre; tel. 1822886; fax 1821876; e-mail petroleum@pilmalawi.mw; f. 2000 following liberalization of the petroleum industry; industry consortium incl. national and international oil cos; imports 80% of the country's fuel requirements; Gen. Man. ROBERT MDEZA.

Pharmanova Ltd: POB 30073, Chichiri, Blantyre 3; tel. 1870633; fax 1870345; Man. Dir YUSUF PATEL.

Plastic Products Ltd: POB 907, Blantyre; tel. 1670455; fax 1670664; 100% owned by the Malawi Devt Corpn; mfrs of polythene bags; Gen. Man. ROBERT KAPYEPYE.

Press Corpn Ltd: Chayamba Bldg, Victoria Ave, POB 1227, Blantyre; tel. 1633569; fax 1633318; e-mail companysec@presscorp.com; internet www.presscorp.com; f. 1983 as Press Group Ltd; revenue 10,978m. (Dec. 2003); holding co operating through 19 subsidiaries and four assoc. cos in distribution, banking, insurance, manufacturing and processing; Chair. DEAN C. LUNGU; Group CEO Dr MATHEWS A. P. CHIKAONDA; 9,500 employees.

Subsidiaries incl. The Foods Co Ltd, Hardware and Gen. Dealers Ltd, People's Trading Centre Ltd, Presscane Ltd and also:

Ethanol Co Ltd (ETHCO): POB 50, Dwangwa; tel. 1295200; e-mail ireneo@ethanolmw.com; internet www.ethanol-malawi.com; f. 1982; producer and distributor of ethanol fuel; 58.9% owned by Press Corpn Ltd; distillery at Dwangwa; Man. Dir S. DANIEL LIWIMBI.

Limbe Leaf Tobacco Co Ltd: Plot 29/125–126, Area 29, POB 40044, Kanengo, Lilongwe 4; tel. 1710355; fax 1710763; e-mail lmuhara@lltcmw.com; internet www.limbeleaf.com; 58% owned by Universal Leaf Corpn, USA, 42% owned by Press Corpn Ltd; Group Chair. Dr M. A. P. CHIKAONDA; Man. Dir K. R. STAINTON.

Macsteel (Malawi) Ltd: Raynor Ave, POB 5651, Limbe, Blantyre; tel. 1841677; fax 1845871; e-mail steel@macsteelmw.com; fmrly Press Steel and Wire Ltd; present name adopted in 2003; 50% owned by Press Corpn Ltd, 50% owned by Macsteel Africa, South Africa; steel processors.

Malawi Pharmacies Ltd: Masauko Chipembere Highway, POB 51041, Limbe; tel. 1642293; fax 1677784; e-mail mpl@mpl.com.mw; 90% owned by Press Corpn Ltd; mfrs and distributors of pharmaceuticals; Man. Dir. DUMISANI P. CHISALA.

Maldeco Aquaculture Ltd: POB 45, Mangochi; tel. 1584300; fax 1584724; e-mail maldeco@malawi.net; f. 2003; 100% subsidiary of Press Corpn Ltd; Operations Man. J. H. MGASA.

Puma Energy Malawi: 8 Independence Dr., POB 469, Blantyre; f. 1963; 50% owned by Puma Energy (Switzerland), 50% owned by Press Corpn Ltd; fmrly BP Malawi Ltd, name changed as above in 2011; fuel and oil distributor; Gen. Man. DAVIS LANJESI.

Raiply Malawi Ltd: Private Bag 1, Chikangawa, Mzimba; tel. 1340212; fax 1340231; e-mail raiplymw@raiplymalawi.com; fmrly Viphya Plywoods and Allied Industries (Viply); f. 1999; acquired by T. S. Rai Ltd, Kenya, in 1999; mfrs of plywood, blockboard, timber, treated poles and furniture; CEO THOMAS OOMMEN; 2000 employees.

Shayona Cement Corpn: Kasungu; Man. Dir JITENDRA KUMAR PATEL.

Toyota Malawi Ltd: Queens Cnr, Masauko Chipembere Highway, POB 430, Blantyre; tel. 1841933; fax 1844424; e-mail customercare@toyotamalawi.com; internet www.toyotamalawi.com; f. 1964; import and distribution of motor vehicles and parts; Man. Dir ROSEMARY M. MKANDAWIRE; 165 employees.

Unilever Malawi Ltd: cnr Tsiranana Rd and Citron Ave, POB 5151, Limbe; tel. 1641100; fax 1645720; e-mail charles.cofie@unilever.com; f. 1963; fmrly Lever Brothers (Malawi) Ltd until 2003; subsidiary of Unilever PLC, United Kingdom; mfrs of soaps, detergents, cooking oils, foods, beverages and chemicals; Chair. MALCOLM HUGHES; Man. Dir RAYMOND BANDA.

Universal Industries Ltd: Ginnery Cnr, Masauko Chipembere Highway, POB 507, Blantyre; tel. 1870055; fax 1871404; e-mail ums@unibisco.com; internet www.universal.co.mw; f. 1957; mfrs of confectionery and beverages; Chair. M. J. AMIN; Man. Dir D. K. AMIN; 1,000 employees.

TRADE UNIONS

According to the Malawi Congress of Trade Unions, in 2005 some 18% of the workforce was unionized.

Congress of Malawi Trade Unions (COMATU): POB 1443, Lilongwe; tel. 1757255; fax 1770885; Pres. THOMAS L. BANDA; Gen. Sec. PHILLMON E. CHIMBALU.

Malawi Congress of Trade Unions (MCTU): POB 1271, Lilongwe; tel. 1752162; fax 1820716; e-mail mctusecretariat@mctumw.com; f. 1995 as successor to the Trade Union Congress of Malawi (f. 1964); Pres. LUTHER MAMBALA; Sec.-Gen. ROBERT JAMES D. MKWEZALAMBA; 113,000 paid-up mems (2008).

Affiliated unions include:

Building Construction, Civil Engineering and Allied Workers' Union (BCCEAWU): c/o MCTU, POB 5094, Limbe; tel. 1620381; fax 1622304; e-mail johnmwafulirwa@yahoo.com; f. 1961; Pres. LAWRENCE KAFERE; Gen. Sec. JOHN O. MWAFULIRWA; 6,401 mems (2006).

Commercial Industrial and Allied Workers' Union (CIAWU): c/o MCTU, POB 5094, Limbe; tel. 1820716; fax

1622303; e-mail mareydzinyemba@yahoo.com; Pres. TRYSON KALANDA; Gen. Sec. MARY DZINYEMBA; 3,075 mems (2006).

Communications Workers' Union of Malawi: Armarsi Odvarji Plaza, 1st Floor, Haille Selassie Rd, Private Bag 186, Blantyre; tel. and fax 1830830; e-mail robertjdm2002@yahoo.com; f. 1997; Pres. DEUS SANDRAM; Gen. Sec. ROBERT JAMES DANIEL MKWEZALAMBA; 3,347 mems (2012).

Electronic Media Workers' Union: POB 30133, Chichiri, Blantyre 3; tel. 1871343; e-mail mmsowoya@hotmail.com; Pres. LASTEN KUNKEYANI; Gen. Sec. MALANI MSOWOYA; 243 mems (2006).

ESCOM Staff Union: POB 2047, Blantyre; tel. 1773447; Pres. OSCAR CHIMWEZI; Gen. Sec. RACHEL CHASWEKA; 1,899 mems (2006).

Hotels, Food and Catering Service Union: c/o MCTU 5094, Limbe; tel. 1820314; fax 1824277; e-mail hfpcwu@sdnp.org.mw; internet www.hotelsunionmalawi.org; Pres. HARVEY CHINGONDO KALIMANJIRA; Gen. Sec. SHAKESPEARE SESANI; 5,000 mems (2006).

Malawi Housing Co-operation Workers' Union: c/o MHC, POB 84, Mzuzu; tel. 1332655; fax 1311529; Pres. MADALO KADIKIRA; Gen. Sec. MALLEN MKANDAWIRE; 236 mems (2006).

Plantation and Agriculture Workers' Union: POB 181, Lucheza; Pres. PATRICK KADYANJI; Gen. Sec. DENNIS BANDA; 2,086 mems (2006).

Private Schools Employees' Union of Malawi (PSEUM): c/o MCTU, Kepell Compton Cres., Area 3/089, POB 1271, Lilongwe; tel. 1755614; fax 1752162; e-mail hendrixbanda@yahoo.com; Pres. SAMUEL NJIWA; Gen. Sec. HENDRIX S. BANDA; 2,670 mems (2008).

Railway Workers' Union of Malawi (Central East African Railway Workers' Union—CEARWU): POB 5393, Limbe; tel. 1640844; e-mail cear@cearcdn.mw; f. 1954; Pres. DINA M'MERA; Gen. Sec. LUTHER MAMBALA; 485 mems (2006).

Sugar Plantation and Allied Workers' Union (SPAWUM): c/o Illovo Sugar (Malawi) Ltd, Private Bag 50, Blantyre; tel. 111425200 (mobile); e-mail spawum@illovo.co.za; Pres. KEEPER GUMBO; Gen. Sec. STEPHEN MKWAPATIRA; 8,598 mems (2006).

Teachers' Union of Malawi: Aphunzitsi Centre, Private Bag 11, Lilongwe; tel. 1727302; fax 1727302; e-mail tum@sdnp.org.mw; Pres. CHAULUKA MUWAKE; Gen. Sec. DENIS KALEKENI; 46,207 mems (2006).

Textile, Garment, Leather and Security Services Workers' Union: POB 5094, Limbe; tel. 888345576 (mobile); e-mail textilegarmentunion@yahoo.com; f. 1995; Gen. Sec. GRACE NYIRENDA; 8,900 mems (2009).

Tobacco Tenants Workers' Union: POB 477, Nkhotakota; tel. 1292288; e-mail tobaccoandalliedworkersu@yahoo.com; f. 1992; Pres. LYTON KAPONGOLA; Gen. Sec. RAPHAEL SANDRAM; 5,579 mems (2006).

Transport and General Workers' Union: POB 2778, Blantyre; tel. 888877795 (mobile); fax 1830219; e-mail ronaldmbewe2002@yahoo.com; f. 1945; Pres. FRANCIS ANTONIO; Gen. Sec. RONALD MBEWE; 3,257 mems (2006).

Water Employees' Trade Union of Malawi (WETUM): c/o Lilongwe Water Board, Madzi House, off Likuni Rd, POB 96, Lilongwe; tel. 1750366; fax 1752294; Pres. ANTHONY A. CHIMPHEPO; Gen. Sec. OLIVIA KUNJE; 1,195 mems (2006).

Transport

RAILWAYS

The Central East African Railways Co (fmrly Malawi Railways) operates between Nsanje (near the southern border with Mozambique) and Mchinji (near the border with Zambia) via Blantyre, Salima and Lilongwe, and between Nkaya and Nayuchi on the eastern border with Mozambique, covering a total of 797 km. The Central East African Railways Co and Mozambique State Railways connect Malawi with the Mozambican ports of Beira and Nacala. There is a rail/lake interchange station at Chipoka on Lake Malawi, from where vessels operate services to other lake ports in Malawi. The construction of a 27-km railway line linking Mchinji with Chipata, Zambia, was completed in 2010.

Central East African Railways Co Ltd (CEAR): Station Rd, POB 5144, Limbe; tel. 1640844; fax 1643496; f. 1994 as Malawi Railways Ltd; owned by the Sociedade de Desenvolvimento do Corredor de Nacala, a consortuim of mining companies of Brazil and Mozambique; freight and passenger service; Dir HENDRYL CHIMWAZA.

ROADS

In 2004 Malawi had a total road network of some 15,500 km, of which 3,600 km was paved. In addition, unclassified community roads total an estimated 10,000 km. All main roads, and most secondary roads, are all-weather roads. Major routes link Lilongwe and Blantyre with Harare (Zimbabwe), Lusaka (Zambia) and Mbeya and Dar es Salaam (Tanzania). A 480-km highway along the western shore of Lake Malawi links the remote Northern Region with the Central and Southern Regions. A project to create a new trade route, or 'Northern Corridor', through Tanzania, involving road construction and improvements in Malawi, was completed in 1992.

Department of Road Traffic: c/o Ministry of Transport and Public Infrastructure, Private Bag 257, Capital City, Lilongwe 3; tel. 1756138; fax 1752592; comprises the Nat. Roads Authority.

National Roads Authority: Functional Bldg, off Chilambula Rd, Private Bag B346, Lilongwe 3; tel. 1753699; fax 1750307; e-mail nra@nramw.com; internet www.ra.org.mw; f. 1997; Chair. INKOSI YA MAKOSI M'BELWA; CEO PAUL JOHN KULEMEKA.

Road Transport Operators' Association: Chitawira Light Industrial Site, POB 30740, Chichiri, Blantyre 3; tel. 1870422; fax 1871423; e-mail rtoa@sdnp.org.mw; f. 1956; Chair. P. CHAKHUMBIRA; Exec. Dir SHADRECK MATSIMBE; 200 mems (2004).

United Bus Co: POB 176, Blantyre; tel. 888863912; fax 1870038; e-mail ubc@ubcmw.com; internet www.ubcmw.com; f. 2008 by fmr employees of Shire Bus Lines Ltd following its liquidation in 2006; operates local and long-distance bus services between Makata, Blantyre, Malangalanga, Mzimba and Mzuzu and rural areas; services to Harare (Zimbabwe) and Johannesburg (South Africa); Chair. Al-haj Sheik ALIDI LIKONDE.

SHIPPING

There are 23 ports and landing points on Lake Malawi. The four main ports are at Chilumba, Nkhata Bay, Chipoka and Monkey Bay. Ferry services carry around 60,000 passengers annually; the principal cargoes transported are sugar, fertilizer, dried fish and maize. A new landing point at Ngala, near Dwangwa, to carry sugar to Chipoka was inaugurated in 2005. Smaller vessels are registered for other activities, including fishing and tourism. Lake Malawi is at the centre of the Mtwara Development Corridor transport initiative agreed between Zambia, Malawi, Tanzania and Mozambique in December 2004.

Department of Marine Services: c/o Department of Transport and Public Works, Private Bag A-81, Lilongwe; tel. 1751531; fax 1756290; e-mail marinedepartment@malawi.net; responsible for vessel safety and control, ports services, and maritime pollution control; Dir LASTON MAKUZULA.

Malawi Lake Services Ltd (MLS): POB 15, Monkey Bay; tel. and fax 1587221; fax 1587309; e-mail ilala@malawi.net; f. 1994; state-owned; operates passenger and freight services to Mozambique, and freight services to Tanzania; Gen. Man. OWEN SINGINI; 9 vessels, incl. 3 passenger and 4 cargo vessels.

CIVIL AVIATION

Kamuzu (formerly Lilongwe) International Airport was opened in 1982. There is also an international airport at Chileka (Blantyre) and domestic airports at Mzuzu and Karonga in the Northern Region and at the Club Makokola resort near Mangochi.

Department of Civil Aviation: c/o Ministry of Transport and Public Infrastructure, Private Bag B311, Lilongwe 3; tel. 1770577; fax 1774986; e-mail aviationhq@malawi.net; Dir L. Z. PHESELE.

Air Malawi Ltd: 4 Robins Rd, POB 84, Blantyre; tel. 1820811; fax 1820042; e-mail enquiries@airmalawi.com; internet www.airmalawi.com; f. 1967; privatization, begun in 1999, was postponed in 2005; scheduled domestic and regional services; owns 5 subsidiary cos, incl. Air Cargo Ltd and Lilongwe Handling Co Ltd; CEO PATRICK CHILAMBE.

Tourism

Fine scenery, beaches on Lake Malawi, big game and an excellent climate form the basis of the country's tourist potential. According to the World Tourism Organization, the number of foreign visitor arrivals was 746,000 in 2010. Receipts from tourism (excluding passenger transport) totalled US $47m. in that year.

Department of Tourism: POB 402, Blantyre; tel. 1620300; fax 1620947; f. 1969; responsible for tourism policy; inspects and licenses tourist facilities, sponsors training of hotel staff and publishes tourist literature; Dir of Tourism Services ISAAC K. MSISKA.

Malawi Tourism Association (MTA): POB 1044, Lilongwe; tel. 1770010; fax 1770131; e-mail mta@malawi.net; internet www.malawi-tourism-association.org.mw; f. 1998; Exec. Dir SAM BOTOMANI.

Defence

As assessed at November 2011, Malawi's defence forces comprised a land army of 5,300, a marine force of 220 and an air force of 200; all form part of the army. There was also a paramilitary police force of 1,500.

Defence Expenditure: Estimated at K6,700m. in 2011.

Commander-in-Chief of the Malawi Defence Force: JOYCE BANDA.

Commander of the Malawi Defence Force: Brig.-Gen. HENRY ODILLO.

Education

Primary education, which is provided free of charge but is not compulsory, begins at six years of age and lasts for eight years. Secondary education, which begins at 14 years of age, lasts for four years, comprising two cycles of two years. According to UNESCO, in 2008/09 primary enrolment included 97% of children in the relevant age-group (males 94%; females 99%), while secondary enrolment in 2009/10 included 28% of children in the relevant age-group (males 28%; females 27%). A programme to expand education at all levels has been undertaken; however, the introduction of free primary education in September 1994 led to the influx of more than 1m. additional pupils, resulting in severe overcrowding in schools. In January 1996 the International Development Association granted US $22.5m. for the training of 20,000 new teachers, appointed in response to the influx. In 2008 there were some 46,333 primary school teachers, of whom 18,026 were female. In 1997 additional funding was provided by the African Development Bank for the construction of primary and secondary schools. The five constituent colleges of the University of Malawi had a total of 6,454 students in 2008, while 1,428 students were enrolled at Mzuzu University, 358 at the Catholic University and 148 at the University of Livingstonia. Some students attend institutions in the United Kingdom and the USA. A small number of students attend the Marine College at Monkey Bay, which was established in 1998. Recurrent expenditure on education in 2008/09 was estimated at 21,413m. kwacha (equivalent to 13.7% of total recurrent expenditure).

Bibliography

Bone, D. (Ed.). *Malawi's Muslims: Historical Perspectives*. Blantyre, Kachere Series, 2001.

Burton, P., Pelser, E., and Gondwe, L. *Understanding Offending: Prisoners and Rehabilitation in Malawi*. Pretoria, Institute for Security Studies, 2005.

Conroy, A. C. (Ed.), *et al. Poverty, AIDS and Hunger: Breaking the Poverty Trap in Malawi*. Basingstoke, Palgrave Macmillan, 2006.

Crosby, C. A. *Historical Dictionary of Malawi*. 2nd edn. Metuchen, NJ, Scarecrow Press, 1993.

De Kok, B. *Christianity and African Traditional Religion: Two Realities of a Different Kind*. Zomba, Kachere Series, 2005.

Englund, H. (Ed.). *A Democracy of Chameleons: Politics and Culture in the New Malawi*. Uppsala, Nordic African Institute; London, Global, 2002.

Gilman, L. *The Dance of Politics: Gender, Performance and Democratization in Malawi*. Philadelphia, PA, Temple University Press, 2009.

Harrigan, J. *From Dictatorship to Democracy*. Aldershot, Ashgate Publishing Ltd, 2000.

Henk, D. *The Botswana Defense Force in the Struggle for an African Environment (Initiatives in Strategic Studies: Issues and Policies)*. Basingstoke, Palgrave Macmillan, 2011.

Immink, B., Lembani, S., Ott, M., and Peters Berries, C. (Eds). *From Democracy to Empowerment: Ten Years of Democratisation in Malawi*. Maputo, Konrad-Adenauer-Stiftung, 2003.

Kalinga, O. J. *Historical Dictionary of Malawi*. 3rd edn. Lanham, MI, Scarecrow Press, 2001.

Kay, L. *And Then I Came Here: Expatriate Women Talk About Living in Malawi and Other Parts of the World*. Cambridge, Cirrus Books, 2005.

Langwe, K. J. *Impact of Structural Adjustment and Stabilisation Programmes in Malawi*. Manchester, University of Manchester, 2005.

Levy, S. *Starter Packs: A Strategy to Fight Hunger in Developing Countries?: Lessons from the Malawi Experience 1998–2003*. Cambridge, MA, CABI Publishing, 2005.

Lwanda, J. L. C. *Kamazu Banda of Malawi: A Study in Promise, Power and Paralysis: Malawi under Dr Banda, 1961 to 1993*. Glasgow, Dudu Nsomba Publrs, 1993.

Promises, Power Politics and Poverty: Democratic Transition in Malawi, 1961–1996. Glasgow, Dudu Nsomba Publrs, 1996.

Politics, Culture and Medicine in Malawi. Zomba, Kachere Series, 2005.

Maliyamkono, T. L., and Kanyongolo F. E. *When Political Parties Clash*. Dar es Salaam, TEMA Publrs, 2003.

Manda, M. A. Z. *State and Labour in Malawi*. Glasgow, Dudu Nsomba Publications, 2000.

Mandala, E. C. *The End of Chidyerano: A History of Food and Everyday Life in Malawi, 1860–2004*. Portsmouth, NH, Heinemann, 2005.

Mawdsley, E., and McCann, G. (Eds). *India in Africa: Changing Geographies of Power*. Oxford, Pambazuka Press, 2011.

McCracken, J. (Ed.). *Twentieth Century Malawi: Perspectives on History and Culture*. Stirling, University of Stirling, 2001.

Mchenga, R. G. *Macroeconomic Stabilisation and Structural Adjustment Programmes: Policy Objectives and Outcomes. A Case Study of Malawi*. Manchester, University of Manchester, 2005.

Meinhardt, H., and Patel, N. *Malawi's Process of Democratic Transition: An Analysis of Political Developments between 1990 and 2003*. Maputo, Konrad-Adenauer-Stiftung, 2003.

Mhone, G. C. Z. (Ed.). *Malawi at the Crossroads: The Post-Colonial Political Economy*. Harare, SAPES Books, 1992.

Muula, A., and Cahnika, E. T. *Malawi's Lost Decade: 1994–2004*. Limbe, Montfort Press, 2005.

Ndalama, J. S. *Impact of Economic Reform Programmes on Economic Growth of Malawi*. Manchester, University of Manchester, 2005.

Nzunda, M. S., and Ross, K. R. (Eds). *Church, Law and Political Transition in Malawi 1992–1994*. Gweru, Mambo, 1995.

Patel, N., and Svasand, L. (Eds). *Government and Politics in Malawi*. Zomba, Kachere Series, 2007.

Phiri, D. D. *History of Malawi: From Earliest Times to the Year 1915*. Blantyre, Christian Literature Assen of Malawi (CLAIM), 2004.

History of the Tumbuka. Blantyre, Dzuka Publishing Co Ltd, 2000.

Power, J. *Political Culture and Nationalism in Malawi*. Rochester, NY, University of Rochester Press, 2010.

Sindima, H. J. *Malawi's First Republic: An Economic and Political Analysis*. Lanham, MD, University Press of America, 2002.

Tengatenga, J. *Church, State and Society in Malawi*. Zomba, Kachere Series, 2006.

Thompson, T. J. (Ed.). *Colonialism to Cabinet Crisis. A Political History of Malawi*. Zomba, Kachere Series, 2009.

White, S. V., Kachika, T., and Chipasula Banda, M. *Women in Malawi: A Profile of Women in Malawi*. Limbe, Women and Law in Southern Africa, Research and Education Trust; Harare, Southern African Research and Documentation Centre, Women in Development Southern Africa Awareness, 2005.

MALI

Physical and Social Geography

R. J. HARRISON CHURCH

With an area of 1.24m. sq km (478,841 sq miles), the Republic of Mali is only slightly smaller than Niger, West Africa's largest state. Like Niger and Burkina Faso, Mali is land-locked. Bordering on seven countries, it extends about 1,600 km from north to south, and roughly the same distance from east to west, with a narrowing at the centre. The population was 14,517,176 according to provisional results of the census of April 2009, and was estimated by the UN at 16,318,894 in mid-2012 (giving an average density of 13.2 inhabitants per sq km). The only large city is the capital, Bamako, which had a population of 2,036,520 in mid-2011, according to UN estimates.

The ancient Basement Complex rocks of Africa have been uplifted in the mountainous Adrar des Iforas of the north-east, whose dry valleys bear witness to formerly wetter conditions. Otherwise the Pre-Cambrian rocks are often covered by Primary sandstones, which have bold erosion escarpments at, for example, Bamako and east of Bandiagara. At the base of the latter live the Dogon people. Where the River Niger crosses a sandstone outcrop below Bamako, rapids obstruct river navigation, giving an upper navigable reach above Bamako, and another one below it from Koulikoro to Ansongo, near the border with Niger.

Loose sands cover most of the rest of the country and, as in Senegal and Niger, are a relic of drier climatic conditions. They are very extensive on the long border with Mauritania and Algeria.

Across the heart of the country flows the River Niger, a vital waterway and source of fish. As the seasonal floods retreat, they leave pasture for thousands of livestock desperate for food and water after a dry season of at least eight months. The retreating floods also leave damp areas for man, equally desperate for cultivable land in an arid environment. Flood water is sometimes retained for swamp rice cultivation, and has been made available for irrigation, particularly in the 'dead' south-western section of the inland Niger delta.

The delta is the remnant of an inland lake, in which the upper River Niger once terminated. In a more rainy era this overflowed to join the then mighty Tilemsi river, once the drainage focus of the now arid Adrar des Iforas. The middle and lower courses of the Tilemsi now comprise the Niger below Bourem, at the eastern end of the consequential elbow turn of the Niger. The eastern part of the delta, which was formed in the earlier lake, is intersected by 'live' flood-water branches of the river, while the relic channels of the very slightly higher western part of the delta are never occupied naturally by flood water and so are 'dead'. However, these are used in part for irrigation water retained by the Sansanding barrage, which has raised the level of the Niger by an average of 4.3 m.

Mali is mainly dry throughout, with a rainy season of four to five months and a total rainfall of 1,120 mm at Bamako, and of only seven weeks and an average fall of 236 mm at Gao. North of this there is no rain-fed cultivation, but only semi-desert or true desert, which occupies nearly one-half of Mali. The exploitation of gold reserves, most of which are located near the borders with Senegal and Guinea, is becoming an increasingly important activity. Modest quantities of diamonds are mined near the border with Senegal.

Distances to the nearest foreign port from most places in Mali are at least 1,300 km, and, not surprisingly, there is much seasonal and permanent emigration.

Recent History

KATHARINE MURISON

The former French colony of Soudan merged with Senegal in April 1959 to form the Federation of Mali, which became independent on 20 June 1960. Senegal seceded two months later, and the Republic of Mali was proclaimed on 22 September. President Modibo Keïta declared the country a one-party state, under his Union Soudanaise—Rassemblement Démocratique Africain (US—RDA). Keïta's Marxist regime severed links with France and developed close relations with the Eastern bloc. In November 1968 Keïta was deposed in an army coup, and a Comité Militaire pour la Libération Nationale was formed, with Lt (later Gen.) Moussa Traoré as President.

THE TRAORÉ PERIOD

The new regime promised a return to civilian rule when Mali's economic problems had been overcome. Relations with France improved, and French budgetary aid ensued. In 1976 a new ruling party, the Union Démocratique du Peuple Malien (UDPM), was established. Traoré, the sole candidate, was elected President at elections in 1979, and a single list of UDPM candidates was elected to the legislature. From 1981 the Traoré regime undertook a programme of economic reform, and Traoré was re-elected to the presidency unopposed in 1985.

At elections to the Assemblée nationale in June 1988, provision was made for up to three UDPM-nominated candidates to contest each of the 82 seats. Doubtlessly influenced by political events elsewhere in the region, in March 1990 Traoré initiated a nation-wide series of conferences to consider the exercise of democracy within and by the ruling party. Mali's first cohesive opposition movements began to emerge that year: among the most prominent were the Comité National d'Initiative Démocratique (CNID) and the Alliance pour la Démocratie au Mali (ADEMA), which organized mass pro-democracy demonstrations in December. In January 1991 Traoré relinquished the defence portfolio to Brig.-Gen. Mamadou Coulibaly, the air force Chief of Staff.

ARMY INTERVENTION AND POLITICAL REFORM

The security forces harshly repressed violent pro-democracy demonstrations in March 1991: 106 people were killed and 708 injured. On 26 March it was announced that Traoré had been deposed. A military Conseil de Réconciliation Nationale (CRN), led by Lt-Col (later Lt-Gen.) Amadou Toumani Touré, assumed power, and the Constitution, Government, legislature and the UDPM were dissolved. The CRN was swiftly succeeded by a 25-member Comité de Transition pour le Salut du Peuple (CTSP), chaired by Touré, whose function was to oversee a transition to a democratic, civilian political system. It was announced that municipal, legislative and presidential elections would be organized by the end of the year, and that the armed forces would withdraw from political life in early 1992. Soumana Sacko, briefly Minister of Finance and Trade in 1987, was appointed to head a transitional, civilian-dominated government.

The CTSP affirmed its commitment to the policies of economic adjustment that had been adopted by the Traoré administration. An amnesty was proclaimed for most political prisoners detained under Traoré, and provision was made for the registration of political parties. The CNID was legalized as the Congrès National d'Initiative Démocratique (led by a prominent lawyer, Mountaga Tall), while ADEMA (chaired by Alpha Oumar Konaré) adopted the additional title of Parti Pan-Africain pour la Liberté, la Solidarité et la Justice, and the US—RDA was revived.

A national conference was convened in Bamako in July 1991, during which some 1,800 delegates prepared a draft Constitution for what was to be designated the Third Republic of Mali, together with an electoral code and a charter governing political parties. In November it was announced that the period of transition to civilian rule was to be extended until 26 March 1992. (The delay was attributed principally to the CTSP's desire first to secure an agreement with Tuareg groups in the north—see below.) The Constitution was approved by 99.8% of those who voted (about 43% of the electorate) in a referendum on 12 January 1992. Municipal elections followed one week later, contested by 23 of the country's 48 authorized parties. ADEMA enjoyed the greatest success, winning 214 of the 751 local seats, while the US—RDA took 130 seats and the CNID 96. The rate of abstention by voters was, however, almost 70%. Legislative elections were held on 23 February and 8 March, amid allegations that the electoral system was unduly favourable to ADEMA. Of the 21 parties that submitted candidates, 10 secured seats in the 129-member Assemblée nationale: ADEMA won 76 seats, the CNID nine and the US—RDA eight. Overall, only about one-fifth of the electorate voted.

Nine candidates contested the first round of the presidential election, on 12 April 1992 (the date for the transition to civilian rule having again been postponed). The largest share of the votes (some 45%) was won by Konaré. A second round of voting, contested by the ADEMA leader and his nearest rival, Tiéoulé Mamadou Konaté of the US—RDA, followed two weeks later, at which Konaré won 69% of the votes cast. Again, participation by voters was little more than 20%.

THE KONARÉ PRESIDENCY

Konaré was sworn in as President of the Third Republic on 8 June 1992. Younoussi Touré, formerly the director in Mali of the Banque Centrale des Etats de l'Afrique de l'Ouest, was designated Prime Minister. While most strategic posts in Touré's Government were allocated to members of ADEMA, the US—RDA and the Parti pour la Démocratie et le Progrès (PDP) were also represented.

Younoussi Touré resigned the premiership in April 1993, following several weeks of student protests against austerity measures. The new Prime Minister, Abdoulaye Sekou Sow, who was not affiliated to any political party, appointed a Council of Ministers dominated by ADEMA and its supporters. A reorganization of the Government in November was prompted by the resignation of ADEMA's Vice-President, Mohamed Lamine Traoré, from his ministerial post. ADEMA remained the majority party in the Government, which also included representatives of the CNID, the PDP and the Rassemblement pour la Démocratie et le Progrès (RDP). The US—RDA withdrew from the coalition shortly afterwards.

Political and social tensions were exacerbated by the 50% devaluation, in January 1994, of the CFA franc. Sow resigned in February, and was replaced as Prime Minister by Ibrahim Boubacar Keïta—since November 1993 the Minister of Foreign Affairs, Malians Abroad and African Integration, a close associate of Konaré and regarded as a member of ADEMA's 'radical' wing. The CNID and the RDP withdrew from the government coalition, protesting that they had not been consulted about the changes; a new, ADEMA-dominated Government was appointed, from which the PDP in turn withdrew.

In September 1994 the election of Keïta to the presidency of ADEMA precipitated the resignation of prominent party members, including Mohamed Lamine Traoré. The Mouvement Patriotique pour le Renouveau (MPR), established following an unsuccessful attempt to revive the UDPM, was granted official status in January 1995. A breakaway movement from the CNID was registered in September 1995 as the Parti pour la Renaissance Nationale (PARENA); ADEMA and PARENA established a political alliance in February 1996, and the Chairman and Secretary-General of PARENA were appointed to the Government in July.

The first round of elections to an enlarged 147-seat Assemblée nationale was held on 13 April 1997, contested by more than 1,500 candidates. As early results indicated a clear victory for ADEMA, the main opposition parties condemned the results as fraudulent and announced that they would boycott the second round, as well as the presidential election. In late April the Constitutional Court annulled the first round of voting on the grounds of irregularities.

The first round of the presidential election was postponed, by one week, until 11 May 1997. Konaré emphasized that he had no wish to be the sole candidate. In early May Mamadou Maribatrou Diaby, the leader of the Parti pour l'Unité, la Démocratie et le Progrès, announced that he was prepared to contest the presidency. However, the so-called 'radical' opposition collective adhered to its demands for the cancellation of the ongoing electoral process, for the complete revision of the voters' register, and, in the mean time, for the resignation of the Government and the appointment of a transitional administration. The Constitutional Court rejected an opposition petition seeking the cancellation of the presidential poll. The final results of voting allocated 95.9% of the valid votes cast to Konaré. Claiming success for its campaign for a boycott of the election, the radical opposition stated that the low rate of participation by voters, 28.4% of the registered electorate, effectively invalidated Konaré's victory. (The turn-out was, none the less, higher than that recorded at the 1992 election.) Konaré's investiture, on 8 June, was marred by violent disturbances in Bamako, and the first round of the legislative elections, due on 6 July, was later postponed by two weeks. While some opposition parties announced their intention to present candidates for the Assemblée nationale, 18 others, including the US—RDA, the MPR and the CNID, grouped in a Collectif des Partis Politiques de l'Opposition (COPPO), reiterated their refusal to re-enter the electoral process unless their demands were met in full.

Legislative voting took place on 20 July 1997, preceded by violent disturbances in Bamako and elsewhere, in which two people were reported to have been killed: a total of 17 parties (including five 'moderate' opposition parties), as well as a small number of independent candidates, contested seats in the Assemblée nationale. As at the presidential election, COPPO claimed that its appeal for a boycott of the poll had been successful, and that the low rate of participation by voters (about 12% of the registered electorate in Bamako, and 22% elsewhere) would render the assembly illegitimate. A second round of voting was held for eight seats on 3 August. The final results allocated 130 of the 147 seats to ADEMA. A new Government was appointed in September, again with Keïta as Prime Minister: the new administration included a number of representatives of the moderate opposition parties.

In February 2000 Keïta submitted his Government's resignation. An extensively reorganized Council of Ministers was subsequently appointed, with Mandé Sidibé as Prime Minister. Sidibé was widely considered to be a supporter of economic reform and of an anti-corruption campaign being undertaken by Konaré.

New legislation approved by the Assemblée nationale in mid-2000 included measures designed to ensure the provision of state funding for political parties, and to encourage greater freedom of the press. The legislature also approved a major revision of the Constitution proposed by President Konaré, although a national referendum on the amendments would be required before their implementation. Notably, under the proposed changes, the electoral system at legislative elections would be reformed to incorporate an element of proportional representation and people of dual nationality would be authorized to contest presidential elections. In July COPPO, which now comprised 15 parties and was led by Almamy Sylla of the RDP, announced that it would henceforth participate in the political process. In August the Assemblée nationale approved electoral legislation, which reportedly envisaged a chamber comprising 150 members, 40 of whom would be elected by a system of proportional representation. However, this legislation was rejected by the Constitutional Court in October.

In October 2000 Keïta resigned as leader of ADEMA; a significant faction within the party opposed the proposed nomination of Keïta as the party's candidate at the presidential election scheduled to be held in 2002. At an extraordinary congress of the party, held in November, Dioncounda Traoré was elected as the new President. In July 2001 a new party led by Keïta, the Rassemblement pour le Mali (RPM), was officially registered.

In November 2001 Konaré indefinitely postponed a referendum (due to take place in the following month) on the constitutional amendments adopted by the Assemblée nationale in July 2000. In January 2002 Soumaïla Cissé, the Minister of Facilities, National Development, the Environment and Town Planning, was elected as the presidential candidate of ADEMA; Cissé consequently stepped down from his ministerial position. In March Sidibé resigned as Prime Minister in order to contest the presidency; Modibo Keïta, hitherto Secretary-General at the presidency, was appointed to the premiership. In early April it was reported that 15 opposition parties, including the CNID, the RPM and the MPR, had formed an electoral alliance, Espoir 2002, agreeing to support a single opposition candidate in the event of a second round of voting. Meanwhile, an alliance of 23 political parties announced its support for the presidential candidacy of Amadou Toumani Touré, the leader of the 1991 coup and subsequent transitional regime, while the RPM formally announced the candidacy of Ibrahim Boubacar Keïta.

AMADOU TOUMANI TOURÉ ELECTED PRESIDENT

At the first round of the presidential election, which was held on 28 April 2002, and contested by 24 candidates, Touré secured the largest share of the votes cast, with 28.7%, followed by Cissé, with 21.3%, and Keïta, with 21.0%. As no candidate had secured an overall majority, Touré and Cissé contested a second round of voting on 12 May. Touré, supported by more than 40 parties (including those of Espoir 2002), won 65.0% of the valid votes cast, defeating Cissé. The electoral process was marred by allegations of fraud and incompetence, which led the Constitutional Court to annul around one-quarter of the votes cast in the first ballot, and reports indicated that the turn-out was very low, particularly in the second round (approximately 25%). Touré was inaugurated as President on 8 June and subsequently formed a new Government, appointing Ahmed Mohamed Ag Hamani as Prime Minister and Minister of African Integration, the first Tuareg to hold the Malian premiership.

Legislative elections, which were held in two rounds on 14 and 28 July 2002, were also marked by a low rate of participation and demonstrated the clear absence of any one dominant political grouping in Mali. The RPM emerged as the single largest party in the new Assemblée nationale, with 46 of the 147 seats (although 20 of its seats had been won in local electoral alliances with other parties of the Espoir 2002 grouping), closely followed by ADEMA, which secured 45 seats. Other parties of Espoir 2002 obtained a further 21 seats, giving a total of 66 to supporters of the RPM, while other constituent parties of the pro-ADEMA Alliance pour la République et la Démocratie won an additional six seats, giving a total of 51. The CNID received 13 seats, while parties belonging to an informal alliance supportive of President Touré, the Convergence pour l'Alternance et le Changement (ACC), including PARENA and the US—RDA, won a total of 10 seats. As had been the case in the presidential election, the Constitutional Court annulled a significant number of votes prior to the publication of the definitive results, amid further allegations of electoral fraud. The results of voting in eight constituencies were declared void, as a result of administrative flaws. President Touré announced his willingness to govern in co-operation with any party that could establish command of the legislature. In early September 19 deputies, comprising those of the ACC parties, several independents and other declared supporters of Touré, formed a grouping, the Bloc Présidentiel, within the legislature. Later in the month Ibrahim Boubakar Keïta was elected President of the Assemblée nationale.

On 16 October 2002 Touré announced the formation of a Government of National Unity. ADEMA increased its representation in the Assemblée nationale to 53 deputies, becoming the single largest party, following its victory in by-elections in all eight constituencies where elections were rerun on 20 October, although the RPM-led Espoir 2002 grouping continued to hold a majority of seats.

Ag Hamani tendered his resignation as premier in April 2004, apparently in response to a request by President Touré. A new administration, headed by Prime Minister Ousmane Issoufi Maïga, hitherto Minister of Equipment and Transport (and not affiliated to any political party), was formed in May. ADEMA was the most successful party at municipal elections held that month, winning 28% of the seats contested, followed by the Union pour la République et la Démocratie (URD—formed by Cissé in 2003, following a split in ADEMA), which secured 14%, and the RPM, with 13%; the rate of participation by the electorate was relatively high, at 43.1%.

In November 2006 it was announced that the first rounds of the presidential and legislative elections would be held on 29 April and 1 July 2007, respectively, with second rounds to take place on 13 May and 22 July if required. Later that month ADEMA's First Vice-President, Soumeylou Boubèye Maïga, was expelled from the party, together with three other members of the party's executive committee, after he suggested that he might stand in the presidential election for a newly formed political movement, Convergence 2007; Maïga subsequently announced his candidature and was formally expelled from ADEMA, which confirmed its support for Touré. Keïta was nominated as the RPM's presidential candidate in January. In the following month Keïta, Maïga and two other presidential candidates formed an electoral coalition, the Front pour la Démocratie et la République (FDR), pledging to support each other in the event of a second round of presidential voting. By the end of February a total of 16 parties and associations had joined the FDR. Touré finally declared his candidature at the end of March.

TOURÉ SECURES SECOND TERM

Eight candidates contested the presidential election on 29 April 2007, six of whom had stood in the 2002 election. Touré was re-elected to the presidency with 71.2% of the votes cast, thus avoiding the need for a second round of voting. Keïta, his nearest rival, secured 19.2%, while a turn-out of 36.2% was recorded. Although officially an independent, Touré had been reportedly supported by more than 40 parties, as well as the former Tuareg rebels who had recently signed peace accords with the Government following an uprising in May 2006 (see below). The FDR refused to recognize the results, alleging that state assets had been used to fund Touré's campaign, that the electoral register had been manipulated to favour the incumbent and that voters had been intimidated, but international observers declared the election to have been largely free and fair. Touré was inaugurated to serve his second and final term on 8 June 2007.

LEGISLATIVE AND MUNICIPAL ELECTIONS

The elections to the Assemblée nationale, which were held on 1 and 22 July 2007, were marked by a low turn-out, recorded at 33% in the first round and reported to be 10%–12% in the second. Parties supportive of President Touré, grouped in the Alliance pour la Démocratie et le Progrès, strengthened their position in the legislature, winning a total of 113 of the 147 seats, of which 51 were secured by ADEMA (becoming the largest single party), 34 by the URD, eight by the MPR and seven by the CNID. Of the opposition parties, the RPM took 11 seats (a poor result compared with the 46 seats it secured in the 2002 polls), while its ally in the FDR, PARENA, obtained four. The non-aligned Parti de la Solidarité Africaine pour la Démocratie et l'Indépendance (SADI) won four seats and independent candidates 15. In September 2007 Dioncounda Traoré, the ADEMA leader, was elected President of the Assemblée nationale.

Prime Minister Maïga resigned on 27 September 2007, and was replaced the following day by Modibo Sidibé, hitherto Secretary-General of the Presidency. The new Council of

Ministers included many new appointees, although the ministers responsible for several key portfolios were retained. The Minister of Energy and Water, Ahmed Sow, resigned in September 2008, reportedly in connection with an ongoing inquiry into his alleged links to a Malian textile company, Fils et Tissus Naturels d'Afrique, which had received a €3.7m. loan from the European Investment Bank on the recommendation of an institution previously headed by Sow, the Centre for the Development of Enterprise (based in Brussels, Belgium). Mamadou Igor Diarra, formerly President and Director-General of the recently privatized Banque Internationale pour le Mali, replaced Sow.

Touré effected a government reorganization in April 2009, replacing the Ministers of Higher Education and Scientific Research and of Education, Literacy and the National Languages. Among other changes, Abou-Bakar Traoré, hitherto Minister of Finance, was appointed to head a new Ministry of Mining, while Sanoussi Touré, the former cabinet director of the Prime Minister, became Minister of the Economy and Finance.

In December 2009 President Touré announced plans for constitutional reform and for further decentralization of the local government system, with the creation of new regions and other administrative divisions. The proposed constitutional changes were revealed in April 2010 and included the establishment of an upper legislative chamber (the Sénat), an Audit Court and new agencies to organize elections and to regulate broadcasting, as well as the reorganization of the Constitutional Court. Also envisaged were revisions to the eligibility conditions for presidential candidates and the appointment of an official Leader of the Opposition, who would be accorded the rank of minister. In June 2011 the Council of Ministers finally adopted a draft law on the amendments to the Constitution, which was approved by the Assemblée nationale in August, but was still to be submitted to a national referendum.

Meanwhile, in July 2010 supporters of President Touré (who had confirmed that he would not seek to modify the Constitution in order to be able to contest a third term) formed a new party, the Parti pour le Développement Économique et la Solidarité (PDES), led by the Minister of Equipment and Transport, Hamed Diane Séméga; some 17 deputies joined the PDES during the following weeks. The Minister of Health, Oumar Ibrahima Touré, was dismissed from the Government in December 2010, following a scandal involving the embezzlement of funds received from the Global Fund to Fight AIDS, Tuberculosis and Malaria. Badara Aliou Macalou, the Minister of Malians Abroad and African Integration, assumed additional responsibility for the health portfolio.

Modibo Sidibé resigned the premiership in March 2011, amid speculation that he intended to contest the presidency in 2012. Cissé Mariam Kaïdama Sidibé, hitherto President of the Administrative Council of the Société Nationale des Tabacs et Allumettes du Mali and unaffiliated to any political party, was appointed as Mali's first female Prime Minister in April 2011. Her new Council of Ministers notably included members of the opposition RPM and PARENA, while Soumeylou Boubèye Maïga, a former Minister of Defence during Konaré's presidency, became Minister of Foreign Affairs and International Co-operation, and Daba Diawara was allocated the newly created portfolio of state reform. In July ADEMA selected its leader, Dioncounda Traoré, the President of the Assemblée nationale, to represent the party at the 2012 presidential election, while the RPM nominated Keïta, and in September Soumaïla Cissé was designated as the URD's candidate. The proposed timetable for the 2012 elections was announced in October 2011: the first round of the presidential ballot would be held concurrently with the constitutional referendum on 29 April 2012, followed by a second round on 13 May and legislative polls on 1 and 22 July. Modibo Sidibé confirmed his presidential candidacy in January 2012.

Amid rising domestic and international pressure to quell the renewed Tuareg rebellion in the north of the country (see Ethnic Tensions), in February 2012 President Touré effected an exchange of portfolios between the two government ministers responsible for defence and security, Gen. Sadio Gassama becoming Minister of Defence and War Veterans and Natié Pléa Minister of Internal Security and Civil Protection. As the violence in the north continued, campaigning for the forthcoming elections was muted.

MILITARY COUP

A group of disaffected soldiers, led by Capt. Amadou Sanogo, attacked the presidential palace and seized control of the state broadcaster on 21 March 2012. This followed a mutiny earlier that day at a military camp in Kati, some 10 km from Bamako, mounted by soldiers angered by Gen. Gassama's failure during a visit to the barracks to address their complaints regarding the perceived weakness of the Government's response to the Tuareg insurgency and the insufficiency of the arms and other supplies provided to troops fighting in the north. The formation of a Comité National pour le Redressement de la Démocratie et la Restauration de l'Etat (CNRDRE), headed by Sanogo, was announced on 22 March, together with the suspension of the Constitution and the dissolution of all state institutions. The CNRDRE pledged to return power to a democratically elected President following the establishment of national unity and territorial integrity. Some 14 members of Touré's deposed Government, including Prime Minister Sidibé and foreign minister Maïga, were detained at the Kati camp, while the whereabouts of the President himself were initially unknown, although it later emerged that he had sought refuge in the Senegalese embassy in Bamako. The coup was widely condemned both regionally and internationally; the African Union (AU) suspended Mali from the organization, while the USA, the World Bank and other foreign governments and international institutions halted non-humanitarian aid to the country. Domestically, ADEMA, the RPM, the URD and 35 other political parties joined with some 20 civil society groups to form a movement opposing the coup, the Front Uni pour la Sauvegarde de la Démocratie et de la République, the SADI being the only parliamentary party to express support for the CNRDRE.

At the beginning of April 2012, following talks with representatives of the Economic Community of West African States (ECOWAS), Sanogo announced the re-entry into force of the Constitution and promised to hold consultations regarding the establishment of transitional organs of power that would prepare for free and democratic elections after an unspecified period. None the less, on the following day ECOWAS, which had placed a stand-by military force on alert for a possible intervention in Mali, fulfilled a threat to impose diplomatic, economic and financial sanctions on the CNRDRE pending the restoration of constitutional order. On 6 April, after further negotiations with ECOWAS, the CNRDRE agreed to the application of the constitutional article providing for the President of the Assemblée nationale temporarily to assume the functions of the President of the Republic in the event of the latter post becoming vacant. In return, ECOWAS was to remove the recently imposed sanctions on the CNRDRE, members of which, together with all other participants in the coup, would be granted an amnesty (which was approved by the Malian legislature in May). Touré formally submitted his resignation as President on 7 April, leaving for exile in Senegal later that month. Dioncounda Traoré took office as interim President on 12 April for an initial period of 40 days. An interim Government was formed later that month, headed by astrophysicist Cheick Modibo Diarra and mainly comprising unaffiliated civilians, although three military officers were allocated the strategic portfolios of defence and war veterans, internal security and civil protection, and territorial administration, decentralization and land affairs. Interim Prime Minister Diarra stated that he was willing to negotiate with the Tuareg and Islamist groups that now effectively controlled northern Mali, having taken advantage of the instability resulting from the coup. At a summit held in late April, ECOWAS leaders proposed an extension in the transition period to 12 months and the deployment of regional troops to Mali to assist the interim authorities. However, the CNRDRE, which retained significant influence despite having officially ceded power, opposed the presence of foreign troops in Mali. Meanwhile, several prominent political and military figures considered to be allies of ousted President Touré, including former Prime Minister Modibo Sidibé, were briefly detained in mid-April, prompting expressions of concern from Amnesty International and political parties, and at the end of the month forces loyal to Touré clashed in Bamako with those supportive of the CNRDRE.

Following further discussions involving ECOWAS, the interim Malian authorities and coup leader Sanogo, it was agreed in late May 2012 that Traoré would remain as interim President for a transitional period of one year, while Sanogo would be accorded the status of a former head of state. However, the extension of Traoré's presidential term angered supporters of the coup, several of whom entered the presidential palace and attacked the interim President. The attack, which prompted Traoré to travel to France for medical treatment (where he remained until July), was widely condemned, although supporters of Sanogo continued to favour his installation as interim President in place of Traoré. In late June the Assemblée nationale voted to prolong the mandate of its deputies until the end of the transition period. Meanwhile, ECOWAS and the AU were seeking the approval of the UN Security Council for the deployment of a 3,300-strong regional force to support the transitional process in Mali and to assist the Malian armed forces in combating the insurgency in the north. However, such an intervention had yet to be sanctioned at mid-September, with the Security Council having requested additional details regarding the proposed mission.

In mid-August 2012 Traoré confirmed his support for Diarra and tasked him with appointing a new, transitional Government, the 31 members of which were confirmed on 20 August.

ETHNIC TENSIONS

Ethnic violence emerged in the north in 1990, as large numbers of light-skinned Tuaregs, who had migrated to Algeria and Libya during periods of drought, began to return to Mali and Niger. In July of that year the Traoré Government, claiming that Tuareg rebels were attempting to establish a secessionist state, imposed a state of emergency in the Gao and Tombouctou regions, and the armed forces began a repressive campaign against the nomads. In January 1991 representatives of the Government and of two Tuareg groups, the Mouvement Populaire de l'Azawad (MPA) and the Front Islamique-Arabe de l'Azawad (FIAA), meeting in Tamanrasset, Algeria, signed a peace accord providing for an immediate cease-fire, and the state of emergency was revoked. Following the overthrow of the Traoré regime, the transitional administration affirmed its commitment to the Tamanrasset accord, and Tuareg representatives were included in the CTSP. However, unrest continued, and in June Amnesty International reported instances of the repression of Tuaregs by the armed forces. Thousands of Tuaregs, Moors and Bella (the descendants of the Tuaregs' black slaves, some of whom remained with the nomads) had fled to neighbouring countries to escape retaliatory attacks by the armed forces and the sedentary black population; there were also many casualties in the Malian armed forces.

During the second half of 1991 the MPA was reported to have lost the support of more militant Tuaregs, and a further group, the Front Populaire de Libération de l'Azawad (FPLA), emerged to claim responsibility for several attacks. In December, at a 'special conference on the north' in Mopti, representatives of the transitional Government and of the MPA, the FIAA, the FPLA and the Armée Révolutionnaire de Libération de l'Azawad (ARLA) agreed in principle to a peace settlement. Negotiations resumed in Algiers, the Algerian capital, in January 1992, at which the Malian authorities and the MPA, the FIAA and the ARLA (now negotiating together as the Mouvements et Fronts Unifiés de l'Azawad—MFUA) formally agreed to implement the Mopti accord; the FPLA was reported not to have attended the Algiers sessions. A truce entered into force in February, and a 'national pact' was signed in April by the Malian authorities and the MFUA. In addition to the provisions of the Mopti accord, the pact envisaged special administrative structures for the country's three northern regions (a new administrative region of Kidal having been established in May 1991), the incorporation of Tuareg fighters into the Malian armed forces, the demilitarization of the north and the instigation of efforts more fully to integrate Tuaregs in the economic and political fields.

Despite sporadic attacks, the implementation of the 'national pact' was pursued: joint patrols were established, and new administrative structures were inaugurated in November 1992. In February 1993 the Malian Government and the MFUA signed a preliminary accord facilitating the integration of Tuaregs into the national army. In May the FPLA's Secretary-General, Rhissa Ag Sidi Mohamed, declared the rebellion at an end and returned to Mali from Burkina Faso. However, in February 1994 the assassination of the MPA's military leader (who had recently joined the Malian army) was allegedly perpetrated by the ARLA, and clashes between the MPA and the ARLA continued for several weeks.

In May 1994, at a meeting in Algiers, agreement was reached by the Malian Government and the MFUA regarding the integration of 1,500 former rebels into the regular army and of a further 4,860 Tuaregs into civilian sectors. The agreement was, however, undermined by an intensification of violence. Meanwhile, the Mouvement Patriotique Malien Ganda Koy ('Masters of the Land'), a resistance movement dominated by the majority ethnic group in the north, the Songhaï, emerged amid rumours of official complicity in its actions against the Tuaregs. Meeting in Tamanrasset in June, the Malian authorities and the MFUA agreed on the need for the reinforcement of the army presence in areas affected by the violence, and for the more effective integration of Tuareg fighters.

In August 1994 agreement was reached on the voluntary repatriation from Algeria of Malian refugees. The accord was welcomed by the MFUA, which reiterated its commitment to the 'national pact'. Following discussions involving Tuareg groups, Ganda Koy and representatives of local communities, in April 1995 an agreement was signed providing for co-operation in resolving hitherto contentious issues. Ministerial delegations, incorporating representatives of the MFUA and Ganda Koy, toured the north of Mali, as well as refugee areas in Algeria, Burkina Faso and Mauritania, with the aim of promoting reconciliation and awareness of the peace programme. In June the FIAA announced an end to its armed struggle.

By February 1996 some 3,000 MFUA fighters and Ganda Koy militiamen had registered and surrendered their weapons at designated centres, under an encampment programme initiated in November 1995 in preparation for the eventual integration of former rebels into the regular army or civilian structures. The MFUA and Ganda Koy subsequently affirmed their adherence to Mali's Constitution, national unity and territorial integrity, and advocated the full implementation of the 'national pact' and associated accords. They further proclaimed the 'irreversible dissolution' of their respective movements. In September 1997 the graduation of MFUA and Ganda Koy contingents in the gendarmerie was reported as marking the accomplishment of the integration of all Malian fighters within the regular armed and security forces.

From 1995 significant numbers of refugees returned to Mali, many voluntarily and some under the supervision of the office of the UN High Commissioner for Refugees (UNHCR). The repatriation of some 42,000 Malian refugees from Mauritania was completed in July 1997. The remaining refugee camps in Burkina Faso (where, in all, 160,000 Malians were reported to have sought shelter at some time during the conflict) were closed in December. In November 1996, meanwhile, Mali, Niger and UNHCR signed an agreement for the repatriation of 25,000 Malian Tuaregs from Niger. In June 1998 the last groups of refugees returned from Algeria.

In November 2000 it was reported that Malian government forces had been dispatched to end widespread banditry by an armed group, led by Ibrahim Bahanga, a former Tuareg rebel, in the Kidal area, near to the border with Algeria. In September 2001 Bahanga reportedly announced that his forces were to cease hostilities, following talks with a state official.

In February 2006 it was reported that Lt-Col Hassan Fagaga, a former member of the MPA, had deserted from the army and was leading a group of young armed Tuaregs in Kidal. His demands included the creation of an autonomous commune in Kidal and an improvement in conditions for former rebels integrated into the army. In May Fagaga was believed to have orchestrated a more serious uprising, when former Tuareg rebels raided weapons depots and attacked three military bases in the north. The armed forces swiftly regained control of the bases as the rebels withdrew, demanding negotiations with the Government on the development of the region. In the days following the attacks, in which six people were killed, an estimated 4,500 residents of Kidal fled the town, while reports of further desertions of Tuareg soldiers from the regular army raised fears of renewed conflict in the region. None the less, both the Tuareg rebels and the Government stated their intention to seek a peaceful resolution to the crisis through international mediation. In early July both sides signed an agreement in Algiers, following talks mediated by Algerian officials, in which the Tuareg rebels, grouped in the Alliance Démocratique du 23 Mai pour le Changement (ADC), pledged to desist from demanding autonomy in return for a special investment programme for northern regions, increased powers for local governments, particularly on development issues, and the reintegration into the army of Tuareg soldiers who had deserted. Later that month the Government launched a US $21m. economic development programme for the regions of Kidal, Gao and Tombouctou, supported by the European Union (EU). Further accords signed by the Malian Government and the ADC in Algiers in February 2007 outlined the measures required to facilitate the implementation of the July 2006 agreement and the disarmament and reintegration into society of the Tuaregs. In addition, special security units were to be established in the Kidal region. A two-day international forum on the development of Kidal, Gao and Tombouctou, which was held in March, resulted in a 10-year plan to undertake 39 projects at an estimated cost of 560,660m. francs CFA.

However, divisions subsequently emerged among the Tuaregs. In May 2007 at least 10 people were killed during an attack on a security post near the Algerian border by a group of armed men reportedly led by Bahanga; the attack was believed to have been prompted by a leadership dispute within the Tuareg movement. The Government and the ADC met in Algiers in August to discuss the implementation of the July 2006 peace agreement. In August the abduction of some 50 government soldiers and several civilians in northern Mali, as well as a series of landmine explosions, were attributed to a Tuareg splinter group, believed to be led by Bahanga. Some of the hostages managed to escape their captors, while others were freed after military reinforcements were dispatched to the region. At the end of the month a truce was brokered between the rebels and the military, and six further hostages were subsequently released. None the less, Tuareg rebels fired on a US military aircraft carrying supplies to Malian government troops in September. Clashes followed between armed Tuaregs and soldiers, marking an end to the cease-fire, and a few days later seven rebels and one soldier were killed in further confrontations.

Following talks with senior Tuareg tribal leaders, Bahanga agreed to a new cease-fire, promising to release the remaining hostages (numbering around 30) and to facilitate the removal of landmines from the area. By the end of September 2007 three soldiers and five civilians had been freed by the rebels. Mediation by the Libyan and Algerian Governments led to the release of further hostages in December and in January 2008, and the final 22 soldiers still being held were freed in early March. In April Libyan-brokered talks between representatives of the Malian Government and Bahanga's Tuareg faction (now styled the Alliance Touareg Nord-Mali pour le Changement—ATNMC) resulted in the signature of a new cease-fire agreement in the Libyan capital, Tripoli. Ongoing discussions on the implementation of the accord subsequently reached an impasse, however, partly owing to disagreement regarding a reduction in the number of troops in the Kidal region, and Tuareg rebel attacks on military targets resumed in May. The most serious incident, at Abeibara (some 150 km north of Kidal), in which 15 soldiers and 17 rebels were killed, prompted an expression of concern from the UN Secretary-General, Ban Ki-Moon.

In July 2008 Algerian-brokered negotiations resulted in a new agreement between the Malian Government and the ADC, with both sides pledging to end hostilities, to release hostages and prisoners, to demine certain areas, to allow the return of those displaced by fighting and to create the special security units originally envisaged in the accords of February 2007, comprising both government soldiers and former Tuareg rebels. However, the ATNMC was not party to the agreement, and Bahanga and a number of his followers reportedly fled to Libya. Further talks on implementing the commitments made in July 2008 were held in Algiers in August. By this time the rebels had freed more than 30 of the 92 soldiers being held captive. The release in Kidal, in September, by the ATNMC of 44 government soldiers (apparently following the intervention of the Libyan leader, Col Muammar al-Qaddafi), leaving only around four still captive, was regarded as an important step in the peace process, while the Government announced that it had freed all Tuareg prisoners in its custody.

Also in September 2008 the military launched an offensive against Ganda Izo ('Children of the Land'), a newly emerged militia group, killing one member and arresting more than 30 others. Mainly comprising ethnic Songhaïs and Peuls, Ganda Izo was suspected of being responsible for the deaths of four Tuareg civilians in the Gao region that month, which had raised fears of renewed inter-ethnic violence. The leader of the militia, former army officer Amadou Diallo, who was believed to have been a member of the defunct Ganda Koy (see above), fled to Niger, but was later detained there and extradited to Mali.

In what was regarded as a positive development for the peace process in northern Mali, it was reported in October 2008 that Bahanga intended to remain in Libya. However, in December, in the first major confrontation since the July peace agreement, nine soldiers and 11 rebels were killed (according to figures from the Ministry of Defence and Veterans) in the northern town of Nampala during an attack on a military base, for which the ATNMC claimed responsibility, Bahanga having apparently returned from Libya; the Ministry claimed that the raid was linked to drugs-trafficking. In early January 2009 it was announced that the three Tuareg rebel groups comprising the ADC had decided to rejoin the peace process. This announcement followed a military offensive against the ATNMC initiated in response to grenade attacks by rebels on the homes of government officials in Gao, in which two people had died. Later that month the Malian Government claimed that the security forces had killed 31 ATNMC rebels in Kidal and seized weapons and ammunition. The remaining soldiers being held captive by the rebels were released in late January. In February the military claimed to have seized control of all ATNMC bases. An official ceremony took place in Kidal in mid-February to mark the return of some 700 rebels, including a number of former followers of Bahanga, from their hideouts in the mountains. Later that month it was reported that Bahanga had been granted refuge in Libya. (Bahanga died in August 2011, reportedly in a car accident.) The cantonment of former Tuareg fighters, and the disposal of their weapons, continued in the following months. At Algerian-mediated talks in July, which were notably held in Bamako for the first time, the ADC agreed to assist government forces in combating the growing threat from Al-Qa'ida in the Islamic Maghreb (AQIM). The various ethnic communities in northern Mali—Tuareg, Moor, Peul and Songhaï—participated in a reconciliation ceremony in Tombouctou in the following month, and in November signed an agreement on the creation of a permanent structure for dialogue. Meanwhile, in September the Government approved draft legislation establishing a fund for investment, development and socio-economic reintegration programmes for Gao, Kidal and Tombouctou. However, at a meeting of the ADC held in Algiers in January 2010, the movement's spokesman, Hama Sid Ahmed, criticized the Government for failing to implement the July 2006 agreement, claiming that the continued lack of development in northern Mali was encouraging young people in the region to engage in criminal activities.

A new Tuareg organization, the Mouvement National pour la Libération de l'Azawad (MNLA), emerged in October 2011, demanding independence for northern Mali (Azawad). Many of its members were heavily armed returnees from Libya, where they had fought in support of forces loyal to the Qaddafi regime in the civil conflict that had erupted in that country in February, while others had previously belonged to movements involved in earlier Tuareg rebellions, such as the MFUA. In December a second new Tuareg group, Ansar al-Din (Defenders of Faith), was formed by a former rebel leader, Iyad Ag Agaly, who was seeking the implementation of Islamic (*Shari'a*) law. Fears of a renewed Tuareg insurgency were realized in 2012, beginning in mid-January with violent clashes in the northern towns of Aguelhoc, Ménaka and Tessalit, during which at least 45 MNLA rebels and two government soldiers were reportedly killed (although the MNLA disputed these figures). By early February the rebels had occupied Ménaka and several other towns, although an army offensive forced them to withdraw from Kidal, amid claims by the army that its focus was on retaining control of larger towns. While attending talks in Algiers, a delegation of the ADC called for a cease-fire, a suggestion that the MNLA Secretary-General, Ag Bilal Sharif, dismissed. In mid-February the UN Secretary-General, Ban Ki-Moon, urged an end to the fighting, which had prompted civilians to flee their homes: the UN estimated that 61,400 had been displaced internally and a further 65,000 had sought refuge in Mauritania, Burkina Faso, Niger and Algeria by late February. The Malian Government claimed that troops had been summarily executed in January, in a manner comparable to that employed by AQIM, but the MNLA strongly refuted any link to the Islamist organization. Meanwhile, the Government was criticized by Amnesty International for 'indiscriminate bombing' in the Kidal area that had resulted in civilian casualties.

After the Touré administration was overthrown in late March 2012 (see Military Coup), the rebels rapidly made significant territorial gains, their position strengthened by the resulting political uncertainty and apparent disarray within the army, and by early April they controlled much of northern Mali, including the towns of Kidal, Gao and Tombouctou. On 6 April the MNLA unilaterally declared the independence of the 'state of Azawad' in a statement that was denounced by Malian officials and by foreign governments and regional and international organizations. Despite their different aims, the MNLA and Ansar al-Din had fought together against the army, but divisions soon emerged between them, with Ansar al-Din asserting its authority over several captured towns in the following months, including Tombouctou, where it reportedly appointed an emir belonging to AQIM as governor and began to impose *Shari'a*. In late May, none the less, it was announced that the MNLA and Ansar al-Din had agreed to merge and to establish the 'Islamic Republic of Azawad'. ECOWAS and the interim Malian Government rejected the accord, which was also unpopular with those members of the MNLA who still favoured a secular Azawad state and Ansar al-Din members who opposed the division of Mali and sought the application of *Shari'a* throughout the country. Tensions continued between the Tuareg and Islamist movements, leading to clashes in mid-June in which five people were seriously injured. Meanwhile, MNLA and Ansar al-Din leaders declared their willingness to engage in negotiations with ECOWAS mediators, who insisted, however, that Ansar al-Din's links with AQIM be severed prior to talks. In mid-July the International Criminal Court, based in The Hague, Netherlands, announced that, at the request of the Malian Government, it was initiating a preliminary inquiry into alleged atrocities committed by armed groups in northern Mali, including executions, rapes and the use of child soldiers; it was also suggested that the recent destruction of Muslim shrines in Tombouctou—regarded as idolatrous and thus sacrilegious by Islamist militants—could constitute a war crime. By late July, according to UNHCR, the number of people who had fled northern Mali to take refuge in Burkina Faso, Mauritania and Niger had risen to more than 253,000, while more than 155,000 Malians were internally displaced.

EXTERNAL RELATIONS AND REGIONAL SECURITY CONCERNS

The presence in neighbouring countries of large numbers of refugees from the conflict in northern Mali, and the attendant issue of border security, dominated Mali's regional relations in the 1990s. Although the process of repatriation of refugees was completed by 1998, the north of the country remained vulnerable to continuing insecurity and, particularly, to cross-border banditry. In May the interior ministers of Mali, Senegal and Mauritania met to strengthen co-operation and border controls, and in December Mali and Senegal decided to reinforce border security. Following a visit by Konaré to Algiers in February 1999, Mali and Algeria also agreed to revive their joint border committee to promote development and stability in the region. In August the Malian, Mauritanian and Senegalese interior ministers agreed to establish an operational unit drawn from the police forces of the three countries in order to ensure security in the area of their joint border.

Renewed concerns about insecurity in the region arose in 2003, following reports, in July, that some 15 German, Swiss and Dutch tourists, who had purportedly been kidnapped in February in southern Algeria by Islamist militants belonging to the Groupe Salafiste pour la Prédication et le Combat (GSPC), had been smuggled into Mali. Following negotiations with the kidnappers, the hostages were released in August. It was later reported that the German Government had paid a large ransom to secure their release. In March 2004 Mali announced that it was to increase anti-terrorism co-operation with the authorities in Algeria, Chad and Niger.

In January 2005 the Presidents of Mali and Mauritania signed an agreement on military co-operation aimed at strengthening border security. Mali dispatched troops to the common border in June, in response to a request from the Mauritanian authorities for assistance in detaining the perpetrators of an attack on one of its military bases in which 15 soldiers had been killed. The GSPC claimed responsibility for the incident. Meanwhile, Mali was one of nine north and west African countries that participated in US-led military exercises aimed at increasing co-operation in combating cross-border banditry and terrorism in the region.

In August 2007 the Malian Minister of Internal Security and Civil Protection, Gen. Sadio Gassama, and his Nigerien counterpart agreed to organize joint patrols along their common border. None the less, insecurity persisted. Two Austrian tourists abducted in Tunisia in February 2008 were believed to be being held in northern Mali. Al-Qa'ida in the Islamic Maghreb (AQIM, as the GSPC had been restyled) claimed responsibility for capturing the Austrians. The Austrians were freed in October; the terms of their release were unclear, although officials denied that a ransom had been paid. In November government ministers from Algeria, Burkina Faso, Chad, Libya, Mali and Niger attended a meeting in Bamako to discuss security and development in the Sahel region. The abduction of a UN envoy to Niger and his assistant near the Malian–Nigerien border in December was followed in January 2009 by that of four European tourists, also in the border area. AQIM claimed responsibility for the kidnappings in February, and released the diplomats and two of the tourists in April; a British and a Swiss tourist remained captive. The Briton was killed in May, after the British Government refused to meet AQIM's demand for the release of a detained Jordanian Islamist or to pay a ransom. In June three members of AQIM were reportedly detained by the security forces in Mali, but a senior Malian military intelligence officer who had been conducting investigations into the militant group (which were thought to have led to the arrests) was subsequently killed in Tombouctou. Later that month 26 militants and 10 soldiers reportedly died during a successful operation by the Malian security forces to capture a suspected AQIM base near the border with Algeria, which provided support to the Malian troops. Further fatalities resulted from clashes between AQIM militants and Malian troops in Gao in early July. The Swiss hostage was released later that month.

In September 2009 military leaders from Algeria, Mali, Mauritania and Niger agreed on a plan for co-operation in combating terrorism and cross-border crime. Military assistance was forthcoming from the USA in October, with the provision to Mali of equipment worth some US $5m. Following further abductions of foreign nationals in Mali and Mauritania in November and December, and reports that those kidnapped in Mauritania had been taken to Mali, in January 2010 the two countries agreed to strengthen their security co-operation. However, relations between Mali and its neighbours became strained in February, when the Malian authorities freed four AQIM prisoners, thus securing the release of a French national abducted in November 2009. The Malian Government insisted that the militants, who had reportedly been arrested in April and recently sentenced to nine months' imprisonment for illegally possessing weapons, had served their sentences, but the Algerian and Mauritanian Governments recalled their ambassadors from Bamako for consultations, accusing Mali of violating agreements on judicial and security co-operation by acceding to AQIM's demands. One of three Spanish hostages kidnapped in Mauritania in November was released in Mali in March 2010, and in the following month two Italians seized in December 2009 were also freed.

In April 2010, seeking to reinforce co-operation, Algeria, Mali, Mauritania and Niger established a joint military command headquarters in Tamanrasset. At a summit earlier that month in the Algerian town, army chiefs from the four countries had agreed to co-ordinate intelligence-gathering and patrols in border areas to combat terrorism, organized crime, arms-trafficking and kidnappings. A US-led military training exercise involving several countries in the Sahel region, including Mali, Mauritania and Niger, was held in May. The remaining two Spanish hostages were released in Mali in August. However, controversy arose over claims that, in return for their release, a ransom had been paid to AQIM and Omar Sid'Ahmed Ould Hamma, a Malian national who had been sentenced in July by a Mauritanian court to 12 years' imprisonment for his involvement in the abduction, had been freed and deported to Mali. In September, shortly after the return of the Mauritanian ambassador to Mali and with Malian agreement, the Mauritanian security forces conducted an offensive against suspected AQIM militants in northern Mali. Also that month seven foreigners (five French nationals, one Togolese and one Malagasy) who had been kidnapped in Niger were reportedly transferred to Mali; the two Africans and a French woman were released in February 2011, reportedly following payment of a ransom. In late September 2010 army chiefs from Algeria, Mali, Mauritania and Niger met in Tamanrasset with the aim of developing a common strategy to combat terrorism and organized crime; it was agreed to establish a joint intelligence centre in Algiers. However, differences in approach remained, with Algerian officials notably opposing the payment of ransoms and the release of imprisoned Islamist militants in exchange for hostages, and the Algerian Government boycotted a meeting held in Bamako in October, at which representatives of regional countries and members of the Group of Eight leading industrialized nations discussed efforts against AQIM. The Malian and Mauritanian armies continued to co-operate closely in counter-terrorism operations in late 2010 and 2011. In June 2011 a joint operation by Mauritanian and Malian forces in western Mali reportedly resulted in the deaths of 15 AQIM members. In the previous month, at a meeting in Bamako of government ministers from Algeria, Mali, Mauritania and Niger, the Malian Government had proposed the formation of a regional task force of up to 75,000 troops to combat AQIM.

The economic impact of insecurity in the region was underlined in July, when it emerged, following a meeting of Mali's defence committee, that the country had lost more than 50,000m. francs CFA in tourism receipts, as well as 8,000 jobs in the tourism sector, during the previous two years. Moreover, fears were expressed during a conference on security held in Algiers in September regarding the new threat posed both by the return to Mali and Niger of former Tuareg rebels who had settled in Libya, where they had recently fought in support of forces loyal to the regime of Col Muammar al-Qaddafi, and by an influx of weapons from Libya. Government ministers from Algeria, Mali, Mauritania and Niger held talks in Washington, DC, USA, in early November, meeting with several senior US officials, with the aim of advancing their aim to establish a regional counter-terrorism partnership. Later that month two French citizens were kidnapped in the town of Hombori, in the region of Mopti, and a German tourist was killed and three other foreigners were abducted in Tombouctou; AQIM subsequently claimed responsibility for the kidnappings. A splinter group of AQIM, the Movement for Oneness and Jihad in West Africa (MOJWA), emerged in December, its members reported to be mainly Malians and Mauritanians. Meanwhile, the EU announced that it would provide €150m. in support of regional efforts aimed at increasing security, and Algerian troops reportedly entered Malian territory in order to assist government forces to combat groups affiliated to al-Qa'ida. Border security was further reinforced in February 2012 in response to the renewed Tuareg insurgency in northern Mali (see Ethnic Tensions). At a summit meeting held in Libya in March, ministers responsible for the interior and defence from Algeria, Chad, Egypt, Libya, Mali, Mauritania, Morocco, Niger, Tunisia and Sudan adopted an action plan on regional co-operation and border control aimed at combating organized crime, drugs- and arms-trafficking, terrorism and illegal immigration; measures agreed included the exchange of security intelligence and increased joint border patrols. In early April the Algerian consul and six of his colleagues were abducted in Gao, the MOJWA later claiming responsibility; three of the seven diplomats were released in July. Also in July, in exchange for the release of two Islamists being detained in Mauritania, the MOJWA freed three European aid workers who had been kidnapped in Algeria in October 2011 and subsequently held hostage in Mali; the MOJWA also claimed to have received a ransom of €15m.

Mali was a founder member, with Libya, of the Community of Sahel-Saharan States, established in Tripoli in 1997, and the two countries have developed close links. Libya has mediated between the Malian Government and Tuareg groups on several occasions (see Ethnic Tensions) and provided Mali with two reconnaissance aircraft to combat insecurity in October 2010. In March 2011 President Touré was one of five regional leaders appointed by the AU to a High-Level Ad Hoc Committee on Libya charged with leading African efforts to resolve the conflict that had emerged in that country in early 2011. The Committee opposed air strikes conducted by the North Atlantic Treaty Organization on Libya (which were aimed at enforcing a UN-imposed no-fly zone over that country and at preventing attacks on civilians), advocating a political solution to the conflict. However, the rebel forces in Libya rejected proposals made by the Committee in April and July, demanding that Qaddafi relinquish power. Following significant advances by the anti-Government forces, which took control of Tripoli in late August, the AU recognized the National Transitional Council as the de facto government of Libya in September.

A visit to Mali by the French Minister of State, Minister of the Interior and Land Management, Nicolas Sarkozy, in May 2006 proved controversial, as it followed immediately after the approval by the French Assemblée nationale of legislation proposed by Sarkozy on 'selective' immigration, which generally introduced stricter conditions for immigrants to France and favoured skilled migrants. A group of 21 Malian deputies issued a statement urging Sarkozy to cancel his visit, describing it as a provocation, and several hundred people marched in Bamako in protest against the new legislation and Sarkozy's arrival. According to the French Ministry of the Interior and Land Management, there were some 45,000 legal immigrants from Mali living in France, and a similar number of illegal Malian immigrants. The legislation was approved by the French Sénat in June. France continued to be Mali's principal source of bilateral economic assistance, and in July agreed to provide 200,000m. francs CFA for the period 2006–10. Sarkozy visited Bamako briefly in February 2010 in order to meet a French citizen who had recently been released by AQIM after three months in captivity (see above); he pledged French support for Mali's counter-terrorism efforts. In January 2011 two people were injured (one later dying from his wounds) in an attack outside the French embassy; in November a Tunisian national, who claimed membership of AQIM, was convicted of perpetrating the attack and sentenced to death. During a visit to Mali in February 2012, the French Minister of Foreign and European Affairs, Alain Juppé, urged the Malian Government to negotiate with Tuaregs who had commenced a renewed offensive in northern Mali in the previous month (see Ethnic Tensions).

Mali has, notably, contributed actively to UN peace-keeping forces, and has been prominent in efforts to establish an African military crisis-response force. In late 1996 and early 1997, moreover, Amadou Toumani Touré led a regional mediation effort to resolve the crisis in the Central African Republic (CAR), and in February 1997 a Malian military contingent was dispatched to the CAR as part of a regional surveillance mission. Malian troops remained in the CAR until February 2000, as part of the UN peace-keeping mission that succeeded the regional force in April 1998. In February 1999 488 Malian troops joined the ECOMOG peace-keeping forces of ECOWAS in Sierra Leone; they were withdrawn later that year, when the ECOMOG forces were succeeded by a UN mission. In mid-2012 Malian military personnel were participating in UN peace-keeping missions in the Democratic Republic of the Congo, Liberia and South Sudan, and in the UN-AU joint operation in the Darfur region of western Sudan. Malian forces had also formed part of the UN mission that had been deployed in the CAR and Chad in 2007–10.

Economy

VICTORIA HOLLIGAN

INTRODUCTION

Mali, the second largest country in francophone West Africa, is sparsely populated (with an estimated population of 16.3m. at mid-2012 representing an average density of 13.2 inhabitants per sq km) and land-locked, and most parts are desert or semi-desert, with the economically viable area confined to the Sahelian-Sudanese regions irrigated by the River Niger, which comprise about one-fifth of the total land area. Despite improved policy performance during the 21st century, Mali remains highly vulnerable to external shocks and to the volatility of prices for its gold and cotton exports and oil and food imports. In terms of human development, Mali ranked 175th out of 187 countries in the UN Development Programme's (UNDP) 2011 Human Development Index. Since 1990 Mali's human development rating has grown by 106%, with life expectancy at birth increasing by 11.8 years and expected years of schooling rising by 6.1 years. Although gross national income (GNI) per head has increased by 52% since 1980, the country still ranks among the world's poorest. GNI per head, on a 2005 purchasing parity basis, was US $1,123 in 2011 according to UNDP. The rate of economic growth in the three decades that followed independence was largely affected by drought and changes in the terms of international trade, as well as political instability. There were thus wide fluctuations in trends in real gross domestic product (GDP) from year to year. Overall, GDP increased at an average annual rate of only 2.8% in the 1980s, compared with an average of 5.0% in the 2000s.

After a period of erratic progress in the early 1990s, stability and growth resumed. The stimulus to the agricultural sector that resulted from the 50% devaluation of the currency in January 1994 coincided with a marked increase in world commodity prices in that year. With the prospect of further expansion in exports of cotton (which accounted for about two-fifths of total export earnings in the mid-1990s) and gold (as new capacity came into production), Mali's immediate prospects for sustained economic growth were good. GDP grew, in real terms, by an average of 5.7% per year in 1996–99, as the agricultural sector prospered and public investment resumed. Nevertheless, in 2000 a decline of 3.2% was recorded, owing to a drought-induced decline in cereal production, an increase in the world price of petroleum, and the decision of farmers to boycott the cotton-growing season. In contrast with previous years, this growth figure was compiled using a new accounting methodology, under which agricultural production in the 2000/01 season was included in GDP for 2000 instead of GDP for 2001. In 2001 GDP increased, in real terms, by 12.1%, following a particularly abundant cotton harvest in the 2001/02 season. In 2002 buoyant activity in mining and cotton-ginning helped to compensate for decreasing agricultural production, with growth attaining 4.3%. Bumper cereal and cotton harvests increased growth to 7.2% in 2003. Growth declined to 2.4% in 2004, because of a decrease in agricultural production resulting from below average rainfalls and the worst locust attack in 15 years. Growth recovered significantly in 2005, to 6.1%, and remained strong in 2006, at an estimated 4.6%, according to the IMF, as a result of improved agricultural performance and increased gold production. A decline in economic growth to 3.0% in 2007 was mainly attributed to decreased cotton and gold production. The international financial crisis led to a reduction in remittances from emigrants and lower foreign direct investment (FDI), yet higher gold prices and the strong performance of cereal production resulted in GDP increasing by 4.9% in 2008, according to the IMF. Economic growth was sustained in 2009 at 4.5%, reflecting a good harvest, high gold export prices and lower oil import prices. Strong gold prices mitigated the negative impact of the international financial and economic crisis, which reduced non-privatization-related FDI and private remittances. GDP rose by 5.8% in 2010, owing to a strong performance in the agricultural sector, which offset a decline in gold production. Stagnant gold output in 2011 was outweighed by a material increase in cotton production, resulting in estimated economic growth of 5.4% in that year according to the IMF. Growth was expected to increase slightly to 5.6% in 2012, driven by the inauguration of new gold mines. However, uncertainty resulting from the coup in early 2012 cast doubt over this forecast.

Beginning in 1981, the Moussa Traoré administration, under pressure from the IMF, the World Bank and bilateral donors, undertook successive programmes of market liberalization and civil service reforms. The unpopularity of the austerity programme contributed to the downfall of Traoré in March 1991. Negotiations with the Bretton Woods institutions resumed following the 50% devaluation, in January 1994, of the CFA franc. The institutions agreed to provide some 207,000m. francs CFA in budgetary support for 1994–96. Continued financial support was subsequently secured under the Enhanced Structural Adjustment Facility (ESAF) of the IMF for 1996–99. Under the supervision of the World Bank and the IMF, Mali's adjustment policies largely concentrated on macroeconomic stabilization; fiscal consolidation and tax reform; the liberalization of price and trade policies; regulatory reform; and the reform of public enterprises and the agricultural sector. In August 1999 Mali was declared eligible for a further three-year ESAF arrangement (for the period 1999–2002), and qualified for concessionary debt relief under the Bretton Woods institutions' initiative for heavily indebted poor countries (HIPCs). As a result of economic difficulties experienced by the Malian Government, particularly the problems in the cotton sector, the consequences of a drought in 2000 and the increase in petroleum prices, the duration of the Poverty Reduction and Growth Facility (PRGF, as the ESAF had been renamed) was extended until August 2003. The new Government formed following the election of Amadou Toumani Touré as President in June 2002 confirmed that it would continue to implement the requirements of the PRGF-supported programme. In June 2004 the IMF approved a new PRGF, worth some US $13.7m., with the three-year programme setting out new measures towards fiscal consolidation, privatization and reforms in the cotton sector. In February 2007 the IMF announced an extension of Mali's PRGF from June to November. Despite the completion of four three-year fund arrangements from 1992–2007, Mali continued to suffer from severe economic problems, especially in the cotton sector. In May 2008 the IMF approved a three-year Extended Credit Facility (ECF), worth $45.7m., to assist in covering the costs of higher oil and food imports. In May 2011 the seventh disbursement under the arrangement was approved to reduce the impact of the crises in Côte d'Ivoire and Libya.

Employment patterns have changed little since independence. Subsistence agriculture and livestock-rearing remain the dominant economic activities. There is still significant seasonal migration (during the agricultural off-season) to Côte d'Ivoire and Senegal, and some 3m. Malians are thought to work abroad, with France also an important host country. However, Mail's economy has been adversely affected by the crisis in Côte d'Ivoire and the conflict in Libya through a loss of remittances, as well as higher transportation costs and lower exports. Wage employment is very low, and is concentrated in the state sector and in formal sector businesses in Bamako, the capital.

AGRICULTURE

Agriculture and livestock dominate Mali's economy. In mid-2012 the sector engaged an estimated 73.6% of the total labour force, according to FAO. Agriculture (including livestock, forestry and fishing) contributed 40% of GDP in 2010 or 1,642,000m. francs CFA according to the African Development Bank (AfDB). The sector recorded a 16.1% growth rate in 2010, compared with growth of 6.4% in the previous year, according to the IMF; the improved performance was attributable to favourable levels of rainfall, as well as government support for farmers through input subsidies. In 2011 sectoral growth remained strong at 8.5%, driven mainly by the cotton sector. Rural development has long been one of the Government's main priorities, with aims to modernize activity in agriculture, livestock-rearing and fishing and bring more land under cultivation.

Agricultural exports, including processed crops (notably cotton) and livestock, account for about 15%–20% of Mali's total exports value, a share that has declined since the 1990s, as gold production picked up to become Mali's leading export. Further development is constrained by the inadequacy of the country's transport infrastructure for the movement of perishable goods over long distances. Pending the improvement of that infrastructure, the Government aims to promote the development of agro-industry in order to increase the proportion of processed goods among agricultural exports.

Millet and sorghum—two basic food crops—are essentially produced at subsistence level, although the output of cereals has recovered since the drought years of the early 1980s, and exportable surpluses were occasionally recorded in some years. During the 2008/09 season nearly 5m. tons of cereals were produced, consisting of 0.7m. tons of maize, 1.4m. tons of millet, and 1.5m. tons of sorghum. Despite cereal production declining by 10% in 2011 to 5.8m. tons (due to an early termination of the rainy season), the harvest was 16% above the average of the previous five years, according to FAO. Nevertheless, food security remained an acute issue in Mali, with over 1.8m. people described as 'food insecure' by FAO in February 2012. The ongoing political turmoil involving Tuareg rebels in the north displaced an estimated 250,000 people, which materially increased food insecurity.

Production of rice has increased steadily since the mid-1980s, partially because the area harvested has also increased markedly, from 135,275 ha in 1980 to a peak of 468,239 ha in 2001, before declining slightly, to 391,869 ha, in 2007. An important factor in the improvement in rice production has been the reform of the parastatal Office du Niger. In 1986 a rehabilitation programme was initiated, which aimed to rationalize the organization's management and to increase the total cultivable area to more than 100,000 ha, of which 46,730 ha were to be planted with rice. In 1988 a programme was inaugurated to improve the irrigation network for the cultivation of rice both on the Office du Niger land and in the inland delta of the Niger in the Ségou region. By 2004 the Office du Niger was estimated to have harvested 458,240 tons of rice on 81,222 ha of cultivated land. There is considerable potential for the export of rice to regional markets, now that self-sufficiency has been achieved. According to FAO figures, 20,000 tons were exported in the marketing year 2005/06. In 2008/09 rice output benefited from both good rainfall and the change in use of arable land from cotton to food production, resulting in production of some 1.7m. tons. The rice initiative has increased the share of rice in total grain production in recent years. The rice sector was a key driver of the strong performance in the agriculture sector, with output growing by some 24% in 2010, compared with 6% in the previous year, according to the IMF.

By far the most important cash crop is cotton. The sector grew by 9.2% in 2010, compared with 16.8% in 2009; however, it increased by some 66% in 2011, according to the IMF. Cotton output was projected to decline in 2012 as a result of production normalization following the bumper 2011 harvest as well as the impact of the coup.

Mali was formerly the leading cotton producer in the Franc Zone but has latterly been replaced in this position by Burkina Faso. Mostly exported, cotton provides a livelihood for some 3.5m. people directly and indirectly. Cultivation is in the southern region, by means of village co-operatives co-ordinated by the parastatal Compagnie Malienne pour le Développement des Textiles (CMDT), in which the French company Dagris holds a 40% interest. Following the 47% rise in the producer price that accompanied the 1994 devaluation of the CFA franc, output increased further, as strong international prices encouraged an expansion in the area cultivated, and a record seed cotton crop of 522,903 metric tons was recorded in 1997. Production declined subsequently, as lower world prices of cotton prompted some producers to plant cereal crops rather than cottonseed. Farmers boycotted cotton production in 2000, in protest against decreasing producer prices and the proposed restructuring of the CMDT. As a result, the recorded crop in that year declined to 242,772 tons—its lowest level for more than a decade. However, higher world and farm-gate cotton prices and improved growing conditions resulted in exceptional output of 620,700 tons in 2003. Production decreased to 590,000 tons in 2004, to 534,100 tons in 2005 and to 428,000 tons in 2006, owing to less favourable growing conditions as well as declining world prices for cotton. During the 2007/08 season cottonseed production contracted by 40%, owing to poor weather conditions combined with a reduction in the area harvested. Declining prices, along with the late arrival of the cotton fertilizer, gave farmers an incentive to diversify production. The 2008/09 season was also characterized by a substantial decline in production as a result of relatively low farm-gate prices and an increase in the price of imported pesticides and fertilizers. Production grew by 17.4% in the 2009/10 season due to adequate rainfall, lower fertilizer prices and government financial support.

The Government has worked closely with the World Bank on reforms to liberalize the cotton sector. The privatization of the CMDT has been postponed repeatedly, however, and in 2005 the Government announced the full liberalization of the sector—in particular the division of the CMDT into four regional companies. The CMDT successfully reduced its workforce and started to refocus on its core activities, notably finding a domestic private sector buyer for a majority stake in its cottonseed oil plant, the Huilerie Cotonnière du Mali (HUICOMA), in that year. However, the CMDT continued to suffer from financial difficulties, aggravated by the decline in cotton production. The CMDT privatization process resumed in 2010, when a tender for bids was launched; the Government selected one investor, from a choice of three bidders, to purchase two of the four regional subsidiaries of CMDT.

Mali, in association with Benin, Burkina Faso and Chad (the 'Cotton-four'), lodged an official complaint with the World Trade Organization (WTO) in September 2003, regarding the use of cotton subsidies by the USA and by the European Union (EU) and the consequent dampening effect on world prices. The WTO ruled in favour of the 'Cotton-four' and asked the USA to eliminate its cotton subsidies, a measure that, if implemented, could be expected to result in a marked increase in world cotton prices. Yet, relief through the WTO is unlikely in the near future. Earnings from Mali's cotton exports amounted to 142,000m. francs CFA in 2006, equivalent to 17.5% of total exports, and to 114,000m. francs CFA in 2007 (15.9% of exports), decreasing to only 66,000m. francs CFA in 2008 (8.0% of exports), according to IMF estimates. In 2010 cotton exports were valued at US $168.0m., representing 8.4% of total shipments.

Other industrial crops are wheat and groundnuts, of which output has risen recently as a result of the Government's policy to diversify agriculture. Groundnut production rose from 307,717 tons in 2007 to 388,400 tons in 2008 as a result of the substitution of arable land from cotton production. Output totalled 300,600 tons in 2009 and 314,500 tons in 2010. Other industrial crops produced are sugar cane, with an output of 359,000 tons in 2010, and sunflowers, with an estimated 50,000 tons produced in the 2008/09 season, according to local sources.

In 2011 livestock-raising, the principal economic activity in the north, accounted for 9% of GDP and employed around 30% of the working population. Livestock numbers decreased significantly during the droughts of the 1970s and early 1980s. Nevertheless, at 9.2m. cattle, 11.9m. sheep and 16.5m. goats, according to FAO in 2010, Mali's herd remained the largest in francophone West Africa. The droughts also tended to move livestock-rearing from the north to the south, where it is geared towards export to Côte d'Ivoire and Ghana. The growth of the livestock sector remained at about 4.3% in both 2009 and 2010, according to the IMF, increasing by 4% in 2011.

In the early 1990s fishing on the River Niger produced an annual catch of about 65,000 metric tons, although this was more than doubled in 1995, and in the following years a catch in the region of 100,000 tons was landed. None the less, the sector remains very vulnerable to drought, to the effects of large-scale dam building on the upper reaches of the river, and to pollution from urban centres. The successful implementation of fish-farming projects in 2007 had a positive impact on growth in the fishing sector in that year, when it grew by 4.3%.

MINING AND POWER

Mining accounted for 6.2% of GDP in 2010 and 7.6% in 2011, and contributed over 75% of Mali's exports, according to the IMF. However, the financial gains are not evenly distributed among the population as less than 1% of the total labour force are employed in the sector and the majority of inputs are imported from abroad rather than sourced locally. After growing by 8.2% in 2006, activity in the mining sector declined by 3.2% in 2007 and by 13.5% in 2008, rising by 1.5% in 2009, only to fall by 16.1% in 2010, according to the AfDB. Yet, owing to sustained high gold prices, the impact on export earnings of lower production was minimal. Deposits of bauxite, copper, iron ore and manganese have been located but not yet exploited, largely because of the country's land-locked position and lack of infrastructure. Uranium is mined at the Samit project, in the Tilemsi Basin, by the Canadian Bayswater Uranium Corpn. Marble is mined at Bafoulabé, and phosphate rock at Gao, but by far the most important mineral currently being exploited is gold. In 2001 Mali became the third largest African producer of gold, after South Africa and Ghana, following the opening of the Morila field in late 2000 and the Yatela field in mid-2001 (see below). Gold production increased to some 66,068 kg in 2002, before declining to 53,998 kg in 2003 and 44,585 kg in 2004, according to the Banque Centrale des Etats de l'Afrique de l'Ouest (BCEAO). Production recovered to 49,121 kg in 2005, largely as a result of accelerated production at Morila and the start of production at a new mine, Loulo, in November of that year. Gold output increased further in 2006, to 61,882 kg, before contracting by 11.5% in 2007. All mines recorded decreases in production in 2007 due to temporary technical difficulties associated with large rock formation, except Tabakoto, where production increased by 1,100 kg to 2,500 kg, according to the AfDB. The commissioning of the Kodieran and Syama (see below) mines was also delayed until 2008. The established mines (all except Syama, Kodieran and artisanal mines) were in a deeper extraction phase in 2008 and 2009, resulting in output moderating to 41,160 kg and 42,364 kg, respectively. Gold production declined to 36,344 kg in 2010. In 2000, for the first time, gold was the principal source of Mali's export earnings, supplanting cotton; by 2002 gold accounted for 67.1% of exports, and has continued to represent an absolute majority of Mali's export trade in recent years, representing 78.3% of exports in 2008, 75% in 2009 and 76% in 2010. The market price of gold, which quadrupled from 2004 to 2011 (increasing from US $410 per troy oz. to over $1,780 per oz.), has significantly boosted gold earnings.

In August 1999 a new mining code was adopted by the Malian Government, which it was hoped would increase foreign investment in the sector. The code limits the Government to a 20% stake in mining companies, and provides an improved legal framework for investment. Taxation of the sector was, however, increased, and new taxes were imposed on the sale, transfer and renewal of mining licences, while new requirements were also introduced in the areas of employment conditions, environmental protection, and worker safety. Currently, royalty tax stands at 3% and profits tax at 35% with a five-year tax holiday after initial production in order that firms can recover capital costs before paying profits tax.

An open-pit gold mine at Syama, in the south, was established in 1992 by a consortium led by BHP-Utah (which took 65% of the shares). In 1996 BHP sold its interest to Randgold of South Africa, which subsequently increased its stake to 80%. Lower international prices for gold and increased operating costs at the mine led Randgold to terminate operations at Syama in early 2001, although it was estimated that some 160,000 kg of gold remained at the mine. In 2004 Randgold sold its stake in the Syama gold mine to Resolute Mining of Australia; the redevelopment of this facility commenced in April 2007, with production of 2,000 kg in 2008. Production increased by 16% in 2010, to 9,980 kg, owing to the rehabilitation of the mine.

One of Mali's largest gold-mining projects, Sadiola Hill, in the Kayes region—a joint venture between the Canadian operator IAMGOLD Corpn and AngloGold of South Africa—started operation in 1997. Output was around 13,000–14,000 kg in the late 2000s, but in 2010 production decreased materially to only 3,345 kg, owing to lower grades. A deep sulphide pre-feasibility study projects an increase in production at Sadiola to between 11,000 kg and 14,000 kg per year according to IAMGOLD Corpn.

Operations commenced at the Morila field, in the south-east, in 2000, with an initial production of 3,500 kg; Morila is now Mali's largest operating gold mine and enjoys some of the lowest operating costs in the world. The mine is operated by a company jointly owned by Randgold, AngloGold (each of which owned a 40% share) and the Malian Government (with the remaining 20%). The mine was expected to yield an average annual output of 14,000 kg in 2002–12, but production of some 23,400 kg and 38,900 kg were recorded in 2001 and 2002, respectively. Production declined thereafter, however, owing to technical difficulties and a management dispute between AngloGold and Randgold and a subsequent decrease in ore grades and a reduction in the ore process capacity. Production reached 14,500 kg in 2008 as a result of a more complex extraction process. In 2009 production fell to 9,700 kg as the mine was converted from open pit to stockpile treatment.

The first output of gold from a further mine, at Yatela, a joint venture between AngloGold and IAMGOLD, was reported in May 2001, with commercial production commencing two months later; total production of 43,500 kg was expected over a period of six years, with output of 5,000 kg and 8,600 kg reported in the years 2001 and 2002, respectively. Yatela's gold output declined from 10,000 kg, in 2006 to 5,200 kg in 2008 and to 2,500 kg in 2009. Operations at Randgold's Loulo deposit began in late 1999, while a new company, Société des Mines d'or de Loulo, in which the Malian Government was to have a 20% share, was formed to exploit the Kodieran deposit. Production at Loulo mine started in November 2005 and output totalled around 6,900 kg in 2006, peaking at 9,800 kg in 2007, before decreasing to 7,600 kg in 2008. Production declined by 59% from 2009 to 2010 to 1,700 kg, as a result of a lower mined gold grade. Production was expected to continue until 2012.

Other Australian, French, British, South African, Japanese, US and Canadian companies are active in both gold exploration and production. Prospecting for other mineral resources has also been conducted. In the mid-2000s a joint venture between Canada's Mink Minerals and Ashton Pty of Australia was investigating kimberlite pipes in the Kéniéba area of the south-west, in the hope of locating exploitable deposits of diamonds. By that time, however, petroleum had become by far the most promising mining activity in Mali. Prospecting activity increased in Mali, following the discovery of commercially viable petroleum reserves in neighbouring Mauritania in 2001. The petroleum code was revised in 2004 and in 2005, and by mid-2007 the Government had awarded 15 prospecting licences on production-sharing terms and three prospecting licences on concessional terms for the 25 designated petroleum blocks. In 2008 the Malian Assemblée nationale extended the exploration phase from 10 years to 12 years to encourage further exploration in the basin. Mali currently imports all of the petroleum it requires.

Mali suffers from a serious shortage of energy. According to the World Bank, only 10% of the population had access to electricity; in many areas there is no supply of electricity, and in others quantities were insufficient to meet the requirements of agriculture and the mining sector. The Government aims to expand electricity supply, notably in rural areas, while reducing the country's reliance on fuel wood. In November 2000 a 39% stake in the electricity utility, Energie du Mali (EdM), was sold to SAUR International, a consortium of the French companies Bouygues and Energie de France, with another 21% being owned by Industrial Promotion Services-West Africa (IPS) and 40% by the Malian Government. There were pledges to rehabilitate and expand the company's facilities, and the Government ensured that EdM reduced electricity tariffs in 2003 and 2004. However, in October 2005 SAUR International announced its withdrawal from EdM owing to an unresolved dispute with the Government. SAUR International's 39% share was subsequently divided between IPS and the Government, which became the majority stakeholder with a 66% share.

Roughly one-half of the electricity generated in 2001 was hydroelectric in origin, mostly provided by the Selingué facility on the Sankarani river, making it subject to drought. None the less, the energy situation in Mali has improved since the Manantali project on the Senegal river began production in 2001. The operation of the Manantali dam (constructed at a cost of some US $600m.) was supervised by the Organisation pour la Mise en Valeur du Fleuve Sénégal, in which both Mauritania and Senegal also participate. Mali has rights to receive 55% of the annual output of the hydroelectric plant (estimated at 800m. kWh). Construction of the dam was completed in 1988, but the installation of generating equipment was delayed by disagreements over supply routes, as well as the deterioration in relations between Mauritania and Senegal in 1989–90, so that the dam was not formally inaugurated until 1992. After further problems with funding and cross-border arrangements, Mali finally began to receive electricity generated at Manantali in December 2001. Manantali could eventually increase Mali's total installed capacity in electricity—which in 2005 comprised 31.4 MW held by EdM, and 19 MW held by various other plants, including CMDT and HUICOMA—by an additional 104 MW. Despite international oil prices more than doubling since 2004, electricity tariffs in Mali have only increased by 4%. Consequently, EdM recorded a loss equivalent to 0.3% of GDP in 2010, as imported fuel oil is the main source of power generation in Mali, according to the IMF. A number of projects were planned to absorb the energy deficit, including network interconnection between Mali and Cote d'Ivoire and a heavy-fuel oil thermal power station, costing 15,000m. francs CFA, financed by the Islamic Development Bank. The Government is also implementing a strategy to increase production by connecting with the grid in Côte d'Ivoire, and developing Mali's hydroelectric potential with the World Bank assistance.

MANUFACTURING

Manufacturing activity is concentrated in Bamako, mainly taking the form of agricultural-processing—according to the Organisation for Economic Co-operation and Development, the agro-industry represents around 45% of Mali's industrial activity and is dominated by HUICOMA—and the manufacture of construction materials and basic consumer goods. Manufacturing contributed 12.0% of GDP in 2007, but only 5.6% in 2008 and 5.7% in 2009, according to the AfDB. Manufacturing GDP increased by 1.0% in 2009, 2.6% in 2010 and an estimated 5.4% in 2011, after an average annual growth rate of 3.4% in 2000–08. A decline in cotton production in 2008 resulted in manufacturing GDP contracting by some 32.6% in that year, according to the AfDB. Following the failure of successive governments to improve its performance, the manufacturing sector has been substantially reorganized, under pressure from the IMF and other foreign creditors. The growth of the sector has, however, been hindered by frequent energy shortages. Trends in manufacturing vary greatly from year to year, and in large part reflect activity in the cotton-ginning sector. Prospects in manufacturing have none the less improved in recent years. The textile industry has started to expand following Mali's qualification for the USA's African Growth and Opportunity Act in December 2003; a new spinning factory, Fils et Tissus Naturels d'Afrique, was subsequently opened near Bamako, and the Industrie Textile du Mali, now renamed Bakary Textile Commerce et Industrie, reopened under private ownership in 2005. A Chinese company, Covec, which already owned the formerly state-owned Compagnie Malienne des Textiles (COMATEX), expressed the intention of opening a further textile plant in the country. After declining by 34% in 2008, the textile industry grew by an estimated 31% in 2011. Other manufacturing activities in Mali include cement, sugar-processing and beverages production. In 2008 the public-private company SUKALA commenced operations on a new sugar production plant. Following a contraction of 30% in 2008, the food-processing sector expanded by 4% in 2010 and an estimated 18% in 2011, according to the IMF.

TRANSPORT

After achieving an average annual growth rate of 10.7% between 2002 and 2009, the transport and communications sector grew by 5.0% in 2010 and 5.9% in 2011. The early 1960s saw very substantial investment (one-fifth of total planned investment spending) in road-building, in particular after Mali's withdrawal from the Franc Zone in 1962 disrupted traditional trading outlets. However, by 2004 road communications remained poor: of some 18,709 km of classified roads, only 3,370 km were paved. Mali's main access to the sea has historically been via the Bamako–Abidjan (Côte d'Ivoire) road, although, as a result of heightened instability in Côte d'Ivoire during the 2000s, an increasing proportion of freight was diverted to other regional ports, including Tema (Ghana), Lomé (Togo) and Nouakchott (Mauritania). A number of construction and maintenance road projects have received significant funding from the European Development Fund (EDF), the World Bank, and the AfDB to help restore some of the vital links in the sub-region, notably Bamako–Dakar (Senegal) and Bamako–Accra (Ghana). An announced increase in the EU's development assistance for 2008–13, through the EDF, will benefit the transport sector, in particular road development. Some road sections, such as the Kayes–Kidira road in the west, have been completed. As part of the 2008–12 sectoral plan, the Government upgraded 290 km of priority roads in 2008. Further transportation projects include improving facilities and equipment at the Bamako international airport, expanding urban roads, and repairing railway infrastructure. The donor-funded programme for the modernization of the transport infrastructure in Mali also aimed to rehabilitate a section of the very dilapidated 1,286-km rail link from Bamako to Dakar. In October 2003 a Franco-Canadian consortium, Canac-Getma, took over the concession to operate the railway from the state-owned Régie du Chemin de Fer du Mali. Owing to the inadequacy of the road and rail facilities, the country's inland waterways are of great importance to the transport infrastructure. The River Niger is used for bulk transport during the rainy season, while traffic on the River Senegal was expected to improve as a result of the completion of measures associated with the Manantali hydroelectric project.

FINANCE

As a result of an improvement in tax collection and higher taxes in the mining sector, the Government exceeded its fiscal target in 2003, with the deficit (excluding grants) declining to 147,200m. francs CFA (5.7% of GDP), or 32,500m. francs CFA, equivalent to 1.3% of GDP, if these factors were included In 2004 overall fiscal performance remained good. The budget deficit (excluding grants) rose to 171,200m. francs CFA (6.6% of GDP), or 67,900m. francs CFA (2.6% of GDP) including grants, in that year, as a result of increased spending in priority sectors, a 14.6% rise in civil servants' salaries, and higher public investment and lending to the CMDT. Tax on petroleum products was, meanwhile, reduced to cushion the impact of rising fuel prices on consumers. The bulk of the deficit was financed through grants and concessionary lending. In 2006 continued efforts by the Government to widen the tax base, improve fiscal administration and reduce tax exemptions were expected to contribute to an increase in revenue; however, increased social and election-related expenditure (in preparation for the 2007 presidential and legislative elections) were estimated to have resulted in an increase in the fiscal deficit (excluding grants) to 7.5% of GDP. In 2007 the Government succeeded in widening the tax base, resulting in a 20,000m. francs CFA increase in tax revenues, which contributed to total government revenue increasing by 3% compared with the previous year, to 581,900m. francs CFA, according to the AfDB. In an attempt to offset higher import costs, the Government used the revenues derived from high gold prices to provide tax breaks for food and fuel imports and increase the wages of civil servants (by 5% in 2008 and a further 5% in 2009), which resulted in the fiscal deficit widening to 8.6% of GDP in 2007, according to the IMF. Volatile commodity markets affected government spending in two ways in 2008: higher prices for oil, fertilizers and rice required government intervention to limit the impact on consumers, whereas other sectors, such as mining, benefited from higher export revenues and taxes. In response to a dispute over value-added tax and customs duty refunds, the Government issued bonds to mine operators amounting to 1.5% of GDP in 2008, leading to a further deterioration in government finances. The basic government budget deficit was equivalent to 2.6% of GDP in 2008. Management of public finances improved in 2009, with the basic budget deficit contracting to 1.4% of GDP. Total revenue increased to 14.5% of GDP, reflecting improved monitoring of the taxation collection department. A fiscal stimulus plan for 2010–12 was formulated, financed mainly by the sale of part of the state telecommunications firm Société des Télécommunications du Mali—Malitel (SOTELMA), and focusing on infrastructure, agriculture, social development, domestic debt repayment and co-financing public investment projects with donors. The fiscal position improved again in 2010, reflecting an increase in total revenue to 17.4% of GDP, resulting in the basic fiscal deficit declining to 1.2% of GDP, according to the IMF. At the same time, current expenditure increased by 0.4% of GDP, due to additional transfers to the electricity company, the costs involved in returning migrants from Côte d'Ivoire and Libya, and increased spending on election preparations. In 2011 the budget deficit contracted slightly to 1% of GDP, mainly due to higher tax revenues. Net expenditure increased by 11%, as a result of additional transfers to the state energy company and spending on the repatriation and settlement of migrant workers from Libya and Côte d'Ivoire. It was expected that the budget deficit would widen dramatically in 2012 due to the costs associated with the election and the ongoing political crisis in northern Mali.

FOREIGN TRADE AND PAYMENTS

Mali's trade deficit has been greatly reduced since the early 1970s, when exports typically represented only six months' of imports. Export earnings were boosted in the late 1990s by the sharp increase in cotton production (in response to much higher local prices), by higher demand from Côte d'Ivoire for Malian livestock, and by enhanced gold production. Import spending, meanwhile, remained contained as a result of higher prices, tight management of demand and improved domestic food supply. The trade balance turned positive in 2002, at US $162.7m., as cotton exports were boosted by a recovery in the international price and bumper harvests, which helped to compensate for lower exports to other countries of the region associated with the onset of conflict in Côte d'Ivoire. Rising international prices for gold and cotton, combined with the strengthening of the CFA franc against the US dollar, helped to finance the petroleum-import bill in 2003. None the less, the trade balance recorded a deficit of $60.5m. in 2003, because of lower gold exports in volume terms and higher imports in capital goods. Similar trends were recorded in 2004, with the trade deficit widening to 62,000m. francs CFA (equivalent to $89m.), according to the IMF. Despite increased gold exports in 2005, higher oil-related imports contributed to a widening of the trade deficit, to an estimated 65,000m. francs CFA (equivalent to $132.2m.). In 2006, although imports remained strong, a dramatic increase in gold exports—reflecting rising production and high international prices—resulted in the trade balance moving to a surplus, projected by the IMF at 28,000m. CFA francs (equivalent to $53.5m. or 15.7% of GDP). In 2007 terms of trade deteriorated with soaring oil and food import prices offsetting the rise in gold export prices and the slight increase in international cotton prices. Exports of the main value items, namely gold and cotton, decreased in 2007, returning the trade balance to a deficit, according to the IMF. In 2009 gold exports represented 70% of the value of total exports, offsetting a 25% reduction in the value of cotton exports, and resulting in the trade deficit declining to 3.2%, compared with 5.5% in 2008.

Mali's services balance has traditionally recorded a structural deficit, as a result of high transport costs and interest repayments on external debt. Grant inflows, but also emigrants' remittances, have helped to fill the financing gap in most years. Workers' remittances often go unrecorded, although evidence points to a decline since the onset of unrest in Côte d'Ivoire in 2002, where, prior to that time, an estimated 2m. Malians worked. The current account deficit (including official transfers) widened to 6.4% of GDP in 2007, but narrowed, to an estimated 6.1% of GDP (including official transfers), in 2008; however, high oil prices coupled with lower cotton exports adversely affected the external sector. The external position deteriorated sharply in 2008, registering a deficit of 9.7% of GDP, mostly financed by private capital inflows, before improving slightly to 7.3% of GDP in 2009, driven by strong gold prices. Proceeds from the divestment of part of SOTELMA, the state telecommunications firm, which had been sold in July 2009 for US $400m. (4% of GDP), combined with funding from the IMF's ECF in August, significantly increased Mali's reserves in the Union Economique et Monétaire Ouest-africaine to $1,602m. in 2009, compared with $1,033m. in the previous year. The current account deficit increased slightly to 7.5% of GDP in 2010, with the positive impact of rising gold and cotton prices being outweighed by higher oil prices and the fall in gold production. As the current account deficit was only partially financed by net capital inflows, the overall balance of payments recorded a deficit of an estimated 86,000m. francs CFA ($174m.). This was financed by drawing on foreign exchange reserves, resulting in Mali's reserves falling to an estimated $1,295m., according to the IMF. Despite remittances from abroad declining in 2011 due to the crises in neighbouring Libya and Côte d'Ivoire, the current account deficit narrowed to an estimated 5.2% of GDP due to a 19.7% increase in exports, driven by the cotton and gold sectors.

Aid inflows generally represent around 10% of GDP and over one-third of government spending. Overseas development assistance inflows peaked at US $541.3m. in 1995 and averaged $389.2m. per year in 1996–2001. All donors disbursed a total of $542.8m. in 2003 and $567.4m. in 2004. France, in particular, has maintained a high level of support for the structural adjustment programme, in the form of budgetary grants as well as loans and debt relief.

In October 1988, following agreement with the IMF on a programme of economic adjustment, Mali became the first debtor country to benefit from a system of exceptional debt relief that had been agreed in principle at that year's summit meeting of industrialized nations, held in Toronto, Canada. In addition, Mali was one of 35 countries that had its official debt to France (equivalent to US $240m.) cancelled at the beginning of 1990. None the less, external debt, which reached $2,468m. by the end of 1990, continued to represent a substantial burden. The debt-service ratio in that year was reduced to a tolerable level—12.3%—only because of the non-payment of some obligations. The 'Paris Club' of Western official creditors agreed in November 1992 to a further round of rescheduling. However, with debt at the end of 1993 equivalent to 108% of GNI, Mali was a prime candidate for the special measures of debt relief that followed the 50% devaluation of the CFA franc in January 1994. Major bilateral aid sources, led by France, cancelled a proportion of debt and rescheduled repayments. Following the approval of a further three-year ESAF allowance in April 1996, further debt relief was granted by Mali's external creditors in May of that year, under the 'Naples terms', although only a small proportion of Mali's debt was deemed eligible, and the net benefit to Mali was estimated to have been around $50m.

In September 2000 the IMF and the World Bank announced that Mali was to receive some US $220m. in debt-service relief under their original HIPC initiative (for which Mali had been deemed eligible in 1998) and a further $650m. under an enhanced framework. Mali reached completion point in March 2003, when full debt relief started. According to the World Bank, Mali's total external debt amounted to $3,320m. at the end of 2004, which was equivalent to 71% of GNI. Mali's total external debt stock declined to $2,969m. at the end of 2005, representing 58.5% of GNI. The annual cost of servicing the debt was equivalent to 5.8% of the value of exports of goods and services in 2003 and 7.3% in 2004. In June 2005 Mali was among 18 countries to be granted 100% debt relief under the Multilateral Debt Relief Initiative agreed by the Group of Eight leading industrialized nations (G8). The IMF, the AfDB and the World Bank subsequently announced debt write-offs worth around $2,000m., contributing to a significant reduction in Mali's external debt stock, from 48.8% of GDP in 2005 to 20% of GDP in 2006. In 2007 the public debt ratio remained constant at 22.6% of GDP, declining to 19.1% in 2008, before increasing to 19.3% in 2009, 24.2% in 2010 and 27.5% in 2011, according to the IMF. In 2008 the cost of debt-servicing was equivalent to 4% of the total value of goods and services exports in that year, increasing to 4.2% in 2009, but, according to IMF estimates, declining to 2.9% in 2010.

Statistical Survey

Source (unless otherwise stated): Direction Nationale de la Statistique et de l'Informatique, rue Archinard, porte 233, BP 12, Bamako; tel. 2022-2455; fax 2022-7145; e-mail cnpe.mali@afribonemali.net; internet www.dnsi.gov.ml.

Area and Population

AREA, POPULATION AND DENSITY

Area (sq km)	1,240,192*
Population (census results)	
17 April 1998†	9,790,492
1 April 2009 (provisional)	
Males	7,202,744
Females	7,314,432
Total	14,517,176
Population (UN estimates at mid-year)‡	
2010	15,369,809
2011	15,839,536
2012	16,318,894
Density (per sq km) at mid-2012	13.2

* 478,841 sq miles.

† Figures are provisional and refer to the *de jure* population.

‡ Source: UN, *World Population Prospects: The 2010 Revision*.

POPULATION BY AGE AND SEX

(UN estimates at mid-2012)

	Males	Females	Total
0–14	3,916,871	3,757,662	7,674,533
15–64	4,102,784	4,190,777	8,293,561
65 and over	142,622	208,178	350,800
Total	8,162,277	8,156,617	16,318,894

Source: UN, *World Population Prospects: The 2010 Revision*.

Ethnic Groups (percentage of total, 1995): Bambara 36.5; Peul 13.9; Sénoufo 9.0; Soninké 8.8; Dogon 8.0; Songhaï 7.2; Malinké 6.6; Diola 2.9; Bobo and Oulé 2.4; Tuareg 1.7; Moor 1.2; Others 1.8 (Source: La Francophonie).

ADMINISTRATIVE DIVISIONS

(*de jure* population at 1998 census, provisional figures)

District		Mopti	1,475,274
Bamako	1,016,167	Kayes	1,372,019
Regions		Tombouctou	461,956
Sikasso	1,780,042	Gao	397,516
Ségou	1,679,201	Kidal	42,479
Koulikoro	1,565,838		

PRINCIPAL TOWNS*

(*de jure* population at 1998 census, provisional figures)

Bamako (capital)	1,016,167	Koutiala	74,153
Sikasso	113,813	Kayes	67,262
Ségou	90,898	Gao	54,903
Mopti	79,840	Kati	49,756

* With the exception of Bamako, figures refer to the population of communes (municipalities).

Mid-2011 ('000, incl. suburbs, UN estimate): Bamako 2,036,520 (Source: UN, *World Urbanization Prospects: The 2011 Revision*).

BIRTHS AND DEATHS

(annual averages, UN estimates)

	1995–2000	2000–05	2005–10
Birth rate (per 1,000)	49.1	49.0	47.6
Death rate (per 1,000)	18.6	17.2	15.5

Source: UN, *World Population Prospects: The 2010 Revision*.

Life expectancy (years at birth): 51.0 (males 49.9; females 52.1) in 2010 (Source: World Bank, World Development Indicators database).

ECONOMICALLY ACTIVE POPULATION

('000 persons, 2004, estimates)

	Males	Females	Total
Agriculture, hunting and forestry	657.7	291.7	949.4
Fishing	33.3	2.0	35.2
Mining	8.4	3.0	11.4
Manufacturing	136.1	136.4	272.5
Electricity, gas and water	5.1	—	5.1
Construction	97.5	4.7	102.1
Wholesale and retail trade; repair of motor vehicles, motorcycles and personal household goods	266.1	402.1	668.1
Hotels and restaurants	1.4	6.3	7.6
Transport, storage and communications	51.8	3.5	55.3
Financial intermediation	4.4	—	4.4
Real estate	3.5	0.6	4.0
Public administration	33.3	6.6	39.9
Education	35.6	18.3	53.9
Health and social work	11.4	9.5	20.9
Other social services	42.6	97.5	140.1
Total employed	1,388.3	982.5	2,370.8
Unemployed	107.0	120.5	227.4
Total labour force	1,495.3	1,103.0	2,598.2

Source: ILO.

Mid-2012 (estimates in '000): Agriculture, etc. 3,198; Total labour force 4,345 (Source: FAO).

Health and Welfare

KEY INDICATORS

Total fertility rate (children per woman, 2010)	6.3
Under-5 mortality rate (per 1,000 live births, 2010)	178
HIV/AIDS (% of persons aged 15–49, 2009)	1.0
Physicians (per 1,000 head, 2008)	0.05
Hospital beds (per 1,000 head, 2010)	0.10
Health expenditure (2009): US $ per head (PPP)	57
Health expenditure (2009): % of GDP	5.5
Health expenditure (2009): public (% of total)	47.2
Access to water (% of persons, 2010)	64
Access to sanitation (% of persons, 2010)	22
Total carbon dioxide emissions ('000 metric tons, 2008)	594.1
Carbon dioxide emissions per head (metric tons, 2008)	<0.1
Human Development Index (2011): ranking	175
Human Development Index (2011): value	0.359

For sources and definitions, see explanatory note on p. vi.

Agriculture

PRINCIPAL CROPS

('000 metric tons)

	2008	2009	2010
Rice, paddy	1,624.2	1,950.8	2,308.2
Maize	695.1	1,477.0	1,403.6
Millet	1,413.9	1,390.4	1,373.3
Sorghum	1,027.2	1,465.6	1,256.8
Fonio	41.3	35.5	52.3
Sweet potatoes	317.1	236.8	204.7
Cassava (Manioc)	71.5	79.6	38.2
Yams	67.1	65.4	90.1
Sugar cane	360.0*	377.0	359.0
Groundnuts, with shell	388.4	300.6	314.5
Karité nuts (Sheanuts)*	190.0	232.1	199.7
Cottonseed†	124.0	144.0	170.0
Tomatoes	57.9	62.2	41.3
Onions, dry*	38.0	39.0	40.0
Guavas, mangoes and mangosteens	48.9	47.4	47.8*
Cotton (lint)*	60.0	72.0	78.0

* FAO estimate(s).

† Unofficial figures.

Aggregate production ('000 metric tons, may include official, semi-official or estimated data): Total cereals 4,814.9 in 2008, 6,334.6 in 2009, 6,418.3 in 2010; Total pulses 106.4 in 2008, 158.6 in 2009, 155.3 in 2010; Total roots and tubers 622.9 in 2008, 472.2 in 2009, 415.5 in 2010; Total vegetables (incl. melons) 472.1 in 2008, 950.9 in 2009, 802.1 in 2010; Total fruits (excl. melons) 353.5 in 2008, 385.6 in 2009, 391.1 in 2010.

Source: FAO.

LIVESTOCK

('000 head, year ending September)

	2008	2009	2010
Cattle	8,637	8,896	9,163
Sheep	10,762	11,300	11,865
Goats	14,986	15,736	16,523
Pigs	75	74	75
Horses	434	478	488
Asses	843	862	881
Camels	887	904	923
Chickens	34,889	35,000	36,750

Source: FAO.

LIVESTOCK PRODUCTS

('000 metric tons, FAO estimates)

	2008	2009	2010
Cattle meat	129.1	136.3	143.7
Sheep meat	40.5	44.5	46.4
Goat meat	62.6	65.8	69.1
Chicken meat	39.4	40.6	40.6
Game meat	20.8	22.1	23.7
Pig meat	2.4	2.5	2.6
Cows' milk	284.0	300.0	308.7
Sheep's milk	142.5	153.0	160.0
Goats' milk	595.4	656.4	689.2
Camels' milk	355.3	295.8	301.9

Source: FAO.

Forestry

ROUNDWOOD REMOVALS

('000 cubic metres, excl. bark, FAO estimates)

	2008	2009	2010
Sawlogs, veneer logs and logs for sleepers	4	4	4
Other industrial wood	409	409	409
Fuel wood	5,203	5,264	5,326
Total	5,616	5,677	5,739

2011: Production assumed to be unchanged from 2010 (FAO estimates).

Source: FAO.

SAWNWOOD PRODUCTION

('000 cubic metres, incl. railway sleepers)

	1987	1988	1989
Total (all broadleaved)	11	13	13*

* FAO estimate.

1990–2011: Production assumed to be unchanged from 1989 (FAO estimates).

Source: FAO.

Fishing

('000 metric tons, live weight)

	2008	2009*	2010
Capture	100.0*	100.0	100.0
Nile tilapia	30.0	30.0	30.0
Elephantsnout fishes	7.0	7.0	7.0
Characins	5.0	5.0	5.0
Black catfishes	4.0	4.0	4.0
North African catfish	25.0	25.0	25.0
Nile perch	6.0*	6.0	6.0
Other freshwater fishes	19.0*	19.0	18.9
Aquaculture	0.8	1.4	2.1*
Total catch	100.8*	101.4	102.1*

* FAO estimate(s).

Source: FAO.

Mining

(metric tons unless otherwise indicated)

	2008	2009	2010
Gold (kg)	41,160	42,364	36,344
Salt*	6,000	6,000	6,000
Semi-precious stones	10,000	10,000	10,000*

* Estimated figure(s).

Source: US Geological Survey.

Industry

SELECTED PRODUCTS

('000 metric tons unless otherwise indicated)

	2006	2007	2008
Raw sugar	34	34	35
Fish (dried, salted or in brine); smoked fish and edible fish meal	5.7	8.8	n.a.
Cigarettes (million)	625.8	546.8	276.3
Electric energy (million kWh)	489	495	508

Cement: 10,000 metric tons in 2000 (Source: US Geological Survey).

Source: mainly UN Industrial Commodity Statistics Database.

Finance

CURRENCY AND EXCHANGE RATES

Monetary Units

100 centimes = 1 franc de la Communauté Financière Africaine (CFA).

Sterling, Dollar and Euro Equivalents (31 May 2012)

£1 sterling = 819.959 francs CFA;
US $1 = 528.870 francs CFA;
€1 = 655.957 francs CFA;
10,000 francs CFA = £12.20 = $18.91 = €15.24.

Average Exchange Rate (francs CFA per US $)

2009 472.19
2010 495.28
2011 471.87

Note: An exchange rate of 1 French franc = 50 francs CFA, established in 1948, remained in force until January 1994, when the CFA franc was devalued by 50%, with the exchange rate adjusted to 1 French franc = 100 francs CFA. This relationship to French currency remained in effect with the introduction of the euro on 1 January 1999. From that date, accordingly, a fixed exchange rate of €1 = 655.957 francs CFA has been in operation.

BUDGET

('000 million francs CFA)*

Revenue†	2009	2010‡	2011§
Budgetary revenue	653.2	727.6	780.3
Tax revenue	624.3	681.8	731.1
Non-tax revenue	28.9	45.8	49.2
Special funds and annexed budgets	71.8	78.7	71.5
Total	725.0	806.3	851.8

Expenditure‖	2009	2010‡	2011§
Budgetary expenditure	1,004.4	971.0	1,175.9
Current expenditure	549.0	601.2	714.8
Wages and salaries	213.5	231.8	269.8
Interest payments (scheduled)	15.7	19.1	28.1
Other current expenditure	319.8	350.3	417.0
Capital expenditure	455.4	369.8	461.1
Externally financed	303.2	187.6	249.2
Special funds and annexed budgets	71.8	78.7	71.5
Total	1,076.2	1,049.7	1,247.4

* Figures represent a consolidation of the central government budget, special funds and annexed budgets.
† Excluding grants received ('000 million francs CFA): 193.9 in 2009; 133.7 in 2010 (estimate); 178.8 in 2011 (programmed figure).
‡ Estimates.
§ Programmed figures.
‖ Excluding net lending ('000 million francs CFA): 21.6 in 2009; 14.7 in 2010 (estimate); –3.1 in 2011 (programmed figure).

Source: IMF, *Seventh Review Under the Extended Credit Facility and Request for a new Three-Year Arrangement Under the Extended Credit Facility—Staff Report; Joint IDA/IMF Debt Sustainability Analysis; Informational Annex; Statement by IMF Staff Representative; Statement by Alternate Executive Director for Mali; and Press Releases* (January 2012).

INTERNATIONAL RESERVES

(excl. gold, US $ million at 31 December)

	2009	2010	2011
IMF special drawing rights	115.0	113.1	112.7
Reserve position in IMF	15.5	15.4	15.4
Foreign exchange	1,473.9	1,215.9	1,250.6
Total	1,604.4	1,344.4	1,378.6

Source: IMF, *International Financial Statistics*.

MONEY SUPPLY

('000 million francs CFA at 31 December)

	2009	2010	2011
Currency outside banks	304.6	312.3	415.4
Demand deposits	495.5	610.7	677.2
Total money (incl. others)	800.5	923.1	1,092.9

Source: IMF, *International Financial Statistics*.

COST OF LIVING

(Consumer Price Index for Bamako: base: 2000 = 100)

	2008	2009	2010
Food, beverages and tobacco	132.6	136.7	103.6
Clothing	105.9	108.7	108.6
Housing, water, electricity and gas	118.2	118.4	116.7
All items (incl. others)	126.3	129.1	130.9

2011: Food, beverages and tobacco 112.8; All items (incl. others) 134.6.

Source: ILO.

NATIONAL ACCOUNTS

(million francs CFA at current prices)

Expenditure on the Gross Domestic Product

	2009	2010	2011*
Government final consumption expenditure	734	788	859
Private final consumption expenditure	2,633	2,831	3,097
Changes in inventories	31	155	32
Gross fixed capital formation	868	986	1,114
Total domestic expenditure	4,266	4,760	5,102
Exports of goods and services	914	1,105	1,254
Less Imports of goods and services	947	1,209	1,345
GDP in purchasers' values	4,233	4,656	5,012

Gross Domestic Product by Economic Activity

	2009	2010	2011*
Agriculture, hunting, forestry and fishing	1,486	1,698	1,761
Mining and quarrying	284	287	351
Manufacturing	219	227	287
Electricity, gas and water	83	91	100
Construction	216	238	263
Wholesale and retail trade, restaurants and hotels	611	669	713
Transport and communications	233	250	268
Finance, insurance, real estate and other business services	315	333	350
Public administration and defence	378	399	427
Sub-total	3,825	4,192	4,520
Less Imputed bank service charges	15	16	23
Indirect taxes, less subsidies	423	480	515
GDP in purchasers' values	4,233	4,656	5,012

* Provisional.

Source: African Development Bank.

BALANCE OF PAYMENTS
(US $ million)

	2008	2009	2010
Exports of goods f.o.b.	2,097.2	1,773.7	2,055.6
Imports of goods f.o.b.	–2,732.9	–1,986.3	–2,730.7
Trade balance	–635.7	–212.6	–675.1
Exports of services	454.3	354.4	383.7
Imports of services	–1,024.3	–825.6	–1,017.1
Balance on goods and services	–1,205.7	–683.9	–1,308.5
Other income received	101.6	81.6	71.7
Other income paid	–414.2	–539.0	–490.7
Balance on goods, services and income	–1,518.3	–1,141.2	–1,727.5
Current transfers received	554.0	648.3	700.8
Current transfers paid	–99.2	–162.0	–163.3
Current balance	–1,063.4	–654.9	–1,189.9
Capital account (net)	328.8	384.1	229.6
Direct investment abroad	–49.2	–28.9	–12.1
Direct investment from abroad	228.9	778.2	410.6
Portfolio investment assets	–117.9	–60.3	–462.2
Portfolio investment liabilities	22.6	21.3	7.2
Financial derivatives assets	3.6	–1.6	–3.9
Other investment assets	205.5	–370.7	304.9
Other investment liabilities	330.4	554.3	507.9
Net errors and omissions	31.0	–175.3	31.1
Overall balance	–79.7	446.3	–177.0

Source: IMF, *International Financial Statistics*.

External Trade

PRINCIPAL COMMODITIES
(distribution by SITC, US $ million)

Imports c.i.f.*	2007	2008	2010†
Food and live animals	252.2	320.1	437.4
Cereals and cereal preparations	91.3	117.9	146.0
Mineral fuels, lubricants, etc.	484.9	713.2	1,221.0
Petroleum, petroleum products and related materials	478.4	704.4	1,211.0
Chemicals and related products	338.9	471.6	692.7
Medicinal and pharmaceutical products	140.2	136.2	336.1
Manufactured goods	399.7	683.1	850.7
Iron and steel	89.0	142.5	188.9
Machinery and transport equipment	534.5	860.2	1,121.6
Road vehicles	158.9	220.5	319.1
Miscellaneous manufactured articles	83.1	162.7	228.6
Total (incl. others)	2,184.8	3,338.9	4,703.5

Exports f.o.b.	2007	2008	2010†
Food and live animals	93.7	127.7	95.8
Crude materials, inedible, excluding fuels	207.4	213.1	177.3
Cotton	198.7	203.1	168.0
Machinery and transport equipment	27.3	58.5	30.8
Road vehicles	5.1	21.7	5.8
Gold, non-monetary, unwrought, in powder or semi-manufactured	1,082.5	1,437.1	1,578.7
Total (incl. others)	1,440.6	1,918.3	1,996.3

* Including commodities and transactions not classified according to kind (US $ million): 492.2 in 2007; 734.0 in 2008; 1,258.9 in 2010.

† Data for 2009 were not available.

Source: UN, *International Trade Statistics Yearbook*.

SELECTED TRADING PARTNERS
(US $ million)

Imports c.i.f.	2007	2008	2010*
Belgium	67.2	86.4	69.9
Benin	97.5	74.6	467.7
Brazil	36.4	58.8	67.0
Burkina Faso	35.8	5.3	n.a.
China, People's Repub.	130.0	342.1	467.4
Côte d'Ivoire	277.0	346.9	371.0
France (incl. Monaco)	325.9	464.8	630.3
Germany	52.3	81.3	111.1
Ghana	65.3	55.7	74.2
India	78.3	66.1	67.7
Italy	21.4	36.9	49.2
Japan	41.1	91.9	121.6
Netherlands	15.8	23.2	110.8
Senegal	432.2	575.7	638.8
South Africa	79.5	151.2	298.0
Thailand	11.2	39.5	16.1
Togo	87.3	45.1	105.4
Ukraine	12.1	37.4	72.8
United Arab Emirates	14.6	40.0	43.6
USA	81.6	221.4	421.3
Total (incl. others)	2,184.8	3,338.9	4,703.5

Exports f.o.b.	2007	2008	2010*
Bangladesh	11.8	5.2	16.1
Belgium	30.4	6.4	7.0
Burkina Faso	10.9	18.5	43.1
China, People's Repub.	32.1	35.4	40.8
Côte d'Ivoire	36.0	49.1	39.9
France (incl. Monaco)	12.6	24.2	22.7
Guinea	11.3	11.8	5.6
Indonesia	25.7	11.8	12.0
Pakistan	30.1	16.5	20.5
Senegal	61.1	131.1	87.8
South Africa	966.0	1,390.1	1,139.2
Switzerland-Liechtenstein	65.6	49.0	241.6
Thailand	27.0	27.2	9.3
United Kingdom	26.5	1.3	15.6
Viet Nam	23.5	21.7	8.7
Total (incl. others)	1,440.6	1,918.3	1,996.3

* Data for 2009 were not available.

Source: UN, *International Trade Statistics Yearbook*.

Transport

RAILWAYS
(traffic)

	1999	2000	2001
Passengers ('000)	778.7	682.3	649.0
Freight carried ('000 metric tons)	535	438	358

Passenger-km (million): 210 in 1999.

Freight ton-km (million): 241 in 1999.

ROAD TRAFFIC
(motor vehicles in use, estimates)

	1994	1995	1996
Passenger cars	24,250	24,750	26,190
Lorries and vans	16,000	17,100	18,240

2009 (motor vehicles in use): Passenger cars 107,194; Vans and lorries 49,074; Motorcycles and mopeds 24,700.

Source: IRF, *World Road Statistics*.

CIVIL AVIATION
(traffic on scheduled services)*

	1999	2000	2001
Kilometres flown (million)	3	3	1
Passengers carried ('000)	84	77	46
Passenger-km (million)	235	216	130
Total ton-km (million)	36	32	19

* Including an apportionment of the traffic of Air Afrique.

Source: UN, *Statistical Yearbook*.

Tourism

FOREIGN VISITORS BY NATIONALITY*

	2007	2008	2009
Austria	988	2,638	660
Belgium, Luxembourg and the Netherlands	10,280	8,166	6,642
Canada	5,076	6,940	10,091
France	57,682	41,778	38,261
Germany	6,962	9,033	5,380
Italy	9,272	8,269	5,307
Japan	1,416	4,672	1,307
Middle Eastern states	1,190	4,176	2,946
Scandinavian states	1,436	3,883	1,791
Spain	7,792	10,164	4,388
Switzerland	2,480	5,037	2,723
United Kingdom	5,224	5,357	4,173
USA	12,488	12,579	16,901
West African states	18,914	15,276	27,408
Total (incl. others)	164,124	189,511	160,012

* Arrivals at hotels and similar establishments.

2010: Total visitors 169,000.

Receipts from tourism (US $ million, excl. passenger transport): 192 in 2009; 205 in 2010.

Source: World Tourism Organization.

Communications Media

	2009	2010	2011
Telephones ('000 main lines in use)	84.8	114.5	104.7
Mobile cellular telephones ('000 subscribers)	4,460.5	7,440.4	10,821.9
Internet subscribers ('000)	19.8	24.4	n.a.
Broadband subscribers ('000)	3.0	2.3	2.4

Personal computers: 100,000 (8.1 per 1,000 persons) in 2007.

Source: International Telecommunication Union.

Television receivers ('000 in use): 160 in 2000 (Source: UNESCO, *Statistical Yearbook*).

Radio receivers ('000 in use): 570 in 1997 (Source: UNESCO, *Statistical Yearbook*).

Daily newspapers (national estimates): 3 (total circulation 12,350 copies) in 1997; 3 (total circulation 12,600) in 1998; 9 in 2004 (Source: UNESCO Institute for Statistics).

Book production: 14 titles (28,000 copies) in 1995 (first editions only, excluding pamphlets); 33 in 1998 (Sources: UNESCO, *Statistical Yearbook*, UNESCO Institute for Statistics).

Education

(2010/11 unless otherwise indicated)

			Students ('000)		
	Institutions*	Teachers	Males	Females	Total
Pre-primary	212	1,618	35.5	35.7	71.2
Primary	2,871	43,629	1,145.3	969.5	2,114.8
Secondary	n.a.	33,220	487.7	332.7	820.4
Tertiary	n.a.	1,112†	57.9‡	23.3‡	81.2‡

* 1998/99 figures.
† 2004/05 figure.
‡ 2009/10 figure.

2005/06: *Pre-primary*: 412 institutions; 1,510 teachers; 51,071 students; *Primary and Secondary (lower)*: 8,079 institutions; 39,109 teachers; 1,990,765 students (1,137,787 males, 852,978 females); *Secondary (higher)*: 121 institutions; 1,904 teachers; 47,279 students (31,724 males, 15,555 females—estimates); *Secondary (technical and vocational)*: 119 institutions; 41,137 students; *Secondary (teacher training)*: 10,467 students (Source: Office of the Secretary-General of the Government, Bamako).

Source: mainly UNESCO Institute for Statistics.

Pupil-teacher ratio (primary education, UNESCO estimate): 48.5 in 2010/11 (Source: UNESCO Institute for Statistics).

Adult literacy rate (UNESCO estimates): 31.1% (males 43.4%; females 20.3%) in 2010 (Source: UNESCO Institute for Statistics).

Directory

The Constitution

The Constitution of the Third Republic of Mali was approved in a national referendum on 12 January 1992. The document upholds the principles of national sovereignty and the rule of law in a secular, multi-party state, and provides for the separation of powers of the executive, legislative and judicial organs of state.

Executive power is vested in the President of the Republic, who is Head of State and is elected for five years by universal adult suffrage. The President appoints the Prime Minister, who, in turn, appoints other members of the Council of Ministers.

Legislative authority is exercised by the unicameral 147-member Assemblée nationale, which is elected for five years by universal adult suffrage.

The Constitution guarantees the independence of the judiciary. Final jurisdiction in constitutional matters is vested in a Constitutional Court.

The rights, freedoms and obligations of Malian citizens are enshrined in the Constitution. Freedom of the press and of association are guaranteed.

The Government

HEAD OF STATE

Interim President: DIONCOUNDA TRAORÉ (took office on 12 April 2012 for an interim period of 40 days, which was subsequently extended to a transitional period of 12 months with effect from 22 May).

COUNCIL OF MINISTERS

(September 2012)

Prime Minister: CHEICK MODIBO DIARRA.

Minister of the Economy, Finance and the Budget: TIÉNA COULIBALY.

Minister of Defence and War Veterans: Maj. YAMOUSSA CAMARA.

Minister of Foreign Affairs and International Co-operation: TIÈMAM COULIBALY.

Minister of Territorial Administration and Decentralization: Col. MOUSSA SINKO COULIBALY.

Minister of the Civil Service, Governance and Administrative and Political Reform, in charge of Relations with the Institutions: MAMADOU NAMORY TRAORÉ.

Minister of Malians Abroad and African Integration: ROKIATOU TRAORÉ GUIKINÉ.

Minister of Internal Security and Civil Protection: Gen. TIÉFING KONATÉ.

Minister of Agriculture: Dr YARANGA COULIBALY.

Minister of Higher Education and Scientific Research: Prof. HAROUNA KANTÉ.

Minister of Education and Literacy: ADAMA OUANE.

Minister of Health: SOUMANA MAKADJI.

Minister of Housing, Town Planning and Land Affairs: FADIMA DIALLO TOURÉ.

Minister of Equipment and Land Settlement: MAMADOU COULIBALY.

Minister of Transport and Road Infrastructure: Lt Col. ABDOULAYE KOUMARÉ.

Minister of Mining: Dr AMADOU BABA SY.

Minister of Justice, Keeper of the Seals: MALICK COULIBALY.

Minister of Labour, Employment and Professional Training: Dr DÉDIA MAHAMANE DIALLO KATTRA.

Minister of Trade and Industry: ABDEL KARIM KONATÉ.

Minister of Stockbreeding and Fisheries: MAKAN TOUNKARA.

Minister of Humanitarian Action, Solidarity and the Elderly: Dr MAMADOU SIDIBÉ.

Minister of Communication: BRUNO MAÏGA.

Minister of Post and New Technologies: BREHIMA TOLO.

Minister of Energy and Water: ALFA BOCAR NAFO.

Minister of Culture: BOUBACAR HAMADOUN KÉBÉ.

Minister of the Environment and Sanitation: DAVID SAGARA.

Minister of Youth and Sports: HAMEYE FOUNÉ MAHALMADANE.

Minister of the Family, the Promotion of Women and Children: ICHATA ALWATA SAHI.

Minister of the Promotion of the National Languages and Civic Education: BOCAR MOUSSA DIARRA.

Minister of Handicrafts and Tourism: OUSMANE AG RHISSA.

Minister of Religious Affairs and Cults: Dr YACOUBA TRAORÉ.

Minister-delegate at the Ministry of the Economy, Finance and the Budget, responsible for the Budget: MARIMPA SAMOURA.

Minister-delegate at the Ministry of Territorial Administration and Decentralization, responsible for Decentralization: DEMBA TRAORÉ.

In addition, there were three special advisers with ministerial rank.

MINISTRIES

Office of the President: BP 1463, Koulouba, Bamako; tel. 2022-2572; fax 2023-0026; internet www.koulouba.pr.ml.

Office of the Prime Minister: Quartier du Fleuve, BP 790, Bamako; tel. 2022-4310; fax 2023-9595; e-mail ecrireaupm@primature.gov.ml; internet www.primature.gov.ml.

Office of the Secretary-General of the Government: BP 14, Koulouba, Bamako; tel. 2022-2552; fax 2022-7050; e-mail sgg@sgg.gov.ml; internet www.sgg.gov.ml.

Ministry of Agriculture, Stockbreeding and Fisheries: BP 1676, Bamako; tel. 2022-2785; e-mail ministere@ma.gov.ml; internet www.maliagriculture.org.

Ministry of the Civil Service, Governance and Administrative and Political Reform: Bamako.

Ministry of Communication, Posts and New Technologies: ave de l'Yser, Quartier du Fleuve, BP 116, Bamako; tel. and fax 2022-2054.

Ministry of Crafts, Culture and Tourism: Badalabougou, Semagesco, BP 2211, Bamako; tel. 2029-6450; fax 2029-3917; e-mail malitourisme@afribone.net.ml; internet www.malitourisme.com.

Ministry of Defence and Veterans: route de Koulouba, BP 2083, Bamako; tel. 2022-5021; fax 2023-2318.

Ministry of the Economy, Finance and the Budget: Bamako; internet www.finances.gov.ml.

Ministry of Education, Literacy and the Promotion of the National Languages: Bamako.

Ministry of Energy, Water and the Environment: Bamako.

Ministry of Equipment, Transport, Housing and Town Planning: Bamako; tel. 2022-3937.

Ministry of the Family, the Promotion of Women and Children: porte G9, rue 109, Badalabougou, BP 2688, Bamako; tel. 2022-6659; fax 2023-6660; e-mail mpfef@cefib.com; internet www.mpfef.gov.ml.

Ministry of Foreign Affairs and International Co-operation: Koulouba, Bamako; tel. 2022-8314; fax 2022-5226.

Ministry of Health: BP 232, Koulouba, Bamako; tel. 2022-5302; fax 2023-0203.

Ministry of Higher Education and Scientific Research: BP 71, Bamako; tel. 2022-5780; fax 2022-2126; e-mail info@education.gov.ml; internet www.education.gov.ml.

Ministry of Humanitarian Action, Solidarity and the Elderly: Bamako; tel. 2023-2301.

Ministry of Internal Security and Civil Protection: BP E 4771, Bamako; tel. 2022-0082.

Ministry of Justice: Quartier du Fleuve, BP 97, Bamako; tel. 2022-2642; fax 2023-0063; e-mail ucprodej@afribone.net.ml; internet www.justicemali.org.

Ministry of Malians Abroad and African Integration: Cité du Niger, route de l'Hotel Mandé, Bamako; tel. 2021-8148; fax 2021-2505; e-mail maliensdelexterieur@yahoo.fr; internet www.maliensdelexterieur.gov.ml.

Ministry of Territorial Administration, Decentralization and Land Affairs: face Direction de la RCFM, BP 78, Bamako; tel. 2022-4212; fax 2023-0247; internet www.matcl.gov.ml.

Ministry of Trade, Mining and Industry: BP 234, Koulouba, Bamako; tel. 2022-5156; fax 2022-0192.

Ministry of Sports: route de Koulouba, BP 91, Bamako; tel. 2022-3153; fax 2023-9067; e-mail mjsports@mjsports.gov.ml; internet www.mjsports.gov.ml.

Ministry of Youth, Labour, Employment and Professional Training: Bamako; tel. 2022-3180.

President and Legislature

PRESIDENT

Presidential Election, 29 April 2007

Candidate	Votes	% of votes
Gen. (retd) Amadou Toumani Touré (Independent)	1,612,912	71.20
Ibrahim Boubacar Keïta (RPM)	433,897	19.15
Tiébilé Dramé (PARENA)	68,956	3.04
Oumar Mariko (SADI)	61,670	2.72
Others	88,048	3.89
Total	2,265,483	100.00

LEGISLATURE

Assemblée nationale

BP 284, Bamako; tel. 2021-5724; fax 2021-0374; e-mail mamou@blonba.malinet.ml.

President: DIONCOUNDA TRAORÉ.

General Election, 1 and 22 July 2007

Party	Seats
Alliance pour la Démocratie au Mali—Parti Pan-africain pour la Liberté, la Solidarité et la Justice (ADEMA)	51
Union pour la République et la Démocratie (URD)	34
Rassemblement pour le Mali (RPM)	11
Mouvement Patriotique pour le Renouveau (MPR)	8
Congrès National d'Initiative Démocratique—Faso Yiriwa Ton (CNID)	7
Parti pour la Renaissance Nationale (PARENA)	4
Parti de la Solidarité Africaine pour la Démocratie et l'Indépendance (SADI)	4
Union pour la Démocratie et le Développement (UDD)	3
Bloc des Alternances pour le Renouveau, l'Intégration et la Coopération Africaine (BARICA)	2
Mouvement pour l'Iindépendance, la Renaissance et l'Intégration Africaine (MIRIA)	2
Parti de la Solidarité et du Progrès (PSP)	2
Bloc pour la Démocratie et l'Intégration Africaine—Faso Jigi (BDIA)	1
Parti Citoyen pour le Renouveau (PCR)	1
Rassemblement National pour la Démocratie (RND)	1
Union Soudanaise—Rassemblement Démocratique Africain (US—RDA)	1
Independents	15
Total	147

Election Commission

Commission Électorale Nationale Indépendante (CENI): Bamako; Pres. MAMADOU DIAMOUTANI.

Advisory Councils

Economic, Social and Cultural Council: BP E 15, Koulouba, Bamako; tel. 2022-4368; fax 2022-8452; e-mail cesc@cefib.com; internet www.cesc.org.ml; f. 1987; Pres. JEAMILLE BITTAR.

High Council of Communities: Bamako; compulsorily advises the Govt on issues relating to local and regional devt; comprises national councillors, elected indirectly for a term of five years; Pres. OUMAROU AG MOHAMED IBRAHIM HAÏDARA.

Political Organizations

In 2007 there were 94 political parties officially registered in Mali, the most active of which included:

Alliance pour la Démocratie au Mali—Parti Pan-africain pour la Liberté, la Solidarité et la Justice (ADEMA): rue Fankélé, porte 145, BP 1791, Bamako-Coura; tel. 2022-0368; internet www.adema-pasj.org; f. 1990 as Alliance pour la Démocratie au Mali; Pres. DIONCOUNDA TRAORÉ; Sec.-Gen. MARIMATIA DIARRA.

Bloc des Alternances pour le Renouveau, l'Intégration et la Coopération Africaine (BARICA): Bamako.

Bloc pour la Démocratie et l'Intégration Africaine—Faso Jigi (BDIA): Bolibana, rue 376, porte 83, BP E 2833, Bamako-Coura; tel. 2023-8202; f. 1993; liberal, democratic; Leader SOULEYMANE MAKAMBA DOUMBIA.

Congrès National d'Initiative Démocratique—Faso Yiriwa Ton (CNID): rue 426, porte 58, Niarela, BP 2572, Bamako; tel. 2021-4275; fax 2023-1861; e-mail mc_tall@hotmail.com; internet www.cnidmali.net; f. 1991; Chair. Me MOUNTAGA TALL; Sec.-Gen. Dr AMADOU SY.

Convention Démocratique et Sociale (CDS): Ouolofobougou-Bolibana, rue 417, porte 46, Bamako; tel. 2029-2625; f. 1996; Chair. MAMADOU BAKARY SANGARÉ.

Convention Parti du Peuple (COPP): Korofina nord, BP 9012, Bamako; fax 2021-3591; e-mail lawyergakou@datatech.toolnet.org; f. 1996; Pres. Me MAMADOU GACKOU.

Mouvement pour l'Indépendance, la Renaissance et l'Intégration Africaine (MIRIA): Dravéla, Bolibana, rue 417, porte 66, Bamako; tel. 2029-2981; fax 2029-2979; e-mail miria12002@yahoo.fr; f. 1994 following split in ADEMA; Pres. MAMADOU KASSA TRAORÉ.

Mouvement National de Libération de l'Azawad (MNLA): internet www.mnlamov.net; f. 2011; Touareg movement seeking independence for the Azawad region; Gen. Sec. BILAL AG ACHERIF.

Mouvement Patriotique pour le Renouveau (MPR): Quinzambougou, BP E 1108, Bamako; tel. 2021-5546; fax 2021-5543; f. 1995; Pres. Dr CHOGUEL KOKALA MAÏGA.

Parti Citoyen pour le Renouveau (PCR): Niaréla II, rue 428, porte 592, Bamako; tel. 6672-0988; internet pcrmali.net; f. 2005; Pres. OUSMANE BEN FANA TRAORÉ.

Parti de la Solidarité Africaine pour la Démocratie et l'Indépendance (SADI): Djélibougou, rue 246, porte 559, BP 3140, Bamako; tel. 2024-1004; f. 2002; Leader CHEICK OUMAR SISSOKO.

Parti de la Solidarité et du Progrès (PSP): rue 552, porte 255, Quinzambougou, Bamako; tel. 2021-9960; f. 1945; Pres. OUMAR HAMMADOUN DICKO.

Parti pour la Démocratie et le Progrès/Parti Socialiste (PDP/PS): Korofina sud, rue 96, porte 437, Bamako; tel. 2024-1675; fax 2020-2314; f. 1991; Leader FRANÇOIS KABORÉ.

Parti pour le Développement Économique et la Solidarité (PDES): Bamako; internet www.pdesmali.net; f. 2010; Pres. HAMED DIANE SÉMÉGA.

Parti pour la Renaissance Nationale (PARENA): rue Soundiata, porte 1397, BP E 2235, Ouolofobougou, Bamako; tel. 2023-4954; fax 2022-2908; e-mail info@parena.org.ml; internet www.parena.org.ml; f. 1995 following split in CNID; Pres. TIÉBILÉ DRAMÉ; Sec.-Gen. AMIDOU DIABATÉ.

Parti pour l'Indépendance, la Démocratie et la Solidarité (PIDS): Hippodrome, rue 250, porte 1183, BP E 1515, Bamako; tel. 2077-4575; f. 2001 by dissidents from US—RDA; Pres. DABA DIAWARA.

Rassemblement National pour la Démocratie (RND): Niaréla, route Sotuba, porte 1892, Hamdallaye, Bamako; tel. 2029-1849; fax 2029-0939; f. 1997 by 'moderate' breakaway group from RDP; Pres. ABDOULAYE GARBA TAPO.

Rassemblement pour la Démocratie et le Progrès (RDP): Niarela, rue 485, porte 11, BP 2110, Bamako; tel. 2021-3092; fax 2024-6795; f. 1991.

Rassemblement pour le Mali (RPM): Hippodrome, rue 232, porte 130, BP 9057, Bamako; tel. 2021-1433; fax 2021-1336; e-mail siegerpmbko@yahoo.fr; internet www.rpm.org.ml; f. 2001; Pres. IBRAHIM BOUBACAR KEÏTA; Sec.-Gen. Dr BOCARY TRETA.

Union des Forces Démocratiques pour le Progrès—Sama-ton (UFDP): Quartier Mali, BP E 37, Bamako; tel. 2023-1766; f. 1991; Sec.-Gen. Col YOUSSOUF TRAORÉ.

Union pour la Démocratie et le Développement (UDD): ave OUA, porte 3626, Sogoniko, BP 2969, Bamako; tel. 2020-3971; f. 1991; Leader Me HASSANE BARRY.

Union pour la République et la Démocratie (URD): Niaréla, rue 268, porte 41, Bamako; tel. 2021-8642; e-mail contact@urd-mali.net; internet www.urd-mali.net; f. 2003; Pres. SOUMAÏLA CISSÉ.

Union Soudanaise—Rassemblement Démocratique Africain (US—RDA): Hippodrome, porte 41, BP E 1413, Bamako; tel. and fax 2021-4522; f. 1946; sole party 1960–68, banned 1968–91; 'moderate' faction split from party in 1998; Leader Dr BADARA ALIOU MACALOU.

Diplomatic Representation

EMBASSIES IN MALI

Algeria: Daoudabougou, BP 02, Bamako; tel. 2020-5176; fax 2022-9374; Ambassador NOUREDDINE AYADI.

Brazil: rue 113, porte 62, Badalabougou Ouest, Bamako; tel. 2022-9817; fax 2022-9906; Ambassador JEORGE JOSÉ FRANTZ RAMOS.

Burkina Faso: ACI-2000, Commune III, BP 9022, Bamako; tel. 2023-3171; fax 2021-9266; e-mail ambafaso@experco.net; Ambassador Prof. SANNÉ MOHAMED TOPAN.

Canada: route de Koulikoro, Immeuble Séméga, Hippodrome, BP 198, Bamako; tel. 2021-2236; fax 2021-4362; e-mail bmako@international.gc.ca; internet www.bamako.gc.ca; Ambassador VIRGINIE SAINT-LOUIS.

China, People's Republic: route de Koulikoro, Hippodrome, BP 112, Bamako; tel. 2021-3597; fax 2022-3443; e-mail chinaemb_ml@mfa.gov.cn; internet ml.china-embassy.org/fra; Ambassador CAO ZHONGMING.

Côte d'Ivoire: square Patrice Lumumba, Immeuble CNAR, 3e étage, BP E 3644, Bamako; tel. 2022-0389; fax 2022-1376; Ambassador SAMUEL OUATTARA.

Cuba: porte 31, rue 328, Niarela, Bamako; tel. 2021-0289; fax 2021-0293; e-mail emcuba.mali@orangemali.net; internet emba.cubaminrex.cu/malifr; Ambassador SIDENIO ACOSTA ADAY.

Denmark: Immeuble UATT, 2ème étage, Quartier du Fleuve, BP E 1733, Bamako; tel. 2023-0377; fax 2023-0194; e-mail bkoamb@um.dk; internet mali.um.dk; Chargé d'affaires ANDERS GARLY ANDERSEN.

Egypt: Badalabougou-est, BP 44, Bamako; tel. 2022-3565; fax 2022-0891; e-mail mostafa@datatech.net.ml; Ambassador HAMED AHMED CHOUKRY HAMED.

France: square Patrice Lumumba, BP 17, Bamako; tel. 4497-5757; fax 2022-3136; e-mail ambassade@france-mali.org.ml; internet www.ambafrance-ml.org; Ambassador CHRISTIAN ROUYER.

Germany: Badalabougou-est, rue 14, porte 330, BP 100, Bamako; tel. 2070-0770; fax 2022-9650; e-mail allemagne@orangemali.net; internet www.bamako.diplo.de; Ambassador KARL FLITTNER.

Ghana: BP 3161, Bamako; Ambassador DONALD ADABERE ADABRE.

Guinea: Immeuble Saybou Maïga, Quartier du Fleuve, BP 118, Bamako; tel. 2022-3007; fax 2021-0806; Ambassador OUSMANE KONATÉ.

India: 101 ave de l'OUA, Badalabougou Est, Bamako; tel. 2023-5420; fax 2023-5417; e-mail hoc.bamako@mea.gov.in; f. 2009; Ambassador K. JOSEPH FRANCIS.

Iran: ave al-Quds, Hippodrome, BP 2136, Bamako; tel. 2021-7638; fax 2021-0731; Chargé d'affaires ABOLMOUHSEN SHARIF MOHAMMADI.

Japan: rue 43 porte 407, Cité du Niger, BP E4227, Bamako; tel. 2070-0150; fax 2021-7785; internet www.ml.emb-japan.go.jp; Ambassador MASAHIRO KAWADA.

Korea, Democratic People's Republic: Bamako; Ambassador KIM PONG HUI.

Libya: Badalabougou-ouest, face Palais de la Culture, BP 1670, Bamako; tel. 2022-3496; fax 2022-6697; Ambassador Dr ALI MUHAMMAD ALMAGOURI.

Mauritania: route de Koulikoro, Hippodrome, BP 135, Bamako; tel. 2021-4815; fax 2022-4908; e-mail ambarimbko@yahoo.fr; Ambassador SIDI MOHAMED OULD HANANA.

Morocco: Badalabougou-est, rue 25, porte 80, BP 2013, Bamako; tel. 2022-2123; fax 2022-7787; e-mail sifamali@afribone.net.ml; Ambassador HASSAN NACIRI.

Netherlands: rue 437, BP 2220, Hippodrome, Bamako; tel. 2021-9572; fax 2021-3617; e-mail bam@minbuza.nl; internet www.mfa.nl; Ambassador MAARTEN BROUWER.

Nigeria: Badalabougou-est, BP 57, Bamako; tel. 2021-5328; fax 2022-3974; e-mail ngrbko@malinet.ml; Ambassador ILIYA ALI DUNIYA NUHU.

Russia: BP 300, Niarela, Bamako; tel. 2021-5592; fax 2021-9926; e-mail ambrusse_mali@orangemali.net; Ambassador ALEXEY G. DOULIAN.

Saudi Arabia: Villa Bal Harbour, 28 Cité du Niger, BP 81, Bamako; tel. 2021-2528; fax 2021-5064; e-mail mlemb@mofa.gov.sa; Ambassador NAHID BIN ABDULRAHMAN AL-HARBI.

Senegal: porte 341, rue 287, angle ave Nelson Mandela, BP 42, Bamako; tel. 2021-0859; fax 2016-9268; Ambassador (vacant).

South Africa: bât. Diarra, Hamdallaye, ACI-2000, BP 2015, Bamako; tel. 2029-2925; fax 2029-2926; e-mail bamako@foreign.gov.za; Ambassador R. W. MOKOU.

Spain: porte 81, rue 13, Badalabougou-est, BP 3230, Bamako; tel. 2023-6527; fax 2023-6524; e-mail emb.bamako@maec.es; Ambassador Dr LOURDES MELÉNDEZ GARCÍA.

Tunisia: Quartier du Fleuve, Bamako; tel. 2023-2891; fax 2022-1755; Ambassador TAREK BEN SALEM.

Turkey: Cité du Niger, M-105/112, Niarela, Bamako; tel. 7770-0007; e-mail ambassade.bamako@mfa.gov.tr; internet bamako.be.mfa.gov.tr; Ambassador KEMAL KAYGISIZ.

USA: ACI 2000, rue 243, porte 297, Bamako; tel. 2070-2300; fax 2070-2479; e-mail webmaster@usa.org.ml; internet mali.usembassy.gov; Ambassador MARY BETH LEONARD.

Venezuela: Badalabougou Ouest, Bamako; tel. 2023-2531; fax 2023-2534; Ambassador JOHNY ERREDDY BALZA ARISMENDI.

Judicial System

The 1992 Constitution guarantees the independence of the judiciary.

High Court of Justice: Bamako; competent to try the President of the Republic and ministers of the Government for high treason and for crimes committed in the course of their duties, and their accomplices in any case where state security is threatened; mems designated by the mems of the Assemblée nationale, and renewed annually.

Supreme Court: BP 7, Bamako; tel. 2022-2406; e-mail csupreme@afribone.net.ml; internet www.cs.insti.ml; f. 1969; comprises judicial, administrative and auditing sections; judicial section comprises five chambers, administrative section comprises two chambers, auditing section comprises three chambers; Pres. NOUHOUM TAPILY; Sec.-Gen. MAMA SININTA.

President of the Bar: Me MAGATTÉ SÈYE.

Constitutional Court: Hamdallaye ACI 2000, Commune IV, BP E 213, Bamako; tel. 2022-5609; fax 2023-4241; e-mail tawatybouba@yahoo.fr; internet www.cc.insti.ml; f. 1994; Pres. AMADI TAMBA CAMARA; Sec.-Gen. BOUBACAR TAWATY.

There are three Courts of Appeal, seven Tribunaux de Première Instance (Magistrates' Courts) and also courts for labour disputes.

Religion

According to UN figures, around 80% of the population are Muslims, while 18% follow traditional animist beliefs and under 2% are Christians.

ISLAM

Association Malienne pour l'Unité et le Progrès de l'Islam (AMUPI): Bamako; state-endorsed Islamic governing body.

Chief Mosque: pl. de la République, Bagadadji, Bamako; tel. 2021-2190.

Haut Conseil Islamique: Bamako; f. 2002; responsible for management of relations between the Muslim communities and the State; Pres. MAHMOUD DICKO.

CHRISTIANITY

The Roman Catholic Church

Mali comprises one archdiocese and five dioceses. Approximately 2% of the total population practices Roman Catholicism.

Bishops' Conference

Conférence Episcopale du Mali, Archevêché, BP 298, Bamako; tel. 2222-5499; fax 2222-5214; e-mail cemali@afribone.net.ml.

f. 1973; Pres. Most Rev. JEAN-BAPTISTE TIAMA (Bishop of Sikasso).

Archbishop of Bamako: JEAN ZERBO, Archevêché, BP 298, Bamako; tel. 2222-5842; fax 2222-7850; e-mail mgrjeanzerbo@afribonemali.net.

Other Christian Churches

There are several Protestant mission centres, mainly administered by US societies.

BAHÁ'Í FAITH

National Spiritual Assembly: BP 1657, Bamako; e-mail ntirandaz@aol.com.

The Press

The 1992 Constitution guarantees the freedom of the press.

DAILY NEWSPAPERS

Les Echos: Hamdallaye, ave Cheick Zayed, porte 2694, BP 2043, Bamako; tel. 2029-6289; fax 2026-7639; e-mail lesechos@jamana.org; internet www.jamana.org/lesechos; f. 1989; daily; publ. by Jamana cultural co-operative; circ. 30,000; Dir ALEXIS KALAMBRY; Editor-in-Chief ABOUBACAR SALIPH DIARRA.

L'Essor: square Patrice Lumumba, BP 141, Bamako; tel. 2022-3683; fax 2022-4774; e-mail info@essor.gov.ml; internet www.essor.gov.ml; f. 1949; daily; pro-Govt newspaper; Editor SALIM TOGOLA; circ. 3,500.

Info Matin: 56 rue 350, Bamako Coura, BP E 4020, Bamako; tel. 7541–4141; fax 2023-8227; e-mail redaction@info-matin.com; internet www.info-matin.com; independent; Dir of Publication and Editor-in-Chief SAMBI TOURÉ.

Le Républicain: 116 rue 400, Dravéla-Bolibana, BP 1484, Bamako; tel. 2029-0900; fax 2029-0933; internet lerepublicain-mali.com; f. 1992; independent; Dir SALIF KONÉ.

PERIODICALS

26 Mars: Badalabougou-Sema Gesco, Lot S13, BP MA 174, Bamako; tel. 2029-0459; f. 1998; weekly; independent; Dir BOUBACAR SANGARÉ.

L'Aurore: Niarela 298, rue 438, BP 3150, Bamako; tel. and fax 2021-6922; e-mail aurore@timbagga.com.ml; f. 1990; 2 a week; independent; Dir KARAMOKO N'DIAYE.

Le Canard Déchaîné: Immeuble Koumara, bloc 104, Centre Commercial, Bamako; tel. 7621-2686; fax 2022-86-86; e-mail maison.presse@afribone.net.ml; weekly; satirical; Dir OUMAR BABI; circ. 3,000 (2006).

Le Carrefour: ave Cheick Zayed, Hamdallaye, Bamako; tel. 2023-9808; e-mail journalcarrefour@yahoo.fr; f. 1997; Dir MAHAMANE IMRANE COULIBALY.

Le Continent: AA 16, Banankabougou, BP E 4338, Bamako; tel. and fax 2029-5739; e-mail le_continent@yahoo.fr; f. 2000; weekly; Dir IBRAHIMA TRAORÉ.

Le Courrier: 230 ave Cheick Zayed, Lafiabougou Marché, BP 1258, Bamako; tel. and fax 2029-1862; e-mail journalcourrier@webmails.com; f. 1996; weekly; Dir SADOU A. YATTARA; also *Le Courrier Magazine*, monthly.

L'Indépendant: Immeuble ABK, Hamdallaye ACI, BP E 1040, Bamako; tel. and fax 2023-2727; e-mail independant@cefib.com; 2 a week; Dir El Hadj SAOUTI LABASS HAÏDARA.

L'Inspecteur: Immeuble Nimagala, bloc 262, BP E 4534, Bamako; tel. 6672-4711; e-mail inspecteurmali@yahoo.fr; f. 1992; weekly; Dir ALY DIARRA.

Jamana—Revue Culturelle Malienne: BP 2043, Bamako; BP E 1040; e-mail infos@jamana.org; f. 1983; quarterly; organ of Jamana cultural co-operative.

Journal Officiel de la République du Mali: Koulouba, BP 14, Bamako; tel. 2022-5986; fax 2022-7050; official gazette.

Kabaaru: Village Kibaru, Bozola, BP 24, Bamako; f. 1983; state-owned; monthly; Fulbé (Peul) language; rural interest; Editor BARRY BELCO MOUSSA; circ. 3,000.

Kibaru: Village Kibaru, Bozola, BP 1463, Bamako; f. 1972; monthly; state-owned; Bambara and three other languages; rural interest; Editor NIANZÉ SAMAKÉ; circ. 5,000.

Liberté: Immeuble Sanago, Hamdallaye Marché, BP E 24, Bamako; tel. 2028-1898; e-mail ladji.guindo@cefib.com; f. 1999; weekly; Dir ABDOULAYE LADJI GUINDO.

Le Malien: rue 497, porte 277, Badialan III, BP E 1558, Bamako; tel. 2023-5729; fax 2029-1339; e-mail lemalien2000@yahoo.fr; f. 1993; weekly; Dir SIDI KEITA.

Match: 97 rue 498, Lafiabougou, BP E 3776, Bamako; tel. 2029-1882; e-mail bcissouma@yahoo.fr; f. 1997; 2 a month; sports; Dir BABA CISSOUMA.

Musow: BP E 449, Bamako; tel. 2028-0000; fax 2028-0001; e-mail musow@musow.com; internet www.musow.com; women's interest.

Nyéléni Magazine: Niarela 298, rue 348, BP 13150, Bamako; tel. 2029-2401; f. 1991; monthly; women's interest; Dir MAÏMOUNA TRAORÉ.

L'Observateur: Galérie Djigué, rue du 18 juin, BP E 1002, Bamako; tel. and fax 2023-0689; e-mail belcotamboura@hotmail.com; f. 1992; 2 a week; Dir BELCO TAMBOURA.

Le Reflet: Immeuble Kanadjigui, route de Koulikoro, Boulkassoumbougou, BP E 1688, Bamako; tel. 2024-3952; fax 2023-2308; e-mail lereflet@afribone.malinet.ml; weekly; fmrly *Le Carcan*; present name adopted Jan. 2001; Dir ABDOUL KARIM DRAMÉ.

Royal Sports: BP 98, Sikasso; tel. 6672-4988; weekly; also *Tatou Sports*, publ. monthly; Pres. and Dir-Gen. ALY TOURÉ.

Le Scorpion: 230 ave Cheick Zayed, Lafiabougou Marché, BP 1258, Bamako; tel. and fax 2029-1862; f. 1991; weekly; Dir MAHAMANE HAMÈYE CISSÉ.

Le Tambour: rue 497, porte 295, Badialan III, BP E 289, Bamako; tel. and fax 2022-7568; e-mail tambourj@yahoo.fr; f. 1994; 2 a week; Dir YÉRO DIALLO.

NEWS AGENCY

Agence Malienne de Presse et de Publicité (AMAP): square Patrice Lumumba, BP 141, Bamako; tel. 2022-3683; fax 2022-4774; e-mail amap@afribone.net.ml; internet www.amap.ml; f. 1977; Dir SOULEYMANE DRABO.

PRESS ASSOCIATIONS

Association des Editeurs de la Presse Privée (ASSEP): BP E 1002, Bamako; tel. 6671-3133; e-mail belcotamboura@hotmail.com; Pres. DRAMANE ALIOU KONÉ.

Association des Journalistes Professionels des Médias Privés du Mali (AJPM): BP E 2456, Bamako; tel. 2022-1915; fax 2023-5478; Pres. MOMADOU FOFANA.

Association des Professionnelles Africaines de la Communication (APAC MALI): porte 474, rue 428, BP E 731, Bamako; tel. 2021-2912; Pres. MASSIRÉ YATTASSAYE.

Maison de la Presse de Mali: 17 rue 619, Darsalam, BP E 2456, Bamako; tel. 2022-1915; fax 2023-5478; e-mail maison.presse@afribone.net.ml; internet www.mediamali.org; independent media assen; Pres. SADOU A. YATTARA.

Union Interprofessionnelle des Journalistes et de la Presse de Langue Française (UIJPLF): rue 42, Hamdallaye Marché, BP 1258, Bamako; tel. 2029-9835; Pres. MAHAMANE HAMÉYE CISSÉ.

Union Nationale des Journalistes Maliens (UNAJOM): BP 1300, Bamako; tel. 2022-1915; fax 2023-5478; e-mail ibrafam@yahoo.fr; Pres. IBRAHIM FAMAKAN COULIBALY.

Publishers

EDIM SA: ave Kassé Keïta, BP 21, Bamako; tel. 2022-4041; fax 2029-3001; e-mail edim@afribone.net.ml; f. 1972 as Editions Imprimeries du Mali; general fiction and non-fiction, textbooks; Chair. and Man. Dir ALOU TOMOTA.

Editions Donniya: Cité du Niger, BP 1273, Bamako; tel. 2021-4646; fax 2021-9031; e-mail imprimcolor@cefib.com; internet www.imprimcolor.cefib.com; f. 1996; general fiction, history, reference and children's books in French and Bambara.

Le Figuier: 151 rue 56, Semal, BP 2605, Bamako; tel. and fax 2023-3211; e-mail lefiguier@afribone.net.ml; f. 1997; fiction and non-fiction.

Editions Jamana: BP 2043, Bamako; tel. 2029-6289; fax 2029-7639; e-mail jamana@timbagga.com.ml; internet www.jamana.org; f. 1988; literary fiction, poetry, reference; Dir BA MAÏRA SOW.

Editions Teriya: BP 1677, Bamako; tel. 2024-1142; theatre, literary fiction; Dir GAOUSSOU DIAWARA.

Broadcasting and Communications

TELECOMMUNICATIONS

At the end of 2011 there were two telecommunications companies in Mali, both of which provided mobile and fixed-line telephone services. In January 2012 a third licence to provide mobile telephone services was awarded to a consortium of Planor and Monaco Telecom. In 2010 there were 80,148 subscribers to fixed-line telephone services and 7.4m. subscribers to mobile telephone services.

Regulatory Authority

Comité de Régulation des Télécommunications (CRT): ACI 2000 Hamdallaye, rue 390, porte 1849, BP 2206, Bamako; tel. 2023-1490; fax 2023-1494; e-mail crtmali@crt.ml; internet www.crt-mali.org; f. 1999; Dir Dr CHOGUEL K. MAÏGA.

Service Providers

Orange Mali SA: Immeuble Orange Mali, Hamdallaye, ACI-2000, BP E 3991, Bamako; tel. 4499-9903; fax 4499-9001; e-mail orange@orangemali.com; internet www.orangemali.com; f. 2003 as Ikatel; repackaged under brand name Orange in 2007; fixed-line and mobile cellular telecommunications; jtly owned by France Télécom and Société Nationale des Télécommunications du Sénégal; Dir-Gen. JEAN-LUC BOHÉ; 1,097 fixed lines and 4.7m. subscribers to mobile cellular telecommunications services (2010).

Société des Télécommunications du Mali—Malitel (SOTELMA): Quartier du Fleuve, près de la BCEAO, BP 740, Bamako; tel. 2021-5280; fax 2021-3022; e-mail segal@sotelma.ml; internet www.sotelma.ml; f. 1990; 51% owned by Itissalat al-Maghrib—Maroc Télécom (Morocco), 20% state-owned; operates fixed-line telephone services, also mobile and cellular telecommunications under the brand name Malitel in Bamako, Kayes, Mopti, Ségou and Sikasso; 79,051 fixed lines and 2.69m. subscribers to mobile cellular telecommunications services (2010); Dir-Gen. NOREDDINE BOUMZEBRA.

BROADCASTING

Radio

Office de Radiodiffusion-Télévision Malienne (ORTM): 287 rue de la Marne, BP 171, Bamako; tel. 2021-2019; fax 2021-4205; e-mail ortm@ortm.ml; internet www.ortm-mali.tv; Dir-Gen. BALLY IDRISSA SISSOKO; Dir of Radio SEYDOU BABA TRAORÉ.

Radio Mali–Chaîne Nationale: BP 171, Bamako; tel. 2021-2019; fax 2021-4205; e-mail ortm@spider.toolnet.org; f. 1957; state-owned; radio programmes in French, Bambara, Peul, Sarakolé, Tamashek, Sonrai, Moorish, Wolof, English.

Chaîne 2: Bamako; f. 1993; radio broadcasts to Bamako.

In 2010 there were an estimated 400 community, commercial and religious radio stations broadcasting in Mali. Signals from Radio France International, the Voice of America, Radio Chine Internationale, the British Broadcasting Corporation (BBC) and Deutsche Welle are also received.

Fréquence 3: Bamako; f. 1992; commercial.

Radio Balanzan: BP 419, Ségou; tel. 2132-0288; commercial.

Radio Bamakan: Marché de Médine, BP E 100, Bamako; tel. and fax 2021-2760; e-mail radio.bamakan@ifrance.com; internet bamakan.net; f. 1991; community station; 104 hours of FM broadcasts weekly; Man. MODIBO DIALLO.

Radio Espoir—La Voix du Salut: Sogoniko, rue 130, porte 71, BP E 1399, Bamako; tel. 2020-6708; e-mail accm@mali.maf.net; f. 1998; broadcasts 16 hours of radio programming daily on topics including Christianity, devt and culture; Dir DAOUDA COULIBALY.

Radio Foko de Ségou Jamana: BP 2043, Bamako; tel. 2132-0048; fax 2022-7639; e-mail radiofoko@cefib.com.

Radio Guintan: Magnambougou, BP 2546, Bamako; tel. 2020-0938; f. 1994; community radio station; Dir RAMATA DIA.

Radio Jamana: BP 2043, Bamako; tel. 2029-6289; fax 2029-7639; e-mail radio@jamana.org; internet www.jamana.org.

Radio Kayira: Djélibougou Doumanzana, BP 3140, Bamako; tel. 2024-8782; fax 2022-7568; internet www.kayira.org; f. 1992; community station; Dir OUMAR MARIKO.

Radio Klédu: Cité du Niger, BP 2322, Bamako; tel. 2021-0018; e-mail rkledudirect@cefib.com; internet www.kleducommunication.com; f. 1992; commercial; Dir-Gen. JACQUES DEZ.

Radio Liberté: BP 5015, Bamako; tel. 2023-0581; f. 1991; commercial station broadcasting 24 hours daily; Dir ALMANY TOURÉ.

Radio Patriote: Korofina-Sud, BP E 1406, Bamako; tel. 2024-2292; f. 1995; commercial station; Dir MOUSSA KEÏTA.

Radio Rurale de Kayes: Plateau, BP 94, Kayes; tel. 2158-0081; e-mail rrk@afribone.net.ml; internet www.radioruraledekayes.net; f. 1988; community stations established by the Agence de Coopération Culturelle et Technique (ACTT); transmitters in Niono, Kadiolo, Bandiagara and Kidal; Dir FILY KEÏTA.

Radio Sahel: BP 394, Kayes; tel. 2152-2187; f. 1991; commercial; Dir ALMAMY S. TOURÉ.

Radio Tabalé: Bamako-Coura, BP 697, Bamako; tel. and fax 2022-7870; internet www.radiotabale.org; f. 1992; independent public-service station; broadcasting 57 hours weekly; Dir TIÉMOKO KONÉ.

La Voix du Coran et du Hadit: Grande Mosquée, BP 2531, Bamako; tel. 2021-6344; f. 1993; Islamic station broadcasting on FM in Bamako; Dir El Hadj MAHMOUD DICKO.

Radio Wassoulou: BP 24, Yanfolila; tel. 2165-1097; internet wassoulou.radio.org.ml; commercial.

Television

Office de Radiodiffusion-Télévision Malienne (ORTM): see Radio; a second channel, Télévision Malienne 2, was launched on 31 December 2011; Dir of Television BALY IDRISSA SISSOKO.

Multicanal SA: Quinzambougou, BP E 1506, Bamako; tel. 2020-2929; e-mail sandrine@multi-canal.com; internet www.multi-canal.com; private subscription broadcaster; relays international broadcasts; Pres. ISMAÏLA SIDIBÉ; Dir-Gen. MOHAMED KEITA.

TV Klédu: 600 ave Modibo Keïta, BP E 1172, Bamako; tel. 2023-9000; fax 2023-7050; e-mail info@tvkledu.com; private cable TV operator; relays international broadcasts; Pres. MAMADOU COULIBALY.

Finance

(cap. = capital; res = reserves; dep. = deposits; m. = million; br(s). = branch(es); amounts in francs CFA)

BANKING

In 2009 there were 13 banks and four other financial institutions in Mali.

Central Bank

Banque Centrale des Etats de l'Afrique de l'Ouest (BCEAO): ave Moussa Travele, BP 206, Bamako; tel. 2022-2541; fax 2022-4786; internet www.bceao.int; f. 1962; HQ in Dakar, Senegal; bank of issue for the mem. states of Union Economique et Monétaire Ouest-Africaine (UEMOA, comprising Benin, Burkina Faso, Côte d'Ivoire, Guinea-Bissau, Mali, Niger, Senegal and Togo); cap. 134,120m., res 1,474,195m., dep. 2,124,051m. (Dec. 2009); Gov. KONÉ TIÉMOKO MEYLIET; Dir in Mali KONZO TRAORÉ; brs at Mopti and Sikasso.

Commercial Banks

Bank of Africa—Mali (BOA—MALI): 418 ave de la Marné, Bozola, BP 2249, Bamako; tel. 2070-0500; fax 2070-0560; e-mail information@boamali.net; internet www.boamali.com; f. 1983; cap. 5,500.0m., res 5,818.0m., dep. 139,178.2m. (Dec. 2009); Pres. BOUREIMA SYLLA; Dir-Gen. MAMADOU SENE; 18 brs.

Banque Commerciale du Sahel (BCS–SA): ave Bozola 127, BP 2372, Bamako; tel. 2021-0535; fax 2021-1660; e-mail dg@bcss.mali.com; f. 1980; fmrly Banque Arabe Libyo-Malienne pour le Commerce Extérieur et le Développement; 96.61% owned by Libyan-Arab Foreign Bank; cap. 7,500m., res 1,046m., total assets. 37,953m. (Dec. 2006); Pres. KABA DIAMINATOU DIALLO; Dir-Gen. IBRAHIM ABOUJAFAR SWEAI; 1 br.

Banque de l'Habitat du Mali (BHM): ACI 2000, ave Kwamé N'Krumah, BP 2614, Bamako; tel. 2022-9190; fax 2022-9350; e-mail bhm@bhm-sa.com; internet www.bhm-sa.com; f. 1990; present name adopted 1996; 25.8% owned by Institut National de Prévoyance Social; cap. and res 5,414.7m., total assets 98,237.5m. (Dec. 2003); Pres. and Dir-Gen. MODIBO CISSÉ; 5 brs.

Banque Internationale pour le Commerce et l'Industrie au Mali (BICI–Mali): blvd du 22 octobre 1946, Quartier du Fleuve, BP 72, Bamako; tel. 2070-0700; fax 2023-3373; e-mail bicim-dg@africa.bnpparibas.com; f. 1998; 85% owned by BNP Paribas BDDI Participations (France); cap. and res 3,678m., total assets 40,076m. (Dec. 2003); Pres. and Dir-Gen. PIERRE BEREGOVOY; 1 br.

Banque Internationale pour le Mali (BIM): ave de l'Indépendance, BP 15, Bamako; tel. 2022-5066; fax 2022-4566; e-mail bim@bim.com.ml; internet www.bim.com.ml; f. 1980; present name adopted 1995; 51% owned by Attijariwafa Bank Group (Morocco), 10.5% state-owned; cap. 4,254m., dep. 120,250m., total assets 131,159m. (Dec. 2006); Pres. and Dir-Gen. MOHAMMED KRISNI; 14 brs.

Ecobank Mali: Immeuble Amadou Sow, pl. de la Nation, Quartier du Fleuve, BP E 1272, Bamako; tel. 2070-0600; fax 2023-3305; e-mail ecobankml@ecobank.com; internet www.ecobank.com; f. 1998; 49.5% owned by Ecobank Transnational Inc, 17.8% by Ecobank Bénin, 14.9% by Ecobank Togo, 9.9% by Ecobank Burkina; total assets 596m. (Dec. 2011); Pres. SAMBA DIALLO; Dir-Gen. BINTA N'DOYE TOURÉ; 2 brs.

Development Banks

Banque de Développement du Mali (BDM-SA): ave Modibo Keita, Quartier du Fleuve, BP 94, Bamako; tel. 2022-2050; fax 2022-5085; e-mail info@bdm-sa.com; internet www.bdm-sa.com; f. 1968; absorbed Banque Malienne de Crédit et de Dépôts in 2001; 27.38% owned by Banque Marocaine du Commerce Extérieur (Morocco), 19.58% state-owned, 15.96% by BCEAO, 15.96% by Banque ouest-africaine de développement; cap. and res 15,658m., total assets 276,148m. (Dec. 2002); Pres. and Dir-Gen. ABDOULAYE DAFFÉ; 14 brs.

Banque Malienne de Solidarité (BMS): ave du Fleuve, Immeuble Dette Publique, 2e étage, BP 1280, Bamako; tel. and fax 2023-5034; e-mail bms-sa@bms-sa.com; f. 2002; cap. 2.4m.; Dir BABALI BAH; 1 br.

Banque Nationale de Développement Agricole—Mali (BNDA—Mali): Immeuble BNDA, blvd du Mali, ACI 2000, BP 2424, Bamako; tel. 2029-6464; fax 2029-2575; e-mail bnda@bndamali.com; internet www.bndamali.com; f. 1981; 36.5% state-owned, 22.8% owned by Agence Française de Développement (France), 21.4% owned by Deutsche Entwicklungsgesellschaft (Germany), 19.4% owned by BCEAO; cap. 12,096.2m., res

2,059.0m., dep. 125,447.5m. (Dec. 2008); Chair., Pres. and Gen. Man. MOUSSA ALASSAME DIALLO; 22 brs.

Financial Institutions

Direction Générale de la Dette Publique: Immeuble ex-Caisse Autonome d'Amortissement, Quartier du Fleuve, BP 1617, Bamako; tel. 2022-2935; fax 2022-0793; management of the public debt; Dir NAMALA KONÉ.

Equibail Mali: rue 376, porte 1319, Niarela, BP E 566, Bamako; tel. 2021-3777; fax 2021-3778; e-mail equip.ma@bkofafrica.com; f. 1999; 50.2% owned by African Financial Holding, 17.5% by Bank of Africa—Benin; cap. 300m. (Dec. 2002); Mems of Administrative Council RAMATOULAYE TRAORÉ, PAUL DERREUMAUX, LÉON NAKA.

Société Malienne de Financement (SOMAFI): Immeuble Air Afrique, blvd du 22 octobre 1946, BP E 3643, Bamako; tel. 2022-1866; fax 2022-1869; e-mail somafi@malinet.ml; f. 1997; cap. and res 96.9m., total assets 3,844.9m. (Dec. 2002); Man. Dir ERIC LECLÈRE.

STOCK EXCHANGE

Bourse Régionale des Valeurs Mobilières (BRVM): Chambre de Commerce et de l'Industrie du Mali, pl. de la Liberté, BP E 1398, Bamako; tel. 2023-2354; fax 2023-2359; e-mail abocoum@brvm.org; f. 1998; nat. branch of BRVM (regional stock exchange based in Abidjan, Côte d'Ivoire, serving the mem. states of UEMOA); Man. AMADOU DJÉRI BOCOUM.

INSURANCE

Allianz Mali: ave de la Nation, BP E4447, Bamako; tel. 2022-4165; fax 2023-0034; e-mail allianz.mali@allianz-ml.com; internet www.allianz-africa.com/mali/index.php; Dir-Gen. OLIVIER PICARD.

Assurances Lafia: Immeuble Assurances Lafia SA, Hamdallaye ACI 2000, ave du Mali, BP 1542, Bamako; tel. 2029-0940; fax 2029-5223; e-mail info@assurancelafia.com; internet www.assurancelafia.com; f. 1983; cap. 1,000m.; Dir-Gen. AMINATA DEMBÉLÉ CISSÉ; 17 brs.

Caisse Nationale d'Assurance et de Réassurance du Mali (CNAR): square Patrice Lumumba, BP 568, Bamako; tel. 2021-3117; fax 2021-2369; f. 1969; state-owned; cap. 50m.; Dir-Gen. F. KEITA; 10 brs.

Colina Mali SA: ave Modibo Keita, BP E 154, Bamako; tel. 2022-5775; fax 2023-2423; e-mail mali@groupecolina.com; internet www.groupecolina.com/fr/ml; f. 1990; cap. 1,000m.; Dir-Gen. MARCUS K. LABAN.

Compagnie d'Assurance Privée—La Soutra: BP 52, Bamako; tel. 2022-3681; fax 2022-5523; f. 1979; cap. 150m.; Chair. AMADOU NIONO.

Compagnie d'Assurance et de Réassurance de Mali: BP 1822, Bamako; tel. 2022-6029.

Compagnie d'Assurance et de Réassurance Sabu Nyuman: rue 350, porte 129, Bamako-Coura, BP 1822, Bamako; tel. 2022-6029; fax 2022-5750; e-mail assur.sn@malinet.ml; f. 1984; cap. 250m.; Pres. MOMADOU SANOGO; Dir-Gen. YAYA DIARRA.

Gras Savoye Mali: Immeuble SOGEFIH, 3ème etage, Quartier du Fleuve, ave Moussa Travele, BP E 5691, Bamako; tel. 2022-6469; fax 2022-6470; e-mail grassavoyemali@ml.grassavoye.com; affiliated to Gras Savoye (France); Man. FAYEZ SAMB.

Nouvelle Alliance d'Assurance (NALLIAS): BP 12671, Bamako; tel. 2022-2244; fax 2022-9422; e-mail contact@nalliasmali.com; f. 2007; Dir-Gen. CHEIKNA DIAWARA.

Nouvelle Société Interafricaine d'Assurance (NSIA Mali): Immeuble du Patronat, derrière le Gouvernorat, ACI 2000, Bamako; tel. 2023-2440; fax 2023-2441; f. 2009; Dir-Gen. GEORGES ALAIN N'GORAN; also (NSIA Vie Mali) ; Dir-Gen. KODJO SALAMI WOROU.

Société Nouvelle d'Assurance—Vie (SONA—VIE): Immeuble Sonavie, ACI 2000, BP E 2217, Bamako; tel. 2029-5400; fax 2029-5501; e-mail sonavie@cefib.com; internet www.sonavie.com; f. 1996; Dir-Gen. MAMADOU TOURÉ.

Trade and Industry

GOVERNMENT AGENCIES

Agence Nationale pour l'Emploi (ANPE): BP 211, Bamako; tel. 2022-3187; fax 2023-2624; e-mail anpe@anpe-mali.org; internet www.anpe-mali.org; f. 2001; Dir-Gen. Prof. MAKAN MOUSSA SISSOKO.

Agence pour la Promotion des Investissements au Mali (API-Mali): Quartier du fleuve, BP 1980, Bamako; tel. 2022-9525; fax 2022-9527; e-mail contact@apimali.gov.ml; internet www.apimali.gov.ml; f. 2005; CEO MANSOUR HAÏDARA.

Autorité Pour la Promotion de la Recherche Petrolière (AUREP): Médina Coura, rue 28, porte 189, BP E 4306, Bamako; tel. 2021-2948; fax 2021-2882; e-mail diawara.baba@aurep.org; internet www.aurep.org; f. 2003; Dir-Gen. BABA DIAWARA.

Direction Nationale des Affaires Economiques (DNAE): BP 210, Bamako; tel. 2022-2314; fax 2022-2256; involved in economic and social affairs.

Direction Nationale des Travaux Publics (DNTP): ave de la Liberté, BP 1758, Bamako; tel. and fax 2022-2902; administers public works.

Guichet Unique–Direction Nationale des Industries: rue Titi Niare, Quinzambougou, BP 96, Bamako; tel. and fax 2022-3166.

Office National des Produits Pétroliers (ONAP): Quartier du Fleuve, rue 315, porte 141, BP 2070, Bamako; tel. 2022-2827; fax 2022-4483; e-mail onapmali@afribone.net.ml; Dir-Gen. TAPA NOUGA NADIO.

Office du Niger: BP 106, Ségou; tel. 2132-0292; fax 2132-0143; e-mail on@office-du-niger.org.ml; internet www.office-du-niger.org.ml; f. 1932; taken over from the French authorities in 1958; restructured in mid-1990s; cap. 7,139m. francs CFA; principally involved in cultivation of food crops, particularly rice; the Office du Niger zone is the western region of the Central Niger Delta; Pres. and Dir-Gen. AMADOU BOYE COULIBALY.

Office des Produits Agricoles du Mali (OPAM): BP 132, Bamako; tel. 2022-3755; fax 2021-0406; e-mail opam@cefib.com; f. 1965; state-owned; manages National (Cereals) Security Stock, administers food aid, responsible for sales of cereals and distribution to deficit areas; cap. 5,800m. francs CFA; Pres. and Dir-Gen. BAKARY DIALLO.

DEVELOPMENT ORGANIZATIONS

Agence pour le Développement du Nord-Mali (ADN): Gao; f. 2005 to replace l'Autorité pour le Développement Intégré du Nord-Mali (ADIN); govt agency with financial autonomy; promotes devt of regions of Tombouctou, Gao and Kidal; br. in Bamako.

Agence Française de Développement (AFD): Quinzambougou, route de Sotuba, BP 32, Bamako; tel. 2021-2842; fax 2021-8646; e-mail afdbamako@groupe-afd.org; internet www.afd.fr; Country Dir HERVÉ BOUGAULT.

Office de Développement Intégré du Mali-Ouest (ODIMO): place Patrice Lumumba, Bamako; tel. 2022-5759; f. 1991 to succeed Office de Développement Intégré des Productions Arachidières et Céréalières; devt of diversified forms of agricultural production; Man. Dir ZANA SANOGO.

Service de Coopération et d'Action Culturelle: square Patrice Lumumba, BP 84, Bamako; tel. 2021-8338; fax 2021-8339; e-mail scac.bamako-amba@diplomatie.gouv.fr; administers bilateral aid from France; Dir YVES GUEYMARD.

CHAMBERS OF COMMERCE

Chambre de Commerce et d'Industrie du Mali (CCIM): pl. de la Liberté, BP 46, Bamako; tel. 2022-5036; fax 2022-2120; e-mail ccim@cimali.org; internet www.ccimmali.org; f. 1906; Pres. JEAMILLE BITTAR; Sec.-Gen. DABA TRAORÉ.

Chambre des Mines du Mali (CMM): Bamako; f. 2004; Pres. ABDOULAYE PONA; Sec.-Gen. SÉKOU DIORO DICKO.

EMPLOYERS' ASSOCIATIONS

Association Malienne des Exportateurs de Légumes (AMELEF): Bamako; tel. 7608-9048; fax 2029-2836; f. 1984; Pres. BAKARY YAFFA; Sec.-Gen. BIRAMA TRAORÉ.

Association Malienne des Exportateurs de Ressources Animales (AMERA): Bamako; tel. 2022-5683; f. 1985; Pres. AMBARKÉ YERMANGORE; Admin. Sec. ALI HACKO.

Conseil National du Patronat du Mali (CNPM): Immeuble du Patronat, Hamdallaye, ACI 2000, derrière le Gouvernorat du District, route de Sotuba, BP 2445, Bamako; tel. 2021-6311; fax 2021-9077; e-mail cnpm@cnpmali.org; internet www.cnpmali.org; f. 1980 as Fédération Nationale des Employeurs du Mali; Pres. MAMADOU SIDIBÉ; 39 professional groups and 5 regional employers' associations.

UTILITIES

Commission de Régulation de l'Électricité et l'Eau: Bamako; f. 2000; Pres. MOCTAR TOURÉ.

Electricity

Agence Malienne pour le Développement de l'Energie Domestique et l'Electrification Rurale (AMADER): colline de Badalabougou, POB E715, Bamako; tel. 2023-8567; fax 2023–8239; e-mail itoure@amadermali.net; internet www.amadermali.org; f. 2003; Pres. and Dir-Gen. ISMAËL O. TOURÉ.

Energie du Mali (EdM): square Patrice Lumumba, BP 69, Bamako; tel. 2022-3020; fax 2022-8430; e-mail sekou.edm@cefib.com; internet www.edm-sa.com.ml; f. 1960; 66% state-owned, 34% owned by Industrial Promotion Services (West-Africa); planning, construction and operation of power-sector facilities; cap. 7,880m. francs CFA; Pres. OUSMANE ISSOUFI MAÏGA; Dir-Gen. SÉKOU ALPHA DJITÈYE.

Enertech GSA: marché de Lafiabougou, BP 1949, Bamako; tel. 2022-3763; fax 2022-5136; f. 1994; cap. 20m. francs CFA; solar energy producer; Dir MOCTAR DIAKITÉ.

Société de Gestion de l'Energie de Manantali (SOGEM): Parcelle 2501, ACI 2000, BP E 4015, Bamako; tel. 2023-3286; fax 2023-8350; generates and distributes electricity from the Manantali hydro-electric project, under the auspices of the Organisation pour la mise en valeur du fleuve Sénégal; Dir-Gen. SALOUM CISSÉ.

Gas

Air Liquide Maligaz: route de Sotuba, BP 5, Bamako; tel. 2022-2394; internet www.ml.airliquide.com; gas distribution.

There are four other gas distributors in Mali: Sodigaz, Fasogaz, Sigaz and Total.

Water

Société Malienne de Gestion de l'Eau Potable (SOMAGEP): Bamako; f. 2010; responsible for the operation of public drinking water supplies; Pres. BOUBACAR KANÉ.

Société Malienne du Patrimoine de l'Eau Potable (SOMAPEP): Bamako; f. 2010; responsible for the management and development of infrastructure for supplying drinking water; Pres. ADAMA TIÉMOKO DIARRA.

MAJOR COMPANIES

The following are among the major private and state-owned companies in terms of capital investment or employment.

Abattoir Frigorifique de Bamako (AFB): Zone Industrielle, BP 356, Bamako; tel. 2022-2467; fax 2022-9903; f. 1965; cap. 339m. francs CFA; transferred to 80% private ownership in 2002; Man. Dir ABDOULAYE KAFO ABDOUL WAHAB.

Bakary Textile Commerce et Industrie (BATEX-CI): Zone Industrielle, BP 299, Bamako; tel. 2022-4647; e-mail batexci2006@yahoo.fr; f. 2005 following purchase of liquidated textile co Industrie Textile du Mali (ITEMA); Pres. and Dir-Gen. BAKARY CISSÉ.

Compagnie Malienne pour le Développement des Textiles (CMDT): BP 487, Bamako; tel. 2021-7919; fax 2021-8141; e-mail cmdt@cmdt.ml; f. 1974; 60% state-owned, 40% owned by Dagris (France); restructured in 2001–03; privatization under way in 2011; cotton cultivation, ginning and marketing; Pres and Dir-Gen. TIÉNA COULIBALY.

Compagnie Malienne des Textiles (COMATEX): route de Markala, BP 52, Ségou; tel. 2132-0183; fax 2132-0123; f. 1994; production of unbleached fibre and textiles; owned by Covec (People's Republic of China); cap. 1,500m. francs CFA; Dir-Gen. LIU ZHEN SHAN; 1,300 employees (2002).

Fils et Tissus Naturels d'Afrique (Fitina): BP E 4024, Bamako; f. 2004; cotton products; Pres. AIMÉ ZINCK; 50 employees (2011).

Grands Moulins du Mali (GMM): BP 324, Bamako; tel. 2021-3664; fax 2022-5874; e-mail groupeami@groupeami.com; f. 1979; mfrs of flour and animal feed; cap. 2,500m. francs CFA; sales US $52.2m. (2006); Pres. GÉRARD ACHCAR; Man. and Dir-Gen. CYRIL ACHCAR.

Groupe Tomota: Immeuble Tomota, ave Cheick Zayed, Hamdallaye, BP 2412, Bamako; tel. 2029–3000; fax 2029–3001; e-mail atomota@groupe-tomota.com; internet www.groupe-tomota.net; Pres. and Dir-Gen. ALIOU TOMOTA.

Graphique Industrie: Immeuble Tomota, ave Cheick Zayed, Hamdallaye, BP 2412, Bamako; tel. 2029–3000; fax 2029–3001; Dir-Gen. ALIOU TOMOTA.

Huilerie Cotonnière du Mali (HUICOMA): Immeuble Graphique Industrie, ave Cheick Zayed, BP 2474, Bamako; tel. 2023-4261; fax 2023-6032; e-mail dc@huicoma.net; f. 1979; cap. 1,500m. francs CFA; majority stake transferred to ownership of Groupe Alou Tomota in 2005; processing of oilseeds; Pres. and Dir-Gen. ALIOU TOMOTA; 800 employees (2004).

Initiative Malienne de Tannerie (IMAT): Zone Industrielle, Commune II, Bamako; tel. 2021-4470; fax 2021-4065; f. 1994; fmrly Tannerie de l'Afrique de l'Ouest; jt venture by private Malian interests and Curtidos Corderroura (Spain); processing of skins and hides; 150 employees.

Pharmacie Populaire du Mali (PPM): ave Houssa Travele, BP 277, Bamako; tel. 2022-5059; fax 2022-9034; f. 1960; majority state-owned; import and marketing of medicines and pharmaceutical products; cap. 400m. francs CFA; Pres. and Dir-Gen. Dr GUINDO AÏCHA YATASSAYE; 157 employees (2002).

Shell Mali: BP 199, Bamako; tel. 2021-2452; fax 2021-7615; f. 1963; subsidiary of Royal Dutch Shell (Netherlands); distribution of petroleum; Gen. Man. IBRA DIENG.

Société des Brasseries du Mali (BRAMALI/BGI): BP 442, Bamako; f. 1981; owned by Groupe Castel (France); cap. 500m. francs CFA; mfrs of beer and soft drinks; Chair. and Man. Dir SEYDOU DJIM SYLLA.

Société d'Equipement du Mali (SEMA): Face Ecole Cathédrale, BP 163, Bamako; tel. 2022-5071; fax 2023-0647; f. 1961; construction and public works; cap. 140m. francs CFA; Dir MAMADOU DIAKITE; 51 employees.

Société d'Exploitation des Mines d'Or de Sadiola (SEMOS): Sadiola; e-mail Rdagenais@semos-sadiola.com; f. 1994; 41% owned by AngloGold Ashanti (South Africa), 41% by IAMGOLD (Canada); devt of gold deposits at Sadiola Hill; Dir-Gen. Dr DAVID RENNER.

Société des Mines d'or de Loulo (SOMILO): Loulo; fax 2022-8187; f. 1987; cap. 2,133m. francs CFA; 51% owned by Randgold Resources (South Africa); exploration and devt of gold deposits at Loulo; Chair. MAMADOU TOURÉ; Man. Dir ROBERT KRUH.

Société des Mines de Morila: Morila, près de Sanso; f. 2000; exploration and devt of gold deposits at Morila; 40% owned by Randgold Resources (South Africa), 40% by AngloGold Ashanti (South Africa), 20% owned by Govt of Mali; Chair. MAMADOU TOURÉ; Dir-Gen. SAMBA TOURÉ.

Société Nationale des Tabacs et Allumettes du Mali (SONATAM): route de Sotuba, Zone Industrielle, BP 59, Bamako; tel. 2021-4965; fax 2022-2372; f. 1968; cap. 12,539m. francs CFA; 25.5% owned by Laico (Libya), 25.5% owned by Imperial Tobacco Group Plc (United Kingdom), 35% state-owned; further transfer to private ownership proposed for 2003; production of cigarettes; Chair. MARIAM KAIDAMA CISSÉ; Gen. Man. RÉMI SPRIET; 145 employees.

Société pour le Développement des Investissements en Afrique (SODINAF): Quartier du Fleuve, ave de l'Yser, porte 345, BP 8012, Bamako; tel. 2022-3786; devt of gold deposits at Kodieran; Pres. and Dir-Gen. ALIOU BOUBACAR DIALLO.

Star Oil Mali: Quartier TSF, Zone Industrielle, Niarela, BP 145, Bamako; tel. 2022-2598; fax 2022-6882; f. 2004 by purchase of Mobil Oil Mali; distribution of petroleum products; Dir-Gen. TIDIANI BEN HOUSSEIN.

Total Mali: ave Kasse Keita, BP 13, Bamako; tel. 2022-2971; fax 2022-8027; e-mail info@totalmali.com; f. 1976; fmrly Elf Oil Mali, subsequently renamed TotalFinaElf Mali; present name adopted 2003; distribution of petroleum; Dir-Gen. PATRICE THIRION.

Usine Malienne de Produits Pharmaceutiques (UMPP): Zone Industrielle, BP 2286, Bamako; tel. 2022-5161; fax 2022-5169; f. 1983; 100% state-owned; 51% transfer to private ownership proposed in late 2006; producer of pharmaceutical products; cap. 2,551m. francs CFA (2006); Gen. Man. OUSMANE DOUMBIA; 187 employees (2003).

TRADE UNION FEDERATION

Union Nationale des Travailleurs du Mali (UNTM): Bourse du Travail, blvd de l'Indépendance, BP 169, Bamako; tel. 2022-3699; fax 2023-5945; f. 1963; 13 nat. and 8 regional unions, and 52 local orgs; Sec.-Gen. SIAKA DIAKITÉ.

There are, in addition, several non-affiliated trade unions.

Transport

RAILWAYS

Mali's only railway runs from Koulikoro, via Bamako, to the Senegal border. The line continues to Dakar, Senegal, a total distance of 1,286 km, of which 729 km is in Mali. The track is in very poor condition, and is frequently closed during the rainy season. In 1995 the Governments of Mali and Senegal agreed to establish a joint company to operate the Bamako–Dakar line, and the line passed fully into private ownership in 2003. Some 358,000 metric tons of freight were handled on the Malian railway in 2001. Plans exist for the construction of a new rail line linking Bamako with Kouroussa and Kankan, in Guinea.

Transrail SA: Immeuble la Roseraie, 310 ave de la liberté, BP 4150, Bamako; tel. 2022-5967; fax 2022-5433; e-mail ericpeiffer@transrailsa.com; f. 2003 on transfer to private management of fmr Régie du Chemin de Fer du Mali; jt venture of Canac (Canada) and Getma (France); Dir-Gen. ERIC PEIFFER.

ROADS

The Malian road network in 2004 comprised 18,709 km, of which about 3,370 km were paved. A bituminized road between Bamako and Abidjan (Côte d'Ivoire) provides Mali's main economic link to the coast; construction of a road linking Bamako and Dakar (Senegal) is to be financed by the European Development Fund. The African Development Bank also awarded a US $31.66m. loan to fund the Kankan–Kouremale–Bamako road between Mali and Guinea. In addition, there are plans to build a road across the Sahara to link Mali with Algeria.

Autorité Routière du Mali: rue 320, Porte 153, Hamdallaye ACI 2000, 03 BP 12, Bamako; tel. 2029-1125; fax 2029-1108; e-mail infos@arfer-mali.net; internet www.arfer-mali.net; f. 2001; Dir-Gen. MORY KANTÉ.

INLAND WATERWAYS

The River Niger is navigable in parts of its course through Mali (1,693 km) during the rainy season from July to late December. The River Senegal was, until the early 1990s, navigable from Kayes to Saint-Louis (Senegal) only between August and November, but its navigability was expected to improve following the inauguration, in 1992, of the Manantali dam, and the completion of works to deepen the river-bed.

Compagnie Malienne de Navigation (COMANAV): BP 10, Koulikoro; tel. 2026-2094; fax 2026-2009; f. 1968; 100% state-owned; river transport; Pres. and Dir-Gen. DEMBÉLÉ GOUNDO DIALLO.

Conseil Malien des Chargeurs (CMC): Dar-salam, BP E 4031, Bamako; tel. 2023-0486; fax 2023-0489; e-mail contact@cmchargeurs.com; internet www.cmchargeurs.com; f. 1999; Pres. OUSMANE BABALAYE DAOU.

Société Navale Malienne (SONAM): Bamako-Coura, BP 2581, Bamako; tel. 2021-6066; fax 2022-6066; f. 1981; transferred to private ownership in 1986; Chair. ALIOUNE KEÏTA.

Société Ouest-Africaine d'Entreprise Maritime (SOAEM): rue Mohamed V, BP 2428, Bamako; tel. 2022-5832; fax 2022-4024; maritime transport co.

CIVIL AVIATION

The principal airport is at Bamako-Senou. The other major airports are at Bourem, Gao, Goundam, Kayes, Kita, Mopti, Nioro, Ségou, Tessalit and Tombouctou. There are about 40 small airfields. Mali's airports are being modernized with external financial assistance. In early 2005 the Malian Government announced the creation of a new national airline, in partnership with the Aga Khan Fund for Economic Development and Industrial Promotion Services.

Aéroports du Mali: Bamako; internet www.aeroportsdumali.com; f. 1970; responsible for commercial exploitation, maintenance and development of airports; Pres. and Dir-Gen. AYA THIAM DIALLO.

Agence Nationale de l'Aviation Civile (ANAC): route de l'Aéroport de Bamako, Sénou, BP 227, Bamako; tel. 2020-5524; fax 2020-6175; e-mail anacmali@hotmail.com; internet www.anac-mali.org; f. 2005 to replace Direction Nationale de l'Aéronautique Civile (f. 1990); Pres. TOURÉ ALIMATA TRAORÉ; Dir-Gen. HADY NIANG.

Air Mali: Immeuble Tomota, ave Cheick Zayed, BP E 2286, Bamako; tel. 2022-2424; fax 2022-7111; e-mail dc.cam@cam-mali.org; internet www.air-mali.com; f. 2005; 51% owned by Fonds Aga Khan pour le Développement Economique (AKAFED), 20% state-owned; domestic and international flights; Dir-Gen. ABDERRAHMANE BERTHÉ.

STA Trans African Airlines: Quartier du Fleuve, BP 775, Bamako; tel. 2022-4444; fax 2021-0981; internet www.sta-airlines.com; f. 1984 as Société des Transports Aériens; privately owned; local, regional and international services; Man. Dir MELHEM ELIE SABBAGUE.

Tourism

Mali's rich cultural heritage is promoted as a tourist attraction. In 2009 169,000 tourists visited Mali, while receipts from tourism totalled some US $205m.

Ministry of Crafts and Tourism: see section on The Government.

Defence

As assessed at November 2011, the active Malian army numbered some 7,350 men. Paramilitary forces numbered 4,800 and there was an inactive militia of 3,000 men. Military service is by selective conscription and lasts for two years.

Defence Expenditure: Estimated at 103,000m. francs CFA in 2010.

Chief of Staff of the Armed Forces: Col. IBRAHIMA DEMBELE.

Chief of Staff of the Air Force: Col MAMADOU TOGOLO.

Chief of Staff of the Land Army: Col MAMADOU ADAMA DIALLO.

Chief of Staff of the National Guard: Col BROULAYE KONÉ.

Education

Education is provided free of charge and is officially compulsory for nine years between seven and 16 years of age. Basic education, which includes six years of primary education, begins at the age of seven and lasts for nine years. Secondary education, from 16 years of age, lasts for a further three years. The rate of school enrolment in Mali is among the lowest in the world. According to UNESCO, in 2009/10 primary enrolment included 62% of children in the appropriate age-group (males 66%; females 57%), while secondary enrolment included only 29% of those in the appropriate age-group (males 35%; females 24%). Tertiary education facilities include the national university, developed in the mid-1990s. In 2009/10 there were some 81,200 students enrolled in tertiary education. Hitherto many students have received higher education abroad, mainly in France and Senegal. In 2005 spending on education represented 14.8% of total budgetary expenditure.

Bibliography

Bah, T. *Mali: le procès permanent.* Paris, L'Harmattan, 2010.

Bastian, D. E., Myers, R. A., and Stamm, A. L. *Mali.* Oxford, ABC-Clio, 1994.

Bertrand, M. *Transition malienne, décentralisation, gestion communale bamakoise: Rapport de recherche, ministère de la coopération, villes et décentralisation en Afrique, novembre 1997.* Paris, Pôle de recherche pour l'organisation et la diffusion de l'information géographique, 1999.

Bingen, R. J., Staatz, J. M., and Robinson, D. (Eds). *Democracy and Development in Mali.* East Lancing, MI, The Michigan State University Press, 2000.

Bocquier, P., and Diarra, T. *Population et société au Mali.* Paris, L'Harmattan, 1999.

Boilley, P. *Les Touaregs Kel Adagh: dépendances et révoltes: du Soudan français au Mali contemporain.* Paris, Editions Karthala, 1999.

Bonneval, P., Kuper, M., Tonneau, J.-P. *et al. L'Office du Niger, grenier à riz du Mali: succès économiques, transitions culturelles et politiques de développement.* Paris, Editions Karthala, 2002.

Brenner, L. *Controlling Knowledge: Religion, Power, and Schooling in a West African Muslim Society.* Bloomington, IN, Indiana University Press, 2001.

Camara, M. M. *Questions brûlantes pour démocratie naissante.* Dakar, Nouvelles éditions africaines du Sénégal, 1998.

Cissé, A. *Mali: Une Démocratie à Refonder.* Paris, L'Harmattan, 2006.

Cissé, Y. T., and Kamissoko, W. *La grande geste du Mali, des origines à la fondation de l'empire.* Paris, Editions Karthala, 1988.

Couloubaly, P. B. *Le Mali d'Alpha Oumar Konaré: ombres et lumières d'une démocratie en gestation.* Paris, L'Harmattan, 2004.

Davies, S. *Adaptable Livelihoods: Coping with Food Insecurity in the Malian Sahel.* New York, St Martin's Press, 1995.

Dayak, M. *Touareg, la tragédie.* Paris, J.-C. Lattès, 1992.

Diakite, Y. *La Fédération du Mali: sa création et les causes de son éclatement.* Bamako, Ecole Normale Supérieure de Bamako, 1985.

Diarrah, C. O. *Le Mali de Modibo Keita.* Paris, L'Harmattan, 1986.

Mali: Bilan d'une gestion désastreuse. Paris, L'Harmattan, 2000.

Foltz, W. J. *From French West Africa to the Mali Federation.* New Haven, CT, Yale University Press, 1965.

Gaudio, A. *Le Mali.* Paris, Editions Karthala, 1988.

Gibbal, J. M. *Genii of the River Niger.* Chicago, IL, University of Chicago Press, 1994.

Grevoz, D. *Les canonnières de Tombouctou: les français à la conquête de la cité mythique 1870–1894.* Paris, L'Harmattan, 1992.

Harrison Church, R. J. *West Africa.* 8th edn. London, Longman, 1979.

Imperato, P. J. *Historical Dictionary of Mali*. 3rd edn. Lanham, MD, Scarecrow Press, 1996.

Jenkins, M. *To Timbuktu: A Journey down the Niger*. New York, William Morrow & Co Inc, 1997.

Jus, C. *Soudan français-Mauritanie: Une géopolitique coloniale (1880–1963)*. Paris, L'Harmattan, 2003.

Klein, M. A. *Slavery and Colonial Rule in French West Africa*. Cambridge, Cambridge University Press, 1998.

Konaré B. A. *Ces mots que je partage: discours d'une Première Dame d'Afrique, avec une introduction sur la parole*. Bamako, Editions Jamana, 1998.

Lucke, L. *Waiting for Rain: Life and Development in Mali, West Africa*. Hanover, MS, Christopher Publishing House, 1998.

Maharaux, A. *L'Industrie au Mali*. Paris, L'Harmattan, 2000.

Maïga, A. B. C. *La politique africaine du Mali de 1960 à 1980*. Bamako, Ecole Normale Supérieure de Bamako, 1983.

Maïga, M. T.-F. *Le Mali: De la secheresse à la rebellion nomade: Chronique et analyse d'un double phénomène du contre-développement en Afrique Sahélienne*. Paris, L'Harmattan, 1997.

Mariko, K. *Les Touaregs Ouelleminden*. Paris, Editions Karthala, 1984.

Roberts, R. L. *Two Worlds of Cotton: Colonialism and the Regional Economy in the French Soudan, 1800–1946*. Stanford, CA, Stanford University Press, 1996.

Snyder, F. G. *One-Party Government in Mali: Transition towards Control*. New Haven, CT, and London, Yale University Press, 1965.

Tag, S. *Paysans, état et démocratisation au Mali: enquête en milieu rural*. Hamburg, Institut für Afrika-Kunde, 1994.

Toulmin, C. *Cattle, Women, and Wells: Managing Household Survival in the Sahel*. Oxford, Clarendon, 1992.

MAURITANIA

Physical and Social Geography

DAVID HILLING

Covering an area of 1,030,700 sq km (397,950 sq miles), the Islamic Republic of Mauritania forms a geographical link between the Arab Maghreb and black West Africa. Moors, heterogeneous groups of Arab/Berber stock, form about two-thirds of the population, which totalled 2,508,159 at the November 2000 census. In mid-2011 the population totalled 3,432,192, according to official estimates, giving an average population density of 3.3 persons per sq km.

The Moors are divided on social and descent criteria, rather than skin colour, into a dominant group, the Bidan or 'white' Moors, and a group, probably of servile origin, known as the Harratin or 'black' Moors. All were traditionally nomadic pastoralists. The country's black African inhabitants traditionally form about one-third of the total population, the principal groups being the Wolof, the Toucouleur and the Fulani (Peul). They are mainly sedentary cultivators and are concentrated in a relatively narrow zone in the south of the country.

During the drought of the 1970s and early 1980s, there was mass migration to the towns, and the urban population increased from 18% of the total in 1972 to as much as 35% in 1984. The population of Nouakchott was 393,300 at the time of the 1988 census, but had risen to 588,195 by the census of 2000. The populations of towns such as Nouadhibou (59,200 in 1988) and Rosso (27,783 in 1988) had increased to 72,337 and 48,922, respectively, by 2000. According to UN figures, the population of Nouakchott had risen to an estimated 786,226 by mid-2011. There has been a general exodus from rural areas and an associated growth of informal peri-urban encampments. In 1963 about 83% of the population was nomadic, and 17% sedentary, but by 1988 only 12% remained nomadic, while 88% were settled, mainly in the larger towns. By 2001 the nomadic population numbered only 128,063, equivalent to less than 5% of the population.

Two-thirds of the country may be classed as 'Saharan', with rainfall absent or negligible in most years and always less than 100 mm. In parts vegetation is inadequate to graze even the camel, which is the main support of the nomadic peoples of the northern and central area. Traditionally this harsh area has produced some salt, and dates and millet are cultivated at oases such as Atar. Southwards, in the 'Sahelian' zone, the rainfall increases to about 600 mm per year; in good years vegetation will support sheep, goats and cattle, and adequate crops of millet and sorghum can be grown. There is evidence that the 250 mm precipitation line has moved 200 km further south since the early 1960s, as Saharan conditions encroach on Sahelian areas. In 1983 rainfall over the whole country reached an average of only 27% of that for the period 1941–70, and was only 13% in the pasturelands of the Hodh Ech Chargui (Hodh Oriental) region. Average annual rainfall in the capital in the 1990s was 131 mm. In the early 1990s the Senegal river was at record low levels, and riverine cultivation in the seasonally inundated *chemama* lands was greatly reduced, although larger areas of more systematic irrigation could be made possible by dams that have been constructed for the control of the river.

Geologically, Mauritania is a part of the vast western Saharan 'shield' of crystalline rocks, but these are overlain in parts with sedimentary rocks, and some 40% of the country has a superficial cover of unconsolidated sand. Relief has a general north-east–south-west trend, and a series of westward-facing scarps separate monotonous plateaux, which only in western Adrar rise above 500 m. Locally these plateaux have been eroded, so that only isolated peaks remain, the larger of these being known as kedias and the smaller as guelbs. These are often minerally enriched; however, reserves of high-grade iron ore in the *djbel le-hadid* ('iron mountains') of the Kédia d'Idjil were nearing exhaustion in the late 1980s, and production ceased in 1992. Mining at a neighbouring guelb, El Rhein (some 40 km to the north), commenced in 1984, while the exploitation of the important M'Haoudat deposit (55 km to the north of Zouïrât) began in 1994. Gypsum, rock salt, gold and copper are also mined on a small scale. Other exploitable mineral resources include diamonds, phosphates, sulphur, peat, manganese and uranium. Many international companies were involved in offshore petroleum exploration in Mauritania in the early 2000s, with reserves at the offshore Shafr el Khanjar and Chinguetti fields estimated at 450m.–1,000m. barrels; production commenced at Chinguetti in 2006.

In 1991 Arabic was declared to be the official language. The principal vernacular languages, Pular, Wolof and Solinké, were, with Arabic, recognized as 'national languages'. French is still widely used, particularly in the commercial sector.

Recent History

KATHARINE MURISON

OULD DADDAH AND THE MPP

Mauritania achieved independence from France on 28 November 1960. Moktar Ould Daddah, whose Mauritanian Assembly Party (MAP) had won all the seats in the previous year's general election, became Head of State. All parties subsequently merged with the MAP to form the Mauritanian People's Party (MPP), and Mauritania was declared a one-party state in 1964. A highly centralized and tightly controlled political system was imposed on a diverse political spectrum. Some elements among the Moorish population favoured union with Morocco and, although each Government included a small minority of black Mauritanians, the southern population feared Arab domination.

In the early 1970s the Ould Daddah Government undertook a series of measures to assert Mauritania's political, cultural and economic independence. In 1973 the country joined the League of Arab States, and in 1974 withdrew from the Franc Zone. In that year the foreign-owned iron-ore mines were nationalized. The period of reform culminated in the adoption, in 1975, of a charter for an Islamic, national, centralized and socialist democracy.

For the next four years Mauritanian political life was dominated by the question of the Spanish-controlled territory of the Western Sahara, sovereignty of which was claimed by both Morocco and Mauritania. In November 1975 Spain agreed to cede the territory in February 1976 for division between Mauritania and Morocco. However, the occupation of the territory by Mauritania and Morocco met with fierce resistance from guerrillas of the Frente Popular para la Liberación de Saguia el-Hamra y Río de Oro (the Polisario Front), which had, with Algerian support, proclaimed a 'Sahrawi Arab

Democratic Republic' (SADR). With the assistance of Moroccan troops, Mauritania occupied Tiris el Gharbia, the province it had been allocated, but resistance by Polisario forces continued. Increasingly dependent on support from Moroccan troops and on financial assistance from France and conservative Arab states, Mauritania was unable to defend itself militarily and its economy was in ruins.

SALEK AND OULD HAIDALLA

In July 1978 Ould Daddah was overthrown in a bloodless military coup. Power was assumed by a Military Committee for National Recovery (MCNR), headed by the Chief of Staff, Lt-Col (later Col) Moustapha Ould Mohamed Salek, which suspended the Constitution and dissolved the National Assembly and MPP. Salek assumed absolute power in March 1979, replacing the MCNR with a Military Committee for National Salvation (MCNS). In May Lt-Col Mohamed Khouna Ould Haidalla was appointed Prime Minister, and in the following month Salek resigned and was succeeded as President by Lt-Col Mohamed Mahmoud Ould Ahmed Louly. In July Polisario announced an end to the cease-fire. Ould Haidalla subsequently declared that Mauritania had no territorial claims in Western Sahara, a decision that was formalized in the Algiers Agreement, signed with Polisario in August. King Hassan of Morocco then announced that his country had taken over Tiris el Gharbia 'in response to local wishes'.

Ould Haidalla displaced Louly as President in January 1980 and dismissed several members of the MCNS. Ould Haidalla formed a civilian Government in December and published a draft constitution with provision for a multi-party system. In April 1981, however, the army Chief of Staff, Lt-Col (later Col) Maawiya Ould Sid'Ahmed Taya, became Prime Minister of a new military Government, and the draft constitution was abandoned.

TAYA ASSUMES POWER

Popular discontent with Ould Haidalla's rule led to a bloodless coup in December 1984, led by Col Taya. The new Government introduced major economic reforms, which attracted support from foreign donors, and sought a political rapprochement with supporters of Ould Daddah.

The second half of the 1980s witnessed growing unrest among the black Mauritanian population—resentful at what they perceived as the increasing Arabicization of the country. Inter-ethnic tensions were highlighted by the arrest, in October 1987, of 51 members of the black Toucouleur ethnic group, following the discovery of a coup plot. Three military officers were sentenced to death and 41 others were imprisoned.

CONSTITUTIONAL REFORM

At a national referendum on 12 July 1991, 97.9% of those who voted (85.3% of the registered electorate) endorsed a new Constitution, which provided for the introduction of a multi-party political system. The new Constitution accorded extensive powers to the President of the Republic, who was to be elected, by universal suffrage, for a period of six years, with no limitation placed on further terms of office. Provision was made for a bicameral legislature—comprising a National Assembly (al-Jamiya al-Wataniyah), to be elected by universal suffrage every five years, and a Senate (Majlis al-Shuyukh), to be indirectly elected by municipal leaders. Arabic was designated as the sole official language. Following the adoption of the Constitution, legislation permitting registration of political parties took effect. Among the first parties to be accorded official status was the pro-Government Democratic and Social Republican Party (DSRP).

The presidential election took place on 17 January 1992. According to official results, Taya obtained 62.7% of the poll (51.7% of the registered electorate voted); his nearest rival, Ahmed Ould Daddah (the half-brother of the country's first President), received 32.8% of the votes cast. At the legislative elections, which took place on 6 and 13 March, the DSRP won 67 of the National Assembly's 79 seats, with all but two of the remaining seats being secured by independent candidates. Other than the DSRP, only one party presented candidates for the Senate, indirect elections to which followed on 3 and 10 April. The DSRP consequently obtained some 36 of the 54 seats. At his inauguration, on 18 April, President Taya designated Sidi Mohamed Ould Boubacar, hitherto Minister of Finance, as Prime Minister, to lead a civilian Government, in which the sole military officer was the Minister of Defence.

Mauritania's first multi-party municipal elections took place in January and February 1994, the DSRP winning control of 172 of the country's 208 districts. Ahmed Ould Daddah's Union of Democratic Forces—New Era (UDF—NE) was the only other party to win control of any districts, with 17. The DSRP's control of the political process was confirmed at elections to renew one-third of the Senate's membership in April and May.

In January 1996 Taya appointed Cheikh el Avia Ould Mohamed Khouna (hitherto Minister of Fisheries and Marine Economy) as Prime Minister, and a new Council of Ministers was formed. At the elections to the National Assembly, held on 11 and 18 October, the DSRP won 71 of the 79 seats. The Rally for Democracy and Unity (RDU), closely allied with the administration, also secured a seat. The Action for Change (AC), which largely represented Harratin ('black' Moors who had formerly been slaves) was the only opposition party to win a seat, and six independent candidates were also elected.

At the presidential election, held on 12 December 1997, Taya was returned to office with 90.9% of the valid votes cast. Opposition parties alleged that there had been widespread electoral fraud and claimed that the official rate of voter participation (73.8% of the registered electorate) was unrealistically high. Taya subsequently appointed Mohamed Lemine Ould Guig, a university academic, as Prime Minister, and a new Council of Ministers was installed.

In March 1998 serious internal divisions in the UDF—NE caused the party to split into two rival factions, led by Ahmed Ould Daddah and Moustapha Ould Bedreddine. In November Khouna, premier in 1996–97, replaced Guig as Prime Minister. In November the pro-Iraqi Baathist National Vanguard Party (Taliaa) was banned by the Government for 'attempted subversion and public order violation', following its criticism of the Mauritanian Government's decision to establish full diplomatic relations with Israel in the previous month.

In October 2000, following violent anti-Israeli protests organized by the UDF—NE in response to renewed violence in the Palestinian Autonomous Areas, the Council of Ministers held an extraordinary session at which the party was officially dissolved, on the grounds that it had incited violence and sought to damage Mauritanian national interests. Several senior members of the UDF—NE were detained in November. The faction of the UDF—NE led by Ould Bedreddine, which remained authorized, restyled itself as the Union of Progressive Forces (UPF).

In January 2001 the National Assembly approved several electoral reforms, introducing an element of proportional representation to legislative elections, with all registered parties to be granted equal state funding and access to the media; moreover, independent candidates were to be prohibited and the number of deputies was to be increased from 79 to 81. Some 15 political parties contested elections to the National Assembly, held on 19 and 26 October 2001, when a turn-out of 54.5% was recorded. The DSRP won 64 of the 81 seats in the National Assembly. The AC took four seats, while the Union for Democracy and Progress (UDP), the RDU, the UPF and the newly formed Rally of Democratic Forces (RDF, which replaced the banned UDF—NE) each won three seats, and the Popular Front (PF) secured one seat. At concurrent municipal elections the DSRP secured control of 184 of the 216 districts. In November Khouna was reappointed as Prime Minister, and a new Council of Ministers was announced.In January 2002 the Government dissolved the AC, accusing the party of racism and extremism, and of attempting to undermine national unity and Mauritania's relations with Senegal.

HEIGHTENED TENSIONS

Widespread demonstrations took place in Mauritania in protest against the commencement in March 2003 of full-scale military operations aimed at ousting the Baathist Iraqi regime of Saddam Hussain by a US-led coalition. As opposition to the

Government's broadly pro-US stance intensified in May, police raided the headquarters of a tolerated—although not officially authorized—Baathist party, the National Renaissance Party (Nouhoudh), arresting three of its leaders; 13 other Baathists were also arrested over a period of four days. Ten of the detainees were charged with attempting to re-establish Taliaa. The Government's increasing intolerance of radical opposition movements also targeted Islamist activists: a senior member of the RDF, Mohamed Jemil Ould Mansour, was one of several prominent Islamists and religious leaders arrested in May. Also in May, a pro-Islamist weekly journal, *Al-Rayah*, was closed, and nine Baathists were convicted of engaging in illegal political activity. In June four Islamic cultural associations were closed down, and, according to opposition reports, more than 100 alleged Islamists were detained, 36 of whom (including Ould Mansour) were charged with plotting against the constitutional order.

The tensions that had been building throughout the first half of 2003 culminated in an attempted coup in June. Fighting in the capital resulted in the deaths of 15 people (including six civilians and the Chief of Staff of the Armed Forces, Col Mohamed Lamine Ould Ndiayane), according to official reports, with a further 68 people injured. Reports named the leaders of the coup as Saleh Ould Hnana, a former colonel and Baathist sympathizer, who had been expelled from the Mauritanian armed forces in 2002, and Mohamed Ould Sheikhna, a squadron leader in the national air force; Taya subsequently stated, however, that Islamists had been responsible for the rebellion. In the days following the restoration of order, at least 12 alleged rebel leaders were arrested, including Ould Sheikhna. In July another suspected coup leader, Lt Didi Ould M'Hamed, who had fled to Senegal, was extradited to Mauritania.

In July 2003 President Taya appointed a new Prime Minister, Sghair Ould M'Bareck, a Harratin. A new Government was subsequently formed. Further arrests of Islamists were reported throughout July and in September it was announced that some 30 members of the military, including 20 senior officers, were to be tried in connection with the June coup attempt.

Six candidates, including Taya, Ahmed Ould Daddah, Ould Boulkheir and former President Ould Haidalla, contested the presidential election held on 7 November 2003. According to official results, Taya won 66.7% of the votes cast, followed by Ould Haidalla, with 18.7%. Some 60.8% of the electorate participated in the election. Opposition candidates accused the Government of perpetrating fraud at the election, which international observers had not been permitted to monitor.

In December 2003 Ould Haidalla and four others were convicted of plotting to overthrow the Head of State; they received five-year suspended sentences, during which time they were forbidden to engage in political activity, and were fined the equivalent of US $1,600 each. Four others received lesser sentences and fines. In April 2004 the Government refused to consider an application for the registration of a new political party, the Party for Democratic Convergence (PDC), filed by supporters of Ould Haidalla, on the grounds that the party leadership comprised Islamist radicals and individuals who were either being sought by the courts or had recently received suspended prison sentences.

The DSRP won 15 of the 18 seats contested at partial elections to the Senate held in April 2004, while its ally, the RDU, secured its first senatorial representation. The opposition Popular Progressive Alliance (PPA) also obtained representation, winning two seats; Ould Boulkheir was elected President of the party in August. In July a new political party opposed to the Taya regime, and apparently supportive of Ould Haidalla, Reward (Sawab), was officially registered.

In August 2004 31 members of the Mauritanian armed forces were arrested in connection with an alleged plot to overthrow Taya. The Minister of National Defence, Baba Ould Sidi, claimed that the conspirators belonged to a group known as the Knights of Change (Fursan at-Taghyir). Later that month the Chief of Staff of the National Gendarmerie, Col Sidi Ould Riha, alleged that Ould Hnana and Ould Sheikhna had organized the coup with assistance from Libya and Burkina Faso. The Governments of both countries denied any involvement in the alleged plot, while opposition leaders suggested that the Mauritanian Government had invented the conspiracy as a pretext to purge the military of opponents.

The Government announced that it had averted a further attempted coup in September 2004. Among those arrested in connection with the latest plot was Capt. Abderahmane Ould Mini, who was also believed to have been one of the leaders of the June 2003 uprising. The Government accused Burkina Faso and Libya of providing logistical and financial support to the rebels through Sidi Mohamed Mustapha Ould Limam Chavi, a Mauritanian-born adviser to President Blaise Compaoré of Burkina Faso. In October Ould Hnana was arrested on the border with Senegal. Also that month Ould Mansour (who had returned to Mauritania in January) and two other Islamist leaders, Mohamed el Hacen Ould Dedew and Moktar Ould Mohamed Moussa, were detained for several days for questioning regarding the September coup plot. Ould Haidallah, Ahmed Ould Daddah and Ould Horma, the President of the PDC, were arrested on suspicion of having given financial assistance to the coup plotters.

In November 2004 the trial of 195 soldiers and civilians accused of participating in the coup attempt of June 2003 and the two more recent plots commenced at a military barracks in Ouad Naga, some 50 km east of Nouakchott. Ould Hnana and Ould Mini were the only defendants to admit to conspiring to overthrow the President. Ould Sheikhna and Chavi were among 19 defendants who were tried *in absentia*. In February 2005 Ould Hnana, Ould Mini, Ould Sheikhna and a fourth army officer, Capt. Mohamed Ould Salek, were sentenced to life imprisonment with hard labour. The court acquitted 111 of the defendants, including Ould Haidallah, Ould Daddah and Ould Horma, while the remainder received prison sentences ranging from 18 months to 15 years. Chavi was sentenced to a 15-year term. (In December 2011 the Mauritanian authorities issued an international arrest warrant for Chavi, who was reportedly accused of financing terrorism and sharing intelligence with terrorist groups.)

In April 2005 police arrested some 20 prominent Islamists (among them Ould Dedew and Ould Mohamed Moussa), who were accused of preparing 'terrorist acts'. At the same time the Government revealed that earlier that month seven Mauritanians had been intercepted on their return from Algeria, where they had allegedly received military training from a radical Islamist militant group, the Groupe Salafiste pour la Prédication et le Combat (GSPC). The seven men were reportedly charged with establishing a criminal association in May. In mid-May further arrests were made during police raids on several mosques in Nouakchott. The Government claimed that weapons had been discovered in the mosques, together with plans to carry out terrorist and subversive acts to destabilize the country. Islamist groups dismissed these claims. In late May 14 Islamists were released without charge, while some 40 others appeared in court, variously charged with leading or belonging to an unauthorized group, fomenting unrest and distributing propaganda in mosques.

In June 2005 15 soldiers were killed, and a further 17 injured, in an attack by some 150 assailants on a military post in Lemgheity, in north-eastern Mauritania. The GSPC claimed responsibility for the attack, describing it as revenge for the imprisonment of Islamists in Mauritania. The Mauritanian Islamist movement condemned the attack.

TAYA OVERTHROWN

On 3 August 2005, while President Taya was absent from Mauritania, a group of army officers seized control of state broadcasting services and the presidential palace in a bloodless coup. A 17-member self-styled Military Council for Justice and Democracy (MCJD) under the leadership of Col Ely Ould Mohamed Vall, the Director of National Security, who had hitherto been regarded as a close ally of Taya, assumed power. The Council stated that it would preside over the country for a transitional period of up to two years, at the end of which democratic elections, in which members of the MCJD and the Government would be prohibited from participating, would be held; the dissolution of the National Assembly was subsequently announced, although the 1991 Constitution, supplemented and amended by the Council's own charter, was to be retained, as were most of the institutions provided for by the Constitution, including the Constitutional Council and judicial bodies. Taya was prevented from re-entering the country and subsequently took up residence in Qatar, where he had been offered political asylum.

On 7 August 2005 Vall appointed Sidi Mohamed Ould Boubacar, hitherto ambassador to France, as Prime Minister, a position that he had held in 1992–96; a new, civilian Government was named on 10 August. In the immediate aftermath of the coup, the African Union (AU) announced the suspension of Mauritania's membership. However, the overthrow of Taya's regime had widespread domestic support. In mid-August a delegation from the AU met members of the MCJD, subsequently announcing the willingness of the Union to co-operate with the new leadership of Mauritania, although the country was to remain suspended from the organization pending democratic elections.

In September 2005 Vall announced a general amnesty for political prisoners; Ould Hnana and Ould Mini were among the first to be freed. Also that month a number of exiled opponents of Taya's regime, including Ould Sheikhna, returned to Mauritania. In October the Ministry of the Interior, Posts and Telecommunications refused to register the PDC, led by Ould Horma and Ould Mansour, on the grounds that legislation on political organizations stipulated that Islam could not be the exclusive ideology of a party. However, Ould Horma subsequently formed a new party, the Rally for Mauritania—TEMAM (RM—TEMAM), that was authorized.

TRANSITION TO CIVILIAN RULE

In November 2005 a 15-member National Independent Electoral Commission was inaugurated, and the MCJD issued a timetable for the transition to democratic rule, commencing with a constitutional referendum in June 2006 and ending with a presidential election in March 2007. In December 2005 the MCJD replaced 12 of the country's regional governors, as well as most prefects and district administrators.

In March 2006 the MCJD approved proposals presented by the transitional Government on constitutional amendments to be put to a national referendum. The principal changes envisaged included: limiting the presidential term of office to five years, renewable only once; stipulating a maximum age of 75 years for presidential candidates; and prohibiting a President from holding any other official post, particularly the leadership of a political party. The proposed reforms were supported by most major political parties, including the Republican Party for Democracy and Renewal (RPDR), as the former ruling DSRP had been renamed). In May the European Union (EU) announced the resumption of co-operation with Mauritania, which had been suspended following the coup in August 2005. An independent human rights commission was established later that month.

The constitutional referendum was held on 25 June 2006, and according to official results, 96.9% of the valid votes cast were in favour of the amendments; a turn-out of 76.5% of the registered electorate was recorded. In late June 11 political parties, including the RDF, the PF, the PPA, the UPF and the RM—TEMAM, announced the formation of the Coalition of Forces for Democratic Change (CFDC) to contest the forthcoming legislative and local elections.

The elections to the National Assembly and to municipal councils took place on 19 November 2006, with a second round of legislative voting held on 3 December. Turn-outs of 73.4% and 69.5% were recorded at the first and second rounds, respectively. The RDF became the largest single party in the National Assembly, winning 15 of the 95 seats, followed by the UPF, which took eight, the former ruling RPDR, with seven, the PPA five, and the Centrist Reformists four. Parties belonging to the CFDC secured a total of 41 seats, while 41 independent candidates also secured legislative representation. In the concurrent local elections, it was reported that parties that had opposed Taya's regime had won 63% of the municipal posts. Independent candidates secured 34 seats in the 56-member Senate at indirect elections held on 21 January and 4 February 2007, while 15 seats were taken by constituent parties of the CFDC.

The first round of the presidential election, which was held on 11 March 2007, was contested by 20 candidates. Sidi Mohamed Ould Cheikh Abdellahi, who had served in the Governments of both Moktar Ould Daddah and Taya, won 24.8% of the votes cast, while the RDF's Ahmed Ould Daddah secured 20.7%, Zeine Ould Zeidane, the former Governor of the central bank, received 15.3% and Ould Boulkheir, of the PPA, took 9.8%. Some 70.1% of the electorate participated in the poll. Ould Cheikh Abdellahi and Ould Daddah proceeded to a second round of voting. Although nominally an independent, Ould Cheikh Abdellahi was favoured by the MCJD and by The Charter (Al-Mithaq), an alliance formed in January 2007 by 18 political parties and movements that had formerly been loyal to Taya. (Dominated by the RPDR and also including 39 of the 41 independent deputies, The Charter held a majority in the legislature.) With the additional support of Ould Zeidane and, more surprisingly, Ould Boulkheir (a member of the CFDC, like Ould Daddah), Ould Cheikh Abdellahi defeated Ould Daddah at the second round, which was held on 25 March, with 52.9% of the votes cast. A turn-out of 67.5% was recorded. International observers declared their satisfaction with the conduct of the election, and in April the AU restored full membership rights to Mauritania.

Ould Cheikh Abdellahi was inaugurated on 19 April 2007, marking the formal transfer of power from the MCJD. On the following day the President appointed Ould Zeidane as Prime Minister, and later that month the formation was announced of a new Council of Ministers, mainly comprising technocrats with no ministerial experience. In late April Ould Boulkheir was elected President of the National Assembly, becoming the first Harratin to hold this position.

In May 2007 the trial of 25 suspected Islamist militants commenced; several of the accused were being tried *in absentia*. Some of the defendants were charged in connection with the attack on a military post in Lemgheity in June 2005 (see above), while others were accused of having received training from the GSPC (which had reportedly restyled itself as al-Qa'ida in the Islamic Maghreb—AQIM). In early June 2007 24 of the defendants were acquitted owing to lack of evidence, and one defendant, who had escaped from prison in April 2006, was sentenced, *in absentia*, to two years' imprisonment for falsifying identity papers. The trial of a second group of 14 alleged militants began in late June 2007. Three were charged with participating in the attack at Lemgheity, while 11 were charged with having links to the GSPC. In July five of the accused were convicted of the lesser charge of using forged documents and sentenced to prison terms ranging from two to five years, while the other nine were acquitted.

In August 2007 the Ministry of the Interior, Posts and Telecommunications announced that it had registered 18 new political parties, the most notable of which was an Islamist party led by Ould Mansour, the National Rally for Reform and Development (Tawassoul—NRRD). Later that month the National Assembly adopted legislation criminalizing slavery, making the practice punishable by up to 10 years' imprisonment. Although slavery had been officially abolished by presidential decree in 1981, criminal legislation to enforce the ban had not been introduced. In November 2009 the UN Special Rapporteur on slavery announced that she had recommended a series of measures to eradicate the practice in Mauritania.

A plan to form a single pro-presidential party provoked considerable controversy during the second half of 2007. Concern was expressed that such a move would represent a setback for democracy, raising the prospect of a return to a one-party state. None the less, the National Pact for Democracy and Development (NPDD), was finally established in January 2008, led by Yahya Ould Ahmed el Waghef, the Secretary-General of the Presidency of the Republic. (The Constitution prohibited President Ould Cheikh Abdellahi from holding the leadership of a political party.)

Three attacks in late 2007 and early 2008 were attributed to groups linked to AQIM, prompting fears of a rise in Islamist extremism in Mauritania. In the first incident, in December 2007, four French tourists were killed by unidentified gunmen near the town of Aleg, some 250 km east of Nouakchott. A few days later three soldiers were killed in an attack on a military base at El-Ghallawiya, about 700 km north of the capital. Finally, in February 2008, three people were injured in a shooting outside the Israeli embassy in Nouakchott; seven people were later charged with participating in this attack. Meanwhile, several people were arrested in connection with the deaths of the French tourists. One of these suspects, Sidi Ould Sidna, escaped from custody in early April, but was recaptured at the end of that month, when several other wanted Islamists were also arrested, including Khadim Ould Seman, who was alleged to have led the Israeli embassy attack. Also in April, the security forces detained Marouf Ould Haiba, who was accused of orchestrating the attack against the French tourists. In May it was announced that Ould Sidna, Ould Haiba, Ould Seman and some 20 others would stand trial on various terrorism-related charges. Ould Sidna, Ould Haiba and Mohammed Ould Chabarnou were sentenced to death in May 2010, having been convicted of the murder of the French tourists.

In May 2008 Ould Zeidane was replaced as Prime Minister by Ould Ahmed el Waghef. The new Council of Ministers was dominated by members of the NPDD and also included members of the opposition UPF and NRRD. However, divisions within the NPDD over the composition of the new Government led to the resignation from the party of 27 senior members, including its Secretary-General, Mohammed Lamine Ould Eby, who claimed that reformist members of the party had been sidelined. At the end of the month 39 deputies, mostly NPDD dissidents, filed a motion of no confidence in the Council of Ministers. In early July Ould Ahmed el Waghef pre-empted a vote on the censure motion by tendering his Government's resignation, but he was immediately reappointed as Prime Minister. Opposition members were excluded from a new Council of Ministers established in mid-July. Political tensions persisted, however, and in early August 48 members of the NPDD resigned from the party.

THE HIGH COUNCIL OF STATE

On 6 August 2008 President Ould Cheikh Abdellahi was deposed in a bloodless coup led by Gen. Mohamed Ould Abdel Aziz, the Presidential Chief of Staff. Ould Abdel Aziz declared himself President of an 11-member military High Council of State (HCS), which assumed interim executive power and pledged to organize a free and fair presidential election 'as soon as possible'. Ould Cheikh Abdellahi and Ould Ahmed el Waghef were among several members of the ousted administration detained by the military immediately following the coup, which was widely condemned by the international community. It was reported that the coup had been carried out in response to Ould Cheikh Abdellahi's decision to dismiss four senior military officials, including Ould Abdel Aziz, owing to their suspected support for NPDD dissidents. The HCS issued a constitutional ordinance, which stated that it would exercise the powers of the President as defined by the Constitution, and granted Ould Abdel Aziz the power to appoint a Prime Minister, military officials and civil servants, but did not dissolve the legislature. The European Commission threatened to withhold aid in response to the coup, and on 9 August the AU announced Mauritania's suspension from participation in the activities of the organization. Ould Ahmed el Waghef was released on 11 August, but was placed under house arrest later that month. A large majority of Mauritania's deputies and senators (106 of 151) signed a statement expressing support for the coup, with 41 of the country's 59 parties reported to be backing Ould Abdel Aziz's assumption of power, while several parties loyal to Ould Cheikh Abdellahi, including the depleted NPDD, formed a new movement, the National Front for the Defence of Democracy (NFDD). In mid-August Moulaye Ould Mohamed Laghdaf, hitherto ambassador to Belgium and the EU, was appointed as Prime Minister. Despite its support for the coup, the RDF was among a number of parties that refused to participate in the new Government, which was appointed on 31 August, citing the absence of assurances regarding the length of the transitional period or the ineligibility of members of the military to contest the presidency.

Responsibility for an attack on a military convoy in northern Mauritania in mid-September 2008, in which 11 soldiers and a guide were killed, was claimed by AQIM, which had condemned the coup in the previous month. Ould Abdel Aziz had pledged to combat terrorism after seizing power, and three 200-strong military units were subsequently established to counter terrorism, particularly at the borders with Algeria and Mali.

In late September 2008 Ould Abdel Aziz rejected an AU ultimatum to reinstate President Ould Cheikh Abdellahi by 6 October, stating that it was an 'unrealistic' demand. In mid-October it was announced that Ould Mohamed Laghdaf would head a commission charged with establishing democratic conditions prior to the restoration of constitutional order. On 20 October a government delegation, led by the Prime Minister, held talks with EU officials in Paris, France, at which the EU demanded the formulation within one month of a plan for a return to civilian rule. Discussions with the EU continued, but on 20 November the Union declared that it would consider 'appropriate measures' against the Mauritanian authorities, deeming their proposals insufficient. Also in November Ould Ahmed el Waghef and four others were charged in connection with the bankruptcy of the national airline in 2008; the former Prime Minister was also charged over the alleged purchase of spoiled foodstuffs under an emergency aid programme in 2007–08.

Following international pressure, Ould Cheikh Abdellahi was freed on 21 December 2008. Political party leaders, legislators, representatives of civil society organizations, religious leaders and diplomats were among the more than 1,000 participants at a national convention held between 27 December and 5 January 2009, although the consultations were boycotted by the NFDD and Ould Cheikh Abdellahi. The convention proposed the organization of a presidential election on 30 May, subject to the approval of the HCS, which subsequently set the polling date for 6 June. A referendum on constitutional amendments reducing the powers of the President and enhancing those of the legislature was expected to be held concurrently.

In early February 2009, following the expiry of another deadline for a return to constitutional order, the AU's Peace and Security Council imposed travel restrictions and a freezing of funds on several members of the HCS and government ministers, while speculation mounted that Ould Abdel Aziz intended to contest the presidential election, despite strong opposition to his candidacy from the NFDD, the RDF and international organizations. The EU rejected the HCS's electoral plan (as did the NFDD and the RDF), describing it as 'unconstitutional and unilateral', and subsequently suspended all non-humanitarian aid to Mauritania. None the less, preparations for the presidential poll proceeded, with the appointment of new members to the National Independent Electoral Commission in early April. Later that month, as anticipated, Ould Abdel Aziz resigned from the military and as President of the HCS in order to stand in the election; three other candidates were also approved by the Constitutional Council. The RDF announced that it would boycott the election, insisting that military officers involved in the coup should not be eligible to run for President. In early May it was reported that Ould Abdel Aziz had been named leader of a new political party, the Union for the Republic (UR), which 83 of the 151 members of the legislature had joined.

Negotiations between representatives of the HCS, the NFDD and the RDF took place in Dakar, Senegal, in late May 2009, under the mediation of the Senegalese Government and with the support of the AU, the EU and other international organizations. The need to reach a consensus was emphasized by rising tensions in Mauritania, where demonstrations by opponents of the military regime were reportedly being violently suppressed. In early June participants in the talks signed an agreement aimed at ending the political crisis, which provided for the formal resignation of Ould Cheikh Abdellahi, the postponement of the presidential election until 18 July and the formation of a transitional unity government. In addition, Ould Ahmed el Waghef was immediately released from detention. In late June, after signing a decree appointing the transitional Government (which comprised both pro- and anti-coup ministers but was still headed by Ould Mohamed Laghdaf), Ould Cheikh Abdellahi resigned the presidency. The HCS was renamed the Superior Council for National Defence and placed under the authority of the new Government.

THE PRESIDENCY OF OULD ABDEL AZIZ

The presidential election was held, as scheduled, on 18 July 2009, contested by 10 candidates. Provisional results released by the Ministry of the Interior on the following day indicated that Ould Abdel Aziz had been elected President in a first round of voting, having received 52.6% of the votes cast. Only two other candidates secured more than 5% of the votes cast: Ould Boulkheir, the PPA leader and President of the National Assembly, representing the NFDD, with 16.3% of the votes, and the RDF's Ould Daddah, with 13.7%. An electoral turn-out of some 64.6% was recorded. Several of Ould Abdel Aziz's challengers alleged that massive fraud had been perpetrated in favour of the former head of the HCS, and the President of the National Independent Electoral Commission resigned from his position, citing doubts regarding the reliability of the vote. None the less, Ould Abdel Aziz's victory was confirmed later that month by the Constitutional Council, which rejected formal challenges from Ould Boulkheir, Ould Daddah and Vall (who had contested the election as an independent, receiving 3.8% of the votes). Ould Abdel Aziz was sworn in as President on 5 August, pledging to combat terrorism and corruption and to reform the army, and on 11 August he reappointed Ould Mohamed Laghdaf to the premiership. A new Government was also installed: Hamadi Ould Hamadi assumed the national defence portfolio, Mohamed Ould Boilil was appointed Minister of the Interior and Decentralization, Kane Ousmane was allocated the finance portfolio, and the leader of the UDP, Naha Mint Mouknass, became Mauritania's first female Minister of Foreign Affairs and Co-operation.

An alliance of the UR and the NRRD secured 13 of the 17 contested seats in partial elections to the Senate held in November 2009. Following their poor performance in the senatorial polls, in mid-December eight opposition parties, including the NPDD, the RDF, the PPA and the UPF, formed a new coalition, the Co-ordination of the Democratic Opposition (CDO). Later that month the CDO organized a rally in Nouakchott, at which leaders condemned the Government's allegedly dictatorial approach and rising insecurity.

The abduction of three Spanish aid workers near the northern city of Nouadhibou in November 2009 was followed in December by the seizure of two Italians in the south-east of the country; AQIM claimed responsibility for both incidents. One of the three Spaniards was released in Mali in March 2010, and in the following month the two Italians were also freed. Several Islamist militants were convicted of terrorist offences in May, with three notably being sentenced to death for the murder of four French tourists in 2007 (see above), while in July Omar Sid'Ahmed Ould Hamma, a Malian citizen who had been extradited from Mali to Mauritania in February, was sentenced to 12 years' imprisonment for his involvement in the abduction of the three Spaniards. However, Ould Hamma was freed and deported to Mali in the following month, apparently in exchange for the release of the remaining two Spanish hostages. In July the National Assembly adopted anti-terrorism legislation that defined which crimes constituted acts of terrorism and granted increased powers to police officers investigating such offences. The legislature had been forced to amend the legislation, which had initially been approved in January, after the Constitutional Council ruled that several of its provisions were unconstitutional and violated human rights.

Meanwhile, in January 2010 the EU decided to normalize relations with Mauritania and to resume full development co-operation. The UR and 10 other parties supportive of President Ould Abdel Aziz announced the formation of a Coalition of Government Parties in early March. Ould Abdel Aziz effected a minor government reorganization in the same month, notably appointing Ahmed Ould Moualaye Ahmed to replace Kane Ousman as Minister of Finance.

The ruling UR held its first congress in mid-July 2010, electing Mohamed Mahmoud Ould Mohamed Lemine as party Chairman. Later that month Ould Abdel Aziz and Ould Daddah held their first meeting since the previous year's presidential election, and in September the RDF unilaterally announced its decision officially to recognize the legitimacy of Ould Abdel Aziz's presidency, prompting speculation regarding divisions within the CDO. The opposition coalition was further weakened in December by the NPDD's declaration that it would work with the UR, although two days later Ould Daddah and Mohamed Ould Maouloud, the President of the UPF, reaffirmed the CDO's commitment to challenging Ould Abdel Aziz and his administration. In June 2011 the NRRD decided to join the CDO, while the PPA terminated its membership of the coalition, citing differences with the other constituent parties.

The Mauritanian authorities intensified their counter-terrorism efforts from mid-2010, while also pardoning and releasing from prison 52 convicted or suspected Islamist militants (not linked to AQIM) to mark Muslim festivals in September and November. Also in November, five young AQIM members surrendered to the army; the anti-terrorism legislation adopted in July granted special conditions to those who did so. The army foiled a planned attack by AQIM on Nouakchott in February 2011, firing on a car containing explosives some 12 km south of the capital. Three militants were killed and several soldiers injured when the vehicle exploded. Two AQIM members arrested in connection with the plot claimed that they had intended to detonate car bombs at the Ministry of National Defence and the French embassy.

President Ould Abdel Aziz reorganized the Council of Ministers in February 2011. Two new ministers entered the Government: Thiam Diombar, hitherto Director-General of the Treasury, as Minister of Finance, and Taleb Ould Abdi Vall, former Director-General of the Société nationale industrielle et minière, as Minister of Petroleum, Energy and Mines. The former Minister of Finance, Amedi Camara, who had only been assigned this portfolio in a minor reshuffle some two months previously, was appointed as Minister-delegate to the Prime Minister, in charge of the Environment and Sustainable Development, replacing Ba Housseinou Hamady, who became Minister of Health. Among further minor changes effected in March, Hamadi Ould Baba Ould Hamadi, hitherto Minister of National Defence, was appointed as Minister of Foreign Affairs and Co-operation, in place of Mint Mouknass, while Ahmedou Ould Idey Ould Mohamed Radhi was allocated the defence portfolio.

Trade unions and a newly formed group of youth activists (Youth of 25 February) organized a series of protests and marches in Nouakchott and other towns in early 2011 over a range of issues, including rapidly rising food prices, working conditions and youth unemployment. In response, the Government announced various measures aimed at appeasing the protesters, such as a programme to distribute land to impoverished people in Nouakchott and plans to create jobs and increase food production. However, in April the Youth of 25 February movement organized a major anti-Government rally in Nouakchott, described as a 'day of anger'. Police used tear gas to prevent demonstrators from entering a square from which they had been barred, arresting some 22 protesters.

Elections to renew one-third of the seats in the Senate were postponed in early April 2011, just over two weeks before they were due to take place; no reason was given for the delay. The senatorial polls were subsequently scheduled to be held concurrently with elections to the National Assembly and to municipal councils on 25 September and 16 October. However, in August the Ministry of the Interior and Decentralization announced the indefinite postponement of the legislative and municipal elections, in response to demands from opposition parties, which had threatened to boycott the polls. A national dialogue between political parties was conducted in September and October, to discuss issues of governance, national unity, the rule of law and the roles of media and civil society, but most members of the CDO, including the RDF and the UPF, declined to participate.

Meanwhile, sporadic protests continued in mid-2011. In August Biram Ould Abeid, the President of an anti-slavery organization, the Initiative for the Resurgence of the Abolitionist Movement in Mauritania (IRA), was sentenced to three months' imprisonment after organizing a sit-in demonstration against child enslavement. Some 56 people were arrested in Nouakchott in the following month after protests in several towns by the black movement Don't Touch My Nationality against a national population census that it deemed racist precipitated violent clashes with the security forces. One demonstrator was killed when protesters were dispersed in the southern town of Maghama. The Mauritanian authorities rejected claims by the movement that the census would lead to discrimination against the black minority and released 25 of the detainees in early October, but protests continued. Ould Abeid of the IRA created considerable controversy in late April 2012, prompting a number of protest marches, when he burned Islamic law texts that he claimed condoned slavery. Ould Abeid was one of 10 IRA activists arrested the day after the incident, and in late May Ould Abeid and six other detainees were charged with threatening state security (the other three being released); their trial commenced in June. Following widespread criticism, Ould Abeid and the IRA apologized for the destruction of the texts.

A series of anti-Government protests organized by the CDO took place from March 2012, in support of demands for the resignation of President Ould Abdel Aziz. In mid-April police used tear gas to disperse protesters in the capital, making several arrests and prompting the CDO to condemn what it termed 'brutal repression'. The protests increased in frequency and intensity in May, with several people reportedly being injured and others detained, when police attempted to quell the dissent. The CDO accused Ould Abdel Aziz of despotism and of failing to adhere to commitments made in the agreement signed in Dakar in June 2009. A new National Independent Electoral Commission was sworn into office in June 2012, some of its members representing four opposition parties that had participated in the national dialogue in September and October 2011. The Commission's first task was to organize the delayed legislative and municipal elections, which had yet to be rescheduled. However, the CDO refused to recognize the legitimacy of the body, holding a further demonstration in July 2012, with protesters reiterating demands for Ould Abdel Aziz's departure from office. A few days earlier one person had been killed in the town of Akjout, 250 km north of Nouakchott, when a protest by mine workers demanding higher wages and improved working conditions escalated into a riot, leading to the intervention of the security forces.

EXTERNAL RELATIONS

The persistence of inter-ethnic tensions within Mauritania was exemplified by the country's border dispute with Senegal. The deaths, in April 1989, of two Senegalese, following a disagreement over grazing rights with Mauritanian livestock-breeders, provoked a crisis that was exacerbated by long-standing ethnic and economic rivalries. In the aftermath of this incident Mauritanian nationals residing in Senegal were attacked. Senegalese nationals in Mauritania, together with black Mauritanians, suffered similar attacks, and several hundred people were killed. Many black Mauritanians fled, or were expelled, to Mali. Mauritania and Senegal suspended diplomatic relations in August 1989. Hopes of a rapprochement were further undermined in late 1990, when the Mauritanian authorities accused Senegal of complicity in an alleged attempt to overthrow Taya.

In July 1991 the foreign ministers of Mauritania and Senegal, meeting in Guinea-Bissau, agreed in principle to the reopening of the Mauritania–Senegal border and the resumption of diplomatic relations between the two countries. Full diplomatic links were restored in April 1992, and the process of reopening the border began in May. In late 1994 the Governments of Mauritania and Senegal agreed measures to facilitate the free movement of goods and people between the two countries, and in early 1995 it was reported that diplomatic initiatives with a view to the repatriation of Afro-Mauritanians from Senegal were in progress. According to figures published by the office of the UN High Commissioner for Refugees (UNHCR), the number of Mauritanian refugees in Senegal declined from 65,485 in 1995 to 19,999 in 1999, but progress with repatriation subsequently stalled. After taking office in April 2007, President Ould Cheikh Abdellahi urged Mauritanian refugees in Senegal and Mali to return, requesting assistance from UNHCR to facilitate their repatriation. A tripartite agreement on the voluntary repatriation and reintegration of the refugees in Senegal was signed by UNHCR and the Mauritanian and Senegalese Governments in November. In January 2008 an official ceremony was held to mark the return of the first group of around 100 refugees. The number of Mauritanian refugees in Senegal declined from 32,292 at the end of 2008 to 19,917 at the end of 2011, according to UNHCR. The repatriation programme ended in March 2012, with UNHCR reporting that some 14,000 Mauritanians had opted to remain in Senegal and would receive support with integration from UNHCR and its partners.

Meanwhile, in June 2000 relations between Mauritania and Senegal deteriorated after Mauritania accused the new Senegalese administration of relaunching an irrigation project that involved the use of joint waters from the Senegal river, in contravention of the Organisation pour la Mise en Valeur du Fleuve Sénégal project. The dispute escalated when the Mauritanian authorities requested that all of its citizens living in Senegal return home and issued the estimated 100,000 Senegalese nationals living in Mauritania with a 15-day deadline by which to leave the country. In mid-June, following mediation by Morocco, The Gambia and Mali, the Mauritanian Minister of the Interior announced that the decision to expel Senegalese citizens had been withdrawn and that Mauritanians living in Senegal could remain there. President Abdoulaye Wade of Senegal visited Mauritania later that month and announced that the irrigation project had been abandoned.

In January 2006 Wade became the first foreign Head of State to visit Mauritania after Vall seized power in August 2005. Both leaders pledged to enhance co-operation in a number of areas, and Wade expressed his support for the transitional process under way in Mauritania. In March 2006 Vall paid a reciprocal visit to Senegal. In the following month the two countries signed an agreement regulating the seasonal migration of Mauritanian cattle into Senegal, an issue that had caused significant disputes in the past, notably in 1989. In mid-2009 the Senegalese Government mediated in the Mauritanian political dispute regarding the restoration of constitutional order following the coup in August 2008.

Relations with Mali were also dominated in the 1990s by the issue of refugees. The problem of Mauritanian refugees in Mali was compounded by the presence in Mauritania of light-skinned Malian Tuaregs and Moors and also Bella (for further details, see the Recent History of Mali), who, the Malian authorities asserted, were launching raids on Malian territory from bases in Mauritania. Following reports that Malian troops had, in turn, crossed into Mauritania in pursuit of rebels, the two countries agreed in early 1993 to establish the precise demarcation of their joint border, which was concluded in September 1993. In April 1994 Mauritania, Mali and UNHCR representatives signed an agreement for the eventual voluntary repatriation of Malian refugees from Mauritania. The Tuareg refugee camp in Mauritania closed in mid-1997, following the repatriation of some 42,000 Malians. According to UNHCR, there were 12,442 Mauritanian refugees in Mali at the end of 2011, some 9,000 of whom had expressed a desire to return to Mauritania. However, a renewed Tuareg rebellion in northern Mali from January 2012 prompted more than 253,000 Malians to flee into neighbouring countries by late July that year, with more than 91,600 having entered Mauritania.

In January 2005 the Presidents of Mali and Mauritania signed an agreement on military co-operation intended to strengthen border security. In response to a request from the Mauritanian authorities following the attack on the military post at Lemgheity (see above), Mali dispatched troops to the common border in June. In mid-2005 both Mali and Mauritania joined seven other North and West African countries in participating in US-led military exercises aimed at increasing co-operation in combating cross-border banditry and terrorism in the region. Although the USA initially condemned the overthrow of Taya's regime in August 2005, US-Mauritanian military co-operation continued. In August 2007 joint US-Mauritanian military exercises were conducted in eastern Mauritania with the aim of training Mauritanian forces in methods of combating terrorism, illegal immigration and drugs-trafficking; in the following month Mauritanian coastguards also received training from the US Department of Defense. The USA responded more forcefully to the coup in August 2008 than to that which ousted Taya, swiftly suspending all non-humanitarian assistance to Mauritania, including funding for peace-keeping training, anti-terrorism activities and military co-operation; in addition, the US Administration placed travel restrictions on leading members of the military regime in October, and decided to terminate trade benefits previously accorded to Mauritania in December. Co-operation resumed following the internationally recognized presidential election of July 2009.

In September 2009, amid increasing concern regarding the activities of AQIM, military leaders from Algeria, Mali, Mauritania and Niger agreed on a plan for co-operation in combating terrorism and cross-border crime. Following further abductions of foreign nationals in Mali and Mauritania in November and December, and reports that those kidnapped in Mauritania had been taken to Mali, in January 2010 the two countries agreed to strengthen their security co-operation. However, relations became strained in the following month, when the Malian authorities freed four AQIM prisoners (one of whom was Mauritanian), thus securing the release of a French national abducted in November 2009. In response, the Mauritanian Government temporarily recalled its ambassador from Mali for consultations, accusing Mali of violating agreements on judicial and security co-operation by acceding to AQIM's demands. Also in February 2010, the Mauritanian armed forces announced the creation of a new military zone along the borders with Algeria and Mali, restricting movement within the area. In April, seeking to reinforce co-operation, Algeria, Mali, Mauritania and Niger established a joint military command headquarters in the southern Algerian town of Tamanrasset. At a summit earlier that month in Tamanrasset, army chiefs from the four countries had agreed to co-ordinate intelligence-gathering and patrols in border areas to combat terrorism, organized crime, arms-trafficking and kidnappings. A US-led military training exercise involving several countries in the Sahel region, including Mali, Mauritania and Niger, was held in May. In September, shortly after the return of the Mauritanian ambassador to Mali and with Malian agreement, the Mauritanian security forces conducted an offensive against suspected AQIM militants in northern Mali; according to official figures, 12 AQIM combatants and six soldiers were killed during the fighting. Later that month army chiefs from Algeria, Mali, Mauritania and Niger, meeting in Tamanrasset, agreed to establish a joint intelligence centre in Algiers to combat terrorism and organized crime. Mauritania also participated in a meeting of representatives of regional countries and members of the Group of Eight leading industrialized nations held in Bamako, Mali, in October, at which efforts against AQIM were discussed.

Meanwhile, the Mauritanian and Malian armies continued to co-operate closely in counter-terrorism activities. In June 2011 a joint operation by Mauritanian and Malian forces in western Mali reportedly resulted in the deaths of 15 suspected AQIM members, although AQIM later claimed to have killed 20 Mauritanian soldiers. In the previous month, at a meeting in Bamako of government ministers from Algeria, Mali, Mauritania and Niger, the Malian Government had proposed the formation of a regional task force of up to 75,000 troops to combat AQIM. The Mauritanian army claimed to have killed six AQIM militants in early July, after the organization attacked an army base near the town of Bassiknou, close to the Malian border. Later that month, at the 12th meeting of their joint co-operation committee, Mali and Mauritania agreed to strengthen co-operation in economic and social areas, as well as in security matters. Fears were expressed during a conference on security held in Algiers in September regarding the new threat posed both by the return to Mali and Niger of former Tuareg rebels who had settled in Libya, where they had recently fought in the civil conflict in support of forces loyal to the regime of Col Muammar al-Qaddafi, and by an influx of weapons to the Sahel region from Libya. In October it was reported that a senior AQIM commander had been killed by Mauritanian air forces during an aerial attack against suspected AQIM bases in Malian territory near the joint border. Government ministers from Algeria, Mali, Mauritania and Niger held talks in Washington, DC, USA, in November, meeting with several senior US officials, in order to advance their aim of establishing a regional counter-terrorism partnership. In December the EU announced that it would provide €150m. in support of regional efforts to increase security. At a summit meeting held in Libya in March 2012, interior and defence ministers from Algeria, Chad, Egypt, Libya, Mali, Mauritania, Morocco, Niger, Tunisia and Sudan adopted an action plan on regional co-operation and border control aimed at combating organized crime, drugs- and arms-trafficking, terrorism and illegal immigration; measures agreed included the exchange of security intelligence and increased joint border patrols. The Mauritanian authorities freed two Islamists from prison in July in order to secure the release by a splinter group of AQIM, the Movement for Oneness and Jihad in West Africa, of three European aid workers who had been kidnapped in Algeria in October 2011 and subsequently held hostage in Mali.

Although France has remained an important source of aid and technical assistance, successive Mauritanian Governments have sought increasingly to enhance links with the other countries of the Maghreb and with the wider Arab world. In February 1989 Mauritania became a founder member, with Algeria, Libya, Morocco and Tunisia, of a new regional economic organization, the Union du Maghreb Arabe (UMA). The member states subsequently formulated 15 regional co-operation conventions. In February 1993, however, it was announced that, given the differing economic orientations of each signatory, no convention had actually been implemented, and the organization's activities were to be 'frozen'. None the less, meetings of UMA leaders continued to be convened annually. Vall paid an official two-day visit to Morocco in November 2005, at the invitation of King Muhammad VI. During the visit, Vall's first outside Mauritania since assuming power in August, agreements were signed on co-operation in the fields of drinking water, maritime fishing and agricultural development. Relations remained strong under President Ould Cheikh Abdellahi, and in July 2007 Mauritania and Morocco signed an agreement on co-operation in the energy sector. In September 2008 the recently appointed Minister of Foreign Affairs and Co-operation, Mohamed Mahmoud Ould Mohamedou, visited King Muhammad to discuss the political situation in Mauritania, following the previous month's coup. The revival of the largely dormant UMA was a major focus of discussions during a four-day visit to Algeria by President Ould Abdel Aziz in December 2011.

Mauritania's relations with France improved significantly in the 1990s. However, relations deteriorated abruptly in 1999, following the arrest by the French authorities in July of Ely Ould Dah, a captain in the Mauritanian army, who was attending a training course in France. Ould Dah was charged with torturing, in 1991, fellow Mauritanian soldiers suspected of participating in the unsuccessful attempt to overthrow the Taya administration in 1990. The charges were brought at the request of human rights organizations under the 1984 International Convention against Torture and Other Cruel, Inhuman or Degrading Treatment or Punishment, to which France is a signatory. The Mauritanian Government responded by suspending military co-operation with France and introducing visas for French nationals visiting Mauritania. In September 1999 a French court ordered Ould Dah's release from custody, although he was required to remain in France until the end of legal proceedings. By April 2000, however, Ould Dah had illicitly returned to Mauritania. Relations with France appeared to improve following the election of a new, centre-right Government there in 2002, and in September of that year the French Minister of Defence, Michèle Alliot-Marie, met Taya in Nouakchott, and affirmed that co-operation between the two countries was to be strengthened. The French Minister of Foreign Affairs, Dominique de Villepin, visited Mauritania in June 2003, shortly after the attempted coup had been suppressed, when he expressed renewed support for the Taya administration; it was announced that French military co-operation with Mauritania was to recommence later in the year. In July 2005 a French court found Ould

Dah guilty of torture, sentencing him *in absentia* to 10 years' imprisonment. During a visit to Mauritania in February 2008, the French Minister of Foreign and European Affairs, Bernard Kouchner, pledged to increase bilateral co-operation on security matters in view of the recent attacks perpetrated by suspected Islamist militants in Mauritania in which French nationals had been killed (see above). In August 2009 a suicide bomber was responsible for an explosion outside the French embassy in Nouakchott, although no other people were seriously injured in the attack. The French Minister of Foreign and European Affairs, Alain Juppé, visited Mauritania in July 2011, discussing efforts to combat AQIM among other issues with President Ould Abdel Aziz.

In November 1995 Mauritania signed an agreement to recognize and re-establish relations with Israel. (The Libyan Government denounced these measures, closed its embassy in Mauritania and severed all economic assistance to the country, although diplomatic relations with Libya were restored in March 1997.) In October 1998 Mauritania's Minister of Foreign Affairs and Co-operation visited Israel and held talks with the Prime Minister, Binyamin Netanyahu. The visit was strongly criticized by the Arab League, which argued that it contravened the League's resolutions on the suspension of the normalization of relations with Israel. Shortly afterwards the Taya administration denied reports that it had agreed to store Israeli nuclear waste in Mauritania. Widespread controversy was provoked by the establishment of full diplomatic relations between Mauritania and Israel in October 1999. (Of Arab countries, only Egypt and Jordan, under their respective peace treaties with Israel, had taken such a step.) The announcement was widely criticized by other Arab nations, particularly Iraq (see above), as well as by opposition groups within Mauritania. Following the resumption of the Palestinian uprising in late September 2000, the Mauritanian Government came under renewed pressure to suspend diplomatic relations with Israel. However, although Taya's Government condemned the use of excessive force by Israeli forces in the Palestinian territories, it did not accede to these demands. A visit by the Mauritanian Minister of Foreign Affairs and Co-operation, Dah Ould Abdi, to Israel in May 2001, when he met the Israeli Prime Minister, Ariel Sharon, and the Minister of Foreign Affairs, Shimon Peres, provoked further controversy, particularly as it followed a violent escalation in the Israeli–Palestinian conflict and an appeal by the Arab League for all member countries to cease political contacts with Israel. A visit to Mauritania by the Israeli Deputy Prime Minister and Minister of Foreign Affairs, Silvan Shalom, in May 2005 was preceded, and followed, by the detention of several Islamists, although the Government denied that the arrests were linked to Shalom's presence. His visit was accompanied by a number of anti-Israeli protests in Nouakchott. Diplomatic relations with Israel were maintained by the transitional administration that took office following the coup of August 2005 and by the Government appointed by newly elected President Ould Cheikh Abdellahi in April 2007. In early March 2008, however, the Mauritanian Government expressed 'deep concern' at the intensification of Israel's military offensive in the Gaza Strip, urging the international community to intervene to end the bloodshed in the territory. The Mauritanian Government had recently come under increasing domestic pressure from several political parties to sever ties with Israel, and in the previous month the Israeli embassy in Nouakchott had been attacked by suspected Islamist militants (see above). Later in March the Palestinian President, Mahmud Abbas, visited Mauritania, where he held talks with Ould Cheikh Abdellahi. None the less, following his appointment as Mauritanian Prime Minister in May, Ould Ahmed el Waghef reportedly stated that breaking off diplomatic relations with Israel was 'not on the agenda'. However, bilateral relations deteriorated after the HCS assumed power in August 2008, and in January 2009 Mauritania recalled its ambassador to Israel in protest against a major military operation by the latter in the Gaza Strip. In March Israel reportedly closed its embassy in Nouakchott at the request of the Mauritanian Government. One year later, in March 2010, the Mauritanian Minister of Foreign Affairs and Co-operation announced that the termination of diplomatic relations with Israel was 'complete and definitive'.

Mauritania's relations with Libya and Burkina Faso were severely strained in August 2004, after the Government accused both countries of supporting a plot to seize power from President Taya (see above). The Government claimed that Burkina Faso and Libya had supplied the insurgents with weapons and funding, while Burkina Faso was also accused of having provided refuge and training to Ould Hnana and Ould Sheikhna after the failed coup attempt of June 2003. Both countries vigorously rejected the allegations, and Burkina Faso requested that the AU establish a commission of inquiry into the charges. In December 2004, during the trial of those accused of participating in the plots to overthrow Taya, Ould Hnana denied receiving assistance from Burkina Faso or Libya. In December 2005 Vall's attendance at the inauguration of President Blaise Compaoré of Burkina Faso, following the latter's re-election in the previous month, appeared to indicate a willingness on both sides to improve bilateral relations, and the two leaders held talks after the ceremony.

In March 2011 President Ould Abdel Aziz was one of five regional leaders appointed by the AU to a High-Level Ad Hoc Committee on Libya charged with leading African efforts to resolve the conflict that had broken out in that country in early 2011. The Committee opposed air strikes conducted by the North Atlantic Treaty Organization (NATO) on Libya (which were aimed at enforcing a UN-imposed no-fly zone over that country and at preventing attacks on civilians), advocating a political solution to the conflict. However, the rebel forces in Libya rejected the proposals of the Committee, its efforts being rendered largely futile by the NATO action. In June Ould Abdel Aziz stated that the Libyan leader, Col Muammar al-Qaddafi, should stand down, although it was not until late November that the Mauritanian Government officially recognized the National Transitional Council as the legitimate government of Libya, Qaddafi's death a month earlier having effectively marked the end of the conflict. Qaddafi's brother-in-law and the former head of Libyan military intelligence, Abdullah al-Senussi, was arrested at Nouakchott airport in March 2012, having flown in from Morocco. The Libyan Government requested Senussi's extradition, which was also sought by the International Criminal Court, based in The Hague, Netherlands, which had accused him of crimes against humanity, and by France, where he had been convicted *in absentia* of involvement in a 1989 attack on an aircraft that killed 170 people. However, in May 2012 Senussi was charged in Mauritania with illegally entering the country using a forged passport. Later that month the Libyan interim President, Mustafa Abd al-Jalil, urged the Mauritanian Government to extradite Senussi, as did Libya's interim Prime Minister, Dr Abd al-Rahim al-Keib, when visiting Mauritania in July. In early August, however, Ould Abdel Aziz asserted that Senussi must be tried in Mauritania on charges of illegal entry before being extradited.

Economy

VICTORIA HOLLIGAN

Mauritania has few natural resources other than minerals and its rich marine fisheries, which benefit from the Canary Current large marine ecosystem. It is hoped that the development of offshore petroleum resources will strengthen the economy in the medium to long term. The commercial part of the economy that contributes to foreign-exchange earnings is based on the exploitation of the country's fishery, petroleum and mineral resources, while the traditional rural economy is based mainly on livestock and agriculture, which is continually exposed to the problems of drought and desertification. Mauritania remains one of the least developed countries in the world, with a ranking of 159th out of 187 countries in the World Bank's 2011 Human Development Index. Despite ranking below the average for countries in Sub-Saharan Africa, Mauritania's Human Development Index value grew by 37% between 1980 and 2011. Specifically, over that period life expectancy increased by 5.5 years, mean years of schooling by 4.2 years, and GNI per capita by 14%, according to the World Bank.

A trend away from a nomadic way of life towards settlement in urban areas has recently been apparent, with 53% of the population living in urban areas in 2010, mainly the capital Nouakchott, compared with 14% in 1970. Around one-half of Mauritania's population is affected by poverty, which is predominantly a rural phenomenon. Although the incidence of poverty decreased from 46% in 2004 to 42% in 2008, unequal income distribution coupled with uncontrolled population growth have prevented the poverty rate from falling at a higher rate towards the World Bank's target of 25% by 2015. The Mauritanian economy remains vulnerable because of its dependence on the mining, fisheries and, more recently, oil sectors, all of which are liable to changes in world market prices.

Overall gross domestic product (GDP) growth has remained solid, increasing by 5.4% in 2005 and by some 11.4% in 2006 owing to the commencement of petroleum production, according to the IMF. GDP grew by only 1% in 2007 due to a steeper-than-expected decline in oil production as a result of technical problems; however, real non-oil GDP increased by 5.9% due to new mining projects and an expansion in agriculture. Although oil production rose in the second half of 2008, production did not recover to 2006 levels owing to technical difficulties on the Chinguetti field, resulting in overall GDP growth of 5.0%. Non-oil GDP growth declined by 1.0% in 2009 as a result of reduced donor financing due to domestic political turmoil, and less demand for Mauritania's main export commodities (iron ore, copper and fish) due to the global recession. Overall economic growth decreased by 1.2% in 2009, but increased by 5.2% in 2010, because of sustained high commodity prices and strong mining exports offsetting food and fuel imports. All sectors of the economy expanded, except the oil sector, resulting in non-oil GDP growth of 5.7% in 2010. The IMF estimated economic growth of 4.8% in 2011, which was contingent on the growth of the manufacturing and mining industries outpacing the drought-related decline in agricultural and livestock production. The revolutions in other Arab countries (dubbed the 'Arab Spring') have not had a material impact on Mauritania's economy, owing to the implementation of policies designed to reduce the impact of high food and energy prices on the poor and an increase in the minimum wage. The IMF forecast that GDP could record growth of 5.5% in 2012 if there was an increase in both manufacturing and mining production.

In the late 1990s donors sought a greater commitment from the Government to create an expanded economic role for the private sector, and it undertook to privatize the state telecommunications and public utility companies, and the national airline. The state telecommunications company, the Société Mauritanienne des Télécommunications, was transferred to majority private ownership in 2001 and was renamed Mauritel. In late 2002 the hitherto majority owner, Maroc Télécom, reduced its stake in the company, and the state again became the owner with the largest proportion of share equity in the company, with 46%. The electricity company, the Société Mauritanienne d'Electricité (SOMELEC), was initially scheduled to be transferred to majority private ownership in 2004; however, in mid-2004, the Government announced that the privatization process was being temporarily suspended, owing to a global recession in the electricity sector, while the overthrow of the regime of President Maawiya Ould Sid'Ahmed Taya in 2005 further delayed progress towards privatization, although the new administration announced the intention of pursuing liberal economic policies.

In May 1999 Mauritania concluded an agreement with the World Bank and the IMF, in accordance with which Mauritania was to receive US $450m. in support. In July the IMF approved a loan equivalent to some $56.5m., under the terms of a three-year Poverty Reduction and Growth Facility (PRGF) to support the Government's 1999–2002 economic programme. A further PRGF arrangement was agreed with the IMF in June 2003. Following a sharp depreciation in the value of the national currency in mid-2004, and a related increase in consumer prices, the ministers responsible for finance, economic affairs and trade were replaced in July, together with the Governor of the central bank. The new authorities took measures to ensure fiscal and monetary stability, although inflation continued to increase, to an estimated annual average of 10.4% in 2004. However, in November the Mauritanian authorities requested the cancellation of the PRGF arrangement, following the publication of revised figures that revealed substantial (and previously unreported) extra-budgetary spending. In early 2006 the IMF determined that Mauritania should repay two non-complying disbursements issued under the 1999–2002 PRGF; the first of these repayments was made to the Fund in April 2006. In the same year the IMF agreed to a Staff Monitored Programme (SMP) as a basis to form a new track record for a second PRGF, on the condition that central bank statements were verified independently and all information available was fully disclosed. Consequently, historical economic and financial data was revised, and a second, three-year Poverty Reduction Strategy Paper (PRSP), valued at $24.2m, was approved by the IMF and World Bank in early 2007. The programme, however, was suspended in early October 2008, following the coup staged by a military junta in August of that year, which caused most bilateral and multilateral donors to suspend non-emergency aid flows. After two months of consultations with the leaders of the military, the European Union (EU) suspended a 2008 aid package worth €156m. on the grounds that the military junta failed to present satisfactory proposals or commitments. The World Bank also suspended $175m. worth of aid for 17 national projects. In July 2009 Gen. Mohamed Ould Abdel Aziz was elected President, enabling international donors to normalize relations with Mauritania. In March 2010 the IMF approved a new, three-year Extended Credit Facility (the replacement for the PRGF) amounting to $118.1m., which was to improve broad-based economic growth and reduce poverty.

AGRICULTURE

As mining has developed, the contribution of agriculture and livestock-rearing to GDP has declined—from about 44% in 1960 to 16.3% in 2011, according to the African Development Bank (AfDB). Favourable weather conditions in 2010 increased the contribution of these sectors to GDP to more than 25%, according to the Banque Nationale de Mauritanie (BNM). However, 2011 was characterized by less favourable weather conditions and a potential severe drought was anticipated in 2012 by the authorities and donors. An estimated 50% of the economically active population are employed in the agricultural sector. Less than 1% of the land receives sufficient rainfall to sustain crop cultivation, which is largely confined to the riverine area in the extreme south. Mauritania is a food-deficient country with annual agricultural production varying substantially, according to weather conditions. Currently, domestic cereal production meets 30% of Mauritania's food needs, according to FAO. During 2000–07, according to the AfDB, agricultural GDP (including fishing) contracted by an average of 0.5% per year, although agricultural GDP increased by 1.9% in 2007, by 1.8% in 2008, by 1.5% in 2009 and by some 19.7% in 2010, before falling by nearly 1% in 2011, according to the IMF.

Production of cereals has fluctuated in recent years: output reached 152,600 tons in 2003, partially reflecting an increase in the area of the crop harvested, but declined in 2004 to 124,600 tons, before reaching 155,000 tons in 2007. Improvements in irrigation led to a rise in rice production from 41,678 tons in 1991 to a record crop of 101,900 tons in 1998. Output declined subsequently and totalled 49,000 tons in 2007, before more than doubling to 110,000 tons in 2010 and falling to 79,000 tons in 2011, according to FAO estimates. Other crops produced included cow peas, dates, fresh fruit, tubers and vegetables. High food import prices coupled with a poor harvest in 2007 heightened food insecurity. In response, FAO provided 500 tons of sorghum, millet, maize and cow pea seeds to the south of the country, and the Government established a Special Intervention Programme to reduce the impact of food shortages. These actions improved food security in 2009, with the UN World Food Programme (WFP) food security survey indicating a 14% decrease in persons living in food insecurity since 2008. Cereal production was estimated by FAO to have increased from 167,000 tons in 2008 to 170,000 tons in 2009, mainly due to a rise in sorghum production of 11% to 100,000 tons. Cereal production increased by 52% to some 259,000 tons in 2010, owing to favourable weather conditions. However, poor rainfall in 2011 caused a dramatic fall in cereal production to only 117,000 tons. In some rain-dependent agricultural zones, cereal production fell by a record 78%, according to the FAO, materially increasing food insecurity. The estimated number of food-insecure people increased from 428,000 in July 2011 to 838,000 in November 2011, according to a WFP/OSA (Observatoire de la Sécurité Alimentaire) survey, and was expected by FAO to rise to some 1.2m. by early 2012. In November 2011 the Government launched Plan EMEL ('Hope') to respond to the burgeoning food crisis by requesting assistance from the international community to subsidize cereal and livestock fodder. Mauritania is still highly dependent on imports of millet and sorghum from neighbours, Senegal and Mali, and wheat purchased on the international market. In 2009 some 508,000 tons of cereals were imported, increasing to 509,000 tons in 2010 and an estimated 514,000 tons in 2011, according to FAO.

Herding is the main occupation of the rural population, and its contribution to GDP was 10.7% in 2009, compared with 9.9% from both fishing and agriculture in the same period. The sector grew by 2.5% in 2010, compared with 3.0% in 2009. In 2010 there were 1.7m. head of cattle, 14.4m. sheep and goats, and 1.4m. camels, according to FAO estimates. The adverse weather conditions in 2011 reduced the availability of cattle food, resulting in an anticipated drastic fall in cattle production, according to the Mauritanian Association of Cattle Breeders.

The Gorgol valley irrigation scheme, funded by the World Bank, the European Community (EC, now the EU), Saudi Arabia, Libya and France, provided irrigation for 3,600 ha of rice, sugar, wheat and maize from the inauguration of the dam in 1985. Two similar projects were in progress: one at Boghé, on the Senegal river, and the other based on a number of small dams in the centre and west of the country. In total, the three schemes were projected to bring some 30,000 ha into cultivation. The construction of dams at Djama, Senegal, (completed in 1985) and at Manantali, Mali, (completed in 1988) under the auspices of the Organisation pour la Mise en Valeur du Fleuve Sénégal (OMVS) increased the amount of land available for irrigation as well as generating power, some of which goes to Nouakchott. In 1996 Mauritania won funding of some US $76.5m. from various donors for a major five-year irrigation project along the Senegal river. In late 1999 the World Bank granted funding worth $102m. to support irrigated agricultural projects in Mauritania. In addition, Mauritania signed a water management agreement with Mali and Senegal concerning water and pollution management within the Senegal river valley.

FISHING

The fisheries sector became increasingly important to the Mauritanian economy during the 1990s, and in 2005 it contributed more than 6% of national GDP and 29% of government receipts. As mining revenues increased from the mid-2000s, the contribution of fishing revenues to GDP decreased to about 5% in 2009, 4% in 2010 and 3% in 2011. According to FAO estimates, the total fishing catch grew by 27.3% from 216,900 metric tons in 2009 to 276,200 tons in 2010. The sector is increasingly regarded as an important potential contributor to national food security and is also the fourth most important source of exports after iron ore, gold and oil. The fishing and mining sectors together account for nearly 80% of total exports, which are mainly destined for Europe and the People's Republic of China. Virtually all the Mauritanian industrial fishing fleet is concentrated in Nouadhibou, in the north, which has both industrial and artisanal fishing ports, the latter constructed with Arab finance and Japanese aid. Artisanal fishing fleets are based along the coast and also in Nouakchott.

In 1996 a five-year fishing agreement was signed with the EU, which increased substantially Mauritania's annual compensation entitlement (including licence fees), from around US $10.7m. in the previous three-year treaty, to $75.4m. The annual catch quota was raised from 76,050 metric tons to 183,392 tons. For the first time, EU vessels were allowed to trawl the deep-water (pelagic) species. As part of the accord, the EU agreed to increase local employment in the industry from around 400 workers to 1,000 and to observe an annual two-month rest period (September and October) to protect species during their peak reproductive season. After prolonged negotiations, Mauritania signed a new fishing agreement with the EU for 2001–06, despite increasing fears that Mauritanian waters were being over-fished. The 2001 agreement with the EU provided for annual financial compensation of €86m., including support for surveillance and the management of fishing licences. In addition, EU vessels were to pay licence fees in accordance with the tonnage captured. A further accord, valid for six years, was concluded by the Mauritanian authorities and the EU in mid-2006; the fishing of sensitive species was to be significantly reduced under the terms of the new agreement. Mauritania was to receive €86m. annually. A further €22m. per year was to be paid by EU vessel owners for licence fees, of which an estimated €10m. was to be used to improve domestic port infrastructures and to modernize the national artisan fleet. A further protocol, concluded in March 2008 and valid from mid-2008 until 2012, aimed to respond to Mauritania's needs in terms of sustainable development of the fisheries sector and accounted for changes in the European fleet operating in Mauritanian waters. Fishing possibilities were reduced by 25% for octopus, by 43% for small pelagic and by 10%–50% for demersal species, resulting in the yearly tonnage being reduced from 440,000 tons to 250,000 tons. Given the reduced fishing possibilities, the EU's contribution has been reduced to €75.3m. annually, with a further €15m. in licence fees. Due to a lack of sectoral support by the Mauritanian Government in 2010, the EU introduced a new mechanism, the Compte d'Affectation Spéciale in early 2011. This special account was expected to contribute towards ensuring that funds from the EU were used to develop port infrastructure, combat illegal fishing and protect marine life.

The value of fish exports generally declined during the late 1990s and 2000s, partly because of the poor state of the Mauritanian fleet, only 60% of which was considered operational at that time, while the potential for fishing to contribute to the national economy has also been challenged by the extent to which catches by EU and other distant-water fleet-fishing vessels from Mauritanian waters are landed outside the country, in centres such as Las Palmas (in Spain's Canary Islands—a major regional entrepôt) or Vigo (Spain). High-value species that are targeted by distant-water fleets and local fishing vessels include octopus, squid, hake and crustaceans. Lower-value small pelagic species (sardines and mackerel) are mainly targeted by vessels from Eastern Europe (the Baltic states,

Poland and Russia), the Netherlands and Ireland. In 2007 fish exports were valued at US $205m., while EU fishing licences and compensation contributed a further $215m. Exports of fish decreased by some 17% from 161,400 metric tons in 2007 to 133,600 tons in 2008, representing an estimated 12% of the total value of exports. Government receipts from fishing increased from UM 41,000m. in 2009 to UM 42,300m. in 2010, before falling to an estimated UM 35,200m. in 2011, according to the IMF.

Effective management of Mauritania's fisheries resources will require closer regional co-ordination, given the importance of migratory species and stocks that straddle national boundaries. Mauritania is a member of regional organizations concerned with fisheries management and surveillance and collaborates with neighbouring maritime states. Notably, in March 2002 Mauritania signed a fisheries pact with Senegal, which was aimed at co-operation in the management of marine resources, fisheries surveillance, bilateral economic ventures, and enhanced collaboration in other fields such as scientific research and education. Representatives from the Fédération Nationale des Pêches of Mauritania and the Conseil National Interprofessionnel de la Pêche Artisanale du Sénégal met in Nouakchott in early 2010 to discuss the renewal of the soon-to-expire bilateral fishing pact. In August 2011 Mauritania signed a co-operation agreement with China to invest more than US $100m. in constructing a fish-processing plant.

MINING AND POWER

While over one-half of the population depends on agriculture and livestock for its livelihood, the country's economic growth prospects were transformed during the 1960s by the discovery and exploitation of reserves of iron ore and copper, which made Mauritania one of West Africa's wealthier countries in terms of per-head income. Moreover, the commencement of petroleum production, in early 2006, was expected to lead to significant economic growth. During 2000–06 industry, on average, represented 30.3% of GDP, and contributed 47% of GDP in 2007, according to the AfDB. In the period following the 2008 coup, mining accounted for 25.4% of GDP in 2009, rising to 34.8% in 2010 and further, to 37.1%, in 2011.

In the early 2000s iron ore accounted for about 11% of Mauritania's gross national income (GNI) and for 50%–60% of the country's exports, although higher international prices for the commodity increased the share of exports accounted for by iron ore to 64.5% in 2005, compared with 52.4% in 2004, despite a small decline (from 11.0m. metric tons to 10.6m. tons) of the quantity exported. In 2008 iron exports were 11.2m. tons, in comparison with 11.8m. tons in 2007, according to the Banque Centrale de Mauritanie (BCM). However, as a result of higher iron prices, the value of iron exports increased from an estimated US $575m. (40% of total exports) in 2007 to $823m. (46% of total exports) in 2008, according to the IMF. Owing to the global reduction in iron ore prices and a 10% decrease in production to 10.2m. tons in 2009, the value of exports declined to $521m. (38% of total exports) before rising to an estimated $997m. (48% of total exports) in 2010, because of increased production (11.5m. tons) and a rebound in prices. Production was estimated by the IMF to have fallen slightly, to 11.4m. tons, in 2011, although the value of exports increased by over 50% to an estimated $1,514m., owing to strong iron ore export prices. The 80% state-owned Société Nationale Industrielle et Minière (SNIM) is the world's seventh largest iron ore exporter. SNIM is involved in several new key projects, at El Agareb, al-Qalb al-Og, Tazadit and Guelb El Rhein, which were expected to increase iron production significantly. Iron ore is transported to the Nouadhibou port on the Atlantic coast by a 700-km rail network, owned by SNIM. The loading and storage facilities located at the port are also owned by SNIM. ArcelorMittal, the world's largest steel maker, signed an agreement in early 2008 with SNIM to develop the El Agareb iron ore mining project, with plans to double iron ore production to some 25 tons per year. Industries Qatar paid $375m. in 2008 for a 49.9% stake in the al-Qalb al-Og project in northern Mauritania, with partners SNIM and Australian Sphere Investment. Tazadit 1 is a project with China's state-owned Minmetals, projecting production of more than 2.5m. tons in 2011. A project costing $1,100m. is under way to expand the capacity of SNIM's Guelb El Rhein mine by a further 4m. tons per year, to build a new mineral seaport, and to modernize the railway connection from the mine to the seaport. Several financial institutions, including the AfDB, the European Investment Bank, the Agence Française de Développement and the Islamic Development Bank (IDB), were to provide funding for this project. As part of the growth projects, SNIM plans to construct a new enrichment plant and invest in human resources, with the aim of reaching a production target of 25m. tons of iron ore by 2018.

In 2010 iron ore was the most valuable mineral export; however, the value of exports of gold was expected to rise from 2012. Gold production increased by 144% in 2008, compared with the previous year, from 82,800 troy oz to 200,200 oz, with exports growing at the same rate, from 79,400 oz to 194,700 oz. These results were mainly due to an increase in the production of the Tasiast Gold Mine, taken over by the Dutch Red Back Mining B.V., which purchased the mining lease under the name Tasiast Mauritanie Limited SA from Lundin Mining Corporation in August 2007 for US $225m. The mine was officially opened by the President of Mauritania in July 2007; it consists of three permit areas totalling 16,222 sq km in area (the Tasiast, Ahmeyim-Tijirit and Karet). Output from the mine increased by nearly 25% from 158,657 oz in 2009 to 267,700 oz in 2010. Gold production growth stabilized at 6.7% in 2010. Kinross acquired a 100% interest in the Tasiast gold mine in September 2010 upon completing its acquisition of Red Back Mining Inc. for $7,100m. and announced investment of $15,000m. over three years in order to expand annual production capacity to 1m. oz. The deposit was estimated to contain nearly 2.2m. metric tons of resources, including 1.3m. tons of proven and probable reserves, in June 2011, according to Kinross. In early 2012 Kinross announced a write-down of $4.,600m. related to goodwill, as well as delays in the expansion project of up to nine months and an increase in labour costs. Meanwhile, the Australian company Drake Resources Ltd acquired two permits covering the southern extensions of the Tasiast greenstone belt in early 2011.

In 2001 a project at Akjoujt, which was being developed by Guelb Moghrein Mines d'Akjoujt, SA, and which contained an estimated 2,600 metric tons of cobalt, 328,000 tons of copper and about 25,700 kg of gold, was put up for sale. In July 2004 First Quantum Minerals Ltd of Canada announced that the Mauritanian Government had approved its involvement in the development of the copper and gold deposits at Akjoujt. A new company, the Société des Mines du Cuivre de Mauritanie, was duly formed, owned by a copper-mining consortium led by First Quantum. Production of some copper and gold at the site commenced in late 2005, and commercial production of 28,700 tons of copper started in 2007 after investment of more than US $104m. Production rose by 15% in 2008 to 33,100 tons, increased to 36,000 tons in 2009 and remained constant in 2011. Upon completion of an optimization programme, production was expected to reach 50,000 tons in 2012, according to First Quantum.

In March 1999 it was reported that geologists had discovered diamond deposits in northern Mauritania. By late 1999 two companies had reported progress with their diamond exploration projects, and in March 2000 the Mauritanian Government granted the US company Brick Capital Corpn a licence to prospect for diamonds in the Tiris Zemmour region. In January 2001 Ashton Mining announced the first discovery of diamond-bearing kimberlite in Mauritania, at Maqetir in the north. In that year BHP Billiton PLC of Australia, De Beers Consolidated Mines Ltd of South Africa, Rex Diamond Mining Corpn of Canada, and Rio Tinto PLC of the United Kingdom were all involved in prospecting for diamonds in the north of the country.

SNIM was involved in prospecting for tungsten (wolfram), iron, petroleum, phosphates and uranium. Phosphate reserves estimated at more than 135m. metric tons have been located at Bofal, near the Senegal river. Société Arabe des Industries Métallurgiques, a subsidiary of SNIM that produces 30,000 tons of gypsum per year, was granted a permit to begin exploiting these reserves in co-operation with foreign partners. In October 1999 highly valuable blue granite deposits were discovered in the north of the country. The Australian company Forte Energy currently holds seven uranium exploration licences covering 8,103 sq km. After making uranium discoveries in 2010, the company has drilled more exploration wells, with the expectation to announce their resource base by the end of 2012.

Exploratory drilling for petroleum began at the offshore Autruche field in 1989. In May 2001 it was announced that exploratory drilling at the offshore Chinguetti field had discovered petroleum-bearing sands; it was subsequently estimated that reserves at the field amounted to 120m. barrels. In June 2004 it was announced that the Government and Woodside Petroleum of Australia had reached a final agreement on the development of the Chinguetti oilfield. The company was to invest US $600m. in the field and commenced production in February 2006, with initial output forecast at 75,000 barrels per day (b/d). The company signed a revised contract with the new authorities in early 2006, which, *inter alia*, would result in a greater share of petroleum revenue being payable to the Government when petroleum prices were high, thereby resolving a dispute between the company and the former regime. However, in mid-2007 Woodside stated that initial output from Chinguetti was somewhat lower than expected, with around 12,000 b/d recorded at that time. Estimated reserves were consequentially reduced by 57% to 53m. barrels. In October Woodside sold its Mauritanian onshore and offshore production and exploration interests to Petronas of Malaysia for $418m. A programme of well interventions and infill drilling was successfully completed in 2008, resulting in production rates in excess of 17,000 b/d by the end of 2008. In line with field expectations, production fell to 7,850 b/d in 2010. A programme of well optimization was undertaken in 2011 to reduce the field decline rate. Other partners in the licence are the national oil company Société Mauritanienne de Hydrocarbures (SMH), Premier, Kufpec, and Tullow Oil, which purchased Roc Oil's share in 2011.

According to the IMF, oil production was 11.2m. barrels in 2006 and 5.5m. barrels in 2007; production was 4.4m. barrels in 2008, according to the BNM, which also certified an improvement in output from July 2008. Earnings from crude petroleum exports slightly increased from US $338.7m. in 2007 to $356.9m. in 2008, representing 17.7% of the total value of exports, owing to higher oil prices in that year. Nevertheless, oil production was characterized by technical difficulties on the Chinguetti oilfield and delays in developing new operating wells resulted in oil production declining further to 4.1m. barrels in 2009. In 2010 oil production fell by 26% to 3m. barrels; owing to well optimization, however, oil production stabilized at 2.9m. barrels in 2011.

Exploration and seismic testing for offshore petroleum and gas has been continuous, with reports of further discoveries, including significant levels of both petroleum and gas, at the offshore Banda in 2002, at Pelican and Tiof in 2003, at Tevet in 2004 and at Faucon in 2005. In January 2011 the Cormoran-1 exploration well successfully appraised the Pelican gas field and discovered two new underlying fields, Cormoran and Petronia. However, outstanding concerns regarding the protection of the marine environment and the avoidance of conflict between the petroleum sector and marine fisheries remained unresolved.

Onshore exploration is being conducted in the Taoudin Basin, where French oil company Total, along with partners Sonatrach of Algeria and Qatar Petroleum, began an exploration programme near the Malian border in 2009. In early 2012 Total secured a further exploration block just north of its existing onshore acreage with state partner SMH.

Reflecting the needs of mineral development, electricity generation expanded rapidly from 38m. kWh in 1967 to 165m. kWh in 2001 and to 277m. kWh in 2006. About one-half of the electricity is now generated by hydroelectric installations built on the Senegal river under the OMVS scheme. SNIM generates electrical power for its production centres from two diesel-powered plants at Zouïrât, and from the Point-Central plant in Nouadhibou. Mauritania receives 15% of the output from the Manantali dam. Additionally, it was intended to connect the dam under construction at Boghé (see above) to the Manantali electricity grid, in a project funded by the Arab Fund for Economic and Social Development. A new power station that was intended to generate 35% of the power needed in the capital was inaugurated in Nouakchott in May 2003. Mauritania has a 10,000-b/d refinery located at Nouadhibou, the Somir Refinery, which processes Algerian crude petroleum and is operated by an Algerian company. Winfield Resources, listed as a Canadian company, is currently attempting to secure financing to build a new 300,000-b/d refinery in the capital.

MANUFACTURING AND SERVICES

As of mid-2010 there was no significant industrial development outside the mining and the fish-processing sectors, although some development has occurred in areas such as construction materials and food processing. Initially, development concentrated on import substitution. However, as income from iron-mining rose during the early 1970s, the Government promoted the development of large-scale, capital-intensive manufacturing projects, in which it participated directly. These included the petroleum refinery at Nouadhibou, which entered production in 1978, with an annual capacity of 1m. metric tons. In the event, this wholly government-financed project was closed by the new regime. An agreement on rehabilitation was reached with Algeria in 1985, and operations resumed in mid-1987. More than three-quarters of its total annual output of 1.5m. tons are exported.

The development of fish-processing units at Nouadhibou, as a result of the Government's fisheries policy, made this sub-sector into the single most important manufacturing activity, accounting for as much as 3.9% of GDP in 2002. However, several plants have closed, mainly because of high utility costs, a lack of skilled labour and inadequate port facilities. In 2011 the manufacturing sector contributed 3.7% of GDP, according to the AfDB. According to the World Bank, manufacturing GDP increased at an average annual rate of 0.4% in 2001–10; it decreased by 0.1% in 2009, but grew by 5.0% in 2010, largely owing to a rise in output in the food-processing sub-sector.

The services sector recorded moderate growth of 4.4% in 2010, fuelled by the hotel, commerce and restaurant sector, after contracting by 0.3% in 2009, according to the BCM. The services sector contributed 38.9% of GDP in 2010, falling slightly to 37.5% in 2011, according to the AfDB.

TRANSPORT, TOURISM AND TELECOMMUNICATIONS

Transport and communications in Mauritania are difficult, with sparse coverage and a lack of maintenance, although infrastructure related to mineral development is of a high standard. The iron ore port of Point-Central can accommodate 150,000-metric ton bulk carriers, while Nouakchott's capacity was expanded to 950,000 tons with the completion, in 1986, of a 500,000-ton deep-water facility, financed and constructed by China. This development reduced the country's dependence on transportation through Senegal, and the excess capacity that the port currently represents could be used for gypsum and copper exports, and for traffic to Mali. Outside the mineral shipment network, communications are at present still poor: Mauritel operates the country's terrestrial telephone network and shares the domestic market for mobile telephone services with three other operators. In 2006 there were some 11,066 km of roads and tracks, of which only 2,966 km were metalled. In early 2004 the construction of a 470-km road linking Nouakchott and Nouadhibou was completed; the new highway was expected to improve prospects for both tourism and external trade. The Senegal river is navigable for 210 km throughout the year, and there are three major river ports, at Rosso, Kaédi and Gouraye. There are international airports at Nouakchott, Nouadhibou and Néma, 13 small regional airports, and a number of other airstrips. A new airline, Mauritania Airways, was established in early 2007, following an agreement signed between TunisAir of Tunisia and the Mauritanian private group Bouamatou. The former national airline, Air Mauritania, was liquidated in January 2008. In November 2010 Mauritania Airways was banned from European airspace owing to reported operational and maintenance deficiencies, and ceased operating in December. A new airline, Mauritania Airlines International, was established in the same month to replace the defunct flag carrier.

GOVERNMENT FINANCE

Mauritania's budget situation was transformed by mineral development. In the late 1970s, until the withdrawal from Western Sahara in 1979, spending increased as a result of the guerrilla war and the administrative costs associated with the annexed territory. Even after this time, the budget remained in deficit. In return for IMF stand-by credits, successive Mauritanian Governments have since 1980 attempted to restrain the level of budgetary spending and to raise current revenue.

Since fiscal policy is dependent on volatile natural resource revenues, fiscal balances are calculated as a percentage of non-oil GDP to determine the vulnerability of the economy and ensure that safeguards are in place against external shocks. The decrease in iron ore prices and the impact of the coup reduced revenue by 5%, to UM 188,500m., in 2009, while the Government lowered expenditure by 7.3%, to UM 242,900m., resulting in an overall deficit of UM 40,700m. or 5.3% of non-oil GDP, compared with a deficit of UM 55,600m., or 7.7%, in the previous year. The budget deficit shrank to UM 19,200m. (2.0% of non-oil GDP) in 2010, mainly as a result of an increase in tax receipts by some 40%. The fiscal deficit widened to an estimated 26,100m. in 2011, or 2.3% of non-oil GDP, due to one-off drought-related expenditures. The fiscal balance was expected to widen further in 2012, as a result of essential increased expenditures on drought-relief programmes initiated to avoid a humanitarian crisis.

FOREIGN TRADE AND PAYMENTS

The balance of trade tremained in surplus from 1992 until 2001, when a deficit of $33.7m. was recorded. The deficit widened in 2002, to an estimated $87.7m., further increasing in 2003 to $223.8m., in 2004 to $483.8m. and in 2005 to $783.3m. The IMF estimated a provisional deficit of $199.6m. in 2006. The sharp increase in the deficit during 2002–05 was principally the consequence of the import of petroleum-related machinery and equipment prior to the coming on-stream of various facilities. Such fluctuations in the trade balance were largely responsible for changes in the deficit on the current account of the balance of payments, which remained substantial into the 2000s. The BCM reported that the balance of payments recorded a deficit of UM 26,000m. in 2008, due to a current account deficit of UM 106,100m. However, the trade surplus was UM 6,100m. owing to high commodity prices. The current account deficit declined from 15.7% of GDP in 2008 to a projected 11.9% in 2009, due to re-engagement with the international community and a more favourable market for commodity exports (iron ore, copper and fish), according to the IMF. In 2010 the value of mining exports, namely iron ore, gold and copper, increased by some 71%, which mitigated the negative impact of food and fuel imports, resulting in the current account deficit shrinking to an estimated 8.8% of GDP. Sustained high prices for mining exports caused the current account deficit to fall again, to an estimated 5.3% of GDP, in 2011.

Foreign reserves stood at UM 51,000m. in 2008 (US $195m.) compared with UM 52,000m. ($208m.) one year earlier. Following sanctions imposed after the coup, foreign reserves were expected to deteriorate significantly in 2009. However, an allocation of Special Drawing Rights from the IMF and the receipt of financial compensation under the fisheries agreement with the EU enabled the BCM to increase foreign exchange reserves to $238m. in that year, according to the IMF. As a result of an increase in foreign direct investment (FDI) to 3.5% of GDP, coupled with foreign loans amounting to 6% of GDP, foreign exchange reserves increased to $288m. in 2010, according to the IMF. Sustained high mining revenues in 2011, combined with strong inflows of FDI (14% of GDP) and foreign loans (6% of GDP), resulted in official reserves increasing to a record high of $445.2m. in that year.

In 2010 the principal source of imports was France (14.1%); other major suppliers were the United Arab Emirates (12.1%), the Netherlands (10.6%) and Belgium (9.9%). The principal markets for exports in that year were China (19.1%), Japan (16.2%) and Spain (15.3%). The principal exports in 2010 were estimated to be: iron ore (44.4%), fish (18.4%) and crude petroleum (14.6%). The principal imports in that year were extraction industry-related machinery and equipment (28.4%), petroleum products (26.6%) and food products (18.2%).

By 1988 Mauritania was classified by the World Bank as 'debt-distressed' and was thus eligible for the system of exceptional debt relief that was agreed in principle at the summit meeting of industrialized nations, held in Toronto, Canada, in June 1988. Accordingly, in June 1989 the 'Paris Club' of Western official creditors agreed to reschedule $52m. of the country's external debt. While the foreign debt continued to rise, to $2,233m. by the end of 1991, debt-rescheduling agreements meant that the debt-service ratio was reduced to 20.4% of the value of exports of goods and services in that year. Nevertheless, debt had risen to $2,396m. by the end of 1995, equivalent to 235.9% of GNI. In early 1995 the IMF approved a $63m. loan, extending an ESAF to support the Government's financial and economic reform programme for 1995–97.

Towards the end of 1996 almost the entire stock of foreign privately contracted commercial debt (of US $92m.) was retired through a discounted buy-back operation funded by the World Bank and other donors. At the end of 1998 total external debt stood at $2,391m., while the cost of debt-servicing was equivalent to 27.7% of the value of exports of goods and services. Total external debt was equivalent to 250.8% of GNI at that time. Debt relief increased considerably, totalling UM 11,603m. in 2001. By 2007 total debt was reduced to 97.2% of GDP from 203.3% of GDP over the period 1997–2006. Notably, debt-financing payments reduced from 15.3% of exports over the period 2000–06 to only 2.4% of exports in 2007, according to the AfDB.

In late 1998 Mauritania concluded a three-year (1999–2001) arrangement that would allow it to reduce its multilateral debt substantially under the initiative for heavily indebted poor countries (HIPC). In return, Mauritania undertook to privatize the posts and telecommunications sectors, public utilities (water and electricity), and the national air carrier, Air Mauritanie. A second phase of the agreement, to be implemented in its final year, related to Mauritania's monetary policies and the control of the exchange market. The agreement was to be complemented by measures to protect fish stocks and reform the country's tax regime. In February 2000 Mauritania became one of the first countries to receive assistance under the HIPC initiative, amounting to a reduction of Mauritania's debt by US $622m. in net present value terms, representing savings of an estimated 40% of annual debt-service obligations. Agreement under the enhanced HIPC initiative was reached in 2002. Additionally, the 'Paris Club' of official creditors agreed in March 2000 to cancel $80m. of Mauritania's external debt; a further sum, equivalent to $188m., was cancelled by the 'Paris Club' in July 2002. In June 2003 another PRGF arrangement was agreed with the IMF. The PRGF was cancelled in late 2004, following the provision of inaccurate information to the Fund (see above), and the IMF emphasized that full disclosure of the mis-stated official reserves for 2000–02, as well as independent verification of the central bank's financial statements, would be required before any further requests for funding would be considered. Following the assumption of power by a new, transitional Government in August 2005, a significant revision of economic and financial data was undertaken, as a result of which marked discrepancies were found between economic data provided to the IMF during much of the 1990s and early 2000s. However, following the repayment of two disbursements issued during 1999–2002 deemed to be non-complying, the authorities entered into a new PRGF-supported programme later in 2006, worth $24.2m. After completion of the first review under the PRGF, the IMF commended Mauritania's progress. The country had met all criteria under the programme, with significant structural reforms carried out, including the adoption of legislation granting greater autonomy to the central bank. Another positive structural reform noted by the Fund was the new foreign exchange market, which was introduced in early 2007.

The support of foreign donors remained essential to stimulate the key sectors of the economy. Net financial flows in 2006 comprised US $187.6m. of overseas development assistance and $23.6m. of FDI, according to the AfDB. In June 2005 Mauritania was among 18 countries to be granted 100% debt relief on multilateral debt agreed by the Group of Eight leading industrialized nations (G8), subject to the approval of the lenders. In April 2007 the IDB granted the Government $18m. in the form of two loans; the money was set aside for road-building and the agricultural sector. A further $15m. was granted by the AfDB in 2007 in the form of a supplementary loan to finance the provision of safe drinking water from the Senegal river (Aftout Essaheli) to Nouakchott. Total external debt declined from $3,123m. in 2009 to $2,432m. in 2010, according to the AfDB. External debt was equivalent to 50.7% of GDP at the end of December 2011, compared with 76.8% in 2010 and about 100% in 2009, owing to debt cancellation by Arab aid donors and a policy of obtaining soft loans. In order to fund investment in the energy sector a standard line of credit was obtained in 2011.

Statistical Survey

Source (unless otherwise stated): Office National de la Statistique, BP 240, Nouakchott; tel. 45-25-28-80; fax 45-25-51-70; e-mail webmaster@ons.mr; internet www.ons.mr.

Area and Population

AREA, POPULATION AND DENSITY

Area (sq km)	1,030,700*
Population (census results)	
5–20 April 1988	1,864,236†
1–15 November 2000‡	
Males	1,241,712
Females	1,266,447
Total	2,508,159
Population (official estimates at mid-year)	
2009	3,456,430
2010	3,340,623
2011	3,432,192
Density (per sq km) at mid-2011	3.3

* 397,950 sq miles.

† Including an estimate of 224,095 for the nomad population.

‡ Figures include nomads, totalling 128,163 (males 66,007; females 62,156), enumerated during 10 March–20 April 2001.

Ethnic Groups (percentage of total, 1995): Moor 81.5; Wolof 6.8; Toucouleur 5.3; Sarakholé 2.8; Peul 1.1; Others 2.5 (Source: La Francophonie).

POPULATION BY AGE AND SEX

(UN estimates at mid-2012)

	Males	Females	Total
0–14	726,389	701,885	1,428,274
15–64	1,053,476	1,042,336	2,095,812
65 and over	41,148	57,728	98,876
Total	1,821,013	1,801,949	3,622,962

Source: UN, *World Population Prospects: The 2010 Revision*.

REGIONS

(census of November 2000)

Region	Area ('000 sq km)	Population*	Chief town
Hodh Ech Chargui	183	281,600	Néma
Hodh el Gharbi	53	212,156	Aïoun el Atrous
Assaba	37	242,265	Kiffa
Gorgol	14	242,711	Kaédi
Brakna	33	247,006	Aleg
Trarza	68	268,220	Rosso
Adrar	215	69,542	Atâr
Dakhlet-Nouadhibou	22	79,516	Nouadhibou
Tagant	95	76,620	Tidjikja
Guidimagha	10	177,707	Sélibaby
Tiris Zemmour	253	41,121	Zouîrât
Inchiri	47	11,500	Akjoujt
Nouakchott (district)	1	558,195	Nouakchott
Total	1,030	2,508,159	

* Including nomad population, enumerated during 10 March–20 April 2001.

PRINCIPAL TOWNS

(population at census of 2000*)

Nouakchott (capital)	558,195	Kiffa	32,716
Nouadhibou	72,337	Bougadoum	29,045
Rosso	48,922	Atâr	24,021
Boghé	37,531	Boutilimit	22,257
Adel Bagrou	36,007	Theiekane	22,041
Kaédi	34,227	Ghabou	21,700
Zouîrât	33,929	Mal	20,488

* With the exception of Nouakchott, figures refer to the population of communes (municipalities), and include nomads.

Mid-2011 (incl. suburbs, UN estimate): Nouakchott 786,226 (Source: UN, *World Urbanization Prospects: The 2011 Revision*).

BIRTHS AND DEATHS

(annual averages, UN estimates)

	1995–2000	2000–05	2005–10
Birth rate (per 1,000)	38.2	36.6	34.8
Death rate (per 1,000)	10.6	10.3	10.1

Source: UN, *World Population Prospects: The 2010 Revision*.

Life expectancy (years at birth): 58.2 (males 56.6; females 60.0) in 2010 (Source: World Bank, World Development Indicators database).

ECONOMICALLY ACTIVE POPULATION

(census of 2000, persons aged 10 years and over, including nomads)

	Males	Females	Total
Agriculture, hunting, forestry and fishing	219,771	94,535	314,306
Mining and quarrying	5,520	249	5,769
Manufacturing	18,301	11,855	30,156
Electricity, gas and water	2,655	182	2,837
Construction	15,251	311	15,562
Trade, restaurants and hotels	83,733	24,799	108,532
Transport, storage and communications	17,225	691	17,916
Financing, insurance, real estate and business services	1,557	454	2,011
Community, social and personal services	72,137	26,583	98,720
Other and unspecified	33,350	22,608	55,958
Total	469,500	182,267	651,767

Mid-2012 (estimates in '000): Agriculture, etc. 782; Total labour force 1,567 (Source FAO).

Health and Welfare

KEY INDICATORS

Total fertility rate (children per woman, 2010)	4.5
Under-5 mortality rate (per 1,000 live births, 2010)	111
HIV/AIDS (% of persons aged 15–49, 2009)	0.7
Physicians (per 1,000 head, 2009)	0.13
Hospital beds (per 1,000 head, 2006)	0.40
Health expenditure (2009): US $ per head (PPP)	79
Health expenditure (2009): % of GDP	4.2
Health expenditure (2009): public (% of total)	52.8
Access to water (% of persons, 2010)	50
Access to sanitation (% of persons, 2010)	26
Total carbon dioxide emissions ('000 metric tons, 2008)	1,998.5
Carbon dioxide emissions per head (metric tons, 2008)	0.6
Human Development Index (2011): ranking	159
Human Development Index (2011): value	0.453

For sources and definitions, see explanatory note on p. vi.

Agriculture

PRINCIPAL CROPS
('000 metric tons)

	2008	2009	2010
Rice, paddy	82.2	53.6	134.4
Maize	15.5	11.8	19.9
Sorghum	85.6	93.6	114.2
Millet	2.3	8.1	3.3
Peas, dry*	10.7	11.6	10.0
Cow peas, dry*	10.4	10.3	11.1
Beans, dry	9.9†	10.0*	10.5*
Dates	19.2	20.0*	19.9*

* FAO estimate(s).
† Unofficial figure.

Aggregate production ('000 metric tons, may include official, semi-official or estimated data): Total cereals 191 in 2008, 172 in 2009, 276 in 2010; Total pulses 51 in 2008–09, 52 in 2010; Total roots and tubers 7 in 2008–10; Total vegetables (incl. melons) 5 in 2008, 4 in 2009, 5 in 2010; Total fruits (excl. melons) 22 in 2008, 23 in 2009–10.

Source: FAO.

LIVESTOCK
('000 head, year ending September)

	2008	2009	2010*
Cattle	1,654	1,678	1,678
Goats	5,261	5,524	5,500
Sheep	7,893	8,287	8,860
Asses*	170	170	170
Horses*	20	20	20
Camels	1,341	1,351	1,351
Chickens*	4,300	4,300	4,300

* FAO estimates.

Source: FAO.

LIVESTOCK PRODUCTS
('000 metric tons, FAO estimates)

	2008	2009	2010
Goat meat	14.6	14.6	14.6
Camel meat	21.6	21.6	24.9
Chicken meat	4.5	4.5	4.5
Camel milk	28.6	29.7	26.3
Cows' milk	136.7	142.2	126.0
Sheep's milk	109.0	113.1	115.5
Goats' milk	115.7	120.1	123.8
Hen eggs	5.9	5.6	5.4

Source: FAO.

Forestry

ROUNDWOOD REMOVALS
('000 cubic metres, excl. bark, FAO estimates)

	2008	2009	2010
Sawlogs, veneer logs and logs for sleepers	1	1	1
Other industrial wood	2	2	2
Fuel wood	1,747	1,791	1,836
Total	1,750	1,794	1,839

2011: Production assumed to be unchanged from 2010 (FAO estimates).

Source: FAO.

SAWNWOOD PRODUCTION
('000 cubic metres, incl. railway sleepers)

	2005	2006	2007*
Broadleaved (hardwood)	7	14	14
Total	7	14	14

* FAO estimates.

2008–11: Production assumed to be unchanged from 2007 (FAO estimates).

Source: FAO.

Fishing

('000 metric tons, live weight)

	2008	2009	2010
Freshwater fishes*	15.0	15.0	15.0
Sardinellas	21.8	89.0*	147.7
European pilchard (sardine)	15.3	13.4	16.7
European anchovy	12.6	7.0	5.0
Jack and horse mackerels	34.2	24.4	33.7
Chub mackerel	6.3	5.1	4.6
Octopuses	7.6	12.3	15.8
Total catch (incl. others)*	195.3	216.9	276.2

* FAO estimate(s).

Source: FAO.

Mining

('000 metric tons)

	2008	2009	2010
Gypsum	44.4	36.9	70.7*
Iron ore: gross weight	10,950	10,275	11,500
Iron ore: metal content*	7,120	6,680	7,480

* Estimate(s).

Source: US Geological Survey.

Industry

SELECTED PRODUCTS
('000 metric tons unless otherwise indicated)

	2008	2009	2010
Cement*	322	340	340†
Crude steel*†	5	5	5
Electric energy (million kWh)	486.9	470.0	516.5

* Data from US Geological Survey.
† Estimated production.

Finance

CURRENCY AND EXCHANGE RATES

Monetary Units
5 khoums = 1 ouguiya (UM).

Sterling, Dollar and Euro Equivalents (30 March 2012)
£1 sterling = 466.102 ouguiyas;
US $1 = 291.150 ouguiyas;
€1 = 388.860 ouguiyas;
1,000 ouguiyas = £2.15 = $3.43 = €2.57.

Average Exchange Rate (ouguiyas per US $)

2009	262.366
2010	275.894
2011	281.118

BUDGET

('000 million ouguiyas)

Revenue*	2008	2009	2010
Tax revenue	115.0	106.6	154.6
Taxes on income and profits	34.9	34.6	43.8
Tax on business profits	19.8	16.9	22.0
Tax on wages and salaries	11.9	14.4	18.3
Taxes on goods and services	59.8	53.8	78.1
Value-added tax	39.5	38.7	48.9
Turnover taxes	13.8	7.7	21.9
Tax on petroleum products	3.9	4.5	2.2
Other excises	1.3	1.7	4.0
Taxes on international trade	17.4	14.2	17.3
Non-tax revenue	67.1	75.8	81.6
Fishing royalties and penalties	38.7	41.0	42.3
Revenue from public enterprises	16.2	18.4	13.3
Capital revenue	1.5	0.7	0.7
Other revenue (incl. special accounts)	6.6	9.0	9.9
Oil revenue	18.0	13.7	13.5
Total	200.2	196.1	249.6

Expenditure†	2008	2009	2010
Current expenditure	191.1	170.1	196.8
Wages and salaries	71.1	77.0	83.7
Equipment maintenance and supplies	53.9	51.7	59.8
Transfers and subsidies	42.8	20.3	27.9
Interest on public debt	16.5	16.2	15.0
Capital expenditure	55.6	36.9	56.4
Domestically financed	43.6	n.a.	n.a.
Financed from abroad	12.0	n.a.	n.a.
Total	246.7	207.0	253.2

* Excluding grants received ('000 million ouguiyas): 3.2 in 2008; 2.4 in 2009; 11.6 in 2010.

† Excluding restructuring and net lending ('000 million ouguiyas): 15.1 in 2008; 21.0 in 2009; 16.6 in 2010.

2011 ('000 million ouguiyas): *Revenue:* Tax revenue 183.7; Non-tax revenue 109.8; Oil revenue 22.9; Grants 7.7; Total revenue (incl. grants) 324.1. *Expenditure:* Current expenditure 238.9 (Wages and salaries 89.1); Capital expenditure and net lending 85.0; Total expenditure (incl. net lending) 324.0.

2012 ('000 million ouguiyas, projections): Total revenue 325.3; Total expenditure 383.9 (Source: IMF, *Islamic Republic of Mauritania: Third Review Under the Three-Year Extended Credit Facility Arrangement—Staff Report; Press Release on the Executive Board Discussion*—December 2011).

INTERNATIONAL RESERVES

(US $ million at 31 December)

	2009	2010	2011
Gold*	12.6	16.1	18.0
IMF special drawing rights	0.2	0.1	1.5
Foreign exchange	225.4	271.7	483.2
Total	238.2	287.9	502.7

* Valued at market-related prices.

Source: IMF, *International Financial Statistics*.

MONEY SUPPLY

(million ouguiyas at 31 December)

	2009	2010	2011
Currency outside banks	82,226	91,252	113,723
Demand deposits at deposit money banks	148,967	172,001	222,926
Total money (incl. others)	232,111	264,517	338,012

Source: IMF, *International Financial Statistics*.

COST OF LIVING

(Consumer Price Index; base: 2000 = 100)

	2008	2009	2010
Food (incl. beverages)	190.6	195.5	223.9
Clothing (incl. footwear)	152.5	163.0	174.1
Rent	169.6	164.3	171.9
All items (incl. others)	170.4	174.1	195.6

2011: Food (incl. beverages) 223.9, All items (incl. others) 195.6.

Source: ILO.

NATIONAL ACCOUNTS

(million ouguiyas at current prices)

Expenditure on the Gross Domestic Product

	2009	2010	2011
Government final consumption expenditure	154,933	165,566	173,626
Private final consumption expenditure	576,563	700,322	792,306
Gross capital formation	195,381	243,948	296,593
Total domestic expenditure	926,877	1,109,836	1,262,525
Exports of goods and services	399,012	602,378	849,802
Less Imports of goods and services	531,703	715,161	965,879
GDP in purchasers' values	794,187	997,054	1,146,447

Gross Domestic Product by Economic Activity

	2009	2010	2011
Agriculture, hunting, forestry and fishing	146,638	157,932	172,377
Mining and quarrying	184,990	320,222	393,514
Manufacturing	29,718	33,822	39,194
Construction	40,726	50,410	58,396
Wholesale and retail trade, restaurants and hotels	81,113	95,814	109,803
Finance, insurance and real estate	92,171	99,092	112,291
Transport and communications	35,071	36,905	39,444
Public administration and defence	116,834	126,894	135,727
Sub-total	727,261	921,091	1,060,746
Indirect taxes, less subsidies	66,925	75,962	85,702
GDP in purchasers' values	794,187	997,054	1,146,447

Source: African Development Bank.

BALANCE OF PAYMENTS
(US $ million)

	2008	2009	2010*
Exports of goods f.o.b.	1,787.6	1,364.2	2,073.5
Imports of goods f.o.b.	–1,910.9	–1,390.9	–1,935.3
Trade balance	–123.3	–26.7	138.2
Services (net)	–626.7	–479.2	–550.9
Balance on goods and services	–750.0	–505.9	–412.7
Other income (net)	30.5	52.1	–68.5
Balance on goods, services and income	–719.5	–453.8	–481.2
Current transfers (net)	196.6	130.8	162.1
Private unrequited transfers (net)	71.7	66.4	59.3
Official transfers	124.9	64.4	102.8
Current balance	–522.9	–323.0	–319.1
Capital account (net)	30.9	0.0	209.0
Direct investment (net)	338.4	–3.1	128.3
Official medium- and long-term loans	200.5	172.6	79.5
Other capital	–161.2	42.6	39.0
Net errors and omissions	68.9	102.5	99.2
Overall balance	–45.4	–8.4	235.9

* Estimates.

Source: IMF, *Islamic Republic of Mauritania: Third Review Under the Three-Year Extended Credit Facility Arrangement—Staff Report; Press Release on the Executive Board Discussion* (December 2011).

External Trade

PRINCIPAL COMMODITIES
('000 million ouguiyas)

Imports	2008	2009	2010
Food products	105.3	96.0	86.5
Cosmetic chemical products	7.5	9.4	10.2
Petroleum products	138.5	70.9	126.0
Construction materials	24.1	26.5	38.8
Road vehicles and parts	27.1	26.0	37.8
Various equipment and appliances	55.8	78.7	134.8
Total (incl. others)	395.1	350.7	474.1

Exports	2008	2009	2010
Iron ore	186.5	142.5	221.1
Fish	66.6	83.9	91.6
Petroleum	78.7	57.3	72.7
Total (incl. others)	392.2	369.0	498.1

2011 (US $ million): Total imports 689.7; Total exports 691.0.

PRINCIPAL TRADING PARTNERS
(US $ million)

Imports c.i.f.	2008	2009	2010
Belgium	24.1	18.9	46.9
Brazil	17.5	18.2	13.1
China, People's Republic	19.3	28.3	32.2
Côte d'Ivoire	1.8	1.7	1.1
France	64.6	64.5	66.9
Germany	12.4	14.1	12.9
Greece	2.1	1.5	1.5
Italy	3.8	3.1	5.2
Japan	12.9	11.0	12.6
Malaysia	8.2	6.83	6.8
Morocco	6.7	4.9	11.0
Netherlands	30.3	18.5	50.4
Singapore	3.8	2.4	21.8
Spain	19.2	9.9	22.4
United Arab Emirates	4.6	4.7	57.4
United Kingdom	4.1	10.1	5.2
USA	12.7	14.2	17.6
Total (incl. others)	395.1	350.7	474.1

Exports c.i.f.*	2008	2010	2010
China, People's Republic	30.6	66.0	38.0
France	64.1	20.0	3.6
Germany	32.2	18.0	0.1
Italy	28.6	34.0	3.8
Japan	21.2	27.5	32.3
Russia	5.1	5.2	8.9
Spain	26.3	30.5	30.4
United Kingdom	8.7	5.3	n.a.
Total (incl. others)	313.5	305.4	199.0

* Excluding exports of petroleum, gold and copper.

2011 (US $ million): Total imports 689.7; Total exports 691.0.

Transport

RAILWAYS
(traffic)

	2009	2010
Passengers carried	12,736	11,874
Freight carried (metric tons)	4,432	5,948

Freight ton-km (million, estimates): 6,720 in 1991; 6,810 in 1992; 6,890 in 1993 (Source: UN Economic Commission for Africa, *African Statistical Yearbook*).

ROAD TRAFFIC
(motor vehicles registered)

	2004	2005	2006
Passenger cars	6,033	6,040	6,182
Government vehicles	251	317	369
Specialist vehicles	413	542	504

SHIPPING

Merchant Fleet
(registered at 31 December)

	2007	2008	2009
Number of vessels	152	155	155
Total displacement ('000 grt)	51.5	52.0	52.0

Source: IHS Fairplay, *World Fleet Statistics*.

International Sea-borne Freight Traffic
(Port of Nouakchott, '000 metric tons)

	2007	2008	2009
Goods loaded	251	267	283
Goods unloaded	2,045	2,051	2,448

Source: Port Autonome de Nouakchott.

CIVIL AVIATION
(traffic on scheduled services)*

	2007	2008	2009
Kilometres flown (million)	1	1	1
Passengers carried ('000)	155	154	142
Passenger-km (million)	68	68	64
Total ton-km (million)	6	7	6

* Including an apportionment of the traffic of Air Afrique.

Source: UN, *Statistical Yearbook*.

Passengers carried ('000): 114 in 2010; 118 in 2011.

Tourism

Tourist arrivals (estimates, '000): 24 in 1999.

Receipts from tourism (US $ million, excl. passenger transport): 28 in 1999 (Source: World Tourism Organization).

Communications Media

	2009	2010	2011
Telephones ('000 main lines in use)	74.5	71.6	72.3
Mobile cellular telephones ('000 subscribers)	2,182.2	2,745.0	3,283.4
Broadband subscribers	5,900	5,600	6,100

Internet subscribers: 9,700 in 2008.

Personal computers: 139,000 (45.4 per 1,000) in 2006.

Television receivers ('000 in use): 247 in 1999.

Radio receivers ('000 in use): 570 in 1997.

Daily newspapers: Estimated average circulation ('000 copies) 12 in 1996; 3 in 2004.

Sources: UNESCO, *Statistical Yearbook*; UN, *Statistical Yearbook*; International Telecommunication Union.

Education

(2010/11 unless otherwise indicated)

	Institutions	Teachers	Students Males	Students Females	Students Total
Pre-primary	n.a.	251*	n.a.	n.a.	4,856*
Primary	2,676†	13,640	264,787	271,189	535,976
Secondary	n.a.	5,869	67,641	55,608	123,249
Tertiary	4‡	379	10,434	4,102	14,536

* 2004/05.

† 1998/99.

‡ 1995/96.

Pupil-teacher ratio (primary education, UNESCO estimate): 37.2 in 2009/10.

Adult literacy rate (UNESCO estimates): 58.0% (males 64.9%; females 51.2%) in 2010.

Sources: mainly UNESCO Institute for Statistics and Ministry of National Education, Nouakchott.

Directory

While no longer an official language, French is still widely used in Mauritania, especially in the commercial sector. Many organizations are therefore listed under their French names, by which they are generally known.

The Constitution

The Constitution of the Islamic Republic of Mauritania was approved in a national referendum on 12 July 1991; amendments were adopted following a referendum conducted on 25 June 2006.

The Constitution vests executive power in the President, who is elected, by universal adult suffrage, for a term of five years, renewable only once. Legislative power is vested in the National Assembly, which is elected by universal suffrage for a period of five years, and in the Senate, which is elected by municipal leaders with a six-year mandate, one-third of its membership being renewed every two years. All elections are conducted in the context of a multi-party political system. The President of the Republic appoints the Prime Minister and, on the recommendation of the latter, the members of the Council of Ministers.

The Constitution states that the official language is Arabic, and that the national languages are Arabic, Pular, Wolof and Solinké.

The Government

HEAD OF STATE

President: MOHAMED OULD ABDEL AZIZ (inaugurated 5 August 2009).

COUNCIL OF MINISTERS

(September 2012)

Prime Minister: MOULAYE OULD MOHAMED LAGHDAF.

Minister, Secretary-General to the President of the Republic: ADAMA SY.

Minister of State for National Education, Higher Education and Scientific Research: AHMED OULD BAHYA.

Minister of Justice: ABIDINE OULD EL KHAIRE.

Minister of Foreign Affairs and Co-operation: HAMADI OULD BABA OULD HAMADI.

Minister of National Defence: AHMEDOU OULD IDEY OULD MOHAMED RADHI.

Minister of the Interior and Decentralization: MOHAMED OULD BOILIL.

Minister of Economic Affairs and Development: SIDI OULD TAH.

Minister of Finance: THIAM DIOMBAR.

Minister of Islamic Affairs and Original Education: AHMED OULD NEINI.

Minister of the Civil Service and the Modernization of the Administration: MATY MINT HAMADY.

Minister of Health: BA HOUSSEINOU HAMADY.

Minister of Petroleum, Energy and Mines: TALEB OULD ABDI VALL.

Minister of Fisheries and the Maritime Economy: GHDAFNA OULD EYIH.

Minister of Trade, Industry, Crafts and Tourism: BAMBA OULD DARAMANE.

Minister of Housing, Urban Development and Land Settlement: ISMAIL OULD BEDDE OULD CHEIKH SIDIYA.

Minister of Rural Development: BRAHIM OULD M'BARECK OULD MOHAMED EL MOCTAR.

Minister of Equipment and Transport: YAHYA OULD HADEMINE.

Minister of Water Resources and Sanitation: MOHAMED LEMINE OULD ABOYE.

Minister of Culture, Youth and Sports: CISSÉ MINT CHEIKH OULD BOYDE.

Minister of Communication and Relations with Parliament: HAMDY OULD MAHJOUB.

Minister of Social Affairs, Childhood and Families: MOULATY MINT EL MOCTAR.

Minister-delegate to the Prime Minister, in charge of the Environment and Sustainable Development: AMEDI CAMARA.

Minister-delegate to the Minister of State for National Education, in charge of Primary Education: HAMED HAMOUNY.

Minister-delegate to the Minister of State for National Education, in charge of Secondary Education: OUMAR OULD MATALLA.

Minister-delegate to the Minister of State for National Education, in charge of Employment, Vocational Training and New Technologies: MOHAMED OULD KHOUNA.

Secretary-General of the Government: OUSMANE BA.

MINISTRIES

Office of the President: BP 184, Nouakchott; tel. and fax 45-25-26-36.

Office of the Prime Minister: BP 237, Nouakchott; tel. 45-25-33-37.

Office of the Secretary-General of the Government: BP 184, Nouakchott.

Ministry of the Civil Service and the Modernization of the Administration: BP 193, Nouakchott; tel. and fax 45-25-84-10.

Ministry of Communication and Relations with Parliament: Nouakchott.

Ministry of Culture, Youth and Sports: BP 223, Nouakchott; tel. 45-25-11-30.

Ministry of Economic Affairs and Development: 303 Ilot C, BP 5150, Nouakchott; tel. 45-25-16-12; fax 45-25-51-10; e-mail nfomaed@mauritania.mr; internet www.economie.gov.mr.

Ministry of Equipment and Transport: BP 237, Nouakchott; tel. 45-25-33-37.

Ministry of Finance: BP 181, Nouakchott; tel. 45-25-20-20; internet www.finances.gov.mr.

Ministry of Fisheries and the Maritime Economy: BP 137, Nouakchott; tel. 45-25-46-07; fax 45-25-31-46; e-mail ministre@mpem.mr; internet www.mpem.mr.

Ministry of Foreign Affairs and Co-operation: BP 230, Nouakchott; tel. 45-25-26-82; fax 45-25-28-60.

Ministry of Health: BP 177, Nouakchott; tel. 45-25-20-52; fax 45-25-22-68; internet www.sante.gov.mr.

Ministry of Housing, Urban Development and Land Settlement: Nouakchott.

Ministry of the Interior and Decentralization: BP 195, Nouakchott; tel. 45-25-36-61; fax 45-25-36-40; e-mail paddec@mauritania.mr; internet www.interieur.gov.mr.

Ministry of Islamic Affairs and Original Education: Nouakchott; internet www.affairesislamiques.gov.mr.

Ministry of Justice: BP 350, Nouakchott; tel. 45-25-10-83; fax 45-25-70-02.

Ministry of National Defence: Nouakchott.

Ministry of National Education, Higher Education and Scientific Research: BP 387, Nouakchott; tel. 45-25-12-37; fax 45-25-12-22.

Ministry of Petroleum, Energy and Mines: Nouakchott; tel. 45-25-71-40.

Ministry of Rural Development: BP 366, Nouakchott; tel. 45-25-15-00; fax 45-25-74-75; internet www.agriculture.gov.mr.

Ministry of Social Affairs, Childhood and Families: Nouakchott.

Ministry of Trade, Industry, Crafts and Tourism: BP 182, Nouakchott; tel. 45-25-35-72; fax 45-25-76-71.

Ministry of Water Resources and Sanitation: BP 4913, Nouakchott; tel. 45-25-71-44; fax 45-29-42-87; e-mail saadouebih@yahoo.fr.

President and Legislature

PRESIDENT

Presidential Election, 18 July 2009

Candidate	Votes	% of votes
Mohamed Ould Abdel Aziz	409,100	52.64
Messaoud Ould Boulkheir	126,782	16.31
Ahmed Ould Mohameden Ould Daddah	106,263	13.67
Mohamed Jemil Ould Brahim Ould Mansour	37,059	4.77
Ibrahima Moktar Sarr	35,709	4.60
Ely Ould Mohamed Vall Ould Eleya	29,681	3.82
Kane Hamidou Baba	11,568	1.49
Saleh Ould Mohamedou Ould Hanena	10,219	1.32
Hamady Ould Abdallahi Meymou	8,936	1.15
Sghair Ould M'Bareck	1,788	0.23
Total	777,105	100.00

Al-Jamiya al-Wataniyah (National Assembly)

ave de l'Indépendance, BP 185, Nouakchott; tel. 45-25-11-30; fax 45-25-70-78; internet www.mauritania.mr/assemblee.

President: MESSOUD OULD BOULKHEIR.

General Election, 19 November and 3 December 2006

Party	Constituency seats	National list seats	Total seats
Rally of Democratic Forces	12	3	15
Union of Progressive Forces	7	1	8
Republican Party for Democracy and Renewal	5	2	7
Popular Progressive Alliance	4	1	5
Centrist Reformists	2	2	4
Mauritanian Party for Union and Change—Hatem	3	1	4
Union for Democracy and Progress	2	1	3
Rally for Democracy and Unity	2	1	3
Democratic Renewal	1	1	2
Alternative	1	—	1
Union of the Democratic Centre	1	—	1
Popular Front	—	1	1
Independents	41	—	41
Total	81	14	95

Majlis ash-Shuyukh (Senate)

ave de l'Indépendance, BP 5838, Nouakchott; tel. 45-25-68-77; fax 45-25-73-73; internet www.senat.mr.

President: BÂ MAMADOU DIT M'BARÉ.

The total number of seats in the Senate is 56 with three seats reserved for representatives of the Mauritanian diaspora. After elections held on 21 January and 4 February 2007, the strength of the parties was as follows:

Party	Seats
Independents	34
Coalition of Forces for Democratic Change	15
Republican Party for Democracy and Renewal	3
Total*	52

* The result from one constituency was annulled by the Constitutional Council and the remaining three reserved seats were yet to be allocated.

Elections to renew 17 seats were held on 8 and 15 November 2009, at which the Union for the Republic secured 13 seats, the Union for Democracy and Progress and the National Rally for Reform and Development (Tawassoul) one seat each and independent candidates won two seats.

Election Commission

National Independent Electoral Commission: Nouakchott; 15 mems; Pres. ABDALLAHI OULD SOUEID AHMED.

Advisory Council

Economic and Social Council: Nouakchott.

Political Organizations

Alliance for Justice and Democracy (AJD): Nouakchott; Leader CISSÉ AMADOU CHIEKHOU.

Alternative (Al-Badil): Nouakchott; f. 2006; mem. of Co-ordination of the Democratic Opposition coalition, formed in 2010; Leader MOHAMED YEHDHIH OULD MOKTAR EL HASSEN.

Centrist Reformists: Nouakchott; f. 2006; mem. of Coalition of Forces for Democratic Change, formed in advance of legislative and local elections in 2006; moderate Islamist grouping.

Democratic Renewal: Nouakchott; f. 2005; mem. of Coalition of Forces for Democratic Change, formed in advance of legislative and local elections in 2006; Pres. MOUSTAPHA OULD ABEIDERRAHMANE.

El Wiam Démocratique et Social: Leader BOIDEIL OULD HOUMEID.

Mauritanian African Liberation Forces—Renovation (MALF—Renovation): Nouakchott; tel. 22-28-77-40 (mobile); internet www.flam-renovation.org; f. 2006 in split from clandestine, exiled, Mauritanian African Liberation Forces; represents interests of Afro- (Black) Mauritanians; mem. of Coalition of Forces for Democratic Change, formed in advance of legislative and local elections in 2006; Leader MAMADOU BOCAR BÂ.

Mauritanian Labour Party: Nouakchott; f. 2001; Leader MOHAMED EL HAFEDH OULD DENNA.

Mauritanian Party for the Defence of the Environment (MPDE—The Greens): Nouakchott; internet pmde.hautetfort .com; ecologist; mem. of Bloc of Parties for Change, formed in advance of legislative and local elections in 2006; Pres. MOHAMED OULD SIDI OULD DELLAHI.

Mauritanian Party for Renewal and Agreement: Nouakchott; f. 2001; Leader MOULAY EL-HASSEN OULD JIYID.

Mauritanian Party for Union and Change—Hatem: Nouakchott; f. 2005 by leadership of the fmr prohibited Knights of Change militia and reformist elements of the fmr ruling Democratic and Social Republican Party; mem. of Coalition of Forces for Democratic Change, formed in advance of legislative and local elections in 2006; Pres. SALEH OULD HNANA; Sec.-Gen. ABDERAHMANE OULD MINI.

Mauritanian People's Rally Party (MPRP): Nouakchott; f. 2009 by parliamentary deputies in support of ruling military junta; Leader Dr LOULEID OULD WEDAD.

National Party for Democracy and Development (NPDD): Nouakchott; Leader YAHYA OULD EL WAGHEF.

National Rally for Reform and Development (NRRD) (Tawassoul): f. 2007; Islamist; mem. of Co-ordination of the Democratic Opposition coalition, formed in 2010; Leader MOHAMED JEMIL OULD MANSOUR.

Party for Liberty, Equality and Justice (PLEJ): Nouakchott; internet www.plej.biz; mem. of Bloc of Parties for Change, formed in advance of legislative and local elections in 2006; mem. of Co-ordination of the Democratic Opposition coalition, formed in 2010; Pres. MAMADOU ALASSANE BÂ.

Popular Front (PF): Nouakchott; f. 1998; social-liberal; mem. of Coalition of Forces for Democratic Change, formed in advance of legislative and local elections in 2006; Leader MOHAMED LEMINE CH'BIH OULD CHEIKH MELAININE.

Popular Progressive Alliance (PPA): Nouakchott; internet www .app.mr; f. 1991; mem. of Coalition of Forces for Democratic Change, formed in advance of legislative and local elections in 2006; mem. of Co-ordination of the Democratic Opposition coalition, formed in 2010; Pres. MESSAOUD OULD BOULKHAR.

Rally for Democracy and Unity (RDU): Nouakchott; f. 1991; supported regime of fmr Pres. Taya; Chair. AHMED OULD SIDI BABA.

Rally of Democratic Forces (RDF): Ilot K, 120, BP 4986, Nouakchott; tel. 45-25-67-46; fax 45-25-65-70; e-mail info@rfd-mauritanie .org; internet www.rfd-mauritanie.org; f. 2001; mem. of Coalition of Forces for Democratic Change, formed in advance of legislative and local elections in 2006; mem. of Co-ordination of the Democratic Opposition coalition, formed in 2010; Pres. AHMED OULD DADDAH.

Republican Party for Democracy and Renewal (RPDR): ZRB, Tevragh Zeina, Nouakchott; tel. 45-29-18-36; fax 45-29-18-00; e-mail info@prdr.mr; internet www.prdr.mr; f. 2006 to replace Democratic and Social Republican Party, the fmr ruling party, prior to coup of August 2005; Leader SIDI MOHAMED OULD MED VALL DIT GHRINY.

Reward (Sawab): Nouakchott; f. 2004; social democratic; Chair. of Central Council MOHAMED MAHMOUD OULD GHOULMA; Pres. Dr CHEIKH OULD SIDI OULD HANENA.

Union for Democracy and Progress (UDP): Ilot V, 70, Tevragh Zeina, BP 816, Nouakchott; tel. 45-25-52-89; fax 45-25-29-95; f. 1993; Pres. NAHA HAMDI MINT.

Union of the Democratic Centre (UDC): Nouakchott; f. 2005 by fmr mems of the Democratic and Social Republican Party, the fmr ruling party; Pres. CHEIKH SID'AHMED OULD BABA.

Union of Democratic Youth (UDY): f. 2008; promotes patriotism and moderate Islamic values, opposes extremism; Pres. JEDDOU OULD AHMAD.

Union of Progressive Forces (UPF) (Ittihad Quwa al-Taqaddum): Nouakchott; e-mail ufpweb2@yahoo.fr; internet www.ufpweb .org; tel. 45-29-32-66; fax 45-24-35-86; e-mail infos@ufpweb.org; f. 2000; mem. of Coalition of Forces for Democratic Change, formed in advance of legislative and local elections in 2006; mem. of Co-ordination of the Democratic Opposition coalition, formed in 2010; Pres. MOHAMED OULD MAOULOUD; Sec.-Gen. MOHAMED EL MOUSTAPHA OULD BEDREDDINE.

Union for the Republic (UR): Nouakchott; f. 2009; Chair. MOHAMED MAHMOUD OULD MOHAMED LEMINE.

Unauthorized, but influential, is the Islamic **Ummah Party** (the Constitution prohibits the operation of religious political organizations), founded in 1991 and led by Imam SIDI YAHYA, and the Baathist **National Vanguard Party (Taliaa)**, which was officially dissolved by the Government in 1999 and is led by AHMEDOU OULD BABANA. The clandestine **Mauritanian African Liberation Forces (MALF)** was founded in 1983 in Senegal to represent Afro-Mauritanians (Point d'ébullition, BP 5811, Dakar-Fann, Senegal; tel. +221 822-80-77; e-mail ba_demba@yahoo .fr; internet members .lycos .co .uk/ flamnet; Pres. SAMBA THIAM); a faction broke away from this organization and returned to Mauritania in early 2006, forming the Mauritanian African Liberation Forces—Renovation. A further group based in exile is the **Arab-African Salvation Front against Slavery, Racism and Tribalism—AASF** (e-mail faas@caramail .com; internet membres .lycos .fr/faas). In August 2007 a further 18 new parties were registered: included were an Islamist party, the **National Rally for Reform and Development**, and two parties led by women, the **National Party for Development**, led by SAHLA BINT AHMAD ZAYID, and the **Mauritanian Hope Party**, led by TAHI BINT LAHBIB.

Diplomatic Representation

EMBASSIES IN MAURITANIA

Algeria: Ilot A, Tevragh Zeina, BP 625, Nouakchott; tel. 45-25-35-69; fax 45-25-47-77; Ambassador ZAHANI ABDEL HAMID.

China, People's Republic: rue 42-133, Tevragh Zeina, BP 257, Nouakchott; tel. 45-25-20-70; fax 45-25-24-62; e-mail chinaemb_mr@ mfa.gov.cn; internet mr.china-embassy.org; Ambassador CHEN GONGLAI.

Congo, Democratic Republic: Tevragh Zeina, BP 5714, Nouakchott; tel. 45-25-46-12; fax 45-25-50-53; e-mail ambardc.rim@ caramail.com; Chargé d'affaires a.i. TSHIBASU MFUAD.

Egypt: Villa 468, Tevragh Zeina, BP 176, Nouakchott; tel. 45-25-21-92; fax 45-25-33-84; Ambassador Dr YOUSSOUF AHMED CHARGHAOUI.

France: rue Ahmed Ould Hamed, Tevragh Zeina, BP 231, Nouakchott; tel. 45-29-96-99; fax 45-29-69-38; e-mail ambafrance .nouakchott-amba@diplomatie.gouv.fr; internet www .france-mauritanie.mr; Ambassador MICHEL VENDEPOORTER.

Germany: Tevragh Zeina, BP 372, Nouakchott; tel. 45-25-17-29; fax 45-25-17-22; e-mail info@nouakchott.diplo.de; internet www .nouakchott.diplo.de; Ambassador DIETMAR BLAAS.

Iraq: Tevragh Zeina, Nord Villa 399, Nouakchott; tel. 45-24-32-52; fax 45-24-32-51; e-mail nokemb@iraqmfamail.com; Ambassador AHMED NAEEF RASHID AL-DULAIMI.

Japan: Tevragh Zeina, BP 7810, Nouakchott; tel. 45-25-09-77; fax 45-25-09-76; Ambassador HIROSHI AZUMA.

Korea, Democratic People's Republic: Nouakchott; Ambassador (vacant).

Kuwait: Tevragh Zeina, BP 345, Nouakchott; tel. 45-25-33-05; fax 45-25-41-45; Ambassador ADNAN ABDELLAH AL-AHMED.

Libya: BP 673, Nouakchott; tel. 45-25-52-02; fax 45-25-50-53; Chargé d'affaires ISSA ALI EL-VENAS.

Mali: Tevragh Zeina, BP 5371, Nouakchott; tel. 45-25-40-81; fax 45-25-40-83; e-mail ambmali@hotmail.com; Ambassador ETHMANE KONÉ.

Morocco: 569 ave de Gaulle, Tevragh Zeina, BP 621, Nouakchott; tel. 45-25-14-11; fax 45-29-72-80; e-mail sifmanktt@mauritel.mr; Ambassador ABDERRAHMANE BENOMAR.

Nigeria: Ilot P9, BP 367, Nouakchott; tel. 45-25-23-04; fax 45-25-23-14; Ambassador Alhaji BALA MOHAMED SANI.

Qatar: BP 609, Nouakchott; tel. 45-25-23-99; fax 45-25-68-87; e-mail nouakchoti@mofa.gov.qa; Ambassador MOHAMMED KURDI TALEB AL-MERRI.

Russia: rue Abu Bakr, BP 221, Nouakchott; tel. 45-25-19-73; fax 45-25-52-96; e-mail ambruss@opt.mr; Ambassador VLADIMIR BAYBAKOV.

Saudi Arabia: Las Balmas, Zinat, BP 498, Nouakchott; tel. 45-25-26-33; fax 45-25-29-49; e-mail mremb@mofa.gov.sa; Ambassador SAOUD BEN ABDEL AZIZ EL-JABIRI.

Senegal: Villa 500, Tevragh Zeina, BP 2511, Nouakchott; tel. 45-25-72-90; fax 45-25-72-91; Ambassador MAHMOUDOU CHEIKH KANE.

South Africa: Hotel Tfeila, Mezzanine Floor, Salon el-Waha, ave Charles de Gaulle, BP 2006, Nouakchott; tel. 45-24-55-90; fax 45-24-55-91; e-mail nouakchott@foreign.gov.za; Ambassador JOHANNES JACOBUS SPIES.

Spain: BP 232, Nouakchott; tel. 45-25-20-80; fax 45-25-40-88; e-mail emb.nouakchott@mae.es; Ambassador ALONSO DEZCALLAR Y MAZARREDO.

Syria: Tevragh Zeina, BP 288, Nouakchott; tel. 45-25-27-54; fax 45-25-45-00; Ambassador SAID EL-BENI.

Tunisia: BP 631, Nouakchott; tel. 45-25-28-71; fax 45-25-18-27; Ambassador CHAFIK HAJJI.

United Arab Emirates: Tafarugh Zeena Quarter, ZRA 742 bis, Nouakchott; tel. 45-25-10-98; fax 45-25-09-92; e-mail embeau@ mauritel.mr; Ambassador ABDULLAH MOHAMMED AT-TAKAWI.

USA: rue Abdallaye, BP 222, Nouakchott; tel. 45-25-26-60; fax 45-25-15-92; e-mail tayebho@state.gov; internet mauritania.usembassy.gov; Ambassador JO ELLEN POWELL.

Yemen: Tevragh Zeina, BP 4689, Nouakchott; tel. 45-25-55-91; fax 45-25-56-39; Ambassador MOHAMED ALI YAHYA SHIBAN.

Judicial System

The Code of Law was promulgated in 1961 and subsequently modified to incorporate Islamic institutions and practices. The main courts comprise three courts of appeal, 10 regional tribunals, two labour tribunals and 53 departmental civil courts. A revenue court has jurisdiction in financial matters. The members of the High Court of Justice are elected by the National Assembly and the Senate.

Shari'a (Islamic) law was introduced in February 1980. A special Islamic court was established in March of that year, presided over by a magistrate of Islamic law, assisted by two counsellors and two *ulemas* (Muslim jurists and interpreters of the Koran). A five-member High Council of Islam, appointed by the President, advises upon the conformity of national legislation to religious precepts, at the request of the President. A High Council of Fatwas and Appeals for Reprieve, comprising nine members, renewable every two years, was established in 2012.

Audit Court (Cour des Comptes): Nouakchott; audits all govt institutions; Pres. SOW ADAMA SAMBA.

Constitutional Council: f. 1992; includes six mems, three nominated by the Head of State and three designated by the Presidents of the Senate and National Assembly; Pres. SGHAIR OULD M'BAREK; Sec.-Gen. SY ADAMA.

High Council of Fatwas and Appeals for Reprieve (Haut Conseil de la Fatwa et des Recours Gracieux): Nouakchott; f. 2012; comprises nine members, renewable every two years; issues fatwas with respect to interpretations of Islamic law; also has the authority to resolve disputes which are not under any court of law; Pres. MOHAMED EL MOCTAR OULD M'BALLA.

High Council of Islam (al-Majlis al-Islamiya al-A'la'): Nouakchott; f. 1992; Pres. MAHFOUDH OULD LEMRABOTT.

High Court of Justice: Nouakchott; f. 1961; comprises an equal number of appointees elected from their membership by the National Assembly and the Senate, following each partial or general renewal of those legislative bodies; competent to try the President of the Republic in case of high treason, and the Prime Minister and members of the Government in case of conspiracy against the State.

Supreme Court: BP 201, Palais de Justice, Nouakchott; tel. and fax 45-25-67-40; internet www.coursupreme.ma; f. 1961; comprises an administrative chamber, two civil and social chambers, a commercial chamber and a criminal chamber; Pres. YAHFDHOU OULD MOHAMED YOUSSEF.

Religion

ISLAM

Islam is the official religion, and the population are almost entirely Muslims of the Malekite rite. The major religious groups are the Tijaniya and the Qadiriya. Chinguetti, in the region of Adrar, is the seventh Holy Place in Islam. A High Council of Islam (Haut Conseil Islamique) supervises the conformity of legislation to Muslim orthodoxy.

Haut Conseil Islamique: BP 5949, Nouakchott; tel. 45-25-19-91; fax 45-25-19-17.

CHRISTIANITY

Roman Catholic Church

Mauritania comprises the single diocese of Nouakchott, directly responsible to the Holy See. The Bishop participates in the Bishops' Conference of Senegal, Mauritania, Cape Verde and Guinea-Bissau, based in Dakar, Senegal. There are an estimated 4,500 adherents, mainly non-nationals, in the country.

Bishop of Nouakchott: Most Rev. MARTIN ALBERT HAPPE, Evêché, BP 5377, Nouakchott; tel. 45-25-04-27; fax 45-25-37-51; e-mail mgrmartinhappe@yahoo.fr.

The Press

Of some 400 journals officially registered in Mauritania in 2004, some 30 were regular, widely available publications, of which the following were among the most important:

Al-Akhbar: ave Charles de Gaulles, BP 5346, Nouakchott; tel. 25-00-28-28; fax 25-00-22-33; e-mail fr.redaction@alakhbar.info; internet fr.alakhbar.info; f. 2003; weekly; Arabic and French.

Biladi: Immeuble BMCI, 5ème étage, apt 508, BP 1122, Nouakchott; tel. and fax 45-24-02-75; e-mail oneina1@gmail.com; internet www.rmibiladi.com; French; weekly; Dir of Publication MOUSSA OULD HAMED; Editor-in-Chief ABDELVETAH OULD MOHAMED.

Le Calame/Al-Qalam: rue 42–62, Tevragh Zeina, 348 Kennedy ave Ouest, BP 1059, Nouakchott; tel. 45-24-08-29; fax 45-24-08-30; e-mail lecalame@yahoo.fr; internet www.lecalame.mr; f. 1993; weekly; Arabic and French; independent; Editors-in-Chief RIYAD OULD AHMED EL-HADI (Arabic edn), AHMED OULD CHEIKH (French edn).

Châab: BP 371, Nouakchott; tel. 45-25-29-40; fax 45-25-55-20; e-mail chaab@ami.mr; internet www.ami.mr; f. 1975; daily; Arabic; also publ. in French *Horizons*; publ. by Agence Mauritanienne de l'Information; Dir of Publication YARBA OULD SGHAÏR.

Challenge: BP 1346, Nouakchott; tel. and fax 45-29-22-46; e-mail challengehebdo@yahoo.fr; internet www.challenge-mr.com; weekly.

Ech-tary: BP 1059, Nouakchott; tel. 45-25-50-65; e-mail info@echtary.net; internet www.echtary.net; fortnightly; Arabic; satirical.

Essirage Hebdo: Nouakchott; tel. 22-01-09-82; e-mail wadiaa@maktoob.com; internet www.essirage.net; weekly.

L'Essor: BP 5310, Nouakchott; tel. 36-30-21-68 (mobile); fax 45-25-95-95; e-mail sidiel2000@yahoo.fr; monthly; the environment and the economy; Dir SIDI EL-MOCTAR CHEÏGUER; circ. 2,500.

L'Eveil-Hebdo: BP 587, Nouakchott; tel. 45-25-67-14; fax 45-25-87-54; e-mail symoudou@yahoo.fr; f. 1991; weekly; independent; Dir of Publication SY MAMADOU.

Journal Officel: BP 188, Nouakchott; tel. 45-25-33-37; fax 45-25-34-74; fortnightly.

Maghreb Hebdo: BP 5266, Nouakchott; tel. 45-25-98-10; fax 45-25-98-11; f. 1994; weekly; Dir KHATTRI OULD DIÈ.

Mauritanies1: Nouakchott; e-mail contact@mauritanies1.com; internet www.mauritanies1.com; monthly.

Al-Mourabit: Nouakchott; tel. 45-24-95-35; e-mail brahimbakar@almourabit.mr; internet www.almourabit.mr; weekly; French; Editor-in-Chief BRAHIM OULD BAKAR OULD SNEIBA.

Nouakchott-Info: Immeuble Abbas, Tevragh Zeina, BP 1905, Nouakchott; tel. 45-25-02-71; fax 45-25-54-84; e-mail aboulmaaly@yahoo.com; internet www.ani.mr; f. 1995; daily; independent; Arabic and French; Dir of Publication and Editor-in-Chief MOHAMED MAHMOUD ABOUL MAALY.

Points Chauds: Ilot L prés de la garde Nationale (face de Mauritanie couleur), Nouakchott; tel. 45-25-06-04; fax 45-29-37-97; e-mail info@pointschauds.info; internet www.pointschauds.info; Editor-in-Chief MOULAY AHMED.

Le Quotidien de Nouakchott: BP 1153 Nouakchott; tel. 45-24–53-74; e-mail khalioubi@yahoo.fr; internet www.quotidien-nouakchott.com; French; Editor-in-Chief KHALILOU DIAGANA.

Al-Rayah (The Banner): Nouakchott; e-mail team@rayah.info; internet www.rayah.info; f. 1997; independent; weekly; pro-Islamist; Editor AHMED OULD WEDIAA.

Tahalil Hebdo: BP 5205, Nouakchott; tel. 45-24-18-00; fax 45-25-80-87; e-mail contact@journaltahalil.com; internet www.journaltahalil.com; weekly; French.

La Tribune: BP 6227, Nouakchott; tel. 46-46-18-82 (mobile); e-mail contact@la-tribune.info; internet www.la-tribune.info; weekly; French; Editor-in-Chief KISSIMA TOCKA DIAGANA.

NEWS AGENCY

Agence Mauritanienne de l'Information (AMI): BP 371, Nouakchott; tel. 45-25-29-40; fax 45-25-45-87; e-mail ami@mauritania.mr; internet www.ami.mr; fmrly Agence Mauritanienne de Presse; state-controlled; news and information services in Arabic and French; Man. Dir YARBA OULD SGHAÏR.

Publishers

Imprimerie Commerciale et Administrative de Mauritanie: BP 164, Nouakchott; textbooks, educational.

Imprimerie Nationale: BP 618, Nouakchott; tel. 45-25-44-38; fax 45-25-44-37; f. 1978; state-owned; Pres. RACHID OULD SALEH; Man. Dir ISSIMOU MAHJOUB.

GOVERNMENT PUBLISHING HOUSE

Société Nationale d'Impression: BP 618, Nouakchott; Pres. MOUSTAPHA SALECK OULD AHMED BRIHIM.

Broadcasting and Communications

In 2011 there were three mobile cellular telephone operators in Mauritania, one of which, Mauritel, also provided fixed-line telephone services. In 2011 there were 3,283,400 subscribers to mobile telephone services and 72,300 subscribers to fixed-line services.

TELECOMMUNICATIONS

Autorité de Régulation: 428 rue 23023 Ksar, BP 4908, Nouakchott; tel. 45-29-12-70; fax 45-29-12-79; e-mail webmaster@are.mr; internet www.are.mr; f. 1999; Pres. NANI OULD CHROUGHA.

SERVICE PROVIDERS

Chinguitel: Carrefour Cité SMAR, Nouakchott; tel. 22-00-02-91 (mobile); internet www.chinguitel.mr; provides mobile cellular, fixed-line and internet services; Dir-Gen. ABDERAHMAN MOHAMED AHMED OUSMANE.

Mauritel: 563 ave du Roi Fayçal, BP 7000, Nouakchott; tel. 45-25-76-00; fax 45-25-17-00; e-mail webmaster@mauritel.mr; internet www.mauritel.mr; fmrly Société Mauritanienne des Télécommunications; provides fixed-line and mobile cellular telephone services; 46% state-owned, 51% owned by the Compagnie Mauritanienne de Communication (created by Maroc Télécom), 3% owned by Mauritel employees; Dir-Gen. KAMAL OKBA.

Société Mauritano-Tunisienne de Télécommunications (Mattel): 441 ave Charles de Gaulle, Tevragh-Zeina, BP 3668, Nouakchott; tel. 45-29-53-54; fax 45-29-81-03; e-mail mattel@mattel.mr; internet www.mattel.mr; f. 2000; privately owned Mauritanian-Tunisian co; operates mobile cellular communications network; Dir-Gen. MOHAMED ALI ESSAHILI.

BROADCASTING

In July 2010 the National Assembly passed legislation allowing the establishment of private broadcasters for the first time in Mauritania, thereby ending almost 50 years of state monopoly. In November 2011 the Haute Autorité de la Presse et de l'Audiovisuel awarded licences to five radio and two television channels: Sahara FM, Radio Cobenni, Mauritanides FM, Radio Tenwir and Radio Nouakchott; Mauri–Vision and Télévision Watanya

Radio

Radio Mauritanie (RM): ave Gamal Abdel Nasser, BP 200, Nouakchott; tel. and fax 45-25-21-64; e-mail rm@radiomauritanie.com; internet www.radiomauritanie.mr; f. 1958; state-controlled; broadcasts two channels; five transmitters; radio broadcasts in Arabic, French, Sarakolé, Toucouleur and Wolof; Dir MOHAMED LEMINE OULD MOULAYE ELY (acting).

Radio Mauritanie also operates 10 local radio stations. Broadcasts from RFI (FM), Africa N°1 and Radio Monte Carlo Doualiya are also received in the country.

Television

Télévision de Mauritanie (TVM): BP 5522, Nouakchott; tel. 45-25-40-67; fax 45-25-40-69; e-mail dgtvm@tvmsat.mr; internet www.tvm.mr; f. 1982; Dir-Gen. MOHAMED DIEH OULD SIDATY.

Finance

(cap. = capital; res = reserves; dep. = deposits; m. = million; br(s).= branch(es); amounts in ouguiyas)

BANKING

In 2010 there were 10 commercial banks, two other financial institutions and some 80 microfinance institutions operating in Mauritania.

Central Bank

Banque Centrale de Mauritanie (BCM): ave de l'Indépendance, BP 623, Nouakchott; tel. 45-25-22-06; fax 45-25-27-59; e-mail info@bcm.mr; internet www.bcm.mr; f. 1973; bank of issue; cap. 200m., res 2,869.7m., dep. 96,225.3m. (2009); Gov. SID'AHMED OULD RAISS; 4 brs.

Commercial Banks

Attijari Bank Mauritanie: 91/92 rue Mamadou Konaté, Nouakchott; tel. 45-29-63-74; fax 45-29-64-40; cap. 3,398m. (Dec. 2010).

Banque El Amana (BEA): rue Mamadou Konaté BP 5559, Nouakchott; tel. 45-25-59-53; fax 45-25-34-95; e-mail info@bea.mr; internet www.bea.mr; f. 1996; 72% privately owned, 27% owned by Société Nationale Industrielle et Minière; cap. 4,790.3m. (March 2011); CEO AHMED SALEM BOUNA MOKHTAR; Gen. Man. AHMED SALEM ELY EL KORY.

Banque pour le Commerce et l'Industrie (BCI): ave Gemal Abdel Nasser, BP 5050, Nouakchott; tel. 45-29-28-76; fax 45-29-28-77; e-mail bci@bci-banque.com; internet www.bci-banque.com; f. 1999; privately owned; cap. 4,000m. (Dec. 2010); Pres. and Dir-Gen. ISSELMOU OULD DIDI OULD TAJEDINE; 11 brs.

Banque pour le Commerce et l'Investissement en Mauritanie (Bacim-Bank): P54, ave du Général Charles de Gaulle 20, rue 42-060, BP 1268, Nouakchott; tel. 45-29-19-00; fax 45-29-13-60; e-mail bacim-bank@mauritel.mr; internet www.bacim.mr; f. 2002; privately owned; cap. 1,500m. (Dec. 2005); Dir-Gen. HENRI CHAINTREUIL; 6 brs.

Banque Mauritanienne pour le Commerce International (BMCI): Immeuble Afarco, ave Nasser, BP 622, Nouakchott; tel. 45-25-28-26; fax 45-25-20-45; e-mail info@bmci.mr; internet www.bmci.mr; f. 1974; 95.82% owned by Group Abbas; cap. 4,000m., res 3,402m., dep. 31,005m. (Dec. 2006); Pres. and Dir-Gen. MOULAY SIDI OULD HACEN OULD ABASS; 18 brs.

Banque Nationale de Mauritanie (BNM): ave Gamal Abdel Nasser, BP 614, Nouakchott; tel. 45-25-26-02; fax 45-25-33-97; e-mail bnm10@bnm.mr; internet www.bnm.mr; f. 1989; privately owned; res 977m., dep. 20,659m. (Dec. 2003); cap. 6,000m. (Dec. 2005); Pres. and Dir-Gen. MOHAMED OULD NOUEIGUED; 10 brs.

Chinguitty Bank: ave Gamal Abdel Nasser, BP 626, Nouakchott; tel. 45-25-21-73; fax 45-25-33-82; e-mail chinguittybank@mauritel.mr; f. 1972; 51% owned by Libyan Arab Foreign Bank, 49% state-owned; cap. and res 4,002.9m., total assets 11,428.7m. (Dec. 2007); Pres. MOHAMED OULD DIDI; Gen. Man. YOUNIS TAHER AS-SOUDI; 2 brs.

Générale de Banque de Mauritanie pour l'Investissement et le Commerce SA (GBM): ave de l'Indépendance, BP 5558, Nouakchott; tel. 45-25-36-36; fax 45-25-46-47; e-mail gbm@gbm.mr.com; f. 1995; 70% privately owned; cap. 7,200m., res 14,037.6m., dep. 15,142.5m. (Dec. 2006); Pres. and Dir-Gen. MOHAMED HMAYEN OULD BOUAMATOU; 1 br.

Société Générale Mauritanie (SGM): ave Charles de Gaulle, BP 5085, Nouakchott; tel. 45-29-70-00; fax 45-24-53-00; internet www.sgm.mr; f. 2005; present name adopted 2007; cap. 4,000m. (Jan. 2006); Pres. and Dir-Gen. JEAN-PHILLIPE EQUILBECQ; 1 br.

Islamic Bank

Banque al-Wava Mauritanienne Islamique (BAMIS): 758, rue 22–018, ave du Roi Fayçal, BP 650, Nouakchott; tel. 45-25-14-24; fax 45-25-16-21; e-mail bamis@bamis.mr; internet www.bamis.mr; f. 1985; fmrly Banque al-Baraka Mauritanienne Islamique; majority share privately owned; cap. 7,000m., dep. 27,487m. (Dec. 2011); Pres. MOHAMED ABDELLAHI OULD ABDELLAHI; Dir-Gen. MOHAMED ABDELLAHI OULD SIDI; Exec. Dir MOHAMED OULD TAYA; 8 brs.

INSURANCE

In 2008 there were eight insurance companies in Mauritania.

Assurances Générales de Mauritanie: BP 2141, ave de Gaulle, TZA Ilot A 667, Nouakchott; tel. 45-29-29-00; fax 45-29-29-11; Man. MOULAYE ELY BOUAMATOU.

Compagnie Nationale d'Assurance et de Réassurance (NASR): 12 ave Nasser, BP 163, Nouakchott; tel. 45-25-26-50; fax 45-25-18-18; e-mail nasr@nasr.mr; internet www.nasr.mr; f. 1994; state-owned; Pres. MOHAMED ABDALLAHI OULD SIDI; Dir-Gen. AHMED OULD SIDI BABA.

Mauritanienne d'Assurances et de Réassurances (MAR): Nouakchott; tel. 45-24-12-18; e-mail mar@mar-assur.mr; internet www.mar-assur.mr; f. 2002.

Société Anonyme d'Assurance et de Réassurance (SAAR): ave J. F. Kennedy, Immeuble El-Mamy, BP 2841, Nouakchott; tel. 45-25-30-56; fax 45-25-25-36; e-mail saar@infotel.mr; f. 1999; Pres. and Dir-Gen. AHMED BEZEID OULD MED LEMINE.

TAAMIN: BP 5164, Nouakchott; tel. 45-29-40-00; fax 45-29-40-02; e-mail info@assurancestaamin.com; internet www.assurancestaamin.com; Pres. and Dir-Gen. MOULAYE EL HASSEN OULD MOCTAR EL HASSEN.

Trade and Industry

DEVELOPMENT ORGANIZATIONS

Agence Française de Développement (AFD): rue Mamadou Kouaté prolongée, BP 5211, Nouakchott; tel. 45-25-25-25; fax 45-25-49-10; e-mail afdnouakchott@afd.fr; internet www.afd.fr; Country Dir PATRICK ABBES.

Service de Coopération et d'Action Culturelle: BP 203, Nouakchott; tel. 45-29-95-59; fax 45-29-96-15; e-mail scac.nouakchott-amba@diplomatie.fr; administers bilateral aid from France; Dir SYLVAIN FOURCASSIE.

Société Nationale pour le Développement Rural (SONADER): BP 321, Nouakchott; tel. 45-21-18-00; fax 45-25-32-86; e-mail sonader@toptechnology.mr; f. 1975; Dir-Gen. MOHAMED OULD AHMAHOULLAH.

CHAMBER OF COMMERCE

Chambre de Commerce, d'Industrie et d'Agriculture de Mauritanie (CCIAM): 303 ave de l'Indépendance, BP 215, Nouakchott; tel. 45-25-22-14; fax 45-25-38-95; e-mail cciam_info@yahoo.fr; internet www.chambredecommerce.mr; f. 1954; Pres. MOHAMEDOU OULD MOHAMED MAHMOUD; Sec.-Gen. ABDEL AZIZ WANE.

EMPLOYERS' ORGANIZATION

Union Nationale du Patronat Mauritanien (UNPM): 824 ave de Roi Fayçal, Ksar, BP 383, Nouakchott; tel. 45-25-33-01; fax 45-25-91-08; e-mail germe@opt.mr; f. 1960; professional asscn for all employers active in Mauritania; Pres. AHMED BABA OULD AZIZI OULD EL MAMY; Sec.-Gen. SEYID OULD ABDALLAHI.

UTILITIES

Electricity

Société Mauritanienne d'Electricité (SOMELEC): 47 ave de l'Indépendance, BP 355, Nouakchott; tel. 45-29-66-04; fax 45-25-39-95; e-mail dahane@somelec.mr; internet www.somelec.mr; f. 2001; state-owned; transfer to majority private sector ownership proposed; production and distribution of electricity; Pres. MEMMED OULD AHMED; Dir-Gen. MOHAMED SALEM OULD BÉCHIR.

Gas

Société Mauritanienne de Gaz (SOMAGAZ): POB 5089, Nouakchott; tel. 45-24-28-58; fax 45-24-29-70; e-mail somagazinfo@somagaz.com; internet www.somagaz.com; f. 1987; production and distribution of butane gas; Dir-Gen. ABDALLAHI OULD BENANE.

Water

Société Nationale d'Eau (SNDE): 106 ave 42-096, Tevragh Zeina, BP 796, Nouakchott; tel. 45-25-52-73; fax 45-25-19-52; e-mail mfoudail@infotel.mr; f. 2001; Pres. CHEIKH OULD BAHA; Dir-Gen. AHMED KHALIVA OULD BEYAH.

MAJOR COMPANIES

The following are some of the largest companies in terms of either capital investment or employment:

Ciment de Mauritanie SA: Zone du Wharf, BP 40029, Nouakchott; tel. 45-25-71-01; fax 45-25-36-83; e-mail abad@asmlgroup.com; internet www.ciment.mr; f. 1979; Pres. and Dir-Gen. AHMED SALECK MOHAMED LAMINE.

Compagnie Mauritano-Coréenne de Pêche (COMACOP): BP 527, Nouakchott; tel. 45-25-37-47; fax 45-25-20-34; f. 1977; cap. UM 230m.; fishing and freezer complex; Pres. and Dir-Gen. ABDOU OULD AL HACHEME.

Entreprise de Bâtiment, Travaux et Routes (EBTR): Zone industrielle de la Foire, BP 5501, Nouakchott; tel. 45-25-82-34; fax 45-25-69-55; e-mail info@ebtr.mr; internet www.ebtr.mr; f. 1992; construction; Pres. and Dir-Gen. MOHAMED LAFDAL BETTAH.

Mauritano-Française des Ciments: Zone du port, lot no 1, BP 5291, Nouakchott; tel. 45-25-82-55; fax 45-25-83-16; e-mail mafci@mauritel.mr; Pres. and Dir-Gen. MOHAMMAD LAMINE OULD ZAIN.

Naftal, SA Mauritanie: BP 73, Nouadhibou; tel. 45-74-52-40; f. 1981 as Société Mauritanienne des Industries de Raffinage (SOMIR); affiliate of Naftec (Algeria); cap. UM 4,600m.; operates a petroleum refinery and negotiates overseas transactions; Chair. ABDELMADJID KAZI TANI; Man. Dir MOHAMED OTHMANI.

Naftec, SA Mauritanie: ave Abdellahi, BP 679, Nouakchott; tel. 45-25-26-51; fax 45-25-25-42; e-mail naftec@toptechnology.mr; internet www.naftec.mr; f. 1980; cap. UM 120m.; majority-owned by Naftec (Algeria), Mauritanian Govt is a minority shareholder; import and distribution of petroleum products; fmrly Société Mauritanienne de Commercialisation des Produits Pétroliers; Dir-Gen. A. GHIMOOZ.

Pact-Industrie: Nouakchott; tel. 45-74-60-56; fax 45-74-60-57; e-mail pactndb@yahoo.fr; Pres. and Dir-Gen. MAURICE BENZA.

Société Arabe du Fer et de l'Acier en Mauritanie (SAFA): BP 114, Nouadhibou; tel. 45-74-53-89; fax 45-74-61-28; e-mail safa@snim.com; f. 1985; cap. UM 450m.; 75% owned by SNIM; steel-rolling mill; Chair. MOHAMED ALI OULD SIDI MOHAMED; Man. Dir MOHAMED YARBANA OULD MOHAMED EL MAMY; 142 employees (2001).

Société Arabe des Industries Métallurgiques (SAMIA): Zone Industrielle el-Mina, route de Rosso, BP 6247-1248, Nouakchott; tel. 45-25-44-55; fax 45-29-05-85; e-mail samia@samia.mr; internet www.samia.mr; f. 1974; cap. UM 762m.; 50% owned by SNIM, 50% owned by Kuwait Real Estate Investment Consortium; extraction of gypsum and production of plaster of Paris; Man. Dir MOHAMED OULD BILAL; 56 employees (2001).

Société Arabe Libyenne-Mauritanienne des Ressources Maritimes (SALIMAUREM): BP 75, Nouadhibou; tel. 45-74-52-41; f. 1978; cap. UM 2,300m.; 50% state-owned, 50% owned by Libyan-Arab Finance Co; fishing and fish-processing; freezer factory; Chair. AHMED OULD GHNAHALLA; Dir-Gen. SALA MOHAMED ARIBI.

Société Arabe des Mines de l'Inchiri (SAMIN): Akjoujt; tel. 45-76-71-04; f. 1981; cap. UM 3,276m.; 75% owned by Wadi Al Rawda Mining (United Arab Emirates); Chair. TAHER TABET; Man. Dir SIDI MALEK.

Société de Construction et de Gestion Immobilière de la Mauritanie (SOCOGIM): BP 28, Nouakchott; tel. 45-25-42-13; e-mail socogim@mauritel.mr; f. 1974; cap. UM 1,088.2m.; 89% state-owned; Chair. DIALLO MAMADOU BATHIA; Dir-Gen. MOHAMED LEMINE OULD KHATTRI.

Société Mauritanienne de Commercialisation de Poissons, SA (SMCP): blvd Median, BP 250, Nouadhibou; tel. 45-74-52-81; fax 45-24-55-66; e-mail info@smcpsa.com; internet www.smcpsa.com; f. 1984; cap. UM 500m.; Govt is a minority shareholder; until 1992 monopoly exporter of demersal fish and crustaceans; Pres. MOHAMED SALEM OULD LEKHAL; Dir-Gen. BOIJEL OULD HEMEID.

Société des Mines du Cuivre de Mauritanie (MCM): BP 5576, Nouakchott; tel. 45-25-64-23; fax 45-25-63-20; f. 2005 to acquire operations of Guelb Moghrein Mines d'Akjoujt (GEMAK); exploitation of copper and other ores at Akjoujt; 80% owned by First Quantum Minerals (Canada); Dir-Gen. MERLIN THOMAS.

Société Nationale d'Importation et d'Exportation (SONIMEX): BP 290, Nouakchott; tel. 45-25-14-72; fax 45-25-30-14; f. 1966; cap. UM 914m.; 74% state-owned; import of foodstuffs and textiles, distribution of essential consumer goods, export of gum arabic; Pres. HAMOUD OULD AHMEDOU; Dir-Gen. MAHFOUDH OULD AGATT.

Société Nationale Industrielle et Minière (SNIM): BP 42, Nouadhibou; tel. 45-74-51-74; fax 45-74-53-96; e-mail snim@snim.com; internet www.snim.com; f. 1972; cap. UM 9,059.5m.; 78.4% state-owned; balance held by Islamic Development Bank (Saudi Arabia) and private Kuwaiti and Jordanian interests; operates mining centre at Zouerate, three open pit cast iron mines, port facilities, and 700-km railway line; Man. Dir MOHAMED ABDALLAHI OULD OUDAA; c. 4,500 employees (2009).

TIVISKI SA: BP 2069, Nouakchott; tel. 45-25-17-56; e-mail contact@tiviski.com; internet www.tiviski.com; f. 1989; dairy products; Dir-Gen. NAGI ICHOUDOU.

Total Mauritanie: E Nord, Lot no 110, BP 4973, Nouakchott; tel. 45-29-00-19; distribution of petroleum; Man. Dir ABDOUL WAHAB.

TRADE UNIONS

Confédération Générale des Travailleurs de Mauritanie: BP 6164, Nouakchott; tel. 45-25-60-24; fax 45-25-80-57; e-mail admin@cgtm.org; internet cgtm.org; f. 1992; obtained official recognition in 1994; Sec.-Gen. ABDALLAHI OULD MOHAMED.

Confédération Libre des Travailleurs de Mauritanie: BP 6902, Nouakchott; fax 45-25-23-16; f. 1995; Sec.-Gen. SAMORY OULD BÉYE.

Confédération Nationale des Travailleurs de Mauritanie (CNTM): Nouakchott; tel. 45-00-17-01; fax 45-24-35-80; e-mail contact@cntm-rim.org; internet www.cntm-rim.org; Sec.-Gen. MOHAMED AHMED OULD SALECK.

Union des Travailleurs de Mauritanie (UTM): Bourse du Travail, BP 630, Nouakchott; f. 1961; Sec.-Gen. ABDERAHMANE OULD BOUBOU; 45,000 mems.

Transport

RAILWAYS

A 704-km railway connects the iron-ore deposits at Zouérate with Nouadhibou; a 40-km extension services the reserves at El Rhein, and a 30-km extension those at M'Haoudat. Motive power is diesel-electric. The Société Nationale Industrielle et Minière (SNIM) operates one of the longest (2.4 km) and heaviest (22,000 metric tons) trains in the world.

SNIM—Direction du Chemin de Fer et du Port: BP 42, Nouadhibou; tel. 45-74-51-74; fax 45-74-53-96; e-mail m.khalifa.beyah@zrt.snim.com; internet www.snim.com; f. 1963; Gen. Man. MOHAMED EL-MOCTAR OULD TALEB.

ROADS

In 2006 there were about 11,066 km of roads and tracks, of which only 2,966 km were paved. The 1,100-km Trans-Mauritania highway, completed in 1985, links Nouakchott with Néma in the east of the country. The construction of a 470-km highway between Nouakchott and Nouadhibou was completed in 2004. Plans exist for the construction of a 7,400-km highway, linking Nouakchott with the Libyan port of Tubruq (Tobruk).

Autorité de Régulation des Transports: Nouakchott; Pres. CHEIKH SID'AHMED OULD BABA.

Entreprise Nationale de l'Entretien Routier: Dir-Gen. MADI OULD TALEB.

Société Mauritanienne des Transports (SOMATRA): Nouakchott; tel. 45-25-29-53; f. 1975; Pres. CHEIKH MALAININE ROBERT; Dir-Gen. MAMADOU SOULEYMANE KANE.

INLAND WATERWAYS

The Senegal river is navigable in the wet season by small coastal vessels as far as Kayes (Mali) and by river vessels as far as Kaédi; in the dry season as far as Rosso and Boghé, respectively. The major river ports are at Rosso, Kaédi and Gouraye.

SHIPPING

The principal port, at Point-Central, 10 km south of Nouadhibou, is almost wholly occupied with mineral exports. There is also a commercial and fishing port at Nouadhibou. The deep-water Port de l'Amitié at Nouakchott, built and maintained with assistance from the People's Republic of China, was inaugurated in 1986, and has a total annual capacity of about 1.5m. metric tons. In 2009 Mauritania's merchant fleet consisted of 155 vessels and had a total displacement of some 52,000 grt.

Mauritanienne de Transport Maritime: Nouakchott; tel. 45-25-44-79; fax 45-25-44-76; e-mail mtm@mtm.mr; internet www.mtm.mr; f. 1996; Pres. and Dir-Gen. A. KADER KAMIL.

Port Autonome de Nouadhibou: BP 236, Nouadhibou; tel. 45-74-51-36; fax 45-74-51-36; e-mail contact@pan.mr; internet www.portndb.com; f. 1973; state-owned; Pres. BAL MOHAMED EL HABIB; Dir-Gen. MOHAMED ABDERRAHMANE OULD BRAHIM.

Port Autonome de Nouakchott (Port de l'Amitié): BP 5103, El Mina, Nouakchott; tel. 45-25-38-59; fax 45-25-16-15; e-mail info@panpa.mr; internet www.panpa.mr; f. 1986; deep-water port; Dir-Gen. AHMEDOU OULD HAMED.

Shipping Companies

Cie Mauritanienne de Navigation Maritime (COMAUNAM): 119 ave Nasser, BP 799, Nouakchott; tel. 45-25-36-34; fax 45-25-25-04; f. 1973; 51% state-owned, 49% owned by Govt of Algeria; nat. shipping co; forwarding agent, stevedoring; Chair. MOHAND TIGHILT; Dir-Gen. KAMIL ABDELKADER.

Société d'Acconage et de Manutention en Mauritanie (SAMMA): BP 258, Nouadhibou; tel. 45-74-52-63; fax 45-74-52-37; e-mail didi.samma@snim.com; internet www.samma.mr; f. 1960; freight and handling, shipping agent, forwarding agent, stevedoring; Man. Dir DIDI OULD BIHA.

Société Générale de Consignation et d'Entreprises Maritimes (SOGECO): 1765 rue 22-002, Commune du Ksar, BP 351, Nouakchott; tel. 45-25-22-02; fax 45-25-39-03; e-mail sogeco@sogeco.sa.mr; internet www.sogecosa.com; f. 1973; shipping agent, forwarding, stevedoring; Man. Dir SID'AHMED OULD ABEIDNA.

Société Mauritanienne pour la Pêche et la Navigation (SMPN): BP 40254, Nouakchott; tel. 45-25-36-38; fax 45-25-37-87; e-mail smpn@toptechnology.mr; Dir-Gen. ABDALLAHI OULD ISMAIL.

VOTRA: route de l'Aéroport, BP 454, Nouakchott; tel. 45-25-24-10; fax 45-25-31-41; e-mail info@votra.net; internet www.votra.net; Dir-Gen. MOHAMED MAHMOUD OULD MAYE.

CIVIL AVIATION

There are international airports at Nouakchott, Nouadhibou and Néma, and 23 smaller airstrips.

Agence Nationale de l'Aviation Civile (ANAC): BP 91, Nouakchott; tel. 45-24-40-06; fax 45-25-35-78; e-mail abseddigh@anac.mr; internet www.anac.mr; f. 2004; Gen. Man. ABOUBEKRINE SEDDIGH OULD MOAMED EL HACEN.

Mauritania Airlines International: Nouakchott; f. 2010.

Tourism

Mauritania's principal tourist attractions are its historical sites, several of which have been listed by UNESCO under its World Heritage Programme, and its game reserves and national parks. Some 24,000 tourists visited Mauritania in 1999. Receipts from tourism in that year totalled an estimated US $28m.

Office National du Tourisme: BP 2884, Nouakchott; tel. 45-29-03-44; fax 45-29-05-28; e-mail ont@tourisme-mauritanie.com; f. 2002; Dir KHADIJÉTOU MINT BOUBOU.

SOMASERT: BP 42, Nouadhibou; tel. 45-74-29-91; fax 45-74-90-43; e-mail somasert@snim.com; internet www.somasert.com; f. 1987; subsidiary of SNIM; responsible for promoting tourism, managing hotels and organizing tours; Dir-Gen. SAAD CHEIK SAAD BOUH.

Defence

As assessed at November 2010, the total armed forces numbered an estimated 15,870 men: army 15,000, navy about 620, air force 250. Full-time membership of paramilitary forces totalled about 5,000. Military service is by authorized conscription, and lasts for two years.

Defence Expenditure: Estimated at UM 30,100m. in 2009.

Chief of Staff of the Armed Forces: Gen. MOHAMED OULD CHEIKH MOHAMED AHMED.

Chief of Staff of the Navy: Col CHEIKH OULD BAYE.

Chief of Staff of the National Gendarmerie: Col N'DIAGA DIENG.

Education

Primary education, which is officially compulsory, begins at six years of age and lasts for six years. In 2009/10 total enrolment at primary schools included 74% of children in the relevant age-group (72% of boys; 76% of girls), according to UNESCO estimates. Secondary education begins at 12 years of age and lasts for seven years, comprising a first cycle of four years and a second of three years. Total enrolment at public secondary schools in 2006/07 included only 16% of children in the appropriate age-group (17% of boys; 15% of girls), according to UNESCO estimates. In 2010/11 a total of 14,536 students were enrolled at Mauritania's higher education institutions (including the Université de Nouakchott, which was opened in 1983). In 2005 spending on education represented 8.3% of total budgetary expenditure.

Bibliography

Abdoul, M., *et al. Regards sur la Mauritanie.* L'ouest saharien: cahiers d'études pluridisciplinaires; Vol. 4. Paris, L'Harmattan, 2004.

Audibert, J. *MIFERMA: Une aventure humaine et industrielle en Mauritanie.* Paris, L'Harmattan, 1991.

Bader, C., and Lefort, F. *Mauritanie, la vie réconciliée.* Paris, Fayard, 1990.

Balta, P., and Rulleau, C. *Le Grand Maghreb, des indépendances à l'an 2000.* Paris, Découverte, 1990.

Belvaude, C. *La Mauritanie.* Paris, Editions Karthala, 1989.

Bonte, P. *La montagne de fer: la SNIM, Mauritanie: une entreprise minière saharienne à l'heure de la mondialisation.* Paris, Editions Karthala, 2001.

Boye, A. H., and Thiam, S. *J'étais à Oualata: le racisme d'Etat en Mauritanie.* Paris, L'Harmattan, 1999.

Calderini, S., Cortese, D., and Webb, J. L. A. *Mauritania.* Oxford, ABC Clio, 1992.

Clausen, U. *Demokratisierung in Mauritanien: Einfuehrung und Dokumente.* Hamburg, Deutsches Orient-Institut, 1993.

de Chassey, C. *Mauritanie 1900–1975: de l'ordre colonial à l'ordre néo-colonial entre Maghreb et Afrique noire.* Paris, Anthropos, 1978.

Désiré-Vuillemin, G. *Histoire de la Mauritanie: des origines à l'indépendance.* Paris, Editions Karthala, 1997.

Devey, M. *La Mauritanie.* Paris, Editions Karthala, 2005.

Diaw, M. *La politique étrangère de la Mauritanie.* Paris, L'Harmattan, 1999.

Garnier, C., and Ermont, P. *Désert fertile: un nouvel état, la Mauritanie.* Paris, Hachette, 1960.

Human Rights Watch, Africa. *Mauritania's Campaign of Terror: State-Sponsored Repression of Black Africans*. New York, Human Rights Watch, 1994.

Jus, C. *Soudan français–Mauritanie, une géopolitique coloniale (1880–1963): tracer une ligne dans le désert*. Paris, L'Harmattan, 2003.

Marchesin, P. *Tribus, ethnies et pouvoir en Mauritanie*. Paris, Editions Karthala, 1992.

McBrewster, J., Miller F. P., and Vandome, A. (Eds). *History of Mauritania*. Mauritius, Alphascript Publishing, 2009.

Ould Ahmed Salem, M. *L'économie mauritanienne: le bilan de la planification économique depuis l'indépendance* (trans. from Arabic by Ould Moulaye Ahmed, A.). Nouakchott, Imprimerie Atlas, 1994.

Ould Beidy, S. *L'administration territoriale et le développement local en Mauritanie*. Paris, L'Harmattan, 2009

Ould Daddah, M. *La Mauritanie contre vents et marées*. Paris, Editions Karthala, 2003.

Ould-May, M. *Global Restructuring and Peripheral States: The Carrot and the Stick in Mauritania*. Lanham, MD, Littlefield Adams, 1996.

Ould Meymoun, M. *La Mauritanie entre le pouvoir civil et le pouvoir militaire*. Paris, L'Harmattan, 2011.

Ould Saleck, El-A. *Les Haratins: La paysage politique mauritanien*. Paris, L'Harmattan, 2003.

Pazzanika, A. G. *Historical Dictionary of Mauritania*. Lanham, MD, Scarecrow Press, 1996.

Robinson, D. *Sociétés musulmanes et pouvoir colonial français au Sénégal et en Mauritanie 1880–1920*. Paris, Editions Karthala, 2004.

Sy, A. A. *L'Enfer d'Inal: Mauritanie—l'horreur des camps*. Paris, L'Harmattan, 2000.

Vandermotten, C. *Géopolitique de la vallée du Sénégal: les flots de la discorde*. Paris, L'Harmattan, 2004.

Wolff, W. J., van der Land, J., Nienhuis, P. H., and de Wilde, P. A. W. J. (Eds). *Ecological Studies in the Coastal Waters of Mauritania*. London, Kluwer Academic Publishers, 1993.

MAURITIUS

Physical and Social Geography

The Republic of Mauritius, comprising the islands of Mauritius and Rodrigues, together with the Agalega Islands and the Cargados Carajos Shoals, lies in the Indian Ocean 800 km east of Madagascar. The island of Mauritius covers 1,865 sq km (720 sq miles) in area. It is a volcanic island, consisting of a plain rising from the north-east to the highest point on the island, Piton de la Rivière Noire (827 m above sea-level) in the south-west, interspersed by abrupt volcanic peaks and gorges, and is almost completely surrounded by a coral reef. Including Rodrigues and its other islands, the republic occupies a land area of 2,040 sq km (788 sq miles).

The climate is sub-tropical maritime, but with two distinct seasons; additionally, the warm dry coastal areas contrast with the cool rainy interior. Mauritius and Rodrigues are vulnerable to cyclones, particularly between September and May.

Rodrigues, a volcanic island of 104 sq km (40 sq miles) surrounded by a coral reef, lies 585 km east of the island of Mauritius. Its population was enumerated at 35,779 in the 2000 census, and was estimated to number 38,039 at December 2011. Mauritius has two dependencies (together covering 71 sq km, with 289 inhabitants at December 2011): Agalega, two islands 935 km north of Mauritius; and the Cargados Carajos Shoals (or St Brandon Islands), 22 islets without permanent inhabitants but used as a fishing station, 370 km north-north-east of Mauritius.

Mauritius claims sovereignty over Tromelin, a small island without permanent inhabitants, 556 km to the north-west. This claim is disputed by Madagascar and France. Mauritius also seeks the return of the Chagos Archipelago (notably the coral atoll of Diego Garcia), about 2,000 km to the north-east. The archipelago was formerly administered by Mauritius but in 1965 became part (and in 1976 all) of the British Indian Ocean Territory.

The population of the Republic of Mauritius was provisionally enumerated at 1,257,900 at the July 2011 census, giving a density of 616.6 inhabitants per sq km. During 2001–10 the population increased at an average annual rate of only 0.7%, owing, in part, to higher emigration and a decline in the birth rate. Almost 42% of the population reside in the urban area extending from Port Louis (the capital and business centre) on the north-west coast, to Curepipe in the island's centre. The population is of mixed origin, including people of European, African, Indian and Chinese descent. English is the official language, and Creole (Kreol), derived from French, the lingua franca. The most widely spoken languages at the 2000 census were Creole (38.6%) and Bhojpuri (30.6%), a Hindi dialect.

Recent History

KATHARINE MURISON

INTRODUCTION

The islands of Mauritius and Rodrigues passed from French into British control in 1810. Subsequent settlement came mainly from East Africa and India, and the European population has remained predominantly francophone.

The Indian community in Mauritius took little part in politics until 1947, when the franchise was extended to adults over the age of 21 years who could establish simple literacy in any language. This expansion of the electorate deprived the Franco-Mauritian and Creole communities of their political dominance, and the Mauritius Labour Party (MLP), led by Dr (later Sir) Seewoosagur Ramgoolam, consolidated the new political role of the Indian community. The Parti Mauricien Social Démocrate (PMSD) emerged to represent traditional Franco-Mauritian and Creole interests, under the leadership of Gaëtan (later Sir Gaëtan) Duval. With impetus from Ramgoolam's MLP, Mauritius proceeded to independence, within the Commonwealth, on 12 March 1968, with Ramgoolam as Prime Minister of a coalition Government that was subsequently extended to include the PMSD.

In November 1965 the United Kingdom transferred the Chagos Archipelago (including the atoll of Diego Garcia), a Mauritian dependency about 2,000 km (1,250 miles) north-east of the main island, to the newly created British Indian Ocean Territory (BIOT, q.v.). Mauritius has subsequently campaigned for the return of the islands, which have been developed as a major US military base.

From 1970 the strongest opposition to the Ramgoolam coalition came from a newly formed left-wing group, the Mouvement Militant Mauricien (MMM), led by Paul Bérenger. Having attracted considerable public support during a period of labour unrest, the MMM emerged as the largest single party in the Legislative Assembly at elections in December 1976, although with insufficient seats to form a government. Ramgoolam was able to form a new coalition with the PMSD.

THE JUGNAUTH COALITIONS, 1982–95

At elections to the Legislative Assembly in June 1982, an alliance of the MMM and the Parti Socialiste Mauricien (PSM) won all 60 elective seats on the main island. Anerood (later Sir Anerood) Jugnauth became Prime Minister and appointed Bérenger as Minister of Finance. In March 1983, however, following discord within the cabinet over Bérenger's stringent economic policies and his attempts to make Creole (Kreol) the official language (despite the Indian descent of the majority of the population), Bérenger and his supporters resigned. Jugnauth formed a new Government, and in April formed a new party, the Mouvement Socialiste Militant (MSM), which subsequently merged with the PSM. However, the new Government lacked a legislative majority, and Jugnauth was obliged to dissolve the Assembly in June.

At a general election in August 1983, an alliance comprising the MSM, the MLP and the PMSD, obtained a decisive majority. Jugnauth remained as Prime Minister, with Duval as Deputy Prime Minister. In December Ramgoolam was appointed Governor-General. The new leader of the MLP, Satcam (later Sir Satcam) Boolell, was dismissed from the cabinet in February 1984, prompting the party to withdraw from the coalition.

At the general election, held on 30 August 1987, an electoral alliance comprising the MSM, the PMSD and the MLP won 39 of the 60 elective seats on the main island, while the MMM, which campaigned in alliance with two smaller parties, won 21 seats. Dr Paramhansa (Prem) Nababsingh subsequently became the leader of the MMM and of the opposition in the Assembly, replacing Bérenger, who had failed to secure a seat. In September Jugnauth appointed a new Council of Ministers. In August 1988, following a disagreement over employment policies, Sir Gaëtan Duval, the leader of the PMSD, left the Government, together with his brother, Hervé Duval, the Minister of Industry.

In July 1990 the MMM and MSM agreed to form an alliance to contest the next general election, and to proceed with constitutional revisions that would allow Mauritius to become a republic within the Commonwealth. However, the draft amendments were opposed by the MLP (in alliance with the two PMSD), prompting Jugnauth to dismiss Boolell, as well as two MSM ministers who had refused to support the proposed reforms. A further three ministers representing the MLP also resigned, leaving only one MLP member in the Government. Boolell subsequently relinquished the leadership of the MLP to Dr Navinchandra (Navin) Ramgoolam (the son of Sir Seewoosagur Ramgoolam, who died in December 1985). In September 1990 Jugnauth formed a new coalition Government, in which the six vacant ministerial posts were awarded to the MMM, while Nababsingh became one of the three Deputy Prime Ministers.

At a general election on 15 September 1991, an alliance of the MSM, the MMM and the Mouvement des Travaillistes Démocrates (MTD) won 57 of the 62 elective seats, while the alliance of the MLP and the PMSD secured only three seats. Members of the Organisation du Peuple Rodriguais (OPR) were returned to the remaining two seats. However, members of the opposition, including Ramgoolam and Sir Gaëtan Duval, alleged electoral malpractice. Jugnauth subsequently formed a new Government, to which nine representatives of the MMM (including Bérenger) and one representative of the MTD were appointed. Later in September Duval resigned from the Legislative Assembly.

In December 1991 the Legislative Assembly approved constitutional amendments providing for Mauritius to become a republic within the Commonwealth on 12 March 1992. Under the terms of the revised Constitution, the Governor-General, Sir Veerasamy Ringadoo, who had been nominated by Jugnauth, became interim President on 12 March 1992, pending the election of a President and Vice-President, for a five-year term, by a simple majority of the legislature (which was renamed the National Assembly). The Constitution vested executive power in the Prime Minister, who would be appointed by the President, and would be the parliamentary member best able to command a majority in the National Assembly. Later that month the Government announced that Cassam Uteem, the Minister of Industry and Industrial Technology and a member of the MMM, was to be nominated to the presidency after a period of three months. Uteem was duly elected President by the National Assembly in June, with Sir Rabindrah Ghurburrun, also of the MMM, as Vice-President.

Jugnauth dismissed Bérenger from the Council of Ministers in mid-1993, on the grounds that he had repeatedly criticized government policy. The removal of Bérenger precipitated a serious crisis within the MMM, the political bureau of which decided that the other nine members of the party who held ministerial portfolios should remain in the coalition Government. Led by Nababsingh, the Deputy Prime Minister, and the Minister of Industry and Industrial Technology, Jean-Claude de l'Estrac, supporters of the pro-coalition faction announced in October that Bérenger had been suspended as Secretary-General of the MMM. Bérenger and his supporters responded by expelling 11 MMM officials from the party, and subsequently obtaining a legal ban on Nababsingh and de l'Estrac using the party name. The split in the MMM led in November to a government reshuffle, in which the remaining two MMM ministers supporting Bérenger were replaced by members of the party's pro-coalition faction.

In April 1994 the MLP and the MMM announced that they had agreed terms for an alliance to contest the next general election. Under its provisions, Ramgoolam was to be Prime Minister and Bérenger Deputy Prime Minister, with cabinet portfolios allocated on the basis of 12 ministries to the MLP and nine to the MMM. In the same month three deputies from the MSM withdrew their support from the Government. Nababsingh and the dissident faction of the MMM formed a new party, the Renouveau Militant Mauricien (RMM), which formally commenced political activity in June.

In November 1994, during the course of a parliamentary debate on electoral issues, Bérenger and de l'Estrac accepted a mutual challenge to resign from their seats in the National Assembly and to contest by-elections. In the following month the MSM indicated that it would not oppose RMM candidates in the two polls. In January 1995, however, Jugnauth unsuccessfully sought to undermine the MLP/MMM alliance by offering electoral support to the MLP. The by-elections, held in February, were both won by MLP/MMM candidates, and Bérenger was returned to the National Assembly. Following these results, Jugnauth opened political negotiations with the PMSD, whose leader, Charles Gaëtan Xavier-Luc Duval (the son of Sir Gaëtan Duval), agreed to enter the coalition as Minister of Industry and Industrial Technology and Minister of Tourism. The post of Attorney-General and Minister of Justice, previously held by Jugnauth, was also allocated to the PMSD, and Sir Gaëtan Duval accepted an appointment as an economic adviser to the Prime Minister. As a result, however, of widespread opposition within the PMSD to participation in the coalition, Xavier-Luc Duval left the Government in October, and Sir Gaëtan Duval subsequently resumed the leadership of the party. The Minister for Rodrigues, representing the OPR, also resigned from the cabinet.

MLP/MMM COALITION

At a general election in December 1995 the MLP/MMM alliance won a decisive victory: of the 62 elected seats, the MLP secured 35, the MMM 25 and the OPR two. Under constitutional arrangements providing representation for unsuccessful candidates attracting the largest number of votes, Sir Gaëtan Duval re-entered the National Assembly, together with two members of the Mouvement Rodriguais (MR) and a representative of Hizbullah, an Islamist fundamentalist group. Ramgoolam became Prime Minister of the new MLP/MMM coalition, with Bérenger as Deputy Prime Minister with responsibility for foreign and regional relations. Sir Gaëtan Duval died in May 1996 and was succeeded in the National Assembly and as leader of the PMSD by his brother, Hervé Duval.

THE MLP IN POWER

Serious divisions within the coalition Government emerged in late 1996, when differences were reported between Ramgoolam and Bérenger over the allocation of ministerial responsibilities. Bérenger's criticism of the coalition's performance intensified in the following months, and culminated in June 1997 in his dismissal from the Government and the consequent withdrawal of the MMM from the coalition. Ramgoolam formed an MLP cabinet, assuming personal responsibility for foreign affairs. Also in June the National Assembly re-elected Uteem to a second five-year term as President. A prominent supporter of the MLP, Angidi Verriah Chettiar, was elected Vice-President.

Following the dissolution of the MLP/MMM alliance, Bérenger sought to consolidate political opposition to the Government, securing the support of two small parties, the Mouvement Militant Socialiste Mauricien (MMSM) and the Rassemblement pour la Réforme (RPR), in August 1997. The alliance was extended to include a breakaway faction of the PMSD, known as the 'Vrais Bleus', under the leadership of Hervé Duval, who had been replaced as party leader by his nephew, Xavier-Luc Duval, an opponent of co-operation with the MMM. In April 1998 the MMM, the MMSM, the RPR and the 'Vrais Bleus' parties formed an electoral coalition, the Alliance Nationale, to contest a by-election for a vacant seat in the National Assembly. The seat, which was retained by the MLP, had also been sought by Jugnauth on behalf of the MSM, which remained unrepresented in the National Assembly. Jugnauth subsequently opened negotiations with Bérenger for an MSM/MMM electoral alliance, and in December both parties agreed terms for a joint list of candidates.

In February 1999 Jugnauth assumed the leadership of the informal MSM/MMM alliance. The appointment of Jugnauth's son, Pravind, as deputy leader of the MSM later that year caused divisions within the alliance, with members of the MMM claiming that Jugnauth was attempting to establish a political dynasty.

A reorganization of the Council of Ministers was carried out in October 1999, following the victory of Xavier-Luc Duval in a by-election the preceding month; the MLP had endorsed the candidature of Duval, who had formed his own party, the Parti Mauricien Xavier-Luc Duval (PMXD), in 1998. Duval was appointed Minister of Industry, Commerce, Corporate Affairs and Financial Services.

THE 2000 GENERAL ELECTION

A general election was held on 11 September 2000. The rate of participation was high, at 81%. The result was a significant victory for the opposition MSM/MMM alliance, also comprising the PMSD, which won a total of 54 of the 62 directly elective seats in the National Assembly, while the MLP/PMXD alliance took six seats and the OPR two. As agreed prior to the election, Jugnauth became Prime Minister again, while Bérenger was appointed Deputy Prime Minister and Minister of Finance. A new Council of Ministers was sworn in on 20 September.

In November 2000 the British High Court of Justice ruled that the eviction of several thousand inhabitants of the Chagos Archipelago between 1967 and 1973, to allow the construction of a US military base on the atoll of Diego Garcia, had been unlawful. The Court overturned a 1971 ordinance preventing the islanders from returning to the Archipelago. (The majority of the displaced islanders had been resettled in Mauritius, which had administered the Chagos Archipelago until its transfer to BIOT in 1965.) Following the ruling, the Mauritian Government declared its right to sovereignty over the islands to be indisputable and sought international recognition of this. Jugnauth stated that he would be prepared to negotiate with the USA over the continued presence of the military base. The United Kingdom reiterated that it would return the islands if, as had been maintained for many years, the USA was prepared to move out of the base on Diego Garcia. In May 2002 legislation allowing the displaced islanders to apply for British citizenship came into effect.

In November 2001 legislation providing for the creation of an 18-member Regional Assembly for Rodrigues received the President's assent. At the first elections to the new Assembly, which were held in September 2002, the OPR won 10 seats and the MR took eight.

PRESIDENTIAL CHANGE

In February 2002 President Uteem resigned in protest at controversial anti-terrorism legislation, which he felt surrendered too great a part of the nation's sovereignty to Western powers and ascribed excessive powers to the authorities, at the expense of the rights of the citizen. Vice-President Chettiar also resigned as his successor when called on to sanction the legislation, which was widely opposed. The bill was finally promulgated by the Chief Justice of the Supreme Court, Arianga Pillay, acting as interim President, as it had already been passed twice by the National Assembly. On 25 February Karl Offman of the MSM was elected President at an extraordinary session of the National Assembly, which was boycotted by opposition deputies. Offman was to relinquish the presidency to Jugnauth in October 2003, as already agreed by his party. In April 2003 Jugnauth resigned from the leadership of the MSM in favour of his son, Pravind.

In August 2003, in preparation for the transfer of governing roles, a constitutional amendment was approved by the National Assembly to increase the powers of the President, giving the incumbent the right to refuse a request from the Prime Minister to dissolve the legislature following a vote of no confidence. Jugnauth resigned as premier on 30 September and was immediately replaced by Bérenger, the first non-Hindu Prime Minister, who appointed a new Council of Ministers. On 1 October, as agreed, Offman resigned from the presidency and Jugnauth was elected as his successor by the National Assembly one week later. Bérenger's Government threatened to pursue its claim of sovereignty over the Chagos Archipelago at the International Court of Justice, on the basis that the separation of the Archipelago from Mauritian territory prior to independence was contrary to international law. In June 2004 the British authorities issued two decrees (known as Orders in Council) effectively prohibiting the islanders and their descendants from returning to live on the Chagos Archipelago, despite the High Court ruling in their favour in 2000. The Chagossians subsequently challenged the validity of these Orders in Council.

In early 2005 Anil Bachoo, the Minister of Public Infrastructure, Land Transport and Shipping, and Mookhesswur Choonee, the Minister of Local Government and Solid Waste Management, resigned from the Government and from the MSM, before founding a new party, the Mouvement Social Démocrate (MSD). The politicians reportedly disapproved of an implicit arrangement between the ruling parties that Bérenger would resign from the premiership at mid-term, in order for Pravind Jugnauth to assume power, just as Jugnauth's father (the incumbent President) had done for Bérenger. The MSD subsequently joined the MLP-led Alliance Sociale (AS), also comprising the MMSM, the Mouvement Républicain and the PMXD, which had been established to contest forthcoming elections to the National Assembly.

THE AS IN GOVERNMENT

At the legislative elections, which were held on 3 July 2005, the AS defeated the incumbent coalition of the MSM/MMM/PMSD, winning 38 of the 62 directly elected seats. The MSM/MMM/PMSD alliance secured 22 seats, and the remaining two were taken by the OPR. The rate of voter participation was 81.5%. Navin Ramgoolam was appointed as Prime Minister, and a new Council of Ministers was sworn into office on 7 July. Xavier-Luc Duval became one of three Deputy Prime Ministers.

The PMSD withdrew from its alliance with the MSM and the MMM in late 2005 The opposition was further weakened in April 2006, when the PMSD announced that it was joining the government coalition and the MSM/MMM alliance collapsed following weeks of increasing tension between Pravind Jugnauth and Bérenger. The MSM withdrew its support from Bérenger as official leader of the opposition. Bérenger was succeeded by Nando Bodha, the Secretary-General of the MSM and a close ally of Pravind Jugnauth (who had failed to retain his seat in the legislature in July 2005), since the MSM held 11 seats in the National Assembly to the MMM's 10. Bodha's nomination was rejected by Ashock Jugnauth, a senior member of the MSM (and uncle of Pravind), who resigned from the party and established a new opposition party, the Union Nationale (UN).

Elections to the Rodrigues Regional Assembly were held in December 2006. The MR secured 10 of the Assembly's 18 seats, while the OPR took eight.

In August 2007 Chettiar returned to the position of Vice-President, succeeding Raouf Bundhun, whose mandate had expired earlier that year. Bérenger replaced Bodha as official leader of the opposition in the following month, after the PMSD's two deputies and Ashock Jugnauth lent their support to the MMM. Prime Minister Ramgoolam assumed additional responsibility for the Ministry of Foreign Affairs, International Trade and Co-operation in March 2008, having dismissed the incumbent minister, Madun Dulloo, the leader of the MMSM, as a result of his public criticism of the Government's performance. In July the MMSM, which had effectively ended its participation in the AS, merged with the MMM.

Ramgoolam effected a government reorganization in mid-September 2008, notably appointing Arvin Boolell, hitherto Minister of Agro-industry and Fisheries, to the reconstituted post of Minister of Foreign Affairs, Regional Integration and International Trade. Other changes included the transfer of Deputy Prime Minister Ahmed Rashid Beebeejaun from the Ministry of Public Infrastructure, Land Transport and Shipping to the newly created Ministry of Renewable Energy and Public Utilities, being replaced in the infrastructure portfolio by Bachoo, who had served as Minister of the Environment since July 2005. On 19 September Jugnauth was unanimously re-elected as President by the National Assembly for a second five-year term. On the following day the Assembly adopted legislation providing for the creation of the title of Vice-Prime Minister, to be allocated to two ministers: Xavier-Luc Duval, the Minister of Tourism, Leisure and External Communications, and Rama Sithanen, the Minister of Finance and Economic Empowerment, assumed these positions, which ranked below that of Deputy Prime Minister.

Ashock Jugnauth's election to the National Assembly in 2005 was nullified in November 2008, when the British Privy

Council upheld a verdict by the Mauritian Supreme Court in March 2007 that he had been guilty of bribery during the election campaign. With the backing of the MLP, the MSM's Pravind Jugnauth was victorious in the resulting by-election, which was held in March 2009, defeating Ashock. In late 2009 the PMXD and the Mouvement Républicain merged into the PMSD, with Xavier-Luc Duval becoming leader of the enlarged party. The PMSD also decided to rejoin the ruling AS, abandoning its opposition alliance with the MMM and the UN. Meanwhile, a new opposition party, the Mouvement Mauricien Social Démocrate (MMSD), was formed by Eric Guimbeau, formerly of the PMSD.

2010 LEGISLATIVE ELECTIONS

Elections to the National Assembly were held on 5 May 2010. A recently formed alliance of Ramgoolam's MLP, the MSM and the PMSD, the Alliance de l'Avenir, secured 41 of the 62 directly elected seats, while the Alliance du Coeur, comprising the MMM, the MMSD and the UN, won 18 seats, the MR two seats and the Front Solidarité Mauricienne one. Seven additional seats were allocated: four to the Alliance de l'Avenir, two to the Alliance du Coeur and one to the OPR. A turn-out of 77.8% was recorded. The MR subsequently joined the ruling coalition, giving it the two-thirds' majority required to adopt constitutional reforms promised during the electoral campaign. Ramgoolam retained the premiership, and on 11 May a new Council of Ministers was sworn into office. Beebeejaun was reappointed as Deputy Prime Minister, while the PMSD leader, Xavier-Luc Duval, retained the position of Vice-Prime Minister, assuming responsibility for the Ministry of Social Integration and Economic Empowerment, and the MSM's Pravind Jugnauth became Vice-Prime Minister, Minister of Finance and Economic Development. Sithanen was excluded from the new Government. Monique Ohsan-Bellepeau, the President of the MLP, was elected as Vice-President of the Republic by the National Assembly in November, following the death of Chettiar in September.

The opposition UN was severely weakened in early 2011, when 11 senior members rejoined the MSM. However, there were persistent rumours of tensions within the ruling coalition, between the MSM and the MLP, during the first half of the year, and in June the MSM's Showkutally Soodhun, hitherto Minister of Industry and Commerce, was effectively demoted, with the transfer of the commerce portfolio to Michaël Yeung Sik Yuen, of the PMSD, who became Minister of Business, Enterprise, Commerce and Consumer Protection. The MSM suffered a further, more significant, reverse in July, when the Minister of Health and Quality of Life, MSM member Santi Bai (Maya) Hanoomanjee, was arrested by the Independent Commission Against Corruption and charged with corruption, following a six-month investigation into a scandal involving the purchase by the Government, for an allegedly inflated sum, of a medical clinic owned by the private company MedPoint. Four days after her arrest Hanoomanjee resigned from the Council of Ministers, as did the five other MSM ministers, in support of their colleague, although Pravind Jugnauth announced that the party would remain part of the ruling coalition. The six vacated portfolios were initially distributed, on an acting basis, to existing ministers. However, following a more comprehensive government reorganization effected in early August, Jugnauth declared that the MSM was entering into opposition, claiming that the party had been forced out of the coalition. Xavier-Luc Duval was notably allocated Jugnauth's former ministerial portfolio, becoming Vice-Prime Minister and Minister of Finance and Economic Development, while Anil Bachoo, the Minister of Public Infrastructure, the National Development Unit, Land Transport and Shipping, was elevated to the office of Vice-Prime Minister. The Government retained a narrow majority in the National Assembly. Jugnauth, a shareholder in MedPoint, was arrested in September and provisionally charged with having a conflict of interest in the Government's decision to acquire the clinic from the company; he denied the charge, asserting that he had declared his interests to the Council of Ministers and withdrawn from a meeting on the matter.

The OPR became the largest party in the Rodrigues Regional Assembly as a result of elections held in February 2012, securing 11 of the 21 seats, while the MR won eight and the Front Patriotique Rodriguais two.

RESIGNATION OF PRESIDENT JUGNAUTH

President Anerood Jugnauth resigned from office at the end of March 2012, following several weeks of disagreements with Prime Minister Ramgoolam, in order to return to party politics. He joined a renewed alliance of the MSM and the MMM, which he was expected to lead as candidate for the premiership in the legislative elections due in 2015. Vice-President Ohsan-Bellepeau assumed the presidency in an acting capacity.

Meanwhile, constitutional reform remained under consideration in 2011–12. In December 2011 a team of international experts commissioned by the Government to consider electoral changes submitted its report to the Prime Minister, proposing, *inter alia*, the replacement of the first-past-the-post system with a form of proportional representation and the abolition of the system of allocating additional seats in the National Assembly (the so-called 'best-loser' system), which was designed to ensure a balance of ethnic groups. However, its recommendations were largely rejected by the main political parties, although reform continued to be a priority for Ramgoolam's administration. In a decision issued in the same month, following a hearing in October, the Privy Council notably declined to rule on a legal challenge to the 'best-loser' system, which had been made by legislative election candidates whose nomination papers had been rejected owing to their refusal to declare to which community they belonged, referring the case back to the Mauritius Supreme Court. The Government's programme for 2012–15, presented in April 2012, included a pledge to conduct a constitutional review that would focus on the electoral system, the financing of political parties and the powers and method of election of the President. Also promised was legislation providing for popular referendums to be held on major constitutional and other issues.

On 20 July 2012 Kailash Purryag, hitherto Speaker of the National Assembly, was elected President of the Republic by the legislature in a vote boycotted by MSM and MMM deputies. Purryag took office on the following day.

RECENT FOREIGN RELATIONS

Enhancing bilateral economic relations was a priority for the AS Government that took office in July 2005. In October Ramgoolam paid a week-long state visit to India, a major source of direct investment in Mauritius, aimed at further strengthening the already close bilateral relationship; eight agreements on economic co-operation were signed during the visit; the Prime Minister made further visits to India in subsequent years, most recently in February 2012. Meanwhile, in August 2005 the first meeting of a joint Indian-Mauritian ministerial committee took place to discuss the possibility of signing a Comprehensive Economic Co-operation and Partnership Agreement between the two countries. Several further rounds of discussions were subsequently held, but negotiations stalled following the refusal of the Mauritian Government to accept Indian-proposed amendments to a bilateral convention on double taxation avoidance; the Indian Government was seeking to tax capital gains made in India by companies registered in Mauritius. An agreement had yet to be reached by mid-2012, although further talks on the renegotiation of the taxation treaty were scheduled to be held in late August, with the Mauritian Government having become keen to resolve the issue, amid concerns that domestic taxation measures planned in India would override the provisions of the existing bilateral agreement, adversely affecting the Mauritian economy. In March 2006 the Indian President, Aavul Pakkiri Jainulabidin Abdul Kalam, attended celebrations to mark National Day during a three-day visit to Mauritius. Bilateral relations were further strengthened in April 2011, during a four-day state visit to Mauritius by Kalam's successor, Pratibha Patil. In September 2006 Mauritius and the USA signed a trade and investment framework agreement, and in July 2007 Mauritius signed a preferential trade agreement with Pakistan, which entered into force in November of that year.

Ramgoolam's Government also sought to improve bilateral relations with Seychelles, signing a wide-ranging agreement on co-operation with that nation in December 2005. In July 2008, after six years of negotiations, the Governments of Mauritius and Seychelles signed a boundary agreement defining the areas of their two exclusive economic zones (that of Mauritius covering some 1.9m. sq km). Following further discussions on the delimitation of the extended continental shelf of the two countries, in December the Governments of Mauritius and Seychelles submitted a joint claim (to approximately 396,000 sq km beyond their respective exclusive economic zones) under the UN Convention on the Law of the Sea. In March 2011 the UN Commission on the Limits of the Continental Shelf confirmed the two countries' joint jurisdiction over the claimed area. In March 2012, during a state visit to Mauritius by the President of Seychelles, James Michel, two bilateral treaties were signed on the joint exercise of sovereign rights in the extended continental shelf and on a framework for the joint management of the area. Relations were further strengthened during a visit to Seychelles by Prime Minister Ramgoolam in June.

Closer ties with the People's Republic of China were also pursued. Chinese President, Hu Jintao, visited Mauritius in February 2009, and agreed to loan Mauritius funds for the extension of the passenger terminal of its international airport. In January 2010 it was reported that China was investing US $700m. in the creation of a special economic zone in Mauritius. Furthermore, in January 2011 the Chinese and Mauritian Governments signed an economic and trade co-operation agreement, under which China was to provide Mauritius with a grant of Rs 200m. and an interest-free loan of Rs 100m. to fund a range of unspecified projects. In March 2012 it was announced that China would provide funding for the construction of a Rs 3,400m. dam at Côte d'Or, in central Mauritius, aimed at addressing water shortages.

Ramgoolam's Government continued with efforts to regain sovereignty over the Chagos Archipelago. A group of 102 Chagossians was permitted to visit the Archipelago in March 2006, accompanied by Deputy Prime Minister Duval and two other government ministers, principally in order to visit the graves of relatives; further such visits took place in 2008 and 2011. In May 2006 the British High Court of Justice overturned the Orders in Council issued by the British Government under the royal prerogative in June 2004, ruling them to be unlawful, and confirmed the right of the islanders to return to the Archipelago without any conditions. In May 2007 the British High Court of Appeal rejected an appeal lodged by the British Government against the High Court's decision. However, in October 2008, in a final appeal, the House of Lords ruled in favour of the British Government, denying the right of the Chagossians to return to their homeland. Following the verdict, the Chagossians filed a complaint against the United Kingdom at the European Court of Human Rights. Representatives of the British and Mauritian Governments held two rounds of discussions on the Archipelago in January and July 2009. A planned third round of talks did not take place, however, owing to the Mauritian Government's displeasure at the British Government's unilateral decision, confirmed in April 2010, to establish a marine protection area (MPA) around the Archipelago. The Chagossians were also concerned by the implications of this plan, which would involve a ban on fishing (an activity considered essential to the viability of any future resettlement of the islands), on their case before the European Court of Human Rights. In December the Mauritian Government announced that it had filed a case against the United Kingdom with the International Tribunal for the Law of the Sea, contesting the compatibility of the creation of the MPA with the UN Convention on the Law of the Sea. The announcement followed the leaking of a confidential US diplomatic cable, detailing discussions that took place between British and US officials in 2009 on the MPA, which suggested that one of the motives behind its establishment was to prevent, or at least hinder, the resettlement of the Archipelago. Meanwhile, the Chagossians also appealed for a judicial review of the decision to create the MPA. During a visit to the United Kingdom in June 2012, Prime Minister Ramgoolam raised the issue of the Chagos Archipelago with his British counterpart, David Cameron. Ramgoolam emphasized the need for formal talks between Mauritius, the United Kingdom and the USA, which he hoped would result in an agreement on Mauritian sovereignty of the Archipelago while allowing the continued use of Diego Garcia as a US military base. The two Prime Ministers also signed an agreement on the transfer of suspected pirates caught by British naval forces to Mauritius for prosecution. The British High Court was due to conduct a judicial review into the legality of the MPA in July, while a ruling by the European Court of Human Rights was also anticipated imminently.

In November 2009 representatives of the Mauritian and French Governments reached agreement on the joint management of economic, scientific and environmental issues concerning the disputed island of Tromelin. Boolell and the French Secretary of State for Co-operation and Francophony, Alain Joyandet, signed a formal accord to this effect in the Mauritian capital, Port Louis, in June 2010. Both countries continued to claim sovereignty of the island.

Economy

DONALD L. SPARKS

The Republic of Mauritius is a small island state, with only 2,040 sq km in land area, and a population of 1.3m. Unlike most other members of the African Union, Mauritius is classified by the World Bank as an 'upper-middle-income' economy. Less than 8% of its population lives below the poverty line. The UN Development Programme's 2011 *Human Development Report* awarded Mauritius the highest rank in sub-Saharan Africa on its Human Development Index: 77th out of 187 countries. This index combines life expectancy (73.4 years), adult literacy (84.4%) and gross national income per head (at US $12,918 on an international purchasing-power parity basis). Also, unlike much of the region, Mauritius has a low 'dependency ratio', with those under 14 years of age (21.8%) and over 65 years of age (7.5%) comprising less than 30% of the total population. The nation's population growth rate, at 0.7%, is also one of the region's lowest.

Mauritius has achieved good rates of economic growth during the past two decades: between 1985 and 1995 the economy grew at an average annual rate of 15.5%, one of the highest in the region, and in 1995–2005 growth averaged 10.3% per year. The Government's Central Statistics Office (CSO) reported gross domestic product (GDP) growth of 5.5% in 2007 and 5.3% in 2008. However, Mauritius did not fully escape the effects of the international financial crisis that began in that year. Its important tourism sector suffered particularly badly, and, while it has recovered to some extent, tourist arrivals were down at the beginning of 2012. The Government's latest data indicated GDP growth of 3.1% for 2009, 4.2% for 2010 and an estimated 4.1% for 2011, bolstered by strong recoveries in the tourism and manufacturing (especially textiles) sectors. In addition, the 2012 budget included a variety of stimulus measures, including increasing capital spending (mostly on infrastructure), extending credit to small firms and reducing taxes. However, while the Governor of the Bank of Mauritius expected growth to continue, at just under 4% in 2012, economists at the Mauritius Commercial Bank cautioned that the rate could fall to 3% as a result of the economic slowdown in Europe, Mauritius' major trade partner.

Mauritius has a four-pillar economy, based upon textiles, tourism, sugar and financial services. However, the Government has recently taken steps aimed at diversifying the economy to enable it better to withstand external shocks and become more competitive in the global economy. Agriculture, fisheries and forestry's contribution to GDP declined from roughly 25% in the 1970s to 4.4% in 2011. In the same year services was the largest component of GDP, comprising 71.8% of total output. Industry accounted for 23.8% of GDP.

INDUSTRY

Until the 1970s the industrial sector was effectively limited to the import-substitution of basic consumer products, such as food, beverages, tobacco, footwear, clothing, metal products, paints and board for furniture. Since then there has been a rapid expansion in manufacturing, with the sector accounting for 23.8% of GDP in 2011. The manufacturing sector grew by 2.2% in 2007 and 3.2% in 2008, but, partly as a result of the global economic downturn, growth declined to an estimated 1.1% in 2009. The overall industrial sector expanded by 2.7% in 2010 and by an estimated 2.9% in 2011.

In view of the limited domestic market, the traditionally high level of unemployment (although the unemployment rate declined to 7.8% in 2011) and the emphasis on reducing dependence on the sugar sector, the Government adopted a policy of export promotion by developing an export-processing zone (EPZ), concentrating on labour-intensive processing of imported goods for the export market. Within the EPZ the Government offers both local and foreign investors attractive incentives, including tax 'holidays', exemption from import duties on most raw materials and capital goods, free repatriation of capital, profits and dividends, low-price electricity, etc. In 1993 there were 554 enterprises in the EPZ, employing about 83,500 workers, the lowest level since 1987. The decline both in new enterprises and employment continued in the mid-1990s, when a total of 494 businesses were employing 82,220 workers. By 2007 404 companies were employing 67,314 workers, of whom 32,973 were foreign workers, mostly from the People's Republic of China, Sri Lanka and India. There has been increasing unrest from foreign labour. For example, in 2007 the Compagnie Mauricienne de Textile, a firm employing some 5,000 workers deported 177 foreign employees who had taken part in demonstrations over what they considered to be poor working conditions. The fastest-growing EPZ sectors have been textiles and clothing, which account for about 71% of total EPZ exports, more than 52% of EPZ enterprises and 82% of EPZ labour.

Other rapidly growing sectors include electronic components and diamond-processing, and emphasis has been put on the development of precision engineering (electronics, watch- and instrument-making, etc.) and skilled crafts (diamond-cutting and -polishing, furniture, quality goods, etc.). Other items produced include toys, razor blades, nails, industrial chemicals, detergents, rattan furniture, plastic goods and tyres.

As a result of increasing labour costs, many firms in the EPZ are using more capital-intensive technologies; this has already affected employment, and will continue to do so over the next few years. The demand for skilled personnel in various business sectors, including marketing, management, accounting and computing, has also exceeded the number of suitable candidates, and the Government began to address this problem in 1999 by expediting the granting of labour permits to non-nationals possessing relevant professional qualifications.

India's and China's membership of the World Trade Organization (WTO) has increased international competition and put Mauritius at a disadvantage within the textile industry. Mauritius qualified to export duty-free textiles and manufactures to the USA under the African Growth and Opportunity Act. It was hoped that this would prove to be a major advantage in the early 2000s, in contrast to the quotas that had previously been imposed by the USA. Indeed, Mauritian exports to the USA increased, from US $275m. in 2001 to $298m. in 2003. However, with the enactment of the third version of the Act in 2004, Mauritius, together with South Africa, was not classified as a 'least developed country' because of its high income levels, and was therefore not eligible for the Third Country Fibre benefit, which allows the sourcing of fabrics from any country. Mauritius and South Africa were obliged to source their fabrics regionally or from the USA in order to qualify for duty-free access to North American markets. Thus, other regional states such as Lesotho, Madagascar and Swaziland, which are classified as 'less-developed countries', began to erode Mauritian textile exports. At least two textile companies made severe retrenchments to their operations in Mauritius following these developments. Mauritius, in conjunction with the other members of the Common Market for Eastern and Southern Africa (COMESA), began negotiating a comprehensive economic partnership agreement with the European Union (EU) in 2008. Indeed, Mauritius continues to receive financial assistance from the EU for restructuring the sugar industry and for a number of other development projects.

Mauritius has a large, and growing, informal sector. Women comprise almost one-third of the economically active population, although they represent up to 65% of the work-force in the EPZ. Unemployment, in the past hardly a major issue, increased from 1991, owing to a structural shift in the economy, whereby rising incomes reduced the number of low-wage jobs. The rate of unemployment has declined slightly since 2005, when it reached 9.3%; it was reduced from 8.8% in 2008 to 7.2% in 2009, but increased to 7.5% in 2010 and 7.8% in 2011. The total labour force amounted to 607,400 in 2011. In 2010 construction and industry employed the greatest percentage of all workers (30%), followed by trade, restaurants and hotels (22%) agriculture and fishing (9%), transport and communications (7%), and finance (6%).

TOURISM

Tourism has become a major component of the economy, and is one of the most important sources of foreign exchange; it has become increasingly important with the decline of contributions from sugar and textiles. Arrivals of foreign tourists increased from 27,650 visitors in 1970 to a record 964,600 in 2011, up from 934,827 in 2010. In 2009 receipts from tourism contributed 8.7% of GDP and 22% of foreign exchange earnings. In 2010 32.3% of visitors were from France, 12.3% from Réunion, 10.4% from the United Kingdom, 8.7% from South Africa, 6.0% from Italy and 5.7% from Germany. Tourism receipts grew by 8.6% in 2011, but are likely to level off in 2012 (see below).

Tourism was dampened in 2006 by the outbreak of Chikungunya (a rare form of mosquito-borne fever which reached the Indian Ocean), although the fever did not actually affect Mauritius. Moreover, as a result of the global economic downturn, tourist arrivals declined in every quarter between late 2007 and mid-2009. Indeed, arrivals in the first half of 2009 declined by 9.3% compared with the corresponding period of 2008. Security concerns were highlighted by the widely reported murder in January 2011 of an Irish tourist at a luxury hotel (despite the fact that violent crimes against tourists fell from 913 incidents in 2005 to 292 in 2010). The recent debt crisis in the euro zone has also affected Mauritius, as the number of tourists fell by 0.6% during the first six months of the 2011/12 tourist season (which runs from November to March). European visitors (who comprise two-thirds of all arrivals) were down by 2.1%. Visitors from France, the largest single market, were down by 1.2%, with declines of 15.5% from Italy, 9.9% from the United Kingdom and 5.6% from Germany. A rise in the number of arrivals from China and India was not enough to compensate for the declines from Europe. Due to this overall decline, the CSO has lowered its forecast of arrivals in 2012 from 1,101,000 to 980,000 (still an increase over 2011). None the less, fewer tourists will have an impact on the construction sector, as the demand for new hotels will decline.

Traditionally, Air Mauritius maintained an arrangement allowing a monopoly of service with French and British routes (via Air France and British Airways), resulting in higher fares and inflexible rates. In an effort to end this monopoly, the Government allowed Virgin Atlantic to operate two flights a week from the United Kingdom to Mauritius, in addition to British Airways flights. By 2006 new flights by Corsair (France) and Virgin Atlantic (United Kingdom) had provided additional competition. Currently some 18 international airlines service the island. In an effort to accommodate environmental considerations with the higher rates of hotel room occupancy, since 1990 the Government has largely ceased issuing permits to construct new hotels, although a Saudi Arabian-owned group, Kingdom Hotel Investment, announced that it was to develop a US $230m. luxury resort in 2006. The overall room occupancy rate for 2008 was 68%, with 11,488 rooms. Tourism provided employment directly for 28,534 people in March 2008. This sector, however, also contributes to the demand for costly imports, especially foodstuffs.

In 2009 the Mauritius Tourism Promotion Authority funded a US $3m. promotional campaign. The industry has yet—and is unlikely—to achieve the Government's 2015 target of 2m. tourist arrivals annually. However, the World Economic Forum ranked Mauritius 53rd of 133 countries in its travel and tourism competitiveness index for 2011. In the short term Mauritius may benefit from political unrest in the competing tourist markets of Egypt and Tunisia.

AGRICULTURE AND FISHERIES

Traditionally, agriculture formed the backbone of the Mauritian economy and sugar dominated the sector. However, the agriculture and fisheries sector's contribution to GDP decreased to 9% in 2011, compared with 20% in 1970. In addition, the sector has become more diversified in recent years: by 2010 the three most significant exports represented less than 20% of total exports (in many sub-Saharan African countries, the ratio is over 80%). Agricultural activity faces a number of difficulties unrelated to adverse weather conditions: Mauritius is prone to cyclonic weather. Labour costs have been rising sharply, as have the prices of agricultural inputs and land. Producer prices have not kept pace with these factors, and the Government generally has not allocated sufficient resources to agricultural expansion and other services.

Sugar remains the dominant crop, accounting for just over one-half of agricultural output, but contributing less than 2% of GDP. By 2010 around 4,800 ha of planted sugar cane was harvested. There are several large privately owned estates, and 11 factories for processing the estate sugar and the cane grown by planters in the surrounding areas. The National Assembly passed the Sugar Industry Efficiency (Amendment) Bill in February 2007, intended to restructure and modernize the industry. In addition, the Multi-Annual Adaptation Strategy Action Plan 2006–15, approved in April 2006, aimed to consolidate output at 520,000 metric tons per year and reduce the number of sugar refineries from 11 to four. The plan envisaged the modernization of the remaining plants, which would be capable of processing sugar and producing biofuel.

Many of the 'small' sugar planters, who are mostly Indo-Mauritian and who cultivate about one-quarter of the total land under cane, have grouped themselves into co-operatives to facilitate the consignment of cane to the factories on the estates. Some 17,800 workers (3.4% of the employed labour force) were employed in the sugar industry in 2008, representing 37.6% of those employed in agriculture. A bulk sugar terminal, opened in 1980 with an annual capacity of 350,000 metric tons, is the third largest in the world. The Mauritius Sugar Syndicate markets all manufactured sugar, while the main estates are grouped into the Mauritius Sugar Producers' Association. Production increased by 3.4% in 2009, to 467,200 tons, but declined by 3.2% in 2010, to 452,473 tons and again, to 435,309 tons, in 2011. However, productivity increased over the year, rising from 79.7 tons per ha compared to 79 tons in 2010. Mauritius no longer exports raw sugar, only the higher valued refined sugar. Sugar exports increased by 13.4% in 2010, according to the CSO.

In 1975 Mauritius acceded to the sugar protocol of the first Lomé Convention, which was signed in that year by the European Community (EC, now the EU) and 46 developing countries. Under this protocol and its successors, Mauritius received a basic annual export quota of 507,000 metric tons of raw cane sugar and is the principal exporter of sugar to the EU, which comprises the main market for Mauritian sugar. Other important customers are the USA, Canada and New Zealand. Until recently, Mauritius has benefited from the EU quota arrangement in that, for these exports, the guaranteed price has been three times higher than the 'spot' price on the world market. The complaint of unfair competition in the sugar trade brought against the EU by Australia, Brazil and Thailand was upheld by the WTO in the same period.

Tea production, once a significant component of the island's economy, has been adversely affected over recent decades by rising production costs and low prices on world markets. None the less, owing to better weather conditions, the production of green tea leaves increased by 21.8% in 2011, from 7,370 metric tons in 2010 to 8,975 tons. Manufactured teas also increased, from 1,467 tons in 2010 to 1,787 tons in 2011. Most tea-growing is carried out by about 1,400 smallholders, grouped into co-operatives. The supervision of the sector is carried out by the Mauritius Tea Factories Co (TeaFac), owned jointly by several state bodies and by tea producer co-operatives. TeaFac operates four factories, which account for about 75% of tea exports, and is responsible for export sales. The tea industry receives support from state subsidies. Following the conversion of tea plots into sugar cane plantations, the area under tea plantation was 651 ha in 2011, compared with 3,000 ha in 1999.

Tobacco is the other main cash crop. Production has been expanded to the point where locally manufactured cigarettes are composed entirely of local tobacco, apart from certain luxury grades. Practically all tobacco is grown and processed by British American Tobacco (BAT—Mauritius). Output during the late 1990s averaged about 700 metric tons per year, but had declined to an estimated 357 tons by 2006. In 2011 there were 222 ha under tobacco cultivation, 4.2% higher than in the previous year. Tobacco production increased by 11.3%, from 310 tons in 2010 to 345 tons in 2011.

Subsistence farming is conducted on a small scale, although the cultivation of food crops is becoming more widespread in view of the need to diversify the economy and reduce food imports. Food accounted for an estimated 16.6% of the total cost of imports in 2007. The expansion of vegetable cultivation and experiments in intercropping with sugar have resulted in self-sufficiency in potatoes and nearly all other vegetables. Other crops being experimentally intercropped with sugar are maize, rice, vanilla and groundnuts. According to the Ministry of Finance and Economic Development, production of food crops increased slightly in 2011, from 114,844 tons in 2010 to 115,618 tons, while the area harvested decreased from 7,570 ha to 7,364 ha over the same period.

Mauritius produces only 8% of its total beef requirements and about 20% of its total consumption of dairy products, the remainder having to be imported, mainly from New Zealand, Australia and South Africa. Mauritius is self-sufficient in pork, eggs and poultry. Most cattle fodder has to be imported, in particular maize from South Africa, at considerable cost. Studies have been conducted on the possible production of high-protein feeding stuffs, as by-products of sugar cane. Local beef production increased by 55% in 2011, from 88 metric tons in 2010 to 136 tons. This increase was due mostly to the schemes financed by the 'Food Security Fund' of the Ministry of Agro-industry and Food Security. The production of poultry increased from 46,600 tons in 2010 to 47,000 tons in 2011, while pork production also increased, from 623 tons to 650 tons.

Mauritius regards the fishing sector as an important part of its economic diversification agenda. In 2007 the value of fish exports comprised 5.8% of total exports. In early 2006 Mauritius joined FAO's South West Indian Ocean Fisheries Commission scheme to increase its oceanic bank fisheries. The programme provides technical assistance for boat repair and maintenance. Vessels from Japan, Taiwan and the Republic of Korea (South Korea) fish in offshore waters and tranship 15,000–16,000 metric tons of fish, mostly tuna, every year. Fish production fell by 2.5%, from 5,547 tons in 2010 to 5,411 tons in 2011. Fisheries exports have increased six-fold from the early 1990s, and provided almost 15% of total export revenue in 2011. Fresh coastal fish catch increased by 3.8% over the same period, while other catch decreased by 6.2%.

In early 2012 Mauritius signed a three-year Fisheries Partnership Agreement with the EU that established the terms for European fishing boats operating in local waters. Under the agreement, the EU will pay Mauritius US $2.8m. for the rights to harvest up to 5,500 metric tons annually. The agreement also calls for more locals to work aboard EU vessels while in Mauritian waters.

TRANSPORTATION, COMMUNICATIONS AND INFORMATION TECHNOLOGY

Mauritius has a very good transportation infrastructure. There are 2,066 km of paved roads, of which 75 km are motorways. The road network is good, considering the mountainous terrain, and about 98% of the roads are paved. A motorway connects Port Louis with the Plaisance international airport. Port Louis, the major commercial port, underwent modernization and expansion during the 1990s, with loan finance from the World Bank. Mauritius was keen to establish itself as a shipping hub—as a possible alternative to Durban, South Africa—for both cargo and cruise shipping; in 2003 the Mauritius Ports Authority formed a long-term regeneration plan for its facilities and development, which had already undergone a decade of investment. The Ports Authority is improving security under the International Ship and Port Facility Service Code to better access US ports.

The international airport at Plaisance is served by 18 airlines. In 2005 the airport handled more than 1m. passengers. A second airport, on the island of Rodrigues, handled 49,500 passengers in 2006.

Mauritius has made the most significant advances in the region in developing the usage of computers, telephones and the internet. The number of telephones per 1,000 people increased from 132.1 in 1995 to 288.4 in 2005, and in that year there were 572.9 mobile telephone subscribers per 1,000 people (one of the region's highest levels, behind Seychelles and South Africa). In 2010 the country had 1.9m. mobile telephone subscribers, compared with 387,700 land-line telephones. In 2004 personal computers per 1,000 people amounted to 162 and internet hosts per 10,000 people increased from virtually nil to 34.4. The number of internet hosts reached a record 51,123 in 2011, up from 4,997 in 2006, and there were 290,000 internet users in 2009. Indeed, Mauritius regards information technology (IT) as an area in which it can establish a comparative advantage. The Government announced its intention to transform the island into an IT free zone (a so-called 'cyber island') and to establish subsidized IT digital parks. One such park, Cyber City, created 173 new jobs during 2004, and the number of firms increased from 60 to 72. At January 2006 there were 107 companies operating in the sector and demand had exceeded supply for occupancy of the facility. In the World Economic Forum's *Global Information Technology Report* covering 2010–11 Mauritius (at 47th) was ranked as the most information and communications technology-ready country in the region, overtaking South Africa (at 61st).

In 2000 the South Africa-Far East underwater fibre optic cable was laid, linking Port Louis to both regions, which was to become the key to the internet infrastructure. Mauritius Telecom undertook an investment programme of US $21m. into new technology, and a second cellular telephone provider, Emtel, invested MRs 250m. in its Global System for Mobile Communications network. Mauritius has hoped to capitalize on the bilingual nature of its work-force in providing IT services to francophone Africa, in co-operation with Indian expertise. From the beginning of 2003 the telecommunications market was opened to competition, and in August the Information and Communication Technologies Authority (ICTA) approved 14 licences (including 10 international licences, one fixed-line licence, one payphone licence, one internet service licence and one mobile communication licence). In early 2006 the ICTA reduced the prices of international private leased circuits and direct dialling charges. Also, Mauritius Telecom's monopoly over fixed phone lines ended in 2005, when an Indian company, MTN, began operations.

POWER AND WATER

Mauritius relies on imports for most of its energy needs, although it is trying to diversify using sugar by-products. The sugar estates generate electricity from bagasse. Bagasse accounted for as much as 93% of the indigenous production of electricity in 2005 (19.0% of the country's total energy requirement), when Mauritius generated an estimated 20% of its own energy (the rest deriving from imported fuels). Owing to the normally abundant rainfall and precipitous water courses, 4%–6% of electricity is generated from hydro sources. Most of the supply, however, is provided by diesel-powered thermal stations (estimated at 94.9% in 2005). Mauritius consumed 2,234,000m. kWh in 2008. Studies on wave power and wind power are also being carried out. Water supply and distribution are well developed, with only 0.75% of the population without piped provision. Subterranean reserves are tapped to supply industry, the principal consumer. Imports of mineral fuels comprised an estimated 16.4% of the value of merchandise imports in 2005. In 2004 the Indian Oil Company (IOC) opened its 15,000-metric-ton petroleum storage terminal, increasing the island's storage capacity by 20%. The IOC planned to build a network of 25 petrol stations at an investment of US $18m. Mauritius consumed an estimated 23,000 barrels of imported oil per day in 2010. There is no natural gas production.

THE EXTERNAL SECTOR

In 2009 exports amounted to US $1,933m. and imports $3,473m., resulting in a trade deficit of $1,540m. Imports declined significantly in 2009 owing to decreased demand. However, as the economy improved in 2010, trade expanded: exports grew to $2,041m., with imports at $3,935m., resulting in a trade deficit of $1,894m. As most of the country's import bills are denominated in US dollars, and its export receipts in euros, the strengthening value of the euro has been beneficial for the external account. Exports of textiles and clothing (representing some 50% of export revenue) have been hampered by reduced world-wide demand, particularly from the United Kingdom and the USA, the principal importers. Exports totalled $2,707m. in 2011, and imports $5,241m., resulting in a trade deficit of $2,234m. The deficit was driven largely by a 24.6% increase in fuel imports.

In 2011 the principal sources of imports were India (23.4%) and China (14%). Europe remains the principal market for exports, accounting for 62.4% of the total, with France (21.3%) and the United Kingdom (14.2%) having the largest shares. It should be noted that if the euro zone crisis continues, Mauritius' exports will probably suffer in 2012. The importance of South Africa in Mauritius' trade with southern Africa is expected to increase significantly when COMESA becomes fully operational. In 2011 the principal domestic exports were manufactured articles, mainly EPZ products, clothing and textiles comprising 25% of the total, followed by sugar and fish. The principal imports in that year were fuels and lubricants (31.9%), food and beverages (26.9%), and machinery and transportation equipment (26.6% of total imports).

Mauritius has actively promoted economic initiatives to advance the trading interests of countries on the Indian Ocean rim, and in 1998 joined the Government of Mozambique in establishing a 100,000-ha special economic zone on the Mozambique mainland. Proposals to establish a second such zone were announced in November. Mauritius maintains an active commitment to the Indian Ocean Commission, the Indian Ocean Rim Association for Regional Co-operation (IOR–ARC) and the South African Development Community (SADC). Indeed, Mauritius was involved in the negotiations with the EU that proposed a free trade zone with SADC before the EU's Cotonou Agreement with African, Caribbean and Pacific countries expired in 2005. In addition, as a member of COMESA, Mauritius is working towards an economic partnership agreement (EPA) with the EU focused primarily on the sugar sector. Another EPA is being negotiated with India. From 2001 until 2004 Mauritius maintained a surplus in the current account. However, in 2004 the current account went into deficit by US $107.5m., and the deficit increased to $152.8m. in 2005. The current account deficit in 2009 was 22% lower than the year before. It fell by $194m., equivalent to 7.7% of GDP, down from 10.4% in 2008. The main reason for this decline was the decrease in the trade deficit. The current account deficit was estimated at $1,339m. in 2011. Mauritius' external debt amounted to $5,205m. at the end of that year. Mauritius has an excellent international credit rating and its debt service ratio stood at around 3% at mid-2011. Its public debt represented 57.3% of GDP at that time.

In recognition of the impact the global economic downturn has had on Mauritius, in late 2008 the Government introduced a US $330m. additional stimulus package (ASP), which was designed to strengthen the economy, create jobs and improve stability during these difficult times. The ASP was adopted in April 2009.

Mauritius' economic advances in the mid-1980s, precipitated by the growth of the EPZ sector, enabled the Government to introduce far-reaching measures to encourage economic expansion. Additional finance was to be obtained from the privatization of state enterprises, and the imposition of a value-added tax from September 1998 to replace the previous sales tax. As part of a long-term strategy to establish Mauritius as an international financial centre, controls on the movement of foreign exchange were relaxed in 1986. By 2000 the Bank of Mauritius sought to continue to allow the rupee to appreciate against the dollar to stem increases in fuel import prices (mostly denominated in dollars). However, such an appreciation damaged Mauritius' textile exports to the USA, and by late 2004 the authorities aimed to devalue the rupee against the dollar. None the less, during 2007 the rupee appreciated by 22% against the US dollar, owing to record tourism earnings, increased inward foreign investment and the general dollar depreciation. That appreciation continued during 2009, when the rupee rose by 16% between March and December. By mid-2012 the exchange rate was US $1 = MRs 29. Mauritius is heavily dependent on food and fuel imports, and global prices in these sectors has an impact on the domestic inflation rate, which was 6.7% in 2011, down from 7.2% in 2010. Should those world prices decline in 2012–13, then the inflation rate is likely to fall.

The economic relationship with China has deepened in recent years: in February 2009 Mauritius was one of only four countries in the region visited by China's President, Hu Jintao. In addition, Mauritius was selected by China as an economic and trade co-operation zone, the largest and one of only three such zones in sub-Saharan Africa. Also, the island has become a significant provider of offshore banking and investment services for a number of South Asian countries (particularly India), as well as for countries in SADC and IOR–ARC groupings. However, in 2003 the Indian authorities began investigating a number of companies claiming residence in Mauritius in order to qualify for the Double Tax Avoidance Treaty between the two countries, exempting them from paying capital gains tax; any threat to the treaty would undermine the Mauritian offshore financial industry. In late 2005 the central bank created the Mauritius Credit Information Bureau to provide credit information to most of the commercial banks; by mid-2006 the programme was operational, and was to help households from succumbing to over-indebtedness.

Foreign direct investment (FDI) reached a record US $453m. in 2010, which exceeded the Government's target and represented an increase of 59% from 2009. A large part of that increase came from India's MRs 2,700m. investment in the medical sector. The United Kingdom was the main source of FDI in 2010, accounting for 33.1% of the total, followed by India (20.7%), France (11.5%) and South Africa (10.5%). However, FDI is estimated to have fallen to $340.7 m. in 2011, according to the Board of Investment. According to the World Bank, Mauritius is one of the world's highest recipients of FDI per caput.

Official development assistance from all donors totalled US $68m. in 2007, and increased to $155,550m. in 2009. In April 2009 the World Bank approved a $100m. development policy loan (DPL). This was the third of four such loans designed to strengthen trade competitiveness and public sector efficiency. In addition to the DPL, the World Bank approved a separate $18m. loan to assist local businesses to reduce their cost of doing business.

The Stock Exchange of Mauritius' (SEM) all-share index has performed remarkably well since the mid-2000s. The index had increased to 1,852.2 by the end of 2007 and reached an all-time high of 2,105.62 in May 2011, representing a 7.0% increase during the year. The largest share of capitalization was from the banking and insurance sectors (39% of the total), followed by hotels (32.2%) and sugar (5.5%). The SEM has 46 companies and authorized mutual funds listed, with a total market capitalization of MRs 170,693m. in 2012, up from MRs 151,212m. in 2009.

ECONOMIC PROSPECTS

Despite its relatively favourable economic performance in recent years, Mauritius faces a number of longer-term problems and uncertainties. Prominent among these is a narrow natural resources base combined with the rate of population growth (0.7%), which projects a population of more than 1.5m. people by 2015. This growth is exclusive of the numbers of émigré Mauritians, estimated at about 50,000, who are expected to return to the island following retirement. In addition, Mauritius had the region's longest life expectancy at birth of 73.4 years in 2011, considerably higher than the region's average of 46 years. This demographic trend is expected to pose considerable economic challenges, especially with employment. Since 2005 the official unemployment rate has been slightly beneath 10%, and it stood at 7.8% in 2011. The EPZ sector, which led the island's industrial expansion during the 1980s and early 1990s has slowed. Mauritius is confronted by increased competition in the international textile market, and any future alteration in its privileged access to the EU markets would necessitate the industry becoming more competitive, with the use of newer, costly technology.

The Government has pursued an aggressive reform approach in its attitude towards business. It has moved from intervention to greater co-operation, including lower taxes, deregulation and tax reforms. Government investment in IT should also reap benefits. The country's expertise in sugar production has resulted in increased technical consulting in a number of nearby sub-Saharan African states. Mauritius continues to strengthen its regional relationships. For example, in 2005 and 2006 it signed a number of bilateral agreements on fisheries, textiles and tourism with Madagascar, and similar (although more limited) agreements with Seychelles.

The Mauritius Offshore Business Activities Authority is keen to promote a better climate to ensure the country's development as a centre for international business. The Government is particularly concerned about its international financial standing and has made efforts to counter the impression of corporate and official corruption. Mauritius' international reputation for financial integrity was questioned in the mid-2000s, when the Swiss-based Forum on Financial Stability placed Mauritius on a list of 25 suspected tax havens or money-laundering sites. However, that perception is changing: in 2011 the non-governmental organization Transparency International ranked Mauritius as the 48th least corrupt nation out of 182 (only Botswana ranked higher in the region); the World Bank's most recent study of governance standards of 209 countries ranks Mauritius among only four African nations with positive scores (the others were South Africa, Namibia and Botswana); and in 2012 the Heritage Foundation awarded Mauritius the highest ranking of sub-Saharan African countries in its economic freedom index. That index included 10 variables, from property rights to the level of corruption, and attempted to rank how friendly a country is towards business (foreign and domestic). Interestingly, Mauritius was the only sub-Saharan African country ranked in the category 'mostly free' (8th out of 184 countries, ahead of Luxembourg and the USA). In 2012 the World Bank ranked Mauritius 23rd world-wide and the best in sub-Saharan Africa in terms of the ease of doing business (for the fourth consecutive year).

As Mauritius is a small, open economy, it is vulnerable to external shocks, and it did not escape the world-wide economic downturn unscathed. However, the Government put expansionary economic policies in place to counter the crisis, and was successful in their implementation in many respects. Certainly, in comparison with any neighbouring country (excluding South Africa), Mauritius' economy has diversified very successfully. In addition, the country has achieved an unusually high level of economic growth and stability and has withstood the challenges of the global economic downturn relatively well. Barring a deeper crisis in the euro zone, Mauritius is likely to experience increased returns from its tourism, finance and IT sectors in the coming years.

Statistical Survey

Source (unless otherwise stated): Central Statistics Office, LIC Bldg, President John F. Kennedy St, Port Louis; tel. 212-2316; fax 211-4150; e-mail cso@mail.gov.mu; internet statsmauritius.gov.mu.

Area and Population

AREA, POPULATION AND DENSITY

Area (sq km)	2,040*
Population (census results)†	
2 July 2000	
Males	583,949
Females	595,188
Total	1,179,137
3-4 July 2011	1,257,900
Density (per sq km) at 2011 census	616.6

* 788 sq miles.

† Excluding adjustment for underenumeration.

POPULATION BY AGE AND SEX

(official estimates at mid-2011)

	Males	Females	Total
0–14	137,682	133,438	271,120
15–64	456,871	462,752	919,623
65 and over	39,171	56,137	95,308
Total	633,724	652,327	1,286,051

Note: Estimates exclude data for Agalega and St Brandon, and have not been revised to take account of the 2011 census.

ISLANDS

	Area (sq km)	Population 2000 census	Population 2011 census
Mauritius	1,865	1,143,069	1,217,175
Rodrigues	104	35,779	40,440
Other islands	71	289	285

Ethnic Groups: Island of Mauritius, mid-1982: 664,480 Indo-Mauritians (507,985 Hindus, 156,495 Muslims), 264,537 general population (incl. Creole and Franco-Mauritian communities), 20,669 Chinese.

LANGUAGE GROUPS

(census of 2 July 2000)*

Arabic	806	Marathi	16,587
Bhojpuri	361,250	Tamil	44,731
Chinese	16,972	Telegu	18,802
Creole	454,763	Urdu	34,120
English	1,075	Other languages	169,619
French	21,171	Not stated	3,170
Hindi	35,782	**Total**	1,178,848

* Figures refer to the languages of cultural origin of the population of the islands of Mauritius and Rodrigues only. The data exclude an adjustment for underenumeration.

POPULATION BY DISTRICT

(official estimates at 1 July 2011)

Black River	77,242	Port Louis	128,319
Flacq	140,670	Riv du Rempart	109,513
Grand Port	115,772	Rodrigues	37,925
Moka	81,431	Savanne	70,526
Pamplemousses	138,904	**Total**	1,286,051
Plaine Wilhems	385,749		

PRINCIPAL TOWNS

(official estimates at 1 July 2011)

Port Louis (capital)	148,380	Vacoas/Phoenix	108,613
Beau Bassin/Rose Hill	111,061	Curepipe	84,756
		Quatre Bornes	82,032

BIRTHS, MARRIAGES AND DEATHS*

	Registered live births Number	Rate (per 1,000)	Registered marriages Number	Rate (per 1,000)	Registered deaths Number	Rate (per 1,000)
2004	19,230	15.5	11,385	9.2	8,475	6.8
2005	18,829	15.1	11,294	n.a.	8,648	7.0
2006	17,605	14.1	11,471	9.1	9,162	7.3
2007	17,034	13.5	11,547	9.1	8,498	6.7
2008	16,372	12.9	11,197	8.8	9,004	7.1
2009	15,344	12.0	10,619	8.3	9,224	7.2
2010	15,005	11.7	10,555	8.2	9,131	7.1
2011	14,701	11.4	10,499	8.1	9,170	7.1

* Figures refer to the islands of Mauritius and Rodrigues only. The data are tabulated by year of registration, rather than by year of occurrence.

Life expectancy (years at birth): 73.0 (males 69.5; females 76.7) in 2010 (Source: World Bank, World Development Indicators database).

ECONOMICALLY ACTIVE POPULATION

('000 persons aged 16 years and over, incl. foreign workers)

	2009	2010	2011*
Agriculture, forestry and fishing	44.9	44.9	44.4
Sugar cane	14.2	13.9	13.5
Mining and quarrying	0.2	0.2	0.2
Manufacturing	115.8	114.5	112.3
Electricity, gas and water	3.1	3.3	3.3
Construction	52.4	54.0	55.0
Wholesale and retail trade, repair of motor vehicles and household goods	85.4	88.8	89.7
Hotels and restaurants	35.8	37.3	38.0
Transport, storage and communications	40.0	40.4	40.2
Financial intermediation	12.6	13.2	13.5
Real estate, renting and business activities	32.4	34.9	35.8
Public administration and defence; compulsory social security	39.4	39.1	38.9
Education	30.1	30.8	31.1
Health and social work	16.7	19.0	19.5
Other services	37.0	37.7	37.8
Total employed	545.8	558.1	559.7
Males	355.3	358.8	358.2
Females	190.5	199.3	201.5
Unemployed	41.5	45.2	46.1
Total labour force	587.3	603.3	605.8

* Provisional.

Health and Welfare

KEY INDICATORS

Total fertility rate (children per woman, 2010)	1.6
Under-5 mortality rate (per 1,000 live births, 2010)	15
HIV/AIDS (% of persons aged 15–49, 2009)	1.0
Physicians (per 1,000 head, 2004)	1.1
Hospital beds (per 1,000 head, 2008)	3.3
Health expenditure (2009): US $ per head (PPP)	714
Health expenditure (2009): % of GDP	5.6
Health expenditure (2009): public (% of total)	37.1
Access to water (% of persons, 2010)	99
Access to sanitation (% of persons, 2010)	89
Total carbon dioxide emissions ('000 metric tons, 2008)	3,953.0
Carbon dioxide emissions per head (metric tons, 2008)	3.1
Human Development Index (2011): ranking	77
Human Development Index (2011): value	0.728

For sources and definitions, see explanatory note on p. vi.

Agriculture

PRINCIPAL CROPS

('000 metric tons)

	2008	2009	2010
Potatoes	14.9	19.8	17.0
Sugar cane	4,533.0	4,669.4	4,365.8
Coconuts	2.2*	1.6*	1.9†
Cabbages and other brassicas	3.7	4.6	4.8
Lettuce and chicory	0.9	0.9	0.0
Tomatoes	11.5	12.6	10.9
Cauliflowers and broccoli	1.2	1.7	1.3
Pumpkins, squash and gourds	13.8	17.1	17.2
Cucumbers and gherkins	8.7	11.1	11.5
Aubergines (Eggplants)	1.8	2.8	2.7
Onions, dry	5.6	4.9	5.9
Carrots and turnips	4.7	7.4	4.5
Bananas	10.5	10.9	11.0
Pineapples	6.4	8.9	6.3
Tea	1.7	1.5	1.5
Tobacco, unmanufactured	0.3	0.3	0.3

* Unofficial figure.

† FAO estimate.

Aggregate production ('000 metric tons, may include official, semi-official or estimated data): Total cereals 0.8 in 2008, 0.8 in 2009, 1.1 in 2010; Total roots and tubers 16.3 in 2008, 21.5 in 2009, 18.6 in 2010; Total vegetables (incl. melons) 59.0 in 2008, 71.7 in 2009, 66.6 in 2010; Total fruits (excl. melons) 20.8 in 2008, 24.3 in 2009, 21.3 in 2010.

Source: FAO.

LIVESTOCK

('000 head, year ending September)

	2008	2009	2010
Cattle	7.3	7.2	7.5
Pigs	13*	14	22
Sheep*	15	20	20
Goats	26	26	28
Chickens*	13,500	13,650	13,650

* FAO estimate(s).

Source: FAO.

LIVESTOCK PRODUCTS

('000 metric tons)

	2008	2009	2010
Cattle meat	2	2	2
Chicken meat	42	44	46
Cows' milk	3	4	4
Hen eggs	11	10	10

Source: FAO.

Forestry

ROUNDWOOD REMOVALS

('000 cubic metres, excl. bark)

	2008*	2009	2010
Sawlogs, veneer logs and logs for sleepers	6	4	4
Other industrial wood	3	6	2
Fuel wood	7	6	9
Total	15	15	15

* FAO estimates.

2011: Production assumed to be unchanged from 2010 (FAO estimates).

Source: FAO.

SAWNWOOD PRODUCTION

('000 cubic metres, incl. railway sleepers)

	2008*	2009	2010
Coniferous (softwood)	2.7	2.0	2.0
Broadleaved (hardwood)	0.3	0.1	0.1
Total	3.0	2.1	2.1

* FAO estimates.

2011: Production assumed to be unchanged from 2010 (FAO estimates).

Source: FAO.

Fishing

(metric tons, live weight)

	2008	2009	2010
Capture	6,642	7,676	7,786
Groupers and seabasses	556	1,033	860
Snappers and jobfishes	404	430	739
Emperors (Scavengers)	3,022	3,454	3,032
Goatfishes	100	497	268
Spinefeet (Rabbitfishes)	111	274	372
Swordfish	308	75	27
Tuna-like fishes	200	100	360
Octopuses	92	89	93
Aquaculture	246	437	568
Red drum	175	330	498
Total catch	6,888	8,113	8,354

Note: Figures exclude aquatic animals, recorded by number rather than weight. The number of Nile crocodiles captured was: n.a. in 2008; 100 in 2009; n.a. in 2011.

Source: FAO.

Industry

SELECTED PRODUCTS

('000 metric tons unless otherwise indicated)

	2009	2010	2011
Fish*	66.1	63.0	54.0
Frozen*	3.5	2.4	2.2
Canned*	61.9	59.8	51.1
Raw sugar*	467.2	452.5	435.3
Molasses*	147.6	143.5	138.6
Beer and stout ('000 hectolitres)*	351.7	367.6	373.7
Iron bars and steel tubes*	31.0	32.0	35.0
Fertilizers*	31.0	24.3	27.0
Electric energy (million kWh)	2,577	2,689	2,730*

* Provisional.

Cigarettes (million): 6 in 2008.

Finance

CURRENCY AND EXCHANGE RATES

Monetary Units

100 cents = 1 Mauritian rupee.

Sterling, Dollar and Euro Equivalents (31 May 2012)

£1 sterling = 46.23 rupees;
US $1 = 29.82 rupees;
€1 = 36.99 rupees;
1,000 Mauritian rupees = £21.63 = $33.53 = €27.04.

Average Exchange Rate (Mauritian rupees per US $)

2009 31.960
2010 30.784
2011 28.706

BUDGET

(million rupees)

Revenue

	2010	2011
Tax revenue	55,209.1	59,180.3
Taxes on income, profits and capital gains	13,976.3	13,619.7
Individual income tax	4,497.1	4,913.3
Corporate tax	8,428.0	7,847.0
Taxes on property	3,904.3	3,939.5
Domestic taxes on goods and services	34,633.4	38,817.9
Excise duties	9,331.0	11,487.1
Value-added tax	21,094.4	22,713.6
Taxes on international trade	1,525.2	1,560.3
Other tax revenue	1,169.9	1,242.9
Non-tax revenue	10,270.4	10,042.9
Social contributions	1,008.2	1,020.4
Grants	1,991.0	2,344.5
Property income	3,812.2	3,312.6
Other non-tax revenue	3,459.0	3,365.4
Total	65,479.5	69,223.2

Expense/Outlays

Expense by economic type	2010	2011
Expenditure	66,983.2	70,975.3
Wages and salaries	17,541.0	18,001.3
Other purchases of goods and services	6,149.6	6,194.5
Interest payments	10,261.9	9,667.1
Subsidies and other current transfers	25,091.9	29,665.2
Transfer to general government units	23,838.3	28,233.2
Social benefits	4,855.8	5,125.4
Other expense	3,083.0	2,321.8
Net Acquisition of non-financial assets	8,076.1	8,632.6
Acquisition of fixed capital assets	7,859.5	8,194.1
Non-produced assets	216.6	438.5
Total	75,059.3	79,607.9

Outlays by function of government	2010	2011
General public services	19,753.6	19,219.6
Public order and safety	6,173.2	7,441.6
Community and social services	38,409.1	41,484.2
Education	10,091.9	10,329.3
Health	7,726.3	7,326.6
Social security and welfare	15,738.5	16,824.5
Housing and community amenities	1,587.0	3,718.7
Recreational, cultural and religious services	649.2	721.8
Environmental protection	2,616.2	2,563.3
Economic services	10,723.4	11,462.5
Agriculture, forestry, fishing and hunting	2,910.9	2,019.3
Fuel and energy	37.4	54.9
Mining, manufacturing, and construction	400.7	262.9
Transportation and communications	4,280.1	3,909.3
Tourism	457.5	540.4
General economic, commercial and labour affairs	458.5	407.6
Other economic affairs	2,178.2	4,268.1
Total expenditure	75,059.3	79,607.9

INTERNATIONAL RESERVES

(US $ million at 31 December)

	2009	2010	2011
Gold (market prices)	124.9	159.6	196.0
IMF special drawing rights	156.7	153.7	153.4
Reserve position in IMF	20.6	34.0	48.4
Foreign exchange	2,001.5	2,254.2	2,380.9
Total	2,303.7	2,601.5	2,778.7

Source: IMF, *International Financial Statistics*.

MONEY SUPPLY

(million rupees at 31 December)

	2009	2010	2011
Currency outside depository corporations	17,152.6	18,975.0	20,307.8
Transferable deposits	70,923.4	70,035.5	73,190.5
Other deposits	207,632.2	227,244.8	236,362.4
Securities other than shares	772.2	2,868.9	4,044.5
Broad money	296,480.4	319,124.2	333,905.2

Source: IMF, *International Financial Statistics*.

COST OF LIVING

(Consumer Price Index; base: July 2006–June 2007 = 100)

	2009	2010	2011
Food and non-alcoholic beverages	129.1	133.9	141.7
Alcoholic beverages and tobacco	116.5	119.8	141.8
Clothing and footwear	115.1	123.6	130.5
Housing, fuel and electricity	105.7	105.4	107.8
Household operations	115.1	119.3	122.6
All items (incl. others)	116.8	120.2	128.1

NATIONAL ACCOUNTS

(million rupees in current prices)

National Income and Product

	2009	2010	2011
Compensation of employees	95,936	101,735	109,949
Operating surplus Consumption of fixed capital	153,450	160,610	172,534
Gross domestic product (GDP) at factor cost	249,386	262,345	282,483
Taxes on production and imports	33,819	37,279	41,768
Less Subsidies	851	840	1,026
GDP in purchasers' values	282,354	298,784	323,225
Primary incomes received from abroad *Less* Primary incomes paid abroad	−1,333	3,656	2,416
Gross national income	281,021	302,440	325,641
Current transfers from abroad *Less* Current transfers paid abroad	6,909	5,630	3,795
Gross national disposable income	287,930	308,070	329,436

Expenditure on the Gross Domestic Product

	2009	2010	2011
Private final consumption expenditure	208,879	220,305	237,148
Government final consumption expenditure	39,751	41,625	43,447
Gross fixed capital formation	74,430	74,395	76,722
Increase in stocks	−14,294	−3,746	5,511
Total domestic expenditure	308,766	332,579	362,828
Exports of goods and services	138,243	156,939	174,962
Less Imports of goods and services	164,655	190,734	214,566
GDP in purchasers' values	282,354	298,784	323,225

Gross Domestic Product by Economic Activity

	2009	2010	2011
Agriculture, hunting, forestry, and fishing	9,800	9,677	10,444
Sugar cane	3,489	3,050	3,594
Mining and quarrying	101	107	106
Manufacturing	47,325	47,764	50,461
Electricity, gas and water	5,398	5,401	5,358
Construction	17,471	18,231	18,608
Wholesale and retail trade, repair of motor vehicles and personal goods	28,770	31,178	33,813
Hotels and restaurants	16,749	18,514	20,268
Transport, storage and communications	24,191	25,257	26,404
Financial intermediation	25,834	26,465	28,806
Real estate, renting and business activities	29,776	32,645	36,995
Public administration and defence; compulsory social security	15,322	16,159	16,981
Education	11,085	11,686	12,596
Health and social work	8,936	9,694	10,808
Other services	10,857	12,050	13,846
Gross value added in basic prices	251,615	264,828	285,494
Taxes, less subsidies, on products	30,739	33,956	37,731
GDP in market prices	282,354	298,784	323,225

BALANCE OF PAYMENTS
(US $ million)

	2008	2009	2010
Exports of goods f.o.b.	2,383.9	1,938.5	2,261.5
Imports of goods f.o.b.	–4,386.0	–3,503.9	–4,157.3
Trade balance	–2,002.1	–1,565.4	–1,895.8
Exports of services	2,543.9	2,239.0	2,695.1
Imports of services	–1,919.9	–1,607.3	–1,983.8
Balance on goods and services	–1,378.1	–933.7	–1,184.5
Other income received	819.9	457.6	456.8
Other income paid	–641.7	–402.6	–255.1
Balance on goods, services and income	–1,200.0	–878.7	–982.9
Current transfers received	411.2	413.1	404.4
Current transfers paid	–187.0	–189.4	–221.1
Current balance	–975.8	–655.0	–799.6
Capital account (net)	–1.4	–1.9	–4.8
Direct investment abroad	–52.4	–37.8	–129.4
Direct investment from abroad	377.7	256.7	431.0
Portfolio investment assets	–92.9	–261.1	–138.6
Portfolio investment liabilities	–76.8	204.8	–45.4
Other investment assets	631.8	–357.7	–3,851.4
Other investment liabilities	155.7	948.9	4,574.2
Net errors and omissions	211.9	287.8	172.9
Overall balance	177.9	384.7	209.0

Source: IMF, *International Financial Statistics*.

External Trade

PRINCIPAL COMMODITIES
(million rupees)

Imports c.i.f.	2009	2010	2011*
Food and live animals	22,051	24,610	26,926
Fish and fish preparations	7,055	7,869	9,213
Mineral fuels, lubricants, etc.	18,557	25,630	31,940
Refined petroleum products	15,293	21,302	26,977
Chemicals	10,711	12,462	12,113
Basic manufactures	21,452	25,087	27,633
Textile yarn, fabrics, etc.	2,012	2,495	3,028
Cotton fabrics	1,965	2,159	2,395
Machinery and transport equipment	27,689	27,239	26,644
Machinery specialized for particular industries	2,614	2,517	2,742
General industrial machinery, equipment and parts	4,704	4,179	3,860
Telecommunications and sound equipment	3,483	4,357	3,925
Other electrical machinery, apparatus, etc.	3,853	4,256	4,071
Road motor vehicles	5,446	6,824	7,156
Miscellaneous manufactured articles	11,028	12,202	12,964
Total (incl. others)	118,444	134,882	148,081

Exports f.o.b.†	2009	2010	2011*
Food and live animals	18,593	20,854	20,838
Basic manufactures	5,106	5,843	6,568
Chemicals and related products	1,957	2,218	2,173
Machinery and transport equipment	1,285	1,687	1,446
Miscellaneous manufactured articles	27,709	29,429	31,283
Total (incl. others)	56,162	61,990	64,688

* Provisional.

† Excluding stores and bunkers for ships and aircraft (million rupees): 5,519 in 2009; 7,560 in 2010; 11,228 in 2011 (provisional).

PRINCIPAL TRADING PARTNERS
(million rupees)*

Imports c.i.f.	2009	2010	2011†
Argentina	1,772	1,908	2,557
Australia	3,344	4,250	3,858
Belgium	1,703	1,256	1,820
China, People's Repub.	14,903	18,033	20,790
France	13,812	11,787	13,117
Germany	3,123	3,256	3,548
India	22,336	29,629	34,671
Indonesia	2,987	2,997	2,966
Italy	2,727	2,980	3,145
Japan	3,823	4,520	3,705
Korea, Repub.	1,440	1,650	2,259
Malaysia	3,417	3,474	3,326
Netherlands	n.a.	1,518	1,719
New Zealand	n.a.	1,668	2,198
South Africa	10,236	11,433	10,484
Spain	2,800	3,680	4,399
Switzerland	1,107	1,366	1,561
Thailand	3,120	3,080	3,187
Turkey	n.a.	1,506	1,429
United Arab Emirates	803	1,231	1,992
United Kingdom	2,925	2,992	3,445
USA	2,576	3,142	2,828
Total (incl. others)	118,444	134,882	148,081

Exports f.o.b.	2009	2010	2011†
Belgium	1,454	1,317	1,453
France	9,317	10,517	9,211
Germany	1,327	1,199	1,386
Italy	3,090	4,609	5,221
Japan	n.a.	666	400
Madagascar	3,587	3,562	4,017
Netherlands	830	840	1,004
Portugal	1,400	313	200
Réunion	2,321	1,981	2,014
Seychelles	n.a.	702	868
South Africa	2,553	3,602	4,993
Spain	2,549	3,921	4,610
Switzerland	758	1,024	1,175
United Kingdom	15,280	13,373	13,790
USA	4,624	6,189	6,784
Total (incl. others)	56,162	61,990	64,688

* Imports by country of origin; exports by country of destination (including re-exports, excluding ships' stores and bunkers).

† Provisional.

Transport

ROAD TRAFFIC
(motor vehicles registered at 31 December)

	2009	2010	2011
Private vehicles:			
Cars	165,036	175,634	185,357
Motorcycles and mopeds	152,935	159,329	165,706
Commercial vehicles:			
Buses	2,803	2,845	2,912
Taxis	6,941	6,924	6,907
Lorries and trucks	12,950	13,186	13,539

SHIPPING

Merchant Fleet
(registered at 31 December)

	2007	2008	2009
Number of vessels	43	47	50
Total displacement ('000 grt)	39.7	41.1	66.2

Source: IHS Fairplay, *World Fleet Statistics*.

Sea-borne Freight Traffic
('000 metric tons)

	2009	2010	2011
Goods unloaded	4,761	5,100	5,386
Goods loaded*	1,117	1,130	1,091

* Excluding ships' bunkers.

CIVIL AVIATION
(traffic)

	2009	2010	2011*
Aircraft landings	9,824	10,160	10,121
Freight unloaded (metric tons)	20,400	23,992	21,707
Freight loaded (metric tons)	21,924	24,267	23,414

* Provisional.

Tourism

FOREIGN TOURIST ARRIVALS

Country of residence	2009	2010	2011*
France	275,599	302,185	302,004
Germany	51,279	52,886	56,331
India	39,252	49,779	53,955
Italy	56,736	56,540	52,747
Réunion	104,946	114,914	113,000
South Africa	74,176	81,458	86,232
Switzerland	15,349	18,577	24,362
United Kingdom	101,996	97,548	88,182
Total (incl. others)	871,356	934,827	964,642

* Provisional.

Tourism earnings (gross, million rupees): 41,213 in 2008; 35,693 in 2009; 39,456 in 2010.

Communications Media

	2009	2010	2011
Telephones ('000 main lines in use)	375.2	387.7	374.6
Mobile cellular telephones ('000 subscribers)	1,086.7	1,190.9	1,294.1
Internet subscribers ('000)	101.0	98.5	n.a.
Broadband subscribers ('000)	68.8	79.2	116.8
Television sets licensed ('000)	315.0	314.8	316.4
Daily newspapers	8	12	11*
Non-daily newspapers	54	56	57*

* Provisional.

Personal computers: 220,000 (45.4 per 1,000 persons) in 2006.

1996: Book production: titles 80, copies ('000) 163.

Sources: partly UNESCO, *Statistical Yearbook*; UN, *Statistical Yearbook*; International Telecommunication Union.

Education

(March 2011)

	Institutions	Teachers	Students*
Pre-primary	1,018	2,550	33,901
Primary	305	5,627	116,068
Secondary	180	7,873	115,289
Technical and vocational	126	634	7,270

* By enrolment.

Pupil-teacher ratio (primary education, UNESCO estimate): 21.5 in 2009/10 (Source: UNESCO Institute for Statistics).

Adult literacy rate (UNESCO estimates): 88.5% (males 90.9%; females 86.2%) in 2010 (Source: UNESCO Institute for Statistics).

Directory

The Constitution

The Mauritius Independence Order, which established a self-governing state, came into force on 12 March 1968, and was subsequently amended. Constitutional amendments providing for the adoption of republican status were approved by the Legislative Assembly (henceforth known as the National Assembly) on 10 December 1991, and came into effect on 12 March 1992. The main provisions of the revised Constitution are listed below:

HEAD OF STATE

The Head of State is the President of the Republic, who is elected by a simple majority of the National Assembly for a five-year term of office. The President appoints the Prime Minister (in whom executive power is vested) and, on the latter's recommendation, other ministers.

COUNCIL OF MINISTERS

The Council of Ministers, which is headed by the Prime Minister, is appointed by the President and is responsible to the National Assembly.

THE NATIONAL ASSEMBLY

The National Assembly, which has a term of five years, comprises the Speaker, 62 members elected by universal adult suffrage, a maximum of eight additional members and the Attorney-General (if not an elected member). The island of Mauritius is divided into 20 three-member constituencies for legislative elections. Rodrigues returns two members to the National Assembly. The official language of the National Assembly is English, but any member may address the Speaker in French.

The Government

HEAD OF STATE

President: KAILASH PURRYAG.

Vice-President: MONIQUE OHSAN-BELLEPEAU.

COUNCIL OF MINISTERS
(September 2012)

Prime Minister, Minister of Defence, Home Affairs and External Communications, Minister of Rodrigues: Dr NAVINCHANDRA RAMGOOLAM.

Deputy Prime Minister and Minister of Energy and Public Utilities: Dr AHMED RASHID BEEBEEJAUN.

Vice-Prime Minister and Minister of Finance and Economic Development: CHARLES GAËTAN XAVIER-LUC DUVAL.

Vice-Prime Minister and Minister of Public Infrastructure, the National Development Unit, Land Transport and Shipping: ANIL KUMAR BACHOO.

Minister of Foreign Affairs, Regional Integration and International Trade: Dr ARVIN BOOLELL.

Minister of Housing and Lands: Dr ABU TWALIB KASENALLY.

Minister of Social Security, National Solidarity and Reform Institutions: SHEILABAI BAPPOO.

Minister of Education and Human Resources: Dr VASANT KUMAR BUNWAREE.

Minister of Agro-industry and Food Security: SATYA VEYASH FAUGOO.

Minister of the Environment and Sustainable Development: DEVANAND VIRAHSAWMY.

Minister of Tertiary Education, Science, Research and Technology: Dr RAJESHWAR JEETAH.

Minister of Youth and Sports: SATYAPRAKASH RITOO.

Minister of Local Government and Outer Islands: LOUIS HERVÉ AIMÉE.

Minister of Arts and Culture: MOOKHESSWUR CHOONEE.

Minister of Information and Communication Technology: TASSARAJEN PILLAY CHEDUMBRUM.

Minister of Fisheries: LOUIS JOSEPH VON-MALLY.

Minister of Labour, Industrial Relations and Employment: SHAKEEL AHMED YOUSUF ABDUL RAZACK MOHAMED.

Attorney-General: YATINDRA NATH VARMA.

Minister of Tourism and Leisure: JOHN MICHAEL TZOUN SAO YEUNG SIK YUEN.

Minister of Health and Quality of Life: LORMUS BUNDHOO.

Minister of Industry, Commerce and Consumer Protection: SAYYAD ABD-AL-CADER SAYED-HOSSEN.

Minister of Social Integration and Economic Empowerment: SURENDRA DAYAL.

Minister of Business, Enterprise and Co-operatives: JANGBAHADOORSING ISWURDEO MOLA ROOPCHAND SEETARAM.

Minister of Gender Equality, Child Development and Family Welfare: MARIA FRANCESCA MIREILLE MARTIN.

Minister of the Civil Service and Administrative Reforms: SUTYADEO MOUTIA.

MINISTRIES

Office of the President: State House, Le Réduit, Port Louis; tel. 454-3021; fax 464-5370; e-mail president@mail.gov.mu; internet www.gov.mu/portal/site/president.

Office of the Prime Minister: New Treasury Bldg, Intendance St, Port Louis; tel. 207-9595; fax 208-8619; e-mail primeminister@mail.gov.mu; internet pm.gov.mu.

Ministry of Agro-industry and Food Security: Renganaden Seeneevassen Bldg, 8th and 9th Floor, cnr Jules Koenig and Maillard Sts, Port Louis; tel. 212-2335; fax 212-4427; e-mail moa-headoffice@mail.gov.mu; internet www.gov.mu/portal/site/moa.

Ministry of Arts and Culture: Renganaden Seeneevassen Bldg, 7th Floor, cnr Pope Hennessy and Maillard Sts, Port Louis; tel. 212-2112; fax 210-0681; e-mail moac@mail.gov.mu; internet www.gov.mu/portal/site/mac.

Ministry of Business, Enterprise and Co-operatives: Air Mauritius Centre, 8th Floor, John F. Kennedy St, Port Louis; tel. 210-3774; fax 201-3289; e-mail Mincom@intnet.mu; internet www.gov.mu/portal/site/commercesite.

Ministry of the Civil Service and Administrative Reforms: New Government Centre, 7th Floor, Port Louis; tel. 201-2886; fax 212-9528; e-mail civser@mail.gov.mu; internet www.gov.mu/portal/site/mcsasite.

Ministry of Defence, Home Affairs and External Communications: New Government Centre, 4th Floor, Port Louis; tel. 201-2409; fax 212-9393; e-mail pmo@mail.gov.mu; internet pmo.gov.mu/dha.

Ministry of Education and Human Resources: IVTB House, Pont Fer, Phoenix; tel. 697-7862; fax 698-3601; e-mail moeps@mail.gov.mu; internet www.gov.mu/portal/site/education.

Ministry of Energy and Public Utilities: Air Mauritius Centre, 10th Floor, John F. Kennedy St, Port Louis; tel. 211-0049; fax 208-6497; e-mail mpu@mail.gov.mu; internet www.gov.mu/portal/site/mpusite.

Ministry of the Environment and Sustainable Development: Ken Lee Tower, cnr Barracks and St Georges Sts, Port Louis; tel. 203-6200; fax 212-8324; e-mail menv@mail.gov.mu; internet www.gov.mu/portal/site/menvsite.

Ministry of Finance and Economic Development: Government House, Ground Floor, Port Louis; tel. 201-1146; fax 211-0096; e-mail mof@mail.gov.mu; internet www.gov.mu/portal/site/MOFSite.

Ministry of Foreign Affairs, Regional Integration and International Trade: Newton Tower, 9th–11th Floors, Sir William Newton St, Port Louis; tel. 201-1648; fax 208-8087; e-mail mfa@mail.gov.mu; internet www.gov.mu/portal/site/mfasite.

Ministry of Gender Equality, Child Development and Family Welfare: CSK Bldg, cnr Remy Ollier and Emmanuel Anquetil Sts, Port Louis; tel. 206-3700; fax 240-7717; e-mail mwfwcd@mail.gov.mu; internet www.gov.mu/portal/site/women-site.

Ministry of Health and Quality of Life: Emmanuel Anquetil Bldg, 5th Floor, Sir Seewoosagur Ramgoolam St, Port Louis; tel. 201-2175; fax 208-7222; e-mail moh@mail.gov.mu; internet www.gov.mu/portal/site/mohsite.

Ministry of Housing and Lands: Moorgate House, Port Louis; tel. 212-6022; fax 212-7482; internet www.gov.mu/portal/site/housing.

Ministry of Industry, Commerce and Consumer Protection: Air Mauritius Centre, 7th Floor, John F. Kennedy St, Port Louis; tel. 210-7100; fax 211-0855; e-mail mind@mail.gov.mu; internet www.gov.mu/portal/site/industry-site.

Ministry of Information and Communication Technology: Air Mauritius Centre, 9th Floor, John F. Kennedy St, Port Louis; tel. 210-0201; fax 212-1673; e-mail mict@mail.gov.mu; internet www.gov.mu/portal/site/telcomit.

Ministry of Labour, Industrial Relations and Employment: Victoria House, cnr St Louis and Barracks Sts, Port Louis; tel. 207-

2600; fax 212-3070; e-mail mol@mail.gov.mu; internet www.gov.mu/portal/site/laboursite.

Ministry of Local Government and Outer Islands: Emmanuel Anquetil Bldg, 3rd Floor, cnr Sir Seewoosagur Ramgoolam and Jules Koenig Sts, Port Louis; tel. 201-2155; fax 208-9729; e-mail mlg@mail.gov.mu; internet www.gov.mu/portal/site/mlge.

Ministry of Public Infrastructure, the National Development Unit, Land Transport and Shipping: Moorgate House, 9th Floor, Sir William Newton St, Port Louis; tel. 208-0281; fax 208-7149; e-mail mpi@mail.gov.mu; internet www.gov.mu/portal/site/mpisite.

Ministry of Social Integration and Economic Empowerment: Port Louis.

Ministry of Social Security, National Solidarity and Reform Institutions: Renganaden Seeneevassen Bldg, 13th Floor, cnr Jules Koenig and Maillard Sts, Port Louis; tel. 207-0625; fax 212-8190; e-mail mss@mail.gov.mu; internet www.gov.mu/portal/site/ssnssite.

Ministry of Tertiary Education, Science, Research and Technology: Wing A, 4th Floor, Cyber Tower 1, Cyber City, Ebene; tel. 4541450; fax 4681440; e-mail tertiary@mail.gov.mu; internet www.gov.mu/portal/site/tertiary.

Ministry of Tourism and Leisure: Air Mauritius Centre, 5th Floor, John F. Kennedy St, Port Louis; tel. 211-7930; fax 208-6776; e-mail mtou@mail.gov.mu; internet www.gov.mu/portal/site/tourist.

Ministry of Youth and Sports: Emmanuel Anquetil Bldg, 3rd Floor, Sir Seewoosagur Ramgoolam St, Port Louis; tel. 201-2543; fax 211-2986; e-mail mys@mail.gov.mu; internet www.gov.mu/portal/site/sportsSite.

Legislature

National Assembly

Port Louis; tel. 201-1414; fax 212-8364; e-mail themace@intnet.mu; internet mauritiusassembly.gov.mu.

Speaker: PEEROO RAZACK.

General Election, 5 May 2010

Party	Seats: Directly elected	Additional*	Total
Alliance de l'Avenir†	41	4	45
Alliance du Coeur‡	18	2	20
Mouvement Rodriguais (MR)	2	—	2
Front Solidarité Mauricienne (FSM)	1	—	1
Organisation du Peuple Rodriguais (OPR)	—	1	1
Total	62	7	69

* Awarded to those among the unsuccessful candidates who attracted the largest number of votes, in order to ensure that a balance of ethnic groups is represented in the Assembly.

† Alliance comprising the Mauritius Labour Party, the Parti Mauricien Social Démocrate and the Mouvement Socialiste Militant.

‡ Alliance comprising the Mouvement Militant Mauricien, the Union Nationale and the Mouvement Mauricien Social Démocrate.

Election Commission

Electoral Commissioner's Office (ECO): Max City Bldg, 4th Floor, cnr Louis Pasteur and Remy Ollier Sts, Port Louis; tel. 240-9690; fax 241-9409; e-mail electcom@mail.gov.mu; internet electoral.gov.mu; under the aegis of the Prime Minister's Office; Commissioner appointed by the Judicial and Legal Service Commission; Electoral Commissioner M. I. ABDOOL RAHMAN.

Political Organizations

Forum des Citoyens Libres (FCL): Leader GEORGES AH-YAN.

Front Solidarité Mauricienne (FSM): Leader CEHL MEEAH.

Mauritius Labour Party (MLP) (Parti Travailliste): 7 Guy Rozemont Sq., Port Louis; tel. 212-6691; fax 210-0189; e-mail info@labourparty.mu; internet www.labourparty.mu; f. 1936; formed part of the Alliance de l'Avenir for the 2010 elections; Leader Dr NAVINCHANDRA RAMGOOLAM; Pres. PATRICK ASSIRVADEN; Sec.-Gen. DEVENAND VIRAHSAWMY.

Mouvement Mauricien Social Démocrate (MMSD): Morcellement Piat, Forest-Side, POB 1, Port Louis; tel. 670-4000; fax 670-1111; e-mail mmsd@orange.mu; internet www.mmsd.mu; f. 2009; formed part of the Alliance du Coeur for the 2010 elections; Leader ERIC GUIMBEAU.

Mouvement Militant Mauricien (MMM): 21 Poudrière St, Port Louis; tel. 212-6553; fax 208-9939; internet www.lemmm.org; f. 1969; socialist; formed part of the Alliance du Coeur for the 2010 elections; Pres. SAM LAUTHAN; Leader PAUL BÉRENGER; Secs-Gen. STEVEN OBEEGADOO, RAJESH BHAGWAN.

Mouvement Rodriguais (MR): Port Mathurin, Rodrigues; tel. 831-1876 (Port Mathurin); tel. and fax 686-8859 (Vacoas); fax 831-2648; e-mail nvmally@intnet.mu; f. 1992; represents the interests of Rodrigues; Leader LOUIS JOSEPH (NICHOLAS) VON-MALLY.

Mouvement Sociale Démocrate (MSD) (Social Democratic Movement): Port Louis; f. 2005; Leader ANIL BACHOO.

Mouvement Socialiste Militant (MSM): Sun Trust Bldg, 1st Floor, 31 Edith Cavell St, Port Louis; tel. 212-8787; fax 212-9334; e-mail info@msmparty.org; internet www.msmparty.com; f. 1983 by fmr mems of the MMM; formed part of the Alliance de l'Avenir for the 2010 elections; Leader Dr PRAVIND KUMAR JUGNAUTH; Pres. JOE LESJONGARD; Sec.-Gen. SHOWKUTALLY SOODHUN.

Organisation du Peuple Rodriguais (OPR): Mont Lubin, Rodrigues; represents the interests of Rodrigues; f. 1976; Leader LOUIS SERGE CLAIR.

Parti Mauricien Social Démocrate (PMSD): Melville, Grand Gaube; internet www.pmsd.mu; centre-right; formed part of the Alliance de l'Avenir for the 2010 elections; Leader CHARLES GAËTAN XAVIER-LUC DUVAL; Sec.-Gen. RAMA VALAYDEN.

Union Nationale (UN) (Mauritian National Union): Port Louis; f. 2006; formed part of the Alliance du Coeur for the 2010 elections; Chair. ASHOCK JUGNAUTH.

Some of the blocs and parties that participated in the 2010 elections include **Les Verts Fraternels/The Greens** (Leader SYLVIO MICHEL), the **Parti du Peuple Mauricien (PPM)**, the **Rezistans ek Alternativ** (Secretary ASHOK SUBRON), **Lalit** (lalitmauritius.com) and the **Tamil Council**.

Diplomatic Representation

EMBASSIES AND HIGH COMMISSIONS IN MAURITIUS

Australia: Rogers House, 2nd Floor, John F. Kennedy St, POB 541, Port Louis; tel. 202-0160; fax 208-8878; e-mail ahc.portlouis@dfat.gov.au; internet www.mauritius.embassy.gov.au; High Commissioner SANDRA VEGTING.

China, People's Republic: Royal Rd, Belle Rose, Rose Hill; tel. 454-9111; fax 464-6012; e-mail chinaemb_mu@mfa.gov.cn; internet www.ambchine.mu; Ambassador BIAN YANHUA.

Egypt: Sun Trust Bldg, 2nd floor, Edith Cavell St, Port Louis; tel. 213-1765; fax 213-1768; Ambassador ABD-AL HAMEED AHMAD MARZOUK.

France: 14 St George St, Port Louis; tel. 202-0100; fax 202-0110; e-mail ambafr.port-louis@hotmail.fr; internet www.ambafrance-mu.org; Ambassador JACQUES MAILLARD.

India: LIC Centre, 6th Floor, John F. Kennedy St, POB 162, Port Louis; tel. 208-8891; fax 208-6859; e-mail hicom.ss@intnet.mu; internet indiahighcom.intnet.mu; High Commissioner MADHUSUDAN GANAPATHI.

Madagascar: Guiot Pasceau St, Floreal, POB 3, Port Louis; tel. 686-5015; fax 686-7040; e-mail madmail@intnet.mu; internet www.ambamad.mu; Chargé d'affaires a.i. RICHARD VIA.

Pakistan: 9A Queen Mary Ave, Floreal, Port Louis; tel. 698-8501; fax 698-8405; e-mail pareportlouis@hotmail.com; High Commissioner Maj.-Gen. (retd) MUHAMMAD SIDDIQUE.

Russia: Queen Mary Ave, Floreal, POB 10, Port Louis; tel. 696-1545; fax 696-5027; e-mail rusemb.mu@intnet.mu; Ambassador VYACHESLAV NIKIFOROV.

South Africa: BAI Bldg, 4th Floor, 25 Pope Hennessy St, POB 908, Port Louis; tel. 212-6925; fax 212-6936; e-mail sahc@intnet.mu; High Commissioner MADUMANE M. MATABANE.

United Kingdom: Les Cascades Bldg, 7th Floor, Edith Cavell St, POB 1063, Port Louis; tel. 202-9400; fax 202-9408; e-mail bhc@intnet.mu; High Commissioner NICK LEAKE.

USA: Rogers House, 4th Floor, John F. Kennedy St, POB 544, Port Louis; tel. 202-4400; fax 208-9534; e-mail usembass@intnet.mu; internet mauritius.usembassy.gov; Chargé d'affaires a.i. TROY FITRELL.

Judicial System

The laws of Mauritius are derived both from the French Code Napoléon and from English Law. The Judicial Department consists of the Supreme Court, presided over by the Chief Justice and such number of Puisne Judges as may be prescribed by Parliament (currently nine), who are also Judges of the Court of Criminal Appeal and the Court of Civil Appeal. These courts hear appeals from the Intermediate Court, the Industrial Court and 10 District Courts (including that of Rodrigues). The Industrial Court has special jurisdiction to protect the constitutional rights of the citizen. There is a right of appeal in certain cases from the Supreme Court to the Judicial Committee of the Privy Council in the United Kingdom.

Supreme Court: Jules Koenig St, Port Louis; tel. 212-0275; fax 212-9946; internet supremecourt.intnet.mu.

Chief Justice: YEUNG KAM JOHN YEUNG SIK YUEN.

Senior Puisne Judge: KESHOE PARSAD MATADEEN.

Religion

Hindus are estimated to comprise more than 50% of the population, with Christians accounting for some 30% and Muslims 17%. There is also a small Buddhist community.

CHRISTIANITY

The Anglican Communion

Anglicans in Mauritius are within the Church of the Province of the Indian Ocean, comprising seven dioceses (five in Madagascar, one in Mauritius and one in Seychelles). The Archbishop of the Province is the Bishop of Antananarivo, Madagascar.

Bishop of Mauritius (also Archbishop of the Province of the Indian Ocean): Most Rev. GERALD JAMES (IAN) ERNEST, Bishop's House, Phoenix; tel. 686-5158; fax 697-1096; e-mail dioang@intnet.mu.

The Presbyterian Church of Mauritius

Minister: Pasteur ANDRÉ DE RÉLAND, cnr Farquhar and Royal Rds, Coignet, Rose Hill; tel. 464-5265; fax 395-2068; e-mail embrau@bow.intnet.mu; f. 1814.

The Roman Catholic Church

Mauritius comprises a single diocese, directly responsible to the Holy See, and an apostolic vicariate on Rodrigues. Some 26% of the total population are Roman Catholics.

Bishop of Port Louis: Rt Rev. MAURICE PIAT, Evêché, 13 Mgr Gonin St, Port Louis; tel. 208-3068; fax 208-6607; e-mail eveche@intnet.mu.

BAHÁ'Í FAITH

National Spiritual Assembly: Port Louis; tel. 212-2179; mems resident in 190 localities.

ISLAM

World Islamic Mission (Mauritius): Shah Noorani Centre, Old Moka Rd, Bell Village, Port Louis; tel. 211-1092; fax 210-9445; e-mail wim@wimmauritius.org; internet www.wimmauritius.org; f. 1975; Gen. Sec. HAMADE AUBDOOLLAH.

The Press

DAILIES

China Times: 24 Emmanuel Anquetil St, POB 325, Port Louis; tel. 240-3067; f. 1953; Chinese; Editor-in-Chief LONG SIONG AH KENG; circ. 3,000.

Chinese Daily News: 32 Rémy Ollier St, POB 316, Port Louis; tel. 240-0472; f. 1932; Chinese; Editor-in-Chief WONG YUEN MOY; circ. 5,000.

L'Express: 3 rue des Oursins, Riche-Terre, Baie du Tombeau, POB 247, Port Louis; tel. 206-8200; fax 247-1010; internet www.lexpress.mu; f. 1963; owned by La Sentinelle Ltd; English and French; Dir of Publication ARIANE CAVALOT DE L'ESTRAC; Editor-in-Chief JÉRÔME BOULLE; circ. 35,000.

The Independent Daily: Port Louis; internet theindependent.mu.

Le Matinal: AAPCA House, 6 La Poudrière St, Port Louis; tel. 207-0909; fax 213-4069; e-mail editorial@lematinal.com; internet www.lematinal.com; f. 2003; in French and English; owned by AAPCA (Mauritius) Ltd; Editor-in-Chief KIRAN RAMSAHAYE.

Le Mauricien: 8 St George St, POB 7, Port Louis; tel. 208-3251; fax 208-7059; e-mail redaction@lemauricien.com; internet www.lemauricien.com; f. 1907; English and French; Dir of Publication JACQUES RIVET; Editor-in-Chief GAËTAN SÉNÈQUE; circ. 35,000.

Le Quotidien: Pearl House, 4th Floor, 16 Sir Virgile Naz St, Port Louis; tel. 208-2631; fax 211-7479; e-mail quotidien@bow.intnet.mu; f. 1996; English and French; Dirs JACQUES DAVID, PATRICK MICHEL; circ. 30,000.

Le Socialiste: Manilall Bldg, 3rd Floor, Brabant St, Port Louis; tel. 208-8003; fax 211-3890; English and French; Editor-in-Chief VEDI BALLAH; circ. 7,000.

WEEKLIES AND FORTNIGHTLIES

5-Plus Dimanche: 3 Brown Sequard St, Port Louis; tel. 213-5500; fax 213-5551; e-mail comments@5plusltd.com; internet www.5plusltd.com; f. 1994; English and French; Editor-in-Chief FINLAY SALESSE; circ. 30,000.

5-Plus Magazine: 3 Brown Sequard St, Port Louis; tel. 213-5500; fax 213-5551; e-mail comments@5plusltd.com; f. 1990; English and French; Editor-in-Chief PIERRE BENOÎT; circ. 10,000.

Bollywood Massala: Le Défi Bldg, Royal Rd, Port Louis; tel. 211-8131; fax 213-0959; e-mail ledefi.plus@intnet.mu; internet www.defimedia.info.

Business Magazine: 3 Brown-Sequard St, 3rd Floor, Port Louis; tel. 202-2300; fax 211-1926; e-mail businessmag@intnet.mu; internet www.businessmag.mu; f. 1992; owned by Business Publications Ltd; English and French; Editor-in-Chief PIERRICK PEDEL; circ. 7,500.

Le Défi-Plus: Le Défi Bldg, Royal Rd, Port Louis; tel. 211-8131; fax 213-0959; e-mail ledefi.plus@intnet.mu; internet www.defimedia.info; Saturdays; Dir of Publication ESHAN KHODABUX.

L'Hèbdo: Le Défi Bldg, Royal Rd, Port Louis; tel. 211-8131; fax 213-0959; e-mail ledefi.plus@intnet.mu; internet www.defimedia.info.

Impact News: 10 Dr Yves Cantin St, Port Louis; tel. 211-5284; fax 211-7821; e-mail farhadr@wanadoo.mu; internet www.impactnews.info; English and French; Editor-in-Chief FARHAD RAMJAUN.

Lalit de Klas: 153B Royal Rd, GRNW, Port Louis; tel. 208-2132; e-mail lalitmail@intnet.mu; internet www.lalitmauritius.org; English, French and Mauritian Creole; Editor RADA KISTNASAMY.

Mauritius Times: 23 Bourbon St, Port Louis; tel. and fax 212-313; e-mail mtimes@intnet.mu; internet www.mauritiustimes.com; f. 1954; English and French; Editor-in-Chief MADHUKAR RAMLALLAH; circ. 15,000.

News on Sunday: Dr Eugen Laurent St, POB 230, Port Louis; tel. 211-5902; fax 211-7302; e-mail newsonsunday@news.intnet.mu; f. 1996; owned by Le Défi Group; weekly; in English; Editor NAGUIB LALLMAHOMED; circ. 10,000.

Le Rodriguais: Saint Gabriel, Rodrigues; tel. 831-1613; fax 831-1484; f. 1989; Creole, English and French; Editor JACQUES EDOUARD; circ. 2,000.

Samedi Plus: Port Louis; Editor-in-Chief DHARMANAND DOOHARIKA.

Star: 38 Labourdonnais St, Port Louis; tel. 212-2736; fax 211-7781; e-mail starpress@intnet.mu; internet www.mauriweb.com/star; English and French; Editor-in-Chief REZA ISSACK.

Sunday: Port Louis; tel. 208-9516; fax 208-7059; f. 1966; English and French; Editor-in-Chief SUBASH GOBIN.

Turf Magazine: 8 George St, POB 7, Port Louis; tel. 207-8200; fax 208-7059; e-mail bdlm@intnet.mu; internet www.lemauricien.com/turfmag; owned by Le Mauricien Ltd.

La Vie Catholique: 28 Nicolay Rd, Port Louis; tel. 242-0975; fax 242-3114; e-mail viecatho@intnet.mu; internet www.laviecatholique.com; f. 1930; weekly; English, French and Creole; Editor-in-Chief DANIÈLE BABOORAM; circ. 8,000.

Week-End: 8 St George St, POB 7, Port Louis; tel. 207-8200; fax 208-3248; e-mail redaction@lemauricien.com; internet www.lemauricien.com/weekend; f. 1966; owned by Le Mauricien Ltd; French and English; Editor JOSIE LEBRASSE; circ. 80,000.

Week-End Scope: 8 St George St, POB 7, Port Louis; tel. 207-8200; fax 208-7059; e-mail wes@lemauricien.com; internet www.lemauricien.com/wes; f. 1989; owned by Le Mauricien Ltd; English and French; Editor-in-Chief JACQUES ACHILLE.

OTHER SELECTED PERIODICALS

CCI–INFO: 3 Royal St, Port Louis; tel. 208-3301; fax 208-0076; e-mail mcci@intnet.mu; internet www.mcci.org; English and French; f. 1995; quarterly; publ. of the Mauritius Chamber of Commerce and Industry; Man. FAEEZA IBRAHIMSAH.

Education News: Edith Cavell St, Port Louis; tel. 212-1303; English and French; monthly; Editor-in-Chief GIAN AUBEELUCK.

Le Message de L'Ahmadiyyat: c/o Ahmadiyya Muslim Assen, POB 6, Rose Hill; tel. 464-1747; fax 454-2223; e-mail darussalaam@intnet.mu; French; monthly; Editor-in-Chief MOUSSA TAUJOO; circ. 3,000.

Le Progrès Islamique: 51B Solferino St, Rose Hill; tel. 467-1697; fax 467-1696; f. 1948; English and French; monthly; Editor DEVINA SOOKIA.

Publishers

Business Publications Ltd: TN Tower, 2nd Floor, St George St, Port Louis; tel. 211-3048; fax 211-1926; internet www.businessmag.mu; f. 1993; English and French; Dir LYNDSAY RIVIÈRE.

Editions de l'Océan Indien: Stanley, Rose Hill; tel. 464-6761; fax 464-3445; e-mail eoibooks@intnet.mu; internet www.eoi-info.com; f. 1977; general, textbooks, dictionaries, literature; English, French and Asian languages; Gen. Man. DEVANAND DEWKURUN.

Editions Le Printemps: 4 Club Rd, Vacoas; tel. 696-1017; fax 686-7302; e-mail elp@bow.intnet.mu; Man. Dir A. I. SULLIMAN.

Editions Vizavi: 9 St George St, Port Louis; tel. 211-3047; e-mail vizavi@intnet.mu; Dir PASCALE SIEW.

Broadcasting and Communications

TELECOMMUNICATIONS

In 2011 there were 374,694 subscribers to fixed-line telephone services and 1.2m. subscribers to mobile cellular telephone services.

Information and Communication Technologies Authority (ICTA): The Celicourt, 12th Floor, 6 Sir Celicourt Antelme St, Port Louis; tel. 211-5333; fax 211-9444; e-mail icta@intnet.mu; internet www.icta.mu; f. 1999; regulatory authority; Chair. TRILOK DWARKA; Exec. Dir Dr KRISHNA OOLUN.

Mauritius Telecom Ltd: Telecom Tower, Edith Cavell St, Port Louis; tel. 203-7000; fax 208-1070; e-mail ceo@mauritiustelecom.com.mu; internet www.mauritiustelecom.com; f. 1992; 60% owned by Govt of Mauritius, State Bank of Mauritius and National Pensions Fund, 40% owned by France Télécom through RIMCOM; privatized in 2000; provides all telecommunications services, including internet and digital mobile cellular services; Chair. APPALSAMY (DASS) THOMAS; CEO SARAT DUTT LALLAH.

Cellplus Mobile Communications Ltd: Telecom Tower, 9th Floor, Edith Cavell St, Port Louis; tel. 208-5057; fax 211-6996; e-mail contact@orange.mu; internet www.orange.mu/mobile; f. 1996; introduced the first GSM cellular network in Mauritius and recently in Rodrigues (Cell-Oh); a wholly owned subsidiary of Mauritius Telecom.

Emtel: 10 Ebene Cyber City, Ebene; tel. 454-5400; fax 454-1010; e-mail emtel@emtelnet.com; internet www.emtel.com; f. 1989; CEO SHYAM ROY.

Outremer Télécom Maurice: Hassamal Bldg, Rémono St, POB 113, Rose Hill; tel. 401-9400; fax 401-9422; e-mail info@outremer-telecom.mu; internet www.outremer-telecom.mu; Man. Dir MICHEL RIGOT.

BROADCASTING

In 1997 the Supreme Court invalidated the broadcasting monopoly held by the Mauritius Broadcasting Corporation.

Independent Broadcasting Authority: The Celicourt, 2nd Floor, 6 Sir Celicourt Antelme St, Port Louis; tel. 213-3890; fax 213-3894; e-mail iba@intnet.mu; internet iba.gov.mu; Chair. TRILOCK DWARKA; Dir DULLIPARSAD SURAJ BALI.

Radio

Mauritius Broadcasting Corpn: 1 Royal Rd, Moka; tel. 402-8000; fax 433-3330; e-mail customercare@mbc.intnet.mu; internet www.mbcradio.tv; f. 1964; parastatal organization operating eight national radio services and nine television channels; Chair. CLAUDE NARAIN; Dir-Gen. DHANJAY CALLIKAN.

Radio One: 3 Brown Sequard St, Port Louis; tel. 211-4555; fax 211-4142; e-mail sales@r1.mu; internet www.r1.mu; f. 2002; owned by Sentinelle media group; news and entertainment; Dir-Gen. NICOLAS ADELSON.

Radio Plus: 4B Labourdonnais St, Port-Louis; tel. 208-6002; fax 212-0047; e-mail radioplus@intnet.mu; internet www.radioplus.mu; f. 2002.

Top FM: The Peninsula, Caudan Bldg, 7th Floor, 2A Falcon St, Caudan, Port Louis; tel. 213-2121; fax 213-2222; e-mail topfm@intnet.mu; internet www.topfmradio.com; f. 2003; Chair. BALKRISHNA KAUNHYE.

Radio France International and France Inter are also broadcast to Mauritius.

Television

Independent television stations commenced broadcasting from 2002, as part of the liberalization of the sector.

Mauritius Broadcasting Corpn: see Radio.

Broadcasts from France 24 and TV5 are received in Mauritius.

Finance

(cap. = capital; res = reserves; dep. = deposits; m. = million; brs = branches; amounts in Mauritian rupees, unless otherwise stated)

BANKING

Central Bank

In 2010 there were 19 commercial banks and 11 non-bank deposit-taking institutions in Mauritius. The first Islamic bank of Mauritius, Century Banking Corpn Ltd, started its operation in 2011.

Bank of Mauritius: Sir William Newton St, POB 29, Port Louis; tel. 202-3800; fax 208-9204; e-mail governor.office@bom.intnet.mu; internet bom.intnet.mu; f. 1966; bank of issue; cap. 1,000.0m., res 19,158.8m., dep. 27,353.7m. (June 2010); Gov. RUNDHEERSING BHEENICK.

Principal Commercial Banks

ABC Banking Corpn Ltd: 7 Duke of Edinburgh Ave, Place d'Armes, Port Louis; tel. 206-8000; fax 208-0088; internet www.abcbanking.mu; f. 2010; Chair. Prof. DONALD AH CHUEN; CEO MOHAMED KHALIL ALKHUSHAIRI.

AfrAsia Bank Ltd: Bowen Square, 10 Dr Ferriere St, Port Louis; tel. 208-5500; fax 213-8850; e-mail afrasia@afrasiabank.com; internet www.afrasiabank.com; f. 2007; Chair. ARNAUD LAGESSE; CEO JAMES BENOIT.

Bank of Baroda: 32 Sir William Newton St, POB 553, Port Louis; tel. 208-1504; fax 208-3892; e-mail info@bankofbaroda-mu.com; internet www.bankofbaroda-mu.com; f. 1962; total assets 2,655,000m. (June 2007); Vice-Pres. (Mauritius Operations) S. K. CHAWLA; 7 brs.

Bank One Ltd: 16 Sir William Newton St, POB 485, Port Louis; tel. 202-9200; fax 210-4712; e-mail info@firstcitybank-mauritius.com; internet www.bankone.mu; f. 1991 as the Delphis Bank Ltd; merged with Union International Bank in 1997; private bank; taken over by consortium in 2002; name changed as above in 2008; 50% owned by Investments & Mortgages Bank Ltd (Kenya), 50% by Ciel Investments Ltd; cap. 491.4m., res 142.1m., dep. 9,481.3m. (Dec. 2009); Chair. SARIT SHAH; CEO RAJ DUSSOYE.

Barclays Bank PLC, Mauritius: Harbour Front Bldg, 8th Floor, John F. Kennedy St, POB 284, Port Louis; tel. 402-1000; fax 467-0618; e-mail barclays.mauritius@barclays.com; f. 1919; absorbed Banque Nationale de Paris Intercontinentale in 2002; cap. 100.0m., res 616.1m., dep. 6,886.7m. (Dec. 2001); Man. Dir RAVIN DAJEE; 16 brs.

Bramer Banking Corpn Ltd: 26 Bourbon St, Port Louis; tel. 208-8826; fax 213-4792; internet www.bramerbank.mu; f. 1989; present name adopted 2008; owned by British American Investment Group (BAI); cap. 200.0m., res 39.9m., dep. 4,301.8m. (Dec. 2009); Chair. HASSAM A. M. VAYID; CEO ASHRAF ESMAEL (acting); 16 brs.

Deutsche Bank Mauritius Ltd: Barkly Wharf East, 4th Floor, Le Caudan Waterfront, POB 615, Port Louis; tel. 202-7878; fax 202-7898; internet www.db.com/mauritius.

Habib Bank Ltd: 30 Louis Pasteur St, Port Louis; tel. 217-7600; fax 216-3829; e-mail habib@intnet.mu; f. 1964; 2 brs.

Hongkong and Shanghai Banking Corpn Ltd (HSBC): HSBC Centre, 5th Floor, 18 Cyber City, Ebene; tel. 403-0701; fax 403-8300; e-mail hsbcmauritius@hsbc.co.mu; internet www.hsbc.co.mu; f. 1916; CEO SANDEEP UPPAL; Man. Dir JAMES BOUCHER.

Investec Bank (Mauritius) Ltd: Dias Pier Bldg, 7th Floor, Le Caudan Waterfront, Port Louis; tel. 207-4000; fax 207-4003; internet www.investec.com; f. 1997; Chair. HUGH S. HERMAN; CEO CRAIG C. MCKENZIE.

Mauritius Commercial Bank Ltd: MCB Centre, 9–15 Sir William Newton St, POB 52, Port Louis; tel. 202-5000; fax 208-7054; e-mail mcb@mcb.co.mu; internet www.mcb.mu; f. 1838; cap. 2,554.9m., res 3,990.0m., dep. 132,569.1m. (June 2010); Pres. GERARD J. HARDY; CEO PIERRE-GUY NOEL; 42 brs.

Mauritius Post and Co-operative Bank Ltd: 1 Sir William Newton St, Port Louis; tel. 207-9999; fax 208-7270; e-mail mpcb@mpcb.mu; internet www.mpcb.mu; f. 2003; 44.3% owned by The Mauritius Post Ltd, 35.7% state-owned, 10% owned by the Sugar Investment Trust; cap. 384.0m., res 119.4m., dep. 7,131.9m. (Dec. 2009); CEO RAJIV KUMAR BEEHARRY; Gen. Man. PAVADAY THONDRAYON.

P. T. Bank Internasional Indonesia (Mauritius): Barkly Wharf, 5th Floor, Caudan Waterfront, Port Louis; tel. 210-6365; fax 210-5458; e-mail biimrt@intnet.mu; internet bii.intnet.mu; f. 1998; CEO SARAH JANE KATE NIRSIMLOO.

SBI Mauritius: SBI Tower Mindspace, 6th and 7th Floors, Bhumi Park, 45 Cyber City, Ebene; tel. 404-4900; fax 454-6890; e-mail info@sbimauritius.com; internet www.sbimauritius.com; f. 1978 as Indian Ocean International Bank Ltd; merged with SBI International in 2008 and renamed as above; cap. 48.6m., res 62.0m., dep. 438.4m. (March 2009); Chair. PRATIP CHAUDHURI; Man. Dir and CEO J. S. HIREMATH; 15 brs.

Standard Chartered Bank (Mauritius) Ltd: Ebene House, 2nd Floor, 33 Cyber City, Ebene; tel. 466-5000; fax 466-5161; e-mail info.scbm@sc.com; internet www.standardchartered.com/mu; wholly owned subsidiary of Standard Chartered Bank PLC; 'offshore' banking unit.

State Bank of Mauritius Ltd: State Bank Tower, 1 Queen Elizabeth II Ave, POB 152, Port Louis; tel. 202-1111; fax 202-1234; e-mail sbm@sbmgroup.mu; internet www.sbmgroup.mu; f. 1973; cap. 303.7m., res 2,975.1m., dep. 61,252.9m. (June 2010); Chair. MUNI KRISHNA REDDY; CEO GAUTAM VIR; 48 brs.

Development Bank

Development Bank of Mauritius Ltd: rue La Chaussée, POB 157, Port Louis; tel. 203-3600; fax 208-8498; e-mail dbm@intnet.mu; internet www.dbm.mu; f. 1964; name changed as above in 1991; 85% govt-owned; cap. 225m., res 1,646.5m., dep. 4,155.9m. (June 2009); Chair. ERIC N. G. PING CHEUN; Man. Dir IQBAL CARRIM (acting); 6 brs.

Principal 'Offshore' Banks

Banque des Mascareignes Ltd: 1 Cathedral Sq., Level 8, 16 Jules Koenig St, POB 43, Port Louis; tel. and fax 207-8600; fax 210-2300; e-mail serviceclient@bm.mu; internet www.banquedesmascareignes.mu; f. 2004; name changed as above 2005; 69.5% owned by Financière Océor (France), 27.7% owned by Banque de la Réunion; cap. 838.7m., res 597.7m., dep. 11,793.0m. (Dec. 2011); Chair. PHILIPPE GARSUAULT; CEO HUY HOANG DANG.

Bank of Baroda, Barclays Bank PLC, AfrAsia Bank Ltd, PT Bank International Indonesia, Investec Bank (Mauritius), Standard Chartered Bank (Mauritius) and HSBC Bank PLC also operate 'offshore' banking units.

Islamic Bank

Century Banking Corpn Ltd: Barkly Wharf, 4th Floor, Le Caudan Waterfront, Port Louis; f. 2010; Pres. HESHAM SHOKRY.

Banking Organization

Mauritius Bankers Association (MBA): Newton Tower, Level 15, Sir William Newton St, Port Louis; tel. 213-2390; fax 213-0968; e-mail mba@mba.mu; internet www.mba.mu; f. 1967; Chair. SOOPAYA PARIANEN; CEO AISHA C. TIMOL; 20 mems.

STOCK EXCHANGE

Financial Services Commission: FSC House, 54 Cyber City, Ebene; tel. 403-7000; fax 467-7172; e-mail fscmauritius@intnet.mu; internet www.fscmauritius.org; f. 2001; regulatory authority for securities, insurance and global business activities; Chair. SAID LALLOO; Chief Exec. (vacant).

Stock Exchange of Mauritius Ltd: 1 Cathedral Sq., 4th Floor, 16 Jules Koenig St, Port Louis; tel. 212-9541; fax 208-8409; e-mail stockex@sem.intnet.mu; internet www.stockexchangeofmauritius.com; f. 1989; 11 mems; Chair. GAETAN LAN HUN KUEN; CEO SUNIL BENIMADHU.

INSURANCE

Albatross Insurance Co Ltd: 22 St George St, POB 116, Port Louis; tel. 207-9007; fax 208-4800; e-mail headoffice@albatross-insurance.com; internet www.albatross-insurance.com; f. 1975; Chair. VAUGHAN HEBERDEN.

Anglo-Mauritius Assurance Society Ltd: Swan Group Centre, 10 Intendance St, POB 837, Port Louis; tel. 202-8600; fax 208-8956; e-mail anglo@intnet.mu; internet www.anglo.mu; f. 1951; Chair. CYRIL MAYER; CEO LOUIS RIVALLAND.

BAI Co (Mauritius) Ltd: BAI Centre, 217 Royal Rd, Curepipe; tel. 602-3000; fax 670-3384; e-mail bai@bai.intnet.mu; internet www.bai.mu; f. 1988 as British American Insurance Co (Mauritius) Ltd; renamed as above in 2010; Pres. and CEO RISHI SOOKDAWOOR.

Indian Ocean General Assurance Ltd: 35 Corderie St, POB 865, Port Louis; tel. 212-4125; fax 212-5850; e-mail info@iogaltd.com; internet iogaltd.com; f. 1971; total assets 221m. (June 2007); Gen. Man. R. L. MATHUR.

Jubilee Insurance (Mauritius) Ltd: Cathedral Sq., Pope Hennessy St, Port Louis; tel. 210-3678; fax 212-7970; e-mail sarah.hossen@jubileemauritius.com; f. 1998; Admin. Officer SARAH HOSSEN.

Lamco International Insurance Ltd: Lamco Bldg, 12 Barracks St, Port Louis; tel. 212-4494; fax 208-0612; e-mail lamco@intnet.mu; internet www.lamcoinsurance.com; f. 1978; Chair. ABOO BAKAR YACOOB ATCHIA; Gen. Man. NAJEEB C. ADIA.

Life Insurance Corpn of India: LIC Centre, John F. Kennedy St, POB 310, Port Louis; tel. 212-5316; fax 208-6392; e-mail liccmm@intnet.mu; f. 1956; Chief Man. NAVIN PRAKASH SINHA.

Mauritian Eagle Insurance Co Ltd: IBL House, 1st Floor, Caudan Waterfront, POB 854, Port Louis; tel. 203-2200; fax 203-2299; e-mail caudan@mauritianeagle.com; internet www.mauritianeagle.com; f. 1973; Chair. PATRICE D'HOTMAN DE VILLIERS; Man. Dir ERIC A. VENPIN.

Mauritius Union Assurance Co Ltd: 4 Léoville l'Homme St, POB 233, Port Louis; tel. 207-5500; fax 212-2962; e-mail info@mauritiusunion.com; internet www.mauritiusuniongroup.com; f. 1948; Chair. DOMINIQUE GALEA; Group Man. Dir KRIS LUTCHMENARRAIDOO.

Mauritius Union Group: 4 Léoville l'Homme St, Port Louis; tel. 207-5500; fax 212-2962; e-mail info@mauritiusunion.com; internet www.mauritiusuniongroup.com; f. 1948; CEO KRIS LUTCHMENARRAIDOO.

New India Assurance Co Ltd: Bank of Baroda Bldg, 3rd Floor, 15 Sir William Newton St, POB 398, Port Louis; tel. 208-1442; fax 208-2160; e-mail niasurance@intnet.mu; internet www.niacl.com; f. 1935; general insurance; Chief Man. S. VAIDESWARAN.

Phoenix Insurance (Mauritius) Co Ltd: 36 Sir William Newton St, POB 852, Port Louis; tel. 208-0056; fax 213-3882; e-mail tilakf@intnet.mu; f. 1977; CEO TILAK FERNANDO (acting).

Rainbow Insurance Co Ltd: 23 Edith Cavell St, POB 389, Port Louis; tel. 202-8800; fax 208-8750; e-mail raininsu@intnet.mu; internet www.rainbowinsurance.mu; f. 1976; Chair. B. GOKULSING; Gen. Man. PRAVIN RAMBURN.

State Insurance Co of Mauritius Ltd (SICOM): SICOM Bldg, Sir Celicourt Antelme St, Port Louis; tel. 203-8400; fax 208-7662; e-mail email@sicom.intnet.mu; internet www.sicom.mu; f. 1975; Man. Dir K. G. BHOOJEDHUR-OBEEGADOO.

Sun Insurance Co Ltd: 2 St George St, Port Louis; tel. 208-0769; fax 208-2052; e-mail suninsco@intnet.mu; f. 1981; Chair. Sir KAILASH RAMDANEE; Man. Dir A. MUSBALLY.

Swan Insurance Co Ltd: Swan Group Centre, 10 Intendance St, POB 364, Port Louis; tel. 207-3500; fax 208-6898; e-mail swan@intnet.mu; f. 1955; Chair. J. M. ANTOINE HAREL; CEO M. E. CYRIL MAYER.

Trade and Industry

GOVERNMENT AGENCIES

Agricultural Marketing Board (AMB): Dr G. Leclézio Ave, Moka; tel. 433-4025; fax 433-4837; e-mail agbd@intnet.mu; internet amb.intnet.mu; f. 1964; operates under the aegis of the Ministry of Agro-industry and Food Security; markets certain locally produced and imported food products (such as potatoes, onions, garlic, spices and seeds); provides storage facilities to importers and exporters; Gen. Man. RODNEY RAMA.

Mauritius Meat Authority: Abattoir Rd, Roche Bois, POB 612, Port Louis; tel. 242-5884; fax 217-1077; e-mail mauritiusmeat@intnet.mu; f. 1974; licensing authority; controls and regulates sale of meat and meat products; also purchases and imports livestock and markets meat products; Gen. Man. A. BALGOBIN.

Mauritius Sugar Authority: Ken Lee Bldg, 2nd Floor, Edith Cavell St, Port Louis; tel. 208-7466; fax 208-7470; e-mail msa@intnet.mu; regulatory body for the sugar industry; Chair. S. HANOOMANJEE; Exec. Dir Dr G. RAJPATI.

Mauritius Tea Board: Wooton St, Curepipe Rd, Curepipe; POB 28, Eau Coulée; tel. 675-3497; fax 676-1445; e-mail teaboard@intnet.mu; internet www.gov.mu/portal/site/teaboard; f. 1975; regulates and controls the activities of the tea industry; Chair. V. GONDEEA; Gen. Man. ATMARAMSINGH SEEPERGAUTH.

Mauritius Tobacco Board: Plaine Lauzun, Port Louis; tel. 212-2323; fax 208-6426; e-mail tobaco@intnet.mu; internet tobaccoboard.intnet.mu; Gen. Man. HEMRAJSINGH RAMAHOTAR.

DEVELOPMENT ORGANIZATIONS

Board of Investment—Mauritius (BOI): 1 Cathedral Sq., 10th Floor, 16 Jules Koenig St, Port Louis; tel. 211-4190; fax 208-2924;

e-mail invest@boi.intnet.mu; internet www.boimauritius.com; f. 2001 to promote international investment, business and services; Chair. of Bd MAURICE LAM; Man. Dir KEN POONOOSAMY.

Enterprise Mauritius: Saint James Court, 7th Floor, Saint Denis St, Port Louis; tel. 212-9760; fax 212-9767; e-mail info@em.intnet.mu; internet www.enterprisemauritius.biz; f. 2004 from parts of the Mauritius Industrial Development Authority, the Export Processing Zones Development Authority and the Sub-contracting and Partnership Exchange—Mauritius; comprises a Corporate Services Unit, a Strategic Direction Unit, a Business Development Unit, a Client-Services Unit and a Special Support Unit (est. from the former Clothing and Textile Centre); Chair. LOUIS AMÉDÉE DARGA; CEO DEV CHAMROO.

Joint Economic Council (JEC): Plantation House, 3rd Floor, pl. d'Armes, Port Louis; tel. 211-2980; fax 211-3141; e-mail jec@intnet.mu; internet www.jec-mauritius.org; f. 1970; the co-ordinating body of the private sector of Mauritius, including the main business orgs of the country; Pres. LOUIS RIVALLAND; Dir RAJ MAKOOND.

Mauritius Freeport Authority (MFA): 1 Cathedral Sq., Level 10, 16 Jules Koenig St, Port Louis; tel. 203-3800; fax 208-2924; e-mail contact@investmauritius.com; internet www.efreeport.com; f. 1990; Asst Dir NANDA NARRAINEN.

National Productivity and Competitiveness Council (NPCC): Alexander House, 4th Floor, Cyber City, Ebene; tel. 467-7700; fax 467-3838; e-mail natpro@intnet.mu; internet www.npccmauritius.com; f. 2000; represents the Govt, the private sector and trade unions; Chair. RAJENDRAPARSAD MUNGUR; Exec. Dir Dr KRISHNALALL COONJAN.

Small Enterprises and Handicraft Development Authority (SEHDA): Industrial Zone, Coromandel; tel. 233-0500; fax 233-5545; e-mail sehda@intnet.mu; internet www.sehda.org; f. 2006 following the merger of the Small and Medium Industries Development Organization and the National Handicraft Promotion Agency; provides support to potential and existing small entrepreneurs; Man. Dir INDIRA SEEBURN.

State Investment Corpn Ltd (SIC): Air Mauritius Centre, 15th Floor, John F. Kennedy St, Port Louis; tel. 202-8900; fax 208-8948; e-mail contactsic@stateinvestment.com; internet www.stateinvestment.com; f. 1984; provides support for new investment and transfer of technology, in agriculture, industry and tourism; Man. Dir MUHAMMAD IQBAL MALLAM-HASHAM; Chair. RAJ DIREVIUM NAGAYA RINGADOO.

CHAMBERS OF COMMERCE

Chinese Chamber of Commerce: Jade Court, Suite 206, Jummah Mosque St, Port Louis; tel. and fax 242-0156; e-mail admin@cccmauritius.org; internet www.cccmauritius.org; f. 1908; Pres. ARMAND AH-KONG.

Mauritius Chamber of Commerce and Industry: 3 Royal St, Port Louis; tel. 208-3301; fax 208-0076; e-mail mcci@intnet.mu; internet www.mcci.org; f. 1850; 400 mems; Pres. CÉDRIC DE SPEVILLE; Sec.-Gen. MAHMOOD CHEEROO.

INDUSTRIAL ASSOCIATIONS

Association of Mauritian Manufacturers (AMM): c/o The Mauritius Chamber of Commerce and Industry, 3 Royal St, Port Louis; tel. 208-3301; fax 208-0076; e-mail amm@mcci.intnet.mu; f. 1995; Pres. VINCENT DE LABAUVE D'ARIFAT.

Mauritius Export Processing Zone Association (MEPZA): Unicorn House, 6th Floor, 5 Royal St, Port Louis; tel. 208-5216; fax 212-1853; f. 1976; consultative and advisory body; Chair. GUILLAUME SUGNIN.

Mauritius Sugar Producers' Association (MSPA): Plantation House, 2nd Floor, Edinburgh Ave, Port Louis; tel. 212-0295; fax 212-5727; e-mail mspa@mspa.intnet.mu; f. 1947; Chair. CYRIL MAYER; Dir JEAN LI YUEN FONG.

EMPLOYERS' ORGANIZATION

Mauritius Employers' Federation: MEF-MCCI Bldg, Cyber City, Ebene; tel. 466-3600; fax 465-8200; e-mail mef@intnet.mu; internet www.mef-online.org; f. 1962; Chair. CLENCY APPAVOO; Dir Dr AZAD JEETUN.

UTILITIES

Electricity

Central Electricity Board: Royal Rd, POB 40, Curepipe; tel. 601-1100; fax 675-7958; e-mail ceb@intnet.mu; internet ceb.intnet.mu; f. 1952; state-operated; Chair. BALRAJ NARROO; Gen. Man. SHIAM KRISHT THANNOO.

Water

Central Water Authority: Royal Rd, St Paul, Phoenix; tel. 601-5000; fax 686-6264; e-mail cwa@intnet.mu; corporate body; scheduled for privatization; f. 1973; Gen. Man. HARRY KISSOON BOOLUCK; Chair. MEGHDUTH CHUMROO.

Waste Water Management Authority: Sir Celicourt Antelme St, Port Louis; tel. 206-3000; fax 211-7007; e-mail wma@intnet.mu; internet wma.gov.mu; f. 2000; Chair. KHUSHAL LOBINE; Gen. Man. MOUSSA ELIAS ALLYBOCUS.

MAJOR COMPANIES

Business Parks of Mauritius Ltd (BPML): NPF Bldg, 10th Floor, route Moka, Rose Hill; tel. 467-6900; fax 467-6907; e-mail bpml@bpmlmauritius.mu; internet www.e-cybercity.mu; f. 2001 by the Government as a private company; develops, constructs and manages high technology business parks, including Ebene Cyber City; Exec. Chair. DHARAM HAUGAH.

Compagnie Mauricienne de Textile International Ltée (CMT): c/o CMT Spinning Mills Ltd, La Tour Koenig, Pointe aux Sables; tel. 234-2898; fax 234-2842; e-mail info@cmt-intl.com; internet www.cmt-intl.com; f. 1983; textiles and pharmaceuticals; subsidiaries in Hong Kong, China, Madagascar and Zimbabwe; Man. Dir KRIS POONOOSAMY; 3,000 employees.

Consolidated Investments and Enterprises Group (CIEL): Ebene Skies, 5th Floor, rue de l'Institut, Ebene; tel. 404-2200; fax 404-2201; e-mail info@cielgroup.com; internet www.cielgroup.com; f. 1977; comprises CIEL Agro-Industry (Deep River—Beau Champ sugar estate), CIEL Investment Ltd and CIEL Textile Ltd; Chair. P. ARNAUD DALAIS; CEO JEAN-PIERRE DALAIS.

Currimjee Jeewanjee and Co Ltd: 38 Royal St, POB 49, Port Louis; tel. 206-6200; fax 240-8133; e-mail contact@currimjee.com; internet www.currimjee.com; f. 1890; media and communications, food and beverages, financial services, real estate, textiles, trading, travel and freight; Chair. BASHIRALI A. CURRIMJEE; 4,500 employees.

ENL Ltd: Swan Group Centre, 7th Floor, Intendance St, Port Louis; tel. 213-3800; fax 208-0968; e-mail enlgroup@intnet.mu; internet www.enl.mu; f. 1944; holding co; fmrly Espitalier Noël Ltd; name changed as above in 2010; agriculture, manufacturing and services; comprises more than 20 companies; notable subsidiaries include Mon Désert Alma Ltd, Savannah Sugar Estate Co Ltd and General Investment & Development Co Ltd (GIDC); Chair. and Group CEO HECTOR ESPITALIER-NOËL; 5,000 employees.

Gamma Civic Ltd: Royal Rd, Chapman Hill, Beau Bassin; tel. 403-8000; fax 454-1592; e-mail headoffice@gamma.mu; internet www.gamma.mu; f. 1961; supply of building materials, civil engineering and construction; CEO CARL AH TECK.

General Construction Co Ltd: POB 503, Port Louis; tel. 202-2000; fax 208-8249; e-mail gcc@gcc.mu; f. 1958; civil engineering and construction; Chair. JEAN-CLAUDE MAINGARD; Man Dir DIDIER ADAM; 4,300 employees.

Groupe Mon Loisir (GML): Swan Group Centre, 11th Floor, 10 Intendance St, Port Louis; tel. 211-1714; fax 208-0134; e-mail corporate@gmlmail.com; internet www.gmltogether.com; tourism, manufacturing, financial services and real estate interests; 117 subsidiaries and affiliates; Chair. THIERRY LAGESSE; Chief Exec. ARNAUD LAGESSE; 12,500 employees.

Flacq United Estates Ltd (FUEL): 4th Floor, IBL House, Caudan Waterfront, Port Louis; tel. 211-1713; fax 208-0134; e-mail corporate@gmlmail.com; internet www.gmltogether.com; f. 1948; investment co; owned by Groupe Mon Loisir; cultivates 8,000 ha of sugar cane plantation; operates the largest sugar factory on the island; supplies electricity derived from bagasse to the national grid; Chair. THIERRY LAGESSE; Chief Exec. JOSEPH VAUDIN.

Harel Mallac and Co Ltd: 18 Edith Cavell St, Port Louis; tel. 207-3000; fax 207-3030; e-mail ho@harelmallac.com; internet www.harelmallac.com; f. 1830; multiple activities, incl. 6 divisions: technologies; office equipment; travel, tourism and retail; reprographics; engineering and outsourcing; Chair. of Bd ANTOINE L. HAREL; Chief Exec. CHRISTOPHER BOLAND; 740 employees.

IndianOil (Mauritius) Ltd (IOML): Terminal, Mer Rouge; tel. 217-2714; fax 217-5500; e-mail indianoil@intnet.mu; internet www.ioml.mu; wholly owned by IndianOil Corpn (India); Man. Dir RANJAN KUMAR MOHAPATRA.

Innodis Ltd: Innodis Bldg, Caudan; tel. 466-5253; fax 466-5253; e-mail info@innodisgroup.com; internet www.innodisgroup.com; distributes and markets dry, chilled and frozen consumer goods; also has chicken farming and processing units; operates five outlets under Supercash, a cash and carry concept, in Mauritius and Rodrigues; f. 1973 as Mauritius Farms Ltd; present name assumed in 2006; owned by Altima Group; Chief Operating Officer JEAN HOW HONG; more than 1,200 employees.

International Distillers (Mauritius) Ltd: POB 661, Plaine Lauzun; tel. 212-6896; fax 208-6076; e-mail idm@idm.intnet.mu; f. 1972; mfrs, importers and distributors of wines and spirits; Chief Exec. JACQUES T. LI WAN PO; Man. Dir W. L. SHEPHERD.

Ireland Blyth Ltd (IBL): IBL House, 5th Floor, Caudan, POB 56, Port Louis; tel. 203-2000; fax 203-2001; e-mail iblinfo@iblgroup.com; internet www.iblgroup.com; f. 1972; marketing and distribution of consumer goods and durables, pharmaceuticals, fertilizers and pesticides, mechanical and electrical engineering and cold storage operations; Chair. THIERRY LAGESSE; Chief Exec. NICOLAS MAIGROT; 7,000 employees.

Lafarge (Mauritius) Cement Ltd: 5 John Kennedy St, POB 60, Port Louis; tel. 240-1925; fax 240-3554; e-mail mpcmru@intnet.mu; CEO VINCENT LENETTE.

Mauritius Chemical and Fertilizer Industry Ltd: Chaussée Tromelin, POB 344, Port Louis; tel. 261-3965; fax 240-9969; e-mail mcficontact@mcfi.intnet.mu; internet www.mcfi.mu; f. 1975; mfrs of agricultural chemicals and fertilizers; Chair. ANTOINE L. HAREL; Man. Dir SÉBASTIEN LAVOIPIERRE.

Mauritius Sugar Terminal Corporation (MSTC): 17 Kwan Tee St, Caudan, Port Louis; tel. 208-1451; fax 208-3225; f. 1979; provides, operates and maintains facilities for storage, sampling, bagging, packing, loading and unloading of sugar and advises on the provisions of adequate means of inland or sea access to the terminal; Gen. Man. KHEEREERAZ MAHADEB (acting).

Mon Trésor et Mon Désert Ltd: Anglo-Mauritius House, 7th Floor, A. de Plevitz St, Port Louis; tel. 212-3252; fax 208-8263; e-mail bm@socrdc.com; internet www.montresor.mu; f. 1926; sugar-cane and energy production; Chair. CYRIL MAYER; Man. Dir GEORGES LEUNG SHING; 4,000 employees.

Omnicane Ltd: 7th Floor, Anglo-Mauritius House, Adolphe de Plevitz St, POB 159, Port Louis; tel. 212-3251; fax 211-7093; e-mail info@omnicane.com; internet www.omnicane.com; sugar, energy and bioethanol; Chair. SUNIL BANYMANDHUB; CEO JACQUES M. D'UNIENVILLE.

Phoenix Beverages Ltd: Phoenix House, Pont-Fer, Phoenix; tel. 601-2000; fax 686-6920; e-mail pbl@pbg.mu; internet www.phoenixbeveragesgroup.com; f. 1960; formerly Mauritius Breweries Ltd, now part of the Phoenix Beverages Group; name changed as above 2004; brews, bottles and distributes alcoholic and soft drinks; Chair. THIERRY LAGESSE; Chief Exec. RICHARD WOODING.

Robert Le Maire Group (RLM): Old Moka Rd, POB 161, Belle Village, Port Louis; tel. 212-1865; fax 208-0112; e-mail headoffice.rlm@rlmgroup.mu; internet www.rlmgroup.mu; importers and merchants, general agents and providers of engineering and contracting services; CEO ROGER KOENIG.

Rogers & Co Ltd: Rogers House, 5 John F. Kennedy St, POB 60, Port Louis; tel. 202-6666; fax 208-3646; e-mail info@rogers.mu; internet www.rogers.mu; f. 1948; aviation, chemicals and pharmaceuticals, construction materials, engineering, food, financial services, property development, shipping, tourism; Chair. TIMOTHY TAYLOR; CEO PHILIPPE ESPITALIER-NOËL; 3 vessels.

Shell Mauritius Ltd: Shell House, Roche Bois, POB 85, Port Louis; tel. 206-1234; fax 240-1043; internet www.shell.com/mu-en; f. 1905; marketing and distribution of petroleum products; Chair. PAWAN K. JUWAHEER.

State Trading Corporation (STC): Fon Sing Bldg, 3rd Floor, 12 Edith Cavell St, Port Louis; tel. 208-5440; fax 208-8359; e-mail stcfin@intnet.mu; internet stc.intnet.mu; f. 1982; responsible for the importation of essential commodities, such as petroleum products, cement, rice and wheat flour and liquefied petroleum gas; Chair. ANURADHA APPADOO; Gen. Man. MEGANATHAN PILLAY.

Sugar Investment Trust (SIT): NG Tower, Ground Floor, Cybercity, Ebene; tel. 406-4747; fax 466-6566; e-mail sitrust@intnet.mu; internet www.sit.intnet.mu; f. 1994; Chair. RITESH SUMPUTH; CEO RAVIN BHOLAH.

Sun Resorts Ltd (SRL): Ebene Skies, rue de l'Institut, Ebene; tel. 402-0000; fax 402-0199; e-mail info@sunresorts.mu; internet www.sunresortshotels.com; f. 1983; holding co, with interests in the hotel business; CEO FELICE FABIO PICCIRILLO; 2,900 employees.

Tamak Textile Ltd: 2 Royal Rd, Coromandel; tel. 233-0020; fax 233-4275; e-mail tamak@tamak.com; f. 1983; mfr of quality casual garments for men, ladies and children; Chair. LILY TSANG MANG KIN; Man. Dir EMMANUEL TSANG MANG KIN.

Terra Mauricia Ltd: 18 Edith Cavell St, POB 317, Port Louis; tel. 208-0808; fax 208-8798; e-mail harelfreres@harelfreres.com; internet terra.co.mu; f. 1960; multiple activities, incl. financial and beverage supplies; Pres. DANIEL NAIRAC; Man. Dir M.E. CYRIL MAYER.

United Basalt Products Ltd (UBP): Trianon, Quatre Bornes; tel. 454-1964; fax 454-8043; e-mail caroline.cure@ubpgroup.com; internet www.ubp.mu; f. 1953; mfrs of building materials; Chair. JACQUES LAGESSE; Gen. Man. JEAN-MICHEL GIRAUD; 720 employees.

TRADE UNIONS

Federations

Federation of Civil Service and Other Unions (FCSOU): Jade Court, Rm 308, 3rd Floor, 33 Jummah Mosque St, Port Louis; tel. 216-1977; fax 216-1475; e-mail f.c.s.u@intnet.mu; internet www.fcsu.org; f. 1957; 72 affiliated unions with 30,000 mems (2006); Pres. TOOLSYRAJ BENYDIN; Sec. (vacant).

General Workers' Federation: 7 Impasse Ruisseau des Creoles, Port Louis; tel. 213-1771; Pres. SERGE JAUFFRET; Sec.-Gen. DEVIANAND NARRAIN.

Mauritius Labour Congress (MLC): 8 Louis Victor de la Faye St, Port Louis; tel. 212-4343; fax 208-8945; e-mail mlcongress@intnet.mu; f. 1963; Pres. HANIFF PEERUN; Gen. Sec. BHOLANATH JEEWUTH.

Mauritius Trade Union Congress (MTUC): Emmanuel Anquetil Labour Centre, James Smith St, Port Louis; tel. 210-8567; f. 1946; Pres. DEWAN QUEDOU.

Principal Unions

Government Servants' Association: 107A Royal Rd, Beau Bassin; tel. 464-4242; fax 465-3220; e-mail gsa@intnet.mu; internet www.gsa.mauritius.org; f. 1945; Pres. RADHAKRISNA SADIEN; Sec.-Gen. POONIT RAMJUG.

Government Teachers' Union: 3 Mgr Gonin St, POB 1111, Port Louis; tel. 208-0047; fax 208-4943; f. 1945; Pres. JUGDUTH SEEGUM; Sec. MOHAMMAD SALEEM CHOOLUN; 4,550 mems (2005).

Nursing Association: 159 Royal Rd, Beau Bassin; tel. and fax 464-5850; e-mail nur.ass@intnet.mu; f. 1955; Pres. BAGOOADUTH KALLOOA; Sec.-Gen. RAM NOWZADICK.

Plantation Workers' Union: 8 Louis Victor de la Faye St, Port Louis; tel. 212-1735; f. 1955; Pres. SIV DABY; Sec. GOPAL BHUJAN.

Port Louis Harbour and Docks Workers' Union: Port Louis; tel. 208-2276; Pres. JOSÉ FRANÇOIS; Sec.-Gen. GERARD BERTRAND.

Union of Employees of the Ministry of Agriculture and other Ministries: 28 Hennessy Ave, Quatre-Bornes; tel. 465-1935; e-mail bruno5@intnet.mu; f. 1989; Sec. BRUNEAU DORASAMI; 2,500 mems (Dec. 2003).

Transport

RAILWAYS

There are no operational railways in Mauritius.

ROADS

In 2009 there were 2,028 km of paved roads, of which 75 km were motorways, 950 km were other main roads, and 592 km were secondary roads. An urban highway links the motorways approaching Port Louis. A motorway connects Port Louis with Plaisance airport.

National Transport Corpn: Bonne Terre Vacoas; tel. 426-2938; fax 426-5489; e-mail cnt.bus@intnet.mu; internet ntc.intnet.mu; Chair. CHETAN RAMBANS DOOKUN; Gen. Man. PRADEEP KUMAR DASH.

SHIPPING

Mauritius is served by numerous foreign shipping lines. In 1990 Port Louis was established as a free port to expedite the development of Mauritius as an entrepôt centre. At 31 December 2009 Mauritius had a merchant fleet of 50 vessels, with a combined displacement of 66,200 grt.

Mauritius Ports Authority: H. Ramnarain Bldg, Mer Rouge, Port Louis; tel. 206-5400; fax 240-0856; e-mail info@mauport.com; internet www.mauport.com; f. 1976; Chair. MAURICE ALLET; Dir-Gen. SHEKUR SUNTAH.

Ireland Blyth Ltd: IBL House, Caudan, Port Louis; tel. 203-2000; fax 203-2001; e-mail iblinfo@iblgroup.com; internet www.iblgroup.com; Chair. THIERRY LAGESSE; CEO NICOLAS MAIGROT.

Mauritius Freeport Development Co Ltd: Freeport Zone 5, Mer Rouge, Port Louis; tel. 206-2000; fax 206-2025; e-mail info@mfd.mu; internet www.mfd.mu; f. 1997; manages and operates Freeport Zone 5, more than 40,000 sq m of storage facility; facilities include dry warehouses, cold warehouses, processing and transformation units, open storage container parks and a container freight station; largest logistics centre in the Indian Ocean region; Chair. RENÉ LECLÉZIO; CEO DOMINIQUE DE FROBERVILLE.

Mauritius Shipping Corpn Ltd: St James Court, Suite 417/418, St Denis St, Port Louis; tel. 208-5900; fax 210-5176; internet www.mauritiusshipping.mu; f. 1985; state-owned; operates two passenger-cargo vessels between Mauritius, Rodrigues, Réunion and Madagascar; Man. Dir Capt. J. PATRICK RAULT.

CIVIL AVIATION

Sir Seewoosagur Ramgoolam International Airport is at Plaisance, 4 km from Mahébourg. From 2006 air routes with France and the United Kingdom were liberalized, allowing new carriers to operate on the routes.

Civil Aviation Department: Sir Seewoosagur Ramgoolam International Airport, Plaine Magnien; tel. 603-2000; fax 637-3164; e-mail civil-aviation@mail.gov.mu; internet civil-aviation.gov.mu; overseen by the Prime Minister's Office (External Communications Division); Dir ANAND GUNGAH.

Air Mauritius: Air Mauritius Centre, John F. Kennedy St, POB 441, Port Louis; tel. 207-7070; fax 208-8331; e-mail contact@airmauritius.com; internet www.airmauritius.com; f. 1967; 51% state-owned; services to 22 destinations in Europe, Asia, Australia and Africa; Chair. APPALSAMY THOMAS; CEO ANDRÉ VILJOEN.

Tourism

Tourists are attracted to Mauritius by its scenery and beaches, the pleasant climate and the blend of cultures. Accommodation capacity totalled 21,072 beds in 2005. The number of visitors increased from 300,670 in 1990 to 964,642 in 2011, when the greatest numbers of visitors were from France (31.3%), Réunion (11.7%) and the United Kingdom (9.1%). Gross revenue from tourism in 2010 was estimated at MRs 39,456m. The Government sought to increase the volume of tourists visiting the country (to some 2m. people by 2015) by improving the jetty facilities in the port in order to welcome cruise ships and by liberalizing air transit routes.

Mauritius Tourism Promotion Authority: Victoria House, 4th and 5th Floor, St Louis St, Port Louis; tel. 210-1545; fax 212-5142; e-mail mtpa@intnet.mu; internet www.tourism-mauritius.mu; f. 1996; Chair. ROBERT DESVAUX; Man. Dir KARL MOOTOOSAMY.

Tourism Authority (TA): Victoria House, 1st and 2nd Floor, St Louis St, Port Louis; tel. 213-1740; fax 213-1738; e-mail contact@tourismauthority.mu; internet www.tourismauthority.mu; f. 2003; parastatal; responsible for licensing, regulating and supervising the activities of tourist enterprises; Dir NIVEN MUNEESAMY.

Defence

The country has no standing defence forces, although as assessed at November 2011 paramilitary forces were estimated to number 2,000, comprising a special 1,500-strong mobile police unit, to ensure internal security, and a coast-guard of 500.

Defence Expenditure: Budgeted at Rs 310m. in 2012.

Education

Education is officially compulsory and free of charge for 11 years between the ages of five and 16. Primary education begins at five years of age and lasts for six years. Secondary education, beginning at the age of 11, lasts for up to seven years, comprising a first cycle of five years and a second of two years. At March 2005 up to 77% of pre-primary schools were privately run institutions. Primary and secondary education are available free of charge and became compulsory in 2005. According to UNESCO estimates, in 2009/10 enrolment at primary schools included 93% of pupils in the relevant age-group (males 92%; females 94%), while the comparable ratio for secondary schools in 2003/04 was 74% (males 74%; females 74%). The education system provides for instruction in seven Asian languages (71% of primary school children and 30% of secondary school children were studying at least one of these in 2005). The Government exercises indirect control of the large private sector in secondary education (in 2005 only 70 of 188 schools were state administered). The University of Mauritius had 7,531 students in 2006/07 (34.3% of whom were part-time students); in addition, many students receive further education abroad. A total of 7,270 students were enrolled in technical and vocational education in 2011. Of total expenditure by the central Government in 2007/08, Rs 6,973.8m. (11.7%) was for education.

Other Islands

RODRIGUES

The island of Rodrigues covers an area of 104 sq km. Its population, which was enumerated at 35,779 at the 2000 census, was officially estimated to number 38,039 at December 2011. Formerly also known as Diego Ruys, Rodrigues is located 585 km east of the island of Mauritius, and is administered by a resident commissioner. Rodrigues is currently represented in the National Assembly by two members. In 2001 a constitutional amendment provided for the establishment of the Rodrigues Regional Assembly (RRA). Elections to the RRA were held in February 2012 at which the Organisation du Peuple Rodriguais secured 11 of the Assembly's 21 seats, while the Mouvement Rodriguais took eight and the Front Patriotique Rodriguais two seats. Fishing and farming are the principal activities, while the main exports are cattle, salt fish, sheep, goats, pigs and onions. The island is linked to Mauritius by thrice-weekly air and monthly boat services.

Rodrigues Regional Assembly: Passenger Terminal Bldg, Fisherman Lane; tel. 831-0686; internet rra.gov.mu; Chair. JOSEPH CHENLYE LAMVOHEE; Chief Commissioner JOHNSON ROUSSETY.

THE LESSER DEPENDENCIES

The Lesser Dependencies (area 71 sq km, population enumerated at 289 in December 2011) are the Agalega Islands, two islands about 935 km north of Mauritius, and the Cargados Carajos Shoals (St Brandon Islands), 22 islets without permanent inhabitants, lying 370 km north-north-east. Mauritius also claims sovereignty over Tromelin Island, 556 km to the north-west. This claim is disputed by Madagascar, and also by France, which maintains an airstrip and weather station on the island.

Bibliography

Addison, J., and Hazareesingh, K. *A New History of Mauritius*. Oxford, ABC; Rose Hill, Editions de l'Océan Indien, 1991.

Benedict, B. *Indians in a Plural Society: A Report on Mauritius*. London, HMSO, 1961.

Bissoonoyal, B. *A Concise History of Mauritius*. Bombay, Bharatiya Vidya, 1963.

Bowman, L. W. *Mauritius: Democracy and Development in the Indian Ocean*. Boulder, CO, Westview Press, 1991.

Cohen, R. *African Islands and Enclaves*. London, Sage Publications, 1983.

Dukhira, C. D. *Mauritius and Local Government Management*. Oxford, ABC; Port Louis, Editions de l'Océan Indien; Bombay, LSG Press, 1992.

Favoreu, L. *L'Île Maurice*. Paris, Berger-Levrault, 1970.

Frankel, J. A. *Mauritius: African Success Story*. National Bureau of Economic Research Working Paper No. 16569, December 2010.

Imam, P. A. and Kohler, R. *Balance Sheet Vulnerabilities of Mauritius During a Decade of Shocks*. IMF Working Paper No. 10/148, June 2010.

Ingrams, W. H. *A Short History of Mauritius*. London, Macmillan, 1931.

Jones, P., and Andrews, B. *A Taste of Mauritius*. London, Macmillan, 1982.

Mahadeo, T. *Mauritian Cultural Heritage*. Port Louis, Editions de l'Océan Indien, 1995.

Prayag, G, Dookhony-Ramphul, K., and Maryeven, M. 'Hotel Development and Tourism Impacts in Mauritius: Hoteliers' Perspectives on Sustainable Tourism' in *Development Southern Africa*, Vol. 27, Issue 5, 2010.

Ramgoolam, Sir S. *Our Struggle: 20th Century Mauritius*. New Delhi, Vision Books, 1982.

Selvon, S. *Historical Dictionary of Mauritius*. 2nd edn. Metuchen, NJ, Scarecrow Press, 1991.

Titmuss, R. M., and Abel-Smith, B. *Social Policies and Population Growth in Mauritius*. Sessional Paper No. 6, 1960. London, Methuen, reprinted by Frank Cass, 1968.

Toussaint, A. *Port Louis, deux siècles d'histoire (1735–1935)*. Port Louis, 1946.

Wright, C. *Mauritius*. Newton Abbot, David and Charles, 1974.

MOZAMBIQUE

Physical and Social Geography

RENÉ PÉLISSIER

The Republic of Mozambique covers a total area of 799,380 sq km (308,641 sq miles). This includes 13,000 sq km of inland water, mainly comprising Lake Niassa, the Mozambican section of Lake Malawi. Mozambique is bounded to the north by Tanzania, to the west by Malawi, Zambia and Zimbabwe, and to the south by South Africa and Swaziland.

With some exceptions towards the Zambia, Malawi and Zimbabwe borders, Mozambique is generally a low-lying plateau of moderate height, descending through a sub-plateau zone to the Indian Ocean. The main reliefs are Monte Binga (2,436 m above sea-level), the highest point of Mozambique, on the Zimbabwe border in Manica province, Monte Namúli (2,419 m) in Zambézia province, the Serra Zuira (2,227 m) in Manica province and several massifs that are a continuation into northern Mozambique of the Shire highlands of Malawi. The coastal lowland is narrower in the north but widens considerably towards the south, so that terrain less than 1,000 m high comprises about 45% of the total Mozambican area. The shore-line is 2,470 km long and generally sandy and bordered by lagoons, shoals and strings of coastal islets in the north.

Mozambique is divided by at least 25 main rivers, all of which flow to the Indian Ocean. The largest and most historically significant is the Zambezi, whose 820-km Mozambican section is navigable for 460 km. Flowing from eastern Angola, the Zambezi provides access to the interior of Africa from the eastern coast.

Two main seasons, wet and dry, divide the climatic year. The wet season has monthly averages of 26.7°C–29.4°C, with cooler temperatures in the interior uplands. The dry season has June and July temperatures of 18.3°C–20.0°C at Maputo. Mozambique is vulnerable to drought and attendant famine, which severely affected much of the country during the 1980s, particularly during the period 1982–84 and again during 1986–87. In 2000 serious flooding affected the centre and south of Mozambique, displacing an estimated 500,000 people and causing severe damage to the country's infrastructure.

The population totalled 20,226,296, according to the results of the 1 August 2007 census, giving a density of 25.3 inhabitants per sq km. The UN estimated the population at 24,475,184 in mid-2012 (30.6 inhabitants per sq km). Mozambique's population increased at an average annual rate of 2.5% during 2001–10, according to World Bank figures.

North of the Zambezi, the main ethnic groupings among the African population, which belongs to the cultural division of Central Bantu, are the Makua-Lomwe groups, who form the principal ethno-linguistic subdivision of Mozambique and are believed to comprise about 40% of the population. South of the Zambezi, the main group is the Thonga, who feature prominently as Mozambican mine labourers in South Africa. North of the Thonga area lies the Shona group, numbering more than 1m. Southern ethnic groups have tended to enjoy greater educational opportunities than those of other regions. The Government has sought to balance the ethnic composition of its leadership, but the executive is still largely of southern and central origin.

Mozambique is divided into 11 administrative provinces, one of which comprises the capital, Maputo, a modern seaport whose population was estimated at 1,099,102 at the census of 2007. The second seaport of the country is Beira. Other towns of importance include Nampula, on the railway line to Niassa province and Malawi, and Matola. By mid-2011, according to UN figures, the population of Maputo had increased to an estimated 1,150,030.

Recent History

ANA NAOMI DE SOUSA

Based on an earlier article by EDWARD GEORGE

The territory now comprising the Republic of Mozambique came under Portuguese control in the 19th century and became a Portuguese 'overseas province' in 1951. Nationalist groups began to form in the early 1960s, eventually uniting in the Frente de Libertação de Moçambique (Frelimo), under the leadership of Eduardo Mondlane, in 1962. In 1964 Frelimo launched a military campaign for independence that subsequently developed into a serious conflict, engaging thousands of Portuguese troops by the early 1970s. Following the assassination of Mondlane in 1969, Samora Machel was elected leader. After the military coup in Portugal in April 1974, the Portuguese authorities agreed to hand over power to a transitional Frelimo-dominated Government, and full independence followed on 25 June 1975, when the People's Republic of Mozambique was declared, with Machel as its President.

The new Frelimo Government implemented a centrally planned economy and one-party state, and in 1977 Frelimo declared itself to be a 'Marxist-Leninist vanguard party'. Despite impressive advances in the fields of public health, social welfare and education, Frelimo's policy of *socialização do campo* (socialization of the countryside) succeeded in antagonizing most of the country's peasantry (which accounted for 80% of the population); collective agriculture was promoted, traditional beliefs and ceremonies were prohibited, *regulos* (tribal kings) were stripped of their powers, and church-run social projects were closed.

CIVIL WAR AND CONFLICT WITH SOUTH AFRICA

In its foreign policy, Frelimo embraced international activism during the late 1970s, implementing sanctions against the white regime in Rhodesia (now Zimbabwe) by cutting off its main transport route via the Mozambican port of Beira. It also allowed Robert Mugabe's Zimbabwe African National Union (ZANU) forces to set up bases on its territory and mount cross-border raids. The Rhodesian authorities responded by arming and providing support to the dissident Movimento Nacional de Resistência de Moçambique (MNR).

After 1980, following the emergence of an independent Zimbabwe, South Africa became the MNR's main supporter; the MNR, now renamed Resistência Nacional Moçambicana (Renamo), rapidly expanded from some 500 to a force of an estimated 8,000 guerrillas. Renamo concentrated its attacks on the symbols of Frelimo achievements, such as schools, health centres, social projects and transport infrastructure, and acquired a reputation for brutality, including mass murders of civilians as well as mutilations.

The high economic cost of the conflict with Renamo prompted Mozambique to enter into discussions with the South African Government in late 1983. Negotiations culminated in the Nkomati Accord, a non-aggression treaty signed in 1984, in which both sides bound themselves not to give material aid to opposition movements in each other's countries, and to establish a joint security commission. Effectively, this meant that Mozambique would prevent the African National Congress of South Africa (ANC) from conducting military operations from its territory, while South Africa would cease to support Renamo. However, the South African Government effectively ignored the Accord, and by August 1984 Renamo forces were active in all of Mozambique's provinces, with the capital increasingly under threat.

The escalating internal conflict led the Frelimo Government to warn South Africa in August 1984 that the Accord was under threat unless Renamo activity was halted. South Africa responded by convening a number of separate but parallel talks with Renamo and Frelimo government representatives, which culminated, in October, in the so-called 'Pretoria Declaration' in which a cease-fire was agreed in principle between the Frelimo Government and the rebels, and a tripartite commission, comprising Frelimo, Renamo and South African representatives, was established to implement the truce. In November, however, Renamo withdrew from the peace negotiation. In April 1985 a joint operational centre dealing with security and other matters relating to the Nkomati Accord was also established on the border between Mozambique and South Africa. However, in the same month, Renamo guerrilla activity effectively severed rail links between the two countries.

The worsening security situation precipitated a meeting in June 1985 in Harare, Zimbabwe, between President Machel, the Prime Minister of Zimbabwe, Robert Mugabe, and President Julius Nyerere of Tanzania, at which it was agreed that Tanzania and Zimbabwe would support Mozambique, and, in particular, that Zimbabwe would augment its military presence in Mozambique. This arrangement resulted in the capture, in August, of the largest Renamo base, the so-called 'Casa Banana' in Sofala province, and of other major rebel bases in the area. Not only were large quantities of weapons captured, but also incriminating documentation concerning South African support for Renamo since the signing of the Nkomati Accord, although the South African Government claimed that its continued contacts with Renamo were designed to promote peace negotiations between the guerrillas and the Frelimo Government. In October Mozambique unilaterally suspended the joint security commission.

In October 1986 a Soviet Tupolev aircraft carrying Machel, on his return from a meeting in Zambia of leaders of the 'front-line' states, crashed just inside South African territory, killing the President and 33 others. Machel was succeeded as President by Joaquim Chissano, the Minister of Foreign Affairs. Controversy has continued to surround the causes of the crash, especially over the strong possibility of South African involvement. In January 1987 a joint report, compiled by Mozambican, Soviet and South African experts, concluded that pilot error, and not sabotage, had caused the accident. In October 2008 a former member of South Africa's special services alleged that he had been part of a covert operation to divert the aircraft off course and cause it to crash. However, there has been little progress with the investigation, as the plot to bring down Machel's aircraft was believed to have involved members of Frelimo and the Mozambican armed forces who were opposed to his rule.

In February 1987 Zimbabwean and Mozambican troops recaptured five towns in northern Mozambique that Renamo had seized in late 1986. This signified a general shift in the balance of power, with Renamo increasing its operations in the south, while government troops registered important successes in the north and along the coastline. Following the death of Machel, Mozambique had applied intense pressure on Malawi, including threats of military action, to induce its neighbour to cease accommodating Renamo, and in December 1987 a joint security agreement was signed between the two states.

An open raid in May 1987 by South African security forces on alleged ANC bases in metropolitan Maputo effectively signalled the demise of the Nkomati Accord. In December President Chissano announced a 'law of pardon', offering to release on parole or shorten the sentences of repentant convicted prisoners; he also offered amnesty for members of Renamo willing to surrender their weapons.

POLITICAL LIBERALIZATION

Fundamental changes in Frelimo's political and economic philosophy began to emerge in 1987, when an economic recovery programme, the Programa de Reabilitação Econômica (PRE), was launched; it included wide-ranging policy reforms designed to move the country away from socialist central planning towards a free-market economy (see Economy). In 1989 the party renounced its Marxist-Leninist orientation, embracing social democracy and opening its membership to all. In January 1990 draft proposals for a new constitution were published, providing for the direct election of the President and Assembléia Popular by universal suffrage. The draft constitution, which was submitted to public debate during 1990, provided for the separation of Frelimo and the state and the independence of the judiciary. The process of political change was further advanced in August, when Frelimo announced that the country's name was to be changed from the People's Republic of Mozambique to the Republic of Mozambique.

The new Constitution was formally approved by the Assembléia Popular (renamed Assembléia da República) in November 1990. Provisions outlawing censorship and enshrining freedom of expression had been added, and the death penalty was abolished. The new Constitution was welcomed by Western aid donors but rejected by Renamo as the product of an unrepresentative, unelected body. One of the first acts of the new legislature, in December, was to approve legislation allowing the formation of new political parties.

After President Chissano had announced in March 1991 that a general election would be held in 1992, new political parties continued to organize. In March 1993 the Government published a draft electoral law proposing the establishment of a 21-member national electoral commission, chaired by a member of the Supreme Court, to organize and supervise the elections.

PEACE INITIATIVES

In June 1989 the Government launched a peace initiative, which demanded the cessation of acts of terrorism, guaranteed the right of political participation to all 'individuals' who renounced violence, recognized the principle that no group should impose its will on another by force and demanded that all parties respect the legitimacy of the state and of the Constitution. In mid-1989 Presidents Daniel arap Moi of Kenya and Robert Mugabe of Zimbabwe agreed to mediate between Renamo and the Mozambique Government. Renamo rejected the plan, demanding its recognition as a political entity, the introduction of multi-party elections and the withdrawal of Zimbabwean troops from Mozambique. However, in July 1990 the first direct talks between the two sides were held in Rome, Italy. The talks culminated in the signing on 1 December of a partial cease-fire agreement, which provided for the withdrawal of Zimbabwean forces to within 3 km of the Beira and Limpopo transport 'corridors'. In exchange, Renamo agreed to cease hostilities and refrain from attacking the 'corridors'. The withdrawal of Zimbabwean troops to the 'corridors' was completed by the end of December.

Although attacks by Renamo resumed in the early months of 1991, peace talks nevertheless continued in Rome, and in October the two sides signed a protocol that was said to represent a recognition by Renamo of the Government's legitimacy. The establishment of a commission to oversee the eventual cease-fire was also agreed. In the following month it was agreed that Renamo would function as a political party immediately after a cease-fire. In mid-January 1992 Mugabe and President Hastings Kamuzu Banda of Malawi held direct discussions with the Renamo leader, Afonso Dhlakama, in Malawi, in an effort to expedite the peace talks. In March a protocol was signed in Rome, establishing the principles for the country's future electoral system. The protocol provided for a system of proportional representation for the legislature, with legislative and presidential elections to take place simultaneously within one year of the signing of a cease-fire. A national electoral commission was to be established to oversee the elections, with one-third of its members appointed by Renamo. The protocol also guaranteed freedom of the press and media as well as of association, expression and movement.

In early August 1992 Chissano and Dhlakama signed a joint declaration in Rome, committing the two sides to a total cease-fire by 1 October, as part of a general peace agreement that would provide for presidential and legislative elections within one year. The two leaders agreed to guarantee the political rights and freedoms and personal security of all Mozambican citizens and political parties, and to accept the role of the international community, particularly the UN, in monitoring the peace agreement.

THE PEACE AGREEMENT

The peace agreement, the Acordo Geral de Paz (AGP), was eventually signed on 4 October 1992. It provided for a general cease-fire to come into force immediately after ratification of the treaty by the Assembléia da República. Both Renamo and government forces were to withdraw to assembly points within seven days of ratification. A new 30,000-strong national defence force, the Forças Armadas de Defesa de Moçambique (FADM), would then be created, drawing on equal numbers from each side, with the remaining troops surrendering their weapons to a UN peace-keeping force within six months. A cease-fire commission, incorporating representatives from the Government, Renamo and the UN, would be established to assume responsibility for supervising the implementation of the truce regulations. In overall political control of the peace process would be the Comissão de Supervisão e Controle (CSC—Supervision and Control Commission), comprising representatives of the Government, Renamo and the UN, with responsibilities including the supervision of the Cease-fire Commission and other commissions charged with establishing the joint armed forces and reintegrating demobilized soldiers into society, as well as verifying the withdrawal of foreign troops from Mozambique. Presidential and legislative elections were to take place, under UN supervision, one year after the signing of the AGP, provided that it had been fully implemented and the demobilization process completed.

In October 1992 the UN Security Council agreed to appoint a special representative for Mozambique, and to dispatch 25 military observers. In December the UN Security Council approved a plan for the establishment of the UN Operation in Mozambique (ONUMOZ), providing for the deployment of some 7,500 troops, police and civilian observers to oversee the process of demobilization and formation of the new national armed forces, and to supervise the forthcoming elections. There were continued delays in the deployment of the peace-keeping force. Renamo, in turn, refused to begin demobilizing its forces until the UN force was in place and withdrew from the CSC and the Cease-fire Commission in March 1993. The first UN troops became operational in the Beira corridor on 1 April, prompting the withdrawal of the Zimbabwean troops guarding the Beira and Limpopo corridors.

Renamo, however, continued to use demands for finance to delay the demobilization process, claiming, in late May 1993, that it needed US $100m. from the international community to transform itself into a political party. In June a meeting in Maputo of the CSC announced a formal postponement of the election date to October 1994 (one year behind the original schedule) and appealed for immediate action on establishing assembly points and commencing the formation of the new national armed forces. The CSC meeting was followed by a meeting of aid donors, which revealed growing impatience among the international community with the repeated delays in implementing the peace agreement and with Renamo's escalating demands for funds. The meeting produced additional promises of support for the peace process, bringing the total pledged by donors to $520m., including support for the repatriation of 1.5m. refugees from neighbouring countries, the resettlement of 4m.–5m. displaced people and the re-integration of some 80,000 former combatants into civilian life, as well as for emergency relief and reconstruction. The UN also agreed to establish a trust fund of $10m. to finance Renamo's transformation into a political party.

In addition, an agreement was signed at a meeting of the CSC in November 1993, which provided for the confinement of troops to begin at the end of that month. In March 1994, in an effort to expedite the confinement process, the Government announced its decision to begin the unilateral demobilization of its troops. Renamo responded by beginning the demobilization of its troops. In April the high command of the FADM was inaugurated. The demobilization processes continued to make slow progress, however, and the deadline for troop confinement was continuously extended. On 16 August, in accordance with the provisions of the AGP, the government Forças Armadas de Moçambique were formally dissolved and their functions transferred to the FADM.

THE 1994 ELECTIONS

In October 1993 the CSC approved a new timetable covering all aspects of the peace process, including the elections in October 1994, and in November consensus was finally reached on the text of the electoral law. The Comissão Nacional de Eleicões (CNE—National Elections Commission) was inaugurated in early February 1994. In August Renamo formally registered as a political party. In the same month three other opposition parties formed an electoral coalition, the União Democrática (UD).

Presidential and legislative elections were held on 27–28 October 1994. Hours before the beginning of the poll Renamo withdrew, claiming that conditions were not conducive to free and fair elections. Following intense international pressure, Renamo abandoned its boycott in the early hours of 28 October, necessitating the extension of the voting by a day. In the presidential election, Chissano secured an outright majority (53.3%) of the votes, thus avoiding the need for a second round of voting. His closest rival was Dhlakama, who received 33.7% of the votes. In the legislative election, Frelimo also secured an overall majority, winning 129 of the 250 seats, while Renamo obtained 112 and the UD the remaining nine seats. The level of participation by the electorate was considerable, with some 80% of all registered voters exercising their right to vote. The UN recognized the occurrence of irregularities, but asserted that these were insufficient to have affected the overall credibility of the poll, which it declared to have been free and fair. Chissano was inaugurated as President on 9 December, and the new Government was sworn in on 23 December; all the portfolios were assigned to members of Frelimo.

In December 1994 the Cease-fire Commission issued its final report, according to which ONUMOZ had registered a combined total of 91,691 government and Renamo troops during the confinement process, of whom 11,579 had enlisted in the FADM (compared with the 30,000 envisaged in the AGP). In practice, demobilization had continued until 15 September, with special cases still being processed the day before the elections. Furthermore, an estimated 3m. internally displaced Mozambicans had been successfully resettled since the signing of the AGP, according to the office of the United Nations High Commissioner for Refugees (UNHCR). In May 1995 UNHCR also reported that a total of 1.7m. refugees had returned to Mozambique from six southern African countries. Expenditure on the repatriation process then totalled some US $152m. In November the process was reported to have been completed.

In February 1996 the Government proposed that municipal elections, which the Constitution stipulated must be conducted no later than October 1996, be held in 1997. Delays had resulted from a dispute between the Government and the opposition regarding the scope of the elections: the opposition demanded simultaneous local elections throughout Mozambique, while the Government sought to hold elections only in those areas that had attained municipal status, which would have excluded almost 60% of the population. In October 1996 the Assembleia da República approved a constitutional amendment differentiating between municipalities (including 23 cities and 116 other district capitals) and administrative posts (numbering 394). Each of these units would have its own elected council and mayor.

In April 1998 Renamo and 15 other opposition parties officially announced their withdrawal from the elections, which had been repeatedly postponed, and Renamo subsequently began a vigorous campaign to dissuade the electorate from voting. In the event, very few opposition parties contested the elections, which took place on 30 June, and Frelimo's main opposition came from independent candidates. Frelimo secured all the mayoral posts and took control of all the municipal authorities contested. However, the rate of voter participation was just 14.6%.

In October 1998 the Government published draft constitutional amendments that envisaged substantial changes to the country's political system, including a reduction in presidential powers and a concomitant increase in those of the Prime Minister, as well as the separation of the jurisdictions of central government and local administration. The amendments would confer the status of Head of Government on the Prime Minister, transferring this from the President—who would remain Head of State. The President would no longer be able to appoint the Prime Minister without first consulting the Assembleia da República, and would dismiss and appoint ministers only on the proposal of the Prime Minister. In addition, a Council of State would be formed as a consultative body to advise the President. The underlying aim of the proposed changes was to make provision for a situation in which a President and government could be drawn from different parties.

THE 1999 ELECTIONS

Under the Constitution, the five-year term of the President and the Assembleia da República was to end in November 1999. However, political disputes and administrative delays made it increasingly unlikely that elections would be held in that year. The delay was caused by Renamo's insistence on the need to re-register the entire electorate and by the late appointment of the CNE. In May the Government announced that voter registration would take place between July and September, thus allowing for elections to take place in November, but Renamo protested that a longer period would be necessary in order to ensure that the majority of the population would be able to register in time. In June Frelimo announced that Chissano would stand as its presidential candidate. In the following month 11 opposition parties, led by Renamo, signed an agreement to contest the forthcoming elections as a coalition, styled Renamo—União Eleitoral (Renamo—UE), presenting a single list of legislative candidates, with Dhlakama as its presidential candidate.

Presidential and legislative elections took place on 3–5 December 1999. In the presidential contest, Chissano defeated Dhlakama (his sole challenger), taking 52.3% of the valid votes cast. Frelimo increased its outright majority in the legislative elections, winning 133 of the 250 seats in the Assembleia da República; Renamo—UE obtained the remaining seats. On 15 January 2000 Chissano was sworn in for a further five-year presidential term and subsequently effected a substantial reorganization of the Council of Ministers. However, Renamo disputed the legitimacy of the newly elected Government.

In May 2000 an attack on a police station in the northern province of Nampula, in which five people were killed, was believed to have been carried out by members of Renamo. At the same time, Dhlakama threatened to regroup demobilized Renamo soldiers and seize control of the country. Tensions worsened in November, when more than 100 people died in riots in the northern parts of the country. While 41 people were killed in the riots themselves, more than 83 died after being arrested and detained in an overcrowded gaol in Montepuez, Cabo Delgado. A parliamentary inquiry, dominated by Frelimo, eventually blamed Renamo for the riots. In January 2002 several Renamo members were found guilty of armed rebellion, but the human rights organization Amnesty International criticized the judicial process for lacking transparency.

The riots brought an abrupt end to the negotiations that had been taking place between Chissano and Renamo since June 2000. Renamo had announced in July that it was to boycott the election of the new CNE, while denouncing the appointment of new provincial governors, all of whom were Frelimo appointees, on the grounds that it did not recognize the Government's legitimacy. In late December Dhlakama and Chissano held talks in an attempt to resolve the growing political tension between their two parties. Dhlakama stated that he was prepared to accept the results of the 1999 elections, and Chissano pledged to discuss the appointment of Renamo governors in the provinces where the latter had won a majority of the votes. Negotiations resumed in January 2001. However, Chissano rejected Dhlakama's demands for an early election and the appointment of Renamo governors. Moreover, at another meeting in March Chissano referred the latter issue to the Assembleia da República, the Frelimo representatives of which were strongly opposed to accommodating Renamo demands. Consequently, in protest, Dhlakama ceased negotiations in April.

At the Renamo party congress, held in October–November 2001, Dhlakama was re-elected as party President, while the party's representative in Portugal, Joaquim Vaz, was elected as the new Secretary-General. However, in July 2002 Dhlakama announced the dismissal of Vaz and the dissolution of the party's national political commission, assuming the position of Secretary-General himself. At the eighth congress of Frelimo, held in mid-June 2002, Armando Guebuza was elected as Frelimo's new Secretary-General, thereby becoming Frelimo's presidential candidate for the 2004 election.

On 19 November 2003, following a postponement of one month owing to administrative and logistical delays, municipal elections were held in 33 of Mozambique's cities and towns. The governing party, Frelimo, was the outright victor, winning a majority of 29 of the 33 municipal councils, and the mayorship in 28 municipalities. Renamo, which had boycotted Mozambique's first municipal elections in 1998, gained control of five urban centres, including the third largest city, Beira, but failed to win a majority on the councils located in its northern and central heartlands.

In February 2004 Pascoal Mocumbi, who had been Prime Minister since 1994, resigned his post to take up an international appointment. In his place, Luísa Dias Diogo was appointed as Mozambique's first female Prime Minister, combining the role with her existing finance portfolio.

THE 2004 ELECTIONS

The legislative and presidential elections, which were held on 1–2 December 2004, were the most controversial since multiparty democracy was established in 1994, and Frelimo was accused of widespread electoral fraud. Voter turn-out was a record low of 36.3%, reflecting disillusionment with and apathy towards the political system among the population. The results, which were announced on 21 December 2004 by the CNE, handed Frelimo a decisive victory, and were in sharp contrast to the closely fought 1999 elections. Guebuza won 63.7% of the votes in the presidential election and Frelimo took 62.0% in the parliamentary election, while Renamo managed just 29.7% of the votes in the parliamentary election, and Dhlakama secured 31.7% of the presidential votes. The smaller parties failed to reach the threshold of 5% of votes and did not gain any seats in the Assembleia da República. Although international observers subsequently endorsed the election results as 'generally free', there were widespread accusations of irregularities, fraud and intimidation of opposition parties during the elections, and both the European Union and the US Carter Center expressed concerns over the results.

Despite the controversy, on 17 January 2005 the Constitutional Council validated the results, and on 2 February Armando Guebuza was sworn in as Mozambique's new President in a ceremony that was boycotted by Renamo. On the same day Joaquim Chissano formally stood down as President after 18 years in power, and one month later he also relinquished his role as President of Frelimo.

THE GUEBUZA PRESIDENCY

Following his inauguration in February 2005, Guebuza announced a new Council of Ministers, replacing 18 of the 22 members of the previous Government. Diogo retained the post of Prime Minister, but relinquished the role as Minister of

Finance to her deputy, Manuel Chang. Other new appointments included Alcinda Abreu as the Minister of Foreign Affairs and Co-operation and José Pacheco as Minister of the Interior. Guebuza identified as the priorities of his presidency an overhaul of the justice system and a campaign against corruption in the police force. He also pledged that his Government would focus strongly on measures to reduce poverty.

In May 2005 controversy over the transparency of the electoral process was reignited when Frelimo's candidate in the mayoral by-election for the northern city of Mocímboa da Praia, Amadeu Pedro, defeated his Renamo rival, Saide Assane, by only 602 votes. An investigation by the CNE revealed an unusually high proportion of invalid votes, which Renamo claimed was the decisive factor in Pedro's victory. However, the CNE subsequently validated the poll, precipitating protests in Mocímboa da Praia in September, and prompting Assane to hold a mock swearing-in ceremony in the city centre, which was dispersed by the security forces. In ensuing clashes, at least eight Renamo supporters were killed and 47 others were injured, after which the army intervened to restore order. In an effort to restore faith in the electoral process, Frelimo proposed amending the system for appointing members to the CNE, reducing the allocation of political parties to the body to one-third, with the remaining two-thirds to be split between appointees from the Government, the judiciary and civil society. However, given Frelimo's strong influence in the Government and over the judiciary, the changes were not expected to have any significant effect.

On 23 December 2005 President Guebuza swore into office the Council of State, a consultative body the creation of which had been authorized by the Assembleia da República in November. Meanwhile, Dhlakama's announcement that he would seek re-election at the Renamo party congress in November provoked disappointment among reformist elements in the party.

In June 2006 Frelimo announced that it would hold its ninth party congress in Quelimane, the capital of Zambézia province, from 10–14 November, with the goal of electing a new central committee and debating the party's political strategy for the forthcoming provincial, municipal and national elections. In late September Frelimo held district conferences to elect delegates who would attend the congress. Angered by Frelimo's choice to hold its congress in Quelimane, as the area was a Renamo stronghold, Renamo announced that it would hold a special conference of war veterans in Quelimane shortly before Frelimo's congress. In November Frelimo's party congress went ahead as planned in Quelimane, unanimously re-electing Guebuza as President and further consolidating his control over the party. Guebuza did, however, cede the party's secretary-generalship to the Governor of Nampula province, Filipe Paúnde. The congress also elected a new and enlarged political commission, which included five new members, notably the Minister of Development and Planning, Aiuba Cuereneia, and the Minister of Education and Culture, Aires Bonifácio Ali. A new central committee, which was expanded from 160 to 180 members, was also elected.

In late November 2006 the Assembleia da República adopted legislation creating directly elected provincial assemblies, a demand that had been pursued by Renamo since negotiations on constitutional changes started in 2004. The new law established 10 provincial assemblies, each with a minimum of 50 elected members, which were to have responsibility for approving and monitoring provincial governments' official programmes. In December 2006 the Assembleia da República approved three revised electoral laws: on the composition of the CNE, voter registration and electoral procedures. The new legislation reduced the CNE's membership from 18 to 13 members, five of whom were to be parliamentary deputies, with the remaining eight coming from civil society, subject to approval by the legislature. A key change in the electoral code was the removal of the 5% threshold required for parties to win seats in the Assembleia; this was expected to benefit the many small parties that had failed to gain seats in previous elections.

In February 2007 the Chinese President, Hu Jintao, made his first official visit to Mozambique as part of a 10-day tour of Africa. The visit followed Guebuza's attendance at the Forum on China-Africa Co-operation in Beijing in November 2006, during which several co-operation agreements were signed. During Hu's visit new agreements worth US $234m. were signed, including a $20m. debt cancellation arrangement, a $40m. loan for infrastructure development, and a $195m. interest-free loan for projects in the agriculture, health and education sectors. In late February 2007 Guebuza dismissed the Minister of Agriculture, Tomás Mandlate, and replaced him with Erasmo Muhate, the former head of Mozambique's cotton institute, the Instituto de Algodão de Moçambique.

After months of bitter wrangling between Frelimo and Renamo, in mid-March 2007 the Assembleia da República approved legislation relating to the election of provincial assemblies. Subsequently, legislation was also adopted governing municipal elections, which were due to be held in 2008. The main change to the code was the provision that voters could still vote if they lost their voting card, provided that their name appeared on the register and that they produced photographic identification.

In March 2007 the suburb of Malhazine in the capital was severely damaged by a series of explosions at a military arsenal. At least 119 people were killed and more than 500 treated for injuries, while over 1,000 homes were severely damaged or destroyed. The explosions provoked angry demonstrations against the military and the Minister of National Defence, Gen. (retd) Tobias Joaquim Dai. In response, the Government established a commission of inquiry, which reported in April that the disaster had been caused by several factors, including obsolete explosives, poor storage conditions and human error. The Government promised to compensate the victims of the blasts and to rebuild damaged or destroyed houses, and in late March it launched a programme to relocate 17 army arsenals away from urban areas. During this operation five soldiers were killed and 10 injured in June, when munitions exploded while being loaded at an arsenal in Moamba, 60 km from Maputo.

In early May 2007 the CNE's five parliamentary members were appointed by the Assembleia da República, three from Frelimo and two from Renamo, and in mid-June Guebuza swore into office the eight other members from civil society. In September, following the delayed start of voter registration, the Government announced that the country's first provincial elections, due in December, would be postponed until 16 January 2008. In October 2007 Renamo announced that it would not take part in the elections as part of the Renamo—UE electoral alliance, with which it had contested the previous legislative elections. Finally, on 8 November the Assembleia da República approved a constitutional amendment, postponing the provincial elections until late 2009.

In early 2008 Mozambique was affected by severe flooding in the Zambezi Valley and central regions, causing 25 deaths, displacing 95,000 people and destroying an estimated 117,000 ha of crops, according to the Instituto Nacional de Gestão de Calamidades (INGC—National Institute for Disaster Management). This was followed in early March by Cyclone Jokwe, which struck Nampula, Cabo Delgado, Zambézia and Sofala provinces, causing 10 deaths, destroying 10,000 buildings and displacing an estimated 200,000 people. The Government was widely praised for its response to the disaster, which was spearheaded by the INGC, with support from donors. In July the Government set up a new agency, the Gabinete de Coordenação da Reconstrução (GACOR), with responsibility for resettling those displaced by national disasters, leaving the INGC to focus on the rescue and emergency phases of disaster response.

In March 2008 Guebuza carried out his largest cabinet reorganization since coming to power in 2005. The Minister of Transport and Communications, António Francisco Mungwambe, was replaced by the former director of the INGC, Paulo Zucula; the Minister of Justice, Esperança Alfredo Machavela, was replaced by Maria Benvida Levy; and the Minister of Environmental Co-ordination, Luciano André de Castro, was replaced by the former Minister of Foreign Affairs and Co-operation, Alcinda Abreu, whose own portfolio was assumed by Oldemiro Baloi. The reorganization was followed in late March by the replacement of the Chief of General Staff, his deputy, and the Minister of National Defence, Dai, whose portfolio was given to Filipe Nhussi, a former director of the national rail company, Portos e Caminhos de Ferro de Moçambique.

Also in March 2008 voter registration for the 2009 presidential election was officially completed, with a total of 8.9m. voters having been registered. In April the Government announced that local elections would take place on 9 November in 43 municipalities, 10 more than in 2003. In August 2008 a supplementary phase of voter registration for those who had missed the first phase due to the flooding and cyclone disruption was concluded, with an additional 2.7m. voters having been registered. In September Frelimo's political commission selected Guebuza to stand as the party's candidate, which according to the Constitution would be the last term he would be allowed to serve as Mozambican President. In mid-November local elections were held in Mozambique, with an estimated 48% turn-out. These resulted in an overwhelming victory for Frelimo, which won control of 41 out of 43 municipalities, including three that had been previously controlled by Renamo, and all of the 10 new municipalities.

The former Minister of the Interior, Almerino Manhenje, was arrested and charged in September 2008 with 49 counts of embezzlement of public funds worth an estimated US $8.8m. during his 10 years in office (1996–2005); a further eight officials at the ministry were arrested for involvement in the fraud. (In May 2011 Manhenje was sentenced to two years' imprisonment; the list of charges against him was reduced on appeal.) In October 2009 the Chairman of Aeroportos de Moçambique (ADM), Diodino Cambaza, was arrested and charged with embezzling public funds; the former Minister of Transport and Communications, António Mungwambe, was subsequently charged with involvement in the ADM fraud. In February 2010 Cambaza was sentenced to 22 years' imprisonment, while Mungwambe and former ADM Director of Finances Antenor Pereira each received 20-year gaol terms for their involvement in the $3.3m. fraud. The sentencing coincided with anti-corruption negotiations between the Government and the country's aid donors, and the revelation that Frelimo had benefited directly from the embezzlement undermined the ruling party's anti-corruption agenda. In May 2011 Mungwabe's sentence was reduced to four years. In April of that year a senior judge and head of the Constitutional Council, Luis Mondlane, resigned, amid media reports that he had misused public funds for personal use, pending a criminal investigation. He was replaced by Hermenegildo Gamito, a prominent businessman and banker.

In January 2009 the Constitutional Court ratified the results of the November local elections, noting some irregularities but ruling that these did not affect the overall outcome. The following month the run-off mayoral election was held in Nacala, resulting in a victory for the Frelimo candidate, Chale Ossufa, who won 54.7% of the vote, defeating the incumbent Renamo candidate, Manuel dos Santos. As a result, Frelimo secured control of 42 out of 43 municipal councils, reducing Renamo's control of municipalities from five to none. Renamo's heavy electoral defeat prompted acute disquiet within the party and raised questions over its future viability.

Widespread rioting was reported in Mogincual district, Nampula province, in February 2009, after rumours that Red Cross workers, who were using chlorine to treat the local water supply, were spreading cholera. Three Red Cross health workers and two policemen were killed in the disturbances, which ended with the arrest of 29 Mozambicans. However, on the night of 16 March, 12 of those arrested suffocated to death after being forced into an overcrowded prison cell; two senior police officers were subsequently suspended, and an inquiry was launched to determine who was at fault for the deaths. The two police officers were sentenced to one year in prison in August.

In March 2009 a new opposition party was launched, the Movimento Democrático de Moçambique (MDM), which elected the mayor of Beira, Daviz Simango, as its leader. The party drew strong support from disaffected Renamo members who began to defect to the MDM in large numbers, including senior party figures such as Renamo's parliamentary leader, Maria Moreno, and the party's official spokesman, Eduardo Namburete. In early April the Assembleia da República approved a new electoral law under which Mozambique's presidential, legislative and provincial elections would be held on the same ballot and later that month President Guebuza announced that the elections would be held on 28 October.

The MDM selected Simango as its presidential candidate, following a party convention in Nampula in June 2009. Later that month there was an alleged assassination attempt on Simango at an MDM rally in Nacala when members of Dhlakama's bodyguard opened fire on Simango's motorcade as it passed. Three people were injured in the ensuing disturbances, including a policeman. Renamo subsequently denied any involvement in the incident, but a police investigation uncovered the weapon believed to have been used in the attempt from Dhlakama's Nacala residence, and the police later accused 10 Renamo members of involvement in the attempt. Meanwhile, also in June, an explosion at Renamo's civil war headquarters in Sofala killed several members of the Renamo 'Presidential Guard'. Dhlakama claimed that mortars had been fired at the base, implicating the army, although no evidence to support this accusation was uncovered.

Dhlakama was overwhelmingly re-elected as party leader at Renamo's delayed party conference, which took place in Nampula in late July 2009, easily defeating his only rival, Rogério Francisco João Vicente, Renamo's information chief in Inhambane province. However, the congress was widely dismissed as lacking legitimacy, as the majority of those in attendance were staunch Dhlakama supporters and did not include many senior Renamo members who had threatened to defect to the MDM. Renamo subsequently struggled to recover from its defeat in the 2008 municipal elections, and was further weakened by infighting and defections to the MDM. The continued leadership of Dhlakama was unpopular with reformist party members, and was seen as a key factor in the emergence of the MDM, which hoped to attract both disillusioned members from the increasingly authoritarian and centralized Frelimo, and key elements from the opposition.

In July 2009 Prime Minister Diogo announced an emergency plan to combat HIV/AIDS in the south of Mozambique, which suffered from the highest HIV infection rates due to its proximity with South Africa and history of cross-border migration. A report on HIV prevalence released in the previous month suggested that the country's HIV infection rate had begun to stabilize, declining among adults by almost 2% in 2004–08, and predicted that the rate would remain at 14% during 2009–10. At the end of 2009 the UN Children's Fund (UNICEF) estimated HIV prevalence among adults at 11.5%, and up to 25% in the southern provinces.

THE 2009 ELECTIONS

In September 2009 the CNE announced that MDM candidates were to be prohibited from standing in the forthcoming elections in nine of Mozambique's 13 constituencies, prompting international criticism. Despite an official appeal launched by the MDM, the decision was not overturned. A further 10 parties and 17 presidential candidates were excluded from various constituencies, with the CNE in all cases citing procedural errors, such as missing documentation, to defend its actions. As a result, Frelimo stood unopposed in several areas. The 45-day campaign period was marred from the outset by sporadic outbreaks of violence and attempts by Frelimo and Renamo to undermine the MDM's threat to their dominance of the political system. On the first day of campaigning, the MDM offices in Chokwe, Gaza province, were attacked and three party workers were injured. The perpetrators were identified by the MDM as Frelimo supporters, and local police initially refused to accept an official complaint. Renamo party bases and staff were attacked in September in Maputo and in Tete province, where the offices were burned down, while Renamo's 'Presidential Guard' attacked alleged Frelimo supporters at a rally marking Dhlakama's first appearance during the campaign. Both the MDM and Renamo complained of obstruction and intimidation tactics from Frelimo and the state during campaigning.

Voting in the legislative and presidential elections took place peacefully on 28 October 2009. The rate of participation by the electorate, at 44%, was an improvement compared with the 2004 elections, but it was still low, indicating continued, widespread disillusionment with the political process. The official results were released by the CNE on 11 November and revealed an overwhelming victory for the ruling party, Frelimo, which won 74.7% of the vote, increasing its majority to 191 of the 250 seats in the Assembleia da República. Renamo suffered a humiliating defeat, gaining just 17.7% of the ballot, which reduced the party's parliamentary representation to 51 seats. The MDM only obtained eight seats (3.9%), but still performed better than any other political party opposing both Frelimo and Renamo since the introduction of multi-party democracy, by attracting educated, urban voters in Beira and Maputo; the results equated to a significant break in the domination of the political scene by the two, older parties. In the concurrent presidential election, the incumbent, Guebuza of Frelimo, won a decisive victory, securing re-election with 75.0% of the votes cast. Dhlakama performed poorly, with the Renamo candidate being awarded just 16.4% of the ballot, while Simango of the MDM won a modest 8.6% share of the vote.

Elections observers accepted the results of both elections as broadly free and fair but criticized Frelimo's misuse of state resources and domination of the media in its campaigns, and noted the disparity between Frelimo's financial capacity and that of the opposition parties. Numerous irregularities were noted in certain provinces, but were not believed to be significant enough to cast doubt over the final results. Observers were strongly critical of the CNE, its management of the elections, and the exclusion of smaller parties and candidates on procedural irregularities.

Immediately after the CNE published the results, Dhlakama denounced the outcome and demanded the creation of a transitional government to organize new elections, and a boycott of the parliamentary swearing-in ceremony, a move supported by 35 Renamo delegates. However, 16 members of Renamo defied Dhlakama and attended the opening ceremony, including Renamo Secretary-General Ossufo Momade. The Constitutional Council rejected Dhlakama's appeals on 7 December 2009, declaring that there was insufficient evidence to support his demands.

GUEBUZA'S SECOND TERM

As a party, Frelimo emerged strengthened from the 2009 elections, having increased its presence in the northern and central regions, which were previously held by Renamo. In contrast with 2004, Guebuza retained most of his cabinet following the elections, with the notable exception of Diogo, who was replaced as Prime Minister by Aires Ali, a Guebuza loyalist, in January 2010. Following discussions on the conduct of the elections, Mozambique's budget support donors suspended funding in December 2009, demanding immediate action on electoral law reform and addressing corruption and conflicts of interests, with particular reference to the unclear divisions between the Frelimo party and the state. Following a series of proposed concessions by the Government, at the end of March 2010 the donor nations announced that they would resume budget support.

In April 2010 the Constitutional Council decided to modify the legislation governing *bancada* or 'bench' status, which in its existing form stated that only parties with a minimum of 11 parliamentary seats had the right to raise questions in the Assembleia da República, to propose legislation and to participate in parliamentary commissions. Despite Renamo opposition, the Council reduced the threshold required to eight seats, allowing the MDM to be officially confirmed as the third *bancada* in the Assembleia da República in May, marking a break from 32 years of bipartisan parliamentary politics. A new opposition party emerged in April, with the creation of the centre-right Partido Humanitário de Moçambique (Pahumo), led by defectors from Frelimo, Renamo and smaller opposition parties. At Pahumo's first convention in June, Cornélio Quivela—previously an MDM candidate who was prevented by the CNE from contesting the 2009 elections—was elected as leader of the party.

In September 2010 Mozambique experienced the most violent rioting since 2008, when protests erupted in Maputo and Manica over the rising costs of basic commodities. At least 14 people were killed and over 400 were injured and dozens of shops and businesses suffered damages. The protests were sparked by increases of up to 30% in the prices of bread, water and electricity in 2010, as the metical fell in value against the South African rand; 178 protesters had received prison sentences by the first half of 2011. The Government initially took an uncompromising stance against the protesters and made no acknowledgement of the demands. The violence escalated, however, and eventually the authorities announced the reinstatement of subsidies in what was widely regarded as an embarrassing reversal of policy. The police were heavily criticized for using live ammunition against protesters, but only one officer, who shot and killed an 11-year old boy, was prosecuted.

In October 2010, one month after the riots, President Guebuza reorganized key positions in his Government. Former Minister of the Interior José Pacheco was appointed Minister of Agriculture, replacing Soares Nhaca. Pacheco was succeeded in the Ministry of the Interior by the former chief of the Police Sciences Academy, Alberto Mondlane. The Minister of Industry and Trade, Antonio Fernando, was replaced with Armando Inroga, formerly President of the Association of Mozambican Economists, and the Minister of Health, Ivo Garrido, with Alexandre Manguele. Earlier in the year, mismanagement of the state's medicine distribution network had led to large quantities of medicines going to waste in storage, contributing to a nation-wide shortage of retroviral drugs and analgesics. As a result, the Government urged people to use certain out-of-date medicines for several months until supplies could be replaced. There were also a large number of reported cases of thefts of medicines that were sold on the black market. In November the World Bank approved US $143m. of funding for Mozambique, part of which was for the improvement of medical supplies.

Despite advances against the spread of HIV, AIDS had become the main cause of death among adults in Mozambique by 2010. Women, and those living in Mozambique's southern provinces, were still disproportionately affected. Meanwhile, malaria was still the biggest cause of death among children, accounting for 42.3% of child mortalities and 19% of all maternal deaths. Malaria cases fell from 6m. in 2007 to 4m. in 2009.

In October 2010 diplomatic relations between Mozambique and Malawi were strained when Malawi attempted to inaugurate a new shipping route from its fluvial port, Nsanje, down the Shire and Zambezi rivers to the Mozambican port of Chine. Plans for the route have been ongoing since 2005, but the Mozambican authorities seized the first Malawian ship to cross the border in October, arresting the Malawian military attaché onboard; the incident prompted an angry response from the Malawian Government. The Mozambican Government stated that further environmental impact assessments on the project were required.

Flooding in Mozambique in the November 2010–March 2011 rainy season was less severe than in previous years, despite unusually heavy rains in January 2011. The Zambezi, Limpopo, Save and Pungue rivers burst their banks, causing at least 11 deaths and widespread evacuations, which were co-ordinated by the INGC. The floods did not cause the large-scale displacement or damage to agriculture sustained in recent years, but outbreaks of cholera followed the flooding in at least 13 districts. In January 2011 there were more attacks on health officials, amid rumours that they were spreading cholera. In Cabo Delgado, a community leader was beaten to death by a mob, which claimed he had collected products that caused cholera. In the same province, youths attacked the houses of people who were accused of storing pills that caused cholera. In Nampula province, health and agricultural workers were accused of spreading cholera and attacked, and three local health centres were targeted. In most of the cases the perpetrators were arrested and received prison sentences.

In February 2011 a boat illegally transporting Somalis and Ethiopians to South Africa sank off the coast of Mozambique, killing 51 people. The following month the Government changed national laws that had previously permitted the free movement, within Mozambique's borders, of asylum seekers and refugees. The amendment was prompted by a heavy influx of refugees from Somalia and Ethiopia, many of whom were leaving the overcrowded Maratane refugee camp in Nampala province, destined primarily for South Africa.

In May 2011 new legislation, which had been proposed by the Frelimo Government, was introduced to provide benefits for the veterans of Mozambique's liberation struggle and the civil war that followed. Parliamentary debates between Frelimo and Renamo reignited accusations of discrimination against the former rebels by the ruling party; the legislation provided for benefits to veterans from both sides of the civil war, but with greater incentives for former Frelimo combatants. In November demobilized soldiers protested in Maputo, demanding increased pensions. An official spokesperson for the demonstrators was arrested and later charged with inciting violence.

In October 2011 Frelimo officially launched a constitutional review process, which was expected to result in a draft revised constitution being presented to the legislature for consideration by mid-2013. Renamo refused to nominate any representatives to the parliamentary commission that was established to investigate proposed constitutional reform and boycotted a subsequent parliamentary session. The commission was dominated by Frelimo, which held the majority in the Assembleia da República and was empowered to approve constitutional change without the support of Renamo. One member from the opposition MDM agreed to participate.

By-elections were held in Quelimane, Pemba and Cuamba in December 2011 after Frelimo forced its mayors in these three cities to resign, allegedly owing to their poor performances in office. Renamo boycotted the elections. The most significant result of the polls was the victory of the MDM's candidate in Quelimane; Frelimo maintained control of Pemba and Cuamba. In May 2012 a mayoral by-election was held in Inhambane following the death of the incumbent. Ten members of the MDM were arrested for illegal campaigning but were later released without charge after the party complained of politically motivated harassment. The Frelimo candidate won the by-election with 78% of the votes.

In March 2012 two people were killed in Nampula during clashes between the police and members of Renamo, some of whom had fired on a police car that had approached Renamo's head office; 34 Renamo activists, mostly demobilized veterans, were arrested but later released. The incident once again raised the issue of Renamo's 'Presidential Guard', which Frelimo regarded as an illegal armed group. In April Dhlakama met with President Guebuza, and further talks between the two were due to take place later in the year.

Economy

ANA NAOMI DE SOUSA

Based on an earlier article by EDWARD GEORGE

INTRODUCTION

Mozambique's post-independence economy has suffered the damaging effects of a guerrilla war, drought, floods, famine, the displacement of population and a severe scarcity of skilled workers and foreign exchange. These difficulties have been compounded by a large visible trade deficit, with export earnings covering less than one-third of import costs, and high levels of debt repayments. As a result, Mozambique has remained heavily reliant on foreign credits. In recent years, however, substantial debt relief has reduced servicing to a more sustainable level, while exports have increased sharply. The discovery of large reserves of coal and natural gas are at the forefront of growing foreign interest in the mining and industrial sectors, bringing with it much-needed investment in infrastructure. Between 2010 and 2011 foreign direct investment (FDI) in Mozambique more than doubled. However, given the country's continued dependence on foreign aid, and despite robust growth, the economy has remained vulnerable to external shocks such as rising global food and oil prices, and economic problems in donor countries.

After 1993 the Mozambican economy became one of the fastest growing in the world, with annual real gross domestic product (GDP) growth averaging 8.3% in 1997–2006, according to estimates by the World Bank. Growth slowed between 2008 and 2009 as a result of the global economic crisis; none the less, real GDP exceeded expectations in 2009 and rose by 6.3%. GDP growth was a relatively moderate 6.5% in 2010, increasing to 7.1% in 2011.

The average rate of inflation has been uneven since 2005, when it decreased to 7.2%, aided by the strengthening of the currency—the metical—against the US dollar, strong monetary discipline and lower food prices. It averaged 13.2% in 2006, before decreasing to 8.2% in 2007 and rising to 10.3% in 2008. In 2009 inflation contracted to an average of 2.5%, the lowest rate in a decade, in response to the decline in international food and energy prices. In 2010 the inflation rate accelerated rapidly, driven by rising international food prices and the devaluation of the metical, reaching 17% in August, shortly before the price rise riots (see below). From August, the central bank increased its key interest rate from 11.5% to 15.5%, to counter rising inflation and increased foreign exchange sales to reduce net internal reserves. As a result, the inflation rate declined to 15% by the end of November; overall, inflation averaged 12.4% in that year. With the Government continuing to pursue restrictive fiscal and monetary policies, and with global food prices easing, inflation decreased further in 2011 to an average of 2.3%, despite a year-on-year rise in consumer prices in the first six months of the year. In response, in March 2012 the central bank reduced the standing lending and standing deposit facility rates.

The value of the national currency stabilized in the early 2000s, averaging US $1 = 22,581 meticais in 2004. However, the introduction of a new foreign-exchange auction system in early 2005 led to sharp periods of volatility, which forced the central bank to introduce a temporary trading band. This helped to stabilize the metical, which depreciated in real terms against the US dollar by only 0.3% during 2006, which enabled the central bank to remove the temporary trading band. On 1 July 2006 the currency was devalued, with one new currency unit—metical da nova família—becoming equivalent to 1,000 of the former units. Most old currency was withdrawn from circulation by the end of 2006, but old notes were to be accepted at banks until the end of 2007 and at the central bank until the end of 2012. After appreciating strongly in 2007, the currency depreciated in 2008, but rose again in 2009. In August 2009 the IMF estimated that the metical was overvalued by between 26% and 41%. According to the IMF, the metical depreciated by over 30% in nominal terms against the US dollar and the South African rand in 2010, but, as a result of government intervention after the September riots, it recovered to previous levels.

ECONOMIC POLICY

Plans to sell a number of major state-owned enterprises were announced in early 1992, and a new investment code was approved by the legislature in 1993, providing identical fiscal and customs benefits to both local and foreign investors. By the end of 1999 over 1,000 state-owned enterprises had been privatized in what was considered to be one of the world's most successful privatization programmes. After it stalled for several years due to opposition from vested interests, in May 2008 the Government revived the process with the sale of 10% of its shares in Companhia Moçambicana de Hidrocarbonetos (CMH) on Maputo's stock exchange, Bolsa de Valores de Moçambique (BVM); the flotation raised US $6.7m.

Following the floods in February 2000, in March the IMF authorized the release of US $50m. under the Poverty Reduction and Growth Facility (PRGF); in June international aid donors pledged an estimated $530m. for 2000, and a further $560m. was pledged for 2001. In June 2002 the IMF authorized the release of an additional tranche worth $11m. In June 2003 the IMF completed its review of Mozambique's performance under the PRGF and approved the drawing of a further $11.8m. from the total fund of $122.9m. The IMF concluded that the Government had achieved higher than expected economic growth, had met the agreed macroeconomic benchmarks and had made satisfactory progress in implementing the policies and measures of its Poverty Reduction Strategy Paper (PRSP). That month the IMF approved a new PRGF programme for 2004–06 worth $17.1m.

In June 2006 the Government launched a new four-year poverty reduction strategy, the Plano de Acção para a Redução da Pobreza Absoluta (PARPA II), covering 2006–09. PARPA II's overall target was to reduce poverty by about 10% to 45% of the population by 2009, through improving governance, investing in human capital and supporting private sector growth.

In January 2007 the IMF completed its fifth PRGF review, judging that policy performance had been positive, that the economy was becoming increasingly diversified, with growth across all sectors, and that increased revenue collection had led to a lower domestic deficit. In June the IMF completed its sixth and final PRGF review, releasing a final US $2.4m. The following month the Fund awarded a three-year Policy Support Instrument (PSI), a new programme guaranteeing Mozambique advice, monitoring and policy endorsement from the IMF, but not financial assistance, which would be provided by donors. The PSI was aimed at maintaining macroeconomic stability as foreign aid was scaled up, implementing a second wave of economic and structural reforms and continuing implementation of the poverty reduction programme outlined in PARPA II. In July 2009 the IMF completed its annual Article IV consultation, agreeing to provide an exceptional $175m. loan under the exogenous shocks facility (ESF), which was designed to assist low-income countries with a strong record of macroeconomic management that were challenged by temporary balance of payments difficulties. In September the IMF completed its fifth PSI review, reporting that the Mozambican economy had remained resilient to the economic downturn, while urging stronger fiscal and monetary policies to control debt levels. The sixth and final PSI review was conducted in March 2010, commending the strong economic performance and low inflation rates of the previous years. In June the IMF announced a new, three-year PSI for the period 2010–12, worth $21m. and aimed at enhancing economic development, reducing poverty and maintaining macroeconomic stability, with a focus on increasing public sector investment and continued support of structural reforms. In a Letter of Intent to the IMF in May 2011, the Government set out its expenditure priorities to encourage private investment, focusing on improving transport and electricity infrastructure and on three major projects: the construction of an international airport at Nacala; the refurbishment of Beira port; and continued expansion of the national road network.

Preliminary sectoral reports into the effectiveness of PARPA II were released in June 2010, showing inconsistent progress. There were improvements in combating child poverty, but malnutrition remained a concern at 48% in 2008, a reduction of just 4% since 2003. Crucially, it was concluded that PARPA II had failed to improve agricultural productivity or rural poverty. In a 2010 report on family expenditure in the period 2008–09, the Ministry of Planning estimated that rural poverty had risen from 55% to 57%, while urban poverty was estimated to have decreased slightly from 52% to 50%. In 2011 the Government announced its third Poverty Reduction Action Plan, PARPA III, for the period 2011–14, with a focus on increasing agricultural and fishing output, promoting employment opportunities, encouraging social development and boosting tax revenues from the exploitation of natural resources.

During 2005–08 the Government increased spending substantially, in particular on public sector wages and priority social sectors, the bulk of which was financed by donor inflows. In December 2008 the Assembleia da República (Assembly of the Republic) approved the 2009 budget, which was also highly expansionary, with large increases in revenue and expenditure. In line with PARPA II, 68.7% of spending was to be on priority sectors. A large rise in expenditure reflected the recruitment of 12,000 teachers, 1,600 police and 1,200 health workers, the construction of 800 new schools, and investment in expanding access to safe drinking water. The 2010 budget increased total spending by 20% to US $3,700m., equal to 38.7% of GDP. For the first time, the Government was to provide for more than one-half of the total budget, while external donors would contribute 44%. The Government's accompanying Plano Económico e Social (PES) targeted real GDP growth of 6.2% in 2010, driven by agriculture and exports, and annual average inflation of 9.5%. The PES set a series of ambitious targets in the agricultural sector, many of which were related to the objectives not met under PARPA II and Proagri (see below).

Following widespread rioting over fuel prices in February 2008, the Government introduced diesel fuel subsidies for private transport operators and in July suspended customs duty and value-added tax (VAT) on imported fuel products for six months. These measures, which cost an estimated 1.2% of GDP, were withdrawn at the end of the year when international oil prices declined. In March 2009 the Government reintroduced fuel subsidies, with a price cap on petrol and diesel. However, following criticism from Mozambique's budget support donors, the Government agreed gradually to remove the subsidies. In May the IMF urged the Government to implement a domestic fiscal stimulus in order to alleviate the impact of the global economic crisis on Mozambique.

In March 2010 the Government announced it was withdrawing generalized subsidies, in accordance with IMF recommendations. It had already begun gradually withdrawing the fuel subsidy, and by the end of June fuel prices had increased by 44%. Further measures were made public in September; electricity rates were to rise by 13% and the price of bread was to increase by over 20%, with immediate effect. The cost of piped water would also rise. The removal of the subsidies coincided with rising international food and oil prices, and with the weakening of the metical, in particular against the South African rand. In the first half of 2010 the price of fruit and vegetables rose by almost 35%. Consumer prices rose by almost 12% from the end of 2009 and inflation accelerated to the highest rates in over a decade. The day after the Government announced the removal of the subsidies, widespread rioting erupted in Maputo. To appease the public outcry, on 7 September the Government held an emergency cabinet meeting and announced that it would reinstate subsidies; two weeks later it pledged to subsidize bakers, provide free electricity for households using up to 100 kWh and reduced the costs of water for small-scale domestic consumption. In the place of a generalized fuel subsidy, subsidies for public transport would be introduced. In order to ease consumer prices, the Government lowered customs duties on certain products imported from South Africa and removed the import duty on rice. In accordance with the emergency measures, the Government announced that it would freeze the salaries of ministers and high-ranking officials. Overall, government expenditure on subsidies declined during 2009–12, totalling 1.2% of GDP, according to the 2012 budget.

Mozambique's 19 main donors (G-19), which provided direct budget support as part of the Programme Aid Partnership (PAP), gave a total of US $1,700m. in budget support in 2004–08. In late 2008 the PAP was expanded to include two more donors—the USA and the UN—neither of which provide budget support but instead fund specific sectoral projects.

In response to donor criticism, in 2007 the Government pledged to reorganize the Gabinete Central de Combate à Corrupção (GCCC) in an attempt to revive the national anti-corruption strategy. As a result of these efforts, overall PAP pledges for the 2009 budget rose slightly, to US $445m., in addition to $329m. for sectoral projects. Following the landslide victory of the Frente de Libertação de Moçambique (Frelimo) in the October 2009 legislative and presidential elections, increasing concerns from the PAP over the Government's conduct culminated in the aid partners imposing a donor strike in December. The PAP demanded electoral law reform and tangible progress on tackling corruption. Sweden and Switzerland reduced funding for the budget, and 13 other countries froze their pledges in real terms, in protest against the Government's lack of progress in improving governance and eradicating official corruption. Following negotiations between the aid donors and the Government, the PAP agreed to resume payments in February 2010. Aid from budget donors reached over $445m. in 2011, including an additional $25m. from the World Bank, increasing the institution's contributions to $85m.; Sweden and Switzerland again decreased funding, in response to growing concerns about the failure of Mozambique's recent poverty reduction strategies and increasingly centralized governance.

The Government pursued further reforms, having already introduced VAT in June 1999, as a condition to the implementation of debt reduction under the IMF and World Bank's initiative for heavily indebted poor countries (HIPC). In an attempt to increase fiscal revenues, in April 2002 the Assembleia da República approved legislation that aimed to overhaul the country's tax system. In December 2005 a centralized tax service, the Autoridade Tributária de Moçambique, was created, combining the tax directorate and the customs service, in an attempt to streamline tax collection and increase revenue collection, and in January 2008 new, simplified tax codes were introduced. This resulted in an increase in the number of taxpayers from 390,000 in 2006 to 770,000 at the end of 2008. In May 2007 the Government established the Gabinete de Informação Financeira de Moçambique to investigate money-laundering and financial crimes. The authorities also introduced new mining and petroleum fiscal regimes, which should substantially increase these sectors' contribution to tax revenues.

In November 2011 the Government released the state budget for 2012, which increased total spending by 15%, to US $5,980m., compared with the previous year. Over one-half of total expenditure was directed towards poverty reduction, with 18% allocated to education. PAP donors agreed to provide $606m. in financial assistance, $344m. of which was direct budgetary support, with the remaining $262m. to be used to fund sectoral programmes; however, the G-19 group of donors issued a renewed appeal for the Government to increase its anti-corruption efforts.

In June 2010 the Portuguese and Mozambican Governments launched the Banco Nacional de Investimentos (BNI) in Maputo, with a share capital of US $500,000m., which aims to finance the country's largest infrastructure projects. Only Portuguese and Mozambican companies have access to the funding. In June 2011 the central bank announced the introduction of new 20, 50 and 100 metical notes, made using polymer. It was hoped that the new notes would cope better with the humidity and last longer in circulation.

Between 2011 and 2012 the Government substantially increased minimum wages in Mozambique, which are divided into 11 economic sectors. Despite a 54% increase, in 2012 employees in agriculture still had the lowest monthly minimum wage at US $83, while the highest minimum wage was $222 for workers in the financial sector. However, only around 30% of Mozambican workers are engaged in the formal economy, with 300,000 people entering the workforce every year.

AGRICULTURE

Agricultural activities engage around 80% of the population, yet Mozambique has the lowest level of commercial agricultural productivity in Southern Africa. Since independence the sector has been adversely affected by the scarcity of skilled labour following the post-independence exodus by the Portuguese, the internal conflict, which prevented nearly 3m. Mozambicans from farming the land, and drought, flooding, cyclones and insect pests, which have combined to destroy food crops in large areas of the country (notably in the south and the Zambézia region). The sector was seriously damaged by the floods of 2000, which affected an estimated 2m. people. Some 127,000 ha of crops (10% of the country's cultivated land) were destroyed, and much livestock was lost. However, the sector subsequently recovered, averaging annual growth of an estimated 7.3% in 2001–10, which contributed to strong GDP growth during this period.

The area of arable land cultivated in Mozambique rose by 47% between 1999/2000 and 2009/10, to 15.6% of the total land area. Agriculture (including fishing) has recovered considerably from the conflict and the floods, accounting for an estimated 25% of Mozambique's GDP in 2011. The major cash crops, representing 5.7% of the total cultivated area, are tobacco, sugar, cotton, sesame and cashew nuts. Prawns remain the principal agricultural export earner, with revenue totalling US $76m. in 2010, having decreased slightly since 2005 in line with international 'total allowable catch' quotas. Maize, bananas, rice, tea, sisal and coconuts are also grown, and the main subsistence crop is cassava. The Ministry of Agriculture estimated that national production of maize totalled 2.1m. metric tons in 2010, but wheat is becoming increasingly popular as a staple, despite less than 1% of the wheat supply coming from domestic production. Mozambique was formerly the world's sixth largest producer of cassava, a staple crop, but most rural farming families are still net importers of cassava, according to FAO. Cassava production rose from 5.0m. tons in 2007 to 9.7m. tons in 2010. However, in 2010 domestic prices of cassava increased by 60%, compared with 2008, presenting a serious risk to food security (see below).

A five-year government programme, Proagri, which aimed to increase state capacity and co-ordination in all areas of agricultural production, began in 1999 with the support of all major donors, at a total cost of US $202m. At the same time, donors strongly urged the introduction of new land legislation and made their approval of the Proagri programme conditional upon certain guarantees for peasant land-tenure rights. In December 2003 the Ministry of Agriculture announced that Proagri had fallen behind schedule, and it was not until February 2007 that donors agreed to fund the second, €45m. phase of the programme, covering 2007–09. The programme's main objectives were to help small farmers increase marketed output and diversify into high-value crops, with the goal of improving food security, developing agro-industries and managing better the country's natural resources. Despite some improvements to procedure and management systems at a ministerial level, by the end of 2009 it was clear that Proagri had failed to produce actual results, and from 2010 there was a shift in donor funding from government-led agricultural development towards direct sector support.

In August 2010 the Ministry of Finance published the Auditoria de Desempenho no Sector Agrario (Performance Audit on the Agriculture Sector), which suggested that the Government was spending too little on agriculture and raised questions over the role of the Fundo Internacional de Desenvolvimento Agricolo (International Fund for Agricultural Development). In December the Government admitted that it needed to increase spending on the sector from 5.6% of total government expenditure in 2009, and committed 10% of future budgets to agriculture. In September 2010 the Government announced the launch of a US $25m. credit line to boost agricultural production, underwritten by the Alliance for Green Revolution in Africa and Standard Bank. The funding was intended to boost production and develop mechanisms to deal with surpluses and shortages, such as improving storage facilities. In February 2011 the World Bank published an Analysis of Public Expenditure in Agriculture in Mozambique. According to the report, the use of improved farming technologies in Mozambican farming was below regional averages, with less than 5% of rural smallholders using chemical pesticides or fertilizers, and only 10% of maize producers and 3% of rice growers using improved seeds. The report concluded that the employment of more advanced technologies could greatly enhance Mozambique's crop output.

In 2010 the United States Agency for International Development, the Agência Brasileira de Cooperação (Brazilian Agency for Co-operation), and the Empresa Brasileira de Pesquisa Agropecuária (Brazilian Agricultural Research Corporation) committed US $20m. to funding development projects aimed at strengthening the capacity of the Instituto de Investigação Agrícola de Moçambique (National Institute of Agrarian Research), with a focus on diversifying farming methods. In 2011 the Government launched the Programa de Desenvolvimento da Agricultura nas Savanas Tropicais de

Moçambique (Programme to Develop Agriculture in Mozambique's Tropical Savannahs), known as ProSavana, in co-operation with the Governments of Brazil and Japan. The US $13.5m. project aimed to diffuse farming technology and provide training to agricultural workers in the Nacala Corridor.

As part of efforts to exploit Mozambique's abundant water resources, in June 2007 rehabilitation was completed of the Massingir dam in Gaza province, at a cost of US $80m., expanding its reservoir capacity to 2,800m. cu m of water. The dam was to irrigate 90,000 ha of land in the Limpopo Valley, and there were plans to build a 25-MW hydroelectric power plant on the dam. However, in May 2008 there was a breach at the dam, causing extensive flooding in the surrounding region. In July 2009 the African Development Bank (AfDB) granted Mozambique a $20.6m. loan to finance the repairs.

Following the implementation of the policy of land seizures in Zimbabwe from 1998, more than 150 white Zimbabwean farmers resettled in Mozambique's sparsely populated central province of Manica. The farmers revived the cultivation of previously defunct crops, in particular tobacco, tea and edible oils (especially from sunflowers). As a result, tobacco production grew by 360% in 2001–05, earning US $41m. in export revenues in 2004. In May 2006 Mozambique Leaf Tobacco opened a $55m. tobacco-processing plant, with a capacity of 50,000 metric tons per year, in Tete; tobacco had previously been sent to Malawi for processing. In 2006 tobacco production rose by 11.8%, to 72,704 tons, with exports reaching $103.6m., the same value as the largest traditional agricultural export, prawns. By 2010 tobacco output had increased to an estimated 86,000 tons and exports had risen to $142.6m. (nearly three times the value of exports of fish, crustaceans and molluscs in that year).

In May 2011, marking a radical departure from its previous approach, the Government unveiled the €1,400m. Plano Estratégico de Desenvolvimento do Setor Agrário (PEDSA—Strategic Agriculture Development Plan), based partly on the regional Comprehensive African Agriculture Development Programme (CAADP). The programme combined two, five-year plans for the periods 2010–14 and 2015–19, and incorporated the Plano de Accao da Producao Agricola (Action Plan for Agricultural Production) for 2008–11. The strategy placed an emphasis on encouraging the development of the private agricultural sector and increasing investor confidence, supported in part by government investment in the private sector of 120m. meticais. The principal aim of the strategy was to move Mozambique from subsistence farming towards supplying domestic needs in a competitive market, and producing crops for export. Around 37,000 smallholders in Mozambique were referred to as emerging farmers, whose semi-commercial activities had the potential for much more efficient production. The key objectives of the PEDSA were to raise growth in the agricultural sector by 7% per year, and for the area of land farmed for basic food produce to increase by 25% by 2019. The PEDSA programme was based on data released in November 2011 and compiled from the Censo Agro-Pecuário 2009/10. According to the census, the number of farms increased moderately from 3.1m. in 1999/2000 to 3.8m. in 2009/10. Less than 5% of farms used fertilizer, pesticides or irrigation. The average farm size at the time of the census was 1.5 ha.

Only 3% of farmland in Mozambique is irrigated, and much of the existing irrigation is in a state of disrepair. Some 60% of the land currently irrigated is used for sugar, and much of the remainder is concentrated on rice fields. In March 2011 the World Bank granted a US $70m. loan for the Government's Programme to Develop Sustainable Irrigation, known as PROIRRI, which targeted the provinces of Zambézia, Sofala and Manica.

Major Crops

More than 50% of cashew cultivation takes place in Nampula province, followed by Zambézia and Inhambane. Production of cashew nuts was 204,000 metric tons in 1974, making the country one of the largest producers in the world. Output decreased sharply after independence and declined to 20,000 tons in 1984, owing to inefficient marketing practices by state enterprises, lack of transportation and the effects of drought. In an attempt to increase production levels, the Government doubled producer prices for the crop that year. Production increased subsequently, but fluctuated according to weather conditions. Output of cashew nuts reached an unusually high 105,337 tons in 2005 (as a result of exceptional climatic conditions), but declined to 64,150 tons by the 2008/09 (October–March) harvest during the global economic downturn, rising to 95,000 tons in 2009/10 and 96,000 tons in 2010/11.

Following demands by the World Bank that the industry be privatized, in 1994–95 the Government sold the cashew-processing factories to six Mozambican trading companies for US $9m. However, by February 1999 all but three of the country's 14 principal cashew-processing plants had closed. By the end of 2000 cashew prices had declined to just over one-half of the 1999 price; this was believed principally to be the result of a collapse in the demand for cashews in India, although it was also suggested that the liberalization of the cashew-processing industry had adversely affected the sector. In 2001 the Mozambican Government responded by placing an embargo on the export of raw cashews to India, in an attempt to save the domestic processing industry from collapse. Since 2003 there has been a revival in the cashew-processing industry with the opening of small plants using labour-intensive methods. By 2006 a total of 23 processing factories were operating in northern Mozambique, processing an annual 33,000 metric tons of nuts. Output progressively increased, and by 2010/11 had reached 112,000 tons. However, in 2011/12 production decreased to its lowest level in a decade, reaching only 64,000 tons, as international demand declined. One of the current problems in Mozambique is the age of its cashew trees, which were planted an average of 40 years ago; the maximum yield of cashew trees occurs at between 25 and 30 years, after which their production declines. In April 2011 the cashew institute, INCAJU, proposed a $172m. investment plan involving the establishment of new cashew tree plantations, which it hoped would raise annual production to over 200,000 tons.

Cotton has traditionally been the main cash crop of northern Mozambique, with more than 500,000 growers in the Cabo Delgado, Niassa, Nampula and Zambézia provinces. Nearly all cotton is cultivated by peasant producers working in concession areas where large companies have sole right of purchase. International cotton demand and prices declined from 2008 as a result of the global economic downturn, and production decreased to 65,000 tons in 2009, only 60,000 tons of which were marketed. In 2010 the downward trend continued, and production fell further to 42,000 tons, of which 99% was exported to Asia. According to a government report, only 71% of the anticipated producers chose to harvest cotton in 2010, owing to lower purchase prices. Furthermore, in January 2010 the Instituto do Algodão de Moçambique (National Cotton Institute) revealed that around 5,000 tons of cotton had been smuggled out of the country, destined mostly for Zimbabwe, where peasant producers were able to secure higher prices for the crops. Owing to a four-fold increase in the international price of cotton, in 2011 the cotton yield rose by 70% to 70,000 tons, generating US $41m. in revenue. In that year Olam Moçambique announced plans to invest $50m. in upgrading a cotton-ginning plant in Nampula province to increase its annual production capacity from 12,000 tons to 60,000 tons. In 2012 the China-Africa Cotton Company opened a cotton-ginning plant in Beira, which could produce up to 40,000 tons per year. However, global prices declined from 2011, and in 2012 the Government reduced the domestic purchasing price of cotton from 15 meticais per kg to 10.5 meticais.

Sugar is a significant plantation crop in Mozambique. Production of sugar cane increased dramatically after the peace agreement, driven by high international prices, from 200,000 metric tons in 1994 to 2.2m. tons in 2007, according to FAO. In the aftermath of the 2000 flooding, Illovo Sugar and Tongaat-Hulett (both of South Africa) and a consortium of Mauritian investors committed US $300m. for four sugar refineries at Maragra, Xinavane, Mafambisse and Marromeu, turning Mozambique into a net sugar exporter in 2002. In November 2004 Illovo Sugar agreed to purchase the abandoned Buzi plantation, south-west of Beira, for $1.2m. The plantation was the last sugar company in state hands, and Illovo resumed production in 2009. In 2006 a French agro-industrial group, Tereos, purchased a 50% stake in Mozambique's largest sugar refinery, Sena Sugar, pledging to invest $30m. in the sugar sector. In June 2007 Tongaat-Hulett announced that it would invest $177m. in expanding production at its sugar factories in Xinavane and Mafambisse, with the aim of raising production from 124,000 tons to 296,000 tons. As part of these plans, in 2007 the $4.3m. Muda-Nhaurire dam was inaugurated, to irrigate sugar cane plantations supplying the Mafambisse mill. In 2007 the Government announced that it would invest $250m. in the sugar sector over the next seven years, with the aim of improving productivity and competition in the sector, and was also investigating a $50m. sugar plantation project in Maputo province, including rehabilitation of the Corumana dam, which would irrigate the plantation, to produce sugar and ethanol. By 2011 all four major refineries were working at full capacity. As a result of major investment in recent years, the national production of refined sugar has risen, reaching 387,784 tons in 2011, owing to increases in the area under cultivation and crop yield. From 2009 Mozambique was entitled to duty-free sugar exports to the European Union (EU), under the Everything But Arms initiative. In 2011 Mozambique exported 194,181 tons of sugar, earning $83.5m.

The Zambézia hills and mountains, close to the Malawi border, are the main producing area for tea. More than 90% of tea produced in Mozambique is exported; the principal markets for Mozambican tea are the United Kingdom and the USA. Production was estimated at 16,256 metric tons in 2007, but had declined considerably by 2011. Copra is produced mainly on immense coconut plantations on the coastal belt of the Zambézia and Nampula provinces. It is also a popular crop among Mozambicans who use the oil and other copra products in daily life, and output reached an estimated 31,000 tons in 2007. However, in the same year there was an outbreak of plague that spread to affect 25% of all copra plantations by 2010. The Government hoped to plant resistant species all over the country by 2013. In the late 1990s significant efforts were made to rehabilitate the vast rice fields between Massingir and Chokwe, in the Limpopo valley, and by 2000 rice production had risen to 200,500 tons, before declining again as a result of poor rains to just 99,173 tons in 2006. According to the Ministry of Agriculture, following heavy government investment in new seeds, machinery and inputs, rice production rose to 260,000 tons in 2008 and 360,000 tons in 2011, although it was still short of Mozambique's annual rice requirement of 600,000 tons. In 2010 the Government secured financing from the People's Republic of China and Libya to develop the sector and increase output and hoped to become self sufficient in rice by 2015. Oil seeds, such as sesame and sunflower, and, above all, groundnuts (production of which was estimated at 70,000 tons in 2010) are exported in limited quantities to Portugal. Bananas (production estimated at 115,000 tons in 2010) and citrus fruits (39,000 tons in 2009) are exported, as well as potatoes (111,000 tons in 2010) and kenaf (a jute-like fibre—production estimated at 2,500 tons in 2009).

Interest in developing a biofuel sector in Mozambique has grown in recent years. According to a study by US company Ecoenergy, the country could produce 40m. litres of biodiesel per year from jatropha and palm and 21m. litres of bio-ethanol from sugar cane, maize and cassava. Ecoenergy drew up a national biofuel strategy, which was implemented in 2009 and was to form the basis of a new law aimed at attracting investment to the sector. In 2011 the Government announced that from 2012 all petrol fuel sold in Mozambique would have to be 10% ethanol and diesel and 3% biodiesel. At the end of 2009 the Government reported that US $250m. had been invested in the sector, and several major projects were under way. Progress in the sector has been slow since 2009, however. In mid-2011 there were 33 projects pending approval and only three large projects in the early stages of implementation. In March Mozambique made its first export of 30 tons of jathropa biofuel to German airliner Lufthansa for an undisclosed price.

Mozambique has to import fresh and prepared meat. Livestock is still of secondary importance, owing partly to the prevalence of the tsetse fly over about two-thirds of the country, but the total number of cattle has increased steadily since the end of the war. Most of the cattle are raised south of the Save river, notably in Gaza province, which has about 500,000 head. There were an estimated 4.8m. goats, 200,000 sheep and 1.4m. pigs in 2010, and 1.5m. head of cattle in 2011. Between 1999 and 2011 livestock increased by 71%. In 2011 the Government announced that it would begin to implement a programme of artificial insemination for cattle and goats and would begin importing bulls to increase the cattle stock. By 2012 Mozambique produced 40,000 metric tons of chicken meat per year, compared with its domestic consumption of 60,000 tons.

Mozambique has 19m. ha of productive forest and, according to government estimates, can annually produce 500,000 cu m of logs. Forestry has developed chiefly along the Beira railway and in the wetter Zambézia province. Some eucalyptus plantations have been established in the south of the country to produce wood for paper; in 2006 work began on two plantation projects in Niassa province, worth US $80m., which were to plant 210,000 ha with eucalyptus and pines. In January 2010 the Government approved a 126,000-ha forest plantation for carbon sequestration, wood and pulp, funded by a Norwegian carbon offset and renewable energy company, Green Resources, at an estimated cost of over $2,000m. The majority of exports are sawn timber and construction timber, with South Africa being the principal market. However, the forestry sector is affected by widespread corruption, with numerous small companies, including Chinese ones, felling hardwood trees indiscriminately, particularly in the central provinces of Zambézia, Manica and Sofala. Between 2002 and 2006 commercial logging production averaged 135,000 cu m per year, although the figure may have been much higher as a result of the increase in unregulated logging. In 2002 the Government banned the export of unprocessed logs, which led to growth in the number of sawmills, from 139 in 2000 to 178 in 2005, increasing annual production of sawn wood, from 28,121 cu m in 2004 to 198,000 cu m in 2010. In 2008 the rate of deforestation was estimated at 0.6% per year, equivalent to 219,000 ha.

In 2011 the US-based Oakland Institute published a detailed study on land concessions, revealing that the Government had granted over 2.5m. ha of land during 2004–09 to foreign investors, 73% for forestry and the remaining 27% for biofuel and agricultural crops. Due to policy disagreements, the Government suspended the sale of land concessions over 1,000 ha between 2009 and 2011. Sales resumed in 2012, with concessions between 1,000 ha and 10,000 ha subject to approval from the Minister of Agriculture, and concessions over 10,000 ha subject to approval from the Council of Ministers. In 2012 the Government granted five large land concessions of between approximately 19,000 ha and 70,000 ha to foreign companies.

Fishing is a relatively recent development along Mozambique's extensive coastline and much of its potential is untapped. Although the country is not self-sufficient in fish, domestic catches cover around one-third of consumption at present, compared with 6% in 1979. Fishing accounts for around 2% of GDP. In 2010, according to FAO, the total fishing catch was estimated at 150,634 metric tons, of which 8,556 tons was shrimp. In December 2006 Mozambique signed a five-year fishing agreement with the EU, which came into effect on 1 January 2007. In exchange for an annual payment of €1.2m., the EU was granted a 10,000-ton quota for tuna and other species, excluding deep-water prawns, which had been included in previous agreements. Fish currently accounts for 3% of Mozambique's exports, annually, with the EU the destination for more than 95% of fish exports (of which more than 70% are shrimp). In June 2011 the Government signed a three-year extension to the fisheries agreement with the EU, which came into force in January 2012. Under the new terms, the 10,000-ton quota was reduced to 8,000 tons, and the EU agreed to make an annual payment of €980,000, together with €460,000 in aid. There was a slight decrease in the number of companies participating, due to the growing risk of piracy in the Indian Ocean. Mozambique has potential to develop aquaculture, and over the last 15 years or so a number of international and local companies have established shrimp-farming projects in the country. A Mozambican aquaculture company in Zambézia exported 200 tons of shrimp to Europe in 2010 and planned to expand to export to China and the USA. In 2010 Mozambique produced 630 tons of fish through aquaculture and in 2011 produced 10,000 tons of farmed prawns.

Food Shortages and Security

Mozambique remains one of the poorest countries in the world, ranking 184th of 187 nations on the UN Development Programme's 2011 Human Development Index. Despite relative progress in the agriculture sector in Mozambique, per caput rural food productivity has remained consistently at approximately 600 kg for the last 20 years or so, according to the World Bank.

In 2002 Mozambique experienced a serious drought, and an estimated 500,000 people required food aid. Surpluses from the north and centre of the country traditionally reached the areas in deficit in the south at greatly inflated prices, owing to high transport costs, making it more cost-effective to import maize from South Africa and to export surpluses to Tanzania and Malawi. Rehabilitation of the commercial networks that link the areas with surplus maize to neighbouring countries and to the ports of Nacala and Beira was an urgent requirement (and was still ongoing around 10 years later). In 2003 cumulative rainfall in the Maputo area was the lowest in 50 years, and 156,000 metric tons of emergency food aid was required. Despite the drought in the south, agricultural production grew by 4.2% in that year, fuelled by strong investment in sugar, tobacco, tea and citrus plantations in the north of the country. A severe drought in the south during 2005 reduced the cereal harvest by 5.2%, to 1.9m. tons, compared with 2004. Following improved rains in late 2005, cereal production increased by 10.5% in 2006, reaching 2.1m. tons. According to the Ministry of Agriculture, cereal output declined to 1.9m. tons in 2007, owing to the adverse effects of flooding and cyclone damage, before recovering to 2.3m. tons in 2008. Cereal output improved further in 2009, rising to 2.6m. tons. However, flooding and drought, which affected the central and southern regions between 2009 and 2010, resulted in the loss of an estimated 12% of the harvest. A huge increase in the price of cassava, a staple food for most rural families, in 2008–09 also jeopardized food security.

As part of efforts to reduce cereal imports, in April 2008 the Government announced that it would import 150 metric tons of wheat seed for distribution to farmers, along with subsidized fertilizer. This increased wheat output from just 3,000 tons in 2007 to 21,300 tons in 2008, although this was still far short of the national wheat requirement, which was estimated at 470,000 tons.

As a result of its dependency on basic food imports, Mozambique was severely affected by the global economic downturn and the international food price rises that followed from 2008. In 2010 the prices of some basic foods increased by up to 50%. In 2008 the Government introduced the three-year Plano de Accao para a Producao de Alimentos (PAPA—Food Production Action Plan) for 2008–11, in response to rising global cereal prices and the increasing deficits in basic food products. The objectives of the plan were to increase the domestic production of basic food crops as a way of reducing Mozambique's dependence on imports and its vulnerability to global price fluctuations. It focused on six crops; maize, wheat, cassava, rice, potatoes and oilseed, as well as poultry and fishing. As part of PAPA, the Government introduced subsidies for agricultural inputs, such as fertilizer and seeds. The US $333m. plan additionally aimed to increase national grain production and to make Mozambique self-sufficient in rice production by 2011. By 2010, however, Mozambique had increased domestic rice production to only 340,000 tons, still far below the national requirement of 600,000 tons. In 2009 FAO launched a two-year, €7m. project to strengthen the provision and distribution of seeds in Mozambique and to support smallholder farmers.

Storage facilities for agricultural produce are insufficient for Mozambique's imports and domestic produce, at 560,000 metric tons. In 2011 the Government announced that it intended to increase the national storage capacity by 143,000 tons by 2012, through construction of silos and warehouses.

Initial figures for 2010/11 indicated that Mozambique had increased cereal production by 4.6% to 2.9m. metric tons; however, in January 2011 an outbreak of mosaic virus in southern Mozambique had affected 20% of the cassava output in the region. An estimated 250,000 Mozambicans required food aid in 2011, owing to rising prices and poor crop performances in the centre and south of the country. According to government figures, 46% of children suffered from chronic malnutrition in 2012, with the highest rates being found in Nampula province. In 2011 the USA-based International Food Policy Research Institute ranked Mozambique 65th out of 81 countries on its Global Hunger Index and described the situation in the country as 'alarming'.

MINING

Mozambique has considerable mineral resources, which have only recently started to be exploited. After many years of limited production, coal-mining is now driving FDI and economic growth. In 2010 the mining sector was worth US $95.6m. and was expected to continue to grow. Tete province contains some of the richest undeveloped coal reserves in the world, from which exports began in 2011.

Until 2010 exploitation was limited by investor concerns over internal unrest. As a result, mining was estimated to have contributed less than 0.5% of GDP in 2006. Until recently, mining production had been small-scale and consisted mainly of marble, granite, gold and bauxite. Exports reached only US $35m. in 2006 (excluding the SASOL pipeline—see below), but had risen to $257m. by 2008. FDI in the sector rose from just $40m. in 2004 to $217m. in 2007, increasing to $788.9m. by the end of 2010. In 2011 mining investment projects were worth $11,600m. By that year the Government had issued a total of 1,125 mining licences, 844 of which were prospecting and research licences and 112 were for coal-mining in Tete province. In 2010, however, it revoked six of the concession licences, on the grounds that there had been no activity on the sites, and in 2011 the Government announced that it would award no further licenses for coal-mining in Tete until it could verify whether or not companies were complying with the terms of their contracts.

Unofficial artisanal production, mainly of gold and precious stones, was estimated to be worth around US $40m.–$60m. per year; large quantities of minerals were believed to be illegally exported, depriving Mozambique of valuable revenue. The Assembleia da República adopted a new mining investment code in 2002, which was drafted with World Bank assistance. However, the IMF recommended that the Government review the tax exemptions offered to companies investing in Mozambique, and in 2007 legislation was approved establishing new tax and environmental regimes for the mining and petroleum sectors. In addition, the Government supported a $33m. project to establish a geological survey of the country. In 2009 the Government established a state-controlled mining company, and in 2012 it was studying the possibility of introducing a new mining code.

Mozambique has the potential to become one of Africa's largest exporters of coal, and could export as much as 100m. metric tons annually by 2020. However, the lack of infrastructure such as sufficient power supplies and transport links to export the coal has negatively affected the speed of development. Mozambique has confirmed coal reserves of 10,000m. tons and estimated reserves of 16,000m. tons, but until 2010 (when coal production reached an estimated 50,000 tons) output was relatively low: 37,700 tons in 2008 and 25,900 tons in 2009.

The country's Tete province is believed to contain undeveloped coal deposits that are among the richest in the world. In 2004 Brazil's Companhia do Vale do Rio Doce, with a 95% stake, and American Metals and Coal International (AMCI), with the remaining 5%, bought the mining rights for the Moatize coal mine, near Tete, which had estimated reserves of 2,500m. metric tons. Construction work at the mine commenced in March 2009. Following delays to the US $1,260m. project, coal production eventually began in May 2011, and was stockpiled in anticipation of the conclusion of the Sena rail line to Beira (see below). The company began exporting in September, utilizing the newly opened rail line, and planned to export 1m. tons in the first year and 4m. tons in the second year. Annual production was initially forecast eventually to reach 11m. tons, potentially rising to 14m. tons. However, in November 2011 Vale announced a $600m. expansion plan, which would increase production to 22m. tons per year. The expanded mine was projected to commence operations in 2014. Also in

November 2011 the Government purchased a 5% stake in the Moatize coal mine from Vale for $21m. In January 2012 hundreds of Moatize residents who had been resettled from the area surrounding the mine held anti-Vale demonstrations.

In November 2011 the Government confirmed plans to build three coal-fired power stations in Tete province, including a 1,500-MW plant at Moatize. As part of the project, reconstruction of the 550-km Moatize–Beira railway had been completed in August. However, the railway's freight capacity was estimated at 5m. metric tons per year, and it was acknowledged early on that Beira port would not be able to accommodate the burgeoning industry in the long term. In October 2009 the Government secured US $500m. in funding from the EU, the Netherlands and Denmark to build a new railway line connecting the Moatize mine with the deep-sea port at Nacala. Construction of the 200-km railroad was expected to take five years to complete. In February 2012 the Government announced plans to build a coal terminal at Nacala, with the capacity to handle 18m. tons per year, to meet growing international demand. The $4,400m. terminal would be funded by Vale and was expected to be completed within three years. In the following month the Government launched a $45m. rehabilitation programme for the Sena railway, which was aimed at increasing annual freight capacity to 6.5m. tons and eventually 12.0m. tons. Meanwhile, in 2011 the Ministry of Public Works and Housing announced the $95m. construction of a new road bridge over the Zambezi river in Tete city, which would take four years to complete.

Other companies are also developing coal concessions, and in 2012 there were 36 mining companies operating in the district of Moatize alone. In February 2006 the Government awarded a licence to Aquila Coal (Australia) to prospect for coal in the Moatize area, and in April another Australian company, Riversdale Mining (purchased in 2011 by the Anglo-Australian mining company Rio Tinto), acquired two coal concessions in the Zambezi valley. Indian steel companies have also invested in the development of Mozambique's coal reserves. In November 2007 ArcelorMittal purchased a 35% stake in coal exploration licences in Tete province. In February 2008 India's Global Steel Holdings purchased two coal licences in Tete province, located close to Vale's Moatize concession, with estimated reserves of 70m. metric tons. In June a joint venture involving Riversdale Mining (65%) and India's Tata Steel (35%) announced plans to invest US $800m. in developing an estimated 4,000m. tons of coal reserves at Benga, in Tete province. The Benga mine began exporting coal from Beira port in May 2012, and the Government and Rio Tinto were negotiating plans to link Benga with the Moatize coal rail terminal by 2015. In 2009 Eurasian Natural Resources Corpn (ENRC) of Kazakhstan acquired Central African Mining and assumed coal exploration under 12 licences in Tete province, where the company expected its Estima project to produce 20m. tons of coal per year by 2015. In 2010 the Ncondenzi Coal Company announced plans to develop 1,800m. tons of coal deposits in Tete province, with an output target of 2m. tons a year from 2015. Another Indian company, GIEP, purchased a 75% stake in 11 coal-mining licences, with estimated reserves of 200m. tons, while several Chinese companies were also granted licences in Cabo Delgado and Niassa provinces. In May 2010 the British company Beacon Hill Resources took control of the Minas Moatize open cast mine (first developed under Portuguese rule), where the reserves were estimated at over 450m. tons. The company increased production from 2,000 tons in 2010 to 8,000 tons in 2011 and expected eventually to export 1.8m. tons a year.

Mozambique has significant reserves of tantalite, with annual production estimated at 712,095 metric tons in 2004. However, only small quantities are exported. In 2010 a Canadian company, Pacific Wildcat Resources, was operating the Muiane tantalite mine, in Zambézia province, which closed during the civil war, and a tantalum-processing plant. In January 2011 the Government announced that an unnamed Canadian company was preparing to invest $6m. in a factory to process tantalite from the Muiane mine. In June 2010 Highland African Mining, a subsidiary of Jersey-based company Noventa, announced plans to invest $20m. to increase production at the nearby Marropino mine. In April 2010 production at the Marropino mine was restarted by the British company Noventa, with the capacity to produce 450,000 lbs of tantalum per year. International prices and demand from conflict-free Mozambique grew in 2010, when the country was the world's second largest producer. In April 2011 a new tantalum-processing plant was inaugurated in Zambézia province, with the capacity to process 30–50 tons per hour. In 2011, however, Noventa revealed that it would need a further $25m. to continue operations at Marropino. In 2012 the Marropino mine was adversely affected by Cyclone Fuso, and the company declared that it needed to raise a further $10m.–$13m. as a result of lower output.

There are deposits of ilmenite (titanium ore) in the area north of the mouth of the Zambezi river. In January 2002 the Government and the Anglo-Irish company Kenmare Resources signed an agreement to develop the Moma Titanium Minerals Project (MTMP) in Nampula province, with estimated heavy mineral reserves of 163m. metric tons. At that time (prior to the 'coal rush'), the MTMP was the largest single mining project in Mozambique since independence. The mine, which had estimated development costs of US $460m., started producing titanium ore in late 2006, reaching full production in May 2009, and was expected to produce 800,000 tons of ilmenite, 56,000 tons of zircon and 21,000 tons of rutile (another titanium ore) per year. In February 2011 the company confirmed plans to expand the mine's output to 1.2m. tons per year by developing reserves in Nantaka, at an estimated cost of €146m. In 2011 Kenmare Resources confirmed the discovery of new mineral deposits, which could come into production in 2018.

In 1999 the largest reserve of titanium in the world (estimated at 100m. metric tons), known as Corridor Sands, was discovered in the district of Chibuto in the province of Gaza. Western Mining Corpn (bought by BHP Billiton of Australia, in 2005) of Australia increased its stake in the venture to 90% in December 2002, and the mine was expected to export up to 370,000 tons per year, starting in 2010. However, in early 2009 BHP Billiton withdrew completely from the project, citing global oversupply and rising construction costs. In October 2010 the Government launched an international tender for the development rights to Corridor Sands for which only two eligible bids were received. The Government chose Canadian company Rock Forage Titanium, and was expected to issue a licence by 2013. However, in November 2011 the concession was cancelled by the Government owing to the failure of Rock Forage Titanium to attract the necessary investment.

Despite estimated reserves of 50 metric tons, gold-mining has only recently begun to attract investors on an industrial scale. The total national official extraction of gold was an estimated mere 68 kg in 2006; by 2010 it had risen to 1,979 kg. Artisanal production by some 60,000 *garimpeiros* (gold panners), including large numbers of migrants from Zimbabwe and Tanzania, accounted for around 90% of national gold output in 2010. In January 2006 the United Kingdom's Pan African Resources gained control of a gold-prospecting licence in Manica province, after acquiring a Mozambican company, Explorator Limitada, and in April 2011 it was awarded a mining licence. The firm planned to construct a 30-m open-pit mine and an underground mine at a cost of US $80m., with production expected to total 850 kg per year. Meanwhile, in early 2006 the United Kingdom's African Eagle Resources started exploration on two gold-mining permits at Majele and Muazua in Nampula province. In September Pan African Mining, now a subsidiary of Canada's African Queen Mines, acquired an 85% stake in the Fingoe and Casula gold prospects in Tete province and pledged to invest at least $150,000 in exploration. A Portuguese-Angolan consortium, Agrupamento Mineiro, started mining for gold in Manica in May 2007 after four years of prospecting at a cost of $15m.; the mine was expected to produce 60 kg of gold per month. In November 2009 the Government granted an exploration licence to the South African company Tsozo Refinery and approved plans for the firm to construct a gold-processing plant, which was completed in April 2010 with a capacity of 11,000 kg per year. African Queen Mines entered into a joint venture with Opti Metal Trading of Switzerland in 2010 for continued exploration and prospective drilling in the Fingoe belt, which it hoped could produce 560 kg of gold per year. In

May 2011 a Chinese company was planning to build three industrial gold-processing plants in Mozambique, which by 2015 could process up to 400 kg per day. In July 2011 the Government revoked the licence of South African company Mambas Mineirais amid accusations that it had contributed to the contamination of the local Nhamucuarara river. The Government later concluded that six rivers in Manica province had become polluted as a result of artisanal gold-panning techniques using mercury and other chemicals.

In 2011 the Government announced that Mozambique would apply to join the Kimberley Process Certification Scheme to govern the exploitation of diamonds. In the same year there were 27 companies exploring for diamonds in the provinces of Sofala, Manica, Niassa and Inhambane.

Annual production from the Montepuez marble quarry in Cabo Delgado province has been projected at 8,100 cu m, with Portugal and South Africa identified as potential export markets. An Israeli company is currently mining emeralds and garnets in Zambézia province.

In mid-2012 Brazilian Vale began a feasibility study for exploration of phosphate (a primary nutrient for plants and a basic fertilizer ingredient) at the Evate mine in Nampula province. The results of the US $20m. study were to be published in 2013. It has been estimated that the Evate mine could produce as much as 42m. metric tons of phosphate per year. The company also planned to build a $3,000m. fertilizer complex at nearby Nacala-a-Velha. Also in mid-2012, the Canadian company SRK Consulting was carrying out environmental impact studies for another phosphate mine in Nampula province; the results were expected in 2013.

PETROLEUM AND GAS

Despite natural gas having being discovered in Mozambique in 1969, the country had no hydrocarbons industry until very recently and continues to import all its petroleum requirements from South Africa. However, oil and, in particular, major gas finds precipitated rapid development and foreign investment from 2010. In 2012 proven gas reserves were 127,400m. cu m, while recoverable gas resources were estimated at over 100,000,000m. cu ft. The state-owned Empresa Nacional de Hidrocarbonetos de Moçambique (ENH) currently holds a 10% stake in three blocks in the Rovuma basin Prosperidade field, and discoveries in 2012 led to projections that the natural gas industry could generate up to an annual US $9,500m. in revenue and taxes in the future. In April 2012 the Government announced plans to update existing legislation to allow the State to hold up to 40% of the shares in hydrocarbon projects, up from 25%.

The domestic oil requirement was estimated at 17,000 barrels per day (b/d) in 2010, while consumption of natural gas was only 3m. gigajoules in 2011. In October 2007 the Government approved a US $5,000m. project by a US company, Ayr Logistics, to build an oil refinery in the port of Nacala, producing 300,000 b/d of refined petroleum products. In 2009 a Mozambican company, OilMoz, announced its intention to construct an oil refinery in Maputo province, producing 350,000 b/d, at an estimated cost of $8,000m. Investors in the Nacala and Maputo projects were adversely affected by the global downturn from 2008, and in 2010 the Government announced that it was considering withdrawing both companies' licences because of huge delays; nevertheless, after the discovery of oil in the same year (see below), it was decided that the projects would continue. OilMoz expected the Maputo refinery to be operational in 2015, with 15% of its output to be used domestically. The state oil company, Petróleos de Moçambique (PETROMOC), would hold an undisclosed stake in the project, and Anglo-Dutch company Shell would participate as a technical partner. As part of efforts to liberalize the energy sector, in 2008 the Government abolished the monopoly on fuel imports held by Importadora Moçambicana de Petróleos (IMOPETRO). In 2009 domestic fuel distribution was dominated by PETROMOC, with a 48% market share, and BP, with 35%, with the remainder being divided between four other companies. In June 2012, rather than launching an international tender, the Government chose PETROMOC to import and distribute domestic gas.

In late 2009 work started on a 450-km pipeline from Maputo to Kendal in South Africa's Gauteng province, which was expected to transport 3,500m. litres of fuel per year by 2011. The consortium developing the US $620m. project, known as Petroline, included Petromoc (40%), South Africa's Gigajoule (15%) and Woesa (20%), and private Mozambican investors (25%). However, following repeated delays, in 2011 Petroline announced the suspension of the project.

Investments in the petroleum industry since independence reached US $4,000m. in 2010; investment in natural gas increased from $362m. in 2009 to $600m. in 2010. In 2011 the Government forecast gas production capacity to increase from 120m. gigajoules to 183m. gigajoules a year.

Petroleum-prospecting has been carried out by international companies, both off shore near the Rovuma river basin and Beira and on the mainland. In 2000 ENH commenced the sale of 14 offshore energy exploration licences to foreign companies. Finally, in 2002 an agreement was signed with Malaysia's Petronas for exploration rights on the 29,000-sq km Zambezi block, opposite the river delta. However, exploration on the block proved disappointing, and in 2007 the company abandoned its only exploration well after finding no evidence of hydrocarbons.

In July 2005 the Instituto Nacional de Petróleo (INP—National Petroleum Institute) launched a licensing round for five exploration blocks in the 60,000-km Rovuma basin, attracting bids from seven oil companies. In December 2007 Mozambique opened its third licensing round, for nine blocks, seven of which were off shore, in the 61,000-sq km area located between the Pande and Temane gas fields. In February 2010 the USA's Anadarko Petroleum Corpn reported the first deep-water gas find in the Rovuma basin. Between November 2010 and February 2011, Andarko made four large discoveries in the Rovuma basin, and in August it presented a proposal to invest $415,000m. in a project that was to produce 1.5m. tons of liquefied natural gas (LNG) a year for export by 2018. Between October 2011 and May 2012 Italy's ENI announced three large gas finds in the Rovuma basin. Also in May 2012, Andarko confirmed the presence of another major gas deposit, which could contain over 20,000,000m. cu ft of gas, and a further find was announced in June. Together, these made Rovuma one of the largest gas discoveries in the world, with exploration still ongoing. ENI expected to start producing liquefied natural gas (LNG) in 2016, while Andarko anticipated that LNG production would begin in 2018. In 2012 ENI announced that it was considering plans to invest up to $50,000m. in the development of the gas industry in Mozambique.

In October 2000 ENH signed a contract with the South African mining company SASOL for the development of the Pande and Temane gas fields and a processing facility in southern Inhambane province, in which SASOL was to hold 70% of the equity and ENH the remainder. The International Finance Corpn, part of the World Bank Group, subsequently acquired a 5% shareholding from ENH. The fields' reserves were estimated at 55,000m. cu m, sufficient for 50 years of production. Construction of an 865-km pipeline was completed in February 2004, primarily to supply the South African market, with a branch also extended to Maputo. The first exports of gas began in that month, totalling 85m. gigajoules of gas per year during 2004–05. In 2004–08 SASOL sold gas and condensate from the Pande and Temane gas fields worth US $230m., comprising $177m. of natural gas and $55m. of condensed gas. In May 2012 SASOL announced the completion of the $220m. expansion of the central gas-processing facility at Temane, increasing its annual capacity from 120m. gigajoules to 183m. gigajoules. Approximately 27m. gigajoules would be exported to South Africa, and 9m. gigajoules would constitute royalty gas for the Mozambique Government.

In 2008 SASOL carried out seismic surveys to test for additional gas reserves in offshore Blocks 16 and 19, in which the company held a 50% stake, along with Petronas (35%) and ENH (15%). In September the Government granted ENH a licence to explore for gas in the Buzi river basin, which had reserves estimated at 10,000m. cu ft–17,000m. cu ft. In April 2009 ENH sold 75% of its shares to Indonesia's PT Kaliala Production. Viability studies were carried out in 2011 after the removal of land mines. In November a further seven blocks were offered in Mozambique's fourth onshore licensing round; however, only one company, Norway's DNO, was successful, securing rights to explore the Lower Zambezi block. The Government had confirmed in February that it would hold another licensing round within two years.

Consumption of liquefied petroleum gas (LPG) in Mozambique, most of which was for domestic cooking use, was estimated at 17,000 metric tons in 2010, and supplies were imported from South Africa. In October 2007 SASOL announced a project, in partnership with PETROMOC, to construct an LPG production plant near the Pande and Temane gas fields. The facility was expected to produce 6,000 tons of LPG per year, potentially increasing to 35,000 tons depending on investment. However, in 2011 the project was delayed as a result of financial and technical issues.

In mid-2012 the state-owned Petroleum, Oil and Gas Corpn of South Africa was engaged in talks with the Mozambican Government to develop a US $4,000m. gas-to-liquids plant, with a projected output of 40,000 barrels per day.

POWER

Mozambique has the capacity to generate around 2,200 MW of hydroelectric power, mainly concentrated in the Zambezi basin. Hydroelectricity accounted for 10% of Mozambique's energy supplies in 2011. Domestic demand for electricity grew from 118 MW in 1977 to 235 MW in 1998 and, by 2006, had more than doubled to 577 MW, while the number of households connected to the national power grid increased from 62,000 in 1998 to 850,000 in 2010. Overall, the demand for power in Mozambique was 1,600 MW in 2012 and was rising by an average of 15% per year, driven by mining projects in the north of the country. This has led to sporadic power outages in the main cities and a dependence on gas oil to fuel emergency power generators. Despite the huge growth in demand, only 18% of the population were connected to the electricity grid in 2012. In September 2011 the Ministry of Energy launched a US $200m. programme to connect all 128 districts of Mozambique to the grid by 2014.

In 2005 the Government established the INP to regulate the energy sector, and to manage the State's joint ventures with foreign companies. Significant finds and development in Mozambique's coal and gas sectors (see above) have driven investment in the country's energy infrastructure since 2010. In February the World Bank granted Mozambique an US $80m. loan under the Energy Development and Access Project, a five-year programme to be implemented by the Ministry of Energy, aimed at developing infrastructure for private sector and rural development.

The main component of the Mozambican power-generating industry is the Cahora Bassa dam, built by the Portuguese authorities during the colonial era, which exports to South Africa and Zimbabwe. However, frequent sabotage of power lines during the civil war halted supplies from the dam to the South African grid. A programme to rehabilitate the lines was carried out in July 1995. Transmission to both South Africa and Zimbabwe has been suspended multiple times as a result of payment delays and disagreements over tariff rates. In 2012 Cahora Bassa supplied 65% of its output to South Africa and 19% to Zimbabwe.

Under a 1984 agreement, Mozambique acquired an 18% stake in the company managing the dam, Hidroelétrica de Cahora Bassa (HCB), with Portugal owning the remainder. In October 2006 an agreement was reached with the Portuguese Government transferring part of its ownership of HCB to Mozambique. Under the deal, Mozambique increased its stake to 85%, leaving Portugal with a 15% stake. In addition, Portugal wrote off an estimated $2,500m. in HCB debt. The repayment to Portugal was completed before the end of 2007, and in November Mozambique formally assumed majority ownership of HCB. In April 2012 the Presidents of Mozambique and Portugal reached an agreement over the sale of Portugal's remaining 15% stake, with the Mozambique Government purchasing 7.5% for $42m. and the private Portuguese energy company Redes Energeticas Nacionais (REN) acquiring the remaining 7.5%. REN had already agreed to sell portions of its stake to the State Grid Corpn of China (25%) and Oman Oil (15%), and in 2012 the company declared that it intended to divest its remaining shares to the Government within two years in exchange for a stake in a new company expected to operate the planned transmission lines from Tete to Maputo (see below). In mid-2012 HCB was pursuing the rehabilitation of the dam spillways and the Songo substation, and was also planning to construct a second dam upstream, the 1,250-MW Cahora Bassa North, which would export electricity to West Africa by 2013, although additional funding was still needed.

Construction, at a cost of US $45m., of a 350-km transmission line to the Zimbabwean capital Harare was completed in January 1998. The new line allowed Zimbabwe to draw 500 MW of electricity from Cahora Bassa—about 25% of the dam's installed capacity. Plans for the construction of further lines to supply Malawi and Swaziland were also being pursued following the signing of agreements between Mozambique and those countries in 1994. In January 2008 HCB temporarily halted power supplies to Zimbabwe because of mounting payment arrears amassed by the Zimbabwe Electricity Supply Authority (ZESA), before restoring them later in the year after part of these were repaid. By mid-2009 arrears had started to accumulate once more, reaching an estimated US $50m., but in July the Mozambican Government announced that it would nevertheless continue to supply power to ZESA as part of efforts to support the country's economic recovery under its new unity Government. In June HCB announced that it would increase electricity exports to Botswana from 30 MW to 75 MW, in response to requests for more power from the Botswana Power Corporation. Mozambique is part of the Southern African Power Pool, a Southern African Development Community (SADC) initiative that aims to implement a cross-border power-trading system, to which it hopes to contribute around 6,000 MW by 2015. Zimbabwe's energy arrears had reached $76m. by 2012; in April the Mozambique Government declared that it would continue to supply power, provided that Zimbabwe reduced its debt to under $40m.

In 2006 HCB won a tender to supply 100 MW–200 MW to Malawi by 2009, eventually rising to 300 MW. In June 2010 the Government announced that the newly created BNI would finance a power line between the Cahora Bassa dam and Malawi, at an estimated cost of $2,400m., as well as a second 100-MW power station at Cahora Bassa North, costing $700m. Relations between Mozambique and Malawi improved after a new Malawian President, Joyce Banda, took office in April 2012. An initial electricity agreement was signed in the following month, which would eventually allow Malawi to receive power from the Cahora Bassa dam.

The Government had long-standing plans to construct a 1,400-km power line from Cahora Bassa to Maputo, at an estimated cost of US $2,500m., which would create a national electricity grid and end the need to re-import Mozambican power through the transmission lines of the state-owned South African electricity provider, the Electricity Supply Commission (ESKOM). However, funding for the ambitious project had yet to be fully secured. In 2011 the Mozambican state electricity supplier Electricidade de Moçambique developed a project, known as CESUL, to construct two, 25,550-km, high-tension transmission lines from Tete to Maputo to carry up to 3,750 MW, marking the first link between the northern and southern grids. One of the lines would carry electricity from Cahora Bassa to Maputo; the second would serve Tete and potentially also the provinces of Maputo, Manica, Sofala, Inhambane and Gaza. By June 2012 the Government had secured funding pledges from the World Bank, the AfDB and other donors, and expected construction to begin in 2014 and to be completed in 2017. It was estimated that the project would cost up to $2,000m.

Mozambique has a hydroelectric potential of 12,500 MW, concentrated around the Zambezi river. Other main hydroelectric plants are on the Revue river in Manica province, at Chicamba Real and Mavúzi, which had a combined capacity of 88 MW. In November 2011 the Government announced plans to build a third, $60m. plant in the province, on the Nhancangare river. In 2012 the Government officially transferred ownership of the Chicamba and Mavúzi dams from a Portuguese company, Sociedade Hidroeléctrica do Revué, inactive since 1978, to the state-owned electricity utility Electricidade de Moçambique (EDM). Further south, on the Limpopo, is the dam that helps to irrigate the colonato (a former Portuguese settler scheme). There is also a coal-fired power station in Maputo with a capacity of 60 MW, which is supplied by importing coal from South Africa. In May 2007 the Chinese Government agreed to finance the construction of a $300m. dam on the Incomati river, which will provide water to Maputo, and the Mphanda Nkuwa dam in the Zambezi valley, at an estimated cost of $3,500m. In November the Government awarded the tender to construct the Mphanda Nkuwa dam to a consortium made up of the Brazilian engineering company Camargo Correa, EDM and a local company, Energia Capital. In April 2009 China's Eximbank agreed to provide $2,000m. in financing for the construction of the Mphanda Nkuwa dam, and an additional $300m. towards the construction of a power line from the dam to Maputo. In 2012 EDM revealed that it had asked ESKOM to enter into a financing partnership in return for power purchases to fund both the Mphanda Nkuwa dam and the Cahora Bassa North project. EDM expected that, at the earliest, Mphanda Nkuwa would begin generating power in 2019, followed around two years later by Cahora Bassa North, with both projects being dependent on the construction of the CESUL transmission lines. In mid-2012 Brazil's Vale was still considering plans to construct an 1,800-MW thermal coke power plant at Moatize as part of its coal-mining project.

In 2012 the British company Aggreko and Shanduka of South Africa revealed plans to construct a 107-MW gas-fired plant in Ressano Garcia, 60 km north-west of Maputo, on the border with South Africa, which would use gas from the South African Temane fields and supply EDM and SASOL for two years. The plant would be built at the same site as the South African Matola Gas and Gigawatt projects, and was expected to be operational in October 2012.

From 2010 the Government began to promote the use of solar power for the electrification of rural areas, through the use of micro-hydro and photovoltaic systems. In November 2011 the Government launched a five-year renewable energy programme, which included a plan to produce low-cost photovoltaic panels and batteries. In 2012 the Government declared that solar power had reached up to 2.8m. people in Mozambique.

INDUSTRY

Industries are mainly devoted to the processing of primary materials, and Mozambique remains dependent on South African industrial products. About one-half of Mozambican manufacturers are located in and around Maputo, although the Government is encouraging decentralization towards Beira and northern Mozambique. Food-processing forms the traditional basis of this sector, with sugar-refining, and cashew- and wheat-processing predominating. Other industries include the manufacture of cement, fertilizers, agricultural implements, textiles, glass, ceramics, paper, tyres and railway carriages. In 2001–10 industrial GDP, according to the World Bank, increased at an estimated average annual rate of 7.4%. Industry contributed 9.1% of GDP in 2006, and 10.0% in 2012, excluding aluminium, which accounted for one-third of all exports. In 2009 the Government introduced tax exemptions for companies investing over US $50,000 in specific sectors, including manufacturing, rural industry and assembly industries.

Mozambique has the potential to produce 500,000 metric tons of raw cotton annually, but currently achieves less than one-fifth of that capacity. Textile production and brewing gained in importance during the 1980s. Cotton-spinning and -weaving are undertaken at Chimoio, at Maputo and in Nampula province. The country's largest textile factory, Texlom, located in the industrial suburb of Matola, ceased operations in the late 1990s, when the industry almost entirely collapsed, but reopened in mid-2009 under the name Moztex following a US $2.5m. investment by the Aga Khan Foundation. Another textile factory, Texmoque, located in Nampula, resumed operations in 2008 following its sale to Tanzanian investors. In 2011 the Government launched a national programme to revive the textile industry, which included plans to invest in three new cotton-ginning plants and in the production of cotton fibre for export. In the same year a cotton-ginning factory in Gaza province, the Companhia Agricola de Fomento do Algodão, began operating, with the capacity to produce 40,000 tons per year. Cotton exports to Asia in 2011 contributed $36m. in revenues. In mid-2012 the Government was still seeking investors to revive production at a third textile factory, Riopele, located in Marracuene district, 30 km north of Maputo.

With generous fiscal incentives from the Government, construction began on the Mozal aluminium smelter at Beloluane, near Maputo, in 1998. The facility was completed in 2000 with an initial output capacity of 250,000 metric tons per year. By 2012 Mozal accounted for one-half of national industrial output. Originally majority-owned by BHP Billiton, the smelter is now a joint venture between Japan's Mitsubishi Corpn (25%), the Industrial Development Corpn of South Africa (24%) and the Mozambique Government (3.9%), with BHP Billiton retaining a 47.1% stake. An electricity consortium, Motraco, consisting of the state electricity company, EDM, and its counterparts in South Africa and Swaziland, was created in November 1998 to supply 435 MW of electricity to Mozal. In June 2001 Mozal announced its decision to undertake a US $860m. expansion, and Mozal II became operational in October 2003. Mozal's impact on the Mozambican economy has been huge: in 2003 its aluminium exports provided 55% of total export earnings and accounted for one-quarter of Mozambique's GDP growth. In 2004 Mozal II doubled its production capacity to 506,000 tons of aluminium ingots per year, becoming one of the largest smelters in the world and driving dramatic growth in the mining sector of 129.8% in the first half of 2005. By 2007 Motraco had boosted its supply of power to Mozal to 900 MW. However, in 2008 BHP Billiton reduced power to Mozal by 4%, due to electricity shortages across the region. As a result, after making a profit of $573m. in 2007, Mozal made a loss of $115m. in 2008. In 2011 Mozal announced that it would need access to an additional 5,000 MW or more in order to increase its capacity by 280,000 tons per year. The Government hoped that the eventual development of the CESUL transmission lines (see above) would allow Mozal to expand.

Cement output increased from 179,000 metric tons in 1996 to 800,000 tons in 2006 and 1.8m. tons in 2012. Domestic demand also expanded, reaching 2.3m. tons per year in 2012, and was expected to continue to rise by 7% per year. In 2007 an Anglo-Mozambican consortium started construction of the country's fourth cement plant at Boane, near Maputo, at a cost of US $99m. In 2011 the Cimentos de Moçambique plant increased its annual capacity by 400,000 tons; in the same year a fifth factory, Cimento Nacional, was under construction, with an annual capacity of 250,000 tons. Four more cement factories were planned, including a plant in Matola with a planned output of 500,000 tons per year. The Government expected the new projects to increase total annual output to 7m. tons by 2014.

In August 2009 Capital Star Steel, a joint venture between Mozambican investors, the Seven Star Group (China) and Capital Africa Steel (South Africa), inaugurated a US $50m. steel tube factory, with planned output of 200,000 matric tons per year.

As a result of the global downturn, international aluminium prices decreased by 35% in 2009. Annual exports in Mozambique declined by 26.6%. in 2010, and export earnings contracted by 37.2%. In September 2009 Arcelor Mittal announced that it was closing its steel-rolling mill in Maputo and suspending construction of a US $40m. steel mill in Belelance. Aluminium prices had increased from the end of 2009, and world demand for the metal rose in 2010–12. In 2011 Mozambique was the continent's second largest producer of aluminium after South Africa, and aluminium accounted for 50% of Mozambique's mineral exports, earning $1,160m.

TRANSPORT

Traditionally, Mozambique's transport system has been based around 'transport corridors', which include rail, road and energy infrastructure, linking the interior and neighbouring countries with the Mozambican ports. There are four main corridors: the 'Beira Corridor' from the Zimbabwean border to the port of Beira, the 'Limpopo Corridor' and the 'Maputo Corridor' from South Africa to Maputo, and the 'Nacala Corridor' from Nacala to Malawi.

After the end of the civil war, more emphasis was placed on individual reconstruction and construction projects than on the four corridors. However, from 2010 there was a renewed focus on the corridor zones amid efforts to integrate road, rail and sea infrastructure to support the country's burgeoning coal industry.

Railways

Prior to independence, Mozambique derived much of its income from transit charges on goods carried between Zimbabwe, Zambia, Malawi, Swaziland and South Africa and its ports. The main lines are: from Maputo, the Ressano Garcia line to the South African border, the Goba line to the Swaziland border and the Chicualacuala line to the Zimbabwe border (the Limpopo rail link) in the south; from Beira, the Beira–Mutare line to the Zimbabwe border, the Trans-Zambézia line to the Malawi border and the Tete line. In the north the main route is the Nacala–Malawi line, with a branch line to Lichinga. All of these lines are intended primarily to export the products of landlocked countries, and secondarily to transport Mozambican goods.

Before independence Mozambique had 3,131 km of track, excluding the Sena Sugar Estates railway (90 km), which served only the company's properties. By 2003 the total length of track was 3,114 km, of which 2,072 km was operational. Most of the international lines are controlled by international conventions, since their effective functioning is vital to Mozambique's neighbours. Passenger traffic rose from 26m. passenger-km in 1992 to 403m. passenger-km in 1997, before declining to 169m. passenger-km in 2005, as a result of deterioration of the network and rolling stock.

In 2002 the state ports and railway company, Portos e Caminhos de Ferro de Moçambique (CFM) was privatized and restructured into divisions overseeing four lines and their connected ports. As a result of privatization, CFM's work-force was reduced from nearly 20,000 in 1998 to 1,863 in 2005. In 2004 an Indian company, Rites, won the tender to operate the rail line from Beira to Zimbabwe, and in 2006 it took over management of the line.

In May 1999 a consortium headed by CFM was given approval to purchase the privatized Malawi Railways. CFM was partnered by the Sociedade de Desenvolvimento do Corredor de Nacala (SDCN—Nacala Corridor Development Co), which consisted of US, French and Mozambican private companies. Payment, of some US $20m., was to be made over a period of 20 years. The assets of the rail company were to belong to the consortium, although the task of upgrading the infrastructure was to remain the duty of the Malawian Government, with World Bank funding. In late February 2000 an agreement was signed providing for the transfer of the management of the port of Nacala to SDCN and the 800-km railway line to Malawi. However, management of the port and railway line was only assumed by SDCN in 2005. Work began on rehabilitating the line in late 2005, but disputes subsequently arose with the Mozambican authorities over interference in the concession's management. In 2010 Brazilian Vale purchased a 51% stake in SDCN—the mining company had been seeking alternatives to the Sena railway to export its coal from Moatize. In April 2011 Vale signed an agreement with the Malawian Government, which would allow 100 km of track to be built from Moatize to Malawi.

In May 2004 an Indian consortium, comprising Rites and Ircon (RICON), won the tender to reconstruct the 550-km Sena railway line running from the port of Beira to the Moatize coal mines in Tete, and in December of that year the World Bank agreed to lend US $110m. to upgrade the railway system. In early 2006 CFM completed rehabilitation of the first 32-km section of the Beira–Tete line, estimating the project's total cost at $200m. In early 2008 CFM completed work on the line as far as Inhaminga, in addition to a new branch line to the country's largest sugar plantation in Marromeu. In November the Sena railway line resumed operations from Dondo to Marromeu; completion of the line was delayed, after the track was found in 2010 to be faulty in numerous locations. As a result, some of the first coal exports from Moatize had to be transported by road, and in 2011 the Government cancelled its contract with RICON. In May 2012 the Government announced plans to launch a tender for the modernization of the Sena line between Beira and Dondo to increase capacity to 6.5m. metric tons per year (and to 20m. tons by 2015).

In response to the demands of the Moatize coal mine, in 2009 the Government announced the construction of a new, 200-km railway line through Nampula province to the deep-sea port at Nacala. The cost of the project was estimated at US $500m. and would be funded by the Government and external donors. In 2011 the Governments of Mozambique, Botswana and Zimbabwe entered into an agreement to revive the Limpopo rail line as part of a $7,000m. project that would include construction of a deepwater harbour (see below). The project was expected to take 10 years to complete, once funding had been secured. In May 2012 the Ministry of Planning and Development launched a strategy to integrate the various projects under way in the Nacala corridor, including the railway and the rehabilitation of the port.

In February 2012 ENRC, which was engaged in Mozambique's coal-mining sector, announced plans for the development of rail and port infrastructure between Nacala and Tete, asserting that they would be cheaper to implement than parallel plans proposed by the Brazilian mining company Vale. However, in July the Corredor Logístico Integrado de Nacala (CLIN), a joint venture between Vale Moçambique (80%) and CFM (20%), was awarded a concession to develop the Nacala corridor. The project would include construction of the railway between Moatize and Malawi and the Nacala-a-Velha branch at an estimated cost of US $1,500m., with a freight capacity of 40m. metric tons per year, 30m. tons of which would be reserved for Vale's coal exports. The scheme also involved the construction of the Nacala-a-Velha Port Terminal (see below). According to the terms of the venture, CFM would increase its stake to 50% at a later stage.

Roads

Railway-dominated Mozambique suffers from a lack of good roads. In 2012 there were only an estimated 30,000 km of roads and tracks, of which only 7,000 km were paved. Furthermore, the main roads are penetration lines towards bordering countries and are grossly insufficient for Mozambique's purposes.

Between 2001 and 2006 the Government spent on average US $140m. a year on the road sector. In June 2007 the Government announced the next phase of the national road programme, PRISE, covering 2007–11. The programme was to cost $1,140m., over one-half of which was to be provided by donors. During 2007–09 the World Bank provided Mozambique with $100m. to support the programme. Priority projects included rehabilitation and extension of the north–south national highway, the construction of 15 new bridges, the rehabilitation of the Beira–Zimbabwe road, and improvements to the Lichinga–Pemba and Milange–Mocuba roads. In September 2007 the World Bank approved a $100m. loan to fund the rehabilitation of the main north–south motorway in Inhambane and Maputo provinces. In June 2008 Japan agreed to construct a new 400-km tarred road from Nampula to Cuamba, in Niassa province. In June 2009 the Government announced that it had invested $1,000m. in improving the road network in 2005–09, including the paving of 2,500 km of roads. Also in that month, the World Bank approved a loan worth $181m. to finance the construction of the first phase of a 1,033-km road corridor from Nacala on the Mozambican coast to Malawi and Zambia. Construction of the first phase began in 2009. In 2010 the AfDB provided $86.5m. of financing for the second phase of the project.

In December 2005 work began on a 2.4-km bridge over the Zambezi river at Caia to replace the ferry service. The US $100m. project was funded by the EU, Sweden, Italy, Japan, and the Mozambican Government, and was inaugurated in August 2009. In October 2005 work began on a bridge over the Rovuma river, which forms the border between Mozambique and Tanzania. The 720-m Unity Bridge, which was to be constructed by a Chinese company, would cost an estimated $25m. However, the project was criticized by donors, who instead suggested upgrading the existing ferry service at far less cost; as a result, the two Governments were to bear the full cost. Following delays with importing construction materials, the bridge was eventually inaugurated in May 2010. In 2008 work was completed on a $14.4m. bridge over the Limpopo river, in Gaza province, funded by the Nordic Development Fund and the Mozambican Government. In October 2008 the bridge over the Lugela river, Zambézia province, which was destroyed by flooding in 2000, reopened to traffic following a $7.3m. rehabilitation project.

In May 2011 the Government announced that it would finance construction of a second, 1.6-km road bridge over the Zambeze river, from Tete to Moatize, supporting further the development of the Nacala Corridor. The construction was estimated at €105m. and would be carried out by a consortium of Portuguese companies, including Mota Engil. It was expected to take over three years to complete. In June the World Bank approved a US $41m. loan to Mozambique towards concluding repairs to three sections of the north–south motorway, which was still incomplete—one section in Maputo city, and the others in Gaza and Inhambane provinces. In the same month the Maputo administration announced that it was investing $7m. to repair and improve roads and pavements in the capital city. In mid-2012 China's Eximbank provided $300m. towards the construction of a 74-km ring road around Maputo city, which would ease congestion and provide a link with the Maputo–South Africa highway. Work commenced in June and was scheduled for completion in 2014.

Ports

The main ports are Maputo (the second largest port in Africa, with its annex at Matola), Beira, Nacala and Quelimane. Maputo and Beira ports exist chiefly as outlets for South Africa, Swaziland, Zimbabwe, Zambia, Malawi and the Democratic Republic of the Congo.

In 2003 the management of the port of Maputo was transferred to the private sector. The Maputo Port Development Co (MPDC), a consortium led by a British company, Mersey Docks and Harbour Co Ltd, and including Sweden's Skanska and some Portuguese investors, as well as a local company, Gestores de Moçambique, acquired a 15-year lease of the facility. The company invested US $45m. in priority works, including the dredging of the harbour and the purchase of new tugs and equipment. However, a proposed $170m. expansion, which would have increased the port's capacity to 17m. metric tons per year by 2010, was put on hold as a result of the company's non-payment of $10m. in annual fixed fees to the Government, which it withheld until rehabilitation work on the Ressano Garcia railway had been completed. In April 2006 a South African shipping company, Grindrod, acquired a 12.2% equity stake in MPDC. In January 2008 Dubai Ports World (DP World) acquired a stake in MPDC and announced that it would invest $32m. to expand Maputo port's container facilities. In 2010 MPDC stated that it would invest $70m. in a three-year refurbishment project for both Maputo port and Matola mineral port, situated outside Maputo. By 2012 DP World, Gestores de Moçambique and Grindrod held 57% of the shares in MPDC, with CFM and the Government holding the remaining 43% stake. Traffic at the port almost doubled between 2003 and 2012, reaching 1,030 ships in the latter year.

In October 2006 Grindrod started work on a US $25m. expansion of the coal terminal at Matola port, boosting its capacity from 1.7m. metric tons per year to 6.0m. tons per year by 2008. The company completed work on a new car terminal in December 2007, as part of $80m. of investments in Maputo port during 2007–09, and a second-phase expansion to accommodate 180,000 cars per year was completed in 2011. Most of the freight in that year comprised vehicles entering the African market from Asia. A third phase, which was expected to take place after 2012, would provide facilities for high and heavy vehicles and increase capacity to 250,000 units. In January 2012 Grindrod announced that it would sell a 35% stake in the coal terminal to the Dutch Vitol group for $67.7m.

In 2005 Denmark financed a US $53m. rehabilitation of the Beira port, expanding its storage facilities and dredging the harbour to enable large-draught ships to moor permanently. In 2005 cargo traffic totalled 1.5m. metric tons, a 12.3% increase on 2004, and this was expected to rise substantially once the second phase of rehabilitation was complete. In July 2009 work began on a $19m. project, with financing from the AfDB and the Islamic Development Bank, to rehabilitate Beira's fishing port (which had closed in 2001), intended to enable it to export up to $90m. worth of fish each year. A second phase of the project would involve the rehabilitation of infrastructure around the fishing port, at an estimated cost of $40m.; however, no financing had been secured by the end of 2009. In June 2012 a new $200m. coal terminal was opened at Beira port with the capacity to handle up to 20m tons a year. The new terminal was expected to go some way to providing the capacity needed for exports from the Moatize mine.

In 2006 the company that manages the port of Nacala, CDN, announced plans to expand the port's facilities to handle Panamax-size vessels weighing up to 200,000 metric tons. In 2007 work began on an $8m. interim project to increase the port's capacity to handle containers. In early 2012 a concession was awarded to the CLIN for the construction of a new port at Nacala, which would be used principally for coal exports and would be served by a new rail link to Moatize and Malawi.

In 2011 the Governments of Mozambique, Botswana and Zimbabwe signed a memorandum of understanding for the construction of a deep-water port in Matutuine, in the south of Mozambique. The port would have cargo and passenger handling capacities and would be built for petroleum exports. The US $5,000m. project included plans for reconstruction of a rail from the port linking all three countries, with construction planned for 2012–16. The sources of funding for the project were not made public, but it was announced that the Governments had secured private funding.

Air

International air transport is operated by the state-owned Linhas Aéreas de Moçambique (LAM), and domestic and regional routes by Sociedade de Transporte e Trabalho Aéreo (TTA). There are 18 airports, of which eight are international—Beira, Maputo, Nampula, Pemba, Ponto Douro, Quelimane, Tete and Vilankulos. Despite opposition from within the ruling party, sustained pressure from the World Bank led the Government to agree to transfer LAM and TTA to private sector ownership. The latter was privatized in May 1997. Efforts to privatize LAM suffered a reverse when the restricted tender, apparently won by a consortium led by the Portuguese airline TAP, was cancelled following renewed opposition from within the ruling party. At the same time, the Government's strategy of preserving LAM's monopoly on lucrative routes until 2003 was challenged in court by TTA. In November 2000 TTA was authorized to begin regional flights. However, TTA was unable to raise enough funding to operate on these routes, which covered the largest cities, such as Maputo and Beira. In 2007 the Government adopted a new civil aviation policy, which authorized foreign or domestic carriers to operate routes that were not serviced by LAM. This led to direct flights from Johannesburg, South Africa, to Inhambane, Pemba and Vilanculos. In 2004 a local company, Air Corridor, started the first domestic services in competition with LAM, flying from its base in Nampula to Maputo, Quelimane, Beira, Pemba and Lichinga. However, the airline closed in 2006 due to operational problems and the Government's refusal to grant it regional routes. In 2010 a private South African carrier, 1Time, began operating between Johannesburg and Maputo, running five flights a week at discounted rates. However, in 2011 1Time ceased flights on the route after being denied authorization to increase the number of weekly flights. In September another South African airline, Comair, was granted 10 flights per week on the same route. In the same year, the private Mozambican carrier KAYA Airlines began operating domestic flights between Maputo, Beira, Tete and Nampula.

In September 2006 the airport authority, Aeroportos de Moçambique (ADM), announced a two-year project, worth US $136m., to rehabilitate and expand the country's main airports. This would include the expansion of Maputo's Mavalane international airport, to more than double its handling capacity, from 495,000 passengers per year to 1m. passengers per year. The Government was also seeking to lease the management of the airport to a private operator. In April 2008 construction started on a new 900,000-passenger terminal at Maputo's international airport, along with the upgrade of the existing terminal. The $75m. project was implemented by a Chinese construction company, An Hui, and was successfully completed in mid-2010. In August 2010 the Government awarded the $36m. contract for construction of a second passenger terminal to An Hui, and the works were due for completion by the end of 2012. In April 2008 LAM announced a $150m. investment programme over three years, involving the upgrade or purchase of new aircraft, and improved training for its pilots and ground staff. In August 2009 the Government declared a new policy to liberalize airport services, such as baggage-handling and tax collection, by authorizing private sector involvement.

In March 2010 the Government announced that it would build a new international airport in Pemba, Cabo Delgado province, to meet growing demand from tourism. A tender for the construction work was launched by ADM in mid-2010. In 2011 the Government signed an agreement with the Brazilian Development Bank to convert the Nacala military air base into a commercial airport, with the capacity to handle up to 500,000 passengers per year, to support the tourism industry. The work would be carried out by the Brazilian company Odebrecht, at an estimated cost of $120m., with the Government providing $40m. of the total. The airport was expected to be operational in 2013.

In 2012 the Government declared that it would need US $500m. during 2012–15 to upgrade the national airports. Although the number of domestic passengers had decreased between 2009 and 2010, the overall volume of passengers and cargo had risen.

TELECOMMUNICATIONS

The telecommunications sector in Mozambique has suffered from years of underinvestment. In 2007 the state monopoly Telecomunicações de Moçambique (TDM) operated a network of just 78,000 fixed lines. However, the new mobile technology and internet industries were key sectors for growth. A mobile cellular telephone company, Moçambique Celular (mCel), a joint venture between TDM and Germany's Deutsche Telekom, was launched in 1997. In June 2002 Vodacom Moçambique (VM), a subsidiary of Vodacom South Africa, paid US $15m. for a second mobile telephone operating licence. However, it was unable to launch services until late 2003 due to a protracted dispute over interconnection fees to other networks operated by TDM and mCel. In 2004 VM launched a $567m. investment programme covering Maputo, the main towns of the south, the road routes to South Africa and Swaziland, and the city of Nampula, before extending its service to other parts of the country. By the end of 2008 there were an estimated 4.8m. mobile telephone subscribers in Mozambique, rising to 7.9m. in 2011, with mCel enjoying a 70% market share, and VM the remaining 30%. Internet usage is low, although it has expanded in recent years in line with improving infrastructure. In July 2007 TDM completed the extension of the country's fibre-optic network from Maputo to Quelimane. According to the International Telecommunication Union, there were 200,000 internet users in 2007, compared with 50,000 in 2002. In 2010 the World Bank estimated that 4.2% of the population had access to the internet, 75% of whom resided in Maputo. In April the Government opened a tender for a third mobile telephone network, setting a reserve price of $25m. Bidding ended in July and in November the Government selected Vietnamese company Viettel to establish Movitel. Viettel said it would invest $400m. in Movitel between 2010 and 2015 and aimed to reach 85% of the population. However, there was criticism about the winning bid, which, at $29m., was not the highest; Viettel is 29% owned by the SPI, the Frelimo party holding company. Movitel launched its network in May 2012, reaching 105 of Mozambique's 128 districts with 2G (second generation) and 3G (third generation) technology.

TOURISM

By the end of the 1990s tourism was the fastest growing sector of the Mozambique economy. In 2003, according to official figures, there were 441,000 tourist arrivals in Mozambique, a sharp increase on 1995 when there were only 150,000 tourists. According to the World Tourism Organization, in 2005 Mozambique's tourism sector grew by 37%, the fastest rate of growth in the world, with nearly US $500m. of projects being approved. Tourist arrivals have grown steadily, reaching 2.6m. in 2008 and 3.1m. in 2009, according to the World Tourism Organization, although receipts declined slightly in the latter year as a result of the global economic downturn. South Africans comprise the bulk of visitors to Mozambique. The central bank estimated that receipts from tourism rose from $108m. in 2005 to $231m. in 2011; however, the true figure could be several times higher, as most tourist transactions are in cash and unrecorded. In 2012 there were over 10,700 hotel rooms in the country and around 42,000 Mozambicans employed in tourism.

Mozambique's beaches and nature and game reserves have become important tourist attractions. In April 1998 the Government launched the development of the 22,000-sq km Niassa reserve in the far north of the country. The most significant development, however, was the extension of South Africa's Kruger National Park into Mozambique, part of a programme, supported by the World Bank, the EU, South Africa's Peace Parks Foundation, and the US and German Governments, to develop five trans-frontier conservation areas. A cross-border park linking territories in Mozambique with the Kruger Park and Gonarezhou park in Zimbabwe, the Great Limpopo Transfrontier Park, created a single conservation area, comprising one of the world's largest wildlife reserves. In December 2002 an international treaty establishing the park was signed, and in 2004 the Government invited tenders for licences to operate hiking trails on the Mozambique side of the park. The park was formally opened in late 2007. In 2005 the Government solicited funding from the World Bank to develop the national tourism infrastructure. With some of these funds, the Government revived the Maputo Elephant Reserve (which was renamed the Maputo Special Reserve), located 120 km south of Maputo, which was a major game park in the colonial era but lost much of its game during the war. The Mozambique Tourism Anchor Investment Program was launched in 2007, with support from the AfDB and a small group of international donor countries. However, it failed to attract the direct investment necessary. A report on the programme released in 2012 attributed its failures to the global economic downturn and difficulties in defining policy and a regulatory framework with the Government.

In December 2009 the Government published a list of 17 priority areas for the development of tourism; most of these were in the northern province of Inhambane. In 2011 the Government declared that it would invest over US $2,000m. in tourism infrastructure development and management until 2015, through the Mozaico do Índico project, based around two key areas—the Arco Norte (Cabo Delgado, Nampula and Niassa) and the Ancora Project (including the Maputo Special Reserve and the Gile Reserve).

TRADE AND DEBT

The beginning of aluminium production at the Mozal smelter almost doubled exports, from US $364m. in 2000 to $726m. in 2001, rising further to $1,043.9m. in 2003. Exports again rose sharply to $1,503.9m. in 2004 as a result of the expansion of the Mozal aluminium smelter and the construction of the SASOL gas pipeline to South Africa; buoyed by high aluminium prices, they increased from $1,745.3m. in 2005 to an estimated $2,200m. in 2010. Imports rose at a slower pace, from $997.3m. in 2001 to $2,811.1m. in 2007. However, due to higher fuel costs, imports rose sharply to $3,457.8m. in 2008 and to $3,335m. in 2010. As a result, the trade deficit, which had declined between 2002 and 2006, rose sharply to $1,390m. in 2009. It recovered slightly in 2010, decreasing to $973m., but the Ministry of Industry and Trade expected the deficit to increase in the short term from 2011 as a result of imports destined for the mega-projects in the coal and natural gas sectors. In 2001 the current account deficit stood at $657.2m., but by 2009 had grown to $1,171m. (equivalent to approximately 11% of GDP), driven by high fuel and food prices and a greater volume of imports resulting from the increase in aid. The deficit declined slightly to $1,113m. in 2010 as prices recovered. The country has historically received large inflows of remittances from expatriates and donor aid.

Mozambique has a diversified set of trading partners. In 2010 the principal source of imports was South Africa (34.4%), followed by the Netherlands (18.0%). In that year the Netherlands was the principal market for exports (52.7%), followed by South Africa (20.8%). Bilateral trade between China and Mozambique has increased rapidly in recent years, from US $23m. in 2001 to $210m. in 2010. In December 2001 the USA first declared Mozambique eligible for the African Growth and Opportunity Act (AGOA), which allows Mozambique duty-free access to the US market for most of its products; its eligibility was renewed in December 2002. The Government has also signed preferential export agreements with China, and in July 2010 the Banco Internacional de Moçambique signed a co-operation accord with the Bank of China. In September China committed to $1,200m. worth of investments in Mozambique and signed a series of new co-operation agreements in mining, energy and agriculture, among other areas. The accords marked a new phase in bilateral relations between the two countries, which were to discuss a further $600m. of investments in the near future.

The prospect of reducing Mozambique's debt burden improved following the decision by the 'Paris Club' of official creditors to admit Russia as a member in 1997. Since Mozambique owed substantial debts to Russia, this cleared the way for Mozambique to benefit from the IMF and World Bank's HIPC debt-reduction initiative. A programme under HIPC terms was approved in April 1998 and took effect in June 1999. Mozambique was to receive US $3,700m. in debt relief under the HIPC initiative, reducing the country's external debt by almost two-thirds.

Following massive flooding in the southern and central regions of the country in February 2000, in mid-March the Paris Club agreed to defer all payments due on the country's external debt, valued at US $73m., for a period of one year. However, a number of conditions were attached to the debt-relief package, including the maintenance of a stable economic environment and the implementation of the poverty reduction strategy in the areas of social development and public sector reform. In April the IMF agreed to grant Mozambique a further $600m. in debt relief under the enhanced terms of the HIPC initiative. The value of the country's debt-stock was reduced to $7,052m. at the end of 2000, and the debt-servicing ratio was reduced to the equivalent of 11.7% of exports in that year.

In 2002 Mozambique attracted US $406m. in FDI, making it the fifth highest destination for FDI in sub-Saharan Africa, according to a report by the UN Conference on Trade and Development. Between 1998 and 2002 total FDI reached $1,420m., much of it related to the expansion of the Mozal project (see above), but declined steadily to an estimated $154m. in 2006. Investment in a second generation of smaller mega-projects helped to increase FDI inflows again. In 2007 a total of 186 FDI projects were approved, worth $7,500m., in the mining, tourism, services and agricultural sectors. In 2008 FDI was estimated at $587.1m. The Government estimated that FDI had increased by an average of 44% a year in 2007–09, totalling €2,700m. In 2010 over 50% of FDI was in the agriculture sector. The level of FDI rose substantially in 2011 as interest in the burgeoning gas and coal sectors escalated.

In May 2004 Mozambique was one of 16 countries selected for access to the US Government's Millennium Challenge Corpn (MCC), the body set up to disburse additional development funding. In 2007 the MCC granted Mozambique US $506.9m. in funding over three years to fund projects to reduce poverty, improve health, and raise incomes and employment, which should benefit 5m. Mozambicans by 2015.

In January 2006, as part of the Multilateral Debt Relief Initiative, the IMF cancelled Mozambique's entire debt to the Fund, an amount worth $153m. It was followed by the AfDB, which waived $370.4m. in debt, and in July by the World Bank, which wrote off $1,359m. in International Development Assistance loans. In May 2007 Mozambique completed a buy-back operation for its entire commercial debt, nominally worth $176m., at less than one-10th of its value; the $16.1m. operation was funded by the Norwegian Government and the World Bank. Given the Government's strong track record of governance, further debt write-offs (by individual countries and by international organizations) ensued. At the end of 2009 Mozambique's total external debt was $4,168m., of which $3,354m. was public and publicly guaranteed debt. In that year, the cost of servicing long-term public and publicly guaranteed debt and repayments to the IMF was equivalent to 1.4% of the value of exports of goods, services and income (excluding workers' remittances).

Statistical Survey

Source (unless otherwise stated): Instituto Nacional de Estatística, Comissão Nacional do Plano, Av. Ahmed Sekou Touré 21, CP 493, Maputo; tel. 21491054; fax 21490384; e-mail webmaster@ine.gov.mz; internet www.ine.gov.mz.

Area and Population

AREA, POPULATION AND DENSITY

Area (sq km)	799,380*
Land	786,380
Inland waters	13,000
Population (census results)	
1 August 1997	15,278,334
1 August 2007	
Males	9,734,678
Females	10,491,618
Total	20,226,296
Population (UN estimates at mid-year)†	
2010	23,390,765
2011	23,929,710
2012	24,475,184
Density (per sq km) at mid-2012	30.6

* 308,641 sq miles.

† Source: UN, *World Population Prospects: The 2010 Revision*.

POPULATION BY AGE AND SEX
(UN estimates at mid-2012)

	Males	Females	Total
0–14	5,377,214	5,332,000	10,709,214
15–64	6,211,370	6,736,062	12,947,432
65 and over	347,568	470,970	818,538
Total	11,936,152	12,539,032	24,475,184

Source: UN, *World Population Prospects: The 2010 Revision*.

PROVINCES
(at census of 1 August 2007)

Province	Area (sq km)	Population	Density (per sq km)
Cabo Delgado	82,625	1,605,649	19.4
Gaza	75,709	1,226,272	16.2
Inhambane	68,615	1,252,479	18.3
Manica	61,661	1,412,029	22.9
City of Maputo	300	1,094,315	3,647.7
Maputo Province	26,058	1,205,553	46.3
Nampula	81,606	3,985,285	48.8
Niassa	129,056	1,169,837	9.1
Sofala	68,018	1,642,636	24.2
Tete	100,724	1,783,967	17.7
Zambézia	105,008	3,848,274	36.6
Total	799,380	20,226,296	25.3

PRINCIPAL TOWNS
(at 2007 census, preliminary)

Town	Population	Town	Population
Maputo (capital)	1,099,102	Nacala-Porto	207,894
Matola	675,422	Quelimane	192,876
Nampula	477,900	Tete	152,909
Beira	436,240	Xai-Xai	116,343
Chimoio	238,976		

Mid-2011 (incl. suburbs, UN estimate): Maputo 1,150,030 (Source: UN, *World Urbanization Prospects: The 2011 Revision*).

BIRTHS AND DEATHS

	2009	2010	2011
Crude birth rate (per 1,000)	41.8	41.6	41.4
Crude death rate (per 1,000)	14.0	13.7	13.5

Source: African Development Bank.

Life expectancy (years at birth): 49.7 (males 48.7; females 50.7) in 2010 (Source: World Bank, World Development Indicators database).

ECONOMICALLY ACTIVE POPULATION
(persons aged 12 years and over, 1980 census)

	Males	Females	Total
Agriculture, forestry, hunting and fishing	1,887,779	2,867,052	4,754,831
Mining and quarrying } Manufacturing	323,730	23,064	346,794
Construction	41,611	510	42,121
Commerce	90,654	21,590	112,244
Transport, storage and communications	74,817	2,208	77,025
Other services*	203,629	39,820	243,449
Total employed	2,622,220	2,954,244	5,576,464
Unemployed	75,505	19,321	94,826
Total labour force	2,697,725	2,973,565	5,671,290

* Including electricity, gas and water.

Source: ILO, *Yearbook of Labour Statistics*.

1997 (percentage distribution of economically active population at census of 1 August): Agriculture, forestry and hunting: 91.3% of females, 69.6% of males; Mining: 0.0% of females, 1.0% of males; Manufacturing: 0.8% of females, 5.5% of males; Energy: 0.0% of females, 0.3% of males; Construction: 0.3% of females, 3.9% of males; Transport and communications: 0.1% of females, 2.3% of males; Commerce and finance: 4.3% of females, 9.7% of males; Services: 2.2% of females, 3.4% of males; Unknown: 0.9% of females, 1.4% of males.

Mid-2012 ('000 persons, estimates): Agriculture, etc. 9,047; Total labour force 11,307 (Source: FAO).

Health and Welfare

KEY INDICATORS

Total fertility rate (children per woman, 2010)	4.9
Under-5 mortality rate (per 1,000 live births, 2010)	135
HIV/AIDS (% of persons aged 15–49, 2009)	11.5
Physicians (per 1,000 head, 2008)	0.03
Hospital beds (per 1,000 head, 2007)	0.8
Health expenditure (2009): US $ per head (PPP)	47
Health expenditure (2009): % of GDP	5.4
Health expenditure (2009): public (% of total)	73.1
Access to water (% of persons, 2010)	47
Access to sanitation (% of persons, 2010)	18
Total carbon dioxide emissions ('000 metric tons, 2008)	2,313.9
Carbon dioxide emissions per head (metric tons, 2008)	0.1
Human Development Index (2011): ranking	184
Human Development Index (2011): value	0.322

For sources and definitions, see explanatory note on p. vi.

Agriculture

PRINCIPAL CROPS
('000 metric tons)

	2008	2009	2010
Rice, paddy	102	179*	180†
Maize	1,285	1,932†	1,878†
Millet	24	49†	50*
Sorghum	187	384†	395*
Potatoes*	105	110	111
Sweet potatoes*	89	90	92
Cassava (Manioc)	5,410*	5,672*	5,700
Cashew nuts, with shell	85	64	67*
Groundnuts, with shell	94	68†	70†
Coconuts*	265	270	278
Sunflower seed	5	7*	7*
Tomatoes*	14	15	16
Bananas*	109	109	115
Oranges*	20	20	21
Grapefruits and pomelos*	11	11	11
Guavas, mangoes and mangosteens*	18	18	19
Pineapples*	9	9	10
Papayas*	41	42	44
Tobacco, unmanufactured	64	63	86*

* FAO estimate(s).
† Unofficial figure.

Aggregate production ('000 metric tons, may include official, semi-official or estimated data): Total cereals 1,600 in 2008, 2,547 in 2009, 2,506 in 2010; Total roots and tubers 6,413 in 2008, 6,691 in 2009, 6,739 in 2010; Total vegetables (incl. melons) 195 in 2008, 207 in 2009, 216 in 2010; Total fruits (excl. melons) 357 in 2008, 359 in 2009, 369 in 2010.

Source: FAO.

LIVESTOCK
('000 head, year ending September)

	2008	2009	2010*
Asses*	45	45	45
Cattle	1,240	1,235†	1,250
Pigs	1,266	1,300*	1,350
Sheep	182	190*	200
Goats	4,325	4,500*	4,800
Chickens*	18,000	18,500	19,000

* Estimate(s).
† Unofficial figure.

Source: FAO.

LIVESTOCK PRODUCTS
('000 metric tons, FAO estimates)

	2008	2009	2010
Cattle meat	19	19	19
Goat meat	21	22	24
Pig meat	91	94	97
Chicken meat	22	22	23
Cows' milk	66	67	67
Goats' milk	8	8	9
Hen eggs	14	14	15

Source: FAO.

Forestry

ROUNDWOOD REMOVALS
('000 cubic metres, excl. bark)

	2008	2009	2010
Sawlogs, veneer logs and logs for sleepers	113	136	225
Other industrial wood	1,191	1,191	1,191
Fuel wood	16,724	16,724	16,724
Total	18,028	18,051	18,140

Source: FAO.

SAWNWOOD PRODUCTION
('000 cubic metres, incl. railway sleepers)

	2008	2009	2010
Coniferous (softwood)	6	6	6
Broadleaved (hardwood)	51	114	192
Total	57	120	198

Source: FAO.

Fishing

(metric tons, live weight)

	2008	2009	2010
Dagaas	10,055	13,131	11,018
Penaeus shrimps	7,482	7,349	7,313
Knife shrimp	1,448	1,163	1,243
Marine fishes	78,457	101,134	105,092
Total catch (incl. others)	119,646	148,049	150,634

Note: Figures exclude crocodiles, recorded by number rather than by weight. The number of Nile crocodiles caught was: 566 in 2008; n.a. in 2009; 2,448 in 2010.

Source: FAO.

Mining

('000 metric tons unless otherwise indicated)

	2008	2009	2010*
Bauxite	5.4	3.6	11.0
Coal	37.7	25.9	50.0
Gold (kilograms)†	298	511	80
Quartz (metric tons)	157.3	140.6	700.0
Gravel and crushed rock ('000 cubic metres)	115.5	1,200.0*	1200.0
Marble (slab) ('000 square metres)	7.9	0.3	n.a.
Salt (marine)*	110	110	110
Natural gas (million cu m)	3,037	2,803	3,100

* Estimate(s).

† Figures exclude unreported gold production; total gold output is estimated at 600 kg–900 kg per year.

Source: US Geological Survey.

Industry

SELECTED PRODUCTS
('000 metric tons, unless otherwise indicated)

	2005	2006	2007
Wheat flour	204	193	182
Raw sugar	164	172	183
Groundnut oil ('000 metric tons)*	14.4	11.8	10.1
Beer ('000 hl)	1,412	n.a.	n.a.
Soft drinks ('000 hl)	1,149	1,170	1,170
Cigarettes (metric tons)	1,735	2,543	2,571
Footwear (excl. rubber, '000 pairs)	37	37	40
Cement	564	774	771
Electric energy (million kWh)	13,285	14,737	16,076

* FAO estimates.

2008: Groundnut oil 12,063 metric tons (FAO estimate); Electric energy (million kWh) 15,127.

2009 ('000 metric tons, FAO estimate): Groundnut oil 7.2.

2010 ('000 metric tons, FAO estimate): Groundnut oil 7.6.

Sources: FAO; UN Industrial Commodity Statistics Database.

Finance

CURRENCY AND EXCHANGE RATES

Monetary Units
100 centavos = 1 metical (plural: meticais).

Sterling, Dollar and Euro Equivalents (30 April 2012)
£1 sterling = 45.08 meticais;
US $1 = 27.72 meticais;
€1 = 36.63 meticais;
1,000 meticais = £22.19 = $36.08 = €27.30.

Average Exchange Rate (meticais per US $)
2009 27.52
2010 33.96
2011 29.07

Note: Between April 1992 and October 2000 the market exchange rate was the rate at which commercial banks purchased from and sold to the public. Since October 2000 it has been the weighted average of buying and selling rates of all transactions of commercial banks and stock exchanges with the public. A devaluation of the metical, with 1 new currency unit becoming equivalent to 1,000 of the former currency, was implemented on 1 July 2006.

BUDGET
('000 million meticais)

Revenue*	2009	2010†	2011†
Taxation	41.47	56.54	71.54
Taxes on income and profits	13.72	18.48	24.89
Domestic taxes on goods and services	22.89	31.69	38.42
Taxes on international trade	4.08	5.26	6.73
Other taxes	0.78	1.10	1.51
Non-tax revenue	5.26	7.94	9.58
Total	46.73	64.48	81.12

Expenditure‡	2009	2010†	2011†
Current expenditure	47.87	59.56	71.50
Compensation of employees	23.62	29.11	35.66
Goods and services	11.72	13.09	15.57
Interest on public debt	1.36	2.67	3.58
Transfer payments	11.17	14.69	16.46
Capital expenditure	34.41	43.70	50.60
Total	82.28	103.30	122.09

* Excluding grants received ('000 million meticais): 25.30 in 2009; 28.34 in 2010 (estimate); 28.63 in 2011 (estimate).

† Estimates.

‡ Excluding net lending ('000 million meticais): 4.42 in 2009; 1.93 in 2010 (estimate); 6.17 in 2011 (estimate).

Source: IMF, *Republic of Mozambique: Fourth Review Under the Policy Support Instrument and Request for Modification of Assessment Criteria—Staff Report; Debt Sustainability Analysis; Press Release on the Executive Board Discussion; and Statement by the Executive Director for Mozambique.* (June 2012).

INTERNATIONAL RESERVES
(US $ million at 31 December)

	2009	2010	2011
IMF special drawing rights	170.34	167.07	165.05
Reserve position in IMF	0.01	0.01	0.01
Foreign exchange	1,928.91	1,992.32	2,303.71
Total	2,099.27	2,159.39	2,468.77

Source: IMF, *International Financial Statistics*.

MONEY SUPPLY
('000 million meticais at 31 December)

	2009	2010	2011
Currency outside depository corporations	13,053.6	17,393.6	17,475.6
Transferable deposits	60,847.7	73,744.5	80,162.5
Other deposits	33,173.7	42,273.7	46,223.3
Broad money	107,075.0	133,411.8	143,861.4

Source: IMF, *International Financial Statistics*.

COST OF LIVING
(Consumer Price Index; base: 1998 = 100)

	2002	2003	2004
Food, beverages and tobacco	151	175	187
Clothing and footwear	126	122	125
Firewood and furniture	190	215	263
Health	119	133	134
Transportation and communications	205	232	234
Education, recreation and culture	145	150	151
Other goods and services	136	154	159
All items	157	179	195

Source: IMF, *Republic of Mozambique: Selected Issues and Statistical Appendix* (August 2005).

All items (Consumer Price Index; base: 2005 = 100): 139.5 in 2009; 157.2 in 2010; 173.5 in 2011 (Source: IMF, *International Financial Statistics*).

NATIONAL ACCOUNTS
('000 million meticais at current prices)

Expenditure on the Gross Domestic Product

	2008	2009	2010
Government final consumption expenditure	29,691	34,368	40,999
Private final consumption expenditure	192,513	214,369	258,540
Change in stocks	2,677	–4,164	–5,438
Gross fixed capital formation	39,614	43,959	47,245
Total domestic expenditure	264,495	288,532	341,346
Exports of goods and services	72,638	73,799	78,931
Less Imports of goods and services	96,775	96,119	107,525
GDP in purchasers' values	240,358	266,213	312,751
GDP at constant 2003 prices	161,635	171,873	183,513

Gross Domestic Product by Economic Activity

	2008	2009	2010
Agriculture, livestock and forestry	60,109	67,425	83,087
Fishing	4,259	4,227	5,047
Mining	3,318	3,566	4,413
Manufacturing	33,610	34,449	37,459
Electricity and water	10,044	11,586	13,277
Construction	6,860	7,533	8,820
Wholesale and retail trade; repairs	33,457	37,735	46,346
Restaurants and hotels	3,781	3,904	4,656
Transport and communications	22,180	24,913	28,881
Financial services	9,522	10,508	11,839
Real estate and business services	13,495	14,254	14,783
Public administration and defence	8,519	9,848	11,379
Education	9,320	10,888	13,010
Health	3,514	4,015	4,537
Other services	3,677	3,874	3,975
Sub-total	225,665	248,725	291,509
Less Financial services indirectly measured	5,688	6,403	6,667
Gross value added in basic prices	219,977	242,322	284,843
Taxes on products *Less* Subsidies on products	20,380	23,891	27,909
GDP in market prices	240,358	266,213	312,751

BALANCE OF PAYMENTS
(US $ million)

	2008	2009	2010
Exports of goods f.o.b.	2,653.3	2,147.2	2,333.3
Imports of goods f.o.b.	–3,643.4	–3,422.0	–3,512.4
Trade balance	–990.2	–1,274.8	–1,179.2
Exports of services	555.0	611.7	646.9
Imports of services	–965.3	–1,069.0	–1,153.2
Balance on goods and services	–1,400.5	–1,732.1	–1,685.5
Other income received	167.1	176.2	162.4
Other income paid	–798.5	–427.2	–247.0
Balance on goods, services and income	–2,031.9	–1,983.2	–1,770.1
Current transfers received	977.5	931.7	817.2
Current transfers paid	–125.1	–168.6	–160.4
Current balance	–1,179.4	–1,220.1	–1,113.3
Capital account (net)	419.9	422.3	345.5
Direct investment abroad	—	–2.8	0.8
Direct investment from abroad	591.6	892.5	789.0
Portfolio investment assets	–8.4	4.4	0.3
Portfolio investment liabilities	0.3	0.1	1.1
Other investment assets	–80.7	–118.6	–179.5
Other investment liabilities	269.7	260.0	157.2
Errors and omissions (net)	107.5	–42.7	66.5
Overall balance	120.6	195.0	67.7

Source: IMF, *International Financial Statistics*.

External Trade

PRINCIPAL COMMODITIES
(US $ million)

Imports c.i.f.	2008	2009	2010
Cereals	244.2	275.6	149.2
Rice	114.5	152.3	74.1
Vegetables, fruits and food preparations	10.5	14.5	10.5
Tomatoes, prepared or preserved	0.5	0.7	0.6
Cucumbers, gherkins and onions preserved by vinegar	0.0	0.0	0.0
Mineral fuels, lubricants, etc.	811.4	582.8	711.0
Petroleum oils	650.8	411.5	520.6
Iron and steel and products thereof	87.7	104.9	102.5
Nuclear reactors, boilers, machinery, etc.	313.4	397.7	360.8
Electrical and electronic equipment	218.7	191.8	152.6
Road vehicles	413.9	452.6	368.6
Trucks and motor vehicles for transport of goods	168.9	180.9	146.6
Total (incl. others)	4,007.8	3,764.2	3,564.2

Exports f.o.b.	2008	2009	2010
Fish, crustaceans, molluscs and preparations thereof	75.7	65.4	56.6
Crustaceans	68.7	60.3	52.3
Tobacco and manufactured tobacco substitutes	195.0	180.6	144.5
Tobacco, unmanufactured	193.0	179.3	142.6
Mineral fuels, lubricants, etc.	287.7	374.2	447.4
Electrical energy	226.4	274.4	276.5
Aluminium and articles thereof	1,452.5	n.a.	1,160.0
Nuclear reactors, boilers, machinery, etc.	53.1	78.6	23.6
Total (incl. others)	2,653.3	2,147.2	2,243.1

Source: Trade Map-Trade Competitiveness Map, International Trade Centre, www.intracen.org/marketanalysis.

PRINCIPAL TRADING PARTNERS
(US $ million)

Imports c.i.f.	2008	2009	2010
Argentina	41.2	26.6	2.6
Bahrain	269.7	14.9	94.7
China, People's Republic	156.1	173.1	130.0
Germany	64.7	66.4	79.5
India	144.4	244.7	201.7
Indonesia	38.9	16.0	14.5
Italy	31.1	56.9	74.7
Japan	127.8	141.6	126.3
Malaysia	52.1	46.3	34.9
Netherlands	698.0	488.2	642.9
Pakistan	38.1	55.1	49.2
Portugal	115.8	142.0	154.2
Saudi Arabia	3.9	49.3	7.1
Singapore	10.2	67.2	7.9
South Africa	1,164.9	1,333.8	1,226.8
Spain	44.6	24.7	10.2
Taiwan	117.6	7.2	n.a.
Thailand	87.0	127.6	52.2
United Arab Emirates	103.6	75.6	47.6
United Kingdom	52.0	28.4	57.4
USA	160.4	134.8	74.4
Yemen	0.3	0.7	—
Total (incl. others)	4,007.8	3,764.2	3,564.2

Exports f.o.b.	2008	2009	2010
China, People's Republic	51.6	74.5	79.6
Germany	24.7	24.8	20.4
India	28.4	56.5	30.4
Malawi	46.8	46.7	27.0
Netherlands	1,476.4	893.9	1,181.9
Poland	17.8	24.3	7.9
Portugal	26.4	32.2	108.3
Russia	24.0	29.5	13.6
Singapore	1.9	28.4	11.0
South Africa	265.5	460.3	467.2
Spain	51.0	31.4	30.6
United Kingdom	10.2	28.7	1.4
USA	18.2	41.4	16.4
Zimbabwe	81.3	73.8	72.1
Total (incl. others)	2,653.3	2,147.2	2,243.1

Source: Trade Map-Trade Competitiveness Map, International Trade Centre, www.intracen.org/marketanalysis.

Transport

RAILWAYS
(traffic)

	2007	2008	2009
Passenger-km (million)	319.6	113.6	163.3
Freight ton-km (million)	736.3	717.9	727.7

ROAD TRAFFIC
(motor vehicles in use)

	2007	2008	2009
Light vehicles	152,536	175,522	203,799
Heavy vehicles	56,010	63,659	72,550
Trailers	4,681	6,511	8,584
Tractors	2,484	2,790	3,422
Motorbikes	38,364	42,125	46,822
Total	254,075	290,607	335,177

SHIPPING

Merchant Fleet
(registered at 31 December)

	2007	2008	2009
Number of vessels	129	130	129
Total displacement ('000 grt)	37.9	38.2	41.3

Source: IHS Fairplay, *World Fleet Statistics*.

Freight Handled
('000 metric tons)

	2006	2007	2008
Goods loaded and unloaded	10,683	11,086	11,521

International Sea-borne Freight Traffic
('000 metric tons)

	2001	2002	2003
Goods loaded	2,962	2,780	2,982
Goods unloaded	3,144	4,062	3,837

CIVIL AVIATION
(traffic on scheduled services)

	2007	2008	2009
Kilometres flown (million)	8	8	8
Passengers carried ('000)	443	463	490
Passenger-km (million)	471	505	552
Total ton-km (million)	48	52	56

Source: UN, *Statistical Yearbook*.

Tourism

TOURIST ARRIVALS BY COUNTRY OF RESIDENCE

Country	2007	2008	2009
Malawi	118,820	72,807	86,814
Portugal	24,585	49,116	85,267
South Africa	398,668	1,084,572	1,288,819
Swaziland	29,093	174,648	207,293
United Kingdom	13,537	36,262	58,450
USA	12,319	32,436	38,702
Zimbabwe	101,895	811,241	965,907
Total (incl. others)	1,259,000	2,617,424	3,110,271

Tourism receipts (US $ million, excl. passenger transport): 196 in 2009; 197 in 2010 (provisional); 231 in 2011 (provisional).

Source: World Tourism Organization.

Communications Media

	2009	2010	2011
Telephones ('000 main lines in use)	82.4	88.1	88.1
Mobile cellular telephones ('000 subscribers)	5,970.8	7,224.2	7,855.3
Internet subscribers ('000)	13.5	n.a.	n.a.
Broadband subscribers ('000)	12.5	14.6	16.3

2004: Daily newspapers 19 (average circulation 54,900); Non-daily newspapers 50 (estimated average circulation 210,250).

Periodicals: 32 (average circulation 83,000) in 1998.

Television receivers ('000 in use): 230 in 2001.

Radio receivers ('000 in use): 730 in 1997.

Personal computers: 282,590 (13.6 per 1,000 persons) in 2005.

Sources: International Telecommunication Union; UN, *Statistical Yearbook*; UNESCO Institute for Statistics.

Education

(2005, unless otherwise indicated)

	Institutions	Teachers	Students
Pre-primary*†	5,689	28,705	1,745,049
Primary‡			
First level	8,696	45,887	3,393,677
Second level	1,320	11,011	452,888
Secondary§			
First level	156	210,128	5,004
Second level	35	25,737	861
Technical	41	1,028	21,752
Teacher training‖	18	n.a.	9,314

* Public education only.
† 1997 figures.
‡ Primary education is divided into two cycles of five years followed by two years.
§ Secondary education is divided into two cycles of three years.
‖ 2002 figures.

Source: mainly Ministry of Education.

Students (2009/10 unless otherwise indicated): Primary 5,277,868; Secondary 671,902; Tertiary 28,298 (2004/05) (Source: UNESCO Institute for Statistics).

Teachers (2009/10 unless otherwise indicated): Primary 90,236; Secondary 19,222; Tertiary 3,009 (2004/05) (Source: UNESCO Institute for Statistics).

Pupil-teacher ratio (primary education, UNESCO estimate): 55.4 in 2010/11 (Source: UNESCO Institute for Statistics).

Adult literacy rate (UNESCO estimates): 56.1% (males 70.8%; females 42.8%) in 2010 (Source: UNESCO Institute for Statistics).

Directory

The Constitution

The Constitution came into force on 30 November 1990, replacing the previous version, introduced at independence on 25 June 1975 and revised in 1978. Its main provisions, as amended in 1996 and 2004, are summarized below. There are 306 articles in the Constitution.

GENERAL PRINCIPLES

The Republic of Mozambique is an independent, sovereign, unitary and democratic state of social justice. Sovereignty resides in the people, who exercise it according to the forms laid down in the Constitution. The fundamental objectives of the Republic include:

the defence of independence and sovereignty;

the defence and promotion of human rights and of the equality of citizens before the law; and

the strengthening of democracy, of freedom and of social and individual stability.

POLITICAL PARTICIPATION

The people exercise power through universal, direct, equal, secret, personal and periodic suffrage to elect their representatives, by referendums and through permanent democratic participation. Political parties are prohibited from advocating or resorting to violence.

FUNDAMENTAL RIGHTS AND DUTIES OF CITIZENS

All citizens enjoy the same rights and are subject to the same duties, irrespective of colour, race, sex, ethnic origin, place of birth, religion, level of education, social position or occupation. In realizing the objectives of the Constitution, all citizens enjoy freedom of opinion, assembly and association. All citizens over 18 years of age are entitled to vote and be elected. Active participation in the defence of the country is the duty of every citizen. Individual freedoms are guaranteed by the State, including freedom of expression, of the press, of assembly, of association and of religion. The State guarantees accused persons the right to a legal defence. No Court or Tribunal has the power to impose a sentence of death upon any person.

STATE ORGANS

Public elective officers are chosen by elections through universal, direct, secret, personal and periodic vote. Legally recognized political parties may participate in elections.

THE PRESIDENT

The President is the Head of State and of the Government, and Commander-in-Chief of the armed forces. The President is elected by direct, equal, secret and personal universal suffrage on a majority vote, and must be proposed by at least 10,000 voters, of whom at least 200 must reside in each province. The term of office is five years. A candidate may be re-elected on only two consecutive occasions, or again after an interval of five years between terms. The President is advised by a Conselho de Estado (Council of State), but is not obliged to follow its advice.

COUNCIL OF STATE

The Conselho de Estado is an advisory body presided over by the President of the Republic. It comprises the President of the Assembleia da República (Assembly of the Republic), the Prime Minister, the President of the Conselho Constitucional (Constitutional Council), the President of the Supreme Court, those former Presidents of the Republic not deposed, the former Presidents of the Assembleia and the second placed candidate in the most recent presidential election. In addition, seven representatives are nominated by the President of the Assembleia for the term of the legislature and four representatives are nominated by the President of the Republic for the duration of the presidential mandate. The Conselho de Estado rules on the dissolution of the Assembleia and the declaration of war and oversees general elections and public referenda.

THE ASSEMBLY OF THE REPUBLIC

Legislative power is vested in the Assembleia da República. The Assembleia is elected by universal direct adult suffrage on a secret ballot, and is composed of 250 Deputies. The Assembleia is elected for a maximum term of five years, but may be dissolved by the President before the expiry of its term. The Assembleia holds two ordinary sessions each year. The Assembleia, with a two-thirds' majority, may impeach the President.

THE COUNCIL OF MINISTERS

The Council of Ministers is the Government of the Republic. The Prime Minister assists and advises the President in the leadership of the Government and presents the Government's programme, budget and policies to the Assembleia da República, assisted by other ministers.

THE JUDICIARY

Judicial functions shall be exercised through the Supreme Court and other courts provided for in the law on the judiciary, which also subordinates them to the Assembleia da República. Courts must safeguard the principles of the Constitution and defend the rights and legitimate interests of citizens. Judges are independent, subject only to the law.

LOCAL STATE ORGANS

The Republic is administered in provinces, municipalities and administrative posts. The highest state organ in a province is the provincial government, presided over by a governor, who is answerable to the central Government. There shall be assemblies at each administrative level.

CONSTITUTIONAL COUNCIL

The Conselho Constitucional rules, inter alia, on the constitutionality of legislation, the eligibility of presidential candidates and the legitimacy of electoral results. The Conselho Constitucional also formally declares the death or deposition of the Head of State and rules on the incapacity of the President of the Republic to remain in office. It comprises seven judges: one nominated by the President of the Republic, five elected by the Assembleia da República according to proportional representation and one nominated by the Supreme Court, each to serve a term of five years, which is renewable. Councillors must be aged 35 years or over.

The Government

HEAD OF STATE

President of the Republic and Commander-in-Chief of the Armed Forces: ARMANDO EMÍLIO GUEBUZA (took office 2 February 2005; re-elected 28 October 2009).

COUNCIL OF MINISTERS
(September 2012)

Prime Minister: AIRES BONIFÁCIO ALI.

Minister of the Interior: ALBERTO MONDLANE.

Minister of Finance: MANUEL CHANG.

Minister of Planning and Development: AIÚBA CUERENEIA.

Minister of Foreign Affairs and Co-operation: OLDEMIRO JÚLIO MARQUES BALOI.

Minister of National Defence: FILIPE JACINTO NHUSSI.

Minister of Justice: MARIA BENVINDA LEVI.

Minister of Environmental Co-ordination: ALCINDA ANTÓNIO DE ABREU.

Minister of Agriculture: JOSÉ CONDUNGUA PACHECO.

Minister of Health: ALEXANDRE MANGUELE.

Minister of Industry and Trade: ARMANDO INROGA.

Minister of Science and Technology: VENÂNCIO SIMÃO MASSINGUE.

Minister of Labour: MARIA HELENA TAÍPO.

Minister of Transport and Communications: PAULO FRANCISCO ZUCULA.

Minister of Public Works and Housing: CADMIEL FILIANE MUTHEMBA.

Minister of Public Service: VITÓRIA DIAS DIOGO.

Minister of Tourism: FERNANDO SUMBANA JÚNIOR.

Minister of State Administration: CARMELITA RITA NAMASHULUA.

Minister of Mineral Resources: ESPERANÇA LAURINDA FRANCISCO NHIUANE BIAS.

Minister of Energy: SALVADOR NAMBURETE.

Minister of Veterans' Affairs: MATEUS ÓSCAR KIDA.

Minister of Education: ZEFERINO DE ALEXANDRE MARTINS.

Minister of Culture: ARMANDO ARTUR JOÃO.

Minister of Fisheries: VICTOR MANUEL BORGES.

Minister of Women's Affairs and Social Welfare Co-ordination: IOLANDA MARIA PEDRO CAMPOS CINTURA.

Minister of Youth and Sport: PEDRITO FULEDA CAETANO.

Minister of Presidential Affairs: ANTÓNIO CORREIA FERNANDES SUMBANA.

Minister in the Presidency with responsibility for Social Affairs: FELICIANO SALOMÃO GUNDANA.

Minister in the Presidency with responsibility for Parliamentary, Municipal and Provincial Assembly Affairs: ADELAIDE ANCHIA AMURANE.

There were also 23 Deputy Ministers.

MINISTRIES

Office of the President: Av. Julius Nyerere 1780, Maputo; tel. 21491121; fax 21492065; e-mail gabimprensa@teldata.mz; internet www.presidencia.gov.mz.

Office of the Prime Minister: Praça da Marinha Popular, Maputo; tel. 21426861; fax 21426881; internet www.portaldogoverno.gov.mz.

Ministry of Agriculture: Praça dos Heróis Moçambicanos, CP 1406, Maputo; tel. 21460011; fax 21460055; internet www.minag.gov.mz.

Ministry of Culture: Rua de Tchamba 86, Maputo; tel. 21492582; fax 21498040.

Ministry of Education: Av. 24 de Julho 167, CP 34, Maputo; tel. 21492006; fax 21492196; internet www.mec.gov.mz.

Ministry of Energy: Av. 25 de Setembro, 1218 3° andar, CP 1831, Maputo; tel. 21303265; fax 21313971; e-mail asi@me.gov.mz; internet www.me.gov.mz.

Ministry of Environmental Co-ordination: Rua Kassoende 167, Maputo; tel. 21492403; e-mail jwkacha@virconn.com; internet www.micoa.gov.mz.

Ministry of Finance: Praça da Marinha Popular, CP 272, Maputo; tel. 21315000; fax 21306261.

Ministry of Fisheries: Rua Consiglieri Pedroso 347, CP 1723, Maputo; tel. 21431266; fax 21425087; internet www.mozpesca.gov.mz.

Ministry of Foreign Affairs and Co-operation: Av. 10 de Novembro 620–640, Maputo; tel. 21327000; fax 21327020; e-mail minec@minec.gov.mz; internet www.minec.gov.mz.

Ministry of Health: Avs Eduardo Mondlane e Salvador Allende 1008, CP 264, Maputo; tel. 21427131; fax 21427133; e-mail mdgedge@dnsdee.misau.gov.mz; internet www.misau.gov.mz.

Ministry of Industry and Trade: Praça 25 de Junho 300, CP 1831, Maputo; tel. 21352600; fax 214262301; e-mail infomic@mic.gov.mz; internet www.mic.gov.mz.

Ministry of the Interior: Av. Olof Palme 46/48, CP 290, Maputo; tel. 21303510; fax 21420084.

Ministry of Justice: Av. Julius Nyerere 33, Maputo; tel. 21491613; fax 21494264.

Ministry of Labour: Av. 24 de Julho 2351, CP 281, Maputo; tel. 21428301; fax 21421881; internet www.mitrab.gov.mz.

Ministry of Mineral Resources: Av. Fernão de Magalhães 34, 1° andar, CP 294, Maputo; tel. 21314843; fax 320618; e-mail msithole .mirem@tvcabo.co.mz; internet www.mirem.gov.mz.

Ministry of National Defence: Av. Mártires de Mueda 280, CP 3216, Maputo; tel. 21492081; fax 21491619.

Ministry of Planning and Development: Av. Ahmed Sekou Touré 21, CP 4087, Maputo; tel. 21490006; fax 21495477; internet www.mpd.gov.mz.

Ministry of Public Service: Av. Julius Nyerere 3, CP 1225, Maputo; tel. 21485558; fax 21485683; internet www.mfp.gov.mz.

Ministry of Public Works and Housing: Av. Karl Marx 606, CP 268, Maputo; tel. 21430028; fax 21421369; internet www.moph.gov .mz.

Ministry of Science and Technology: Av. Patrice Lumumba 770, Maputo; tel. 21352800; fax 21352860; e-mail secretariado@mct.gov .mz; internet www.mct.gov.mz.

Ministry of State Administration: Rua da Rádio Moçambique 112, CP 4116, Maputo; tel. 21426666; fax 21428565; internet www .mae.gov.mz.

Ministry of Tourism: Av. 25 de Setembro 1018, CP 4101, Maputo; tel. 21306210; fax 21306212; internet www.mitur.gov.mz.

Ministry of Transport and Communications: Av. Mártires de Inhaminga 336, CP 276, Maputo; tel. 21430152; fax 21431028; internet www.mtc.gov.mz.

Ministry of Veterans' Affairs: Rua General Pereira d'Eça 35, CP 3697, Maputo; tel. 21490601.

Ministry of Women's Affairs and Social Welfare Co-ordination: Rua de Tchamba 86, CP 516, Maputo; tel. 21490921; fax 21492757; internet www.mmas.gov.mz.

Ministry of Youth and Sport: Av. 25 de Setembro 529, CP 2080, Maputo; tel. 21312172; fax 21300040; e-mail mjd@tvcabo.co.mz; internet www.mjd.gov.mz.

PROVINCIAL GOVERNORS

(September 2012)

Cabo Delgado Province: ELISEU JOAQUIM MACHAVA.

Gaza Province: RAIMUNDO MAICO DIOMBA.

Inhambane Province: AGOSTINHO ABACAR TRINTA.

Manica Province: ANA COMOANA SOFALA.

Maputo Province: MARIA ELIAS JONAS.

Nampula Province: FELISMINO ERNESTO TOCOLI.

Niassa Province: DAVID NGOANE MARIZANE.

Sofala Province: CARVALHO MUARIA.

Tete Province: ALBERTO CLEMENTINO ANTÓNIO VAQUINA.

Zambézia Province: FRANCISCO ITAE MEQUE.

City of Maputo: LUCÍLIA JOSÉ MANUEL NOTA HAMA.

President and Legislature

PRESIDENT

Presidential Election, 28 October 2009

Candidate	Votes	% of votes
Armando Guebuza (Frelimo)	2,974,627	75.01
Afonso Macacho Marceta Dhlakama (Renamo)	650,679	16.41
Daviz Simango (MDM)	340,579	8.59
Total*	3,965,885	100.00

* Excluding 175,553 invalid votes and 264,655 blank votes.

LEGISLATURE

Assembleia da República: CP 1516, Maputo; tel. 21400826; fax 21400711; e-mail cdi@sortmoz.com.

Chair.: VERONICA MACAMO.

General Election, 28 October 2009

Party	Votes	% of votes	Seats
Frelimo	2,907,335	74.66	191
Renamo	688,782	17.69	51
MDM	152,836	3.93	8
PLD	26,929	0.69	—
PDD	22,410	0.58	—
PVM	19,577	0.50	—
Others	75,989	1.95	—
Total*	3,893,858	100.00	250

* Excluding 143,893 invalid votes and 349,499 blank votes.

Election Commission

Comissão Nacional de Eleições (CNE): Maputo; internet www .stae.org.mz; f. 1997; 13 mems; Pres. JOÃO LEOPOLDO DA COSTA.

Political Organizations

The following political organizations were successful in gaining approval from the Comissão Nacional de Eleições to contest the November 2009 legislative and presidential elections.

Aliança Democrática de Antigos Combatentes para o Desenvolvimento (ADACD): Maputo; f. 2009; coalition comprising the Partido do Progresso do Povo de Moçambique (PPPM), the Partido Socialisa de Moçambique (PSM), the Partido do Congresso Democrático (PACODE) and the Partido da União para a Reconciliação (PUR); Leader JOÃO LIKALAMBA.

Aliança Independente de Moçambique (ALIMO): f. 1998; Leader KHALID HUSSEIN SIDAT.

Coligação União Eleitoral (UE): f. 1999; Co-ordinator MANECA DANIEL.

Partido Ecologista de Moçambique (PEMO): Maputo.

Partido de Unidade Nacional (PUN): TV Sado 9, Maputo; tel. 21419204; Pres. HIPOLITO COUTO.

Frente de Libertação de Moçambique (Frelimo): Rua Pereira do Lago 10, Bairro de Sommerschield, Maputo; tel. 21490181; fax 21490008; e-mail info@frelimo.org.mz; internet www.frelimo.org .mz; f. 1962 by merger of three nationalist parties; reorg. 1977 as a 'Marxist-Leninist vanguard movement'; in 1989 abandoned its exclusive Marxist-Leninist orientation; Pres. ARMANDO EMÍLIO GUEBUZA.

Movimento Democrático de Moçambique (MDM): Maputo; f. 2009; Pres. DAVIZ SIMANGO; Sec.-Gen. ISMAEL MUSSA.

Movimento Patriótico para Democracia (MPD): f. 2009; Leader MATIAS DIANHANE BANZE.

Partido Ecologista—Movimento da Terra (ECOLOGISTA—MT): Leader JOÃO PEDRO MASSANGO.

Partido Humanitário de Moçambique (Pahumo): Nampula; f. 2010 by fmr mems of the Frente de Libertação de Moçambique (Frelimo), Resistência Nacional Moçambicana (Renamo) and Partido para a Paz, Democracia e Desenvolvimento (PDD); Pres. CORNÉLIO QUIVELA; Sec.-Gen. JOSÉ LOPES.

Partido de Liberdade e Desenvolvimento (PLD): f. 2009; Pres. CAETANO SABILE.

Partido Nacional dos Operários e Camponeses (PANAOC): f. 1998; Leader ARMANDO GIL SUEIA.

Partido para a Paz, Democracia e Desenvolvimento (PDD): Av. Amilcar Cabral 570, Maputo; tel. 21486759; fax 21486765; e-mail pdd@tvcabo.co.mz; internet www.pdd.org.mz; f. 2003; liberal; Leader RAÚL DOMINGOS.

Partido Popular Democrático (PPD): f. 2004; Leader MARCIANO FIJAMA.

Partido de Reconciliação Democrática Social (PRDS): f. 1998; Leader ARMANDO GIL SUEIA.

Partido de Reconciliação Nacional (PARENA): Maputo; f. 2004; Leader ANDRÉ BALATE.

Partido de Solidariedade e Liberdade (PAZS): f. 2004; Leader CARLOS INÁCIO COELHO.

Partido Trabalhista (PT): f. 1993; Pres. MIGUEL MABOTE; Sec.-Gen. LUÍS MUCHANGA.

Partido os Verdes de Moçambique (PVM): f. 1997; Leader BRUNO SAPEMBA.

Resistência Nacional Moçambicana (Renamo): Av. Julius Nyerere 2541, Maputo; tel. 21493107; internet www.renamo.org.mz; also known as Movimento Nacional da Resistência de Moçambique (MNR); f. 1976; fmr guerrilla group, in conflict with the Govt between 1976 and Oct. 1992; obtained legal status in 1994; Pres. AFONSO MACACHO MARCETA DHLAKAMA; Sec.-Gen. OSSUFO MOMADE.

União dos Democratas de Moçambique—Partido Popular (UDM—PP): f. 2009; Leader JOSÉ RICARDO VIANA.

União Nacional de Moçambique (UNAMO): f. 1987; breakaway faction of Renamo; social democratic; obtained legal status 1992; Pres. CARLOS ALEXANDRE DOS REIS.

União para a Mudança (UM): f. 1993; Leader FRANCISCO MAINDANE MUARIVA.

Diplomatic Representation

EMBASSIES AND HIGH COMMISSIONS IN MOZAMBIQUE

Algeria: Rua de Mukumbura 121–125, CP 1709, Maputo; tel. 21492070; fax 21490582; e-mail ambalgmaputo@tvcabo.co.mz; Ambassador AHMED LAKHDAR TAZIR.

Angola: Av. Kenneth Kaunda 783, CP 2954, Maputo; tel. 21493139; fax 21493930; Ambassador ISAÍAS JAIME VILINGA.

Brazil: Av. Kenneth Kaunda 296, CP 1167, Sommerschield, Maputo; tel. 21484800; fax 21484806; e-mail ebrasil@teledata.mz; internet www.ebrasil.co.mz; Ambassador ANTONIO JOSÉ MARIA DE SOUZA E SILVA.

China, People's Republic: Av. Julius Nyerere 3142, CP 4668, Maputo; tel. 21491560; fax 21491196; e-mail chinaemb_mz@mfa.gov.cn; Ambassador HUANG SONGFU.

Congo, Democratic Republic: Av. Kenneth Kaunda 127, CP 2407, Maputo; tel. 21497154; fax 21494929; Ambassador ANTOINE KOLA MASALA NE BEBY.

Congo, Republic: Av. Kenneth Kaunda 783, CP 4743, Maputo; tel. 21490142; Chargé d'affaires a.i. MONSEGNO BASHA OSHEFWA.

Cuba: Av. Kenneth Kaunda 492, CP 387, Maputo; tel. 21492444; fax 21491905; e-mail embacuba.mozambique@tvcabo.co.mz; internet emba.cubaminrex.cu/mozambique; Ambassador RAFAEL ARÍSTIDES JIMENO LÓPEZ.

Denmark: Av. Julius Nyerere 1162, CP 4588, Maputo; tel. 21480000; fax 21480010; e-mail mpmamb@um.dk; internet www.ambmaputo.um.dk; Ambassador JOHNNY FLENTØ.

Egypt: Av. Mao Tse Tung 851, CP 4662, Maputo; tel. 21491118; fax 21491489; e-mail egypt@tvcabo.co.mz; Ambassador ABDEL KADER TANTAWY ES-SAYED.

Finland: Av. Julius Nyerere 1128, CP 1663, Maputo; tel. 21482400; fax 21491662; e-mail sanomat.map@formin.fi; internet www.finland.org.mz; Ambassador MATTI KÄÄRIÄINEN.

France: Av. Julius Nyerere 2361, CP 4781, Maputo; tel. 21484600; fax 21491727; e-mail ambafrancemz@tvcabo.co.mz; internet www.ambafrance-mz.org; Ambassador CHRISTIAN DAZIANO.

Germany: Rua Damião de Góis 506, CP 1595, Maputo; tel. 21482700; fax 21492888; e-mail info@maputo.diplo.de; internet www.maputo.diplo.de; Ambassador ULRICH KLOECKNER.

Holy See: Av. Kwame Nkrumah 224, CP 2738, Maputo; tel. 21491144; fax 21492217; Apostolic Nuncio Most Rev. ANTONIO ARCARI (Titular Archbishop of Caeciri).

Iceland: Av. Zimbabwe 1694, Maputo; tel. 21483509; fax 21483511; e-mail mozambique@iceida.is; internet www.iceland.org/mo; Chargé d'affaires MARGRÉT EINARSDÓTTIR.

India: Av. Kenneth Kaunda 167, CP 4751, Maputo; tel. 21492437; fax 21492364; e-mail hicomind@tvcabo.co.mz; internet www.hicomind-maputo.org; High Commissioner ASHOK KUMAR AMROHI.

Ireland: Av. Julius Nyerere 3332, Maputo; tel. 21491440; fax 21493023; e-mail maputoembassy@dfa.ie; Ambassador RUAIRÍ DE BURCA.

Italy: Av. Kenneth Kaunda 387, CP 976, Maputo; tel. 21492229; fax 21490503; e-mail ambasciata.maputo@esteri.it; internet www.ambmaputo.esteri.it; Ambassador CARLO LO CASCIO.

Japan: Av. Julius Nyerere 2832, CP 2494, Maputo; tel. 21499819; fax 21498957; internet www.mz.emb-japan.go.jp; Ambassador EJI HASHIMOTO.

Korea, Democratic People's Republic: Rua da Kaswende 167, Maputo; tel. 21491482; Ambassador PAK KUN GWANG.

Malawi: Av. Kenneth Kaunda 75, CP 4148, Maputo; tel. 21492676; fax 21490224; High Commissioner MARTIN O. KANSICHI.

Mauritius: Rua Dom Carlos 42, Av. de Zimbabwe, Sommerschield, Maputo; tel. 21494624; fax 21494729; e-mail maputo@mail.gov.mu; High Commissioner JEAN HAREL LAMVOHEE.

Netherlands: Av. Kwame Nkrumah 324, CP 1163, Maputo; tel. 21484200; fax 21484248; e-mail map@minbuza.nl; internet www.hollandinmozambique.org; Ambassador FRÉDÉRIQUE DE MAN.

Nigeria: Av. Kenneth Kaunda 821, CP 4693, Maputo; tel. and fax 21490991; High Commissioner MATILDA KWASHI.

Norway: Av. Julius Nyerere 1162, CP 828, Maputo; tel. 21480100; fax 21480107; e-mail emb.maputo@mfa.no; internet www.norway.org.mz; Ambassador TOVE BRUVIK WESTBERG.

Portugal: Av. Julius Nyerere 720, CP 4696, Maputo; tel. 21490316; fax 21491172; e-mail embaixada@embpormaputo.org.mz; Ambassador MÁRIO GODINHO DE MATOS.

Russia: Av. Vladimir I. Lénine 2445, CP 4666, Maputo; tel. 21417372; fax 21417515; e-mail embrus@tvcabo.co.mz; internet www.mozambique.mid.ru; Ambassador IGOR V. POPOV.

South Africa: Av. Eduardo Mondlane 41, CP 1120, Maputo; tel. 21243000; fax 21493029; e-mail ritterb@dirco.gov.za; High Commissioner D. MOOPELOA.

Spain: Rua Damião de Góis 347, CP 1331, Maputo; tel. 21492025; fax 21494769; e-mail emb.maputo@maec.es; Ambassador EDUARDO LÓPEZ BUSQUETS.

Swaziland: Av. Kwame Nkrumah, CP 4711, Maputo; tel. 21491601; fax 21492117; High Commissioner Prince TSHEKEDI.

Sweden: Av. Julius Nyerere 1128, CP 338, Maputo; tel. 21480300; fax 21480390; e-mail ambasseden.maputo@foreign.ministry.se; internet www.swedenabroad.se/maputo; Ambassador TORVALD ÅKESSON.

Switzerland: Av. Ahmed Sekou Touré 637, CP 135, Maputo; tel. 21315275; fax 21315276; e-mail map.vertretung@eda.admin.ch; internet www.eda.admin.ch/maputo; Ambassador THERESA ADAM.

Tanzania: Ujamaa House, Av. dos Mártires da Machava 852, CP 4515, Maputo; tel. 21490110; fax 21494782; e-mail ujamaa@zebra.eum.mz; High Commissioner ISSA MOHAMED ISSA.

Timor-Leste: Av. do Zimbabwe 1586, Maputo; tel. 21493644; fax 21493544; e-mail embrdtl@tvcabo.co.mz; Ambassador MARINA RIBEIRO ALKATIRI.

United Kingdom: Av. Vladimir I. Lénine 310, CP 55, Maputo; tel. 21356000; fax 21356060; e-mail bhcgeneral@gmail.com; internet ukinmozambique.fco.gov.uk; High Commissioner ANTHONY SHAUN CLEARY.

USA: Av. Kenneth Kaunda 193, CP 783, Maputo; tel. 21492797; fax 21490114; e-mail maputoirc@state.gov; internet maputo.usembassy.gov; Ambassador LESLIE V. ROWE.

Zambia: Av. Kenneth Kaunda 1286, CP 4655, Maputo; tel. 21492452; fax 21491893; e-mail zhcmmap@zebra.uem.mz; High Commissioner SIMON GABRIEL MWILA.

Zimbabwe: Av. Kenneth Kaunda 816, CP 743, Maputo; tel. 21490404; fax 21492237; e-mail maro@isl.co.mz; Ambassador AGRIPA MUTAMBARA.

Judicial System

The Constitution of November 1990 provides for a Supreme Court and other judicial courts, an Administrative Court, courts-martial, customs courts, maritime courts and labour courts. The Supreme Court consists of professional judges, appointed by the President of the Republic, and judges elected by the Assembleia da República. It acts in sections, as a trial court of primary and appellate jurisdiction, and, in plenary session, as a court of final appeal. The Administrative Court controls the legality of administrative acts and supervises public expenditure.

President of the Supreme Court: OSIAS PONDJA.

Attorney-General: AUGUSTO PAULINO.

Conselho Constitucional: Rua Mateus Sansão Muthemba 493, CP 2372, Maputo; tel. 21487431; fax 21487432; e-mail correiocc@cconstitucional.org.mz; internet www.cconstitucional.org.mz; f. 1990; Pres. HERMENEGILDO GAMITO.

Tribunal Administrativo: Rua Mateus S. Muthemba 65, CP 254, Maputo; tel. 21490170; fax 21498890; e-mail ta@ta.gov.mz; internet www.ta.gov.mz; Pres. MACHATINE PAULO MARRENGANE MUNGUAMBE.

Religion

There are an estimated 5m. Christians and 4m. Muslims, as well as small Hindu, Jewish and Bahá'í communities. In 2004 over 100 religious groups were officially registered.

CHRISTIANITY

There are many Christian organizations registered in Mozambique.

Conselho Cristão de Moçambique (CCM) (Christian Council of Mozambique): Av. Agostinho Neto 1584, CP 108, Maputo; tel. 21322836; fax 21321968; f. 1948; 22 mems; Pres. Rt Rev. ARÃO MATSOLO; Gen. Sec. Rev. DINIS MATSOLO.

The Roman Catholic Church

Mozambique comprises three archdioceses and nine dioceses. The number of adherents represents some 22% of the total population.

Bishops' Conference

Conferência Episcopal de Moçambique (CEM), Secretariado Geral da CEM, Av. Paulo Samuel Kankhomba 188/RC, CP 286, Maputo; tel. 21490766; fax 21492174.

f. 1982; Pres. Most Rev. LÚCIO ANDRICE MUANDULA (Bishop of Xai-Xai).

Archbishop of Beira: Most Rev. CLAUDIO DALLA ZUANNA, Cúria Arquiepiscopal, Rua Correia de Brito 613, CP 544, Beira; tel. 23322313; fax 23327639; e-mail arquidbeira@teledata.mz.

Archbishop of Maputo: Most Rev. FRANCISCO CHIMOIO, Paço Arquiepiscopal, Avda Eduardo Mondlane 1448, CP 258, Maputo; tel. 21326240; fax 21321873.

Archbishop of Nampula: Most Rev. TOMÉ MAKHWELIHA, Paço Arquiepiscopal, CP 84, 70100 Nampula; tel. 26213024; fax 26214194; e-mail arquidiocesenpl@teledata.mz.

The Anglican Communion

Anglicans in Mozambique are adherents of the Anglican Church of Southern Africa (formerly the Church of the Province of Southern Africa). There are two dioceses in Mozambique. The Metropolitan of the Province is the Archbishop of Cape Town, South Africa.

Bishop of Lebombo: Rt Rev. DINIS SALOMÃO SENGULANE, CP 120, Maputo; tel. 21734364; fax 21401093; e-mail bispo_sengulane@virconn.com.

Bishop of Niassa: Rev. MARK VAN KOEVERING, CP 264, Lichinga, Niassa; tel. 27112735; fax 27112336; e-mail bishop.niassa@gmail.com.

Other Churches

Baptist Convention of Mozambique: Av. Maguiguane 386, CP 852, Maputo; tel. 2126852; Pres. Rev. BENTO BARTOLOMEU MATUSSE; 78 churches, 25,000 adherents.

The Church of Jesus Christ of the Latter-Day Saints: Maputo; 9 congregations, 1,975 mems.

Evangelical Lutheran Church in Mozambique: Av Kim II Song 520, CP 1488, Sommerschield, Maputo; tel. 212489200; fax 212489201; e-mail mabasso.ielm@tvcabo.co.mz; Sen. Pastor JOSE MABASSO; 12,606 mems (2010).

Free Methodist Church: Pres. Rev. FRANISSE SANDO MUVILE; 214 churches, 21,231 mems.

Igreja Congregational Unida de Moçambique: Rua 4 Bairro 25 de Junho, CP 930, Maputo; tel. 21475820; Pres., Sec. of the Synod A. A. LITSURE.

Igreja Maná: Rua Francisco Orlando Magumbwe 528, Maputo; tel. 21491760; fax 21490896; e-mail adm_mocambique@igrejamana.com; Bishop DOMINGOS COSTA.

Igreja Reformada em Moçambique (IRM) (Reformed Church in Mozambique): CP 3, Vila Ulongue, Anogonia-Tete; f. 1908; Gen. Sec. Rev. SAMUEL M. BESSITALA; 60,000 mems.

Presbyterian Church of Mozambique: Av. Ahmed Sekou Touré 1822, CP 21, Maputo; tel. 21421790; fax 21428623; e-mail ipmoc@zebra.uem.mz; f. 1887; 100,000 adherents; Pres. of Synodal Council Rev. ORIENTE SIBANE.

Seventh-Day Adventist Church: Av. Maguiguana 300, CP 1468, Maputo; tel. and fax 21427200; e-mail victormiconde@teledata.co.mz; 937 churches, 186,724 mems (2004).

Other denominations active in Mozambique include the Church of Christ, the Church of the Nazarene, the Greek Orthodox Church, the United Methodist Church of Mozambique, the Wesleyan Methodist Church, the Zion Christian Church, and Jehovah's Witnesses.

ISLAM

Comunidade Mahometana: Av. Albert Luthuli 291, Maputo; tel. 21425181; fax 21300880; internet www.paginaislamica.8m.com/pg1.htm; Pres. SALEEM AHMED.

Congresso Islâmico de Moçambique (Islamic Congress of Mozambique): represents Sunni Muslims; Chair. ASSANE ISMAEL MAQBUL.

Conselho Islâmico de Moçambique (Islamic Council of Mozambique): Pres. ABDUL CARIMO.

The Press

DAILIES

Correio da Manha: Av. Filipe Samuel Magaia 528, CP 1756, Maputo; tel. 21305322; fax 21305321; e-mail refi@virconn.com; f. 1997; published by Sojornal, Lda; also publishes weekly Correio Semanal; Dir REFINALDO CHILENGUE.

Diário de Moçambique: Av. 25 de Setembro 1509, 2° andar, CP 2491, Beira; tel. and fax 23427312; f. 1981; under state management since 1991; Dir EZEQUIEL AMBRÓSIO; Editor FARUCO SADIQUE; circ. 5,000 (2003).

Expresso da Tarde: Av. Patrice Lumumba 511, 1° andar, Maputo; tel. 21314912; subscription only; distribution by fax; Dir SALVADOR RAIMUNDO HONWANA.

Mediafax: Av. Amílcar Cabral 1049, CP 73, Maputo; tel. 21301737; fax 21302402; e-mail mediafax@tvcabo.co.mz; f. 1992 by co-operative of independent journalists Mediacoop; news-sheet by subscription only, distribution by fax and internet; Editor BENEDITO NGOMANE.

Notícias de Moçambique: Rua Joaquim Lapa 55, CP 327, Maputo; tel. 21420119; fax 21320120; internet www.jornalnoticias.co.mz; f. 1926; morning; f. 1906; under state management since 1991; Pres. ESSELINA MACOME; Dir ROGÉRIO SITOE; circ. 12,793 (2003).

Further newspapers available solely in e-mail or fax format include Diário de Notícias and Matinal.

WEEKLIES

Campeão: Av. 24 de Julho 3706, CP 2610, Maputo; tel. and fax 21401810; sports newspaper; Dir RENATO CALDÉIRA; Editor ALEXANDRE ZANDAMELA.

Correio Semanal: Av. Filipe Samuel Magaia 528, CP 1756, Maputo; tel. 21305322; fax 21305312; Dir REFINALDO CHILENGUE.

Desafio: Rua Joaquim Lapa 55, Maputo; tel. 21305437; fax 21305431; Dir ALMIRO SANTOS; Editor BOAVIDA FUNJUA; circ. 3,890 (2003).

Domingo: Rua Joaquim Lapa 55, CP 327, Maputo; tel. 21431026; fax 21431027; f. 1981; Sun.; Dir JORGE MATINE; circ. 15,000 (2007).

Fim de Semana: Rua da Resistência 1642, 1° andar, Maputo; tel. and fax 21417012; e-mail fimdomes@tvcabo.co.mz; internet www.fimdesemana.co.mz; f. 1997; independent.

Savana: Av. Amílcar Cabral 1049, CP 73, Maputo; tel. 21301737; fax 21302402; e-mail savana@mediacoop.co.mz; internet www.savana.co.mz; f. 1994; owned by mediacoop, SA; CEO FERNANDO LIMA; Publr KOK NAM; Editor FERNANDO GONÇALVES; circ. 15,000 (2009).

Tempo: Av. Ahmed Sekou Touré 1078, CP 2917, Maputo; tel. 21426191; f. 1970; magazine; under state management since 1991; Dir ROBERTO UAENE; Editor ARLINDO LANGA; circ. 40,000.

Zambeze: Rua José Sidumo, Maputo; tel. 21302019; Dir ANGELO MUNGUAMBE; circ. 2,000 (2003).

@Verdade: Av. Mártires da Machava 905, Maputo; tel. 843998624; e-mail averdademz@gmail.com; internet www.verdade.co.mz; f. 2008; Dir ERIK CHARAS; Editor-in-Chief RUI LAMARQUES.

PERIODICALS

Agora: Afrisurvey, Lda, Rua General Pereira d'Eça 200, 1° andar, CP 1335, Maputo; tel. 21494147; fax 21494204; internet www.agora.co.mz; f. 2000; monthly; economics, politics, society; Pres. MARIA DE LOURDES TORCATO; Dir JOVITO NUNES; Editor-in-Chief ERCÍLIA SANTOS; circ. 5,000.

Agricultura: Instituto Nacional de Investigação Agronómica, CP 3658, Maputo; tel. 2130091; f. 1982; quarterly; publ. by Centro de Documentação de Agricultura, Silvicultura, Pecuária e Pescas.

Aro: Av. 24 de Julho 1420, CP 4187, Maputo; f. 1995; monthly; Dir POLICARTO TAMELE; Editor BRUNO MACAME, Jr.

Arquivo Histórico: Av. Filipe Samuel Magaia 715, CP 2033, Maputo; tel. 21421177; fax 21423428; f. 1934; Editor JOEL DAS NEVES TEMBE.

Boletim da República: Av. Vladimir I. Lénine, CP 275, Maputo; govt and official notices; publ. by Imprensa Nacional da Moçambique.

Moçambique–Novos Tempos: Av. Ahmed Sekou Touré 657, Maputo; tel. 21493564; fax 21493590; f. 1992; Dir J. MASCARENHAS.

Mozambiquefile: c/o AIM, Rua da Radio Moçambique, CP 896, Maputo; tel. 21313225; fax 21313196; e-mail aim@aim.org.mz; internet www.sortmoz.com/aimnews; monthly; Dir GUSTAVO MAVIZ; Editor PAUL FAUVET.

Mozambique Inview: c/o Mediacoop, Av. Amílcar Cabral 1049, CP 73, Maputo; tel. 21430722; fax 21302402; e-mail inview@savana.co.mz; internet www.mediacoop.odline.com; f. 1994; 2 a month; economic bulletin in English; Dir KOK NAM.

Portos e Caminhos de Ferro: CP 276, Maputo; English and Portuguese; ports and railways; quarterly.

Revista Maderazinco: CP 477, Maputo; tel. 823004770; e-mail maderazinco@yahoo.com; internet www.tropical.maderazinco.co.mz; f. 2002; quarterly; literature; Editor ROGÉRIO MANJATE.

Revista Médica de Moçambique: Instituto Nacional de Saúde, Ministério da Saúde e Faculdade de Medicina, Universidade Eduardo Mondlane, CP 264, Maputo; tel. 21420368; fax 21431103; e-mail mdgedge@malarins.uem.mz; f. 1982; 4 a year; medical journal; Editor MARTINHO DGEDGE.

NEWS AGENCY

Agência de Informação de Moçambique (AIM): Rua da Rádio Moçambique, CP 896, Maputo; tel. 21313225; fax 21313196; e-mail aim@aim.org.mz; f. 1975; daily reports in Portuguese and English; Dir GUSTAVO LISSETIANE MAVIE.

Publishers

Arquivo Histórico de Moçambique (AHM): Av. Filipe Samuel Magaia 715, CP 2033, Maputo; tel. 21421177; fax 21423428; internet www.ahm.uem.mz; Dir JOEL DAS NEVES TEMBE.

Central Impressora: c/o Ministério da Saúde, Avs Eduardo Mondlane e Salvador Allende 1008, CP 264, Maputo; tel. 21427131; fax 21427133; owned by the Ministry of Health.

Centro de Estudos Africanos: Universidade Eduardo Mondlane, CP 1993, Maputo; tel. 21490828; fax 21491896; f. 1976; social and political science, regional history, economics; Dir Col SERGIO VIEIRA.

Editora Minerva Central: Rua Consiglieri Pedroso 84, CP 212, Maputo; tel. 2122092; fax 21328816; e-mail geral@minerva.co.mz; internet www.minerva.co.mz; f. 1908; stationers and printers, educational, technical and medical textbooks; Man. Dir J. F. CARVALHO.

Editorial Ndjira, Lda: Av. Ho Chi Minh 85, Maputo; tel. 21300180; fax 21308745; f. 1996.

Empresa Moderna, Lda: Av. 25 de Setembro, CP 473, Maputo; tel. 21424594; f. 1937; fiction, history, textbooks; Man. Dir LOUIS GALLOTI.

Fundo Bibliográfico de Língua Portuguesa: Av. 25 de Setembro 1230, 7° andar, Maputo; tel. 21429531; fax 21429530; e-mail palop@zebra.uem.mz; f. 1990; state owned; Pres. LOURENÇO ROSÁRIO.

Imprensa Universitária: Universidade Eduardo Mondlane, Praça 19 de Maio, Maputo; internet www.uem.mz/imprensa_universitaris; university press.

Instituto Nacional do Livro e do Disco: Av. 24 de Julho 1921, CP 4030, Maputo; tel. 21434870; govt publishing and purchasing agency; Dir ARMÉNIO CORREIA.

Moçambique Editora: Rua Armando Tivane 1430, Bairro de Polana, Maputo; tel. 21495017; fax 21499071; e-mail info@me.co.mz; internet www.me.co.mz; f. 1996; educational textbooks, dictionaries.

Plural Editores: Av. Patrice Lumumba 765, Maputo; tel. 21360900; fax 21308868; e-mail plural@pluraleditores.co.mz; internet www.pluraleditores.co.mz; f. 2003; educational textbooks; part of the Porto Editora Group.

GOVERNMENT PUBLISHING HOUSE

Imprensa Nacional de Moçambique: Rua da Imprensa, CP 275, Maputo; tel. 21427021; fax 21424858; internet www.imprensanac.gov.mz; part of Ministry of State Administration; Dir VENÂNCIO T. MANJATE.

Broadcasting and Communications

TELECOMMUNICATIONS

Regulatory Authority

Instituto Nacional das Comunicações de Moçambique (INCM): Av. Eduardo Mondlane 123–127, CP 848, Maputo; tel. 21490131; fax 21494435; e-mail info@incm.gov.mz; internet www.incm.gov.mz; regulates post and telecommunications systems; Pres. ISIDORO PEDRO DA SILVA.

Major Telecommunications Companies

TDM's monopoly on the provision of fixed-line services was ended in December 2007, although it remained the sole fixed-line operator at early 2012. There were also three mobile telephone operators in early 2012.

Moçambique Celular (mCel): Rua Belmiro Obadias Muianga 384, CP 1483, Maputo; tel. 21351100; fax 21351117; internet www.mcel.co.mz; f. 1997 as a subsidiary of TDM; separated from TDM in 2003; mobile cellular telephone provider; Pres. SALVADOR ADRIANO.

Telecomunicações de Moçambique, SARL (TDM): Rua da Sé 2, CP 25, Maputo; tel. 21431921; fax 21431944; e-mail scatdm@tdm.mz; internet www.tdm.mz; f. 1993; Chair. JOAQUIM RIBEIRO PEREIRA DE CARVALHO; Man. Dir MAMUDO IBRAIMO.

Vodacom Moçambique (VM): Time Square Complex, Bloco 3, Av. 25 de Setembro, Maputo; tel. 840900000; fax 840901775; e-mail yumna.bhikha@vm.co.mz; internet www.vm.co.mz; f. 2002; mobile cellular telephone provider; owned by Vodacom Group (South Africa) and local shareholders; Chair. SALIMO ABDULA; Man. Dir JOSÉ DOS SANTOS.

BROADCASTING

Radio

Rádio Encontro: Av. Francisco Manyanga, CP 366, Nampula; tel. 26215588; fax 26215878; e-mail radioencontro@teledata.mz.

Rádio Feba Moçambique: Av. Julius Nyerere 441A, CP 1648, Maputo; tel. 21440002; fax 21440009; e-mail febamoz@org.ue.mz; internet febamoz.go.co.mz.

Rádio Maria: Rua Igreja 156A, Machava Sede, Matola, Maputo; tel. 21750505; fax 21752124; e-mail info.moz@radiomaria.org; internet www.radiomaria.org.mz; f. 1995; evangelical radio broadcasts; Dir Fr JOÃO CARLOS H. NUNES.

Rádio Miramar: Rede de Comunicação, Av. Julius Nyerere 1555, Maputo; tel. 21486311; fax 21486813; e-mail jose.guerra@tvcabo.co.mz; owned by Brazilian religious sect, the Universal Church of the Kingdom of God.

Rádio Moçambique: Rua da Rádio 2, CP 2000, Maputo; tel. 21431687; fax 21321816; e-mail sepca_mz@yahoo.com.br; internet www.rm.co.mz; f. 1975; programmes in Portuguese, English and vernacular languages; Chair. RICARDO MADAUANE MALATE.

Rádio Terra Verde: Av. Eduardo Mondlane 2623, 5° andar, Maputo; tel. and fax 21302083; fmrly Voz da Renamo; owned by former rebel movement Renamo; transmitters in Maputo and Gorongosa, Sofala province.

Rádio Trans Mundial Moçambique: Av. Eduardo Mondlane 2998, CP 1526, Maputo; tel. 21440003; fax 21440004; e-mail rtransmundial@isl.co.mz.

Television

Rádio Televisão Klint (RTK): Av. Agostinho Neto 946, Maputo; tel. 21422956; fax 21493306; Dir CARLOS KLINT.

RTP África: Rua Pero de Anaia 248, Maputo; tel. (21) 497344; fax (21) 487347; e-mail rtp.a.moc@teledata.mz.

Televisão Miramar: Rua Pereira Lago 221, Maputo; tel. 21486311; fax 21486813; owned by Brazilian religious sect, the Igrega Universal do Reino de Deus (Universal Church of the Kingdom of God).

Televisão de Moçambique, EP (TVM): Av. 25 de Setembro 154, CP 2675, Maputo; tel. 21308117; fax 21308122; e-mail tvm@tvm.co.mz; internet www.tvm.co.mz; f. 1981; Pres. of Administrative Council ARMINDO CHAVANA.

TV Cabo Moçambique: Av. dos Presidentes 68, CP 1750, Maputo; tel. 21480550; fax 21480501; e-mail tvcabo@tvcabo.co.mz; internet www.tvcabo.co.mz; cable television and internet services in Maputo.

Finance

(cap. = capital; res = reserves; dep. = deposits; m. = million; brs = branches; amounts in meticais, unless otherwise stated)

BANKING

In 2009 there were 14 banks and three microfinance institutions in Mozambique.

Central Bank

Banco de Moçambique: Av. 25 de Setembro 1695, CP 423, Maputo; tel. 21354600; fax 21323247; e-mail gpi@bancomoc.mz; internet www.bancomoc.mz; f. 1975; bank of issue; cap. 248.9m., res 845.2m., dep. 43,260.2m. (Dec. 2009); Gov. ERNESTO GOUVEIA GOVE; 4 brs.

National Banks

Banco de Desenvolvimento e de Comércio de Moçambique, SARL (BDCM): Av. 25 de Setembro 420, 1° andar, sala 8, Maputo; tel. 21313040; fax 21313047; f. 2000; 42% owned by Montepio Geral (Portugal).

Banco Mercantil e de Investimento, SARL (BMI): Av. 24 de Julho 3549, Maputo; tel. 21407979; fax 21408887.

Banco Nacional de Investimentos (BNI): Maputo; f. 2010; 49.5% owned by the Govt of Mozambique, 49.5% owned by the Govt of

Portugal, 1% owned by Banco Comercial e de Investimentos, SARL; cap. US $500,000m.; Exec. Dir ADRIANO MALEIANE.

Banco Terra: Av. Samora Machel 341 R/C, CP 69, Maputo; tel. 21359300; fax 21316120; internet www.bancoterra.co.mz; f. 2008; provides access to a full range of financial services to the rural and peri urban population in Mozambique; cap. 185m., dep. 100.3m. (Dec. 2007); 30.7% owned by Rabobank (Netherlands); Pres. H. MERTENS; CEO KARL MOURSOND.

Barclays Bank Mozambique SA: Av. 25 de Setembro 1184, CP 757, Maputo; tel. 21351700; fax 21323470; internet www.bancoaustral.co.mz; f. 1995 as Banco Popular de Desenvolvimento (BPD); name changed to Banco Austral SARL in 1998; name changed as above in 2007; 80% owned by Amalgamated Banks of South Africa, 20% owned by União, Sociedade e Participacões, SARL, which represents employees of the bank; cap. 315m., res 311.7m., dep. 5,347.5m. (Dec. 2008); Chair. CASIMIRO FRANCISCO; Man. Dir PAUL NICE; 58 brs and agencies.

BCI Fomento (BCI) (Banco Comercial e de Investimentos, SARL): Edif. John Orr's, Av. 25 de Setembro 1465, CP 4745, Maputo; tel. 21353700; fax 21309831; e-mail bci@bci.co.mz; internet www.bci.co.mz; f. 1996; renamed as above following 2003 merger between Banco Comercial e de Investimentos and Banco de Fomento; 51% owned by Caixa Geral de Depósitos (Portugal), 30% Banco Português de Investimento, 18% owned by INSITEC; cap. 319.8m., res 516.7m., dep. 11,996.4m. (Dec. 2006); Chair. CELSO ISMAEL CORREIA; CEO IBRAIMO IBRAIMO; 68 brs.

ICB-Banco Internacional de Comércio, SARL: Av. 25 de Setembro 1915, Maputo; tel. 21311111; fax 21314797; e-mail icbm@icbank-mz.com; internet www.icbank-mz.com; f. 1998; cap. and res 44,923,748m., total assets 164,773,569m. (Dec. 2003); Chair. JOSEPHINE SIVARETNAM; CEO LEE SANG HUAT; 4 brs.

Millennium bim: Av. 25 de Setembro 1800, CP 865, Maputo; tel. 21354496; fax 21354415; e-mail scheman@millenniumbim.co.mz; internet www.millenniumbim.co.mz; f. 1995; name changed from Banco Internacional de Moçambique in 2005; 66.7% owned by Banco Comercial Português, 17.4% by the state; cap. 741.0m., res 2,291.0m., dep. 29,744.7m. (Dec. 2008); Pres. MÁRIO FERNANDES DA GRAÇA MACHUNGO; CEO JOÃO FILIPE DE FIGUEIREDO JÚNIOR; 86 brs.

Moza Banco: Av. Kwame Nkrumah 97, CP 1012, Maputo; tel. 21480800; fax 21480801; e-mail info@mozabanco.co.mz; internet www.mozabanco.co.mz; f. 2008; cap. US $15m.; Chair. PRAKASH RATILAL.

Novo Banco, SARL: Av. do Trabalho 750, Maputo; tel. and fax 21407705; f. 2000; cap. and res 51,995m., total assets 108,847m. (Dec. 2003).

Standard Bank, SARL (Moçambique): Praça 25 de Junho 1, CP 2086, Maputo; tel. 21352500; fax 21426967; e-mail camal.daude@standardbank.co.mz; internet www.standardbank.co.mz; f. 1966 as Banco Standard Totta de Mozambique; 98.14% owned by Stanbic Africa Holdings, UK; cap. 1,294.0m., res 430.6m., dep. 14,362.1m. (Dec. 2011); Man. Dir ANTONIO COUTINHO; 24 brs.

Foreign Banks

African Banking Corporation (Moçambique), SA: ABC House, Av. Julius Nyerere 99, Polana, CP 1445, Maputo; tel. 21482100; fax 21487474; e-mail abcmoz@africanbankingcorp.com; internet www.africanbankingcorp.com; f. 1999; 100% owned by African Banking Corpn Holdings Ltd (Botswana); fmrly BNP Nedbank (Moçambique), SARL; changed name as above after acquisition in 2002; cap. 148m., res 101m., dep. 3,598.9m. (Dec. 2009); Chair. BENJAMIM ALFREDO; Man. Dir JOSEPH SIBANDA; 2 brs.

African Banking Corporation Leasing, SARL: Rua da Imprensa 256, 7° andar, CP 4447, Maputo; tel. 21300451; fax 21431290; e-mail ulcmoz@mail.tropical.co.mz; 66% owned by African Banking Corpn Holdings Ltd (Botswana); fmrly ULC (Moçambique); changed name as above in 2002; Chair. ANTÓNIO BRANCO; Gen. Man. VICTOR VISEU.

Mauritius Commercial Bank (Moçambique) SA: Av. Friedrich Engels 400, Maputo; tel. 21481900; fax 21498675; e-mail contact@mcbmozambique.com; internet www.mcbmozambique.com; f. 1999; name changed as above in June 2007; 81% owned by Mauritius Commercial Bank Group; total assets US $46,777m. (Dec. 2006); Chair. PIERRE GUY NOEL; Gen. Man. PETER HIGGINS.

DEVELOPMENT FUND

Fundo de Desenvolvimento Agrário: Rua Joaquim Lapa 192, 2º andar, Maputo; tel. 21302814; fax 21430044; e-mail antonio.andre@ffa.org.mz; f. 2006 to provide credit for small farmers and rural co-operatives; promotes agricultural and rural devt; Sec. ANTÓNIO ANDRÉ.

STOCK EXCHANGE

Bolsa de Valores de Moçambique: Av. 25 de Setembro 1230, Prédio 33, 5° andar, Maputo; tel. 21308826; fax 21310559; e-mail bvm@bvm.co.mz; internet www.bolsadevalores.co.mz; f. 1999; Chair. Dr JUSSUB NURMAMAD.

INSURANCE

In December 1991 the Assembleia da República approved legislation terminating the state monopoly of insurance and reinsurance activities. In 2005 five insurance companies were operating in Mozambique.

Companhia de Seguros de Moçambique, IMPAR: Rua da Imprensa 625, Prédio 33, Maputo; tel. 21429695; fax 21430640; f. 1992; Pres. INOCÊNCIO A. MATAVEL; Gen. Man. MANUEL BALANCHO.

Empresa Moçambicana de Seguros, EE (EMOSE): Av. 25 de Setembro 1383, CP 1165, Maputo; tel. 21356300; fax 21424526; e-mail comercial@emose.co.mz; internet www.emose.co.mz; f. 1977 as state insurance monopoly; took over business of 24 fmr cos; 80% govt-owned, 20% private; cap. 150m.; Chair. VENÂNCIO MONDLANE.

Seguradora Internacional de Moçambique: Av. 25 Setembro 1800, Maputo; tel. 21430959; fax 21430241; e-mail simseg@zebra.uem.mz; Pres. MÁRIO FERNANDES DA GRAÇA MACHUNGO.

Trade and Industry

GOVERNMENT AGENCIES

Centro de Promoção de Investimentos (CPI) (Investment Promotion Centre): Rua da Imprensa 332, CP 4635, Maputo; tel. 21313295; fax 21313325; e-mail cpi@cpi.co.mz; internet www.cpi.co.mz; f. 1987; encourages domestic and foreign investment and IT ventures with foreign firms; evaluates and negotiates investment proposals; Dir LOURENÇO SAMBO.

Instituto do Algodão de Moçambique (IAM): Av. Eduardo Mondlane 2221, 1° andar, CP 806, Maputo; tel. 21424264; fax 21430679; e-mail iampab@zebra.uem.mz; internet www.iam.gov.mz; responsible for promotion and devt of the cotton industry; Dir NORBERTO MAHALAMBE.

Instituto do Fomento do Cajú (INCAJU): Maputo; internet incaju.gov.mz; national cashew institute; Dir FILOMENA MAIOPUE.

Instituto Nacional de Açúcar (INA): Rua da Gávea 33, CP 1772, Maputo; tel. 21326550; fax 21427436; e-mail gpsca.ina@tvcabo.co.mz; Chair. ARNALDO RIBEIRO.

Instituto Nacional de Petróleo (INP): Av. Fernão de Magalhães 34, 1º/2ºandar, CP 4724, Maputo; tel. 21320935; fax 21320932; e-mail info@inp.gov.mz; internet www.inp.gov.mz; f. 2005; regulates energy sector; Pres. ARSÉNIO MABOTE.

Instituto para a Promoção de Exportações (IPEX): Av. 25 de Setembro 1008, 2° andar, CP 4487, Maputo; tel. 21307257; fax 21307256; e-mail ipex@tvcabo.co.mz; internet www.ipex.gov.mz; f. 1990 to promote and co-ordinate national exports abroad; Pres. Dr JOÃO MACARINGUE.

Unidade Técnica para a Reestruturação de Empresas (UTRE): Rua da Imprensa 256, 7° andar, CP 4350, Maputo; tel. 21426514; fax 21421541; implements restructuring of state enterprises; Dir MOMADE JUMAS.

CHAMBERS OF COMMERCE

Câmara de Comércio de Moçambique (CCM): Rua Mateus Sansão Muthemba 452, CP 1836, Maputo; tel. 21491970; fax 21490428; e-mail ccm@tvcabo.co.mz; internet www.ccmoz.org.mz; f. 1980; Pres. JOÃO AMÉRICO MPFUMO; Sec.-Gen. MANUEL NOTIÇO.

Mozambique-USA Chamber of Commerce: Rua Matheus Sansão Muthemba 452, Maputo; tel. 21492904; fax 21492739; e-mail ccmusa@tvcabo.co.mz; internet www.ccmusa.co.mz; f. 1993; Sec. PETER MUCHIRI.

South Africa-Mozambique Chamber of Commerce (SAMOZACC): tel. 768548303; fax 866049050; e-mail info@samozacc.co.za; internet www.samozacc.co.za; f. 2005; Chair. (Mozambique) DAVID ROBBETZE.

TRADE ASSOCIATIONS

Associação das Indústrias do Cajú (AICAJU): Maputo; cashew processing industry asscn; Chair. CARLOS COSTA; 12 mem. cos.

Confederação das Associações Económicas de Moçambique (CTA): Rua de Fernando Ganhão 120, CP 2975, Maputo; tel. 21491914; fax 21493094; internet www.cta.org.mz; Pres. SALIMO ABDULA; Sec. OLGA TIMBA; 58 mem. cos.

STATE INDUSTRIAL ENTERPRISES

Empresa Nacional de Hidrocarbonetos de Moçambique (ENH): Av. Fernão de Magalhães 34, CP 4787, Maputo; tel. 21429456; fax 21421608; controls concessions for petroleum exploration and production; Dir MÁRIO MARQUES.

Petróleos de Moçambique (PETROMOC): Praça dos Trabalhadores 9, CP 417, Maputo; tel. 21427191; fax 21430181; internet www.petromoc.co.mz; f. 1977 to take over the Sonarep oil refinery and its associated distribution co; formerly Empresa Nacional de Petróleos de Moçambique; state directorate for liquid fuels within Mozambique, incl. petroleum products passing through Mozambique to inland countries; CEO JOSÉ MATEUS MUÁRIA KATHUPA.

UTILITIES

Electricity

Electricidade de Moçambique (EDM): Av. Agostinho Neto 70, CP 2447, Maputo; tel. 21490636; fax 21491048; e-mail ligacaoexpresso@edm.co.mz; internet www.edm.co.mz; f. 1977; 100% state-owned; production and distribution of electric energy; in 2004 plans were announced to extend the EDM grid to the entire country by 2020, at an estimated cost of US $700m; Pres. MANUEL JOÃO CUAMBE; Dir PASCOAL BACELA; 2,700 employees.

Companhia de Transmissão de Moçambique, SARL (MOTRACO) (Mozambique Transmission Co): Av. 25 de Setembro 420, Prédio JAT, 4° andar, Maputo; tel. 21313427; fax 21313447; e-mail asimao@motraco.co.mz; internet www.motraco.co.mz; f. 1998; jt venture between power utilities of Mozambique, South Africa and Swaziland; electricity distribution; Gen. Man. FRANCIS MASAWI.

Water

Direcção Nacional de Águas: Av. 25 de Setembro 942, 9° andar, CP 1611, Maputo; tel. 21420469; fax 21421403; e-mail watco@zebra.uem.mz; internet www.dnaguas.gov.mz; Dir AMÉRICO MUIANGA.

MAJOR COMPANIES

BP Moçambique Lda: Av. dos Mártires da Inhaminga 170, CP 854, Maputo; tel. 21325025; fax 21326042; internet www.bp.com; f. 1981; distribution of petroleum products; Gen. Man. MARTINHO GUAMBE; 150 employees.

British American Tobacco (BAT) (Sociedade Agricola de Tabacos Lda): CP 713, Maputo; tel. 21496011; fax 21491397; internet www.bat.com; production of cigarettes; Gen. Man. LUIZ RIBEIRO.

Cervejas de Moçambique, SARL (CDM): Rua do Jardim 1329, CP 3555, Maputo; tel. 21475007; fax 21475120; brewery; Dir-Gen. GRANT LIVERSAGE.

Cimentos de Moçambique, SA (CM): Av. 24 de Julho 7, 9° andar, Maputo; tel. 21482500; fax 21487869; e-mail idiniz@cimpor.com; f. 1994; owned by Cimentos de Portugal; cement; Chair. STEFFEN KASA; Dir FRANCISCO ILÍDIO DINIZ; 470 employees.

Coca Cola Sabco (Mozambique), SARL: Av. OUA 270, Maputo; tel. 21400190; fax 21400375; internet www.cocacolasabco.com; f. 1994; bottling co; Country Man. SAIDER SIBANDA.

Comércio Grossista de Produtos Alimentares (COGROPA): Av. 25 de Setembro 916, CP 308, Maputo; tel. and fax 21420153; food supplies; transfer pending to private ownership; Dir ANTÓNIO BAPTISTA DO AMARAL.

Companhia de Desenvolvimento Mineiro, SARL (CDM): Av. 24 de Julho 1895, CP 1152, Maputo; tel. 214205889; fax 21428921; e-mail ljossene@teledata.mz; f. 1989; mineral exploration and mineral trade; Pres. LUÍS JOSSENE.

Companhia Industrial do Monapo, SARL: Av. do Trabalho 2106, CP 1248, Maputo; tel. 21400290; fax 21401164; animal and vegetable oils and soap; CEO CARMEN RAMOS.

Construtora do Tâmega: Rua da Tâmega, Machava, CP 1238, Maputo; tel. 21750012; fax 21750174; e-mail tamega@tamega.co.mz; f. 1946; civil engineering and construction; Chair. JOAQUÍM DA MOTA; Man. Dir JOAQUÍM CORDEIRO; 1,450 employees.

Custódio e Irmão, Lda (CIL): Av. de Angola 2351, CP 2495, Maputo; tel. 21465225; fax 21465677; f. 1972; concrete, wood and steel construction materials; Chair. LEONEL CUSTÓDIO.

Embalagens Mondipak, Lda: CP 303, Maputo; tel. 21750372; fax 21750044; e-mail mondipak@teledata.mz; f. 1969 as Embalagens Holdains, Lda; present name adopted in 2006; packaging materials; Gen. Man. NURO MOMEDE MULÁ.

Empresa de Construções Metálicas (ECOME): Av. das Indústrias-Machava, CP 1358, Maputo; tel. 214020114; fax 21417176; agricultural equipment; Dir JUSTINO LUCAS.

ENACOMO, SARL (Empresa Nacional de Comércio): Av. Samora Machel 285, 1° andar, CP 698, Maputo; tel. 21427471; fax 21427754; e-mail enacomo-sede@virconn.net; f. 1976; imports, exports, acquisition, investment, tourism; Man. Dir CARLOS PACHECO FARIA.

Forjadora, SARL (Fábrica de Equipamentos Industriais): Av. de Angola 2850, CP 3078, Maputo; tel. 21465537; fax 21465211; motor vehicle and truck bodies; Chair. CARLOS SIMBINE; Man. Dir JORGE MORGADO.

Hidroeléctrica de Cahora Bassa, SARL (HCB): CP 263, Songo; tel. 25282291; fax 25282364; e-mail cas.sng@hcb.co.mz; internet www.hcb.co.mz; Mozambican Govt (85%), Portuguese Govt (15%); further 5% of Portuguese share to be purchased by Mozambican Govt; production and transmission of electricity; Chair. PAULO MUXANGA.

Higest: Estrada Velha da Moamba, Km 15, Machava, Maputo; tel. 21750034; fax 21750391; e-mail expedição@higest.co.mz; internet www.higest.co.mz; produces poultry feed, chickens and eggs; Dir-Gen. LUÍS GONÇALVES.

Indústria Moçambicana de Aço, SARL (IMA): Av. 24 de Julho 2373, 12° andar, CP 2566, Maputo; tel. 21421141; fax 21420087; f. 1970; steel; Dir MANUEL JOSÉ SEREJO.

Lojas Francas de Moçambique (INTERFRANCA): Rua Timor Leste 106, CP 1206, Maputo; tel. 21425199; fax 21431044; music equipment, motor cars, handicrafts, furniture; Gen. Dir CARLOS E. N. RIBEIRO.

MEDIMOC SA: Av. Julius Nyerere 500, 1° andar, CP 600, Maputo; tel. 21491211; fax 21490168; f. 1977 as Empresa Estatal de Importação e Exportação de Medicamentos (MEDIMOC); pharmaceuticals, medical equipment and supplies; Gen. Dir RENATO RONDA; 230 employees.

Mozal: Parque Industrial Beluluane, Boane, CP 1235, Maputo; tel. 21735000; fax 21735082; internet www.mozal.com; in 2004 Mozal II reached full production level; aluminium smelting and production; 47% owned by BHP Billiton; Gen. Man. CARLOS MESQUITA; 1,150 employees.

Riopele Têxteis de Moçambique, SARL: Rua Joaquim Lapa 21, CP 1658, Maputo; tel. 21331331; fax 21422902; textiles; Dir CARLOS RIBEIRO.

Sociedade de Pesca de Mariscos, Lda (PESCAMAR): Rua Joaquim Lapa 192, Maputo; tel. 21424568; fax 21306801; fishing trawlers; subsidiary of Pescanova SA, Spain; 608 employees; Man. Dir FELISBERTO MANUEL.

Vidreira de Moçambique, SARL: Talhão 77, Av. das Indústrias, Machava, Maputo; tel. 21750353; fax 21750371; e-mail vidreira@teledata.mz; 45% govt-owned; production of glass; Chair. CARLOS MOREIRA DA SILVA; Gen. Man. CARLOS NEVES; 525 employees.

TRADE UNIONS

Freedom to form trade unions, and the right to strike, are guaranteed under the 1990 Constitution.

Confederação de Sindicatos Livres e Independentes de Moçambique (CONSILMO): Sec.-Gen. JEREMIAS TIMANE.

Organização dos Trabalhadores de Moçambique—Central Sindical (OTM—CS) (Mozambique Workers' Organization—Trade Union Headquarters): Rua Manuel António de Sousa 36, Maputo; tel. 21426786; fax 21421671; internet www.otm.org.mz; f. 1983; Pres. CARLOS MUCAREIA; Sec.-Gen. ALEXANDRE MUNGUAMBE; 15 affiliated unions with over 94,000 mems including:

Sindicato Nacional dos Empregadores Bancários (SNEB): Av. Fernão de Magalhães 785, 1° andar, CP 1230, Maputo; tel. 21428627; fax 21303274; e-mail snebmoz@tvcabo.co.mz; internet www.snebmoz.co.mz; f. 1992; Sec.-Gen. ROLANDO LOPES NGULUBE.

Sindicato Nacional da Função Pública (SINAFP): Av. Ho Chi Min 365, Maputo; Sec.-Gen. LEONEL COANA.

Sindicato Nacional dos Profissionais da Estiva e Ofícios Correlativos (SINPEOC): Av. Paulo Samuel Kakhomba 1568, Maputo; tel. and fax 21309535; Sec.-Gen. BENTO MADALA MAUNGUE.

Sindicato Nacional dos Trabalhadores Agro-Pecuários e Florestais (SINTAF): Av. 25 de Setembro 1676, 1° andar, CP 4202, Maputo; tel. 21306284; f. 1987; Sec.-Gen. EUSÉBIO LUÍS CHIVULELE.

Sindicato Nacional dos Trabalhadores da Aviação Civil, Correios e Comunicações (SINTAC): Av. 25 de Setembro 1509, 2° andar, Porta 5, Maputo; tel. 21309574; e-mail sintacnacional@tdm.co.mz; Sec.-Gen. JOÃO FABIÃO MACHAVA.

Sindicato Nacional dos Trabalhadores do Comércio, Seguros e Serviços (SINECOSSE): Av. Ho Chi Minh 365, 1° andar, CP 2142, Maputo; tel. 21428561; Sec.-Gen. AMÓS JÚNIOR MATSINHE.

Sindicato Nacional dos Trabalhadores da Indústria do Açúcar (SINTIA): Av. das FPLM 1912, Maputo; tel. 21461772; fax 21461975; f. 1989; Sec.-Gen. ALEXANDRE CÂNDIDO MUNGUAMBE.

Sindicato Nacional dos Trabalhadores da Indústria Alimentar e Bebidas (SINTIAB): Av. Eduardo Mondlane 1267, CP 394, Maputo; tel. 21324709; fax 21324123; f. 1986; Gen. Sec. SAMUEL FENIAS MATSINHE.

Sindicato Nacional dos Trabalhadores da Indústria de Cajú (SINTIC): Rua do Jardim 574, 4° andar, Maputo; tel. 21477732; Sec.-Gen. BOAVENTURA MONDLANE.

Sindicato Nacional dos Trabalhadores da Indústria Metalúrgica, Metalomecânica e Energia (SINTIME): Av. Samora Machel 30, 6°, Maputo; Sec.-Gen. MATEUS MUIANGA.

Sindicato Nacional dos Trabalhadores da Indústria Química e Afins (SINTIQUIAF): Av. Olof Palme 255, CP 4439, Maputo; tel. 21320288; fax 21321096; e-mail sintiquigra@tvcabo.co.mz; f. 2008 by merger of SINTEVEC and SINTIQUIGRA; clothing, leather and footwear workers' union; Sec.-Gen. JÉSSICA GUNE.

Sindicato Nacional dos Trabalhadores da Marinha Mercante e Pesca (SINTMAP): Rua Joaquim Lapa 22, 5° andar, No. 6, Maputo; tel. 21305593; Sec.-Gen. DANIEL MANUEL NGOQUE.

Sindicato Nacional dos Trabalhadores dos Portos e Caminhos de Ferro (SINPOCAF): Av. Guerra Popular, esquina Av. 25 de Setembro, CP 2158, Maputo; tel. 21403912; fax 21303839; Sec.-Gen. SAMUEL ALFREDO CHEUANE.

Sindicato Nacional de Jornalistas (SNJ): Av. 24 de Julho 231, Maputo; tel. 21492031; fax 823015912; f. 1978; Sec.-Gen. EDUARDO CONSTANTINO.

Transport

Improvements to the transport infrastructure since the signing of the Acordo Geral de Paz (General Peace Agreement) in 1992 have focused on the development of 'transport corridors', which include both rail and road links and promote industrial development in their environs. The Beira Corridor, with rail and road links and a petroleum pipeline, runs from Manica, on the Zimbabwean border, to the Mozambican port of Beira, while the Limpopo Corridor joins southern Zimbabwe and Maputo. Both corridors form a vital outlet for the land-locked southern African countries, particularly Zimbabwe. The Maputo Corridor links Ressano Garcia in South Africa to the port at Maputo, and the Nacala Corridor runs from Malawi to the port of Nacala. Two further corridors were planned: the Mtwara Development Corridor was to link Mozambique, Malawi, Tanzania and Zambia, while the Zambezi Corridor was to link Zambézia province with Malawi.

RAILWAYS

In 2003 the total length of track was 3,114 km, of which 2,072 km was operational. There are both internal routes and rail links between Mozambican ports and South Africa, Swaziland, Zimbabwe and Malawi. During the hostilities many lines and services were disrupted. In the early 2000s work commenced on upgrading the railway system and private companies were granted non-permanent concessions to upgrade and run the railways. In 2009 plans were announced for the construction of a line connecting Moatize with the Malawian railway south of Blantyre. There were also plans for a line to connect Mutarara with Malema. Reconstruction of the 670-km Sena railway line linking Beira with Moatize was expected to be completed by early 2013.

Beira Railway Co: Dondo; f. 2004; 51% owned by Rites & Ircon (India), 49% owned by CFM; rehabilitating and managing Sena and Zimbabwe railway lines.

Portos e Caminhos de Ferro de Moçambique (CFM): Praça dos Trabalhadores, CP 2158, Maputo; tel. 21327173; fax 21427746; e-mail cfmnet@cfmnet.co.mz; internet www.cfmnet.co.mz; fmrly Empresa Nacional dos Portos e Caminhos de Ferro de Moçambique; privatized and restructured in 2002; Chair. ROSÁRIO MUALEIA; comprises four separate systems linking Mozambican ports with the country's hinterland, and with other southern African countries, including South Africa, Swaziland, Zimbabwe and Malawi:

CFM—Centro (CFM—C): Largo dos CFM, CP 236, Beira; tel. 23321000; fax 23329290; lines totalling 994 km linking Beira with Zimbabwe and Malawi, as well as link to Moatize (undergoing rehabilitation); Exec. Dir JOAQUIM VERÍSSIMO.

CFM—Norte: Av. do Trabalho, CP 16, Nampula; tel. 26214320; fax 26212034; lines totalling 872 km, including link between port of Nacala with Malawi; management concession awarded to Nacala Corridor Development Co (a consortium 67% owned by South African, Portuguese and US cos) in January 2000; Dir of Railways MANUEL MANICA.

CFM—Sul: Praça dos Trabalhadores, CP 2158, Maputo; tel. and fax 21430894; lines totalling 1,070 km linking Maputo with South Africa, Swaziland and Zimbabwe, as well as Inhambane–Inharrime and Xai-Xai systems; Exec. Dir JOAQUIM ZUCULE.

CFM—Zambézia: CP 73, Quelimane; tel. 24212502; fax 24213123; 145-km line linking Quelimane and Mocuba; Dir ORLANDO J. JAIME.

ROADS

In 2006 there were an estimated 17,805 km of roads in Mozambique, of which 5,083 km were paved.

Administraçao Nacional de Estradas (ANE): Av. de Moçambique 1225, CP 1294, Maputo; tel. 21475157; fax 21475290; internet www.ane.gov.mz; f. 1999 to replace the Direcção Nacional de Estradas e Pontes; implements government road policy through the Direcção de Estradas Nacionais (DEN) and the Direcção de Estradas Regionais (DER); Pres. Eng. LUCIANO DE CASTRO; Dir-Gen. CECÍLIO GRACHANE.

SHIPPING

Mozambique has three main sea ports, at Nacala, Beira and Maputo, while inland shipping on Lake Niassa and the river system remain underdeveloped. At December 2009 Mozambique's registered merchant fleet consisted of 129 vessels, totalling 41,300 grt.

Portos e Caminhos de Ferro de Moçambique (CFM-EP): Praça dos Trabalhadores, CP 2159, Maputo; tel. 21427173; fax 21427746; e-mail cfmnet@cfmnet.co.mz; internet www.cfmnet.co.mz; fmrly Empresa Nacional dos Portos e Caminhos de Ferro de Moçambique; privatized and restructured in 2002; Chair. ROSÁRIO MUALEIA; Port Dir CFM-Sul Eng. ANTÓNIO FRANCISCO MANUEL BIÉ; Port Dir CFM-Norte Eng. FRANCO CATUTULA; Port Dir CFM-Centro Dr CÂNDIDO JONE.

Agência Nacional de Frete e Navegação (ANFRENA): Rua Consiglieri Pedroso 396, CP 492, Maputo; tel. 21427064; fax 21427822; Dir FERDINAND WILSON.

Empresa Moçambicana de Cargas, SARL (MOCARGO): Rua Consiglieri Pedroso 430, 1°–4° andares, CP 888, Maputo; tel. 21428318; fax 21302067; e-mail msamaral@mocargo.com; internet www.mocargo.co.mz; f. 1982; shipping, chartering and road transport; Man. Dir MANUEL DE SOUSA AMARAL.

Manica Freight Services, SARL: Praça dos Trabalhadores 51, CP 557, Maputo; tel. 21356500; fax 21431084; e-mail fdimande@manica.co.mz; internet www.manica.co.mz; international shipping agents; Man. Dir AHMAD Y. CHOTHIA.

Maputo Port Development Co, SARL (MPDC): Port Director's Building, Porto de Maputo, CP 2841, Maputo; tel. 21313920; fax 21313921; e-mail info@portmaputo.com; internet www.portmaputo.com; f. 2002; private sector international consortium with concession (awarded 2003) to develop and run port of Maputo until 2018; Pres. RONNIE HOLTSHAUSEN; CEO JORGE FERRAZ.

Mozline, SARL: Av. Karl Marx 478, 2° andar, Maputo; tel. 21303078; fax 21303073; e-mail mozline1@virconn.com; shipping and road freight services.

Navique, SARL: Av. Mártires de Inhaminga 125, CP 145, Maputo; tel. 21312705; fax 21426310; e-mail smazoi@navique.co.mz; internet www.navique.com; f. 1985; Chair. J. A. CARVALHO; Man. Dir PEDRO VIRTUOSO.

CIVIL AVIATION

In 2010 there were eight international airports.

Instituto de Aviação Civil de Moçambique (IACM): Maputo; civil aviation institute; Dir ALBERTO MABJAIA.

Air Corridor, SARL: Av. Eduardo Mondlane 945, Nampula; tel. 26213333; fax 26213355; e-mail fagadit@aircorridor.com.mz; internet www.aircorridor.co.mz; f. 2004; domestic carrier and cargo transport; Chair. MOMADE AQUI RAJAHUSSEN; Commercial Dir FARUK ALY GADIT.

Linhas Aéreas de Moçambique, SARL (LAM): Aeroporto Internacional de Maputo, CP 2060, Maputo; tel. 21465137; fax 21422936; e-mail jrviegas@lam.co.mz; internet www.lam.co.mz; f. 1980; 80% state-owned; operates domestic services and international services to South Africa, Tanzania, Mayotte, Zimbabwe and Portugal; CEO MARLENE MENDES MANAVE.

Sociedade de Transportes Aéreos/Sociedade de Transporte e Trabalho Aéreo, SARL (STA/TTA): Rua da Tchamba 405, CP 665, Maputo; tel. 21491765; fax 21491763; e-mail sta.tta@sta.co.mz; f. 1991; domestic airline and aircraft charter transport services; acquired Empresa Nacional de Transporte e Trabalho Aéreo in 1997; Chair. JOSÉ CARVALHEIRA; Dir of Operations FERNANDO CARREIRA.

Other airlines operating in Mozambique include Serviço Aéreo Regional, South African Airlines, Moçambique Expresso, SA—Airlink International, Transairways (owned by LAM) and TAP Air Portugal.

Tourism

Tourism, formerly a significant source of foreign exchange, ceased completely following independence, and was resumed on a limited scale in 1980. There were only 1,000 visitors in 1981 (compared with 292,000 in 1972 and 69,000 in 1974). With the successful conduct of multi-party elections in 1994 and the prospect of continued peace, there was considerable scope for development of this sector. By the late 1990s tourism was the fastest growing sector of the Mozambique economy, and in 2000 it was announced that a comprehensive tourism development plan was to be devised, assisted by funding from the European Union. In 2005 there were 5,030 hotels in Mozambique. The opening of the Great Limpopo Transfrontier Park, linking territories in Mozambique with South Africa and Zimbabwe, was expected to attract additional tourists. Further national parks were planned. There were 3.1m. foreign tourist arrivals in 2009 and tourism receipts in 2011 totalled an estimated US $231m.

Fundo Nacional do Turismo: Av. 25 de Setembro 1203, CP 4758, Maputo; tel. 21307320; fax 21307324; internet www.futur.org.mz; f. 1993; hotels and tourism; CEO Dr ZACARIAS SUMBANA.

Defence

As assessed at November 2011, total active armed forces were estimated at 11,200 (army 10,000, navy 200, air force 1,000).

Defence Expenditure: Budgeted at an estimated 2,020,000m. meticais in 2010.

Commander-in-Chief of the Armed Forces: Pres. ARMANDO EMÍLIO GUEBUZA.

Chief of General Staff: Brig. PAULO MACARINGUE.

Deputy Chief of General Staff: Gen. OLIMPIO CAMBONA.

Education

Primary Education is officially compulsory for seven years from the age of six. It is divided into two cycles, of five and two years. Secondary schooling, from 13 years of age, lasts for five years and comprises a first cycle of three years and a second of two years. According to UNESCO estimates, in 2009/10 92% of children in the relevant age-group were enrolled at primary schools (males 94%; females 89%), while secondary enrolment included only 16% of children in the relevant age-group (males 17%; females 15%). There were 28,298 students in tertiary education in 2004/05. Two privately owned higher education institutions, the Catholic University and the Higher Polytechnic Institute, were inaugurated in 1996. In 2003 it was announced that education would no longer take place solely in Portuguese, but also in some Mozambican dialects. In 2006 some US $39m. was granted by international donors to develop educational resources. Education was allocated 20.2% of total current expenditure in that year.

Bibliography

Abrahamsson, H., and Nilsson, A. *Mozambique: The Troubled Transition from Socialist Construction to Free Market Capitalism*. London, Zed Books, 1995.

Alden, C. *Mozambique and the Construction of the New African State: From Negotiations to Nation Building*. Basingstoke, Palgrave Publishers, 2001.

Armon, J., *et al.* (Eds). *Accord: The Mozambique Peace Process in Perspective*. London, Conciliation Resources, 1998.

Tragedy and Triumph: Mozambique Refugees in Southern Africa, 1977–2001. Westport, CT, Greenwood Publishing Group, 2002.

Bekoe, D. *Implementing Peace Agreements: Lessons from Mozambique, Angola, and Liberia*. Basingstoke, Palgrave Macmillan, 2008.

Berman, E. *Managing Arms in Peace Processes: Mozambique*. New York, United Nations, 1996.

Bowen, M. L. *The State Against the Peasantry (Rural Struggles in Colonial and Postcolonial Mozambique)*. Charlottesville, VA, University Press of Virginia, 2000.

Cabrita, J. *Mozambique (The Tortuous Road to Democracy)*. Basingstoke, Palgrave Publishers, 2001.

Cann, J. P. *Counter-insurgency in Africa: The Portuguese Way of War 1961–1974*. Westport, CT, Greenwood Press, 1997.

Chan, S. *War and Peace in Mozambique*. Basingstoke, Macmillan, 1998.

Chissano, J. A. *Peace and Reconstruction*. Harare, Southern African Research and Documentation Centre, 1997.

Christie, F., and Hanlon, J. *Mozambique and the Great Flood of 2000*. Bloomington, IN, Indiana University Press, 2001.

Clement, J. A. P., and Peiris, S. J. *Post-stabilization Economics in Sub-Saharan Africa: Lessons from Mozambique*. Washington, DC, IMF Publications, 2007.

Englund, H. *From War to Peace on the Mozambique–Malawi Borderlands*. New York, Columbia University Press, 2002.

Finnegan, W. A. *A Complicated War: The Harrowing of Mozambique*. Berkeley, CA, University of California Press, 1992.

Fox, L. *Beating the Odds: Sustaining Inclusion in Mozambique's Growing Economy*. Washington, DC, World Bank Publications, 2009.

Geffray, C. *La Cause des Armes au Mozambique—Anthropologie d'une guerre civile*. Paris, Editions Karthala, 1990.

Hanlon, J. *Apartheid's Second Front: South Africa's War Against its Neighbours*. Harmondsworth, Penguin, 1986.

Hanlon, J., and Smart, T. *Do Bicycles Equal Development in Mozambique?* London, James Currey, 2010.

Harrison, G. *The Politics of Democratisation in Rural Mozambique (Grassroots Governance in Mecufi)—African Studies, 55*. Lampeter, Edwin Mellen Press, 2000.

Hoile, D. *Mozambique: Propaganda, Myth and Reality*. London, Mozambique Institute, 1991.

Mozambique: Resistance and Freedom: A Case for Reassessment. London, Mozambique Institute, 1994.

Isaacman, A., and Isaacman, B. *Mozambique from Colonialism to Revolution, 1900–82*. Boulder, CO, Westview Press, 1983.

Ishemo, S. L. *The Lower Zambezi Basin in Mozambique (A Study in Economy and Society, 1850–1920)—The Making of Modern Africa*. Aldershot, Avebury, 1995.

Knauder, S. *Globalization, Urban Progress, Urban Problems, Rural Disadvantages (Evidence from Mozambique)*. Aldershot, Ashgate Publishing Ltd, 2000.

Macqueen, N. *The Decolonization of Portuguese Africa: Metropolitan Revolution and the Dissolution of Empire*. Harlow, Longman, 1997.

Manning, C. *The Politics of Peace in Mozambique*. Westport, CT, Praeger Publishers, 2002.

Mario, M., Fry, P., Levy, L., and Chilundo, A. *Higher Education in Mozambique: A Case Study*. London, James Currey, 2003.

Mazula, B. *Mozambique: Elections, Democracy and Development*. Maputo, Manila, 1996.

Minter, W. *Apartheid's Contras: An Inquiry into the Roots of War in Angola and Mozambique*. London, Zed Press, 1994.

Ndege, G. O. *Culture and Customs of Mozambique*. Westport, CT, Greenwood Publishing Group, 2006.

Newitt, M. *A History of Mozambique*. Bloomington, IN, Indiana University Press; London, Hurst, 1993.

Pitcher, A. *Transforming Mozambique: The Politics of Privatization, 1975–2000*. Cambridge, Cambridge University Press, 2002.

Rafael, S. D. *Dicionário Toponímico, Histórico, Geográfico e Etnográfico de Moçambique*. Maputo, Arquivo Histórico de Moçambique, 2002.

Saul, J. (Ed.). *A Difficult Road: The Transition to Socialism in Mozambique*. New York, Monthly Review Press, 1985.

Schafer, J. *Soldiers at Peace: The Post-war Politics of Demobilized Soldiers in Mozambique*. Basingstoke, Palgrave MacMillan, 2007.

Sheldon, K. *Pounders of Grain: A History of Women, Work, and Politics in Mozambique*. Westport, CT, Greenwood Publishing Group, 2002.

Soderbaum, F. *Regionalism and Uneven Development in Southern Africa: The Case of the Maputo Development Corridor*. Aldershot, Ashgate, 2003.

Torp, J. E. *Mozambique: Politics, Economics, Society*. London, Pinter, 1989.

Trindade, J. C., and Meneses, M. P. *Law and Justice in a Multicultural Society: The Case of Mozambique*. Dakar, CODESRIA, 2006.

Vail, L., and White, L. *Capitalism and Colonialism in Mozambique*. London, Heinemann Educational, 1995.

Vines, A. *No Democracy Without Money: The Road to Peace in Mozambique (1981–1992)*. London, Catholic Institute for International Relations, 1994.

Renamo: Terrorism in Mozambique. 2nd edn. London, James Currey, 1996.

Young, T., and Hall, M. *Confronting Leviathan: Mozambique Since Independence*. London, Hurst, 1997.

NAMIBIA

Physical and Social Geography

A. MacGREGOR HUTCHESON

The Republic of Namibia, lying across the Tropic of Capricorn, covers an area of 825,615 sq km (318,772 sq miles). It is bordered by South Africa on the south and south-east, by Botswana on the east and Angola on the north, while the narrow Caprivi Strip, between the two latter countries, extends Namibia's boundaries to the Zambezi river and a short border with Zambia.

The Namib Desert, a narrow plain 65 km–160 km wide and extending 1,600 km along the entire Atlantic seaboard, has a mean annual rainfall of less than 100 mm; long lines of huge sand dunes are common and it is almost devoid of vegetation. Behind the coastal plain the Great Escarpment rises to the plateau, which forms the rest of the country. Part of the Southern African plateau, it has an average elevation of 1,100 m above sea-level, but towards the centre of the country it rises to altitudes of 1,525 m–2,440 m. A number of mountain masses rise above the general surface throughout the plateau. Eastwards the surface slopes to the Kalahari Basin and northwards to the Etosha Pan. Much of Namibia's drainage is interior to the Kalahari. There are no perennial rivers apart from the Okavango and the Cuando, which cross the Caprivi Strip, and the Orange, Kunene and Zambezi, which form parts of the southern and northern borders.

Temperatures in the coastal areas are modified by the cool Benguela Current, while altitude modifies plateau temperatures (Walvis Bay, sea level: January 19°C, July 14.5°C; and Windhoek, 1,707 m: January 24°C, July 14°C). Average annual rainfall varies from some 50 mm on the coast to 550 mm in the north. Most rain falls during the summer (September–March), but is unreliable and there are years of drought. Grasslands cover most of the plateau; they are richer in the wetter north, but merge into poor scrub in the south and east.

Most of the population (which totalled some 2,104,900, according to the preliminary results of the census of 28 August 2011) reside on the plateau. Figures for the density of population (2.5 inhabitants per sq km at 28 August 2011) are misleading, as the better-watered northern one-third of the plateau contains more than one-half of the total population and about two-thirds of the African population, including the Ovambo (the largest single ethnic group), Kavango, East Caprivians and Kaokovelders. Almost the entire European population (80,000 in 1988, including the European population of Walvis Bay, an exclave of South Africa that was ceded to Namibia in March 1994) are concentrated in the southern two-thirds of the plateau, chiefly in the central highlands around Windhoek, the capital, together with the other main ethnic groups, the Damara, Herero, Nama, Rehoboth and Coloured. Excluding ports and mining centres in the Namib, and apart from small numbers of Bushmen (San) in the Kalahari, the desert regions are largely uninhabited.

Namibia possesses scattered deposits of valuable minerals, and its economy is dominated by the mining sector. Of particular importance are the rich deposits of alluvial diamonds, which are exploited by surface mining, notably in the area between Oranjemund and Lüderitz. Furthermore, new diamond fields off shore have also been developed with much success. Uranium ore (although of a low grade) is mined open-cast at Rössing, 39 km north-east of Swakopmund, which, on a global scale, is the largest open-pit uranium oxide complex and the third-largest producer of uranium oxide. There is another, smaller uranium deposit, thought to be of a higher grade, about 80 km south of Rössing. Tin, copper, rock salt, lead and zinc are also mined, and Namibia is believed to have significant reserves of coal, iron ore and platinum, although these have yet to be assessed. Other minerals currently produced or awaiting exploitation include vanadium, manganese, gold, silver, tungsten (wolfram), cadmium and limestone. There are also considerable reserves of offshore natural gas. In mid-2011 the Government announced that sizeable deposits of petroleum had been discovered off the southern coast of Namibia. Commercial production was not scheduled to commence for several years, but, once it did so, was expected to benefit the country enormously in the form of significant amounts of revenue.

Despite the limitations imposed by frequent drought, agriculture is a significant economic activity. With the help of water from boreholes, large areas are given over to extensive ranching. Rivers, notably the Orange, Kunene and Okavango, are potential water resources for irrigation and hydroelectric power, while swamps, such as those situated in the Caprivi Strip, could be drained to enhance arable output.

Namibia possesses potentially the richest inshore and deep-water fishing zones in tropical Africa, as a consequence of the rich feeding provided by the Benguela Current. Measures are being taken to counter the effects of decades of overfishing by both domestic and foreign fleets.

Recent History

CHRISTOPHER SAUNDERS

HISTORICAL BACKGROUND

The origins of the modern territory of Namibia lay in the protectorate established by the German Government in 1884. The present boundaries, which in the north cut through the Ovambo-speaking peoples, were demarcated in the late 19th and early 20th centuries. The port of Walvis Bay, initially ruled by the United Kingdom, was from 1884 part of the Cape Colony and therefore of the Union of South Africa from 1910. Following the outbreak of the First World War, South African forces occupied the German colony of South West Africa (SWA). After the war the League of Nations awarded South Africa a mandate to administer the territory. No trusteeship agreement was concluded with the UN after the Second World War, and the refusal of that organization in 1946 to agree to South Africa's request to annex SWA marked the beginning of a protracted legal dispute regarding the status of the territory. In 1950 the International Court of Justice (ICJ) ruled that South Africa did not have to place the territory under the UN trusteeship system, but could not alter the legal status of the territory unilaterally. In 1966, after the ICJ had failed to make a substantive judgment on whether South Africa's rule of the territory was illegal, the UN General Assembly voted to terminate South Africa's mandate and to assume responsibility for the territory; a Council for South West Africa was appointed in 1967, and in the following year the UN resolved that the territory should be renamed Namibia. This had no immediate practical effect, however, as South Africa remained in firm occupation of the territory. Another result of the ICJ's 'non-decision' was that the South West Africa People's Organisation

(SWAPO), which had been founded in 1960 under the leadership of Sam Nujoma, began an armed insurgency in the north of the territory in August 1966.

A turning point came in 1971 when the ICJ issued an advisory opinion that South Africa's presence in Namibia was illegal and that it should withdraw. In December 1973 the UN General Assembly recognized SWAPO as the 'authentic representative of the people of Namibia', and appointed the first UN Commissioner for Namibia to undertake 'executive and administrative tasks'. South Africa's unsuccessful military intervention in Angola in the second half of 1975 set the scene for the escalation of the Namibian armed struggle. With support from the new Government in Angola, the military wing of SWAPO, the People's Liberation Army of Namibia (PLAN), was able to establish bases close to Namibia's borders. South Africa reacted to this threat by greatly expanding counter-insurgency forces in the territory and taking initiatives on the political front. In September 1975 a constitutional conference was convened to discuss the territory's future. The Turnhalle Conference, as it became known (after a historic building in the Namibian capital, Windhoek), designated 31 December 1978 as the target date for Namibian independence, and in March 1977 it produced a draft constitution for a pre-independence interim government. This constitution, providing for 11 ethnic administrations, was denounced by the UN and SWAPO, which issued its own constitutional proposals based on a parliamentary system with universal adult suffrage.

In order to persuade South Africa to reject the Turnhalle proposals in favour of a plan that would be acceptable to the UN, a 'contact group' comprising the five Western members of the UN Security Council was established in 1977. In September South Africa appointed an Administrator-General for Namibia, and the territory's representation in the South African Parliament was terminated. By April 1978 the 'contact group' was able to present proposals for a settlement providing for UN-supervised elections, a reduction in the numbers of South African troops in Namibia and the release of political prisoners. These proposals were accepted by South Africa in April and by SWAPO in July. The proposals were then incorporated into UN Security Council Resolution 435 on 28 September 1978. South Africa insisted on holding its own election for a Namibian Constituent Assembly in the territory in December of that year; with SWAPO boycotting the election, 41 of the 50 seats were won by the Democratic Turnhalle Alliance (DTA), a conservative coalition of the ethnic groups involved in the conference. The DTA leader, Dirk Mudge, became Chairman of a Ministerial Council, which was granted limited executive powers.

In January 1981 the UN convened a conference in Geneva, Switzerland, which was attended by SWAPO, South Africa, the DTA and other internal parties. The 'contact group' and the 'front-line' states (Angola, Botswana, Mozambique, Tanzania, Zambia and Zimbabwe) were present as observers. However, South Africa and the internal parties would not agree on a cease-fire date and the implementation of the UN plan, so the conference was abortive. Under US chairmanship, the Western 'contact group' then resumed consultations with South Africa and SWAPO during 1981. In July 1982 both agreed to constitutional guidelines providing that the constitution for an independent Namibia should include a bill of rights and be approved by two-thirds of the members of a constituent assembly. Although South Africa for a time refused to agree that the election should be conducted wholly on the basis of proportional representation, the UN Secretary-General was able to report that all other points at issue had been resolved.

By then, however, a more formidable obstacle to the implementation of the UN plan had arisen. South Africa insisted that the Cuban troops who had supported the Angolan Government from 1975 withdraw from that country before it would agree to the implementation of Resolution 435. The idea of linking South Africa's withdrawal from Namibia with the withdrawal of Cuban military forces from Angola was introduced by the US Administration under President Ronald Reagan in 1981, in an attempt to persuade the South African Government to agree to withdraw from Namibia. SWAPO and its allies, however, saw this 'linkage' as giving South Africa an excuse not to implement Resolution 435, for as long as South African forces were active in southern Angola there seemed no likelihood that the Angolan Government and the Cubans would agree to withdraw the Cuban military force.

In February 1984 a cease-fire agreement was concluded in Lusaka, Zambia, following talks between South African and US government officials. Under the terms of the agreement, a joint commission was established to monitor the withdrawal of South African troops from Angola, and Angola undertook to permit neither SWAPO nor Cuban forces to move into the area vacated by South African troops. SWAPO declared that it would abide by the agreement, but made it clear that it would continue PLAN operations until a cease-fire was established in Namibia as the first stage in the implementation of UN Resolution 435. In November, in response to US proposals, President José Eduardo dos Santos of Angola suggested a timetable for the withdrawal of Cuban troops from the south of Angola, but in the mid-1980s the possibility of a settlement involving the implementation of UN Resolution 435 seemed remote.

The South African administration took advantage of the delay in the transition to independence to build an anti-SWAPO front. The DTA was weakened in early 1982 by losing support among the Ovambo, the largest ethnic group in Namibia, and after many disputes with the South African Government over the future role of the DTA, Mudge resigned as Chairman of the Ministerial Council in January 1983, and the Council was dissolved. The Administrator-General, in turn, dissolved the National Assembly, and assumed direct rule of Namibia on behalf of the South African Government. He then promoted the establishment of a multi-party conference (MPC), made up of the DTA and smaller internal parties. On 17 June 1985 the South African Government formally installed a 'Transitional Government of National Unity' in Windhoek, which consisted of a Cabinet and a National Assembly. Neither was elected: appointments were made from among the constituent parties of the MPC. A 'bill of rights', drawn up by the MPC, prohibited racial discrimination, and a Constitutional Council was established, under a South African judge, to prepare a constitution for an independent Namibia. South Africa retained responsibility for foreign affairs, defence and internal security.

With the Cold War winding down, and the Soviet Union making it clear that it would work to settle regional conflicts in which it was engaged, Angola and Cuba accepted, in principle, US demands for a complete withdrawal of Cuban troops from Angola in January 1988. In March proposals for the withdrawal were rejected by South Africa, but South African troops were unable to gain the upper hand against the Angolan and Cuban forces at Cuito Cuanavale, in southern Angola, and the Cuban forces began moving southwards to the Namibian border. With the threat of a major confrontation between the Cuban and South African armies looming, South Africa agreed to participate in tripartite negotiations with Angola and Cuba, with the USA acting as mediator: these began in May. South Africa agreed to implement Resolution 435, providing that a timetable for the withdrawal of Cuban troops could be agreed. By mid-July the participants in the negotiations had accepted a document containing 14 'essential principles' for a peaceful settlement, and in early August it was agreed that the implementation of Resolution 435 would begin on 1 November. South African troops were withdrawn from southern Angola by the end of August. The November deadline was not met, however, owing to disagreement on an exact schedule for the evacuation of Cuban troops. In mid-November these arrangements were agreed in principle, although their formal ratification was delayed until mid-December, owing to South African dissatisfaction with verification procedures.

On 22 December 1988 South Africa, Angola and Cuba signed an agreement designating 1 April 1989 as the implementation date for Resolution 435. Another treaty, signed by Angola and Cuba, required the evacuation of all Cuban troops from Angola by July 1991. A joint commission was established to monitor the implementation of the trilateral treaty. Under the terms of Resolution 435, South African forces in Namibia were to be confined to their bases, and their numbers reduced to 1,500 by 1 July 1989; all South African troops were to have been withdrawn from Namibia one week after the election. A multinational UN observer force, the UN Transition Assistance Group (UNTAG), was to monitor the South African withdrawal and supervise the election, and the UN Secretary-General's Special Representative, Martti Ahtisaari of Finland, would have to declare whether the election was free and fair.

IMPLEMENTATION OF THE UN INDEPENDENCE PLAN

By the implementation date of 1 April 1989, the day the cease-fire took effect, few of the UNTAG forces (which were eventually to comprise 4,650 troops, with a further 500 police and about 1,000 civilian observers) had arrived. On that day PLAN forces began to reveal themselves in Ovamboland. They probably hoped to be settled in bases under UN supervision, but the South African Government obtained Ahtisaari's agreement to the release of its forces from their base, and more than 300 PLAN troops were killed in the subsequent fighting. On 9 April the joint commission produced conditions for an evacuation of the PLAN forces, after Sam Nujoma, President of SWAPO, had ordered their withdrawal to Angola. At a meeting of the joint commission on 19 May, the cease-fire was certified to be in force. In June most racially discriminatory legislation was repealed, and an amnesty was granted to Namibian refugees and exiles. By September nearly 42,000 of those who had gone into exile, including Nujoma, had returned to Namibia.

The pre-independence election was conducted peacefully in November 1989, with more than 95% of the electorate turning out to vote. SWAPO received 57.3% of all votes cast and won 41 of the 72 seats in the Constituent Assembly, while the DTA, with 28.6% of the votes, secured 21 seats. Ahtisaari pronounced the election to have been 'free and fair', after which the remaining South African troops left Namibia, and SWAPO's bases in Angola were disbanded.

In February 1990 the Constituent Assembly unanimously adopted a draft Constitution, which provided for a multi-party political system based on universal adult suffrage, with an independent judiciary and a 'bill of rights'. Executive power was to be vested in a President, who was permitted to serve a maximum of two five-year terms, while a 72-member National Assembly was to have legislative power. The Constituent Assembly subsequently elected Nujoma as Namibia's first President. On 21 March 1990 Namibia became independent: the Constituent Assembly became the National Assembly, and the President and his Cabinet (headed by Hage Geingob, the Prime Minister, who had been Chairman of the Constituent Assembly) took office.

SWAPO IN GOVERNMENT

Namibia became a full member of the Southern African Customs Union (SACU), having previously been a de facto member; the South African Development Co-ordination Conference (SADCC), which sought to reduce the dependence of southern African states on South Africa; the UN; the Organization of African Unity (from 2002 the African Union—AU); and the Commonwealth. Full diplomatic relations were established with many states, and partial diplomatic relations with South Africa, with which negotiations began over the future of Walvis Bay. These led to a joint administration of the port and then its incorporation into Namibia in early 1994. In August 1992 Namibia joined the other SADCC members in recreating the organization as the Southern African Development Community (SADC), to which South Africa was admitted in August 1994.

In November 1991 the DTA, formerly a coalition of ethnically based interests, reorganized itself as a single party, but its support continued to dwindle. In November and December 1992 the first elections were held for the country's 13 regional councils and 48 local authorities. SWAPO won nine regional councils, while the DTA won three (in the remaining council there was no clear majority). SWAPO thus secured control of the newly established second house of parliament, the National Council, which comprised two members from each regional council; it began its work in May 1993.

Namibia's first post-independence presidential and legislative elections took place on 7–8 December 1994, and resulted in overwhelming victories for Nujoma and SWAPO. Nujoma was elected for a second term as President, securing 76.3% of the votes cast; his only challenger was Mudge's successor as President of the DTA, Mishake Muyongo. SWAPO secured 53 of the elective seats in the National Assembly, obtaining 73.9% of the valid votes cast. Although SWAPO thus had a two-thirds' majority in the National Assembly, Nujoma gave assurances that no amendments would be made to the Constitution without prior approval by national referendum. He was sworn in for his second presidential term on 21 March 1995. The previous day, as part of a major reorganization of cabinet portfolios, he assumed personal responsibility for home affairs and the police. Geingob remained as Prime Minister.

In May 1997, at SWAPO's second party congress since independence, a resolution endorsing the proposal that Nujoma should seek re-election for a third term as President was justified on the grounds that he had initially been chosen by the Constituent Assembly, and had only once been elected President on a popular mandate. Hifikepunye Pohamba, one of Nujoma's closest associates in the years of exile, replaced Moses Garoëb as Secretary-General of the party. In a minor reshuffle of the Cabinet in December 1997, Pohamba was appointed Minister without Portfolio.

REGIONAL CONCERNS

With the resumption of the civil war in Angola in late 1992, the Namibian Government's concerns about security along its northern border increased. In March 1993 the Angolan insurgent movement União Nacional para a Independência Total de Angola (UNITA) alleged that members of the Namibian Defence Force had crossed the border into southern Angola to assist Angolan government forces in offensives against it. The Namibian authorities denied any involvement in the Angolan civil conflict, but in 1996 a special field force of the Namibian police was deployed along the Okavango river on the Angolan border to deter possible UNITA attacks. In August 1996 Namibian and Angolan officials agreed on further measures to increase border security.

In 1996 Namibia and Botswana referred their dispute over the demarcation of their joint border on the Chobe river (specifically, the issue of the sovereignty of the sparsely inhabited island of Kasikili-Sedudu) for adjudication by the ICJ. In December 1997 a new dispute began concerning two further islands, Situngu and Luyondo, when Botswanan soldiers allegedly harvested crops planted on the islands by Namibian villagers. In May 1998 the two countries signed an accord establishing a joint technical commission to demarcate their border on the Chobe river.

In August 1998 President Nujoma ordered the dispatch of Namibian troops in support of President Laurent-Désiré Kabila of the Democratic Republic of the Congo (DRC) against rebel forces supported by Uganda and Rwanda. Within weeks almost 2,000 Namibian troops were fighting in the DRC alongside troops from Angola and Zimbabwe, helping to secure the Matadi corridor from Kinshasa, DRC, to the sea. Although Nujoma asserted that Namibian involvement was an act of solidarity and support for the territorial integrity of the DRC in the face of external aggression, many observers considered that he hoped participation in the war might allow Namibia to benefit from future mineral exploitation in the DRC. Nujoma played a prominent role in efforts towards a negotiated settlement, helping to persuade Kabila to enter talks with the rebels and Uganda to discuss withdrawal from the DRC. He continued to deny that there were any Namibian troops supporting the Angolan Government against UNITA, but stated that, if requested, Namibia would assist its neighbour under the auspices of SADC. In April Namibia signed a regional defence pact with Angola, the DRC and Zimbabwe, providing for mutual assistance in the event of aggression against any of the signatories.

Efforts to resolve the conflict in the DRC were accelerated in early 2001, following the assassination of Laurent-Désiré Kabila and the succession to the presidency of his son, Maj.-Gen. Joseph Kabila. Proposals for the withdrawal of the foreign troops stationed in the DRC, including the Namibian contingent, were subsequently approved by the participating countries, under the aegis of the UN Security Council, and the withdrawal of Namibian forces from the DRC was completed in September.

Relations with Botswana were further complicated from late 1998, when refugees began entering that country from the Caprivi Strip, a thin section of Namibian territory extending from the north-eastern corner of that country and bordering Angola, Zambia and Botswana. Beginning in October a stream of refugees fled to Botswana, citing police harassment, after a man was reportedly killed at a secret military training base that the Namibian Government alleged was being used by the secessionist Caprivi Liberation Movement (CLM). The people of Caprivi had long sought closer links with their neighbours to the east, believing that the Government in Windhoek was ignoring the development of their region because they did not support SWAPO. It emerged that the leading refugee figure was Muyongo, and in August 1998 the DTA's executive suspended Muyongo as President, and dissociated the party from Muyongo's overt support for the secession of the Caprivi Strip. With 14 other members of the CLM, he sought, and was granted, asylum by the Botswana Government in February 1999. Nujoma, who had at first sought the extradition of the refugees so that they could be tried as terrorists, made a state visit to Botswana in March, during which he agreed with President Festus G. Mogae that the secessionist leaders could be accorded refugee status, on condition that they be resettled in a third country; the remaining refugees, who by then numbered some 2,500 (including many San Bushmen), would be able to return without fear of punishment or persecution. This agreement was subsequently ratified by the two countries and the office of the UN High Commissioner for Refugees (UNHCR). Muyongo and another leader of the movement, Boniface Mamili (a chief of the Mafwe), were granted political asylum in Denmark.

In early August 1999, however, an unanticipated attack by members of what was styled the Caprivi Liberation Army (CLA) on the regional capital of Caprivi, Katima Mulilo, resulted in 12 deaths. The Namibian Government imposed a state of emergency in Caprivi, and was offered support by Zimbabwe and Zambia against the separatists. The CLA, which had bases in western Zambia, was said to have close links with the separatist Barotse Patriotic Front in that country. It was widely suspected that UNITA had given the CLA military training and supported the attack because of the Namibian Government's close ties with the Angolan Government. Although the state of emergency was revoked in late August, human rights groups in Namibia produced evidence that Namibian troops had committed acts of brutality against those believed to support the rebels. More than 120 of those arrested appeared in court in 2001, charged with high treason, murder and sedition, but their trial was postponed. In July 2007 10 of the alleged secessionists were finally convicted of high treason and sentenced to prison terms of 30–32 years.

Tensions along the Namibia–Angola border escalated from late 1999, after the two countries began joint patrols targeting UNITA, and the Namibian Government authorized the Angolan armed forces to launch attacks against UNITA from Namibian territory. UNITA responded by launching sporadic attacks in the Caprivi Strip. By June 2000 more than 50 Namibians had been killed in cross-border raids by the Angolan rebels. However, following the death of Jonas Savimbi, the UNITA leader, and the signing of a cease-fire between the Angolan Government and UNITA in April 2002, the situation in the north-east of Namibia improved considerably. As Angola became more peaceful, its trade with Namibia increased, and in August 2002 Namibian refugees in Botswana began to be repatriated. In that month the return of Angolan refugees in Namibia to their country began; about 20,000 returned home in the second half of 2003, under the auspices of UNHCR.

At a meeting held in March 1999 Presidents Nujoma and Mogae confirmed that Namibia and Botswana would each respect the judgment of the ICJ regarding sovereignty of Kasikili-Sedudu. In December the judgment was finally made in Botswana's favour. The two countries then established a joint commission to settle the remaining disputes in the Chobe river area, and agreed that its decisions would be binding on both Governments. In March 2003 the two Governments accepted the commission's demarcation of their joint border along the Kwando, Linyanti and Chobe rivers. The issue of Namibia's border with South Africa remained unresolved: Namibia claimed that its southern border extended to the middle of the Orange river, while South Africa claimed its territory stretched to the northern bank. How the boundary ran out to sea (and thus to diamond deposits) was also disputed.

One of the most significant developments on the country's borders occurred in 2004 when President Nujoma and his Zambian counterpart, Levy Mwanawasa, opened the Sesheke bridge across the Zambezi river. This linked the Trans-Caprivi Highway to the Zambian Copperbelt, and made it possible for exports from Zambia and the southern DRC to be sent to the Namibian port of Walvis Bay. By mid-2012 progress was also being made with the SADC-inspired Kunene Transboundary Water Supply Project, designed to benefit 700,000 people in southern Angola and northern Namibia by providing water for domestic consumption, irrigation and industry. In addition, SADC promoted the so-called 'Western Power Corridor' from South Africa through Namibia to Angola; the boldest proposal was to route the delivery of power from the Inga hydroelectric dam in the DRC through Angola to Namibia. Moreover, in 2012 Namibia was part of an SADC group that was attempting to formulate a common policy on the Economic Partnership Agreement proposed by the European Union (EU). However, with the deadline of January 2014 approaching, it was feared that negotiations with the EU would prove unsuccessful and that Namibia's favourable terms of access to the European market would consequently revert to the Generalised System of Preferences, which excluded beef and table grapes, both important Namibian exports to the EU.

NUJOMA'S THIRD TERM

Meanwhile, in October 1998 an exceptional amendment to the Constitution, allowing Nujoma to seek a third presidential term, was approved by the requisite two-thirds' majority in the National Assembly; in the following month it was endorsed by the National Council.

A potential challenge to SWAPO's dominance emerged with the establishment in March 1999 of a new political party under a former trade union leader and senior SWAPO official, Ben Ulenga. Ulenga had resigned from his post as Namibia's High Commissioner to the United Kingdom in August 1998, in protest against SWAPO's decision to alter the Constitution to allow Nujoma to seek a third term as President. Ulenga also opposed Namibia's involvement in the conflict in the DRC, and was critical of the SWAPO Government's failure to address the issue of unemployed former combatants adequately. Ulenga established a new party, the Congress of Democrats (CoD). Unlike the DTA, the CoD was not tainted with a history of collaboration with South Africa under apartheid. Concerned about the CoD's prospects in the presidential and general elections due in late 1999, Nujoma swiftly appointed two key figures from the labour movement as deputy ministers, and the Government set aside N $255m. in the 1999/2000 budget for the social integration of about 9,000 former combatants, who were to be offered employment in the public service. A number were given posts in the police, and a national youth service scheme was also proposed.

The elections, which were held on 30 November and 1 December 1999, resulted in an overwhelming victory for Nujoma and SWAPO. The support won by Ulenga and the CoD was mainly at the expense of the DTA. In the presidential election Nujoma was returned for a third (and final) term of office, with 76.8% of the votes cast, while Ulenga took 10.5% and the President of the DTA 9.6%. SWAPO won 55 of the elective seats in the National Assembly, with 76.1% of the votes cast (thus ensuring that it retained the two-thirds' majority enabling it to amend the Constitution); the CoD and the DTA each won seven seats (taking, respectively, 9.9% and 9.5% of the total votes cast), but the DTA was able to retain its status as the official opposition by forming an alliance with the Damara-based United Democratic Front (UDF), which secured two seats. Geingob was reappointed Prime Minister in a reorganization of the Cabinet announced by Nujoma in March 2000. Pohamba relinquished his post as Minister without Portfolio, but remained Secretary-

General of SWAPO until the party's congress in 2002 when he was elevated to the position of party Vice-President. In January 2001 he had been appointed Minister of Lands, Resettlement and Rehabilitation. In what was widely seen as a way of removing a potential successor, in August 2002 Nujoma suddenly dismissed Geingob as Prime Minister and replaced him with the long-serving Minister of Foreign Affairs, Theo Ben-Gurirab.

As Namibia entered the new millennium, one of its major problems was HIV/AIDS. By 2003 21.3% of Namibia's adult population (aged between 15 and 49 years) were estimated to be living with HIV, and the Government responded tardily to the pandemic. In 2002 the effect of AIDS in reducing the agricultural labour force and production was cited as one of the reasons for the serious food crisis that had developed by the middle of that year, when an estimated 70,000 people in the north-eastern Caprivi region needed urgent food aid. In August UN agencies, government officials and other organizations undertook a joint assessment of food supplies throughout the country. Severe flooding in the Caprivi region in May 2003 necessitated further food aid, this time supplied by the International Committee of the Red Cross. The decision by the Namibian Government to allocate more than N $80m. in the 2003/04 budget for the purchase of antiretroviral drugs for people infected with HIV was widely welcomed, as was the announcement in May 2003 that the Government was to support the manufacture of generic medication for the treatment of HIV/AIDS.

There was much speculation that Nujoma would seek a fourth term as the country's President, but there was significant opposition to that idea, which would have required a further constitutional amendment, and in April 2004 at a special meeting of SWAPO's central committee he confirmed that he would not stand again. Hidipo Hamutenya was widely viewed as his likely successor, but Nujoma dismissed him from the Cabinet and Pohamba was chosen as SWAPO's presidential candidate. Hamutenya later broke with SWAPO (see below).

After Zimbabwe's President Robert Mugabe allowed the forcible seizure of land from white farmers and its redistribution to the black population, the issue of land reform gained more prominence on the Namibian Government's agenda. The Government remained firm that it would not permit land invasions, and by 2000 only 35,000 black farmers had been settled on land obtained from white farmers. However, during a visit to Germany in mid-2002, Nujoma sought financial aid for the purchase of land from white commercial farmers for landless blacks. In August of that year Nujoma warned white farmers to co-operate with the Government's scheme for land redistribution. Representatives of the Herero people, meanwhile, proceeded with cases against the German Government, Deutsche Bank AG and Woermann Line (a shipping firm), from which they demanded compensation of some US $4,000m. for their involvement in the dispossession of the Herero and the atrocities committed against them under German colonial rule. The Namibian Government refused to support this claim, declaring that it was in Namibia's interests to continue to work harmoniously with the German Government and industry.

The Namibian Government had long maintained that it would target farms owned by foreigners for expropriation, and in 2003 a list of 192 farms owned by foreigners, mostly South Africans and Germans, had been compiled. In February 2004 the Government announced that it had lost patience with the slow pace of land reform under the 'willing buyer, willing seller' programme and would now consider using compulsory expropriation to speed up the process of redistributing land to the estimated 240,000 landless people. By 2004 some 700 farms had been sold to the Government for land-reform purposes over a decade, and some 4,000 white commercial farmers owned about 30m. ha of land, although much of that was arid and unsuitable for peasant agriculture. In March Pohamba wrote to 15 landowners informing them that they were required to sell their property to the State, and giving them 14 days to respond. The Namibia Agricultural Union stated that it would accept expropriation providing it was carried out within the country's legal and constitutional framework, which required that compensation should be paid at market value and that those targeted should have the right to have recourse to the law to contest expropriation. Expropriation with compensation meant that budgetary constraints would determine the rate of redistribution, and some Namibians spoke out against paying for land that had been seized in the process of colonial settlement. Many farmers feared that their land would be forcibly seized, as in Zimbabwe, and Nujoma's continued support for Mugabe added to the farmers' concerns. In May Nujoma confirmed that his Government was not only targeting underused land, but would expropriate land as a punitive step against whites who maltreated their labourers. The CoD pointed out that those who most deserved to benefit from land reform were San and Herero, not wealthy SWAPO members, and that the expropriation process would create uncertainty and dissuade potential foreign investors.

THE POHAMBA PRESIDENCY

In the legislative elections held on 15–16 November 2004, SWAPO won 76.1% of the national vote and retained its 55 seats in the 72-seat National Assembly. Pohamba overwhelmingly defeated his opponents in the presidential election, in which there was a turn-out of 85% of registered voters, taking 76.4% of the votes cast. Following the elections the CoD, which became the official opposition, with five seats (one more than the DTA), and the Republican Party (RP), which won a seat for the first time, alleged widespread voting irregularities and instigated proceedings at the High Court. In March 2005 the High Court ordered a recount of the results. However, although the recount resulted in all parties, with the exception of the CoD, receiving a smaller number of votes, the allocation of seats remained unchanged.

In regional elections held in November 2004 the turn-out was much lower than in the general election, though higher than in the previous regional election. SWAPO won 96 of the 107 constituencies, and gained control of 12 of the 13 regional authorities. The CoD failed to secure a single seat, and the DTA was able to win seats only in Kunene, the only region not held by SWAPO. As each regional authority nominated two members to the 26-member National Council (the upper house of the legislature), SWAPO's majority in that house was now greater than before. Parliament as a whole was increasingly marginalized, and unable to provide any effective check on executive power.

On 21 March 2005, at celebrations to mark the 15th anniversary of independence, Pohamba was inaugurated as President. He appointed Nahas Angula, the former Minister of Higher Education, Training and Employment Creation, as the new Prime Minister, and Dr Libertina Amathila as Deputy Prime Minister. Both were veterans of the liberation struggle, and Angula, one of the country's leading intellectuals, had been influential in securing support for Pohamba. Nujoma remained SWAPO President.

Implementation of the Government's land-reform programme continued to be slow and frustrating both for the authorities and for those seeking land. By mid-2006 only 10,000 people had been resettled on some 150 commercial farms. In many cases of resettlement the new owners were not able to operate the farms commercially, and valuable equipment was stolen or lay idle. The Government made available about US $7.7m. annually to buy commercial farms, and all farms for sale had to be offered to the State in the first instance. In the year to March 2006 one-half of the money allocated was spent on resettling 150 families on 19 farms, three of which were expropriated. Although an Affirmative Action Loan Scheme (see Economy) allowed individual black Namibians to buy commercial farms on preferential terms, in many cases those who bought under this scheme were not able to keep up their loan repayments.

Namibia remained among the most unequal societies in the world. While the country had moved up to 125th place out of the 177 countries in the 2005 UN Human Development Report, with over 90% of children of primary school age attending school, and water and electricity reaching over 80% of the population, 35% of the country's 2m. people still lived on less than US $1 per day, and nearly 56% on less than US $2 per day. The Government claimed that it could not afford to introduce the Basic Income Grant for which many in the non-governmental sector appealed. HIV prevalence was estimated at 19.6% among adults nationally, but among antenatal clinic attendees it was 42% in Katima Mulilo, the main town in the Caprivi Strip, and it ranged between 22% and 28% in the port cities of Lüderitz, Swakopmund and Walvis Bay. Of the estimated 230,000 Namibians who were HIV-positive in 2007, it was believed that 50,000 required antiretroviral medication, but that only 22,000 were receiving such treatment. One year later, however, another report claimed that 88% of those needing the medication were receiving it. HIV remained the leading cause of the continued decline in life expectancy, which was estimated by the World Health Organization to be 57 years in 2009. By 2012 the adult prevalence rate had declined to 15%, largely owing to an education campaign and the greater availability of antiretroviral drugs.

President Pohamba spoke of promoting 'zero tolerance' for corruption soon after taking up office and appointed an Anti-Corruption Commission, which began its work in 2006. However, that body was given very limited resources and was not able to prevent large-scale self-enrichment or bring to account all those responsible for corruption in a number of state agencies, including the Social Security Commission and the Ministry of Defence. The Namibia Development Corporation admitted in April 2007 that tens of millions of Namibian dollars given as credits to black empowerment initiatives would never be repaid, and a scandal involving a large oil contract was nullified at a senior level. Despite all this, Namibia ranked near the top of tables on African governance, including the Mo Ibrahim Foundation Index and the World Bank Governance Index.

For much of 2007 SWAPO was deeply divided over whether Nujoma should stand for re-election as the party's President. Some party members wanted him to stand so that he could again be the party's candidate for the national presidency in 2009. Nujoma did not make clear his intentions until he announced in October 2007 that the party's fourth congress, to be held in Windhoek in November, should elect his successor as President of SWAPO. Pohamba was then elected to that post. In his first government reorganization, in April 2008, Pohamba appointed former Prime Minister Geingob as Minister of Trade and Industry, while Namibia's ambassador to Germany, Peter Katjavivi, became Director-General of the National Planning Commission.

Before the November 2007 SWAPO congress, Hamutenya had established a breakaway party, the Rally for Democracy and Progress (RDP). This created further political tensions, and when the RDP was heavily defeated in a local government election, it blamed widespread intimidation and maintained that the election had not been free and fair; Hamutenya claimed that he had received death threats. As the country moved towards the 2009 general election, there were a number of cases of intimidation and violence, especially between supporters of SWAPO and the RDP. While SWAPO spent over N $8m. on its campaign, both the DTA and the CoD were severely weakened by in-fighting, factionalism and breakaways.

THE 2009 ELECTIONS AND BEYOND

The results of the presidential and legislative elections held on 27–28 November 2009 were not released until 4 December, after much criticism of the inefficiency of the Electoral Commission of Namibia, which had at various times released very different figures for the number of registered voters. Nevertheless, the outcome was another massive victory for SWAPO, which won 75.3% of the vote for the National Assembly and 54 of the 72 seats—the third time in a row that it had gained over two-thirds of the votes. President Pohamba fared even better, receiving 76.4% of the vote in the presidential election. The RDP, contesting its first general election, won 11.3% of the vote and eight seats in the Assembly, and thus became the official opposition. Its presidential candidate, Hidipo Hamutenya, obtained 11.1% of the vote in that election. Seven other smaller parties obtained seats in the legislature. The opposition parties, led by the RDP, challenged the result in the High Court, claiming that they had evidence of electoral fraud. They pointed to the fact that some non-registered persons had been allowed to vote, and that voter turn-out in some constituencies was higher than the number of registered voters. After the High Court dismissed the challenge on a technicality and awarded costs against the litigants, the parties appealed to the Supreme Court. The RDP, DTA and RP members boycotted the opening of the fifth Parliament in late March 2010 because their legal challenge was ongoing. In February 2011 the Judge President, while acknowledging irregularities in the election, dismissed the case. The nine parties again stated their intention to appeal against the verdict.

Meanwhile, on 21 March 2010, the 20th anniversary of independence, President Pohamba announced the formation of a new Government, again headed by Prime Minister Angula, in which only five new ministers were appointed. Utoni Nujoma, son of the founding President, became Minister of Foreign Affairs, replacing Dr Marco Hausiku, who was appointed Deputy Prime Minister. Nujoma was a potential successor to Pohamba, although Geingob, who remained Minister of Trade and Industry, was, as Vice-President of SWAPO, next in line, despite not being of Ovambo descent. The SWAPO congress, due to be held in late 2012, was expected to decide on the succession to Pohamba. Some members of SWAPO suggested that Geingob should not automatically succeed Pohamba, but that there should be an open contest. There was speculation that Angula might present himself as a candidate. Although official campaigning was not scheduled to commence until August 2012, unofficial campaigning became increasingly intense in that year, with Geingob and the Secretary-General of SWAPO, Pendukeni Iivula-Ithana, clearly canvassing for support. Some observers claimed that this electioneering was adversely affecting the business of government.

Meanwhile, Tom Alweendo, the former Governor of the Bank of Namibia who took over as Director-General of the National Planning Commission, promoted Vision 2030, which envisaged that by that year Namibia might have successfully dealt with the problems of poverty and inequality. With the official unemployment rate rising to over 50%, in March 2011 the Government launched a two-year Targeted Intervention Programme for Employment and Economic Growth (at a projected cost of N $15,000m.), which was intended to create thousands of jobs in the transportation, tourism, construction and agriculture sectors, as well as in housing and sanitation. However, implementation was very uneven, with some ministries remaining unaware of the programme. The Namibian Institute for Public Policy Research identified a lack of skilled labour as the main obstacle to economic growth.

On 19 April 2010 the ruling party held a rally to mark 50 years since its foundation. Although much was made of Namibia's undoubted achievements since independence, some of those arrested at the time of the Caprivi secession in 1999 remained in gaol more than 10 years later without having been convicted. Appeals for them to be granted an amnesty were ignored by the authorities, though some claims against the Government for human rights abuses in the Caprivi Strip at the time of the secession attempt were settled out of court. In March 2011 the presiding judge refused to admit any new evidence in the main trial, but the case continued none the less. By mid-2012 21 of those detained had died in gaol, while Muyongo remained in exile in Denmark.

In the regional and local elections held in November 2010, SWAPO retained control of all the councils that it held previously, but voter turn-out was only 38%, compared with 54% in the 2005 elections, and SWAPO failed to secure the Kunene region. Although the RP dissolved itself prior to the elections, and urged its supporters to vote for the RDP, that party fared poorly, despite winning the Windhoek East constituency. New legislation introduced in advance of the elections provided for the selection of regional Governors by presidential nomination, rather than by election by the regional councils as had hitherto been the case; critics claimed that the new process was undemocratic. Meanwhile, in late 2010 the Government announced that payments of N $50,000 would be made to 40,000 war veterans over a three-year period, at an estimated total cost of N $3,400m.

The Economist Intelligence Unit classifies Namibia as a 'flawed democracy' in its democracy index, chiefly owing to

SWAPO's perceived political intolerance. Although the Anti-Corruption Commission continues its work, it has failed to resolve many high-profile cases, such as that relating to the suspension of the head of the Namibian Defence Force, following allegations that he had received vast sums of money while serving as Namibia's High Commissioner to Botswana; a government contract for the provision of security scanning equipment, which was linked to prominent Chinese investors; and the write-off by the Government Institutions Pension Fund of some N $660m. that had been lent to a group of entrepreneurs with close ties to SWAPO. Moreover, many heavily subsidized state-owned enterprises are in serious financial trouble, and there have been numerous allegations of fraud and corruption, especially in relation to railway construction projects undertaken by TransNamib, the Chief Executive Officer of which was dismissed in April 2012. Furthermore, it has also been claimed that Chinese firms are winning tenders for contracts in Namibia by undercutting locals and paying workers less than the minimum wage.

In early 2011 the Minister of Mines and Energy declared that the Government intended to impose a windfall tax on the profits of mines and wished to increase its involvement in the mining industry. This announcement prompted concerns that nationalization might be imminent, while appeals for more land and businesses to be transferred to black ownership further weakened investor confidence. In July, however, the Cabinet abandoned plans for a mining tax, and also in that month the Minister of Mines and Energy announced that petroleum had been discovered off the southern Namibian coast. With deposits estimated at over 11,000m. barrels, Namibia appeared set to become one of the leading oil-producing countries on the continent. Commercial production was not scheduled to commence for several years, but it was expected to have enormous consequences for a country regarded by some analysts as the world's most unequal nation.

Economy

DONALD L. SPARKS

INTRODUCTION

Namibia is relatively prosperous in African terms: its gross domestic product (GDP) per head was US $7,300 in 2011. The World Bank classifies Namibia as a 'lower middle income country'. It should be noted, however, that Namibia has one of the world's most unequal income distributions, with a Gini coefficient of 0.7 (Gini coefficients measure income inequalities, with zero indicating perfect equality and a score of one indicating maximum inequality; in developed countries it is usually about 0.3). According to the UN Development Programme (UNDP), 55.8% of the population lived below the international poverty line of US $2 per day during 1990–2005. The reason for this imbalance principally lies in the economic structure that was imposed in colonial times. Ranches were established as settlers displaced Africans on two-thirds of the viable farmland. From the African 'reserves' came a stream of migrant workers, on whose low wages the development of the early mines and ranches depended. In the diamond and uranium mines, where profits have been high and the wage bill a small proportion of costs, the situation has changed, and these enterprises now pay the highest wages in the country. Elsewhere, particularly on the ranches, wages remain extremely low.

The UNDP's 2011 Human Development Index, a compilation of life expectancy, adult literacy, education and GDP per head, ranked Namibia 120th out of 187 countries, with a score of 0.606—slightly ahead of South Africa (at 123rd) but behind Botswana (118th). Some 92% of Namibia's population has access to improved water sources, according to the UN Children's Fund (UNICEF), and the Government spends US $189 per head on health care, compared with the average for sub-Saharan Africa of US $45. However, HIV/AIDS has had a devastating effect on the nation's economy; 13.1% of its adult population, some 180,000 people, were living with HIV/AIDS in 2009. It should be noted, however, that the HIV prevalence rate declined from 22% in 2002, attributed largely to the National Awareness Campaign. Also, during 2003 the Government was able to provide public antiretroviral (ART) drugs to cover approximately 40,000 patients (equivalent to some 70% of those patients who could benefit from ART treatment). As a result of these and other recent improvements, life expectancy at birth increased from 54.0 years in 1982 to 62.5 years in 2012.

Namibia's comparative wealth reflects a large and fairly diversified mining sector, producing diamonds, uranium and base metals for export. Despite frequent drought, large ranches generally provide significant exports of beef and karakul sheepskins. Yet the economy is highly extractive and poorly integrated. About 80% of the goods that Namibia produces are exported, and about 70% of the goods that are used in the country, including about one-half of the food, are imported.

The Namibian economy has made significant strides since independence, and has become more diversified in recent years. In 2011 services made the largest contribution to the economy, accounting for 61.3% of GDP, followed by industry (22.4%), and agriculture and fishing (16.3%). Overall GDP increased, in real terms, at an average annual rate of 4.6% in 2000–09. The Ministry of Finance's Macroeconomic Framework for 2008/09–2010/11, which forecast real GDP growth of 5.2% annually during 2008–11, turned out to be somewhat optimistic. Real GDP increased by 3.3% in 2008, but declined by 0.8% in 2009 owing to the worldwide economic downturn and lower commodity prices. Diamond prices, for example, contracted by 30% during 2008, following decreased demand for retail diamond jewellery in the USA (Namibia's largest market) and Europe. Furthermore, Namibia reduced its rough diamond output by 57% in 2009. However, the diamond sector has since made a strong recovery (see Minerals and Mining), and the overall economy recovered from the declines of 2008–09, with growth of about 4.0% in 2011. The Ministry of Finance projected that the economy would grow by 4.4% in 2012, again buoyed by higher diamond output and increased public infrastructure spending. Unlike many of its neighbours, Namibia would not be severely affected by recession in the eurozone, as the majority of its shipments of diamonds and uranium are exported to the USA and Asia.

FINANCE

Before Namibia's independence, South Africa was an important source of public finance for Namibia. South Africa made its final contribution, of R83m., at independence in 1990 and ceased acting as guarantor of Namibian loans. Since then revenue from the Southern African Customs Union (SACU) has been an important source of revenue for the Government. The Customs Union was renegotiated in 2002 and a new SACU secretariat was established in Windhoek. The new agreement, which came into effect in July 2004, guarantees a duty rate of 17%, reducing the yearly fluctuations of the past. In addition, each country now receives customs revenues based on its relative share of SACU GDP, of which Namibia has 2.4%. SACU receipts accounted for an estimated 27% of total government revenue in 2011/12 and were expected to increase to 39% in 2012/13. This was, in part, a result of a N $2,500m. windfall payment from the SACU common revenue pool to compensate Namibia for past underpayments. However, this source of revenue has been volatile. Accordingly, in an effort to reduce dependence on SACU receipts, Namibia was planning to revise its corporate income tax structure for diamond-mining (see below), and to institute a carbon tax on vehicles and a new tax on the export of natural resources.

By the end of 2011 Namibia's total outstanding debt amounted to US $2,370m., up from US $2,180m. in 2010 and US $800m. in 2009. The debt-service ratio to exports increased from 8.7% in 2008 to 11.6% in 2009, before declining slightly to an estimated 11.2% in 2010. Compared with most of its neighbours, Namibia's overall debt situation is reasonable. About one-quarter of its debt is denominated in South African rand (thus avoiding exchange rate risk), about one-half in euros and only 7% in US dollars. As Namibia's GDP per caput is higher than the qualifying threshold, it does not receive loans (denominated in dollars) from the International Development Association. In 2007 the World Bank made its first loan to Namibia: US $7.5m. was granted to support the Government's training and education sector.

Namibia's current economic policy is based on the fourth five-year development plan, which was launched in 2012. Its major goals included poverty reduction, increased private sector employment, greater income equality, economic diversification and fighting HIV/AIDS. The new five-year plan incorporated provisions from the New Equitable Economic Empowerment Framework, which was due to be implemented in 2012. The budget for 2012/13 projected total government spending at N $40,000m., up from N $37,100m. in the previous year. Total revenues were forecast at N $35,420m., resulting in an anticipated budgetary deficit of N $4,737m. (4.6% of GDP).

In 1910 Namibia (then under German rule and called South West Africa) established a short-lived stock exchange at Lüderitz. After independence a new Namibian Stock Exchange (NSX) was created (in 1992), with initial funding coming from 36 leading Namibian businesses. It continues to expand, although perhaps more slowly than anticipated; at mid-2011 there were 43 members. The market value of shares traded on the exchange increased substantially in the late 1990s, establishing NSX as sub-Saharan Africa's second largest stock exchange in capital value, although 98% of it was provided by dual-listed shares in South African firms, and trading volumes, while on the increase, remained relatively modest. From April 1998 dual-listing was permitted with all other stock exchanges of the Southern African Development Community (SADC). Namibia is continuing its efforts to establish itself as a leading offshore financial centre in the region. The new investment regime will allow investors to bypass some restrictions on foreign exchange transactions imposed by the South African Reserve Bank (SARB) with which Namibia had hitherto been obliged to comply, as a member of the Common Monetary Area. The Namibian dollar, linked at parity to the South African rand, was valued at US $1 = 8.17 in May 2012. Namibia's foreign exchange reserves totalled US $1,758m. in 2011.

As most of Namibia's imports are from South Africa, its domestic inflation rate is heavily influenced by South African price levels. The annual rate of inflation has been volatile in recent years: it rose to 7.2% by July 2007, its highest level since 2002. The rate had increased to 10.3% by late 2008, and averaged 11.5% in January–March 2009, up 3% over the same period a year before. Much of this increase was attributed to higher domestic fuel prices. The annual rate of inflation stood at 8.8% in 2009, owing to lower international fuel and food prices and the downward inflation trend in South Africa, since Namibia imports most of its consumer goods from that country. Inflation declined to 4.5% in 2010, the lowest level since 2006. The rate was reported to have risen to 5.3% in 2011, largely driven by wage increases, higher electrical tariffs, and food and transport price growth.

The South African central bank's sustained policy of monetary restraint curbs inflation in Namibia (as Namibia's monetary policies are effectively controlled by South Africa). Generally, the Bank of Namibia follows the SARB's changes in repo (interest) rates. However, in December 2007 the Bank of Namibia (for the first time since 2004) did not match the SARB's increase and rates remained unchanged at 10.5%. None the less, in recognition of the world economic downturn, and in an effort to stimulate the economy, the Bank of Namibia lowered the interest rate by 100 basis points, to 8%, in April 2009, the second reduction that year. A year later the repo rate was 7%, although South Africa reduced its rate to 6.5%, the lowest since 1981. This meant that Namibia's interest rates were higher than South Africa's for the first time in a decade. By early 2012 the repo rate stood at 6.0%, still above South Africa's 5.5%.

Unemployment remains a serious problem for Namibia (it has had the highest unemployment rate in SADC), both in the light industrial sector and in urban areas, and there were serious concerns as to how jobs would be found for recent school leavers. By 2004 unemployment in the formal sector stood at 22% (and at 44% for urban 20–24 year olds), but that had increased to 37% in 2007, according to the Namibia Economic Society. In 2011 the unemployment rate reached 51%, but was expected to decline following the implementation of a N $15,200m. public job creation programme during 2011/12–13/14. The formal labour force grew from 429,000 workers in 1980 to 803,700 in 2011. The services sector was the largest employer, with 61% of total workers, followed by industry (22%) and agriculture (16%); however, these figures did not take into account Namibia's informal sector, which included large numbers of subsistence farmers. A new labour bill was introduced in 2006, which included an increase in the minimum wage and a new 45-hour working week, and provided all workers with 20 days of annual leave each year.

Following independence Namibia began to receive financial assistance from the international donor community. Germany, the USA and Scandinavian countries are the principal bilateral donors. Total official development assistance (ODA) declined from US $192m. in 1995 to $145m. in 2006, while increasing to US $207m. in 2008 and US $326m. in 2009, according to the World Bank. On a per caput basis, Namibia receives more than the average for sub-Saharan Africa: in 2009 aid per caput amounted to US $95.50. In 2007 the People's Republic of China announced a N $1,000m. loan and a N $720m. line of credit for the purchase of Chinese goods and services. China had extended a N $18m. interest-free loan in 2006 and a N $45m. interest-free loan for Namibia's small-scale farming sector. However, there has recently been a backlash against Chinese economic activity, as more than 500 small retail shops are owned by Chinese business persons.

MINERALS AND MINING

By almost any standards Namibia is mineral-rich, and it is the world's biggest miner of offshore diamonds. Indeed, Namibia is the world's leading producer of gem-quality diamonds, traditionally accounting for some 30% of total world output. In addition, Namibia has the world's largest uranium mine (see below) and was the world's fourth-largest producer of uranium in 2011. Namibia is Africa's second-largest producer of zinc, its third-largest producer of lead and fourth-largest source of copper. Other important minerals include hydrocarbons, tungsten, vanadium, silver, gold, columbite-tantalite (coltan), germanium and beryl; there are also significant reserves of tin, lithium and cadmium. Under the Minerals (Prospecting and Mining) Act, which came into operation in early 1994, the Government has taken action to diversify the mining sector. There has been a general increase in mining exploration in recent years. In 1980 mining accounted for about one-half of Namibia's GDP, but this had declined to 15.9% by 2008. However, minerals account for more than one-half of total exports, and in 2005 diamonds accounted for 41% of total export earnings. The GDP of the mining sector declined by 29.4% during 2009, owing to lower diamond and copper prices. For example, copper prices declined to US $3,500 per metric ton, compared with US $8,686 per ton in 2008. However, copper prices started to pick up in late 2009, increasing to around US $6,000 per ton, and had reached a record US $10,000 per ton by 2011.

Diamonds form a key component of Namibia's economy. Diamond-mining has historically contributed approximately 70% of the sector's GDP and some 10% of national GDP. The ownership of Namibia's most important diamond mine, centred on Oranjemund, underwent a significant reorganization in late 1994, when a new operating company, Namdeb Diamond Corpn (owned in equal shares by the Namibian Government and the Switzerland-based De Beers Centenary

AG), acquired the diamond assets of Consolidated Diamond Mines, the De Beers subsidiary that had previously held sole exploitation rights to Namibian alluvial diamond deposits. Namdeb accounted for 97% of the country's total output of 1.9m. carats in 2004. About 98% of the diamonds recovered in Namibia are of gem quality, and under the new arrangements these stones continue to be marketed by De Beers through the Central Selling Organisation. Total production was 2.1m. carats in 2006, an increase of 17.5% compared with 2005. Of that amount, 1.0m. carats was onshore production, with 1.1m. carats produced off shore. However, diamond prices fell by 30% from mid-2008 until late 2009, following decreased demand for retail diamond jewellery in the USA (Namibia's largest market) and Europe. The actual volume of exports declined by 29% in 2008, to 2.2m. carats. This lack of sales resulted in a large stockpile of unsold diamonds. Output fell once again during 2009, with production standing at 939,000 carats, amounting to N $3,818m. However, production and sales of rough cut diamonds recovered dramatically in early 2010, with prices rising to 80% of their pre-crash height. According to the Ministry of Mines and Energy, diamond production increased by 57%, to 1.48m. carats, in 2010. In the same year gem sales rose by 12%, to 1.52m. carats, earning N $5,580m. DeBeers estimated that its diamond production contracted by 9% in 2011, to 1.3m. carats. However, higher prices (driven by rising demand) increased the value of sales by 23%, to N $6,500m. The USA is the largest market, comprising 38% of the total share, followed by China (11%) and India (10%). With the US economy in recovery, diamond prices were expected to remain high during 2012. Moreover, offshore production was projected to increase in that year due to the relaunching of one of the five marine mining vessels following repairs.

A new Diamond Act, to succeed legislation in force since before independence in 1939, was approved by the Namibian parliament in mid-1999; the Act allows individuals to apply for licences to trade in, import or export diamonds, subject to criminal penalties for unauthorized dealing. Namibia is co-operating in international efforts to ensure that diamonds from conflict areas are not used to support continued warfare (so-called 'conflict diamonds'). In 2011 the Government launched a new minerals policy, under which mining rights for six strategic minerals (including uranium and gold) would be exclusively reserved for the state-owned Epangelo Mining Company. However, the Government announced in 2012 that the new requirements would not apply to current licence holders or applications already under way.

The Government implemented a new marketing agreement in 2010 to allow firms to buy uncut stones directly from Namdeb. This new arrangement should allow local firms to cut more locally-mined stones: N $2,000m. worth of local rough diamonds were to be available by the end of 2009, equal to about 13% of total diamond production. In addition, a new 50:50 joint venture between the Government and De Beers, the Namibian Diamond Trading Company, was to be responsible for sorting, establishing value and marketing Namdeb's output to the local firms as well as to the world market. The Government also placed a moratorium in 2007 on new licences for cutting and polishing diamonds.

The huge, although low-grade, Rössing uranium mine came into production in 1976. After an initial period of profitability for its owner, the Rio Tinto-Zinc group, the mine suffered from the depression in the uranium market. The Rössing mine's uranium is sold by means of long-term contracts to European Union (EU) countries, Japan and Taiwan, but the persistently weak 'spot' price of uranium has forced renegotiations of the contract prices. Rössing's output in 2003 declined by 13%, from 1,887 metric tons to 1,647 tons. Rössing recorded a 13-year record output of 3,600 tons of uranium oxide in 2004, owing in part to new equipment coming online and additional contracts. This was a 49% increase over 2003 output, and was equivalent to US $124m. Production stood at 3,617 tons in 2006, before fluctuating moderately in subsequent years; output totalled 3,600 tons in 2010 and 2,631 tons in 2011. Rio Tinto (which owns a 69% equity share of Rössing) estimated that leaching from the lower-grade ore could more than double the annual capacity to 10,400 tons.

In 2003 an Australian company, Paladin Resources, began developing a uranium operation south of Rössing at Langer Heinrich. Construction began in September 2005, at a cost of US $92m. The mine was officially opened in March 2007, and production reached 1,200 metric tons in that year. In the first quarter of 2010 the Langer Heinrich mine produced a record 421 tons, an increase of 35% compared with the same period a year before. However, owing to heavy rains, output declined dramatically in the first quarter of 2011. The mine had a final stage of expansion, which was expected to result in a total capacity of 2,359 tons per year by the end of 2011. When the Langer Heinrich and Rössing mines are producing at full capacity, Namibia is able to export over 5,000 tons annually, placing Namibia as Africa's largest uranium producer, and fourth in the world, behind Canada, Australia and Kazakhstan. Furthermore, the Valencia uranium mine, 35 km east of Rössing, commenced output in 2011. The proposed Husab uranium project was under consideration at mid-2012, but there were several issues to be resolved, one of which was the projected US $1,700m. cost.

A new company, Rosh Pinah Zinc Corpn, was established in May 1999 as a joint venture between ISCOR and PE Minerals, which holds the mineral rights to the Rosh Pinah zinc-lead mine. Zinc is on the way to becoming Namibia's second largest source of export revenues (after diamonds). The Skorpion Zinc mine, opened in 2000 at a cost of US $454m., produced 47,000 metric tons in 2003, all of which was exported. Production of zinc concentrates has increased since then, and in 2009 output reached a record 150,000 tons. Skorpion's sales are now the third most important source of export earnings, after Namdeb and Rössing. Its parent company, Anglo American, announced the sale of its zinc operations to Vedanta Resources (headquartered in London, United Kingdom) in May 2010 for a total of US $1,338m., of which US $707m. was for the Skorpion mine. Copper from the Tsumeb smelter has resumed production (following a temporary closure at the end of 2009), and is expected to double capacity when the expansion is completed.

Namibia is believed to have considerable offshore reserves of natural gas, estimated at as much as 560,000m. cu m in the Kudu gas field off Lüderitz. Exploration rights for the offshore Kudu gas fields were held by a consortium led by Shell, which planned to pipe gas to power stations to be constructed in Namibia and South Africa. Chariot Oil and Gas raised over US $100m. to fund drilling in 2012, while Tower Resources has raised over US $5m. to start its first offshore well by the end of 2012. In July 2004 Energy Africa and South Africa's Electricity Supply Commission (ESKOM) reached a joint development agreement with the National Petroleum Corpn of Namibia and NamPower (Namibia Power Corpn—see below) to develop a N $6,400m. gas-fired power plant that would make Namibia self-sufficient in energy. Tullow Oil, the owner of the Kudu 'gas-to-power' facility, announced the completion of its financial study in early 2005. In the same year the Chinese oil firm China Shine acquired a majority stake in the inland Etosha concession, with plans to spend US $50m. on petroleum exploration. A Canadian company, EnerGulf Resources, estimated that its concession along the Namibia–Angola border contained some 3,200m. barrels of reserves. In July 2011 the Minister of Mines and Energy announced that large, commercially-viable deposits of petroleum had been discovered off the southern Namibian coast. With deposits estimated at over 11,000m. barrels, Namibia could potentially become one of the leading oil-producing countries on the continent.

AGRICULTURE AND FISHING

Drought, overgrazing and unscientific farming methods have had an adverse effect on the agricultural sector. Namibia has a fragile, desert ecology, and most of the land can support only livestock. The major agricultural activities are the processing of meat and other livestock products, and more than 90% of commercial agricultural output comprises livestock production. The most important agricultural product is beef, with beef production representing some 87% of Namibia's gross non-fishing agricultural income. The only large-scale commercial arable farming is in the Karstveld around Tsumeb, and on the Hardap irrigation scheme in the south. Subsistence crops include beans, potatoes and maize. The country usually imports about one-half of its cereals requirement, but in the drought-free years it is able to provide some 70% of local demand. In an effort to diversify agricultural production, seedless-grape plantations are being developed on the banks of the Orange river bordering South Africa.

Colonial history bequeathed Namibia three different agricultural sectors: about 4,000 large commercial ranches, almost all white-owned; 20,000 African stock-raising households, compressed into central and southern reserves; and 120,000 black families practising mixed farming on just 5% of the viable farmland in the far north. The planted area is currently estimated at 241,000 ha.

The Government has plans to transfer some communal lands (mostly in the north) to private ownership, although there is considerable opposition from traditional leaders. At the time of Namibia's independence about 50% of the country's commercial farms were owned by absentee landlords, and the possible redistribution of such land was an important political issue. In 1992 the Government initiated the National Resettlement Policy (NRP), which was designed to redistribute 7.3m. ha of farmland owned by absentee landowners or otherwise underutilized; this represented almost one-quarter of the 32m. ha owned by commercial (mostly white) farmers at independence. The Namibian Government, through Agribank, began to grant low-interest loans (under the Affirmative Action Loan Scheme—AALS) to farmers in 1994. By the end of 2003 the Government had acquired some 829,500 ha of land and had redistributed about 1% annually since the beginning of the NRP; by contrast, in the same period more than 3.1m. ha of land had been bought with individual AALS loans.

The Government was facing increasing pressure to take possession of commercial farmland without paying full compensation, a development that would require an amendment of the Constitution, which stipulates that market prices be paid for land. In early 2004 the Prime Minister announced that the Government would expand the programme to include domestically-owned commercial farms. The Government's declared target was to resettle more than 243,000 people within the following five years; at that time some 37,000 people had been given land since 1990. Namibia is mindful of the negative consequences Zimbabwe has experienced from such actions, and in mid-2004 there were demands to revise the AALS to concentrate on building new farms. In early 2005 the Government adopted a new land tenure law covering reforms in urban areas, communal resettlement and compensation policies, although no changes to previous policies have yet been made. Heavy rains in much of north-central Namibia and the Caprivi region in early 2008 caused significant damage not only to crops, but also to roads, bridges and homes. A flood emergency office was established in Oshakati, in the north, to help the 70,000 displaced persons of Omusati, Oshikoto, Oshana and Ohangwena due to flooding. The Namibia Early Warning and Food Information Unit predicted that the year's millet and maize harvest would be 14% lower than the 119,000 metric tons produced in 2007 (which was down 40% from the previous year due to drought). In addition, waterlogged fields could well result in stunted growth of grain crops in the communal, subsistence areas.

Owing to the cold, nutrient-rich Benguela Current, Namibia has one of the richest fisheries in the world. Indeed, the country is Africa's primary exporter of fish and fish products, and the industry currently employs some 24,000 workers (of whom 43% are seagoing personnel and 57% are engaged in onshore processing). Prior to independence, however, Namibia received no tax or licence fees from fishing because the illegal occupation of the territory deprived it of an internationally recognized fishing zone within the usual limit of 200 nautical miles (370 km). There are, in fact, two separate fisheries off Namibia: in shore and off shore. The inshore fishery, for pilchard, anchovy and rock lobster, is controlled by Namibian and South African companies, based at Lüderitz and Walvis Bay. Other important species include hake, horse mackerel and crab. Following independence the Namibian authorities enforced a 370-km exclusive economic zone (EEZ), thereby achieving considerable success in restocking its overfished waters. Fish stocks have since recovered, and many foreign commercial companies are pressing the Government to increase the annual 30,000-metric-ton interim catch limit. The Minister of Fisheries and Marine Resources maintained that the one-month moratorium on hake fishing in 2006 was successful, as the catch levels had increased, and the value of fish landings had risen from N $3,700m. in 2005 to N $3,900m. in 2006. However, some in the industry claimed that the moratorium had resulted in numerous job losses. After three years of declines, fish landings rose to 394,000 tons in 2009, a 6% increase over 2008. None the less, this was nearly one-third below the level in 2005, reflecting both declining stocks and the reductions in the total allowable catch.

The fishing industry is an important source of employment and export earnings (70% of its output is sold to Europe, with Spain being the largest customer). There is considerable scope for job creation in the sector, particularly in fish-processing. None the less, the fishing sector has suffered during the past few years. The sector is faced with increased operational costs, a strengthening Namibian dollar (making exports less attractive), poor catches and smaller fish being caught.

OTHER ECONOMIC SECTORS

Namibia's manufacturing sector is small. It provided 15.5% of GDP in 2010, and consists mainly of processing fish, minerals and meat for export, and production of basic consumer products, such as beer and bread. Food products account for about 70% of all goods produced in Namibia. The development of the manufacturing sector has been limited by fluctuations in the supply of cattle and fish, by the small domestic market, by the high cost of energy and transport, and by the lack of an educated entrepreneurial class. Furthermore, Namibia's traditional dependence on South Africa for most manufactured goods has resulted in the underdevelopment of the sector. The Export Processing Zone Act was approved in 1995, establishing an export processing zone (EPZ) in Walvis Bay and allowing others to follow. Only three EPZ factories were operating in Walvis Bay in 1999. During 2005 a number of firms in the EPZ closed, including Rhino Garments Namibia, resulting in a loss of 1,700 jobs. In 2004 there were 32 firms, and only 25 by the end of 2005. Employment likewise declined, from 10,057 workers to 6,967. Total investment in the EPZ reached US $785m. by mid-2005, according to the Offshore Development Company.

A Malaysian company, Ramatex, established a N $900m. integrated textile and garment facility in Windhoek in 2002, although it closed its operations in March 2008, resulting in the loss of some 3,000 jobs. The closure has been attributed to the ending of the Multi-fibre Arrangement (MFA), which made its exports to the USA less attractive than those from Asian producers. Exports were to be primarily to the USA, as a result of the US African Growth and Opportunity Act (AGOA), which allows duty-free access for certain textiles from sub-Saharan Africa. Owing to the high demand for cotton inputs, the Government hoped to be able to stimulate the country's small cotton industry and envisaged the creation of some 20,000 jobs in the textile industry by 2005. Under the AGOA, from 2007 African firms had to obtain raw materials such as cotton from within Africa.

SAB Miller, a South African brewer, had been scheduled to begin construction of a N $34m. brewery in Okahandja in 2010, but the project was delayed due to problems with a land transfer deal from the Okahandja municipality. None the less, when completed, it will have an annual capacity of 260,000 hectolitres of beer. The brewery will be 60% owned by SAB Miller and 40% owned by local partners. SAB Miller already has a 22% share of the domestic market. Namibia's largest brewery is NamBrew, the turnover of which increased by 20% in 2009.

Construction contributed only 4.3% of GDP in 2010. Following the 1993–94 expansion in commercial and residential property developments, growth in the GDP of the construction sector slowed to 2.8% in 1995. New employment opportunities in the construction sector were provided in 2001 by the new Skorpion Zinc mine (see above) and government-financed infrastructure projects in the southern part of the country. The country's major new construction project was an expansion of a shopping mall outside Windhoek, at a cost of US $28m.

The electricity, gas and water sectors (which represented 2.3% of GDP in 2008) are somewhat more integrated and extensive than might be expected. The principal mines and towns are linked in a national grid, which can be fed by the 120-MW Van Eck power station outside Windhoek, the hydroelectric station at Ruacana (which has a generating capacity of up to 320 MW) on the Kunene river, and the 45-MW Paratus scheme at Walvis Bay. There is a link to the system operated by South Africa's ESKOM, and the Zambia Electricity Supply Corpn provides electricity to the Caprivi region.

In 1991 Namibia and Angola signed an agreement on the further development of the Kunene river as a source of energy, in spite of concerns that the dam would disrupt the area's ecology and displace the Himba people. There is, however, a significant difference in approach between the two governments, which may delay the project indefinitely. While Namibia prefers the construction of a reservoir at Epupa Falls, at an estimated cost of N $539m., Angola favours a smaller, slightly more costly, but less ecologically damaging site at Baynes Mountains. Work began in 1999 on a second power interconnector to the South African grid, at a cost of N $870m.; this was to be Namibia's largest post-independence construction project. In August 2002 it was also announced that NamPower would collaborate with Zambia on the construction of a power interconnector between the two countries, and an agreement was finalized in July 2004. In 2007 Namibia agreed to an interest-free loan to the Zimbabwe Electricity Supply Authority, to allow it to rehabilitate Zimbabwe's Hwange coal-fired plant in return for a guaranteed supply. Some 40% of Namibia's electricity is produced locally, the remainder being imported. ESKOM accounts for 68% of Namibia's electricity imports (with Zimbabwe's Hwange supplying most of the remainder). In 2006 Russia offered to help Namibia build a nuclear power plant, as the Government pledged to become self-sufficient in energy within three years.

Tourism is playing an increasingly important role in the economy. In 2009 nearly 1m. tourists visited Namibia, and receipts totalled N $11,500m. The 2010 Fédération Internationale de Football Association (FIFA) World Cup tournament in neighbouring South Africa provided a boost to tourism, and it was estimated that in that year too some 1m. tourists visited the country. The Government has promoted the development of 'eco-tourism' in Namibia. The Namibian authorities appear to intend to introduce a liberalized air policy, with the minister responsible for transport deciding not to object to a proposal by Kalahari Express Airlines that services operate between Windhoek, and Cape Town and Johannesburg, South Africa, despite strong criticism from Air Namibia, the state airline. Besides several local and regional connections, Air Namibia also flies to Frankfurt, Germany. In mid-2005 Air Namibia resumed its Windhoek–London direct flights, after a three-year suspension. As the United Kingdom is Namibia's second major source of European visitors (after Germany), this service was expected to prove successful, especially as there was no competition on this route. In 2006 a N $550m. joint venture between Namibian-, Kuwaiti- and Swiss-based hotel firms was formed to construct three five-star hotels in Namibia. Operating under the Kempinski name, these have all now opened.

The Trans-Kalahari Highway, which was officially opened in 1998, has proved an important development for regional trade and economic integration. The Highway provides a link between Walvis Bay and South Africa's important Gauteng industrial area. However, until Walvis Bay's harbour development programme is completed, the port is likely to remain under-utilized. Currently, Walvis Bay attracts only a 1% share of container traffic to southern Africa, because it is too shallow. A project to deepen the port to 12.8 m began in February 2000. When completed, it should enable Walvis Bay to receive container vessels with a capacity of 2,200–2,400 metric tons, allowing the port to attract at least some of the business currently using the South African ports of Cape Town and Durban.

Access to telephones, computers and the internet has increased more rapidly in Namibia than in most neighbouring countries. In 2010 Namibia had 157,000 land-line telephones, 1.53m. mobile cellular telephones and more than 127,000 internet users.

FOREIGN TRADE, BALANCE OF PAYMENTS AND AID

Namibia's principal trading partners traditionally include South Africa, the United Kingdom, Germany, Japan and the USA. In 2011 exports amounted to US $4,568m., compared with US $4,277m. in 2010, while imports were US $5,345m., compared with US $5,152m., resulting in a trade deficit of US $765m. In 2008 Namibia sold 31.8% of its exports to South Africa. By far its largest supplier in that year was also South Africa (which accounted for 67.8% of all imports). Principal exports in 2009 were minerals (40% of the total, of which diamonds and uranium comprised the bulk), manufactured products (23%) and food and live animals (12%). Namibia's principal imports in 2008 were machinery and transport equipment (31.1% of total imports), petroleum and petroleum products (13.0%), chemicals and related equipment (10.9%), and food and live animals (10.8%).

The current account surplus declined to US $129m. in 2009 (down from a record US $1,158m. in 2006), and a deficit of US $187m. was recorded in 2010. The current account registered another surplus, of US $108.7m., in 2011. Net foreign direct investment increased by 42% in 2010 to reach a record N $6,300m. Official ODA has fluctuated over the past few years: Namibia received US $151.7m. in 2006, US $217.4m. in 2007, US $206.8m. in 2008 and US $326.2m. in 2010.

ECONOMIC PROSPECTS

Namibia will continue to be dominated economically by its large neighbour, South Africa, for the foreseeable future. South Africa is the source of the vast majority of Namibia's imports; in addition, South Africa has significant control over Namibia's transport infrastructure, as Namibia's only external rail links are with South Africa.

The Government has committed the nation to a mixed-market economy and is trying to encourage private sector investment and export-orientated manufacturing industries. In 2000 the National Assembly approved a plan from the Ministry of Finance and the Ministry of Trade and Industry to begin a privatization programme. The Government established a council for state-owned enterprises, with a divestiture sub-committee that was to work on privatization details. The World Bank's 2012 *Doing Business* survey ranked Namibia 78th out of 183 countries, with positive ratings by business in a number of key areas. Transparency International ranked Namibia joint 57th out of 182 countries in its 2012 Corruption Index—slightly ahead of South Africa (which ranked joint 64th) and well ahead of most of the region. The 2010–11 Global Competitiveness Index showed Namibia moving up the index to 74th out of the 133 countries ranked (from 80th out of 134 in 2008–09). The Heritage Foundation's 2012 Index of Economic Freedom ranked Namibia 76th out of 184 nations, placing it in the 'moderately free' category, slightly behind South Africa but ahead of most other countries in the region.

Namibia's natural beauty (for tourism), abundant mineral reserves and rich fisheries are expected to form the basis of the nation's potential economic prosperity. However, this relatively narrow base can be viewed as a liability, and volatility in all three sectors presents major vulnerabilities. The economic development of the impoverished northern region of the country remains a priority. Economic advance has hitherto been accomplished primarily by the extractive industries and has not yet filtered through to the wider economy in terms of increased employment, more equitable income distribution or higher income per head. Indeed, the fourth five-year national development plan (2012–16) appealed for reducing poverty and income inequality, stimulating economic growth, creating employment, promoting economic empowerment, and a renewed effort to prevent the spread of HIV/AIDS. Namibia appears to have recovered from the worldwide economic downturn of 2008–09. It has experienced some 22 years of independence with relatively little social or economic upheaval, relatively sound public economic policies, and a physical infrastructure that should eventually lead to long-term development and growth. Perhaps its biggest challenge will be to ensure that such growth is distributed more evenly and in such a way that it will be sustainable.

Statistical Survey

Source (unless otherwise indicated): Central Bureau of Statistics, National Planning Commission, Government Office Park, Block D2, Luther St, Windhoek; PMB 13356, Windhoek; tel. (61) 2834056; fax (61) 237620; e-mail info@npc.gov.na; internet www.npc.gov.na.

Area and Population

AREA, POPULATION AND DENSITY

Area (sq km)	825,615*
Population (census results)	
28 October 2001	1,826,854
28 August 2011 (preliminary)*	
Males	1,021,600
Females	1,083,300
Total	2,104,900
Density (per sq km) at 2011 census	2.5

* 318,772 sq miles.
* Data rounded to nearest 100 persons.

POPULATION BY AGE AND SEX
(UN estimates at mid-2012)

	Males	Females	Total
0–14	423,141	415,778	838,919
15–64	714,119	721,640	1,435,759
65 and over	38,508	51,245	89,753
Total	1,175,768	1,188,663	2,364,431

Note: Estimates not adjusted to take account of results of 2011 census.

Source: UN, *World Population Prospects: The 2010 Revision*.

ETHNIC GROUPS
(population, 1988 estimates)

Ovambo	623,000	Caprivian	47,000
Kavango	117,000	Bushmen	36,000
Damara	94,000	Baster	31,000
Herero	94,000	Tswana	7,000
White	80,000	Others	12,000
Nama	60,000	**Total**	1,252,000
Coloured	51,000		

REGIONS
(population at 2011 census, preliminary)

	Area (sq km)	Population*	Density (per sq km)
Caprivi	14,785	90,100	6.1
Erongo	63,539	150,400	2.4
Hardap	109,781	79,000	0.7
Karas	161,514	76,000	0.5
Kavango	48,742	222,500	4.6
Khomas	36,964	340,900	9.2
Kunene	115,260	88,300	0.8
Ohangwena	10,706	245,100	22.9
Omaheke	84,981	70,800	0.8
Omusati	26,551	242,900	9.1
Oshana	8,647	174,900	20.2
Oshikoto	38,685	181,600	4.7
Otjozondjupa	105,460	142,400	1.4
Total	825,615	2,104,900	2.5

* Data are rounded to nearest 100 persons.

PRINCIPAL TOWNS
(population at 2011 census, preliminary)

Windhoek	322,500	Rehoboth	28,800
Rundu	61,900	Katima Mulilo	28,200
Walvis Bay	61,300	Otjiwarongo	28,000
Swakopmund	44,700	Okahandja	22,500
Oshakati	35,600	Ondangwa	21,100

Note: Data are rounded to nearest 100 persons.

BIRTHS AND DEATHS
(annual averages, UN estimates)

	1995–2000	2000–05	2005–10
Birth rate (per 1,000)	32.9	29.9	27.4
Death rate (per 1,000)	9.3	10.6	8.6

Source: UN, *World Population Prospects: The 2010 Revision*.

Life expectancy (years at birth): 62.1 (males 61.5; females 62.7) in 2010 (Source: World Bank, World Development Indicators database).

EMPLOYMENT
(persons aged 15 to 69 years, 2004 labour force survey)

	Males	Females	Total
Agriculture, hunting and forestry	64,991	37,645	102,636
Fishing	7,933	4,787	12,720
Mining and quarrying	5,909	1,653	7,562
Manufacturing	12,082	11,673	23,755
Electricity, gas and water	5,031	1,120	6,151
Construction	18,296	1,309	19,605
Wholesale and retail trade, repair of motor vehicles, motorcycles and personal and household goods	27,004	26,891	53,895
Restaurants and hotels	5,889	7,243	13,132
Transport, storage and communications	12,744	3,117	15,861
Financial intermediation	3,506	4,076	7,582
Real estate, renting and business activities	5,280	4,095	9,375
Public administration and defence; compulsory social security	20,216	10,469	30,685
Education	12,313	18,855	31,168
Health and social work	3,533	10,477	14,010
Other community, social and personal services	7,480	5,152	12,632
Private households with employed persons	4,067	20,014	24,081
Extra-territorial organizations and bodies	72	—	72
Sub-total	216,346	168,576	384,922
Not classifiable by economic activity	305	102	407
Total employed	216,651	168,678	385,329

Source: ILO.

Mid-2012 ('000 persons, FAO estimates): Agriculture, etc. 271; Total labour force 842 (Source: FAO).

Health and Welfare

KEY INDICATORS

Total fertility rate (children per woman, 2010)	3.2
Under-5 mortality rate (per 1,000 live births, 2010)	40
HIV/AIDS (% of persons aged 15–49, 2009)	31.1
Physicians (per 1,000 head, 2004)	0.3
Hospital beds (per 1,000 head, 2006)	3.3
Health expenditure (2009): US $ per head (PPP)	448
Health expenditure (2009): % of GDP	7.2
Health expenditure (2009): public (% of total)	55.0
Access to water (% of persons, 2010)	93
Access to sanitation (% of persons, 2010)	32
Total carbon dioxide emissions ('000 metric tons, 2008)	3,967.7
Carbon dioxide emissions per head (metric tons, 2008)	1.8
Human Development Index (2011): ranking	120
Human Development Index (2011): value	0.625

For sources and definitions, see explanatory note on p. vi.

Agriculture

PRINCIPAL CROPS
('000 metric tons)

	2008	2009	2010*
Wheat	14.5	12.4	12.5
Maize	58.1	57.3	58.0
Millet	35.5	37.3	40.0
Sorghum	4.4	4.7	5.0
Grapes	19.8*	20.0*	21.5

* FAO estimate(s).

Aggregate production ('000 metric tons, may include official, semi-official or estimated data): Total cereals 112.5 in 2008, 111.7 in 2009, 115.5 in 2010; Total roots and tubers 329.2 in 2008, 293.9 in 2009, 342.5 in 2010; Total vegetables (incl. melons) 56.2 in 2008, 55.7 in 2009, 60.0 in 2010; Total fruits (excl. melons) 39.8 in 2008, 39.6 in 2009, 42.2 in 2010.

Source: FAO.

LIVESTOCK
('000 head, year ending September, FAO estimates)

	2008	2009	2010
Horses	45	45	45
Asses	140	140	140
Cattle	2,400	2,380	2,400
Sheep	2,700	2,700	2,800
Goats	2,000	2,000	2,100
Pigs	55	60	65
Chickens	4,900	5,000	5,100

Source: FAO.

LIVESTOCK PRODUCTS
('000 metric tons)

	2008	2009	2010
Cattle meat	36.2	36.0	36.5*
Sheep meat*	12.1	12.1	12.2
Chicken meat*	11.0	11.2	11.6
Cows' milk*	109.0	110.0	114.6
Hen eggs*	3.5	3.3	3.4
Wool, greasy*	1.4	1.3	1.4

* FAO estimate(s).

Source: FAO.

Forestry

Separate figures are not yet available. Data for Namibia are included in those for South Africa.

Fishing

('000 metric tons, live weight)*

	2008	2009	2010†
Capture†	372.8	370.3	370.0
Cape hakes (Stokvisse)	126.3	136.9	140.0
Kingklip	3.7	4.5	4.4
Devil anglerfish	8.6	n.a.	n.a.
Southern African pilchard	20.7	13.7	14.0
Cape horse mackerel (Maasbanker)	192.7	198.3	198.0
Aquaculture†	0.5	0.5	0.5
Total catch†	373.3	370.9	370.5

* Figures include quantities caught by licensed foreign vessels in Namibian waters and processed in Lüderitz and Walvis Bay. The data exclude aquatic mammals (whales, seals, etc.). The number of South African fur seals caught was: 47,115 in 2008; 47,403 in 2009; n.a. in 2010.

† FAO estimate(s).

Source: FAO.

Mining

(metric tons unless otherwise indicated)

	2008	2009	2010
Copper ore†	7,471	—	—
Lead concentrates†	14,062	10,129	10,140
Zinc concentrates†	38,319	48,856	53,624
Silver ore (kilograms)*†	30,000	30,000	30,000
Uranium oxide	4,838	5,600	5,473
Gold ore (kilograms)†	2,126	2,057	2,683
Fluorspar (Fluorite)‡	118,263	80,857	104,494
Salt (unrefined)	732,000	807,348	770,636
Diamonds ('000 metric carats)	2,435	1,192	1,693

* Estimate.

† Figures refer to the metal content of ores and concentrates.

‡ Figures (on a wet-weight basis) refer to acid-grade material.

Source: US Geological Survey.

Industry

SELECTED PRODUCTS
(metric tons)

	2006	2007	2008
Unrefined (blister) copper (unwrought)	21,918	20,600*	16,271
Electrical energy (million kWh)	1,491	1,694	2,097

* Estimate.

2009: Unrefined (blister) copper (unwrought) 21,543.

2010: Unrefined (blister) copper (unwrought) 25,019.

Sources: US Geological Survey; UN Industrial Commodity Statistics Database.

Finance

CURRENCY AND EXCHANGE RATES

Monetary Units
100 cents = 1 Namibian dollar (N $).

Sterling, US Dollar and Euro Equivalents (31 May 2012)
£1 sterling = N $13.228;
US $1 = N $8.532;
€1 = N $10.582;
N $100 = £7.56 = US $11.72 = €9.45.

Average Exchange Rate (N $ per US $)
2009 8.4737
2010 7.3212
2011 7.2611

Note: The Namibian dollar was introduced in September 1993, replacing (at par) the South African rand. The rand remained legal tender in Namibia.

CENTRAL GOVERNMENT BUDGET
(N $ million, year ending 31 March)

Revenue*	2008/09	2009/10	2010/11†
Taxation	19,884.8	22,272.7	21,055.8
Taxes on income and profits	7,354.0	8,136.6	9,357.6
Taxes on property	167.0	221.9	238.0
Domestic taxes on goods and services	3,712.0	5,162.3	5,286.3
Taxes on international trade and transactions	8,501.8	8,585.2	5,975.3
Other taxes	150.0	166.7	198.6
Non-tax revenue	1,348.6	1,568.5	1,377.8
Entrepreneurial and property income	815.6	1,112.0	895.6
Fines and forfeitures	24.0	35.1	40.4
Administrative fees and charges	475.5	421.4	430.9
Return on capital from lending and equity	33.5	4.6	10.9
Total	21,233.4	23,845.8	22,433.6

Expenditure	2008/09	2009/10	2010/11†
Current expenditure	17,401.0	19,499.8	22,552.6
Personnel expenditure	7,709.0	9,045.0	10,963.7
Expenditure on goods and other services	3,731.0	4,064.9	4,318.3
Interest payments	1,331.0	1,427.1	1,316.9
Subsidies and other current transfers	4,630.0	4,962.8	5,953.7
Capital expenditure	5,064.1	4,337.8	5,605.9
Capital investment	3,775.4	2,763.1	4,507.6
Capital transfers	159.4	900.0	561.5
Total lending and equity participation	1,129.3	674.7	536.8
Statistical discrepancy	—	1,071.3	–414.3
Total	22,465.1	24,908.9	27,744.2

* Excluding grants received from abroad (N $ million): 141.0 in 2008/09; 200.8 in 2009/10; 265.1 in 2010/11 (estimate).

† Estimates.

2010/11 (N $ million, year ending 31 March, revised estimates): *Revenue:* Taxation 21,518.0 (Taxes on income and profits 9,910.4, Taxes on property 138.5, Domestic taxes on goods and services 5,284.7, Taxes on international trade and transactions 5,975.9, Other taxes 208.4); Non-tax revenue 1,697.9; Return on capital from lending and equity 4.2; Total revenue 23,220.1 (excl. grants 23.5). *Expenditure:* Current expenditure 22,411.0; Capital expenditure 4,143.1; Interest payments 965.5; Total expenditure (incl. others) 27,552.7.

2011/12 (N $ million, year ending 31 March, estimates): *Revenue:* Taxation 25,405.8 (Taxes on income and profits 10,412.1, Taxes on property 233.1, Domestic taxes on goods and services 7,393.9, Taxes on international trade and transactions 7,137.0, Other taxes 229.8); Non-tax revenue 1,402.4; Return on capital from lending and equity 20.4; Total revenue 26,828.6 (excl. grants 24.2). *Expenditure:* Current expenditure 27,801.1; Capital expenditure 8,070.0; Interest payments 1,279.8; Total expenditure (incl. others) 37,165.8.

Source: Bank of Namibia, *Annual Report 2010* and *Annual Report 2011*.

INTERNATIONAL RESERVES

(excluding gold, US $ million at 31 December)

	2009	2010	2011
IMF special drawing rights	204.44	200.83	8.09
Reserve position in IMF	0.12	0.12	0.12
Foreign exchange	1,846.37	1,494.74	1,778.48
Total	2,050.93	1,695.69	1,786.69

Source: IMF, *International Financial Statistics*.

MONEY SUPPLY

(N $ million at 31 December)

	2009	2010	2011
Currency outside depository corporations	1,156.7	1,292.7	1,697.7
Transferable deposits	19,741.5	22,760.4	26,152.8
Other deposits	27,642.1	29,141.9	32,678.7
Securities other than shares	3.9	—	—
Broad money	48,544.2	53,194.9	60,529.2

Source: IMF, *International Financial Statistics*.

COST OF LIVING

(Consumer Price Index; base: December 2001 = 100)

	2009	2010	2011
Food and non-alcoholic beverages	192.6	198.9	209.0
Alcoholic beverages and tobacco	187.2	205.8	218.8
Clothing and footwear	122.6	126.7	127.9
Housing, fuel and power	148.8	157.4	172.8
Health	124.5	130.4	137.8
Transport	181.2	192.0	202.1
Communications	123.5	125.1	126.7
Recreation and culture	139.4	144.0	149.5
Education	174.6	183.8	193.2
All items (incl. others)	165.4	172.7	181.5

NATIONAL ACCOUNTS

(N $ million at current prices)

National Income and Product

	2008	2009	2010
Compensation of employees	28,480	31,030	33,536
Operating surplus	29,813	28,546	30,318
Domestic factor incomes	58,293	59,576	63,854
Consumption of fixed capital	8,776	9,735	10,498
Gross domestic product (GDP) at factor cost	67,070	69,312	74,352
Taxes, less subsidies, on production and imports	5,877	6,367	7,157
GDP in purchasers' values	72,946	75,679	81,509
Primary income received from abroad	1,870	1,752	1,185
Less Primary income paid abroad	3,666	2,442	4,291
Gross national income	71,149	74,989	78,403
Less Consumption of fixed capital	8,776	9,735	10,498
National income in market prices	62,373	65,254	67,905
Other current transfers from abroad	9,762	11,245	9,668
Less Other current transfers paid abroad	484	632	640
National disposable income	71,651	75,867	76,933

Expenditure on the Gross Domestic Product

	2008	2009	2010
Government final consumption expenditure	14,851	17,215	18,583
Private final consumption expenditure	41,946	48,019	50,490
Change in stocks	661	229	–843
Gross fixed capital formation	17,838	17,871	18,169
Total domestic expenditure	75,296	83,334	86,399
Exports of goods and services	38,777	35,663	36,363
Less Imports of goods and services	39,850	41,656	40,647
Statistical discrepancy	–1,277	–1,663	–606
GDP in purchasers' values	72,946	75,679	81,509
GDP in constant 2004 prices	51,037	50,816	54,170

Gross Domestic Product by Economic Activity

	2008	2009	2010
Agriculture and forestry	2,969	2,988	3,362
Fishing	2,411	2,523	2,177
Mining and quarrying	11,772	8,063	7,174
Diamond mining	5,500	2,749	3,992
Manufacturing	9,405	10,119	11,725
Electricity and water	1,590	1,928	2,089
Construction	2,880	2,915	3,243
Wholesale and retail trade, repairs, etc.	7,682	8,610	9,708
Hotels and restaurants	1,283	1,399	1,382
Transport, storage and communications	3,395	3,708	4,334
Financial intermediation	2,849	3,619	4,205
Real estate and business services	5,415	5,987	6,435
Public administration and defence	6,143	7,047	7,209
Education	5,202	5,944	6,613
Health	2,229	2,441	2,719
Community, social and personal services	2,193	2,455	2,531
Private households with employed person	492	559	598
Sub-total	67,930	70,305	75,504
Less Financial services indirectly measured	840	993	1,153
GDP at basic prices	67,070	69,312	74,352
Taxes, less subsidies, on products	5,877	6,367	7,157
GDP in purchasers' values	72,946	75,679	81,509

Source: Bank of Namibia, *Quarterly Bulletin*.

BALANCE OF PAYMENTS
(US $ million)

	2008	2009	2010
Exports of goods f.o.b.	3,116.4	3,535.3	4,129.0
Imports of goods f.o.b.	−3,833.2	−4,518.8	−4,914.7
Trade balance	−716.9	−983.5	−785.7
Exports of services	554.7	521.5	853.3
Imports of services	−588.7	−609.0	−705.1
Balance on goods and services	−750.9	−1,071.0	−637.5
Other income received	303.1	339.3	228.5
Other income paid	−457.6	−409.3	−792.4
Balance on goods, services and income	−905.4	−1,141.0	−1,201.5
Current transfers received	1,009.3	1,063.9	974.8
Current transfers paid	−59.0	−83.8	−87.5
Current balance	44.9	−161.0	−314.2
Capital account (net)	77.2	66.7	112.5
Direct investment abroad	−6.2	3.0	−4.4
Direct investment from abroad	409.0	490.2	795.9
Portfolio investment assets	−1,023.4	−533.2	−695.1
Portfolio investment liabilities	3.9	−58.7	4.4
Other investment assets	−111.8	−401.1	−470.2
Other investment liabilities	−169.5	−172.1	−101.0
Net errors and omissions	676.1	186.3	−378.9
Overall balance	−99.9	−579.8	−1,051.0

Source: IMF, *International Financial Statistics*.

External Trade

PRINCIPAL COMMODITIES
(US $ million)

Imports c.i.f.	2006	2007	2008
Food and live animals	335.7	502.8	506.1
Mineral fuels and lubricants	86.7	416.4	637.7
Petroleum and petroleum products	83.1	399.4	610.0
Chemicals and related products	294.4	368.4	510.7
Basic manufactures	472.3	671.1	876.5
Non-metallic mineral manufactures	80.7	133.2	254.6
Metal products	152.6	247.5	267.2
Machinery and transport equipment	1,082.0	1,383.5	1,456.5
Machinery specialized for particular industries	135.0	167.2	225.4
General industrial machinery, equipment and parts	106.2	119.6	167.6
Telecommunications and sound equipment	104.4	111.2	108.8
Telecommunications equipment, parts and accessories	80.4	80.3	77.1
Electrical machinery, apparatus, etc.	124.8	143.1	156.6
Road vehicles	413.4	485.2	597.5
Passenger motor vehicles (excl. buses)	243.7	286.9	287.1
Other transport equipment	92.4	169.0	38.0
Miscellaneous manufactured articles	366.7	513.4	477.5
Clothing and accessories	86.8	130.6	115.8
Total (incl. others)	2,798.5	4,026.0	4,688.6

Exports f.o.b.	2006	2007	2008
Food and live animals	746.2	807.9	852.5
Fish, shellfish and preparations thereof.	434.7	458.9	527.7
Fresh or frozen fish	415.4	431.7	493.2
Beverages and tobacco	111.9	137.7	195.8
Beverages	107.1	135.6	149.6
Alcoholic beverages	100.7	126.4	136.7
Beer made from malt	85.4	110.5	114.8
Crude materials (inedible) except fuels	336.1	647.9	1,042.5
Metal ores and scrap	188.6	474.5	840.0
Ores and concentrates of uranium and thorium	163.0	350.3	741.7
Basic manufactures	1,516.8	1,556.5	1,314.7
Non-metallic mineral manufactures	911.7	723.0	798.8
Pearl, precious and semi-precious stones	900.8	705.0	780.6
Diamonds	900.4	704.6	780.0
Machinery and transport equipment	121.0	280.3	288.6
Miscellaneous manufactured articles	362.0	422.1	890.7
Printed matter	292.7	357.0	807.3
Total (incl. others)	3,375.9	4,040.3	4,729.3

Source: UN, *International Trade Statistics Yearbook*.

PRINCIPAL TRADING PARTNERS
(US $ million)

Imports c.i.f.	2006	2007	2008
China, People's Repub.	96.8	101.5	153.3
Germany	62.4	83.9	96.6
South Africa	2,305.3	3,143.0	3,179.8
Spain	19.8	91.4	22.3
United Kingdom	23.6	45.2	373.3
USA	41.6	54.8	94.9
Total (incl. others)	2,798.5	4,026.0	4,688.6

Exports f.o.b.	2006	2007	2008
Angola	192.9	260.9	405.6
Belgium	12.2	12.9	50.8
Canada	127.6	199.3	334.2
Congo, Democratic Republic of	45.4	43.1	51.2
France	53.7	106.4	126.7
Germany	109.0	99.8	48.9
Italy	243.5	570.9	63.9
Netherlands	36.7	74.8	76.0
South Africa	829.2	1,172.3	1,505.0
Spain	202.0	242.8	242.4
United Kingdom	865.2	682.9	709.7
USA	81.7	102.1	260.8
Total (incl. others)	3,375.9	4,040.3	4,729.3

Source: UN, *International Trade Statistics Yearbook*.

Transport

RAILWAYS

	2002/03	2003/04
Freight (million net ton-km)	1,244.6	1,247.4
Passengers carried	125,656	112,033

Source: TransNamib Holdings Ltd, *2004 Annual Report*.

ROAD TRAFFIC
(motor vehicles in use at 31 December)

	2008	2009
Passenger cars	107,825	100,460
Buses and coaches	2,396	3,012
Lorries and vans	117,410	120,978
Motorcycles and mopeds	4,792	5,356

Source: IRF, *World Road Statistics*.

SHIPPING

Merchant Fleet
(at 31 December)

	2007	2008	2009
Number of vessels	173	166	168
Displacement (gross registered tons)	126,062	122,076	121,579

Source: IHS Fairplay, *World Fleet Statistics*.

Sea-borne Freight Traffic
('000 freight tons*, year ending 30 August, unless otherwise indicated)

	2007/08	2008/09	2009/10
Port of Lüderitz:			
Goods loaded	56.8	26.0	120.1
Goods unloaded	126.5	124.9	138.7
Goods transshipped (freight tons)	29	—	—
Containers handled (total TEUs)	13,019	15,401	8,576
Port of Walvis Bay:			
Goods loaded	1,251.3	1,219.8	1,239.5
Goods unloaded	2,702.4	2,994.3	2,638.2
Goods transshipped	439.0	824.0	1,023.5
Containers handled (total TEUs)	170,586	250,262	247,743

* One freight ton = 40 cu ft (1.133 cu m) of cargo capacity.

Source: Namibian Ports Authority.

CIVIL AVIATION
(traffic on scheduled services)

	2007	2008	2009
Kilometres flown (million)	12	12	12
Passengers carried ('000)	431	452	455
Passenger-km (million)	1,683	1,723	1,668
Total ton-km (million)	164	175	171

Source: UN, *Statistical Yearbook*.

Tourism

FOREIGN TOURIST ARRIVALS*

Country of origin	2006	2007	2008
Angola	278,058	336,045	310,395
Botswana	24,720	25,649	26,378
Germany	68,214	80,418	81,543
South Africa	239,886	250,038	243,038
United Kingdom	24,736	28,214	28,111
Zimbabwe	30,623	26,764	29,281
Total (incl. others)	833,344	928,914	931,110

* Excluding same-day visitors: 127,000 in 2006; 119,000 in 2007; 148,000 in 2008.

Tourism receipts (US $ million, incl. passenger transport, unless otherwise indicated): 484 in 2008; 469 in 2009; 438 in 2010 (excl. passenger transport, provisional).

Source: World Tourism Organization.

Communications Media

	2008	2009	2010
Telephones ('000 main lines in use)	145.4	148.7	157.0
Mobile cellular telephones ('000 subscribers)	1,052.0	1,217.0	1,534.5
Internet users ('000)	113.5	127.5	n.a.
Broadband subscribers ('000)	0.3	0.4	9.6

Personal computers: 500,000 (239.4 per 1,000 persons) in 2007.

Television receivers ('000 in use): 67 in 2000.

Source: International Telecommunication Union.

Daily newspapers (2004): 4 (average circulation 55,800) (Source: UNESCO, *Statistical Yearbook*).

Non-daily newspapers (2004): 3 (average circulation 240,000) (Source: UNESCO, *Statistical Yearbook*).

Education

(2008/09 unless otherwise indicated)

	Teachers	Students		
		Males	Females	Total
Pre-primary	1,314*	16,414†	16,322†	32,736†
Primary	13,516	206,011	200,909	406,920
Secondary	7,031	78,414	90,976	169,390
Tertiary‡	1,204	8,594	11,376	19,970

* Estimate for 1999/2000.
† 2005/06.
‡ 2007/08.

Source: UNESCO, Institute for Statistics.

Pupil-teacher ratio (primary education, UNESCO estimate): 30.1 in 2008/09 (Source: UNESCO Institute for Statistics).

Adult literacy rate (UNESCO estimates): 88.8% (males 89.0%; females 88.5%) in 2010 (Source: UNESCO Institute for Statistics).

Directory

The Constitution

The Constitution of the Republic of Namibia took effect at independence on 21 March 1990. Its principal provisions are summarized below:

THE REPUBLIC

The Republic of Namibia is a sovereign, secular, democratic and unitary State and the Constitution is the supreme law.

FUNDAMENTAL HUMAN RIGHTS AND FREEDOMS

The fundamental rights and freedoms of the individual are guaranteed regardless of sex, race, colour, ethnic origin, religion, creed or social or economic status. All citizens shall have the right to form and join political parties. The practice of racial discrimination shall be prohibited.

THE PRESIDENT

Executive power shall be vested in the President and the Cabinet. The President shall be the Head of State and of the Government and the Commander-in-Chief of the Defence Force. The President shall be directly elected by universal and equal adult suffrage, and must receive more than 50% of the votes cast. The term of office shall be five years; one person may not hold the office of President for more than two terms.*

THE CABINET

The Cabinet shall consist of the President, the Prime Minister and such other ministers as the President may appoint from members of the National Assembly. The President may also appoint a Deputy Prime Minister. The functions of the members of the Cabinet shall include directing the activities of ministries and government departments, initiating bills for submission to the National Assembly, formulating, explaining and assessing for the National Assembly the budget of the State and its economic development plans, formulating, explaining and analysing for the National Assembly Namibia's foreign policy and foreign trade policy and advising the President on the state of national defence.

THE NATIONAL ASSEMBLY

Legislative power shall be vested in the National Assembly, which shall be composed of 72 members elected by general, direct and secret ballots and not more than six non-voting members appointed by the President by virtue of their special expertise, status, skill or experience. Every National Assembly shall continue for a maximum period of five years, but it may be dissolved by the President before the expiry of its term.

THE NATIONAL COUNCIL

The National Council shall consist of two members from each region (elected by regional councils from among their members) and shall have a life of six years. The functions of the National Council shall include considering all bills approved by the National Assembly, investigating any subordinate legislation referred to it by the National Assembly for advice, and recommending legislation to the National Assembly on matters of regional concern.

OTHER PROVISIONS

Other provisions relate to the administration of justice (see under Judicial System), regional and local government, the public service commission, the security commission, the police, defence forces and prison service, finance, and the central bank and national planning commission. The repeal of, or amendments to, the Constitution require the approval of two-thirds of the members of the National Assembly and two-thirds of the members of the National Council; if the proposed repeal or amendment secures a majority of two-thirds of the members of the National Assembly, but not a majority of two-thirds of the members of the National Council, the President may make the proposals the subject of a national referendum, in which a two-thirds' majority is needed for approval of the legislation.

* In late 1998 the National Assembly and National Council approved legislation whereby the Constitution was to be exceptionally amended to allow the incumbent President to seek a third term of office.

The Government

HEAD OF STATE

President and Commander-in-Chief of the Defence Force: HIFIKEPUNYE POHAMBA (elected by direct suffrage 15–16 November 2004; took office 21 March 2005; re-elected 27–28 November 2009).

THE CABINET
(September 2012)

President: HIFIKEPUNYE POHAMBA.

Prime Minister: NAHAS ANGULA.

Deputy Prime Minister: Dr MARCO HAUSIKU.

Minister of Presidential Affairs and Attorney-General: ALBERT KAWANA.

Minister of Home Affairs and Immigration: ROSALIA NGHIDINWA.

Minister of Safety and Security: NANGOLO MBUMBA.

Minister of Defence: Maj.-Gen. (retd) CHARLES NAMOLOH.

Minister of Foreign Affairs: UTONI NUJOMA.

Minister of Information and Communication Technology: JOEL KAAPANDA.

Minister of Education: Dr ABRAHAM IYAMBO.

Minister of Mines and Energy: ISAK KATALI.

Minister of Justice: PENDUKENI IVULA-ITHANA.

Minister of Trade and Industry: Dr HAGE GEINGOB.

Minister of Agriculture, Water and Forestry: JOHN MUTORWA.

Minister of Finance: SAARA KUUGONGELWA-AMADHILA.

Minister of Health and Social Services: Dr RICHARD KAMWI.

Minister of Labour and Social Welfare: IMMANUEL NGATJIZEKO.

Minister of Regional and Local Government and Housing and Rural Development: JERRY EKANDJO.

Minister of Environment and Tourism: NETUMBO NANDI-NDAITWAH.

Minister of Works, Transport and Communications: ERRKI NGHINTINA.

Minister of Lands, Resettlement and Rehabilitation: ALPHEUS NARUSEB.

Minister of Fisheries and Marine Resources: BEN ESAU.

Minister of Gender Equality and Child Welfare: DOREEN SIOKA.

Minister of Youth, National Service, Sport and Culture: KAZENAMBO KAZENAMBO.

Minister of Veteran Affairs: Dr NICKEY IYAMBO.

Also attending Cabinet

Dir-Gen. of the Namibia Central Intelligence Agency: Lt-Gen. (retd) LUCAS HANGULA.

Dir-Gen. of the National Planning Commission: TOM K. ALWEENDO.

MINISTRIES

Office of the President: State House, Robert Mugabe Ave, PMB 13339, Windhoek; tel. (61) 2707111; fax (61) 221780; e-mail angolo@op.gov.na; internet www.op.gov.na.

Office of the Prime Minister: Robert Mugabe Ave, PMB 13338, Windhoek; tel. (61) 2879111; fax (61) 226189; internet www.opm.gov.na.

Ministry of Agriculture, Water and Forestry: Government Office Park, PMB 13184, Windhoek; tel. (61) 2087111; fax (61) 221733; internet www.mawf.gov.na.

Ministry of Defence: PMB 13307, Windhoek; tel. (61) 2049111; fax (61) 232518; e-mail psecretary@mod.gov.na; internet www.mod.gov.na.

Ministry of Education: Government Office Park, PMB 13186, Windhoek; tel. (61) 2933358; fax (61) 2933368; internet www.mec.gov.na.

Ministry of Environment and Tourism: 2nd Floor, FGI House, Post St Mall, PMB 13346, Windhoek; tel. (61) 2842111; fax (61) 2842216; e-mail kshangula@met.gov.na; internet www.met.gov.na.

Ministry of Finance: Fiscus Bldg, John Meinert St, PMB 13295, Windhoek; tel. (61) 2099111; fax (61) 227702; internet www.mof.gov.na.

Ministry of Fisheries and Marine Resources: Uhland and Goethe Sts, PMB 13355, Windhoek; tel. (61) 2059111; fax (61) 233286; e-mail mfmr@mfmr.gov.na; internet www.mfmr.gov.na.

Ministry of Foreign Affairs: Govt Bldgs, Robert Mugabe Ave, PMB 13347, Windhoek; tel. (61) 2829111; fax (61) 223937; e-mail headquarters@mfa.gov.na; internet www.mfa.gov.na.

Ministry of Gender Equality and Child Welfare: Juvenis Bldg, Independence Ave, PMG 13359, Windhoek; tel. (61) 2833111; fax (61) 238941; e-mail genderequality@mgecw.gov.na; internet www.mgecw.gov.na.

Ministry of Health and Social Services: Old State Hospital, Harvey St, PMB 13198, Windhoek; tel. (61) 2032000; fax (61) 227607; e-mail doccentre@mhss.gov.na; internet www.healthnet.org.na.

Ministry of Home Affairs and Immigration: Cohen Bldg, Kasino St, PMB 13200, Windhoek; tel. (61) 2922111; fax (61) 2922185; internet www.mha.gov.na.

Ministry of Information and Communication Technology: PMB 13344, Windhoek; tel. (61) 2839111; fax (61) 222343; internet www.mict.gov.na.

Ministry of Justice: Justitia Bldg, Independence Ave, PMB 13248, Windhoek; tel. (61) 2805111; fax (61) 221615.

Ministry of Labour and Social Welfare: 32 Mercedes St, Khomasdal, PMB 19005, Windhoek; tel. (61) 2066111; fax (61) 212323; internet www.mol.gov.na.

Ministry of Lands, Resettlement and Rehabilitation: Brendan Simbwaye Bldg, Goethe St, PMB 13343, Windhoek; tel. (61) 2852111; fax (61) 254240.

Ministry of Mines and Energy: 1st Aviation Rd, PMB 13297, Windhoek; tel. (61) 2848111; fax (61) 238643; e-mail info@mme.gov.na; internet www.mme.gov.na.

Ministry of Presidential Affairs: Windhoek.

Ministry of Regional and Local Government and Housing and Rural Development: PMB 13289, Windhoek; tel. (61) 2975111; fax (61) 226049; internet www.mrlgh.gov.na.

Ministry of Safety and Security: Brendan Simbwaye Bldg, Goethe St, PMB 13323, Windhoek; tel. (61) 2846111; fax (61) 233879.

Ministry of Trade and Industry: Block B, Brendan Simbwaye Sq., Goethe St, PMB 13340, Windhoek; tel. (61) 2837111; fax (61) 220227; e-mail tic@mti.gov.na; internet www.mti.gov.na.

Ministry of Veteran Affairs: PMB 13407, Windhoek; tel. (61) 222330; fax (61) 221615.

Ministry of Works, Transport and Communications: 6719 Bell St, Snyman Circle, PMB 13341, Windhoek; tel. (61) 2088111; fax (61) 224381; e-mail jngweda@mwtc.gov.na; internet www.mwtc.gov.na.

Ministry of Youth, National Service, Sport and Culture: NDC Bldg, Goethe St, PMB 13391, Windhoek; tel. (61) 270611; fax (61) 2706303.

President and Legislature

PRESIDENT

Presidential Election, 27–28 November 2009

Candidate	Votes	% of votes
Hifikepunye Pohamba (SWAPO)	611,241	76.42
Hidipo Hamutenya (RDP)	88,640	11.08
Katuutire Kaura (DTA)	24,186	3.02
Kuaima Riruako (NUDO)	23,735	2.97
Justus Garoeb (UDF)	19,258	2.41
Others	32,810	4.10
Total	799,870*	100.00

* Excluding 12,363 invalid votes.

NATIONAL ASSEMBLY

Speaker: THEO-BEN GURIRAB.

General Election, 27–28 November 2009

Party	Votes	% of votes	Seats
SWAPO	602,580	75.27	54
RDP	90,556	11.31	8
DTA	25,393	3.17	2
NUDO	24,422	3.05	2
UDF	19,489	2.43	2
APP	10,795	1.35	1
RP	6,541	0.82	1
CoD	5,375	0.67	1
SWANU	4,989	0.62	1
Others	10,427	1.30	—
Total	800,567*	100.00	72†

* Excluding 10,576 invalid votes.

† In addition to the 72 directly elected members, the President of the Republic is empowered to nominate as many as six non-voting members.

NATIONAL COUNCIL

Chairman: ASSER KUVERI KAPERE.

The second chamber of parliament is the advisory National Council, comprising two representatives from each of the country's 13 Regional Councils, elected for a period of six years.

Election Commission

Electoral Commission of Namibia (ECN): 11 Goethe St, POB 13352, Windhoek; tel. (61) 376200; fax (61) 237618; e-mail mndjarakana@opm.gov.na; internet www.ecn.gov.na; f. 1992; independent; Chair. VICTOR L. TONCHI; Dir of Elections and CEO MOSES K. NDJARAKANA.

Political Organizations

All People's Party of Namibia (APP): f. 2008 in Kavango region; splinter group of the CoD, which split in late 2007; Pres. IGNATIUS SHIXWAMENI.

Congress of Democrats (CoD): 8 Storch St, POB 40905, Windhoek; tel. (61) 256954; fax (61) 256980; internet www.cod.org.na; f. 1999 after split from SWAPO; Pres. BEN ULENGA; Nat. Chair. ARNOLD LOSPER; Sec.-Gen. TSUDAO GURIRAB.

Democratic Party of Namibia (DPN): Windhoek; f. 2008; Interim Pres. SALOMON DAWID ISAACKS; Sec.-Gen. ADAM ISAAK.

Democratic Turnhalle Alliance of Namibia (DTA): Rand St, Khomasdal, POB 173, Windhoek; tel. (61) 238530; fax (61) 226494; e-mail m.venaani@parliament.gov.na; internet www.dtaofnamibia.org.na; f. 1977 as a coalition of 11 ethnically based political groupings; reorg. in 1991 to allow dual membership of coalition groupings and the main party; Pres. KATUUTIRE KAURA; Chair. JOHAN DE WAAL; Sec.-Gen. MCHENRY VENAANI.

Monitor Action Group (MAG): POB 80808, Olympia, Windhoek; tel. (61) 252008; fax (61) 229242; e-mail mag@iway.na; f. 1991 by mems of the National Party of South West Africa alliance; Leader and Chair. J. W. F. (KOSIE) PRETORIUS.

Namibia Democratic Movement for Change (NDMC): POB 60043, Katutura; tel. and fax (61) 297795; f. 2004; Pres. FRANS GOAGOSEB; Sec.-Gen. JOSEPH KAUANDENGE.

National Democratic Party of Namibia (NDP): Daily Park, POB 2438, Ngweze, Katima Mulilo; f. 2004; Pres. MARTIN LUKATO.

National Unity Democratic Organization (NUDO): Clemence Kapuuo St, Plot 1881, POB 62691, Soweto, Katutura; tel. and fax (61) 211550; e-mail nudoparty@iway.na; internet www.nudoofnamibia.org.na; f. 1964 by the Herero Chiefs' Council; joined the DTA in 1977; broke away from the DTA in 2003; Pres. Chief KUAIMA RIRUAKO; Sec.-Gen. ASSER MBAI.

Rally for Democracy and Progress (RDP): POB 83141, Olympia, Windhoek; tel. (61) 255973; e-mail info@rdp.org.na; internet www.rdp.org.na; f. 2007 by fmr mems of ruling SWAPO party; absorbed the Republican Party in Oct. 2010; Pres. HIDIPO HAMUTENYA; Sec.-Gen. JESAYA NYAMU.

South West African People's Organization of Namibia (SWAPO): Hans-Dietrich Genscher St, Plot 2464, Katutura, POB 1071, Windhoek; tel. (61) 238364; fax (61) 232368; internet www.swapoparty.org; f. 1957 as the Ovamboland People's Congress; renamed South West Africa People's Organisation in 1960; Pres. HIFIKEPUNYE POHAMBA; Vice-Pres. HAGE GEINGOB; Sec.-Gen. PENDUKENI IIVULA-ITHANA.

South West African National Union (SWANU): POB 2976, Windhoek; e-mail swanu@swanu.org.na; internet www.swanu.org.na; f. 1959 by mems of the Herero Chiefs' Council; formed alliance with the Workers' Revolutionary Party in 1999; Pres. USUTUAIJE MAAMBERUA; Vice-Pres. B. B. DE CLERK.

United Democratic Front (UDF): POB 20037, Windhoek; tel. (61) 230683; fax (61) 237175; f. 1989 as a centrist coalition of eight parties; reorg. as a single party in 1999; Nat. Chair. ERIC BIWA; Pres. JUSTUS GAROEB.

The **Caprivi Liberation Army (CLA)**, f. 1998 as the Caprivi Liberation Movement, seeks secession of the Caprivi Strip; conducts military operations from bases in Zambia and Angola; political wing operates from Denmark as the **Caprivi National Union**, led by MISHAKE MUYONGO and BONIFACE MAMILI.

Diplomatic Representation

EMBASSIES AND HIGH COMMISSIONS IN NAMIBIA

Algeria: 24 Robert Mugabe Ave, POB 3079, Windhoek; tel. (61) 221507; fax (61) 236376; e-mail Ambalg.w@mweb.com; Ambassador YOUCEF DELILECHE.

Angola: Angola House, 3 Dr Agostinho Neto St, Ausspannplatz, PMB 12020, Windhoek; tel. (61) 227535; fax (61) 221498; Ambassador MANUEL A. D. RODRIGUEZ.

Botswana: 101 Nelson Mandela Ave, POB 20359, Windhoek; tel. (61) 221941; fax (61) 236034; internet www.botnam.com.na; High Commissioner NORMAN MOLEBOGE.

Brazil: 52 Bismarck St, POB 24166, Windhoek; tel. (61) 237368; fax (61) 233389; e-mail brasemb@mweb.com.na; internet www.brazilianembassy.org.na; Ambassador MARCIO ARAUJO LAGE.

China, People's Republic: 13 Wecke St, POB 22777, Windhoek; tel. (61) 372800; fax (61) 225544; e-mail chinaemb_na@mfa.gov.cn; internet na.chineseembassy.org; Ambassador XIN SHUNKANG.

Congo, Republic: 9 Korner St, POB 22970, Windhoek; tel. (61) 257517; fax (61) 240796; Ambassador PATRICE NDOUNGA.

Cuba: 37 Quenta St, Ludwigsdorf, POB 23866, Windhoek; tel. (61) 227072; fax (61) 231584; e-mail embajada@cubanembassy.net; internet www.cubadiplomatica.cu/namibia; Ambassador CARLOS MANUEL ROJAS LAGO.

Egypt: 10 Berg St, POB 11853, Windhoek; tel. (61) 221501; fax (61) 228856; e-mail embassy.windhoek@mfa.gov.eg; internet www.mfa.gov.eg/windhoek_emb; Ambassador HAZEM RAMADAN.

Finland: 2 Crohn St (cnr Bahnhof St), POB 3649, Windhoek; tel. (61) 221355; fax (61) 221349; e-mail sanomat.win@formin.fi; internet www.finland.org.na; Chargé d'affaires a.i. ANNE SALORANTA.

France: 1 Goethe St, POB 20484, Windhoek; tel. (61) 2276700; fax (61) 231436; e-mail contact@ambafrance-na.org; internet www.ambafrance-na.org; Ambassador JEAN-LOUIS ZOËL.

Germany: Sanlam Centre, 6th Floor, 154 Independence Ave, POB 231, Windhoek; tel. (61) 273100; fax (61) 222981; e-mail germany@iway.na; internet www.windhuk.diplo.de; Ambassador EGON KOCHANKE.

Ghana: 5 Nelson Mandela Ave, POB 24165, Windhoek; tel. (61) 221341; fax (61) 221343; e-mail ghanahc@iwwn.com.na; High Commissioner AFUA DAAKU.

India: 97 Nelson Mandela Ave, POB 1209, Windhoek; tel. (61) 226037; fax (61) 237320; e-mail hicomind@mweb.com.na; internet www.highcommissionofindia.web.na; High Commissioner SATYA PAL MANN.

Indonesia: 103 Nelson Mandela Ave, POB 20691, Windhoek; tel. (61) 2851000; fax (61) 2851231; e-mail kbri@iafrica.com.na; internet www.kemlu.go.id/windhoek; Ambassador LEONARDUS WIDAYATMO.

Kenya: Kenya House, 5th Floor, 134 Robert Mugabe Ave, POB 2889, Windhoek; tel. (61) 226836; fax (61) 221409; e-mail kenyanet@mweb.com.na; High Commissioner PETER GITAU.

Libya: 69 Burg St, Luxury Hill, POB 124, Windhoek; tel. (61) 234454; fax (61) 234471; Chargé d'affaires a.i. ENNAS A. A. ENAAS.

Malawi: 56 Bismarck St, POB 13254, Windhoek 9000; tel. (61) 221391; High Commissioner F. CHIKUTA.

Malaysia: 63 Joseph Mukwayu Ithana St, Ludwigsdorf, POB 312, Windhoek; tel. (61) 259342; fax (61) 259343; e-mail malwdhoek@kln.gov.my; internet www.kln.gov.my/perwakilan/windhoek; Chargé d'affaires MUSTAFA HJ MANSOR.

Nigeria: POB 23547, Windhoek; tel. (61) 232101; fax (61) 221639; e-mail nhcnam@mweb.com.na; internet www.nhcwindhoek.org; High Commissioner BIODUN OLORUNFEMI.

Russia: 4 Christian St, POB 3826, Windhoek; tel. (61) 228671; fax (61) 229061; e-mail rusemnam@mweb.com.na; Ambassador NIKOLAI M. GRIBKOV.

South Africa: RSA House, cnr Jan Jonker St and Nelson Mandela Ave, POB 23100, Windhoek; tel. (61) 2057111; fax (61) 224140; e-mail dibem@foreign.gov.za; High Commissioner YVETTE MAVIVI MYAKAYAKA-MANZINI.

Spain: 58 Bismarck St, POB 21811, Windhoek-West; tel. (61) 223066; fax (61) 227209; e-mail emb.windhoek@mae.es; internet www.mae.es/embajadas/windhoek/es/home; Ambassador ALFONSO BARNUEVO SEBASTIÁN DE ERICE.

United Kingdom: 116 Robert Mugabe Ave, POB 22202, Windhoek; tel. (61) 274800; fax (61) 228895; e-mail general.windhoek@fco.gov.uk; internet www.ukinnamibia.fco.gov.uk; High Commissioner MARIANNE YOUNG.

USA: 14 Lossen St, PMB 12029, Windhoek; tel. (61) 2958500; fax (61) 2958603; internet windhoek.usembassy.gov; Ambassador WANDA L. NESBITT.

Venezuela: Southern Life Tower, 3rd Floor, 39 Post St Mall, PMB 13353, Windhoek; tel. (61) 227905; fax (61) 227804; Chargé d'affaires a.i. JORGE JIMÉNEZ.

Zambia: 22 Mandume Ndemufayo St, POB 22882, Windhoek; tel. (61) 237610; fax (61) 228162; e-mail zahico@iway.na; internet www.zahico.iway.na; High Commissioner MAVIS MUYUNDA.

Zimbabwe: cnr Independence Ave and Grimm St, POB 23056, Windhoek; tel. (61) 228134; fax (61) 226859; e-mail zimbabwe@mweb.com.na; Ambassador CHIPO ZINDOGA.

Judicial System

Judicial power is exercised by the Supreme Court, the High Court, and a number of Magistrate and Lower Courts. The Constitution provides for the appointment of an Ombudsman.

The Supreme Court: Private Bag 13398, Windhoek; tel. (61) 279900; fax (61) 224979; e-mail cjudge@iway.na; internet www.superiorcourts.org.na/supreme; f. 1990; Chief Justice PETER SHIVUTE; Additional Judge JOHANNES DAWID GERHARDUS MARITZ.

The High Court: Private Bag 13179, Windhoek; tel. (61) 2921111; fax (61) 221686; e-mail chiefregistrar@mtcmobile.com.na; internet www.superiorcourts.org.na/high; Judge Pres. PETRUS DAMASEB.

Additional Judges of the High Court: SYLVESTER MAINGA, ELTON HOFF, KATO VAN NIEKERK, LOUIS MULLER, COLLINS PARKER, NATE NDAUENDAPO, CHRISTI LIEBENBURG, JOHAN SWANEPOEL, NAOMI SHIVUTE, MARLENE TOMASSI, ALFRED SIBOLEKA.

Religion

It is estimated that about 90% of the population are Christians.

CHRISTIANITY

Council of Churches in Namibia: 8 Mont Blanc St, POB 41, Windhoek; tel. (61) 374054; fax (61) 62786; e-mail ccn.gensec@mweb.com.na; f. 1978; eight mem. churches; Pres. Bishop ERICH HERTEL; Gen. Sec. Rev. MARIA KAPERE.

The Anglican Communion

Namibia comprises a single diocese in the Anglican Church of Southern Africa (formerly the Church of the Province of Southern Africa). The Metropolitan of the Province is the Archbishop of Cape Town, South Africa. In 2006 there were an estimated 110,000 Anglicans in the country.

Bishop of Namibia: Rt Rev. NATHANIEL NDAXUMA NAKWATUMBAH, POB 57, Windhoek; tel. (61) 238920; fax (61) 225903; e-mail shirley@mweb.com.na.

Dutch Reformed Church

Dutch Reformed Church in Namibia (Nederduitse Gereformeerde Kerk in Namibië): 46A Schanzen Rd, POB 389, Windhoek; tel. (61) 374350; fax (61) 227287; e-mail clem@ngkn.com.na; internet www.ngkerk.org.za/namibie; f. 1898; Sec. Rev. CLEM MARAIS; 21,169 mems in 44 congregations (2011).

Evangelical Lutheran

Evangelical Lutheran Church in Namibia (ELCIN): POB 2018, Ondangwa; tel. (65) 240241; fax (65) 240472; e-mail gen.sec@elcin.org.na; internet www.elcin.org.na; f. 1870; became autonomous in 1954; Presiding Bishop Dr SHEKUTAAMBA V. V. NAMBALA; Gen. Sec. Rev. ELIKAIM N. K. SHAANIKA; 703,893 mems (2010).

Evangelical Lutheran Church in the Republic of Namibia (ELCRN) (Rhenish Mission Church): POB 5069, 6 Church St, Ausspanplatz, 9000 Windhoek; tel. (61) 224531; fax (61) 226775; e-mail bishop@elcrnam.org; f. 1957; became autonomous in 1972; Pres. Bishop Dr ZEPHANIA KAMEETA; 420,000 mems (2010).

German Evangelical-Lutheran Church in Namibia (ELCIN—GELC): POB 233, 12 Fidel Castro St, Windhoek; tel. (61) 224294; fax (61) 221470; e-mail bishop-office@elcin-gelc.org; internet www.elcin-gelc.org; Pres. Bishop ERICH HERTEL; 5,100 mems (2010).

Methodist

African Methodist Episcopal Church: POB 798, Keetmanshoop; tel. (63) 222347; fax (63) 223026; e-mail erikke5@hotmail.com; bishop resident in Cape Town, South Africa; Rep. Rev. Dr ANDREAS BIWA; c. 8,000 mems in 33 churches.

Methodist Church of Southern Africa: POB 143, Windhoek; tel. (61) 228921; fax (61) 229202; e-mail central@iway.na; internet www.methodist.org.za; Rep. Rev. KEVIN ENDRES.

The Roman Catholic Church

Namibia comprises one archdiocese, one diocese and one apostolic vicariate. Some 18% of the population are Roman Catholics.

Bishops' Conference

Namibian Catholic Bishops' Conference, POB 11525, Windhoek 9000; tel. (61) 224798; fax (61) 228126; e-mail ncbc@windhoek.org.na.

f. 1996; Pres. LIBORIUS NDUMBUKUTI NASHENDA (Archbishop of Windhoek).

Archbishop of Windhoek: LIBORIUS NDUMBUKUTI NASHENDA, POB 272, Windhoek 9000; tel. (61) 227595; fax (61) 229836; e-mail rcarch@iafrica.com.na; internet www.rcchurch.na.

Other Christian Churches

Among other denominations active in Namibia are the Evangelical Reformed Church in Africa, the Presbyterian Church of Southern Africa, Seventh Day Adventists and the United Congregational Church of Southern Africa. At mid-2000 there were an estimated 820,000 Protestants and 192,000 adherents professing other forms of Christianity.

JUDAISM

Windhoek Hebrew Congregation: POB 563, Windhoek; tel. (61) 221990; fax (61) 226444.

BAHÁ'Í FAITH

National Spiritual Assembly: POB 20372, Windhoek; tel. (61) 302663; e-mail bahainamibia@iway.na; Sec. ROSI STEVENSON; mems resident in 215 localities.

The Press

The African Magazine: NCCI, 2 Jenner St, POB 1770, Windhoek; tel. and fax (61) 255018; e-mail info@theafricanmagazin.org; internet www.theafricanmagazin.org.

AgriForum: 114A Robert Mugabe Ave, Private Bag 13255, Eros, Windhoek; tel. (61) 237838; fax (61) 220193; e-mail agriforum@agrinamibia.com.na; internet www.agrinamibia.com.na; f. 1978; monthly; Afrikaans and English; publ. by the Namibia Agricultural Union; Editor MARIETJIE VAN STADEN; circ. 4,000.

Allgemeine Zeitung: 11 Gen. Murtala Muhammed Ave, POB 86695, Eros, Windhoek; tel. (61) 225822; fax (61) 220225; e-mail azinfo@az.com.na; internet www.az.com.na; f. 1916; publ. by Newsprint Namibia; daily; German; Editor-in-Chief STEFAN FISCHER; circ. 5,000.

Caprivi Vision: Windhoek; tel. (61) 253162; monthly; Editor VISCO LUMAMEZI.

Informanté: POB 11363, Windhoek; tel. (61) 2754000; fax (61) 2754090; e-mail informante1@tqi.na; internet www.informante.web.na; weekly; Editor NGHIDIPO NANGOLO.

Insight Namibia: IMLT Bldg, 70–72 Dr Frans Indongo St, POB 86058, Windhoek; tel. (61) 301438; fax (61) 240385; e-mail editor@insight.com.na; internet www.insight.com.na; f. 2004; monthly; business and current affairs; Editor ROBIN SHERBOURNE.

Namib Times: 8 Sam Nujoma Ave, POB 706, Walvis Bay; tel. (64) 205854; fax (64) 204813; e-mail ntimes@iway.na; internet www.namibtimes.net; f. 1958; 2 a week; Afrikaans, English, German and Portuguese; Editor FLORIS STEENKAMP; circ. 4,300.

Namibia Brief: Independence Ave, POB 2123, Windhoek; tel. (61) 251044; fax (61) 237251; e-mail cblatt@iafrica.com.na; 2 a year; English; Editor CATHY BLATT; circ. 7,500.

Namibia Economist: 7 Schuster St, POB 49, Windhoek 9000; tel. (61) 221925; fax (61) 220615; e-mail info@economist.com.na; internet www.economist.com.na; f. 1986; weekly; English; business, finance and economics; Editor DANIEL STEINMANN; circ. 7,000.

Namibiamagazin: Sudetenland-Str. 18, 37085 Goettingen, Germany; tel. and fax (551) 7076870; e-mail redaktion@namibia-magazin.info; publ. by Klaus Hess Verlag; German; politics, tourism, culture, economics, and German-Namibian relations; Rep. KLAUS A. HESS.

Namibia Review: Directorate Print Media and Regional Offices, Regular Publications, Turnhalle Bldg, Bahnhof St, PMB 13344, Windhoek; tel. (61) 2839111; fax (61) 224937; e-mail bupe@webmail.co.za; f. 1992; publ. by the Ministry of Information and Communication Technology; monthly; information on govt policy and developmental issues; Editor ELIZABETH KALAMBO-M'ULE; circ. 5,000.

Namibia Sport: Unit 3, 14 Liliencron St, POB 1246, Windhoek; tel. (61) 224132; fax (61) 224613; e-mail editor@namibiasport.com.na; internet www.namibiasport.com.na; f. 2002; monthly; Editor HELGE SCHUTZ; circ. 2,000.

Namibia Today: 21 Johan Albrecht St, POB 24669, Windhoek; tel. (61) 276730; fax (61) 276381; e-mail editor@namibiatoday.com.na; 2 a week; Afrikaans, English, Otjiherero and Oshiwambo; publ. by SWAPO; Editor ASSER NTINDA; circ. 5,000.

The Namibian: 42 John Meinert St, POB 20783, Windhoek; tel. (61) 279600; fax (61) 279602; e-mail editor@namibian.com.na; internet www.namibian.com.na; daily; English; Editor TANGENI AMUPADHI; circ. 23,000 (Mon.–Thur.), 32,000 (Fri.).

Namibian Sun: 11B Gen. Murtala Muhammad Ave, Eros, POB 86829, Windhoek; tel. (61) 383400; fax (61) 306853; e-mail sun@namibiansun.com; internet www.namibiansun.com; Mon. to Fri.; English; Editor TABBY MOYO.

NCCI Namibia Business Journal: NCCI Head Office, 2 Jenner St, POB 9355, Windhoek; tel. (61) 228809; fax (61) 228009; publ. by the Namibia Chamber of Commerce and Industry; 6 a year; English; CEO TARAH SHAANIKA; Editor CHARITY MWIYA; circ. 4,000.

New Era: Daniel Tjongarero House, cnr Kerby and W. Kulz Sts, PMB 13364, Windhoek; tel. (61) 273300; fax (61) 220584; e-mail editor@newera.com.na; internet www.newera.com.na; f. 1991; daily; publ. by the Ministry of Information and Communication Technology; English; Chair. MATTHEW GOWASEB; CEO SYLVESTER BLACK; Editor RAJAH MUNAMAVA; circ. 10,000.

Plus Weekly: POB 21506, Windhoek; tel. (61) 233635; fax (61) 230478; e-mail info@namibiaplus.com; publ. by Feddersen Publications; Afrikaans, English and German.

Republikein: 11 Gen. Murtala Muhammed Ave, POB 3436, Eros, Windhoek; tel. (61) 2972000; fax (61) 223721; e-mail republikein@republikein.com.na; internet www.republikein.com.na; f. 1977; daily; Afrikaans and English; owned by Democratic Media Holdings; Editor ESTELLE DE BRUYN; circ. 21,000.

Sister Namibia: 163 Nelson Mandela Ave, POB 86753, Windhoek; tel. (61) 230618; fax (61) 236371; e-mail director@sisternamibia.org; internet www.sisternamibia.org; f. 1989; 4 a year; publ. by Sister Namibia human rights org.; women's rights and gender equality issues; Dir LAURA SASMAN; circ. 6,000.

The Southern Times: cnr Dr W. Külz and Kerby Sts, POB 32235, Windhoek; tel. (61) 301094; fax (61) 301095; internet www.southerntimesafrica.com; f. 2004; weekly (Sun.); owned by New Era and Zimpapers, Zimbabwe; printed in Namibia and Zimbabwe; regional; CEO PETER MIETZNER.

Space Magazine: Sanlam Centre, 3rd Floor, POB 3717, Windhoek; tel. (61) 225155; e-mail space@mweb.com.na; monthly; English; family life; Publr ESTER SMITH; Editor YANNA SMITH.

Windhoek Observer: 6 Schuster St, POB 2255, Windhoek; tel. (61) 221737; fax (61) 226098; e-mail whkob@africaonline.com.na; f. 1978; weekly; English; Editor KUVEE KANGUEEHI; circ. 14,000.

NEWS AGENCY

Namibia Press Agency (Nampa): cnr Keller and Eugene Marais Sts, POB 26185, Windhoek 9000; tel. (61) 374000; fax (61) 221713; e-mail admin@nampa.org; internet www.nampa.org; f. 1991; Chair. REGGIE DIERGAARDT; CEO NGHIDINUA HAMUNIME.

PRESS ASSOCIATION

Press Club Windhoek: POB 2032, Windhoek; tel. (61) 2796000; fax (61) 279602; e-mail carmen@namibian.com.na; Chair. CARMEN HONEY.

Publishers

ELOC Printing Press: PMB 2013, Oniipa, Ondangwa; tel. (65) 240211; fax (65) 240536; e-mail elocbook@iway.na; internet www.elocbook.iway.na; f. 1901; Exec. Dir JOEL AKUDHENGA.

Gamsberg Macmillan Publishers (Pty) Ltd: 19 Faraday St, POB 22830, Windhoek; tel. (61) 232165; fax (61) 233538; e-mail gmp@iafrica.com.na; internet www.macmillan-africa.com; imprints incl. New Namibia Books and Out of Africa; Man. Dir HERMAN VAN WYK.

Longman Namibia: POB 9251, Eros, Windhoek; tel. (61) 231124; fax (61) 224019; Publr LINDA BREDENKAMP.

National Archives of Namibia: 1–9 Eugène Marais St, PMB 13250, Windhoek; tel. (61) 2935211; fax (61) 2935217; e-mail natarch@mec.gov.na; f. 1939; Chief Archivist WERNER HILLEBRECHT.

PUBLISHERS' ASSOCIATION

Association of Namibian Publishers: POB 40219, Windhoek; tel. (61) 228284; fax (61) 231496; f. 1991; Chair. Dr H. MELBER.

Broadcasting and Communications

TELECOMMUNICATIONS

State-owned Telecom Namibia Ltd (Telecom) has a monopoly on the provision of fixed-line services.

Regulatory Authority

Communications Regulatory Authority of Namibia (CRAN): Communication House, 56 Robert Mugabe Ave, Windhoek; Private Bag, 13309, Windhoek; tel. (61) 222666; fax (61) 238646; e-mail cran@cran.na; internet www.cran.na; f. 2011; issues broadcasting licences, supervises broadcasting activities and programme content; Chair. LAZARUS JACOBS; CEO STANLEY SHANAPINDA.

Service Providers

Leo Namibia: POB 40799, Windhoek; tel. 0855550000 (mobile); e-mail info@leo.na; internet www.leo.na; f. 2007; fmrly Cell One, name changed as above in 2009; CEO GERHARD MAY.

Mobile Telecommunications Ltd (MTC): cnr Mosé Tjitendero and Hamutenya Wanahepo Ndadi Sts, Olympia, Windhoek; POB 23051, Windhoek; tel. (61) 2802000; fax (61) 2802124; e-mail feedback@mtc.com.na; internet www.mtc.com.na; f. 1995 as jt venture between Namibia Post and Telecommunications Holdings (NPTH), Telia and Swedfund; 34% owned by Portugal Telecom, 64% by NPTH; Chair. DIRK CONRADIE; Man. Dir MIGUEL GERALDES.

Telecom Namibia Ltd (Telecom): 9 Lüderitz St, POB 297, Windhoek; tel. (61) 2012221; fax (61) 239844; e-mail ndoromaaf@telecom.na; internet www.telecom.na; f. 1992; operates fixed-line and fixed wireless network; state-owned; Chair. J. IITA; Man. Dir FRANS NDOROMA.

BROADCASTING

Radio

In 2007 there were a total of 14 radio stations broadcasting from Windhoek, including:

Namibian Broadcasting Corpn (NBC): Pettenkofer St, Windhoek West, POB 321, Windhoek; tel. (61) 2919111; fax (61) 215767; e-mail tnandjaa@nbc.com.na; internet www.nbc.com.na; f. 1990; runs 10 radio stations, broadcasting daily to 90% of the population in English (24 hours), Afrikaans, German and eight indigenous languages (10 hours); Chair. SVEN THIEM; Dir-Gen. ALBERTUS AOCHAMUB.

Channel 7/Kanaal 7: POB 20500, Windhoek; tel. (61) 235815; fax (61) 240190; e-mail channel7@k7.com.na; internet www.k7.com.na; Christian community radio station; English and Afrikaans; Man. NEAL VAN DEN BERGH.

Katutura Community Radio: Clemence Kapuuo St, POB 70448, KHD, Katutura, Windhoek; tel. (61) 263726; fax (61) 236371; f. 1995 by non-governmental orgs; Dir FREDERICK GOWASEB.

Kudu FM: 158 Jan Jonker St, POB 5369, Windhoek; tel. (61) 247262; fax (61) 247259; e-mail radiokudu@radiokudu.com.na; internet www.radiokudu.com.na; f. 1998; commercial station affiliated to Omulunga Radio; English, Afrikaans and German.

Ninety Nine FM (Pty) Ltd (99 FM): POB 11849, Klein-Windhoek, Windhoek; tel. (61) 383450; fax (61) 230964; e-mail 99@99fm.com.na; f. 1994; CEO CHRISNA GREEFF.

Omulunga Radio: POB 40789, Windhoek; tel. (61) 239706; fax (61) 247259; e-mail omulunga@omulunga.com.na; internet www.omulunga.com.na; f. 2002; Ovambo interest station affiliated to Kudu FM; Oshiwambo and English.

Radio Energy (Radio 100): Energy House 17, cnr Bismark and Church Sts, Windhoek West; POB 676, Windhoek; tel. (61) 256380; fax (61) 256379; e-mail energy@iway.na; internet www.energy100fm.com; f. 1996; commercial radio station; Man. Dir JOHN WALENGA.

Other radio stations included: Kosmos Radio, Radio France International (via relay), Radio 99 and Radio Wave. There were six community radio stations including: Radio Ecclesia (Catholic), Live FM (in Rehoboth), Ohangwenga Community Radio, and UNAM Radio (University of Namibia). A further four community stations were planned in 2005 at Oshakti, Gobabis, Keetmanshoop and Swakopmund.

Television

Namibian Broadcasting Corpn (NBC): Cullinan St, Northern Industrial, POB 321, Windhoek; tel. (61) 2913111; fax (61) 216209; internet www.nbc.com.na; f. 1990; broadcasts television programmes in English to 45% of the population, 18 hours daily; Chair. SVEN THIEME; Dir-Gen. ALBERTUS AOCHAMUB.

Multi-Choice Namibia: Kenya House, Robert Mugabe Ave, POB 2662, Windhoek; tel. (61) 2705261; fax (61) 2705247; commercial television channels; Gen. Man. KOBUS BEZUIDENHOUT.

One Africa TV: 79 Hosea Kutako Dr., POB 21593, Windhoek; tel. (61) 2891500; fax (61) 259450; internet www.oneafrica.tv.

Trinity Broadcasting Namibia: POB 1587, Swakopmund; tel. (64) 401100; fax (64) 403752; e-mail comments@tbnnamibia.tv; internet www.tbnnamibia.tv; f. 2002; CEO COENIE BOTHA.

Finance

(cap. = capital; res = reserves; dep. = deposits; m. = million; brs = branches; amounts in Namibian dollars)

BANKING

In 2010 there were five commercial banks in Namibia.

Central Bank

Bank of Namibia: 71 Robert Mugabe Ave, POB 2882, Windhoek; tel. (61) 2835111; fax (61) 2835067; e-mail jerome.mutumba@bon.com.na; internet www.bon.com.na; f. 1990; cap. 40.0m., res 1,662.9m., dep. 10,930.5m. (Dec. 2009); Gov. IPUMBU WENDELINUS SHIIMI; Dep. Gov. P. HARTMAN.

Commercial Banks

Bank Windhoek Ltd: Bank Windhoek Bldg, 262 Independence Ave, POB 15, Windhoek; tel. (61) 2991223; fax (61) 223188; e-mail info@bankwindhoek.com.na; internet www.bankwindhoek.com.na; f. 1982; cap. 4.8m., res 1,229.4m., dep. 4,182.2m. (June 2010); Chair. J. C. 'KOOS' BRANDT; Man. Dir JAMES HILL; 32 brs.

FIDES Bank Namibia: Windhoek; internet www.fidesbank.co.na; Chair. MARIA GAOMAS.

First National Bank of Namibia Ltd: 209–211 Independence Ave, POB 195, Windhoek; tel. (61) 2992111; fax (61) 2220979; e-mail info@fnbnamibia.com.na; internet www.fnbnamibia.com.na; f. 1987 as First Nat. Bank of Southern Africa Ltd; present name adopted 1990; res 1,703.6m., dep. 12,179.3m. (June 2010); Chair. H. DIETER VOIGTS; CEO L. J. HAYNES; 28 brs and 12 agencies.

Nedbank Namibia Ltd: 12–20 Dr Frans Indongo St, POB 1, Windhoek; tel. (61) 2959111; fax (61) 2952046; e-mail service@nedbank.com; internet www.nedbank.com.na; f. 1973; fmrly Commercial Bank of Namibia Ltd; subsidiary of Nedbank Ltd, South Africa; cap. 16m., res 110m., dep. 4,436m. (Dec. 2007); Chair. T. J. FRANK; Man. Dir ERASTUS HOVEKA; 16 brs and 3 agencies.

Standard Bank Namibia Ltd: Standard Bank Centre, cnr Werner List St and Post St Mall, POB 3327, Windhoek; tel. (61) 2942126; fax (61) 2942583; e-mail info@standardbank.com.na; internet www.standardbank.com.na; f. 1915; controlled by Standard Bank Africa; cap. 2.0m., res 1,137.7m., dep. 10,969.5m. (Dec. 2009); Chair. LEAKE S. HANGALA; Man. Dir MPUMZI PUPUMA; 23 brs.

Agricultural Bank

Agricultural Bank of Namibia (AgriBank): 10 Post St Mall, POB 13208, Windhoek; tel. (61) 2074111; fax (61) 2074289; e-mail info@agribank.com.na; internet www.agribank.com.na; f. 1922; state-owned; total assets 739.1m. (March 2001); Chair. HANS-GUENTHER STIER; CEO LEONARD N. IIPUMBU.

Development Bank

Development Bank of Namibia (DBN): 12 Daniel Munamava St, POB 235, Windhoek; tel. (61) 2908000; fax (61) 2908049; e-mail info@dbn.com.na; internet www.dbn.com.na; f. 2004; Chair. SVEN THIEME; CEO DAVID NUYOMA.

STOCK EXCHANGE

Namibian Stock Exchange (NSX): Robert Mugabe Ave 4, POB 2401, Windhoek; tel. (61) 227647; fax (61) 248531; e-mail info@nsx.com.na; internet www.nsx.com.na; f. 1992; CEO JOHN D. MANDY; Operations Man. MANDA STEYNBERG.

INSURANCE

In 2010 there were 18 long-term and 13 short-term insurance companies operating in Namibia.

Corporate Guarantee and Insurance Co of Namibia Ltd (CGI): Corporate House, Ground Floor, 17 Lüderitz St, POB 416, Windhoek; tel. (61) 259525; fax (61) 255213; e-mail info@corporateguarantee.com; internet www.corporateguarantee.com; f. 1996; wholly owned subsidiary of Nictus Group Ltd since 2001; Chair. F. R. VAN STADEN; Man. Dir and Principal Officer P. J. DE W. TROMP.

Insurance Co of Namibia (INSCON): POB 2877, Windhoek; tel. (61) 275900; fax (61) 233808; f. 1990; short-term insurance; Chair. CHARLES KAURAISA; Man. Dir FERDINAND OTTO.

Legal Shield: 140–142 Robert Mugabe Ave, POB 11363, Windhoek; tel. (61) 2754200; fax (61) 2754090; internet www.legalshield.na; f. 2000; legal, funeral and medical insurance; Man. Dir SANDRA MILLER.

Metropolitan Namibia: Metropolitan Pl., 1st Floor, cnr Bülow and Stubel Sts, POB 3785, Windhoek; tel. (61) 2973000; fax (61) 248191; internet www.metropolitan.com.na; f. 1996; subsidiary of Metropolitan Group, South Africa; acquired Channel Life in 2004; Chair. M. L. SMITH; Man. Dir JASON NANDAGO.

Mutual and Federal Insurance Co Ltd: Mutual and Federal Centre, 5th–7th Floors, 227 Independence Ave, POB 151, Windhoek; tel. (61) 2077111; fax (61) 2077205; f. 1990; subsidiary of Mutual and Federal, South Africa; acquired CGU Holdings Ltd in 2000 and FGI Namibia Ltd in 2001; Man. Dir G. KATJIMUNE; Gen. Man. J. W. B. LE ROUX.

Namibia National Reinsurance Corpn Ltd (NamibRE): Capital Centre, 2nd Floor, Levinson Arcade, POB 716, Windhoek; tel. (61) 256905; fax (61) 256904; e-mail info@namibre.com; internet www.namibre.com; f. 2001; 100% state-owned; Man. Dir ANNA NAKALE-KAWANA.

Old Mutual Life Assurance Co (Namibia) Ltd: Mutual Platz, 5th Floor, Post St Mall, POB 165, Windhoek; tel. (61) 2993999; fax (61) 2993520; e-mail infonamibia@oldmutual.com; internet www.oldmutual.com.na; Chair. G. S. VAN NIEKERK; Chief Exec. BERTIE VAN DER WALT.

Sanlam Namibia: 154 Independence Ave, POB 317, Windhoek; tel. (61) 2947418; fax (61) 2947416; e-mail marketing@sanlam.com.na; internet www.sanlam.com.na; f. 1928; subsidiary of Sanlam Ltd, South Africa; merged with Regent Life Namibia, Capricorn Investments and Nam-Mic Financial Services in Dec. 2004; Chair. KOOS BRANDT; CEO TERTIUS STEARS.

Santam Namibia Ltd: Ausspannplaza Complex, Ausspannplatz, POB 204, Windhoek; tel. (61) 2928000; fax (61) 235225; 60% owned by Santam, South Africa; 33.3% owned by Bank Windhoek Holdings Ltd; acquired Allianz Insurance of Namibia Ltd in 2001; Chief Exec. RIAAN LOUW.

Swabou Insurance Co Ltd: Swabou Bldg, Post St Mall, POB 79, Windhoek; tel. (61) 2997528; fax (61) 2997551; internet www.fnbnamibia.com.na; f. 1990; acquired by FNB Namibia Holdings Ltd in 2004; short-term insurance; Man. Dir RENIER TALJAARD.

Swabou Life Assurance Co Ltd: 209–211 Independence Ave, POB 79, Windhoek; tel. (61) 2997502; fax (61) 2997550; e-mail tgurirab@fnbnamibia.com.na; internet www.fnbnamibia.com.na; f. 1990; acquired by FNB Namibia Holdings Ltd in 2004; life assurance; CEO GERHARD MANS.

Trade and Industry

GOVERNMENT AGENCIES

Karakul Board of Namibia—Swakara Fur Producers and Exporters: PMB 13300, Windhoek; tel. (61) 237750; fax (61) 231990; e-mail swakara@agra.com.na; internet www.swakara.net; f. 1982; promotes development of karakul wool and the pelt industry; Chair. RAIMAR VAN HASE; Man. WESSEL H. VISSER.

Meat Board of Namibia: POB 38, Windhoek; tel. (61) 275830; fax (61) 228310; e-mail info@nammic.com.na; internet www.nammic.com.na; f. 1935; facilitates export of livestock, meat and processed meat products; Chair. POENA POTGIETER; Gen. Man. PAUL STRYDOM.

Meat Corpn of Namibia (Meatco Namibia): POB 3881, Windhoek; tel. (61) 3216400; fax (61) 3217045; e-mail hoffice@meatco.com.na; internet www.meatco.com.na; f. 1986; processors of meat and meat products at four abattoirs and one tannery; CEO KOBUS DU PLESSIS.

Namibian Agronomic Board: 30 David Merero St, POB 5096, Ausspannplatz, Windhoek; tel. (61) 379500; fax (61) 225371; e-mail nabdesk@nammic.com.na; internet www.nab.com.na; f. 1985; Chair. GERNOT EGGERT; CEO CHRISTOF BROCK.

National Petroleum Corpn of Namibia (NAMCOR): Petroleum House, 1 Aviation Rd, PMB 13196, Windhoek; tel. (61) 2045000; fax (61) 2045061; e-mail info@namcor.com.na; internet www.namcor.com.na; f. 1965 as Southern Oil Exploration Corpn (South-West Africa) (Pty) Ltd—SWAKOR; present name adopted 1990; state petroleum co; responsible for importing 50% of national oil requirements; Chair. F. KISTING; Man. Dir SAMUEL BEUKES.

DEVELOPMENT ORGANIZATIONS

Namibia Investment Centre (NIC): Ministry of Trade and Industry, Brendan Simbwaye Sq., Block B, 6th Floor, Goethe St, PMB 13340, Windhoek; tel. (61) 2837335; fax (61) 220278; e-mail nic@mti.gov.na; f. 1990; promotes foreign and domestic investment; Exec. Dir BERNADETTE ARTIVOR.

Namibia Non-Governmental Organisations' Forum Trust (NANGOF Trust): 9 Strauss St, off Beethoven St, POB 70433, Khomasdal, Windhoek; tel. (61) 212503; fax (61) 211306; e-mail info@nangoftrust.org.na; internet www.nangoftrust.org.na; f. 1991 as NANGOF; renamed NANGOF Trust in July 2007; CEO IVIN LOMBARDT.

National Housing Enterprise: 7 Gen. Murtala Muhammed Ave, Eros, POB 20192, Windhoek; tel. (61) 2927111; fax (61) 222301; internet www.nhe.com.na; f. 1993; replaced Nat. Building and Investment Corpn; provides low-cost housing; manages Housing Trust Fund; 100% state-owned; Chair. V. R. RUKORO; CEO VINCENT HAILULU.

CHAMBERS OF COMMERCE

Chamber of Mines of Namibia (CoM): Channel Life Tower, 4th Floor, Post St Mall, POB 2895, Windhoek; tel. (61) 237925; fax (61) 222638; e-mail dmeyer@chamberofmines.org.na; internet www.chamberofmines.org.na; f. 1979; Pres. MIKE LEECH; Gen. Man. VESTON MALANGO; 60 mems (2009).

Namibia Chamber of Commerce and Industry (NCCI): 2 Jenner St, cnr Simpson and Jenner Sts, POB 9355, Windhoek; tel. (61) 228809; fax (61) 228009; e-mail ncciinfo@ncci.org.na; internet www.ncci.org.na; f. 1990; Chair. JOHN ENDJALA; CEO TARAH SHAANIKA; c. 3,000 mems (2008).

EMPLOYERS' ORGANIZATIONS

Construction Industries Federation of Namibia: cnr Stein and Schwabe Sts, POB 1479, Klein Windhoek; tel. (61) 230028; fax (61) 224534; e-mail info@cif.namibia.na; internet www.cifnamibia.com; Pres. KARL HEINZ SCHULZ; Gen. Man. BÄRBEL KIRCHNER; 71 contracting mems, 21 small and medium enterprises members, 17 trade mems, 7 affiliated mems.

Namibia Agricultural Union (NAU): PMB 13255, Windhoek; tel. (61) 237838; fax (61) 220193; e-mail nau@agrinamibia.com.na; internet www.agrinamibia.com.na; f. 1947; represents commercial farmers; Pres. RYNO VAN DER MERWE; Exec. Man. SAKKIE COETZEE.

Namibia National Farmers' Union (NNFU): 4 Axalie Doeseb St, Windhoek West; POB 3117, Windhoek; tel. (61) 271117; fax (61) 271155; e-mail info@nnfu.org.na; internet www.nnfu.org.na; f. 1992; represents communal farmers; Pres. PINTILE DAVIDS.

Namibia Professional Hunting Association (NAPHA): 318 Sam Nujoma Dr., Klein Windhoek; POB 11291, Windhoek; tel. (61) 234455; fax (61) 222567; e-mail napha@mweb.com.na; internet www.napha.com.na; f. 1974; represents hunting guides and professional hunters; Pres. JOHANNES BRAND; c. 470 mems.

UTILITIES

Electricity

Electricity Control Board: 8 Bismarck St, ECB House, POB 2923, Windhoek; tel. (61) 374300; fax (61) 374304; e-mail info@ecb.org.na; internet www.ecb.org.na; f. 2000; CEO SISEHO C. SIMASIKU.

Namibia Power Corpn (Pty) Ltd (NamPower): NamPower Centre, 15 Luther St, POB 2864, Windhoek; tel. (61) 2054111; fax (61) 232805; e-mail paulinus.shilamba@nampower.com.na; internet www.nampower.com.na; f. 1964; state-owned; Chair. ANDRIES LEEVI HUNGAMO; Man. Dir PAULINUS SHILAMBA.

Water

Namibia Water Corporation Ltd (NamWater): 176 Iscor St, Northern Industrial Area, POB 13389, Windhoek; tel. (61) 710000; fax (61) 713000; e-mail shigwedhaj@namwater.com.na; internet www.namwater.com.na; f. 1997; state-owned; CEO Dr VAINO SHIVUTE.

MAJOR COMPANIES

CIC Holdings Ltd: United House, cnr Solingen and Iscor Sts, Northern Industrial Area, POB 98, Windhoek; tel. (61) 2855800; internet www.cicholdings.co.za; fax (61) 2855884; f. 1946 as J. J. van Zyl (Pty) Ltd; 30% owned by Super Group Ltd, South Africa; provides logistical and administrative services to consumer goods industry; Chair. BRYAN KENT; CEO TREVOR P. ROGERS.

Namdeb Diamond Corpn Ltd: POB 35, Oranjemund; tel. (63) 235493; fax (63) 235401; f. 1994; 50% state-owned, 50% owned by De Beers Centenary AG, Switzerland; operates alluvial diamond mine at Oranjemund; also recovers marine diamonds; Chair. NICHOLAS F. OPPENHEIMER; Man. Dir I. ZAAMWANI; 2,953 employees.

Namibia Breweries Ltd (Nambrew): Iscor St, Northern Industrial Area, Windhoek; POB 206, Windhoek; tel. (61) 320499; fax (61) 263327; internet www.nambrew.com; f. 1920 as South West Breweries Ltd; present name adopted 1990; 56% owned by Olfitra, 29% jtly owned by Diageo PLC, United Kingdom, and Heineken NV, Netherlands; producers and distributors of beer, spirits and soft drinks; sales N $509.2m. (2000); Chair. SVEN THIEME; Man. Dir H. VAN DER WESTHUIZEN; 700 employees.

Namibia Sea Products (NamSea): POB 2715, Walvis Bay; tel. (64) 203497; fax (64) 203498; e-mail namsea@iafrica.com.na; 35% owned by Namibia Fishing Industries, 28.6% by Standard Bank Nominees, 2.3% by NamSea Share Trust; fishery, cannery, and producers of fish meal and fish oil; sales N $91.8m. (2004); Chair. C. L. R. HAIKALI; Sec. P. A. SCHWIEGER.

Nictus Group: POB 13231, Windhoek; tel. (61) 229558; fax (61) 227320; e-mail ncs@nictus.com.na; f. 1964; furniture, carpet and motor retail, and financial services; Chair. J. L. OLIVIER; CEO NICO TROMP.

Ohorongo Cement (Pty) Ltd: Schanzenweg 35, Klein Windhoek POB 86842, Eros; tel. (61) 248485; fax (61) 247878; internet www.ohorongo-cement.com; f. 2011; Chair. GERHARD HIRTH; Man. Dir HANS-WILHELM SCHÜTTE.

Rosh Pinah Zinc Corpn (RPZC): Rosh Pinah Mine, Rosh Pinah; tel. (63) 274201; f. 1999 to succeed Imcor Zinc (Pty) Ltd; lead and zinc producers; owned and operated by Kumba Resources, South Africa (fmrly Iscor Mining); Chair. R. MYBURGH; Mine Man. CHRISTO ASPELING; 493 employees.

Rössing Uranium Ltd: 28 Hidipo Hamuntenya Ave, Private Bag 5005, Swakopmund; tel. (64) 5209111; fax (64) 5203017; e-mail yourcontact@rossing.com.na; internet www.rossing.com; f. 1970; began production in 1976; operates world's largest open-pit uranium mine in the Namib Desert; Chair. REHABEAM HOVEKA; Man. Dir CHRIS SALISBURY; 930 employees (2006).

Skorpion Zinc: Skorpion Zinc Mine, Private Bag 2003, Rosh Pinah; tel. (63) 2712100; fax (63) 2712331; e-mail Recruitment@skorpionzinc.com.na; internet www.skorpionzinc.com.na; f. 2000; entered commercial production 2004; owned and operated by Anglo Base Metals (Anglo American PLC—UK); producers of zinc; Mine Man. GERALD BOTING; 615 employees.

Weatherly Mining Namibia: Ausspann Plaza, Unit 4, Ground Floor, Dr Agostinho Neto Rd, Ausspannplatz, Windhoek; tel. (61) 2931010; internet www.weatherlyplc.com; f. 2006 after acquisition of Ongopolo Mining and Processing Ltd assets by Weatherly International; copper producers; Man. Dir and COO CRAIG THOMAS.

TRADE UNIONS

In 2004 there were 27 unions representing more than 100,000 workers.

Trade Union Federations

National Union of Namibian Workers (NUNW): Mungunda St, Katutura; POB 50034, Windhoek; tel. (61) 215037; fax (61) 215589; f. 1972; affiliated to the SWAPO party; Pres. ELIAS MANGA; Sec.-Gen. EVILASTUS KAARONDA; c. 70,000 mems.

The NUNW has 10 affiliates, which include:

Metal and Allied Namibian Workers' Union (MANWU): Mingunda St, POB 22771, Windhoek 9000; tel. (61) 263100; fax (61) 264300; e-mail manwu@mweb.com.na; internet www.manwu.com.na; f. 1987; Pres. JACOBUS SHIRUNGA; Gen. Sec. BERNARD MILINGA; 5,500 mems.

Mineworkers' Union of Namibia (MUN): POB 1566, Windhoek; tel. (61) 261723; fax (61) 217684; f. 1986; Pres. JOHN NDEUTEPO; Sec.-Gen. JONAS LUMBU; 12,500 mems.

Namibia Farm Workers' Union (NAFWU): NUNW Centre, Mungunda Street, Katutura; POB 21007, Windhoek; tel. (61) 218653; e-mail nafwu@iafrica.com.na; internet nafwu.com; f. 1994; Pres. ASSER HENDRICKS; Sec.-Gen. ALFRED ANGULA; 5,700 mems (2009).

Namibia Financial Institutions Union (NAFINU): POB 61791, Windhoek; tel. (61) 239917; fax (61) 215589; f. 2000; Pres. DAVID SHIKULO; Gen. Sec. ASNATH ZAMUEE.

Namibia Food and Allied Workers' Union (NAFAU): Mungunda St, Katutura; POB 1553, Windhoek; tel. (61) 218213; fax (61) 263714; e-mail nafau@mweb.com.na; f. 1986; Pres. ABEL KAZONDUNGE; Gen. Sec. KIROS SACKARIAS; 12,000 mems.

Namibia National Teachers' Union (NANTU): Mungunda St, POB 61009, Katutura, Windhoek; tel. (61) 262247; fax (61) 261926; e-mail nantu@nantu.org.na; internet www.nantu.org.na; f. 1989; Pres. SIMEON KAVILA; Gen. Sec. BASILIUS G. M. HAINGURA.

Namibia Public Workers' Union (NAPWU): POB 50035, Bachbrecht, Windhoek; tel. (61) 261961; fax (61) 263100; e-mail napwu@namibnet.com; f. 1987; Pres. ELIPHAS NDINGARA; Sec.-Gen. PETRUS NEVONGA; 11,000 mems.

Namibia Transport and Allied Workers' Union (NATAU): POB 7516, Katutura, Windhoek; tel. (61) 218514; fax (61) 263767; f. 1988; Pres. DAWID TJOMBE; Gen. Sec. JOHN KWEDHI; 7,500 mems.

Trade Union Congress of Namibia (TUCNA): POB 2111, Windhoek; tel. (61) 246143; fax (61) 212828; f. 2002 following the merger of the Namibia People's Social Movement (f. 1992 as the Namibia Christian Social Trade Unions) and the Namibia Fed. of Trade Unions (f. 1998); Pres. PAULUS HANGO; c. 45,000 mems (2005).

TUCNA has 14 affiliates, including:

Namibia Seamen and Allied Workers' Union (NASAWU): Nataniel Maxuilli St, Walvis Bay; POB 1341, Walvis Bay; tel. (64) 204237; fax (64) 205957; Pres. PAULUS HANGO.

Namibia Wholesale and Retail Workers' Union (NWRWU): 19 Verbena St, Khomasdal; POB 22769, Windhoek; tel. (61) 212378; fax (61) 212828; Sec.-Gen. JOSHUA MABUKU.

Public Service Union of Namibia (PSUN): 45–51 Kroon Rd, Khomasdal, Windhoek; POB 21662, Windhoek; tel. (61) 213083; fax (61) 213047; e-mail psun@iway.na; internet www.psun.com.na; f. 1991; successor to the Govt Service Staff Assen; Pres. JOHANES HOESEB; Sec.-Gen. VICTOR KAZONJATI.

Teachers' Union of Namibia (TUN): PSUN Bldg, Dollar St 4551, Khomasdal, POB 30800, Windhoek; tel. (61) 229115; fax (61) 246360; e-mail tun@mweb.com.na; Pres. MAHONGORA KAVIHUHA.

Transport

RAILWAYS

The main line runs from Nakop, at the border with South Africa, via Keetmanshoop to Windhoek, Kranzberg, Tsumeb, Swakopmund and Walvis Bay. There are three branch lines, from Windhoek to Gobabis, Otavi to Grootfontein and Keetmanshoop to Lüderitz. The total rail network covers 2,382 route-km. Under phase one of the Northern Railway Line Extension Project, the Kranzberg–Tsumeb line was extended by 248 km to Ondangwa in 2006. Work subsequently commenced on phase two of the project, a further 60-km extension of this line to Oshikango, with the eventual aim of constructing an international link with Oshakati, Angola, under phase three. In 2010 plans were under way for the construction of a trans-Kalahari railway linking Walvis Bay with the Mmamabula coal deposits in Botswana. There were also plans for a railway line connecting the Namibian railway system with Mulobezi, Zambia.

TransNamib Holdings Ltd: TransNamib Bldg, cnr Independence Ave and Bahnhof St, PMB 13204, Windhoek; tel. (61) 2982437; fax (61) 2982386; e-mail pubrelation@transnamib.com.na; internet www.transnamib.com.na; f. 1998; state-owned; Chair. FOIBE JACOBS; CEO TITUS HAIMBILI.

ROADS

Between 2000 and 2002 the total road network decreased from 66,467 km to 42,237 km of roads, of which 12.8% was paved in 2002. A major road link from Walvis Bay to Jwaneng, northern Botswana, the Trans-Kalahari Highway, was completed in 1998, along with the Trans-Caprivi Highway, linking Namibia with northern Botswana, Zambia and Zimbabwe. The Government is also upgrading and expanding the road network in northern Namibia.

Roads Authority: Snyman Circle, Ausspannplatz, Windhoek; tel. (61) 2847000; fax (61) 2847158; e-mail pr@ra.org.na; internet www.ra.org.na; Chair. HILENI KAIFANUA; CEO CONRAD LUTOMBI (acting).

SHIPPING

The ports of Walvis Bay and Lüderitz are linked to the main overseas shipping routes and handle almost one-half of Namibia's external trade. Walvis Bay has a container terminal, built in 1999, and eight berths; it is a hub port for the region, serving landlocked countries such as Botswana, Zambia and Zimbabwe. In 2005 NAMPORT added a N $30m. floating dock to the Walvis Bay facilities with a view to servicing vessels used in the region's expanding petroleum industry. Traditionally a fishing port, a new quay was completed at Lüderitz in 2000, with two berths, in response to growing demand from the offshore diamond industry. At the end of 2009 Namibia's merchant fleet comprised 168 vessels, with a combined displacement of 121,579 gross registered tons.

African Portland Industrial Holdings (APIH): Huvest Bldg, 1st Floor, AE/Gams Centre, Sam Nujoma Dr., POB 40047, Windhoek; tel. (61) 248744; fax (61) 239485; e-mail jacques@apiholdings.com; f. 1994; 80% owned by Grindrod (South Africa); bulk port terminal operator; Man. Dir ATHOL EMERTON; Sec. JACQUES CONRADIE.

Namibian Ports Authority (NAMPORT): 17 Rikumbi Kandanga Rd, POB 361, Walvis Bay; tel. (64) 2082207; fax (64) 2082320; e-mail jerome@namport.com.na; internet www.namport.com; f. 1994; Chair. MIKE VAN DER MEER; Man. Dir GERSON ADOLF BISEY UIRAB.

CIVIL AVIATION

There are international airports at Windhoek (Hosea Kutako) and Walvis Bay (Rooikop), as well as a number of other airports throughout Namibia and numerous landing strips.

Directorate of Civil Aviation: POB 12003, Windhoek; tel. (61) 702212; fax (61) 702244; e-mail director@dca.com.na; internet www.dca.com.na; Dir ANGELINE SIMANA PAULO.

Air Namibia: TransNamib Bldg, cnr Independence Ave and Bahnhof St, POB 731, Windhoek; tel. (61) 2996000; fax (61) 2996101; e-mail aarickerts@airnamibia.com.na; internet www.airnamibia.com.na; f. 1946 as South West Air Transport; present name adopted in 1991; state-owned; part-privatization postponed indefinitely in 2003; services to Angola, Botswana, Ghana, South Africa, Zimbabwe, Germany and the United Kingdom; Chair. HINYANGERWA PIUS ASHEEKE; Man. Dir THEO NAMASES (acting).

Kalahari Express Airlines (KEA): POB 40179, Windhoek; tel. (61) 245665; fax (61) 245612; f. 1995; domestic and regional flights; Exec. Dir PEINGONDJABI SHIPOH.

Namibia Airports Company (NAC) Limited: 5th Floor, Sanlam Centre Independence Ave, POB 23061, Windhoek; tel. (61) 2955000; fax (61) 2955022; e-mail pr@airports.com.na; internet www.airports.com.na; f. 1998; Chair. NDEUHALA KATONYALA; CEO TOSKA SAM (acting).

Tourism

Namibia's principal tourist attractions are its game parks and nature reserves, and the development of 'eco-tourism' is being promoted. Tourist arrivals in Namibia in 2008 totalled 931,110. In 2010 tourism receipts amounted to an estimated US $438m.

Namibia Tourism Board: 1st Floor, Channel Life Towers, 39 Post Street Mall, Private Bag 13244, Windhoek; tel. (61) 2906000; fax (61) 254848; e-mail info@namibiatourism.com.na; internet www.namibiatourism.com.na; Chair. ERICKA AKUENJE; CEO DIGU NAOBEB.

Defence

As assessed at November 2011, the Namibian Defence Force numbered an estimated 9,000 men; there was also a 200-strong navy, operating as part of the Ministry of Fisheries and Marine Resources, and a paramilitary force of 6,000.

Defence Expenditure: Budgeted at N $3,130m. for 2012.

Commander-in-Chief of the Defence Force: Pres. HIFIKEPUNYE POHAMBA.

Acting Chief of Staff of the Defence Force: Lt-Gen. EPAPHRAS DENGA NDAITWAH.

Acting Commander of the Army: Brig.-Gen. TOMAS HAMUNYELA.

Education

Education is officially compulsory and free of charge for 10 years between the ages of six and 16 years, or until primary education has been completed (whichever is the sooner). Under the Education Act of 2001, free basic education was extended to grade 12, although it is not compulsory beyond the limits set in the Constitution. Primary education begins at six years of age and lasts for seven years. Secondary education, beginning at the age of 13, lasts for up to five years, comprising a first cycle of three years and a second of two. According to UNESCO estimates, in 2008/09 enrolment at primary schools included 85% of children in the relevant age-group (males 83%; females 88%), while the comparable ratio for secondary enrolment in 2006/07 was 54% (males 48%; females 60%). Higher education is provided by the University of Namibia, the Technicon of Namibia, a vocational college and four teacher-training colleges. In 2007/08 19,970 students were enrolled in tertiary education. Various schemes for informal adult education are also in operation in an effort to combat illiteracy. In 2009/10 education received an estimated 18.6% of total government expenditure.

Bibliography

Arcadi de Saint-Paul, M. *Namibie: Une Siècle d'Histoire*. Paris, Albatron, 1984.

Bley, H. *Namibia under German Rule*. Uppsala, Nordiska Afrikainstitutet, 1997.

Cliffe, L., *et al. The Transition to Independence in Namibia*. Boulder, CO, Lynne Rienner Publishers, 1994.

Cros, G. *Chroniques Namibiennes: La Dernière Colonie*. Paris, Présence Africaine, 1983.

Dale, R. *The UN and the Independence of Namibia: The Longest Decolonization, 1946–1990*. 1994.

Diescho, J. *The Namibian Constitution in Perspective*. Windhoek, Gamsberg Macmillan, 1994.

Du Pisani, A. *SWA / Namibia: The Politics of Continuity and Change*. Johannesburg, Jonathan Ball, 1986.

Du Pisani, A., Kössler, R., and Lindeke, W. (Eds). *The Long Aftermath of War: Reconciliation and Transition in Namibia*. Freiburg, Arnold-Bergstraesser-Institut, 2010.

Du Pisani, A., and Otaala, B. *UNAM HIV / AIDS Policy*. Windhoek, University of Namibia Press, 2002.

Duggal, N. K. (Ed.). *Namibia: Perspectives for National Reconstruction and Development*. Lusaka, UN Institute for Namibia, 1986.

Freeman, L. 'Contradictions of Independence: Namibia in Transition' in *Transformation*, No. 17, 1992.

Gewald, J. *Herero Heroes: A Socio-Political History of the Herero of Namibia, 1890–1923*. London, James Currey Publishers, 1999.

Green, R. H. *From Sudwesafrika to Namibia: The Political Economy of Transition*. Uppsala, Scandinavian Institute for African Studies, 1981.

Grotpeter, J. J. *Historical Dictionary of Namibia*. Metuchen, NJ, Scarecrow Press, 1994.

Hayes, P., Silvester, J., Wallace, M., and Hartmann, W. *Namibia under South African Rule*. London, James Currey Publishers, 1998.

Heribert, W., and Matthew, B. (Eds). *The Namibian Peace Process: Implications and Lessons for the Future*. Freiburg, Arnold-Bergstraesser-Institut, 1994.

Hishongwa, N. *The Contract Labour System and its Effects on Social and Family Life in Namibia*. Windhoek, Gamsberg Macmillan, 1992.

Hohn, S. 'International Justice and Reconciliation in Namibia: The ICC Submission and Public Memory' in *African Affairs*, Vol. 109, Issue 436, 2010.

Hofnie, K., Friedman, S., and Iipinge, S. *The Relationship Between Gender Roles and HIV Infection in Namibia*. Windhoek, University of Namibia, 2004.

Hopwood, G. *Guide to Namibian Politics*. Windhoek, Namibia Institute for Democracy, 2007.

Katjavivi, P. H. *A History of Resistance in Namibia*. London, James Currey Publishers, 2004.

LeBeau, D. *Namibia: Ethnic Stereotyping in a Post-Apartheid State*. Windhoek, University of Namibia, 1991.

Leys, C., and Saul, J. S. *Namibia's Liberation Struggle: The Two-Edged Sword*. London, James Currey Publishers, 1995.

Lush, D. *Last Steps to Uhuru: An Eye-Witness Account of Namibia's Transition to Independence (1988–1992)*. Ibadan, Spectrum Books, 1993.

Mans, M. *Music as Instrument of Diversity and Unity: Notes On A Namibian Landscape*. Uppsala, Nordic Africa Institute, 2003.

Mbuende, K. *Namibia: The Broken Shield: Anatomy of Imperialism and Revolution*. Uppsala, Scandinavian Institute for African Studies, 1986.

Melber, H. *Re-Examining Liberation in Namibia: Political Culture since Independence*. Uppsala, Nordiska Afrikainstitutet, 2003.

Cross-examining Transition in Namibia: Socio-economic and Ideological Transformation since Independence. Uppsala, Nordiska Afrikainstitutet, 2006.

Melber, H. (Ed.). *Transitions in Namibia: Which Changes for Whom?* Uppsala, Nordiska Afrikainstitutet, 2007.

Namibian Economic Policy Unit. *2009 Namibia Economic Review and Prospects for 2010*. Windhoek, NEPRU, 2010.

Omar, G., *et al. Introduction to Namibia's Political Economy*. Cape Town, Southern Africa Labour and Development Research Unit, 1990.

Otaala, B. *HIV/AIDS: The Challenge for Tertiary Institutions in Namibia*. Windhoek, University of Namibia, 2000.

Otaala, B. (Ed.). *Government Leaders in Namibia Responding to the HIV/AIDS Epidemic*. Windhoek, University of Namibia, 2003.

Peltola, P. *The Lost May Day: Namibian Workers' Struggle for Independence*. Uppsala, Finnish Anthropological Society and Nordiske Afrikainstitutet, 1995.

Rena, R. 'Namibian Economy: Recent Developments and Future Expectations' in *Journal of Social and Economic Policy*, Vol. 7, Issue 1, 2010.

Saunders, C. 'The Role of the UN in the Independence of Namibia' in *History Compass*, Vol. 5, Issue 3, 2007.

Soggot, D. *Namibia: The Violent Heritage*. London, Collings, 1986.

Soiri, I. *Radical Motherhood: Namibian Women's Independence Struggle*. Uppsala, Nordiske Afrikainstitutet, 1996.

Sparks, D. L., and Green, D. *Namibia: The Nation after Independence*. Boulder, CO, Westview Press, 1992.

Thornberry, C. *A Nation is Born: The Inside Story of Namibia's Independence*. Windhoek, Gamsberg Macmillan, 2004.

Torreguitar, E. *National Liberation Movements in Office: Forging Democracy with African Adjectives in Namibia*. New York, Peter Lang, 2009.

Totemeyer, G., *et al.* (Eds). *Namibia in Perspective*. Windhoek, Council of Churches in Namibia, 1987.

Tsokodayi C. J. *Namibia's Independence Struggle*. Bloomington, IN, Xlibris, 2011.

Uys, S. 'Namibia: The Socialist Dilemma' in *African Affairs*, Vol. 81, Issue 325, 1982.

Vergau, H-J. *Negotiating the Freedom of Namibia: The Diplomatic Achievement of the Western Contact Group*. Basel, Basler Afrika Bibliographien, 2011.

Wallace, M. *A History of Namibia: From the Beginning to 1990*. London, C. Hurst & Co, 2011.

Walther, D. J. *Creating Germans Abroad: Cultural Policies and National Identity in Namibia*. Athens, OH, Ohio University Press, 2002.

Winterfeldt, V., Fox, T., and Mufune, P. (Eds). *Namibia: Society, Sociology*. Windhoek, University of Namibia, 2002.

Zimmerer, J., and Zeller, J. (Eds). *Genocide in German South West Africa: the Colonial War (1904–1908) in Namibia and its Aftermath*. Monmouth, Merlin Press, 2008.

NIGER

Physical and Social Geography

R. J. HARRISON CHURCH

The land-locked Republic of Niger is the largest state in West Africa. With an area of 1,267,000 sq km (489,191 sq miles), it is larger than Nigeria, its immensely richer southern neighbour, which is Africa's most populous country. The relatively small size of Niger's population, 11,060,291 at the census of May 2001, rising to 16,644,338 by mid-2012, according to UN estimates, is largely explained by the country's aridity and remoteness. Population density in mid-2012 averaged 13.1 persons per sq km. Two-thirds of Niger consists of desert, and most of the north-eastern region is uninhabitable. The only large city is Niamey, which had a population of 1,297,160 in mid-2011. Hausa tribespeople are the most numerous (representing some 55.4% of Nigerien citizens in 2001), followed by the Djerma and Sonraï (together amounting for a total of 21.0%), Tuareg (9.3%) and Peulh (8.5%).

In the north-centre is the partly volcanic Aïr massif, with many dry watercourses remaining from earlier wetter conditions. Agadez, in Aïr, receives an average annual rainfall of no more than about 180 mm. None the less, the Tuaregs keep considerable numbers of livestock by moving them seasonally to areas further south, where underground well-water is usually available. Further south, along the Niger–Nigeria border, are sandy areas where annual rainfall is just sufficient for the cultivation of groundnuts and millet by Hausa farmers. Cotton is also grown in small, seasonally flooded valleys and depressions.

In the south-west is the far larger, seasonally flooded Niger valley, the pastures of which nourish livestock that have to contend with nine months of drought for the rest of the year. Rice and other crops are grown by the Djerma and Sonraï peoples as the Niger flood declines.

Niger thus has three very disparate physical and cultural focuses. Unity has been encouraged by French aid and by economic advances, but the attraction of the more prosperous neighbouring state of Nigeria is considerable. Distances to the nearest ports (Cotonou, in Benin, and Lagos, in Nigeria) are at least 1,370 km, both routes requiring breaks of bulk.

Recent History

KATHARINE MURISON

Formerly a part of French West Africa, Niger became a self-governing republic within the French Community in December 1958, and proceeded to full independence on 3 August 1960. Control of government passed to the Parti Progressiste Nigérien (PPN), whose leader, Hamani Diori, favoured the retention of close economic links with France.

The period 1968–74 was overshadowed by the Sahelian drought. Widespread civil disorder followed allegations that some government ministers were misappropriating stocks of food aid, and in April 1974 Diori was overthrown by the Chief of Staff of the Armed Forces, Lt-Col (later Maj.-Gen.) Seyni Kountché. A Conseil Militaire Suprême (CMS) was established, and the legislature was replaced by a consultative Conseil National de Développement (CND). Although political parties were outlawed, exiled opposition activists were permitted to return to the country.

THE KOUNTCHÉ REGIME

The military Government maintained generally amicable relations with France and formed new links with Arab states. Domestically, there was a renewal of political activism, and plots to remove Kountché were thwarted in 1975 and 1976. In January 1983 a civilian Prime Minister, Oumarou Mamane, was appointed, although he was removed from the post in November of that year. Economic adjustment efforts were impeded by the recurrence of drought in 1984–85 and by the closure of the land border with Nigeria in 1984–86, with the result that Niger's dependence on external financial assistance was increased.

A draft 'national charter' was overwhelmingly approved (by some 99.6% of voters) at a national referendum in June 1987. The charter provided for the establishment of non-elective, consultative institutions at both national and local levels.

SAÏBOU AND THE SECOND REPUBLIC

Kountché died in November 1987 and the Chief of Staff of the Armed Forces, Col (later Brig.) Ali Saïbou, was inaugurated as Chairman of the CMS and Head of State on 14 November. Diori was received by Saïbou, an appeal was made to exiled Nigeriens to return, and an amnesty was announced for political prisoners. Although the military continued to play a prominent role in government, Oumarou Mamane was reappointed as Prime Minister in July 1988.

In August 1988 Saïbou announced an end to the 14-year ban on political organizations, with the formation of a new ruling party, the Mouvement National pour la Société de Développement (MNSD). In May 1989 the constituent congress of the MNSD elected a Conseil Supérieur d'Orientation Nationale (CSON) to replace the CMS. A constitutional document, drafted by the CND, which provided for the continued role of the armed forces in what was to be designated the Second Republic, was endorsed by 99.3% of voters in a national referendum in September. As President of the CSON, Saïbou was the sole candidate at a presidential election in December, when he was confirmed as Head of State, for a seven-year term, by 99.6% of voters. At the same time a single list of 93 CSON-approved deputies to a new Assemblée nationale (to succeed the CND) was endorsed by a similar margin. The post of Prime Minister was abolished later in December, but was restored in March 1990, when it was allocated to a prominent industrialist, Aliou Mahamidou, in an extensive government reorganization.

In November 1990 Saïbou announced that a multi-party political system would be established. Interim provision was made for the registration of political parties (the Constitution was amended to this effect in April 1991).

THE TRANSITION PERIOD

In March 1991 it was announced that the armed forces were to withdraw from political life, and serving military officers were, accordingly, removed from the Council of Ministers. In July Saïbou resigned as Chairman of the MNSD—Nassara (as the MNSD had been restyled), in order to distance himself from party politics in preparation for a national conference on the country's political evolution. He was succeeded as party leader by Col (retd) Mamadou Tandja.

The National Conference, convened on 29 July 1991, was attended by about 1,200 delegates, including representatives of the organs of state, 24 political organizations, professional, women's and students' groups. Declaring the Conference sovereign, delegates voted to suspend the Constitution and to dissolve its organs of state: Saïbou was to remain in office as interim Head of State. The Government was dissolved, and in October the Conference appointed Amadou Cheiffou (a regional official of the International Civil Aviation Organization) to head a transitional Government pending the installation (scheduled for early 1993) of elected democratic institutions. The Conference ended in November 1991; its Chairman, André Salifou (a dean of the University of Niamey), was designated Chairman of a 15-member Haut Conseil de la République (HCR), which was to function as an interim legislature.

A constitutional referendum took place on 26 December 1992, when the new document was approved by 89.8% of those who voted (56.6% of the electorate). At elections to the new 83-member Assemblée nationale, which were held on 14 February 1993 and contested by 12 political parties, the MNSD—Nassara won the greatest number of seats (29), but was prevented from resuming power by the rapid formation of the Alliance des Forces de Changement (AFC), which grouped six parties with a total of 50 seats. Principal members of the AFC were the Convention Démocratique et Sociale—Rahama (CDS), the Parti Nigérien pour la Démocratie et le Socialisme—Tarayya (PNDS) and the Alliance Nigérienne pour la Démocratie et le Progrès Social—Zaman Lahiya (ANDP).

The MNSD—Nassara was similarly frustrated at the presidential election. At the first round, on 27 February 1993, Tandja won the greatest proportion of the votes cast (34.2%), followed by Mahamane Ousmane, the leader of the CDS (26.6%). Ousmane was elected President at a second round on 27 March by 55.4% of those who voted (just over 35% of the electorate), aided by the support of four of the six other candidates at the first round, who were members of the AFC.

OUSMANE AND THE THIRD REPUBLIC

Ousmane was inaugurated as President of the Third Republic on 16 April 1993 and appointed a presidential candidate, Mahamadou Issoufou of the PNDS, to the post of Prime Minister. In May Moumouni Adamou Djermakoye (the leader of the ANDP and another presidential candidate) was elected Speaker of the Assemblée nationale.

In September 1994 the PNDS withdrew from the AFC, and Issoufou resigned as Prime Minister, in protest against the perceived transfer of some of the premier's powers to the President. A new minority Government, led by Souley Abdoulaye of the CDS, failed to withstand a parliamentary motion of no confidence proposed by the MNSD—Nassara and the PNDS in October. Ousmane dissolved the Assemblée nationale.

Legislative elections were held on 12 January 1995. The results indicated that the MNSD—Nassara, combining its 29 seats with those of its allies, would be able to form a 43-strong majority group in the legislature. While Ousmane's CDS increased its representation to 24 seats, the AFC (having lost the support of the PNDS and also that of the PPN) held 40 seats. However, Ousmane declined to accept the new majority's nominee as Prime Minister, Hama Amadou (the Secretary-General of the MNSD—Nassara), appointing instead another member of that party, Amadou Boubacar Cissé, a former official of the World Bank. Cissé was expelled from the MNSD—Nassara, and the party and its allies announced that they would not co-operate with his administration. His position was further undermined by the election of Issoufou to the post of Speaker of the Assemblée nationale. A parliamentary motion of censure against Cissé was narrowly approved, and Ousmane was obliged to accept Amadou as Prime Minister.

Difficulties of 'cohabitation' precipitated an institutional crisis from July 1995, when Ousmane apparently refused to chair a session of the Council of Ministers at which Amadou's nominations for new senior executives of state-owned organizations were to have been adopted. The Government ordered the deployment of security forces at the premises of state enterprises, thereby preventing the incumbent executives from performing their duties. The crisis over the delineation of responsibilities between the President and Prime Minister deepened in subsequent months.

MILITARY TAKE-OVER

On 27 January 1996 the elected organs of state were overthrown by the military, under the command of Col (later Brig.-Gen.) Ibrahim Baré Maïnassara (Chief of Staff of the Armed Forces since March 1995). The coup leaders, who formed a 12-member Conseil de Salut National (CSN), chaired by Maïnassara, asserted that their seizure of power had been necessitated by Niger's descent into political chaos. The CSN suspended the Constitution, dissolving the Assemblée nationale and other institutions; political parties were suspended, and a state of emergency was imposed. The coup was generally condemned internationally. The CSN appointed Boukary Adji, the Deputy Governor of the Banque Centrale des Etats de l'Afrique de l'Ouest (BCEAO) and a former finance minister, as Prime Minister. Adji's transitional Government was composed entirely of civilians. In mid-February Ousmane, Amadou and Issoufou signed a joint text, in Maïnassara's presence, which effectively endorsed the legitimacy of the CSN.

Two independent consultative bodies were established in late February 1996: the advisory Conseil des Sages (which elected Saïbou as its Chairman); and the Co-ordinating Committee of the National Forum. The National Forum for Democratic Renewal, which was convened in April, adopted constitutional revisions that aimed to guarantee greater institutional stability, essentially by conferring executive power solely on the President of the Republic and requiring the Prime Minister to implement a programme stipulated by the Head of State.

Despite Maïnassara's earlier assurances that he had no personal political ambitions, by May 1996 he had confirmed reports of his intention to seek election to the presidency. The revised Constitution was approved by 92.3% of voters on 12 May; only 35% of the electorate were reported to have voted, however. The ban on activities by political organizations was revoked shortly afterwards. Ousmane, Issoufou, Tandja and Djermakoye swiftly announced their intention to contest the presidential election, scheduled for July.

Voting in the presidential election commenced on 7 July 1996, but was quickly halted in Niamey and in other areas where preparations were incomplete: polling took place in these areas the following day. Controversy arose when, shortly before the end of voting, the authorities announced the dissolution of the electoral supervisory body, the Commission Électorale Nationale Indépendante (CENI), in response to what they termed its 'obvious and deliberate' obstruction of the electoral process. A new commission was appointed to collate the election results. Maïnassara secured an outright victory, with some 52.2% of the votes cast; Ousmane had won 19.8%, and Tandja 15.7%.

THE FOURTH REPUBLIC

Maïnassara was installed as President of the Fourth Republic on 7 August 1996. The new Government, under Adji, included former Prime Ministers Abdoulaye and Cissé. Members of the CDS, the MNSD—Nassara and the PNDS who accepted government posts were subsequently expelled from their parties.

The legislative elections, held on 23 November 1996, were contested by 11 parties and movements, as well as by independent candidates. The Front pour la Restauration et la Défense de la Démocratie (FRDD), formed by eight opposition parties (including the CDS, the MNSD—Nassara and the PNDS) in September, boycotted the vote. According to official results, the pro-Maïnassara Union Nationale des Indépendants pour le Renouveau Démocratique (UNIRD) took 52 of the 83 seats in the Assemblée nationale. (The Supreme Court later upheld complaints of fraud in three constituencies won by the UNIRD, annulling the results there.) The CSN was formally dissolved on 12 December. A new Government was appointed shortly afterwards, with Cissé as Prime Minister. The

FRDD leaders had rejected an invitation by Maïnassara to join the Government, and the deputy leader of the CDS, Sanoussi Jackou, was expelled from the party after accepting a ministerial post.

In November 1997 Maïnassara dismissed the Government; by this time a resumption of hostilities in the north had been compounded by chronic food insecurity, further labour unrest and ongoing political agitation. Maïnassara appointed Ibrahim Hassane Maiyaki, hitherto Minister of Foreign Affairs and Co-operation, as Prime Minister and named a new Council of Ministers in December.

In February 1998 the Parti Nigérien pour l'Autogestion—al Umat, the Parti pour l'Unité Nationale et le Développement—Salama and the ANDP formed the Alliance des Forces Démocratiques et Sociales (AFDS). However, the AFDS subsequently protested that it was being marginalized in the political process and by the state media; the alliance thereafter became increasingly associated with the opposition. Political tensions escalated from April, as clashes in Tahoua between the security forces and FRDD activists, who were demanding Maïnassara's resignation, were followed by violent protests in Maradi and in Zinder, where opposition activists allegedly attacked vehicles and property belonging to the pro-Maïnassara Rassemblement pour la Démocratie et le Progrès—Djamaa (RDP).

In July 1998 the Government and the opposition parties of the FRDD and the AFDS signed an agreement aimed at ending two years of political crisis. Revisions were outlined to electoral procedures and institutions, as well as to the manner in which senior appointments were made to the Supreme Court and to the presidency of the CENI. However, the opposition challenged the appointment by Maïnassara of Lawali Mahamane Danda to head the electoral body. The remaining members of the CENI were appointed by presidential decree in September.

DEATH OF MAÏNASSARA

On 9 April 1999 Maiyaki made a broadcast to the nation, announcing the death of Maïnassara in an "unfortunate accident' at a military airbase in Niamey. The Prime Minister stated that the defence and security forces would continue to be the guarantors of republican order and national unity, and announced the dissolution of the Assemblée nationale, as well as the temporary suspension of all party political activity. Despite the official explanation for his death, it was generally perceived that Maïnassara had been assassinated by members of his presidential guard. On 11 April the Constitution was suspended, and its institutions dissolved. A military Conseil de Réconciliation Nationale (CRN), under the chairmanship of Maj. Daouda Mallam Wanké (hitherto head of the presidential guard), was to exercise executive and legislative authority during a nine-month transitional period. A new constitution was to be prepared, for submission to a national referendum, prior to the restoration of civilian rule and the installation of elected organs of state on 31 December. Maiyaki was reappointed as Prime Minister on 12 April, and a transitional Council of Ministers was named shortly afterwards.

Although the military take-over was condemned by the parties that had supported Maïnassara, the incoming regime was broadly welcomed, in its initial stages, by the FRDD and the AFDS. However, Niger's creditors strongly denounced the apparent coup, as did the Economic Community of West African States (ECOWAS).

THE FIFTH REPUBLIC

The draft Constitution of what was to be designated the Fifth Republic envisaged a balance of powers between the President, Government and legislature, although the President was to be politically liable only in the case of high treason. The Government, under an appointed Prime Minister, was to be responsible to the Assemblée nationale, which would be competent to remove the Prime Minister by vote of censure. The draft document was submitted to a referendum on 18 July 1999, when it was approved by 89.6% of those who voted (about one-third of the registered electorate). Wanké promulgated the new Constitution on 9 August.

The first round of the presidential election, contested by seven candidates, took place on 17 October 1999. Voting was considered to have been largely transparent and peaceful. Tandja (MNSD—Nassara) won 32.3% of the votes cast, followed by Issoufou (PNDS), with 22.8%, and former President Ousmane (CDS), with 22.5%. The rate of participation by voters was 43.7%. Having secured the support of Ousmane, Tandja was elected President at a second round of voting, held on 24 November, defeating Issoufou with 59.9% of the votes cast. The rate of participation was about 39% of the registered electorate. The MNSD—Nassara was similarly successful in concurrent elections to the Assemblée nationale, winning 38 of the 83 seats; the CDS took 17, the PNDS 16, the RDP eight and the ANDP four.

Tandja was inaugurated as President on 22 December 1999. Amadou was subsequently appointed Prime Minister, and a new Council of Ministers was announced in January 2000. In January the Assemblée nationale adopted draft amnesty legislation, as provided for in the Constitution but opposed by the RDP. In March 12 opposition parties, led by the PNDS, formed the Coordination des Forces Démocratiques (CFD). Similarly, 17 parties loyal to the President, chief among them the MNSD—Nassara and CDS, formed the Alliance des Forces Démocratiques (AFD) in July.

Tandja Re-elected

The first round of the presidential election, which was held on 16 November 2004, was contested by six candidates, four of whom (Djermakoye, Issoufou, Ousmane and Tandja) were standing for a fourth time. Tandja won 40.7% of the votes cast, followed by Issoufou, with 24.6%, and Ousmane, with 17.4%. The rate of voter participation was 48.2%. Tandja succeeded in securing the support of all four eliminated candidates ahead of the second round, which took place on 4 December. As in 1999, Tandja comfortably defeated Issoufou, with 65.5% of the votes cast. Turn-out at the second round was 45.0%. The ruling MNSD—Nassara also performed well at concurrent elections to the enlarged 113-member Assemblée nationale, winning 47 seats, while five other parties loyal to Tandja secured a further 41 seats, including 22 taken by the CDS. The opposition PNDS and its allies won a total of 25 seats. Amadou was reappointed to the premiership in late December 2004, and the formation of a new Council of Ministers, composed of members of the MNSD—Nassara and its allies, was announced.

Public Discontent

In mid-March 2005 up to 20,000 people protested in Niamey against rising prices, following the introduction of a 19% value-added tax on basic commodities. The demonstration was organized by the Coalition Contre la Vie Chère (CCVC), comprising some 30 groups, including trade unions, human rights organizations and consumer movements. In the following week, after the Government refused to authorize a second protest march, the Coalition staged a one-day strike, which halted most activity in the capital. The authorities subsequently agreed to hold talks with the CCVC. However, before a meeting could take place, five leaders of the CCVC were arrested and accused of establishing an unauthorized association and plotting against state security. Several of them had appeared on private radio and television stations, appealing to religious leaders to hold prayers in order to save Niger from misery, in what the Government Spokesman, Mohamed Ben Omar, described as a 'veiled call to rebellion'. The radio station Alternative FM, the director of which, Moussa Tchangari, was one of those charged, was also closed by police, prompting protests from international press freedom groups. During a further one-day strike, held a few days later, protesters erected barricades and burned tyres in Maradi and Tahoua, leading to further arrests. A third strike was suspended by the CCVC in early April in the hope that a compromise could be reached with the Government. Two days later the five leaders of the CCVC were released, and the Government and the Coalition subsequently reached an agreement on measures to mitigate the effect of the 19% tax.

None the less, public discontent with the Government arose again in mid-2005 over severe food shortages. The Government, which had been supplying cereals at subsidized prices in the most stricken areas, appealed for international assistance and announced plans to 'loan' grain to farmers most at risk until they could reimburse the Government after the harvest later in the year. Following widespread international media coverage of the food shortages in late July, donors substantially increased their contributions and the Government agreed to distribute free food to those worst affected.

A parliamentary motion of censure against Amadou's Government was approved in May 2007, when a number of deputies representing movements hitherto loyal to the ruling MNSD—Nassara voted against the Government. The opposition had proposed the vote in protest at Amadou's refusal to testify before an inquiry into the misappropriation of education funds. Three days later Tandja appointed a new Prime Minister, Seyni Oumarou, hitherto Minister of State and Minister of Infrastructure. Despite opposition complaints that Oumarou was too closely associated with his predecessor, the new Prime Minister was officially sworn into office on 7 June. Several senior ministers retained their positions in the new Government.

In December 2007 it was reported that at least 14 public officials, including the mayor of Niamey, Aboubacar Ganda, and allies of former Prime Minister Amadou, had been detained on suspicion of corruption and were awaiting trial. In June 2008 Amadou himself was arrested, his immunity from prosecution having been lifted by the Assemblée nationale. Amadou denied allegations that he had embezzled 100m. francs CFA of state funds intended for the development of the press, claiming that the accusations were a politically motivated attempt to prevent him from contesting the presidency in 2009. The former Prime Minister retained significant support within the ruling MNSD—Nassara, of which he remained President, raising the possibility of a split within the party. Several thousand protesters, including a number of MNSD—Nassara deputies, demonstrated in Niamey in October 2008 to demand Amadou's release.

Tandja Attempts to Retain Power

Speculation that Tandja might seek to extend his presidential mandate beyond the two terms permitted by the Constitution mounted in late October 2008, when a demonstration took place in Zinder in support of a third term of office for the President; similar rallies were held in other towns in the following month. At the end of November, however, nearly 5,000 people were reported to have participated in a counter-demonstration, organized by a civil society group opposed to a third mandate for Tandja. The campaign to prolong Tandja's presidency gained further momentum in December, as Prime Minister Oumarou and leaders of several political parties allied to the Government were among thousands of participants at a rally in Niamey aimed at securing a three-year extension for Tandja. One week later opponents of such a move again held a counter-demonstration.

An extraordinary congress of the MNSD—Nassara, held in Zinder in February 2009, designated Oumarou as President of the party, replacing Amadou, whose supporters declared the change of leadership to be 'illegal' on the grounds that it contravened party regulations. Amadou was released from prison in April, owing to ill health, although he was still to stand trial. Meanwhile, Tandja stated in March that he would be willing to remain in power after the end of his second term, but that he would not revise the Constitution in order to do so. In early May the President declared his intention to organize a referendum on the extension of his mandate. In mid-May the CENI announced that local elections would take place on 25 October, followed by a presidential election on 14 November and legislative elections on 28 November.

A political crisis swiftly developed over Tandja's referendum plan, which was criticized by opposition parties, several pro-presidential parties, non-governmental organizations (NGOs) and trade unions. As part of a government reorganization in mid-May 2009, ministers from the ANDP, which opposed a referendum, were notably replaced. Later that month, after the Constitutional Court ruled that a referendum on his retention of power would be illegal, the President dissolved the Assemblée nationale. In early June Tandja created a committee to draft a new constitution (of what was to be designated the Sixth Republic) that would enable him to remain in office for a transitional period of three years if endorsed at a national referendum (subsequently scheduled for 4 August). However, in mid-June the Constitutional Court annulled the decree on the organization of the referendum. Two days later thousands of protesters attended a demonstration in Niamey against Tandja's plan for a referendum. The CENI subsequently declared that legislative elections would take place on 20 August, while allies of Amadou announced the formation of a new political party, the Mouvement Démocratique Nigérien (Moden), and the CDS withdrew its eight ministers from the Government, stating that it could not be associated with a project deemed illegal by the Constitutional Court. The CDS and some 10 other parties later formed a coalition, the Mouvement pour la Défense de la Démocratie et la République (MDDR), under the leadership of Ousmane, with the stated aim of defending the Constitution and democracy.

Following the Constitutional Court's refusal to review its decision regarding the referendum, in late June 2009 Tandja assumed emergency powers to rule by decree (claiming that Niger's independence was under threat), dissolved the Court and suspended the Constitution. Opposition leaders accused Tandja of staging a coup and trade unions called a one-day general strike in protest, which was only partially observed. Amid mounting international concern, in early July the European Commission threatened to suspend aid to Niger; ECOWAS had also earlier threatened economic and diplomatic sanctions, while other international donors and organizations, including the UN, France and the USA, urged the Nigerien Government to respect the constitutional order. Undeterred, Tandja appointed members to a new Constitutional Court and again decreed that a constitutional referendum would be held on 4 August. In mid-July the European Commission postponed the payment of budgetary assistance to Niger. Later in July a joint delegation of the UN, the African Union (AU) and ECOWAS visited Niamey in an effort to resolve the political crisis, but the President remained defiant in his determination to proceed with the referendum, which was held, as scheduled, on 4 August. According to the CENI, 92.5% of those who participated in the vote (68.3% of the electorate) were in favour of the new Constitution, which, in addition to prolonging Tandja's mandate by three years, provided for the removal of the limit on presidential terms, the significant expansion of the powers of the President and the creation of a Senate. The results, particularly the turn-out, were disputed by the Coordination des Forces pour la Démocratie et la République (CFDR)—an alliance formed in July by the MDDR, the Front de Défense de la Démocratie (led by Mahamadou Issoufou of the PNDS), the civil society organization Front pour la République et la Démocratie and seven trade union federations—which had urged voters to boycott the referendum.

THE SIXTH REPUBLIC

The Constitution of the Sixth Republic entered into force on 18 August 2009. On the following day Oumarou's Government was reappointed, and it was announced that legislative elections would be held on 20 October. Several former deputies were arrested in early September on suspicion of embezzling public funds. The CFDR demanded the release of its members, claiming that the investigation that had led to their detention had been conducted on Tandja's orders and had deliberately targeted deputies who were seeking the reinstatement of the Assemblée nationale. Oumarou and two other ministers resigned later that month in order to contest the forthcoming elections. Ali Badjo Gamatié, hitherto Deputy Governor of the BCEAO, was appointed as Prime Minister on 2 October.

The main opposition parties boycotted the elections to the Assemblée nationale, which took place, as scheduled, on 20 October 2009, despite a demand for an indefinite postponement issued three days earlier by ECOWAS leaders at a special summit held in Abuja, Nigeria. According to results released by the CENI on 24 October and endorsed by the Constitutional Court in November, the MNSD—Nassara secured 76 of the 113 seats, while the Rassemblement Social-démocratique—Gaskiya (which had been formed following a split in the CDS) won 15 seats, independent candidates 11 and the RDP seven. A turn-out of 51.3% was recorded. On the day after the election ECOWAS suspended Niger from membership of the organization pending a restoration of constitutional order, and in November the European Union (EU) suspended development aid to the country.

Tens of thousands of protesters attended a demonstration organized by the CFDR in mid-December 2009 in support of demands that Tandja should step down from office by 22 December, when his presidential mandate would have ended under the previous Constitution. On 23 December the US State Department announced the suspension of non-humanitarian assistance to Niger and the imposition of travel restrictions on members and supporters of Tandja's regime. Meanwhile, talks between the Government and the opposition commenced in Niamey, mediated by former Nigerian President Abdulsalami Abubakar under the aegis of ECOWAS. In January 2010 Abubakar proposed a plan to resolve the political crisis, which provided for Tandja to retain power for a transitional period and the formation of a 'government of national reconciliation'. However, government and opposition representatives failed to reach agreement on the plan, and the negotiations were abandoned in mid-February. Some 10,000 people subsequently participated in an anti-Government demonstration in Niamey.

TANDJA OUSTED

On 18 February 2010 members of the armed forces seized power, capturing President Tandja and his government ministers during an attack on the presidential palace in which some 10 people were killed. Citing the need to resolve Niger's 'tense political situation' as their motivation for ousting Tandja's administration, the coup leaders formed a Conseil Suprême pour la Restauration de la Démocratie (CSRD), headed by Squadron Commdr Salou Djibo, and announced the suspension of the Constitution and the dissolution of all state institutions. The CSRD pledged to engage in dialogue with the main political and civil organizations, prior to drafting a new constitution and holding national elections at the end of a transitional period, the length of which was still to be determined. The coup was generally condemned internationally, with the AU suspending Niger's membership of the organization, but the CFDR declared its support for the CSRD, organizing a well attended rally in Niamey to demonstrate this. On 22 February Djibo was officially designated as Head of State and Head of Government, and on the following day Mahamadou Danda was appointed as acting Prime Minister. Hitherto a political adviser at the Canadian embassy in Niamey, Danda was not affiliated to any political party and had served in Wanké's transitional administration after the April 1999 coup. On 2 March Djibo announced the formation of a 20-member interim Council of Ministers, largely comprising civilian technocrats who were regarded as being politically neutral or had been resident abroad, as well as five military officers. It was decreed that members of the CSRD and the transitional Government would be barred from contesting elections. Also in March, Djibo appointed military officers to replace civilian regional governors who had been dismissed following the coup, and installed a 131-member advisory council for the transitional period, the Conseil Consultatif National, chaired by civil society activist Marou Amadou. In late March Oumarou and 13 other former ministers and officials loyal to Tandja (who remained in detention in the presidential buildings in Niamey) were arrested and accused of involvement in 'subversive activities' aimed at undermining the transitional process; they were released several days later.

In April 2010 Djibo appointed a 16-member committee to draft a new constitution, electoral law and charter governing political parties. In May, in an announcement that was welcomed by ECOWAS, the CSRD confirmed that the transition to civilian rule would be completed by 18 February 2011, following a constitutional referendum and local, legislative and presidential elections. A new CENI was inaugurated in June 2010, under the chairmanship of a judge, Abdourahmane Ghousmane. On 3 July Ghousmane announced that a constitutional referendum would take place on 31 October, followed by local elections on 27 November, and legislative elections and the first round of the presidential election on 3 January 2011. On the same day ECOWAS decided to permit Niger to attend meetings of the organization as an observer. In early August 2010 Oumarou and three others were charged with embezzlement of public funds. One week later, despite the charges against him, the former Prime Minister was selected as the MNSD—Nassara's presidential candidate following a party congress. The CENI announced a revised electoral timetable in September, delaying the polls owing to organizational and financial difficulties. The local elections were to be held on 8 January 2011, the legislative elections and the first round of the presidential ballot on 31 January, and a second round of presidential voting on 12 March. Meanwhile, in late September 2010 the Council of the EU approved a proposal by the European Commission for a gradual resumption of development aid to Niger, conditional on continued progress towards the restoration of constitutional order in the country. Humanitarian assistance had been maintained throughout the political crisis, with €15m. having been allocated by the Commission in June to address severe food shortages.

Four senior army officers, including Col Abdoulaye Badié, Djibo's Permanent Secretary, were arrested in October 2010 on suspicion of involvement in a foiled plot to overthrow the transitional administration. In addition, Col Amadou Diallo, one of the few military officers in the Government, was dismissed as Minister of Equipment.

TRANSITION TO CIVILIAN RULE

The constitutional referendum was held, as scheduled, at the end of October 2010, despite the arrests earlier that month. The Constitution of the Seventh Republic, which provided for a five-year presidential term (renewable only once) and an amnesty for the perpetrators of February's coup, was approved by 90.2% of those who participated in the vote (some 52.7% of the electorate). Previously envisaged provisions setting an upper age limit for presidential candidates and requiring that they possess a university degree were notably excluded from the new charter, which was promulgated by Djibo in late November. In the following month Tandja's immunity from prosecution was withdrawn, and in January 2011 the former President was moved from house arrest to prison, after being formally charged with corruption. Municipal and regional elections took place on 11 January, having been postponed for three days owing to logistical problems.

Observation missions from the AU, the EU and ECOWAS praised the overall conduct of the legislative and presidential elections held on 31 January 2011, at which respective turn-outs of 51.6% and 49.2% were recorded. Of the Assemblée nationale's 113 seats, the PNDS secured 39, while the MNSD—Nassara won 26 and Moden 24; five other parties also gained representation. Four of the 10 presidential candidates attracted more than 5% of the votes cast: PNDS leader Issoufou, with 36.2%, Oumarou, with 23.2%, former Prime Minister Amadou, with 19.8%, and former President Ousmane, with 8.3%. At the second round of the presidential ballot, on 12 March, Issoufou defeated Oumarou, securing 57.9% of the votes cast. Amadou and four other unsuccessful candidates from the first round had declared their support for Issoufou, although Ousmane had notably backed Oumarou. A participation rate of some 49.0% was recorded. In March both the AU and ECOWAS lifted Niger's suspension from membership of those organizations. Issoufou was sworn in as President on 7 April 2011, marking a return to civilian rule.

ISSOUFOU'S PRESIDENCY

Following his inauguration, President Issoufou immediately appointed as Prime Minister Brigi Rafini, a Tuareg and a member of the RDP (which had supported Issoufou's candidacy in the run-off vote), who had served as a government minister during Maïnassara's presidency. The 24-member Council of Ministers, formed later in April 2011, was largely composed of members of the PNDS and other parties that had supported Issoufou in the second round of the election, which together held a comfortable legislative majority; Oumarou declined an invitation to join the Government. Three senior ministers were appointed: Bazoum Mohamed, the Vice-President of the

PNDS, as Minister of State, Minister of Foreign Affairs, African Integration and Nigeriens Abroad; former Prime Minister Cissé, the President of the Union pour la Démocratie et la République—Tabbat, as Minister of State, Minister of Planning, Land Settlement and Community Development; and Abdou Labo, a dissident member of the CDS, as Minister of State, Minister of the Interior, Public Security, Decentralization and Religious Affairs. Priorities identified by President Issoufou for the Government included the modernization of the agricultural and livestock sectors and an increase in expenditure on education, which was to be provided free of charge up to the age of 16 years. Meanwhile, Amadou was elected as President of the Assemblée nationale.

Former President Tandja was released from prison in May 2011, after the Court of Appeal in Niamey quashed the charges against him. Later that month the Assemblée nationale approved legislation according an amnesty to those responsible for ousting Tandja from office in February 2010, as envisaged in the Constitution. The EU confirmed the full resumption of development co-operation with Niger in June 2011, with the European Commission releasing a payment of €25m. in July and further funds being granted in November.

Three senior finance officials, all of whom had been appointed by the CSRD, were dismissed in June 2011, after it was discovered that some 1,500m. francs CFA of public funds had been misappropriated. In August President Issoufou confirmed reports that an attempted coup had been foiled in the previous month, stating that 10 people had been arrested on suspicion of involvement. Issoufou also pledged to curb corruption—appearing to link the coup plot to his Government's recent action against embezzlement—and announced plans to create a state authority for this purpose. Meanwhile, the PNDS, Moden and the ANDP were among some 30 political parties (holding a total of 84 of the Assemblée nationale's 113 seats) that formed an alliance in support of the President, the Mouvance pour la Renaissance du Niger. A minor reorganization of the Council of Ministers was effected in September, mainly in anticipation of production commencing at an oilfield in Agadem, in the Diffa region, and a refinery near Zinder: notably, Foumakoye Gado, hitherto Minister of Mines and Energy, was appointed as Minister of Petroleum and Energy, while Omar Hamidou Tchiana joined the Government as Minister of State, Minister of Mines and Industrial Development. Six senior security officials, including the heads of the police, domestic intelligence and security services, were dismissed in December, following the deaths of two people in clashes between demonstrators and police in Zinder. The disturbances had been prompted by the trial of an opposition politician, Aboubacar Mahamadou, who was accused (and later acquitted) of preparing protests against President Issoufou, who had visited the town in late November to open the oil refinery.

In early April 2012 the Assemblée nationale voted to revoke the immunity from prosecution of eight opposition deputies who were accused of embezzling public funds during Tanja's presidency. Meanwhile, Issoufou implemented government changes affecting three ministries. The Minister of Finance, Ouhoumoudou Mahamadou, and the Minister of Equipment, Kalla Hankoraou, were dismissed after the Constitutional Court ruled that they had violated the Constitution by awarding a government contract to a member of the Assemblée nationale; they were replaced by Jules Bayé and Sadi Soumaïla, respectively, and Ibrahim Yacouba suceeded Salami Maïmouna as Minister of Transport. Shortly afterwards the legislature rejected a motion of censure in the Council of Ministers proposed by the opposition, only 29 deputies voting against the Government.

ETHNIC CONFLICT

As in neighbouring Mali, ethnic unrest was precipitated by the return to Niger, beginning in the late 1980s, of large numbers of Tuareg nomads, who had migrated to Libya and Algeria earlier in the decade to escape the drought. In May 1985, following an armed incident near the Niger–Libya border, all non-Nigerien Tuaregs were expelled from the country. In May 1990 Tuaregs launched a violent attack on the prison and gendarmerie at Tchin-Tabaraden, in north-eastern Niger. The alleged brutality of the armed forces in quelling the raid provoked considerable disquiet. In April 1991 44 Tuaregs were acquitted of involvement in the attack on Tchin-Tabaraden. Rebels mounted a renewed offensive in October, and in the months that followed numerous violent attacks were directed at official targets in the north, and clashes took place between Tuareg rebels and the security forces. In early 1992 the transitional Government intensified security measures in northern Niger, formally recognizing, for the first time, that there was a rebellion in that area and acknowledging the existence of a Tuareg movement, the Front de Libération de l'Aïr et l'Azaouad (FLAA). The leader of the FLAA, Rhissa Ag Boula, stated that the Tuareg rebels were seeking the establishment of a federal system, in which each ethnic group would have its own administrative entity.

A two-week truce, agreed in May 1992 by the Government and FLAA, failed. Tuareg attacks subsequently resumed, precipitating a major offensive, in August, against the rebellion. Some 186 Tuaregs were arrested, according to official figures, by September. Military authority was intensified by the appointment, in October, of senior members of the security forces to northern administrative posts. In November a commission appointed by the transitional Government to consider the Tuareg issue recommended a far-reaching programme of decentralization, according legal status and financial autonomy to local communities. In January 1993 five people were killed in a Tuareg attack on an MNSD—Nassara meeting in the northern town of Abala. Although he escaped injury, the principal target of the attack was said to have been Mamadou Tandja, who had been Minister of the Interior at the time of the suppression of the Tchin-Tabaraden raid. Although Tuareg attacks and acts of sabotage persisted, later in January 81 Tuaregs were released from detention (57 others had been released in December 1992), and a Minister of State for National Reconciliation, whose main responsibility would be to seek a resolution of the dispute, was appointed to the Government. In February 1993 30 people were reported to have been killed in raids by Tuaregs (for which the FLAA denied responsibility) around Tchin-Tabaraden.

The Ousmane administration identified the resolution of the Tuareg dispute as a major priority, and, in June 1993 a formal, three-month truce agreement, providing for the demilitarization of the north and envisaging negotiations on the Tuaregs' political demands, was signed in Paris, France. Financial assistance was promised to facilitate the return of Tuareg refugees from Algeria, and for the development of northern areas. However, a new Tuareg group, the Armée Révolutionnaire de Libération du Nord-Niger (ARLN), emerged to denounce the accord, and by July a further split was evident between supporters of the truce (led by Mano Dayak, the Tuareg signatory to the agreement), who broke away from the FLAA to form the Front de libération de Tamoust (FLT), and its opponents (led by Ag Boula), who stated that they could not support any agreement that contained no specific commitment to discussion of federalism. In September the FLT and the Government agreed to extend the truce for a further three months. Although the FLAA and the ARLN refused to sign the accord, in October they joined the FLT in a Coordination de la Résistance Armée (CRA), with the aim of presenting a cohesive programme in future negotiations.

There was an escalation of violence during May 1994, with as many as 40 deaths recorded. Negotiations reopened in Paris in June, but there was renewed unrest in August and September, including attempts by Tuaregs to disrupt power supplies to uranium mines. A grenade attack on a meeting in Agadez of the mainly Tuareg Union pour la Démocratie et le Progrès Social—Amana (UDPS), which Tuareg groups attributed to government forces, resulted in six deaths. At a meeting in Ouagadougou, Burkina Faso, in September, none the less, the CRA presented Nigerien government negotiators with what it termed a 'comprehensive and final' plan for a restoration of peace. A new peace accord was signed on 9 October, which, while emphasizing that Niger was 'unitary and indivisible', proposed the establishment of elected assemblies or councils for territorial communities, to which would be delegated responsibility for the implementation of economic, social and cultural policies. The Government was to take immediate measures to ensure the rehabilitation and security of areas affected by the conflict. Provisions were also to be made to facilitate the return and resettlement of refugees. A renewable three-month truce was to take immediate effect, to be monitored by French and Burkinabè military units. By the time of the conclusion of the Ouagadougou agreement the number of deaths since the escalation of the Tuareg rebellion in late 1991 was officially put at 150.

In January 1995 a commission was established to consider the administrative reorganization of the country. Shortly afterwards representatives of the Nigerien Government, the CRA, Algeria, Burkina Faso and France agreed to a three-month renewal of the truce. Further talks were briefly delayed by a split in the Tuareg movement. Ag Boula, who in January had withdrawn from the CRA (having repeatedly criticized Dayak's negotiating stance) and refused to participate in the decentralization committee, emerged as the leader of the Tuareg delegation (now renamed the Organisation de la Résistance Armée, ORA) in Ouagadougou. In April it was announced that a lasting peace agreement had been reached. The accord, which essentially confirmed the provisions of the October 1994 agreement, provided for the establishment of a special peace committee, to be overseen by representatives of the three mediating countries, whose task would be to ensure the practical implementation of the accord. Demobilized rebels were to be integrated into the Nigerien military and civil sectors, and special military units were to be accorded responsibility for the security of the northern regions; particular emphasis was to be placed on the development of the north, and the Government undertook to support the decentralization process. There was to be a general amnesty for all parties involved in the Tuareg rebellion and its suppression, and a day of national reconciliation was to be instituted in memory of the victims of the conflict. The peace agreement, which envisaged the implementation of its provisions within a period of six months, was formally signed by Ag Boula and the Nigerien government negotiator, Mai Maigana, in Niamey on 24 April 1995. A cease-fire took effect the following day.

Meanwhile, there was increasing evidence in late 1994 and early 1995 of ethnic unrest in the Lake Chad region of south-east Niger, where several thousand (mainly Toubou) Chadian refugees had settled since the overthrow of President Hissène Habré in late 1990. Clashes between settled Toubous and nomadic Peulh resulted in numerous deaths. The Front Démocratique du Renouveau (FDR), which emerged in October 1994 to demand increased autonomy for south-eastern regions, was believed to be responsible for many of the deaths.

Although the ORA expressed concern at the slow implementation of the April 1995 peace agreement, its provisions were gradually enacted: the Comité Spécial de la Paix (CSP) was inaugurated in May and a military observer group, comprising representatives of Burkina Faso and France, was deployed in the north in July. The amnesty decree was signed by Hama Amadou in July, and all Tuareg prisoners were reported to have been released shortly afterwards. The peace process was undermined following a clash in the north between Tuaregs and an Arab militia unit, as a result of which a Tuareg leader and at least 12 others were killed. Moreover, there was evidence that Dayak and other Tuareg groups in a revived CRA were making common cause with the FDR in demanding autonomy for their regions. Talks between representatives of the Tuareg movements and the FDR, which took place in northern Niger in September–October, failed either to reunite the CRA and the ORA, or to establish the principle of the FDR's adherence to the April peace accord. In October clashes in the north-east involving rebel Tuaregs and the armed forces were attributed to elements of the CRA. Dayak subsequently stated that the CRA would not join the peace process until the authorities and the ORA recognized all groups within the CRA. In December Dayak was killed in an air crash. In January 1996 the new leader of the FLT (and acting leader of the CRA), Mohamed Akotai, indicated that his movement favoured inter-Tuareg reconciliation and a dialogue with the Government.

Following the coup of January 1996, the CSN quickly expressed its commitment to the peace process. In March agreements were signed by the Nigerien authorities, the office of the UN High Commissioner for Refugees (UNHCR) and the Governments of Algeria and Burkina Faso regarding the repatriation of Tuareg refugees. Shortly afterwards the CRA, including the FDR, affirmed its recognition of the April 1995 agreement, and in April 1996 the Government and the CRA signed an agreement formalizing the latter's adherence to the 1995 accord. In May 1996 the ORA and the CRA agreed to establish a joint committee to co-ordinate their activities and represent their interests in negotiations with the authorities.

In July 1996 preliminary agreement was reached between the CSP and the resistance movements regarding the integration of demobilized fighters into regular military and civilian sectors. In September joint peace-keeping patrols of the Nigerien armed forces and former rebels were inaugurated in the north. In late September, however, Ag Boula, denouncing the inadequacy of arrangements for the reintegration of demobilized fighters, announced that the ORA was no longer bound by the peace treaty. The authorities asserted that this abandonment of the 1995 accord was linked primarily to the arrest of ORA members in connection with the diversion, some months previously, of a large consignment of cigarettes bound for the north. In an apparent gesture of reconciliation, however, the detainees were released at the end of October 1996 and the ORA surrendered the consignment to the authorities. In November it was reported that a new group had emerged from among the ORA and the CRA; led by Mohamed Anako, the Union des Forces de la Résistance Armée (UFRA) affirmed its commitment to the peace accord. A meeting between the High Commissioner for the Restoration of Peace and 10 of the reported 12 resistance groups was followed in December by the signing of a protocol for the encampment of some 5,900 former fighters, prior to their disarmament and reintegration into regular armed forces and civilian structures. The ORA, however, remained excluded from this process.

Following a meeting in Niamey between Maïnassara and Ag Boula in January 1997, and assurances regarding the implementation of provisions of the 1995 accord, the ORA declared its renewed support; it was announced, moreover, that the FLAA and FLT would establish a joint patrol aimed at combating insecurity and banditry. In February 1997 the UFRA joined members of the regular armed forces, the CRA and the Comité de Vigilance de Tassara (CVT) in a peace-keeping patrol in Agadez. In April Maïnassara signed a decree establishing a commission to oversee the process of encampment and reintegration of former fighters.

Insecurity persisted in early 1997, however, particularly in the east. In June it was announced that Toubous and Arabs of the Forces Armées Révolutionnaires du Sahara (FARS) had, following negotiations in Chad, agreed to join the peace process. It was reported that large numbers of armed Toubous had fled to north-eastern Nigeria following the defeat of the FARS. In July the FDR announced its withdrawal from the peace process, stating that Nigerien and Chadian military units had attacked one of its bases in the Lake Chad region, although the Nigerien authorities denied that any engagement had taken place.

A further meeting of the parties to the peace process took place in September 1997, at which agreement was reached on several areas regarding the integration of former fighters into the armed and security forces. At this time, however, elements of the UFRA, apparently frustrated at the slow progress of the implementation of the peace process, had taken up arms again.

The conclusion of the disarmament process was officially celebrated in Tchin-Tabaraden in October 1997. The armed forces subsequently undertook an offensive against positions held by dissident fronts. In November, following two weeks of talks, a peace accord, incorporating an immediate cease-fire, was signed in Algeria between the Nigerien Government, the UFRA and the FARS. In March 1998 the ORA and CRA surrendered their weapons stocks at Agadez. The handover of armaments was attended by Ag Boula (who had been appointed Minister-delegate responsible for Tourism in the Government named in late 1997) and, on behalf of the CRA, Mohamed Akotai. Voluntary repatriations of Nigerien refugees from Algeria, under the supervision of UNHCR and the Algerian Red Crescent, began in March 1998.

In April 1998 Maiyaki chaired a meeting in Niamey of the peace monitoring and implementation committee, now charged with overseeing the implementation of the April 1995 peace agreement and what was termed the November 1997 Algiers addendum protocol. In June 1998 it was reported that the last units of the UFRA had disarmed at a ceremony near Agadez. Negotiations in Chad resulted in the signing of a peace agreement in August by the Government of Niger and the FDR.

Following the death of President Maïnassara, in April 1999, the military CRN gave assurances that the peace process would be continued. Ag Boula was promoted to the rank of minister in the transitional Government, while Mohamed Anako was appointed as special adviser to Wanké. Ag Boula retained his post in the new Government of Hama Amadou, formed in January 2000. In June the final groups of fighters from the UFRA and other resistance movements participating in the peace process were disarmed near Agadez, prior to their intended integration into the national forces. In September more than 1,200 guns, surrendered by the disarmed factions, were ceremoniously burned in Agadez. At the ceremony, Anako announced the dissolution of several of the rebel groups and militias. In September 2001 Chahayi Barkaye, the leader of the FARS, the only ethnic rebel group to have refused disarmament, was killed in heavy fighting with Nigerien soldiers near the Libyan border.

Ag Boula retained his ministerial post until February 2004, when he was dismissed and charged with complicity in the murder of an MNSD—Nassara activist; in order to maintain Tuareg representation in the Government, Anako was appointed as a Minister-delegate at the Ministry of the Economy and Finance. In June concerns emerged of a renewed rebellion in northern Niger, following reports of attacks on vehicles in the region, the desertion of former Tuareg rebels who had been integrated into the national security forces and the declaration by some former combatants that they had reconstituted the FLAA and planned to resume hostilities. The UN imposed restrictions on the movements of its staff in the area in response to increasing insecurity, although the Minister of the Interior and Decentralization dismissed suggestions that a Tuareg rebellion had recommenced and rejected reports of mass desertions of former Tuareg rebels from the army. None the less, in mid-August armed men attacked three buses on the Agadez–Arlit road, killing three passengers, and in October five people died in clashes in northern Niger between government forces and apparent Tuareg rebels, who also took four soldiers hostage. Mohamed Ag Boula, the brother of Rhissa Ag Boula, claimed responsibility for the attacks, stating that he was leading an insurgent force of 200 Tuareg, Toubou and Semori nomads, who were seeking the full implementation of the 1995 peace agreement and the release of all former rebels. However, the Government insisted that the perpetrators were not rebels, describing them rather as bandits. The four soldiers were freed in January 2005, following Libyan mediation. In March Rhissa Ag Boula was released from prison, where he had been awaiting trial. The authorities reportedly denied Ag Boula's release was linked to that of the hostages, although Mohamed Ag Boula had previously refused to free the kidnapped soldiers while his brother remained in detention. According to reports, in July Mohamed Ag Boula surrendered weapons to the Libyan leader, Col Muammar al-Qaddafi, and around 500 former combatants of the FLAA joined the Libyan army; however, Libya denied having enlisted the former rebels. In August Rhissa Ag Boula was elected Chairman of the UDPS. An economic assistance programme for more than 3,000 former Tuareg rebels was launched in northern Niger in October.

There was evidence of continued activity by ethnic rebel groups in Niger in 2006, which escalated in 2007–08. The Toubou-dominated FARS claimed responsibility for the kidnapping of more than 20 foreign tourists in south-east Niger in August 2006. Most of the tourists were released shortly afterwards, but two were held hostage until October, when they were finally freed following Libyan mediation. A new Tuareg militia group, the Mouvement des Nigériens pour la Justice (MNJ), emerged in February 2007, when it claimed responsibility for an attack on an army base near Iférouane, some 1,000 km north of Niamey, in which three soldiers were killed and two kidnapped. As with previous incidents, the Government sought to minimize the significance of the attack, blaming it on bandits rather than rebels. It was reported that the MNJ, led by Aghali Alambo, was demanding an increased role for Tuaregs in Niger's institutions and in the mining sector and a more equitable distribution of revenue from mineral resources. Meanwhile, the FARS was reported to have demanded the expulsion of a group of Chinese petroleum prospectors from the north-east of the country. In April a security guard at a uranium exploration site owned by the French company AREVA was killed in an attack by heavily armed men claiming to belong to the MNJ.

Insecurity in northern Niger intensified in mid-2007. After mounting a largely unsuccessful raid on the airport in Agadez, the MNJ attacked a military base in Tazerzait in June, claiming to have killed 15 government soldiers and captured 72 others. Meanwhile, President Tandja refused to recognize the MNJ as a rebel group, continuing to attribute the growing unrest in the north to acts of banditry perpetrated by arms- and drugs-traffickers. In late June the Government dispatched additional troops to northern Niger, while political parties, human rights groups and former Tuareg rebels urged Tandja to negotiate with the MNJ. In July the Nigerien Government expelled AREVA's head of operations in Niger, amid accusations (strongly denied by both AREVA and the French Government) that the company had provided support to the MNJ in a bid to discourage potential competitors. (Relations between AREVA and the Nigerien Government subsequently improved, leading to a renewal of their partnership in uranium mining.)

Following a further deterioration in the security situation in the north, with the deaths of 11 soldiers and gendarmes in three landmine explosions and of two civilians during an apparent attack on a fuel depot in Agadez, in late August 2007 Tandja declared a three-month state of emergency in the region, granting the security forces additional powers of detention. (As the conflict continued, the state of emergency was regularly extended.) Two civilians were killed in early September 2007 when their vehicle hit a landmine near Iférouane; the MNJ and the army each accused the other of planting mines. A few days later the MNJ took six soldiers hostage during an attack on a military post in Adharous, some 80 km north of Agadez. However, a further 14 of those captured in June were released in September, again following Libyan mediation.

Press freedom groups expressed concern at restrictions imposed on the media in relation to coverage of the Tuareg unrest in September 2007, while it was reported that 10 civilians (said to be critics of the Government's policy of not negotiating with the MNJ) had been detained since the imposition of the state of emergency. Clashes between the MNJ and government troops continued, with the MNJ claiming to have killed more than 30 soldiers in October and November. In mid-December the Ministry of National Defence announced that seven civilians had been accidentally killed by government forces fighting MNJ rebels in Tiguidit, some 80 km south-east of Agadez, although the MNJ denied that any such confrontation had occurred. Two human rights organizations, Amnesty International and Human Rights Watch, alleged that both the army and the MNJ were committing abuses against civilians, accusing the former of extrajudicial killings and the latter of laying landmines indiscriminately. It was reported that residents of Iférouane had fled the town en masse owing to the ongoing insecurity. The deaths of three civilians in landmine explosions in the southern towns of Maradi, Tahoua and Niamey in December and in January 2008 prompted fears that the conflict was spreading. Later in January the MNJ attacked the town of Tânout (some 150 km north of Zinder), killing at least three soldiers and abducting the town's prefect and four soldiers. In March Libyan officials secured the release of 25 hostages being held by the MNJ. Fighting persisted none the less: the MNJ claimed later that month to have killed three members of the security forces in a raid on a military post in Bani-Bangou in the south-west of Niger and 15 soldiers in the northern region of Tidène, while the armed forces announced that 10 rebels had died in army operations targeting hideouts in the Aïr mountains (although the MNJ asserted that the dead were all civilians).

The MNJ expanded its activities to the south-eastern region of Diffa in early April 2008, joining forces with Toubou insurgents in clashes with a tripartite border force involving troops from Niger, Nigeria and Chad. Later that month the FARS stated that it had killed seven government troops during further skirmishes in Diffa. Claims by the MNJ in early May that it had killed five soldiers and shot down a military reconnaissance plane near the northern town of Gougaram were rejected by the Government. Later that month the army launched a major offensive against the MNJ in Iférouane, in which 11 rebels and five soldiers died, according to official figures (disputed by the MNJ). Internal divisions within the MNJ led to the formation at the end of May of a breakaway group, the Front des Forces de Redressement (FFR), led by Mohamed Aoutchiki Kriska (a leading member of the FLT in the 1990s); Rhissa Ag Boula, living in exile in France, was named as the FFR's Commissioner of War. In July Ag Boula was convicted *in absentia* of ordering the murder of an MNSD—Nassara activist in January 2004 and sentenced to death. Meanwhile, in late June 2008 the MNJ abducted four French employees of AREVA in northern Niger and held them captive for several days, stating that its intention was to demonstrate the Government's inability to fulfil a promise to protect foreign workers. Following the release of the French nationals, heavy fighting between the army and the MNJ around the northern town of Tazerzait reportedly resulted in significant casualties on both sides, including the death of Mohamed Acharif, a leading MNJ member.

In August 2008 the MNJ refuted a government claim that it had agreed to a cease-fire following talks with Qaddafi, but declared its willingness to engage in discussions with the Government if they were conducted outside Niger. Later that month the FARS ended its rebellion, although a ceremony to mark this decision, at which hundreds of weapons were surrendered to the authorities, was overshadowed by the explosion of an anti-tank mine, which killed one person and injured 40 more. After several weeks of relative peace, hostilities resumed in October, when the MNJ attacked government troops at Eroug, near Gougaram, causing a number of fatalities. In December a claim, attributed to Ag Boula, that the FFR was responsible for the abduction of the UN Secretary-General's special envoy to Niger, Robert Fowler, and two others (see Foreign Relations, below) was swiftly denied by Mohamed Aoutchiki Kriska.

Hopes for an end to the Tuareg rebellion were raised during 2009. In March the Front Patriotique du Niger (FPN), which had been formed following a split in the MNJ, requested Libyan mediation to initiate peace negotiations with the Government. During a visit to Niamey in mid-March, Qaddafi appealed to all Tuareg rebel groups to lay down their arms and engage in a peace process, and handed over six hostages, previously held by the MNJ, whose freedom he had secured. After two days of Libyan-sponsored talks held in early April, delegates from the Nigerien Government (headed by the Minister of State, Minister of the Interior, Public Security and Decentralization, Albadé Abouba), the MNJ, the FPN and the FFR reportedly committed themselves to restoring peace in the north. President Tandja held talks with representatives of the three Tuareg groups for the first time in early May in Agadez, offering an amnesty if the rebels disarmed; shortly beforehand the MNJ announced the release of the last remaining hostage. The softening of Tandja's previously hardline stance towards the rebels was linked by some observers to the economic importance attached to AREVA's development of a uranium mine (expected to become the second largest in the world) at Imouraren, in the Agadez region, construction of which was about to commence. In mid-May the MNJ and the FPN were reported to have agreed to a cease-fire during discussions with Prime Minister Oumarou, which were, however, boycotted by the FFR. In early October, in response to Tandja's offer of amnesty, around 1,000 FPN rebels reportedly surrendered their weapons in northern Niger, as did members of the MNJ at a symbolic ceremony in southern Libya attended by Qaddafi and Alambo. However, there was continued evidence of divisions within the MNJ—notably a statement posted on the MNJ's website in September announcing the removal of Alambo as its leader, citing his continued presence in Libya and failure to consult the movement's other leaders—with some members seemingly unwilling to lay down their weapons. None the less, in November the repatriation of some 800 former MNJ militants from Libya to Niger commenced and the state of emergency in Agadez was revoked. An official MNJ disarmament ceremony took place near Arlit in January 2010, with the MNJ stating that 3,000 of its members had renounced the armed struggle. It was reported that the FFR had also agreed to surrender. The leaders of the main Tuareg movements returned to Niamey after Tandja was overthrown in February to seek involvement in the transitional process and to apply pressure on the new military authorities to accelerate the reintegration of former rebels. Ag Boula was arrested in the capital in March in connection with his 2008 conviction. However, the charges against him were dismissed in late 2010, and in September 2011 he was appointed as a special adviser to President Issoufou. In March 2012 Alambo, who had been accorded the role of special adviser to Hama Amadou, the President of the Assemblée nationale, was arrested on suspicion of involvement in smuggling arms and explosives from Libya.

The return to Niger and Mali of former Tuareg rebels who had settled in Libya, where they had recently fought in support of forces loyal to the Qaddafi regime, prompted fears of renewed instability during the second half of 2011. After these fears were realized in northern Mali in January 2012, Issoufou expressed concern that the renewed Tuareg insurgency in that country would spread to Niger, voicing strong support in mid-2012 for AU and ECOWAS efforts to secure the approval of the UN Security Council for a proposed regional military intervention in Mali (where a coup had additionally taken place in March). Furthermore, by early August more than 260,000 Malians had fled the unrest into neighbouring countries, with some 55,000 having entered Niger, which was already suffering severe food shortages following an extremely poor harvest in 2011.

FOREIGN RELATIONS AND REGIONAL SECURITY CONCERNS

Relations with the USA, which had deteriorated markedly following the 1996 presidential election and the death of Maïnassara in early 1999, appeared to improve after the reinstallation of an elected Government in January 2000, and in March the USA announced an end to the sanctions imposed after Maïnassara's death. In January 2003 US President George W. Bush, during the annual State of the Union address, asserted that the Iraqi regime of Saddam Hussain had sought to obtain illicit supplies of uranium, for an alleged nuclear weapons programme, from an unnamed African state, which was subsequently revealed to be Niger. The Nigerien Government denied having provided any such assistance to the Iraqi authorities, and in June the US Assistant to the President for National Security Affairs, Condoleezza Rice, stated that the evidence for Nigerien association with the regime of Saddam Hussain lacked credibility. In July an Italian newspaper, *La Repubblica*, published facsimiles of the documents that had apparently provided the basis for the allegations made in the State of the Union address; these documents, which contained several flaws and inaccuracies, were widely considered to be forgeries by this time. The USA, together with several other donor countries and international organizations, was critical of President Tandja's attempt to extend his mandate in mid-2009 (see above). In December, as Tandja remained in office, the USA suspended non-humanitarian assistance to Niger. Bilateral assistance was resumed fully in mid-2011, following the return to civilian rule in Niger.

Niger's relations with Libya were generally close during Tandja's presidency. In January 2000 Tandja undertook an official visit to Libya and held talks with Qaddafi. Qaddafi made a reciprocal visit to Agadez in July, where he pledged support for the peace process involving the Tuaregs. In October 2008 the Governments of Niger and Libya agreed to establish a joint committee of security officials to co-operate in combating organized crime, drugs-trafficking, illegal migration and terrorism; a bilateral agreement on securing the border against such activities was signed in April 2009. Niger received an influx of some 200,000 migrants fleeing Libya in 2011, following the outbreak of civil conflict in that country in February. The Nigerien Government confirmed in September that more than 30 Qaddafi loyalists, including one of his sons, Saadi Qaddafi, had been permitted to enter Niger from Libya on humanitarian grounds. In late August the Government had formally recognized the National Transitional Council (NTC) formed by the anti-Qaddafi forces as the 'only authority representing the Libyan people'. Saadi Qaddafi was placed under house arrest in Niger in February 2012, following the broadcast of a television interview in which he vowed to return to Libya and claimed that he was in contact with armed groups opposed to the NTC. During a visit to Libya in May, Prime Minister Brigi Rafini stated that the Nigerien authorities would consider a request from Libya for the extradition of Libyan supporters of the deposed Qaddafi regime who had taken refuge in Niger.

In May 2000 a long-term dispute between Niger and Benin regarding the ownership of a number of small islands along their common border at the Niger river escalated, reportedly following the sabotage of a Beninois administrative building on the island of Lété, apparently by Nigerien soldiers. A meeting between representatives of the two Governments failed to resolve the dispute, which was subsequently referred to the Organization of African Unity (now the AU) for arbitration. In April 2002 the two Governments ratified an agreement (signed in June 2001) to refer the issue of ownership of the islands to the International Court of Justice (ICJ) at The Hague, Netherlands. In July 2005 a five-member Chamber formed by the ICJ to consider the case issued its judgment on the delineation of the border between Benin and Niger, ruling that 16 of the 25 disputed islands, including Lété, belonged to Niger. Niger officially took ownership of Lété in February 2007, in a ceremony held on the island. In February 2009 the Governments of Niger and Burkina Faso signed an agreement on seeking arbitration by the ICJ over the demarcation of part of their common border; the dispute was jointly submitted to the Court in July 2010, with public hearings in the case due to be held in October 2012.

In June 2001 Niger and Nigeria announced that joint patrols of their common frontier would be instigated, in order to combat increasing cross-border crime and smuggling in the region. Further concerns regarding regional security were raised in early 2004, when Islamist militants belonging to the Algerian-based Groupe salafiste pour la prédication et le combat (GSPC) reportedly attacked a group of tourists in northern Niger. In March clashes between the militants and Chadian and Nigerien troops resulted in the deaths of some 43 GSPC fighters in northern Niger. It was reported in that month that the Governments of Algeria, Chad, Mali and Niger were to reinforce security co-operation in the regions of their common borders. A further four GSPC members were reportedly killed by Nigerien troops near the Malian border in April. In June the Nigerian police force announced that it had established a committee to co-ordinate joint border patrols with the security forces of Cameroon, Chad and Niger. In June 2005 Niger, Algeria, Chad, Mali and Nigeria were among nine North and West African countries that participated in US-led military exercises aimed at increasing co-operation in combating cross-border banditry and militancy in the region. At a meeting in March 2006 government officials from Mali and Niger agreed on the need to heighten security at their common border. In the following month Niger's Minister of the Interior and Decentralization, Moukaïla Modi, visited Algeria to attend a two-day session of the bilateral Algeria–Niger border committee, which had first met in January 2004. In June 2006 government ministers and officials responsible for security from Benin, Burkina Faso and Niger agreed to establish border patrols in an attempt to curb cross-border crime. Meanwhile, Islamist militants remained active in the region. The abduction of the UN Secretary-General's special envoy to Niger, Robert Fowler, his assistant and their driver about 40 km north-west of Niamey, near the border with Mali, in mid-December 2008 was followed in January 2009 by that of four European tourists, also in the border area. In February al-Qa'ida in the Islamic Maghreb (AQIM, as the GSPC had been restyled) claimed to be holding those kidnapped; the driver was released in March and the diplomats and two of the tourists in April, all in Mali, where they had been held, but a British and a Swiss tourist remained captive. The group was subsequently believed to have killed the British hostage after the United Kingdom rejected a demand for the release of a detained Jordanian Islamist, but released the Swiss national in July. Amid increasing concern regarding the activities of AQIM, in September military leaders from Algeria, Mali, Mauritania and Niger agreed on a plan for co-operation in combating terrorism and cross-border crime.

In April 2010, seeking to reinforce co-operation, Algeria, Mali, Mauritania and Niger established a joint military command headquarters in the southern Algerian town of Tamanrasset. At a summit earlier that month in Tamanrasset, army chiefs from the four countries had agreed to co-ordinate intelligence-gathering and patrols in border areas to combat terrorism, organized crime, arms-trafficking and kidnappings. Also in April, a French national and his Algerian driver were abducted in northern Niger, near the Algerian border, with AQIM later claiming responsibility; the driver was released later that month, but the French citizen was killed in Mauritania in July. Meanwhile, a US-led military training exercise involving several countries in the Sahel region, including Mali, Mauritania and Niger, was held in May. In mid-September seven foreigners (five French nationals, one Togolese and one Malagasy) were kidnapped near the northern Nigerien town of Arlit, before being transferred by their captors to Mali; AQIM claimed responsibility for the abductions. The French Government deployed 80 military personnel to Niamey to assist in the search for the hostages, who were employees of the French company AREVA and one of its contractors. At a meeting of army chiefs from Algeria, Mali, Mauritania and Niger, held in Tamanrasset in late September, it was agreed to establish a joint intelligence centre in Algiers to combat terrorism and organized crime. Niger also participated in a meeting of representatives of regional countries and members of the Group of Eight leading industrialized nations held in Bamako, Mali, in October, at which efforts against AQIM were discussed. In January 2011 two Frenchmen who had been seized in Niamey by suspected AQIM militants died when an operation mounted by Nigerien troops and French special forces to rescue them failed. Also that month the US Peace Corps, which had been operating in Niger since 1962, suspended its activities in the country and withdrew its volunteers as a result of security concerns. Three of the seven hostages abducted in September 2010 (the two Africans and a French woman) were released in February 2011.

Further meetings to discuss joint counter-terrorism efforts took place in Bamako between army chiefs from Algeria, Mali, Mauritania and Niger in April and between government ministers from the four countries in May. Meanwhile, Niger's Chief of General Staff of the Armed Forces and his Nigerian counterpart pledged to strengthen military co-operation in order to combat terrorism and banditry. Clashes between Nigerien troops and AQIM militants some 80 km north of Arlit resulted in the deaths of one soldier and one militant in June. The militants were reported to have entered Niger from Libya in vehicles containing large quantities of arms and explosives, prompting President Issoufou to express concern in the following month regarding the impact of the Libyan conflict on Niger's security and economy owing to the influx of weapons and the need to support Nigerien migrants returning from Libya (whose remittances had previously been an important source of income for their families in Niger). These concerns were reiterated at a conference on security held in Algiers in early September, amid fears that AQIM would gain access to weapons from Libya, and further explosives were seized later that month in a security operation in border area between Algeria and Niger. In mid-September one soldier and three AQIM fighters were killed in a clash in northern Niger. Government ministers from Algeria, Mali, Mauritania and Niger held talks in Washington, DC, USA, in November, meeting with several senior US officials, with the aim of advancing their aim to establish a regional counter-terrorism partnership. Meanwhile, at least 14 people were reportedly killed in a clash near the town of Assamaka, in northern Niger, between Nigerien troops and an armed group including Malian Tuaregs formerly allied to Qaddafi who were believed to be en route from Libya to Mali. In December the EU announced that it would provide €150m. in support of regional efforts aimed at increasing security. At a summit meeting held in Libya in March 2012, ministers responsible for the interior and defence from Algeria, Chad, Egypt, Libya, Mali, Mauritania, Morocco, Niger, Tunisia and Sudan adopted an action plan on regional co-operation and border control aimed at combating organized crime, drugs- and arms-trafficking, terrorism and illegal immigration; measures agreed included the exchange of security intelligence and increased joint border patrols.

The Government provoked controversy in October 2006 when it announced its intention to expel Mahamid Arabs from Niger and return them to Chad. The Mahamids, believed to number up to 150,000, had first crossed into Niger in large numbers in 1974 to escape severe drought conditions, and more had followed in the 1980s, fleeing conflict. Most had settled in the Diffa region, where the Government claimed they now posed a threat to security owing to their possession of firearms and poor relations with the local population. Amid protests from Chad and within Niger, most notably from legislative deputies of Arab origin, the Government insisted that only those without the correct documentation would be removed, estimating that at most 4,000 people would be affected, and subsequently suspended the expulsions altogether, stating that the Mahamids would instead be moved to regions where water and grazing land were more plentiful. However, this reversal of policy prompted demonstrations in Diffa by several thousand people opposed to the continued presence in Niger of the Mahamids.

The People's Republic of China has sought to develop strong economic relations with Niger in recent years, increasing bilateral trade and investing heavily in uranium mining. In June 2008 the China National Oil and Gas Exploration and Development Corpn signed an agreement with the Nigerien Government, reported to be worth US $5m. over a three-year period, on oil exploration and drilling rights in Agadem, in the Diffa region, and on the construction of a pipeline and refinery at Olléwa, near Zinder; the refinery was officially inaugurated in November 2011. In September 2008, during a six-day visit to China, Nigerien Prime Minister Oumarou held talks with his Chinese counterpart, Wen Jiabao, after which a bilateral agreement on economic and technological co-operation was signed.

Economy

VICTORIA HOLLIGAN

INTRODUCTION

The UN's Human Development Index (HDI), which takes into account life expectancy and conditions in health and education, has continuously ranked Niger close to last of all the countries surveyed; in the 2011 index, Niger was ranked 186th out of 187 countries, just below Burundi and above the Democratic Republic of the Congo. Poverty remains widespread, and, at only US $661 per head (according to estimates by the World Bank on a purchasing-power parity basis) in 2011, gross national income is among the lowest in the world. The country is greatly influenced by its economic relations with its southern neighbour, Nigeria, and substantial unrecorded trade, particularly the smuggling of fuel from Nigeria into Niger, flourishes across the 2,000-km border. The informal, or 'grey', economy is unusually large in Niger, and the World Bank estimates that it represents up to 70% of all economic activity. However, indicators for health and education have improved—evident through the fact that Niger's HDI has increased by 67% since 1980, as a function of life expectancy at birth increasing by 15 years and the mean years of schooling increasing by one year—and it was hoped that anticipated increases in petroleum and uranium production would further economic and social development. Niger's oil and mining exports were projected to triple between 2011 and 2016, boosting government revenue from natural resources. The provision, in 2007, of free access to health services for children under the age of five and pregnant women had a favourable impact on social and poverty indicators, with infant and maternal health coverage expanding. The rate of poverty declined from 62% of the population in 2005 to 59.5% in 2008, according to an IMF household survey.

The economy contracted in almost every year of the 1980s, owing to a combination of weakening earnings from uranium, drought and economic turmoil in neighbouring Nigeria. There was a long-term decline in international demand and prices for uranium, while the traditional rural economy remained subject to the vagaries of the Sahelian climate. It was hoped that the enhanced flows of aid and measures of debt relief that followed the devaluation of the CFA franc in January 1994 would help to achieve the objectives of the development programme for 1994–96. The targeted gross domestic product (GDP) growth of 4% in 1994 and of more than 5% annually thereafter were not met, with growth averaging 3.4% per year in 1994–96. The potentially very damaging boycott by aid donors after the military coup in January 1996 came to an end relatively rapidly: the signing of an Enhanced Structural Adjustment Facility (ESAF) agreement with the IMF in June was followed by pledges of funding from the World Bank, the African Development Bank (AfDB), the European Union (EU), France and Japan. The programme, supported by the ESAF, aimed to achieve average annual GDP growth of 4.5% in 1997–98. Economic performance was slightly below this level (at 3.4%) in 1997, but exceptional growth, of 10.4%, was recorded in 1998, following a recovery in agriculture. Meanwhile, the disposal of state assets accelerated, with the privatization of three state enterprises in 1998: the textiles company, Société Nigérienne des Textiles; the dairy, Office du Lait du Niger; and the cement plant, Société Nigérienne de Cimenterie.

In March 1999 a joint mission of the World Bank and IMF reported 'significant progress' in Niger's meeting of commitments under the ESAF (which was due to expire at the end of June), raising the prospect that another such facility would be accorded, and that Niger would be declared eligible for debt reduction under the initiative for heavily indebted poor countries (HIPC). This progress was jeopardized by the presumed assassination of President Ibrahim Baré Maïnassara in April 1999 and his replacement by another military head of state, Maj. Daouda Mallam Wanké. Niger's most important donors—France, the IMF and the World Bank, and the EU—all suspended aid, and GDP declined by 0.6% in 1999. The staging in October–November of that year of presidential and legislative elections that were deemed fair and transparent facilitated the resumption of aid in 2000. The new administration of President Mamadou Tandja committed itself to reinstating the programme of public sector reform and privatization, and was successful, in December 2000, in securing a Poverty Reduction and Growth Facility (PRGF—the successor to the ESAF) worth US $78m. for 2001–03. The programme had foreseen respective growth rates of 3.0% in 2000 and 3.7% in 2001. In the event, GDP declined by 1.4% in 2000, as a result of a drought in the second half of the year.

Improved agricultural production and sustained activity in construction and trade supported GDP growth of 3.0% in 2002 and 4.0% in 2003. Economic performance weakened in 2004, as a result of drought, a locust infestation and higher energy prices, and the rate of growth was reduced to 0.9%. In February 2005 the IMF approved a new three-year PRGF, worth US $10m., in view of the Government's overall strong policy performance. Following difficulties early in that year, when inflation surged as a result of the 2004 drought, growth for

2005 as a whole increased to 7.0%, with a good harvest recorded in the last quarter of the year. Growth in 2006 remained relatively strong, at 4.8%, while inflationary pressures decreased as a result of satisfactory harvests for the second consecutive year, but slowed to 3.2% in 2007, largely owing to a disappointing harvest. In 2008 GDP growth accelerated to 9.5%, bolstered by unprecedented levels of agricultural production, coupled with increased electricity production and robust performances by the telecommunications and transport sectors. According to the IMF, GDP increased at an average annual rate of 4.8% over the period 2000–08.

In June 2008 a new PRGF worth US $37.5m. was approved by the IMF. The PRGF was subsequently replaced by the Extended Credit Facility, and by early 2010 some $20m. had been disbursed by the Fund. After contracting by 0.9% in 2009, GDP grew by an estimated 8% in 2010 thanks to an abundant harvest, according to the IMF. The military coup that deposed President Mamadou Tandja and installed the self-designated Conseil Suprême pour la Restauration de la Démocratie in February 2010 had a negative impact on external donor financing. Yet, with the reintroduction of democratic rule in April 2011 and the election of Mahamadou Issoufou as President, relations with donors were expected to normalize. The new Government has pledged to further economic development and reduce corruption in the extractive industry sector, while improving security conditions. Niger's economy was estimated to have grown by 3.8% in 2011, with an expansion in the mining, trade and service industries offsetting the reduction in remittances from tens of thousands of Nigerian workers leaving war-torn Libya and the impact of a poor harvest. Yet economic prospects for 2012 were expected to improve materially with the start-up of the country's first oil project; the IMF forecast GDP growth to reach 14%. The rise in resource-related government revenues in the oil and uranium industries is expected to boost development spending in infrastructure, health and education, and thus to reduce poverty in the medium term.

THE TRADITIONAL ECONOMY

Although only a small proportion of Niger's land is capable of supporting settled farming, agriculture, livestock, forestry and fishing contribute just under 50% of GDP and employ an estimated 80% of the working population, according to FAO. The agriculture sector grew at an average annual rate of 5.3% in 1995–2006 and by 4% in 2007. In 2008 the sector expanded by some 25% owing to good rainfall; record harvests of millet, sorghum, wheat, rice, corn, fonoi and cow peas were recorded in that year. In 2009 the sector declined by 6.8% due to adverse weather conditions. Despite the bumper harvest of 2010, as a result of which the agriculture sector grew by an estimated 30% in real terms, food insecurity remains high, with 6m. Nigeriens being subject to severe food shortages in early 2012.

Principal staple products are millet, sorghum and cassava, all grown mainly for household consumption. Rice is also produced, on the small area that is under modern irrigation, while cow peas, cotton, groundnuts and onions are the principal cash crops. Cereal output rose to a new record of 3.3m. metric tons in 2002, before declining slightly, to 3.1m. tons, in 2003; the harvests in both years reflected improved climatic conditions. A food crisis emerged in 2004–05, as a result of drought and a locust invasion. Commercial purchases and food aid totalled 454,600 tons of cereals for the 2004/05 marketing year, with both the Government and the UN World Food Programme appealing for food aid. Production consequently recovered from 2.7m. tons in 2004 to 3.7m. tons in 2005. In 2006 cereal production was officially estimated at 4.0m. tons, creating a cereal surplus in the country of over 450,000 tons. Several years without drought have enabled the Government to accumulate a national stock of cereal, yet vulnerability to desertification and climate change still threatens food security. Higher imported food prices in 2008, mainly for rice and vegetable oil, necessitated the suspension of taxes on imported rice for three months to protect the urban population, at an estimated cost of 4,000m. francs CFA. In 2009 cereal production fell by 30%, from 5m. tons to 3.5m. tons, due to adverse weather conditions, with rainfall an estimated 70% below normal conditions. Food insecurity increased further as sustained high food prices reduced the purchasing power of Nigerien households, resulting in a severe famine in 2010, with over 50% of the population facing food shortages, according to officials. Despite flooding, cereal production increased to an estimated 5.3m. tons in 2010 (against a mid-year forecast of 6.4m. tons) as a result of a successful harvest and the distribution of 3,400 quality seeds to farmers, according to FAO. In the same year the Ministry of Agricultural Development announced that Niger's gross national cereal balance was the highest for 20 years, reaching some 1.5m. tons. Erratic rains and long dry spells coupled with pest attacks resulted in cereal production falling by 27% to 3.8m. tons in 2011. Specifically, millet production fell by 24% to 2.9m. tons and sorghum by 38% to 0.8m tons, according to FAO. Despite food being available at the national level, FAO remains concerned that the majority of households in Niger lack access to food. The crisis in neighbouring Libya has further exacerbated food insecurity through the return of an estimated 84,000 Nigerien economic migrants (according to the International Organisation for Migration in November 2011) and, consequently, a dramatic fall in remittances.

Cow pea output, estimated at 1.5m. metric tons in 2008 and 787,000 tons in 2009, is the second largest in the world after Nigeria, according to the AfDB. The value of cow pea exports more than doubled in 2008, reaching 41,800m. francs CFA, from 19,200m. francs CFA in 2007; however, exports declined by 19.9% in 2009, to 33,500m. francs CFA. Onion exports were projected at 46,600m. francs CFA in 2009, up from 37,700m. francs CFA in 2006. After an abundant harvest of 209,369 tons in 2003/04 (according to unofficial figures), groundnut production had stabilized at about 150,000 tons annually, increasing to 307,800 tons in 2008 before declining to 253,000 tons in 2009. Annual production of cotton has recovered in recent years, ranging between 8,000 tons and 10,000 tons.

The most important traditional activity in Niger after crop farming is livestock-rearing. Cattle are the second most significant export, in terms of foreign exchange earnings, after uranium, with a significant—if largely unrecorded—trade across the border with Nigeria. In 2009 cattle accounted for an estimated 11.8% of export earnings, compared with 12.3% in the previous year. Pastoralists' terms of trade have been adversely affected recently by the sustained high cattle feed prices and falling livestock prices. The Government has been unable to promote either intensive commercial livestock operations or dairy farming, in part owing to Niger's ecological conditions. Moreover, in 2010 the famine and severe flooding in the Agadez, Diffa and Zinder regions killed thousands of cattle, resulting in fodder supply falling 66% below normal conditions. Yet efforts are being made to improve the health of livestock, with an estimated 1m. head of cattle being vaccinated in the northern Agadez region by the Ministry of Stockbreeding, assisted by the International Committee of the Red Cross.

With about 90% of cultivable land believed to have been lost to drought in the 20th century, and losses recently averaging 200,000 ha per year, the anti-desertification campaign is a priority for the Nigerien Government, and a programme of afforestation and environmental protection is proceeding. Niger gained access to funds from the Climate Investment Fund's Pilot Program for Climate Resilience to reduce desertification and food insecurity in 2010. A portion of the funds will be used to fight against desert encroachment and drought, with the objective of allowing Niger to achieve its development goals in a sustainable manner. In terms of forestry, a new forestry code was adopted in June 2004 and better conservation through behavioural changes led to some success in recovering hundreds of thousands of hectares of forest.

MINING AND POWER

There has been renewed foreign interest in Niger's mineral resources in recent years. The mining code was updated in August 2006 and, as part of the new Constitution of 2011, mandated that all mining contracts must be published. In March 2011 the Council of the Extractive Industries Transparency Initiative declared Niger to be a compliant country. The mining and export of uranium has played a very significant role in Niger's formal economy and until recently represented a steady source of budgetary revenue and foreign exchange earnings. In 2008 Niger ranked third, after Canada and Australia, among the world's principal producers of uranium and is expected to rise to second place in 2013, when production commences at the Imouraren mine in the Agadez region. Niger's uranium industry has witnessed a renaissance in recent years, owing to rising demand from the People's Republic of China. Uranium revenue represented 1.8% of GDP in 2009, 1.7% in 2010, an estimated 1.9% in 2011, and was forecast by the IMF to account for 2.1% of GDP in 2012. Improving processing technology at existing mines and the development of new mines were expected to result in an almost two-fold increase in uranium output by 2013. Prospecting and exploitation of the country's other mineral resources, including gold, petroleum, iron ore, copper, phosphates, coal and salt, have been slow to pick up. Petroleum and gold have, none the less, received increased attention from foreign prospectors in recent years, and gold was produced on a commercial scale for the first time in 2004. Oil production at the Agadem block, north of Lake Chad (see below), was expected to commence in 2012 and to contribute 1.7% of GDP, according to the IMF.

The mining of uranium began in 1971 at Arlit, in the desolate Aïr mountains. The Compagnie Générale des Matières Nucléaires (COGEMA—a subsidiary of the French Government's Commissariat à l'Énergie Atomique, now the French public multinational AREVA NC) and French private interests hold a majority share in the mining company, Société des Mines de l'Aïr (SOMAÏR), with the Nigerien Government's Office National des Ressources Minières du Niger (ONAREM) holding a 36.6% share. Production at the country's second uranium mine, at Akouta, was begun in 1978 by a consortium—the Compagnie Minière d'Akouta (COMINAK)—of the Government, AREVA, the Japanese Overseas Uranium Resources Development and the Spanish Empresa Nacional del Uranio. Operating costs at the mine are high, owing to the remoteness of the sites. Although international demand declined following the end of the Cold War and the scaling down of nuclear power programmes, plans to increase capacity, which had hitherto been postponed indefinitely, have been revived as a result of a recovery in the world price of uranium since late 2002. The recovery in world uranium prices reflected a renewed interest in nuclear energy, not only because of concerns over carbon dioxide emissions, but also because of electricity shortages in fast-growing Asian countries, which prompted the construction of new nuclear power plants. Annual production in Niger reached an average of 3,114 tons in 2002–05, which was roughly in line with the existing capacity of COMINAK and SOMAÏR. SOMAÏR was in the process of expanding output by about 35%, and COMINAK expected yields to increase through the use of improved processing technology. The Government has actively awarded new uranium-mining concessions to Canadian (Global Uranium Corpn, Semafo Inc, Cameco Corpn), Chinese (Chinese National Nuclear Corpn), Indian (Dharni Sampda Private Ltd) and French (AREVA) interests since 2006, with new discoveries first being announced in 2007. These investments were expected to increase output from 3,241 tons in 2009 to 9,600 tons in 2015.

In 2007 Société des Mines d'Azelik (SOMINA), a joint venture between China Nuclear International Uranium Corpn (SinoU) (33%), the Nigerien Government (24.8%), ZXJOY Invest of China (24.8%) and Trendfield Holding Ltd of the Chinese Special Administrative Region of Hong Kong (5%), began to develop the Azelik deposits in the Agadez region, with production at the Teguidda mine commencing in late 2010. Output at this mine was expected to reach a maximum capacity of 700 metric tons per year in 2012. Niger secured a 650m. yuan preferential loan from the Export-Import Bank of China to fund its share of the development of the mine. Nigerien labourers—many of whom are Tuaregs—complained about conditions at the mine where rooms are located in illegally close proximity to the open-pit workings. In January 2009 AREVA signed an agreement with the Government to invest €1,200m. over a five-year period to develop the Imouraren uranium-mining site in the Agadez region; following protracted delays, output was expected finally to commence in late 2013 and ultimately to reach 5,000 tons annually in 2016, making the site the second largest open-pit mine in the world. AREVA was to own 66.7% of the project, with the Government, through ONAREM, holding the remainder in a joint venture. In February 2010 AREVA signed an agreement with Korea Electric Power Company (Kepco), providing for the acquisition by the South Korean firm of a 10% stake in the mine. In late 2010 the Canadian Global Atomic Fuels Corporation announced positive results of the metallurgical and economic studies on the Dasa open-pit uranium project located on the Adrar Emoles concession.

In 2009 export earnings from uranium represented 45% of total exports, with revenues of 198,000m. francs CFA. In 2010 and 2011 export earnings from uranium represented 50% of total exports, with revenues of 242,300m. francs CFA and 301,300m. francs CFA, respectively; they were forecast by the IMF to increase to 360,500m. francs CFA in 2012.

The price of uranium has fluctuated since 2007, although the general trend has been downward. In August 2007 it was US $109.6/lb, but by June 2012 the price had declined to $50.4/lb.

Niger's gold reserves, most of which are located in the Liptako region, near the border with Burkina Faso, have been exploited on a small scale since the early 1980s. Gold reserves are estimated at 50,000 metric tons. Canadian, Ghanaian and South African interests are all active in this sector. Production at the Samira Hill gold mine, in which Etruscan Resources and Semafo, of Canada, have an interest, started in September 2004. The country's gold production subsequently increased from 1,531 kg in 2004 to an estimated 5,300 kg in 2005. As further exploration projects came on line, export earnings from gold rose from 23,900m. francs CFA in 2006 to 25,500m. francs CFA in 2007, according to the IMF. The value of gold exports represented an estimated 6.6% of total exports in 2008 (26,300m. francs CFA), increasing to an estimated 8.2% in 2009 (34,700m. francs CFA), according to the IMF.

Coal deposits, estimated at 6m. metric tons, have been located at Anou-Anaren, to the north-west of Agadez. Annual production, which began in 1981, has generally been in the region of 160,000–200,000 tons, most of which is used for uranium-processing in Arlit and Akokan. Reserves of some 30m. tons of coal deposits were discovered at Salkadamna, 600 km north-east of Niamey, in 2006.

Deposits of petroleum, located in the south-west, were for a long time not deemed commercially exploitable. However, there was a marked increase in petroleum exploration activity in the late 1990s, with TG World Energy (of Canada) taking on a concession in the central region of Ténéré in 1997 and Hunt Oil (of the USA) starting exploratory drilling near the border with Libya in late 1999. The China National Oil and Gas Exploration and Development Corporation (CNODC) also owns an exploration permit in the Ténéré region. In January 2005 a consortium led by ExxonMobil (of the USA) and Petronas (of Malaysia) announced its first discovery of petroleum in Niger, less than one year after it drilled three exploratory wells in the Agadem region. CNODC signed a production-sharing agreement in June 2008 with the Government to develop the Agadem field, with estimated reserves of 320m. barrels, to construct a refinery in Zinder near the Nigerian border with a capacity of 20,000 barrels per day, and to build a 460-km pipeline linking the field with the refinery. Oil production was expected to start in 2012; however, given that some 100 wells were to be to drilled over a three-year period, this start-up date could be delayed. Consistent with mining and petroleum laws, the Government has a 15% ownership in the Agadem field; drilling costs borne by the Government were expected to amount to US $25m. per year on average. The capital cost of the oilfields and pipeline are financed by CNODC, with the Nigerien Government repaying the financing cost of its share through future cash flows of the project. The refinery in Zinder, which was estimated to be capable of producing 7,000m. barrels of petroleum products, was to be managed as a corporation, with the Government contributing 40% of the capital costs, equivalent to about $40m., funded through a concessional loan from the Bank of China. Given that domestic consumption represents about one-third of the output of the refinery, exports of petroleum products to neighbouring countries, mainly Nigeria, were being arranged in advance of the refinery's expected start date of 2012. The national oil company, SONIDEP, will market domestic production. The Chinese company has been criticized by Nigerien civil society groups, such as GREN (Group for Reflection and Action in Niger's Extractive Industries), for dangerous working conditions on the project site and for failing to compensate villagers who have been negatively affected by the construction of the pipeline.

According to the most recent estimates, electricity production in Niger, which is entirely thermal, totalled 204,000 MW in 2009. As a result, some 340,000 MW had to be imported from hydroelectric supplies from Nigeria to cover the country's consumption needs, the major consumers being uranium companies. Access to electricity was estimated at just 7% of the population in 2005. Owing to the unreliability of the Nigerian supply, construction of a hydroelectric facility at Kandadji, on the Niger river, began in 2009 with a scheduled completion date of 2014. The 165-MW facility (originally proposed to be 230 MW) was expected to cost 140,000m. francs CFA (US $280m.), financed by the Government and loans from a number of multinational agencies, including the AfDB, the Islamic Development Bank, the Organization of the Petroleum Exporting Countries Fund, the Arab Bank for Economic Development in Africa, the Kuwaiti Fund, the Saudi Fund and the West African Development Bank, all at concessional rates. This project would regulate the water flow for the benefit of downstream areas, increasing the irrigation potential in the Niger delta up to a maximum of 45,000 ha. The Government was also involved in a programme to expand domestic electricity production to mitigate the risk of Nigeria not exporting electricity through the existing interconnected transmission system. This project resulted in the contribution to GDP of electricity, gas and water increasing from 3.3% in 2007 to 9.5% in 2008. A regional project to enhance the electricity grid connection between Burkina Faso, Niger and Nigeria was envisaged in the medium term. Long-standing plans to privatize the national electricity company, the Société Nigérienne d'Electricité, and the petroleum distribution parastatal, Société Nigérienne de Distribution des Produits Pétroliers, were abandoned in 2007, ostensibly owing to the lack of foreign interest. This came as a surprise, given the Government's commitment to accelerate its programme of privatization under the PRGF programme agreed for 2005–08.

MANUFACTURING

As in most other West African countries, manufacturing takes the form of the processing of agricultural commodities and import substitution. According to the AfDB, the manufacturing sector grew at an average annual rate of 1.8% in 1995–2006, and expanded by 2.3% in 2007, 3.9% in 2008 and 8.5% in 2009. The sector contributed 3.2% to GDP in 2009. There is a groundnut oil extraction plant, as well as a brewery, cotton ginneries, rice mills, flour mills and tanneries. Import substitution has been stimulated by the very high cost of transport. A textile plant, the Entreprise Nigérienne de Textile, with output of 5.6m. metres in 2003, and a cement works, the Société Nigérienne de Cimenterie (with an annual capacity of 60,000 metric tons), are in operation; both were transferred from state to majority private ownership in the late 1990s. There are also light industries serving the very limited local market. Activity in the sector remains predominantly small scale and artisanal, and, in that it draws on local inputs, was stimulated by the currency devaluation, which made foreign manufactures correspondingly expensive.

TRANSPORT, TOURISM AND TELECOMMUNICATIONS

The transport system is still poorly developed. Road rehabilitation heavily depends on funding from donors. In 2006 there were 18,550 km of classified roads, of which 3,803 km were paved. There is, at present, no railway. Long-mooted plans to extend the Cotonou–Parakou line from Benin have recently elicited some renewed interest from India, which pledged US $500m. for the 10-year construction project in 2006. Most foreign trade is shipped through Cotonou, via the Organisation commune Bénin-Niger des Chemins de Fer et des Transports (OCBN). The Niger river provides transport from Niamey to Benin, but is only navigable for between four and five months a year. The emphasis in transport development is on diversifying and improving access to the seaports of Lomé, Togo, via Burkina Faso, as well as extending the Trans-Sahara Highway. There are international airports at Niamey, Agadez and Zinder, and three major domestic airports.

Tourist arrivals increased from 39,190 in 1997 to 59,920 in 2005, when Niger hosted the Games of La Francophonie (comprising both sporting and other cultural events). However, instability in the north of the country together with a series of kidnappings have recently prompted a significant reduction in tourist arrivals. A Canadian UN diplomat along with his assistant and driver were kidnapped near to a part Canadian-owned uranium plant, Samira, 40 km from the capital, in December 2008, and four tourists were kidnapped (and one was later executed) on the Niger–Mali border in January 2009. Tourist arrivals totalled 74,278 in 2010, compared with 65,875 in the previous year.

Telecommunications in Niger expanded with the arrival of three mobile cellular telephone and two internet service providers. The Société Nigérienne des Télécommunications (SONITEL), the national telecommunications operator established in March 1997 following the merger of telecommunications and post office parastatals, was privatized in 2001, with a majority stake being sold to Chinese and Libyan interests. A new telecommunications licence was granted in 2007 worth 31,000m. francs CFA (1.6% of GDP), according to the IMF. In 2010 there were 3.8m. mobile cellular telephone subscribers.

FINANCE

The fundamental problem in Nigerien public finances is the gross inadequacy of tax revenue, as successive governments have failed to bring most of the economy into the tax 'net'. However, improvements in the collection of customs duties, company profit taxes, and value-added tax (VAT), coupled with receipts from selling uranium licences, allowed total revenues to account for an estimated 19.9% of GDP in 2009, compared with 13.0% in 2006, according to the IMF.

The Government of Hama Amadou, from January 2000, was confronted with a severe financial crisis, and all payments on its domestic and external debt were suspended, pending the preparation of a new budget. The new administration recommitted Niger to a wide-ranging privatization programme, and in March 2000 civil service reforms were pushed through, resulting in the early retirement of some 2,400 public servants. As relations with external creditors were regularized and external debt payment arrears settled, the budget deficit (on a cash basis) increased to 156,800m. francs CFA by the end of 2000, equivalent to 12.2% of GDP. The deficit narrowed in 2001, to 53,400m. francs CFA, equivalent to 4.1% of GDP, as resumed external assistance and tax reforms—notably the introduction of VAT—helped boost revenue. Public finances remained constant in 2002, with a budgetary deficit of 58,700m. francs CFA, equivalent to 4.1% of GDP. Tight control over spending was maintained in 2003, after the Government took some measures to compensate for a loss in revenue related to lower transfers from the Union Economique et Monétaire Ouest-Africaine and the repeated closure, during the course of the year, of the border with Nigeria. None the less, the budget deficit was reduced slightly, to 51,000m. francs CFA, equivalent to 3.6% of GDP.

While fiscal performance in 2004 (when both presidential and legislative elections were held) was in line with expectations, budgetary performance in 2005 was revised to account for a shortfall in domestic revenues as a result of the drought. According to the Banque Centrale des Etats de l'Afrique de l'Ouest estimates, the budget deficit (including grants) decreased from 69,100m. francs CFA (4.7% of GDP) in 2005 to 47,000m. francs CFA in 2006 (2.7% of GDP). Continued progress was made in reducing domestic payment arrears in 2006. In 2007 the basic budget deficit decreased to 0.9% of GDP owing to uranium licence receipts and a general broadening of the tax base, according to the IMF. In 2008 total government revenue of an estimated 407,000m. francs CFA (17.5% of GDP), comprised mainly of tax revenue, was exceeded by total government expenditure of 564,500m. francs CFA (24.2% of GDP), resulting in an estimated basic budget deficit of 14,900m. francs CFA (0.6% of GDP). The basic budget deficit widened to 4.1% of GDP in 2009 owing to costs of 19,500m. francs CFA (0.8% of GDP) associated with construction of the Zinder refinery. In 2010 the basic budget deficit contracted to 3.0% of GDP, after a reduction in government expenditure from 24.6% to 21.5% of GDP offset the reduction in external financing in the first half of the year (owing to the political situation). However, the budget deficit was expected to increase to 4% of GDP in 2012 as a function of government capital expenditures increasing from 8% to 10.6% of GDP as a result of ongoing extractive industry commitments.

Public and private investment grew in 2008 as a result of increased investment in uranium-mining; petroleum exploration and construction of the refinery; and an expansion of electricity production capacity and the Kandaji dam project. Thus, the investment-to-GDP ratio rose from below 14% in 2000–04 to 26% in 2008, according to the Ministry of the Economy and Finance. Capital spending in 2009 was characterized by investments in the oil industry, with expenditure totalling 12.1% of GDP, representing 50% of total budgetary expenditure. In 2010 capital expenditure fell by 40% in absolute terms to 8% of GDP (37% of budgetary expenditure) owing to a reduction in external finance related to the political situation. In 2011 capital expenditure was expected to increase by 30% in absolute terms, to 10.6% of GDP (40% of budgetary expenditure), with external finance nearly doubling to 206,000m. francs CFA owing to the stabilization of the political environment. Private investment, mainly from China, grew from 25.2% of GDP in 2009 to an estimated 41.1% of GDP in 2010.

FOREIGN TRADE AND PAYMENTS

Rising oil prices, food requirements and the increasing demand for capital equipment have all put pressure on the import bill since 2002. This was in part compensated for by the depreciation of the US dollar against the franc CFA in January 1994. On the export side, the onset of armed conflict in Côte d'Ivoire in September 2002 put a temporary halt to Niger's exports in livestock and onions, until other alternative trade routes were found. Stronger international prices for gold and uranium—and the beginning of commercial gold production in 2004—have improved Niger's prospects; however, uranium export prices have remained substantially below world prices, which, combined with upward pressures on the oil import bill, led to an increase in the trade deficit each year from 2002 to 2005; in the latter year the deficit stood at 94,800m. francs CFA, equivalent to 5.5% of GDP. From 2006 to 2008 both imports and exports increased by 53%; the former, mainly driven by petroleum and food imports, and the latter, driven by uranium exports, increased to 409,000m. francs CFA. Over the same period the trade balance widened from 7% to 9% of GDP, according to the AfDB. In 2009 the trade deficit widened to 15.3% of GDP as a result of increased imports of capital goods, petroleum and food offsetting uranium exports, according to the IMF. After contracting to 13.9% in 2010, the trade deficit was estimated by the IMF to have widened to 15.3% in 2011, resulting mainly from increased capital goods imports.

With merchandise trade normally in deficit, and the high transportation costs arising from the country's landlocked position, the annual current account of the balance of payments has been in persistent deficit, restricted to manageable levels only by inflows of official aid. Statistics on the current account balance vary greatly from one source to another, however. In 2005 a current account deficit (including grants) of 124,100m. francs CFA was recorded, equivalent to 6.3% of GDP. During the period 2005–07 the current account deficit averaged the equivalent of 8.5% of GDP. In 2007 it was estimated at 7.7% of GDP, including grants (13.5% excluding grants), according to the IMF. In the same year the value of key imports (food and petroleum) exceeded that of key exports (uranium, cattle and gold), resulting in a balance of goods deficit of 75,700m. francs CFA. The current account widened to 12.6% of GDP (13.6% excluding grants) in 2008, attributable to capital goods imports related to uranium developments (Imouraren and Azelik projects) and the rise in oil and food imports. A signature bonus related to the Agadem oilfield of 5.4% of GDP increased Niger's official reserves of foreign currency. In 2009 the current account (excluding grants) widened to some 25% of GDP owing to further imports of capital goods financed by foreign direct investment (FDI) in the uranium and petroleum sectors. The size of these imports, some 13% of GDP, outweighed the positive impact of strong agricultural and mining exports and of a reduction in the value of oil and food imports. In 2010 the current account deficit (excluding grants) remained large, yet narrowed to 21% of GDP due to the rise in uranium exports somewhat offsetting the increase in imports of petroleum, food and capital goods. In 2011 the current account deficit widened further to an estimated 27.5% of GDP, reflecting substantial oil and uranium mining imports financed by FDI associated with the Imouraren mine and the Agadem oilfield. Yet the deficit remained sustainable due to the high levels of foreign aid, which doubled to 12% of GDP. When refined petroleum products are exported and the SOMINA uranium and Immouraren mines maximize production, the current account deficit is expected to decline sharply to an estimated 13.4% of GDP in 2014.

External borrowing to compensate for the chronic deficit on the current account resulted in a sharp escalation in Niger's foreign debt in the late 1970s and 1980s. With a debt-service ratio of 41% in 1988, Niger was classified as 'debt-distressed' by the World Bank, and hence at the December rescheduling of debt by the 'Paris Club' of official creditors, the highly concessionary 'Toronto terms' for debt relief were applied. The cancellation by France of debts of US $320m. in 1990, further 'Paris Club' rescheduling and a 'buy-back', supported by the World Bank, of $108m. in commercial debt reduced the debt-service ratio to 12% of foreign earnings by 1992.

After the devaluation of the CFA franc in January 1994 doubled the cost in local currency terms of repayment of and interest on debt, exceptional measures of debt relief were required. In March a new agreement with the 'Paris Club' rescheduled 85,000m. francs CFA in debt, and France cancelled one-half of Niger's liabilities. Another round of rescheduling on the more concessionary 'Naples terms' (which effectively allowed two-thirds of eligible debt to be written off) followed agreement of the ESAF in 1996. Niger's debt remained in the region of US $1,600m. in 1995–2001. Interim debt relief under the HIPC initiative also started in 2001, following the negotiation of a PRGF, which took effect from December 2000, and the declaration of Niger's eligibility for the initiative. Under the HIPC, Niger's foreign debt was to be reduced by $1,200m. in nominal terms, with $680.2m. being provided by multilateral creditors. Total debt relief was achieved in April 2004, when the country reached completion point. As a result, the 'Paris Club' agreed to cancel $160m. of Niger's debt and reschedule the remaining $90m. In June 2005 Niger was among 18 countries to be granted 100% debt relief on multilateral debt agreed by the Group of Eight (G8) leading industrialized nations. As a result of these initiatives, the debt-to-GDP ratio declined substantially from 52% in 2005 to 10.9% in 2009, before rising to an estimated 11.8% in 2010, according to the IMF. However, as Niger finances its share of capital costs in uranium, petroleum and hydroelectric projects, the IMF estimated that the debt-to-GDP ratio would increase to an average of 17% over the 2011–28 period. Correspondingly, the debt service ratio as a percentage of government revenue was expected to increase from 3.9% in 2010 to an estimated 6.0% in 2011.

Statistical Survey

Source (unless otherwise stated): Institut national de la Statistique, Immeuble sis à la Rue Sirba, derrière la Présidence de la république, BP 720, Niamey; tel. 20-72-35-60; fax 20-72-21-74; e-mail insniger@ins.ne; internet www.stat-niger.org.

Area and Population

AREA, POPULATION AND DENSITY

Area (sq km)	1,267,000*
Population (census results)	
20 May 1988	7,248,100
20 May 2001	
Males	5,516,588
Females	5,543,703
Total	11,060,291
Population (UN estimates at mid-year)†	
2010	15,511,953
2011	16,068,992
2012	16,644,338
Density (per sq km) at mid-2012	13.1

* 489,191 sq miles.

† Source: UN, *World Population Prospects: The 2010 Revision.*

POPULATION BY AGE AND SEX

(UN estimates at mid-2012)

	Males	Females	Total
0–14	4,170,245	3,963,489	8,133,734
15–64	4,033,070	4,102,633	8,135,703
65 and over	174,428	200,473	374,901
Total	8,377,743	8,266,595	16,644,338

Source: UN, *World Population Prospects: The 2010 Revision.*

ETHNIC GROUPS

(2001 census, Nigerien citizens only)

	Population	%
Hausa	6,069,731	55.36
Djerma-Sonraï	2,300,874	20.99
Tuareg	1,016,883	9.27
Peulh	935,517	8.53
Kanouri-Manga	513,116	4.68
Toubou	42,172	0.38
Arab	40,085	0.37
Gourmantché	39,797	0.36
Others	5,951	0.05
Total	10,964,126	100.00

ADMINISTRATIVE DIVISIONS

(2011)

Agadez	511,188	Niamey (city)	1,302,910
Diffa	489,531	Tahoua	2,741,922
Dosso	2,078,339	Tillabéri	2,572,125
Maradi	3,117,810	Zinder	2,916,929

PRINCIPAL TOWNS

(population at 2001 census)

Niamey (capital)	707,951	Agadez	78,289
Zinder	170,575	Tahoua	73,002
Maradi	148,017	Arlit	69,435

Mid-2011 (incl. suburbs, UN estimate): Niamey 1,297,160 (Source: UN, *World Urbanization Prospects: The 2011 Revision*).

BIRTHS AND DEATHS

(annual averages, UN estimates)

	1995–2000	2000–05	2005–10
Birth rate (per 1,000)	53.5	51.3	49.5
Death rate (per 1,000)	19.3	16.2	13.8

Source: UN, *World Population Prospects: The 2010 Revision.*

2011: Birth rate 48.2 per 1,000; Death rate 12.6 per 1,000 (Source: African Development Bank).

Life expectancy (years at birth): 54.3 (males 53.8; females 54.7) in 2010 (Source: World Bank, World Development Indicators database).

EMPLOYMENT

('000 persons at 31 December)

	2008	2009	2010
Agriculture, hunting, forestry and fishing	157	128	158
Mining and quarrying	86	29	31
Manufacturing	950	907	1,012
Electricity, gas and water	112	161	181
Construction	433	490	603
Trade, restaurants and hotels	871	704	1,419
Transport, storage and communications	369	502	635
Financing, insurance, real estate and business services	220	205	224
Community, social and personal services	963	1,096	1,315
Total	4,161	4,222	5,578

2001 census (persons aged 10 years and over): Total employed 4,015,951 (males 2,706,910, females 1,309,041), Unemployed 64,987 (males 49,437, females 15,550), Total labour force 4,080,938 (males 2,756,347, females 1,324,591).

Health and Welfare

KEY INDICATORS

Total fertility rate (children per woman, 2010)	7.1
Under-5 mortality rate (per 1,000 live births, 2010)	143
HIV/AIDS (% of persons aged 15–49, 2009)	0.8
Physicians (per 1,000 head, 2008)	0.02
Hospital beds (per 1,000 head, 2005)	0.3
Health expenditure (2009): US $ per head (PPP)	37
Health expenditure (2009): % of GDP	5.4
Health expenditure (2009): public (% of total)	50.3
Access to water (% of persons, 2010)	49
Access to sanitation (% of persons, 2010)	9
Total carbon dioxide emissions ('000 metric tons, 2008)	850.7
Carbon dioxide emissions per head (metric tons per, 2008)	0.1
Human Development Index (2011): ranking	186
Human Development Index (2011): value	0.295

For sources and definitions, see explanatory note on p. vi.

Agriculture

PRINCIPAL CROPS
('000 metric tons)

	2008	2009	2010
Wheat	8.8	8.6*	8.7*
Rice, paddy	32.5	20.1	30.0
Millet	3,522	2,678	3,843
Sorghum	1,226	739	1,305
Potatoes	22.6	34.0	35.0*
Sweet potatoes	58	49	58*
Cassava (Manioc)	110	108	110*
Sugar cane	188	212	212*
Cow peas, dry	1,543.9	787.5	1,773.4
Groundnuts, with shell	308.5	253.5	406.2
Sesame seed	50	76	86
Cottonseed*	7	4	5
Cabbages and other brassicas	171	112	150*
Lettuce and chicory	77	66	70*
Tomatoes	90	56	67*
Chillies and peppers, green	26	16	19*
Onions, dry	374	384	390*
Garlic	8	2	2*
Beans, green*	29	23	30
Carrots and turnips	10	7	8*
Dates	17	38	39*
Tobacco, unmanufactured*	1.0	1.0	1.1

* FAO estimate(s).

Aggregate production ('000 metric tons, may include official, semi-official or estimated data): Total cereals 4,804 in 2008, 3,452 in 2009, 5,204 in 2010; Total roots and tubers 191 in 2008, 190 in 2009, 203 in 2010; Total vegetables (incl. melons) 905 in 2008, 763 in 2009, 835 in 2010; Total pulses 1,573 in 2008, 817 in 2009, 1,804 in 2010.

Source: FAO.

LIVESTOCK
('000 head, year ending September)

	2008	2009	2010
Cattle	8,737	9,262	9,817
Sheep	10,191	10,548	10,917
Goats	12,641	13,147	13,673
Pigs*	40	40	40
Horses	237	240	242
Asses	1,567	1,599	1,631
Camels	1,627	1,654	1,680
Chickens*	11,200	11,500	12,000

* FAO estimates.

Source: FAO.

LIVESTOCK PRODUCTS
('000 metric tons, FAO estimates)

	2008	2009	2010
Game meat	24	26	28
Horse meat	1	1	1
Goat meat	52.8	58.2	61.2
Sheep meat	35.2	44.8	48.0
Chicken meat	10.8	11.0	11.5
Hen eggs	7.6	8.0	8.3

Source: FAO.

Forestry

ROUNDWOOD REMOVALS
('000 cubic metres, excl. bark, FAO estimates)

	2004	2005	2006
Industrial wood	579	701	701
Fuel wood	2,857	2,857	2,857
Total	3,436	3,558	3,558

2007–11: Production assumed to be unchanged from 2006 (FAO estimates).

Source: FAO.

SAWNWOOD PRODUCTION
('000 cubic metres, incl. railway sleepers, FAO estimates)

	1991	1992	1993
Total (all broadleaved)	0	1	4

1994–2011: Figures assumed to be unchanged from 1993 (FAO estimates).

Source: FAO.

Fishing

(metric tons, live weight)

	2007	2008	2009
Capture (freshwater fishes)	29,728	29,960	29,884
Aquaculture	40	40	70*
Total catch	29,768	30,000	29,954*

* FAO estimate.

2010: Catch assumed to be unchanged from 2009 (FAO estimates).

Source: FAO.

Mining

('000 metric tons unless otherwise indicated)

	2008	2009	2010
Hard coal	182.9	225.1	246.6*
Tin (metric tons)*†‡	n.a	5.9	5.7
Uranium (metric tons)	2,993	3,241	4,198*
Gold (kg)	2,314	2,067	1,929
Gypsum*	8.7	19.7	7.6

* Provisional.
† Data refer to the metal content of ore.
‡ Artisanal production only.

Industry

SELECTED PRODUCTS
('000 metric tons, unless otherwise indicated)

	2005	2006	2007
Raw sugar*	10	10	10
Cement	83.4	62.0	42.0
Soap	9.4	9.4	9.4
Textile fabrics (million metres)	2.0	1.9	2.6
Beer ('000 bottles)	94.9	97.5	99.9
Electric energy (million kWh)*	202	194	195

* Source: UN Industrial Commodity Statistics Database.

2008: Electric energy (million kWh) 213; Raw sugar 10,000 metric tons (Source: UN Industrial Commodity Statistics Database).

2009: Electric energy (million kWh) 234 (Source: UN Industrial Commodity Statistics Database).

Source: partly IMF, *Niger: Selected Issues and Statistical Appendix* (February 2009).

Finance

CURRENCY AND EXCHANGE RATES

Monetary Units

100 centimes = 1 franc de la Communauté Financière Africaine (CFA).

Sterling, Dollar and Euro Equivalents (31 May 2012)

£1 sterling = 819.959 francs CFA;
US $1 = 528.870 francs CFA;
€1 = 655.957 francs CFA;
10,000 francs CFA = £12.20 = $18.91 = €15.24.

Average Exchange Rate (francs CFA per US $)

2009	472.186
2010	495.277
2011	471.866

Note: An exchange rate of 1 French franc = 50 francs CFA, established in 1948, remained in force until January 1994, when the CFA franc was devalued by 50%, with the exchange rate adjusted to 1 French franc = 100 francs CFA. This relationship to French currency remained in effect with the introduction of the euro on 1 January 1999. From that date, accordingly, a fixed exchange rate of €1 = 655.957 francs CFA has been in operation.

BUDGET

('000 million francs CFA)

Revenue*	2009	2010	2011
Tax revenue	343.0	361.7	403.8
Income and profits	102.3	86.9	101.3
Goods and services	99.0	109.9	98.8
International trade	116.6	135.0	177.9
Other taxes	25.1	29.9	25.8
Non-tax revenue	20.6	23.9	32.4
Total	363.6	385.6	436.2

Expenditure†	2009	2010	2011
Current expenditure	276.5	346.1	370.3
Wages and salaries	93.6	103.2	122.6
Materials and supplies	83.9	94.2	94.9
Subsidies and transfers	97.2	135.5	142.1
Other	1.8	13.2	10.7
Capital expenditure	309.1	217.8	321.0
Exceptional expenses	24.3	20.1	28.8
Total	609.9	584.0	720.1

* Excluding grants received ('000 million francs CFA): 110.9 in 2009; 130.2 in 2010; 217.3 in 2011.

† Excluding lending minus repayment ('000 million francs CFA): 0.0 in 2009–10; 38.9 in 2011.

2012 ('000 million francs CFA, budget projections): *Revenue:* Tax revenue 539.8, Non-tax revenue 66.2; Total 606.0. *Expenditure:* Current expenditure 412.2; Capital expenditure 582.4; Total 994.7 (Source: IMF, *Niger: Request for a New Three-Year Arrangement Under the Extended Credit Facility - Staff Report; Press Release on the Executive Board Discussion; and Statement by the Executive Director for Niger*—May 2012).

INTERNATIONAL RESERVES

(US $ million at 31 December, excl. gold)

	2009	2010	2011
IMF special drawing rights	85.1	83.6	83.3
Reserve position in IMF	13.5	13.3	13.3
Foreign exchange	556.9	663.4	576.5
Total	655.5	760.3	673.0

Source: IMF, *International Financial Statistics*.

MONEY SUPPLY

('000 million francs CFA at 31 December)

	2009	2010	2011
Currency outside banks	187.9	234.9	269.6
Demand deposits at deposit money banks*	166.6	214.1	204.7
Checking deposits at post office	1.7	1.4	1.8
Total money (incl. others)*	356.4	450.5	476.4

* Excluding the deposits of public enterprises of an administrative or social nature.

Source: IMF, *International Financial Statistics*.

COST OF LIVING

(Consumer Price Index for Niamey, annual averages; base: 2000 = 100 unless otherwise indicated)

	2009	2010	2011
Food*	132.1	132.5	137.0
Clothing	101.0	n.a.	n.a.
Rent	115.7	n.a.	n.a.
All items (incl. others)	131.9	128.2	132.0

* Base: 2006 = 100.

Source: ILO.

NATIONAL ACCOUNTS

('000 million francs CFA at current prices)

Expenditure on the Gross Domestic Product

	2009	2010	2011*
Government final consumption expenditure	423.2	422.2	510.7
Private final consumption expenditure	1,860.0	1,976.4	2,194.8
Gross fixed capital formation	838.8	973.6	964.9
Changes in inventories	1.5	34.4	2.2
Total domestic expenditure	3,123.4	3,406.5	3,672.6
Exports of goods and services	517.9	572.6	684.7
Less Imports of goods and services	1,108.0	1,170.0	1,346.4
GDP at purchasers' values	2,533.4	2,809.1	3,010.9

Gross Domestic Product by Economic Activity

	2009	2010	2011*
Agriculture, hunting, forestry and fishing	987.0	1,182.1	1,189.6
Mining and quarrying	159.9	164.9	189.0
Manufacturing	128.3	137.6	147.8
Electricity, gas and water supply	28.6	32.7	34.4
Construction	64.1	71.5	77.1
Wholesale and retail trade; restaurants and hotels	384.2	396.6	423.4
Finance, insurance and real estate	131.0	137.8	144.0
Transport and communications	156.5	164.4	177.1
Public administration and defence	224.8	226.7	286.3
Other services	105.2	107.7	118.4
Sub-total	2,369.6	2,622.0	2,787.1
Less Imputed bank service charge	21.7	23.7	24.6
Indirect taxes (net)	185.5	210.9	248.3
GDP at purchasers' values	2,533.4	2,809.1	3,010.9

* Estimates.

BALANCE OF PAYMENTS
('000 million francs CFA)

	2009	2010*	2011†
Exports of goods f.o.b.	470.7	508.7	605.4
Imports of goods f.o.b.	–847.2	–887.3	–1,049.3
Trade balance	–376.5	–378.6	–443.8
Services (net)	–299.7	–397.1	–483.2
Balance on goods and services	–676.2	–775.7	–927.1
Income (net)	–16.3	–15.8	–29.2
Balance on goods, services and income	–692.6	–791.5	–956.3
Private unrequited transfers (net)	53.9	72.9	36.5
Public unrequited transfers (net)	17.3	153.2	116.0
Current balance	–621.3	–565.5	–803.8
Capital account (net)	120.3	95.8	162.5
Direct investment (net)	345.4	495.3	478.3
Portfolio investment (net)	7.4	17.9	1.3
Other investment (net)	65.5	61.0	123.6
Net errors and omissions	–7.1	—	—
Overall balance	–89.8	104.5	–38.1

* Preliminary.

† Projections.

Source: IMF, *Niger: Request for a New Three-Year Arrangement Under the Extended Credit Facility - Staff Report; Press Release on the Executive Board Discussion; and Statement by the Executive Director for Niger* (May 2012).

External Trade

PRINCIPAL COMMODITIES
(distribution by SITC, US $ million)

Imports c.i.f.	2008	2009	2010
Food and live animals	247.8	187.0	272.0
Dairy products and birds' eggs	32.4	28.4	25.4
Milk and cream	31.9	28.0	24.9
Milk and cream, preserved, concentrated or sweetened	31.2	27.1	23.2
Cereals and cereal preparations	141.7	90.3	151.7
Rice, semi-milled or wholly milled	106.1	61.7	66.1
Rice, semi-milled or milled (unbroken)	89.5	49.8	55.8
Sugar, sugar preparations and honey	28.2	23.8	25.2
Beverages and tobacco	29.1	37.6	43.0
Cigarettes	25.5	32.3	38.1
Crude materials (inedible) except fuel	87.0	76.5	67.7
Textile fibres (not wool tops) and their wastes (not in yarn)	56.1	49.0	44.3
Bulk textile waste, old clothing, traded in bulk or in bales	55.4	49.0	44.3
Mineral fuels, lubricants, etc. (incl. electric current)	207.2	194.2	286.3
Petroleum, petroleum products, etc.	189.2	176.2	261.0
Petroleum products, refined	185.9	172.5	258.1
Animal and vegetable oils, fats and waxes	32.4	28.2	31.1
Fixed vegetable oils and fats	27.4	25.9	26.2
Palm oil	19.2	20.9	16.4
Chemicals and related products	175.1	145.8	142.6
Medicinal and pharmaceutical products	118.7	63.0	37.9
Basic manufactures	161.1	282.2	571.4
Textile yarn, fabrics, made-up articles, etc.	26.3	47.0	23.8
Cotton fabrics, woven (not incl. narrow or special fabrics)	18.0	22.3	12.8
Machinery and transport equipment	251.6	525.3	757.6
Telecommunications, sound recording and reproducing equipment	24.9	55.7	30.9
Road vehicles	76.4	149.6	209.6
Passenger motor vehicles (excl. buses)	29.7	31.5	34.0
Miscellaneous manufactured articles	56.2	150.3	118.3
Total (incl. others)	1,247.5	1,627.2	2,290.0

Exports f.o.b.	2008	2009	2010
Food and live animals	85.9	179.4	78.2
Live animals chiefly for food	46.3	132.7	47.2
Animals of the bovine species (incl. buffaloes), live	21.0	51.3	26.9
Sheep and goats, live	18.4	70.2	14.7
Fish, crustaceans and molluscs, and preparations thereof	0.4	n.a.	n.a.
Vegetables and fruit	17.8	37.8	15.0
Vegetables, fresh or simply preserved; roots and tubers	17.1	37.3	14.2
Other fresh or chilled vegetables	12.2	33.4	10.6
Beverages and tobacco	8.1	5.6	6.8
Cigarettes	7.8	5.4	6.5
Crude materials (inedible) except fuels	321.9	361.0	255.2
Textile fibres (not wool tops) and their wastes (not in yarn)	30.8	11.2	11.0
Ores and concentrates of uranium and thorium	289.4	348.7	242.9
Mineral fuels, lubricants, etc., (incl. electric current)	16.4	7.2	7.6
Petroleum, petroleum products, etc.	16.3	7.2	7.6
Basic manufactures	24.8	13.8	13.9
Fabrics, woven, 85% plus of cotton, bleached, dyed, etc., or otherwise finished	22.7	12.7	12.9
Total (incl. others)	503.1	628.0	483.5

Source: UN, *International Trade Statistics Yearbook*.

2011 (million francs CFA): Total imports 854,405; Total exports 424,586.

PRINCIPAL TRADING PARTNERS
(US $ million)

Imports c.i.f.	2008	2009	2010
Argentina	13.0	10.9	11.4
Belgium	31.1	19.7	32.1
Benin	12.0	5.9	19.7
Brazil	25.4	24.1	19.8
Burkina Faso	10.7	18.8	12.6
Cameroon	13.2	n.a.	n.a.
China, People's Republic	156.8	499.1	1,002.5
Côte d'Ivoire	62.5	62.6	51.5
France (incl. Monaco)	164.1	219.7	252.5
Germany	26.8	42.4	46.7
Ghana	17.7	13.2	17.7
India	29.0	26.2	11.1
Italy	14.2	19.5	16.8
Japan	44.5	70.4	75.4
Malaysia	26.0	21.0	21.9

Imports c.i.f.—*continued*	2008	2009	2010
Netherlands	89.4	70.2	73.4
Nigeria	58.1	82.0	88.4
Pakistan	42.3	22.1	13.0
South Africa	11.2	15.0	8.0
Thailand	43.7	n.a.	n.a.
Togo	49.4	42.0	52.0
United Kingdom	40.3	44.0	118.4
USA	95.4	79.2	138.9
Viet Nam	18.4	15.2	22.3
Total (incl. others)	1,247.5	1,627.2	2,290.0

Exports f.o.b.	2008	2009	2010
Belgium	3.8	1.3	1.6
Benin	0.9	2.5	1.2
Brazil	7.6	3.2	6.6
Burkina Faso	3.8	3.0	3.0
Cameroon	2.9	3.2	2.5
China, People's Republic	5.5	3.1	37.6
Côte d'Ivoire	17.9	11.5	8.9
France (incl. Monaco)	167.3	295.7	43.5
Germany	2.3	3.8	5.7
Ghana	7.1	24.1	6.6
Italy	3.7	n.a.	n.a.
Japan	49.8	0.6	80.0
Korea, Democratic People's Republic	6.4	3.2	3.0
Mali	0.1	n.a.	n.a.
Netherlands	8.7	0.8	3.7
Nigeria	59.2	139.1	53.6
South Africa	—	1.5	—
Spain	8.5	13.5	19.9
Switzerland-Liechtenstein	21.8	44.3	75.5
Thailand	10.0	3.6	5.8
Togo	0.3	1.1	0.3
United Kingdom	0.5	n.a.	n.a.
USA	88.7	49.2	80.6
Total (incl. others)	503.1	628.0	483.5

Source: UN, *International Trade Statistics Yearbook*.

2011 (million francs CFA): Total imports 854,405; Total exports 424,586.

Transport

ROAD TRAFFIC
(motor vehicles in use at 31 December, estimates)

	2007	2008	2009
Passenger cars	75,697	84,675	93,118
Buses and coaches	4,019	4,560	5,066
Tractors and semi-trailers	6,024	7,429	9,053

CIVIL AVIATION
(traffic on scheduled services)

	2008	2009	2010
Aircraft movements	4,556	5,647	5,022
Passengers carried ('000)	121.3	154.5	156.3
Freight carried (metric tons)	3,216	3,327	1,891
Mail (metric tons)	90	103	n.a.

Tourism

FOREIGN TOURIST ARRIVALS BY NATIONALITY*

	2008	2009	2010
Africa	46,981	42,312	44,702
America	4,528	4,078	4,589
East Asia and the Pacific	3,507	3,158	3,560
Europe	18,138	16,335	18,416
France	14,667	13,209	14,892
Total (incl. others)	73,154	65,883	74,278

* Figures refer to arrivals at national borders.

Receipts from tourism (US $ million, excl. passenger transport): 66.0 in 2009; 79.0 in 2010.

Source: World Tourism Organization.

Communications Media

	2009	2010	2011
Telephones ('000 main lines in use)	76.3	83.6	90.0
Mobile cellular telephones ('000 subscribers)	2,599.0	3,805.6	4,339.9
Internet users ('000)	115.9	n.a.	n.a.
Broadband subscribers	1,000	1,500	1,800

* Estimated figure.

Personal computers: 10,000 (0.8 per 1,000 persons) in 2005.

Television receivers ('000 in use): 395 in 2000.

Radio receivers ('000 in use): 680 in 1997.

Daily newspapers: 1 (average circulation 2,000 copies) in 1997; 1 (average circulation 2,000 copies) in 1998; 1 (average circulation 2,500 copies) in 2004.

Non-daily newspapers: 5 (average circulation 14,000 copies) in 1996; 28 (average circulation 34,000 copies) in 2004.

Books published (first editions): titles 5; copies 11,000 in 1991.

Sources: UNESCO, *Statistical Yearbook*; UNESCO Institute for Statistics; UN, *Statistical Yearbook*; International Telecommunication Union.

Education

(2009/10 unless otherwise indicated)

	Institutions	Teachers	Students
Pre-primary	826	2,119	67,678
Primary	12,623	44,710	1,726,452
Secondary	859	9,724	286,709
Tertiary*	7	278	4,953
University	2	304	11,292

* 2004/05 figures.

Pupil-teacher ratio (primary education, UNESCO estimate): 39.0 in 2010/11 (Source: UNESCO Institute for Statistics).

Adult literacy rate (UNESCO estimates): 30.4% (males 44.3%; females 16.4%) in 2007 (Source: UNESCO Institute for Statistics).

Directory

The Constitution

On 31 October 2010 90.2% of those who voted in a national referendum approved the text of the Constitution of the Seventh Republic. On 25 November the new Constitution was promulgated by the President of the Conseil Suprême pour la Restauration de la Démocratie, Salou Djibo. The main provisions are summarized below:

The President of the Republic is the Head of State and is elected by direct, universal suffrage for a term of five years, renewable only once. Candidates for the presidency must be at least 35 years of age. The President appoints a Prime Minister, upon whose recommendation he appoints the members of the Government. The Prime Minister is the Head of Government.

Legislative power is exercised by the Assemblée nationale, members of which are elected by direct, universal suffrage for terms of five years.

The judiciary is independent and consists of a Constitutional Court, a Court of Cassation, a Council of State, a Court of Auditors, and other courts and tribunals instituted by law.

The Constitution also makes provision for an Economic, Social and Cultural Council (Conseil Économique, Social et Culturel) and a Higher Council of Communications (Conseil Superieur de la Communication).

The initiative for the revision of the Constitution belongs jointly to the President of the Republic and members of the Assemblée nationale, four-fiths of whom must approve the proposed amendment (and three-quarters of the members must vote).

French is the official language.

The Government

HEAD OF STATE

President: MAHAMADOU ISSOUFOU (inaugurated 7 April 2011).

COUNCIL OF MINISTERS

(September 2012)

Prime Minister: BRIGI RAFINI.

Minister of State, Minister of Foreign Affairs, African Integration and Nigeriens Abroad: BAZOUM MOHAMED.

Minister of State, Minister of Planning, Land Settlement and Community Development: AMADOU BOUBACAR CISSÉ.

Minister of State, Minister of the Interior, Public Security, Decentralization and Religious Affairs: ABDOU LABO.

Minister of State, Minister of Mines and Industrial Development: OMAR HAMIDOU TCHIANA.

Minister of Public Health: SOUMANA SANDA.

Minister of Petroleum and Energy: FOUMAKOYE GADO.

Minister of Justice, Keeper of the Seals and Government Spokesperson: MAROU AMADOU.

Minister of Equipment: SADI SOUMAILA.

Minister of Town Planning, Housing and Sanitation: MOUSSA BAKO ABDOULKARIM.

Minister of Trade and the Promotion of the Private Sector: SALEY SAIDOU.

Minister of Communication and New Information Technology: SALIFOU LABO BOUCHÉ.

Minister of Population, the Promotion of Women and the Protection of Children: MAIKIBI KADIDIATOU DAN DOBI.

Minister of National Defence: KARIDJO MAHAMADOU.

Minister of Finance: JULES BAYÉ.

Minister of Professional Training and Employment: NGADÉ NANA HADIZA NOMA KAKA.

Minister of Higher Education and Scientific Research: MAMADOU YOUBA DIALLO.

Minister of National Education, Literacy and the Promotion of National Languages: ALI MARIAMA ELHADJ IBRAHIM.

Minister of Agriculture: OUHA SAIDOU.

Minister of Water Resources and the Environment: ISSOUFOU ISSAKA.

Minister of Stockbreeding: MAHAMANE ELHADJ OUSMANE.

Minister of Transport: IBRAHIM YACOUBA.

Minister of Youth, Sports and Culture: HASSANE KOUNOU.

Minister of Handicrafts and Tourism: YAHAYA BAARÉ HAOUA ABDOU.

Minister of the Civil Service and Labour: SABO FATOUMA ZARA BOUBACAR.

Minister, in charge of Relations with the Institutions: ELHADJ LAOUALI CHAÏBOU.

MINISTRIES

Office of the President: BP 550, Niamey; tel. 20-72-23-80; fax 20-72-33-96; internet www.presidence.ne.

Office of the Prime Minister: BP 893, Niamey; tel. 20-72-26-99; fax 20-73-58-59.

Ministry of Agriculture: BP 12091, Niamey; tel. 20-73-35-41; fax 20-73-20-08.

Ministry of the Civil Service and Labour: BP 11107, Niamey; tel. 20-73-22-31; fax 20-73-61-69; e-mail sani.yakouba@caramail.com.

Ministry of Communication and New Information Technology: Niamey.

Ministry of Equipment: Niamey.

Ministry of Finance: BP 389, Niamey; tel. 20-72-23-74; fax 20-73-59-34.

Ministry of Foreign Affairs, African Integration and Nigeriens Abroad: BP 396, Niamey; tel. 20-72-29-07; fax 20-73-52-31.

Ministry of Handicrafts and Tourism: BP 480, Niamey; tel. 20-73-65-22; fax 20-72-23-87; internet www.niger-tourisme.com.

Ministry of Higher Education and Scientific Research: BP 628, Niamey; tel. 20-72-26-20; fax 20-72-40-40; e-mail mesnt@intnet.ne.

Ministry of the Interior, Public Security and Decentralization: BP 622, Niamey; tel. 20-72-32-62; fax 20-72-21-76.

Ministry of Justice: BP 466, Niamey; tel. 20-72-31-31; fax 20-72-37-77.

Ministry of Mines and Industrial Development: BP 11700, Niamey; tel. 20-73-45-82; fax 20-73-27-59.

Ministry of National Defence: BP 626, Niamey; tel. 20-72-20-76; fax 20-72-40-78.

Ministry of National Education, Literacy and the Promotion of National Languages: BP 557, Niamey; tel. 20-72-28-33; fax 20-72-21-05; e-mail scdameb@intnet.ne.

Ministry of Petroleum and Energy: Niamey.

Ministry of Planning, Land Settlement and Community Development: BP 403, Niamey; tel. 20-73-53-57; fax 20-72-21-71.

Ministry of Population, the Promotion of Women and the Protection of Children: BP 11286, Niamey; tel. 20-72-23-30; fax 20-73-61-65.

Ministry of Professional Training and Employment: Immeuble ex-HCCT, blvd Mali Béro, BP 628, Niamey; tel. 20-72-59-51; fax 20-73-67-81.

Ministry of Public Health: BP 623, Niamey; tel. 20-72-28-08; fax 20-73-35-70.

Ministry of Relations with the Institutions: Niamey.

Ministry of Stockbreeding: BP 12091, Niamey; tel. 20-73-79-59; fax 20-73-31-86.

Ministry of Town Planning, Housing and Sanitation: BP 403, Niamey; tel. 20-73-53-57; fax 20-72-21-71.

Ministry of Trade and the Promotion of the Private Sector: BP 480, Niamey; tel. 20-73-29-74; fax 20-73-21-50; e-mail nicom@intnet.ne.

Ministry of Transport: BP 12130, Niamey; tel. 20-72-28-21; fax 20-73-36-85.

Ministry of Water Resources and the Environment: BP 257, Niamey; tel. 20-73-47-22; fax 20-72-40-15.

Ministry of Youth, Sports and Culture: BP 215, Niamey; tel. 20-72-32-35; fax 20-72-23-36.

President and Legislature

PRESIDENT

Presidential Election, First Round, 31 January 2011

Candidate	Votes	% of votes
Mahamadou Issoufou (PNDS—Tarayya)	1,192,945	36.16
Seyni Oumarou (MNSD—Nassara)	766,215	23.23
Hama Amadou (Moden)	653,737	19.82
Mahamane Ousmane (CDS)	274,676	8.33
Cheiffou Amadou (RSD—Gaskiya)	134,732	4.08
Others*	276,336	8.38
Total	3,298,641	100.00

* There were five other candidates.

Second Round, 12 March 2011, provisional results

Candidate	Votes	% of votes
Mahamadou Issoufou (PNDS—Tarayya)	1,820,639	57.95
Seyni Oumarou (MNSD—Nassara)	1,321,248	42.05
Total	3,141,887	100.00

LEGISLATURE

Assemblée nationale

pl. de la Concertation, BP 12234, Niamey; tel. 20-72-27-38; fax 20-72-43-08; e-mail an@assemblee.ne; internet www.assemblee.ne.

President: HAMA AMADOU.

General Election, 31 January 2011, provisional results

Party	Votes	% of votes	Seats
PNDS—Tarayya	1,143,263	33.02	39
MNSD—Nassara	707,191	20.43	26
Moden	684,583	19.77	24
ANDP—Zaman Lahiya	252,857	7.30	8
RDP—Djamaa	232,105	6.70	7
UDR—Tabbat	185,473	5.36	6
CDS—Rahama	109,536	3.16	2
RSD—Gaskiya	60,048	1.73	—
UNI	32,277	0.93	1
Others	54,552	1.58	—
Total	3,461,885	100.00	113*

* Including eight special seats, five of which were allocated to the PNDS—Tarayya, two to Moden and one to the MNSD—Nassara.

Election Commission

Commission Électorale Nationale Indépendante (CENI): Niamey; internet www.ceni-niger.net; Pres. ABDOURAHMANE GHOUSMANE.

Political Organizations

A total of 23 political parties contested the legislative elections of January 2011.

Alliance Nigérienne pour la Démocratie et le Progrès Social—Zaman Lahiya (ANDP—Zaman Lahiya): Quartier Abidjan, Niamey; tel. 20-74-07-50.

Alliance pour la Démocratie et le Progrès—Zumunci (ADP): Niamey; tel. 20-73-67-57; e-mail adp@zumunci.com; internet www.adpzumunci.com; f. 1992; Chair. ISSOUFOU BACHAR.

Convention Démocratique et Sociale—Rahama (CDS—Rahama): BP 11973, Niamey; tel. 20-74-19-85; f. 1991; mem. of Alliance des Forces Démocratiques (AFD); Pres. MAHAMANE OUSMANE.

Mouvement Démocratique Nigérien (Moden): Niamey; e-mail mdnloumana@gmail.com; internet mdn-lumana.populus.org; f. 2009 by supporters of former Prime Minister Hama Amadou; Pres. HAMA AMADOU; Sec.-Gen. OMAR HAMIDOU TCHIANA.

Mouvement National pour la Société de Développement—Nassara (MNSD—Nassara): rue Issa Beri 30, cnr blvd de Zarmaganda, porte 72, BP 881, Niamey; tel. 20-73-39-07; fax 20-72-41-74; e-mail presi@mnsd-nassara.org; internet www.mnsd.ne; f. 1988; sole party 1988–90; restyled as MNSD—Nassara in 1991; Chair. Col (retd) MAMADOU TANDJA; Pres. SEYNI OUMAROU.

Mouvement des Nigériens pour la Justice (MNJ): ; e-mail mnj.contact@gmail.com; internet m-n-j.blogspot.com; f. 2007; Pres. AGHALI ALAMBO.

Parti des Masses pour le Travail—al Barka (PMT—al Barka): Niamey; tel. 20-74-02-15; MAMALO ABDOULKARIM.

Parti Nigérien pour la Démocratie et le Socialisme—Tarayya (PNDS—Tarayya): pl. Toumo, Niamey; tel. 20-74-48-78; internet pnds-tarayya.net; f. 1990; Pres. MAHAMADOU ISSOUFOU; Sec.-Gen. FOUMAKOYE GADO.

Parti Social-démocrate Nigérien—Alheri (PSDN): tel. 20-72-28-52; Pres. LABO ISSAKA.

Rassemblement pour la Démocratie et le Progrès—Djamaa (RDP—Djamaa): pl. Toumo, Niamey; tel. 20-74-23-82; party of late Pres. Maïnassara; Chair. HAMID ALGABID; Sec.-Gen. MAHAMANE SOULEY LABI.

Rassemblement des Patriotes Nigériens—al Kalami (RPN—al Kalami): Niamey; f. 2009; Pres. OUSMANE ISSOUFOU OUBANDAWAKI.

Rassemblement Social-démocratique—Gaskiya (RSD—Gaskiya): Quartier Poudrière, Niamey; tel. 20-74-00-90; f. 2004 following split in the CDS; Pres. CHEIFFOU AMADOU.

Rassemblement pour un Sahel Vert—Ni'ima (RSV): BP 12515, Niamey; tel. and fax 20-74-11-25; e-mail agarba_99@yahoo.com; f. 1991; Pres. ADAMOU GARBA.

Union pour la Démocratie et le Progrès Social—Amana (UDPS): internet www.udps-amana.com; represents interests of Tuaregs; Chair. RHISSA AG BOULA.

Union pour la Démocratie et la République—Tabbat (UDR—Tabbat): Quartier Plateau, Niamey; f. 2002; Pres. AMADOU BOUABACAR CISSÉ.

Union des Nigeriens Indépendants (UNI): Quartier Zabarkan, Niamey; tel. 20-74-23-81; Leader AMADOU DJIBO.

Union des Patriotes Démocratiques et Progressistes—Shamuwa (UPDP): Niamey; tel. 20-74-12-59; Chair. Prof. ANDRÉ SALIFOU.

Union des Socialistes Nigériens—Talaka (USN): f. 2001 by mems of the UFPDP; Leader ISSOUFOU ASSOUMANE.

Diplomatic Representation

EMBASSIES IN NIGER

Algeria: route des Ambassades-Goudel, BP 142, Niamey; tel. 20-72-35-83; fax 20-72-35-93; Ambassador HAMID BOUKRIF.

Benin: BP 11544, Niamey; tel. 20-72-28-60; Ambassador AWAHOU LABOUDA.

Chad: POB 12820, Niamey; tel. 20-75-34-64; fax 20-72-43-61; Ambassador MAHAMAT NOUR MALLAYE.

China, People's Republic: BP 873, Niamey; tel. 20-72-32-83; fax 20-72-32-85; e-mail embchina@intnet.ne; Ambassador XIA HUANG.

Cuba: rue Tillaberi, angle rue de la Cure Salée, face lycée Franco-Arabe, Plateau, BP 13886, Niamey; tel. 20-72-46-00; fax 20-72-39-32; e-mail embacuba@niger.cubaminrex.cu; internet emba.cubaminrex.cu/nigerfr; Ambassador ROBERTO RODRÍGUEZ PENA.

Egypt: Terminus Rond-Point Grand Hôtel, BP 254, Niamey; tel. 20-73-33-55; fax 20-73-38-91; Ambassador BELAL ELMASSRY.

France: route de Tondibia, Quartier Yantala, BP 10660, Niamey; tel. 20-72-24-32; fax 20-72-25-18; e-mail webmestre@mail.com; internet www.ambafrance-ne.org; Ambassador ALAIN HOLLEVILLE.

Germany: 71 ave du Général de Gaulle, BP 629, Niamey; tel. 20-72-35-10; fax 20-72-39-85; e-mail amb-all-ny@web.de; Ambassador RÜDIGER JOHN.

India: BP 201, Niamey; tel. 20-37-00-29; fax 20-20-37-01; e-mail amb.niamey@mea.gov.in; Ambassador Y. P. SINGH.

Iran: 11 rue de la Présidence, BP 10543, Niamey; tel. 20-72-21-98; fax 20-72-28-10; e-mail aliakbar_100@yahoo.com; Ambassador MOHAMAD NIKKHAH.

Korea, Democratic People's Republic: Niamey; Ambassador PAK SONG IL.

Libya: route de Goudel, BP 683, Niamey; tel. 20-72-40-19; fax 20-72-40-97; e-mail boukhari@intnet.ne; Ambassador (vacant).

Morocco: ave du Président Lubke, face Clinique Kaba, BP 12403, Niamey; tel. 20-73-40-84; fax 20-73-80-27; e-mail ambmang@intnet.ne; Ambassador TAYEB RAOUF.

Nigeria: rue Goudel, BP 11130, Niamey; tel. 20-73-24-10; fax 20-73-35-00; e-mail embnig@intnet.ne; Ambassador ALIYU ISA SOKOTO.

Pakistan: 90 rue YN 001, ave des Zarmakoye, Yantala Plateau, BP 10426, Niamey; tel. 20-75-32-57; fax 20-75-32-55; e-mail parepniamey@yahoo.com; internet www.brain.net.pk/~farata; Ambassador (vacant).

Saudi Arabia: route de Tillabery, BP 339, Niamey; tel. 20-75-32-15; fax 20-75-24-42; e-mail neemb@mofa.gov.sa; Ambassador SAOUD BIN ABDUL AZIZ AL-DAYIL.

Spain: 151 rue de la Radio, BP 11888, Niamey; tel. 20-75-59-61; e-mail emb.niamey@maec.es; Ambassador MARÍA SOLEDAD FUENTES GÓMEZ.

USA: rue des Ambassades, BP 11201, Niamey; tel. 20-73-31-69; fax 20-73-55-60; e-mail NiameyPASN@state.gov; internet niamey.usembassy.gov; Ambassador BISA WILLIAMS.

Judicial System

According to the Constitution of the Seventh Republic, promulgated on 25 November 2010, the judiciary is independent and consists of a Constitutional Court, a Court of Cassation, a Council of State, a Court of Auditors, and any other courts and tribunals instituted by law.

Constitutional Court: BP 10779, Niamey; internet cour-constitutionnelle-niger.org; 7 mems; Pres. FATIMATA SALIFOU BAZEYE.

Religion

It is estimated that some 95% of the population are Muslims, 0.5% are Christians and the remainder follow traditional beliefs.

ISLAM

The most influential Islamic groups in Niger are the Tijaniyya, the Senoussi and the Hamallists.

Association Islamique du Niger: BP 2220, Niamey; tel. 20-74-08-90; Dir CHEIKH OUMAROU ISMAEL.

CHRISTIANITY

The Roman Catholic Church

Niger comprises one archdiocese and one diocese. The Archbishop and Bishop participate in the Bishops' Conference of Burkina Faso and Niger (based in Ouagadougou, Burkina Faso).

Archbishop of Niamey: Rt Rev. MICHEL CHRISTIAN CARTATÉGUY, Evêché, BP 10270, Niamey; tel. 20-73-32-59; fax 20-73-80-01; e-mail cartateguymi@voila.fr; internet eglisecatholiqueauniger.org.

Bishop of Maradi: Rt Rev. AMBROISE OUÉDRAOGO, Evêché, BP 447, Maradi; tel. and fax 20-41-03-30; fax 20-41-13-86; e-mail evechemi@intnet.ne.

The Press

The following were among those newspapers and periodicals believed to be appearing regularly in the early 2010s:

L'Action: Quartier Yantala, Niamey; tel. 96-96-92-22; e-mail action_ne@yahoo.fr; internet www.tamtaminfo.com/action.pdf; f. 2003; fortnightly; popular newspaper intended for youth audience; Dir of Publication BOUSSADA BEN ALI; circ. 2,000 (2003).

L'Actualité: Quartier Terminus, BP 383, Niamey; tel. 20-73-30-91; e-mail actualite98@yahoo.fr; internet lactualite-niger.com; f. 2010; weekly; Dir of Publication MAHAROU HABOU OUMAROU; circ. 1,500.

L'Alternative: BP 10948, Niamey; tel. 20-74-24-39; fax 20-74-24-82; e-mail alter@intnet.ne; internet www.alternative.ne; f. 1994; weekly; in French and Hausa; Dir MOUSSA TCHANGARI; Editor-in-Chief ABDRAMANE OUSMANE.

Anfani: Immeuble DMK, rue du Damagaram, BP 2096, Niamey; tel. 20-74-08-80; fax 20-74-00-52; e-mail anfani@intnet.ne; f. 1992; 2 a month; Editor-in-Chief IBBO DADDY ABDOULAYE; circ. 3,000.

Le Canard Déchainé: BP 383, Niamey; tel. 93-92-66-64; satirical; weekly; Dir of Publication ABDOULAYE TIÉMOGO; Editor-in-Chief IBRAHIM MANZO.

Le Canard Libéré: BP 11631, Niamey; tel. 20-75-43-52; fax 20-75-39-89; e-mail canardlibere@caramail.com; satirical; weekly; Dir of Publication TRAORÉ DAOUDA AMADOU; Editorial Dir OUMAROU NALAN MOUSSA.

Le Démocrate: 21 rue 067, NB Terminus, BP 11064, Niamey; tel. 20-73-24-25; e-mail le_democrate@caramail.com; internet www.tamtaminfo.com/democrate.pdf; weekly; independent; f. 1992; Dir of Publication ALBERT CHAÏBOU; Editor-in-Chief OUSSEINI ISSA.

Les Echos du Sahel: Villa 4012, 105 Logements, BP 12750, Niamey; tel. and fax 20-74-32-17; e-mail ecosahel@intnet.ne; f. 1999; rural issues and devt; quarterly; Dir IBBO DADDY ABDOULAYE.

L'Enquêteur: BP 172, Niamey; tel. 93-90-18-74 (mobile); e-mail lenqueteur@yahoo.fr; fortnightly; Publr TAHIROU GOURO; Editor IBRAHIM SOULEY.

Haské: BP 297, Niamey; tel. 20-74-18-44; fax 20-73-20-06; e-mail webmaster@planetafrique.com; internet www.haske.uni.cc; f. 1990; weekly; also Haské Magazine, quarterly; Dir CHEIKH IBRAHIM DIOP.

Journal Officiel de la République du Niger: BP 116, Niamey; tel. 20-72-39-30; fax 20-72-39-43; f. 1960; fortnightly; govt bulletin; Man. Editor BONKOULA AMINATOU MAYAKI; circ. 800.

Libération: BP 10483, Niamey; tel. 96-97-96-22 (mobile); f. 1995; weekly; Dir BOUBACAR DIALLO; circ. 1,000 (2003).

Le Républicain: Nouvelle Imprimerie du Niger, pl. du Petit Marché, BP 12015, Niamey; tel. 20-73-47-98; fax 20-73-41-42; e-mail webmasters@republicain-niger.com; internet www.republicain-niger.com; f. 1991; weekly; independent; Dir of Publication MAMANE ABOU; circ. 2,500.

La Roue de l'Histoire: Zabarkan, rue du SNEN, BP 5005, Niamey; tel. 20-74-05-69; internet www.tamtaminfo.com/roue.pdf; weekly; Propr SANOUSSI JACKOU; Dir ABARAD MOUDOUR ZAKARA.

Le Sahel Quotidien: BP 13182, ONEP, Niamey; tel. 20-73-34-87; fax 20-73-30-90; e-mail onep@intnet.ne; internet www.lesahel.org; f. 1960; publ. by Office National d'Edition et de Presse; daily; Dir IBRAHIM MAMANE TANTAN; Editor-in-Chief ALASSANE ASOKOFARE; circ. 3,000; also Sahel-Dimanche, Sundays; circ. 5,000.

Sauyi: BP 10948, Niamey; tel. 20-74-24-39; fax 20-74-24-82; e-mail sarji@alternative.ne; fortnightly; Hausa; publ. by Groupe Alternative; Hausa; rural interest; Dir SAÏDOU ARJI.

La Source: Academie des Arts, BP 5320, Niamey; tel. 96-53-95-77 (mobile); e-mail amanimb9@yahoo.fr; weekly; Dir of Publication AMANI MOUNKAÏLA; circ. 1,000.

Stadium: BP 10948, Niamey; tel. 96-96-73-07 (mobile); e-mail abbarimi@gmail.com; sports; 2 a month; Editor ABBA KIARI.

Le Témoin: BP 10483, Niamey; tel. 96-96-58-51; e-mail istemoin@yahoo.fr; internet www.tamtaminfo.com/temoin.pdf; 2 a month; Dir of Publication IBRAHIM SOUMANA GAOH; Editors AMADOU TIÉMOGO, MOUSSA DAN TCHOUKOU, I. S. GAOH; circ. 1,000 (2005).

Ténéré Express: BP 13600, Niamey; tel. 20-73-35-76; fax 20-73-77-75; e-mail tenerefm@intnet.ne; daily; independent; current affairs; Dir ABDOULAYE MOUSSA MASSALATCHI.

Le Trophée: BP 2000, Niamey; tel. 20-74-12-79; e-mail strophee@caramail.com; sports; 2 a month; Dir ISSA HAMIDOU MAYAKI.

Le Visionnaire: quartier Plateau, Niamey; tel. 98-15-62-40; weekly; Dir of Publication SALIFOU SOUMAÏLA ABDOULKARIM; circ. 1,000.

NEWS AGENCIES

Agence Nigérienne de Presse (ANP): BP 11158, Niamey; tel. 20-74-08-09; e-mail anpniger@intnet.ne; f. 1987; state-owned; Dir YAYE HASSANE.

Sahel—Office National d'Edition et de Presse (ONEP): BP 13182, Niamey; tel. 20-73-34-86; f. 1989; Dir MAHAMADOU ADAMOU.

PRESS ASSOCIATION

Association Nigérienne des Editeurs de la Presse Indépendante (ANEPI): Niamey; Pres. IBRAHIM SOUMANA GAOH; Sec.-Gen. IBRAHIM MANZO DIALLO.

Publishers

La Nouvelle Imprimerie du Niger (NIN): pl. du Petit Marché, BP 61, Niamey; tel. 20-73-47-98; fax 20-73-41-42; e-mail imprim@intnet.ne; f. 1962 as Imprimerie Nationale du Niger; govt publishing house; brs in Agadez and Maradi; Dir MAMAN ABOU.

Réseau Sahélien de Recherche et de Publication: Niamey; tel. 20-73-36-90; fax 20-73-39-43; e-mail resadep@ilimi.uam.ne; press of the Université Abdou Moumouni; Co-ordinator BOUREIMA DIADIE.

Broadcasting and Communications

TELECOMMUNICATIONS

In 2011 there were five licensed providers of telecommunications services in Niger: three mobile cellular telephone operators, one fixed-line operator and one dual operator.

Regulatory Authorities

Autorité de Régulation Multisectorielle: 64 rue des bâtisseurs, BP 13179, Niamey; tel. 20-73-90-08; fax 20-73-85-91; e-mail arm@armniger.org; internet www.armniger.org; f. 1999; Pres. AMINATA GARBA.

Conseil National de Régulation: Niamey; Pres. ALMOUSTAPHA BOUBACAR.

Infrastructure and Development

Haut Commissariat à l'Informatique et aux Nouvelles Technologies de l'Information et de la Communication: Niamey; High Commissioner SOUMANA HAMMA BEIDI.

Service Providers

Airtel Niger: route de l'Aéroport, BP 11922, Niamey; tel. 20-73-23-46; fax 20-73-23-85; e-mail info.ne@zain.com; internet africa.airtel.com/niger; f. 2001 as Zain Niger; present name adopted in 2010; Dir-Gen. ALAIN KAHASHA.

Moov Niger: route de l'aéroport, 720 blvd du 15 Avril, BP 13379, Niamey; tel. 20-74-19-54; fax 20-74-19-39; internet www.moov.ne; f. 2001; 68% owned by Orascom Telecom (Egypt); Dir CHEIKH BEN HAÏDARA.

Orange Niger: 1282 blvd Mali Bero, BP 2874, Niamey; tel. 90-22-22-22; e-mail service.client@orange-niger.ne; internet www.orange.ne; provides mobile, fixed-line and internet services; Dir-Gen. BRELOTTE BA.

Société Nigérienne des Télécommunications (SONITEL): ave du Général de Gaulle, BP 208, Niamey; tel. 20-72-29-98; fax 20-72-24-78; e-mail info@sonitel.ne; internet www.sonitel.ne; f. 1998; 51% jtly owned by ZTE Corpn (People's Republic of China) and Laaico (Libya), 46% state-owned; Dir-Gen. MOUSSA BOUBACAR.

Sahel Com: BP 208, Niamey; internet www.sahelcom.ne; f. 2002; mobile cellular telecommunications in Niamey.

BROADCASTING

Regulatory Authority

Observatoire National de la Communication (ONC): rue Presidence, BP 9999, Niamey; internet www.csc-niger.ne; f. 2010 to replace Conseil Supérieur de la Communication (CSC); Pres. ABDOURAHAMANE OUSMANE; 13 mems.

Radio

Independent radio stations have been permitted to operate since 1994, although the majority are concentrated in the capital, Niamey. In 2000 the first of a network of rural stations, RURANET, which were to broadcast mainly programmes concerned with development issues, mostly in national languages, was established.

Anfani FM: blvd Nali-Béro, BP 2096, Wadata, Niamey; tel. 20-74-08-80; fax 20-74-00-52; e-mail anfani@intnet.ne; private radio station, broadcasting to Niamey, Zinder, Maradi and Diffa; Dir ISMAËL MOUTARI.

Office de Radiodiffusion-Télévision du Niger (ORTN): BP 309, Niamey; tel. 20-72-31-63; fax 20-72-35-48; internet www.ortn.ne; f. 1967; state broadcasting authority; Dir-Gen. LOÏC CRESPIN.

Ténéré FM: BP 13600, Niamey; tel. 20-73-65-76; fax 20-73-46-94; e-mail tenerefm@intnet.ne; f. 1998; Dir ABIBOU GARBA; Editor-in-Chief SOULEYMANE ISSA MAÏGA.

La Voix du Sahel: BP 361, Niamey; tel. 20-72-22-02; fax 20-72-35-48; e-mail ortny@intnet.ne; internet www.ortn.ne; f. 1958; govt-controlled radio service; programmes in French, Hausa, Djerma, Kanuri, Fulfuldé, Tamajak, Toubou, Gourmantché, Boudouma and Arabic; Dir IBRO NA-ALLAH AMADOU.

RURANET: Niamey; internet membres.lycos.fr/nigeradio; f. 2000; network of rural radio stations, broadcasting 80% in national languages, with 80% of programmes concerned with devt issues; 31 stations operative in April 2002.

La Voix de l'Hémicycle: BP 12234, Niamey; f. 2002 as the radio station of the Assemblée nationale; broadcasts parliamentary debates and analysis for 15 hours daily in French and national languages to Niamey and environs.

Sudan FM: Dosso; auth. 2000; private radio station; Dir HIMA ADAMOU.

RFI, BBC, la Voix de l'Amérique, Deutsch Welle and Radio Chine Internationale are also broadcast to Niger.

Television

Office de Radiodiffusion-Télévision du Niger (ORTN): see Radio.

Tal TV: BP 309, Niamey; f. 2001; broadcasts 72 hours of programmes each week.

Télé-Sahel: BP 309, Niamey; tel. 20-72-31-55; fax 20-72-35-48; govt-controlled television service; broadcasts daily from 13 transmission posts and six retransmission posts, covering most of Niger; Dir-Gen. ABDOU SOULEY.

Radio Télévision Bonferey: rue du Collège Mariama, BP 2260, Niamey; tel. 20 74 1717; e-mail bonferey@yahoo.fr; internet www.bonferey.net; f. 2007; Dir-Gen. MAHAMANE CHAIBOU.

Télévision Ténéré (TTV): BP 13600, Niamey; tel. 20-73-65-76; fax 20-73-77-75; e-mail tenerefm@intnet.ne; f. 2000; independent broadcaster in Niamey; Dir ABIBOU GARBA.

Other television channels include Dounia, Canal 3 and Bonferey. The independent operator, Télé Star, broadcasts several international or foreign channels in Niamey and environs, including TV5 Monde, Canal Horizon, CFI, RTL9, CNN and Euro News. Canal+Media Overseas, another independent operator, broadcasts over 50 television channels, both international and African, as well as a number of radio channels.

Finance

(cap. = capital; res = reserves; dep. = deposits; m. = million; brs = branches; amounts in francs CFA)

BANKING

In 2009 there were 10 commercial banks and one financial institution in Niger.

Central Bank

Banque Centrale des Etats de l'Afrique de l'Ouest (BCEAO): rue de l'Uranium, BP 487, Niamey; tel. 20-72-24-91; fax 20-73-47-43; HQ in Dakar, Senegal; f. 1962; bank of issue for the mem. states of the Union Economique et Monétaire Ouest-Africaine (UEMOA, comprising Benin, Burkina Faso, Côte d'Ivoire, Guinea-Bissau, Mali, Niger, Senegal and Togo); cap. 134,120m., res 1,474,195m., dep. 2,124,051m. (Dec. 2009); Gov. KONÉ TIÉMOKO MEYLIET; Dir in Niger ABDOULAYE SOUMANA; brs at Maradi and Zinder.

Commercial Banks

Bank of Africa—Niger (BOA—Niger): Immeuble BOA, rue du Gawèye, BP 10973, Niamey; tel. 20-73-36-20; fax 20-73-38-18; e-mail information@boaniger.com; internet www.boaniger.com; f. 1994 to acquire assets of Nigeria International Bank Niamey; 42.6% owned by African Financial Holding; cap. 3,500m., res 4,072m., dep. 92,026m. (Dec. 2009); Pres. PAUL DERREUMAUX; Dir-Gen. MAMADOU SÉNÉ; 8 brs.

Banque Atlantique Niger: BP 375, Rond Point Liberté, Niamey; tel. 20-73-98-88; fax 20-73-98-91; e-mail ban@banqueatlantique.net; internet www.banqueatlantique.net; f. 2005; 73% owned by Atlantic Financial Group, Lomé; total assets US $19.5m. (Dec. 2006); Chair. KONE DOSSONGUI; Man. Dir AMADOU MOUSTAPHA DIOUF.

Banque Commerciale du Niger (BCN): rue du Combattant, BP 11363, Niamey; tel. 20-73-39-15; fax 20-73-21-63; e-mail info@bcn.ne; internet www.bcn-niger.com; f. 1978; 83.15% owned by Libyan Arab Foreign Bank, 16.85% state-owned; cap. and res 1,477m., total assets 14,618m. (Dec. 2003); Administrator BASHIR M. SAMALOUS.

Banque Internationale pour l'Afrique au Niger (BIA—Niger): ave de la Mairie, BP 10350, Niamey; tel. 20-73-31-01; fax 20-73-35-95; e-mail bia@intnet.ne; internet www.bianiger.com; f. 1980; 35% owned by Groupe Belgolaise (Belgium); cap. 2,800m., res –25m., dep. 78,367m. (Dec. 2008); Pres. AMADOU HIMA SOULEY; Dir-Gen. OUHOUMOUDOU MAHAMADOU; 11 brs.

Banque Islamique du Niger pour le Commerce et l'Investissement (BINCI): Immeuble El Nasr, BP 12754, Niamey; tel. 20-73-27-30; fax 20-73-47-35; e-mail binci@intnet.ne; f. 1983; fmrly Banque Masraf Faisal Islami; 33% owned by Dar al-Maal al-Islami (Switzerland), 33% by Islamic Development Bank (Saudi Arabia); cap. 1,810m., total assets 7,453m. (Dec. 2003); Pres. ABDERRAOUF BENESSAÏAH; Dir-Gen. AISSANI OMAR.

Ecobank Niger: blvd de la Liberté, angle rue des Bâtisseurs, BP 13804, Niamey; tel. 20-73-71-81; fax 20-73-72-04; e-mail ecobankni@ecobank.com; internet www.ecobank.com; f. 1999; 99.85% owned by Ecobank Transnational Inc, Lomé; total assets 100,385m. (Dec. 2009); Chair. IBRAHIM IDDI ANGO; Dir-Gen. MOUKARAMOU CHANOU.

Société Nigérienne de Banque (SONIBANK): ave de la Mairie, BP 891, Niamey; tel. 20-73-47-40; fax 20-73-46-93; e-mail sonibank@intnet.ne; internet www.sonibank.net; f. 1990; 25% owned by Société Tunisienne de Banque; cap. 5,000m., res 7,355m., dep. 92,222m. (Dec. 2010); Pres. ILLA KANÉ; Dir-Gen. MOUSSA HAITOU; 6 brs.

Development Banks

Caisse de Prêts aux Collectivités Territoriales (CPCT): route Torodi, BP 730, Niamey; tel. 20-72-34-12; fax 20-72-30-80; f. 1970; 100% state-owned (94% by organs of local govt); cap. and res 744m., total assets 2,541m. (Dec. 2003); Administrator ABDOU DJIBO (acting).

Crédit du Niger (CDN): 11 blvd de la République, BP 213, Niger; tel. 20-72-27-01; fax 20-72-23-90; e-mail cdb-nig@intnet.ne; f. 1958; 54% state-owned, 20% owned by Caisse Nationale de Sécurité Sociale; transfer to full private ownership pending; cap. and res 1,058m., total assets 3,602m. (Dec. 2003); Administrator ABDOU DJIBO (acting).

Fonds d'Intervention en Faveur des Petites et Moyennes Entreprises Nigériennes (FIPMEN): Immeuble Sonara II, BP 252, Niamey; tel. 20-73-20-98; f. 1990; state-owned; cap. and res 124m. (Dec. 1991); Chair. AMADOU SALLA HASSANE; Man. Dir IBRAHIM BEIDARI.

Savings Bank

FINAPOSTE: BP 11778, Niamey; tel. 20-73-24-98; fax 20-73-35-69; fmrly Caisse Nationale d'Epargne; Chair. Mme PALFI; Man. Dir HASSOUME MATA.

STOCK EXCHANGE

Bourse Régionale des Valeurs Mobilières (BRVM): c/o Chambre de Commerce et d'Industrie du Niger, pl. de la Concertation, BP 13299, Niamey; tel. 20-73-66-92; fax 20-73-69-47; e-mail imagagi@brvm.org; internet www.brvm.org; f. 1998; national branch of BRVM (regional stock exchange based in Abidjan, Côte d'Ivoire, serving the member states of UEMOA); Man. IDRISSA S. MAGAGI.

INSURANCE

Agence Nigérienne d'Assurances (ANA): pl. de la Mairie, BP 423, Niamey; tel. 20-72-20-71; f. 1959; cap. 1.5m.; owned by L'Union des Assurances de Paris; Dir JEAN LASCAUD.

Caren Assurance: BP 733, Niamey; tel. 20-73-34-70; fax 20-73-24-93; e-mail carenas@intnet.ne; insurance and reinsurance; Dir-Gen. IBRAHIM IDI ANGO.

Leyma—Société Nigérienne d'Assurances et de Réassurances (SNAR—Leyma): BP 426, Niamey; tel. 20-73-57-72; fax 20-73-40-44; f. 1973; restructured 2001; Pres. AMADOU HIMA SOULEY; Dir-Gen. GARBA ABDOURAHAMANE.

La Nigérienne d'Assurance et de Réassurance: BP 13300, Niamey; tel. 20-73-63-36; fax 20-73-73-37; Dir-Gen. OUMAROU ALMA.

Union Générale des Assurances du Niger (UGAN): rue de Kalley, BP 11935, Niamey; tel. 20-73-54-06; fax 20-73-41-85; f. 1985; cap. 500m.; Pres. PATHÉ DIONE; Dir-Gen. MAMADOU TALATA; 7 brs.

Trade and Industry

GOVERNMENT AGENCIES

Centre National d'Energie Solaire (ONERSOL): BP 621, Niamey; tel. 20-72-39-23; e-mail cnes@intnet.ne; frmly Office National de l'Energie Solaire (ONERSOL), present name adopted 1998; govt agency for research and devt, commercial production and exploitation of solar devices; Dir ABDOUSSALAM BA.

Office des Eaux du Sous-Sol (OFEDES): BP 734, Niamey; tel. 20-74-01-19; fax 20-74-16-68; govt agency for the maintenance and devt of wells and boreholes; Pres. DJIBO HAMANI.

Office du Lait du Niger (OLANI): BP 404, Niamey; tel. 20-73-23-69; fax 20-73-36-74; f. 1971; devt and marketing of milk products; transferred to majority private ownership in 1998; Dir-Gen. M. DIENG.

Office National des Ressources Minières du Niger (ONAREM): Rond-Point Kennedy, BP 12716, Niamey; tel. 20-73-59-28; fax 20-73-28-12; f. 1976; govt agency for exploration, exploitation and marketing of all minerals; Pres. MOUDY MOHAMED; Dir-Gen. A. A. ASKIA.

Office des Produits Vivriers du Niger (OPVN): pl. du petit Marché, BP 474, Niamey; tel. 20-73-44-43; fax 20-73-24-68; e-mail opvn@opvn.net; internet www.opvn.net; govt agency for developing agricultural and food production; Dir-Gen. SEYDOU SADOU.

Riz du Niger (RINI): BP 476, Niamey; tel. 20-71-13-29; fax 20-73-42-04; f. 1967; cap. 825m. francs CFA; 30% state-owned; transfer to 100% private ownership proposed; production and marketing of rice; Pres. YOUSSOUF MOHAMED ELMOCTAR; Dir-Gen. M. HAROUNA.

DEVELOPMENT ORGANIZATIONS

Agence Française de Développement (AFD): 203 ave du Gountou-Yéna, BP 212, Niamey; tel. 20-72-33-93; fax 20-72-26-05; e-mail afdniamey@groupe-afd.org; internet www.afd.fr; Country Dir EMMANUEL DEBROISE.

Stichting Nederlandse Vrijwilligers Niger (SNV): ave des Zarmakoye, BP 10110, Niamey; tel. 20-75-36-33; fax 20-75-35-06; e-mail snvniger@snv.ne; internet www.snvniger.org; present in Niger since 1978; projects concerning food security, agriculture, the environment, savings and credit, marketing, water and communications; operations in Tillabéri, Zinder and Tahoua provinces; Dir-Gen. NIKO PATER.

CHAMBER OF COMMERCE

Chambre de Commerce d'Agriculture, d'Industrie et d'Artisanat du Niger: BP 209, Niamey; tel. 20-73-22-10; fax 20-73-46-68; e-mail cham209n@intnet.ne; internet www.ccaian.org; f. 1954; comprises 80 full mems and 40 dep. mems; Pres. IBRAHIM IDI ANGO; Sec.-Gen. SADOU AISSATA.

INDUSTRIAL AND TRADE ORGANIZATIONS

Centre Nigérien du Commerce Extérieur (CNCE): pl. de la Concertation, BP 12480, Niamey; tel. 20-73-22-88; fax 20-73-46-68; f. 1984; promotes and co-ordinates all aspects of foreign trade; Dir AÏSSA DIALLO.

Société Nationale de Commerce et de Production du Niger (COPRO-Niger): Niamey; tel. 20-73-28-41; fax 20-73-57-71; f. 1962; monopoly importer of foodstuffs; cap. 1,000m. francs CFA; 47% state-owned; Man. Dir DJIBRILLA HIMA.

EMPLOYERS' ORGANIZATIONS

Syndicat des Commerçants Importateurs et Exportateurs du Niger (SCIMPEXNI): Chambre de Commerce, d'Agriculture, d'Industrie et d'Artisanat du Niger, Niamey; tel. 20-73-33-17; Pres. M. SILVA; Sec.-Gen. INOUSSA MAÏGA.

Syndicat National des Petites et Moyennes Entreprises et Industries Nigériennes (SYNAPEMEIN): Chambre de Commerce, d'Agriculture, d'Industrie et d'Artisanat du Niger, Niamey; tel. 20-73-50-97; Pres. ALZOUMA SALEY; Sec.-Gen. HASSANE LAWAL KADER.

Syndicat Patronal des Entreprises et Industries du Niger (SPEIN): BP 415, Niamey; tel. 20-73-24-01; fax 20-73-47-07; f. 1994; Pres. AMADOU OUSMANE; Sec.-Gen. NOUHOU TARI.

UTILITIES

Electricity

Société Nigérienne d'Electricité (NIGELEC): 46 ave du Gen. de Gaulle, BP 11202, Niamey; tel. 20-72-26-92; fax 20-72-32-88; e-mail nigelec@intnet.ne; f. 1968; 95% state-owned; 51% transfer to private ownership proposed; production and distribution of electricity; Dir-Gen. ALHASSANE HALID.

Water

Société d'Exploitation des Eaux du Niger (SEEN): blvd Zarmaganda, BP 12209, Niamey; tel. 20-72-25-00; fax 20-73-46-40; fmrly Société Nationale des Eaux; 51% owned by Veolia Environnement (France); production and distribution of drinking water; Pres. ABARY DAN BOUZOUA SOULEYMENE; Dir-Gen. SEYNI SALOU.

Société de Patrimoine des Eaux du Niger: Immeuble Sonara II, 6ème étage, BP 10738, Niamey; tel. 20-73-43-40; fax 20-73-46-40; e-mail infos@spen.ne; internet www.spen.ne; f. 2000; Dir-Gen. ISSAKA HASSANE DJÉGOULÉ.

MAJOR COMPANIES

The following are among the largest companies in terms of either capital investment or employment.

Compagnie Minière d'Akouta (COMINAK): Immeuble Sonora, rond-point Kennedy, BP 10545, Niamey; tel. 20-73-45-86; fax 20-73-28-55; f. 1974; 34% owned by AREVA NC (France), 31% by ONAREM (Niger govt), 25% by Overseas Uranium Resources Development (Japan), 10% by Enusa Industrias Avanzadas (Spain); mining and processing of uranium at Akouta; cap. 3,500m. francs CFA; sales €66.3m. (2000); Chair. El Hadj ALLELE HABIBOU; 1,054 employees (2002).

Entreprise Nigérienne de Textile (ENITEX): route de Kolo, BP 10735, Niamey; tel. 20-73-25-11; f. 1997; cap. 1,000m. francs CFA; textile complex at Niamey; fmrly Société Nouvelle Nigérienne des Textiles (SONITEXTIL); 80% owned by China Worldbest Group (People's Rep. of China), 20% by Nigerien interests; sales 2,300m. francs CFA (2005); Chair. SAIDOU MAMANE; Man. Dir ZHANG ZHI QIANG; 920 employees (2002).

Les Moulins du Sahel (MDS): route de Kalmaharo, BP 12710, Niamey; tel. 20-74-26-07; fax 20-74-26-19; milling of flour; Dir-Gen. IBRAHIM BOLHO; 25 employees (2005).

Office National des Produits Pharmaceutiques et Chimiques (ONPPC): BP 11585, Niamey; tel. 20-74-27-92; fax 20-74-26-34; e-mail onppc@intnet.ne; f. 1962; cap. 440m. francs CFA; state-owned; Dir MARIAMA SAMBO.

Société des Brasseries et Boissons Gazeuses du Niger (BRANIGER): BP 11245, Niamey; tel. 20-74-26-83; fax 20-74-29-48; e-mail braniger@intnet.ne; f. 1967; cap. 1,482.3m. francs CFA; mfrs of beer and other soft drinks; Chair. JEAN-CLAUDE PALU; Dir-Gen. CYRIL BRUNEL; 114 employees (2009).

Société des Mines de l'Aïr (SOMAÏR): BP 10545, Niamey; tel. 20-72-29-70; fax 20-72-51-13; f. 1971; cap. 4,349m. francs CFA; 56.9% owned by AREVA NC (France), 36.6% by ONAREM (Niger Govt); uranium mining at Arlit; Chair. FREDERIC TONA; Dir-Gen. SERGE MARTINEZ; 571 employees (2003).

Société des Mines du Liptako (SML): BP 11583, Niamey; tel. 20-75-30-32; fax 20-75-30-40; e-mail smlniger@hotmail.com; internet www.etruscan.com/s/SamiraHill.asp; f. 2004; 80% owned by African GeoMin Mining Development Corpn (jtly owned by Etruscan Resources—Canada and Semafo—Canada), 20% by Nigerian Govt; operates gold mine at Samira Hill.

Société Nigérienne du Charbon (SONICHAR): BP 51, Agadez; tel. 20-44-02-48; fax 20-44-03-49; e-mail sonichar@intnet.ne; internet www.sonichar.com; f. 1975; cap. 19,730m. francs CFA; 69.3% state-owned, 10.1% owned by the Islamic Development Bank (Saudi Arabia), 15.8% by COMINAK and SOMAÏR; exploitation of coal reserves at Anou Araren and generation of electricity; Dir-Gen. ALKASSOUM MOUSSANA; 290 employees (2003).

Société Nigérienne de Cimenterie (SNC): BP 03, Malbaza; tel. 20-64-04-49; fax 20-64-04-50; e-mail snc_dfc@intnet.ne; internet malbazacement.com; f. 1963; privatized 1998; cap. 900m. francs CFA; 93% owned by Damnaz Cement Co Ltd (Nigeria); production and marketing of cement at Malbaza; Chair. IDI ANGO IBRAHIM; Dir-Gen. BO WALLANDER; 125 employees (2004).

Société Nigérienne de Distribution des Produits Pétroliers (SONIDEP): BP 11702, Niamey; tel. 20-73-33-34; fax 20-73-43-28; e-mail sonidep@intnet.ne; internet www.sonidep.com; f. 1977; 100% state-owned; transfer to 51% private ownership proposed; distribution of petroleum products; cap. 1,000m.; sales 45,018m. (2001); Dir-Gen. IDI ANGO OUSMANE; 160 employees (2001).

Société Nigérienne de l'Urbanisme et de Construction Immobilière (SONUCI): BP 532, Niamey; tel. 20-72-28-12; fax 20-72-36-25; Dir-Gen. ABDOULKARIM DAN MALAM.

Total Niger: route de l'Aéroport, BP 10349, Niamey; tel. 20-38-28-81; distribution of petroleum.

TRADE UNION FEDERATIONS

Confédération Démocratique des Travailleurs du Niger (CDTN): 1046 ave de l'Islam, BP 10766, Niamey; tel. 20-74-38-34; fax 20-74-28-55; e-mail c_cdtn@yahoo.fr; f. 2000; Sec.-Gen. ISSOUFOU SIDIBE.

Confédération des Travailleurs du Niger (CTN): Niamey; Sec.-Gen. MAMADOU SAKO.

Entente des Travailleurs du Niger (ETN): Bourse du Travail, BP 388, Niamey; tel. and fax 20-73-52-56; f. 2005 by merger of Confédération Nigérienne du Travail, Union Generale des Travailleurs du Niger and Union des Syndicats des Travailleurs du Niger.

Transport

ROADS

Niger is crossed by highways running from east to west and from north to south, giving access to neighbouring countries. A road is under construction to Lomé, Togo, via Burkina Faso, and the 428-km Zinder–Agadez road, scheduled to form part of the Trans-Sahara Highway, has been upgraded. In 2006 there were 18,550 km of classified roads, of which 3,803 km were paved.

Société Nationale des Transports Nigériens (SNTN): BP 135, Niamey; tel. 20-72-24-55; fax 20-74-47-07; e-mail stratech@intnet.ne; f. 1963; operates passenger and freight road-transport services; 49% state-owned; Chair. MOHAMED ABDOULAHI; Man. Dir BARKE M. MOUSTAPHA.

RAILWAYS

There are as yet no railways in Niger.

Organisation Commune Bénin-Niger des Chemins de Fer et des Transports (OCBN): BP 38, Niamey; tel. 20-73-27-90; f. 1959; 50% owned by Govt of Niger, 50% by Govt of Benin; manages the Benin-Niger railway project (begun in 1978); also operates more than 500 km within Benin (q.v.); extension to Niger proposed; transfer to private ownership proposed; Dir-Gen. RIGOBERT AZON.

INLAND WATERWAYS

The River Niger is navigable for 300 km within the country. Access to the sea is available by a river route from Gaya, in south-western Niger, to the coast at Port Harcourt, Nigeria, between September and March. Port facilities at Lomé, Togo, are used as a commercial outlet for land-locked Niger.

Société Nigérienne de Transit (NITRA): Zone Industrielle, BP 560, Niamey; tel. 20-73-22-53; fax 20-73-26-38; f. 1974; 48% owned by SNTN; customs agent, freight-handling, warehousing, etc.; manages Nigerien port facilities at Lomé, Togo; Pres. MOUNKAILA SEYDOU; Man. Dir SADE FATIMATA.

Société Nigérienne des Transports Fluviaux et Maritimes (SNTFM): Niamey; tel. 20-73-39-69; river and sea transport; cap. 64.6m. francs CFA; 99% state-owned; Man. Dir BERTRAND DEJEAN.

CIVIL AVIATION

There are international airports at Niamey (Hamani Diori), Agadez (Mano Dayak) and Zinder, and major domestic airports at Diffa, Maradi and Tahoua.

Agence Nationale de l'Aviation Civile (ANAC-NIGER): BP 1096, Niamey; fax 20-73-58-95; f. 2010; Dir-Gen. AMADOU SEYDOU YAYE.

Air Inter Afrique: Niamey; tel. 20-73-85-85; fax 20-73-69-73; f. 2001; operates services within West Africa; CEO CHEIKH OUSMANE DIALLO.

Nigeravia: BP 10454, Niamey; tel. 20-73-30-64; fax 20-74-18-42; e-mail nigavia@intnet.ne; internet www.nigeravia.com; f. 1991; operates domestic, regional and international services; Pres. and Dir-Gen. JEAN SYLVESTRE.

Sahel Airlines: rue de Rivoli, BP 10154, Niamey; tel. 20-73-65-71; fax 20-73-65-33; e-mail sahelair@intnet.ne; Dir-Gen. ABDOUL AZIZ LARABOU.

Société Nigérienne des Transports Aériens (SONITA): Niamey; f. 1991; owned by private Nigerien (81%) and Cypriot (19%) interests; operates domestic and regional services; Man. Dir ABDOULAYE MAIGA GOUDOUBABA.

Tourism

The Aïr and Ténéré Nature Reserve, covering an area of 77,000 sq km, was established in 1988. In 2010 74,278 tourists entered Niger, while receipts from tourism totalled $79m.

Centre Nigerien de Promotion Touristique (CNPT): ave de Président H. Luebke, BP 612, Niamey; tel. 20-73-24-47; fax 20-73-28-07; e-mail CNPT2@yahoo.fr; internet www.maisontourism-niger.com; Dirs BOULOU AKANO, IBRAHIM HALIDOU, KIEPIW TOYÉ FANTA.

Defence

As assessed at November 2011, Niger's armed forces totalled 5,300 men (army 5,200; air force 100). Paramilitary forces numbered 5,400 men, comprising the gendarmerie (1,400 men), the republican guard (2,500) and the national police force (1,500). Conscription is selective and lasts for two years.

Defence Expenditure: Estimated at 23,400m. francs CFA in 2010.

Chief of General Staff of the Armed Forces: Brig.-Gen. SOULEYMANE SALOU.

Chief of General Staff of the Land Army: Col SALIFOU MODY.

Chief of General Staff of the Air Force: Col HASSANE MOSSI.

Education

Education is available free of charge, and is officially compulsory for eight years between the ages of seven and 15 years. Primary education begins at the age of six or seven and lasts for six years. Secondary education begins at the age of 13 years, and comprises a four-year cycle followed by a three-year cycle. According to UNESCO estimates, primary enrolment in 2009/10 included 57% of children in the appropriate age-group (boys 63%; girls 51%). Secondary enrolment in 2007/08 included only 10% of the relevant age-group (boys 13%; girls 8%). The Abdou Moumouni University (formerly the University of Niamey) was inaugurated in 1973, and the Islamic University of Niger, at Say (to the south of the capital), was opened in 1987. Some 11,292 students were enrolled at those institutions in 2009/10. In December 2001 the Assemblée nationale approved legislation providing for the introduction of teaching in all local languages, with the aim of improving the literacy rate—one of the lowest in the world. Expenditure on education in 2008 represented 15.5% of total spending.

Bibliography

Abdourhame, B. *Crise institutionnelle et démocratisation au Niger*. Talance, Université de Bordeaux IV, 1997.

Adji, B. *Dans les méandres d'une transition politique*. Paris, Editions Karthala, 1998.

Asiwaju, A. I., and Barkindo, B. M. (Eds). *The Nigerian-Niger Transborder Co-operation*. Lagos, Malthouse Press, 1993.

Azam, J.-P. *Le Niger: la pauvreté en période d'ajustement*. Paris, L'Harmattan, 1993.

Bernus, E. *Touaregs, un peuple du désert*. Paris, Robert Laffont, 1996.

Carlier, M. *Meharistes au Niger*. Paris, L'Harmattan, 2001.

Charlick, R. B. *Niger: Personal Rule and Survival in the Sahel*. Boulder, CO, Westview Press, 1991.

Decalo, S. *Historical Dictionary of Niger*. 3rd edn. Metuchen, NJ, Scarecrow Press, 1996.

Decoudras, P.-M., and Souleymane, A. *La rébellion touarègue au Niger: actes des négociations avec le Gouvernement*. Bordeaux, Centre d'Etude d'Afrique Noire, Institut d'Etudes Politiques de Bordeaux, 1995.

Deschamps, A. *Niger 1995: Révolte touaregue: Du cessez-le-feu provisoire à la "paix définitive"*. Paris, L'Harmattan, 2000.

Fluchard, C. *Le PPN/RDA et la décolonisation du Niger 1946–1960*. Paris, L'Harmattan, 1996.

Frère, M.-S. *Presse et démocratie en Afrique francophone: les mots et les maux de la transition au Bénin et au Niger*. Paris, Editions Karthala, 2000.

Gilliard, P. *L'extrême pauvreté au Niger: mendier ou mourir?*. Paris, Editions Karthala, 2005.

Grégoire, E. *Touaregs du Niger: Le Destin d'un mythe*. Paris, Editions Karthala, 2000.

Hamani, A. *Les femmes et la politique au Niger*. Paris, L'Harmattan, 2001.

Harrison Church, R. J. *West Africa*. 8th edn, London, Longman, 1979.

Koré, L. *La rébellion touareg au Niger*. Paris, L'Harmattan, 2010.

Idrissa, K. (Ed.). *Le Niger: Etat et démocratie*. Paris, L'Harmattan, 2001.

Lund, C. *Law, Power and Politics in Niger: Land Struggles and the Rural Code*. Uppsala, Nordiska Africainstitutet, 1998.

Luxereau, A., and Roussel, B. *Changements économiques et sociaux au Niger*. Paris, L'Harmattan, 1998.

Maignan, J.-C., *et al*. *La difficile démocratisation du Niger*. Paris, Centre des hautes études sur l'Afrique et l'Asie modernes (CHEAM), 2000.

Mamadou, A. *A la conquête de la souveraineté populaire: les élections au Niger 1992–1999*. Niamey, Nouvelle Imprimerie de Niger, 2000.

Mayaki, I. A. *Le Caravane Passe*. Paris, Odilon Média, 1999.

Salifou, A. *La question touarègue au Niger*. Paris, Editions Karthala, 1993.

Le Niger. Paris, L'Harmattan, 2002.

Séré de Rivières, E. *Histoire du Niger*. Paris, Berger-Levrault, 1966.

Zakari, M. *L'islam dans l'espace nigérien. De 1960 aux années 2000*. (2 vols) Paris, L'Harmattan, 2010.

NIGERIA

Physical and Social Geography

AKIN L. MABOGUNJE

The Federal Republic of Nigeria covers an area of 909,890 sq km (351,310 sq miles) on the shores of the Gulf of Guinea, with Benin to the west, Niger to the north, Chad to the north-east, and Cameroon to the east and south-east. The population was enumerated at 140,003,542, according to provisional results of the census of March 2006, giving an average density of 157.2 persons per sq km. The population was estimated by the UN to have risen to 166,629,385 by mid-2012.

Nigeria became independent on 1 October 1960, and in 1968 adopted a new federal structure comprising 12 states. A federal capital territory was created in 1979. The number of states was increased to 19 in 1976, to 21 in 1987, to 30 in 1991, and to 36 in 1996.

PHYSICAL FEATURES

The physical features of Nigeria are of moderate dimensions. The highest lands are along the eastern border of the country and rise to a maximum of 2,040 m above sea-level at Vogel Peak, south of the Benue river. The Jos plateau, which is located close to the centre of the country, rises to 1,780 m at Shere Hill and 1,698 m at Wadi Hill. The plateau is also a watershed, from which streams flow to Lake Chad and to the rivers Niger and Benue. The land declines steadily northwards from the plateau; this area, known as the High Plains of Hausaland, is characterized by a broad expanse of level sandy plains, interspersed by rocky dome outcrops. To the south-west, across the Niger river, similar relief is represented in the Yoruba highlands, where the rocky outcrops are surrounded by forests or tall grass and form the major watershed for rivers flowing northwards to the Niger and southwards to the sea. Elsewhere in the country, lowlands of less than 300 m stretch inland from the coast for over 250 km and continue in the trough-like basins of the Niger and Benue rivers. Lowland areas also exist in the Rima and Chad basins at the extreme north-west and north-east of the country, respectively. These lowlands are dissected by innumerable streams and rivers flowing in broad sandy valleys.

The main river of Nigeria is the Niger, the third longest river of Africa. Originating in the Fouta Djallon mountains of north-east Sierra Leone, it enters Nigeria for the last one-third of its 4,200 km course. It flows first south-easterly, then due south and again south-easterly to Lokoja, where it converges with its principal tributary, the Benue. From here the river flows due south until Aboh, where it merges with the numerous interlacing distributaries of its delta. The Benue rises in Cameroon, flows in a south-westerly direction into the Niger, and receives on its course the waters of the Katsina Ala and Gongola rivers. The other main tributaries of the Niger within Nigeria are the Sokoto, Kaduna and Anambra rivers. Other important rivers in the country include the Ogun, the Oshun, the Imo and the Cross, many of which flow into the sea through a system of lagoons. The Nigerian coastline is relatively straight, with few natural indentations.

CLIMATE

Nigeria has a climate which is characterized by relatively high temperatures throughout the year. The average annual maximum varies from 35°C in the north to 31°C in the south; the average annual minimum from 23°C in the south to 18°C in the north. On the Jos plateau and the eastern highlands altitude moderates the temperatures, with the maximum no more than 28°C and the minimum sometimes as low as 14°C.

The annual rainfall total decreases from over 3,800 mm at Forcados on the coast to under 650 mm at Maiduguri in the north-east of the country. The length of the rainy season ranges from almost 12 months in the south to under five months in the north. Rain starts in January in the south and moves gradually across country. June, July, August and September are the rainiest months country-wide. In many parts of the south, however, there is a slight break in the rains for some two to three weeks in late July and early August. No such break occurs in the northern part of the country, and the rainy season continues uninterrupted for three to six months.

SOILS AND VEGETATION

The broad pattern of soil distribution in the country reflects both the climatic conditions and the geological structure; heavily leached, reddish-brown, sandy soils are found in the south, and light or moderately leached, yellowish-brown, sandy soils in the north. The difference in colour relates to the extent of leaching the soil has undergone.

The nutrient content of the soil is linked to the geological structure. Over a large part of the northern and south-western areas of the country the geological structure is that of old crystalline Basement complex rocks. These are highly mineralized and give rise to soils of high nutrient status, although variable from place to place. On the sedimentary rocks found in the south-east, north-east and north-west of the country the soils are sandy and less variable but are deficient in plant nutrients. They are highly susceptible to erosion.

The vegetation displays clear east-west zonation. In general, mangrove and rainforests are found in the south, occupying about 20% of the area of the country, while grassland of various types occupies the rest. Four belts of grassland can be identified. Close to the forest zone is a derived savannah belt, which is evidently the result of frequent fires in previously forested areas. This belt is succeeded by the Guinea, the Sudan and the Sahel savannah northwards in that order. The height of grass and density of wood vegetation decrease with each succeeding savannah belt.

RESOURCES

Although nearly 180,000 sq km of Nigeria is in the forest belt, only 23,000 sq km account for most of its timber resources. These forests are mainly in Ondo, Bendel and Cross River States. Nigeria exports a wide variety of tropical hardwoods, and internal consumption has been growing rapidly.

Cattle, goats and, to a lesser extent, sheep constitute important animal resources. Most of the cattle are found in the Sudan grassland belt in the far north. Poultry and pigs are increasing in importance.

Coastal waters are becoming important fishing grounds. Traditionally, however, major sources of fish have been Lake Chad in the extreme north-east, the lagoons along the coast, the creeks and distributaries of the Niger Delta and the various rivers in the country.

Mineral resources are varied, although considerable exploration remains to be carried out. Tin and columbite are found in alluvial deposits on the Jos plateau. Extensive reserves of medium-grade iron ore exist, and iron and steel production is being developed.

Fuel resources include deposits of lignite and sub-bituminous coal, exploited at Enugu since 1915; however, total reserves are small. More significant are the petroleum reserves, estimates of which alter with each new discovery in the offshore area. The oil produced, being of low sulphur content and high quality, is much in demand on the European and US markets. Since Libya restricted production in 1973, Nigeria has been Africa's leading producer of petroleum. Natural gas is also found in abundance, and has been undergoing development since the mid-1980s.

POPULATION

The Nigerian population is extremely diverse. There are more than 500 spoken languages, and well over 250 ethnic groups, some numbering fewer than 10,000 people. Ten groups, notably Hausa-Fulani, Yoruba, Ibo, Kanuri, Tiv, Edo, Nupe, Ibibio and Ijaw, account for nearly 80% of the total population. Much of the population is concentrated in the southern part of the country, as well as in the area of dense settlement around Kano in the north. Between these two areas is the sparsely populated Middle Belt.

Urban life has a long history in Nigeria, with centres of population such as Kano, Benin and Zaria dating from the Middle Ages. Recent economic development, however, has stimulated considerable rural–urban migration and led to the phenomenal growth of such cities as Lagos, Ibadan, Kaduna and Port Harcourt. In December 1991 the federal capital was formally transferred to Abuja (which then had an estimated population of 107,069); however, a number of government departments and non-government institutions have remained in the former capital, Lagos. According to UN estimates, at mid-2010 Lagos had 10.5m., Kano 3.4m., Ibadan 2.8m., and Kaduna 1.6m. inhabitants.

Recent History

RALPH YOUNG

The territory comprising the Federal Republic of Nigeria was colonized by the United Kingdom during the second half of the 19th and the first decade of the 20th centuries. Much of the administration remained under the control of traditional rulers, supervised by the colonial authorities. In 1947 the United Kingdom introduced a new Nigerian Constitution, establishing a federal framework based on three regions and aimed at accommodating the interests of Nigeria's diverse ethnic groups: notably the Ibo (in the east), the Yoruba (in the west) and the Hausa and Fulani (in the north). The Northern Region, whose inhabitants were mainly Muslims, contained around one-half of Nigeria's total population.

Politically, the Eastern Region was dominated by the National Council for Nigeria and the Cameroons, led by Dr Nnamdi Azikiwe, with mainly Ibo support, while in the Western Region Obafemi Awolowo's Action Group drew upon mainly Yoruba support. The Northern Region was dominated by the Northern People's Congress (NPC), representing the traditional and mercantile Hausa-Fulani élite; its leader was the region's premier, the Sardauna of Sokoto, Ahmadu (later Sir Ahmadu) Bello. Abubakar (later Sir Abubakar) Tafawa Balewa, a former schoolteacher and Bello's key lieutenant, became the first federal Prime Minister in 1957.

In 1954 the federation became self-governing, and, following federal legislative elections in 1959 in which the NPC obtained the largest representation, the Federation of Nigeria achieved independence on 1 October 1960, initially as a constitutional monarchy, with Tafawa Balewa as Prime Minister and Minister of Foreign Affairs. In June 1961 the northern section of the neighbouring UN Trust Territory of British Cameroons, formerly part of the German protectorate of Kamerun, was incorporated into Nigeria's Northern Region. In October 1963 the country was renamed the Federal Republic of Nigeria, remaining a member of the Commonwealth. Azikiwe took office as Nigeria's first (non-executive) President.

MILITARY INTERVENTION AND CIVIL WAR, 1966–76

Nigeria's regional rivalries were reflected in the federal armed forces. In January 1966 Tafawa Balewa's Government was overthrown by junior (mainly Ibo) army officers; Balewa was killed, together with the finance minister and several senior military officers. Maj.-Gen. (later Gen.) Johnson Aguiyi-Ironsi, the army's Commander-in-Chief and an Ibo, took control. The coup was followed by serious anti-Ibo riots in Northern urban centres in May. In July Aguiyi-Ironsi himself was killed in a counter-coup by northern troops. Power was transferred to the Chief of Army Staff, Lt-Col (later Gen.) Yakubu Gowon, a Christian northerner. Gowon restored some degree of discipline to the armed forces, but in May 1967 the Eastern Region's military Governor, Lt-Col Chukwuemeka Odumegwu-Ojukwu, proclaimed its independence as the 'Republic of Biafra'. In July fighting commenced, and in the ensuing civil war between 500,000 and 2m. civilians died, mainly from starvation, before Biafra's surrender in January 1970. Gowon subsequently implemented a strategy of reconciliation, and initiated preparations to return the country to civilian rule. These were seriously impeded by the failure of the 1973 population census to produce credible results. Having announced in October 1974 that the return to civilian rule, scheduled for 1976, had been indefinitely postponed, in July 1975 Gowon was forcibly 'retired', and was succeeded as Head of Government by Brig. (later Gen.) Murtala Ramat Muhammed. He proceeded to order major administrative reforms, including the creation of new states, bringing the total from 12 to 19.

FROM OBASANJO TO SHAGARI AND THE SECOND REPUBLIC, 1976–83

Muhammed was assassinated in February 1976 by disaffected army officers, and power was transferred to Muhammed's deputy, Lt-Gen. (later Gen.) Olusegun Obasanjo, who promised the return to civilian rule by October 1979. During 1976 legislation to reform the structure of local government was introduced, and a Constituent Assembly was created in August 1977. The new Constitution, promulgated in September 1978, envisaged an executive presidency and a bicameral legislature. To win the presidential election, a candidate would need to obtain an outright majority of the national vote while winning at least 25% of the votes in two-thirds of the states. Executive governors and legislatures were to be elected in each state. The ending of the state of emergency in September 1978 spurred political party activity, but, of the 19 associations that eventually applied for registration, only five received approval by the Federal Election Commission (FEDECO).

Among these five, the Unity Party of Nigeria (UPN) was led by Chief Obafemi Awolowo, a prominent First Republic politician and Yoruba leader. The National Party of Nigeria (NPN) included such veteran NPC politicians as Alhaji Shehu Shagari (later selected as its presidential candidate). The People's Redemption Party, the northern-based opposition to the NPN, was led by Alhaji Aminu Kano. The Nigerian People's Party (NPP) chose ex-President Azikiwe as its presidential candidate, while the Greater Nigeria People's Party, a breakaway faction of the NPP, selected Alhaji Waziri Ibrahim. At elections in July 1979 to the National Assembly, and for State Assemblies and State Governors, the NPN received the most widespread support, securing 37% of the seats in the House of Representatives, 38% in the Senate and 36% in the State Assemblies; it also captured seven of the 19 state governorships. At the presidential election in August, Shagari obtained the mandatory 25% of the vote in 12, rather than the required 13, states; the Supreme Court upheld his election, however. On 1 October, the new Constitution came into force, and Shagari took office as President of the Second Republic.

National and state elections took place in August–September 1983. In the presidential poll Shagari was returned for a second term, receiving 47% of the total votes cast. The NPN attained a decisive majority in the elections to the Senate (60 seats out of 96) and the House of Representatives (264 seats out of 450), and won 13 of the 19 state governorships. However, the credibility of the elections was undermined by evidence of widespread malpractice.

THE RETURN OF MILITARY RULE

On 31 December 1983 Shagari was deposed in a bloodless coup led by Maj.-Gen. Muhammadu Buhari, a former military Governor of Borno State and Federal Commissioner for Petroleum during 1976–78. All political parties were banned, FEDECO was dissolved, and all bank accounts were temporarily frozen. The new regime consisted of a reconstituted Supreme Military Council (SMC), headed by Buhari; a National Council of States, presided over by military Governors; a Federal Executive Council; and State Executive Councils. The authorities stated that there was no schedule for a return to civilian rule, and prohibited all debate on Nigeria's political future.

In August 1985 Buhari's regime was overthrown by Maj.-Gen. (later Gen.) Ibrahim Babangida, the Chief of Army Staff. The SMC was replaced by a 28-member Armed Forces Ruling Council (AFRC), headed by Babangida. A Council of Ministers was formed, together with a reconstituted Council of States. State governorships were redistributed, and Buhari's ministers were removed. Babangida declared a national economic emergency in October 1985 and assumed extensive powers over the economy. Although formal negotiations with the IMF were suspended, preparations were made during 1986 for the introduction of a structural adjustment programme that received World Bank support. In January 1986 Babangida announced that power would be transferred to civilian hands on 1 October 1990.

In February 1986 Babangida announced that Nigeria's application for full membership of the Organization of the Islamic Conference had been accepted, sparking unrest among the non-Muslim sector of the population. In May some 15 people, mostly students, were shot dead by police during demonstrations at the Ahmadu Bello University, in Zaria. In March 1987 violent clashes erupted between Muslim and Christian youths in Kaduna State, causing some 30 deaths. In April the AFRC formed an Advisory Council on Religious Affairs, comprising Muslim and Christian leaders, to investigate the causes of the violence, and the authorities issued decrees banning religious organizations in schools and universities.

In July 1987 the AFRC announced that the transfer of power to civilian hands would be delayed until 1992. In September the number of states was increased from 19 to 21, while the AFRC proscribed all categories of former politicians and its own membership from contesting the future elections. The AFRC also established a constitutional review committee and a new National Electoral Commission (NEC). Babangida subsequently announced that the new Constitution would be promulgated in 1989, with a Constituent Assembly to debate its terms. Accordingly, in April 1988 newly elected local government councillors elected 450 members to the Constituent Assembly, while the AFRC nominated a further 117, to represent various interest groups. Debate over the new draft Constitution threatened to founder when Muslims demanded the inclusion of *Shari'a* courts, forcing Babangida to ban further debate on this topic. The Assembly then presented its draft Constitution the following April.

With the ban on political parties lifted in May 1989, the Constitution was promulgated and was due to be enacted in October 1992. Elections for the Government of the Third Republic were to be contested only by political parties approved by the AFRC from a list compiled by the NEC. A total of 13 parties succeeded in fulfilling the substantial registration requirements. In October, however, after the NEC had recommended six of the 13 associations, Babangida announced the AFRC's decision to dissolve all 13 because they lacked distinctive ideologies and were allied to discredited civilian politicians. In their place the AFRC created two new political parties, the Social Democratic Party (SDP) and the National Republican Convention (NRC). In December the NEC published draft constitutions and manifestos for both. An abortive coup took place in April 1990, when junior officers from the Middle Belt attempted to seize Dodan Barracks in Lagos. In August Chief Tom Ikimi, a southerner, was elected Chairman of the NRC, while Baba Kingibe, a northerner, was installed as SDP Chairman.

Following the April 1990 coup attempt, Babangida announced that the presidency would be restructured in preparation for civilian rule, and that the size of the armed forces would be substantially reduced. In September three military officers were retired from the Government, leaving Maj.-Gen. Sani Abacha, the Minister of Defence, as the only serving officer. Twenty-one civilian Deputy Governors were appointed at state level, pending gubernatorial elections in 1991. In December local government elections took place, although only an estimated 20% of registered voters participated.

The democratic transition was overshadowed by growing ethnic and religious conflict. In October 1990 the Movement for the Survival of the Ogoni People (MOSOP) was formed to oppose Shell's exploitation of petroleum reserves in the Ogoni territory in Rivers State. Following demonstrations organized by MOSOP, some 80 Ogonis were killed by security forces. In April 1991 several demonstrations by Muslims in the northern state of Katsina, in protest against a newspaper article regarded as blasphemous, resulted in violence. In the same month around 130 people, mainly Christians, were killed in riots in Bauchi and other predominantly Muslim states. Some 120 Muslims were reportedly killed by troops sent to restore order. In late 1991 violence erupted in Taraba, in the east, due to a long-standing land dispute between the Tiv and Jukun ethnic groups; this caused an estimated 5,000 fatalities by March 1992.

In September 1991 the creation of nine new states, to bring the total to 30, exacerbated rather than eased tensions, prompting several violent demonstrations. In October primary elections took place to select candidates for the forthcoming gubernatorial and state assembly elections. In November, following allegations of fraud, the results were annulled in nine states, and 12 candidates were disqualified. The resulting controversy led to increased divisions in both parties, and especially the SDP.

Federal Capital Moves to Abuja

In December 1991 the seat of federal government was formally transferred from Lagos to Abuja. In gubernatorial and state assembly elections that month, the SDP gained a majority in 16 State Assemblies, while the NRC won 14; however, NRC candidates were elected as Governors in 16 of the 30 states, including those in the south-east of Nigeria, where the SDP had previously received support. In May 1992 widespread rioting broke out after sharp increases in transport fares, while further riots occurred following the arrest of Dr Beko Ransome-Kuti, Chairman of the Campaign for Democracy (CD), an alliance of 25 civil society organizations. The Government subsequently banned all associations with a religious or ethnic base.

At the National Assembly elections in July 1992 the SDP gained a majority in both chambers, securing 52 seats to the NRC's 37 in the Senate and 314 seats to the NRC's 275 in the House of Representatives. However, the legislature's formal inauguration was postponed until 2 January 1993, when the full installation of civilian rule was planned. Primary elections for the NRC and SDP presidential candidates commenced on 1 August 1992, but were suspended owing to widespread irregularities. A further attempt took place on 12, 19 and 26 September. By the end of the second round of voting four leading candidates had emerged: Gen. (retd) Shehu Musa Yar'Adua and Chief Olu Falae (SDP), and Alhaji Umaru Shinkafi and Adamu Ciroma (NRC). However, 10 of the original 23 aspirants (including Falae) withdrew from the third stage of polling, alleging fraudulent practices. Yar'Adua claimed to have won the SDP nomination, while Shinkafi and Ciroma were to contest a final poll for the NRC candidacy on 10 October.

On 6 October 1992 the AFRC suspended the primaries, and when the NEC reported malpractices Babangida disqualified all 23 contestants from standing again. The presidential election (scheduled for 5 December) was postponed until 12 June 1993, and the transition to civilian rule until 27 August. Under new arrangements, the AFRC was to be replaced by a National

Defence and Security Council (NDSC), and the Council of Ministers by a civilian Transitional Council. In December 1992 the bicameral National Assembly was formally convened in Abuja. On 2 January 1993 the 14-member NDSC and Transitional Council took office. The former was chaired by Babangida, and the latter by Chief Ernest Shonekan, a prominent businessman who was designated as Head of Government.

Disputed Outcome of the 1993 Election

National party congresses took place, as scheduled, during 27–29 March 1993: the NRC selected Alhaji Bashir Othman Tofa, an economist and businessman, as its presidential candidate, while Chief Moshood Kashimawo Olawale Abiola, a wealthy publisher, emerged as the SDP's choice. In April Abiola chose the former SDP chairman Baba Kingibe as his vice-presidential candidate, and Tofa selected Dr Sylvester Ugoh, who had served in the Shagari administration. Voter participation in the presidential election on 12 June 1993 was low, but international monitors reported few problems. The initial results, released by the NEC, indicated that Abiola had a clear lead. The NEC then withheld the remaining results until further notice. Widespread confusion followed, and the NDSC was accused of sabotaging the elections. Later in June the Campaign for Democracy issued election results indicating that Abiola had won a majority of votes in 19 states.

On 23 June 1993 the NDSC declared the election invalid, halted related court proceedings, suspended the NEC, and repealed all decrees regulating the transition to civilian rule. New electoral regulations were introduced that effectively precluded Abiola and Tofa from contesting a further poll. Babangida maintained that the election was marred by corruption and other irregularities, while insisting that he remained committed to the transition on 27 August; in order to meet this schedule, a reconstituted NEC was to supervise the selection of two new presidential candidates. Abiola, however, continued to claim that he had been legitimately elected to the presidency. The United Kingdom announced a review of its relations with Nigeria, and imposed a number of military sanctions, while the USA immediately suspended all assistance to the Government. In early July 1993 a demonstration, organized by the CD, led to rioting. Although order was restored by the security forces, sporadic unrest continued. The NDSC announced that a new presidential election was to take place on 14 August in order to fulfil the pledge to transfer power on 27 August, but the SDP declared its intention to boycott any electoral process that superseded its victory on 12 June.

'Interim National Government'

In late July 1993 Babangida announced that an Interim National Government (ING) was to be created, given the insufficient time to meet the 27 August deadline. A committee comprising officials of the two parties and senior military officers was established to determine the ING's composition. Abiola immediately declared his intention of forming a 'parallel government'; following alleged death threats, he fled abroad to solicit international support for his claim to the presidency. In August the CD continued its campaign of civil disobedience over the election's annulment, calling a three-day general strike (which was widely observed in the south-west, where Abiola enjoyed strong support). Several prominent members of the CD were arrested, while additional restrictions were imposed on the press. Later in August Babangida unexpectedly announced his resignation, reportedly because of pressure from within the NDSC. On 27 August a 32-member Interim Federal Executive Council, headed by Chief Shonekan, was installed; the new administration, which included several members of the former Transitional Council, was to supervise preparations for local government elections later that year and a presidential election in early 1994; the transitional period for the return to civilian rule was extended to 31 March 1994. The inclusion in the ING of several members of the dissolved NDSC, including Abacha—appointed to the new post of Vice-President—prompted strikes, which caused widespread economic disruption.

As the new head of state, Shonekan pledged his commitment to the democratic process, and initiated negotiations with the Nigerian Labour Congress (NLC); he also released several journalists and CD figures. In early September 1993 the NLC and the National Union of Petroleum Workers and Natural Gas (NUPENG) provisionally suspended strike action, after the ING agreed to consider their demands. A series of military appointments, which included the nomination of Lt-Gen. Oladipo Diya as Chief of Defence Staff, effectively removed Babangida's supporters from key positions within the armed forces, thereby strengthening Abacha's position. Diya, who had reportedly opposed the election's annulment, declared that the military's political involvement would cease, and in the same month Abiola returned to Lagos amid popular acclaim. Later in September the NRC and SDP agreed to a new electoral timetable, with local government elections and a presidential election taking place concurrently in February 1994. The CD announced the resumption of strike action in support of demands for the installation of Abiola as President.

Abacha and the PRC, 1993–98

Shonekan announced his resignation as head of state on 17 November 1993, following a meeting with senior military officials, and transferred power to Abacha. The following day Abacha dissolved all organs of state and bodies established under the transitional process, replaced the State Governors with military administrators, prohibited political activity (thereby proscribing the NRC and the SDP), and announced the formation of a Provisional Ruling Council (PRC) comprising senior military officials and the principal members of a new Federal Executive Council (FEC). He promised, however, to transfer power to a civilian government, and pledged to convene a conference mandated to determine Nigeria's constitutional future. On 21 November Abacha introduced legislation restoring the 1979 Constitution. To counter domestic and international criticism, several prominent supporters of Abiola, including Kingibe and four former members of the ING, were appointed to the PRC and the FEC, which were installed on 24 November. Abacha also held discussions with Abiola, while the NLC agreed to abandon strike action after the Government acted to limit proposed price increases for petroleum products.

In April 1994 the Government announced the establishment of the National Constitutional Conference (NCC) to prepare a new draft constitution by late October; the ban on political activity was to end in January 1995. In May 1994 the National Democratic Coalition (NADECO), a new pro-democracy organization including former politicians, retired military officers and human rights activists, demanded Abacha's resignation by the end of May, and urged a boycott of the NCC. Nevertheless, elections took place that month at local government levels to select the 273 conference delegates, although the boycott was widely observed in the south-west. Also in May Ken Saro-Wiwa, the MOSOP leader, was arrested in connection with the deaths of four Ogoni electoral candidates. At the end of May Abiola announced his intention of forming a government of national unity by 12 June (the anniversary of the presidential election). Violent anti-Government protests followed the expiry of the date stipulated by NADECO for the military regime's resignation.

In early June 1994 several former Senate members were charged with treason, after they reconvened and declared the Government illegal. Following a symbolic ceremony in the same month at which Abiola was publicly inaugurated as head of a parallel government, he was arrested and charged with treason, prompting protests from pro-democracy organizations and criticism from both the British and US Governments.

NUPENG initiated strike action in July 1994 to demand Abiola's release and installation as President; the strike was subsequently joined by the Petroleum and Natural Gas Senior Staff Association of Nigeria (PENGASSAN). Government troops distributed fuel in an attempt to ease the resultant national shortage, while senior officials of NUPENG and PENGASSAN were arrested. In early August the trial of Abiola was adjourned, after a defence appeal that the High Court in Abuja had no jurisdiction over an offence allegedly committed in Lagos. Abiola, however, refused to accept bail, since the conditions required him to refrain from political activity. Later that month Abacha replaced the senior officials of NUPENG and PENGASSAN, and ordered petroleum workers to end strike action; the effects of the strike soon began to recede. In September Abacha promulgated legislation extending the period of detention without trial to three months and prohibited legal action challenging government decisions. The Minister of Justice was subsequently dismissed, after protesting that he had not been consulted. The trial of Saro-Wiwa and a further 14 MOSOP activists, on charges of complicity in the murder of the four Ogoni traditional leaders, commenced in January 1995. In March some 150 military officers were arrested, indicating widespread disaffection within the armed forces. The authorities subsequently claimed to have uncovered a coup conspiracy, and arrested the former head of state, Gen. (retd) Olusegun Obasanjo, and his former deputy, Maj.-Gen. (retd) Shehu Musa Yar'Adua, together with other prominent critics.

The constitutional proposals approved in late 1994 were endorsed by the NCC in April 1995. At the end of that month, however, the conference reversed its previous decision that a civilian government be installed on 1 January 1996, since the timetable was untenable. In June 1995 about 40 people, including several civilians, were arraigned before a special military tribunal in connection with the alleged coup attempt in March; it was reported that Obasanjo and Yar'Adua had also been secretly charged. Further arrests of pro-democracy activists occurred that month to pre-empt protests on the anniversary of the annulled election; nevertheless, a one-day general strike, supported by the CD, was widely observed. At the end of June reports emerged that the military tribunal had sentenced Obasanjo to 25 years' imprisonment, while Yar'Adua and 13 other military officers received the death penalty, prompting an international outcry. In early October the PRC commuted the death sentences and reduced the terms of imprisonment, although the capital charges against Abiola remained. Concurrently, Abacha announced a three-year programme for transition to civilian rule, with a new President to be inaugurated on 1 October 1998, following elections at local, state and national level.

At the end of October 1995 Saro-Wiwa and a further eight Ogoni activists were sentenced to death by the special military tribunal for inciting the 1994 killing of the Ogoni election candidates; six other defendants, including MOSOP's Deputy President, were acquitted. An international campaign against the convictions ensued, led by Saro-Wiwa's son. However, on 10 November (coinciding with a Commonwealth summit in Auckland, New Zealand) the nine convicted Ogonis were executed. Nigeria was suspended from the Commonwealth and threatened with expulsion if democracy was not restored within two years. Later that month the European Union (EU) reaffirmed the sanctions imposed in 1993 (notably an embargo on exports of military equipment), and extended visa restrictions to civilian members of the regime; the EU also announced the suspension of development co-operation with Nigeria. The Governments of the USA, South Africa and EU member states recalled their diplomatic representatives in protest at the executions. Additional security forces were dispatched to Ogoniland to deter protests, while a further 19 Ogonis were charged with complicity in the May 1994 murders.

Nigerian officials met the Commonwealth Ministerial Action Group (CMAG) in June 1996 in an attempt to avert the imposition of sanctions; shortly before, the Government released a number of political prisoners and promulgated legislation regarding the registration of political parties. The Nigerian delegation demanded that Nigeria be readmitted to the Commonwealth, in exchange for the Government's adoption of a programme for transition to civilian rule by October 1998. Though rejecting this as unsatisfactory, the Commonwealth remained divided over further measures. It was finally agreed that the Commonwealth would suspend the adoption of sanctions, with the situation being reviewed at a September meeting of the CMAG.

In October 1996 the creation of a further six states increased the Federation to 36. An Ijaw demonstration in Warri, Delta State's economic capital, in March 1997, in protest at the relocation of local government headquarters from Ijaw to Itsekiri territory, precipitated violent clashes. Protesters seized Shell installations and took some 100 employees hostage. By mid-April it was reported that about 90 people had been killed, while the disruption in petroleum production had contributed to a national fuel shortage, effectively halting the transportation system in much of the country. Later in May a commission of inquiry was established to investigate the cause of the clashes and submit recommendations for restoring order in the region.

In May 1997 some 22 pro-democracy and human rights organizations, including MOSOP and the CD, formed a loose alliance, the United Action for Democracy, to press for the restoration of democracy. In July the authorities announced a new electoral timetable, with elections to the State Assemblies taking place in December and those for the National Assembly in April 1998; gubernatorial and presidential elections would occur that August. The United Nigerian Congress Party proved to be the most successful party at the December 1997 elections, winning control of 29 of the 36 State Assemblies, with a total of 637 of the 990 contested seats.

A CMAG report on Nigeria, prepared for the Commonwealth Heads of Government summit in October 1997, criticized the Government's record on human rights and the inadequacies of the planned transition process. With Nigeria having enhanced its reputation by pressurizing the military rulers in Sierra Leone, another Commonwealth member, to restore the democratically elected Government there, the Commonwealth members postponed the threat of more severe economic sanctions and Nigeria's expulsion for a further year, reiterating demands that democracy be restored by 1 October 1998.

In December 1997 Maj.-Gen. Yar'Adua died in suspicious circumstances in prison, and an assassination attempt occurred at Abuja airport against Abacha's deputy, Diya, who was known to favour the military's complete withdrawal from government. Diya and several others were then arrested and charged with planning a coup. A special military tribunal commenced proceedings in February 1998 against some 30 defendants. In April Diya and five others were sentenced to death; a further four defendants received terms of life imprisonment, while five received shorter sentences and 15 were acquitted. Clemency appeals were made by foreign governments and prominent Nigerians.

By early March 1998 the Government was clearly manoeuvring to create support for an Abacha presidency. The five registered political parties all proceeded to nominate Abacha at special government-funded conventions in mid-April. Public rejection of Abacha was reflected, however, in the widespread boycott of the 25 April legislative elections. The political atmosphere became increasingly volatile from late April when some 10 people were killed in bomb attacks in Ife and Lagos. In the course of anti-Government protests in early May, security forces killed several demonstrators and made numerous arrests. Attempts at constructing a united pro-democracy alliance saw the formation in May of a Joint Action Committee of Nigeria (JACON), comprising 45 groups which opposed the regime.

Abubakar and Transition, 1998–99

On 8 June 1998 Abacha died unexpectedly. Senior military officers rapidly asserted authority, and the Chief of Defence Staff, Maj.-Gen. Abdulsalami Abubakar, was designated as Abacha's successor. The regime pledged to continue the Abacha Government's transition to civilian rule. Abubakar, promoted to the rank of General, was formally installed as head of state on 9 June 1998. The Commonwealth Secretary-General announced that sanctions against Nigeria would remain pending democratic elections. In early July, following discussions with UN officials, the new authorities freed Abiola, who, on his release, collapsed and subsequently died. Rioting ensued amid speculation over official responsibility; however, an autopsy indicated that Abiola had died of heart failure. Abubakar promised to release other political prisoners and to complete the transition to civilian rule on 29 May 1999. The Government dissolved the five existing political parties. In early August 1998 a new 31-member Federal Executive Council was appointed, including civilian members, along with an Independent National Electoral Commission (INEC). The INEC soon announced that local government elections would occur in

December and state elections in January 1999, with national legislative and presidential elections in February.

Abubakar also initiated discussions with opposition groupings; however, JACON activists rejected any continuation of military rule and NADECO leaders demanded a government of national unity and the holding of a sovereign national conference. Abubakar continued to release political prisoners (including Obasanjo, freed in June), and to urge exiles to return home. (Wole Soyinka and the MOSOP leader, Ledum Mitee, eventually returned in October 1998, although others remained abroad.) When the INEC had commenced proceedings in late August 1998, numerous political groupings applied for registration, including the People's Democratic Party (PDP), established by northern politicians who had urged Abacha not to seek election in March. The All People's Party (APP) was created by a coalition of associations that had received considerable support during Abacha's rule, while the Alliance for Democracy (AD) was formed by politicians linked to NADECO and committed to Nigeria's political restructuring. Of the 29 parties applying for registration, the INEC approved nine in late October.

At local elections on 5 December 1998 the PDP gained control of about 60% of municipal councils. The INEC ruled that only the PDP, APP and AD had received sufficient votes to be allowed to contest the state and federal elections in early 1999. At the state elections on 9 January the PDP secured the most votes overall. The APP fared well in the Middle Belt and in parts of the north, while the AD performed strongly in the south-west. The PDP won 21 of the 36 governorships. Afterwards, the AD and APP agreed to establish an alliance for the federal elections.

Violent protests in the Niger Delta resumed in late 1998, with clashes also occurring between the Ijaw and Itsekiri communities. Nigeria's daily petroleum production was at times seriously affected by occupations of petroleum installations and abductions of oil workers. In December Ijaw activists adopted the 'Kaiama Declaration' demanding the withdrawal of petroleum companies from the region.

Olusegun Obasanjo emerged as the PDP's presidential nominee, with Atiku Abubakar as vice-presidential candidate, while the AD–APP alliance adopted Olu Falae of the AD as its candidate and the APP's Umaru Shinkafi as his running mate. There was a turn-out of only 40% for the National Assembly elections on 20 February 1999. The PDP secured 208 seats in the 360-member House of Representatives and 60 seats in the 109-member Senate; the AD took 76 seats in the House and 20 in the Senate, while the APP won 69 and 24 seats in the House and Senate, respectively; and few seats in both chambers remained unfilled due to the Delta unrest. On 27 February Obasanjo won the presidential election, with 62.8% of votes cast.

RETURN TO CIVILIAN GOVERNMENT

The new Constitution, based on the 1979 Constitution, came into effect on 29 May 1999, when Obasanjo was inaugurated as President. His new Government ensured representation for each of the 36 states, as constitutionally required, and incorporated several members of former military and civilian administrations, including Gen. (retd) Theophilus Danjuma as Minister of Defence, Adamu Ciroma as Minister of Finance and Bola Ige (of the opposition AD) as Minister of Power and Steel. Among his senior advisers, Obasanjo also appointed Rilwanu Lukman (the Secretary General of the Organization of the Petroleum Exporting Countries—OPEC) and Phillip Asiodu, with extensive experience of government policy-making. Obasanjo initiated a major shake-up of military postings, and promoted officers from southern and Middle Belt states to counterbalance the existing northern dominance in senior ranks. All military officers who had previously held political positions were retired.

As civilian government returned, there was an upsurge in inter-ethnic violence, first in Warri, where some 200 people were killed in early June 1999 during fighting between three rival communities, and then in July in Lagos and Kano, with violent clashes between the Hausa and Yoruba communities. Renewed unrest also occurred in Bayelsa State in November, when Ijaw militants killed several policemen in Odi; the response by Nigerian troops—burning the town, resulting in the deaths of many inhabitants—attracted widespread condemnation. A further eruption of anti-Hausa violence occurred in the same month in Lagos State, this time with the clear involvement of a militant Yoruba group, the Odua People's Congress (OPC). (Following renewed attacks against northerners in Lagos in October 2000, the Government banned it and other militia groups.) The Government's solution to the Delta crisis was to introduce a Niger Delta Development Commission (NDDC) and to increase the allocation to the petroleum-producing states to 13% of the federal budget. After considerable resistance in the National Assembly, the NDDC bill was approved in May 2000.

In October 1999 the Government brought murder charges against Mohammed Abacha, the late ruler's son. Among the murders cited was the assassination of Abiola's wife Kudirat in 1996 and the suspected murder of Shehu Musa Yar'Adua in detention in December 1997. Two retired generals, Ishaya Bamaiyi and Jeremiah Useni, the former Inspector-General of Police, Ibrahim Coomassie, and Abacha's head of security, Hamza al-Mustapha, were also arrested. Also in October 1999 the Swiss authorities agreed to order banks to freeze the accounts of Abacha's family and of several senior officials; many residences acquired by these officials during the Abacha era were confiscated.

HEIGHTENED RELIGIOUS AND ETHNIC DIVISIONS

The adoption of *Shari'a* law in northern states caused increasing religious tensions from December 1999 onwards. In Ilorin (Kwara State) 14 churches were burnt. Christians in Kaduna city staged demonstrations, with the resulting skirmishes escalating into intercommunal violence that left more than 1,000 dead during early 2000. Revenge attacks against Muslims occurred in southern cities, notably in Aba (Abia State). A decision by northern state Governors in late February to suspend the application of *Shari'a* came too late to calm the situation. Further religious clashes occurred in Kaduna in May, with an estimated 150 killed. Although the state governments adopting *Shari'a* agreed that month to revert to the penal code, this proved only a temporary measure; by mid-2001 *Shari'a* law had been introduced in 12 northern states, with many ordering the closure of establishments selling alcohol and the arrest of prostitutes. In early September more intercommunal violence erupted in the Middle Belt city of Jos, in Plateau State, where *Shari'a* had not been adopted and where many people had taken refuge from the anticipated imposition of the Islamic code. Further unrest was precipitated in Kano in October, when, in response to the first US bombardment of Afghanistan, demonstrators burned British and US flags. The *Shari'a* issue was to complicate the relationship between the states and the Federal Government. Although the Obasanjo administration did not attempt to prevent states from adopting *Shari'a*, it repeatedly expressed its reservations and encouraged legal challenges to *Shari'a*-based judgments. International opinion also served to restrain the courts in the implementation of the harshest penalties.

Ethnic tensions also remained high in several parts of the country. In June 2001 there was serious fighting between the Tiv and Azara communities in the Middle Belt state of Nassarawa. In neighbouring Benue State, in October, Tiv militia killed 19 soldiers, provoking brutal reprisals. There were also confrontations between Itsekiri and Urhobo communities in Warri and between Yoruba and Hausa residents in Lagos. The increasing ethnic polarization was accompanied by the emergence of unofficial militia and vigilante groups. Some, like OPC in the south-western states, acted in defiance of the authorities, while others appeared to be in the pay of state governments, or of individual state governors, such as the 'Bakassi boys' (employed to enforce control in several south-eastern towns).

Plans by the Minister of Defence, Gen. (retd) Theophilus Danjuma, to reduce the size of the armed forces were abandoned in late 2000. Nevertheless, a considerable number of senior military officers were retired or replaced in February and April 2001. With the upsurge of religious and ethnic conflict in the second half of 2001, troops were deployed in at least six different states, although the army's reputation was damaged by reports of human rights violations, notably the reprisals against civilians in Benue State in October, for which Obasanjo issued an apology.

OBASANJO'S SECOND TERM

With federal and state elections approaching, most of the larger parties chose well-known former military figures as their presidential candidates. Within the ruling PDP significant divisions existed between the presidency and the party's legislators in the National Assembly, culminating in efforts in early August 2002 to impeach Obasanjo for alleged breaches of the Constitution. The PDP national executive sought to resolve the conflicts between the two branches, and mediation by former President Shagari eased tensions. Due to the influence of Vice-President Atiku Abubakar in many northern and eastern states, Obasanjo was reselected in January 2003 as the PDP's presidential candidate. The APP, now renamed the All Nigeria People's Party (ANPP), chose Gen. (retd) Muhammadu Buhari, while the National Democratic Party was represented by Gen. (retd) Ike Nwachukwu. Former 'Biafran' leader Ojukwu Chukwuemeka Odumegwu stood on behalf of the All Progressives Grand Alliance (APGA).

Federal and state elections were held during April–May 2003. The PDP emerged with convincingly large majorities, securing 213 seats in the House of Representatives and 73 in the Senate. The ANPP won only 95 seats in the House and 28 in the Senate, while the five other parties were poorly represented. In the presidential election Obasanjo won 61.9% of the votes and Buhari 32.2%. In state governorship contests the PDP obtained 28 states, the ANPP won seven northern states, while the AD only took Lagos state. Although most international observers endorsed the results, leading representatives of the opposition persisted in contesting the election results; however, a legal challenge by Buhari was rejected by the federal Court of Appeal.

Obasanjo's new Government incorporated some high-profile economic reformers, and proved more effective than its predecessor. However, the Government still faced the challenge of maintaining security. The most acute problems arose in the Niger Delta states, where tensions mounted after the 2003 elections. During the election campaign Delta politicians had recruited informal militias from the pool of unemployed youths, who subsequently merged with militant groups already engaging in the theft and sale of crude petroleum, using the proceeds for sophisticated weapons. Following violent incidents in Port Harcourt in September 2004, an Ijaw-supported movement emerged, the Niger Delta People's Volunteer Force (NDPVF), under the leadership of Mujahid Dokubo-Asari, demanding the recognition of Ijaw economic and political rights and the departure of all foreign nationals. The threat of greater turmoil prompted Obasanjo to invite Dokubo-Asari to Abuja for peace talks in October, when it was agreed that the NDPVF would disarm. Although some weapons were surrendered, violent incidents against oil industry workers continued in 2005, with a sharp escalation following Dokubo-Asari's arrest in September and his arraignment on treason charges. A new group, the Movement for the Emancipation of the Niger Delta (MEND), claimed responsibility for a series of attacks, starting in December, on oil installations near Port Harcourt and kidnappings of foreign workers; the latter were normally released unharmed after ransoms were paid by the oil companies. MEND allied itself with demands for the release not only of Dokubo-Asari but also the detained Governor of Bayelsa State, Diepreye Alamieyeseigha, who had been impeached by his State Assembly in December after fleeing from the United Kingdom, where he faced charges of money-laundering.

A high-level conference on Nigeria's federal structure and its democratic institutions opened in Abuja in February 2005. Disagreements arose particularly over oil revenue derivation issues. When the conference closed in July, it had established little more than general principles regarding the involvement of oil-producing areas in the management of their resources. The majority of delegates favoured the retention of the existing arrangement of two four-year terms in office for the President and State Governors. Even as these issues appeared resolved, Obasanjo's supporters began to demand a constitutional amendment allowing him to seek a third term. The ruling PDP soon became deeply divided on the issue, with Vice-President Atiku Abubakar's supporters opposing the initiative. In May 2006, after a motion proposing this was defeated in the Senate, the 'third term' campaign was abandoned, leaving the rift between Obasanjo and Abubakar irreparable.

In September 2006 Obasanjo requested that the Senate commence impeachment proceedings following a report by the Economic and Financial Crimes Commission (EFCC) alleging that Abubakar had made unauthorized use of US $125m. to finance the business interests of close associates. Following his expulsion from the PDP, although retaining the post of Vice-President, Abubakar announced that he would stand as a presidential candidate, and in November was adopted by the newly formed Action Congress (AC). The ANPP again selected Buhari as its candidate. After much manoeuvring behind the scenes, the PDP chose Umaru Musa Yar'Adua, the Katsina State Governor and younger brother of the late Shehu Musa Yar'Adua. A Niger Delta politician, Goodluck Jonathan, was selected as his running mate. Like Yar'Adua, Jonathan had limited experience of national politics.

In mid-February 2007 the EFCC sent letters to all political parties listing 130 electoral candidates for various offices who were liable to be charged with corruption; the list included Vice-President Abubakar. The PDP agreed to replace 52 of its candidates, but Abubakar dismissed the move and won several legal rulings permitting him to continue to stand. The AC's campaign was hampered by the INEC's attempt to disqualify Abubakar, whose candidature was eventually approved by a high court ruling shortly before voting took place.

CONTROVERSIAL 2007 ELECTIONS

Both rounds of elections, at state level on 14 April 2007 and at federal level on 21 April, proved controversial, producing considerable criticism from international observers and the Nigerian press over widespread malpractice. Violence also marred the elections in some areas. In 27 states various national and state legislative contests (and one gubernatorial election) were re-run on 28 April. Obasanjo himself insisted that while the elections had not been 'perfect', the overall result was not invalidated. Requiring at least 25% of the vote in two-thirds of the states, Yar'Adua secured a landslide victory with 70% of the vote; Buhari received 18.6% and Abubakar 7.2%, while 21 other candidates shared the remainder. The PDP also emerged comfortably from the legislative contests, winning 263 of 360 seats in the House of Representatives and 87 of 109 in the Senate. The ANPP took 63 and 14, respectively, while Abubakar's AC obtained 30 House seats and six in the Senate. The remaining places were taken by minor parties. At state level, the PDP maintained its supremacy with 26 governorships. The ANPP secured seven governorships in northern states, and the AC took Lagos; the LP and the APGA won three governorships between them.

Yar'Adua took office on 29 May 2007, his legitimacy undermined by an election controversy that denied him a clear popular mandate. Obasanjo's prominent campaign role and his continuing position as chairman of the PDP's Board of Trustees left Yar'Adua vulnerable to being viewed as his 'puppet'. Yar'Adua's unscheduled trip abroad during the campaign for medical treatment sparked rumours about his health. Although the Obasanjo regime had left a positive economic legacy, the agenda of urgent economic and political problems was formidable. Yar'Adua's transition team was headed by Dr Aliyu Modibo, a seasoned politician at national level; Baba Kingibe, a former diplomat and Abiola's running mate in the annulled 1993 elections (who subsequently served Gen. Abacha as both Foreign and Interior Minister) became Secretary to the Government. Maj.-Gen. (retd) Abdullahi Mohammed, Obasanjo's Chief of Staff and political 'gatekeeper' since 1999, was retained. The appointments of key military officials that Obasanjo made two days before stepping down were also upheld, including Gen. Owoye Andrew Azazi as Chief of Defence Staff.

Yar'Adua's caution was also evident when his new Cabinet was announced. Only two of the 39 ministers were identifiable as close allies, although only four of Obasanjo's ministers were included. Yar'Adua's pledge to create a 'government of national unity' bore fruit when the ANPP accepted two ministerial posts. The new President continued Obasanjo's precedent by assuming responsibility for the energy portfolio, committing his Government to prioritizing addressing the country's frequent power and fuel shortages.

Buhari and Abubakar initially considered organizing mass demonstrations to contest the results, but turned to the courts instead. By June 2008 10 PDP governors had had their elections nullified by state-level tribunals (pending appeals) as had several senators, including David Mark, the Senate's President and the person who would temporarily assume the presidency if Yar'Adua's own election had to be re-run.

One month after his inauguration, Yar'Adua published records showing his personal assets and those of his wife—a gesture no previous Nigerian head of state had made. In June 2008 the Government announced its intention to conduct an audit of the 2007 petroleum block licensing round, and also launched a US $3,500m. case against Pfizer, the world's largest pharmaceutical company, for conducting illegal drug trials in Kano. (The case was settled out of court in May 2009 through a $75m. compensation payment to Kano State; the federal Government's claim was abandoned.) A massive building contract for new health clinics was cancelled, and the sale of two state-owned refineries was placed under review, the first of several privatizations by the Obasanjo regime to be cancelled that would include, in April 2008, the Ajaokuta Steel Company and the National Iron Ore Mining Company. Electoral reform was placed on the agenda in August 2007 with the selection of a 22-member review panel, headed by former Chief Justice Mohammed Uwais. Also in August an extensive management reorganization at the Nigerian National Petroleum Corporation (NNPC) was announced, with the Government preparing to divide the NNPC into several smaller companies subject to closer oversight.

THE YAR'ADUA PRESIDENCY

In his inauguration speech, Yar'Adua had recognized that the future growth of Nigeria's petroleum output required a solution to the Niger Delta unrest. The choice of Jonathan, the Bayelsa State Governor, as his Vice-President indicated a new political resolve. Prior to the elections there had been an escalation of attacks on oil installations and incidents of hostage-taking, and these intensified in early May 2007. In late May MEND declared a temporary cease-fire to encourage the Government to signal its intentions. At the insistence of the region's newly elected governors, and with pressure from MEND, the NDPVF leader, Dokubo-Asari, was released on 14 June.

Jonathan, to whom Yar'Adua had delegated a leading role, visited the Niger Delta region in late June 2007, and the fragile truce continued. On 3 September the Angolan Government arrested Henry Okah, a senior MEND leader, on charges of weapons-trafficking. In late September MEND ended its cease-fire, warning that its attacks on oil installations would continue until Okah's release, but Okah was extradited to Nigeria in February 2008 to face charges of treason and other crimes. A new 'action plan' for the Delta had been announced in October; although not differing significantly from that which Obasanjo had produced in 2004, it did offer substantial additional funding to the NDDC. After an attempt to organize a Delta conference in December 2007, the political momentum slowed; in late May 2008 Yar'Adua promised that the long-delayed conference would take place (although no date was indicated). On 4 June Yar'Adua instructed Shell to cease operations in the Ogoni territories in Rivers State, blaming its failure to develop a sustainable relationship with the Ogoni community. Shell had ceased production from its Ogoniland wells in 1993, after the outbreak of violent protests by Ogoni activists, and was now judged negligent of its contractual obligations; the NNPC assumed control of its installations in late June 2008.

Yar'Adua's low-key presidential style contrasted with Obasanjo's more interventionist approach, and earned him the sobriquet 'Baba Go Slow'. However, Obasanjo's own influence soon began to wane. Several regime figures involved in approving oil and gas contracts were named in foreign courts for receiving bribes from Western companies, while legislative committees in Nigeria uncovered scandals in the oil and power sectors, with both of which Obasanjo had been closely associated; before the end of 2007 the EFCC commenced its own investigations. At the PDP conference in March 2008 Obasanjo's candidate was defeated for the party chairmanship. In April his daughter, Senator Iyabo Obasanjo-Bello, was among those charged by the EFCC in connection with attempts to defraud the Ministry of Health.

The replacement in May 2008 of the presidential Chief of Staff, Maj.-Gen. (retd) Abdullahi Mohammed, marked the beginning of an extensive government reorganization. In August President Yar'Adua replaced the Chief of Defence Staff and all three service chiefs. Then, in early September, after returning from his second trip abroad in recent months for medical treatment, Yar'Adua dismissed Baba Kingibe as Secretary to the Government, while on 10 September he commenced a cabinet reshuffle with a significant restructuring of ministries that included splitting the Ministry of Energy into its petroleum and power components and creating a new ministry with responsibility for Niger Delta affairs. No fewer than 20 ministers and ministers of state were relieved of their posts. Among the newcomers was Rilwanu Lukman, a former OPEC Secretary-General and the architect of the planned restructuring of the oil and gas industries, who took over the petroleum portfolio. Among those retaining their positions was the Attorney-General and Minister of Justice, Michael Aondoakaa.

On 12 December 2008 the Supreme Court ended the uncertainties over the April 2007 presidential election, dismissing the appeals of both Abubakar and Buhari. However, with legal challenges to the PDP gubernatorial victories in Ondo and Edo States being upheld (in favour of the Labour Party and the AC, respectively), the number of governorships controlled by the PDP decreased to 26. Local elections in Jos (Plateau State) on 27 November 2008 provoked the worst sectarian and communal violence since 2001, after ANPP (Muslim) candidates lost all 17 wards to the Christian-dominated PDP in Jos. The two days of bloodshed left an estimated 400 dead and much destroyed property. In Bauchi, the capital of neighbouring Bauchi State, further Muslim–Christian fighting in February 2009 resulted in 14 deaths.

However, it was the ongoing unrest in the Niger Delta that appeared to represent the greater threat to the country's security. The attacks by militant groups on oil pipelines and other facilities had reduced oil production by over one-fifth, while significant amounts were also being pilfered through illegal 'bunkering' operations. In June 2008, after a daring attack on the large-scale Bonga oil facility 120 km off the coast, MEND called a cease-fire to allow negotiations with the Government. However, both militants and civil society spokesmen objected to the Government's choice of UN Under-Secretary-General Ibrahim Gambari to chair these talks; as Nigeria's then UN representative, Gambari had vigorously defended Saro-Wiwa's execution. On 17 July the Government cancelled its plans for a 'Delta summit', and by early May 2009 had not revived efforts to bring the militants to the negotiating table. MEND's seemingly unstable mix of militant political activism and criminality left uncertainties over its cohesion.

In mid-September 2008, in response to an army raid in Rivers State, MEND unleashed a six-day 'oil war', with attacks on pipelines and other facilities, before once again declaring a truce. MEND operations declined noticeably after this point until mid-May 2009, when the capture of an oil tanker and a cargo ship (plus 15 hostages) triggered a large-scale (and clearly long-planned) operation to dismantle MEND forces in Delta and Bayelsa States controlled by the warlord Tompolo (the *nom de guerre* of Ijaw leader Government Ekpemupolo). Although Tompolo eluded capture, the Government undermined his political base by revealing captured documents that detailed the network of politicians, civil servants, security personnel and oil company officials with whom he secretly dealt and the banks that laundered his funds. With MEND in apparent disarray, President Yar'Adua announced on 25 June a '60-day amnesty' from 6 August until 4 October, geared to both the disarmament and the rehabilitation of militant groups. He also promised the release of Henry Okah, as soon as the Angolan authorities (who had arrested Okah in 2007 on gun-running charges) signalled their agreement.

On 8 June 2009 Royal Dutch Shell agreed to a US $15.5m. out-of-court settlement over claims by the families of Saro-Wiwa and the other Ogoni activists executed by the Abacha regime 14 years earlier. Faced with a US court action alleging complicity in human rights abuses by Shell and its former director in Nigeria, the corporation, while denying the charges, agreed to offer the families of the 'Ogoni 9' $10.5m., with an additional $5m. for community development projects in Ogoniland.

In July 2007 the EFCC had brought corruption charges against six former PDP governors who, having left office at the April elections, lost their immunity from prosecution; in December the EFCC added a seventh, James Ibori, the influential former Governor of Delta State and a major contributor to PDP funds. In May 2008 British police arrested Ibori's wife, Theresa, on charges of money-laundering, and placed Ibori himself under investigation. The refusal by Nigeria's Ministry of Justice to respond to British extradition requests for the pair paralleled its earlier response to French authorities, who were seeking the extradition of the former Minister of Petroleum, Dan Etete; Etete was tried *in absentia* in 2007 for money-laundering. The US Justice Department had been investigating the US $6,000m. liquefied natural gas (LNG) project on Nigeria's Bonny Island, and in September 2008 Albert 'Jack' Stanley, the third most senior executive of the US engineering corporation Halliburton, confessed to using a secret account to bribe senior Nigerian officials, including three former heads of state (not publicly named). On 11 February 2009 Kellog Brown and Root, a Halliburton subsidiary, pleaded guilty to five counts of violating the Foreign Corrupt Practices Act, and was fined $579m.

The Yar'Adua Government was seemingly slow to react to the unfolding scandal, and in fact had sent out contrary signals over corruption. In December 2007 Nuhu Ribadu, the EFCC's Chairman, had been sent on a nine-month 'study leave' shortly after the EFCC had charged James Ibori. In June 2008 he was replaced permanently (by Farida Waziri, a retired assistant Inspector-General of Police). In December 2008, having finished his course at the Nigerian Institute of Police and Strategic Studies, Ribadu was summarily dismissed for indiscipline and insubordination. Ribadu, who had escaped an assassination attempt the previous September, fled into exile in the United Kingdom. Meanwhile, as the Bonny Island issue emerged, no follow-up action was initiated in Nigeria; it was only in April 2009 that a committee of senior police and security officials was appointed to investigate the charges.

Ongoing efforts to recover the public funds, estimated at around US $3,000m., allegedly looted by the late ruler Sani Abacha were rewarded in November 2009 when a Swiss court ordered the seizure of assets worth $350m. from his family; the total thus far recovered by the Nigerian government stood at around $2,000m. In December a Nigerian court cleared former Delta State Governor James Ibori of all outstanding corruption charges. However, after fleeing to Dubai, in the United Arab Emirates, Ibori was eventually extradited to the United Kingdom in March 2011 to face money-laundering charges.

The impasse over the Niger Delta remained the abiding regional threat to the country's stability. The military offensive in Rivers State in May 2009 had destabilized Tompolo's forces, but they soon regrouped; during July Nigeria's oil production declined to 1.3m. barrels per day, around one-half of its production capacity. Yet MEND leaders in the eastern Delta region indicated their acceptance of the amnesty programme. With Henry Okah finally freed on 13 July, MEND declared a 60-day cease-fire in mid-July, which was extended for another 30 days on 16 September. In July MEND established the Aaron Team to conduct its negotiations; this body included Wole Soyinke, a Nobel Prize laureate for literature, and two senior retired military officers (including ex-Chief of General Staff Owoye Azazi). Tompolo himself accepted disarmament and an amnesty for his fighters on 3 October, just before the amnesty's deadline. After an initial meeting between President Yar'Adua, Henry Okah and the Aaron Team on 21 October, MEND declared an indefinite cease-fire on 25 October. Ultimately, over 17,000 militants appeared at the three designated reception centres, far more than anticipated, and probably including many unemployed youths, but the haul of weaponry was disappointing. While greatly reducing the attacks on oil installations, the amnesty did not entirely end them. Nor was it clear that it would arrest either the growth of piracy in the Gulf of Guinea, which appeared partly independent of the militant groups, and the spread of kidnapping for ransom beyond the Delta region.

FURTHER RELIGIOUS TENSIONS

Although encouraging progress towards resolution of the Niger Delta conflict was evident, the northern states emerged anew as an arena of ethnic and religious divisions. On 28 December 2009 some 40 people died in Bauchi city following intracommunal violence among members of Kala-Kato, a small Islamic sect. This incident followed the brief but bloody upsurge of violence the previous July in Bauchi and three other northern states by another Islamic sect, Boko Haram (also known as Jama'atu Ahlus Sunnah lid Da'awati wal Jihad); like Kala-Kato, this sect recruited largely from the large pool of unemployed youths. Four days of fighting between sect members and security forces in Maiduguri, the Borno State capital, resulted in some 1,000 fatalities. The sect's leader, Mohammed Yusuf, who called for the eradication of Western education, was captured and killed by police.

In mid-January 2010 four days of intercommunal fighting broke out in Jos, the Plateau State capital, leaving up to 450 dead. With the army summoned to maintain security, the second outbreak of fighting in early March, comprising a series of reprisal raids, was centred on the mainly Christian villages outside Jos, and led to several hundred fatalities. As in November 2008, the January conflagration was widely suspected to reflect political manipulation by groups contending for control of the local government, but the violence in rural Jos was clearly linked to competition over access to land between Christian Berom farming communities and incoming Muslim Fulani pastoral communities searching for new pasturage because of environmental degradation further north.

THE DECLINE AND DEATH OF YAR'ADUA

Concerns that poor health might prevent President Yar'Adua from completing his tenure had persisted. His delay in returning from medical treatment in Saudi Arabia in September 2008 briefly sparked rumours of his death; a press report in mid-September that he would step down after the cabinet reorganization also gained momentary traction. In November 2009 Yar'Adua again left for medical treatment in Saudi Arabia, resulting in Nigeria's most serious political crisis since the restoration of democracy in 1999. Since he had failed formally to transfer power to his Vice-President, a power vacuum emerged, with the FEC unable to take decisions. Only his own family and medical staff were allowed access to Yar'Adua and until he gave a telephone interview with the British Broadcasting Corporation on 12 January 2010, in which he promised his early return to Nigeria, his only official action had been to sign a supplementary budget measure. With demands from the media and civil society for a transfer of power to Goodluck Jonathan, there were also pressures from abroad, particularly the USA, along with signs of restiveness in the Delta.

The impasse at the centre was essentially political. The diverse regional interests originally combining to establish the PDP had agreed that the presidential nominee would rotate every two presidential elections between the north and the south. With Olosegun Obasanjo, a southerner, having served two terms, Yar'Adua had been expected, health permitting, to be renominated for the 2011 elections. If Goodluck Jonathan, a Christian from the Delta state of Bayelsa, was to complete Yar'Adua's term, this delicate arrangement would be disturbed; if he then captured the PDP nomination for 2011, the ruling party might split. A coterie of senior northern politicians determined to block Jonathan's accession to power coalesced around Yar'Adua's wife Turai.

The Federal High Court broke the deadlock on 13 January 2010 when it ordered Jonathan to exercise the functions of the president until Yar'Adua's return, although a subsequent judgment on 29 January rejected his formal recognition as interim president. After all 36 State Governors on 4 February unanimously supported Jonathan's assumption of this role, both chambers of the National Assembly then voted to secure this outcome on 9 February. Yet the formal succession remained uncertain. On the evening of 23 February Yar'Adua arrived back in Abuja. Two Presidents now occupied Aso Rock, the presidential residence, who were neither meeting nor even speaking; Yar'Adua's actual state of health remained unknown. Jonathan, in stages, asserted his authority, first demoting the controversial Minister of Justice, Michael Aondoakaa, and then dismissing the head of the INEC, a move welcomed by both media and opposition parties. On 17 March he dismissed the entire Cabinet, which had split into factions during the extended transition. A new FEC, with 38 members, was sworn in on 5 April.

On 5 May 2010 President Yar'Adua died of a heart condition complicated by long-standing kidney problems. The following day Goodluck Jonathan was inaugurated as Nigeria's 14th head of state, and promised the country that he would continue Yar'Adua's reform programme: above all, consolidating peace in the Niger Delta, revitalizing the power sector, ensuring that the bill restructuring the petroleum sector became law, and completing the Uwais panel's electoral reform programme.

The 52-year-old former zoology professor had only entered politics in 1999. Although some saw him as lacking the forceful personality required to dominate Nigeria's turbulent political scene, he had shown sound judgement in stabilizing public affairs during a politically sensitive transition. His first serious test would come in November 2010, when a PDP congress was to select a presidential candidate for national elections due in early 2011. By early June 2010 a range of candidates were mobilizing support to challenge the incumbent; the person President Jonathan had selected on 18 May as his substantive Vice-President, Mohammed Namadi Sambo, the Governor of Kaduna State, was not among them. Jonathan's own ambitions remained unclear.

In Yar'Adua's absence the settlement process had lost momentum. On 16 March 2010 MEND ended its cease-fire by detonating two large bombs in Warri; the explosions were intended to disrupt an important conference on the Delta region's future prospects. Meanwhile, in the same month a new grouping emerged, the Joint Revolutionary Council, which claimed responsibility for several recent attacks. With Jonathan's final accession to power, however, a meeting in Abuja in mid-May with some 100 Delta notables, including the key MEND leaders, produced strong support for the amnesty programme and for the Government's plans for the region's development.

THE PRESIDENCY OF GOODLUCK JONATHAN

As President Jonathan consolidated his position, he changed his service chiefs in September 2010, promoting the Chief of Air Staff, Air Marshall Oluseyi Petinrin, to become Chief of Defence Staff. Meanwhile, action over the alleged bribery by foreign firms involved in the Bonny Island LNG scheme gained momentum. In mid-2010 the Government had commenced legal action in the US courts against Halliburton, and in early December charges were also filed against Dick Cheney, the former head of Halliburton and US Vice-President under President George W. Bush. In mid-December the charges against Cheney were withdrawn after Halliburton agreed to pay a fine of US $250m. No Nigerian politicians or officials involved in the case were prosecuted, however.

With national and state elections expected in January 2011, Prof. Attahirura Jega, a respected academic and democracy activist, was appointed as the INEC's new Chairman in June 2010; he promised a thorough revision of the electoral roll and the introduction of biometric identity cards. These reforms required a postponement of the elections until April 2011.

By January 2011 the main candidates in the presidential electoral contest were in place. Having declared his candidacy in September 2010, Jonathan had secured the PDP's nomination at the party's primary election in January 2011, unexpectedly winning by an overwhelming majority against Abubakar, the candidate on whom the party's northern élite had finally agreed in November 2010. His success left the PDP divided. Since it disrupted the zoning arrangement for rotating presidential candidates, the party's National Executive Committee had only reluctantly approved his candidacy in August (and without endorsing it). His nomination prompted protests in several northern cities.

In October 2010 over 30 opposition parties formed the Patriotic Electoral Alliance of Nigeria to support a single presidential candidate, but this project soon fell apart. By late 2010 Muhammadu Buhari, the ANPP's candidate in 2003 and 2007, who had severed ties with the party in March 2010 and cofounded the Congress for Progressive Change (CPC), was mobilizing popular support in northern states. To replace Buhari, the ANPP selected the Governor of Kano State, Ibrahim Shekarau. The Action Congress of Nigeria (ACN), as the AC had been redesignated, nominated Nuhu Ribadu, the former EFCC Chairman, who had returned from exile in the United Kingdom after Jonathan became President. The new registration of voters took place in January 2011 and produced an electoral list of nearly 74m. voters.

If the opposition appeared resurgent, Jonathan's political base in the Delta states looked rather less secure. Complaints by militants over the late payment of monthly grants, and resentment at the pay-offs awarded to their former commanders, led to two groups returning to their former bases in August and November 2010. MEND threatened a return to violence, and attacks on oil pipelines and facilities increased. It also claimed responsibility for two car bombs in Abuja, which killed 12 people and wounded 38 others during Nigeria's 50th Independence Day celebrations. Henry Okah, the former MEND leader now living in exile in South Africa, was detained by South African police and charged with arms-trafficking. The rise in tensions signified the approach of elections, reflecting the blurred boundaries between violence and party politics in the Delta.

In the north, tensions between the Christian and Muslim communities remained evident in Jos, while intercommunal violence also briefly erupted in neighbouring Taraba State. In July 2010 Boko Haram announced that Mohammed Shekau, who was believed to have been killed during the sect's 'uprising' the previous July, had taken command of the group. Boko Haram had, it emerged, allied itself in February 2010 with al-Qa'ida in the Islamic Maghreb (AQIM), a militant Islamist group based in Algeria, which offered it both weapons and training. In September Boko Haram activists stormed the Bauchi State prison and released some 700 inmates (including 150 Boko Haram prisoners), precipitating a period of attacks on political figures, the police and unsympathetic Muslim clerics in Borno, Bauchi and Yobe States. On 24 December, the Christian holiday of Christmas Eve, four bombs exploded in Jos, targeting Christian areas, while three churches were attacked in Maiduguri. On 31 December, New Year's Eve, bombs exploded at a church and a bar near an army barracks in Abuja. Over 100 people died in these attacks.

Legislative elections took place on 9 April 2011, followed by the presidential ballot on 16 April and gubernatorial voting on 26 April. The elections were held in an atmosphere of calm, with few violent incidents reported. Voter turn-out was 53.7%. Jonathan secured a clear first-round victory in the presidential election, taking 22.5m. votes (58.6%) to Buhari's 12.2m. (32.0%). Ribadu received 2.1m. votes (5.4%), while Shekarau gained 917,012 (2.4%). Crucially, Jonathan crossed the 25% threshold in 31 of the 36 states, whereas Buhari did so in only 13 (and in none outside the north). In the Senate, Jonathan could rely on a comfortable PDP majority, while in the House of Representatives the PDP appeared likely to retain a narrow majority. The ACN was the largest opposition group in both chambers.

Of the 26 state governorships being contested, the PDP won 19, but at a special election in May 2011 in the south-eastern state of Imo the PDP lost to the APGA, giving it 23 governorships overall; the ACN held six, the ANPP three, the APGA two, and the CPC and LP one apiece. In January 2012 the Supreme Court reversed a lower court ruling and declared that five PDP governors originally elected in 2007 but then forced to undergo re-run elections in 2008, should have faced election in 2011. New elections were quickly organized, with the PDP retaining the governorship in all five states.

Meanwhile, the outcome of the presidential election prompted three days of violence across 14 northern states, leaving an estimated 800 people dead and over 70,000 displaced; the rioters' targets included the Zaria home of Namadi Sambo, Jonathan's vice-presidential nominee, and the properties of traditional leaders who supported the PDP's presidential campaign. President Jonathan dismissed the Minister of the Interior on 18 April 2011. Although observers judged the elections to have been fair and transparent, Buhari challenged the results.

A new Government of 42 ministers was assembled in July and August 2011, after President Jonathan's nominees received Senate approval. Ten ministers, including the Minister of Petroleum Resources, Diezani Alison-Madueke, retained their posts, and another two ministers received new portfolios. Many new appointees were evidently being rewarded for their supporting roles in the President's re-election. However, the key ministries were allocated to capable and experienced figures. As Minister of Finance, the President appointed Ngozi Okonjo-Iweala, the World Bank's Managing Director for Africa and a former finance minister under President Obasanjo who was credited with negotiating the cancellation of US $18,000m. of Nigeria's foreign debt.

In November 2011 Jonathan dismissed the EFCC's Chairwoman, Farida Waziri, after criticism of its performance caused Western donors to reduce the funding available to support the agency's work; she was replaced by Ibrahim Lamorde, hitherto Chief of Operations. Even under its first Chairman, Nuhu Ribadu, the EFCC's record had been disappointing: of 35 prominent politicians against whom charges had been brought, few had been gaoled and none had served lengthy sentences. According to Transparency International's 2011 Corruption Perception Index, Nigeria ranked 143rd among 182 states, a significant worsening of its position since the end of the Obasanjo regime.

At the start of 2012 the Government provoked a political crisis over its economic strategy by withdrawing the existing subsidy on fuel. This subsidy had been introduced to cushion the cost of importing refined petroleum products, in turn necessitated by the Government's continued inability to maintain sufficient domestic refining capacity to meet local demand. The Obasanjo Government had tried and failed to end this costly measure in 2003. Although the fuel subsidy reform was announced in October 2011, and the subsidy itself was not included in the 2012 budget statement in November, the announcement of its actual withdrawal on 1 January 2012 and the immediate doubling of fuel prices were unexpected. Protests quickly broke out, and on 9 January the two leading trade union federations launched a general strike when the Government refused to reverse its decision. Much of Nigeria's economy was paralysed for eight days, and there were widespread demonstrations organized by civil society groups and opposition party activists. The strike was ended on 16 January, when President Jonathan offered to compromise by restoring one-half of the subsidy. The Government could make a strong case that the fuel subsidy had become unaffordable; in 2011 it had consumed almost one-quarter of federal expenditure, and was more than 700% above the amount budgeted. However, public anger was reignited in April 2012 when a parliamentary committee issued a report showing that rampant corruption in the subsidy programme had cost the state thousands of millions of dollars. President Jonathan's announcement in late May that the EFCC had been ordered to intervene failed to dispel the furore.

In December 2011 security forces were forced to intervene after intercommunal clashes over conflicting land claims in the south-eastern Ebonyi State and Benue State in the north had each caused several dozen deaths. However, the Niger Delta region remained relatively calm. MEND claimed a single attack on an oil pipeline in February 2012. By this time most of MEND's former leaders were either engaged in private business or held government posts. Meanwhile, piracy in the Gulf of Guinea, for which Delta criminal gangs were largely responsible, had extended its reach to the waters off Benin and Togo. In August 2011 the British insurer Lloyds of London classified the area as a 'war risk' zone. Ban Ki-moon, the UN Secretary-General, promised to send a special team to assess the Gulf's security problems. In October Nigeria agreed to mount joint naval patrols with Benin. Plans were also announced in the 2012 budget to add 24 ships to the Nigerian navy over the next three years.

Meanwhile, following Jonathan's inauguration as President, Boko Haram rapidly escalated its activities, and by July 2011 the security situation appeared to be drifting out of control. The sect's growing sophistication and ruthlessness were underlined by the suicide bombings of the national police headquarters in Abuja on 16 July and the UN's headquarters in the capital on 26 August. While Borno State, and especially its capital, Maiduguri, remained the epicentre of its activities, Boko Haram spread its attacks widely across the northern states, with police facilities, the army, churches, banks and beer parlours providing key targets. Overall, the group staged 115 attacks during 2011, killing at least 550 people. On 20 January 2012, days after local Muslim and Christian leaders in the northern city of Kano signed a 'covenant' to maintain peaceful inter-community relations, Boko Haram staged its bloodiest raid thus far, launching co-ordinated bomb attacks on eight government and police buildings and leaving 185 dead.

The Government's response echoed the strategy deployed in the Niger Delta. Though the group's links with external militant Islamist groups—including AQIM and possibly also al-Shabaab in Somalia—remained of concern, Boko Haram was approached primarily as a problem having local roots, and one amendable to a domestic solution: firm security measures to contain the violence, the offer of negotiations when the Government felt sufficiently secure, and an amnesty programme including training programmes to reintegrate its activists into normal society. The 2012 budget raised security spending to around 20% of federal expenditure. Troop levels in northern states were rapidly increased, and in late July 2011 a Joint Task Force (modelled on that deployed in the Delta region) was created in an attempt to defeat Boko Haram in Maiduguri. This approach was then extended to five other northern states, despite concerns that indiscriminate reprisals by soldiers were alienating local communities. On 31 December, however, President Jonathan was forced to declare a state of emergency in Borno State and three other northern states, and closed Nigeria's borders in the affected areas. In a radio address in January 2012 he warned that Boko Haram had supporters in every branch of the state, including the security services. In March the President dismissed the Inspector-General of Police, Hafiz Ringim, after his deputy was judged to have been responsible for the escape from custody of a leading member of Boko Haram. In June the Minister of Defence, Dr Haliru Mohammed Bello, was dismissed along with the National Security Adviser, Maj.-Gen. Azazi; the latter, a fellow Ijaw from Jonathan's home state, was replaced by Sambo Dasuki, a retired army colonel and the son of a former prominent northern traditional ruler, to bolster the regime's links with disaffected northern élites.

Boko Haram had revealed its demands for a cessation of violence in June 2011; these included the imposition of strict *Shari'a* law in all states with a majority Muslim population and punishment for those involved in the killing in 2009 of Mohammed Yusuf, the group's founding leader, while in police custody. The Government's counter-offer in early July 2011 of talks requiring a prior end to attacks was promptly rejected by Boko Haram. On 14 September former President Obasanjo secretly met with representatives of the sect in Maiduguri, and offered himself as an intermediary with the federal Government. However, it was not until March 2012 that reliable reports emerged that the start of negotiations had been agreed—only for Boko Haram to back away when the details of the talks were leaked to the press. In early June a senior northern Muslim cleric told the media that Boko Haram had accepted him as a intermediary for planned negotiations, but the group immediately rejected his claim, and within 48 hours a new wave of bombings and shootings had begun.

FOREIGN RELATIONS

Nigeria has long played a leading role in African affairs and is a prominent member of the Economic Community of West African States (ECOWAS) and other regional organizations. Nigeria contributed a significant number of troops to the ECOWAS Monitoring Group (ECOMOG) deployed in Liberia from August 1990 after the outbreak of large-scale armed conflict. ECOMOG forces were partially withdrawn in early 1998, following democratic elections. However, the Liberian civil war resumed in August 2003, and 1,500 Nigerian peace-keeping troops were redeployed under an ECOWAS mandate. The Liberian President, Charles Taylor, had accepted Obasanjo's offer of asylum earlier that month. Nigeria subsequently contributed the largest West African contingent (numbering 1,651 at August 2004) to the UN Mission in Liberia (UNMIL—see chapter on Liberia).

In 1993 Nigerian troops were also dispatched to Sierra Leone after a formal request by its Government to help repulse the rebel Revolutionary United Front. Following a coup by the Sierra Leonean army in May 1997, Nigerian forces were soon in conflict with the new junta; in February 1998 Nigerian troops gained control of Freetown, ousting the coup leaders. In March the democratically elected Sierra Leonean President, Alhaji Ahmed Tejan Kabbah, was formally reinstalled. However, Nigerian forces suffered heavy casualties, particularly during a concerted rebel assault on Freetown in January 1999. Following a UN Security Council decision in October to authorize the deployment of the UN Mission in Sierra Leone (UNAMSIL), ECOMOG formally withdrew in April 2000. n October 2004 Nigerian troops joined the African Union (AU) peace-keeping force dispatched to protect communities displaced by the uprising in Sudan's Darfur region.

After Nigeria's aborted presidential election of June 1993, the United Kingdom, together with other European governments and the USA, imposed military sanctions, with further sanctions adopted in late 1995 (see above). After the death of Abacha, Nigeria's relations with the United Kingdom, the Commonwealth and the EU improved rapidly. At the transition to civilian rule on 29 May 1999 Nigeria was automatically readmitted to Commonwealth membership. The return of civilian government led to stronger relations with the USA, and President Bill Clinton visited Abuja in August 2000. Also during 2000 US military staff arrived to train Nigerian contingents for UN peace-keeping operations, while the Government received advice from a US military contractor on institutionalizing civilian control of the military and restructuring the armed forces. After late 2001 the Bush Administration provided substantial additional support for Nigeria's military in line with its 'war on terror'.

In 1991 Nigeria claimed that Cameroonian troops had occupied several fishing settlements in Cross River State (in south-eastern Nigeria), following a long-standing border dispute concerning the Bakassi peninsula in the Gulf of Benin. Cameroon's claim, based on a 1913 treaty ceding the peninsula to the German protectorate of Kamerun, was recognized by an unratified agreement in 1975, but subsequent attempts to resolve the dispute achieved little progress. In December 1993 some 500 Nigerian troops were dispatched after incidents in which Nigerian nationals were killed by Cameroonian security forces; the two Governments agreed to establish joint patrols in the disputed area. In February 1994, after the Nigerian Government increased its troop levels, Cameroon decided to submit the dispute for adjudication by the UN, the Organization of African Unity (now the AU), and the International Court of Justice (ICJ), and requested French military assistance. Regional and international diplomacy contained the tensions, although several armed clashes occurred between late 1994 and January 2002.

In October 2002 the ICJ endorsed Cameroon's case, while upholding Nigeria's own offshore boundary claims. Although critical of the judgment, the Nigerian Government agreed to establish a joint commission to defuse tension. A separate agreement on the demarcation of the Cameroon border in the Lake Chad region was reached in December 2003, when Nigeria ceded 33 villages to Cameroonian control. However, Nigeria's planned withdrawal from the Bakassi peninsula, in September 2004, was opposed in the House of Representatives, which instead demanded a UN-supervised referendum. Eventually, in June 2006 Obasanjo and Cameroon's President Paul Biya signed an agreement at the UN, confirming the transfer of the Bakassi region to Cameroon. The withdrawal of some 3,000 Nigerian troops from the region, monitored by German, British, French and US officials, began in early August. Cameroon agreed not to deploy a military presence in the peninsula for five years; in November 2007, however, 21 Cameroonian soldiers died when their post on Bakassi was attacked by unidentified assailants. Nigeria was initially blamed, but several dissident groups (both Nigerian and Cameroonian) subsequently claimed responsibility. With the transfer of the peninsula scheduled for August 2008, two Nigerian militant groups opposed to the hand-over process intensified their activities, including several raids on Cameroonian military posts on the Bakassi peninsula between June and October 2008. However, the hand-over was completed on 14 August 2008 with an official flag-exchange ceremony that, for security reasons, took place in the city of Calabar, over 100 miles from the peninsula. Earlier that year, on 14 March, Nigeria and Cameroon had also reached an agreement over their long-disputed maritime boundary.

Nigeria's religious problems spilled over into its foreign relations when, on 25 December 2009, a 24-year-old Nigerian, Umar Farouk Abdulmutallab, attempted to detonate a bomb onboard a transatlantic airliner as it approached Detroit airport in the USA. The son of a prominent Nigerian banker (and former government minister), Abdulmutallab had received training from a Yemeni group connected to the militant Islamist al-Qa'ida network. Nigeria protested against its inclusion on an official list published in January 2010 of 14 countries whose citizens would be subject to strict screening procedures when travelling to the USA. Following the Jos violence in early March 2010, Col Muammar al-Qaddafi, the Libyan leader, publicly recommended that Nigeria be split into two states, reflecting its Muslim–Christian divide. This intervention provoked a heated public response, while the Government withdrew its ambassador in Tripoli; however, tensions soon eased. Although Nigeria's representative on the UN Security Council had supported the establishment of an air exclusion zone over Libya in March 2011, following the outbreak of hostilities in that country, Nigeria subsequently criticized the North Atlantic Treaty Organization aerial campaign as 'disproportionate'.

The coup in Mali on 22 March 2012 was to raise more immediately pressing concerns, for the rebellion by Tuareg groups in the north of Mali which had triggered the army's intervention swiftly exploited the ensuing political chaos to seize control of the northern half of the country and declare, on 6 April, the independent state of Azawad. With this challenge to regional stability, Nigeria joined the efforts of ECOWAS to force the new military junta to restore power to civilian hands. At the same time, a mediation channel was established through the Government of Burkina Faso (with Nigeria, Algeria and Mauritania in support) to pursue negotiations with the Tuareg leadership, although most energy was instead consumed in resolving the ongoing impasse between the political and military leadership in the Malian capital, Bamako. Planning was also set in motion for a possible military intervention force of around 3,000 troops—to which Nigeria, Niger and Senegal agreed to contribute. As of early September, the UN Security Council had still not given ECOWAS approval to undertake such an enterprise. By then, a fundamental shift of power had occurred within Azawad; the Mouvement National pour la Libération de l'Azawad, which had led the Tuareg rebellion, had been eclipsed by its main ally, the radical Islamist Harakat Ansar al-Din (Movement of Religious Supporters) and two other Islamist groups, including AQIM, known to have already been training Boko Haram fighters at camps in Mali's remote northern regions.

Economy

LINDA VAN BUREN

Revised for this edition by OBI IHEME

INTRODUCTION

One of the greatest challenges faced by successive Nigerian presidents has been contentious relations between the executive and legislative branches, and animosity with the powerful State Governors, especially concerning any economic reforms that have attempted to alter the way in which petroleum revenues are distributed to the states and, thereafter, to each of Nigeria's 774 local government areas. Such a situation was forecast to continue throughout 2012. Furthermore, the perennial lack of electricity has long been regarded as the greatest impediment to Nigeria's economic growth, particularly in the non-oil sector.

Nigeria has long based its annual national budgets—and therefore also the federal, state and local budgets—on conservative forecasts of each year's oil revenues. It is thus not unusual for actual oil revenues to exceed the forecasts on which the budget was based, in many years resulting in a substantial windfall. The 36 state budgets and the 774 local budgets are funded by allocations from the federal budget. Since the late 1970s most Nigerian governments, whether military or civilian, have been painfully aware of the vagaries of the oil price and so have set their federal budgets on conservative forecasts of oil revenue. For example, *BusinessDay* magazine stated that the 2012 federal budget presented to the National Assembly in December 2011 was based on an oil price of US $72 per barrel, and the Federal Government planned to raise 55% of its projected fiscal revenues from oil income. The environment for the Government to meet its revenue targets is favourable, and Renaissance Capital, an investment bank focused on emerging markets, believed that the average oil price in 2012 will be $110 per barrel. The 2011 federal budget was predicated on an oil export volume of 2.3m. barrels per day (b/d), on a price of US $65 per barrel, and on an exchange rate of ₦65 = $1.

Security factors on the ground in Nigeria, more than quotas set by the Organization of Petroleum Exporting Countries (OPEC), place a limit on the country's oil export volume. Any excess oil revenue is treated as a windfall, to be placed into an Excess Crude Account (ECA). In years when budgetary revenue from petroleum falls short of the forecast, withdrawals are then made from the ECA to make up the difference. When the ECA is full, as was the case at the end of 2008, Nigeria's foreign exchange reserves are high. The ECA is not to be used to cover overspending; its purpose is to stabilize revenue levels.

Despite significant agricultural and mineral resources, Nigeria is ranked by the World Bank as a low-income country. Per caput assessments of one of Africa's most powerful economies remain problematic because the population of Nigeria has long been disputed. The 2006 Nigerian census found that the country's population was 140,003,542, whereas the 1991 Nigerian census had concluded that the population was 88,992,220. Either the population had been growing by 3.6% per year over the 16 years, or one or both of the censuses were inaccurate. The IMF estimated Nigeria's gross domestic product (GDP) per caput at US $1,490 in 2011. The development of the petroleum industry, which began in the late 1950s and gained momentum in the late 1960s and the 1970s, radically transformed Nigeria from an agriculturally based economy to a major oil exporter. Nigeria became a member of OPEC in 1971, 11 years after the organization was founded in 1960. Increased earnings from petroleum exports generated high levels of real economic growth, and by the mid-1970s Nigeria ranked as the dominant economy in sub-Saharan Africa and as the continent's major exporter of petroleum. Following declines in world petroleum prices, however, successive governments became increasingly over-extended financially, with insufficient revenue from petroleum to pay the rising cost of imports or to finance major development projects. The decline in Nigeria's foreign exchange earnings led to an accumulation of arrears in trade debts and to import shortages, which, in turn, resulted in a sharp fall in economic activity, with Nigerian industry struggling to operate at a fraction of installed capacity without essential imported raw materials and spare parts. Poor harvests, an overvalued currency and a widening budget deficit compounded the problem.

Meanwhile, measures undertaken under the structural adjustment programme, with the aim of attracting private capital from abroad, proved largely unsuccessful; investors were deterred by the country's reputation for corruption and by the Government's failure to control expenditure. The budget deficit began to expand rapidly, increasing to more than 12% of GDP. Economic instability was also reflected in persistently high inflation; the annual average rate was 56% in 1995. In 2006 inflation fell below 10% for the first time in five years. With rising food prices, inflation reached 13.5% in 2008, although it subsequently fell to an annual average rate of 12.3% in 2011. The Economist Intelligence Unit (EIU) forecast inflation to be 12.7% in 2012, then to decline to 9.6% by 2014. The increase in the 2012 rate was due to a reduction in the fuel price subsidy, which caused the cost of production inputs and consumer prices to rise, and to the introduction of a new minimum wage law.

AGRICULTURE

Until Nigeria attained independence in 1960, agriculture was the most important sector of the economy, accounting for more than one-half of GDP and at least three-quarters of export earnings. However, with the rapid expansion of the petroleum industry, the agricultural sector entered a relative decline. Between the mid-1960s and the mid-1980s Nigeria moved from a position of self-sufficiency in basic foodstuffs to one of heavy dependence on imports. Under-investment, a steady drift away from the land to urban centres, increased consumer preference for imported foodstuffs and outdated farming techniques continued to keep the level of food production well behind the rate of population growth. Agriculture's role in the country's exports dwindled to a tiny proportion; nevertheless, the sector still contributed an estimated 35.2% of Nigeria's GDP in 2010.

In August 2011 the Minister of Agriculture and Natural Resources, Dr Akinwunmi Adesina, launched the Federal Government's Agricultural Transformation Action Plan, which aims to transform the sector into a more profitable business sector by increasing opportunities along the value chains of agricultural products, and to add 20m. metric tons of food to Nigeria's domestic food supply. Other important targets are to create 1.3m. jobs along the cassava value chain and to enhance food's nutritional value and the health of Nigerians. Cassava is the staple food, and Nigeria is the world's largest producer of this root crop; more recently, it has also been promoted as a source of biofuel. The Nigeria Cassava Growers' Association estimated in June 2008 that ethanol made from cassava could save the country US $6,100m. annually by 2012. Although it might seem that Nigeria would have little need for biofuel substitution, while it is certainly rich in resources of crude petroleum, the country does not refine enough oil to meet its own requirements for fuel products such as petrol and kerosene; imports of refined fuel products cost the country $7,900m. in 2010. Experiments were under way in 2011 to stimulate production, for export purposes and also for supplementing 10% cassava flour, also known as *gari*, in wheat-flour-based products such as bread.

Traditional smallholder farmers, who use simple techniques of production and the bush fallow system of cultivation, account for about two-thirds of Nigeria's total agricultural production. Subsistence food crops (mainly cassava, yams, maize, sorghum, millet and rice) are grown in the central and western areas of Nigeria and are traded largely outside the cash economy. Of the total cereal crop in 2010, maize represented the largest share (totalling some 7.30m. metric tons), followed by sorghum (4.78m. tons), millet (4.13m. tons) and paddy rice (3.22m. tons). Cash crops (mainly oil palm, followed by groundnuts, palm kernels, plantains, sugarcane, karité nuts, cotton, cashew nuts, coconuts, cocoa, rubber, kola nuts, sesame seed and coffee) are cultivated in the mid-west and north of the country, with the cocoa belt lying mainly in the south-east. Output of cocoa beans rose by 69% in 1988 following the abolition of the Cocoa Marketing Board in 1987 and reached a record 485,000 tons in 2007; it declined to 364,000 tons in 2009, but increased again, to 428,000 tons, in 2010. Among the cash crops, only cocoa makes any significant contribution to exports. Recent emphasis has been placed on encouraging domestic cocoa-processing to provide higher-value products for export.

The production and export of oil palm products declined dramatically during the last decades of the 20th century and amounted to about 8.5m. metric tons per year in 2005–10. Output of palm kernels was about 1.32m. tons in 2010, while palm oil production was 1.09m. tons. Nigeria is by far the largest producer of palm kernels and oil palm in Africa and is the third largest producer in the world (after Malaysia and Indonesia).

In 1990 Nigeria overtook Liberia as the largest rubber producer in Africa. Production reached 143,000 metric tons in 2010. Nigeria had about 345,000 ha of rubber plantations in 2009. Local demand from the tyre and footwear industries continued to exceed domestic supply.

Production of raw cotton fluctuates. Output amounted to 501,300 metric tons in 2009, yielding 177,020 tons of cotton lint and 235,366 tons of cottonseed. Incentives for local textile companies and higher tariffs on imported cotton in the early 2000s stimulated local production, but textile manufacturers prefer the higher quality of legally or illegally imported cotton from neighbouring countries.

One crop exhibiting significant growth in production from the mid-1990s was cashew nuts; the area devoted to this crop more than doubled between 1995 and 2005 and amounted to 335,000 ha in 2009. Output of this up-market tree crop amounted to a record 727,603 metric tons of cashew nuts in shells in 2008, but totalled some 594,000 tons in 2010.

According to FAO, Nigeria's national herd in 2010 comprised 56.5m. goats, 35.5m. sheep, 16.6m. cattle, 7.5m. pigs and 192.3m. chickens, while the total fish catch amounted to 751,000 metric tons in 2009.

Some 20% of the land area is forested, but exports of timber (mostly obeche, abura and African mahogany) are relatively small, earning about US $10m. per year. Deforestation, particularly in the Niger Delta area, remains a major problem. About 12% of the country's total land area is threatened by the encroaching Sahara desert in the north, and a National Committee on Arid Zone Afforestation was formed to lead Nigeria's anti-desertification programme. As is common in Africa, more trees by far are felled for fuel wood than for any other use in Nigeria. Fuel wood is still the main source of domestic energy and accounts for more than 60% of commercial primary energy consumption, in this country of huge petroleum and gas reserves.

The 1978 Land Use Decree stipulated that land be vested in the State Governors, who would hold it in trust for all Nigerians. The Government agreed to amend the Decree, in response to protests from smallholder farmers, who claimed that it discriminated against them. The other key issues facing the agricultural sector are environmental degradation; inadequate storage facilities and transport, leading to massive post-harvest losses; lack of research and training facilities for the transfer of new technologies; and the absence of credit facilities for smallholder farmers. Nigeria's resources are not fully exploited, and many parts of the country remain very poorly developed. Inadequate provision of economic infrastructure, such as power, water supply, roads and telecommunications, especially in rural areas, has proved an impediment to both agricultural and industrial investment.

PETROLEUM

According to BP, in 2011 Nigeria was the 12th largest oil producer in the world and the largest in Africa. At the end of 2011 Nigeria had proven petroleum reserves of about 37,200m. barrels (1 barrel = 42 US gallons = 158.973 litres), the 10th largest in the world, representing 2.3% of the global total and with a projected reserve life of 41 years. The first commercial discoveries of petroleum were made in 1956 in the Niger River Delta region. Exports began in 1958, and production advanced rapidly. By the early 1970s the petroleum industry had become the dominant sector of the Nigerian economy and the major determinant of the country's economic growth. The petroleum sector accounted for 34.5% of GDP in 2009, and for 80% of government revenue and 92.0% of exports by value in 2008. The international price of petroleum has a direct and powerful effect not only on the Nigerian economy as a whole but on the national budget, which is based on projected earnings from petroleum exports.

Nigeria is a member of OPEC and accounts for about 8% of the Organization's total petroleum production. Since Libya restricted output in 1973, Nigeria has been Africa's leading petroleum-producing country. Being of low sulphur content and high quality, its petroleum is much in demand on the European and North American markets. Nigeria's two main types of petroleum are Bonny Light crude and Forcados crude; other types include Qua Ibo crude and Brass River crude.

Revenues from exports of petroleum, which are shared in decreasing proportions between federal, state and local governments, have largely determined the pace of Nigeria's economic development. Successive governments based their five-year plans on predicted earnings from petroleum. From the 1990s onwards, foreign exchange revenue from sales of petroleum has been virtually the sole means of meeting the country's import needs and debt-servicing commitments, and the size of these earnings varies widely from year to year. Production costs for Nigerian petroleum are up to seven times as high as those in the Middle East, but the Nigerian product's low sulphur content places it at the upper end of OPEC's price scale. The Niger Delta remains Nigeria's main petroleum-producing region, containing more than 200 oil-fields, the largest of which is Forcados Yokri. Forcados alone can produce about 380,000 b/d, in optimum circumstances. However, sabotage, including damage to the TransForcados trunkline at Chanomi Creek, caused Shell to declare *force majeure* on Forcados exports for three months during 2009.

The USA is the major market for Nigeria's petroleum, taking, on average, about one-half of total exports; Spain, Germany, France, Portugal and the United Kingdom are also important customers. In 2005 US stocks were reported to be at a low level, and the continuing precarious nature of political relations between the USA and Iran placed upward pressure on demand, thereby contributing to the rise in the international price of petroleum. Nigeria was well placed to benefit from this, provided that it could maintain regular supplies. Militant activity succeeded in suspending some output from the country's total production, but new installations came on stream in 2005–06 to compensate, and more capacity was under construction. In addition, a policy shift favoured liftings from offshore wells, in the belief that they could be protected from sabotage more effectively. Nevertheless, in May 2010 Shell briefly closed the Trans Niger pipeline at Bodo West and Bera, after illegal siphoning of crude oil resulted in leaks and fire incidents.

In 1988 the Nigerian National Petroleum Corpn (NNPC) was restructured as a holding company, with 12 subsidiaries: the National Petroleum Investment Management Services, the Nigerian Petroleum Development Co, the Nigeria Gas Co, the Products and Pipelines Marketing Co, Integrated Data Services Limited, Nigerian Liquefied Natural Gas (NLNG), National Engineering and Technical Co, Hydrocarbon Services Nigeria, Warri Refinery and Petrochemical Co, Kaduna Refinery and Petrochemical Co (KRPC), Port Harcourt Refining Co (PHRC) and Eleme Petrochemicals Co. On 17 May 2007 the outgoing Government of Olusegun Obasanjo controversially approved the privatization of 51% of PHRC and KRPC. This unpopular sale became a major factor in the June general strike in the first month of the Government of Alhaji Umaru

Musa Yar'Adua. The buyer of the 51% share in these two refineries was Bluestar Oil Services Ltd, a consortium comprising Sinopec of the People's Republic of China and three Nigerian firms, Dangote Oil and Gas, Transnational Corpn of Nigeria Ltd (Transcorp) and Zenon Oil. The Yar'Adua Government tasked the Bureau of Public Enterprises (BPE) with reviewing the refinery privatization, in a bid to placate the Nigeria Labour Congress and avert the general strike. On 21 June the BPE announced that 10% of the equity of the two refineries would be retained for the refinery workers and that another 10% would be reserved for the local 'host communities'. All four refineries continued to be held by the NNPC in mid-2012.

Since 1993 security in the onshore Niger Delta has been difficult. Pipelines and manifolds have been sabotaged, spilling oil into the surrounding environment, and foreign hostages have been regularly taken and released a few days later. The focus of attention thus shifted to offshore production, and construction was carried out with consideration for security. The greatest benefit to Nigeria's oil output came on 25 November 2005 with the beginning of production at the Bonga field, 120 km off shore, in water over 1,000 m deep. This 60-sq-km technologically advanced field comprises 16 wells and cost US $3,600m. to develop to first production. Its designated capacity is 225,000 barrels of oil and 150m. cu ft of gas per day. The deep-water Bonga field boasts one of the world's largest Floating Production, Storage and Offloading (FPSO) vessels as well as extensive underwater operating facilities. The Erha field, 97 km off shore, in water 1,200 m deep, began production in May 2006, with a designated capacity of about 210,000 barrels of oil and 300m. cu ft of gas per day. In February 2005 the NNPC signed a $1,000m. contract for an FPSO vessel for the 45,000-acre Agbami deep offshore field, where reserves were estimated at more than 800m. barrels. Agbami, in which the NNPC held 50% of the equity and Chevron Texaco 32%, entered production in July 2008 and was expected to produce 250,000 b/d of crude oil and 450m. cu m of gas per day.

Nigeria has four petroleum refineries: Port Harcourt A, Port Harcourt B, Warri and Kaduna. Port Harcourt B, the newest, was designed to refine for export; owing to problems at the other three refineries, however, there have been times when Port Harcourt B's entire production has been for domestic consumption. The Warri refinery, Nigeria's oldest, was closed in January 2006 after militants bombed the pipeline supplying it with crude oil; it reopened in January 2008. The Kaduna refinery, closed in February 2006, reopened in April 2008 but was closed again for maintenance from November to February 2010. It shut down again in March, since 47 acts of vandalism had already occurred on the pipelines feeding the Kaduna and Warri refineries; the Kaduna refinery was subsequently reopened, but shut down again in November after its feeder pipelines were damaged in attacks attributed to the Movement for the Emancipation of the Niger Delta, a prominent insurgency group.

Government subsidization of petroleum products for the domestic market reportedly amounted to US $192m. in the first quarter of 2000 alone, and these subsidies are strongly discouraged by the IMF and the World Bank. Smuggling is a continuing problem; despite popular discontent with the price increases, in neighbouring countries petrol is sold for the equivalent of ₦45 per litre, providing a substantial incentive for cross-border trafficking.

On 1 January 2012 the Federal Government announced a 100% increase in the price of petroleum products, owing to its overnight removal of the petroleum subsidy. This caused nation-wide protests, given the severe economic impact that the fuel price increase would have not only on transportation, but, as a critical factor of production, on many other products and services. The subsidy was eventually reinstated, but at a lower level, after negotiations with labour unions.

Development of an integrated petrochemicals industry has been a priority of successive governments since 1977. Nigeria has a carbon-black plant near Warri, a polypropylene plant also near Warri and a linear alkyl benzene plant at Kaduna. The units use feedstock from the nearby refineries. The Eleme Petrochemical Complex has a design capacity of 250,000 metric tons per year of polyethylene and 80,000 tons per year of polypropylene, but it has reportedly operated far below capacity since its construction in 1995.

Despite continuing uncertainty over the implementation of the Petroleum Industry Bill (PIB) and how it will affect multinational oil companies, there is still appetite for investing in Nigeria's oil sector. In May 2012 the NNPC announced a US $1,500m. financing deal with its joint venture partner ExxonMobil to increase oil reserves by 85m. barrels and production by 55,000 b/d.

NATURAL GAS

Besides its petroleum resources, Nigeria possesses the largest deposits of natural gas in sub-Saharan Africa. Proven reserves are assessed at 5,100,000m. cu m, most of which is located with petroleum deposits in and around the Niger Delta. Other gas reserves were estimated at a further 1,800,000m. cu m. In a bid to curtail the wasteful flaring of gas, the Government in 1985 issued a decree penalizing petroleum companies for this practice. Although the decree affected only 69 of the 155 petroleum-producing fields, many of the large operators began to install gas reinjection facilities. Some 18,000m. cu m of gas was flared each year, at a market cost of over US $4,000m., according to petroleum companies; domestic consumption was estimated at only 3,000m. cu m per year. Utilization of gas increased substantially in 1990 when the Warri associated gas project, under which 17m. cu m per day was piped from the Niger Delta to Igbin power station near Lagos, came into operation. Nevertheless, the flaring of gas was a major source of contention between the Ogoni ethnic group and Shell (see Recent History) in the 1990s. The Nigerian Government failed to meet its target of ending all gas flaring by 31 December 2008; this objective would not only have positive environmental effects but would also increase the amount of gas available for export. In 1996 the Shell Petroleum Development Co of Nigeria Ltd awarded a £320m. contract for a new gas-processing plant at Soku, in Rivers State. The plant was to enable Shell to flare less gas in the Niger Delta and was to supply the liquefied natural gas (LNG) plant that was then under construction at Bonny Island (see below). The plant at Soku, upon completion, was to be capable of delivering 12.7m. cu m of gas per day. However, the Soku plant suffered from its inception, as a result of illegal siphoning from the pipelines feeding the plant. Those incidents increased in frequency and magnitude in 2009, and Shell had to plug more than 50 illegal valves in August and September alone. By January 2010 these breaches in security had prompted Shell to announce the temporary closure of the Soku plant. The Agbami offshore field was expected to produce about 450m. cu m of gas per day, in addition to its output of crude oil (see above). Shell's offshore gas-gathering system delivered its first gas to NLNG in January 2006.

In September 1995 Nigeria joined Benin, Togo and Ghana in signing an agreement to proceed with the construction of a West African Gas Pipeline (WAGP) from Nigeria; they signed a memorandum of understanding in respect of the WAGP in 1999, and later that year a consortium comprising Chevron and Shell, led by Chevron, signed a joint venture agreement with the national petroleum companies of the four signatory countries. In May 2003 Nigeria and partner countries signed a further agreement for the creation of the West African Pipeline Company to operate the pipeline. The pipeline had been expected to deliver its first methane gas in late 2006; however, the delivery was delayed until late 2007, after Niger Delta militants sabotaged the Escravos segment of the pipeline. Lying partly on shore in Nigeria and partly off shore in the Gulf of Guinea, the pipeline was to transport gas overland from the Escravos gasfield to Lagos, after which it continues under water. The offshore part of the pipeline parallels the shoreline and carries gas westward, delivering it through to the cities of Cotonou, in Benin, Lomé, in Togo, and three Ghanaian ports, Tema (serving Accra), Takoradi and Effasu.

In 1988 the Government announced a new US $2,000m. scheme to construct a pipeline from gasfields in eastern Nigeria to what is now the NLNG plant at Bonny Island. The six trains in operation by 2008 were capable of delivering 22m. cu m of LNG per year. The scheme was to use gas associated with oilfields in the Niger Delta, which at the time was being flared. NLNG was initially owned 49% by the NNPC, 25.6% by Shell Gas Nigeria, 15% by Elf Aquitaine Gaz's affiliate Cleag Ltd, and 10.4% by Agip International of Italy. In May 2010 Shell announced new associated gas-gathering projects, costing $2,000m., which were designed to cover 26 flow stations and reduce gas flaring to 25%.

Meanwhile, Chevron began developing the US $1,000m. Escravos facility to manufacture liquid fuels from natural gas. This scheme would have the dual advantage of supplying fuel to the region and reducing the wasteful flaring of natural gas. Phase One of this project entered into production in 1997, supplying primarily the domestic Nigerian market. In June 1999 South Africa's SASOL and Chevron agreed to proceed with Phase Two of the Escravos scheme, having conducted a feasibility study to assess the suitability of SASOL's gas-to-liquids technology there. The output of Phase Two was allocated for regional distribution via the WAGP. Also aimed at using Nigeria's gas reserves were the Warri refinery extension and the Delta steel plant at Aladja. Gas is also planned to be used as a feedstock for the second phase of the NNPC chemicals complex near Port Harcourt.

The Minister of Trade and Investment, Olusegun Aganga, stated in May 2012 that Nigeria had obtained US $40,000m. in new investments in the key Onne oil and gas zone, highlighting the continued interest in the sector despite ongoing security problems.

COAL AND OTHER MINERALS

Nigeria is West Africa's most important producer of coal. The country possesses substantial deposits of lignite but has yet to exploit their full potential. The Government estimates Nigeria's coal reserves at 3,000m. metric tons, situated in 17 coalfields. Nevertheless, coal accounts for only about 0.2% of Nigeria's total energy consumption. Nigerian coal is low in ash and sulphur content and so is more environmentally friendly than many other types of coal. However, in a country where attention focuses on petroleum and gas, coal takes a relatively low priority for domestic use, and export sales are hindered by the high cost of transport to countries with strict environmental criteria to meet. Coal is mined by the Nigerian Coal Corpn and is used mainly by the railway, by traditional metal industries and for the generation of electricity. There are long-term plans to exploit the Lafia/Obi coal deposits (estimated at more than 270m. tons) for use at the Ajaokuta steel complex. Deposits of bitumen near Akure have been developed under the Government's Bitumen Implementation Project.

Nigeria's output of tin concentrates has been in decline since the late 1960s, and these exports have reflected the depressed conditions in world tin prices since the late 1980s. Production peaked at 357,000 metric tons in 1995, but then declined; output amounts to around 230,000 tons per year. The country has two tin smelters, with a combined capacity well in excess of total ore production. In the late 2000s the BPE was seeking investment partners to develop several of the country's unexploited or underexploited hard minerals, including bentonite, gypsum (in Bauchi State), kaolin (in Plateau State), rock salt, barytes (in Nassarawa State), phosphates, talc, manganese, copper, bitumen, gold and tin. Gold is found mostly in south-western Nigeria and comprises both primary gold in a schist belt and alluvial gold. Nigeria also mines modest amounts of gemstones, mainly in Plateau, Bauchi and Kaduna States. The potential exists for profitable exploitation of sapphires, rubies, emeralds, aquamarines, topazes, tourmalines, amethysts, garnets and zircons. Gem-quality sapphires are mined at Nisama Jama'a, in Kaduna State.

The Aluminium Smelter Co of Nigeria (ALSCON) built an aluminium smelter at Ikot Abasi, in Akwa Ibom State, at a cost of US $2,500m. with a capacity of 90,000 metric tons per year. It came on stream in 1997 but produced only 36,000 tons of aluminium ingots in two years, so was closed in 1999. In 2004 the Obasanjo Government invited investors to privatize and reopen the smelter. A tripartite agreement was signed in May between the BPE, the BFI Group Corpn (BFIG) of the USA and UC Rusal of Russia. In order to demonstrate transparency, the BPE announced the opening of bids on a live national television broadcast. BFIG, based in California, USA, but with participation by businessmen of Nigerian origin, submitted the highest bid, at $410m., while Rusal added a conditional bid of $5m. The BFIG bid was very publicly acknowledged to be the highest, but the BPE, claiming that BFIG had not met its other commitments under the agreement, subsequently reopened negotiations with Rusal, the world's largest aluminium company. These discussions culminated in Rusal's acquisition in February 2007 of a 77.5% share of ALSCON for $250m.; the price also included costs for the dredging of a river. The Nigerian Government retained a 15% share, while Germany's Ferrostaal AG took the remaining 7.5%. Rusal embarked on a three-year $150m. rehabilitation of the smelter. ALSCON was relaunched in February 2008 and produced its first 1,000 ingots in May.

MANUFACTURING AND CONSTRUCTION

Manufacturing contributed an estimated 2.2% of GDP in 2010 and grew by 8.5% in 2009. Despite its contribution to the overall economy having fallen slightly, prospects in the sector are high. In June 2012 US-based Procter and Gamble announced its intention to invest US $250m. in a factory in Nigeria's Ogun State. Manufacturers' interests are represented by the Manufacturers' Asscn of Nigeria (MAN), which comprises more than 2,000 member companies. In 2010 manufacturing activities included 11 sectoral groups and 72 sub-sectoral groups.

Manufacturing has traditionally been heavily reliant on imported raw materials and components. Efforts to lessen that reliance have been largely unsuccessful. The combination of import restrictions, over-pricing and industrial disputes favoured cheaper foreign goods and encouraged smuggling and 'black-market' activities. Manufacturers asserted that inadequate development funds and the Government's stringent fiscal policy had constrained the sector, which was estimated to be operating at less than one-third of its capacity in 2009. Despite successive governments' efforts to encourage industrial dispersal, most manufacturing plants are still based in Lagos State. The Agbara industrial estate, in Ogun State, has attracted some industries, although most of the heavily import-based companies are reluctant to move from Lagos State since some 70% of all industrial materials are still handled at its ports. In 2004 MAN estimated that 55% of all imports into Nigeria evaded Nigerian customs. These imports, having circumvented any protective tariffs and quotas, posed formidable competition in the Nigerian market for locally produced goods.

The creation of an integrated iron and steel industry has been a high priority of successive development plans. The Delta steel complex at Aladja, which has an annual capacity of 1m. metric tons and operates the direct reduction system, supplies billets and wire rods to three steel-rolling mills at Oshogbo, Katsina and Jos. Each of the three mills has an initial annual capacity of 210,000 tons of steel products. In 2005 an Indian company began a US $50m. rehabilitation of the Ajaokuta Steel Company Ltd, including the sintering mill and the rolling mill, to produce steel wire rods. By mid-2006 the company reported that it had produced 128,000 tons of rolled products. Both Ajaokuta and the National Iron Ore Mining Co were not operating in 2010, pending a loan of some ₦650m. to finance the resumption of production. In February 2011 President Goodluck Jonathan pledged to resuscitate the two ailing firms, and in mid-2012 the Government affirmed its intention to press ahead with the privatization of Nigeria's steel companies.

The assembly of motor vehicles in Nigeria is dominated by Peugeot in passenger cars and Mercedes in commercial vehicles. Local demand remains well above supply; the cost of components and the difficulties in obtaining import licences have reduced output. Peugeot Automobile Nigeria in November 2009 commissioned a new assembly line for the Peugeot 307 sedan, with the capacity to produce 22 units per day or 7,000 units per year. The country has three tyre manufacturers.

A 208,847-ha export-processing zone at the port city of Calabar, in Cross River State, has attracted investors in 14 sectors, including textiles and garments, wood-processing, tyres, food-processing, electrical products, light-truck assembly, packaging, carpets and rugs, iron and steel, and cocoa-processing. In 2007 the Zone was offering a streamlined one-step approval of applications by the Nigerian Export Processing Zone Authority 'to the exclusion of other government agencies'.

POWER

Power blackouts are a frequent occurrence in Nigeria, and it is estimated that an injection of US $12,000m. is needed to meet the country's electricity needs. The Yar'Adua Government estimated in November 2009 that total generating capacity was 5,000 MW. Planned targets to add 10,000 MW to the national grid through the use of national independent power producers and independent power producers (IPPs) by December 2007 and then late 2008 were both missed. The National Electricity Regulatory Commission, established in 2006, granted generating licences in June 2007 to 20 IPPs that were to add 8,237.5 MW to the national grid. Meanwhile, the Nigeria Atomic Energy Commission announced plans to generate a minimum of 1,000 MW of electricity using nuclear power plants by 2017.

The principal supplier of electricity in Nigeria was the Power Holding Company of Nigeria (PHCN, formerly National Electric Power Authority—NEPA, which was earmarked for privatization in the 1990s). PHCN was to oversee the distribution of NEPA assets to the six generating companies and 11 distribution companies that came into existence with the restructuring of NEPA, in preparation for its privatization. Power generation facilities include the 1,320-MW Chinese-built thermal power station at Egbin, in Lagos State (fuelled with natural gas piped from the Escravos field); the Kainji hydroelectric installation (capacity 760 MW, using eight turbines); the gas- and oil-fuelled thermal installations at Afam, in Rivers State (742 MW, using 18 units, several of which were not producing) and at Sapele, in Delta State (696 MW); and the coal-fuelled thermal plant on the Oji River (150 MW).

In 2001 Shell Petroleum Development Co of Nigeria (SPDC) acquired 15-year contracts for two gas-fuelled power projects at Afam, valued at US $540m. The first project was to refurbish, operate and transfer the Afam IV plant, and the other was to lease, operate and transfer the Afam V plant. Under a separate contract, SPDC, in a joint venture, was to raise the capacity of Afam VI (which became fully operational in July 2009, using three gas turbines) from 450 MW to 650 MW. The new combined cycle turbine entered into operation in May 2010. The national grid in theory supplied electricity to 43% of all Nigerians in 1999, and PHCN then failed to meet a target of bringing mains electricity to 85% of the population by the end of 2010 (which would have required a large capital investment to fund 16 proposed new power plants and 14,500 km of new transmission lines, as well as ancillary services). Plans were under consideration for the construction of new installations at Onitsha, Kaduna, Makurdi, Oron, Katsina and Mambilla. While electricity generation was once viewed as a 'strategic' industry where foreigners were not welcome, the Obasanjo Government in 1999 invited overseas investment, particularly on build, own and operate (BOO) terms. Examples of proposed BOO projects were a 350-MW gas-fuelled power station in Rivers State and a power plant in Ondo State. The West African Portland Cement Company, which operates a cement factory (with annual production of 1m. metric tons) at Ewekoro in Ogun State and has a requirement for some 20 MW of power, entered into a BOO agreement in 2001 with a private sector company for electricity supply over a 15-year period. The country's manufacturers sometimes lose as much as two-thirds of working hours from power cuts, and official sources cite unreliable electricity supplies as one of the principal factors impeding growth in the manufacturing sector.

President Goodluck Jonathan's plans to privatize PHCN, as those of at least two of his predecessors, have faced intense opposition from numerous quarters. First, powerful vested interests want to maintain the *status quo*, as many businesses are making enormous sums of money from Nigeria's poor power generation. Second, labour unions fear massive job losses if a private company, wishing to maximize its profits, were to reduce its workforce. Third, the public fear that a private enterprise managing the country's electricity grid would seek to maximize its profits in part by raising tariffs. Nevertheless, the Federal Government has pursued its privatization plans; the Minister of Power, Prof. Barth Nnaji, stated that the 23 October 2012 deadline for the sale of all PHCN's 17 subsidiaries would be met, and the BPE also confirmed that it was on track to meet this target. The PHCN had been formally dissolved in early 2012, although its successor companies were yet to be established by September. Meanwhile, in August Nnaji was obliged to resign from his post as a result of an alleged conflict of interest in the privatization process.

TRANSPORT

In comparison with most other West African states, Nigeria has a well-developed transport system. However, congestion, lack of maintenance and poor planning have resulted in services that are unreliable and often dangerous. Approximately 95% of all goods and passengers travel by road, principally to and from the major ports. In 2011 the road network totalled 198,000 km, of which some 9,660 km were paved. Road safety standards in Nigeria are virtually non-existent, and driving licences are distributed indiscriminately. On average, 30,000 accidents are reported each year, with the loss of over 8,000 lives.

The railway network covers 3,505 km. The two main narrow-gauge lines run from Lagos to Nguru and from Port Harcourt to Kaura Namoda, with extensions from Kafanchan, through Jos, to Maiduguri, and from Minna to Baro. A new 52-km railway line for iron ore traffic was constructed between the Ajaokuta steel complex and Itakpe in the 1990s. In 2005 it was reported that the Nigerian Railway Corpn was operating at only 20% of its capacity. As part of a streamlining exercise to prepare it for commercialization, it was announced that the company would have to lose 50% of its workforce. A project to rehabilitate the Lagos–Jebba line was completed in February 2011. In mid-2012 the Nigerian Railway Corpn remained on the BPE's list of state enterprises to be privatized. Achieving a serviceable rail infrastructure was one of the principal objectives established by former President Yar'Adua.

There are international airports at Ikeja (Lagos), Kano and Abuja, as well as 11 domestic airports. The Abuja airport has 10 terminals, three of which were to handle international traffic, while the other seven were to serve the domestic market. Murtala Mohammed International Airport in Lagos received new cargo-handling equipment, valued at US $4m., in 2000. In mid-2011 both the Federal Airports Authority of Nigeria and the Nigerian Aviation Handling Co Ltd were on the BPE's privatization list. The parastatal Nigeria Airways' domestic monopoly was ended in the early 1980s, and several private charter airlines commenced operations. International traffic is dominated by foreign airlines. Successive military governments put increasing pressure on Nigeria Airways to improve its standard of service and reduce its costs, but the carrier continued to incur substantial financial losses. Owing to Nigeria Airways' difficulties, it was announced that private airlines would be allowed to offer international services if they satisfied safety requirements. In September 2004 Virgin Nigeria airlines was established, with Virgin Atlantic of the United Kingdom owning 49% and private sector Nigerian shareholders owning the majority 51% share. Despite being totally privately owned, Virgin Nigeria was to become the new national flag carrier. Its flights between Lagos and London began in June 2005, and its Lagos–Dubai service commenced in June 2006. Virgin Nigeria also operates regional services linking Lagos to Accra (Ghana) and Douala (Cameroon), and its domestic services link Lagos to Abuja, Kano and Port Harcourt. In May 2003 the liquidation of Nigeria Airways was announced, this being confirmed by two court orders in February 2004. Nevertheless, the BPE has identified a dozen or so former Nigeria Airways assets that could be sold to investors, ranging from cargo sheds to Skypower Aviation and Handling Co Ltd.

Nigeria's principal seaports for general cargo are Apapa, Tin Can Island (both of which serve Lagos), Port Harcourt, Warri, Sapele and Calabar. The main ports for petroleum shipments are Bonny and Burutu. CPCS Transcom Ltd of Canada was appointed in 2003 to oversee the Nigeria Ports Authority privatization. The entity was to be dismantled into 24 concessions, and in 2005 94 companies and consortia were prequalified to bid for them. In 2009 the unbundled Nigeria Ports Authority was on the BPE's privatization list, but any divestiture was on hold pending new legislation.

TRADE

Nigeria, as a petroleum exporter, traditionally operates a visible trade surplus. In recent years, sabotage by political dissidents in the Niger Delta has resulted in disruption to liftings, causing Nigeria to fall as much as 10% short of fulfilling its OPEC export quota. In 2010 total export revenue on a free-on-board (f.o.b.) basis amounted to an estimated US $74,600m. Crude oil, gas and petroleum products accounted for $72,300m., or 96.9% of the total, in 2010. Visible imports in the same year, also on an f.o.b. basis, cost an estimated $41,200m., of which $7,900m., or 19% of the total, was for the import of refined oil products. The resulting visible trade surplus was an estimated $33,400m. The current account of the balance of payments demonstrated a surplus of some $14,200m. in 2010. The overall balance of payments, however, showed a deficit of $8,300m. At 31 December 2010 Nigeria held gross external reserves of $34,100m., sufficient to cover the cost of 6.6 months of visible imports. These reserves were boosted by the ECA (see above), which contained large amounts of windfall oil revenue from the mid-2008 period of exceptional oil prices. In 2010 Nigeria's main export clients were the USA (53.1%), Brazil (7.8%) and Spain (7.6%), while its principal import suppliers were China (11.8%), the Netherlands (8.7%), the USA (8.5%), the Republic of Korea (5.4%) and the United Kingdom (5.1%).

The national currency is the naira. During the year to 19 June 2009, the naira depreciated against the US dollar by 20%, largely because the US currency, in which oil prices are denominated, was strengthening. The Nigerian currency regained its stability in the year to 28 May 2011, appreciating by 2% from ₦151.01 = US $1 on 29 May 2010 to ₦156.30 = $1 on 29 May 2011. At 31 May 2012 the rate was ₦155.25 = $1.

The recent increase in public spending on infrastructure was expected to result in an increase in imports, and strong economic growth will mean higher consumption by the public of imported goods. The EIU estimated a current account surplus of 7.6% of GDP in 2012 and an average of 3.6% of GDP during 2013–16 due to increased imports and steadily declining oil prices.

DEBT

In 2005 the 'Paris Club' of public sector creditors signed debt reduction agreements with Nigeria, whereby its debt would be reduced by US $18,000m., in exchange for an agreement to pay back the remaining $12,000m. by March 2006. Nigeria did indeed make the final payment, whereupon the debt reduction commitments came into force on 21 April 2006, entirely eliminating Nigeria's debt to the 'Paris Club'. However, domestic debt stocks remained above levels that were acceptable to the IMF and the World Bank. Even so, the budget for 2010 allocated ₦517,070m. to debt-servicing payments, more than one-half of which were to service domestic debt. According to the IMF, Nigeria's total external debt stood at $4,800m. at 31 December 2010, up from $4,000m. at 31 December 2009. The figure at the end of 2010 was equivalent to 2.2% of GDP, and external debt-servicing payments as a percentage of exports of goods and services in 2010 stood at 6.2%. Total domestic debt was equivalent to 15% of GDP.

PUBLIC FINANCE

Since the early 1970s the channelling of earnings from petroleum exports, import and excise duties and other forms of tax revenue through the federal, state and local governments has been the main impetus of economic activity in Nigeria. Budgets in the 1990s were characterized by overly ambitious and ultimately unattainable targets. In an attempt to avoid a repetition of the protracted dissent that had met earlier budgets, Obasanjo introduced greater transparency into the budgeting exercise, implementing the concept of 'core revenue', whereby, from 2001, 'budget call circulars' to ministries would specify in advance the levels of current and capital expenditure to be allocated to each. A lengthy procedure for adopting financial legislation developed, in which the World Bank and the IMF negotiated with the President and his executive team to agree a strategy for economic reform, while the legislature subsequently rejected their recommendations and followed a different course. Fiscal discipline at all levels of government, greater transparency and improved accountability were widely regarded as crucial for economic progress. Obasanjo's economic planners received praise from the World Bank for their National Economic Empowerment and Development Strategy programme, which was complemented by equivalent programmes at the state and local level; all three programmes received funding pledges. The strong increase in petroleum revenues in 2005–06 made it possible for Nigeria to eliminate its huge 'Paris Club' debts, thereby allowing the Government henceforth to divert resources to spending on social needs, poverty reduction and infrastructural development. The World Bank declared that 'fiscal spending would have to leave room for the private sector to be the driver of growth in Nigeria', a principle that both the Obasanjo and the Yar'Adua Governments embraced.

The Ministry of Finance wants to reduce public expenditure in the short term, but faces pressure from the National Assembly to spend more on building modern infrastructure, which Nigeria badly needs. However, a perennial problem is the mismanagement and theft of public funds by the very officials entrusted to manage them. Public officials often collude with private individuals or companies to commission useless public projects in a bid to receive large financial rewards, or sometimes embezzle public money. This undoubtedly influences the Ministry's plans to rein in public spending.

As mentioned above, international oil prices largely dictate the size of Nigeria's state revenues, although lately the non-oil sectors have also driven a lot of economic growth. While oil prices were relatively high at mid-2012, if Western nations suffered another recession—the USA alone accounts for about one-half of Nigeria's oil exports—this, combined with the possibility of reduced growth in China (another source of high demand), as well as the precarious security situation in the Niger Delta, could have a negative effect on oil exports and thus government revenues.

With the legislature continuing to demand higher public spending, the target deficit of 1% of GDP by 2015 forecast by Nigeria's Medium-Term Expenditure Framework will likely be missed and a 2% deficit will be the reality. However, this can be sustained as long as the expenditure results in higher growth, which likely means a focus on capital, rather than recurrent, expenditure.

ECONOMIC PROSPECTS

When Nigeria first began to receive revenue from petroleum in the 1960s and 1970s, opportunities to utilize those earnings for economic development were spectacularly missed. Now, Nigeria has a further opportunity to benefit from its position as Africa's major petroleum exporter, in a global climate of oil prices that remain high. Disruption to supply by militants has indeed had an adverse impact, a factor which the Yar'Adua Government sought to address with its peace initiative in the Niger Delta region in 2008 (see Recent History). Even outside the hydrocarbons sector, the IMF described the prospects for Nigeria's non-oil economy as 'robust', its agricultural growth as 'solid' and its performance in the financial and telecommunications sectors as 'strong'. Goodluck Jonathan, who became President in May 2010 following the death of Yar'Adua, has proposed reforms that the IMF regards as 'welcome'; however, some of them are sufficiently far-reaching that they may prove difficult to implement in the face of parliamentary and trade union opposition.

Overall, the Government is focusing on more prudent fiscal and monetary policies. Positive oil prices will aid an improved fiscal policy through higher revenues, which in turn will lower inflation. On the other hand, controlling public spending will be difficult. Strong performance in non-oil sectors will help Nigeria's economic performance overall and GDP, which was forecast by the EIU to grow by about 6.4% in 2012 and to average 7% during 2013–16. Also important are government efforts to improve Nigeria's business environment. While Nigeria's ranking of 133rd out of 185 countries in the World Bank's 2012 *Doing Business* report is an improvement on its 137th place in 2011, much work still remains to be done to ease business procedures and reduce bureaucracy. Conflicting policies among government agencies, the inefficiency of public institutions, and the constant need drastically to reduce the over-reliance on corrupt business practices all deter potential investors.

Although oil prices are currently strong, other factors could still dampen the sector's performance. Ongoing unrest in the Niger Delta frequently results in armed militants attacking oil installations, stealing oil—frequently in collusion with public and security officials—and kidnapping expatriate oil workers, which leads either to shutdowns or slowdowns of production. Furthermore, the proposed PIB, under debate for several years, aims to transform the oil industry in favour of domestic companies and to extract higher royalties for the Federal Government. Uncertainty over the bill's final implementation has caused several multinational oil companies to postpone plans to invest in Nigeria. Investment in northern Nigeria could also be affected by the recent increase in violence being perpetrated by the militant Islamist sect Boko Haram (see Recent History). Its campaign of fatal gun and bomb attacks on the police, churches, mosques and the general public could deter both foreign and local investment and affect the production of some goods and services.

These risks highlight the importance of continuing the process of economic diversification in Nigeria. Although during the last decade other industries besides petroleum have experienced high growth and have been performing well, many opportunities still exist. The telecommunications sector has continued to experience very high growth rates, and the agricultural, construction, manufacturing and banking sectors are also expected to continue to perform strongly. Opportunities also exist in the production and distribution side of Nigeria's successful film industry, known as Nollywood, as well as in its burgeoning music industry.

Statistical Survey

Sources (unless otherwise stated): National Bureau of Statistics, Plot 762, Independence Avenue, Central Business District, PMB 127, Garki, Abuja; tel. (9) 2731085; fax (9) 2731084; internet www.nigerianstat.gov.ng; Central Bank of Nigeria, Central Business District, PMB 187, Garki, Abuja; tel. (9) 61639701; fax (9) 61636012; e-mail info@cenbank.org; internet www.cenbank.org.

Area and Population

AREA, POPULATION AND DENSITY

Area (sq km)	909,890*
Population (census results)	
28–30 November 1991†	88,992,220
21–27 March 2006	
Males	71,345,488
Females	69,086,302
Total	140,431,790
Population (UN estimates at mid-year)‡	
2010	158,423,182
2011	162,470,733
2012	166,629,385
Density (per sq km) at mid-2012	183.1

* 351,310 sq miles.
† Revised 15 September 2001.
‡ Source: UN, *World Population Prospects: The 2010 Revision*.

POPULATION BY AGE AND SEX
(UN estimates at mid-2012)

	Males	Females	Total
0–14	36,439,844	34,842,923	71,282,767
15–64	45,304,584	44,348,123	89,652,707
65 and over	2,653,819	3,040,092	5,693,911
Total	84,398,247	82,231,138	166,629,385

Source: UN, *World Population Prospects: The 2010 Revision*.

STATES
(population at 2006 census)

	Area (sq km)	Population	Density (per sq km)	Capital
Abia	4,900	2,845,380	581	Umuahia
Adamawa	38,700	3,178,950	82	Yola
Akwa Ibom	6,900	3,902,051	556	Uyo
Anambra	4,865	4,177,828	859	Awka
Bauchi	49,119	4,653,066	95	Bauchi
Bayelsa	9,059	1,704,515	188	Yenogoa
Benue	30,800	4,253,641	138	Makurdi
Borno	72,609	4,171,104	57	Maiduguri
Cross River	21,787	2,892,988	133	Calabar
Delta	17,108	4,112,445	240	Asaba
Ebonyi	6,400	2,176,947	340	Abakaliki
Edo	19,187	3,233,366	169	Benin City
Ekiti	5,435	2,398,957	441	Ado-Ekiti
Enugu	7,534	3,267,837	434	Enugu
Gombe	17,100	2,365,040	138	Gombe
Imo	5,288	3,927,563	743	Owerri
Jigawa	23,287	4,361,002	187	Dutse
Kaduna	42,481	6,113,503	144	Kaduna
Kano	20,280	9,401,288	464	Kano
Katsina	23,561	5,801,584	246	Katsina
Kebbi	36,985	3,256,541	88	Birnin Kebbi
Kogi	27,747	3,314,043	119	Lokoja
Kwara	35,705	2,365,353	66	Ilorin
Lagos	3,671	9,113,605	2,483	Ikeja
Nassarawa	28,735	1,869,377	65	Lafia
Niger	68,925	3,954,772	57	Minna
Ogun	16,400	3,751,140	229	Abeokuta
Ondo	15,820	3,460,877	219	Akure
Osun	9,026	3,416,959	379	Oshogbo
Oyo	26,500	5,580,894	211	Ibadan
Plateau	27,147	3,206,531	118	Jos
Rivers	10,575	5,198,716	492	Port Harcourt
Sokoto	27,825	3,702,676	133	Sokoto
Taraba	56,282	2,294,800	41	Jalingo
Yobe	46,609	2,321,339	50	Damaturu
Zamfara	37,931	3,278,873	86	Gusau
Federal Capital Territory (Abuja)	7,607	1,406,239	185	Abuja
Total	909,890	140,431,790	154	—

PRINCIPAL TOWNS
(unrevised census of November 1991)

Lagos (federal capital)*	5,195,247	Enugu	407,756
Kano	2,166,554	Oyo	369,894
Ibadan	1,835,300	Warri	363,382
Kaduna	933,642	Abeokuta	352,735
Benin City	762,719	Onitsha	350,280
Port Harcourt	703,421	Sokoto	329,639
Maiduguri	618,278	Okene	312,775
Zaria	612,257	Calabar	310,839
Ilorin	532,089	Katsina	259,315
Jos	510,300	Oshogbo	250,951
Aba	500,183	Akure	239,124
Ogbomosho	433,030	Bauchi	206,537

* Federal capital moved to Abuja (population 107,069) in December 1991.

Mid-2011 ('000 incl. suburbs, UN estimate): Abuja 2,153 (Source: UN, *World Urbanization Prospects: The 2011 Revision*).

BIRTHS AND DEATHS
(annual averages, UN estimates)

	1995–2000	2000–05	2005–10
Birth rate (per 1,000)	42.2	41.5	40.4
Death rate (per 1,000)	18.7	16.7	15.1

Source: UN, *World Population Prospects: The 2010 Revision*.

Life expectancy (years at birth): 51.4 (males 50.6; females 52.2) in 2010 (Source: World Bank, World Development Indicators database).

EMPLOYMENT
('000 persons aged 14 years and over)

	2005	2006	2007
Agriculture, hunting, forestry and fishing	29,017	30,682	31,278
Mining and quarrying	69	73	81
Manufacturing	908	960	821
Electricity, gas and water	427	451	n.a.
Construction	273	289	n.a.
Wholesale and retail trade; repairs of motor vehicles and motorcycles and personal and household articles	104	110	140
Hotels and restaurants	96	102	130
Transport, storage and communications	416	440	1,108
Financial intermediation	281	297	303
Real estate, renting and business activities	60	64	81
Public administration, defence and compulsory social security	5,067	5,358	5,338
Education	9,473	10,017	10,444
Health and social welfare	296	313	308
Other community, social and personal service activities	2,999	3,171	3,280
Total employed	49,486	52,327	54,030

Mid-2012 (estimates in '000): Agriculture, etc. 12,293; Total labour force 52,552 (Source: FAO).

Health and Welfare

KEY INDICATORS

Total fertility rate (children per woman, 2010)	5.5
Under-5 mortality rate (per 1,000 live births, 2010)	143
HIV/AIDS (% of persons aged 15–49, 2009)	3.6
Physicians (per 1,000 head, 2008)	0.4
Hospital beds (per 1,000 head, 2004)	0.5
Health expenditure (2009): US $ per head (PPP)	136
Health expenditure (2009): % of GDP	6.1
Health expenditure (2009): public (% of total)	35.1
Access to water (% of persons, 2010)	58
Access to sanitation (% of persons, 2010)	31
Total carbon dioxide emissions ('000 metric tons, 2008)	95,756.4
Carbon dioxide emissions per head (metric tons, 2008)	0.6
Human Development Index (2011): ranking	156
Human Development Index (2011): value	0.459

For sources and definitions, see explanatory note on p. vi.

Agriculture

PRINCIPAL CROPS
('000 metric tons)

	2008	2009	2010
Wheat	53	50*	51*
Rice, paddy	4,179	3,403	3,219
Maize	7,525	7,339	7,306
Millet	9,064	4,885	4,125
Sorghum	9,318	5,271	4,784
Potatoes	1,105	915*	900*
Sweet potatoes	3,318	2,747*	2,704*
Cassava	44,582	36,804	37,504
Taro (Coco yam)	5,387	2,985	2,594
Yams	35,017	29,092	29,148
Sugar cane	1,412	1,402	1,414
Cow peas, dry	2,916	2,370	2,243
Cashew nuts*	728	650	650
Kolanuts	140*	162	170
Soybeans (Soya beans)	591	574	394
Groundnuts, with shell	2,873	2,969	2,636
Coconuts	234	194†	170*
Oil palm fruit*	8,500	8,500	8,500
Sesame seed	122	120	116
Melonseed	493	370	361
Tomatoes	1,701	1,334*	1,861*
Chillies and peppers, green*	725	453	500
Onions and shallots, green*	226	180	236
Onions, dry*	621	638	640
Carrots and turnips*	284	199	213
Okra	1,039	826*	956*
Maize, green*	677	538	706
Plantains	2,727	2,911*	2,733*
Citrus fruits*	3,400	3,769	3,488
Guavas, mangoes and mangosteens*	750	831	790
Pineapples*	810	875	910
Papayas*	689	764	704
Cocoa beans	367	364	360*
Ginger	175	169	162
Tobacco, unmanufactured	12	14*	17*
Natural rubber*	110	145	144

* FAO estimate(s).

† Unofficial figure.

Aggregate production ('000 metric tons, may include official, semi-official or estimated data): Total cereals 30,209 in 2008, 20,996 in 2009, 19,529 in 2010; Total roots and tubers 89,409 in 2008, 72,542 in 2009, 72,850 in 2010; Total vegetables (incl. melons) 10,978 in 2008, 8,704 in 2009, 11,056 in 2010; Total fruits (excl. melons) 9,352 in 2008, 10,232 in 2009, 9,838 in 2010.

Source: FAO.

LIVESTOCK
('000 head, year ending September)

	2008	2009	2010
Horses*	208	208	211
Asses*	1,065	1,065	1,200
Cattle	16,293	16,435	16,013
Camels*	19	19	19
Pigs	6,908	7,184	7,472
Sheep	33,874	34,687	35,520
Goats	53,800	55,145	56,524
Chickens	174,434	183,156	192,313

* FAO estimates.

Source: FAO.

LIVESTOCK PRODUCTS
('000 metric tons, FAO estimates)

	2008	2009	2010
Cattle meat	293.8	298.4	301.6
Sheep meat	145.3	148.8	150.7
Goat meat	277.4	284.3	291.3
Pig meat	217.6	226.3	234.0
Chicken meat	243.3	256.5	268.0
Game meat	135.8	144.9	155.0
Cows' milk	420	472	496
Hen eggs	581	613	623

Source: FAO.

Forestry

ROUNDWOOD REMOVALS
('000 cubic metres, excluding bark, FAO estimates)

	2008	2009	2010
Sawlogs, veneer logs and logs for sleepers	7,100	7,100	7,100
Pulpwood	39	39	39
Other industrial wood	2,279	2,279	2,279
Fuel wood	62,389	62,793	63,215
Total	71,807	72,211	72,633

2011: Production assumed to be unchanged from 2010 (FAO estimates).

Source: FAO.

SAWNWOOD PRODUCTION
('000 cubic metres, including railway sleepers)

	1995	1996	1997
Broadleaved (hardwood)	2,356	2,178	2,000

1998–2011: Broadleaved (hardwood) production as in 1997.

Source: FAO.

Fishing

('000 metric tons, live weight)

	2008	2009	2010
Capture	601.4	598.2	617.0
Tilapias	47.6	54.2	56.6
Elephant snout fishes	22.4	22.6	23.0
Torpedo-shaped catfishes	32.8	35.2	37.8
Sea catfishes	20.8	18.4	17.2
West African croakers	11.3	9.2	7.5
Sardinellas	63.5	67.5	67.6
Bonga shad	22.1	23.4	24.8
Southern pink shrimp	11.4	9.4	7.7
Other shrimps and prawns	1.9	11.5	13.5
Aquaculture	143.2	152.8	200.5
Total catch	744.6	751.0	817.5

Source: FAO.

Mining

(metric tons unless otherwise indicated)

	2008	2009	2010
Coal, bituminous	500,000	450,000	450,000*
Kaolin	100,000	100,000	100,000
Gypsum	300,000	300,000	320,000*
Crude petroleum ('000 barrels)	768,800	780,348	896,043
Tin concentrates	240	237	230

* Estimate.

† Metal content.

Source: US Geological Survey.

Natural gas (million cu m, excl. gas flared or recycled): 24,796 in 2009; 36,588 in 2010; 39,864 in 2011 (Source: BP, *Statistical Review of World Energy*).

Industry

SELECTED PRODUCTS
('000 metric tons unless otherwise indicated)

	2008	2009	2010
Palm oil*†	1,330	1,380	1,350
Beer of barley*‡	1,540	1,600	1,760
Plywood ('000 cubic metres)†§	56	56	56
Wood pulp*†	23	23	23
Paper and paperboard*†	19	19	19
Raw sugar§	21	n.a.	n.a.
Liquefied petroleum gas ('000 barrels)†	1,900	1,200	1,900
Motor spirit—petrol ('000 barrels)	5,958	3,102	6,400†
Kerosene ('000 barrels)	5,179	2,530	5,000†
Gas-diesel (distillate fuel) oil ('000 barrels)	8,698	4,168	7,000†
Residual fuel oils ('000 barrels)	9,629	4,060	6,600†
Cement	5,000	5,000	5,400†
Electric energy (million kWh)§	21,110	19,777.	n.a.

* Source: FAO.

† Estimates.

‡ Unofficial figure.

§ Source: UN Industrial Commodity Statistics Database.

Source (unless otherwise indicated): US Geological Survey.

2011 ('000 metric tons unless otherwise indicated, FAO estimates): Plywood 56 ('000 cubic metres); Wood pulp 23; Paper and paperboard 19 (Source: FAO).

Finance

CURRENCY AND EXCHANGE RATES

Monetary Units
100 kobo = 1 naira (₦).

Sterling, Dollar and Euro Equivalents (31 May 2012)
£1 sterling = 240.700 naira;
US $1 = 155.250 naira;
€1 = 192.557 naira;
1,000 naira = £4.155 = $6.441 = €5.193.

Average Exchange Rate (naira per US $)
2009 148.902
2010 150.298
2011 153.903

FEDERAL BUDGET
(₦ '000 million)

Revenue	2009	2010*	2011*
Petroleum revenue	1,079	2,193	2,951
Non-petroleum revenue	535	659	788
Import and excise duties	134	141	153
Companies' income tax	264	313	388
Value-added tax	63	79	97
Total	1,614	2,852	3,739

Expenditure	2009	2010*	2011*
Recurrent expenditure	2,294	3,444	3,211
Goods and services	1,712	1,896	1,881
Personnel and pension	1,148	1,360	1,547
Overhead cost	564	536	334
Interest payments	283	475	612
Transfers	299	366	278
Capital expenditure	658	1,158	1,083
Total	2,952	4,602	4,294

* Projections.

Source: IMF, *Nigeria: 2010 - Article IV Consultation-Staff Report; Debt Sustainability Analysis; Informational Annex; Public Information Notice on the Executive Board Discussion; and Statement by the Executive Director for Nigeria* (February 2011).

INTERNATIONAL RESERVES
(US $ million at 31 December)

	2009	2010	2011
Gold (national valuation)	0	0	0
IMF special drawing rights	2,380	2,580	2,572
Foreign exchange	42,382	32,339	32,640
Total	44,763	34,919	35,212

Source: IMF, *International Financial Statistics*.

MONEY SUPPLY
(₦ '000 million at 31 December)

	2009	2010	2011
Currency outside depository corporations	927.2	1,082.4	1,245.1
Transferable deposits	3,575.5	4,137.6	4,906.0
Other deposits	5,708.0	5,941.4	6,526.2
Broad money	10,210.7	11,161.4	12,677.2

Source: IMF, *International Financial Statistics*.

COST OF LIVING
(Consumer Price Index at May; base: May 2003 = 100)

	2009	2010	2011
Food (excl. beverages)	201.6	227.9	255.5
Alcoholic beverages, tobacco and kola	165.7	172.8	191.7
Clothing (incl. footwear)	159.6	174.8	195.1
Rent, fuel and light	228.7	247.5	293.8
Household goods and maintenance	167.6	193.7	220.2
Medical care and health	167.5	177.0	197.0
Transport	184.0	203.8	221.9
Education	223.8	263.4	271.4
All items (incl. others)	201.0	227.0	254.9

NATIONAL ACCOUNTS
(₦ '000 million at current basic prices)

Expenditure on the Gross Domestic Product

	2009	2010*	2011*
Government final consumption expenditure	3,213.2	4,963.9	5,356.6
Private final consumption expenditure	18,859.6	20,408.9	19,908.8
Increase in stocks	1.8	2.2	2.1
Gross fixed capital formation	3,048.0	4,663.6	5,991.4
Total domestic expenditure	25,122.6	30,038.7	31,259.0
Exports of goods and non-factor services	7,766.2	15,640.7	18,650.9
Less Imports of goods and non-petroleum services	7,663.6	11,354.6	12,081.7
GDP in basic prices	25,225.1	34,324.8	37,828.1
GDP in constant basic 1990 prices	594.2	609.9	608.2

Gross Domestic Product by Economic Activity

	2009	2010*	2011*
Agriculture, hunting, forestry and fishing	9,186.3	10,310.7	11,590.1
Mining and quarrying	7,458.8	14,551.5	15,328.1
Crude petroleum	7,418.1	14,505.8	15,275.7
Manufacturing	612.3	643.1	694.7
Electricity, gas and water	62.1	70.3	80.7
Construction	347.7	394.7	456.0
Wholesale and retail trade	4,082.4	4,648.7	5,388.0
Hotels and restaurants	99.0	113.8	130.8
Transport and communications	762.7	791.6	858.7
Finance, insurance	444.2	507.8	574.3
Real estate and business services	1,213.0	1,348.2	1,515.3
Government services	255.4	292.7	333.1
Other community, social and personal services	270.3	311.8	353.6
GDP at factor cost	24,794.2	33,984.8	37,303.4
Indirect taxes (net)†	430.9	340.0	524.7
Total GDP in basic prices	25,225.1	34,324.8	37,828.1

* Provisional.
† Figures obtained as residuals.

BALANCE OF PAYMENTS
(US $ million)

	2009	2010	2011
Exports of goods f.o.b.	56,120	76,450	92,470
Imports of goods f.o.b.	–30,779	–46,203	–61,630
Trade balance	25,341	30,247	30,840
Exports of services	2,218	3,081	3,386
Imports of services	–18,697	–21,332	–24,564
Balance on goods and services	8,862	11,995	9,661
Other income received	935	998	897
Other income paid	–15,339	–20,438	–23,673
Balance on goods, services and income	–5,541	–7,445	–13,115
Current transfers received	19,825	21,183	22,273

—continued	2009	2010	2011
Current transfers paid	–464	–478	–472
Current balance	13,821	13,260	8,686
Direct investment abroad	–1,525	–912	–817
Direct investment from abroad	8,555	6,026	8,839
Portfolio investment assets	–822	–1,117	–1,609
Portfolio investment liabilities	476	3,703	5,148
Other investment assets	–6,488	–13,449	–17,388
Other investment liabilities	1,799	–2,142	730
Net errors and omissions	–26,331	–15,063	–3,284
Overall balance	–10,515	–9,693	306

Source: IMF, *International Financial Statistics*.

External Trade

PRINCIPAL COMMODITIES
(distribution by HS, ₦ '000 million)

Imports c.i.f.	2009	2010	2011
Live animals and animal products	157.0	190.0	567.4
Vegetable products	268.6	270.8	1,169.7
Prepared foodstuffs; beverages, spirits and vinegar and tobacco	176.9	207.7	1,430.2
Mineral products	118.1	176.6	1,059.1
Chemicals and related products	434.7	476.3	510.1
Plastics, rubber and articles thereof	392.3	490.1	659.8
Base metals and articles thereof	531.4	598.2	604.7
Machinery and mechanical appliances	1,449.0	1,931.0	1,924.3
Vehicles, aircraft, vessels and associated transport equipment	1,003.8	1,404.5	1,199.9
Total (incl. others)	5,047.9	6,648.5	9,892.6

Exports f.o.b.	2009	2010	2011
Prepared foodstuffs; beverages, spirits and vinegar and tobacco	240.0	240.1	224.4
Mineral products	6,720.2	11,415.9	17,335.6
Plastics, rubber and articles thereof	49.1	147.5	1,177.5
Raw hides and skins, leather, furskins and articles thereof	76.6	461.1	121.1
Total (incl. others)	7,434.5	13,009.9	19,440.4

PRINCIPAL TRADING PARTNERS
(₦ '000 million)*

Imports c.i.f.	2009	2010	2011
Brazil	168.0	216.9	549.0
China, People's Republic	893.2	1,100.8	1,461.0
France (incl. Monaco)	292.1	388.7	444.3
Germany	45.4	30.8	466.0
Italy	99.0	300.2	278.4
Japan	144.1	171.8	447.1
Netherlands	31.3	52.8	233.9
Spain	10.8	48.8	149.7
United Kingdom	229.5	185.6	262.8
USA	303.7	1,192.8	1,781.0
Total (incl. others)	5,047.9	6,648.5	9,892.6

Exports f.o.b.	2009	2010	2011
Brazil	593.5	908.0	1,632.8
Canada	261.4	382.5	225.2
China, People's Republic	78.1	216.5	392.6
France (incl. Monaco)	407.4	526.9	1,140.1
Germany	67.7	84.3	197.2
Italy	309.7	458.0	991.0
Netherlands	199.4	591.6	414.5
Spain	324.3	425.3	1,146.0
United Kingdom	156.6	190.5	1,210.6
USA	2,026.6	4,471.4	4,381.3
Total (incl. others)	7,434.5	13,009.9	19,440.4

* Imports by country of consignment; exports by country of destination.

Transport

RAILWAYS
(traffic)

	2006	2007	2008
Passenger journeys ('000)	708.8	1,478.7	1,996.3
Passenger-km (million)	256.6	535.3	722.7
Freight ('000 metric tons)	41,219	31,405	47,409
Net freight ton-km (million)	34.3	26.0	41.1

ROAD TRAFFIC
(motor vehicles in use, estimates)

	1995	1996
Passenger cars	820,069	885,080
Buses and coaches	1,284,251	903,449
Lorries and vans	673,425	912,579
Motorcycles and mopeds	481,345	441,651

2007 ('000 motor vehicles in use): Passenger cars 4,560; Motorcycles and mopeds 3,040.

Source: IRF, *World Road Statistics*.

SHIPPING

Merchant Fleet
(registered at 31 December)

	2007	2008	2009
Number of vessels	379	470	516
Displacement ('000 grt)	407.7	611.6	679.2

Source: IHS Fairplay, *World Fleet Statistics*.

International Sea-borne Freight Traffic
(estimates, '000 metric tons)

	1991	1992	1993
Goods loaded	82,768	84,797	86,993
Goods unloaded	10,960	11,143	11,346

Source: UN Economic Commission for Africa, *African Statistical Yearbook*.

CIVIL AVIATION
(traffic on scheduled services)

	2007	2008	2009
Kilometres flown (million)	18	24	23
Passengers carried ('000)	1,365	1,461	1,365
Passenger-km (million)	1,528	1,978	1,873
Total ton-km (million)	143	179	169

Source: UN, *Statistical Yearbook*.

Passengers carried ('000): 1,555 in 2010 (Source: World Bank, World Development Indicators database).

Tourism

ARRIVALS BY NATIONALITY*

Country	2007	2008	2009
Benin	740,367	822,695	855,605
Cameroon	201,586	223,984	233,274
Chad	160,290	178,100	185,527
France	116,704	129,668	134,609
Germany	113,842	126,488	131,309
Ghana	39,078	43,420	45,157
Italy	123,697	137,473	142,712
Liberia	202,638	225,153	234,160
Niger	1,101,959	1,224,399	1,273,378
Sudan	118,916	132,130	137,128
Total (incl. others)	5,238,545	5,820,497	6,053,318

* Figures refer to arrival at frontiers of visitors from abroad, including same-day visitors (excursionists).

Total tourist arrivals ('000): 1,555 in 2010.

Tourism receipts (US $ million, excl. passenger transport): 602 in 2009; 571 in 2010; 601 in 2011 (provisional).

Source: World Tourism Organization.

Communications Media

	2009	2010	2011
Telephones ('000 main lines in use)	1,482.0	1,050.2	719.4
Mobile cellular telephones ('000 in use)	74,518.3	87,297.8	95,167.3
Internet subscribers ('000)	188.0	222.2	n.a.
Broadband subscribers ('000)	82.0	99.1	215.7

Radio receivers ('000 in use): 23,500 in 1997.

Television receivers ('000 in use): 12,000 in 2001.

Book production (titles, including pamphlets): 1,314 in 1995.

Daily newspapers: 25 (estimated average circulation 2,760,000 copies) in 1998.

Personal computers: 1,200,000 (8.5 per 1,000 persons) in 2005.

Sources: International Telecommunication Union; UNESCO Institute for Statistics.

Education

(2008, unless otherwise specified)

	Institutions	Teachers	Students		
			Males	Females	Total
Primary*	54,434	586,930	11,483,943	9,810,575	21,294,518
Secondary*	18,238	270,650	3,682,141	2,943,802	6,625,943
Poly/ Monotechnic†	178	16,499	n.a.	n.a.	237,708
University	95	23,535†	n.a.	n.a.	724,856†

* Provisional.

† 2005 figure.

Pupil-teacher ratio (primary education, UNESCO estimate): 36.0 in 2009/10 (Source: UNESCO Institute for Statistics).

Adult literacy rate (UNESCO estimates): 61.3% (males 72.1%; females 50.4%) in 2010 (Source: UNESCO Institute for Statistics).

Directory

The Constitution

The Constitution of the Federal Republic of Nigeria was promulgated on 5 May 1999, and entered into force on 31 May. The main provisions are summarized below:

PROVISIONS

Nigeria is one indivisible sovereign state, to be known as the Federal Republic of Nigeria. Nigeria is a Federation, comprising 36 States and a Federal Capital Territory. The Constitution includes provisions for the creation of new States and for boundary adjustments of existing States. The Government of the Federation or of a State is prohibited from adopting any religion as a state religion.

LEGISLATURE

The legislative powers of the Federation are vested in the National Assembly, comprising a Senate and a House of Representatives. The 109-member Senate consists of three Senators from each State and one from the Federal Capital Territory, who are elected for a term of four years. The House of Representatives comprises 360 members, representing constituencies of nearly equal population as far as possible, who are elected for a four-year term. The Senate and House of Representatives each have a Speaker and Deputy Speaker, who are elected by the members of the House from among themselves. Legislation may originate in either the Senate or the House of Representatives, and, having been approved by the House in which it originated by a two-thirds majority, will be submitted to the other House for approval, and subsequently presented to the President for assent. Should the President withhold his assent, and the bill be returned to the National Assembly and again approved by each House by a two-thirds majority, the bill will become law. The legislative powers of a State of the Federation will be vested in the House of Assembly of the State. The House of Assembly of a State will consist of three or four times the number of seats that the State holds in the House of Representatives (comprising not less than 24 and not more than 40 members).

EXECUTIVE

The executive powers of the Federation are vested in the President, who is the Head of State, the Chief Executive of the Federation and the Commander-in-Chief of the Armed Forces of the Federation. The President is elected for a term of four years and must receive not less than one-quarter of the votes cast at the election in at least two-thirds of the States in the Federation and the Federal Capital Territory. The President nominates a candidate as his associate from the same political party to occupy the office of Vice-President. The Ministers of the Government of the Federation are nominated by the President, subject to confirmation by the Senate. Federal executive bodies include the Council of State, which advises the President in the exercise of his powers. The executive powers of a State are vested in the Governor of that State, who is elected for a four-year term and must receive not less than one-quarter of votes cast in at least two-thirds of all local government areas in the State.

JUDICIARY

The judicial powers of the Federation are vested in the courts established for the Federation, and the judicial powers of a State in the courts established for the State. The Federation has a Supreme Court, a Court of Appeal and a Federal High Court. Each State has a High Court, a *Shari'a* Court of Appeal and a Customary Court of Appeal. Chief Judges are nominated on the recommendation of a National Judicial Council.

LOCAL GOVERNMENT

The States are divided into 774 local government areas. The system of local government by democratically elected local government councils is guaranteed, and the Government of each State will ensure their existence. Each local government council within the State will participate in the economic planning and development of the area over which it exercises authority.

Federal Government

HEAD OF STATE

President and Commander-in-Chief of the Armed Forces, Minister responsible for Power: Dr GOODLUCK EBELE JONATHAN (sworn in 6 May 2010; re-elected 16 April 2011).

Vice-President: NAMADI SAMBO.

CABINET
(September 2012)

Minister of Labour and Productivity: CHUKWUEMEKA NGOZI WOGU.

Minister of Women's Affairs: Hajiya ZAINAB MAINA.

Minister of Science and Technology: Prof. ITA OKON BASSEY EWA.

Minister of Aviation: STELLA ODUAH-OGIEMWONYI.

Minister of the Federal Capital Territory: BALA MOHAMMED.

Minister of Petroleum Resources: DEZIANI ALISON-MADUEKE.

Minister of the Interior: ABBA MORO.

Minister of Niger Delta Affairs: PETER GODSDAY ORUBEBE.

Minister of Health: Prof. CHRISTIAN OTU ONYEBUCHI.

Minister of Works: MIKE ONOLEMEMEN.

Minister of Police Affairs: Capt. CALEB OLUBOLADE.

Minister of Power: (vacant).

Minister of Education: Prof. RUQAYYATU RUFAI.

Minister, Chairman of the National Planning Commission: Dr SHAMSUDEEN USMAN.

Minister of Mines and Steel Development: MUSA MOHAMMED SADA.

Minister of Defence: (vacant).

Attorney-General and Minister of Justice: MOHAMMED BELLO ADOKE.

Minister of Sports: Mallam BOLAJI ABDULLAHI.

Minister of Trade and Investment: OLUSEGUN OLUTOYIN AGANGA.

Minister of Information and Communication: LABARAN MAKU.

Minister of Foreign Affairs: OLUGBENGA ASHIRU.

Minister of Transport: IDRIS A. UMAR.

Minister of Agriculture and Natural Resources: Dr AKINWUNMI AYO ADESINA.

Minister of Culture and Tourism: EDEM DUKE.

Minister of the Environment: HADIZA IBRAHIM MAILAFA.

Minister of Finance: NGOZI OKONJO-IWEALA.

Minister of Communication Technology: OMOBOLA JOHNSON OLUBUSOLA.

Minister of Lands and Housing: AMA PEPPLE.

Minister of Water Resources: SARAH RENG OCHEPKE.

There were, in addition, 11 Ministers of State.

MINISTRIES

Office of the Head of State: New Federal Secretariat Complex, Shehu Shagari Way, Central Area District, Abuja; tel. (9) 5233536.

Ministry of Agriculture and Natural Resources: Area 11, Secretariat Complex, Garki, PMB 135, Abuja; tel. (9) 3141931; e-mail aruma@nigeria.gov.ng.

Ministry of Aviation: New Federal Secretariat Complex, Shehu Shagari Way, Central Area District, PMB 146, Abuja; tel. (9) 5237487.

Ministry of Commerce and Industry: Area 1, Secretariat Complex, Garki, PMB 88, Abuja; e-mail fmi@fmind.gov.ng; tel. (9) 2341662.

Ministry of Culture and Tourism: Phase II Federal Secretariat, Block A, 1st Floor, Shehu Shagari Way, Abuja; tel. (9) 2348311; fax (9) 23408297; e-mail akayode@nigeria.gov.ng; internet www.visit-nigeria.gov.ng.

Ministry of Defence: Ship House, Central Area, Abuja; tel. (9) 2340534; fax (9) 2340714; e-mail mamed@nigeria.gov.ng.

Ministry of Education: New Federal Secretariat Complex, Shehu Shagari Way, Central Area District, PMB 146, Abuja; tel. (9) 5237838; e-mail enquires@fme.gov.ng; internet www.fme.gov.ng.

Ministry of Energy: Annex 3, Federal Secretariat Complex, Shehu Shagari Way, Central Area, PMB 278, Garki, Abuja; tel. (9) 5239462; fax (9) 5236652; e-mail info@mpr.gov.ng.

Ministry of the Environment: Federal Secretariat Towers, Shehu Shagari Way, Central Area, PMB 468, Garki, Abuja; tel. (9) 5234014; fax (9) 5211847; e-mail haloa@nigeria.gov.ng; internet www.environmentnigeria.org.

Ministry of the Federal Capital Territory: Kapital St, off Obafemi Awolowo St, Garki Area 11, PMB 25, Garki, Abuja; tel. (9) 2341525; fax (9) 3143859; e-mail presunit@fct.gov.ng; internet www.fct.gov.ng.

Ministry of Finance: Ahmadu Bello Way, Central Area, PMB 14, Garki, Abuja; tel. (9) 2346290; e-mail susman@nigeria.gov.ng; internet www.fmf.gov.ng.

Ministry of Foreign Affairs: Sir Tafawa Balewa House, Federal Secretariat, PMB 130, Abuja; tel. (9) 5230570; e-mail omaduekwe@nigeria.gov.ng; internet www.mfa.gov.ng.

Ministry of Health: New Federal Secretariat Complex, Ahmadu Bello Way, Central Business District, PMB 083, Garki, Abuja; tel. (9) 5238362; e-mail agrange@nigeria.gov.ng.

Ministry of Housing: Mabushi District, Garki, Abuja; tel. (9) 2346550; fax (9) 2340174.

Ministry of Information and Communication: New Federal Secretariat Complex, Shehu Shagari Way, Central Area District, PMB 1278, Abuja; tel. (9) 5237183; e-mail jodey@nigeria.gov.ng.

Ministry of the Interior: Area 1, Secretariat Complex, Garki, PMB 16, Abuja; tel. (9) 2341934; fax (9) 2342426; e-mail gabbe@nigeria.gov.ng; internet www.fmia.gov.ng.

Ministry of Justice: New Federal Secretariat Complex, Shehu Shagari Way, Central Area, PMB 192, Garki, Abuja; tel. (9) 5235208; fax (9) 5235194.

Ministry of Labour and Productivity: New Federal Secretariat Complex, Shehu Shagari Way, Central Area, PMB 04, Garki, Abuja; tel. (9) 5235980; e-mail hlawal@nigeria.gov.ng.

Ministry of Mines and Steel Development: New Federal Secretariat Complex, Shehu Shagari Way, Central Area, PMB 107, Garki, Abuja; tel. (9) 5235830; fax (9) 5235831.

Ministry of Niger Delta Affairs: Abuja.

Ministry of Petroleum Resources: 1st and 2nd Floors, New Federal Secretariat Complex, Shehu Shagari Way, Garki, Abuja; tel. (9) 5230763.

Ministry of Police Affairs: 8th Floor, New Federal Secretariat Complex, Shehu Shagari Way, Garki, Abuja; tel. (9) 2340422; internet www.policeaffairs.gov.ng.

Ministry of Power: Abuja.

Ministry of Science and Technology: New Federal Secretariat Complex, Shehu Shagari Way, Central Area, PMB 331, Garki, Abuja; tel. (9) 5233397; fax (9) 5235204.

Ministry of Special Duties: Block 3, 3rd Floor, Phase II New Federal Secretariat Complex, Shehu Shagari Way, Garki, Abuja.

Ministry of Transport: Dipcharima House, Central Business District, off 3rd Ave, PMB 0336, Garki, Abuja; tel. (9) 2347451; fax (9) 2347453; e-mail info@fmt.gov.ng; internet www.fmt.gov.ng.

Ministry of Water Resources: Area 11, Secretariat Complex, Garki, PMB 135, Abuja; tel. (9) 3141931; e-mail aruma@nigeria.gov.ng.

Ministry of Women's Affairs: New Federal Secretariat Complex, Shehu Shagari Way, Central Area, PMB 229, Garki, Abuja; tel. (9) 5237112; fax (9) 5233644; e-mail sbungudu@nigeria.gov.ng; internet www.fmwa.gov.ng.

Ministry of Works: Mabushi District, Garki, Abuja; tel. (9) 2346550; fax (9) 2340174.

Ministry of Youth Development and Sports: Federal Secretariat, Phase II, Shehu Shagari Way, PMB 229, Abuja; tel. (9) 5237112; fax (9) 5233644; e-mail aolasunkanmi@nigeria.gov.ng.

National Planning Commission: Old Central Bank Bldg, 4th Floor, Garki, PMB 234, Abuja; e-mail info@nigerianeconomy.com; internet www.npc.gov.ng.

National Sports Commission: New Federal Secretariat Complex, Shehu Shagari Way, Maitama, Abuja; tel. (9) 5235905; fax (9) 5235901; e-mail agimba@nigeria.gov.ng.

President and Legislature

PRESIDENT

Presidential Election, 16 April 2011, provisional results

Candidate	Votes	% of votes
Goodluck Ebele Jonathan (People's Democratic Party)	22,495,187	58.87
Muhammadu Buhari (Congress for Progressive Change)	12,214,853	31.97
Malam Nuhu Ahmed Ribadu (Action Congress of Nigeria)	2,079,151	5.44
Ibrahim Shekarau (All Nigeria People's Party)	917,012	2.40
Mahmud Mudi Waziri (People For Democratic Change)	82,243	0.22
Others*	421,532	1.10
Total	38,209,978	100.00

* There were 15 other candidates.

NATIONAL ASSEMBLY

House of Representatives

Speaker of the House of Representatives: AMINU WAZIRI TAMBUWAL.

Election, 9 April 2011

Party	Seats
People's Democratic Party	152
Action Congress of Nigeria	53
Congress for Progressive Change	31
All Nigeria People's Party	23
Others	20
Total	279*

* There are 360 seats; however results in 81 constituencies were not immediately made available.

Senate

Speaker of the Senate: DAVID MARK.

Election, 9 April 2011

Party	Seats
People's Democratic Party	53
Action Congress of Nigeria	18
Congress for Progressive Change	6
All Nigeria People's Party	4
Others	4
Total	85*

* There are 109 seats; however, full results of the senatorial elections were not immediately made available.

Election Commission

Independent National Electoral Commission (INEC): Plot 436 Zambezi Cres., Maitama District, PMB 0184, Garki, Abuja; tel. (9) 2224632; e-mail contact@inecnigeria.org; internet www.inecnigeria.org; f. 1998; Chair. Prof. ATTAHIRU JEGA.

Political Organizations

Following the death of the military Head of State in June 1998, the existing authorized political parties were dissolved. The Government established a new Independent National Electoral Commission (INEC), which officially approved three political parties to contest elections in February 1999. Prior to legislative and presidential elections in April 2003, three political associations were granted registration in June 2002, as were a further 24 in December. According to the INEC, by 2011 63 parties had been officially registered.

Action Congress of Nigeria (ACN): PMB 141, Garki, Abuja; tel. (9) 2730102; internet www.acnigeria.com; f. 2006 by a merger of the Alliance for Democracy, the Justice Party, the Advanced Congress of Democrats and several minor parties; Chair. Dr USMAN BUGAJE; Nat. Sec. Chief BISI AKANDE.

Advanced Congress of Democrats (ACD): Suite 35/36, Mazafala Complex, Kuru, Abuja; tel. 8044107989 (mobile); Chair. YUSUF BABA; Nat. Sec. Dr KENNETH KALU.

Alliance for Democracy (AD): Plot 2096, Bumbona Close, Zone 1, Wuse, Abuja; tel. (9) 5239357; e-mail info@alliancefordemocracy.org; f. 1998; Chair. MOJISOLUWA AKINFEWA.

All Nigeria People's Party (ANPP): Bassan Plaza, Plot 759, Central Business Area, Abuja; tel. (9) 2347556; f. 1998; Chair. Chief OKEY NWOSU; Nat. Sec. SAIDU KUMOR.

All Progressives Grand Alliance (APGA): House 4, Rd 116, Gwarimpa Housing Estate, Abuja; e-mail feedback@apganigeria.com; internet apganigeria.com; regd June 2002; Chair. VICTOR C. UMEH; Nat. Sec. Alhaji SHIKAFI .

Congress for Progressive Change (CPC): Suite 212, Banex Plaza, Plot 750, Aminu Kano Cres., Zone A7, Wuse II, Abuja; Nat. Chair. RUFAI HANGA; Nat. Sec. BADMUS MUTALLIB.

Democratic People's Party (DPP): 20 Oro Ago St, opp. Holy Trinity Hospital, off Muhammadu Buhari Way, old CBN, Garki II, Abuja; Chair. BIODUN OGUNBIYI; Nat. Sec. Dr ADEMOLA ADEBO.

Fresh Democratic Party: 4 Park Close, Aguyi Ironsi St, Maitma, Abuja; Chair. Rev. CHRIS OKOTIE; Nat. Sec. SOLA SALAKO.

Movement for the Actualization of the Sovereign State of Biafra (MASSOB): Okwe, Imo; tel. 7039015000 (mobile); e-mail massob_1999@yahoo.com; f. 1999; Leader Chief RALPH UWAZURIKE.

Movement for the Emancipation of the Niger Delta (MEND): f. 2005; main Ijaw militant group operating in the Niger Delta; Leader Maj.-Gen. GODSWILL TAMUNO.

Movement for the Survival of the Ogoni People (MOSOP): 17 Kenule St, Bori, Khana Local Govt Area, Ogoni; tel. (84) 233907; e-mail info@mosop.org; internet www.mosop.org; f. 1990 to organize opposition to petroleum production in Ogoni territory; Pres. LEDUM MITEE; Sec.-Gen. MOSES DAMGBOR.

National Conscience Party (NCP): 18 Phase 1 Low Cost Housing Estate, Lake City Ave, Gwagwalada, Abuja; tel. (9) 4937279; internet www.nigeriancp.net; Leader GANI FAWEHINMI; Chair. OSAGIE OBAYUWANA.

National Democratic Party (NDP): Plot 39, Durban St, off Ademola Adetokunbo Cres., Wuse II, Abuja; tel. (9) 6704070; regd June 2002; Chair. Alhaji ALIYU HABU FARI; Nat. Sec. ADEMOLA AYOADE.

Niger Delta People's Volunteer Force (NDPVF): prominent Ijaw militant group operating in the Niger Delta; Leader Alhaji MUJAHID DOKUBO-ASARI.

People For Democratic Change (PDC): Kalabari St, Karu Site, Karu, Abuja; Nat. Chair. MAHMUD MUDI WAZIRI; Nat. Sec. BENJAMIN EMEKA IGWE.

People's Democratic Party (PDP): Wadata Plaza, Michael Okpara Way, Zone 5, Wuse, Abuja; tel. (9) 5232589; e-mail info@peopledemocraticparty.org; internet www.peopledemocraticparty.org; f. 1998; supports greater federalism; ruling party; Chair. Alhaji BAMANGA TUKUR; Nat. Sec. Alhaji ABUBAKAR BARAJE.

People's Redemption Party (PRP): City Plaza, Area 11, Garki, Abuja; tel. 8033495403 (mobile); regd Dec. 2002; Chair. Alhaji ABDULKADIR B. MUSA; Nat. Sec. Dr E. NGOZI OKAFOR.

People's Salvation Party (PSP): 451 Oron St, Wuse Zone 1, Abuja; tel. (9) 5235359; regd Dec. 2002; Chair. Dr JUNAIDU MOHAMMED; Nat. Sec. Dr V. A. AMOSU.

Progressive People's Alliance (PPA): 36 Moses A. Majekodunmi Cres., Utako District, Abuja; tel. 7038263544 (mobile); internet ppanigeria.com; Chair. SAM NKIRE; Nat. Sec. DAHIRU MUSA MOHAMMED.

United Nigeria People's Party (UNPP): Plot 1467, Safana Close, Garki 11, Abuja; tel. (9) 2340091; regd June 2002; Chair. MALLAM SALEH JAMBO; Nat. Sec. Dr UKEJE NWOKEFORO.

Diplomatic Representation

EMBASSIES AND HIGH COMMISSIONS IN NIGERIA

Algeria: Plot 203, Etim Inyang Cres., POB 55238, Falomo, Lagos; tel. (1) 612092; fax (1) 2624017; Ambassador HAFRAD ALI.

Angola: 5 Kasumu Ekomode St, Victoria Island, POB 50437, Falomo Ikoyi, Lagos; tel. (1) 611702; fax (1) 618675; Ambassador EVARISTO DOMINGOS KIMBA.

Argentina: 1611 Yusuf Maitama Sule St, Asokoro District, Abuja; tel. (9) 7800651; fax (9) 3148683; e-mail enige@mrecic.gov.ar; internet www.nigeria.embajada-argentina.gov.ar; Ambassador MARIA SUSANA PATARO.

Australia: 5th Floor, Oakland Centre, 48 Aguiyi Ironsi St, Maitama, Abuja; PMB 5152, Abuja; tel. (9) 4612780; fax (9) 4612782; e-mail ahc.abuja@dfat.gov.au; internet www.nigeria.embassy.gov.au; High Commissioner IAN MCCONVILLE.

Austria: Plot 9, Usuma St, Maitama, Abuja; tel. 7064183226 (mobile); fax (9) 4612715; e-mail abuja-ob@bmeia.gv.at; Ambassador Dr STEFAN SCHOLZ.

Belarus: Sheraton Abuja Hotel, RM 317, Ladi Kwali Street, Maitama, Abuja; tel. 8092349803; e-mail nigeria@mfa.gov.by; Ambassador VYACHESLAV BESKOSTY.

Belgium: 9 Usuma St, Maitama, Abuja; tel. (9) 4131859; fax (9) 4132015; e-mail abuja@diplobel.fed.be; internet www.diplomatie.be/abuja; Ambassador DIRK VERHEYEN.

Benin: 4 Abudu Smith St, Victoria Island, POB 5705, Lagos; tel. (1) 2614411; fax (1) 2612385; Ambassador PATRICE HOUNGAVOU.

Brazil: Plot 173, Mississippi St, Maitama, Abuja; tel. (9) 4134067; fax (9) 4134066; Ambassador ANA CANDIDA PEREZ.

Bulgaria: 10 Euphrates St, off Aminu Kano Cres., Maitama, Abuja; tel. (9) 4130034; fax (9) 4132741; e-mail bulembassy@yahoo.com; internet www.mfa.bg/abuja; Ambassador MIROSLAV NIKOLAEV KOMAROV.

Burkina Faso: No. 4, Freetown St, off Ademola Adetokunbo Cres., Wuse II, Abuja; tel. (9) 4130491; fax (9) 4130492; e-mail ebfn@nova.net.ng; Ambassador DRAMANE YAMÉOGO.

Cameroon: 469, Lobito Cres., Wuse II, Abuja; tel. (1) 4611355; e-mail haucocamabuja@yahoo.fr; High Commissioner ABBAS IBRAHIMA SALAHEDDINE.

Canada: 15 Bobo St, Maitama, POB 5144, Abuja; tel. (9) 4612900; fax (9) 4612901; e-mail abuja@international.gc.ca; internet www.canadainternational.gc.ca/nigeria; High Commissioner CHRISTOPHER COOTER.

Chad: 10 Mississippi St, PMB 488, Abuja; tel. (9) 4130751; fax (9) 4130752; Ambassador MAHAMAT HABIB DOUTOUM.

China, People's Republic: Plot 302–303, Central Area, Abuja; tel. (9) 4618661; fax (9) 4618660; e-mail chinaemb_ng@mfa.gov.cn; internet ng.china-embassy.org; Ambassador DENG BOQING.

Congo, Republic: 447 Lobito Cres., Abuja; tel. (9) 4137407; fax (9) 4130157; Ambassador PETER NGUI.

Côte d'Ivoire: 2630 Gourara St, Abuja; tel. (9) 4133087; fax (9) 4133137; e-mail cotedivoire@micro.com.ng; Ambassador MAMAN TOURÉ.

Cuba: Plot 339, Diplomatic Zone, Area 10, Garki, Abuja; tel. (9) 4614821; fax (9) 4614820; e-mail embajada@ng.embacuba.cu; internet emba.cubaminrex.cu/nigeriaing; Ambassador ELIO SAVÓN OLIVA.

Czech Republic: Plot 1223, 5 Gnassingbé Eyadéma St, Asokoro District, POB 4628, Abuja; tel. (9) 3141245; fax (9) 3141248; e-mail abuja@embassy.mzv.cz; internet www.mzv.cz/abuja; Ambassador JAROSLAV SIRO.

Egypt: 8 Buzi Close, off Amazon St, Maitama, Abuja; PMB 5069, Wuse, Abuja; tel. (9) 4136091; fax (9) 4132602; Ambassador YOUSSEF HASSAN SHAWKI.

Equatorial Guinea: 20 Dakala St, off Parakou Cres., off Aminu Kano Cres., Wuse II, Abuja; tel. and fax (9) 7816867; e-mail egembassyabj@hotmail.com; Ambassador JOB OBIANG ESONO MBENGONO.

Eritrea: Plot 1510, Yedseram St, off IBB Way, Maitama, Abuja; tel. 8139856889 (mobile); fax (9) 4136085; e-mail eriemba_nigeria@yahoo.com; Ambassador MOHAMMED ALI OMARO.

Ethiopia: 19 Ona Cres., Maitama, POB 2488, Abuja; tel. (1) 4131691; fax (1) 4131692; e-mail etabuja@primair.net; Ambassador YOHANESS GENDA.

Finland: 9 Iro Dan Musa St, Asokoro, Abuja; tel. (9) 3147256; fax (9) 3147252; e-mail sanomat.aba@formin.fi; internet www.finlandnigeria.org; Ambassador ANNELI VUORINEN.

France: 37 Udi Hills St, off Aso Dr., Abuja; tel. (9) 5235510; fax (9) 5235482; e-mail sec-amb.abuja-amba@diplomatie.gouv.fr; internet www.ambafrance-ng.org; Ambassador JEAN-MICHEL DUMOND.

Gabon: 8 Norman Williams St, SW Ikoyi, POB 5989, Lagos; tel. (1) 684566; fax (1) 2690692; Ambassador CORENTIN HERVO-AKENDENGUE.

The Gambia: 7 Misratah St, off Parakou Cres., Wuse II, PMB 5058, Abuja; tel. (9) 5241224; fax (9) 5241228; e-mail ghcabuja@yahoo.com; High Commissioner ANGELA COLLEY.

Germany: 9 Lake Maracaibo Close, off Amazon St, Maitama, Abuja; tel. (9) 4130962; fax (9) 4130949; e-mail info@abuja.diplo.de; internet www.abuja.diplo.de; Ambassador DOROTHEE JANETZKE-WENZEL.

Ghana: 21–25 King George V Rd, POB 889, Lagos; tel. (1) 2630015; fax (1) 2630338; High Commissioner ALHAJI BABA KAMARA.

Greece: 6 Seguela St, Wuse II, POB 11525, Abuja; tel. (9) 4612775; fax (9) 4612778; e-mail gremb.abj@mfa.gr; internet www.mfa.gr/abuja; Ambassador HARALAMBOS DAFARANOS.

Guinea: No. 349, Central Business District, opp. United Nations Premises, POB 591, Abuja; tel. (9) 4618612; fax (9) 4618611; e-mail ambaguinig@yahoo.com; Ambassador Dr CHEICK ABDOUL CAMARA.

Holy See: Pope John Paul II Cres., Maitama, PMB 541, Garki, Abuja; tel. (9) 4138381; fax (9) 4136653; e-mail nuntiusabj@hotmail.com; Apostolic Nuncio AUGUSTINE KASUJJA (Titular Archbishop of Caesarea in Numidia).

Hungary: 61 Jose Marti Cres., Asokoro, POB 5299, Abuja; tel. 7064786188 (mobile); e-mail mission.abv@kum.hu; internet www.mfa.gov.hu/emb/abuja; Chargé d'affaires a.i. JÁNOS KOVÁCS.

India: 15 Rio Negro Close, off Yedseram St, Maitama, Abuja; tel. (9) 4602800; fax (9) 4602805; e-mail hoc.abuja@mea.gov.in; internet www.indianhcabuja.com; High Commissioner MAHESH SACHDEV.

Indonesia: 5B Anifowoshe St, Victoria Island, POB 3473, Marina, Lagos; tel. (1) 2614601; fax (1) 2613301; e-mail unitkomigs@hyperia.com; Ambassador SUDIRMAN HASENG.

Iran: 1 Udi Hills St, off Aso Dr., Maitama, Abuja; tel. (1) 5238048; fax (1) 5237785; e-mail iranabuja@gmail.com; Ambassador SAEED KOOZECHI.

Ireland: 11 Negro Cres., Maitama District, Abuja; tel. (9) 4620611; fax (9) 4620613; e-mail abujaembassy@dfa.ie; internet www.embassyofireland.org.ng; Ambassador KYLE O'SULLIVAN.

Israel: Plot 12, Mary Slessor St, Asokoro, POB 10924, Abuja; tel. (9) 4605500; e-mail info@abuja.mfa.gov.il; internet abuja.mfa.gov.il; Ambassador MOSHE RAM.

Italy: 21st Cres., off Constitution Ave, Central Business District, Abuja; tel. (9) 4614722; fax (9) 4614709; e-mail ambasciata.abuja@esteri.it; internet www.ambabuja.esteri.it; Ambassador ROBERTO COLAMINÈ.

Jamaica: Plot 247, Muhammadu Buhari Way, Central Area District, Abuja; tel. and fax (9) 2345107; e-mail jamaicanembassy@yahoo.com; High Commissioner ANN SCOTT.

Japan: 9 Bobo St, off Gana St, Maitama, PMB 5070, Abuja; tel. (9) 4138898; fax (870) 600-315-545 (satellite); Ambassador RYUICHI SHOJI.

Kenya: 18 Yedseram St, Maitama, PMB 5160, Abuja; tel. (9) 4139155; fax (9) 4139157; e-mail abuja@mfa.go.ke; High Commissioner DANIEL MEPUKORI KOIKAI.

Korea, Democratic People's Republic: Plot 350, Central Area, Cadastral Zone, AO, POB 407, Garki, Abuja; tel. (9) 2347200; fax (9) 2347199; Ambassador JONG HAK SE.

Korea, Republic: 9 Ovia Cres., off Pope John Paul St, Maitama, POB 6870, Abuja; tel. (9) 4612701; fax (9) 4612702; e-mail emb-ng@mofat.go.kr; internet nga-abuja.mofat.go.kr; Ambassador CHOI JONG-HYUN.

Liberia: 3 Idejo St, Plot 162, off Adeola Odeku St, Victoria Island, POB 70841, Lagos; tel. (1) 2618899; Ambassador Prof. AL-HASSAN CONTEH.

Libya: Plot 1591, Mike Okoye Cl., off George Sowemimo St, Asokoro Ext., POB 435, Garki, Abuja; tel. (9) 3148356; fax (9) 3148354; Ambassador Eng. MANSOUR O. OSMAN.

Malaysia: 4A, Plot 2232B, Rio Negro Close, off Yedseram St, Maitama, PMB 5217, Wuse, Abuja; tel. (9) 7809379; internet www.kln.gov.my/abuja; e-mail malabuja@kln.gov.my; High Commissioner NIK MUSTAFA KAMAL NIK AHMAD.

Mexico: 39 Usuma St, off Ghana St, Maitama District, PMB 718, Garki, Abuja; tel. (9) 4620630; e-mail embnigeria@sre.gob.mx; Ambassador MARCO BARCO.

Morocco: 5 Mary Slessor St, off Udo Udoma Cres., Asokoro, Abuja; tel. (9) 8746697; fax (9) 3141959; e-mail mcherkaoui45@yahoo.fr; Ambassador MUSTAPHA BOUH.

Namibia: Plot 1738, T. Y. Danjuma St, Cadasdral Zone, A4 Asokoro, Abuja; tel. (9) 7809441; e-mail namibiahighcomabuja@yahoo.com; internet www.namibiahc.com.ng; High Commissioner SELMA ASHIPALA-MUSAVYI.

Netherlands: 21st Cres., off Constitution Ave, Central Business District, Abuja; tel. (9) 4611200; fax (9) 4611240; e-mail abj@minbuza.nl; internet nigeria.nlembassy.org; Ambassador BERT RONHAAR.

Niger: 15 Adeola Odeku St, Victoria Island, PMB 2736, Lagos; tel. (9) 4136206; fax (9) 4136205; Ambassador MOUSSA ELHADJI IBRAHIM.

Norway: 54 T.Y. Danjuma St, Asokoro, Abuja; tel. (9) 8746989; fax (9) 3149309; e-mail emb.abuja@mfa.no; internet www.emb-norway.com.ng; Ambassador KJELL LILLERUD.

Pakistan: 4 Samora Machel Street, Asokoro, Abuja; tel. (9) 3141650; fax (9) 3141652; e-mail pahicabuja@yahoo.com; High Commissioner ASIF DURAIZ AKHTAR.

Philippines: 2 Kainji St, cnr Lake Chad Cres., Maitama, Abuja; tel. (9) 4137981; fax (9) 4137650; e-mail pe.abuja@dfa.gov.ph; Ambassador NESTOR NABAYRA PADALHIN.

Poland: 10 Ona Cres., off Lake Chad Cres., Maitama, 900271, Abuja; tel. 8052000204 (mobile); e-mail contact@abuja-polemb.net; internet www.abuja.polemb.net; Ambassador PRZEMYSŁAW NIESIOŁOWSKI.

Portugal: 27B Gana St, Maitama, Abuja; tel. (9) 4137211; fax (9) 4137214; e-mail portemb@rosecom.net; Ambassador MARIA DE FÁTIMA DE PINA PERESTRELLO.

Romania: Nelson Mandela St, No. 76, Plot 498, Asokoro, Abuja; tel. (9) 3142304; fax (9) 3142306; e-mail romembabujaconsularsection@gmail.com; internet www.romnig.com; Chargé d'affaires a.i. MIRCEA LEUCEA.

Russia: 5 Walter Carrington Cres., Victoria Island, POB 2723, Lagos; tel. (1) 2613359; fax (1) 4619994; Ambassador ALEXANDER DIMITRIEVICH POLYAKOV.

Rwanda: Abuja; High Commissioner JOSEPH HABINEZA.

Saudi Arabia: Plot 347H, off Adetokunbo Ademola Cres., Wuse II, Abuja; tel. (9) 4131880; fax (9) 4134906; Ambassador ANWAR A. ABD-RABBUH.

Senegal: 14 Kofo Abayomi Rd, Victoria Island, PMB 2197, Lagos; tel. (1) 2611722; Ambassador SAOUDATOU NDIAYE SECK.

Serbia: 11, Rio Negro Close, off Yedseram St, Cadastral Zone A6, Maitama District, Abuja; tel. 8059738141 (mobile); fax (9) 4130078; e-mail mail@ambnig.com; Ambassador RIFAT RONDIC.

Sierra Leone: Plot 308 Mission Rd, opp Ministry of Defence (Ship House), Diplomatic Zone, Central Business District, Abuja; tel. (9) 8704241; fax (9) 8725413; e-mail slhcnig@yahoo.com; High Commissioner HENRY O. MACAULEY.

Slovakia: POB 1290, Lagos; tel. (1) 2621585; fax (1) 2612103; e-mail obeo.sk@micro.com.ng; Ambassador MIROSLAV HACEK.

Somalia: Plot 1270, off Adeola Odeka St, POB 6355, Lagos; tel. (1) 2611283; Ambassador M. S. HASSAN.

South Africa: 71 Usuma St, off Gana St, Maitama, Abuja; tel. (9) 4133776; fax (9) 4133829; e-mail sahcabuja@yahoo.co.uk; High Commissioner J. N. K. MAMABOLO.

Spain: 8 Bobo Close, Maitama, PMB 5120, Wuse, Abuja; tel. (9) 4613258; fax (9) 4613259; e-mail emb.abuja@maec.es; internet www.maec.es/embajadas/abuja; Ambassador ALVARO CASTILLO AGUILAR.

Sudan: Plot 337, Misson Rd Zone, Central Area District, Abuja; tel. (9) 6700668; fax (9) 2346265; e-mail sudaniabj@hotmail.com; Ambassador AHMED ALTIGANI SALEH.

Sweden: PMB 569, Garki, Abuja; tel. (9) 8746913; fax (870) 782-248-789 (satellite); e-mail ambassaden.abuja@foreign.ministry.se; internet www.swedenabroad.com/abuja; Ambassador SVANTE KILANDER.

Switzerland: 157 Adetokumbo Ademola Cres., Wuse II, Abuja; tel. (9) 4610540; fax (9) 4610548; e-mail abu.vertretung@eda.admin.ch; internet www.eda.admin.ch/abuja; Ambassador Dr ANDREAS BAUM.

Syria: 25 Kofo Abayomi St, Victoria Island, Lagos; tel. (1) 2615860; Chargé d'affaires a.i. MUSTAFA HAJ-ALI.

Tanzania: 8 Agoro Odiyan St, Victoria Island, POB 6417, Lagos; tel. (1) 613604; fax (1) 610016; e-mail tanabuja@lytos.com; High Commissioner ABDUL CISCO MTIRO.

Thailand: 24 Tennesse Cres., off Panama St, Maitama, Abuja; tel. (9) 8723746; fax (9) 4135193; e-mail thaiabj@mfa.go.th; Ambassador N. SATHAPORN.

Togo: Plot 976, Oju Olobun Close, Victoria Island, POB 1435, Lagos; tel. (1) 2617449; fax (1) 617478; Ambassador FOLI-AGBENOZAN TETTEKPOE.

Trinidad and Tobago: 7 Casablanca St, off Nairobi St, off Amino Kano Cres., Wuse II, Abuja; tel. (9) 6411118; fax (9) 4611117; e-mail trinitobagoabj@yahoo.co.uk; internet www.ttmissionsnigeria.com; High Commissioner NYAHUMA MENTHUHOTEP OBIKA.

Turkey: 5 Amazon St, Minister's Hill, Maitama, Abuja; tel. (9) 4139787; fax (9) 4139457; e-mail embassy.abuja@mfa.gov.tr; internet www.abuja.emb.mfa.gov.tr; Ambassador ALI RIFAT KÖKSAL.

Ukraine: Plot 15, Moundou St, Wuse II, Abuja; tel. (9) 5239577; fax (9) 5239578; e-mail emb_ng@mfa.gov.ua; internet www.mfa.gov.ua/nigeria; Ambassador VALERII VASYLIEV.

United Kingdom: Dangote House, Aguiyi Ironsi St, Wuse, Abuja; tel. (9) 4132010; fax (9) 4623223; e-mail information.abuja@fco.gov.uk; internet www.ukinnigeria.fco.gov.uk; High Commissioner ANDREW LLOYD.

USA: Plot 1075, Diplomatic Dr., Central District Area, Abuja; tel. (9) 4614000; fax (9) 4614171; e-mail consularabuja@state.gov; internet abuja.usembassy.gov; Ambassador TERENCE PATRICK MCCULLEY.

Venezuela: Plot 1361 Hon, Justice Sowemino St, Asokoro District, Abuja; tel. (9) 3140900; fax (9) 3140903; e-mail evenigeria@yahoo.com; Ambassador BORIS ENRÍQUEZ MARTÍNEZ.

Zambia: 351 Mission Rd, Central Area District, Garki, Abuja; tel. (9) 4618605; fax (9) 4618602; e-mail zambiahc@yahoo.com; High Commissioner GEORGE MPOMBO.

Zimbabwe: 19 Tiamiyu Savage St, POB 50247, Victoria Island, Lagos; tel. (1) 2619328; e-mail zimabuja@yahoo.co.uk; High Commissioner Dr JOHN SHUMBA MVUNDURA.

Judicial System

Supreme Court

Three Arms Complex, Central District, PMB 308, Abuja; tel. (9) 2346594.

Consists of a Chief Justice and up to 15 Justices, appointed by the President, on the recommendation of the National Judicial Council (subject to the approval of the Senate); has original jurisdiction in any dispute between the Federation and a state, or between states, and hears appeals from the Federal Court of Appeal.

Chief Justice: ALOMA MARIAM MUKHTAR.

Court of Appeal: consists of a President and at least 35 Justices, of whom three must be experts in Islamic (*Shari'a*) law and three experts in Customary law; has 12 divisions in various states.

Federal High Court: Abuja; internet www.fhc-ng.com; Chief Judge ABDULLAHI MUSTAPHA.

Each state has a **High Court**, consisting of a Chief Judge and a number of judges, appointed by the Governor of the state on the recommendation of the National Judicial Council (subject to the approval of the House of Assembly of the state). If required, a state may have a **Shari'a Court of Appeal** (dealing with Islamic civil law) and a **Customary Court of Appeal**. **Special Military Tribunals** have been established to try offenders accused of crimes such as corruption, drugs-trafficking and armed robbery; appeals against rulings of the Special Military Tribunals are referred to a **Special Appeals Tribunal**, which comprises retired judges.

Religion

ISLAM

According to the 2003 Nigeria Demographic and Health Survey, Muslims comprised 50.5% of the total population.

Spiritual Head: Col MUHAMMADU SA'AD ABUBAKAR (the Sultan of Sokoto).

CHRISTIANITY

According to the 2003 Nigeria Demographic and Health Survey, 48.2% of the population were Christians.

Christian Council of Nigeria: 139 Ogunlana Dr., Surulere, POB 2838, Lagos; tel. (1) 7923495; f. 1929; 15 full mems and six assoc. mems; Pres. Most Rev. EMMANUEL UDOFIA; Gen. Sec. Rev. IKECNUKWU OKORIE.

The Anglican Communion

Anglicans are adherents of the Church of the Province of Nigeria, comprising 139 dioceses. Nigeria, formerly part of the Province of West Africa, became a separate Province in 1979; in 1997 it was divided into three separate provinces and a 10-Province structure for the Church of Nigeria (Anglican Communion) was proclaimed in January 2003.

Primate, Archbishop of the Province of Abuja: Most Rev. NICHOLAS DIKERIEHI OROGODO OKOH, Bishopscourt, Cable Point, POB 216, Asaba; tel. (56) 280682; e-mail primate@anglican-nig.org; internet www.anglican-nig.org.

Archbishop of the Province of Bendel and Bishop of Esan: Most Rev. FRIDAY JOHN IMAEKHAI, 24 Douala St, Wuse Zone 5, POB 212, Abuja; tel. (9) 5236950; fax (9) 5230986.

Archbishop of the Province of Ibadan and Bishop of Ibadan: Most Rev. JOSEPH AKINFENWA, POB 3075, Mapo; tel. (2) 8101400; fax (2) 8101413; e-mail ibadan@anglican.skannet.com.ng.

Archbishop of the Province of Jos and Bishop of Maiduguri: Most Rev. EMMANUEL KANA MANI, Bishopscourt, off Lagos St, GRA POB 1693, Maiduguri; tel. (76) 234010; e-mail maiduguri@anglican-nig.org.

Archbishop of the Province of Kaduna and Bishop of Kaduna: Most Rev. JOSIAH IDOWU-FEARON, POB 72, Kaduna; tel. (62) 240085; fax (62) 244408; e-mail manasoko@infoweb.abs.net.

Archbishop of the Province of Lagos and Bishop of Lagos: Most Rev. EPHRAIM ADEBOLA ADEMOWO, 29 Marina, POB 13, Lagos; tel. (1) 2636026; fax (1) 2636536; e-mail lagos@anglican.skannet.com.ng.

Archbishop of the Province of the Niger and Bishop of Awka: Most Rev. MAXWELL SAMUEL CHIKE ANIKWENWA, Bishopscourt, Ifite Rd, POB 130, Awka; tel. (48) 550058; fax (48) 550052; e-mail angawka@infoweb.abs.net.

Archbishop of the Niger Delta and Bishop of Aba: Most Rev. UGOCHUCKWU UWAOMA EZUOKE, Bishopscourt, 70/72 St Michael's Rd, POB 212, Aba; tel. (82) 227666; e-mail aba@anglican-nig.org.

Archbishop of the Province of Ondo and Bishop of Ekiti: Most Rev. SAMUEL ADEDAYE ABE, Bishopscourt, POB 12, Okesa St, Ado-Ekiti, Ekiti; tel. (30) 250305; e-mail ekiti@anglican.skannet.com.ng.

Archbishop of the Province of Owerri and Bishop of Orlu: Most Rev. BENNETT C. I. OKORO, Bishopscourt, POB 260, Nkwerre; tel. (82) 440538.

General Secretary: Ven. EMMANUEL ADEKUNLE, 24 Douala St, Wuse Zone 5, POB 212, Abuja; tel. (9) 5236950; fax (9) 5230987; e-mail general_secretary@anglican-nig.org.

The Roman Catholic Church

Nigeria comprises nine archdioceses, 41 dioceses and two Apostolic Vicariates. An estimated 15% of the population were Roman Catholics.

Catholic Bishops' Conference of Nigeria

Plot 459, Cadastral Zone B2, Southern Park, Durumi 1, Garki, POB 6523, Abuja; tel. (9) 5239413; fax (9) 5230881; e-mail cathsec1@infoweb.abs.net; internet www.cbcn-ng.org.

f. 1976; Pres. Most Rev. FELIX ALABA ADEOSIN JOB (Archbishop of Ibadan); Sec.-Gen. of Secretariat Rev. Fr MATTHEW HASSAN KUKAH.

Archbishop of Abuja: Most Rev. JOHN OLORUNFEMI ONAIYEKAN, Archdiocesan Secretariat, POB 286, Garki, Abuja; tel. (9) 2340661; fax (9) 2340662; e-mail onaiyekan7@hotmail.com.

Archbishop of Benin City: AUGUSTINE OBIORA AKUBEZE, Archdiocesan Secretariat, POB 35, Benin City, Edo; tel. (52) 253787; fax (52) 255763; e-mail cadobc@infoweb.abs.net.

Archbishop of Calabar: Most Rev. JOSEPH EDRA UKPO, Catholic Secretariat, PMB 1044, 1 Bishop Moynagh Ave, Calabar, Cross River; tel. (87) 231666; fax (87) 239177; e-mail archdical@yahoo.com.

Archbishop of Ibadan: Most Rev. FELIX ALABA JOB, Archbishop's House, PMB 5057, 8 Bale Latosa Rd, Onireke, Ibadan, Oyo; tel. (22) 2413544; fax (22) 2414855; e-mail archdiocese.ibadan@skannet.com.

Archbishop of Jos: Most Rev. IGNATIUS AYAU KAIGAMA, Archdiocesan Secretariat, 20 Joseph Gomwalk Rd, POB 494, Jos, Plateau; tel. (73) 452878; fax (73) 451547; e-mail josarch@hisen.org.

Archbishop of Kaduna: Most Rev. MATTHEW MAN-OSO NDAGOSO, Archbishop's House, 71 Tafawa Balewa Way, POB 248, Kaduna; tel. (62) 246076; fax (62) 240026; e-mail catholickaduna@yahoo.com.

Archbishop of Lagos: Most Rev. ALFRED ADEWALE MARTINS, Archdiocesan Secretariat, 19 Catholic Mission St, POB 8, Lagos; tel. (1) 2635729; fax (1) 2633841; e-mail arclagos@yahoo.com.

Archbishop of Onitsha: Most Rev. VALERIAN OKEKE, Archdiocesan Secretariat, POB 411, Onitsha, Anambra; tel. (46) 413298; fax (46) 413913; e-mail secretariat@onitsha-archdiocese.org.

Archbishop of Owerri: Most Rev. ANTHONY JOHN VALENTINE OBINNA, Villa Assumpta, POB 85, Owerri, Imo; tel. (83) 250115; fax (83) 230760; e-mail owcatsec@owerriarchdiocese.org.

Other Christian Churches

Brethren Church of Nigeria: c/o Kulp Bible School, POB 1, Mubi, Adamawa; f. 1923; Gen. Sec. Rev. JINATU WAMDEO; 100,000 mems.

Church of the Lord (Aladura) Worldwide: 10/12 Primate Oshitelu St, Ogere-Remo, POB 71 Shagamu, Ogun; tel. (803) 3307288; fax (805) 2321578; e-mail cla_primate@yahoo.com; internet www.aladura.info; f. 1925; Primate Most Rev. Dr RUFUS OKIKIOLA OSITELU; 3.8m. mems.

Lutheran Church of Christ in Nigeria: POB 21, Hospital Rd, Numan, Adamawa; tel. (75) 772330; fax (75) 625093; e-mail nemuelbabba@hotmail.com; Pres. Archbishop CHRISTIAN EKONG; 1.9m. mems (2010).

Lutheran Church of Nigeria: POB 49, Obot Idim Ibesikpo, Uyo, Akwa Ibom; tel. (85) 200505; fax (85) 200451; e-mail chrisekonglcn@yahoo.com; internet www.lutheranchurchnigeria.org; f. 1936; Pres. Most Rev. CHRISTIAN EKONG; 142,000 mems (2010).

Methodist Church Nigeria: Wesley House, 21–22 Marina, POB 2011, Lagos; tel. (1) 2702563; fax (1) 2702710; 483,500 mems; Patriarch Rev. Dr SUNDAY OLA KAKINDE.

Nigerian Baptist Convention: Baptist Bldg, PMB 5113, Ibadan; tel. (2) 2412267; fax (2) 2413561; e-mail baptconv@nigerianbaptist.org; internet nigerianbaptist.org; Pres. Rev. Dr REUBEN I. CHUGA; Gen. Sec. Dr SAMSON OLASUPO AYOKUNLE; 3.5m. mems.

The Presbyterian Church of Nigeria: 26–29 Ehere Rd, Ogbor Hill, POB 2635, Aba, Imo; tel. (82) 222551; f. 1846; Moderator Rt Rev. Dr UBON B. USUNG; Synod Clerk Rev. NDUKWE NWACHUKWU EME; 1m. mems.

The Redeemed Church of Christ, the Church of the Foursquare Gospel, the Qua Iboe Church and the Salvation Army are prominent among numerous other Christian churches active in Nigeria.

AFRICAN RELIGIONS

The beliefs, rites and practices of the people of Nigeria are very diverse, varying between ethnic groups and between families in the same group.

The Press

DAILIES

Al-Mizan: internet almizan.faithweb.com; Hausa; Editor IBRAHIM MUSA.

Aminiya: 20 POW Mafemi Cres., off Solomon Lar Way, Utako, Abuja; tel. (9) 6726241; internet aminiya.dailytrust.com; Hausa; Editor-in-Chief MANNIR DAN ALI.

BusinessDay: 72 Festac Link Rd, Amuwo Odofin, Lagos; tel. 8034694482 (mobile); internet www.businessdayonline.com; Editor PHILLIP ISAKPA.

Daily Champion: Isolo Industrial Estate, Oshodi-Apapa, Lagos; fax (1) 4526011; e-mail letters@champion-newspapers.com; internet www.champion-newspapers.com; Man. Editor UGO ONUOHA.

Daily Independent: Independent Newspapers Ltd, Block 5, Plot 7D, Wempco Rd, Ogba, PMB 21777, Ikeja, Lagos; tel. (1) 4962136; e-mail newseditor@idailyindependentnig.com; internet www.dailyindependentnig.com; f. 2001; Editor IKECHUKWU AMAECHI.

Daily Triumph: Triumph Publishing Co Ltd, Gidan Sa'adu Zungur, PMB 3155, Kano; tel. (64) 633875; fax (64) 630273; internet www.triumphnewsng.com; Editor Dr MUKHTARI MAGAJI.

Daily Trust: 20 POW Mafemi Cres., off Solomon Lar Way, Utako, Abuja; tel. (9) 6726241; e-mail dailytrust@yahoo.co.uk; internet www.dailytrust.com; f. 2001; Editor HABEEB PINDIGA.

The Guardian: Guardian Newspapers Ltd, Rutam House, Isolo Expressway, Isolo, PMB 1217, Oshodi, Lagos; tel. (1) 4524111; fax (1) 4524080; e-mail editday@ngrguardiannews.com; internet www.ngrguardiannews.com; f. 1983; independent; Editor-in-Chief EMEKA IZEZE; Editor DEBO ADESINA; circ. 80,000.

Leadership: 8A Umuozu Close, off Samuel Ladoke Akintola Blvd, POB 9514, Garki, Abuja; tel. (9) 2345055; fax (9) 2345360; e-mail leadershipnigeria@yahoo.com; internet leadershipnigeria.com.

The Nation: Vintage Press Ltd, 27B Fatai Atere Way, Matori, Mushin, Lagos; tel. (1) 8168361; e-mail info@thenationonlineng.com; internet www.thenationonlineng.net; f. 2006; Editor GBENGA OMOTOSO.

National Daily: e-mail editor@nationaldailyngr.com; internet www.nationaldailyngr.com; f. 2006; Exec. Editor SYLVESTER EBHODAGHE; circ. 50,000.

New Age: Lagos; e-mail ebiz@newage-online.com; internet www.newage-online.com; Editor STEVE OSUJI.

New Nigerian: New Nigerian Newspapers Ltd, 4/5 Ahmadu Bello Way, POB 254, Kaduna; tel. (62) 245220; fax (62) 245221; internet www.newnigeriannews.com; f. 1965; govt-owned; Editor-in-Chief NDANUSA ALAO; circ. 80,000.

Nigerian Compass: 10 Western Industrial Ave, Compass Media Village, Isheri, Ogun; tel. (1) 7400001; internet www.compassnews.net; Editor GABRIEL AKINADEWO.

Nigerian Observer: Bendel Newspaper Co Ltd, 24 Airport Rd, PMB 1334, Benin City; tel. (52) 240050; e-mail info@nigerianobservernews.com; internet nigerianobservernews.com; f. 1968; Editor TONY IKEAKANAM; circ. 150,000.

Nigerian Tribune: African Newspapers of Nigeria Ltd, Imalefalafi St, Oke-Ado, POB 78, Ibadan; tel. (2) 2312844; e-mail editornigeriantribune@yahoo.com; internet www.tribune.com.ng; f. 1949; Editor EDWARD DICKSON; circ. 109,000.

Peoples Daily: 35 Ajose Adeogun St, Peace Park Plaza, 1st Floor, Utako, Abuja; tel. (9) 9702136; e-mail editor@peoplesdaily-online.com; internet www.peoplesdaily-online.com; Editor AHMED SHEKARAU.

The Port Harcourt Telegraph: NUJ Bldg, Ernest Ikoli Press Centre, Moscow Rd, Port Harcourt; tel. 8036002239 (mobile); e-mail phtelegraph@yahoo.com; internet www.phctelegraphnews.com; 3 a week; Editor-in-Chief OGBONNA NWUKE.

The Punch: 1 Olu Aboderin St, Onipetesi, PMB 21204, Ikeja, Lagos; tel. (1) 7748081; e-mail editor@punchontheweb.com; internet www.punchng.com; f. 1976; Editor-in-Chief ADEMOLA OSINUBI; circ. 150,000.

The Sun: The Sun Publishing Ltd, 2 Coscharis St, Kirikiri Industrial Layout, Apapa, PMB 21776 Ikeja, Lagos; tel. (1) 5875560; fax (1) 5875561; e-mail thesun@sunnewsonline.com; internet www.sunnewsonline.com; f. 2003; Editor STEVE NWOSU.

This Day: 35 Creek Rd, Apapa, Lagos; tel. 8022924721; fax (1) 4600276; e-mail info@thisdayonline.com; internet www.thisdaylive.com; f. 1995; Editor IJEOMA NWOGWUGWU.

The Tide: Rivers State Newspaper Corpn, 1 Ikwerre Rd, POB 5072, Port Harcourt; tel. 8034780061 (mobile); e-mail webmaster@thetidenewsonline.com; internet www.thetidenewsonline.com; f. 1971; Editor SOYE WILSON JAMABO; circ. 30,000.

Vanguard: Kirikiri Canal, PMB 1007, Apapa; e-mail vanguard@linkserve.com.ng; internet www.vanguardngr.com; f. 1984; Editor MIDENO BAYAGBON; circ. 130,000.

SUNDAY NEWSPAPERS

New Nigerian on Sunday: 4/5 Ahmadu Bello Way, POB 254, Kaduna; tel. (62) 245220; fax (62) 245221; e-mail auduson@newnigerian.com; internet www.newnigeriannews.com/sunday; f. 1981; weekly; Editor MALAM TUKUR ABDULRAHMAN; circ. 120,000.

Next on Sunday: Timbuktu Media, 235 Igbosere Rd, Lapal Plaza, 2nd Floor, Lagos; tel. (1) 8977685; e-mail MediaRelations@TimbuktuMedia.com; internet 234next.com; Editor MUFU OGUNBUNMI.

Sunday Compass: 10 Western Industrial Ave, Compass Media Village, Isheri, Ogun; tel. (1) 7400001; internet www.compassnews.net; Editor DOTUN OLADIPO.

Sunday Observer: Bendel Newspapers Co Ltd, 24 Airport Rd, PMB 1334, Benin City; e-mail info@nigerianobservernews.com; internet www.nigerianobservernews.com; f. 1968; Editor T. O. BORHA; circ. 60,000.

Sunday Sun: The Sun Publishing Ltd, 2 Coscharis St, Kirikiri Industrial Layout, Apapa, PMB 21776 Ikeja, Lagos; tel. 5875560; fax (1) 5875561; e-mail thesun@sunnewsonline.com; internet www.sunnewsonline.com; Editor FUNKE EGBEMODE.

Sunday Tide: Rivers State Newspaper Corpn, 4 Ikwerre Rd, POB 5072, Port Harcourt; f. 1971; Editor AUGUSTINE NJOAGWUANI.

Sunday Tribune: Imalefalafi St, POB 78, Oke-Ado, Ibadan; tel. (2) 2310886; e-mail editornigeriantribune@yahoo.com; internet www.tribune.com.ng; Editor DEBO ABDULLAHI.

Sunday Triumph: Triumph Publishing Co Ltd, Gidan Sa'adu Zungur, PMB 3155, Kano; tel. (64) 633875; fax (64) 630273; internet www.triumphnewspapers.com; Editor MUSA AHMAD TIJJANI.

WEEKLIES

Business Hallmark: 109B Adeniyi Jones Ave, Ikeja, Lagos; tel. (1) 8034026226 (mobile); fax (1) 7397008; e-mail info@bizhallmark.com; internet bizhallmark.com; Editor-in-Chief PRINCE EMEKA OBASI.

Business World: 7B Regina Omolara St, off Opebi Rd, Opebi, Lagos; tel. (1) 8742199; e-mail info@businessworldng.com; internet businessworldng.com/web; Editor NIK OGBULI.

The News: 27 Acme Rd, Agidingbi, PMB 21531, Ikeja, Lagos; tel. (1) 7939286; e-mail info@thenewsng.com; internet thenewsng.com; independent; Editor-in-Chief JENKINS ALUMONA.

Newswatch: 3 Billingsway Rd, Oregun, Ikeja, Lagos; tel. (1) 7619660; e-mail newswatch@newswatchngr.com; internet www.newswatchngr.com; f. 1985; English; CEO RAY EKPU; Editor-in-Chief DAN AGBESE.

Nigerian Newsworld: A1 AMAC Plaza, Zone 3, Wuse, Abuja; tel. (9) 7816987; internet nigeriannewsworld.com; f. 2010; Editor-in-Chief DENNIS O. SAMI.

Technology Times: 9 Olufunlola Okikiolu St, off Toyin St, Ikeja, Lagos; tel. (1) 8968161; e-mail info@technologytimes.com.ng; internet www.technologytimes.com.ng; 2004; Man. Editor SHINA BADARU.

Tell Magazine: PMB 21749, Ikeja, Lagos; tel. (1) 7747910; e-mail newsroom@tellng.com; internet www.tellng.com; f. 1991; Editor AYO AKINKUOTU.

Truth (The Muslim Weekly): 45 Idumagbo Ave, POB 418, Lagos; tel. (1) 2668455; f. 1951; Editor S. O. LAWAL.

Weekly Insight: 33 Oron Road, Uyo; contemporary issues; Editor AUGUSTINE DAVID; circ. 5,000.

Weekly Trust: 20 POW Mafemi Cres., off Solomon Lar Way, Utako, Abuja; tel. (9) 6726241; internet www.weekly.dailytrust.com; Editor ABDULKAREEM BABA AMINU (acting).

ENGLISH-LANGUAGE PERIODICALS

The Catholic Ambassador: PMB 2011, Iperu-Remo, Ogun; tel. 8023503748; e-mail ambassadorpublications@yahoo.com; internet www.mspfathers.org; f. 1980; quarterly; Roman Catholic; Editor-in-Chief Rev. Fr PATRICK EBITO AKEKPE; circ. 20,000.

Economic Confidential: Abuja; e-mail info@economicconfidential.com; internet www.economicconfidential.net; f. 2007; monthly; Editor SANYA ADEJOKUN.

Financial Standard: 2 IPM Ave, CBD, Alausa-Ikeja, Lagos; tel. (1) 4934894; fax (1) 4934891; e-mail info@financialstandardnews.com; internet www.financialstandardnews.com; f. 1999; Mon.–Fri.; Editor-in-Chief SUNDAY SAMUEL ADEBOLA ONANUGA; circ. 60,000.

The Leader: 19A Assumpta Press Ave, Industrial Layout, PMB 1017, Owerri, Imo; tel. 8088227344 (mobile); e-mail leaderpress@yahoo.com; internet www.leadernewspaperowerri.com; f. 1956; weekly; Roman Catholic; Editor-in-Chief Rev. CHIMARAOKE SAMUEL OFFURUM.

Nigerian Journal of Economic and Social Studies: Nigerian Economic Society, c/o Dept of Economics, University of Ibadan, PMB 22004, Ibadan, Oyo; tel. (2) 8700395; e-mail journaleditor@nigerianeconomicsociety.org; internet www.nigerianeconomicsociety.org; f. 1957; 3 a year; Editor Prof. ABDUL GANIYU GARBA.

Nigerian Journal of Science: Science Asscn of Nigeria, c/o Dept of Computer Science, University of Ibadan, POB 4039, Ibadan, Oyo; tel. 8023382550 (mobile); e-mail editor@sciencenigeria.org; internet www.sciencenigeria.org; publ. of the Science Asscn of Nigeria; f. 1966; 2 a year; Editor Prof. I. FAWOLE; circ. 1,000.

Nigerian Medical Journal: Office of the Nigerian Medical Journal, Paediatric Surgery Unit, Department of Surgery, Jos University Teaching Hospital, PMB 2076, Jos, Plateau; e-mail nmj@nigeriannma.org; internet nigeriamedj.com; quarterly; Editor Prof. FRANCIS A. UBA.

VERNACULAR PERIODICAL

Gaskiya ta fi Kwabo: New Nigerian Newspapers Ltd, 4/5 Ahmadu Bello Way, POB 254, Kaduna; tel. (62) 245220; fax (62) 245221; internet www.newnigeriannews.com; f. 1939; 3 a week; Hausa; Editor ALHAJI NASIRU GARBA TOFA (acting).

NEWS AGENCY

News Agency of Nigeria (NAN): Independence Avenue, Central Business District, PMB 7006, Garki, Abuja; tel. (9) 6732189; e-mail nanhq@nanngr.com; internet www.nannewsngr.com; f. 1976; state-owned; Man. Dir OLUREMI OYO; Editor-in-Chief DIPO OGBEDE.

Publishers

Africana First Publishers Ltd: Book House Trust, 1 Africana-First Dr., PMB 1639, Onitsha; tel. (46) 485031; f. 1973; study guides, general science, textbooks; Chair. RALPH O. EKPEH; Man. Dir J. C. ODIKE.

Ahmadu Bello University Press: PMB 1094, Zaria; tel. (69) 550054; f. 1972; history, Africana, social sciences, education, literature and arts; Man. Dir SA'IDU HASSAN ADAMU.

Albah International Publishers: 100 Kurawa, Bompai-Kano, POB 6177, Kano City; f. 1978; Africana, Islamic, educational and general, in Hausa; Chair. BASHARI F. ROUKBAH.

Cassava Republic: Abuja; e-mail info@cassavarepublic.biz; internet www.cassavarepublic.biz; f. 2006; Publishers BIBI BAKARE-YUSUF, JEREMY WEATE.

Daar Communications PLC: Daar Communications Centre, Kpaduma Hills, off Gen. T. Y. Danjuma St, Asokoro, Abuja; tel. (9) 3144802; fax (9) 3300512; broadcasting and information services; Man. Dir LADI LAWAL.

Evans Brothers (Nigeria Publishers) Ltd: Jericho Rd, PMB 5164, Ibadan; tel. (2) 2414394; fax (2) 2410757; f. 1966; general and educational; Chair. Dr ADEKUNLE OJORA; Man. Dir GBENRO ADEGBOLE.

Fourth Dimension Publishing Co Ltd: 16 Fifth Ave, City Layout, PMB 01164, Enugu; tel. (42) 459969; fax (42) 456904; e-mail nwankwov@infoweb.abs.net; internet www.fdpbooks.com; f. 1977; periodicals, fiction, verse, educational and children's; Chair. ARTHUR NWANKWO; Man. Dir V. U. NWANKWO.

HEBN Publishers PLC: 1 Ighodaro Rd, Jericho, PMB 5205, Ibadan; tel. (2) 2412268; fax (2) 2411089; e-mail info@hebnpublishers.com; internet www.hebnpublishers.com; f. 1962; educational, law, medical and general; Chair. AIGBOJE HIGO; Man. Dir AYO OJENIYI.

Heritage Books: The Poet's Cottage, Artistes Village, Ilogbo-Eremi, Badagry Expressway, POB 610, Apapa, Lagos; tel. (1) 5871333; f. 1971; general; Chair. NAIWU OSAHON.

Ibadan University Press: Publishing House, University of Ibadan, PMB 16, IU Post Office, Ibadan; tel. (2) 400550; e-mail iup-unibadan@yahoo.com; f. 1951; scholarly, science, law, general and educational; Dir F. A. ADESANOYE.

Literamed Publications Ltd (Lantern Books): Plot 45, Alausa Bus-stop, Oregun Industrial Estate, Ikeja, PMB 21068, Lagos; tel. (1) 7901129; fax (1) 7936521; e-mail information@lantern-books.com; internet www.lantern-books.com; f. 1969; children's, medical and scientific; Chair. O. M. LAWAL-SOLARIN.

Longman Nigeria Ltd: 52 Oba Akran Ave, PMB 21036, Ikeja, Lagos; tel. (1) 4978925; fax (1) 4964370; e-mail longman@linkserve.com; f. 1961; general and educational; Man. Dir J. A. OLOWONIYI.

Macmillan Nigeria Publishers Ltd: Ilupeju Industrial Estate, 4 Industrial Ave, POB 264, Yaba, Lagos; tel. (1) 4962185; e-mail macmillan@hotmail.com; internet www.macmillan.nigeria.com; f. 1965; educational and general; Exec. Chair. J. O. EMANUEL; Man. Dir Dr A. I. ADELEKAN.

Northern Nigerian Publishing Co Ltd: Gaskiya Bldg, POB 412, Zaria; tel. (69) 332087; fax (69) 331348; internet www.nnpchausa.com; f. 1966; general, educational and vernacular texts; Gen. Man. MAHMUD BARAU BAMBALE.

Obobo Books: The Poet's Cottage, Artistes Village, Ilogbo-Eremi, Badagry Expressway, POB 610, Apapa, Lagos; tel. and fax (1) 5871333; e-mail theendofknowledge@yahoo.com; internet www.theendofknowledge.com; f. 1981; children's books; Editorial Dir BAKIN KUNAMA.

Ogunsanya Press Publishers and Bookstores Ltd: SW9/1133 Orita Challenge, Idiroko, POB 95, Ibadan; tel. (2) 310924; f. 1970; educational; Man. Dir Chief LUCAS JUSTUS POPO-OLA OGUNSANYA.

Spectrum Books Ltd: Spectrum House, Ring Rd, PMB 5612, Ibadan; tel. (2) 2310058; fax (2) 2318502; e-mail admin1@spectrumbooksonline.com; internet www.spectrumbooksonline.com; f. 1978; educational and fiction; Chair. JOOP BERKHOUT; Man. Dir SINA OKEOWO.

University of Lagos Press: University of Lagos, POB 132, Akoka, Yaba, Lagos; tel. (1) 825048; e-mail library@rcl.nig.com; university textbooks, monographs, lectures and journals; Man. Dir S. BODUNDE BANKOLE.

University Publishing Co: 11 Central School Rd, POB 386, Onitsha; tel. (46) 210013; f. 1959; primary, secondary and university textbooks; Chair. E. O. UGWUEGBULEM.

West African Book Publishers Ltd: Ilupeju Industrial Estate, 28–32 Industrial Ave, POB 3445, Lagos; tel. (1) 7754518; fax (1) 2799127; e-mail w_bookafricapubl@hotmail.com; internet www.wabp.com; f. 1963; textbooks, children's, periodicals and general; Chair. B. A. IDRIS-ANIMASHAUN; Man. Dir FOLASHADE B. OMO-EBOH.

PUBLISHERS' ASSOCIATION

Nigerian Publishers' Association: Book House, NPA Permanent Secretariat, Jericho G.R.A., POB 2541, Ibadan; tel. (2) 2413396; f. 1965; Pres. S. B. BANKOLE.

Broadcasting and Communications

TELECOMMUNICATIONS

In early 2012 there were five mobile cellular telephone operators and 16 fixed-line or fixed wireless operators. At December 2011 there were 719,406 subscribers to fixed-line and fixed wireless telephone services, and 90,566,238 subscribers to mobile telephone services. In addition, there were 4.6m. subscribers to CDMA telephone services, provided by four operators.

Nigerian Communications Commission (NCC): Plot 423, Aguiyi Ironsi St, Maitama, Abuja; tel. (9) 4617000; fax (9) 4617514; e-mail ncc@ncc.gov.ng; internet www.ncc.gov.ng; f. 1932 as an independent regulatory body for the supply of telecommunications services and facilities; Chair. PETER EGBE IGOH; Exec. Chair. and CEO Dr EUGENE JUWAH.

Airtel Nigeria: Plot L2, Banana Island, Foreshore Estate, Ikoyi, Lagos; tel. 8021900000; fax (1) 3200477; e-mail customercare.ng@airtel.com; internet www.ng.airtel.com; f. 2000; fmrly Celtel Nigeria, subsequently Zain Nigeria, present name adopted in 2010; CEO RAJAN SWAROOP; 18m. subscribers (Dec. 2011).

EMTS Ltd (Etisalat): tel. 8090000200 (mobile); fax 8090000201 (mobile); e-mail care@etisalat.com.ng; internet www.etisalat.com.ng; f. 2007; 10m. subscribers (Dec. 2011).

Globacom Nigeria Ltd: Mike Adenuga Towers, 1 Mike Adenuga Cl., off Adeola Odeku, Victoria Island, Lagos; tel. 8050020121 (mobile); e-mail customercare@gloworld.com; internet www.gloworld.com; f. 2003; Chair. Dr MIKE ADENUGA, Jr; 19m. subscribers (Dec. 2011).

MTN Nigeria Communications Ltd: Golden Plaza Bldg, Awolowo Rd, Falomo, Ikoyi, PMB 80147, Lagos; tel. 8032005638 (mobile); fax 8039029636 (mobile); e-mail info@mtnnigeria.net; internet www.mtnonline.com; f. 2001; CEO BRETT GOSCHEN; 41m. subscribers (Dec. 2011).

Multi-Links Telecommunication Ltd: 231 Adeola Odeku St, Victoria Island, POB 3453, Marina, Lagos; tel. (1) 7740000; fax (1) 7912345; internet www.multilinks.com; f. 1994; owned by Telkom SA; Chair. MARTINS DIRKS; 70,795 subscribers (Dec. 2011).

Nigerian Mobile Telecommunications Ltd (M-TEL): 2 Bissau St, off Herbert Macaulay Way, Wuse Zone 6, Abuja; tel. (9) 5233031; internet www.mtelnigeria.com; f. 1996; Chair. OLULADE ADEGBOYEGA; 258,520 subscribers (Dec. 2011).

Nigerian Telecommunications Ltd (NITEL): 2 Bissau St, off Herbert Macaulay Way, Wuse Zone 6, Abuja; tel. (9) 5233021; f. 1984; 51% owned by Transnational Corporation of Nigeria PLC, 49% govt-owned; Chair. Dr MARTINS IGBOKWE; 58,750 subscribers (Dec. 2011).

Reliance Telecoms (Zoom): Zoom Mobile House 8A, Adeola Odeku St, Victoria Island, Lagos; tel. 07074800211; fax 07074800241; e-mail corporatecomm@zoomnigeria.com; f. 1998; fixed wireless and CDMA; CEO EDWIN MOMIFE; 43,784 fixed and 315,619 subscribers (Dec. 2011).

Starcomms: Starcomms House, Plot 1261 Bishop Kale Close, off Saka Tinubu St, Victoria Island, Lagos; tel. (1) 8041234; fax (1) 8110301; e-mail customerservice@starcomms.com; internet www.starcomms.com; f. 1999; fixed wireless and CDMA; Chair. Chief MANN LABABIDI; CEO LOGAN PATHER; 367,367 fixed wireless and 980,109 CDMA subscribers (Dec. 2011).

Telnet (Nigeria) Ltd: Plot 242, Kofo Abayomi St, Victoria Island, POB 53656, Falomi Ikoyi, Lagos; tel. (1) 4611747; e-mail contact@iteco.com; internet www.telnetng.com; f. 1985; telecommunications engineering and consultancy services; Group Exec. Dir BENJAMIN ISHAKU.

21st Century Technologies: 249A, Muri Okunola St, Victoria Island, Lagos; tel. (1) 2710083; e-mail commercial@21ctl.com; internet www.21ctl.com; fixed-line services; Chair. TUNDE AJISOMO; CEO WALE AJISEBUTU; 70,087 subscribers (Dec. 2011).

BROADCASTING

According to the National Broadcasting Commission, there are 100 radio stations and 147 television stations in the country.

Regulatory Authority

National Broadcasting Commission: Plot 20, Ibrahim Taiwo St, Asokoro District, POB 5747, Garki, Abuja; tel. (9) 7805730; fax (9) 3147522; e-mail infonbc@nbc.gov.ng; internet www.nbc.gov.ng; Dir-Gen. Eng. YOMI BOLARINWA.

Radio

Federal Radio Corpn of Nigeria (FRCN): Radio House, Herbert Macaulay Way, Area 10, PMB 452, Garki, Abuja; tel. (9) 2345230; fax (9) 2346486; e-mail info@radionigeria.net; internet www.radionigeria.net; f. 1976; controlled by the Fed. Govt and divided into five zones: Lagos (English); Enugu (English, Igbo, Izon, Efik and Tiv); Ibadan (English, Yoruba, Edo, Urhobo and Igala); Kaduna (English, Hausa, Kanuri, Fulfulde and Nupe); Abuja (English, Hausa, Igbo and Yoruba); Dir-Gen. YUSUF NUHU.

Imo Broadcasting Corpn: Egbu Rd, PMB 1129, Owerri, Imo; tel. (42) 250327; operates one radio station in Imo State; CEO SAMFO NWANKWO.

Ray Power Radio 100.5 FM: Abeokuta Express Way, Ilapo, Alagbado, Lagos; tel. (1) 2644814; fax (1) 2644817; 100% owned by DAAR Communications Ltd; commenced broadcasting Sept. 1994; commercial; Chair. Chief ALEOGHO RAYMOND DOKPESI.

Voice of Nigeria (VON): 6th and 7th Floor, Radio House, Herbert Macaulay Way, Area 10, Garki, Abuja; tel. (9) 2344017; fax (9) 2346970; e-mail info@voiceofnigeria.org; internet www.voiceofnigeria.org; f. 1990; controlled by the Fed. Govt; external services in English, French, Arabic, Ki-Swahili, Hausa and Fulfulde; Dir-Gen. Alhaji ABUBAKAR BOBBOYI JIJIWA.

Television

Nigerian Television Authority (NTA): Television House, Area 11, Garki, PMB 13, Abuja; tel. (9) 2345907; fax (9) 2345914; f. 1976; controlled by the Fed. Govt; operates a network of 31 terrestrial broadcasters, which share national programming but also broadcast local programmes; also operates c. 70 regional channels; Chair. BENSON ABOUNU; Dir-Gen. Dr MAGAWATA MOHAMMED USMAN.

Africa Independent Television (AIT): Kpaduma Hill, off T. Y. Danjuma, Asokoro Extension, Abuja; e-mail info@daargroup.com; internet www.daargroup.com; f. 1994; 100% owned by DAAR Communications Ltd; Exec. Chair. Dr ALEOGHO RAYMOND DOKPESI.

Minaj Broadcast International (MBI): Minaj Media Group, 130/132, Ladipo St, Matori, Mushin, POB 70811, Victoria Island, Lagos; tel. (1) 4529203; fax (1) 4528500; e-mail info@minajmedia.com; internet www.minajmedia.com; provides free-to-air services; Chair. Chief MIKE AJEGBO.

Murhi International Television (MITV): MITV Plaza, Ikeja Central Business District, Obafemi Awolowo Way, Alausa, Lagos; tel. (1) 4931271; fax (1) 4931272; e-mail mitv@murhi-international.com; Chair. MURI GBADEYANKA BUSARI.

Finance

(cap. = capital; res = reserves; dep. = deposits; m. = million; brs = branches; amounts in naira)

BANKING

In early 2011 there were 24 commercial banks and five development finance institutions in Nigeria. In June Stanbic IBTC Bank PLC received a preliminary licence to provide Islamic banking services. Jaiz International PLC was also granted approval, in principle, to open the country's first Islamic bank.

Central Bank

Central Bank of Nigeria: Plot 33, Abubakar Tafawa Balewa Way, Central Business District, Cadestral Zone, PMB 0187, Garki, Abuja; tel. (9) 46239701; fax (9) 46236012; e-mail info@cenbank.org; internet www.cenbank.org; f. 1958; bank of issue; cap. 5,000m., res 320,165m., dep. 4,971,643m. (Dec. 2006); Gov. SANUSI LAMIDO AMINU SANUSI; 28 brs.

Commercial Banks

Access Bank: Plot 1665, Oyin Jolayemi St, Victoria Island, Lagos; tel. (1) 2805628; e-mail contactcenter@accessbankplc.com; internet www.accessbankplc.com; Chair. GBENGA OYEBODE; CEO AIGBOJE AIG-IMOUKHUEDE.

Citibank Nigeria Ltd: 27 Kofo Abayomi St, Victoria Island, POB 6391, Lagos; tel. (1) 2798400; fax (1) 2618916; internet www.citibanknigeria.com; f. 1984; cap. 2,793.7m., res 34,900.5m., dep. 97,969.5m. (Dec. 2008); Chair. OLAYEMI CARDOSO; Country Officer EMEKA EMUWA; 4 brs.

Diamond Bank PLC: Plot 1261, Adeola Hopewell St, Victoria Island, POB 70381, Lagos; tel. (1) 2701500; fax (1) 2619728; e-mail info@diamondbank.com; internet www.diamondbank.com; f. 2005 by merger with Lion Bank of Nigeria PLC; cap. 6,579.6m., res. 100,941.0m., dep. 410,094.0m. (April 2008); Chair. IGWE NNAEMEKA ALFRED ACHEBE; Man. Dir and CEO ALEX OTTI.

Enterprise Bank Ltd: 143 Ahmadu Bello Way, Victoria Island, Lagos; tel. (1) 2623780; internet www.springbankplc.com; f. 2004 by merger of ACB International Bank PLC, Citizens International Bank PLC, Fountain Trust Bank PLC, Guardian Express Bank PLC, Omegabank (Nigeria) PLC and Trans International Bank PLC; acquired by Platinum Habib Bank Group in 2008; name changed as above following nationalization in August 2011; Chair. EMEKA ONWUKA; Man. Dir AHMED KURU.

First Bank of Nigeria PLC: Samuel Asabia House, 35 Marina, POB 5216, Lagos; tel. (1) 2665900; fax (1) 2669073; e-mail firstcontact@firstbanknigeria.com; internet www.firstbanknigeria.com; f. 1894 as Bank of British West Africa; cap. 12,432m., res. 338,622m., dep. 1,150,816m. (March 2009); Chair. Dr OBA OTUDEKO; CEO and Man. Dir STEPHEN OLABISI ONASANYA; 302 brs.

Guaranty Trust Bank PLC: Plot 635, Akin Adesola St, PMB 75455, Victoria Island, Lagos; tel. (1) 2715227; e-mail corpaff@gtbank.com; internet www.gtbank.com; f. 1990; cap. 9,326.9m., res 160,507.5m., dep. 728,859.7m. (Dec. 2009); Chair. OLUWOLE S. ODUYEMI; 161 brs.

Keystone Bank Ltd: 1 Bank PHB Cres., Victoria Island, Lagos; tel. (1) 4485742; e-mail phblink@bankphb.com; internet www.bankphb.com; frmly Bank PHB, name changed following nationalization in August 2011; Chair. JACOB AJEKIGBE; Man. Dir OTI IKOMI.

Mainstreet Bank Ltd: 51–55 Broad St, PMB 12021, Lagos; tel. (1) 2641566; fax (1) 2669763; e-mail info@afribank.com; internet www.afribank.com; f. 1969 as International Bank for West Africa Ltd; fmrly Afribank Nigeria Ltd, name changed as above following nationalization in August 2011; cap. 3,065.0m., res 31,822.0m., dep. 280,290.1m. (March 2008); Chair. FALALU BELLO; Man. Dir and CEO FAITH TUEDOR-MATTHEWS; 137 brs.

Skye Bank PLC: 3 Akin Adesola St, Victoria Island, Lagos; tel. (1) 2701600; e-mail info@skyebankng.com; internet www.skyebankng.com; Chair. MORONKEJI ONASANYA; Group Man. Dir KEHINDE DUROSINMI-ETTI.

Stanbic IBTC Bank PLC: I.B.T.C. Place, Walter Carrington Cres., POB 71707, Victoria Island, Lagos; tel. (1) 2712400; fax (1) 2806998; e-mail customercarenigeria@stanbic.com; internet www.ibtc.com/portal/site/nigeria; f. 1989 as Investment Banking & Trust Co Ltd; name changed as above 2008 following merger with Stanbic Bank (Nigeria) Ltd; cap. 9,375.0m., res 67,241.7m., dep. 181,093.1m. (Dec. 2008); Chair. ATEDO N. A. PETERSIDE; CEO SOLA DAVID-BORHA; 57 brs.

Sterling Bank: Sterling Towers, 20 Marina, POB 12735, Lagos; tel. (1) 2600420; fax (1) 2633294; e-mail tradeservices@sterlingbankng.com; internet www.sterlingbankng.com; f. 2005 following merger of Indo-Nigerian Bank Ltd, Magnum Trust Bank, NAL Bank PLC, NBM Bank and Trust Bank of Africa Ltd; cap. 6,281.5m., res. 23,957.3m., dep. 184,730.2m. (Sept. 2008); Chair. Alhaji SULEIMAN ADEBOLA ADEGUNWA; Man. Dir RAZACK ADEYEMI ADEOLA.

Union Bank of Nigeria Ltd: 36 Marina, PMB 2027, Lagos; tel. (1) 2630361; fax (1) 2669873; e-mail info@unionbankng.com; internet www.unionbankng.com; f. 1969 as Barclays Bank of Nigeria Ltd; cap. 101,049m., res 1,493m., dep. 482,382m. (March 2007); Chair. Prof. MUSA G. YAKUBU; Man. Dir and CEO OLUNFUNKE IYABO OSIBODU; 235 brs.

United Bank for Africa (Nigeria) Ltd: UBA House, 57 Marina, POB 2406, Lagos; tel. (1) 2808822; fax (1) 2808448; e-mail cic@ubagroup.com; internet www.ubagroup.com; f. 1961; cap. 8,622m., res 179,533m., dep. 1,258,035m. (Sept. 2008); Chair. FERDINAND NGOGO ALABRABA; Man. Dir TONY O. ELUMELU; 428 brs.

Unity Bank PLC: Plot 785, Herbert Macaulay Way, Central Business District, POB 52463, Abuja; tel. (9) 4616700; fax (9) 4616730; e-mail we_care@unitybankng.com; internet www.unitybankng.com; f. 2005; cap. 21,752.9m., res. 9,015.0m., dep. 79,683.5m. (June 2006); Chair. Prof. AKIN L. MABOGUNJE; Man. Dir and CEO Alhaji FALALU BELLO.

Wema Bank Ltd: Wema Towers, PMB 12862, 54 Marina, Lagos; tel. (1) 2668043; fax (1) 2669236; e-mail info@wemabank.com; internet www.wemabank.com; f. 1945; cap. 5,035.0m., res 19,781.7m., dep. 125,476.0m. (March 2007); Chair. Chief SAMUEL BOLARINDE; Man. Dir SEGUN OLOKETUYI; 146 brs.

Zenith Bank PLC: Plot 84, Ajose Adeogun St, Victoria Island, POB 75315, Lagos; tel. (1) 2788000; fax (1) 2618212; e-mail enquiry@zenithbank.com; internet www.zenithbank.com; f. 1990; name changed as above in 2004; cap. 8,372.4m., res. 330,111.7m., dep. 1,167,335.2m. (Sept. 2008); Man. Dir JIM OVIA.

Merchant Banks

FBN Capital Ltd: 16 Keffi St, off Awolowo Rd, Ikoyi, Lagos; tel. (1) 2798300; fax (1) 2633600; e-mail info@fbncapital.com; internet www.fbncapital.com; Chair. OYEKANMI HASSAN-ODUKALE; Man. Dir and CEO KAYODE AKINKUGBE.

Fidelity Bank PLC: 2 Kofo Abayomi St, Victoria Island, Lagos; tel. (1) 2713487; fax (1) 2610414; e-mail info@fidelitybankplc.com; internet www.fidelitybankplc.com; f. 1988; cap. 14,481.3m., res 114,892.5m., dep. 356,137.3m. (June 2009); Chair. Chief CHRISTOPHER EZEH; CEO REGINALD IHEJIAHI; 20 brs.

First City Monument Bank Ltd: Primrose Tower, 17A Tinubu St, POB 9117, Lagos; tel. (1) 2665944; fax (1) 2665126; e-mail fcmb@fcmb-ltd.com; internet www.firstcitygroup.com; f. 1983; cap. 8,136.0m., res 119,322.0m., dep. 349,441.8m. (April 2009); Chair. Dr JONATHAN A. D. LONG; Man. Dir and CEO LADI BALOGUN; 12 brs.

Development Finance Institutions

Bank of Industry (BOI) Ltd: 23 Marina, POB 2357, Lagos; tel. (1) 2665528; fax (1) 2665286; e-mail info@boi-ng.com; internet www.boinigeria.com; f. 1964 as the Nigerian Industrial Development Bank Ltd to provide medium and long-term finance to industry, manufacturing, non-petroleum mining and tourism; name changed as above Oct. 2001; cap. 6,585.1m., dep. 3,500m. (Dec. 2005); Chair. Alhaji ABDULSAMAD RABIU; Man. Dir Dr EVELN N. OPUTU; 8 brs.

The Federal Mortgage Bank of Nigeria (FMBN): Mortgage House, Plot 266, Cadastral AO, Central Business District, PMB 2273, Garki, Abuja; tel. (9) 4602102; e-mail info@fmbnigeria.org; internet www.fmbnigeria.org; f. 1956 as Nigerian Building Society (NBS); Chair. Alhaji ADEDAMOLA ATTA; Man. Dir GIMBA YA'U KUMO.

Nigerian Agricultural, Co-operative and Rural Development Bank Ltd (NACRDB): Yakubu Gowoh, PMB 2155, Kaduna; tel. (62) 244417; fax (62) 244612; e-mail nacb@infoweb.abs.net; internet www.nacrdb.com; f. 1973 for funds to farmers and co-operatives to improve production techniques; name changed as above Oct. 2000, following merger with People's Bank of Nigeria; cap. 1,000m. (2002); Chair. Chief GORDON BOZIMO; Man. Dir Dr MOHAMMED SANTURAKI; 200 brs.

The Nigerian Export-Import Bank (NEXIM): NEXIM House, Plot 975, Cadastral Zone AO, Central Business District, PMB 276, Garki, Abuja; tel. (9) 6281630; fax (9) 6281640; e-mail neximabj@neximbank.com.ng; internet www.neximbank.com.ng; f. 1991; CEO ROBERTS U. ORYA.

The Urban Development Bank of Nigeria PLC (UDBN): Plot 977, Central Business Area, PMB 272, Garki, Abuja; tel. (9) 6710863; e-mail enquiries@udbng.com; internet www.udbng.com; f. 1992; Chair. HAKEEM O. SANUSI.

Bankers' Association

Chartered Institute of Bankers of Nigeria: PC 19 Adeola Hopewell St, POB 72273, Victoria Island, Lagos; tel. (1) 2703494; fax (1) 4618930; e-mail cibn@cibng.org; internet www.cibng.org; Chair. JOSEPH LAOYE JAIYEOLA; CEO Dr UJU M. OGUBUNKA.

STOCK EXCHANGE

Securities and Exchange Commission (SEC): SEC Towers, Plot 272, Samuel Adesujo Ademulegun St, Central Business District, PMB 315, Garki, Abuja; tel. (9) 6330000; fax (9) 2346276; internet www.sec.gov.ng; f. 1979 as govt agency to regulate and develop capital market and to supervise stock exchange operations; Chair. UDOMA UDO UDOMA; Dir-Gen. DAISY EKINEH.

Nigerian Stock Exchange: Stock Exchange House, 2–4 Customs St, POB 2457, Lagos; tel. (1) 2660287; fax (1) 2668724; e-mail info@nigerianstockexchange.biz; internet www.nigerianstockexchange.com; f. 1960; Pres. ALIKO DANGOTE; CEO OSCAR ONYEMA; 6 brs.

INSURANCE

In 2011 the insurance sector comprised 51 registered companies, seven life insurance companies, 23 non-life insurance companies, 19 composite companies and two reinsurance companies. Since 1978 they have been required to reinsure 20% of the sum insured with the Nigeria Reinsurance Corpn.

Regulatory Authority

National Insurance Commission (NAICOM): Shippers Plaza, Micheal Okpara St, Wuse Zone 5, PMB 457, Garki, Abuja; tel. (9) 6733520; fax (9) 6735649; e-mail info@naicom.gov.org; internet www.naicom.gov.ng; f. 1992 as National Insurance Supervisory Board; present name adopted 1997; Chair. Hajia INNA MARYAM CIROMA; Commr for Insurance FOLA DANIEL.

Insurance Companies

African Alliance Insurance Co Ltd: 112 Broad St, POB 2276, Lagos; tel. (1) 7227666; fax (1) 2660943; e-mail info@africanallianceinsurance.com; internet www.africanallianceinsurance.com; f. 1960; life assurance and pensions; Man. Dir ALPHONSUS OKPOR; 30 brs.

Aiico International Insurance (AIICO): AIICO Plaza, Plot PC 12, Afribank St, Victoria Island, POB 2577, Lagos; tel. (1) 2610651; fax (1) 2799800; e-mail info@aiicoplc.com; internet www.aiicoplc.com; CEO S. D. A SOBANJO.

Ark Insurance Group: Glass House, 11A Karimu Kotun St, Victoria Island, POB 3771, Marina, Lagos; tel. (1) 2615826; fax (1) 2615850; e-mail info@arkinsurancegroup.com; internet www.arkinsurancegroup.com; Chair. FRANCIS OLUWOLE AWOGBORO.

Continental Reinsurance Co Ltd: St. Nicholas House, 8th Floor, 6 Catholic Mission St, POB 2401, Lagos; tel. (1) 2665350; fax (1) 2665370; e-mail info@continental-re.com; internet www.continental-re.com; Chair. S. A. LAGUDA; CEO Dr FEMI OYETUNJI.

Cornerstone Insurance Co PLC: POB 75370, Victoria Island, Lagos; tel. (1) 2631832; fax (1) 2633079; e-mail marketing@cornerstone.com.ng; internet www.cornerstone.com.ng; f. 1991; Chair. ADEDOTUN SULAIMAN; Man. Dir and CEO LIVINGSTONE MAGORIMBO.

CrystaLife: 12th and 13th Floor, Eleganza House, 15B Joseph St, POB 1514, Lagos; tel. (1) 2636800; fax (1) 2637095; e-mail equilifekn@equity-lifeinsurance.com; internet www.crystalifeassurance.com; Chair. AKINSOLA AKINFEMIWA; Man. Dir and CEO OLUSEYI IFATUROTI.

Equity Assurance PLC: 19 Circular Road, Presidential Estate, POB 2709, Port Harcourt; tel. (84) 236114; fax (84) 236115; e-mail portharcourt@equityassuranceplc.com; f. 1991; Chair. OLUFEMI SOMOLU; COO OLUMIDE FALOHUN.

Great Nigeria Insurance Co PLC: 8 Omo-Osaghie St, off Obafemi Awolono Rd, Ikoyi S/W, Ikoyi, POB 2314, Lagos; tel. (1) 2695805; fax (1) 2693483; e-mail info@gniplc.com; internet www.gniplc.com; f. 1960; all classes; Chair. SEGUN OLOKETUYI; Man. Dir CECILIA O. SIPITAN.

Guinea Insurance PLC: Reinsurance Bldg, 10th Floor, 46 Marine, POB 1136, Lagos; tel. (1) 2665201; e-mail info@guineainsurance.com; internet www.guineainsurance.com; f. 1958; all classes; Man. Dir and CEO SOJI EMIOLA.

Industrial and General Insurance Co Ltd: Plot 741, Adeola Hopewell St, PMB 80181, Victoria Island, Lagos; tel. (1) 6215010; fax (1) 2621146; e-mail info@iginigeria.com; internet www.iginigeria.com; Chair. YAKUBU GOWON.

Law Union and Rock Insurance PLC: 14 Hughes Ave, Alagomeji, Yaba, POB 944, Lagos; e-mail enquiry@lur-ng.com; tel. (1) 8995010; fax (1) 3425077; internet www.lawunioninsurance.com; fire, accident and marine; Chair. AKINSOLA AKINFEMIWA; Man. Dir and CEO YINKA BOLARINWA; 6 brs.

Leadway Assurance Co Ltd: 121/123 Funsho Williams Ave, Iponri, Lagos; tel. (1) 2700700; fax (1) 2700800; e-mail insure@leadway.com; internet www.leadway.com; f. 1970; all classes; Man. Dir OYEKANMI ABIODUN HASSAN-ODUKALE.

Lion of Africa Insurance Co Ltd: St Peter's House, 3 Ajele St, POB 2055, Lagos; tel. (1) 2600950; fax (1) 2636111; internet thelionofafrica.org; f. 1952; all classes; Man. Dir and CEO PETER MONYE.

National Insurance Corpn of Nigeria (NICON): 5 Customs St, POB 1100, Lagos; tel. (1) 2640230; fax (1) 2666556; f. 1969; all classes; cap. 200m.; Chair. JIMOH IBRAHIM; 28 brs.

N.E.M. Insurance Co (Nigeria) Ltd: 138/146 Broad St, POB 654, Lagos; tel. (1) 5861920; internet www.nem-insurance.com; all classes; Chair. Chief ADEWALE TELUWO; Man. Dir TOPE SMART.

Niger Insurance PLC: 48/50 Odunlami St, POB 2718, Marina, Lagos; tel. (1) 2631329; fax (1) 2662196; e-mail info@nigerinsurance.com; internet www.nigerinsurance.com; f. 1962; all classes; Chair. BALA ZAKARIYA'U; Man. Dir Dr JUSTUS URANTA; 6 brs.

Nigeria Reinsurance Corpn: 46 Marina, PMB 12766, Lagos; tel. (1) 2667049; fax (1) 2668041; e-mail info@nigeriare.com; internet www.nigeriareinsurance.com; all classes of reinsurance; Man. Dir T. T. MIRILLA.

Royal Exchange PLC: New Africa House, 31 Marina, POB 112, Lagos; tel. (1) 7404158; e-mail info@royalexchangeplc.com; internet portal.royalexchangeplc.com; 1921; all classes; Chair. KENNETH EZENWANI ODOGWU; Man. Dir CHIKE MOKWUNYE; 25 brs.

UnityKapital Assurance PLC: 497 Abogo Largema St, off Constitution Ave, Central Business District, POB 2044, Abuja; tel. (9) 4619900; fax (9) 4619901; e-mail info@unitykapital.com; internet www.unitykapital.com; f. 1973; Chair. Alhaji FALALU BELLO; CEO MOHAMMED KARI.

Unity Life and Fire Insurance Co Ltd: 25 Nnamdi Azikiwe St, POB 3681, Lagos; tel. (1) 2662517; fax (1) 2662599; all classes; Man. Dir R. A. ODINIGWE.

West African Provincial Insurance Co: WAPIC House, 119 Awolowo Rd, POB 55508, Falomo-Ikoyi, Lagos; tel. (1) 2672770; fax (1) 2693838; e-mail wapic@alpha.linkserve.com; Man. Dir D. O. AMUSAN.

Insurance Association

Nigerian Insurers' Association (NIA): 42 Saka Tinubu St, Victoria Island, POB 9551, Lagos; tel. (1) 7743813; fax (1) 2621298; e-mail info@nigeriainsurers.org; internet www.nigeriainsurers.org; f. 1971; Chair. REMI OLOWUDE; Dir-Gen. SUNDAY THOMAS.

Trade and Industry

GOVERNMENT AGENCIES

Bureau of Public Enterprises: The Presidency, Bureau of Public Enterprises, 11 Osun Cres., off IBB Way, Maitama District, PMB 442, Garki, Abuja; tel. (9) 4604400; fax (9) 4604411; e-mail bpe@bpeng.org; internet www.bpeng.org; Dir-Gen. BOLANLE ONAGORUWA.

Corporate Affairs Commission: Plot 420, Tigris Cres., off Aguiyi Ironsi St, Maitama, PMB 198, Garki, Abuja; tel. (9) 4618594; fax (9) 2342669; e-mail info@cac.gov.ng; internet www.cac.gov.ng; Chair. Chief Dr JIMOH IBRAHIM; Registrar-Gen./CEO BELLO MAHMUD.

National Council on Privatisation: Bureau of Public Enterprises, NDIC Bldg, Constitution Ave, Central Business District, PMB 442, Garki, Abuja; tel. (9) 5237405; fax (9) 5237396; e-mail bpegen@micro.com.ng; internet www.bpe.gov.ng; Chair. NAMADI SAMBO.

Nigeria Export Processing Zones Authority (NEPZA): 2 Zambezi Cres., Cadastral Zone A6, off Aguiyi Ironsi St, Maitama, PMB 037, Garki, Abuja; tel. (9) 4131598; fax (9) 4131550; e-mail info@nepza.gov.ng; internet www.nepza.gov.ng; Man. Dir SINA A. AGBOLUAJE.

Nigeria Sovereign Investment Authority: Abuja; f. 2011; Chair. Alhaji MAHEY RASHEED; Man. Dir UCHE ORJI.

DEVELOPMENT ORGANIZATIONS

Chad Basin Development Authority (CBDA): Dikwa Rd, PMB 1130, Maiduguri; tel. (76) 232015; f. 1973; irrigation and agriculture-allied industries; Man. Dir Dr ABUBAKAR GARBA ILLIYA; Gen. Man. Alhaji BUNU S. MUSA.

Cross River Basin Development Authority (CRBDA): 32 Target Rd, PMB 1249, Calabar; tel. (87) 223163; f. 1976; Gen. Man. SIXTUS ABETIANBE.

Federal Institute of Industrial Research, Oshodi (FIIRO): FIIRO Rd, by Cappa Bus Stop, off Agege Motor Rd, Oshodi, Ikeja, PMB 21023, Lagos; tel. (1) 4701846; fax (1) 4525880; e-mail info@fiiro.gov.ng; internet www.fiiro-ng.org; f. 1956; plans and directs scientific research for industrial and technological development; provides tech. assistance and information to industry; specializes in foods, minerals, textiles, natural products and industrial intermediates; Dir-Gen. Dr GLORIA NWAKAEGHO ELEMO.

Industrial Training Fund: 1, Kufang Village, Miango Rd, PMB 2199, Jos, Plateau; tel. and fax (73) 462395; e-mail dp@itf-nigeria.com; internet www.itf-nigeria.com; f. 1971 to promote and encourage skilled workers in trade and industry; Dir-Gen. Prof. OLU E. AKEREJOLA.

Kaduna Industrial and Finance Co Ltd: Investment House, 27 Ali Akilu Rd, PMB 2230, Kaduna; tel. 8037035577 (mobile); fax (62) 290781; e-mail info@kadunainvest.com; internet www.kadunainvest.com; f. 1989; provides devt finance; Man. Dir and CEO ALHAJI SHEHU MUHAMMAD SHITU.

Kwara State Investment Corpn: Charlets, 109–112 Fate Rd, PMB 1344, Ilorin, Kwara; tel. (31) 220510.

Lagos State Development and Property Corpn: 2/4 Town Planning Way, Ilupeju Industrial Estate, PMB 21050, Lagos; tel. (1) 7621424; e-mail info@lsdpc.gov.ng; internet www.lsdpc.gov.ng; f. 1972; planning and devt of Lagos; Man. Dir BIODUN OKI.

New Nigerian Development Co Ltd: 18/19 Ahmadu Bello Way, Ahmed Talib House, PMB 2120, Kaduna; tel. (62) 249355; fax (62) 245482; e-mail nndc@skannet.com.ng; f. 1949; owned by the govts of 19 northern states; investment finance; 8 subsidiaries, 83 assoc. cos; Chair. Prof. HALIDU IBRAHIM ABUBAKAR.

Niger Delta Development Commission (NDDC): 167 Aba Rd, Port Harcourt; e-mail info@nddc.gov.ng; internet www.nddc.gov.ng; f. 2000; Chair. Dr TARILAH TEBEPAH; Man. Dir Dr CHRISTIAN OBOH.

Odu'a Investment Co Ltd: Cocoa House Complex, Oba Adebimpe Rd, PMB 5435, Ibadan; tel. (2) 2001037; fax (2) 413000; e-mail odua@oduainvestmentcompany.com; internet www.oduainvestmentcompany.com; f. 1976; jtly owned by Ogun, Ondo and Oyo States; Man. Dir A. K. JIMOH.

Projects Development Institute (PRODA): Emene Industrial Layout, Proda Rd, POB 01609, Enugu; tel. 7098811745 (mobile); fax (42) 457691; e-mail info@proda-ng.org; internet proda-ng.org; f. 1970; promotes the establishment of new industries and develops industrial projects utilizing local raw materials; Dir BASIL K. C. UGWA.

Raw Materials Research and Development Council (RMRDC): Plot 427, Aguiyi, Ironsi St, Maitama District, PMB 232, Garki, Abuja; tel. (9) 4134716; fax (9) 4136034; e-mail icsd_liaison@rmrdc.gov.ng; internet www.rmrdc.gov.ng; f. 1988; Dir.-Gen. Prof. AZIKIWE PETER ONWUALU.

Rubber Research Institute of Nigeria (RRIN): PMB 1049, Benin City; tel. 8033197241; e-mail rubberresearchnig@yahoo.com; internet www.rrin.org; f. 1961; conducts research into the production of rubber, gum arabic and other latex bearing plants of economic importance; Exec. Dir OSAYANMO I. EGUAVOEN; Chair Air Cdre JOHN A. EHIWERE.

CHAMBERS OF COMMERCE

Nigerian Association of Chambers of Commerce, Industry, Mines and Agriculture (NACCIMA): 8A Oba Akinjobi Way, PMB 12816, Lagos; tel. (1) 4964727; fax (1) 4964737; e-mail contact@naccima.com; internet www.naccima.com; f. 1960; Pres. Dr HERBERT ADEMOLA AJAYI; Dir-Gen. JOHN ISEMEDE.

Aba Chamber of Commerce and Industry: UBA Bldg, Ikot Expene Rd/Georges St, POB 1596, Aba; tel. (82) 352084; fax (82) 352067; f. 1971; Pres. Chief KALU OMOJI KALU.

Abeokuta Chamber of Commerce and Industry: Commerce House, Nr Govt House, Oke Igbehin, Ibaha, POB 937, Abeokuta; tel. (39) 241230; Pres. Chief S. O. AKINREMI.

Abuja Chamber of Commerce, Industry, Mines & Agriculture: International Trade Fair Complex, KM8, Airport Rd, PMB 86, Garki, Abuja; tel. 8033139347 (mobile); e-mail abuccima@hotmail.com; f. 1986; Pres. DELE KELVIN OYE.

Adamawa Chamber of Commerce and Industry: c/o Palace Hotel, POB 8, Jimeta, Yola; tel. (75) 255136; Pres. Alhaji ISA HAMMANYERO.

Akure Chamber of Commerce and Industry: 57 Oyemekun Rd, POB 866, Akure; tel. (34) 242540; f. 1984; Pres. OMOLADE OWOSENI.

Awka Chamber of Commerce and Industry: 220 Zik Ave, POB 780, Awka; tel. (45) 550105; Pres. Lt-Col (retd) D. ORUGBU.

Bauchi Chamber of Commerce and Industry: 96 Maiduguri Rd, POB 911, Bauchi; tel. (77) 43727; f. 1976; Pres. Alhaji MAGAJI MU'AZU.

Benin Chamber of Commerce, Industry, Mines and Agriculture: 10 Murtala Muhammed Way, POB 2087, Benin City; tel. (52) 255761; Pres. Chief SIMON UDUIGHO EKWENUKE.

Benue Chamber of Commerce, Industry, Mines and Agriculture: Suite 7, IBB Sq, High Level, PMB 102344, Makurdi; tel. (44) 32573; Chair. Col (retd) R. V. I. ASAM.

Borno Chamber of Commerce and Industry: Grand Stand, Ramat Sq., off Central Bank, PMB 1636, Maiduguri; tel. (76) 232832; e-mail bsumar@hotmail.com; f. 1973; Pres. Alhaji MOHAMMED RIJYA; Sec.-Gen. BABA SHEHU BUKAR.

Calabar Chamber of Commerce and Industry: Desan House Bldg, 38 Ndidem Iso Rd, POB 76, Calabar, Cross River; tel. (87) 221558; 92 mems; Pres. Chief TAM OFORIOKUMA.

Enugu Chamber of Commerce, Industry, Mines and Agriculture (ECCIMA): International Trade Fair Complex, Abakaliki Rd, POB 734, Enugu; tel. (42) 290481; e-mail enuguchamber@yahoo.com; internet www.enuguchamber.net; f. 1963; Pres. THEO OKONKWO; Dir-Gen. EMEKA OKEREKE.

Franco-Nigerian Chamber of Commerce: 5th Floor, Big Leaf House, 7 Oyin Jolayemi St, POB 70001, Victoria Island, Lagos; tel. (1) 4611201; fax (1) 4613501; e-mail fncci@ccife.org; internet franco-nigerian.com; f. 1985; Pres. MARCEL HOCHET; Gen. Man. AKIN AKINBOLA.

Gongola Chamber of Commerce and Industry: Palace Hotel, POB 8, Jimeta-Yola; tel. (75) 255136; Pres. Alhaji ALIYU IBRAHIM.

Ibadan Chamber of Commerce and Industry: Commerce House, Ring Rd, Challenge, PMB 5168, Ibadan; tel. 7056778489 (mobile); e-mail ibdcci@yahoo.com; internet ibadanchamberofcommerce.org; Pres. DIIMEJI MIKE-FOWOWE.

Ijebu Chamber of Commerce and Industry: 51 Ibadan Rd, POB 604, Ijebu Ode; tel. (37) 432880; Pres. DOYIN DEGUN.

Ikot Ekpene Chamber of Commerce and Industry: 47 Aba Rd, POB 50, Ikot Ekpene; tel. (85) 400153; Pres. G. U. EKANEM.

Kaduna Chamber of Commerce, Industry, Mines and Agriculture: POB 728, Rigachikun, Kaduna; tel. 7023228854 (mobile); fax 7023228908 (mobile); e-mail kadunachamberofcommerce@yahoo.com; internet www.kadccima.org.ng; f. 1973; Pres. UMAR YAHAYA.

Kano Chamber of Commerce, Industry, Mines and Agriculture: Trade Fair Complex, Zoo Rd, POB 10, Kano City, Kano; tel. (64) 666936; fax (64) 667138; Pres. Alhaji AHMAD RABIU.

Katsina Chamber of Commerce and Industry: IBB Way, POB 789, Katsina; tel. (65) 31974; Pres. ABBA ALI.

Kwara Chamber of Commerce, Industry, Mines and Agriculture: 9A Kwara Hotel Premises, Ahmadu Bello Ave, POB 1634, Ilorin; tel. 8035888047 (mobile); fax (31) 224131; e-mail kwaccima@yahoo.com; internet www.kwaccima.com; f. 1965; Pres. Dr HEZEKIAH ADEDIJI.

Lagos Chamber of Commerce and Industry: Commerce House, 1 Idowu Taylor St, Victoria Island, POB 109, Lagos; tel. (1) 7746617; fax (1) 2701009; e-mail inform@micro.com.ng; internet www.lagoschamber.com; f. 1888; 1,500 mems; Pres. Chief OLUSOLA FALEYE.

Niger Chamber of Commerce and Industry: Trade Fair Site, Paiko Rd, POB 370, Minna; tel. (66) 223153; Pres. Alhaji U. S. NDANUSA.

Nnewi Chamber of Commerce, Industry, Mines and Agriculture: 31A Nnobi Rd, POB 1471, Nnewi, Anambra State; tel. (70) 35187662; f. 1987; Pres. PRINCE EMEKA A. AYABAZU.

Osogbo Chamber of Commerce and Industry: Obafemi Awolowo Way, Ajegunle, POB 870, Osogbo, Osun; tel. (35) 231098; Pres. Prince VICTOR ADEMLE.

Owerri Chamber of Commerce and Industry: OCCIMA Secretariat, 123 Okigwe Rd, POB 1439, Owerri; tel. (83) 234849.

Oyo Chamber of Commerce and Industry: Ogbomosho Rd, opp. Apaara Methodist Church, POB 588, Oyo; tel. (38) 240691; Pres. B.A. LASEBIKAN.

Plateau State Chambers of Commerce, Industry, Mines and Agriculture: POB 74, 21A Nassarawa Rd, Jos; tel. (73) 453918; f. 1976; Pres. SILAS JANGA.

Port Harcourt Chamber of Commerce, Industry, Mines and Agriculture: Alesa Eleme, POB 585, Port Harcourt; tel. (84) 239536; f. 1952; Pres. VINCENT FURO.

Remo Chamber of Commerce and Industry: 7 Sho Manager Way, POB 1172, Shagamu; tel. (37) 640962; Pres. Chief ADENIYI OGUNSANYA.

Sapele Chamber of Commerce and Industry: 144 New Ogorode Rd, POB 154, Sapele; tel. and fax (54) 42323; Pres. Chief DAVID IWETA.

Sokoto Chamber of Commerce and Industry: 12 Racecourse Rd, POB 2234, Sokoto; tel. (60) 231805; Pres. Alhaji ALIYU WAZIRI BODINGA.

Umahia Chamber of Commerce: 44 Azikiwe Rd, Umahia; tel. (88) 223373; fax (88) 222299; Pres. GEORGE AKOMAS.

Uyo Chamber of Commerce and Industry: 141 Abak Rd, POB 2960, Uyo, Akwa Ibom; Pres. Chief DANIEL ITA-EKPOTT.

Warri Chamber of Commerce, Industry, Mines and Agriculture: Block 1, Edewor Shopping Centre, PMB 302, Warri; tel. (53) 253709; internet www.waccima.com; f. 1963; Pres. AUSTIN E. EGBEGBADIA.

INDUSTRIAL AND TRADE ASSOCIATIONS

Federation of Agriculture Commodity Associations of Nigeria (FACAN): Lagos; f. 2011; Pres. Dr VICTOR IYAMA; AKIN GBADAMOSI.

National Cashew Association of Nigeria (NCAN): 32/35 Calcutta Cres., Apapa-Lagos; tel. (1) 5870966; Pres. OLATUNJI OWOEYE.

National Coffee and Tea Association of Nigeria: Old NRC Bldg, Gembu, Taraba; tel. (75) 624486.

National Cotton Association of Nigeria (NACOTAN): 48/50 Namagwatse House, Ahmadu Bello Way, Kaduna; Pres. Alhaji ALIYU ISAH DANMARAYA.

Nigerian Export Promotion Council (NEPC): Plot 40, Blantyre St, Wuse 2, Abuja; tel. (9) 5230932; fax (9) 5230931; e-mail info@nepc.gov.ng; internet www.nepc.gov.ng; f. 1977; Chair. Alhaji ISIAKA ADELEKE; CEO DAVID ADULUGBA.

Nigerian Investment Promotion Commission (NIPC): Plot 1181, Aguiyi Ironsi St, Maitama District, PMB 381, Garki, Abuja; tel. (9) 4134380; e-mail infodesk@nipc.gov.ng; internet www.nipc.gov.ng; Chair. FELIX OMOIKHOJE AIZOBEOJE OHIWEREI; Exec. Sec. Alhaji MUSTAFA BELLO.

Potato Growers, Processors and Marketers Association of Nigeria (POGPMAN): Lagos; Pres. BAYO AJIBADE.

EMPLOYERS' ORGANIZATIONS

Association of Advertising Agencies of Nigeria (AAAN): Plot 8, Otunba Jobi Fele-Way, Central Business District, Alausa, Ikeja, Lagos; tel. and fax (1) 4970842; e-mail lekan@aaanigeria.com; internet www.aaanigeria.com; Pres. FUNMI ONABOLU; CEO LEKAN FADOLAPO.

Chartered Institute of Bankers of Nigeria: PC 19 Adeola Hopewell St, POB 72273, Victoria Island, Lagos; tel. (1) 2703494; fax (1) 4618930; e-mail cibn@cibng.org; internet www.cibng.org; Chair. JOSEPH LAOYE JAIYEOLA; CEO Dr UJU M. OGUBUNKA.

Institute of Chartered Accountants of Nigeria: Plot 16, Professional Layout Centre, Idowu Taylor St, Victoria Island, POB 1580, Lagos; tel. (1) 7642294; fax (1) 7642295; e-mail info.ican@ican.org.ng; internet www.ican-ngr.org; f. 1965; CEO and Registrar ADEDOYIN OWOLABI; Pres. SEBASTIAN ACHULIKE OWUAMA.

Nigeria Employers' Consultative Association: NECA House, Plot A2, Hakeem Balogun St, Central Business District, Alausa, Ikeja, POB 2231, Marina, Lagos; tel. (1) 7746352; fax (1) 7912941; e-mail neca@necang.org; internet www.necang.org; f. 1957; Pres. R. U. UCHE; Dir-Gen. O. A. OSHINOWO.

Nigerian Institute of Architects (NIA): 2 Kukawa Close, off Gimbiya St, Area 11, Garki, Abuja; tel. (9) 4802518; e-mail info@niarchitects.org; internet niarchitects.org; f. 1960; Pres. OLATUNJI OLUMIDE BOLU.

Nigerian Institute of Building (NIOB): House No 24, Road 37, Gwarinpa Housing Estate, Abuja; tel. and fax (9) 7831243; e-mail niob@niobuilding.org; internet www.niobuilding.org; f. 1967; Pres. DACHOLLOM DALYOP JAMBOL.

Nigerian Institution of Estate Surveyors and Valuers: Plot 759, BASSAN Plaza, Wing C, Last Floor, Central Business District, Independence Ave, PMB 5147 Abuja; tel. (9) 4604710; e-mail admin@niesv.org.ng; internet www.niesv.org.ng; f. 1969; Pres. BODE ADEDIJI; Nat. Sec. ROWLAND E. ABONTA.

Nigerian Society of Engineers (NSE): National Engineering Centre, Plot 1035 Cadastral, off National Mosque-Labour House Rd, Central Business Area, PMB 13866, Abuja; tel. (9) 6735096; e-mail info@nseng.org; internet www.nse.org.ng; f. 1958; Pres. MUSTAPHA BALARABE SHEHU.

UTILITIES

Electricity

Following the liberalization of the electricity sector in 2005, the Power Holding Company of Nigeria (PHCN), the national producer and distributor of electricity, was dissolved in early 2012, and its assets and responsibilities were transferred to 17 successor companies. The privatization process was scheduled to be completed by October.

Nigerian Electricity Regulatory Commission (NERC): Adamawa Plaza, Plot 1099, First Ave, off Shehu Shagari Way, Central Business District, PMB 136, Garki, Abuja; tel. (9) 6700991; e-mail info@nercng.org; internet www.nercng.org; f. 2005; Chair. and CEO Dr SAM AMADI.

Gas

Nigeria Liquefied Natural Gas Co Ltd (NLNG): C. & C. Towers, Plot 1684, Sanusi Fafunwa St, Victoria Island, PMB 12774, Marina, Lagos; tel. (1) 2624190; fax (1) 2616976; internet www.nigerialng.com; f. 1989; Man. Dir CHIMA IBENECHE.

MAJOR COMPANIES

The following are some of the largest companies in terms either of capital investment or employment.

African Timber and Plywood (AT & P): PMB 4001, Sapele; f. 1935; a division of UAC of Nigeria Ltd and an assoc. co of UAC International Ltd, London; loggers and mfrs of plywood, particleboard, flushdoors, lumber and machined wood products; Gen. Man. L. HODGSON.

British American Tobacco Nigeria: PC 35 Idowu Taylor St, POB 137, Lagos; tel. (1) 4617103; fax (1) 4617514; internet www.batnigeria.com; f. 2000, merged with the Nigerian Tobacco Co. the same year; cap. ₦200m.; mfrs of tobacco products; Man. Dir BEVERLEY SPENCER-OBATOYINBO; 696 employees.

Camela Vegetable Oil Co Ltd: 126 Okigwe Road, POB 852, Owerri; tel. 803300089 (mobile); production of vegetable oil products; Chair. Chief OKEY IKORO.

Chellarams PLC: 2 Goriola St, Victoria Island, Lagos; tel. (1) 2627880; fax (1) 2622458; e-mail head.office@chellaramsplc.com; internet www.chellaramsplc.com; f. 1923; Chair. ASIWAJU SOLOMON KAYODE ONAFOWOKAN OON; Man. Dir Chief SURESH M. CHELLARAM.

Chemical and Allied Products PLC (CAP PLC): 2 Adeniyi Jones Ave, PMB 21072, Ikeja, Lagos; tel. 7098733733 (mobile); fax (1) 2707592; internet www.capplc.com; mfrs of paints, pesticides and pharmaceuticals, distributors of chemicals, dyestuffs, explosives, plastic raw materials and associated products; Chair. LARRY ETTAH; Man. Dir OMOLARA ELEMIDE.

Conoil PLC: Bull Plaza, 38–39 Marina, PMB 2052, Lagos; tel. 8059293211 (mobile); f. 1975; fmrly Shell Nigeria Ltd, subsequently National Oil and Chemical Marketing PLC; 74.4% owned by Conpetro Ltd; Chair. MIKE ADENUGA, Jr; Man. Dir JOHN VASIKARAN (acting).

Consolidated Tin Mines of Nigeria Ltd: PMB 2036, Jos; tel. (73) 80634; f. 1986 by merger of Amalgamated Tin Mines of Nigeria Ltd and five other mining cos operating on the Jos plateau; privatization pending; production of tin concentrate from alluvial tin ore and separation of columbite, zircon and monazite; Chair. (vacant).

Dangote Group: Union Marble House, 1 Alfred Rewane Rd, PMB 40032, Falomo, Ikoyi, Lagos; tel. (1) 4480815; fax (1) 2702893; e-mail communications@dangote-group.com; internet www.dangote-group.com; conglomerate with interests in cement, sugar, flour, salt, etc.; Pres. Alhaji ALIKO ALIKO DANGOTE; COO OLAKUNLE ALAKE.

Dangote Cement: Obajana; Man. Dir JAGATH RATHEE.

Dangote Flour Mills: Terminal E, Administrative Bldg, Apapa Port Complex, Lagos; tel. (1) 2712200; fax (1) 5878019; f. 1999; Man. Dir ROHIT CHAUDHRY.

Dangote Sugar Refinery PLC: Modandola House, 42/44 Warehouse Rd, Apapa, Lagos; tel. (1) 5804646; fax (1) 2714466; internet www.dangote-sugar.com; f. 2000; Man. Dir Eng. ABDULLAHI A. SULE.

National Salt Co. of Nigeria PLC (NASCON): 15B Ikosi Rd, Oregun Industrial Estate, Oregun-Ikeja, Lagos; tel. (1) 2712212; e-mail nascon@dangote-group.com; f. 1973; Man. Dir ADEJINLE O. ADENIJI.

Delta Steel Co PLC: Ovwian-Aladja, PMB 1220, Warri; tel. 8063384579 (mobile); e-mail patejuleigh@yahoo.com; internet www.deltasteelcompany.com; f. 1979; owned by Global Steel Holdings Ltd (GSHL); operates direct-reduction steel complex with eventual annual capacity of 1m. tons; Group Man. Dir Dr SAMUEL NWABUOKEI.

Eastern Bulkcem Co Ltd: 11 Awolowo Rd, Flat 5, Block 2, Ikoyi, Lagos; tel. and fax (1) 2691114; e-mail ebc@eaglecement.com; internet www.eaglecement.com; f. 1977; Exec. Dir CYNTHIA ADAORA OKOLO.

Flour Mills of Nigeria PLC (FMN): 2 Old Dock Rd, POB 341, Apapa, Lagos; tel. 5803370; fax 5871602; e-mail info@fmnplc.com; internet www.fmnplc.com; f. 1960; conglomerate with interests in cement, wheat products, pasta, packaging, fertilizer, etc.; Chair. GEORGE S. COUMANTAROS; Group Man. Dir EMMANUEL A. UKPABI.

Forte Oil PLC: 13 Walter Carrington Cres., Victoria Island, POB 512, Lagos; tel. (1) 2776100; fax (1) 2776129; e-mail corp-comm@forteoilplc.com; internet www.forteoilplc.com; cap. ₦72m.; fmrly BP Nigeria Ltd, subsequently African Petroleum Ltd; present name adopted 2011; markets lubricants, fuel oil, automotive gas oil, motor spirits, liquefied petroleum gas and kerosene; Chair. FEMI OTEDOLA; Acting CEO AKINWUNMI AKINFEMIWA.

Guinness (Nigeria) Ltd: Oba Akran Ave, Ikeja, PMB 1071, Lagos State; tel. (1) 4971560; fax (1) 4970560; f. 1950; cap. p.u. ₦25m.; brewers; breweries in Ogba (700,000 hl) and Benin (900,000 hl); Man. Dir KEITH TAYLOR.

Henry Stephens Group: Head Office: 90 Awolowo Rd, SW Ikoyi, POB 2480, Lagos; tel. (1) 603460; subsidiary cos include:

Henry Stephens Engineering Co Ltd: 2 Ilepeju By-Pass, Ikeja, PMB 21386, Lagos; tel. (1) 3222483; fax (1) 33489300; e-mail henrystephen@hotvoice.com; for construction machinery, motors and agricultural equipment; Chair. Chief OLADELE FAJEMIROKUN.

IBRU: 33 Creek Rd, PMB 1155, Apapa, Lagos; tel. (1) 876634; agricultural equipment, machinery and service; fishing and frozen fish distribution, civil and agricultural engineering; Man. Dir OSKAR IBRU.

Julius Berger Nigeria PLC: 10 Shettima A. Munguno Cres., Utako, Abuja; tel. (9) 6110000; fax (9) 6114444; e-mail info@julius-berger.com; internet www.julius-berger.com; construction and civil engineering; Chair. Dr MOHAMMED NURUDDEEN IMAM; Man. Dir Eng. WOLFGANG GOETSCH; 18,000 Nigerian employees.

Lafarge Cement WAPCO Nigeria PLC: Elephant Cement House, 237–239 Ikorodu Rd, Ikeja Central Business District, Alausa, POB 1001, Lagos; tel. (1) 7745088; internet www.lafargewapco.com; f. 1959; name changed as above in 2007; production and sale of cement and decorative materials; cap. p.u. ₦60.3m.; Chair. CHIEF OLUSEGUN OLADIPO OSUNKEYE OON; Man. Dir/CEO JOSEPH HUDSON; 812 employees.

Lenoil: Icon House, Idejo St, Lagos; tel. (1) 610447; fax (1) 2615284; CEO LENO ADESANYA.

A. G. Leventis Group: Iddo House, Iddo, POB 159, Lagos; tel. (1) 800220; fax (1) 860574; internet www.agleventisplc.com; activities include wholesale and retail distribution, vehicle assembly, food production and farming, manufacture of glass, plastics, beer, technical and electrical equipment, property investment and management; Chair. Chief JOSEPH BABATUNDE OKE; Man. Dir. ARTHUR BOUREKAS.

Mandilas Group Ltd: 35 Simpson St, POB 35, Lagos; tel. (1) 7404781; fax (1) 2662605; e-mail mandilas@mandilasng.com; internet www.mandilasng.com; subsidiaries include Mandilas Enterprises Ltd, Mandilas Travel Ltd, Norman Industries Ltd, Electrolux-Mandilas Ltd, Phoenix of Nigeria Assurance Co Ltd, Sulzer Nigeria Ltd, Mandilas Ventures Ltd, Original Box Co Ltd; Chair. T. A. MANDILAS.

Mobil Oil Nigeria: PMB 12054, 1 Lekki Express Way, Victoria Island, Lagos; tel. (1) 2621640; fax (1) 2621733; a subsidiary of ExxonMobil; offshore petroleum production; Chair. and Man. Dir DUKE KEISER.

MRS Nigeria PLC: 8 McCarthy St, Lagos; tel. (1) 4614500; fax (1) 2630647; internet www.texaco.com; f. 1913; petroleum marketing; Chair. M. D. FINNEGAN.

Nigerian Breweries Ltd: Iganmu House, 1 Abebe Village Rd, Iganmu, POB 545, Lagos; tel. (1) 2717400; fax (1) 5852067; e-mail info@nbplc.com; internet www.nbplc.com; f. 1946; also facilities at Aba, Kaduna, Ibadan and Enugu; Chair. Chief K. B. JAMODU; Man. Dir NICO A. VERVELDE; 3,683 employees.

Nautilus (Nigeria) Engineering and Construction Co Ltd (NNEC): 5 Idowu Taylor St, 5th Floor, Victoria Island, Lagos; tel. (1) 2610809; fax (1) 3200749; e-mail info@nnecltd.com; internet www.nnecltd.com; engineering and construction.

Nigerian National Petroleum Corpn (NNPC): NNPC Towers, Herbert Macauley Way, Central Business District, PMB 190, Garki, Abuja; tel. (9) 20081133; fax (9) 2340029; e-mail contactus@nnpcgroup.com; internet www.nnpcgroup.com; f. 1977; reorg. 1988; holding corpn for Fed. Govt's interests in petroleum cos; 11 operating subsidiaries; Man. Dir ANDREW YAKUBU.

Port Harcourt Refining Co Ltd: Alesa Eleme, POB 585, Port Harcourt, Rivers State; tel. (84) 777821; fax (84) 766951; e-mail phrc@nnpc-group.com; f. 1965; Man. Dir BASHIR ABDULLAHI.

Warri Petrochemical and Refining Co. (WRPC): PMB 44, Effuron, Warri; tel. (53) 254161; fax (53) 252535; e-mail wrpc@nnpc.com.na; Man. Dir ANDY YAKUBU.

Oando Plc: Stallion House, 8th–10th Floor, 2 Ajose Adeogun St, Victoria Island, Lagos; tel. (1) 2601290; fax (1) 2633939; e-mail info@oandoplc.com; internet www.oandoplc.com; f. 1956 as ESSO; rebranded in 1976 as Unipetrol Nigeria Ltd; merged with Agip Nigeria Plc in 2003 and assumed present name; Chair. OBA M. A. GBADEBO; CEO JUBRIL ADEWALE TINUBU.

Peugeot Automobile Nigeria Ltd: Plot 1144, Mallam Kulbi Rd, Kakuri Industrial Estate, PMB 2266, Kaduna; tel. (62) 231131; fax (62) 232503; e-mail customerservice@peugeotnigeria.com; internet www.peugeotnigeria.com; f. 1972; engaged in the manufacture and marketing of fully built Peugeot automobiles through appointed network of distributors; 54.87% owned by ASD Motors-Nig, 10% owned by Automobiles Peugeot, Govt of Nigeria and Bank of India, Nigeria; Man. Dir Alhaji SHEHU SANI DAUDA.

Reynolds Construction Co Nigeria Ltd: Plot 1682, Sanusi Fafunwa St, Victoria Island, Lagos; tel. (1) 2611635; fax (1) 2611635; e-mail md@rcc-nigeria.com; internet www.rcc-nigeria.com; f. 1969; Chair. Chief S. O. FADAHUNSI.

SCOA Nigeria PLC: 157 Apapa Oshodi Expressway, Isolo, POB 2318, Lagos; tel. 8034004141 (mobile); e-mail info@scoaplc.com; internet www.scoaplc.com; cap. ₦44.8m.; vehicle assembly and maintenance, distribution and maintenance of heavyweight engines, industrial air-conditioning and refrigeration, home and office equipment, textiles, tanning, general consumer goods, mechanized farming; Chair. HENRY H. AGBAMU; Man. Dir Dr MASSA F. BOULOS.

Shell Petroleum Development Company of Nigeria Ltd: Freeman House, 21–22 Marina, PMB 2418, Lagos; tel. (1) 2769999; fax (1) 2636791; e-mail shellnigeria@shell.com; internet www.shell.com.ng; the largest petroleum operation in Nigeria; carries out onshore and offshore exploration and production; 55% govt-owned; Man. Dir MUTIU SUNMONU.

Total Premier Services Nigeria Ltd (TPSNL): Plot 5, Chief Yesuf Abiodun Way, off Ozumba Mbadiwe Way, Victoria Island, Lagos; internet www.tpsnl.com; supplier of oil country tubular goods (OCTGs); Chair. JAMES SIMMONS.

Triana Ltd: 18–20 Commercial Rd, PMB 1064, Apapa, Lagos; tel. (1) 8105132; e-mail trianaltd@yahoo.com; internet www.trianaltd.com; f. 1970; shipping, clearing and forwarding, warehousing, airfreighting; Dir Alhaji R. A. O. MAJEKODUNMI.

UAC of Nigeria Ltd: Niger House, 1–5 Odunlami St, POB 9, Lagos; tel. (1) 2663176; fax (1) 2662628; e-mail info@uacnplc.com; internet www.uacnplc.com; fmrly United Africa Co; divisions include brewing, foods, electrical materials, packaging, business equipment, plant hire, timber; Chair. UDOMA UDO UDOMA; CEO LARRY EPHRAIM ETTAH.

Grand Cereals and Oil Mills Ltd: KM 17, Zawan Roundabout, POB 13462, Jos, Plateau; tel. (73) 280317; fax (73) 280014; e-mail info@grandcereals.com; internet www.grandcereals.com; a subsidiary of UAC of Nigeria Ltd; Man. Dir LAYIWOLA RAMONI OYATOKI.

United Cement Company of Nigeria Ltd (UNICEM): Spring Rd, Diamond Hill, PMB 1017, Calabar; tel. (703) 4090955; Man. Dir DIDIER TRESARRIEU.

Unilever (Nigeria) PLC: 15 Dockyard Rd, POB 15, Apapa, Lagos; tel. (1) 5803300; fax (1) 5803711; f. 1923; cap. ₦112.0m.; mfrs of detergents, edible fats and toilet preparations; Chair. NNAEMEKA ALFRED ACHEBE; Man. Dir THABO MABE.

TRADE UNIONS

Federations

Nigerian Labour Congress (NLC): Labour House, Plot 820/821, Central Business District, Abuja; tel. (9) 6276042; fax (9) 6274342; e-mail gsec@nlcng.org; internet www.nlcng.org; f. 1978; comprised 36 affiliated industrial unions in 2009; Pres. ABDULWAHED IBRAHIM OMAR; Gen. Sec. OWEI LAKEMFA.

Trade Union Congress of Nigeria (TUC): Express House, 338 Ikorodu Rd, Maryland, Lagos; tel. (1) 4701699; e-mail info@tucnigeria.org; internet www.tucnigeria.org; Pres.-Gen. PETER ESELE; Gen. Sec. JOHN KOLAWOLE; 24 mem. orgs.

Principal Unions

Amalgamated Union of Public Corpns, Civil Service, and Technical and Recreational Services Employees (AUPCTRE): 9 Aje St, PMB 1064, Yaba, Lagos; tel. (1) 5863722; Gen. Sec. SYLVESTER EJIOFOR.

National Union of Journalists: Lagos; Pres. LANRE OGUNDIPE; Sec. MOHAMMED KHALID.

National Union of Petroleum Workers and Natural Gas (NUPENG): 9 Jibowu St, off Ikorodu Rd, Yaba, Lagos; tel. (1) 8770277; fax (1) 3425310; e-mail headoffice@nupeng.org; internet nupeng.org; f. 1977; Gen. Sec. ELIJAH OKOUGBO.

Nigerian Union of Civil Engineering, Construction, Furniture and Woodworkers: 51 Kano St, Ebute Metta, PMB 1064, Lagos; tel. (1) 5800263.

Nigerian Union of Mine Workers: 95 Enugu St, POB 763, Jos; tel. (73) 52401.

Petroleum and Natural Gas Senior Staff Association of Nigeria (PENGASSAN): U. M. Okoro House, 288 Ikorodu Rd, Anthony, Lagos; tel. (1) 2790715; fax (1) 2790717; e-mail headoffice@pengassan.org; internet www.pengassan.org; f. 1978; Gen. Sec. M. A. OLOWOSHILE.

Transport

RAILWAYS

In 2005 there were about 3,528 km of mainly narrow-gauge railways. The two principal lines connect Lagos with Nguru and Port Harcourt with Maiduguri. In 2010 there were plans for the construction of a 21-km monorail in Enugu. There were also plans for a light rail project in Lagos.

Nigerian Railway Corpn: PMB 1037, Ebute-Metta, Lagos; tel. (1) 7747320; fax (1) 5831367; e-mail info.nrc@nrc-ng.org; internet www.nrc-ng.org; f. 1955; restructured in 1993 into three separate units: Nigerian Railway Track Authority; Nigerian Railways; and Nigerian Railway Engineering Ltd; Chair. Dr BELLO HALIRU MOHAMMED; Man. Dir ADESEYI SIJUWADE.

ROADS

In 2011 the Nigerian road network totalled 198,000 km, including 15,688 km of highways and 18,719 km of secondary roads; some 9,660 km were paved.

Federal Roads Maintenance Agency (FERMA): Plot 163, Aminu Kano Cres., Wuse II, Abuja; e-mail information@ferma.ng.gov; internet www.ferma.gov.ng; f. 2002; Chair. Eng. ABDULKHADIR A. KURE; Man. Dir and CEO Eng. SANI HALIRU.

Nigerian Road Federation: Ministry of Transport, National Maritime Agency Bldg, Central Area, Abuja; tel. (9) 5237053.

Road Transport Employers'Association of Nigeria (RTEAN): Plot 2082, Harper Cres., Beside Police Officers Mess, Wuse Zone 7, FCT, Abuja; internet rtean.com; Pres. JOSIAH OLUFEMI OLUFEMI AJEWOLE; Sec.-Gen. Alhaji DANLAMI GARBA NAVOM.

INLAND WATERWAYS

National Inland Waterways Authority (NIWA): PMB 1004, Adankolo, Lokoja, Kogi State; tel. (58) 2220965; internet niwagovng.com; f. 1997; responsible for all navigable waterways; Man. Dir AHMED AMINU YAR'ADUA.

SHIPPING

The principal ports are the Delta Port complex (including Warri, Koko, Burutu and Sapele ports), Port Harcourt and Calabar; other significant ports are situated at Apapa and Tin Can Island, near Lagos. The main petroleum ports are Bonny and Burutu. In 2009 Nigeria's merchant fleet comprised 516 vessels, with a total displacement of 679,200 gross registered tons. Some 101 shipping companies were registered in 2010.

Nigerian Maritime Administration and Safety Agency (NIMASA): 4 Burma Rd, Apapa; tel. 5452843; e-mail info@nimasa.gov.ng; internet nimasa.gov.ng; f. 2007 following merger of National Maritime Authority and Joint Maritime Labour Industrial Council; Chair. ALHAJI AHMADU ADAMU MU'AZU; Dir-Gen. ZAIKEDE PATRICK AKPOBOLOKEMI.

Nigerian Ports Authority: 26/28 Marina, PMB 12588, Lagos; tel. (1) 2600620; fax (1) 2636719; e-mail telnpo@infoweb.abs.net; internet www.nigerianports.org; f. 1955; Man. Dir OMAR SULEIMAN.

Nigerian Green Lines Ltd: Yinka Folawiyo Plaza, 38 Yinka Folawiyo Ave (fmrly Warehouse Rd), Apapa; tel. (1) 5450436; fax (1) 5450204; f. 1972; Yinka Folawiyo Group; 2 vessels totalling 30,751 grt; Chair. Alhaji W. I. FOLAWIYO.

Association

Nigerian Shippers' Council: Shippers' Tower, 4 Park Lane, Apapa, Lagos; tel. (1) 5452307; fax (1) 5452906; e-mail info@shipperscouncil.com; internet www.shipperscouncil.com; Chair. Chief Dr MARIAN ALI; CEO Capt. ADAMU A. BIU.

CIVIL AVIATION

The principal international airports are at Lagos (Murtala Mohammed Airport), Kano, Port Harcourt and Abuja. There are also 18 airports servicing domestic flights.

Federal Airports Authority of Nigeria (FAAN): Murtala Mohammed Airport, PMB 21607, Ikeja, Lagos; tel. (1) 4970335; fax (1) 4970342; e-mail contact@faannigeria.org; internet www.faannigeria.org; Chair. EBITIMI BANIGO; CEO GEORGE ESEZOBOR URIESI.

Nigerian Civil Aviation Authority (NCAA): Nnandi Azikwe International Airport, Abuja; e-mail info@ncaa.gov.ng; internet www.ncaa.gov.ng; Dir-Gen. HAROLD OLUSEGUN DEMUREN.

Principal Airlines

Air Nigeria: 3rd Floor, Ark Towers, Plot 17, Ligali Ayorinde St, Victoria Island Extension, Ikeja, Lagos; tel. (1) 4600505; internet www.flyairnigeria.com; f. Sept. 2004, name changed as above in 2010; private flag carrier; owned by Air Nigeria Development Ltd; scheduled domestic regional and international services; operations suspended owing to financial difficulties in September 2012; Chair. JIMOH IBRAHIM; CEO KINFE KAHASSAYE.

Arik Air: Murtala Mohammed Airport, POB 10468, Ikeja, Lagos; tel. (1) 2799900; fax (1) 4975940; e-mail info@arikair.com; internet www.arikair.com; f. 2002; Chair. JOSEPH ARUMEMI-IKHIDE; Group CEO Dr MICHAEL ARUMEMI-IKHIDE.

Chanchangi Airlines Nigeria Ltd: Kaduna; f. 1994; domestic scheduled services; Chair. Alhaji AHMADU CHANCHANGI; Man. Dir TREVOR WORTHINGTON.

Dana Air: 51 Allen Ave, Ikeja, Lagos; tel. (1) 2809888; e-mail contact@flydanaair.com; internet www.flydanaair.com; CEO JACKY HATHIRAMANI.

IRS Airlines Ltd: 62 Micheal Otedola Cres., off Joel Ogunnaike GRA, Ikeja, Lagos; tel. (1) 2704486; fax (1) 2704486; e-mail rirabiu@flyirsairlines.com; internet www.flyirsairlines.com; f. 2001; domestic services; Chair. Alhaji ISYAKU RABIU.

Tourism

Potential attractions for tourists include fine coastal scenery, dense forests and the rich diversity of Nigeria's arts. A total of 6.1m. tourists visited Nigeria in 2009. Receipts from tourism in 2011 amounted to US $601m.

Nigerian Tourism Development Corpn: Old Federal Secretariat, Area 1, Garki, PMB 167, Abuja; tel. (9) 2342764; fax (9) 2342775; e-mail ntdc@metrong.com; internet www.nigeria.tourism.com; Chair. Prince ADESUYI HAASTRUP; CEO OMOTAYO OMOTOSHO.

Defence

As assessed at November 2011, the total strength of the armed forces was 80,000: the army totalled 62,000 men, the navy 8,000 and the air force 10,000. There was also a paramilitary force of 82,000. Military service is voluntary. In 2011 a total of 4,949 Nigeria troops were stationed abroad, of which 88 were observers.

Defence Expenditure: Budgeted at ₦348,000m. in 2011.

Commander-in-Chief of the Armed Forces: Dr GOODLUCK EBELE JONATHAN.

Chief of Defence Staff: Air Marshall OLUSEYI PETINRIN.

Chief of Army Staff: Maj.-Gen. O. A. IHEJIRIKA.

Chief of Naval Staff: Rear-Adm. O. S. IBRAHIM.

Chief of Air Staff: Air Vice-Marshal M. D. UMAR.

Education

Education is partly the responsibility of the state governments, although the Federal Government has played an increasingly important role since 1970. Primary education begins at six years of age and lasts for six years. Secondary education begins at 12 years of age and lasts for a further six years, comprising two three-year cycles. Education to junior secondary level (from six to 15 years of age) is free and compulsory. According to UNESCO estimates, in 2009/10 primary enrolment was equivalent to 83% of children in the relevant age-group (males 87%; females 79%), while the comparable ratio for secondary enrolment in that year was equivalent to 44% (males 47%; females 41%). In 2005 724,856 students were enrolled at Nigerian universities. Expenditure on education by the Federal Government in 2005 was ₦82,797m., equivalent to 5.0% of total spending in the federal budget.

Bibliography

Achebe, C. *There Was A Country: A Personal History of Biafra.* London, Penguin, 2012.

Adalemo, I. A., *et al.* (Eds). *Giant in the Tropics: A Compendium.* Lagos, Gabumo, 1993.

Adamokekun, L. *The Fall of the Second Republic.* Ibadan, Spectrum Books, 1985.

Adejumobi, S., and Momah, A. (Eds). *The Political Economy of Nigeria under Military Rule, 1984–1993.* Nigeria, Southern Africa Printing and Publishing House, 1995.

The Enigma of Military Rule in Africa. Harare, SAPES Books, 1995.

Adibe, J. *Negotiating the Nigeria-Nation: Essays on State, Governance and Development.* London, Adonis & Abbey, 2012.

Nigeria without Nigerians? Boko Haram and the Crisis in Nigeria's Nation-Building Project. London, Adonis & Abbey, 2012.

Agbaje, A., Diamond, L., and Onwudiwe, E. (Eds). *Nigeria and the Struggle for Democracy and Good Governance.* Ibadan, Ibadan University Press, 2004.

Anyanwu, U. D., and Aguwa, J. C. U. (Eds). *The Igbo and the Tradition of Politics.* Enugu, Fourth Dimension, 1993.

Apter, A. *The Pan-African Nation: Oil and the Spectacle of Culture in Nigeria.* Chicago, IL, University of Chicago Press, 2005.

Ate, B. E., and Akinterinwa, B. A. (Eds). *Nigeria and its Immediate Neighbours: Constraints and Prospects of Sub-Regional Security in the 1990s.* Lagos, Nigerian Institute of International Affairs, 1992.

Ayeni, V., and Soremekun, K. (Eds). *Nigeria's Second Republic.* Lagos, Daily Times Publications, 1988.

Babatope, E. *Murtala Muhammed: A Leader Betrayed.* Enugu, Roy and Ezete Publishing Co, 1986.

The Abacha Regime and the 12 June Crisis. London, Beacons Books, 1995.

The Abacha Years: What Went Wrong? Lagos, Ebino Topsy, 2003.

Babawale, T. (Ed.). *Urban Violence, Ethnic Militias and the Challenge of Democratic Consolidation in Nigeria.* Lagos, Malthouse Press, 2003.

Bakarr Bah, A. *Breakdowns and Reconstitution: Democracy, the Nation-State, and Ethnicity in Nigeria.* Lanham, MD, Lexington Books, 2005.

Bangura, Y. *Intellectuals, Economic Reform and Social Change: Constraints and Opportunities in the Formation of a Nigerian Technocracy.* Dakar, CODESRIA, 1994.

Campbell, J. *Nigeria: Dancing on the Brink.* Lanham, MD, Rowman and Littlefield, 2010.

Collier, P., Soludo, C. C., and Pattillo, C. (Eds). *How Economic Choices Will Determine Nigeria's Future.* Basingstoke, Palgrave Macmillan, 2007.

Cruise O'Brien, D. B., Dunn, J., and Rathbone, R. (Eds). *Contemporary West African States.* Cambridge, Cambridge University Press, 1989.

Cyprian Nwagwu, E. O. *Taming the Tiger: Civil-Military Relations Reform and the Search for Political Stability in Nigeria.* Lanham, MD, University Press of America, 2003.

Dibie, R. A. *Public Management and Sustainable Development in Nigeria: Military-Bureaucracy Relationship.* London, Ashgate Publishing Company, 2003.

Dike, V. E. *The Osu Caste System in Igboland: A Challenge for Nigerian Democracy.* Kearney, NE, Morris Publishing, 2002.

Ejiogu, E. *The Roots of Political Instability in Nigeria.* Farnham, Ashgate, 2011.

Elaigwu, J. I. *The Politics of Federalism in Nigeria.* London, Adonis & Abbey, 2007.

Enwerem, I. M. *Dangerous Awakening: The Politicization of Religion in Nigeria.* Ibadan, FRA, 1996.

Ezegbobelu, E. E. *Challenges of Interreligious Dialogue: Between the Christian and the Muslim Communities in Nigeria.* New York, Peter Lang, 2009.

Falola, T., and, Heaton, M. *A History of Nigeria.* Cambridge, Cambridge University Press, 2008.

Forrest, T. *Politics and Economic Development in Nigeria.* Boulder, CO, Westview Press, 1993.

The Advance of African Capital: The Growth of Nigerian Private Enterprise. Charlottesville, VA, University Press of Virginia, 1994.

Forsyth, F. *The Biafra Story: the Making of an African Legend.* Barnsley, Leo Cooper, 2002.

Gould, M. *The Struggle for Modern Nigeria: The Biafran War 1967-1970.* London, I.B. Tauris, 2011.

Graf, W. D. *The Nigerian State: Political Economy, State, Class and Political System in the Post-Colonial Era.* London, James Currey, 1988.

Hill, J. *Nigeria Since Independence: Forever Fragile?* Basingstoke, Palgrave Macmillan, 2012.

Hunt, J. T. *Politics of Bones: Dr. Owens Wiwa And The Struggle For Nigeria's Oil.* Toronto, McClelland & Stewart, 2005.

Ihonvbere, J. O. *Nigeria: The Politics of Adjustment and Democracy.* New Brunswick, NJ, Transaction, 1993.

Ihonvbere, J. O., and Shaw, T. M. (Eds). *Illusions of Power; Nigeria in Transition.* Africa World Press, 1998.

Ikpuk, J. S. *Militarism of Politics and Neo-colonialism: The Nigerian Experience 1966–1990.* London, Janus Publishing Co, 1995.

Iweriebor, E. E. G. *Radical Politics in Nigeria, 1945–1950: The Significance of the Zikist Movement.* Zaria, Ahmadu Bello University Press, 1996.

Jeyifo, B. (Ed.). *Perspectives on Wole Soyinka: Freedom and Complexity.* Jackson, MS, University Press of Mississippi, 2001.

Wole Soyinka: History, Politics and Colonialism. Cambridge, Cambridge University Press, 2003.

Korieh, C. *Religion, History, and Politics in Nigeria: Essays in Honor of Ogbu U. Kalu.* Lanham, MD, University Press of America, 2005.

Maier, K. *This House Has Fallen: Midnight in Nigeria.* Public Affairs, 2000.

This House Has Fallen: Nigeria in Crisis. Boulder, CO, Westview Press, 2003.

Mathews, M. P. (Ed.). *Nigeria: Current Issues and Historical Background.* Hauppauge, NY, Nova Science Publishers, 2002.

Mbadiwe, K. O. *Rebirth of a Nation.* Oxford ABC, Enugu, Fourth Dimension Publishing, 1991.

Momah, S., and Momah, A. (Eds). *Political Economy of Nigeria under Military Rule, 1894–1993.* Harare, SAPES Books, 1995.

Na'Allah, A. R. (Ed.). *Ogoni's Agonies: Ken Saro-Wiwa and the Crisis in Nigeria.* Africa World Press, 1998.

Nnoli, O. *Ethnicity and Development in Nigeria.* Aldershot, Avebury, 1995.

Nwabueze, B. O., and Akinola, A. (Eds). *Military Rule and Social Justice in Nigeria.* Ibadan, Spectrum Books, 1993.

Nwankwo, A. A. *The Nationalities Question in Nigeria: The Class Foundation of Conflicts.* Enugu, Fourth Dimension, 1990.

Nigeria: The Political Transition and the Future of Democracy. Enugu, Fourth Dimension, 1993.

Obasanjo, O. *My Command: An Account of the Nigerian Civil War 1967–1970.* London, Heinemann, 1981.

Obi, C., and Rustrad, S. *Oil and Insurgency in the Niger Delta: Managing the Complex Politics of Petroviolence.* London, Zed Books, 2011.

Ogbondah, C. W. *Military Regimes and the Press in Nigeria, 1968–1993; Human Rights and National Development.* Lanham, MD, University Press of America, 1993.

Ogwu, U. J., and Olaniyan, R. O. (Eds). *Nigeria's International Economic Relations: Dimensions of Dependence and Change.* Lagos, Nigerian Institute of International Affairs, 1990.

Olaniyan, R. A. *The Amalgamation and its Enemies: An Interpretive History of Modern Nigeria.* Ile-Ife, Obafemi Awolowo University Press, 2003.

Olowu, D., and Soremekun, K. *Governance and Democratisation in Nigeria.* Ibadan, Spectrum Books, 1995.

Olupona, J. (Ed.). *Religion and Peace in Multi-Faith Nigeria.* Ile-Ife, Obafemi Awolowo University Press, 1992.

Oluwakayode Adekson, A. *The 'Civil Society' Problematique: Deconstructing Civility and Southern Nigeria's Ethnic Radicalisation.* London, Routledge, 2003.

Omeje, K. *High Stakes and Stakeholders: Oil Conflict and Security in Nigeria.* Aldershot, Ashgate, 2006.

Omoweh, D. A. *Shell Petroleum Development Company, the State and Underdevelopment of Nigeria's Niger Delta: a Study in Environmental Degradation.* Lawrenceville, NJ, Africa World Press, 2005.

Osaghae, E. E. *Crippled Giant: Nigeria Since Independence.* London, Hurst, 1998.

Paden, J. N. *Muslim Civic Cultures And Conflict Resolution: The Challenge Of Democratic Federalism In Nigeria.* Washington, DC, Brookings Institution Press, 2005.

Peel, J. D. Y. *Ijeshas and Nigerians: The Incorporation of a Yoruba Kingdom*. Cambridge, Cambridge University Press, 1983.

Religious Encounter and the Making of the Yoruba (African Systems of Thought). Bloomington, Indiana University Press, 2001.

Peel, M. *A Swamp Full of Dollars: Pipelines and Paramilitaries at Nigeria's Oil Frontier*. London, IB Tauris, 2011.

Peters, J. *The Nigerian Military and the State*. London, Tauris, 1997.

Rotberg, R. I. *Crafting The New Nigeria: Confronting The Challenges*. Boulder, CO, Lynne Rienner Publications, 2004.

Smith, D. J. *A Culture of Corruption: Everyday Deception and Popular Discontent in Nigeria*. Princeton, NJ, Princeton University Press, 2007.

Soyinka, W. *The Open Sore of a Continent: a Personal Narrative of the Nigerian Crisis (W. E. B. Du Bois Institute Series)*. Oxford University Press, 1998.

The Burden Of Memory, the Muse of Forgiveness (W. E. B. Du Bois Institute Series). Oxford University Press, 1998.

Suberu, R. T. *Federalism and Ethnic Conflict in Nigeria*. Washington, DC, United States Institute for Peace, 2002.

Synge, R. *Nigeria, the Way Forward*. London, Euromoney Books, 1993.

Tijani, H. *Britain, Leftist Nationalists and the Transfer of Power in Nigeria, 1945–1965*. Abingdon, Routledge, 2006.

Udogu, E. I. *Nigeria in the Twenty-First Century: Strategies for Political Stability and Peaceful Coexistence*. Lawrenceville, NJ, Africa World Press, 2005.

Watson, R. *Civil Disorder is the Disease of Ibadan: Chieftaincy and Civic Culture in a Colonial City (Western African Studies)*. Columbus, OH, Ohio University Press, 2002.

West, D. L. *Governing Nigeria: Continuing Issues After the Elections*. Cambridge, MA, World Peace Foundation, 2003.

Wright, S. *Nigeria: Struggle for Stability and Status*. Boulder, CO, Westview Press, 1999.

RÉUNION

Physical and Social Geography

Réunion is a volcanic island in the Indian Ocean lying at the southern extremity of the Mascarene Plateau. Mauritius lies some 190 km to the north-east and Madagascar about 800 km to the west. The island is roughly oval in shape, being about 65 km long and up to 50 km wide; the total area is 2,507 sq km (968 sq miles). Volcanoes have developed along a north-west to south-east angled fault; Piton de la Fournaise (2,624 m) most recently erupted in October 2010. The others are now extinct, although their cones rise to 3,000 m and dominate the island. The heights and the frequent summer cyclones help to create abundant rainfall, which averages 4,714 mm annually in the uplands, and 686 mm at sea-level. Temperatures vary greatly according to altitude, being tropical at sea-level, averaging between 20°C (68°F) and 28°C (82°F), but much cooler in the uplands, with average temperatures between 8°C (46°F) and 19°C (66°F), owing to frequent winter frosts.

The population of Réunion has more than doubled since the 1940s, reaching 808,250 at the January 2008 census; the estimated population in mid-2012 was 865,480, giving a population density of 345.2 inhabitants per sq km. Between the censuses of 1999 and 2008, Réunion's population increased at an average annual rate of 1.6%. According to UN estimates, at mid-2011 25.3% of Réunion's population was under 14 years of age, while 66.1% of the population was aged between 15 and 64 years. The capital is Saint-Denis, with 131,649 inhabitants at the March 1999 census; this figure was estimated to have risen to 144,794 by mid-2011. Other major towns include Saint-Paul, with 99,291 inhabitants, and Saint-Pierre and Le Tampon, with 74,480 and 69,849 inhabitants, respectively, in 2006. The population is of mixed origin, including people of European, African, Indian and Chinese descent.

Recent History

Revised by the editorial staff

Réunion (formerly known as Bourbon) was first occupied in 1642 by French settlers expelled from Madagascar, and was governed as a colony until 1946, when it received full departmental status. In 1974 it became an Overseas Department (Département d'outre-mer) with the status of a region. Réunion administered the small and uninhabited Indian Ocean islands of Bassas da India, Juan de Nova, Europa and the Iles Glorieuses, which are also claimed by Madagascar, and Tromelin, which is also claimed by both Madagascar and Mauritius, until January 2005 when they were placed under the authority of the Prefect, Chief Administrator of the French Southern and Antarctic Territories.

In 1982 the French Government proposed a decentralization plan, envisaging the dissolution of the Conseils généraux and régionaux (Regional and General Councils) in the Overseas Departments and the creation in each department of a single assembly, to be elected on the basis of proportional representation. However, this proposal received considerable opposition in Réunion and the other Overseas Departments, and the plan was eventually abandoned. Revised legislation on decentralization in the Overseas Departments was approved by the French Assemblée nationale (National Assembly) in December.

In the elections to the French Assemblée nationale, which took place in March 1986 under a system of proportional representation, the number of deputies from Réunion was increased from three to five. The Parti Communiste Réunionnais (PCR) won two seats, while the Union pour la Démocratie Française (UDF), the Rassemblement pour la République (RPR) and a newly formed right-wing party, France-Réunion-Avenir (FRA), each secured one seat. In the concurrent elections to the Conseil régional the centre-right RPR-UDF alliance and FRA together received 54.1% of the votes cast, winning 18 and eight of the 45 seats, respectively, while the PCR won 13 seats.

In the second round of the French presidential election, which took place in May 1988, François Mitterrand, the incumbent President and a candidate of the Parti Socialiste (PS), received 60.3% of the votes cast in Réunion. At the ensuing general election for the French Assemblée nationale in June, the system of single-member constituencies was reintroduced. As in the previous general election, the PCR won two of the Réunion seats, while the UDF, the RPR (these two parties allying to form the Union du Rassemblement du Centre) and the FRA each won one seat.

In September 1990 a number of right-wing movements, including the UDF and the RPR, announced the creation of an informal alliance, known as Union pour la France (UPF), to contest the regional elections in 1992.

In March 1990 violent protests took place in support of a popular, but unlicensed, island television service, Télé Free-DOM, following a decision by the French national broadcasting commission, the Conseil Supérieur de l'Audiovisuel (CSA), to award a broadcasting permit to a rival company. In February 1991 the seizure by the CSA of Télé Free-DOM's broadcasting transmitters prompted further violent demonstrations in Saint-Denis. The violence was officially ascribed to widespread discontent with the island's social and economic conditions, and a parliamentary commission was established to ascertain the background to the riots.

In March 1991 the commission of inquiry attributed the riots in February to the inflammatory nature of television programmes, which had been broadcast by Télé Free-DOM in the weeks preceding the disturbances, and blamed the station's director, Dr Camille Sudre, who was also a deputy mayor of Saint-Denis. However, the commission refuted allegations by right-wing and centrist politicians that the PCR had orchestrated the violence.

In March 1992 the mayor of Saint-Denis, Gilbert Annette, expelled Sudre from the majority coalition in the municipal council, after Sudre presented a list of independent candidates to contest regional elections later that month. In the elections to the Conseil régional, which took place on 22 March, Sudre's list of candidates secured 17 seats, while the UPF obtained 14 seats, the PCR nine seats and the PS five seats. In concurrent elections to the Conseil général (which was enlarged to 47 seats), right-wing candidates secured 29 seats, the number of PCR deputies increased to 12, and the number of PS deputies to six; Boyer retained the presidency of the Conseil. Shortly after the elections, Sudre's independent candidates (known as Free-DOM) formed an alliance with the PCR, whereby members of the two groups held a majority of 26 of the 45 seats in the Conseil régional. On 27 March, with the support of the PCR, Sudre was elected as President of the Conseil régional by a majority of 27 votes. The UPF and the PS rejected Sudre's offer to join the Free-DOM-PCR coalition. The PS subsequently appealed against the results of the regional elections, on the grounds that, in contravention of regulations, Sudre's privately owned radio station, Radio Free-DOM, had campaigned on his behalf prior to the elections.

As President of the Conseil régional, Sudre announced that Télé Free-DOM was shortly to resume broadcasting. However, the CSA maintained that if transmissions were resumed Télé Free-DOM would be deemed illegal, and would be subject to judicial proceedings. Jean-Paul Virapoullé, a deputy to the French Assemblée nationale, subsequently proposed the adoption of legislation that would legalize Télé Free-DOM and would provide for the establishment of an independent media sector outside the jurisdiction of the CSA. In April 1992 Télé Free-DOM transmitters were returned, and at the end of May broadcasting was resumed (without the permission of the CSA).

In September 1992 the PCR advocated a boycott of the French referendum on the ratification of the Treaty on European Union, which was to be conducted later that month, in protest at the alleged failure of the French Government to recognize the needs of the Overseas Departments. At the referendum only 26.3% of the registered electorate voted, of whom 74.3% approved the ratification of the treaty. Later that month Boyer and Pierre Lagourgue were elected as representatives to the French Sénat (Senate). The RPR candidate, Paul Moreau, retained his seat.

At the elections to the French Assemblée nationale, which took place in late March 1993, Sudre was defeated by Virapoullé in the second round of voting, while another incumbent right-wing deputy, André Thien Ah Koon, who contested the elections on behalf of the UPF, also retained his seat. The number of PCR deputies in the Assemblée was reduced from two to one (Paul Vergès), while the PS and RPR each secured one of the remaining seats.

In May 1993 the results of the regional elections of March 1992 were annulled, and Sudre was prohibited from engaging in political activity for one year, on the grounds that programmes broadcast by Radio Free-DOM prior to the elections constituted political propaganda. Sudre subsequently selected his wife, Margie, to assume his candidacy in fresh elections to the Conseil régional. In the elections, which took place in June 1993, the Free-DOM list of candidates, headed by Margie Sudre, secured 12 seats, while the UDF obtained 10, the RPR eight, the PCR nine and the PS six seats. Margie Sudre was subsequently elected as President of the Conseil régional, with the support of the nine PCR deputies and three dissident members of the PS, by a majority of 24 votes.

At elections to the Conseil général, which took place in March 1994, the PCR retained 12 seats, while the number of PS deputies increased to 12. The number of seats held by the RPR and UDF declined to five and 11, respectively (compared with six and 14 in the incumbent Conseil). The RPR and UDF subsequently attempted to negotiate an alliance with the PCR; despite long-standing inter-party dissension, however, the PCR and PS established a coalition within the Conseil général, thereby securing a majority of 24 of the 47 seats. In April a member of the PS, Christophe Payet, was elected President of the Conseil général by a majority of 26 votes, defeating Sinimalé; the right-wing parties (which had held the presidency of the Conseil for more than 40 years) boycotted the poll. The PS and PCR signed an agreement, whereby they were to control the administration of the Conseil général jointly, and indicated that centrist deputies might be allowed to enter the alliance. In July Boyer's prison sentence was reduced on appeal to a term of one year.

In November 1994 an official visit to Réunion by Edouard Balladur, the French Prime Minister (and declared candidate for the presidential election in 1995), provoked strike action in protest at his opposition to the establishment of social equality between the Overseas Departments and metropolitan France. Jacques Chirac, the official presidential candidate of the RPR, visited the island in December 1994, when he was endorsed by the organ of the PCR, *Témoignages*, after declaring his commitment to the issue of social equality. In the second round of the presidential election, which took place in May 1995, the socialist candidate, Lionel Jospin, secured 56% of votes cast on Réunion, while Chirac won 44% of the votes (although Chirac obtained the highest number of votes in total); the PCR and Free-DOM had advised their supporters not to vote for Balladur, because of his opposition to the principle of social equality.

With effect from the beginning of 1996 the social security systems of the Overseas Departments were aligned with those of metropolitan France. Paul Vergès, joint candidate of the PCR and the PS, was elected to the French Sénat in April, securing 51.9% of the votes cast. Fred K/Bidy won 40.0% of the votes, failing to retain Eric Boyer's seat for the RPR. In the by-election to replace Paul Vergès, which took place in September, Claude Hoarau, the PCR candidate, was elected with 56.0% of the votes cast, while Margie Sudre obtained 44.0%. A new majority alliance between Free-DOM, the RPR and the UDF was subsequently formed in the Conseil régional, with the re-election of its 19-member permanent commission in October.

In October 1996 the trial of a number of politicians and business executives, who had been arrested in 1993–94 on charges of corruption, took place, after three years of investigations. Annette was convicted and, in December of that year, received a prison sentence, although it was reduced on appeal in December 1997. Jacques de Châteauvieux, the Chairman of Groupe Sucreries de Bourbon, was found guilty of bribery and was also jailed. Some 20 others were also found guilty of corruption.

Four left-wing candidates were successful in elections to the French Assemblée nationale held in May and June 1997. Claude Hoarau (PCR) retained his seat and was joined by Huguette Bello and Elie Hoarau, also both from the PCR, and Michel Tamaya (PS), while André Thien Ah Koon, representing the RPR-UDF coalition, was re-elected.

In February 1998 the PCR (led by Paul Vergès), the PS and several right-wing mayors presented a joint list of candidates, known as the Rassemblement, to contest forthcoming elections. In the elections to the Conseil régional, which took place on 15 March, the Rassemblement secured 19 seats, while the UDF obtained nine seats and the RPR eight, with various left-wing candidates representing Free-DOM winning five. Vergès was elected President of the Conseil régional on 23 March, with the support of the deputies belonging to the Rassemblement and Free-DOM groups. In concurrent elections to an expanded 49-member Conseil général, right-wing candidates (including those on the Rassemblement's list) secured 27 seats, while left-wing candidates obtained 22 seats, the PCR and the PS each winning 10 seats. At the end of the month Jean-Luc Poudroux of the UDF was elected President of the Conseil général, with the support of two left-wing deputies.

In October 1998 Réunion's three PCR deputies to the French Assemblée nationale proposed legislation providing for the division of the island into two departments, with Saint-Pierre to gain equal status with Saint-Denis as the chief town of a department. In December 1999, while attending the Heads of State summit of the Indian Ocean Commission (IOC) on the island, President Chirac announced that he supported the creation of a second department on Réunion, as part of a number of proposed changes to the institutional future and socio-economic development of the French Overseas Departments. In March 2000 the French Secretary of State for Overseas Departments and Territories declared that Réunion was to be divided into two departments, Réunion South and Réunion North, as of 1 January 2001. However, both the proposed date and the geographical division of the island were rejected by the PS, although it stated that it remained in favour of the creation of a second department. Virapoullé, now President of the UDF, expressed his opposition to the proposals. Demonstrations both for and against the division of the island took place in March 2000. It was subsequently agreed that the proposals would not be effected until 1 January 2002, and changes were made to the initial plans regarding the geographical division of the island. However, on 15 June 2000 the creation of a second department was rejected by the French Sénat by 203 votes to 111. In November the Assemblée nationale definitively rejected the creation of a second department, but approved the changes to the institutional future of the Overseas Departments, which were finally ratified by the Constitutional Council in December. Also in that month Paul Vergès was arrested on charges of forgery and fraud in connection with his election to the Sénat in 1996.

At municipal elections, held in March 2001, the left-wing parties experienced significant losses. Notably, the PS mayor of Saint-Denis, Michel Tamaya, was defeated by the RPR candidate, René-Paul Victoria. The losses were widely interpreted as a general rejection of Jospin's proposals to create a second department on the island. At elections to the Conseil général, held concurrently, the right-wing parties also made substantial gains, obtaining 38 of the 49 seats; the UDF retained its majority and Jean-Luc Poudroux was re-elected as President. In July Elie Hoarau was obliged to resign from the French Assemblée nationale, following his conviction on charges of electoral fraud, as a result of which he received a one-year prison sentence and a three-year interdiction on holding public office.

In the first round of the presidential election, which was held on 21 April 2002, Jospin secured 39.0% of the valid votes cast in the department (although he was eliminated nationally), followed by Chirac, who received 37.1%. In the second round, on 5 May, Chirac overwhelmingly defeated the candidate of the extreme right-wing Front National, Jean-Marie Le Pen, with 91.9% of the vote. At elections to the Assemblée nationale in June, André Thien Ah Koon, allied to the new Union pour la Majorité Présidentielle (UMP, which had recently been formed by the merger of the RPR, Démocratie Libérale and elements of the UDF), and Bello were re-elected. Tamaya lost his seat to Victoria of the UMP, Claude Hoarau lost to Bertho Audifax of the UMP, while Elie Hoarau, who was declared ineligible to stand for re-election, was replaced by Christophe Payet of the PS. In November the UMP was renamed the Union pour un Mouvement Populaire.

In elections to the Conseil régional, which took place on 21 and 28 March 2004, the Alliance, a joint list of candidates led by the PCR, secured 27 seats. The UMP won 11 seats, and an alliance of the PS and Les verts Réunion obtained seven seats. Following concurrent elections to the Conseil général, to renew 25 of the 49 seats, right-wing candidates held 30 seats, while left-wing candidates held 19. On 1 April Nassimah Dindar of the UMP was elected to succeed Poudroux as President of the Conseil général. Paul Vergès was re-elected as President of the Conseil régional on the following day. In February 2005 Gélite Hoarau replaced Paul Vergès as the PCR's representative to the Sénat.

In late May 2005 a national referendum on ratification of the proposed constitutional treaty of the European Union was held, at which 59.9% of Réunion's electorate joined with a majority of French voters in rejecting the treaty; voter turn-out on the island was around 53%.

In the first round of the French presidential election, held on 22 April 2007, Ségolène Royal of the PS secured 46.2% of the votes cast in Réunion, while Nicolas Sarkozy of the UMP received 25.1%. Both therefore proceeded to the second round of voting, which took place on 6 May. Sarkozy claimed victory in the second round ballot at national level; however, voting on Réunion again went in favour of Royal, who received 63.6% of the island vote. Legislative elections took place in June in which Victoria and Bello both retained their seats in the Assemblée nationale, but Audifax lost his seat to Jean-Claude Fruteau of the PS. Didier Robert of the UMP defeated Paul Vergès, while Patrick Lebreton of the PS was also elected. In March 2008 Dindar was re-elected to the presidency of the Conseil général.

In January 2009 workers in Guadeloupe, a French overseas territory in the Caribbean, went on strike to protest at rising fuel and food prices and the deterioration of living conditions on the island. The unrest soon spread to other Departments, including Réunion, where unemployment had reached 25.2% in February and living costs had increased significantly. In early March thousands of workers took to the streets of Saint-Denis, demanding a 20% reduction in the price of basic goods, and a wage increase of €200 per month for low-paid workers. The protests turned violent as demonstrators began throwing stones and police responded by firing tear gas to disperse the crowds.

In January 2010 President Sarkozy visited Réunion for the first time since his election to the presidency. Also in that month Michel Lalande replaced Pierre-Henry Maccioni as Prefect. Elections to the Conseil régional took place on 14 and 21 March, at which the La Réunion en Confiance alliance led by Robert won 27 seats. The Liste de l'Alliance, headed by Paul Vergès' PCR, took 12 seats, while the PS-led Pour une Réunion Plus Juste avec l'Union des Socialistes Alliance secured six seats. On 26 March Robert was elected to succeed Vergès as President of the Conseil régional.

In October 2011 a fire broke out in Maïdo forest in the National Park, threatening areas of endemic plants, rare wildlife species and key micro-habitats for biodiversity. (The site was inscribed on the UNESCO World Heritage List in July 2010). The French authorities were heavily criticized by local and metropolitan officials for taking six days to react and their delay in sending fire-fighting planes; some 2,824 ha of land were destroyed before the fire could be brought under control.

In early 2012 several nights of social unrest were reported; initially the protests were directed at the high cost of fuel prices with transporters blocking fuel outlets, but subsequently protests at the generally high cost of living spread across the island and security forces were brought in from France to quell the violence. Negotiations between local politicians, civil society representatives, transporters and petrol companies were held by Lalande and an agreement was reached to lower prices of fuel and electricity for households on modest income and to freeze prices for 60 staple products from 1 March onwards.

In the first round of the French presidential election, held on 22 April 2012, François Hollande (of the PS) secured 53.3% of the votes cast on Réunion, while incumbent President Sarkozy won 17.96%; both proceeded to a second round of voting, which took place on 6 May. In the second ballot, Hollande secured a resounding victory, winning 71.49% of the vote, compared with 28.5% for Sarkozy. Hollande was inaugurated on 15 May in Paris, France. General elections to the French Assemblée nationale were held in June, at which Thierry Robert (representing the Mouvement Démocrate, part of the Le Centre pour la France coalition) was elected with 66.9% of the votes cast on Réunion, defeating Jean-Claude Lacouture (of the UMP), who received 33.1%. In August Jean-Luc Marx replaced Lalande as Prefect.

In January 1986 France was admitted to the IOC, owing to its sovereignty over Réunion. Réunion was given the right to host ministerial meetings of the IOC, but is not eligible to occupy the presidency, owing to its non-sovereign status.

Economy

Revised by the editorial staff

As a result of its connection with France, Réunion's economy is relatively developed, especially in comparison with its sub-Saharan African neighbours. Réunion's gross national income in 1995 was estimated at 29,200m. French francs, equivalent to about 44,300 francs per head. Between the censuses of 1999 and 2008, Réunion's population increased at an average annual rate of 1.6%. According to UN estimates, the population at mid-2012 totalled 865,480, giving a population density of 345.2 per sq km. In 2010, according to official figures, Réunion's gross domestic product (GDP), measured at current prices, was €14,900m.; in 2009 GDP per head totalled €18,250. GDP increased, in real terms, at an average annual rate of 5.9% in 2000–09; growth in 2008 was 7.0%.

The economy has traditionally been based on agriculture, but in 2007 the sector directly contributed only 1.3% of GDP and, in 2008, salaried agricultural workers accounted for only 1.6% of the economically active population. (In 2006 some 10.9% of the economically active population was unsalaried.) Agricultural GDP increased at an average annual rate of 3.9% during 1990–2000; growth in 2001 was 3.1%. At 31 December 2003 there were 7,621 farmers, compared to 14,699 in 1989; similarly, agricultural land area had decreased from 54,510 ha in 1989 to 48,233 ha in 2003. In recent years some 19.0% of the total land area has been cultivated; around a further 21% of land is classified as agricultural but remains uncultivated, mainly because of the volcanic nature of the soil, but also owing to increasing urbanization. Sugar cane is the principal crop and has formed the basis of the economy for over a century; the secondary usage of agricultural land is for fodder, and this sector is growing, with relatively high yields. In 2007 sugar accounted for 37.9% of export earnings, and although export quantities fell in 2009 they grew by 4.4% in 2010. According to provisional figures, in 2004 some 53% of the arable land was used for sugar plantations. The cane is grown on nearly all the good cultivable land up to 800 m above sea-level on the leeward side of the island, except in the relatively dry north-west, and up to 500 m on the windward side. The sugar cane harvest was consistently above 1.8m. metric tons between 2000–02 despite the damage caused by cyclones. However, heavy rains reduced the sugar content of the cane: during the same period, raw sugar production fell from 204,000 tons to 194,313 tons; by 2003 this figure had recovered to 207,668 tons. Sugar production reached just over 221,000 tons in 2004, a lower yield than might have been expected, owing to heavy rains and low sunshine levels. Output declined to 202,342 tons in 2005, but preliminary figures suggested a mild improvement in the late 2000s; in 2009 production rose to an estimated 207,000 tons. According to official figures 1.8m. tons of sugar canes was harvested in 2008.

Geraniums, vetiver and ylang ylang are grown for the production of aromatic essences. Exporters of oil of geranium and vetiver have experienced difficulty in competing with new producers whose prices are much lower. Output of oil of geranium declined to 8.8 metric tons in 2000 and by 2007 production had fallen to 2.0 tons. Output of vetiver totalled 12.1 tons in 1987, but subsequently declined to less than 0.5 tons in 2004. An agreement between Réunion, Madagascar and the Comoros concerning price and export quotas on vanilla ended in 1992 and production in that year reached 116.5 tons. However, between 1997 and 2003 annual production averaged just over 32 tons. In 2004 output of vanilla was reported at 25 tons and production remained low in subsequent years: falling to 21 tons in 2005 before rising, slightly, to an estimated 22 tons in 2006. Tobacco cultivation (introduced at the beginning of the century) produced a crop of 192.8 tons in 1988. Cyclone damage destroyed 115 of the island's 400 tobacco drying sheds in 1989/90 and production declined sharply, to 107.8 tons in 1990, to 73.3 tons in 1991, and to 22 tons in 1992; production between 2000–04 remained at an estimated 20 tons. A variety of tropical fruits is grown for export, including pineapples, lychees, bananas and mangoes, and the island is self-sufficient in cattle and pigs, both of which demonstrated strong growth at the end of the 1990s, and 80% self-sufficient in vegetables. Overall, however, substantial food imports are necessary to supply the dense population.

Although fish are not abundant off Réunion's coast, the commercial fishing industry is an important source of income and employment, especially in the deep-sea sector. The largest fishing vessels make voyages lasting several months, to catch spiny lobsters (langoustes) that breed in the cold waters near Antarctica. In an attempt to preserve resources, the fishing quota for 1989 was reduced, and the total catch declined to 1,725 metric tons. The total catch increased substantially thereafter, reaching 4,703 tons by 1998, before declining again; the total catch in 2010 was 3,200 tons.

In 2007 industry (including manufacturing, construction and power) contributed 16.6% of GDP and salaried workers within the sector accounted for 16.0% of the salaried population in 2008. According to the UN, industrial GDP increased at an average annual rate of 4.3% during 1990–99; growth in 2001 was 3.7%. A Law of Adjustment for Overseas Territories had a favourable effect on the overall number of enterprises in 2001, as 4,500 were created, while 2,900 were closed down. In 2003 of the 292 companies registered in the industry sector more than one-half were involved in producing intermediary goods (including metal items, construction materials, and paper, card and plastic), just under one-quarter were involved in food-processing and a slightly smaller number in the production of other consumables (including textiles and furnishings, printed materials, and pharmaceuticals).

No mineral resources have been identified in Réunion and imports of refined petroleum products comprised 12.5% of the value of total imports in 2011. In 2003 the island imported 83.5% of its fuel requirements. Energy is derived principally from thermal and hydroelectric power. Power plants at Bois-Rouge and Le Gol produce around 45% of the island's total energy requirements; almost one-third of the electricity generated is produced using a mixture of coal and bagasse, a by-product of sugar cane. Total electricity production in 2011 was 2,750m. kWh.

Services (including transport, communications, trade and finance) contributed 82.0% of GDP in 2007 and employed 82.4% of the salaried population in 2008. The public sector accounts for more than two-thirds of employment in the services sector. In 2002 the 10 largest companies in terms of revenue were all from the services sector, eight of them involved in volume retail and distribution (principally of consumables but also automobiles). In terms of employment eight of the 10 largest companies provided services, while the other two were involved in construction. The development of tourism is actively promoted, and it is hoped that increased investment in this sector will lead to higher receipts and will help to reduce the trade deficit, as well as provide new jobs. In 1988 Réunion received aid from the European Community (now the European Union—EU) to stimulate the sector. Tourist arrivals subsequently increased considerably, rising by an average of 9.2% per year in 1990–97. In 2005 409,000 tourists visited Réunion and tourism receipts totalled €308.8m. in that year. However, a dramatic decline occurred in 2006 following an epidemic of the 'chikungunya' virus, and hotels were reporting that reservations during the peak season were down by 60%. The figure was not as substantial as feared, although the 279,000 visitors in 2006 did represent a 31.8% decline on the previous year's results. A recovery was experienced in 2007 with 380,500 tourists visiting Réunion and receipts totalled €292.9m.; tourist arrivals increased further, totalling 471,300 by 2011 (81.0% of whom were from metropolitan France).

In 2011 Réunion recorded a trade deficit of €4,488.3m. The principal sources of imports in 2010 were France (54.2%), Singapore and the People's Republic of China. The principal market for exports in 2010, were France (31.6%), Mayotte, Madagascar and Spain. The principal exports in 2011 were prepared foodstuffs (59.8% of total exports), electrical and electronic equipment and components, and transport equipment. The principal imports in that year were electrical and electronic equipment and components (18.8% of total imports), transport equipment, prepared foodstuffs and refined petroleum products. The contribution of exports to GDP declined from 12% at the beginning of the 1970s to 2% in 1992, owing partly to a decline in world sugar prices, and stood at 1.9% in 2010. In 1998 the volume of goods passing through the ports increased, exceeding 3m. metric tons for the first time, principally as a result of a rise in imports; the figure has remained consistently above 3m. tons since that time. Fuel imports were boosted by the growing number of motor vehicles and a greater number of direct flights from Réunion.

The close connection with France protects the island from the dangers inherent in the narrowness of its economic base. Nevertheless, unemployment and inflation, compounded after 1974 by a number of bankruptcies among small sugar planters, have been the cause of major social and economic problems. The annual rate of inflation averaged 1.8% in 2001–10; consumer prices increased by 1.5% in 2010 and by 2.4% in 2011. An estimated 23.6% of the labour force were unemployed in December 2008. Unemployment among Réunion's youth (aged 15–24) has remained high—from 49.1% in 2005 it continued to increase to 49.6% in 2009 and to 55.3% in mid-2010. Since 1980 the Government has invested significant sums in a series of public works projects in an effort to create jobs and to alleviate the high level of seasonal unemployment following the sugar cane harvest. However, large numbers of workers emigrate in search of employment each year, principally to France.

The French Government has increased its infrastructural spending in Réunion, particularly on improvements to health services, housing, electricity supply and communication facilities for low-income families. In January 1989 legislation that established a guaranteed minimum income was introduced. In November 1990 the French Government announced measures aimed at establishing parity of the four Overseas Departments with metropolitan France in social and economic programmes. The reforms included the standardization by 1992 of minimum wage levels in Réunion with those operating in the other three Overseas Departments. It was envisaged that minimum wages in the Overseas Departments would be equal with those in metropolitan France by 1995, although this was to be achieved by way of trade union negotiations with employers rather than by government wage guarantees.

In April 1991 representatives of the four Overseas Departments in the French Assemblée nationale and Sénat formed an interparliamentary group to safeguard and promote the agricultural economies of these territories. In July 1992, however, the French Government announced an increase in minimum income of 3.3%, and in family allowance of 20% (far less than required to establish parity with metropolitan France). In September the Conseil régional adopted an economic development programme, known as the emergency plan, which provided for the creation of an export free zone (EFZ). Under the emergency plan, the French Government would subsidize wages and some employers' contributions of companies operating within the EFZ. By 1993 levels of family allowance in the Overseas Departments had reached parity with those in force in metropolitan France, as envisaged. In early 1994, however, the French Government indicated that it intended to give priority to the reduction of unemployment rather than the standardization of minimum wage levels, and announced a programme of economic and social development for the Overseas Departments, whereby approximately one-third of the unemployed population were to be involved in community projects; enterprises were to receive incentives to engage the unemployed, and a number of economic sectors that had been disadvantaged by international competition were to be exempted from certain taxes. In June the Conseil régional drafted a five-year development plan, at a projected cost of 10,000m. French francs, of which 4,900m. francs were to be financed by the EU: these funds were principally designated to support export initiatives and to improve infrastructure and the environment; allocations were also made to the tourism sector.

In early 1995 the minimum wage level in Réunion was about 14% below that in metropolitan France. However, by 1 January 1996 the minimum wage in Réunion was equal to that in metropolitan France, having increased on average by 23% since the end of 1993. In May 2000 the French Government announced that it had agreed to equalize the minimum taxable wage in the Overseas Departments with that of metropolitan France, within a period of three years; the current minimum taxable wage in Réunion was 20% lower than that of metropolitan France. This measure was approved by the French Sénat in June. In early 2001 the French Government announced that it was to spend €84m. on improving educational facilities in Réunion, as part of a major programme of investment in the Overseas Territories and Departments.

In early 2009 thousands of Réunionnais demonstrated in cities calling for lower prices for essential items and a salary increase of €200 a month for the lowest paid workers, following similar successful protests in the French Caribbean islands of Guadeloupe and Martinique. During a visit to Réunion in January 2010 the French President, Nicolas Sarkozy, announced plans to create a 'green laboratory' on Réunion with the intention of making the island energy self-sufficient by 2030. (A consequent injection of public subsidies into solar projects led to a 21.7% rise in the creation of enterprises on the island; the French Institut National de la Statistique et des Études Économiques, however, noted that 96.2% of these enterprises had no salaried workers.) It was proposed that Réunion would harness its considerable solar and thermal power potential and would introduce electric cars (produced by the French company Renault, in alliance with Nissan of Japan) and solar-powered charging stations. In August 2011 a study was presented by the French Commissioner for Indian Ocean Development to the island authorities that highlighted a lack of international opening on an economic level, the small size of undercapitalized local companies and an absence of 'risk culture'. The report recommended the rationalizing of aid for international companies to create an export platform for a shared strategy for 2012 and 2013.

Statistical Survey

Source (unless otherwise indicated): Institut National de la Statistique et des Études Économiques, Service Régional de la Réunion, 15 rue de l'Ecole, 97490 Sainte-Clotilde; tel. 262-48-81-00; fax 262-41-09-81; internet www.insee.fr/fr/insee_regions/reunion.

AREA AND POPULATION

Area: 2,507 sq km (968 sq miles).

Population: 706,180 (males 347,076, females 359,104) at census of 8 March 1999; 816,364 at census of 1 January 2009. Note: According to new census methodology, data in 2009 refer to median figures based on the collection of raw data over a five-year period (2006–11). *1 January 2011:* 840,000. *Mid-2012* (UN estimate): 865,480 (Source: UN, *World Population Prospects: The 2010 Revision*).

Density (at mid-2012): 345.2 per sq km.

Population by Age and Sex (UN estimates at mid-2012): *0–14:* 219,343 (males 111,204, females 108,139); *15–64:* 572,107 (males 280,076, females 292,031); *65 and over:* 74,030 (males 32,465, females 41,565); *Total* 865,480 (males 423,745, females 441,735) (Source: UN, *World Population Prospects: The 2010 Revision*).

Principal Towns (population at census of January 2006): Saint-Denis (capital) 138,314; Saint-Paul 99,291; Saint-Pierre 74,480; Le Tampon 69,849; Saint-André 51,817; Saint-Louis 49,455. *Mid-2011* (incl. suburbs, UN estimate): Saint-Denis 144,794 (Source: UN, *World Urbanization Prospects: The 2011 Revision*).

Births, Marriages and Deaths (2010 unless otherwise indicated): Registered live births 14,146 (birth rate 17.4 per 1,000); Registered marriages (2009) 2,919 (marriage rate 3.6 per 1,000); Registered deaths 4,220 (death rate 5.1 per 1,000).

Life Expectancy (years at birth, 2008): Males 74.6; females 82.1.

Economically Active Population (persons aged 15 years and over, 1999 census): Agriculture, hunting, forestry and fishing 9,562; Mining, manufacturing, electricity, gas and water 13,424; Construction 11,003; Wholesale and retail trade 24,658; Transport, storage and communications 5,494; Financing, insurance and real estate 4,851; Business services 11,225; Public administration 39,052; Education 23,325; Health and social work 17,376; Other services 13,707; *Total employed* 173,677 (males 100,634, females 73,043); Unemployed 124,203 (males 63,519, females 60,684); *Total labour force* 297,880 (males 164,153, females 133,727). Figures exclude 967 persons on compulsory military service (males 945, females 22). *2008* (salaried workers at 1 January, preliminary): Agriculture 3,262; Industry (incl. energy) 14,431; Construction 18,658; Trade 27,112; Transport 7,718; Financial activities and real estate 6,102; Private services 19,484; Business services 19,819; Health and welfare 18,340; Education 23,474; Public administration 48,174; Total employed 206,574. Note: Total excludes 26,626 non-salaried workers. *Unemployed* (at 1 January 2008): 72,133.

HEALTH AND WELFARE

Key Indicators

Total Fertility Rate (children per woman, 2008): 2.5.

Physicians (per 1,000 head, 2011): 2.1.

Hospital Beds (per 1,000 head, 2000): 3.7.

For definitions, see explanatory note on p. vi.

AGRICULTURE, ETC.

Principal Crops ('000 metric tons, 2010, FAO estimates): Maize 13.8; Potatoes 7.4; Sugar cane 1,930.0; Cabbages and other brassicas 2.7; Lettuce and chicory 4.5; Tomatoes 11.8; Cauliflowers and broccoli 5.2; Pumpkins, squash and gourds 0.8; Eggplants (Aubergines) 0.8; Onions and shallots, green 4.7; Beans, green 3.8; Carrots and turnips 2.0; Bananas 7.2; Tangerines, mandarins, clementines and satsumas 3.4; Mangoes, mangosteens and guavas 2.5; Pineapples 17.6. *Aggregate Production* ('000 metric tons, may include official, semi-official or estimated data): Total vegetables (incl. melons) 46.3; Total fruits (excl. melons) 59.4.

Livestock ('000 head, 2010, FAO estimates): Cattle 33.2; Pigs 80.7; Sheep 1.0; Goats 40.0; Chickens 15,000.

Livestock Products ('000 metric tons, 2010, FAO estimates): Cattle meat 1.7; Pig meat 12.0; Chicken meat 16.8; Rabbit meat 2.1; Cow's milk 29.8; Hen eggs 6.7.

Forestry ('000 cu m, 1991): *Roundwood Removals:* Sawlogs, veneer logs and logs for sleepers 4.2; Other industrial wood 0.9 (FAO estimate); Fuel wood 31.0 (FAO estimate); Total 36.1. *Sawnwood Production:* 2.2. *1992–2010:* Annual production assumed to be unchanged from 1991 (FAO estimates).

Fishing (metric tons, live weight, 2010, all capture, FAO estimates): Albacore 600; Yellowfin tuna 475; Bigeye tuna 507; Swordfish 942; Common dolphinfish 60; *Total catch* (incl. others) 3,200.

Source: FAO.

INDUSTRY

Selected Products (metric tons, 2011, unless otherwise indicated): Sugar 206,000; Oil of geranium 2 (2007); Oil of vetiver root 0.4 (2002); Rum (hl) 93,704 (2010); Electric energy (million kWh) 2,750 (Source: partly Institut d'Emission des Départements d'Outre-mer, *Rapport Annuel 2011*).

FINANCE

Currency and Exchange Rates: The French franc was used until the end of February 2002. Euro notes and coins were introduced on 1 January 2002, and the euro became the sole legal tender from 18 February. Some of the figures in this Survey are still in terms of francs. For details of exchange rates, see Mayotte.

Budget (€ million): *Regional Budget* (2009): Revenue 750 (Taxes 293, Transfers received 324, Loans 133); Expenditure 750 (Current expenditure 284, Capital 466). *Departmental Budget* (2009): Revenue 1,415.0 (State endowments 884.5, Direct and indirect taxes 392.3, Loans 60.0, Other subsidies—Europe and other bodies) 39.4, Other revenues and receipts 38.8); Expenditure 1,415.0 (Social welfare 843.2, General services 278.8, Development 56.2, Teaching 62.0, Networks and infrastructure 43.9, Security 53.2, Planning and environment 10.6, Culture, societies, youth and sports 10.7, Traffic 56.3). Source: Conseil général, *Le Budget du Département*.

Money Supply (million francs at 31 December 1996): Currency outside banks 4,050; Demand deposits at banks 7,469; Total money 11,519.

Cost of Living (Consumer Price Index; base: 2000 = 100): All items 118.8 in 2009; 120.6 in 2010; 123.5 in 2011. Source: ILO.

Expenditure on the Gross Domestic Product (€ million at current prices, 2010): Private final consumption expenditure 9,590; Government final consumption expenditure 5,720; Gross capital formation 3,150; *Total domestic expenditure* 18,460; Exports of goods 280; *Less* Imports of goods 4,260; Tourist expenditure 300; Statistical discrepancy 120; *GDP in market prices* 14,900.

Gross Domestic Product by Economic Activity (€ million at current prices, 2007): Agriculture, forestry and fishing 177; Mining, manufacturing, electricity, gas and water 917; Construction 1,274; Wholesale and retail trade 1,182; Transport and communications 820; Finance and insurance 704; Public administration 1,521; Education, health and social work 3,128; Other services (incl. hotels and restaurants) 3,472; *Sub-total* 13,196; *Less* Financial intermediation services indirectly measured 462; *Gross value-added at basic prices* 12,734; Taxes on products, *less* subsidies on products 1,235; *GDP in market prices* 13,969.

EXTERNAL TRADE

Principal Commodities (€ million, 2011): *Imports:* Agriculture, forestry and fishing 101.2; Mining and quarrying 77.1 (Natural hydrocarbons 76.9); Prepared foodstuffs 699.3; Refined petroleum products 597.1; Electrical and electronic equipment and components 895.6 (Information products and electronics 342.4, Electronic equipment and household electrical goods 295.5, Industrial and agricultural machinery 257.6); Transport equipment 737.4; Other industrial products 1,608.5 (Textiles and footwear 250.2, Paper and paperboard 142.1, Chemicals and perfumes 224.0, Pharmaceutical products 267.5, Plastic products 231.0, Metal products 252.5, Miscellaneous manufactured products 241.3); Printed books 58.1; Total 4,775.2. *Exports:* Agriculture, forestry and fishing 3.3; Industrial and household waste 25.7; Prepared foodstuffs 171.5; Refined petroleum products 2.0; Electrical and electronic equipment and components 30.4 (Information products and electronics 15.7, Electronic equipment and household electrical goods 3.7, Industrial and agricultural machinery 11.0); Transport equipment 25.7; Other industrial products 26.8 (Textiles and footwear 2.6, Paper and paperboard 1.3, Chemicals and perfumes 6.6, Pharmaceutical products 0.9, Plastic products 1.5, Metal products 9.8, Miscellaneous manufactured products 3.8); Total 286.9. Note: Totals may not be equal to the sum of components, owing to rounding (Source: Source: Institut d'Emission des Départements d'Outre-mer, *Rapport Annuel 2011*).

Principal Trading Partners (€ million, 2010): *Imports:* Belgium 52.1; China, People's Republic 287.5; France 2,312.8; Germany 200.6; Italy 89.8; Singapore 389.8; South Africa 100.0; Spain 62.0; Total (incl. others) 4,265.2. *Exports f.o.b.:* France 88.9; Hong Kong 13.4; Italy 6.7; Japan 10.5; Madagascar 15.1; Mauritius 7.4; Mayotte 26.5; Spain 18.0; USA 8.4; Total (incl. others) 281.5.

TRANSPORT

Road Traffic (1 January 2005): Motor vehicles in use 338,500.

Shipping: *Merchant Fleet* (total displacement at 31 December 1992): 21,000 grt (Source: UN, *Statistical Yearbook*); *Traffic* (2007): Passenger arrivals 14,667; Passenger departures 16,225; Vessels entered 709; Freight unloaded 3,652,600 metric tons; Freight loaded 559,500 metric tons; Containers unloaded 111,952 TEUs; Containers loaded 112,921 TEUs.

Civil Aviation (2011): Passenger arrivals 1,096,610; Passenger departures 1,095,644; Freight unloaded 47,868 metric tons; Freight loaded 8,011 metric tons (Source: Institut d'Emission des Départements d'Outre-mer, *Rapport Annuel 2011*).

TOURISM

Tourist Arrivals: 421,900 in 2009; 420,300 in 2010; 471,300 in 2011 (Source: Institut d'Emission des Départements d'Outre-mer, *Rapport Annuel 2011*).

Arrivals by Country of Residence (2011): France (metropolitan) 381,600; Other EU 19,600; Mauritius 18,200; Total (incl. others) 471,300 (Source: Institut d'Emission des Départements d'Outre-mer, *La Réunion: Rapport Annuel 2011*).

Tourism Receipts (€ million): 308.8 in 2005; 224.8 in 2006; 292.9 in 2007.

COMMUNICATIONS MEDIA

Television Receivers ('000 in use, 1998): 130 in use. Source: UNESCO, *Statistical Yearbook*.

Telephones ('000 main lines in use, 2010): 480.9. Source: International Telecommunication Union.

Mobile Cellular Telephones ('000 subscribers, 2008): 579.2. Source: International Telecommunication Union.

Personal Computers ('000 in use, 2004): 279. Source: International Telecommunication Union.

Internet Users ('000, 2009): 300. Source: International Telecommunication Union.

Broadband Subscribers ('000, 2009): 185. Source: International Telecommunication Union.

Book Production (1992): 69 titles (50 books; 19 pamphlets). Source: UNESCO, *Statistical Yearbook*.

Daily Newspapers (1996): 3 (estimated average circulation 55,000 copies). Source: UNESCO, *Statistical Yearbook*.

Non-daily Newspapers (1988, estimate): 4 (average circulation 20,000 copies). Source: UNESCO, *Statistical Yearbook*.

EDUCATION

Pre-primary and Primary (2010/11, unless otherwise indicated): Schools 532 (pre-primary 174, primary 358 in 2003/04); public sector pupils 112,452 (pre-primary 41,111, primary 71,341); private pupils 9,192 (pre-primary 3,293, primary 5,899).

Secondary (2010/11, unless otherwise indicated): Schools 121 (112 public sector, 9 private) (2005/06); pupils 100,995 (public sector 94,269, private 6,726).

University (2009/10): Institution 1; students 11,659.

Other Higher (2006/07): Students 4,988.

Teaching Staff (31 December 2007): Pre-primary and primary 6,866; Secondary 9,178; University 498; Other higher 476.

Directory

The Government

(September 2012)

HEAD OF STATE

President: FRANÇOIS HOLLANDE.

Prefect: JEAN-LUC MARX, Préfecture, pl. du Barachois, 97405 Saint-Denis Cédex; tel. 262-40-77-77; fax 262-41-73-74; e-mail courrier@reunion.pref.gouv.fr; internet www.reunion.pref.gouv.fr.

DEPARTMENTAL ADMINISTRATION

President of the Conseil général: NASSIMAH DINDAR (UMP), Hôtel du Département, 2 rue de la Source, 97488 Saint-Denis Cédex; tel. 262-90-30-30; fax 262-90-39-99; internet www.cg974.fr.

President of the Conseil régional: DIDIER ROBERT (UMP), Hôtel de Région Pierre Lagourgue, ave René Cassin, Moufia, BP 7190, 97719 Saint-Denis Cédex 9; tel. 262-48-70-00; fax 262-48-70-71; e-mail region.reunion@cr-reunion.fr; internet www.regionreunion.com.

Election, Conseil Régional, 14 and 21 March 2010

Party	Seats
La Réunion en Confiance*	27
Liste de l'Alliance†	12
Pour une Réunion Plus Juste avec l'Union des Socialistes‡	6
Total	45

* An alliance led by the UMP.
† An alliance led by the PCR.
‡ An alliance led by the PS.

REPRESENTATIVES TO THE FRENCH PARLIAMENT

Deputies to the French National Assembly: ERICKA BAREIGTS (PS), HUGUETTE BELLO (Divers Gauche), JEAN JACQUES VLODY (PS), PATRICK LEBRETON (PS), JEAN-CLAUDE FRUTEAU (PS), MONIQUE ORPHÉ (PS), THIERRY ROBERT (Le Centre pour la France/MoDem).

Representatives to the French Senate: JACQUELINE FARREYROL (UMP), MICHEL FONTAINE (UMP), PAUL VERGÈS (PCR), MICHEL VERGOZ (PS).

GOVERNMENT OFFICES

Direction des Actions de Solidarité et d'Intégration (DASI): 26 ave de la Victoire, 97488 Saint-Denis Cédex; tel. 262-90-35-44; fax 262-90-39-94.

Direction de l'Aménagement et du Développement Territorial: ave de la Victoire, 97488 Saint-Denis Cédex; tel. 262-90-86-86; fax 262-90-86-70.

Direction des Déplacements et de la Voirie (DDV): 6 allée Moreau, Le Chaudron, 97490 Sainte-Clotilde; tel. 262-20-38-08; fax 262-94-17-90; e-mail dtransports@cg974.fr.

Direction du Développement Rural, de l'Agriculture et de la Forêt (DDRAF): ave de la Victoire, 97488 Saint-Denis Cédex; tel. 262-90-35-24; fax 262-90-39-89.

Direction de l'Eau: 14 allée de la forêt, 97400 Saint-Denis Cédex; tel. 262-30-84-84; fax 262-30-84-85; e-mail office@eaureunion.fr; internet www.eaureunion.fr.

Direction de l'Environnement et de l'Energie (DEE): 16 rue Jean Chatel, 97400 Saint-Denis Cédex; tel. 262-90-24-00; fax 262-90-24-19.

Direction des Finances: ave de la Victoire, 97488 Saint-Denis Cédex; tel. 262-90-39-39; fax 262-90-39-92; e-mail d.finances@cg974.fr; internet www.cg974.fr.

Direction Générale des Services (DGS): 2 rue de la Source, 97488 Saint-Denis Cédex; tel. 262-90-30-92; fax 262-90-39-99.

Direction de l'Informatique (DI): 19 route de la Digue, 97488 Saint-Denis Cédex; tel. 262-90-32-90; fax 262-90-32-99.

Direction de la Logistique (DL): 2 rue de la Source, 97488 Saint-Denis Cédex; tel. 262-90-31-38; fax 262-90-39-91.

Direction du Patrimoine (DP): 6 bis rue Rontaunay, 97488 Saint-Denis Cédex; tel. 262-90-86-81; fax 262-90-86-90.

Direction de la Promotion Culturelle et Sportive (DPCS): 18 rue de Paris, 97488 Saint-Denis Cédex; tel. 262-94-87-00; fax 262-94-87-26.

Direction des Ressources Humaines (DRH): 2 rue de la Source, 97488 Saint-Denis Cédex; tel. 262-90-34-65; fax 262-90-34-91.

Direction de la Vie Educative: ave de la Victoire, 97488 Saint-Denis Cédex; tel. 262-90-36-96; fax 262-90-37-21.

Political Organizations

Mouvement Démocrate (MoDem): Saint-Denis; internet www.mouvementdemocrate.fr; f. 2007; fmrly Union pour la Démocratie Française (UDF); centrist.

Mouvement pour l'Indépendance de la Réunion (MIR): f. 1981 to succeed the fmr Mouvement pour la Libération de la Réunion; grouping of parties favouring autonomy; Leader ANSELME PAYET.

Parti Communiste Réunionnais (PCR): Saint-Denis; f. 1959; Pres. PAUL VERGÈS; Sec.-Gen. ELIE HOARAU.

Mouvement pour l'Égalité, la Démocratie, le Développement et la Nature: affiliated to the PCR; advocates political unity; Leader RENÉ PAYET.

Parti Socialiste (PS)—Fédération de la Réunion (PS): 190 route des Deux Canons Immeuble, Futura, 97490 Saint-Clotilde; tel. 262-29-32-06; fax 262-28-53-03; e-mail psreunion@wanadoo.fr; internet www.parti-socialiste.fr; left-wing; Sec. ANNETTE GILBERT.

Union pour un Mouvement Populaire (UMP)—Fédération de la Réunion: 6 bis blvd Vauban, BP 11, 97461 Saint-Denis Cédex; tel. 262-20-21-18; fax 262-41-73-55; f. 2002; centre-right; local branch of the metropolitan party; Departmental Sec. DIDIER ROBERT.

Les Verts Réunion: Apt 30, Res ARIAL, 132 rue Général de Gaulle, 97400 Saint-Denis; tel. 262-55-73-52; fax 262-25-03-03; e-mail sr-verts-reunion@laposte.net; internet lesverts.fr; ecologist; Regional Sec. VINCENT DEFAUD.

Judicial System

Cour d'Appel: Palais de Justice, 166 rue Juliette Dodu, 97488 Saint-Denis; tel. 262-40-58-58; fax 262-20-16-37; Pres. JEAN-FRANÇOIS GABIN.

There are two Tribunaux de Grande Instance, one Tribunal d'Instance, two Tribunaux pour Enfants and two Conseils de Prud'hommes.

Religion

A substantial majority of the population are adherents of the Roman Catholic Church. There is a small Muslim community.

CHRISTIANITY

The Roman Catholic Church

Réunion comprises a single diocese, directly responsible to the Holy See. The number of adherents was equivalent to 80% of the population.

Bishop of Saint-Denis de la Réunion: Mgr GILBERT GUILLAUME MARIE-JEAN AUBRY, Evêché, 36 rue de Paris, BP 55, 97461 Saint-Denis Cédex; tel. 262-94-85-70; fax 262-94-85-73; e-mail eveche .lareunion@wanadoo.fr; internet www.diocese-reunion.org.

The Press

DAILIES

Journal de l'Ile de la Réunion: Centre d'affaires Cadjee, 62 blvd du Chaudron, BP 40019, 97491 Sainte-Clotilde Cédex; tel. 262-48-66-00; fax 262-48-66-50; internet www.clicanoo.re; f. 1951; CEO and Dir of Publication JEAN-BAPTISTE MARIOTTI; Editor-in-Chief YVES MONT-ROUGE; circ. 35,000.

Quotidien de la Réunion et de l'Océan Indien: BP 303, 97712 Saint-Denis Cédex 9; tel. 262-92-15-10; fax 262-28-25-28; e-mail laredaction@lequotidien.re; internet www.lequotidien.re; f. 1976; Dir MAXIMIN CHANE KI CHUNE; circ. 38,900.

Témoignages: 6 rue du Général Emile Rolland, BP 1016, 97828 Le Port Cédex; tel. 262-55-21-21; e-mail temoignages@wanadoo.fr; internet www.temoignages.re; f. 1944; affiliated to the Parti Communiste Réunionnais; daily; Dir JEAN-MAX HOARAU; Editor-in-Chief ALAIN ILAN CHOJNOW; circ. 6,000.

PERIODICALS

Al-Islam: Centre Islamique de la Réunion, BP 437, 97459 Saint-Pierre Cédex; tel. 262-25-45-43; fax 262-35-58-23; e-mail centre-islamique-reunion@wanadoo.fr; internet www .islam-reunion.com; f. 1975; 4 a year; Dir ISSAC GANGAT.

L'Eco Austral: Technopole de la Réunion 2, rue Emile Hugot, BP 10003, 97801 Saint-Denis Cédex 9; tel. 262-41-51-41; fax 262-41-31-14; internet www.ecoaustral.com; f. 1993; monthly; regional economic issues; Editor ALAIN FOULON; circ. 50,000.

L'Economie de la Réunion: c/o INSEE, Parc Technologique, 10 rue Demarne, BP 13, 97408 Saint-Denis Messag Cédex 9; tel. 262-48-89-00; fax 262-48-89-89; e-mail dr974–dir@insee.fr; internet www.insee .fr/reunion; 4 a year; Dir of Publication VALERIE ROUX; Editor-in-Chief CLAIRE GRANGE.

Lutte Ouvrière—Ile de la Réunion: BP 184, 97470 Saint-Benoît; fax 262-48-00-98; e-mail contact@lutte-ouvriere-ile-de-la-reunion .org; internet www.lutte-ouvriere.org/en-regions/la-reunion; monthly; Communist; digital.

Le Mémento Industriel et Commercial Réunionnais: 80 rue Pasteur, BP 397, 97468 Saint-Denis; tel. 262-21-94-12; fax 262-41-10-85; e-mail memento@memento.fr; internet www.memento.fr; f. 1970; monthly; Editor-in-Chief GEORGES-GUILLAUME LOUAPRE-POTTIER; circ. 20,000.

La Réunion Agricole: Chambre d'Agriculture, 24 rue de la Source, BP 134, 97463 Saint-Denis Cédex; tel. 262-94-25-94; fax 262-21-06-17; e-mail herve.cailleaux@reunion.chambagri.fr; f. 2007; monthly; Dir JEAN YVES MINATCHY; Chief Editor HERVÉ CAILLEAUX; circ. 8,000.

Leader Réunion: 14 rue de la Guadeloupe, ZA Foucherolles, 97490 Sainte-Clotilde; tel. 262-92-10-60; Dir of Publication CAROLE MAN-OTE.

Visu: 97712 Saint-Denis Cédex 9; tel. 262-90-20-60; fax 262-90-20-61; weekly; Editor-in-Chief PHILIPPE PEYRE; circ. 53,000.

NEWS AGENCY

Imaz Press Réunion: 12 rue Victor MacAuliffe, 97400 Saint-Denis; tel. 262-20-05-65; fax 262-20-05-49; e-mail ipr@ipreunion.com; internet www.ipreunion.com; f. 2000; photojournalism and news agency; Dir RICHARD BOUHET.

Broadcasting and Communications

TELECOMMUNICATIONS

Orange Réunion: 35 blvd du Chaudron, BP 7431, 97743 Saint-Denis Cédex 9; tel. 262-20-02-00; fax 262-20-67-79; internet reunion .orange.fr; f. 2000; subsidiary of Orange France; mobile cellular telephone operator.

Société Réunionnaise du Radiotéléphone (SRR): 21 rue Pierre Aubert, 97490 Sainte-Clotide; BP 17, 97408 Saint-Denis, Messag Cédex 9; tel. 262-48-19-70; fax 262-48-19-80; internet www.srr.fr; f. 1995; subsidiary of SFR Cegetel, France; mobile cellular telephone operator; CEO JEAN-PIERRE HAGGAÏ; 431,719 subscribers in Réunion, 46,341 in Mayotte (as Mayotte Télécom Mobile) in 2003.

BROADCASTING

Réunion 1ère: 1 rue Jean Chatel, 97716 Saint-Denis Cédex; tel. 262-40-67-67; fax 262-21-64-84; internet reunion.la1ere.fr; acquired by Groupe France Télévisions in 2004; fmrly Réseau France Outre-mer, present name adopted in 2010; radio and television relay services in French; broadcasts two television channels (Télé-Réunion and Tempo) and three radio channels (Radio-Réunion, France-Inter and France-Culture); Dir-Gen. GENEVIÈVE GIARD; Regional Dir ROBERT MOY.

Radio

In 2005 there were 46 licensed private radio stations. These included:

Antenne Réunion Radio: Saint-Denis; e-mail direction@ antennereunion.fr; internet www.antennereunion.fr; f. 2011.

Cherie FM Réunion: 3 rue de Kerveguen, 97400 Sainte-Clotilde; tel. 262-97-32-00; fax 262-97-32-32; Editor-in-Chief LEA BERTHAULT.

NRJ Réunion: 3 rue de Kerveguen, 97490 Sainte-Clotilde; tel. 262-97-32-00; fax 262-97-51-10; e-mail c.duboc@h2r.re; commercial radio station; Station Man. SYLVAIN PEGUILLAN.

Radio Festival: 3 rue de Kerveguen, 97490 Sainte-Clotilde; tel. 262-97-32-00; fax 262-97-32-32; e-mail redaction@radiofestival.fr; internet www.radiofestival.re; f. 1995; commercial radio station; Pres. MARIO LECHAT; Editor-in-Chief JEAN-PIERRE GERMAIN.

Radio Free-DOM: 131 rue Jules Auber, BP 666, 97400 Saint-Denis Cédex; tel. 262-41-51-51; fax 262-21-68-64; e-mail freedom@freedom .fr; internet www.freedom.fr; f. 1981; commercial radio station; Dir Dr CAMILLE SUDRE.

Television

Antenne Réunion: rue Emile Hugot, BP 80001, 97801 Saint-Denis Cédex 9; tel. 262-48-28-28; fax 262-48-28-26; e-mail direction@ antennereunion.fr; internet www.antennereunion.fr; f. 1991; broadcasts 10 hours daily; Pres. CHRISTOPHE DUCASSE; Dir-Gen. PHILIPPE ROUSSEL.

Canal Réunion: 6 rue René Demarne, Technopole de la Réunion, 97490 Sainte-Clotilde; tel. 262-97-98-99; fax 262-97-98-90; e-mail contact@canalreunion.net; internet www.canalreunion.com; subscription television channel; broadcasts a minimum of 19 hours daily; Chair. JEAN-NOEL TRONC; Dir JEAN-BERNARD MOURIER.

TV-4: 8 chemin Fontbrune, 97400 Saint-Denis; tel. 262-52-73-73; broadcasts 19 hours daily.

Other privately owned television services include TVB, TVE, RTV, Télé-Réunion and TV-Run.

Finance

(cap. = capital; res = reserves; dep. = deposits; m. = million; brs = branches)

BANKING

Central Bank

Institut d'Émission des Départements d'Outre-mer: 4 rue de la Compagnie des Indes, 97487 Saint-Denis Cédex; tel. 262-90-71-00; fax 262-21-41-32; e-mail agence@iedom-reunion.fr; internet www .iedom.fr/reunion; Dir ARNAUD BELLAMY-BROWN.

Commercial Banks

Banque Française Commerciale Océan Indien (BFCOI): 60 rue Alexis de Villeneuve, BP 323, 97466 Saint-Denis Cédex; tel. 262-40-55-55; fax 262-25-21-47; e-mail webmaster@bfcoi.com; internet www.bfcoi.com; f. 1976; cap. €16.7m., res €65.9m., dep. €1,302.4m. (Dec. 2008); Pres. PIERRE GUY-NOEL; Gen. Man. ROGER MUNOZ; 8 brs.

Banque Nationale de Paris Intercontinentale: 67 rue Juliette Dodu, BP 113, 97463 Saint-Denis; tel. 262-40-30-02; fax 262-41-39-09; e-mail contactreunion@bnpparibas.com; internet www.bnpgroup

.com; f. 1927; 100% owned by BNP Paribas; Chair. MICHEL PEBEREAU; Man. Dir DANIEL DEGUIN; 16 brs.

Banque de la Réunion (BR), SA: 27 rue Jean Chatel, 97711 Saint-Denis Cédex; tel. 262-40-01-23; fax 262-40-00-61; internet www.banquedelareunion.fr; f. 1853; owned by Groupe Banque Populaire et Caisse d'Epargne (France); cap. €65.4m., res €112.0m., dep. €2,010.8m. (Dec. 2008); Pres. BRUNO DELETRE; Gen. Man. BENOÎT CATEL; 20 brs.

BRED-Banque Populaire: 33 rue Victor MacAuliffe, 97461 Saint-Denis; tel. 262-90-15-60; fax 262-90-15-99.

Crédit Agricole de la Réunion: Parc Jean de Cambiaire, Cité des Lauriers, BP 84, 97462 Saint-Denis Cédex; tel. 262-40-81-81; fax 262-40-81-40; internet www.ca-reunion.fr; f. 1949; total assets €2,564m. (Dec. 2004); Chair. CHRISTIAN DE LA GIRODAY; Gen. Man. PIERRE MARTIN.

Development Bank

Société Financière pour le Développement Economique de la Réunion (SOFIDER): 3 rue Labourdonnais, BP 867, 97477 Saint-Denis Cédex; tel. 262-40-32-32; fax 262-40-32-00; internet www.sofider.re; part of the Agence Française de Développement; Dir-Gen. CLAUDE PÉRIOU.

INSURANCE

More than 20 major European insurance companies are represented in Saint-Denis.

AGF Vie La Réunion: 185 ave du Général de Gaulle, BP 797, 97476 Saint-Denis Cédex; tel. 262-94-72-23; fax 262-94-72-26; e-mail agfoi-vie@agfoi.com.

Capma & Capmi: 18 rue de la Cie des Indes, 97499 Saint-Denis; tel. 262-21-10-56; fax 262-20-32-67.

Groupama Océan Indien et Pacifique: 13 rue Fénelon, BP 626, 97473 Saint-Denis Cédex; tel. 262-26-12-61; fax 262-41-50-79; Chair. DIDIER FOUCQUE; Gen. Man. MAURICE FAURE (acting).

Trade and Industry

GOVERNMENT AGENCIES

Agence de Gestion des Initiatives Locales en Matière Européenne (AGILE)—Cellule Europe Réunion: 3 rue Felix Guyon, 97400 Saint-Denis; tel. 262-90-10-80; fax 262-21-90-72; e-mail celleurope@agile-reunion.org; internet www.agile-reunion.org; responsible for local application of EU structural funds; Dir SERGE JOSEPH.

Agence Régionale de Santé Océan Indien (ARS-OI): 2 bis ave Georges Brassens, CS 60050, 97408 Saint-Denis Messag Cédex 9; tel. 262-97-90-00; e-mail ars-oi-delegation-reunion@ars.sante.fr; internet www.ars.ocean-indien.sante.fr; f. 2010; responsible for implementation of health policies in Réunion and Mayotte; Dir-Gen. CHANTAL DE SINGLY.

Conseil Economique Social et Environnemental Régional (CESER): 10 rue du Béarn, BP 7191, 97719 Saint-Denis Messag Cédex; tel. 262-97-96-30; fax 262-97-96-31; e-mail cesr-reunion@cesr-reunion.fr; internet www.cesr-reunion.fr; f. 1984; Pres. JEAN-RAYMOND MONDON.

Direction de la Jeunesse, des Sports et de la Cohésion Sociale de la Réunion (DJSCS): 14 allée des Saphirs, 97487 Saint-Denis Cédex; tel. 262-20-96-40; fax 262-20-96-41; e-mail dd974@jeunesse-sports.gouv.fr; internet www.reunion.drjscs.gouv.fr; Dir RÉGIS BERTOGLI.

Direction Régionale des Affaires Culturelles de la Réunion (DRAC): 23 rue Labourdonnais, BP 224, 97464 Saint-Denis Cédex; tel. 262-21-91-71; fax 262-41-61-93; e-mail drac-la.reunion@culture.gouv.fr; internet www.reunion.pref.gouv.fr/drac; f. 1992; responsible to the French Ministry of Culture; Regional Dir JEAN-MARC BOYER.

Direction Régionale du Commerce Extérieur (DRCE): 3 rue Serge Ycard, 97490 Sainte-Clotilde; tel. 262-92-24-70; fax 262-92-24-76; e-mail reunion@missioneco.org; internet www.missioneco.org/reunion; Dir PHILIPPE GENIER.

Direction de l'Environnement, de l'Aménagement et du Logement (DEAL): 2 rue Juliette Dodu, 97706 Saint-Denis; tel. 262-40-26-26; fax 262-40-27-27; internet www.reunion.developpement-durable.gouv.fr; Regional Dir BERTRAND GALTIER.

Direction Régionale de l'Industrie, de la Recherche et de l'Environnement: 130 rue Léopold Rambaud, 97495 Sainte-Clotilde Cédex; tel. 262-92-41-10; fax 262-29-37-31; internet www.reunion.drire.gouv.fr; Reg. Dir JEAN-CHARLES ARDIN; Sec.-Gen. JACQUELINE LECHEVIN.

DEVELOPMENT ORGANIZATIONS

Agence de Développement de la Réunion (AD): rue Serge Ycart, BP 33, 97490 Sainte-Clotilde Cedex; tel. 262-92-24-92; fax 262-92-24-88; e-mail info@adreunion.com; internet www.adreunion.com; Chair. JISMY SOUPRAYENMESTRY.

Agence Française de Développement (AFD): 44 rue Jean Cocteau, BP 2013, 97488 Saint-Denis Cédex; tel. 262-90-00-90; fax 262-21-74-58; e-mail afdstdenis@re.groupe-afd.org; internet www.afd.fr; Dir MARC DUBERNET.

Association pour le Développement Industriel de la Réunion: 8 rue Philibert, BP 327, 97466 Saint-Denis Cédex; tel. 262-94-43-00; fax 262-94-43-09; e-mail adir@adir.info; internet www.adir.info; f. 1975; Pres. MAURICE CERISOLA; Sec.-Gen. FRANÇOISE DELMONT DE PALMAS; 190 mems.

Chambre d'Agriculture de la Réunion: 24 rue de la Source, BP 134, 97463 Saint-Denis Cédex; tel. 262-94-25-94; fax 262-21-06-17; e-mail president@reunion.chambagri.fr; internet www.reunion.chambagri.fr; Pres. JEAN-YVES MINATCHY; Gen. Man. JEAN-FRANÇOIS APAYA.

Jeune Chambre Economique de Saint-Denis de la Réunion: 25 rue de Paris, BP 1151, 97483 Saint-Denis; internet saintdenis.jcer.fr; f. 1963; Chair. SYLVIE CRESPO; 30 mems.

CHAMBERS OF COMMERCE

Chambre de Commerce et d'Industrie de la Réunion (CCIR): 5 bis rue de Paris, BP 120, 97463 Saint-Denis Cédex; tel. 262-94-20-00; fax 262-94-22-90; e-mail sg.dir@reunion.cci.fr; internet www.reunion.cci.fr; f. 1830; Pres. ERIC MAGAMOOTOO; Dir MOHAMED AHMED.

Chambre de Métiers et de l'Artisanat: 42 rue Jean Cocteau, BP 261, 97465 Saint-Denis Cédex; tel. 262-21-04-35; fax 262-21-68-33; e-mail cdm@cm-reunion.fr; internet www.cm-reunion.fr; f. 1968; Pres. BERNARD PICARDO; Sec. BENJAMINE DE OLIVEIRA; 14 mem. orgs.

EMPLOYERS' ASSOCIATIONS

Conseil de l'Ordre des Pharmaciens: 1 bis rue Sainte Anne, Immeuble le Concorde, Appt. 26, 1er étage, 97400 Saint-Denis; tel. 262-41-85-51; fax 262-21-94-86; e-mail delegation_reunion@ordre.pharmacien.fr; Pres. CHRISTIANE VAN DE WALLE.

Fédération Régionale des Coopératives Agricoles de la Réunion (FRCA): 8 bis, route de la Z. I. No. 2 97410, Saint-Pierre; tel. 262-96-24-40; fax 262-96-24-41; internet www.frca-reunion.coop; f. 1979; Pres. JEAN-FLORE BARRET; Sec.-Gen. RITO FERRERE; 27 mem. orgs.

Coopérative Agricole des Huiles Essentielles de Bourbon (CAHEB): 83 rue de Kerveguen, 97430 Le Tampon; BP 43, 97831 Le Tampon; tel. 262-27-02-27; fax 262-27-35-54; e-mail caheb@geranium-bourbon.com; f. 1963; represents producers of essential oils; Pres. MARIE ROSE SEVERIN; Sec.-Gen. LAURENT JANCI.

Société Coopérative Agricole Fruits de la Réunion: 18 Bellevue Pâturage, 97450 Saint-Louis; fax 262-91-41-04; f. 2002; Pres. CHRISTIAN BARRET.

Union Réunionnaise des Coopératives Agricoles (URCOOPA): Z. I. Cambaie, BP 90, 97862 Saint-Paul Cedex; tel. 262-45-37-10; fax 262-45-37-05; e-mail urcoopa@urcoopa.fr; internet www.urcoopa.fr; f. 1982; represents farmers; comprises Coop Avirons (f. 1967), Société Coopérative Agricole Nord-Est (CANE), SICA Lait (f. 1961), and CPPR; Pres. ARY MONDON; Dir-Gen. OLIVIER RONIN.

Mouvement des Entreprises de France Réunion (MEDEF): 14 rampes Ozoux, BP 354, 97467 Saint-Denis; tel. 262-20-01-30; fax 262-41-68-56; e-mail medef.reunion@wanadoo.fr; Pres. FRANÇOIS CAILLÉ.

Ordre National de Médecins: 3 résidence Laura, 4 rue Milius, 97400 Saint-Denis; tel. 262-20-11-58; fax 262-21-08-02; e-mail reunion@974.medecin.fr; internet www.odmreunion.net; Pres. Dr YVAN TCHENG.

Syndicat des Pharmaciens de la Réunion: 1 ave Marcel Hoarau, 97490 Sainte-Clotilde; tel. 262-28-53-60; fax 262-28-79-67; e-mail synd974@resopharma.fr; Pres. FRÉDE SAUTRON.

Syndicat des Producteurs de Rhum de la Réunion: chemin Frédéline, BP 354, 97453 Saint-Pierre Cédex; tel. 262-25-84-27; fax 262-35-60-92; Chair. OLIVIER THIEBLIN.

Syndicat du Sucre de la Réunion: BP 50109, 40 route Gabriel Macé, 97492 Sainte-Clotilde, Cedex; tel. 262-47-76-76; fax 262-21-87-35; internet www.sucre.re; f. 1908; Pres. PHILIPPE LABRO.

MAJOR COMPANIES

Brasseries de Bourbon: 60 Quai Ouest, BP 420, 97468 Saint-Denis; internet www.brasseriesdebourbon.fr; 85.6% owned by Heineken NV, Netherlands; brewery and distributor of alcoholic beverages and soft drinks; Pres. EDWIN BOTTERMAN; Man. EUGÈNE UBALIJORO.

Caltex Oil (Réunion) Ltd: BP 103, 97823 Le Port Cédex; tel. 262-42-76-76; fax 262-43-23-11; subsidiary of ChevronTexaco Corpn, USA; retail and distribution of petroleum products; revenue c. €90m. (2002).

Compagnie Laitière des Mascareignes (CILAM): 56 Quai Ouest, BP 264, 97400 Saint-Denis; tel. 262-90-27-27; fax 262-41-89-95; f. 1965; 80% owned by mems of SICA Lait; dairy products; Pres. PAUL MARTINEL; Dir-Gen. GILLES ESPITALIER-NOËL; c. 180 employees.

Coopérative d'Achats des Détaillants Réunionnais SA (CADRE): 3 rue Simone Morin, Zone Industrielle les Tamarins, 97420 Le Port; tel. 262-42-93-93; fax 262-42-92-50; retail distribution; Chair. DAVID SOUI MINE.

Distridom: 23 rue de Bordeaux, 97420 Le Port; f. 1993; supermarket retail (Leader Price); revenue €80.0m. (2003); Pres. PASCAL THIAW KINE; Man. Dir LAURENT THIAW KINE.

Groupe Caillé: 31 rue Jean Chatel, 97400 Saint-Denis; tel. 262-94-00-44; internet www.groupe-caille.com; Pres. FRANÇOIS CAILLÉ.

Jules Caillé Auto: 1 rue Edouard Manès, Z.I. du Chaudron, BP 51, 97408 Denis Messagerie Cedex 9; tel. 262-48-86-00; fax 262-48-86-02; internet www.peugeot-reunion.fr; f. 1919; agent for Peugeot motor vehicles; Chair. FRANÇOIS CAILLÉ; c. 320 employees.

Grands Travaux de l'Océan Indien (GTOI): Z. I. No. 2, BP 2016, 97824 Le Port Cédex; tel. 262-42-85-85; fax 262-71-05-21; e-mail standard@gtoi.fr; internet www.gtoi.fr; construction and civil engineering; revenue €171.1m. (2005); CEO CHRISTOPHE GUY; Gen. Man. JEAN-PIERRE PONS; c. 1,100 employees (2005).

Hyper Soredeco: 75 rue du Karting la Jamaique, 97490 Saint-Denis; supermarket retail (Carrefour); Chair. JACQUES CAILLÉ; c. 300 employees.

Ravate Distribution: 131 rue Maréchal Leclerc, BP 450, 97400 Saint-Denis; tel. 262-21-06-63; fax 262-41-26-63; retailers of construction materials, wood, hardware; Chair. ISSOP RAVATE; Dir ADAM RAVATE; c. 440 employees.

SEMS SA: 5 impasse du Grand Prado; supermarket retail; revenue €249.0m. (2004); more than 1,000 employees.

Société Bourbonnaise de Travaux Publics et de Constructions (SBTPC): 28 rue Jules Verne, BP 2013, 97824 Le Port; tel. 262-42-45-00; fax 262-43-49-80; e-mail sbtpc@sbtpc.fr; internet www.sbtpc.com; subsidiary of Vinci Construction Filiales Int., France; construction and civil engineering; revenue €91m. (2004); Man. BERNARD LENFANT; c. 500 employees.

Société Foucque: 69 blvd du Chaudron, BP 300, 97490 Sainte-Clotilde; tel. 262-97-49-74; fax 262-48-24-61; internet www.foucque.fr; agent for Citroën motor vehicles, and farming machinery; revenue €100m. (2004); Man. Dir RÉMY BRIATTE; c. 300 employees.

Société Réunionnaise de Produits Pétroliers (SRPP): Zone Industrielle N1, 97420 Le Port; BP 2015, 97824 Le Port Cédex; tel. 262-42-07-11; fax 262-42-11-34; storage and retail of petroleum products; revenue €191m. (2004); Chair. ROBERT LAUROUA; CEO MOMAR NGUER; c. 100 employees.

Sodexpro: 10 rue Theodore Drouet, BP 123, 97420 Le Port; supermarket retail; revenue €78.0m. (2001); Pres. FRANÇOIS CAILLÉ; c. 100 employees.

Tereos Océan Indien: 23 rue Raymond Vergès, 97441 Sainte-Suzanne; tel. 262-58-82-82; fax 262-77-82-98; internet tereos-oceanindien.com; f. 1923; fmrly Groupe Quartier Français; Pres. PHILIPPE LABRO; Comprises:

Distillerie Rivière du Mât: chemin Manioc, Z. I. Beaufonds, 97470 Saint-Benoît; tel. 262-67-46-41; fax 262-50-27-32; e-mail visitedistillerie@gqf.com; internet www.rdm.gqf.com; Dir TEDDY BOYER.

Eurocanne: La Mare, 97438 Sainte-Marie; tel. 262-43-27-79; fax 262-43-51-39; e-mail choarau@tereos.com; storage, packing and distribution; exports 85% of production; Dir PATRICK LORCET.

Mascarin: 1 rue Claude Chappe, ZAC 2000, BP 134, 97420 Le Port Cédex; tel. 262-55-10-20; fax 262-43-99-45; storage, packing and distribution; exports 90% of production; Chair. PHILIPPE LABRO; Man. Dir JEAN-PIERRE DANIEL SIX.

Sucrerie de Bois-Rouge: 2 chemin Bois-Rouge, BP 1017, Cambuston, 97440 Saint-André; tel. 262-58-83-30; fax 262-58-83-31; e-mail sucrerie.br@bois-rouge.fr; internet www.bois-rouge.fr; f. 1817; 51% owned by Tereos, 39% owned by Groupe Quartier Français; produces, refines and exports sugar; fmrly Groupes Sucreries de Bourbon, acquired by Tereos in 2001; Pres. and Dir-Gen. JEAN-FRANÇOIS MOSER; 150 permanent and 100 seasonal employees; processes c. 1m. metric tons of sugar cane per campaign; comprises.

Sucrerie du Gol: 23 rue Raymond Vergès, BP 95, 97441 Saint-Louis; tel. 262-58-82-82; fax 262-46-53-01; e-mail communication-oi@tereos.com; internet www.tereos-oceanindien.com; Pres. PHILIPPE LABRO; 200 permanent and 200 seasonal employees; processes c. 1.1m. metric tons of sugar cane per campaign.

Total Réunion: 3 rue Jacques Prévert, Rivière des Galets, BP 286, 97827 Le Port Cédex; tel. 262-55-20-20; fax 262-55-20-21; e-mail total-reunion@totalreunion.fr; internet www.totalreunion.fr; retail and distribution of petroleum products; revenue €137.m. (2004); Pres. ALAIN CHAMPEAUX; Dir-Gen. PHILLIPE BODILIS; c. 30 employees.

TRADE UNIONS

CFE-CGC de la Réunion: 1 Rampes Ozoux, Résidence de la Rivière, Appt 2A, BP 873, 97477 Saint-Denis Cédex; tel. 262-90-11-95; fax 262-90-11-99; e-mail union@cfecgcreunion.com; internet www.cfecgcreunion.com; departmental br. of the Confédération Française de l'Encadrement-Confédération Générale des Cadres; represents engineers, teaching, managerial and professional staff and technicians; Pres. ALAIN IGLICKI; Sec.-Gen. DANIEL THIAW-WING-KAI.

Confédération Générale du Travail de la Réunion (CGTR): 144 rue du Général de Gaulle, BP 1132, 97482 Saint-Denis Cédex; Sec.-Gen. GEORGES MARIE LEPINAY.

Fédération Départementale des Syndicats d'Exploitants Agricoles de la Réunion (FDSEA): 105 rue Amiral Lacaze, Terre Sainte, 97410 Saint-Pierre; tel. 262-96-33-53; fax 262-96-33-90; e-mail fdsea-reunion@wanadoo.fr; affiliated to the Fédération Nationale des Syndicats d'Exploitants; Sec.-Gen. JEAN-BERNARD HOARAU.

Fédération Réunionnaise du Bâtiment et des Travaux Publics: angle rue du Pont et rue de la Boulangerie, BP 108, 97462 Saint-Denis Cédex; tel. 262-41-70-87; fax 262-21-55-07; internet www.frbtp.re; Pres. STÉPHANE BROSSARD.

Fédération Syndicale Unitaire Réunion (FSU): 4 rue de la Cure, BP 279, 97494 Sainte-Clotilde Cédex; tel. 262-86-29-46; fax 262-22-35-28; e-mail fsu974@fsu.fr; internet sd974.fsu.fr; f. 1993; departmental br. of the Fédération Syndicale Unitaire; represents public sector employees in sectors incl. teaching, research, and training, and also agriculture, justice, youth and sports, and culture; Sec. CHRISTIAN PICARD.

Union Départementale Confédération Française des Travailleurs Chrétiens (UD CFTC): Résidence Pointe des Jardins, 1 rue de l'Atillerie, 97400 Saint-Denis; tel. 262-41-22-85; fax 262-41-26-85; e-mail usctr@wanadoo.fr.

Union Départementale Force Ouvrière de la Réunion (FO): 81 rue Labourdonnais, BP 853, 97477 Saint-Denis Cédex; tel. 262-21-31-35; fax 262-41-33-23; e-mail eric.marguerite@laposte.net; Sec.-Gen. ERIC MARGUERITE.

Union Interprofessionnelle de la Réunion (UIR-CFDT): 58 rue Fénelon, 97400 Saint-Denis; tel. 262-90-27-67; fax 262-21-03-22; e-mail uir.cfdt@wanadoo.fr; affiliated to the Confédération Française Démocratique du Travail; Sec.-Gen. JEAN-PIERRE RIVIERE.

Affiliated unions incl.:

FEP-CFDT Réunion: 58 rue Fénélon, 97400 Saint-Denis; tel. 262-90-27-67; fax 262-21-03-22; e-mail jpmarchau@uir-cfdt.org; affiliated to the Fédération Formation et Enseignement Privés; represents private sector teaching staff.

SGEN-CFDT: 58 rue Fénélon, 97400 Saint-Denis; tel. 262-90-27-72; fax 262-21-03-22; e-mail reunion@sgen.cfdt.fr; internet www.sgen-cfdt-reunion.org; mem. of Union Interprofessionnelle de la Réunion; represents teaching staff; Sec.-Gen. JEAN-LOUIS BELHÔTE.

Union Régionale UNSA-Education: BP 169, 97464 Saint-Denis Cédex; tel. 262-20-02-25; fax 262-21-58-65; e-mail urreunio@unsa.org; represents teaching staff; Sec.-Gen. ERIC CHAVRIACOUTY.

Transport

ROADS

A route nationale circles the island, generally following the coast and linking the main towns. Another route nationale crosses the island from south-west to north-east linking Saint-Pierre and Saint-Benoît. In 1994 there were 370 km of routes nationales, 754 km of departmental roads and 1,630 km of other roads; 1,300 km of the roads were bituminized. Discussions began in the mid-2000s regarding a proposed 'tram-train' network that would link Saint-Benoît to Saint-Joseph via Saint-Denis. However, by mid-2012 no progress had been made with this project.

Société d'Economie Mixte des Transports, Tourisme, Equipements et Loisirs (SEMITTEL): 24 chemin Benoite-Boulard, 97410 Saint-Pierre; tel. 262-55-40-60; fax 262-55-49-56; e-mail contact@

semittel.re; f. 1984; bus service operator; Pres. MARRIE PERIANAYAGOM.

Société des Transports Départementaux de la Réunion (SOTRADER): 2 allée Bonnier, 97400 Saint-Denis; tel. 262-94-89-40; fax 262-94-89-50; f. 1995; bus service operator; Dir-Gen. FRÉDÉRIC DELOUYE.

SHIPPING

In 1986 work was completed on the expansion of the Port de la Pointe des Galets, which was divided into the former port in the west and a new port in the east (the port Ouest and the port Est), known together as Port Réunion. In 2009 some 3.3m. metric tons of freight were unloaded and 594,700 tons loaded at the two ports. The Chambre de Commerce et d'Industrie de la Réunion also manages three yachting marinas.

Port Authority (Concession Portuaire): rue Evariste de Parny, BP 18, 97821 Le Port Cédex; tel. 262-42-90-00; fax 262-42-47-90; internet www.reunion.port.fr; Dir BRUNO DAVIDSEN.

CMA CGM Réunion: 85 rue Jules Verne, Z.I. No. 2, BP 2007, 97822 Le Port Cédex; tel. 262-55-10-10; fax 262-43-23-04; e-mail lar.genmbox@cma-cgm.com; internet www.cmacgm.com; f. 1996 by merger of Cie Générale Maritime and Cie Maritime d'Affrètement; shipping agents; Man. Dir VALÉRIE SEVENO.

Mediterranean Shipping Co France (Réunion), S.A. (MSC): 1 bis, Gustave Eiffel, Z.A.C. 2000, BP 221, 97825 Le Port Cédex; tel. 262-42-78-00; fax 262-42-78-10; e-mail msclareunion@mscfr.mscgva.ch; internet www.mscreunion.com.

Réunion Ships Agency (RSA): 17 rue R. Hoareau, BP 10186, 97825 Le Port Cédex; tel. 262-43-33-33; fax 262-42-03-10; e-mail rsa@indoceanic.com; internet www.indoceanic.com; f. 1975; subsidiary of Indoceanic Services; Man. Dir HAROLD JOSÉ THOMSON.

Société d'Acconage et de Manutention de la Réunionnaise (SAMR): 3 ave Théodore Drouhet, Z.A.C. 2000, BP 40, 97821 Le Port Cédex; tel. 262-55-17-55; fax 262-55-17-62; stevedoring; Pres. DOMINIQUE LAFONT; Man. MICHEL ANTONELLI.

Société de Manutention et de Consignation Maritime (SOMACOM): 3 rue Gustave Eiffel, Zac 2000, BP 97420, Le Port; tel. 262-42-60-00; fax 262-42-60-10; stevedoring and shipping agents; Gen. Man. DANIEL RIGAT.

Société Réunionnaise de Services Maritimes (SRSM): 3 ave Théodore Drouhet, Z.A.C. 2000, BP 2006, 97822 Le Port Cédex; tel. 262-55-17-55; fax 262-55-17-62; e-mail n.hoarau@dri-reunion.com; freight only; Man. MICHEL ANTONELLI.

CIVIL AVIATION

Réunion's international airport, Roland Garros-Gillot, is situated 8 km from Saint-Denis. A programme to develop the airport was completed in 1994. In 1997 work commenced on the extension of its terminal, at a cost of some 175m. French francs, and the project was completed in 2002. The Pierrefonds airfield, 5 km from Saint-Pierre, commenced operating as an international airport in December 1998 following its development at an estimated cost of nearly 50m. French francs. Air France, Corsair and Air Austral operate international services. In 2009 Roland Garros-Gillot handled some 1.75m. passengers, while Pierrefonds airport handled 126,651 passengers.

Air Austral: 4 rue de Nice, 97400 Saint-Denis; tel. 262-90-90-91; fax 262-29-28-95; e-mail reservation@air-austral.com; internet www.airaustral.com; f. 1975; subsidiary of Air France; Dir-Gen. GÉRARD ETHEVE.

Tourism

Réunion's attractions include spectacular scenery and a pleasant climate. In January 2010 the island had some 2,090 hotel rooms. In 2011 some 471,300 tourists visited Réunion. Receipts from tourism in 2009 were €305.8m.

Délégation Régionale au Commerce, à l'Artisanat et au Tourisme: Préfecture de la Réunion, 97400 Saint-Denis; tel. 262-40-77-58; fax 262-50-77-15; Dir PHILIPPE JEAN LEGLISE.

L'Île de la Réunion Tourisme (IRT): pl. du 20 décembre 1848, BP 615, 97472 Saint-Denis Cédex; tel. 262-21-00-41; fax 262-21-00-21; e-mail ctr@la-reunion-tourisme.com; internet www.reunion.fr; fmrly Comité du Tourisme de la Réunion; name changed as above in 2009; Pres. JACQUELINE FARREYROL.

Office du Tourisme Intercommunal du Nord: 2 pl. Etienne Regnault, 97400 Saint-Denis; tel. 262-41-83-00; fax 262-21-37-76; e-mail info@ot-nordreunion.com; Pres. FRÉDÉRIC FOUCQUE; Dir CATHERINE GLAVNIK.

Defence

Réunion is the headquarters of French military forces in the Indian Ocean and French Southern and Antarctic Territories. As assessed at November 2009, there were 1,000 French troops stationed on Réunion and Mayotte, including a gendarmerie.

Education

Education is modelled on the French system, and is compulsory for 10 years between the ages of six and 16 years. Primary education begins at six years of age and lasts for five years. Secondary education, which begins at 11 years of age, lasts for up to seven years, comprising a first cycle of four years and a second of three years. In the academic year 20010/11 there were 44,404 pupils enrolled at pre-primary schools and 77,240 at primary schools. In the academic year 20010/11 there were 100,995 pupils enrolled at secondary schools. There is a university, with several faculties, providing higher education in law, economics, politics, and French language and literature, and a teacher-training college. In 2009/10 11,659 students were enrolled at the university.

Bibliography

Boléguin, V. *La Réunion: une jeunesse tiraillée entre tradition et modernité. Les 16-30 ans au chômage*. Paris, L'Harmattan, 2011.

Cohen, P. *Le cari partagé: Anthropologie de l'alimentation à l'île de la Réunion*. Paris, Karthala, 2000.

Delval, R. *Musulmans français d'origine indienne: Réunion, France métropolitaine, anciens établissements français de l'Inde*. Paris, CHEAM, 1987.

Dracius, S., Samlong, J-F., and Theobald, G. *La crise de l'outre-mer français: Guadeloupe, Martinique, Réunion*. Paris, L'Harmattan, 2009.

Ho, H. Q. *Contribution à l'histoire économique de l'île de la Réunion (1642–1848)*. Paris, L'Harmattan, 2000.

La Réunion (1882-1960): Histoire économique Colonage, salariat et sous-développement. Paris, L'Harmattan, 2008.

Maestri, E. *Les îles du sud-ouest de l'Océan Indien et la France de 1815 à nos jours*. Paris, L'Harmattan, 1994.

Martinez, E. *Le Département français de La Réunion et la coopération internationale dans l'Océan Indien*. Paris, L'Harmattan, 1988.

Paillat-Jarousseau, H. *Une terre pour cultiver et habiter: anthropologie d'une localité de l'île de la Réunion*. Paris, L'Harmattan, 2001.

Payet, J. V. *Histoire de l'esclavage à l'île Bourbon (Réunion)*. Paris, L'Harmattan, 2000.

Wong-Hee-Kam, E. *La diaspora chinoise aux Mascareignes: le cas de la Réunion*. Paris, L'Harmattan, 1996.

RWANDA

Physical and Social Geography

PIERRE GOUROU

The Rwandan Republic, like the neighbouring Republic of Burundi, is distinctive both for the small size of its territory and for the density of its population. Covering an area of 26,338 sq km (10,169 sq miles), Rwanda had an enumerated population of 7,142,755 at the census of 15 August 1991, with a density of 271 inhabitants per sq km. However, political and ethnic violence during 1994 was estimated to have resulted in the death or external displacement of 35%–40% of the total population. Prior to these events, the population had been composed of Hutu (about 85%), Tutsi (about 14%) and Twa (1%). According to the results of a national census, published in December 2002, Rwanda's population had recovered to about 8.1m., indicating an increase of 12% since the 1991 census. At mid-2012, according to UN estimates, the population totalled 11,271,785, with a density of 428.0 inhabitants per sq km. The official languages are French, English (which is widely spoken by the Tutsi minority) and Kinyarwanda, a Bantu language with close similarities to Kirundi, the main vernacular language of Burundi.

It seems, at first sight, strange that Rwanda has not been absorbed into a wider political entity. Admittedly, the Rwandan nation has long been united by language and custom and was part of a state that won the respect of the east African slave-traders. However, other ethnic groups, such as the Kongo, Luba, Luo and Zande, which were well established in small territorial areas, have not been able to develop into national states. That Rwanda has been able to achieve this is partly the result of developments during the colonial period. While part of German East Africa, Rwanda (then known, with Burundi, as Ruanda-Urundi) was regarded as a peripheral colonial territory of little economic interest. After the First World War it was entrusted to Belgium under a mandate from the League of Nations. The territory was administered jointly with the Belgian Congo, but was not absorbed into the larger state. The historic separateness and national traditions of both Rwanda and Burundi have prevented their amalgamation.

Although the land supports a high population density, physical conditions are not very favourable. Rwanda's land mass is very rugged and fragmented. It is part of a Pre-Cambrian shelf from which, through erosion, the harder rocks have obtruded, leaving the softer ones submerged. Thus very ancient folds have been raised and a relief surface carved out with steep gradients covered with a soil poor in quality because of its fineness and fragility. Rwanda's physiognomy therefore consists of a series of sharply defined hills, with steep slopes and flat ridges, which are intersected by deep valleys, the bottoms of which are often formed by marshy plains. The north is dominated by the lofty and powerful chain of volcanoes, the Virunga, whose highest peak is Karisimbi (4,519 m) and whose lava, having scarcely cooled down, has not yet produced cultivable soil.

The climate is tropical, although tempered by altitude, with a daily temperature range of as much as 14°C. Kigali, the capital (1,003,570 inhabitants at mid-2011, according to UN estimates), has an average temperature of 19°C and 1,000 mm of rain. Altitude is a factor that modifies the temperature (and prevents sleeping sickness above about 900 m), but such a factor is of debatable value for agriculture. Average annual rainfall (785 mm) is only barely sufficient for agricultural purposes, but two wet and two relatively dry seasons are experienced, making two harvests possible.

Recent History

PHIL CLARK and ZACHARY D. KAUFMAN

HUTU ASCENDANCY

Rwanda was not an artificial creation of colonial rule. When Rwanda and Burundi were absorbed by German East Africa in 1899, they had been established kingdoms for several centuries. In 1916, during the First World War, Belgian forces occupied the region. From 1920 Rwanda formed part of Ruanda-Urundi, administered by Belgium under a League of Nations mandate and later as a UN Trust Territory. In 1961 it was decided by referendum to replace Rwanda's monarchy with a republic, to which full independence was granted on 1 July 1962. Political life in the new Republic was dominated by its first President, Grégoire Kayibanda, and the governing party, the Mouvement Démocratique Républicain (MDR), also known as the Parti de l'Émancipation du Peuple Hutu (Parmehutu). Tensions between the majority Hutu (comprising about 85% of the population) and their former Belgian-imposed overlords, the Tutsi (14%), which had sporadically erupted into serious violence during 1963–65, recurred in late 1972 and early 1973. These tensions were the seeds of the 1994 genocide, perpetrated by Hutu, of between 800,000 and 1m. people, mostly Tutsi but also some Hutu and Twa who were considered to be Tutsi sympathizers.

In July 1973 the Minister of Defence and head of the National Guard, Maj.-Gen. Juvénal Habyarimana, deposed Kayibanda, proclaimed a Second Republic and established a military Government under his leadership. In 1975 a new ruling party, the Mouvement Révolutionnaire National pour le Développement (MRND), was formed. A referendum in December 1978 approved a new Constitution, aimed at returning the country to civil government in accordance with an undertaking by Habyarimana in 1973 to end the military regime within five years. Habyarimana was elected President in the same month. Elections to the legislature, the Conseil National du Développement (CND), were held in December 1981 and in December 1983, in which month Habyarimana was re-elected President.

In the presidential election of December 1988 Habyarimana, as sole candidate, reportedly secured 99.98% of the votes cast. Elections for the CND were also held in that month. During 1989 economic conditions deteriorated sharply, and the introduction of an economic austerity programme in December increased public discontent. In July 1990 Habyarimana announced that a national commission would be appointed to investigate the issue of political reform. The Commission Nationale de Synthèse (CNS) was duly established in September with a mandate to make recommendations for political renewal. However, these measures did little to alleviate the acute sense of political crisis.

REBEL INVASION AND POLITICAL UPHEAVAL

On 1 October 1990 an estimated force of 10,000 militia, representing the exiled, Tutsi-dominated Front Patriotique

Rwandais (FPR), crossed the border from Uganda into north-eastern Rwanda, where they swiftly occupied several towns. The troops were primarily Tutsi refugees, but they also included significant numbers of disaffected elements of Uganda's ruling National Resistance Army (NRA, now the Uganda People's Defence Force—UPDF). The invasion force was led by Maj.-Gen. Fred Rwigyema, a former Ugandan Deputy Minister of Defence. In response to a request for assistance from Habyarimana, Belgian and French paratroopers were dispatched to the Rwandan capital, Kigali, to protect foreign nationals and to secure evacuation routes. A contingent of troops sent by Zaire (now the Democratic Republic of the Congo—DRC) assisted the small Rwandan army in turning back the FPR some 70 km from Kigali.

The conflict continued into 1992, as the FPR made frequent guerrilla forays into Rwanda. Both sides reported thousands of casualties; many civilians resident in the border regions were killed, and as many as 100,000 displaced. Increasing ethnic tensions, exacerbated by the war, resulted in a series of unprovoked attacks upon Tutsi civilians, and prompted accusations of government involvement, particularly in the Bugesera region of southern Rwanda. In July it was reported that the warring parties had negotiated a cease-fire, providing for the establishment of a 'neutral area'.

The FPR invasion accelerated the political reform process initiated in 1990. Following widespread public discussion of proposals put forward by the CNS in December, the Commission published its report and a draft constitution in March 1991. The new Constitution, providing for the legalization of political parties, entered into force in June. Full freedom of the press was declared, leading to the establishment of a number of magazines and newspapers critical of government policy. In April 1992, following a series of unsuccessful attempts to negotiate a transitional government, the composition of a broad-based coalition Government, incorporating four opposition parties—the revived MDR, the Parti Social-démocrate (PSD), the Parti Liberal (PL) and the Parti Démocratique Chrétien (PDC)—together with the Mouvement Républicain National pour la Démocratie et le Développement (MRNDD—the new party name adopted by the MRND in 1991), was announced. The new administration was to be headed by Dismas Nsengiyaremye of the MDR as Prime Minister, a post established by the Constitution. Multi-party elections for municipalities, the legislature and the presidency were to take place before April 1993. In late April 1992, in compliance with a new constitutional prohibition of the armed forces' participation in the political process, Habyarimana relinquished his military title and functions.

The coalition Government and FPR representatives initiated a new dialogue in May 1992 and conducted formal discussions in Paris, France, during June. Further negotiations, in Arusha, Tanzania, in July resulted in an agreement on the implementation of a new cease-fire, to take effect from the end of that month, and the creation of a military observer group (GOM) sponsored by the Organization of African Unity (OAU, now the African Union—AU), to comprise representatives from both sides, together with officers drawn from the armed forces of Nigeria, Senegal, Zimbabwe and Mali. However, by October subsequent negotiations had failed to resolve outstanding problems concerning the creation of a 'neutral zone' between the Rwandan armed forces and the FPR (to be enforced by the GOM), the incorporation of the FPR in a Rwandan national force, the repatriation of refugees, and the demands of the FPR for full participation in the transitional Government and legislature.

A resurgence in violence followed the breakdown of negotiations in early February 1993, resulting in the deaths of hundreds on both sides. An estimated 1m. civilians fled southwards and to neighbouring Uganda and Tanzania, as the FPR advanced as far as Ruhengeri and seemed, for a time, on the verge of capturing Kigali. Belgium, France and the USA denounced the FPR's actions. In late February the Government accepted FPR terms for a cease-fire in return for an end to attacks against FPR positions and on Tutsi communities, and the withdrawal of foreign troops. Although fighting continued with varying intensity, new peace negotiations were convened in March in Arusha.

Negotiations conducted during April 1993 failed to produce a solution to the crucial issue of the structure of future unitary Rwandan armed forces. In the same month the five participating parties in the ruling coalition agreed to a three-month extension of the Government's mandate in order to facilitate a peace accord. Further talks in May between the Government and the FPR in the northern town of Kinihira produced significant progress, including an agreed schedule for the demobilization of the 19,000-strong security forces. In June an agreed protocol outlined the repatriation of all Rwandan refugees resident in Uganda, Tanzania and Zaire, including recommendations that compensation be made to those forced into exile more than 12 years earlier. In June the UN Security Council approved the creation of the UN Observer Mission Uganda-Rwanda (UNOMUR), to be deployed on the Ugandan side of the border for an initial period of six months, in order to block FPR military supply lines.

In July 1993 Habyarimana met representatives of the five parties represented in the coalition Government and sought a further extension to its mandate. However, the Prime Minister's insistence that the FPR should be represented in any newly mandated government exacerbated existing divisions within the MDR, prompting Habyarimana to conclude the agreement with a conciliatory group of MDR dissidents, including the Minister of Education, Agathe Uwilingiyimana, who was appointed as Rwanda's first female Prime Minister on 17 July. The Council of Ministers was reorganized to replace the disaffected MDR members.

Habyarimana and Col Alex Kanyarengwe of the FPR formally signed a peace accord in Arusha on 4 August 1993. A new transitional Government, to be headed by a mutually approved Prime Minister (later named as the MDR moderate faction leader, Faustin Twagiramungu), was to be installed by 10 September. A multi-party general election was to take place after a 22-month period, during which the FPR would participate in a transitional government and national assembly. In mid-August the Government revoked the curfew in Kigali and removed military road-blocks from all but three northern prefectures. By the end of the month, however, the Prime Minister was forced to make a national appeal for calm, following reports of renewed outbreaks of violence in Kigali and Butare, Rwanda's second largest city. The Government and the FPR attributed the failure to establish a transitional government and legislature by the September deadline to the increasingly fragile security situation, and both sides urged the prompt dispatch of a neutral UN force to facilitate the implementation of the Arusha Accord. Meanwhile, relations between the Government and the FPR deteriorated, following the rebels' assertion that the Government had violated the Accord by attempting to dismantle and reorganize those departments assigned to the FPR under the terms of the agreement.

UN INTERVENTION

On 5 October 1993 the UN Security Council adopted Resolution 872, endorsing the creation of the UN Assistance Mission for Rwanda (UNAMIR), under the leadership of Canadian Lt-Gen. Roméo Dallaire, to be deployed in Rwanda for an initial period of six months, with a mandate to: monitor observance of the cease-fire; contribute to the security of the capital; and facilitate the repatriation of refugees. UNAMIR, incorporating UNOMUR and GOM, was formally inaugurated on 1 November, and comprised some 2,500 personnel. In December the UN declared that it was satisfied that conditions had been sufficiently fulfilled to allow for the introduction of the transitional institutions by the end of the month. In that month UNAMIR officials escorted a 600-strong FPR battalion to Kigali (as detailed in the Arusha Accord) to ensure the safety of FPR representatives selected to participate in the transitional Government and legislature. On 5 January 1994 Habyarimana was invested as President of a transitional Government, for a 22-month period, under the terms of the Arusha Accord. (His previous term of office, in accordance with the Constitution, had expired on 19 December 1993.)

Dallaire reported in early 1994 that the Habyarimana Government was increasing anti-Tutsi propaganda across

Rwanda, stockpiling weapons and training youth militias. He emphasized that anti-Tutsi sentiment was increasing rapidly, and that violence against Tutsi was likely in the coming months. In March the Prime Minister-designate, Twagiramungu, declared that he had fulfilled his consultative role as established by the Arusha Accord, and announced the composition of a transitional Government, in an attempt to accelerate the installation of the transitional bodies. However, political opposition to the proposed Council of Ministers persisted, and Habyarimana insisted that the list of proposed legislative deputies, newly presented by Uwilingiyimana, should be modified to include representatives of additional political parties, including the Coalition pour la Défense de la République (CDR). CDR participation was strongly opposed by the FPR, owing both to its alleged failure to accept the code of ethics for the behaviour of political parties, and to its policies advocating ethnic discrimination. This prompted a further postponement of the formation of a transitional administration.

In April 1994 the UN Security Council (which in February had warned that the UN presence in Rwanda might be withdrawn in the absence of swift progress in implementation of the Arusha Accord) agreed to extend UNAMIR's mandate for four months, pending a review of progress made in implementing the Accord.

COLLAPSE OF CIVIL ORDER AND GENOCIDE

On 6 April 1994 the presidential aircraft, returning from a regional summit in Dar es Salaam, Tanzania, was fired upon over Kigali, and exploded on landing. All 10 passengers were killed, including Habyarimana, President Cyprien Ntaryamira of Burundi, two Burundian cabinet ministers, and the Chief of Staff of the Rwandan armed forces. In Kigali, although it was unclear who had been responsible for the attack, the presidential guard obstructed UNAMIR officials attempting to investigate the crash site, and immediately initiated a brutal campaign of retributive violence against political opponents of the late President. As politicians and civilians fled the capital, the brutality of the political assassinations was compounded by attacks on the clergy, UNAMIR personnel and Tutsi civilians. Hutu civilians were instructed to murder their Tutsi neighbours. The mobilization of the Interahamwe, or unofficial militias (allegedly affiliated with the MRNDD and the CDR), apparently committed to the massacre of government opponents and Tutsi civilians, was encouraged by the presidential guard (with support from some factions of the armed forces) and by inflammatory broadcasts from Radio-Télévision Libre des Mille Collines in Kigali. The Prime Minister, the President of the Constitutional Court, the Ministers of Labour and Social Affairs and of Information, and the Chairman of the PSD were among the prominent politicians assassinated, or declared missing and presumed dead, within hours of Habyarimana's death.

The Speaker of the CND, Dr Théodore Sindikubwabo, announced on 8 April 1994 that he had assumed the office of interim President of the Republic, in accordance with the provisions of the 1991 Constitution. The five remaining participating political parties and factions of the Government selected a new Prime Minister, Jean Kambanda, and a new Council of Ministers (largely comprising MRNDD members). The FPR immediately challenged the legality of the new administration, claiming that the CND's constitutional right of succession to the presidency had been superseded by Habyarimana's inauguration as President in January under the terms of the Arusha Accord. The legitimacy of the new Government, which had fled to the town of Gitarama to escape escalating violence in the capital, was subsequently rejected by factions of the PL and MDR (led by Twagiramungu), and by the PDC and the PSD, which in May announced that they had allied themselves as the Democratic Forces for Change.

FPR Offensives and the Refugee Crisis

In mid-April 1994 the FPR resumed military operations from its northern stronghold, with the stated intention of relieving its beleaguered battalion in Kigali, restoring order to the capital and halting the massacre of Tutsi civilians. Grenade attacks and mortar fire intensified in the capital, prompting the UN to mediate a fragile 60-hour cease-fire, during which small evacuation forces from several countries escorted foreign nationals out of Rwanda. Belgium's UNAMIR contingent of more than 400 troops was also withdrawn, after Hutu militiamen killed 10 Belgian peace-keepers sent to protect Prime Minister Uwilingiyimana, who was also murdered.

As the political violence incited by the presidential guard and the Interahamwe gathered momentum, the militia's identification of all Tutsi as political opponents of the state promoted ethnic polarization, resulting in a pogrom against Tutsi. Reports of mass Tutsi killings and unprovoked attacks on fleeing Tutsi refugees, and on those seeking refuge in schools, hospitals and churches, elicited unqualified international condemnation and outrage, and promises of financial and logistical aid for an estimated 2m. displaced Rwandans (some 250,000 had fled across the border to Tanzania in a 24-hour period in late April 1994), many of whom were killed by famine and disease in makeshift camps. By late May attempts to assess the full scale of the humanitarian catastrophe in Rwanda were complicated by unverified reports that the FPR (which claimed to control more than one-half of the country) was carrying out retaliatory atrocities against Hutu militias and civilians. Unofficial estimates at that time indicated that between 200,000 and 500,000 Rwandans had been killed since early April.

On 21 April 1994, in the context of intensifying violence in Kigali, and the refusal of the Rwandan armed forces to agree to the neutral policing of the capital's airport (subsequently secured by the FPR), the UN Security Council resolved to reduce its force in Rwanda to 270 personnel, a move that attracted criticism from the Rwandan Government, the FPR and international relief organizations. However, on 16 May, following intense international pressure and the disclosure of the vast scale of the humanitarian crisis in the region, the Security Council approved Resolution 917, providing for the eventual deployment of some 5,500 UN troops with a revised mandate, including the policing of Kigali's airport and the protection of refugees in designated 'safe areas'. In late May the UN Secretary-General criticized the failure of UN member states to respond to his invitation to participate in the enlarged force (only Ghana, Ethiopia and Senegal had agreed to provide small contingents). Further UN-sponsored attempts to negotiate a cease-fire failed, and the FPR made significant territorial gains in southern Rwanda, forcing the Government to flee Gitarama and seek refuge in the western town of Kibuye.

In early June 1994 the UN Security Council adopted Resolution 925, extending the mandate of the revised UN mission in Rwanda (UNAMIR II) until December. However, the Secretary-General continued to encounter considerable difficulty in securing equipment and armaments requested by the participating African countries. By mid-June confirmed reports of retributive murders committed by FPR members (including the massacre, in two separate incidents in early June, of 22 clergymen, among them the Roman Catholic Archbishop of Kigali), and the collapse of a fragile OAU-negotiated truce, prompted the French Government to announce its willingness to lead an armed police action, endorsed by the UN, in Rwanda. Although France insisted that its military presence (expected to total 2,000 troops) would maintain strict political neutrality and operate, from the border regions, in a purely humanitarian capacity pending the arrival of a multinational UN force, the FPR contended that the French administration's maintenance of high-level contacts with representatives of the self-proclaimed Rwandan Government indicated political bias. On 23 June the first contingent of 150 French marine commandos launched Operation Turquoise, entering the western town of Cyangugu, in preparation for a large-scale operation to protect refugees in the area. By mid-July the French initiative had successfully relieved several beleaguered Tutsi communities and had established a temporary 'safe haven' for the displaced population in the south-west, through which a mass exodus of Hutu refugees began to flow, encouraged by reports (disseminated by supporters of the defeated interim Government) that the advancing FPR forces were seeking violent retribution against Hutu. An estimated 1m. Rwandans sought refuge in the Zairean border town of Goma, while a similar number attempted to cross the border elsewhere in the south-west. The

FPR had swiftly secured all major cities and strategic territorial positions, but had halted its advance several kilometres from the boundaries of the French-controlled neutral zone, requesting the apprehension and return for trial of those responsible for the recent atrocities.

The first report of the UN Special Rapporteur on human rights in Rwanda confirmed at the end of June 1994 that at least 500,000 Rwandans had been killed since April, and urged the establishment of an international tribunal to investigate allegations of genocide. In early July the UN announced the creation of a commission of inquiry for this purpose.

THE FPR TAKES POWER

On 19 July 1994 Pasteur Bizimungu, a Hutu, was inaugurated as President for a five-year term. In November a multi-party protocol of understanding was concluded, providing for a number of amendments to the terms of the August 1993 Arusha Accord, relating to the establishment of a transitional legislature. Among the new provisions was the exclusion from the legislative process of members of those parties implicated in alleged acts of genocide during 1994. A 70-member National Transitional Assembly was installed on 12 December. On 5 May 1995 the new legislature announced its adoption of a new Constitution based on selected articles of the 1991 Constitution, the terms of the August 1993 Arusha Accord, the FPR's victory declaration of July 1994 and the November 1994 protocol of understanding.

In July 1999 Rwanda announced the end of the five-year transitional Government and its replacement by a four-year national unity Government. The new transitional period would allow the Government to complete the national reconciliation process, restore internal security, improve the economy and social services, and establish a democratic system. Critics rejected the unilateral extension of political power and claimed that the Government's action revealed its undemocratic and dictatorial nature.

The increasingly stringent policies of the Government, which was now dominated by supporters of the Vice-President and FPR Chairman, Paul Kagame, prompted a number of prominent figures to flee Rwanda. A notable case involved the popular Speaker of the Transitional National Assembly, Kabuye Sebarenzi, who had campaigned for good governance and official accountability. After moving from the FPR to the PL and drawing attention to government ministers accused of corruption, Sebarenzi's political fortunes gradually waned. In December 1999 the PL President, Pio Mugabo, postponed the vote for a new party President, reportedly on orders from Kagame. Sebarenzi had been expected to be elected to this post, which would have strengthened his chances of winning the election for the national presidency. In January 2000 the Transitional National Assembly forced Sebarenzi's resignation on apparently fabricated charges of official misconduct, organizing genocide survivors against the Government and supporting the 'army of the king'. Later that month Sebarenzi, fearing assassination by the Government, fled to Uganda, then Europe, and finally to the USA. Bizimungu resigned as President on 23 March and subsequently relocated to the USA. Kagame served as provisional President until 17 April, when members of the legislature and the Government elected him, by 81 votes to five, as the first Tutsi President since independence in 1962. Kagame, who was to serve for the remainder of the transition period, until legislative and presidential elections in 2003, pledged to facilitate political decentralization, expedite the trials of some 125,000 genocide suspects in prison and conduct local government elections.

Meanwhile, in September 1999 a legislative commission of inquiry implicated several government ministers in cases of corruption, some of whom subsequently resigned. A further parliamentary inquiry discovered that, when serving as Minister of Education in 1995, the Prime Minister, Pierre-Célestin Rwigyema, had been implicated in the diversion of funds from a World Bank education programme almost exclusively to his home town of Gitarama. Rwigyema survived a motion of censure in the Transitional National Assembly in December 1999, but he resigned two months later. In March 2004 the Auditor-General informed the legislature that some 60 public institutions reported that tenders for 2002 valued at US $5.8m. had not been processed by the national tender board as scheduled. Moreover, $7m. of government spending was unaccounted for during that year and, of 44 cases of alleged embezzlement of government funds, only nine were referred for trial and only two cases had been heard. However, the authorities did dismiss 139 police officers in March 2004 for a series of crimes, including bribery and corruption.

In June 2000 the Ministry of Local Government and Social Affairs introduced legislation on decentralization, which aimed to make the district (*akarere*) the principal organ of local government. Apart from providing judicial services, the *akarere* was to assume responsibility for agriculture, forestry and veterinary services, as well as stimulating local trade and managing the provision of education, health, water, roads and other facilities. A legislative council and an executive committee, aided by an executive secretary, were to govern the *akarere*. This initiative was the most ambitious political scheme ever undertaken in post-independence Rwanda. Its success depended on the availability of donor aid, the authorities' ability to collect taxes, and the central Government's willingness to transfer adequate funds and power to the *akarere*. Many donors insisted that, in order to receive foreign aid, Rwanda must shed its authoritarian culture and near-total concentration of power in the central Government.

ELECTIONS AND THE END OF THE TRANSITIONAL PERIOD

On 6 March 2001 Rwanda conducted nation-wide elections for local officials. President Kagame claimed that the ballot represented a significant measure towards democratization. However, Rwandan government statistics indicated that about 45% of the districts were contested by only one candidate. International human rights organizations condemned the elections as unfair; many voters claimed that they had participated in the polls only for fear of receiving fines or other penalties, while local and international election monitors had received the requisite documentation late on 5 March, making it impossible to observe pre-election procedures, such as registration, and difficult to reach distant polling stations.

Some 93.4% of the electorate approved a new Constitution on 26 May 2003. The European Union (EU) Electoral Observation Mission in Rwanda subsequently reported that the referendum had been conducted in 'satisfactory conditions'. The Constitution mandated a bicameral legislature, which would comprise an 80-member Chamber of Deputies and a 26-member Senate. Also in that month the Government endorsed a parliamentary report that urged the banning of the MDR for propagating a 'divisive' ideology and the prosecution of 47 of its members and supporters for 'ethnic extremism'. The human rights organization Amnesty International accused the Rwandan authorities of orchestrated suppression of political opposition, and Human Rights Watch maintained that the Government was seeking to eliminate any opposition prior to Rwanda's presidential and parliamentary elections, scheduled for August and September, respectively. The new Constitution entered into effect on 4 June. However, the International Federation for Human Rights claimed that it would inhibit multi-party pluralism and freedom of expression.

On 25 August 2003 Kagame won the first presidential election to take place in Rwanda since the 1994 genocide, with 95.1% of the valid votes cast. Former Prime Minister Twagiramungu (most of whose supporters were members of the opposition in exile) won 3.6% of the votes, and the only other opposition candidate, Jean-Népomuscène Nayinzira, 1.3%. Twagiramungu subsequently accused the authorities of electoral malpractice, and submitted a challenge against the official results to the Supreme Court. EU monitors confirmed that irregularities had occurred, although a South African observer mission declared that the poll had been 'free and fair'. In early September the Supreme Court rejected Twagiramungu's appeal. Kagame was officially inaugurated on 12 September. On 30 September 218 candidates (representatives submitted by eight political parties and 19 independents) contested legislative elections for 53 of 80 seats in the Chamber of

Deputies. Official figures indicated that some 96% of registered voters participated in the election, although independent observers maintained that the number of voters was less than that for the presidential poll. The FPR won 33 seats; the PSD secured seven seats, the PL six, the Parti Démocrate Centriste three, the Parti Démocrate Idéal two, the Parti Socialiste Rwandais one and the Union Démocratique du Peuple Rwandais one. The new Constitution reserved the remaining seats in the Chamber of Deputies for 'special groups' (24 representatives of women, two of youth and one of disabled persons). On 2 October some 20,000 representatives of provincial women's groups contested the 24 seats reserved for women, while local government officials and academic representatives contested 14 of the 26 Senate seats. On 9 October President Kagame appointed eight senators, as authorized by the Constitution. (A further four senators were nominated by a regulatory body, the Parties' Forum.) The EU assessed that there were serious irregularities in the legislative elections.

In 2004–05 the Kagame administration accused several government officials of promoting the 'ideology of genocide'. In July 2004 the Chamber of Deputies published a report accusing several local civil society organizations, including the Ligue Rwandaise pour la Promotion et la Défense des Droits de l'Homme (LIPRODHOR), one of Rwanda's largest human rights organizations, of supporting such an ideology. The report also rebuked some international non-governmental organizations (NGOs), such as CARE International and Trócaire Overseas Development Agency, for supporting these groups. The EU condemned the findings, and the Government rejected the legislature's recommendation for a ban on all suspect organizations. Eight LIPRODHOR officials fled to Uganda, claiming that they were in danger from government agents. In September LIPRODHOR's general assembly, having been obliged by the Government to conduct an internal investigation, issued a statement denouncing some of its members for 'genocide-related acts'. In January 2005 the legislature renewed its accusations that LIPRODHOR was propagating a genocidal ideology and ethnic divisionism. Several senior LIPRODHOR members then fled Rwanda, while the organization issued a formal apology to the people of Rwanda. The Government again declined to close LIPRODHOR as the legislature's report had recommended, although it ordered a further internal investigation. The subsequent chaos forced LIPRODHOR to cease operations.

POST-GENOCIDE CRIMINAL JUSTICE

On 8 November 1994 the UN Security Council adopted Resolution 955, establishing the UN International Criminal Tribunal for Rwanda (ICTR) to be convened in Arusha, despite the negative vote of Rwanda, which held a non-permanent seat on the Council in 1994. The ICTR began formal proceedings in November 1995, and the first trial began in January 1997. By 29 July 2011, the date of the ICTR's most recent annual report to the UN General Assembly and Security Council, the ICTR had completed judgments at the first instance of 58 people and judgments at the appellate level of 35 people. Several of these decisions established important international criminal law precedents concerning the definition of crimes and the accountability of perpetrators, regardless of their official position. The ICTR was the first international war crimes tribunal to receive a guilty plea for genocide; it passed the first genocide conviction; it indicted and subsequently convicted the first head of state and the first woman for genocide; it defined rape in international law and held that it could constitute genocide; and it approved the first genocide conviction of journalists. As at 11 May 2012, according to the ICTR report on the implementation of its completion strategy, the ICTR had completed work at trial level in respect of 83 of 93 indictments. This included 52 first-instance judgments involving 72 accused, six referrals to national jurisdictions, two withdrawn indictments, and three indictees who had died prior to, or in the course of, proceedings. Appeal proceedings had been concluded in respect of 43 persons.

In February 1996 the Rwandan Prime Minister announced the creation of special courts within the country's existing judicial system. Under these arrangements, Rwanda's Supreme Court Chief Prosecutor began investigations in each of the country's 10 districts, and established three-member judicial panels in each district to consider cases. The panels were to comprise some 250 lay magistrates, who received four months' legal training. Additionally, 320 judicial police inspectors, all of whom had attended a three-month training course, compiled dossiers on those detained for allegedly committing genocide. Newly established assessment commissions reviewed possible detentions on the basis of available evidence.

In August 2004 the ICTR Chief Prosecutor, Hassan Bubacar Jallow, who had been appointed by the UN Security Council on 15 September 2003, visited Rwanda to review the Government's proposal that at least some of those convicted by the ICTR of committing atrocities should serve their sentences in Rwandan prisons. The ICTR had initially opposed this strategy as Rwanda at that time employed the death penalty, while the maximum ICTR sentence is life imprisonment. In June 2007 the Rwandan legislature removed the death penalty from all national statutes. In response, the ICTR commenced proceedings to transfer suspects from Arusha to the national courts in Kigali. The ICTR chambers initially denied some of the ICTR Prosecutor's requests for referral of cases to Rwanda for trial, noting concerns about obtaining witnesses, ensuring a fair trial and the risk of solitary confinement in Rwanda. More recently, however, the ICTR chambers have approved the referral of some suspects—the first being Jean-Bosco Uwinkindi, whose appeal against transfer was rejected in April 2012—to the Rwandan courts, which in turn instituted a special chamber in the High Court to handle the transfer and extradition of genocide suspects. In addition, the ICTR Chief Prosecutor has provided assistance to Rwanda's judicial system in its efforts to try other suspects whom the ICTR investigated but did not indict. The ICTR chambers have referred additional cases and transferred some convicted individuals to other states, such as France and Italy. Various countries, including the United Kingdom, Sweden, Germany and Finland, extradited or at least considered extraditing Rwandan genocide suspects to Rwanda or third-party countries such as France. Some countries refusing to extradite suspects to Rwanda cited their concern that they would not receive a fair trial, although the ICTR's decision to transfer cases has begun to change international practice in this regard.

During his 2004 visit to Rwanda, Jallow declined to answer questions about whether the ICTR intended to prosecute anyone from the FPR for crimes against humanity. In October 2004 unidentified assailants killed an ICTR prosecution witness in the province of Gikongoro. Many suspected that the incident had been related to the testimony that he had provided at the ICTR trial over genocide charges concerning Col Aloys Simba. In November Jallow revealed that 14 alleged *génocidaires* (perpetrators of the 1994 genocide) had taken refuge in the DRC and accused the Congolese authorities of failing to make any effort to apprehend them. In December the ICTR's Appeals Chamber upheld the convictions of two defendants who had been sentenced in February 2003 to 10 and 25 years' imprisonment, respectively, for their role in the genocide in the province of Kibuye. In January 2005 Jallow announced that he was ready to proceed with 17 new genocide trials, which would be conducted at the same time as 25 ongoing trials. He also indicated that national courts would conduct some of these trials, and that his office had completed investigations into another 16 cases, some of which concerned alleged FPR atrocities. In mid-2005 the ICTR renewed its demand for prosecutions against members of the FPR for war crimes. The alleged implication of the FPR in shooting down the aircraft of President Habyarimana in 1994 was of particular interest to the Tribunal. In response, Aloys Mutabingwa, Rwanda's ICTR representative, demanded that the ICTR charge French government officials for their role in the events that precipitated the genocide. Despite such declarations, no prosecutions of FPR or French officials have occurred. In 2009 Finland became the first foreign country to conduct a genocide trial *in situ* in Rwanda, in the case of François Bazaramba.

The Rwandan national courts, operating concurrently to the ICTR, have played a major role in prosecuting genocide suspects. This has been a difficult undertaking, in view of the decimation of the Rwandan judiciary by the genocide. Despite significant reconstruction of the judiciary since then, the system had difficulties in dealing with the immense number of imprisoned genocide suspects awaiting trial. On 1 August 2003 a court in Gikondo convicted 105 people of genocide, sentencing 73 to life imprisonment and 11 to death. The remainder received custodial terms, ranging from one to 25 years, while the court acquitted 37 suspects. By late 2003 Rwandan courts had convicted approximately 6,500 suspects, of whom 600–700 received death sentences.

To relieve the pressure on its courts and to facilitate a communal dialogue on the root causes of the genocide as a means to reconciliation, the Rwandan Government instituted the *gacaca* community-based judicial system, based partly on a traditional model of participative justice, to deal with the majority of genocide cases. In October 2000 the Transitional National Assembly adopted legislation providing for the creation of *gacaca* courts. This was approved by the Constitutional Court on 18 January 2001, and in October voters elected approximately 260,000 *gacaca* judges, who were to: facilitate the community's evidence-gathering process during open-air hearings; evaluate evidence; and impose judgments on genocide suspects. Suspects who confessed to their crimes early enough were able to benefit from the *gacaca* courts' plea-bargaining structure, which incorporated community service for certain lower-level crimes related to the genocide to reintegrate convicted *génocidaires* into the community. The Government pledged that all court proceedings would be publicized and all court decisions subject to appeal.

On 18 June 2002 the authorities formally inaugurated the *gacaca* system. For the first three years of operation, however, *gacaca* trials involved only the community's recording of basic information related to the events of the genocide, rather than specific evidence related to particular genocide suspects. Some 673 community courts commenced operations throughout the country in November, followed by a further 8,258 in March 2003.

The Government had undertaken to begin trials for 750 genocide suspects in September 2004 using the *gacaca* system, but this process was delayed until 2005. Meanwhile, in December 2004 the National Service of Gacaca Jurisdictions reported that it would use lists of genocide suspects that the Netherlands-based NGO Penal Reform International had earlier rejected as inadmissible on the grounds of presumed guilt. Hearings of genocide suspects' cases before nearly 9,000 *gacaca* tribunals ultimately commenced on 10 March 2005. Defendants included several current government officials, and while in office Prime Minister Bernard Makuza and Minister of Defence Gen. Marcel Gatsinzi provided testimony. It appeared that Makuza would not be liable for prosecution, but Gatsinzi, a former commander of the École des Sous-officiers in Butare, was accused of providing weapons to Hutu troops to kill Tutsi. Gatsinzi admitted that some military personnel under his command had been involved in killings, but rejected allegations that he had assisted them.

The Rwandan Government asserted that as many as 1m. suspects might eventually be charged with genocide during *gacaca* hearings, causing the Prosecutor-General to warn that the system would be unable to process so many cases. *Gacaca* hearings were further complicated in early 2005 when thousands of Hutu reportedly fled to neighbouring countries to avoid possible prosecution. In Burundi, for example, the office of the UN High Commissioner for Refugees (UNHCR) initially granted refugee status to some 2,000 recently arrived Rwandans. However, after complaints from the Rwandan Government, Burundi indicated that the Rwandans would not be granted refugee status, that it would urge them to return home, and that it would initiate extradition proceedings against those who refused. Additionally, in October 2006 France, Belgium and the Netherlands agreed to seek those who had taken up residence in those countries and bring them to trial.

In July 2006 phase two of the *gacaca* system began. The process was initially scheduled for completion in mid-2009—much of early 2009 having been spent prosecuting those accused of Category 1 genocide crimes, including local orchestrators of the genocide and individuals suspected of committing sexual crimes. The most recent version of the *gacaca* law (adopted in May 2008) shifted to the jurisdiction of the *gacaca* courts the remainder of Category 1 genocide cases still awaiting trial in the national courts, which were struggling to try the thousands of day-to-day cases before them. The Government proposed that, after their genocide caseload had been completed, the *gacaca* courts should be maintained as a community-based legal system designed to consider minor infractions, leaving the national courts to prosecute more serious crimes such as corporate fraud and murder.

By June 2011 the *gacaca* courts had completed their backlog of genocide cases in all but a few jurisdictions. The Minister of Justice and Attorney-General, Tharcisse Karugarama, announced that the *gacaca* jurisdictions would be officially closed by December, with a government evaluation report on the impact of the entire *gacaca* process due to be completed soon thereafter. The Government officially opened a documentation centre in Kigali containing the handwritten records of around 1m. *gacaca* trials from around the country, making it the world's largest repository of evidence relating to a mass crime. The authorities also announced that new legislation was being considered that would enable the future prosecution through the national courts of any remaining genocide suspects not prosecuted through *gacaca*. Furthermore, the Government was reviewing the controversial genocide ideology law and various media laws, which human rights commentators had argued were routinely used to silence critics of the FPR.

The Rwandan Government officially closed *gacaca* proceedings on 18 June 2012, the 10th anniversary of their commencement. In its report presented at the closing of *gacaca*, the National Service of Gacaca Jurisdictions stated that *gacaca* had tried 1,958,634 suspects, convicting 1,681,648 (86%) and acquitting 277,066 (14%). This number appeared to refer to the number of genocide cases rather than suspects prosecuted under the *gacaca* system, which would indicate a significantly lower number of suspects than that specified by the Government. The *gacaca* courts reportedly heard appeals from 178,741 (9%) of those tried, affirming 132,902 (74%) and reversing 45,839 (26%).

2008 LEGISLATIVE ELECTIONS

On 15 September 2008, at only the second legislative election to be held since the 1994 genocide, the FPR secured a resounding victory, winning 78.8% of the votes cast and 42 of the 53 directly elected seats; the PSD took seven seats; and the PL four. For the first time, women outnumbered men in the legislature, occupying some 56% of the seats. Turn-out for the elections was estimated at more than 98%. In October Rose Mukantantabana was nominated as Speaker of the Chamber of Deputies, becoming the first woman in Rwanda to hold that position.

2010 PRESIDENTIAL ELECTION

On 9 August 2010 Rwanda held its second presidential election since the genocide. According to official results released by the National Electoral Commission, Paul Kagame secured an overwhelming victory, winning 93.1% of the votes cast. His closest challenger, Dr Jean Damascene Ntawukuriryayo of the PSD, took just 5.2% of the votes, while Prosper Higiro of the PL secured 1.4% and Alvera Mukabaramba of the Parti du Progrès et du Concorde 0.4%. Some 97.5% of the registered electorate participated in the poll. In the build-up to the election there were several grenade attacks in Kigali, and the FPR cracked down against opposition politicians, journalists and dissident military officials. Gen. Faustin Kayumba Nyamwasa was shot in an attack in Johannesburg, South Africa, and *Umuvugizi* journalist Jean-Léonard Rugambage and the Vice-President of the opposition Parti Démocratique Vert, André Kagwa Rwisereka, were both murdered—the FPR was widely suspected of involvement. Kagame's principal challenger for the presidency, Victoire Ingabire, the leader of the Forces Démocratiques Unifiées—Inkingi party, and her US lawyer were arrested and imprisoned (both on charges of genocide denial and, in Ingabire's case, also of collaborating with Hutu rebels in the DRC). The Government also suspended *Umuvugizi* and another Kinyarwanda newspaper, *Umuseso*, until after the election, following the publication of articles interpreted as inciting public discord. Assistant Secretary Johnnie Carson, of the US Department of State's Bureau of African Affairs, stated that the US Administration had concerns over human rights abuses committed during the presidential campaign. Kagame was inaugurated for a second seven-year term on 6 September, and his Government was reappointed unchanged eight days later.

In January 2011 the High Military Court sentenced two former senior army officers to 24 years' imprisonment *in absentia*, and two former officials in Kagame's administration to 20 years *in absentia*, for threatening state security, after they had issued a document, in September 2010, denouncing Kagame's Government as authoritarian, corrupt and repressive.

2011 GOVERNMENT CHANGES

President Kagame effected a reorganization of the Council of Ministers on 6 May 2011. Notable changes included the mergers of the Ministry of Environment and Lands with that of Forestry and Mines, and the Ministry of Youth with that of Sports and Culture. The former Governor of the Banque Nationale du Rwanda, François Kanimba, was appointed as Minister of Trade and Industry, while Dr Agnes Binagwaho became Minister of Health. On 7 October Kagame appointed Pierre Damien Habumuremyi, hitherto Minister of Education, as Prime Minister, after Bernard Makuza was nominated to the Senate. A new Government, in which the majority of ministers from the previous administration were retained, was subsequently formed.

The trial of Victoire Ingabire, on six charges including genocide denial, involvement in terrorist activities, planning state insecurity and divisionism, which had begun in August 2011, was concluded in late April 2012, with the prosecution demanding a life sentence. (Ingabire was boycotting the trial at this time, accusing the presiding judge of bias.) It was announced in late June that the verdict had been adjourned until 7 September. In January, meanwhile, four senior armed forces officers, including the head of military intelligence, were arrested on charges of involvement in illegal business dealings in the DRC.

HUMAN RIGHTS AND REFUGEE ISSUES

According to the US Department of State's human rights report for 2011, released on 24 May 2012, the Rwandan authorities continued to commit abuses and to restrict the right of citizens to change their government. The report asserted that the country's most significant human rights problems were 'lack of respect for the integrity of the person, particularly illegal detention, torture, and disappearance of persons detained by SSF [state security forces]; unwarranted restrictions on the freedoms of speech and press, particularly harassment, violence, and arrest of journalists, political dissidents, and human rights advocates; and societal violence and discrimination against women and children'. The report also raised concerns about allegations of attempted assassinations of government opponents, conditions within prison and detention facilities, and restrictions on freedoms of association and religion. Other areas of concern cited in the report included official corruption, child labour, human-trafficking, and discrimination and violence against ethnic minorities, particularly the Twa, and against members of the lesbian, gay, bisexual and transgender communities.

The record of the Armée Patriotique Rwandaise (APR—the FPR's military wing) in eastern DRC has alarmed many international human rights organizations, owing to long-standing reports of the APR's involvement in executions, rape, forcible removal of people and other abuses. An increasing number of people from the Kivu provinces of eastern DRC, especially non-Banyarwanda, strongly oppose the APR because of its harsh treatment of local populations. Many non-Banyarwanda have joined anti-Rwandan Mai-Mai militias to combat the APR and its Banyarwanda allies. In June 2003 Rwanda and Burundi agreed to co-operate in bringing stability to the Great Lakes region by supporting peace efforts in Burundi and the DRC. In October Rwanda announced that it would create a commission of inquiry to investigate two cases of alleged resource exploitation in the DRC, but the Government continued to dismiss reports of human rights violations by Rwandan troops in the DRC as uninformed and biased. In April 2004 Rwanda deployed troops along its border with Burundi and the DRC, in anticipation of possible attacks from Hutu rebels. Burundi accused Rwandan government forces of invading Ruhororo and Kaburantwa Valley, in the north-western province of Cibitoke, and succeeded in persuading them to withdraw.

REGIONAL CONCERNS

Rwanda's 1997 military intervention in the DRC marked a turning point in Central Africa's history. The Kagame Government justified its actions by claiming that its armed forces sought only to eliminate Hutu extremist elements there. However, it soon became evident that Rwandan and Ugandan troops had also started a systematic campaign to loot the region's resources. Efforts by the UN to prevent this illegal exploitation failed.

Meanwhile, by 2004 various international human rights organizations believed that more than 4m. had died in eastern DRC as a result of warfare, disease and starvation. In June Col Jules Mutebutsi, a Congolese Tutsi rebel commander, and a number of his troops had sought refuge in Rwanda, after clashing with personnel of the UN Observer Mission in the Democratic Republic of the Congo (MONUC) in Bukavu. UNHCR refused to grant refugee status to Mutebutsi and his troops until it received proof that they were no longer combatants. In August the Rwandan Government sought to placate the UN by moving Mutebutsi and his soldiers from the temporary Ntendezi camp near the DRC border to the Coko camp in a remote district of Gikongoro province. However, this measure failed to allay UN concerns that Mutebutsi and his followers remained combatants. The UN also accused the Kagame administration of arming dissident militias in the DRC's Ituri district in Orientale province, and of operating a military training camp in Kibungo province for abductees from the Kiziba and Gihembe refugee camps. In the same month Rwanda blamed the Forces Démocratiques pour la Libération du Rwanda (FDLR), regarded as the successor force to the former Rwandan army and containing Interahamwe militia members who fled to the DRC after the 1994 genocide, for killing 152 Congolese Tutsi refugees in the Burundian Gatumba refugee camp, near the border with the DRC. The Rwandan Government threatened to deploy troops in the DRC unless MONUC and the Congolese authorities took action, and additionally demanded that MONUC abandon its ineffective voluntary disarmament programme for the FDLR. MONUC responded that its efforts to disarm the FDLR had failed because Rwanda and its DRC-based allies continued to carry out disruptive military operations in eastern DRC. MONUC also accused Rwanda of using FDLR activities as justification for reintervention in the DRC.

In September 2004 the UN announced that the Rwandan and DRC Governments had agreed to launch a Joint Verification Mechanism (JVM) to enhance border security. Both countries pledged to take reports of fighting to the JVM for verification before they were released to the media. In November the DRC armed forces and MONUC commenced joint missions in the Walungu district of Sud-Kivu province to persuade the FDLR to disarm and return home. Shortly afterwards the FDLR launched a rocket attack on Rwanda's Gisenyi province from Nord-Kivu. Kagame warned the AU that Rwandan troops would intervene in the DRC if the armed forces and MONUC failed to disarm the FDLR. The UN, the EU, the United Kingdom, the USA, Belgium and South Africa cautioned Kagame against intervening in the DRC, while many donors, including the Swedish Government, suspended aid to the Rwandan Government. On 1 December MONUC reported that there were around 100 Rwandan troops in the Virunga mountains along the Rwanda–DRC–Uganda border. Although the Rwandan Government denied that it had any forces in the DRC, the DRC authorities asserted that the troops had been fighting the FDLR in Nord-Kivu for at least a week. DRC armed reinforcements subsequently clashed with military units of dissidents loyal to the pro-Rwanda Rassemblement Congolais pour la Démocratie (RCD) in Kanyabayonga, Nord-Kivu. However, the DRC Government maintained that the incident involved its armed forces and invading Rwandan troops. The JVM was unable to confirm whether Rwandan troops had participated in the fighting. Nevertheless, MONUC suspected that Rwanda provided military aid to the RCD. On 20 December the Rwandan Government responded to growing international criticism by announcing that it would no longer intervene in the DRC. On 31 March 2005 the FDLR unexpectedly condemned the 1994 genocide, pledged to co-operate with the ICTR, and announced that it was willing to end its armed struggle, begin disarmament on 5 May, and eventually return to Rwanda. These concessions resulted from secret discussions in Rome, Italy, between the rebels and Rwandan officials under the auspices of the Roman Catholic Sant'Egidio community. None the less, the FDLR subsequently continued its campaign of violence in the Kivu provinces, aimed mainly at the Congolese Tutsi population.

In January 2009 Rwanda and the DRC mounted an unprecedented joint operation in the Kivu provinces in an attempt to eradicate the FDLR. The joint forces succeeded in capturing from the FDLR Katoyi, Kibua, Kirambo, Gitoyi, Rubugu and Panamo in the Rutshuru district of Nord-Kivu. However, soon after Rwanda withdrew its forces in February—as dictated by a bilateral agreement—the FDLR regained much of its lost territory and increased its attacks against Tutsi civilians, perpetrating crimes including mass rape and murder. Also in January 2009 Rwanda arrested Laurent Nkunda, President of the Congrès National pour la Défense du Peuple (CNDP)—the largest Rwanda-backed rebel group operating in the Kivu provinces. The arrest was seen as further proof of Rwanda's dedication to improving relations with the DRC. However, Nkunda's departure failed to halt the CNDP's operations in eastern DRC. By mid-2012 Nkunda remained under house arrest in Rwanda, where the authorities disregarded demands by the Congolese Government that he be extradited for trial.

In April 2012 former CNDP rebels who had been integrated into the DRC army mutinied under the banner of a new armed force named M23, in reference to the peace agreement concluded on 23 March 2009 between the CNDP and the Government of the DRC. The mutineers claimed the DRC authorities had violated the agreement by threatening to divide and disperse CNDP integrated brigades away from Nord- and Sud-Kivu. Between April and the beginning of August 2012 M23 captured various towns in Nord-Kivu and threatened to attack the provincial capital, Goma. Fighting between M23 and the DRC army, the latter supported by the UN Organization Stabilization Mission in the Democratic Republic of Congo (MONUSCO—as MONUC had become in July 2010), led to the deaths of hundreds of DRC civilians and the displacement of an estimated 250,000 people. An interim report by the UN Group of Experts on the DRC, released in June 2012, accused the Rwandan Government of fomenting the M23 rebellion and supplying the rebels with training, equipment and recruits, in violation of international protocols barring support for rebel groups in eastern DRC. In response, several major donors withdrew or withheld aid to Rwanda.

Rwanda–Uganda relations have often been tense, primarily since the Ugandan authorities believed that the Rwandan Government was aiding the self-styled People's Redemption Army (PRA), a rebel group with alleged links to the Ugandan opposition leader Col Kizza Besigye. In November 2004 Uganda expelled a Rwandan diplomat, James Wizeye, for espionage and co-operation with the PRA, which supposedly aimed to overthrow President Museveni's Government. Rwanda retaliated by expelling a Ugandan diplomat. Shortly afterwards Ugandan security forces arrested three UPDF soldiers for selling information to Wizeye. Rwandan officials denied these charges, and accused Ugandan government elements of seeking to damage bilateral relations. In April 2005 Rwanda announced that it had detained a UPDF officer, Capt. David Mugambe, on espionage charges. Mugambe claimed to be fleeing political persecution in Uganda, but the Ugandan Government maintained that he was sought by the authorities for providing weapons to criminals. In 2011–12, however, meetings between Presidents Paul Kagame and Yoweri Museveni (of Uganda) and their advisers appear to have substantially improved Rwanda–Uganda relations.

INTERNATIONAL RELATIONS

Despite Rwanda's alleged poor record in the areas of governance and human rights, the Government retained the support of much of the international community. However, relations with France and Belgium remained uneven, largely owing to the legacies of the 1994 genocide. In March 2004 the French daily newspaper *Le Monde* reported that a French magistrate's study had determined that Kagame had ordered the shooting down of President Habyarimana's aircraft, which had precipitated the genocide. In response, Kagame asserted that France 'supplied weapons, and, working alongside Hutu Government extremists, gave orders, to the perpetrators of the genocide'. In October 2006 the Rwandan Government established a commission, headed by former Prosecutor-General Jean de Dieu Mucyo, to investigate France's alleged role in the Rwandan genocide. The Mucyo commission published its report in August 2008, detailing the involvement of senior French government and military officials in arming and training genocidal militias in 1994. The French Government maintained that French peace-keeping troops had saved 'several hundred thousand lives' during the genocide.

In November 2008 a French judge, Jean-Louis Bruguière, issued arrest warrants for Kagame and nine of his associates, alleging their involvement in Habyarimana's assassination. Rwanda immediately severed relations with France, ordering the French ambassador and other diplomats in Rwanda to leave the country. To further demonstrate its split from France and its historic sphere of influence in Africa, in December Rwanda stated its desire to join the Commonwealth—a goal it achieved in November 2009, with strong support from the United Kingdom. However, also in November it was announced that, following extensive consultations and negotiations between the two countries, Rwanda and France were to restore diplomatic relations. In January 2010 Laurent Contini, hitherto France's ambassador to Zimbabwe, was appointed to Rwanda, and days later the French Minister of Foreign and European Affairs, Bernard Kouchner, visited Kigali for further discussions regarding the normalization of relations. Rwanda officially reopened its embassy in Paris in February, immediately prior to a visit by French President Nicolas Sarkozy to Kigali. During the visit, Sarkozy admitted that France had made a number of 'serious errors of judgement' (although without admitting responsibility) in the period following the assassination of Habyarimana, and pledged to bring to justice any person resident in France suspected of involvement in the genocide. The Rwandan Government welcomed a decision taken by the French authorities the previous month to create a special investigative unit, as part of the Tribunal de Grande Instance in Paris, to expedite the prosecution of genocide crimes.

In October 2010 a UN mapping report was published into atrocities committed in the DRC in 1993–2003. The report included details of grave human rights violations committed by a number of regional actors, including the FPR. By this time, there were signs that some of Rwanda's international support was beginning to wane. In early 2011 questions were raised over Rwanda's relations with the United Kingdom, following reports that the Rwandan Government had issued death threats against British-based Rwandan dissidents and had allegedly hired a contract killer to assassinate two Rwandan opposition members living in the capital, London. UN allegations in 2012 regarding Rwandan support for the M23 rebellion in eastern DRC led to the withdrawal or withholding of substantial aid to Rwanda by the the USA, the United Kingdom, the Netherlands and Germany. This was the first time that the USA and the United Kingdom had withdrawn budget support to Rwanda and issued warnings to the Rwandan Government concerning its alleged operations in the DRC.

In April 2004 Rwandan soldiers were the first foreign troops to arrive in the Darfur region of western Sudan, where they were to protect the AU observer mission and defend Sudanese civilians (see the chapter on Sudan). The Rwandan Government was widely commended internationally for its participation. By November Rwanda's total personnel strength in the AU mission had risen to around 400 troops. In February 2005, during a visit to Darfur, Kagame held discussions with the Sudanese President, Lt-Gen. Omar Hassan Ahmad al-Bashir. The Rwandan President maintained that he was acting in co-operation with Sudan to resolve the Darfur crisis, while al-Bashir declared that the two countries were linked by a 'common concern' for peace. On his return to Rwanda, Kagame urged the AU to increase the number of troops in Darfur, claiming that, after the experiences of Rwanda in 1994, the international community must not allow another genocide to occur. By September 2010 a total of 3,300 Rwandan soldiers and 86 police officers were serving with the AU/UN Hybrid operation in Darfur (UNAMID), the Force Commander of which was a Rwandan, Lt.-Gen. Patrick Nyamvumba. After a draft of the UN mapping report (see above) was leaked in August of that year, accusing Rwandan troops of committing grave crimes in the DRC, Rwanda temporarily threatened to withdraw its peace-keepers from Darfur.

Economy

DUNCAN WOODSIDE

INTRODUCTION

Rwanda's economy has undergone spectacular development over the last decade, despite the tiny country's land-locked status, extreme population density and the catastrophic legacy of the 1994 genocide. Over just three years between 2008 and the end of 2010, the economy increased in size, in real terms, by close to one-quarter, despite the fact that the developed world was experiencing recession for much of this period. In 2010 gross domestic product (GDP) expanded by 7.4%, in real terms, according to the Ministry of Finance and Economic Planning. The services sector was a strong contributor to growth, expanding by 8.1%, in real terms; this was due in part to the increasing popularity of the country as a tourist destination, amid significant efforts to promote gorilla safaris and lake-based holidays. Tourist arrivals in Rwanda totalled 666,000 in 2010, and earned the country US $200m. in revenue, according to President Paul Kagame. The consistently strong performance extended into 2011, when GDP growth again exceeded 8.0%, according to preliminary estimates by the IMF in early 2012. The IMF forecast that 2012 and 2013 would see real annual growth of 7.5%–8.0%. Despite the prospect of further difficulties in global markets (in the shape of an intensification of the protracted debt crisis in the euro area, the central Banque Nationale du Rwanda (BNR)—confirming GDP growth of 8.6% for 2011—announced in May 2012 that it expected a further acceleration in the growth rate in that year.

Rwanda has attracted significant investment and foreign aid in recent years, thanks in part to a business-friendly environment and a successful projection of an intolerant attitude to corruption. In 2009 the World Bank designated Rwanda as the world's leading reformer in its annual *Doing Business* report, which praised the country for enhancing transparency and simplifying the procedures involved in establishing a business. Registered investment in the country increased by 41% during 2009, to a total of US $1,110m., according to the Rwanda Development Board, with foreign investment accounting for $524m. (or 47.6%) of this total. In what could amount to a significant further boost, Rajesh Exports, an Indian company with a significant influence in the global jewellery trade, announced in May 2011 that it was considering investing up to $1,000m. in the country's incipient gold and diamond trade.

The high level of economic growth in recent years appears to have been achieved without generating substantial imbalances. Inflation has been kept under control (consumer price growth was just 2.3% in 2010, according to the IMF). Meanwhile, deficits on the trade and current accounts, while nominally substantial, have been comfortably financed by capital inflows from donors and foreign investors. In order to prevent excess demand and an overheating of the economy, the BNR raised its benchmark interest rate by 1%, to 7%, during 2011. None the less, inflation at year-end was running at 8.3% year-on-year, indicating the need to keep a continued tight rein on monetary policy. The currency retained its remarkable long-standing stability against the US dollar throughout 2011 and into 2012, with the Rwanda franc trading at less than 600 per dollar in late May 2012.

The pace of Rwanda's recent economic development is all the more remarkable given the two huge obstacles to economic development: the extreme population density and the distance from the sea. Rwanda's economy took a long time to recover from the 1994 genocide, which, among other shocks, saw around one-quarter of the country's population flee to neighbouring countries and almost wiped out the cattle stock. Hundreds of thousands of exiled Tutsis fled to Rwanda from neighbouring Uganda after the genocide was halted, but it took until 2001 for GDP to recover to pre-genocide levels, according to the Government. From low base figures, overall GDP increased, in real terms, at an average annual rate of 6.8% in 1996–2006.

Four major foreign investment projects were agreed in 2009. In the telecommunications sector, Sweden's Millicom International Cellular invested US $100m.; in the alternative fuels sector, deals worth a combined $250m. were signed with the US company Eco-Fuel Global and the United Kingdom's Eco Positive; and, in the gas sector, the Government signed a $300m. agreement with ContourGlobal of the USA. The latter was Rwanda's largest foreign investment deal to date, and involved a 100-MW power project utilizing methane gas from beneath Lake Kivu.

However, despite this progress, Rwanda remains an extremely poor country, with the vast majority of its people living in poverty (particularly outside the capital, Kigali). The UN Development Programme (UNDP)'s 2011 Human Development Index, which ranks countries in a league table based on education, income and access to health care, placed Rwanda 166th out of 187 countries, and firmly within the category of 'low' human development.

In January 2010 a full customs union came into force throughout the East African Community (EAC), comprised of Kenya, Uganda, Tanzania, Rwanda and Burundi. In effect, this meant that tariffs between member states were eliminated (creating a free trade area), completing a phased reduction which began in 2005. Rwanda did not join the EAC until June 2007, giving the country less time to adjust to full competition with Kenya (the region's most competitive exporter), with implications for the terms of trade. A common market came into effect in July 2010, entailing the free circulation of services, citizens and capital.

AGRICULTURE

Agricultural Production

The IMF stated in February 2008 that commitment to agricultural reform was crucial to the outlook for Rwanda's economy, with Deputy Managing Director Murilo Portugal underlining that modernizing the industry to ensure food security and develop farming infrastructure represented particularly important challenges. This followed the release of a report by UNDP in July 2007, which maintained that the country needed to deal urgently with the problems generated by deficient agriculture investment and high population growth. Rwanda's population stood at 11.27m. by mid-2012, according to UN estimates, with annual population growth averaging 2.6% in 2001–10, and it is the most densely populated country in Africa. In this context, the IMF reported in July 2008 that the Rwandan Government was formulating a broad-based agricultural reform plan, elements of which would include soil conservation.

Some 89% of the labour force were employed in the agricultural sector in 2012, according to FAO. About 95% of the total value of agricultural production is provided by subsistence crops. Since the late 1970s the area of land annually made available for subsistence crops has increased only marginally, and, moreover, crop yields have declined in many areas, owing to erosion and the traditional intensive cultivation methods used. (The problem of erosion was exacerbated during 1990–94 by the felling by displaced Rwandans of trees for timber and charcoal.) Attempts to increase the yield of small farm plots have included a recent initiative to cultivate climbing beans.

The principal food crops are bananas, sweet potatoes, potatoes, cassava, beans, sorghum, rice, maize and peas. In general terms, production of cereals—particularly maize and sorghum—is strong. In 2005 the Government launched a 10-year rice development programme. Rice, then grown on approximately 7,455 ha in Butare, Kibungo and Umutara provinces, was selected as a 'priority crop' since it performs well in flood-prone valleys and eases pressure on hillside land for other crops, and also because domestic demand is high. It was planned to increase the cultivated area to 66,000 ha by 2016, through improved management of new areas in the marshlands, with the aim of meeting domestic requirements by 2009 and generating about US $170m. in export earnings. Confronted with adverse climatic conditions in 2004, the Government concentrated on improving service delivery (agricultural extension, seed availability and education in land conservation). It also pursued a tree-planting and environmental awareness campaign, partly through the introduction of a monthly *Umuganda* community service to plant trees and improve the environment.

The country recorded a significant increase in food output in 2008, of 16%, according to figures from the BNR, owing to a combination of favourable weather and an ongoing programme to raise yields. This followed a 15% rise in food production in 2007 and a 0.7% increase in 2006. More than 10,000 metric tons of high-yielding seeds were distributed under the Government's Crop Intensification Project in 2008. Small-scale farmers have been encouraged to pool land, share equipment and use fertilizers in order to increase yields. This ongoing commercialization of agriculture was reported by the Rwanda Agricultural Development Authority to have resulted in particular success in the maize sector, with average yields reaching 7 tons per acre in 2008.

One sector that the Government has sought to promote from a low base is the horticulture industry. Land devoted to producing flowers for export expanded from 2 ha in 2005 to 42 ha in 2008. The authorities planned a further increase, to 200 ha, by 2010, with the industry expected to earn some US $21m. by that stage, mainly from European markets.

Land Reform

The Government argues that land reform, aimed at freezing the dismantling of agricultural plots and promoting the transformation of marshes and swamps into suitable land for agriculture, will contribute to an increase in food production. Land reforms under consideration in 2004 envisaged encouraging the development of more viable plots: the current average size of less then 0.7 ha was considered too small. Agricultural research undertaken at the US Michigan State University, however, has demonstrated that small farms in Rwanda are more productive (in terms of yield per unit of land) than large farms. The land reform programme also has an important political component, as poor Hutu farmers fear that they will lose or have to sell their land to rich urban Tutsi in the process of land consolidation. Furthermore, the state policy of displacing a large number of rural poor to government-designated sites, which had been initiated in 1997 and pursued until early 2000, was criticized by foreign human rights organizations in 2001. The basic aim of the reform was to substitute the dispersed habitat and create larger landholdings in order to boost productivity. However, human rights activists, while agreeing that making agriculture more productive was imperative, considered that such reforms should not be made at the expense of the poor. The US-based Human Rights Watch accused military officers and businessmen with government connections of having appropriated large holdings of land from the poor.

Coffee

Revenue from coffee fluctuates considerably from year to year. After a disappointing crop in 2007, which totalled just 15,000 metric tons, Rwanda produced 22,000 tons of coffee in 2008, according to the Office des Cultures Industrielles du Rwanda—Café, owing to favourable weather conditions. The 2009 coffee crop totalled 24,000 metric tons, according to the Rwanda Coffee Development Authority (RCDA). This was lower than the original forecast, due to the impact of drought in coffee-growing regions.

Part of the reason for the poor crop in 2007 had been over-picking and a high preponderance of mature coffee trees in 2006—with many of these giving way to new trees, which initially bring a lower yield. A further 40m. new seedlings were due to be planted in 2008. Other long-term factors supported the outlook for the coffee industry, enabling the country to move up the value-added chain. Investment was being made in washing stations, as fully washed coffee commands higher prices than unwashed coffee on international markets.

In December 2007, furthermore, the US company Starbucks announced that it was opening a Starbucks Farmer Support Center for East Africa in Rwanda. The centre, which opened in 2009, was to be staffed by a full-time agronomist, who would work with farmers to increase yields and quality. In a further recognition of Rwanda's ability to produce quality coffee, Starbucks announced that it would start selling premium Rwanda Blue Bourbon Coffee in European markets for the first time in March 2008. This particular coffee is grown at between 1,700 m and 2,000 m above sea level in Cyangugu province. Starbucks also announced in June 2009 that it would begin selling Rwandan coffee certified as 'fair trade', which ensures a minimum income for farmers, in the United Kingdom and Ireland.

Despite a national target of 40,000 metric tons for 2011, which had been set two years earlier, Rwanda produced only 20,000 tons of coffee that year, according to the National Agricultural Export Development Board (NAEB). The poor harvest was attributed to weak management and adverse weather in parts of the country. However, despite the low level of production, annual export earnings rose to US $75m. in 2011, from $56m. in 2010, because of high international coffee prices. For 2012 the national output target for the sector was 24,000 tons. Although this represented an increase of 20% on the 2010 level, the long-standing pattern for the crop of a bad year followed by a good year (and vice versa) meant this target was considered achievable.

Tea

As with the coffee industry, the tea industry in Rwanda is notoriously volatile, owing to fluctuations in production and international prices. The two-and-a-half-year period from the beginning of 2006 to mid-2008 neatly encapsulated how volatile resultant tea earnings can be. In 2007 tea output rose by 25%, to 20,000 metric tons, from 16,000 tons in 2006, but a regional supply glut meant that earnings for 2007 were less, at US $31.6m., compared with $31.9m. in 2006, according to estimates made by the IMF in July 2008. However, earnings in the first six months of 2008 were $26m., almost comparable with total earnings in 2007. While improved output played a part, a recovery of prices was a bigger factor in the high revenues recorded in the first half of 2008. Indeed, average prices at the weekly auction in Kenya's Mombasa port reached $2.2 per kg in the first half of 2008, compared with $1.7 per kg in 2007. Poor rainfall affected Kenya (which generally accounts for some 75% of regional tea output) more than Rwanda, depressing regional supply and sending prices higher.

The 2008 tea crop was supported by both favourable weather and very buoyant international tea prices. Export earnings from the crop were registered at US $47.6m., according to IMF estimates, compared with $31.6m. in 2007 and $31.9m. in 2006. Despite drought affecting the tea crop in early 2009, higher prices meant that the harvest, which declined to 20,300 metric tons, earned a total of $48m. during the calendar year, according to the Rwanda Tea Authority. Earnings from tea exports in the first six months of 2011 reached $34.3m. The NAEB announced in December 2011 that it was targeting a sustained increase in exports of the commodity, in line with a drive to increase areas under tea cultivation. In 2010 tea plants covered 15,000 ha, yielding 23,349 tons in that year, but the aim was to raise tea output to at least 31,460 tons by 2014, and to 41,873 tons in 2017. By the latter year, land under tea cultivation was targeted to rise 31,588 ha, and tea exports were projected to bring in annual receipts of $147m. However, the historic volatility in global commodity markets made the export earnings target particularly vulnerable to sharp fluctuations in the price of tea. Following an earlier, largely successful privatization initiative, the private sector was expected to be the key driver of rising production. A 90% share of Rwanda's five privately owned tea factories is now accounted for by moderate-sized companies, with the remaining 10% of holdings being operated by small-scale co-operatives. In total, Rwanda had 11 tea factories as of late 2011.

Livestock

By mid-1994 the livestock sector was in extreme crisis, and the majority of the country's livestock had been lost (although some cattle were introduced by refugees returning from Uganda). However, between 1998 and 2000 livestock numbers increased from 657,137 to 732,123 head of cattle, from 192,344 to 248,345 sheep, from 481,145 to 756,522 goats and from 120,928 to 177,220 pigs. In an attempt to stimulate dairy production and increase household income, the Government and UNDP began working with communities in Mutara prefecture. Since 2000 farmers have been encouraged to produce yoghurt, cheese and cooking fat. By early 2005 some livestock numbers were approaching pre-war levels. According to government statistics, the numbers of cattle and poultry had reached 88% and 70% of the levels recorded in 1994, respectively, but the proportion was just 30% for goats. In order to boost milk output, Rwanda has imported several hundred cows from Germany and South Africa; these are more productive than the local Ankole breed but also more vulnerable to disease. In 2010, according to FAO data, livestock numbers were 1.2m. head of cattle, 743,000 sheep, 2.7m. goats and 602,000 pigs.

The poultry sector is expanding rapidly. Fish production is also accelerating, with the development of fisheries projects in Lake Kivu and in other smaller lakes throughout the country. From 1,300 metric tons in 1994, FAO estimated that the total catch increased to 9,678 tons in 2010.

INDUSTRY

The industrial sector followed the usual pattern for less-developed African states, and food-based industries predominated, with the major companies prior to 1994 being BRALIRWA, the Rwandan subsidiary of a Dutch brewery, the Régie Sucrière de Kibuy (sugar-processing) and the Office de la Valorisation Industrielle de la Banane du Rwanda, producing banana wine and liquors. By mid-1994 activity in the sector had been suspended, with factories and plants looted, destroyed or abandoned, although the BRALIRWA plant had resumed production by October.

In 2008 BRALIRWA gave notice of its intention significantly to expand operations. This was in response to an increase in both domestic and regional demand, including in the Democratic Republic of the Congo (DRC)'s eastern provinces and Uganda. Beer production was projected to increase to more than 700,000 hl, from 600,000 hl, while the rise in soft drinks production would be from 390,000 hl to 420,000 hl. The increased volumes were accommodated by investment in fermentation and bottling capacity, including a new soft drinks plant in Nyamyumba, in north-west Rwanda (close to the border with the DRC). Further expansion was envisaged, including a move into the Tanzanian market. BRALIRWA generated earnings of 6,000m. Rwanda francs in 2008, and in March 2009 announced a rebranding to celebrate the 50th anniversary of Primus, a significant local beer brand. The company produced 1.25m. hl of alcoholic and soft drinks in 2009, and was targeting an increase to 1.35m. hl in 2010.

In April 2010 the Government announced that its remaining 30% stake in BRALIRWA would be sold before the end of the year: 5% would be sold to Heineken, the Dutch brewer that already held a 70% stake, and 25% to the public, in the first initial public offering (IPO) on Rwanda's stock market. The IPO proceeded in November and December 2010. In January 2011 the Minister of Finance and Economic Planning, John Rwangombwa, announced that the offering was heavily oversubscribed: US $80m. worth of bids were received, whereas the Government was seeking to raise $29.5m. The funds from the IPO would be placed in a state account for infrastructure investment. When BRALIRWA commenced trading on the Rwanda Stock Exchange, on 31 January 2011, its share price surged in value by 62%, to 220 Rwanda francs, from a pre-opening price of 136 Rwanda francs.

BRALIRWA announced in January 2012 that it was to increase the retail price of soft drinks—including Coca Cola, three Fanta sub-brands and Sprite—by 50 Rwanda francs to 300 francs, to offset a rise in production expenses (including high global fuel prices, which had persistently stoked distribution and transport costs). However, this was the first price rise for the company's soft drinks line since 2008, and the increase put the retail cost of locally bottled Coca-Cola back on a par with the price for the rival brand Pepsi-Cola. Also in early 2012 BRALIRWA extended its relationship with the Coca-Cola Company by signing a new five-year bottling agreement. BRALIRWA's financial performance in 2011 was strong, as net profit increased by 42% year-on-year, to 14,700m. Rwanda francs, propelled partly by a rise in sales, which increased 16.3% by volume. The company anticipated a further expansion in the demand for both soft drinks and alcoholic beverages, including Guinness and Amstel, in 2012, reflecting the continued strong growth of the overall economy.

Amid rising demand for cement—reflecting a long-running construction boom in the capital, together with government investment in public infrastructure nation-wide—local company Cimenterie du Rwanda (CIMERWA) announced in March 2012 that it was seeking a US $105m. loan in order to build a new plant. The loan was being arranged by Banque de Kigali, and would entail a US dollar-denominated foreign currency component (provisionally priced at 6% above the London Interbank Offered Rate—LIBOR) and a Rwanda franc-denominated tranche (costed initially at a nominal 16%). The financing arrangement represented one of the most ambitious undertaken in Rwanda, but, if successful, it would enable CIMERWA to fund the completion of a factory with an annual output capacity totalling 600,000 metric tons per year. Construction of the new plant, at Bugarama, in south-west Rwanda, was scheduled to begin in the second quarter of 2012, and eventual completion would allow the firm to close its old factory, where annual production capacity was limited to 100,000 tons.

SERVICES

A key emerging sector in Rwanda is the financial services industry, as the country integrates more closely with fellow members of the EAC and benefits from trade with the DRC. This has led to a rise in both commercial and personal incomes, which in turn has boosted bank deposits. Banque de Kigali, Rwanda's largest commercial lender, has played a leading role in the expansion of the banking sector. In the 18 months to the end of March 2011, the bank increased its branch network from 18 to 33, with a further 10 planned to open later that year. The bank was also investing in extending the availability of mobile telephone banking, debit cards and automatic teller machines (ATMs), in an effort to increase its retail customer base from 70,000 to 500,000 by early 2013. In order to help fund this continued expansion, Banque de Kigali conducted an IPO in June 2011. In September shares in Banque de Kigali began trading on the Rwanda Stock Exchange, after an IPO that saw the sale of a 45% stake in the bank. Underlining investors' strong appetite for the offering, the bank's shares increased in value by 8% on the first day of trading, to reach 135 Rwanda francs per share. The shares later peaked at 200 Rwanda francs, before correcting, to trade at around 125 Rwanda francs per share by April 2012. In that month Banque de Kigali announced that it intended to begin an expansion into Kenya and Uganda before the end of the year.

In an additional boost to Rwanda's financial sector, the global credit and international payment facilitator Visa announced in December 2011 that it was to extend its operations into the country. Visa would introduce basic facilities for processing card payments, including local clearing infrastructure.

None the less, the Governor of the BNR, Claver Gatete, stated in February 2012 that the pace of growth in the banking sector was likely to slow in that year, because of its deliberate tightening of liquidity, indicating that the central bank detected a threat of overheating. This situation stood in stark contrast to that in parts of the developed world, with credit seizing up in parts of the euro area once again in mid-2012 as a result of the intensifying sovereign debt crisis in Greece and pressure on the Spanish banking sector.

Rwanda's inflation rate reached 8.3% year-on-year in December 2011, up from just over 2% for 2010 as a whole. Additionally, although the BNR raised the key lending rate by an aggregate 1.0% in 2011 (in two increments of 0.5%, in October and November, so that the key rate reached 7.0%), the IMF cautioned in January 2012 that the inflationary environment would be likely to necessitate additional tightening in that year. In this context, Gatete released central bank figures in February forecasting that growth in commercial loans would slow to 16.6% in 2012, from 28.4% in 2011.

Meanwhile, an additional factor that bodes well for the development of Rwanda's banking industry—and, by extension, the country's private sector as a whole—was the approval of Kenya Commercial Bank's (KCB) application for a licence in the country. KCB had already opened branches in Tanzania, Uganda and South Sudan. Rwanda's decision to grant market entry to the bank was interpreted as a positive development, which would help to intensify local competition and improve services for local entrepreneurs. After a difficult year for the local venture, KCB Rwanda recorded a loss of 1,700m. Rwanda francs in 2010, but 2011 was substantially better, with the subsidiary posting a net profit of 475m. Rwanda francs. Its local loan book surged by 22,000m. Rwanda francs year-on-year, to 35,000m. Rwandan francs in 2011. The bank aimed to achieve a 50% increase in net profit in 2012. Illustrating its successful integration into the local banking market, KCB was co-operating with Banque de Kigali to arrange dollar-denominated funding for the cement company CIMERWA in early 2012.

In October 2008 anti-money-laundering legislation was ratified by Rwanda's legislature. The legislation provided for the establishment of a financial intelligence unit to track, receive, process and evaluate banking data in the pursuit of terrorists and illicit funds associated with other criminal activities. The IMF meanwhile continued to urge further reform of the banking sector. A Financial Sector Development Plan had been finalized in May 2007. Its core aims were: to increase the affordability of financial services (including extending the provision of microfinance); to enhance savings mobilization; to modernize the regulatory framework; and to restructure the national payments system. The IMF assessed in February 2009 that weaknesses in the system remained, emphasizing a need fully to implement the Financial Sector Development Plan. In particular, the Fund stated that adequate credit was still not being provided to the agriculture sector. As part of efforts to address these concerns, the Rwandan Government encouraged foreign banks to establish operations in the country. In March 2011 Equity Bank, Kenya's biggest bank by market value, announced that it would open five branches in Rwanda, having received a licence to operate in the country. The Rwandan authorities were co-operating with local banks to extend the banking sector's reach beyond Kigali, with a particular emphasis on increasing the number of branches and ATMs. In mid-2011 the Governor of the BNR announced that the authorities were aiming to ensure that 80% of Rwanda's population would have access to credit by 2017, compared with 21% of the population at that stage.

The authorities are encouraging the development of a local securities exchange as a means of opening up an additional source of funding for businesses. Rwanda's second IPO and the subsequent trading of Banque de Kigali shares on the Rwanda Stock Exchange from September 2011, after BRALIRWA floated in January of that year (see Industry, above), represented a major step forward, as the development of the local securities market had been slow initially, and had been largely restricted to trading in bonds rather than company shares.

MINING

Cassiterite (a tin-bearing ore) is Rwanda's principal mineral resource (exports of cassiterite were valued at US $37.6m. in the first 10 months of 2008), followed by wolframite (a tungsten-bearing ore), columbo-tantalite (coltan) and gold. Cassiterite exports accounted for 46% of total mineral exports, which reached $81.9m. in the first 10 months of 2008.

On 12 April 2001 a UN panel of experts on the illegal exploitation of neighbouring DRC's natural resources recommended that the UN Security Council impose an embargo on all Rwandan mineral exports. The report alleged that much of Rwanda's exported coltan, cassiterite, gold and diamonds included Congolese products, which were exploited and exported in illicit circumstances. The panel adopted this conclusion by comparing Rwandan official statistics for 1995 and 2000, which demonstrated a dramatic rise in gold exports, from 1 kg to 10 kg, in cassiterite exports, from 247 metric tons to 437 tons, and in coltan exports, from 54 tons to 87 tons.

Rwanda's exports of minerals have continued to outstrip domestic production. However, Rwanda's domestic production prospects improved following the announcement of the discovery of gold deposits by TransAfrika Resources of Mauritius in February 2009. In November of that year another Mauritius-based company, Gatumba Mining Concessions, announced that it would invest at least US $2.5m. and build 10 small coltan-processing plants in the country during 2010–15. The company was also considering the feasibility of two 'medium-sized' open-cast mines to extract coltan.

In September 2010 the Rwandan Geology and Mines Authority (OGMR) announced that it would start tracing and certifying the sources of its cassiterite, in response to legislation adopted in the USA in July. The US Congress gave the Securities and Exchange Commission (SEC), which regulates financial markets (and therefore the activity of listed firms) in the USA, nine months to design a certification scheme, in an effort to counteract the trade in 'conflict minerals.' This legislation would oblige US firms to certify whether minerals purchased from the DRC and nine neighbouring countries (including Rwanda) were sourced from areas of the DRC controlled by illegal armed groups. The Director-General of OGMR, Michael Biryabarema, raised concerns that Rwanda's mineral exports could suffer from an indiscriminate aversion among buyers to the whole region. The US legislation relates to cassiterite, gold, wolframite and coltan purchases. The proposals would require companies using these minerals in their products to investigate their supply chains, to ascertain where materials are sourced, and to disclose their conclusions (with an explanation of the investigatory process). In the event that a company verifiably concluded that a product did not contain 'conflict minerals', it would be permitted to label the relevant product 'DRC conflict-free'. The Electronic Industry Citizenship Coalition (EICC)—a not-for-profit association of companies including Apple, Hewlett-Packard, Intel and Microsoft—undertook to stop using minerals in cases where the supply chain had not been fully traced.

While the SEC's proposals on 'conflict minerals' had been set to enter force in April 2011, the USA's financial regulator stated in that month that it had postponed adoption of the new regulations until at least August. The SEC pledged that a final draft would be confirmed between August and December. Ahead of the implementation of the legislation, Rwanda's income from mineral exports rose to US $60m. in 2010, from $54.6m. in 2009, according to an estimate by the OGMR in December 2010. In the first quarter of 2011 earnings from tin, tungsten and tantalum reached $35.3m. Export volumes of tin alone during this three-month period increased by 115% year on year, yielding export revenues of $21.5m. for Rwanda. In April 2011, in a further apparent effort to offset the potential negative effect of the SEC regulations and to meet the supply chain requirements of the EICC, Rwanda's then Minister of Forestry and Mines, Christophe Bazivamo, announced that the country had banned the sale of minerals originating from conflict-affected parts of the DRC.

As a further signal of good faith, Rwanda handed over to the DRC authorities 82 metric tons of confiscated illicit output, including cassiterite and coltan, in November 2011. The move represented part of an extended rapprochement between the two countries. In January 2012 four senior Rwandan army officers were dismissed, due to alleged illegal business dealings in the DRC's minerals industry. Rwanda's head of military intelligence, Brig.-Gen. Richard Rutatina, was among those removed from office.

India-based jewellery trader Rajesh Exports announced in May 2011 that it was considering investing up to US $1,000m. in Rwanda, through the establishment of a gold refinery and a diamond trading operation. The company stated that it was in talks with the Rwandan Government about the viability of establishing the country as a continental centre for processing gold output, while it was also examining the possibility of setting up a trading and processing centre for uncut diamonds.

Natural Gas

Another important mineral to be exploited is natural gas, which was discovered beneath Lake Kivu on the border with the DRC. Reserves of an estimated 60,000m. cu m (about one-half of which are in the DRC) are believed to be among the largest in the world. In May 2000 Rwanda's water, electricity and gas parastatal, Electrogaz, initiated talks with the South African company Mossgas to discuss the possibility of exploiting the Lake Kivu methane and gas resources. Two pilot installations, funded by the European Union (EU), produce gas, but here again the small size of the potential market casts doubt on the likely profitability of large-scale processing. However, Electrogaz hopes to receive Belgian funding for a programme to increase its daily output of gas from 5,000 cu m to 25,000 cu m. The overall electricity generation potential from natural gas resources was estimated at 200 MW by a private consultant, and at 700 MW by the Rwandan Government. In 2006 the British firm Dane Associates entered into a £48m. partnership with the Rwandan Government. A 30-MW power plant was expected to result, which would tap Lake Kivu's renewable methane deposit. Plans to supply natural gas to the cement and other industries were also under consideration.

In 2004 the World Bank was also planning to finance consultant support for the Unité de Promotion et d'Exploitation du Gaz du Lac Kivu (UPEGAZ) parastatal, considering that the medium-term development of the power sector was 'inextricably linked' to the exploitation of Lake Kivu's methane reserves. According to Bank sources, a Strategic Social and Environmental Assessment of Power Development Options for Rwanda, Burundi and western Tanzania concluded that power generation from Kivu gas was competitive with comparable hydroelectricity options. Meanwhile, the World Bank was also considering financing the construction of a transmission link to connect potential new generation at Lake Kivu. Recent developments in the sector have included demonstrations of methane extraction technology to the Government and potential investors by engineers from a South African firm, Murray & Roberts, at a pilot plant near Gisenyi. Cogelgaz, a joint venture between BRALIRWA and the Banque de Commerce, de Développement et d'Industrie, had commissioned the company to undertake the technical improvement of its existing gas plant. Rwandan projects planned by Murray & Roberts included the supply of methane gas to urban areas.

In June 2008 the Minister of State in charge of Energy, Albert Butare, stated that the Government was poised to launch a 5-MW pilot project from the methane gas reserves. He added that the Government was in talks with a US investor for a 100-MW project, and claimed that the potential power generation from Lake Kivu stood at 350 MW. The US firm ContourGlobal subsequently signed an agreement with the Government to develop the US $325m. power project, which, according to the company, would involve extracting gas from a lake-based platform from a depth of 350 m. The gas would then be processed and carried through a pipeline to a proposed onshore plant, which would be situated close to the lake-shore, in the town of Kibuye.

ENERGY

Rwanda has long suffered power shortages. In 2007 the country generated 165.4 GWh of electricity, but total demand stood at 248.7 GWh, according to government statistics. Fossil fuels accounted for just over one-half (54%) of electricity generation, while the remaining 46% was sourced from hydroelectric power. The land relief is considered ideal for power generation. According to studies undertaken under the auspices of the Economic Community of the Great Lake Countries (CEPGL), the Ruzizi river alone offers potential generating capacity totalling 500 MW, of which only a fraction is currently being used. By the end of 2010 only 6% of the country's population of some 10m. was connected to electricity (up only marginally from 5% in 2007); however, the Ministry of Infrastructure stated in February 2011 that it was aiming to increase connectivity to 50% of the population within five years. In order to meet this ambitious target, the Government was seeking new funds totalling US $290m.

In January 2011 Rwanda began commissioning at the Rukarara hydroelectric power plant. The plant would have the capacity to generate electricity of 9.5 MW, after an initial testing phase when it was producing between 2.5 MW and 6 MW, according to the Ministry of Infrastructure. In March Tunisia's Société Tunisienne de l'Electricité et du Gaz secured a US $68.6m. contract to connect 50,000 homes in Rwanda to the national electricity grid over the following two years. The Rwandan authorities would pay for the project over a period of five years.

Rwanda planned to build a hydropower plant on the Nyabarongo river from 2008, and requested a modification of its Poverty Reduction and Growth Facility (PRGF) with the IMF to accommodate construction of the project. The total cost of the project—which was to take four years—was to be US $112.7m., or approximately 3% of GDP. The IMF expressed misgivings after the authorities failed to secure borrowing on concessional terms for one-half of the project, but the Rwandan Government stated its determination to press ahead with construction, which it regarded as crucial to the country's future development. To help finance construction, the Government secured $80m. in funding, including credit from Exim Bank of India.

Rwanda's power sector received an investment boost when Egypt's Orascom Construction Industries announced in September 2011 that it would invest up to US $130m. in building a 50-MW methane power plant. The project, located on Lake Kivu, would take three to four years to complete and would substantially increase Rwanda's installed generating capacity, which stood at just 69 MW in 2009. Furthermore, the Belgian Development Agency (BTC) has pledged to invest €55m. over a three-year period in geothermal energy exploration. The agency was to carry out drilling work in order to confirm whether heat can be sourced from Rwanda's sector of the East African Rift. Early expectations were that 300 MW of energy could be sourced from Rwanda's share of the territory.

TRANSPORT AND COMMUNICATIONS

Internal communications in Rwanda are operated almost exclusively along the relatively well-developed road system (14,008 km in 2004), as there are no railways nor navigable waterways (except Lake Kivu). Asphalted highways link Rwanda with Burundi, Uganda, the DRC and Tanzania. They also connect the principal towns. Tarmac roads extend to just over 1,000 km, which, given the small size of the country, is one of the highest densities in Africa.

Rwanda's external trade is heavily dependent on the ports of Mombasa (Kenya), Dar es Salaam (Tanzania) and Matadi (DRC), and about 80% of Rwandan exports and imports pass through Uganda and Kenya.

Feasibility studies have been conducted for a railway network to link Uganda, Rwanda, Burundi and Tanzania. The Rwandan business community showed renewed interest in the sector in 2000, dispatching a delegation to the railway terminal of Isaka (Tanzania) to discuss with the local authorities and the Tanzania Railway Corporation plans to make greater use of this central corridor, combining a road link from Kigali to Isaka (500 km) and the railway line from Isaka to the port of Dar es Salaam (1,300 km). Burundi, Rwanda and Tanzania expressed their renewed intention to seek funds to build the railway link between Isaka and Kigali, with a possible extension to Burundi. In January 2008 Tanzania announced that it expected work to begin on the Isaka–Kigali link before the end of the year. The office of Tanzania's President Jakaya Kikwete stated that the work was envisaged to be completed by 2013.

Rwanda's national carrier, Rwandair Express offers services to Kenya, Uganda and Burundi on a daily basis, while also flying to the United Arab Emirates (UAE) and South Africa three times a week. In March 2012 Canada-listed Bombardier Aerospace announced that it was to sell two of its CRJ900 NextGen aircraft to Rwandair for a total of US $89m. The deal included an option to increase the order to four jets, which if exercised, would entail a total price of $185m. Six months earlier ambitious plans were made public for a new international airport in Rwanda. A government document called for bids to construct, fund and operate the airport—to belocated at Bugesera, about 25 km south-east of Kigali—on a 25-year lease. The schedule envisaged the airport opening by 2016, following the construction of passenger and cargo terminals, together with a 4.2-km runway. A subsequent expansion, with the aim of mirroring Nairobi's status as a regional air traffic hub, would involve building a second runway and additional terminals, enabling the airport to accommodate 3m. passengers per year by 2030.

In 2004 more than 300 secondary schools were provided with internet connectivity. In February 2005 President Paul Kagame stated, at the African Information Communications Technologies conference in Accra, Ghana, that all of the country's secondary schools were to be connected to the internet by 2017. Kagame also announced that broadband infrastructure was in place in Rwanda, that there was fibre-optic infrastructure in Kigali and most other towns, and that the authorities planned to extend this to other areas of the country. Rwanda, like other East and Central African countries, relies on satellite as a sole medium for international connectivity. However, the Government did, through Rwandatel, subscribe to the East African Submarine Cable System. The number of internet centres was increasing rapidly in the country. In early 2005, for example, farmers at Maraba were using such facilities to communicate with other coffee producers from the rest of the world.

The Government announced in July 2008 that it would invest 1,500m. Rwanda francs in telecommunications infrastructure in rural areas in 2008. The funding came from a 2% tax on the total turnover of landline operator Rwandatel and the main cellular operator MTN Rwandacell (a privately owned South Africa-Rwanda partnership). A state-sponsored company, New Artel, was to use the money to invest in areas that the two main telecommunications operators did not reach. New Artel has a strong focus on increasing internet connectivity.

In 2008 only 9% of the population had access to telephony. A third combined 15-year fixed and mobile licence was secured in December 2008 by Swedish operator Millicom, which started operations in the country with its Tigo Rwanda brand in November 2009. The mobile penetration rate in January 2010 was 24% of the population. The Rwanda Utilities Regulatory Agency (RURA) aimed to increase this rate further by promoting enhanced competition and by reducing the retail price of the cheapest mobile phones, from 8,000 Rwanda francs to 2,000 Rwanda francs, with plans to subsidize 50% of the cost of each phone. As a result, mobile penetration accelerated at an extraordinary rate in 2010, as the number of users increased by 50%, from 2.4m. to 3.6m. (36% of the population), according to RURA. The agency was targeting a 50% penetration rate by 2015.

Rwandatel had its cellular licence revoked in April 2011 by the regulatory authority, on the grounds that the company was failing to compete effectively against rival firms MTN and Tigo, and was thereby jeopardizing an industry-wide expansion target. Rwandatel had fewer than 444,000 subscribers as of August 2010, whereas newcomer Tigo had already attracted close to 530,000, while MTN had 2.2m. customers. In September 2011 a further operator entered Rwanda's mobile phone market: Bharti Airtel, which launched services in March 2012, stated its intention to invest US $100m. in Rwanda over three years. By the end of 2011 MTN's subscriber base had reached 2.9m., while Tigo's had surged to 1.55m., resulting in respective market shares nearing 65% and 35%. To illustrate the relative gain made by Tigo, a year earlier it had just 19% of the local market, while MTN's share stood at 72%. By the end of 2011 the mobile penetration rate in Rwanda was almost 42%, reaching a total of 4.45m. people.

DEVELOPMENT PLANNING

Despite criticisms of Rwanda's involvement in the conflict in the DRC and the illegal exploitation of Congolese mineral resources (including Rwanda's hostile invasions of 1996 and 1998–2002, and Kigali's sponsoring of proxy armed groups for many years), Paul Kagame's administration has received the continued support of donors. This is partly due to long-standing sentiments of remorse within the international community and among non-governmental organizations over the failure to prevent the 1994 genocide, but is also a consequence of the Government's willingness to effect political reforms and to manage donor funds in a highly transparent manner.

In 2002 the US Agency for International Development (USAID) planned to support the three priority areas: development relief and conflict prevention; global health; and economic growth. USAID also announced its intention to increase its efforts to counter HIV/AIDS by expanding awareness activities, working with other donors to prevent mother-to-child transmission, and providing counselling and other support to infected persons. In that year USAID was in the early stages of implementing a three-year, multifaceted effort to stimulate agricultural production and promote broad-based economic growth, complemented by a substantial development-orientated Food for Peace programme. Components of the programme included human resources development at the principal agricultural research, training and educational institutions, agricultural policy advice, and the expansion of agribusiness and export opportunities.

In January 2001 Rwanda, which had been declared eligible to benefit from the IMF- and World Bank-sponsored initiative for heavily indebted poor countries (HIPC), obtained debt relief of US $810m., which was to contribute substantially to the alleviation of the country's debt burden. Total outstanding external debt was estimated at $1,324m. by the end of 2000, equivalent to 73% of GDP. More than 87% of Rwandan external debt was owed to multilateral partners, principally the World Bank Group, at $998.4m., followed by the African Development Bank (AfDB) ($208.4m.). The main bilateral creditors were France ($35.2m.), the People's Republic of China ($32.2m.), Saudi Arabia ($29.8m.), Kuwait ($29.4m.) and Japan ($13.6m.). The Government estimated that annual cash flow savings from this relief would be about $20m.–$30m., equivalent to 1.5% of GDP, in 2001–10.

In February 2008 the IMF authorized disbursement of US $1.8m. from the country's $12.7m. PRGF, taking total loans under the three-year programme to $7.2m. The IMF's fourth review under the PRGF, published in July, pointed to continued, uninterrupted multilateral support. This review stated that the planned large-scale hydroelectric power project (see Energy, above) should have a 'manageable' impact on debt sustainability, while helping to alleviate infrastructure bottlenecks. This followed a positive evaluation of the project's viability by the World Bank.

A 24% rise in spending was proposed in the 2009/10 budget, taking expenditure from 676,000m. Rwanda francs to 838,000m. Rwanda francs, including recurrent expenditure of 481,000m. Rwanda francs, development spending of 342,000m. Rwanda francs, and 15,000m. Rwanda francs for redressing payment arrears and other items. Revenues, meanwhile, were projected at 770,000m. Rwanda francs (including 344,000m. Rwanda francs in donor funds), resulting in a forecast budget deficit of 68,000m. Rwanda francs, which would be offset by loans, including bilateral lending from Asia and the Middle East. According to the IMF, in 2009/10 total expenditure was projected at 814,900m. Rwanda francs, slightly below the budgeted level, while total revenue was forecast at 779,600m. Rwanda francs, marginally above the amount initially budgeted.

Following completion of three consecutive PRGF programmes (and significant debt relief), the Government requested a three-year Policy Support Instrument (PSI), which amounts to a voluntary surveillance mechanism without providing loans. In June 2010 the IMF Executive Board approved a three-year, which would focus on three key areas: fiscal consolidation (including efforts to generate higher revenues); monetary and exchange rate reforms (centred on a more flexible exchange rate and inflation-targeting); and structural reforms (focusing on the elimination of infrastructure bottlenecks, enhanced regulation of the financial sector and an expansion of the export base). President Kagame and US President George W. Bush signed a bilateral investment treaty in February 2008. The treaty's details included the free transfer of investment-related funds, non-discriminatory treatment for companies working in one another's countries, and provisions for compensation in the event of expropriation. Bilateral trade flows increased during 2007, with Rwanda's exports to the USA increasing by 43%, to US $13m., and Rwanda's imports from the USA increasing by 37%, to $16m.

In an article for the British newspaper *Financial Times* in May 2009, President Kagame argued that aid often left recipient populations 'unstable, distracted and more dependent'. He added that a 'discussion' needed to take place on 'when to end aid and how best to end it'. However, at that stage, Rwanda remained a long way from terminating its dependence on foreign aid. The 2008 budget was 49% funded by foreign donors, according to the country's 2008–10 budget framework paper. The World Bank and the United Kingdom's Department for International Development were the biggest aid donors for the 2008 budget.

A 'mini-budget' for the first six months of 2009 was approved by Rwanda's Council of Ministers in October 2008. From 1 July 2009 the country would align its financial year (hitherto the calendar year) with the July/June fiscal period followed by other EAC members. The EAC is an intergovernmental body comprising Burundi, Kenya, Rwanda, Tanzania and Uganda, and is designed to promote regional integration and trade. The January–June 2009 budget amounted to US $687.2m., and prioritized four key development areas: governance and sovereignty; human development and social sectors; infrastructure; and capacity-building.

In its fourth review of the PSI, completed in June 2012, the IMF commended Rwanda on its continued strong macroeconomic performance, after real economic growth registered more than 8% in 2011. Moreover, Rwanda's rate of inflation, at around 8%, was the lowest in the region, showing the central bank's ability to maintain monetary discipline in the context of pressures from high imported food and fuel costs. The Fund emphasized that planned government reforms to revenue collection should help to underpin a stronger fiscal profile, which would also be supported by tackling long-standing debt management issues.

FOREIGN TRADE

Like many emerging markets, Rwanda has maintained a trade deficit, as it imports significant volumes of capital goods to help develop its economy. In 2007 the deficit amounted to US $404m, according to the IMF. Exports amounted to $177m. in 2007, compared with an import bill of $581m. By the end of 2010 the annual trade deficit had increased to $846m. Although exports in that year reached an estimated $455m. (an increase of 24% compared with 2009), imports stood at $1,300m., according to the Rwanda Development Board. In January 2011 the IMF estimated that the current account deficit, excluding official transfers, stood at $981m. in 2010, up from an estimated $968m. in 2009 and $676.1m. in 2008.

However, in its January 2011 country report, the IMF was not overly concerned by this upward trajectory. Rwanda's trade deficit remained manageable because of significant donor support and foreign direct investment (FDI). Including official transfers in the current account balance generated a relatively modest estimated deficit of US $380.8m. in 2010, following a deficit of $443.6m. in 2009. Meanwhile, strong FDI levels bolstered the capital account, which remained in surplus, thereby helping to fund the country's trade and current account deficits. The capital account recorded an estimated surplus of $207.5m. in 2010, up from $200m. in 2009, according to IMF estimates published in January 2011.

The trade and current account deficits widened further in 2011, according to preliminary statistics published by the IMF in January 2012. Although exports rose from a revised US $297.3m. in 2010 to $404.4m. in 2011—in large part owing to the impact of high global commodity prices on coffee export revenues—this improvement was more than offset by a surge in imports, which climbed from a revised $1,084m. in 2010 to a provisional $1,576m. in 2011. The trade deficit therefore widened from a revised $787m. in 2010 to a provisional $1,171m. in 2011, taking the current account deficit (excluding official transfers) from $988m. to $1,311m.

Rwanda's principal export destination in 2011 was Kenya, which received 36.6% of the country's shipments, officially followed by the DRC (14.7%), China (9.1%), Swaziland (5.9%), the USA (5.3%) and Pakistan (4.6%). Kenya was also Rwanda's main source of imports, providing 19.6% of the country's externally sourced goods, followed by Uganda (17.7%), the UAE (8.4%), Tanzania (5.7%) and China (5.3%).

In March 2004 negotiations commenced between the EU and the Eastern and Southern Africa group of countries (including Rwanda) for a World Trade Organization-compatible free trade Economic Partnership Agreement (EPA). In November 2007 EAC member states initialled an interim EPA with the EU on market access. Negotiations on a full EPA were ongoing in 2012.

A customs union was established by the EAC in 2005, although Rwanda, which had long maintained high import tariffs on certain goods, in order to generate revenues and suppress the trade deficit, did not become a member until July 2007. A cabinet paper in late 2008 estimated the loss of revenues from joining the customs union to be an annual US $10.9m. The Minister of Finance and Planning attributed these losses to the application of the customs union's common external tariff, which would replace the national tariff structure. The national tariff had applied as follows: 0% import tax on raw materials, 5% on goods of 'economic importance', 10% on intermediate goods and 30% on fully finished products. By contrast, the EAC's common external tariff was to apply the following structure: 0% import tax on raw materials, 15% on intermediate goods and 25% on fully finished products. With the entry into force of a full EAC customs union in January 2010, however, certain exemptions were granted to the common market (and the customs union) on *ad hoc* basis. Rwanda, for example, received a six-month extension of a waiver on sugar duties in March 2012, having, owing to supply constraints, been unable fully to exploit an earlier allowance to import 50,000 metric tons of this commodity. Ordinarily, sugar imports entering the EAC are taxed at a rate of 100%. It was estimated that Rwanda would import 38,000 tons of sugar during the new six-month grace period. However, operators in Rwanda would be deterred from profiteering through exports of the anticipated additional sugar imports to its partner states, since any such activity would be subject, at 100%, to the EAC's Common External Tariff.

Statistical Survey

Source (unless otherwise stated): National Institute of Statistics of Rwanda (NISR); tel. 250571037; e-mail info@statistics.gov.rw; internet www.statistics.gov.rw.

Area and Population

AREA, POPULATION AND DENSITY

Area (sq km)	26,338*
Population (census results)	
15 August 1991	7,142,755
16 August 2002	
Males	3,879,448
Females	4,249,105
Total	8,128,553
Population (UN estimates at mid-year)†	
2010	10,624,005
2011	10,942,952
2012	11,271,785
Density (per sq km) at mid-2012	428.0

* 10,169 sq miles.
† Source: UN, *World Population Prospects: The 2010 Revision.*

POPULATION BY AGE AND SEX

(UN estimates at mid-2012)

	Males	Females	Total
0–14	2,408,990	2,422,804	4,831,794
15–64	2,990,352	3,143,250	6,133,602
65 and over	138,284	168,105	306,389
Total	5,537,626	5,734,159	11,271,785

Source: UN, *World Population Prospects: The 2010 Revision.*

PREFECTURES

(population at 1991 census)

	Area (sq km)	Population*	Density (per sq km)
Butare	1,830	765,910	418.5
Byumba	4,987	779,365	159.2
Cyangugu	2,226	517,550	232.5
Gikongoro	2,192	462,635	211.1
Gisenyi	2,395	728,365	304.1
Gitarama	2,241	849,285	379.0
Kibungo	4,134	647,175	156.5
Kibuye	1,320	472,525	358.0
Kigali }	3,251	921,050	355.2
Kigali-Ville }		233,640	
Ruhengeri	1,762	765,255	434.3
Total	26,338	7,142,755	271.2

* Source: UN, *Demographic Yearbook.*

2002 census (population): Butare 725,914; Byumba 707,786; Cyangugu 607,495; Gikongoro 489,729; Gisenyi 864,377; Gitarama 856,488; Kibungo 702,248; Kibuye 469,016; Kigali 789,330; Kigali-Ville 603,049; Ruhengeri 891,498; Umutara 421,623; *Total* 8,128,553.

PRINCIPAL TOWNS

(population at 1978 census)

Kigali (capital)	117,749	Ruhengeri	16,025
Butare	21,691	Gisenyi	12,436

Mid-2011 (incl. suburbs, UN estimate): Kigali 1,003,570 (Source: UN, *World Urbanization Prospects: The 2011 Revision*).

BIRTHS AND DEATHS

(annual averages, UN estimates)

	1995–2000	2000–05	2005–10
Birth rate (per 1,000)	40.7	39.8	40.7
Death rate (per 1,000)	19.9	14.4	12.3

Source: UN, *World Population Prospects: The 2010 Revision.*

Life expectancy (years at birth): 55.1 (males 53.8; females 56.4) in 2010 (Source: World Bank, World Development Indicators database).

ECONOMICALLY ACTIVE POPULATION

(persons aged 14 years and over, at census of August 2002)

	Males	Females	Total
Agriculture	1,218,181	1,731,411	2,949,592
Fishing	3,374	94	3,468
Industrial activities	3,692	1,636	5,328
Production activities	32,994	10,649	43,643
Electricity and water	2,390	277	2,667
Construction	41,641	1,244	42,885
Trade reconstruction	56,869	32,830	89,699
Restaurants and hotels	4,525	2,311	6,836
Transport and communications	29,574	1,988	31,562
Financial intermediaries	1,560	840	2,400
Administration and defence	22,479	5,585	28,064
Education	22,688	17,046	39,734
Health and social services	7,521	7,054	14,575
Sub-total	1,447,488	1,812,965	3,260,453
Activities not adequately defined	69,042	39,458	108,500
Total employed	1,516,530	1,852,423	3,368,953

Source: IMF, *Rwanda: Selected Issues and Statistical Appendix* (December 2004).

Mid-2012 (estimates in '000): Agriculture, etc. 4,618; Total labour force 5,187 (Source: FAO).

Health and Welfare

KEY INDICATORS

Total fertility rate (children per woman, 2010)	5.4
Under-5 mortality rate (per 1,000 live births, 2010)	64
HIV/AIDS (% of persons aged 15–49, 2009)	2.9
Physicians (per 1,000 head, 2004)	0.05
Hospital beds (per 1,000 head, 2007)	1.6
Health expenditure (2009): US $ per head (PPP)	111
Health expenditure (2009): % of GDP	10.1
Health expenditure (2009): public (% of total)	48.6
Access to water (% of persons, 2010)	65
Access to sanitation (% of persons, 2010)	55
Total carbon dioxide emissions ('000 metric tons, 2008)	704.1
Carbon dioxide emissions per head (metric tons, 2008)	0.1
Human Development Index (2011): ranking	166
Human Development Index (2011): value	0.429

For sources and definitions, see explanatory note on p. vi.

Agriculture

PRINCIPAL CROPS
('000 metric tons)

	2008	2009	2010
Maize	167.0	285.5	432.4
Sorghum	144.0	174.5	161.2
Potatoes	1,162.0	1,287.4	1,789.4
Sweet potatoes	826.0	801.4	840.1
Cassava (Manioc)	978.5	2,019.7	2,377.2
Taro (Cocoyam)	130.4	136.8	186.0
Sugar cane	63.0	63.0*	63.0*
Beans, dry	308.0	326.5	327.5
Peas, dry	21.7	33.8	38.0
Groundnuts, with shell	11.5	15.4	14.4
Pumpkins, squash and gourds*	169.7	209.3	210.4
Plantains	2,604.0	2,993.5	2,749.2
Coffee, green	20.7	28.0†	26.0†
Tea	20.0	20.0*	24.5*

* FAO estimate(s).
† Unofficial figure.

Aggregate production ('000 metric tons, may include official, semi-official or estimated data): Total cereals 466 in 2008, 651 in 2009, 746 in 2010; Total roots and tubers 3,111 in 2008, 4,261 in 2009, 5,208 in 2010; Total pulses 330 in 2008, 360 in 2009, 365 in 2010; Total vegetables (incl. melons) 368 in 2008, 421 in 2009, 419 in 2010; Total fruits (excl. melons) 2,800 in 2008, 3,202 in 2009, 2,941 in 2010.

Source: FAO.

LIVESTOCK
('000 head, year ending September)

	2008	2009	2010
Cattle	1,548.5	1,194.9	1,218.5
Pigs	310.8	586.6	602.3
Sheep	704.0	718.2	743.2
Goats	1,736.2	2,519.8	2,735.5
Chickens	2,000*	2,000	2,848

* FAO estimate.

Source: FAO.

LIVESTOCK PRODUCTS
('000 metric tons)

	2008	2009	2010
Cattle meat*	36.9	35.4	36.4
Goat meat*	6.1	7.2	7.3
Pig meat*	5.7	6.9	7.6
Chicken meat*	2.4	2.4	2.4
Game meat*	11.0	11.9	13.2
Cows' milk	118.8	145.0	183.7*
Sheep's milk*	2.6	2.7	2.7
Goats' milk*	27.9	28.9	29.8
Hen eggs*	2.8	2.5	2.9

* FAO estimate(s).

Source: FAO.

Forestry

ROUNDWOOD REMOVALS
('000 cubic metres, excluding bark, FAO estimates)

	2007	2008	2009
Sawlogs, veneer logs and logs for sleepers	245	961	962
Other industrial wood	250	250	250
Fuel wood	5,000	5,000	5,000
Total	5,495	6,211	6,212

2010–11: Production assumed to be unchanged from 2009 (FAO estimates).

Source: FAO.

SAWNWOOD PRODUCTION
('000 cubic metres, including railway sleepers)

	2007	2008	2009
Coniferous (softwood)	22	40	50
Non-coniferous (hardwood)	57	81	85
Total	79	121	135

2010–11: Production assumed to be unchanged from 2009 (FAO estimates).

Source: FAO.

Fishing

(metric tons, live weight, FAO estimates)

	2008	2009	2010
Capture	9,050	9,050	9,050
Nile tilapia	3,950	3,950	3,950
Aquaculture	388	488	628
Nile tilapia	300	400	500
Total catch	9,438	9,538	9,678

Source: FAO.

Mining

(metric tons, estimates)

	2008	2009	2010
Tin concentrates*	1,500	1,700	2,500
Tungsten concentrates*	1,708	874	843
Columbo-tantalite†	600	480	380

* Figures refer to the metal content of ores and concentrates.
† Figures refer to the estimated production of mineral concentrates. The metal content (metric tons, estimates) was: Niobium (Columbium) 190 in 2008, 150 in 2009, 120 in 2010; Tantalum 150 in 2008, 120 in 2009, 93 in 2010.

Source: US Geological Survey.

Industry

SELECTED PRODUCTS

	2001	2002	2003
Beer ('000 hectolitres)	479	539	412
Soft drinks ('000 hectolitres)	228	n.a.	n.a.
Cigarettes (million)	278	391	402
Soap (metric tons)	7,056	5,571	4,456
Cement (metric tons)	83,024	100,568	105,105

Source: IMF, *Rwanda: Statistical Annex* (August 2002) and IMF, *Rwanda: Selected Issues and Statistical Appendix* (December 2004).

Cement ('000 metric tons): 103.2 in 2008; 92.1 in 2009; 95.1 in 2010 (Source: US Geological Survey).

Electric energy (million kWh): 170.0 in 2006; 169.0 in 2007; 234.0 in 2008 (Source: UN Industrial Commodity Statistics Database).

Finance

CURRENCY AND EXCHANGE RATES

Monetary Units

100 centimes = 1 franc rwandais (Rwanda franc).

Sterling, Dollar and Euro Equivalents (31 May 2012)

£1 sterling = 944.668 Rwanda francs;
US $1 = 609.306 Rwanda francs;
€1 = 755.722 Rwanda francs;
10,000 Rwanda francs = £10.59 = $16.41 = €13.23.

Average Exchange Rate (Rwanda francs per US $)

2009	568.281
2010	583.131
2011	600.307

Note: Since September 1983 the currency has been linked to the IMF special drawing right (SDR). Until November 1990 the mid-point exchange rate was SDR 1 = 102.71 Rwanda francs. In November 1990 a new rate of SDR 1 = 171.18 Rwanda francs was established. This remained in effect until June 1992, when the rate was adjusted to SDR 1 = 201.39 Rwanda francs. The latter parity was maintained until February 1994, since when the rate has been frequently adjusted. In March 1995 the Government introduced a market-determined exchange rate system.

BUDGET

('000 million Rwanda francs)

Revenue*	2009/10	2010/11†	2011/12‡
Tax revenue	376.4	463.8	519.7
Direct taxes	148.8	180.9	207.3
Taxes on goods and services	195.0	245.1	271.4
Taxes on international trade	32.6	37.8	41.0
Non-tax revenue	15.0	20.6	45.4
Total	391.4	484.4	565.1

Expenditure§	2009/10	2010/11†	2011/12‡
Current expenditure	459.2	527.0	596.3
Wages and salaries	106.9	122.0	131.2
Purchases of goods and services	106.3	124.1	148.3
Interest payments	14.7	15.6	16.0
Domestic debt	10.1	10.9	10.1
External debt	4.6	4.7	5.9
Transfers	179.6	197.2	223.9
Exceptional expenditure	51.6	68.1	76.9
Capital expenditure	316.7	438.6	508.6
Domestic	159.3	218.9	248.9
External	157.4	219.7	259.7
Total	775.9	965.6	1,104.9

* Excluding grants received ('000 million Rwanda francs): 409.3 in 2009/10; 379.0 in 2010/11 (preliminary); 463.5 in 2011/12 (projection).

† Preliminary.

‡ Projections.

§ Excluding lending minus repayments ('000 million Rwanda francs): 28.2 in 2009/10; 18.7 in 2010/11 (preliminary); 0.7 in 2011/12 (projection).

Source: IMF, *Rwanda: Fourth Review Under the Policy Support Instrument and Request for Modification of Assessment Criteria—Staff Report; Press Release* (June 2012).

INTERNATIONAL BANK RESERVES

(US $ million at 31 December)

	2009	2010	2011
IMF special drawing rights	130.92	128.55	127.58
Foreign exchange	611.82	684.21	922.46
Total	742.74	812.76	1,050.04

Source: IMF, *International Financial Statistics*.

MONEY SUPPLY

(million Rwanda francs at 31 December)

	2003	2004	2005
Currency outside banks	29,246	36,512	46,277
Demand deposits at deposit money banks	52,220	62,604	82,524
Total money (incl. others)	82,305	99,941	129,326

2006: Currency outside banks 52,620.

Source: IMF, *International Financial Statistics*.

COST OF LIVING

(Consumer Price Index for Kigali; base: 2000 = 100)

	2007	2008	2009
Food (incl. non-alcoholic beverages)	185.0	215.2	248.3
Clothing	119.2	n.a.	n.a.
Rent	200.6	n.a.	n.a.
All items	164.2	189.5	210.8

2010: Food (incl. non-alcoholic beverages) 254.4; All items (incl. others) 214.0.

2011: Food (incl. non-alcoholic beverages) 271.0; All items (incl. others) 226.1.

Source: ILO.

NATIONAL ACCOUNTS

('000 million Rwanda francs at current prices)

Expenditure on the Gross Domestic Product

	2009	2010	2011
Government final consumption expenditure	454	524	580
Private final consumption expenditure } Changes in inventories	2,464	2,742	3,160
Gross fixed capital formation	644	688	818
Total domestic expenditure	3,562	3,954	4,558
Exports of goods and services	303	329	514
Less Imports of goods and services	881	1,003	1,244
GDP in purchasers' values	2,985	3,280	3,828
GDP in constant 2006 prices	2,182	2,339	2,540

Gross Domestic Product by Economic Activity

	2009	2010	2011
Agriculture, hunting, forestry and fishing	1,012	1,058	1,223
Mining and quarrying	16	21	48
Manufacturing	190	218	252
Electricity, gas and water	6	7	8
Construction	218	244	317
Wholesale and retail trade, restaurants and hotels	446	500	564
Finance, insurance, real estate and business services	346	373	415
Transport and communications	223	256	288
Public administration and defence	128	151	181
Education	140	167	210
Health	44	51	53
Other personal services	30	33	34
Sub-total	2,799	3,079	3,593
Less Imputed bank service charges	41	50	69
Indirect taxes, less subsidies	226	249	306
GDP in purchasers' values	2,985	3,280	3,828

Note: Totals may not be equal to the sum of components, owing to rounding.

BALANCE OF PAYMENTS
(US $ million)

	2008	2009	2010
Exports of goods f.o.b.	257	188	297
Imports of goods f.o.b.	–880	–961	–1,084
Trade balance	–623	–772	–787
Exports of services	408	341	310
Imports of services	–521	–519	–557
Balance on goods and services	–736	–950	–1,033
Other income received	28	15	13
Other income paid	–62	–52	–59
Balance on goods, services and income	–771	–987	–1,079
Current transfers received	558	655	714
Current transfers paid	–40	–51	–56
Current balance	–252	–383	–421
Capital account (net)	210	200	286
Direct investment from abroad	103	119	42
Portfolio investment assets	–19	—	—
Portfolio investment liabilities	—	—	21
Other investment assets	–88	–19	–28
Other investment liabilities	—	143	117
Net errors and omissions	–5	3	–6
Overall balance	–51	63	10

Source: IMF, *International Financial Statistics*.

External Trade

PRINCIPAL COMMODITIES
(US $ million)

Imports c.i.f.	2008	2009	2010
Food and live animals	78.5	97.4	133.3
Cereals and cereal preparations	37.3	55.8	66.8
Rice	6.9	11.8	16.7
Vegetables and fruit	3.9	4.2	7.1
Sugar, sugar preparations and honey	19.1	23.4	39.5
Crude materials, inedible, except fuels	45.9	34.2	51.4
Textile fibres and their wastes	22.0	13.8	11.4
Mineral fuels, lubricants and related materials	64.5	89.8	52.9
Petroleum, petroleum products and related materials	63.6	88.9	51.7
Animal and vegetable oils, fats and waxes	30.8	36.0	40.2
Chemicals and related products	133.3	187.6	170.3
Medicinal and pharmaceutical products	46.8	79.2	63.1
Basic manufactures	238.2	224.1	265.4
Iron and steel	85.4	56.5	64.7
Machinery and transport equipment	301.4	340.5	449.2
Telecommunications, sound recording and reproducing equipment	42.7	89.0	50.4
Electric machinery, apparatus and appliances, and parts	47.4	78.7	76.0
Road vehicles	73.9	66.0	178.6
Miscellaneous manufactured articles	37.0	34.8	37.7
Total (incl. others)	1,035.6	1,112.0	1,273.8

Exports f.o.b.	2008	2009	2010
Coffee, tea, cocoa, spices, and manufactures thereof	—	109.6	92.8
Coffee	—	33.9	58.4
Tea	—	75.6	34.4
Crude materials, inedible, except fuels	140.7	71.6	105.0
Metalliferous ores and metal scrap	136.3	67.9	98.6
Tin ores and concentrates	78.6	34.2	66.9
Ores and concentrates of other non-ferrous base metals	17.0	11.2	10.5
Ores of molybdenum, niobium and titanium	38.0	20.4	20.3
Total (incl. others)	250.2	260.7	237.8

Source: UN, *International Trade Statistics Yearbook*.

PRINCIPAL TRADING PARTNERS
(US $ million)

Imports	2008	2009	2010
Bahrain	11.3	4.6	2.4
Belgium	59.4	42.3	50.7
Burundi	3.5	3.3	26.0
China, People's Republic	99.5	92.0	76.0
Congo, Democratic Republic	6.1	6.0	63.0
Denmark	10.1	37.5	47.0
Egypt	13.6	16.0	25.0
France (incl. Monaco)	32.9	29.5	41.3
Germany	39.2	41.8	50.9
India	48.4	54.3	55.6
Italy	7.6	10.2	15.4
Japan	39.1	35.0	59.9
Kenya	128.4	123.9	79.6
Korea, Republic	9.2	34.0	40.0
Netherlands	11.5	22.8	8.3
Saudi Arabia	17.5	11.5	19.2
South Africa	39.2	36.6	43.0
Spain	14.1	2.5	13.0
Sweden	30.9	54.2	120.0
Switzerland-Liechtenstein	6.2	13.7	13.3
Tanzania	25.4	54.6	75.0
Uganda	148.5	143.0	52.6
UAE	84.4	69.5	89.4
United Kingdom	24.6	22.3	14.9
USA	36.5	43.3	31.8
Total (incl. others)	1,035.6	1,112.0	1,273.8

Exports	2008	2009	2010
Angola	—	3.6	—
Belgium	65.0	29.5	26.7
Burundi	6.2	5.4	4.7
China, People's Republic	5.9	7.7	17.6
Congo, Democratic Republic	17.5	12.7	16.4
Germany	7.9	3.3	3.7
Hong Kong	25.8	16.0	19.1
India	13.0	1.4	0.4
Italy	3.7	1.1	2.5
Kenya	31.7	83.1	39.3
South Africa	12.0	5.5	3.2
Swaziland	14.4	23.6	11.8
Switzerland-Liechtenstein	7.5	12.2	54.4
Tanzania	1.1	4.1	4.3
Uganda	6.8	5.6	6.8
United Kingdom	13.4	4.8	11.0
USA	4.9	3.9	7.6
Total (incl. others)	250.2	260.7	237.8

Source: UN, *International Trade Statistics Yearbook*.

Transport

ROAD TRAFFIC
(motor vehicles in use at 31 December, estimates)

	1995	1996
Passenger cars	12,000	13,000
Lorries and vans	16,000	17,100

2008 (motor vehicles in use at 31 December): Passenger cars 22,251; Buses and coaches 4,776; Vans and lorries 10,827; Motorcycles and mopeds 24,013.

Source: IRF, *World Road Statistics*.

CIVIL AVIATION
(traffic on scheduled services)

	2008	2009	2010
Passengers carried	276,115	266,946	313,327
Freight carried (metric tons)	8,544	6,724	6,352

Tourism

(by country of residence)

	2000	2001*
Africa	93,058	99,928
Burundi	20,972	9,455
Congo, Democratic Republic	10,450	28,514
Kenya	2,050	2,243
Tanzania	18,320	18,697
Uganda	38,897	38,472
Americas	2,250	2,785
Europe	6,412	8,395
Belgium	1,866	2,057
Total (incl. others)	104,216	113,185

* January–November.

Total tourist arrivals ('000): 764 in 2008; 646 in 2009; 619 in 2010.

Tourism receipts (US $ million, excl. passenger transport): 174 in 2009; 202 in 2010; 252 in 2011 (provisional).

Source: World Tourism Organization.

Communications Media

	2009	2010	2011
Telephones ('000 main lines in use)	33.5	39.7	38.9
Mobile cellular telephones ('000 subscribers)	2,429.3	3,548.8	4,446.2
Internet subscribers ('000)	15.2	16.7	n.a.
Broadband subscribers ('000)	2.2	2.6	3.7

Personal computers: 28,000 (3.0 per 1,000 persons) in 2006.

Radio receivers ('000 in use): 601 in 1997.

Daily newspapers: 1 in 1998.

Non-daily newspapers: 25 in 2004.

Sources: International Telecommunication Union; UN, *Statistical Yearbook*; UNESCO, *Statistical Yearbook*.

Education

(2009/10)

		Students		
	Teachers	Males	Females	Total
Pre-primary	4,107	47,034	49,900	96,934
Primary	35,583	1,132,556	1,166,770	2,299,326
Secondary	14,477	209,926	215,661	425,587
Tertiary	2,829	35,242	27,492	62,734

Source: UNESCO Institute for Statistics.

Pupil-teacher ratio (primary education, UNESCO estimate): 58.1 in 2010/11 (Source: UNESCO Institute for Statistics).

Adult literacy rate (UNESCO estimates): 71.1% (males 74.8%; females 67.5%) in 2010 (Source: UNESCO Institute for Statistics).

Directory

The Constitution

A new Constitution was approved at a national referendum on 26 May 2003 and entered into effect on 4 June. The main provisions are summarized below:

PREAMBLE

The state of Rwanda is an independent sovereign Republic. Fundamental principles are: the struggle against the ideology of genocide and all its manifestations; the eradication of all ethnic and regional divisions; the promotion of national unity; and the equal sharing of power. Human rights and personal liberties are protected. All forms of discrimination are prohibited and punishable by law. The state recognizes a multi-party political system. Political associations are established in accordance with legal requirements, and may operate freely, providing that they comply with democratic and constitutional principles, without harm to national unity, territorial integrity and state security. The formation of political associations on the basis of race, ethnicity, tribal or regional affiliation, sex, religion or any other grounds for discrimination is prohibited.

LEGISLATURE

Legislative power is vested in a bicameral Parliament, comprising a Chamber of Deputies and a Senate. The Chamber of Deputies has 80 deputies, who are elected for a five-year term. In addition to 53 directly elected deputies, 27 seats are allocated, respectively, to two youth representatives, one disabilities representative, and 24 female representatives, who are indirectly elected. The Senate comprises 26 members, of whom 12 are elected by local government councils in the 12 provinces, and two by academic institutions, while the remaining 12 are nominated (eight by the President and four by a regulatory body, the Parties' Forum). Members of the Senate serve for eight years.

PRESIDENT

The President of the Republic is the Head of State, protector of the Constitution, and guarantor of national unity. He is the Commander-in-Chief of the armed forces. Presidential candidates are required to be of Rwandan nationality and aged a minimum of 35 years. The President is elected by universal suffrage for a seven-year term, and is restricted to two mandates. He signs into law presidential decrees in consultation with the Council of Ministers.

GOVERNMENT

The President nominates the Prime Minister, who heads the Council of Ministers. Ministers are proposed by the Prime Minister and appointed by the President.

JUDICIARY

The judiciary is independent and separate from the legislative and executive organs of government. The judicial system is composed of the Supreme Court, the High Court of the Republic, and provincial, district and municipal Tribunals. In addition, there are specialized judicial organs, comprising *gacaca* and military courts. The *gacaca* courts try cases of genocide or other crimes against humanity committed between 1 October 1990 and 31 December 1994. Military courts (the Military Tribunal and the High Military Court) have jurisdiction in military cases. The President and Vice-President of the Supreme Court and the Prosecutor-General are elected by the Senate two months after its installation.

The Government

HEAD OF STATE

President: Maj.-Gen. PAUL KAGAME (took office 22 April 2000; re-elected 25 August 2003 and 9 August 2010).

COUNCIL OF MINISTERS
(September 2012)

Prime Minister: PIERRE DAMIEN HABUMUREMYI.

Minister of Agriculture and Animal Resources: Dr AGNES KALIBATA.

Minister of the East African Community: MONIQUE MUKARULIZA.

Minister of Health: Dr AGNES BINAGWAHO.

Minister of Internal Security: MUSSA FAZIL HARERIMANA.

Minister of Defence: Gen. JAMES KABAREBE.

Minister of Lands, the Environment, Forestry and Mines: STANISLAS KAMANZI.

Minister of Finance and Economic Planning: JOHN RWANGOMBWA.

Minister of Disaster Preparedness and Refugee Affairs: Gen. MARCEL GATSINZI.

Minister of Local Government: JAMES MUSONI.

Minister in the Office of the Prime Minister, in charge of Gender and Family Promotion: ALOYSIA INYUMBA.

Minister of Youth, Sports and Culture: PROTAIS MITALI KABANDA.

Minister of Justice and Attorney-General: THARCISSE KARUGARAMA.

Minister in the Office of the President: VENANTIA TUGIREYEZU.

Minister of Education: Dr VINCENT BIRUTA.

Minister of Public Service and Labour: ANASTASE MUREKEZI.

Minister of Foreign Affairs: LOUISE MUSHIKIWABO.

Minister in the Office of the President, in charge of ICT: Dr IGNACE GATARE.

Minister in the Office of the Prime Minister, in charge of Cabinet Affairs: PROTAIS MUSONI.

Minister of Trade and Industry: FRANCOIS KANIMBA.

Minister of Infrastructure: ALBERT NSENGIYUMVA.

Minister of State in the Ministry of Local Government, in charge of Social Affairs and Community Development: ALVERA MUKABARAMBA.

Minister of State in the Ministry of Infrastructure, in charge of Energy and Water: EMMA FRANÇOISE ISUMBINGABO.

Minister of State in the Ministry of Education, in charge of Primary and Secondary Education: Dr MATHIAS HABAMUNGU.

MINISTRIES

Office of the President: BP 15, Kigali; tel. 59062000; fax 572431; e-mail info@presidency.gov.rw; internet www.presidency.gov.rw.

Office of the Prime Minister: Kigali; tel. 252585444; fax 252583714; e-mail primature@gov.rw; internet www.primature.gov.rw.

Ministry of Agriculture and Animal Resources: BP 621, Kigali; tel. 250585008; fax 250585057; e-mail info@minagri.gov.rw; internet www.minagri.gov.rw.

Ministry of Defence: BP 23, Kigali; tel. 250577942; fax 250576969; e-mail info@mod.gov.rw; internet www.mod.gov.rw.

Ministry of Disaster Management and Refugee Affairs: POB 4386 Blue Star House, Kacyiru, Kigali; e-mail info@midimar.gov.rw; internet www.midimar.gov.rw.

Ministry of the East African Community: BP 267, Kigali; tel. 250599122; internet www.mineac.gov.rw.

Ministry of Education: BP 622, Kigali; tel. 250583051; fax 250582161; e-mail info@mineduc.gov.rw; internet www.mineduc.gov.rw.

Ministry of Finance and Economic Planning: blvd de la Révolution, opp. Kigali City Council, BP 158, Kigali; tel. 250576701; fax 250577581; e-mail mfin@minecofin.gov.rw; internet www.minecofin.gov.rw.

Ministry of Foreign Affairs: Kimihurura, 5th and 6th Floors, ave du lac Muhazi, BP 179, Kigali; tel. 250599128; fax 250599129; e-mail info@minaffet.gov.rw; internet www.minaffet.gov.rw.

Ministry of Gender and Family Promotion: Kigali; tel. 250577626; fax 250577543; internet www.migeprofe.gov.rw.

Ministry of Health: BP 84, Kigali; tel. 250577458; fax 250576853; e-mail info@moh.gov.rw; internet www.moh.gov.rw.

Ministry of Infrastructure: BP 24, Kigali; tel. 250585503; fax 250585755; e-mail info@mininfra.gov.rw; internet www.mininfra.gov.rw.

Ministry of Internal Affairs: BP 446, Kigali; tel. 250586708; e-mail sec_cent@mininter.gov.rw; internet www.mininter.gov.rw.

Ministry of Justice: BP 160, Kigali; tel. 250586561; fax 250586509; e-mail mjust@minijust.gov.rw; internet www.minijust.gov.rw.

Ministry of Lands, the Environment, Forestry and Mines: BP 3052, Kigali; tel. 250582628; fax 250582629; e-mail info@minirena.gov.rw; internet www.minirena.gov.rw.

Ministry of Local Government: BP 790, Kigali; tel. 250585406; fax 250582228; e-mail webmaster@minaloc.gov.rw; internet www.minaloc.gov.rw.

Ministry of Public Service and Labour: BP 403, Kigali; tel. 250585714; fax 250583621; e-mail mifotra@mifotra.gov.rw; internet www.mifotra.gov.rw.

Ministry of Trade and Industry: BP 73, Kigali; tel. 250599103; fax 250599101; e-mail albert.bizimana@minicom.gov.rw; internet www.minicom.gov.rw.

Ministry of Youth, Sports and Culture: BP 1044, Kigali; tel. 250583531; fax 250583518; e-mail info@minispoc.gov.rw; internet www.minispoc.gov.rw.

President and Legislature

PRESIDENT

Presidential Election, 9 August 2010

Candidate	Votes	% of votes
Paul Kagame	4,638,560	93.08
Jean Damascene Ntawukuriryayo	256,488	5.15
Prosper Higiro	68,235	1.37
Alivera Mukabaramba	20,107	0.40
Total	4,983,390	100.00

CHAMBER OF DEPUTIES

Speaker: ROSE MUKANTANTABANA.

General Election, 15 September 2008

Party	Votes	% of votes	Seats
Front Patriotique Rwandais*	3,655,956	78.76	42
Parti Social-démocrate	609,327	13.12	7
Parti Libéral	348,186	7.5	4
Independent	27,848	0.6	—
Total	4,641,317	100.00	80†

* Contested the elections in alliance with the Parti Démocrate Chrétien, the Parti Démocratique Islamique, the Union Démocratique du Peuple Rwandais, the Parti de Prospérité et de Solidarité and the Parti Socialiste Rwandais.

† In addition to the 53 directly elected deputies, 27 seats are allocated, respectively, to two youth representatives, one disabilities representative and 24 female representatives, who are indirectly elected.

SENATE

Speaker: Dr VINCENT BIRUTA.

The Senate comprises 26 members, of whom 12 are elected by local government councils in the 12 provinces and two by academic institutions, while the remaining 12 are nominated (eight by the President and four by a regulatory body, the Parties' Forum).

Election Commission

National Electoral Commission: BP 6449, Kigali; tel. 250597800; fax 250597851; e-mail comelena@rwanda1.com; internet www

.comelena.gov.rw; f. 2000; independent; Chair. Prof. CHRYSOLOGUE KARANGWA.

Political Organizations

Under legislation adopted in June 2003, the formation of any political organization based on ethnic groups, religion or sex was prohibited.

Democratic Green Party: BP 6334, Kigali; tel. 788563039 (mobile); e-mail info@rwandagreendemocrats.org; internet www.rwandagreendemocrats.org; f. 2009; Pres. FRANK HABINEZA.

Front Patriotique Rwandais (FPR): internet www.rpfinkotanyi.org; f. 1990; also known as Inkotanyi; comprises mainly Tutsi exiles, but claims multi-ethnic support; commenced armed invasion of Rwanda from Uganda in Oct. 1990; took control of Rwanda in July 1994; Chair. Maj.-Gen. PAUL KAGAME; Vice-Chair. CHRISTOPHE BAZIVAMO; Sec.-Gen. FRANÇOIS NGARAMBE.

Parti Démocrate Chrétien (PDC): BP 2348, Kigali; tel. 250576542; fax 250572237; f. 1990; Chair. AGNES MUKABARANGA.

Parti Démocratique Islamique (PDI): Tresor Bldg, 2nd Floor, Kigali; f. 1991; Leader SHEIKH HARERIMANA MUSSA FAZIL.

Parti Démocratique Rwandais (Pader): Kigali; f. 1992; Sec. JEAN NTAGUNGIRA.

Parti Libéral (PL): BP 1304, Kigali; tel. 252577916; fax 252577838; f. 1991; restructured 2003; Chair. PROSPER HIGIRO; Sec.-Gen. Dr ODETTE NYIRAMIRIMO.

Parti du Progrès et de la Concorde (PPC): f. 2003; incl. fmr mems of Mouvement démocratique républicain; Leader Dr CHRISTIAN MARARA.

Parti de Prospérité et de Solidarité (PSP): Kigali.

Parti Social-démocrate (PSD): Kigali; f. 1991 by a breakaway faction of fmr Mouvement Révolutionnaire National pour le Développement; Leader Dr VINCENT BIRUTA.

Parti Social Imberakuri (PS Imberakuri): Nyamirambo, Kigali; tel. 788307145 (mobile); e-mail ntagandab@yahoo.fr; internet www.imberakuri.org; f. 2009; Pres. BERNARD NTAGANDA; Sec.-Gen. THEOBALD MUTARAMBIRWA.

Parti Socialiste Rwandais (PSR): BP 827, Kigali; tel. 252576658; f. 1991; workers' rights; Chair. JEAN-BAPTISTE RUCIBIGANGO.

Other political organizations have been formed by exiled Rwandans and operate principally from abroad; these include:

Rassemblement Républicain pour la Démocratie au Rwanda (RDR): Postbus 3124, 2280 GC, Rijswijk, Netherlands; tel. (31) 623075674; fax (31) 847450374; e-mail info@rdrwanda.org; internet www.rdrwanda.org; f. 1995; prin. opposition party representing Hutu refugees in exile; Pres. VICTOIRE UMUHOZA INGABIRE.

Diplomatic Representation

EMBASSIES AND HIGH COMMISSIONS IN RWANDA

Belgium: rue Nyarugenge, BP 81, Kigali; tel. 250575551; fax 250573995; e-mail kigali@diplobel.fed.be; internet www.diplomatie.be/kigali; Ambassador MARC PECSTEEN DE BUYTSWERVE.

Burundi: rue de Ntaruka, BP 714, Kigali; tel. 250575010; Ambassador Col REMY SINKAZI.

China, People's Republic: BP 1345, 44 blvd de la Revolution, Kigali; tel. 250570843; fax 250570848; e-mail chinaemb_rw@mfa.gov.cn; internet rw.chineseembassy.org; Ambassador SHU ZHAN.

Congo, Democratic Republic: 504 rue Longue, BP 169, Kigali; tel. 250575289; Ambassador NORBERT NKULU KILOMBO.

Egypt: BP 1069, Kigali; tel. and fax 28082686; e-mail egypt@rwanda1.com; Ambassador KHALED ABD AL-RAHMAN.

France: rue du Député Kamunzinzi, BP 441, Kigali; tel. 252551800; fax 252551820; e-mail ambafrance.kigali-amba@diplomatie.gouv.fr; internet www.ambafrance-rw.org; Ambassador LAURENT CONTINI; recalled Feb. 2012.

Germany: 10 ave Paul VI, BP 355, Kigali; tel. 250575141; fax 502087; e-mail info@kigali.diplo.de; internet www.kigali.diplo.de; Ambassador ELMAR TIMPE.

Holy See: 49 ave Paul VI, BP 261, Kigali (Apostolic Nunciature); tel. 252575293; fax 252575181; e-mail na.rwanda@diplomat.va; internet www.vatican.va; Apostolic Nuncio Mgr LUCIANO RUSSO.

Japan: 1236, Kacyiru South Gasabo, BP 874, Kigali; tel. 250500884; internet www.rw.emb-japan.go.jp; Ambassador KUNIO HATANAKA.

Kenya: BP 1215, Kigali; tel. 250583332; fax 250510919; e-mail kigali@mfa.go.ke; High Commissioner ROSE MAKENA MUCHIRI.

Korea, Democratic People's Republic: Kigali; Ambassador KIM PONG GI.

Libya: BP 1152, Kigali; tel. 250576470; Secretary of the People's Bureau MOUSTAPHA MASAND EL-GHAILUSHI.

The Netherlands: blvd de l'Umuganda, Kacyiru, BP 6613, Kigali; tel. 252584711; e-mail kig@minbuza.nl; Ambassador LEONI CUELENAERE.

Nigeria: Kigali; High Commissioner AYIBAKURO OGIDI-OKE.

Russia: 19 ave de l'Armée, BP 40, Kigali; tel. 250575286; fax 250503322; e-mail ambruss@rwandatel1.rwanda1.com; internet www.rwanda.mid.ru; Ambassador MIRGAYAS M. SHIRINSKII.

South Africa: 1370 blvd de l'Umuganda, POB 6563, Kacyiru-Sud, Kigali; tel. 250583185; fax 250583191; e-mail saemkgl@rwanda1.com; internet www.saembassy-kigali.org.rw; High Commissioner GEORGE NKOSINATI TWALA (designate).

Sweden: Aurore House, Kacyiru, 1st Floor, Kigali; tel. 252597400; fax 252597459; e-mail ambassaden.kigali@sida.se; internet www.swedenabroad.com/kigali; Ambassador ANN DISMORR.

Uganda: 31 ave de la Paix, BP 656, Kigali; tel. and fax 250503537; e-mail embassy@ugandaembassy.rw; internet www.ugandaembassy.rw; High Commissioner RICHARD KABONERO.

United Kingdom: Parcelle 1131, blvd de l'Umuganda, Kacyiru, BP 576, Kigali; tel. 250584098; fax 250582044; e-mail bhc.kigali@fco.gov.uk; internet ukinrwanda.fco.gov.uk/en; High Commissioner BENEDICT LLEWELLYN-JONES.

USA: 2657 ave de la Gendarmerie, Kacyiru, BP 28, Kigali; tel. 252596400; fax 252596771; e-mail irckigali@state.gov; internet rwanda.usembassy.gov; Ambassador DONALD W. KORAN.

Judicial System

The judicial system is composed of the Supreme Court, the High Court of the Republic, and provincial, district and municipal Tribunals. In addition, there are specialized judicial organs, comprising *gacaca* and military courts. The *gacaca* courts were established to try cases of genocide or other crimes against humanity committed between 1 October 1990 and 31 December 1994. Trials for categories of lesser genocide crimes were to be conducted by councils in the communities in which they were committed, with the aim of alleviating pressure on the existing judicial system. Trials under the *gacaca* court system formally commenced on 25 November 2002 and the system closed in June 2012, having tried almost 2m. suspects. Military courts (the Military Tribunal and the High Military Court) have jurisdiction in military cases. The President and Vice-President of the Supreme Court and the Prosecutor-General are elected by the Senate.

Supreme Court

BP 2197, Kigali; tel. 252517649; fax 252582276; e-mail info@supremecourt.gov.rw; internet www.supremecourt.gov.rw.

The Supreme Court comprises five sections: the Department of Courts and Tribunals; the Court of Appeals; the Constitutional Court; the Council of State; and the Revenue Court.

President of the Supreme Court: ALOYSIA CYANZAIRE.

Vice-President: Prof. SAM RUGEGE.

President of the High Court: JOHNSTON BUSINGYE.

Prosecutor-General: MARTIN NGOGAEU.

Religion

AFRICAN RELIGIONS

About one-half of the population hold traditional beliefs.

CHRISTIANITY

Union des Eglises Rwandaises: BP 79, Kigali; tel. 28085825; fax 28083554; f. 1963; fmrly Conseil Protestant du Rwanda.

The Roman Catholic Church

Rwanda comprises one archdiocese and eight dioceses. About 49% of the total population is Roman Catholic.

Bishops' Conference

Conférence Episcopale du Rwanda, BP 357, Kigali; tel. 250575439; fax 250578080; e-mail cerwanda@rwanda1.com.

f. 1980; Pres. Rt Rev. SMARAGDE MBONYINTEGE (Bishop of Kabgayi).

Archbishop of Kigali: Most Rev. THADDÉE NTIHINYURWA, Archevêché, BP 715, Kigali; tel. 250575769; fax 250572274; e-mail kigarchi@yahoo.fr.

The Anglican Communion

The Church of the Province of Rwanda, established in 1992, has nine dioceses.

Archbishop of the Province and Bishop of Gasabo: Most Rev. ONESPHORE RWAJE, BP 61, Kigali; tel. and fax 250576340; e-mail ek@rwanda1.com.

Provincial Secretary: Rev. EMMANUEL GATERA, BP 61, Kigali; tel. and fax 250576340; e-mail egapeer@yahoo.com.

Protestant Churches

Eglise Baptiste: Nyantanga, BP 59, Butare; Pres. Rev. DAVID BAZIGA; Gen. Sec. ELEAZAR ZIHERAMBERE.

Eglise Luthérienne du Rwanda: BP 3099, Kigali; tel. 755110035 (mobile); fax 250519734; e-mail luthchurchlcr@yahoo.com; Bishop GEORGE W. KALIISA; 40,000 mems (2010).

There are about 250,000 other Protestants, including a substantial minority of Seventh-day Adventists.

BAHÁ'Í FAITH

National Spiritual Assembly: BP 652, Kigali; tel. 250572550; e-mail asnbaha@rwanda1.com.

ISLAM

There is a small Islamic community.

The Press

REGULATORY AUTHORITY

Media High Council: Revolution Ave, POB 6929, Kigali; tel. 250570333; fax 250570334; e-mail info@mhc.gov.rw; internet www.mhc.gov.rw; f. 2002; Pres. ARTHUR ASIIMWE; Exec. Sec. EMMANUEL MUGISHA (acting).

DAILY

The New Times: Immeuble Aigle Blanc, BP 4953, Kigali; tel. 788301166; fax 250574166; e-mail editorial@newtimes.co.rw; internet www.newtimes.co.rw; f. 1995; daily; English; CEO and Editor-in-Chief COLLIN HABA (acting).

PERIODICALS

Bulletin Agricole du Rwanda: OCIR—Café, BP 104, Kigali-Gikondo; f. 1968; quarterly; French; Pres. of Editorial Bd Dr AUGUSTIN NZINDUKIYIMANA; circ. 800.

Etudes Rwandaises: Université Nationale du Rwanda, Rectorat, BP 56, Butare; f. 1977; quarterly; pure and applied science, literature, human sciences; French; Pres. of Editorial Bd CHARLES NTAKIRUTINKA; circ. 1,000.

Hobe: BP 761, Kigali; f. 1955; monthly; children's interest; circ. 95,000.

Inkingi: BP 969, Kigali; tel. 250577626; fax 250577543; monthly.

Inkoramutima: Union des Eglises Rwandaises, BP 79, Kigali; quarterly; religious; circ. 5,000.

Kinyamateka: 5 blvd de l'OUA, BP 761, Kigali; tel. 250576164; e-mail km@rwanda1.com; internet www.kinyamateka.org.rw; f. 1933; fortnightly; economics; circ. 11,000; Dir Fr PIERRE CLAVER NKUSI.

La Nouvelle Relève: Office Rwandais d'Information, BP 83, Kigali; tel. 250575735; e-mail lnr2020@yahoo.fr; internet www.orinfor.gov.rw; f. 1963; bi-weekly; politics, economics, culture, education, sport, justice, health, society and environment; French; Dir GÉRARD RUGAMBWA; circ. 1,700.

Nouvelles du Rwanda: Université Nationale du Rwanda, BP 117, Butare; every 2 months.

Nyabarongo—Le Canard Déchaîné: BP 1585, Kigali; tel. 250576674; monthly.

Le Partisan: BP 1805, Kigali; tel. 250573923; fortnightly.

La Patrie—Urwatubyaye: BP 3125, Kigali; tel. 250572552; monthly.

Rwanda Herald: Kigali; f. Oct. 2000; owned by Rwanda Independent Media Group.

Rwanda Libération: BP 398, Kigali; tel. 250577710; monthly; Dir and Editor-in-Chief ANTOINE KAPITENI.

Rwanda Renaître: BP 426, Butare; fortnightly.

Rwanda Rushya: BP 83, Kigali; tel. 250572276; fortnightly.

Le Tribun du Peuple: BP 1960, Kigali; bi-monthly; Owner JEAN-PIERRE MUGABE.

Umucunguzi: Gisenyi; f. 1998; Kinyarwanda and French; Chief Editor EMILE NKUMBUYE.

Umuhinzi-Mworozi: OCIR—Thé, BP 1334, Kigali; tel. 250514797; fax 250514796; f. 1975; monthly; circ. 1,500.

Umusemburo—Le Levain: BP 117, Butare; monthly.

Umuseso: Kigali; independent; weekly; Kinyarwanda; publ. suspended in April 2010; Editor CHARLES KABONERO.

Urunana: Grand Séminaire de Nyakibanda, BP 85, Butare; tel. 250530793; e-mail wellamahoro@yahoo.fr; f. 1967; 3 a year; religious; Pres. WELLAS UWAMAHORO; Editor-in-Chief DAMIEN NIYOYIREMERA.

NEWS AGENCIES

Office Rwandais d'Information (Orinfor): BP 83, Kigali; tel. 250575735; fax 250576539; internet www.orinfor.gov.rw; f. 1973; Dir JOSEPH BIDERI.

Rwanda News Agency (RNA): BP 453, Kigali; tel. 250587215; fax 250587216; internet www.rnanews.com; f. 1975.

Publishers

Editions Rwandaises: Caritas Rwanda, BP 124, Kigali; tel. 250575786; fax 250574254; e-mail caritas1@rwanda1.com; Man. Dir Abbé CYRIAQUE MUNYANSANGA; Editorial Dir ALBERT NAMBAJE.

Implico: BP 721, Kigali; tel. 250573771.

Imprimerie de Kabgayi: BP 66, Gitarama; tel. 250562252; fax 250562345; e-mail imprikabgayi@yahoo.fr; f. 1932; Dir Abbé CYRILLE UWIZEYE.

Imprimerie de Kigali, SARL: 1 blvd de l'Umuganda, BP 956, Kigali; tel. 250582032; fax 250584047; e-mail impkig@rwandatel1.rwanda1.com; f. 1980; Dir LÉONCE NSENGIMANA.

Pallotti-Presse: BP 863, Kigali; tel. 250574084.

GOVERNMENT PUBLISHING HOUSES

Imprimerie Nationale du Rwanda: BP 351, Kigali; tel. 250576214; fax 250575820; f. 1967; Dir JUVÉNAL NDISANZE.

Régie de l'Imprimerie Scolaire (IMPRISCO): BP 1347, Kigali; e-mail imprisco@rwandatel1.rwanda1.com; f. 1985; Dir JEAN DE DIEU GAKWANDI.

Broadcasting and Communications

TELECOMMUNICATIONS

At November 2011 there were 4,446,194 mobile subscribers and 38,901 fixed-line subscribers.

REGULATORY AUTHORITY

Rwanda Utilities Regulatory Agency (RURA): POB 7289, Kigali; tel. 252584562; fax 252584563; e-mail info@rura.gov.rw; internet www.rura.gov.rw; f. 2001; also responsible for regulation of electricity, water, sanitation, gas and transportation sectors; Chair. EUGÈNE KAZIGE; Dir-Gen. REGIS FRANCOIS GATARAYIHA.

SERVICE PROVIDERS

Airtel Rwanda: Airtel Head Office, near Amahoro National Stadium, Kigali; tel. 730000456; e-mail customer.care@rw.airtel.com; internet www.africa.airtel.com; f. 2011; commenced operations in April 2012; Country Man. MARCELLIN PALUKU.

MTN Rwandacell: BP 264, MTN Centre, Nyarutarama, Kigali; tel. 250586863; fax 250586865; e-mail customercare@mtn.co.rw; internet www.mtn.co.rw; f. 1998; provides mobile cellular and fixed-line telephone services; CEO KHALED MIKKAWI; 2,892,827 mobile subscribers and 10,014 fixed-line subscribers.

Rwandatel: Ecobank Bldg, 7th Floor, ave de La Paix, BP 1332, Kigali; tel. 252555555; fax 252582300; e-mail info@rwandatel.rw; internet www.rwandatel.rw; national telecommunications service; privatized 2007; licence for cellular services revoked in April 2011; liquidation pending; provides fixed-line telephone services.

Tigo Rwanda: 9801 Nyarutarama, POB 6979, Kigali; tel. 722123000 (mobile); internet www.tigo.co.rw; provides mobile cellular telephone and internet services; CEO DIEGO CAMBEROS (acting).

BROADCASTING

Radio

Radio Rwanda: BP 83, Kigali; tel. 250575665; fax 250576185; f. 1961; state-controlled; daily broadcasts in Kinyarwanda, Swahili, French and English; Dir of Programmes DAVID KABUYE.

Deutsche Welle Relay Station Africa: Kigali; daily broadcasts in German, English, French, Hausa, Swahili, Portuguese and Amharic.

Television

Télévision Rwandaise (TVR): Kigali; fax 250575024; f. 1992; transmissions reach more than 60% of national territory; broadcasts for 10 hours daily in Kinyarwanda, French and English.

A second television station, TVI0, was to commence operations in July 2012.

Finance

(cap. = capital; res = reserves; dep. = deposits; m. = million; brs = branches; amounts in Rwanda francs)

BANKING

In 2010 there were 12 banks in Rwanda.

Central Bank

Banque Nationale du Rwanda (BNR): ave Paul VI, BP 531, Kigali; tel. 250575282; fax 250572551; e-mail info@bnr.rw; internet www.bnr.rw; f. 1964; bank of issue; cap. 7,000m., res 21,183.0m., dep. 297,242.9m. (Dec. 2009); Gov. CLAVER GATETE.

Commercial Banks

Following the privatization of two commercial banks, government control of the banking section was reduced from 45% in 2003 to 22% in 2005, although the three largest banks continued to control two-thirds of the system's assets, valued at US $365m. (equivalent to 34% of GDP).

Access Bank (Rwanda) Ltd: UTC Bldg, 3rd Floor, 1232 ave de la Paix, BP 2059, Kigali; tel. 250500091; fax 250575761; e-mail bancor@rwanda1.com; internet www.accessbankplc.com/rw; f. 1995 as Banque à la Confiance d'Or; fmrly Bancor SA; name changed as above in 2009 when acquired by private investors; 75% owned by Access Bank (Nigeria); cap. and res 3,417.1m., total assets 34,549.3m. (Dec. 2005); Chair. NICHOLAS WATSON.

Banque Commerciale du Rwanda, SA: BP 354, 11 blvd de la Révolution, Kigali; tel. 250595200; fax 250573395; e-mail bcr@rwanda1.com; internet www.bcr.co.rw; f. 1963; privatized Sept. 2004; cap. 5,000m., res 749m., dep. 74,559m. (Dec. 2009); Chair. Dr NKOSANA MOYO; Man. Dir DAVID KUWANA; 6 brs.

Banque de l'Habitat du Rwanda: ave de la Justice, BP 1034, Kigali; tel. 250573843; fax 250572799; e-mail bhr@rwanda1.com; internet www.bhr.co.rw; f. 1975 as Caisse Hypothécaire du Rwanda; name changed as above in 2005; 56% state-owned; cap. 778.2m., total assets 6,966.8m. (Dec. 2003); Pres. FRANÇOIS RUTISHASHA; Dir-Gen. GERVAIS NTAGANDA.

Banque de Kigali, SA: 63 ave du Commerce, BP 175, Kigali; tel. 250593100; fax 250573461; e-mail bk@bk.rw; internet www.bk.rw; f. 1966; cap. 5,005.0m., res 10,892.3m., dep. 124,586.8m. (Dec. 2009); Chair. LADO GURGENIDZE; Man. Dir JAMES GATERA; 33 brs.

Compagnie Générale de Banque: blvd de l'Umuganda, BP 5230, Kigali; tel. 250597500; fax 250503336; e-mail cogebank@cogebank.com; internet www.cogebank.com; f. 1999; cap. and res 1,210.8m., total assets 7,297.4m. (Dec. 2003); Pres. ANDRÉ KATABARWA; 13 brs.

Ecobank Rwanda: ave de la Paix, BP 3268, Kigali; tel. 250503580; fax 250501319; e-mail contact@ecobank.com; internet www.ecobank.com; cap. and res 3,158.4m., total assets 45,950.9m. (Dec. 2003); Man. Dir DANIEL SACKEY.

Fina Bank SA: 20 blvd de la Révolution, BP 331, Kigali; tel. 250598600; fax 250573486; e-mail info@finabank.co.rw; internet www.finabank.com; f. 1983 as Banque Continentale Africaine (Rwanda); name changed 2005; cap. 5,000.6m., res 634.6m., dep. 40,885.6m. (Dec. 2009); privatized; Chair. ROBERT BINYON; Man. Dir STEPHEN CALEY; 5 brs.

Development Banks

Banque Rwandaise de Développement, SA (BRD): blvd de la Révolution, BP 1341, Kigali; tel. 250575079; fax 250573569; e-mail brd@brd.com.rw; internet www.brd.com.rw; f. 1967; 56% state-owned; cap. and res 4,104.6m., total assets 13,920.7m. (Dec. 2003); CEO JACK NKUSI KAYONGA.

Banques Populaires du Rwanda (Banki z'Abaturage mu Rwanda): BP 1348, Kigali; tel. 250573559; fax 250573579; e-mail info@bpr.rw; internet www.bpr.rw; f. 1975; cap. and res 1,180.5m., total assets 20,433.8m. (Dec. 2002); Pres. MANASSÉ TWAHIRWA; CEO HERMAN KLAASSEN; 145 brs.

STOCK EXCHANGE

Rwanda Stock Exchange (RSE): Kigali; f. 2011.

INSURANCE

In 2010 there were five insurance companies in Rwanda.

Compagnie Générale d'Assurances et de Réassurances au Rwanda (COGEAR): ave de l'Armée, BP 2753, Kigali; tel. 250576041; fax 250576082; Dir-Gen. ANASTASE MUNYANDAMUTSA.

Société Nationale d'Assurances du Rwanda (SONARWA): 2417 blvd de la Révolution, BP 1035, Kigali; tel. 250572101; fax 250572052; e-mail sonarwa@rwandatel1.rwanda1.com; internet www.sonarwa.co.rw; f. 1975; 35% owned by Industrial and General Insurance Co Ltd (Nigeria); cap. 500m.; Pres. FRANÇOIS NGARAMBE; Dir-Gen. HOPE MURERA.

SORAS Group Ltd: blvd de la Révolution, BP 924, Kigali; tel. 788185300 (mobile); fax 250573362; e-mail infogroup@soras.co.rw; internet www.soras.co.rw; f. 1984; cap. 2,505m. (2012); Pres. CHARLES MHORANYI.

Trade and Industry

GOVERNMENT AGENCIES

Capital Markets Authority: Ecobank Bldg, 5th Floor, ave de la Paix, POB 6136, Kigali; tel. 250500335; e-mail info@cma.rw; internet www.cma.rw; f. 2007; Exec. Dir ROBERT MATHU.

National Agricultural Export Development Board (NAEB): POB 104, Kigali; tel. 252575600; e-mail info@naeb.gov.rw; internet www.naeb.gov.rw; f. 2011; formulates policies and strategies for developing exports of agricultural and livestock products; Dir Gen. ALEX KANYANKOLE.

Rwanda Agricultural Development Authority (RADA): BP 538, Kigali; tel. 755102618 (mobile); e-mail infos@rada.gov.rw; internet www.rada.gov.rw; f. 2006; contributes towards the growth of agricultural production through the development of appropriate technologies, providing advisory, outreach and extension services to stakeholders in agriculture; Dir-Gen. NORBERT SENDEGE (acting).

Rwanda Investment and Export Promotion Agency: Kimihurura, ave du Lac Muhazi, POB 6239, Kigali; tel. 250510248; fax 250510249; e-mail info@rwandainvest.com; internet www.rwandainvest.com; f. 1998 as Rwanda Investment Promotion Agency; Dir-Gen. FRANCIS GATARE.

Rwanda Public Procurement Authority: ave de la Paix, POB 4276, Kigali; tel. 250501403; fax 250501402; e-mail rppa1@rwanda1.com; internet www.rppa.gov.rw; f. 2008 to replace the Nat. Tender Bd (f. 1998); organizes and monitors general public procurement; Chair. DAMIEN MUGABO; Dir AUGUSTUS SEMINEGA.

Rwanda Revenue Authority (RRA): ave du Lac Muhazi, POB 3987, Kimihurura, Kigali; tel. 250595520; fax 250578488; e-mail cg@rra.gov.rw; internet www.rra.gov.rw; f. 1998 to maximize revenue collection; Commissioner-Gen. MARY BAINE.

DEVELOPMENT ORGANIZATIONS

Coopérative de Promotion de l'Industrie Minière et Artisanale au Rwanda (COOPIMAR): BP 1139, Kigali; Dir DANY NZARAMBA.

Institut de Recherches Scientifiques et Technologiques (IRST): BP 227, Butare; tel. 250530395; fax 250530939; e-mail irst@irst.ac.rw; internet www.irst.ac.rw; Dir-Gen. Dr JEAN BAPTISTE NDUWAYEZU.

Institut des Sciences Agronomiques du Rwanda (ISAR): 47 rue du Député Kamunzinzi, POB, 5016 Kigali; tel. 250530642; fax 250530644; e-mail info@isar.rw; internet www.isar.rw; for the devt of subsistence and export agriculture; Dir DAPHROSE GAHAKWA; 12 centres.

Office National pour le Développement de la Commercialisation des Produits Vivriers et des Produits Animaux (OPROVIA): BP 953, Kigali; privatization pending; Dir DISMAS SEZIBERA.

Régie d'Exploitation et de Développement des Mines (REDEMI): BP 2195, Kigali; tel. 250573632; fax 250573625; e-mail ruzredem@yahoo.fr; f. 1988 as Régie des Mines du Rwanda; privatized in 2000; state org. for mining tin, columbo-tantalite and wolfram; Man. Dir JEAN-RUZINDANA MUNANA.

Rwanda Development Board: Gishushu, Nyarutarama Rd, POB 6239, Kigali; tel. 250580804; e-mail info@rdb.rw; internet www.rdb.rw; f. 2008 to replace eight govt agencies (RIEPA, ORTPN, Privatization Secretariat, Rwanda Commercial Registration Services Agency, Rwanda Information and Technology Authority, Centre for Support to Small and Medium Enterprises, Human Resource and Institutional Capacity Development Agency, and Rwanda Environmental Management Authority); CEO JOHN GARA.

Société de Pyrèthre au Rwanda (SOPYRWA): BP 79, Ruhengeri; tel. and fax 250546364; e-mail info@sopyrwa.com; internet www.sopyrwa.com; f. 1978; cultivation and processing of pyrethrum; post-war activities resumed in Oct. 1994; current production estimated at 80% pre-war capacity; Dir SYLVAIN NZABAGAMBA.

INDUSTRIAL ASSOCIATIONS

Association des Industriels du Rwanda: BP 39, Kigali; tel. and fax 250575430; Pres. YVES LAFAGE; Exec. Sec. MUGUNGA NDOBA.

Private Sector Federation (PSF): Gikonda Magerwa, POB 319, Kigali; tel. 250252570650; fax 250583574; e-mail info@rpsf.org.rw; internet psf.org.rw; f. 1999 to replace the Chambre de Commerce et d'Industrie de Rwanda; promotes and represents the interests of the Rwandan business community; CEO HANNINGTON NAMARA.

UTILITIES

Rwanda Utilities Regulatory Agency (RURA): see Telecommunications.

Rwanda Electricity Corpn and Rwanda Water and Sanitation Corpn (RECO & RWASCO): POB 537, Kigali; tel. 252598400; e-mail fgatanazi@electrogaz.co.rw; internet www.electrogaz.co.rw; f. 1976 as Electrogaz; changed name as above in 2009 after company was split, although it is managed as one institution; state-owned water and electricity supplier; Man. Dir YVES MUYANGE; Dir of Electricity CHARLES KANYAMIHIGO; Dir of Water THEONESTE MINANI.

MAJOR COMPANIES

BP-Fina Rwanda: BP 144, Kigali; tel. 250572428; fax 250574998; wholesale trade in petroleum products; Man. Dir GEORGES BOSSERT.

BRALIRWA: BP 131, Kigali; tel. 252587200; e-mail bralirwa@heineken.com; internet www.bralirwa.com; f. 1959; 70% owned by Heineken NV, Netherlands; mfrs and bottlers of beer in Nyamyumba and soft drinks in Kigali; Chair. JEAN PAUL VAN HOLLEBEKE; Man. Dir JONATHAN HALL.

Cimenterie du Rwanda (CIMERWA): POB 21, Cyangugu; tel. 255105882; internet www.cimerwa.rw; f. 1984; mfrs of cement; post-war activities resumed in Aug. 1994; 1995 production estimated at 60% of pre-war capacity; Man. Dir ROLF ANTTILA.

Kabuye Sugar Works SARL: BP 373; Kigali; tel. 250575468; fax 250572865; f. 1969; privatized 1997; owned by the Madhvani Group, Uganda; Gen. Man. M. S. V. RAO.

Kigali Cement Co.: ave de Poids Lourds, Kigali; tel. 788301985 (mobile).

Rwigass Cigarettes Co: BP 1286, Kigali; tel. 250575535; fax 250575516; production of cigarettes; Man. Dir R. ASSINAPOL.

SHER Consult Ltd: rue de l'Akagera, Parcelle 3925, Nyarugenge, BP 1526, Kigali; tel. and fax 250578630; fax 250578851; e-mail info@sherconsult.com; internet sher.sherconsult.com; f. 1985; rural devt; Chair. and Man. Dir PAUL GATIN; Rwandan Rep. EGBERT HAMEL.

Société Emballage—Rwanda: BP 1009, Kigali; tel. 250575705; export of fruit and fruit products; production of soya- and cereal-based foods since 1997.

Société Rwandaise pour la Production et la Commercialisation du Thé (SORWATHE), SARL: SOMECA Bldg, 1st Floor, blvd de la révolution, POB 1436, Kigali; tel. 252578516; fax 252575461; e-mail sorwathe@rwanda1.com; f. 1978; tea.

Tôlerie Industrielle du Rwanda (TOLIRWA): BP 521, Kigali; tel. 572129; produces sheet metal; Dir-Gen. JAFFER.

TRADE UNIONS

Centrale des Syndicats des Travailleurs du Rwanda (CESTRAR): BP 1645, Kigali; tel. 783266262; e-mail cestrar@rwanda1.com; f. 1985; Sec.-Gen. ERIC MANZI.

Congrès du Travail et de la Fraternité au Rwanda: BP 1576, Kigali; tel. 788635536 (mobile); e-mail cotraf_rw@yahoo.fr; internet www.cotraf.org; f. 2003; Pres. DOMINIQUE BICAMIMPAKA.

Conseil National des Organisations Syndicales Libres (COSYLI): BP 4866, Kigali; tel. 725102374; Pres. FLORIDA MUKARUGAMBWA.

Transport

Rwanda Transport Development Agency (RTDA): Kucukiro Pension Plaza, 4th Floor, African Union Blvd, POB 6674, Kigali; e-mail info@rtda.gov.rw; internet www.rtda.gov.rw; f. 2010; manages day-to-day aspects of the transport sector; Pres. ELIAS TWAGIRA MATHANIYA.

RAILWAYS

There are no railways in Rwanda, although plans exist for the construction of a line linking Kigali and Isaka in Tanzania, with possible extensions to Bujumbura in Burundi and the Democratic Republic of the Congo. Rwanda has access by road to the Tanzanian railways system. In 2011 the African Development Bank approved US $8.5m. in loans and grants to finance a multinational railway project study in Rwanda, Tanzania and Burundi.

ROADS

In 2004 there were an estimated 14,008 km of roads, of which 2,662 km were paved. There are road links with Uganda, Tanzania, Burundi and the Democratic Republic of the Congo.

Office National des Transports en Commun (ONATRACOM): BP 619, Kigali; tel. 250575411; fax 250576126; e-mail onatraco@rwanda1.com; f. 1978; Dir-Gen. BENJAMIN NTAGANIRA.

INLAND WATERWAYS

There are services on Lake Kivu between Cyangugu, Gisenyi and Kibuye, including two vessels operated by ONATRACOM.

CIVIL AVIATION

The Kanombe international airport at Kigali can process up to 500,000 passengers annually. There is a second international airport at Kamembe, near the border with the Democratic Republic of the Congo. Bugesera International Airport, currently under construction, was expected to receive its first flight in 2015. There are airfields at Butare, Gabiro, Ruhengeri and Gisenyi, servicing internal flights.

Rwandair: Kigali Int. Airport Bldg, Top Floor, BP 7275, Kigali; tel. 250503687; fax 250503686; e-mail info@rwandair.com; internet www.rwandair.com; f. 2002 as Rwandair Express; renamed 2009; international services; CEO JOHN MIRENGE.

Tourism

Attractions for tourists include the wildlife of the national parks (notably mountain gorillas), Lake Kivu and fine mountain scenery. Since the end of the transitional period in late 2003, the Government has increased efforts to develop the tourism industry. In 2010 a total of 619,000 tourists visited Rwanda. Total receipts from tourism were estimated at $252m. in 2011.

Office Rwandais du Tourisme et des Parcs Nationaux (ORTPN): blvd de la Révolution 1, BP 905, Kigali; tel. 250576514; fax 250576515; e-mail info@rwandatourism.com; internet www.rwandatourism.com; f. 1973; govt agency; Dir-Gen. ROSETTE RUGAMBA.

Defence

As assessed at November 2011, the total strength of the Rwandan armed forces was estimated at 33,000, comprising an army of 32,000 and an air force of 1,000. In addition, there were an estimated 2,000 local defence forces. A programme to restructure the army, which was expected to be reduced in size to number about 25,000, was planned and a Rwanda Demobilization and Reintegration Commission was mandated to facilitate the reintegration of discharged military personnel into civilian life. In 2011 a total of 3,256 troops were stationed abroad, of which 16 were observers.

Defence Expenditure: Budgeted at 46,400m. Rwanda francs in 2012.

Chief of Defence Staff: Lt-Gen. CHARLES KAYONGA.

Chief of Staff, Land Forces: Lt-Gen. CAESAR KAYIZARI.

Chief of Staff of the Air Force: JOSEPH DEMALI (acting).

Education

Primary education, beginning at seven years of age and lasting for six years, is officially compulsory. Secondary education, which is not compulsory, begins at the age of 14 and lasts for a further six years, comprising two equal cycles of three years. In 2003, however, the Government announced plans to introduce a nine-year system of basic education, including three years of attendance at lower secondary schools. Schools are administered by the State and by Christian missions. In 2009/10 99% of children in the relevant age-group were enrolled in primary schools, according to UNESCO estimates, while secondary enrolment in that year was equivalent to 32% of children in the appropriate age-group (males 32%; females 32%). The Ministry of Education established 94 new secondary schools in 2003, and a further 58 in 2005. Rwanda has a university, with campuses at Butare and Ruhengeri, and several other institutions of higher education, but some students attend universities abroad, particularly in Belgium, France or Germany. In 2009/10 the number of students in tertiary education (there were six public higher education institutions and seven private higher institutions) was 62,734. At the beginning of the 2011 school year English became the language of instruction in all public Rwandan educational establishments. In 2008 spending on education represented 20.4% of total budgetary expenditure.

Bibliography

Abdulai, N. (Ed.). *Genocide in Rwanda: Background and Current Situation*. London, Africa Research and Information Centre, 1994.

Adelman, H., and Suhrke, A. (Eds). *The Path of a Genocide: The Rwanda Crisis from Uganda to Zaire*. Piscataway, NJ, Transaction Publishers, 2000.

African Rights. *Rwanda: Not So Innocent: When Women Become Killers*. London, African Rights, 1995.

Rwanda: Killing the Evidence: Murder, Attacks, Arrests, and Intimidation of Survivors and Witnesses. London, African Rights, 1996.

Barnett, M. N. *Eyewitness to a Genocide: The United Nations and Rwanda*. Ithaca, NY, Cornell University Press, 2002.

Berry, J. A. (Ed.). *Genocide in Rwanda: A Collective Memory*. Washington, DC, Howard University Press, 1999.

Braekman, C. *Rwanda: histoire d'un génocide*. Paris, Fayard, 1994.

Brauman, R. *Devant le mal. Rwanda, un génocide en direct*. Paris, Arléa, 1994.

Chrétien, J. P. *Rwanda, les Médias du génocide*. Paris, Editions Karthala, 1995.

Clark, P. *The Gacaca Courts, Post-Genocide Justice and Reconciliation in Rwanda: Justice without Lawyers*. Cambridge, Cambridge University Press, 2010.

Clark, P., and Kaufman Z. (Eds) *After Genocide: Transitional Justice, Post-Conflict Reconstruction and Reconciliation in Rwanda and Beyond*. New York, Columbia University Press and Hurst & Co., 2009.

Dallaire, R. *Shake Hands with the Devil: The Failure of Humanity in Rwanda*. Ontario, Random House of Canada Ltd, 2003.

Des Forges, A. *'Leave None to Tell the Story': Genocide in Rwanda*. New York, Human Rights Watch, 1999.

Destexhe, A. *Rwanda and Genocide in the Twentieth Century*. London, Pluto Press, 1994.

Dorsey, L. *Historical Dictionary of Rwanda*. Lanham, MD, Scarecrow Press, 1999.

Dupaquier, J.-F. (Ed.). *La justice internationale face au drame rwandais*. Paris, Editions Karthala, 1996.

Eltringham, N. *Accounting for Horror: Post-Genocide Debates in Rwanda*. London, Pluto Press, 2004.

Gourevitch, P. *We Wish to Inform You That Tomorrow We Will Be Killed With Our Families: Stories from Rwanda*. New York, Picador, 1999.

Grünfeld, F., and Huijboom, A. *The Failure to Prevent Genocide in Rwanda: The Role of Bystanders*. Boston, MA, Martinus Nijhoff, 2007.

Guichaoua, A. (Ed.). *Les crises politiques au Burundi et au Rwanda (1993–1994)*. Paris, Editions Karthala, 1995.

Harrell, P. E. *Rwanda's Gamble: Gacaca and a New Model of Transitional Justice*. Lincoln, NE, iUniverse, 2003.

Jones, B. D. *Peacemaking in Rwanda: The Dynamics of Failure (Project of the International Peace Academy)*. Boulder, CO, Lynne Rienner Publishers, 2001.

Kamukama, D. *Rwanda Conflict: Its Roots and Regional Implications*. Kampala, Fountain Publishers, 1993.

Khan, S. M., and Robinson, M. *The Shallow Graves of Rwanda*. London, I. B. Tauris & Co Ltd, 2001.

Kinzer. S. *A Thousand Hills: Rwanda's Rebirth and the Man Who Dreamed It*. New Jersey, John Wiley & Sons, 2008.

Kuperman, A. J. *The Limits of Humanitarian Intervention: Genocide in Rwanda*. Washington, DC, Brookings Institution, 2001.

Mamdani, M. *When Victims Become Killers: Colonialism, Nativism and the Genocide in Rwanda*. Princeton, NJ, Princeton University Press, 2001.

Melvern, L. *A People Betrayed: the Role of the West in Rwanda's Genocide*. London, Zed Books, 2000.

Conspiracy to Murder: The Rwandan Genocide. London, Verso, 2006.

Minear, L., and Guillot, P. *Soldiers to the Rescue: Humanitarian Lessons from Rwanda*. Paris, OECD, 1996.

Misser, F. *Vers un nouveau Rwanda?—Entretiens avec Paul Kagame*. Brussels, Editions Luc Pire, 1995.

Mwakikagile, G. *Identity Politics and Ethnic Conflicts in Rwanda and Burundi: A Comparative Study*. Dar es Salaam, New Africa Press, 2012.

Mushikiwabo, L., and Kramer, J. *Rwanda Means the Universe: A Native's Memory of Blood and Bloodlines*. New York, St Martin's Press, 2006.

Omaar, R. *Rwanda: Death, Despair and Defiance*. London, African Rights, 1994.

Pierce, J. R. *Speak Rwanda*. New York, Picador USA, 2000.

Prunier, G. *The Rwanda Crisis 1959–1964: History of a Genocide*. London, Hurst, 1995.

Reyntjens, F. *Pouvoir et droit au Rwanda: droit public et évolution politique 1916–1973*. Tervuren, Musée royal de l'Afrique centrale, 1985.

L'Afrique des grands lacs en crise. Paris, Editions Karthala, 1994.

Rudakemwa, F. *Rwanda: à la recherche de la vérité historique pour une réconciliation nationale*. Paris, L'Harmattan, 2007.

Sabarenzi, J., and Mullane, L. *God Sleeps in Rwanda: A Personal Journey of Transformation*. New York, Atria, 2009.

Scherrer, C. P. *Genocide and Crisis in Central Africa: Conflict Roots, Mass Violence and Regional War*. Westport, CT, Praeger, 2001.

Sparrow, J. *Under the Volcanoes: Rwanda's Refugee Crisis*. Geneva, Federation of Red Cross and Red Crescent Societies, 1994.

Straus, S. and L. Waldorf (Eds). *Remaking Rwanda: State Building and Human Rights after Mass Violence*. Madison, WI, University of Wisconsin Press, 2011.

Twagilimana, A. *The Debris of Hate: Ethnicity, Regionalism, and the 1994 Genocide*. Lanham, MD, University Press of America, 2003.

Uzabakiliho, F. *Flight for Life: A Journey from Rwanda*. New York, Vantage Press, 2001.

Waller, D. *Rwanda: Which Way Now?* Oxford, Oxfam, 1993.

Waugh, C. M. *Paul Kagame and Rwanda: Power, Genocide and the Rwandan Patriotic Front*. Jefferson, NC, McFarland and Co, 2004.

SAINT HELENA, ASCENSION AND TRISTAN DA CUNHA

Physical and Social Geography

Saint Helena, a rugged and mountainous island of volcanic origin, lies in the South Atlantic Ocean, latitude 16° S, longitude 5° 45' W, 1,131 km south-east of Ascension and about 1,930 km from the south-west coast of Africa. The island is 16.9 km long and 10.5 km broad, covering an area of 121 sq km (47 sq miles). The highest elevation, Diana's Peak, rises to 823 m above sea-level. The only inland waters are small streams, few of them perennial, fed by springs in the central hills. These streams and rainwater are sufficient for domestic water supplies and a few small irrigation schemes.

The cool South Atlantic trade winds are continuous throughout the year. The climate is sub-tropical and mild: the temperature in Jamestown, on the sea-coast, is 21°C–29°C in summer and 18°C–24°C in winter. Inland it is some 5°C cooler. Annual rainfall varies from 200 mm to 760 mm in the centre of the island.

At the census of 10 February 2008 the population was enumerated at 4,257, giving a density of 35.2 inhabitants per sq km. Jamestown, the capital, is the only town and had a population of 699 in mid-2009. The language of the island is English and the majority of the population belong to the Anglican Communion.

Saint Helena has one of the world's most equable climates. Industrial pollution is absent from the atmosphere, and there are no endemic diseases of note. The island is of interest to naturalists for its rare flora and fauna; there are about 40 species of flora that are unique to Saint Helena.

The island of Ascension, with a population of 710 at the February 2008 census, lies in the South Atlantic Ocean (7° 55' S, 14° 20' W), 1,131 km north-west of Saint Helena. The island, which covers an area of 88 sq km (34 sq miles), is a barren, rocky peak of purely volcanic origin, which was previously destitute of vegetation except above 450 m on Green Mountain (which rises to 875 m). The mountain supports a small farm producing vegetables and fruit. Since 1983 an alteration has taken place in the pattern of rainfall in Ascension. Total average annual rainfall has increased and the rain falls in heavy showers and is therefore less prone to evaporation. Grass, shrubs and flowers have grown in the valleys. Some topsoil has been produced by the decay of previous growth and root systems.

Tristan da Cunha, with a population of 264 at the February 2008 census, lies in the South Atlantic Ocean, 2,800 km west of Cape Town, South Africa and 2,300 km south-west of Saint Helena. Also in the group are Inaccessible Island, 37 km west of Tristan; the three Nightingale Islands, 37 km south; and Gough Island (Diego Alvarez), 425 km south. Tristan is volcanic in origin and nearly circular in shape, covering an area of 98 sq km (38 sq miles) and rising in a cone to 2,060 m above sea-level. The climate is typically oceanic and temperate. Rainfall averages 1,675 mm per year on the coast. The island provides breeding-grounds for albatrosses, rock-hopper penguins and seals, and a number of unique species, including the flightless land rail.

Recent History

Revised by the editorial staff

SAINT HELENA

The then uninhabited island of Saint Helena was discovered on 21 May 1502 by a Portuguese navigator, João da Nova, who named it in honour of St Helena, whose festival falls on that day. The British East India Co first established a settlement there in 1659, in order that the island might serve as a distant outpost from which to protect England's trade interests. The island was captured and briefly held by the Dutch in 1673. In that year a charter to occupy and govern Saint Helena was issued by King Charles II to the East India Co. In this charter the King confirmed the status of the island as a British outpost, and bestowed full rights of British citizenship on all those who settled on the island and on their descendants in perpetuity (see below). During 1815–21 the British Government temporarily assumed direct control of the island, owing to the exile there at Longwood House of Napoleon Bonaparte. In 1834 control over the island's affairs was transferred on a permanent basis from the East India Co to the British Government. Its importance as a port of call on the trade route between Europe and India ceased with the opening of the Suez Canal in 1869.

At the general election held in 1976, all but one of the 12 members elected to the Legislative Council strongly supported a policy of maintaining close economic links with the United Kingdom. This policy has been advocated by almost all members of the Legislative Council brought to office at subsequent elections (normally held every four years) up to and including that of November 2009.

In October 1981 the Governor announced the appointment of a commission to review the island's constitutional arrangements. The commission reported in 1983 that it was unable to find any proposal for constitutional change that would command the support of the majority of the islanders. In 1988, however, the Government obtained the introduction of a formal Constitution to replace the Order in Council and Royal Instructions under which Saint Helena was governed. This Constitution entered into force on 1 January 1989.

Owing to the limited range of economic activity on the island, Saint Helena is dependent on development and budgetary aid from the United Kingdom. From 1981, when the United Kingdom adopted the British Nationality Act, which effectively removed the islanders' traditional right of residence in the United Kingdom, opportunities for overseas employment were limited to contract work, principally in Ascension and the Falkland Islands. In 1992 an informal 'commission on citizenship' was established by a number of islanders to examine Saint Helena's constitutional relationship with the United Kingdom, with special reference to the legal validity of the 1981 legislation as applied to Saint Helena. In April 1997 the commission obtained a legal opinion from a former acting Attorney-General of Saint Helena to the effect that the application of the Act to the population of Saint Helena was in contravention of the royal charter establishing British sovereignty in 1673. The commission indicated that it intended to pursue the matter further. In July 1997 private legislation was introduced in the British Parliament to extend full British nationality to 'persons having connections with' Saint Helena. In the following month the British Government indicated that it was considering arrangements under which islanders would be granted employment and residence rights in the United Kingdom. In February 1998, following a conference held in

London, United Kingdom, of representatives of the British Dependent Territories, it was announced that a review was to take place of the future constitutional status of these territories, and of means whereby their economies might be strengthened. It was subsequently agreed that the operation of the 1981 legislation in relation to Saint Helena would also be reviewed. As an immediate measure to ameliorate the isolation of Saint Helena, the British Government conceded permission for civilian air landing rights on Ascension Island, which, with the contemplated construction of a small airstrip on Saint Helena, could facilitate the future development of the island as a tourist destination.

On 21 May 2002 Saint Helenians celebrated both the 500th anniversary of the island's discovery and the restoration of British citizenship under the British Overseas Territories Act, which reinstated those rights removed in 1981. In September 2002 an independent constitutional adviser visited Saint Helena and consulted extensively with the island's residents on the options for future constitutional development.

On 4 February 2002 a referendum was held in Saint Helena, Ascension Island, the Falkland Islands and on RMS *Saint Helena* on future access to Saint Helena; 71.6% of votes cast were in favour of the construction of an airport (the remainder of voters opted for a shipping alternative). Plans for the airport and associated commercial developments were cancelled in February 2003, on the grounds of unprofitability and environmental concerns; however, following protests by islanders, in April the Executive Council invited tenders for the construction of the airport. In mid-2006 all three of the final contractors for the project declared that some of the commercial risks associated with the terms of the tender were unfeasible. A procurement review was commissioned immediately, and by February 2007 four contractors had expressed formal interest in bringing air access to Saint Helena; towards the end of that year two bids were received for the design, build and operation contract for the airport. However, in February 2008 it was revealed that none of the shortlisted companies had provided an appropriate solution, and further negotiations would be necessary for the commencement of the project. Despite an initial commitment to bringing the airport into operation by 2012, in April 2009 the British Department for International Development (DfID) announced a further consultation on future access to Saint Helena. In December it was announced that as a result of 'current economic conditions' the British Government had decided that it would not be appropriate to proceed with the airport project 'at this time'. However, a further analysis of potential cost savings to the airport contract which might be enabled by recent technological developments, and of options for funding the capital cost of the airport through a public-private partnership, was to be carried out during 2010. In July it was decided that construction of the airport would go ahead, although no details on the budget or timescale for completion were made immediately available. In December DfID and the Saint Helena Government signed a memorandum of understanding detailing the reforms required in order to prepare for the construction of the airport. In November 2011 it was confirmed that these conditions had been met and a contract for the construction of the airport was signed with a South African company, Basil Read (Pty) Ltd. The total cost of the project was reported to be some £247m., a 20% reduction of the original quote received prior to the earlier cancellation of the project. Preparatory work for the project commenced in mid-2012; recent investigations to determine the suitability of existing infrastructure found that increased water supplies would be needed during the construction and in June 121 Drilling, a South African company contracted by Basil Read, began a drilling programme. If the drilling were to discover insufficient supplies of fresh water, desalinated water would be required to sustain the building project, which was due to reach its peak activity in March 2013. In July 2012 the Government announced the first Variation Order under the airport construction project, which was to amend the runway design and allow for greater flexibility and the possibility of expanding the runway at a later date to accommodate larger aircraft. In August the new design for the terminal was unveiled.

Meanwhile, a consultative poll on the draft for a new constitution, which, *inter alia*, proposed the creation of a ministerial form of government, took place on 25 May 2005. The draft document was rejected by 52.6% of voters. Concern was expressed at the low rate of voter participation, recorded at 43% of registered voters. Nevertheless, some elements of the rejected constitution were adopted, including the division of Saint Helena into two electoral constituencies. The British Government subsequently stated that it wished to identify any possible improvements to the existing Constitution in conjunction with the new Executive Council, which took office following the elections held on 31 August. A new Governor, Andrew Gurr, was appointed in November 2007, and in April 2008 he outlined proposals for a new constitution that would be drafted following a full consultation process, which he envisaged would be completed by mid-2009. He suggested that the previous draft constitution had been rejected due to the proposed introduction of ministerial government, and that consequently a number of potential improvements in other areas had been lost.

On 1 September 2009 the St Helena, Ascension and Tristan da Cunha Constitution Order 2009 entered into force. Under the new Constitution, Ascension and Tristan da Cunha were no longer referred to as 'Dependencies' and the territory was henceforth to be known as St Helena, Ascension and Tristan da Cunha. The new Constitution also established fundamental rights and freedoms for each of the three islands, which were to share the same Governor, Attorney-General, Supreme Court and Court of Appeal. St Helena was to be represented by a Legislative Council and an Executive Council, while Ascension and Tristan da Cunha were to be represented by Island Councils. Legislative elections were held in early November, following which the new councils were formed. The Legislative Council subsequently appointed chairmen to head the eight Council Committees responsible for overseeing policy formation.

In May 2008 a number of British newspapers reported that the United Kingdom, seeking to take advantage of its possessions in the South Atlantic, had submitted claims for the extension of the territorial waters surrounding Saint Helena, Ascension and Tristan da Cunha. This was attributed to the sharp increase in global petroleum prices and the possibility of securing areas of sea-bed that could, in future years, be drilled for oil, gas and mineral resources. The UN Convention on the Law of the Sea permits countries to lay claim to an area of sea-bed with a radius of up to 350 nautical miles around their territory.

A new Governor, Mark Capes, was appointed in July 2011 and took office in October, upon the retirement of Gurr. Colin Owen was designated as Financial Secretary and was scheduled to take office at the end of August 2012, when incumbent Paul Blessington was to leave the island.

Meanwhile, in April 2012 a package of land reform policies was adopted, including a revised Land Development Control Plan (LDCP), which had initially come into effect in 2007. The revised LDCP placed greater emphasis on facilitating development rather than restricting it and highlighted the importance of both natural and built heritage for the tourism sector. A greater importance for higher environmental standards was also outlined. A new Housing Strategy, included in the package, focused on ensuring residents have access to affordable housing and that it is suitable for the long-term needs of the island. In November 2011 Tony Earnshaw was appointed as Lands Executive, for a term of two years, to oversee land reforms.

In July 2012 the Government signed a 10-year deal with Cable & Wireless South Atlantic Ltd, based in the Falkland Islands. Cable & Wireless agreed to invest £1.5m. in improved infrastructure to provide faster internet speeds and increase the amount of data customers can use. Internet charges, which were among the highest world-wide, would decrease from January 2013, while the cost of international telephone calls would also be reduced. In a second contract, the number of television channels available would increase from three to 15, although no date for the upgrade was given.

ASCENSION

The island of Ascension was discovered by a Portuguese expedition on Ascension Day 1501. The island was uninhabited until the arrival of Napoleon, the exiled French Emperor, on Saint Helena in 1815, when a small British naval garrison was placed there. Ascension remained under the supervision of the British Admiralty until 1922, when it was made a dependency of Saint Helena. (This status was revoked under the new Constitution which entered into force on 1 September 2009.)

The island is famous for green turtles, which land there from December to May to lay their eggs in the sand. It is also a breeding ground of the sooty tern, or 'wideawake', vast numbers of which settle on the island every 10 months to lay and hatch their eggs. All wildlife except rabbits and cats is protected by law. Shark, barracuda, tuna, bonito, marlin and other game fish are plentiful in the surrounding ocean. Following the decision by the British Government in February 1998 to open airfield facilities on Ascension to civilian flights, a modest eco-tourism sector is being developed.

The population in March 2001 was 982 (excluding British military personnel), of whom 760 were St Helenians. The majority of the remainder were expatriate civilian personnel of Merlin Communications International (MCI), which operates the British Broadcasting Corpn (BBC) Overseas World Service Atlantic relay station, Cable & Wireless PLC, which provides international communications services and operates the 'Ariane' satellite tracking station of the European Space Agency, and the US military base. Ascension does not raise its own finance; the costs of administering the island are borne collectively by the user organizations, supplemented by income from philatelic sales. Some revenue, which is remitted to the Saint Helena administration, is derived from fishing licences. On 31 March 2001 the joint venture between the BBC and Cable & Wireless, dating from 1984, to provide public services to the island was dissolved. The Ascension Island Government took over responsibility for health and education, the Ascension Island Works and Services Agency, a statutory body, was established to maintain transport and infrastructure, and any remaining services were taken over by the new Ascension Island Commercial Services Ltd (AICS) company. AICS was jointly owned by the Ascension Islands Government, the BBC and Cable & Wireless and had the declared aim of privatizing the new enterprises by 2002. This development was regarded as highly significant in that it reorientated public-service provision to the demands of the resident population, rather than towards the needs of those organizations using the island.

Dissent developed among the resident population in June 2002, following the decision of the Foreign and Commonwealth Office to impose taxes for the first time on the island. The primary objection of the population was that this was 'taxation without representation', as the islanders do not possess the right to vote, to own property or even to live on the island. (Protests took the form of a petition and the threat of legal action under the European Convention on Human Rights.) The Governor responded with plans to introduce a democratically elected council that would have a purely advisory function and no decision-making powers. On 22–23 August a vote on the democratic options took place on the island, with 95% of the votes cast being in favour of an Island Council, rather than an Inter-Island Council plus Island Council structure; 50% of those eligible to vote did so. The Council was to be chaired by the Administrator, on behalf of the Governor, and was to comprise seven elected members, the Attorney-General, the Director of Finance and one or two appointed members. Elections for councillors took place in October, and the Island Council was inaugurated in the following month. A joint consultative council was also to be established, with representatives from both Ascension and Saint Helena, in order to formulate policy relating to economic development and tourism common to both islands.

The British Government subsequently stated its intention to enact legislation granting the islanders right of abode and the right to own property. However, following a visit to the island by a delegation of British officials in November 2005, it was announced that the proposed reforms would not be carried out, on the basis that there was no indigenous population and that residents only lived and worked on the island for the duration of their employment contracts. The British Government cited its reluctance to change fundamentally the nature of the territory and also maintained that granting such rights would impose greater financial liabilities on British taxpayers, and would bring an unacceptable level of risk to the United Kingdom. In January 2006 the Island Council announced that it intended to seek clarification regarding the legality of the British Government's decision, observing that some residents had lived on the island for more than 40 years.

In May 2007 the Island Council was suspended and the Ascension Island Advisory Group was established to provide advice to the Administrator on certain policy issues. It was anticipated that the Advisory Group would meet on a monthly basis, to be supplemented by informal meetings as necessary. Consultation papers were issued to encourage the people of Ascension to participate in the decision-making process, such as that published by Governor Andrew Gurr in February 2008, which outlined the future responsibilities and operation of the Island Council. The suspension was initially expected to last until elections in May 2008, but after public consultation Gurr postponed the elections until later in that year; they were eventually held in October and a new Island Council was sworn in that month.

In 1942 the US Government, by arrangement with the British Government, established an airbase, Wideawake, which it subsequently reoccupied and extended by agreement with the British Government in 1956, in connection with the extension of the long-range proving ground for guided missiles, centred in Florida. A further agreement in 1965 allowed the USA to develop tracking facilities on the island in support of the National Aeronautics and Space Administration's 'Apollo' space programme. This operation was terminated in 1990. In October 2003 the British Government concluded negotiations with the US authorities over the signing of an agreement to allow US air-charter access to the airfield.

TRISTAN DA CUNHA

The British navy took possession of Tristan da Cunha in 1816 during Napoleon's residence on Saint Helena, and a small garrison was stationed there. When the garrison was withdrawn, three men elected to remain and became the founders of the present settlement. Because of its position on a main sailing route the colony thrived until the 1880s, but with the replacement of sail by steam a period of decline set in. No regular shipping called and the islanders suffered at times from a shortage of food. Nevertheless, attempts to move the inhabitants to South Africa were unsuccessful. The islanders were engaged chiefly in fishing and agricultural pursuits.

The United Society for the Propagation of the Gospel has maintained an interest in the island since 1922, and in 1932 one of its missionary teachers was officially recognized as Honorary Commissioner and magistrate. In 1938 Tristan da Cunha and the neighbouring uninhabited islands of Nightingale, Inaccessible and Gough were made dependencies of Saint Helena. (This status was revoked under the new Constitution which entered into force on 1 September 2009.) In 1950 the office of Administrator was created. The Island Council was established in 1952.

The island is remote, and regular communications are restricted to about six calls each year by vessels from Cape Town (usually crayfish trawlers), an annual visit from a British vessel, the RMS *St Helena*, from Cape Town and the annual call by a South African vessel with supplies for the island and the weather station on Gough Island. There is, however, a wireless station on the island which is in daily contact with Cape Town. A satellite system, which provides direct dialling for telephone and fax facilities, was installed in 1992. The cost of international communications was to diminish greatly from mid-2006, with the installation of a satellite internet and telephone exchange, part of the British Foreign and Commonwealth Office telecommunications network.

An assessment was carried out on the island's harbour in 2006, as its location means that it is vulnerable to extreme weather conditions which threaten its structural integrity in the long term. Plans to relocate the harbour, however, proved too expensive and it was renovated early in 2008. This was paid for by the British Department for International Development and was completed in March with the help of Royal Engineers from the United Kingdom. The island is largely self-sufficient.

Economy

Revised by the editorial staff

SAINT HELENA

From the 1980s increased benefits were made available to private farmers in a major effort to encourage greater local production, local utilization and farming efficiency. Grants, loans (of capital and labour) and free technical assistance have been offered and an increasing number of full-time smallholders have taken advantage of the scheme. Two major irrigation schemes using butyl-lined reservoirs have been completed. Following a notable rise in food production in the early 1980s, more land was rented or leased from the Government for this purpose. Commonage grazing areas are now made available by the Government to private stock owners on a per head per month basis. Individuals hold land either in fee simple or by lease. Immigrants require a licence to hold land. Crown land may be leased on conditions approved by the Governor. At the 2008 census 7.3% of the employed labour force were engaged in agriculture and fishing. Saint Helena was developing a reputation for niche organic products, such as coffee, and a project to develop honey production was also underway. It was also hoped that an integrated pest-management programme would lead to a greater range and output of agricultural production.

A major reafforestation programme was begun during the mid-1970s, aimed at replacing flax and fostering land reclamation. A sawmill/timber treatment plant produces a proportion of the timber needed for construction and fencing requirements, but most timber continues to be imported. Timber sales amounted to 390 cu m in 1999. No mineral resources have been identified.

Fish of many kinds are plentiful in the waters around Saint Helena, and a fisheries corporation exists to exploit this resource. The total catch amounted to 864 metric tons in 2010. A freezing/storage unit is capable of storing 20 tons, allowing fish to be frozen for export as well as the local market. Fish exports comprise tuna—skipjack and dried salted skipjack—and in 2000 totalled 43.1 tons, with earnings amounting to £113,000. (Wild fish products from the island's inshore fishery recently became some of the first to receive organic certification from the British Soil Association.) A small quantity of coffee is the only other commodity exported.

In terms of offshore fishery, the Government has previously gained up to 20% of its revenue from the sale of licences to international companies. International sales of the territory's postal stamps also comprise a significant proportion of local income (£89,000 in 2008/09).

Unemployment is a serious problem, and a large proportion of the labour force is forced to seek employment overseas, principally on Ascension and the Falkland Islands. In March 2001 551 Saint Helenians were working on Ascension, and in December 1999 371 were working on the Falkland Islands; approximately 1,700 members of the work-force were employed offshore at the end of 2005. However, a benefit of this arrangement was the volume of remittances entering the economy (see below). In 2004 the rate of unemployment (including community work scheme placements) was estimated at 7.6%, but by November 2008 this rate was estimated to have fallen to 2.3% of the labour force. Unemployment has resulted in widespread reliance on welfare benefit payments and a concurrent decline in living standards for the majority of the population. Nearly 70% of employment on the island is provided by the Government (all key services and infrastructure, excluding telecommunications), although policies are actively being implemented to develop the private sector.

The main imports in 2009/10, by value, were food and live animals, machinery and equipment and mineral fuels, lubricants etc. Total imports for that period were valued at £10.3m.; these were mainly supplied by South Africa (£5.4m.) and the United Kingdom (£4.7m.). This figure was significantly greater than that of exports in the same year of some £321,000. The main export commodity is fish.

In 2009/10 Saint Helena was budgeted to receive £7.7m. in British aid. Local revenue was budgeted at £1.7m. in that year and total expenditure at £23.4m. Approximately one-third of the Government's annual recurrent budget and most capital investment is funded by the United Kingdom. Remittances from increasing offshore employment contributed some £3.4m. in 2009/10. Official estimates put gross domestic product (GDP) at £19.0m. in 2009/10, while GDP was estimated to have decreased, in real terms, by an annual average of 1.6% during 1999/2000–2005/06; a decline of 10.1%, in real terms, was recorded for 2005/06. The population declined by an annual average of 3.2% during 1999/2000–2005/06, and, largely as a result of this, per caput GDP increased, in real terms, by an annual average of 1.9% over the same period. The annual rate of inflation, according to retail prices, averaged 4.4% in 2000–09, and the rate, influenced to a large extent by the prevailing rates in its two most important trading partners, South Africa and the United Kingdom, had remained relatively stable (around 3%–5%) during 2003–07, although consumer prices increased by 8.0% in both 2008 and 2009.

The Saint Helena Growers' Co-operative Society is the only such association on the island. It is both a consumers' and a marketing organization, and provides consumer goods, such as seeds, implements and feeding stuffs, to its members, and markets their produce, mainly vegetables, locally, to visiting ships and to Ascension Island. The local market is limited and is soon over-supplied, and this, together with the decrease in the number of ships calling over recent years, has inhibited the growth of this enterprise.

The only port in Saint Helena is Jamestown, which is an open roadstead with a good anchorage for ships of any size. In 1978, with the establishment of the Saint Helena Shipping Co, the Saint Helena Government assumed responsibility for the operation and maintenance of a charter vessel (known as the RMS *Saint Helena*, which entered operation in 1990), which carries cargo and passengers six times a year between Saint Helena and Cardiff, United Kingdom, via Vigo, Spain, and nine times a year between Saint Helena and Cape Town, South Africa (with calls at the Canary Islands); in addition, there are around 16 visits a year to Ascension Island, and one to Tristan da Cunha. The Saint Helena Shipping Co receives an annual subsidy from the British Government. There is a bulk fuel farm at Rupert's Valley, which is supplied at approximately three-month intervals with fuel from Europe.

There is no airport or airstrip as yet on Saint Helena and no railway, although in April 2003 the Executive Council invited tenders for the construction of an airport, which was initially expected to be completed by 2012. However, in April 2009 the British Department for International Development announced a further consultation on future access to Saint Helena, thus casting doubt on whether the project would actually proceed. Nevertheless, this development represented the potential to expand significantly both the private sector and the economy as a whole, and plans included extensive infrastructural development to support the potential inflow of people and cargo. In July 2010 it was decided that construction of the airport would go ahead and preparatory work began in early 2012 (see Recent History). New tourism and investment policies took effect in January 2007, aimed at increasing competitiveness in an open economy and making Saint Helena an attractive option for international investment. Receipts from tourism amounted to £707,000 in 2009/10, an increase from the £414,000 recorded in 2007/08. There are 118 km of all-weather roads, and a further 20 km of earth roads, which are used mainly by animal transport and are usable by motor vehicles only in dry weather. All roads have steep gradients and sharp curves.

In early 2012 The Saint Helena authorities published a Sustainable Economic Development Plan (SEDP) for 2012/13–2021/22, which aimed to introduce a 'tourism driven economy' in conjunction with the construction of the airport. The SEDP stated that a 'relatively modest' number of visitors (totalling 30,000 per year) was required in order to make Saint Helena financially self-sustaining, and plans were already advanced with regard to the construction of a number of large tourism resorts on the island. Furthermore, based on the visitor number projections, average wages on the island were predicted to double in real terms by 2021/22, while an increase in GDP, to £117m. by 2022 (compared with 15.6m. in 2009/10), was also projected. Also in March 2012 the National Strategy for the Development of Statistics was formally endorsed to provide a framework for enhancing St Helena's statistical systems.

Meanwhile, in August 2011 the state-owned St Helena Broadcasting (Guarantee) Corporation Ltd (SHBC) was registered and in 2012 a new community-owned media services organization was in the process of being established. It was envisaged that the SHBC would broadcast three FM radio stations (one of which would be a relay of the British Broadcasting Corporation's World Service). Existing radio station Saint FM was invited to join the corporation but declined. The island's other radio station, Radio St Helena, was scheduled to cease broadcasting in August 2012. The final edition of *The St Helena Herald* was published in early March, to be replaced by the SHBC's new weekly newspaper, *The Sentinal*, which published its first issue later that month. (Saint FM also publishes the weekly *St Helena Independent*, and this was to continue.)

ASCENSION

Ascension does not raise its own finance; the costs of administering the island are borne collectively by the user organizations, supplemented by income from philatelic sales. The island is developing a modest eco-tourism sector. Some revenue, which is remitted to the Saint Helena administration, is derived from fishing licences (estimated to be around £1m. in 1999). Facilities on Ascension underwent rapid development in 1982 to serve as a major staging post for British vessels and aircraft on their way to the Falkland Islands (q.v.), and the island has continued to provide a key link in British supply lines to the South Atlantic.

As of early 2004 Ascension Island had a balanced fiscal budget, although with minimal reserves. Government expenditure funds one school, one hospital (offering limited services), police and judicial services; these services are provided without charge to local tax-payers. The Saint Helena-based firm Solomons has a primary role in the incipient private sector and a sports-fishing industry was in the process of being established.

TRISTAN DA CUNHA

The island's major source of revenue derives from a royalty for the crayfishing concession, supplemented by income from the sale of postage stamps and other philatelic items, and handicrafts. The fishing industry and the administration employ all of the working population. Some 20 power boats operating from the island land their catches to a fish-freezing factory built by the Atlantic Islands Development Corpn, the fishing concession of which was transferred in January 1997 to a new holder, Premier Fishing (Pty) Ltd, of Cape Town, and later to another South African company, Ovenstone (Pty) Ltd. In February 2008, however, a fire destroyed the factory completely, along with the island's power plant. This was expected to have severe negative effects on the 2008–09 fishing season. Ovenstone resumed operations in mid-2009 in a new factory built to European Union standards. The power plant was scheduled to be commissioned during the fourth quarter of 2008, but it was anticipated that its construction would also be delayed. The island's harbour was also renovated in 2008, in a project funded by the British Department for International Development (DfID), and undertaken with the help of Royal Engineers from the United Kingdom.

Budget estimates for 2005/06 projected a deficit of £147,507. Development aid from the United Kingdom ceased in 1980, leaving the island financially self-sufficient. The United Kingdom, however, has continued to supply the cost of the salaries and passages of the Administrator, a doctor and visiting specialists (a dentist every two years and an optician every two years). In April 2008, prompted by concerns surrounding the island's dwindling capital reserves, Administrator David Morley warned that the island could be bankrupt within four years unless economic austerity measures were implemented immediately. Chief among these proposals was the introduction, with effect from 1 June 2008, of an incremental system of income tax (with a maximum rate of 13%). It was reported in May 2008 that the United Kingdom Government had registered a claim with the UN Commission for the Limits of the Continental Shelf to extend its territorial waters around Tristan da Cunha. It was hoped that these areas of seabed could be secured with the possibility of drilling for petroleum, gas and mineral resources in future years.

Statistical Survey

Sources (unless otherwise indicated): Development and Economic Planning Dept, Government of Saint Helena, Saint Helena Island, STHL 1ZZ; tel. 2777; fax 2830; e-mail depd@helanta.sh; Saint Helena Development Agency (SHDA), POB 117, No. 2 Main St, Jamestown, Saint Helena Island, STHL 1ZZ; tel. 2920; fax 2166; e-mail enquiries@shda.co.sh; internet www.shda.co.sh.

Note: Unless otherwise indicated, figures in this Statistical Survey relate only to the island of Saint Helena.

AREA AND POPULATION

Area: 411 sq km (159 sq miles). St Helena 121 sq km (47 sq miles); Ascension Island 88 sq km (34 sq miles); Tristan da Cunha 98 sq km (38 sq miles); Inaccessible Island 10 sq km (4 sq miles); Nightingale Islands 2 sq km (1 sq mile); Gough Island 91 sq km (35 sq miles).

Population: 5,157 at census of 8 March 1998; 4,257 (enumerated total) at census of 10 February 2008, 3,981 (resident population) at census of 10 February 2008. *Ascension Island* (enumerated total at 2008 census): 710. *Tristan da Cunha* (enumerated total at 2008 census): 264. *2011* (estimate at 31 December); Saint Helena 4,250. Note: There are no indigenous inhabitants on Ascension Island, but several hundred personnel and employees and their families are permanently resident (mostly nationals of Saint Helena, with some 200 UK nationals and 150 US nationals). There is a small weather station on Gough Island, staffed, under agreement, by personnel employed by the South African Government.

Density (at 2008 census): 35.2 per sq km.

Population by Age and Sex (resident population at 2008 census): *0–14:* 600 (males 317, females 283); *15–64:* 2,677 (males 1,378, females 1,299); *65 and over:* 703 (males 326, females 377); *Total* 3,981 (males 2,022, females 1,959). Note: Total includes one male of undetermined age.

Principal Town (UN estimate, incl. suburbs): Jamestown (capital), population 673 in mid-2011 (Source: UN, *World Urbanization Prospects: The 2011 Revision*).

Births and Deaths (2011): Registered live births 34 (8.5 per 1,000); Registered deaths 49 (11.5 per 1,000).

Employment (2008 census): Agriculture, hunting and related activities 122; Fishing 33; Mining and quarrying 8; Manufacturing 115; Electricity, gas and water 113; Construction 190; Wholesale and retail trade, etc. 385; Hotels and restaurants 36; Transport, storage and communications 237; Financial intermediation 20; Real estate, renting and business activities 185; Public administration and defence 157; Education 112; Health and social work 178; Other community services 217; Private household 17; Extra-territorial organizations 5; *Total employed* 2,130 (males 1,174; females 956) (Source: ILO). *Unemployed* (2007/08, incl. community work scheme) 66.

AGRICULTURE, ETC.

Livestock (livestock census, 2009): Cattle 598; Sheep 651; Pigs 386; Goats 773; Asses 46; Chickens 4,421.

Livestock Products (metric tons, 2009): Cattle meat 40.9; Pig meat 67.2; Sheep meat 0.8.

Fishing (metric tons, live weight, including Ascension and Tristan da Cunha, 2010): Skipjack tuna 250; Yellowfin tuna 65; Tristan da Cunha rock lobster 403; Total catch (incl. others) 864. Figures include catches of rock lobster from Tristan da Cunha during the 12 months ending 30 April of the year stated (Source: FAO).

INDUSTRY

Electric Energy (production, kWh million): 8.5 in 2008; 8.8 in 2009; 9.1 in 2010.

FINANCE

Currency and Exchange Rate: 100 pence (pennies) = 1 Saint Helena pound (£). *Sterling, Dollar and Euro Equivalents* (31 May 2012): £1 sterling = Saint Helena £1; US $1 = 64.50 pence; €1 = 80.00 pence; £10 = $15.50 = €12.50. *Average Exchange Rate* (£ per US dollar): 0.6419 in 2009; 0.6472 in 2010; 0.6241 in 2011. Note: The Saint Helena pound is at par with the pound sterling.

Budget (£ million, 2009/10): Total revenue 9.4 (excluding United Kingdom budgetary aid 7.7); Total expenditure (incl. trading accounts) 23.4. *Ascension Island* (£ million, year ending 31 March 2004, estimates): Total revenue 4.3; Total expenditure 4.0 (recurrent 3.3, capital 0.7). *Tristan da Cunha* (£ million, 2005/06, estimates): Total revenue 0.7; Expenditure 0.9 (with excess expenditure financed from capital reserves of 1.2).

Gross National Product (£ million at current prices): 20.32 in 2007/08; 21.47 in 2008/09; 19.04 in 2009/10.

Gross Domestic Product (£ million at current prices): 17.28 in 2007/08; 17.39 in 2008/09; 15.55 in 2009/10.

Expenditure on the Gross Domestic Product (£ million at current prices, 2009/10): Government expenditure 20.22; Private expenditure 14.25; Changes in stocks 0.21; *Total domestic expenditure* 34.68; Exports of goods and services 1.19; *Less* Imports of goods and services 20.32; *GDP in purchasers' values* 15.55.

Money Supply (£ '000, 2006/07): Currency in circulation 3,618 (excl. commemorative coins valued at 514).

Cost of Living (Retail Price Index; base: February 2002 = 100): 121.6 in 2007; 131.3 in 2008; 141.8 in 2009.

EXTERNAL TRADE

Principal Commodities (£ '000, 2009/10): *Imports:* Total 10,267 (Food and live animals 2,617; Mineral fuels, lubricants, etc. 1,349; Machinery and transport equipment 1,896). *Exports:* Total 321 (mostly fish). Note: Trade is mainly with the United Kingdom (imports 4,732 in 2009/10) and South Africa (imports 5,431 in 2009/10).

TRANSPORT

Road Traffic (2009): 2,391 licensed vehicles (incl. 1,459 passenger motor cars).

Shipping: *Vessels Entered* (2009): 235. *Merchant Fleet* (31 December 2009): 2 vessels; Total displacement 2,232 grt (Source: IHS Fairplay, *World Fleet Statistics*).

TOURISM

Visitor Arrivals: 2,595 (tourists 1,113) in 2007; 2,589 (tourists 825) in 2008; 2,452 (tourists 847) in 2009.

Receipts from Tourism (£ '000, estimates): 414 in 2007/08; 320 in 2008/09; 707 in 2009/10.

COMMUNICATIONS MEDIA

Radio Receivers ('000 in use, 1997): 3 (Source: UNESCO, *Statistical Yearbook*).

Television Subscribers (April 2007): 1,161.

Telephones (main lines in use, 2011): 2,400 (Source: International Telecommunication Union).

Broadband Subscribers (2011): 800 (Source: International Telecommunication Union).

EDUCATION

Primary (2006/07): 2 schools; 14 teachers; 115 pupils.

Amalgamated School (2006/07): 1 school; 15 teachers; 116 pupils.

Intermediate (2006/07): 2 schools; 17 teachers; 119 pupils.

Secondary (2006/07): 1 school; 42 teachers; 324 pupils.

2009/10 (all levels): 7 schools; 88 teachers; 516 enrolled pupils.

Directory

The Constitution

The St Helena, Ascension and Tristan da Cunha Constitution Order 2009, which entered into force on 1 September 2009, replaced the Saint Helena Constitution Order 1988 of 1 January 1989. While separate territories, St Helena, Ascension and Tristan da Cunha form a single territorial grouping under the British Crown and are represented by a single Governor.

Executive authority is reserved to the British Crown, but is exercised on behalf of Her Majesty Queen Elizabeth II by the Governor, either directly or through officers subordinate to him or her. Executive authority of Ascension is exercised by the Governor, either directly or through the Administrator of Ascension. Executive authority of Tristan da Cunha is exercised by the Governor, either directly or through the Administrator of Tristan da Cunha. The Executive Council for St Helena is presided over by the Governor and consists of five of the elected members of the Legislative Council (the elected members of the Legislative Council choose from among themselves those who will also be members of the Executive Council) and three ex officio members (the Chief Secretary, the Financial Secretary and the Attorney-General).

Legislative authority for Saint Helena is vested in the Legislature, consisting of Her Majesty Queen Elizabeth II and the Legislative Council, which has the power to make laws for the peace, order and good government of Saint Helena. The Legislative Council consists of a Speaker and Deputy Speaker, 12 elected members and three ex officio members (the Chief Secretary, the Financial Secretary and the Attorney-General). Legislative authority on Ascension and on Tristan da Cunha is vested in the Governor, who acts after consultation with the respective Island Councils, although he or she is not obliged to act in accordance with this advice.

The Government

HEAD OF STATE

Queen: HM Queen ELIZABETH II.

Governor: MARK CAPES.

The Governor of Saint Helena, in his capacity as Governor of Ascension and Tristan da Cunha, is represented by an Administrator on those islands. The Governor, either directly, or through the Administrator, exercises executive authority on behalf of Her Majesty Queen Elizabeth II. The Governor, acting after consultation with the Island Councils, whose advice he or she is not obliged to follow, may make laws for the peace, order and good government of Ascension and Tristan da Cunha.

Administrator of Ascension: COLIN WELLS.

Administrator of Tristan da Cunha: SEAN BURNS.

EXECUTIVE COUNCIL

(September 2012)

President: MARK CAPES (The Governor).

Chief Secretary: OWEN O'SULLIVAN.

Financial Secretary: COLIN OWEN.

Attorney-General: KENNETH BADDON.

Elected Members: RODNEY BUCKLEY, CYRIL GUNNELL, MERVYN YON, ANTHONY GREEN, STEDSON FRANCIS.

LEGISLATIVE COUNCIL
(September 2012)

The Legislative Council consists of the Speaker, the Deputy Speaker, 12 elected members and three ex officio members (the Chief Secretary, the Financial Secretary and the Attorney-General).

Speaker: CATHY HOPKINS.

Deputy Speaker: ERIC BENJAMIN.

Committee Chairmen

Access and Transport: JOHN CRANFIELD.

Economy and Finance: (vacant).

Education and Employment: RODNEY BUCKLEY.

Health and Social Welfare: CYRIL GUNNELL.

Home and International: DEREK THOMAS.

Infrastructure and Utilities: MERVYN YON.

Natural Resources, Development and Environment: RAYMOND WILLIAMS.

Tourism and Leisure: BERNICE OLSSON.

GOVERNMENT OFFICES

Office of the Governor: The Castle, Jamestown, STHL 1ZZ; tel. 2555; fax 2598; e-mail pagovernor@sainthelena.gov.sh; internet www.sainthelena.gov.sh.

Office of the Chief Secretary: The Castle, Jamestown, STHL 1ZZ; tel. 2470; fax 2598; e-mail ocs@cwimail.sh.

Office of the Financial Secretary: The Castle, Jamestown, STHL 1ZZ; tel. 2470; fax 2020; e-mail pafinancialsecretary@sainthelena.gov.sh.

Office of the Administrator of Ascension: The Residency, Georgetown, Ascension, ASCN 1ZZ; tel. 7000; fax 6152; e-mail aigenquiries@ascension.gov.ac; internet www.ascension-island.gov.ac.

Office of the Administrator of Tristan da Cunha: The Administrator's Office, Edinburgh of the Seven Seas, Tristan da Cunha, TDCU 1ZZ; tel. (20) 30142000; fax (satellite) (20) 30142000; e-mail tristandcadmin@gmail.com; internet www.tristandc.com/administator.php.

Political Organizations

There are no political parties in Saint Helena. Elections to the Legislative Council, the latest of which took place in November 2009, are conducted on a non-partisan basis.

Judicial System

The legal system is derived from English common law and statutes. There is a Supreme Court and a Court of Appeal, and provision was made in the 2009 Constitution for the establishment of other subordinate courts. The Supreme Court is presided over by a Chief Justice. The Court of Appeal consists of a President and two or more Justices of Appeal. There is also a four-member Judicial Services Commission, presided over by the Chief Justice.

The Attorney-General of Saint Helena is the principal legal adviser to the Government of Saint Helena. The Attorney-General of Ascension and of Tristan da Cunha is the principal legal adviser to the Government of Ascension and to the Government of Tristan da Cunha and is the person for the time being holding or acting in the office of Attorney-General of St Helena. The courts of Ascension and of Tristan da Cunha are the Supreme Court of St Helena, the Court of Appeal of St Helena, and such courts subordinate to the Supreme Court as may be established by law.

Chief Justice: CHARLES W. EKINS.

Attorney-General: KENNETH BADDON.

Sheriff: GRETA PAT MUSK.

Religion

The majority of the population belongs to the Anglican Communion. Ascension forms part of the Anglican diocese of Saint Helena, which normally provides a resident chaplain who is also available to minister to members of other denominations. There is a Roman Catholic chapel served by visiting priests, as well as a small mosque. Adherents of the Anglican church predominate on Tristan da Cunha, which is within the Anglican Church of Southern Africa, and is under the jurisdiction of the Archbishop of Cape Town, South Africa.

CHRISTIANITY

The Anglican Communion

Anglicans are adherents of the Anglican Church of Southern Africa (formerly the Church of the Province of Southern Africa). The Metropolitan of the Province is the Archbishop of Cape Town, South Africa. St Helena forms a single diocese.

Bishop of Saint Helena: Rt Rev. RICHARD FENWICK, Bishopsholme, POB 62, Saint Helena, STHL 1ZZ; tel. and fax 4471; e-mail bishop@helanta.sh; diocese f. 1859; has jurisdiction over the islands of Saint Helena and Ascension.

The Roman Catholic Church

The Church is represented in Saint Helena, Ascension and Tristan da Cunha by a Mission, established in August 1986. There were an estimated 100 adherents in the islands at 31 December 2007.

Superior: Rev. Fr MICHAEL MCPARTLAND (also Prefect Apostolic of the Falkland Islands); normally visits Tristan da Cunha once a year and Ascension Island two or three times a year; Rev. Fr MICHAEL DAVID GRIFFITHS, Sacred Heart Church, Jamestown, STHL 1ZZ; tel. and fax 2535.

Other Christian Churches

The Salvation Army, Seventh-day Adventists, Baptists, New Apostolics and Jehovah's Witnesses are active on the island.

BAHÁ'Í FAITH

There is a small Bahá'í community on the island.

The Bahá'í Community of St Helena: Moon Bldg, Napoleon St, POB 49, Jamestown; tel. 4525; fax 4924; e-mail enquiries@sthelenabahai.org; internet www.sthelenabahai.org; f. 1954; Chair. BASIL GEORGE.

The Press

The St Helena Independent: St Helena Media Productions Ltd, 2nd Floor, Association Hall, Main St, Jamestown, STHL 1ZZ; tel. 2660; e-mail independent@cwimail.sh; internet www.saint.fm; f. 2005; independent; weekly.

The Sentinel: The Livery Stables, Nr The Market Clock, Jamestown, STHL 1ZZ; tel. 2727; e-mail news@shbc.sh; internet www.shbc.sh/sentinel; f. 2012.

Broadcasting and Communications

TELECOMMUNICATIONS

Cable & Wireless (St Helena) PLC: POB 2, Bishops Rooms, Jamestown, STHL 1ZZ; tel. 2155; fax 2206; e-mail webmaster@helanta.sh; internet www.cw.com/sthelena; f. 1899; provides national and international telecommunications.

BROADCASTING

In 2012 a new community-owned media services organization was in the process of being established. The government-funded Saint Helena Broadcasting (Guarantee) Corporation (SHBC) was to broadcast three FM radio stations (one of which would be a relay of the British Broadcasting Corporation's World Service), and which were scheduled to be operational by late 2012 at which time Radio St Helena was to cease broadcasting. SHBC also introduced a weekly newspaper; the Sentinel published its first edition on 29 March 2012, replacing the Saint Helena Herald.

Cable & Wireless PLC: The Moon, Jamestown, STHL 1ZZ; tel. 2200; f. 1995; provides a 3-channel television service 24 hours daily from 5 satellite channels.

Saint Helena Broadcasting (Guarantee) Corporation (SHBC): The Livery Stables, Nr The Market Clock, Jamestown, STHL 1ZZ; tel. 2727; e-mail news@shbc.sh; internet www.shbc.sh; f. 2011; CEO DARRIN HENRY.

Saint FM: Association Hall, Main St, Jamestown, STHL 1ZZ; tel. 2660; e-mail fm@helanta.sh; internet www.saint.fm; f. 2004; independent FM radio station; also broadcasts on Ascension Island, Falkland Islands and Tristan da Cunha; Dir MIKE OLSSON.

Radio St Helena: Saint Helena Information Office, Broadway House, Jamestown, STHL 1ZZ; tel. 4669; fax 4542; e-mail radio.sthelena@cwimail.sh; internet www.sthelena.se/radioproject; independent service; providing broadcasts for 24 hours per day; local programming and relays of British Broadcasting Corporation World Service programmes; Station Man. GARY WALTERS.

Finance

BANK

Bank of Saint Helena: Post Office Bldg, Main St, Jamestown, STHL 1ZZ; tel. 2390; fax 2553; e-mail jamestown@sthelenabank.com; internet www.sainthelenabank.com; f. 2004; replaced the Government Savings Bank; total assets £42,369,292 (31 March 2010); Chair. LYN THOMAS; Man. Dir ROSEMARY BARGO; 1 br. on Ascension.

INSURANCE

Solomon & Co PLC: Jamestown, STHL 1ZZ; tel. 2380; fax 2423; e-mail generalenquiries@solomons.co.sh; internet www.solomons-sthelena.com; f. 1790; Sbusiness operating units include: mercantile, procurement, shipping and travel agents, stevedoring, insurance, livestock and arable farming (including coffee production), bakery, butchery, bulk fuel management, vehicle inspection, autoshop, construction works and information technology and administration services; CEO MANDY PETERS.

Trade and Industry

GOVERNMENT AGENCY

St Helena Development Agency: 2 Main St, POB 117, Jamestown, STHL 1ZZ; tel. 2920; fax 2166; e-mail enquiries@shda.co.sh; internet www.shda.co.sh; f. 1995; Chair. GEORGE STEVENS; Man. Dir LINDA HOUSTON.

CHAMBER OF COMMERCE

St Helena Chamber of Commerce: POB 34, Jamestown, STHL 1ZZ; tel. 2258; fax 2598; e-mail secretary@chamberofcommerce.org.sh; internet www.chamberofcommerce.org.sh; 60 mems; Pres. STUART MOORS; Sec. BRENDA MOORS-CLINGHAM.

CO-OPERATIVE

St Helena Growers' Co-operative Society: Jamestown, STHL 1ZZ; tel. and fax 2511; vegetable marketing; also suppliers of agricultural tools, seeds and animal feeding products; 108 mems (1999); Chair. STEDSON FRANCIS; Sec. PETER W. THORPE.

MAJOR COMPANIES

Argos Atlantic Cold Stores Ltd: POB 151, Jamestown; tel. 2333; fax 2334; f. 2000; processes, freezes and exports fish; owns five fishing vessels; head office in the Falkland Islands.

Island of St Helena Coffee Company Ltd: POB 119, Post Office, Main Street, Jamestown, STHL 1ZZ; tel. and fax 4944; e-mail info@st-helena-coffee.sh; internet www.st-helena-coffee.sh; f. 1994; organic Arabica coffee, also sells chocolates online; Head DAVID R. HENRY.

St Helena Fisheries Corpn: Rupert's Valley, STHL 1ZZ; tel. 2430; fax 2552; e-mail shfc@helanta.sh; f. 1979; Gen. Man. TERRY RICHARDS.

St Helena Leisure Corpn Ltd (Shelco): Jamestown, STHL 1ZZ; e-mail joe.terry@shelco.sh; internet www.shelco.sh; f. 2002; Chair. NIGEL THOMPSON.

Solomon & Co (St Helena) PLC: Main St, Jamestown, STHL 1ZZ; tel. 2380; fax 2423; e-mail generalenquiries@solomons.co.sh; internet www.solomons-sthelena.com; f. 1790; business operating units include: mercantile, procurement, shipping and travel agents, stevedoring, insurance, livestock and arable farming (including coffee production), bakery, butchery, bulk fuel management, vehicle inspection, autoshop, construction works and information technology and administration services; CEO MANDY PETERS.

W. A. Thorpe & Sons: Market St, POB 4, Jamestown, STHL 1ZZ; tel. 2781; fax 2318; e-mail office@thorpes.sh; internet www.thorpes.sh; f. 1865; imports groceries and hardware and maintains small cattle farm; 40 employees.

Transport

There are no railways in Saint Helena.

AIR

The construction of an airport on Saint Helena was first proposed in 2002. Despite an initial commitment to bringing the airport into operation by 2012, in April 2009 the British Department for International Development announced a further consultation on future access to Saint Helena. In December it was announced that as a result of 'current economic conditions' the British Government had decided that it would not be appropriate to proceed with the airport project 'at this time'. However, in July 2010 it was announced that construction of the airport would proceed, and it was expected to be operational by 2015. A twice-weekly Royal Air Force Tristar service between the United Kingdom and the Falkland Islands transits Ascension Island both southbound and northbound. There is a weekly US Air Force military service linking the Patrick Air Force Base in Florida with Ascension Island, via Antigua and Barbuda. There is no airfield on Tristan da Cunha.

ROADS

In 2002 there were 118 km of bitumen-sealed roads, and a further 20 km of earth roads, which can be used by motor vehicles only in dry weather. All roads have steep gradients and sharp bends.

SHIPPING

The St Helena Line Ltd serves Ascension Island with a two-monthly passenger/cargo service between Cardiff, in the United Kingdom, and Cape Town, in South Africa. A vessel under charter to the British Ministry of Defence visits the island monthly on its United Kingdom–Falkland Islands service. A US freighter from Cape Canaveral calls at three-monthly intervals. The St Helena Line Ltd, the MV *Hanseatic*, and MS *Explorer* and the SA *Agulhas* each visit Tristan da Cunha once each year, and two lobster concession vessels each make three visits annually, remaining for between two and three months. Occasional cruise ships also visit the island.

St Helena Line Ltd: Andrew Weir Shipping, Dexter House, 2 Royal Mint Court, London, EC3N 4XX, United Kingdom; tel. (20) 7265-0808; fax (20) 7481-4784; internet www.aws.co.uk; internet www.rms-st-helena.com; 5-year govt contract renewed in August 2006; service subsidized by the British Govt by £1.5m. annually; operates 2-monthly passenger/cargo services by the RMS *St Helena* to and from the United Kingdom and Cape Town, South Africa, calling at the Canary Islands, Ascension Island and Vigo, Spain, and once a year at Tristan da Cunha; also operates programme of shuttle services between Saint Helena and Ascension Island and the St Helena Liner Shipping Service; Chair. GARRY HOPCROFT.

Tourism

Although Saint Helena possesses flora and fauna of considerable interest to naturalists, as well as the house (now an important museum) in which the French Emperor Napoleon I spent his final years in exile, the remoteness of the island, which is a two-day sea voyage from Ascension Island, has inhibited the development of tourism. The potential construction of an airport on Saint Helena would greatly increase the island's accessibility to the limited number of visitors that can currently be accommodated. A total of 847 tourists visited Saint Helena in 2009. There are three hotels and a range of self-catering facilities. Small-scale eco-tourism is encouraged on Ascension Island, although accommodation is limited and all visits require written permission from the Administrator. Access is available by twice weekly flights operated from the United Kingdom by the Royal Air Force (see above), and by the RMS *St Helena*. Permission from the Administrator and the Island Council is required for visits to Tristan da Cunha. Facilities for tourism are limited, although some accommodation is available in island homes.

St Helena Tourism: Main St, Jamestown, STHL 1ZZ; tel. 2158; fax 2159; e-mail melissa.fowler@tourism.gov.sh; internet www.sthelenatourism.com; f. 1998; provides general information about the island; Customer Services Man. MELISSA FOWLER.

Education

Education is compulsory and free for all children between the ages of five and 15 years, although power to exempt after the age of 14 can be exercised by the Education Committee. The standard of work at the secondary comprehensive school is orientated towards the requirements of the General Certificate of Secondary Education and the General Certificate of Education Advanced Level of the United Kingdom. During the second half of the 1980s the educational structure was reorganized from a two-tier to a three-tier comprehensive system, for which a new upper-school building was constructed.

There is a free public library in Jamestown, financed by the Government and managed by a committee, and a mobile library service in the country districts. There is also a Teacher Education Centre in Jamestown.

Bibliography

Ashmole, P., and Ashmole, M. *St Helena and Ascension Island: A Natural History*. Oswestry, Anthony Nelson, 2000.

Blackburn, J. *The Emperor's Last Island: A Journey to St Helena*. London, Secker & Warburg, 1992.

Blakeston, O. *Isle of Helena*. London, Sidgwick & Jackson, 1957.

Booy, D. M. *Rock of Exile: A Narrative of Tristan da Cunha*. London, Dent, 1957.

Castell, R. *St Helena: Island Fortress*. Old Amersham Byron Publicity Group, 1977.

Christopherson, E. (Ed.). *Results of the Norwegian Scientific Expedition to Tristan da Cunha, 1937–1938*, 16 parts. Oslo, Oslo University Press, 1940–62.

Cohen, R. (Ed.). *African Islands and Enclaves*. London, Sage Publications, 1983.

Cross, T. *St Helena: with chapters on Ascension and Tristan da Cunha*. Newton Abbot, David & Charles, 1981.

Day, A. (Ed.). *St Helena, Ascension and Tristan da Cunha* (World Bibliographical Series, Vol. 197). Santa Barbara, CA, ABC-Clio, 1997.

Eriksen, R. *St Helena Lifeline*. Norfolk, Mallett & Bell, 1999.

Gosse, P. *St Helena, 1502–1938*. London, Thomas Nelson, 1990 (reissue).

Hart-Davis, D. *Ascension: The Story of a South Atlantic Island*. London, Constable, 1972.

Mabbett, B. J. *St Helena: The Postal, Instructional and Censor Markings, 1815–2000*. Reading, West Africa Study Circle, 2002.

Mackay, M. M. *Angry Island: The Story of Tristan da Cunha (1506–1963)*. London, Barker, 1963.

Munch, P. A. *Crisis in Utopia: The Ordeal of Tristan da Cunha*. New York, Cromwell, 1971.

Royle, S. A. *A Geography of Islands: Small Island Insularity*. London, Routledge, 2001.

'Historic Communities: On a Desert Isle (Tristan da Cunha)', in *Communities, Journal of Co-operative Living*, No. 105, 1999.

Schreier, D., and Lavarello-Schreier, K. *Tristan da Cunha: History, People, Language*. London, Battlebridge Publishers, 2003.

The St Helena Research Group. *A Strategic Profile of St Helena, 2000 Edition* (Strategic Planning Series). Icon Group International Inc, 2000.

SÃO TOMÉ AND PRÍNCIPE

Physical and Social Geography

RENÉ PÉLISSIER

The archipelago forming the Democratic Republic of São Tomé and Príncipe is, after the Republic of Seychelles, the smallest independent state in Africa. Both the main islands are in the Gulf of Guinea on a south-west/north-east axis of extinct volcanoes. The boundaries take in the rocky islets of Caroço, Pedras and Tinhosas, off Príncipe, and, south of São Tomé, the Rôlas islet, which is bisected by the line of the Equator. The total area of the archipelago is 1,001 sq km (386.5 sq miles), of which São Tomé occupies an area of 859 sq km.

São Tomé is a former plantation island where the eastern slopes and coastal flatlands are covered by huge cocoa estates (*roças*) formerly controlled by Portuguese interests, alongside a large number of local smallholders. These plantations have been carved out of an extremely dense mountainous jungle that dominates this equatorial island. The highest point is the Pico de São Tomé (2,024 m), surrounded by a dozen lesser cones above 1,000 m in height. Craggy and densely forested terrain is intersected by numerous streams. The coast of Príncipe is extremely jagged and indented by many bays. The highest elevation is the Pico de Príncipe (948 m). Both islands have a warm and moist climate, with an average yearly temperature of 25°C. Annual rainfall varies from over 5,100 mm on the south-western mountain slopes to under 1,020 mm in the northern lowlands. The dry season, known locally as *gravana*, lasts from June to September.

The total population was 117,504 at the census of 4 August 1991, when São Tomé had 112,033 inhabitants and Príncipe 5,471. The population was 137,599 at the census of September 2001. In mid-2012, according to UN estimates, the population was 171,880, giving a density of 171.7 inhabitants per sq km. During 2001–10, according to the World Bank, the population increased at an average annual rate of 1.6%. The capital city is São Tomé, with an estimated 59,851 inhabitants in mid-2009, according to the UN. It is the main export centre of the island. Inland villages on São Tomé are mere clusters of houses of native islanders. Príncipe has only one small town of about 1,000 people, Santo António.

The native-born islanders (*forros*) are the descendants of imported slaves and southern Europeans who settled in the 16th and 17th centuries. Intermarriage was common, but subsequent influxes of Angolan and Mozambican contract workers until about 1950 re-Africanized the *forros*. Descendants of slaves who escaped from the sugar plantations from the 16th century onwards (known as Angolares), are now mainly fishermen.

The widespread exodus of skilled Portuguese plantation administrators, civil servants and traders during the period just prior to independence in July 1975, together with the departure of most of the Angolan and Mozambican workers and the repatriation of more than 10,000 São Tomé exiles from Angola, caused considerable economic dislocation, the impact of which continues to be felt.

Recent History

GERHARD SEIBERT

INTRODUCTION

São Tomé and Príncipe were colonized by Portugal in the 16th century. A nationalist group, the Comité de Libertação de São Tomé e Príncipe, was formed in 1960 and became the Movimento de Libertação de São Tomé e Príncipe (MLSTP) in 1972, under the leadership of Dr Manuel Pinto da Costa. Following the military coup in Portugal in April 1974, the Portuguese Government recognized the right of the islands to independence. In December Portugal appointed a transitional Government that included members of the MLSTP, which was recognized as the sole legitimate representative of the people. At elections for a Constituent Assembly held in July 1975, the MLSTP won all 16 seats. Independence as the Democratic Republic of São Tomé and Príncipe took effect on 12 July, with Pinto da Costa as President and Miguel Trovoada as Prime Minister. The Constitution promulgated in November effectively vested absolute power in the President and the political bureau of the MLSTP.

MLSTP GOVERNMENT

During 1976–82 serious ideological as well as personal divisions arose within the MLSTP, and in March 1978 Angolan soldiers were brought to the islands, following an alleged attempt to overthrow the Government. In 1979 Trovoada was dismissed as Prime Minister, arrested and detained without trial until 1981, when he was permitted to leave the islands.

In its foreign relations, São Tomé and Príncipe avoided any formal commitment to the Eastern bloc, although close economic ties existed with the People's Republic of China and the German Democratic Republic. Gabon, the islands' nearest mainland neighbour, viewed these developments with disquiet, and relations consequently deteriorated. However, São Tomé and Príncipe extended the range of its international contacts by joining the IMF and the World Bank in 1977, acceding to the Lomé Convention in 1978, and participating in the foundation of the francophone Communauté économique des états de l'Afrique centrale (CEEAC) in 1983. The bulk of the country's trade continued to be transacted with Western Europe, and relations with Portugal remained generally cordial. In 1985, confronted by the threat of a complete economic collapse, Pinto da Costa began to abandon economic ties with the Eastern bloc in favour of capitalist strategies.

Political Change

In October 1987 the Central Committee of the MLSTP announced major political and constitutional changes, including the election by universal suffrage of the head of state, and of members of the legislative Assembleia Popular Nacional by secret ballot, as well as the admission of different political currents within the party. In January 1988 the post of Prime Minister was reintroduced, to which Celestino Rocha da Costa was appointed. Carlos Monteiro Dias da Graça, who had been pardoned in 1985 for an attempted coup orchestrated from Gabon in 1978, was appointed Minister of Foreign Affairs. However, Trovoada, who had been invited to return from exile, remained in France, stating that the changes were insufficient. By 1987 three small overseas opposition groups were already in existence.

Increasingly concerned by the country's economic problems, and encouraged by a progressive faction within the party, the MLSTP embarked, in late 1989, on a transition to full multi-party democracy. In August 1990, in a national referendum, the electorate overwhelmingly approved the introduction of the new Constitution, proposed by the MLSTP Central Committee, which provided for a multi-party political system, and a maximum of two five-year terms of office for the President. At the MLSTP party congress, held in October 1990, da Graça succeeded Pinto da Costa as Secretary-General. In addition, the party's name was amended to the Movimento de Libertação de São Tomé e Príncipe—Partido Social Democrata (MLSTP—PSD). Also in that year the Frente Democrata Cristã (FDC) was founded by members of a former opposition group based in Libreville, Gabon, and the Partido Democrático de São Tomé e Príncipe—Coligação Democrática de Oposição (PDSTP—CODO), a merger of two other opposition groups formerly in exile, was formed, under the leadership of Albertino Neto. However, the major challenge to the ruling party came from the Partido de Convergência Democrática—Grupo de Reflexão (PCD—GR), a coalition of former MLSTP dissidents, independents and young professionals, under the leadership of Leonel d'Alva.

At elections to the new Assembleia Nacional, held on 20 January 1991, the MLSTP—PSD secured only 30.5% of the total votes and 21 seats, while the PCD—GR obtained 54% of the votes and 33 seats; the PDSTP—CODO took the one remaining seat. In February a transitional Government, headed by Daniel Daio, was installed, pending the forthcoming presidential election; President Pinto da Costa confirmed his decision not to run in the election, and two of the three remaining candidates subsequently withdrew from the contest. On 3 March Trovoada, the sole remaining contender, was elected President, receiving 82% of the votes cast. Trovoada took office the following month and officially inaugurated the PCD—GR Government, headed by Daio.

THE TROVOADA PRESIDENCY

A political crisis erupted in early 1992, when co-operation between the Government and the presidency began to break down after the PCD—GR attempted to introduce a constitutional amendment limiting presidential powers. Meanwhile, in June 1991 stringent austerity measures were imposed by the IMF and the World Bank as preconditions for economic assistance, which contributed to a sharp decline in the islanders' living standards. Following two mass demonstrations held in April 1992 to protest against the austerity programme, Trovoada dismissed the Daio Government. The PCD—GR, which initially condemned Trovoada's actions as an 'institutional coup', was invited to designate a new Prime Minister. In May Norberto Costa Alegre became Prime Minister and formed a new administration.

In April 1994 the Assembleia Nacional began discussion of a draft bill providing local autonomy for the island of Príncipe. Its proposals, approved later that year, included provision for the creation of a regional assembly and a five-member regional government. In March 1995 the first elections to a new seven-member Assembleia Regional (Regional Assembly) and five-member Regional Government were conducted on Príncipe, resulting in victory for the MLSTP—PSD, which won an absolute majority. The new Regional Government began functioning in April.

In early 1994 relations between the Government and the presidency again began to deteriorate. In April Trovoada publicly dissociated himself from government policy, and in July dismissed the Alegre administration citing 'institutional conflict'. On 4 July Trovoada appointed Evaristo do Espírito Santo de Carvalho (Minister of Defence and Security in the outgoing administration) as Prime Minister. The PCD—GR, which refused to participate in the new Government, subsequently expelled Carvalho from the party. On 10 July, in an attempt to resolve the political crisis, Trovoada dissolved the Assembleia Nacional and announced that a legislative election would be held on 2 October.

This election resulted in a decisive victory for the MLSTP—PSD, which secured 27 seats, one short of an absolute majority. The PCD—GR and the Acção Democrática Independente (ADI) each obtained 14 seats. The level of voter participation, which was as low as 52%, was believed to reflect public disillusionment at the failure of democracy to realize expectations of a transformation in the country's social and economic prospects. In late October 1994 da Graça was appointed Prime Minister and subsequently announced his intention to form a government of national unity with those parties represented in the legislature. However, both the ADI and the PCD—GR rejected the proposal. The new Council of Ministers was thus composed almost entirely of members of the MLSTP—PSD.

On 15 August 1995, following a period of social unrest, a group of some 30 soldiers staged a coup and detained Trovoada. The insurgents cited widespread corruption and political incompetence as justification for the coup. Following negotiations, the military insurgents and the Government signed a 'memorandum of understanding', providing for the reinstatement of Trovoada and the restoration of constitutional order. In return, the Government gave an undertaking to restructure the armed forces, and the Assembleia Nacional granted a general amnesty to all those involved in the coup.

Consensus Government

At the end of December 1995 Armindo Vaz d'Almeida was appointed Prime Minister, at the head of a coalition Government of the MLSTP—PSD, the ADI and the PDSTP—CODO. At the presidential election of 30 June 1996 no candidate secured an absolute majority. Consequently, a second ballot, between the two leading candidates, was conducted on 21 July, at which Trovoada defeated Pinto da Costa by winning 52.7% of the votes. In mid-September the Vaz d'Almeida administration was dissolved, following its defeat in a confidence motion in the Assembleia Nacional. The motion had been proposed by Vaz d'Almeida's own party, the MLSTP—PSD, which accused the Government of inefficiency and corruption, and had received the support of the PCD—GR. In late October the two parties signed an accord providing for the establishment of a nine-member coalition Government. In mid-November the President appointed Raúl Wagner da Conceição Bragança Neto, Assistant Secretary-General of the MLSTP—PSD, as Prime Minister. The new Government, which included five members of the MLSTP—PSD, three members of the PCD—GR and one independent, was inaugurated later that month.

The Premiership of Pósser da Costa

At an extraordinary congress of the MLSTP—PSD held in May 1998, the former President and party leader, Manuel Pinto da Costa, was elected unopposed as President of the party.

Legislative elections were held on 8 November 1998, at which the MLSTP—PSD secured an absolute majority, with 31 seats, while the ADI won 16 seats and the PCD—GR obtained the remaining eight seats. In December Guilherme Pósser da Costa was appointed Prime Minister. A new Council of Ministers was installed on 5 January 1999.

PRESIDENTIAL AND LEGISLATIVE ELECTIONS

A presidential election took place on 29 July 2001. Among the five candidates hoping to succeed Trovoada were Pinto da Costa of the MLSTP—PSD and Fradique de Menezes, a businessman standing for the ADI, who received the support of outgoing President Trovoada. In the event, de Menezes was elected to the presidency, winning 56.3% of the votes cast, while Pinto da Costa secured 38.7%. Later in July de Menezes appointed a Council of Ministers composed entirely of members of the parliamentary opposition, including the ADI's Evaristo de Carvalho as Prime Minister. De Menezes was inaugurated in early September.

The MLSTP—PSD boycotted the Assembleia Nacional in early November 2001, and urged President de Menezes to restore constitutional order by returning the Government to the majority party or announcing early elections. In December Carlos Neves, hitherto leader of the ADI, and several of his followers left the party, following Trovoada's announcement of his candidacy for the party leadership. Later that month the dissident ADI members took leading positions in a new party created by supporters of de Menezes, the Movimento Democrático Força da Mudança (MDFM). Meanwhile, the President and representatives of political parties signed a pact advocating the formation of an all-party government after legislative elections, which were scheduled for 3 March 2002, in order to guarantee political stability. At the elections, the MLSTP—PSD won 24 seats in the Assembleia Nacional and an alliance of the MDFM and the PCD (the suffix Grupo de Reflexão had been dropped the previous year) secured 23, while Uê Kédadji (UK—an alliance comprising the ADI and four smaller parties) obtained only eight seats. Following negotiations with the leader of the MLSTP—PSD, President de Menezes appointed Gabriel da Costa, a lawyer and hitherto ambassador to Portugal, as Prime Minister. In April a Government of National Unity, which included members of the MLSTP—PSD, the MDFM-PCD and UK, as well as a number of independents, was installed.

In August 2002 the four deputies of the ADI left UK and formed a legislative group of independents. In mid-September a member of the Supreme Defence Council accused de Menezes of having illegally promoted the Minister of Defence and Internal Affairs, Victor Monteiro, to the highest rank of Lt-Col, since the minister had not met the necessary legal requirements. This affair provoked an open conflict between Monteiro and Prime Minister da Costa, who refused to continue working with the defence minister. Finally, on 27 September President de Menezes dismissed the da Costa Government, claiming that the conflict had created political instability. In October de Menezes appointed Maria das Neves de Souza of the MLSTP—PSD, hitherto Minister of Trade, Industry and Tourism, as Prime Minister.

In late October 2002 the Assembleia Nacional initiated a revision of the Constitution in order to clarify ambiguous articles that had provoked conflicts between the President and the Government since 1991. The proposed amendments curbed the powers of the President and strengthened the position of government and the legislature. President de Menezes fiercely condemned the proposed legislation and threatened to dissolve the legislature, if it could not reach consensus with him on the new Constitution. In early December 2002 the Assembleia Nacional unanimously approved the amendments to the Constitution, which were to come into effect after the end of the President's term in 2006. Following the refusal of the legislature to submit the amendments to a popular referendum, on 17 January 2003 de Menezes vetoed the new Constitution. On 22 January he dissolved the Assembleia Nacional and called early legislative elections for 13 April. However, Prime Minister das Neves and Alice de Carvalho, the President of the Supreme Court, successfully mediated in the conflict. On 24 January a memorandum of understanding was signed by the President and representatives of the parliamentary parties, according to which de Menezes revoked the dissolution of the legislature and promulgated the constitutional amendments, while the Assembleia Nacional agreed to submit the new Constitution to a popular referendum at the end of the President's mandate in 2006.

CIVIL UNREST AND MILITARY COUP

In mid-April 2003 a group of citizens published an open letter, signed by 80 people, which accused the Government and the President of having failed to improve living conditions and expressed concern over a lack of transparency in the country's petroleum negotiations. Furthermore, it accused the President of failing to explain the remittance of US $100,000 by Chrome Oil Services to the Belgian bank account of his company, CGI, in February 2002 and of having conceded to his brother, João de Menezes, resident in Portugal, the exclusive rights for the exploitation of casinos and the airport in São Tomé. In response, President de Menezes held a controversial press conference, during which he accused a number of the signatories of the document of having committed acts of corruption themselves in the past. He declared that the payment of $100,000 from the Nigerian petroleum company was a donation to the MDFM-PCD campaign for the legislative elections.

On 16 July 2003, while President de Menezes was on a private visit to Nigeria, a group of military officers, led by Maj. Fernando Pereira ('Cobó'), together with the FDC, initiated a bloodless coup and detained a number of government ministers in the military barracks. Pereira and the leaders of the FDC, Sabino dos Santos and Alércio Costa, established a Military Junta of National Salvation. The coup plotters claimed to have acted in response to continued corruption and the widening gap between the small wealthy minority and the impoverished majority. The coup was quickly condemned by regional and world powers and organizations, which demanded the restitution of the constitutional order. On the fourth day of the rebellion the Military Junta commenced negotiations with international mediators from the Comunidade dos Países de Língua Portuguesa (CPLP), the CEEAC, the African Union (AU), Nigeria, the USA and South Africa. On 22 July President de Menezes returned to São Tomé, accompanied by the Nigerian President, Olusegun Obasanjo, and on the same day the coup was ended when a memorandum of understanding was signed by de Menezes and Pereira. The agreement provided for a general amnesty for the coup leaders; the restoration of President de Menezes; respect by the President for the Constitution and the separation of powers; the formation of a new Government; the approval of a law on the proper use of petroleum revenue by the Assembleia Nacional; the sound and transparent management of public funds by the Government; the improvement of the conditions of the armed forces; and the prohibition of foreign military intervention. A 13-member Commission, headed by a representative of the CEEAC, was created to monitor the implementation of the agreement. At the beginning of August Prime Minister das Neves resigned in preparation for the installation of a new administration. Das Neves was subsequently reappointed as Prime Minister, heading a Government comprising representatives from the MLSTP—PSD, the MDFM and the ADI.

In January 2004 the Tribunal de Contas (Audit Office), which had begun operations in early 2003 and was headed by Francisco Fortunato Pires, submitted its first report on government accounts to the Assembleia Nacional. The report criticized various irregularities in the management of public funds during 2003 and denounced the absence of record-keeping and of an inventory of state property.

The unauthorized actions of two ministers of the President's party provoked a governmental crisis in March 2004. It emerged that Tomé Vera Cruz, the Minister of Natural Resources and the Environment, had signed a controversial petroleum agreement with Energem Petroleum, while the Minister of Foreign Affairs, Mateus Rita, had tried to sign an air transport agreement with the Angolan Government, both without the consent of Prime Minister das Neves. As a result of the affair, the MDFM resigned from the Government and UK joined the coalition. In April 2004, at an extraordinary meeting, the MDFM re-elected Vera Cruz as party leader and renamed the party MDFM—Partido Liberal (PL).

In mid-June 2004 de Menezes inaugurated the National Forum of Reconciliation that had been stipulated as part of the memorandum of understanding of 22 July 2003, bringing together 600 delegates of political parties and civil society to debate the country's problems. Thereafter, the Forum organized 55 meetings to listen to the population's concerns and expectations. At the Forum's closing ceremony on 12 July 2004 a long list of recommendations and conclusions on a wide range of political and social-economic issues was presented.

DAS NEVES DISMISSED

In August 2004 an audit report of the accounts of the food aid agency, Gabinete de Gestão da Ajuda (GGA), embarrassed the country's political élite. The GGA was created in 1993 to administer the counterpart funds in dobras stemming from the local sale of foreign food aid. The report, covering the years 2001–04, revealed a series of irregularities, including the illegal concession of credits, the payment of fictitious services, and illicit financial transfers to the finance and economy ministries for extra-budgetary expenditure. In total, funds of US $1.9m. were diverted to local politicians and office holders. According to the document, Prime Minister das Neves had also taken various amounts from the GGA accounts. Although she denied the allegations, in mid-September 2004 das Neves and her coalition Government were dismissed by President de Menezes, who subsequently asked the MLSTP—PSD to form a new government. Days later a new Council of Ministers was installed by presidential decree, which, like the previous administration, was a coalition of the MLSTP—PSD, the

ADI and two independents. Damião Vaz de Almeida, the former Minister of Labour, Employment and Solidarity, was appointed Prime Minister.

In early 2005 the Assembleia Nacional agreed to lift the parliamentary immunity of five deputies—namely former Prime Ministers Pósser da Costa and das Neves, and ex-ministers Arzemiro dos Prazeres (of the PCD), Basílio Diogo (MDFM), and Júlio Silva (ADI)—allowing them to be questioned about their alleged involvement in the GGA scandal. All five suspects denied any wrongdoing. In May the public prosecutor formally charged das Neves and dos Prazeres with embezzlement, while the three other suspects were acquitted from any criminal responsibility. In October 2006 the Government dissolved the GGA. In April 2007 a judge dismissed the case against das Neves and dos Prazeres owing to a lack of evidence. However, in June the public prosecutor filed an appeal against this decision at the Supreme Court.

Meanwhile, at the fourth party congress of the MLSTP—PSD in February 2005 Pósser da Costa was elected party President, replacing Manuel Pinto da Costa. Dionísio Dias, the current President of the Assembleia Nacional, was elected party Vice-President, while Homéro Salvaterra became Secretary-General. Following the approval, in April, of the budget for that year by the Assembleia Nacional, trade unions representing public sector workers demanded an increase of the minimum salary from 300,000 dobras (US $30) to 1m. dobras ($100) per month. Citing budgetary constraints, the Government presented a proposal of only 428,000 dobras ($43), and on 30 May the unions commenced a five-day general strike. President de Menezes declared that the Government was responsible for the action, and on the fourth day of the strike Prime Minister Vaz d'Almeida abruptly resigned, accusing de Menezes of a lack of institutional solidarity with the Government and of having ratified petroleum block awards on 31 May to Nigerian companies of doubtful credibility (see Economy). The ruling MLSTP—PSD, having first asked for early elections, under pressure from donor countries to minimize instability in the country, acceded to the President's request that the party nominate a new Prime Minister.

On 9 June 2005 the Governor of the central bank (the Banco Central de São Tomé e Príncipe—BCSTP), Maria do Carmo Silveira, was sworn in as Prime Minister, along with a new MLSTP—PSD Government, for the remaining nine-month term of the legislature. The ADI did not participate in the new Government, but promised to support it in the Assembleia Nacional. In late June, at the request of the public prosecutor, the Assembleia Nacional lifted the parliamentary immunity of Alcino Pinto, the parliamentary leader of the MLSTP—PSD. Pinto, the managing director of Air São Tomé e Príncipe, was charged with the alleged embezzlement of funds from the company's accounts. In early July the Government's legislative programme, which focused on sustainable development and improvement in the social sector, was approved by the Assembleia Nacional, and by early August a preliminary agreement on a 29% pay rise had been agreed between the Government and trade unions.

THE 2006 ELECTIONS

In January 2006 the PCD and the MDFM formally renewed their electoral alliance for the legislative elections scheduled for 26 March. Prior to the elections, President de Menezes ordered an audit of the computer system of the Comissão Eleitoral Nacional (CEN—National Electoral Commission) to impede possible electoral fraud. Nevertheless, the election campaign was marked by persistent reports of vote-buying. In 13 localities, some 9,600 out of the 89,850 registered voters were unable to vote owing to roadblocks erected by the local population in protest against poor access roads and the lack of other basic infrastructure. Elections in those localities were repeated on 2 April. In early April the Constitutional Court decided to recount all ballots to reconfirm the results announced by the CEN, despite MDFM-PCD opposition. On 28 April final election results were announced. The pro-de Menezes MDFM-PCD won 23 seats, the MLSTP—PSD and the ADI obtained 20 seats and 11 seats, respectively, while the newly established Novo Rumo took one seat. The MDFM-PCD subsequently formed a minority Government led by Prime Minister Vera Cruz, the Secretary-General of the MDFM.

Also in late April 2006 President de Menezes announced that a presidential election would be held on 30 July, with local elections scheduled to take place on 9 July. In early June the Supreme Court refused to acknowledge 10 candidatures presented for the local elections since they had been submitted after the deadline of 25 May. The ADI and the MLSTP—PSD had not presented candidatures, and demanded that local elections be held after the presidential election. Following a protest by hundreds of demonstrators in Príncipe, led by the opposition União para a Mudança e Progresso do Príncipe (UMPP), against the court's decision, on 12 June the head of the island's Regional Government, Zeferino dos Prazeres (of the MLSTP—PSD), resigned. Subsequently, the central Government appointed João Paulo Cassandra, the leader of the revolt, as head of a provisional Regional Government pending the holding of the regional elections. In early July the elections were postponed until 27 August.

At the election presidential election, which took place on 30 July, de Menezes secured 60.6% of the votes cast, while Trovoada won 38.8% and a third candidate, Nilo de Oliveira Guimarães, received 0.6%. Some 64.9% of the 91,119 registered voters participated in the election, which was praised by international monitors as having been 'free and fair'.

In the local elections of 27 August 2006, the first since December 1992, the MDFM-PCD secured control in five of São Tomé's six district councils, while the MLSTP—PSD obtained the majority in the Lembá district. In Príncipe, where regional elections had not been held since March 1995, the UMPP, headed by José Cassandra, gained an absolute majority.

Immediately after the local elections MLSTP—PSD leader Pósser da Costa resigned from his post following the consecutive electoral defeats suffered by his party. At an extraordinary congress held in February 2007 Rafael Branco became the party's new President. At the MDFM convention in May Prime Minister Vera Cruz was re-elected as the party's Secretary-General, while President de Menezes was elected as Chairman of the MDFM, despite the country's Constitution forbidding the head of state to exercise other public functions. Having accepted the function, however, de Menezes opted not to assume the role publicly as long as he remained President. At the fifth congress of the PCD in November Albertino Bragança was elected party President, replacing Leonel Mário d'Alva, while the then Minister of Public Works and Infrastructure, Delfim Santiago das Neves, became Secretary-General.

On 8 October 2007 some 30 officers of the 100-man rapid-reaction police force seized the police headquarters and took hostage about two dozen policemen. The Ninjas, as they were known, demanded the payment of outstanding subsidies, allegedly promised by the Government during their nine-month training in 2003–04. On the second day of the revolt the mutineers released the hostages. On 17 October the Ninjas refused a government ultimatum to leave the police headquarters and threatened to defend themselves if attacked by the military. That day the President of the Assembleia Nacional, Francisco da Silva, initiated negotiations with the Ninjas and the Government. The Government subsequently accepted an agreement mediated by da Silva, according to which the financial demands of the Ninjas were met. However, the policemen who participated in the revolt were to be dismissed. On 2 November the Ninjas again seized the police headquarters and demanded the payment of the subsidies within three days. They accused the Government of failing to meet the 15-day term for setting a date for the payments to be made. Two days later the armed forces occupied the police headquarters, detained 10 rebel leaders and urged the rebels to withdraw and surrender their weapons. During the siege one member of the rapid-reaction police force was killed and two other rebels were wounded. Subsequently, the unit was dissolved and most of its members, who had not participated in the revolt, were reintegrated in the police force. In January 2008 the Supreme Court ruled that the arrest of seven Ninjas, who had been kept in detention since November 2007, was illegal and ordered their immediate release. Meanwhile, later in November, at a consultation meeting presided over by President de Menezes, Vera Cruz was compelled to reorganize his Government. On 20 November Vera Cruz presented his new cabinet, in which several key ministers were replaced.

THE RESIGNATION OF VERA CRUZ

In late January 2008 the Prime Minister withdrew the national budget for 2008, estimated at US $90m., to avoid its rejection by the MLSTP—PSD and the ADI, which together held a majority of 31 seats. The opposition criticized the budget proposal for not including sufficient investment in agriculture, fishing and tourism. Consequently, on 7 February Vera Cruz resigned. On 13 February the MDFM, the PCD and the ADI signed a coalition agreement valid until 2014. The following day the ADI leader Patrice Trovoada was sworn in as Prime Minister of a coalition Government of the MDFM, the PCD and his own party, with a parliamentary majority of more than 30 seats.

A revised national budget for 2008, amounting to US $86m, was submitted to the Assembleia Nacional in April. Despite criticism from the coalition parties, the budget was eventually approved. However, following the vote, the MLSTP—PSD presented a motion of no confidence against Prime Minister Trovoada. On 20 May the motion was carried, supported by members of the MLSTP—PSD and the PCD, which accused Trovoada of lacking transparency in government affairs. Subsequently, the MDFM denounced the party alliance with the PCD, making the MLSTP—PSD the majority party in the Assembleia Nacional. Following three days of talks, on 9 June the four major parties agreed to request that President de Menezes entrust the leader of the MLSTP—PSD, Rafael Branco, with the formation of a new government. Consequently, on 21 June President de Menezes appointed Branco at the head of a coalition Government composed of the MLSTP—PSD, the PCD and the MDFM. In mid-October Branco dismissed the Minister of Natural Resources, Energy and the Environment, Agostinho Rita (of the MDFM), following accusations of corruption.

In February 2009 the police detained Arlércio Costa, the leader of the FDC, and 39 other individuals with links to that party for allegedly having attempted to destabilize public order. Subsequently, a judge committed for trial 27 of the detained, including Costa, a former member of the infamous South African Buffalo Battalion and one of the leaders of the 2003 coup in São Tomé, on a charge of having threatened state security. In July 2009 a judge ordered the release from custody of 15 of those detained. In November Costa was found guilty of rebellion and illegal possession of weapons and sentenced to a five-year prison term, another defendant received a two-year suspended sentence, while the others were acquitted. However, in early January 2010 President de Menezes granted amnesty to Costa, who, during the trial, had accused de Menezes of having invented the plot in response to their competing private business interests.

Meanwhile, in March 2009 a local court sentenced Diógenes Moniz, the former director of the GGA, and Aurélio Aguiar, the GGA treasurer, to nine and seven years' imprisonment, respectively, after they were found guilty of forgery and harmful management as part of the embezzlement of some US $4m. of funds stemming from the sale of Japanese food aid. The trial and its outcome provoked controversy, particularly since senior politicians, allegedly involved in the GGA scandal that was discovered in 2004, had ultimately not been tried.

At an extraordinary congress of the MDFM in mid-December 2009, de Menezes was elected by acclamation as President of the party. Although de Menezes declared that he would not officially assume this position until his presidential term ended in September 2011, the other members of the coalition, the MLSTP—PSD and the PCD, accused him of violating the Constitution, which stated that the office of President was incompatible with any other public or private function. In response, de Menezes ordered the withdrawal of the four MDFM ministers from the Government. However, two of the ministers, Justino Veiga and Cristina Dias, refused to accede to this demand, although Branco's attempt to retain the two ministers in a reshuffled cabinet was vetoed by de Menezes. In mid-January 2010 President de Menezes inaugurated Branco's new Government, composed of the MLSTP—PSD and the PCD. Two days later, in an unexpected development, de Menezes publicly retracted his acceptance of the MDFM leadership, but denied that his decision had been influenced by political pressure.

In March 2010 President de Menezes announced that local elections would be held on 25 July and legislative elections on 1 August. The local elections, originally scheduled for August 2009, had allegedly been postponed owing to a lack of funding. At these polls the MLSTP—PSD obtained a majority in the four district councils of Lobata, Lembá, Cantagalo and Caué, while the ADI gained the majority in the two most populated districts of Água Grande (with the capital São Tomé) and Mé-Zóchi. The UMPP, headed by Tozé Cassandra, won all seven seats of the Regional Assembly of Príncipe.

The ADI secured victory in the legislative elections of 1 August 2010, obtaining 26 seats in the Assembleia Nacional. The MLSTP—PSD of Prime Minister Branco won 21 seats, while his coalition partner, the PCD, secured only seven seats. Surprisingly, the MDFM received only one seat, down from 12 in the previous election in 2006. It was the fourth time since 1991 that an opposition party had won the legislative elections in São Tomé. Even combined, the ADI and the MDFM were one seat short of the total required for an absolute majority in parliament. Trovoada was appointed Prime Minister on 10 August 2010, and on 14 August de Menezes approved the installation of a new Government, which included a number of independent members. During the inauguration ceremony Trovoada promised to implement the changes that he had proposed during the election campaign, to combat corruption and to present concrete results in the short and medium term.

At the fifth extraordinary congress of the opposition MLSTP—PSD, held in January 2011, local businessman Aurélio Martins was elected as the new party leader. Xavier Mendes, a former Minister of Agriculture, became the new President of the PCD in the following month. At a meeting of the MLSTP—PSD's National Council in early April, the party endorsed Martins as its candidate in the presidential election due to be held in July.

THE 2011 PRESIDENTIAL ELECTION

At the presidential election, which was held as scheduled on 17 July 2011 and was contested by 10 candidates, the country's first President, Manuel Pinto da Costa (standing as an independent), won 35.8% of the votes. His closest rivals were Evaristo de Carvalho (representing the ADI), who took 21.8%, Maria das Neves (of the MLSTP—PSD) and Delfim Neves (of the PCD), who secured 14.0% and 13.9%, respectively. Aurélio Martins, the official candidate of the MLSTP—PSD, received only 4.2% of the votes, the poorest score of the party's four candidates. As no candidate had secured an overall majority, Pinto da Costa and Carvalho contested a run-off on 7 August, at which Pinto da Costa secured 52.9% of the valid votes cast, according to results released by the CEN. Pinto da Costa was sworn in as President on 3 September.

In early December 2011 anonymous protestors in Príncipe burnt the national flag in front of the seat of the island's Regional Government and left behind pamphlets bearing anti-Government slogans. The protest occurred while José Cassandra, head of Príncipe's Regional Government, was renegotiating with the Government of Patrice Trovoada the terms of an eco-tourism development project signed in May between the Regional Government and Here Be Dragons (HBD), a venture capital company owned by the South African millionaire Mark Shuttleworth. The central Government contested the legality of several terms of the US $70m. agreement, which included the concession of the Sundy estate that in 2010 had already been assigned to SOCFINCO (a subsidiary of the Belgium-based Société Financière des Caoutchoucs Luxembourg—SOCFIN). After several rounds of negotiations, the final agreement with HBD was signed in March 2012.

At an extraordinary congress held in early June 2012, the opposition MLSTP—PSD elected by acclamation Jorge Amado, São Tomé's ambassador to the Republic of China (Taiwan), as the new party leader. He replaced Aurélio Martins, whose position had become untenable following his poor performance in the 2011 presidential election.

FOREIGN RELATIONS

Following President Trovoada's unilateral decision in May 1997 to establish diplomatic relations with Taiwan, the People's Republic of China suspended diplomatic relations with São Tomé, ceased all development co-operation and demanded the repayment of bilateral debts amounting to US $17m. In exchange for diplomatic recognition, Taiwan promised São Tomé $30m. in development aid over a three-year period. Trovoada declared that, in view of the economic condition of São Tomé, the Taiwanese aid could not be rejected. However, the Government declared that this aid could not compensate for the loss of the long-standing co-operation enjoyed with China. Consequently, the Government refused to accept $4.3m. in aid offered by Taiwan and prohibited its officials from receiving the four high-ranking diplomats appointed to represent Taiwan in São Tomé. In October, in order to avoid an open conflict with Trovoada, the Government withdrew its opposition to the diplomatic recognition of Taiwan and subsequently accepted the Taiwanese development aid. In January 1998 Taiwan's ambassador presented his credentials to Trovoada. In July 2002 the Taiwanese President, Chen Shui-bian, made a three-day visit to São Tomé. During the visit President de Menezes declared his Government's support for Taiwan's application for membership of the UN and other international organizations. In September 2007 President de Menezes participated in the first Taiwan-Africa leadership summit in the Taiwanese capital, Taipei, his sixth visit to Taiwan. Before his departure he gave assurances that during his mandate São Tomé would not sever ties with Taiwan, a country that maintains diplomatic relations with only four other African nations. In return for Taiwanese aid, in his speech at the 62nd General Assembly in New York, USA, de Menezes requested the readmission of Taiwan to the UN.

At the request of the US European Command (EUCOM), in March 2004 US security company Military Professional Resources Incorporated dispatched a retired US colonel on a one-year mission to São Tomé to conduct an assessment of the local defence requirements. One of the objectives was to provide the country with the adequate naval equipment to patrol its Exclusive Economic Zone and the Joint Development Zone. In February 2006 the USA donated a nine-crew patrol boat for São Tomé's coastguard. In June the US Navy selected São Tomé as the regional centre of its Marine Domain Awareness, a surveillance radar programme for the identification and monitoring of shipping traffic to be shared among the neighbouring countries in the Gulf of Guinea region; installation of the system began in December. In Libreville in August 2006 the summit of the heads of state and government of the eight-country Gulf of Guinea Commission (GGC), which had been established in 1999, designated São Tomé as the GGC's Executive Secretary for a three-year period. Subsequently, President de Menezes appointed Carlos Gomes, the former Chairman of the Joint Development Authority in Abuja, Nigeria, as the Secretary of the GGC, based in Luanda, Angola.

In March 2007 30 French soldiers based in Gabon held joint manoeuvres with 35 local military officers in São Tomé. The objective was to prepare the local armed forces for a peace-keeping unit in Central Africa financed by France. In the same month the guided-missile frigate USS *Kauffman* paid a four-day visit to São Tomé to strengthen the US maritime partnership with the archipelago. During the visit sailors of the frigate held joint exercises with São Tomé's coast guard. In May Vice-Adm. John Stufflebeem, Commander of the US Sixth Fleet based in the Mediterranean, promised US support to monitor the country's waters during a visit to São Tomé. In the same month the Nigerian Minister of Defence, Thomas I. Aguiyi-Ironsi, announced the establishment of a Gulf of Guinea Guard by Nigeria, Cameroon, Equatorial Guinea, São Tomé, Gabon, Angola, and the Democratic Republic of the Congo to protect their common maritime interests in the region.

In January 2008 the Africa Partnership Station, a US initiative to promote maritime security in West and Central Africa that included sailors from Africa, Europe and the USA aboard the amphibious dock landing ship USS *Fort McHenry*, paid a 10-day visit to São Tomé. Furthermore, São Tomé and Príncipe became the first African country to receive global maritime traffic information from the US Navy's Regional Maritime Awareness Capability surface surveillance programme. In May 2012 President Pinto da Costa received the commander of the United States Africa Command (AFRICOM), Gen. Carter F. Ham, who considered the archipelago's strategic position to be an important component for security in the Gulf of Guinea region. However, Gen. Ham denied rumours concerning alleged plans to establish US military bases in São Tomé.

In July 1996 São Tomé and Príncipe was among the five lusophone African countries that, together with Portugal and Brazil, formed the Comunidade dos Países de Língua Portuguesa (CPLP, a Portuguese-speaking commonwealth seeking to achieve collective benefits from co-operation in technical, cultural and social matters). In July 2004 São Tomé hosted the fifth summit of the heads of state and government of the CPLP. At the end of the meeting Brazilian President Luís Inácio 'Lula' da Silva passed the CPLP's rotating presidency for the following two years to President de Menezes. In August 2010 the new Government of Patrice Trovoada announced plans to reorientate the country's foreign policy towards closer co-operation within the Central African region.

Economy

GERHARD SEIBERT

INTRODUCTION

The economy of São Tomé and Príncipe, which until recently was based almost exclusively on the export of cocoa, has experienced a long period of decline since independence in 1975. The sudden loss of protected markets in Portugal and the mass exodus of skilled personnel were compounded by the negative effects of systematic nationalization and the relentless decline in the world price of cocoa after 1979.

President Manuel Pinto da Costa decided at independence to nationalize virtually all enterprises of any size. The Government also took a monopoly of foreign trade, and controlled prices and distribution through a network of 'people's shops'. São Tomé became a member of the IMF and the World Bank in 1977, and introduced a new currency unit, the dobra, to replace the Portuguese escudo at par. The dobra became increasingly overvalued, placing considerable strain on the balance of payments.

In 1985, confronted by the threat of economic collapse, the President initiated a process of economic liberalization. Following discussions during 1986 with the World Bank and the IMF, the Government widened the scope of its reforms with the introduction in 1987 of a three-year structural adjustment programme. This aimed to reduce the large trade and budget deficits, increase agricultural production, stimulate exports, and increase foreign earnings from tourism and fishing. Price controls were abolished on many goods, trade was liberalized, wages, taxes and duties were increased, and the dobra was devalued. The value of the dobra drifted downwards towards parallel rates, while further adjustments to controlled prices were made to bring these rates closer to market levels. In recognition of these reforms, a donors' meeting in Geneva,

Switzerland, in 1989 pledged new loans and a rescheduling of debts, and in June the IMF approved a three-year SDR 2.8m. Structural Adjustment Facility (SAF). However, in 1990 the Government subordinated economic concerns to its own survival, causing the IMF to suspend payments. The budget deficit increased to US $4.5m., inflation reached 47%, and foreign exchange reserves were severely depleted.

The currency was repeatedly devalued, and by June 1993 the dobra was trading officially at approximately US $1 = 425 dobras, while 'black market' rates stood at about $1 = 600 dobras. By mid-1992 the IMF indicated that enough progress had been made for payments under the SAF to be resumed. This was a precondition to addressing the problem of the country's high level of external debt, which, in 1993 stood at $254m., of which $225.8m. was long-term debt.

In 1994 the current account of the balance of payments registered a deficit equivalent to 9.6% of GDP, while annual inflation doubled to 40%. By September 1994 none of the public finance targets set by the IMF had been met. In order to reverse the negative trend, in December the Government increased fuel prices by some 30%. In addition, the official and free-market exchange rates were unified. Successive devaluations of the currency implemented during 1994 totalled some 50%.

In 1995, following negotiations with a joint mission of the IMF and the World Bank, the Government announced a series of austerity measures aimed at facilitating the disbursement of a third tranche of credit under the SAF. With the implementation of successive increases in fuel prices in March and September, the structural adjustment credit of US $3.2m. was disbursed in early 1996. Further increases in fuel prices were imposed in February and May. In mid-1996 the Government announced a series of measures aimed at stemming the rapid depreciation of the currency and reducing the annual rate of inflation from 48% to about 25% by the end of the year. By October the current fiscal balance (excluding donations) had reached a deficit of 7,800m. dobras, compared with a targeted surplus for the year of 4,400m. dobras. The deficit resulted from low revenues, owing to tax evasion, the exemption of import duties on 73% of all imports, and excessive public spending.

In May 1997 the IMF advised the Government to take urgent measures to curb inflation and to stem the rapid devaluation of the currency. However, in April 1998 an IMF mission to São Tomé found that government expenditure had risen, owing to salary increases, while revenue had remained low. In addition, due to extra-budgetary spending, monetary financing of the budget was as high as 12,300m. dobras. As a result, the IMF announced that São Tomé would not qualify for debt cancellation under the initiative for heavily indebted poor countries (HIPC).

As a consequence of vigorous adjustment measures imposed by the IMF, the country's economic and fiscal performance improved considerably in 1998. There was a surplus in the primary budget (excluding externally financed capital outlays) equivalent to 0.7% of GDP, compared with a deficit of 2.2% in 1997. The average inflation rate was reduced from 68.5% in 1997 to 42.3% in 1998, while the differential between the official rate of exchange of the dobra and the 'black market' rate was narrowed from 6.5% in 1996 to less than 1% in 1998. Private investment increased to the equivalent of 18.4% of GDP in 1998. Following the reduction in inflation, the central bank reduced its reference interest rate from 55% to 29.5% in November 1998, again, to 24.5%, in February 1999, and finally to 19% in May. The measure was expected to encourage investment and thus lead to greater economic growth.

In March 1999 the Government presented a memorandum of economic and financial policies outlining its objectives for 1999–2002. The programme included the development of a more prudent fiscal policy aimed at broadening the tax base, prioritizing expenditure on infrastructure and the social sector, the creation of a social programme to reduce poverty and improve educational and health services, the implementation of a tight monetary policy, and the introduction of accelerated structural reforms in an attempt to boost private sector development and achieve sustainable economic growth.

In April 2000 the Government presented an interim Poverty Reduction Strategy Paper (PRSP) for 2000–02. According to the document, at least 40% of the local population lived below the poverty line, while some 33% were considered to live in extreme poverty, with an income sufficient to cover only one-half of minimum household food requirements. In late April 2000 the IMF granted São Tomé and Príncipe a three-year Poverty Reduction and Growth Facility (PRGF), worth some US $8.9m. The successful implementation of the Government's three-year programme was a precondition for future debt reduction within the framework of the HIPC initiative. In May the 'Paris Club' group of donors agreed to reduce the interest on São Tomé and Príncipe's external debt by 95% until 2003, worth an estimated $26m.

Economic policy performance under the PRGF-supported programme in 2000 was negatively affected by a 1.5% deterioration in terms of trade, owing to lower cocoa prices and higher petroleum prices. However, as a result of growth in food crop production, tourism and construction, real GDP growth for 2000 was estimated at 3.0%. Consumer prices increased by an average of 12.2% in that year, while the primary fiscal surplus rose to 2.1%. Influenced by higher petroleum prices and the nominal devaluation of the dobra, government revenue (excluding grants) increased by 19%, to 80,000m. dobras (21.7% of GDP), in 2000. The difference between the official and parallel exchange rate rose to 2.4%.

In November 2000 the IMF declared São Tomé and Príncipe eligible for assistance under the enhanced HIPC initiative, and in mid-December released a second disbursement of the PRGF worth US $1.2m. The IMF and the World Bank granted the country debt service relief worth $200m. in nominal terms under the enhanced HIPC initiative. Nominal debt relief savings for the following 20 years were estimated at $131m., or about $6.5m. per year. In April 2001 the African Development Bank (AfDB) conceded São Tomé an 80% reduction in debt service payments, equivalent to debt relief of $34.2m. The resources created by this reduction were to be directed primarily to health, education, infrastructure, poverty reduction and improved governance. São Tomé was to receive full debt relief assistance, if it took a series of agreed measures to achieve economic growth and poverty reduction, including at least one year's satisfactory implementation of the complete PRSP.

Following the Government's failure to observe structural performance criteria and other measures recommended by the IMF, in late 2001 the Fund suspended its PRGF-supported programme. The IMF had also criticized the lack of transparency in the negotiation of petroleum contracts in that year. In order to secure a new PRGF medium-term programme, the Government was obliged to execute a six-month staff-monitored IMF programme (SMP), ending in June 2002. The debt-rescheduling that Paris Club donor countries had agreed in May 2000 became inoperative until the approval of a new PRGF arrangement.

Real GDP growth in 2001 achieved the targeted 4%. However, owing to higher petroleum prices, combined with a 5% devaluation of the dobra, the inflation rate was 9%. The overall fiscal deficit (on a commitment basis, including official grants) reached 15% of GDP, while the primary budget deficit (including HIPC-financed social spending) was 7% of GDP. The external current account deficit (including official transfers) was reduced from 21% of GDP in 2000 to 11% of GDP in 2001. The difference between the official exchange rate and the parallel market rate was about 1% in 2001. There was a considerable increase in customs and consumption tax collection in that year, although overspending resulted in a primary budget deficit of more than 3% of GDP.

Government performance under the SMP during the first half of 2002 was disappointing. Spending was higher than forecast, owing to wage demands, and higher energy and utility costs, while expenditure related to the March 2002 elections more than offset higher revenue. Consequently, the primary fiscal deficit (including HIPC-financed social expenditure) increased to 3.2% of GDP, compared with a targeted deficit of 1.6% of GDP. The Government agreed to extend the SMP to December in order to re-establish a satisfactory track record of policy implementation. As part of the structural reforms, the Government had to apply mechanisms by which adjustments in the consumer prices of fuel, water and electricity reflected import and distribution costs; implement a privatization programme for the Empresa de Água e Electricidade (EMAE); adopt a revised investment code to strengthen incentives in the private sector; and submit to the Assembleia Nacional (National Assembly) a draft law on the management of petroleum resources and the establishment of a reserve fund. An IMF mission that visited São Tomé in July 2003 declared that the Government had fulfilled the required conditions for discussion of a new PRGF agreement and could benefit from a debt reduction of 83% (some US $200m.), as part of the enhanced HIPC initiative, in the first quarter of 2004.

In March 2004 the IMF recognized that the Government had made progress in macroeconomic management during 2002–03. The Government observed five out of nine quantitative benchmarks and four out of six structural benchmarks. In 2003 real GDP growth was 4.5%, while the average inflation rate was 9.8%. The primary fiscal deficit (including HIPC-financed social outlays) was 12% of GDP. As a result of increased exports and modestly higher imports, the external current account was estimated at 45% of GDP. In August 2005 the IMF approved a new three-year PRGF worth US $4.3m.

In March 2006 the IMF considered performance under the PRGF arrangement satisfactory and released US $600,000. In May the Minister of Planning and Finance declared that due to the lax financial policies of the former Government the country had failed to reach the HIPC conclusion point scheduled for June. Nevertheless, in June an IMF mission declared that the country was close to reaching the conclusion point, provided that the action plan to contain expenditure presented by the new Government was implemented.

In March 2007 the Assembleia Nacional approved the annual budget for 2007 of US $96m., of which 81% was externally financed. In the same month the IMF and the World Bank announced that the country had now met the economic reform targets and was eligible for debt cancellation equivalent to $317m. under the enhanced HIPC initiative. In May the Paris Club creditors agreed to write off bilateral debts of $24m. in nominal terms, thus reducing São Tomé's debt to Paris Club creditors to $600,000. Germany and France cancelled bilateral debts of €4.6m. in August 2007, and of €7.6m. in March 2008, respectively.

Following the completion of the third review of the PRGF agreement in January 2007, the IMF released US $600,000, although the Fund criticized insufficient pro-poor spending. After having completed the fourth review in June, the IMF released a further $600,000. According to the Fund, the country had made significant progress in macroeconomic stabilization with regard to GDP growth and lower inflation. Following the fifth review, which assessed encouraging economic performance, in December another $700,000 was released, bringing the total of payments under the agreement to some $4m. In addition, the IMF disbursed HIPC assistance of about $1.4m. In March 2008 an IMF mission conducted the final review of the three-year PRGF agreement. The mission concluded that the Government had met all quantitative performance criteria, except the criteria on the domestic primary fiscal deficit and the banking system's credit to the Government. In the opinion of the IMF, economic growth had been considerable in the previous two years, with real GDP growth of 6% in 2007, due to foreign investments in tourism. However, the country's production and export base remained very narrow and extremely vulnerable to external shocks.

In December 2008 the Assembleia Nacional approved the 2009 national budget, which included public investments totalling US $100m. in health and education (25%), agriculture and fishing (20%), water and energy (16%), and infrastructure (15%). The budget also included an increase of the minimum wage from 650,000 dobras to 1.2m. dobras and an average 35% rise in public sector salaries. External donors were expected to finance some 80% of the budget. In March 2009 the IMF released $540,000 as part of a new three-year PRGF, totalling $3.8m. and covering the period 2009–11, which had been approved in the same month. The new PRGF aimed to achieve average annual GDP growth of 6.3%, reduce inflation below 10% until 2011, implement sustainable public finances and further structural reform of public enterprises, and improve the overall business environment. GDP grew by 5.8% in 2008.

In December 2009 the Assembleia Nacional approved the 2010 national budget of US $153m., which allocated $50m. for current expenditures and $103m. for capital expenditures. Some 90% of the budget was to be financed by external donors. Public works and infrastructure projects represented 19% of the budget, while education, health and agriculture received 13%, 11% and 8%, respectively.

In February 2010 the IMF released a further US $570,000 as part of the new Extended Credit Facility (ECF) arrangement, which had been approved in March 2009. In November 2010 the IMF carried out the second and third reviews of the ECF arrangement. The mission was concerned that, despite considerable debt relief granted by international donors, the country remained at high risk of returning to unsustainable debts because of its poor export and production performance. In January 2011 the Assembleia Nacional approved the 2011 national budget of $153m., of which 93% was expected to be financed by foreign donors.

In mid-December 2011 the Assembleia Nacional approved the 2012 national budget of US $152m. with the 26 votes of the ruling Acção Democrática Independente (ADI) and the vote of the Movimento Democrático Força da Mudança deputy, while the opposition parties the Movimento de Libertação de São Tomé e Príncipe—Partido Social Democrata (MLSTP—PSD) and the Partido de Convergência Democrática abstained. The public sector wage bill represented 44.3% of current expenditures (34.8% of the total), while transfers and goods and services accounted for 25.0% and 24.6%, respectively. Capital expenditures depended largely on financing by external donors.

AGRICULTURE

According to the African Development Bank (AfDB), agriculture (including fishing) contributed 18.0% of GDP in 2008, and, according to FAO estimates, employed 56.7% of the total labour force in mid-2012. At independence, São Tomé inherited a plantation economy, dominated by cocoa and partially protected from international price movements by a guaranteed home market. Most land was farmed by large Portuguese-owned enterprises. In 1975 the Government nationalized all landholdings of over 200 ha and grouped them into state enterprises, which covered over 80% of the cultivable land area. The nationalization of the estates led to the exodus of many of the skilled agricultural personnel. The state farms incurred substantial deficits and, within a decade, were brought to the point of financial collapse.

In 1985 the Government initiated a policy of partial privatization. Ownership of the estates was kept in the hands of the State, but foreign aid was sought to rehabilitate the plantations and foreign companies were invited to tender for management contracts of 15–20 years' duration. Privatization proceeded slowly under this system, and was confined to the prime land in the north-east of São Tomé island. By the early 1990s the strategy of estate management contracts was in crisis. Declining cocoa prices stifled the optimism of the late 1980s.

An alternative strategy of breaking up the estates into smallholdings has been pursued since 1985. About 10,000 ha of land were distributed to small farmers during 1985–89. The Government viewed these areas as suitable only for domestic food production. At the instigation of the World Bank, which was providing finance of US $17.2m. for the process of land reform, the Government announced that some 20,000 ha of land would be transferred to smallholders between 1993 and 1998. Land distributed to smallholders since 1985 that had not been cultivated would be repossessed and redistributed by the State. Financing was subsequently forthcoming from international donors.

In December 2000 the Land Reform Programme, financed by the World Bank, ended. However, agrarian reform continued, as not all estate lands had been redistributed. In November the Government announced that a new support programme for some 11,000 smallholders, fishermen and market women was to commence in March 2002. The 12-year programme, which was expected to benefit some 58,000 people, was financed by the International Fund for Agricultural Development (IFAD) with US $13m. and was to replace the smallholder support project financed by France and the IFAD since 1995. According to figures provided by the IMF in 2004, only 43,522 ha were distributed in 1993–2003 to a total of 8,735 beneficiaries. The average size of the plots was 3.2 ha.

Following independence cocoa regularly accounted for well over 90% of exports by value. Cocoa covered 61% of the cultivated area on the 15 large estates in 1986. However, production declined to around 4,000 metric tons per year in the 1980s, and export earnings from cocoa decreased by 67% between 1979 and 1988. As cocoa prices declined still further in the early 1990s, production drifted down to a low of 3,193 tons in 1991 and there has been no discernible recovery since. According to unofficial estimates, production in 2010 was 2,000 tons. Low yields were caused in part by an infestation of the insect *Heliothrips rubrocintus*, which affected 40% of the cocoa crop. The World Bank blamed the Government's poor provision of agricultural services for the spread of the infestation. Nevertheless, in 2010 cocoa still accounted for 75.4% of total exports, illustrating the failure of the Government's export diversification programme. Some 60% of the arable land is still planted with cocoa, and in the medium term cocoa will remain the main cash crop for both rural incomes and export production. In 2007 cocoa exports represented an income of US $3.5m. Owing to higher prices in 2008 and 2009, cocoa exports accounted for $4.9m. In terms of quantity, cocoa exports reached 2,728 tons in 2009. In 2011 cocoa exports of 2,208 tons accounted for income of US $5.1m., 8% less than in 2010, when 2,413 tons were sold for $5.5m. Despite the decrease in production, in 2011 cocoa still represented 96% of all agricultural exports. In 2010 organic cocoa produced by 2,200 small farmers accounted for about 600 tons of total production.

The islands' principal secondary crops are copra, coffee, and palm oil and kernels. In 1986 coconut palms covered 23% of the cultivated area on the 15 state-owned estates, and copra was the country's only export of any significance apart from cocoa. By 1998 production of copra had decreased to 162 metric tons. By 2000, however, production had increased to 882 tons, although this declined to only 400 tons in 2003, according to FAO estimates. Oil palms accounted for 10% of the cultivated area on the estates in 1986 and coffee for 3%, but exports of these commodities ceased altogether in the latter half of the 1980s. Coffee output increased from 14 tons in 1992 to 36 tons in 1998, then declined to an estimated 20 tons in 2006, before rising slightly, to 30 tons, in 2008. Exports of taro (also known as cocoyam, or matabala), plantains and citrus fruit to Gabon were also targeted for development, and in 2008 27,000 tons were produced.

Self-sufficiency in basic food crops has eluded the Government since independence, despite the high fertility of the islands' volcanic soils, the long growing season, the variety of micro-climates and abundant rainfall. The apportionment of centrally fixed planning targets for food production among the nationalized estates proved unsuccessful, and by the mid-1980s the country was estimated to be importing 90% of its food requirements. By 1992 it was estimated that imports of food had decreased to around 45% of consumption. From the early 1980s the European Community (EC, now the European Union—EU) provided funds to plant 610 ha of high-yielding oil palms and to establish a publicly owned palm oil factory on the 1,500-ha Ribeira Peixe estate in the south-east of São Tomé island. By 1992 the project was producing about 80,000 litres of oil a month and was able to meet the country's internal requirements. However, in April 2005, of the original 610 ha of palm trees only one-third were being exploited, and there were only 93 workers left of the 300 formerly employed. Despite the capacity to produce 500 litres of palm oil per hour, the actual production level was only 4,000 litres per week. Owing to a lack of demand, the palm oil manufacturer EMOLVE experienced difficulties selling even this small quantity on the local market. In July 2009 the French consortium SOCSINCO announced the investment of US $50m. in the rehabilitation of EMOLVE and in the construction of a new palm oil factory on the Sundy estate on Príncipe. Palm oil production was expected to start within three to five years. In the same month the Government and the Libyan company African Investment Company (Atico) signed a 20-year concession contract for the Monte Café estate (239 ha). Atico promised to invest $3m. in the first four years in the renewal of the coffee and cocoa plantations and the rehabilitation of the outdated infrastructure of the state-owned plantation. In October the Libyan authorities donated five tractors (as well as drivers and fuel) to several small farming communities, in support of the Government's 'Nova Agricultura' programme.

The greatest obstacles to self-sufficiency in food are the virtual absence of a smallholder tradition, due to the plantation economy, and the impossibility of growing wheat for a population increasingly accustomed to eating bread and other wheat-based products. Average food consumption in the country is 300 metric tons per month, comprising mainly local food crops including plantains, bread-fruit, taro, cassava, sweet potatoes and vegetables.

In October 2010 a €1.1m. food security project, financed mainly by the EU, was inaugurated. The scheme, which was to continue until 2012, was expected to provide more than 1,000 small-scale farmers in 27 agricultural communities with technical and material support to encourage the diversification and expansion of food crop production.

In February 2012 the African Union's Comprehensive Africa Agriculture Development Programme was officially launched in São Tomé and Príncipe, which became the sixth country in the Central African sub-region where the World Bank-financed programme was implemented. One of the programme's goals was to increase annual agricultural production by 5% through the allocation of 10% of the national budget to agriculture.

The livestock sector has been seriously affected by the decline in veterinary services since independence and periodic outbreaks of swine fever. In 2003 swine fever reduced the number of pigs to some 2,500. Goats are widely reared, and are sometimes exported to Gabon. In 2000 there were 26,253 head of goat and sheep, and 63 metric tons of goat and sheep meat were produced; however, stocks in 2010 stood at only 3,000 sheep and 5,200 goats, with goat meat production of 19 tons. The islands are free of tsetse fly, but cattle have been badly affected by bovine tuberculosis. Beef production increased, however, from 12 tons in 1992 to an estimated 130 tons in 2010; the national herd numbered around 4,800 head in the latter year.

Similar difficulties have beset the fishing sector, a priority area for economic diversification. In the early 1990s fishing was the second largest source of foreign exchange, due principally to revenue from fishing licences, and employed some 10% of the economically active population. A state-owned fishing company, Empesca, with two modern trawlers, was formed at independence. In June 1978 the Government established an Exclusive Economic Zone (EEZ) around the islands of 370 km (200 nautical miles), although the trawlers actually spent most of their time fishing in Angolan waters. In the late 1980s lack of maintenance on the trawlers led to a rapid decline in the sector, and the industrial catch in 1988 was only 1 metric ton. In the long term, the Government is basing its hopes for the fishing industry on the tuna resources of the area, and it is estimated that tuna catches could reach 17,000 tons a year without affecting stocks. In 2009 the total catch was estimated at 4,250 tons. In 2002 there were 4,687 fishermen and a total of 2,524 boats, of which 884 had an outboard motor. A fish-processing plant, the Sociedade Nacional de Comércio e Pesca, financed with US $2m. of private capital, began operations in September 1995 in Ribeira Funda, some 20 km from the capital. Production was mainly destined for export.

In March 2007 São Tomé signed a new four-year fishing agreement with the EU that became effective on 1 June. In return for a payment of €663,000, the agreement allowed 43 boats from Spain, France and Portugal to fish in the country's waters. In July the Government announced that Japan would grant a loan of US $6.9m. for the development of the fishing sector during 2008–09. The funds were allocated to support artisanal fishermen, improve fish storage and processing facilities, and acquire boats. In March 2008 the São Tomé authorities signed a one-year fishing agreement with the Japanese Government that allowed Japanese trawlers to catch tuna in the islands' waters in exchange for technical support for artisanal fishing. In April 2011 the EU and São Tomé signed a new three-year fishing agreement, which allowed 40 trawlers to operate in the archipelago's waters. In exchange, the EU paid a total of €2.05m., including €682,500 to support the islands' fisheries policy.

São Tomé and Príncipe's considerable forestry resources have been neglected, although it was estimated in 1984 that two-thirds of the country's energy consumption came from fuel wood and most housing is of wooden construction. Colonial legislation for the protection of forests was replaced by a new law in 1979, but it was not enforced and no barriers were placed on the uncontrolled cutting of trees. A commission was set up in 1988 to study the problems of forest preservation and reafforestation, and it began by drawing up a national forest inventory with foreign assistance. This revealed that 29% of the country was still covered in primary forest (*obó*), mainly in the inaccessible south-western quadrant of both islands. Some 245 sq km on São Tomé island and 45 sq km on Príncipe were identified as needing to be demarcated as 'ecological reserves', in areas where commercial agriculture is uneconomic. In addition, the inventory noted the existence of 30,000 ha of secondary forest, largely on abandoned plantation land, and 32,000 ha of 'shade forest', covering commercial crops. The resources exploitable on a sustainable basis outside the 'ecological reserves' were estimated at between 70,000 cu m and 105,000 cu m of construction wood and between 43,000 cu m and 65,000 cu m of fuel wood per year. However, it was also estimated that the country needed 20,000 cu m of fuel wood for dry-processing cocoa, copra and other commercial crops, and a further 140,000 cu m for domestic purposes.

In 1990 São Tomé was included in the Programme for Conservation and Rational Utilization of Forest Ecosystems in Central Africa (ECOFAC), an EC-funded Central African forest conservation project that was intended to lead to the demarcation and enforcement of forest reserves covering 32% of the total land area. The programme of land distribution to smallholders led to increasing deforestation, with the new occupants arbitrarily felling trees. With the assistance of the UN Environment Programme, the Government formulated legislation, which was approved by the Assembleia Nacional in 1998, concerning management of the environment in order to address increasing problems of this kind. In January 2006 the European Commission granted São Tomé €930,000 as part of a new support programme for tropical rain forests, ECOFAC IV, which amounted to a total of €38m. for seven countries. In August the two laws approved by the Assembleia Nacional in 2004 that created the Obô National Parks in São Tomé and on Príncipe, respectively, came into effect.

MANUFACTURING AND SERVICES

According to the AfDB, industry (including mining, manufacturing, construction and power) contributed an estimated 18.8% of GDP in 2008. The secondary sector comprises some 50 small and medium-sized enterprises and several hundred microenterprises. Many basic manufactured products are still imported, especially from Portugal. The Government aims to develop food-processing and the production of construction materials. All industrial companies were originally scheduled for privatization by the end of 1993. By early 1995 10 non-agricultural public enterprises had been privatized, liquidated or placed under foreign management. In mid-1997 the Government announced the sale of its minority shares in three enterprises: the brick manufacturer Cerámica de São Tomé, the clothing manufacturer Confecções Agua Grande Lda, and the construction materials supplier Cunha Gomes, SA. In November 1998 the Government liquidated the pharmaceutical company Empresa Nacional de Medicamentos, and the slaughterhouse Empresa de Transformação de Carnes. Enterprises to remain under state control were the palm oil manufacturer, EMOLVE, the water and electricity utility, EMAE, the ports administration, the Empresa Nacional de Administração dos Portos, the airport administration company, the Empresa Nacional de Aeroportos e Segurança Aérea (ENASA), the telecommunications company, the Companhia Santomense de Telecomunicaçoes (CST—49%), and the airline Air São Tomé e Príncipe (35%), all of which were to be transformed into limited liability companies.

In March 2012 São Tomé's first pharmaceutical company, Empharma, was created as a joint venture between the Santomean State (holding 37% of the shares), the Cape Verdean company Impharma (36%) and local pharmacies (21%).

The privately owned Banco Comercial do Equador (BCE), which in 2000 represented some 50% of bank credit conceded and about 40% of deposits in the country, was declared bankrupt in December 2002. In January 2003 the multinational air freight carrier Panalpina, which provided supplies to oil companies, ceased its weekly operations from Luxembourg to São Tomé and moved to Malabo, Equatorial Guinea. With the departure of Panalpina, São Tomé lost annual revenue of more than US $1m. The expected petroleum wealth in the country attracted new investments in the banking sector. In December a branch office of the Cameroonian Afriland First Bank, with a capital stock of $1.8m., opened in São Tomé. The bankrupt BCE was recapitalized and renamed as Banco Equador SARL in 2004, with a stock capital of $3m. Later in the same month President Fradique de Menezes inaugurated the National Investment Bank (NIB), owned by the private Portuguese airline Air Luxor (90%) and its subsidiaries in São Tomé and Cape Verde (5% each). The NIB announced plans to increase its capital of $2.5m. to $50m. within five years. In February 2005 Island Bank, SA, a subsidiary of the Nigerian Hallmark Bank, became the fifth commercial bank to open a branch office in São Tomé. In July the Cameroonian Commercial Bank Group inaugurated the Commercial Bank—São Tomé e Príncipe with a stock capital of $3m. In July 2007 the private Togo-based Ecobank that operates in Central and West Africa opened a branch with an initial capital of $1.5m. in São Tomé. In August 2008 President de Menezes inaugurated a local branch office of the Nigerian Oceanic Bank Group, the seventh commercial bank operating in São Tomé and Príncipe, Africa's smallest economy. Also in 2008 the country's second insurance company, NICON Seguros STP, a subsidiary of the Nigerian company NICON Insurance, was inaugurated in São Tomé. In the same year the central bank requested that commercial banks increase their stock capital to $5m.

In April 2011 Afriland First Bank inaugurated a new office building in São Tomé. In August the central bank withdrew the licence of the NIB owing to a five-year period of inactivity arising from a legal dispute. In March 2012 the Gabonese BGFI Bank opened a local branch office in São Tomé with a stock capital of 4,600m. francs CFA.

ENERGY

There are no mineral resources on the islands, but offshore prospecting for hydrocarbons since the late 1980s has produced encouraging preliminary findings. In May 1997 the Government signed an accord with the Environmental Remedial Holding Corp (ERHC) of the USA and the South African Procura Financial Consultants (PFC) concerning the exploration and exploitation of petroleum, gas and mineral reserves in São Tomé's territory. The agreement, which was valid for 25 years, provided for an initial payment to the Government of US $5m. ERHC and the PFC were then to finance the evaluation of the petroleum reserves, and a petroleum company was to be established with the Government, from which the State would receive 40% of the revenue. In November the Government submitted details of the country's 370-km EEZ, drafted by ERHC, to the UN and the Gulf of Guinea Commission. In March 1998 São Tomé approved a law establishing the boundaries of the EEZ, which was presented to the UN Law of the Sea Commission in May. In July the Government and ERHC established a joint-venture petroleum company, Sociedade Nacional de Petróleos de São Tomé e Príncipe (STPETRO), with the Government holding 51% of the shares. In June President Miguel Trovoada and the President of Equatorial Guinea, Teodoro Obiang Nguema Mbasogo, signed a bilateral agreement on the delimitation of the two countries' maritime borders. In March the Government assured the IMF of transparency in all future operations concerning petroleum exploration activities and promised to consult the international monetary institutions in all its negotiations with petroleum companies. Petroleum products were imported from Angola at concessionary rates after independence, but are now being supplied at commercial prices. At the request of the World Bank, in early 1998 the Government sold a 49% share of the state fuel company, Empresa Nacional de Combustíveis e Óleos (ENCO), of which 40% was acquired by the Angolan petroleum company SONANGOL and 9% by local investors.

In October 1999 the Government rescinded the 1997 agreement with ERHC, on the grounds that the company had not met a number of commitments included in the contract. In May 2001, as part of an agreement brokered by the Nigerian Government, São Tomé settled the conflict with ERHC, which, in the mean time, had been taken over by the Nigerian company Chrome Energy Corporation. In exchange for the settlement, the Government conceded to ERHC far-reaching financial advantages, including working interests in licences, a share in signature bonuses and profit oil, and an overriding royalty in production.

In August 2000 Nigeria and São Tomé achieved an agreement on the joint exploration of petroleum in the oil-rich waters disputed by the two countries. According to the agreement, Nigeria was to receive 60% of the profits of the joint zone and São Tomé 40%. In February 2001 Presidents Obasanjo and Trovoada signed a treaty on the joint management of the waters lying between the two countries. The treaty demarcated the borders of a common development zone, which was to be managed by a joint commission and was to be jointly exploited. In March São Tomé allowed Nigeria exploitation rights in Block 246, which had been explored by Nigeria for several years and is situated in the Joint Development Zone (JDZ), in exchange for compensation. In January 2002 a Joint Development Authority (JDA), based in Abuja, was created to direct the affairs of the JDZ. In the first half of 2002 it was agreed that São Tomé would receive 60,000 barrels per day (b/d) from Block 246. In July the Government received an advance payment of US $5m. on future signature bonuses from Nigeria. In February 2001 the Government and the Norwegian company Petroleum Geo-Services (PGS) signed an agreement on the execution of seismic studies outside Blocks 1–22, which had been conceded by ExxonMobil of the USA; the studies commenced in November. In April 2002 PGS confirmed the country's oil potential and stated that the identified blocks were commercially viable. In April 2001 São Tomé also reached an agreement with Gabon on the delimitation of the maritime borders between the two countries.

Following a critical assessment of São Tomé's oil agreements by US lawyers, conducted at the request of the IMF, in May 2002 President de Menezes demanded renegotiations of all oil contracts signed by previous governments with Nigeria, ERHC/Chrome, ExxonMobil and PGS. In November the Nigerian Government suspended the licensing round for nine blocks in the JDZ until São Tomé clarified the contentious issue of the agreement with third parties. In February 2003 Nigeria declared null and void the memorandum of understanding that promised São Tomé and Príncipe compensation for Block 246, 10% of which was located within the JDZ. In exchange, this part of Block 246 was returned to the JDZ. In the preceding months Nigeria had reduced the amount of petroleum it intended to supply from 60,000 b/d to 10,000 b/d. Nigeria had also failed to adhere to a number of other promises made in the memorandum, such as the concession of scholarships and the construction of a refinery. The three principal contracts with third parties were all renegotiated in early 2003. The new agreement with ExxonMobil, signed in January, gave the company pre-emptive rights to stakes of 40% in one block and 25% each in two other blocks of its choice from any offered in the JDZ, while it was obliged to match signature bonuses and terms offered by other bidders. This was much more favourable to São Tomé than ExxonMobil's previous contract. The new agreement with PGS was concluded in early March, but no details were revealed. Finally, in mid-March ERHC/Chrome relinquished its rights to an overriding royalty interest, a share of signature bonuses and a share of profit in the JDZ. According to the new agreement, ERHC/Chrome increased its rights to participate in the JDZ from a total of 30% working interest in two blocks to a total of 125% working interest spread over six blocks, ranging from 15% to 30% each. In addition, the Nigerian company was not required to pay signature bonuses on four of the blocks. Analysts considered the new agreement excessively generous to ERHC/Chrome and out of line with international practice. In April the licensing round of the first nine of the 25 blocks in the JDZ was launched in Abuja.

In October 2003 Nigeria conceded a daily allocation of 30,000 b/d of crude petroleum to São Tomé and Príncipe at a guaranteed margin of US $0.13 per barrel until the end of 2004, for sale on the international market. The Government entrusted the Japanese-owned oil-trading company Arcadia with the sale of the crude. The country expected to earn $1.4m. annually through the agreement. Also in October at a ceremony in São Tomé 19 oil companies submitted 31 valid bids for seven of the nine oil blocks in the JDZ that had been put out for public tender in April. In mid-April 2004 ERHC/Chrome exercised four signature bonus-free options of 15%, 20%, 25% and 30%, respectively, in Blocks 6, 3, 4 and 2, and took another two stakes of 15% and 20% in Blocks 5 and 9, for which signature bonuses were payable. The four signature bonus-free options would cost São Tomé lost income of $75m. Later in April at a meeting of the Nigeria-São Tomé Joint Ministerial Council (JMC) in Abuja it was disclosed that the exploration rights for Block 1 were jointly awarded to ChevronTexaco of the USA (51%), ExxonMobil (40%) and Equity Energy Resources (9%). The JMC decided to postpone the allocation of the remaining blocks to avoid attributing the blocks to companies with uncertain financial and technical capacities. De Menezes announced the execution of new seismic studies by PGS before a new licensing round for the remaining eight blocks would be held. The sale of Block 1 entitled São Tomé to a signature bonus of $49m., much less than the $200m. expected from the auction. ChevronTexaco promised to sign a product-sharing agreement with the JDA in August and start drilling in 2005. However, the eight-year Product Sharing Contract for Block 1 was only signed in February 2005. In June Presidents Obasanjo and de Menezes signed a nine-point agreement on transparency in payments, expenditure and other dealings in the transactions in the JDZ. The Abuja Joint Declaration adopted guidelines for reporting promulgated by the United Kingdom's Extractive Industries Transparency Initiative (EITI).

In October 2004 the Government replaced the National Oil Commission with a 15-member Conselho Nacional de Petróleo (National Petroleum Council—CNP). Its members included the Head of State, the Prime Minister and various government ministers, although de Menezes resigned from the body in May 2005. At the same time, the Agência Nacional de Petróleo de São Tomé e Príncipe (ANP—National Petroleum Agency of São Tomé e Príncipe) was created as the regulatory body of the petroleum sector. The World Bank financed 50% of the ANP's US $1.3m. budget for 2005. In December 2004 President de Menezes signed legislation on petroleum revenue management, which included provisions for control of oil receipts, transparency, conflict of interests, frequent auditing of accounts and a permanent reserve fund. The law upheld the transparency principles of the Abuja Joint Declaration.

In November 2004 the JDA organized a new licensing round for Blocks 2–6. In April 2005 the JMC approved the awarding of the five blocks. However, the announcement was delayed by vehement accusations of irregularities by the MLSTP—PSD in São Tomé. In a report, the ANP accused the JDA of having carried out insufficient checks into bidders' backgrounds, and expressed fears that awards given to inexperienced Nigerian firms could discourage reputable petroleum companies. Patrice Trovoada, the leader of the ADI and the presidential petroleum adviser, demanded a higher percentage for Equator Exploration. In response, President de Menezes dismissed Trovoada from his post, allegedly on the grounds that he had abused his function in order to conduct private business. Under pressure from Nigerian President Obasanjo, on 31 May de Menezes approved the JMC's award recommendations unchanged. A consortium of ERHC and Devon Energy/Pioneer Natural Resources won a 65% stake of Block 2, while Block 4 was awarded to a consortium of ERHC and Noble Energy. Anadarko Petroleum Corpn received 51% of Block 3. An Iranian-Nigerian consortium was awarded the right to operate Block 5, while a Nigerian company became operator of Block 6. The five signature bonuses totalled US $283m. However, owing to ERHC's bonus-free options, São Tomé would only receive $57.2m.

In July 2005 Devon Energy withdrew from the consortium with ERHC, owing to the low interest the company received as one of the three partners. In November the Geneva-based Addax Petroleum replaced Noble Energy in the ERHC/Noble consortium of Block 4. In February 2006 Pioneer Natural Resources withdrew from the operatorship of Block 2 and was replaced by the Chinese state company Sinopec and Addax. In the same month ERHC entered into a participation agreement with Addax Nigeria in Block 3.

An investigation report into the second licensing round requested by the Assembleia Nacional in May 2005 and submitted by the Attorney-General, Adelino Pereira, to the local authorities in December revealed serious irregularities in the process of block awards, including vague selection criteria and the attribution of concessions to petroleum companies with doubtful technical and financial qualifications. Furthermore, the document stated that ERHC's preferential rights would result in a loss of US $60m. in signature bonuses for São Tomé and suggested that the company had made illegal payments to Santomean officials. The Attorney-General asked the US authorities to investigate the contracts awarded to ERHC. In response to the report, President de Menezes declared that it was impossible to cancel the block awards without Nigerian consent. The Nigerian Minister of Petroleum Resources, Edmund Dakoru, rejected the report's allegations as based on deficient information and a result of internal political wrangling in São Tomé. As a result of the report, in May 2006 a search warrant issued by a US court was executed on ERHC, and the signature of the production-sharing contracts for the five blocks suffered considerable delays. Only in mid-March did the JDZ sign production-sharing contracts with Addax and other consortium winners Conoil (20%), Gosonic Oil (5%), Hercules/Centurion (10%), and Overt (5%) of Block 4, with operator Anadarko and ERHC and other parties of Block 3, and with operator Sinopec, Addax, ERHC, A. and Hatman (Nigeria), Momo, and Equator Exploration in Block 2. The signature bonuses for these blocks were $90m., $40m., and $71m., respectively. As a result of ERHC's bonus-free options, São Tomé received only $28.6m. of the total amount. Owing to a lack of interest by bidders in April, the JDA withdrew Blocks 7, 8, and 9 from the licensing round.

In January 2006 ChevronTexaco started drilling the first exploration well in Block 1. Drilling was completed in March; Chevron announced the discovery of oil and gas in May. In mid-April Addax increased its interest in Block 4 to 38.3% by acquiring the 5% stake held by the Nigerian Overt Ventures for US $10m. Later in that month Equator Exploration increased its share in Block 2 from 6% to 9% by acquiring, together with ONGC Videsh Ltd, a 7.5% interest held by A. and Hatman. In March 2007 the British Geological Service re-evaluated the seismic data on possible oil deposits in the country's EEZ produced by the Norwegian PGS in the early 2000s. Also in March 2007 Addax and Sinopec announced plans to drill five exploration wells in Blocks 2 and 4 in the period from 2008–13, at an estimated cost of at $74m. Later that month the JMC increased the annual budget for the JDA in Abuja by 44%, from $9m. in 2006 to $13m. in 2007.

Addax Petroleum announced in September 2007 that it had agreed to acquire ExxonMobil's 40% stake in Block 1 for US $77.6m. and 2% of Addax's share of profitable oil produced in Block 1. At the same time it became known that Chevron had assigned 5.1% of its original 51% stake in Block 1 to South Africa's SASOL. In January 2008 the privately owned company Dana Gas, based in the United Arab Emirates, acquired the 10% participating interest in Block 4 from Hercules/Centurion.

In February 2008 São Tomé was accepted as one of seven new applicant countries for the implementation of the EITI, created in 2002. However, in April 2010 the EITI board excluded São Tomé and Príncipe from the application process for failing to implement the established minimum requirements for candidate countries. In July 2008 the JMC rejected property claims of ERHC for JDZ Blocks 5 and 6. In response, ERHC filed a lawsuit in Abuja against the JDZ in an attempt to secure its 15% interests in each of the blocks. In addition, in November ERHC requested the London Court of International Arbitration (LCIA) to clarify that these interests remain untouched. In another arbitration with Addax concerning a 9% portion of JDZ Block 4, in July the LCIA awarded 7.2% to Addax Petroleum and 1.8% to ERHC. In January 2009 Nigeria agreed to resume the supply of 30,000 b/d of crude petroleum to São Tomé initiated in 2003 that had been suspended in 2007 after former President Obasanjo had been succeeded in office by President Alhaji Umaru Musa Yar'Adua.

Sinopec and Addax Petroleum started exploratory drilling in Blocks 2 and 4 in August 2009. In October Addax drilled an exploratory well in Block 3, where the company had acquired Anadarko's 51% stake and operatorship in August. In November and December, respectively, Addax drilled another two wells in Block 4. Hydrocarbons were allegedly discovered, but official drilling results were not disclosed. The JDA granted the two companies a six-month extension of the exploration period in March 2010. Following successive extensions, the exploration phase ended in March 2012. However, Sinopec and Addax did not report any discovery of commercially viable petroleum.

Meanwhile, in October 2009 Sinopec became the largest stakeholder in the JDZ after completing the takeover of Addax for US $7,300m. In November President Menezes promulgated the new oil operations law. The amendments allowed the Government in certain circumstances to concede drilling rights in the country's EEZ directly to oil companies, without the obligation to hold a licensing round to sell exploration concessions.

In March 2010 the ANP launched the first licensing round for seven of 19 delineated blocks in the EEZ. Earlier in February ERHC and Equator Exploration, which had acquired PGS's pre-emption rights in 2004, had exercised their preferential options, obtaining Blocks 4 and 11 and Blocks 5 and 12, respectively. In November the French oil company Total acquired Chevron's 45.9% stake in Block 1 of the JDZ. Despite an extension of the licensing round, in late November the ANP announced that only six small companies had submitted bids for the seven blocks. In May 2011 the Government awarded the exploration licence for EEZ Block 3 to the Nigerian company Oranto Petroleum; licences for the other six blocks were not allocated. In October the Government signed a 28-year production-sharing contract with Oranto that included the payment of a signature bonus of US $2 m. In December, during a meeting with the JDA in São Tomé, Total announced plans to invest $200m. in exploration drillings in two wells of the JDZ's Block 1, which were scheduled for the first quarter of 2012.

In February 2012 the JDA signed a production-sharing contract with the Iranian company ICC-EOC for Block 6 of the JDZ, which had been awarded in 2005. Following a long dispute with other shareholders, ERHC transferred its 15% share in Block 5 to the Government of São Tomé and Príncipe. Consequently, São Tomé had to contribute 15% of the signature bonus of US $15m., of which it was entitled to receive 40%. In April 2012 the Government and Equator Exploration signed a 28-year production-sharing contract for Block 5 of the EEZ that included the payment of a signature bonus of $2m.

The São Tomé Government sold 35% of its 51% stake in ENCO to SONANGOL for US $32m. in September 2008. Shortly before, a private shareholder had sold 3% to SONANGOL, which increased the Angolan company's share in ENCO from 40% to 75%, while the State retained 16% of the shares and private investors 6%. The Government used $10m. of the proceeds to settle ENCO's debt with SONANGOL, while $22m. were earmarked to finance the 2009 budget. In February 2009 SONANGOL and the Government signed an agreement on the construction of a $30m. regional fuel supply station for ships in Neves.

In March 2012 the Government and the Geneva-based Russian oil trading company Gunvor signed an agreement on the construction of fuel deposits and an oil harbour at Praia Esprainha, involving investments of US $200m.

In 2000 some 74% of electricity generation was derived from thermal sources, and 26% from hydroelectric sources. The capital city's generators still rely on fuel oil, and power cuts have become increasingly frequent as fuel prices have risen. EMAE, which was scheduled for privatization in 2001 at the instigation of the IMF, incurred substantial budgetary deficits during the early 2000s, which the Government was obliged to pay off.

The expansion of the electricity grid on Príncipe commenced in the second half of 2002, financed by the Portuguese Agency for Development Aid and including 13 km of power lines running from Picão in the north to Terreiro Velho in the south, with an extension to the airport through Santo Cristo. In January 2003 EMAE increased electricity tariffs by 5.6% to cover production costs. Despite higher tariffs, since December 2002 EMAE had been unable to pay for the fuel supplied by ENCO. When, in April 2004, the debts had reached some US $1m., ENCO stopped supplies, causing frequent energy cuts. EMAE claimed that it could not pay ENCO since the Government had not paid its energy bill. In turn, the Government created a commission to tackle EMAE's chronic problems. Prime Minister Maria das Neves de Souza announced the establishment of both a new thermal power plant outside the city and the construction of a hydroelectric dam at the Yô Grande river in the south of São Tomé by 2006 to increase the country's energy supply. In mid-2004 the Government and Synergie Investments (of the United Kingdom) signed a contract for the construction of a 25-GW hydroelectric power plant on the Yô Grande and the repair of the small hydroelectric plant at the Contador river. In December the Government conceded Synergie Investments the concession for the exploration of the plant on the Contador river that produces some 20% of the country's electricity.

By July 2005 ENCO had accumulated debts of US $3m. with the Angolan supplier SONANGOL. In November ENCO announced plans to increase the supply price of petrol for EMAE from 6,000 dobras per litre to 8,000 dobras per litre. At that time EMAE's debts with ENCO amounted to 26,800m. dobras. Consequently, ENCO ceased to concede credits to EMAE and did not pay tax debts of 14,000m. dobras to the treasury. In April 2006, owing to higher fuel prices, EMAE increased the electricity tariffs by 33% for private customers, by 50% for embassies and international institutions, and by 60% for governmental departments. In May the new Government succeeded in convincing ENCO to pay part of the tax debts. In turn, the Government used this revenue to settle its own debts of 8,000m. dobras with EMAE. In November a criminal investigation was launched after EMAE revealed that for several years some 40% of its monthly fuel supplies had been diverted.

Owing to the rapid rises in international oil prices, in September 2007 the Government approximately doubled the prices per litre for petrol, diesel and kerosene to 20,000 dobras, 18,000 dobras and 8,000 dobras, respectively. ENCO claimed to have incurred debts of 90,000m. dobras due to the differential between the purchase price and the resale price in the country. In October 2007 EMAE increased the electricity tariffs by 68%. The company, which produces 80% of energy by thermal power, accumulated debts of some 50,000m. dobras with ENCO. As a result of the unsettled debts, in September ENCO had ceased the fuel supplies on credit to EMAE, which resulted in frequent power cuts. On 16 October the two companies reached a deal to regularize the debts.

In April 2008 the Italian company Italbrevetti established a thermal power plant of three groups of generators, with a capacity of 3 MW, in Bobô Fôrro, 3 km north of the capital. In exchange for the €4.2m. investment, the Government granted that company the exploration and management rights of the hydroelectric dam of Contador for a 20-year period. In addition, the Government allowed the construction of another thermal power plant with a production capacity of 12 MW. In July two of the generators broke down, contributing to the ongoing power cuts in the country. Due to the continuous energy crisis, in August the Government dismissed the administration of EMAE and announced its intention to restructure the state-owned company. EMAE produced only 12 MW, while national demand was estimated at 15 MW. In November a former defence minister, Lt-Col Óscar Sacramento e Sousa, was appointed as the new Director-General of EMAE. In October the Government announced its intention to launch a public tender for the construction of a 30-MW thermal power plant to be run by a concessionaire.

In April 2009 the International Court of Arbitration in Paris, France, ruled that the Government would have to pay Synergie Investments €3m. in compensation for having unilaterally abrogated in 2005 the contract to construct a hydroelectric plant, signed in 2004. Meanwhile, in October 2009 a fire destroyed two generator groups in EMAE's central thermal power station, reducing its capacity from 13.7 MW to 5 MW. Prime Minister Rafael Branco complained that, despite making available some US $10m. in funding, EMAE had made little progress. During the following months some 70% of the island was without electricity. In late December Taiwan started the construction of a new $15m. thermal power station in Santo Amaro, with a total capacity of 8.5 MW. In the same month Hidroeléctrica, a majority Portuguese-owned consortium, sent six generators, which were installed in Bobô Fôrro and expected to produce 5 MW. The Santo Amaro power station was inaugurated in October 2010. Taiwan Electrical and Mechanical Engineering Services was entrusted to manage the plant during the first two years.

In March 2011 the Government approved an increase in fuel prices, the first since 2008. The prices per litre for diesel and petrol rose from 18,000 dobras to 21,500 dobras and from 22,000 dobras to 26,000 dobras, respectively.

TRANSPORT, TOURISM AND COMMUNICATIONS

In January 2008 the Government created a Maritime and Port Administration Institute to supervise navigation in the country's EEZ. The new institution was expected to regularize the situation of 439 ships world-wide using the country's flag. However, the country received only 10% of the potential registration fees. In August the Government and Terminal Link SA, the local subsidiary of French consortium CMA CGM, signed a €260m. contract on the construction of a 80-ha deep-sea port at Fernão Dias with a container terminal for the Gulf of Guinea region. The port was expected to employ some 1,000 people directly and indirectly create another 3,000 jobs. The construction works were scheduled to start in early 2011, but were subsequently postponed indefinitely due to CMA CGM's failure to secure funding for the project.

Air São Tomé e Príncipe, which began operations in 1993, was dissolved and replaced by the newly created company STP-Airways owned by the Government (35%) and private investors (65%). In February 2007 STP-Airways inaugurated a twice-weekly direct flight to Luanda, Angola, operated by TAAG—Linhas Aéreas de Angola. However, shortly afterwards the European authorities prohibited TAAG from entering European airspace. In March the Nigerian Airline Aero Contractors, locally represented by Linhas Aéreas São-tomenses, inaugurated a weekly flight to Lagos, Nigeria. In January 2008 the Dutch-owned SCD-Aviation inaugurated regular flights between São Tomé, Príncipe, Libreville (Gabon), Port Gentil (Gabon) and Douala (Cameroon). In May the Government and SCD-Aviation signed a €5m. agreement on the modernization and management of the airport on Príncipe and the maintenance of an air link to both islands.

After investing US $1m. in the modernization of air control, in July 2007 the ENASA assumed the control and commercial exploration of the country's airspace that had been controlled by Ghana due to a lack of technical means.

In May 2008 the Portuguese company EuroAtlantic announced that it had taken a 37% stake in STP-Airways, while the Government maintained 35%, the local Banco Equador, owned by the Angolan groups Mombaka and António Mosquito, and the Grupo de Investimentos e de Apoio aos Serviços both took 14%. EuroAtlantic assumed the management of STP-Airways. In June the Equato-Guinean airline Ceiba Internacional inaugurated a weekly air service between São Tomé and Malabo. Ceiba, created in 2007, was subject to a ban by the European Aviation Safety Agency. In August 2008 STP-Airways inaugurated a regular weekly flight from São Tomé to Lisbon, Portugal; in June 2009 a weekly domestic flight to Príncipe island commenced, and in August the company inaugurated a weekly flight from São Tomé to Luanda.

In November 2009 the European Commission included all airlines registered in São Tomé on a 'black list' of airlines banned from European airspace for safety reasons. Despite repeated warnings, São Tomé's Instituto Nacional de Aviação Civil (National Institute of Civil Aviation) had not fulfilled the international security norms demanded by the EU. However, STP-Airways continued operations to Lisbon, since its plane was registered in Portugal.

In April 2011 the Government signed a 30-year concession agreement with SONANGOL on the management and exploitation of São Tomé's port of Ana Chaves and the country's international airport. The agreement included the establishment of a private management company, jointly owned by SONANGOL (80%) and the Santomean State (20%), to administer the two facilities. SONANGOL promised to invest US $5m. in the port and another $7m. in the airport.

In August 2011 Air Nigeria inaugurated a weekly flight between Lagos and São Tomé. The flight was operated via Douala, Cameroon, and was subsequently extended to Libreville, Gabon.

In 1990 the telecommunications company CST was established as a joint venture between the State (49%) and the Portuguese Rádio Marconi (51%). In March 1997 an internet service was officially launched. In April 2003 CST extended the mobile cellular telephone service to Santo António on Príncipe. At the instigation of the IMF, in February 2004 a law on the liberalization of the local telecommunications market was approved, which, since 1989, had been a monopoly of the CST. Due to this monopoly, São Tomé's international telephone rates were among the highest in the world. Under the new legislation, the CST would maintain the exclusive right to operate the international telecommunications service and mobile phone service until the end of 2005, allowing the company to recoup investments in modernization made over the last 15 years. However, the implementation of this legislation was delayed and it was not until 2006 that the Government set up the Autoridade Geral de Regulação, the communication regulatory authority. In April 2004 the CST introduced an automatic roaming service for mobile telephone connections with the Portuguese TDM, a subsidiary of Portugal Telecom. By December the CST operated 7,050 telephone lines and had 7,745 mobile phone subscribers, representing telephone density rates of 4.9% and 5.4%, respectively. By March 2008 the CST had increased the number of clients of the mobile phone service to 32,000, accounting for 60% of the company's receipts. In July the Government and Portugal Telecom SGPS signed an agreement that allowed the CST to participate with an investment of US $15m. in the international consortium West African Festoon System (WAFS), which constructed an optic fibre submarine cable link between Luanda and Accra, Ghana. The country would connect to the WAFS project through a ground station in Libreville and the SAT3 submarine cable. The undersea link was expected to provide the islands with improved international communication links. By December 2010 the CST had 100,000 mobile phone clients, representing some 61% of the country's population.

In May 2011 the Government, the CST and Africatel Holding (a subsidiary of Portugal Telecom) signed an agreement on the country's connection to another optical fibre submarine cable. STP Cabo, a new company jointly owned by the CST (74.5%) and the Government (24.5%), was established to manage the undersea link. In November the submarine cable arrived at Praia Melão. In March 2012 CST commenced mobile broadband services using the G3 network, as well as video calling and data transmission.

The improvement in communications has been of great importance in sustaining efforts to develop tourism. The islands benefit from spectacular volcanic mountains and craters, beaches, unique bird life and flora, and have ample potential for game-fishing. However, the high rainfall during most of the year limits the duration of the tourist season, and the sea is usually dangerous to bathe in because of strong currents. In addition, the development of the industry has been hampered by high malaria incidence, expensive air fares and inadequate government policies. Nevertheless, the first modern tourist hotel, the Miramar, was completed in 1986 with a capacity of 50 beds; it has attracted mainly European expatriates and wealthy Gabonese. Although tourism has been identified as a growth sector for many years, a lack of development has confined its contribution to GDP to only 3%. The number of foreign visitors increased from 9,609 in 2003 to 15,746 in 2005, but decreased to 12,266 in 2006. In 2007 the number of foreign visitors declined further, to 11,815, but rose again, to 14,456, in 2008.

In July 2002 the Government and local tour operators created a National Tourist Council to co-ordinate tourism promotion. In March 2004 the Government announced plans to sell by public tender old plantation houses, in order to promote rural tourism and attempt to save from ruin the mostly dilapidated colonial architecture. Potential investors were obliged to maintain the original tropical architecture of the estate buildings. In early May the Government held a round-table conference on tourism development to present a strategy for the development of the country's tourism to local and foreign investors. The priorities for tourism development identified by the local authorities included improving and diversifying the market, upgrading infrastructure, building capacity of local tourism agents, training of human resources, and the promotion of São Tomé's tourism potential. However, the event attracted very few potential investors from Europe's large tourist markets. At the end of that month the Pestana Group, Portugal's largest hotel group, signed an agreement with the Government regarding the establishment of a five-star hotel in the country's capital. This investment was estimated at €25m. and was expected to employ some 600 local people. In September 2005 Pestana commenced construction works. In 2006 Dutch investor Rombout Swanborn purchased the Bombom Island resort in Príncipe and the Marlin Beach Hotel in São Tomé. In May 2008 Pestana inaugurated its hotel in São Tomé with 115 rooms, a casino and a discothèque.

In February 2011 the South African investor Mark Shuttleworth purchased the Bom Bom Island Resort in Príncipe from the Dutch businessman Rombout Swanborn, director of the tour operator Africa's Eden. In May Príncipe's Regional Government granted Shuttleworth's local company HBD Boa Vida the concession of the Sundy estate. Shuttleworth promised to invest in sustainable development based on luxury eco-tourism, agriculture and agro-forestry. HBD Boa Vida also received from the Regional Government a concession for the beach Praia Uva, and acquired the Paciência estate and two tourist complexes at Praia Macaco and at Praia Boi from foreign concessionaires. However, the agreement signed by Principe's Regional Government was contested by the central Government led by Prime Minister Patrice Trovoada, since in 2010 the Sundy estate had already been assigned under another agreement to SOCFINCO (a subsidiary of the Belgium-based Société Financière des Caoutchoucs Luxembourg—SOCFIN) Consequently, SOCFINCO was compensated with lands in São Tomé and, after several rounds of negotiations, a final agreement was signed between the central Government and HBD.

Portugal, the USA and the Government launched a 10-year malaria eradication campaign, financed with US $16m., in 2001. In December 2005 the health authorities started a national anti-malaria campaign financed predominantly by Taiwan. By April 2006 mortality by malaria had been reduced by more than 50% over the previous two years. The number of hospital admissions due to malaria decreased from 13,230 in 2004 to 5,560 in 2005. In March 2007 the health authorities announced that malaria cases had declined from 67,156 in 2004 to 9,106 in 2006. Malaria mortality was reduced from 169 deaths from the disease in 2004 (19% of total mortality) to 26 in 2006 (3%). In the following years malaria mortality and morbidity further decreased; however, recently the rate of infection has begun to increase again. In May 2012 the director of the National Anti-Malaria Programme, Maria de Jesus Trovoada, reported 3,647 cases of malaria infection between January and April, considerably more than the 2,103 cases registered during the same period of 2011.

FOREIGN TRADE AND PAYMENTS

Owing to the importance of cocoa and tourism, the islands' economic life is entirely dependent on external markets. Until 1980 the trade balance was usually positive because of the small value of imports. However, since then low world cocoa prices and low cocoa production, combined with the higher cost of food imports, have led to a continuing trade deficit. The deficit reached a record total of US $22.9m. in 2002. Shortages of essential supplies, especially fuel, have become more frequent. Portugal is the country's main supplier of goods, accounting for 60.9% of total imports in 2010, although there are considerable annual fluctuations. Since the mid-1980s São Tomé has sold its cocoa mainly to Germany and the Netherlands. In 2010 the Netherlands accounted for 10.5% of total exports. In 2011 São Tomé's exports were worth US $5.7 m., while imports accounted for $130.7m., resulting in a trade balance deficit of $125m.

Over the years the UN Development Programme (UNDP), the World Bank, the EU, Portugal, France, Italy, Japan, the People's Republic of China and Arab countries have been especially prominent as donors. In 1997 Taiwan, which provides US $10m. in assistance annually, replaced China as a major donor country. However, the institutional weakness of the country and the lack of co-ordination between donors has led to problems in the efficiency with which aid is utilized. The influx of aid has helped to deal with the deficit on the current account, but it has distorted prices. According to UN figures, in 1993 São Tomé received official development assistance of $378 per head, the highest level of any developing country. In 2002 outstanding debt totalled $264.8m. Multilateral and bilateral medium- and long-term debt amounted to $177.0m. and $82.8m., respectively. In June the AfDB granted São Tomé and Príncipe a credit of $5.7m. to finance the development of human resources as part of poverty reduction measures. In July Taiwan signed a third three-year co-operation agreement with São Tomé and Príncipe, worth $35m. for the period 2003–06. Taiwan designated 60% of this funding for projects that would have considerable socio-economic impact, 20% for small projects, 10% for agriculture and 10% for small and medium-sized enterprises. In June 2004 Nigeria conceded São Tomé a third interest-free $5m. loan, bringing to $15m. the total owed by São Tomé to Nigeria. The amount would be deducted from future petroleum signature bonus payments. In October the World Bank granted a $5m. loan for strengthening the Government's economic, financial, and budgetary management capacities, particularly with regard to the oil revenue management law. Two months later Portugal and São Tomé signed a new co-operation agreement of €41m. for the period 2005–07.

In late 2004 the World Bank conceded an International Development Association (IDA) credit of US $4.5m. and an IDA grant of $1.5m. for a five-year Social Sector Support Project focusing on basic health and education services. In March 2005 the EU granted a European Development Fund (EDF) credit of $10.3m. for the improvement of the country's road network and road maintenance. In July the AfDB announced a grant of $7.5m. for agriculture and good government. At a UNDP sponsored round-table donor conference in Brussels, Belgium, in December, the Government requested $130m. for poverty reduction and infrastructure projects; however, only $60m. was pledged. In February 2006 the World Food Programme announced a new five-year food aid programme worth $5.2m. Public investments declined by 33% from $28m. in 2004 to $19m. in 2005, of which 78% was financed by external donors. Taiwan contributed $7m., while the EU paid $3.4m. According to a World Bank report in May 2006, the country's total nominal debt represented 1,655% of the value of the export of goods and services or 666% of GDP, while debt service payments were equivalent to 44% of the export of goods. In December the Government held a round-table donor conference for the infrastructure, education and good governance sectors in São Tomé. The donors pledged $52m., considerably less than the $121m. requested by the Government.

In March 2007 the EU promised EDF financing of €13m. during the period 2008–13 for infrastructure improvement and road construction. In November São Tomé and the USA signed a two-year $8.7m. Millennium Challenge Corporation (MCC) threshold programme aimed at improving the country's performance on the MCC Economic Freedom Indicators, particularly with regard to improved tax and customs revenue collection and a reduction of the time required to start a business. Investments executed under the Public Investment Programme in 2007 totalled $19.2m., a decrease of 23% compared with the previous year. Of the total amount spent, $5.1m. was raised internally, while foreign donors provided $14.1m., of which $11.5m. were donations and $2.6m. loans. The public administration absorbed 27% of total public investments, while 15% was spent on health and education and a further 12% on fisheries. In January 2009 the Portuguese construction company Mota-Engil and the Government signed an agreement on the construction of a new water supply system for the capital. The $5.8m. project was co-financed by the AfDB ($2.7m.), the EDF ($2.5m.) and the Government ($600,000). In February Portugal approved a €50m. credit line for São Tomé to finance Portuguese exports as part of the projects included in the archipelago's Public Investment Programme. As part of its Education for All—Fast Track Initiative, in March the World Bank granted the Government $3.6m. for pre-primary and primary education projects. In June the Nigerian Senate approved a $10m. loan for São Tomé as advanced payment of signatures bonus payments for oil blocks of the JDZ. In the same month Libya granted São Tomé $1m., of which $250,000 was destined for the payment of scholarships of students abroad and $750,000 for the import of food products. São Tomé's total external debt was $186m. at the end of 2009, of which $172m. was long-term public debt. In that year, the cost of servicing public debt and repayments to the IMF was equivalent to 5.5% of the value of exports of goods, services and income (excluding workers' remittances).

In July 2009 São Tomé and Portugal signed an exchange rate parity agreement that allowed the national currency to be pegged to the euro. The agreement, supported by a credit line of up to €25m. from Portugal to reinforce the archipelago's foreign exchange reserves, became effective in January 2010. The fixed exchange rate was expected to contribute to macroeconomic and financial stability in São Tomé and Príncipe by attracting direct foreign investments.

Japan announced in September 2009 the donation of 4,000 metric tons of rice, worth €3.4m. In October the Angolan Government promised the release of US $5m., the second tranche of an $11.5m. loan agreed earlier in the year. In December India pledged $1m. for the establishment of a small industries development centre, conceded a credit line of $5m. for priority projects in the areas of agriculture, capacity building and infrastructure, and granted $213,000 for the acquisition of pharmaceutical products.

In 2009 São Tomé received foreign aid worth US $43.4m. ($23.4m. of donations and $20m. of loans). The major donor was Taiwan, with $13m. (55% of the total), followed by Portugal with $3m. and the EU with $2m. In terms of loans, Portugal was the major creditor with $10m., followed by Angola with $6.9m. and the Arab Bank for Economic Development in Africa with $1.1m.

In January 2010 Japan granted São Tomé additional food aid worth €1.9m. In February the International Finance Corporation (part of the World Bank Group) promised a loan of US $5m.–$10m. to finance the development of the energy sector. In March São Tomé and Brazil signed an agreement on development aid worth $5.8m., with São Tomé obliged to finance 10% of the total amount. In June the Government and the EU signed a three-year co-operation agreement worth €13.8m. to improve road maintenance and financial planning. In the same month the AfDB granted São Tomé $11m. in support for 2010–11, of which $3.7m. was for capacity building in the planning and finance sector and for poverty reduction, and $7.4m. was for financing a food security project. In 2010 Portugal provided São Tomé with bilateral development assistance of €19.4m.

The Government announced in March 2011 that the World Bank would directly support the country's 2011 national budget with US $2m., while in May the Gabonese Government granted São Tomé a credit of $5m. to finance the budget. In November the AfDB granted São Tomé $7m. to finance a food security programme aimed at increasing agricultural and fishing production in the country.

In January 2012 UNDP promised São Tomé US $22m. to finance aid programmes in the areas of good government, poverty reduction, environment and sustainable development during 2012–16. In February 2012 the Government signed a co-operation agreement worth $11m. with the UN Population Fund (UNFPA) and the UN Children's Fund (UNICEF) for the period 2012–16. In the same month the EU approved financial aid of €4.7m. for 2012 destined for the health and environment sectors. In March, during a visit by President Pinto da Costa to Malabo, the Government of Equatorial Guinea pledged São Tomé a credit of $2m. to help finance the national budget. In the same month the World Bank approved an IDA grant worth $4.2m. to finance the first in a series of three tranches under the designation of Governance and Competitiveness Development Policy Operations to improve transparency and effectiveness of public expenditures. In April Russia cancelled bilateral debts worth €4m. During a visit by President Pinto da Costa to Luanda in June, the Angolan Minister of Foreign Affairs, George Chicoty, promised São Tomé financial aid worth $10m. that was earmarked for the financing of agriculture and infrastructure projects.

Statistical Survey

Source (unless otherwise stated): Instituto Nacional de Estatística, CP 256, São Tomé; tel. 221982; internet www.ine.st.

AREA AND POPULATION

Area: 1,001 sq km (386.5 sq miles); São Tomé 859 sq km (331.7 sq miles), Príncipe 142 sq km (54.8 sq miles).

Population: 117,504 at census of 4 August 1991; 137,599 (males 68,236, females 69,363) at census of September 2001; 160,821 (males 79,027, females 81,794) at mid-2009 (official estimate). *Mid-2012* (UN estimate): 171,880 (Source: UN, *World Population Prospects: The 2010 Revision*).

Density (mid-2012): 171.7 per sq km.

Population by Age and Sex (UN estimates at mid-2012): *0–14:* 67,878 (males 34,289, females 33,589); *15–64:* 97,682 (males 48,175, females 49,507); *65 and over:* 6,320 (males 2,695, females 3,625); *Total* 171,880 (males 85,159, females 86,721) (Source: UN, *World Population Prospects: The 2010 Revision*).

Population by District (2006): Água-Grande 56,492, Mé-Zochi 38,668, Cantagolo 14,681, Caué 6,324, Lembá 11,759, Lobata 17,251, Pagué (Príncipe) 6,737; Total 151,912.

Principal Towns (population at census of 1991): São Tomé (capital) 42,300; Trindade 11,400; Santana 6,200; Santo Amaro 5,900; Neves 5,900. Source: Stefan Helders, *World Gazetteer* (internet www.world-gazetteer.com). *Mid-2011* (incl. suburbs, UN estimate): São Tomé (capital) 63,952 (Source: UN, *World Urbanization Prospects: The 2011 Revision*).

Births, Marriages and Deaths (2006): Registered live births 5,072 (birth rate 33.40 per 1,000); Registered marriages 171 (marriage rate 1.2 per 1,000) (2003); Registered deaths 1,111 (death rate 7.3 per 1,000). *2011:* Birth rate 30.7 per 1,000; Death rate 7.6 per 1,000 (Source: African Development Bank).

Life Expectancy (years at birth): 64.3 (males 63.0; females 65.8) in 2010. (Source: World Bank, World Development Indicators database).

Economically Active Population (census of 2001): Agriculture and fishing 13,518; Industry, electricity, gas and water 2,893; Public works and civil construction 4,403; Trade, restaurants and hotels 8,787; Transport, storage and communications 792; Public administration 3,307; Health 776; Education 1,373; Other activities 7,088; *Total employed* 42,937. *2006:* Total employed 53,725 (males 28,729, females 24,996); Unemployed 8,894 (males 4,276, females 4,618); Total labour force 62,619 (males 33,005, females 29,614). *Mid-2012* ('000, estimates): Agriculture, etc. 34; Total labour force 60 (Source: FAO).

HEALTH AND WELFARE

Key Indicators

Total Fertility Rate (children per woman, 2010): 3.7.

Under-5 Mortality Rate (per 1,000 live births, 2010): 80.

Physicians (per 1,000 head, 2004): 0.5.

Hospital Beds (per 1,000 head, 2006): 3.2.

Health Expenditure (2009): US $ per head (PPP): 144.

Health Expenditure (2009): % of GDP: 7.2.

Health Expenditure (2009): public (% of total): 40.1.

Access to Water (% of persons, 2010): 89.

Access to Sanitation (% of persons, 2010): 26.

Total Carbon Dioxide Emissions ('000 metric tons, 2008): 128.3.

Carbon Dioxide Emissions Per Head (metric tons, 2008): 0.8.

Human Development Index (2011): ranking: 144.

Human Development Index (2011): value: 0.509.

For sources and definitions, see explanatory note on p. vi.

AGRICULTURE, ETC.

Principal Crops (metric tons, 2010, FAO estimates, unless otherwise indicated): Bananas 33,400; Maize 3,600; Cassava (Manioc) 7,300; Taro 27,500; Yams 1,900; Cocoa beans 2,000 (unofficial figure); Coconuts 26,400; Oil palm fruit 15,000; Coffee, green 30; Cinnamon 60.

Livestock (head, 2010, FAO estimates): Cattle 4,800; Sheep 3,000; Goats 5,200; Pigs 2,620; Chickens 420,000.

Livestock Products (metric tons, 2010, FAO estimates): Cattle meat 130; Pig meat 182; Sheep meat 6; Goat meat 19; Chicken meat 704; Hen eggs 490; Cows' milk 170.

Forestry ('000 cubic metres, 2010): Roundwood removals 116.4; Sawnwood production 5.4.

Fishing (metric tons, live weight of capture, 2010, FAO estimates): Total catch 4,650 (Croakers and drums 170; Pandoras 200; Threadfins and tasselfishes 130; Wahoo 241; Little tunny 193; Atlantic sailfish 121; Flyingfishes 830; Jacks and crevalles 180; Sharks, rays and skates 102).

Source: FAO.

INDUSTRY

Production (metric tons, unless otherwise indicated): Bread and biscuits 3,768 (1995); Soap 261.1 (1995); Beer (litres) 529,400 (1995); Coconut oil 280 (2010, FAO estimate); Palm oil 2,000 (2010, FAO estimate); Electric energy (million kWh) 33 (2008). Sources: IMF, *Democratic Republic of São Tomé and Príncipe: Selected Issues and Statistical Appendix* (September 1998, February 2002, April 2004 and September 2006); UN Industrial Commodity Statistics Database; FAO.

FINANCE

Currency and Exchange Rates: 100 cêntimos = 1 dobra (Db). *Sterling, Dollar and Euro Equivalents* (31 May 2012): £1 sterling = 30,625.5 dobras; US $1 = 19,753.3 dobras; €1 = 24,500.0 dobras; 100,000 dobras = £3.27 = $5.06 = €4.08. *Average Exchange Rate* (dobras per US $): 16,208.5 in 2009; 18,498.6 in 2010; 17,624.2 in 2011.

Budget ('000 million dobras, 2010): *Revenue:* Taxation 617; Non-tax revenue 80; Grants 719; Total 1,417. *Expenditure:* Current expenditure 737 (Personnel costs 309, Goods and services 191, Interest on external debt 16, Transfers 192, Other current expenditure 29); Capital expenditure 1,066; HIPC-related social expenditure 21; Total 1,824. *2011* (estimates): Total revenue and grants 1,315; Total expenditure 2,075. Source: IMF, *Democratic Republic of São Tomé and Príncipe: Staff Report for the 2011 Article IV Consultation* (February 2012).

International Reserves (US $ million at 31 December 2011): IMF special drawing rights 5.78; Foreign exchange 45.69; *Total* 51.47. Source: IMF, *International Financial Statistics*.

Money Supply ('000 million dobras at 31 December 2011): Currency outside depository corporations 177.1; Transferable deposits 918.8; Other deposits 435.6; *Broad money* 1,531.5. Source: IMF, *International Financial Statistics*.

Cost of Living (Consumer Price Index; base: 2000 = 100): 372.9 in 2009; 421.0 in 2010; 459.6 in 2011. Source: African Development Bank.

Gross Domestic Product ('000 million dobras at current prices): 1,952 in 2007; 2,361 in 2008; 2,739 in 2009 (Source: Banco Central de São Tomé e Príncipe).

Expenditure on the Gross Domestic Product ('000 million dobras at current prices, 2009, provisional): Government final consumption expenditure 446.9; Private final consumption expenditure 3,761.6; Gross capital formation 589.4; *Total domestic expenditure* 4,797.9; Exports of goods and services 288.5; *Less* Imports of goods and services 1,876.9; *GDP in purchasers' values* 3,209.5. Source: African Development Bank.

Gross Domestic Product by Economic Activity ('000 million dobras at current prices, 2009, provisional): Agriculture 549.0; Mining and quarrying 19.4; Manufacturing 215.2; Electricity, gas and water 69.2; Construction 265.7; Trade, restaurants and hotels 850.3; Finance, insurance and real estate 528.6; Transport and communications 454.1; Public administration and defence 109.5; Other services 156.5; *GDP at factor cost* 3,217.5; Taxes on products 273.3; *Less* Imputed bank service charge 281.2; *GDP at market prices* 3,209.5. Source: African Development Bank.

Balance of Payments (US $ million, 2010): Exports of goods f.o.b. 12.05; Imports of goods f.o.b. −99.42; *Trade balance* −87.37; Exports of services 12.00; Imports of services –34.25; *Balance on goods and services* −109.62; Other income received 1.89; Other income paid –2.26; *Balance of goods, services and income* –109.99; Current transfers received 8.98; Current transfers paid –6.37; *Current balance* −107.38; Capital account (net) 40.30; Direct investment abroad –0.11; Direct investment from abroad 24.64; Other investment assets 18.82; Other investment liabilities 17.64; Net errors and omissions 2.25; *Overall balance* –3.84. Source: IMF, *International Financial Statistics*.

EXTERNAL TRADE

Principal Commodities (US $ million, 2011): *Imports f.o.b.:* Foodstuffs 30.3; Beverages 11.6; Petroleum and petroleum products 20.2; Machinery 21.7; Transport equipment 12.0; Construction materials 8.7; Total (incl. others) 131.6. *Exports f.o.b.:* Cocoa 5.3 Total (incl. others) 5.9.

Principal Trading Partners (US $ million, 2011): *Imports c.i.f.:* Angola 12.6; Belgium 2.3; Brazil 1.4; China, People's Republic 2.6; France 3.2; Gabon 2.7; Japan 3.3; Portugal 77.5; Spain 1.6; Thailand 1.8; Total (incl. others) 131.6. *Exports f.o.b.:* Angola 0.1; Belgium 1.7; France 0.1; Netherlands 2.2; Portugal 0.8; Spain 0.1; Total (incl. others) 5.9. Source: Banco Central de São Tomé e Príncipe.

TRANSPORT

Road Traffic (registered vehicles, 2007, estimates): Passenger cars 305; Lorries and vans 37. Source: IRF, *World Road Statistics*.

Shipping: *International Freight Traffic* (estimates, metric tons, 1992): Goods loaded 16,000; Goods unloaded 45,000. *Merchant Fleet* (registered at 31 December 2009): Number of vessels 28; Total displacement 22,025 grt (Source: IHS Fairplay, *World Fleet Statistics*).

Civil Aviation (traffic on scheduled services, 2009): Kilometres flown (million) 0.1; Passengers carried ('000) 51; Passenger-km (million) 20; Total ton-km (million) 2. Source: UN, *Statistical Yearbook*.

TOURISM

Foreign Tourist Arrivals: 14,456 in 2008; 15,000 in 2009 (rounded figure); 8,000 in 2010 (rounded figure).

Arrivals by Country of Residence (2008, unless otherwise indicated): Angola 1,141; Brazil 248 (2006); Cape Verde 25; France 593; Gabon 170; Germany 467 (2006); Nigeria 445; Portugal 4,835; Spain 107; USA 158; Total (incl. others) 14,456.

Tourism Receipts (US $ million, excl. passenger transport): 7.7 in 2008; 8.3 in 2009; 10.0 in 2009.

Source: World Tourism Organization.

COMMUNICATIONS MEDIA

Radio Receivers (1998): 45,000 in use. Source: UNESCO, *Statistical Yearbook*.

Television Receivers (1999): 33,000 in use. Source: UNESCO, *Statistical Yearbook*.

Newspapers and Periodicals (2000, unless otherwise indicated): Titles 14 (1997); Average circulation 18,500 copies.

Telephones ('000 main lines, 2011): 8.0 in use. Source: International Telecommunication Union.

Mobile Cellular Telephones ('000 subscribers, 2011): 115.0. Source: International Telecommunication Union.

Personal Computers: 6,000 (39.3 per 1,000 persons) in 2005.

Internet Users (2009): 26,700. Source: International Telecommunication Union.

Broadband Subscribers (2011): 700. Source: International Telecommunication Union.

EDUCATION

Pre-primary (2010/11 unless otherwise indicated): 8,591 pupils (males 4,226, females 4,365); 330 teachers (2009/10).

Primary (2010/11): 35,250 pupils (males 18,045, females 17,205); 1,183 teachers.

Secondary (2010/11): 11,884 pupils (males 5,594, females 6,290); 601 teachers.

Tertiary (2009/10 unless otherwise indicated): 1 polytechnic (2000/01); 95 teachers; 766 pupils.

Source: UNESCO Institute for Statistics; *Carta Escolar de São Tomé e Príncipe,* Ministério de Educação de Portugal.

Pupil-teacher Ratio (primary education, UNESCO estimate): 29.8 in 2010/11. Source: UNESCO Institute for Statistics.

Adult Literacy Rate (UNESCO estimates): 89.2% (males 93.9; females 84.7) in 2010. Source: UNESCO Institute for Statistics.

Directory

The Constitution

A new Constitution came into force on 4 March 2003, after the promulgation by the President of a draft approved by the Assembleia Nacional (National Assembly) in December 2002. A 'memorandum of understanding', which was signed in January 2003 by the President and the Assembleia Nacional, provided for the scheduling of a referendum on the system of governance in early 2006. However, the referendum did not take place. The following is a summary of the main provisions of the Constitution:

The Democratic Republic of São Tomé and Príncipe is a sovereign, independent, unitary and democratic state. Sovereignty resides in the people, who exercise it through universal, equal, direct and secret vote, according to the terms of the Constitution. There shall be complete separation between Church and State. There shall be freedom of thought, expression and information and a free and independent press, within the terms of the law.

Executive power is vested in the President of the Republic, who is elected for a period of five years by universal adult suffrage. The President's tenure of office is limited to two successive terms. He is the Supreme Commander of the Armed Forces and is accountable to the Assembleia Nacional. In the event of the President's death, permanent incapacity or resignation, his functions shall be assumed by the President of the Assembleia Nacional until a new President is elected.

The Council of State acts as an advisory body to the President and comprises the President of the Assembleia Nacional, the Prime Minister, the President of the Constitutional Tribunal, the Attorney-General, the President of the Regional Government of Príncipe, former Presidents of the Republic who have not been dismissed from their positions, three citizens of merit nominated by the President and three elected by the Assembleia Nacional. Its meetings are closed and do not serve a legislative function.

Legislative power is vested in the Assembleia Nacional, which comprises 55 members elected by universal adult suffrage. The Assembleia Nacional is elected for four years and meets in ordinary session twice a year. It may meet in extraordinary session on the proposal of the President, the Council of Ministers or of two-thirds of its members. The Assembleia Nacional elects its own President. In the period between ordinary sessions of the Assembleia Nacional its functions are assumed by a permanent commission elected from among its members.

The Government is the executive and administrative organ of state. The Prime Minister is the Head of Government and is appointed by the President. Other ministers are appointed by the

President on the proposal of the Prime Minister. The Government is responsible to the President and the Assembleia Nacional.

Judicial power is exercised by the Supreme Court and all other competent tribunals and courts. The Supreme Court is the supreme judicial authority and is accountable only to the Assembleia Nacional. Its members are appointed by the Assembleia Nacional. The right to a defence is guaranteed.

The Constitutional Tribunal, comprising five judges with a mandate of five years, is responsible for jurisdiction on matters of constitutionality. During periods prior to, or between, the installation of the Constitutional Tribunal, its function is assumed by the Supreme Court. The Constitution may be revised only by the Assembleia Nacional on the proposal of at least three-quarters of its members. Any amendment must be approved by a two-thirds' majority of the Assembleia Nacional. The President does not have right of veto over constitutional changes.

Note: In 1994 the Assembleia Nacional granted political and administrative autonomy to the island of Príncipe. Legislation was adopted establishing a seven-member Assembleia Regional and a five-member Regional Government; both are accountable to the Government of São Tomé and Príncipe.

The Government

HEAD OF STATE

President and Commander-in-Chief of the Armed Forces: Dr Manuel Pinto da Costa (took office 3 September 2011).

COUNCIL OF MINISTERS
(September 2012)

The Government comprises members of the Acção Democrática Independente (ADI) and independents.

Prime Minister: Patrice Emery Trovoada (ADI).

Minister of Foreign Affairs and Communities: Manuel Salvador dos Ramos (Ind.).

Minister of Defence and Public Security: Carlos Olímpio Stock (ADI).

Minister of Justice and State Reform: Elísio Osvaldo d'Alva Teixeira (ADI).

Minister of Parliamentary Affairs and Decentralization: Arlindo Ramos (ADI).

Minister, Secretary-General of the Government: Afonso da Graça Varela da Silva (Ind.).

Minister of Finance and International Co-operation: Américo d'Oliveira dos Ramos (Ind.).

Minister of Planning and Development: Agostinho Quaresma dos Santos Fernandes (ADI).

Minister of Public Works and Natural Resources: Carlos Manuel Vila Nova (Ind.).

Minister of Health and Social Affairs: Ângela dos Santos José da Costa Pinheiro (ADI).

Minister of Education, Culture and Vocational Training: Olinto da Silva de Sousa Daio (Ind.).

Secretary of State of Youth and Sports: Abnildo d'Oliveira (ADI).

Provisional Government of the Autonomous Region of Príncipe
(September 2012)

President: José Cardoso Cassandra.

Secretary for Social and Cultural Affairs: Felícia Fonseca de Oliveira e Silva.

Secretary for Economic and Financial Affairs: Hélio Lavres.

Secretary for Infrastructure and the Environment: Tiago Rosamonte.

Secretary for Political, Organizational and Institutional Affairs: (vacant).

MINISTRIES

Office of the President: Palácio Presidêncial, São Tomé; internet www.presidencia.st.

Office of the Prime Minister: Rua do Município, CP 302, São Tomé; tel. 223913; fax 224679; e-mail gpm@cstome.net.

Ministry of Defence and Public Security: Av. 12 de Julho, CP 427, São Tomé; tel. 222041; e-mail midefesa@cstome.net.

Ministry of Education, Culture and Vocational Training: Rua Misericórdia, CP 41, São Tomé; tel. 222861; fax 221466; e-mail mineducal@cstome.net.

Ministry of Finance and International Co-operation: São Tomé.

Ministry of Foreign Affairs and Communities: Av. 12 de Julho, CP 111, São Tomé; tel. 222309; fax 223237; e-mail minecoop@cstome.net; internet www.mnecc.gov.st.

Ministry of Health and Social Affairs: Av. Patrice Lumumba, CP 23, São Tomé; tel. 241200; fax 221306; e-mail msaude@cstome.net; internet saude.gov-stp.net.

Ministry of Justice and State Reform: Av. 12 de Julho, CP 4, São Tomé; tel. 222318; fax 222256; e-mail emilioma@cstome.net.

Ministry of Parliamentary Affairs and Decentralization: São Tomé.

Ministry of Planning and Development: Largo Alfândega, CP 168, São Tomé; tel. 224173; fax 222683; e-mail mpfc@cstome.net.

Ministry of Public Works and Natural Resources: São Tomé.

Ministry of Youth and Sports: Rua Misericórdia, CP 41, São Tomé; tel. 222861; fax 221466.

President and Legislature

PRESIDENT

Presidential Election, First Round, 17 July 2011

Candidate	Votes	% of votes
Dr Manuel Pinto da Costa	20,960	35.82
Evaristo do Espírito Santo de Carvalho	12,767	21.82
Maria das Neves de Souza	8,208	14.03
Delfim Neves	8,127	13.89
Elsa Pinto	2,661	4.55
Aurélio Martins	2,431	4.15
Filinto Costa Alegre	2,420	4.14
Jorge Coelho	375	0.64
Helder Barros	369	0.63
Manuel de Deus Lima	204	0.35
Total	58,522	100.00

Presidential Election, Second Round, 7 August 2011

Candidate	Votes	% of votes
Dr Manuel Pinto da Costa	35,110	52.88
Evaristo do Espírito Santo de Carvalho	31,287	47.12
Total	66,397	100.00

ASSEMBLEIA NACIONAL

Assembleia Nacional: Palácio dos Congressos, CP 181, São Tomé; tel. 222986; fax 222835; e-mail romao.couto@parlamento.st; internet www.parlamento.st.

President: Evaristo do Espírito Santo de Carvalho.

General Election, 1 August 2010

Party	Seats
Acção Democrática Independente	26
Movimento de Libertação de São Tomé e Príncipe—Partido Social Democrata	21
Partido de Convergência Democrática	7
Movimento Democrático Força da Mudança	1
Total	55

Election Commission

Comissão Eleitoral Nacional (CEN): Av. Amílcar Cabral, São Tomé; tel. 225497; fax 224116; e-mail censtome@cstome.net; Pres. Victor Correia.

Political Organizations

Acção Democrática Independente (ADI): Av. Marginal 12 de Julho, Edif. C. Cassandra, São Tomé; tel. 222201; f. 1992; Pres. Patrice Trovoada.

Frente Democrata Cristã—Partido Social da Unidade (FDC—PSU): São Tomé; f. 1990; Pres. ARLÉCIO COSTA.

Geração Esperança (GE): São Tomé; f. 2005; Leader EDMILZA BRAGANÇA.

Movimento Democrático Força da Mudança (MDFM): São Tomé; f. 2001; Pres. FRADIQUE DE MENEZES; Sec.-Gen. RAUL CRAVID.

Movimento de Libertação de São Tomé e Príncipe—Partido Social Democrata (MLSTP—PSD): Estrada Riboque, Edif. Sede do MLSTP, São Tomé; tel. 222253; f. 1972 as MLSTP; adopted present name in 1990; sole legal party 1972–90; Pres. JORGE AMADO; Sec.-Gen. JOSÉ VIEGAS.

Novo Rumo: São Tomé; f. 2006 by citizens disaffected by current political parties; Leader JOÃO GOMES.

Partido de Coligação Democrática (CÓDÓ): São Tomé; f. 1990 as Partido Democrático de São Tomé e Príncipe—Coligação Democrática da Oposição; renamed as above June 1998; Leader MANUEL NEVES E SILVA.

Partido de Convergência Democrática (PCD): Av. Marginal 12 de Julho, CP 519, São Tomé; tel. and fax 223257; f. 1990 as Partido de Convergência—Grupo de Reflexão; formed alliance with MDFM to contest legislative elections in 2006; Pres. XAVIER MENDES; Sec.-Gen. DELFIM SANTIAGO DAS NEVES.

Partido Popular do Progresso (PPP): São Tomé; f. 1998; Leader FRANCISCO SILVA.

Partido de Renovação Democrática (PRD): São Tomé; tel. 903109; e-mail prd100@hotmail.com; f. 2001; Pres. ARMINDO GRAÇA.

Partido Social e Liberal (PSL): São Tomé; f. 2005; promotes devt and anti-corruption; Leader AGOSTINHO RITA.

Partido Social Renovado (PSR): São Tomé; f. 2004; Leader HAMILTON VAZ.

Partido Trabalhista Santomense (PTS): CP 254, São Tomé; tel. 223338; fax 223255; e-mail pascoal@cstome.net; f. 1993 as Aliança Popular; Leader ANACLETO ROLIN.

União para a Democracia e Desenvolvimento (UDD): São Tomé; f. 2005; Leader MANUEL DIOGO.

União Nacional para Democracia e Progresso (UNDP): São Tomé; f. 1998; Leader PAIXÃO LIMA.

The União para a Mudança e Progresso do Príncipe (UMPP), led by JOSÉ CARDOSO CASSANDRA, operates on the island of Príncipe and there is also a local civic group, O Renascimento de Água Grande, in the district of Agua Grande, which includes the city of São Tomé.

Diplomatic Representation

EMBASSIES IN SÃO TOMÉ AND PRÍNCIPE

Angola: Av. Kwame Nkrumah 45, CP 133, São Tomé; tel. 222400; fax 221362; e-mail embrang@cstome.net; Ambassador ALFREDO EDUARDO MANUEL MINGAS.

Brazil: Av. Marginal de 12 de Julho 20, São Tomé; tel. 226060; fax 226895; e-mail brasembsaotome@cstome.net; Ambassador CARLOS DE ARAÚJO LEITÃO.

Equatorial Guinea: Av. Kwame Nkrumah, São Tomé; tel. 225427; Ambassador ANTÓNIO EBADE AYINGONO.

Gabon: Rua Damão, CP 394, São Tomé; tel. 224434; fax 223531; e-mail ambagabon@cstome.net; Ambassador CORENTIN BERNARDIN MBOUROU HERVO AKENDENGUE.

Nigeria: Av. Kwame Nkrumah, CP 1000, São Tomé; tel. 225404; fax 225406; e-mail nigeria@cstome.net; Ambassador SUNDAY DOGONYARO OON.

Portugal: Av. Marginal de 12 de Julho, CP 173, São Tomé; tel. 221130; fax 221190; e-mail eporstp@cstome.net; Ambassador MARIA PAULA DA SILVA CEPEDA.

South Africa: Av. da Independencia, No. 7 Representanção da República da Africa de Sul, CP 555, São Tomé; tel. 227568; e-mail consuafricasul@cstome.net; Chargé d'affaires a.i. T. E. MAMUREMI.

Taiwan (Republic of China): Av. Marginal de 12 de Julho, CP 839, São Tomé; tel. 223529; fax 221376; e-mail rocstp@cstome.net; Ambassador JOHN-C. CHEN.

Judicial System

Judicial power is exercised by the Supreme Court of Justice and the Courts of Primary Instance. The Supreme Court is the ultimate judicial authority. There is also a Constitutional Court, which rules on election matters.

Supremo Tribunal de Justiça: Av. Marginal de 12 de Julho, CP 04, São Tomé; tel. 222615; fax 222329; e-mail info@stj.st; internet www.stj.st; Pres. SILVESTRE LEITE.

Religion

According to the 2001 census more than 80% of the population are Christians, almost all of whom are Roman Catholics.

CHRISTIANITY

The Roman Catholic Church

São Tomé and Príncipe comprises a single diocese, directly responsible to the Holy See. An estimated 72% of the population are adherents. The bishop participates in the Episcopal Conference of Angola and São Tomé (based in Luanda, Angola).

Bishop of São Tomé and Príncipe: Rt Rev. MANUEL ANTÓNIO MENDES DOS SANTOS, Centro Diocesano, CP 104, Rua P. Pinto da Rocha 1, São Tomé; tel. 223455; fax 227348; e-mail diocese@cstome.net.

Other Churches

Igreja Adventista do 7° Dia (Seventh-Day Adventist Church): Rua Barão de Água Izé, São Tomé; tel. 2222270; e-mail sdastp@gmail.com; Pres. JOSÉ MARQUES.

Igreja Evangélica: Rua 3 de Fevereiro, São Tomé; tel. 221350.

Igreja Evangélica Assembléia de Deus: Rua 3 de Fevereiro, São Tomé; tel. and fax 222442; e-mail iead@cstome.net.

Igreja Maná: Av. Amílcar Cabral, São Tomé; tel. and fax 224654; e-mail imana@cstome.net.

Igreja do Nazareno: Vila Dolores, São Tomé; tel. 223943; e-mail nszst@cstome.net.

Igreja Nova Apostólica: CP 220, Vila Maria, São Tomé; tel. and fax 222797; e-mail j.cunha@ina-stp.org; internet ina-stp.org.

Igreja Universal do Reino de Deus: Travessa Imprensa, São Tomé; tel. 224047.

The Press

Correio da Semana: Av. Amílcar Cabral 382, São Tomé; tel. 225299; e-mail correiodasemana@cstome.net; f. 2005; weekly; Dir JUVENAL RODRIGUES; circ. 3,000.

Diário da República: Cooperativa de Artes Gráficas, Rua João Devs, CP 28, São Tomé; tel. 222661; internet dre.pt/stp; f. 1836; official gazette; Dir OSCAR FERREIRA.

Jornal Maravilha: São Tomé; tel. 911690; f. 2006; Dir NELSON SIGNO.

Jornal Tropical: Rua Padre Martinho Pinto da Rocha, São Tomé; tel. 923140; e-mail jornaltropical06@hotmail.com; internet www.jornaltropical.st; Dir OCTÁVIO SOARES.

O Parvo: CP 535, São Tomé; tel. 221031; f. 1994; weekly; Publr AMBRÓSIO QUARESMA; Editor ARMINDO CARDOSO.

Téla Nón: Largo Água Grande, Edif. Complexo Técnico da CST, São Tomé; tel. 225099; e-mail diario_digital@cstome.net; internet www.telanon.info; f. 2000; provides online daily news service; Chief Editor ABEL TAVARES DE VEIGA.

Online newspapers include the Jornal de São Tomé e Príncipe (www.jornal.st), Jornal Horizonte (www.cstome.net/jhorizonte) and Vitrina (www.vitrina.st).

PRESS ASSOCIATION

Associação Nacional de Imprensa (ANI): São Tomé; Pres. MANUEL BARRETO.

NEWS AGENCY

STP-Press: Av. Marginal de 12 de Julho, CP 12, São Tomé; tel. 2222087; e-mail stp-press@hotmail.com; internet www.stp-press.st; f. 1985; Dir MANUEL DEMDÊ.

Broadcasting and Communications

TELECOMMUNICATIONS

Companhia Santomense de Telecomunicações, SARL (CST): Av. Marginal 12 de Julho, CP 141, São Tomé; tel. 222226; fax 222500; e-mail webmaster@cstome.net; internet www.cstome.net; f. 1989 by Govt of São Tomé (49%) and Grupo Portugal Telecom (Portugal, 51%) to facilitate increased telecommunications links and television reception via satellite; in March 1997 CST introduced internet services; Rádio Marconi's shares subsequently assumed by Portugal Telecom SA; introduced mobile cellular telephone service in 2001; Pres. FELISBERTO AFONSO L. NETO; Sec. JORGE LIMA D'ALVA TORRES; 120,000 mobile subscribers (2010).

BROADCASTING

Portuguese technical and financial assistance in the establishment of a television service was announced in 1989. Transmissions commenced in 1992 and the service currently broadcasts seven days a week. In 1995 Radio France Internationale and Rádio Televisão Portuguesa Internacional began relaying radio and television broadcasts, respectively, to the archipelago. In 1997 Voice of America, which had been broadcasting throughout Africa since 1993 from a relay station installed on São Tomé, began local transmissions on FM. In 2004 there were plans for Televisão Pública de Angola to begin transmitting by the end of the year. The liberalization of the sector was approved by the Government in early 2005 and Rádio Jubilar, Rádio Tropicana (operated by the Roman Catholic Church) and Rádio Viva FM subsequently began broadcasting. The French television channel TV5 commenced broadcasting in December 2007.

Radio

Rádio Jubilar: Av. Kwam Kruman-Edifício da Catequese, CP 104, São Tomé; tel. 223868; e-mail radiojubilar@cstome.net; f. 2005; operated by the Roman Catholic Church; Dir LEONEL PEREIRA.

Rádio Nacional de São Tomé e Príncipe: Av. Marginal de 12 de Julho, CP 44, São Tomé; tel. 223293; fax 221973; e-mail rnstp@cstome.net; internet www.rnstp.st; f. 1958; state-controlled; home service in Portuguese and Creole; Dir MÁXIMO CARLOS.

Rádio Tropicana: Travessa João de Deus, CP 709, São Tomé; tel. 226856; f. 2005; Dir AGUINALDO SALVATERRA.

Television

Televisão Santomense (TVS): Bairro Quinta de Santo António, CP 393, São Tomé; tel. 221041; fax 2226392; e-mail medeiros450@hotmail.com; state-controlled; Dir ÓSCAR MEDEIROS.

Finance

(cap. = capital; res = reserves; dep. = deposits; m. = million; br(s). = branch(es); amounts in dobras, unless otherwise indicated)

BANKING

Central Bank

Banco Central de São Tomé e Príncipe (BCSTP): Praça da Independência, CP 13, São Tomé; tel. 243700; fax 222777; e-mail bcstp@bcstp.st; internet www.bcstp.st; f. 1992 to succeed fmr Banco Nacional de São Tomé e Príncipe; bank of issue; cap. 108,721.2m., res 175,726.5m., dep. 1,286,443.2m. (Dec. 2009); Gov. MARIA DO CARMO SILVEIRA.

Commercial Banks

Afriland First Bank/STP: Praça da Independência, CP 202, São Tomé; tel. 226749; fax 226747; e-mail stp@afrilandfirstbank.com; internet www.afrilandfirstbank.com; f. 2003; private bank; owned by Afriland First Bank, SA, Cameroon; cap. US $1.8m.; Gen. Man. AUGUSTIN DIAYO; Administrator-Delegate JOSEPH TINDJOU.

Banco Equador SARL: Rua de Moçambique 3B, CP 361, São Tomé; tel. 226150; fax 226149; e-mail be@bancoequador.st; internet www.bancoequador.st; f. 1995 as Banco Comercial do Equador; restructured and name changed to above in 2004; owned by Monbaka, Angola (40%) and Grupo António Mbakassi (40%); cap. US $3m.; Pres. DIONÍSIO MENDONÇA; Gen. Man. RUI MENDONÇA; 1 br.

Banco Internacional de São Tomé e Príncipe (BISTP) (International Bank of São Tomé and Príncipe): Praça da Independência 3, CP 536, São Tomé; tel. 243100; fax 222427; e-mail bistp@cstome.net; internet www.bistp.st; f. 1993; 48% govt-owned, 27% by Caixa Geral de Depósitos (Portugal), 25% by Banco Africano de Investimentos SARL (Angola); cap. 12,546.0m., res 201,953.5m., dep. 689,557.5m. (2009); CEO JOÃO CARLOS AGUIAR CRISTÓVÃO; 3 brs.

Commercial Bank—São Tomé e Príncipe: Av. Marginal 12 de Julho, CP 1109, São Tomé; tel. 227678; fax 227676; e-mail cobstp@cstome.net; internet www.cbc-bank.com; f. 2005; 42% owned by Groupe FOTSO (Cameroon); cap. US $3m. (2005); Chair. YVES MICHEL FOTSO; Gen. Man. JAQUES PAUL WOUENDJI.

Ecobank São Tomé: Edificio HB, Traversa de Pelorinho, CP 316, São Tomé; tel. 222141; fax 222672; e-mail ecobankstp@cstome.net; f. 2007; cap. US $1.5m.

Island Bank, SA: Rua de Guiné, CP 1044, São Tomé; tel. 227484; fax 227490; e-mail ceo@islandbanksa.com; internet www.islandbanksa.com; f. 2005; cap. US $1.8m. (2005); Pres. MARC WABARA; Man. Dir EDWIN F. B. KRUKRUBO.

Oceanic Bank STP: Rua Dr Palma Carlos, CP 1175, São Tomé; tel. 222689; fax 222641; f. 2008; cap. US $5.0m. (Dec. 2008); Dir PETER NWACHUKWU.

INSURANCE

Instituto de Segurança Social: Rua Soldado Paulo Ferreira, São Tomé; tel. 221382; e-mail inss@cstome.net; f. as Caixa de Previdência dos Funcionários Públicos, adopted present name 1994; insurance fund for civil servants; Pres. of Admin. Bd ALBINO GRAÇA DA FONSECA; Dir JUVENAL DO ESPÍRITO SANTO.

NICON Seguros STP: Av. 12 de Julho 997, CP556, São Tomé; tel. and fax 227057; e-mail niconseguros@cstome.net; f. 2008; cap. US $1.3m.; Dir TOWOJO PIUS AGBOOLA.

SAT INSURANCE: Av. Amílcar Cabral, CP 293, São Tomé; tel. 226161; fax 226160; e-mail satinsuran@cstome.net; f. 2001; general insurance; cap. US $1.0m.; Dir MICHEL SOBGUI.

Trade and Industry

GOVERNMENT AGENCIES

Agência Nacional do Petróleo de São Tomé e Príncipe (ANP—STP): Av. Nações Unidas, CP 1048, São Tomé; tel. 226940; fax 226937; e-mail anp_geral@cstome.net; internet www.anp-stp.gov.st; f. 2004; manages and implements govt policies relating to the petroleum sector; Exec. Dir LUÍS PRAZERES.

Nigeria-São Tomé and Príncipe Joint Development Authority (JDA): Plot 1101, Aminu Kano Cres., Wuse II, Abuja, Nigeria; Praça da UCCLA, São Tomé; tel. (234) 95241069; fax (234) 95241061; e-mail enquiries@nigeriasaotomejda.com; internet www.nigeriasaotomejda.com; f. 2002; manages devt of petroleum and gas resources in Joint Development Zone; Exec. Dir Dr JORGE PEREIRA DOS SANTOS.

DEVELOPMENT ORGANIZATION

Instituto para o Desenvolvimento Económico e Social (INDES): Travessa do Pelourinho, CP 408, São Tomé; tel. 222491; fax 221931; e-mail indes@cstome.net; f. 1989 as Fundo Social e de Infrastructuras; adopted present name 1994; channels foreign funds to local economy; Dir HOMERO JERÓNIMO SALVATERRA.

CHAMBER OF COMMERCE

Câmara do Comércio, Indústria, Agricultura e Serviços (CCIAS): Av. Marginal de 12 de Julho, CP 527, São Tomé; tel. 222723; fax 221409; e-mail ccias@cstome.net; internet www2.cciastp.org; Pres. ABÍLIO AFONSO HENRIQUES.

UTILITIES

Electricity and Water

Empresa de Água e Electricidade (EMAE): Av. Água Grande, CP 46, São Tomé; tel. 222096; fax 222488; e-mail emae@cstome.net; f. 1979; state electricity and water co; privatized in 2004; Dir-Gen. Lt-Col ÓSCAR SOUSA.

MAJOR COMPANIES

Empresa Industrial de Madeiras (EIM): Fruta Fruta, CP 137, Água Grande; tel. 222475; fax 222925; e-mail eim@cstome.net; mfrs of wood products.

Empresa Nacional de Combustíveis e Óleos (ENCO): Rua da Guiné, CP 50, São Tomé; tel. 222275; fax 222972; e-mail enco_1@cstome.net; Dir JOSÉ GOMES BARBOSA.

Flora Speciosa: Roça de São José; e-mail informacoes@floraspeciosa.com; internet www.floraspeciosa.com; f. 2003; production and international distribution of tropical flowers.

Sociedade de Construção Civil, SA (CONSTROMÉ): Av. 12 de Julho, CP 551, São Tomé; tel. 221775; e-mail constrome@cstome.net; construction.

TRADE UNIONS

Federação Nacional dos Pequenos Agricoltores (FENAPA): Rua Barão de Água Izé, São Tomé; tel. 224741; Pres. COSME CABEÇA.

Organização Nacional de Trabalhadores de São Tomé e Príncipe (ONTSTP): Rua Cabo Verde, São Tomé; tel. 222431; e-mail ontstpdis@cstome.net; Sec.-Gen. JOÃO TAVARES.

Sindicato de Jornalistas de São Tomé e Príncipe (SJS): Rua 3 de Fevereiro, São Tomé; Pres. VICTOR CORREIA.

Sindicato dos Trabalhadores do Estado (STE): São Tomé; Sec.-Gen. AURÉLIO SILVA.

União Geral dos Trabalhadores de São Tomé e Príncipe (UGSTP): Av. Kwame Nkrumah, São Tomé; tel. 222443; e-mail ugtdis@cstome.net; Sec.-Gen. COSTA CARLOS.

Transport

RAILWAYS

There are no railways in São Tomé and Príncipe.

ROADS

In 1999 there were an estimated 320 km of roads, of which 218 km were asphalted. In 2005 the European Union granted €930,000 towards upgrading the road network.

SHIPPING

The principal ports are at São Tomé city and at Neves on São Tomé island. At December 2009 São Tomé and Príncipe's registered merchant fleet comprised 28 vessels, totalling 22,025 grt.

Companhia Santomense de Navegação, SA (CSN): CP 49, São Tomé; tel. 222657; fax 221311; e-mail csn@setgrcop.com; shipping and freight forwarding.

Empresa Nacional de Administração dos Portos (ENAPORT): Largo Alfândega, CP 437, São Tomé; tel. 221841; fax 224949; e-mail enaport@cstome.net; internet www.enaport.st; Pres. ANTERO DE OLIVEIRA.

Navetur-Equatour: CP 277, Rua Viriato da Cruz, São Tomé; tel. 223781; fax 222122; e-mail navequatur@cstome.net; internet www.navetur-equatour.st; Dir-Gen. LUÍS BEIRÃO.

Transportes e Serviços, Lda (TURIMAR): Rua da Caixa, CP 48, São Tomé; tel. 221869; fax 222162; e-mail turimar@cstome.net; Man. ALBERTO PEREIRA.

CIVIL AVIATION

There is an international airport at São Tomé.

Empresa Nacional de Aeroportos e Segurança Aérea (ENASA): Aeroporto, CP 703, São Tomé; tel. 221878; fax 221154; e-mail enasa@cstome.net; Dir ARISTIDES BAROS.

Linhas Aéreas São-tomenses (LAS): Rua Santo António do Príncipe, São Tomé; tel. 227282; fax 227281; e-mail hba.saotome@gmail.com; f. 2002; owned by Aerocontractors, Nigeria; Dir ANTÓNIO AGUIAR.

SCD-Aviation: Omali Lodge Luxury Hotel, São Tomé; tel. 222350; fax 221814.

STP-Airways: Av. Marginal 12 de Julho, São Tomé; tel. 221160; fax 223449; e-mail stp-airways@cstome.net; internet www.stpairways.st; f. 2006; 35% govt-owned; Dir FELISBERTO NETO.

Tourism

The islands benefit from spectacular mountain scenery, unspoilt beaches and unique species of flora and wildlife. Although still largely undeveloped, tourism is currently one of the sectors of the islands' economy attracting most foreign investment. However, the high level of rainfall during most of the year limits the duration of the tourist season, and the expense of reaching the islands by air is also an inhibiting factor. There were 14,456 tourist arrivals in 2008, and receipts totalled some US $8.3m. in 2009.

Defence

In early 2005 the armed forces were estimated to number some 300. Military service, which is compulsory, lasts for 30 months. There is also a presidential guard numbering some 160. In 2000 Portugal and São Tomé renewed the military agreement for the stationing of the 'Aviocar' and a crew of the Portuguese Air Force in the country. Since April 1988 the aeroplane has provided humanitarian emergency flights from Príncipe to São Tomé, as well as rescue operations for local fishermen along the coast. In 2004 a paramilitary unit, trained by the Angolan Government and comprising 200 men, was created. In mid-2006 army recruitment was broadened to include women.

Defence Expenditure: Budgeted at 1,100m. dobras (excl. capital expenditure) in 2000.

Commander-in-Chief of the Armed Forces: MANUEL PINTO DA COSTA.

Chief of General Staff of the Armed Forces: Lt-Col IDALÉCIO PACHIRE.

Education

Education is officially compulsory between six and 14 years of age. It starts at the age of six and lasts for six years, comprising a first cycle of four years and a second of two years. Secondary education lasts for a further six years, comprising two cycles of three years each. According to UNESCO estimates, in 2009/10 enrolment at primary schools included 98% of children in the relevant age-group (males 97%; females 100%), while the comparable ratio for secondary enrolment in 2006/07 was 32% (males 30%; females 34%). The country's first university, Universidade Lusíada, was inaugurated in October 2006. In 2000 public investment in education (including culture and sport) amounted to US $1.3m., equivalent to 6.7% of total public investment. The budget for 2005 allocated 13.4% of total government expenditure to education.

Bibliography

Becker, K. *São Tomé and Príncipe.* Chalfont St Peter, Bradt Travel Guides, 2008.

Caldeira, A. M. *Mulheres, Sexualidade e Casamento no Arquipelago de São Tomé e Príncipe* (Seculos XV a XVII). Lisbon, Edições Cosmos, 1999.

Viagens de um piloto português do século XVI à costa de África e á São Tomé. Lisbon, Comissão Nacional para as Comemorações dos Descobrimentos Portugueses, 2000.

Cardoso, M. *Cabo Verde e São Tomé e Príncipe. Educação e infra-estruturas como factores de desenvolvimento.* Oporto, Afrontamento, 2007.

Ceita, A. *Economia de S.Tomé e Príncipe. Entre o regime do partido único e o multipartidarismo.* Lisbon, Edições Colibri, 2008.

S. Tomé e Príncipe. Problemas e Perspectivas para o seu Desenvolvimento. Lisbon, Edições Colibri, 2009.

Chabal, P., Birmingham, D., Forrest, J., Newitt, M., Seibert, G., and Andrade, E. S. *History of Postcolonial Lusophone Africa.* Bloomington, IN, Indiana University Press, and London, Hurst, 2002.

Deus Lima, J. *História do Massacre de 1952 em São Tomé e Príncipe: Em Busca de Nossa Verdadeira História.* São Tomé, 2002.

Espírito Santo, C. *A Coroa do Mar.* Lisbon, Editorial Caminho, 1998.

Almas da Elite Santomense. Lisbon, Cooperação, 2000.

Aires de Menezes—O Leão. Lisbon, Cooperação, 2001.

Enciclopédia Fundamental de São Tomé e Príncipe. Lisbon, Cooperação, 2001.

A Guerra da Trindade. Lisbon, Cooperação, 2003.

O Nacionalismo Político São-tomense. 2 vols. Lisbon, Edições Colibri, 2012.

Eyzaguirre, P. B. 'The Independence of São Tomé e Príncipe and Agrarian Reform', in *Journal of Modern African Studies,* April 1989.

'The Ecology of Swidden Agriculture and Agrarian History in São Tomé', in *Cahiers d'Etudes africaines*, Vol. XXVI, No. 101–102, 1986.

'Competing Systems of Land Tenure in an African Plantation Society', in Downs, R. E., and Reyna, S. P. (Eds), *Land and Society in Contemporary Africa.* Hanover, NH, University Press of New England, 1988.

Frynas, J. G., Wood, G., and Soares de Oliveira, R. M. S. 'Business and Politics in São Tomé and Príncipe: From Cocoa Monoculture to Petro-State', in *African Affairs*, No. 102, 2003.

Gallet, D. *São Tomé et Príncipe: Les îles du milieu du monde.* Paris, Editions Karthala, 2001.

Garfield, R. *A History of São Tomé Island 1470–1655: The Key to Guinea.* New York, Edwin Mellen Press, 1992.

Graça, C. *Memórias Políticas de um Nacionalista Santomense Sui Generis.* São Tomé, UNEAS, 2011.

Gründ, F. *Tchiloli: Charlemagne à São Tomé sur l'île du milieu du monde.* Paris, Editions Magellan & Cie, 2006.

Guedes, A. M. *Litígios e Legitimação: Estado, Sociedade Civil e Direito em São Tomé e Príncipe.* Coimbra, Almedina, 2002.

Henriques, I. C. *São Tomé e Príncipe: A Invenção de uma Sociedade.* Lisbon, Vega Editora, 2000.

Hipólito dos Santos, J. *O Desenvolvimento e a Mulher. Um outro mundo é possível.* Lisbon, SEIES, 2003.

Hodges, T., and Newitt, M. *São Tomé and Príncipe: From Plantation Colony to Microstate.* Boulder, CO, Westview Press, 1988.

Jones, P. J., Burlison, J. P., and Tye, A. *Conservação dos ecossistemas florestais da República Democrática de São Tomé e Príncipe.* Gland and Cambridge, UICN, 1991.

Liba, M. (Ed.). *Jewish Child Slaves in São Tomé.* Wellington, New Zealand Jewish Chronicle Publications, 2003.

Lloyd-Jones, S., and Costa Pinto, A. *The Last Empire. Thirty Years of Portuguese Decolonization.* Bristor and Portland, OR, Intellect Books, 2003.

Loude, J.-Y. *Coup de théâtre à São Tomé. Carnet d'enquête aux îles du milieu du monde.* Arles, Actes Sud, 2007.

Mata, I. *Polifonias Insulares. Cultura e Literaturas de São Tomé e Príncipe.* Lisbon, Edições Colibri, 2010.

Nascimento, A. *Poderes e Quotidiano nas Roças de São Tomé e Príncipe de finais de oitocentos a meados do novecentos.* Lisbon, 2002.

Órfãos de Raça: Europeus Entre a Fortuna e a Desventura no São Tomé e Príncipe Colonial. São Tomé, Instituto Camões—Centro Cultural Português, 2002.

O Sul da Diaspora: Cabo-Verdianos em Plantações de São Tomé e Príncipe e Moçambique. Praia, Presidência da República da Cabo Verde, 2003.

Desterro e Contrato: Moçambicanos a caminho de São Tomé e Príncipe (Anos 1940 a 1960). Maputo, Arquivo Histórico de Moçambique, 2003.

A Misericórdia na Voragem das Ilhas. Fragmentos da trajectória das Misericórdias de São Tomé e do Príncipe. Lisbon, 2003.

O Fim do Caminhu Longi. Mindelo, Ilhéu Editora, 2007.

Vidas de São Tomé segundo vozes de Soncente. Mindelo, Ilhéu Editora, 2008.

São Tomé e Príncipe. Atlas da Lusofonia. Lisbon, Prefácio, 2008.

Histórias da Ilha do Príncipe. Oeiras, Município de Oeiras, 2010.

Oliveira, J. E. *A Economia de São Tomé e Príncipe.* Lisbon, Instituto de Investigação Científica Tropical, 1993.

Pélissier, R. *Le Naufrage des Caravelles (1961–75).* Orgeval, Editions Pélissier, 1979.

Explorar. Voyages en Angola et autres lieux incertains. Orgeval, Editions Pélissier, 1980.

Pereira, P. A. *Das Tchiloli von São Tomé: Die Wege des karolinischen Universums.* Frankfurt am Mein, Iko Verlkag, 2002.

Pinto da Costa, M. *Terra Firme.* Porto, Afrontamento, 2011.

Ramos, J. *Quem é Quem em São Tomé e Príncipe. Who's Who.* 3rd edn. São Tomé, 2007.

Ratelband, K. *Nederlanders in West-Afrika 1600–1650: Angola, Kongo en São Tomé.* Walburg Pers, Zutphen, 2000.

da Rosa, L. C. *Die lusographe Literatur der Inseln São Tomé und Príncipe: Versuch einer literaturgeschichtlichen Darstellung.* Frankfurt am Main, TFM/Domus Editoria Euroaea, 1994.

Santos, H. *Olhares Discretos.* São Tomé, Instituto Camões—Centro Cultural Português, 2002.

Seibert, G. 'São Tomé e Príncipe: Military Coup as a Lesson?', in *Lusotopie, Enjeux contemporains dans les espaces lusophones*, Vol. 1996.

'The February 1953 Massacre in São Tomé: Crack in the Salazarist Image of Multiracial Harmony and Impetus for Nationalist Demands for Independence', in *Portuguese Studies Review*, No. 10 (2), 2003.

'The Bloodless Coup of July 16 in São Tomé e Príncipe', in *Lusotopie. Enjeux contemporains dans les espaces lusophones*, Vol. 2003.

'São Tomé e Príncipe: The Difficult Transition from International Aid Recipient to Oil Producer', in *Resource Politics in Sub-Saharan Africa.* Hamburg, IAK, 2005

Comrades, Clients and Cousins: Colonialism and Democratization in São Tomé and Príncipe. 2nd edn. Leiden, Brill Academic Publishers, 2006.

'São Tomé and Príncipe: The Troubles of Oil in an Aid-Dependent Micro-State', in *Extractive Economies and Conflicts in the Global South: Multi-regional Perspectives on Rentier Politics.* Aldershot, Ashgate Publishing, 2008.

Serafim, C. M. S. *As Ilhas de São Tomé no século XVII.* Centro de História de Além-mar, Universidade Nova de Lisboa, 2000.

Shaw, C. S. *São Tomé and Príncipe.* Oxford, Clio Press (World Bibliographical Series, Vol. 172), 1994.

Silva, O. *São Tomé et Príncipe: Ecos da Terra do Ossobó.* Lisbon, Colibri, 2004.

de Sousa Campos, F. R. *As Relações entre Portugal e São Tomé e Príncipe. Do Passado Colonial à Lusofonia.* Lisbon, Edições Colibri, 2011.

Tournadre, M. *São Tomé et Príncipe.* Aurillac, Editions Regads, 2000.

Valverde, P. *Máscara, Mato e Morte em São Tomé.* Oeiras, Celta Editora, 2000.

SENEGAL

Physical and Social Geography

R. J. HARRISON CHURCH

The Republic of Senegal, the most westerly state of mainland Africa, covers an area of 197,021 sq km (76,070 sq miles). The *de jure* population was 9,855,338, according to the census of December 2002, and had increased, according to official estimates, to 12,855,153 by mid-2011, giving a population density of 65.0 per sq km. According to the provisional results of the 2002 census, the capital, Dakar, the largest city in the country, had a population of 955,897, while Pikine, near Dakar, had a population of 768,826. Other large cities included Rufisque (284,263), Guediawaye (also near Dakar) 258,370, Thiès (237,849), Kaolack (172,305), Saint-Louis (154,555) and Mbour (153,503). In the early 2000s the authorities announced the intention of constructing a new capital city at Kébémer, north of Dakar. Senegal's southern border is with Guinea-Bissau, to the west, and with Guinea on the northern edge of the Primary sandstone outcrop of the Fouta Djallon. In the east the border is with Mali, in the only other area of bold relief in Senegal, where there are Pre-Cambrian rocks in the Bambouk mountains. The northern border with Mauritania lies along the Senegal river, navigable for small boats all the year to Podor and for two months to Kayes (Mali). The river has a wide flood plain, annually cultivated as the waters retreat. The delta soils are saline, but dams for power, irrigation and better navigation are being built or proposed. The commissioning in 1985 of the Djama dam has considerably improved navigability at the Senegal river delta. The Manantali scheme, completed in 1988, will eventually extend the all-year navigability of the river from 220 km to 924 km, as far as Kayes.

The Gambia forms a semi-enclave between part of southern Senegal and the sea, along the valley of the navigable Gambia river. This has meant that, since the colonial delimitation of the Gambia–Senegal borders in 1889, the river has played no positive role in Senegal's development and that the Casamance region, in the south, was isolated from the rest of Senegal until the opening of the Trans-Gambian Highway in 1958.

The Cap Vert (Cape Verde) peninsula, on which the capital, Dakar, stands, is of verdant appearance, resulting from exposure to south-westerly winds, and thus contrasts with the yellow dunes to the north. Basalt underlies much of Dakar, and its harbour was constructed in a sandy area east of (and sheltered by) the basaltic plateau. South of the peninsula, particularly in Casamance, the coast is a drowned one of shallow estuaries.

Apart from the high eastern and south-eastern borderlands most of the country has monotonous plains, which in an earlier period were drained by large rivers in the centre of the country. Relic valleys, now devoid of superficial water, occur in the Ferlo desert, and these built up the Sine Saloum delta north of The Gambia. In a later dry period north-east to south-west trending sand dunes were formed, giving Senegal's plains their undulating and ribbed surfaces. These plains of Cayor, Baol and Nioro du Rip are inhabited by Wolof and Serer cultivators of groundnuts and millet. The coast between Saint-Louis and Dakar has a broad belt of live dunes. Behind them, near Thiès, calcium phosphates are quarried (aluminium phosphates are also present) and phosphatic fertilizer is produced.

Although Senegal's mineral resources are otherwise relatively sparse, there are potentially valuable reserves of gold, in the south-east (production of which began in mid-1997), as well as deposits of high-grade iron ore, in considerable quantity, in the east. Reserves of natural gas are exploited offshore from Dakar, and there is petroleum off the Casamance coast.

Senegal's climate is widely varied, and the coast is remarkably cool for the latitude (Dakar 14° 38' N). The Cap Vert peninsula is particularly breezy, because it projects into the path of northerly marine trade winds. Average temperatures are in the range 18°C–31°C, and the rainy season is little more than three months in length. Inland both temperatures and rainfall are higher, and the rainy season in comparable latitudes is somewhat longer. Casamance lies on the northern fringe of the monsoonal climate. Thus Ziguinchor (12° 35' N) has four to five months' rainy season, with average annual rainfall of 1,626 mm, nearly three times that received by Dakar. The natural vegetation ranges from Sahel savannah north of about 15° N, through Sudan savannah in south-central Senegal, to Guinea savannah in Casamance, where the oil palm is common.

Recent History

KATHARINE MURISON

Following three centuries of French rule, Senegal became a self-governing member of the French Community in 1958. The Mali Federation with Soudan (now Mali) was formed in April 1959 and became independent in June 1960. However the Federation collapsed after only two months. The Republic of Senegal was proclaimed on 5 September, with Léopold Sédar Senghor, the founder of the Union Progressiste Sénégalaise (UPS), as its first President. After his Prime Minister, Mamadou Dia, was convicted of plotting a coup, Senghor assumed the premiership himself in late 1962. A new Constitution, strengthening the powers of the President, was approved in a referendum in March 1963. Later in the year the UPS won a decisive victory in elections to the Assemblée nationale, and other parties were either outlawed or absorbed into the UPS, which by 1966 was the sole legal party.

In 1970 the office of the Prime Minister was revived and assigned to a young provincial administrator, Abdou Diouf. Elections in January 1973 returned both Senghor and the UPS with substantial majorities. In 1976 Senghor announced the creation of a three-party system, comprising the UPS (later renamed the Parti Socialiste du Sénégal, PS), the Parti Démocratique Sénégalais (PDS) and a Marxist-Leninist party. At elections in February 1978 the PS won 83 of the 100 seats in the Assemblée nationale, while Senghor overwhelmingly defeated the PDS leader, Abdoulaye Wade, in the presidential election.

DIOUF'S LEADERSHIP, 1981–2000

A period of economic decline and resultant austerity measures, in conjunction with intense pressure for political reform, led to Senghor's resignation in December 1980. Diouf assumed the presidency in January 1981 and undertook to reorganize the political system, by removing restrictions on political activity and allowing the official registration of previously unofficial parties.

In February 1983 Diouf led the PS to a clear victory in presidential and legislative elections. Diouf received 83.5% of the votes cast, and the PS candidates for the enlarged Assemblée nationale secured 111 of the 120 seats.

Preliminary results of the February 1988 presidential and legislative elections indicated decisive victories for both Diouf and the PS. The PDS alleged widespread fraud, and Wade and Amath Dansokho, the leader of the Marxist-Leninist Parti de l'Indépendance et du Travail (PIT), were arrested, together with other opposition activists. The official results allocated 73.2% of the votes cast in the presidential election to Diouf and 25.8% to Wade, while the PS returned 103 deputies to the Assemblée nationale and the PDS 17. Trials began in April for incitement to violence and attacks on the internal security of the State. Dansokho and five others were acquitted, but in May Wade received a one-year suspended prison sentence, while three other PDS activists received prison terms of between six months and two years. However, all those who had been convicted of involvement in the post-election violence were included in a presidential amnesty later in the month.

In October 1989 the Assemblée nationale approved a series of electoral reforms. Changes to the electoral code were intended to ensure a fair system of voter registration; a new system of partial proportional representation was to be introduced for legislative elections; and opposition parties were to be granted access to the state media. Many parties boycotted municipal and rural elections in November 1990 (at which the PS reportedly received the support of 70% of voters), claiming that Senegal's electoral code still permitted widespread malpractice.

Constitutional Concessions

In March 1991 the Assemblée nationale approved several constitutional amendments, notably the restoration of the post of Prime Minister. It was also agreed that opposition parties would, henceforth, be allowed to participate in government. Accordingly, in April Habib Thiam, a former premier, was restored to the post. His Government included four representatives of the PDS, among them Wade, as well as Dansokho. In September the Assemblée nationale adopted a series of amendments to the electoral code. Under the amended code, the presidential election would, henceforth, take place every seven years, in two rounds if necessary (to ensure that the President would be elected by at least one-quarter of registered voters and by an absolute majority of votes cast), and an individual would be limited to a maximum of two terms of office. In October 1992 the PDS ministers resigned from the Government, stating that they had been excluded from the governmental process.

Eight candidates contested the presidential election of February 1993. According to official results, Diouf was re-elected, with 58.4% of the votes cast (51.6% of the electorate had voted), while Wade secured 32.0%.

Post-election Unrest

The PS won 84 seats at elections to the Assemblée nationale on 9 May 1993, while the PDS, with considerable support in urban areas, took 27 seats. Participation by voters was only 40.7%. Shortly after the announcement of the results the Vice-President of the Constitutional Council, Babacar Sèye, was assassinated. Although an organization styling itself the Armée du Peuple claimed responsibility, Wade and three other PDS leaders were detained for three days in connection with the murder. Four people suspected of involvement in Sèye's murder were subsequently arrested: among those detained were Samuel Sarr, a close associate of Wade, and a PDS deputy, Mody Sy.

Wade and the PDS were excluded from Thiam's new Government, which was formed in June 1993. Dansokho, who had supported Diouf's presidential campaign, retained his position in the Council of Ministers, while other ministerial appointments included Abdoulaye Bathily, the leader of the Ligue Démocratique—Mouvement pour le Parti du Travail (LD—MPT), and Serigne Diop, the leader of a PDS splinter group, the Parti Démocratique Sénégalais—Rénovation (PDS—R).

In October 1993 Wade was charged with complicity in the assassination of Sèye, and Wade's wife and a PDS deputy were charged with 'complicity in a breach of state security', although none was detained. In November Ousmane Ngom and Landing Savané, the leader of And Jëf—Parti Africain pour la Démocratie et le Socialisme (AJ—PADS), were among those arrested following a protest in Dakar to demand the cancellation of austerity measures introduced three months earlier. Ngom, Savané and more than 80 others were convicted of participating in an unauthorized demonstration and received six-month suspended prison sentences.

Diouf was regarded as a principal architect of the 50% devaluation, in January 1994, of the CFA franc, and the opposition accused the President of responsibility for resultant hardships. A demonstration in Dakar in February degenerated into serious rioting, as a result of which eight people were killed. Wade, Savané and more than 70 others were subsequently detained and charged with attacks on state security. Legal proceedings against them and 140 others implicated in the unrest were dismissed in July on the grounds of insufficient evidence. In May charges against Wade and his associates in connection with the murder of Sèye had also been dismissed. In October three of those accused of Sèye's murder were convicted and sentenced to between 18 and 20 years' imprisonment, with hard labour.

During the latter part of 1994 both the Government and opposition expressed their desire to restore a national consensus. In March 1995 Thiam named a new Council of Ministers, which included five PDS members, with Wade designated Minister of State at the Presidency.

Elections and Political Sequels

In January 1996 Diouf announced that a Sénat was to be established as a second chamber of the legislature. At regional, rural and municipal elections in November, the PS won control of all regions, all principal towns and the majority of rural communities.

An electoral verification body, the Observatoire National des Élections (ONEL), which was to operate under the aegis of the Ministry of the Interior was created in August 1997; its nine members were to be appointed by the President, after consultations with various interested parties. Although the proposed new body fell short of the opposition's demands for a fully independent electoral commission, the Assemblée nationale overwhelmingly approved legislation providing for the creation of the ONEL.

In late 1997 serious divisions within the PS emerged, with the creation of a dissident grouping led by Kâ. In response to indications that the group was intending to present an independent list of candidates in the 1998 legislative elections, 11 of its leading members, including Kâ, were suspended from the PS for three months. In March 1998 Kâ and his associates duly submitted a separate list of candidates for the elections, under the name Union pour le Renouveau Démocratique (URD), and resigned from the PS. The URD formed an electoral alliance with two left-wing parties and the Alliance pour le Progrès et la Justice—Jëf-Jël (APJ—JJ). Also in March, the Assemblée nationale voted to increase the number of deputies from 120 members to 140, despite opposition from the PDS. Wade announced in late March that the PDS had withdrawn from the Government.

Following the legislative elections, which took place on 24 May 1998 and were contested by a total of 18 parties and coalitions, the PS held 93 seats in the enlarged parliament, while the number of PDS deputies was reduced to 23; Kâ's URD-APJ—JJ alliance secured 11 seats. The rate of participation by voters was only 39% of the registered electorate. Ngom resigned from the PDS in June 1998, following his demotion from the party's deputy chairmanship by Wade, and subsequently formed the Parti Libéral Sénégalais (PLS).

In July 1998 Thiam resigned as Prime Minister; he was replaced by Mamadou Lamine Loum, the Minister of the Economy, Finance and Planning. Loum appointed a Council of Ministers that contained only one non-PS minister (Serigne Diop, Secretary-General of the PDS—R, as Keeper of the Seals, Minister of Justice).

In August 1998 the Assemblée nationale voted to revise the Constitution to remove the clause restricting the President to a maximum of two terms of office. The requirement that a President be elected by more than 25% of all registered voters was also removed. The opposition parties, which described the reforms as a constitutional coup, boycotted the vote on the reforms.

The PS won all 45 seats contested in elections to the new 60-member Sénat on 24 January 1999; these 45 senators were elected by members of the Assemblée nationale, together with local, municipal and regional councillors. In addition, 12 senators, including two opposition leaders, were chosen by the President of the Republic, and three were elected by Senegalese resident abroad. Only the PS, the PLS and a coalition of the PIT and AJ—PADS participated in the elections. The main opposition parties had urged a boycott of the poll, describing the new chamber as unnecessary and costly.

In March 1999 a left-wing alliance of AJ—PADS, the PIT, the PDS and the LD—MPT agreed to nominate Wade as their joint candidate in the presidential election scheduled for 2000. In June 1999 Moustapha Niasse, a former Minister of Foreign Affairs and Senegalese Abroad, also announced his intention of contesting the election. Niasse, a founder member of the PS, published a document criticizing the policies of Diouf and accusing the party of corruption; he subsequently formed his own party, the Alliance des Forces de Progrès (AFP).

THE WADE PRESIDENCY

Campaigning for the February 2000 presidential election began in earnest with Wade's return to Senegal in October 1999 after a year of voluntary exile. Wade quickly succeeded in winning an endorsement from influential members of the Islamic Mouride brotherhood.

In the presidential election, held on 27 February 2000, Diouf failed to win an overall majority, and Diouf and Wade therefore proceeded to a second round of voting. The three most successful candidates were Diouf with 41.3%, Wade with 31.0% and Niasse with 16.8%. Overall turn-out was estimated at 61.0%. In the following weeks Wade succeeded in gathering the support of Niasse and of the other opposition candidates, with the exception of Kâ, who lent his support to Diouf. At the second round of the election, held on 19 March, Wade gained a substantial victory, winning 58.5% of the vote. Turn-out was estimated at 60.1%. Wade's Government was inaugurated in April, with Niasse as Prime Minister and Maj.-Gen. Mamadou Niang as Minister of the Interior.

Early in his tenure, Wade declared his priorities to be restoring peace in Casamance, applying the principle of transparency to the administration and guaranteeing the independence of the judiciary. He also promised to reform the agricultural sector, to attract foreign investment and to solve the country's youth unemployment problems. However, with the PS remaining the largest party in the Assemblée nationale and the Sénat, there remained the prospect of an institutional crisis. In May 2000 Wade promised to submit his preferred constitutional revisions to a referendum, with a view to calling new legislative elections in 2001.

Approval of a New Constitution

The new draft of the Constitution presented to a national referendum on 7 January 2001 included the following significant revisions: a reduction in the presidential term of office from seven to five years; a transfer of some powers from the President to the Prime Minister; the abolition of the Sénat; a reduction in the number of Assemblée nationale seats (from 140 to 120); the reintroduction of the requirement that a President be elected by more than 25% of all registered voters; and the introduction of a revised system of partial proportional representation (using a combination of national and regional lists of candidates). The major parties, including the PS, endorsed these amendments and, in the event, some 94.0% of those voting (65.8% of the registered electorate) supported the changes.

In March 2001 Wade dismissed Niasse and other members of the AFP from the Government, effectively forcing the party into opposition ahead of the parliamentary elections. Mame Madior Boye, hitherto Minister of Justice and a non-partisan member of the Government, was appointed Prime Minister, becoming the first female premier of Senegal. In the general election of 29 April the PDS-led Sopi (Change) Coalition won a resounding victory, with a substantial majority of seats (89 of 120). The AFP and the PS won 11 and 10 seats, respectively. Electoral participation was measured at 67.5%. Boye was reappointed as Prime Minister, leading a 24-member Government comprising 11 members of the PDS, nine representatives of civil society, and two members each of AJ—PADS and the LD—MPT.

The sinking of a state-owned passenger ferry, the MV *Joola*, in September 2002, *en route* from Ziguinchor, the principal city of Casamance, to Dakar led to a national political crisis, even before the final death toll of the accident, subsequently enumerated at 1,863 people, became apparent. In early October the Minister of Capital Works and Transport, Youssouph Sakho, and the Minister of the Armed Forces, Yoba Sambou, resigned in response to the tragedy, as it became clear that the vessel had been severely overloaded; only 64 survivors were reported. Later in the month the head of the navy was dismissed, and Wade announced that the Government accepted responsibility for the disaster. In November Wade dismissed Boye and her Government. Shortly afterwards an inquiry into the incident found that safety regulations had been widely violated on the *Joola*, and that the dispatch of rescue equipment and staff to the ship by the armed forces had been inexplicably delayed. Idrissa Seck, a close ally of Wade and previously a senior official in the PDS, was appointed as the new Prime Minister. In August 2003 the Chief of Staff of the Armed Forces and the Chief of Staff of the Air Force were dismissed as a result of disciplinary action related to the response to the sinking of the *Joola*.

Political tensions intensified in early 2004 as several parties that had supported Wade's candidacy in the presidential election of 2000 and had ministerial representation in the Government, including the LD—MPT and AJ—PADS, declined to participate in celebrations organized to mark the fourth anniversary of Wade's accession to power. In April 2004 Wade dismissed Seck's Government, appointing Macky Sall, hitherto Minister of State, Minister of the Interior and Local Communities, Government Spokesperson, as the new premier.

In January 2005 the Assemblée nationale approved controversial legislation granting amnesty to perpetrators of election-related or politically motivated offences committed between 1983 and 2004, irrespective of whether they had been tried or not, and to all those involved in the murder of Babacar Sèye in May 1993 (see above). In February 2005 the Constitutional Council rejected an opposition appeal to declare the general amnesty unconstitutional, but ruled that the article specifically relating to Sèye's assassination did not conform with the Constitution. Wade subsequently promulgated the general amnesty law. (The three people convicted in October 1994 of Sèye's murder had been pardoned by Wade in February 2002.)

The two LD—MPT members of the Council of Ministers were dismissed and replaced with members of the PDS in March 2005, leaving AJ—PADS as the only party (other than the PDS) to retain ministerial representation from the alliance that supported Wade's presidential candidacy in 2000. The dismissals followed several months of discord between the PDS and the LD—MPT over the latter's criticism of Wade's presidency and its opposition to the amnesty legislation. Amid tensions within the PDS, a further reorganization of the Government in May was interpreted as an attempt to strengthen support for the President, ahead of legislative elections due in 2006. New appointees included Awa Fall Diop, of AJ—PADS, as Minister of Relations with the Institutions, while the party's leader, Landing Savané, hitherto Minister of State, Minister of Industry and Crafts, became a Minister of State at the Presidency. Abdoulaye Diop remained Minister of the Economy and Finance, but was elevated to the position of Minister of State.

Seck was questioned by police in mid-July 2005, after he was accused by President Wade of overspending on work to upgrade roads in Thiès, where he served as mayor. The former Prime Minister refuted any suggestion that he had misappropriated government funds intended for the project. Later that month Seck was formally charged with endangering national security; there was no immediate explanation of the charges, which Seck's defence lawyers claimed to be politically motivated. In August the Assemblée nationale ruled that Seck and the Minister of Property, Housing and Construction, Salif Bâ, should be tried on embezzlement charges by the High Court of Justice, which is convened only to judge cases concerning offences allegedly committed by government members in the exercise of their duties. A few days later Bâ resigned from the Council of Ministers; he was replaced by Oumar Sarr in an ensuing minor reshuffle. Meanwhile, Seck and three other party officials close to the former Prime Minister were expelled from the PDS, having been accused of engaging in divisive activities. In October Seck was additionally charged with illegally sending correspondence from prison.

Despite strong resistance from opposition parties, in December 2005 the Assemblée nationale approved a proposal by Wade to extend deputies' mandates until February 2007, to allow legislative and presidential elections to be held concurrently. Opposition leaders claimed that the postponement was intended to give the PDS more time to resolve ongoing friction within the party.

Seck was released from prison in February 2006 after the High Court of Justice partially dismissed the charges of corruption and embezzlement against him owing to insufficient evidence; he had been cleared of endangering national security in the previous month. Bâ had been provisionally freed in January for health reasons. (The charges against Bâ were reportedly dismissed in January 2008 on the grounds of insufficient evidence.) In April 2006 Seck declared his candidacy for the presidential election, and in September he formed a new political party, Rewmi (Nation). Meanwhile, several opposition parties, including the AFP, the LD—MPT, the PIT, the PR and the PS, announced the formation of the Coalition Populaire pour l'Alternative (CPA) to contest the legislative and presidential elections.

In November 2006 the Assemblée nationale adopted a constitutional amendment abolishing the requirement that a presidential candidate receiving a majority of votes in an election also secure the support of at least one-quarter of all registered voters to be elected at a first round of voting. A few days later the legislature also approved an increase in the number of deputies from 120 to 150. President Wade appointed several new ministers from minor opposition parties to the Government in late November.

The elections to the Assemblée nationale were further postponed in January 2007, until 3 June, after the Council of State ruled that the distribution of legislative seats between constituencies had been inequitable. Opposition parties had complained that the President had allocated more seats to certain constituencies despite their populations being lower than those of others. In late January the Assemblée nationale approved the re-establishment of the Sénat, six years after its abolishment owing to economic concerns; 65 of its 100 members were to be appointed by the President.

Presidential and Legislative Elections of 2007

The presidential election, which took place, as scheduled, on 25 February 2007, was contested by 15 candidates and marked by a high turn-out of 70.6%. Wade won 55.9% of the valid votes cast, thus securing re-election without the need for a second round of voting. His closest rivals were Seck, with 14.9%, Ousmane Tanor Dieng, the First Secretary of the PS, with 13.6%, and the AFP's Niasse, with 5.9%. Wade was sworn in to serve a second term of office on 3 April.

Seventeen opposition parties, including the AFP, the LD—MPT, the PIT, the PS and Rewmi, grouped in an alliance styled the Front Siggil Sénégaal (FSS, Restoring Dignity to Senegal), boycotted the legislative elections. The PDS-led Sopi Coalition consequently secured an overwhelming majority in the enlarged Assemblée nationale on 3 June 2007, winning 131 of the 150 seats. Twelve of the other 13 parties and coalitions that participated in the polls secured legislative representation, although none of them took more than three seats. The lack of effective opposition and the extremely low turn-out, of 34.7%, threatened to undermine the legitimacy of the new legislature. On 19 June, following Macky Sall's resignation, the President appointed a new Prime Minister, Cheikh Hadjibou Soumaré, hitherto Minister-delegate at the Office of the Minister of State, Minister of the Economy and Finance, responsible for the Budget. The appointment of Soumaré, who was unaffiliated to any political party, was regarded as an attempt by Wade to ease tensions within the PDS over the question of who would succeed him at the end of his second, and final, term in office. Sall was subsequently elected as President of the Assemblée nationale.

Deputies and local, municipal and regional councillors elected 35 of the 100 members of the Sénat on 19 August 2007. The polls were boycotted by the FSS, which opposed the reinstatement of the second chamber, notably on the grounds that Wade was to appoint nearly two-thirds of its membership. The PDS secured 34 of the elective seats, while AJ—PADS took one. The Sénat was installed in September, following Wade's nomination of the remaining 65 senators. In October Pape Diop, President of the Assemblée nationale in 2001–07 and mayor of Dakar since 2002, was elected unopposed as the President of the Sénat.

Wade's Second Term

There was evidence of divisions within the PDS in late 2007. In November the leadership of the party decided to abolish the position of PDS Deputy Secretary-General, which was held by Sall. Relations between Wade and Sall had reportedly been strained since Sall had summoned Wade's son, Karim, the President of the Agence Nationale de l'Organisation de la Conférence Islamique, to appear before the Assemblée nationale to answer questions regarding road and hotel construction projects being managed by the agency in preparation for the summit of the Organisation of the Islamic Conference being held in Dakar in March 2008. Meanwhile, there was speculation that Wade favoured Karim as his successor at the head of the PDS and the country.

Wade reorganized the Council of Ministers at the end of March 2008. Among other changes, Ousmane Ngom, hitherto Minister of State, Minister of the Interior, was appointed as Minister of State, Minister of Mines, Industry and Small and Medium-sized Enterprises, being replaced by Cheikh Tidiane Sy, while Madické Niang, a close ally of Wade, who was hitherto responsible for mines and industry, succeeded Sy as Minister of State, Keeper of the Seals, Minister of Justice.

In October 2008 Wade promulgated a constitutional amendment extending the presidential term of office from five years to seven (with effect from the next election, due in 2012). Opposition parties had denounced the revision, insisting that it should be subject to a popular referendum. A PDS-proposed reduction in the mandates of the Presidents of the Assemblée nationale and the Sénat from five years to a renewable term of one year (which was to be applied to the incumbents) was also approved in October. The vote was boycotted by opposition legislators and supporters of Sall, who believed that the amendment was solely intended to marginalize the former Prime Minister. In the following month the Assemblée nationale voted in favour of a resolution to remove Sall from his post. Sall immediately resigned from the PDS and from the positions to which he had been elected as a representative of the PDS (deputy and mayor of Fatick), accusing the party's leadership of attempting to undermine his potential candidacy at the presidential election due in 2012, and subsequently formed a new political party, the Alliance pour la République (APR)—Yakaar (Hope). Mamadou Seck, a former government minister reported to be close to Wade, was elected as the new President of the Assemblée nationale. A Supreme Court was inaugurated in November, replacing the Court of Cassation and the Council of State.

Joining forces in the coalition Benno Siggil Senegaal (Unite for a Strong Senegal), the opposition performed well at the local elections on 22 March 2009, gaining control of Dakar and several other major towns, while Sall was re-elected as mayor of Fatick, representing the APR. None the less, Karim Wade was elected to public office for the first time, winning a seat on the municipal council of Dakar as a candidate of the ruling Sopi Coalition. The opposition's strong performance was attributed to public discontent with rising consumer prices and power shortages. Soumaré tendered his Government's resignation in April, and was replaced as Prime Minister by Souleymane Ndéné Ndiaye, hitherto Minister of State, Minister of the Maritime Economy, Maritime Transport, Fisheries and Fishbreeding. Karim Wade was notably included in the new Council of Ministers appointed in May, as Minister of State, Minister of International Co-operation, Land Settlement, Air Transport and Infrastructure. In mid-May the Assemblée nationale adopted a constitutional amendment providing for the creation of the post of Vice-President, to be appointed by the President; the legislation was approved by the Sénat a few days later. Following speculation that Karim Wade was being prepared as a potential successor to his father, in September President Wade declared his intention to seek a third term in office at the presidential election due in 2012.

Cheikh Tidiane Gadio, Minister of Foreign Affairs since Wade came to power in 2000, was replaced by Madické Niang, hitherto Minister of State, Minister of Justice and Keeper of the Seals, in a government reorganization in early October 2009. Although no official reason was given for Gadio's departure, observers noted his apparently difficult relationship with Karim Wade and his purported disagreement with President Wade's controversial support for the military junta that seized power in neighbouring Guinea in December 2008. (In May 2010 Gadio established a new opposition party, the Mouvement Politique Citoyen.) Further government changes were effected in mid-October 2009: Abdoulaye Baldé, the mayor of Ziguinchor, was appointed as Minister of State, Minister of the Armed Forces, succeeding Bécaye Diop (also from Casamance), who was allocated the interior portfolio, which Cheikh Tidiane Sy had relinquished on health grounds.

President Wade again reorganized the Council of Ministers in June 2010. Tidiane Sy notably returned to the Government as Minister of State, Minister of Justice and Keeper of the Seals, following the dismissal of Amadou Sall, who had only held the post since December 2009. Wade reshuffled three of his ministers of state in September: Ngom resumed the post of Minister of the Interior, Diop became Minister of the Armed Forces and Baldé moved to the Ministry of Mines, Industry, Agro-industry and Small and Medium-sized Enterprises. In a further change in October, Samuel Sarr was dismissed as Minister of State, Minister of Energy, following several weeks of protests against persistent power cuts. Karim Wade was allocated the energy portfolio, becoming Minister of State, Minister of International Co-operation, Air Transport, Infrastructure and Energy, while an audit into the state electricity company was also announced.

Debate surrounding the legality of Wade's desire to contest a third term in office intensified from mid-2010. Although the 2001 Constitution imposed a two-term limit, the PDS maintained that, as Wade had first been elected in 2000, under the previous Constitution (from which a clause restricting the President to a maximum of two terms of office had been removed in 1998), he was entitled to stand for a further presidential mandate in 2012. In August 2010 the PS condemned the appointment of Cheikh Tidiane Diakhaté, a purported ally of Wade, as President of the Constitutional Council, the institution that would be responsible for resolving any dispute over the constitutionality of a third term. Despite the controversy, in November the management committee of the PDS endorsed Wade's candidacy for the presidential election scheduled for 26 February 2012; only former Prime Minister Idrissa Seck, who had rejoined the party in 2009, and two other members of the committee dissented, with the remaining 63 in favour. None the less, further indications of opposition to Wade's intention to contest the 2012 election emerged from within the PDS in 2011. Seck, who had continued to challenge Wade's presidential candidacy, was expelled from the PDS in April.

Meanwhile, amid rising social tensions, four people were detained for several days in March 2011 in connection with an alleged conspiracy to overthrow the Government, before being released without charge. Opposition parties claimed that the arrests were designed to disrupt planned anti-Government demonstrations, which none the less proceeded, together with a number of pro-Government rallies, on 19 March, marking the 11th anniversary of Wade's election in 2000. Tidiane Sy, who had announced the alleged coup plot, resigned as Minister of State, Minister of Justice and Keeper of the Seals in May, while magistrates were participating in a four-day 'go-slow' protest in support of their demand for greater judicial independence. However, he was reappointed to the post several days later as part of a minor government reorganization.

Further controversy arose in mid-June 2011, when the Council of Ministers adopted draft constitutional amendments creating an elected post of Vice-President (with an automatic right of succession in the event of the President's death) and lowering the threshold required for an outright victory in the first round of a presidential election from 50% to 25%. Opposition and civil society organizations denounced the proposals, claiming that Wade hoped to pass power to Karim Wade through the establishment of a vice-presidency and to facilitate his own re-election in February 2012 by avoiding a run-off ballot. However, following violent protests outside the Assemblée nationale on 23 June, as deputies were debating the proposed changes, the Government withdrew the draft legislation. Around 100 people were reportedly injured in clashes with the security forces, which had fired tear gas and rubber bullets in an attempt to disperse the demonstrators.

In July 2011, as the newly formed Mouvement du 23 Juin (M23) prepared to protest against Wade's re-election bid, the Government announced a ban on demonstrations in central Dakar, citing security reasons. The rally organized by M23, which comprised various civil society and opposition groups, was moved to an alternative location, while a pro-Government demonstration also took place on the same day. In late July Wade transferred responsibility for the organization of elections from Minister of State, Minister of the Interior Ngom to a newly appointed Minister in charge of Elections, Cheikh Guèye. The dismissal of Ngom was one of M23's principal demands.In November expected opposition presidential candidates Ousmane Tanor Dieng and Moustapha Niasse, who had come third and fourth in the 2007 contest, rejected an offer from Wade of cabinet positions in a post-election administration in exchange for co-operation in the forthcoming poll.

Wade was unanimously nominated as the PDS presidential candidate at a party conference in Dakar in December 2011. On the previous day one person had been killed in clashes between supporters of Wade and opposition members. Barthélémy Dias, the PS mayor of the Mermoz Sacré-Cœur district of the capital, was subsequently arrested and charged with murder, assault and illegal possession of a weapon in connection with the death; Dias claimed that he had fired in self-defence at PDS activists attacking his office. (Dias was provisionally released in May 2012 and elected to the Assemblée nationale at the legislative elections held in July.) The inclusion of Wade among the 14 presidential candidates approved by the Constitutional Court in January 2012 prompted further violent unrest in Dakar and elsewhere, in which one police officer was killed in the capital and an elderly woman and a teenager were reportedly shot dead by the security forces in the northern town of Podor. The candidacies of Dieng, Niasse and former Prime Ministers Macky Sall and Idrissa Seck were also endorsed, but that of popular musician Youssou N'Dour was notably rejected, on the grounds that his application was not supported by the required number of verifiable signatures. Protests against Wade's participation in the election continued in February, in defiance of a ban on demonstrations, leading to several arrests and further reported casualties.

THE 2012 PRESIDENTIAL AND LEGISLATIVE ELECTIONS

Despite the unrest of the preceding few months, the first round of the presidential election took place in largely peaceful conditions on 26 February 2012, as scheduled. Wade won the largest share of the valid votes cast, with 34.8%, followed by Sall, representing the APR, who secured 26.6%, Niasse (13.3%), Dieng (11.3%) and Seck (7.9%); the remaining nine candidates each received less than 2% of the vote. A turn-out of 51.6% was recorded. As Wade failed to win an overall majority, he and Sall contested a second round of polling on 25 March, at which Sall, having secured the support of the other main opposition candidates, was victorious, taking 65.8% of the valid votes cast. Wade swiftly conceded defeat, thus easing fears of continued political tensions. The turn-out at the run-off vote was 55.0%.

Sall was inaugurated as President on 2 April 2012. Although elected to serve a seven-year term, he pledged to reduce the presidential term of office to five years and to maintain the two-term limit. The new President also promised to focus on poverty alleviation, vowing to lower the prices of basic goods by cutting public expenditure through measures such as halving the size of the Government and reducing Senegal's diplomatic representation. Sall appointed Abdoul Mbaye, a former banker who was not affiliated to any political party, as his Prime Minister. The new Council of Ministers comprised 25 members, compared with the 40 ministers in the outgoing administration, and included Amadou Kane, also a banker, as Minister of the Economy and Finance, Alioune Badara Cissé as Minister of Foreign Affairs and Senegalese Nationals Abroad and N'Dour as Minister of Culture and Tourism. Shortly after taking office Sall's Government initiated a probe into potential wrongdoing by members of Wade's administration.

Elections to the Assemblée nationale took place on 1 July 2012, having been postponed from 17 June to allow more time for preparations. Although 13 of the 24 parties and alliances that participated in the elections secured representation, a coalition of some 12 parties supporting President Sall, Benno Bok Yakaar (United in Hope), won a strong majority, with a total of 119 of the 150 seats. The previously dominant PDS took only 12 seats, while a breakaway group from the former ruling party, Bokk Gis Gis (led by the President of the Sénat, Pape Diop), obtained four seats, as did Bës du Niak. At 36.7%, the turn-out was significantly lower than those recorded in the two rounds of presidential voting, but slightly higher than at the 2007 legislative elections, which had been boycotted by most opposition parties. As a result of legislation adopted in 2010 that provided for gender parity in the candidates presented by each party, 64 women were elected to the new parliament, compared with 27 in the 2007 polls. Former Prime Minister Niasse, the leader of the AFP (a member of the presidential coalition), was elected as President of the Assemblée nationale at the end of July 2012, defeating Oumar Sarr of the PDS. Senatorial elections were scheduled to be held on 16 September. However, in mid-September members of the Assemblée nationale voted to abolish the upper chamber (and the position of Vice-President). Sall had suggested the change as a cost saving measure and intended to use the funds to provide assistance to the victims of recent flooding.

SEPARATISM IN CASAMANCE

The emergence in the early 1980s of the separatist Mouvement des Forces Démocratiques de la Casamance (MFDC) presented the Senegalese authorities with considerable security difficulties in the southern region of Casamance, which is virtually isolated from the rest of Senegal by The Gambia. After demonstrations in the regional capital, Ziguinchor, in December 1982, several leaders of the MFDC were detained without trial. In January 1986 a leading Casamance independence campaigner was sentenced to life imprisonment, while other demonstrators received prison sentences ranging from two to 15 years. However, almost 100 detainees were provisionally released in April 1987, and a further 320 separatists reportedly benefited under the conditions of the May 1988 presidential amnesty.

The MFDC initiated an offensive in 1990 with a series of attacks in the Casamance region. Tensions escalated when military reinforcements were dispatched to the region, and in September 1990 a military Governor was appointed for Casamance. By April 1991 at least 100 people were reported to have been killed as a result of violence in the region. In that month renewed action by separatists violated a truce that had apparently been negotiated by leaders of the MFDC and the new Thiam Government. The release of more than 340 detainees who had been arrested in connection with the unrest in Casamance (including Fr Augustin Diamacouné Senghor, the Secretary-General and executive leader of the MFDC) facilitated the conclusion, at talks in Guinea-Bissau, of a cease-fire agreement by representatives of the Senegalese Government and the MFDC in May. In June, as part of the demilitarization envisaged in the cease-fire accord, the military Governor was replaced by a civilian. An amnesty was ratified by the Assemblée nationale later in June, benefiting some 400 Casamançais (including separatists released in the previous month).

In January 1992 a peace commission, comprising government representatives and members of the MFDC, was established, with mediation by Guinea-Bissau. However, a resurgence of violence from July prompted the Government to redeploy armed forces in the region. This gave rise to MFDC protests that the 'remilitarization' of Casamance was in contravention of the cease-fire agreement. Evidence emerged of a split within the MFDC. The 'Front nord' and the MFDC Vice-President, Sidi Badji, appealed to the rebels to lay down their arms. The other faction, known as the 'Front Sud', led by Diamacouné Senghor (himself now based in Guinea-Bissau), appeared determined to continue the armed struggle.

After an escalation of the conflict in late 1992 and early 1993, in which more than 500 people were killed and tens of thousands forced to leave their homes, a new round of negotiations resulted in the signing of a cease-fire agreement, known as the Ziguinchor Accord, in July 1993. Guinea-Bissau was to act as a guarantor of the agreement, and the Government of France was to be asked to submit an historical arbitration regarding the Casamance issue. In December France issued its judgment that Casamance had not existed as an autonomous territory prior to the colonial period, and that independence for the region had been neither demanded nor considered at the time of decolonization.

From early 1995 renewed violence near the border with Guinea-Bissau indicated a re-emergence of divisions between the two factions of the MFDC. Rebels in the south were reportedly frustrated at the slow progress of the dialogue between the MFDC and the authorities, and accused the Senegalese armed forces of violating the provisions of the Ziguinchor Accord. Diamacouné Senghor was placed under house arrest in Ziguinchor in April, and the other members of the MFDC 'Political Bureau' were transported to Dakar and imprisoned. In June MFDC rebels announced an end to their cease-fire, again accusing the government forces of violating the 1993 Accord. Renewed violence in the south-west resulted in some 60 deaths.

In September 1995 the Government established a Commission Nationale de Paix (CNP). Violence intensified, however. In December Diamacouné Senghor made a televised appeal to the MFDC rebels to lay down their arms. He proposed that preliminary talks between his organization and the CNP take place in early 1996, to be followed by peace negotiations in a neutral country. The members of the MFDC 'Political Bureau' were released from house arrest in December 1995. Salif Sadio, the MFDC military leader, confirmed observance of a truce in January 1996, and preliminary discussions between the MFDC and the CNP took place in that month. After disagreements over the terms and location of further peace talks, there was a breakdown in negotiations in April.

There was renewed optimism regarding the possible resumption of negotiations between a united MFDC and the authorities, following discussions in July 1996 between Diamacouné Senghor and Diouf's personal Chief of Staff in Ziguinchor. However, in March 1997 more than 40 rebels and two members of the armed forces were killed in clashes near the border with Guinea-Bissau. The MFDC denied that it had ended its cease-fire, stating that it would investigate these incidents. In September the armed forces launched a new offensive, in which rebel forces were reported to have sustained heavy losses. A further armed forces offensive in October, the largest such operation in Casamance since the 1995 cease-fire, involved as many as 3,000 soldiers and resulted in the deaths of 12 soldiers and 80 rebels in clashes near the border with Guinea-Bissau, according to Senegalese military sources.

In January 1998 Diamacouné Senghor appealed to MFDC supporters to cease fighting and indicated that his organization would be prepared to abandon its demand for independence, on condition that the Government institute measures to ensure greater economic and social development in Casamance. However, from May 1999 dissident elements within the MFDC, whom Diamacouné Senghor accused of seeking to sabotage the peace process, launched a series of mortar attacks near Ziguinchor.

In June 1999 talks between various MFDC factions began in Banjul, the Gambian capital, although the leaders of several factions did not attend, claiming that Diamacouné Senghor was effectively a hostage of the Senegalese Government. At the meeting Léopold Sagna was confirmed as the head of the armed forces of the MFDC in place of Sadio, who was reportedly less prepared to compromise with government demands. The Senegalese authorities subsequently acceded to the MFDC's demand that Diamacouné Senghor be freed from house arrest, although his movements remained restricted.

At a meeting held in Banjul in December 1999, the Senegalese Government and the MFDC agreed to an immediate cease-fire and to create the conditions necessary to bring about lasting peace; the Governments of The Gambia and of Guinea-Bissau were to monitor the situation in the region; a further meeting between the two parties took place in January 2000. Following his election as President in March, Abdoulaye Wade announced that he would continue negotiations, but that his preference was to conduct direct dialogue with the MFDC. Wade also declared that Diamacouné Senghor would henceforth be permitted full freedom of movement.

In November 2000 members of a peace commission, headed by the Minister of the Interior, Maj.-Gen. Mamadou Niang, and by Diamacouné Senghor, signed a joint statement that envisaged a series of official meetings between the Senegalese Government and the MFDC. The Government simultaneously warned that legal action would be taken against any person actively promoting separatism. The first meeting, in mid-December, was boycotted by representatives of the 'Front Sud' of the MFDC, led by Ali Badji. However, a senior MFDC official present at the onset of negotiations, Alexandre Djiba (who had long been resident outside Senegal), subsequently reportedly met Ali Badji's representatives in Guinea-Bissau. The Senegalese Minister of the Armed Forces, Yoba Sambou, himself a native of Casamance, meanwhile stated that the Government preferred the rebels to unite into a single faction, so that more militant factions within the MFDC would not dispute the peace talks.

In February 2001 Diamacouné Senghor announced that, in order to accelerate the peace process, several senior members of the MFDC, including Sidi Badji and Djiba, had been removed from their positions. However, Sidi Badji rejected the legitimacy of his dismissal. Also in mid-February, in what was reportedly the most serious attack on civilian targets in Casamance for several years, separatist rebels killed some 13 civilians in an ambush. Both Sidi Badji and Diamacouné Senghor denied any knowledge of their supporters' involvement. In early March Diamacouné Senghor accused Sadio of being implicated in the recent killings of civilians; in mid-March the Senegalese Government issued an international arrest warrant for Sadio, who had recently been removed from Guinea-Bissau.

In mid-March 2001 Niang and Diamacouné Senghor signed a cease-fire agreement at a meeting in Ziguinchor, which provided for the release of detainees, the return of refugees, the removal of landmines (which had been utilized in the region since 1998) and for economic aid to reintegrate rebels and to ameliorate the infrastructure of Casamance. Some 16 prisoners were released several days later. The Gambian Government issued a communiqué in which it promised to prevent armed rebel groups from operating on Gambian territory. Later in March Niang and Diamacouné Senghor signed a further agreement, which provided for the disarmament of rebel groups and the confinement to barracks of military forces in Casamance. In April Wade and Sambou participated in negotiations with Diamacouné Senghor, at which other MFDC leaders, including Sidi Badji, were also present.

In May 2001, however, fighting was reported on the border with Guinea-Bissau between separatist forces and troops from Guinea-Bissau, reportedly in response to MFDC raids on villages in the region. As a result of the renewed conflict, Diamacouné Senghor postponed a proposed reconciliation forum, intended to unite the various factions of the MFDC, and a number of members of the movement, including Djiba, were expelled. As tensions between factions within the MFDC intensified, Diamacouné Senghor was removed from the position of Secretary-General of the MFDC in August, at the much-delayed reconciliation forum, and appointed as honorary President. Jean-Marie François Biagui, who had previously been involved in the French-based section of the MFDC, became Secretary-General and de facto leader. Sidi Badji, who continued to question the tactics of Diamacouné Senghor, was appointed as the organization's head of military affairs and became the dominant force in the movement.

Despite these personnel changes within the MFDC, President Wade met Diamacouné Senghor at the presidential palace in Dakar in September 2001. In response to this meeting, it was reported that the new leadership of the MFDC had suspended all further negotiations with the Government. Following further attacks by rebels, Biagui resigned as Secretary-General in November. Sidi Badji was announced as Biagui's successor, in an acting capacity, although Diamacouné Senghor rejected this appointment. In November and December MFDC rebels launched numerous attacks on civilians in Casamance.

In January 2002 Niang held talks with Diamacouné Senghor and Sidi Badji, although no date for the resumption of peace negotiations with the Government was forthcoming. In March mediators from The Gambia and Guinea-Bissau met with MFDC representatives, with the intention of establishing a timetable for the resumption of peace talks. Following continued fighting, in which several civilians were killed, some 9,000 Casamançais were reported to have fled to The Gambia by the end of June.

In August 2002, following a joint declaration signed by Diamacouné Senghor and Sidi Badji urging the resumption of peace talks between the rebels and the Government, Wade appointed an official delegation, chaired by the Second Vice-President of the Assemblée nationale and President of Ziguinchor Regional Council, Abdoulaye Faye, and including among its membership Niang and Sambou, to undertake negotiations with the MFDC. Meanwhile, the holding of an intra-Casamance conference, in early September, appeared to indicate a decline in support for separatist aspirations, as the conference produced a declaration, signed by representatives of 10 ethnic groups resident in the region, in favour of a 'definitive peace in Casamance', and which referred to the region as 'belonging to the great and single territory of Senegal'. However, the absence from the meeting of the MFDC faction loyal to Sidi Badji appeared to refute reports that the various wings of the MFDC had effectively reunited. In mid-September a further meeting between Faye and Niang, representing the Government, and Diamacouné Senghor and Sidi Badji, for the MFDC, was held in Ziguinchor. In late September five civilians, including the brother of Sambou, were killed in an attack attributed to separatist rebels north of Ziguinchor. The internal disunity of the MFDC was emphasized in October, when Biagui publicly demanded forgiveness from the people of Casamance and Senegal for the actions of the organization in a statement that was emphatically rejected by Sidi Badji. In spite of further discussions between the government commission and Diamacouné Senghor and Sidi Badji in January 2003, intermittent conflict and banditry continued in Casamance in early 2003, although by the end of April all members of the MFDC who had been imprisoned on charges other than murder had been released on bail.

In May 2003 President Wade, meeting with a delegation of MFDC leaders, including Diamacouné Senghor, at the Republican Palace in Dakar, announced that several substantive measures towards the normalization of the political and economic situation in Casamance were to be implemented, notably major infrastructural projects and the rehabilitation of damaged villages. The Assemblée nationale was to consider an amnesty for all those implicated in crimes related to the conflict, following a convention of the MFDC, to be held, at an unspecified date, in Guinea-Bissau, prior to the conclusion of final peace talks between the MFDC and the Government. Mine-clearing operations were also to commence. (Sidi Badji, who had been a notable absentee from the delegation present at the meeting, died from natural causes in late May.)

An MFDC convention, which had been postponed on two occasions, was finally held in Ziguinchor in October in the absence of hardline factions loyal to Djiba. Both Diamacouné Senghor and Biagui issued statements confirming that the conflict had ended, and announced that what was termed the emancipation of Casamance did not necessarily entail its independence from Senegal. Following the restoration of peace in Casamance, it was anticipated that some 15,000 displaced persons would return to their home villages in the Ziguinchor administrative region. In March 2004 Diamacouné Senghor removed Biagui from the post of Secretary-General of the MFDC.

In April 2004, after many months of relative peace in Casamance, it was reported that three members of the armed forces had been killed while carrying out mine-clearing operations in Guidel, some 18 km south-east of Ziguinchor, in an attack attributed to the MFDC. The MFDC held a convention in Ziguinchor in May, at which it proposed the cantonment of its combatants while observing a unilateral one-month cease-fire, in return for the withdrawal of government troops deployed in Casamance since 1982. In July the Assemblée nationale adopted legislation providing for an amnesty for all MFDC combatants; however, MFDC leaders claimed that their members had done nothing from which they required amnesty.

In September 2004 delegates at a general assembly of the MFDC dismissed Diamacouné Senghor as leader of the movement, designating him honorary President, as in 2001, and reappointed Biagui as Secretary-General and de facto leader. Biagui announced his intention to transform the MFDC into a political party, which would seek the establishment of a federal system of government, rather than full independence for Casamance. However, the MFDC remained divided. Its armed wing, known as Atika, rejected Biagui's proposals, insisting that independence remained the aim of the movement. Furthermore, Abdoulaye Diédhiou, the head of Atika, claimed that he was the sole legitimate leader of the movement on the grounds that he had the support of its fighters. Nevertheless, the Government continued to regard Diamacouné Senghor as the MFDC's leader.

On 30 December 2004 a general peace accord was signed at a ceremony in Ziguinchor by the Minister of the Interior, Ousmane Ngom, on behalf of the Government, and by Diamacouné Senghor, representing the MFDC. However, at least three factions of the MFDC—Atika, the 'Front Nord' and more hardline elements of the diaspora based in France, led by Mamadou Nkrumah Sané—refused to sign or participate in the implementation of the agreement, which provided for a cease-fire, to be followed by negotiations on political and economic development. Under the terms of the accord, the MFDC committed itself to disarming its fighters, who would be granted amnesty by the Government and integrated into paramilitary units on a voluntary basis. President Wade, who attended the ceremony, pledged that 80,000m. francs CFA from the Government and donor agencies would finance reconstruction and development programmes in Casamance. Negotiations aimed at achieving a definitive resolution of the conflict in Casamance were opened by Prime Minister Sall in February 2005 in the central town of Foundiougne, some 160 km south-east of Dakar, but were boycotted by Biagui and Diédhiou, who reportedly favoured further dialogue within the MFDC before engaging in talks with the Government. Both sides agreed to establish joint technical commissions to address reconstruction, economic and social development, and disarmament, demobilization and demining.

In June 2005 Diamacouné Senghor appointed Ansoumana Badji, formerly the MFDC's representative in Portugal, as Secretary-General of the movement. Biagui rejected Badji's appointment, and in March 2006 was reappointed by Diamacouné Senghor as Secretary-General. Meanwhile, in mid-2005 a number of attacks in Casamance were variously attributed to dissident members of the MFDC or to bandits. In October Salif Sadio, who had not participated in the recent peace negotiations, stated his intention to continue fighting for Casamance's independence. Stalled talks between the MFDC and the Government were scheduled to resume in December, but were postponed at the request of the movement, which was attempting to reconcile its various factions. One year after the signing of the peace accord, the number of armed attacks in Casamance was reported to be increasing. In March 2006 fierce fighting erupted in the border region with Guinea-Bissau between rival MFDC factions, with fighters led by Ismaïla Magne Dieme and César Badiate targeting territory held by Sadio and his supporters. The Guinea-Bissau armed forces subsequently intervened against Sadio's faction, which had established bases in northern Guinea-Bissau (see below), and by late April Sadio's forces had been expelled from Guinea-Bissau. Factional fighting continued in Casamance, however, and in June it was reported that Sadio had seized control of several villages along the Gambian border from Dieme. The Senegalese armed forces mounted an offensive against Sadio's faction in mid-August, prompting an estimated 4,500 Senegalese to cross into The Gambia to escape the unrest, while several thousand others were thought to have been internally displaced within Casamance. The army took control of Sadio's main base in October, although further clashes followed. Diamacouné Senghor died in January 2007 in a French military hospital. Later in January, following clashes between Senegalese government troops and rebels belonging to Badiate's faction near the border with Guinea-Bissau, more than 100 Senegalese were reported to have fled to northern Guinea-Bissau. After several months of relative calm, in December a member of a government-appointed committee charged with bringing peace to Casamance was one of two people killed by unidentified armed men in the village of Mahmouda, some 70 km north-west of Ziguinchor. Biagui condemned the attack.

An upsurge in violent robberies in Casamance in early 2008 was attributed to MFDC dissidents. In May two soldiers were killed in clashes with a group of armed men during a military operation to destroy a field of cannabis near Djibidione, close to the border with The Gambia. Meanwhile, the MFDC remained deeply divided following Diamacouné Senghor's death, undermining efforts to achieve a definitive peace. A further deterioration in the security situation in Casamance was reported in May and June 2009, again attributed to elements of the MFDC. The Government imposed a night-time curfew on the region's two main highways in response to the resumption of violence. Clashes took place between government forces and MFDC dissidents in Casamance in August, and in September the military bombed MFDC bases in response to the killing of a soldier. The renewed violence prompted some 600 people to flee their homes on the outskirts of Ziguinchor. In October six soldiers were killed in a grenade attack near the border with Guinea-Bissau. Two leaders of dissident factions of the MFDC were arrested in mid-March 2010, shortly before the military initiated a further offensive against rebel bases. Later that month Badiate urged the Government to resume negotiations with the MFDC, while Wade reportedly also stated his willingness to engage in talks with rebels seeking peace. None the less, the violence continued, intensifying towards the end of the year. In December, in the worst incident since October 2009, seven soldiers were killed in clashes with MFDC rebels some 35 km from Ziguinchor. Further troops and rebels were killed in heavy fighting in January and February 2011, amid concerns that the MFDC had acquired more sophisticated weaponry.

There was an increase in violence in Casamance in late 2011, believed to be linked to the presidential election scheduled to be held in late February 2012 (see above). Ten civilians were killed by rebels in November 2011, and in the following month an estimated 30 soldiers were reported to have died in a series of MFDC attacks on military positions in the region. Meanwhile, the disunity within the MFDC was apparent in mid-December when hardline separatists boycotted a conference at which Biagui announced plans to transform the MFDC into a political party. Further attacks on the security forces and civilians took place in January and February 2012. Two weeks before the presidential vote, during a visit to Casamance, President Wade announced a new peace plan for the region, entailing disarmament, demining and agricultural projects. However, dissident MFDC leaders rejected Wade's proposal, expressing scepticism regarding the timing of the announcement and the sincerity of the offer, and in the following days four soldiers were killed and nine injured in clashes with MFDC fighters near Sindian, around 100 km north of Ziguinchor, while suspected MFDC rebels looted businesses in Baghagha, some 25 km east of the regional capital. A further three soldiers were killed in early March by MFDC dissidents near the town of Sédhiou. Following his inauguration as Wade's successor in early April, President Sall identified the peaceful resolution of the conflict in Casamance as a major priority for his administration. In late June Sall stated his readiness to open a dialogue with the MFDC factions that continued to fight, led by Sadio, Badiate and Ousmane Niantang Diatta, all three of whom responded positively, although Badiate urged the MFDC to resolve its internal divisions prior to negotiations with the Government, which Sadio insisted should take place outside Africa with international mediation.

REGIONAL AND INTERNATIONAL RELATIONS

From 1989 Senegal's traditional policy of peaceful coexistence with neighbouring countries was severely undermined by a series of regional disputes. Senegal's relations with both The Gambia and Guinea-Bissau were dominated by issues relating to the conflict in Casamance, which also led large numbers of displaced persons to seek refuge in neighbouring countries.

Senegal continues to have good relations with France, which maintained a military presence in Senegal following Senegalese independence in 1960. Following his election as French President in May 2007, Nicolas Sarkozy visited Senegal in July, when he offered to assist Senegal in organizing the trial of Hissène Habré (see below). In October, however, President Wade criticized controversial new French legislation increasing restrictions on immigration, which would introduce voluntary DNA testing of would-be immigrants seeking to join relatives resident in France. A judicial dispute between France and Senegal emerged in September 2008, when a French judge issued international arrest warrants for nine Senegalese officials, including former Prime Minister Boye, in connection with the 2002 *Joola* ferry disaster (see above), in which 22 French nationals had died. The Senegalese Government retaliated by initiating legal proceedings against the French judge, whom it accused of abuse of authority and bringing Senegalese institutions into disrepute. In February 2010, as the 50th anniversary of Senegal's independence approached, it was announced that the Senegalese and French Governments had reached an agreement on the closure of the French military base in Dakar and a gradual reduction in the number of French troops based in Senegal from some 1,200 to around 300. A joint ceremony to mark the return of the base from French to Senegalese control took place in June. During a visit to France by President Macky Sall in April 2012, some two weeks after his inauguration, a new bilateral defence accord was signed (which confirmed the planned reduction in French troops in Senegal), as well as an agreement on a loan of €130m. from France to Senegal.

In October 2005 Senegal severed diplomatic links with Taiwan, which had been maintained since 1996, in order to restore relations with the People's Republic of China. Senegal and China subsequently exchanged ambassadors, and ties were further strengthened during a six-day state visit by Wade to China in June 2006, when several bilateral agreements were signed. Economic relations between the two countries were enhanced in 2008, with the signing of a free trade agreement in October and an economic and technical co-operation agreement in November. Further bilateral accords were concluded during a visit to Senegal by Chinese President Hu Jintao in February 2009.

Following an influx of illegal immigrants into Spain's Canary Islands from Senegal (and other West African countries), in 2006 the Spanish and Senegalese Governments agreed to co-operate on the establishment of a system of legal Senegalese emigration in an effort to discourage illegal migration; joint patrols of Senegal's coast were also to be carried out. During a visit to Dakar by the Spanish Prime Minister, José Luis Rodríguez Zapatero, in December, bilateral agreements were signed on increasing political and economic co-operation and on promoting legal migration. Zapatero also confirmed an earlier commitment to provide €20m. in funding for projects to create employment opportunities within Senegal. The number of African migrants reaching the Canary Islands declined from more than 31,000 in 2006 to 2,246 by 2009, partly owing to improved surveillance, but also because an economic slowdown in Spain had reduced employment opportunities in that country.

Senegal is a significant contributor to peace-keeping activities in sub-Saharan Africa. In early 2003 it was announced that Senegal was to contribute some 650 troops to the Economic Community of West African States (ECOWAS) military mission in Côte d'Ivoire (ECOMICI); Senegalese troops also participated in the UN Operation in Côte d'Ivoire (UNOCI) that assumed the responsibilities of ECOMICI from April 2004. Meanwhile, in August 2003 some 260 Senegalese troops were dispatched to serve in the ECOWAS Mission in Liberia (ECOMIL), which was replaced by the UN Mission in Liberia (UNMIL) in October. In August 2005 Senegal deployed 538 soldiers in the Darfur region of western Sudan as part of the enhanced African Union (AU) Mission in Sudan (AMIS). Senegal increased the number of its troops in Darfur to 1,600 when the AU/UN hybrid operation in Darfur (UNAMID) replaced AMIS on 31 December 2007. In March 2008 Senegalese troops participated in an AU military mission to assist the federal Government of the Comoros to regain control of the island of Nzwani. Senegal has also provided military personnel to successive UN missions in the Democratic Republic of the Congo, the most recent of these, authorized in July 2010, being the UN Organization Stabilization Mission in the Democratic Republic of the Congo (MONUSCO).

In November 2010 Côte d'Ivoire recalled its ambassador to Senegal, accusing the Senegalese Government of interfering in its internal affairs after President Wade met Alassane Ouattara, the Ivorian opposition leader who was to challenge the incumbent Ivorian President, Laurent Gbagbo, in the second round of a presidential election in that country later that month. Once Ouattara was finally inaugurated as President of Côte d'Ivoire in May 2011, his first foreign visit was notably to Senegal.

Senegal recalled its ambassador to Iran in December 2010 in connection with the discovery in October of 13 containers of weapons at the Nigerian port of Lagos that were allegedly being transported from Iran to The Gambia, amid speculation that the arms were ultimately to have been smuggled to MFDC rebels in Casamance. Following a visit to Senegal by the Iranian Minister of Foreign Affairs, the Senegalese Government decided to reinstate its envoy in January 2011, but severed bilateral relations again in the following month, citing further evidence that Iran was supplying weapons to MFDC rebels.

In July 2006 the AU decided that Hissène Habré, President of Chad during 1982–90, should be prosecuted in Senegal (where he had fled after being deposed in 1990) over alleged human rights abuses committed during his presidency. Earlier attempts to prosecute Habré in Senegal had failed, prompting his alleged victims to seek his extradition to stand trial in Belgium under its universal jurisdiction law. The Senegalese Government had referred Habré's case to the AU in November 2005, after a Senegalese court declared that it was not competent to rule on a Belgian extradition request. In February 2007 the Assemblée nationale adopted legislation permitting the Senegalese judiciary to prosecute cases of genocide, crimes against humanity, war crimes and torture, even if the crimes were not committed in Senegal. In May 2008 a senior judge was designated to co-ordinate Habré's trial, and in July the approval of legislation allowing the 2007 law to be applied retroactively seemingly removed the final legal obstacle to the trial being conducted in Senegal. In September 14 Senegalese and Chadian citizens lodged complaints of human rights abuses against Habré with the Senegalese courts. In the following month Habré filed a case with the ECOWAS Community Court of Justice challenging Senegalese plans to prosecute him. With the Senegalese Government apparently reluctant to proceed with a trial, which it estimated would cost some 18,000m. francs CFA (US $35m.) to conduct, in February 2009 the Belgian Government appealed to the International Court of Justice (ICJ) in The Hague, Netherlands, to compel Senegal either to try Habré or to extradite him to Belgium. In mid-November 2010 the ECOWAS Community Court of Justice ruled that Senegal could not try Habré in its own courts, through the retroactive application of its 2007 legislation, but could fulfil the AU mandate for his prosecution by hosting an ad hoc international tribunal. Later that month international donors, meeting with representatives of the AU and the Senegalese Government in Dakar, offered $11.7m. to conduct the trial. In April 2011, under pressure from the AU, the Senegalese Government agreed to the creation of the proposed tribunal, but in the following month its delegates withdrew from further negotiations on the issue with the Union. In July the Government announced that it intended to extradite Habré to Chad, where he had been sentenced to death, *in absentia*, in 2008, but reversed its decision in response to an appeal by the UN High Commissioner for Human Rights, Navanethem Pillay, who expressed concern that Habré might be subjected to torture if returned to Chad. The Belgian Government subsequently again requested that Senegal extradite Habré to stand trial in Belgium, but this was rejected by a Senegalese court in January 2012. In July the ICJ issued its judgment in the case brought by Belgium, ruling that Senegal should commence procedures to prosecute Habré 'without further delay' or, failing that, extradite him to Belgium. Meanwhile, in June the Government of Macky Sall, who favoured trying Habré in Senegal, had established a working group to consider the logistics of organizing a trial with AU support. After four days of talks in Dakar, held immediately following the announcement of the ICJ's verdict in July, the Senegalese authorities agreed to an AU proposal to try Habré before a special court presided over by African judges appointed by the Union. It was envisaged that Habré would be charged only with the most serious of the crimes that he was suspected of committing in order to limit the duration and complexity of the planned trial.

Relations with Mauritania

In April 1989 the deaths of two Senegalese farmers, following a disagreement with Mauritanian livestock-breeders regarding grazing rights in the border region between the two countries, precipitated a crisis that was fuelled by long-standing ethnic and economic rivalries. Mauritanian nationals residing in Senegal were attacked and their businesses ransacked (the retail trade in Senegal had hitherto been dominated by an expatriate community of mainly light-skinned Mauritanians, estimated to number about 300,000), and Senegalese nationals in Mauritania suffered similar attacks. By early May it was believed that several hundred people, mostly Senegalese, had been killed. Operations to repatriate nationals of both countries were undertaken with international assistance, and Senegal granted asylum to Afro-Mauritanians who feared official persecution. None the less, diplomatic relations were severed in August. Renewed outbreaks of violence were reported in late 1989, while in early 1990 attempts at mediation were thwarted by military engagements in the border region. In March 1991 several deaths were reported to have resulted from a military engagement, on Senegalese territory, between members of the two countries' armed forces, following an incursion by Senegalese troops into Mauritania.

Diplomatic links, at ambassadorial level, were restored in April 1992, and the process of reopening the border began in May. None the less, the issues of border demarcation and the status of Mauritanian refugees in Senegal remained to be resolved. In December 1994, however, the Governments of Senegal and Mauritania agreed new co-operation measures, including efforts to facilitate the free movement of goods and people between the two countries. In January 1995, moreover, the Governments of Senegal, Mauritania and Mali undertook to co-operate in resolving joint border issues and in combating extremism, the smuggling of arms and drugs-trafficking. In October the Mauritanian authorities gave assurances that Mauritanian refugees in Senegal were free to return home. According to figures published by the office of the UN High Commissioner for Refugees (UNHCR), the number of Mauritanian refugees in Senegal declined from 65,485 in 1995 to 19,999 in 1999, although progress with repatriation subsequently stalled. In May 1999 Mauritania and Senegal signed an agreement on the joint exploitation of fisheries, while in August Senegal, Mauritania and Mali agreed to establish a joint operational force in order to combat the ongoing insecurity in the border region.

In early June 2000 a new dispute broke out between Mauritania and Senegal, after the former accused the latter of threatening its interests by relaunching an irrigation programme in the fossil valleys area of the River Senegal. Claiming that the project would deprive its own lands of water, Mauritania instructed Senegalese nationals to leave the country within 15 days. Of the 345,000 Senegalese resident in Mauritania, some 25,000 returned home before the order was rescinded on 10 June. Wade immediately visited Nouakchott, the Mauritanian capital, and announced the cancellation of the irrigation project. However, following renewed negotiations, the visit of President Maawiya Ould Sid'Ahmed Taya of Mauritania to Dakar in April 2001 was widely regarded as indicating an improvement in relations between the countries. The extradition of one of the suspected coup plotters from Senegal to Mauritania was also interpreted as an indication of improved relations between the countries, as was the Mauritanian Government's decision to accord 270 temporary fishing licences to Senegalese fishermen in June 2004.

In January 2006 Wade became the first foreign Head of State to visit Mauritania since the overthrow of Taya's regime in August 2005. Wade and Col Ely Ould Mohamed Vall, who had assumed the leadership of Mauritania, as President of a self-styled Military Council for Justice and Democracy, announced that their Governments would henceforth hold regular joint committee meetings, and Wade expressed his support for the transitional process under way in Mauritania. Vall paid a reciprocal visit to Senegal in March 2006. IFollowing democratic elections and a return to civilian rule in Mauritania, in April 2007 the newly elected President, Sidi Mohammed Ould Cheikh Abdellahi, urged the refugees in Senegal to return to Mauritania. A tripartite agreement on the voluntary repatriation and reintegration of the refugees in Senegal was signed by UNHCR and the Mauritanian and Senegalese Governments in November. The first group of around 100 refugees returned to Mauritania in January 2008. The number of Mauritanian refugees in Senegal declined from 32,292 at the end of 2008 to 19,917 at the end of 2011, according to UNHCR. The repatriation programme ended in March 2012, with UNHCR reporting that some 14,000 Mauritanians had opted to remain in Senegal and would receive support with integration from UNHCR and its partners. Meanwhile, after Ould Cheikh Abdellahi was overthrown in August 2008, President Wade opposed the imposition of sanctions against Mauritania's new military administration, headed by Gen. Mohamed Ould Abdel Aziz. In December Senegal's Minister of State, Minister of Foreign Affairs, Cheikh Tidiane Gadio, visited Mauritania to hold talks with Ould Abdel Aziz and Ould Cheikh Abdellahi. In mid-2009 the Senegalese Government mediated in the Mauritanian political dispute regarding the restoration of constitutional order. In March 2010 the Senegalese and Mauritanian authorities agreed to reinforce security co-operation along the joint border.

Relations with Guinea-Bissau

A dispute with Guinea-Bissau regarding the sovereignty of a maritime zone believed to contain reserves of petroleum, together with valuable fishing grounds, caused tensions between the two countries in the late 1980s and early 1990s. In July 1989 an international arbitration panel (to which the issue had been referred in 1985) judged the waters to be part of Senegalese territory. However, the Government of Guinea-Bissau refused to accept the judgment, and referred the matter to the ICJ. In November 1991 the ICJ ruled that the existing delimitation of the maritime border remained valid, and Senegal and Guinea-Bissau signed a treaty recognizing this judgment in February 1993.

Although Guinea-Bissau (together with France) played an important role in the formulation of the 1991 cease-fire agreement between the Senegalese Government and the MFDC, relations were again strained in late 1992. In December an offensive by the Senegalese armed forces against MFDC strongholds close to the border with Guinea-Bissau resulted in the deaths of two nationals of that country. The Guinea-Bissau Government formally protested against Senegalese violations of its airspace. Although Senegal apologized for the incident, a further violation was reported in January 1993. None the less, Guinea-Bissau was again active in efforts to bring about a new cease-fire agreement between Senegal and the MFDC in mid-1993. In October of that year, moreover, the two countries signed a major 20-year agreement regarding the joint exploitation and management of fishing and petroleum resources in their maritime zones.

Renewed operations by the Senegalese military against MFDC rebels in southern Casamance, from early 1995, again affected relations with Guinea-Bissau. In April Guinea-Bissau temporarily deployed as many as 500 troops near the border with Senegal, as part of attempts to locate four missing French tourists. The October 1993 treaty on the joint exploration of maritime wealth was ratified in December 1995: fishing resources were to be shared equally between the two countries, while Senegal was to benefit from a majority share (85%) of petroleum deposits.

In January 1998 it was announced that the authorities in Guinea-Bissau had intercepted a consignment of armaments destined for MFDC rebels and that some 15 officers of the Guinea-Bissau armed forces had been arrested and suspended from duty, including their leader, Brig. (later Gen.) Ansumane Mané. In June, however, troops loyal to Mané rebelled, and civil war broke out in Guinea-Bissau. Senegalese troops intervened in support of the forces loyal to the Government, and were subsequently reinforced to number more than 2,500. Senegal's involvement became the subject of controversy, with Guinea-Bissau refugees accusing Senegalese troops of brutality against civilians. In July the Guinea-Bissau insurgents signed a cease-fire agreement with their Government. Under the terms of an agreement brokered by ECOWAS in November 1998, the final 800 Senegalese soldiers withdrew from Guinea-Bissau in March 1999.

Tensions between the two countries resurfaced in April 2000, when an armed group, reportedly composed of members of the MFDC operating from within Guinea-Bissau, attacked a Senegalese border post. In late April the common border was temporarily closed. In May Wade stated that he feared the prospect of an invasion by forces from Guinea-Bissau, calling on France to supply Senegal with military equipment in order to strengthen the country's position, and requesting that UN military observers be sent to the border area. The Government of Guinea-Bissau continued to deny supporting the MFDC rebels. In August the revision was announced of the agreement on the joint exploitation of petroleum resources; henceforth Guinea-Bissau was to receive 20% rather than 15% of the revenue generated. Relations between Senegal and Guinea-Bissau improved significantly following the killing of Mané during a failed coup attempt in Guinea-Bissau in November 2000, and Guinea-Bissau forces launched a new offensive against MFDC rebel bases in early 2001. Following a subsequent period of transitional rule in Guinea-Bissau, during the first half of 2005 President Wade assumed a mediatory role between rival candidates contesting a presidential election in that country in June and July of that year.

In March 2006, following increasing instability along its border with Senegal, as rival factions of the MFDC clashed (see above), the Guinea-Bissau armed forces launched an offensive against bases established by Salif Sadio around the Guinea-Bissau town of São Domingos. Fighting between Guinea-Bissau troops and MFDC rebels continued until late April, leading to the displacement of several thousand Guinea-Bissau civilians, many of whom fled across the border to Ziguinchor. In January 2007 Guinea-Bissau deployed additional troops in its border area with Senegal, in response to reported clashes between Senegalese troops and forces belonging to César Badiate's MFDC faction. Senegal reinforced security at the border with Guinea-Bissau in November 2008, following a failed coup attempt in that country; the suspected leader of the mutiny was arrested in Dakar in December. President Wade condemned the assassination of his Guinea-Bissau counterpart in March 2009, amid concerns that instability in Guinea-Bissau would lead to a deterioration in the security situation in Casamance. Following a subsequent increase in violence in Casamance, François Diatta, an alleged leader of the MFDC reported to be allied to Mamadou Nkrumah Sané, was arrested in Guinea-Bissau in July. Tension arose in October when the Government of Guinea-Bissau placed its troops on alert along the border with Senegal, accusing the Senegalese authorities of having sold plots of land and removed border posts in a coastal border area claimed by Guinea-Bissau to be part of its territory. At a meeting held in Guinea-Bissau later that month to discuss the dispute, representatives of both countries agreed to revive a joint border commission that had not convened for 16 years. According to UNHCR, at the end of 2011 Guinea-Bissau hosted 7,658 Senegalese refugees from the Casamance region, the number having remained relatively stable over the preceding decade.

Relations with The Gambia

In August 1981, following a coup in The Gambia, President Diouf despatched Senegalese troops to restore the deposed Gambian President, Sir Dawda Jawara, to power. Senegalese forces were subsequently asked to remain, and Diouf and Jawara swiftly established a confederation of the two states, with co-ordinated policies in defence, foreign affairs and economic and financial matters. The agreement establishing the Senegambian Confederation came into effect in February 1982. Diouf was designated permanent President of a Joint Council of Ministers, and a Confederal Assembly was established. However, The Gambia resisted attempts by Senegal to proceed towards the full political and economic integration of the two countries.

In August 1989 the Diouf Government announced the withdrawal of 1,400 Senegalese troops from The Gambia, apparently in protest against a request by Jawara that his country be accorded more power within the Senegambian confederal agreement. Later that month Diouf stated that, in view of The Gambia's reluctance to proceed towards full political and economic integration with Senegal, the functions of the Confederation should be suspended, and the two countries should endeavour to formulate more attainable co-operation accords. The Confederation was formally dissolved in September. In January 1991 the foreign ministers of the two countries signed a bilateral treaty of friendship and co-operation.

Following the coup in The Gambia in July 1994, and the assumption of power by Yahya A. J. J. Jammeh, Jawara was initially granted asylum in Senegal. Despite the presence in Senegal of prominent opponents of the Gambian military regime, in January 1996 the two countries signed an agreement aimed at increasing bilateral trade and at minimizing cross-border smuggling. A further accord, concluded in April 1997, was to facilitate the trans-border movement of goods destined for re-export. In June the two countries agreed to take joint measures to combat insecurity, illegal immigration and trafficking in arms and illegal drugs. In early 1998 President Jammeh offered to act as a mediator between the Senegalese Government and the MFDC (see above) and subsequently hosted regular meetings between the Government and the MFDC.

None the less, intermittent disputes relating to transportation issues between the two countries have occurred. Tensions arose in August 2005, for example, when The Gambia Ports Authority doubled the cost of using the ferry across the Gambia river. Many Senegalese lorry drivers refused to pay the increased fare, opting instead to take a long detour around The Gambia (aided by fuel subsidies granted by the Senegalese Government), while others blockaded the main border crossings between the two countries. At talks mediated by President Olusegun Obasanjo of Nigeria, under the aegis of ECOWAS, in October, Jammeh agreed to reverse the price increase that took effect in August pending further consultations, while Wade pledged to end the blockade of the border. Agreement was also reached on the construction of a bridge over the Gambia river. In December the Gambian and Senegalese Governments decided that the bridge project should be a regional initiative, to be undertaken by the Gambia River Basin Development Organization. Plans for the establishment of a permanent secretariat for bilateral co-operation were also announced.

In August 2006 UNHCR reported that more than 4,500 people had fled to The Gambia from Senegal that month, following renewed fighting in Casamance between Salif Sadio's faction of the MFDC and Senegalese government forces (see above); some 1,600 Senegalese had crossed into The Gambia earlier that year. The total number of Senegalese refugees registered with UNHCR in The Gambia had risen to 6,946 by the end of 2006, and increased further in 2007, to 7,546 by the end of the year; the number had declined slightly, to 7,359, by the end of 2010, but rose to 8,359 at the end of 2011. Nine members of Sadio's MFDC faction were found guilty of terrorism charges by a court in The Gambia in April 2008; they subsequently appealed against their convictions. A visit to The Gambia by President Wade in January 2010 followed claims made by Jammeh in the previous month that the Senegalese Government aided and hosted Gambian dissidents and allegations by the Gambian newspaper *The Daily Observer* that Senegal was seeking to destabilize The Gambia. Wade dismissed the accusations and signed a joint communiqué with Jammeh, in which they pledged to enhance peace and security and reaffirmed their commitment to implement the earlier agreements to construct a bridge over the Gambia river and to establish a permanent secretariat for bilateral co-operation. Tensions arose again in late 2010, however, amid Senegalese concerns that weapons allegedly being smuggled from Iran to The Gambia were intended for MFDC rebels in Casamance. Gambian-Senegalese relations had improved by February 2011, however, when The Gambia acknowledged having received weapons from Iran, but claimed that they were to be used to ensure Gambian national security. At the same time the Gambian and Senegalese Governments agreed to create the long-awaited permanent secretariat later that year and to organize joint military manoeuvres and border patrols. Nevertheless, a renewed dispute regarding the fees charged to Senegalese lorry drivers seeking to cross Gambian territory disrupted cross-border trade and movement for some three months from March. President Macky Sall visited The Gambia shortly after his inauguration in April 2012, notably requesting Jammeh's assistance in resolving the conflict in Casamance. The permanent secretariat had yet to become operational.

Economy

RALPH YOUNG

INTRODUCTION

Senegal retains some of the economic advantages derived from its leading position in pre-independence French West Africa. In 2010 Senegal's per caput gross national income (GNI), according to the World Bank, was US $1,090, one of the highest levels in West Africa. However, with a population estimated at 12.6m. in mid-2011, poverty remained widespread. About one-half of the population was still living below the national poverty line; life expectancy was 59 years; and the adult literacy rate was around 50%. Senegal nevertheless had registered progress between 2000 and 2009 on the UN's Millennium Development Goals relating to overall poverty reduction and education, though not on those relating to health. Its ranking on the UN Development Programme's 2011 Human Development Index was 155th out of 179 countries.

Economic performance was strong for the 15 years straddling the turn of the 21st century. The economy responded positively to the major devaluation of the CFA franc in 1994, which, with the accompanying government reform programme, produced one of the best economic performances in sub-Saharan Africa between 1995 and 2006. Real growth in gross domestic product (GDP) averaged 4.1% per year, peaking at 6.7% in 2003 but remaining strong thereafter, at 5.9% in 2004 and 5.6% in 2005. However, reflecting the economy's continuing vulnerability to internal constraints as well as unfavourable external economic conditions, growth fell sharply in 2006 to 2.5%, owing to a substantial fall in phosphate output, before recovering to 4.9% in 2007. In late 2007 and the first half of 2008 rapid increases in imported food and fuel prices provoked popular unrest as inflation rose from 0.5% in 2006 to 4% in 2007 and 6% in 2008. From late 2008 the global financial crisis caused growth to slow significantly, as earnings from tourism and remittances from Senegalese working abroad declined and foreign investment diminished; from 3.3% in 2008, GDP growth fell to 1.5% in 2009. The economy rebounded in 2010 to achieve GDP growth of 4.0%. However, the impact of drought on agricultural production and the disruptive effects of problems in the energy sector caused overall growth to fall to 2.6% in 2011. The IMF remained confident that this figure would climb back to around 4.0% in 2012, and that inflation, which stood at 3.4% in 2011, would moderate to 2.5%. GDP stood at US $12,855m. in 2010.

Although economic reforms under the guidance of the IMF and the World Bank began in the 1980s, it was only after the 1994 devaluation that the programme of economic liberalization gained momentum, with the progressive dismantling of artificial protection barriers and the promotion of market-oriented incentives, often in the face of considerable resistance from entrenched interest groups. These efforts were intensified in 2003 following the introduction of a World Bank-supported programme designed to encourage new private investment and to reform a wide range of fiscal policies and incentives. A law authorizing the privatization of state-owned enterprises had been approved in 1987, and limited divestiture activities had begun in 1989. An ambitious privatization programme was adopted in the mid-1990s, with 20 state-owned companies offered for sale and restructuring, including those dealing with water and electricity services, telecommunications, the railways and national airline, the groundnut and cotton sectors, and Dakar port. A further round of privatization commenced in 2003 under IMF pressure, but, apart from the privatization of the country's groundnut oil producer, has since advanced slowly.

Abdoulaye Wade, on becoming President in 2000, wasted little time in declaring his intention to make Senegal achieve 'emergent country' status. His Government intensified the economic reforms begun by its predecessors, with the emphasis on further liberalizing markets, transforming the peasant economy into a private sector-driven centre of agro-industry and services, and capitalizing on Senegal's relative proximity to Europe to make the country a regional trading centre. The Government sought to attract private capital as well as donor support for an ambitious infrastructure programme, including a new international airport, road networks, port facilities, and irrigation and afforestation schemes. However, the economy still shows limited diversification and remains dependent on public spending to provide a growth momentum; formal sector employment has been in gradual decline.

AGRICULTURE AND FISHING

Over 40% of Senegal's population is now urban; the capital, Dakar, with 0.3% of the nation's land area, accounts for over 60% of its economic activities. Yet agriculture continues to be the predominant sector for employment, engaging around 70% of the total labour force; the groundnut sector alone provides employment for up to 1m. (mostly small-scale) farmers. The agricultural sector's contribution to GDP declined steadily from the mid-1980s. Almost 25% in 1987, it had slipped below 20% by 2000, and in 2010 it stood at 17.4%. High levels of rural poverty—not least in the politically sensitive Casamance region in the south—and limited access to rural infrastructure and basic services have spurred migration to the urban areas. The agricultural base of the economy was eroded by periodic droughts and the gradual desertification of large tracts of land. In June 2010 Senegal joined 10 other countries bordering the Sahel desert in a project to construct a 'green wall' of trees stretching some 7,100 km from Senegal to Djibouti; the Fund for the Environment promised US $119m. for this project.

Groundnuts are the leading cash crop, but, because of external price fluctuations, drought or locust plagues, annual acreage planted and production have fluctuated. After exceeding 1m. metric tons in both 1999 and 2000, production fell sharply to 260,723 tons in 2002; the acreage planted in these years was, respectively, 916,000 ha, 1.1m ha and 813,000 ha. Production recovered to 440,709 tons in 2003, 602,621 tons in 2004 and 703,373 tons in 2005. However, owing to a prolonged dispute between the sector's trade unions, the main groundnut oil producer and the Government, the acreage planted fell to around 594,000 ha in 2006, while production only reached 460,481 tons, before falling further to 331,195 tons in 2007. It rebounded to 646,964 tons in 2008, and, with good rains, it reached 1.0m. tons in 2009 and a record 1.3m. tons in 2010 (on 1.2m. ha). Groundnuts are exported either as groundnut oil (30,891 tons in 2009) or groundnut cake for animal feed (14,952 tons); these two sources earned Senegal over US $41m. in 2009. Yet earnings from groundnuts have fallen in recent years, since world demand for groundnut oil has declined through competition with other, healthier vegetable oils (based on soya or palm oils).

Two initial attempts, in 1995 and 1999, to privatize the principal groundnut oil producer, the Société Nationale de Commercialisation des Oléagineux du Sénégal (SONACOS), were unsuccessful; however, its divestiture was eventually agreed in December 2004. Yet despite such measures, the Government continued to intervene in the decisions of the Comité National Interprofessionel de l'Arachide (responsible for fixing the producer price each season); it also sought to levy import taxes (despite strong World Bank and IMF criticism) on imports of refined vegetable oils in order to protect SONACOS' falling share of the domestic market. In January 2007 SONACOS was renamed SUNEOR (Wolof for 'Our Gold').

The Government has attempted to reduce dependence on groundnuts by diversifying cash and food crops, in particular by expanding output of cotton, rice, sugar and market-garden produce. Production of unginned cotton rose rapidly, from only 460 metric tons in 1961 to 50,577 tons in 1991. Recently, however, output has declined, from 52,027 tons in 2006 to 38,810 tons in 2008 and 22,090 tons in 2009, although it increased again slightly, to 26,045 tons, in 2010. Senegal exported 8,621 tons of cotton lint worth over US $12m. in 2010. Cashew nut production was only modest until 1998, when three successive seasons saw production reach 7,000 tons or more; however, this has since stabilized at lower levels, and in 2010 was around 5,700 tons. Sugar is produced at the Richard Toll complex in the north, near Saint-Louis. Annual output of sugar cane, all of which is for domestic consumption, reached 829,500 tons in 2006 and a steady 836,000 tons from 2007 to 2010.

Output of rice has fluctuated widely. The average annual output of 169,686 metric tons recorded in 1990–96 fell far short of domestic demand. Production by 2005 had risen to 279,000 tons before falling to 212,000 tons in 2006 and 193,379 tons in 2007; in 2008, however, production rose to almost 370,000 tons, and it increased sharply again in 2009 and 2010, to 502,104 tons and 604,043 tons, respectively. The shortfall is met by cheap imports of rice from the Far East—in both 2007 and 2008, over 1m. tons, although this figure fell to 766,403 tons in 2009. Such imports seriously jeopardize local producers, who no longer attract a state subsidy. Various small- and medium-scale projects, supported by foreign aid and boosted by the Manantali dam in Mali, have extended the area under irrigation for rice—to 147,208 ha, though still only one-quarter of the potentially irrigable area; the production level per hectare nearly doubled between 2000 and 2010. Market gardening began in 1971 and by 2010 the production of horticultural produce and tropical fruits reached 831,656 tons, though most of this services the domestic market. Exports of horticultural produce in 2007 and 2008 were around 27,000 tons, in the latter year being worth almost US $36m.; in 2010 Senegal produced 24,086 tons (worth $23m.). Another agricultural initiative was the experimental introduction of bio-fuel crops, including jatropha, castor oil and sunflowers, over large tracts of land near Kolda and Tambacounda, to explore possibilities for large-scale production.

Besides rice, the principal food crops are millet, sorghum and maize. The traditional food sector has suffered reverses from recurring droughts. Production of millet and sorghum declined substantially from 818,213 metric tons in 2004 to an estimated 318,822 tons in 2007, owing to poor rains and lack of inputs; however, with better conditions the combined harvest for both rose in 2008 to 789,048 tons, over 1m. tons in 2009 and 975,894 tons in 2010. Maize production averaged 87,996 tons per year in 1993–2002, increasing dramatically to 400,907 tons in 2003 following the introduction of hybrid seeds, fertilizer, herbicides and insecticides, as well as a significant increase in the area harvested, from 108,114 ha in 2002 to 175,575 ha in 2003. Maize production in fell to 182,000 tons in 2006 and to 158,266 tons in 2007 before rising to 453,678 tons in 2008 (with over 227,000 ha in production); it stood at 328,644 tons in 2009, but declined to 186,511 tons in 2010. The attainment of food self-sufficiency remained a major priority; in April 2008, following popular unrest over escalating food prices, the Government launched the Grande Offensive Agricole pour la Nourriture et l'Abondance, which aimed to boost rice and maize output to 2.5m. tons by 2015.

Livestock is a significant sector of the traditional economy (although less important than in Senegal's neighbours), and is the base for the dairy and meat-processing industries. In 2010 the cattle herd totalled 3.3m. head, sheep 5.6m., goats 4.8m., pigs 347,000 and horses 528,000. Only some 5% of the country's meat requirements are currently imported. Senegal's exports of 4,207 metric tons of cattle hides in 2007 fell to 2,999 tons in 2008, before disappearing from the list of the country's 20 principal exports in 2009.

Agricultural production is supplemented by output from fishing—a sector that, including processing, regularly accounts for around 25% of merchandise exports, though the industry suffers from problems of overfishing and from high costs compared with its Asian competitors. The value of fish exports (including crustaceans and molluscs) was 113m. francs CFA in 2009. Annual catches averaged 450,000 metric tons in 2002–05. However, in 2006 the artisanal catch by local fishermen fell significantly, reducing the total catch to 379,127 tons, 8.1% lower than in 2005. The total catch recovered to 457,155 tons in 2009, but declined again, to 409,656 tons, in 2010. The annual sustainable catch has been estimated at around 420,000 tons per year. While industrial fishing is practised by both national and foreign operators, small-scale fishing by about 45,000 fishermen continues to predominate. The fishing sector as a whole provides a livelihood for as many as 600,000 people, including those engaged in local canning factories. Although the political insecurity in the southern Casamance region (the main fishing area) has at times adversely affected the sector, fishing remains Senegal's leading source of foreign exchange, constituting 33.7% of total exports in 2006. The Government has announced ambitious plans to develop large-scale aquaculture by 2015 to help supply the country's needs; only 78 tons was produced by such methods in 2010.

After 1979 regular fishing agreements were concluded with the European Community (now the European Union—EU), for which Senegal received financial compensation of about €48m. in 1997–2001; part of the catch made by EU vessels was also landed for processing locally. Some 78 EU boats were licensed to fish in Senegalese waters, but the agreement was not renewed in 2001, following government concerns that industrial fishing activities were depleting stocks and undermining the artisanal fishing sector. However, a new agreement was signed between Senegal and the EU in June 2002 enabling Senegal to receive €64m. in 2002–06; several conditions intended to protect fish stocks were included in the new agreement, including an annual two-month rest period. However, negotiations for a successor accord became deadlocked, and in June 2006 EU ships stopped fishing in Senegalese waters, though a small number continue under Senegalese registration. Factory fishing ships from several non-EU countries also work under license.

MINING

The mining sector's contribution to GDP was 3.5% in 2010. However, including processed derivatives, the sector is the country's second largest source of merchandise export earnings. Mining in Senegal is dominated by the extraction of phosphates, with reserves of calcium phosphates estimated at 100m. metric tons and reserves of aluminium phosphates at 50m.–70m. tons. Phosphate output peaked at 2.3m. tons in

1988; it declined to 1.8m. tons in 2003, and then fell dramatically, to just 584,000 tons in 2006, before recovering to 700,000 tons in 2008, 952,000 tons in 2009 and 976,000 tons in 2010. Phosphate extraction was undertaken by two companies, the Compagnie Sénégalaise des Phosphates de Taïba (CSPT) and the Société Sénégalaise des Phosphates de Thiès (SSPT, privatized in March 1998). A third company, the Compagnie Sénégalaise d'Etude et de Réalisation des Phosphates de Matam (SERPM), began operations in 2009; established as a state enterprise in 2007 (though with private interests holding 51% of the shares), it was subsequently fully privatized to a Senegalese entrepreneur. The phosphate rock has been processed by Industries Chimiques du Sénégal (ICS). The ICS complex produced 630,000 tons of phosphoric acid in 2003 and 504,000 tons in 2005; production then fell sharply to 180,000 tons in 2006 before recovering to 283,000 tons in 2009 and 312,000 tons in 2010. In 2009 ICS also produced 44,000 tons of fertilizer, while in 2010 production reached 45,000 tons. Exports to the EU declined, partly because of the high cadmium content of Senegalese phosphates but, more importantly, because of India's increasing domination of the export market. Expansion was planned both at existing facilities and at new ones at Tobène; a plant for the recovery of phosphates from tailings was constructed at the ICS fertilizer complex, with World Bank support.

As a result of falling market prices and rising costs of fuel and essential imports, ICS was declared bankrupt in 2006 (also threatening CSPT, with which ICS had merged in 1996). The Government (with 47% of the shares) came under pressure to reach agreement with other shareholders, particularly the Indian Farmers' Fertiliser Co-operative (IFFCO), purchaser of some 80% of the phosphate and phosphoric acid produced by ICS, and the Indian Government, which were seeking to increase their joint equity stake from 26% to 51%. New finance was pledged on condition that control was transferred to Indian management and debts were restructured. The Government eventually finalized an agreement in January 2008 whereby IFFCO would provide 91,000m. francs CFA (US $200m.) of new capital for ICS in return for management control and an increase in IFFCO's stake to 85%; in March ICS reached an agreement with its creditors allowing it to repay its debts, estimated at €300m., over 12 years. Under the arrangement, IFFCO would obtain 85% of the ICS output, with the remainder being devoted to fertilizer production to service Senegalese and regional markets. ICS returned to profitability during 2008.

An estimated 391m. metric tons of high-grade iron ore were located in the east, at Falémé, and an additional 250m. tons at Farangalia and Goto. Reflecting an increase in world demand for iron ore, in January 2006 Mittal Steel (of the Netherlands) signed a memorandum of understanding with the Government to develop the production of iron ore at Falémé. The company planned to invest US $2,200m. to develop the deposits, and to construct a new port and railway line. Production was expected to start in 2011, with projected annual output of 15m.–25m. tons. However, the future of the project was put in doubt after Kumba Resources of South Africa claimed that it held rights to the property and threatened to take legal action if the Government did not reaffirm its rights. With this dispute still unresolved, ArcelorMittal (as Mittal Steel had become) announced in July 2009 that, given unfavourable market prospects, it was temporarily suspending the project's development; in response, the Government in November 2011 submitted a case to the Cour d'Arbitrage de la Chambre de Commerce Internationale de Paris demanding compensation of $700m. from the company.

Significant gold deposits were discovered at Sabodala, in the south-east of Senegal, where artisanal production estimated at 600 kg annually had long occurred. The Société Minière de Sabodala began operations in 1997, but a dispute over legal titles halted production in 1998. A new agreement was reached in 2004 with the Australian company Mineral Deposits Ltd (MDL), which thereby acquired a 70% stake in the company); the Canadian firm Teranga Gold Corporation then acquired 90% control in November 2009. From 2005 the Government awarded exploration rights in the Sabodala area to several additional companies. Oromin Explorations of Canada, in partnership with two Saudi Arabian companies, was expected to begin gold production at Masato, in the same region, in 2012. The operational life expectancy of all these mines is relatively short-term—from nine to 15 years. Gold production in 2010 was 4,381 kg.

Exploration for diamonds is also in progress. Commercially viable reserves of titanium were discovered in 1991: workable ores are estimated at some 10m. metric tons. In 2007 the Government awarded a 50-year licence to MDL (for a fee of US $370m.) to develop deposits of zircon and titanium-related minerals used in the paint, jewellery, ceramic and civil engineering industries, in the coastal area between Dakar and Saint-Louis. The Grande Côte Mineral Sands Project was expected to begin production in 2013.

Deposits of petroleum, estimated at 100m. metric tons, were located in the Dôme Flore field, off the Casamance coast, but initially the development of these reserves appeared economically unfeasible. Disagreement with Guinea-Bissau regarding sovereignty of waters in this region was a further obstacle until an agreement was signed in October 1993, providing for the joint management of their maritime zones. To operate for an initial 20-year period, the agreement provided for an 85%:15% division of petroleum resources between Senegal and Guinea-Bissau, respectively; this was altered to 80%:20% in August 2000. The Agence de Gestion et Coopération was created to administer petroleum and fishing activity in the 100,000-sq km joint area. The Senegal–Guinea-Bissau Joint Exploration Zone is divided into two sections, with the Cheval Marin zone operated by the Italian company ENI and the Croix du Sud zone operated by an Australian firm, Fusion Oil. All companies work in partnership with the majority state-owned Société Nationale des Pétroles du Sénégal (PETROSEN). In 1997 PETROSEN announced the discovery of a natural gas deposit, with reserves estimated at 10,000m. cu m, in the Thiès region. The Government adopted a new petroleum code and a new mining code in 1997 and 1998, respectively, to encourage further exploitation of Senegal's mineral resources. The incentives included generous exploration rights if a deposit was located, with no requirement for government equity participation. In 2004 the US oil company, ExxonMobil, acquired a 37% stake in Cheval Marin. By 2008 nine international oil companies were exploring Senegal's offshore areas. In 2009 Senegal was producing 12,000 cu m of natural gas. Oil production, which commenced in 2006, stood at 398,000 barrels in 2010, or an estimated 1,090 barrels per day (b/d).

The energy sector remains critical to Senegal's development, but imposes heavy burdens on the balance of payments. The import expenditures on petroleum and petroleum products can be only partly offset by exports of refined petroleum to neighbouring countries; the net costs amounted to 411,000m. francs CFA in 2007 and around 377,000m. francs CFA in 2008. Senegal's own annual domestic requirement for refined petroleum products was estimated at 39,000 b/d in 2009.

POWER

Most of Senegal's electric power comes from power stations dependent on oil. The addition in 2001 of 90 MW from the Manantali hydroelectric dam and the subsequent gain of 52 MW from an independent producer brought total generating capacity to 698.5 MW in 2008. The installed capacity services mainly urban areas, but since 2005 rural electrification has been rapidly extended. The sale of 34% of the shares of the Société Nationale d'Electricité (SENELEC) in 1999 to Hydro-Quebec and the French firm Elyo was annulled by the new Government of Abdoulaye Wade in 2000; it was decided in 2003 to restructure the company before introducing private equity. The company remained a significant burden on government finances and, with SENELEC experiencing problems with aging equipment and facing rising costs, extensive power cuts began to affect urban centres in March 2006; frequent and at times prolonged cuts continued, resulting in an IMF warning in October 2011 that the power outages had been a serious constraint on Senegal's economic prospects. The power cuts also became a highly charged political issue, as the regime faced, from September 2009, recurring popular protests, initially triggered by frustration at the slow response to the flooding affecting many of Dakar's poorer districts in August, but since then focusing on the ongoing outages; in June 2011 serious rioting occurred, spreading from Dakar to other urban centres.

Senegal had in fact been undertaking significant public investment in boosting its power capacity. In June 2007 an Iranian bank agreed a €32m. loan for the construction of a power transmission line to Tobène, Touba, Tivaouane and Kaolack, while in July the People's Republic of China agreed a preferential loan worth US $48m. for a new electricity transmission centre in Dakar. In January 2008 a new power plant opened in Kounoune, with a generating capacity of 67.5 MW, providing power for an additional 200,000 households With the re-emergence of significant electricity supply problems in mid-2010, Karim Wade, the President's son who already controlled several important economic ministries, assumed the energy portfolio in October, and in December arranged additional technical support from the French power giant EDF and a detailed assessment by the McKinsey consultancy. Its report became the basis of Plan TAKKAL ('Light Yourself Up' in Wolof), which was presented to the National Assembly on 31 March 2011 and which recommended expenditure of $1,500m. during 2011–15, and included a special Energy Support Fund to deal with short-term energy supply problems as well as substantial investments to enhance SENELEC's longer-term capacity. By late September 2011 the mobilization of additional funds through fresh borrowing and budgetary reallocations, as well as the renting of two supplementary power stations (on barges), stabilized the power supply; by the end of the year there was a sufficient fuel reserve for the power stations of 35 days.

It was intended during 2012 to push ahead rapidly with installing additional power capacity—to be bolstered later by a coal-fired generating station—while modernizing the distribution system. A plan for the financial and operation overhauling of SENELEC was expected by February. Although the presidential election in February–March saw the defeat of the Wade Government, the new administration, led by newly elected President Macky Sall, confirmed that it would uphold the outgoing Government's commitments.

MANUFACTURING

Senegal has the most developed manufacturing sector in francophone West Africa after Côte d'Ivoire. In 2007 manufactured products had an export value of over US $330m. The main activity is light industry (mostly located in or near Dakar). The agro-industrial sector is dominated by fish-canning and vegetable oil production, but also includes sugar-refining, flour-milling, tobacco, dairy products and drinks. Extractive industries (mainly the processing of phosphates) constitute a second important branch of activity. Leather goods production is also significant, as are paper and packaging, the manufacture of wood products and building materials, and the chemicals industry (including soap, paints, insecticides, plastics, pharmaceuticals and petroleum products). In the mid-1970s Senegal was the region's main textile exporter, but since 1985 the textile sector is estimated to have lost one-half of its companies and 60% of its jobs owing to competition from Asian imports; the state shareholding in the national textile company, the Société de Développement et des Fibres Textiles (SODEFITEX) was reduced from 60.0% to 46.5% in November 2003, after the French company Dacris acquired a majority stake. In the past, low labour productivity, infrastructural weaknesses and problems of access to credit limited the competitiveness of Senegalese industry and constrained its potential as a growth stimulus. However, over the past decade its role has expanded considerably: in 2010 industry's value added came to $1,543m. (compared with around $700m. in 2000), and it accounted for 16.3% of GDP.

Senegal's only cement plant at Rufisque, with an annual capacity of 1.5m. metric tons, was supplemented in 2002 by a second plant at Kirène, near Thiès, with an initial output of 600,000 tons, rising to 1.2m. tons. With cement a promising export commodity, these plants had increased their output to 3.3m. tons in 2009. Senegal's only refinery, the Société Africaine de Raffinage (SAR), at M'Bao, near Dakar, produced 896,000 tons of petroleum products in 2008, though production dropped to 739,000 tons in 2009 and 617,000 tons in 2010. In late 2006 the Government increased its stake in SAR to 57.2%, with the remainder being held by France's Total, the multinational Royal Dutch Shell, and ExxonMobile. Although SAR is Senegal's largest enterprise, a debt overhang caused the Government to invite the Saudi firm, Binladen Group, to acquire a 34% stake in May 2010 in return for 7,000m. francs CFA; this group planned to raise its future stake to 51% through an investment of 250,000m. francs CFA, in order to increase the refinery's annual capacity to 3m.–4m. tons to enable it to supply other West African markets.

In 2003 Senegal's first vehicle-assembly plant in Thiès, a joint venture between the Government and India's Tata International, started producing buses. In 2008 a car-assembly plant, 60% owned by Iran's Khodro, 20% by the state and 20% by private investors, commenced production of Samand cars. There are also truck and bicycle assembly plants.

TRANSPORT INFRASTRUCTURE

Industrial development was stimulated by, and in turn boosted, the port at Dakar. Container-handling facilities were increased from 29,000 metric tons to more than 100,000 tons when a new terminal was inaugurated in 1988; these were extended in 1993. Port activity then expanded when the renewed civil war in Côte d'Ivoire in 2002 forced Mali to divert much of its traffic there. Between 2007 and 2009 the import and export trade averaged over 10.5m. tons. annually. Improvements to Dakar's fishing port also occurred. In June 2007 the Government selected Dubai Port World to operate and develop the container terminal with a potential capacity of 1.5m. containers annually. The company planned to invest €100m. in doubling the port's handling capacity and a further €300m. on a new container terminal, which was inaugurated in November 2011.

Senegal possesses an extensive road network. In 2007 there were 14,600 km of classified roads, of which about 4,200 km were surfaced; by 2009 one-half of the population was living within 5 km of a paved road. Construction of the 31.5-km Dakar–Diamniadio toll highway was begun in 2010, with a second stage to Mtour 60 km from Dakar announced in October 2011. The route was to be a private-public partnership linking the city with the new Blaise-Diagne international airport and a new special economic zone being built by the Dubai firm Jebel Ali; it was expected to cost $600m. As well as receiving a loan of $69.85m. from the African Development Bank (AfDB), the Government issued a successful five-year $200m. bond appeal in December 2009. A second successful appeal—for $500m., covering a 10-year period—was made in May 2011. However, IMF concern over the level of Senegal's non-concessional borrowing led to agreement in early 2011 to rephase this project so that funds could be diverted to meeting the energy sector's restructuring.

The rail infrastructure includes 922 km of track, although only 70 km of this is two-way. The two main lines run west to east from Dakar to Kidira, and across the Malian border to Bamako, and from Dakar, via Thiès, to Saint-Louis in the north. In 1995 the Senegalese and Malian Governments established a joint company to operate the Dakar–Bamako line, with a 25-year concession granted in 2003 to a French/Canadian consortium, CANAC-Getmar, for which the company paid US $26.7m., in addition to making investments estimated at $70m. to upgrade operations; managed by its subsidiary, Transrail, freight traffic was more than doubled to an estimated 45,000 tons per month by 2005. Divestiture plans in 2009 envisaged the sale of a 51% share to a private investor.

Dakar's Léopold Sédar Senghor International Airport handles 1.6m. passengers and over 30,000 metric tons of freight annually; in addition, there are 12 secondary airports and several smaller airfields. After several years of delay, construction by the Binladen Group started in 2007 of the new Balaise-Digne International Airport at Ndiass, 50 km east of Dakar. With twice the capacity of the existing airport, it should provide 15,000 jobs directly or indirectly, mostly in the Thiès region; its completion was scheduled for 2012. Air Sénégal, the national carrier, was partially privatized in 1999, with Royal

Air Maroc (RAM) taking a 51% stake; in 2001 the company was renamed Air Sénégal International (ASI). With rising competition and fuel costs, ASI accumulated significant losses; in October 2007 the Government regained control of ASI, increasing its share from 49% to 75% and providing €35m. in new capital. However, in May 2009 the Government and RAM agreed to close ASI (by then technically bankrupt). In November the formation of its successor, Sénégal Airline, was announced, with RAM replaced by Emirates Airways as the new technical and strategic partner. Some 64% of the shares were acquired by Senegalese private investors; the Government held 16% and other public agencies 15%, with the remaining 5% going to airline staff. With a working capital of US $25m. and two Airbus 320 airplanes, Sénégal Airline began limited operations in January 2011; when a third Airbus 320 arrived in June, the number of destinations served increased to 14. To reduce competition, the Government denied the Togolese airline Asky landing rights at Dakar and prevented the Belgian company Brussels Airlines from using Dakar as a West African regional hub; the latter decision caused Belgium to withdraw its ambassador and threaten retaliatory measures through the EU. In November 2011, following a decision by the Guinean authorities to ground a Senegal Airlines plane in Conakry over unpaid bills of the disbanded ASI, the Government banned planes travelling to or from Guinea from using Senegal's airspace.

COMMUNICATIONS

In mid-1997 the national telecommunications company, Société Nationale des Télécommunications du Sénégal (SONATEL), was partially privatized, with France Télécom subsidiary France Câbles et Radio purchasing 33.3% of its capital. A further 10% of the shares were sold to SONATEL employees, with 18% of SONATEL's shares being sold on the regional stock exchange in Abidjan, Côte d'Ivoire. Following the recapitalization of SONATEL in 1999, France Câbles et Radio increased its stake to 42.3%, reducing the Government's share to 30%; in April 2009 its participation increased to 52.2%, after a further sale of government shares. After 1997 SONATEL experienced rapid growth, and having moved into the mobile phone market, it had 11m. subscribers in Senegal and three neighbouring countries by 2010. With only 2.2 fixed telephone lines per 100 inhabitants in 2007, the installation of a national digital and fibre-optic network stimulated the rapid development of the telecommunications sector. The penetration of mobile phone usage reached 57% of the population by 2009, and was expected to reach 70% by 2015; internet access was estimated at 16% in 2010. In 2009 a dispute emerged between the Government and the US firm Millicom, which owned, through its Tigo marque, Senegal's most important mobile phone network (with 1.8m. subscribers). Millicom faced pressure to accept an increase in its licence fee from the modest US $100,000 paid in 1998 to $200m., the amount that the Sudanese firm Sudatel had reportedly paid in September 2007 to become Senegal's fourth mobile service provider; Millicom took the dispute to the International Centre for Settlement of Investment Disputes in Paris, with a judgment still pending.

TOURISM

Beginning with a Club Med resort in Casamance in the 1970s, tourism developed as a leading source of foreign exchange, with 246,000 tourist arrivals already by 1990. These reached 769,000 in 2005 and 875,000 in 2009, but fell sharply in 2010 and 2011, with the decline especially marked among French visitors (who normally accounted for one-half of the total). The sector was estimated in 2011 to provide direct employment for 133,000 people.

In 2002 President Wade had set a target of 1.5m. tourists annually by 2010. While this target was revised to 2015, the Government put considerable resources into stimulating and diversifying the sector, heretofore largely dependent on the 'beach holiday' market. In 2007 the Government also lowered value added tax (VAT) on tourism-related activities from 18% to 10%, and ended visa requirements for EU citizens. Senegal currently possesses an estimated 45,000 hotel beds of international tourist standard, and Dakar is an important international conference centre. However, although there have been significant investments in the luxury hotel sector, other parts of the industry have suffered from relative neglect, and the high costs of tourism in Senegal (compared with other destinations), as well as the recently acquired association with sex tourism, have damaged the country's image. Tourism receipts declined from 21.6% of GDP in 2007 to 15.2% in 2009, falling further, to 12.2%, in 2011. An enduring peace settlement in Casamance—a popular destination for holidaymakers—should offer a tourism dividend.

INVESTMENT AND FINANCE

There was an upward trend in private investment from 2000, both in industry and in services, with Senegalese private investment playing an increasingly significant (if secondary) role to external investment. The latter grew dramatically, rising from US $63m. in 2000 and $44.6m. in 2005 to $297.4m. in 2007 and $397.6m. in 2008; it declined to $331m. in 2009, before declining sharply, to $237m., in 2010. Investment from Middle Eastern sources became prominent in sectors such as construction, tourism and communications, while Indian finance underpinned mining development. The Chinese investment presence also expanded. Despite the presence of 235 subsidiaries of French firms, French investment, which accounted for 90% of the total in 2000, represented only 5% in 2008. The World Bank's Doing Business 2009 report included Senegal among the top 10 reformers for 2007/08, with improvements moving its ranking from 168th to 149th of 181 countries; in 2011 it slipped slightly back to 154th out of 183.

Since independence, Senegal has benefited from consistent support by Western donors, which were keen to assist its relatively stable, conservative governments. In 2010 Senegal received official aid worth $931m., with 59% from bilateral sources. Remittances from Senegalese working either in Europe or North America proved an increasingly significant factor, though these underwent a marked fall of 8.6% in 2009, to 660,000m. francs CFA.

Considerable progress was made in the early 1980s in curbing Senegal's budget deficit, although prior to the major devaluation in 1994, the currency's overvaluation had had a negative impact on government revenues. In recent years revenue performance has improved, owing to tax reforms and tightened financial management. Between 2008 and 2011 domestic tax revenue has fluctuated between 18.6% of GDP (in 2009) and 20.4% (2011). On the other hand, the overall fiscal deficit increased sharply between 2003 and 2006 (from 1.4% to 6.0% of GDP), under pressure particularly from rising food and fuel subsidies. Declining to 4.0% in 2007—the IMF's medium-term target—it remained in this range during 2010, before rising to 5.7% in 2011 and to a possible 8.0% in 2012, due to the crisis in the energy sector and the impact of drought on the agricultural sector. The private banking system is burdened by non-performing loans; in 2010 these stood at nearly 20% of total bank loans, although the banks were able to meet the higher minimum capital requirements introduced in that year.

In March 1994 Senegal was the first franc zone member to reach agreement with the IMF on new funding following the devaluation of the CFA franc. A new Enhanced Structural Adjustment Facility (ESAF) was approved in August 1994. Senegal received another three-year ESAF (later known as the Poverty Production and Growth Facility—PRGF), equivalent to about $144m., in April 1998. A further PRGF, equivalent to $33m., for the period 2003–06, was granted in April 2003. Following lengthy negotiations, in November 2007 the IMF awarded Senegal a three-year Policy Support Instrument (PSI). This did not include financial support, but rather focused on maintaining macroeconomic stability and enhancing fiscal governance and transparency. In December 2008 the IMF approved further financial support to Senegal, worth around $112m., under the Exogenous Shocks Facility, to help the Government to cope with rising food and fuel prices. Although a budgetary crisis of mid-2008 briefly endangered the PSI programme's survival, the IMF's overall satisfaction with the Government's response to very challenging circumstances was underlined in May 2011 by the approval of a second PSI in December 2010.

FOREIGN TRADE AND PAYMENTS

Over the past 25 years Senegal's foreign trade and current account balance have been consistently in deficit. However, the fluctuations have tended to narrow, as exports of phosphates and fishery products expanded alongside groundnuts. In nominal CFA franc terms, the value of both imports and exports increased substantially following the currency's 50% devaluation in January 1994, by 119% for exports and 84% for imports. The value of both increased steadily thereafter. In 2007 the trade deficit totalled 958m. francs CFA before increasing to 971m. francs CFA in 2010, and to an estimated 1,192m. francs CFA in 2011. Total exports stood at 990,000m. francs CFA in 2009, 1,087,000m. francs CFA in 2010 and a projected 1,231,000m. francs CFA in 2011. In 2009 the five leading markets for Senegal's exports were Mali (20.6%), India (9.6%), France (4.5%), Italy (4.2%) and The Gambia (4.2%).

After the late 1970s the Government increased its borrowing abroad, and external long-term debt, standing at US $1,114m. in 1980, reached $4,051m. in 2003. Commercial bank debt was negligible following a World Bank-initiated 'buy-back' of 'London Club' debt (at 16% of its face value) in December 1996. Substantial debt relief, in accordance with the 'Trinidad terms', was approved by the 'Paris Club' in March 1994, while France agreed to cancel one-half of Senegal's bilateral debt. Further concessionary relief was granted by the 'Paris Club' in June 1998, in accordance with the 'Naples terms', permitting the cancellation or rescheduling of up to 67% of public debt.

In mid-2000 Senegal became eligible for debt relief under the initiative for heavily indebted poor countries (HIPC). A debt relief programme for Senegal was subsequently announced, which, with the support of official creditors, was equivalent to some US $800m. Debt relief provided by the World Bank represented a 50% reduction in Senegal's obligations to that organization over the following nine years, while that given by the IMF represented 20% of obligations to the Fund over the following seven years. Senegal reached 'completion point' under its HIPC arrangements in March 2004, becoming the 12th developing country to do so. Total debt relief was $488m. in net present value terms. Subsequently, various official creditors, including France, announced significant debt write-offs. In July 2005 Senegal was among 18 countries to be granted substantial further debt relief under the Multilateral Debt Relief Initiative (MDRI) agreed by the Group of Eight leading industrialized nations. As a result of the debt write-offs, the country's total external debt, according to the World Bank, had fallen from $3,883m. in 2005 to $1,644m. in 2006 (17.8% of GDP); it then rose again to $2,384m. in 2008 (19.7%), $2,961m. in 2009 (27%) and $3,483m. in 2010 (27.5%). Some 60% of external debt was owed on concessional terms to multilateral institutions, especially the World Bank and the AfDB; the major bilateral lenders include France, Kuwait, Spain, China and India.

Statistical Survey

Source (unless otherwise stated): Agence nationale de la Statistique et de la Démographie, blvd de l'Est, Point E, BP 116, Dakar; tel. 33-824-0301; fax 33-824-9004; e-mail statsenegal@yahoo.fr; internet www.ansd.sn.

Area and Population

AREA, POPULATION AND DENSITY

Area (sq km)	197,722*
Population (census results)†	
27 May 1988	6,896,808
8 December 2002	
Males	4,846,126
Females	5,009,212
Total	9,855,338
Population (annual averages, official estimates)	
2009	12,171,264
2010	12,509,434
2011	12,855,153
Density (per sq km) at 2011	65.0

* 75,955 sq miles.

† Figures for 1988 and 2002 refer to the *de jure* population. The de facto population at the 1988 census was 6,773,417, and at the 2002 census was 9,552,442.

POPULATION BY AGE AND SEX

(UN estimates at mid-2012)

	Males	Females	Total
0–14	2,870,697	2,805,394	5,676,091
15–64	3,484,502	3,635,822	7,120,324
65 and over	146,147	165,381	311,528
Total	6,501,346	6,606,597	13,107,943

Source: UN, *World Population Prospects: The 2010 Revision.*

POPULATION BY ETHNIC GROUP

(at 1988 census)

Ethnic group	Number	%
Wolof	2,890,402	42.67
Serere	1,009,921	14.91
Peul	978,366	14.44
Toucouleur	631,892	9.33
Diola	357,672	5.28
Mandingue	245,651	3.63
Rural-Rurale	113,184	1.67
Bambara	91,071	1.34
Maure	67,726	1.00
Manjaag	66,605	0.98
Others	320,927	4.74
Total	6,773,417	100.00

Source: UN, *Demographic Yearbook.*

REGIONS

(population estimates, 2010)

	Area (sq km)	Population	Density (per sq km)
Dakar	546	2,592,191	4,747.6
Diourbel	4,862	1,356,796	279.1
Fatick	7,049	724,345	102.8
Kaffrine*	11,041	558,041	50.5
Kaolack	5,265	795,906	151.2
Kedougou*	16,825	129,908	7.7
Kolda	13,721	603,961	44.0
Louga	25,644	857,944	33.5
Matam	28,852	542,201	18.8
Saint-Louis	18,981	894,000	47.1

—*continued*	Area (sq km)	Population	Density (per sq km)
Sedhiou*	7,346	431,238	58.7
Tambacounda	42,638	651,018	15.3
Thiès	6,597	1,658,445	251.4
Ziguinchor	7,355	713,440	97.0
Total	196,722	12,509,434	63.6

* Region created in March 2008.

PRINCIPAL TOWNS
(2002 census, provisional results)

Dakar (capital)	955,897	Mbour	153,503
Pikine	768,826	Diourbel	95,984
Rufisque	284,263	Louga	73,662
Guediawaye	258,370	Tambacounda	67,543
Thiès	237,849	Kolda	53,921
Kaolack	172,305	Mbacké	51,124
Saint-Louis	154,555		

Note: Data given pertain to communes, except for Dakar, Pikine, Rufisque and Guediawaye, where the population figure given is that of the département.

Mid-2011 (incl. suburbs, UN estimate): Dakar 3,035,470 (Source: UN, *World Urbanization Prospects: The 2011 Revision*).

BIRTHS AND DEATHS
(annual averages, UN estimates)

	1995–2000	2000–05	2005–10
Birth rate (per 1,000)	40.8	39.8	38.6
Death rate (per 1,000)	11.6	10.6	9.5

Source: UN, *World Population Prospects: The 2010 Revision*.

2011: Birth rate 36.8 per 1,000; Death rate 8.8 per 1,000 (Source: African Development Bank).

Life expectancy (years at birth): 59.0 (males 57.9; females 60.0) in 2010 (Source: World Bank, World Development Indicators database).

ECONOMICALLY ACTIVE POPULATION
('000 persons, 2006)

	Males	Females	Total
Agriculture, hunting and forestry	631.9	354.6	986.5
Fishing	66.5	10.4	76.9
Mining and quarrying	11.5	2.6	14.1
Manufacturing	203.7	41.7	245.4
Electricity, gas and water supply	18.5	3.3	21.8
Construction	179.7	6.9	186.6
Wholesale and retail trade; repair of motor vehicles, motorcycles and personal household goods	388.0	397.9	785.9
Hotels and restaurants	12.2	16.4	28.6
Transport, storage and communication	135.9	5.8	141.7
Financial intermediation	11.8	4.9	16.7
Public administration and defence; compulsory social security; education; health and social work	118.7	39.0	157.7
Extra-territorial organizations and bodies	3.3	3.7	7.0
Sub-total	1,781.7	887.2	2,668.9
Not classified by economic activity	266.5	217.5	484.0
Total	2,048.1	1,104.8	3,152.9
Unemployed	174.5	176.8	351.4
Total labour force	2,222.6	1,281.6	3,504.3

Source: ILO.

Mid-2012 (estimates in '000): Agriculture, etc. 4,047; Total labour force 5,819 (Source: FAO).

Health and Welfare

KEY INDICATORS

Total fertility rate (children per woman, 2010)	4.8
Under-5 mortality rate (per 1,000 live births, 2010)	75
HIV/AIDS (% of persons aged 15–49, 2009)	0.9
Physicians (per 1,000 head, 2008)	0.06
Hospital beds (per 1,000 head, 2008)	0.3
Health expenditure (2009): US $ per head (PPP)	106
Health expenditure (2009): % of GDP	5.7
Health expenditure (2009): public (% of total)	54.5
Access to water (% of persons, 2010)	72
Access to sanitation (% of persons, 2010)	52
Total carbon dioxide emissions ('000 metric tons, 2008)	4,976.1
Carbon dioxide emissions per head (metric tons, 2008)	0.4
Human Development Index (2011): ranking	155
Human Development Index (2011): value	0.459

For sources and definitions, see explanatory note on p. vi.

Agriculture

PRINCIPAL CROPS
('000 metric tons)

	2008	2009	2010
Rice, paddy	408.2	502.1	604.0
Maize	397.3	328.6	186.5
Millet	678.2	810.1	813.3
Sorghum	251.5	225.0	162.6
Cassava (Manioc)	920.9	265.5	181.2
Sugar cane*	836.0	836.0	836.0
Cashew nuts*	5.1	4.0	5.7
Groundnuts, with shell	731.2	1,032.7	1,286.9
Oil palm fruit*	71	71	71
Tomatoes	43.8	150.0	165.0
Onions, dry	150.0	160.0	160.0
Watermelons	327.3	190.6	240.8
Oranges	30.0	40.0	40.0
Guavas, mangoes and mangosteens	100.0	100.0	100.0

* FAO estimates.

Aggregate production ('000 metric tons, may include official, semi-official or estimated data): Total cereals 1,739.7 in 2008, 1,868.9 in 2009, 1,767.8 in 2010; Total pulses 126.5 in 2008, 86.7 in 2009, 49.0 in 2010; Total roots and tubers 963.7 in 2008, 340.5 in 2009, 266.2 in 2010; Total vegetables (incl. melons) 659.3 in 2008, 613.1 in 2009, 713.6 in 2010; Total fruits (excl. melons) 189.3 in 2008, 203.1 in 2009, 202.7 in 2010.

Source: FAO.

LIVESTOCK
('000 head, year ending September)

	2008	2009	2010
Cattle	3,208	3,294	3,346
Sheep	5,241	5,388	5,576
Goats	4,471	4,598	4,754
Pigs	326	337	347
Horses	522	523	528
Asses	441	477	481
Camels	5	5	5
Chickens	39,407	40,268	46,262

Source: FAO.

LIVESTOCK PRODUCTS
('000 metric tons)

	2008	2009	2010
Cattle meat	65.9	82.4	83.8
Sheep meat	20.9	18.3	19.2
Goat meat	13.7	12.5	12.9
Pig meat	10.6	10.9*	11.4*
Horse meat*	7.2	7.2	7.2
Chicken meat	41.1	39.4	49.2
Cows' milk	125.6	140.9	143.1
Sheep's milk	9.4	11.6	11.8
Goats' milk	11.7	13.6	13.9
Hen eggs*	28	27	30

* FAO estimate(s).

Source: FAO.

Forestry

ROUNDWOOD REMOVALS
('000 cubic metres, excl. bark, FAO estimates)

	2008	2009	2010
Sawlogs, veneer logs and logs for sleepers*	40	40	40
Other industrial wood†	754	754	754
Fuel wood	5,366	5,396	5,427
Total	6,160	6,190	6,221

* Annual output assumed to be unchanged since 1986 (FAO estimates).
† Annual output assumed to be unchanged since 1999 (FAO estimates).

2011: Production assumed to be unchanged from 2010 (FAO estimates).

Source: FAO.

SAWNWOOD PRODUCTION
('000 cubic metres, incl. railway sleepers)

	1989	1990	1991
Total (all broadleaved)	15	22	23

1992–2011: Annual production assumed to be unchanged from 1991 (FAO estimates).

Source: FAO.

Fishing

('000 metric tons, live weight)

	2008	2009	2010
Capture	425.8	442.3*	409.6*
Freshwater fishes	7.4	14.0*	20.0*
Sea catfishes	10.2	13.3	8.8
Round sardinella	165.1	143.0	126.0
Madeiran sardinella	86.0	93.5	83.0
Bonga shad	17.6	12.7	19.2
Octopuses	3.7	3.8	3.3
Aquaculture	0.1	0.1	0.1
Total catch	425.9	442.4*	409.7*

* FAO estimate.

Source: FAO.

Mining

('000 metric tons unless otherwise stated)

	2008	2009	2010
Crude petroleum ('000 barrels)	99	249	398
Gold (kg)	600*	5,354	4,381
Cement, hydraulic	3,084	3,320	4,066
Calcium phosphates	645	948	976
Aluminium phosphates	4	4†	n.a.
Fuller's earth (attapulgite)	167	181	204
Salt (unrefined)	241	222	231

* Government estimates of unreported production of artisanal gold.
† Estimate.

Source: US Geological Survey.

Industry

PETROLEUM PRODUCTS
('000 metric tons)

	2007	2008	2009
Jet fuels	48	99	68
Motor gasoline (petrol)	77	68	83
Kerosene	5	4	3
Gas-diesel (distillate fuel) oils	339	409	n.a.
Residual fuel (Mazout) oils	188	243	191

Source: UN, *Industrial Commodity Statistics Yearbook* and Database.

SELECTED OTHER PRODUCTS
('000 metric tons unless otherwise indicated)

	2009	2010	2011
Wheat flour	297.6	305.7	350.8
Sugar cubes	12.8	18.1	12.1
Salt	222.3	231.6	258.3
Soap	17.8	17.9	19.3
Phosphates	947.8	1,079.2	1,437.2
Fertilizers	44.0	44.9	37.0
Cement	3,327.2	4,065.8	4,722.3
Electricity (million kWh)	2,494.6	2,783.2	2,730.5

Finance

CURRENCY AND EXCHANGE RATES

Monetary Units

100 centimes = 1 franc de la Communauté Financière Africaine (CFA).

Sterling, Dollar and Euro Equivalents (31 May 2012)

£1 sterling = 819.959 francs CFA;
US $1 = 528.870 francs CFA;
€1 = 655.957 francs CFA;
10,000 francs CFA = £12.20 = $18.91 = €15.24.

Average Exchange Rate (francs CFA per US $)

2009 472.19
2010 495.28
2011 471.87

Note: An exchange rate of 1 French franc = 50 francs CFA, established in 1948, remained in force until January 1994, when the CFA franc was devalued by 50%, with the exchange rate adjusted to 1 French franc = 100 francs CFA. This relationship to French currency remained in effect with the introduction of the euro on 1 January 1999. From that date, accordingly, a fixed exchange rate of €1 = 655.957 francs CFA has been in operation.

BUDGET
('000 million francs CFA)

Revenue*	2011	2012†	2013‡
Tax revenue	1,287	1,411	1,495
Income tax	346	379	384
Taxes on goods and services (excl. petroleum)	729	830	835
Taxes on petroleum products	212	202	277
Non-tax revenue	50	50	78
Energy sector support fund operations	39	35	35
Total	1,376	1,497	1,608

Expenditure§	2011	2012†	2013‡
Current expenditure	1,233	1,250	1,274
Wages and salaries	428	450	467
Other operational expenses	702	690	682
Transfers and subsidies	335	312	291
Goods and services	356	366	379
Capital expenditure	718	913	906
Domestically financed	475	504	507
Externally financed	244	409	398
Total	1,952	2,163	2,179

* Excluding grants received ('000 million francs CFA): 150 in 2011; 196 in 2012 (programmed); 204 in 2013 (projections).

† Programmed figures.

‡ Projections.

§ Excluding net lending ('000 million francs CFA): 28 in 2011; –8 in 2012 (programmed); 0 in 2012 (projections).

Source: IMF, *Senegal: Third Review Under the Policy Support Instrument and Request for Modification of Assessment Criteria—Staff Report; Informational Annex; Press Release; and Statement by the Executive Director for Senegal* (August 2012).

INTERNATIONAL RESERVES
(excluding gold, US $ million at 31 December)

	2009	2010	2011
IMF special drawing rights	204.4	200.7	199.9
Reserve position in IMF	2.7	2.8	2.8
Foreign exchange	1,916.1	1,844.0	1,742.9
Total	2,123.2	2,047.5	1,945.7

Source: IMF, *International Financial Statistics*.

MONEY SUPPLY
('000 million francs CFA at 31 December)

	2009	2010	2011
Currency outside banks	494.8	561.8	589.4
Demand deposits at deposit money banks	856.6	980.3	1,051.0
Checking deposits at post office	14.6	6.1	7.9
Total money (incl. others)	1,366.9	1,549.2	1,649.7

Source: IMF, *International Financial Statistics*.

COST OF LIVING
(Consumer Price Index; base: 2000 = 100)

	2006	2007	2008
Food (incl. tobacco)	116.0	124.5	136.4
Clothing	85.9	88.4	86.3
Electricity, gas and other fuels	112.0	123.2	n.a.
Rent	108.2	119.1	120.8
All items (incl. others)	110.0	116.4	123.1

2009: Food (incl. tobacco) 132.3; All items (incl. others) 121.8.

2010: All items 121.9.

2010: All items 126.0.

Source: ILO.

NATIONAL ACCOUNTS
(million francs CFA at current prices)

Expenditure on the Gross Domestic Product

	2009	2010	2011
Government final consumption expenditure	871,000	944,000	1,007,500
Private final consumption expenditure	4,843,523	4,980,518	5,312,500
Gross fixed capital formation	1,388,000	1,414,000	1,540,100
Changes in inventories	–56,000	29,000	92,700
Total domestic expenditure	7,046,523	7,367,518	7,952,800
Exports of goods and services	1,472,000	1,538,000	1,611,600
Less Imports of goods and services	2,490,000	2,536,000	2,724,800
Statistical discrepancy	—	–400	140
GDP at purchasers' values	6,028,523	6,369,118	6,839,740

Gross Domestic Product by Economic Activity

	2009	2010	2011
Agriculture, hunting, forestry and fishing	907,000	971,000	1,041,900
Mining and quarrying	106,000	123,000	154,100
Manufacturing	740,000	781,000	847,700
Electricity, gas and water	153,000	171,000	173,800
Construction	244,000	246,000	267,800
Trade, restaurants and hotels	1,002,580	1,036,518	1,093,000
Finance, insurance and real estate	524,849	553,194	580,000
Transport and communications	635,541	646,486	696,100
Public administration and defence	613,382	652,736	693,861
Other services	514,670	539,583	573,579
Sub-total	5,441,022	5,720,517	6,121,840
Indirect taxes	722,000	791,600	868,300
Less imputed bank service charge	134,500	143,000	150,400
GDP at purchasers' values	6,028,523	6,369,118	6,839,740

Source: African Development Bank.

BALANCE OF PAYMENTS
(US $ million)

	2007	2008	2009
Exports of goods f.o.b.	1,673.8	2,206.0	2,096.8
Imports of goods f.o.b.	–4,163.8	–5,606.0	–4,125.0
Trade balance	–2,489.9	–3,400.0	–2,028.2
Exports of services	1,200.9	1,294.1	1,022.1
Imports of services	–1,238.4	–1,414.5	–1,151.1
Balance on goods and services	–2,527.4	–3,520.4	–2,157.2
Other income received	138.2	235.4	160.2
Other income paid	–212.1	–283.3	–341.0
Balance on goods, services and income	–2,601.2	–3,568.3	–2,338.0
Current transfers received	1,557.5	1,985.9	1,756.8
Current transfers paid	–268.0	–301.3	–283.6
Current balance	–1,311.7	–1,883.7	–864.8
Capital account (net)	332.7	239.5	305.1
Direct investment abroad	–24.7	–126.3	–77.1
Direct investment from abroad	297.4	397.6	331.1
Portfolio investment assets	6.4	51.6	–91.3
Portfolio investment liabilities	24.7	20.9	–1.6
Financial derivatives assets	—	0.2	—
Financial derivatives liabilities	25.6	–0.2	—
Other investment assets	84.4	147.7	–128.2
Other investment liabilities	421.7	599.7	451.4
Net errors and omissions	12.8	–13.5	–171.3
Overall balance	–130.8	–566.5	–246.8

Source: IMF, *International Financial Statistics*.

External Trade

PRINCIPAL COMMODITIES
('000 million francs CFA)

Imports c.i.f.	2009	2010	2011
Rice	163.8	130.8	175.7
Animal and vegetable oils and fats	68.6	59.9	79.8
Crude petroleum	186.7	224.4	255.1
Other petroleum products	214.2	312.9	389.4
Pharmaceutical products	64.8	62.6	71.6
Artificial plastic materials	73.5	52.1	77.0
Common metals	86.2	101.5	122.4
Agricultural and industrial machinery	312.0	271.3	307.4
Vehicles	69.6	69.7	71.1
Total (incl. others)	2,137.4	2,196.3	2,544.2

Exports f.o.b.	2009	2010	2011
Fresh fish	73.5	78.8	89.5
Crustaceans, molluscs and other shellfish	33.2	35.2	51.1
Frozen fish	5.8	2.0	1.5
Peanut oil	18.1	28.4	36.9
Hydraulic cement	70.6	99.7	112.2
Petroleum products	207.6	215.9	176.5
Phosphoric acid	69.8	98.5	160.7
Total (incl. others)	890.5	978.2	1,138.8

PRINCIPAL TRADING PARTNERS
('000 million francs CFA)

Imports c.i.f.	2009	2010	2011
Argentina	45.6	48.2	47.6
Belgium-Luxembourg	49.9	46.5	40.6
Brazil	80.8	54.3	87.2
China, People's Republic	192.0	195.1	177.9
Côte d'Ivoire	63.3	50.9	74.0
France (incl. Monaco)	425.5	441.4	460.3
Germany	74.9	54.8	48.5
India	47.5	59.1	50.9
Ireland	10.8	12.3	10.7
Italy	69.6	47.3	80.1
Japan	39.0	52.0	40.5
Morocco	37.8	27.8	26.2
Netherlands	61.7	96.1	122.3
Nigeria	197.4	230.8	256.3
South Africa	42.3	40.1	47.7
Spain	92.2	84.9	93.7
Thailand	116.9	73.9	96.8
Turkey	27.7	40.5	94.3
Ukraine	22.4	57.4	37.1
United Kingdom	40.1	58.4	87.2
USA	64.3	61.5	121.2
Viet Nam	33.4	27.8	54.0
Total (incl. others)	2,137.4	2,196.3	2,544.2

Exports f.o.b.	2009	2010	2011
Benin	5.8	10.2	9.8
Burkina Faso	10.1	12.4	19.0
Cameroon	7.8	15.6	22.8
Côte d'Ivoire	26.8	25.5	24.9
France (incl. Monaco)	51.7	47.2	53.0
The Gambia	33.4	33.7	37.5
Greece	12.1	8.1	8.3
Guinea	28.3	34.6	55.1
Guinea-Bissau	21.5	20.6	23.7
India	73.2	103.8	168.2

Exports f.o.b.—*continued*	2009	2010	2011
Italy	24.5	23.2	32.6
Japan	1.5	2.0	4.9
Mali	171.5	247.7	181.0
Mauritania	25.9	23.4	31.4
Netherlands	13.5	10.9	11.8
Spain	20.7	28.9	35.0
Switzerland	74.1	82.0	104.4
Togo	8.8	10.0	13.2
United Arab Emirates	13.0	18.0	15.5
Total (incl. others)	890.5	978.2	1,138.8

Transport

RAILWAYS
(traffic)

	2002	2003	2004
Passenger-km (million)	105	129	122
Net ton-km (million)	345	375	358

Passengers ('000): 4,789 in 1999.

Freight carried ('000 metric tons): 2,017 in 1999.

ROAD TRAFFIC
(motor vehicles in use)

	2006	2007	2008
Passenger cars	178,977	187,838	196,074
Buses and coaches	14,787	14,110	15,969
Lorries and vans	27,948	33,212	53,852
Motorcycles and mopeds	9,201	10,656	12,403

Source: IRF, *World Road Statistics*.

SHIPPING

Merchant Fleet
(vessels registered at 31 December)

	2007	2008	2009
Number of vessels	186	186	189
Total displacement ('000 grt)	46.4	46.5	47.3

Source: IHS Fairplay, *World Fleet Statistics*.

International Sea-borne Freight Traffic
('000 metric tons)

	2006	2007	2008
Goods loaded	2,279	2,322	2,232
Goods unloaded	7,651	8,787	8,358

Source: Port Autonome de Dakar.

CIVIL AVIATION
(traffic on scheduled services)*

	2007	2008	2009
Kilometres flown (million)	13	20	19
Passengers carried ('000)	539	567	573
Passenger-km (million)	993	1,017	985
Total ton-km (million)	97	103	101

* Including an apportionment of the traffic of Air Afrique.

Source: UN, *Statistical Yearbook*.

Tourism

FOREIGN TOURIST ARRIVALS BY NATIONALITY*

	2005	2006	2007
African states	87,565	106,396	97,398
Belgium, Luxembourg and the Netherlands	21,712	23,896	17,717
East Asian and Pacific states	3,837	3,846	3,620
France	191,580	184,376	171,452
Germany	9,615	8,708	6,973
Italy	11,493	13,705	13,953
Spain	15,353	17,021	19,039
United Kingdom	4,380	5,582	5,416
USA	11,080	12,404	20,482
Total (incl. others)	386,565	405,827	386,793

* Figures refer to arrivals at hotels and similar establishments.

Total tourist arrivals ('000): 810 in 2009; 900 in 2010.

Receipts from tourism (US $ million, excl. passenger transport): 463 in 2009; 453 in 2010.

Source: World Tourism Organization.

Communications Media

	2009	2010	2011
Telephones ('000 main lines in use)	278.8	341.9	346.4
Mobile cellular telephones ('000 subscribers)	6,901.5	8,343.7	9,352.9
Internet subscribers ('000)	59.7	78.6	n.a.
Broadband subscribers ('000)	58.7	78.6	92.7

Personal computers: 250,000 (22.2 per 1,000 persons) in 2005.

Television receivers ('000 in use): 380 in 2000.

Radio receivers ('000 in use): 1,240 in 1997.

Daily newspapers: 1 (average circulation 45,000 copies) in 1996; 13 in 2004.

Non-daily newspapers: 6 (average circulation 37,000 copies) in 1995.

Sources: mainly International Telecommunication Union; UNESCO, *Statistical Yearbook*, UNESCO Institute for Statistics.

Education

(2009/10 unless otherwise indicated)

	Institutions*	Teachers	Students ('000) Males	Females	Total
Pre-primary	1,725	6,009	70.1	76.7	146.8
Primary	7,939	50,369	832.1	862.9	1,695.0
Secondary	1,122	22,437	389.5	335.7	725.2
Tertiary	n.a.	n.a.	57.8	34.3	92.1

* 2008/09 (Source: Ministry of Education, Dakar).

Source: UNESCO Institute for Statistics.

Pupil-teacher ratio (primary education, UNESCO estimate): 33.7 in 2009/10 (Source: UNESCO Institute for Statistics).

Adult literacy rate (UNESCO estimates): 49.7% (males 61.8%; females 38.7%) in 2009 (Source: UNESCO Institute for Statistics).

Directory

The Constitution

The Constitution of the Republic of Senegal was promulgated following its approval by popular referendum on 7 January 2001, and entered into force thereafter, with the exception of those sections relating to the Assemblée nationale and the relations between the executive and legislative powers (articles 59–87), which took effect following legislative elections on 29 April 2001. The main provisions (including subsequent amendments) are summarized below:

PREAMBLE

The people of Senegal, recognizing their common destiny, and aware of the need to consolidate the fundaments of the Nation and the State, and supporting the ideals of African unity and human rights, proclaim the principle of national territorial integrity and a national unity respecting the diverse cultures of the Nation, reject all forms of injustice, inequality and discrimination, and proclaim the will of Senegal to be a modern democratic State.

THE STATE AND SOVEREIGNTY

Articles 1–6: Senegal is a secular, democratic Republic, in which all people are equal before the law, without distinction of origin, race, sex or religion. The official language of the Republic is French; the national languages are Diola, Malinké, Pular, Sérère, Soninké, Wolof and any other national language that may be so defined. The principle of the Republic is 'government of the people, by the people and for the people'. National sovereignty belongs to the people who exercise it, through their representatives or in referenda. Suffrage may be direct or indirect, and is always universal, equal and secret. Political parties and coalitions of political parties are obliged to observe the Constitution and the principles of national sovereignty and democracy, and are forbidden from identifying with one race, one ethnic group, one sex, one religion, one sect, one language or one region. All acts of racial, ethnic or religious discrimination, including regionalist propaganda liable to undermine the security or territorial integrity of the State are punishable by law. The institutions of the Republic are: the President of the Republic; the Parlement (comprising the Assemblée nationale and the Sénat); the Government and the Constitutional Council; the Council of State; the Final Court of Appeal (Cour de Cassation); the Revenue Court (Cour de Comptes); and Courts and Tribunals.

PUBLIC LIBERTIES AND THE HUMAN PERSON; ECONOMIC AND SOCIAL RIGHTS AND COLLECTIVE RIGHTS

Articles 7–25: The inviolable and inalienable rights of man are recognized as the base of all human communities, of peace and justice in the world, and are protected by the State. All humans are equal before the law. The Republic protects, within the rule of law, the right to free opinion, free expression, a free press, freedom of association and of movement, cultural, religious and philosophical freedoms, the right to organize trade unions and businesses, the right to education and literacy, the right to own property, to work, to health, to a clean environment, and to diverse sources of information. No prior authorization is required for the formation of an organ of the press. Men and women are guaranteed equal rights to possess property.

Marriage and the family constitute the natural and moral base of the human community, and are protected by the State. The State is obliged to protect the physical and moral health of the family, in particular of the elderly and the handicapped, and guarantees to alleviate the conditions of life of women, particularly in rural areas. Forced marriages are forbidden as a violation of individual liberty.

The State protects youth from exploitation, from drugs, and from delinquency.

All children in the Republic have the right to receive schooling, from public schools, or from institutions of religious or non-religious communities. All national educational institutions, public or private, are obliged to participate in the growth of literacy in one of the national languages. Private schools may be opened with the authorization of, and under the control of, the State.

Freedom of conscience is guaranteed. Religious communities and institutions are separate from the State.

All discrimination against workers on grounds of origins, sex, political opinions or beliefs are forbidden. All workers have the right to join or form trade or professional associations. The right to strike is recognized, under legal conditions, as long as the freedom to work is not impeded, and the enterprise is not placed in peril. The State guarantees sanitary and human conditions in places of work.

THE PRESIDENT OF THE REPUBLIC

Articles 26–52: The President of the Republic is elected, for a term of seven years, by universal direct suffrage. The mandate may be renewed once. Candidates for the presidency must be of solely Senegalese nationality, enjoy full civil and political rights, be aged 35 years or more on the day of elections, and must be able to write, read and speak the official language fluently. All candidates must be presented by a political party or a legally constituted coalition of political parties, or be accompanied by a petition signed by at least 10,000 electors, including at least 500 electors in each of six administrative regions. Candidates may not campaign predominately on ethnic or regional grounds. Each political party or coalition of political parties may present only one candidate. If no candidate receives an absolute majority of votes cast in the first round, representing the support of at least one-quarter of the electorate, a second round of elections is held between the two highest-placed candidates in the first round. In the case of incapacity, death or resignation, the President's position is assumed by the President of the Sénat, and in the case of his or her incapacity, by the President of the Assemblée nationale, in all cases subject to the same terms of eligibility that apply to the President. The President presides over the Council of Ministers, the Higher Council of National Defence, and the National Security Council, and is the Supreme Chief of the Armed Forces. The President appoints a Prime Minister, and appoints ministers on the recommendation of the Prime Minister.

THE GOVERNMENT

Articles 53–57: The head of the Government is the Prime Minister. In the event of the resignation or removal from office of a Prime Minister, the entire Government is obliged to resign.

THE OPPOSITION

Article 58: The Constitution guarantees the right to oppose political parties that are opposed to Government policy, and recognizes the existence of a parliamentary opposition.

THE PARLEMENT

Article 59–66: Deputies of the Assemblée nationale are elected by universal direct suffrage, for a five-year mandate, subject only to the dissolution of the Assemblée nationale. Any serving deputy who resigns from his or her party shall have his or her mandate removed. Deputies enjoy immunity from criminal proceedings, except with the authorization of the bureau of the Assemblée nationale. The Assemblée nationale votes on the budget. Deputies vote as individuals and must not be obligated to vote in a certain way. Except in exceptional and limited circumstances, sessions of the Assemblée nationale are public.

The members of the Sénat are elected by universal direct suffrage, for a five-year mandate. Two-fifths of the members of the Sénat must be women.

RELATIONS BETWEEN THE EXECUTIVE AND LEGISLATIVE POWERS

Articles 67–87: The Parlement is the sole holder of legislative power. The Assemblée nationale votes on the budget and authorizes a declaration of war. The President of the Republic may, having received the opinion of the Prime Minister and the President of the Assemblée nationale, pronounce by decree the dissolution of the Assemblée nationale, except during the first two years of any Assemblée.

INTERNATIONAL TREATIES

Articles: 88–91: The President of the Republic negotiates international engagements, and ratifies or approves them with the authorization of the Parlement. The Republic of Senegal may conclude agreements with any African State that would comprise a partial or total abandonment of national sovereignty in order to achieve African unity.

JUDICIAL POWER

Articles 92–98: The judiciary is independent of the legislature and the executive power. The judiciary consists of the Constitutional Council, the Council of State, the Court of Final Appeal, the Revenue Court and Courts and Tribunals. The Constitutional Council comprises five members, including a President, a Vice-President and three judges. Each member serves for a mandate of six years (which may not be renewed) with partial renewals occurring every two years. The President of the Republic appoints members of the Constitutional Council, whose decisions are irreversible.

THE HIGH COURT OF JUSTICE

Articles 99–101: A High Court of Justice, presided over by a magistrate and comprising members elected by the Assemblée nationale and the Sénat, is instituted. The President of the Republic can only be brought to trial for acts accomplished in the exercise of his duties in the case of high treason. The High Court of Justice tries the Prime Minister and other members of the Government for crimes committed in the exercise of their duties.

LOCAL GOVERNMENT

Article 102: Local government bodies operate independently, by means of elective assemblies, in accordance with the law.

ON REVISION

Article 103: The Prime Minister proposes any amendments to the Constitution to the President of the Republic after they have been approved by both the Assemblée nationale and the Sénat. Amendments may be approved by referendum or, at the initiative of the President of the Republic, solely by approval by the Parlement, in which case a three-fifths' majority must be in favour.

The Government

HEAD OF STATE

President: MACKY SALL (took office 2 April 2012).

COUNCIL OF MINISTERS

(September 2012)

Prime Minister: ABDOUL MBAYE.

Minister of Foreign Affairs and Senegalese Nationals Abroad: ALIOUNE BADARA CISSÉ.

Minister of the Interior: MBAYE NDIAYE.

Minister of Health and Social Action: EVA MARIE COLL SECK.

Minister of the Armed Forces: AUGUSTIN TINE.

Minister of Justice, Keeper of the Seals: AMINATA TOURÉ.

Minister of the Economy and Finance: AMADOU KANE.

Minister of Culture and Tourism: YOUSSOU N'DOUR.

Minister of Women, Childhood and Female Entrepreneurship: MARIAMA SARR.

Minister of National Education: IBRAHIMA SALL.

Minister of Agriculture and Rural Equipment: BENOÎT SAMBOU.

Minister of Land Settlement and Local Communities: CHEIKH BAMBA DIÈYE.

Minister of Trade, Industry and Handicrafts: MATA SY DIALLO.

Minister of Stockbreeding: AMINATA MBENGUE NDIAYE.

Minister of Fishing and Maritime Affairs: PAPE DIOUF.

Minister of Infrastructure and Transport: MOR NGOM.

Minister of Energy and Mines: ALY NGOUILLE NDIAYE.

Minister of Youth, Professional Training and Employment: ALY KOTO NDIAYE.

Minister of Sport: EL HADJI MALICK GACKOU.

Minister of Town Planning and Housing: KHOUDIA MBAYE.

Minister of Higher Education and Research, Government Spokesperson: Prof. SERIGNE MBAYE THIAM.

Minister of Ecology and the Protection of Nature: ALI HAÏDAR.

Minister of the Civil Service, Labour and Relations with the Institutions: MANSOUR SY.

Minister of Hydraulics and Sanitation: OUMAR GUÈYE.

Minister of Communication and Information and Communication Technologies: ABOU LÔ.

Minister-delegate to the Minister of the Economy and Finance, in charge of the Budget: ABDOULAYE DAOUDA DIALLO.

Minister of State, Secretary-General of the Presidency: AMINATA TALL.

MINISTRIES

Office of the President: ave Léopold Sédar Senghor, BP 168, Dakar; tel. 33-880-8080; internet www.presidence.sn.

Office of the Prime Minister: Bldg Administratif, 9e étage, ave Léopold Sédar Senghor, BP 4029, Dakar; tel. 33-889-6969; fax 33-823-4479; internet www.gouv.sn.

Ministry of Agriculture and Rural Equipment: Bldg Administratif, 3e étage, BP 4005, Dakar; tel. 33-849-7000; fax 33-823-3268; internet www.agriculture.gouv.sn.

Ministry of the Armed Forces: Bldg Administratif, 8e étage, ave Léopold Sédar Senghor, BP 4041, Dakar; tel. 33-849-7612; fax 33-823-6338; internet www.forcesarmees.gouv.sn.

Ministry of the Civil Service, Labour and Relations with the Institutions: Bldg Administratif, 1er étage, BP 4007, Dakar; tel. 33-849-7000; fax 33-823-7429; e-mail mineladiallo@yahoo.fr; internet www.fonctionpublique.gouv.sn.

Ministry of Communication and Information and Communication Technologies: 58 blvd de la République, BP 4027, Dakar; tel. 33-823-1065; fax 33-821-4504; internet www.telecom.gouv.sn.

Ministry of Culture and Tourism: Bldg Administratif, 3e étage, ave Léopold Sédar Senghor, BP 4001, Dakar; tel. 33-822-4303; fax 33-822-1638; internet www.culture.gouv.sn.

Ministry of the Economy and Finance: rue René Ndiaye, BP 4017, Dakar; tel. 33-889-2100; fax 33-822-4195; e-mail i_diouf@minfinances.sn; internet www.finances.gouv.sn.

Ministry of Ecology and the Protection of Nature: Bldg Administratif, 2e étage, BP 4055, Dakar; tel. 33-889-0234; fax 33-822-2180; e-mail ministereenvironnement@gmail.com; internet www.environnement.gouv.sn.

Ministry of Energy and Mines: 122 bis ave André Peytavin, BP 4037, Dakar; tel. 33-822-9994; fax 33-822-5594; e-mail mindpme@msn.com; internet www.industrie.gouv.sn.

Ministry of Fishing and Maritime Affairs: Bldg Administratif, 4e étage, BP 4050, Dakar; tel. 33-849-5073; fax 33-823-8720; e-mail abdoumbodj@yahoo.fr; internet www.ecomaritime.gouv.sn.

Ministry of Foreign Affairs and Senegalese Nationals Abroad: pl. de l'Indépendance, BP 4044, Dakar; tel. 33-889-1300; fax 33-823-5496; e-mail maeuase@senegal.diplomatie.sn; internet www.diplomatie.gouv.sn.

Ministry of Health and Social Action: Fann Résidence, rue Aimé Césaire, BP 4024, Dakar; tel. 33-869-4242; fax 33-869-4269; e-mail mdseck@minsante.sn; internet www.sante.gouv.sn.

Ministry of Higher Education and Research: rue Docteur Calmette, BP 4025, Dakar; tel. 33-849-7556; fax 33-822-4563; internet www.recherche.gouv.sn.

Ministry of Hydraulics and Sanitation: blvd Dial Diop, pl. de l'ONU, BP 2372, Dakar; tel. 33-869-1526; fax 33-864-5932.

Ministry of Infrastructure and Transport: Bldg Administratif, Dakar; tel. 33-849-7000; fax 33-842-0292.

Ministry of the Interior: pl. Washington, BP 4002, Dakar; tel. 33-889-9100; fax 33-821-0542; e-mail mint@primature.sn; internet www.interieur.gouv.sn.

Ministry of Justice: Bldg Administratif, 7e étage, ave Léopold Sédar Senghor, BP 4030, Dakar; tel. 33-849-7000; fax 33-823-2727; e-mail justice@justice.gouv.sn; internet www.justice.gouv.sn.

Ministry of Land Settlement and Local Communities: Dieuppeul Derklé, rue DD, 142 BP 4002, Dakar; tel. 33-869-4700; fax 33-869-4713.

Ministry of National Education: 56 ave Lamine Gueye, Dakar; tel. 33-849-5402; fax 33-821-8930; internet www.education.gouv.sn.

Ministry of Sport: Bldg Administratif, Dakar.

Ministry of Stockbreeding: VDN, blvd du Koweit, BP 45677, Dakar; tel. 33-859-0630; fax 33-864-6311.

Ministry of Town Planning and Housing: 54 ave Georges Pompidou X Raffenel, Immeuble Plazza, 1er étage, Dakar; tel. 33-889-0730.

Ministry of Trade, Industry and Handicrafts: Bldg Administratif, Dakar; tel. 33-822-9542; fax 33-822-4669.

Ministry of Women, Childhood and Female Entrepreneurship: Bldg Administratif, 6e étage, BP 4050, Dakar; tel. 33-849-7061; fax 33-822-9490; e-mail communication@famille.gouv.sn; internet www.famille.gouv.sn.

Ministry of Youth, Professional Training and Employment: Rue C X 100, Zone B, Dakar; tel. 33-859-3877; fax 33-829-2428; internet www.jeunesse.gouv.sn.

President and Legislature

PRESIDENT

Presidential Election, First Round, 26 February 2012

Candidate	Valid votes	% of valid votes
Abdoulaye Wade	942,546	34.82
Macky Sall	719,369	26.57
Moustapha Niasse	357,347	13.20
Ousmane Tanor Dieng	305,980	11.30
Idrissa Seck	212,848	7.86
Cheikh Mamadou Abiboulah Dièye	52,196	1.93
Ibrahima Fall	48,950	1.81
Others*	67,820	2.51
Total	2,707,056†	100.00

* There were seven other candidates.
† In addition, there were 28,350 invalid votes.

Presidential Election, Second Round, 25 March 2012

Candidate	Valid votes	% of valid votes
Macky Sall	1,909,244	65.80
Abdoulaye Wade	992,556	34.20
Total	2,901,800*	100.00

* In addition, there were 14,093 invalid votes.

LEGISLATURE

Assemblée nationale

pl. Soweto, BP 86, Dakar; tel. 33-823-1099; fax 33-823-6708; e-mail assnat@assemblee-nationale.sn; internet www.assemblee-nationale.sn.

President: MOUSTAPHA NIASSE.

General Election, 1 July 2012

Party	Votes	% of votes	Seats
Benno Bokk Yaakaar (BBY)	1,040,899	53.06	119
Parti Démocratique Sénégalais (PDS)	298,846	15.23	12
Bokk Gis Gis (BGG)	143,180	7.30	4
Bës du Niak	113,321	5.78	4
Mouvement de la Réforme pour le Développement Social (MRDS)	70,655	3.60	2
Parti de la Vérité pour le Développement (PVD)	48,553	2.47	2
Union pour le Renouveau Démocratique (URD)	21,964	1.12	1
Mouvement Patriotique du Sénégal/Faxas	21,868	1.11	1
Convergence Patriotique pour la Justice et l'Équité/Nay Leer	20,762	1.06	1
Tekki 2012	20,671	1.05	1
Deggo Soxali Transport Ak Commerce	18,859	0.96	1
Leeral	17,791	0.91	1
And Jëf—Parti africain pour la Démocratie et le Socialisme (AJ—PADS)	15,889	0.81	1
Others	108,518	5.53	—
Total	1,961,776	100.00	150

Sénat

President: PAPE DIOP.

Election, 19 August 2007

Party	Seats
Parti Démocratique Sénégalais (PDS)	34
And Jëf—Parti Africain pour la Démocratie et le Socialisme (AJ—PADS)	1
Total	100*

* The remaining 65 members are appointed by the President.

Election Commission

Commission Électorale Nationale Autonome (CENA): BP 28900, Dakar; internet www.cena.sn; f. 2005; Pres. DEMBA KANDJI.

Political Organizations

A total of 24 parties and coalitions contested the legislative elections held in July 2012.

Alliance des Forces de Progrès (AFP): rue 1, angle rue A, point E, BP 5825, Dakar; tel. 33-869-7595; fax 33-825-7770; e-mail afp.net@yahoo.fr; internet www.afp-senegal.org; f. 1999; Sec.-Gen. MOUSTAPHA NIASSE.

Alliance Jëf-Jël: Villa 5, rue 1, Castors Front de Terre, Dakar; tel. 77-652-2232; e-mail tallasylla@hotmail.com; f. 1997; Pres. TALLA SYLLA.

And Defar Sénégal Coalition: Kolda; Leader LANDING SAVANÉ.

And Jëf—Parti Africain pour la Démocratie et le Socialisme (AJ—PADS): Villa 1, Zone B, BP 12136, Dakar; tel. and fax 33-864-4130; e-mail webmaster@ajpads.org; internet ajpads.com; f. 1992; Sec.-Gen. LANDING SAVANÉ.

Benno Bokk Yaakaar (BBY): Dakar; coalition comprising 80 political organizations.

Alliance pour la République (APR—Yaakaar): Dakar; f. 2008; Leader MACKY SALL.

Bës du Niak: Leader SERIGNE MANSOUR MANSOUR SY DJAMIL.

Bokk Gis Gis (BGG): Dakar; coalition of political organizations.

Bloc des Centristes Gaïndé (BCG): Villa 734, Sicap Baobabs, Dakar; tel. 33-825-3764; e-mail issa_dias@sentoo.sn; f. 1996; Pres. and Sec.-Gen. JEAN-PAUL DIAS.

Convergence Patriotique pour la Justice et l'Équité/Nay Leer: Dakar; Leader DEMBA DIOP.

Convergence pour le Renouveau et la Citoyenneté (CRC): 7 ave Bourguiba, Industrial Zone, Sodida, Dakar; tel. 33-824-4900; e-mail info@crc-sn.org; internet www.crc-sn.org; Sec.-Gen. ALIOU DIA.

Deggo Soxali Transport Ak Commerce: Dakar; Leader ALASSANE NDOYE.

Front pour le Socialisme et la Démocratie—Benno Jubël (FSD—BJ): contested 2001 election as mem. of Sopi Coalition; Sec.-Gen. BAMBA DIÈYE.

Leeral: Dakar; Leader EL HADJI DIOUF.

Ligue Démocratique—Mouvement pour le Parti du Travail (LD—MPT): ave Bourguiba, Dieuppeul 2, Villa 2566, BP 10172, Dakar Liberté; tel. 33-825-6706; fax 33-827-4300; e-mail jallarbi@sentoo.sn; internet www.ldmpt.sn; regd 1981; social-democrat; Sec.-Gen. ABDOULAYE BATHILY.

Mouvement pour la Démocratie et le Socialisme—Naxx Jarinu (MDS—NJ): Unité 20, Parcelles Assainies, Villa 528, Dakar; tel. 33-869-5049; f. 2000; Leader OUMAR KHASSIMOU DAI.

Mouvement Patriotique du Sénégal/Faxas (MPS/Faxas): Ouest Foire, en face du CICES, prés de la Station Shell, Dakar; tel. 77-568-27-87; e-mail info@mpsfaxas.com; internet www.mpsfaxas.com; Leader SERIGNE KHADIM THIOUNE.

Mouvement de la Réforme pour le Développement Social (MRDS): HLM 4, Villa 858, Dakar; e-mail sgmrds@mrds.sn; internet www.mrds.sn; f. 2000; Pres. IMAM MBAYE NIANG; Sec.-Gen. Imam IYANE SOW.

Mouvement Républicain Sénégalais (MRS): Résidence du Cap-Vert, 10e étage, 5 pl. de l'Indépendance, BP 4193, Dakar; tel. 33-822-0319; fax 33-822-0700; e-mail agaz@omnet.sn; Sec.-Gen. DEMBA BA.

Mouvement pour le Socialisme et l'Unité (MSU): HLM 1, Villa 86, Dakar; tel. 33-825-8544; f. 1981 as Mouvement Démocratique Populaire; National Co-ordinator-Gen. MOUHAMADOU BAMBA N'DIAYE.

Parti Africain de l'Indépendance (PAI): Maison du Peuple, Guediewaye, BP 820, Dakar; tel. 33-837-0136; f. 1957; reorg. 1976; Marxist; Sec.-Gen. MAJMOUT DIOP.

Parti Démocratique Sénégalais (PDS): blvd Dial Diop, Immeuble Serigne Mourtada Mbacké, Dakar; tel. 33-823-5027; fax 33-823-1702; e-mail cedobe@aol.com; internet www.sopionline.com; f. 1974; liberal democratic; Sec.-Gen. Me ABDOULAYE WADE.

Parti de l'Indépendance et du Travail (PIT): route front de terre, BP 10470, Dakar; tel. 33-827-2907; fax 33-820-9000; regd 1981; Marxist-Leninist; Sec.-Gen. AMATH DANSOKHO.

Parti Libéral Sénégalais (PLS): 13 ave Malick Sy, BP 28277, Dakar; tel. and fax 33-823-1560; f. 1998 by breakaway faction of PDS; Leader Me OUSMANE NGOM.

Parti Populaire Sénégalais (PPS): Quartier Escale, BP 212, Diourbel; tel. 33-971-1171; regd 1981; populist; Sec.-Gen. Dr OUMAR WANE.

Parti pour le Progrès et la Citoyenneté (PPC): Quartier Merina, Rufique; tel. 33-836-1868; Sec.-Gen. Me MBAYE JACQUES DIOP.

Parti pour la Renaissance Africaine—Sénégal (PARENA): Sicap Dieuppeul, Villa 2685/B, Dakar; tel. 77-636-8788; fax 33-823-5721; e-mail mariamwane@yahoo.fr; f. 2000; Sec.-Gen. MARIAM MAMADOU WANE LY.

Parti de la Renaissance et de la Citoyenneté: Liberté 6, Villa 7909, Dakar; tel. 33-827-8568; f. 2000; Sec.-Gen. SAMBA DIOULDÉ THIAM.

Parti Social-démocrate—Jant Bi (PSD—JB): Leader MAMOUR CISSE.

Parti Aocialiste Authentique (PSA): internet psa-senegal.org; Leader SOUTY TOURRE.

Parti Socialiste du Sénégal (PS): Maison du Parti Socialiste Léopold Sédar Senghor, Colobane, BP 12010, Dakar; tel. and fax 33-824-7744; e-mail senegalpartisocialiste@gmail.com; internet www.ps-senegal.com; f. 1958 as Union Progressiste Sénégalaise; Sec.-Gen. OUSMANE TANOR DIENG.

Parti de la Vérité pour le Développement (PVD): Dakar; f. 2004; Leader CHEIKH MOUHAMADOU KARA.

Rassemblement des Écologistes du Sénégal—Les Verts (RES): rue 67, angle rue 52, Gueule Tapée, BP 25226, Dakar-Fann; tel. and fax 33-842-3442; f. 1999; Sec.-Gen. OUSMANE SOW HUCHARD.

Rassemblement National Démocratique (RND): Sacré-Coeur III, Villa no 9721, Dakar; tel. 765808617 (mobile); f. 1976; legalized 1981; mem. of opposition Bennoo Siggil Senegal (f. 2009); Sec.-Gen. MADIOR DIOUF.

Rassemblement Patriotique Sénégalais—Jammi Rewmi (RPS—JR): Leader ELY MADIODO FALL FALL.

Rassemblement des Travailleurs Africains—Sénégal (RTA—S): Immeuble Seydou Nourou Tall, Apt. B6, 2ème étage, 12 rue 14 angle P, BP 13725, Derklé, Grand-Yoff, Dakar; tel. 33-827-1579; e-mail rtas@rtasenegal.org; internet www.rtasenegal.org; f. 1997; Sec.-Gen. El Hadji MOMAR SAMBE.

Takku Defaraat Sénégal Coalition: VDN à côté de la Poste; tel. 33-860-5019; fax 33-860-5020; f. 2000; Leader ROBERT SAGNA.

Tekki 2012: Zone B, Villa 23A, Bis, Dakar; tel. 33-868-43-33; e-mail tekki@sentoo.sn; internet www.tekki.org; Leader MAMADOU LAMINE DIALLO.

Union Nationale Patriotique (UNP): Leader NDÈYE FATOU TOURÉ.

Union pour le Renouveau Démocratique (URD): Bopp Villa 234, rue 7, Dakar; tel. 33-864-7431; fax 33-820-7317; e-mail urd@urdsenegal.sn; internet www.urdsenegal.sn; f. 1998 by breakaway faction of PS; Sec.-Gen. DJIBO LEÏTY KÂ.

The **Mouvement des Forces Démocratiques de la Casamance (MFDC)** was founded in 1947; it had paramilitary and political wings and formerly sought the independence of the Casamance region of southern Senegal. The MFDC is not officially recognized as a political party (the Constitution of 2001 forbids the formation of parties on a geographic basis) and waged a campaign of guerrilla warfare in the region from the early 1980s. Representatives of the MFDC have participated in extensive negotiations with the Senegalese Government on the restoration of peace and the granting of greater autonomy to Casamance, and in December 2004 a cease-fire agreement was signed between the two sides, pending further peace negotiations. The Honorary President of the MFDC, Fr AUGUSTIN DIAMACOUNÉ SENGHOR, died in January 2007; the post of Secretary-General was disputed between JEAN-MARIE FRANÇOIS BIAGUI and ANSOUMANA BADJI.

Diplomatic Representation

EMBASSIES IN SENEGAL

Algeria: 5 rue Mermoz, Plateau, POB 3233, Dakar; tel. 33-849-5700; fax 33-849-5701; e-mail ambalgdak@orange.sn; f. 1963; Ambassador ABDERRAHMANE BENGUERAH.

Austria: 18 rue Emile Zola, BP 3247, Dakar; tel. 33-849-4000; fax 33-849-4370; e-mail dakar-ob@bmaa.gv.at; Ambassador Dr GERHARD DEISS.

Belgium: ave des Jambaars, BP 524, Dakar; tel. 33-889-4390; fax 33-889-4398; e-mail dakar@diplobel.fed.be; internet www.diplomatie.be/dakar; Ambassador JOHAN VERKAMMEN.

Brazil: Immeuble Fondation Fahd, 4e étage, blvd Djily Mbaye, angle rue Macodou Ndiaye, BP 136, Dakar; tel. 33-823-1492; fax 33-823-

7181; e-mail embdakar@sentoo.sn; Ambassador MARIA ELISA THÉÓFILO DE LUNA.

Burkina Faso: Sicap Sacré Coeur III, Extension VDN No. 10628B, BP 11601, Dakar; tel. 33-864-5824; fax 33-864-5823; e-mail ambabf@sentoo.sn; Ambassador SALAMATA SAWADOGO.

Cameroon: 157–9 rue Joseph Gomis, BP 4165, Dakar; tel. 33-849-0292; fax 33-823-3396; Ambassador EMMANUEL MBONJO-EJANGUE.

Canada: rue Galliéni angle rue Amadou Cissé Dia, BP 3373, Dakar; tel. 33-889-4700; fax 33-889-4720; e-mail dakar@international.gc.ca; internet www.canadainternational.gc.ca/senegal; Ambassador PERRY CALDERWOOD.

Cape Verde: 3 blvd El-Hadji Djilly M'Baye, BP 11269, Dakar; tel. 33-822-4285; fax 33-821-0697; e-mail acvc.sen@metissacana.sn; Ambassador FRANCISCO PEREIRA DA VEIGA.

China, People's Republic: rue 18 prolongée, Fann Résidence, BP 342, Dakar; tel. 33-864-7775; fax 33-864-7780; Ambassador GONG YUANXING.

Congo, Democratic Republic: 16 rue Léo Frobénus, Fann Résidence, Dakar; tel. 33-824-6574; fax 33-864-6576; Chargé d'affaires a.i. FATAKI NICOLAS LUNGUELE MUSAMBYA.

Congo, Republic: Statut Mermoz, Pyrotechnie, BP 5242, Fann Résidence, Dakar; tel. 33-824-8398; fax 33-825-7856; Ambassador VALENTIN OLLESSONGO.

Côte d'Ivoire: ave Birago Diop, BP 359, Dakar; tel. 33-869-0270; fax 33-825-2115; e-mail cmrci@ambaci-dakar.org; internet www.ambaci-dakar.org; Ambassador EDOUARD TIAPÉ KASSARATÉ.

Cuba: 43 rue Aimé Césaire, BP 4510, Fann Résidence, Dakar; tel. 33-869-0240; fax 33-864-1063; e-mail embacubasen@sentoo.sn; Ambassador VILMA REYES VALDESPINO.

Egypt: 22 ave Brière de l'Isle, Plateau, BP 474, Dakar; tel. 33-889-2474; fax 33-821-8993; e-mail ambegydk@telecomplus.sn; Ambassador HESHAM MUHAMMAD MAHER.

Ethiopia: 18 blvd de la République, BP 379, Dakar; tel. 33-821-9896; fax 33-821-9895; e-mail ethembas@sentoo.sn; Ambassador ATO HASSEN ABDULKADIK.

France: 1 rue El Hadj Amadou Assane Ndoye, BP 4035, Dakar; tel. 33-839-5100; fax 33-839-5181; internet www.ambafrance-sn.org/france_senegal/spip.php?rubrique1; Ambassador NICOLAS NORMAND.

Gabon: ave Cheikh Anta Diop, cnr Fann Résidence, BP 436, Dakar; tel. 33-865-2234; fax 33-864-3145; e-mail ambgabon@refer.sn; Ambassador VINCENT BOULE.

The Gambia: 11 rue Elhadji Ismaïla Guèye (Thiong), BP 3248, Dakar; tel. 33-821-4416; fax 33-821-6279; e-mail gambit.high.commission@gmail.com; Ambassador GIBRIL SEMAN JOOF.

Germany: 20 ave Pasteur, angle rue Mermoz, BP 2100, Dakar; tel. 33-889-4884; fax 33-822-5299; e-mail info@daka.diplo.de; internet www.dakar.diplo.de; Ambassador CHRISTIAN CLAGES.

Ghana: Lot 27, Parcelle B, Almadies, BP 25370, Dakar; tel. 33-869-1990; fax 33-820-1950; e-mail info@ghembsen.org; Ambassador ABDULAI YAKUBU.

Guinea: rue 7, angle B&D, point E, BP 7123, Dakar; tel. 33-824-8606; fax 33-825-5946; Ambassador Elhadj MADIFING DIANÉ.

Guinea-Bissau: rue 6, angle B, point E, BP 2319, Dakar; tel. 33-823-0059; fax 33-825-2946; Ambassador (vacant).

Holy See: rue Aimé Césaire, angle Corniche-Ouest, Fann Résidence, BP 5076, Dakar; tel. 33-824-2674; fax 33-824-1931; e-mail vatemb@orange.sn; Apostolic Nuncio Most Rev. LUIS MARIANO MONTEMAYOR (Titular Archbishop of Illici).

India: 5 rue Carde, BP 398, Dakar; tel. 33-849-5875; fax 33-822-3585; e-mail indiacom@orange.sn; internet www.ambassadeinde.sn; Ambassador M. K. J. FRANCIS.

Indonesia: ave Cheikh Anta Diop, BP 5859, Dakar; tel. 33-825-7316; fax 33-825-5896; e-mail kbri@sentoo.sn; Ambassador ANDRADJATI.

Iran: 17 ave des Ambassadeurs, Fann Résidence, BP 735, Dakar; tel. 33-825-2528; fax 33-824-2314; e-mail ambiiran@telecomplus.sn; Ambassador JAHAN BAKHSHE HASANZADE.

Iraq: point E, rue 6, angle B, à coté de la Croix Rouge Internationale, BP45448, Dakar; tel. 33-869-7799; fax 33-824-0909; e-mail dkremb@iraqmfamail.com; Ambassador MOHAMMED HAKIM AL-ROBAI'EE.

Italy: rue Alpha Achamiyou Tall, BP 348, Dakar; tel. 33-889-2636; fax 33-821-7580; e-mail ambasciata.dakar@esteri.it; internet www.ambdakar.esteri.it; Ambassador ARTURO LUZZI.

Japan: blvd Martin Luther King, Corniche-Ouest, BP 3140, Dakar; tel. 33-849-5500; fax 33-849-5555; Ambassador HIROSHI FUKADA.

Korea, Republic: Villa Hamoudy, rue Aime Cesaire, Fann Résidence, BP 5850, Dakar; tel. 33-824-0672; fax 33-824-0695; e-mail senegal@mofat.go.kr; internet sen.mofat.go.kr; Ambassador KIM HYUNG-KUK.

Kuwait: blvd Martin Luther King, Dakar; tel. 33-824-1723; fax 33-825-0899; e-mail q8embassydkr@sentoo.sn; Ambassador HAMAD BURAHAMAH.

Lebanon: 56 ave Jean XXIII, BP 6700 Dakar-Etoile, Dakar; tel. 33-822-0255; fax 33-823-5899; e-mail ambaliban@orange.sn; internet www.ambaliban.org; Ambassador MICHEL HADDAD.

Liberia: 146 Ouest-Foire, BP 5845, Dakar-Fann; tel. 33-869-4019; fax 33-820-8223; e-mail libembdkr1@yahoo.com; Ambassador JOHNNY A. MCCLAIN.

Libya: route de Ouakam, Dakar; tel. 33-824-5710; fax 33-824-5722; Ambassador AL HADY SALEM HAMMAD.

Madagascar: Immeuble rue 2, angle Ellipse, Point E, BP 25395, Dakar; tel. 33-825-2666; fax 33-864-4086; e-mail ambamad@sentoo.sn; internet www.ambamad.sn; Ambassador RICHARD AUGUSTE PARAIN.

Malaysia: 7 Extension VDN, Fann Mermoz, BP 15057, Dakar; tel. 33-825-8935; fax 33-825-4719; e-mail maldakar@kln.gov.my; Ambassador Dato' JAMAIYAH MOHAMED YUSOF.

Mali: Fann Résidence, Corniche-Ouest, rue 23, BP 478, Dakar; tel. 33-824-6252; fax 33-825-9471; e-mail ambamali@sentoo.sn; Ambassador N'TJI LAÏCO TRAORÉ.

Mauritania: 37 blvd Charles de Gaulle, Dakar; tel. 33-823-5344; fax 33-823-5311; Ambassador MOHAMMED VALL OULD BELLAL.

Morocco: 73 ave Cheikh Anta Diop, BP 490, Dakar; tel. 33-824-6927; fax 33-825-7021; e-mail ambmadk@sentoo.sn; Ambassador TALEB BERRADA.

Netherlands: 37 rue Jaques Bugnicourt, BP 3262, Dakar; tel. 33-849-0360; fax 33-821-7084; e-mail dak@minbuza.nl; internet www.nlambassadedakar.org; Ambassador PIETER JAN KLEIWEG DE ZWAAN.

Nigeria: 8 ave Cheikh Anta Diop, BP 3129, Dakar; tel. 33-869-8600; fax 33-825-8136; e-mail info@nigeriandakar.sn; internet www.nigeriandakar.sn; Ambassador KAYTEN CATHERINE JACKDEN.

Oman: Villa 7062, Stéle Mermoz, BP 2635; tel. 33-824-6136; e-mail dakar@mofa.gov.om; Ambassador AHMED BARAKAT ABDULLAH AL-IBRAHIM.

Pakistan: Stèle Mermoz, Villa 7602, BP 2635, Dakar; tel. 33-824-6135; fax 33-824-6136; e-mail parepdakar@gmail.com; internet www.mofa.gov.pk/senegal; Ambassador ABDUL MATEEN KHAN.

Portugal: 6 Villa Martha, Fann Résidence, BP 281, Dakar; tel. 33-864-0317; fax 33-864-0322; e-mail ambportdakar@sentoo.sn; Ambassador RUI ALBERTO MANUPPELLA TERENO.

Qatar: 25 blvd Martin Luther King, BP 5150, Dakar; tel. 33-820-9559; fax 33-869-1012; Ambassador ALI ABDUL LATIF AHMED AL-MASALAMANI.

Romania: rue A prolongée, point E, BP 3171, Dakar; tel. 33-825-2068; fax 33-824-9190; e-mail romania.consul@orange.sn; internet dakar.mae.ro; Ambassador SIMONA CORLAN-IOAN.

Russia: ave Jean Jaurès, angle rue Carnot, BP 3180, Dakar; tel. 33-822-4821; fax 33-821-1372; e-mail ambrus@orange.sn; internet www.senegal.mid.ru; Ambassador VALERY NESTERUSHKIN.

Rwanda: Dakar; Ambassador GÉRARD NTWARI.

Saudi Arabia: 10 route de Ngor n° 10, BP 15150, Dakar; tel. 33-869-8390; fax 33-820-6553; e-mail snemb@mofa.gov.sa; Ambassador HAMAD SAEED AL-ZAABI.

South Africa: Memoz SUD, Lotissement Ecole de Police, BP 21010, Dakar-Ponty; tel. 33-865-1959; fax 33-864-2359; e-mail ambafsud@orange.sn; internet www.saesenegal.info; Ambassador S. S. KOTANE.

Spain: 18–20 ave Nelson Mandela, BP 2091, Dakar; tel. 33-821-1178; fax 33-821-6845; e-mail emb.dakar@mae.es; Ambassador CRISTINA DIAZ FERNANDEZ-GIL.

Sudan: 31 route de la Pyrotechnie, Mermoz, Fann-Résidence, BP 15033, Dakar; tel. 33-824-9853; fax 33-824-9852; e-mail sudembse@sentoo.sn; Ambassador MAHMOUD HASSAN EL-AMIN.

Switzerland: rue René N'Diaye, angle rue Seydou, BP 1772, Dakar; tel. 33-823-0590; fax 33-822-3657; e-mail dak.vertretung@eda.admin.ch; internet www.eda.admin.ch/dakar; Ambassador MURIEL BERSET.

Syria: rue 1, point E, angle blvd de l'Est, BP 498, Dakar; tel. 33-824-6277; fax 33-824-9007; e-mail syrdak@orange.sn; Ambassador (vacant).

Thailand: 10 rue Léon Gontran Damas, Angle F, Fann Résidence BP 3721, Dakar; tel. 33-869-3290; fax 33-824-8458; e-mail thaidkr@sentoo.sn; internet www.mfa.go.th/web/2366.php; Ambassador KANYA CHAIMAN.

Tunisia: rue Alpha Hachamiyou Tall, BP 3127, Dakar; tel. 33-823-4747; fax 33-823-7204; e-mail at.dakar@sentoo.sn; Ambassador CHOUKRI HERMASSI.

Turkey: ave des Ambassadeurs, Fann Résidence, BP 6060, Etoile, Dakar; tel. 33-869-2542; fax 33-825-6977; e-mail trambdkr@sentoo.sn; Ambassador ASLI ÜĞDÜL.

United Kingdom: 20 rue du Dr Guillet, BP 6025, Dakar; tel. 33-823-7392; fax 33-823-2766; e-mail britembe@orange.sn; internet ukinsenegal.fco.gov.uk; Ambassador JOHN MARSHALL.

USA: ave Jean XXIII, angle rue Kleber, BP 49, Dakar; tel. 33-829-2100; fax 33-822-2991; e-mail usadakar@state.gov; internet dakar.usembassy.gov; Ambassador LEWIS LUKENS.

Zimbabwe: rue de Louga, angle rue 31, Point E, BP 25342, Fann, Dakar; tel. 33-825-4131; fax 33-825-4016; e-mail zimdakar@yahoo.com; Ambassador TRUDY STEVENSON.

Judicial System

The Supreme Court was re-established in 2008, replacing the Court of Cassation and the Council of State. The Supreme Court is the highest court of appeal, and regulates the activities of subordinate courts and tribunals. It also judges complaints brought against the Executive and resolves electoral disputes. The Constitutional Council verifies that legislation and international agreements are in accordance with the Constitution; decides disputes between the Executive and the Legislature. The Revenue Court supervises the public accounts.

Supreme Court: blvd Martin Luther King, Dakar; tel. 33-889-1010; fax 33-823-7894; f. 2008; Pres. PAPE OMAR SAKHO.

Constitutional Council: BP 45732, Dakar; tel. 33-822-5252; fax 33-822-8187; e-mail magou_51@hotmail.com; internet www.gouv.sn/institutions/conseil_const.html; 5 mems; Pres. CHEIKH TIDIANE DIAKHATÉ.

Revenue Court (Cour des Comptes): 15 ave Franklin Roosevelt, BP 9097, Peytavin, Dakar; tel. 33-849-4001; fax 33-849-4362; e-mail amdjibgueye@courdescomptes.sn; internet www.courdescomptes.sn; f. 1999; Pres. ABDOU BAME GUEYE; Sec.-Gen. El Hadji ABDOUL MADJIB GUEYE; Pres. of Chambers ABBA GOUDIABY, MAMADOU TOURE, MAMADOU HADY SARR; Chief Administrator ABDOURAHMANE DIOUKNANE.

High Court of Justice: Dakar; competent to try the Prime Minister and other members of the Government for crimes committed in the exercise of their duties; The President of the Republic may only be brought to trial in the case of high treason; mems elected by the Assemblée nationale.

Religion

At the time of the 1988 census almost 94% of the population were Muslims, while some 5% professed Christianity (the dominant faith being Roman Catholicism); a small number, mostly in the south, followed traditional beliefs.

ISLAM

There are four main Islamic brotherhoods active in Senegal: the Tidjanes, the Mourides, the Layennes and the Qadiriyas.

Association pour la Coopération Islamique (ACIS): Dakar; f. 1988; Pres. Dr THIERNAO KÂ.

Grande Mosquée de Dakar: Dakar; tel. 33-822-5648; Grand Imam El Hadj ALIOUNE MOUSSA SAMB.

CHRISTIANITY

The Roman Catholic Church

Senegal comprises one archdiocese and six dioceses. Roman Catholics represented about 5% of the total population.

Bishops' Conference

Conférence des Evêques du Sénégal, de la Mauritanie, du Cap-Vert et de Guinée-Bissau, BP 941, Dakar; tel. 33-836-3309; fax 33-836-1617; e-mail archevchedkr@sentoo.sn.

f. 1973; Pres. Most Rev. JEAN-NOËL DIOUF (Bishop of Tambacounda).

Archbishop of Dakar: Cardinal THÉODORE-ADRIEN SARR, Archevêché, ave Jean XXIII, BP 1908, Dakar; tel. 33-889-0600; fax 33-823-4875; e-mail archevechedkr@sentoo.sn.

The Anglican Communion

The Anglican diocese of The Gambia, part of the Church of the Province of West Africa, includes Senegal and Cape Verde. The Bishop is resident in Banjul, The Gambia.

Protestant Church

Église Luthérienne du Sénégal: BP 9, Fatick, Niakhar; tel. 33-949-1171; fax 33-949-1385; e-mail elsfk@orange.sn; Pres. Rev. ABDOU THIAM.

Eglise Protestante du Sénégal: 65 rue Wagane Diouf, BP 22390, Dakar; tel. 33-821-5564; fax 33-821-7132; internet www.epsenegal.org; f. 1862; Pastor JUPITER GUEYE; Sec.-Gen. SANDRA FONKUI.

BAHÁ'Í FAITH

National Spiritual Assembly: Point E, rue des Ecrivains, impasse 2 à droite après la Direction de la Statistique, BP 1662, Dakar; tel. 33-824-2359; e-mail bahai@sentoo.sn; internet www.sn.bahai.org; regd 1975; Sec. ABOUBAKRINE BA.

The Press

DAILY NEWSPAPERS

L'Actuel: route du Front de Terre, angle ave Bourguiba, Immeuble Dramé, BP 11874, Dakar; tel. 33-864-2601; fax 33-864-2602; e-mail lactuel@sentoo.sn; Editor-in-Chief ABDOURAHMANE SY.

Dakar Soir: Point Presse Sarl, 3e étage, 108 Hann Maristes, BP 21548, Dakar; tel. and fax 33-832-1093; f. 2000; Editor-in-Chief ALAIN NDIAYE.

Frasques Quotidiennes: 51 rue du Docteur Thèze, BP 879, Dakar; tel. 33-842-4226; fax 33-842-4277; e-mail frasques@arc.sn.

L'Info 7: Sicap rue 10, BP 11357, Dakar; tel. and fax 33-864-2658; e-mail comsept@sentoo.sn; f. 1999.

Le Matin: route de l'Aéroport Léopold Sédar Senghor, Yoff, BP 6472, Dakar; tel. 33-869-1270; fax 33-820-1181; e-mail lematin@metissacana.sn; internet www.lematindelafrique.com; daily; independent; Editor-in-Chief ALIOUNE FALL.

L'Observateur: Immeuble Elimane Ndour, rue 15, angle Corniche, Dakar; tel. 33-849-1644; fax 33-849-1645; e-mail info@futursmedias.net; internet www.lobservateur.sn; Editor-in-Chief SERIGNE SALIOU SAMB.

L'Office: 9 rue de Thann, Dakar; tel. 33-824-2115; fax 33-824-2108; e-mail loffice@loffice.sn; internet www.loffice.sn; Editor-in-Chief LAMINE NDOUR.

Le Populaire: ave Bourguiba, Immeuble Baye Ndama, BP 11357, Dakar; tel. 33-869-6363; fax 33-824-2446; e-mail popxibaar@yahoo.fr; internet www.popxibaar.com; f. 2000; Dir of Publication DAOUDA DIARRA; Editor-in-Chief HAROUNA DÈME.

Le Quotidien: 12 Cité Adama Diop, Yoff Routes de Cimétieres, BP 25221, Dakar; tel. 33-869-8484; fax 33-820-7297; e-mail lequotidien@lequotidien.sn; internet www.lequotidien.sn; f. 2003; Dir MAMADOU BIAYE.

Le Soleil: Société sénégalaise de presse et de publications, route du Service géographique, Hann, BP 92, Dakar; tel. 33-859-5959; fax 33-832-0886; e-mail lesoleil@lesoleil.sn; internet www.lesoleilmultimedia.com; f. 1970; Editors-in-Chief HABIB DEMBA FALL, SIDY DIOP; circ. 25,000 (2009).

Sud Quotidien: Amitié II, angle blvd Bourguiba, BP 4130, Dakar; tel. 33-824-3306; fax 33-824-3322; e-mail info@sudonline.sn; internet www.sudonline.sn; independent; Dir ABDOULAYE NDIAGA SYLLA; circ. 30,000.

Tract: 13 rue de Thann, BP 3683, Dakar; tel. and fax 33-823-4725; e-mail tract.sn@laposte.net; f. 2000.

Wal Fadjri/L'Aurore (The Dawn): Sicap Sacré-Coeur 8542, BP 576, Dakar; tel. 33-824-2343; fax 33-824-2346; e-mail walf@walf.sn; internet www.walf.sn; f. 1984; Exec. Dir MBAYE SIDY MBAYE; circ. 15,000.

24 Heures Chrono: Sacré coeur 3, Villa 10595; tel. 77-576-0358; internet www.24sn.com; Editor SAMBA BIAGUI.

PERIODICALS

Le Cafard Libéré: 10 rue Tolbiac, angle Autoroute, Soumédioune, BP 7292, Dakar; tel. 33-822-4383; fax 33-822-0891; f. 1987; weekly; satirical; Editor PAPE SAMBA KANE; circ. 12,000.

Le Courrier du Sud: BP 190, Ziguinchor; tel. 33-991-1166; weekly.

Dakar Life: Dakar; tel. 77-638-85-85 (mobile); Dir of Publication MASSAMBA MBAYE; circ. 15,000.

Démocratie: Liberté V, 5375 M, 71 rue du rond-point Liberté V et VI, Dakar; tel. 33-824-8669; fax 33-825-1879.

Eco Hebdo: rue 22, Médina, BP 11451, Dakar; tel. and fax 33-837-1414; weekly.

Emergence Plus: Dakar; tel. 33-867-67-05; fax 33-867-46-99; e-mail emergencemag@orange.sn; Dir of Publication MOUMINA AÏDA KANE.

Ethiopiques: BP 2035, Dakar; tel. 33-849-1414; fax 33-822-1914; e-mail senghorf@orange.sn; internet www.refer.sn/ethiopiques; f. 1974; literary and philosophical review; publ. by Fondation Léopold Sédar Senghor; Editor BASSIROU DIENG.

Icone: Dakar; monthly; Dir of Publication MANSOUR DIENG.

Le Journal de l'Economie: 15 rue Jules Ferry, BP 2851, Dakar; tel. 33-823-8733; fax 33-823-6007; e-mail lejeco@sentoo.sn; weekly.

Journal Officiel de la République du Sénégal: Rufisque; tel. 33-849-1817; internet www.jo.gouv.sn; f. 1856; weekly; govt journal.

Nord Ouest: Immeuble Lonase, BP 459, Louga; tel. 76-680-7943; e-mail lenordouest@yahoo.fr; f. 2000; regional monthly; Dir of Publication PAPE MOMAR CISSÉ.

Nouvel Horizon: Liberté II, Villa 1589, BP 10037, Dakar; tel. 33-864-1152; fax 33-864-1150; e-mail nh-thiof@sentoo.sn; weekly; Editor-in-Chief ISSA SALL.

Le Politicien: 8123 Terminus Liberté VI, BP 11018, Dakar; tel. and fax 33-827-6396; f. 1977; weekly; satirical.

Promotion: BP 1676, Dakar; tel. 33-825-6969; fax 33-825-6950; e-mail giepromo@telecomplus.sn; f. 1972; fortnightly; Dir BOUBACAR DIOP; circ. 5,000.

République: BP 21740, Dakar; tel. 33-822-7373; fax 33-822-5039; e-mail republike@yahoo.fr; f. 1994; weekly.

Sopi (Change): 5 blvd Dial Diop, Dakar; tel. 33-824-4950; fax 33-824-4700; f. 1988; weekly; publ. by PDS; Editor CHEIKH KOUREYSSI BA.

Station One: Immeuble Cheikh Tall Dioum, 5éme étage, 58 ave Bourguiba, Dakar; tel. 77-633-50-40 (mobile); f. 2008; monthly; Dir of Publication MOUSTAPHA SOW; 20,000.

Le Témoin: Gibraltar II, Villa 310, Dakar; tel. 33-822-3269; fax 33-821-7838; f. 1990; weekly; Editor-in-Chief MAMADOU OUMAR NDIAYE; circ. 5,000.

Thiof: BP 10037, Dakar; tel. 33-864-11-51; monthly; Editor-in-Chief SOULEYMANE THIAM; circ. 15,000.

Le 221: BP 11600, Dakar; tel. 33-860-45-15; fax 33-867-67-79; internet agenda.au-senegal.com; Editor-in-Chief SELLY WANE; circ. 25,000.

Vive La République: Sicap Amitié III, Villa 4057, Dakar; tel. 33-864-0631; weekly.

Weekend Magazine: 12 Cité Adama Diop, Yoff Routes de Cimétieres, BP 25221, Dakar; tel. 33-869-8484; fax 33-869-84-99; e-mail weekend@weekend.sn; internet www.weekend.sn; f. 2007; publ. by Groupe Avenir Communication, which also publishes the daily Le Quotidien; Dir of Publication PAPA SAMBA DIARRA; circ. 9,000.

Xareli (Struggle): BP 12136, Dakar; tel. 33-822-5463; fortnightly; publ. by AJ—PADS; circ. 7,000.

NEWS AGENCIES

Agence Panafricaine d'Information—PANA-Presse SA: ave Bourjuiba, BP 4056, Dakar; tel. 33-869-1234; fax 33-824-1390; e-mail marketing@panapress.com; internet www.panapress.com; f. 1979 as Pan-African News Agency (under the auspices of the Organization of African Unity), restructured as 75% privately owned co in 1997; Dir-Gen. BABACAR FALL.

Agence de Presse Sénégalaise: 58 blvd de la République, BP 117, Dakar; tel. 33-823-1667; fax 33-822-0767; e-mail aps@aps.sn; internet www.aps.sn; f. 1959; govt-controlled; Dir-Gen. DOUDOU SARR NIANG.

PRESS ORGANIZATION

Syndicat des Professionnels de l'Information et de la Communication du Sénégal (SYNPICS): BP 21722, Dakar; tel. 33-842-4256; fax 33-842-0269; e-mail synpics@yahoo.fr; Sec.-Gen. DIATA CISSÉ.

Publishers

Africa Editions: BP 1826, Dakar; tel. 33-823-4880; fax 33-822-5630; f. 1958; general, reference; Man. Dir JOËL DECUPPER.

Agence de Distribution de Presse: km 2.5, blvd du Centenaire de la Commune de Dakar, BP 374, Dakar; tel. 33-832-0278; fax 33-832-4915; e-mail adpresse@telecomplus.sn; f. 1943; general, reference; Man. Dir PHILIPPE SCHORP.

Centre Africain d'Animation et d'Echanges Culturels Editions Khoudia: BP 5332, Dakar-Fann; tel. 33-821-1023; fax 33-821-5109; f. 1989; fiction, education, anthropology; Dir AISSATOU DIA.

Editions Clairafrique: 2 rue El Hadji Mbaye Guèye, BP 2005, Dakar; tel. 33-822-2169; fax 33-821-8409; f. 1951; politics, law, sociology, anthropology, literature, economics, devt, religion, school books.

Editions des Ecoles Nouvelles Africaines: ave Cheikh Anta Diop, angle rue Pyrotechnie, Stèle Mermoz, BP 581, Dakar; tel. 33-864-0544; fax 33-864-1352; e-mail eenas@sentoo.sn; youth and adult education, in French.

Editions Juridiques Africaines (EDJA): 18 rue Raffenel, BP 22420, Dakar-Ponty; tel. 33 821-6689; fax 33 823-2753; e-mail edja.ed@orange.sn; internet www.edja.sn; f. 1987; law; Dir NDÉYE NGONÉ GUÉYE.

Editions des Trois Fleuves: blvd de l'Est, angle Cheikh Anta Diop, BP 123, Dakar; tel. 33-825-7923; fax 33-825-5937; f. 1972; general non-fiction; luxury edns; Dir GÉRARD RAZIMOWSKY; Gen. Man. BERTRAND DE BOISTEL.

Enda—Tiers Monde Editions (Environmental Development Action in the Third World): 54 rue Carnot, BP 3370, Dakar; tel. 33-822-9890; fax 33-823-5157; e-mail editions@enda.sn; internet www.enda.sn; f. 1972; Third-World environment and devt; Dir RAPHAËL NDIAYE; Exec. Sec. JOSÉPHINE OUÉDRAOGO.

Grande Imprimerie Africaine (GIA): 9 rue Amadou Assane Ndoye, Dakar; tel. 33-822-1408; fax 33-822-3927; f. 1917; law, administration; Man. Dir CHEIKH ALIMA TOURÉ.

Institut fondamental d'Afrique noire (IFAN)—Cheikh Anta Diop: BP 206, Campus universitaire, Dakar; tel. 33-825-9890; fax 33-824-4918; internet www.afrique-ouest.auf.org; f. 1936; scientific and humanistic studies of Black Africa, for specialist and general public.

Nouvelles éditions africaines du Sénégal (NEAS): 10 rue Amadou Assane Ndoye, BP 260, Dakar; tel. 33-822-1580; fax 33-822-3604; e-mail neas@telecomplus.sn; f. 1972; literary fiction, schoolbooks; Dir-Gen. SAYDOU SOW.

Per Ankh: BP 2, Popenguine; e-mail perankheditions@arc.sn; internet www.perankhbooks.com; history.

Société Africaine d'Édition: 16 bis rue de Thiong, BP 1877, Dakar; tel. 33-821-7977; f. 1961; African politics and economics; Man. Dir PIERRE BIARNES.

Société d'Édition 'Afrique Nouvelle': 9 rue Paul Holle, BP 283, Dakar; tel. 33-822-3825; f. 1947; information, statistics and analyses of African affairs; Man. Dir ATHANASE NDONG.

Société Nationale de Presse, d'Édition et de Publicité (SONAPRESS): Dakar; f. 1972; Pres. OBEYE DIOP.

Sud-Communication: BP 4100, Dakar; operated by a journalists' co-operative; periodicals.

Xamal, SA: BP 380, Saint-Louis; tel. 33-961-1722; fax 33-961-1519; general literature, social sciences, in national languages and in French; Dir ABOUBAKAR DIOP.

GOVERNMENT PUBLISHING HOUSE

Société Sénégalaise de Presse et de Publications—Imprimerie nationale (SSPP): route du Service géographique, BP 92, Dakar; tel. 33-832-4692; fax 33-832-0381; f. 1970; 62% govt-owned; Dir SALIOU DIAGNE.

Broadcasting and Communications

TELECOMMUNICATIONS

At the end of 2011 there were three providers of mobile cellular telephone services in Senegal. Two of them also provided fixed-line services. At September 2011 there were 361,020 subscribers to fixed-line telephone services and 9.6m. subscribers to mobile telephone services.

Regulatory Authority

Agence de Régulation des Télécommunications et des Postes (ARTP): route des Almadies Angle Dioulikayes, BP 14130, Dakar-Peytavin; tel. 33-869-0369; fax 33-869-0370; e-mail contact@artp.sn; internet www.artp.sn; f. 2001; Pres. Prof. ABDOULAYE SAKHO; Dir-Gen. NDONGO DIAO.

Service Providers

Excaf Telecom: Domaine Industriel SODIDA, rue 14 Prolongée, BP 1656, Dakar; tel. 33-824-2424; fax 33-824-2191; e-mail dunyaa@excaf.com; internet www.excaf.com; f. 1972 as L'Agence Africaine de Commercialisation Artistique; name changed as above in 1992; Pres. and Dir-Gen. IBRAHIMA DIAGNE.

Expresso Sénégal: Dakar; internet www.expressotelecom.com; f. 2007; Pres. and Dir-Gen. EL AMIR AHMED EL AMIR YOUSIF.

Société Nationale des Télécommunications du Sénégal (SONATEL): 46 blvd de la République, BP 69, Dakar; tel. 33-839-1118; fax 33-823-6037; internet www.sonatel.sn; f. 1985; 52.2% owned by France Câbles et Radio (France Télécom, France), 27.67% owned by Govt; Pres. MICHEL HIRSCH; Man. Dir ALIOUME N'DIAYE; 2,340 employees (2007).

Orange Sénégal: 46 ave de la République, en face de la Cathédrale, BP 2352, Dakar; tel. 33-839-1771; fax 33-839-1754; internet www.orange.sn; f. 1996 as Sonatel Mobiles; fmrly known as Alizé.

Télécom Plus SARL: 20 rue Amadou Assane Ndoye, BP 21100, Dakar; tel. 33-839-9700; fax 33-823-4632; telecommunications products and services.

Tigo: 15 route de Ngor, BP 146, Dakar; tel. 33-869-7420; fax 33-820-6788; internet www.tigo.sn; fmrly Sentel Sénégal GSM; name changed as above in 2005; mobile cellular telephone operator in Dakar, most western regions, and in selected localities nation-wide; 75% owned by Millicom International Cellular (Luxembourg), 25% by Senegalese private investors; Gen. Man. YOUVAL ROSH; 250,000 subscribers (2003).

BROADCASTING

Regulatory Authority

Haut Conseil de l'Audiovisuel: Immeuble Fahd, Dakar; tel. and fax 33-823-4784; f. 1991; Pres. AMINATA CISSÉ NIANG.

Radio

Radiodiffusion-Télévision Sénégalaise (RTS): Triangle sud, angle ave Malick Sy, BP 1765, Dakar; tel. 33-849-1212; fax 33-822-3490; e-mail rts@rts.sn; internet www.rts.sn; f. 1992; state broadcasting co; broadcasts 2 national and 8 regional stations; Dir-Gen. BABACAR DIAGNE.

Radio Sénégal Internationale: Triangle sud, angle ave El Hadj Malick Sy, BP 1765, Dakar; tel. 33-849-1212; fax 33-822-3490; f. 2001; broadcasts news and information programmes in French, English, Arabic, Portuguese, Spanish, Italian, Soninké, Pulaar and Wolof from 14 transmitters across Senegal and on cable; Dir CHÉRIF THIAM.

RST1: Triangle sud, angle ave El Hadj Malick Sy, BP 1765, Dakar; tel. 33-849-1212; fax 33-822-3490; f. 1992; broadcasts in French, Arabic and 6 vernacular languages from 16 transmitters across Senegal; Dir MANSOUR SOW.

JDP FM (Jeunesse, Développement, Paix): Dakar; tel. 33-991-4813; e-mail abdousarr@orange.sn; Dir ABDOU SARR.

Oxy-Jeunes: Fojes BP 18303, Pikine, Dakar; tel. 33-834-4919; fax 33-827-3215; e-mail cheikh_seck@eudoramail.com; f. 1999; youth and community radio station supported by the World Asscn of Community Radio Stations and the Catholic Organization for Development and Peace.

Radio Nostalgie Dakar: BP 21021, Dakar; tel. 33-821-2121; fax 33-822-2222; e-mail nostafric@globeaccess.net; f. 1995; music; broadcasts in French and Wolof; Gen. Man. SAUL SAVÎOTE.

Radio PENC-MI: BP 51, Khombole; tel. 33-957-9103; fax 33-824-5898; e-mail rdoucoure@oxfam.org.uk.

Radio Rurale FM Awagna de Bignona: BP 72, Bignona; tel. 33-994-1021; fax 33-994-1909; e-mail mksonko2000@yahoo.fr.

Sud FM: Immeuble Fahd, 5e étage, BP 4130, Dakar; tel. 33-865-0888; fax 33-822-5290; e-mail info@sudonline.sn; internet www.sudfm.net; f. 1994; operated by Sud-Communication; regional stations in Saint-Louis, Kaolack, Louga, Thiès, Ziguinchor and Diourbel; Dir-Gen. OUMAR-DIOUF FALL.

Wal Fadjri FM: Sicap Sacré-Coeur no 8542, BP 576, Dakar; tel. 33-824-2343; fax 33-824-2346; internet www.walf.sn/radio; f. 1997; Islamic broadcaster; Exec. Dir MBAYE SIDY MBAYE.

Senegal also receives broadcasts from Radio France Internationale (RFI), the French service of the British Broadcasting Corporation (BBC) and Radio Chine Internationale.

Television

Radiodiffusion-Télévision Sénégálaise (RTS): see Radio; Dir of Television BABACAR DIAGNE.

Canal Horizons Sénégal: 31 ave Albert Sarrault, BP 1390, Dakar; tel. 33-889-5050; fax 33-823-3030; e-mail infos@canalhorizons.sn; internet www.canalhorizons.com; f. 1990; private encrypted channel; 18.8% owned by RTS and Société Nationale des Télécommunications du Sénégal, 15% by Canal Horizons (France); Man. Dir BÉNÉDICTE CHENUET.

Réseau MMDS-EXCAF Télécom: rue 14 prolongée, HLM 1, Domaine Industriel SODIDA, BP 1656, Dakar; tel. 33-824-2424; fax 33-824-2191; broadcasts selection of African, US, European and Saudi Arabian channels.

The French television stations, France-2, TV5 and Arte France, are also broadcast to Senegal.

Finance

(cap. = capital; res = reserves; dep. = deposits; m. = million; br(s). = branch(es); amounts in francs CFA)

BANKING

In 2009 there were 18 commercial banks and three other financial institutions in Senegal.

Central Bank

Banque Centrale des États de l'Afrique de l'Ouest (BCEAO): blvd du Général de Gaulle, angle rue 11, BP 3159, Dakar; tel. 33-889-4545; fax 33-823-5757; e-mail akangni@bceao.int; internet www.bceao.int; f. 1962; bank of issue for mem. states of the Union Économique et Monétaire Ouest Africaine (UEMOA, comprising Benin, Burkina Faso, Côte d'Ivoire, Guinea-Bissau, Mali, Niger, Senegal and Togo); cap. 134,120m., res 1,474,195m., dep. 2,124,051m. (Dec. 2009); Gov. KONÉ TIÉMOKO MEYLIET; Dir in Senegal FATIMATIOU ZAHRA DIOP; brs at Kaolack and Ziguinchor.

Commercial Banks

Bank of Africa—Sénégal: Résidence Excellence, 4 ave Léopold Sédar Senghor, BP 1992, Dakar; tel. 33-849-6240; fax 33-842-1667; e-mail information@boasenegal.com; internet www.boasenegal.com; f. 2001; cap. 2,750m., res 82,011m., dep. 48,703m. (Dec. 2007); Pres. PAUL DERREUMAUX; Dir-Gen. FAUSTIN AMOUSSOU; 8 brs.

Banque Internationale pour le Commerce et l'Industrie du Sénégal (BICIS): 2 ave Léopold Sédar Senghor, BP 392, Dakar; tel. 33-839-0390; fax 33-823-0737; e-mail bicis@africa.bnpparibas.com; internet www.bicis.sn; f. 1962; 54.11% owned by Groupe BNP Paribas (France); cap. 5,000m., res 21,473m., dep. 272,099m. (Dec. 2008); Chair. LANDING SANÉ; Dir-Gen. AMADOU KANE; 17 brs.

CBAO Groupe Attijariwafa bank: 1 pl. de l'Indépendance, BP 129, Dakar; tel. 33-33-849-9696; fax 33-823-2005; e-mail cbao@cbao.sn; internet www.cbao.sn; fmrly Compagnie Bancaire de l'Afrique Occidentale (CBAO), name changed as above in 2008 following merger with Attijari bank Sénégal; 100% owned by Attijariwafa Bank Group (Morocco); cap. 11,450m., res 48,171m., dep. 551,272m. (Dec. 2008); Pres. BOUBKER JAÏ; Dir-Gen. ABDELKRIM RAGHNI.

Citibank Senegal SA: Immeuble SDIH, 4e étage, 2 pl. de l'Indépendance, BP 3391, Dakar; tel. 33-849-1104; fax 33-823-8817; e-mail thioro.ba@citicorp.com; f. 1975; wholly owned subsidiary of Citibank NA (USA); cap. 1,626m., total assets 84,864m. (Dec. 2001); Pres. JOHN REED; Man. KEVIN A. MURRAY; 1 br.

Compagnie Ouest Africaine de Crédit Bail (LOCAFRIQUE): Immeuble Coumaba Castel, 11 rue Galandou Diouf, BP 292, Dakar; tel. 33-849-8100; fax 33-822-0894; e-mail locafrique@arc.sn; f. 1977; cap. 579m., total assets 1,241m. (Dec. 2003); Dir-Gen. AMADOU SY.

Crédit du Sénégal (CLS): blvd El Hadji Djily Mbaye, angle rue Huart, BP 56, Dakar; tel. 33-849-0000; fax 33-823-8430; e-mail cl_senegal@creditdusenegal.com; internet www.creditdusenegal.com; f. 1989 by acquisition of USB by Crédit Lyonnais (France); name changed as above in 2007 following merger with Crédit Agricole (France); 95% owned by Attijariwafa Bank Group (Morocco); cap. 2,000m., res 9,099m., dep. 107,497m. (Dec. 2009); Pres. and Chair. BOUBKER JAÏ; Dir-Gen. MOHAMED EL-GHAZI; 5 brs.

Ecobank Sénégal: 8 ave Léopold Sédar Senghor, BP 9095, Dakar; tel. 33-849-2000; fax 33-823-4707; e-mail ecobanksn@ecobank.com; internet www.ecobank.com; 41.45% owned by Ecobank Transnational Inc (Togo, operating under the auspices of the Economic Community of West African States), 17.0% by Ecobank Bénin, 12.43% by Ecobank Côte d'Ivoire, 4.56% by Ecobank Niger, 4.56% by Ecobank Togo; cap. 10,463m., res 3,351m., dep. 229,122m. (Dec. 2009); Pres. MAHENTA BIRIMA FALL; Dir-Gen. BOATIN KWASI.

International Commercial Bank (Senegal) SA: 18 ave Léopold Sédar Senghor, BP 32310, Dakar; tel. 33-823-5647; fax 33-842-2585; e-mail mail@icbank-senegal.com; internet www.icbank-senegal.com; f. 2006; CEO S. GANESH KUMAR; 1 br.

Société Générale de Banques au Sénégal (SGBS): 19 ave Léopold Sédar Senghor, BP 323, Dakar; tel. 33-839-5500; fax 33-823-9036; e-mail sgbs@sentoo.sn; internet www.sgbs.sn; f. 1962; 57.72% owned by Société Générale (France), 35.23% owned by private Senegalese investors; cap. 4,527m., res 28,301m., dep. 366,361m. (Dec. 2006); Pres. PAPA-DEMBA DIALLO; Dir-Gen. DANIEL TERUIN; 30 brs and sub-brs.

Development Banks

Banque de l'Habitat du Sénégal (BHS): 69 blvd du Général de Gaulle, BP 229, Dakar; tel. 33-839-3333; fax 33-823-8043; e-mail bdld10@calva.com; internet www.bhs.sn; f. 1979; cap. and res 19,661.0m., total assets 132,554.6m. (Dec. 2003); Pres. AHMED YÉRO DIALLO; Dir-Gen. BOCAR SY; 5 brs in Senegal and 5 brs abroad.

Caisse Nationale de Crédit Agricole du Sénégal (CNCAS): pl. de l'Indépendance, Immeuble ex-Air Afrique, 31–33 rue El Hadji Asmadou Assane Ndoye, angle ave Colbert, BP 3890, Dakar; tel. 33-839-3636; fax 33-821-2606; e-mail cncas@cncas.sn; internet www.cncas.sn; f. 1984; 23.8% state-owned; cap. 5,500m., res 2,065m., dep. 101,944m. (Dec. 2009); Pres. ABDOULAYE DIACK; Dir-Gen. ARFANG BOUBACAR DAFFE; 13 brs.

Société Financière d'Equipement (SFE): 2e étage, Immeuble Sokhna Anta, rue Dr Thèze, BP 252, Dakar; tel. 33-823-6626; fax 33-823-4337; 59% owned by Compagnie Bancaire de l'Afrique Occidentale; cap. and res 388m., total assets 6,653m. (Dec. 1999); Pres. ARISTIDE ORSET ALCANTARA; Dir-Gen. MOHAMED A. WILSON.

Islamic Bank

Banque Islamique du Sénégal (BIS): Immeuble Abdallah Fayçal, rue Huart, angle rue Amadou Ndoye, BP 3381, 18524 Dakar; tel. 33-849-6262; fax 33-822-4948; e-mail contact@bis-bank.com; internet www.bis-bank.com; f. 1983; 44.5% owned by Dar al-Maal al-Islami (Switzerland), 33.3% by Islamic Development Bank (Saudi Arabia), 22.2% state-owned; cap. 2,706m., res 1,335m., dep. 44,798m. (Dec. 2007); Pres. of Bd of Administration BADER EDDINE NOUIOUA; Dir-Gen. AZHAR S. KHAN; 4 brs.

Banking Association

Association Professionnelle des Banques et des Etablissements Financiers du Sénégal (APBEF): 5 rue Calmette, angle A. Assane Ndoye, BP 6403, Dakar; tel. 33-823-6093; fax 33-823-8596; e-mail apbef@orange.sn; Pres. ARFANG BOUBACAR DAFFÉ.

STOCK EXCHANGE

Bourse Régionale des Valeurs Mobilières (BRVM): BP 22500, Dakar; tel. 33-821-1518; fax 33-821-1506; e-mail nksy@brvm.org; internet www.brvm.org; f. 1998; national branch of BRVM (regional stock exchange based in Abidjan, Côte d'Ivoire, serving the member states of UEMOA); Man. NDÈYE KHADY SY.

INSURANCE

In 2010 the insurance sector comprised 22 companies: 13 non-life insurance companies, seven life insurance companies, one reinsurance company and one agricultural insurance company.

Allianz Sénégal Assurances: rue de Thann, angle ave Abdoulaye Fadiga, BP 2610, Dakar; tel. 33-849-4400; fax 33-823-1078; e-mail allianz.senegal@allianz-sn.com; internet www.allianz-senegal.com; name changed as above in 2009; Dir-Gen. OLIVIER MALÂTRE; also **Allianz Sénégal Assurances Vie**; life insurance.

AMSA Assurances: 43 ave ave Hassan II, BP 225, Dakar; tel. 33-839-3600; fax 33-823-3701; e-mail amsa-sn@amsa-group.com; internet amsa-group.com; f. 1977; fmrly Assurances Générales Sénégalaises (AGS); cap. 2,990m.; Dir-Gen. AÏDA DJIGO WANE; also **AMSA Assurances Vie**; life insurance.

Assurances La Sécurité Sénégalaise (ASS): BP 2623, Dakar; tel. 33-849-0599; fax 33-821-2581; e-mail ass.dk@orange.sn; internet ass-assurances.com; f. 1984; cap. 1,000m. (2007); Pres. MOUSSA SOW; Man. Dir MBACKÉ SENE.

AXA Assurances Sénégal: 5 pl. de l'Indépendance, BP 182, Dakar; tel. 33-849-1010; fax 33-823-4672; internet www.axa.sn; e-mail info@axa.sn; f. 1977; fmrly Csar Assurances; 51.5% owned by AXA (France); cap. 2,116m. (June 2011); Dir-Gen. ALIOUNE DIAGNE.

Compagnie d'Assurances-Vie et de Capitalisation (La Nationale d'Assurances-Vie): 7 blvd de la République, BP 3853, Dakar; tel. 33-822-1181; fax 33-821-2820; f. 1982; cap. 80m.; Pres. MOUSSA DIOUF; Man. Dir BASSIROU DIOP.

Compagnie Générale d'Assurances (CGA): 10 ave Léopold Sédar Senghor, angle rue Félix Faure, BP 50184, Dakar; tel. 33-889-6200; fax 33-821-3363; e-mail cgasen@orange.sn; internet www.cga.sn; f. 2007; Pres. MAMADOU LAMINE LOUM; Dir-Gen. MAMADOU MOUSTAPHA NOBA.

Compagnie Nationale d'Assurance Agricole du Sénégal: BP 15297, Dakar; tel. 33-869-7800; fax 33-860-6880; e-mail cnaas@cnaas.sn; internet www.cnaas.sn; f. 2008; agricultural insurance; Dir-Gen. AMADOU NDIAYE.

Compagnie Nationale d'Assurance et de Réassurance des Transporteurs: Rocade Fann Bel-Air, pl. Bakou, BP 22545, Dakar; tel. 33-831-0606; fax 33-832-1205; e-mail cnart@cnart.sn; internet www.cnart.sn; f. 2000; Dir-Gen. MOR ADJ.

Compagnie Sénégalaise d'Assurances et de Réassurances (CSAR): 5 pl. de l'Indépendance, BP 182, Dakar; tel. 33-823-2776; fax 33-823-4672; f. 1972; cap. 945m.; 49.8% state-owned; Pres. MOUSTAPHA CISSÉ; Man. Dir MAMADOU ABBAS BA.

Gras Savoye Sénégal: Immeuble Isocèle au Point E, rue de Diourbel, angle Rond-Point de l'Ellipse, BP 9, Dakar; tel. 33-859-4051; fax 33-824-9392; e-mail gs.senegal@sn.grassavoye.com; Man. THIERRY LABBÉ.

Intercontinental Life Insurance Co (ILICO): 16 rue de Thing, angle rue Moussé Diop, BP 1359, Dakar; tel. 33-889-8787; fax 33-822-0449; e-mail dakar@ilico.sn; internet www.ilico.sn; f. 1993; life insurance; fmrly American Life Insurance Co; Dir-Gen. YACINE DIOP DJIBO.

La Nationale d'Assurances: 5 ave Albert Sarrault, BP 3328, Dakar; tel. 33-822-1027; fax 33-821-2820; f. 1976; fire, marine, travel and accident insurance; Pres. AMSATA DIOUF; also **La Nationale d'Assurances—Vie**; life insurance.

Nouvelle Société Interafricaine d'Assurances Sénégal (NSIA): 18–20 ave Léopold Sédar Senghor, BP 18524, Dakar; tel. 33-889-6060; fax 33-842-6464; e-mail nsiasenegal@orange.sn; f. 2002; Dir-Gen. SIDY FAYE; also **Nouvelle Société Interafricaine d'Assurances Vie Sénégal**; Dir-Gen. RAMATOULAYE NDIAYE.

Salama Assurances Sénégal: 67 blvd de la République, BP 21022, Dakar; tel. 33-849-4800; fax 33-822-9446; e-mail salama@orange.sn; internet www.salama.sn; f. 1987; fmrly Sosar al amane, name changed as above in 2008; Dir-Gen. MAMADOU FAYE.

Société Africaine d'Assurances: Dakar; tel. 33-823-6475; fax 33-823-4472; f. 1945; cap. 9m.; Dir CLAUDE GERMAIN.

Société Nationale d'Assurance Mutuelle Vie (SONAM Vie): 6 ave Léopold Sédar Senghor, angle Carnot, BP 210, Dakar; tel. 33-889-8900; fax 33-823-6315; e-mail sonam@sonam.sn; f. 1973; Dir-Gen. SOULEYMANE NIANE; also **Société Nationale d'Assurance Mutuelle Assurances** ; Dir-Gen. MAMADOU DIOP.

Société Sénégalaise de Courtage et d'Assurances (SOSECODA): 16 ave Léopold Sédar Senghor, BP 9, Dakar; tel. 33-823-5481; fax 33-821-5462; f. 1963; cap. 10m.; 55% owned by SONAM; Man. Dir A. AZIZ NDAW.

Société Sénégalaise de Réassurances SA (SENRE): 39 ave Georges Pompidou, BP 386, Dakar; tel. 33-822-8089; fax 33-821-5652; e-mail moussadiaw@senre.sn; internet www.senre.sn; cap. 600m; Pres. MAREME MBENGUE; Dir-Gen. MOUSSA DIAW.

Union des Assurances du Sénégal Vie (UASen-Vie): 4 ave Léopold Sédar Senghor, BP 182, Dakar; tel. 33-889-0040; fax 33-823-1108; e-mail uasenvie@uasen.com; Dir-Gen. ADJARATOU KHADY N'DAW SY.

Insurance Association

Fédération Sénégalaise des Sociétés d'Assurances (FSSA): 43 ave Hassan II, BP 1766, Dakar; tel. 33-889-4864; fax 33-821-4954; e-mail fssa@orange.sn; internet www.fssa.sn; f. 1967; fmrly Comité des Sociétés d'Assurances du Sénégal; Pres. MOR ADJ; Sec.-Gen. VADIOUROU DIALLO; 24 mems.

Trade and Industry

GOVERNMENT AGENCIES

Agence de Développement et d'Encadrement des Petites et Moyennes Entreprises (ADEPME): 9 Fenêtre Mermoz, ave Cheikh Anta Diop, BP 333, Dakar-Fann; tel. 33-869-7071; fax 33-860-1363; e-mail adepme@orange.sn; internet www.adepme.sn; f. 2001; assists in the formation and operation of small and medium-sized enterprises; Dir-Gen. MARIE THÉRÈSE DIEDHIOU.

Agence Nationale Chargée de la Promotion de l'Investissement et des Grands Travaux (APIX): 52–54 rue Mohamed V, BP 430, 18524 Dakar; tel. 33-849-0555; fax 33-823-9489; e-mail contact@apix.sn; internet www.investinsenegal.com; f. 2000; promotes investment and major projects; Dir-Gen. AMINATA NIANE.

Agence Sénégalaise de Promotion des Exportations (ASEPEX): Amitié 3, No. 4426, Sotrac Mermoz, BP 14709, Dakar; tel. 33-869-2021; fax 33-869-2022; e-mail asepex@asepex.sn; internet www.asepex.sn; f. 2005; promotes exports; Dir-Gen. SAGAR DIOUF TRAORÉ.

Société de Développement Agricole et Industriel (SODAGRI): Immeuble King Fahd, 9e étage, BP 222, Dakar; tel. 33-821-0426; fax 33-822-5406; e-mail contats@sodagri.net; internet www.sodagri.net; f. 1974; cap. 120m. francs CFA; agricultural and industrial projects; Dir-Gen. BOUBACAR SY.

Société de Gestion des Abattoirs du Sénégal (SOGAS): BP 14, Dakar; tel. 33-854-0740; fax 33-834-2365; e-mail sogas@sentoo.sn; f. 1962; cap. 619.2m. francs CFA; 28% state-owned; livestock farming; Dir-Gen. TALLA CISSÉ.

Société Internationale des Etudes de Développement en Afrique (SONED—AFRIQUE): Parc à Mazout, Immeuble Ndiaga Diop, Colobane, BP 2084, Dakar; tel. 33-825-8802; fax 33-825-8881; e-mail sonedaf@orange.sn; internet www.soned-afrique.org; f. 1974; cap. 150m. francs CFA; Pres. ABDOUL EL MAZIDE NDIAYE.

Société Nationale d'Aménagement et d'Exploitation des Terres du Delta du Fleuve Sénégal et des Vallées du Fleuve Sénégal et de la Falémé (SAED): 200 ave Insa Coulibaly-Sor, BP 74, Saint-Louis; tel. 33-961-1533; fax 33-961-1463; e-mail saed@orange.sn; internet www.saed.sn; f. 1965; cap. 2,500m. francs CFA; 100% state-owned; controls the agricultural devt of more than 40,000 ha around the Senegal river delta; Dir-Gen. MAMOUDOU DEME.

DEVELOPMENT ORGANIZATIONS

Agence Française de Développement (AFD): 15 ave Nelson Mandela, BP 475, Dakar; tel. 33-849-1999; fax 33-823-4010; e-mail afddakar@groupe-afd.org; internet www.afd.fr; Country Dir DENIS CASTAING.

Centre International du Commerce Extérieur du Sénégal (CICES): route de l'Aéroport, BP 8166, Dakar-Yoff, Dakar; tel. 33-827-5414; fax 33-827-5275; e-mail cices@sn.ecobiz.ecowas.com; internet cicesfidak.com; Pres. MATAR GUEYE; Dir-Gen. BAÏDY SOULEYMANE NDIAYE.

Conseil des Investisseurs Européens au Sénégal (CIES): 2 pl. de l'Indépendance, BP 130, Dakar; tel. 33-823-6272; fax 33-823-8512; e-mail cies@orange.sn; f. 1993; Pres. GÉRARD SENAC.

France Volontaires: BP 1010, route de la VDN, Sacré coeur 3, Villa no 8908, Dakar; tel. 33-824-5295; fax 33-824-5390; e-mail afvp.dn@sentoo.sn; internet www.france-volontaires.org; f. 1972; name changed as above in 2009; Regional Delegate for Senegal, Cape Verde, Guinea, Guinea-Bissau, Mali and Mauritania JEAN-LOUP CAPDEVILLE; Nat. Delegate MAMADOU NDOUR CAMARA.

Groupements Economiques du Sénégal (GES): 21 ave Faidherbe, BP 282, Dakar; tel. 33-822-2821; Pres. MOR MATY SARR.

Service de Coopération et d'Action Culturelle: BP 2014, Dakar; tel. 33-839-5100; fax 33-839-5359; administers bilateral aid from France; fmrly Mission Française de Coopération et d'Action Culturelle; Dir JEAN-LUC LE BRAS.

CHAMBERS OF COMMERCE

Union Nationale des Chambres de Commerce, d'Industrie et d'Agriculture du Sénégal (UNCCIA): 1 pl. de l'Indépendance, BP 118, Dakar; tel. 33-823-7169; fax 33-823-9363; f. 1888; restructured 2002; Pres. MAMADOU LAMINE NIANG.

Chambre de Commerce, d'Industrie et d'Agriculture de Dakar (CCIAD): 1 pl. de l'Indépendance, BP 118, Dakar; tel. 33-823-7189; fax 33-823-9363; e-mail cciad@orange.sn; internet www.cciad.sn; f. 1888; Pres. MAMADOU LAMINE NIANG; Sec.-Gen. ALY MBOUP.

Chambre de Commerce, d'Industrie et d'Agriculture de Diourbel: 744 ave Léopold Sédar Senghor, BP 7, Diourbel; tel. 33-971-1203; fax 33-971-3849; e-mail mamandiaye@hotmail.com; f. 1969; Pres. MOUSTAPHA CISSÉ LO; Sec.-Gen. MAMADOU NDIAYE.

Chambre de Commerce, d'Industrie et d'Agriculture de Fatick: BP 66, Fatick; tel. and fax 33-949-1425; e-mail ccfatick@cosec.sn; Pres. BABOUCAR BOP; Sec.-Gen. SEYDOU NOUROU LY.

Chambre de Commerce, d'Industrie et d'Agriculture de Kaolack: BP 203, Kaolack; tel. 33-941-2052; fax 33-941-2291; e-mail cciak@netcourrier.com; internet www.cciak.fr.st; Pres. IDRISSA GUÈYE; Sec.-Gen. SALIMATA S. DIAKHATÉ.

Chambre de Commerce d'Industrie et d'Agriculture de Kolda: BP 23, Quartier Escale, Kolda; tel. 33-996-1230; fax 33-996-1068; Pres. AMADOU MOUNIROU DIALLO; Sec.-Gen. YAYA CAMARA.

Chambre de Commerce, d'Industrie et d'Agriculture de Louga: 2 rue Glozel, BP 26, Louga; tel. 33-967-1114; fax 33-967-0825; e-mail ccial@orange.sn; Pres. CHEIKH MACKÉ FAYE; Sec.-Gen. CHEIKH SENE.

Chambre de Commerce, d'Industrie et d'Agriculture de Matam: BP 95, Matam; tel. and fax 33-966-6591; Pres. MAMADOU NDIADE; Sec.-Gen. BOCAR BA.

Chambre de Commerce, d'Industrie et d'Agriculture de Saint-Louis: 10 rue Blanchot, BP 19, Saint-Louis; tel. 33-961-1088; fax 33-961-2980; f. 1879; Pres. El Hadj ABIBOU DIEYE; Sec.-Gen. MOUSSA NDIAYE.

Chambre de Commerce, d'Industrie et d'Agriculture de Tambacounda: 120 blvd Diogoye, BP 127, Tambacounda; tel. 33-981-1014; fax 33-981-2995; Pres. DJIBY CISSÉ; Sec.-Gen. TENGUELLA BA.

Chambre de Commerce, d'Industrie et d'Agriculture de Thiès: 96 ave Lamine Guèye, BP 3020, Thiès; tel. 33-951-1002; fax 33-951-1397; e-mail ccthies@cosec.sn; f. 1883; 38 mems; Pres. ATTOU NDIAYE; Sec.-Gen. ABDOULKHADRE CAMARA.

Chambre de Commerce, d'Industrie et d'Agriculture de Ziguinchor: rue du Gen. de Gaulle, BP 26, Ziguinchor; tel. 33-991-1310; fax 33-991-5238; f. 1908; Pres. JEAN PASCAL EHEMBA; Sec.-Gen. MAMADOU LAMINE SANE.

EMPLOYERS' ASSOCIATIONS

Association des Industries et Prestataires de Services de la Zone Franche Industrielle de Dakar: km 18, route de Rufisque, BP 3857, Dakar; tel. 33-839-8484; fax 33-821-2609; Pres. MANSOUR GUEYE.

Chambre des Métiers de Dakar: route de la Corniche-Ouest, Soumbedioune, Dakar; tel. 33-821-7908; e-mail dakarmetiers@orange.sn; Pres. MAGATTE MBOW; Sec.-Gen. MBAYE GAYE.

Confédération Nationale des Employeurs du Sénégal: 5 ave Carde, Rez de Chaussée, BP 3819, Dakar; tel. 33-823-0974; fax 33-822-9658; e-mail cnes@sentoo.sn; internet www.cnes.sn; Pres. MANSOUR KAMA.

Conseil National du Patronat du Sénégal (CNP): 7 rue Jean Mermoz, BP 3537, Dakar; tel. 33-889-6565; fax 33-822-2842; e-mail cnp@orange.sn; internet www.cnp.sn; Pres. BAÏDY AGNE; Sec.-Gen. HAMIDOU DIOP.

Groupement Professionnel de l'Industrie du Pétrole au Sénégal (GPP): rue 6, km 4.5, blvd du Centenaire de la Commune de Dakar, BP 479, Dakar; tel. 33-849-3115; fax 33-832-5212; e-mail noeljp@orange.sn; Pres. BERNARD LACAZE; Sec.-Gen. JEAN-PIERRE NOËL.

Organisation des Commerçants, Agriculteurs, Artisans et Industriels: 52 rue Paul Holl, angle rue Tolbiac, Dakar; tel. 33-823-6794; fax 33-823-6550; Pres. ALASSANE SECK.

Rassemblement des Opérateurs Economiques du Sénégal (ROES): BP 5001/2, Dakar; tel. 33-825-5717; fax 33-825-5713; Pres. KHADIM BOUSSO.

Syndicat des Commerçants Importateurs, Prestataires de Services et Exportateurs de la République du Sénégal (SCIMPEX): 7 rue Jean Mermoz, BP 806, Dakar; tel. 33-821-3662; fax 33-842-9648; e-mail scimpex@orange.sn; f. 1943; Pres. PAPA ALSASSANE DIENG; Sec.-Gen. MAURICE SARR.

Syndicat Patronal de l'Ouest Africain des Petites et Moyennes Entreprises et des Petites et Moyennes Industries: BP 3255, 41 blvd Djily M'Baye, Dakar; tel. 33-821-3510; fax 33-823-3732; e-mail mactarniang@yahoo.fr; f. 1937; Pres. BABACAR SEYE; Sec.-Gen. MACTAR NIANG.

Syndicat Professionnel des Entrepreneurs de Bâtiments et de Travaux Publics du Sénégal: ave Abdoulaye Fadiga, BP 1520, Dakar; tel. 33-832-4708; fax 33-832-5071; f. 1930; 130 mems; Pres. OUMAR SOW.

Syndicat Professionnel des Industries du Sénégal (SPIDS): BP 593, Dakar; tel. 33-823-4324; fax 33-822-0884; e-mail spids@spids.sn; internet www.spids.sn; f. 1944; 110 mems; Pres. CHRISTIAN BASSE.

Union des Entreprises du Domaine Industriel de Dakar: BP 10288, Dakar-Liberté; tel. 33-825-0786; fax 33-825-0870; e-mail snisa@orange.sn; Pres. ARISTIDE TINO ADEDIRAN.

Union Nationale des Chambres de Métiers: Domaine Industriel SODIDA, ave Bourguiba, BP 30040, Dakar; tel. 33-825-0588; fax 33-824-5432; e-mail uncm@orange.sn; internet www.artisanat-senegal.org; f. 1981; Pres. El Hadj SEYNI SECK; Sec.-Gen. BABOUCAR DIOUF.

Union Nationale des Commerçants et Industriels du Sénégal (UNACOIS): ave Cheikh Ahmadou Bamba 3780, BP 3698, Dakar; tel. 33-821-6080; fax 33-822-0185; e-mail unacois.as@orange.sn; internet www.unacois.org; Pres. IDY THIAM; Sec.-Gen MAME BOU DIOP.

UTILITIES

Electricity

Commission de Régulation du Secteur de l'Electricité: Ex-Camp Lat Dior, BP 11701, Dakar; tel. 33-849-0459; fax 33-849-0459; e-mail crse@orange.sn; internet www.crse.sn; f. 1998; regulatory authority; Pres. MAÏMOUNA NDOYE SECK.

Agence Sénégalaise d'Électrification Rurale (ASER): Ex-Camp Lat Dior, BP 11131, Dakar; tel. 33-849-4717; fax 33-849-4720; internet www.aser.sn; Dir-Gen. ALIOU NIANG.

Société Nationale d'Electricité (SENELEC): 28 rue Vincent, BP 93, Dakar; tel. 33-839-3030; fax 33-823-1267; e-mail webmaster@senelec.sn; internet www.senelec.sn; f. 1983; 100% state-owned; Pres. CHEIKH TIDIANE MBAYE; Dir-Gen. SEYDINA KANE.

Water

Société Nationale des Eaux du Sénégal (SONES): route de Front de Terre, BP 400, Dakar; tel. 33-839-7800; fax 33-832-2038; e-mail sones@sones.sn; internet www.sones.sn; f. 1995; water works and supply; state-owned; Pres. ABDOUL ALY KANE; Dir-Gen. Dr IBRAHIMA DIALLO.

Sénégalaise des Eaux (SDE): Centre de Hann-Route du Front de Terre, BP 224, Dakar; tel. 33-839-3737; fax 33-839-3705; e-mail eau@sde.sn; internet www.sde.sn; f. 1996; subsidiary of Groupe Saur International (France); water distribution services; Pres. ABDOULAYE BOUNA FALL; Dir-Gen. MAMADOU DIA.

MAJOR COMPANIES

The following are some of the largest companies in terms of either capital investment or employment.

AfricaMer: Nouveau Quai de Pêche-Môle 10, BP 8214, Dakar; tel. 33-821-6893; fax 33-821-4426; e-mail africamer@cyg.sn; fishing and export of frozen fish and seafood; sales US $17.0m. (2001); Dir-Gen. EMMANUEL GIORGIO GABRIELLI; 2,700 employees (2002).

Compagnie Commerciale et Industrielle du Sénégal (CCIS): route du Front de Terre, angle Service géographique, BP 137, Dakar; tel. 33-849-3939; fax 33-849-3814; e-mail ccis@arc.sn; internet www.ccis.sn; f. 1972; cap. 1,969.6m. francs CFA; mfrs of PVC piping and plastic for shoes; Man. Dir NAYEF DERWICHE.

Compagnie Sucrière Sénégalaise (CSS): ave Félix Eboué, BP 2031, Dakar; tel. 33-832-2886; fax 33-832-9192; e-mail css@sentoo.sn; internet www.css.sn; f. 1970; cap. 13,586m. francs CFA; sales 48,955.8m. francs CFA (2001); growing of sugar cane and refining of cane sugar; Dir-Gen. ANDRÉ FROISSARD; 5,222 employees (April 2002).

Crown Sénégal: route du Service Géographique, Hann, BP 3850, Dakar; tel. 33-849-3232; fax 33-832-3725; f. 1959; cap. 900m. francs CFA; 77% owned by Crown Holding (France); fmrly CarnaudMetalbox Sénégal; mfrs of metal packaging; Chair. LAURENT DONDIN; Man. Dir MICHEL BOREAU.

Les Grands Moulins de Dakar (GMD): ave Félix Eboué, BP 2068, Dakar; tel. 33-839-9797; fax 33-832-8947; e-mail gmd@gmd.sn; internet www.gmd.sn; f. 1946; cap. 1,180m. francs CFA; sales US $96.8m. (2004); production of wheat flour and animal food; Chair. JEAN-CLAUDE MIMRAN; Dir EMILE ELMALEM; 300 employees (2004).

Industries Chimiques du Sénégal (ICS): Km 18, Route de Rufisque, BP 3835, Dakar; tel. 33-879-1000; fax 33-834-0814; e-mail icssg@ics.sn; internet www.ics.sn; f. 1975; cap. 130,000m. francs CFA; majority-owned by Govt of India, 10% state-owned; mining of high-grade calcium phosphates at Taïba, production of sulphuric and phosphoric acid at two factories at Darou, fertilizer factory at M'Bao; Man. Dir ALASSANE DIALLO; 2,000 employees (2001).

Lesieur Afrique (Dakar): pl. Amílcar Cabral, BP 236, Dakar; tel. 33-823-1066; f. 1942; cap. 1,796m. francs CFA; subsidiary of Lesieur Afrique (Morocco); groundnut-shelling plant (annual capacity: 350,000 metric tons) and vegetable oil refining plant (capacity: 30,000 tons) at Dakar; Man. Dir MAMBAYE DIAW.

Manufacture de Tabacs de l'Ouest Africain (MTOA): km 2.5, blvd du Centenaire de la Commune de Dakar, BP 76, Dakar; tel. 33-849-2500; fax 33-849-2555; f. 1951; mfrs of tobacco products; Pres. PIERRE IMBERT; Dir-Gen. HENRI LUQUET; 300 employees.

Mobil Oil Sénégal: blvd du Centenaire de la Commune de Dakar, BP 227, Dakar; tel. 33-859-3000; fax 33-859-3100; subsidiary of ExxonMobil (USA); marketing and sale of petroleum and petroleum products; Pres. MOULAYE ALI HAIDARA; Dir-Gen. RICHARD WILLEMS; 80 employees (2002).

Nestlé Senegal: km 14, route de Rufisque, BP 796, Dakar; tel. 33-839-8300; fax 33-834-1702; e-mail nestle-senegal.senegal@nestle.com; f. 1960; cap. 1,620m. francs CFA; mfrs of sweetened and unsweetened condensed milk and culinary products; wholly owned by Nestlé (Switzerland); sales US $34.2m. (2001); Dir-Gen. ALVARO LABARCA.

La Rochette Dakar (LRD): km 13.7, blvd du Centenaire de la Commune de Dakar, BP 891, Dakar; tel. 33-839-8282; fax 33-834-2826; e-mail contact@rochette.sn; internet www.rochette.sn; f. 1946; cap. 500m. francs CFA; mfrs of paper and cardboard packaging; Chair. and Man. Dir ADEL SALHAB; 166 employees (2002).

Senbus Industries: près du Chemin de fer, Dakar; tel. 33-952-0039; 93% owned by SIE—Société d'intervention financière, 7% state-owned; f. 2003; assembly of passenger coaches and buses; Pres. and Dir-Gen. OUSMANE JOSEPH DIOP.

Sénégal Pêche: Môle 10, Pont de Pêche, BP 317, Dakar; tel. 33-822-3035; owned by China International Fisheries Corpn.

Shell Sénégal: route des Hydrocarbures, BP 144, Dakar; tel. 33-849-3737; fax 33-832-8730; internet www.shell.com/home/Framework?siteId=sn-en; f. 1961; marketing and distribution of petroleum and gas; Dir-Gen. EBENEZER FAULKNER; 193 employees (2002).

Société Africaine de Raffinage (SAR): BP 203, Dakar; tel. 33-834-8439; fax 33-821-1010; f. 1963; 46% state-owned, 34% owned by Saudi Binladin Group (Saudi Arabia) and 20% by Total (France); cap. 1,000m. francs CFA; petroleum refinery at M'Bao; Pres. AYMÉROU NGINGUE; Dir-Gen. OMAR KASSOU; 220 employees (2002).

Société des Brasseries de l'Ouest Africain (SOBOA): route des Brasseries, BP 290, Dakar; tel. 33-832-0190; fax 33-832-5469; f. 1928; cap. 820m. francs CFA; mfrs of beer and soft drinks; Man. Dir PIERRE TRAVERSA.

Société de Conserves Alimentaires du Sénégal (SOCAS): 50 ave Lamine Guèye, BP 451, Dakar; tel. 33-839-9000; fax 33-823-8069; e-mail socas@orange.sn; internet www.socas-senegal.com; f. 1969; mfrs of tomato concentrate, vegetable canning, export of fresh vegetables; Pres. DONALD BARON; Dir-Gen. ERIC BINSON; 315 employees (2003).

Société de Développement et des Fibres Textiles (SODEFITEX): km 4.5, blvd du Centenaire de la Commune de Dakar, BP 3216, Dakar; tel. 33-889-7950; fax 33-832-0675; e-mail dg@sodefitex.sn; internet www.sodefitex.sn; f. 1974; 51.0% owned by Geocoton (France), 46.5% state-owned; responsible for planning and development of cotton industry and rural sustainable development; cap. 3,000m. francs CFA; Pres. YOUSSOU DAOU; Dir-Gen. AHMED BACHIR DIOP.

Société Industrielle Moderne des Plastiques Africains (SIMPA): 50 ave du Président Lamine Guèye, BP 451, Dakar; tel. 33-823-4325; fax 33-821-8069; f. 1958; cap. 551m. francs CFA; mfrs of injection-moulded and extruded plastic articles; Chair. and Man. Dir RAYMOND GAVEAU.

Société Industrielle de Papeterie au Sénégal (SIPS): km 11, route de Rufisque, BP 1818, Dakar; tel. 33-834-0929; fax 33-834-2303; f. 1972; cap. 750m. francs CFA; mfrs of paper goods; Chair. OMAR ABDEL KANDER GHANDOUR; Man. Dir ALI SALIM HOBALLAH.

Société Minière de Sabodala (SMS): 7 rue Mermoz, BP 268, Dakar; tel. 33-821-9560; fax 33-823-3864; 70% owned by Mineral Deposits Ltd (Australia), 30% owned by private Senegalese interests; exploration and exploitation of gold mines in Sabodala region; Dir-Gen. GUY ALAIN PREIRA.

Société Nationale des Pétroles du Sénégal (PETROSEN): route du Service Géographique, Hann, POB 2076, Dakar; tel. 33-839-9298; fax 33-832-1899; e-mail petrosen@petrosen.sn; internet www.petrosen.sn; f. 1981; 90% state-owned; exploration and exploitation of hydrocarbons; Pres. IBRAHIMA KHALIL DIEYE; Dir-Gen. IBRAHIMA MBODJI.

Société Nouvelle des Salins du Sine Saloum (SNSS): BP 200, Diohrane, Kaolack; tel. 33-941-1904; fax 33-941-1629; e-mail salins@orange.sn; f. 1965; 51% owned by Salins (Compagnie des Salins du Midi—France), 49% state-owned; production and marketing of sea-salt; cap. 563m. francs CFA; Dir LUC LEROY.

Société de Produits Industriels et Agricoles (SPIA): 56 ave Faidherbe, BP 3806, Dakar; tel. 33-869-3269; fax 33-820-1773; internet spia-sn.com; f. 1980; cap. 640m. francs CFA; mfrs of plant-based medicines at Louga; Chair. DJILLY MBAYE; Dir-Gen. CHEIKH DEMBA KAMARA.

Société Sénégalaise des Phosphates de Thiès (SSPT): 39 ave Jean XXIII, BP 241, Dakar; tel. 33-823-3283; fax 33-823-8384; e-mail miller@telecomplus.sn; f. 1948; cap. 1,000m. francs CFA; owned by TOLSA SA (Spain); production of phosphates and attapulgite, mfrs of phosphate fertilizers; Chair. MÍREN LARREA; Man. EDUARDO MILLER MENDEZ.

Société Textile de Kaolack (SOTEXKA): Dakar; tel. 33-821-8999; fax 33-821-2301; f. 1977; cap 8,628m. francs CFA; 63% state-owned; transfer pending to private ownership; textile and garment-assembling complex; Man. Dir LAMINE NDOYE FALL.

SUNEOR: 32–36 rue du Dr Calmette, BP 639, Dakar; tel. 33-849-1700; fax 33-821-9970; internet www.suneor.sn; f. 1975 as Société Nationale de Commercialisation des Oléagineux du Sénégal (SONACOS); cap. 22,626.6m. francs CFA; majority share owned by Advens (France); comprises five factories, processing and export of edible oils, cattle feed, bleach and vinegar; Pres. ABBAS JABER; Dir-Gen. THIENDIATÉ BOUYO NDAO; 339 permanent and 201 seasonal employees (2007).

Total Sénégal: Km 3, blvd du Centenaire de la Commune de Dakar, BP 355, Dakar; tel. 33-839-5454; fax 33-832-5974; e-mail total@total.sn; internet www.total-senegal.com; distribution of petroleum; Dir-Gen. (vacant).

Société des Produits Pétroliers (SPP): Zone des Hydrocarbures, Terre Plein Nord-Est, Port de Commerce, BP 97, Dakar; tel. 33-849-3200; Total Sénégal is sole shareholder; import, storage and distribution of petroleum products, mfrs of lubricating oil.

TRADE UNIONS

Confédération Nationale des Travailleurs du Sénégal (CNTS): 7 ave du Président Laminé Gueye, BP 937, Dakar; tel. 33-821-0491; fax 33-821-7771; e-mail cnts@orange.sn; internet cnts-senegal.net; f. 1969; affiliated to PS; Sec.-Gen. MODY GUIRO.

Confédération Nationale des Travailleurs du Sénégal—Forces de Changement (CNTS—FC): Dakar; f. 2002 following split from CNTS; Sec.-Gen CHEIKH DIOP; 31 affiliated asscns.

Confédération des Syndicats Autonomes (CSA): BP 10224, Dakar; tel. 33-835-0951; fax 33-893-5299; e-mail csasenegal@yahoo.com; organization of independent trade unions; Sec.-Gen. Mamadou Diouf.

Union Démocratique des Travailleurs du Sénégal (UDTS): BP 7124, Médina, Dakar; tel. 33-835-3897; fax 33-854-1070; 18 affiliated unions; Sec.-Gen. Malamine Ndiaye.

Union Nationale des Syndicats Autonomes du Sénégal (UNSAS): BP 10841, HLM, Dakar; fax 33-824-8013; Sec.-Gen. Mademba Sock.

Transport

RAILWAYS

There are 922 km of main line, including 70 km of double track. One line runs from Dakar north to Saint-Louis (262 km), and the main line runs to Bamako (Mali). All the locomotives are diesel-driven. In 2009 plans were announced for the construction of a 10,000-km transcontinental railway linking Dakar with Port Sudan (Sudan).

Société Nationale des Chemins de Fer du Sénégal (SNCS): BP 175A, Thiès; tel. 33-939-5300; fax 33-951-1393; f. 1905; state-owned; operates passenger and freight services on Dakar–Thiès and Djourbel–Kaoulack lines, following transfer of principal Dakar–Bamako (Mali) line to private management in 2003; suburban trains operate on Dakar–Thiès route as 'Le Petit Train Bleu'; Pres. Drame Alia Diene; Man. Dir Diouf Mbaye.

ROADS

In 2007 there were 14,800 km of roads, of which some 4,800 km were paved. A 162.5-km road between Dialakoto and Kédougou, the construction of which (at a cost of some 23,000m. francs CFA) was largely financed by regional donor organizations, was inaugurated in 1996. The road was to form part of an eventual transcontinental highway linking Cairo (Egypt) with the Atlantic coast, via N'Djamena (Chad), Bamako (Mali) and Dakar. In 1999 new highways were completed in the east of Senegal, linking Tambacounda, Kidira and Bakel.

Comité Executif des Transports Urbains de Dakar (CETUD): Résidence Fann, route du Front de Terre Hann, BP 17265 Dakar; tel. 33-859-4720; fax 33-832-5686; e-mail cetud@cetud.sn; internet www.cetud.sn; f. 1997; regulates the provision of urban transport in Dakar; Pres. Ousmane Thiam.

Dakar-Bus: Dakar; f. 1999; operates public transport services within the city of Dakar; owned by RATP (France), Transdev (France), Eurafric-Equipment (Senegal), Mboup Travel (Senegal) and Senegal Tours (Senegal).

Dakar Dem Dikk: km 4.5, ave Cheikh Anta Diop, Dakar; tel. 33-865-1555; fax 33-860-3193; internet www.demdikk.com; f. 2001; Dir-Gen. Moussa Diagne.

Fonds d'Entretien Routier Autonome (FERA): Dakar; f. 2007.

INLAND WATERWAYS

Senegal has three navigable rivers: the Senegal, navigable for three months of the year as far as Kayes (Mali), for six months as far as Kaédi (Mauritania) and all year as far as Rosso and Podor, and the Saloun and the Casamance. Senegal is a member of the Organisation de mise en valeur du fleuve Gambie and of the Organisation pour la mise en valeur du fleuve Sénégal, both based in Dakar. These organizations aim to develop navigational facilities, irrigation and hydroelectric power in the basins of the Gambia and Senegal rivers, respectively.

SHIPPING

The port of Dakar is the second largest in West Africa, after Abidjan (Côte d'Ivoire), and the largest deepwater port in the region, serving Senegal, Mauritania, The Gambia and Mali. It handled more than 10m. metric tons of international freight in 2008. The port's facilities include 40 berths, 10 km of quays, and also 53,000 sq m of warehousing and 65,000 sq m of open stocking areas. In addition, there is a container terminal with facilities for vessels with a draught of up to 11 m. In March 2005 the Governments of Mauritania, Morocco and Senegal agreed that a shipping line linking the three countries and to transport merchandise was to commence operations, following the completion of a tendering process. At 31 December 2009 Senegal's merchant fleet numbered 189 vessels and amounted to 47,300 gross registered tons.

Dakarnave: blvd du Centenaire de la Commune, 2POB 438, Dakar; tel. 33-849-1001; fax 33-823-8399; e-mail commercial@dakarnave.sn; internet www.dakarnave.com; responsible for Senegalese shipyards; owned by Chantier Navals de Dakar, SA (Dakarnave), a subsidiary of Lisnave International, Portugal; CEO Frederico J. Spranger.

Maersk Sénégal: route de Rufisque, BP 3836, Dakar; tel. 33-859-1111; fax 33-832-1331; e-mail senmkt@maersk.com; internet www.maersksealand.com/senegal; f. 1986.

SDV Sénégal: 47 ave Albert Sarrault, BP 233, Dakar; tel. 33-839-0000; fax 33-839-0069; e-mail sdv.shipping@sn.dti.bollore.com; f. 1936; 51.6% owned by Groupe Bolloré (France); shipping agents, warehousing; Pres. André Guillabert; Dir-Gen. Bernard Fraud.

Société Maritime de l'Atlantique (SOMAT): c/o Port Autonome de Dakar, BP 3195, Dakar; internet www.somat.sn; f. 2005; 51% owned by Compagnie Marocaine de Navigation, COMANAV (Morocco), 24.5% by Conseil Sénégalais des Chargeurs, COSEC, 24.5% by Société Nationale de Port Autonome de Dakar, PAD; operates foot passenger and freight ferry service between Dakar and Ziguinchor (Casamance).

Société Nationale de Port Autonome de Dakar (PAD): 21 blvd de la Libération, BP 3195, Dakar; tel. 33-823-4545; fax 33-823-3606; e-mail pad@portdakar.sn; internet www.portdakar.sn; f. 1865; state-owned port authority; Pres. and Dir-Gen. Bara Sady.

SOCOPAO-Sénégal: BP 233, Dakar; tel. 33-823-1001; fax 33-823-5614; e-mail socopao@sn.dti.bollore.com; f. 1926; warehousing, shipping agents, sea and air freight transport; Man. Dir Gilles Cuche.

TransSene: 1 blvd de l'Arsenal, face à la gare ferroviaire, Dakar; tel. 33-823-0290; fax 33-821-1431; e-mail transsene@transsene.com; internet www.transsene.com; f. 1978; CEO Cheikh Diop.

CIVIL AVIATION

The international airport is Dakar-Léopold Sédar Senghor. There are other major airports at Saint-Louis, Ziguinchor and Tambacounda, in addition to about 15 smaller airfields. A new international airport, near Ndiass, some 45 km south-east of Dakar, was expected to be operational in early 2014.

Agence Nationale de l'Aviation Civile du Sénégal (ANACS): BP 8184, Dakar; tel. 33-869-5335; fax 33-820-0403; e-mail daviacivile@sentoo.sn; internet www.anacs.sn; civil aviation authority; Dir-Gen. Mathiaco Bessane.

Sénégal Airlines: Immeuble La Rotonde, rue Amadou Assane Ndoye, Dakar; e-mail contact@senegalairlines.aero; internet www.senegalairlines.aero; f. 2010; 36% state-owned; domestic and regional services; Dir-Gen. Edgardo Badiali.

Tourism

Senegal's attractions for tourists include six national parks (one of which, Djoudj, is listed by UNESCO as a World Heritage Site) and its fine beaches. The island of Gorée, near Dakar, is of considerable historic interest as a former centre for the slave trade. In 2010 some 900,000 visitor arrivals were recorded; receipts from tourism in that year were US $453m.

Ministry of Culture and Tourism: Bldg Administratif, 3e étage, ave Léopold Sédar Senghor, BP 4001, Dakar; tel. 33-822-4303; fax 33-822-1638; internet www.culture.gouv.sn.

Defence

As assessed at November 2011, Senegal's active armed forces comprised a land army of 11,900, a navy of 950, and an air force of 770. There was also a 5,000-strong paramilitary gendarmerie. Military service is by selective conscription and lasts for two years. France and the USA provide technical and material aid. In April 2010 President Abdoulaye Wade announced that Senegal was to reclaim all military bases held by France, although in November of that year 761 French troops remained in Senegal, despite Wade's assertion that this number would be reduced to just 300. In 2011 a total of 1,601 Senegalese troops were deployed abroad, of which 56 were observers.

Defence Expenditure: Estimated at 98,800m. francs CFA in 2010.

Chief of Staff of the Armed Forces: Gen. Abdoulaye Fall.

Education

Primary education, which usually begins at seven years of age, lasts for six years and is officially compulsory. In 2009/10 primary enrolment included 75% of children in the relevant age-group (males 73%; females 78%), according to UNESCO estimates. Secondary education usually begins at the age of 13, and comprises a first cycle of four years (also referred to as 'middle school') and a further cycle of three years. According to UNESCO estimates, in 2009/10 secondary enrolment was equivalent to 37% of children in the relevant age-group (males 40%; females 35%). There are three universities in Senegal: the Université Cheikh Anta Diop and the Université du Sahel in Dakar, and the Université Gaston Berger in Saint-Louis. Some 92,100 students were enrolled in tertiary education in 2009/10.

Since 1981 the reading and writing of national languages has been actively promoted, and is expressly encouraged in the 2001 Constitution. According to official figures, in 2010 spending on education represented 40% of total budgetary expenditure, a rise of some 202% since 2000. However, the World Bank disputed these figures and estimated the spending at 32%.

Bibliography

Adedeji, A., Senghor, C., and Diouf, A. *Towards a Dynamic African Economy*. Ilford, Frank Cass Publishers, 1989.

Beck, L. *Brokering Democracy in Africa: The Rise of Clientelist Democracy in Senegal*. Basingstoke, Palgrave Macmillan, 2008.

Bellitto, M. *Une histoire du Sénégal et de ses entreprises publiques*. Paris, L'Harmattan, 2002.

Biondi, J.-P. *Senghor, ou, la tentation de l'universel: l'aventure coloniale de la France*. Paris, Denoël, 1993.

Boubacar, B. *Agriculture et Sécurité Alimentaire au Sénégal*. Paris, L'Harmattan, 2008.

Camara, A. *La philosophie politique de Léopold Sédar Senghor*. Paris, L'Harmattan, 2002.

Clark, A. F., and Phillips, L. C. *Historical Dictionary of Senegal*. 2nd edn. Metuchen, NJ, Scarecrow Press, 1994.

Copans, J. *Islam, mysticisme et marginalité: les Baay Faal du Sénégal*. Paris. L'Harmattan, 2008.

Coulibaly, A. L. *Le Sénégal à l'épreuve de la démocratie: Enquête sur 50 ans de lutte et de complots au sein de l'élite socialiste*. Paris, L'Harmattan, 1999.

Wade, un opposant au pouvoir: L'alternance piégée. Dakar, Editions Sentinelles, 2003.

Coulon, C. *Le Marabout et Le Prince: Islam et Pouvoir en Sénégal*. Paris, A. Pedone, 1981.

Cruise O'Brien, D. B. *The Mourides of Senegal: The Political and Economic Organization of an Islamic Brotherhood*. Oxford, Clarendon, 1971.

Cruise O'Brien, D. B., Diop, M. C., and Diouf, M. *La construction de l'Etat au Sénégal*. Paris, Editions Karthala, 2002.

Cruise O'Brien, D. B., Dunn, J., and Rathbone, R. (Eds). *Contemporary West African States*. Cambridge, Cambridge University Press, 1989.

de Benoist, J. R. *Histoire de l'Eglise catholique au Sénégal: Du milieu du XVe siècle à l'aube du troisième millénaire*. Paris, Editions Karthala, 2008.

Diagne, A. *Abdou Diouf, le maître du jeu*. Dakar, Agence Less Com, 1996.

Diagne, A., and Daffé, G. (Eds). *Le Sénégal en quête d'une croissance durable*. Paris, Editions Karthala, 2002.

Diallo, M. L. *Le Sénégal, un lion économique?* Paris, Editions Karthala, 2004.

Diop, A.-B. *La société Wolof*. Paris, Editions Karthala, 1983 (reissue).

Diop, M.- C. (Ed.). *Senegal: Essays in Statecraft*. Dakar, CODESRIA, 1993.

La société sénégalaise entre le local et le global. Paris, Editions Karthala, 2002.

Le Sénégal contemporain. Paris, Editions Karthala, 2003.

Le Sénégal à l'heure de l'information: Technologies et Société. Paris, Editions Karthala, 2003.

Gouverner le Sénégal: Entre ajustement structurel et développement durable. Paris, Editions Karthala, 2004.

Diouf, M. *Sénégal, les ethnies et la nation*. Paris, UN Research Institute for Social Development, Forum du Tiers-Monde and L'Harmattan, 1994.

L'Endettement puis l'ajustement: L'Afrique des institutions Bretton-Woods. Paris, L'Harmattan, 2002.

Dreyfus, M., and Juillard, C. *Le plurilinguisme au Sénégal: Langues et identités en devenir*. Paris, Editions Karthala, 2005.

Eades, J., and Dilley, R. *Senegal*. Santa Barbara, CA, ABC Clio, 1993.

Fauvelle, F. X. *L'Afrique de Cheikh Anta Diop: histoire et idéologie*. Paris, Editions Karthala, 1996.

Gaye, M. *Le Sénégal sous Abdoulaye Wade: Banqueroute, corruption et liberticide*. Paris, L'Harmattan, 2011.

Gellar, S. *Senegal: An African Nation between Islam and the West*. 2nd edn. Boulder, CO, Westview Press, 1995.

Getz, T. R. *Slavery and reform in West Africa: toward emancipation in nineteenth-century Senegal and the Gold Coast*. Athens, OH, Ohio University Press, 2004.

Harrison Church, R. J. *West Africa*. 8th edn. London, Longman, 1979.

Harvey, C., and Robinson, M. *The Design of Economic Reforms in the Context of Economic Liberalization: The Experience of Mozambique, Senegal and Uganda*. Brighton, Institute of Development Studies, 1995.

Hesseling, G. *Histoire politique du Sénégal*. Paris, Editions Karthala, 1983.

Hymans, J. L. *Léopold Sédar Senghor*. Edinburgh University Press, 1972.

Johnson, G. W. *Naissance du Sénégal contemporain*. Paris, Editions Karthala, 1991.

Jus, C. *Soudan français–Mauritanie, une géopolitique coloniale (1880–1963): tracer une ligne dans le désert*. Paris, L'Harmattan, 2003.

Lambert, M. *Longing for Exile: Migration and the Making of a Translocal Community in Senegal, West Africa*. Westport, CT, Greenwood Press, 2002.

Leymarie, I. *Les griots wolof du Sénégal*. Paris, Maisonneuve & Larose, 1999.

Linares, O. *Power, Prayer and Production: The Jola of Casamance*. Cambridge, Cambridge University Press, 1993.

Loum, N. *Médias et l'état au Sénégal: L'impossible autonomie*. Paris, L'Harmattan, 2003.

Magassouba, M. *L'Islam au Sénégal: Demain les Mollahs?* Paris, Editions Karthala, 1985.

Makédonsky, E. *Le Sénégal: La Sénégambie*. 2 vols, Paris, L'Harmattan, 1987.

Mbacke, K., Hunwick, J., and Ross, E. (transl.) *Sufism and Religious Brotherhoods in Senegal*. Princeton, NJ, Markus Wiener, 2005.

Milcent, E., and Sordet, M. *Léopold Sédar Senghor et la naissance de l'Afrique moderne*. Paris, Editions Seghers, 1969.

Robinson, D. *Sociétés musulmanes et pouvoir colonial français au Sénégal et en Mauritanie 1880–1920*. Paris, Editions Karthala, 2004.

Roche, C. *Histoire de la Casamance: conquête et résistance, 1850–1920*. Paris, Editions Karthala, 1985.

Le Sénégal à la conquête de son indépendance: 1939–1960: chronique de la vie politique et syndicale, de l'Empire français à l'indépendance. Paris, Editions Karthala, 2001.

Saint-Martin, Y.-J. *Le Sénégal sous le second empire*. Paris, Editions Karthala, 1989.

Sarr, P. *Le Sénégal: Des idées pour une nouvelle donne*. Paris, L'Harmattan, 2012.

Schaffer, F. C. *Democracy in Translation: Understanding Politics in an Unfamiliar Culture*. Ithaca, NY, Cornell University Press, 2000.

Seck, A. *Sénégal émergence d'une démocratie moderne, 1945–2005: Un itinéraire politique*. Paris, Editions Karthala, 2005.

Senghor, L. S. *Liberté I, Négritude et Humanisme; Liberté II, Nation et voie africaine du socialisme*. Editions du Seuil, 1964 and 1971.

Snipe, T. *Arts and Politics in Senegal, 1960–1996*. Lawrenceville, NJ, Africa World Press Inc, 1997.

Souane, L. *Sénégal: histoire d'une démocratie confisquée*. Paris, L'Harmattan, 2012.

Sweeney, P. (Ed.). *The Gambia and Senegal*. London, APA, 1996.

Vaillant, J. G. *Vie de Léopold Sédar Senghor: Noir, Français et Africain*. Paris, Editions Karthala, 2006.

Vandermotten, C. *Géopolitique de la vallée du Sénégal: les flots de la discorde*. Paris, L'Harmattan, 2004.

Villalon, L. *Islamic Society and State Power in Senegal: Disciples and Citizens in Fatick*. Cambridge, Cambridge University Press, 1995.

Wade, A. *Un destin pour l'Afrique*. Paris, Editions Karthala, 1992.

Wane, A. M. *Le Sénégal entre deux naufrages?: Le Joola et l'Alternance*. Paris, L'Harmattan, 2003.

Wolf, F. *Senegal: Entwicklungsland im Globalisierungswettlauf*. Frankfurt am Main, Peter Lang, 2004.

Yansané, A. Y. *Decolonization in West African states, with French Colonial Legacy: Comparison and Contrast: Development in Guinea, the Ivory Coast, and Senegal, 1945–1980*. Cambridge, MA, Schenkman Publishing Co, 1984.

Zarour, C. *La Coopération arabo-sénégalaise*. Paris, L'Harmattan, 2000.

SEYCHELLES

Physical and Social Geography

The Republic of Seychelles comprises a scattered archipelago of granitic and coralline islands, lying about 1,600 km east of continental Africa and ranging over some 1m. sq km of the western Indian Ocean. The exact number of islands is unknown, but has been estimated at 115, of which 41 are granitic and the remainder coralline. The group also includes numerous rocks and small cays. At independence in June 1976, the Aldabra Islands, the Farquhar group and Desroches (combined area 28.5 sq km, or 11 sq miles), part of the British Indian Ocean Territory since 1965, were reunited with Seychelles, thus restoring the land area to 308 sq km (119 sq miles). Including the Aldabra lagoon, the country's area is 455.3 sq km (175.8 sq miles).

The islands take their name from the Vicomte Moreau de Séchelles, Controller-General of Finance in the reign of Louis XV of France. The largest of the group is Mahé, which has an area of about 148 sq km (57 sq miles) and is approximately 27 km long from north to south. Mahé lies 1,800 km due east of Mombasa, Kenya, 3,300 km south-west of Mumbai, India, and 1,100 km north of Madagascar. Victoria, the capital of Seychelles and the only port of the archipelago, is on Mahé. It is the only town in Seychelles of any size and had an estimated population of 26,609 (including suburbs) in mid-2011; Mahé itself had an estimated population of 72,100 at mid-2004 (with Praslin accounting for 7,200 people and La Digue and the outer islands some 3,200 people). The islanders have a variety of ethnic origins—African, European, Indian and Chinese. In 1981 Creole (Seselwa), the language spoken by virtually all Seychellois, replaced English and French as the official language. The total population was enumerated at 90,945 at the August 2010 census, giving a density of 199.7 persons per sq km.

The granitic islands, which are all of great scenic beauty, rise fairly steeply from the sea, and Mahé has a long central ridge, which at its highest point, Morne Seychellois, reaches 912 m. Praslin, the second largest island in the group, is 43 km from Mahé and the other granitic islands are within a radius of 56 km. The coral islands are reefs in different stages of formation, rising only marginally above sea-level.

For islands so close to the Equator, the climate is surprisingly equable. Maximum shade temperature at sea-level averages 29°C, but during the coolest months the temperature may fall to 24°C. There are two seasons, hot from December to May, and cooler from June to November while the south-east trade winds are blowing. Rainfall varies over the group; the greater part falls in the hot months during the north-west trade winds, and the climate then tends to be humid and somewhat enervating. The mean annual rainfall in Victoria is 2,360 mm and the mean average temperature nearly 27°C. All the granitic islands lie outside the cyclone belt.

Recent History

KATHARINE MURISON

The archipelago now forming the Republic of Seychelles was occupied by French settlers in 1770. Following its capture in 1811 by British naval forces, Seychelles was formally ceded by France to Britain in 1814. The islands were administered as a dependency of Mauritius until 1903, when Seychelles became a separate Crown Colony.

During the 1960s political activity was focused on the socialist-orientated Seychelles People's United Party (SPUP), led by France Albert René, and the centre-right Seychelles Democratic Party (SDP), led by James (later Sir James) Mancham, who became the islands' Chief Minister in 1970. The two parties formed a coalition Government in 1975, and the independent Republic of Seychelles, with Mancham as President and René as Prime Minister, was proclaimed on 29 June 1976.

SINGLE-PARTY GOVERNMENT

In June 1977 supporters of the SPUP staged an armed coup while Mancham was absent in the United Kingdom, and installed René as President. René claimed that Mancham had intended to postpone the 1979 elections (a charge that Mancham denied), but there was little doubt that the ex-President's extravagant lifestyle and capitalist philosophy had displeased many of the islanders.

A new Constitution was promulgated in 1979. The SPUP, now redesignated the Seychelles People's Progressive Front (SPPF), was declared the sole legal party, and legislative and presidential elections were held to legitimize the new political order. The Government's socialist programme, however, led to discontent, particularly among the small middle class. Plots to overthrow René were suppressed in 1978, 1981, 1982 and 1983. This sustained anti-Government activism was blamed by the Government on pro-Mancham exiled groups, although Mancham denied any involvement in the conspiracies.

Until the early 1990s exiled opposition to René remained split among a number of small groups based principally in the British capital, London. In July 1991 five of these parties, including the Rassemblement du Peuple Seychellois pour la Démocratie (subsequently renamed the Seychelles Christian Democrat Party, SCDP), founded by Dr Maxime Ferrari, established a coalition, the United Democratic Movement (UDM), under Ferrari's leadership. During 1991 the René Government came under increasing pressure from France and the United Kingdom, the islands' principal aid donors, to return Seychelles to a democratic political system. Internally, open opposition to the SPPF was voiced by the newly formed Parti Seselwa (PS), led by a Protestant clergyman, Wavel Ramkalawan. In August Ferrari returned from exile, and in November René invited all political dissidents to return to the islands.

RESUMPTION OF MULTI-PARTY POLITICS

In December 1991 the SPPF conceded its political monopoly, and agreed that political groups numbering at least 100 members could be granted official registration, and that multi-party elections would take place in July 1992 for a constituent assembly. The Constituent Assembly's proposals for constitutional reform would be submitted to a national referendum, with a view to holding multi-party parliamentary elections in December. In April Mancham returned from exile to lead the New Democratic Party.

The draft Constitution, which required the approval of at least 60% of voters, was endorsed by only 53.7% at a referendum held in November 1992. A revised draft Constitution was drawn up, in which a compromise plan was reached on the electoral formula for a new National Assembly. With the joint endorsement of René and Mancham, the draft Constitution was approved by 73.9% of voters at a national referendum in

June. Opponents of the new constitutional arrangements comprised the PS, the Seychelles National Movement (SNM) and the National Alliance Party (NAP). At the presidential and legislative elections that followed in July, René received 59.5% of the vote, against 36.7% for Mancham and 3.8% for Philippe Boullé, who was representing an alliance of the PS, the SCDP, the SNM and the NAP. In the legislative elections, the SPPF secured 28 of the 33 seats, while the Democratic Party (DP, as the New Democratic Party had been renamed) took four and the PS one.

Following the 1993 elections, the Government began to promote a gradual transition from socialism to free-market policies, aimed at maximizing the country's potential as an 'offshore' financial and business centre. State-owned port facilities were transferred to private ownership in 1994, when plans were also announced for the creation of a duty-free international trade zone to provide transshipment facilities. Arrangements also proceeded during 1995 for the privatization of government activities in tourism, agriculture and tuna-processing.

In July 1996 the SPPF introduced a series of constitutional amendments, creating the post of Vice-President, to which James Michel, the Minister of Finance, Communications and Defence and a long-standing political associate of René, was appointed in August. The constitutional changes also provided for revisions in constituency boundaries, which were generally interpreted as favouring SPPF candidates in future legislative elections. Measures were also implemented whereby the number of directly elected members of the National Assembly was to be increased from 22 to 25, and the number of seats allocated on a proportional basis reduced from 11 to a maximum of 10.

ELECTIONS OF 1998 AND 2001–02

In January 1998 René announced that presidential and legislative elections would be held in March, and that he was to seek a second term. The outcome of the elections provided the SPPF with a decisive victory. René obtained 66.7% of the presidential ballot, while his party secured 30 of the 34 seats in the enlarged National Assembly. Ramkalawan, with 19.5% of the presidential vote, substantially exceeded support for Mancham, who received 13.8%. In the National Assembly the United Opposition (UO), which had been formed in 1995 by the amalgamation of the PS, the SNM, the SCDP and the NAP as a single party, under the leadership of Ramkalawan, increased its representation from one seat to three seats, with the DP losing three of the four seats previously held. Mancham, who lost his seat, announced his temporary withdrawal from active politics. In July 1998 the UO changed its name to the Seychelles National Party (SNP).

In July 2001 René announced that the presidential election was to be held two years before it was due, in order to reassure investors of the political stability of the country, which was suffering from a lack of foreign earnings and a decline in tourism. At the election, which was held on 31 August–2 September, René was re-elected as President, with 54.2% of the valid votes cast, defeating the SNP's Ramkalawan, who secured 45.0%. Philippe Boullé, the first independent candidate in the country's history (who had contested the presidential election in July 1993 for an opposition alliance), secured only 0.9% of the votes.

Legislative elections, which were due in 2003, were also held early, on 4–6 December 2002. The SPPF retained its majority in the National Assembly, but with the loss of seven seats, securing 23 of the 34 seats; the SNP, with 11 seats, won significantly more than in the previous election. In early 2003, for the first time, President René officially acknowledged Vice-President Michel as his successor, also announcing that he was to relinquish certain presidential duties to Michel.

THE MICHEL PRESIDENCY

On 14 April 2004 René officially resigned from the presidency; Michel was inaugurated as President of the Republic on the same day and Joseph Belmont subsequently succeeded him as Vice-President. (However, René remained President of the SPPF, to which position he was re-elected in May 2005.)

Michel won a narrow victory at a presidential election held on 28–30 July 2006, securing his first elected term in office, with 53.7% of the votes cast. Ramkalawan, who was supported by the DP, as well as his own SNP, received 45.7% of the vote, while Boullé, standing again as an independent, took only 0.6%. A turn-out of 88.7% of the electorate was recorded. President Michel was sworn in to serve a five-year term on 1 August. A new Government, which included three new ministers, was inaugurated on 9 August.

In March 2007, in response to a five-month boycott of the legislature by the SNP, Michel dissolved the National Assembly. Early elections were held on 10–12 May, at which a turn-out of 85.9% was recorded. The SPPF secured 23 of the 34 seats, the same number it had held in the previous legislature, while an alliance of the SNP and the DP took the remaining 11 seats. Michel restructured the Government in July, reducing the number of ministries from 10 to eight.

Economic concerns came to the fore in late 2008. The Government was forced to seek emergency assistance from the IMF, as a shortage of foreign exchanges reserves, resulting partly from the international financial crisis, left Seychelles unable to service its substantial external debt. As part of a comprehensive economic reform programme introduced in November, the rupee was allowed to float freely and all controls on foreign exchange were removed. The IMF and the World Bank approved further assistance for Seychelles in late 2009, praising the Government's implementation of the reform programme, and the economy recovered strongly in 2010–11. Several debt cancellation and restructuring agreements were also reached with foreign donors in 2009–11, significantly reducing the debt burden.

Meanwhile, the ruling SPPF and the opposition DP both adopted new names in June 2009: the former was restyled the Parti Lepep (People's Party) and the latter, no longer in alliance with the SNP, became the New Democratic Party (NDP). Michel, hitherto Secretary-General of the SPPF, was elected President of the Parti Lepep (René being accorded the title Founding President), while Ralph Volcere was confirmed as leader of the NDP, having assumed the leadership of the DP in March, following the resignation of Paul Chow.

In December 2009 a committee established in April 2008 to review the Constitution submitted its report to President Michel. In March 2010 Michel charged the Attorney-General, Ronny Govinden, with undertaking the task of drafting amendments to the Constitution and associated legislation.

President Michel announced a reorganization of the Council of Ministers in June 2010, prompted by the imminent retirement of Vice-President Belmont and by the resignation of the Minister of Social Development and Health, Marie-Pierre Lloyd. Among the changes, three new ministers joined the Government: Jean-Paul Adam, previously Secretary of State in the Office of the President, as Minister of Foreign Affairs; Erna Athanasius as Minister of Health; and Peter Sinon, hitherto an Executive Director at the African Development Bank, as Minister of Investment, Natural Resources and Industry, a newly created post. Danny Faure, the Minister of Finance, succeeded Belmont as Vice-President on 1 July, retaining the finance portfolio and assuming additional responsibility for trade, information technology and public administration.

Michel was re-elected as President in an election held on 19–21 May 2011, securing 55.5% of the valid votes cast. His closest rival, contesting the presidency for a fourth time, was Ramkalawan, who received 41.4% of the votes, while Boullé, also participating in his fourth presidential ballot, took 1.7% and Volcere only 1.4%. A turn-out of 85.3% of the electorate was recorded. President Michel was sworn in to serve a second elected term in office on 24 May. Volcere offered his resignation as leader of the NDP following his poor performance in the election, but this was rejected by the party.

In July 2011 the National Assembly approved a constitutional amendment providing for the creation of a five-member Electoral Commission to replace the office of Electoral Commissioner. The SNP criticized the legislation on the grounds that the Commission's members were to be appointed by the President, albeit from among seven candidates proposed by the Constitutional Appointments Authority, and demanded the establishment of an independent body. Also in July, the National Assembly approved a motion for its own dissolution; sittings of the Assembly had been boycotted since late May by the SNP, which disputed the results of that month's presidential vote, alleging irregularities. Early legislative elections, which had not been due until May 2012, were subsequently scheduled for September 2011. In August, however, the SNP and the NDP announced that they would boycott the polls, urging a postponement to allow the reform of the electoral system, which, they claimed, favoured the Government. Following this announcement, David Pierre, hitherto Deputy Secretary-General of the SNP, formed a new party, the Popular Democratic Movement (PDM).

The elections, which took place on 29 September–1 October 2011, were contested by Parti Lepep, the PDM and an independent candidate. A turn-out of 74.3% of the electorate was recorded, compared with 85.9% in 2007, while 31.9% of the votes cast were invalid or blank. Electoral observers from the Southern African Development Community (SADC) none the less concluded that the elections had been conducted in a free and fair manner. The Parti Lepep was initially the only party to secure representation in the National Assembly, winning all 25 constituency seats and an additional six on the basis of proportional representation. However, the PDM appealed to the Constitutional Court, arguing that the number of proportional seats allocated should be based on the percentage of valid votes gained rather than the percentage of total votes. The party had received 10.9% of the valid votes cast, but only 7.4% of the total votes, with a 10% share of the vote being required to qualify for additional seats. The PDM's appeal was rejected by the Constitutional Court in late October, but the Court of Appeal reversed this ruling in December, ordering the Electoral Commission to award two further PR seats to Parti Lepep and one to the PDM. Parti Lepep declined to nominate additional members, but Pierre took up the PDM seat, becoming Leader of the Opposition and bringing the total number of seats in the National Assembly to 32.

A major government reorganization was effected in March 2012, with the appointment of six new ministers and the restructuring of several portfolios. Pierre Laporte, hitherto Governor of the Central Bank, was notably appointed Minister of Finance, Trade and Investment, combining portfolios previously held by Vice-President Faure and Sinon, who retained responsibility for information technology and public administration, and natural resources and industry, respectively. Mitcy Larue replaced Athanasius as Minister of Health.

A Forum for Electoral Reform, comprising representatives of all registered political parties and chaired by the Electoral Commission, held several meetings during the first half of 2012 to consider changes to the electoral and political system.

EXTERNAL RELATIONS

Seychelles, a member of the Commonwealth, the African Development Bank (AfDB), the Common Market for Eastern and Southern Africa, the African Union and SADC, has traditionally pursued a policy of non-alignment in international affairs. In July 2003 the country announced its withdrawal from SADC and the Indian Ocean Rim Association for Regional Co-operation with effect from July 2004, as part of a five-year macroeconomic plan. However, Seychelles was formally readmitted to SADC at a summit in South Africa in August 2008. President Michel had sought to rejoin the Community in an effort to increase trade and encourage foreign investment.

In 1983 Seychelles, Madagascar and Mauritius agreed to form an Indian Ocean Commission (IOC) with the aim of increasing regional co-operation. The first such agreement under the IOC was signed by the three countries in January 1984. The Comoros joined the IOC in 1985.

President Michel continued to foster strong relations with India, paying a state visit to the country in July 2005, following which India pledged a US $10m. aid package to assist the Government's economic reform programme and agreed to reschedule the debt owed by Seychelles. It was hoped that the establishment by Seychelles of a high commission in the Indian capital, New Delhi, in early 2008 would further enhance bilateral ties. During a visit to New Delhi by Michel in June 2010 the Indian Government agreed to a further rescheduling of Seychelles' debt and a Bilateral Investment Protection and Promotion Agreement was signed with the aim of expanding economic links.

In July 2008, after six years of negotiations, the Governments of Mauritius and Seychelles signed a boundary agreement defining the areas of their two exclusive economic zones (EEZs—that of Seychelles covering some 1.4m. sq km). Following further discussions on the delimitation of the extended continental shelf of the two countries, in December the Governments of Mauritius and Seychelles submitted a joint claim (to approximately 396,000 sq km beyond their respective EEZs) under the UN Convention on the Law of the Sea. In March 2011 the UN Commission on the Limits of the Continental Shelf confirmed the two countries' joint jurisdiction over the claimed area. In March 2012, during a state visit to Mauritius by Michel, two bilateral treaties were signed on the joint exercise of sovereign rights in the extended continental shelf and on a framework for the joint management of the area. Relations were further strengthened during a visit to Seychelles by the Prime Minister of Mauritius, Navinchandra Ramgoolam, in June.

Michel's Government sought to encourage further investment from the People's Republic of China, hoping to capitalize on that country's greatly expanded Africa programme. Relations with China were strengthened during a state visit to that country by Michel in November 2006, when he held talks with the Chinese President, Hu Jintao, and Premier, Wen Jiabao, and attended the summit of the Forum on China-Africa Co-operation. President Hu paid a reciprocal visit to Seychelles in February 2007. In September Seychelles officially opened an embassy in the Chinese capital, Beijing, the first resident ambassador to China having presented his credentials to President Hu in May. Bilateral relations were further enhanced in May 2010, during a second state visit by Michel to China, when Hu pledged to provide Seychelles with some US $6m. for development projects. Following a visit to Seychelles by the Chinese Minister of National Defence, Liang Guanglie, in December 2011, the Seychelles Government announced that it was to provide facilities to resupply Chinese naval ships operating in the Indian Ocean. The Chinese Government subsequently downplayed speculation in the Indian and US media that it intended to establish a military base in Seychelles.

Attacks by Somali pirates on ships off the coast of Seychelles became of increasing concern from 2009. In response, the Seychelles Government sought international assistance to combat piracy and protect fishing fleets in its territorial waters, receiving financial and military support from countries including the People's Republic of China, France, India, the United Kingdom, the USA and the United Arab Emirates. In November 2009, moreover, Seychelles signed an agreement with the European Union (EU) allowing the deployment of EU troops on its territory to counter attacks. Amendments to the penal code were adopted in March 2010 to enable the prosecution of suspected pirates, including those apprehended by foreign naval forces, and in July, in the first case of its kind in Seychelles, 11 Somalis were sentenced to 10 years' imprisonment by the Supreme Court, having been convicted of piracy-related offences. Further such convictions followed in subsequent years.

Economy

DONALD L. SPARKS

INTRODUCTION

Seychelles, with a population of just over 90,000, is a small but prosperous country in the African context and is classified by the World Bank as an 'upper-middle-income economy', one of only five states in the region thus designated. In 2011 Seychelles' gross domestic product (GDP) per head was US $24,700 (using purchasing-power parity measurements, i.e. adjusting for cost of living, exchange rate fluctuations, etc.). This is the highest ranking in all of sub-Saharan Africa. In addition, its life expectancy, which was 73.7 years at birth in 2011, is (along with that of Mauritius) the region's highest (compared with a sub-Saharan African average of 50.5 years), and 97% of its population has access to safe water and sanitation (compared with a regional average of about 50%). The services sector (tourism, transport and communications) has dominated the economy in recent years and traditionally accounts for about 70% of GDP. The nation's GDP increased, in real terms, at an average annual rate of 1.1% during 1996–2006, according to the IMF. However, Seychelles did not escape the effects of the world-wide economic recession that began in 2008. In 2009 the country's GDP declined by 7.6%, although this decline was tempered somewhat by a better-than-expected performance in tourism. In 2010 real GDP grew by 6.2%, with the tourist market again experiencing strong growth: tourist arrivals increased by 11% to reach an all-time high of almost 175,000. Growth continued at an estimated 5% in 2011, fuelled by yet another record-breaking year of visitors, which numbered 194,476.

TOURISM

The economy is heavily dependent on tourism, which employs almost one-third of the labour force and provides more than 70% of hard currency earnings. In addition, the tourism sector has significant 'positive spillovers' into the rest of the economy, boosting demand for ancillary services. However, it has been estimated that more than 60% of gross earnings from tourism leaves the country as payment for imported food and other goods, and by way of remittances to tour operators.

The tourism industry began in 1971 with the opening of Mahé International Airport. In that year there were only 3,175 visitors; by 1981 the number had risen to 60,425. Tourist arrivals remained fairly constant during the mid- and late 1990s, and had increased to 130,046 by 2000. In 2009 tourism earnings rose to US $203m., while the number of tourist arrivals declined slightly, to 157,541 visitors; Europe remained the largest source of tourists, with 60% of the total (largely from France, Italy, Germany, the United Kingdom and Switzerland). The number of arrivals increased to a record 174,529 visitors in 2010. Arrivals from Europe grew relatively slowly, by 8% (owing principally to the continued economic weakness in the euro area); the leading markets were France (35,026 visitors), Italy (25,602), Germany (21,311), the United Kingdom (12,322), South Africa (10,425) and Russia (8,942). Growth has continued into 2011; arrivals were 12% higher in January than in the corresponding month of 2010. However, as almost three-quarters of visitors come from Europe, a double-dip recession in the European Union (EU) will dampen the chances for the economy to continue its recent growth.

Seychelles has developed an extensive network of international air links. According to the Seychelles Tourism Board, there are direct links from 18 different foreign cities (including new links with Qatar), and Air Seychelles has direct flights to London (United Kingdom), Frankfurt (Germany), Paris (France), Milan and Rome (Italy), Johannesburg (South Africa), Bangkok (Thailand) and Port Louis (Mauritius). In 2011 Transaero began a direct air service to Russia and Blue Panorama to Italy, which follows Etihad's entry in 2010. Charter flights, which had been discouraged previously, are now welcome.

The Government estimated the islands' maximum tourist capacity, without detriment to the environment, at 200,000 visitors annually. It was hoped to attract an increasing proportion of visitors interested in the ecological aspects of the archipelago, and to this end attention was focused in the late 1990s on the tourism potential of the outlying islands. A conglomerate based in Dubai, the United Arab Emirates (UAE), purchased land near Victoria with a view to constructing a marina village, to include yachting facilities, a golf course, a conference centre and a 320-room hotel. In 2006 the Hilton group acquired the £28m. Northolme resort on Mahé, adding further to the high-end range of hotel brands available, which included the Shangri-La group, Le Méridien, the Four Seasons and Lemuria. In 2010 the Hilton group acquired another resort on Silhouette Island, while Kingdom Hotel Investments group of Saudi Arabia opened a US $145m. luxury resort on Praslin Island, under the management of the Raffles group.

AGRICULTURE, FISHERIES AND MINERALS

Until tourism began, agriculture was a major contributor to the economy. However, by 2011 the sector accounted for just under 2% of GDP and 3% of the total work-force. As the area of cultivable land is limited to about 6,000 ha of Seychelles' total land area and the soil is often poor, it is unlikely that the country will ever become self-sufficient in agriculture. (In 2006 FAO declared that fewer than 3,000 ha were available for agricultural production, compared with 12,000 ha in the 1980s.) The islands are heavily dependent on imported food, which, together with drink and tobacco, has generally accounted for up to 25% of the total import bill, although this proportion was slowly reduced. The Government is seeking to stimulate greater self-sufficiency in vegetables, fruit, meat and milk. There are a number of large farms and about 650 small farms and numerous smallholdings, about one-half of them run by 'part-time' farmers. The main agricultural exports have traditionally been coconuts (especially for copra), frozen fish and cinnamon (exported as bark). Cup copra is processed locally into oil, and the by-product made into animal feed. Tea is grown for domestic consumption, and there is a small surplus for export. Seychelles is self-sufficient in eggs and poultry, and there has been a large increase in the number of pigs, although animal feed has to be imported. The islands possess a fruit and vegetable canning plant and an integrated poultry unit.

Seychelles' small artisanal fish catch fell by 3% in 2006, to 4,237 metric tons. However, in 2007 Japan granted the Seychelles Fisheries Association US $400,000 to develop small-scale artisanal fishing and processing. In 2005 the fisheries sector earned $290m., a 16% increase over the previous year. A modern fishing industry, operated by the Fishing Development Co, is concentrating on industrial tuna fishing through operations including the Société Thonière de Seychelles (of which 49% is owned by French interests), which has two freezer ships, and a tuna-canning plant at Victoria that began operation in 1987 as a joint venture between the Governments of Seychelles and France.

In 1987, the first year of its production, canned tuna became the most significant export commodity. By 2007 Seychelles' canned tuna exports totalled US $183m., compared with only $4m. worth of fresh and frozen fish and prawns. In 2009 canned tuna production stood at 29,110 metric tons, while exports generated $221m. The value of canned tuna exports declined slightly, to $213m., in 2010, but it none the less remains the country's largest export earner. In 2006 the US multinational foods group H. J. Heinz sold its European seafood division, which included a 60% share in the Seychelles Indian Ocean Tuna Co (IOT) cannery, for US $505m. About 99% of tuna produced at the factory is exported to Europe through the port at Victoria, which has become the principal centre in the Indian Ocean for tuna transshipment. Although Victoria is still responsible for shipping nearly 90% of the region's tuna, it was likely to lose business to neighbouring states (especially

Mauritius and Madagascar) because of the poor service being offered to the foreign fishing fleets.

In 1978 Seychelles declared an exclusive economic zone (EEZ), extending 370 km (200 nautical miles) from the coast, to curtail the activities of large foreign fleets, which until then had been freely catching almost 24,000 metric tons per year of deep-sea tuna. Agreements were thereafter concluded with several foreign governments. A new three-year fisheries agreement with the EU—which guarantees Seychelles US $4m. annually for the tuna catch up to 52,000 tons (lower than the previous 55,000 limit), and an additional $93 per ton for catches in excess of that amount—came into effect in January 2011. The agreement commits 35% of revenue for developing sustainable fisheries. In addition, any EU fishing vessel will have to employ two Seychellois workers (or pay a penalty of $40 per day). The new agreement allows for 60 fishing vessels in total (48 purse seiners and 12 surface longliners), compared with 52 previously. The EU also increased its annual development grant to $3.1m., up from $1.7m. previously.

Assistance in expanding the fishing industry sector has been forthcoming from the African Development Bank (AfDB), France, Japan and the United Kingdom. In 1991 Seychelles joined Madagascar and Mauritius to form a tuna-fishing association. According to the Indian Ocean Tuna Commission (IOTC), the regional tuna catch substantially exceeds sustainable limits and there were fears of stock depletion. Tuna caught in the Seychelles' EEZ accounts for 25% of the total Indian Ocean catch made by European vessels. In early 2004 the EU began funding a US $17m. tuna-tagging programme in conjunction with the IOTC. The programme was to tag about 100,000 fish over a 30-month period to determine their migration and thus assist in the fight against illegal fishing.

The islands' sole mineral export is guano. In 2007 the Government began investigating the possibility of processing local coral into lime for a cement factory. India has collaborated in surveys for polymetallic nodules in the EEZ. Several petroleum companies have conducted exploration operations in Seychelles waters over the years, although thus far without success. In early 2005, however, the Seychelles National Oil Co Ltd signed an agreement with the US firm Petroquest to begin explorations for a nine-year period over an area covering 30,000 sq km. With higher petroleum prices and new exploration technologies, Seychelles has become a more attractive possibility for findings.

INFRASTRUCTURE, ENERGY AND MANUFACTURING

The network of roads is generally good. Seychelles had 508 km of roads in 2011, of which 490 km were paved. Most surfaced roads are on Mahé and Praslin. The international airport on Mahé has been expanded, its runway has been strengthened to bear Boeing 747s, and a new domestic terminal has been built. There are a total of eight airstrips with paved runways, and six with unpaved runways, mostly located on several outlying islands.

Seychelles' major infrastucture project, the Mahé east coast development plan, includes the modernization and expansion of Victoria port and the construction of a new road linking Victoria to the airport. Another major project is the five-year construction of the 56 ha Eden Island, at a cost of US $450m. Almost completed, this resort will have 450 luxury villas (with prices of over $1.2m. each), a hotel complex and a marina. The project is located on reclaimed land near Victoria, and will require a $2.6m. causeway to link it with the mainland. The commercial port can accommodate vessels of up to 214 m in length, but there is only one berth. Additional berthing capacity is planned, with some facilities for containerization, and possibly a repair dock.

Commercial energy in Seychelles comes from imported petroleum, of which over one-half is used in the transportation and construction sectors, and the remaining converted into electricity. The Seychelles Petroleum Co Ltd, a parastatal, is in charge of oil imports, with Malaysia's Petronas being the major supplier. In late 2008 Dubai-based company Black Marlin Energy signed an agreement with the Seychelles Petroleum Co Ltd on a large offshore exploration project, covering 15,000 sq km of continental shelf. The company planned to sink its first well in 2012. As Seychelles did not intend to build a refinery, any output and exports would be in the form of crude petroleum.

The Seychelles Electricity Corpn was established in 1980 as a parastatal organization that was to finance its own recurrent costs. The extension of electricity supply to the islands of Mahé, Praslin and La Digue has been completed. Power supplies are generated entirely from petroleum. In 2007 Seychelles imported 7,653 barrels of oil per day; however, the vast majority of fuel imports are re-exported, mainly as bunker sales to visiting ships and aircraft. Seychelles generated US $210m. in petroleum re-exports in 2011. Some 250m. kWh of electricity was produced in 2008. Studies have been conducted on the use of windmills, and solar and wave power for electricity generation, and in October 2009 a renewable energy company from the UAE, Masdar, announced an agreement with the Seychelles Government to carry out an evaluation study for a proposed wind power project on Mahé Island. In April 2011 it was reported that the Government of the UAE emirate Abu Dhabi had disbursed a $37m. grant to finance the development of the wind power plant and a housing project on the island. In 2012 the Government proposed a new energy law that would open up the Public Utilities Corporation, a monopoly, to competition, and would also encourage investment in renewable energy.

Seychelles has a well-developed telecommunications infrastructure, and is thus well positioned to attract additional investment. In 2010 Alcatel-Lucent of France signed an agreement with the Seychelles Government under the terms of which the telecoms company would lay a US $30m., 1,900-km submarine fibre optic cable from Victoria to the Tanzanian capital, Dar es Salaam. Upon completion, scheduled for 2012, the project will increase broadband capacity and reduce costs (as it lessens the dependence on the expensive satellite links). The nation ranks highest in sub-Saharan Africa in terms of its number of mobile telephone users: 83 per 100 people (tied with South Africa), compared with a regional average of 17.5. There were 159,700 mobile phone subscriptions in 2010 (a 37% increase over the previous year), out of a population of only 89,188. Seychelles also ranks highest for landline telephone usage, with 28,676 subscribers in 2010 (up by 12% from 2009). It is also the regional leader in personal internet usage: in 2008 the internet was used by 40.4 per 100 people, compared with a regional average of 5.9 (Mauritius had the second highest usage, at 21.8 per 100 people). In 2009 some 32,000 people were internet users.

Manufacturing's contribution to GDP has increased in recent years and accounted for 15.8% in 2006, before declining to 8.9% in 2009. During 2000–10 manufacturing contributed, on average, 15% of GDP. Several small industries have been established in Seychelles, including brewing, plastic goods, salt, coconut oil, cinnamon essence distilling, soft drinks, detergents, cigarettes, soap, boat-building, furniture, printing and steel products, as well as animal feed, meat- and fish-processing, dairy products, paints, television assembly, and handicrafts for the tourism industry.

TRADE, FINANCE, DEBT AND FOREIGN INVESTMENT

Seychelles traditionally sustains a substantial visible trade deficit. However, this deficit is partly offset by earnings from tourism and by capital inflows in the form of aid and private investment. The current account has generally been in deficit in recent years; the deficit was US $351m. in 2010, but it declined to $216.3m. in 2011. Seychelles' total external debt stood at $1,374m. in 2010. Its debt service ratio (as a percentage of exports) rose from 6.6% in 2008 to 12.8% in 2009, and was expected to reach 28% in 2011. In 2011 Seychelles' exports amounted to $505m. and imports totalled $877m., resulting in a trade deficit of $372m. The previous year's trade deficit was $367m. In 2010 its main suppliers were Saudi Arabia (32.7% of total imports), South Africa (13.0%), France (10.5%), Spain (10.3%) and Singapore (9.2%). Seychelles' principal export markets were the United Kingdom (17.9% of the total, including re-exports), France (16.7%), Italy (10.5%), Japan (10.5%)

and Thailand (6.6%). Seychelles' most significant export was canned tuna ($246m.), while its principal import was mineral fuels ($268m.).

In 1993 Seychelles joined the Preferential Trade Area for Eastern and Southern Africa (PTA, which in 1994 became the Common Market for Eastern and Southern Africa—COMESA) and benefits from the clearing house function, which facilitates the use of member countries' currencies for regional transactions. This has reduced the pressure on foreign exchange resources, particularly from trade with Mauritius. In late 2007 Seychelles signed an interim trade agreement with the EU (along with several other COMESA members). This agreement, which became effective in 2008, guarantees special trading privileges for Seychelles' exports into the EU, especially fisheries products. On the negative side, the deal will expose Seychelles to greater competition from the EU by 2012 when Seychelles will be forced to liberalize 62% of its imports. Trade between Seychelles and other members of the Indian Ocean Commission (IOC) accounts for only 2%–3% of the country's total official trade, owing principally to Seychelles' high import duties. In 2004 Seychelles withdrew from membership of both the Southern African Development Community (SADC) and the Indian Ocean Rim Association for Regional Co-operation, claiming that the benefits were not commensurate with the costs; however, Seychelles rejoined SADC in August 2008. In 1995 Seychelles applied for full membership of the World Trade Organization (at which it currently has observer status), and it is expected to become a member by 2014.

Seychelles recorded a budget deficit of SR 12.8m. in 2007. Total revenue was SR 2,539.4m. and expenditure amounted to SR 2,552.2m. The deficit was blamed on higher imported fuel and food costs and higher debt-servicing due to the depreciation of the rupee. Revenue was US $183.9m. in 2009, with expenditure of $195.8m., resulting in a budget deficit of $11.9m. Aided primarily by the introduction in 2010 of stringent austerity measures (partly as a result of the IMF adjustment programme—see below), in that year the deficit was reversed and a surplus of $6m. was recorded (with revenues of $316.5m. and expenditures of $310.3m.). In 2011 the Government estimated a surplus of 4.5% of GDP.

In 2009 the Government introduced sweeping tax reforms with the intention of making taxation fairer and more transparent, broadening the tax base, and bringing the tax system in line with international standards. Business cuts were to be implemented, and the top business tax rate capped at 33% (down from a high of 40%). In July 2010 a new personal income tax was introduced at a rate of 18.75%. In addition, an excise tax for four consumer categories—vehicles, fuel, cigarettes and alcohol—was launched. A value-added tax (VAT) was to be introduced in mid-2012 to replace the general sales tax (GST).

Owing to its relatively high GDP per head, Seychelles has never been particularly favoured for international aid. None the less, Seychelles does receive development assistance from a wide variety of sources, including the World Bank, the EU (particularly France) and other Western European countries, the AfDB, the Banque Arabe pour le Développement Economique en Afrique, the USA, India, Canada, Arab countries and the People's Republic of China. Total official development assistance averaged US $11.8m. during 2000–04. Aid from all donors was $3m. in 2007, but increased to $12.1m. in 2008 and further to $23.2m. in 2009, according to the World Bank.

In late 2008 the IMF approved a two-year, US $26m. stand-by arrangement for Seychelles to assist with the balance of payments crisis and support the Government's economic reform programme. Under the programme, the Government allowed the rupee to float freely on foreign exchange markets, which resulted in a 50% devaluation of the currency (from SR 8.5 = $1 to SR 17 = $1). In late 2009 the IMF approved a new three-year programme worth $31m. In addition, the Government reduced public spending, especially on the public sector work-force, eliminated subsidies to the parastatal Seychelles Trading Co, and raised public transit fares and taxes. While these reforms were painful (inflation increased, the rupee's value was decimated and households saw their buying power eroded), the IMF's approval of the Government's reform plans sent strong positive signals for debt relief. In early 2010 most of the country's creditors accepted an offer by the Government to repay approximately one-half of its outstanding debt, with the other half to be rescheduled. The restructuring of this commercial debt, together with $70m. of debt relief from the April 2009 'Paris Club', reduced Seychelles' debt burden to 73% of GDP, down from 98.5% in the previous year. The country's external debt declined to $1,374m. in 2010, from $1,422m. in 2008, and by 2012 amounted to less than 50% of GDP.

The Seychelles rupee was linked to the IMF special drawing right (SDR) in 1979, and this remained in effect until February 1997, when the fixed link with the SDR was ended. The exchange rate was US $1 = SR 5.45 at June 2006, virtually unchanged from 2003–05. However, the rupee depreciated dramatically following its flotation in November 2008. The exchange rate had stabilized by mid-2012 to $1 = SR 13.9. With government price controls on fuel and certain food items, inflation traditionally remained low: annual increases were 0.9% in 2005 and 0.4% in 2006. Indeed, by late 2009 inflation had turned into deflation as consumer prices fell by 2.5% year-on-year in December, driven largely by the appreciation of the rupee, which helped to contain import costs. However, as a result of higher food and fuel prices, the inflation rate rose to 5.6% in early 2012. Inflation was exacerbated by the rupee's depreciation against the US dollar, which resulted in increased import prices.

Foreign direct investment (FDI) increased from US $46m. in 1995 to $350m. in 2008. Owing in large part to the world-wide economic recession, FDI declined to $242m. in 2009. However, the IMF estimated that FDI (primarily directed at the tourism sector) increased to a record $411m. in 2010. In 1996 the Government launched a controversial scheme called the Economic Citizenship Programme, whereby foreign nationals could buy, for $25,000, Seychelles citizenship and passports. Nevertheless, the Seychelles' international reputation has recovered to a large extent. Indeed, the country ranks relatively well in Transparency International's Corruption Perceptions Index: in 2012 it was placed 50th out of 178 countries, and third in the region (behind Mauritius and Cape Verde, but ahead of South Africa). In addition, in 2009 Seychelles moved from the Organisation for Economic Co-operation and Development's 'grey list' to its 'white list' (which measures transparency in tax and other standards). Over the past two years Seychelles has signed a number of tax agreements with European and other nations that will eliminate double taxation.

ECONOMIC PROSPECTS

Since the early 1990s the Government has sought to diversify the economy by encouraging foreign investment, both public and private, particularly in tourism, farming, fisheries and small-scale manufacturing. However, Seychelles' desire to become an international business centre has gained limited momentum. Measures to promote the development of an international business centre for financial services, trading and transhipment commenced in 1995 with the formation of the Seychelles International Business Authority as the regulatory authority (although many local economic activities, such as taxis, tour operators, small-scale agriculture and fishing, internet providers and other small businesses, were to be reserved for local investors only). In 2004 Seychelles established the Seychelles Investment Bureau (SIB), which has approved investments amounting to some US $51m. According to the Government, 58 projects (mostly in the tourism sector) worth SR 1,400m. have been attracted under the SIB, of which 94% were from foreign investors. In addition, Barclays Bank of the United Kingdom opened the nation's first 'offshore' bank in early 2005. The Financial Intelligence Unit, established in 2006, was charged with pursuing cases of financial fraud in the offshore banking sector.

For over a decade the Seychelles Government has strived to liberalize the economy: price controls on imported goods (except foodstuffs) were lifted in early 2008, and the 12.5% tax on basic foodstuffs removed. In 2006 the Government finally relaunched its privatization programme with the sale of the state-owned insurance firm State Assurance Corporation of Seychelles, which was subsequently renamed the Seychelles Assurance Co Ltd. In March 2009 the Government reported to the IMF that it had divested the Agro-Industries Co and the animal feed factory and had liquidated the Coetivy Prawns Co (all previously part of the former Seychelles Marketing Board). The Fund reacted favourably to these developments, welcoming the authorities' broad-based reform strategy.

Seychelles is subject to a variety of external shocks, from adverse weather to the fluctuating euro to piracy. Indeed, Somalia-based piracy remains a significant concern as it adds to the uncertainty and costs of shipping, tourism and fishing. The Ministry of Finance has estimated the total costs of piracy at nearly US $17m. (freight and insurance $4.5m., tourism—because of cancellations and fewer cruise ships—$8m. and fishing $4m.). By 2012 Seychelles had 61 pirates in detention.

While Seychelles was not left unscathed by the recent worldwide economic downturn (with tourism and FDI especially adversely affected), the country has recovered well and performed better than most of its regional neighbours. Real GDP grew by 6.2% in 2010 and by an estimated 5% in 2011, primarily as a result of record tourism earnings. None the less, should the EU enter into a double-dip recession, Seychelles' tourism sector, and eventually the rest of its economy, will slow.

However, in the long term Seychelles has the potential to become a regional player in e-commerce, given its high literacy rate, well-developed telecommunications infrastructure and the ability of most citizens to speak three languages (English, French and Creole). Should recent political and policy changes translate into lasting economic reform, the country may well be within reach of further increases in incomes and an extended period of sustained economic growth and development.

Statistical Survey

Source (unless otherwise stated): Statistics and Database Administration Section, Management and Information Systems Division, POB 206, Victoria; e-mail misdstat@seychelles.net; internet www.nsb.gov.sc.

AREA AND POPULATION

Area: 455.3 sq km (175.8 sq miles), incl. Aldabra lagoon (145 sq km).

Population: 81,755 at census of 26 August 2002; 90,945 (males 46,912, females 44,033) at census of 26 August 2010.

Density (at 2010 census): 199.7 per sq km.

Population by Age and Sex (official estimates at mid-2012): *0–14:* 19,689 (males 9,908, females 9,781); *15–64:* 61,625 (males 30,628, females 30,997); *65 and over:* 6,989 (males 2,777, females 4,212); *Total* 88,303 (males 43,313, females 44,990). Note: Estimates not adjusted to take account of 2010 census.

Principal Town: Victoria (capital), estimated population 60,000 (incl. suburbs) in 1994. *Mid-2011* (incl. suburbs, UN estimate): Victoria 26,609. (Source: UN, *World Urbanization Prospects: The 2011 Revision*).

Births, Marriages and Deaths (registrations, 2011): Live births 1,625 (birth rate 18.6 per 1,000); Marriages (of residents) 466 (marriage rate 5.3 per 1,000); Deaths 691 (death rate 7.9 per 1,000).

Life Expectancy (years at birth, official estimates): 72.6 (males 67.7; females 78.0) in 2011.

Employment (2011, averages): Agriculture, forestry and fishing 506; Manufacturing 4,670; Electricity and water 1,080; Construction (with quarrying) 6,147; Trade, restaurants and hotels 14,522; Transport, storage and communications 4,747; Other services 18,219; *Total* 49,891.

HEALTH AND WELFARE

Key Indicators

Total Fertility Rate (children per woman, 2010): 2.3.

Under-5 Mortality Rate (per 1,000 live births, 2010): 14.

Physicians (per 1,000 head, 2004): 1.51.

Hospital Beds (per 1,000 head, government establishments only, 2010): 3.6.

Health Expenditure (2009): US $ per head (PPP): 712.

Health Expenditure (2009): % of GDP: 3.3.

Health Expenditure (2009): public (% of total): 92.7.

Access to Water (% of persons, 2004): 88.

Total Carbon Dioxide Emissions ('000 metric tons, 2008): 682.1.

Carbon Dioxide Emissions Per Head (metric tons, 2008): 7.8.

Human Development Index (2011): ranking: 52.

Human Development Index (2011): value: 0.773.

For sources and definitions, see explanatory note on p. vi.

AGRICULTURE, ETC.

Principal Crops (metric tons, 2010): Coconuts 1,700*; Vegetables (incl. melons) 2,400*; Bananas 1,400*; Other fruits (excl. melons) 1,850*; Tea 49; Cinnamon 49.
* FAO estimate.

Livestock (head, 2010, FAO estimates): Cattle 350; Pigs 5,363; Goats 5,300.

Livestock Products (metric tons, 2010, FAO estimates): Pig meat 305; Chicken meat 658; Hen eggs 1,250.

Fishing ('000 metric tons, live weight, 2010): Capture 87.1 (Skipjack tuna 43.8; Yellowfin tuna 26.0; Bigeye tuna 10.7); Aquaculture 0.3* (Giant tiger prawn 0.3*); *Total catch* 87.4*.
* FAO estimate.

Source: FAO.

INDUSTRY

Industrial Production (2011): Canned tuna 30,152 metric tons; Beer and stout ('000 litres) 5,400; Soft drinks ('000 litres) 6,984; Cigarettes 55m.; Electric energy 324m. kWh.

FINANCE

Currency and Exchange Rates: 100 cents = 1 Seychelles rupee (SR). *Sterling, Dollar and Euro Equivalents* (30 March 2012): £1 sterling = 22.471 rupees; US $1 = 14.037 rupees; €1 = 18.747 rupees; 100 Seychelles rupees = £4.45 = $7.12 = €5.33. *Average Exchange Rate* (Seychelles rupees per US $): 13.6099 in 2009; 12.0678 in 2010; 12.3810 in 2011. Note: In November 1979 the value of the Seychelles rupee was linked to the IMF's special drawing right (SDR). In March 1981 the mid-point exchange rate was set at SDR 1 = 7.2345 rupees. This remained in effect until February 1997, when the fixed link with the SDR was ended.

Budget (SR million, 2011): *Revenue:* Tax revenue 4,232.3 (Taxes on income, etc. 612.4; Domestic taxes on goods and services 1,208.4; Excise tax 420.9); Non tax revenue 570.0; Total 4,802.4, excl. grants received (278.9). *Expenditure:* Current expenditure 3,713.3 (Wages and salaries 891.2; Goods and services 994.2; Interest 383.5; Transfers 1,423.4); Capital expenditure 1,060.5; Total 4,773.8, excl. lending minus repayments (8.6). *2012* (budget estimates): Total revenue 4,985.2 (excl. grants 440.1); Total expenditure 5,172.6 (excl. lending minus repayment 8.5). Note: Figures represent the consolidated accounts of the central Government, covering the operations of the Recurrent and Capital Budgets and of the Social Security Fund (Source: Ministry of Finance, Victoria).

International Reserves (US $ million at 31 December 2011): IMF special drawing rights 10.39; Reserve position in IMF 0.81; Foreign exchange 241.11; Total 252.31. Source: IMF, *International Financial Statistics*.

Money Supply (SR million at 31 December 2011): Currency outside depository corporations 623.5; Transferable deposits 5,707.8; Other deposits 1,264.4; *Broad money* 7,595.7. Source: IMF, *International Financial Statistics*.

Cost of Living (Consumer Price Index; base: 2005 = 100): All items 189.4 in 2009; 184.8 in 2010; 189.6 in 2011. Source: IMF, *International Financial Statistics*.

Expenditure on the Gross Domestic Product (SR million at current prices, 2010): Government final consumption expenditure 3,176.9; Private final consumption expenditure 6,997.0; Gross capital formation 6,093.8; *Total domestic expenditure* 16,267.7; Exports of goods and services 10,384.9; *Less* Imports of goods and services 15,358.3; Statistical discrepancy 327.1; *GDP in purchasers' values* 11,621.3. Source: UN National Accounts Main Aggregates Database.

Gross Domestic Product by Economic Activity (SR million at current prices, 2010, provisional): Agriculture, forestry and fishing 264.6; Manufacturing 863.2; Electricity and water 157.0; Construction 534.0; Wholesale and retail trade, and repair of motor vehicles and motorcycles 929.1; Trade, restaurants and hotels 1,994.2; Transport, storage and communications 1,168.3; Finance, insurance, real estate and business services 2,493.2; Education 273.2; Public administration and defence, and social security 521.3; Other services 639.5; *Sub-total* 9,837.7; Import duties, less subsidies 1,965.5; *Less* Imputed bank service charge 181.9; *GDP in purchasers' values* 11,621.3.

Balance of Payments (US $ million, 2010): Exports of goods f.o.b. 400.2; Imports of goods f.o.b. –736.8; *Trade balance* –336.5; Exports of services 591.8; Imports of services –441.1; *Balance on goods and services* –185.9; Other income received 7.6; Other income paid –72.2; *Balance on goods, services and income* –250.4; Current transfers received 43.0; Current transfers paid –17.6; *Current balance* –225.1; Capital account (net) 275.3; Direct investment abroad –6.2; Direct investment from abroad 167.3; Portfolio investment assets 27.2; Portfolio investment liabilities –2.5; Other investment assets 8.5; Other investment liabilities 44.8; Net errors and omissions 13.2; *Overall balance* 302.5. Source: IMF, *International Financial Statistics*.

EXTERNAL TRADE

Principal Commodities (distribution by SITC, SR million, 2010, provisional): *Imports c.i.f.:* Food and live animals 1,941.8; Mineral fuels 2,693.3; Basic manufactures 2,664.7; Machinery and transport 2,661.9; Total (incl. others) 11,881.2. *Exports f.o.b.:* Canned tuna 2,382.5; Fish (fresh/frozen) 31.0; Frozen prawns 0.0; Fish meal 87.4; Medicaments, etc. 32.5; Total (incl. others) 4,818.1 (of which domestic exports SR 2,654.6m. and re-exports SR 2,163.6m.).

Principal Trading Partners (SR million, 2010, provisional): *Imports c.i.f.:* France 706.1; Italy 423.3; Singapore 726.4; South Africa 753.6; Spain 930.1; United Arab Emirates 4,673.0; United Kingdom 547.8; Total (incl. others) 11,881.2. *Exports f.o.b.:* France 803.9; Germany 118.6; Italy 441.4; Netherlands 119.8; Sri Lanka 30.0; United Kingdom 859.8; Total (incl. others) 4,818.1 (of which domestic exports SR 2,654.6m. and re-exports SR 2,163.6m.).

TRANSPORT

Road Traffic (registered motor vehicles, 2010): Private 10,146; Commercial 2,878; Taxis 278; Self-drive 1,647; Motorcycles 74; Omnibuses 293; *Total* 15,316.

Shipping: *Merchant Fleet* (registered at 31 December 2009): Vessels 50; Total displacement 203,192 grt (Source: IHS Fairplay, *World Fleet Statistics*); *International Sea-borne Freight Traffic* (2010): Freight ('000 metric tons): Imports 404; Exports 5,879; Transshipment (of fish) 163.

Civil Aviation (traffic on scheduled services, 2009): Kilometres flown 17m.; Passengers carried 565,000; Passenger-km 1,428m.; Total ton-km 165m. (Source: UN, *Statistical Yearbook*). *2010:* Aircraft movements 4,480; Passengers embarked 229,000; Passengers disembarked 229,000; Freight embarked 2,601 metric tons; Freight disembarked 6,641 metric tons.

TOURISM

Foreign Tourist Arrivals ('000): 157.5 in 2009; 174.5 in 2010; 194.5 in 2011.

Arrivals by Country of Residence (2011): France 39,370; Germany 23,706; Italy 25,674; Russia 8,840; South Africa 10,559; Switzerland 7,644; United Kingdom 13,291; Total (incl. others) 194,476.

Tourism Receipts (SR million, central bank estimates): 2,841 in 2009; 2,451 in 2010; 2,750 in 2011.

COMMUNICATIONS MEDIA

Radio Receivers (1997): 42,000 in use. Source: UNESCO, *Statistical Yearbook*.

Television Receivers (2000): 16,500 in use. Source: International Telecommunication Union.

Telephones (2011): 27,900 main lines in use. Source: International Telecommunication Union.

Mobile Cellular Telephones (2011): 126,600 subscribers. Source: International Telecommunication Union.

Personal Computers: 18,000 (211.7 per 1,000 persons) in 2007. Source: International Telecommunication Union.

Internet Subscribers (2010): 7,900 accounts. Source: International Telecommunication Union.

Broadband Subscribers (2011): 7,800. Source: International Telecommunication Union.

Book Production (1980): 33 titles (2 books, 31 pamphlets).

Daily Newspapers (2010): 2.

Non-daily Newspapers (2010): 3.

EDUCATION

Pre-primary (2011): 33 schools; 221 teachers; 2,903 pupils.

Primary (2011): 27 schools; 686 teachers (males 105, females 581); 8,643 pupils (males 4,324, females 4,319).

Secondary (2011): 13 schools; 569 teachers (males 226, females 343); 7,064 pupils (males 3,523, females 3,541).

Post-secondary (2011): 9 schools; 182 teachers; 2,198 pupils.

Vocational (2004): 7 institutions; 82 teachers; 1,099 pupils.

Special Education (2010): 2 institution; 23 teachers; 55 pupils.

Pupil-teacher Ratio (primary education): 13 in 2011.

Adult Literacy Rate (official estimate): 94% (males 94%; females 95%) in 2010.

Directory

The Constitution

The independence Constitution of 1976 was suspended after the coup in June 1977 but reintroduced in July with substantial modifications. A successor Constitution, which entered into force in March 1979, was superseded by a new Constitution, approved by national referendum on 18 June 1993.

The President is elected by popular vote simultaneously with elections for the National Assembly. The President fulfils the functions of Head of State and Commander-in-Chief of the armed forces and may hold office for a maximum period of three consecutive five-year terms. The National Assembly is elected for a term of five years;. 25 members are directly elected and a maximum of 10 seats are proportionally allocated. There is provision for an appointed Vice-President. The Council of Ministers is appointed by the President and acts in an advisory capacity to him. The President also appoints the holders of certain public offices and the judiciary.

The Government

HEAD OF STATE

President: JAMES ALIX MICHEL (took office 14 April 2004, elected 28–30 July 2006; re-elected 19–21 May 2011).

Vice-President: DANNY FAURE.

COUNCIL OF MINISTERS

(September 2012)

President, with additional responsibility for Defence, Legal Affairs, Youth and Hydrocarbons: JAMES MICHEL.

Vice-President, Minister of Information Technology and Public Administration: DANNY FAURE.

Minister of Community Development, Social Affairs and Sports: VINCENT MERITON (Designated Minister).

Minister of Home Affairs and Transport: JOEL MORGAN.

Minister of Education: MACSUZY MONDON.

Minister of Foreign Affairs: JEAN-PAUL ADAM.

Minister of Natural Resources and Industry: PETER SINON.

Minister of the Environment and Energy: DR ROLPH PAYET.

Minister of Finance, Trade and Investment: PIERRE LAPORTE.

Minister of Tourism and Culture: ALAIN ST ANGE.

Minister of Health: MITCY LARUE.

Minister of Land Use and Housing: CHRISTIAN LIONNET.

Minister of Labour and Human Resource Development: IDITH ALEXANDER.

MINISTRIES

Office of the President: State House, POB 55, Victoria; tel. 4224155; fax 4224985; internet www.statehouse.gov.sc.

Office of the Vice-President: State House, POB 1303, Victoria; tel. 4286800; fax 4225152; e-mail jbelmont@statehouse.gov.sc.

Ministry of Community Development and Sports: Oceangate House, POB 731, Victoria; tel. 4225477; fax 4224081; e-mail oplg@seychelles.net; internet www.localgovernment.gov.sc.

Ministry of Education: POB 48, Mont Fleuri; tel. 4283283; fax 4224859; e-mail ps@eduhq.edu.sc; internet www.education.gov.sc.

Ministry of the Environment and Energy: Victoria; f. .

Ministry of Finance, Trade and Investment: Liberty House, POB 113, Victoria; tel. 4382006; fax 4225265; e-mail psf@finance.gov.sc; internet www.finance.gov.sc.

Ministry of Foreign Affairs: Maison Quéau de Quinssy, POB 656, Mont Fleuri; tel. 4283500; fax 4224845; e-mail mfapesey@seychelles.net; internet www.mfa.gov.sc.

Ministry of Health: POB 52, Mont Fleuri; tel. 4388000; fax 4226042; internet www.moh.gov.sc.

Ministry of Home Affairs and Transport: Independence House, POB 199, Victoria; tel. 4670504; fax 4323651; internet www.env.gov.sc.

Ministry of Labour and Human Resource Development: Independence House, 1st Floor, POB 1097, Victoria; tel. 4297200; fax 4325326; e-mail contact@employment.gov.sc; internet www.employment.gov.sc.

Ministry of Land Use and Housing: Victoria; tel. 4284444; fax 4225187; e-mail mluh@mluh.gov.sc.

Ministry of Natural Resources and Industry: Victoria.

Ministry of Tourism and Culture: Victoria.

President and Legislature

PRESIDENT

Election, 19–21 May 2011

Candidate	Votes	% of votes
James Alix Michel (Parti Lepep)	31,966	55.46
Wavel Ramkalawan (SNP)	23,878	41.43
Philippe Boullé (Independent)	956	1.66
Ralph Volcere (NDP)	833	1.45
Total	57,633	100.00

NATIONAL ASSEMBLY

Speaker: PATRICK HERMINIE.

Election, 29 September–1 October 2011

Party	Valid votes cast	% of valid votes	Seats*
Parti Lepep	31,123	88.56	31
Popular Democratic Movement (PDM)	3,828	10.89	—
Independent	194	0.55	—
Total	35,145†	100.0	31

* Of the Assembly's 31 seats, 25 were filled by direct election and six by allocation on a proportional basis. The election was boycotted by the Seychelles National Party (SNP), the main opposition party of Seychelles. On 9 December 2011 the Court of Appeal directed the Election Commission to compute the number of proportional seats based on the number of valid votes (rather than the number of actual votes—including invalid or spoiled votes), and thus two further proportional seats were awarded to Parti Lepep and one seat was awarded to the PDM. Parti Lepep, however, declined to nominate additional members, and consequently the total number of seats in the National Assembly was increased to 32.

† Excludes 16,447 invalid votes (31.87% of the total votes cast).

Election Commission

Electoral Commission: Suite 203, Aarti Bldg, Mont Fleuri, POB 741, Victoria; tel. 4295555; fax 4225474; e-mail hendrick@seychelles.net; internet www.ecs.sc; f. 1993; Electoral Commissioner HENDRICK PAUL GAPPY.

Political Organizations

New Democratic Party (NDP): POB 169, Mont Fleuri; tel. 4224916; fax 4224302; e-mail management@dpseychelles.com; internet www.dpseychelles.com; f. 1992; successor to the Seychelles Democratic Party (governing party 1970–77); Leader RALPH VOLCERE.

Parti Lepep (People's Party): POB 1242, Victoria; tel. 4284900; fax 4225070; e-mail admin@sppf.sc; internet www.partilepep.com; fmrly the Seychelles People's United Party (f. 1964), which assumed power in 1977; renamed Seychelles People's Progressive Front in 1978; sole legal party 1978–91; assumed present name in 2009; Pres. JAMES ALIX MICHEL; Sec.-Gen. DANNY FAURE.

Seychelles National Party (SNP): Arpent Vert, Mont Fleuri, POB 81, Victoria; tel. 4224124; fax 4225151; e-mail secretariat@snpseychelles.sc; internet www.snpseychelles.sc; f. 1995 as the United Opposition, comprising the fmr mem. parties of a coalition formed to contest the 1993 elections; adopted present name in 1998; Leader Rev. WAVEL RAMKALAWAN; Sec.-Gen. NICHOLAS PREA.

Other political parties active in Seychelles include: the Popular Democratic Movement (f. 2011; Leader David Pierre) and the Seychelles Freedom Party (f. 2011; Leader Christopher Gill).

Diplomatic Representation

EMBASSIES AND HIGH COMMISSIONS IN SEYCHELLES

China, People's Republic: POB 680, St Louis; tel. 4671700; fax 4671730; e-mail china@seychelles.net; internet sc.china-embassy.org/eng; Ambassador SHI ZHONGJUN.

Cuba: Bel Eau, POB 730, Victoria; tel. 4224094; fax 4224376; e-mail cubasey@seychelles.net; internet emba.cubaminrex.cu/seychellesing; Ambassador MARIA AIDA NOGALES JIMÉNEZ.

France: La Ciotat Bldg, Mont Fleuri, POB 478, Victoria; tel. 4382500; fax 4382510; e-mail ambafrance@intelvision.net; internet www.ambafrance-sc.org; Ambassador PHILLIPE DELACROIX.

India: Le Chantier, POB 488, Francis Rachel St, Victoria; tel. 4610301; fax 4610308; e-mail hicomind@seychelles.net; internet www.seychelles.net/hicomind; High Commissioner ASIT KUMAR NAG.

Russia: Le Niol, POB 632, St Louis; tel. 4266590; fax 4266653; e-mail rfembsey@seychelles.net; Ambassador MIKHAIL I. KALININ.

United Kingdom: 3rd Floor, Oliaji Trade Centre, Francis Rachel St, POB 161, Victoria; tel. 4283666; fax 4283657; e-mail bhcvictoria@fco.gov.uk; internet ukinseychelles.fco.gov.uk/en; High Commissioner LINDSAY SKOLL.

Judicial System

The legal system is derived from English Common Law and the French Code Napoléon. There are three Courts: the Court of Appeal, the Supreme Court and the Magistrates' Courts. The Court of Appeal hears appeals from the Supreme Court in both civil and criminal cases. The Supreme Court is also a Court of Appeal for the Magistrates' Courts as well as having jurisdiction at first instance. The Constitutional Court, a division of the Supreme Court, determines matters of a constitutional nature, and considers cases bearing on civil liberties. There is also an industrial court and a rent tribunal.

Supreme Court: POB 157, Victoria; tel. 4285800; fax 4224197; e-mail judiciary@seychelles.sc; Chief Justice FREDERICK EGONDE-ENTENDE.

President of the Court of Appeal: FRANCIS MACGREGOR.

Justices of Appeal: JACQUES HODOUL, SATYABHOOSUN GUPT DOMAH, ANTHONY FERNANDO, MATHILDA TWOMEY.

Attorney-General: RONNY GOVINDEN.

Religion

The majority of the inhabitants are Christians, of whom more than 85% are Roman Catholics and about 8% Anglicans. Hinduism, Islam, and the Bahá'í Faith are also practised.

CHRISTIANITY

The Anglican Communion

The Church of the Province of the Indian Ocean comprises six dioceses: four in Madagascar, one in Mauritius and one in Seychelles. The Archbishop of the Province is the Bishop of Antananarivo, Madagascar.

Bishop of Seychelles: Rev. JAMES RICHARD WONG YIN SONG, POB 44, Victoria; tel. 4321977; fax 4323879; e-mail angdio@seychelles.net.

The Roman Catholic Church

Seychelles comprises a single diocese, directly responsible to the Holy See. An estimated 85% of the total population are Roman Catholics.

Bishop of Port Victoria: Rt Rev. DENIS WIEHE, Bishop's House-Evêché, Olivier Maradan St, POB 43, Victoria; tel. 4322152; fax 4324045; e-mail rcchurch@seychelles.net.

Other Christian Churches

Pentecostal Assemblies of Seychelles: Victoria; tel. 4224598; e-mail paos@seychelles.net; Pastor HERMITTE FREMINOT; 700 mems.

The Press

L'Echo des Iles: POB 12, Victoria; tel. 4322262; fax 4321464; e-mail echo@seychelles.net; bi-monthly; French, Creole and English; Roman Catholic; Editor Fr EDWIN MATHIOT; circ. 2,800.

The People: Maison du Peuple, Revolution Ave, Victoria; tel. 4224455; internet www.thepeople.sc; owned by Parti Lepep; monthly; Creole, French and English; circ. 1,000.

Seychelles Nation: Information Technology and Communication Division, POB 800, Victoria; tel. 4225775; fax 4321006; e-mail seynat@seychelles.net; internet www.nation.sc; f. 1976; govt-owned; Mon.–Sat.; English, French and Creole; the country's only daily newspaper; Dir DENIS ROSE; circ. 3,500.

Seychelles Review: POB 29, Victoria; tel. 4241881; fax 4241545; e-mail surmer@seychelles.net; internet www.seychellesreview.com; f. 1994; monthly; business, politics, real estate and tourism; Editor ROLAND HOARAU.

Seychelles Weekly: POB 308, Victoria; e-mail editor@seychellesweekly.com; internet www.seychellesweekly.com; supports democracy in Seychelles; Editor (vacant).

Seychellois: POB 32, Victoria; f. 1928; publ. by Seychelles Farmers Assen; quarterly; circ. 1,800.

Vizyon: Arpent Vert, Mont Fleuri, Victoria; tel. 4224507; fax 4224987; internet www.snpseychelles.sc/vizyon.htm; f. 2007; political fortnightly magazine of the opposition SNP; successor to weekly Regar; Creole, English and French; Editor ROGER MANCIENNE.

Broadcasting and Communications

TELECOMMUNICATIONS

Cable and Wireless (Seychelles) Ltd: Mercury House, Francis Rachel St, POB 4, Victoria; tel. 4284000; fax 4322777; e-mail cws@seychelles.net; internet www.cwseychelles.com; f. 1990; Chief Exec. CHARLES HAMMOND.

Atlas Seychelles Ltd (XNET): POB 903, Victoria; tel. 4304060; fax 4324565; e-mail atlas@seychelles.net; internet www.seychelles.net; f. 1996 by a consortium of Space95, VCS and MBM; acquired by Cable and Wireless (Seychelles) Ltd in 2005; internet service provider; Gen. Man. ANTHONY DELORIE.

Telecom Seychelles Ltd (Airtel): POB 1358, Providence; tel. 4600609; fax 4601602; internet africa.airtel.com/seychelles; f. 1998; 100% owned by Bharti Airtel (India); provides fixed-line, mobile and satellite telephone and internet services; Chief Exec. VINOD SUD.

BROADCASTING

Radio

Seychelles Broadcasting Corpn (SBC): Hermitage, POB 321, Victoria; tel. 4289600; fax 4225641; e-mail sbcradtv@seychelles.sc; internet www.sbc.sc; f. 1983; reorg. as independent corpn in 1992; programmes in Creole, English and French; Man. Dir ANTOINE ONEZIME.

SBC Radio: Union Vale, POB 321, Victoria; tel. 4289600; fax 4289720; e-mail sbcradtv@seychelles.sc; internet www.sbc.sc; f. 1941; programmes in Creole, English and French; Man. Dir IBRAHIM AFIF.

Television

Seychelles Broadcasting Corpn (SBC): see Radio.

SBC TV: Hermitage, POB 321, Victoria; tel. 4224161; fax 4225641; e-mail sbcradtv@seychelles.sc; f. 1983; programmes in Creole, English and French; Head of TV Production JUDE LOUANGE.

Finance

(cap. = capital; res = reserves; dep. = deposits; m. = million; brs = branches; amounts in Seychelles rupees)

BANKING

In 2009 there were seven banks operating in Seychelles, of which two conducted 'offshore' business. Five of these seven banks were foreign-owned, whereas the Government of Seychelles had a majority stake in the other two banks.

Central Bank

Central Bank of Seychelles (CBS): Independence Ave, POB 701, Victoria; tel. 4282000; fax 4226104; e-mail enquiries@cbs.sc; internet www.cbs.sc; f. 1983; bank of issue; cap. 97.7m., res 172.0m., dep. 2,787.1m. (Dec. 2010); Gov. CAROLINE ABEL.

National Banks

Development Bank of Seychelles: Independence Ave, POB 217, Victoria; tel. 4294400; fax 4224274; e-mail devbank@dbs.sc; internet www.dbs.sc; f. 1977; 55.5% state-owned; cap. 39.2m., res 43.9m., dep. 137.4m. (Dec. 2009); Chair. ANTONIO LUCAS; Man. Dir ROGER TOUSSAINT.

Seychelles International Mercantile Banking Corporation Ltd (Nouvobanq) (SIMBC): Victoria House, State House Ave, POB 241, Victoria; tel. 4293000; fax 4224670; e-mail nvb@nouvobanq.sc; internet www.nouvobanq.sc; f. 1991; 78% state-owned, 22% by Standard Chartered Bank (United Kingdom); cap. 100.0m., res 103.0m., dep. 2,774.0m. (Dec. 2009); Chair. AHMED AFIF; Pres. AHMED SAEED; 2 brs.

Seychelles Savings Bank Ltd (SSB): Kingsgate House, POB 531, Victoria; tel. 4294000; fax 4224713; e-mail ssb@savingsbank.sc; f. 1902; state-owned; term deposits, savings and current accounts; cap. and res 7.8m. (Dec. 1992); Man. Dir MICHAEL BENSTRONG; 4 brs.

Foreign Banks

Bank of Baroda (India): Trinity House, Albert St, POB 124, Victoria; tel. 4610333; fax 4324057; e-mail ce.seychelles@bankofbaroda.com; internet www.bankofbaroda.com/seychelles.asp; f. 1978.

Barclays Bank (Seychelles) Ltd (United Kingdom): Independence Ave, POB 167, Victoria; tel. 4383838; fax 4324054; e-mail barclays@seychelles.sc; f. 1959; Seychelles Dir LOGANADEN SIDAMBARAM; 3 brs and 4 agencies.

Habib Bank Ltd (Pakistan): Frances Rachel St, POB 702, Victoria; tel. 4224371; fax 4225614; e-mail habibsez@seychelles.net; f. 1976; Vice-Pres. and Chief Man. SOHAIL ANWAR.

Mauritius Commercial Bank (Seychelles) Ltd (MCB Seychelles): POB 122, Manglier St, Victoria; tel. 4284555; fax 4322676; e-mail contact@mcbseychelles.com; internet www.mcbseychelles.com; f. 1978 as Banque Française Commerciale (BFCOI); changed name in 2003; cap. 20.0m., res 20.0m., dep. 1,232.6m. (Dec. 2009); Man. Dir JOCELYN AH-YU; 5 brs.

Offshore Bank

BMI Offshore Bank: Office 12, Marina House, Eden Island, POB 672, Victoria; tel. 4345660; e-mail enquiries@bmi.com.sc; internet www.bmi.com.sc; Dir-Gen. JAMAL ALI AL-HAZEEM.

INSURANCE

In 2010 there were four domestic and three non-domestic insurance companies in Seychelles.

H. Savy Insurance Co Ltd (HSI): Maison de la Rosière, 2nd Floor, Palm St, POB 887, Victoria; tel. 4322272; fax 4321666; e-mail insurance@mail.seychelles.net; f. 1995; all classes; majority-owned by Corvina Investments; Gen. Dir JEAN WEELING-LEE.

Seychelles Assurance Co Ltd (SACL): Pirate's Arms Bldg, POB 636, Victoria; tel. 4225000; fax 4224495; e-mail sacos@sacos.sc; internet www.sacos.sc; f. 1980; 37% owned by Opportunity Investment Company, 20% state-owned; all classes of insurance; subsidiaries include SUN Investments (Seychelles) Ltd, property-development company; fmrly State Assurance Corporation of Seychelles—SACOS; current name adopted 2006; Chair. and Man. Dir ANTONIO A. LUCAS.

Trade and Industry

GOVERNMENT AGENCIES

National Economic Council: Victoria; f. 2012; advisory body comprising the President as Chairman, the Vice-President as

Vice-Chairman and also ministers, the Governor of the Central Bank and the CEOs of several banks and govt organizations.

Seychelles Fishing Authority (SFA): POB 449, Fishing Port, Victoria; tel. 4670300; fax 4224508; e-mail management@sfa.sc; internet www.sfa.sc; f. 1984; assessment and management of fisheries resources; Chair. VÉRONIQUE HERMINIE; Man. Dir RONDOLPH PAYET.

Seychelles Trading Co Ltd (STC): Latanier Rd, POB 634, Victoria; tel. 4285000; fax 4224735; e-mail mail@stcl.sc; internet stcl.sc; f. 1984; replaced import and distribution arm of the fmr Seychelles Marketing Board (SMB) in 2008; manufacturing and marketing of products, retailing, trade; Chair. COLIN JEAN-LOUIS; CEO PATRICK VEL.

Small Business Financing Agency (SBFA): Victoria; Chair. DOREEN ARNEPHY; CEO ROSANDA ALCINDOR.

DEVELOPMENT ORGANIZATIONS

Indian Ocean Tuna Commission (IOTC) (Commission de Thons de l'Océan Indien): Le Chantier Mall, 2nd Floor, POB 1011, Victoria; tel. 4225494; fax 4224364; e-mail secretariat@iotc.org; internet www.iotc.org; f. 1996; an inter-governmental organization mandated to manage tuna and tuna-like species in the Indian Ocean and adjacent seas; to promote co-operation among its members with a view to ensuring, through appropriate management, the conservation and optimum utilization of stocks and encouraging sustainable development of fisheries based on such stocks; Exec. Sec. ALEJANDRO ANGANUZZI.

Seychelles International Business Authority (SIBA): Industrial Trade Zone, Bois de Rose Ave, Roche Caiman, POB 991, Victoria; Bois de Rose Ave, Roche Caiman; tel. 4380800; fax 4380888; e-mail siba@seychelles.net; internet www.siba.net; f. 1995 to supervise registration of companies, transshipment and 'offshore' financial services in an international free-trade zone covering an area of 23 ha near Mahé International Airport; CEO WENDY PIERRE.

Seychelles Investment Board (SIB): POB 1167, Caravelle House, 2nd floor, Manglier St, Victoria; tel. 4295500; fax 4225125; e-mail sib@seychelles.sc; internet www.sib.gov.sc; f. 2004; CEO SHERIN RENAUD.

Small Enterprises Promotion Agency (SEnPA): Camion Hall Bldg, Victoria; tel. 4323151; fax 4324121; e-mail senpa@senpa.sc; internet www.senpa.sc; f. 2004; fmrly the Seychelles Industrial Development Corpn, f. 1988; promotes and develops small enterprises, crafts and cottage industries; CEO SYLVIANE VALMONT.

CHAMBER OF COMMERCE

Seychelles Chamber of Commerce and Industry: Ebrahim Bldg, 2nd Floor, POB 1399, Victoria; tel. 4323812; fax 4321422; e-mail scci@seychelles.int; Chair. VAITHUNASAMY RAMADOSS; Sec.-Gen. NICHOLE TIRANT-GHÉRARDI.

EMPLOYERS' ORGANIZATION

Federation of Employers' Associations of Seychelles (FEAS): POB 214, Victoria; tel. 4324969; fax 4324996; Chair. BASIL SOUNDY.

UTILITIES

Electricity

Public Utilities Corporation (Electricity Division): Electricity House, POB 174, Roche Caiman; tel. 4678000; fax 4321020; e-mail pmorin@puc.sc; Man. Dir PHILIPPE MORIN.

Seychelles Energy Commission: Room 205, Aarti Chambers, POB 1488, Victoria; tel. 4421700; e-mail mrazanajatovo@sec.sc; f. 2010; Chair. WILLS AGRICOLE.

Water

Public Utilities Corporation (Water and Sewerage Division): Unity House, POB 34, Victoria; tel. 4322444; fax 4325612; e-mail pucwater@seychelles.net; Man. Dir STEPHEN ROUSSEAU.

MAJOR COMPANIES

Abhaye Valabhji (PTY) Ltd: POB 175, Victoria; tel. 4373881; fax 4373848; e-mail md@avgroup.sc; internet www.avgroup.sc; f. 1964; furniture, household appliances, marine engines and motor vehicles; Chair. ABHAYE VALABHJI; Man. Dir ANIL VALABHJI.

Allied Builders (Seychelles) Ltd: POB 215, Les Mamelles, Victoria; tel. 4344600; fax 4344560; e-mail allied@seychelles.net; internet www.alliedbuilders-seychelles.com; f. 1980; building and civil engineering construction; Chair. KALYAN KURJI PATEL; Man. Dir PRAVIN DARAD; 400 employees.

Amalgamated Tobacco Co (Seychelles) Ltd: Anse des Genêts, POB 679, Victoria; tel. 4373118; fax 4373322; e-mail atc@seychelles.net; mfrs of cigarettes; Man. Dir R. LATIMER; Gen. Man. J. Y HIPWAYE.

Corvina Investment Co Ltd: POB 738, Maison la Rosière, Victoria; tel. 4321655; e-mail corvina@seychelles.net; f. 1998; holds investments in 30 Seychelles companies and one in Mauritius; holds interests in shipping, tourism, trading, manufacturing, and financial and management services; Chair. GUY ADAM; Man. Dir ABOO AUMEERUDDY.

Diamond SA (Seychelles) Ltd: POB 1283, Victoria; tel. 4224440; fax 4224430; e-mail info@diamondsa.sc.

Gondwana Granite Co Ltd: POB 977, Victoria; tel. 4373737; fax 4373647; e-mail granite@gondwana.sc; internet www.gondwana.sc; Chair. Dr SELWYN GENDRON.

Indian Ocean Tuna Co: POB 676, Victoria; tel. 4282500; fax 4224628; e-mail iotmdpa@seychelles.net; fmrly Conserveries de l'Océan Indien; reorg. 1995; 40% govt-owned; tuna-processing; largest private sector employer in Seychelles, with c. 2,000 employees; Gen. Man. TONY LAZAZZARA.

Oceana Fisheries Co Ltd: POB 71, Victoria; tel. 4224712; fax 4224661; e-mail oceana@seychelles.net; exports fish; Dir ANTOINE TIRANT.

Paradise Computer Services (Pty) Ltd: Victoria House, POB 847, Victoria; tel. 4289565; fax 4321389; e-mail pcs@seychelles.net; internet www.paradisecomputer.sc; f. 1996; distributor of computers, laptops, printers, peripherals, accessories and cables, office equipment and supplies; Man. Dir RAJA RAMANI.

Seychelles Breweries (SeyBrew) Ltd: O'Brien House, Le Rocher, POB 273, Victoria; tel. 4382600; fax 4382680; e-mail seybrew@seychelles.net; internet www.seybrew.com; sole producer of beer and soft drinks; Chair. DAVID HAMPSHIRE.

Seychelles National Oil Co Ltd (SNOC): Maison du Peuple, POB 230, Victoria; tel. 4225182; fax 4225177; internet www.snoc.sc; f. 1984; merged with Seychelles Petroleum Co (SEPEC) in June 2003, retaining its own name; petroleum exploration in the exclusive economic zone; Chair. GUY ADAM; Man. Dir PATRICK R. JOSEPH.

Seychelles Petroleum Co Ltd (SEYPEC): New Port Rd, POB 222, Victoria; tel. 4290600; fax 4224456; e-mail e.belle@seypec.com; internet www.seypec.com; f. 1985; merged with Seychelles National Oil Co in June 2003, only to retain its name for international transactions; distributing fuel and lubricants; state-owned; Dep. CEO EDDY BELLE.

Seychelles Timber Co (SEYTIM): Grande Anse; tel. 4278343; logging, timber sales, joinery and furniture; operates sawmill at Grande Anse.

United Concrete Products (Seychelles) Ltd (UCPS): POB 382, Anse Des Genets, Victoria; tel. 4373100; fax 4373142; e-mail adeel@ucps-seychelles.com; f. 1970; manufactures concrete products; Exec. Dir J. ALBERT; Gen. Man. S. PAYET.

Victoria Computer Services (Pty) Ltd: POB 724, Victoria; tel. 4323790; fax 4324056; e-mail vcs@seychelles.net; f. 1991; computers and accessories, internet service provider, computer training, telecommunications; Chair. K. MASON; Man. Dir MARC HOUAREAU.

TRADE UNION

Seychelles Federation of Workers' Unions (SFWU): Maison du Peuple, Latanier Rd, POB 154, Victoria; tel. 4224455; fax 4225351; e-mail sfwu@seychelles.net; f. 1978 to amalgamate all existing trade unions; affiliated to Parti Lepep; 25,200 mems; Pres. OLIVIER CHARLES; Gen. Sec. ANTOINE ROBINSON.

Transport

RAILWAYS

There are no railways in Seychelles.

ROADS

In 2008 there were 508 km of roads, of which 490 km were surfaced. Most surfaced roads are on Mahé and Praslin.

Seychelles Public Transport Corpn (SPTC): POB 610, Mahé; tel. 4280280; fax 4322425; internet www.sptc.sc; f. 1977; covers 66 routes on Mahé; CEO GEFFY ZIALOR.

SHIPPING

Privately owned ferry services connect Victoria, on Mahé, with the islands of Praslin and La Digue. At 31 December 2009 Seychelles' merchant fleet numbered 50 vessels, totalling 203,192 grt.

Seychelles Ports Authority (SPA): POB 47, Mahé Quay, Victoria; tel. 4224701; fax 4224004; e-mail enquiries@seychellesports.sc;

internet www.spa.sc; Chair. Capt. GUY ADAM; CEO Lt Col ANDRÉ D. CISEAU.

Aquarius Shipping Agency Ltd: POB 865, Victoria; tel. 4225050; fax 4225043; e-mail aqua@seychelles.net; Gen. Man. ANTHONY SAVY.

Hunt, Deltel and Co Ltd: Trinity House, Albert St, POB 14, Victoria; tel. 4380300; fax 4225367; e-mail hundel@seychelles.net; internet www.hundel.sc; f. 1937; Man. Dir E. HOUAREAU.

Mahé Shipping Co Ltd: Maritime House, POB 336, Victoria; tel. 4380500; fax 4380538; e-mail mail@maheship.sc; internet www.maheship.sc; f. 1969; shipping agents; Chair. Capt. G. C. C. ADAM.

Seychelles Shipping Line Ltd: POB 977, Providence, Victoria; tel. 4373737; fax 4373647; e-mail ssl@gondwana.sc; f. 1994; operates freight services between Seychelles and Durban, South Africa; Chair. SELWYN GENDRON; Man. Dir HASSAN OMAR.

CIVIL AVIATION

Seychelles International Airport is located at Pointe Larue, 10 km from Victoria. A new international passenger terminal and aircraft parking apron were constructed in the mid-2000s on land reclaimed in 1990; the existing terminal (which underwent SR 3m. in renovations in 2002) was to be converted into a cargo terminal. The airport also serves as a refuelling point for aircraft traversing the Indian Ocean. There are airstrips on several outlying islands.

Seychelles Civil Aviation Authority (SCAA): POB 181, Victoria; tel. 4384000; fax 4384009; e-mail secretariat@scaa.sc; internet www.scaa.sc; f. 1970; formerly Directorate of Civil Aviation; responsible for the Flight Information Region of 2.6m. sq km of Indian Ocean airspace; Chair. Capt. DAVID SAVY; CEO GILBERT FAURE.

Air Seychelles: The Creole Spirit Bldg, Quincy St, POB 386, Victoria; tel. 4381002; fax 4224305; e-mail airseymd@seychelles.net; internet www.airseychelles.net; f. 1979; operates scheduled internal flights from Mahé to Praslin; also charter services to Bird, Desroches and Denis Islands and to outlying islands of the Amirantes group; international services to Europe were discontinued in Jan. 2012, but a twice-weekly service to Abu Dhabi commenced in March 2012 and flights to the People's Republic of China were due to start in Jan. 2013; Chair. JOEL MORGAN; CEO CRAMER BALL.

Tourism

Seychelles enjoys an equable climate, and is renowned for its fine beaches and attractive scenery. The islands are home to a unique endemic flora and fauna, including several rare species of birds. Most tourist activity is concentrated on the islands of Mahé, Praslin and La Digue, although the potential for ecological tourism of the outlying islands has received increased attention. It is government policy that the development of tourism should not blight the environment, and strict laws govern the location and construction of hotels. In 1998 the Government indicated that up to 200,000 visitors (although not more than 4,000 at any one time) could be accommodated annually without detriment to environmental quality. However, several new luxury resorts were constructed in the early 2000s, and the yachting sector was also under development. Receipts from tourism totalled an estimated SR 2,451m. in 2010. In 2011 there were 194,500 tourist arrivals; most visitors are from Europe.

Compagnie Seychelloise de Promotion Hotelière Ltd: POB 683, Victoria; tel. 4224694; fax 4225291; e-mail cosproh@seychelles.net; promotes govt-owned hotels.

Seychelles Tourism Board (STB): POB 1262, Victoria; tel. 4671300; fax 4620620; e-mail info@seychelles.travel; internet www.seychelles.travel; f. 1998 as Seychelles Tourism Marketing Authority; merged with Seychelles Tourism Office in 2005; Chair. BARRY FAURE; CEO ELSIA GRANDCOURT.

Defence

As assessed at November 2011, the army numbered 200 men. Paramilitary forces comprised a 250-strong national guard and a 200-strong coast guard. Seychelles contributes servicemen to the East African Stand-by Brigade, a part of the African Union stand-by peace-keeping force.

Defence Expenditure: Budgeted at SR 292m. in 2011 (including capital expenditure).

Commander-in-Chief of Seychelles Armed Forces: Brig. LÉOPOLD PAYET.

Education

Education is free and compulsory for children between six and 16 years of age. A programme of educational reform, based on the British comprehensive schools system, was introduced in 1980. The language of instruction in primary schools is English. The duration of primary education is six years, while that of general secondary education is five years (of which the first four years are compulsory), beginning at 12 years of age. Pre-primary and special education facilities are also available. According to UNESCO estimates, in 2008/09 enrolment at primary schools included 94% of children (males 93%; females 95%) in the relevant age-group, while the comparable ratio for secondary enrolment in that year was 97% (males 95%; females 99%). There were 2,198 students in post-secondary (non-tertiary) education in 2011. A number of students study abroad, principally in the United Kingdom. Government expenditure on education in 2009 was SR 229.2m., equivalent to about 6.0% of total spending.

Bibliography

Benedict, B. *People of the Seychelles.* London, HMSO, 1966.

Benedict, M., and Benedict, B. *Men, Women and Money in Seychelles.* Berkeley, CA, University of California Press, 1982.

Bennett, G., and Bennett, P. R. *Seychelles* (World Bibliographical Series). Santa Barbara, CA, ABC-Clio, 1993.

Bowden, A., *et al. The Economic Costs of Maritime Piracy.* One Earth Future Foundation Working Paper, December 2010.

Bradley, J. T. *History of Seychelles.* Victoria, Clarion Press, 1940.

Central Bank of Seychelles. *Quarterly Review.* Victoria, Central Bank of Seychelles.

Cohen, R. (Ed.). *African Islands and Enclaves.* London, Sage Publications, 1983.

Franda, M. *Quiet Turbulence in the Seychelles: Tourism and Development.* Hanover, NH, American Field Staff Reports, Asia Series No. 10, 1979.

Gabby, R., and Ghosh, R. N. *Seychelles Marketing Board: Economic Development in a Small Island Economy.* Singapore, Academic Press International, 1992.

Lee, C. *Seychelles: Political Castaways.* London, Hamish Hamilton, 1976.

Lionnet, G. *The Seychelles.* Newton Abbot, David and Charles, 1972.

Mancham, Sir J. R. *Paradise Raped: Life, Love and Power in the Seychelles.* London, Methuen, 1983.

Island Splendour. London, Methuen, 1984.

Nieuwkerk, A., and Bell, W. *Seychelles.* International Development Research Centre, 2007.

Payet, R. 'Climate Change and the Tourism-Dependent Economy of the Seychelles' in Leary, N., *et al* (Eds) *Climate Change and Vulnerability.* London, Earthscan, 2008.

Scarr, D. *Seychelles since 1770: History of a Slave and Post-Slavery Society.* New Jersey, NJ, Africa World Press, Inc, 2000.

Skerrett, J., and Skerrett, A. *Seychelles.* London, APA, 1994.

Thomas, A. *Forgotten Eden.* London, Longman, 1968.

Toussaint, A. *History of the Indian Ocean.* London, Routledge and Kegan Paul, 1966.

USA International Business Publications. *Seychelles Country Study Guide* (World Country Study Guide). 2000.

Webb, A. W. T. *Story of Seychelles.* Seychelles, 1964.

SIERRA LEONE

Physical and Social Geography

PETER K. MITCHELL

The Republic of Sierra Leone, which covers an area of 71,740 sq km (27,699 sq miles), rises from the beaches of the south-west to the broad plateaux of the Atlantic/Niger watershed at the north-eastern frontier. Despite the general horizontal aspect of the landscapes, developed over millennia upon largely Pre-Cambrian structures, there are a number of abrupt ascents to older uplifted erosion surfaces—most impressively along sections of a major escarpment, 130 km inland, separating a western lowland zone (c. 120 m above sea-level) from the country's more elevated interior half (c. 500 m). Incised valleys, interspersed by minor waterfalls, carry drainage south-westwards; only locally or along a coastal sedimentary strip do rivers flow through open terrain.

A geologically recent submergence of major floodplains, particularly north of Cape St Ann, has brought tide-water into contact with the rocky margins of the ancient shield, impeding up-river navigation. Water-borne trade has found compensation in sheltered deep-water anchorages, notably off Freetown, the principal port and capital, where a line of coastal summits rising to almost 900 m above sea-level facilitates an easy landfall.

Intrusive gabbros form the peninsular range; elsewhere, isolated blocks or hill groups consist of rock-bare granites or the metamorphic roots of long-vanished mountain chains, which provide mineral deposits: iron, chromite, gold, rutile and bauxite. Reserves of kimberlite in the southern high plateaux are approaching exhaustion. The pipes and dikes of kimberlite may provide the basis for future deep mining.

Differences in seasonal and regional incidence of humidity and rainfall are important. Prolonged rains (May to October, with heaviest rains from July to September) are bracketed by showery weather with many squally thunderstorms, such spells beginning earlier in the south-east. Consequently, the growing season is longest here (although total rainfall—over 5,000 mm locally—is greater along the coast) and the 'natural' vegetation is tropical evergreen forest; the cultivation of cash crops such as cocoa, coffee, kola and oil-palm is successful in this area, and the more productive timber areas, although limited, are concentrated here. The savannah-woodlands of the north-east have less rain (1,900 mm–2,500 mm), a shorter period for plant growth and a dry season made harsh by harmattan winds, with cattle-rearing, groundnuts and tobacco as potential commercial resources. Semi-deciduous forest occupies most intervening areas, but long-term peasant occupation has created a mosaic of short-term cropland, fallow regrowth plots and occasional tracts of secondary forest.

Permanent rice-lands have been created from mangrove swamp in the north-west, and much encouragement is being given to the improvement of the many small tracts of inland valley swamp throughout the east. Such innovation contrasts with a widespread bush-fallowing technique, giving low yields of rain-fed staples, normally rice, but cassava (especially on degraded sandy soils) and millet in the north.

Sierra Leone's fourth national census, which was held in December 2004, enumerated 4,976,871 inhabitants, representing a population density of 69 inhabitants per sq km. At mid-2012, according to UN estimates, Sierra Leone had 6,126,453 inhabitants and a population density of 85.4 inhabitants per sq km.

Traditional *mores* still dominate, in spite of the Westernizing influences of employment in mining, of education and of growing urbanization. A large proportion of the population follows animist beliefs, although there are significant Islamic and Christian communities. Extended family, exogamous kin-groups and the paramount chieftaincies form a social nexus closely mirrored by a hierarchy of hamlet, village and rural centre: some 29,000 non-urban settlements, including isolated impermanent homesteads. The towns, however, are expanding. Greater Freetown, which it was assumed was equivalent to the Western Area Urban District, had 772,873 inhabitants at the 2004 census, while Koindu, the centre of the Kono diamond fields, had 80,025 inhabitants; other towns are also growing. Bo included 149,957 and Kenema 128,402 inhabitants at the 2004 census. By mid-2011 the population of Freetown was estimated by the UN to have increased to 940,683. Diamond-mining has attracted settlers to many villages in the mining areas.

The official language of the country is English, while Krio (Creole), Mende, Limba and Temne are also widely spoken.

Recent History

BHAIRAV RAJA

Based on an earlier article by EDWARD GEORGE

In 1896 a British protectorate was proclaimed over the hinterland of the coastal colony of Sierra Leone, which had been under British administration since 1787. In 1951, following the introduction of a Constitution, elections were won by the Sierra Leone People's Party (SLPP), led by Dr (later Sir) Milton Margai, who became Chief Minister in 1953 and Prime Minister in 1958. On 27 April 1961 Sierra Leone became an independent state within the Commonwealth. The SLPP retained power in elections in 1962. Sir Milton died in 1964 and was succeeded as Prime Minister by his half-brother, Dr (later Sir) Albert Margai. The main opposition party, the All-People's Congress (APC), led by Dr Siaka Stevens, gained a parliamentary majority at general elections in 1967, but was prevented from taking power by a military coup. Following an army mutiny in April 1968, a civilian Government was restored, with Stevens as Prime Minister. A period of political instability followed, culminating in an attempted military coup in March 1971, which was suppressed with the aid of troops from neighbouring Guinea. In April a republican Constitution was introduced, with Stevens as executive President. The SLPP offered no candidates in the 1973 general elections, and Stevens, as sole candidate, was elected to a further presidential term.

In 1978 the APC was constitutionally established as the sole legal party, upon which a number of prominent supporters of the SLPP joined the APC and received ministerial posts. The Government encountered increasing opposition in 1981, following a scandal involving several officials and cabinet ministers in the misappropriation of public funds. Amid serious outbreaks of violence, general elections took place in May 1982 and a new Government was formed.

In April 1985 Stevens announced that he was to leave office upon the expiry of his existing mandate later that year. At a conference of the APC in August, Maj.-Gen. Joseph Saidu Momoh, a cabinet minister and the Commander of the Armed Forces, was nominated as sole candidate for the presidency and for the party leadership. In October Momoh received 99% of votes cast in a presidential election, and was inaugurated as President on 28 November. Although retaining his military affiliation, Momoh installed a civilian Cabinet, which included several members of the previous administration. Elections to the House of Representatives took place in May 1986.

By early 1990 there was widespread popular support for the restoration of a multi-party system. Having initially rejected this, in August Momoh conceded the necessity of electoral reforms, and announced an extensive review of the Constitution. The Central Committee of the APC approved a number of proposed amendments to the Constitution, and in November Momoh appointed a 30-member National Constitutional Review Commission, which, in March 1991, submitted a draft Constitution, providing for the restoration of a plural political system. The maximum duration of the President's tenure of office was to be two five-year terms. The President was to appoint the Cabinet, which was to include one Vice-President, rather than two. Legislative power was to be vested in a bicameral legislature, elected by universal adult suffrage for a term of five years. The Government subsequently accepted the majority of the Commission's recommendations. It presented the draft Constitution to the House of Representatives and announced that the parliamentary term, which was due to end in June, was to be extended for a further year, owing to the disruption caused by the conflict between government forces and Liberian rebels in the south of the country. The general elections, which were scheduled for May, were also to be postponed for a year to allow time for the transition to a plural political system. However, political activity by parties other than the APC remained illegal until the new Constitution took effect. At a national referendum, which was conducted during 23–30 August, the new Constitution was approved by 60% of voters, with 75% of the electorate participating.

REBEL ACTIVITY AND MILITARY RULE

Repeated border incursions by Liberian rebels, reported to be members of the National Patriotic Front of Liberia (NPFL), resulted in the deaths of several Sierra Leoneans in March 1991. The Sierra Leone Government, which had already committed 500 of its troops to the peace-keeping operation in Liberia authorized by the Economic Community of West African States (ECOWAS) Monitoring Group (ECOMOG), subsequently deployed another 2,150 troops on the Liberian border and, in April, attacked rebel bases in Liberian territory. The Government alleged that the rebel offensive had been instigated by the NPFL leader, Charles Taylor, in an attempt to force Sierra Leone's withdrawal from ECOMOG. The newly created Revolutionary United Front (RUF), which was apparently led by a former Sierra Leone army photographer, Cpl Foday Sankoh, began to support the NPFL in its attacks against Sierra Leone army positions. In mid-1991 Sierra Leonean troops, by now assisted by military units from Nigeria and Guinea, initiated a counter-offensive against the RUF rebels, and succeeded in recapturing several towns in the east and south of the country. Government forces were also joined by some 1,200 former members of the Liberian armed forces, who had fled to Sierra Leone in September 1990, while a number of other countries, including the United Kingdom and the USA, provided logistical support to Sierra Leone.

In September 1991 six newly created political associations demanded that the Government give way to an interim administration. Shortly afterwards the first Vice-President, Abubakar Kamara, and the second Vice-President, Salia Jusu-Sheriff, resigned from both the APC and the Government. In December Momoh and leaders of the registered political parties agreed to co-operate in the establishment of a multi-party system.

In April 1992 Capt. Valentine Strasser declared that the Momoh Government had been replaced by a five-member military junta. Momoh fled to Guinea, and Strasser announced the formation of a National Provisional Ruling Council (NPRC), while making pledges about the introduction of a multi-party system and an end to the conflict, and assuring ECOWAS of the continued participation of Sierra Leone in ECOMOG. The NPRC suspended the Constitution, dissolved the House of Representatives, imposed a state of emergency and curfew, and temporarily closed the country's air, sea and land borders.

On 1 May 1992 the NPRC (which comprised 18 military officers and four civilians) was formally convened under Strasser's chairmanship. All political activity was suspended, and it was subsequently reported that some 55 people, including members of the former Cabinet, had been arrested. On 6 May Strasser was sworn in as head of state. Later that month the new Government established a commission of inquiry to investigate the activities of members of the former regime. In August Strasser announced the establishment of an advisory council, which, among its other functions, was to review the provisions of the 1991 Constitution. In December 1992 Capt. Solomon Musa was appointed Chief Secretary of State and the Government announced that it had foiled a coup attempt by a group known as the Anti-Corruption Revolutionary Movement (which included former members of the army and security forces). Shortly afterwards nine of those accused of involvement in the conspiracy were tried by a military tribunal and were summarily executed. In January 1993 the United Kingdom announced the suspension of economic aid to Sierra Leone, in protest against the executions. Later that month the military regime released several former members of the Momoh Government, who had been detained since May 1992.

Strasser announced in April 1993 that a programme providing for a return to civilian Government by 1996 had been adopted. He also stated that measures were being taken to reduce the powers of the security services. In a government reorganization in July 1993, Musa was replaced as Deputy Chairman of the NPRC and Chief Secretary of State by Capt. Julius Maada Bio, ostensibly on the grounds that false allegations against him had proved detrimental to the stability of the administration. Musa (who was widely blamed for the repressive measures undertaken by the Government) took refuge in the Nigerian High Commission in Freetown, and subsequently sought refuge in the United Kingdom.

In January 1994 the Government claimed that it had regained control of a number of rebel bases, but the RUF managed to regroup and the fighting subsequently intensified in the south and east of Sierra Leone. In April it was reported that the RUF, which had been joined by disaffected members of the armed forces, had initiated attacks in the north of the country.

Meanwhile, in November 1993 Strasser announced a two-year transitional programme, which provided for the installation of a civilian government by January 1996. In December 1993 a five-member Interim National Electoral Commission (INEC), under the chairmanship of Dr James Jonah (the assistant Secretary-General of the UN, in charge of political affairs), was established to organize the registration of voters and the demarcation of constituency boundaries, in preparation for the forthcoming local government elections. In the same month the National Advisory Council submitted several constitutional proposals (which included a number of provisions similar to those of the 1991 Constitution), stipulating that only Sierra Leonean nationals of more than 40 years of age were to qualify to contest a presidential election (thereby precluding Strasser and the majority of members of the NPRC). In April 1994 several senior members of the armed forces were dismissed, following criticism of the Government's failure to end the RUF rebellion; by this time there were widespread rumours of collusion between military officers and the rebels.

In March 1995 Musa was apparently ordered to retire from the armed forces after Strasser rejected his proposal for the installation of a transitional civilian government. Lt-Col Akim Gibril became Chief Secretary of State, replacing Bio, who was appointed Chief of the Defence Staff. In late April, on the third anniversary of the NPRC coup, Strasser announced that the ban on political activity would be lifted and that a National Consultative Conference was to be convened to discuss the transitional process. He indicated that elections would take place by the end of the year, with the installation of a civilian government in January 1996. The ban on political parties was formally rescinded on 21 June. The RUF, which was making large advances, refused to participate in the political process.

Continued atrocities perpetrated against civilians were increasingly attributed to 'sobels', disaffected members of the armed forces who engaged in acts of looting, banditry and indiscriminate killing. By early 1995 some 900,000 civilians had been displaced as a result of the intensification of the civil conflict. Despite successful counter-offensives by government forces, the RUF made some advances towards Freetown and initiated attacks against towns in the vicinity (including Songo, which was situated only 35 km east of Freetown), apparently prior to besieging the capital. The Governments of Guinea and Nigeria dispatched additional troops to Sierra Leone, while it was reported that mercenaries recruited from South Africa were assisting the authorities with military training and logistics. The RUF indicated that humanitarian organizations would be prevented from operating in territory that the movement controlled, and there were increasing reports of massacres and other violations of human rights perpetrated by the rebels against the civilian population. In November the RUF regained control of Kailahun, and a further 10 towns in Moyamba District. In December an Organization of African Unity (OAU, now the African Union) mission conducted negotiations with RUF representatives in Abidjan, Côte d'Ivoire.

FALL OF STRASSER AND ELECTION OF KABBAH

In December 1995 it was announced that the presidential and legislative elections were to take place concurrently in February 1996. In January, however, Strasser was deposed by military officers, led by Bio, in a bloodless coup. Bio, who assumed the office of head of state, announced that the coup had been instigated in response to efforts by Strasser to remain in power. A reconstituted Supreme Council of State and Council of Secretaries were formed, and, following a meeting of the new military leadership, and representatives of the political parties and the INEC, it was announced that the elections would proceed as scheduled. Following the refusal of Bio to accede to the RUF's request for a postponement of the elections pending a peace agreement, the rebels abandoned a cease-fire in early February and subsequently launched a series of attacks in various parts of the country, killing large numbers of civilians.

The presidential and legislative elections took place on 26 February 1996. The reconstituted SLPP secured 36% of votes cast in the legislative elections, while its presidential candidate, Ahmed Tejan Kabbah, also received most support, with 36% of votes. Seven of the political parties, including the National Unity Party (which had supported Bio), demanded that the results be annulled, owing to the disruption of the elections in several regions caused by rebel violence. Since none of the candidates had achieved the requisite majority of 55% of the votes, a second round of the presidential election, which took place on 15 March, was contested by Kabbah and the candidate of the United National People's Party (UNPP), John Karefa-Smart (who had obtained 23% of votes cast in the first round): Kabbah was elected President by 60% of the votes. Later in March seats in the new 80-member Parliament were allocated on a basis of proportional representation, with the SLPP securing 27, the UNPP 17, the People's Democratic Party 12 and the reconstituted APC only five; the 12 provincial districts were represented in the legislature by Paramount Chiefs. Kabbah was inaugurated on 29 March, when the military Government officially relinquished power to the new civilian administration. In July the Parliament adopted legislation that formally reinstated the Constitution of 1991.

Following discussions between President Kabbah and the rebel leader, Foday Sankoh, in April 1996, both the Government and the RUF made a commitment to a cessation of hostilities, and announced the establishment of three joint committees, which would consider issues regarding the demobilization of rebel forces. Sankoh refused, however, to recognize the legitimacy of the new Government, and demanded that a transitional administration be installed, pending further elections. At further discussions between the Government and the rebel leadership in July, Sankoh demanded that members of the RUF be allocated ministerial posts as a precondition to the cessation of hostilities.

MILITARY AND RUF IN ALLIANCE

On 25 May 1997 dissident members of the armed forces, led by Maj. Johnny Paul Koroma, seized power, deposing Kabbah, who fled to Guinea. Koroma claimed that the coup, which prompted international condemnation, was in response to the Government's failure to implement a peace agreement with the RUF, reached in November 1996. The Nigerian Government demanded that the junta relinquish power, and increased its military strength in Freetown. The new authorities imposed a curfew in Freetown, following widespread violent looting by armed factions; most foreign nationals were evacuated. In early June 1997 Nigerian forces initiated a naval bombardment of Freetown in an effort to force the new military leaders to resign. However, forces loyal to the coup leaders, assisted by RUF members, succeeded in repelling Nigerian attacks. Koroma announced the establishment of a 20-member Armed Forces Revolutionary Council (AFRC), with himself as Chairman and Sankoh as Vice-Chairman (*in absentia*, since he was being detained in Abuja by the Nigerian authorities). The AFRC (which was not internationally recognized as the legitimate Government) included a further three members of the RUF and several civilians. All political activity, the existing Constitution and government bodies were suspended, although Koroma pledged that democratic rule would be restored following new elections.

In mid-June 1997 the AFRC announced that it had suppressed a coup attempt, following the arrest of 15 people, including several senior military officers. In the same month it was reported that troops supporting the junta had repulsed an attack by Kamajors, who remained loyal to Kabbah, at the town of Zimmi, 250 km south-east of Freetown. On 17 June Koroma was formally installed as the self-proclaimed head of state. However, despite appeals from Koroma, civilians continued to observe a campaign of civil disobedience, which had been organized by the labour congress in protest against the coup. In the same month members of the disbanded legislature, who had met in defiance of the ban on political activity, proposed a peace agreement, under which a government of national unity representing all political parties and the RUF would be established, and ECOMOG and UN forces would be deployed throughout the country.

By July 1997 the new military Government had become completely isolated by the international community. The Commonwealth Ministerial Action Group (which had been established to respond to unlawful activities by member states) suspended Sierra Leone from meetings of the Commonwealth, pending the restoration of constitutional order and the reinstatement of a democratically elected government. The UN Security Council also condemned the coup, and expressed support for ECOWAS efforts to resolve the situation. A four-nation committee, comprising representatives of Nigeria, Côte d'Ivoire, Guinea and Ghana, which had been established by ECOWAS to monitor a return to constitutional rule, urged the Government to relinquish power during a series of negotiations with an AFRC delegation. In an apparent effort to consolidate power, Koroma formed a Cabinet, known as the Council of Secretaries, comprising representatives of the RUF and the army, together with a number of civilians.

Following further reports of clashes between Kamajors and government forces in the south of the country, in late July 1997 AFRC representatives and the ECOWAS committee, meeting in Abidjan, Côte d'Ivoire, agreed to an immediate cease-fire; negotiations were to continue, with the aim of restoring constitutional order; however, Nigeria subsequently accused the AFRC of violating the cease-fire. At the end of August ECOWAS members agreed to impose a total embargo on all supplies of petroleum products, armaments and military equipment to the junta. The UN Security Council subsequently approved the adoption of sanctions against Sierra Leone. The ECOMOG military presence at Lungi airport was increased, and a base was established at Jui, on the principal road linking Freetown to the rest of the country. ECOMOG enforced the economic blockade on Freetown by launching aerial bombardments against merchant ships in the port. During September there was an escalation of hostilities between the AFRC's forces and ECOMOG, resulting in numerous deaths; thousands of Freetown residents subsequently fled from the capital.

Amid increasing ECOMOG military pressure and mounting popular resistance, the military junta apparently acceded to ECOWAS demands that the AFRC relinquish power by 22 April 1998, as part of an agreement that also provided for the imposition of a cease-fire, and the disarmament and demobilization of combatant forces. However, subsequent major disagreements over the terms of the accord prompted further confrontations between the AFRC and ECOMOG. Despite Koroma's demands that ECOMOG begin to withdraw its forces as a precondition for his adherence to the agreement, ECOMOG's Nigerian forces were strengthened. There was no progress on the disarmament programme, which had been scheduled to begin in December.

KABBAH'S RESTORATION TO POWER

International efforts to restore Kabbah to power intensified during January 1998, when the United Kingdom appointed a former ambassador to Angola, John Flynn, to co-operate with the UN and ECOWAS officials to this end. According to subsequent reports in the British media, Kabbah contracted a British military consultancy, Sandline International, to undertake the supply of armaments, and to provide military support and training, both to Sierra Leonean forces loyal to the ousted Government and to ECOMOG. Following armed clashes near the ECOMOG base at Jui at the end of January, the ECOMOG Force Commander, Col Maxwell Khobe, ordered a final offensive against the capital in early February. The presidential mansion was captured after several days of fighting, and full control of Freetown was achieved by mid-February; it was estimated that about 100 people had been killed during the operation.

Following the seizure of the capital, ECOMOG ended the military embargo and opened Lungi airport to commercial traffic. A special task force was established to supervise government activities and to expedite the delivery of humanitarian aid. International donors pledged to provide emergency food and medical supplies, and mine-clearance expertise. The Kamajor forces (now operating under the name of Civil Defence Forces) initially seized Bo and Koidu in mid-February 1998; however, intensive fighting for control of the area ensued, while violence and looting continued in many parts of the country. Some AFRC officers were quickly captured by ECOMOG, while others fled to the northern region; Koroma was reported to have taken refuge in a village in the south-east of the country. Many refugees, including RUF activists, fled into Liberia. Nigerian troops undertook most of the operations to suppress continuing rebel activity, ousting the RUF from Kenema and forcing AFRC troops to surrender in Makeni. ECOMOG only finally gained control of Bo in late February, but fighting continued in the surrounding countryside for some weeks thereafter. On 10 March Kabbah returned to Freetown and was formally inaugurated. Although international donors pledged substantial support, the stability of his Government was initially dependent on the continued presence of the ECOMOG forces. In mid-April Kabbah appointed Khobe as Chief of National Security. During April the reinstated Government charged a total of 59 people, including the former President, Joseph Momoh, with treason and collaboration with the AFRC.

In May 1998 government and ECOMOG troops continued to launch attacks against rebel forces, which remained in control of Kailahun District and part of Kono District. In late July the UN Security Council established a 70-member UN Observer Mission in Sierra Leone (UNOMSIL); the force, which had an initial six-month mandate, was to monitor the security situation and the disarmament of former combatants based in secure regions of the country. In August 16 people were convicted and sentenced to death for their involvement in the May 1997 coup. After appeals for clemency, their sentences were reviewed, but in October 1998 24 former members of the armed forces were executed, after having been convicted of collaborating with the ousted junta. At the end of October Sankoh, who had in July been returned from detention in Nigeria, was convicted and sentenced to death for treason and murder, owing to his support for the May 1997 coup; he immediately launched an appeal. In November 1998 a further 15 civilians were sentenced to death for treason, and ex-President Momoh received a 10-year prison sentence.

The death sentence imposed on Sankoh prompted an upsurge in attacks by RUF forces, in alliance with former AFRC members, after October 1998. There were increased reports of atrocities being perpetrated against civilians as the rebels began the systematic recruitment and abduction of minors, both to act as combatants and to transport ammunition and goods. Despite a rapid reinforcement of the ECOMOG contingent to 15,000 troops, and the deployment of Kamajors, the rebels seized Koidu in the east and the northern town of Makeni, before advancing into Lunsar and Waterloo, closer to Freetown. Fighting subsequently erupted throughout the capital in early January 1999; the rebels attacked civilians and forced them to flee towards the city centre, thus securing cover for a rapid advance. Over a period of three weeks an estimated 5,000 people were killed in Freetown, including thousands of civilians, at least 800 ECOMOG troops and hundreds of RUF rebels, while many thousands of city residents were assaulted or mutilated. A subsequent investigation by a human rights organization concluded that these widespread abuses were authorized at a high level within the RUF's command structure. The investigation also identified violations of human rights committed by ECOMOG forces, especially with regard to their policy of summary execution of captured rebels.

As the rebels withdrew from the city they set alight buildings and caused widespread destruction. ECOMOG was eventually able to restore a semblance of order to Freetown, but in view of an implied threat of a complete withdrawal by the Nigerian forces, owing to the heavy losses they had suffered, there was a renewed international initiative for negotiations with the RUF. With mediation by the UN, the OAU, the Commonwealth, the United Kingdom and the USA, the discussions began in Lomé, Togo, following a UN-supervised release of Sankoh in April 1999. In May the Sierra Leonean Government and the RUF signed a cease-fire agreement, although violations were subsequently reported. Continuing negotiations on the proposed participation of the RUF in a transitional administration followed. In early July the Government and the RUF reached a power-sharing agreement, after the Government acceded to rebel demands that Sankoh be appointed Vice-President, with responsibility for the mineral resources industry, and the RUF be allocated a further eight cabinet posts. The accord provided for the release of civilians who had been abducted by the rebels, and the disarmament and reintegration into the armed forces of former combatants; the RUF was to be reconstituted as a political organization. However, the UN High Commissioner for Refugees and human rights organizations objected to a general amnesty for perpetrators of human rights violations granted under the provisions of the peace agreement.

In early October 1999 Sankoh issued a prepared apology for atrocities committed during the war, but under questioning from journalists, he continued to deny most accusations that had been levelled against the RUF. Negotiations ensued on the composition of the Government, in which the former AFRC junta had expected to be allocated senior posts. Sankoh was eventually ceded powers equivalent to those of a Vice-President, as well as the chairmanship of a new commission for strategic resources, national reconstruction and development, while four RUF members were allocated government positions, with the AFRC effectively excluded from participation in the new administration.

UN AND BRITISH MILITARY DEPLOYMENT

The political climate was already highly uncertain by the time the UN Security Council eventually approved the UN Mission to Sierra Leone (UNAMSIL) on 22 October 1999, and tension increased as the UN peace-keeping force, at first mainly comprising troops from Commonwealth countries, began to arrive and be deployed in the country during November. UNAMSIL was to consist of 6,000 troops, who were to join the remaining 5,000-strong Nigerian ECOMOG contingent. In accordance with the Lomé agreement, the RUF was registered as a political party in November, but Sankoh showed little inclination to moderate the aggressive culture of the movement or to oblige it to adhere to the disarmament timetable, which was considerably behind schedule. In January 2000 the UN Secretary-General, Kofi Annan, asked the Security Council to increase the size of UNAMSIL to 11,000 troops, to allow for the complete replacement of ECOMOG.

The disarmament process, which had been scheduled to end in December 1999, did not proceed as planned, with most RUF combatants refusing to relinquish their weapons and some being rearmed through supply lines from Liberia, especially after the joint border between the two countries was opened in November. Only 2,500 of an estimated 45,000 former combatants surrendered any armaments. The rate of disarmament accelerated only in those areas that were controlled by the AFRC; by early 2000 some 12,000 combatants had complied. In January there were confrontations between ECOMOG and RUF forces, and these were followed in February by the RUF's refusal to allow Indian and Ghanaian UNAMSIL forces to be deployed in the east of the country.

Nigeria agreed in January 2000 to suspend the progressive withdrawal of its ECOMOG troops from Sierra Leone, on the understanding that many of them would be transferred to UNAMSIL control at the end of April. While the RUF became increasingly aggressive, it was also undergoing division between Sankoh's loyalists and those of Sam Bockarie and other leaders operating from bases in Liberia. The formal ending of the ECOMOG mission on 30 April was accompanied by a severe loss of control by UNAMSIL. At the same time the leadership of the Sierra Leone army was also thrown into confusion by the unexpected death, in April, of its Nigerian Chief of Staff, Brig.-Gen. Khobe.

By the end of April 2000 it was estimated that about 20,000 armed RUF rebels were still able to operate freely in the country. The UN force at this stage amounted to only 8,500 troops, many of them on unarmed monitoring duties. At the beginning of May the RUF clashed with the UN forces, and after a few days some 500 UN troops were reported missing, presumed kidnapped. This development prompted the British Government to start preparations for a rescue mission, on behalf of both the UN and the Sierra Leone armed forces. On 8 May the United Kingdom dispatched a force of 800 paratroopers, with strong air force and naval support. After first securing the airport, the British forces were deployed throughout Freetown and surrounding areas, pre-empting an RUF offensive against Waterloo, near the capital, on 11 and 12 May. A renewed RUF attempt to advance on Freetown was successfully repelled, while Sankoh, after a brief disappearance, was arrested and detained on behalf of the Government on 17 May.

In mid-May 2000 British forces declared Freetown to be secure, and it was reported that the RUF had commenced the release of some of its hostages, after Liberian mediation. ECOWAS defence chiefs agreed to resume sending troops to the country, but under a changed command structure that would reflect the military role played by Nigeria and would expand the mandate from peace-keeping to peace enforcement. In mid-May the UN Security Council approved a further increase in the size of UNAMSIL, to 13,000, by immediately deploying 3,000 West African and 800 Bangladeshi troops. The RUF released most of the UN hostages.

Many of the British forces were withdrawn in mid-June 2000, although some 250 British troops subsequently remained in Sierra Leone. In early July the UN Security Council adopted a resolution, proposed by the United Kingdom, for an international embargo on the purchase of diamonds mined from RUF-controlled regions. Later that month some 233 peace-keeping personnel (mainly Indian) held hostage by the RUF at Kailahun were rescued in a military operation, staged by UNAMSIL, with the endorsement of the UN Security Council. Meanwhile, increasing divisions in the pro-Government forces were reported. In late August one of the most notorious of the militia groups supporting the former AFRC junta, the West Side Boys (WSB), abducted 11 British military personnel and one member of the Sierra Leone army. The WSB subsequently issued a number of demands, including the release from detention of their leader, as a precondition to freeing the hostages. Five of the British personnel were released a few days later, but additional British troops were dispatched to Sierra Leone following the failure of negotiating officials to secure an agreement over the remaining hostages. In early September about 150 British troops attacked the WSB base, and succeeded in freeing the remaining hostages; one British serviceman and 25 WSB members were killed during the rescue mission. Later that month the Indian Government announced that the Indian contingent, numbering 3,073, was gradually to be withdrawn from UNAMSIL. The overall British military presence was again reinforced by an increase in the number of ground troops to about 600, and it was also disclosed that about 5,000 British troops were being held in reserve for possible rapid deployment if necessary.

These military arrangements constituted the background to the signing of a new cease-fire agreement between the Government and RUF in Abuja, Nigeria, on 11 November 2000; under its terms, the RUF was committed to return the weapons and ammunition that it had previously seized, as well as to commence a comprehensive programme of disarmament, demobilization and reintegration of troops. With Sankoh under arrest, the leadership of the RUF had been assumed by the movement's military commander, 'Gen.' Issa Sesay, although his authority was reportedly challenged by a commander based in Makeni, known as 'Strongman' Mingo, who was believed to be largely responsible for the creation of close links with dissidents from neighbouring Guinea. With RUF support, these Guinean rebels established a series of bases along the border, most of them inside Sierra Leone itself. Thus, a new conflict situation, involving the armed forces of Guinea, developed rapidly in the second half of 2000.

ADVANCES IN PACIFICATION, DISARMAMENT AND ELECTIONS

In early 2001 the RUF continued to exert its control over rather more than one-half of the country, especially the north and east, including, for a short period, the entire border region with Guinea. The rebel movement continued to demand the release of Sankoh and control of the eight ministerial posts that it had been promised under the Lomé peace agreement. However, Kabbah appointed leading members of other opposition parties to the government posts, and in February requested that Parliament defer elections, scheduled to take place later that month, for six months. There were subsequent indications that the RUF might be preparing to contest the elections. The movement appointed a new leader, Omrie Golley, who represented those in favour of reviving the peace process. In May the demobilization and disarmament process was resumed, with the formal surrender to UNAMSIL of 10,000 armaments in Freetown. At the same time hundreds of the RUF's child soldiers were transferred to the authority of UNAMSIL and humanitarian agencies. In the following weeks RUF combatants began to disarm much more rapidly than ever before and also relinquished control of the regions bordering Guinea. Disarmament commenced in July in the diamond-producing region at Kono, and UNAMSIL was soon able to deploy forces across most of Sierra Leone. A Pakistani battalion was deployed in Kono from the beginning of August, while Bangladeshi forces were stationed in Kabala and Koinadugu. The overall troop strength of UNAMSIL was reinforced to its authorized total of 17,500, including 260 military observers and 60 civilian police.

The Kabbah Government agreed in August 2001 to postpone elections for a further period, in order to allow for the prior completion of the disarmament process. Meetings of a specially convened National Consultative Forum succeeded in bringing together all sides of political opinion and in achieving compromises in some of the more difficult political issues before a resumption of more normal political processes. More than 20 political associations were represented at an important meeting of the Forum in November, where new electoral measures were discussed. It was agreed that elections would be organized on a constituency basis, rather than by proportional representation.

By the end of 2001 a total of 36,000 combatants had been disarmed, both from the RUF and the Civil Defence Forces (CDF—constituted from the Kamajors). The transfer of armaments had also commenced in the RUF strongholds of Kailahun and Tongo Field. In January 2002, as the disarmament process was being finally concluded, Golley declared the war to be ended. The now officially dissolved RUF established the Revolutionary United Front Party (RUFP), with the aim of contesting the forthcoming elections with other political associations, including the ruling SLPP, the revived APC and the newly formed Peace and Liberation Party (PLP) of Johnny Paul Koroma.

The election campaign commenced in April 2002, with Kabbah again nominated as the SLPP presidential candidate, Ernest Bai Koroma representing the APC and Pallo Bangura standing for the RUFP. The elections, which took place on 14 May, were conducted almost entirely peacefully. Kabbah was overwhelmingly re-elected as President, with 70.1% of the vote, and the SLPP won 83 seats, thereby securing a comfortable majority of the 112 elective seats in Parliament. The APC won 27 seats and the PLP two, while the RUFP failed to secure any representation in the legislature. The UN declared that the elections had proceeded successfully, but also indicated that it did not envisage an early withdrawal of its peacekeeping forces. On 20 May Kabbah was officially inaugurated for a second term in office. Solomon Berewa (hitherto Minister of Justice) became Vice-President, and a reorganized Cabinet was installed. In July a seven-member Truth and Reconciliation Commission (TRC) was established.

With a measure of peace returning to the country during 2002 and 2003, allowing a gradual reduction in the UN military presence, the Government attempted to establish the conditions for economic recovery, and to restore health and education facilities. The national disarmament process was eventually concluded in February 2004, following the demobilization of 72,490 combatants, of whom 6,845 were child soldiers. The majority of the former combatants had been given short-term allowances and some education or vocational training to assist their return to civilian life, with the total cost of the programme estimated at US $36.5m. The UNAMSIL force was reduced to 3,200 troops during 2005. Prior to the termination of its mandate at the end of that year, the UN Security Council unanimously approved the establishment of a successor operation, the UN Integrated Office for Sierra Leone (UNIOSIL) from January 2006, with an initial mandate of 12 months. UNIOSIL's primary responsibilities would be to: help the Government reinforce human rights; ensure the holding of free and fair elections in 2007; co-ordinate efforts against arms- and human-trafficking; and assist in providing security for the UN-sponsored Special Court (see below).

The TRC conducted its hearings during 2003, receiving statements from about 9,000 individuals and organizations relating to the abuses committed during the 10 years of civil conflict. Its provisional final report, published in October 2004, concluded that the origins of conflict lay in the 'bad governance, endemic corruption and the denial of basic human rights' of earlier years. The Commission blamed the leaderships of the RUF, AFRC and CDF alike for their authorization, instigation or tolerance of human rights abuses, but discovered that the RUF leaders were the worst offenders in this respect. It also noted that both Libya and Liberia had played a key role in supporting the RUF rebellion, and proposed that Libya should pay compensation. The TRC made several 'imperative' recommendations, including the abolition of the death penalty, judicial reforms and the renewal of efforts to end corruption in the mining industry and in government administration. The SLPP Government suffered a reverse during local government elections in May 2005, when, in what was widely regarded as a vote of protest against the continuing poor state of the economy and the Government's failure to address corruption, the opposition APC won majorities in the municipal councils of both Freetown and Makeni. Subsequently, the Chairman of the Electoral Commission, Eugene Davis, complained of 'political interference' and resigned. When the SLPP held its delegates' conference in September, Vice-President Solomon Berewa was elected party leader and therefore the party's presidential candidate in the 2007 election. One of his leading rivals for the position, Charles Margai, the son of Sierra Leone's second Prime Minister, Sir Albert Margai, left the party shortly afterwards and established his own association, the People's Movement for Democratic Change (PMDC), potentially weakening support for the SLPP in the south and east of the country. Margai's challenge took on an additional dimension when in February 2006 he adopted, in his professional capacity as a lawyer, the case of three RUF supporters who had been arrested in late January and accused of conspiring to overthrow the Government.

Kabbah hoped to stage a referendum on his preferred constitutional changes (including establishing an upper chamber in Parliament) to coincide with the 2007 elections. However, a combination of organizational and political factors appeared to rule out any referendum, while the elections themselves were postponed from late July until 11 August to allow time for political campaigning and for the opening of new polling booths to reduce the difficulties of voting during the rainy season. The National Electoral Commission (NEC, which had replaced the INEC in March 2000) completed the process of voter registration in May and the registration of seven political parties taking part in the elections, along with their presidential candidates, in mid-July.

THE APC RETURNS TO POWER

On 11 August 2007 the APC, led by Ernest Koroma, secured a comprehensive victory in the parliamentary election, ending more than a decade in power for the SLPP. According to the NEC, the APC secured 53% of the national vote, winning 59 seats in Parliament. The SLPP took 43% of the vote and 43 seats, and the PMDC 9% of the vote and 10 seats. However, as most of the 12 traditional chiefs who were allocated parliamentary seats were believed to be SLPP supporters, the APC did not secure an overall majority. Voter turn-out was high, at 75%, and international observers declared the voting free and fair. In the first round of the presidential election, held on the same day, Koroma secured 44.3% of the vote, ahead of Solomon Berewa of the SLPP, with 38.3%. Koroma secured the backing of the third-placed candidate, Charles Margai, for the second round against Berewa, held on 15 September, which Koroma won, with 54.6% of the vote.

In November 2007 a new Government took office, which was dominated by APC members and included several technocrats, notably David Carew as Minister of Finance and Development. Although four PMDC members were awarded cabinet posts, the SLPP was not invited to join the Government. On 15 November Koroma was sworn in as President, appointing a new head of the Anti-Corruption Commission, Abdul Tejan Cole, and replacing the Chief Justice and the heads of several civil service departments. Koroma also promised to implement the recommendations of the TRC, which included compensating victims of the war, although it remained unclear how this would be financed.

The APC further strengthened its grip on power in March 2008, with four by-election victories in the northern and eastern regions, its heartland of support. The by-elections resulted from four deputies giving up their seats in Parliament to take up cabinet posts, including the newly appointed Minister of Justice, Abdul Serry-Kamal. The APC's victories increased its representation in the legislature to 61, leaving it just short of an overall majority.

In March 2008 UNIOSIL began to scale down its operations ahead of its scheduled closure in September. UNIOSIL was to be replaced by a UN peace-building office (UNIPSIL) in October, with responsibility for co-ordinating all UN projects in the country; this was approved by UN Security Council Resolution No. 1829 in August. In May the UN Peacebuilding Fund announced a grant of US $1m. to boost youth employment in Sierra Leone, which would fund food-for-work projects run by the United Nations Development Programme (UNDP) and the World Food Programme in conjunction with the Ministry of Education, Youths and Sports.

The APC won a resounding victory in local elections held in Sierra Leone's 13 municipalities in July 2008. According to the

NEC, the APC won seven out of 13 district councils, while the SLPP won the remaining six. In the mayoral elections the APC won in six municipalities, compared with two for the SLPP and one for the PMDC. Both of the main parties fared well in their heartlands of support, the APC in the Western Area and the north of the country, and the SLPP in the Southern and Eastern regions, while the APC's overall level of support rose slightly. A total of 796,000 valid votes were cast, with the APC securing 44.8% of the vote, the SLPP 36% and the PMDC 10.2%. Although the election was widely reported to have been free and fair, over 150 legal challenges were made of alleged ballot-rigging and illicit removal of ballot boxes. Given the APC's political dominance, during the second half of 2009 the leadership of the SLPP and PMDC held exploratory talks on a merger of the two parties, with the aim of creating a political force capable of challenging the APC, although no agreement had emerged by the end of the year.

In July 2008 the Government suffered a major set-back when a Venezuelan-registered aircraft was seized after landing without authorization at Freetown's international airport, and the police discovered 600 kg of cocaine and a cache of assault rifles on board. A total of 61 people were arrested in the subsequent investigation, including Sierra Leoneans and several South Americans, although at least 13 were quickly released owing to lack of evidence. The arrest of the brother of the Minister of Transport and Aviation, Kemoh Sesay, in connection with the incident raised suspicions of government involvement. Despite protests of innocence by Sesay, he was dismissed by President Koroma, who launched a full-scale investigation into the affair. The increasing use of Sierra Leone as a hub for drugs-trafficking operations is of growing concern to the Government, and it has pledged to seek donor funding to improve airport security. In a further move to clamp down on the traffickers, in September a new National Drugs Act was adopted, which was drawn up with the assistance of the UN Office of Drug Control. The new law introduced mandatory prison sentences for manufacturers and dealers of hard drugs, rather than the previous US $1,000 fine, as well as penalties for the laundering of illicit funds.

The Government stepped up its efforts to combat official corruption in September 2008, when Parliament approved the Anti-Corruption Act. The new law significantly increased the powers of the Anti-Corruption Commission (ACC), which had proved ineffective since its creation in 2000, giving it full independence in its operations, and the authority to investigate 29 offences, including conflicts of interest, receiving or giving gifts, and the laundering of illicit funds. The ACC would have the power to pursue Sierra Leonean citizens living abroad who were suspected of corruption, as well as to investigate both the existing and previous regimes, and it was to conduct its operations in co-ordination with international anti-corruption agencies. The Government also created a commission of inquiry, which was to work alongside the ACC, to investigate misconduct by members of the previous SLPP regime. The SLPP denounced the move as a 'witch-hunt' aimed at undermining and dividing the opposition, but the Government insisted that it was essential to shed light on the malpractices of the former administration in order to improve governance and ensure continued donor support. In October 2008 the Government appointed four commissioners to undertake these investigations, but it was unclear how long they would take or whether their final report would be made public.

In February 2009 President Koroma reorganized the Cabinet in an attempt to revitalize the Government after a series of corruption scandals and rising unpopularity due to the impact of the global downturn on Sierra Leone's economy. Most notably, the former Governor of the Bank of Sierra Leone, Samura Kamara, took over the finance and development portfolio from David Carew, who was moved to head the Ministry of Trade and Industry. In the following month Koroma was re-elected as party leader at the APC convention. Also in March the SLPP elected party veteran John Benjamin as Chairman, replacing Alhaji Sulaiman Jah, who had been interim party leader since Solomon Berewa's resignation in the aftermath of the party's 2007 legislative election defeat.

In June 2009 the parliamentary Speaker appointed 10 deputies to investigate allegations made against the majority leader, Turay, and Dauda Dumbuya, of involvement in the illegal sale of public land. In August a violent demonstration revealed the political animosity that existed between the APC and the SLPP. Armed men, allegedly aligned with the APC, attacked the headquarters of the SLPP. Jacob Jusu Saffa, the SLPP Secretary-General, claimed that party offices all over the country had been attacked and that party supporters had been beaten on many occasions.

CORRUPTION AND GOVERNANCE

In December 2009 Benjamin publicly accused President Koroma of nepotism and failing to tackle corruption. Despite Koroma's campaign pledges to end corruption and revitalize the economy, critics argued that two years into his presidency little progress had been made. Poverty was widespread, infant and maternal mortality rates were the highest in the world, and the country was still situated (with Niger) at the bottom of UNDP's Human Development Index. The TRC noted that corruption, marginalization, and regional and ethnic divides were key factors that precipitated the civil war in 1991, and warned that a relapse could lead to renewed conflict. The exclusion of perceived opposition supporters from government was considered to be an obstacle to national reconciliation. With more than 50% of Sierra Leone's revenue coming from donor assistance, and with 'donor fatigue' setting in, the Government urgently needed to generate substantial funds internally, which would necessitate combating corruption and increasing government transparency and accountability in order to attract investment.

Nevertheless, there were some signs that corruption was being addressed. During 2009 27 public officials were indicted for corruption, including judges and the heads of the post office and the national broadcasting service, while the number of prosecutions increased from nine in 2008 to 29 in 2009. Transparency International's 2009 Corruption Perceptions Index showed Sierra Leone rising up the rankings, albeit only to 146th out of the 180 countries surveyed. It was suggested that Abdul Tejan Cole, the head of the ACC, had been instrumental in delivering change. In 2008 he had introduced a system whereby all public officials were obliged to declare their assets. He also persuaded Parliament to increase the ACC's powers, enabling the Commission to launch prosecutions on its own, without having to refer cases to the Attorney-General, a political appointee.

In August 2010 Sierra Leone was the fastest rising nation on the Mo Ibrahim Index, which ranks African countries according to governance quality. With the assistance of the British Department for International Development (DFID), many reforms have taken place in the police force and the military. Democratic institutions have functioned well, and the country has enjoyed relative peace. However, analysts have suggested that one of the main threats to stability in Sierra Leone is the continuous unrest in neighbouring Guinea, following the seizure of power in December 2008 by a military junta led by Capt. Moussa Dadis Camara. Sierra Leone has been urged to strengthen its borders to prevent infiltration from renegade fighters in Guinea.

INDICTMENTS AND REGIONAL CHANGES

The UN and the Government reached agreement in 2002 on the establishment of a Special Court to apply both local and international law to cases of crimes against humanity, in co-operation with the TRC. In March the Special Court issued the first indictments against seven former leaders of the combatant groups, notably Sankoh, Bockarie, Johnny Paul Koroma and Hinga Norman. However, Sankoh died in custody shortly after the indictments and Bockarie was reported to have been killed in Liberia in May 2003, while Koroma was missing and presumed dead. In June Charles Taylor was officially indicted for crimes against humanity, resulting from his involvement in the Sierra Leone conflict, and an international warrant was issued for his arrest, but he accepted an offer of asylum in Nigeria shortly afterwards. In January 2004 the Special Court judges decided to try the nine indictees already in custody in three separate groups, according to the organizations with which they were identified. The CDF group comprised

Norman, Moinina Fofana and Allieu Kondewa, the RUF group Issa Hassan Sesay, Morris Kallon and Augustine Gbao, and the AFRC group Alex Tamba Brima, Brima Bazzy Kamara and Santigie Borbor Kanu. Norman's trial did not get fully under way until January 2006; when he gave testimony to answer the charges against him, he argued that he could not be held responsible for the acts of the CDF, since he was only the organization's civilian co-ordinator, and that many people, including President Kabbah and senior foreign diplomats, had been in active support of the Kamajor combatants, who were closely allied to the CDF. The verdict in Norman's case had not been delivered when he died in February 2007, after being flown to Senegal for surgery.

Taylor was finally surrendered to the Special Court in March 2006, after the Liberian Government formally requested that the Nigerian authorities extradite him (see chapter on Liberia). In late April the Court petitioned the International Criminal Court in The Hague, Netherlands, to make its facilities available for Taylor's trial, because of security concerns in Freetown. The United Kingdom agreed to allow Taylor to serve his term in a British prison if he were convicted, and Taylor was transferred to the facilities of the International Criminal Court in The Hague in June; his trial eventually commenced on 4 June 2007. Taylor had been charged with 11 counts of war crimes and, if found guilty, would face life imprisonment. In late June the Special Court found Brima, Kamara and Kanu guilty of war crimes and crimes against humanity, and in July sentenced them to a total of 145 years in prison; their appeal against the sentences was subsequently rejected. In August Fofana and Kondewa were found guilty of war crimes; they appealed against their convictions, but these appeals were dismissed by the Special Court.

In March 2008 Taylor's former chief of operations, Joseph Marzah, testified against Taylor, implicating him in war crimes that included the murder of civilians and prisoners of war, and selling weaponry to rebels in Sierra Leone in return for diamonds. In October Taylor's son, Charles McArthur Emmanuel, was convicted by a court in the USA of ordering and committing acts of torture in Liberia in 1999–2003, when he was head of a special military unit; in January 2009 he was sentenced to 97 years in prison, but planned to appeal against his conviction. In late January the prosecution concluded its case against Charles Taylor, after calling a total of 91 witnesses to testify against him. The defence commenced its case in mid-July, and was expected to appeal for Taylor's acquittal or an adjournment that would enable him to testify in his own defence. Finally, on 30 May 2012 the Special Court sentenced Taylor to 50 years in prison, after he had been convicted of crimes including 'aiding and abetting' murder and violent sexual acts committed by the forces under his command, as well as illegally recruiting child soldiers, during the Sierra Leone conflict of 1996–2002.

The Government announced in June 2009 that it was to open an investigation into the 1992 killings of 29 people whom the military junta then in power had accused of plotting a coup. Minister of Justice Abdul Serry-Kamal argued that the victims had been killed illegally, without standing trial. Many of the junta's leaders had since assumed senior positions within the SLPP, including Julius Maada Bio, who subsequently secured his party's nomination for the 2012 presidential election (see below), and the SLPP claimed that the proposed investigation was politically motivated. No date was given for the start of the inquest and at mid-2012 no official investigation had yet been launched.

At the end of October 2009 the Special Court transferred to Rwanda eight prisoners, including both rebel and pro-Government militia fighters, who it had convicted of various serious crimes committed during the civil war. They were to serve their sentences, ranging from 15 to 22 years, in Rwanda as there was no prison in Sierra Leone that met the standards required. Those transferred included Sesay, Kallon and Gbao, the most senior surviving commanders of the RUF, whose appeals had been rejected by the Court. Brima, Kamara and Kanu, of the AFRC, and Fofana and Kondewa, former leaders of the CDF who had been sentenced in 2008, were also sent to Rwanda.

Twelve years after they were first deployed during Sierra Leone's civil war, the last UN troops withdrew from the country on 17 February 2011 (following the departure of the main UN peace-keeping contingent in 2005). However, a detachment of UN troops remained to guard the Special Court. Also in February 2011 the Assistant Minister of Foreign Affairs of the People's Republic of China assured Sierra Leone's Minister of Foreign Affairs and International Co-operation, Joseph Bandabla Dauda, of his country's continued assistance to Sierra Leone. China had been providing support to the UN Peacebuilding Commission (established in December 2005 to assist post-conflict states) through the UN Security Council.

In July 2012 Sierra Leone's Government signed a memorandum of understanding with its Kenyan counterpart for a working relationship to pursue insurgents from the militant Islamist al-Shabaab organization in Somalia. Sierra Leone subsequently deployed 850 troops to join the Kenya Defence Forces in southern Somalia as part of the African Union Mission to Somalia (AMISOM).

CIVIL UNREST IN THE RUN-UP TO THE 2012 ELECTIONS

In September 2011 there were reports of political violence in Kono District, involving two senior elders of the ruling APC party of President Koroma. Party supporters loyal to Vice-President Samuel Sam-Sumana allegedly assaulted the bodyguards of the Minister of Internal Affairs, Musa Tarawalli, when both of the politicians were attending a funeral in Kono District. The incident precipitated widespread publicity, and presented a severe challenge to the nation in its preparations for the 2012 presidential and legislative elections (which were later scheduled for 17 November). The country appeared to be far from removing the stigma of political violence, which was among the factors that continued to impede good governance and the development of the country. The spate of violence in Kono District was considered by one report to be reminiscent of past elections, when politicians hired thugs under the pretext of engaging them to carry out illicit diamond-mining. Most of these illicit miners were considered to be present for reasons of engaging in electoral fraud when elections were imminent. The Kono incident occurred amid speculation that the retirement of President Koroma as APC leader would be followed by an intensive struggle to decide his successor.

In June 2012 the opposition National Democratic Alliance (NDA) demanded that the Government immediately disarm all police officers armed with weapons, with claims that they were 'killing people indiscriminately'. The NDA raised serious concerns over the Government's purchase of weapons for the Sierra Leone police, and also questioned the professionalism of the police in responding to emergency situations. This followed a series of incidents (in Sierra Leone's second city of Bo, as well as in the towns of Bumbuna and Wellington) involving the security forces in which innocent civilians were reportedly killed, which raised questions about the ability of the police to manage the forthcoming elections. Indeed, the polls were expected to test just how far the nation had actually progressed during a decade of relative stability.

Since the end of Sierra Leone's civil war some 10 years earlier, large amounts of international aid had been invested to reform the country's security forces. For example, between 2005 and 2011 DFID had spent £27m. on a 'justice sector development programme'. In April 2012 the UN Security Council warned Sierra Leone to 'respond proportionately to threats to security', after the police purchased US $4.5m. of weaponry, including heavy machine guns and grenade launchers. Following diplomatic negotiations, the heavier weaponry was transferred to the army.

HEALTH CARE PROBLEMS

According to the UN, one woman in eight dies giving birth in Sierra Leone, making the country among the worst places in the world for antenatal and post-natal care. According to UN figures, life expectancy at birth in 2010 was just 47 years. Reasons cited for such a low life expectancy were the lack of access to basic health supplies as well as the consequences of the civil war. The average has also been substantially lowered owing to maternal deaths during or following child birth, particularly in rural areas. Sierra Leone is one of 12 countries in Africa where the reduction in child mortality has reversed. In mid-March 2010 a nation-wide, 10-day health workers' strike over pay and conditions severely impeded an already weak health care system. The strike was ended in late March after President Koroma announced a pay increase for health workers, but many of their grievances remained unresolved. In April the Government launched a free health care programme for lactating mothers, pregnant women and children under five years of age, potentially benefiting up to 230,000 pregnant women and 1m. young children annually. The Government anticipated that this would lead to a reduction in maternal and child illnesses and deaths, although there were concerns regarding the shortage of pharmaceutical drugs in the country, particularly in rural areas.

In February 2011, as part of the free health care programme, Sierra Leone's First Lady, Sia Nyama Koroma, launched the free pneumococcal vaccination campaign for children under one year of age. In June the ACC announced the commencement of an investigation into numerous complaints made regarding the blatant misuse of drugs intended for the Government's free health care policy. Doctors from Cuba, Nigeria and South Africa were recruited to assist with the implementation of the initiative, to cover an acute shortage of medical personnel. In 2010 there were just three doctors per 100,000 people; the World Health Organization recommends at least 228. As part of its £16m. commitment to health care in Sierra Leone for the period 2009–12, DFID provided £5.5m. to fund the purchase of essential drugs and supplies. In July 2012 Saudi Arabia sent a consignment of drugs towards the health care initiative. The Sierra Leone health system is heavily subsidized by international donors, which could be a concern for long-term sustainability. Capacity constraints were made evident by the Minister of Health and Sanitation, Zainab Bangura, who stated that the country needed 54 gynaecologists, but had only four. Likewise, she highlighted that there were only two paediatricians in a nation of over 5m. people.

An Amnesty International report in September 2011 suggested that Sierra Leone's free health care plan for pregnant women and young children was 'dysfunctional and hobbled by corruption and a lack of accountability'. The country has been facing huge public accountability concerns, after the UN Children's Fund (UNICEF) claimed that large amounts of drugs destined for the programme had gone missing. In some cases, medicines intended for the project were discovered in private health care facilities and pharmacies. Corruption was a particular problem at the Freetown port, where officials demanded money to clear shipments of medication or expedite processing. In June civil society organizations in Sierra Leone reported that 43 containers of drugs were at ports awaiting clearance, some of which had been there since 2010.

An additional health concern to those presented through giving birth is the incidence of tuberculosis, due to the fact that it is an airborne disease. Malaria is another serious burden upon the health service, responsible for approximately 2,000 deaths each day, mostly children, the vast majority of which are preventable. The United Kingdom provided 1m. bed nets to support the Government's aim of ensuring every household in the country had protection against malaria by November 2010. In addition, the Government waived taxes on all imported malaria drugs. During 2010 3.2m. insecticide-treated bed nets were distributed free of charge throughout the country. This resulted in a considerable decrease in the number of people suffering from malaria, with the overall mortality rate for children under five falling from 73.2% in 2009 to 47.0% in 2010, and with the number of deaths caused by malaria dropping from 32% to 16% over the same period. However, maternal health and child mortality remain the gravest threats to the population.

Economy

JOSEPH LAKE

INTRODUCTION

Sierra Leone is one of the poorest economies in the world, owing to decades of political instability, corruption and the mismanagement of its abundant natural resources. The civil war that took place between 1991 and 2002 destroyed the country's economic prospects during that period, although considerable progress has been made since then. Much of Sierra Leone's infrastructure was destroyed during the conflict, and GDP contracted at an average annual rate of 2.2% during the 1990s. However, economic growth returned in 2000, and agricultural output increased significantly following the end of the civil war. Real GDP growth averaged 11.5% per year during 2000–06, as the improved security situation allowed farmers to return to their land and resume the cultivation of crops, and mining operations were restarted.

The average annual growth rate declined to a less spectacular (yet still robust) 5.2% in 2007–11 for two principal reasons: the global economic downturn led to a large fall in the prices of Sierra Leone's main exports—diamonds, rutile and bauxite—and the post-war years of 'catch-up growth' ended. Nevertheless, according to the World Bank, life expectancy rose from just 37 years in 1995 to 47 in 2010, and the Government is currently adopting policies to seek to achieve faster growth. Sierra Leone's 'Agenda for Change', which has been supported by the World Bank, lists human development as its priority and identifies three sectors as primary growth drivers: agriculture, energy and transport infrastructure. The Government is also attempting to make the business environment more attractive to investors. Its success in this regard was reflected in the World Bank's annual 'ease of doing business' index, where Sierra Leone was ranked as one of the 12 leading reformers for 2012. Improvements in the ease of paying taxes, trading across borders and enforcing contracts moved Sierra Leone up from 150th to 141th place in the overall rankings of 183 countries.

Sierra Leone's economy was poorly developed even prior to the civil conflict of the 1990s. The lack of progress in infrastructural development, both before and after the war, has rendered large areas of the country untouched by monetization or formal trade. A majority of the population survive by subsistence agriculture and by informal trading activities, which suffered much disruption during the civil conflict. Poor implementation of economic policies meant that modernization projects often failed, even before the conflict, which destroyed much of the remaining infrastructure and caused severe disruption to the traditional economy, as well as to the mining operations that earned foreign exchange. At about the same time as the world began to draw a distinction between conflict diamonds and other diamonds, civil conflict erupted in Sierra Leone.

By the 1980s Sierra Leone suffered high inflation, an acute shortage of foreign exchange and heavy external debt, while the country's natural mineral resources remained underutilized. Official revenue from exports (particularly diamonds) was adversely affected by smuggling, which was encouraged by government policies on price controls and the exchange rate. In 1986 the Government of Maj.-Gen. Joseph Saidu Momoh (1985–92) implemented an economic reform programme, based on IMF recommendations, which included the introduction of a 'floating' exchange rate, the elimination of government subsidies on rice and petroleum, the liberalization of trade, and increases in producer prices, with the aim of encouraging self-sufficiency in rice and other foods. In 1988, however, the IMF withdrew its support for the programme, declaring Sierra Leone ineligible for assistance until arrears in repayments were received. This pattern of payment arrears and unsustainable levels of debt continued to plague Sierra Leone for the next 17 years.

Internal unrest throughout the 1990s impeded government efforts to achieve economic stability. In 1994 the regime of Capt. Valentine Strasser initiated an extensive privatization programme, involving 19 enterprises; it was announced that a certain percentage of shares would be reserved for Sierra Leone citizens, while the State would also place shares on the international market. The civil conflict, which had affected mainly the southern and eastern regions of the country, escalated in 1995, forcing the closure of the bauxite and rutile mining operations, which formed the principal sources of official export earnings. Major long-term foreign investors withdrew from the country. With the disruption of nearly all export activity, Sierra Leone became increasingly dependent on the small amounts of foreign assistance that were available from the World Bank's International Development Association and the European Union, as well as on emergency humanitarian aid.

AGRICULTURE AND FISHING

The agricultural sector, which currently employs around 59% of the population, according to FAO figures, was devastated by the civil war. The majority of refugees were able to return to return to their land by 2003, and harvests improved from 2004 onwards. While the majority of the population earn their living from the land, much of this is in the form of subsistence farming. In 2010, according to the African Development Bank (AfDB), agriculture, hunting, forestry and fishing contributed 60.1% of GDP.

Some 70 different crops are cultivated in the country. The majority of farmers are engaged in the production of food crops, including the main staple, rice, as well as cassava, sorghum and millet. Prior to the civil conflict of the 1990s, about three-quarters of farmers cultivated rice. Harvests fell significantly during the civil war, but recovered well thereafter. Rice output increased from 199,134 metric tons in 2000 to more than 1m. tons in 2006—the largest rice harvest in Sierra Leone's history. Production declined to 680,100 tons in 2008, but then rose to 784,700 tons in 2009 and to some 909,200 tons in 2010. The poor condition of commercial farming in Sierra Leone means that it remains a net importer of staple foods; for example, rice imports cost US $72m. in 2010. Cocoa and coffee (principally of the robusta variety) are the main cash crops and, together with a few other crops such as palm kernels, groundnuts and piassava (a fibre crop), are grown for export.

The fishing sector, particularly marine fisheries, was seriously affected by the civil conflict, although the sector quickly recovered. The total catch improved from 119,000 metric tons in 2002 to 227,000 tons in 2004, and has since stayed at around this level, totalling an estimated 200,000 tons in 2010, according to FAO figures. Nevertheless, overfishing by foreign vessels within Sierra Leone's coastal waters has depleted the available stocks of sardinellas and other formerly common species. In the early 2010s the country's fishermen continued to campaign to gain a viable share of its coastal waters. Most fishing is still artisanal. Sierra Leonean coastal waters harbour an abundance of fish (including tuna, mackerel and snapper) and shellfish (including shrimps, crabs and lobsters), while the estuaries of the rivers Sherbro and Kittam are significant breeding grounds for tarpon fish.

ENERGY

Large sections of Sierra Leone still have no access to the electricity grid, and even Freetown experiences extensive daily power cuts, to the detriment of industry, as well as the disruption of general economic and social activity. Many businesses and residences are, therefore, dependent on diesel generators for their electricity needs. The long-awaited Bumbuna hydroelectric power station on the Seli river in the Northern Province was finally completed in 2009, more than 30 years after construction work first started. The building of the power station was delayed because of corruption, stolen equipment and the civil war. Phase I was inaugurated in November 2009—the cost of US $200m. was met by the World Bank and other international donors—and it supplies 50 MW of power during the rainy season (supply falls as low as 20 MW during the dry season). Total electricity generating capacity in Sierra Leone is 76.5 MW. Phase II of the Bumbuna project was scheduled for completion in 2017 and would increase the country's generating capacity to 400 MW. While the Bumbuna plant was a notable political success for the Government of Ernest Bai Koroma, demand for electricity still far outstrips capacity, while poor distribution networks mean that supply remains unreliable and limited.

A number of hydrocarbon discoveries off the Sierra Leonean coast have led to speculation that the country might have petroleum reserves that could boost its energy capacity. Oil was first discovered off shore in September 2009 by a consortium led by US-listed Anadarko Petroleum; its Venus exploration well discovered more than 45 ft of hydrocarbons. This prompted further exploration, and in February 2012 it was announced that the Jupiter-1 exploration well, also owned by a consortium led by Anadarko, had encountered 98 ft of oil and gas. However, despite speculation that the reserves could be a 'bookend' to an oilfield stretching along the West African coast to Ghana, the amounts found thus far are insufficient to be commercially viable, and further discoveries will be required if offshore hydrocarbon reserves are to boost the energy sector in Sierra Leone.

MINING

Mining began in Sierra Leone in the 1930s and has since been the country's main source of export revenue and foreign exchange. The sector is of crucial importance to the economy, and an important source of revenue for the Government, although its capital-intensive nature means that it employs far fewer people than agriculture and exposes the country to fluctuations in sometimes volatile global commodity prices. The most important commodities that are mined are diamonds, bauxite, rutile, iron ore and, to a lesser extent, gold. In 2010 Sierra Leone's export earnings were worth US $342m., of which these minerals alone accounted for 57%, divided between diamonds (33%), rutile (12%), bauxite (9%) and gold (3%). Exports of iron ore resumed for the first time in 30 years in the final quarter of 2011, and were expected to become the country's largest export earner in 2012.

The diamond sector has been the most important source of export revenue for most of the past few decades and control of diamond earnings has, at times, been a matter of military importance. The majority of miners are artisanal, and the sector is a significant employer. During the civil war diamond-smuggling escalated and, in an attempt to bring the problem under control, UN sanctions were imposed, banning the export of diamonds. This embargo was lifted in 2003 when the country joined the Kimberley Process, an initiative aimed at preventing the sale of 'blood diamonds' on international markets. Nevertheless, diamond-smuggling remains widespread because of the weak monitoring capacity of the Government and the small size of diamonds, which makes them easy to smuggle—informal estimates suggest that only around one-third of diamond exports pass through official channels and that the remaining two-thirds are smuggled. The combined effects of export tariff reductions and the Kimberley Process Certification Scheme helped to boost official diamond export revenue from just US $1.5m. in 1999 to $148m. in 2008. Prices fell significantly during the global economic downturn, and diamond exports were worth $114m. in 2011. Sierra Leone has produced two of the world's 10 largest diamonds. The 968.9-carat 'Star of Sierra Leone', discovered in 1972, is the third largest rough diamond ever found. The sixth largest was the 'Woyie River Diamond', at 770 carats, an alluvial diamond discovered in 1943. A South African company, Koidu Holdings, is the largest diamond operator in the country. It operates the Koidu mine, in Kono District in eastern Sierra Leone, which is the country's most important production centre, with estimated reserves of 2.4m. carats and the capacity to produce 250,000 carats per year.

There are two main bauxite-mining areas in Sierra Leone: Gondama, south-east of Freetown, and Port Loko, north-east of the capital. Bauxite-mining began at Mokanji in 1964, but most of these operations moved a further 35 km south-east to

Gondama District in the early 1980s. Rebels overran the mines in 1995 and operations ceased for more than a decade. Sierra Mineral Holdings Limited (SMHL), then a subsidiary of Titanium Resources Group (TRG), began efforts to resume bauxite-mining in south-western Sierra Leone and to rehabilitate existing related infrastructure at Gondama and at the port of Nitti. The mines are estimated to have reserves of 31m. metric tons, with an annual export capacity of around 1.4m. tons. TRG sold SMHL to aluminium group Vimetco NV in 2008 for US $40m. Bauxite exports resumed in March 2006, and amounted to $32.7m. in 2007. However, weak demand during the global economic downturn reduced total bauxite exports to $18.7m. in 2009, before recovering to $31.0m. in 2010. The Sierra Leone Exploration and Mining Company (Slemco), a subsidiary of Singapore's Varada Resources, confirmed in mid-2010 an estimated 321m. tons of bauxite reserves near the northern town of Port Loko.

Sierra Leone has the world's largest deposit of rutile, an essential ingredient of paint pigment. Prior to the disruption resulting from the civil conflict, Sierra Leone was, after Australia, the world's second largest producer of rutile, and the reserves at the Sierra Rutile-owned mine are reported to be the largest and highest-grade natural rutile resource in the world. With the return of peace, the Government of Ahmed Tejan Kabbah announced that the resumption of production at Sierra Rutile was a priority. Exports of rutile resumed in 2006 and the sector currently employs around 1,000 workers. Rutile export earnings increased from US $29m. in 2006 to $38m. in 2007; they have since remained at around that level, reaching $40m. in 2010.

There are two main iron ore sites in Sierra Leone: Tonkolili, which has reserves estimated at 12,800m. metric tons; and Marampa, which has reserves of around 1,000m. tons. Neither site was mined for over three decades because of low global prices, until production recommenced in 2011 at Tonkolili, which is operated by the British company African Minerals. The first consignment of iron ore from the mine was exported in the final quarter of that year, and African Minerals expects annual production of around 20m. tons. Production was also restarted at Marampa by the United Kingdom's London Mining in December 2011, 35 years after the mine was originally shut down. The company forecast production of around 1.5m tons in 2012, but had plans to invest US $3,000m., with the aim of eventually increasing annual production to 16m. tons. The revival of iron ore production is transforming the country's economy and was the most important factor in making Sierra Leone the world's fastest growing economy in 2012; the IMF predicted that revenue from exports of iron ore would reach $1,200m. during the year. The buoyant sector has also raised local expectations, and a strike at Tonkolili mine in April 2012 over workers' salaries and conditions escalated into a violent protest in the course of which one person was killed and several injured.

MANUFACTURING AND TRANSPORT

The manufacturing sector was severely affected by the 1997 coup, which forced most operators to shut down; widespread looting and destruction of factories occurred during the nine-month period in government of the junta. The damage was so extensive that many companies did not reopen after peace was restored. Among the industrial activities that resumed after mid-1999 were the manufacture of plastic footwear, paint, confectionery, soap, cement and soft drinks. According to the AfDB, industry (including mining, manufacturing, construction and power) accounted for only 5.4% of GDP in 2010; the manufacturing sector contributed 1.9% of GDP in that year.

The manufacturing sector is hindered by supply-side constraints, such as poor infrastructure and a lack of skilled labour. Two large land-leasing deals have recently been agreed, which have the potential to benefit the manufacturing sector but which have also provoked protests from those who believe that they are not in the best interests of the local population. The Government signed a US $200m. agreement with Addax Bioenergy in January 2010 to lease 20,234 ha of land in northern Sierra Leone to produce biofuels. Addax's plans included the construction of an ethanol distillery, a sugar cane-crushing facility and a 32-MW biomass power plant. It aimed to produce 960,000 metric tons of sugar cane, starting in 2013, which would be used to provide 83m. litres of ethanol and 165 GWh of electricity, making it the largest sugar cane-ethanol plant in Africa. In addition, the Government signed a $112m. deal in 2011 with French company Socfin to lease 12,500 ha of land for palm oil production; this deal has also encountered local and political opposition.

Sierra Leone's longest railway, the 292-km narrow-gauge government line, closed in 1971. The prospect of iron ore production prompted the recent repair of the disused 74-km railway line from the port of Pepel to Lunsar. A further 126 km of new line is currently being constructed from Lunsar to the iron ore mine at Tonkolili.

The country had 11,300 km of classified roads in 2002, including 2,138 km of main roads and 1,950 km of secondary roads; however, only about 904 km of the network was paved. Rehabilitating the infrastructure is a priority, and key road projects include reconstruction of the Makeni–Matotaka, Kenema–Koindu and Port Loko–Lungi roads, as well as the road leading from Freetown to the Guinean capital, Conakry.

Inland waterways and coastal shipping are important features of internal transport. There are almost 800 km of established routes for launches, which include the coastal routes from Freetown northward to the areas served by the Great and Little Scarcies rivers and southward to the important seaport of Bonthe. Although some of the upper reaches of the rivers are navigable only between July and September, there is a considerable volume of river traffic. The Mano River Bridge, between Sierra Leone and Liberia, reopened in June 2007.

The services and facilities of the international airport at Lungi, north of Freetown, were improved once peace returned, with the addition of duty-free shopping. In mid-2012 British Midland International of the United Kingdom operated a service twice a week from London Heathrow to Lungi, and Belgium's Brussels Airlines operated a service twice a week from Brussels to Lungi.

EXTERNAL TRADE AND DEBT

Sierra Leone runs a structural trade and current account deficit, according to official figures. However, a large amount of economic activity in the informal sector, particularly the large-scale smuggling of diamonds, finances much of this deficit while going unrecorded. According to the IMF, official exports amounted to an estimated US $359.4m. in 2010, of which diamonds contributed 36%. Export revenue covered 53% of the cost of imports in 2010, and the trade deficit was $322.9m., equivalent to 16.9% of GDP. This was largely financed on the capital account by strong flows of foreign direct investment (FDI), which amounted to $485.9m. Gross international reserves stood at $409m. at 31 December 2010, largely unchanged from the previous year. The IMF estimated that both the trade and current account deficits widened in 2011, as capital imports for the iron ore sector increased. However, the Fund predicted that these deficits would fall in the coming years as iron ore exports, which recommenced at the end if 2011, began to have a significant impact. Indeed, the IMF forecast that export revenue would increase four-fold in 2012, owing to iron ore production.

As a result of its protracted foreign exchange crisis, Sierra Leone had a poor record of servicing its foreign debt and had little access to loans at concessional rates until 2001. In December 2006 Sierra Leone was granted debt relief under the initiative for heavily indebted poor countries (HIPC); the decision reduced Sierra Leone's total external bilateral debt from an estimated US $1,197.6m. at 31 December 2005 to $483m. at 31 December 2006. In January 2007 the 'Paris Club' of official creditors cancelled the entire remaining Sierra Leonean debt to official multilateral and bilateral creditors, and the IMF and the World Bank urged private sector creditors to follow suit. Even so, Sierra Leone's total external debt ncreased again, to $778m., by the end of 2010. However, given the rapid economic growth in the mean time, the relative debt burden remained reasonable: the debt-to-GDP ratio was 40.7% at the end of 2010, compared with 141.3% at the end of 2005. The IMF expected commercial creditors to deliver their share of debt relief under the HIPC initiative through a debt buy-back operation in 2012, which was forecast to reduce external commercial debt ($232m. at the end of 2010) by more than 90%.

PUBLIC FINANCE

The development of the state has been consistently hampered by corruption, political instability and economic mismanagement. Fiscal policy was derailed during the civil war, when public resources were redirected to the war effort while the provision of public services collapsed. Since the peace process, progress has been made in stabilizing the economy, and current economic policy is guided by the Government's Agenda for Change (2008–12), as well as the Extended Credit Facility with the IMF (2010–13). The 2012 budget, presented to Parliament by the Minister of Finance and Economic Development, Dr Samura Kamara, in November 2011, marked a decisive new chapter in the country's fiscal history. It was based on the assumption of real GDP growth of 50% (the IMF forecast real GDP growth of 36%), largely driven by the iron ore sector. While this would dramatically alter the shape of Sierra Leone's economy, the IMF did not expect it to have a large impact on public finances until 2013. In 2012 most of the companies operating in the iron ore industry were likely to benefit from tax exemptions, and the Fund did not expect their taxable income to become positive until 2013. As a result, the size of the government revenue would shrink in relation to the size of the economy in 2012, before expanding again in 2013.

In the 2012 budget, the Government forecast that, as a percentage of GDP, spending would fall to 24.2% from the 26.7% recorded the previous year, while revenue would decrease to 19.8% from 22.8% in 2011. The fiscal deficit (including grants) was budgeted to be 4.4% of GDP, which was in line with past performance. The Government recently introduced several changes to the tax code, including tax relief for tourism companies, a reduction in import duty on raw materials from 5% to 3%, and a decrease in corporation tax for mining companies from 37.5% to 30.0%. The Government subsidizes fuel prices, which local reports have claimed cost it up to US $50m. annually. This policy has become a focus of negotiations with the IMF, which wanted the Government fully to pass on the cost of higher global fuel prices to consumers. The Government, fearful that this could spark public opposition, agreed a compromise policy in 2011: any increase in imported fuel prices up to 5% compared with the price level at the end of May 2011 would be absorbed by fuel marketing companies, while any increase above 5% would be passed on to domestic consumers.

One of the major recent fiscal reforms was the implementation of a Goods and Services Tax (GST) in January 2010. At an initial rate of 15%, the GST replaced no fewer than seven different taxes. This outgoing plethora of taxes had, according to the Government, been costly for businesses to account for. In order not to place an excessive burden on the country's poorest, certain items were proclaimed exempt from the GST, including rice, piped water, fuel, books, and educational, medical and pharmaceutical services. The introduction of the GST had some disadvantages, not least the effect of increasing inflation from 10.8% in December 2009 to 17.0% in February 2010.

ECONOMIC PROSPECTS

According to the IMF, Sierra Leone was the eighth poorest country in the world in 2010, with a per caput GDP of just US $807. In that year 53.4% of all Sierra Leoneans lived on less than $1.25 a day, and 76.1% lived on less than $2 a day. The country's lengthy and frequent power cuts are not only inconvenient for Freetown residents, but are also expensive for manufacturing companies. A return to regular supplies of electricity in the capital would have a positive real effect on the economy, as well as improving the morale of the citizens who have suffered so much hardship for so many years. The fact that Phase I of the Bumbuna hydroelectric power station entered into production in November 2009 has helped significantly, but more progress is necessary. The Government has signed an agreement with a US energy company, Joule, to increase capacity at the Bumbuna plant from 50 MW to 400 MW by 2017, but this is subject to delays. The Koroma Government enjoys good relations with the IMF and other donors, who provide around one-half of the nation's budget. They will continue to support the Government to make faster progress in the strengthening of revenue collection, spending restraint, transparency in public procurement contracts and in the mining sector, and achieving more effective results from the Anti-Corruption Commission. Iron ore production will radically alter the economic landscape in the coming years. The first consignment of iron ore since the 1970s was exported in November 2011. The IMF forecast that iron ore production would increase economic growth to 36% in 2012 and have a lasting impact in subsequent years. Sierra Leone will benefit through higher FDI, export earnings and tax revenue, as well as better infrastructure. However, on the down side, higher employment expectations among the local population could also lead to protests (such as the strike at the Tonkolili mine in April 2012 which culminated in the death of one protester).

Statistical Survey

Source (unless otherwise stated): Central Statistics Office, PMB 595, Tower Hill, Freetown; tel. (22) 223287; fax (22) 223897; internet www.sierra-leone.org/cso.html and www.statistics-sierra-leone.org.

Area and Population

AREA, POPULATION AND DENSITY

Area (sq km)	71,740*
Population (census results)†	
14 December 1985	3,515,812
4 December 2004	
Males	2,420,218
Females	2,556,653
Total	4,976,871
Population (UN estimates at mid-year)‡	
2010	5,867,536
2011	5,997,487
2012	6,126,453
Density (per sq km) at mid-2012	85.4

* 27,699 sq miles.

† Excluding adjustment for underenumeration, estimated to have been 9% in 1985.

‡ Source: UN, *World Population Prospects: The 2010 Revision*.

POPULATION BY AGE AND SEX
(UN estimates at mid-2012)

	Males	Females	Total
0–14	1,295,907	1,317,459	2,613,366
15–64	1,640,493	1,755,829	3,396,322
65 and over	59,811	56,954	116,765
Total	2,996,211	3,130,242	6,126,453

Source: UN, *World Population Prospects: The 2010 Revision*.

ADMINISTRATIVE DISTRICTS
(population at 2004 census)

	Population
Bo	463,668
Bombali	408,390
Bonthe	129,947
Kailahun	358,190
Kambia	270,462
Kenema	497,948
Koinadugu	265,758
Kono	335,401
Moyamba	260,910
Port Loko	453,746
Pujehun	228,392
Sherbo	9,740
Tonkolili	347,197
Western Area Rural District	174,2489
Western Area Urban District	772,873
Total	4,976,871

PRINCIPAL TOWNS
(population at 2004 census)

Freetown (capital)	772,873*	Makeni	82,840
Bo	149,957	Koindu	80,025
Kenema	128,402		

* Western Area Urban District.

Mid-2011 (incl. suburbs, UN estimate): Freetown 940,683 (Source: UN, *World Urbanization Prospects: The 2011 Revision*).

BIRTHS AND DEATHS
(annual averages, UN estimates)

	1995–2000	2000–05	2005–10
Birth rate (per 1,000)	44.6	42.7	40.6
Death rate (per 1,000)	24.9	20.8	16.9

Source: UN, *World Population Prospects: The 2010 Revision*.

Life expectancy (years at birth): 47.4 (males 46.8; females 48.0) in 2010 (Source: World Bank, World Development Indicators database).

ECONOMICALLY ACTIVE POPULATION
(persons aged 10 years and over, 2004 census)

	Male	Female	Total
Agriculture, hunting and forestry	617,928	654,306	1,272,234
Fishing	33,317	17,822	51,139
Mining and quarrying	59,311	9,663	68,974
Manufacturing	7,397	2,015	9,412
Electricity, gas and water supply	7,104	1,243	8,347
Construction	28,239	10,829	39,068
Wholesale and retail trade; Repair of motor vehicles, motorcycles, and personal and household goods	102,212	167,283	269,495
Hotels and restaurants	2,619	2,312	4,931
Transport, communications and storage	14,425	1,257	15,682
Financial intermediation	3,993	2,941	6,934
Real estate, renting and business activities	5,475	5,310	10,785
Public administration and defence; compulsory social security	21,126	4,853	25,979
Education	23,254	11,326	34,580
Health and social work	9,852	9,976	19,828
Other community, social and personal service activities	44,423	39,063	83,486
Households with employed persons	3,983	4,306	8,289
Extra-territorial organizations and bodies	2,508	1,338	3,846
Total employed	987,166	945,843	1,933,009
Unemployed	45,936	22,316	68,252
Total labour force	1,033,102	968,159	2,001,261

Source: ILO.

Mid-2012 (estimates in '000): Agriculture, etc. 1,360; Total labour force 2,308 (Source: FAO).

Health and Welfare

KEY INDICATORS

Total fertility rate (children per woman, 2010)	5.0
Under-5 mortality rate (per 1,000 live births, 2010)	174
HIV/AIDS (% of persons aged 15–49, 2009)	1.6
Physicians (per 1,000 head, 2008)	0.02
Hospital beds (per 1,000 head, 2006)	0.4
Health expenditure (2009): US $ per head (PPP)	110
Health expenditure (2009): % of GDP	13.9
Health expenditure (2009): public (% of total)	10.5
Access to water (% of persons, 2010)	55
Access to sanitation (% of persons, 2010)	13
Total carbon dioxide emissions ('000 metric tons, 2008)	1,334.8
Carbon dioxide emissions per head (metric tons, 2008)	0.2
Human Development Index (2011): ranking	180
Human Development Index (2011): value	0.336

For sources and definitions, see explanatory note on p. vi.

Agriculture

PRINCIPAL CROPS
('000 metric tons)

	2008	2009	2010
Rice, paddy	680.1	784.7	909.2
Maize	23.5	29.6	37.8
Millet*	20	23	27
Sorghum*	23.0	26.7	31.0
Sweet potatoes*	30.3	28.8	25.5
Cassava (Manioc)*	396.6	349.6	361.3
Sugar cane*	70	70	70
Groundnuts, with shell	59.7	75.1	94.4
Oil palm fruit*	195.0	195.0	195.0
Tomatoes*	19.7	15.7	19.3
Plantains*	40.8	43.5	41.9
Citrus fruit*	100.9	111.9	108.4
Coffee, green*	20.5	18.9	13.7
Cocoa beans	10.5†	10.0†	14.0

* FAO estimates.
† Unofficial figure.

Aggregate production ('000 metric tons, may include official, semi-official or estimated data): Total cereals 750.7 in 2008, 867.5 in 2009, 1,008.4 in 2010; Total roots and tubers 429.8 in 2008, 381.0 in 2009, 388.4 in 2010; Total vegetables (incl. melons) 313.1 in 2008, 249.0 in 2009, 325.0 in 2010; Total fruits (excl. melons) 226.8 in 2008, 249.7 in 2009, 241.5 in 2010.

Source: FAO.

LIVESTOCK
('000 head, year ending September)

	2008	2009	2010
Cattle	391	470*	494
Pigs	36	43	45
Sheep	470	620	651
Goats	550	730	767
Chickens*	7,700	7,800	7,800
Ducks*	75	75	75

* FAO estimate(s).

Source: FAO.

LIVESTOCK PRODUCTS
('000 metric tons, FAO estimates)

	2008	2009	2010
Chicken meat	11.7	11.9	11.9
Pig meat	1.7	2.1	2.1
Game meat	3.2	3.4	3.6
Cows' milk	20.1	20.9	21.1
Hen eggs	9.0	9.0	9.0

Source: FAO.

Forestry

ROUNDWOOD REMOVALS

('000 cubic metres, excl. bark, FAO estimates)

	2008	2009	2010
Sawlogs, veneer logs and logs for sleepers*	3.6	3.6	3.6
Other industrial wood†	120.0	120.0	120.0
Fuel wood	5,508.8	55,43.7	5,581.6
Total	5,632.4	5,667.3	5,705.2

* Annual output assumed to be unchanged since 1993.

† Annual output assumed to be unchanged since 1980.

Source: FAO.

SAWNWOOD PRODUCTION

('000 cubic metres, incl. railway sleepers)

	1991	1992	1993
Total (all broadleaved)	9.0	9.0*	5.3

* FAO estimate.

1994–2010: Annual production as in 1993 (FAO estimates).

Source: FAO.

Fishing

('000 metric tons, live weight of capture)

	2007	2008	2009*
Freshwater fishes*	14.0	14.0	14.0
West African ilisha	3.9	7.8	7.7
Tonguefishes	1.2	1.3	1.2
Bobo croaker	8.7	12.2	12.0
Sardinellas	16.6	20.2	19.8
Bonga shad	52.7	86.0	84.4
Tuna-like fishes	2.3	2.7	2.7
Penaeusus shrimps	1.4	1.0	1.0
Marine molluscs	0.9	0.8	0.8
Total catch (incl. others)*	144.5	203.6	200.0

* FAO estimates.

2010: Catch assumed to be unchanged from 2009 (FAO estimates).

Source: FAO.

Mining

(metric tons, unless otherwise indicated)

	2008	2009	2010
Cement (hydraulic)	254,160	236,240	300,980
Bauxite ('000 metric tons)	954	757	1,090
Diamonds ('000 carats)	371	401	438
Ilmenite	17,528	15,161	18,206
Rutile	78,908	63,864	68,198

Source: US Geological Survey.

Industry

PETROLEUM PRODUCTS

('000 metric tons, estimates)

	2006	2007	2008
Jet fuels	22	22	22
Motor spirit (petrol)	33	33	33
Kerosene	11	11	12
Distillate fuel oils	60	60	60
Residual fuel oils	40	40	40

Source: UN Industrial Commodity Statistics Database.

SELECTED OTHER PRODUCTS

('000 metric tons unless otherwise indicated)

	2005	2006	2007
Beer and stout ('000 crates)	1,012	832	780
Soft drinks ('000 crates)	1,908	2,089	2,432
Confectionery ('000 kg)	2,074.3	2,329.9	3,141.0
Soap (metric tons)	417	n.a.	n.a.
Paint ('000 litres)	135	649	714
Cement*	172.1	234.4	235.8

* Source: US Geological Survey.

Cement: 254.2 in 2008; 236.2 in 2009, 301.0 in 2010 (Source: US Geological Survey).

Source: mainly IMF, *Sierra Leone: Selected Issues and Statistical Appendix* (January 2009).

Finance

CURRENCY AND EXCHANGE RATES

Monetary Units

100 cents = 1 leone (Le).

Sterling, Dollar and Euro Equivalents (31 May 2012)

£1 sterling = 6,730.04 leones;
US $1 = 4,340.84 leones;
€1 = 5,383.94 leones;
10,000 leones = £1.45 = $2.27 = €1.69.

Average Exchange Rate (leones per US $)

2009 3,385.65
2010 3,978.09
2011 4,349.16

CENTRAL GOVERNMENT BUDGET

(Le '000 million)

Revenue*	2010	2011†	2012†
Tax	916	1,315	1,497
Personal income tax	204	305	313
Goods and services tax	246	335	408
Import duties	190	283	344
Excise duties	133	68	23
Non-tax revenue	92	111	110
Total	1,008	1,426	1,607

Expenditure	2010	2011†	2012†
Current expenditure	1,286	1,564	1,810
Wages and salaries	536	650	798
Goods and services	426	351	361
Transfer and subsidies	165	326	391
Interest	159	237	260
Capital expenditure	787	995	1,001
Total	2,074	2,558	2,811

* Excluding grants received (Le '000 million):544 in 2010; 757 in 2011 (projected); 697 in 2012 (projected).

† Projected.

Source: IMF, *Sierra Leone: Second and Third Reviews Under the Three-Year Arrangement Under the Extended Credit Facility, Request for Waivers of Nonobservance of Performance Criteria, Request for Modification of Performance Criteria, and Financing Assurances Review—Staff Report; Press Release on the Executive Board Discussion; and Statement by the Executive Director for Sierra Leone.* (December 2011).

INTERNATIONAL RESERVES
(US $ million at 31 December)

	2008	2009	2010
IMF special drawing rights	30.4	189.6	184.2
Foreign exchange	189.7	215.3	224.8
Total	220.2	405.0	409.0

2011: IMF special drawing rights 178.9.

Source: IMF, *International Financial Statistics*.

MONEY SUPPLY
(Le million at 31 December)

	2009	2010	2011
Currency outside banks	420,921	557,262	641,832
Demand deposits at commercial banks	359,688	454,007	526,779
Total money (incl. others)	807,479	1,048,055	1,209,324

Source: IMF, *International Financial Statistics*.

COST OF LIVING
(Consumer Price Index; base: 2003 = 100)

	2008	2009	2010
Food (incl. beverages)	186.4	203.2	243.1
Clothing	131.7	143.7	n.a.
Rent	200.1	207.5	n.a.
All items (incl. others)	182.6	199.0	238.8

2011: Food 295.7; All items (incl. others) 277.2.

Source: ILO.

NATIONAL ACCOUNTS
(Le million at current prices)

Expenditure on the Gross Domestic Product

	2008	2009	2010*
Government final consumption expenditure	941,478	1,103,894	1,798,606
Private final consumption expenditure	4,890,660	5,891,034	6,539,564
Gross fixed capital formation	428,359	504,900	643,552
Changes in inventories	1,537,383	912,197	1,020,872
Total domestic expenditure	7,797,880	8,412,025	10,002,594
Exports of goods and services	1,082,595	1,059,017	1,645,869
Less Imports of goods and services	2,342,461	2,130,118	3,082,034
GDP in purchasers' values	6,538,014	7,340,924	8,566,429

Gross Domestic Product by Economic Activity

	2008	2009	2010*
Agriculture, hunting, forestry and fishing	3,721,762	4,306,282	4,904,307
Mining and quarrying	171,161	132,382	142,111
Manufacturing	128,082	122,316	154,206
Electricity, gas and water	16,917	19,948	24,833
Construction	95,936	85,364	119,354
Wholesale and retail trade, restaurants and hotels	583,990	584,236	680,114
Finance, insurance, real estate and business services	317,536	348,224	396,264
Transport and communications	424,827	475,009	560,867
Public administration and defence	215,951	244,668	313,897
Other services	609,696	728,319	870,323
Sub-total	6,285,858	7,046,748	8,166,276
Less Imputed bank service charges	105,210	126,328	166,329
Indirect taxes, less subsidies	357,365	420,503	566,482
GDP in purchasers' values	6,538,014	7,340,924	8,566,429

* Provisional figures.

Source: African Development Bank.

BALANCE OF PAYMENTS
(US $ million)

	2008	2009	2010
Exports of goods f.o.b.	273.5	270.4	362.9
Imports of goods f.o.b.	–471.2	–511.9	–735.9
Trade balance	–197.7	–241.5	–373.0
Exports of services	61.4	58.2	60.0
Imports of services	–125.4	–122.5	–143.6
Balance on goods and services	–261.7	–305.8	–456.6
Other income received	17.7	11.3	9.7
Other income paid	–92.4	–46.9	–58.2
Balance on goods, services and income	–336.5	–341.5	–505.2
Current transfers received	43.9	53.8	63.4
Current transfers paid	–7.4	–3.4	–41.1
Current balance	–300.0	–291.0	–482.9
Capital account (net)	61.4	68.6	22.7
Direct investment (net)	57.6	74.3	86.6
Portfolio investment assets	—	–26.0	–22.1
Portfolio investment (net)	1.6	5.6	3.0
Other investment assets	–2.8	21.7	–11.8
Other investment liabilities	39.0	236.6	45.7
Net errors and omissions	–21.6	–186.0	37.4
Overall balance	–164.8	–96.1	–321.4

Source: IMF, *International Financial Statistics*.

External Trade

PRINCIPAL COMMODITIES
(US $'000)

Imports c.i.f.	2008	2009	2010
Food and live animals	116,083.5	104,509.7	104,894.0
Beverages and tobacco	22,139.5	25,255.6	19,487.5
Crude materials (inedible) except fuels	14,345.3	16,142.2	13,267.3
Mineral fuels, lubricants, etc.	200,641.8	126,459.4	171,414.2
Animal and vegetable oils and fats	4,719.7	7,764.1	9,435.1
Chemicals	24,515.9	33,682.7	43,837.9
Basic manufactures	56,875.9	67,746.2	110,535.5
Machinery and transport equipment	75,586.7	95,085.7	248,698.2
Miscellaneous manufactured articles	19,231.3	43,659.2	18,217.6
Miscellaneous transactions and commodities	—	—	30,250.2
Total	534,139.6	520,304.8	770,037.5

Exports f.o.b.	2008	2009	2010
Bauxite	28,063.1	18,678.0	31,061.1
Coffee	1,487.6	13,123.6	1,698.2
Cocoa beans	14,982.0	20,544.6	37,051.2
Diamonds	98,803.7	78,374.0	113,514.7
Rutile	36,658.7	35,920.4	40,567.2
Total (incl. others)*	200,911.5	207,100.3	317,780.7

* Including re-exports: 14,755.6 in 2008; 23,561.9 in 2009; 23,445.7 in 2010.

2011: Total imports 1,707,944.6; Total exports (incl. re-exports 33,199.0) 349,653.7.

Source: Bank of Sierra Leone.

PRINCIPAL TRADING PARTNERS
(Le million)

Imports c.i.f.	2006	2007	2008
China, People's Repub.	115,451.1	174,865.4	233,933.1
Côte d'Ivoire	140,820.1	123,869.0	152,358.8
Germany	36,348.6	53,783.9	42,616.6
USA	116,243.5	165,403.2	176,288.8
Total (incl. others)	1,040,180.0	1,180,481.0	1,404,925.0

Exports	2006	2007	2008
Belgium	354 620.5	436,257.7	291 015.4
France	59,754.0	101,826.2	96,328.2
Germany	70,164.7	94,728.3	42,150.4
India	5,970.9	10,952.3	149,813.9
USA	129,994.1	174,698.0	168,149.9
Total (incl. others)	775,658.0	862,346.0	815,532.0

Source: African Development Bank.

Transport

ROAD TRAFFIC
(motor vehicles in use at 31 December)

	2000	2001	2002
Passenger cars	2,045	2,263	11,353
Buses and coaches	2,597	3,516	4,050
Goods vehicles	2,309	2,898	3,565
Motorcycles	1,398	1,532	1,657

2008 (motor vehicles in use at 31 December): Passenger cars 25,376; Buses and coaches 6,197; Vans and lorries 2,279; Motorcycles and mopeds 9,474.

Source: IRF, *World Road Statistics*.

SHIPPING

Merchant Fleet
(registered at 31 December)

	2007	2008	2009
Number of vessels	302	365	330
Displacement (gross registered tons)	486,843	612,448	628,490

Source: Lloyd's Register-Fairplay, *World Fleet Statistics*.

International Sea-borne Freight Traffic
(estimates, '000 metric tons)

	1991	1992	1993
Goods loaded	1,930	2,190	2,310
Goods unloaded	562	579	589

Source: UN Economic Commission for Africa, *African Statistical Yearbook*.

CIVIL AVIATION
(traffic on scheduled services)

	2007	2008	2009
Kilometres flown (million)	2	2	2
Passengers carried ('000)	20	21	22
Passenger-km (million)	108	110	107
Total ton-km (million)	19	19	18

Source: UN, *Statistical Yearbook*.

Tourism

TOURIST ARRIVALS BY REGION OF RESIDENCE

	2009	2010	2011
Africa	11,637	10,806	15,652
Americas	7,348	7,406	10,474
Asia	3,515	3,516	5,360
Europe	12,815	10,295	13,807
Middle East	948	2,667	3,485
Not specified	512	3,925	3,664
Total	36,775	38,615	52,442

Tourism receipts (US $ million, excl. passenger transport): 34 in 2008; 25 in 2009; 26 in 2010 (Source: World Tourism Organization).

Communications Media

	2008	2009	2010
Telephones ('000 main lines in use)	31.5	32.8	14.0
Mobile cellular telephones ('000 subscribers)	1,008.8	1,160.0	2,000.0
Internet users ('000)	13.9	14.9	n.a.

2011: Mobile cellular telephones ('000 subscribers) 2,137.0.

Daily newspapers: 1 (average circulation 20,000) in 1996.

Radio receivers ('000 in use): 1,120 in 1997.

Television receivers ('000 in use): 64 in 2006; 65 in 2007.

Sources: UNESCO, *Statistical Yearbook*; UN, *Statistical Yearbook*; and International Telecommunication Union.

Education

(2010/11 unless otherwise indicated)

			Number of pupils		
	Schools*	Teachers	Males	Females	Total
Pre-primary	n.a.	2,167	18,247	19,104	37,351
Primary	2,704	38,125	582,899	611,604	1,194,503
Secondary	246	10,024†	141,418†	98,161†	239,579†
Tertiary*	n.a.	1,198	6,439	2,602	9,041

* 2001/02.
† 2006/07.

Source: mainly UNESCO Institute for Statistics.

Pupil-teacher ratio (primary education, UNESCO estimate): 31.3 in 2010/11 (Source: UNESCO Institute for Statistics).

Adult literacy rate (UNESCO estimates): 42.1% (males 53.6%; females 31.4%) in 2010 (Source: UNESCO Institute for Statistics).

Directory

The Constitution

Following the transfer of power to a democratically elected civilian administration on 29 March 1996, the Constitution of 1991 (which had been suspended since April 1992) was reinstated. The Constitution provided for the establishment of a multi-party system, and vested executive power in the President, who was to be elected by the majority of votes cast nationally and by at least 25% of the votes cast in each of the four provinces. The maximum duration of the President's tenure of office was limited to two five-year terms. The President was to appoint the Cabinet, subject to approval by the Parliament. The Parliament was elected for a five-year term and comprised 124 members, 112 of whom were elected by a system of proportional representation, in 14 constituencies, while 12 Paramount Chiefs also represented the provincial districts in the legislature. Members of the Parliament were not permitted concurrently to hold office in the Cabinet.

The Government

HEAD OF STATE

President and Commander-in-Chief of the Armed Forces: ERNEST BAI KOROMA (elected 8 September 2007; inaugurated 15 November 2007).

Vice-President: SAHR SAM-SUMANA.

CABINET

(September 2012)

The Government is formed by members of the All-People's Congress.

Minister of Finance and Economic Development: Dr SAMURA KAMARA.

Minister of Foreign Affairs and International Co-operation: JOSEPH BANDABLA DAUDA.

Minister of Justice and Attorney-General: FRANKLYN BAI KARBGO.

Minister of Information and Communications: Alhaji IBRAHIM BEN KARGBO.

Minister of Health and Sanitation: (vacant).

Minister of Agriculture, Food Security and Forestry: Dr SAM SESAY.

Minister of Works, Housing and Infrastructure: ALIMAMY P. KOROMA.

Minister of Education, Science and Technology: Dr MINKAILU BAH.

Minister of Political and Public Affairs: Alhaji ALPHA SAHID BAKAR KANU.

Minister of Lands, Country Planning and the Environment: Capt. ALLIEU PAT SOWE.

Minister of Defence: Maj. (retd) ALFRED PALO CONTEH.

Minister of Local Government and Rural Development: DAUDA SULAIMAN KAMARA.

Minister of Internal Affairs: MUSA TARAWALLI.

Minister of Marine Resources and Fisheries: Dr SOCCOH KABIA.

Minister of Energy and Water Resources: OLUNIYI ROBBIN-COKE.

Minister of Tourism and Cultural Affairs: VICTORIA SAIDU KAMARA.

Minister of Youth Employment and Sports: PAUL KAMARA.

Minister of Mineral Resources: Alhaji MINKAILU MANSARAY.

Minister of Labour and Social Security: (vacant).

Minister of Trade and Industry: Dr RICHARD CONTEH.

Minister of Transport and Aviation: VANDI CHIDI MINAH.

Minister of Social Welfare, Gender and Children's Affairs: STEPHEN GAOJIA.

Minister of State, Office of the Vice-President: Dr KOMBA KONO.

Special Adviser to the President: KEMOH SESAY.

Resident Minister, Eastern Region: WILLIAM JUANA SMITH.

Resident Minister, Southern Region: MOIJUE KAIKAI.

Resident Minister, Northern Region: ALIE KAMARA.

There were also 24 Deputy Ministers.

MINISTRIES

Office of the President: Freetown; tel. (22) 232101; fax (22) 231404; e-mail info@statehouse-sl.org; internet www.statehouse.gov.sl.

Ministry of Agriculture, Food Security and Forestry: Youyi Bldg, 3rd Floor, Brookfields, Freetown; tel. (22) 222242; fax (22) 241613.

Ministry of Defence: State Ave, Freetown; tel. (22) 227369; fax (22) 229380.

Ministry of Education, Science and Technology: New England, Freetown; tel. (22) 240881; fax (22) 240137.

Ministry of Energy and Water Resources: Electricity House, 4th Floor, Siaka Stevens St, Freetown; tel. (22) 226566; fax (22) 228199; e-mail info@energyandpower.gov.sl; internet www.energyandpower.gov.sl.

Ministry of Foreign Affairs and International Co-operation: Gloucester St, Freetown; tel. (22) 223260; fax (22) 225615; e-mail mfaicsl@yahoo.com.

Ministry of Health and Sanitation: Youyi Bldg, 4th Floor, Brookfields, Freetown; tel. (22) 240187; e-mail info@health.sl; internet www.health.sl.

Ministry of Information and Communications: Youyi Bldg, 8th Floor, Brookfields, Freetown; tel. (22) 240339; fax (22) 241757.

Ministry of Internal Affairs: Liverpool St, Freetown; tel. (22) 226979; fax (22) 227727.

Ministry of Justice: Guma Bldg, Lamina Sankoh St, Freetown; tel. (22) 227444; fax (22) 229366.

Ministry of Labour and Social Security: New England Ville, Freetown; tel. (22) 78341246; fax (22) 228472.

Ministry of Lands, Country Planning and the Environment: Youyi Bldg, 4th Floor, Brookfields, Freetown; tel. (22) 242013.

Ministry of Local Government and Rural Development: New England, Freetown; tel. (22) 226589; fax (22) 222409.

Ministry of Marine Resources and Fisheries: Marine House, 11 Old Railway Line, Brookfields, Freetown; tel. (22) 242117.

Ministry of Mineral Resources: Youyi Bldg, 5th Floor, Brookfields, Freetown; tel. and fax (22) 240467; e-mail contact@mmr-sl.org; internet www.mmr-sl.org.

Ministry of Political and Public Affairs: State House, State Ave, Freetown; tel. (22) 228698; fax (22) 222781.

Ministry of Social Welfare, Gender and Children's Affairs: New England, Freetown; tel. (22) 241256; fax (22) 242076.

Ministry of Tourism and Cultural Affairs: Ministerial Bldg, George St, Freetown; tel. (22) 222588.

Ministry of Trade and Industry: 6th Floor, Youyi Bldg, Brookfields, Freetown; tel. (22) 225127; e-mail info@trade.gov.sl; internet www.trade.gov.sl.

Ministry of Transport and Aviation: Ministerial Bldg, George St, Freetown; tel. (22) 221245; fax (22) 227337.

Ministry of Works, Housing and Infrastructure: New England, Freetown; tel. (22) 240937; fax (22) 240018.

Ministry of Youth Employment and Sports: New England, Freetown; tel. (22) 240881; fax (22) 240137.

President and Legislature

PRESIDENT

Presidential Election, First Round, 11 August 2007

Candidate	Votes	% of votes
Ernest Bai Koroma (APC)	815,523	44.34
Solomon Berewa (SLPP)	704,012	38.28
Charles Margai (PMDC)	255,499	13.89
Others	64,174	3.48
Total	1,839,208	100.00

Presidential Election, Second Round, 8 September 2007

Candidate	Votes	% of votes
Ernest Bai Koroma (APC)	859,144	60.22
Solomon Berewa (SLPP)	567,449	39.78
Total	1,426,593	100.00

PARLIAMENT

Speaker: Justice E. K. COWAN.

General Election, 11 August 2007

Party	Seats
All-People's Congress (APC)	59
Sierra Leone People's Party (SLPP)	43
People's Movement for Democratic Change (PMDC)	10
Total	112*

* A further 12 seats were allocated to Paramount Chiefs, who represented the 12 provincial districts.

Election Commission

National Electoral Commission (NEC): NEC Bldg, 15 Industrial Estate, Wellington, Freetown; tel. 76547299 (mobile); internet www.nec-sierraleone.org; f. 2000; Chair. CHRISTIANA AYOKA MARY THORPE.

Political Organizations

A ban on political activity was rescinded in June 1995. Numerous political parties were officially granted registration prior to elections in May 2002.

All-People's Congress (APC): 137H Fourah Bay Rd, Freetown; e-mail info@new-apc.org; internet apcparty.org; f. 1960; sole authorized political party 1978–91; merged with the Democratic People's Party in 1992; reconstituted in 1995; Leader ERNEST BAI KOROMA.

Citizens United for Peace and Progress (CUPP): e-mail info@cupp.org; internet www.cupp.org; f. 2002; Chair. ABUBAKARR YANSSANEH.

Peace and Liberation Party (PLP): Freetown; f. 2002; Nat. Chair. Rev. DARLINGTON MORRISON; Interim Leader SYL JUXON SMITH.

People's Democratic Party (PDP): Freetown; supported Sierra Leone People's Party in May 2002 elections; Leader OSMAN KAMARA.

People's Movement for Democratic Change (PMDC): 9A Hannah Benka-Coker St, Freetown; e-mail karamohslylhorg@aol.com; internet www.pmdcsl.net; f. April 2006 by fmr mems of Sierra Leone People's Party; Leader CHARLES F. MARGAI; Sec.-Gen. ANSU B. LANSANA.

Sierra Leone People's Party (SLPP): 15 Wallace Johnson St, Freetown; tel. and fax (22) 2256341; e-mail info@slpp.ws; internet www.slpp.ws; f. 1951; Nat. Chair. JOHN BENJAMIN.

United National People's Party (UNPP): Leader Dr JOHN KAREFA-SMART.

Young People's Party (YPP): 19 Lewis St, Freetown; tel. (22) 232907; e-mail info@yppsl.org; internet www.yppsl.org; f. 2002; Leader SYLVIA BLYDEN; Sec.-Gen. ABDUL RAHMAN YILLA.

Diplomatic Representation

EMBASSIES AND HIGH COMMISSIONS IN SIERRA LEONE

China, People's Republic: 29 Wilberforce Loop, POB 778, Freetown; tel. and fax (22) 231797; e-mail chinaemb_sl@mfa.gov.cn; internet sl.china-embassy.org; Ambassador KUANG WEILIN.

Egypt: 174C Wilkinson Rd, POB 652, Freetown; tel. (22) 231245; fax (22) 234297; Ambassador GAMAL TAWFIK ABDULLAH.

The Gambia: 6 Wilberforce St, Freetown; tel. (22) 225191; fax (22) 226846; High Commissioner DEMBO BADJIE.

Ghana: 13 Walpole St, Freetown; tel. (22) 223461; fax (22) 227043; High Commissioner ELIZABETH MILLS-ROBERTSON.

Guinea: 6 Wilkinson Rd, Freetown; tel. (22) 232584; fax (22) 232496; Ambassador MOHAMED LAMIN SOMPARE.

Lebanon: 22A Spur Rd, Wilberforce, Freetown; tel. (22) 222513; fax (22) 234665; Ambassador GHASSAN ABDEL SATER.

Liberia: 10 Motor Rd, Brookfields, POB 276, Freetown; tel. (22) 230991; Ambassador THOMAS N. BRIMA.

Libya: 1A and 1B P. Z. Compound, Wilberforce, Freetown; tel. (22) 235231; fax (22) 234514; Chargé d'affaires a.i. Dr AHMED ABUDABBOUS.

Nigeria: 37 Siaka Stevens St, Freetown; tel. (22) 224224; fax (22) 2242474; High Commissioner EYO ASUQUO.

United Kingdom: 6 Spur Rd, Wilberforce, Freetown; tel. (22) 232565; fax (22) 232070; e-mail freetown.consular.enquiries@fco.gov.uk; internet ukinsierraleone.fco.gov.uk; High Commissioner IAN HUGHES.

USA: South Ridge, Hill Station, Freetown; tel. (22) 515000; fax (22) 515355; e-mail TaylorJB2@state.gov; internet freetown.usembassy.gov; Ambassador MICHAEL S. OWEN.

Judicial System

The Supreme Court

The Supreme Court is the ultimate court of appeal in both civil and criminal cases. In addition to its appellate jurisdiction, the Court has supervisory jurisdiction over all other courts and over any adjudicating authority in Sierra Leone, and also original jurisdiction in constitutional issues.

Chief Justice: UMU HAWA TEJAN JALLOH.

Supreme Court Justices: SHAHINEH BASH-TAQI, SALAMATU KOROMA, PATRICK HAMILTON.

The Court of Appeal

The Court of Appeal has jurisdiction to hear and determine appeals from decisions of the High Court in both criminal and civil matters, and also from certain statutory tribunals. Appeals against its decisions may be made to the Supreme Court.

Justices of Appeal: S. C. E. WARNE, C. S. DAVIES, S. T. NAVO, M. S. TURAY, E. C. THOMPSON-DAVIS, M. O. TAJU-DEEN, M. O. ADOPHY, GEORGE GELAGA KING, Dr A. B. Y. TIMBO, VIRGINIA A. WRIGHT.

High Court

The High Court has unlimited original jurisdiction in all criminal and civil matters. It also has appellate jurisdiction against decisions of Magistrates' Courts.

Judges: FRANCIS C. GBOW, EBUN THOMAS, D. E. M. WILLIAMS, LAURA MARCUS-JONES, L. B. O. NYLANDER, A. M. B. TARAWALLIE, O. H. ALGHALI, W. A. O. JOHNSON, N. D. ALHADI, R. J. BANKOLE THOMPSON, M. E. T. THOMPSON, C. J. W. ATERE-ROBERTS (acting).

Magistrates' Courts: In criminal cases the jurisdiction of the Magistrates' Courts is limited to summary cases and to preliminary investigations to determine whether a person charged with an offence should be committed for trial.

Local Courts have jurisdiction, according to native law and custom, in matters that are outside the jurisdiction of other courts.

Religion

A large proportion of the population holds animist beliefs, although there are significant numbers of Islamic and Christian adherents.

ISLAM

In 1990 Islamic adherents represented an estimated 30% of the total population.

Ahmadiyya Muslim Mission: 15 Bath St, Brookfields, POB 353, Freetown; Emir and Chief Missionary SAID UR-RAHMAN.

Kankaylay (Sierra Leone Muslim Men and Women's Association): 15 Blackhall Rd, Kissy, POB 1168, Freetown; tel. 33635205; fax (22) 224439; e-mail kankaylay@yahoo.com; internet www.kankaylay.com; f. 1972; 500,000 mems; Pres. Alhaji IBRAHIM ALPHA TURAY; Lady Pres. Haja MARIAM TURAY.

Sierra Leone Muslim Congress: POB 875, Freetown; f. 1928; Pres. Alhaji MUHAMMAD SANUSI MUSTAPHA.

CHRISTIANITY

Council of Churches in Sierra Leone: 4A King Harman Rd, Brookfields, POB 404, Freetown; tel. (22) 240569; fax (22) 421109; f. 1924; 17 mem. churches; Pres. Rev. MOSES B. KHANU; Gen. Sec. ALIMAMY P. KOROMA.

The Anglican Communion

Anglicans in Sierra Leone are adherents of the Church of the Province of West Africa, comprising 12 dioceses, of which two are in Sierra Leone. The Archbishop of the Province is the Bishop of Koforidua, Ghana.

Bishop of Bo: Rt Rev. SAMUEL SAO GBONDA, MacRobert St, POB 21, Bo, Southern Province; e-mail bishop@sierratel.sl.

Bishop of Freetown: Rt Rev. JULIUS O. PRINCE LYNCH, Bishopscourt, Fourah Bay Rd, POB 537, Freetown; tel. (22) 251307; fax (22) 251306; e-mail bishop@sierratel.sl.

Baptist Churches

Sierra Leone Baptist Convention: POB 64, Lunsar; 119 mem. churches; 994 mems; Pres. Rev. JOSEPH S. MANS; Sec. Rev. N. T. DIXON.

The Nigerian Baptist Convention is also active.

Methodist Churches

Methodist Church Sierra Leone: Wesley House, George St, POB 64, Freetown; tel. (22) 222216; fax (22) 227539; e-mail mcsl@ymail.com; autonomous since 1967; Pres. of Conf. Rt Rev. ARNOLD C. TEMPLE; Sec. Rev. MUSA J. JAMBAWAI; 26,421 mems.

United Methodist Church: Freetown; tel. 76444100 (mobile); e-mail sierraleoneannualconference@yahoo.com; f. 1880; Presiding Bishop JOHN K. YAMBASU; 225,000 mems.

Other active Methodist bodies include the African Methodist Episcopal Church, the Wesleyan Church of Sierra Leone, the Countess of Huntingdon's Connexion and the West African Methodist Church.

The Roman Catholic Church

Sierra Leone comprises one archdiocese and three dioceses. An estimated 5% of the total population are Roman Catholics.

Inter-territorial Catholic Bishops' Conference of The Gambia and Sierra Leone

Santanno House, POB 893, Freetown; tel. (22) 228240; fax (22) 228252.

f. 1971; Pres. Rt Rev. GEORGE BIGUZZI (Bishop of Makeni).

Archbishop of Freetown: Most Rev. EDWARD TAMBA CHARLES, Santanno House, 10 Howe St, POB 893, Freetown; tel. (22) 224590; fax (22) 224075; e-mail jhg3271@sierratel.sl.

Other Christian Churches

The following are represented: the Christ Apostolic Church, the Church of the Lord (Aladura), the Evangelical Church, the Evangelical Lutheran Church in Sierra Leone, the Missionary Church of Africa, the Sierra Leone Church and the United Brethren in Christ.

AFRICAN RELIGIONS

There is a diverse range of beliefs, rites and practices, varying between ethnic and kinship groups.

The Press

DAILIES

For di People: Freetown; independent; Editor PAUL KAMARA.

The Sierra Leone Daily Mail: 29–31 Rawdon St, POB 53, Freetown; tel. (22) 223191; internet www.sierraleonedailymail.com; f. 1931; state-owned; currently online only; Editor-in-Chief CHRISTIAN F SESAY, Jr; circ. 10,000.

PERIODICALS

The Catalyst: Christian Literature Crusade Bookshop, 92 Circular Rd, POB 1465, Freetown; tel. (22) 224382; Editor JUSU-WAI SAWI.

Concord Times: 51 Krootown Rd, Freetown; tel. (22) 229199; e-mail info@concordtimessl.com; internet www.concordtimessl.com; 3 a week; Editor DOROTHY GORDON.

Leonean Sun: 49 Main Rd, Wellington, Freetown; tel. (22) 223363; f. 1974; monthly; Editor ROWLAND MARTYN.

Liberty Voice: 139 Pademba Rd, Freetown; tel. (22) 242100; Editor A. MAHDIEU SAVAGE.

The New Citizen: 7 Wellington St, Freetown; tel. (22) 228693; e-mail info@thenewcitizen-sl.com; internet www.thenewcitizen-sl.com; f. 1982; Man. Editor SAMUEL B. CONTEH.

The New Globe: 49 Bathurst St, Freetown; tel. (22) 228245; weekly; Man. Editor SAM TUMOE; circ. 4,000.

The New Shaft: 60 Old Railway Line, Brookfields, Freetown; tel. (22) 241093; 2 a week; independent; Editor FRANKLIN BUNTING-DAVIES; circ. 10,000.

The Pool Newspaper: 1 Short St, 5th Floor, Freetown; tel. and fax (22) 220102; e-mail pool@justice.com; f. 1992; 3 a week; independent; Man. Dir CHERNOR OJUKU SESAY; circ. 3,000.

Progress: 1 Short St, Freetown; tel. (22) 223588; weekly; independent; Editor FODE KANDEH; circ. 7,000.

Sierra Leone Chamber of Commerce Journal: Sierra Leone Chamber of Commerce, Industry and Agriculture, Guma Bldg, 5th Floor, Lamina Sankoh St, POB 502, Freetown; tel. (22) 226305; fax (22) 228005; monthly.

Unity Now: 82 Pademba Rd, Freetown; tel. (22) 227466; Editor FRANK KPOSOWA.

The Vision: 60 Old Railway Line, Brookfields; tel. (22) 241273; Editor SIAKA MASSAQUOI.

Weekend Spark: 7 Lamina Sankoh St, Freetown; tel. (22) 223397; f. 1983; weekly; independent; Editor ROWLAND MARTYN; circ. 20,000.

NEWS AGENCY

Sierra Leone News Agency (SLENA): 15 Wallace Johnson St, PMB 445, Freetown; tel. (22) 224921; fax (22) 224439; f. 1980; Man. Dir AUGUSTUS KAMARA.

Publishers

Njala University Publishing Centre: Njala University College, PMB, Freetown; science and technology, university textbooks.

Sierra Leone University Press: Fourah Bay College, POB 87, Freetown; tel. (22) 22491; fax (22) 224439; f. 1965; biography, history, Africana, religion, social science, university textbooks; Chair. Prof. ERNEST H. WRIGHT.

United Christian Council Literature Bureau: Bunumbu Press, POB 28, Bo; tel. (32) 462; books in Mende, Temne, Susu; Man. Dir ROBERT SAM-KPAKRA.

Broadcasting and Communications

TELECOMMUNICATIONS

In early 2012 there were three GSM mobile cellular telephone operators in Sierra Leone, while state-owned SIERRATEL was the sole fixed-line operator. SIERRATEL also provided mobile telephone services using CDMA (code division multiple access) technology.

Regulatory Authority

National Telecommunications Commission (NATCOM): Freetown; tel. 76604359 (mobile); fax 22235981; e-mail its@natcomsl.com; internet www.natcomsl.com; f. 2006; manages radio spectrum; Chair. and Commissioner SIRAY A. TIMBO.

SERVICE PROVIDERS

Africell: 1 Pivot St, Wilberforce, Freetown; tel. 77777777 (mobile); e-mail info@africell.sl; internet www.africell.sl; f. 2005; CEO SHADI EI-GERJAWI; 1,500,000 subscribers (Aug. 2012).

Airtel Sierra Leone: Zain House, 42 Main Motor Rd, Wilberforce, Freetown; tel. (22) 233222; e-mail info.africa@airtel.com; internet africa.airtel.com/sierra; f. 2000; fmrly Zain Sierra Leone, present name adopted in 2010; Man. Dir RAJVARDHAN SINGH BHULLAR.

Comium (SL) Ltd: Comium Bldg, 30D Wilkinson Rd, Freetown; tel. 33333030 (mobile); fax 33333060 (mobile); e-mail info@comium.com.sl; internet www.comium.com.sl; f. 2005; mobile cellular telephone and broadband internet provider; CEO MIKE CAROLL.

Sierra Leone Telecommunications Co (SIERRATEL): 7 Wallace Johnson St, POB 80, Freetown; tel. (22) 222801; fax (22) 224439; internet www.sierratel.sl; state-owned telecommunications operator; Chair. Dr TOM OBALEH KARGBO; Man. Dir ALPHA SESAY.

BROADCASTING

Sierra Leone Broadcasting Corpn (SBC): New England, Freetown; tel. (22) 240403; f. 1934; name changed as above in 2010 following merger of Sierra Leone Broadcasting Service and UN Radio in Sierra Leone; state-controlled; programmes mainly in English and the four main Sierra Leonean vernaculars: Mende, Limba, Temne and Krio; weekly broadcast in French; television service established 1963; Dir-Gen. ELVIS GBANABOM HALLOWELL.

Finance

(cap. = capital; res = reserves; dep. = deposits; m. = million; br(s). = branch(es); amounts in leones)

BANKING

In 2010 there were 12 commercial banks and six community banks in Sierra Leone.

Central Bank

Bank of Sierra Leone: Siaka Stevens St, POB 30, Freetown; tel. (22) 226501; fax (22) 224764; e-mail info@bankofsierraleone.com; internet www.bsl.gov.sl; f. 1964; cap. 50,000.0m., res –352,030.6m., dep. 419,113.6m. (Dec. 2009); Gov. Dr SHEKU S. SESAY; Dep. Gov. ANDRINA ROSA COKER; 1 br.

Other Banks

Access Bank Sierra Leone Ltd: 30 Siaka Stevens St, Freetown; e-mail info@accessbanksierraleone.com; f. 2007.

Ecobank Sierra Leone Ltd: 7 Lightfoot Boston St, POB 1007, Freetown; tel. (22) 221704; fax (22) 229450; e-mail info@ecobanksl.com; internet www.ecobank.com; Chair. KEILI ANDREW KARMOH; Man. Dir CLEMENT DODOO.

First International Bank (SL) Ltd: 2 Charlotte St, Freetown; tel. (22) 220038; fax (22) 221970; e-mail fib@sierratel.sl; internet fibsl.biz; f. 1998; Chair. CHRISTIAN J. SMITH; Man. Dir CHRIS UCHENDU.

Guaranty Trust Bank: Sparta Bldg, 12 Wilberforce St, POB 1168, Freetown; tel. (22) 228493; fax (22) 228318; internet www.gtb.sl; f. Feb. 2002 through the acquisition of 90% of shareholding of First Merchant Bank of Sierra Leone by Guaranty Trust Bank of Nigeria; cap. 2,261.0m., total assets 17,769.0m. (Dec. 2003); Chair. JIDE OGUNDARE; Man. Dir ADE BURAIMO; 3 brs.

International Commercial Bank (Sierra Leone) Ltd: 22 Rawdon St, POB 515, Freetown; tel. (22) 222877; fax (22) 220376; e-mail enquiry@icbank-sl.com; internet www.icbank-sl.com; f. 2004; 1 br.

National Development Bank Ltd: Leone House, 6th Floor, 21–23 Siaka Stevens St, Freetown; tel. (22) 226792; fax (22) 224468; f. 1968; 99% state-owned; provides medium- and long-term finance and tech. assistance to devt-orientated enterprises; cap. 1,604.3m., total assets 2,200m. (Dec. 2003); Chair. MURRAY E. S. LAMIN; Man. Dir MOHAMED M. TURAY; 3 brs.

Rokel Commercial Bank (Sierra Leone) Ltd: 25–27 Siaka Stevens St, POB 12, Freetown; tel. (22) 222501; fax (22) 222563; e-mail rokelsl@sierratel.sl; internet www.rokelsl.com; f. 1971; cap. 15,116.5m., res 29,772.8m., dep. 312,619.4m. (Dec. 2009); 51% govt-owned; Chair. BIRCH M. CONTE; Man. Dir HENRY AKINTOTA MACAULEY; 11 brs.

Sierra Leone Commercial Bank Ltd: Christian Smith Bldg, 29–31 Siaka Stevens St, Freetown; tel. (22) 225264; fax (22) 225292;

e-mail slcb@slcb.biz; internet www.slcb.biz; f. 1973; state-owned; cap. 12,000.0m., res 22,891.9m., dep. 274,726.8m. (Dec. 2008); Chair. SHEIKI G. BANGURA; Man. Dir CHRISPIN BISHOP DEIGH; 8 brs.

Skye Bank Sierra Leone Ltd: 31 Siaka Stevens St, Freetown; tel. (22) 220095; fax (22) 221773; internet www.skyebanksl.com; Chair. PATRICK COKER; Man. Dir OLUMIDE OLATUNJI.

Standard Chartered Bank Sierra Leone Ltd: 9–11 Lightfoot-Boston St, POB 1155, Freetown; tel. (22) 225021; fax (22) 225760; e-mail scbsl@sierratel.sl; internet www.standardchartered.com/sl; f. 1894; cap. 15,255.7m., res 18,399.8m., dep. 221,661.7m. (Dec. 2009); Chair. ALEX B. KAMARA; CEO and Man. Dir ALBERTO R. SALTSON; 3 brs.

Union Trust Bank Ltd: Lightfoot-Boston St, PMB 1237, Freetown; tel. (22) 226954; fax (22) 226214; e-mail info@utb.sl; internet www.utb.sl; fmrly Meridien BIAO Bank Sierra Leone Ltd; adopted present name in 1995; cap. 7,477.9m., res 8,275.1m., total assets 60,720.1m. (Dec. 2007); Chair. Alhaji Dr SHEKU TEJAN KAMARA; Man. Dir and CEO JAMES SANPHA KOROMA; 7 brs.

United Bank For Africa Sierra Leone Ltd: 15 Charlotte St, Freetown; tel. (22) 228099; fax (22) 225395; e-mail cicsl@ubagroup.com; internet www.ubagroup.com; f. 2008; 4 brs.

Zenith Bank Sierra Leone Ltd: 18–20 Rawdon St, Freetown; tel. (22) 225400; fax (22) 225070; e-mail enquiry@zenithbank.com.sl; f. 2007; Chair. EDDY MARTINS EGWUENU; Man. Dir ADEWALE ADENIYI.

INSURANCE

In 2010 there were nine insurance companies in Sierra Leone.

Aureol Insurance Co Ltd: Kissy House, 54 Siaka Stevens St, POB 647, Freetown; tel. (22) 223435; fax (22) 229336; e-mail info@aureolinsurance.com; internet aureolinsurance.com; f. 1986; Chair. Dr PATRICK E. COKER; Man. Dir SOLOMON J. SAMBA.

National Insurance Co Ltd: 18–20 Walpole St, PMB 84, Freetown; tel. (22) 222535; fax (22) 226097; e-mail nic@sierratel.sl; f. 1972; state-owned; Chair. P. J. KUYEMBEH; CEO ARTHUR NATHANIEL YASKEY.

New India Assurance Co Ltd: 18 Wilberforce St, POB 340, Freetown; tel. (22) 226453; fax (22) 222494; e-mail niasl@sierratel.sl; Man. Dir A. CHOPRA.

Reliance Insurance Trust Corpn Ltd: 24 Siaka Stevens St, Freetown; tel. (22) 225115; fax (22) 228051; e-mail oonomake@yahoo.com; f. 1985; Chair. MOHAMED B. COLE; Man. Dir ALICE M. ONOMAKE.

Sierra Leone Insurance Co Ltd: 3 Howe St, POB 836, Freetown; tel. (22) 224920; fax (22) 222115; e-mail office@slico.com.sl; internet www.slico.com.sl; f. 1983; Man. Dir and CEO ALI-DAUSY MASSALLY.

Trade and Industry

GOVERNMENT AGENCIES

Government Gold and Diamond Office (GGDO): c/o Bank of Sierra Leone, Siaka Stevens St, Freetown; tel. (22) 222600; fax (22) 229064; f. 1985; govt regulatory agency for diamonds and gold; combats illicit trade; Chair. Alhaji M. S. DEEN.

National Commission for Privatisation: Lotto House, OAU Dr., Tower Hill, POB 56, Freetown; tel. (22) 227759; fax (22) 227935; e-mail info@ncp.gov.sl; internet ncp.gov.sl; f. 2001; Chair. ABU BANGURA.

CHAMBER OF COMMERCE

Sierra Leone Chamber of Commerce, Industry and Agriculture (SLCCIA): Guma Bldg, 5th Floor, Lamina Sankoh St, POB 502, Freetown; tel. 76483017 (mobile); e-mail info@chamberofcommerce.sl; internet www.chamberofcommerce.sl; f. 1961; 300 mems; Pres. GLADYS STRASSER-KING.

TRADE AND INDUSTRIAL ASSOCIATIONS

Sierra Leone Investment and Export Promotion Agency (SLIEPA): Standard Chartered Bank Bldg, 3rd Floor, Lightfoot-Boston St, Freetown; tel. (22) 220788; e-mail info@sliepa.org; internet www.sliepa.org; f. 2007; fmrly Sierra Leone Export Development and Investment Corporation; Man. Dir CHRIS JASABE.

Small-Medium Scale Businesses Association (Sierra Leone): O.A.U. Dr., Tower Hill, PMB 575, Freetown; tel. (22) 222617; fax (22) 224439; Dir ABU CONTEH.

EMPLOYERS' ORGANIZATIONS

Sierra Leone Chamber of Mines: POB 456, Freetown; tel. (22) 226082; f. 1965; mems comprise the principal mining concerns; Pres. JOHN SISAY; Exec. Officer N. H. T. BOSTON.

Sierra Leone Employers' Federation: POB 562, Freetown; Chair. AMADU B. NDOEKA; Exec. Officer L. E. JOHNSON.

UTILITIES

Electricity

National Power Authority: Electricity House, 36 Siaka Stevens St, Freetown; tel. (22) 229868; fax (22) 227584; e-mail Sierra_Leone@iaeste.org; supplies all electricity in Sierra Leone.

Water

Guma Valley Water Co: Guma Bldg, 13/14 Lamina Sankoh St, POB 700, Freetown; tel. (22) 25887; e-mail gumasl@yahoo.co.uk; f. 1961; responsible for all existing water supplies in Freetown and surrounding villages, including the Guma dam and associated works.

MAJOR COMPANIES

Aureol Tobacco Co Ltd: Wellington Industrial Estate, POB 109, Freetown; tel. (22) 223435; fax (22) 263138; f. 1959; cigarette mfrs; Chair. Prof. K. KOSO-THOMAS; Man. Dir A. D. A. M'CORMACK; 75 employees.

Bata Shoe Co Sierra Leone Ltd: Wallace Johnson St, POB 111, Freetown; footwear mfrs and distributors. Assoc. co:

Plastic Manufacturing Sierra Leone Ltd: Wilkinson Rd, POB 96, Freetown; footwear mfrs.

Chanrai Sierra Leone Ltd: Wellington Industrial Estate, POB 57, Freetown; tel. (22) 263292; fax (22) 263305; f. 1893; importers of motor spares, air-conditioners, refrigerators, building materials, textiles and provisions; mfrs of soaps and polyethylene bags; Dir R. K. LAKHANPAL; 115 employees.

Dalcon International: Spiritus House, 8 Howe St, Freetown; tel. (22) 228325; fax (22) 228223; e-mail dalcon_c@yahoo.com; f. 1991; export trade in cocoa and coffee; Chair. IBRAHIM K. TURAY.

The Diamond Corpn (West Africa) Ltd: 25–27 Siaka Stevens St, POB 421, Freetown; purchase and export of diamonds; Dir S. L. MATTURI.

KPMG Peat Marwick: Bicentenary House, 17 Wallace-Johnson St, POB 100, Freetown; tel. (22) 222061; fax (22) 228149; internet www.kpmg.com; f. 1960; accounting and consultancy services; Dir DAVID CAREW.

Rokel Leaf Tobacco Development Co Ltd: POB 29, Makeni; f. 1974; production of leaf tobacco; Chair. J. T. SHORT.

Sierra Leone Bottling Co. Ltd: George Brook, POB 412, Freetown; tel. 76315777 (mobile); e-mail iokujagu@eccbc.com; Country Man. ISRAEL OKUJAGU.

Sierra Leone Brewery Ltd: Wellington Industrial Estate, POB 721, Freetown; tel. (22) 263384; fax (22) 263118; internet www.slbrewery.com; e-mail albert.collier@heineken.com; f. 1961; 45% owned by Heineken Technisch Beheer (Netherlands); brewing and marketing of Guinness stout and Star lager; Man. Dir V. L. THOMAS.

Sierra Leone National Petroleum Co: NP House, Cotton Tree, POB 277, Freetown; tel. (22) 225040; fax (22) 226892; petroleum products; Chair. MICHAEL A. CARROL; CEO MOHAMED BABAIUDE COLE.

Sierra Leone Ore and Metal Co (SIEROMCO): POB 725, Freetown; tel. (22) 226777; fax (22) 227276; mining of bauxite; operations suspended since 1995; Chair. K. WOLFENSBERGER; Man. Dir JAMES WESTWOOD.

Sierra Rutile Ltd: PMB, Freetown; tel. and fax (22) 228144; f. 1971; jtly owned by US and Australian interests; mining of rutile and ilmenite (titanium-bearing ores); Dir JOHN B. SISAY; 1,600 employees.

TRADE UNIONS

Artisans', Ministry of Works Employees' and General Workers' Union: 4 Pultney St, Freetown; f. 1946; 14,500 mems; Pres. IBRAHIM LANGLEY; Gen. Sec. TEJAN A. KASSIM.

Sierra Leone Labour Congress: 35 Wallace Johnson St, POB 1333, Freetown; tel. (22) 226869; f. 1966; 51,000 mems in 19 affiliated unions; Pres. MOHAMED A. DEEN; Sec.-Gen. Alhaji KANDEH YILLA; 25,000 mems (2007).

Principal affiliated unions:

Clerical, Mercantile and General Workers' Union: 35 Wallace Johnson St, Freetown; f. 1945; 3,600 mems; Pres. M. D. BENJAMIN; Gen. Sec. M. B. WILLIAMS.

Sierra Leone Association of Journalists: 31 Garrisson Street, Freetown; tel. 76605811; e-mail slajalone@hotmail.com; Pres. UMARU FOFANA; Sec.-Gen. ISHMAIL KOROMA.

Sierra Leone Dockworkers' Union: 165 Fourah Bay Rd, Freetown; f. 1962; 2,650 mems; Pres. ABDUL KANISURE; Gen. Sec. A. C. CONTEH.

Sierra Leone Motor Drivers' Union: 10 Charlotte St, Freetown; f. 1960; 1,900 mems; Pres. A. W. HASSAN; Gen. Sec. ALPHA KAMARA.

Sierra Leone Teachers' Union: Regaland House, Lowcost Step—Kissy, POB 477, Freetown; f. 1951; 18,500 mems; Pres. ABDULAI BRIMA KOROMA; Sec.-Gen. DAVIDSON KUYATEH.

Sierra Leone Transport, Agricultural and General Workers' Union: 4 Pultney St, Freetown; f. 1946; 1,600 mems; Pres. S. O. SAWYERR-MANLEY; Gen. Sec. S. D. KARGBO.

United Mineworkers' Union: 35 Wallace Johnson St, Freetown; f. 1944; 6,500 mems; Gen. Sec. EZEKIEL DYKE.

Also affiliated to the Sierra Leone Labour Congress: the **General Construction Workers' Union**, the **Municipal and Local Government Employees' Union** and the **Sierra Leone National Seamen's Union**.

Transport

RAILWAYS

There are no passenger railways in Sierra Leone.

Marampa Mineral Railway: Delco House, POB 735, Freetown; tel. (22) 222556; 84 km of track linking iron ore mines at Marampa (inactive since 1985) with Pepel port; Gen. Man. SYL KHANU.

ROADS

In 2002 there were an estimated 11,300 km of classified roads, including 2,138 km of main roads and 1,950 km of secondary roads; about 904 km of the total network was paved.

Sierra Leone Road Transport Corpn (SLRTC): Blackhall Rd, POB 1008, Freetown; tel. (22) 250442; fax (22) 250000; f. 1965; state-owned; operates transport services throughout the country; Gen. Man. BOCKARIE LEWIS KAMARA.

Sierra Leone Road Transport Authority: Blackhall Rd, PMB 1324, Freetown.

INLAND WATERWAYS

Established routes for launches, which include the coastal routes from Freetown northward to the Great and Little Scarcies rivers and southward to Bonthe, total almost 800 km. Although some of the upper reaches of the rivers are navigable only between July and September, there is a considerable volume of river traffic.

SHIPPING

Freetown, the principal port, has full facilities for ocean-going vessels.

Sierra Leone National Shipping Co Ltd: 45 Cline St, POB 935, Freetown; tel. (22) 229883; fax (22) 229513; f. 1972; state-owned; shipping, clearing and forwarding agency; representatives for foreign lines; Chair. Alhaji B. M. KOROMA; Man. Dir SYLVESTER B. FOMBA.

Sierra Leone Ports Authority: Queen Elizabeth II Quay, PMB 386, Cline Town, Freetown; tel. (22) 226480; fax (22) 226443; e-mail sierraleoneports@yahoo.com; f. 1965; parastatal body, supervised by the Ministry of Transport and Aviation; operates the port of Freetown; Gen. Man. HUBERT A. BLOOMER (acting).

Sierra Leone Shipping Agencies Ltd: Deep Water Quay, Clinetown, POB 74, Freetown; tel. (22) 221709; fax (22) 293111; e-mail fna.otal@bollore.com; f. 1949; Man. Dir MICHEL MEYNARD.

CIVIL AVIATION

There is an international airport at Lungi.

Directorate of Civil Aviation: Ministry of Transport and Aviation, Ministerial Bldg, George St, Freetown; tel. (22) 222106; fax (22) 228488; Dir GEORGE GBONGBOR.

Sierra National Airlines: Leone House, 25 Pultney St, POB 285, Freetown; tel. (22) 222075; fax (22) 222026; f. 1982; state-owned; operates domestic and regional services, and a weekly flight to Paris, France; operations resumed, following civil conflict, in Nov. 2000; Chair. TAMBA MATTURI; Man. Dir ADAM CORMACK.

Tourism

The main attractions for tourists are the coastline, the mountains and the game reserves. Civil conflict throughout most of the 1990s effectively suspended tourist activity. By 2011, however, tourist arrivals had increased to 52,442, compared with 10,615 in 1999. Receipts from tourism totalled an estimated US $26m., according to the World Tourism Organization, in 2010.

Sierra Leone National Tourist Board: Cape Sierra Hotel, Room 100, Aberdeen, POB 1435, Freetown; tel. (22) 236620; fax (22) 236621; e-mail info@welcometosierraleone.org; internet www.welcometosierraleone.org; f. 1990; Gen. Man. CECIL J. WILLIAMS.

Defence

As assessed at November 2011, the armed forces of the Republic of Sierra Leone numbered about 10,500, with a navy of 200. In October 1999 the UN Security Council adopted a resolution establishing the UN Mission in Sierra Leone (UNAMSIL), which was to supervise the implementation of a peace agreement between the Government and rebel forces, signed in July of that year. Following the completion of disarmament in January 2002, a new army, restructured with British military assistance, was established. In September 2004 UNAMSIL transferred primary responsibility for security to the armed forces, but retained its own rapid intervention capacity. Some 100 British troops remained in the country to support peace-keeping operations and to continue reorganization of the Sierra Leone armed forces. The mandate of UNAMSIL (which had been reduced from nearly its maximum authorized strength of 17,500 to about 3,400) was completed at the end of 2005. Following a UN Security Council resolution in August, the United Nations Integrated Office in Sierra Leone (UNIOSIL) was established in the capital, Freetown, on 1 January 2006 for an initial period of one year, extended in December until the end of 2007. In December of that year, UNIOSIL's mandate was extended until September 2008. In October the United Nations Integrated Peacebuilding Office in Sierra Leone (UNIPSIL) officially replaced UNIOSIL with an initial mandate of one year; this was subsequently extended until September 2012. Preparations were under way in the early 2010s to reduce the size of the armed forces.

Defence Expenditure: Estimated at Le 57,600m. in 2011.

Commander-in-Chief of the Armed Forces: Pres. ERNEST BAI KOROMA.

Chief of Defence Staff: Maj.-Gen. SAMUEL OMARU WILLIAMS.

Education

Primary education begins at five years of age and lasts for seven years. Secondary education, beginning at the age of 12, also lasts for a further seven years, comprising a first cycle of five years and a second cycle of two years. In 1987 tuition fees for government-funded primary and secondary schools were abolished. In 2000/01 primary enrolment was equivalent to 92.8% of children in the relevant age-group, while about 26% of children of the relevant age-group were enrolled at secondary schools (males 30%; females 20%) in 2006/07. There is one university, which comprises six colleges. A total of 9,041 students were enrolled in tertiary education in 2001/02. Budgetary expenditure on education by the central Government in 2002 was Le 36,400m.

Bibliography

Abdullah, I. *Between Democracy and Terror: The Sierra Leone Civil War*. Muckleneuk, Unisa Press, 2004.

Ashby, P. *Against All Odds: Escape from Sierra Leone*. London, St Martin's Press, 2004.

Beah, I. *A Long Way Gone: Memoirs of a Boy Soldier*. New York, Farrar, Straus & Giroux, 2007.

Bergner, D. *In the Land of Magic Soldiers: A Story of White and Black in West Africa*. New York, Farrar Straus & Giroux, 2003.

Bundu, A., and Karefa-Smart, J. *Democracy by Force? A Study of International Military Intervention in the Conflict in Sierra Leone from 1991–2000*. Parkland, FL, Universal Publishers, 2001.

Campbell, G. *Blood Diamonds: Tracing the Deadly Path of the World's Most Precious Stones*. Boulder, CO, Westview Press, 2003.

Châtaigner, J-M. *L'ONU dans la crise en Sierra Leone : Les méandres d'une négociation*. Paris, Editions Karthala, 2005.

Conteh-Morgan, E., and Dixon-Fyle, M. *Sierra Leone at the End of the Twentieth Century: History, Politics and Society*. Berne, Peter Lang, 1999.

Cox, T. S. *Civil-Military Relations in Sierra Leone: A Case Study of African Soldiers in Politics*. Bridgewater, NJ, Replica Books, 2001.

Cubitt, C. *Local and Global Dynamics of Peacebuilding: Post-conflict Reconstruction in Sierra Leone*. Abingdon, Routledge, 2011.

Daramy, S. B. *Constitutional Developments in the Post-Colonial State of Sierra-Leone 1961–1984*. Lewiston, NY, Edwin Mallen, 1993.

Denov, M. *Child Soldiers: Sierra Leone's Revolutionary United Front*. Cambridge, Cambridge Universiy Press, 2010.

Fowler, W. *Operation Barras: The SAS Rescue Mission Sierra Leone 2000*. London, Cassell, 2005.

Francis, D. J. *The Politics of Economic Regionalism: Sierra Leone in ECOWAS (The International Political Economy of New Regionalisms)*. Burlington, VT, Ashgate Publishing Co, 2002.

Gberie, L. *A Dirty War in West Africa: The RUF and the Destruction of Sierra Leone*. London, Hurst & Co., 2005.

Rescuing a Fragile State: Sierra Leone 2002-2008. Waterloo, ON, Wilfrid Laurier University Press, 2009.

Greenhalgh, P. *West African Diamonds: An Economic History 1919–83*. Manchester, Manchester University Press, 1985.

Hirsch, J. L. *Sierra Leone: Diamonds and the Struggle for Democracy (International Peace Academy Occasional Paper Series)*. Boulder, CO, Lynne Rienner Publishers, 2001.

Karamoh, K. *A Mother's Saga: An Account of the Rebel War in Sierra Leone*. New South Wales, Universal Publishers, 2003.

Kargbo, M. *British Foreign Policy and the Conflict in Sierra Leone, 1991–2001*. Oxford, Peter Lang, 2006.

Keen, D. *Conflict and Collusion in Sierra Leone*. New York, Palgrave Macmillan, 2005.

Kelsall, T. *Culture under Cross-Examination: International Justice and the Special Court for Sierra Leone*. Cambridge, Cambridge University Press, 2009.

Land, J. *Blood Diamonds*. New York, Tor Books, 2002.

Marda, M., and Bangura, J. (Eds). *Sierra Leone beyond the Lome Peace Accord*. New York, Palgrave Macmillan, 2010.

Megill, E. L. *Sierra Leone Remembered*. Bloomington, IN, Authorhouse, 2004.

Olonisakin, F. *Peacekeeping in Sierra Leone: The Story of UNAMSIL*. Boulder, CO, Lynne Rienner Publishers, 2007.

Osagie, I. F. *The Amistad Revolt: Memory, Slavery and the Politics of Identity in the United States and Sierra Leone*. Athens, GA, University of Georgia Press, 2003.

Peeters, P., Cunningham, W., Acharya, G., and Van Adams, A. *Youth Employment in Sierra Leone: Sustainable Livelihood Opportunities in a Post-conflict Setting*. Washington DC, World Bank Publications, 2009.

Peters, K. *War and the Crisis of Youth in Sierra Leone*. Cambridge, Cambridge University Press, 2011.

Reno, W. *Corruption and State Politics in Sierra Leone*. Cambridge, Cambridge University Press, 2008.

Richards, P. *Fighting for the Rain Forest: War, Youth and Resources in Sierra Leone*. Oxford, James Currey, 1996.

Schwartz, P. *Sustainable Development and Mining in Sierra Leone*. Dartford, Pneuma Springs Publishing, 2006.

Shaw, R. *Memories of the Slave Trade: Ritual and the Historical Imagination in Sierra Leone*. Chicago, IL, University of Chicago Press, 2002.

Thompson, B. *The Constitutional History and Law of Sierra Leone, 1961–1995*. Lanham, MD, University Press of America, 1997.

Turay, E. D. A., and Abraham, A. *The Sierra Leone Army: A Century of History*. London, Macmillan, 1988.

Voeten, T. *How de Body? One Man's Terrifying Journey Through an African War*. New York, Thomas Dunne Books, 2002.

Wang, L. *Education in Sierra Leone: Present Challenges, Future Opportunities*. Washington, DC, World Bank Publications, 2007.

Wundah, M. *Sierra Leone's Corridors of Power*. New York, Strategic Book Publishing, 2009.

Wyse, A. *The Krio of Sierra Leone: An Interpretive History*. London, Hurst, 1989.

H. C. Bankole-Bright and Politics in Colonial Sierra Leone, 1919–1958. Cambridge, Cambridge University Press, 2003.

SOMALIA

Physical and Social Geography

I. M. LEWIS

The Federal Republic of Somalia covers an area of 637,657 sq km (246,201 sq miles). It has a long coastline on the Indian Ocean and the Gulf of Aden, forming the 'Horn of Africa'. To the north, Somalia faces the Arabian peninsula, with which it has had centuries of commercial and cultural contact. To the north-west, it is bounded by the Republic of Djibouti, while its western and southern neighbours are Ethiopia and Kenya. The country takes its name from its population, the Somali, a Muslim Cushitic-speaking people who stretch into these neighbouring states.

Most of the terrain consists of dry savannah plains, with a high mountain escarpment in the north, facing the coast. The climate is hot and dry, with an average annual temperature of 27°C, although temperate at higher altitudes and along the coast during June–September, with annual rainfall rarely exceeding 500 mm in the most favourable regions. Only two permanent rivers—the Juba and Shebelle—water this arid land. Both rise in the Ethiopian highlands, but only the Juba regularly flows into the sea. The territory between these two rivers is agriculturally the richest part of Somalia, and constitutes a zone of mixed cultivation and pastoralism. Sorghum, millet and maize are grown here, while along the rivers, on irrigated plantations, bananas (the mainstay of Somalia's exports) and citrus fruits are produced. This potentially prosperous zone contains remnants of Bantu groups—partly of ex-slave origin—and is also the home of the Digil and Rahanwin, who speak a distinctive dialect and are the least nomadic element in the population. Of the other Somali clans—the Dir, Isaaq, Hawiye and Darod, primarily pastoral nomads who occupy the rest of the country—the Hawiye along the Shebelle valley are the most extensively engaged in cultivation. A small subsidiary area of cultivation (involving Dir and Isaaq) also occurs in the north-west highlands.

In this predominantly pastoral country, permanent settlements are small and widely scattered, except in the agricultural regions, and for the most part are tiny trading centres built around wells. There are few large towns. Mogadishu, the capital, which dates from at least the 10th century as an Islamic trading post, had an estimated population of 1,554,000 in mid-2011. The other main centres are Kismayu and Berbera, the main southern and northern ports, respectively. The northern town of Hargeysa was declared the capital of the secessionist 'Republic of Somaliland' in 1991.

According to the census of 1986, the population of Somalia was 7,114,431. According to UN estimates, the mid-year population in mid-2012 was 9,797,444, giving a density of 15.4 inhabitants per sq km. Important demographic changes took place from the later decades of the 20th century, beginning with the serious drought that affected the north of the country in 1974–75 and led to the resettlement of large numbers of people in the south. During 1980–88 successive influxes of refugees from Ethiopia created a serious refugee problem before repatriations began in 1990. Of greatest consequence, however, has been the dislocation of Somalia's population during the civil unrest that has raged since the late 1980s; by late 2010 there were an estimated 1.6m. internally displaced Somalis. More than 770,000 refugees from Somalia were resident outside the country at the end of 2011, including an estimated 351,773 in Kenya, 179,845 in Yemen, 81,247 in Ethiopia and 23,839 in the United Kingdom.

Recent History

WALTER S. CLARKE

INTRODUCTION

Following years of humanitarian crisis, Somalia now has an opportunity to break from its past and to demonstrate that it can build a future. Although Somalia still suffers from drought and displacement, the UN was able to announce in February 2012 that the country was no longer in a famine situation. During 2011 the concerted efforts of the Somali army, supported by troops from other African states, have succeeded in driving the al-Qa'ida-allied al-Shabaab out of Mogadishu and nearly all the towns and villages that the insurgent group had occupied in previous years. On the broader international level, the plight of Somalia attracted assistance from some new sources, including the United Kingdom and Turkey, which both organized international conferences to draw attention to Somalia's immediate and future needs. International agencies developed a 'road map' to keep the attention of all interested parties focused on ending the Somali Government's 'transitional' status and moving towards democratic elections and responsible government.

It is important to specify the differing international perspectives on the recovery of the Somali state. For both Ethiopia and Kenya, Somalia must become a viable but not necessarily strong state. For Djibouti and Uganda, a troubled Somalia presents a threat to their own productivity and general welfare. The European Union (EU) and its trading partners around the world hope that disciplined Somalia authorities could bring the scourge of piracy in the Gulf of Aden and the Indian Ocean under control. The US Government believed that it could restore order in Somalia in 1993–95 by eliminating famine without becoming involved in 'nation-building'. Since that time, the USA has defined its interests in Somalia in terms of the 'global war on terror' and of piracy.

Most foreign analysts are sceptical about the chances of success of the new national institutions that are being established. In general, they decry the speed at which the new organs are being created, and express concerns that the new Constitution was drafted by just a few Somalian and international technocrats to the exclusion of most of the Somalian people and that the central authorities are likely to be weaker than most sub-national political bodies. The British Royal Institute of International Affairs (Chatham House) published a study in June 2012 warning that 'the end of the roadmap will not signal an end to Somalia's transition'. Other academics state simply that the complicated process of meetings and negotiations are at best a 'transition to a transition'.

The policy of the US Government toward Somalia changed after the terrorist attacks against the USA on 11 September 2001. The prospect of a vast territory populated mainly by Muslims without a viable national government, strategically located near the vital lines of communication connecting the oil fields of the Middle East to Europe and North America, required a critical response. Thus was born the concept of 'ungoverned territories', areas without authority. The USA continues to view Somalia primarily from the perspective of anti-(Islamic) terrorism. In addition, analysts and observers from both sides of the civil-military divide speak vaguely of unknown perpetrators, whose presence presumably presents a threat to the success of whatever is being planned.

None the less, the Somali people retain a common language, religion and customs. Whether the current transition ends positively or not, Somalis will continue to cleave to what has been termed by academics as 'governance without government'. Traditional clan leaders, clerics, professionals, *Shari'a* (Islamic) courts and civic associations are available to communities when national government is either weak or non-existent. It is from this perspective that the designation of 'ungoverned territories' appears unsatisfactory and misleading.

INDEPENDENCE AND PAN-SOMALISM

On 26 June 1960 British Somaliland became the first Somali dependency to be accorded independence. The Italian UN Trust Territory of Somalia received its independence on 1 July and, as the result of earlier agreements with Somaliland leaders, joined with the former British Somaliland to form the Somali Republic. The Italians held the Trust Territory's first election in March 1959, in which the Somali Youth League (SYL) took 83 of the 90 seats in the Legislative Assembly. British Somaliland had experienced largely decentralized governance and indirect rule, which left the traditional roles of chiefs and religious leaders relatively undisturbed; the former Italian trusteeship had seen more direct rule with policies aimed at diminishing the roles of clan chiefs and religious leaders. The two new partners decided that the presidency would be held by a figure from the former Italian side; the premiership would be the responsibility of a Somali from the former British territory. A coalition was built between the SYL and the two leading northern parties after independence. The early years of the new Somali Republic were not easy, and the original coalition developed many cleavages and the SYL split into competing factions.

National elections were held in 1967 in which Dr Abd al-Rashid Ali Shermarke was elected President and Mohamed Ibrahim Egal, a highly respected politician from Somaliland, was named Prime Minister. The National Assembly became highly fractured as clan-based factions formed; confidence in the Government was waning. Following indecisive legislative elections in 1969, Shermarke was assassinated, effectively ending Somalia's democratic experiment.

After the death of Shermarke, it appeared that a replacement closely allied to Egal might become President. Justifying its action as an effort to prevent chaos, the military assumed control of the Government and a Supreme Revolutionary Council (SRC) was formed. The country was renamed the Somali Democratic Republic. The President of the SRC, a former national police chief, Maj.-Gen. Mohammed Siad Barre, became Head of State. The selection of a military dictator in 1967 marked the end of good and effective government in Somalia.

The ill-health of the aged Ethiopian Emperor Haile Selassie, the coming independence of the French Territory of the Afars and Issas (as Djibouti was then known), and rising opposition to his arbitrary rule encouraged Siad Barre to imagine that it was the right time to bring the Somali populations of the Ethiopian Ogaden under his protection. In 1976 he restructured the Western Somali Liberation Front (WSLF) to prepare it for insurgency operations in the Ogaden. As Siad Barre prepared for war—efforts that did not escape the attention of Soviet military advisers attached to his army—the USSR attempted to mediate between Siad Barre and Lt-Col Mengistu Haile Mariam of Ethiopia, in order to bring the whole of the Horn into the Soviet sphere of influence. The Soviet efforts were summarily rejected by Siad Barre, and the Soviets reluctantly removed their military advisers (many of whom went directly to Ethiopia) and ended their military supply relationship with Somalia. Seeking to counterbalance its political losses in Addis Ababa, the USA reactivated an earlier military agreement and provided some support to the Somalis. In May 1977 the WSLF blew up three bridges on the rail line connecting Djibouti to Addis Ababa. Somali regular forces entered the Ogaden in support of the WSLF in July and advanced quickly to the foothills of the Ethiopian plateau in the vicinity of Harar. The USSR used its vast logistical resources to bring in Cuban military forces (from Angola) and supplies, and more advisers, stopping the Somali military advance in January 1978. Exhausted, demoralized and ill-supplied, Somali forces returned to Somalia, and in March the Ethiopians claimed total victory over the invaders.

DETERIORATION OF THE SOMALI STATE

The abject defeat of Somali forces in the Ogaden ignited opposition to Siad Barre throughout the country. The peoples of the former British Somaliland were deeply resentful of the costly human and financial losses brought about by the war. Opposition groups were formed, including the Somali Salvation Democratic Front (SSDF), a Mijertein-based group, and the Somali National Movement (SNM), rooted in the Isaaq sub-clan in Somaliland. Siad Barre made peace with Mengistu in 1988 by restoring diplomatic relations, and the SNM was ordered to vacate its Ogaden bases. The SNM subsequently captured Burao and occupied a part of Hargeysa, the regional capital. Siad Barre ordered his former son-in-law, Gen. Mohamed Siad 'Morgan', to make an example of the northern dissidents. Using South African mercenary pilots and heavy artillery to bombard the city, Morgan's forces systematically killed and raped the Somali population of the city and then mined the ruins. An estimated 40,000 Somalis were killed by their own Government in this operation and some 400,000 refugees fled to Ethiopia.

By early 1990 the power of the President was so circumscribed that he was referred to as the 'Mayor of Mogadishu'. While the President desperately searched for a formula to assuage the forces gathering to overthrow his inept rule, the opposition was growing in strength. Siad Barre's military experienced a few minor victories over the SNM in the north, but more significantly, the Hawiye, Somalia's largest clan group, was preparing for major operations against him. Hawiye forces initiated large-scale attacks on government installations and military facilities in and around Mogadishu in November. Gen. Mohamed Farah Aidid, who had been imprisoned early in the Siad Barre presidency and subsequently released and appointed ambassador to India, gathered troops while marching south from Galkayo. He advanced steadily on Siad Barre's positions in Mogadishu. Unable to stand up to Aidid's United Somali Force and other Hawiye forces and abandoned by all but his family, Siad Barre left Mogadishu on 26 January 1991, fleeing south with his family and the remnants of his army. The deposed President made an abortive attempt to recapture Mogadishu in mid-1991, but was pushed back over the Kenyan border. Having failed to obtain political asylum in Kenya, Siad Barre took exile in Nigeria, where he died of natural causes in January 1995.

The people of Somalia gained little from the fall of Siad Barre. The administration of the country had largely evaporated, and the exultant victors of the battles of Mogadishu and elsewhere had little governmental experience. The business community in Mogadishu feared Aidid; many of them joined in establishing the 'manifesto group' within the United Somali Congress (USC). In January 1991 this group selected Ali Mahdi Mohamed, a respected Hawiye Abgal businessman and former government minister, as the new leader of Somalia. Aidid could not accept this action, and in February his followers in the USC elected Omar Arteh Ghalib, an Isaaq, as head of Somalia.

Bitter fighting broke out between sub-clan militia groups as Ali Mahdi's Hawiye Abgal fighters confronted Aidid's Hawiye Habr Gedir forces. Mogadishu was soon separated by a rubble-filled 'green line' demarcating the largely north–south sub-clan ethnic boundaries of the shattered city. In the 1991–92 civil war that consumed most of Mogadishu it was estimated that some 35,000 civilians were killed and many more thousands displaced. In southern Somalia fighting broke out between sub-clan groups vying for control of the strategic port city of Kismayu.

In March 1992 the UN Security Council supported an effort to achieve a cease-fire in Somalia, and in April it authorized a very limited observation operation under the title UN

Operation in Somalia (UNOSOM). The Secretary-General sent his personal representative, Muhammad Sahnoun, a well-respected Algerian diplomat, to Mogadishu in May to work with the faction leaders to achieve a cease-fire. Aidid by that time was the master of southern Mogadishu, with control of the airport. He was firmly opposed to any international mandates to intervene in Somali affairs and restricted UN peace-keepers' access to the airport.

Continued battles in Mogadishu and in the south, combined with the policies of Aidid and other warlords to prevent the distribution of food and medicine to the region known as the 'triangle of death', bordered by Merca, south of Mogadishu, Baidoa and Kismayu, led to hundreds of thousands of deaths between mid-1991 and late 1992. Persons displaced by Aidid's takeover of southern Mogadishu were mostly government officials and businessmen associated with the Siad Barre regime. For Aidid, who had used the seized properties as rewards to his commanders, there was no question of permitting the displaced Marehan to return to Mogadishu to regain their properties, and he had no scruples about using starvation to keep them in place.

INTERNATIONAL MILITARY INTERVENTION

In August 1992 US President George H. W. Bush authorized a humanitarian operation to fly food from Mombasa, Kenya, to airports in Somalia. Subsequently, in an arrangement between the US Government and the UN Security Council, a US-led UN peace-keeping operation was authorized to enter Somalia to relieve the starvation situation and restore order. The first US troops of the Unified Task Force (UNITAF) landed at Mogadishu in early December as part of 'Operation Restore Hope'. More than 20 nations contributed troops to UNITAF, and by 28 December, one month ahead of schedule, UNITAF controlled Mogadishu, had opened the warehouses in the port of Mogadishu, cleared the routes to the interior and quickly restored food flows. Aidid was displeased with these developments, but the incoming forces established confidence with him by assuring him that their mission was limited and they did not expect to be present in the country for a long period of time. Both Aidid and Ali Mahdi, still in power in north Mogadishu, were accorded judicial and police powers in their areas, thereby relieving UNITAF from asserting those responsibilities.

UNITAF handed over the operation to a UN-led peace-keeping force headed by Gen. Çevik Bir of Turkey on 4 May 1993. Although 30 countries contributed to UNOSOM II, the UN force was about one-half of the size of UNITAF at its peak (approximately 30,000 at the end of January). Aidid was dissatisfied at the open-ended international operation, and in early June, having been advised of a UN inspection of a weapons site at the former national radio station under his control, his forces launched an ambush of the Pakistani military unit after the inspection was completed. There was also a simultaneous ambush of a lightly armed Pakistani food distribution detail. In these confrontations, 24 Pakistanis were killed and dozens more were seriously injured, as a result of Aidid's order to his force to continue firing on those downed. On the following day the UN Security Council held an emergency session in New York, USA, to condemn the Mogadishu attack and to call for punishment of the unnamed perpetrators. There was little doubt regarding responsibility for this unprovoked attack, and UNOSOM II launched a number of unsuccessful operations to find Aidid. In a US-led helicopter operation on 4 October to capture Aidid's followers meeting at the Olympic Hotel in Mogadishu, two helicopters were shot down and 18 US military personnel were killed. Lacking heavily armoured vehicles, the US response force took several hours to bring relief to the survivors of the helicopter crashes and to recover the dead. Under heavy pressure from the US Congress, President Bill Clinton decided to withdraw US forces from Somalia, and the US element of the operation ended in March 1994. UNOSOM II concluded its operations in February 1995 when the remaining troops were removed under the protection of a combined US-Italian task force.

The international effort to rescue Somalia from itself was a failure. In the West, many excuses were offered for the inability of the international forces to knit Somalia back together. Peculiarly, the most frequent one involved the alleged unplanned expansion of the nation-building tasks ('mission creep') beyond the missions acceptable to the intervening forces ('mission shrink'). When the genocide in Rwanda began in April 1994, barely one month after the final departure of US forces from Somalia, the world's initial response was to reduce the number of peace-keeping forces in beleaguered Rwanda; Somalia had drained all enthusiasm for humanitarian intervention from the world community.

Despite the presence of the international force, the Somali clans and sub-clans maintained their internal rivalries. Aidid's Somali National Alliance (SNA) began to dissipate as Aidid attempted to make leadership changes. Sporadic gunfights between members of the two groups followed during May and August 1996. On 1 August, while participating in a battle with rival forces in Mogadishu's suburbs, Aidid was reportedly shot and died the following day. His son, Hussein Mohamed Aidid, raised in California, USA, and a former US Marine Corps reservist, was elected leader of the SNA, and factional fighting continued.

RECONCILIATION CONFERENCES IN ADDIS ABABA

From the time of the collapse of the Siad Barre regime in 1991 until the present day, some 16 national reconciliation conferences have been convened, sponsored variously by the UN, the OAU, the Intergovernmental Authority on Development (IGAD), the USA, Kenya, Ethiopia and Egypt, to devise a resolution that might facilitate co-operation between leaders. In every case, there was insufficient trust among the leaders to find a formula upon which a national political consensus could be built. Some of the more notable international reconciliation efforts are listed below.

UNITAF facilitated two reconciliation conferences (in January and March 1993), both in Addis Ababa, during its five-month deployment in Somalia. There was little time to prepare the Somali political terrain for these hurried meetings, a problem that was exacerbated when Aidid was accorded virtual veto power over the attendance lists. UNITAF imposed the issuance of invitations to the conferences to a large contingent of Somali women and civil society. In the first Addis Ababa meeting (4–8 January 1993), the various warlord protagonists in Somalia's burgeoning civil war focused on defining the issues, especially a cease-fire, possible disarmament modalities and how to organize future national reconciliation conferences. In the second round in Addis Ababa in 15–27 March, 15 clan-based factions agreed on certain fundamentals to be developed, including a transition mechanism which would include a Transitional National Council (TNC), a central executive department and supporting regional and local district councils. The establishment of a transitional charter-drafting committee was also planned. The agreements made at Addis Ababa in early 1993 were never implemented, as Aidid believed that no negotiation could ever be more satisfying than a military victory.

The Ethiopian Government convened a conference, with 41 leaders representing 26 factions, at the resort of Sodere from November 1996 to January 1997. Only 'Somaliland' was not represented at the meeting. Hussein Aidid, who had become a strident foe of Ethiopia, also boycotted the conference. For the Ethiopian Government, alarmed by evidence of al-Qa'ida interest in cultivating closer relations with more fundamentalist groups such as the Islamic Union Party (al-Ittihad al-Islam—AIAI), the Sodere meeting declared its interest in the situation in Somalia. The Sodere meetings introduced two potentially useful concepts into the reconciliation process—the principle of proportional representation of clans and the '4.5 formula', which ensured that the four major clans would be required to give the smaller clan groups (grouped within the '.5') representation in the negotiations.

MEDIATION EFFORTS BY DJIBOUTI

In 2000 Ismaïl Omar Guelleh, the newly elected President of Djibouti, involved himself in the reconciliation process, perceiving this as an opportunity to follow a tradition established by his predecessor of attempting to resolve the Somali problem. Believing that the power of the warlords needed to be diluted if there was to be any chance of success, he invited 1,500 Somalis from all branches of society to attend a national reconciliation conference in the town of Arta, west of Djibouti city. Representatives from the self-declared regions of 'Somaliland' and 'Puntland' (see below) refused to attend. Guelleh's plan was to have the delegates elect a new national legislature that would be established in Mogadishu. The legislature would then elect a President who would appoint a Prime Minister. The Arta discussions opened on 2 May. It took several weeks for the delegations to agree on an electoral formula: each of the four major clan families (Darod, Dir, Rahanwin and Hawiye) would be allocated 24 seats in a Transitional National Assembly (TNA), and an equal number would be made available to the smaller clan groups. An additional 25 seats would be reserved for women, with each of the five previous groups enjoined to select five women to hold seats in the TNA. To overcome the impasse in the negotiations after long discussions of the manner of allocation of legislative seats between clans and sub-clans, the delegations requested that President Guelleh intervene. He was asked to apportion an additional 20 seats, thereby raising the number of legislators to 245. This last-minute effort to assuage the ambitions of representatives of smaller clan and sub-clan groups was successful.

The TNA met for the first time on 13 August 2000 with 166 delegates present. In a subsequent session, Abdallah Deerow Isa, formerly director of the political wing of the Rahanwin Resistance Army was elected Speaker. On 26 August Abdulkasim Salad Hasan, a Hawiye who had held several ministerial positions in the Siad Barre regime, was elected interim President of Somalia by the TNA with 145 of 245 votes. His principal opponent was Abdullah Ahmed Adow, a former ambassador to the USA, who received 92 votes. Attending the ceremonies were the heads of government of Eritrea, Ethiopia, Sudan, Yemen and Djibouti. Representatives of the UN, the EU, the Arab League, the OAU, France, Italy, Kuwait and Libya were also present. President Abdulkasim flew to Mogadishu on 30 August, where he was reportedly met by a welcoming crowd of 100,000 Somalis. After wide-ranging consultations with clan leaders, on 8 October the new President appointed Ali Khalif Galaydh, a Dulbahante from Burao in 'Somaliland', as Prime Minister. Later that month Galaydh announced the composition of a 32-member Transitional National Government (TNG).

Somalia's TNA began debating a motion of no confidence in the TNG in mid-October 2001. The major issue concerned the inability or unwillingness of the Prime Minister and his Government to promote national reconciliation. The motion also noted that in one year, the TNG had failed to constitute a single regional administration. The Prime Minister was also accused of corruption in handing out 1,600 mobile cellular telephones to friends and political colleagues, which resulted in a cost to the treasury of US $700,000. After one week of debate in the Assembly, the Government lost the vote of no confidence by 141 votes to 29.

THE ELDORET-MBAGATHI RECONCILIATION CONFERENCE

In mid-August 2002 IGAD announced that a Somali national reconciliation conference would convene at Eldoret, Kenya, on 15 October. The Kenyan Minister of Foreign Affairs, Marsden Madoka, told the press that the conference was expected to last two weeks, but, in fact, the process was to take two years.

President Daniel arap Moi of Kenya opened the 14th Somali national reconciliation conference in Eldoret on 15 October 2002 by welcoming the many delegations and expressing hope that this would be the last such conference. The UN Secretary-General's representative promised the gathered Somali leaders that if they could produce a peaceful environment, the UN would provide increased development assistance and humanitarian aid. Somali delegations in Eldoret included the TNG, representatives of 'Puntland', the Somali Reconciliation and Restoration Council (SRRC), the Juba Valley Alliance, and various Mogadishu warlords including Hussein Aidid and Yalahow. Other representatives included some from civil society, women's groups and the Somali diaspora. The rules of procedure were adopted on the second day, although IGAD technical committee chairman Mwangale observed that not all groups were present. Mwangale also noted that the number of registrations on the second day of the conference totalled 450, a significant increase from the 300 invited. In a press conference on the third day of the conference, Mwangale stated that the number of delegations was well beyond expectations, but he was encouraged by the numbers and believed that the conference could reach discussion of constitutional and governing structures within a month rather than the three months originally planned.

Following elections in Kenya in which President Moi was defeated, a new Government was established, and on 18 January 2003 Kenya announced that a retired diplomat, Bethwel Kiplagat, would replace Mwangale as special envoy to Somalia. Kiplagat was introduced to the conference on 22 January and he promised more consultation and transparency with the delegations. In early February the talks broke down when the available delegates in Eldoret could not constitute a quorum. The Kenyan authorities decided to move the conference from Eldoret to Nairobi. An EU-financed professional administrative and financial management team was contracted to put the conference on a more solid path.

The conference moved to Nairobi on 17 February 2003, where it was housed in a renovated trade school at Mbagathi, an industrial suburb of the Kenyan capital. Despite the change of locale, there remained a continuing dispute over seats in the conference. Kiplagat announced the creation of an arbitration committee to resolve seating issues, comprising representatives of Somalia's clans. Each clan group was to select three people such as elders and other leaders to employ traditional Somali mediation techniques to resolve such problems. Kiplagat claimed that he had been involved in mediation issues every day from morning to night, and that henceforth all such problems would be referred to the Somali arbitration committee.

On 15 September 2003 the delegates at the reconciliation conference adopted a Transitional Federal Charter (TFC), which would lead to the establishment of a Transitional Federal Parliament (TFP) with a mandate of four years. Its membership would be selected by traditional elders and politicians invited to the talks. President Abdulkasim and Yalahow's representatives continued their opposition to the new charter. Their protestations were rejected by the collected delegates. The organizers announced that the conference had entered its third and last phase on 16 September.

In a press conference on 26 October 2003, Abdulkasim blamed the IGAD technical committee for what he termed 'the total breakdown' of the Nairobi conference. He claimed that the Kenyan organizers gave Ethiopia too significant a role in the running of the conference. As a result of the machinations of the organizers, he observed, the official delegates of the TNG became a minority group in the face of a dozen factions created and supported by Ethiopia.

However, progress was made on a number of contentious issues: the TFP would comprise 275 members, with 12% of seats allocated to women; they would be selected for a period of five years by the political leaders who were party to the original Declaration on Cessation of Hostilities, and politicians were officially invited to take part in the technical committees, in consultation with traditional leaders. Each of the four major clans would select 61 members, and 31 positions would be allocated to the minority clans. Once formed, the Parliament would choose a President, who would nominate a Prime Minister to lead a government. The amended TFC was signed on 29 January 2004 by the TNG and the assembled political faction chiefs. One of the signatories was Asha Haji Ilmi, a civil society leader and the first Somali woman to sign a peace agreement.

The amended agreement was to enter into effect after its adoption by the plenary session in Nairobi and the existing TNA in Mogadishu. Agreement to the new charter was soon achieved in Nairobi, and on 8 February 2004, after only three days of debate, the TNA gave its approval. At the vote, 155 members of the 245-member TNA were present; of those, 136 members voted in favour, one voted against, and 18 members abstained. The positive vote of the TNA was echoed by 60 elders representing all Hawiye sub-clans. After the parliamentary vote, President Abdulkasim signed a decree making the charter legal and binding on his administration, which was reconstituted as the Transitional Federal Government (TFG).

On 16 September 2004 11 candidates presented themselves for election as Speaker of the TFP. A businessman, Sharif Hasan Sheikh Adan, won with 161 of the 267 votes cast. His closest opponent, Adan Muhammad Nur, received 105 votes and protested alleged electoral irregularities.

Election of a new President of Somalia began on 10 October 2004 in Nairobi. After the first round, the three leading candidates were Abdullahi Yussuf Ahmed, former warlord in the self-declared breakaway region of 'Puntland', Abdullahi Addou, former finance minister, and Mogadishu warlord Qanyare Afrah. Yussuf secured victory in the second round. In 1998 he had led the north-eastern Somali provinces in the formation of 'Puntland', and his record there did not demonstrate a strong commitment to democracy. The new President took his oath of office in Nairobi on 14 October 2004. On 4 November President Yussuf appointed Ali Mohammed Ghedi as transitional Prime Minister.

On 1 December 2004 Prime Minister Ghedi announced a Cabinet that would consist of 31 ministers, 31 deputy ministers and five ministers of state. The Cabinet appeared to be inclusive, with all clan groups appropriately represented, but regional analysts observed that it was much too large for Somalia's requirements and that the TFG could not afford to maintain so many ministers. The Cabinet was later rejected by the TFP. In mid-January 2005 a new Cabinet that included many former warlords was announced. Hussein Aidid was made Deputy Prime Minister and Minister of the Interior and Security. Qanyare Afrah became Minister of National Security. Other familiar names on the cabinet list included Yalahow, Osman 'Ato', Shatigadud and Nur. Abdullahi Shaykh Isma'il was appointed Minister of Foreign Affairs.

The President and the parliamentarians moved to Baidoa in February 2006. Although it was initially denied by TFG officials, it was reported that Ethiopian forces had already entered Somalia to provide protection for the new administration in Baidoa.

THE RISE OF THE ISLAMIC COURTS

Although many foreign policy experts appeared surprised when the Union of Islamic Courts (UIC) emerged in 2006, and assumed that it was a move engineered by al-Qa'ida, the religious authorities had been a factor in Somali lives for some years. According to a study by Chatham House, the Islamic Courts owed their origin to the early 1990s when Abgal politicians in north Mogadishu saw the need for an institution to restore law and order to the chaotic city. They turned to local Hawiye clerics who co-operated by founding a *Shari'a* court. The Chatham study emphasized that the origin of the UIC was more due to the communal need for justice and security than out of an Islamist imperative.

In June 2001 the TFG announced that it would 'nationalize' the Islamic Courts. This was announced by President Abdulkasim as he presided over the incorporation of some judges from the Islamic Courts into the normal judiciary. Soon after the 11 September attacks in New York and Washington, DC, the US Government froze AIAI assets in the USA. The alleged affiliation of AIAI with al-Qa'ida came as a surprise to most regional observers. AIAI was widely credited with having established some Islamic Courts in Mogadishu in recent years, but it was believed to have handed those courts over to the Government in June 2002.

The Islamic judges were assigned to the High Court as Islamic *qadis* responsible for adjudicating family affairs. The Islamic Court in Mogadishu, also known as the Shirkole Islamic Court, had been set up in south Mogadishu in the mid-1990s along clan lines in order to combat the dramatic increase in crime that followed the collapse of the Siad Barre regime. Each Shirkole court maintained its own militia to deal with criminals and to provide local protection. The Islamic Court militia was set to be absorbed by official security services. In spite of efforts to nationalize all of the Islamic Courts, some of them continued to operate independently in Mogadishu, especially in the northern sectors.

The rapid takeover of Mogadishu and most of Somalia south of Galkayo by the UIC in 2006 alarmed many foreign powers and dramatically altered the course of Somali politics. The rising strength of the Islamic Courts contributed to the decision of the USA to facilitate the establishment of the Alliance for the Restoration of Peace and Counter-Terrorism in March. The warlord collaborators in this venture did not have any successes to show for their efforts, but the event served as a rallying cry for the subsequent explosive offensive launched by the Islamic Courts in March and April. The UIC militias were relentless in fighting against the so-called anti-terrorist forces. Warlord resistance collapsed in early June, and the UIC declared itself victorious. Sheikh Sharif Sheikh Ahmed was selected by the militia heads as Chairman of the UIC on 6 June. Early evidence of the success of the UIC was the reopening of the city of Mogadishu to both its inhabitants and the outside world. The international airport reopened in August for the first time since 1995, and the UIC administration also reopened the port. Journalists flocked to the city, while residents marvelled at the disappearance of road-blocks and bandits. There were 11 Islamic Court groups within the UIC, and they represented a number of different Islamic tendencies. For most Mogadishu residents, the few months of Islamic control in 2006 represented the only real period of peace and relative security since early in the Siad Barre years. In late June, at a meeting in Khartoum sponsored by the Arab League, the Islamists and the TFG signed a series of accords, in which they agreed to recognize each other and to work towards peace. On 27 June a UIC delegation met with representatives of the US embassy in Khartoum. The Islamists laid out a list of complaints (the restrictions imposed on charities and financial organizations and US backing of warlords) and recent favourable actions (the creation of the Contact Group on Somalia and positive comments about the Arab League-sponsored meeting with the TFG).

The Islamist group with the clearest international ties was al-Shabaab ('the Youth'). It was founded in Somalia in 2004 by Aden Hashi 'Ayro', who reportedly had received training with al-Qa'ida and the Taliban in Afghanistan; he was also the military chief within the UIC group. Al-Shabaab had a certain appeal to Somali youth: it was highly disciplined, and it had lofty goals (to establish a 'caliphate' in Somalia). Many members received military and technical training in Eritrea. 'Ayro' was killed by a US drone missile in May 2008 in Musa Mareb. Western powers and Ethiopia saw only the negative possibilities of an Islamic republic in Somalia, and they failed to offer any support to Sheikh Sharif Sheikh Ahmed, a moderate within the Islamist movement.

THE ETHIOPIAN INVASION AND OCCUPATION

The downfall of the Islamists came more quickly than their earlier victory over the warlords. On 12 December 2006 the leaders of the military wing of the Supreme Somali Islamic Courts Council—SSICC, as the UIC had been renamed. SSICC issued an ultimatum to the Ethiopian Government, granting it one week to withdraw from the Baidoa area or be forced out. On 20 December there was an exchange of fire between Ethiopian and SSICC forces near Baidoa, and the Islamists retreated. Ethiopian forces pressed south and east, first capturing the town of Bandiiradley, about 60 km south of Galkayo, and then sweeping through towns and villages before marching unopposed into Mogadishu on 28 December. Under Ethiopian protection, the TFG moved to the capital. For TFG President Abdullahi Yussuf Ahmed and most of his Government, it was the first time that they had set foot in the capital since their election in 2004. By 13 January 2007 the Ethiopian army had driven most of the remnants of the SSICC forces into the southern tip of Somalia at Ras Kamboni where the Islamists were attacked by US air and sea forces and Kenyan ground units with undetermined results.

Some of the Islamist leaders were able to flee to Yemen and others to Saudi Arabia, while the foot soldiers simply blended back into the population. In March 2007 the SSICC and others angered by the Ethiopian presence regrouped and attacked Ethiopian positions throughout the capital area. In July fighting erupted in the Bakhara market, the lifeblood of the city's economy. The port of Kismayu also remained a critical part of the southern Somali economy, but following the takeover of the port by Marehan forces in April 2007, the TFG-appointed local administrator was expelled, and the TFG lost all authority in Kismayu. In the lower Shebelle region, TFG forces continued to come under fire from militia groups claiming allegiance to a previous administration. The location of Sheikh Hassan Dahir Aweys, the radical Chairman of the SSICC, remained unknown, prompting concerns over how to respond should he re-emerge on the local political scene. The moderate head of the SSICC, Sheikh Ahmed, escaped the round-up of Islamist leaders in Somalia and turned himself in to the Kenyan authorities. He was granted political asylum by Yemen in February 2007.

The Ethiopian force proved to be more than a match for the Islamists, warlords and any other opponents who appeared against them. By the end of April 2007 fighting in Mogadishu had diminished, although the fighting caused a reported 300,000 to flee the city. The TFG had done little to effect any kind of reconciliation, and both the European community and international humanitarian agencies complained to the TFG that they were unable to provide relief to the needy victims of Somalia's disorder. The Ethiopian military utilized heavy tanks and artillery to return sniper fire, and despite better equipment and training, there was a large toll of civilians caught in the cross-fire between Islamists and Ethiopians.

The Ethiopian forces succeeded in suppressing the Islamist forces; however, al-Shabaab refused to accept defeat, and it soon followed extremist elements and became radicalized. No longer a subordinate force within the SSICC, al-Shabaab became the symbol of resistance to the Ethiopian invasion. In the absence of government, it provided goods and services that no other entity could provide the population. Recruitment rose, and al-Shabaab built paramilitary training camps in the broad areas of (mostly southern) Somalia which were beyond regular Ethiopian control. During this period, al-Qa'ida assumed greater leadership of the movement through its access to cash and weaponry.

FURTHER RECONCILIATION EFFORTS

By mid-2007 there was talk of holding another national reconciliation conference, this time in Mogadishu. The organizing chairman was Ali Mahdi Mohamed, a familiar name in Somali business and politics and former nemesis of Mohamed Farah Aidid. A competing national conference was also organized in Asmara, where opponents of the TFG and the Ethiopian troop presence, miscellaneous clan dissidents, SSICC refugees and Ogadeni separatists were given refuge.

The reconciliation conference opened, after inevitable delays, in Mogadishu on 15 July 2007. The opening ceremony was boycotted by Hawiye elders, Islamists and anti-Ethiopian militants. The talks lasted six weeks, and opinion was divided over the success of the negotiations. Some 2,000 delegates attended the conference, which appeared to run peacefully, although it was periodically interrupted by gunfire and mortar fire. Hawiye elders maintained that the conference was not inclusive and that little progress was made in ending violence in Somalia, with hundreds reported to have been killed in fighting during the talks. The final resolutions appealed for a negotiated truce between clans, agreements on the sharing of natural resources, and elections in 2009.

At the rump reconciliation conference held in Asmara, about 400 Somali oppositionists met for one week and decided to create a united opposition party under the title Alliance for the Re-liberation of Somalia (ARS). A central committee of some 191 members was set up to guide the campaign against the TFG. At the heart of the agreements secured among dissidents in Asmara were fundamental cleavages that appear to be inherent in Somali politics. Notably, the Asmara conference was attended by Dahir Aweys, who reappeared after going into hiding after the Ethiopian invasion of Somalia.

By mid-October 2007 it appeared that the TFG was splitting along clan lines. On one side was President Abdullahi Yussuf, a seemingly unreconstructed warlord who brought his own presidential guard with him when he came from 'Puntland'. He tended to depend upon his private bodyguard rather than use the police drawn from the local Hawiye population. Yusuf's bodyguards acted with total impunity, and members of Yussuf's administration acted out of fear of them. Prime Minister Ali Mohammed Ghedi, a Hawiye, had some support from the local population, but little from members of his own Government. On 11 October 22 members of his Government signed a statement demanding a vote of no confidence in the Prime Minister. Ghedi handed in his letter of resignation to the President on 29 October and immediately left the country to explain the reasons for his departure to the Government of Kenya, which had been instrumental in bringing him into the Government in November 2004.

On 22 November 2007 President Yussuf named Nur Hassan Hussein as Prime Minister. Hussein was in his seventies, had trained as a lawyer, and was a former police chief who, until his appointment, had since 1991 been Secretary-General of the Somali Red Crescent Society. Like his predecessor, his ethnic affiliation was Hawiye Abgal. According to an unnamed civil society source, Hussein possessed the quality of not having belonged to any known political or ethnic faction and 'had left no fingerprints anywhere'. As some observers had hoped, Hussein used his new post and flawless background to invite a dialogue with the Islamists, oppositionists and opportunists in Asmara.

AFRICAN UNION PEACE-KEEPING TROOPS INTERVENE

The first troops to arrive for the operation designated the AU Mission in Somalia (AMISOM) were from Uganda, deploying to Mogadishu in early March 2007. They were followed some months later by forces from Burundi. These troops were designed to replace the Ethiopian military in Mogadishu, but they arrived amid a serious increase in confrontations between the SSICC and TFG and Ethiopian forces that began in March. The increased fighting in the city in April initiated the largest displacement of civilians from Mogadishu observed in the 16-year history of the post-Siad Somali civil war.

The AMISOM troops were in Somalia on the basis of a UN Security Council resolution that authorized the AU to deploy up to 8,000 military personnel to assist the TFG. The resolution was made under Article 6 of the UN Charter, which restricted AMISOM to peace-keeping purposes only and the activities of AMISOM were largely confined to protecting the TFG. No forces from a country contiguous to Somalia could be accepted. AMISOM did not co-ordinate its activities with the Ethiopian military forces. Until their departure from Somalia in January 2008, the Ethiopian Government stated that its forces would stay until AMISOM reached its authorized deployment level of 8,000. (This level, in fact, was not achieved until much later.)

While the TFG attempted to govern in Mogadishu under the protection of the Ethiopians and AMISOM, much of the opposition leadership took refuge outside of the country. SSICC and other anti-TFG leaders accepted the invitation of the Eritrean leader to stay in Asmara.

THE DJIBOUTI ACCORDS

Hoping to profit from the signs of dissension within Islamist and extremist ranks, the TFG called for a meeting in Mogadishu of moderates and those political activists who feared Somalia coming under the control of al-Shabaab and other groups either affiliated with al-Qa'ida or espousing conservative Wahhabism. The goal of the meeting was to broaden the TFG's appeal at a time that appeared favourable.

In April 2008 Sheikh Ahmed commended the international community for its efforts to bring the TFG and the opposition to the negotiating table. Other leaders within the SSICC were less charitable, referring to Sheikh Ahmed's efforts to secure wide support as simple 'tourism'. In the event, the TFG and the moderate factions of the SSICC participated in the peace talks, held in April in Djibouti, that country again acting as neutral arbiter in the search for some kind of Somali peace arrangement. When the talks ended in late May, both sides hoped that public opinion would believe that they had succeeded in initiating a helpful dialogue. The reality was quite different.

The Ethiopian Government supported Yussuf from the very beginning because he was not a pan-Somali believer in liberating the Somalis in the Ogaden. Seeing little return on their investment, the Ethiopians gradually lost enthusiasm for someone who had not progressed much beyond being a limited warlord from 'Puntland'.

The Djibouti conference was again opened, and the two sides discussed their options with a UN team. Ultimately, the most that could be obtained was an agreement for a three-month cease-fire, during which time other matters could be agreed upon. There were two major events during the course of 2008 which indicated that Somali politics were turning strongly towards ideological lines. The first was the killing (by a US drone) of Aden Hashi 'Ayro', who was near to becoming recognized as the head of the Islamist movement in Somalia. Even more significantly, Sheikh Ahmed finally decided to end speculation about his ideological wavering and take the leadership of the moderate ARS—D.

THE DOWNFALL OF YUSSUF

In July 2008 the Prime Minister dismissed the mayor of Mogadishu, Mohamed Dheere, a warlord who had for a long time been one of Yussuf's closest friends and confidants. Dheere reacted with contempt for the Prime Minister's action. Many people believed that his sense of personal impunity and careless inability to provide assistance and security for his citizens was one of the principal reasons for the displacement of approximately one-half of the city's population during 2008. On 12 August Yussuf formally reinstated Dheere to his former position. In late August the President and Prime Minister met publicly and pledged to work together to defeat the SSICC. Yussuf indicated that the poor relations between him and the Prime Minister had contributed to the lack of progress in the political scene.

On 28 November 2008 Ethiopia announced that it would remove its troops from Somalia by the end of the year, irrespective of UN or AU troops being present. At the time of the Ethiopian announcement, there were only 3,400 AMISOM peace-keeping troops in Somalia. The more radical opposition forces were having increasing success in southern Somalia. It appeared to some observers that al-Qa'ida's foreign component was gaining in size, and the assumption was that these new fighters were being smuggled into the country through Kismayu, which had been under al-Shabaab control for many months. On 16 December President Yussuf dismissed Prime Minister Nur Hassan and, as required by the Transitional Charter, he called upon the TFP to approve the action. Instead, the TFP voted overwhelmingly to reinstate the Prime Minister. On the basis of the favourable vote, the Prime Minister reportedly planned to present a reconciliation plan that would give one-half of the seats in the TFP to opposition groups, including moderate Islamists. On the following day President Yussuf named Mohamed Mohamud Guled as the new Prime Minister, but no action was taken by the TFP. Yussuf left office on 21 December and, with his bodyguards, friends and family, he fled back to 'Puntland'. TFP President Sheikh Adan became acting President pending the election of a new President. Although Ethiopia had long ago abandoned the ineffective Yussuf, it began its withdrawal from Somalia on 3 January 2009, and the last Ethiopian convoy departed Baidoa and Somalia on 26 January. Immediately after the last Ethiopian vehicle left the town, al-Shabaab troops entered Baidoa. An al-Shabaab spokesman called a meeting in a stadium and appealed for an end to looting and disorder, proclaiming that henceforth *Shari'a* law would be imposed.

A NEW PRESIDENT AND A NEW GOVERNMENT

According to the Transitional Charter, the TFP had 30 days to elect a new President by secret ballot. Its first major political action came on 28 January 2009, when, meeting in Djibouti, the TFP voted to expand its membership from 275 to 550. There were 211 votes in favour, 11 opposed and three abstentions. Of the 275 new seats, 200 were allocated to supporters of Sheikh Sharif Sheikh Ahmed, with the remaining 75 reserved for civil society or the leadership of any new parties that might emerge during the transition.

On 30 January 2009 Sheikh Ahmed was elected President of Somalia in the second ballot. Defeated in the first round was former Vice-President Nur Hassan Hussein, who withdrew when he obtained only 59 votes. The unsuccessful candidate in the second round was Gen. Maslah Mohamed Siad, son of the late dictator. In his acceptance speech, the new President pledged to run a loyal and neutral Government and appealed to Somalis to join him. When the election results became known in Mogadishu, large crowds celebrated in the streets. The 45-year-old cleric had left many fond memories of his six-month period in 2006 as coup leader in Mogadishu.

One week after his arrival in Mogadishu, Sheikh Ahmed named Omar Abdirashid Ali Sharmarke, the son of Abdirashid Ali Sharmarke, the first elected President of Somalia, as Prime Minister. The nomination was ratified by the TFP by a vote of 414 to nine. Ali Sharmarke grew up in the USA and Canada and holds Canadian citizenship. He worked for the UN in Darfur, Sudan, and served briefly in Washington, DC, as Somali ambassador-designate.

Although the TFG's area of real authority was over only a few neighbourhoods in Mogadishu and the airport, a number of more moderate Islamist administrations around the country opted to establish ties with the new Government, and it gained control over some new parts of Mogadishu. Under a programme developed by the French Government, several hundred Somalis were sent to Djibouti for police training. Sheikh Sharif Sheikh Ahmed proclaimed Somalia an Islamic Republic as a means to counteract al-Shabaab propaganda, but he failed to take advantage of the initial shock his elevation to the presidency caused al-Shabaab and other hardline Islamists. For instance, a moderate group, the Ahlu Sunnah Wal Jam'a (Followers of the Prophetic Way and Consensus), formed in reaction to the harsh fundamentalism of al-Shabaab, was regarded as a possible ally for the President, but, reportedly, he was unwilling to co-operate with them.

In mid-May 2010 the TFP convened for the first time since December 2009, although during the session the parliament building came under attack from al-Shabaab and it was reported that at least 24 people had been killed. Nevertheless, proceedings continued and Sheikh Adan claimed that a vote of no confidence in Prime Minister Ali Sharmarke had been approved by 280 of the deputies present. However, it was later stated that the vote of no confidence had actually been taken on Sheikh Adan's position and the following day he announced his resignation as Speaker. Ali Sharmarke maintained that he would remain in his post and that President Sheikh Ahmed, who had indicated that he would seek to dismiss the premier, did not have the power to effect his removal. On 20 May 2010 Sheikh Ahmed confirmed that Ali Sharmarke and his Government would remain in office. On 28 May Sheikh Adan was again elected Speaker of the TFP.

The power struggle between Ali Sharmarke and Sheikh Ahmed continued during mid-2010, however, and on 21 September the Prime Minister announced his resignation. The Deputy Prime Minister and Minister of Energy and Fuel, Abdiwahid Ilmi Gonjeh, was appointed to replace Ali Sharmarke as premier on an acting basis.

In October 2010 President Sheikh Ahmed attended the opening of the General Assembly session in New York, as a new African head of state. While he was in New York, he agreed to meet a Somali-American, who had not returned to Somalia for over 20 years; Mohamed Abdullahi Mohamed 'Formajo', hitherto an officer for the New York State Department of Transportation, impressed the Somali President, who decided to make him the country's next Prime Minister.

Upon his arrival in Mogadishu, and with a mandate from the President, Abdullahi Mohamed immediately instituted radical reforms, reducing the size of the Cabinet from 39 to 18 members. His choices for ministers focused on technocrats, and he disregarded clan-balancing formulas. He took measures to ensure that civil servants and soldiers regularly received their pay, reorganized the accounting office and arranged that the Government pay its bills. He also ordered that the roads be repaired and schools reopened. His insistence on fiscal probity antagonized many politicians, particularly TFP Speaker Sheikh Adan.

Prime Minister Abdullahi Mohamed was fully aware of the 'clannism' that permeated all political activities in Somalia; his choices for the new administration favoured the supporters of President Sheikh Ahmed. However, Sheikh Adan was fearful that the relative inexperience of its members was a ruse to extend the mandate of the Government beyond the August 2011 date stipulated at the latest Djibouti meetings. The growing enmity between the President and Speaker brought renewed external intervention, and under pressure from the USA, the UN, Ethiopia and Uganda, a conference was held in Kampala on 9 June to discuss the modalities for ending the transition by the scheduled date in August. Until the Kampala meeting there was no enthusiasm within the highly corrupt TFG to fulfil this earlier obligation. The TFP had recently and overwhelmingly adopted a resolution extending the mandate of the legislature for a further three years. At Kampala, it was agreed that the August date for the transition to a permanent government would be impossible to arrange in the limited time available and the end of transition was postponed until August 2012.

Differences between President Sheikh Ahmed and Speaker Sheikh Adan continued, however, mostly surrounding Prime Minister Abdullahi Mohamed, whose efforts to establish a proper accounting system were a substantial aggravation to the Speaker and other members of Government. In order for Sheikh Ahmed to secure Sheikh Adan's agreement to the proposed extension, the Prime Minister was obliged to submit his resignation within 30 days. Abdullahi Mohamed was permitted to select his successor.

When the results of the Kampala talks were announced, crowds in Mogadishu protested at the departure of the popular Prime Minister, the first time that any Somali cabinet minister had received such public acclaim. Abdullahi Mohamed subsequently helped to establish a new political organization, the Somali Justice and Peace Party (known as Tayo), in which he holds office as Secretary-General. The Somali Justice and Peace Party is chaired by Dr Mariam Qasim, Abdullahi Mohamed's former Minister of Women's Affairs, and the first woman to head a Somali political party.

Abdullahi Mohamed's choice for the next Prime Minister of Somalia was Abdiweli Mohamed Ali, who was appointed on 23 June 2011. Also a Somali with dual US nationality, Abdiweli Mohamed Ali had hitherto been employed as a university professor at Niagara College in New York. His Cabinet, comprising 18 newly appointed ministers, was established on 21 July. In principle, this administration was to remain in place until 20 August 2012, when the transition would end and a permanent government would take its place.

To ensure compliance with the plan, the UN Special Representative for Somalia, Augustine Mahiga of Tanzania, negotiated a 'road map' for full Somali governmental autonomy by 20 August 2012. Mahiga held the first meeting on ending the transition in Somalia, attended by government leaders and representatives of international and regional organizations, on 4–6 September 2011. Several further meetings took place during the course of the following year, in addition to two large international conferences that were intended to mobilize the resources necessary for the post-transition period (see below). Among the essential tasks to be achieved by the scheduled date were the drafting of a new constitution, the arrangement of a system under which clan elders would select a Constituent Assembly, the selection of a parliamentary Speaker and the organization of a presidential election. Despite some minor time slippage at the end of the period, the programme in general proceeded as planned. Although comprehensive, the new Somali Constitution was drafted quickly, and little about it was made known to the public and a number of important politicians before it was accepted.

THE LONDON CONFERENCE

The United Kingdom had shown little interest in the Somalia disaster until late 2011 (although it provided some assistance to 'Somaliland'), and had no formal diplomatic representative based in Mogadishu. However, British Foreign Secretary William Hague, who visited Somalia on 2 February 2012 to co-ordinate the forthcoming conference in the British capital, London, announced the reopening of the United Kingdom embassy. The London Conference, which was held on 23 February, was a significant event for Somalia. Delegates from more than 54 nations (including Ethiopia, Kenya, Uganda and France) and organizations were present, probably the largest gathering that had been staged on Somalia since its independence. 'Somaliland' and 'Puntland' were both represented at the conference.

The conference was addressed by British Prime Minister David Cameron and other international leaders, including UN Secretary-General Ban Ki-Moon and US Secretary of State Hillary Clinton. A lengthy communiqué, which was published on 24 February, projected an overall positive attitude towards providing urgent assistance for Somalia. The interests of most participants encompassed security, food, business and investments. There was some disappointment at the level of financial commitments (amounting to US $300m. instead of billions of dollars), but the engagement demonstrated by the British Government was generally applauded by the Somali people.

TURKISH ASSISTANCE

Amidst the ongoing humanitarian crisis, in August 2011 Turkish Prime Minister Recep Tayyip Erdoğan, who was accompanied by his family, five ministers, and various relief experts, made a significant visit to Somalia. While meeting President Sheikh Ahmed, Erdoğan announced that a new Turkish ambassador to Somalia was to be appointed, the first in 20 years. The Turkish Prime Minister and his entourage then made a tour of Mogadishu, including refugee camps. Within days of Erdoğan's visit, Turkey pledged US $250m. in humanitarian relief for Somalia.

On 4 October 2011 al-Shabaab staged a bomb attack at the University of Mogadishu, which was targeted at students preparing to take examinations for scholarships to Turkey. The blast killed over 100 students and wounded many more. The Turkish Government sent an aircraft to Mogadishu to transport the most severely injured for special medical treatment in Turkey.

On 31 May–1 June 2012 the Turkish Government organized a conference in İstanbul, with the theme 'Preparing Somalia's Future: Goals for 2015'. Prime Minister Erdoğan headed the conference, which was attended by Ban and representatives from 57 countries and 11 international organizations. The conference issued a communiqué that generally reiterated the objectives issued by the London Conference of peace, security, co-operation, and adherence to the 'road map'.

THE TRANSITIONAL 'ROAD MAP'

The first task at the end of the transitional process required 135 carefully selected elders to agree on the 825 members of the Constituent Assembly, which was to approve the draft constitution. The criteria for selection were developed to exclude major figures such as warlords who had perpetuated the country's civil conflict. The first obstacle in the final transitional stage emerged when the elders insisted on reviewing the draft constitution first. They proposed some changes (including an increase in the new parliament from 225 to 275 members, and the establishment of an upper house), which were ignored. An Elders' Arbitration Committee was responsible for establishing the members of the Constituent Assembly.

The National Constituent Assembly, according to the 'road map', was scheduled to convene on 12 July 2012, but this was delayed owing to the elders' desire to revise the draft constitution. It appeared that certain elders were withholding the names of eligible Constituent Assembly members until the desired constitutional changes were implemented. As a result, it was agreed that the number of parliamentary deputies would be increased to 275. The Constituent Assembly finally met on 25 July. The Provisional Constitution was overwhelmingly approved in 1 August, with 621 delegates of the total 825 voting in favour and 13 against. (Adoption of the Provisional Constitution was dependent on the outcome of a future referendum.) A list of members of the new Parliament was eventually approved by the Constituent Assembly on 24 August, although several deputies selected by the Constituent Assembly were rejected by the Technical Selection Committee. The new members of the Federal Parliament included 30 women, a large number for Somalia, but still significantly fewer than the 30% stipulated in the new Constitution.

The election of the parliamentary Speaker and two Deputy Speakers was delayed until 28 August 2012. Six candidates contested the poll for the post of Speaker. The second round of voting was won by Mohamed Osman Jawari, a former Minister of Labour of the Siad Barre period and Chairman of the committee that had drafted the new Constitution.

THE 2012 PRESIDENTIAL ELECTION

The election of the new President was, of course, the most important part of the transitional process. Some 25 presidential candidates successfully registered to contest the poll. The new Constitution specified precise criteria for presidential eligibility: candidates were required to be Muslim, over the age of 40 and without a criminal record; they were also to pay a US $10,000 registration fee. Among the most high-profile candidates were incumbent President Sheikh Ahmed, Prime Minister Abdiweli Mohamed Ali, former Speaker Sheikh Adan and former premier Abdullahi Mohamed. Other candidates included: Abdirahman Abdullahi Baadiyow, the co-founder of Mogadishu University; Hassan Sheikh Mohamud, an academic and civic activist, Abdullah Ahmed Adow, a defeated presidential candidates in 2000 and a former ambassador to the USA; Ahmed Ismail Samatar, a prominent academic; and Yusuf Garaad Omar, the former head of the BBC Somali Service in London

In various Somali commentaries about the forthcoming presidential election, most believed that Sheikh Ahmed and Abdiweli Mohamed Ali had the best chances of election, although Abdullahi Mohamed still had a strong following from his tenure as Prime Minister. However, the President had a serious disadvantage in that he and his administration were specified as corrupt in a confidential UN Monitoring Group report of 27 June 2012, which was made public on the internet shortly afterwards. The report stated that 'systematic embezzlement, pure and simple misappropriation of funds and theft of public money have become government systems'. The UN estimated that only 30% of tax collections and other payments ever reached the treasury. Sheikh Ahmed denied the charges against his Government. Sheikh Ahmed also ordered the release of over 200 prisoners, including several senior al-Shabaab members, to celebrate the *Id al-Fitr* holiday. In another questionable action, he provided a diplomatic permit for a high-level al-Shabaab officer.

The presidential election took place on 10 September 2012 at the Police Academy in Mogadishu, with 271 of the 275 members of parliament present. Sheikh Ahmed narrowly won the first round, with 64 votes, followed by Hassan Sheikh Mohamud, with 60 votes, and Abdiweli Mohamed Ali, with 32 votes, no candidate therefore securing the necessary two-thirds of votes cast. Abdiweli and a fourth candidate withdrew from the election prior to the second poll. In the second round of voting on the same day Hassan Sheikh Mohamud was overwhelming elected, receiving 190 votes, while Sheikh Ahmed took 79. The outgoing President Sheikh Ahmed conceded defeat, lauding the transparency of the election process, and pledged to work with the new President. Two days after the presidential election, al-Shabaab staged a suicide bomb attack at the Jazeera Hotel, near the airport, where Mohamud was holding a joint press conference with the visiting Kenyan foreign minister. Three hotel workers and a security guard died in the attack.

Mohamud was formally inaugurated as President on 16 September 2012, at a ceremony attended by many regional heads of state. Under the terms of the new Constitution, for the transitional process to be completed he was to appoint a Prime Minister within 30 days; the new premier would then be tasked to form a new administration within 60 days.

AL-SHABAAB AND THE STRUGGLE FOR NATIONAL SURVIVAL

Many native Somali members of al-Shabaab tend to organize themselves along clan lines largely as a means of increasing their access to power and to profit. The few hundred foreign organizers and jihadis confer upon themselves the title of *muhajirin* (or émigrés) and the locals are *ansars* ('helpers') from the Koranic legend of the trek from Mecca to Medina. According to an International Crisis Group study of Somali Islamists, the foreign elements consolidated their control of al-Shabaab by moving the group closer to the orbit of al-Qa'ida.

In April 2010 Human Rights Watch (HRW) published a report, part of which focused on al-Shabaab beliefs and actions, which presents a grim picture of a group wishing to control every aspect of the lives of the people under its command. The report noted that many of the practices contravene regional and international human rights standards. Al-Shabaab generally prohibits all gatherings (including wedding parties), ring tones on mobile cellular telephones, Western music and films, and, in some areas, the wearing of bras, seen as a 'Western deception'. Smoking and the use of qat, a mildly addictive narcotic herb used heretofore by nearly all Somali males and some women, were totally forbidden. Al-Shabaab did not permit Somalis to watch televised coverage of the 2010 Fédération Internationale de Football Association (FIFA) World Cup matches held in South Africa.

The almost whimsical nature of beliefs and punishments appear to vary from one area to another, apparently dependent upon the notions and moods of the local 'emirs' (al-Shabaab leaders). The range of punishments varies from confiscations of offending mobile phones and the shaving of heads to beatings and lashes to amputations and executions. Failure to attend prayers at the local mosque was nearly always punished with lashings. The heaviest burdens of al-Shabaab imperatives target Somali women who are punished for appearing in public without the heavy *abayas* that cover every part of their bodies from head to toe. Women were punished for travelling without a male escort (who is not permitted to occupy the same row of seats as the woman). Women can no longer practice a trade, a real hardship in a community in which a large number of male providers have been killed in wars or gone abroad to find work. According to the Associated Press, households in southern Somalia were required to contribute a male child to the militants' ranks; childless families had to pay US $50, equivalent to an annual income. Seemingly intent on making more misery for the lives of Somalis, al-Shabaab outlawed a number of UN and Western aid agencies operating in Somalia, an action contributing to the hardships resulting from the 2011 famines in southern Somalia.

These actions have served to erode al-Shabaab's stature and credibility. A suicide bombing at a medical school graduation ceremony in Mogadishu in December 2009 killed more than 20 people, including TFG ministers and some of the graduates. It was ascribed to foreign jihadists working with al-Shabaab, and according to an International Crisis Group report, the incident led to some high-level defections and acute public resentment.

Al-Shabaab mounted its first attack outside Somalia in July 2010, when it detonated bombs at two sites in Kampala, Uganda, during screenings of the 2010 FIFA World Cup final. The bombs killed 74 people and left a further 70 injured. Al-Shabaab claimed responsibility for the bombings and stated that they were revenge for allegedly indiscriminate artillery fire by AMISOM Ugandan troops in Mogadishu. The Kampala attacks had broad repercussions at the AU summit which opened in Kampala barely two weeks later.

As reinforced AMISOM and government forces increased pressures on al-Shabaab during 2010–11, the Islamist hold on Mogadishu became more tenuous. By July 2011 observers believed that the TFG controlled as much as 85% of the capital. In a quite unexpected move, on 6 August most Somali al-Shabaab forces withdrew from Mogadishu, heading south towards Kismayu with 50 or more trucks and other vehicles. Most of the senior foreign fighters flew out of Balidogle airfield north of Mogadishu.

Since that time, al-Shabaab has been in decline. Its last stronghold in the Mogadishu area (Maslah camp) was seized on

1 March 2012. The insurgent forces have lost control of the southern towns of Afgoye, Balad, Baidoa, Hudur, Baledwayne, Merca and Barawe, and the last significant town under al-Shabaab control, Kismayu, is under threat. Al-Shabaab is preparing bases and camps in the jungle areas of the lower Juba and in the Golis mountains overlooking the Gulf of Aden.

Al-Shabaab's defeat was attributed to a number of factors, which may also reflect the movement's ongoing internal disputes: drought, famine and falling receipts from its 'taxes' on shipments in and out of Kismayu reportedly caused cash problems for the group; the 'Arab Spring' of revolutionary protests in North Africa and the Middle East affected countries that had been generous with their contributions to al-Qa'ida and al-Shabaab in the past, and donations fell; the Islamists suffered from growing unpopularity caused by the capricious and harsh rules introduced by their leaders; al-Shabaab had a serious 'image problem', with recent executions of women and children and the expulsion of Western aid groups; Western efforts to control fund-raising by Islamic radical groups showed some success; and some critical leaders were killed by Western drones or in confrontations with TFG forces, hampering control of the organization. Defections are increasing, and the Somali Government and AMISOM have recently jointly published the 'National Disengagement Framework for former al-Shabaab members'. There are reports of al-Shabaab executions of its own members for fear of their collaboration with foreign intelligence services. Al-Shabaab formally joined al Qa'ida on 12 February 2012, perhaps showing a need for support.

'THE REPUBLIC OF SOMALILAND'

'The Republic of Somaliland' comprises the territory of the former British protectorate of the same name. It has a population of approximately 3.5m., and it has been self-governing since 1991. The region has a bicameral Government with an upper house, the *guurti*, and a house of representatives. Long before the collapse of the Siad Barre regime in January 1991, the primary desire for the people of the former British Somaliland was to revoke their voluntary 1960 association with the Republic of Somalia. 'Somaliland' now celebrates 19 May 1991 as the date of its second independence. Without international recognition, it first proved difficult to attract aid, and this in turn meant the Government had no means to settle the claims of ex-guerrilla fighters, nor could it afford to demobilize them. Only assistance from non-governmental organizations enabled the Government to begin the work of repairing the war-damaged infrastructure of the region, and some progress was made in the removal of mines (it was estimated that there were approximately 2m. such devices to be cleared), souvenirs of the repressive Siad Barre regime.

Since 1991 the single fundamental issue of 'Somaliland's' foreign policy has been the quest for international recognition, a goal that continues to elude the Government. 'Somaliland's' relations with its neighbours have vacillated between confrontation and co-operation. The representatives of 'Somaliland' show great imagination in their quest, and frequently receive invitations to attend international meetings and festivities. The only meetings that the Government of 'Somaliland' resolutely refuses to attend are those that involve Somali national reconciliation or integration.

The AU remains bound by the principle of respect of borders existing at the time of independence. 'Somaliland' rejects this interpretation because it first gained independence on 26 June 1960, four days before it voluntarily joined the Somali Republic, when that territory was granted independence. 'Somaliland's' first President was Abidirahman Mohamed Ali 'Tur'. The 'Somalilanders' turned to their traditional elders to select a new 'national' leader to succeed 'Tur'. After protracted discussions at Borama, the elders selected Mohamed Ibrahim Egal, an elder statesman who served as the first Prime Minister of the Republic of Somalia in 1960 and served in several governments in Somalia before the central administration dissolved in 1991. Egal was successful in negotiating with the 'Somaliland' clans, was able to disarm factions and set the candidate state on a solid path. After Egal's death in 2002, he was succeeded by his Vice-President, Kahin. Without the approval of the AU, Western governments were unlikely to recognize 'Somaliland' as an independent state. In December 2005 President Kahin submitted an application for 'Somaliland' membership of the AU, but it was not accepted.

Relations with Djibouti have historically been strained because of former President Egal's refusal to participate in the Djibouti-sponsored Somali national reconciliation process. Looking back to the pre-colonial period, 'Somaliland' would like to re-establish Berbera as an alternative port for Ethiopia. There have also been a number of political disagreements and minor border disputes between 'Somaliland' and its neighbours. Relations with 'Puntland' suffer because of disputed ownership of the regions of Sanaag and Sool, which were part of British Somaliland, but the inhabitants of which, the Harti, are more closely related to clans in 'Puntland'. Since the late 1990s the dispute over Sanaag and Sool has caused numerous low-level armed confrontations. In late October 2004 fighting erupted at the village of Adi-Addeye, north of Sool's capital, Las Anod, which resulted in the deaths of 109 people. 'Somaliland' protested to the AU, IGAD, the UN Security Council and various foreign governments, and accused TFG President Yussuf (the former leader of 'Puntland') of engineering the violence to justify his request for international peace-keepers in Somalia.

'Somaliland's desire to be recognized as a democratic model was negatively affected by former President Kahin's various contrived delays in holding elections in 2008, and again in early 2009. There are three political parties in 'Somaliland', and after the second delay in April 2009, they all agreed to hold elections on 27 September. However, it was not until 26 June 2010 that elections were finally held. The incumbent President Kahin was soundly defeated by Ahmad Muhammad Silanyo, who took 49.9% of overall votes against Kahin's 33.2%. The new President was sworn in on 27 July.

While remaining focused on asserting its own independence, 'Somaliland' is attempting to suppress the separatist aims of the recently self-declared 'Khatumo state', which is located in the northern regions of Sool, Sanaag and Ayn, on the border of 'Somaliland'. The Khatumo militia in August 2012 twice attacked 'Somaliland' forces near the northern town of Buhodle. However, this situation may change. In early September it was reported that the commander of the Khatumo militia force had defected and surrendered to the 'Somaliland' authorities.

THE AUTONOMOUS STATE OF 'PUNTLAND'

In May 1998 delegates from three north-eastern regions of Somalia met in Garowe to establish a single administration for the area as an autonomous state within Somalia. They named the region 'Puntland' or Land of Frankincense, one of its main exports, and designated Garowe as its capital. In July the delegates elected Abdullahi Yussuf Ahmed, a former leader of the SSDF and later President of Somalia, as their President, and Muhammad Abdi Hashi as Vice-President. In August Yussuf established a 69-member parliament and a nine-member Cabinet. In February 2001 a group of 78 elders, intellectuals and other prominent members of society issued a statement that accused the 'Puntland' Government of committing human rights violations, concluding secret marine agreements, secretly joining the pro-Ethiopian and southern-controlled SRRC Council, printing counterfeit money and sabotaging peace in the region.

The 'Puntland' Government of President Abdirahman Mohamed Farole generally co-operates with the Somalian authorities in the hope of receiving its share of significant political positions and consideration, while it defends itself against any incursions from 'Somaliland'. In January 2011 President Farole announced that 'Puntland' had suspended all co-operation with the TFG, after complaining that there were too many unfulfilled promises and impediments to 'Puntland's aspirations. Farole objected strongly to Prime Minister Mohamed Abdullahi Mohamed's questioning of the legality of the 'Puntland' administration. To demonstrate the anger of the 'Puntland' administration, Farole dismissed four ministers for having 'too close ties' with the TFG. Orders were given that prohibited any TFG aircraft from landing at any of 'Puntland's airports.

Relations improved significantly in June 2011, however, after the appointment of a new Somali Prime Minister, Abdiweli Mohamed Ali, who is a Majertein, as are Farole and most people in 'Puntland'. A new rapprochement was evidently made when President Sheikh Ahmed and a large delegation flew to Garowe on 28 August for an official visit. It was assumed that the regime change in Mogadishu in September 2012 would be acceptable to the 'Puntland' authorities.

Economy

WALTER S. CLARKE

A TIME OF POSITIVE CHANGE

Just one year ago, Somalia was undergoing a national humanitarian emergency more grave than anything experienced before. As a result of the effects of the worst drought in 50 or 60 years, more than 4m. people, or 53% of the national population, were in crisis, with 3.3m. in need of rescue assistance. Of the 4m. in crisis, 3m. lived in the south, which was largely controlled by the militant Islamist al-Shabaab. With better rains, the winter crop situation improved considerably, and UN agencies announced in February 2012 that the country was no longer considered to be in a state of famine. By March the Somali army, supported by African Union (AU) forces, was able to complete its efforts to drive all al-Shabaab military units out of Mogadishu, although total security in the capital was still not ensured. Despite continued al-Shabaab suicide bomb attacks in Mogadishu, a presidential election was successfully conducted on 10 September and the new President, Hassan Sheikh Mohamud, was installed on 16 September (see Recent History).

A NEW ERA IN MOGADISHU

According to recent visitors, Mogadishu is rapidly returning to normalcy, and businesses are gradually reopening. Following the improvement in the security situation, Somalis are more likely to pursue a social life in the capital, and many small shops, bars, restaurants and internet cafés remain open until past midnight, in contrast to the period when al-Shabaab controlled sections of the city.

UN personnel returned to their offices in Mogadishu from Nairobi in February 2012. The Turkish Government reopened its embassy in the Somali capital on 1 November 2011, not long after a visit to the capital by Turkish Prime Minister Recep Tayyip Erdoğan and a large delegation in August. Soon afterwards, Turkish Airlines established weekly flights between İstanbul and Mogadishu. Twice-weekly service began on 8 September 2012. The British Foreign Secretary, who visited Somalia in February 2012, also announced that the United Kingdom embassy was to be reopened. The US ambassador and US Special Representative to Somalia, James Swan, continued to co-ordinate all US activities in Somalia from Nairobi.

CHALLENGES FOR THE NEW GOVERNMENT

The new President of Somalia will find that there are virtually no state finances once he appoints a new Prime Minister and a new government is formed. According to a UN Monitoring Group report, which was published officially on 30 July 2012, the Transitional Federal Government (TFG) administration, established eight years earlier, engaged in management practices described as 'chaotic and opaque ... the product of deliberate, systematic and often sophisticated behaviour intended to prevent transparency or accountability'. The TFG President, the parliamentary Speaker of Parliament, successive Prime Ministers and cabinet officials from ministers to district commissioners were all involved to a certain degree. In a World Bank report, issued in May, it was reported that about 68% of all revenues in 2009–10 were unaccounted for. The Monitoring Group report included details on multiple passport selling and currency forgery schemes that generated huge profits for various officials, of between US $130m. and $150m., and nothing for the state. In 2009, under pressure from transitional financial institutions and international partners, the then Prime Minister Omar Abdirashid Ali Sharmarke, established a Public Financial Management Unit (PFMU) to introduce accountability and transparency to the TFG government structures. After one annual and two quarterly reports which provided credible insights into TFG misadministration, the TFG Minister of Finance closed the PFMU.

The UN Monitoring Group Report offers insights into potential sources of income for the new Somali administration. At present, the most dependable sources of income are import taxes and port fees. The port of Mogadishu is the most important source of official funds, with reported revenue in the 2011 financial year of nearly US $12m. Unfortunately for the state, the port-docking and -handling fees are received directly by the port authority to pay for labour costs and port upkeep. The UN Monitoring Report suggested that taxes on the narcotic qat, and telecommunications and remittance companies could represent new sources of state income. It is hoped that the new administration formed by President Mohamud and his Prime Minister will be able to address effectively what the UN terms the 'corrupt and incoherent' official financial accounting system.

There are no reliable figures for the number of Somalis living overseas, but they are a very important source of funds for families in Somalia. It is believed that at least 1.5m. Somalis reside outside the country, with large populations in the United Kingdom, Canada and the USA, but with the most significant populations in Saudi Arabia, the United Arab Emirates (UAE) and Yemen. At a December 2005 conference in Washington, DC (USA), sponsored by the World Bank and the UN Development Programme (UNDP), it was estimated that 1m. expatriate Somalis remitted between US $825m. and $1,000m. to Somalia during 2004. More than 50% of remittances were believed to be destined for consumption, but a significant portion went into investment.

At the heart of the foreign remittance process in Somalia is the *hawala* system, which relies on trusted agents at both ends to effect informal money transfers. Although *hawala* was practised for many years before the 11 September 2001 attacks, US investigators were suspicious that it allowed funds for terrorism to circulate and in November the USA closed the al-Barakat money-transfer company, which operated in 40 countries, and seized its assets, worth some US $43m., owing to its suspected links to terrorist organizations. At the time al-Barakat was Somalia's biggest employer, with radio and telecommunications interests in addition to its remittance business. After several years of investigation by international banking authorities, a single employee in Scandinavia was found to have suspicious ties and, after his dismissal in 2005, al-Barakat was permitted to reopen.

REFUGEES AND INTERNALLY DISPLACED PERSONS

With the restoration of order in Mogadishu and the departure of al-Shabaab from most cities and towns in Somalia by mid-2012, many internally displaced persons (IDPs and refugees, who had fled owing to the conflict or drought conditions, were expected to return home. International agencies estimate that at least 1.5m. Somalis are IDPs. There are an estimated 500,000 Somali refugees at the Dadaab refugee complex in north-eastern Kenya. Another 130,000 Somali refugees have taken refuge in Ethiopia.

In October 2011 the Government of Kenya prevented new Somalian refugees from entering the Dadaab complex, on the grounds that the three camps there were filled to capacity and that more refugees would constitute a threat to Kenya's security. The Somali authorities are concerned about the financial costs necessary to house and feed potential large numbers of returning refugees, and that their resettlement might provoke ethnic tensions and discontent. The Government of Kenya, aware of the al-Shabaab retreat from many towns and villages, has urged refugee agencies to close down Dadaab and repatriate the Somalians.

THE ECONOMICS OF PIRACY

Intensive surveillance, more participant vessels and better intelligence-sharing have proved effective in combating high sea piracy. Three naval forces have now been established to interdict piracy in the Gulf of Aden and the Indian Ocean: the European Union (EU) Naval Force Somalia (NAVFOR), the North Atlantic Treaty Organization (NATO) Operation Atalanta and Task Force 151. After closely integrated campaigns in 2011, they reported that pirate activity appears to be in decline.

Modern piracy in the Horn of Africa began in 2005, when four ships were attacked: three ships (a liquefied natural gas carrier, a freighter and a bulk carrier) were captured. Two paid ransoms (reportedly just over US $1m.), while one was released without payment. The fourth, a luxury cruise ship, effectively outran the pirate skiffs. From this modest beginning emerged a fairly extensive industry, with a number of ships and hundreds of crewmen held in ships or onshore of small coastal towns, including Hobyo and Eyl in 'Puntland', as well as similar villages near Mogadishu and Kismayu. Now involved in the piracy business are businessmen with access to ship itineraries, capacities, cargo, crew and defences, located in London, the United Kingdom, and the UAE. Pirate syndicates sell shares to finance their investments in boats, weapons and personnel. Ship ransoms have grown exponentially each year, as have the number of attacks. The average ship ransom in 2005 was $150,000; in 2010 the average payment was $5.4m. The total ransoms paid in 2010 were $238m. and total losses to shippers using the Red Sea and the Gulf of Aden in that year amounted to about $12,000m., when the costs of extra fuel, insurance and security were included.

Co-ordinated attacks sometimes involve two or three large ships (usually captured fishing boats) and several small boarding skiffs, which are taken to a favoured mooring near the villages mentioned above. Lawyers in the UAE then negotiate the ransom payment. During the negotiations, which can last for months, the crews are usually well cared for, but there are now several reports of crews being beaten and otherwise mistreated.

The distribution of the proceeds follows a fairly standard formula: one-half goes to pirate gang leaders, local warlords and the legal negotiators and intermediaries, while one-quarter goes to the gang that seizes the ship, with a special share going to the first pirate who boards the victim ship. The pirates who watch the ship and take care of the crews until the ransom is paid receive 10% and the local village receives 10%. Despite the fact that unseen businessmen and lawyers take the greatest share, there is no lack of volunteers to take up piracy. For the pirate who actually boards the ship, the cash reward can be as much as US $150,000.

Reflecting the apparent decline in piracy activity, it was reported that in the first half of 2012 there were 69 attacks involving Somali pirates, compared with 163 during the same period in 2011. In February 2012 seven ships and 177 hostages were being held, compared with 30 ships and 682 crewmen held a year earlier. The NATO Deputy Chief of Staff reported that there was no sign that pirate bases in 'Puntland' were building up logistical supplies, and attributed much of the success to the use of armed guards, as well as improved co-ordination within the counter-piracy fleet. In the most recent indication that the fleet had moved to an offensive position, in early September an EU NAVFOR helicopter attacked a pirate land base, damaging a number of the pirate vessels.

AL-SHABAAB'S BUSINESS MODEL

Al-Shabaab began its operations in Somalia in early 2007 as a radical off-shoot of the Union of Islamic Courts, most of whose members had scattered in response to the Ethiopian invasion a few months earlier. Al-Shabaab wished to be seen as a defender of the Somali people by attacking Ethiopian forces while establishing a strict *Shari'a*-based justice system. As masters of a quasi-state, al-Shabaab distributed money and food in public ceremonies that were widely publicized. It also organized an all-inclusive taxation system in which uniform taxes were applied to trade, services, domestic agriculture and all imported goods. Under regional emirs (al-Shabaab military personnel), taxes were collected from throughout its area of control and remitted to the most senior al-Shabaab leaders. Some local funds were retained to build roads, regulate the activities of non-governmental organizations (NGOs) and generally enforce onerous application of extremely arbitrary interpretations of Islamic law. Efforts were made through contacts in the Somali diaspora to attract young recruits to the new Islamic state. Within months of its creation, al-Shabaab's area of control included most of south and central Somalia; it also controlled most of Mogadishu, with the exception of a few blocks in the centre of the city held somewhat tenuously by the Government.

Once it had most of the accoutrements of a centralized state, al-Shabaab attempted to control what its population could learn about the outside world. It banned Western music, films, television and internet news sources. Listening to BBC or the Voice of America news services was totally prohibited and any effort to contravene these regulations could lead to torture or death. Even school children fall within the financial tentacles of al-Shabaab. In April 2011 the al-Shabaab commander responsible for finance in Jowhar, the capital of the Middle Shabelle region, ordered all school teachers to report the exact number of students in their schools. After the registration is completed, each student will be required to contribute one US dollar a month to the *jihad*. Lacking funds, students will be obliged to contribute themselves to the *jihad*. In the absence of either contribution, the student will be seen as anti-Islamic.

After al-Shabaab's draconian style became better known in the West, there was an immediate fall in donations from the diaspora. Al-Shabaab's efforts to control the work of NGOs operations in south and central Somalia led some humanitarian groups to leave the country voluntarily; others, including World Food for Peace (WFP), were forced to leave. The two major sources of funds for al-Shabaab by 2010 were proceeds from the port of Kismayu and the sale of illegal firewood through the port of Kismayu.

In a recent study of the situation in Somalia, a UN Monitoring Group outlined al-Shabaab's revenue sources in descending order of importance, as follows: taxation and extortion; commerce, trade and contraband; diaspora support; and external support. The UN Monitoring Group observed that al-Shabaab 'is evolving from an armed faction into a lucrative consortium of business interests'. The report also stated that al-Shabaab's taxation system was 'far more sophisticated and comprehensive than that of any other Somali authority, including the administrations of Puntland and Somaliland'. The tax collections are made personally by representatives of al-Shabaab from owners of general stores; businesses are taxed on the basis of size and profitability; businesses also pay a flat 2.5% on annual profits; farmers who may not have cash are taxed in kind on the basis of tonnage of product, as well as a levy of US $10 per acre under cultivation; ad hoc 'contributions' are also imposed for specific military operations. These are known as '*jihad* war contributions'.

A separate study estimated that al-Shabaab operations generated between US $70m. and $100m. per year before the ongoing government campaign to force the insurgents out of Kismayu. Annual Kismayu port revenues were estimated at $30m.–$60m. However, the loss of economic control over the Bakara market in Mogadishu also severely affected al-Shabaab finances.

FOREIGN AID AND DEVELOPMENT

In January 2004 the UN, in co-operation with the World Bank, UNDP and several other UN agencies, released a new socio-economic survey for Somalia, the first since the collapse of the Siad Barre regime in 1991. Reliable data were expected to assist donors to divert funds to those sectors in most need of development. (In the mid-2000s Somalia received some US $100m. in assistance each year.) Some key findings in the report were that 43% of Somalis lived on income of $1 per day or less and that 'Somaliland' and 'Puntland' had better income levels than the rest of the country because the degree of conflict in those territories was lower than in the south. In July a new Coca-Cola beverage factory opened in Mogadishu. Somali businessmen had invested $8.3m. in the factory, which employed 150 people; some 70 others were employed with distributors for the company. The factory was capable of producing 36,000 bottles per hour. A subsequent World Bank report was published in early 2006: *Somalia: From Resilience towards Recovery and Development. A Country Economic Memorandum for Somalia*. This survey examined many issues of the Somali failed state and supplemented the statistics provided in the earlier report.

FOREIGN TRADE

There are no reliable recent trade statistics, meaningful figures being impossible to produce in the absence of anything resembling proper administration. Despite a considerable narrowing of the trade deficit in 1988, to US $157.6m., Somalia's foreign trade deficit (almost entirely financed by foreign aid) was estimated at $278.6m. in 1989, with the deficit on the current account of the balance of payments increasing from $98.5m. in 1988 to $156.7m. in 1989. In 2003 Somalia's main export destinations were believed to include the UAE ($37m.), Yemen ($22m.), Oman ($10m.), Nigeria ($4m.), Bahrain ($3m.) and India ($3m.). The main suppliers of imports included Kenya ($58m.), Djibouti ($26m.), Brazil ($25m.), India ($12m.), Thailand ($16m.) and the United Kingdom ($6m.).

'SOMALILAND'

The relative stability of the self-proclaimed 'Republic of Somaliland', following its secession in 1991, contributed to improvements in the economy of that territory. More than one-half of the 3.5m. population of 'Somaliland' comprises nomadic pastoralists. As in Somalia proper, a substantial portion of regional income was derived from remittances. Population growth, drought and general poverty ensured that the agricultural sector was unable to sustain real development. The lack of international recognition effectively closed access to international financial institutions such as the World Bank and the IMF. However, 'Somaliland' has received assistance from the EU and has a number of bilateral agreements, listed below.

In March 2005 the Berbera Port Authority and the Ethiopian Maritime and Transit Services Enterprise concluded an agreement to increase Ethiopian transit trade through Berbera. In 2010 2.5m. cattle were exported through the Berbera Port, about 78% of the total to Saudi Arabia, 20% to Yemen and the remainder to Egypt and Oman. The local authorities are seeking investors to finance dredging of the port to a depth of 20 m from its current depth of 11.5 m. The port director estimates that the expansion will cost US $60m. To date, the largest private investment in 'Somaliland' is a $17m. Coca Cola bottling plant outside Hargeysa, which employs 57 workers and produces 11,000 bottles per hour. It has 120 clients in 'Somaliland', 'Puntland' and Mogadishu. The largest private sector company in 'Somaliland' is the Dahabshil group of remittance offices. Funds received from the 'Somaliland' diaspora through these affiliates have financed hospitals, schools and infrastructure projects.

Officials also explored ways to improve trade between Somalia and 'Somaliland'. In June 2005 the UN rehabilitated the Berbera and Dhoqoshey police stations in 'Somaliland' and offered training courses for the Internal Control Unit, the Special Protection Unit and the Criminal Investigations Department. Additionally, the UN supported the territory's Law Review Commission and the University of Hargeysa Legal Clinic. In July 2012 the 'Somaliland' authorities announced that both the Hargeysa and Berbera airports were to be upgraded; the project was to be partially financed with Kuwaiti government funds.

In January 2000 President Egal approved a plan for Total Red Sea, the local subsidiary of the French oil company, to assume management responsibility for the port of Berbera's petroleum-storage facilities. On 18 April 2001 a 'Somaliland' newspaper announced that a British company, Rovagold, had received permission to commence prospecting for offshore petroleum. Rovagold, which had signed agreements in 1999 with two Chinese companies, Continental Petroleum Engineering Co and China Petrochemical Corpn, planned to start exploration activities off the coast of Berbera. In mid-October 2002 'Somaliland' signed an agreement with the Seminal Copenhagen Group to begin petroleum exploration in late 2002.

In Hargeysa, a pirate's prison, which was refurbished with a UN grant of US $1.5m., was opened in November 2010. In August 2012 it held 313 prisoners, including, under an agreement between the Presidents of 'Somaliland' and Seychelles, a group of 17 pirates who were convicted in Seychelles.

In spite of its status as a state without formal international recognition, 'Somaliland' has concluded a number of arrangements with the EU, several of which have been active for years. According to the EU, these include 27 projects in governance (€21.9m.); 13 projects in the education sector (€11.2m.); 13 projects designed to spur economic growth (€15.1m.); and nine projects in other sectors (€8.5m.) such as health, water and sanitation. The 2011 EU report cites the Sheikh Veterinary School and livestock quarantine station in Berbera as a special project in a sector that provides employment to 63% of the people and generates about 40% of 'Somaliland's' GDP. The EU expert also notes that school enrolment in 'Somaliland' grew from 38.6% in 2006 to an estimated 60% in 2010. The EU also plans to provide technical experts to assist in developing a sustainable solution to a recently announced Free Primary Education Policy.

'Somaliland' receives assistance from many international financial institutions, as well as bilateral assistance from Western states. British Secretary of State Andrew Mitchell visited Hargeysa in January 2011, where he publicly announced that 40% of the United Kingdom's aid to Somalia would go to 'Somaliland'. The USA also provides assistance to 'Somaliland', primarily through international agencies and NGOs.

'PUNTLAND'

The regional administration of 'Puntland' was established as an autonomous region in August 1998. 'Puntland' occupies about one-third of the total land area of Somalia, incorporating the areas of Bari and Nugaal, and parts of Mudug, Sanaag and Sool regions. The main economic activity of 'Puntland' at that time was cattle-rearing, while frankincense and Gum Arabica were also principal exports.

Although most state officials decry the fact that most Somali pirates operate from 'Puntland', the authorities seldom take any direct action to cause the pirate combines much concern. There was some international relief in March 2012, when 'Puntland' President Abdirahman Mohamed Farole welcomed the EU decision allowing NAVFOR ships to fire at pirate bases on shore. There has been some previous co-operation from the 'Puntland' Government on counter-piracy activity, which was instrumental in forcing pirates out of the coastal towns of Garaad and Eyl.

The possibility of profitable oil exploitation in 'Puntland' now appears less likely. The Horn Petroleum Corpn of Canada announced in August 2012 that it would plug and abandon its Shabeel North-1 well in the Dharoor valley, after the exploratory operation proved unsuccessful. The company is now considering seismic studies in the Dharoor valley.

The main port and commercial centre in 'Puntland' is Bossaso. Thousands of Somalis, Ethiopians and other travellers traditionally have used the port of Bossaso as a route to Yemen and ultimately to the states of the Persian (Arabian) Gulf states and Europe. People-smuggling is an historic trade in the Gulf of Aden. Many smugglers throw passengers overboard when they fear being apprehended by Yemeni patrols, and each year hundreds of migrants, including women and children, are drowned.

Statistical Survey

Sources (unless otherwise stated): Economic Research and Statistics Dept, Central Bank of Somalia, Mogadishu, and Central Statistical Dept, State Planning Commission, POB 1742, Mogadishu; tel. (1) 80385.

Area and Population

AREA, POPULATION AND DENSITY

Area (sq km)	637,657*
Population (census results)†	
7 February 1975	3,253,024
February 1986 (provisional)	
Males	3,741,664
Females	3,372,767
Total	7,114,431
Population (UN estimates at mid-year)‡	
2010	9,330,872
2011	9,556,872
2012	9,797,444
Density (per sq km) at mid-2012	15.4

* 246,201 sq miles.

† Excluding adjustment for underenumeration.

‡ Source: UN, *World Population Prospects: The 2010 Revision*.

POPULATION BY AGE AND SEX
(UN estimates at mid-2012)

	Males	Females	Total
0–14	2,206,089	2,188,453	4,394,542
15–64	2,533,661	2,603,364	5,137,025
65 and over	120,216	145,661	265,877
Total	4,859,966	4,937,478	9,797,444

Source: UN, *World Population Prospects: The 2008 Revision*.

PRINCIPAL TOWNS
(estimated population in 1981)

Mogadishu (capital)	500,000	Berbera	65,000
Hargeysa	70,000	Merca	60,000
Kismayu	70,000		

Mid-2011 ('000, including suburbs, UN estimate): Mogadishu 1,554 (Source: UN, *World Urbanization Prospects: The 2011 Revision*).

BIRTHS AND DEATHS
(annual averages, UN estimates)

	1995–2000	2000–05	2005–10
Birth rate (per 1,000)	45.9	45.7	44.2
Death rate (per 1,000)	17.9	16.2	15.5

Source: UN, *World Population Prospects: The 2010 Revision*.

Life expectancy (years at birth): 50.9 (males 49.4; females 52.5) in 2010 (Source: WHO, *World Health Statistics*).

ECONOMICALLY ACTIVE POPULATION
(estimates, '000 persons, 1991)

	Males	Females	Total
Agriculture, etc.	1,157	1,118	2,275
Industry	290	46	336
Services	466	138	604
Total labour force	1,913	1,302	3,215

Source: UN Economic Commission for Africa, *African Statistical Yearbook*.

2002 (percentage distribution): Agriculture 66.9; Industry 12.0; Services 21.1 (Source: The World Bank and United Nations Development Programme, *Socio-Economic Survey 2002 Somalia*).

Mid-2012 (estimates in '000): Agriculture, etc. 2,545; Total labour force 3,938 (Source: FAO).

Health and Welfare

KEY INDICATORS

Total fertility rate (children per woman, 2010)	6.3
Under-5 mortality rate (per 1,000 live births, 2010)	180
HIV/AIDS (% of persons aged 15–49, 2009)	0.7
Physicians (per 1,000 head, 2006)	0.04
Hospital beds (per 1,000 head, 1997)	0.42
Health expenditure (2001): US $ per head (PPP)	18
Health expenditure (2001): % of GDP	2.6
Health expenditure (2001): public (% of total)	44.6
Total carbon dioxide emissions ('000 metric tons, 2008)	649.1
Carbon dioxide emissions per head (metric tons, 2008)	0.1
Access to water (% of persons, 2010)	29
Access to sanitation (% of persons, 2010)	23

For sources and definitions, see explanatory note on p. vi.

Agriculture

PRINCIPAL CROPS
('000 metric tons, FAO estimates)

	2008	2009	2010
Rice, paddy	16.6	16.5	14.6
Maize	100	112	120
Sorghum	75	86	100
Sweet potatoes	7	7	6
Cassava (Manioc)	79	83	78
Sugar cane	200	230	230
Groundnuts, with shell	5	5	6
Sesame seed	54	64	71
Watermelons	10	11	11
Grapefruit and pomelos	7	7	6
Bananas	41	41	37
Oranges	9	9	9
Lemons and limes	7	8	8
Dates	12	12	11

Aggregate production ('000 metric tons, may include official, semi-official or estimated data): Total cereals 193 in 2008, 215 in 2009, 236 in 2010; Total roots and tubers 86 in 2008, 90 in 2009, 84 in 2010; Total vegetables (incl. melons) 87 in 2008, 101 in 2009, 103 in 2010; Total fruits (excl. melons) 213 in 2008, 215 in 2009, 193 in 2010.

Source: FAO.

LIVESTOCK
('000 head, year ending September, FAO estimates)

	2007	2008	2009
Cattle	4,815	4,800	4,780
Sheep	11,790	11,780	11,760
Goats	11,430	11,420	11,400
Pigs	4	4	4
Asses and mules	44	44	n.a.
Camels	7,000	7,000	7,000
Chickens	3	3	3

2010: Figures assumed to be unchanged from 2009 (FAO estimates).

Source: FAO.

LIVESTOCK PRODUCTS
('000 metric tons, FAO estimates)

	2008	2009	2010
Cows' milk	438	452	573
Goats' milk	382	395	501
Sheep's milk	451	466	590
Cattle meat	59	58	58
Sheep meat	43	43	43
Goat meat	38	38	38
Hen eggs	2	2	2

Source: FAO.

Forestry

ROUNDWOOD REMOVALS
('000 cubic metres, excl. bark, FAO estimates)

	2008	2009	2010
Sawlogs, veneer logs and logs for sleepers*	28	28	28
Other industrial wood	82	82	82
Fuel wood	11,806	12,163	12,532
Total	11,916	12,273	12,642

* Annual output assumed to be unchanged since 1975.

2011: Production assumed to be unchanged from 2010 (FAO estimates).

Source: FAO.

SAWNWOOD PRODUCTION
('000 cubic metres, incl. railway sleepers)

	1973	1974	1975
Total (all broadleaved)	15*	10	14

* FAO estimate.

1976–2011: Production assumed to be unchanged from 1975 (FAO estimates).

Source: FAO.

Fishing

('000 metric tons, live weight, FAO estimates)

	2004	2005	2006
Marine fishes	28.7	23.9	28.7
Total catch (incl. others)	30.0	25.0	30.0

2007–10: Figures assumed to be unchanged from 2006 (FAO estimates).

Source: FAO.

Mining

('000 metric tons, estimates)

	2002	2003	2004
Salt	1	1	1
Gypsum	2	2	2

Source: US Geological Survey.

Industry

SELECTED PRODUCTS
('000 metric tons, unless otherwise indicated)

	1986	1987	1988
Sugar*	30.0	43.3	41.2
Canned meat (million tins)	1.0	—	—
Canned fish	0.1	—	—
Pasta and flour	15.6	4.3	—
Textiles (million yards)	5.5	3.0	6.3
Boxes and bags	15.0	12.0	5.0
Cigarettes and matches	0.3	0.2	0.1
Petroleum products	128	44	30

* Data from FAO.

Raw sugar ('000 metric tons): 20 in 2006–08 (Source: UN Industrial Commodity Statistics Database).

Electric energy (million kWh): 307 in 2006; 326 in 2007–08 (Source: UN Industrial Commodity Statistics Database).

Finance

CURRENCY AND EXCHANGE RATES

Monetary Units

100 cents = 1 Somali shilling (So. sh.).

Sterling, Dollar and Euro Equivalents (30 April 2012)

£1 sterling = 39,514.23 Somali shillings;
US $1 = 24,300.00 Somali shillings;
€1 = 32,110.02 Somali shillings;
100,000 Somali shillings = £2.53 = $4.12 = €3.11.

Average Exchange Rate (Somali shillings per US $)

1987	105.18
1988	170.45
1989	490.68

Note: A separate currency, the 'Somaliland shilling', was introduced in the 'Republic of Somaliland' in January 1995. The exchange rate was reported to be US $1 = 2,750 'Somaliland shillings' in March 2000.

CURRENT BUDGET
(million Somali shillings)

Revenue	1986	1987	1988
Total tax revenue	8,516.4	8,622.4	12,528.1
Taxes on income and profits	1,014.8	889.7	1,431.0
Income tax	380.5	538.8	914.8
Profit tax	634.3	350.9	516.2
Taxes on production, consumption and domestic transactions	1,410.4	1,274.2	2,336.4
Taxes on international transactions	6,091.2	6,458.5	8,760.6
Import duties	4,633.2	4,835.2	6,712.1
Total non-tax revenue	6,375.2	8,220.4	7,623.4
Fees and service charges	274.1	576.1	828.8
Income from government property	633.4	656.4	2,418.9
Other revenue	5,467.2	6,987.9	4,375.7
Total	14,891.6	16,842.8	20,151.5

Expenditure	1986	1987	1988
Total general services	11,997.7	19,636.7	24,213.6
Defence	2,615.9	3,145.0	8,093.9
Interior and police	605.0	560.7	715.4
Finance and central services	7,588.3	14,017.8	12,515.6
Foreign affairs	633.0	1,413.9	2,153.1
Justice and religious affairs	248.5	290.2	447.0
Presidency and general administration	93.0	148.0	217.4
Planning	189.0	24.9	24.3
National Assembly	25.0	36.2	46.9
Total economic services	1,927.6	554.1	600.3
Transportation	122.2	95.2	94.5
Posts and telecommunications	94.3	76.7	75.6
Public works	153.9	57.5	69.8

Expenditure—*continued*	1986	1987	1988
Agriculture	547.2	59.4	55.3
Livestock and forestry	459.0	89.5	109.9
Mineral and water resources	318.8	85.2	93.1
Industry and commerce	131.0	45.1	43.9
Fisheries	101.2	45.5	58.2
Total social services	1,050.5	900.1	930.8
Education	501.6	403.0	478.1
Health	213.8	203.5	255.2
Information	111.5	135.0	145.8
Labour, sports and tourism	139.6	49.3	51.7
Other	84.0	109.3	.
Total	14,975.8	21,091.0	25,744.7

1989 (estimates): Budget to balance at 32,429.0m. Somali shillings.

1990 (estimates): Budget to balance at 86,012.0m. Somali shillings.

1991 (estimates): Budget to balance at 268,283.2m. Somali shillings.

CENTRAL BANK RESERVES
(US $ million at 31 December)

	1987	1988	1989
Gold*	8.3	7.0	6.9
Foreign exchange	7.3	15.3	15.4
Total	15.6	22.3	22.3

* Valued at market-related prices.

Source: IMF, *International Financial Statistics*.

MONEY SUPPLY
(million Somali shillings at 31 December)

	1987	1988	1989
Currency outside banks	12,327	21,033	70,789
Private sector deposits at central bank	1,771	1,555	5,067
Demand deposits at commercial banks	15,948	22,848	63,971
Total money	30,046	45,436	139,827

Source: IMF, *International Financial Statistics*.

COST OF LIVING
(Consumer Price Index; base: 2000 = 100)

	2001	2002	2003
All items	111.5	133.8	133.8

2004–06: Consumer prices assumed to be unchanged from 2003.

Source: African Development Bank.

NATIONAL ACCOUNTS
('000 million Somali shillings at current prices, estimates)

Expenditure on the Gross Domestic Product

	2008	2009	2010
Government final consumption expenditure	3,260	3,430	2,985
Private final consumption expenditure	27,176	28,569	24,839
Gross fixed capital formation	7,512	7,863	6,797
Changes in inventories	22	22	18
Total domestic expenditure	37,970	39,884	34,639
Exports of goods and services	115	120	104
Less Imports of goods and services	631	661	573
GDP at purchasers' values	37,456	39,343	34,171

Gross Domestic Product by Economic Activity

	2008	2009	2010
Agriculture, hunting, forestry and fishing	19,795	20,802	18,075
Mining and quarrying	222	233	203
Manufacturing	817	859	746
Construction	1,381	1,451	1,261
Trade, restaurants and hotels	3,495	3,671	3,190
Transport and communications	3,103	3,234	2,821
Public administration and defence	4,088	4,311	3,740
Sub-total	32,902	34,560	30,036
Indirect taxes (net)	4,554	4,782	4,135
GDP at purchasers' values	37,456	39,343	34,171

Source: African Development Bank.

BALANCE OF PAYMENTS
(US $ million)

	1987	1988	1989
Exports of goods f.o.b.	94.0	58.4	67.7
Imports of goods f.o.b.	−358.5	−216.0	−346.3
Trade balance	−264.5	−157.6	−278.6
Imports of services	−127.7	−104.0	−122.0
Balance on goods and services	−392.2	−261.6	−400.6
Other income paid	−52.0	−60.6	−84.4
Balance on goods, services and income	−444.2	−322.2	−485.0
Current transfers received	343.3	223.7	331.2
Current transfers paid	−13.1	—	−2.9
Current balance	−114.0	−98.5	−156.7
Investment liabilities	−22.8	−105.5	−32.6
Net errors and omissions	39.0	22.4	−0.8
Overall balance	−97.9	−181.7	−190.0

Source: IMF, *International Financial Statistics*.

External Trade

SELECTED COMMODITIES
(US $ million)

Imports c.i.f.	2007	2008	2009
Vegetables and vegetable products	69	95	173
Vegetables, fresh or chilled	0	49	124
Wheat or meslin flour	29	50	31
Refined sugar, solid	53	59	74
Foliage, branches, etc.	29	62	1
Total (incl. others)	920	1,180	1,021

Exports f.o.b.	2007	2008	2009
Livestock	66	55	127
Goats	44	28	48
Sheep	6	11	42
Cattle	16	16	37
Wood charcoal	20	27	16
Gold, waste and scrap	1	27	—

Note: No data were available for total exports (estimated at US $69m. in 2000).

Source: African Development Bank.

SELECTED TRADING PARTNERS
(US $ million)

Imports c.i.f.	2007	2008	2009
Brazil	19	9	58
Ethiopia	73	77	135
Kenya	124	187	145
United Arab Emirates	300	194	256
Total (incl. others)	920	1,180	1,021

Exports f.o.b.	2007	2008	2009
Nigeria	48	7	0
Oman	8	14	63
United Arab Emirates	41	63	81
Yemen	36	43	42

Note: No data were available for total exports (estimated at US $69m. in 2000).

Source: African Development Bank.

Transport

ROAD TRAFFIC
(estimates, '000 motor vehicles in use)

	1994	1995	1996
Passenger cars	2.8	2.0	1.0
Commercial vehicles	7.4	7.3	6.4

Source: International Road Federation, *World Road Statistics*.

SHIPPING

Merchant Fleet
(registered at 31 December)

	2007	2008	2009
Number of vessels	18	16	15
Total displacement ('000 grt)	9.9	6.0	5.2

Source: IHS Fairplay, *World Fleet Statistics*.

International Sea-borne Freight Traffic
('000 metric tons)

	1989	1990	1991
Goods loaded	325	324	n.a.
Goods unloaded	1,252*	1,118	1,007*

* Estimate.

Source: UN Economic Commission for Africa, *African Statistical Yearbook*.

CIVIL AVIATION
(traffic on scheduled services)

	1989	1990	1991
Kilometres flown (million)	3	3	1
Passengers carried ('000)	89	88	46
Passenger-km (million)	248	255	131
Freight ton-km (million)	8	9	5

Source: UN, *Statistical Yearbook*.

Tourism

	1996	1997	1998
Tourist arrivals ('000)	10	10	10

Source: World Bank.

Communications Media

	2008	2009	2010
Telephones ('000 main lines in use)*	100	100	100
Mobile cellular telephones ('000 subscribers)	627	641	648
Internet users ('000)	102	106	n.a.

* Estimates.

2011: Mobile cellular telephones ('000 subscribers) 655.

Radio receivers ('000 in use): 470 in 1997.

Television receivers ('000 in use): 135 in 1997.

Daily newspapers (number of titles): 2 in 1996.

Sources: UNESCO, *Statistical Yearbook*; International Telecommunication Union.

Education

(1985, unless otherwise indicated)

	Institutions	Teachers	Pupils
Pre-primary	16	133	1,558
Primary	1,224	10,338	196,496
Secondary:			
general	n.a.	2,149	39,753
teacher training	n.a.	30*	613*
vocational	n.a.	637	5,933
Higher	n.a.	817†	15,672†

* Figure refers to 1984.
† Figure refers to 1986.

Source: UNESCO, *Statistical Yearbook*.

1990 (UN estimates): 377,000 primary-level pupils; 44,000 secondary-level pupils; 10,400 higher-level pupils.

1991: University teachers 549; University students 4,640.

2006/07 (UNESCO estimates): *Pupils:* Primary 457,132; Secondary 86,929 (General 86,929) *Teachers:* Primary 12,870; Secondary 4,504 (General 4,504 (Source: UNESCO Institute for Statistics).

Pupil-teacher ratio (primary education, UNESCO estimate): 35.5 in 2006/07 (Source: UNESCO Institute for Statistics).

Adult literacy rate (UNESCO estimates): 24.0% in 2002 (Source: UN Development Programme, *Human Development Report*).

Directory

The Constitution

The Constitution promulgated in 1979 and amended in 1990 was revoked following the overthrow of President Siad Barre in January 1991. In July 2000 delegates at the Somali national reconciliation conference in Arta, Djibouti, overwhelmingly approved a Transitional National Charter, which was to serve as Somalia's constitution for an interim period of three years. The Charter, which was divided into six main parts, guaranteed Somali citizens the freedoms of expression, association and human rights, and distinctly separated the executive, the legislature and the judiciary, as well as guaranteeing the independence of the latter. The Charter provided for the creation of a Transitional National Assembly (TNA), which was to exercise legislative power in Somalia during the interim period. The 245-member TNA was inaugurated in August and elected a President of Somalia. Despite the expiry of its mandate in August 2003, the TNA remained in place, pending the election of a new legislative body. In February 2004, following protracted negotiations in Kenya, a new Transitional Federal Charter (replacing the previous Charter) was approved by the TNA; it provided for the establishment of a new 275-member Transitional Federal Parliament (TFP), to comprise 61 representatives from each of the four major clans and 31 from an alliance of smaller clans. The TFP elected a national President in October, who, in turn, nominated a Prime Minister. In January 2009 the composition of the TFP (which remained based in Baidoa, owing to the adverse security situation in Mogadishu) was increased by an additional 275 members.

On 1 August 2012 a new Provisional Constitution was adopted by the National Constituent Assembly, a body comprising 825 elders drawn from traditional Somali clans. The main provisions are summarized below:

THE FEDERAL REPUBLIC OF SOMALIA

Somalia is a federal, sovereign and democratic republic founded on inclusive representation of the people, a muliti-party system and social justice.

THE TERRITORY OF THE FEDERAL REPUBLIC OF SOMALIA

The boundaries of the Federal Republic of Somalia shall be those described in the 1960 Constitution of the Republic of Somalia and are to the north: The Gulf of Aden; to the north-west: Djibouti; to the west: Ethiopia; to the south-west: Kenya; to the east: the Indian Ocean.

STATE AND RELIGION

Islam is the religion of the State. No religion other than Islam can be propagated in the country. No law which is not compliant with the general principles of *Shari'a* (Islamic) law can be enacted. The official language of the Federal Republic of Somalia is Somali and Arabic is the second language.

THE STRUCTURE OF GOVERNMENT

The structure of the Government in the Federal Republic of Somalia is composed of two levels of government: the Federal Government level; and the Federal Member States level, which is comprised of the Federal Member State Government, and the local governments. No single region can stand alone. Until such time as a region merges with another region(s) to form a new Federal Member State, a region shall be directly administered by the Federal Government for a maximum period of two years.

THE FEDERAL PARLIAMENT

The Federal Parliament of the Federal Republic of Somalia consists of: the House of the People; and the Upper House. The term of office of the Federal Parliament is four years from the day of the announcement of the election results.

The members of the House of the People shall be elected by the citizens of the Federal Republic of Somalia in a direct, secret and free ballot. The number of ordinary members of the House of the People shall be 225. The House of the People is empowered to pass, amend or reject legislation tabled before it.

The members of the Upper House shall be elected through a direct, secret and free ballot by the people of the Federal Member States, and their number shall be no more than 54 members based on the 18 regions that existed in Somalia before 1991. All Federal Member States should have an equal number of representatives in the Upper House. The Upper House represents the Federal Member States, and its legislative duties include: participation in the process of the amending the Constitution; passing, amending, or rejecting the laws that are tabled before it.

THE PRESIDENT OF THE FEDERAL REPUBLIC OF SOMALIA

Any Somali citizen is eligible for the position of President of the Federal Republic of Somalia, as long as he or she is a Muslim and at least 40 years of age.

The Houses of the Federal Parliament shall elect the President of the Federal Republic of Somalia in a joint session. A minimum of two-thirds of the members of each House of the Federal Parliament must be present when electing the President. Candidatures must be proposed to the joint session of the Houses of the Federal Parliament by a minimum of 20 members of the House of the People, or a minimum of one Federal Member State.

The election of the President shall be conducted by secret ballot. Any candidate who gains a two-thirds majority vote of the total membership of the two Houses of the Federal Parliament shall be elected President of the Federal Republic of Somalia. If no candidate gains the necessary two-thirds majority in the first round, a second round of voting shall be conducted for the four candidates with the greatest number of votes from the first round, and any candidate who gains a two-thirds majority vote of the total membership of the two Houses of the Federal Parliament in the second round shall be elected President of the Federal Republic of Somalia. If no candidate gains the necessary two-thirds majority in the second round, a third round of voting shall be conducted between the two candidates with the greatest number of votes from the second round, and the candidate who gains the greatest number of votes in the third round shall be elected President of the Federal Republic of Somalia.

The President serves as Commander-in-Chief of the Armed Forces, appoints the Prime Minister, and dismisses ministers, state ministers and deputy ministers on the recommendation of the Prime Minister. The President shall hold office for a term of four years.

THE EXECUTIVE

The executive power of the Federal Government shall be vested in the Council of Ministers, which is the highest executive authority of the Federal Government and consists of the Prime Minister, the Deputy Prime Minister(s), ministers, state ministers and deputy-ministers. The Prime Minister is the Head of the Federal Government and appoints the Deputy Prime Minister(s), ministers, state ministers, and deputy ministers. Those eligible for membership of the Council of Ministers may be, but shall not be limited to, members of the House of the People. Vacancy in the office of the Prime Minister caused by the resignation, dismissal, failure to fulfil responsibility, or death of the Prime Minister shall lead to the dissolution of the Council of Ministers.

The Council of Ministers has the powers to: formulate the overall government policy and implement it; approve and implement administrative regulations, in accordance with the law; prepare draft laws, and table them before the House of the People of the Federal Parliament.

JUDICIAL AUTHORITY

The judiciary is independent of the legislative and executive branches of government whilst fulfilling its judicial functions. Members of the judiciary shall be subject only to the law. The national court structure shall be of three levels, which are: the Constitutional Court; the Federal Government level courts; and the Federal Member State level courts. The highest court at the Federal Government level shall be the Federal High Court, whilst the highest court at the Federal Member State level shall be the Federal Member State High Court.

The Government

HEAD OF STATE

President: HASSAN SHEIKH MOHAMUD (inaugurated 16 September 2012).

CABINET

(September 2012)

The newly elected President, Hassan Sheikh Mohamud, was to appoint a new Cabinet before the end of September 2012. The outgoing Government is listed below.

Prime Minister: Dr ABDIWELI MOHAMED ALI.

Deputy Prime Minister and Minister of Agriculture and Livestock: HUSSEIN SHEIKH MOHAMMAD HUSEIN.

Deputy Prime Minister and Minister of Defence: HUSSEIN ARAB ISSE.

Deputy Prime Minister and Minister of Commerce and Industry: ABDIWAHAB HUSSEIN KALIF.

Minister of Justice, Religious Affairs and Endowment: AHMED HASSAN GABOBE.

Minister of the Interior and National Security: ABDISAMED MOHAMUD SHEIKH HASSAN.

Minister of Finance and the Treasury: ABDINASIR MOHAMED ABDULLE.

Minister of Women's Development and Family Welfare: ASHA OSMAN AQIL.

Minister of Health and Human Services: ABDIASIS SHEIKH YUSUF.

Minister of Information, Posts and Telecommunications: ABDULKADIR MOHAMED AHMED.

Minister of Youth, Sports and Labour: MAHMUD JIRDE HUSAYN.

Minister of Fisheries, Marine Resources and the Environment: ABDURAHMAN SHEIKH IBRAHIM.

Minister of Land, Air and Sea Transport: ADAM ABDULLAHI ADAM.

Minister of Constitutional and Federal Affairs: ABDIRAHMAN HOSH JIBRIL.

Minister of Public Works and Reconstruction: JEYLANI NUR IKAR.

Minister of Minerals Resources, Water, Energy and Petroleum: ABDULKADIR MOHAMED DHI'ISOW.

Minister of Education, Higher Education and Culture: Dr AHMED AIDID IBRAHIM.

Minister of Planning and International Co-operation: ABDULLAHI GODAH BARRE.

There were also nine Ministers of State and 26 Deputy Ministers.

MINISTRIES

Office of the President: 1 Villa Baidao, 2525 Baydhabo; e-mail president@president.somaligov.net; internet www.president.somaligov.net.

Office of the Prime Minister: 1 Villa Somalia, 2525 Mogadishu; tel. (5) 543050; fax (5) 974242; e-mail primeminister@opm.somaligov.net; internet www.opm.somaligov.net.

Ministry of Agriculture and Livestock: 1 Villa Somalia, 2525 Mogadishu; internet www.moa.somaligov.net.

Ministry of Commerce and Industry: 1 Villa Somalia, 2525 Mogadishu; internet www.moin.somaligov.net.

Ministry of Constitutional and Federal Affairs: Mogadishu.

Ministry of Defence: Mogadishu; internet www.mod.somaligov.net.

Ministry of Education, Higher Education and Culture: Mogadishu.

Ministry of Finance and the Treasury: 1 Villa Somalia, 2525 Mogadishu; tel. (5) 404240; internet www.mof.somaligov.net.

Ministry of Fisheries, Marine Resources and the Environment: 1 Villa Somalia, 2525 Mogadishu; internet www.mminfisherysom.org.

Ministry of Foreign Affairs: 1 Villa Somalia, 2525 Mogadishu; tel. and fax (5) 424640; internet www.mfa.somaligov.net.

Ministry of Health and Human Services: 1 Villa Somalia, 2525 Mogadishu; tel. and fax (5) 424640; internet www.moh.somaligov.net.

Ministry of Information, Posts and Telecommunications: 1 Villa Somalia, 2525 Mogadishu; tel. and fax (5) 424640; internet www.moi.somaligov.net.

Ministry of the Interior and National Security: 1 Villa Somalia, 2525 Mogadishu; internet www.mois.somaligov.net.

Ministry of Justice, Religious Affairs and Endowment: Mogadishu.

Ministry of Land, Air and Sea Transport: Mogadishu.

Ministry of Minerals Resources, Water, Energy and Petroleum: Mogadishu.

Ministry of Planning and International Co-operation: 2525 Mogadishu.

Ministry of Public Works and Reconstruction: 1 Villa Somalia, 2525 Mogadishu; internet www.mopwh.somaligov.net.

Ministry of Women's Development and Family Welfare: 1 Villa Somalia, 2525 Mogadishu; internet www.mowfa.somaligov.net.

Ministry of Youth, Sports and Labour: 1 Villa Somalia, 2525 Mogadishu; internet www.moys.somaligov.net.

Legislature

FEDERAL PARLIAMENT

Speaker: MOHAMED OSMAN JAWARI.

The Federal Parliament of the Federal Republic of Somalia consists of: the House of the People; and the Upper House. The term of office of the Federal Parliament is four years from the day of the announcement of the election results. The members of the House of the People shall be elected by the citizens of the Federal Republic of Somalia in a direct, secret and free ballot. The number of ordinary members of the House of the People shall be 225. The House of the People is empowered to pass, amend or reject legislation tabled before it. The members of the Upper House shall be elected through a direct, secret and free ballot by the people of the Federal Member States, and their number shall be no more than 54 members based on the 18 regions that existed in Somalia before 1991. All Federal Member States should have an equal number of representatives in the Upper House. The Upper House represents the Federal Member States, and its legislative duties include: participation in the process of the amending the Constitution; passing, amending, or rejecting the laws that are tabled before it.

Election Commission

The Provisional Constitution adopted on 1 August 2012 provided for the establishment of a National Independent Electoral Commission, within 60 days of the formation of the Council of Ministers. The Commission was to be responsible for the organization of all elections and was to be composed of no more than nine members.

Political Organizations

Alliance for the Re-liberation of Somalia (ARS): f. 2007; split into two factions in 2008; 'Djibouti wing' led by SHEIKH SHARIF SHEIKH AHMED signed a peace agreement with the TNG, while the 'Asmara wing' led by SHEIKH HASSAN DAHIR AWEYS remained in conflict with the Government.

Islamic Party (Hizb al-Islam): radical Islamist party; Chair. SHEIKH AHMAD QASIM.

Islamic Union Party (al-Ittihad al-Islam): aims to unite ethnic Somalis from Somalia, Ethiopia, Kenya and Djibouti in an Islamic state.

Juba Valley Alliance (JVA): f. 1999; alliance of militia and businessmen from the Habr Gedir and Marehan clans; Pres. BARE ADAN SHIRE.

National Democratic League: Beled Weyne; f. 2003; Chair. Dr ABDIRAHMAN ABDULLE ALI; Sec.-Gen. ABDIKARIM HUSAYN IDOW.

Peace and Development Party (PDP): Mogadishu; f. 2011; Chair. HASSAN SHEIKH MOHAMUD.

Rahanwin Resistance Army (RRA): guerrilla force active around Baidoa; Chair. HASAN MUHAMMAD NUR SHATIGADUD.

Al-Shabaab (The Youth): f. 2007 by former members of the Union of Islamic Courts; Leader IBRAHIM HAJI JAMA.

Somali Democratic Alliance (SDA): f. 1989; represents the Gadabursi ethnic grouping in the north-west; opposes the Isaaq-dominated SNM and its declaration of an independent 'Republic of Somaliland'; Leader MOHAMED FARAH ABDULLAH.

Somali Justice and Peace Party (Tayo Political Party): Maka, al-Mukarrama, Mogadishu; e-mail mqasim@tayoparty.org; internet tayoparty.org; f. 2012; Sec.-Gen. MOHAMED ABDULLAHI MOHAMED 'FARMAJO'.

Somali National Salvation Council: f. 2003; Chair. MUSE SUDI YALAHOW.

Somali Patriotic Movement (SPM): f. 1989 in southern Somalia; represents Ogadenis (of the Darod clan) in southern Somalia; this faction of the SPM has allied with the SNF in opposing the SNA; Chair. Gen. ADEN ABDULLAHI NOOR ('Gabio').

Somali Reconciliation and Restoration Council (SRRC): f. 2001 by faction leaders opposed to the establishment of the Hasan administration; aims to establish a rival national govt; Co-Chair. HUSSEIN MOHAMED AIDID, HILOWLE IMAN UMAR, ADEN ABDULLAHI NOOR, HASAN MOHAMED NUR, ABDULLAHI SHAYKH ISMA'IL; Sec.-Gen. MOWLID MA'ANEH MOHAMED.

Somali Revolutionary Socialist Party (SRSP): f. 1976 as the sole legal party; overthrown in Jan. 1991; conducts guerrilla operations in Gedo region, near border with Kenya; Sec.-Gen. (vacant); Asst Sec.-Gen. AHMED SULEIMAN ABDULLAH.

Somali Solidarity Party: Mogadishu; f. 1999; Chair. ABD AL-RAHMAN MUSA MOHAMED; Sec.-Gen. SA'ID ISA MOHAMED.

Southern Somali National Movement (SSNM): based on coast in southern Somalia; Chair. ABDI WARSEMEH ISAR.

Supreme Somali Islamic Courts Council: formerly the Union of Islamic Courts; seeks to create a Somali state under the guiding principles of *Shari'a* (Islamic) law; Chair. Sheikh HASSAN DAHIR AWEYS.

United Somali Congress (USC): f. 1989 in cen. Somalia; overthrew Siad Barre in Jan. 1991; party split in 1991, with this faction dominated by the Abgal sub-clan of the Hawiye clan, Somalia's largest ethnic group; Leader ABDULLAHI MA'ALIN; Sec.-Gen. MUSA NUR AMIN.

United Somali Congress—Somali National Alliance (USC—SNA): f. 1995 by dissident mems of the SNA's USC faction; represents the Habr Gedir sub-clan of the Hawiye; Leader OSMAN HASSAN ALI 'ATO'.

United Somali Congress—Somali Salvation Alliance (USC—SSA): Leader MUSE SUDI YALAHOW.

United Somali Party (USP): opposes the SNM's declaration of the independent 'Republic of Somaliland'; Leader MOHAMED ABDI HASHI.

Diplomatic Representation

EMBASSIES IN SOMALIA

Note: Following the overthrow of Siad Barre in January 1991, all foreign embassies in Somalia were closed and all diplomatic personnel left the country. Some embassies were reopened, including those of France, Sudan and the USA, following the arrival of the US-led Unified Task Force (UNITAF) in December 1992; however, nearly all foreign diplomats left Somalia in anticipation of the withdrawal of the UN peace-keeping force, UNOSOM, in early 1995. In September 2011 Turkey reopened its embassy in Mogadishu. In early 2012 the United Kingdom also appointed its first ambassador to Somalia in 21 years. However, the ambassador was to be based in Nairobi, Kenya until security conditions improved in Somalia.

Cuba: Mogadishu.

Djibouti: Mogadishu; Ambassador DAYIB DOUBAD ROBLEH.

Korea, Democratic People's Republic: Via Km 5, Mogadishu; Ambassador KIM RYONG SU.

Ethiopia: POB 368, Mogadishu; Ambassador ABDULAZIZ AHMED ADAM.

Libya: Via Medina, POB 125, Mogadishu; Ambassador SAID RABIC.

Pakistan: Via Afgoi, Km 5, POB 339, Mogadishu; tel. (1) 80856.

Sudan: Via al-Mukarah, POB 552, Mogadishu; Chargé d'affaires a.i. FADIL AL-JASULI MUSTAFA.

Turkey: Via Km 6, POB 2833, Mogadishu; tel. (1) 81975; reopened Sept. 2011; Ambassador CEMALETTIN KANI TORUN.

United Arab Emirates: Via Afgoi, Km 5, Mogadishu; tel. (1) 23178.

Yemen: K4, Mogadishu; Ambassador AHMED HAMID ALI UMAR.

Judicial System

According to the draft Provisional Constitution adopted on 1 August 2012, the judiciary is independent of the legislative and executive branches of government. No law which is not compliant with the general principles of *Shari'a* (Islamic) law can be enacted. The national court structure shall be of three levels, which are: the Constitutional Court; the Federal Government level courts; and the Federal Member State level courts. The highest court at the Federal Government level shall be the Federal High Court, whilst the highest court at the Federal Member State level shall be the Federal Member State High Court. If a case is presented before a court, and the case concerns the Federal Government, the court shall refer the case to the Federal Government level court. If a case is presented before a court and the case concerns a constitutional matter, the court may refer the case to the Constitutional Court. Any court with judicial powers can decide on whether a matter brought before it is a constitutional matter or not, if this will not contradict the exclusive powers of the Constitutional Court. The Constitutional Court is the final authority in constitutional matters and is composed of five judges including the Chief Judge and the Deputy Chief Judge.

Religion

ISLAM

Islam is the state religion. Most Somalis are Sunni Muslims.

Imam: Gen. MOHAMED ABSHIR.

CHRISTIANITY

The Roman Catholic Church

Somalia comprises a single diocese, directly responsible to the Holy See. The total number of Roman Catholics in Somalia was estimated at just 100.

Bishop of Mogadishu: (vacant), POB 273, Ahmed bin Idris, Mogadishu; tel. (1) 20184; e-mail evechcat@intnet.dj.

The Anglican Communion

Within the Episcopal Church in Jerusalem and the Middle East, the Bishop in Egypt has jurisdiction over Somalia.

The Press

The Country: POB 1178, Mogadishu; tel. (1) 21206; f. 1991; daily.

Dalka: POB 388, Mogadishu; tel. (1) 500533; e-mail dalka@somalinternet.com; internet www.dalka-online.com; f. 1967; current affairs; weekly.

Heegan Times (Vigilance): POB 1178, Mogadishu; tel. 6126369706 (mobile); e-mail abdiaziz.hassan@heegantimes.com; internet heegantimes.com; weekly; online newspaper; English; Editor ABDIAZIZ HASSAN.

Horseed: POB 1178, Mogadishu; tel. (1) 21206; e-mail horseednet@gmail.com; internet www.horseednet.com; weekly; in Somali and English.

Huuriya (Liberty): Hargeysa; daily.

Jamhuuriya (The Republic): Hargeysa; e-mail webmaster@jamhuuriya.info; internet www.jamhuuriya.info; independent; daily; Editor-in-Chief HASSAN SAÏD FAISAL ALI; circ. 2,500.

Al-Mujeehid: Hargeysa; weekly.

New Era: POB 1178, Mogadishu; tel. (1) 21206; quarterly; in English, Somali and Arabic.

Qaran Press (Maalinle Madaxbannaan): Mogadishu; tel. (1) 215305; financial information; daily; in Somali; Editor ABDULAHI AHMED ALI; circ. 2,000.

Riyaaq (Happiness): Bossasso.

Sahan (Pioneer): Bossasso; Editor MUHAMMAD DEEQ.

Somalia Times: POB 555, Mogadishu BN 03040; e-mail info@somalpost.com; internet www.somaliatimes.com; Somali; weekly; circ. 50,000.

NEWS AGENCIES

Horn of Africa News Agency: Mogadishu; e-mail info@hananews.org; f. 1990.

Somali National News Agency (SONNA): POB 1748, Mogadishu; tel. (1) 24058; Dir MUHAMMAD HASAN KAHIN.

Publishers

Government Printer: POB 1743, Mogadishu.

Somalia d'Oggi: Piazzale della Garesa, POB 315, Mogadishu; law, economics and reference.

Broadcasting and Communications

TELECOMMUNICATIONS

Since the collapse of the central Government in 1991 there has been no authority in place to regulate the telecommunications sector. No licence is required to set up a telecommunications network or provide telephone services. In early 2012 there were three major telecommunications operators in the country.

Hormuud Telecom Somalia Inc.: Mogadishu; internet www.hortel.net; f. 2002; fixed-line and mobile cellular telecommunications operator.

NationLink Telecom: Mogadishu; internet www.nationlinktelecom.com; f. 1997; fixed-line and mobile cellular telecommunications operator; Pres. ABDIRIZAK IDO.

Somali Telecom (Olympic Telecommunications): Mogadishu.

Somaliland Telecommunications Corpn: Hargeysa; Dir MOHAMED ARWO.

Telcom Somaliland: Telcom Somaliland Bldg, Togdheer St, Hargeysa; tel. (2) 300161; fax (2) 300162; e-mail info@telcomsomaliland.com; internet www.telcomsomaliland.com; f. 2003; provides local, national long distance and int. telecommunications, mobile communications and data services.

BROADCASTING

In 2011 there were some 15 private radio stations operating in Mogadishu.

Radio

Holy Koran Radio: Mogadishu; f. 1996; religious broadcasts in Somali.

Radio Awdal: Boorama, 'Somaliland'; operated by the Gadabursi clan.

Radio Banaadir: Tahlil Warsame Bldg, 4 Maka al-Mukarama Rd, Mogadishu; tel. (5) 2960268; e-mail rbb@radiobanadir.com; internet www.radiobanadir.com; f. 2000; serves Mogadishu and its environs.

Radio Free Somalia: tel. (5) 630838; e-mail admin@radiofreesomalia.com; internet www.radiofreesomalia.com; f. 1993; operates from Galacaio in north-eastern Somalia; relays humanitarian and educational programmes.

Radio Gaalkayco: operates from 'Puntland'.

Radio Hargeysa, the Voice of the 'Republic of Somaliland': POB 14, Hargeysa; tel. 155; e-mail radiohargeysa@yahoo.com; internet www.radiosomaliland.com/radiohargeisa.html; serves the northern region ('Somaliland'); broadcasts in Somali, and relays Somali and Amharic transmission from Radio Mogadishu; Dir of Radio IDRIS EGAL NUR.

Radio HornAfrique: Mogadishu; f. 1999; commercial independent station broadcasting music and programmes on social issues; Dir (vacant).

Radio Mogadishu, Voice of the Masses of the Somali Republic: southern Mogadishu; f. 1993 by supporters of Gen. Aidid after the facilities of the fmr state-controlled radio station, Radio Mogadishu (of which Gen. Aidid's faction took control in 1991), were destroyed by UNOSOM; broadcasts in Somali, Amharic, Arabic, English and Swahili; Chair. FARAH HASAN AYOBOQORE.

Radio Mogadishu, Voice of Somali Pacification: Mogadishu; f. 1995 by supporters of Osman Hassan Ali 'Ato'; broadcasts in Somali, English and Arabic; Dir-Gen. MUHAMMAD DIRIYEH ILMI.

Radio Mogadishu, Voice of the Somali Republic: Ministry of Information Bldg, nr Villa Somalia, 00252 Mogadishu; e-mail radiomogadishu@gmail.com; internet radiomuqdisho.net; f. 1951; state-owned.

Radio Shabelle: Mogadishu; tel. 7894261398 (mobile); e-mail ali.dahir@shabelle.net; internet www.shabelle.net; f. 2002; Chair. and CEO ABDIMAALIK YUSUF.

Radio Somaliland: internet www.radiosomaliland.com.

Voice of Peace: Galkayo; tel. 90795026 (mobile); e-mail codkanabadda@gmail.com; internet www.codkanabadda.com; f. 1993; aims to promote peace and reconstruction in Somalia; receives support from UNICEF and the AU.

Some radio receivers are used for public address purposes in small towns and villages.

Note: In January 2007 the Transitional National Government was granted emergency powers to proscribe four media companies in an attempt to restore order in Mogadishu. HornAfrique Media and Shabelle Media were believed to have ceased operations, although others condemned the ban and refused to close.

Television

A television service, financed by Kuwait and the United Arab Emirates, was inaugurated in 1983. Programmes in Somali and Arabic are broadcast for three hours daily, extended to four hours on Fridays and public holidays. Reception is limited to a 30-km radius of Mogadishu.

Somali National Television (SNTV): Mogadishu; re-launched 2011 after 20 years' hiatus; state-owned; broadcasts 24 hrs a day.

Somali Television Network (STN): Mogadishu; f. 1999; broadcasts 22 channels in Somali, English, French, Hindi, Gujarati, Bengali, Punjabi, Italian and Arabic; Man. Dir ABURAHMAN ROBLEY ULAYEREH.

Television HornAfrique: Mogadishu; f. 1999; broadcasts 6 channels in Somali and Arabic; CEO ALI IMAN SHARMARKEH.

Finance

(cap. = capital; res = reserves; m. = million; brs = branches; amounts in Somali shillings unless otherwise stated)

BANKING

Central Bank

Central Bank of Somalia: 1 Villa Somalia, Mogadishu; tel. (1) 657733; fax (1) 215026; internet www.somalbanca.org; Chair. ABDULLAHI JAMA ALI.

A central bank (with 10 branches) is also in operation in Hargeysa (in the self-proclaimed 'Republic of Somaliland').

Commercial Banks

Commercial Bank of Somalia: Via Primo Luglio, POB 203, Mogadishu; tel. (1) 22861; f. 1990 to succeed the Commercial and Savings Bank of Somalia; state-owned; cap. 1,000m. (May 1990); 33 brs.

Universal Bank of Somalia: Mogadishu; f. 2002; cap. US $10m.; Gen. Man. MAHAD ADAN BARKHADLE (acting).

Private Bank

Somali-Malaysian Commercial Bank: Mogadishu; f. 1997; cap. US $4m.

Development Bank

Somali Development Bank: Via Primo Luglio, POB 1079, Mogadishu; tel. (1) 21800; f. 1968; state-owned; cap. and res 2,612.7m. (Dec. 1988); Pres. MOHAMED MOHAMED NUR; 4 brs.

INSURANCE

State Insurance Co of Somalia: POB 992, Mogadishu; f. 1974; Gen. Man. ABDULLAHI GA'AL; brs throughout Somalia.

Trade and Industry

DEVELOPMENT ORGANIZATIONS

Agricultural Development Corpn: POB 930, Mogadishu; f. 1971 by merger of fmr agricultural and machinery agencies and grain marketing board; supplies farmers with equipment and materials and purchases growers' cereal and oil seed crops; Dir-Gen. MOHAMED FARAH ANSHUR.

Livestock Development Agency: POB 1759, Mogadishu; f. 1966; Dir-Gen. HASSAN WELI SHEIKH HUSSEN; brs throughout Somalia.

Somali Co-operative Movement: Mogadishu; Chair. HASSAN HAWADLE MADAR.

Somali Oil Refinery: POB 1241, Mogadishu; Chair. NUR AHMED DARAWISH.

Water Development Agency: POB 525, Mogadishu; Dir-Gen. KHALIF HAJI FARAH.

CHAMBER OF COMMERCE

Somali Chamber of Commerce and Industry (SCCI): Somali Chamber Bldg, nr Banadir Hotel, Shibis District, Mogadishu; tel. (1) 643081; fax (1) 221560; e-mail info@somalicci.com; f. 1970; Pres. IMAN ALI.

TRADE ASSOCIATION

National Agency of Foreign Trade: POB 602, Mogadishu; tel. (1) 120485; major foreign trade agency; state-owned; brs in Berbera and over 150 centres throughout Somalia; Dir-Gen. JAMA AW MUSE.

UTILITIES

Water Development Agency: POB 525, Mogadishu; Dir-Gen. KHALIF HAJI FARAH.

TRADE UNION

National Union of Somali Journalists (NUSOJ): Tree Biano Bldg, Via al-Mukarah Km 4, Mogadishu; fax (1) 859944; e-mail nusoj@nusoj.org; internet www.nusoj.org; f. 2002 as Somali Journalists' Network (SOJON); name changed as above in 2005; Chair. BURHAN AHMED DAHIR; Sec.-Gen. MOHAMED IBRAHIM; 6 brs across Somalia.

Transport

RAILWAYS

There are no railways in Somalia.

ROADS

In 2000 there were an estimated 22,100 km of roads, of which some 11.8% were paved.

SHIPPING

Merca, Berbera, Mogadishu and Kismayu are the chief ports. An EU-sponsored development project for the port of Berbera (in 'Somaliland') was announced in February 1996. It was reported that the port of Mogadishu, which had been largely closed since 1995, was reopened to commercial traffic in August 2006. There was a large increase in piracy off the coast of Somalia during the late 2000s.

Berbera Port Authority: Berbera; tel. (2) 740198; fax (2) 770224; e-mail bportadm@telesom.net; Gen. Man. ALI OMER MOHAMED.

Somali Ports Authority: POB 935, Mogadishu; tel. (1) 30081; Port Dir AHMED HAGI ALI ADANI.

Juba Enterprises Beder & Sons Ltd: POB 549, Mogadishu; privately owned.

Puntland Shipping Service: Bossasso.

Shosman Commercial Co Ltd: North-Eastern Pasaso; privately owned.

CIVIL AVIATION

Mogadishu has an international airport. There are airports at Hargeysa and Baidoa and six other airfields. It was reported that a daily service had been inaugurated in April 1994 between Hargeysa (in the self-declared 'Republic of Somaliland') and Nairobi, Kenya. Mogadishu international airport (closed since 1995) was officially reopened in mid-1998, but continuing civil unrest hampered services. In August 2006 the airport reopened to commercial flights.

Air Somalia: Mogadishu; f. 2001; operates internal passenger services and international services to destinations in Africa and the Middle East; Chair. ALI FARAH ABDULLEH.

Jubba Airways: POB 6200, 30th St, Mogadishu; tel. (1) 217000; fax (1) 227711; e-mail jubbaair@emirates.net.ae; internet www.jubba-airways.com; f. 1998; operates domestic flights and flights to destinations in Djibouti, Saudi Arabia, the United Arab Emirates and Yemen; Man. Dir ABDULLAHI WARSAME.

Defence

Of total armed forces of 64,500 in June 1990, the army numbered 60,000, the navy 2,000 and the air force 2,500. In addition, there were 29,500 members of paramilitary forces, including 20,000 members of the People's Militia. Following the overthrow of the Siad Barre regime in January 1991, there were no national armed forces. Somalia was divided into areas controlled by different armed groups, which were based on clan, or sub-clan, membership. Following his election to the presidency in August 2000, Abdulkasim Salad Hasan announced his intention to recruit former militiamen into a new national force: by December some 5,000 Somalis had begun training under the supervision of Mogadishu's Islamic courts. However, efforts to establish a new national armed force have made little progress since the Government's return to Somalia from exile in 2005. In November 2011 it was estimated that the armed forces of the Transitional Federal Government numbered around 2,000. The total armed forces of the self-proclaimed 'Republic of Somaliland' were estimated to number 15,000, while the armed forces of 'Puntland' were believed to number around 5,000–10,000. The AU Mission in Somalia had an estimated 9,605 troops present in the country (mostly from Burundi and Uganda) in late 2011.

Chief of General Staff: Col ABDI AHMAD GULED.

Air Force Commander: NUR ILMI ADAWE.

Navy Commander: Col MUSE SA'ID MOHAMED.

Army Commander: Gen. MUHAMMAD GHELLE KAHIYE.

Commander of Rapid Reaction Forces: Gen. ABDI'AZIZ ALI BARRE.

Education

Following the overthrow of Mohamed Siad Barre's Government in January 1991 and the ensuing internal disorder, Somalia's education system collapsed. In January 1993 a primary school was opened in the building of Somalia's only university, the Somali National University in Mogadishu (which had been closed in early 1991). A number of schools operating in the country were under the control of fundamentalist Islamist groups. According to a UNICEF survey, there were 1,172 primary schools operating in 2003/04, with a total enrolment of over 285,574 children representing a 19.9% gross enrolment ratio (data from Lower Jubba Region, El Waq district of Gedo Region and Jilib district of Middle Jubba Region were not collected).

Bibliography

Abdi Elmi, A. *Understanding the Somalia Conflagration: Identity, Political Islam and Peacebuilding.* London and New York and Oxford, Pluto Press and Pambazuka Press, 2010.

Ahmed, A. J. (Ed.). *The Invention of Somalia.* Lawrenceville, KS, Red Sea Press, 1995.

Bahadur, J. *The Pirates of Somalia: Inside their Hidden World.* New York, Pantheon Books, 2011.

Beachey, R. *The Warrior Mullah: The Horn Aflame 1892–1920.* London, Bellew Publishing, 1990.

Besteman, C., and Cassanelli, L. V. (Eds). *The Struggle for Land in Southern Somalia: The War Behind the War.* Boulder, CO, and Oxford, Westview Press, 1996.

Bongartz, M. *The Civil War in Somalia: Its Genesis and Dynamics.* Uppsala, Scandinavian Institute for African Studies, 1991.

Burnett, John S. *Where Soldiers Fear to Tread: At Work in the Fields of Anarchy.* London, William Heinemann, 2005.

Cassanelli, L. V. *The Shaping of Somali Society: Reconstructing the History of a Pastoral People, 1600–1900.* Philadelphia, PA, Pennsylvania University Press, 1982.

Clarke, W., and Herbst, J. (Eds). *Learning from Somalia: The Lessons of Armed Humanitarian Intervention.* Boulder, CO, Westview Press, 1997.

Contini, P. *The Somali Republic: An Experiment in Legal Integration.* 1969.

DeLong, K., and Tuckey, S. *Mogadishu: Heroism and Tragedy.* Westport, CT, and London, Praeger, 1994.

de Waal, R., and de Waal, A. *Somalia: Crimes and Blunders.* London, James Currey Publishers, 1995.

Drysdale, J. *Whatever Happened to Somalia?* London, Haan Associates, 1994.

Dualeh, H. A. *From Barre to Aidid: The Story of Somalia and the Agony of a Nation.* Nairobi, Stellagraphics, 1994.

Farah, A. O., Muchie, M., and Gundel, J. *Somalia: Diaspora and State Reconstitution in the Horn of Africa.* London, Adonis & Abbey Publishers, 2007.

Fitzgerald, N. J. *Somalia: History, Issues and Bibliography.* Hauppauge, NY, Nova Science Publishers, 2002.

Ghalib, J. M. *The Cost of Dictatorship. The Somali Experience.* New York, and Oxford, Lilian Barber Press, 1995.

Harper, M. *Getting Somalia Wrong? Faith, War and Hope in a Shattered State.* London and New York, Zed Books, 2012.

Hashim, A. B. *The Fallen State: Dissonance, Dictatorship and Death in Somalia.* Lanham, MD, University Press of America, 1997.

Hess, R. L. *Italian Colonialism in Somalia.* 1966.

Hirsch, J. L., and Oakley, R. B. *Somalia and 'Operation Restore Hope': Reflections on Peacemaking and Peacekeeping.* Washington, DC, United States Institute of Peace Press, 1995.

Human Rights Watch. *Harsh War, Harsh Peace: Abuses by al-Shabaab, the Transitional Federal Government and AMISON in Somalia.* New York, April 2010.

'You Don't Know Who to Blame'. War Crimes in Somalia. August 2011.

Issa-Salwe, A. M., and Cissa-Salwe, C. *The Collapse of the Somali State.* London, Haan Associates, 1994.

Kusow, A. (Ed.). *Putting the Cart before the Horse: Contested Nationalism and the Crisis of the Nation-state in Somalia.* Lawrenceville, NJ, Red Sea Press, 2005.

Laitin, D. D., and Saïd, S. S. *Somalia: Nation in Search of a State.* Boulder, CO, Westview Press, 1987.

Lewis, I. M. *A Modern History of Somalia: Nation and State in the Horn of Africa.* Boulder, CO, Westview Press, 1988.

Blood and Bone: The Call of Kinship in Somali Society. Trenton, NJ, Red Sea Press, 1994.

Saints and Somalis: Popular Islam in a Clan-Based Society. Lawrenceville, NJ, Red Sea Press, 1998.

Little, P. D. *Somalia: Economy without State (African Issues).* London, James Currey Publishers, 2003.

Lyons, T., and Samatar, A. I. *Somalia: State Collapse, Multilateral Intervention and Strategies for Political Reconstruction.* Washington, DC, Brookings Institution, 1995.

Makinda, S. M. *Seeking Peace from Chaos: Humanitarian Intervention in Somalia.* Boulder, CO, Lynne Rienner Publishers, 1993.

Mburu, N. *Bandits on the Border: The Last Frontier in the Search for Somali Unity.* Lawrenceville, NJ, Red Sea Press, 2005.

Morin, D. *Littérature et politique en Somalie.* Talenco Cedex, Université Montesquieu—Bordeaux IV, 1997.

Mubarak, J. A. *From Bad Policy to Chaos in Somalia: How an Economy Fell Apart.* Westport, CT, and London, Praeger, 1996.

An Economic Policy Agenda for Post-Civil War Somalia: How to Build a New Economy, Sustain Growth and Reduce Poverty. Lewiston, NY, The Edwin Mellen Press, 2006.

Mukhtar, M. H. *Historical Dictionary of Somalia: New Edition.* Metuchen, NJ, Scarecrow Press, 2003.

Nenova, T., and Harford, T. 'Anarchy and Invention: How does Somalia's Private Sector Cope without Government?', in *Public Policy Journal*, Note No. 280. Washington, DC, World Bank, Nov. 2004.

Omar, M. O. *Somalia: A Nation Driven to Despair.* New Delhi, Somali Publications, 1996.

Somalia: Past and Present. Mogadishu, Somali Publications, 2004.

Osman, A. A., and Souare, I. K. *Somalia at the Crossroads: Challenges and Perspectives in Reconstituting a Failed State.* London, Adonis & Abbey Publishers, 2007.

Pankhurst, E. S. *Ex-Italian Somaliland.* New York, Philosophical Library, 1951.

Rutherford, K. R. *Humanitarianism Under Fire: The US and UN Intervention in Somalia.* Sterling, VA, Kumarian Press, 2008.

Sahnoun, M. *Somalia: The Missed Opportunities.* Washington, DC, United States Institute of Peace Press, 1994.

Salih, M. A. M., and Wohlgemuth, L. (Eds). *Crisis Management and the Politics of Reconciliation in Somalia.* Uppsala, Scandinavian Institute for African Studies, 1994.

Samatar, A. I. (Ed.). *The Somali Challenge: From Catastrophe to Renewal?* Boulder, CO, Lynne Rienner, 1994.

Samatar, S. S. *Somalia: A Nation in Turmoil.* London, Minority Rights Group, 1991.

Simons, A. *Networks of Dissolution: Somalia Undone.* Boulder, CO and Oxford, Westview Press, 1995.

Stevenson, J. *Losing Mogadishu: Testing US Policy in Somalia.* Annapolis, MD, Naval Institute Press, 1995.

United Nations, Dept of Public Information. *The United Nations and Somalia 1992–1996.* New York, United Nations, 1996.

Report of the Monitoring Group on Somalia and Eritrea Pursuant to Security Council Resolution 2002 (2011). New York, United Nations, 2012.

van Notten, M. (Edited by Heath MacCallum S.) *The Law of the Somalis: A Stable Foundation for Economic Development in the Horn of Africa.* Trenton, NJ, Red Sea Press, 2006.

Wam, P. E. *Conflict in Somalia: Drivers and Dynamics.* Herndon, VA, World Bank Publications, 2005.

World Bank. *Somalia: From Resilience Towards Recovery and Development. A Country Economic Memorandum for Somalia.* Report No. 34356. Washington, DC, World Bank, 2006.

SOUTH AFRICA

Physical and Social Geography

A. MacGREGOR HUTCHESON

The Republic of South Africa occupies the southern extremity of the African continent and, except for a relatively small area in the northern Transvaal, lies poleward of the Tropic of Capricorn, extending as far as latitude 34° 51' S. The republic covers a total area of 1,220,813 sq km (471,358 sq miles) and has common borders with Namibia to the north-west, with Botswana to the north, and with Zimbabwe, Mozambique and Swaziland to the north-east. Lesotho is entirely surrounded by South African territory, lying within the eastern part of the republic.

PHYSICAL FEATURES

Most of South Africa consists of a vast plateau with upwarped rims, bounded by an escarpment. Framing the plateau is a narrow coastal belt. The surface of the plateau varies in altitude from 600 m to 2,000 m above sea-level. It is highest in the east and south-east and dips fairly gently towards the Kalahari Basin in the north-west. The relief is generally monotonous, consisting of undulating to flat landscapes over wide areas. Variation is provided occasionally by low ridges and *inselberge* (or *kopjes*) made up of rock more resistant to erosion. There are three major sub-regions:

(i) the Highveld between 1,200 m and 1,800 m, forming a triangular area which occupies the southern Transvaal and most of the Free State;

(ii) a swell over 1,500 m high, aligned WNW–ESE, part of which is known as the Witwatersrand, rising gently from the plateau surface to the north of the Highveld and forming a major drainage divide; and

(iii) the Middleveld, generally between 600 m and 1,200 m, comprising the remaining part of the plateau.

The plateau's edges, upwarped during the Tertiary Period, are almost everywhere above 1,500 m. Maximum elevations of over 3,400 m occur in the south-east in Lesotho. From the crests the surface descends coastwards by means of the Great Escarpment, which gives the appearance of a mountain range when viewed from below, and which is known by distinctive names in its different sections. An erosional feature, dissected by seaward-flowing rivers, the nature of the Escarpment varies according to the type of rock which forms it. Along its eastern length it is known as the Drakensberg; in the section north of the Olifants river fairly soft granite gives rise to gentle slopes, but south of that river resistant quartzites are responsible for a more striking appearance. Further south again, along the KwaZulu/Natal–Lesotho border, basalts cause the Drakensberg to be at its most striking, rising up a sheer 1,800 m or more in places. Turning westwards the Great Escarpment is known successively as the Stormberg, Bamboes, Suurberg, Sneeuberg, Nieuwveld and Komsberg. The Great Escarpment then turns sharply northwards through the Roggeveld mountains, following which it is usually in the form of a simple step until the Kamiesberg are reached; owing to aridity and fewer rivers the dissection of this western part of the Escarpment is much less advanced than in the eastern (Drakensberg) section.

The Lowland margin that surrounds the South African plateau may be divided into four zones:

(i) the undulating to flat Transvaal Lowveld, between 150 m and 600 m above sea-level, separated from the Mozambique coastal plain by the Lebombo mountains in the east, and including part of the Limpopo valley in the north;

(ii) the south-eastern coastal belt, a very broken region descending to the coast in a series of steps, into which the rivers have cut deep valleys. In northern KwaZulu/Natal the Republic possesses its only true coastal plain, some 65 km at its widest;

(iii) the Cape ranges, consisting of the remnants of mountains folded during the Carboniferous era, and flanking the plateau on the south and south-west. On the south the folds trend E–W and on the south-west they trend N–S, the two trends crossing in the south-western corner of the Cape to produce a rugged knot of mountains and the ranges' highest elevations (over 2,000 m). Otherwise the Cape ranges are comparatively simple in structure, consisting of parallel anticlinal ridges and synclinal valleys. Narrow lowlands separate the mountains from the coast. Between the ridges and partially enclosed by them, e.g. the Little Karoo, is a series of steps rising to the foot of the Great Escarpment. The Great Karoo, the last of these steps, separates the escarpment from the Cape ranges; and

(iv) the western coastal belt is also characterized by a series of steps, but the slope from the foot of the Great Escarpment to the coast is more gentle and more uniform than in the south-eastern zone.

The greater part of the plateau is drained by the Orange river system. Rising in the Drakensberg within a short distance of the Escarpment the Orange flows westward for 1,900 km before entering the Atlantic Ocean. However, the western part of its basin is so dry that it is not unknown for the Orange to fail to reach its mouth during the dry season. The large-scale Orange River Project, a comprehensive scheme for water supply, irrigation and hydroelectric generation, aids water conservation in this western area and is making possible its development. The only other major system is that of the Limpopo, which rises on the northern slopes of the Witwatersrand and drains most of the Limpopo Province to the Indian Ocean. Apart from some interior drainage to a number of small basins in the north and north-west, the rest of the Republic's drainage is peripheral. Relatively short streams rise in the Great Escarpment, although some rise on the plateau itself, having cut through the escarpment, and drain directly to the coast. With the exception of riparian strips along perennial rivers, most of the country relies for water supplies on underground sources supplemented by dams.

CLIMATE AND NATURAL VEGETATION

Except for a small part of Limpopo Province the climate of South Africa is subtropical, although there are important regional variations within this general classification. Altitude and relief forms have an important influence on temperature and on both the amount and distribution of rainfall, and there is a strong correlation between the major physical and the major climatic regions. The altitude of the plateau modifies temperatures and because there is a general rise in elevation towards the Equator there is a corresponding decrease in temperature, resulting in a remarkable uniformity of temperature throughout the Republic from south to north (mean annual temperatures: Cape Town, 16.7°C; and Pretoria, 17.2°C). The greatest contrasts in temperature are, in fact, between the east coast, warmed by the Mozambique Current, and the west coast, cooled by the Benguela Current (respectively, mean monthly temperatures: Durban, January 24.4°C, July 17.8°C; and Port Nolloth, January 15.6°C, July 12.2°C). Daily and annual ranges in temperature increase with distance from the coast, being much greater on the plateau (mean annual temperature range: Cape Town, 8°C; Pretoria, 11°C).

The areas of highest annual rainfall largely coincide with the outstanding relief features, over 650 mm being received only in the eastern third of South Africa and relatively small areas in the southern Cape. Parts of the Drakensberg and the seaward slopes of the Cape ranges experience over 1,500 mm. West of the Drakensberg and to the north of the Cape ranges there is a marked rain-shadow, and annual rainfall decreases progressively westwards (Durban 1,140 mm, Bloemfontein 530 mm, Kimberley 400 mm, Upington 180 mm, Port Nolloth 50 mm).

Virtually all the western half of the country, apart from the southern Cape, receives less than 250 mm and the western coastal belt's northern section forms a continuation of the Namib Desert. Most of the rain falls during the summer months (November to April) when evaporation losses are greatest, brought by tropical marine air masses moving in from the Indian Ocean on the east. However, the south-western Cape has a winter maximum of rainfall with dry summers. Only the narrow southern coastal belt between Cape Agulhas and East London has rainfall distributed uniformly throughout the year. Snow may fall occasionally over the higher parts of the plateau and the Cape ranges during winter, but frost occurs on an average for 120 days each year over most of the interior plateau, and for shorter periods in the coastal lowlands, except in KwaZulu/Natal, where it is rare.

Variations in climate and particularly in annual rainfall are reflected in changes of vegetation, sometimes strikingly, as between the south-western Cape's Mediterranean shrub type, designed to withstand summer drought and of which the protea—the national plant—is characteristic, and the drought-resistant low Karoo bush immediately north of the Cape ranges and covering much of the semi-arid western half of the country. The only true areas of forest are found along the wetter south and east coasts—the temperate evergreen forests of the Knysna district and the largely evergreen subtropical bush, including palms and wild bananas, of Eastern Cape and KwaZulu/Natal, respectively. Grassland covers the rest of the Republic, merging into thornveld in the north-western Cape and into bushveld in Limpopo Province.

MINERAL RESOURCES

South Africa's mineral resources, outstanding in their variety, quality and quantity, overshadow all the country's other natural resources. They are mainly found in the ancient Pre-Cambrian foundation and associated intrusions and occur in a wide curving zone which stretches from Limpopo Province through the Free State and Northern Cape to the west coast. To the south of this mineralized zone the Pre-Cambrian rocks are covered by Karoo sedimentaries, which generally do not contain minerals, with the exception of extensive deposits of bituminous coal. These deposits occur mainly in the eastern Transvaal Highveld, the northern Free State and northern KwaZulu/Natal, mostly in thick, easily worked seams fairly near to the surface. Coal is of particular importance to South Africa because of relatively low production elsewhere in the continent south of the Equator, and South Africa's current dependence on imported petroleum.

The most important mineral regions are the Witwatersrand and the northern Free State, producing gold, silver and uranium; the diamond areas centred on Kimberley, Pretoria, Jagersfontein and Koffiefontein; and the Transvaal bushveld complex containing multiple occurrences of a large number of minerals, including asbestos, chrome, copper, iron, magnesium, nickel, platinum, tin, uranium and vanadium. In the Northern Cape important deposits of manganese, iron ore and asbestos occur in the Postmasburg, Sishen and Kuruman areas, while in the north-western Cape reserves of lead, zinc, silver and copper are being exploited. This list of occurrences and minerals is by no means exhaustive, and prospecting for new mineral resources is continuing. In 1988 exploitable petroleum deposits were discovered off the western Cape coast, and a substantial reserve of natural gas and petroleum was discovered south-west of Mossel Bay, off the south coast of the Cape.

ETHNIC GROUPS AND POPULATION

Five major ethnic groups make up South Africa's multiracial society. The 'Khoisan' peoples—Bushmen, Hottentots and Bergdamara—are survivors of the country's earliest inhabitants. The negroid Bantu-speaking peoples fall into a number of tribal groupings. The major groups are formed by the Nguni, comprising Zulu, Swazi, Ndebele, Pondo, Tembu and Xhosa on the one hand, and by the Sotho and Tswana on the other. The European or 'white' peoples, who once dominated the political and social organization of the Republic and continue to exercise considerable economic influence, are descended from the original 17th-century Dutch settlers in the Cape, refugee French Huguenots, British settlers from 1820 onwards, Germans, and more recent immigrants from Europe and ex-colonial African territories. The remainder of the population comprises Coloureds (people of mixed race) and Asians, largely of Indian origin. At the October 2001 census the total population was 44,819,778, while the ethnic composition of the total population was: Africans (blacks) 79.0%; Europeans (whites) 9.6%; Coloureds 8.9%; and Asians 2.5%. The official languages are Afrikaans, English, isiNdebele, Sesotho sa Leboa, Sesotho, siSwati, Xitsonga, Setswana, Tshivenda, isiXhosa and isiZulu.

The overall density of the population was 36.8 inhabitants per sq km at the census of October 2001, but its distribution is extremely uneven. It is generally related to agricultural resources, more than two-thirds living in the wetter eastern third of the Republic and in the southern Cape. The heaviest concentrations are found in the Witwatersrand mining area—at mid-2010 some 3,669,725 people were estimated to be living in the Johannesburg Metropolitan Area—and in and around the major ports of Cape Town (3,404,807 at mid-2010) and Durban (2,879,233 at mid-2010). The fourth largest city is Pretoria (the greater Metropolitan Area had an estimated population of 1,428,987 at mid-2010). Cape Town is the legislative capital of the country, Pretoria the administrative capital and Bloemfontein the judicial capital. Europeans have a widespread geographical distribution, but more than 80% reside in towns. The majority of African live in the former tribal reserves, which extend in a great horseshoe along the south-eastern coast and up to Limpopo Province and then south-westwards to the north-eastern Cape. The Coloured population is mainly resident in the Cape, and the Asian population is concentrated largely in KwaZulu/Natal and the Witwatersrand. The total population was estimated at 50,586,757 at mid-2011, giving a population density of 41.4 per sq km.

Recent History

CHRISTOPHER SAUNDERS

HISTORICAL BACKGROUND

Hunter-gatherers lived in many parts of South Africa for hundreds of thousands of years, leaving behind evidence of their activities in rock art. About 2,000 years ago descendants of the San (Bushman) people who had acquired sheep arrived from the north. These pastoralists, the Khoikhoi (Hottentot), were the first indigenous people to interact with European seafarers along the coast from the late 15th century. From about 1,500 years ago Bantu-speaking, iron-working farmers moved into the northern parts of South Africa. Growing their own crops, they rapidly increased in numbers and began to develop small kingdoms. Trading routes began to link the coastal areas with the interior. Over time these farmers spread southwards into what is now the Transkei in the Eastern Cape province and the Free State. In the early 19th century a process of political centralization led to the emergence, in what is today KwaZulu/Natal, of the relatively large Zulu state. The Zulu and other black African peoples fought to resist white encroachment during much of the 19th century.

The Dutch East India Company established a settlement at the Cape in 1652. About 150 years later the British took over a sizeable white-ruled colony from the Dutch. Friction between the British authorities at the Cape and the Dutch (Afrikaner or Boer) frontier farmers led many of the latter, after the abolition of slavery in 1834, to embark upon a northward trek to establish an independent polity. Britain subsequently annexed the trekker Republic of Natalia (now part of the province of KwaZulu/Natal), but permitted the creation of two independent Boer republics, the Orange Free State (OFS), between the Orange and Vaal rivers, and the South African Republic or Transvaal. When a large diamond deposit was discovered at what became known as Kimberley in 1871, the British intervened to bring the contested diamond-rich territory under their rule. The rapid development of gold-mining in the Transvaal after 1886, together with the emergence of the South African Republic as the most powerful state in the region, were perceived by British interests as a threat to their paramountcy; the consequent exertion of pressure on the Transvaal and the OFS provoked the Anglo–Boer (or South African) war of 1899–1902. During the war the Boer republics passed under British control, and on 31 May 1910 the Union of South Africa, comprising the two conquered Boer republics and the two British colonies of the Cape and Natal, was formally declared a dominion under the British crown.

The Constitution of the new Union gave the franchise to white males only, except in the Cape, where the existing non-racial voting rights, based on a qualified franchise, were protected. However, in 1936 black Africans in the Cape were stripped of their right to vote, and only whites could be members of the Union Parliament. The two Afrikaner parties in the ex-republics amalgamated with the Cape's South Africa Party to form the national South Africa Party (SAP). Led by two Boer generals, Louis Botha and Jan Smuts, the SAP formed the first Government of the new Union. In 1912 another general, J. B. M. Hertzog, broke away to found the National Party (NP), devoted to the exclusive interests of Afrikaners. In the same year members of the African élite, under the leadership of Pixley Seme, established the South African Native National Congress, soon renamed the African National Congress (ANC). The Congress protested in vain against the 1913 Land Act, which denied Africans the right to buy land outside the Native Reserves or to lease white-owned land, and other legislation imposing racial segregation. As a consequence of the economic crisis of the early 1930s, Hertzog's NP, in power from 1924, entered a coalition with the SAP under Smuts, and the two parties subsequently merged to form the United Party. A small group of Afrikaner nationalists, under Daniel Malan, rejected the coalition and merger, and formed a 'purified' NP.

APARTHEID

Afrikaner farmers, who feared the loss of their low-wage African labour to the towns, and Afrikaner workers in the towns, who feared black competition for their jobs, supported the intensification of racial segregation, which the NP called 'apartheid'. In the 1948 general election the NP secured a narrow parliamentary majority. Malan formed a Government and began putting apartheid into practice. In 1954 he was replaced by the hardline J. G. Strydom, who in 1958 was succeeded by Hendrik Verwoerd, apartheid's chief architect and leading ideologue. Verwoerd believed that each race should be kept apart so that each could develop along its own lines. Each racial group was to have its own territorial area within which to develop its unique cultural personality. Of the areas envisaged for the African peoples, the overwhelming majority were the poverty-stricken Native Reserves, comprising only 13% of the national territory.

The period 1948–59 saw the introduction of a series of interrelated laws and measures aimed at restructuring South African society to conform to apartheid doctrine. The Population Registration Act provided for the classification of the entire population on the basis of race. Inter-racial marriages were forbidden, and the Immorality Act, banning sexual relations between whites and blacks, was extended to include relations between whites and Coloureds. The Group Areas Act of 1950 provided for the designation of particular residential areas for specific races. Existing provisions for the reservation of categories of employment for particular races were strengthened. Race segregation in public places, trains and buses, post-offices, hospitals and even ambulances was introduced wherever it had not been previously practised. Under the terms of the Separate Amenities Act, amenities provided for different races did not have to be of equal standard. The Extension of University Education Act removed the right of non-white students to attend the previously open universities of Cape Town and the Witwatersrand. To strengthen its hand against radical opposition, the Government introduced the Suppression of Communism Act, which forced the Communist Party of South Africa to disband, only to regroup underground as the South African Communist Party (SACP).

The repressive policies of the NP prompted the ANC to embark on a programme of mass civil disobedience. After the Defiance Campaign of 1952, a Congress Alliance was formed, which drew together the ANC and other Congresses, including the South African Indian Congress. At the Congress of the People held in June 1955, a Freedom Charter was adopted, setting out a vision of a new South Africa. Some within the ANC did not approve of the Congress Alliance's assertion that South Africa belonged to all who lived in it, regardless of colour, and in 1958 the Africanists in the ANC, led by Robert Sobukwe, broke away and, in April 1959, formed the Pan-Africanist Congress (PAC).

In March 1960 police in the township of Sharpeville, south of Johannesburg, opened fire on a crowd of unarmed black Africans who were surrounding the police station in response to a PAC demonstration, killing 69 people. The Sharpeville massacre aroused international indignation to an unprecedented degree: South Africa sustained a net outflow of foreign investment capital, and appeals for military, economic and sporting boycotts began to be given serious attention. In 1961, following a referendum among white voters in October 1960, South Africa became a republic, and left the Commonwealth.

In response to demonstrations within South Africa in protest against the Sharpeville massacre, the Government banned both the ANC and the PAC. In 1961 some within the ANC, together with white members of the SACP, formed a military organization, Umkhonto we Sizwe (MK—'Spear of the Nation'). Under the leadership of Nelson Mandela, it aimed to force the Government to negotiate by attacking white-owned property, while avoiding harm to people. Mandela was arrested in 1962 and, along with others, sentenced to life imprisonment on charges of sabotage in 1964. In the following decades the ANC in exile gradually organized a global campaign against apartheid, while at the same time trying to build up a guerrilla army. It was not until after 1976, however, that members of MK were able to return to carry out armed attacks within the country.

Verwoerd argued that the Native Reserves constituted the historic 'homelands' (Bantustans) of different African nations. The 'homelands' were to be led to self-government under constitutions giving scope to the elective principle, but with the balance of power in the hands of government-appointed chiefs. Transkei was accorded 'self-government' under such a system in 1963. Ciskei, Bophuthatswana, Lebowa, Venda, Gazankulu, Qwaqwa and KwaZulu followed in the early 1970s. As explicit racism was replaced by separate nationality as a rationale for the denial of civil rights to black Africans, so stricter controls were imposed to prevent Africans acquiring permanent residence in urban areas. Wherever possible, jobs were given to migrant labourers, and a massive campaign was launched to rid the white areas of 'surplus Bantu', who were to be forced into the overcrowded 'homelands'. In the 1960s more than 1.5m. people were forcibly resettled. These measures were more drastic than those of the first phase of apartheid, and under John Vorster, the Minister of Justice, the powers of the security police were massively extended. Vorster succeeded Verwoerd as Prime Minister in 1966 when Verwoerd was assassinated.

South Africa took control of South West Africa (later to become Namibia) in 1915 and after the First World War ruled the territory as a mandate under the League of Nations. After the Second World War South Africa's application to annex the territory was rejected by the new United Nations, and in 1960 Ethiopia and Liberia brought a case before the International Court of Justice (ICJ) in which they claimed that South Africa was violating the mandate and should therefore withdraw from South West Africa. South Africa fought the case, but at the same time began to introduce the Bantustan system in the territory. After the ICJ dismissed the case in 1966, the UN General Assembly resolved to revoke South Africa's mandate and place the territory under direct UN administration. This was subsequently confirmed by the Security Council, but South Africa refused to co-operate. From 1966 South Africa fought a low-intensity war in northern Namibia against guerrillas of the South West Africa People's Organization (see the chapter on Namibia).

INTERNAL PRESSURES FOR CHANGE

With violent resistance crushed, the most important internal opposition to apartheid from the late 1960s was the Black Consciousness Movement, founded by Steve Biko. His ideas of black assertion gave a new self-confidence to black university students and high school youth. In 1973 black workers in the Durban-Pinetown area began a series of strikes which ultimately led to the formation of new trade unions. Meanwhile, the South African Government endeavoured to confer formal independence on the Bantustans. Transkei accepted this status in 1976, Bophuthatswana in 1977, Venda in 1979 and Ciskei in 1981. All remained dependent on South African financial support and their 'independence' was not internationally recognized. The imposition of 'independence' was resisted by KwaNdebele and KwaZulu. The head of the latter, Chief Mangosuthu Buthelezi, used the political immunity conferred by his position to attack the apartheid system. He founded Inkatha, which began as a Zulu cultural movement but evolved into a significant political force.

In June 1976 the agglomeration of segregated African townships to the south-west of Johannesburg known as Soweto (South-West Townships) erupted, after police opened fire on school children protesting against being forced to use Afrikaans as the medium of instruction for some of their school subjects. Resistance spread not only to other black townships around the Rand and Pretoria but to Natal and the Cape, where Coloured and Indian youths joined in. Repeatedly and violently repressed, the uprisings were not brought under control until the end of the year. Thousands of young people were arrested but many others escaped across the borders to join the liberation movements. The ANC proved far more successful than the PAC in attracting this cadre of prospective freedom fighters, thus consolidating its political hold over the loyalties of the majority. Biko was arrested by the police and died in police custody in September 1977. At the subsequent inquest into his death, details were revealed of how he been had tortured, and the national and international outcry led the Government to ban the black consciousness organizations in October and the UN to impose a mandatory arms embargo on South Africa in November.

P. W. Botha, who had been Minister of Defence and who took over from Vorster as Prime Minister in 1978, altered the balance of influence within the state security network in favour of the armed forces, as opposed to the police. The State Security Council, which brought together politicians and key officials in the security forces, became the main decision-making organ, with the roles of the NP and Parliament (where the Progressive Federal Party—PFP—now led the opposition) increasingly reduced. In the face of the increasing pressure on the apartheid regime, Botha introduced some reforms. Racial job restrictions were gradually abolished and trade union rights extended to black Africans. Restrictions on multiracial sports were reduced, and the laws against inter-racial marriage and extra-marital sexual relations were repealed. The ineffective Senate was replaced by a President's Council, which proposed the establishment of a tricameral Parliament, comprising separate houses for whites, Coloureds and Indians. However, any sharing of power with non-whites was rejected by the hardliners in the NP, who broke away and formed the Conservative Party (CP). Nevertheless, in November 1983 white voters approved the creation of a tricameral legislature in a referendum. Elections for the Coloured House of Representatives and the Indian House of Delegates followed in August 1984, and in September Botha became the country's first executive President.

The introduction of the new Constitution was the catalyst for a large-scale rebellion in the black townships, which was supported by strikes, notably in the economically crucial mining industry. Resistance to apartheid had been galvanized by the coming together of hundreds of local civic and other groups in the United Democratic Front. The Congress of South African Trade Unions (COSATU), a federation of black trade unions that were politically aligned with the ANC, was formed in December 1985, and demanded the abolition of pass restrictions, the withdrawal of foreign investment and the release of Mandela. The township rebellion escalated in March, when the police opened fire on an unarmed African procession in Uitenhage, killing 20 people. Demands intensified for the Government to introduce major reforms, but in August Botha rejected outside interference in dealing with the country's problems. With US banks refusing to roll over short term loans, the currency declined rapidly and business leaders met with the ANC in exile in Zambia. As internal resistance escalated, in June 1986 the Government extended the state of emergency to cover the whole country. This led European banks to suspend new lending to South Africa, and the European Community (EC, now the European Union—EU) and the USA introduced limited sanctions.

Among Afrikaner intellectuals, professionals and businessmen and within the NP itself, opinion was already growing that apartheid would have to be abandoned and an accommodation reached with an effective African leadership. While liberal Afrikaner opinion was moving towards this view, a proliferation of movements on the extreme right expressed the growing desperation of the poorer sections of the white community at the erosion of their privileged position. A paramilitary organization, the Afrikaanse Weerstandsbeweging, founded in 1977 and led by Eugene Terre'Blanche, actively recruited among the security forces.

A general election to the white House of Assembly in 1987 saw the NP emerge with a secure majority but a considerably reduced vote. The CP obtained more seats than the PFP and became the official opposition. In 1989 the PFP was reconstituted as the Democratic Party (DP). In January that year, Botha suffered a stroke and decided to relinquish the NP leadership, while remaining State President. The NP members of Parliament then elected F. W. de Klerk as the new NP leader. Botha met with Mandela—still serving a life sentence—in July, thus effectively recognizing the ANC leader's position as a potential alternative head of government. Botha's colleagues forced him to relinquish the presidency in August. In the September parliamentary elections the opposition parties made considerable gains but the NP retained a clear majority. Upon becoming State President, de Klerk downgraded the State Security Council and the role of the military, and ordered the country's nuclear weapons to be dismantled. He allowed a massive march in Cape Town, then released key ANC leaders. De Klerk now accepted that apartheid was unsustainable and that the ANC must be accepted as a negotiating partner. The ANC, meanwhile, lost its military facilities in Angola as part of the agreement that brought Namibia its independence in March 1990, and had to move its camps even further away from South Africa. The winding down of the Cold War and then the collapse of communism in Eastern Europe in late 1989 meant that the ANC's armed struggle lost its main foreign support base. De Klerk was quick to realize that this gave him the opportunity to revoke the ban on the ANC, which had long been demonized because of its close ties with the SACP.

THE NEGOTIATED SETTLEMENT

Addressing the three Houses of Parliament on 2 February 1990, President de Klerk made the dramatic announcement that Nelson Mandela would be released and that the ban had been lifted on the ANC, the PAC, the SACP and 33 other organizations. It was the Government's intention to open negotiations with black leaders, with a view to devising a new constitution based on universal franchise. Equality of all citizens, regardless of race, was to be guaranteed by an independent judiciary, and protection for individual rights entrenched. On 11 February Mandela was freed after 27 years in prison. ANC refugees soon began to return from exile.

However, the ANC faced major problems in bringing the spontaneous loyalties of the great majority of the black population within a disciplined organizational framework. It urged the continuation of sanctions until the abandonment of apartheid had become demonstrably irreversible.

When the ANC and the Government met in August 1990 to continue discussions on the opening of full constitutional negotiations, the ANC agreed to the formal suspension of its guerrilla activities. In February 1991 de Klerk announced that all the remaining legislation enshrining apartheid, including the Group Areas Act and the Population Registration Act, was to be repealed. By the end of June this legal revolution was complete. The NP even changed its own constitution to open membership to all. The EC and the USA abandoned most sanctions, and contacts between South Africa and black African states expanded. In early July, at its national congress, the ANC elected a new National Executive. Mandela became President, and the leader of the National Union of Mineworkers, Cyril Ramaphosa, Secretary-General.

The main obstacle impeding constitutional negotiations was the continuing violence between Inkatha and ANC supporters and the suspicion that elements of the state security forces were involved. In April 1991 the ANC threatened to withdraw from negotiations if the Government failed to take effective action to stop the violence, and demanded the dismissal of the Minister of Defence, Magnus Malan, and the Minister of Law and Order, Adriaan Vlok. In July it was admitted that secret payments had been made from government funds to Inkatha during 1989–90, and Malan and Vlok were demoted to minor cabinet posts.

A multi-party conference, the Convention for a Democratic South Africa (CODESA), met to begin drafting a new constitution in December 1991. The commencement of constitutional discussions intensified the hostility of the extreme right, and, after losing a parliamentary by-election to the CP, de Klerk called a referendum of white voters. The Government achieved a more than two-thirds' majority in support of continuing negotiations towards a democratic constitution. However, after the Government insisted on provisions that appeared to give it a veto, the CODESA talks again came to an impasse, after which the ANC appealed for a campaign of non-violent mass action by its supporters to put pressure on the Government. Then, on 17 June 1992, a number of residents of the settlement of Boipatong, including women and children, were massacred by Inkatha supporters. The ANC broke off negotiations with the Government, and demanded the disbandment of groups involved in covert operations. In September the armed forces of the nominally independent 'homeland' of Ciskei fired on a procession of ANC supporters, killing 28 people. The ANC blamed the Government for the massacre, but accepted the need for the dialogue to continue.

The multi-party negotiating forum was reconvened in April 1993. Buthelezi, who protested vigorously against the bilateral agreements between the Government and the ANC, initiated meetings between representatives of Inkatha, a number of movements based in the 'homelands' and the CP. By mid-year it had been decided that the elections would be held in April 1994, and that a set of constitutional principles would have to be observed in the final constitution. The interim Constitution was finalized in November, and embodied major compromises by both the main negotiating partners. Its regional proposals provided for some measure of federalism, but not enough to persuade Buthelezi to accept them. There were now to be nine provinces: Western Cape, Eastern Cape, Northern Cape, Orange Free State (renamed Free State in June 1995), North-West, Natal (soon redesignated KwaZulu/Natal), Eastern Transvaal (subsequently renamed Mpumalanga), Northern Transvaal (renamed Northern Province in June 1995 and Limpopo in February 2002) and Pretoria, Witwatersrand and Vereeniging (subsequently renamed Gauteng). The former 'homelands', including those purported to be 'independent', were absorbed into one or more of the new provinces. The national legislature, consisting of a House of Assembly of 400 members and a Senate of 90 members, was also to act as a Constitutional Assembly charged with drafting the country's final constitution within two years. Adoption of the constitution required a two-thirds' majority of the Assembly.

Buthelezi was persuaded to register his Inkatha Freedom Party (IFP) for the April 1994 election, in return for the enhancement of the status of the Zulu monarchy by the transfer of extensive state lands to a trust in the name of the Zulu monarch, King Goodwill Zwelithini. In the general election, the ANC gained an overwhelming majority at national level, although it fell short of the two-thirds' majority needed to write the final Constitution unilaterally. It also gained control of seven of the nine provinces. The NP, the only other grouping to secure more than 20% of the votes, won control of the Western Cape Province. Inkatha won 10% of the votes cast, and was credited with a 51% victory in KwaZulu/Natal. The PAC, with its radical Africanist approach, and the white-led DP each received less than 2% of the votes. On 10 May Mandela was inaugurated as head of state and a Government of National Unity (GNU) was formed, in which the ANC, NP and IFP were represented in proportion to the seats they had won. Thabo Mbeki of the ANC and de Klerk became Deputy Presidents.

THE MANDELA PRESIDENCY

Following the installation of a democratic Government, South Africa was admitted into the Organization of African Unity (OAU—subsequently the African Union—AU), the Commonwealth and the Southern African Development Community (SADC), and resumed its seat in the General Assembly of the UN. The arms embargo that the UN had imposed in 1977 was finally removed.

The GNU focused on the maintenance of stability and the promotion of economic growth, with initial emphasis laid on a Reconstruction and Development Programme (RDP). However, in early 1996 a new macroeconomic policy called the Growth, Employment and Redistribution programme (GEAR), was adopted. This placed attracting foreign investment to stimulate economic growth above issues of redistribution. Although the Government's schemes to provide electricity and clean water to all were initially successful, unemployment remained very high in the townships and many communities continued to refuse to pay for services and rents.

A number of communities began to use vigilante methods in response to the police force's apparent inability to combat an increase in violent crime, which also prompted demands for the restoration of the death penalty, outlawed by the new Constitutional Court in June 1995. The process of transforming the police into a force that was regarded by the public as legitimate and credible was hindered by evidence that emerged about the measures that had, during the apartheid and transitional periods, been used against opponents of that system. Col Eugene de Kock, the former head of a clandestine police base near Pretoria from which political assassinations had been carried out, was put on trial and sentenced to over 200 years in gaol, but Magnus Malan, the former Minister of Defence, and prominent officials in the former armed forces were acquitted of complicity in a massacre perpetrated in KwaZulu in 1987.

The Constitutional Assembly, comprising the two houses of Parliament, approved a final Constitution in May 1996. This was then ratified by the Constitutional Court and signed into law by President Mandela at Sharpeville on 10 December. A National Council of Provinces replaced the Senate as the upper house of Parliament, and socio-economic rights were extended. Following the drafting of the new Constitution, the NP announced that it was to leave the GNU at the end of June in order to form a parliamentary opposition. The Government's former chief negotiator, Roelf Meyer, concerned by the NP's inability to attract black African voters, left the NP and in September 1997 formed a new political party, the United Democratic Movement (UDM), with Bantu Holomisa, the former ruler of Transkei. By mid-1998 Holomisa had become leader of the party, with Meyer his deputy, and the UDM began to attract significant support, most notably in Transkei. After de Klerk resigned as leader of the NP, that party continued to decline under its new leader Marthinus van Schalkwyk.

At the ANC congress in December 1997 Mandela resigned as party President and was succeeded by Thabo Mbeki. Jacob Zuma (hitherto the party Chairman) was elected Deputy

President. Although Mandela remained active as head of state, Mbeki was already effectively in control of government administration. The Mandela Government maintained cordial relations with regimes that had provided substantial support to the ANC during the apartheid era, most notably Iran, Cuba and Libya, but South Africa's links with the USA strengthened following the transition to democracy. Mandela's personal stature enhanced South Africa's prestige internationally. In November 1996 he announced that South Africa would transfer diplomatic recognition from Taiwan (Republic of China) to the People's Republic of China, with effect from the end of 1997. This decision was influenced by the return of Hong Kong to Chinese rule in 1997 and South Africa's wish to secure a permanent seat on an enlarged UN Security Council. After becoming Chairman of SADC in September 1996, Mandela pursued a more active foreign policy, frequently intervening personally in an effort to resolve regional problems. In early 1997 he was involved in intensive diplomatic activity aimed at ending the civil war in Zaire (now the Democratic Republic of the Congo—DRC), and he also sought to mediate in the civil conflict in southern Sudan.

In 1995 Parliament finally approved the establishment of a Truth and Reconciliation Commission (TRC). President Mandela appointed Archbishop Desmond Tutu to head the TRC, and in October 1998 Tutu submitted to Mandela a five-volume report, after the ANC had failed in an attempt to delay publication of the report, on the grounds that it 'criminalized' its role in the struggle against apartheid. The work of the TRC's amnesty committee, which had considered applications by perpetrators of human rights abuses and granted amnesty to those who gave a full account of their actions, finally came to an end in May 2001. While the TRC's reparations committee had recommended that R3,000m. be granted to compensate victims, the Government made only about R65m. available, which equated to a one-off payment of about R30,000 to the 22,000 victims identified by the TRC. President Mbeki rejected the suggestion of a wealth tax to pay for reparations, and voiced strong disapproval of the cases being brought against multinational companies for their alleged complicity in apartheid, on the grounds that such cases would threaten future foreign investment. For many, the Government's response to the recommendations of the TRC was grossly inadequate.

THE MBEKI PRESIDENCY

In the later years of the Mandela presidency Mbeki increasingly assumed responsibility for government administration. One of his major achievements was to contribute to the restoration of relative peace in KwaZulu/Natal, and to improve relations between the ANC and Inkatha. Although he lacked Mandela's personal charisma, he proved to be a competent campaigner for the ANC in the 1999 general election campaign. On 2 June almost 17m. voters participated in the polls, which were judged to be substantially 'free and fair' by domestic and international observers. The ANC obtained 266 seats, narrowly failing to secure a two-thirds' majority in the National Assembly. Support for the opposition fragmented, with the NP, reconstituted as the New National Party (NNP), winning only 28 seats; it lost Coloured support to the ANC and white support to the DP under the leadership of Tony Leon. The latter increased its representation in the National Assembly from seven to 38 seats (thus becoming the official opposition). The IFP, which won 34 seats in the National Assembly, entered into a coalition with the ANC, and Buthelezi remained Minister of Home Affairs. Zuma, long a close associate of Mbeki, became Deputy President. As a result of the coalition, the ANC achieved much more than a two-thirds' majority in the legislature.

On 16 June 1999 Mbeki was formally inaugurated as President. He signalled his intention to pursue the macroeconomic strategies on which the Mandela Government had embarked, but pledged to accelerate the privatization of parastatal companies while also encouraging private investment in state-owned enterprises. One of Mbeki's main aims in foreign policy was to secure a peaceful settlement in the DRC. He assisted in the arrangement of a cease-fire there in June, and South Africa agreed to contribute a small number of troops to the UN peace-keeping force. South African soldiers were also deployed in peace-keeping missions in Burundi and Sudan. Mbeki sought to strengthen links with states such as Cuba, Libya and Iraq, while at the same time travelling to Western countries to win support for his Millennium African Recovery Plan, a programme for good governance and economic reform for the continent, subsequently incorporated into the New Partnership for Africa's Development (NEPAD).

At many international forums Mbeki emphasized the importance of eliminating global poverty and bringing debt relief to poorer countries. In June 2002 he presented NEPAD to the meeting of the Group of Eight leading industrialized countries (G8) in Canada, in an attempt to attract increased foreign aid to the continent. In July Mbeki presided over a conference in Durban, at which the OAU was relaunched as the AU, of which he became the first Chairman. By July 2003 Mbeki had handed over the chairmanship of both the Non-aligned Movement and the AU, but the latter asked him to mediate in the crisis in Côte d'Ivoire. In that he was not successful, and he took advantage of South Africa's election as a non-permanent member of the UN Security Council to withdraw from his role in that country. From 2004 it was a major concern of the Government to secure a permanent seat on an enlarged UN Security Council. However, when South Africa took up its non-permanent seat in January 2007, it came under much criticism for arguing that the Council was overreaching itself and for voting not to take a stand against human rights abuses in countries such as Myanmar and Zimbabwe.

When the invasion of white-owned farms in neighbouring Zimbabwe began, Mbeki not only failed to criticize the Zimbabwean President, Robert Mugabe, but he delayed announcing clearly that the seizure of land by violent means would not be tolerated in South Africa. Identifying land inequalities as a major issue to be addressed, he stated his preference of implementing 'quiet diplomacy' with Mugabe, to influence him to hold a free and fair election and to deal with the land issue peacefully. Mbeki agreed reluctantly to recommend the suspension of Zimbabwe from the Commonwealth, but still refused to criticize Mugabe's increasingly authoritarian rule and the extreme measures taken against both white farmers and supporters of the Zimbabwean opposition Movement for Democratic Change (MDC). In June 2003 Mbeki stated publicly that the Zimbabwean crisis would be resolved by June 2004, but then had to admit that his policy of quiet diplomacy, which aimed to bring the MDC into a unity government, had thus far been unsuccessful. Mbeki ignored those who argued that his failure to condemn Mugabe's rule was threatening to undermine his entire NEPAD strategy. When the Mugabe regime destroyed homes and made hundreds of thousands homeless in 2005, Mbeki again offered no public criticism. In 2007 he stated that South Africa would have to live with the millions of refugees from Zimbabwe who crossed the border, but in March was deputed by SADC to mediate in the crisis.

As the Zimbabwean crisis continued, some foreign investors began to fear that land invasions might occur in South Africa—as happened on a small scale in mid-2001—and that the Government might not stand firm on the rule of law. The programme for land restitution in South Africa proceeded slowly, mainly owing to a cumbersome bureaucratic process. By mid-2007 5,100 claims remained to be settled, but they were the most difficult ones, and it appeared that the deadline of completing the process by 2008 would not be met. Of the 73,000 claims that had been settled, most had been resolved by monetary compensation rather than the return of land. Meanwhile, the Communal Land Rights Act of 2004 aimed to clarify the tenure rights of 15m. people in the former 'homelands'. An estimated 86% of all rural land remained in the hands of approximately 60,000 white commercial farmers, and attacks on white farmers continued at a high level.

It was on the subject of HIV/AIDS that Mbeki was most severely criticized by the national and international media, owing to statements he made in support of dissident scientists who questioned whether AIDS was caused by HIV, and for promoting the idea that an indigenous cure might be found for the disease. While there was widespread support for his view that AIDS must be considered in the context of poverty in Africa, his often ambiguous statements served to divert attention from the question of how best to tackle the pandemic. By the end of 2001 an estimated 4.7m. South Africans were infected with HIV, about one-fifth of the population aged between 15 and 49 years. While the Ministry of Health claimed in mid-2002 that the rate of infection was slowing, others believed that it was gaining momentum. Although the lobby group Treatment Action Campaign (TAC) won a court case in late 2001 in which the Government was ordered to provide antiretroviral drugs for pregnant women, the Mbeki Government argued that both the system of monitoring required and the drugs themselves were too expensive. In 2003 the Government reluctantly accepted that it should make antiretrovirals freely available, but the roll-out proceeded slowly. The TAC continued to demand the dismissal of the Minister of Health. It was not until 2006 that the Government committed itself to a new AIDS policy that the TAC could support. Although Mbeki retained the incompetent Minister of Health, the TAC found that it could work with the new Deputy President, and accepted that the Government had abandoned its previous tardy approach to the pandemic.

Although the level of overall crime remained high, with some particularly violent crimes having an apparent racial aspect to them, certain categories of crime declined in the early 2000s, in part because of the establishment of a new élite anti-crime unit, the Directorate of Special Operations, known as the Scorpions. The underfunded police were often unable to detain offenders, there were numerous escapes from gaols, and those detained were often released back into society because of the inadequacy of the justice system. State agents did, however, successfully infiltrate a right-wing extremist group, members of which were put on trial for plotting to overthrow the State, in a trial that is still not concluded. White emigration increased as a result of rising crime and the impact of events in Zimbabwe, and as a consequence of legislation that required all companies and organizations to set targets for making their workforce more representative of the demographics of the country. Many young white males saw no prospect of employment. A small, well-connected, black élite benefited massively from the Government's Black Economic Empowerment programme (see Economy), and Mbeki defended the rapid emergence of a black bourgeoisie as a means to greater social stability.

The alliance formed by the DP and the NNP in the Western Cape in June 1999 led in mid-2000 to the establishment of the Democratic Alliance (DA), which linked the two parties nationally, under the leadership of Tony Leon, with the NNP leader van Schalkwyk as his deputy. Although the DP claimed that it held firm to its liberal principles, there were few black Africans in the new Alliance and the ANC was able to present the DA as an anti-African front. When municipal elections were held in late 2000 to replace the more than 800 existing local government structures with 284 new municipalities, the main urban centres became 'uni-cities', each under one authority. Cape Town's was controlled initially by the DA. In KwaZulu/Natal the loose alliance between the ANC and IFP brought relative stability, although the chiefs (*inkosi*), who were now paid by the Government, feared that the new local government system would reduce their powers, and sought unsuccessfully to challenge the demarcation of the new structures. In late 2001 a series of crises in the Western Cape, involving alleged corruption by the mayor of Cape Town, provided an opportunity for the NNP faction of the DA, led by van Schalkwyk, to suspend its participation in the alliance and enter into a partnership with the ANC instead. These two parties then entered into a power-sharing agreement in the Western Cape, and van Schalkwyk became Premier of the Western Cape. The NNP was weakened, however, by legislation adopted in June 2002 enabling elected members of Parliament and of local government bodies to change parties without the need to seek re-election. As a result, the UDM, which had opposed the floor-crossing legislation, lost most of its members of Parliament to other parties. The DA gained members from the NNP, and the ANC was able to take power in the Western Cape at local level. Although many expected the ANC also to gain a majority in the KwaZulu/Natal legislature, the IFP managed to remain in power in that province until the 2004 elections.

Perhaps the single most important decision of the Mbeki Government was to purchase aircraft, submarines and corvettes for the South African National Defence Force from the United Kingdom, Germany and Sweden, despite much criticism that they were extremely expensive and unnecessary. The purchase was justified in part by the promised 'offsets', which were supposed to bring foreign capital into the country and create jobs. However, critics alleged that there had been massive corruption in the arms-procurement process. For a time the Government refused to allow the Special Investigation Unit, set up by Mandela, to probe the matter. Eventually in 2001, public hearings were held in Pretoria, under the auspices of the Auditor-General, the National Director of Public Prosecutions (NDPP) and the Public Protector. The report issued in November failed to find evidence of serious wrongdoing, but opposition parties accused the ANC of manipulating and suppressing certain parts of the text. The ANC's chief whip, Tony Yengeni, was subsequently forced to resign, following allegations that he had received favours from one of the contractors in the arms deal while Chairman of the Parliamentary Defence Committee. He was sentenced to four years' imprisonment in March 2003 for defrauding the Government. The Scorpions then began to investigate allegations that Jacob Zuma, the Deputy President, had solicited a bribe from a French manufacturer bidding for an arms contract that was part of the multi-million rand arms deal. The NDPP, Bulelani Ngcuka, in August 2003 announced that there was a *prima facie* case of corruption, but insufficient evidence to convict Zuma, and thus he would not be prosecuted. Zuma lodged a complaint against Ngcuka with the Public Protector, and a number of Zuma's associates claimed that Ngcuka had worked for the apartheid Government. A judicial commission was appointed by President Mbeki, but it could find no evidence to substantiate the claims.

In 2004 South Africa celebrated 10 years of democracy, and a relatively peaceful transition from apartheid to an apparently stable democratic order. The celebration coincided with the holding of the third democratic elections in April. Of the 20m. registered voters (an estimated 7m. eligible persons had not registered), 5m. did not vote. The ANC won 279 of the National Assembly's 400 seats, with 69.7% of the valid votes cast. The DA took 50 seats, with 12.4% of votes cast, and the IFP 28, with 7.0%. For the first time the ANC won control of all nine provincial governments, although it failed to win outright majorities in KwaZulu/Natal and Western Cape. On 23 April the new National Assembly voted unanimously to re-elect Mbeki to the presidency, and he was sworn in to serve a second term on 27 April. He reshuffled the Cabinet, retaining Zuma as Deputy President and Manto Tshabalala-Msimang as Minister of Health, despite her record on HIV/AIDS. Van Schalkwyk was appointed Minister of Environmental Affairs and Tourism.

In the aftermath of the election, the NNP, which won only 1.7% of the vote, decided to disband: van Schalkwyk joined the ANC, but most NNP support was transferred to the DA. The loss of KwaZulu/Natal precipitated a major crisis in the IFP, which continued to be headed by the marginalized Buthelezi. In the Western Cape the ANC had taken power before the election after entering into an alliance with the NNP, and remained in control of the province. Holomisa's UDM, which had lost support to the ANC and other parties, especially during the window period for floor-crossing, emerged from the 2004 election with nine seats and one deputy minister. Patricia de Lille, formerly a prominent member of the PAC, had broken away from that party to form the Independent Democrats (ID), which won seven seats, most of them in the Western Cape. After the local government elections held in March 2006, no clear winner emerged in Cape Town; however, the DA and a coalition of small parties defeated the ANC, allied with the ID, by one vote. Helen Zille of the DA was elected mayor, and she dismissed the ANC-appointed city manager and began a more efficient and open administration. In January 2007 she was able to forge a multi-party coalition with the ID to strengthen her position as mayor. When Leon stepped down as DA leader in May, Zille was elected in his place, combining the post with that of mayor.

Meanwhile, in May 2005 the Public Protector issued a report criticizing the NDPP for improperly prejudicing the Deputy President, whom many saw as the natural successor to Mbeki.

The crisis over the corruption allegations involving Zuma came to a head during the lengthy trial of his long-term acquaintance and financial adviser, the Durban businessman Schabir Shaik. In June Shaik was found guilty of corruption and fraud and sentenced to 15 years' imprisonment by the Durban High Court. The Court found that there had been a 'generally corrupt relationship' between Shaik and Zuma, and that a series of payments made by Shaik on behalf of Zuma were intended to influence Zuma to benefit Shaik's business. The trial revealed that Zuma had been party to a bid to solicit a bribe from the French defence company Thales, one of the contractors in the controversial arms deal (see above). Mbeki subsequently 'released' Zuma from his duties as Deputy President of the country, although he retained the ANC deputy premiership. Mbeki appointed Phumzile Mlambo-Ngcuka, hitherto the Minister of Energy and Mineral Affairs, and the wife of the former NDPP, to replace Zuma. The new NDPP subsequently issued a summons against him on two charges of corruption, but when the trial began the judge dismissed the case. The National Prosecuting Authority (NPA) then tried to assemble more evidence against him, allegedly to show that he had accepted a bribe. While this was going on, Zuma was charged with rape. In court, he claimed that the sex, with an HIV-positive young family friend, had been consensual. Zuma, a former head of the South African National AIDS Council, shocked observers by arguing that he believed there was little danger of his contracting HIV, and health professionals feared that his testimony would undermine prevention campaigns against the HIV virus. When he was acquitted, his supporters claimed that the trial had been part of a political conspiracy to prevent him from succeeding Mbeki as President. By now, Mbeki was much disliked for his aloofness and arrogance, and those on the left of the tripartite alliance, who saw him as the mastermind of the GEAR policy, accused him of having betrayed the struggle and even of ruling dictatorially. Others, more sympathetic to his economic policy, could not understand why he failed to remove cabinet ministers who were clearly incompetent.

Mbeki insisted on standing for a third term as ANC President at the party's 52nd national conference held at Polokwane in December 2007. However, at that event Zuma was elected as the party's new President with 60% of the delegates' votes, and opponents of Mbeki assumed the key party posts. The new ANC Secretary-General, Gwede Mantashe, was the national Chairman of the SACP, and other appointees were mostly from the left of the tripartite alliance, raising the prospect of the ANC forcing the Government to follow more interventionist economic policies. Some regarded the change of leadership as a rejection of Mbeki's secretive and remote leadership style. One of the conference's most controversial decisions was that the Scorpions, the unit that had raided Zuma's premises in search of material to prosecute him, should be disbanded. It was replaced by a new police unit, the Directorate for Priority Crime Investigation (known as the Hawks),which the Constitutional Court later said had to be reconstituted to fulfil constitutional requirements.

Despite repeated demands that he step down as the country's President after his defeat at Polokwane, Mbeki remained in office but as an increasingly isolated and discredited figure. He was very slow to condemn the xenophobic violence that broke out in a series of townships in May 2008, in which over 60 people were killed and tens of thousands were displaced by local mobs angry at the large influx of immigrants from neighbouring countries such as Mozambique. It was widely accepted that in the same way as lack of service delivery and a flawed immigration policy lay behind the violence, failures in government policy and lack of planning were at least in part to blame for the electricity crisis of early 2008, when the state-owned utility ESKOM could not supply the electricity the country needed.

During Mbeki's second term numerous scandals were exposed. It was discovered that a company that had obtained petroleum from Iraq had paid a large sum to the ANC before the 2004 election. Some 200 members of Parliament were implicated in the use of travel vouchers for fraudulent purposes, and over 20,000 government employees were found to have received social grants to which they were not entitled. Furthermore, in September 2007 Mbeki dismissed the NDPP, Vusi Pikoli, citing a breakdown in the relationship between Pikoli and the Minister of Justice, but the dismissal was ostensibly related to Pikoli having obtained an arrest warrant for the National Commissioner of Police, Jackie Selebi, who was alleged to have had close connections with criminals. Selebi was suspended prior to facing trial. In 2008 the Constitutional Court complained that the Judge President of the Cape had tried to influence the court in a matter relating to warrants for the seizure of documents from Zuma. The Judge President, already the subject of investigations, then sought to clear his name. Zuma and his supporters made statements that could be interpreted as suggesting that the independence of the judiciary was at risk. The NPA, meanwhile, had again charged Zuma, this time for fraud, corruption, tax evasion and money-laundering, after the Polokwane conference. Zuma went to great lengths to prevent the case from coming to court, and his lawyers argued that the NPA wanted to prevent him becoming President and that he would not be granted a fair trial. In September a Pietermaritzburg court found that he should have been given the opportunity to make representations before being recharged, and the judge spoke of there having been political interference in charging Zuma. The ANC's National Executive Committee then met and agreed that Mbeki should be recalled as the country's President. He agreed to resign and Kgalema Motlanthe, the Deputy President of the party, was sworn in as South Africa's new President on 25 September. Although the Supreme Court of Appeal overturned the September judgment and the charges against Zuma were reinstated, three weeks before the April 2009 election the Acting Director of Public Prosecutions announced that new evidence, from recorded telephone conversations involving the former head of the Scorpions and Bulelani Ngcuka, had come to light showing interference in the process, and thus all charges against Zuma were dropped. This cleared the way for him to take over as President after the election.

THE ZUMA PRESIDENCY

Dissatisfied with what had happened at Polokwane and with Mbeki's recall, in late 2008 some members of the ANC formed the breakaway Congress of the People (Cope). Its two main figures, the former Minister of Defence and the former Premier of Gauteng, agreed to let the relatively unknown Bishop Mvume Dandala become the party's presidential candidate. In the fourth democratic legislative election, held on 22 April 2009, in which the ANC, as expected, won another overwhelming victory (although just fractionally short of two-thirds of the vote), Cope was only able to gain 7.4% of the vote, and subsequently fell into disarray, with its two leaders trying to oust each other. In the 2009 election the DA increased its share of the vote to 16.7% and regained control of the Western Cape from the ANC. Zille, who remained leader of the opposition, became Premier of the Western Cape. She and others realized that only a coalition of opposition forces could threaten the ANC's majority, and in mid-2010 she announced that the ID, which now enjoyed little support, would join the DA. Although the DA presented itself as a genuinely multi-racial party, and in 2012 Lindiwe Mazibuko, a black African, was elected as its leader in Parliament, it did not enjoy the 'struggle credentials' of the ANC and attracted relatively little black African support.

Zuma was inaugurated as President on 9 May 2009 and the next day announced his new Government and the reorganization of a number of ministries. A National Planning Commission (NPC) and a performance monitoring and evaluation competency were created within the presidency, to be led by Trevor Manuel (the long-serving Minister of Finance) and Collins Chabane, respectively. Appointments made to the enlarged administration included Motlanthe as Deputy President, Pravin Gordhan as Minister of Finance, and Jeff Radebe as Minister of Justice and Constitutional Development; Nkosazana Dlamini-Zuma was moved from Foreign Affairs to Home Affairs. Also of note was the appointment of the leader of the Afrikaner nationalist Vryheidsfront Plus party, Dr Pieter Mulder, as Deputy Minister of Agriculture, Forestry and Fisheries. The NPC finally began its work in

2010. In May 2011 it issued a diagnostic report that identified the major challenges confronting South Africa, and in November handed a National Development Plan to President Zuma, which set out a vision of how the country could eliminate poverty and reduce inequality by 2030. However, despite attempts to publicize the Plan and secure responses to it, it seemed likely to remain more a statement of intent than a guide to practical action.

The ANC continued to be wracked by infighting, and tensions grew between the ANC and its alliance partners, COSATU and the SACP. Some of this factionalism was ideologically based, with those of a nationalist and populist persuasion dominating the ANC Youth League, but personality clashes played a major part, as did the scramble for access to state resources. Although Zuma succeeded in holding his party and the alliance together, he soon showed himself to be a weak and indecisive leader. In February 2010 he apologized to the nation when it emerged that he had fathered an illegitimate child (thought to be his 20th) with the daughter of a leading sports administrator. For a long time the leader of the ANC Youth League, Julius Malema, was allowed to make highly provocative statements that increased racial tensions. After Eugene Terre'blanche, the leader of the extreme right-wing Afrikaner Resistance Movement, was murdered in April, the ANC forced Malema to stop publicly singing an anti-apartheid song that many believed encouraged the killing of Afrikaners. In June the Fédération Internationale de Football Association World Cup for a brief time drew the nation together, and a large police presence kept crime under control during the event. However, although the World Cup, which cost South Africa over R40,000m. to stage, improved the country's image abroad and left behind some impressive infrastructure, it did not produce a tourism boom, while the lavish stadiums built for it promised to remain white elephants. Many argued that the World Cup distracted attention from the country's main problems—the lack of jobs and mass poverty.

The Zuma Government acknowledged that unemployment was a key issue confronting the country. A public works programme, begun in 2004, had failed to bring unemployment down, and over 1m. people lost their jobs as a result of the global economic slowdown from late 2008. A so-called New Growth Path was unveiled in 2010 with the aim of creating 5m. new jobs within 10 years, largely in the public sector, and in 2012 the Government announced a vast infrastructure building programme; by mid-2012, however, there was no sign of unemployment decreasing. While joblessness and poverty increased, so did evidence of lavish expenditure by state officials and of massive wastage of public funds and gross mismanagement in parastatals and state departments. Corruption and misappropriation of funds became ever more blatant. In July 2011 the trial of the former national commissioner of police, Jackie Selebi, finally came to an end, when he was found guilty of having entered into a corrupt relationship with a prominent drug-dealer. While Selebi then languished in prison, his successor as national commissioner, Bheki Cele, who like Selebi was a political appointment, was found to have engaged in corrupt practices and eventually dismissed.

While the media and civil society exposed many cases of corruption, leading figures in both the ANC and the SACP supported curbs on media freedom and the creation of a media appeals tribunal, both of which were widely seen as a response to press reports detailing incidents of self-enrichment by the new political class. When the Government's Protection of State Information Bill proposed very harsh penalties for revealing classified information, a massive public campaign, led by the Right2Know coalition, was mounted against what was dubbed the Secrecy Bill. Some of its more draconian aspects were subsequently removed, but critics continued to claim that the Bill would put freedom of expression at risk and would, when it became law, need to be challenged in the Constitutional Court. President Zuma had, however, in September 2011 appointed a new Chief Justice, Mogoeng Mogoeng, who many believed was not the best candidate for the post. There was much subsequent speculation whether the Court would retain its independence under Mogoeng's leadership. Other legislation proposed by the Government in 2012, which provided for state control over the legal profession, also seemed to threaten judicial independence.

South Africa's image in the world was adversely affected by the Government's failure to act against oppression in both Zimbabwe and Swaziland while it held a non-permanent seat on the UN Security Council. Mbeki could take credit for persuading the parties in Zimbabwe to form a Government of national unity in 2008, but neither he nor Zuma, his successor as SADC mediator on Zimbabwe, openly criticized Mugabe when he continued to use violence against his political opponents and failed to honour the terms of the power-sharing agreement. In March 2011 Zuma prepared a more critical report on Zimbabwe for SADC, but the SADC tribunal was disbanded shortly afterwards since it had ruled against the Zimbabwean Government. South Africa was elected for a second time as a non-permanent member of the UN Security Council for 2011–12, and in 2011 it was invited to join the Brazil-Russia-India-China (BRIC) group of countries, mainly because it was viewed as a gateway to the rest of Africa. After becoming a BRIC member, South Africa hoped that its relations with China in particular, which had now become its largest trading partner, would grow closer and result in increased investment. In January 2012 South African Airways, the national airline, began direct, non-stop flights from Johannesburg to Beijing. However, Chinese imports continued to have a profound negative effect on South Africa's textile industry, which was now the most labour-intensive sector of the economy. Meanwhile, Zuma's mediation efforts during the crises in Côte d'Ivoire and Libya, on behalf of the AU, met with little success. South Africa aroused further divisions on the continent when it nominated Dlamini-Zuma to be Chairperson of the AU Commission. In January 2012 she failed to attract sufficient votes to secure the post, but the Government refused to withdraw her candidacy and continued to lobby intensively on her behalf.

In 2011 racial polarization seemed to increase, particularly when Malema was put on trial for singing 'Kill the Boer'. By the time local government elections were held in May, there had been thousands of protests in townships and squatter settlements against the Government's poor 'service delivery'. The DA secured 24% of the votes cast, up from 16% at the previous election, and it won an outright majority in Cape Town, where De Lille now became mayor. Though the ANC's liberation credentials were clearly on the wane, and the ruling party lost Indian and Coloured support, it was still able to win 62% of the vote, increasing its share of the ballot in KwaZulu/Natal, where the IFP had been weakened by internal discord. Malema, who was re-elected as leader of the ANC Youth League after the election, demanded the nationalization of the mines and banks and the expropriation of white-owned property without compensation. While COSATU supported nationalization, the SACP did not, reflecting the deep divisions within the alliance, which were linked to the succession battle in the ANC. In August Malema was charged with various violations of the ANC constitution, including bringing the ANC into disrepute, after stating that the Youth League would work to effect regime change in Botswana. Violent clashes between supporters of Malema and the security forces took place outside the ANC headquarters in Johannesburg.

Eventually Malema was expelled from the ANC, as Zuma tried to consolidate his position ahead of the key ANC congress to be held at Mangaung (Bloemfontein) in December 2012. Although in theory there were no other candidates for the ANC presidency, a fierce struggle ensued between those who supported Zuma and those who said he should be succeeded by Deputy President Motlantle. This struggle virtually paralysed some aspects of government, and its policy conference held in June 2012 once again revealed the deep divisions within the ANC. Zuma now blamed white males for the failings of the delivery of basic services. Although the idea of greater state intervention in the economy was widely shared, a super tax on mining profits now seemed more likely than nationalization, and expropriation of land with compensation was set to replace the previous 'willing buyer, willing seller' policy. Meanwhile, many state sectors remained dysfunctional. For example, while the Minister of Health promoted a grandiose National Health Insurance Scheme, public healthcare facilities were in a dire state, with basic equipment often not available as a result of mismanagement and corruption.

Long-standing discontent among platinum miners in North West province came to a head in August 2012 when a group at the Lonmin mine near Marikana went on strike and killed two policemen in the ensuing confrontation. The police responded by opening fire on the miners, killing 34. The industrial action then intensified and spread to other mines beyond those producing platinum. Malema, having earlier been expelled by the ANC, exploited the situation and called for President Zuma's resignation. The Government in turn accused Malema of inciting violence and in September he was charged with money laundering offences. Zuma appointed a judicial commission of enquiry to investigate the events at Marikana, but there was speculation that the way in which he handled the crisis might weaken his bid to secure re-election at the December ANC congress.

While the inequalities between the races had lessened since 1994, South Africa remained one of the most unequal societies in the world. Around 10% of black Africans had by 2012 joined the middle class, and a few had become very wealthy indeed. However, although black Africans constituted almost 80% of the population, their income remained only 40% of the country's total. Social spending had increased greatly, to over R50,000m. per year, and by 2012 as many as 15m. people (27% of the population) were receiving social grants, more people than were in formal employment. Over 20m. people lived in poverty, more than a decade earlier. Despite the construction by the State of over 2m. new houses since 1994, many millions continued to live in squatter settlements. Although over 1m. HIV-positive people were receiving anti-retroviral drugs, hundreds were still dying from HIV/AIDS every day. The country's land reform programme had stalled due to bureaucratic impediments, and there were few examples of successful redistribution of land. Ongoing township protests suggested increasing discontent among the poor, who saw the new élite exploiting opportunities for personal enrichment, and resented the continuing legacy of apartheid and the failure of the post-1994 order to address the country's socio-economic problems effectively. With so much government attention focused on the ANC's forthcoming congress in December 2012, many wondered whether South Africa's aspirant constitutional democracy could survive in the face of the severe challenges the country faced.

Economy

LINDA VAN BUREN

Revised for this edition by OBI IHEME

INTRODUCTION

The global economic crisis of 2008 and 2009 took its toll on the South African economy. The value of the South African rand fell by 16.6% in the first quarter of 2008 alone and by 27.6% in the year as a whole. Meanwhile, annual inflation rose to 11.6% in 2008. In a microeconomic context, South African households felt the effects of higher inflation, rising electricity tariffs and—especially surprising in a country accustomed to an abundance of electricity—power rationing. Unplanned emergency maintenance to the power infrastructure in January 2008, coupled with a decline in stocks of coal, led to power cuts that were extensive enough to disrupt both production and exports, especially of mineral products. This reduction in mineral exports widened both the trade and current account deficits, in the latter case causing the depreciation of the rand. In addition, the power rationing caused many manufacturers to curtail their output, and this too had an adverse effect on the trade and current account balances.

However, there was a significant economic recovery in 2010, with real gross domestic product (GDP) growth of 2.8% being recorded. The recovery was bolstered by strong international prices for South Africa's export commodities, by lower global interest rates and by faster world-wide growth. Also, after five consecutive quarters of decline, gross fixed capital formation (GFCF) exhibited positive growth in both the second and the third quarters of 2010, with growth projected at 3.9% in 2011 and at 6.8% in 2013.

As the economic recovery continued into 2011, the Economist Intelligence Unit (EIU) estimated that real GDP grew by 3.1% in that year and projected a deceleration in the growth rate to 2.8% in 2012, mainly due to decreasing domestic demand for goods and services, and the effects of the global economic crisis, which were weakening demand for South Africa's minerals and other exports. However, the growth rate is forecast to rise to as high as 4.1% in 2016, as both domestic and international demand are bolstered by an expected improvement in economic conditions. Inflation was projected by the EIU to be 5.5% in 2012—higher than in the previous period, but still within the South African Reserve Bank's annual target band of 3%–6%. This higher inflation was caused mainly by a weaker rand, rising electricity rates and increases in wages, especially in the public sector. However, the EIU expects inflation to fall to between 4% and 5% by 2016, as South African growth begins to decelerate, world-wide commodity prices come down, and investments in infrastructure yield economic efficiencies. Meanwhile, the depreciation of the rand was forecast to continue during 2012, owing to the persistent current account deficit—which was projected to reach 4.8% of GDP—and higher inflation.

The first quarter of 2012 saw real GDP growth slow to 2.1% from the previous corresponding period, due mainly to a contraction of 1.2% in the industrial sector, and despite the fact that the services sector grew by 3.3%. Particularly acute was a shrinkage in the mining sector—which accounted for 9.8% of GDP in 2011—of 9.9%, largely as the result of a six-week strike in the platinum sub-sector, which, with a 27% share of the mining sector as a whole, is the largest sub-sector. Reduced demand for mined commodities from traditional European customers due to the eurozone economic crisis also contributed greatly to the mining sector's poor performance compared with the first quarter of 2011. On the other hand, services, which contributed 67% of GDP in 2011, grew from the previous period by an estimated 2.5%, and government services by 4.1%.

Economic policy is expected to remain the same in the foreseeable future, given that the key members of the powerful ruling African National Congress (ANC) will most probably retain their currents posts. The main challenge confronting the South African economy is the high rate of unemployment, which rose from 21.9% of the labour force in 2008 to 24.9% in 2010. The unemployment rate was negatively affected by the global recession, and 1m. workers lost their jobs in the first three quarters of 2009 alone. The unemployment rate was not expected to return to 2008 levels before 2015. South Africa's employment rate is the lowest in the G20 group of leading industrial nations and is almost 20 percentage points below the G20 median. A reduction in the level of unemployment could be one of the best ways of countering the country's high crime rate. Both the Government and the private sector have introduced job creation schemes and initiatives such as Black Economic Empowerment, as well as various training and skills programmes. However, at the end of any training course a worker still needs to find employment, and their chances are limited if growth remains moderate.

NATURAL RESOURCES

South Africa's diverse climate permits the cultivation of a wide range of crops, but despite improvements in farming methods and conservation techniques, it remains a relatively poor crop-raising country. This situation also imposes limits on animal husbandry, for which South Africa is better suited, although even here the carrying capacity of the land is fairly low by international standards. Nevertheless, owing to a high degree of specialization, experience and advanced methods, along with considerable capital investment, certain branches of farming, such as the fruit and wool sectors, continue to make a substantial contribution to the economy and to exports.

It is in mineral deposits, though, that South Africa's greatest wealth lies. The discovery, first of diamonds and then, more importantly, of gold, during the latter part of the 19th century formed the basis of the country's modern economic development. A huge complex of heavy and light industry, based initially on the gold-mining sector, grew up in the interior, although South Africa's share in the volume of world gold production (excluding the former USSR) declined from 70% in 1980 to 20% in 2000, owing to a fall in the average grade of ore mined and to increases in output in other parts of the world. Nevertheless, at the start of the 21st century South Africa remained the world's largest gold producer, supplying one-fifth of the global total. By 2010 the country had been overtaken by the People's Republic of China, but was still the world's second largest gold producer and was home to seven of the 13 biggest gold mines, measured by volume output. South Africa has two of the 10 largest gold-mining companies in the world, measured by capitalization in US dollar terms: AngloGold Ashanti (formerly Anglo American Corpn), which ranks fourth, and Gold Fields of South Africa, which ranks ninth. The country also has abundant deposits of many other important minerals. South Africa has the world's largest proven reserves not only of gold but also of platinum group metals, manganese, vanadium, vermiculite, chrome and alumino-silicates. The production of minerals other than gold accounts for 50% of the total value of mining output in most years; more than 50 different minerals are commercially exploited. There are huge reserves of coal—30,408m. metric tons, the eighth largest in the world—with a pit-head price that is probably the lowest in the world, which is why the power rationing of 2008 came as such a surprise. The country's iron ore reserves rank ninth in the world. South Africa possesses about three-quarters of the world's reserves of manganese ore, more than two-thirds of the world's chromium, more than one-half of global reserves of platinum group metals in general and more than one-quarter of its zirconium group minerals, plus a significant proportion of the world's titanium minerals and fluorspar. In addition, South Africa is a major producer of copper, lead, zinc, antimony and uranium.

South Africa's long coastline has few natural harbours, but close to its shores are some of the richest fishing areas in the world. The catch includes Southern African anchovy, Cape hakes, Southern African pilchard, Cape horse mackerel and Whitehead's round herring. Demand for Cape hakes in southern European markets grew significantly in 2006, after European hake stocks became depleted and the European Union (EU), in December 2005, implemented strict quotas on the fishing of this species in European waters. South Africa's total marine fish catch was 623,900 metric tons in 2010, according to FAO.

POPULATION

The chief characteristic of South Africa's population, and the one that dominates its society, is the great racial, linguistic and cultural heterogeneity of its people, with Africans, Asians, Europeans and mixed-race citizens making up the population of the 'Rainbow Nation'.

South Africa's total population as recorded in the October 2001 national census was 44,819,778. A census was held in October 2011; however, final results are not yet available. In the censuses people are no longer officially classified according to race, as they were during apartheid, but, in order to gain some idea of the figures involved, in the 2001 census South Africans were invited to classify themselves. The result was that 79% of those enumerated described themselves as African (black), 10% as white, 9% as Coloured (of mixed race) and 2% as Asian. Official mid-2011 estimates put the population at 50,586,757, of whom 79.5% were African, 9.0% were white, 9.0% were Coloured and 2.5% were Asian. Also present were an estimated 5m. illegal immigrants, of whom 3m. were Zimbabweans.

NATIONAL INCOME

Despite an improvement in the racial distribution of personal income from the 1990s onwards, income remains very unevenly distributed in South Africa. It was estimated in 1988 that the 13% of South Africans who were white received about 54% of total personal income, while the 76% of the population classified as Africans received only 36% of the wealth. The income tax threshold is set at a level that requires only 4m. South Africans to be registered as income tax payers; however, other, more regressive taxes, such as value-added tax (VAT), take in a much wider tax base. The contribution to national income of the three main productive sectors—manufacturing, mining and agriculture—has changed markedly over the years. The most drastic structural change in the economy has been the sharp decline in the proportion of the population engaged in agriculture, hunting, forestry and fishing; from 28% at the 1970 census, the number employed in the sector had fallen to some 639,000 in 2010, 4.9% of the economically active population. In 2011 manufacturing contributed 13.4% of GDP, mining and quarrying contributed 9.8%, and agriculture, fishing and forestry contributed only 2.4%. The services sector accounted for 67.0%, the highest such proportion in Africa.

INVESTMENT AND SAVING

Since the discovery of diamonds and gold in the 19th century, foreign investment has played a vital role in developing these industries and the wider economy. In 2011 foreign direct investment (FDI) was strongest in the information technology and electronics sector, followed by the metals and automotive sector, the tourism sector, the clothing and textiles sector and the chemicals sector. The global economic recession led to large capital outflows as investors withdrew from emerging market economies (EMEs), including South Africa. However, according to the IMF, financing through FDI had been relatively low in South Africa during 2000–09, at about 1% of total financing, compared with the overall average for EMEs, at about 3%.

GFCF grew by at least 8% per year in 2003–05; this declined during the global economic recession, and the forecast was for GFCF growth of 3.9% in 2011 and 6.8% in 2013. The level of debt rose steadily after 2000. Preliminary figures for 2009/10 indicated that South Africa's foreign debt was equivalent to 4.2% of GDP, and this was forecast to increase slightly, to 4.3%, in 2010/11. The country's national government net debt was expected to rise from R526,000m. in 2009 to more than R1,300,000m. in 2013/14. However, the IMF in September 2010 described this debt level as 'manageable'.

TOURISM

The tourism sector showed strong growth in 2006, with 8.5m. tourist arrivals in that year. There were 9.2m. tourist arrivals in 2007, an increase of 8.2%; the number of arrivals also grew, but at a slower rate, in 2008 (9.7m.) and 2009 (10.1m.). Another peak occurred when South Africa hosted the Fédération Internationale de Football Association (FIFA) World Cup between 11 June and 11 July 2010. Of the 1.4m. tourist arrivals in June–July 2010, 309,554 indicated that the purpose of their visit was to watch the World Cup. In a bid to boost tourism and ease movement of visitors to South Africa and Mozambique, the countries' respective Ministers of Tourism announced in 2011 that they would begin issuing a single visitor's visa for the two nations.

MANUFACTURING INDUSTRY

Unlike its counterparts in the rest of Africa, South Africa's manufacturing industry is the largest of the productive sectors of the national economy, measured in terms of contribution to

GDP (13.4% in 2011). In 2011 the sector employed 1.85m. workers, or about 13.3% of the employed labour force. Growth in manufacturing output weakened in 2008, owing to the cumulative effects of the global economic downturn, past monetary tightening and power shortages. In 2009/10 manufacturing output contracted by 12%, and mining output declined by 7%. The IMF observed in 2010 that both manufacturing and mining 'seemed to have bottomed out'. In 2011 both sectors recorded growth: manufacturing output expanded by 2.4% and mining by 0.2%. Industry is heavily concentrated in four industrial areas: Gauteng, Western Cape, Durban-Pinetown and Port Elizabeth-Uitenhage. More than 50% of the country's industry is now located in Gauteng alone, and the tendency has been for this concentration to increase at the expense of the ports and the rural areas. However, in the future, limitations in the availability of water in Gauteng may shift the main growth focus to other manufacturing locations (see below). Furthermore, the sector will continue to be hampered until at least 2013 by power shortages, with intermittent halts in production. Manufacturing growth slowed in April 2012 for the second consecutive month, which reflected a decrease in demand from European countries, South Africa's main trading partners. South Africa's *BusinessDay* newspaper reported that the purchasing managers' index, which is widely accepted as an accurate measure of the sector's performance, decreased in April by 1.4 points to 53.7 points. Furthermore, the global consultancy Deloitte believes that a skills shortage, which is made worse by emigration, as well as high labour costs, are hindering the manufacturing sector's good performance.

Metal Products and Engineering

This field comprises the largest sector of industry (including basic metals, metal products, machinery and transport equipment), employing about 470,000 workers in 2011. The steel industry is the most important branch of this sector, with production of crude steel valued at some R14,000m. per year. ArcelorMittal South Africa produces around 6.4m. metric tons of liquid steel per year, and is the largest steel producer in Africa. It has four locations: two in Gauteng province, one in KwaZulu/Natal province, and one, at Saldanha, in Western Cape. With favourable costs of location, raw materials and labour, and with an efficient scale of production, South African steel is among the cheapest in the world. The country also produces manganese, aluminium and platinum-group metals.

The Chief Economist of the Steel and Engineering Industries Federation of South Africa, Henk Langenhoven, believes that, despite the sector's cost increases and sales price decreases, the growth in fixed capital formation from –1.6% in 2010 to a forecast 5.0% in 2012 portends the improved performance of public sector investments.

The motor industry is another important branch of the engineering sector. The vast majority of new cars contain at least 66% local content by weight, thereby qualifying for special tariff rates as 'locally manufactured' models. In common with this industry in other developing countries, vehicle manufacturing faces the problem of rising costs with increasing local content, because of the lack of those economies of scale that are enjoyed in the major producing countries. With its potential market size of over 50m. people, South Africa would offer better opportunities to achieve economies of scale if incomes were more evenly distributed and a larger proportion of the population could afford to buy basic luxuries such as motor vehicles. In June 2009 a total of 21,315 new passenger cars were sold in South Africa. This figure was 17.5% lower than in June 2008 but was 12.9% higher than in May 2009. In 2004 Volkswagen announced that a new R750m. production line was to be installed at its South African plant at Uitenhage in the Eastern Cape. In 2008 Volkswagen South Africa won a R12,000m. 'centre of excellence' contract to supply diesel particulate filters to the entire Volkswagen group all over the world for a five-year period.

Food, Beverages and Tobacco

Industries processing local farm produce were among the first to develop in South Africa and contribute significantly to exports. Food, beverages and tobacco accounted for about 24% of the value of manufacturing output in 2010. The end of the apartheid era created suitable conditions for South African Breweries (SAB) to become, in a short space of time, the second largest brewing company in the world. SAB embarked on a period of rapid expansion, taking over existing breweries elsewhere in Africa before expanding into Asia, with a major investment in India, and also into the USA, with the acquisition of a 64% stake in the US brewer Miller from Philip Morris for US $5,600m. in May 2002; the conglomerate that resulted was renamed SABMiller, headquartered in the United Kingdom. In 2010 SABMiller had primary brewing and beverage operations in six continents; in Africa it had brewing operations in 10 countries and seven breweries in South Africa. The country's wine industry was established in the 17th century by Protestant immigrants from France. The industry experienced a rapid growth in exports in the post-apartheid era, and its reputation for quality continues. South Africa is the ninth largest wine exporter in the world, exporting over 350m. litres per year.

The Department of Trade and Industry has created a R5,800m. incentive scheme called the Manufacturing Competitiveness Enhancement Programme, which is designed to increase the competitiveness of manufacturing businesses, and has identified the food-processing industry as a priority for South Africa's economy.

Clothing and Textiles

The clothing industry, which was well established before the Second World War, by the 2000s supplied 90% of local demand and employed more than 100,000 workers. The textile industry (other than clothing) was essentially a post-war development; it met 60% of the country's textile needs. Textiles, wearing apparel and footwear contributed about 8% of the value of manufacturing output in 2009. The South African textile industry faces the challenge of lowering its costs in order to compete with low-cost Asian competitors. In mid-2012 the Southern African Clothing and Textile Workers' Union was preparing to launch strike action, after talks broke down with the Apparel Manufacturers of South Africa following the union's claim that employers had reneged on a deal to create more jobs in the sector by paying new workers 30% less than established employees.

Chemicals

South Africa's chemical industry employed about 115,000 workers in 2011, and chemical manufactures contribute about 4% of GDP. The industry had an early beginning, with the manufacture of explosives for the gold mines; the Modderfontein factory, near Johannesburg, is now one of the world's largest privately owned explosives factories. Production of fertilizers is also a significant branch of this industry. However, the most important development in the second half of the 20th century was the establishment by the state-owned South African Coal, Oil and Gas Corpn (SASOL) of its first oil-from-coal plant (SASOL 1), which began production in the northern part of the then Orange Free State (later Free State) in 1955. Based on cheap, low-grade coal with a high ash content, this establishment was, until the commissioning of SASOL 2 and SASOL 3, the largest plant of its kind in the world. Besides producing a small but significant percentage of South Africa's petrol requirements, SASOL's development of synthetic fuel production led to the establishment of a huge petrochemicals complex capable of manufacturing about 110 products, some of which, like coal-tar products, were only by-products of a coal-using process. SASOL was privatized in 1979. The three SASOL plants in full production provide about 40% of South Africa's fuel requirements. In June 2009 SASOL opened a new R70m. fuels application centre in Cape Town, aimed at testing the company's range of fuels on vehicle emissions and performance.

AGRICULTURE

Agriculture's role as a source of income in the South African economy is a declining one, despite major successes in some sub-sectors. Maize is the staple food of the African population and the most important single item in South African farming; this New World crop was introduced into South Africa during the colonial period. There was a 31-year record harvest of

12.8m. metric tons in 2010. The country's annual maize demand is about 8m.–9m. tons. Sorghum production fluctuates: it amounted to 276,500 tons in 2009, a large increase compared with output of 96,000 tons in 2006 but below the record 373,000 tons achieved in 2004. Output of 196,500 tons was recorded in 2010. In 2006 the South African Government rejected an application from a US company to grow genetically modified sorghum in the country. Wool, although prone to wide fluctuations in price, is one of South Africa's most important agricultural exports (along with maize, fruit and cane sugar). The country grows a wide range of cash crops, fruits and vegetables both for domestic consumption and for the export market. The low overall productivity of farming, relative to other sectors, was also reflected in the fact that the sector contributed only 2.4% of GDP in 2011, owing principally to poor crop yields obtained by large numbers of inefficient African subsistence farmers in the former 'homelands'. However, even commercial farms, which were relatively efficient, obtained comparatively low yields by international standards.

The ruling ANC has introduced a new policy that will allow the Government to expropriate agricultural land not in production and obtained illegally or unethically, in a bid to make amends for the forced removal of people from land under the apartheid-era Land Act of 1913.

Nevertheless, the agriculture sector is also receiving new investment. South African seed company Pannar Seed is set to merge with Pioneer Hi-Bred International, a subsidiary of US-based DuPont in a deal (the financial terms of which are not yet disclosed) that will provide technology and research investment, enabling South Africa to remain a continental leader in this sector.

MINING

Despite having given way to manufacturing as the leading sector, mining is still of great importance in external trade. The sector contributed 9.8% of GDP in 2011. South Africa is the world's second largest gold producer, after China, which overtook it in 2008 after South Africa had held the top spot for over a century, from 1905. Since 1945 new gold mines in the Free State, Far West Rand, Klerksdorp and Evander areas not only replaced output from the worked-out mines on the old Rand but also greatly increased total production. In the absence of new discoveries, however, gold output was expected to continue the decline that began in the early 1970s, after a record 1,000 metric tons was mined in 1970. This was largely a result of a policy by the industry of lowering the grade of ore mined as the price rose. (Unless there is a compensating increase in tonnage milled, output falls when the average grade of ore mined is lowered.) Of the 48 gold-mining companies in South Africa in 1994, only 11 were still operating in 2004, most having been merged into one of four major companies: AngloGold Ashanti, Gold Fields, Harmony Gold or Durban Roodeport Deep. The global financial turbulence propelled the gold price to US $964 per oz in July 2008, an increase of 47% in a single year. By July 2009 the global gold price had settled back to about $930 per oz, but one year later, after uncertainties about the high debt levels of Greece and other countries in the eurozone, the precious metal's price trajectory was upward again, reaching $1,483 per oz in July 2011. In South Africa the gold sub-sector's role as an employer fluctuated along similar lines.

The output of other minerals rapidly gained in importance after 1945. Gold accounted for about 80% of South Africa's mineral production in 1946 but for only 50% by 1993 and 27% by 2006. A great expansion took place in the output of uranium, platinum, palladium, nickel, copper, coal, antimony, diamonds, vanadium, asbestos, iron ore, fluorspar, chromium, manganese and limestone, to name only the most important. South Africa's platinum group mines employed more than 100,000 workers in 2010. Power interruptions and temporary platinum mine closures in South Africa in the first half of 2008 drove the global platinum price up and led to pronounced price volatility. The platinum price reached a record US $2,276 per oz in March 2008. It subsequently decreased, but recovered to $1,715 in July 2011. Diamonds were traditionally the country's second most important export commodity after gold, but by the 1980s they had been overtaken by coal, and by 2001 South Africa ranked only fifth in the world in terms of natural rough-diamond production. The largest of South Africa's seven diamond mines is Venetia, in Limpopo Province, operated by De Beers. Trivalence Mining Corpn's 2,082-ha, open-pit kimberlite concession at Palmietgat, about 70 miles (113 km) north of Pretoria, entered production in 2000 and consisted of six kimberlite pipes. According to the US Geological Survey, South African diamond production totalled 15.3m. carats in 2007, declining to 12.9m. carats in 2008 and more than halving to 6.1m. carats in 2009.

South Africa ranked sixth in the world in terms of coal production in 2009 (with 250.6m. metric tons), ninth in the world in terms of proven recoverable reserves at the end of 2008 (30,156m. tons) and fifth in the world in terms of export volume in 2009 (73.8m. short tons). Almost all of South Africa's reserves are of anthracite and bituminous coal, with little or no lignite. The life of its reserves is assessed at 119 years. About 50% of South Africa's 26 major collieries are underground and 50% open-pit. There are also numerous smaller collieries. Major coal-mining companies include BHP Billiton, Anglo American Coal and Xstrata Coal. Anglo Coal also owns 27% of the Richards Bay Coal Terminal, through which its export coal leaves the country.

South Africa is the continent's leading producer of iron ore; exports to China are of particular importance. Kumba Iron Ore, owned by Anglo American, operates the Sishen, Thabazimbi and Kolomela iron-ore mines. Sishen, with reserves of 2,455m. metric tons, is one of the largest open-pit mines in the world and has a projected life span of 27 years. Thabazimbi produces 2.6m. tons per annum and sells exclusively to the ArcelorMittal steel group. Kolomela commenced production in mid-2012; annual output was expected to reach 9m. tons in 2013. A railway line from the high-grade deposits of the Sishen area, in the Northern Cape, carries iron ore to Saldanha Bay.

South Africa has proven petroleum reserves of just 29.4m. metric tons. SASOL produces 155,000 barrels per day (b/d) at its oil-from-coal plant (see above), but domestic consumption of oil is more than three times that level. Imports of petroleum cost South Africa US $14,769.4m. in 2010 and comprised 18.4% of the total import bill. The Petroleum Oil and Gas Corpn of South Africa directs exploration for petroleum and natural gas and operates the world's largest commercial gas-to-liquids plant, at Mossel Bay, with a capacity of 45,000 b/d. In 2003 the Government approved the Minerals and Petroleum Resources Development Act, providing a structured framework for oil and gas exploration. Petroleum exploration continues, with particular interest in waters off the west coast of South Africa.

Large-scale strikes were likely to continue to have a negative effect on the mining sector in 2012; the strike action was due to continuing demands by the Congress of South African Trade Unions for employers to increase workers' salaries and to safeguard their jobs. Additional factors were high costs and reduced demand. In June 2012 Royal Bafokeng Platinum and Aquarius Platinum announced that it was significantly downgrading its production.

TRANSPORT AND COMMUNICATIONS

South Africa has an extensive and modern transport and communications network. In transport, apart from air and roads, the umbrella organization is the parastatal Transnet Ltd. In 2011 Transnet comprised the national ports authority, a port and cargo terminal operations managing division, a freight rail division, a rolling-stock maintenance division, and a fuel and gas pipeline division. The largest section was Transnet Freight Rail, which in 2011 employed 25,000 workers; it operated 80% of the rail network of the entire African continent and was active in 17 African countries. Domestically, Transnet Freight Rail oversees a rail network which covered 31,400 route-km in 2000 (about one-third of all the railway track length in sub-Saharan Africa). Some 87% of the South African rail network is electrified. Transnet turned a profit, before tax, interest and depreciation, of R15,800m. in the year to 31 March 2011.

Transnet is custodian of six commercial ports: Durban, Richards Bay, East London, Port Elizabeth, Cape Town and

Saldanha Bay. In 2011 a new deep-water port was under construction at Ngqura, 7 km from Port Elizabeth. Transnet's container terminals are situated at Durban, Cape Town and Port Elizabeth, and Durban also has a dedicated car terminal. Transnet Port Terminals handled 15.8m. metric tons of bulk and break-bulk cargo in 2009, with 46% of it at Richards Bay (mostly bulk cargo); Durban predominates in break-bulk cargo. The ratio of exports to imports for this cargo, by volume, is about three-to-one in favour of exports (however, the value of imports exceeds the value of exports—see below). The entrance channel to the port of Durban is being widened from 110 m to 220 m, and its depth is to be a minimum of 16 m. In addition, the country's ports handled 3.7m. 20-foot equivalent units (TEUs) of container freight in 2007. Of the total, Durban handled 67%, followed by Cape Town with 21% and Port Elizabeth with 11%. Although Richards Bay handles more bulk and break-bulk cargo, Durban is still the country's largest port in terms of ship arrivals. Of the 13,152 vessels that called at South African ports in 2007, 4,608, or 35%, arrived at Durban, followed by 23% at Cape Town.

In 2011 the country's 10 major airports, including its seven international airports, were under the management of the Airports Co South Africa (ACSA) Ltd, which was 100% owned by the Government but was, nevertheless, operating the airports on a commercial basis. The new greenfield site King Shaka International Airport near Durban opened in May 2010. The new airport has a runway 3,700 m long, capable of handling the latest new-generation large aircraft such as the A380 Airbus. The Ilembe consortium was the principal contractor. The cost was initially assessed at R2,500m., and ACSA, for its part, had a budget of R5,200m.; the final cost was an estimated R7,900m. The main gateway airport is O. R. Tambo International Airport (ORTIA) in Johannesburg. The other five international airports, besides Tambo and King Shaka, are Cape Town International Airport (CTIA); Pilanesberg International, which serves the resort of Sun City; Port Elizabeth International; Bloemfontein International; and Upington International, which only provides international services for cargo. The three 'national' airports are East London, George and Kimberley. ACSA built a new terminal at ORTIA which opened in April 2009, upgraded Bloemfontein Airport in 2007 and 2008 at a cost of R35m, and expanded and upgraded George Airport, serving the Garden Route, at a cost of R39m. (completed in April 2007). CTIA and East London airports were both given new and upgraded terminals in time for the 2010 FIFA World Cup. Upington, a small airport with a very long runway in the north of the country, has been singled out as a cargo hub to serve the rest of Africa and is to become a specialist airport for the parking and storage of mothballed aircraft from all over the world. The national carrier is South African Airways (SAA), one of the world's oldest airlines, founded in 1934. The airline sector was deregulated in 1990, and SAA is now exposed to competition from private sector carriers, both on domestic and on international routes. In March 2007 SAA announced that, following 'several years of continued losses', it was embarking on a 'deep and fundamental restructuring', to be managed by Seabury Airline Planning Group of the USA. SAA posted a net profit of R581m. for the year ending 31 March 2010, up from R398m. the previous year. More than 20 private sector airlines provided about 70 routes to 546 towns in South Africa in 2011.

Freight Dynamics, formerly Autonet, oversees an extensive road network, with more than 500,000 km of classified roads. While this figure includes some motorways, less than 25% of all roads were paved in 2005. In 2009, according to the International Road Federation, there were 5.4m. registered passenger motor vehicles, 2.3m. lorries and vans, 328,158 buses and coaches, and 362,400 motorcycles and mopeds. Private long-distance road haulage was for many years restricted by government legislation designed to protect the railways. The illegal haulage of freight by road is an ongoing problem.

The telecommunications network is fairly extensively developed, with an estimated 4.1m. telephone landlines in use in 2011. The use of mobile cellular telephones increased dramatically from the late 1990s; between 1998 and 2008 the number of mobile subscribers increased from 3.3m. to 45m., for a penetration rate of 92%. By 2011 the number of mobile subscribers had risen to 64m. In 2008 there were also 106.3 internet hosts per 10,000 inhabitants; the number of users rose from 3.6m. in total in that year to 17.5m. in 2008, of whom 8m. accessed the internet via computers and 9.5m. accessed it via mobile telephones.

The Transnet Group is currently investing R33,000m. into its Transnet Port Terminals business unit, with most of the investment going to the Durban and Richards Bay commodity terminals. Transnet states that Durban's container gross crane moves per hour—an important marker of efficiency—will increase by 52% after the investment.

POWER AND WATER

Electricity

The government-owned Electricity Supply Commission (ESKOM) produces 95% of South Africa's electricity and claims to be one of the lowest-cost generators of electricity in the world. In addition to generating, transmitting and distributing electricity in South Africa, ESKOM wholly owns ESKOM Enterprises, which supplies electricity elsewhere in Africa, as far away as Uganda, Nigeria and Mali. ESKOM's highly diversified network of 22 power stations in South Africa was capable of producing 237,430 GWh in 2011, most of it from its 13 coal-fired generators. In fact, ESKOM is the world's largest single buyer of coal, burning a projected 124.7m. metric tons of coal in 2011. The abundance of domestic resources means that coal is likely to remain the country's main power source until the 2020s, by which time the coal-fired stations will be due for decommissioning. However, concerns that the country is too dependent on coal, as well as increasing environmental issues, have prompted the Government to investigate alternative energy supplies. The remaining 11% of ESKOM's output currently comes from its mix of nuclear, pumped-storage, hydroelectric and petroleum-fired gas-turbine power stations. In 1976 ESKOM commissioned the building of the 1,800-MW Koeberg nuclear power station at Duynefontein, between Cape Town and Saldanha Bay, by a French consortium. The 900-MW pressurized water reactor (PWR) Koeberg I was commissioned in 1984, followed by the 900-MW PWR Koeberg II in 1985. The Koeberg reactors have remained the only nuclear reactors in Africa. In 2004 the Mbeki Government gave its support to a 10-year project to develop a new pebble-bed modular reactor (PBMR) at Koeberg, by Pebble Bed Modular Reactor (Pty) Ltd of South Africa, in co-operation with France, the United Kingdom and the USA. In July 2009 the Minister of Public Enterprises, Barbara Hogan, reconfirmed the commitment of Jacob Zuma's Government to the project. Environmental groups, however, have long opposed the scheme. In September the demonstration power plant was postponed indefinitely, and in February 2010 the Government halted funding for the programme. If the project does go ahead, the PBMR would not enter production before 2020. Some peak-load power is provided by the hydroelectric stations of the Orange River Project; ESKOM also entered into an agreement in 1998 to buy 900 MW of power from the Cahora Bassa dam in Mozambique, an amount which increased to 2,000 MW by 2007. ESKOM also returned three renovated generating plants to service, adding 3,600 MW to the national grid in 2009 and 2010. These plants' absence from the national grid accounted in part for the power rationing that began in January 2008. In addition, open-cycle gas-turbine technology was to be introduced at the Atlantis and Mossel Bay stations. Plans to privatize ESKOM were put on hold in mid-2004. Two new coal-fired plants, at Medupi in Lephalale and at Kusile (formerly Bravo) near Witbank, were each to produce 4,500 MW and were to cost at least R80,000m. Medupi was scheduled to come on stream in 2012, followed by Kusile in 2013. The Government extended a R60,000m. loan, disbursed in tranches, to ESKOM to fund its expansion plans and to help alleviate the need for costly power rationing in the country from early 2008 onwards. In June 2012 it was reported that ESKOM, in order to aid its investment planning and stabilize prices, had applied for fixed price increases over a five-year period, although the actual amounts were undisclosed. ESKOM stated that the 29.2% increase in energy costs in March 2012 was largely the result of higher coal prices.

Water

Water supply is increasingly becoming a problem for the future location of industry. The Vaal river, which is the main source of water supply for the large concentration of manufacturing industry and mining in Gauteng and the northern Free State, is nearing the limit of its capacity. Even with planned increases in supply to the Vaal from the Tugela basin in KwaZulu/Natal, it is unlikely that this river will meet future requirements for much longer. It is likely, therefore, that KwaZulu/Natal, with its much greater water supply, will have a higher rate of growth of industry than Gauteng in the future. In March 1988 South Africa and Lesotho signed the final protocols for the Lesotho Highlands Water Project (LHWP); the arrangements were reconfirmed in the mid-1990s after South Africa's change of leadership. The first water deliveries flowed in 1997, and South Africa made the first annual royalty payment, of R110m., in that year. In February 2006 90% of all households in South Africa were within 200m of a piped water source. South Africa needs an estimated R537,000m. of investment in water infrastructure over the next 10 years, although its budgeted amount is only 44% of that, according to the Chief Operations Officer of the Ministry of Water and Environmental Affairs, Trevor Balzer. This shortfall threatens the continued access to water of both households and businesses.

FOREIGN TRADE

South Africa is highly dependent on international trade, especially on exports from its mining sector and imports of essential goods and commodities. According to IMF assessments, the value of merchandise imports rose from US $81,862m. in 2010 to $100,442m. in 2011, signalling a continuing recovery from the weaker domestic demand for imports during the economic recession. The value of visible exports also grew, from $85,700m. in 2010 to $102,858m. in 2011. The surplus on the visible trade balance decreased from $3,838m. in 2010 to $2,416m. in 2011. Of total exports in 2010, just under 10%, or $7,100m., was contributed by gold, compared with $6,300m. in 2009 and $5,900m. in 2008. The current account of the balance of payments remained in deficit in 2011, at $13,683m., compared with $10,117m. in 2010 and $11,327m. in 2009. The current account was last in surplus in 2003 and has been in deficit most years since 1995. Indeed, the IMF forecast in 2009 a continued widening of the current account deficit every year until at least 2015. However, the current account deficits have been small enough not to place undue pressure on the overall balance of payments in most years, and the overall balance has continually carried a surplus, albeit a small one. The overall balance showed an estimated surplus of $4,708m. in 2011, up from $3,796m. in 2010. The EIU forecast a current account deficit in 2012 equivalent to 4.8% of GDP, as well as a decrease in export volume. This was due to weakening demand in South Africa's most important markets, namely the members of the Organisation for Economic Co-operation and Development, and lower commodity prices. However, a projected increase in exports during 2013–16 was expected to lower the current account deficit; it was forecast to be 4.4% of GDP in 2013 and to decline further, to 3.8% of GDP, by 2015. The country remains heavily dependent on manufacturing, on agriculture and especially on mining to pay for imports. South Africa is a member of the Southern African Development Community (SADC).

FINANCE

The South African currency is the rand, issued by the South African Reserve Bank. Its exchange rate fluctuates against a basket of currencies; the rate was R6.68 = US $1 in July 2011, compared with R7.71 = $1 a year earlier, an annual depreciation of 12.3%. The rand was forecast by the EIU to fall within the range of R7.5–R8.5 = $1 in 2012, and gradually to depreciate during 2012–16, largely as a result of the continuing current account deficit and increased inflation. At 31 May 2012 the rate was R8.53 = $1.

Public finance is conducted along orthodox lines, although there has been a steady trend for public spending to grow as a proportion of GDP, despite repeated attempts to prevent further increases in real terms. From 1994 economies in outlays on defence expenditure have been more than offset by large increases in social expenditure on housing, health and education for the African population, which, together with the weak performance of the economy, led to stagnating revenues and spiralling deficits. The 2011/12 budget, presented to parliament by Minister of Finance Pravin Gordhan in February 2011, appealed for total revenue of R729,858m. and for total expenditure of R888,338m., leaving a budget deficit of R158,480m., equivalent to about 5.4% of GDP. The 2012/13 budget was also expected to be in deficit given the anticipated large investments by the Government in social welfare, infrastructure and in salary increases for public sector workers. These pressures were particularly acute given that President Zuma was widely expected to stand for re-election in 2014. Nevertheless, the EIU still anticipated that over the next few years the National Treasury would curb expenditure as much as it could, and would hold the budget deficit to around 3.1% of GDP in 2015/16 and to 2.4% in 2016/17.

ECONOMIC OUTLOOK

Job creation, economic growth and higher investment are critical priorities for South Africa in the coming years. When Zuma assumed the presidency in May 2009, he and his team of economic planners were confronted by the challenge of finding a way to increase the country's wealth and to redistribute it in a way that was effective, without deterring private sector investors, whose funds were badly needed. Progress on this front was debated during the Mbeki years (1999–2008) and continues to be debated today. The achievements that had been made in job creation were negated by the 2008–09 global recession, when 1m. South African jobs were lost, an estimated 900,000 of them in the manufacturing sector. Through all means possible, the Zuma Government will have to create sustainable jobs in even larger numbers. New investment, both by local companies and by foreign enterprises, would be an essential element of any strategy to achieve that goal. Even with apartheid laws no longer in place, a bitter legacy of that system remains in the extreme polarization of incomes. In some respects, the South African economy can boast of spectacular global successes, in terms of diamond- and gold-mining, minerals and brewing. Yet, far more needs to be done to create business opportunities inside South Africa. Former Minister of Finance Trevor Manuel acknowledged this need in the 2009 budget, by raising the threshold for VAT collection from R300,000 to R1m. With a market of 50m. potential consumers, sales of products such as motor vehicles and household goods could be much larger, if every South African household had the means to buy them, a situation that was unrealizable in the 2000s. Even a modest achievement towards lifting more households above the poverty level would provide an impetus not only to badly needed investment but also to the job creation that such investment could bring. However, the persistent fundamental problems affecting the economy, such as skills shortages and the effect of HIV/AIDS on the labour market, prevent high growth in the South African sectors that rely heavily on labour, such as mining and manufacturing.

As mentioned earlier, real GDP was expected to grow by just 2.8% in 2012, due to lower consumer and international spending. However, in 2013 it was forecast to rise by 3.8% as the result of an improvement in world-wide economic conditions. None the less, in addition to skills shortages, inefficient government agencies, corruption, crime and high unemployment were expected significantly to slow down economic growth in 2014, with the EIU forecasting a GDP growth rate of 3.2% for that year. However, the commencement of operations of the Government's infrastructural investments, namely new transportation networks and power stations, was projected to help to boost GDP growth to about 3.7% in 2015 and 4.1% in 2016.

Statistical Survey

Source (unless otherwise indicated): Statistics South Africa, Private Bag X44, Pretoria 0001; tel. (12) 3108911; fax (12) 3108500; e-mail info@statssa.pwv.gov.za; internet www.statssa.gov.za.

Area and Population

AREA, POPULATION AND DENSITY

Area (sq km)	1,220,813*
Population (census results)	
9 October 1996	40,583,573
9 October 2001	
Males	21,434,041
Females	23,385,737
Total	44,819,778
Population (official estimates at mid-year)	
2009	49,320,500
2010	49,991,300
2011	50,586,757
Density (per sq km) at mid-2011	41.4

* 471,358 sq miles.

POPULATION BY AGE AND SEX

(official estimates at mid-2011)

	Males	Females	Total
0–14	7,969,880	7,842,388	15,812,268
15–64	15,538,934	16,696,600	32,235,534
65 and over	1,006,222	1,532,733	2,538,955
Total	24,515,036	26,071,721	50,586,757

ETHNIC GROUPS

(at mid-2011, estimates)

	Number	% of total
Africans (Blacks)	40,206,275	79.5
Europeans (Whites)	4,565,825	9.0
Coloureds	4,539,790	9.0
Asians	1,274,867	2.5
Total	50,586,757	100.0

PROVINCES

(official estimates of population at mid-2011)

	Area (sq km)	Population	Density (per sq km)	Capital
Eastern Cape	168,966	6,829,958	40.4	Bisho
Free State*	129,825	2,759,644	21.3	Bloemfontein
Gauteng†	18,178	11,328,203	623.2	Johannesburg
KwaZulu/Natal	94,361	10,819,130	114.7	Pietermaritzburg
Limpopo‡	125,754	5,554,657	44.2	Pietersburg
Mpumalanga§	76,495	3,657,181	47.8	Nelspruit
Northern Cape	372,889	1,096,731	3.0	Kimberley
North-West	104,882	3,253,390	31.0	Mmabatho
Western Cape	129,462	5,287,863	40.8	Cape Town
Total	1,220,813	50,586,757	41.4	

* Formerly the Orange Free State.

† Formerly Pretoria-Witwatersrand-Vereeniging.

‡ Known as Northern Province (formerly Northern Transvaal) until February 2002.

§ Formerly Eastern Transvaal.

Note: Figures for population are rounded estimates based on the cohort-component compilation method.

PRINCIPAL TOWNS

(metropolitan areas, population at 2001 census)

Johannesburg	3,225,812	Springs	80,776
Durban	3,090,122	Vanderbijlpark	80,201
Cape Town*	2,893,247	Vereeniging	73,288
Pretoria*	1,985,983	Uitenhage	71,668
Port Elizabeth	1,005,779	Rustenburg	67,201
Soweto	858,649	Kimberley	62,526
Tembisa	348,687	Brakpan	62,115
Pietermaritzburg	223,518	Witbank	61,092
Botshabelo	175,820	Somerset West	60,609
Mdantsane	175,783	Klerksdorp	59,511
Boksburg	158,650	Midrand	44,566
East London	135,560	Newcastle	44,119
Bloemfontein*	111,698	Welkom	34,158
Benoni	94,341	Potchefstroom	26,725
Alberton	89,394	Carletonville	18,362
Krugersdorp	86,618	Westonaria	8,440

* Pretoria is the administrative capital, Cape Town the legislative capital and Bloemfontein the judicial capital.

Mid-2011 (incl. suburbs, UN estimates): Cape Town 3,562,470; Pretoria 1,500,960; Bloemfontein 467,778 (Source: UN, *World Urbanization Prospects: The 2011 Revision*).

BIRTHS AND DEATHS

(annual averages, UN estimates)

	1995–2000	2000–05	2005–10
Birth rate (per 1,000)	25.1	24.0	21.9
Death rate (per 1,000)	10.4	13.9	15.2

Source: UN, *World Population Prospects: The 2010 Revision*.

Registered live births ('000): 1,278 in 2008; 1,255 in 2009; 1,295 in 2010.

Registered deaths: 603,094 in 2007; 592,073 in 2008; 572,673 in 2009.

Registered marriages: 186,522 in 2008; 171,989 in 2009; 170,826 in 2010.

Life expectancy (years at birth): 52.1 (males 51.4; females 52.8) in 2010 (Source: World Bank, World Development Indicators database).

IMMIGRATION AND EMIGRATION

	2001	2002	2003
Immigrants:			
Africa	1,419	2,472	4,961
Europe	1,714	1,847	2,567
Asia	1,289	1,738	2,328
Americas	213	244	354
Oceania	51	65	99
Total (incl. others and unspecified)	4,832	6,545	10,578
Emigrants:			
Africa	1,584	1,461	2,611
Europe	5,316	4,637	6,827
Asia	226	218	445
Americas	1,713	1,473	2,090
Oceania	2,912	2,523	3,248
Total (incl. others and unspecified)	12,260	10,890	16,165

Immigrants (2004): Africa 5,235; Europe 2,638; Asia 2,225; Americas 343; Total (incl. others) 10,714.

Note: Data are for documented migration only; emigrant figures are based on self-declaration.

ECONOMICALLY ACTIVE POPULATION
('000 persons aged 15 to 65 years, annual labour force survey)*

	2008	2009	2010
Agriculture, hunting, forestry and fishing	786	686	639
Mining and quarrying	330	317	305
Manufacturing	1,990	1,853	1,739
Electricity, gas and water	97	98	90
Construction	1,161	1,133	1,060
Trade, restaurants and hotels	3,179	2,975	2,927
Transport, storage and communications	785	764	774
Financing, insurance, real estate and business services	1,691	1,768	1,656
Community, social and personal services	2,634	2,670	2,727
Private households	1,209	1,187	1,140
Total employed	13,867	13,455	13,061
Unemployed	4,104	4,215	4,332
Total labour force	17,971	17,670	17,393

* Figures have been assessed independently, so totals are not always equal to the sum of the component parts.

Health and Welfare

KEY INDICATORS

Total fertility rate (children per woman, 2010)	2.5
Under-5 mortality rate (per 1,000 live births, 2010)	57
HIV/AIDS (% of persons aged 15–49, 2009)	17.8
Physicians (per 1,000 head, 2004)	0.8
Hospital beds (per 1,000 head, 2005)	2.8
Health expenditure (2009): US $ per head (PPP)	930
Health expenditure (2009): % of GDP	9.2
Health expenditure (2009): public (% of total)	43.8
Access to water (% of persons, 2010)	91
Access to sanitation (% of persons, 2010)	79
Total carbon dioxide emissions ('000 metric tons, 2008)	435,878.0
Carbon dioxide emissions per head (metric tons, 2008)	8.9
Human Development Index (2011): ranking	123
Human Development Index (2011): value	0.619

For sources and definitions, see explanatory note on p. vi.

Agriculture

PRINCIPAL CROPS
('000 metric tons)

	2008	2009	2010
Wheat	2,130	1,958	1,465
Barley	192.0	216.0	200.0
Maize	12,700	12,050	12,815
Oats	27.0	37.0	27.0
Sorghum	255.0	276.5	196.5
Potatoes	2,040.0	1,866.7	2,071.9
Sweet potatoes	52.5	63.0	63.2
Sugar cane	19,255.4	18,655.1	16,015.6
Beans, dry	59.0	67.0	52.3
Soybeans (Soya beans)	282.0	516.0	566.0
Groundnuts, with shell	88.8	99.5	88.0
Sunflower seed	872.0	801.0	490.0
Seed cotton	26.5	22.7	20.8
Cabbages and other brassicas	152.9	136.0	148.9
Tomatoes	540.5	533.2	544.5
Pumpkins, squash and gourds	166.1	158.3	170.9
Onions, dry	496.4	461.5	518.1
Carrots and turnips	170.5	148.1	141.8
Maize, green*	363	352	402
Watermelons	55.6	72.2	139.4
Bananas	393.1	370.8	393.3
Oranges	1,522.5	1,369.5	1,415.1
Tangerines, mandarins, clementines and satsumas*	139.1	145.0	142.5
Lemons and limes	229.9	204.3	216.0
Grapefruit and pomelos	340.9	406.6	343.2

—*continued*	2008	2009	2010
Apples	770.7	815.8	740.5
Pears	345.1	348.4	366.2
Apricots	61.2	50.1	58.9
Peaches and nectarines	182.8	159.3	152.2
Plums and sloes	62.6	61.2	59.5
Grapes	1,865.3	1,748.6	1,712.7
Mangoes, mangosteens and guavas	78.4	42.5	47.6
Avocados	83.5	76.7	82.5
Pineapples	144.8	123.0	92.9
Tobacco, unmanufactured	9.0	9.6	11.1

* FAO estimates.

Aggregate production ('000 metric tons, may include official, semi-official or estimated data): Total cereals 15,338.4 in 2008, 14,576.7 in 2009, 14,733.3 in 2010; Total roots and tubers 2,092.5 in 2008, 1,929.7 in 2009, 2,135.1 in 2010; Total vegetables (incl. melons) 2,454.0 in 2008, 2,363.2 in 2009, 2,601.9 in 2010; Total fruits (excl. melons) 6,321.5 in 2008, 6,016.5 in 2009, 5,914.4 in 2010.

Source: FAO.

LIVESTOCK
('000 head, year ending September)

	2008	2009	2010
Cattle	13,865	13,761	13,731
Pigs	1,615	1,613	1,594
Sheep	25,094	24,989	24,501
Goats	6,529	6,358	6,275
Horses*	295	300	300
Asses*	151	151	151
Chickens*	150,000	163,000	125,500
Ducks*	370	375	380
Geese and guinea fowls*	135	135	135
Turkeys*	510	515	520

* FAO estimates.

Source: FAO.

LIVESTOCK PRODUCTS
('000 metric tons)

	2008	2009	2010
Cattle meat	783	768	884
Sheep meat	135.1	139.3	139.8
Goat meat*	37.2	36.3	35.5
Pig meat	296.3	313.0	338.0*
Chicken meat	1,327.6	1,387.6	1,471.6
Cows' milk	3,137	3,104	3,233
Hen eggs	473	450	453
Wool, greasy	42	43	41

* FAO estimate(s).

Source: FAO.

Forestry

ROUNDWOOD REMOVALS
('000 cubic metres, excl. bark, FAO estimates)

	2007	2008	2009
Sawlogs, veneer logs and logs for sleepers	4,367.4	5,093.4	4,374.8
Pulpwood	13,875.6	13,661.7	12,940.7
Other industrial wood	1,268.8	1,112.2	1,572.1
Fuel wood	12,000.0	12,000.0	12,000.0
Total	31,511.8	31,867.3	30,887.6

2010: Production assumed to be unchanged from 2009 (FAO estimates).

Source: FAO.

SAWNWOOD PRODUCTION
('000 cubic metres, incl. railway sleepers)

	2007	2008	2009
Coniferous (softwood)	1,845.3	1,878.3	1,753.3
Broadleaved (hardwood)	149.6	177.5	122.3
Total	1,995.0	2,055.8	1,875.6

2010: Production assumed to be unchanged from 2009 (FAO estimates).

Source: FAO.

Fishing

('000 metric tons, live weight)

	2008	2009	2010
Capture*	644.7	512.3	623.9
Cape hakes (Stokvisse)	132.4	107.5	109.0
Southern African pilchard	91.0	94.4	112.4
Whitehead's round herring	64.7	40.6	88.6
Southern African anchovy	265.8	174.5	217.0
Cape horse mackerel	30.5	35.2	33.4
Aquaculture	3.6	3.4*	3.1*
Total catch*†	648.2	515.7	627.1

* FAO estimate(s).

† Excluding aquatic plants ('000 metric tons, FAO estimates): 1.8 in 2008; 1.9 in 2009; 2.0 in 2010.

Note: Figures exclude aquatic animals, recorded by number rather than weight. The number of Nile crocodiles captured was: 40,197 in 2008; 24,988 in 2009; 70,208 in 2010.

Source: FAO.

Mining

('000 metric tons unless otherwise indicated)

	2007	2008	2009
Hard coal	247,666	252,699	250,582
Crude petroleum ('000 barrels)	2,559	1,976	1,070
Natural gas	1,900*	2,111	2,000*
Iron ore†	26,500	30,800	34,800
Copper ore (metric tons)†	97,000	109,000	105,000*
Nickel ore (metric tons)†	37,917	31,675	34,605
Lead concentrates (metric tons)†	41,857	46,440	49,149
Zinc ore (metric tons)†	30,859	29,002	28,159
Manganese ore and concentrates (metallurgical and chemical)‡	5,995	6,806	4,576
Chromium ore‡	9,665	9,682	6,865
Vanadium ore (metric tons)‡	23,486	20,295	14,353
Zirconium concentrates (metric tons)*	398,000	398,000	387,000
Antimony concentrates (metric tons)†	3,354	3,370	2,400*
Cobalt ore (metric tons)*†	400	400	400
Silver (kg)	68,919	75,199	77,780
Uranium oxide (metric tons)	619	654	629
Gold (kg)	252,598	212,571	197,628
Platinum-group metals (kg)	304,032	275,677	271,393
Kaolin	50.8	39.2	31.0
Magnesite—crude	80.7	83.9	78.0*
Phosphate rock‡	2,556	2,287	2,237
Fluorspar	285	299	140
Salt	411.5	429.9	408.4
Diamonds ('000 carats)	15,250	12,895	6,119
Gypsum—crude	627.4	571.3	597.6
Mica (metric tons)	437	426	299
Talc (metric tons)	14,281	5,145	4,718
Pyrophyllite (metric tons)	123,573	80,704	114,889

* Estimated figure(s).

† Figures refer to metal content of ores and concentrates.

‡ Gross weight.

Source: US Geological Survey.

Industry

SELECTED PRODUCTS
('000 metric tons unless otherwise indicated)

	2006	2007	2008
Wheat flour*	2,217	2,242	2,237
Chemical wood pulp	1,306	1,394	1,394
Newsprint	343	349	349
Motor spirit (petrol)	7,910	7,874	8,176
Kerosene	624	610	621
Jet fuel	1,695	1,687	1,769
Distillate fuel oils	9,873	6,219	6,764
Petroleum bitumen—asphalt	519	554	693
Cement (sales)†	14,257	15,316	14,869
Pig-iron†	6,159	5,358	5,350
Crude steel†	9,718	9,098	8,269
Refined copper—unwrought†	104.1	113.2	93.0
Electric energy (million kWh)	254,075	263,479	258,291

* Twelve months ending September.

† Source: US Geological Survey.

2009: Cement (sales) 13,000 (estimate); Pig-iron 4,376; Crude steel 7,484; Refined copper—unwrought 89,453 (Source: US Geological Survey).

Source: mostly UN Industrial Commodity Statistics Database.

Finance

CURRENCY AND EXCHANGE RATES

Monetary Units

100 cents = 1 rand (R).

Sterling, Dollar and Euro Equivalents (31 May 2012)

£1 sterling = 13.23 rand;
US $1 = 8.53 rand;
€1 = 10.58 rand;
100 rand = £7.56 = $11.72 = €94.50.

Average Exchange Rate (rand per US $)

2009	8.4737
2010	7.3212
2011	7.2611

BUDGET
(million rand, year ending 31 March)

Revenue	2010/11	2011/12*	2012/2013*
Tax revenue (gross)	674,183.1	738,734.8	826,401.1
Taxes on incomes and profits	379,941.2	423,805.0	475,729.3
Individuals	226,925.0	249,700.0	285,969.7
Companies (including secondary tax)	150,079.9	171,500.0	186,888.6
Retirement funds	2.8	—	—
Other	2,933.6	2,605.0	2,871.0
Taxes on payroll and workforce	8,652.3	10,100.0	11,131.2
Taxes on property	9,102.3	7,870.0	8,627.1
Domestic taxes on goods and services	249,490.4	264,649.8	294,554.2
Value-added tax	183,571.4	190,815.0	209,674.9
Excise duties	24,563.8	27,694.6	30,772.3
Levies on fuel	34,417.6	37,180.0	42,775.5
Air departure tax	647.8	730.1	750.3
Other	1,293.3	1,800.0	1,979.7
Stamp duties and fees	3.1	—	—
State Miscellaneous Revenue	16.7	—	—
Taxes on international trade and transactions	26,977.1	32,310.0	36,359.3
Departmental revenue	13,460.1	17,579.5	15,091.0
Sub-total	687,643.2	756,314.3	841,492.1
Less SACU payments†	14,991.3	21,763.2	42,151.3
Other adjustments	−2,914.4	—	—
Total	669,737.5	734,551.0	799,340.8

Expenditure	2010/11	2011/12*	2012/2013*
Central government administration	61,690.6	66,960.7	75,820.0
The Presidency	958.7	1,005.8	1,018.0
Parliament	1,198.9	1,249.7	1,333.3
Cooperative governance and traditional affairs	41,821.4	46,177.3	54,715.6
Foreign affairs	4,417.2	5,153.4	5,116.6
Home affairs	6,521.7	5,850.8	5,296.3
Performance monitoring and evaluation	47.3	98.9	174.2
Public works	6,615.5	7,281.7	7,993.8
Women, children and people with disabilities	109.9	143.1	172.2
Financial and administrative services	41,441.5	26,895.6	25,682.4
Government communication and information system	352.2	360.5	429.1
National treasury	38,226.2	21,817.3	21,551.1
Public Enterprises	540.0	353.3	1,249.1
Public services and administration	628.2	690.2	731.5
Statistics South Africa	1,694.9	3,674.3	1,721.6
Social services	154,308.7	176,635.5	193,271.6
Arts and culture	2,248.8	2,411.2	2,685.7
Education	32,430.3	41,929.2	47,844.0
Health	22,520.3	25,622.1	27,557.0
Labour	1,826.3	1,998.1	2,119.7
Social development	94,031.0	103,858.9	112,216.8
Sport and Recreation South Africa	1,252.0	816.0	848.4
Justice and protection services	109,484.2	120,820.7	130,987.2
Correctional services	14,698.8	16,203.1	17,732.2
Defence	30,442.4	34,349.1	37,493.0
Independent complaints directorate	128.4	153.5	197.0
Justice and constitutional development	10,684.9	11,564.5	13,079.6
Safety and security	53,529.7	58,550.5	62,485.4
Economic services and infrastructure	88,667.8	111,320.5	117,868.8
Agriculture and forestry	3,850.7	4,964.4	5,798.8
Communications	1,426.5	2,002.9	1,712.3
Economic development	400.7	567.6	672.7
Energy	5,505.4	6,098.8	6,805.9
Environmental affairs	3,279.5	4,201.6	4,512.2
Human settlements	18,916.5	22,645.5	25,263.2
Mineral resources	994.7	1,039.0	1,169.1
Rural development and land reform	7,122.9	8,136.7	8,877.6
Tourism	1,143.5	1,265.0	1,367.3
Science and technology	4,051.9	4,407.0	4,955.9
Trade and industry	5,796.7	6,876.5	9,092.1
Transport	29,155.1	41,450.0	38,829.0
Water affairs	7,023.7	7,665.5	8,812.7
Sub-total	455,592.8	502,633.0	543,629.5
State debt costs	66,226.8	76,644.9	89,388.1
Provincial equitable share	265,139.4	291,735.5	309,057.4
Skills levy and seats	8,379.3	9,148.7	9,606.1
Members' remuneration	346.0	355.1	430.1
Judges' salaries	1,910.2	2,104.2	2,401.9
President and deputy-president salary	4.0	3.8	2.7
General fuel levy sharing with metros	7,542.4	8,573.1	9,039.7
Unallocated	—	—	30.0
Contingency reserve	—	—	5,780.0
Total	805,141.0	891,198.7	969,365.5

* Estimates.

† Payments to Botswana, Lesotho, Namibia and Swaziland, in accordance with Southern African Customs Union agreements.

Source: National Treasury, Pretoria.

INTERNATIONAL RESERVES
(US $ million at 31 December)

	2009	2010	2011
Gold (national valuation)	4,438	5,654	6,272
IMF special drawing rights	2,803	2,754	2,745
Reserve position in IMF	2	2	3
Foreign exchange	32,432	35,419	39,847
Total	39,675	43,829	48,867

Source: IMF, *International Financial Statistics*.

MONEY SUPPLY
(million rand at 31 December)

	2009	2010	2011
Currency outside depository corporations	61,784	65,079	75,396
Transferable deposits	361,281	408,363	437,816
Other deposits	1,154,303	1,217,424	1,419,445
Securities other than shares	370,544	392,113	322,641
Broad money	1,947,911	2,082,980	2,255,298

Source: IMF, *International Financial Statistics*.

COST OF LIVING
(Consumer Price Index; base: 2000 = 100)

	2006	2007	2008
Food	147.8	163.1	190.0
Clothing	84.6	76.8	87.7
Housing	118.2	129.7	142.2
Electricity, gas and other fuels	141.9	153.3	182.8
All items (incl. others)	134.0	143.5	160.0

2009: Food 109.5; All items (incl. others) 171.4.

2010: Food 111.0; All items (incl. others) 178.7.

2011: Food 118.9; All items (incl. others) 187.7.

Source: ILO.

NATIONAL ACCOUNTS
(million rand at current prices, preliminary)

National Income and Product

	2009	2010	2011
Compensation of employees	1,077,833	1,201,990	1,317,655
Net operating surplus	731,204	821,783	937,150
Consumption of fixed capital	332,584	350,982	376,422
Gross domestic product (GDP) at factor cost	2,141,621	2,374,755	2,631,227
Taxes on production	280,658	310,201	362,872
Less Subsidies	24,124	23,522	29,838
GDP at market prices	2,398,155	2,661,434	2,964,261
Primary incomes received from abroad	34,075	34,099	38,118
Less Primary incomes paid abroad	87,593	87,022	104,689
Gross national income at market prices	2,344,637	2,608,511	2,897,690
Current transfers received from abroad	10,334	9,089	11,287
Less Current transfers paid abroad	32,762	25,851	25,486
Gross national disposable income at market prices	2,322,209	2,591,749	2,883,491

Expenditure on the Gross Domestic Product

	2009	2010	2011
Government final consumption expenditure	502,492	573,470	636,446
Private final consumption expenditure	1,460,911	1,575,930	1,737,277
Increase in stocks	–50,744	–3,425	25,067
Gross fixed capital formation	521,707	520,434	559,888
Residual item	–15,095	298	23,598
Total domestic expenditure	2,419,271	2,666,707	2,982,276
Exports of goods and services	657,192	727,721	854,343
Less Imports of goods and services	678,308	732,994	872,358
GDP at market prices	2,398,155	2,661,434	2,964,261
GDP at constant 2005 prices	1,786,637	1,838,263	1,895,668

Gross Domestic Product by Economic Activity

	2009	2010	2011
Agriculture, forestry and fishing	63,655	58,644	63,984
Mining and quarrying	196,521	227,117	260,381
Manufacturing	331,702	332,470	357,756
Electricity, gas and water	60,402	71,403	78,532
Construction (contractors)	86,522	102,801	120,420
Wholesale and retail trade, catering and accommodation	298,511	342,750	386,430
Transport, storage and communication	199,276	203,673	220,060
Finance, insurance, real estate and business services	464,846	522,048	565,224
Government services	338,903	385,307	434,224
Other community, social and personal services	134,174	166,277	183,493
Gross value added at basic prices	2,174,513	2,412,491	2,670,504
Taxes, less subsidies, on products	223,643	248,944	293,757
GDP at market prices	2,398,156	2,661,435	2,964,261

BALANCE OF PAYMENTS
(US $ million)

	2009	2010	2011
Exports of goods f.o.b.	66,542	85,700	102,858
Imports of goods f.o.b.	–66,009	–81,862	–100,442
Trade balance	534	3,838	2,416
Exports of services	12,020	14,003	14,823
Imports of services	–14,808	–18,456	–19,664
Balance on goods and services	–2,254	–615	–2,425
Other income received	3,988	4,651	5,304
Other income paid	–10,377	–11,876	–14,590
Balance on goods, services and income	–8,643	–7,839	–11,711
Current transfers received	1,242	1,247	1,541
Current transfers paid	–3,926	–3,525	–3,513
Current balance	–11,327	–10,117	–13,683
Capital account (net)	26	31	33
Direct investment abroad	–1,311	161	500
Direct investment from abroad	5,354	1,224	5,718
Portfolio investment assets	–1,746	–4,613	–6,308
Portfolio investment liabilities	13,368	14,386	6,678
Other investment assets	3,101	–3,215	–60
Other investment liabilities	–2,489	892	4,416
Net errors and omissions	–804	5,048	7,414
Overall balance	4,171	3,796	4,708

Source: IMF, *International Financial Statistics*.

External Trade

PRINCIPAL COMMODITIES
(distribution by SITC, US $ million)

Imports c.i.f.	2008	2009	2010
Food and live animals	3,184.8	2,873.1	3,171.8
Crude materials (inedible) except fuels	2,891.0	1,261.8	1,635.0
Mineral fuels, lubricants, etc.	19,555.0	13,663.3	15,722.5
Petroleum, petroleum products, etc.	18,512.8	12,949.0	14,769.4
Crude petroleum oils, etc.	14,957.2	10,294.4	11,199.5
Chemicals and related products	8,549.9	6,673.8	8,662.9
Basic manufactures	9,048.1	6,611.5	8,688.5
Non-metallic mineral manufactures	1,936.1	1,234.7	1,639.6
Machinery and transport equipment	30,670.0	22,201.3	28,400.4
Power generating machinery and equipment	2,627.8	1,762.0	2,128.7
Machinery specialized for particular industries	4,417.2	2,605.1	2,758.8
General industrial machinery, equipment and parts	4,271.9	3,341.7	3,795.9
Office machines and automatic data-processing equipment	3,020.8	2,452.4	3,223.4
Telecommunications and sound equipment	3,913.3	3,172.3	4,397.8
Other electrical machinery, apparatus, etc.	3,627.7	2,987.7	3,580.6
Road vehicles	6,161.2	4,339.8	6,856.0
Passenger motor vehicles (excl. buses)	2,749.7	2,335.8	4,067.2
Other transport equipment	2,038.2	1,107.8	1,219.7
Miscellaneous manufactured articles	6,468.1	5,729.1	7,122.3
Total (incl. others)	87,593.1	63,766.1	80,139.3

Exports f.o.b.	2008	2009	2010
Food and live animals	4,124.1	4,132.8	4,757.3
Vegetables and fruit	2,050.9	2,076.8	2,678.1
Beverages and tobacco	1,078.1	1,132.9	1,219.4
Crude materials (inedible) except fuels	10,624.6	8,448.0	13,078.6
Metalliferous ores and metal scrap	8,252.7	6,806.7	10,892.1
Mineral fuels, lubricants, etc.	7,120.3	6,022.7	7,197.7
Coal, lignite and peat	4,785.5	4,215.1	5,474.0
Petroleum, petroleum products, etc.	2,198.7	1,675.5	1,562.0
Chemicals and related products	5,723.7	4,100.2	5,077.5
Basic manufactures	26,946.0	17,535.4	24,584.1
Non-metallic mineral manufactures	2,647.1	1,588.8	2,298.8
Pearl, precious and semi-precious stones, unworked or worked	2,339.0	1,307.1	1,955.5
Diamonds (non-industrial), not mounted or set	2,282.5	1,300.8	1,944.4
Iron and steel	8,859.7	5,116.2	7,735.0
Pig-iron, etc.	5,954.6	2,912.7	4,976.8
Non-ferrous metals	12,578.3	8,614.0	11,973.2

Exports f.o.b.—*continued*	2008	2009	2010
Silver, platinum and other platinum group metals	9,817.6	6,769.7	9,394.9
Platinum group metals, unwrought, unworked or semi-manufactured	9,801.0	6,766.6	9,377.1
Aluminium	2,071.0	1,464.3	1,889.7
Aluminium and aluminium alloys, unwrought	1,348.4	1,004.2	1,235.5
Machinery and transport equipment	16,229.1	10,786.6	13,450.8
General industrial machinery, equipment and parts	4,078.9	2,489.2	3,211.0
Road vehicles	7,522.3	5,096.1	6,545.7
Passenger motor vehicles (excl. buses)	4,535.6	3,062.5	4,116.9
Miscellaneous manufactured articles	1,777.4	1,408.1	1,699.7
Total (incl. others)	73,965.5	53,863.9	71,484.3

Source: UN, *International Trade Statistics Yearbook*.

PRINCIPAL TRADING PARTNERS
(US $ million)*

Imports f.o.b.	2008	2009	2010
Angola	2,686.5	1,370.6	1,998.2
Argentina	1,003.2	858.2	919.4
Australia	1,630.4	1,083.0	1,312.7
Belgium	1,128.2	927.2	1,147.1
Brazil	1,661.1	1,242.2	1,353.8
China, People's Repub.	9,909.3	8,325.3	11,499.2
France (incl. Monaco)	2,502.6	1,993.2	2,334.0
Germany	9,914.0	7,438.3	9,051.1
India	2,261.9	1,811.6	2,839.4
Iran	3,290.4	2,599.1	3,148.0
Ireland	857.5	n.a.	n.a.
Italy	2,133.8	1,608.2	2,008.4
Japan	4,882.6	3,093.7	4,245.3
Korea, Repub.	1,437.1	1,135.3	1,747.2
Malaysia	1,084.6	865.8	1,166.0
Netherlands	1,213.2	1,157.9	1,414.2
Nigeria	1,892.4	1,839.0	2,200.8
Saudi Arabia	5,523.0	3,204.1	3,243.5
Singapore	887.9	575.8	870.9
Spain	1,063.7	756.9	1,257.9
Sweden	1,614.7	1,104.3	1,403.7
Thailand	1,756.1	1,352.5	1,829.9
United Kingdom	3,556.2	2,526.1	3,019.8
USA	7,038.0	4,949.4	5,837.6
Total (incl. others)	87,593.1	63,766.1	80,139.3

Exports f.o.b.	2008	2009	2010
Angola	897.8	682.0	700.1
Australia	1,494.4	725.8	952.0
Belgium	2,046.6	1,282.2	1,801.2
China, People's Repub.	4,309.8	5,670.1	8,132.4
Congo, Democratic Repub.	1,125.2	573.8	865.8
France (incl. Monaco)	1,447.2	841.3	978.7
Germany	5,748.9	3,512.7	5,529.4
Hong Kong	645.1	963.4	966.5
India	2,279.5	2,067.7	2,980.6
Israel	841.4	575.5	718.0
Italy	1,595.2	1,080.6	1,425.3
Japan	8,119.6	4,096.1	6,425.0
Kenya	709.9	872.4	785.3
Korea, Repub.	1,506.7	900.8	1,713.3
Mozambique	1,609.0	1,606.6	1,893.9
Netherlands	3,463.6	2,036.6	2,284.6
Nigeria	955.0	678.1	622.8
Spain	1,876.6	1,088.5	1,102.9
Switzerland-Liechtenstein	1,556.4	2,273.3	2,276.9
United Arab Emirates	769.9	610.4	850.7
United Kingdom	4,905.9	3,002.1	3,703.5
USA	7,987.4	4,859.7	7,060.8
Zambia	1,965.4	1,416.0	1,750.9
Zimbabwe	1,689.0	1,608.0	2,156.1
Total (incl. others)	73,965.5	53,863.9	71,484.3

* Imports by country of origin; exports by country of destination.

Source: UN, *International Trade Statistics Yearbook*.

Transport

RAILWAYS
(traffic, preliminary)

	2009	2010	2011
Passengers ('000)	649,787	524,560	530,872
Total freight ('000 metric tons)	181,482	183,934	196,561

ROAD TRAFFIC
(registered motor vehicles at 31 December)

	2006	2007	2009*
Passenger cars	4,574,972	5,160,844	5,411,093
Buses and coaches	288,513	316,540	328,158
Lorries and vans	1,824,088	2,125,784	2,267,896
Motorcycles and mopeds	237,556	312,046	362,400

* Data for 2008 were not available.

Source: IRF, *World Road Statistics*.

SHIPPING

Merchant Fleet
(vessels registered at 31 December)

	2007	2008	2009
Number of vessels	250	261	273
Displacement ('000 grt)	192.6	195.1	202.9

Source: IHS Fairplay, *World Fleet Statistics*.

International Sea-borne Freight Traffic

	2003	2004	2005
Goods loaded (metric tons)	128,477,183	124,370,762	127,408,557
Goods unloaded (metric tons)	42,845,843	43,820,161	43,847,748
Containers loaded (TEU)	1,194,400	1,290,883	1,484,009
Containers unloaded (TEU)	1,220,167	1,341,888	1,530,227

Source: National Ports Authority of South Africa.

CIVIL AVIATION
(traffic on scheduled services)

	2007	2008	2009
Kilometres flown (million)	222	226	217
Passengers carried ('000)	12,870	12,989	12,504
Passenger-km (million)	29,893	28,953	26,926
Total ton-km (million)	3,690	3,386	3,108

Source: UN, *Statistical Yearbook*.

2010: Passengers carried ('000) 16,779 (Source: World Bank, World Development Indicators database).

Tourism

FOREIGN VISITOR ARRIVALS*

Country of origin	2007	2008	2009
Botswana	821,070	807,292	838,931
France	118,175	131,512	120,327
Germany	259,856	243,578	216,076
Lesotho	2,171,954	2,165,505	2,100,366
Mozambique	1,085,556	1,228,979	1,363,178
Namibia	221,360	222,817	217,476
Netherlands	130,878	130,083	124,512
Swaziland	1,041,235	1,090,056	1,090,559
United Kingdom	506,481	493,415	495,441
USA	282,062	292,884	268,753
Zambia	184,358	193,677	165,776
Zimbabwe	977,101	1,248,043	1,599,795
Total (incl. others and unspecified)	9,207,697	9,728,860	10,098,306

* Figures include same-day visitors (excursionists), but exclude arrivals of South African nationals resident abroad. Border crossings by contract workers are also excluded.

Total visitor arrivals: 8,074,000 in 2010; 8,339,000 in 2011 (provisional).

Tourism receipts (US $ million, excl. passenger transport): 9,070 in 2010; 9,547 in 2011 (provisional).

Source: World Tourism Organization.

Communications Media

	2009	2010	2011
Telephones ('000 main lines in use)	4,320	4,225	4,127
Mobile cellular telephones ('000 subscribers)	46,436	50,372	64,000
Internet users ('000)	4,420	n.a.	n.a.
Broadband subscribers ('000)	481	743	907

* Estimate.

Book production: 5,418 titles in 1995.

2001: Radio receivers ('000 in use): 11,696; Television receivers ('000 in use): 7,708.

Daily newspapers: 18 (total average circulation 1,408,000) in 2004.

Non-daily newspapers: 314 (total average circulation 7,630,000) in 2004.

Personal computers: 3,966,000 (84.6 per 1,000 persons) in 2005.

Sources: partly UNESCO, *Statistical Yearbook*; UN, *Statistical Yearbook*; International Telecommunication Union.

Education

(2010)*

	Institutions	Teachers	Students
Primary	14,456	187,520	5,992,863
Secondary	6,231	142,181	3,821,763
Combined	4,425	67,281	2,025,105
Intermediate and middle	738	21,127	420,368
ABET centres†‡§	2,395	15,657	297,900
ELSEN centres‖	423	8,781	104,633
Further education and training†§	49	6,255	420,475
ECD¶	4,313	12,504	279,476
Higher education†§	23	16,320	837,779

* Figures for public and independent institutions, unless otherwise indicated.

† Figures for 2009.

‡ Adult basic education and training.

§ Figures refer to public institutions only.

‖ Education for learners with special needs.

¶ Early childhood development.

Source: Department of Education.

Pupil-teacher ratio (primary education, UNESCO estimate): 30.7 in 2008/09 (Source: UNESCO Institute for Statistics).

Adult literacy rate (UNESCO estimates): 89.0% (males 89.9%; females 88.1%) in 2008 (Source: UNESCO Institute for Statistics).

Directory

The Constitution

The Constitution was adopted by the Constitutional Assembly (comprising the National Assembly and the Senate) on 8 May 1996, and entered into force on 4 February 1997. Its main provisions are summarized below:

FOUNDING PROVISIONS

The Republic of South Africa is one sovereign democratic state founded on the following values: human dignity, the achievement of equality and advancement of human rights and freedoms; non-racialism and non-sexism; supremacy of the Constitution and the rule of law; universal adult suffrage, a national common voters' roll, regular elections, and a multi-party system of democratic government, to ensure accountability, responsiveness and openness. There is common South African citizenship, all citizens being equally entitled to the rights, privileges and benefits, and equally subject to the duties and responsibilities of citizenship.

BILL OF RIGHTS

Everyone is equal before the law and has the right to equal protection and benefit of the law. The state may not unfairly discriminate directly or indirectly against anyone on one or more grounds, including race, gender, sex, pregnancy, marital status, ethnic or social origin, colour, sexual orientation, age, disability, religion, conscience, belief, culture, language and birth. The rights that are enshrined include: protection against detention without trial, torture or any inhuman form of treatment or punishment; the right to privacy; freedom of conscience; freedom of expression; freedom of assembly; political freedom; freedom of movement and residence; the right to join or form a trade union or employers' organization; the right to a healthy and sustainable environment; the right to property, except in the case of the Government's programme of land reform and redistribution, and taking into account the claims of people who were dispossessed of property after 19 June 1913; the right to adequate housing; the right to health care, food and water and social security assistance, if needed; the rights of children; the right to education in the official language of one's choice, where this is reasonably practicable; the right to use the language and to participate in the cultural life of one's choice, but not in a manner inconsistent with any provision of this Bill of Rights; access to state information; access to the courts; the rights of people who have been arrested or detained; and the right to a fair trial.

CO-OPERATIVE GOVERNMENT

Government is constituted as national, provincial and local spheres of government, which are distinctive, interdependent and interrelated. All spheres of government and all organs of state within each sphere must preserve the peace, national unity and indivisibility of the Republic; secure the well-being of the people of the Republic; implement effective, transparent, accountable and coherent government for the Republic as a whole; respect the constitutional status, institutions, powers and functions of government in the other spheres; not assume any power or function except those conferred on them in terms of the Constitution.

PARLIAMENT

Legislative power is vested in a bicameral Parliament, comprising a National Assembly and a National Council of Provinces. The National Assembly has between 350 and 400 members and is elected, in general, by proportional representation. National and provincial legislatures are elected separately, under a 'double-ballot' electoral system. Each provincial legislature appoints six permanent delegates and nominates four special delegates to the 90-member National Council of Provinces, which is headed by a Chairperson, who is elected by the Council and has a five-year term of office. Parliamentary decisions are generally reached by a simple majority, although constitutional amendments require a majority of two-thirds.

THE NATIONAL EXECUTIVE

The Head of State is the President, who is elected by the National Assembly from among its members, and exercises executive power in consultation with the other members of the Cabinet. No person may hold office as President for more than two terms. Any party that holds a minimum of 80 seats in the National Assembly (equivalent to 20% of the national vote) is entitled to nominate an Executive Deputy President. If no party, or only one party, secures 80 or more seats, the party holding the largest number of seats and the party holding the second largest number of seats in the National Assembly are each entitled to designate one Executive Deputy President from among the members of the Assembly. The President may be removed by a motion of no confidence or by impeachment. The Cabinet comprises a maximum of 27 ministers. Each party with a minimum of 20 seats in the National Assembly (equivalent to 5% of the national vote) is entitled to a proportional number of ministerial portfolios. The President allocates cabinet portfolios in consultation with party leaders, who are entitled to request the replacement of ministers. Cabinet decisions are reached by consensus.

JUDICIAL AUTHORITY

The judicial authority of the Republic is vested in the courts, which comprise the Constitutional Court; the Supreme Court of Appeal; the High Courts; the Magistrates' Courts; and any other court established or recognized by an Act of Parliament. (See Judicial System.)

PROVINCIAL GOVERNMENT

There are nine provinces: Eastern Cape, Free State (formerly Orange Free State), Gauteng (formerly Pretoria-Witwatersrand-Vereeniging), KwaZulu/Natal, Limpopo (formerly Northern Transvaal, subsequently Northern Province), Mpumalanga (formerly Eastern Transvaal), Northern Cape, North-West and Western Cape. Each province is entitled to determine its legislative and executive structure. Each province has a legislature, comprising between 30 and 80 members (depending on the size of the local electorate), who are elected by proportional representation. Each legislature is entitled to draft a constitution for the province, subject to the principles governing the national Constitution, and elects a Premier, who heads a Cabinet. Parties that hold a minimum of 10% of seats in the legislature are entitled to a proportional number of portfolios in the Cabinet. Provincial legislatures are allowed primary responsibility for a number of areas of government, and joint powers with central government in the principal administrative areas.

LOCAL GOVERNMENT

The local sphere of government consists of municipalities, with executive and legislative authority vested in the Municipal Council. The objectives of local government are to provide democratic and accountable government for local communities; to ensure the provision of services to communities; to promote social and economic development, and a safe and healthy environment; and to encourage the involvement of communities and community organizations in the matters of local government. The National Assembly is to determine the different categories of municipality that may be established, and appropriate fiscal powers and functions for each category. Provincial Governments have the task of establishing municipalities, and of providing for the monitoring and support of local government in each province.

STATE INSTITUTIONS SUPPORTING CONSTITUTIONAL DEMOCRACY

The following state institutions are designed to strengthen constitutional democracy: the Public Protector (whose task is to investigate any conduct in state affairs, or in the public administration in any sphere of government, that is alleged or suspected to be improper); the Human Rights Commission; the Commission for the Protection and Promotion of the Rights of Cultural, Religious and Linguistic Communities; the Commission for Gender Equality; the Auditor-General; and the Electoral Commission.

TRADITIONAL LEADERS

The institution, status and role of traditional leadership, according to customary law, are recognized, subject to the Constitution. A traditional authority that observes a system of customary law may function subject to any applicable legislation and customs. National and provincial legislation may provide for the establishment of local or provincial houses of traditional leaders; the National Assembly may establish a national council of traditional leaders.

The Government

HEAD OF STATE

President: JACOB ZUMA (inaugurated 9 May 2009).

Deputy President: KGALEMA MOTLANTHE.

THE CABINET

(September 2012)

Minister of Agriculture, Forestry and Fisheries: TINA JOEMAT-PETTERSSON.

Minister of Arts and Culture: PAUL MASHATILE.

Minister of Basic Education: MATSIE ANGIE MOTSHEKGA.

Minister of Communications: DINA PULE.

Minister of Co-operative Governance and Traditional Affairs: RICHARD BALOYI.

Minister of Correctional Services: SBUSISO JOEL NDEBELE.

Minister of Defence and Military Veterans: NOSIVIWE MAPISA-NQAKULA.

Minister of Economic Development: EBRAHIM PATEL.

Minister of Energy: ELIZABETH DIPUO PETERS.

Minister of Finance: PRAVIN JAMNADAS GORDHAN.

Minister of Health: Dr PAKISHE AARON MOTSOALEDI.

Minister of Higher Education and Training: Dr BONGINKOSI EMMANUEL 'BLADE' NZIMANDE.

Minister of Home Affairs: Dr NKOSAZANA CLARICE DLAMINI-ZUMA.

Minister of Human Settlements: TOKYO MOSIMA GABRIEL SEXWALE.

Minister of International Relations and Co-operation: MAITE M. NKOANA-MASHABANE.

Minister of Justice and Constitutional Development: JEFFREY THAMSANQA RADEBE.

Minister of Labour: MILDRED OLIPHANT.

Minister of Mineral Resources: SUSAN SHABANGU.

Minister of Police: NATHI MTHETHWA.

Minister of Public Enterprises: MALUSI KNOWLEDGE NKANYEZI GIGABA.

Minister of Public Service and Administration: LINDIWE NONCEBA SISULU.

Minister of Public Works: THEMBELANI 'THULAS' NXESI.

Minister of Rural Development and Land Reform: GUGILE NKWINTI.

Minister of Science and Technology: GRACE NALEDI MANDISA PANDOR.

Minister of Social Development: BATHABILE OLIVE DLAMINI.

Minister of Sport and Recreation: FIKILE APRIL MBALULA.

Minister of State Security: SIYABONGA CYPRIAN CWELE.

Ministers in the Presidency: TREVOR ANDREW MANUEL (National Planning Commission), OHM COLLINS CHABANE (Performance Monitoring, Evaluation and Administration).

Minister of Tourism: MARTHINUS VAN SCHALKWYK.

Minister of Trade and Industry: Dr ROB DAVIES.

Minister of Transport: BEN MARTINS.

Minister of Water and Environmental Affairs: BOMO EDNA MOLEWA.

Minister of Women, Youth, Children and People with Disabilities: LULAMA XINGWANA.

In addition, there were 31 Deputy Ministers.

MINISTRIES

The Presidency: Union Bldgs, West Wing, Government Ave, Pretoria 0001; Private Bag X1000, Pretoria 0001; tel. (12) 3005200; fax (12) 3238246; e-mail president@po.gov.za; internet www.thepresidency.gov.za.

Ministry in The Presidency: National Planning Commission: Union Bldgs, 2nd Floor, Government Ave, Pretoria 0001; Private Bag X1000, Pretoria 0001; tel. (12) 3005277; fax (12) 3238246; e-mail minister@po.gov.za; internet www.thepresidency.gov.za.

Ministry in The Presidency: Performance Monitoring, Evaluation and Administration in The Presidency: Union Bldgs, 2nd Floor, Government Ave, Pretoria 0001; Private Bag X1000, Pretoria 0001; tel. (12) 3005331; fax (12) 3218870; e-mail samson@po.gov.za; internet www.thepresidency.gov.za.

Ministry of Agriculture, Forestry and Fisheries: Agriculture Bldg, 20 Beatrix St, Arcadia, Pretoria 0002; Private Bag X250, Pretoria 0001; tel. (12) 3197317; fax (12) 3197856; e-mail cco@nda.agric.za; internet www.doa.agric.za.

Ministry of Arts and Culture: 481 Church St, 10th Floor, cnr Church and Beatrix Sts, Kingsley Centre, Arcadia, Pretoria; Private Bag X899, Pretoria 0001; tel. (12) 4413709; fax (12) 4404485; e-mail sandile.memela@dac.gov.za; internet www.dac.gov.za.

Ministry of Basic Education: Sol Plaatje House, 123 Schoeman St, Pretoria 0002; Private Bag X603, Pretoria 0001; tel. (12) 3125501; fax (12) 3235989; internet www.education.gov.za.

Ministry of Communications: Nkululeko House, iParioli Office Park, 399 Duncan St, cnr Park St, Hatfield, Pretoria 0083; Private Bag X860, Pretoria 0001; tel. (12) 4278177; fax (12) 3626915; e-mail joe@doc.gov.za; internet www.doc.gov.za.

Ministry of Co-operative Governance and Traditional Affairs: 87 Hamilton St, Arcadia, Pretoria 0001; Private Bag X802, Pretoria 0001; tel. (12) 3340705; fax (12) 3264478; internet www.cogta.gov.za.

Ministry of Correctional Services: Poyntons Bldg, West Block, cnr Church and Schubart Sts, Pretoria 0002; Private Bag X853, Pretoria 0001; tel. (12) 3072000; fax (12) 3286149; e-mail communications@dcs.gov.za; internet www.dcs.gov.za.

Ministry of Defence and Military Veterans: Armscor Bldg, Block 5, Nossob St, Erasmusrand 0181; Private Bag X427, Pretoria 0001; tel. (12) 3556101; fax (12) 3470118; e-mail mil@mil.za; internet www.dod.mil.za.

Ministry of Economic Development: DTI Campus, 3rd Floor, Block A, 77 cnr Meintjies and Esselen Sts, Sunnyside, Pretoria; Private Bag X149, Pretoria 0001; tel. (12) 3941006; fax (86) 3940255.

Ministry of Energy: Mineralia Centre, 234 Visagie St, Pretoria 0002; Private Bag X59, Pretoria 0001; tel. (12) 3178000; fax (12) 3223416; internet www.dme.gov.za.

Ministry of Health: 226 Prinsloo St, Pretoria 0001; Private Bag X399, Pretoria 0001; tel. (12) 3120546; fax (12) 3255526; e-mail bhengu@health.gov.za; internet www.doh.gov.za.

Ministry of Higher Education and Training: Sol Plaatje House, 123 Schoeman St, Pretoria 0002; Private Bag X893, Pretoria 0001; tel. (12) 3125555; fax (12) 3235618; internet www.education.gov.za.

Ministry of Home Affairs: cnr Maggs and Petroleum Sts, Watloo, Pretoria; Private Bag X114, Pretoria 0001; tel. (12) 8108039; fax (12) 8107312; e-mail csc@dha.gov.za; internet www.home-affairs.gov.za.

Ministry of Human Settlements: Govan Mbeki House, 240 Walker St, Sunnyside, Pretoria 0002; Private Bag X644, Pretoria 0001; tel. (12) 4211310; fax (12) 3418513; e-mail mareldia@housing.gov.za; internet www.housing.gov.za.

Ministry of International Relations and Co-operation: Union Bldgs, East Wing, 1 Government Ave, Arcadia, Pretoria 0002; Private Bag X152, Pretoria 0001; tel. (12) 3511000; fax (12) 3291000; e-mail minister@foreign.gov.za; internet www.dfa.gov.za.

Ministry of Justice and Constitutional Development: Momentum Centre, 329 Pretorius St, cnr Pretorius and Prinsloo Sts, Pretoria 0001; Private Bag X276, Pretoria 0001; tel. (12) 313578217; fax (12) 3151749; e-mail znqayi@justice.gov.za; internet www.doj.gov.za.

Ministry of Labour: Laboria House, 215 Schoeman St, Pretoria 0002; Private Bag X117, Pretoria 0001; tel. (12) 3094000; fax (12) 3094030; e-mail page.boikanyo@labour.gov.za; internet www.labour.gov.za.

Ministry of Mineral Resources: Trevenna Campus, Bldg 2C, Meintje and Schoeman St, Sunnyside, Pretoria; Private Bag X59, Arcadia 0007, Pretoria; tel. (12) 4443000; fax (12) 3223416; e-mail enquiries@dmr.gov.za; internet www.dmr.gov.za.

Ministry of Police: Wachthuis, 7th Floor, 231 Pretorius St, Pretoria; Private Bag X463, Pretoria 0001; tel. (12) 3932810; fax (12) 3932812; e-mail bloemb@saps.org.za.

Ministry of Public Enterprises: Infotech Bldg, Suite 401, 1090 Arcadia St, Hatfield, Pretoria 0083; Private Bag X15, Hatfield 0028; tel. (12) 4311000; fax (86) 5012624; e-mail info@dpe.gov.za; internet www.dpe.gov.za.

Ministry of Public Service and Administration: Batho Pele House, 116 Proes St, Pretoria 0001; Private Bag X916, Pretoria 0001; tel. (12) 3361701; fax (12) 3267802; e-mail natasha@dpsa.gov.za; internet www.dpsa.gov.za.

Ministry of Public Works: AVN Bldg, 6th Floor, cnr Skinner and Andries Sts, Pretoria 0002; Private Bag X65, Pretoria 0001; tel. (12) 3105951; fax (12) 3105184; internet www.publicworks.gov.za.

Ministry of Rural Development and Land Reform: Old Bldg, 184 cnr Jacob Mare and Paul Kruger Sts, Pretoria; Private Bag X833, Pretoria 0001; tel. (12) 3128911; fax (12) 3236072; internet www.ruraldevelopment.gov.za.

Ministry of Science and Technology: DST Bldg (No. 53), Meiring Naude Rd, Brummeria 0001; Private Bag X894, Pretoria 0001; tel. (12) 8436300; fax (12) 3242687; e-mail nelvis.qekema@dst.gov.za; internet www.dst.gov.za.

Ministry of Social Development: HSRC Bldg, North Wing, 134 Pretorius St, Pretoria 0002; Private Bag X901, Pretoria 0001; tel. (12) 3127500; fax (12) 3122502; e-mail lakelak@dsd.gov.za; internet www.dsd.gov.za.

Ministry of Sport and Recreation: cnr Vermeulen and Queen Sts, 66 Queen St, Pretoria; Private Bag X896, Pretoria 0001; tel. (12) 3045000; fax (12) 3230795; e-mail stofile@srsa.gov.za; internet www.srsa.gov.za.

Ministry of State Security: Bogare Bldg, 2 Atterbury Rd, Menlyn, Pretoria; POB 1037, Menlyn 0077; tel. (12) 3670700; fax (12) 3670749; e-mail lornad@mweb.co.za; internet www.intelligence.gov.za.

Ministry of Tourism: Fedsure Forum Bldg, North Tower, 1st and 2nd Floors, 315 Pretorius St, cnr Pretorius and van der Walt Sts, Pretoria 0001; Private Bag X424, Pretoria 0001; tel. (12) 3103611; fax (12) 3220082; internet www.tourism.gov.za.

Ministry of Trade and Industry: 77 Meintjies St, Sunnyside, Pretoria 0002; Private Bag X84, Pretoria 0001; tel. (12) 3949500; fax (12) 3949501; e-mail contactus@thedti.gov.za; internet www.thedti.gov.za.

Ministry of Transport: Forum Bldg, 159 Struben St, Pretoria 0002; Private Bag X193, Pretoria 0001; tel. (12) 3093000; fax (12) 3283194; e-mail khozac@dot.gov.za; internet www.transport.gov.za.

Ministry of Water and Environmental Affairs: Sedibeng Bldg, 10th Floor, 185 Schoeman St, Pretoria 0002; Private Bag X313, Pretoria 0001; tel. (12) 3368733; fax (12) 3367817; e-mail pagel@dwaf.gov.za; internet www.dwaf.gov.za.

Ministry of Women, Youth, Children and People with Disabilities: Union Buildings, Room 290A, Government Ave, Pretoria; Private Bag X1000, Pretoria 0001; tel. (12) 3005575; e-mail tseleng@po.gov.za.

National Treasury: 40 Church Sq., Pretoria 0002; Private Bag X115, Pretoria 0001; tel. (12) 3155372; fax (12) 3233262; e-mail dumisa.jele@treasury.gov.za; internet www.treasury.gov.za.

Legislature

PARLIAMENT

National Council of Provinces

Chairman: MNINWA JOHANNES MAHLANGU.

The National Council of Provinces (NCOP), which replaced the Senate under the new Constitution, was inaugurated on 6 February 1997. The NCOP comprises 90 members, with six permanent delegates and four special delegates from each of the nine provinces.

National Assembly

Speaker: MAX VUYISILE SISULU.

General Election, 22 April 2009

Party	Votes	% of votes	Seats
African National Congress	11,650,748	65.90	264
Democratic Alliance	2,945,829	16.66	67
Congress of the People	1,311,027	7.42	30
Inkatha Freedom Party	804,260	4.55	18
Independent Democrats	162,915	0.92	4
United Democratic Movement	149,680	0.85	4
Vryheidsfront Plus	146,796	0.83	4
African Christian Democratic Party	142,658	0.81	3
United Christian Democratic Party	66,086	0.37	2
Pan-Africanist Congress of Azania	48,530	0.27	1
Minority Front	43,474	0.25	1
Azanian People's Organization	38,245	0.22	1
African People's Convention	35,867	0.20	1
Others	134,614	0.76	—
Total	17,680,729	100.00	400

Provincial Governments

(September 2012)

EASTERN CAPE

Premier: NOXOLO KIVIET (ANC).

Speaker of the Legislature: FIKILE XASA (ANC).

FREE STATE

Premier: ACE MAGASHULE (ANC).

Speaker of the Legislature: MOEKETSI SESELE (ANC).

GAUTENG

Premier: NOMVULA PAULA MOKONYANE (ANC).

Speaker of the Legislature: LINDIWE MASEKO (ANC).

KWAZULU/NATAL

Premier: DR ZWELI LAWRENCE MKHIZE (ANC).

Speaker of the Legislature: NELISWA PEGGY NKONYENI (ANC).

LIMPOPO

Premier: CASSEL MATHALE (ANC).

Speaker of the Legislature: RUDOPH PHALA (ANC).

MPUMALANGA

Premier: DAVID D. MABUZA (ANC).

Speaker of the Legislature: JACKSON MTHEMBU (ANC).

NORTHERN CAPE

Premier: HAZEL JENKINS (ANC).

Speaker of the Legislature: GHOOLAM ACHARWARAY (ANC).

NORTH-WEST

Premier: THANDI MODISE (ANC).

Speaker of the Legislature: NONO DUMILE MALOY (ANC).

WESTERN CAPE

Premier: HELEN ZILLE (DA).

Speaker of the Legislature: SHAHID ESAU (DA).

Election Commission

Electoral Commission of South Africa (IEC): Election House, Riverside Office Park, 1303 Heuwel Ave, Centurion, Pretoria; tel. (12) 6225700; fax (12) 6225863; e-mail iec@elections.org.za; internet www.elections.org.za; f. 1996; Chair. PANSY TLAKULA.

Political Organizations

A total of 26 parties contested the elections to the National Assembly in April 2009, while 38 parties presented candidates in the concurrent provincial elections.

African Christian Democratic Party (ACDP): Stats Building, 1st Floor, 2 Fore St, POB 1677, Alberton; tel. (11) 8693941; fax (86) 6564411; e-mail office@acdp.org.za; internet www.acdp.org.za; f. 1993; Leader Rev. KENNETH MESHOE.

African National Congress of South Africa (ANC): 54 Sauer St, Johannesburg 2001; POB 61884, Marshalltown 2107; tel. (11) 3761000; fax (11) 3761100; e-mail nmtyelwa@anc.org.za; internet www.anc.org.za; f. 1912; in alliance with the South African Communist Party (SACP) and the Congress of South African Trade Unions (COSATU); governing party since April 1994; Pres. JACOB ZUMA; Deputy Pres. KGALEMA MOTLANTHE; Sec.-Gen. GWEDE MANTASHE.

African People's Convention (APC): Dr Neil Aggett House, 4th Floor, 90 President St, between Kruis and Small Sts, Johannesburg 2001; tel. (11) 4985535; fax (11) 4985938; e-mail mmazibuko@gpl.gov.za; internet www.theapc.org.za; f. 2008; Pres. THEMBA GODI; Sec.-Gen. HLABIRWA R. D. MATHUME.

Afrikaner Weerstandsbeweging (AWB) (Afrikaner Resistance Movement): POB 274, Ventersdorp 2710, Johannesburg; tel. and fax (18) 2642516; e-mail awb@awb.co.za; internet www.awb.co.za; f. 1973; Afrikaner (Boer) nationalist group seeking self-determination for the Afrikaner people in South Africa; Leader STEYN VAN RONGE.

Al Jama-ah: The Business Hub, 1A Forest Pl., Pinelands, Cape Town 7405; tel. (21) 5314273; internet www.aljama.co.za; Muslim party; Leader MOGAMAD GANIEF EBRAHIM HENDRICKS.

Azanian People's Organization (AZAPO): 141 Commissioner St, Kine Centre, 19th Floor, Johannesburg 2001; POB 4230, Johannesburg 2000; tel. (11) 3316430; fax (11) 3316433; e-mail azapo@mail.ngo.za; internet www.azapo.org.za; f. 1978; to seek the establishment of a unitary, democratic, socialist republic; excludes white mems; Pres. JACOB DIKOBO; Nat. Chair. ZITHULELE NYANGANA ABSALOM CINDI.

Boerestaat Party (Boer State Party): POB 4995, Luipaardsvlei 1743; tel. (11) 7623841; fax (11) 7623842; e-mail info@boerestaatparty.co.za; internet www.boerestaatparty.co.za; f. 1988; seeks the reinstatement of the Boer Republics in a consolidated Boerestaat; Leader COEN VERMAAK.

Christian Democratic Alliance (CDA): Cape Town; tel. (21) 4033518; fax (21) 4033518; e-mail national.office@cda.org.za; internet www.cda.org.za; f. 2008; Leader LOUIS MICHAEL GREEN; Sec.-Gen. KEVIN SOUTHGATE.

Congress of the People (COPE): Braampark, 1st Floor, Forum II, 33 Hoofd St, Braamfontein, Johannesburg 2000; tel. (11) 3396060; fax (11) 3396064; e-mail info@congressofthepeople.org.za; internet www.congressofthepeople.org.za; f. 2008 following split in the ANC; Pres. MOSIUOA LEKOTA.

Democratic Alliance (DA): POB 1475, Cape Town 8000; Theba Hosken House, 2nd Floor, cnr Breda and Mill Sts, Gardens, Cape Town; tel. (21) 4651431; fax (21) 4615559; e-mail info@da.org.za; internet www.da.org.za; f. 2000 by opposition parties, incl. the Democratic Party, the Federal Alliance and the New National Party (NNP), to contest that year's municipal elections; NNP withdrew in late 2001; Leader HELEN ZILLE; Chair. JOE SEREMANE.

Herstigte Nasionale Party (HNP): 199 Neethling St, Eloffsdal, POB 1888, Pretoria 0001; tel. (12) 3358523; fax (12) 3358518; e-mail info@hnp.org.za; internet www.hnp.org.za; f. 1969 by fmr mems of the National Party; advocates 'Christian Nationalism'; Leader ANDRIES BREYTENBACH; Gen. Sec. LOUIS J. VAN DER SCHYFF.

Independent Democrats (ID): Rm 28, Marks Bldg, Parliament Plein St, POB 751, Cape Town 8000; tel. (21) 4038696; fax (21) 4032350; e-mail id@id.org.za; internet www.id.org.za; f. 2003; announced intention in 2010 to merge with the Democratic Alliance by the 2014 legislative elections; Pres. PATRICIA DE LILLE; Chair. MERVYN CIROTA.

Inkatha Freedom Party (IFP): 2 Durban Club Pl., Durban, 4000; POB 4432, Durban 4000; tel. (31) 3651300; fax (31) 3074964; e-mail ifpinfo@iafrica.com; internet www.ifp.org.za; f. 1975 as Inkatha National Cultural Liberation Movement with mainly Zulu support; reorg. in 1990 as a multiracial political party; Pres. Chief MANGOSUTHU GATSHA BUTHELEZI; breakaway faction entitled the National Freedom Party was established under the leadership of Zanele Magwaza-Msibi in Jan. 2011.

Minority Front: 330 Florence Nightingale Dr., Westcliff, Chatsworth; tel. (31) 4033360; fax (31) 4033354; e-mail office@mf.org.za; internet www.mf.org.za; f. 1993; Indian support; Leader SHAMEEN THAKUR.

National Democratic Convention (NADECO): 1615 Commercial City, 40 Commercial Rd, Durban 4001; tel. (31) 3042098; fax (31) 3042944; e-mail mbathah@nadeco.org; internet www.nadeco.org; f. 2005; Pres. Rev. HAWU MBATHA; Chair. THEMBA MBUTHO.

Pan-Africanist Congress of Azania (PAC): 10th Floor, Renaissance House, 16–22 New St, Ghandi Sq., Johannesburg; POB 6010, Johannesburg 2000; tel. (11) 8389380; fax (11) 8389384; e-mail pacazania@telkomsa.net; internet www.panafricanperspective

.com/pac/index.html; f. 1959; Pres. Dr MOTSOKO PHEKO; Nat. Exec. Sec. MFANELO SKWATSHA.

Progressive Independent Party (PIP): Indian support; Leader FAIZ KHAN.

South African Communist Party (SACP): Cosatu House, 3rd Floor, 1 Leyds St, Braamfontein; POB 1027, Johannesburg 2000; tel. (11) 3393633; fax (11) 3396880; e-mail info@sacp.org.za; internet www.sacp.org.za; f. 1921; reorg. 1953; supports the ANC; Chair. GWEDE MANTASHE; Gen. Sec. BLADE NZIMANDE.

United Christian Democratic Party (UCDP): POB 3010, Mmabatho; tel. (18) 3815691; fax (18) 3817346; e-mail ucdpheadoff@ucdp.org.za; internet www.ucdp.org.za; f. 1972 as the Bophuthatswana Nat. Party; name changed to Bophuthatswana Dem. Party in 1974; present name adopted in 1991; multiracial; Pres. ISAAC SIPHO MFUNDISI; Sec.-Gen. J. B. S. MOLABI; Nat. Chair. IPUSENG CELIA DITSHETELO.

United Democratic Movement (UDM): Tomkor Bldg, 2nd Floor, cnr Vermeulen and Du Toit Sts, Pretoria; POB 26290, Arcadia 0007; tel. (12) 3210010; fax (12) 3210014; e-mail info@udm.org.za; internet www.udm.org.za; f. 1997; multiracial support; demands effective measures for enforcement of law and order; Pres. BANTU HOLOMISA; Sec.-Gen. BONGANI MSOMI.

Vryheidsfront Plus (Freedom Front Plus—VF Plus/FF Plus): Blok 8, Highveld Office Park, Highveld, Centurion Pretoria; POB 67391, Highveld, 0169; tel. (12) 6650564; fax (12) 6652420; e-mail info@vf.co.za; internet www.vryheidsfront.co.za; f. 1994 as Freedom Front; name changed after incorporating the Conservative Party and Afrikaner Eenheidsbeweging in Sept. 2003; right-wing electoral alliance; Leader Dr PIETER W. A. MULDER; Chair. PIETER GROENEWALD.

Diplomatic Representation

EMBASSIES AND HIGH COMMISSIONS IN SOUTH AFRICA

Algeria: 950 Arcadia St, Hatfield, Pretoria 0083; POB 57480, Arcadia 0007; tel. (12) 3425074; fax (12) 3426479; Ambassador MOHAMED LAMINE LAABAS.

Angola: 1030 Schoeman St, Hatfield, Pretoria 0083; POB 8685, Pretoria 0001; tel. (12) 3420049; fax (12) 3427039; Ambassador MIGUEL GASPAR FERNANDES NETO.

Argentina: 200 Standard Plaza, 440 Hilda St, Hatfield, Pretoria 0083; POB 11125, Pretoria 0028; tel. (12) 4303524; fax (12) 4303521; e-mail argembas@global.co.za; Ambassador CARLOS SERSALE DI CERISANO.

Australia: 292 Orient St, Arcadia, Pretoria 0083; Private Bag X150, Pretoria 0001; tel. (12) 4236000; fax (12) 3428442; e-mail pretoria.info@dfat.gov.au; internet www.southafrica.embassy.gov.au; High Commissioner ANN JACQUELINE HARRAP.

Austria: Momentum Office Park, 1109 Duncan St, Brooklyn, Pretoria 0181; POB 95572, Waterkloof 0145; tel. (12) 4529155; fax (12) 4601151; e-mail pretoria-ob@bmeia.gv.at; internet www.bmeia.gv.at/pretoria; Ambassador Dr OTTO DITZ.

Azerbaijan: POB 56014, Hatfield 0083; tel. 721412755 (mobile); fax 724429094 (mobile); Ambassador ELKHAN POLUKHOV.

Bangladesh: 410 Farenden St, Sunnyside, Pretoria 0002; tel. (12) 3432105; fax (12) 3435222; e-mail bangladeshpta@iburst.co.za; High Commissioner MUHAMMAD TOUHID HOSSAIN.

Belarus: 327 Hill St, Arcadia, Pretoria 0083; POB 4107, Pretoria 0001; tel. (12) 4307709; fax (12) 3426280; e-mail rsa@mfa.gov.by; internet www.rsa.mfa.gov.by; Ambassador ANDREI MOLCHAN.

Belgium: 625 Leyds St, Muckleneuk, Pretoria 0002; tel. (12) 4403201; fax (12) 4403216; e-mail pretoria@diplobel.fed.be; internet www.diplomatie.be/pretoria; Ambassador JOHAN MARICOU.

Benin: 900 Park St, cnr Orient and Park Sts, Arcadia, Pretoria 0083; POB 26484, Arcadia 0007; tel. (12) 3426978; fax (12) 3421823; e-mail pretoria@embbeninsa.org.za; internet www.maebenin.bj/Pretoria.htm; Ambassador CLAUDE RUBEN FASSINOU.

Botswana: 24 Amos St, Colbyn, Pretoria 0083; POB 57035, Arcadia 0007; tel. (12) 4309640; fax (12) 3421845; High Commissioner MOTLHAGODI MOLOMO.

Brazil: Hillcrest Office Park, Woodpecker Pl., 1st Floor, 177 Dyer Rd, Hillcrest, Pretoria 0083; POB 3269, Pretoria 0001; tel. (12) 3665200; fax (12) 3665299; e-mail pretoria@brazilianembassy.org.za; internet www.brazilianembassy.org.za; Ambassador PEDRO LUIZ CARNEIRO DE MENDONÇA.

Bulgaria: 1071 Church St, Hatfield, Pretoria 0083; POB 29296, Arcadia 0007; tel. (12) 3423720; fax (12) 3423721; e-mail embulgsa@iafrica.com; internet www.bulgarianembassy.co.za; Ambassador VOLODYA CHANEV NEYKOV.

Burundi: 20 Glyn St, Colbyn, Pretoria 0083; POB 12914, Hatfield 0028; tel. (12) 3424881; fax (12) 3424885; Ambassador REGINE RWAMIBANGO.

Cameroon: 800 Duncan St, Brooklyn, Pretoria 0075; POB 13790, Hatfield 0028; tel. (12) 3624731; fax (12) 3624732; e-mail hicocam@cameroon.co.za; High Commissioner ADRIEN KOUAMBO JOMAGUE.

Canada: 1103 Arcadia St, cnr Hilda St, Hatfield, Pretoria 0083; Private Bag X13, Hatfield 0028; tel. (12) 4223000; fax (12) 4223052; e-mail pret@international.gc.ca; internet www.dfait-maeci.gc.ca/southafrica/menu-en.asp; High Commissioner ADÈLE DION.

Chile: Delmondo Office Park, 169 Garsfontein Rd, Ashlea Gardens, Pretoria 0081; POB 2449, Brooklyn Sq. 0075; tel. (12) 4608090; fax (12) 4608093; e-mail chile@iafrica.com; internet www.embchile.co.za; Ambassador FRANCISCO JAVIER MARAMBIO.

China, People's Republic: 965 Church St, Arcadia, Pretoria 0083; POB 95764, Waterkloof 0145; tel. (12) 4316500; fax (12) 3424244; e-mail reception@chinese-embassy.org.za; internet www.chinese-embassy.org.za; Ambassador ZHONG JIANHUA.

Colombia: Park Corner Bldg, 3rd Floor, 1105 Park St, Hatfield, Pretoria 0083; POB 12791, Hatfield 0028; tel. (12) 3420211; fax (12) 3420216; e-mail info@embassyofcolombia.co.za; Ambassador EDGAR JOSÉ PEREA-ARIAS.

Comoros: 817 Thomas St, cnr Church and Eastwood Sts, Arcadia, Pretoria 0083; tel. (12) 3439483; fax (12) 3420138; Ambassador AHMED MOHAMED THABIT.

Congo, Democratic Republic: 791 Schoeman St, Arcadia, Pretoria 0083; POB 28795, Sunnyside 0132; tel. (12) 3446475; fax (12) 3444054; e-mail rdcongo@lantic.net; Ambassador BENE M'POKO.

Congo, Republic: 960 Arcadia St, Arcadia, Pretoria 0083; POB 40427, Arcadia 0007; tel. (12) 3425508; fax (12) 3425510; Ambassador ROGER ISSOMBO.

Côte d'Ivoire: 795 Government Ave, Arcadia, Pretoria 0083; POB 13510, Hatfield 0028; tel. (12) 3426913; fax (12) 3426713; Chargé d'affaires a.i. MICHEL A. KODJO.

Croatia: 1160 Church St, Colbyn, Pretoria 0083; POB 11335, Hatfield 0028; tel. (12) 3421206; fax (12) 3421819; internet za.mfa.hr; Ambassador IVAN PICUKARIĆ.

Cuba: 45 Mackenzie St, Brooklyn, Pretoria 0181; POB 11605, Hatfield 0028; tel. (12) 3462215; fax (12) 3462216; e-mail sudafri@iafrica.com; internet emba.cubaminrex.cu/sudafricaing; Ambassador ANGEL VILLA HERNÁNDEZ.

Cyprus: cnr Church St and Hill St, Arcadia, Pretoria 0083; POB 14554, Hatfield 0028; tel. (12) 3425258; fax (12) 3425596; e-mail cyprusjb@mweb.co.za; High Commissioner ARGYROS ANTONIOU.

Czech Republic: 936 Pretorius St, Arcadia, Pretoria 0083; POB 13671, Hatfield 0028; tel. (12) 4312380; fax (12) 4302033; e-mail pretoria@embassymzv.cz; internet www.mzv.cz/pretoria; Ambassador MARTIN POHL.

Denmark: iParioli Office Park, Block B2, Ground Floor, 1166 Park St, Hatfield, Pretoria; POB 11439, Hatfield 0028; tel. (12) 4309340; fax (12) 3427620; e-mail pryamb@um.dk; internet www.ambpretoria.um.dk; Ambassador DAN E. FREDERIKSEN.

Dominican Republic: 276 Anderson St., Brooklyn, Pretoria 0181; tel. (12) 3602463; fax (12) 5679613; e-mail dominicanembassy@gmail.com; Ambassador RAÚL FERNANDO BARRIENTOS-LARA.

Ecuador: Suite 3, 36 Selati St, Selati Park, Alphen Park, Pretoria; tel. (12) 3461662; fax (12) 3467082; e-mail eecusudafrica@mmrree.gov.ec; Ambassador Dr JOSÉ VALENCIA.

Egypt: 270 Bourke St, Muckleneuk, Pretoria 0002; POB 30025, Sunnyside 0132; tel. (12) 3431590; fax (12) 3431082; e-mail egyptemb@global.co.za; Ambassador MOHAMED BADR ELDIN MOSTAFA ZAYED.

Equatorial Guinea: 48 Florence St, Colbyn, Pretoria; POB 12720, Hatfield 0028; tel. (12) 3429945; fax (12) 3427250; Ambassador F. EDU NGUA.

Eritrea: 1281 Cobham Rd, Queenswood, Pretoria 0186; POB 11371, Queenswood 0121; tel. (12) 3331302; fax (12) 3332330; Ambassador SALIH OMAR ABDU.

Ethiopia: 47 Charles St, Bailey's Muckleneuk, Brooklyn 0181; POB 11469, Hatfield 0028; tel. (12) 3463542; fax (12) 3463867; e-mail ethiopia@sentechsa.com; Ambassador Dr YESHIMEBRAT MERSHA.

Fiji: Pretoria; High Commissioner BEN SALACAKAU.

Finland: 628 Leyds St, Muckleneuk, Pretoria 0002; POB 443, Pretoria 0001; tel. (12) 3430275; fax (12) 3433095; e-mail sanomat.pre@formin.fi; internet www.finland.org.za; Ambassador PETRI SALO.

France: 250 Melk St, cnr Melk and Middle Sts, New Muckleneuk, Pretoria 0181; tel. (12) 4251600; fax (12) 4251689; e-mail france@ambafrance-rsa.org; internet www.ambafrance-rsa.org; Ambassador JACQUES LAPOUGE.

Gabon: 921 Schoeman St, Arcadia, Pretoria 0083; POB 9222, Pretoria 0001; tel. (12) 3424376; fax (12) 3424375; Ambassador SANNI AOUDOU AÏCHATOU.

Germany: 180 Blackwood St, Arcadia, Pretoria 0083; POB 2023, Pretoria 0001; tel. (12) 4278900; fax (12) 3433606; e-mail GermanEmbassyPretoria@gonet.co.za; internet www.pretoria.diplo.de; Ambassador HORST FREITAG.

Ghana: 1038 Arcadia St, Hatfield, Pretoria 0083; POB 12537, Hatfield 0028; tel. (12) 3425847; fax (12) 3425863; Chargé d'affaires a.i. S. J. K. PARKER-ALLOTEY.

Greece: Hadefields Office Park, 1st Floor, 1267 Church St, Block G, Hatfield, Pretoria 0001; tel. (12) 3427136; e-mail gremb.pre@mfa.gr; internet www.mfa.gr/pretoria; Ambassador SPYRIDON THEOCHAROPOULOS.

Guinea: 336 Orient St, Arcadia, Pretoria 0083; POB 13523, Hatfield 0028; tel. and fax (12) 3427348; e-mail embaguinea@iafrica.com; Ambassador GAOUSSOU TOURÉ.

Haiti: 808 George St, Arcadia, Pretoria 0007; POB 14362, Hatfield 0028; tel. (12) 4307560; fax (12) 3427042; Ambassador YOLETTE AZOR-CHARLES.

Holy See: Argo St, Waterkloof Ridge, Pretoria 0181; POB 95200, Waterkloof 0145; tel. (12) 3464235; fax (12) 3461494; e-mail nunziosa@iafrica.com; Apostolic Nuncio Most Rev. MARIO ROBERTO CASSARI (Titular Archbishop of Truentum).

Hungary: 959 Arcadia St, Hatfield, Pretoria 0083; POB 13843, Hatfield 0028; tel. (12) 4303030; fax (12) 4303029; e-mail mission.prt@mfa.gov.hu; internet www.mfa.gov.hu/emb/pretoria; Ambassador BELA LASZLO.

India: 852 Schoeman St, Arcadia, Pretoria 0083; POB 40216, Arcadia 0007; tel. (12) 3425392; fax (12) 3425310; e-mail polinf@hicomind.co.za; internet www.indiainsouthafrica.com; High Commissioner VIRENDRA GUPTA.

Indonesia: 949 Schoeman St, Arcadia, Pretoria 0082; POB 13155, Hatfield, Pretoria 0028; tel. (12) 3423350; fax (12) 3423369; e-mail fpanggabean@indonesia-pretoria.org.za; internet www.indonesia-pretoria.org.za; f. 1995; Ambassador SJAHRIL SABARUDDIN.

Iran: 1002 Schoeman St, Hatfield, Pretoria 0083; POB 12546, Hatfield 0083; tel. (12) 3425880; fax (12) 3421878; e-mail office@iranembassy.org.za; internet www.iranembassy.org.za; Ambassador ASGHAR EBRAHIMI ASL.

Iraq: 803 Duncan St, Brooklyn, Pretoria 0181; POB 11089, Hatfield 0028; tel. (12) 3622048; fax (12) 3622027; Ambassador Dr HISHAM ALI AKBAR IBRAHIM AL-ALAWI.

Ireland: Southern Life Plaza, 1st Floor, 1059 Schoeman St, cnr Festival and Schoeman Sts, Arcadia, Pretoria 0083; POB 4174, Arcadia 0001; tel. (12) 3425062; fax (12) 3424752; e-mail pretoria@dfa.ie; internet www.embassyireland.org.za; Ambassador BRENDAN MCMAHON.

Israel: 428 King's Hwy, Elizabeth Grove St, Lynnwood, Pretoria; Private Bag X50, Menlo Park 0102; tel. (12) 4703500; fax (12) 4703555; e-mail publicaffairs@pretoria.mfa.gov.il; internet pretoria.mfa.gov.il; Ambassador DOV SEGEV-STEINBERG.

Italy: 796 George Ave, Arcadia, Pretoria 0083; tel. (12) 4230001; fax (12) 4305547; e-mail segreteria.pretoria@esteri.it; internet www.ambpretoria.esteri.it; Ambassador ELIO MENZIONE.

Jamaica: 1119 Burnett St, Hatfield, Pretoria 0083; tel. (12) 3626667; fax (12) 3668510; e-mail jhcpretoria@telkomsa.net; High Commissioner NORMA TAYLOR-ROBERTS.

Japan: 259 Baines St, cnr Frans Oerder St, Groenkloof, Pretoria 0181; Private Bag X999, Pretoria 0001; tel. (12) 4521500; fax (12) 4603800; e-mail info@embjapan.org.za; internet www.japan.org.za; Ambassador TOSHIRO OZAWA.

Jordan: 252 Olivier St, Brooklyn, Pretoria 0075; POB 14730, Hatfield 0028; tel. (12) 3468615; fax (12) 3468611; e-mail embjordpta@telkomsa.net; Ambassador O. J. NADIF.

Kenya: 302 Brooks St, Menlo Park, Pretoria 0081; POB 35954, Menlo Park 0012; tel. (12) 3622249; fax (12) 3622252; e-mail info@kenya.org.za; internet www.kenya.org.za; High Commissioner THOMAS AMOLO.

Korea, Democratic People's Republic: 958 Waterpoort St, Faerie Glen, Pretoria; POB 1238, Garsfontein 0042; tel. (12) 9918661; fax (12) 9918662; e-mail dprkembassy@lantic.net; Ambassador JO YONG MAN.

Korea, Republic: Greenpark Estates, Bldg 3, 27 George Storrar Dr., Groenkloof, Pretoria 0081; POB 939, Groenkloof 0027; tel. (12) 4602508; fax (12) 4601158; e-mail embsa@mofat.go.kr; internet zaf.mofat.go.kr; Ambassador YOON LEE.

Kuwait: 890 Arcadia St, Arcadia, Pretoria 0083; Private Bag X920, Pretoria 0001; tel. (12) 3420877; fax (12) 3420876; e-mail safarku@global.co.za; Ambassador HASSAN BADER KAREEM AL-OQAB.

Lebanon: 788 Government St, Pretoria; POB 941, Groenkloof 0027; tel. (12) 4302130; fax (12) 4302238; e-mail embassyoflebanon@telkomsa.net; Ambassador MICHEL THOMAS KATRA.

Lesotho: 391 Anderson St, Menlo Park, Pretoria 0081; POB 55817, Arcadia 0007; tel. (12) 4607648; fax (12) 4607469; High Commissioner LINEO LYDIA KHECHANE-NTOANE.

Liberia: Suite 9 Section 7, Schoeman St Forum, 1157 Schoeman St, Hatfield, Pretoria; POB 14082, Hatfield, Pretoria; tel. (12) 3422734; fax (12) 3422737; e-mail libempta@pta.lia.net; Chargé d'affaires a.i. BEN SIE-TOE COLLINS.

Libya: 900 Church St, Arcadia, Pretoria 0083; POB 40388, Arcadia 0007; tel. (12) 3423902; fax (12) 3423904; e-mail libyasa@telkomsa.net; Ambassador (vacant).

Madagascar: 90B Tait St, Colbyn, Pretoria; POB 11722, Queenswood 0120; tel. (12) 3420983; fax (12) 3420995; e-mail consul@infodoor.co.za; Ambassador DENIS ANDRIAMANDROSO.

Malawi: 770 Government Ave, Arcadia, Pretoria 0083; POB 11172, Hatfield 0028; tel. and fax (12) 3421759; fax (12) 3420147; e-mail highcommalai@telkomsa.net; High Commissioner (vacant).

Malaysia: 1007 Schoeman St, Arcadia, Pretoria 0083; POB 11673, Hatfield 0028; tel. (12) 3425990; fax (12) 4307773; internet www.kln.gov.my/web/zaf_pretoria; High Commissioner M. KENNEDY JAWAN.

Mali: 876 Pretorius St, Arcadia 0083; POB 12978, Hatfield, Pretoria 0028; tel. (12) 3427464; fax (12) 3420670; Ambassador BALLADJI DIAKITE.

Mauritania: 146 Anderson St, Brooklyn, Pretoria; tel. (12) 3623578; fax (12) 3623304; e-mail rimambapretoria@webmail.co.za; Ambassador MOHAMED OULD HANNANI.

Mauritius: 1163 Pretorius St, Hatfield, Pretoria 0083; tel. (12) 3421283; fax (12) 3421286; e-mail mhcpta@mweb.co.za; High Commissioner MOHAMED ISMAEL DOSSA.

Mexico: 570 Ferhsen St, Parkdev Bldg, Ground Floor, Brooklyn Bridge, Pretoria 0181; POB 9077, Pretoria 0001; tel. (12) 4601004; fax (12) 4600973; e-mail info@embamexsud.org; internet www.embamexsud.org; Ambassador HÉCTOR HUMBERTO VALEZZI ZAFRA.

Morocco: 799 Schoeman St, cnr Farenden St, Arcadia, Pretoria 0083; POB 12382, Hatfield 0028; tel. (12) 3430230; fax (12) 3430613; e-mail sifmapre@mwebbiz.co.za; Chargé d'affaires DRISS ISBAYENE.

Mozambique: 529 Edmund St, Arcadia, Pretoria 0083; POB 40750, Arcadia 0007; tel. (12) 4010300; fax (12) 3266388; e-mail highcomm@embamoc.co.za; High Commissioner FERNANDO ANDRADE FAZENDA.

Myanmar: 201 Leyds St, Arcadia, Pretoria 0083; POB 12121, Queenswood 0121; tel. (12) 3412557; fax (12) 3412553; e-mail euompta@global.co.za; Ambassador HLAIMGN PHONE MYINT.

Namibia: 197 Blackwood St, Arcadia, Pretoria 0083; POB 29806, Sunnyside 0132; tel. (12) 4819100; fax (12) 3445998; e-mail secretary@namibia.org.za; High Commissioner MARTEN NENKETE KAPEWASHA.

Nepal: 453 Fehersen St, Baileys Muckleneuk, Pretoria; tel. (12) 346 2399; fax (12) 3460521; Ambassador ARUN PRASAD DHITAL.

Netherlands: 210 Queen Wilhelmina Ave, New Muckleneuk 0181, Pretoria; tel. (12) 4254500; fax (12) 4254511; e-mail pre@minbuza.nl; internet www.dutchembassy.co.za; Ambassador ANDRÉ HASPELS.

New Zealand: 125 Middel St, Muckleneuk, Pretoria 0181; Private Bag X25, Brooklyn Sq. 0075; tel. (12) 4359000; fax (12) 4359002; e-mail enquiries@nzhc.co.za; internet www.nzembassy.com/south-africa; High Commissioner RICHARD MANN.

Nigeria: 971 Schoeman St, Arcadia, Pretoria 0083; POB 27332, Sunnyside 0132; tel. (12) 3420805; fax (12) 3421668; High Commissioner Brig.-Gen. (retd) MOHAMMED BUBA MARWA.

Norway: Ozmik House, 165 Lynnwood Rd, Brooklyn 0181, Pretoria; POB 11612, Hatfield 0028; tel. (12) 3643700; fax (12) 3643799; e-mail emb.pretoria@mfa.no; internet www.norway.org.za; Ambassador KARI MAREN BJØRNSGAARD.

Oman: 42 Nicholson St, Muckleneuk, Pretoria 0081; POB 2650, Brooklyn 0075; tel. (12) 3460808; fax (12) 3461660; e-mail sult-oman@telkom.net; Ambassador KHALID BIN SULAIMAN BIN ABDUL RAHMAN BA'OMAR.

Pakistan: 312 Brooks St, Menlo Park, Pretoria 0181; POB 11803, Hatfield 0028; tel. (12) 3624072; fax (12) 3623967; e-mail pareppretoria@worldonline.co.za; High Commissioner ZAIGHAMUDDIN AZAM.

Panama: 229 Olivier St, Brooklyn, Pretoria; tel. (12) 4606677; fax (12) 3465474; e-mail panamaembassy@bodamail.co.za; Ambassador RODRIGO GUILLERMO CHIARI.

Paraguay: 189 Strelitzia Rd, Waterkloof Heights, Pretoria 0181; POB 95774, Waterkloof 0145; tel. (12) 3471047; fax (12) 3470403; e-mail embaparsudafrica@mre.gov.py; Ambassador JOSÉ MARTÍNEZ LEZCANO.

Peru: 200 Saint Patrick St, Muckleneuk Hill, Pretoria 0083; POB 907, Groenkloof 0027; tel. (12) 4401030; fax (12) 4401054; e-mail embaperu2@telkomsa.net; internet www.embassyofperu.co.za; Ambassador DAÚL MATUTE-MEJÍA.

Philippines: 54 Nicholson St, Muckleneuk, Pretoria 0181; POB 2562, Brooklyn Sq. 0075; tel. (12) 3460451; fax (12) 3460454; e-mail pretoriape@mweb.co.za; internet www.pretoriape.org; Ambassador CONSTANCIO R. VINGNO, Jr.

Poland: 14 Amos St, Colbyn, Pretoria 0083; POB 12277, Queenswood 0121; tel. (12) 4302631; fax (12) 4302608; e-mail amb.pol@pixie.co.za; internet www.pretoria.polemb.net; Ambassador MARCIN KUBIAK.

Portugal: 599 Leyds St, Muckleneuk, Pretoria 0002; POB 27102, Sunnyside 0132; tel. (12) 3412340; fax (12) 3413975; e-mail portemb@global.co.za; Ambassador GABRIELA SOARES DE ALBERGARIA.

Qatar: 355 Charles St, Waterkloof, Pretoria 0181; Private Bag X13, Brooklyn Sq. 0075; tel. (12) 4521700; fax (12) 3466732; e-mail qatar-emb@lantic.net; Ambassador Dr BASHIR ISSA AL-SHIRAWI.

Romania: 117 Charles St, Brooklyn, Pretoria 0181; POB 11295, Hatfield 0028; tel. (12) 4606941; fax (12) 4606947; e-mail pretoria@mae.ro; internet pretoria.mae.ro; Ambassador RADU GABRIEL SAFTA.

Russia: 316 Brooks St, Menlo Park, Pretoria 0081; POB 36034, Pretoria 0102; tel. (12) 3621337; fax (12) 3620116; e-mail ruspospr@mweb.co.za; internet www.russianembassy.org.za; Ambassador MIKHAIL PETRAKOV.

Rwanda: 983 Schoeman St, Arcadia, Pretoria; POB 55224, Arcadia 0007; tel. (12) 3426536; fax (12) 3427106; e-mail ambapretoria@minaffet.gov.rw; internet www.southafrica.embassy.gov.rw; Ambassador VINCENT KAREGA.

Saudi Arabia: 711 Duncan St, cnr Lunnon St, Hatfield, Pretoria 0083; POB 13930, Hatfield 0028; tel. (12) 3624230; fax (12) 3624239; Chargé d'Affaires a.i. ABDULRAHMAN AL-NAJJAR.

Senegal: Charles Manor, 57 Charles St, Baileys Muckleneuk, Pretoria 0181; POB 2948, Brooklyn Sq. 0075; tel. (12) 4605263; fax (12) 3465550; e-mail ambassenepta@telkomsa.za; Ambassador CHEIKH NIANG.

Serbia: 163 Marais St, Brooklyn, Pretoria; POB 13026, Hatfield 0028; tel. (12) 4605626; fax (12) 4606003; e-mail info@srbembassy.org.za; internet www.srbembassy.org.za; Ambassador GORAN VUJIČIĆ.

Singapore: 980 Schoeman St, Arcadia, Pretoria 0083; POB 11809, Hatfield 0028; tel. (12) 4306035; fax (12) 3424425; e-mail sporehc@mweb.co.za; High Commissioner BERNARD WILLIAM BAKER.

Slovakia: 930 Arcadia St, Pretoria 0083; POB 12736, Hatfield 0028; tel. (12) 3422051; fax (12) 3423688; e-mail slovakemb@telkomsa.net; internet www.mfa.sk/zu; Ambassador LADISLAV STRAKA.

Spain: Lord Charles Bldg, 337 Brooklyn Rd, Menlo Park, Pretoria 0181; POB 35353, Pretoria 0001; tel. (12) 4600123; fax (12) 4602290; e-mail emb.pretoria@mae.es; internet www.maec.es/subwebs/Embajadas/Pretoria; Ambassador JUAN IGNACIO SELL SANZ.

Sri Lanka: 410 Alexander St, Brooklyn, Pretoria 0181; tel. (12) 4607690; fax (12) 4607702; e-mail srilanka@global.co.za; internet www.srilanka.co.za; High Commissioner DHARMASENA WIJESINGHE.

Sudan: 1203 Pretorius St, Hatfield, Pretoria 0083; POB 25513, Monument Park 0105; tel. (12) 3424538; fax (12) 3424539; internet www.sudani.co.za; Ambassador ALI YOUSIF AHMED.

Suriname: Suite No. 4, Groenkloof Forum Office Park, 57 George Storrar Drive, Groenkloof, 0181 Pretoria; POB 149, Pretoria; tel. (12) 3467627; fax (12) 3460802; e-mail embsur@lantic.net; Ambassador Dr WILFRIED RAMON ROSEVAL.

Swaziland: 715 Government Ave, Arcadia, Pretoria 0007; POB 14294, Hatfield 0028; tel. (12) 3441910; fax (12) 3430455; Ambassador SOLOMON MNUKWA DLAMINI.

Sweden: iParioli Bldg, 1166 Park St, Hatfield 0083; POB 13477, Hatfield 0028; tel. (12) 4266400; fax (12) 4266464; e-mail sweden@iafrica.com; internet www.swedenabroad.com/pretoria; Ambassador PETER TEJLER.

Switzerland: 225 Veale St, Parc Nouveau, New Muckleneuk, Pretoria 0181; POB 2508, Brooklyn Sq. 0075; tel. (12) 4520660; fax (12) 3466605; e-mail pre.vertretung@eda.admin.ch; internet www.eda.admin.ch/pretoria; Ambassador CHRISTIAN MEUWLY.

Syria: 963 Schoeman St, Arcadia, Pretoria 0083; POB 12830, Hatfield 0028; tel. (12) 3424701; fax (12) 3424702; e-mail syriaemb@telkomsa.net; Ambassador BASSAM DARWISH.

Tanzania: 822 George Ave, Arcadia, Pretoria 0007; POB 56572, Arcadia 0007; tel. (12) 3424393; fax (12) 4304383; e-mail thc@tanzania.org.za; internet www.tanzania.org.za; High Commissioner RADHIA NAIMA MTENGETI MSUYA.

Thailand: 428 cnr Hill and Pretorius Sts, Arcadia, Pretoria 0028; POB 12080, Hatfield 0083; tel. (12) 3424600; fax (12) 3424805; e-mail info@thaiembassy.co.za; internet www.thaiembassy.co.za; Ambassador N. BURANASIRI.

Trinidad and Tobago: 258 Lawley St, Waterkloof, 0181 Pretoria; POB 95872, Waterkloof, Pretoria 0145; tel. (12) 4609688; fax (12) 3467302; e-mail tthepretoria@telkomsa.net; High Commissioner HARRY PARTAP.

Tunisia: 850 Church St, Arcadia, Pretoria 0083; POB 56535, Arcadia 0007; tel. (12) 3426282; fax (12) 3426284; Ambassador MOHAMED FADHEL AYARI.

Turkey: 1067 Church St, Hatfield, Pretoria 0083; POB 56014, Arcadia 0007; tel. (12) 3426055; fax (12) 3426052; e-mail pretbe@global.co.za; internet www.turkishembassy.co.za; Ambassador AHMET VAKUR GÖKDERNIZLER.

Uganda: 882 Church St, Pretoria 0083; POB 12442, Hatfield 0083; tel. (12) 3426031; fax (12) 3426206; e-mail ugacomer@mweb.co.za; High Commissioner KWERONDA RUHEMBA.

Ukraine: 398 Marais St, Brooklyn, Pretoria 0181; POB 57291, Menlo Park 0102; tel. (12) 4601943; fax (12) 4601944; e-mail emb_za@mfa.gov.ua; Ambassador VALERY HREBENIUK.

United Arab Emirates: 992 Arcadia St, Arcadia, Pretoria 0083; POB 57090, Arcadia 0007; tel. (12) 3427736; fax (12) 3427738; e-mail uae@mweb.co.za; Ambassador HAMAD HAREB AL-HABSI.

United Kingdom: 255 Hill St, Arcadia, Pretoria 0002; tel. (12) 4217600; fax (12) 4217555; e-mail media.pretoria@fco.gov.uk; internet ukinsouthafrica.fco.gov.uk; High Commissioner Dr NICOLA BREWER.

USA: 877 Pretorius St, Arcadia, Pretoria 0083; POB 9536, Pretoria 0001; tel. (12) 4314000; fax (12) 3422299; e-mail embassypretoria@state.gov; internet southafrica.usembassy.gov; Ambassador DONALD HENRY GIPS.

Uruguay: 301 MIB House, 3rd Floor, Hatfield Sq., 1119 Burnett St, Hatfield, Pretoria 0083; POB 14818, Pretoria 0028; tel. (12) 3626521; fax (12) 3626523; Ambassador LUIS BERMUDEZ ALVAREZ.

Venezuela: Hatfield Gables South Bldg, 1st Floor, Suite 4, 474 Hilda St, Pretoria 0083; POB 11821, Hatfield 0028; tel. (12) 3626593; fax (12) 3626591; e-mail embasudaf@icon.co.za; Ambassador ANTONIO MONTILLA-SALDIVIA.

Viet Nam: 87 Brooks St, Brooklyn, Pretoria 0181; POB 13692, Hatfield 0028; tel. (12) 3628119; fax (12) 3628115; e-mail embassy@vietnam.co.za; Ambassador MANH HUNG NGUYEN.

Yemen: 329 Main St, Waterkloof 0181; POB 13343, Hatfield 0028; tel. (12) 4250760; fax (12) 4250762; e-mail info@yemenembassy.org.za; internet www.yemenembassy.org.za; Chargé d'affaires MOHAMED JAMIL MUHARRAM.

Zambia: 570 Ziervogel St, Arcadia, Pretoria 0083; POB 12234, Hatfield 0028; tel. (12) 3261854; fax (12) 3262140; High Commissioner BIZWAYO NEWTON NKUNIKA.

Zimbabwe: Zimbabwe House, 798 Merton St, Arcadia, Pretoria 0083; POB 55140, Arcadia 0007; tel. (12) 3425125; fax (12) 3425126; e-mail zimpret@lantic.net; Ambassador PHELEKEZELA MPHOKO.

Judicial System

The common law of the Republic of South Africa is the Roman-Dutch law, the uncodified law of Holland as it was at the time of the secession of the Cape of Good Hope in 1806. The law of England is not recognized as authoritative, although the principles of English law have been introduced in relation to civil and criminal procedure, evidence and mercantile matters.

The Constitutional Court, situated in Johannesburg, consists of a Chief Justice, a Deputy Chief Justice and nine other justices. Its task is to ensure that the executive, legislative and judicial organs of government adhere to the provisions of the Constitution. It has the power to reverse legislation that has been adopted by Parliament. The Supreme Court of Appeal, situated in Bloemfontein, comprises a President, a Deputy President and a number of judges of appeal, and is the highest court in all but constitutional matters. There are also High Courts and Magistrates' Courts. A National Director of Public Prosecutions is the head of the prosecuting authority and is appointed by the President of the Republic. A Judicial Service Commission makes recommendations regarding the appointment of judges and advises central and provincial government on all matters relating to the judiciary.

Constitutional Court: cnr Queen and Sam Hancock/Hospital Sts, Constitution Hill, Braamfontein 2017; tel. (11) 3597400; fax (11) 4036524; e-mail cases@concourt.org.za; internet www.constitutionalcourt.org.za; f. 1995; Chief Justice MOGOENG MOGOENG.

Supreme Court of Appeal: cnr Elizabeth and President Brand Sts, Bloemfontein 9301; POB 258, Bloemfontein 9300; tel. (51) 4127437; fax (86) 6445991; e-mail astreet@justice.gov.za; internet www.supremecourtofappeal.gov.za; f. 1910; Pres. LEX MPATI.

Religion

Some 80% of the population profess the Christian faith. Other religions that are represented are Hinduism, Islam, Judaism and traditional African religions.

CHRISTIANITY

At mid-2000 there were an estimated 12.4m. Protestants and 18.7m. adherents of other forms of Christianity.

South African Council of Churches: POB 62098, Marshalltown 2107; tel. (11) 2417800; fax (11) 4921448; internet www.sacc.org.za; f. 1968; 26 mem. churches; Pres. Prof. TINYIKO MALULEKE; Gen. Sec. EDDIE MAKUE.

The Anglican Communion

Most Anglicans in South Africa are adherents of the Anglican Church of Southern Africa (formerly the Church of the Province of Southern Africa), comprising 25 dioceses (including Angola, Lesotho, Namibia, St Helena, Swaziland and two dioceses in Mozambique). The Church had an estimated 4.5m. communicant members at mid-2006.

Archbishop of Cape Town and Metropolitan of the Province of Southern Africa: Most Rev. THABO CECIL MAKGOBA, 20 Bishopscourt Dr., Bishopscourt, Claremont, Cape Town 7700; tel. (21) 7612531; fax (21) 7614193; e-mail archbish@bishopscourt-cpsa.org.za; internet www.anglicanchurchsa.org.

The Dutch Reformed Church (Nederduitse Gereformeerde Kerk—NGK)

In 2005/06, including confirmed and baptized members, the Dutch Reformed Churches in South Africa consisted of: the Dutch Reformed Church, with 1,155,001 (mainly white) members; the Uniting Reformed Church, with 1,039,606 (mainly Coloured and black) members; the Reformed Church in Africa, with 1,708 Indian members; and the Dutch Reformed Church in Africa, with an estimated 150,000 (mainly black) members. All congregations were desegregated in 1986.

General Synod: POB 13528, Hatfield, Pretoria 0028; tel. (12) 3420092; fax (12) 3420370; e-mail algemenesinode@ngkerk.org.za; internet www.ngkerk.org.za; Moderator Prof. NELUS NIEMANDT; Gen. Sec. Dr KOBUS GERBER.

The Lutheran Churches

Lutheran Communion in Southern Africa (LUCSA): 24 Geldenhuys Rd, POB 7170, Bonaero Park 1619; tel. (11) 9731086; fax (11) 3951615; e-mail info@lucsa.org; internet www.lucsa.org; f. 1991; co-ordinating org. for the Lutheran churches in southern Africa, incl. Angola, Botswana, Malawi, Mozambique, Namibia, South Africa, Swaziland, Zambia and Zimbabwe; 1,618,720 mems (1999); Exec. Dir Bishop J. M. RAMASHAPA.

Evangelical Lutheran Church in Southern Africa (ELCSA): POB 7231, 1622 Bonaero Park; tel. (11) 977137; fax (86) 5026891; e-mail elcsaadmin@mweb.co.za; f. 1975 by merger of four non-white churches; seven dioceses, each headed by a bishop; Presiding Bishop Rt Rev. LOUIS SIBIYA; 615,000 mems (2011).

Evangelical Lutheran Church in Southern Africa (Cape Church): POB 3466, 7602 Matieland; tel. (21) 8869747; fax (21) 8869748; e-mail rohwernj@afrihost.co.za; Pres. Bishop NILS ROHWER; 4,347 mems (2010).

Evangelical Lutheran Church in Southern Africa (N-T): Church Council, 24 Geldenhuys Rd, Bonaero Park, Johannesburg; POB 7095, Bonaero Park 1622; tel. (11) 979 7137; fax (86) 5026891; e-mail bishop@elcsant.org.za; internet www.elcsant.org.za; f. 1981; Pres. Bishop HORST MUELLER; 9,855 mems (2011).

Free Evangelical Lutheran Synod in South Africa: POB 21559, Mayors Walk 3208; 15 Greenwood Rd, Boughton, Pietermaritzburg; tel. (33) 3443238; e-mail felsisamail@gmail.com; internet www.felsisa.org.za; Bishop of the Synodical Council Dr DIETER REINSTORF.

Lutheran Church in Southern Africa: POB 117, 1851 Meadowlands, Soweto; tel. (11) 9888227; fax (11) 9890762; e-mail tswaedi@gmail.com; Bishop DAVID P. TSWAEDI; 20,000 mems (2010).

Moravian Church in Southern Africa: 63 Albert Rd, POB 24111, Lansdowne 7779; tel. (21) 7614030; fax (21) 7614046; e-mail mcsa@iafrica.com; f. 1737; Pres. LENNOX MCBUSI; 50,000 mems (2010).

The Roman Catholic Church

Some 6% of the total population are Roman Catholics.

Southern African Catholic Bishops' Conference (SACBC) 399 Khanya House, Paul Kruger St, POB 941, Pretoria 0001; tel. (12) 3236458; fax (12) 3266218; e-mail sacbclib@wn.apc.org; internet www.sacbc.org.za.

f. 1947mems representing South Africa, Botswana and Swaziland; Pres. JOSEPH BUTI TLHAGALE (Archbishop of Johannesburg); Sec.-Gen. Fr VINCENT BRENNAN.

Archbishop of Bloemfontein: JABULANI ADATUS NXUMALO, Archbishop's House, 7A Whites Rd, POB 362, Bloemfontein 9300; tel. (51) 4481658; fax (51) 4472420; e-mail bfnarch@mweb.co.za.

Archbishop of Cape Town: Most Rev. STEPHEN BRISLIN, Cathedral Place, 12 Bouquet St, Cape Town; POB 2910, Cape Town 8000; tel. (21) 4622417; fax (21) 4619330; e-mail info@catholic-ct.org.za; internet www.catholic-ct.co.za.

Archbishop of Durban: Cardinal WILFRID NAPIER, Archbishop's House, 154 Gordon Rd, Durban 4001; POB 47489, Greyville 4023; tel. (31) 3031417; fax (31) 3121848; e-mail vg@catholic-dbn.org.za.

Archbishop of Johannesburg: Most Rev. BUTI JOSEPH TLHAGALE, Archbishop's House, PMB X10, Doornfontein 2028; tel. (11) 4026400; fax (11) 4026406; e-mail catholic@icon.co.za.

Archbishop of Pretoria: Most Rev. WILLLIAM SLATTERY, Jolivet House, 140 Visagie St, Pretoria 0002; POB 8149, Pretoria 0001; tel. (12) 3265311; fax (12) 3253994; e-mail ptadiocese@absamail.co.za.

Other Christian Churches

In addition to the following Churches, there are a large number of Pentecostalist groups, and more than 4,000 independent African Churches.

African Gospel Church: POB 32312, 4060 Mobeni; tel. (31) 9074377; Moderator Rev. F. D. MKHIZE; Gen. Sec. O. MTOLO; 100,000 mems.

Afrikaanse Protestantse Kerk (Afrikaans Protestant Church): 109 Brooks St, Brooklyn, Pretoria 0028; POB 11488, Hatfield 0028; tel. (12) 3621390; fax (12) 3622023; internet www.apkerk.co.za; f. 1987 by fmr mems of the Dutch Reformed Church (Nederduitse Gereformeerde Kerk) in protest at the desegregation of church congregations; c. 33,623 mems.

Apostolic Faith Mission of South Africa: Bldg No. 14, Central Office Park, 257 Jean Ave, Centurion; POB 9450, Centurion 0046; tel. (12) 6440490; fax (12) 6440732; e-mail admin@afm-ags.org; internet www.afm-ags.org; f. 1908; Pres. Dr ISAK BURGER; Gen. Sec. Pastor M. G. MAHLABO; 136,000 mems.

Assemblies of God: POB 4547, Tyger Valley 7536; tel. (21) 9144386; fax (21) 9144387; e-mail brian@assemblies.org.za; internet www.assemblies.org.za; f. 1915; Chair. Rev. ISAAC HLETA; Gen. Sec. Rev. C. P. WATT; 300,000 mems.

Baptist Union of Southern Africa: Private Bag X45, Wilropark 1731; tel. (11) 7685980; fax (11) 7685983; e-mail secretary@baptistunion.org.za; internet www.baptistunion.org.za; f. 1877; Pres. Rev. STUART OWEN CRANNA; Gen. Sec. Rev. ANGELO SCHEEPERS; 44,574 mems (2011).

Black Dutch Reformed Church: POB 137, Bergvlei 2012; Leader Rev. SAM BUTI; c. 1m. mems.

Church of England in South Africa (CESA): POB 2180, Clareinch 7740; tel. (21) 6717070; fax (86) 2739764; e-mail cameronb@cesa.org.za; internet www.cesa.org.za; Presiding Bishop Rt Rev. DESMOND INGLESBY; Gen Sec. Rev. BRIAN CAMERON; 207 churches.

Evangelical Presbyterian Church in South Africa: POB 31961, Braamfontein 2017; tel. (11) 3391044; fax (11) 4034144; e-mail secretary@epcsa.org.za; internet www.epcsa.org.za; f. 1875; Moderator Rev. H. DIXON MASANGU; Gen. Sec. Rev. Dr TITUS R. MOBBIE; 60,000 mems.

The Methodist Church of Southern Africa: 450A Che Guevara Rd, Glenwood, Durban; POB 50216, Musgrave 4062; tel. (31) 2024214; fax (31) 2017674; e-mail general@mco.org.za; internet www.methodist.org.za; f. 1883; Pres. Bishop I. M. ABRAHAMS; Gen. Sec. Rev. VUYANI G. NYOBOLE; 800,000 mems.

Nederduitsch Hervormde Kerk van Afrika: POB 2368, Pretoria 0001; tel. (12) 3228885; fax (12) 3227909; e-mail elmar@nhk.co.za; internet www.nhk.co.za; f. 1652; Gen. Sec. F. J. LABUSCHAGNE; 123,534 mems.

Nederduitse Gereformeerde Kerk in Afrika: Portland Pl., 37 Jorissen St, 2017 Johannesburg; tel. (11) 4031027; 6 synods (incl. 1 in Swaziland); Moderator Rev. S. P. E. BUTI; Gen. Sec. W. RAATH; 350,370 mems.

Presbyterian Church of Africa: POB 72, Nyanga, Cape Town 7755; tel. (21) 3850687; e-mail faleni@absamail.co.za; internet www.presbyterianchurchofafrica.co.za; f. 1898; 8 presbyteries (incl. 1 in Malawi and 1 in Zimbabwe); Moderator Rev. G. M. MOKABO; 1,231,000 mems.

Reformed Church in South Africa (Die Gereformeerde Kerke): POB 20004, Noordbrug 2522, Potchefstroom; tel. (18) 2973986; fax (18) 2931042; e-mail direkteur@gksa.org.za; internet www.gksa.org.za; f. 1859; Prin. Officer Dr C. J. SMIT; 158,973 mems.

Seventh-day Adventist Church: POB 468, Bloemfontein 9300; tel. (51) 4478271; fax (51) 4488059; e-mail sau.president@adventist

.org.za; internet www.adventist.org.za; Pres. Dr T. LETSELI; Sec. Pastor T. KUNENE; 126,175 mems.

United Congregational Church of Southern Africa: POB 96014, Brixton 2019; tel. and fax (11) 8379997; fax (11) 8372570; e-mail admin@uccsa.co.za; internet www.uccsa.co.za; f. 1967; Gen. Sec. Rev. Dr PRINCE DIBEELA; 500,000 mems in 450 churches.

Uniting Presbyterian Church in Southern Africa: 28 Rhodes Ave, Parktown 2193; POB 96188, Brixton 2019; tel. (11) 7273500; fax (11) 7273506; e-mail gensec@presbyterian.org.za; internet www.upcsa.org.za; f. 1999; Moderator Rt Rev. GEORGE MARCHINKOWSKI; Gen. Sec. Rev. Dr JERRY PILLAY; Clerk of the Assembly TOM COULTER; 130,000 mems.

Zion Christian Church: Zion City, Moria; f. 1910; South Africa's largest black religious group; Leader Bishop BARNABAS LEKGANYANE; c. 4m. mems.

ISLAM

In 2003 there were some 455 mosques and 408 Muslim colleges in South Africa.

United Ulama Council of South Africa (UUCSA): POB 4118, Cape Town 8000; tel. (21) 6965150; fax (21) 6968502; internet www.uucsa.net; f. 1994; Pres. ABDUL HAMIED GHABIER; Sec.-Gen. MOULANA YUSUF PATEL.

JUDAISM

According to the South African Jewish Board of Deputies, in 2006 there were about 80,000 Jews in South Africa, and around 200 organized Jewish communities.

African Jewish Congress: POB 87557, Houghton 2041; tel. (11) 6452556; fax (11) 4854325; e-mail moshe@beyachad.co.za; internet www.africanjewishcongress.com; f. 1994; co-ordinating body representing Jewish communities in sub-Saharan Africa; Pres. MERVYN SMITH; Spiritual Leader and Exec. Dir Rabbi MOSHE SILBERHAFT.

South African Jewish Board of Deputies: POB 87557, Houghton 2041; tel. (11) 6452500; fax (11) 6452559; e-mail sajbod@beyachad.co.za; internet www.jewishsa.co.za; f. 1903; the representative institution of South African Jewry; Chair. ZEV KRENGEL; Nat. Dir WENDY KAHN.

BAHÁ'Í FAITH

National Spiritual Assembly: 209 Bellairs Dr., North Riding 2169, POB 932, Banbury Cross 2164; tel. (11) 8013100; fax (11) 4620129; e-mail nsa.sec@bahai.org.za; internet www.bahai.org.za; f. 1956; Gen. Sec. KULLY ZIPHETHE; 11,000 mems resident in 320 localities.

The Press

Government Communication and Information System (GCIS): Midtown Bldg, cnr Vermeulen and Prinsloo Sts, Pretoria; Private Bag X745, Pretoria 0001; tel. (12) 3142911; fax (12) 3252030; e-mail information@gcis.gov.za; internet www.gcis.gov.za; govt agency; CEO PHUMLA WILLIAMS (acting).

South African Press Ombudsman: 7 St Davids's Park, 2nd Floor, St Davids Place, Parktown 2193; POB 47221, Parklands 2121, Johannesburg; tel. (11) 4843612; fax (11) 4843619; e-mail pressombudsman@ombudsman.org.za; internet www.presscouncil.org.za; Ombudsman JOE THLOLOE.

DAILIES

Eastern Cape

Die Burger (Oos-Kaap): 52 Cawood St, POB 525, Port Elizabeth 6001; tel. (41) 5036111; fax (41) 5036138; e-mail kontak@dieburger.com; internet www.dieburger.com; f. 1937; morning; Afrikaans; Publr ANDRE OLIVIER; circ. 23,849.

Daily Dispatch: 35 Caxton St, POB 131, East London 5200; tel. (43) 7022000; fax (43) 7435155; e-mail letters@dispatch.co.za; internet www.dispatch.co.za; f. 1872; publ. by Dispatch Media (Pty) Ltd; afternoon; also publ. *Weekend Dispatch* (Sat.); English; Editor BRENDAN BOYLE; circ. 33,338 (Mon.–Fri.), 27,927 (Sat.).

The Herald: Newspaper House, 19 Baakens St; POB 1117, Port Elizabeth 1; tel. (41) 5047238; fax (41) 5854966; e-mail heraldletters@avusa.co.za; internet www.theherald.co.za; f. 1845; fmrly *Eastern Province Herald*; publ. by Johnnic Publishing Ltd; morning; English; Editor HEATHER ROBERTSON; circ. 29,719 (Mon.–Fri.), 25,000 (Sat.).

Free State

Die Volksblad: 79 Voortrekker St, POB 267, Bloemfontein 9300; tel. (51) 4047600; fax (51) 4306949; e-mail nuus@volksblad.com; internet www.volksblad.com; f. 1904; publ. by Media 24; morning; Afrikaans; Editor JONATHAN CROWTHER; circ. 29,018 (Mon.–Fri.), 23,000 (Sat.).

Gauteng

Beeld: Media Park, Kingsway 69, Auckland Park, Johannesburg; POB 333, Auckland Park 2006; tel. (11) 7139000; fax (11) 7139960; e-mail nuus@beeld.com; internet www.beeld.com; f. 1974; publ. by Media 24; morning; weekly: *Kampus-Beeld*, student news and information, and *JIP* youth supplement; Afrikaans; Editor-in-Chief PEET KRUGER; Editor TIM DU PLESSIS; circ. 105,618 (Mon.–Fri.), 88,402 (Sat.).

Business Day: POB 1745, Saxonwold 2132; tel. (11) 2803000; fax (11) 2805505; internet www.bday.co.za; f. 1985; publ. by BDFM Publrs (Pty) Ltd; afternoon; English; financial; incl. *Wanted* arts and leisure magazine; Editor PETER BRUCE; circ. 40,451 (Mon.–Fri.).

The Citizen: POB 43069, Industria 2042; tel. (11) 2486000; fax (11) 2486213; e-mail info@citizen.co.za; internet www.citizen.co.za; f. 1976; publ. by Caxton Publrs & Printers Ltd; Mon.–Sat., morning; English; Editor M. WILLIAMS; circ. 76,183 (Mon.–Fri.), 57,935 (Sat.).

The Daily Sun: POB 121, Auckland Park 2006; tel. (11) 8776000; fax (11) 8776020; e-mail info@redink.co.za; internet www.dailysun.co.za; Editor MAZWI XABA.

The New Age: 52 Lechwe St, Corporate Park, Old Pretoria Rd, Midrand 1685; tel. (11) 5421222; fax (86) 7337000; e-mail info@thenewage.co.za; internet www.thenewage.co.za; f. 2010; Editor RYLAND FISHER.

The Pretoria News: 216 Vermeulen St, Pretoria 0002; POB 439, Pretoria 0001; tel. (12) 3002000; fax (12) 3257300; e-mail pta.newsdesk@inl.co.za; internet www.iol.co.za/pretoria-news; f. 1898; publ. by Independent Newspapers Gauteng Ltd; afternoon; English; Editor VAL BOJÉ; circ. 28,690 (Mon.–Fri.), 17,406 (Sat.).

Sowetan: 4 Biermann Ave, Rosebank, Johannesburg 2196; POB 6663, Johannesburg 2000; tel. (11) 2803732; fax (11) 4748834; e-mail editor@sowetan.co.za; internet www.sowetanlive.co.za; f. 1981; publ. by New Africa Publs (NAP) Ltd; morning; English; Editor (vacant); circ. 4,122,825 (Mon.–Fri.).

The Star: 47 Sauer St, POB 1014, Johannesburg 2000; tel. (11) 6339111; fax (11) 8343918; e-mail starnews@star.co.za; internet www.iol.co.za/the-star; f. 1887; publ. by Independent Newspapers Gauteng Ltd; morning; English; also publ. *The Saturday Star*; Editor MOEGSIEN WILLIAMS; circ. 166,461 (Mon.–Fri.), 137,385 (Sat.).

KwaZulu/Natal

The Daily News: 18 Osborne St, Greyville 4001; POB 47549, Greyville 4023; tel. (31) 3082106; fax (31) 3082185; internet www.iol.co.za; f. 1878; Mon.–Fri., afternoon; English; Editor ALAN DUNN; circ. 33,011.

The Mercury: 18 Osborne St, Greyville 4001; POB 47397, Greyville 4023; tel. (31) 3082472; fax (31) 3082662; e-mail mercnews@inl.co.za; internet www.iol.co.za/mercury; f. 1852; publ. by Independent Newspapers KZN; morning; English; Editor PHILANI MGWABA; circ. 34,541 (Mon.–Fri.).

The Witness: 45 Willowton Rd, POB 362, Pietermaritzburg 3200; tel. (33) 3551111; fax (33) 3551122; e-mail angela.quintal@witness.co.za; internet www.witness.co.za; f. 1846; publ. by Natal Witness Printing and Publishing Co Ltd; morning; English; also publ. *Weekend Witness*; Editor ANGELA QUINTAL; circ. 23,700 (Mon.–Fri.), 29,000 (Sat.).

Northern Cape

Diamond Fields Advertiser: POB 610, cnr Bean and Villiers Sts, Kimberley 8300; tel. (53) 8326261; fax (53) 8328902; e-mail pbe@independent.co.za; internet www.iol.co.za; publ. by Independent Newspapers Gauteng Ltd; morning; English; Editor KEVIN RITCHIE; circ. 8,948 (Mon.–Fri.).

North-West

Rustenburg Herald: 13 Coetzer St, POB 2043, Rustenburg 0299; tel. (14) 5928329; fax (14) 5921869; e-mail rustenburgweb@gmail.com; internet www.northwestnewspapers.co.za/herald; f. 1924; English and Afrikaans; Man. Editor WALDIE WOLSCHENK; circ. 20,368.

Western Cape

Die Burger: 40 Heerengracht, POB 692, Cape Town 8000; tel. (21) 4062222; fax (21) 4062913; e-mail kontak@dieburger.com; internet www.dieburger.com; f. 1915; publ. by Media 24; morning; Afrikaans; Editor BUN BOOYENS; circ. 104,102 (Mon.–Fri.), 117,092 (Sat.).

Cape Argus: 122 St George's St, POB 56, Cape Town 8000; tel. (21) 4884911; fax (21) 4884075; e-mail argusnews@ctn.independent.co.za; internet www.iol.co.za/capeargus; f. 1857; publ. by Independent Newspapers Cape Ltd; afternoon; English; also publ. *Weekend Argus*;

Editor CHRIS WHITFIELD; circ. 73,230 (Mon.–Fri.), 103,953 (Sat. and Sun.).

Cape Times: Newspaper House, 122 St George's Mall, Cape Town 8001; POB 11, Cape Town 8000; tel. (21) 4884776; fax (21) 4884744; e-mail alide.dasnois@inl.co.za; internet www.iol.co.za/capetimes; f. 1876; publ. by Independent Newspapers Cape Ltd; morning; English; Dep. Editor ALIDE DASNOIS; circ. 49,526 (Mon.–Fri.).

WEEKLIES AND FORTNIGHTLIES

Eastern Cape

Weekend Post: 19 Baakens St, Private Bag X6071, Port Elizabeth 6000; tel. (41) 5047311; fax (41) 5854966; e-mail weekendpost .easterncape@gmail.com; internet theweekendpost.com; publ. by Johnnic Publishing Co Ltd; English; Editor JEREMY MCCABE; circ. 33,372 (Sat.).

Free State

Vista: POB 1027, Welkom 9460; tel. (57) 3571304; fax (57) 3532427; e-mail mwill@volksblad.com; internet www.media24.com/en/ newspapers/community-newspapers/central-newspapers/vista .html; f. 1971; weekly; English and Afrikaans; Editor MARTI WILL; circ. 38,000 (2005).

Gauteng

City Press: POB 3413, Johannesburg 2000; tel. (11) 7139002; fax (11) 7139977; e-mail news@citypress.co.za; internet www.citypress .co.za; f. 1983; publ. by RCP Media Bpk; weekly; English; Editor-in-Chief FERIAL HAFFEJEE; circ. 173,922 (Sun.).

Engineering News/Mining Weekly: POB 75316, Garden View 2047; tel. and fax (11) 6223744; fax (11) 6229350; e-mail newsdesk@ engineeringnews.co.za; internet www.miningweekly.com; f. 1981; publ. by Creamer Media; weekly; Editor TERENCE CREAMER; circ. 20,000.

Financial Mail: Johncom Bldg, 4 Biermann Ave, Rosebank 2196; POB 1744, Saxenwold 2132; tel. (11) 2805808; fax (11) 2805800; e-mail fmmail@fm.co.za; internet www.fm.co.za; weekly; English; Editor BARNEY MTHOMBOTHI; circ. 33,000.

Mail and Guardian: POB 91667, Auckland Park 2006; tel. (11) 2507300; fax (11) 2507303; e-mail newsdesk@mg.co.za; internet www.mg.co.za; publ. by M&G Media (Pty) Ltd; weekly; English; CEO GOVIN REDDY; Editor NIC DAWES; circ. 40,162 (Fri.).

Noordwes Gazette: POB 515, Potchefstroom 2520; tel. (18) 2930750; e-mail potchherald@media24.com; weekly; English and Afrikaans; Editor H. STANDER; circ. 35,000.

Northern Review: 16 Grobler St, POB 45, Pietersburg 0700; tel. (152) 2959167; fax (152) 2915148; weekly; English and Afrikaans; Editor R. S. DE JAGER; circ. 10,300.

Potchefstroom and Ventersdorp Herald: POB 515, Potchefstroom 2520; tel. (18) 2930750; fax (18) 2930759; e-mail potchherald@media24.com; internet www.potchefstroomherald.co .za; f. 1908; Friday; English and Afrikaans; Editor H. STANDER; Man. Dir RASSIE VAN ZYL; circ. 8,000.

Rapport: POB 333, Auckland Park 2006; tel. (11) 7139628; fax (11) 7139977; e-mail briewe@rapport.co.za; internet www.rapport.co.za; publ. by RCP Media; weekly; Afrikaans; Sr Gen. Man. and Publr SAREL DU PLESSIS; Editor BOKKIE GERBER; circ. 322,731 (Sun.).

South African Jewish Report: POB 84650, Greenside 2034; tel. (11) 2741400; fax (11) 8864202; e-mail sharon@sajewishreport.co.za; internet www.sajewishreport.co.za; weekly; publ. by SA Jewish Report (Pty) Ltd; Editor GEOFF SIFRIN.

Springs Advertiser: 48, 5th Ave, POB 761, Springs 1560; tel. (11) 8124800; fax (11) 8124823; e-mail springseditorial@caxton.co.za; internet www.looklocal.co.za; f. 1916; English and Afrikaans; Editor LEANDI CAMERON; circ. 26,000.

Sunday Times: POB 1742, Saxonwold 2132; tel. (11) 2805155; fax (11) 2805111; e-mail feedback@avusa.co.za; internet www.timeslive .co.za/sundaytimes; f. 1906; weekly; English; also published in Zulu; Editor RAY HARTLEY; circ. 505,402 (Sun.).

Vaalweekblad: 27 Ekspa Bldg, D. F. Malan St, POB 351, Vanderbijlpark 1900; tel. (16) 817010; fax (16) 810604; e-mail rfichat@ media24.com; internet www.vaalweekblad.com; weekly; Afrikaans and English; Editor RETHA FICHAT; circ. 16,000.

Die Vrye Afrikaan: POB 675, Durbanville 7551; tel. (12) 3268646; e-mail redakteur@vryeafrikaan.co.za; internet www.vryeafrikaan .co.za; f. 2004; weekly; Afrikaans; Editor JOHANN ROUSSOUW; circ. 13,000.

KwaZulu/Natal

Farmers' Weekly: 368 Jan Smuts Ave, Craighall, Johannesburg 2196; tel. (11) 8890836; fax (11) 8890862; e-mail farmersweekly@ caxton.co.za; internet www.farmersweekly.co.za; f. 1911; weekly; agriculture and horticulture; Editor ALITA VAN DER WALT; circ. 17,000.

Ilanga: 19 Timeball Blvd, The Point, Durban 4001; POB 2159 Durban 4000; tel. (31) 3346700; fax (31) 3379785; e-mail peterc@ ilanganews.co.za; internet www.ilanganews.co.za; f. 1903; publ. by Mandla Matla Publishing Co (Pty) Ltd; 2 a week; also publ. *Ilanga Lange Sonto* (Sun. circ. 87,000); Zulu; Editor SIPHO NGOBESE; circ. 107,000; circ. 100,000 (Mon. and Thur.).

Independent On Saturday: 18 Osborne St, Greyville 4001; POB 47397, Greyville 4023; tel. (31) 3082900; fax (31) 3082185; e-mail satmail@inl.co.za; internet www.iol.co.za/ios; f. 1878; publ. by Independent Newspapers KZN; English; Editor DEON DELPORT; circ. 56,216.

Ladysmith Gazette: 3 Keate St, POB 10019, Ladysmith 3370; tel. (36) 6376801; fax (36) 6372283; f. 1902; weekly; English, Afrikaans and Zulu; Editor DIANA PROCTER; circ. 7,000.

Post: 18 Osborne St, Greyville, Durban 4000; POB 47397, Greyville 4023; tel. (31) 3082400; fax (31) 3082427; e-mail post@inl.co.za; internet www.iol.co.za/thepost; f. 1955 as *Golden City Post*; publ. by Independent Newspapers KZN; weekly; English; focus on the Indian community; Editor AAKASH BRAMDEO; circ. 45,500 (Wed.).

Sunday Tribune: 18 Osborne St, POB 47549, Greyville 4023; tel. (31) 3082911; fax (31) 3082662; e-mail tribunenews@inl.co.za; internet www.iol.co.za/sunday-tribune; f. 1937; publ. by Independent Newspapers KZN; weekly; English; Editor ALAN DUNN; circ. 109,774 (Sun.).

Umafrika: Media House, 43 Imvubu Park Place, Riverhorse Valley, Business Estate, Durban 4017; tel. (31) 5337600; fax (31) 5337940; e-mail editor@umafrika.co.za; f. 1911; owned by Izimpoondo Communications; Friday; Zulu; Editor and Publisher FRASER MTSHALI; circ. 20,000.

Northern Cape

Die Gemsbok: POB 60, Upington 8800; tel. 27017; fax 24055; English and Afrikaans; Editor D. JONES; circ. 8,000.

Western Cape

Drum: Naspers Bldg, 7th Floor, 5 Protea Place, Sandown 2096; POB 653284, Benmore 2010; tel. (11) 3220885; fax (11) 3220891; e-mail khosi@drum.co.za; f. 1951; English and Zulu; Editor MAKHOSAZANA ZWANE SIGUQA; Publr NERISA COETZEE; circ. 79,895 (2006).

Eikestadnuus: 44 Alexander St, POB 28, Stellenbosch 7600; tel. (2231) 72840; fax (2231) 99538; e-mail eikestad@eikestadnuus.com; internet www.eikestadnuus.co.za; weekly; English and Afrikaans; Editor ELSABÉ RETIEF; circ. 7,000.

Fair Lady: POB 1802, Cape Town 8000; tel. (21) 4081278; fax (21) 4051042; e-mail flmag@fairlady.com; internet www.fairlady.com; fortnightly; English; Editor SUZY BROKENSHA; circ. 103,642.

Huisgenoot: 40 Heerengracht, POB 1802, Cape Town 8000; tel. (21) 4062115; fax (21) 4063316; e-mail hgnbrief@huisgenoot.com; internet www.huisgenoot.com; f. 1916; weekly; Afrikaans; Editor JULIA VILJOEN; circ. 355,487.

Move! Magazine: Media City, 10th Floor, 1 Heerengracht St, Foreshore, Cape Town 8001; tel. (21) 4461232; fax (21) 4461206; e-mail move@media24.com; f. 2005; weekly; English; Editor NOLUTHANDO GWEBA-PHILISANE.

The Southern Cross: POB 2372, Cape Town 8000; tel. (21) 4655007; fax (21) 4653850; e-mail editor@scross.co.za; internet www.scross.co.za; f. 1920; publ. by Catholic Newspapers and Publishing Co Ltd; weekly; English; Roman Catholic interest; Editor GÜNTHER SIMMERMACHER; circ. 11,000 (Wed.).

tvplus: Media City, 10th Floor, 1 Heerengracht St, Cape Town 8001; POB 7197, Roggebaai 8012; tel. (21) 4461222; fax (21) 4461206; e-mail tvplus@media24.com; internet www.tvplus.co.za; f. 2000; weekly; English and Afrikaans; Editor ANDRÉ NEVELING.

Tyger-Burger: Bloemhof Bldg, 112 Edward Rd, Bellville 7530; tel. (21) 9106500; e-mail mmeyer@tygerburger.co.za; internet www .tygerburger.co.za; weekly; Afrikaans and English; Editor MARITA MEYER.

Weekend Argus: 122 St George's Mall, POB 56, Cape Town 8000; tel. (21) 4884911; fax (21) 4884762; internet www.iol.co.za; f. 1857; Sat. and Sun.; English; Editor CHRIS WHITFIELD; circ. 108,294.

You Magazine: Naspers Bldg, 7th Floor, 40 Heerengracht St, Cape Town 8001; POB 7167, Roggebaai 8012; tel. (21) 4062116; fax (21) 4062937; e-mail letters@you.co.za; internet www.you.co.za; f. 1987; weekly; English; Editor LINDA PIETERSEN; circ. 222,845 (2004).

MONTHLIES

Free State

Wamba: POB 1097, Bloemfontein; publ. in seven vernacular languages; educational; Editor C. P. SENYATSI.

Gauteng

Boxing World: 5A Dover St, Randburg, Gauteng; tel. (11) 8868558; e-mail info@boxingworld.co.za; f. 1976; Editor PETER LEOPENG; circ. 10,000.

Nursing News: POB 1280, Pretoria 0001; tel. (12) 3432315; fax (12) 3440750; f. 1978; English and Afrikaans; magazine of the Dem. Nursing Org; circ. 76,000.

KwaZulu/Natal

Bona: POB 32083, Mobeni 4060; tel. (31) 422041; fax (31) 426068; f. 1956; English, Sotho, Xhosa and Zulu; Editor (vacant); circ. 256,631.

Living and Loving: CTP Caxton Magazines, 4th Floor, Caxton House, 368 Jan Smuts Ave, Craighall Park, Johannesburg; tel. (11) 8890621; fax (11) 8890668; e-mail livingandloving@caxton.co.za; internet www.livingandloving.co.za; f. 1970; publ. by Caxton Magazines; English; parenting magazine; Editor CLARE HUISAMEN; circ. 33,000.

Rooi Rose: POB 412982, Craighall 2024; tel. (11) 8890665; fax (11) 8890975; e-mail rooirose@caxton.co.za; internet www.rooirose.co.za; f. 1942; Afrikaans; women's interest; Editor MARTIE PANSEGROUW; circ. 122,296.

World Airnews: POB 35082, Northway 4065; tel. (31) 5641319; fax (31) 5637115; e-mail info@airnews.co.za; internet www.airnews.co.za; f. 1973; owned by TCE Publications; monthly; aviation news; Man. Editor TOM CHALMERS; circ. 12,140 (2012).

Your Family: POB 473016, Parklands 2121; tel. (11) 8890749; fax (11) 8890642; e-mail yourfamily@caxton.co.za; internet www.yourfamily.co.za; f. 1973; English; cooking, crafts, DIY; Editor JANINE COLLINS; circ. 164,115.

Western Cape

Car: Ramsay, Son & Parker (Pty) Ltd, Digital Publishing, 3 Howard Dr., Pinelands, Cape Town; POB 180, Howard Place 7450; tel. (21) 5303100; fax (21) 5322698; e-mail car@rsp.co.za; internet www.cartoday.com; English; Editor J. BENTLEY; circ. 99,411 (2008).

Femina: 21 St John's St, POB 3647, Cape Town 8000; tel. (21) 4646248; fax (21) 4612501; Editor ROBYNNE KAHN; circ. 68,591.

Reader's Digest (South African Edition): 5 Protea Pl., Protea Park, Sandown, Johannesburg 2146; POB 785266, Sandton 2146; tel. (11) 3220700; fax (11) 8839495; e-mail magazine.sa@readersdigest.com; internet www.readersdigest.co.za; f. 1948; English; Editor ANTHONY JOHNSON; circ. 62,399.

Sarie: POB 785266, Sandton 2146; tel. and fax (21) 4083090; fax (86) 5308712; e-mail mvanbre@sarie.com; internet www.media24.com/en/magazines/womens-interest/sarie.html; monthly; Afrikaans; women's interest; Editor MICHELLE VAN BREDA; circ. 137,970 (2004).

South African Medical Journal: MASA House, Central House, Private Bag X1, Pinelands 7430; tel. (21) 5306520; fax (21) 5314126; e-mail danjn@telkomsa.net; internet www.samj.org.za; f. 1884; publ. by the South African Medical Asscn; Editor-in-Chief DANIEL J. NCAYIYANA; circ. 20,000.

Die Voorligter: Private Bag, Tyger Valley 7536; tel. (21) 9177000; fax (21) 9141333; e-mail lig@cnw-inter.net; internet www.christene.co.za; f. 1937; journal of the Dutch Reformed Church of South Africa; Editor Dr F. M. GAUM; circ. 50,000.

Wineland Magazine: VinPro, POB 1411, Suider-Paarl 7624; tel. (21) 8634524; fax (21) 8634851; e-mail in@wineland.co.za; internet www.wineland.co.za; f. 1931; publ. by VinPro wine producers' org.; viticulture and the wine and spirit industry; incorporates *Wynboer* technical guide for wine producers; Editor CASSIE DU PLESSIS; circ. 7,000.

The Wisden Cricketer: POB 16368, Vlaeberg 8018; tel. (21) 4083813; e-mail aevlambi@touchline.co.za; internet www.wisdencricketer.co.za; f. 2005; Publr NIC WIDES; Editor ROB HOUWING.

Woman's Value: POB 1802, Cape Town 8000; tel. (21) 4062629; fax (21) 4062929; e-mail wvdited@womansvalue.com; internet www.women24.com; English; Editor and Publr TERENA LE ROUX; circ. 134,749.

PERIODICALS

Eastern Cape

African Journal of AIDS Research (AJAR): Centre for AIDS Development, Research and Evaluation, Institute of Social and Economic Research, 11th Floor, Braamfontein Centre, 23 Jorissen St, Braamfontein, Johannesburg 2001; tel. (11) 3392611; fax (11) 3392615; e-mail ajar@ru.ac.za; internet www.cadre.org.za; f. 2002; quarterly; Man. Editor KEVIN KELLY.

Gauteng

Africa Insight: Africa Institute of South Africa, POB 630, Pretoria 0001; tel. (12) 3049700; fax (12) 3213164; e-mail ngobenis@ai.org.za; internet www.ai.org.za; f. 1960; quarterly; journal of the Africa Institute of South Africa; Editor SOLANI NGOBENI; circ. 1,200.

Africanus: Unisa Press, POB 392, UNISA, 0003 Pretoria; tel. (12) 4292953; fax (12) 4293449; e-mail delpoa@unisa.ac.za; 2 a year; journal of the Centre for Development Studies, Unisa; African and Third World developmental issues; Editor LINDA CORNWELL.

Codicillus: Unisa Press, POB 392, UNISA, 0003 Pretoria; tel. (12) 4292953; fax (12) 4293449; e-mail delpoa@unisa.ac.za; 2 a year; journal of the School of Law at the Univ. of South Africa; South African and international law; Editor Prof. H. C. ROODT.

The ScienceScope: POB 395, Pretoria 0001; tel. (12) 8412911; fax (12) 3491153; e-mail callcentre@csir.co.za; internet www.csir.co.za; f. 1991 as *Technobrief*; quarterly; publ. by the South African Council for Scientific and Industrial Research; Editor THABO DITSELE; circ. 6,000.

South African Journal of Economics: 4.45 EBW Bldg, University of Pretoria, Pretoria 0002; POB 73354, Lynnwood Ridge 0040; tel. (12) 4203525; fax (12) 3625266; e-mail saje@up.ac.za; internet www.essa.org.za; f. 1933; quarterly; English and Afrikaans; journal of the Economic Soc. of South Africa; publ. by Blackwells; Editorial Sec. TITIA ANTONITES.

KwaZulu/Natal

South African Journal of Chemistry: POB 407, WITS 2050, Johannesburg; tel. (11) 7176741; fax (11) 7176779; e-mail sajc@saci.co.za; internet search.sabinet.co.za/sajchem; f. 1921; publ. by the South African Chemical Institute; digital; Co-ordinating Editor GRAHAM JACKSON.

North-West

Historia: c/o Dept of Historical and Heritage Studies, Faculty of Humanities, Humanities Bldg (Main Campus), University of Pretoria, Pretoria 0002; tel. (12) 4202323; fax (12) 4202656; e-mail moutofa@unisa.ac.za; f. 1956; 2 a year; journal of the Historical Asscn of South Africa; South African and African history; Co-ordinating Editor ALEX MOULTON.

Western Cape

Economic Prospects: Bureau for Economic Research, Economics and Management Sciences Bldg, 7th Floor, Bosman St, Stellenbosch 7600; Private Bag 5050, Stellenbosch 7599; tel. (21) 8872810; fax (21) 8839225; e-mail hhman@sun.ac.za; quarterly; forecast of the South African economy for the coming 18–24 months; Man. Editor H. PIENAAR.

Ecquid Novi: c/o South African Journal for Journalism Research, POB 106, Stellenbosch 7599; tel. (21) 8082625; fax (21) 8083488; e-mail novi@sun.ac.za; internet www.sun.ac.za/ecquidnovi; f. 1980; 2 a year; focus on role of the media in southern Africa and Africa; Man. Editor ARNOLD S. DE BEER.

The Motorist: Highbury Monarch Pty, 8th Floor, Metlife Centre, 7 Coen Steytler Ave, Foreshore, 8001 Cape Town; tel. (21) 4160141; fax (21) 4187312; e-mail themotorist@monarchc.co.za; f. 1966; journal of the Automobile Asscn of SA; Editor FIONA ZERBST; circ. 131,584 (2000).

NEWS AGENCIES

East Cape News (ECN) Pty Ltd: POB 897, Grahamstown 6140; tel. (46) 6361050; e-mail editor@ecn.co.za; internet www.ecn.co.za; f. 1997; fmrly East Cape News Agencies; Dir MIKE LOEWE.

South African Press Association (SAPA): Cotswold House, Greenacres Office Park, cnr Victory and Rustenburg Rds, Victory Park; POB 7766, Johannesburg 2000; tel. (11) 7821600; fax (11) 7821587; e-mail comms@sapa.org.za; internet www.sapa.co.za; f. 1938; Man. WIM J. H. VAN GILS; Editor MARK A. VAN DER VELDEN; 40 mems.

PRESS ASSOCIATIONS

Foreign Correspondents' Association of South Africa: POB 1136, Auckland Park 2006; tel. and fax (11) 6467649; e-mail fca@onwe.co.za; internet www.fcasa.co.za; represents 175 int. journalists; Chair. KIM NORGAARD; Sec. MARTINA SCHWIKOWSKI.

Newspaper Association of South Africa: Nedbank Gardens, 5th Floor, 33 Bath Ave, Rosebank 2196, Johannesburg; POB 47180, Parklands 2121; tel. (11) 7213200; fax (11) 7213254; e-mail na@printmedia.org.za; internet www.printmedia.org.za; f. 1882; represents 42 national daily and weekly newspapers, and 178 community newspapers; Pres. PRAKASH DESAI.

Print Media SA: 2nd Floor, 7 St David's, St David's Office Park, St David's Place, Parktown 2193; POB 47180, Parklands 2121; tel. (11) 5519600; fax (11) 5519650; e-mail printmedia@printmedia.org.za; internet www.printmedia.org.za; f. 1995 following the restructuring of the Newspaper Press Union of Southern Africa; represents all aspects of the print media (newspapers and magazines); over 700 mems; Pres. HOOSAN KARJIEKER.

Publishers

Acorn Books: POB 4845, Randburg 2125; tel. (11) 8805768; fax (11) 8805768; e-mail acornbook@iafrica.com; f. 1985; Africana, general, natural history; Propr and Publr ELEANOR-MARY CADELL.

Jonathan Ball Publishers: 10–14 Watkins St, Denver Ext. 4, Johannesburg 2094; POB 33977, Jeppestown 2043; tel. (11) 6222900; fax (11) 6018183; e-mail orders@jonathanball.co.za; internet www.jonathanball.co.za; acquired by Via Afrika (Naspers Group) in 1992; fiction, reference, bibles, textbooks, general; imprints incl. AD Donker (literature), Delta (general fiction and non-fiction) and Sunbird; Man. Dir JONATHAN BALL.

Bible Society of South Africa: Bible House, 134 Edward St, POB 5500, Tyger Valley 7536; tel. (21) 9108777; fax (21) 9108799; e-mail biblia@biblesociety.co.za; internet www.biblesociety.co.za; f. 1820; bibles and religious material in 11 official languages; CEO Rev. G. S. KRITZINGER.

Brenthurst Press (Pty) Ltd: Federation Rd, POB 87184, Houghton 2041; tel. (11) 5445400; fax (11) 4861651; e-mail orders@brenthurst.co.za; internet www.brenthurst.org.za; f. 1974; Southern African history; Dir MARCELLE GRAHAM.

Christelike Uitgewersmaatskappy (CUM): POB 1599, Vereeniging 1930; tel. (16) 4407000; fax (16) 4211748; e-mail orders@cabooks.co.za; internet www.cum.co.za; religious fiction and non-fiction.

Clever Books: POB 13816, Hatfield 0028; tel. (12) 3423263; fax (12) 4302376; e-mail info@cleverbooks.co.za; internet www.cleverbooks.co.za; f. 1981; subsidiary of Macmillan Publrs; Gen. Man. ELNA HARMSE.

Fisichem Publishers: 19 Hofmeyer St, Private Bag X3, Matieland 7602; tel. (21) 8870900; fax (21) 8839635; e-mail info@fisichem.co.za; internet fisichem.co.za; f. 1985; owned by FRJ Trust; science, maths and accounting study guides; Man. RETHA JORDAAN.

Flesch Publications: 11 Peninsula Rd, Zeekoevlei, Cape Town 7941; POB 31353, Grassy Park 7888; tel. (21) 7054317; fax (21) 7060766; e-mail sflesch@iafrica.com; f. 1954; biography, cookery, aviation; CEO STEPHEN FLESCH.

Fortress Books: POB 2475, Knysna 6570; tel. (44) 3826805; fax (44) 3826848; e-mail fortress@iafrica.com; internet www.uys.com/fortress; f. 1973; military history, biographies, financial; Man. Dir I. UYS.

Heinemann Publishers (Pty) Ltd: Heinemann House, Grayston Office Park, Bldg 3, 128 Peter Rd, Atholl Ext. 12, Sandton 2196; POB 781940, Sandown, Sandton 2146; tel. (11) 3228600; fax (11) 3228715; e-mail customerliaison@heinemann.co.za; internet www.heinemann.co.za; educational; incl. imprints Lexicon, Isando and Centaur; Man. Dir ORENNA KRUT.

Home Economics Publishers (Huishoudkunde Uitgewers): POB 7091, Stellenbosch 7599; tel. and fax (21) 8864722; e-mail mcv1@sun.ac.za; Man. M. C. VOSLOO.

HSRC Press: Human Sciences Research Council Private, Bag X9182, Cape Town 8000; tel. (21) 4668000; fax (21) 4610836; e-mail publishing@hsrc.ac.za; internet www.hsrcpress.ac.za; Chair. Prof. DAN NCAYIYANA.

Juta and Co Ltd: POB 14373, Lansdowne 7780, Cape Town; tel. (21) 6592300; fax (21) 6592360; e-mail cserv@juta.co.za; internet www.juta.co.za; f. 1853; academic and professional development, education, trade, law, electronics; imprints incl. UCT Press (scholarly and academic); CEO LYNNE DU TOIT.

LAPA Publishers (Lees Afrikaans Praat Afrikaans): 380 Bosman St, POB 123, Pretoria 0001; tel. (12) 4010700; fax (12) 3244460; f. 1996 as the publishing arm of the Afrikaans Language and Culture Asscn; present name adopted in 2000; Afrikaans; general fiction and non-fiction; CEO WIM DE WET.

Lemur Books (Pty) Ltd (The Galago Publishing (1999) (Pty) Ltd): POB 1645, Alberton 1450; tel. (11) 9072029; fax (11) 8690890; e-mail lemur@mweb.co.za; internet www.galago.co.za; f. 1980; military, political, history, hunting, general; Man. Dir F. STIFF.

LexisNexis Butterworths SA: 215 North Ridge Rd, Morningside, Durban 4001; POB 792, Durban 4000; tel. (31) 2683111; fax (31) 2683108; e-mail customercare@lexisnexis.co.za; internet www.lexisnexis.co.za; f. 1948 as Butterworths; adopted LexisNexis name in 2001; jtly owned by Reed Elsevier, USA, and Kagiso Media; law, tax, accountancy; Chair. W. ROGER JARDINE; CEO WILLIAM J. LAST.

Lux Verbi-BM: POB 5, Wellington 7654; tel. (21) 8648210; fax (21) 8648295; e-mail jmc@luxverbi-bm.co.za; internet www.luxverbi-bm.com; f. 1818 as the Dutch Reformed Church Publishing Co; merged with Bible Media in 1999; subsidiary of the Naspers Group; imprints incl. Hugenote, NG Kerk Uitgewers, Protea, and Waterkant; Christian media; Man. Dir H. S. SPIES; Editor-in-Chief W. BOTHA.

Maskew Miller Longman (Pty) Ltd: cnr Forest Dr. and Logan Way, Pinelands 7405; POB 396, Cape Town 8000; tel. (21) 5326000; fax (21) 5310716; e-mail customerservices@mml.co.za; internet www.mml.co.za; f. 1893 as Miller Maskew; merged with Longman in 1983; jtly owned by Pearson Education and Caxton Publrs and Printers Ltd; imprints incl. Kagiso Publishing (f. 1994; fmrly De Jager-HAUM) and Phumelela Books; educational and general; CEO JAPIE PIENAAR.

Methodist Publishing House: POB 13128, Woodstock, Cape Town 7915; tel. (21) 4483640; fax (21) 4483716; e-mail george@methbooks.co.za; f. 1894; Christian books and church supplies; Gen. Man. GEORGE VINE.

Nasou—Via Afrika: 40 Heerengracht, Cape Town 8001; POB 5197, Cape Town 8000; tel. (21) 4063005; fax (21) 4063086; e-mail CGillitt@nasou.com; internet www.nasou-viaafrika.com; f. 1963; subsidiary of Via Afrika (Naspers Group); educational; imprints incl. Acacia, Action Publrs, Afritech, Afro, Atlas, Era, Juta, KZN Books, Gariep, Idem, Phoenix Education, Shortland and Y-Press Grade R-3; Man. Dir CLIVE GILLITT.

NB Publishers: Naspers Bldg, 12th Floor, 40 Heerengracht, Roggebai 8012; POB 879, Cape Town 8000; tel. (21) 4063033; fax (21) 4063812; e-mail nb@nb.co.za; internet www.nb.co.za; English, Afrikaans, Xhosa and Zulu; Human & Rousseau (f. 1959; general, children's and youth literature, cookery and self-help), Kwela (f. 1994; fiction), Pharos (dictionaries), Tafelberg (f. 1950; fiction and non-fiction, politics, children's and youth literature) and Best Books (educational texts); Head of Publishing C. T. BREYTENBACH.

Oxford University Press: POB 12119, N1 City, Cape Town 7463; tel. (21) 5962300; fax (21) 5961234; e-mail oxford.za@oup.com; internet www.oxford.co.za; f. 1914; Man. Dir LIEZE KOTZE.

Protea Book House: 1067 Burnett St, Hatfield, Pretoria; POB 35110, Menlo Park, 0102 Pretoria; tel. (12) 3623444; fax (12) 3625688; e-mail protea@intekom.co.za; internet www.proteaboekhuis.co.za; f. 1997; art and photography, Afrikaans fiction, South African history, spiritual, academic and general; Dir NICOL STASSEN.

Random House Struik (Pty) Ltd South Africa: POB 2002, Houghton 2041; tel. (11) 4843538; fax (11) 4846180; e-mail ruthc@randomstruik.co.za; f. 1966; general fiction and non-fiction (lifestyle, nature, sport, politics, general reference, travel and heritage); Man. Dir S. E. CONNOLLY.

Shuter & Shooter Publishers (Pty) Ltd: 110CB Downes Rd, Pietermaritzburg; POB 13016, Cascades, Pietermaritzburg 3202; tel. (33) 8468700; fax (33) 8468701; e-mail sales@shuters.com; internet www.shuters.com; f. 1921; educational, general and African languages and trade books; Man. Dir PRIMI CHETTY.

University of KwaZulu-Natal Press (UKZN Press): Private Bag X01, Scottsville 3209; tel. (33) 2605226; fax (33) 2605801; e-mail books@ukzn.ac.za; internet www.ukznpress.co.za; academic and scholarly; Publr DEBRA PRIMO.

Van Schaik Publishers: 1064 Arcadia St, POB 12681, Hatfield 0028; tel. (12) 3422765; fax (12) 4303563; e-mail vanschaik@vanschaiknet.com; internet www.vanschaiknet.com; f. 1915; acquired by Nasionale Pers, latterly Via Afrika-Naspers Group in 1986; English and Afrikaans; academic and scholarly; CEO LEANNE MARTINI.

Wits University Press: PO Wits, Johannesburg 2050; tel. (11) 4845910; e-mail Veronica.Klipp@wits.ac.za; internet witspress.co.za; f. 1922; general trade, non-fiction and scholarly; Publr VERONICA KLIPP.

PUBLISHERS' ASSOCIATION

Publishers' Association of South Africa (PASA): Suite 305, 2nd Floor, The Foundry, Prestwich St, Green Point, Cape Town 8005; tel. (21) 4252721; fax (21) 4213270; e-mail pasa@publishsa.co.za; internet www.publishsa.co.za; f. 1992; promotes and protects the rights and responsibilities of the independent publishing sector in South Africa; Exec Dir. DUDLEY H. SCHROEDER.

Broadcasting and Communications

REGULATORY AUTHORITY

Independent Communications Authority of South Africa (ICASA): Pinmill Farm, Blocks A, B, C and D, 164 Katherine St, Sandton 2146; Private Bag X10002, Marlboro 2063; tel. (11) 5663000;

fax (11) 4441919; e-mail info@icasa.org.za; internet www.icasa.org.za; f. 2000 as successor to the Independent Broadcasting Authority (f. 1993) and South African Telecommunications Regulatory Authority (f. 1996); regulates telecommunications and broadcasting; Chair. Dr STEPHEN SIPHO MNCUBE; CEO THEMBA DLAMINI.

TELECOMMUNICATIONS

At the end of 2011 there were two providers of fixed-line telephone services and five providers of mobile telephone services in South Africa. In 2011 there were 4.1m. fixed-line subscribers and 64m. mobile subscribers.

Cell C (Pty) Ltd: 150 Rivonia Rd, Sandown 2196; Private Bag X36, Benmore 2010, Johannesburg; tel. (11) 3244000; fax (11) 3244009; e-mail customerservice@cellc.co.za; internet www.cellc.co.za; f. 2000; subsidiary of 3C Telecommunications (60% owned by Oger Telecom South Africa, 40% by CellSAf); mobile cellular telecommunications provider; Chair. SIMON DUFFY; CEO ALAN KNOTT-CRAIG.

Mobile Telephone Networks (Pty) Ltd (MTN): 3 Alice Lane, Ext. 38, PMB 9955, Sandton 2146; tel. (11) 3016000; fax (11) 3018448; internet www.mtn.co.za; f. 1994; mobile cellular telecommunications provider; operations in 21 countries in Africa and the Middle East; 11m. subscribers in South Africa (2006); Chair. MATAMELA CYRIL RAMAPHOSA; CEO SIFISO DABENGWA.

Neotel: 44 Old Pretoria Main Rd, Midrand, Johannesburg; PostNet Suite 612, Private Bag X29, Gallo Manor, Johannesburg, 2052; tel. (11) 5851000; fax (80) 0333636; e-mail info@neotel.co.za; internet www.neotel.co.za; Chair. SRINATH NARASIMHAN; Man. Dir and CEO SUNIL JOSHI.

Telkom SA Ltd: Telkom Towers North, 152 Proes St, Pretoria 0002; POB 925, Pretoria 0001; tel. (12) 3111007; fax (12) 3114031; e-mail letlapll@telkom.co.za; internet www.telkom.co.za; f. 1991; 38% govt-owned; ICT solutions service provider; Chair. LAZARUS ZIM; Group CEO NOMBULELO MOHOL.

Telkom Mobile: Telkom Towers North, 152 Proes St, Pretoria 0001; Private Bag X148, Centurion 0046; tel. 081180; internet www.8ta.com; f. 2010; operates under the brand name '8ta'; owned by Telkom SA Ltd; Man. Dir AMITH MAHARAJ.

Virgin Mobile South Africa (Pty) Ltd (VMSA): CitiGroup Bldg, 2nd Floor, 145 West St, Sandton, Johannesburg; POB 78331, Sandton 2146; tel. (11) 3244000; fax (11) 3244113; e-mail CustomerCare@virginmobile.co.za; internet www.virginmobile.co.za; f. 2006; jt venture btwn Cell C and Virgin Mobile Telecoms Ltd, United Kingdom; mobile cellular telecommunications provider; CEO STEVE BAILEY.

Vodacom Group (Pty) Ltd: Vodacom Corporate Park, 082 Vodacom Blvd, Vodavalley, Midrand 1685; tel. (11) 6535000; e-mail corporate.affairs@vodacom.co.za; internet www.vodacom.co.za; f. 1993; 50% owned by Telkom SA Ltd, 50% by Vodafone Group PLC, United Kingdom; subsidiaries in the DRC (f. 2002), Lesotho (f. 1996), Mozambique (f. 2003) and Tanzania (f. 1999); Chair. MTHANDAZO PETER MOYO; CEO PIETER UYS.

BROADCASTING

Radio

South African Broadcasting Corpn (SABC)—Radio: Private Bag X1, Auckland Park 2006, Johannesburg; tel. (11) 7149111; fax (11) 7149744; e-mail rpsales@sabc.co.za; internet www.sabc.co.za; f. 1936; comprises 15 public radio stations and three commercial radio stations broadcasting in 11 languages; Chair. Dr BEN NGUBANE; Group CEO LULAMA MOKHOBO.

Domestic Services

SAfm; Afrikaans Stereo; 5 FM; Radio 2000; Good Hope Stereo; Radio Kontrei; RPN Stereo; Jacaranda Stereo; Radio Algoa (www.algoafm.co.za; regional services); Radio Lotus (Indian service in English); Radio Metro (African service in English); Thobela FM; Ikwekwezi FM; Radio Sesotho; Setswana Stereo; Radio Swazi; Radio Tsonga; Radio Xhosa; Radio Zulu; Lesedi FM; Ligwalagwala FM; Motsweding FM; Phaphala FM; Radio Sonder Grense (Afrikaans); Tru FM; Ukhozi FM; Umhlobo Wenene FM; X-K FM.

External Services

567 CapeTalk: Suite 7D, Somerset Sq., Highfield Rd, Cape Town; Private Bag 567, Vlaeberg 8018; tel. (21) 4464700; fax (21) 4464800; e-mail 567webmaster@capetalk.co.za; internet www.capetalk.co.za; Man. COLLEEN LOUW.

Channel Africa Network: POB 91313, Auckland Park 2006; tel. (11) 7142255; fax (11) 7142072; e-mail molotod@sabc.co.za; internet www.channelafrica.org; f. 1966; external service of SABC; broadcasts 217 hours per week in English, French, Portuguese, Kiswahili, Chinyanja and Silozi; Gen. Man. DAVID MOLOTO.

Classic FM: Jorissen Place, 6th Floor, 66 Jorissen St, Braamfontein; POB 782, Auckland Park 2006; tel. (11) 4031027; fax (11) 4035451; e-mail info@classicfm.co.za; internet www.classicfm.co.za.

East Coast Radio: Durban; tel. (31) 5709495; fax (86) 6794951; e-mail news@ecr.co.za; internet www.ecr.co.za.

94.7 Highveld Stereo: Primedia Place, 5 Gwen Lane, cnr Gwen Lane and Fredman Dr., Sandown, Gauteng; POB 3438, Rivonia 2128; tel. (11) 5063947; fax (11) 5063393; e-mail comments@highveld.co.za; internet www.highveld.co.za.

Jacaranda 94.2: 1 Samrand Ave, Kosmosdal, POB 11961, Centurion 0046; tel. 800609942; e-mail enquiries@jacarandafm.com; internet www.jacarandafm.com.

Kaya FM 95.9: 1 Central Pl., 30 Jeppe St, Newtown, Johannesburg; POB 434, Newtown 2113; tel. (11) 6349500; fax (11) 6349574; e-mail pr@kayafm.co.za; internet www.kayafm.co.za; f. 1997.

Talk Radio 702: Primedia House, 2nd Floor, 5 Gwen Lane, Sandown, Sandton; POB 5572, Rivonia 2128; tel. (11) 5063702; e-mail 702webmaster@702.co.za; internet www.702.co.za.

YFM 99.2: Albury Rd, Dunkeld Cres., South West Blocks, Dunkeld West, Ext. 8, Sandton 2196; tel. (11) 2807070; fax (11) 2807556; e-mail webmaster@yfm.co.za; internet www.yworld.co.za; f. 1997; Man. Dir and CEO KANTHAN PILLAY.

Television

In February 2007 the Government announced that the country would begin digital terrestrial broadcasting in November 2008 and that the country's analogue signal would be switched off by December 2013.

e.tv: 5 Summit Rd, Hyde Park, Johannesburg 2196; Private Bag, X9944, Sandton 2146; tel. (11) 5379300; e-mail info@etv.co.za; internet www.etv.co.za; f. 1998; CEO MARCEL GOLDING.

Naspers: 40 Heerengracht, Cape Town 8001; tel. (21) 4062121; e-mail GKGreen@multichoice.co.za; internet www.naspers.co.za; provides subscription television through Multichoice, M-Net and SuperSport packages; Chair. TON VOSLOO; Chief Executive KOOS BEKKER.

South African Broadcasting Corpn (SABC)—Television: Private Bag X41, Auckland Park 2006; tel. (11) 7149111; fax (11) 7145055; e-mail enterpri@sabc.co.za; internet www.sabc.co.za; transmissions began in 1976; broadcasts television services in 11 languages over three channels; SABC1 broadcasts in English, isiZulu, isiXhosa, isiNdebele and siSwati; SABC2 broadcasts in English, Afrikaans, Sesotho, Setswana, Sepedi, Xitsonga and Tshivendi; SABC3 broadcasts documentaries, educational programmes and sport in English; Chair. Dr BEN NGUBANE; Group CEO LULAMA MOKHOBO.

Finance

(cap. = capital; auth. = authorized; res = reserves; dep. = deposits; m. = million; brs = branches; amounts in rand)

BANKING

In early 2011 the South African banking sector comprised 19 registered banks, two mutual banks, 13 local branches of foreign banks and 41 foreign banks with approved local representative offices. The five largest banks—Standard Bank, Nedbank, ABSA, FirstRand and Investec—controlled some 90% of total banking assets.

Central Bank

South African Reserve Bank: 370 Church St, POB 427, Pretoria 0002; tel. (12) 3133911; fax (12) 3133197; e-mail info@resbank.co.za; internet www.reservebank.co.za; f. 1921; cap. 2.0m., res 9,875.2m., dep. 181,196.5m. (March 2010); Gov. GILL MARCUS; Sen. Dep. Gov. X. P. GUMA; 7 brs.

Commercial Banks

ABSA Bank Ltd: ABSA Towers East, 3rd Floor, 170 Main St, Johannesburg 2001; POB 7735, Johannesburg 2000; tel. (11) 3504000; fax (11) 3504009; e-mail absa@absa.co.za; internet www.absa.co.za; subsidiary of Barclays Bank PLC; cap. 303m., res 17,675m., dep. 597,772m. (Dec. 2009); Chair. GARTH GRIFFIN; Group Chief Exec. MARIA RAMOS; 726 brs.

African Bank Ltd: 59 16th Rd, Private Bag X170, Midrand 1685; tel. (11) 2569000; fax (11) 2569217; e-mail ymistry@africanbank.co.za; internet www.africanbank.co.za; f. 1975; owned by African Bank Investments Ltd; cap. 121m., res 3,096m., dep. 16,794m. (Sept. 2009); CEO LEONIDAS KIRKINIS; 268 brs.

Albaraka Bank Ltd: 2 Kingsmead Blvd, Kingsmead Office Park, Stalwart Simelane St, Durban 4001; POB 4395, Durban 4000; tel. (31) 3649000; fax (31) 3649001; e-mail marketing@albaraka.co.za; internet www.albaraka.co.za; f. 1989; operates according to Islamic principles; cap. 150.0m., dep. 1,624.2m., total assets 1,870.7m. (Dec. 2008); Chair. Adnan Ahmed Yousif; CEO Shabir Chohan.

Capitec Bank: 1 Quantum St, Techno Park, Stellenbosch 7600; tel. (21) 8095900; e-mail clientcare@capitecbank.co.za; internet www.capitecbank.co.za; f. 2001; Chair. Michiel Scholtz du Pré le Roux; CEO Riaan Stassen.

Bidvest Bank Ltd: Rennie House, 11th Floor, 19 Ameshoff St, Braamfontein 2001, Johannesburg; POB 185, Johannesburg 2000; tel. (11) 4073000; fax (11) 4073322; e-mail letstalk@bidvestbank.co.za; internet www.bidvestbank.co.za; f. 1850 as Rennies Bank Ltd; renamed as above in 2007; subsidiary of Bidvest Group Ltd; foreign exchange, trade finance and related activities; cap. 1.8m., res 603.1m., dep. 873.8m. (June 2009); Chair. J. L. Pamensky; Man. Dir A. C. Salomon; over 60 brs.

FirstRand Bank Ltd: 4 First Place, 4th Floor, cnr Fredman Dr. and Rivonia Rd, Bank City, Sandton 2196; POB 786273, Sandton 2146; tel. (11) 2821808; fax (11) 2828088; e-mail information@firstrand.co.za; internet www.firstrand.co.za; f. 1971 as First National Bank of Southern Africa; merged with Rand Bank in 1998; cap. 4m., res 13,965m., dep. 496,512m. (June 2010); CEO Sizwe Nxasana; 600 brs.

GBS Mutual Bank: 18–20 Hill St, Grahamstown 6139; POB 114, Grahamstown 6140; tel. (46) 6227109; fax (46) 6228855; e-mail gbs@gbsbank.co.za; internet www.gbsbank.co.za; f. 1877; total assets 850.0m. (Dec. 2011); Chair. T. C. S. Tagg; CEO A. M. Vorster; 4 brs.

Habib Overseas Bank Ltd: N77 Oriental Plaza, Fordsburg, Johannesburg 2092; POB 62369, Marshalltown, Johannesburg 2107; tel. (11) 8347441; fax (11) 8347446; e-mail habib@global.co.za; internet www.habiboverseas.co.za; f. 1992; cap. 20m., dep. 691m., total assets US $102m. (Dec. 2009); Chair. Habib Mohamed D. Habib; 5 brs.

HBZ Bank Ltd: 135 Jan Hofmeyr Rd, Westville, Durban 3631; POB 1536, Wandsbeck 3631; tel. (31) 2674400; fax (31) 2671193; e-mail sazone@hbzbank.co.za; internet www.hbzbank.co.za; f. 1995; subsidiary of Habib Bank Ltd; cap. 10.0m., res 141.9m., dep. 1,746.1m. (Dec. 2009); Chair. Muhammad Habib; CEO Zafar Alam Khan; 6 brs.

Mercantile Bank Ltd: Mercantile Lisbon House, 142 West St, Sandown 2196; POB 782699, Sandton 2146; tel. (11) 3020300; fax (11) 3020700; internet www.mercantile.co.za; f. 1965; subsidiary of Mercantile Lisbon Bank Holdings; cap. 1,483.3m., res 74.2m., dep. 4,265.0m. (Dec. 2009); Chair. Dr Joaquim A. S. de Andrade Campos; CEO D. J. Brown; 14 brs.

Nedbank Ltd: 135 Rivonia Rd, Sandown 2196, Johannesburg 2001; tel. (11) 2944444; fax (11) 2946540; e-mail Jackiek@nedbank.co.za; internet www.nedbankgroup.co.za; f. 1988; name changed from Nedcor Bank Ltd in 2002; subsidiary of Nedbank Group Ltd; cap. 27m., res 24,856m., dep. 513,609m. (Dec. 2011); Chair. Reuel J. Khoza; CEO Mike Brown; 472 brs.

South African Bank of Athens Ltd: Bank of Athens Bldg, 116 Marshall St, Johannesburg 2001; POB 7781, Johannesburg 2000; tel. (11) 6344300; fax (11) 8381001; e-mail info@bankofathens.co.za; internet www.bankofathens.co.za; f. 1947; 99.51% owned by National Bank of Greece; cap. 13.9m., res 166.5m., dep. 1,058.1m. (Dec. 2009); Chair. A. Leopoulos; CEO Hector Zarca; 11 brs.

The Standard Bank of South Africa Ltd: Standard Bank Centre, 5 Simmonds St, Johannesburg 2001; POB 7725, Johannesburg 2000; tel. (11) 2994701; fax (11) 6364207; e-mail information@standardbank.co.za; internet www.standardbank.co.za; f. 1862; cap. 60m., res 43,147m., dep. 696,805m. (Dec. 2009); Chair. Derek E. Cooper; CEO J. H. Maree; 1,000 brs.

Ubank Ltd: Sanhill Park, 1 Eglin Rd, Sunninghill; Private Bag X101, Sunninghill 2157; tel. (11) 5185000; fax (86) 5457966; e-mail corpcomm@tebabank.com; internet www.tebabank.co.za; f. 2000; fmrly Teba Bank Ltd, name changed as above in 2010; specializes in microfinance and providing financial services to mining communities; total assets 2,639m. (Feb. 2008); Chair. Ayanda Mjekula; CEO Mark Williams; 90 brs, 29 agencies.

Merchant Bank

Grindrod Bank Ltd: 1st Floor North, 20 Kingsmead Blvd, Kingsmead Office Park, Durban 4001; POB 3211, Durban 4001; tel. (31) 3336600; fax (31) 5710505; internet www.grindrodbank.co.za; f. 1994; present name adopted 2006; Man. Dir David Polkinghorne.

Investment Banks

Cadiz Holdings: Fernwood House, 1st Floor, The Oval, 1 Oakdale Rd, Newlands 7700; POB 44547, Claremont 7735; tel. 6578300; fax 6578301; e-mail reception@cadiz.co.za; internet www.cadiz.co.za; f. 1993; 15% owned by Investec, 11% by Makana Financial Services; total assets 298.1m. (Dec. 2003); Chair. Ray Cadiz; CEO Fraser Shaw.

Investec Bank Ltd: 100 Grayston Dr., Sandown, Sandton 2196; POB 785700, Sandton 2146; tel. (11) 2867000; fax (11) 2867777; e-mail investorrelations@investec.com; internet www.investec.com; f. 1974; cap. 25,703m., res 18,837m., dep. 154,772m. (Mar. 2011); CEO Stephen Koseff; 6 brs.

Sasfin Bank Ltd: 29 Scott St, Waverley 2090; POB 95104, Grant Park 2051; tel. (11) 8097500; fax (11) 8872489; e-mail info@sasfin.com; internet www.sasfin.com; f. 1951; subsidiary of Sasfin Holdings Ltd; cap. 1.7m., res 383.5m., dep. 925.1m. (June 2009); Chair. Norman Axten; CEO Roland Sassoon.

Development Bank

Development Bank of Southern Africa (DBSA): 1258 Lever Rd, Headway Hill; POB 1234, Halfway House, Midrand 1685; tel. (11) 3133911; fax (11) 3133086; e-mail info@dbsa.org; internet www.dbsa.org; total assets 23,684.5m. (March 2004); f. 1983; Chair. Jabu Moleketi; CEO Paul Baloyi.

Bankers' Association

Banking Association South Africa: Sunnyside Office Park, Bldg D, 3rd Floor, 32 Princess of Wales Terrace, Parktown 2193; tel. (11) 6456700; fax (11) 6456800; e-mail webmaster@banking.org.za; internet www.banking.org.za; f. 1993; fmrly Banking Council of South Africa; name changed as above in 2005; 15,000 mems; Chair. Stephen Koseff; Man. Dir Cassim Coovadia.

STOCK EXCHANGE

JSE Ltd: One Exchange Sq., 2 Gwen Lane, Sandown, Sandton; Private Bag X991174, Sandton 2146; tel. (11) 5207000; fax (11) 5208584; e-mail info@jse.co.za; internet www.jse.co.za; f. 1887 as Johannesburg Stock Exchange; present name adopted in 2005; in late 1995 legislation was enacted providing for the deregulation of the Stock Exchange; automated trading commenced in June 1996; demutualized in July 2005 and became a listed co in June 2006; CEO Nicky Newton-King.

INSURANCE

In 2010 South Africa was served by 100 short-term and 81 long-term insurers, and 13 reinsurance firms.

Allianz Insurance Ltd: 40 Ashford Rd, Parkwood, Johannesburg 2001; POB 62228, Marshalltown 2107; tel. (11) 4421111; fax (11) 4421125; e-mail baini@allianz.co.za; internet www.allianz.co.za; Chair. D. du Preez; Man. Dir Ian Bain.

Clientèle Life Assurance Co: Clientèle House, Morning View Office Park, cnr Rivonia and Alon Rds, Morningside, Johannesburg; POB 1316, Rivonia 2128; tel. (11) 3203333; e-mail services@clientelelife.com; internet www.clientelelife.com; f. 1997; subsidiary of Hollard Insurance Group; Chair. Gavin Routledge; Man. Dir Basil William Reekie.

Credit Guarantee Insurance Corpn of Africa Ltd: 31 Dover St, POB 125, Randburg 2125; tel. (11) 8897000; fax (11) 8861027; e-mail info@cgic.co.za; internet www.creditguarantee.co.za; f. 1956; Chair. Peter Todd; Man. Dir Mike C. Truter.

Discovery: 16 Fredman Dr., Sandton 2146; POB 784262, Sandton 2146; tel. (11) 5292888; fax (11) 5293590; e-mail worldinfo@discovery.co.za; internet www.discoveryworld.co.za; f. 1992; 64% owned by FirstRand; health and life assurance; Chair. Monty Hilkowitz; CEO Adrian Gore.

Liberty Life: Liberty Life Centre, 1 Ameshoff St, Braamfontein, Johannesburg 2001; POB 10499, Johannesburg 2000; tel. (11) 4083911; fax (11) 4082109; e-mail info@liberty.co.za; internet www.liberty.co.za; f. 1958; Chair. Saki Macozoma; CEO Bruce Hemphill.

Old Mutual (South African Mutual Life Assurance Society): Mutualpark, Jan Smuts Dr., POB 66, Cape Town 8001; tel. (21) 5099111; fax (21) 5094444; e-mail contact@oldmutual.com; internet www.oldmutual.com; f. 1845; Chair. Michael J. Levett; CEO James Sutcliffe.

Regent Insurance Co Ltd: 146 Boeing Rd East, Elma Park, POB 674, Edenvale 1609; tel. (11) 8795000; fax (11) 4539533; e-mail email@bob.co.za; internet www.regent.co.za; f. 1989; 100% owned by Imperial Holdings; Gen. Man. Jono Soames.

Santam Ltd: Santam Head Office, 1 Sportica Cres., Bellville 7530; POB 3881, Tyger Valley 7536; tel. (21) 9157000; fax (21) 9140700; e-mail info@santam.co.za; internet www.santam.co.za; f. 1918; Chair. D. K. Smith; CEO Ian Kirk.

South African National Life Assurance Co Ltd (SANLAM): 2 Strand Rd, Bellville; POB 1, Sanlamhof 7532; tel. (21) 9479111; fax (21) 9479440; e-mail life@sanlam.co.za; internet www.sanlam.co.za; f. 1918; Chair. Dr J. van Zyl.

Zurich Insurance Co South Africa Ltd: 70 Fox St, Johannesburg 2001; tel. (11) 3709111; fax (11) 8368018; e-mail info@insurance.za.org; internet www.saeagle.co.za; fmrly South African Eagle Insurance Co Ltd; rebranded as above in 2007; Chair. M. C. South; CEO N. V. Beyers.

Association

South African Insurance Association (SAIA): JCC House, 3rd Floor, 27 Owl St, Milpark; POB 30619, Braamfontein 2017; tel. (11) 7265381; fax (11) 7265351; e-mail adele@saia.co.za; internet www.saia.co.za; f. 1973; represents short-term insurers; Chair. RONNIE NAPIER; CEO BARRY SCOTT.

Trade and Industry

GOVERNMENT AGENCIES

National Empowerment Fund: West Block, 187 Rivonia Rd, Morningside 2057; POB 31, Melrose Arch, Melrose North 2076; tel. (11) 3058000; fax (11) 3058001; e-mail info@nefcorp.co.za; internet www.nefcorp.co.za; f. 1998; Chair. RONNIE NTULI; CEO PHILISIWE BUTHELEZI.

Small Enterprise Development Agency (SEDA): DTI Campus, Block G, 77 Meintjies St, Sunnyside, POB 56714, Pretoria; tel. (12) 4411000; e-mail info@seda.org.za; internet www.seda.org.za; f. 2004; CEO HLONELA NELISA LUPUWANA.

DEVELOPMENT ORGANIZATIONS

Business Partners Ltd: 37 West St, Houghton Estate, Johannesburg 2198; POB 7780, Johannesburg 2000; tel. (11) 7136600; fax (11) 7136650; e-mail enquiries@businesspartners.co.za; internet www.businesspartners.co.za; f. 1981 as Small Business Devt Corpn; invests in, and provides services to, small and medium-sized enterprises; Chair. THEO VAN WYK; Man. Dir NAZEEM MARTIN.

Independent Development Trust: Glenwood Office Park, cnr Oberon and Sprite Sts, Faerie Glen, Pretoria; POB 73000, Lynnwood Ridge 0043; tel. (12) 8452000; fax (12) 3480894; e-mail info@idt.org.za; internet www.idt.org.za; f. 1990; advances the national devt programme working with govt and communities in fields incl. poverty relief, infrastructure, empowerment, employment and capacity building; CEO THEMBI NWEDAMUSTWU.

Industrial Development Corpn of South Africa Ltd (IDC): 19 Fredman Dr., Sandown 2196; POB 784055, Sandton 2146; tel. (11) 2693000; fax (11) 2693116; e-mail callcentre@idc.co.za; internet www.idc.co.za; f. 1940; promotes entrepreneurship and competitiveness; total assets 90,421m. (March 2008); Chair. MONHLA HLAHLA; CEO M. G. QHENA.

Productivity SA: International Business Gateway, cnr New and Sixth Rds, Midrand; Private Bag 235, Midrand 1685; tel. (11) 8485300; fax (11) 8485555; e-mail info@productivitysa.co.za; internet www.productivitysa.co.za; f. 1968; Chair. ALWYN NEL; CEO Dr BONGANI COKA.

CHAMBERS OF COMMERCE

Cape Chamber of Commerce and Industry: Cape Chamber House, 19 Louis Gradner St, Foreshore, Cape Town 8001; tel. (21) 4024300; fax (21) 4024302; e-mail info@capechamber.co.za; internet www.capechamber.co.za; f. 1804; Pres. MICHAEL BAGRAIM; Exec. Dir VIOLA MANUEL; 3,000 mems.

Chamber of Commerce and Industry–Johannesburg: JCC House, 6th Floor, 27 Owl St, cnr Empire Rd, Milpark; Private Bag 34, Auckland Park 2006; tel. (11) 7265300; fax (11) 4822000; e-mail info@jcci.co.za; internet www.jcci.co.za; f. 1890; Pres. LAURENCE SAVILLE; CEO KEITH BREBNOR; 3,800 mems.

Durban Chamber of Commerce and Industry: Chamber House, 190 Stanger St, POB 1506, Durban 4000; tel. (31) 3351000; fax (31) 3321288; e-mail chamber@durbanchamber.co.za; internet www.durbanchamber.co.za; CEO ANDREW LAYMAN; 3,500 mems.

Gauteng North Chamber of Commerce and Industry (GNCCI): Tshwane Events Centre, Soutter St, Pretoria; POB 2164, Pretoria 0001; tel. (12) 3271487; fax (12) 3271490; internet www.gncci.co.za; f. 1929; fmrly Pretoria Business and Agricultural Centre; merged with Pretoria Sakekamer in 2004; Chair. BERT BADENHORST; CEO WIM DU PLESSIS; over 900 mems.

Mangaung Chamber of Commerce and Industry (MCCI): 104 Zastron St, Bloemfontein; POB 87, Bloemfontein 9301; tel. (51) 4473368; fax (51) 4475064; e-mail info@bcci.co.za; internet www.bcci.co.za; f. 2004; Pres. NANCY DE SOUSA; c. 550 mems (2010).

Nelson Mandela Bay Business Chamber: KPMG House, 200 Norvic Dr., Greenacres, Port Elizabeth 6045; POB 63866, Greenacres 6057; tel. (41) 3731122; fax (41) 3731142; e-mail info@nmbbusinesschamber.co.za; internet nmbbusinesschamber.co.za; f. 1994; fmrly Port Elizabeth Regional Chamber of Commerce and Industry, present name adopted 2011; Pres. BRYAN DOWLEY; CEO KEVIN HUSTLER; 814 mems.

Pietermaritzburg Chamber of Business (PCB): Chamber House, Royal Showgrounds, Chief Albert Luthuli Rd, Pietermaritzburg 3201; POB 11734, Dorpspruit, Pietermaritzburg 3206; tel. (33) 3452747; fax (33) 3944151; e-mail pcb@pcb.org.za; internet www.pcb.org.za; f. 2002 as successor to the Pietermaritzburg Chamber of Commerce and Industries (f. 1910); Pres. PARIS DLAMINI; CEO MELANIE VENESS; 880 mems.

South African Chamber of Commerce and Industry (SACCI): 24 Sturdee Ave, Rosebank, Johannesburg 2196; POB 213, Saxonwold 2132; tel. (11) 4463800; fax (11) 4463850; e-mail info@sacci.org.za; internet www.sacci.org.za; f. 1990 by merger of Asscn of Chambers of Commerce and Industry and South African Federated Chamber of Industries; fmrly known as South African Chamber of Business; Pres. Prof. ALWYN LOUW; CEO NEREN RAU.

Wesvaal Chamber of Business (WESCOB): POB 7167, Flamwood 2572; tel. (18) 4683750; fax (86) 6936365; e-mail chamber@gds.co.za; internet www.wesvaalchamber.co.za; f. 1898; Pres. BEN MOSALA; c. 200 mems.

INDUSTRIAL AND TRADE ORGANIZATIONS

Association of Cementitious Material Producers (ACMP): POB 168, Halfway House 1685; tel. (11) 2073037; fax (12) (11) 3150315; e-mail naudek.acmp@mweb.co.za; internet www.acmp.co.za; f. 2002; Exec. Dir DHIRAJ B. K. RAMA.

Cape Wools: Wool House, 18 Grahamstown Rd, North End, Port Elizabeth 6001; POB 2191, Port Elizabeth 6056; tel. (41) 544301; fax (41) 546760; e-mail capewool@capewools.co.za; internet www.capewools.co.za; f. 1997; Section 21 service company; seven mems: three appointed by wool producer orgs, two by the Wool Textile Council, one by Wool Brokers and Traders and one by Labour; Chair. GEOFF KINGWILL; Gen. Man. ANDRÉ STRYDOM.

Chamber of Mines of South Africa: Chamber of Mines Bldg, 5 Hollard St, POB 61809, Marshalltown 2107; tel. (11) 4987100; fax (11) 8341884; e-mail webmaster@bullion.org.za; internet www.bullion.org.za; f. 1889; Pres. Dr XOLANI HUMPHREY MKHWANAZI; CEO BHEKI SIBIYA.

Clothing Trade Council (CloTrade): 35 Siemers Rd, 6th Floor, Doornfontein; POB 2303, Johannesburg 2000; tel. (11) 4020664; fax (11) 4020667; f. 2002; successor to the Clothing Fed. of South Africa; Pres. JACK KIPLING.

Grain Milling Federation: Embankment Park, 194 Kwikkie Cres., Centurion 0046; POB 7262, Centurion 0046; tel. (12) 6631660; fax (12) 6633109; e-mail gmf@grainmilling.org.za; internet www.grainmilling.org.za; f. 1944; Exec. Dir JANNIE DE VILLIERS.

Master Builders South Africa (MBSA): POB 1619, Halfway House, Midrand 1685; tel. (11) 2059000; fax (11) 3151644; e-mail info@mbsa.org.za; internet www.mbsa.org.za; f. 1904; fmrly known as Building Industries Fed. South Africa; Pres. DANIE HATTING; Exec. Dir ITUMELENG DLAMINI; 4,000 mems.

Master Diamond Cutters' Association of South Africa: Private Bag X1, Suite 105, Excom 2023; tel. (11) 3341930; fax (11) 3341933; e-mail info@masingita.co.za; f. 1928; Pres. MACDONALD TEMANE; 76 mems.

National Association of Automobile Manufacturers of South Africa: Nedbank Plaza, 1st Floor, cnr Church and Beatrix Sts, Pretoria 0002; POB 40611, Arcadia 0007; tel. (12) 3232980; fax (12) 3263232; e-mail naamsa@iafrica.com; internet www.naamsa.co.za; f. 1935; Dir N. M. W. VERMEULEN; 19 full mems and 23 assoc. mems.

National Chamber of Milling, Inc: POB 7262, Centurion 0046; tel. (12) 6631660; fax (12) 6633109; e-mail info@grainmilling.org.za; internet www.grainmilling.org.za; f. 1936; Exec. Dir JANNIE DE VILLIERS.

National Textile Manufacturers' Association: POB 81, New Germany 3620; tel. (31) 7104410; fax (31) 7056257; f. 1947; Sec. PETER MCGREGOR; 9 mems.

Plastics Federation of South Africa: 18 Gazelle Rd, Corporate Park South, Old Pretoria Rd, Midrand; Private Bag X68, Halfway House, Midrand 1685; tel. (11) 3144021; fax (11) 3143764; internet www.plasticsinfo.co.za; f. 1979; Exec. Dir DAVID HUGHES; 10 mems.

Printing Industries Federation of South Africa (PIFSA): Block D, The Braids, 113 Bowling Ave, Gallo Manor 2191; POB 1396, Gallo Manor 2052; tel. (11) 2871160; fax (11) 2871179; e-mail pifsa@pifsa.org; internet www.pifsa.org; f. 1916; CEO PATRICK LACY; c. 820 mems (representing 65% of printers in South Africa); six additional regional brs.

Retail Motor Industry Organization (RMI): POB 2940, Randburg 2125; tel. (11) 8866300; fax (11) 7894525; e-mail rmi@rmi.org.za; internet www.rmi.org.za; f. 1908; affiliates throughout southern Africa; CEO JEFF OSBORNE; 7,400 mems.

South African Dairy Foundation: POB 72300, Lynnwood Ridge, Pretoria 0040; tel. (12) 3485345; fax (12) 3486284; e-mail dairy-foundation@pixie.co.za; f. 1980; Sec. S. L. VAN COLLER; 59 mems.

South African Federation of Civil Engineering Contractors (SAFCEC): 12 Skeen Blvd, POB 644, Bedfordview 2008; tel. (11) 4090900; fax (11) 4501715; e-mail admin@safcec.org.za; internet www.safcec.org.za; f. 1939; Exec. Dir H. P. LANGENHOVEN; 300 mems.

South African Fruit and Vegetable Canners' Association (Pty) Ltd (SAFVCA): Hoofstraat 258 Main St, POB 6175, Paarl 7620; tel. (21) 8711308; fax (21) 8725930; e-mail info@safvca.co.za; internet www.safvca.co.za; f. 1953; Gen. Man. JILL ATWOOD-PALM; 9 mems.

South African Inshore Fishing Industry Association (Pty) Ltd: POB 2066, Cape Town 8000; tel. (21) 4252727; e-mail safish@new.co.za; f. 1953; Chair. W. A. LEWIS; Man. S. J. MALHERBE; 4 mems.

South African Oil Expressers' Association: Cereal Centre, 6th Floor, 11 Leyds St, Braamfontein 2017; tel. (11) 7251280; f. 1937; Sec. Dr R. DU TOIT; 14 mems.

South African Paint Manufacturers' Association: POB 751605, Gardenview, Johannesburg 2047; tel. (11) 4552503; e-mail sapma@sapma.org.za; internet www.sapma.org.za; Chair. TERRY ASHMORE; 100 mems.

South African Petroleum Industry Association (SAPIA): ABSA Centre, 14th Floor, Adderley St, Cape Town 8001; POB 7082, Roggebai 8012; tel. (21) 4198054; fax (21) 4198058; internet www.sapia.co.za; f. 1994; represents South Africa's six principal petroleum cos; Chair. JAMES SEUTLOADI; Dir AVHAPFANI TSHIFULARO.

South African Sugar Association (SASA): 170 Flanders Dr., POB 700, Mount Edgecombe 4300; tel. (31) 5087000; fax (31) 5087199; internet www.sugar.org.za; Exec. Dir M. K. TRIKAM.

Includes:

South African Sugar Millers' Association NPC (SASMA): POB 1000, Mt Edgecombe 4300; tel. (31) 5087300; fax (31) 5087310; e-mail sasmal@sasa.org.za; represents interests of sugar millers and refiners within the operations of SASA; Exec. Dir D. P. ROSSLER; 6 mem. cos.

Sugar Manufacturing and Refining Employers' Association (SMREA): POB 1000, Mount Edgecombe 4300; tel. (31) 5087300; fax (31) 5087310; e-mail sasmal@sasa.org.za; f. 1947; regulates relations between mems and their employees; participates in the Bargaining Council for the sugar manufacturing and refining industry; Chair. B. V. LANE; 6 mem. cos.

South African Wool Textile Council: POB 2201, North End, Port Elizabeth 6056; tel. (41) 4845252; fax (41) 4845629; Sec. BEATTY-ANNE STARKEY.

Steel and Engineering Industries Federation of South Africa (SEIFSA): 42 Anderson St, POB 1338, Johannesburg 2000; tel. (11) 2989400; fax (11) 2989500; e-mail info@seifsa.co.za; internet www.seifsa.co.za; f. 1943; Exec. Dir BRIAN ANGUS; 38 affiliated trade asscns representing 2,350 mems.

VinPro (SA): POB 1411, Suider-Paarl 7624; tel. (21) 8073322; fax (21) 8632079; e-mail info@vinpro.co.za; internet www.vinpro.co.za; f. 1979; represents wine producers; Chair. ABRIE BOTHA; Exec. Dir JOS LE ROUX.

UTILITIES

Electricity

Electricity Supply Commission (ESKOM): POB 1091, Johannesburg 2000; tel. (11) 8008111; fax (11) 8004390; e-mail PAIA@eskom.co.za; internet www.eskom.co.za; f. 1923; state-controlled; Chair. ZOLA TSOTSI; CEO BRIAN DAMES.

Gas

SASOL Gas: POB 4211, Randburg 2125; tel. (11) 8897600; fax (11) 8897955; e-mail gascustomercare@sasol.com; internet www.sasol.com; f. 1964; Man. Dir HANS NAUDÉ.

Water

Umgeni Water: 310 Burger St, Pietermaritzburg 3201; POB 9, Pietermaritzburg 3200; tel. (331) 3411111; fax (331) 3411167; e-mail info@umgeni.co.za; internet www.umgeni.co.za; f. 1974; CEO MZIMKULU MSIWA.

Water Research Commission: Private Bag X03, Gezina 0031; tel. (12) 3300340; fax (12) 3312565; e-mail orders@wrc.org.za; internet www.wrc.org.za; Chair. Prof. J. B. ADAMS; CEO Dr RIVKA KFIR.

MAJOR COMPANIES

The following are among the leading companies in South Africa:

AECI Ltd: Private Bag X21, Gallo Manor 2052; tel. (11) 8068700; fax (11) 8068701; e-mail groupcommunication@aeci.co.za; internet www.aeci.co.za; f. 1924; cap. and res R9,845m., sales R13,397m. (Dec. 2011); mfrs of speciality chemicals for the mining and manufacturing sectors; large land holding for redevelopment; publicly owned; Chair. SCHALK ENGELBRECHT; CEO G. N. EDWARDS; 7,100 employees.

African Micro Mills: 1–2, Reelin Office Park, 20 Nollsworth Park, La Lucia Ridge, Office Estate, Durban 4051; POB 2040, Mount Edgecombe Country Club 4301; tel. (31) 5846250; fax (31) 5846253; internet www.africanmicromills.com; f. 2004; suppliers of agricultural milling equipment; Man. Dir SÉ HIGGINS.

Afrisam: Holcim Bldg, Constantia Park, cnr 14th Avenue and Hendrik Potgieter Rd, POB 6367, Weltevredenpark 1715; tel. (11) 6705500; fax (11) 6705793; internet www.afrisam.co.za; f. 1934; fmrly Holcim (South Africa) (Pty); present name adopted in 2009; major producer of cement, stone aggregates, lime, industrial minerals and ready-mixed concrete, with extensive interests in manufacture of paper sacks and fertilizers; CEO Dr STEPHAN OLIVIER; 3,500 employees.

Barloworld Ltd: 180 Katherine St, POB 782248, Sandton 2146; tel. (11) 4451000; fax (11) 4443643; e-mail barlowpr@barloworld.com; internet www.barloworld.com; f. 1902; total assets R27,842m. (Sept. 2004); conducts industrial brand management in 31 countries; represents principals incl. Caterpillar (machines and engines), Hyster (lift trucks), Freightliner (trucks) and other motor vehicle mfrs; subsidiary producers incl. PPC Surebuild (cement), Plascon, Taubmans, Bristol and White Knight (coatings), Melles Griot (photonics) and Bibby Sterilin (laboratory equipment); Avis licensee for southern Africa; Chair. DUMISA NTSEBEZA; CEO BRADNEY THOMSON; c. 12,500 employees (South Africa).

Denel (Pty) Ltd: POB 8322, Centurion 0046; tel. (12) 6712700; fax (12) 6712751; e-mail marketing@denel.co.za; internet www.denel.co.za; manufacturer of defence equipment; Chair. ZOLI KUNENE.

Grinaker-LTA: Block A, Jurgens St, Jet Park, Boksburg 1459; POB 1517, Kempton Park 1620; tel. (11) 5786000; fax (11) 5786161; e-mail enquiry@grinaker-lta.co.za; internet www.grinaker-lta.com; f. 2000 by merger of LTA Ltd and Grinaker Holdings; 75% owned by Aveng Ltd, 25% owned by Qakazana Investment Holdings (Pty) Ltd (Tiso Group); total assets R5,000m., sales R9,500m. (Dec. 2008); multi-disciplinary construction and engineering group specializing in infrastructure, energy and mining; Chair. ROGER JARDINE; Man. Dir GRAHAME MCCAIG; 15,000 employees.

ICS Holdings Ltd: Harrowdene Office Park, Bldg 4, Western Service Rd, Woodmead, POB 783854, Sandton 2146; tel. (11) 8045780; fax (11) 8044173; f. 1902; cap. R10.7m.; processes and distributes red meat, poultry and meat products, milk and milk products, ice cream, fish; Chair. R. A. WILLIAMS; Man. Dir R. V. SMITHER; 14,400 employees.

Illovo Sugar Ltd: Illovo Sugar Park, 1 Montgomery Dr., Mount Edgecombe; POB 194, Durban 4000; tel. (31) 5084300; fax (31) 5084499; e-mail gdknox@illovo.co.za; internet www.illovosugar.com; f. 1891; 51.5% owned by Associated British Foods PLC; revenue R8,108m. (March 2011); Africa's largest sugar producer (annual output of some 2.0m. metric tons of raw and refined sugar in Southern Africa); downstream producer of syrup, furfural and its derivatives, ethyl alcohol and lactulose; agricultural, manufacturing and other interests in six southern African countries; Man. Dir GRAHAM CLARK; 12,059 permanent employees.

Irvin and Johnson Ltd: 1 Davidson St, Woodstock, Cape Town 7925; Private Bag X1, Lyndhurst 2106; tel. (21) 4407800; fax (21) 4407800; e-mail international@ij.co.za; internet www.ij.co.za; f. 1910; trawler operators; processors, distributors and exporters of frozen fish; Man. Dir RONALD FASOL; 3,500 employees.

Malesela Taihan Electric Cable (Pty) Ltd: 1 Steel Rd, Peacehaven, Vereeniging, 1930 Gauteng; tel. (16) 4508000; fax (16) 4508202; e-mail info@m-tec.co.za; internet www.m-tec.co.za; f. 1911 as Union Steel Corpn of South Africa; mfr of copper and aluminium conductor and associated products; Chair. M. K. MADUNGANDABA; CEO YOUNG MIN KIM; 354 employees.

Nampak Ltd: 114 Dennis Rd, Athol Gardens, POB 784324, Sandton 2146; tel. (11) 7196300; fax (11) 4445761; e-mail mcleishsa@nampak.co.za; internet www.nampak.co.za; f. 1968; total assets 12,435.6m. (2006); mfrs of packaging in various forms based on paper, paper board, metal, glass and plastics; there are subsidiaries in the service area and fields allied to packaging; CEO ANDREW MARSHALL; Man. Dir Africa NEIL CUMMING; 15,345 employees.

Petroleum, Oil and Gas Corporation of South Africa (Pty) Ltd (PetroSA): 151 Frans Conradie Drive, Parow 7500; Private Bag X5, Parow 7499; tel. (21) 9293000; fax (21) 9293144; e-mail petrosa@petrosa.co.za; internet www.petrosa.co.za; f. 2002 by merger of Mossgas, Soekor and parts of the Strategic Fuel Fund Asscn; undertakes exploration and production of oil and natural gas off the coast of South Africa; Chair. BENNY MOKABA; Pres. and CEO NOSIZWE NOCAWE NOKWE.

Pretoria Portland Cement Co Ltd: PPC Bldg, 180 Katherine St, Barlow Park ext., Sandton; POB 787416, Sandton 2146; tel. (11) 3869000; fax (11) 3869001; e-mail contactus@ppc.co.za; internet www.ppc.co.za; f. 1892; mfrs and distributors of cement, lime and limestone products, paper sacks and other containers; also mines and markets gypsum; Chair. BHEKI LINDINKOSI SIBIYA; CEO PAUL STUIVER; 3,004 employees.

Protea Holdings Cape (Pty) Ltd: POB 3839, Cape Town 8000; tel. (21) 512357; f. 1963; Man. Dir A. WOLFAARDT; 100 employees.

Protea Hospitality Corporation (Pty) Ltd: cnr Arthur's Rd and Main Rd, Sea Point; POB 75, Sea Point; tel. (21) 4305000; fax (21) 4305320; e-mail info@proteahotels.com; internet www.proteahotels.com; f. 1988; operates the largest hotel group in Africa; Chair. OTTO J. STEHLIK; CEO ARTHUR G. GILLIS.

SAPPI Ltd: Sappi House, 48 Ameshoff St, Braamfontein, Johannesburg 2001; POB 31560, Braamfontein 2017; tel. (11) 4078111; fax (11) 3391846; internet www.sappi.com; f. 1936; sales US $5,304m. (2007); supplies coated fine paper and chemical cellulose; 20 pulp and paper mills; Chair. DANIËL CHRISTIAAN CRONJÉ; CEO RALPH BOËTTGER; 15,200 employees.

SASOL Ltd: POB 5486, Johannesburg 2000; tel. (11) 4413111; fax (11) 7885092; e-mail sasol.internet@sasol.com; internet www.sasol.com; f. 1950; operating profit R34,000.0m. (Sept. 2008); group of cos operating the world's largest complex of oil-from-coal petrochemical installations; produces 120 products; Chair. HIXONIA NYASULU; CEO DAVID E. CONSTABLE; 31,000 employees.

South African Breweries Ltd: 65 Park Lane, Sandown; POB 782178, Sandton 2146; tel. (11) 8818111; fax (11) 3391830; internet www.sab.co.za; f. 1895; owned by SABMiller PLC; largest non-mining industrial group in sub-Saharan Africa; brewing and marketing of beer; mfrs, wholesalers and retailers of furniture, footwear, domestic appliances, plate glass, textiles, natural fruit juices and soft drinks; discount department, food and fashion chain stores; also owns and operates hotels; Chair. and Man. Dir NORMAN ADAMI; 8,600 employees.

Stewarts and Lloyds Trading (Pty) Ltd: Block B, Ground Floor, Pellmeadow Office Park, 60 Civin Rd, Bedfordview; POB 79458, Senderwood 2145; tel. (11) 5538500; fax (11) 4931440; e-mail info@sltrading.co.za; internet www.stewartsandlloyds.co.za; f. 1903; acquired by Stockwell in 2001; cap. R12m.; suppliers of metal products and services to the engineering, mining, water, chemical and petro-chemical, automotive, construction and agricultural industries; Export Man. P. KEMP.

L. Suzman Ltd: 2 Elray St, Raedene POB 2188, Johannesburg 2192; tel. (11) 4851020; fax (11) 6401325; f. 1889; cap. R2.1m.; wholesale distribution of tobacco products and other consumer products; operates 26 brs in South Africa; Chair. P. R. S. THOMAS; Man. Dir C. J. VAN DER WALT; 1,000 employees.

Tongaat-Hulett Group Ltd: Amanzimnyama Hill Rd, Tongaat 4400; POB 3, Tongaat 4400; tel. (32) 4394000; fax (32) 9453333; e-mail info@tongaat.co.za; internet www.tongaat.co.za; f. 1892; total assets R9,056m. (Jan. 2007); incorporating Hulett Aluminium, African Products (starch and glucose mfrs), Tongaat-Hulett Sugar, and Moreland (property devt); 38% owned by Anglo South Africa Capital (Pty) Ltd; agri-processing business incl. integrated components of land management, property development and agriculture; Chair. J. B. MAGWAZA; CEO PETER STAUDE; 30,000 employees (2006).

Mining Companies

African Rainbow Minerals (ARM): ARM House, 29 Impala Rd, Chislehurston, POB 786136, Sandton 2146; tel. (11) 7791300; fax (11) 7791312; e-mail ir.admin@arm.co.za; internet www.arm.co.za; f. 2004; formed through merger of Ubuntu-Ubuntu Commercial Enterprises Ltd and Anglovaal Mining Ltd; interests in gold, copper, ferrous metals, platinum group metals and coal; Exec. Chair. PATRICE MOTSEPE; CEO MIKE SCHMIDT.

Anglo American Corpn of South Africa Ltd: 44 Main St, Johannesburg; POB 61587, Marshalltown 2107; tel. (11) 6389111; fax (11) 6383221; internet www.angloamerican.co.za; f. 1917; wholly owned subsidiary of Anglo American PLC; mining and natural resource group; a world leader in gold, platinum group metals and diamonds, with significant interests in coal, base and ferrous metals, industrial minerals, forestry and financial services; Chair. Sir MARK MOODY-STUART; CEO CYNTHIA CARROLL.

AngloGold Ashanti Ltd: 76 Jeppe St, Newtown, Johannesburg 2001; POB 62117, Marshalltown 2107; tel. (11) 6376000; e-mail jjones@anglogoldashanti.com; internet www.anglogoldashanti.co.za; total assets R76,202m. (Dec. 2008); world's largest gold producer; 20 operations located in 10 countries; Chair. TITO MBOWENI; CEO MARK CUTIFANI; 63,000 employees.

De Beers Consolidated Mines Ltd: Private Bag X01, Southdale 2135; tel. (11) 3747000; fax (11) 3747700; internet www.debeersgroup.com; f. 1888; cap. and res R23,349m., sales R15,957m. (Dec. 1998); group of diamond mining cos and allied interests; reorg. 1990, when foreign interests were transferred to De Beers Centenary AG, Switzerland; CEO PHILIPPE MELLIER; 14,000 employees.

Gencor Ltd: Postnet Suite 222, Private Bag X30500, Houghton 2041; tel. (11) 6476200; fax (11) 4841654; f. 1895; fmrly General Mining Union Corpn; diversified group with investments in several cos, incl. GENMIN, which administers mines producing coal, platinum, ferro-alloys, and ENGEN, which has interests in petroleum refining and retail petrol sales; Chair. A. S. DU PLESSIS.

Gold Fields: 150 Helen Rd, Sandown, Sandton, 2196 Johannesburg; Postnet Suite 252, Private Bag X30500, Houghton 2041; tel. (11) 6442460; fax (11) 4840639; e-mail info@goldfields.co.za; internet www.goldfields.co.za; Chair. Dr MAMPHELA RAMPHELE; Man. Dir NICHOLAS HOLLAND.

Palabora Mining Co Ltd: 1 Copper Rd, POB 65, Phalaborwa 1390; tel. (15) 7802911; fax (15) 7810448; e-mail keith.mathole@palabora.co.za; internet www.palabora.co.za; 49% owned by Rio Tinto, 30% owned by Anglo American; mining of copper, with by-products of magnetite, zirconia metals, uranium oxide, anode slimes, nickel sulphate, sulphuric acid and vermiculite; produces c. 80,000 metric tons of refined copper per year; Chair. CLIFFORD N. ZUNGU; Man. Dir ANTHONY W. LENNOX; c. 2,000 employees.

Randgold and Exploration Co Ltd: 3rd Floor, Sandton City Office Tower, 158 Fifth St, Sandton 2196; tel. (71) 5803739; fax (86) 2359863; e-mail info@randgoldexp.co.za; internet www.randgoldexp.co.za; f. 1992 to acquire gold-mining interests of Rand Mines Ltd; mineral exploration and devt; Chair. DAVID CHAIM KOVARSKY.

TRADE UNIONS

According to COSATU, some 40% of workers were unionized at March 2005. Under amendments to the Labour Relations Act (LRA), 1995, introduced in 2002, the Government sought to eliminate illegitimate trade unions and employers' organizations. The provisions of the LRA also stipulated that organizations that failed to provide annual audited financial accounts would be deregistered.

Trade Union Federations

Confederation of South African Workers' Unions (CONSAWU): 21 Adriana Cres., Gateway Industrial Park, Rooishuiskraal X25, Centurion; tel. (12) 6614265; fax (12) 6611793; e-mail consawu@mweb.co.za; internet www.consawu.co.za; f. 2003; Pres. MAGGIE MAKGOBA (acting); Gen. Sec. PIET DU PLOOY; 290,000 mems (2007).

Affiliates with 20,000 or more mems include:

National Union of Public Service and Allied Workers (NUPSAW): NUPSAW House, 814 Church St, Eastwood, Pretoria; POB 11459, Tramshed 0126; tel. (12) 3421674; fax (86) 6724354; e-mail generalsecretary@nupsaw.co.za; internet www.nupsaw.co.za; f. 1998; Pres. EZRA MFINGWANA; Gen. Sec. SUCCESS MATAITSANE; c. 42,000 mems (2005).

Other organizations affiliated to CONSAWU include: the Asscn of Metal, Iron and General Workers' Union; the Asscn Trade Union of South African Workers; the Brick and General Workers' Union; Building, Wood and Allied Workers' Union of South Africa; the Building Workers' Union; the Food and Gen. Workers' Union; the Commercial Workers' Union of South Africa; the Food, Cleaning and Security Workers' Union; the Fed. Council of Retail and Allied Workers; the Hotel and Allied Restaurant Workers' Union; the Movement for Social Justice; the Nat. Certified Fishing and Allied Workers' Union; the Nat. Construction, Building and Allied Workers' Union; the Nat. Union of Tertiary Education of South Africa; the Professional Educators' Union; the Professional Employees' Trade Union of South Africa; the Progressive Gen. Employees' Asscn of South Africa; the Progressive Trade Union of South Africa; Solidarity; the South African Building and Allied Workers' Org.; the South African Domestic and Gen. Workers' Union; the South African Food, Retail and Agricultural Workers' Union; the Transport Action, Retail and Gen. Workers' Union; the Trawler and Line Fishermen's Union; the Westcoast Workers' Union; and the Workers' Labour Council–South Africa.

Congress of South African Trade Unions (COSATU): COSATU House, 110 Jorissen St, cnr Simmonds, Braamfontein 2017; POB 1019, Johannesburg 2000; tel. (11) 3394911; fax (11) 3396940; e-mail patrick@cosatu.org.za; internet www.cosatu.org.za; f. 1985; 21 trade union affiliates representing c. 1.8m. paid-up mems; Pres. SDUMO DLAMINI; Gen. Sec. ZWELINZIMA VAVI.

Affiliates with 20,000 or more mems include:

Chemical, Energy, Paper, Printing, Wood and Allied Workers' Union (CEPPWAWU): Kopano House, 2 Melle St, Braamfontein, Johannesburg 2001; POB 3219, Johannesburg 2000; tel. (11) 7120300; fax (11) 4030262; e-mail secretariat@ceppwawu.org.za; internet www.ceppwawu.org.za; f. 1999 by merger of the Chemical Workers' Industrial Union and Paper, Printing, Wood and the Allied Workers' Union; represents workers in the petrochemical, consumer chemical, rubber, plastics, glass and ceramics, printing, pulp and paper, furniture and woodworking industries; Pres. THAMSANQA MHLONGO; Gen. Sec. SIMON MOFOKENG; Nat. Treas. THULASIZWE SIBANDE; 81,149 mems (2012).

Communication Workers' Union (CWU): 222 Smit St, Braamfontein 2017; POB 10248, Johannesburg 2000; tel. (11) 7200131; fax (11) 7200384; e-mail reception@cwu.org.za; internet www.cwu.org.za; f. 1996 by merger of the Post Office Employees' Asscn, the Post and Telecommunication Workers' Asscn and the South African Post Telecommunication Employees' Asscn; Pres. CECIL MOKHANTSO; Gen. Sec. GALLANT ROBERTS; 18,666 mems (2012).

Democratic Nursing Organisation of South Africa (DENOSA): 605 Church St, Pretoria 0001; POB 1280, Pretoria 0001; tel. (12) 3432315; fax (12) 3440750; e-mail info@denosa.org.za; internet www.denosa.org.za; f. 1996; Pres. DOROTHY MATEBENI; Gen. Sec. THEMBEKA T. GWAGWA; 64,165 mems (2006).

Food and Allied Workers' Union (FAWU): Vuyisile Mini Centre, cnr NY1 and NY110, Guguletu, Cape Town; POB 1234, Woodstock 7915; tel. (21) 6379040; fax (21) 6379190; e-mail admin@fawu.org.za; internet www.fawu.org.za; Pres. ATWELL NAZO; Gen. Sec. KATISHI MASEMOLA; 111,029 mems (2006).

National Education, Health and Allied Workers' Union (NEHAWU): 56 Marshall St, Marshalltown, Johannesburg; POB 10812, Johannesburg 2001; tel. (11) 8332902; fax (11) 8330757; e-mail bongi@nehawu.org.za; internet www.nehawu.org.za; f. 1987; Pres. MZWANDILE MICHAEL MAKWAYIBA; Gen. Sec. FIKILE MAJOLA; 192,739 mems (2006).

National Union of Metalworkers of South Africa (NUMSA): NUMSA Bldg, 153 Bree St, cnr Becker St, Newtown, Johannesburg 2001; POB 260483, Excom 2023; tel. (11) 6891700; fax (11) 8336408; e-mail mziwakheh@numsa.org.za; internet www.numsa.org.za; represents workers in the engineering, motor, tyre, rubber and automobile assembly industries; Pres. CEDRIC SABELO GINA; Gen. Sec. IRVIN JIM; 216,808 mems (2006).

National Union of Mineworkers (NUM): 7 Rissik St, cnr Frederick St, Johannesburg 2000; POB 2424, Johannesburg 2000; tel. (11) 3772002; fax (11) 8360367; e-mail Tmlabatheki@num.org.za; internet www.num.org.za; f. 1982; represents workers in the mining, energy, construction, building material manufacturing, civil engineering and building industries; Pres. SENZENI ZOKWANA; Gen. Sec. FRANS BALENI; 262,042 mems (2006).

Police and Prisons Civil Rights Union (POPCRU): 1 Marie Rd, Auckland Park 0183; tel. (11) 2424600; fax (86) 6253054; e-mail gs@popcru.org.za; internet www.popcru.org.za; Pres. ZIZAMELE CEBEKHULU; Gen. Sec. NKOSINATHI THELEDI; 95,864 mems (2006).

SASBO: The Finance Union: SASBO House, Fourmall Office Park West, Roos St, Fourways, Johannesburg; Private Bag X84, Bryanston 2021; tel. (11) 4670192; fax (11) 4670188; e-mail otism@sasbo.org.za; internet www.sasbo.org.za; f. 1916 as the South African Soc. of Bank Officials; Gen. Sec. SHAUN OELSCHIG; 68,357 mems (2010).

Southern African Clothing and Textile Workers' Union (SACTWU): Industria House, 350 Victoria Rd, Salt River, Cape Town; POB 1194, Woodstock 7915; tel. (21) 4474570; fax (21) 4474593; e-mail headoffice@sactwu.org.za; internet www.sactwu.org.za; Pres. THEMBA KHUMALO; Gen. Sec. ANDRE KRIEL; 110,216 mems (2006).

South African Commercial, Catering and Allied Workers' Union (SACCAWU): SACCAWU House, 11 Leyds St, Braamfontein; POB 10730, Johannesburg 2000; tel. (11) 4038333; fax (11) 4030309; e-mail secretariatadmin@saccawu.org.za; internet www.saccawu.org.za; f. 1975; represents workers in the service industry, commercial, catering, tourism, hospitality and finance sectors; Pres. AMOS MOTHAPO; Gen. Sec. BONES SKULU; 107,553 mems (2006).

South African Democratic Teachers' Union (SADTU): Matthew Goniwe House, cnr Goud and Marshall Sts, Johannesburg 2000; POB 6401, Johannesburg 2000; tel. (11) 3344830; fax (11) 3344836; e-mail dmbetse@sadtu.org.za; internet www.sadtu.org.za; f. 1990; Pres. THOBILE NTOLA; Gen. Sec. MUGWENA MALULEKE; 224,387 mems (2006).

South African Municipal Workers' Union (SAMWU): Trade Union House, 8 Beverly St, Athlone, Cape Town; Private Bag X9, Athlone 7760; tel. (21) 6971151; fax (21) 6969175; e-mail soraya.solomon@samwu.org.za; internet www.samwu.org.za; f. 1987; Pres. SAM MOLOPE; Gen. Sec. MTHANDEKI NHLAPO; 118,973 (2006).

South African Transport and Allied Workers' Union (SATAWU): Marble Towers, 6th Floor, cnr Jeppe and Von Wielligh Sts, Johannesburg 2000; POB 9451, Johannesburg 2001; tel. (11) 3336127; fax (11) 3338918; e-mail cecilia@satawu.org.za; internet www.satawu.org.za; f. 2000; Pres. EZROM MABYANA; Gen. Sec. ZENZO MAHLANGU; 134,000 mems (2006).

Other organizations affiliated to COSATU include: the Musicians' Union of South Africa; the Performing Arts Workers' Equity; the Public and Allied Workers' Union of South Africa; the South African Democratic Nurses' Union; the South African Football Players' Union; the South African Medical Association; and the South African State and Allied Workers' Union.

Federation of Unions of South Africa (FEDUSA): Fedusa House, 10 Kingfisher St, Horizon Park, Roodepoort 1725; POB 7779, Westgate 1734; tel. (11) 2791800; fax (11) 2791821; e-mail dennis@fedusa.org.za; internet www.fedusa.org.za; f. 1997 by merger of the Fed. of South African Labour Unions and Fed. of Civil Servants; 22 mem. unions; politically non-aligned; proposed 'super fed.' with the Nat. Council of Trade Unions and Confed. of South African Workers' Unions delayed in 2006; Pres. KOOS BEZUIDENHOUT; Gen. Sec. DENNIS GEORGE; 500,000 mems (2012).

Affiliated unions with 10,000 or more mems include:

Health and Other Service Personnel Trade Union of South Africa (HOSPERSA): POB 231, Kloof 3640, Durban, Pretoria 0121; tel. (12) 6646353; fax (12) 6646302; e-mail officegs@hospersa.co.za; internet www.hospersa.co.za; f. 1958; represents workers in the public and private health, welfare and services sectors, and the public safety and security and education sectors; Pres. GODFREY SELEMATSELA; Gen. Sec. NOEL DESFONTAINES; 72,000 mems (2009).

National Security and Unqualified Workers' Union (NASAWU): United Bldg, 10th Floor, 58 Field St, Durban; POB 63015, Bishopsgate, Durban 4008; tel. (31) 3059320; fax (31) 3059621; Gen. Sec. HAROLD MDINEKA; 13,000 mems (2006).

National Union of Leather and Allied Workers (NULAW): 33 Selbourne Rd, Umbilo, Durban 4075; POB 59088, Durban 4075; tel. (31) 2060105; fax (31) 2060109; e-mail nulaw@mweb.co.za; internet www.nulaw.org.za; Gen. Sec. ASHLEY BENJAMIN; 13,180 mems (2005).

Professional Transport Workers' Union (PTWU): Sable Centre, 3rd Floor, 41 De Korte St, Braamfontein, Johannesburg; POB 31415, Braamfontein 2017; tel. (11) 3394249; fax (11) 6820444; e-mail ptwu@wol.co.za; represents workers in the road freight, private security and cleaning sectors; Gen. Sec. RECKSON BALOYI; c. 10,000 mems (2002).

South African Typographical Union (SATU): SATU House, 166 Visagie St, Pretoria 0001; POB 1993, Pretoria 0001; tel. (12) 3382021; fax (12) 3264196; e-mail martind@satu.co.za; internet www.satu.co.za; f. 1982; represents workers in the printing, newspaper and packaging industries; Gen. Sec. MARTIN DEYSEL; 17,796 mems (2001).

Suid-Afrikaanse Onderwysersunie (SAOU) (South African Teachers' Union): SAOU Bldg, 278 Serene St, Garsfontein, Pretoria; POB 90120, Garsfontein 0042; tel. (12) 3489641; fax (12) 3489658; e-mail saou@saou.co.za; internet www.saou.co.za; Pres. JOPIE BREED; CEO CHRIS KLOPPER; 24,247 (2006).

UASA—The Union: UASA Office Park, 42 Goldman St, Florida 1709; POB 565, Florida 1710; tel. (11) 4723600; fax (11) 6744057; e-mail andre.venter@uasa.org.za; internet www.uasa.org.za; f. 1998 by merger of the Administrative, Technical and Electronic Asscn of South Africa and Officials' Asscn of South Africa; fed. of 31 unions incl. the fmr Nat. Employees' Trade Union; represents workers in the mining, motor, transport, manufacturing and engineering industries; fmrly United Association of South Africa; CEO J. P. L. 'KOOS' BEZUIDENHOUT; 73,000 mems (2011).

Other organizations affiliated to FEDUSA include: the Airline Pilots' Association of South Africa; the Care, Catering and Retail Allied Workers' Union of South Africa; the Construction and Engineering Industrial Workers' Union; the Insurance and Banking Staff Association; the Internal Staff Association; the Jewellers and Goldsmiths' Union; the Millennium Workers' Union; the Mouth Peace Workers' Union; the National Democratic Change and Allied Workers' Union; the National Teachers' Union; the National Union of Hotel, Restaurant, Catering, Commercial, Health and Allied Workers; the South African Communications Union; the South African Parastatal and Tertiary Institutions Union; the United National Public Servants' Association of South Africa and Allied Workers' Union; and the United Transport and Allied Trade Union.

National Council of Trade Unions (NACTU): Metropolitan Life Centre, 4th Floor, 108 Fox St, Johannesburg; POB 10928, Johannesburg 2000; tel. (11) 8331040; fax (11) 8331032; e-mail info@nactu.org.za; internet www.nactu.org.za; f. 1986 by merger of the Council of Unions of South Africa and Azanian Confed. of Trade Unions; fed. of 22 African trade unions; aligned to the Pan-Africanist Congress of Azania party; Pres. JOSEPH MAQHEKENI; Gen. Sec. MANENE SAMELA; 310,000 mems (2007).

Affiliates with 10,000 or more mems include:

Building, Construction and Allied Workers' Union (BCAWU): Glencairn Bldg, 8th Floor, 73 Market St, Johannesburg; POB 96, Johannesburg 2000; tel. (11) 3339180; fax (11) 3339944; e-mail bcawu@netactive.co.za; f. 1974; Gen. Sec. NARIUS MOLOTO; c. 25,000 mems (2003).

Media Workers' Association of South Africa (MWASA): 208-212 cnr Jeppe and von Wielligh Sts, POB 11136, Johannesburg;

tel. (11) 3371019; fax (11) 3371806; internet www.mwasa.org.za; f. 1978 as the Writers' Asscn of South Africa, successor to the Union of Black Journalists; present name adopted in 1986; applied to become a political party in 2005; Pres. LUNGILE LUSHOZI; Gen. Sec. ERNEST DLAMINI (acting); c. 27,000 mems (1998).

Metal and Electrical Workers' Union of South Africa (MEWUSA): Nedbank Bldg, 7th Floor, 145 Commissioner St, Johannesburg; POB 3669, Johannesburg 2000; tel. and fax (11) 3366740; e-mail mewusa@lantic.net; internet www.mewusa.org.za; f. 1989; Pres. DANIEL LENGOABALA; Gen. Sec. EDWARD THOBEJANE; c. 10,000 paid-up mems (2005).

National Union of Food, Beverages, Wine, Spirit and Allied Workers (NUFBWSAW): 8 Stannic Bldg, 4th Floor, New St, South Ghandi Sq., Johannesburg; POB 5718, Johannesburg 2000; tel. (11) 8331140; fax (11) 8331503; Pres. ARMSTRONG NTOYAKHE; Nat. Organizer ANTHONY HENDRICKS; c. 10,000 mems (2005).

South African Chemical Workers' Union (SACWU): 29 Klerk St, btwn Harrison and Dirk Sts, 11th Floor, Johannesburg; POB 236, Johannesburg 2000; tel. (11) 8386581; fax (11) 8386622; e-mail samela@sacwu.co.za; Pres. JOSEPH MAQHEKENI; c. 40,000 mems (2003).

Other organizations affiliated to NACTU include: the Banking, Insurance and Finance Workers' Union; the Hospitality Industry and Allied Workers' Union; the Hotel, Liquor, Catering, Commercial and Allied Workers' Union of South Africa; the Municipality, Education, State, Health and Allied Workers' Union; the National Clothing and Textile Workers' Union of South Africa; the National Services and Allied Workers' Union; the National Union of Farm Workers; the National Union of Furniture and Allied Workers; the Parliamentary Staff Union; the Transport and Allied Workers Union; and the Transport and Omnibus Workers' Union.

Non-affiliated Union

Public Servants' Association of South Africa (PSA): PSA Head Office Bldg, 563 Belvedere St, Arcadia, Pretoria; POB 40404, Arcadia 0007; tel. (12) 3036500; fax (12) 3036652; e-mail ask@psa.co.za; internet www.psa.co.za; withdrew affiliation from FEDUSA in 2006; Chair. PAUL SELLO; Pres. RASHEID DANIELS; Gen. Man. DANNY ADONIS; 185,500 mems (2006).

Transport

Most of South Africa's railway network, and the harbours and airways are administered by the state-owned Transnet Ltd. There are no navigable rivers. Private bus services are regulated to complement the railways.

Transnet Ltd: Carlton Centre, 150 Commissioner St, Johannesburg 2001; POB 72501, Parkview 2122; tel. (11) 3083000; fax (11) 3082638; e-mail unathi.mgobozi@transnet.net; internet www.transnet.net; CEO BRIAN MOLEFE.

RAILWAYS

With the exception of commuter services, the South African railways system is operated by Transnet Freight Rail Ltd (formerly Spoornet), the rail division of Transnet. The network comprised some 34,000 track-km in 2010, of which 16,946 km was electrified. Extensive rail links connect Transnet Freight Rail with the rail networks of neighbouring countries. In 2010 construction of the 80-km rapid rail network Gautrain was under way in the province of Gauteng. The first phase of the system linking O. R. Tambo International Airport and Sandton was opened for commercial service in June 2010. The second phase linking Pretoria and Johannesburg was completed in August 2011 (with the exception of Johannesburg Park Station).

Transnet Freight Rail: Inyanda House, 21 Wellington Rd, Parktown 2193; Private Bag X47, Johannesburg 2000; tel. (11) 5449368; fax (11) 5449599; e-mail dan.motaung@transnet.net; internet www.spoornet.co.za; fmrly Spoornet; renamed as above in 2007; CEO SIYABONGA GAMA; 25,347 employees.

ROADS

In 2001 there were an estimated 364,131 km of classified roads, including 239 km of motorways. The S'hamba Sonke Programme, which aimed to repair and restore the secondary road network in the country, commenced in April 2011 and was scheduled for completion in 2014.

South African National Roads Agency Ltd (SANRAL): Ditsela Pl., 1204 Park St, cnr Duncan St, Hatfield, Pretoria; POB 415, Pretoria 0001; tel. (12) 4266000; fax (12) 3622116; e-mail info@nra.co.za; internet www.nra.co.za; f. 1998; responsible for design, construction, management and maintenance of 16,150 km of the national road network (2008); Chair. MADUKE LOT NDLOVU; CEO NAZIR ALLI.

SHIPPING

The principal harbours are at Richards Bay, Durban, Saldanha, Cape Town, Port Elizabeth, East London, Ngqura (Coega), and Mossel Bay. The deep-water port at Richards Bay has been extended and its facilities upgraded. Both Richards Bay and Saldanha Bay are major bulk-handling ports, while Saldanha Bay also has an important fishing fleet. More than 30 shipping lines serve South African ports.

South African Maritime Safety Authority (SAMSA): 161 Lynnwood Rd, cnr Duncan St, Brooklyn, Pretoria 0181; POB 13186, Hatfield 0028; tel. (12) 3662600; fax (12) 3662601; e-mail services@samsa.org.za; internet www.samsa.org.za; f. 1998; advises the Govt on matters connected with sea transport to, from or between South Africa's ports, incl. safety at sea, and prevention of pollution by petroleum; Chair. Z. C. NGIDI; CEO TSIETSI MOKHELE.

Transnet National Ports Authority: POB 32696, Braamfontein 2017; tel. (11) 3519001; fax (11) 3519023; internet www.transnetnationalportsauthority.net; f. 2000; fmrly part of Portnet; subsidiary of Transnet; controls and manages the country's seven major seaports; CEO TAU MORWE.

Transnet Port Terminals: Kingsmead Office Park, cnr Stalwart and Stanger Sts, Durban 4001; tel. (31) 3088300; fax (31) 3088302; e-mail tptwebmaster@transnet.net; internet www.transnetportterminals.net; f. 2000 as South African Port Terminals, renamed as above in 2008; fmrly part of Portnet; subsidiary of Transnet; operates 13 container, bulk, breakbulk and car terminals at six of the country's major ports; CEO KARL SOCIKWA.

CIVIL AVIATION

Civil aviation is controlled by the Minister of Transport. The Chief Directorate: Civil Aviation Authority at the Department of Transport is responsible for licensing and control of domestic and international air services.

Airports Company South Africa (ACSA): 24 Johnson Rd, The Maples, Office Park-Bedfordview, Johannesburg; POB 75480, Gardenview 2047; tel. (11) 7231400; fax (11) 4539353; internet www.airports.co.za; f. 1993; owns and operates South Africa's 10 principal airports, of which four (at Johannesburg, Cape Town, Durban and Pilanesburg) are classified as international airports; Chair. BUSISIWE MABUZA; Man. Dir BONGANI MASEKO (acting).

Civil Aviation Authority (CAA): Ikhaya Lokundiza, Bldg 16, Treur Close, Waterfall Park, Bekker St, Midrand; Private Bag X73, Halfway House 1685; tel. (11) 5451000; fax (12) 5451465; e-mail mail@caa.co.za; internet www.caa.co.za; Chair. DESMOND GOLDING (acting); Dir ZAKHELE THWALA (acting).

Airlink Airline: No.3, Greenstone Hill Office Park, Emerald Blvd, Greenstone Hill, Modderfontein; POB 7529, Bonaero Park 1622; tel. (11) 4517300; fax (11) 4517367; e-mail info@flyairlink.com; internet www.saairlink.co.za; f. 1992; internal and external scheduled services and charters in Southern Africa; Man. Dirs RODGER FOSTER, BARRIE WEBB.

COMAIR Ltd: 1 Marignane Dr., Bonaero Park 1619; POB 7015, Bonaero Park 1622; tel. (11) 9210111; fax (11) 9733913; e-mail cr@comair.co.za; internet www.comair.co.za; f. 1946; scheduled domestic, regional and international services; Chair. D. NOVICK; Jt CEOs ERIK VENTER, GIDON NOVICK.

Interair South Africa: Finance House, 1st Floor, Ernest Oppenheimer Rd, Bruma Lake Office, Bruma, Johannesburg; Private Bag 8, OR Tambo Int. Airport, Johannesburg 1627; tel. (11) 6160636; fax (11) 6160930; e-mail info@interair.co.za; internet www.interair.co.za; Exec. Chair. DAVID P. TOKOPH.

Mango Airlines: POB 1273, Kempton Park 1627; tel. (11) 3591222; e-mail enquiries@flymango.com; internet www.flymango.com; CEO NICO BEZUIDENHOUT.

Safair (Pty) Ltd: Northern Perimeter Rd, Bonaero Park 1619; POB 938, Kempton Park 1620; tel. 9280000; fax 3951315; e-mail marketing@safair.co.za; internet www.safair.co.za; f. 1965; part of the ASL Aviation Group; aircraft leasing, engineering and maintenance services; Man. Dir DAVE ANDREW.

South African Airways (SAA): Airways Park, Jones Rd, Private Bag X13, Johannesburg 1627; tel. (11) 9782888; fax (11) 9789567; e-mail voyager@flysaa.com; internet www.flysaa.com; f. 1934; state-owned; internal passenger services linking all the principal towns; international services to Africa, Europe, North and South America and Asia; CEO SIZA MZIMELA.

South African Express Airways (SA Express): Tambo International Airport, Johannesburg; tel. (11) 9789905; fax (11) 9785578; e-mail reservations@flyexpress.aero; internet www.flyexpress.aero; f. 1994; CEO INATI NTSHANGA.

Tourism

Tourism is an important part of South Africa's economy. The chief attractions for visitors are the climate, scenery and wildlife reserves. In 2011 some 8.3m. tourists visited South Africa and receipts from tourism amounted to an estimated US $9,547m.

South African Tourism: Bojanala House, 90 Protea Rd, Chislehurston, Johannesburg 2196; Private Bag X10012, Sandton 2146; tel. (11) 8953000; fax (11) 8953001; internet www.southafrica.net; f. 1947; 11 overseas brs; CEO MOEKETSI MOSOLA.

Defence

As assessed at November 2011, the South African National Defence Force (SANDF) totalled about 62,082: army 37,141, navy 6,244, air force 10,653 and a medical corps numbering 8,044. The SANDF comprised members of the former South African armed forces, together with personnel from the former military wings of the ANC and the Pan-Africanist Congress, and the former 'homelands' militias. In 2011 a total of 2,015 South African troops were stationed abroad; of these, 15 were observers.

Defence Expenditure: Budgeted at R37,493m. in 2012/13.

Chief of the South African National Defence Force: Lt-Gen. GODFREY NHLANHLA NGWENYA.

Chief of the South African Air Force: Lt-Gen. CARLO GAGIANO.

Chief of the South African Army: Maj.-Gen. SOLLY ZACHARIA SHOKE.

Chief of the South African Navy: Vice-Adm. JOHANNES REFILOE MUDIMU.

Education

School attendance is compulsory for children of all population groups between the ages of seven and 16 years. From 1991 state schools were permitted to admit pupils of all races, and in 1995 the right to free state education for all was introduced. According to UNESCO estimates, in 2008/09 enrolment at primary schools included 85% of pupils in the relevant age-group (males 85%; females 85%), while enrolment at secondary schools was equivalent to 94% of pupils in the relevant age-group (males 92%; females 96%). In 2009 there were 23 higher education institutions, with a total of 837,779 students. Initial budget estimates for 2012/13 indicated the allocation of R47,844m. (4.9% of total expenditure) to education.

Bibliography

Abel, R. L. *Politics by Other Means: Law in the Struggle Against Apartheid, 1980–1994.* London, Routledge, 1995.

Adam, H., *et al. Comrades in Business: Post-Liberation Politics in South Africa.* Cape Town, Tafelberg, 1997.

Adebajo, A., *et al.* (Eds). *South Africa in Africa: the post-apartheid era.* Pietermaritzburg, University of KwaZulu-Natal Press, 2007.

Alden, C., and Le Pere, G. *South Africa's Post-apartheid Foreign Policy: From Reconciliation to Revival?* Oxford, Oxford University Press for the International Institute for Strategic Studies, 2003.

Beinart, W. *Twentieth-Century South Africa.* Cape Town, Oxford University Press, 1994.

Butler, A. *Contemporary South Africa.* 2nd edn. Basingstoke, Palgrave Macmillan, 2009.

Callinicos, L. *People's History of South Africa.* 3 vols. Johannesburg, Ravan Press, 1981–93.

Chan, S. *Southern Africa: Old Treacheries and New Deceits.* New Haven, CT, Yale University Press, 2011.

Clark, N. L., and Worger, H. *South Africa: The Rise and Fall of Apartheid.* Harlow, Longman, 2004.

Davenport, R. and Saunders, C. *South Africa A Modern History.* 5th edn. London, Macmillan, 2000.

Davies, R. *Afrikaners in the New South Africa: Identity Politics in a Globalised Economy.* London and New York, I. B. Tauris, 2009.

Devenish, G. *The South African Constitution.* Durban, Lexis Nexus Butterworths, 2005.

Du Pre, R. H. *Separate but Unequal: The 'Coloured' People of South Africa: A Political History.* Johannesburg, Jonathan Ball, 1994.

Feinstein, C. *An Economic History of South Africa.* Cambridge, Cambridge University Press, 2005.

Forde, F. *An Inconvenient Youth: Julius Malema and the 'New' ANC.* Johannesburg, Picador, 2011.

Gevisser, M. *Thabo Mbeki. The Dream Deferred.* Johannesburg, Jonathan Ball, 2009.

Giliomee, H. *The Afrikaners: Biography of a People.* London, C. Hurst & Co, 2003.

Giliomee, H. and Mbenga, B. (Eds). *New History of South Africa.* Cape Town, Tafelberg, 2007.

Hall, M. *The Changing Past: Farmers, Kings and Traders in Southern Africa, 1800–1860.* Cape Town, David Philip, 1987.

Hentz, J. J. *South Africa and the Logic of Regional Co-operation.* Bloomington, IN, Indiana University Press, 2005.

Jeffrey, A. *People's War.* Johannesburg, Jonathan Ball, 2009.

Johnson, R. W. *South Africa: The First Man, the Last Nation.* London, Weidenfeld & Nicolson, 2004.

Johnson, R. W., and Schlemmer, L. (Eds). *Launching Democracy in South Africa: The First Open Election, April 1994.* New Haven, CT, Yale University Press, 1996.

South Africa's Brave New World. London, Allen Lane, 2009.

Laband, J. P. C. *Rope of Sand: The Rise and Fall of the Zulu Kingdom in the Nineteenth Century.* Johannesburg, Jonathan Ball, 1995.

Landsberg, C. *The Diplomacy of Transformation.* Johannesburg, Macmillan, 2010.

Lipton, M. *Capitalism and Apartheid: South Africa 1910–1984.* Aldershot, Maurice Temple Smith/Gower, 1985.

Lodge, T. *Politics in South Africa: From Mandela to Mbeki.* Cape Town, David Philip; and Oxford, James Currey, 2003.

Sharpeville: an apartheid massacre and its consequences. Oxford, Oxford University Press, 2011.

Maharaj, B., Desai, A., and Bond, P. *Zuma's Own Goal: losing South Africa's 'war on poverty'.* Trenton, NJ, Africa World Press, 2011.

Marais, H. *Pushed to the Limit.* Cape Town, University of Cape Town Press, 2010.

Marks, S., and Trapido, S. *The Politics of Race, Class and Nationalism in Twentieth Century South Africa.* London and New York, Longman, 1987.

Maylam, P. *History of the African People of South Africa.* Cape Town, David Philip, 1986.

Meli, F. *South Africa Belongs To Us: A History of the ANC.* London, James Currey; Cape Town, David Philip; and Bloomington, IN, Indiana University Press, 1989.

Nattrass, N. *The Moral Economy of AIDS in South Africa.* Cambridge, Cambridge University Press, 2004.

Nattrass, N., and Ardington, E. (Eds). *Political Economy of South Africa.* Cape Town, Oxford University Press, 1990.

O'Meara, D. *Forty Lost Years: The Apartheid State and the Politics of the National Party.* Johannesburg, Ravan Press, 1996.

Purkitt, H. E. *South Africa's Weapons of Mass Destruction.* Bloomington, IN, Chesham/Indiana University Press, Combined Academic, 2005.

Russell, A. *After Mandela. The Battle for the Soul of South Africa.* London, Hutchinson, 2009.

Saunders, C., and Southey, N. *Dictionary of South African History.* Cape Town, David Philip, 1998.

Schrire, R. (Ed.). *Wealth or Poverty: Critical Choices for South Africa.* Cape Town, Oxford University Press, 1992.

Seegers, A. *The Military in the Making of Modern South Africa.* London, I. B. Taurus, 1997.

Simon, D. (Ed.). *South Africa in Southern Africa: Reconfiguring the Region.* Athens, OH, Ohio University Press, 1998.

South African Democracy Education Trust. *The Road to Democracy in South Africa.* 3 Vols. Cape Town and Pretoria, Zebra Press and UNISA Press, 2004–08.

Southall, R. and Daniel, J. (Eds). *Zunami! The 2009 South African Election.* Cape Town, Jacana Media, 2009.

Sparks, A. *Tomorrow is Another Country: The Inside Story of South Africa's Road to Change.* New York, Hill & Wang, 1995.

Beyond the Miracle. Inside the New South Africa. Johannesburg, Jonathan Ball, 2003.

Spence, J. and Welsh, D. *Ending Apartheid (Turning Points).* London, Longman, 2010.

Terreblanche, S. *A History of Inequality in South Africa 1652–2002.* Scottsville, University of Natal Press, 2003.

Thompson, L. *The Unification of South Africa 1902–1910.* Oxford, Clarendon Press, 1960.

History of South Africa. New Haven, CT, Yale University Press, 1990.

United Nations. *United Nations and Apartheid 1984–1994.* New York and Geneva, United Nations Publications, 1995.

Venter, A., and Landsberg, C. *Government and Politics in South Africa.* 4th edn. Pretoria, Van Schaik, 2011.

Walker, C., *et al.* (Eds). *Land, Memory, Reconstruction and Justice: perspectives on land claims in South Africa.* Scottsville, University of KwaZulu-Natal Press, 2011.

Welsh, D. *The Rise and Fall of Apartheid.* Johannesburg, Jonathan Ball, 2009.

Wilson, M., and Thompson, L. (Eds). *The Oxford History of South Africa.* Oxford, Clarendon Press, 1969–71.

Wilson, R. *The Politics of Truth and Reconciliation in South Africa: Legitimizing the Post-Apartheid State.* Cambridge, Cambridge University Press, 2001.

World Economic Forum. *South Africa at 10: Perspectives by Political, Business and Civil Leaders.* Cape Town, Human & Rousseau, 2004.

SOUTH SUDAN

Physical and Social Geography

The territory of the Republic of South Sudan comprises all lands that constituted the three former Sudanese provinces of Bahr El-Ghazal, Equatoria and Upper Nile in their boundaries as they stood on 1 January 1956, and the Abyei Area, as defined by the Abyei Arbitration Tribunal Award of July 2009. South Sudan is bordered by Sudan to the north, by Ethiopia to the east, by Kenya and Uganda to the south, by the Democratic Republic of the Congo to the south-west, and by the Central African Republic to the west.

According to the Sudan Population and Housing Census of April 2008, the population of South Sudan was 8,260,490. South Sudan had an area of 644,329 sq km (248,777 sq miles), equating to a population density of 12.8 per sq km in 2008. The country is divided into 10 states and the capital is Juba. It was, however, announced in September 2011 that the capital was to be relocated to Ramciel in the centre of the country.

South Sudan is generally a flat, featureless plain reflecting the proximity to the surface of the ancient Basement rocks of the African continent. The Basement is overlain by the Umm Ruwaba formation which holds groundwater bodies of agricultural significance. No point in the country is very high above sea-level, although elevations rise to 3,187 m on Mt Kinyeti, near the border with Uganda.

Average temperatures and rainfall change steadily from month to month, except where the effect of the Ethiopian highlands disturbs the east–west trend in the climatic belts in the south-east. Rainfall reaches over 1,000 mm per year at the southern border and generally occurs in the period April–October. Potential evaporation is always over 1,400 mm per year, even in the humid south.

The River Nile is the dominant geographic feature in South Sudan, flowing across the country. South Sudan is home to the world's largest swamp, the Sudd, which covers a total area of 30,000 sq km. The Nile and its many tributaries also provide access to almost unlimited sources of water which services the land, making it fertile to support diverse vegetation and crops. The flooded areas of the Sudd and Machar and environs support swamp vegetation and grassland. On the uplands of the southern border, rainfall is sufficient to support tropical rainforest.

South Sudan is predominantly Christian and this cultural difference from the largely Arabic Sudan, added to the ethnic separateness and its extreme remoteness, has been expressed in economic backwardness and a tendency to political distinctness. These factors have been the main causes of persistent unrest in southern Sudan and ultimately culminated in the secession of South Sudan from Sudan.

English is the official language, although Arabic is the lingua franca around Juba. Other major languages are Dinka (spoken by 2m.–3m. people), Nuer and Shilluk.

Recent History

DUNCAN WOODSIDE

INTRODUCTION

A new nation state, the Republic of South Sudan, was created on 9 July 2011 when the semi-autonomous region of Southern Sudan seceded from Sudan as a whole, following a referendum held between 9 January and 15 January. The referendum was the central pillar of a 2005 peace agreement that ended 22 unbroken years of civil war between Sudan's Arab-dominated central government and a guerrilla army in the largely Christian and animist south. Secession had become all but inevitable when Sudan's President Lt-Gen. Omar Hassan Ahmad al-Bashir announced on 7 February 2011 that he would accept the choice that southerners had made, after final results released by the Southern Sudan Referendum Commission (SSRC) showed that some 98.8% of registered voters in southern Sudan had opted in favour of independence.

Secession was greeted with jubilation in Juba, the southern capital, when a countdown clock in the city centre reached midnight and heralded the start of 9 July 2011. Celebrations continued throughout this historic day, as tens of thousands of people—many of them war veterans—observed official proceedings. UN Secretary-General Ban Ki-Moon and approximately 30 African heads of state, including al-Bashir, attended the ceremonies. Lt-Gen. Salva Kiir Mayardit, hitherto the President of semi-autonomous Southern Sudan and the leader of its ruling party, the Sudan People's Liberation Movement (SPLM), signed into force a new interim Constitution, under which he became President of the new state. The south's former guerrilla army—the Sudan People's Liberation Army (SPLA)—was formally reconstituted as the national army of the new country. The Republic of South Sudan was immediately recognized by principal world powers, including the USA, the United Kingdom and the People's Republic of China, before it became the 193rd member state of the UN on 14 July.

However, South Sudan faced multiple challenges. There were widespread fears among informed observers that it could quickly degenerate into a failed state, due to an inability to fulfil the fundamental task of guaranteeing a minimal level of security to its citizens. The new nation was bedevilled by multiple internal renegade movements, which had emerged in response to the SPLM's tendency to centralize power and its reluctance to work with opposition parties. Additionally, despite Sudan's official recognition of the new nation's sovereignty, explosive bilateral disagreements threatened to provoke a return to a north–south war. The main points of disagreement were: the failure to agree on the status of the disputed Abyei region; the lack of a mutually agreed wider border between the two sovereign territories; the absence of a deal on the sharing of the south's oil revenues; and the emergence of a new conflict in oil-rich Southern Kordofan State, located in the southernmost part of Sudan.

A year after independence, none of the outstanding bilateral disagreements alluded to above had been resolved. In fact, there had been a dramatic further deterioration in relations between South Sudan and Sudan, raising yet more questions about the viability of the former as a nation state. The SPLA and Sudan Armed Forces (SAF) came into renewed direct conflict in the Heglig oilfields in March and April 2012, causing a breakdown of bilateral negotiations under the auspices of the African Union High Implementation Panel (AUHIP) in the Ethiopian capital, Addis Ababa. A threat of sanctions against both countries by the UN Security Council, in the form of the unanimously agreed Resolution 2046, was required in order to force the two sides back from the brink of renewed full-scale war. Meanwhile, Sudan's Government continued to accuse its counterpart in Juba of supporting rebels in South Kordofan, as well as Blue Nile State. Similarly, South Sudan's Government persisted in alleging that the north was backing armed rebel proxy forces south of the border. Although there was a de-escalation of anti-Government insurgent activity in South Sudan in late 2011 and the first half of 2012—due in part to the death of the principal rebel leader, George Athor—there was an upsurge in localized cattle-related conflict, particularly between the minority Murle and Lou Nuer communities in Jonglei State.

THE FIRST NORTH–SOUTH CIVIL WAR

There is no consensus as to when Sudan's first north–south civil war began. Some observers date it from the 1955 Torit mutiny, when southern soldiers rebelled against northern control in the garrison town of Torit in the Equatoria region. The mutiny came before Sudan's independence from the United Kingdom was formalized on 1 January 1956, but already it was clear that northern Sudanese nationalists intended to establish a quasi-colonial structure in the south after the British left. National elections took place in 1954, but while southerners participated—and largely backed the newly established Liberal Party—the north's National Union Party (NUP) became the largest single party and thus formed the Government in Sudan's capital, Khartoum. Shortly after the elections, the outcome of a Sudanization Commission, which had been set up to establish a post-colonial political structure, generated significant anger, because northerners were installed in all key positions in the south. In a context where southerners had been demanding federalism, this development was a huge disappointment.

Without an external supply of arms, it took some years before the southern rebellion gained any momentum. As such, some observers trace the start of the first civil war not to 1955, but to some time between 1960 and 1962. Even then, it was 1964 before attacks against the northern army became anything more than sporadic, owing largely to the ambush of convoys of weapons that were being dispatched by Sudan's Government to supply the Simba rebellion in Congo. The rebels in southern Sudan were able to establish a moderate arsenal as a result of such ambushes, before further benefiting when the Simbas were driven into southern Sudan in 1965, allowing their remaining weapons to be largely acquired by the south's guerrillas. However, political divisions among southern Sudanese exiles (mainly based in Uganda) and guerrilla commanders on the ground undermined the coherence of the rebels' campaign, at least until Col Joseph Lagu brought together disparate factions with the formation of the Southern Sudan Liberation Front (SSLF) in 1970. His authority was strengthened by military support from Israel, which began arming the southern rebels as a counterweight against the Sudanese Government, in response to the latter's support for radical Arab causes.

The first civil war was brought to an end with the negotiation of the February 1972 Addis Ababa Agreement between the Sudanese Government and the Southern Sudan Liberation Movement (previously the SSLF). Faced with an increasingly powerful rebel movement, which engaged with Sudan's army in 1970 and 1971, the Government made significant overtures towards the rebels. The Government's more conciliatory disposition had begun after a 1969 coup, which brought to power Col Gaafar Muhammad Nimeri. President Nimeri's regime was determined to achieve a political settlement with the southern rebels, in part to bolster its military and political authority, which was tenuous and under constant threat from those whom he had deposed. The 1972 agreement provided for regional autonomy in southern Sudan, allowing a tentative peace to prevail between north and south for the next 11 years.

THE 1983–2005 NORTH–SOUTH WAR

The political accommodation between Nimeri and the south's former rebels disintegrated during the course of 1983. The Sudanese President was coming under increasing domestic pressure to create an Islamic state, which was clearly anathema to regional autonomy for the largely Christian and animist south. The leader of the radical Muslim Brothers, Hassan al-Turabi, was released from jail in 1977 and brought within Nimeri's governing circle, enabling him to exert influence in favour of a theocracy. The creation of an Islamic state became a reality in September 1983 and the south's regional autonomy was terminated. Moreover, external events encouraged Nimeri to dismantle his relationship with southern Sudan's political class. Following the election of Ronald Reagan as the US President in 1980 the Cold War reintensified, and Sudan was regarded by the USA as a counterweight to the Soviet-backed regime then existing under Lt-Col Mengistu Haile Mariam in neighbouring Ethiopia. The USA therefore became a key supplier of arms, which Nimeiri was able to use against the south, once the inevitable new rebellion got under way.

The beginning of the second southern rebellion can be traced to a refusal in January 1983 by Battalion 105 of Sudan's army to redeploy north from garrisons in Pibor, Bor and Pochalla. These units were commanded by southern officers who had taken part in the first rebellion. Fighting broke out in Bor in May, when northern loyalist army units attacked the dissenting troops, who fled, with other southern mutineers, to rear bases in Ethiopia, under the protection of Mengistu. A unified rebel politico-military command was quickly established, under the leadership of Col John Garang, an ethnic Dinka (the Dinkas came to dominate the second rebellion). The new rebel group became known as the SPLA, and its political wing the SPLM. The ultimate objective of the rebels at this time was to overthrow Nimeri and establish a secular state in Sudan, rather than secure independence for the south.

The new rebellion was slow to gain momentum, largely due to a mismatch of the protagonists' external support. While the Sudanese Government could count on the support of the USA, the SPLA had very limited external support and depended overwhelmingly on Mengistu. However, the fortunes of the war oscillated significantly for the two sides over the course of the next 20 years or so. The SPLA made significant gains at the end of the 1980s and in 1990, but it was unable to capitalize fully on the end of the Cold War and other events that caused the Sudanese authorities to become increasingly isolated internationally. With the lifting of the Soviet threat, the USA reduced its support for Sudan, before President al-Bashir's regime, which had come to power in a 1989 coup, alienated any remaining goodwill by backing Saddam Hussain's Government in Iraq and various extremist Islamist causes. Yet, the SPLA itself became paralyzed by an internal split that emerged in August 1991, when two influential southern rebels, Dr Riek Machar Teny-Dhurgon and Lam Akol, mutinied against the authority of Garang, who had shifted the main focus of the SPLA's military operations to the Equatoria regions, from the northern reaches of southern Sudan. Machar remained based in the north of Upper Nile State, leaving him and his units virtually cut off and therefore vulnerable to potential attacks by Sudan's army. Despite declaring their objective to be the secession of the south, the Machar-Akol mutiny came to receive backing from the Sudanese Government in a clear policy of 'divide and rule' by Sudan's central authorities. The SPLA clashed with Machar's renegades several times, with particularly severe fighting taking place in Bor and Kongor in November 1991. Largely due to the poor discipline of the renegades, there were heavy civilian casualties, which generated concerns about human rights and to a great extent extinguished Machar's hopes of securing backing from external sources other than Sudan's Government. With the renegades so dependent on support from the Government, they were unable to generate any lasting credibility in the south, but the split in the SPLA was only resolved in January 2002. Tensions between Machar's ethnic group, the Nuer, and the Dinka continued to simmer for years later, even after southern independence was gained in 2011.

With the election of George W. Bush as US President in 2000 the international community intensified efforts to mediate an end to the north–south civil war. In September 2003 Garang and Ali Osman Muhammad Taha, a key aide to al-Bashir, began direct talks in Kenya, before the signing of a wealth-sharing protocol in January 2004.

THE 2005 COMPREHENSIVE PEACE AGREEMENT

On 9 January 2005 the Government and the SPLM signed the Comprehensive Peace Agreement (CPA) in Nairobi, Kenya, thus opening a new chapter in Sudan's history and officially ending the civil war in the south that had lasted for more than two decades, during which at least 2m. people had been killed and more than 4m. displaced. The accord comprised eight protocols, including agreements that political power and Sudan's national wealth would be shared between the national Government and the south; that the SAF and the SPLA would remain separate forces within the national army, in addition to contributing equally to new Joint Integrated Units (JIU) that would be deployed on both sides of the north–south border; and that all militias would be disbanded within a year. Furthermore, the south's oil revenues would be shared equally between the north and a semi-autonomous south; the SPLM and other southern groups would hold 30% of government positions in the north, while holding 70% in the south; and the contested Nuba Mountains region, together with Blue Nile State, would be governed by an administration in which 55% of the seats would be taken by northern government officials and 45% by the SPLM. Meanwhile, the disputed Abyei region would be granted special status under the presidency. Additionally, the application of *Shari'a* (Islamic) law would be limited to the north and Garang would become Sudan's First Vice-President, President of Southern Sudan and head of the SPLA forces during the six-year transition period, after which a referendum on secession would be held in the south.

The Interim National Constitution was promulgated on 9 July 2005, in accordance with the terms stipulated in the CPA. On 1 August, however, Garang was killed in a helicopter accident while en route to Rumbek, in southern Sudan, from Uganda. The announcement of Garang's death was followed by several days of rioting in Khartoum, during which more than 130 people were killed. Garang was replaced as leader of the SPLA/SPLM by Commdr (later Lt-Gen.) Salva Kiir Mayardit, hitherto deputy leader of the organization. Salva Kiir was subsequently appointed First Vice-President in Sudan's national Government and assumed the presidency of the new Government of Southern Sudan (GOSS). In September a Government of National Unity was established, which was dominated by al-Bashir's National Congress Party (NCP) and the SPLM. By the end of the year a new National Assembly was functioning, and the process of nominating national commissions to implement the CPA in a number of policy areas had also begun.

THE NORTH–SOUTH POLITICAL TRANSITION

In addition to the GOSS, a new Transitional Southern Sudan Legislative Assembly was established and regional administrations were created. In December 2005 a new transitional Constitution for the south was promulgated. Security remained a difficult issue. As well as the forces of the SPLA, a number of other rebel groups were known to be active in the south, including the Southern Sudan Defense Force (SSDF), the members of which predominantly came from the Nuer people of Upper Nile region. The exiled Ugandan Lord's Resistance Army (LRA) had also carried out attacks in the south. It was suggested that both groups enjoyed the support of the NCP in an attempt to undermine the power base of the SPLA/SPLM. However, after the signing of the CPA, Salva Kiir reached agreement with the main SSDF leader, Paulino Matip, while the Vice-President of the GOSS, Riek Machar, met with LRA leader Joseph Kony in an attempt to facilitate peace talks between the LRA and the Ugandan Government. There were also concerns about the capacity of the SPLA/SPLM to transform itself from an armed force into a solely political entity and the repatriation of refugees and internally displaced persons (IDPs) in northern Sudan and neighbouring Uganda. In December 2005 the Office of the UN High Commissioner for Refugees (UNHCR) announced that it would begin to repatriate some 500,000 refugees from neighbouring countries; earlier that month 90,000 refugees had returned to southern Sudan from northern Kenya under UNHCR auspices. In addition, many southerners who had been displaced to the north of the country began to return to their homes in the south, although the rate of return was comparatively slow and facilities to receive those who did go back were very limited.

In accordance with the CPA, a commission, headed by the former US ambassador to Sudan, Donald Petterson, was established to draw the boundaries of the Abyei region. In July 2005 the Abyei Boundary Commission duly released its report, which defined the region as covering areas east from the provincial border of Bahr El-Ghazal State to the border with Upper Nile State, and north to the settlements of Turda, Edd Dibekir and Umm Sakina. Despite having earlier pledged to abide by the Commission's final judgment, President al-Bashir stated that he disagreed with its conclusions (as did the nomadic cattle-herding Misseriya Arabs, which had been used as a military proxy by the north during the civil war). The Misseriya's principal underlying concern was the fact that their seasonal access to grazing lands in Abyei would be cut off, in the event that the region later voted to become part of an independent south. Abyei's permanent residents are largely Ngok Dinka people, closely aligned to the SPLM, but the Misseriya migrate into the region each year in order to find pasture, when their lands to the north are too dry. The CPA provided for two secession referendums in 2011: a main plebiscite, covering all regions of southern Sudan except Abyei; and a second poll, to be held concurrently in Abyei. The latter would give the people of the Abyei region the opportunity to decide whether to remain a part of Sudan, or become part of an independent southern Sudan, in the event that the outcome of the main referendum was a vote in favour of secession.

The two other disputed areas of the Blue Nile and the Nuba Mountains were, at this stage, less problematic but still presented challenges. Observers feared that tension over the border issue could increase in the period leading up to the referendum, particularly with regard to petroleum reserves, much of which lie in the disputed border areas.

In October 2007 disagreement over a number of divisive issues in the CPA led to the SPLM withdrawing from the Government of National Unity. The main points of contention were delays in the redeployment of northern troops from the south, the postponement of border demarcation between north and south, the still unresolved status of Abyei, transparency on the sharing of oil revenues between north and south, and a delay to a national census. The SPLM's withdrawal from the coalition yielded sufficient progress on these issues for it to return as an uneasy partner in the Government before the end of the year. In April 2008 there was a further crisis over Abyei with a violent clash leading to a number of deaths; once again, however, crisis produced compromise with agreement that the Abyei question be referred to a new international arbitration process under the International Court of Justice (ICJ) at The Hague, in the Netherlands. Nevertheless, trust between the two parties in the Government remained low. The NCP clearly wished to retain the unity of Sudan, while seeking to restrain the SPLM as a junior partner focused on the south. Within the SPLM differences persisted over the extent to which it sought to mount a national challenge to the NCP, uniting other marginalized areas such as Darfur and eastern Sudan under the banner of the 'New Sudan', or to concentrate its efforts on consolidating its power base in the south, with a view to seceding in 2011.

The continued mistrust between the two sides was also reflected by a fresh build-up of arms. The SPLM was reported to have received several shipments of both heavy weapons and small arms via the port in Mombasa, Kenya, in 2007 and 2008. In October 2008 loyalists to Sudan's Government seized an Ethiopian cargo plane, which they claimed was carrying light arms and ammunition, in Juba. In the same month Sudan's Government withdrew its ambassadors from Kenya and Ethiopia in response to the two incidents highlighted above. Meanwhile, a report by Human Rights Watch identified Russia, China, India and Iran as all shipping arms to the SAF.

In February 2009 fighting broke out within a JIU in Malakal (the capital of the contentious, oil-rich Upper Nile State), involving troops from supposedly mixed units of the SAF and SPLA. At least 62 people were reportedly killed and 94 injured. The fighting was prompted by the arrival in Malakal of Gabriel Tang-Ginya, a controversial SAF major-general who had previously commanded some of the JIU troops based in Malakal as a militia leader. The clash in Malakal was just one of several in southern Sudan during early 2009, with significant fighting also taking place in Jonglei State in January, March and April that year. The clashes in April, ostensibly over cattle, reportedly resulted in over 1,000 people being killed.

Despite the SPLM's return to the power-sharing Government, major provisions of the CPA remained either unfulfilled or under dispute. Although a census belatedly took place in April 2008, the results were disputed by the SPLM. The party had expected the south's population to be at least one-third of Sudan's national population, but the results gave southern Sudan 21% of a final total of 39.2m. The Southern Sudan Centre for Census and Statistics accused the north's Central Bureau of Statistics of refusing to share information when it tried to verify the latter's data, creating further north–south tension ahead of the planned national polls, which were postponed from July 2009 until February 2010, and subsequently until April 2010. Given its natural southern constituency, under-representation of the south would reduce the SPLM's chances of replacing the NCP as the main national party at the elections.

In addition to the controversial census, one of the few CPA-related achievements in 2008 was the selection of an electoral commission. In a rare instance of unity, the nine-member panel was selected by President al-Bashir, Vice-President Ali Osman Muhammad Taha and GOSS President Salva Kiir, before being approved in November by the National Assembly. This followed the adoption in July 2008 of an electoral law that guaranteed women 25% of seats in the legislature in a voting system based on proportional representation.

The Hague's Permanent Court of Arbitration ruled on the status of Abyei in July 2009. Crucially, the ruling placed the Heglig oilfield outside the region, which reassured the NCP. Even if Abyei became a part of an independent southern Sudan, the north could control this asset, because, it claimed, it would fall within the boundaries of Southern Kordofan State (a northern province). Yet, while the NCP and SPLM accepted the Court of Arbitration's judgment, the Misseriya rejected the ruling. Further complicating matters, SPLM authorities in Unity State claimed that the Court's decision to place the Heglig oilfield outside Abyei meant that it would be located in Unity State (i.e. part of southern Sudan), rather than Southern Kordofan. The lack of clarity about the status of Heglig would have significant negative implications after the south's secession in July 2011.

Sudan's Government and the GOSS continued to delay the preparations for the 2011 secession referendum, with many of the crucial prerequisites stipulated by the CPA still not in place by mid-2010. The same critical issues remained unresolved: the demarcation of the north–south border, the post-referendum status of Southern Kordofan and Blue Nile, the formation of referendum commissions for southern Sudan and Abyei, and the negotiation of a post-secession oil-sharing agreement. There were also delays to the appointment of joint north-south commissions, to oversee the preparations for the referendum and the polling itself. These commissions had to be established before financial and operational planning, including logistics, education of the electorate and poll personnel, and voter registration, could be executed.

The registration of more than 16m. voters in late 2009 was accompanied by heightened political tension, as both national and southern Sudanese authorities suppressed peaceful assemblies and intimidated opposition candidates and activists. In the weeks immediately preceding the polls, Sudan's Government extended national security laws, which drastically restricted the freedom of opposition parties to assemble and campaign. In response to this and other concerns, including the impartiality of the National Elections Commission (NEC), the two main opposition challengers for the presidency—Yasir Saeed Arman of the SPLM and Sadiq al-Mahdi, leader of the Umma National Party—withdrew their candidacies just days before the polls. These boycotts, together with those of smaller parties, including the Sudan Communist Party and the Umma Reform and Renewal Party, brought the credibility of the electoral process into question.

Nevertheless, the first multi-party elections for more than two decades finally took place on 11–15 April 2010. The electorate voted in concurrent presidential, legislative and gubernatorial ballots. As anticipated, incumbent President al-Bashir was re-elected, with 68.2% of the votes cast. In the south, Salva Kiir retained the presidency, securing 93.0% of the ballot. The release of the legislative election results was delayed, but it was later announced that the NCP had secured 312 of the 450 seats, of which 132 were elected by proportional representation. The NCP's nearest rival in the legislative ballot was the SPLM, which won a total of 99 seats. Voting in 16 constituencies was postponed, the result in one seat was not released and one seat was declared vacant. Following the announcement of the results, several opposition parties denounced the elections as fraudulent. While observer missions dispatched by the European Union and the US Carter Center, a monitoring group established by former US president Jimmy Carter, declared that the elections had failed to meet international standards, they refused to corroborate opposition allegations of widespread electoral malpractice. Nevertheless, the Carter Center stated that the polls in the south were characterized by 'a high incidence of intimidation.'

In mid-June 2010 al-Bashir announced a new 35-member coalition Government, which included nine members of the SPLM, two more than required under the terms of the CPA. Lual Achwel Deng of the SPLM, Minister of Foreign Affairs in the previous administration, was appointed as Minister of Petroleum. This represented a conciliatory gesture, designed to placate southern suspicions following the alleged siphoning of oil revenues under the previous Government. Meanwhile, President Salva Kiir named the 32 ministers of a new GOSS Cabinet. An unequivocal advocate of full independence, Salva Kiir's choice of appointments was a reflection of his determination to achieve this objective. Deng Alor Kuol, a former Sudan Minister of Foreign Affairs and a senior member of the SPLM, was appointed as the South Sudan Minister of Regional Co-operation, a key position in managing the referendum preparations. The Secretary-General of the SPLM, Pagan Amum, was named as South Sudan's Minister of Peace and CPA Implementation, giving him a central role in negotiations with Sudan's Government over issues that needed to be settled prior to the referendum. Riek Machar continued as Vice-President, in a bid to preserve some semblance of a Dinka-Nuer ethnic balance within the SPLM leadership, against a background in which ethnic minorities had long perceived that the Dinka had too much control over the SPLM and SPLA.

THE JANUARY 2011 REFERENDUM

For many years, it was unclear whether the SPLM would seek to extend its political influence over the whole country and preserve the unity of Sudan, or press in favour of secession by the south. Garang, who espoused the vision of a 'New Sudan,' which was designed to usher in a new era of countrywide democratic governance, had favoured the former option. A significant constituency within the SPLM continued to hold to this vision after his death. However, under Salva Kiir, the secessionists gradually became politically ascendant, so that by the time the SPLM's presidential candidate was announced for the April 2010 elections, it was clear that the objective of a 'New Sudan' was defunct. In January Arman, the Deputy Secretary-General of the SPLM in northern Sudan, was selected to stand against NCP incumbent al-Bashir in the presidential election. Salva Kiir's decision not to contest the national presidency—and instead focus his energies on retaining the presidency of the south—signalled that the SPLM's political strategy was now focused squarely on secession.

There were significant fears that the referendum would be characterized by chaos and conflict, given the failure of the NCP and SPLM to agree on key secession-related issues and delays to the logistical planning of the voting exercise. Owing to a long dispute over the composition of a body to oversee the vote, this key organ—the Southern Sudan Referendum Commission (SSRC)—was not ready to start work until August 2010. Agreement on the status of Abyei, a common border and a post-secession sharing of the south's oil revenues had still not been reached, as voting got under way.

In the end, however, the referendum proceeded remarkably smoothly. Voting took place over a week—from 9 January to 15 January 2011—and was peaceful and disciplined in all areas. The one caveat to this success was Abyei; the special plebiscite for this disputed region was postponed until an undetermined future date and violent clashes took place between the Dinka and Misseriya in the first half of January.

Crucially, the main referendum's legitimacy was endorsed by SSRC Chairman Mohammed Ibrahim Khalil, a Muslim lawyer from the north. Since the NCP had given its blessing to Khalil as the Chairman of the SSRC, this made it very difficult for the north's ruling party to then question the legitimacy of the polling exercise. The SSRC duly announced on 7 February 2011 that the vote had resulted in 98.8% of participants opting in favour of secession. Al-Bashir formally accepted the outcome on the same day.

POST-SECESSION NORTH–SOUTH TENSIONS

Barely one month ahead of secession, a new conflict broke out between the SAF and the SPLA/SPLA-aligned elements in Southern Kordofan State, which is Sudan's most oil-rich remaining province. Although located in what remains of Sudan, it is home to a significant constituency of southerners. Fighting broke out in early June 2011, after a dispute about the results of an election for the state governorship. Incumbent NCP Governor Ahmed Haroun, who had been indicted by the International Criminal Court (ICC) for alleged war crimes in Sudan's western Darfur provinces, was declared the winner of Southern Kordofan's gubernatorial poll by the NEC, but the defeated SPLM candidate, Abdelaziz al-Hilu, claimed that the contest was marred by fraud. The authorities then demanded that all non-SAF military units disarm, against a background where Southern Kordofan—and in particular the Nuba Mountains—had long been a location of thousands of SPLA soldiers and aligned militia. The refusal of these elements to disarm sparked fighting, which, according to the UN, caused more than 70,000 people to flee over the next month. Most of those fleeing were ethnic Nubans, amid a bombing campaign by Sudan's air force. South Sudan's Vice-President Riek Machar claimed that ethnic cleansing was taking place. The African Union (AU) brokered a preliminary agreement between the NCP and the SPLM over Southern Kordofan in late June, involving pledges to disarm non-SAF elements without the use of force. However, President al-Bashir was subsequently quoted in the state media as declaring that the military campaign in this state would continue.

Although hostilities escalated quickly in Southern Kordofan, the emergence of conflict did not surprise informed analysts. The refusal of SPLA troops and aligned militias to demobilize (albeit in the face of Haroun's hard-line reputation), together with the local SPLM's questioning of the NCP's authority, was viewed as a provocation by Sudan's ruling party. Moreover, Southern Kordofan holds some of the most lucrative oilfields outside South Sudan, making the NCP particularly intolerant of attempts to undermine its authority in this area. As far as Sudan's ruling party was concerned, the message was clear: that the independence of South Sudan should not be interpreted as a precursor to additional secessions and that the Government would hold firm over its remaining territory.

Whilst not as severe as the situation in Southern Kordofan, the Abyei region remained tense in the immediate post-secession period. The SAF had occupied Abyei town in late May 2011, after an attack on one of its military convoys outside the town by the SPLA. Abyei is officially a demilitarized zone and had been due to hold a plebiscite on whether to remain part of Sudan or become a part of Southern Sudan at the same time as the main referendum in January 2011. However, the vote in Abyei was postponed indefinitely, owing to a failure of the SPLM and the NCP to agree on who would be eligible to vote (the NCP insisted that the nomadic Misseriya were eligible, while the SPLM insisted that only permanent residents should vote). The SAF's military occupation from May saw the town 'virtually emptied' of its some 50,000 (largely Ngok Dinka) permanent inhabitants, according to UNHCR. The military takeover had been preceded by intermittent clashes for five months from January, largely between pro-SPLM/SPLA Ngok Dinka residents and the Misseriya.

Following negotiations mediated by the AU, in June 2011 both the SPLM and the NCP accepted the planned deployment of 4,200 peace-keeping troops in Abyei, under the auspices of a new UN mission, the UN Interim Security Force for Abyei (UNISFA). However, although tensions were calmed there, the key issues of contention between the NCP and SPLM over the future of the region remained unresolved. Whilst the SPLM maintained (in accordance with the 2005 CPA) that a referendum must be held in Abyei, al-Bashir insisted on 11 July that Abyei would remain part of Sudan, unless the Khartoum-aligned Misseriya nomads consented to it becoming part of the south. This hardened position on the part of the NCP clearly undermined the prospects for the Abyei referendum ever taking place. In the months after secession, there was still no agreement on the permanent status of Abyei, despite the best efforts of the AUHIP to foster an agreement between the two sides in negotiations based in Addis Ababa. Representatives of the two countries could not even agree on the composition of an interim administration for Abyei, which would govern the region until a full agreement. However, whilst post-secession conflict broke out elsewhere, the deployment of UNISFA acted as a stabilizing influence in the Abyei region in the year after secession. In the first annual migration of Misseriya cattle herders after southern independence, UNISFA, which by the second quarter of 2012 had reached a near-capacity force strength of 3,800 (Ethiopian) troops, played a leading role in negotiating access for the Arab nomads to grazing lands and water, in order to avoid fresh conflict with the Dinka community in the areas surrounding Abyei town.

More generally, with the SPLM and NCP failing to agree on the demarcation of a wider border, it remained possible that conflict could break out anywhere along the 2,100 km that stretches from the Central African Republic in the west to Ethiopia in the east. The other main potential trigger for an escalation of north–south conflict was the expiry of an oil-sharing deal. Until 9 July 2011 revenues from the south's oilfields were shared equally between Sudan's central Government and the south. Following secession, the South Sudanese authorities took control of territory that had accounted for three-quarters of Sudan's oil output. In the immediate post-independence era, Sudan's oil production therefore fell from around 490,000 barrels per day to just over 120,000 barrels per day, while South Sudan's output initially totalled more than 360,000 barrels per day. Furthermore, a new agreement needed to be negotiated, predicated either on a diminished share of oil revenues for Sudan, or a replacement of 'revenue sharing' with a system whereby landlocked South Sudan would pay fees to Sudan's central Government, in order to use the latter's pipelines to transport oil to Port Sudan on the Red Sea coast. Even before secession, in June 2011, al-Bashir threatened to terminate South Sudan's access to Sudan's pipelines, unless a satisfactory agreement was forged. In August agreement on this contentious issue appeared to remain a long way off. Whilst South Sudan was offering a pipeline fee of just US $0.41 per barrel of oil transported through the north, Sudan's Government insisted on $22.80 per barrel. SPLM Secretary-General Pagan Amum therefore accused the authorities in Khartoum of 'daylight robbery', against a background in which pipeline fee structures between other countries in sub-Saharan Africa (and elsewhere in the world) were substantially less onerous than those proposed by Sudan. (For example, at that time landlocked Chad paid Cameroon $0.40 for every barrel of oil piped through the latter's territory.)

In late 2011, although South Sudan offered to pay US $1 per barrel of oil transported through the north's pipelines, the Sudanese Government's negotiating position hardened still further, as it raised its demand for pipeline fees to $36.00 per barrel. It also demanded a one-off grant of $7,400m. from South Sudan, in order to cushion its economy against the huge budgetary impact of the post-secession loss of its oilfields. In its defence, Sudan justified its demands on the basis that South Sudan had not contributed to the original cost of building any of the pipeline infrastructure, while global oil prices had risen significantly in the years since other countries' fee structures for pipelines were negotiated. South Sudan sought a degree of compromise, but this was still not enough to satisfy Sudan. Whilst the South Sudanese Government was willing to waive $2,800m. of what it termed payment arrears by Sudan, together with a $2,600m. grant to guarantee pipeline access, it offered to pay the latter only over the course of four years, and demanded that its earlier proposed $1 per barrel transport fee be deductible from this grant.

To a large extent, South Sudan's bargaining position was constrained by its overwhelming dependence on Sudan's pipeline infrastructure. Juba investigated alternative export routes in 2011, culminating in the signing of a preliminary agreement with the Kenyan Government in January 2012 for a pipeline to the coastal town of Lamu. South Sudan predicted that the new pipeline could be constructed and operational within 18 months. However, as of mid-2012 Kenya and South Sudan were yet to finalize agreement on cost-sharing for the venture, which would have to precede the securing of financing for the ambitious project. Use of the pipeline would also depend heavily on the associated building of deepwater port facilities in Lamu. In interviews in May 2012, industry experts estimated that the 18-month timetable was not realistic, thus leaving South Sudan dependent on Sudan for some time to come.

Predictably, the ongoing huge gulf between the negotiating positions of Sudan and South Sudan led to rising tensions on the ground. South Sudan reported on 30 November 2011 that Sudan had delayed the maritime loading of 600,000 barrels of the former's oil at Port Sudan on the Red Sea. By late January 2012 Sudan had expropriated around US $815m. of southern oil, according to President Kiir. He further accused Sudan of clandestinely building a diversionary pipeline, in order to sequester up to 120,000 barrels per day of southern oil. As a result, South Sudan suspended production at its oilfields, in an effort to force the international community to put pressure on Sudan to adopt a more reasonable stance, against a background in which the shutdown would limit supply to the international market and force oil prices upwards, with negative implications for the import costs of four out of five of the UN Security Council's permanent members. However, this tactic yielded no results in the short- to medium-term, as the Sudanese Government adhered to its negotiating position on pipeline fees.

Despite the impasse over oil, progress was made in February 2012 on a separate issue, under the auspices of the AUHIP-sponsored bilateral talks. Representatives of the two countries agreed on a draft citizenship law as follows: 'nationals of each state shall enjoy in the other state . . . freedom of residence, freedom of movement, freedom to undertake economic activity and freedom to acquire and dispose [of] property.' The agreement was due to be finalized during a visit to Juba by President al-Bashir in early April, but his trip was cancelled shortly beforehand. As a result, the draft law remained unsigned, putting the status of South Sudanese citizens who had remained in Sudan in limbo, after a long-standing Sudan-imposed repatriation deadline elapsed on 8 April.

The cancellation of al-Bashir's official visit to Juba—which would have been his first since South Sudan achieved independence—was triggered by renewed north–south conflict. In late March 2012 the SPLA advanced into Heglig town and surrounding oilfields, which were controlled by Sudan in the immediate post-secession period, despite South Sudan's own long-standing claim to this territory. The incursion was staged as the SAF orchestrated an aerial bombing campaign in Unity State. Initially, the SPLA occupied Heglig town for only two days, before withdrawing, but it advanced again the next month, taking control of Heglig from 10 April to 20 April. The latter occupation was accompanied by fierce fighting between the two national armies, marking a significant military escalation from mere mutual accusations of supporting armed proxies. The SPLA withdrew amid intensive pressure from the international community, which culminated in UN Security Council Resolution 2046. This resolution, agreed in early May, compelled the two national armies to cease hostilities within 48 hours, while the respective Governments were obliged to resume their negotiations in Addis Ababa. The SPLA's move into Heglig was officially condemned as a 'seizure and occupation'; equally, Sudan was condemned for the SAF's aerial bombardments of Unity State, which had allegedly involved the targeting of civilians and South Sudan's own oil facilities.

In wording agreed by all five permanent UN Security Council members, a failure by either of the two countries to abide by Resolution 2046's conditions would result in a new meeting to consider the imposition of multilateral sanctions. Substantial damage was sustained by oil infrastructure around Heglig during this conflict, which resulted in its oilfields ceasing production. Although there was a partial resumption of oil production by Sudan in Heglig after the SPLA withdrew, output was considerably below the pre-conflict level of 55,000 barrels per day, when these oilfields had accounted for nearly one-half of the north's post-secession output. Russia therefore called for an investigation to be launched into the cause of the damage to the Heglig facilities and supported Sudan's claims that South Sudan should provide compensation. However, South Sudan claimed that the damage to Heglig had been caused not by its own forces, but by SAF aerial bombing of SPLA units during the latter's temporary deployment in the area.

In addition to the diplomatic pressure by the UN Security Council, financial imperatives gave an incentive for both sides to moderate their negotiating positions, particularly in terms of the expensive oil impasse. While the shutdown meant that Sudan was deprived of royalties from southern oilfields, South Sudan's Government was faced with the eventual prospect of being forced to suspend most of its activities, since it had depended on oil revenues for 98% of its annual budget. This indicated that further bilateral compromise, at least on the oil dispute, would be required, particularly by South Sudan, which faced a clear danger of state collapse, the longer the crisis continued.

However, achieving a genuinely comprehensive settlement was expected to prove much more difficult. Two of the greatest impediments to the latter were the absence of an officially demarcated north-south border and the new conflict in Sudan's Southern Kordofan State, which spread to Blue Nile in September 2011. The rebellion was led by local elements that had supported the SPLA during the 1983 to 2005 civil war, and had remained in Southern Kordofan's Nuba Mountains and in parts of Blue Nile during the 2005–11 political transition. In effect, these forces retained a local SPLA command structure, but abandoned all pretence of co-operation with the SAF after the May 2011 gubernatorial election dispute. In view of South Sudan's secession, the SPLA units in Southern Kordofan officially became known as the SPLA-North (SPLA-N). Likewise, local SPLM members formally adopted a new political identity, as the SPLM-North (SPLM-N). The ruling SPLM party in South Sudan therefore claimed that these entities were entirely separate from the south's political establishment and army, and denied all reports of cross-border support to the insurgents. The Sudanese Government, however, alleged in April 2012 that SPLA artillery units were backing the SPLA-N as far north as Talodi, 100 km north-west of Heglig (deep within Southern Kordofan State).

Sudan's claims were corroborated by Russia's representative to the UN, Vitalii Churkin, who described the sections of Resolution 2046 that welcomed South Sudan's withdrawal from Heglig as inappropriate, since armed groups in Southern Kordofan and Blue Nile were, with external support, continuing to foment destabilization in Sudan. This followed a claim by the Sudanese Government that the SPLA was providing material support to another Sudan-based rebel group, the Justice and Equality Movement (JEM), which had begun an insurgency in the Darfur provinces in 2003. The SPLA-N and JEM had, along with other anti-Government factions in the north, merged to form the Sudan Revolutionary Front (SRF) in November 2011. The stated aim of this new alliance of northern rebel forces was to remove the ruling NCP from power, before establishing an inclusive democracy in Sudan.

Despite its deep historical ties, South Sudan persisted with its claim that it had nothing to do with the ongoing rebellions in the north. Moreover, it continued to accuse Sudan of supporting insurgencies on its own territory, particularly that of the South Sudan Democratic Army (SSDA). In April 2012, this militia clashed with the SPLA in Upper Nile State. The group, reportedly under the command of Maj. Gen Yohannes Ukich, claimed to have surrounded Malakal, the capital of oil-rich Upper Nile State. A spokesman for the SPLA, Philip Aguer, attributed the insurgent activity to 'Khartoum-backed militias fighting [a] proxy war' and claimed that South Sudan's military had repulsed this particular attack.

There was a small political breakthrough after the April 2012 north–south crisis. South Sudan ordered its police force to withdraw from Abyei, in compliance with a 16 May deadline imposed by Resolution 2046. This was followed by the withdrawal of all SAF forces from Abyei town, in accordance with UNISFA's mandate to act as the sole provider of security in the disputed region.

INTERNAL POLITICAL TENSIONS

The SPLM's domination of political life in the south—both during the 2005–11 transition period and post-secession—generated genuine grievances among opposition groups. The ratification of a post-secession Transitional Constitution by South Sudan's Legislative Assembly on 7 July 2011 did little to address the opposition's concerns about the centralization of power. The new Constitution mandated the President to appoint 66 new members to the Legislative Assembly by decree. On 2 July the Carter Center warned that the new Constitution appeared likely to 'concentrate power in the central government'.

As outlined above, a principal source of tensions between Sudan and newly independent South Sudan has been the existence of renegade movements in the south. Several such factions splintered from the SPLA over the year or so prior to secession, blighting security in Unity State, Jonglei State, Upper Nile State and Warrap State. The SPLM/SPLA consistently alleged that the NCP was supporting these renegade movements, in a bid to destabilize the south's ability to govern itself. However, while Khartoum had clearly pursued a 'divide and rule' approach in order to buy off commanders and weaken the SPLA during the civil war, no hard evidence had been presented to confirm the claims of such tactics during and immediately after secession.

The biggest threat to the authority of South Sudan around the time of independence came from George Athor Deng, a former Deputy SPLA Chief of Staff who lost as an independent candidate in the April 2010 gubernatorial election for oil-rich Jonglei State. He ran against SPLM candidate Kuol Manyang Juuk but alleged that he had been defeated only as a result of fraud. On 3 May Athor demanded that Kuol be removed from the post. He launched his rebellion the same month and although he agreed a cease-fire a few days before the January 2011 referendum, the truce was broken when his forces clashed with the SPLA in Fangak town, Jonglei State, on 9–10 February that year. The SPLM claimed that 197 people died over these two days, while local officials estimated the death toll at 241 and stated that the majority of victims were civilians. Both sides blamed the other for the renewed fighting. Later that month 110 people were killed in further fighting, according to Athor, while the SPLA's spokesperson Col Philip Aguer declared the figure to be lower, at about 40. However, the SPLA acknowledged that Athor was in control of a significant force, of around 2,000 men.

Athor's renegade movement was bolstered by alliances with several other disaffected officers, including Gen. Bapiny Monituel and Capt. Uluak Olony. Monituel was an ethnic Nuer who had expressed discontent about the domination of the SPLM by the Dinka ethnic group. Olony was part of the Shilluk ethnic group and became active in Upper Nile State after the April 2010 elections. Whilst Athor himself was a Dinka, he was able to draw on the support of disaffected ethnic minorities because of his own opposition to the largely Dinka establishment. Athor's loose grouping of rebel forces operated under an umbrella known as the South Sudan Democratic Army/Movement (SSDA/M).

Athor's death was reported in December 2011. The SPLA announced that he had been killed in combat, but allied insurgents declared that he had been assassinated. Whilst the military stated that he had been killed in Marobo county, which is in Central Equatoria State and close to the national border with the neighbouring Democratic Republic of the Congo (DRC), Athor's supporters claimed that he was shot in Kampala, the capital of Uganda, where he was allegedly to meet President Museveni as a prelude to a political agreement between the rebels and South Sudan's Government. A communiqué issued by the insurgents stated that an enhanced rebel alliance had been established, in response to Athor's death. Apart from the SSDA, the communiqué was signed by representatives of three other insurgent groups: the South Sudan Liberation Army (SSLA), the National Democratic Front (NDF) and the South Sudan Defence Force (SSDF). This apparent further coalescence of rebel factions was headed by Brig.-Gen. James Nuot Puot (of the SSDA), Maj.-Gen. James Gai Yoach (SSLA), Lt.-Gen. Gordon Koang Chol (SSDF) and Maj-Gen. Thomas Thiel (NDF). The cited signatories, some of whose titles were self-proclaimed, declared jointly that they had agreed that the manner of Athor's death—and its occurrence at a time when he was prepared to reach a political agreement—represented an intolerable escalation by South Sudan's Government, which precluded any future peace negotiations with any of those rebel groups.

The SSLA had formed a second key rebel front against the south's new establishment, although its significance became debatable in the early days of independence. This force was initially led by Gen. Peter Gatdet Yak, a highly influential officer who rebelled in April 2011. In April 2011 Gatdet published a statement on the website of the *Sudan Tribune*, accusing the SPLM of corruption and discriminating against non-Dinka ethnic groups. Although Gatdet signed a cease-fire on 4 August, the SSLA released a statement in which it declared that its struggle would persist. The SSLA thus disowned its erstwhile leader and replaced him with Maj.-Gen. Yoach.

Overall, rebel activity declined in late 2011 and the first few months of 2012, despite the aggressive joint statement issued after Athor's death. The SSDA suffered a reverse in February 2012, when its new leader, Puot, defected to the side of the authorities, after being offered incentives by the Government. Whilst this further depleted the SSDA, which was already struggling after the loss of the veteran Athor, renewed clashes were reported near Malakal, the capital of Upper Nile State, in April. By this time, Uluak Olony appeared to be leading the SSDA, or at least a splinter group from this organization, as he reportedly commanded a group of up to 800 men in skirmishes with the SPLA.

Of greater concern than anti-SPLM insurgent forces in the year after independence, was a rise in the severity of inter-communal violence among ethnic militias. Cattle-raiding by South Sudan's various pastoralist communities has long been habitual in rural areas, where the possession of livestock is the primary determinant of wealth and status. For many young males, participating in a raid is a rite of passage to full manhood. However, there was a particularly violent attack by a Lou Nuer militia against the Murle community in Pibor county, Jonglei State, in late December 2011. Although thousands of Lou Nuer militia were tracked aerially by the UN as they advanced from their homeland in Akobo county in the first half of December, the peace-keeping presence on the ground in Pibor—together with local detachments of the SPLA—proved powerless to intervene, as hundreds of women and children were massacred. Moreover, nearly the entire cattle stock of the Murle was looted. The Murle's male population subsequently launched several retaliatory raids against Lou Nuer cattle camps in Akobo county during the first quarter of 2012, thereby partially replenishing their cattle stocks.

The SPLA orchestrated a new disarmament campaign in Jonglei State after the December 2011 massacres, but both the Murle and Lou Nuer communities were reluctant to hand over their weapons, due to fears that to do so would leave them even more vulnerable to attack by their rivals. The Murle proved particularly resistant to a 'voluntary' stage of the disarmament campaign, owing to concerns about the deployment of Lou Nuer SPLA troops in their territory during the December crisis. More forceful attempts at disarmament by the SPLA were met with allegations of human rights abuses, including torture. The disarmament programme was further complicated by the fact that cattle-raiding is a regional problem, which crosses national frontiers. As a result, even if the SPLA were successful in disarming South Sudan's community militias, indigenous pastoralist communities would remain vulnerable to attacks from Ethiopia, Kenya and Uganda. Key pastoralist communities outside South Sudan include the Merile, originating from Ethiopia, Uganda's Karamojong groups and Kenya's Turkana population, which all have long-held traditions of practising cattle-raiding. The various conflicts have become more serious in recent decades, due to the high regional prevalence of cheap semi-automatic weapons.

EXTERNAL RELATIONS

South Sudan's most important bilateral ally is the USA. Upon gaining independence, South Sudan was confirmed to be no longer subject to the US Treasury Department's Sudanese Sanctions Regime. The United Kingdom is another principal ally of South Sudan. On 9 July British Foreign Secretary William Hague opened an embassy in Juba. The Foreign and Commonwealth Office announced that the United Kingdom would provide £90m. (US $145m.) in bilateral aid during the first year of the new country's existence.

China has also invested in its bilateral relationship with South Sudan, despite being a long-standing ally of Sudan. China's diplomatic ties with Sudan were established in the 1990s and have been characterized by strong investment, including arms sales. China formally recognized South Sudan on the day it declared independence, after having opened a consulate in Juba nearly three years earlier. After the south's secession, China was faced with an increasingly difficult task in balancing its respective relationships between the Governments in Khartoum and Juba. South Sudan's Government complained that it was still being treated as a province of Sudan, with most of China's diplomatic and commercial concessions being directed towards Sudan. Reflecting these anxieties and the growing row between Juba and Khartoum over oil revenues, South Sudan expelled the Chinese President of the Petrodar oil consortium, Liu Yingcai, in February 2012. State-owned China National Petroleum Corporation (CNPC) has long maintained a 40% stake in Petrodar, which operates in South Sudan's oilfields, and Liu's diplomatic rank equated to ministerial status in China. South Sudan justified Liu's expulsion on the grounds of alleged 'non cooperation'. This came in a context in which unnamed oil companies were accused of colluding with Sudan in the alleged theft of southern oil in December 2011 and January 2012. Nevertheless, China's ambassador to Sudan, Luo Xiaoguang, had asserted that Sudan's seizure of southern oil was 'unjustified', even in the context of South Sudan allegedly failing to pay pipeline fees to the Sudanese authorities.

The status of CNPC in South Sudan—and supply of oil to China—was undermined by the former's decision to suspend oil production in January 2012. Chinese state interests were then affected in the Heglig oilfields by the fighting between the SPLA and SAF in April, when damage was sustained to hydrocarbon infrastructure. In a bid to protect its assets on both sides of the undemarcated border, China used its status as one of the UN Security Council five permanent member nations to take an increasingly assertive multilateral role in 2012, agreeing to the content of Resolution 2046 and the threat to consider the imposition of sanctions in the event of the two countries failing to end hostilities or to resume dialogue. Previously, China had sought in late 2011 and early 2012 to influence South Sudan through offering the prospect of a huge bilateral economic package, including grants and a loan of US $1,000m. for infrastructure investment.

Meanwhile, the relationship between South Sudan's Government and its US counterpart was redefined in 2012. Despite the two Administrations of President George W. Bush having frequently defended South Sudan's interests—both in the later years of the 1983–2005 civil war and during the subsequent north–south political transition—the Obama Administration adopted an increasingly assertive tone in response to the rising military tensions between South Sudan and Sudan in the first half of 2012. The US delegation to the UN Security Council was principal in drafting Resolution 2046. The Obama Administration's ambassador to the UN, Susan Rice, condemned South Sudan's occupation of Heglig as 'illegal' under international law and declared that it 'must not happen again', despite South Sudan continuing to profess its own diplomatic claim to this disputed territory.

In terms of South Sudan's relations with its immediate neighbours, the most important of these relationships—that with Sudan—has been covered in detail above. Relations with other neighbouring countries in the immediate post-secession period were cordial. Kenyan President Mwai Kibaki, Ethiopian Prime Minister Meles Zenawi and Ugandan President Yoweri Museveni all attended the independence celebrations in Juba on 9 July 2011. Given its low level of economic development, the new country relied heavily on imports and skilled labour arriving from Uganda and Kenya in particular. In the immediate post-secession period, there was much speculation that South Sudan would join the East African Community (EAC), which at that time comprised Kenya, Uganda, Rwanda, Tanzania and Burundi. However, membership of this regional economic bloc would need to be a phased process for South Sudan, given the competitive rigours entailed by the EAC's customs union and common market. Fortunately, there is a precedent within the EAC for 'opt-outs' and 'slow-track' integration, as Tanzania and Burundi have been granted more time than other member states to adjust their economies to the EAC's requirements regarding a number of issues. South Sudan's application was considered at the EAC's first biannual summit meeting of 2012, when delegates received an initial report on it by the bloc's ministers, and decided that evaluation of the bid would be completed in November.

South Sudan appeared likely to remain dependent on the largesse of the international community for many years after it formally gained independence. Such assistance would be multilateral, as well as bilateral. On 9 July 2011 a new peace-keeping force, the UN Mission in the Republic of South Sudan (UNMISS), became operational in South Sudan. This multinational peace-keeping body replaced the UN Mission in Sudan (UNMIS), which had been mandated to operate in both the semi-autonomous region of Southern Sudan and in the north before secession. However, the Sudanese Government announced in May that it was not willing to allow UNMIS peace-keeping troops to continue operating in its territories following secession. UNMISS in effect took over UNMIS' role in South Sudan, using the same personnel and structure. UNMISS received an initial one-year mandate, with the expectation that this mandate would be renewed annually several times thereafter; in early July 2012 the UN Security Council renewed the mission's mandate, for the first time, for a further year.

Alongside local insurgencies and associated bilateral tensions with Sudan, external rebellions continued to undermine security in South Sudan in the post-secession era. Chief among these rebel groups was the LRA. Although Uganda's army estimated in late 2011 that this notoriously brutal rebel group's fighting capability had declined to only around 200 men, the LRA continued to kidnap children and terrorize rural communities in the DRC, Central African Republic and South Sudan. In an attempt to combat this threat, South Sudan's Government permitted Uganda's army to maintain a base at Nzara, near Yambio, the capital of Western Equatoria State. The SPLA also tolerated the armed status of the local 'Arrow Boys' militia in Western Equatoria, which, through the use of rifles and traditional weapons, provided a frontline defence for local communities against LRA raids. While the LRA have come under increasing military pressure in recent years, the South Sudanese authorities continued to insist in early 2012 that the exiled Ugandan rebels were receiving support from the Government of Sudan.

Economy

DUNCAN WOODSIDE

INTRODUCTION

With the official secession of the semi-autonomous region of Southern Sudan from Sudan as a whole on 9 July 2011, a new nation with considerable economic potential was created. The fully independent Republic of South Sudan possesses significant oil reserves, particularly in Unity State, Upper Nile State and Jonglei State. When secession occurred, close to 370,000 barrels of oil were being produced each day in southern territories, compared to just over 120,000 barrels in the remainder of Sudan. Based on an average price of around US $114.50 per barrel for Sudan's Nile Blend in June, South Sudan's potential gross annual revenue from oil output in the immediate post-secession period equated to an annual $15,463m.

Yet, while oil revenues placed per caput income at a moderate US $1,000 dollars per year (approximately $2.70 per day, higher than in other regional countries), the distribution of wealth was spectacularly uneven. Most people had yet to benefit from the oil industry's earnings, despite the south having already accrued revenues for six years during the 2005–11 political transition. In part, this was due to the need to build national infrastructure from a base of zero, but there were also strong indications of high-level corruption in the latter years of the transition. In June 2012 South Sudanese President Lt-Gen. Salva Kiir Mayardit stated in a letter to selected public employees that an estimated $4,000m. in funds had been stolen by current and former public officials. Upon independence, approximately one-half of the population was living below the global poverty line, on less than $1 per day. A huge 75% of the adult population were illiterate, according to UN figures. In July 2011 South Sudan's Ministry of General Education and Instruction estimated the adult illiteracy rate to be only marginally lower than the UN estimate, at 73%. Only 10% of children were completing primary education, prior to independence. The high levels of poverty and illiteracy were attributable to the long periods of civil war that blighted the south, with the first war beginning in the early 1960s and finishing in 1973, before a second war fought against the Arab-dominated north from 1983 to 2005. Owing to the conflicts, schooling for the greater part of two generations was limited largely to military training, with the result that hundreds of thousands of men with few marketable skills were seeking work in a post-war economy that almost entirely lacked formal employment opportunities. Foreign professionals took most opportunities in the oil sector, while a construction boom in the capital, Juba, largely benefited foreign contractors, engineers and architects. This localized boom did create some demand for unskilled local labourers, but, essentially, beyond public sector employment, there remained few formal jobs available to most South Sudanese citizens.

Even after six years of post-war reconstruction, the country was still faced with huge infrastructure challenges when it achieved full independence. Paved roads did not exist outside the capital in the immediate post-secession period, making travel between Juba and the provincial capitals perilous, even outside the rainy seasons. In the absence of even a basic manufacturing industry or organized agriculture, most goods and non-subsistence produce were imported from neighbouring Uganda and Kenya. Basic items on sale in Juba's market, including tomatoes and other staples, largely originated from Uganda, as European Commission experts discovered during various assessment visits in 2011. The journey from Nimule, on the Ugandan border, to Juba, took six hours, even when travelling at a dangerously fast rate on perilous dirt roads.

The Government of the newly independent country was therefore faced with huge challenges, in terms of attempting to meet the economic hopes of a population that fully expected a peace and independence dividend, after the end of what it regarded as exploitation by the Arab-dominated Government in the north. Despite the high per caput level of oil output, it was difficult to see how the authorities in the newly independent south would be able to meet these expectations. First, while the nominal level of oil output was high, the gross annual revenue estimated above was substantially reduced when taking costs into account. In the case of South Sudan, such costs did not merely involve paying for deep-soil extraction and skilled oil workers through contractual relationships with international oil companies. South Sudan is land-locked and possesses no pipeline network to carry its output to the sea. As such, it depends entirely on Sudan to pipe its oil to Port Sudan on the Red Sea, in order to feed its output to the international market. This gave Sudan's Government enormous power over its southern neighbour, against a background where the former had received a 50% share of revenues from southern oilfields during the 2006–11 post-war transition (see Mineral Resources and Private Investment, below).

South Sudan's economy underwent a huge negative shock in January 2012, when President Kiir ordered Minister of Petroleum and Mining Stephen Dhieu Dau to shut down oil production in the country, in response to what the Government alleged was the theft of US $815m. of its hydrocarbon exports by Sudan's Government. The main accusations from Juba were twofold: that Sudan's security forces had expropriated southern oil destined for the People's Republic of China at the point of export in Port Sudan; and that it was illegally building a clandestine pipeline, which was designed to divert oil from southern pipelines in Unity State. Sudan denied the theft of South Sudan's oil but announced that it had seized exports in order to compensate for an alleged failure to pay pipeline fees. By that time Sudan was demanding a fee of $32.20 per barrel for use of its pipelines and port, while the Government in Juba was offering just $1.00 per barrel. As of July 2012 South Sudan had yet to resume oil production, due to a failure to resolve the expropriation dispute, and the continuing absence of an agreement on pipeline royalties. Just a month after South Sudan suspended oil production, the World Bank warned the Government that the shutdown, if it persisted for more than a few months, would provoke a massive recession. Moreover, the absence of oil revenues generated the risk of a currency collapse and a descent into hyperinflation. Although this warning was contained in a confidential briefing to the Government, it was subsequently leaked, inducing additional risk aversion among traders towards the national currency. On the black market, the South Sudanese pound lost more than one-third of its value in the first six months of 2012, as it fell from 3.5 to the US dollar in late 2011 to nearly 5.0 to the dollar. By March 2012 year-on-year inflation in South Sudan had risen to 50.9%.

South Sudan had been investigating alternative export routes to Sudan's pipeline infrastructure in 2011, culminating, in January 2012, in the signing of a preliminary agreement with Kenya's Government for the construction of a pipeline running south-east to the Kenyan coastal town of Lamu. South Sudan predicted that the new pipeline could be constructed and operational within 18 months. However, as of mid-2012 Kenya and South Sudan were yet to finalize agreement on cost-sharing for the venture. Another impediment to bringing this project to fruition would be the cost of funding. Although South Sudan's Government planned to offer future exports as collateral for international financing, it was highly uncertain whether the Kenya pipeline was feasible over the medium term, especially in view of an intensifying liquidity crisis in global debt markets in 2012. Use of the pipeline would also depend heavily on the associated building of deepwater port facilities in Lamu. In May 2012 industry experts assessed that the 18-month timetable projected by the Government was wholly unrealistic. Adding further doubt to the viability of the project, South Sudan's oil output was predicted by various experts to diminish significantly towards the end of the current decade. This would make investment in brand new pipeline infrastructure difficult to justify financially, a fact that Sudan clearly recognized and factored into its own aggressive negotiating position.

More generally, continued heavy military spending—not all of which was included on official government balance sheets, according to the Small Arms Survey, an international research group—represented a severe drain on South Sudan's budgetary resources, especially in the light of persisting post-war tensions with Sudan. After the end of the civil war in 2005, the two sides engaged in an arms race, with South Sudan reportedly making significant purchases of heavy and light weapons in 2007 and 2008, while Sudan was, according to Human Rights Watch, being supplied by China, Russia and India. In the immediate post-secession period, the Sudan Armed Forces (SAF) and elements strongly aligned to the south's military, the Sudan People's Liberation Army (SPLA), were engaged in clashes in Southern Kordofan State, the most oil-rich province in what remained of Sudan. Given these tensions, it appeared unlikely that newly independent South Sudan would choose to reduce military spending in the near future. The prospects for a redistribution of spending from arms to other national priorities worsened further, when the SPLA clashed with the SAF in the Heglig oilfields in March and April 2012.

South Sudan therefore faced huge obstacles in its bid to bring its level of socio-economic and human development up to even the modest standards of regional peers, including Ethiopia, Uganda and Kenya. One of the biggest priorities would be investment in education, in order to ensure that at least a significant minority of the next generation learned the basic skills required to conduct trade and contribute to the creation of a sustainable domestic economy.

MACROECONOMIC OVERVIEW

With South Sudan only becoming a fully independent nation in July 2011, macroeconomic data was extremely limited in the immediate post-secession period. There were no figures for the trade account or balance of payments. Also, since South Sudan and Sudan had still to agree on a post-secession division of the latter's (largely unserviced) US $35,700m. of foreign debt, there was a similar absence of data for the new country's debt burden and payment schedules. However, South Sudan's Ministry of Finance and Economic Planning did, at that time, preside over fiscal accounts, since the south's Government had been responsible for managing its own budget during the six years (2005–11) that it had been semi-autonomous from the north.

According to provisional figures published by the semi-autonomous Government of Southern Sudan in March 2011, a central government budget surplus was recorded in the 2010 calendar year. Total revenue amounted to 5,757m. Sudanese pounds, of which oil revenue contributed 5,630m. Sudanese pounds. Total central government expenditure in 2010 was 5,576m. Sudanese pounds, with 2,206m. spent on salaries, 2,280m. on operating expenses and 1,091m. on capital expenditure. This resulted in a budget surplus of 180m. Sudanese pounds, according to the Government. The 2011 approved budget anticipated an increase in total government spending to 5,767m. Sudanese pounds, with 2,433m. allocated to salaries, 2,076m. to operating expenses and 1,258m. to capital spending. The priority areas for government expenditure were security, road construction, primary health care, basic education, water and production. Revenue was expected to rise only slightly in 2011, to 5,767m. Sudanese pounds, resulting in a projected balanced budget (i.e. no deficit or surplus) in 2011. Oil revenues were forecast to increase only marginally, to 5,656m. Sudanese pounds (a rise of 0.5% year on year), despite South Sudan no longer being required to split its hydrocarbon earnings with Sudan from 9 July. This cautious projection allowed for potential difficulties in negotiating a post-secession north-south oil agreement and the fact that oil prices were high in 2010, compared with historical levels, with the OPEC basket—a global benchmark—averaging US $77.40 per barrel that year. However, with oil prices moving even higher in the first half of 2011 due largely to the civil war in Libya and popular uprisings in the Middle East, South Sudan's 2011 budget started to appear very conservative.

In early June 2011, one month before independence, Southern Sudan's Ministry of Finance and Economic Planning forecast that the economy would expand by 6%, in real terms, in 2011, followed by an expected acceleration of growth to 7.2% in 2012. When South Sudan first became independent, the IMF did not provide its own forecasts or historical data for the country, but the Fund had announced in April 2011 that the Government was seeking to become a member. The multilateral body was in the process of setting up a trust fund to help the new country establish a national financial architecture. The IMF envisaged that US $10.6m. would be required over nearly four years, to ensure that South Sudan had a chance of building a system with the statistical, analytical and policy-making capabilities sufficient to manage a national process of monetary, fiscal and regulatory decision-making. In April 2012 South Sudan became the IMF's 188th member, with an initial quota of 123m. in Special Drawing Rights (equivalent to $189.3m.).

In the days following secession, the new nation was already facing macroeconomic policy difficulties. A new currency, the South Sudan pound, was released to banks on 18 July 2011, to replace the Sudanese pound but, around the same time, the Sudanese Government also introduced a new currency. The latter's move to introduce its own new pound generated a risk that South Sudan's holdings of old Sudanese pounds would become worthless, unless Sudan's central bank agreed to allow the old currency to remain legal tender during an extended transition period (i.e. long enough for South Sudan's own central bank to withdraw all old Sudanese pounds from circulation in the south, and exchange them in the north for Sudan's new currency, or for US dollars). Pagan Amum, the Secretary-General of South Sudan's ruling party, the Sudan People's Liberation Movement, accused Sudan of launching 'economic war' against his country, and claimed that his nation could lose US $700m. as a result of the move. Although Sudan's National Congress Party (NCP) sought to reassure the South Sudanese Government, with a spokesman, Rabie Atti, stating that Sudan's adoption of its own new currency would be gradual, a deadline for exchanging the old notes was not, at that stage, announced by the north. Adding to the concerns within the South Sudanese Government, the Governor of Sudan's central bank, Mohammad Khair al-Zubair, appeared to contradict Atti's words, stating on 23 July that the change to the new currency in the north would be effected 'as quickly as possible'.

When introducing its own new currency, South Sudan's central bank announced that it would operate a managed float, with the South Sudan pound initially set at 1:1 with the old Sudanese pound. The old Sudanese pound had come under pressure in the months ahead of secession, amid concerns about the impact of the impending loss of oil revenues on Sudan's fiscal and trade accounts. The official exchange rate stood at close to 2.70 to the US dollar by the time secession occurred in July 2011, but this was considerably out of line with the parallel market value, which had reached 3.50 to the US dollar. Against this background, the President of South Sudan's central bank, Elijah Malok, announced that the south's new currency would not, beyond the initial post-secession valuation, remain fixed to its northern counterpart; instead, its value would track a basket of regional currencies and also depend on the global oil price. The rationale for this semi-flexible exchange rate policy was that South Sudan has a strong trade relationship with neighbouring Uganda and Kenya, while the price of oil—its principal export—is notoriously volatile. An entirely fixed exchange rate regime would be too restrictive, since the central bank would be likely to encounter difficulties in combating pressures to devalue during periods of falling oil prices, and conversely, pressures to revalue in times of rising oil prices. A managed float had the advantage of being able partially to respond to inevitable 'oil shocks', while at the same time mitigating the adverse effect of excessive swings in the value of the exchange rate on the conduct of regional trade.

The South Sudan pound came under significant pressure, as a result of the shutdown of oil production in January 2012. The black market exchange rate reached nearly 5.0 to the US dollar before mid-2012. The Ministry of Finance and Economic Planning had claimed in February that it had accumulated enough foreign exchange reserves to cover between seven months and one year of imports, in the event of a failure to resume oil production. However, it was impossible to substantiate this claim, since neither the Government nor the central bank had published verified data on currency holdings at that stage. The Ministry of Finance and Economic Planning announced that it would be reducing government department budgets in response to the decline in national revenue. By February the Government had approved an emergency programme, which amounted to a 25% cut in expenditure, in real terms, according to the Deputy Minister of Finance and Economic Planning. However, further substantial reductions would be precluded by the fact that core salary payments accounted for 50% of the state budget.

The Government aimed to fund the inevitable huge fiscal gap through borrowing externally and domestically. International borrowing would ideally be characterized largely by discounted loans and grants by key multilateral lenders and bilateral donors, but the volume of funds on offer would be constrained by rising fiscal deficits in many developed countries. Although the other external funding route was to use private international markets, any loans offered in this area would be accompanied by a considerable interest rate, and it was by no means guaranteed that such opportunities would be available, given the effect on confidence caused by an intensifying sovereign debt crisis in the eurozone. Domestic borrowing, meanwhile, would largely centre on loans provided by local commercial banks and sales of local currency denominated treasury bills. Borrowing from banks in South Sudan would be difficult, since the domestic network remained undeveloped and foreign banks would likely be averse to providing loans to the Government. Treasury bills, meanwhile, would prove equally unattractive to investors, even with a high nominal rate of return, because of the expectations of spiralling inflation and currency depreciation.

Acknowledging the extent of the escalating fiscal crisis, the Government extended its spending reduction targets. As of March the emergency budget stipulated cuts of 650m. South Sudanese pounds, which were then increased to more than 800m. South Sudanese pounds in April. However, a report in the *Los Angeles Times* quoted a senior state official as confiding that the Government was failing dismally in its attempts to meet these targets, in part due to the cost of the SPLA's incursion into the Heglig oilfields. At that time no reduction in military spending, including the huge cost of army wages, was envisaged, but it was increasingly uncertain whether such core expenditures could be maintained.

MINERAL RESOURCES AND PRIVATE INVESTMENT

The oil industry is absolutely crucial to South Sudan's economy, accounting for 98% of the semi-autonomous Government of Southern Sudan's revenues in 2010. Moreover, with the expiry, upon the south's secession, of a transitional agreement whereby 50% of Southern Sudan's oil revenues were awarded to Sudan's central Government, the newly independent South Sudan's oil revenues were expected to grow significantly.

Yet, despite the six-year long political transition—and the increasing inevitability of southern secession, in the later years of that transition—a new oil deal between Sudan and South Sudan had not been reached by independence. A new agreement was crucial to both countries, since South Sudan was dependent on its northern counterpart's pipeline infrastructure in order to transport its oil to Port Sudan on the Red Sea. There was, at that time, no other means for South Sudan to convey its oil to the international market. Plans had been announced to build a pipeline to Lamu, on the coast of Kenya, and two days before independence, Southern Sudan's Director-General of Energy, Arkangelo Okwang, projected the cost of constructing the 1,400-km pipeline at between US $1,400m. and $1,500m. However, in a media interview, he acknowledged that negotiations with the Kenyan Government about sharing these costs had not even begun and declined to provide an estimated completion date for the project. In January 2012 the two Governments signed a memorandum of understanding and South Sudan announced that it expected the new pipeline to be operational within 18 months, but the viability of this aim was undermined by a lack of financing for the project (see above). A memorandum of understanding was also signed with the Ethiopian Government in an attempt to provide a second alternative to reliance on Sudan's oil transport infrastructure, in the form of a proposed pipeline running west through Ethiopia and Djibouti to a point of export in the Gulf of Aden. Yet, financing prospects for the latter plan were equally uncertain. If the planned pipelines were ever to be completed, then their operations would be at risk from insecurity, including the possible vandalism of infrastructure (and siphoning of oil) by insurgent groups in the more remote parts of South Sudan and by cattle-herding militias in the hinterlands of Kenya and Ethiopia. There was also the danger that an export point at the Gulf of Aden would be subject to a high risk of piracy, given the large number of Somali pirates operating close to these waters.

Sudan's central Government therefore had a very strong bargaining position. As of mid-August 2011 Sudan was demanding a US $22.80 fee for every barrel of southern oil piped through the north to Port Sudan (nearly 20% of the market price of each barrel, before costs). For its part, the South Sudanese Government was, at that time, proposing a fee of just $0.41 per barrel, which was based, it declared, on an arrangement between Chad and Cameroon on pipeline access. Given the strong position of the Sudanese Government, which could, if it wished, simply refuse South Sudan access to its pipelines in the absence of what it regarded as a satisfactory agreement, it was conceivable that any final consensus on pipeline fees would be closer to the position of Sudan than that of the authorities in Juba. When South Sudan suspended its oil production in January 2012, the respective final bargaining positions of the two sides stood at $1.00 per barrel (offered by the Government in Juba) and $32.20 per barrel (demanded by Sudan).

Tensions between the Governments of Sudan and South Sudan over their respective entitlements to South Sudan's oil revenues pre-date secession. In August 2010 Southern Sudan's Minister of Finance and Economic Planning, David Deng Athorbei, criticized the Sudanese Government for starting to pay the south's share of oil revenues in Sudanese pounds, instead of US dollars, from July that year. Pre-independence, earnings from Southern Sudan's oil exports were aggregated in Khartoum, before the central Government disbursed the south's share to Juba. Sudan's move to local currency payments took place against a background where foreign exchange reserves at Sudan's central bank were under pressure, as was the Sudanese pound. The Government of Southern Sudan objected to being paid in Sudanese pounds, since the official rate for the local currency—at that stage 2.43 to the US dollar—was substantially less than the true market rate (at that time 3.10 to the US dollar). This dispute was eventually resolved to the satisfaction of the south, but the disagreement did little to build confidence in the likelihood of smooth post-secession co-operation over hydrocarbon issues.

In September 2009 Global Witness—an international campaign group which lobbies in favour of transparency in developing countries' natural resource industries—presented alleged discrepancies in oil figures published by the Sudanese Government and those of other sources. For example, it issued data showing that official government figures for oil output in Blocks 1, 2 and 4 in 2007 were 9% lower than the statistics provided by the China National Petroleum Corporation (CNPC), which operated large shares of these concessions through the Petrodar consortium.

Less than one week after independence was formalized, South Sudan's Government and its national oil company, Nile Petroleum, according to a media report, formed a joint venture with international commodities trader Glencore, to be known as Petronile International, which was to develop the country's hydrocarbons sector and market its crude oil. However, shortly afterwards, South Sudan's Director-General of Energy, Arkangelo Okwang, stated that the Government had not empowered Glencore to market the country's oil; instead, the sovereign state would retain the authority to market the oil itself. For its part, Glencore countered that it had been authorized to market South Sudan's oil and claimed that the agreement had been signed by Nile Petroleum and Okwang.

Prior to independence, the Government of Southern Sudan sought to rebalance its relationship with a key existing investor in oil facilities in its territories. In March 2011 the Government signed a two-year memorandum of understanding with Malaysia's Petroliam Nasional Berhad (Petronas). The agreement saw the two sides pledge to establish frameworks to share information and encourage indigenous capacity building in Southern Sudan's oil industry. This followed a July 2010 agreement between Petronas and the semi-autonomous Government, which allowed the former to keep its stake in Block 5B, in Jonglei State, according to a report in the *Sudan Tribune*. This deal was predicated upon allowing Moldova's Ascom a share in the concession, which covers over 20,000 sq km and also involves Nile Petroleum, India's ONGC Videsh, Sweden's Lundin and Sudan's state-owned Sudapet.

The position of international oil companies in South Sudan came under heavy scrutiny by the Government in Juba during late 2011 and early 2012. The Chinese head of the Petrodar consortium, Liu Yingcai, was expelled from South Sudan by Minister of Petroleum and Mining Stephen Dhieu Dau in February 2012, for alleged 'non-cooperation'. The Government also accused unnamed oil companies of colluding with Sudan's security services in the alleged theft of southern oil. The various foreign companies operating in South Sudan—which, in addition to CNPC and ONGC Videsh, included China Petrochemical Corporation (Sinopec) and Malaysia's Petronas—were severely affected by the country's production shutdown. Ahead of the closure, international experts acting on behalf of South Sudan's Government made legal provisions to ensure that it would not be liable to court proceedings initiated by international oil companies. The Government also retained contractual discretion over whether to extend oil companies' contracts by a time period equivalent to the shutdown.

Before the oil shutdown, South Sudan had been close to securing funding from China that amounted to US $1,000m. in concessional loans, which were designated for the development of the former's infrastructure. In addition to the proposed establishment of alternative pipeline routes through neighbouring countries, an infrastructure priority for the Government at that stage was the construction of refining facilities on its own territory. Such investment would be expected to add considerable value to the local oil industry. However, information on any further discussions of this proposed infrastructure agreement between the two Governments—which, if ever finalized, was likely to involve significant contracts for Chinese construction companies—failed to emerge over the next few months, amid the tensions generated by the shutdown of oil production and the SPLA's incursion into the Heglig oilfields, where CNPC maintained significant interests.

Beyond oil, there is also potential for gold extraction in South Sudan. The chief executive of US-listed AngloGold Ashanti, Mark Cutifani, announced in August 2011 that his company was interested in exploring in the country, given its gold-mining interests in neighbouring Democratic Republic of Congo, Ethiopia and Eritrea. However, he expressed concern that exploration plans might be hindered by the US sanctions against Sudan, which have existed since 1997 (ostensibly because of the Sudanese Government's alleged sponsorship of terrorist causes). Such sanctions would prohibit the US-listed firm from exporting gold through Sudan. Given South Sudan's land-locked status and poor infrastructure, exporting output through routes other than Sudan would be costly and expensive.

South Sudan's Ministry of Petroleum and Mining announced in July 2011 that it intended to establish a Mining Act by October that year, in an effort to attract rapid foreign investment in the extraction of natural resources. A draft of the bill was, at that stage, ready for consideration by the country's legislature. The ministry declared that the proposed legislation included a 'friendly' tax code and flexible revenue-sharing provisions, with the relative earnings of the Government and foreign investors to be determined on a case-by-case basis, together with environmental provisions and safeguards for local communities. As well as oil and gold, South Sudan's potential natural resources include coal, chromium ore, uranium, diamonds, tungsten, quartz, zinc, silver, copper and iron ore, according to the Government.

The beginnings of a retail sector had emerged in Juba by the time that independence was secured. Kenya-based conglomerate JIT Group was one of the first companies to become involved, establishing a moderate sized retail outlet in Juba, in addition to its existing regional interests in food, consumer durables and jewellery. In April 2012 regional supermarket chain Nakumatt, also headquartered in Kenya, announced that it would open an outlet in South Sudan. The company stated that it had identified a suitable location and that it was not concerned about renewed conflict between South Sudan and Sudan, which it believed would diminish ahead of construction of the store. Moreover, Nakumatt confirmed that the establishment of a supermarket in the country formed a main part of its expansion strategy for the following 12 to 18 months.

AGRICULTURE

At independence, South Sudan's agricultural industry remained drastically underdeveloped. As a result of the long periods of civil war, stretching from at least the early 1960s to 1973, and then from 1983 to 2005, the south of Sudan had been unable to build even a modestly organized agricultural sector. A further factor that has discouraged the emergence of a crop-based agriculture industry is the strong traditional preference for pastoralism. As in neighbouring Kenya's Turkana region (and Karamoja, in the north-east of Uganda), communities in Southern Sudan have long depended on nomadic cattle and goat-herding. Indeed, even in the aforementioned regions of Uganda and Kenya (both relatively developed and peaceful countries), crop-growing is minimal, since the Turkana and Karamojong people adhere to their pastoralist heritage. Around 75% of families in Southern Sudan owned livestock in 2009, according to a report by the US Agency for International Development (USAID).

What little crop-based agricultural activity that existed in South Sudan in the initial post-secession period was largely centred on family-based subsistence farming, with negligible use of fertilizer or insecticides. In Juba, much of the fruit and vegetables on sale in the market were imported from Uganda, despite the absence of anything more than a dirt track to the Ugandan border.

South Sudan therefore remained dependent on food aid, in order to supply part of its population. In 2010 and 2011 FAO distributed aid to 250,000 internally displaced people and returnees from the north, who migrated into the south prior to independence. Approximately 2.5m. people were affected by food insecurity in Southern Sudan in 2010, according to the Famine Early Warning Systems Network, a USAID-funded project.

However, following independence, there was considerable long-term potential to develop South Sudan's agricultural sector, so that it could not only feed the entire country, but also eventually generate export earnings. The south of the country is predominantly covered by savannah, wetlands and equatorial forests. The most fertile states in South Sudan are the country's three southernmost states: Western Equatoria, Central Equatoria and Eastern Equatoria. In the aforementioned 2009 USAID report, it was estimated that around 90% of land is suitable for agriculture, with around one-half of this land of prime quality, with soil and climatic conditions suitable for ground nuts, sorghum, rice, cassava, maize and sesame. This estimate was made despite the still-extensive presence of landmines planted during the civil war, which resulted in some potentially cultivable land being off-limits in the post-war period, as the UN painstakingly carried out a demining programme. No more than 2% of Southern Sudan's land mass has been under cultivation at any one time, according to the 2009 USAID report. In mid-2011 FAO drew up an Interim Assistance Plan for South Sudan's agricultural sector, with the aim of securing funding of US $50m.

There were huge food shortages in 2012, arising from renewed conflict along the undemarcated border between Unity State and Southern Kordofan and inter-communal fighting in Pibor and Akobo counties, in Jonglei State. There were large displacements of refugees from fighting and aerial bombardment in Sudan's Nuba Mountains and Blue Nile provinces, with thousands of people from the former fleeing to Yida camp, in Unity State. At least 1m. people in South Sudan were suffering the effects of food insecurity by April, while a further 3.7m. were 'at risk' of food insecurity, according to the World Food Programme (WFP) and the UN's Office for the Co-ordination of Humanitarian Affairs (OCHA).

Significant pre-independence acquisitions of land by foreign investors indicated that areas under cultivation would increase considerably following secession. A study prepared for Norwegian People's Aid in March 2011 estimated that 26,400 sq km had been purchased by foreign firms, governments and individuals, between 2007 and 2010. One United Arab Emirates-registered company, Al Ain Wildlife, leased the 22,800 sq km Boma National Park, according to Norwegian People's Aid. The aid organization expressed concern that large-scale purchases—often in areas with significant local populations—could lead to conflict and exacerbate food insecurity, given an alleged lack of consultation ahead of the land sales. This echoed the warnings of a 2010 report by FAO, which cautioned that the wholesale and unchecked selling of land to foreign interests by governments in Africa could fuel socio-economic grievances. Prior to independence, a huge land agreement was reached between a local administration in South Sudan's Central Equatoria State and US-based Nile Trading & Development, giving the latter control of 600,000 ha of land on a 49-year lease, with an option to extend territory by a further 400,000 ha. In a March 2008 agreement that was worth just US $25,000 dollars to the indigenous Mukaya Payam Cooperative, Nile Trading & Development was granted an unrestricted licence to grow and harvest timber (and benefit from associated trading of carbon credits), cultivate biofuel crops, and drill for oil and other mineral resources. The lease was granted over ancestral land by a Paramount Mukaya Chief, according to the Oakland Institute, a non-governmental organization which scrutinizes natural resource and environmental practices in the developing world.

FOREIGN AID AND DEVELOPMENT

In the immediate post-independence era, South Sudan relied heavily on international aid, in order to provide food and shelter for internally displaced populations. The USA was a particularly important donor, under the auspices of USAID. As of late July 2011 a total of US $152.7m. was to be disbursed in the 2011 fiscal year, largely as a result of UN agencies and other international organizations operating on the ground.

Another important donor was the United Kingdom, which opened an embassy in Juba on 9 July 2011 (the day that South Sudan seceded from Sudan). The British Foreign and Commonwealth Office announced in the same month that it would provide £90m. (US $150m.) over the next year in humanitarian and development aid.

At the multilateral level, the UN Development Programme (UNDP) has been heavily involved in South Sudan since the 2005 peace agreement. UNDP took a key role in the post-war demobilization and reintegration programme, as the international community and Government sought to rationalize the oversized military and provide skills for soldiers re-entering civilian life. However, this US $55m. programme was widely criticized. An internal UNDP report, leaked to the international media in December 2010, castigated the agency for spending excessively on office equipment and hiring international consultants, many of whom were not approved. This profligate expenditure limited the funds available for retraining former combatants; by the end of July 2011 only 12,500 former combatants had been demobilized, compared with a target figure of 90,000 by 9 July. Of those demobilized, less than 7,500 had completed retraining, with the consequence that the programme had done little to address South Sudan's massive skills deficit. However, the government-run South Sudan Disarmament, Demobilization and Re-integration Commission (SSDDRC) stated in July that UNDP would be likely to head the second phase of the programme funded by the international community. The second phase was expected to be launched in the latter half of 2012 and was to target 150,000 former combatants, making it the largest and the most ambitious such programme world-wide.

As well as bilateral assistance and the involvement of UN agencies, the World Bank and IMF were also poised to take a significant role in South Sudan's development. The IMF announced in July 2011 that it was prepared to support the country in establishing and developing economic institutions, particularly the central bank, after the Government had approached the multilateral lender for technical assistance. The same month the World Bank's Acting Country Director for South Sudan, Ian Bannon, stated that the establishment of effective government institutions in the country would be likely to take 20 years. Earlier in the year, the World Bank's Vice-President for Africa, Obiageli Ezekwesili, had cautioned Southern Sudan's Government against hastily implementing a development strategy without consulting local communities, declaring in February, after South Sudan's ruling party had been accused by the opposition of over-centralizing power, that: 'The elite cannot determine the vision of the nation all on their own. They need to involve their citizens early on.'

However, despite the country's low level of development and persistent insecurity, both in border areas and internally, the International Finance Corpn (IFC), a division of the World Bank, stated in May 2011 that Southern Sudan was making progress toward eliminating its image as an 'astronomical risk' investment destination. By this time 9,000 businesses had registered in the semi-autonomous region, against a background where establishing a business took an average of just 15 days, according to the IFC.

INFRASTRUCTURE

There were less than 100 km of paved roads in South Sudan upon independence. According to the World Bank, around 4,000 km of road were considered to be 'all weather quality', while an additional 13,000 km of tracks were largely impassable for parts of the year. The land-locked country did not possess its own oil pipeline infrastructure and it depended heavily on imports by dirt road from neighbouring Kenya and Uganda.

In February 2011 a project to tarmac the 192-km road between Juba and Nimule (on the Ugandan border) was inaugurated by President Salva Kiir and the US Consul-General to Southern Sudan, R. Barrie Walkley. The US $225m. project was funded by USAID and at that stage a feasibility study, together with the removal of roadside mines, had been completed. The World Bank provided a further loan of $38m. in May 2012, in order to improve dirt roads in rural areas with high agricultural potential.

By contrast, airport infrastructure was relatively well developed. It was possible to connect with regular commercial flights to Addis Ababa (Ethiopia), Entebbe (Uganda) and Jomo Kenyatta International Airport (Kenya) from Juba International Airport, where a new terminal was under construction as the country gained independence in July 2011. Regional operators Fly 540, Kenya Airways, Air Uganda, Ethiopian Airlines and Jetlink all maintained regular services to and from Juba.

In the absence of proper roads, it was also possible to connect to South Sudan's provincial capitals via landing strips, designed to cater for UN humanitarian flights, including by the WFP. The settlements of Wau, Torit, Rumbek, Yambio, Yei, Malakal, Bentiu, Nasir, Maridi, Padak, Nimule, Aweil, Renk and Kajo-Keji all offered operational airports at the time of independence.

The principal telecommunications companies active in South Sudan upon independence were Lebanon's Vivacell, South Africa's MTN, Kuwait's Zain and Libya's GEMTEL. Vivacell was owned by the Fattouch Investment Group, while Gemtel was bought by the Libyan Arab Investment Portfolio from Uganda Telecom in February 2010. Network coverage was erratic outside provincial capitals and many of those people who could afford mobile telephones kept SIM cards for two or more of these companies, due to geographic variations in the quality of the different networks. The Vivacell network, for example, was ineffective in Pibor county, in Jonglei State, at early 2012, although it was possible to make telephone calls via MTN there. The overall quality of South Sudan's networks deteriorated after independence, with complications arising from the adoption of a new dialling code (+211 instead of +249, which was retained by Sudan). Some networks maintained +249 numbers, due to better coverage, while it became difficult to connect +211 numbers to +249 numbers, thereby constraining cellular traffic and adversely affecting company revenues.

At July 2011, only 1m. of South Sudan's 8m. population had mobile telephones, although strong growth was expected following independence, due to an influx of returnees and oil-led economic growth. In April 2011 Vivacell alone aimed to secure a subscriber base of 3m. by 2014, compared with a targeted 1m. by the end of that year. In July Zain announced that it would be willing to pay a fee, in order to continue its services in the newly independent South Sudan. The company had earlier paid €200m. to the Sudanese Government for the right to a licence across the whole country before secession. Separately, the company planned to invest a total of US $110m. in expanding its 3G services in South Sudan in 2011.

Seacom Limited, which specializes in operating fibre-optic networks, announced in June 2011 that it intended to expand its regional network to include South Sudan. At that time, the company maintained operations in Djibouti, Ethiopia, Kenya, Rwanda, Tanzania and Uganda. Seacom stated that it planned to extend into Burundi first, before creating a network in South Sudan within one year of the latter's independence.

Statistical Survey

Source (unless otherwise stated): National Bureau of Statistics, Near South Sudan High Court, May Street, Juba; e-mail contact.ssnbs@gmail.com; internet www.ssnbs.org; Bank of South Sudan, Juba; tel. 249811820218; fax 249811820211; e-mail info@bankofsouthernsudan.org; internet www.bankofsouthernsudan.org.

Note: The Republic of South Sudan achieved independence from Sudan on 9 July 2011 following a referendum held in January at which voters overwhelmingly approved the secession of South Sudan. More detailed statistical information on pre-secession Sudan can be found in that country's chapter.

Area and Population

AREA, POPULATION AND DENSITY

Area (sq km)	644,329*
Population (census results)	
22 April 2008	
Males	4,287,300
Females	3,973,190
Total	8,260,490
Population (official projections at mid-year)	
2010	9,415,421
2011	9,897,118
2012	10,386,101
Density (per sq km) at mid-2012	16.1

* 248,777 sq miles.

POPULATION BY AGE AND SEX
(population at 2008 census)

	Males	Females	Total
0–14	1,945,033	1,722,860	3,667,893
15–64	2,216,427	2,157,893	4,374,320
65 and over	125,840	92,437	218,277
Total	4,287,300	3,973,190	8,260,490

STATES
(population at 2008 census)

	Area (sq km)	Population	Density (per sq km)
Upper Nile	77,283	964,353	12.5
Jonglei	122,581	1,358,602	11.1
Unity	37,837	585,801	15.5
Warrap	45,567	972,928	21.4
Northern Bahr El-Ghazal	30,543	720,898	23.6
Western Bahr El-Ghazal	91,076	333,431	3.7
Lakes	43,595	695,730	16.0
Western Equatoria	79,343	619,029	7.8
Central Equatoria	43,033	1,103,557	25.6
Eastern Equatoria	73,472	906,161	12.3
Total	644,329	8,260,490	12.8

PRINCIPAL TOWNS
(population at 2008 census)

Juba (capital)	368,436	Uror	178,519
Aweil East	309,921	Magwi	169,826
Gogrial West	243,921	Aweil West	166,217
Bor South	221,106	Tonj North	165,222
Luakpiny/Nasir	210,002	Kapoeta East	163,997
Twic	204,905	Rumbek Centre	153,550
Yei	201,443	Yambio	152,257
Kajo-Keji	196,387	Wau	151,320

BIRTHS AND DEATHS
(official figures)

	2008	2009*	2010*
Births	338,453	347,136	355,099
Birth rate (per 1,000)	39.9	38.8	37.7
Deaths	87,673	89,050	90,262
Death rate (per 1,000)	10.4	10.0	9.6

* Projections.

Life expectancy (years at birth): 58.2 (males 56.9; females 59.5) in 2008.

Health and Welfare

KEY INDICATORS

Total fertility rate (children per woman, 2008)	5.5
Under-5 mortality rate (per 1,000 live births, 2010)	105
Access to water (% of persons, 2010)	67
Access to sanitation (% of persons, 2010)	7

For sources and definitions, see explanatory note on p. vi.

Agriculture

Principal Crop ('000 metric tons): Total cereals 1,068 in 2008; 660 in 2009; 695 in 2010.

Livestock ('000 head): Cattle 10,860 in 2008; 11,735 in 2009; 11,814 in 2010.

Finance

CURRENCY AND EXCHANGE RATES Note: A new currency, the South Sudan pound was introduced, at par with the former new Sudanese pound (see the chapter on Sudan), in July 2011.

CENTRAL GOVERNMENT BUDGET
(million new Sudanese pounds)

Revenue	2009	2010	2011
Oil revenue	4,121.5	5,630.3	4,782.1
Non-oil revenue	118.3	126.6	107.0
Total	4,239.8	5,756.8	4,889.1

Expenditure	2009	2010	2011
Current expenditure	3,232.6	4,485.3	3,480.7
Wages and salaries	1,977.3	2,205.7	1,334.9
Operating	1,255.3	2,279.6	2,145.8
Capital expenditure	1,002.0	1,090.9	943.4
Total	4,234.7	5,576.1	4,424.1

MONEY SUPPLY
(million new Sudanese pounds at 31 December)

	2008	2009
Currency in circulation	963	4,254
Demand deposits	318	766
Total	1,281	5,020

COST OF LIVING
(Consumer Price Index; base: June 2011 = 100)

	2009	2010	2011
Food and non-alcoholic beverages	69.1	69.6	106.8
Housing and fuels	83.0	80.3	101.0
Furnishings and household equipment	76.1	81.5	129.1
Transport	76.1	79.8	107.7
Recreation and culture	86.2	94.6	108.5
All items (incl. others)	73.5	74.4	109.6

NATIONAL ACCOUNTS
(million new Sudanese pounds in current prices)

Expenditure on the Gross Domestic Product
(provisional estimates)

	2008	2009	2010
Government final consumption expenditure	4,644	3,978	5,674
Private final consumption expenditure	9,619	10,493	11,145
Gross capital formation	4,816	3,921	4,005
Total domestic expenditure	19,079	18,392	20,824
Exports of goods and services	21,325	16,837	21,973
Less Imports of goods and services	11,898	10,284	12,310
GDP in purchasers' values	28,505	24,946	30,488

Education

	2008	2009	2010
Permanent schools	6,794	9,884	n.a.
Teachers	25,972	26,575	26,658
Pupil-teacher ratio	50	52	53

Student enrolment: *Primary:* 1,284,252 (males 809,519, females 474,733) in 2007/08; 1,380,580 (males 871,804, females 508,776) in 2008/09; 1,401,874 (males 880,208, females 521,666) in 2009/10. *Secondary:* 44,027 (males 31,977, females 12,050) in 2008/09; 34,487 (males 24,498, females 9,989) in 2009/10.

Adult literacy rate (15 years and over): 27% in 2009.

Directory

Note: Although South Sudan was assigned the international telephone code 211 by the International Telecommunication Union in July 2011, many mobile and fixed-line telephone services continued to be provided using either Sudanese (249) or Ugandan (256) networks. Therefore, all telephone numbers given below include the full international dialling code.

The Constitution

The Transitional Constitution of the Republic of South Sudan was approved by the South Sudan Legislative Assembly on 7 July 2011 and entered into force on 9 July 2011 at South Sudan's formal secession from Sudan.

The President of the Republic of South Sudan is the Head of State and of Government, the Commander-in-Chief of the Sudan People's Liberation Army and the Supreme Commander of all the other regular forces.

Legislative authority is vested in and exercised by the National Legislature, which consists of the 170-member Legislative Assembly and the Council of States. The term of the National Legislature is five years.

The territory of South Sudan is divided into 10 states, each of which has a State Government, consisting of a State Assembly and a State Executive. The latter is headed by a State Governor elected directly by popular vote.

The Government

HEAD OF STATE

President: Lt-Gen. SALVA KIIR MAYARDIT (took office on 11 August 2005 as President of the Government of Southern Sudan).

Vice-President: Dr RIEK MACHAR TENY-DHURGON.

COUNCIL OF MINISTERS
(September 2012)

Minister of Cabinet Affairs: DENG ALOR KUOL.

Minister of Defence and Veteran Affairs: Gen. JOHN KONG NYUON.

Minister of Foreign Affairs and International Co-operation: NHIAL DENG NHIAL.

Minister in the Office of the President: EMMANUEL LOWILLA.

Minister in the Office of the President, Responsible for National Security: Gen. OYAY AJAK.

Minister of Justice: JOHN LUYK JOK.

Minister of the Interior: Gen. ALISON MANANI MAGAYA.

Minister of Parliamentary Affairs: MICHAEL MAKUEI LUETH.

Minister of Finance and Economic Planning: KOSTI MANIBE NGAI.

Minister of Labour, Public Service and Human Resource Development: KWONG DANHIER GATLUAK (acting).

Minister of Health: Dr MICHAEL MILLY HUSSEIN.

Minister of Information and Broadcasting: Dr BARNABA MARIAL BENJAMIN.

Minister of Agriculture and Forestry: Dr BETTY ACHAN OGWARO.

Minister of Roads and Bridges: GIER CHUANG ALUONG.

Minister of Transport: AGNES PONI LOKUDU.

Minister of General Education and Instruction: USTAZ JOSEPH UKEL ABANGO.

Minister of Higher Education, Science and Technology: Dr PETER ADWOK NYABA.

Minister of Commerce, Industry and Investment: GARANG DIING AKUANG.

Minister of the Environment: ALFRED LADO GORE.

Minister of Housing and Physical Planning: JEMA NUNU KUMBA.

Minister of Telecommunications and Postal Services: MADUT BIAR YEL.

Minister of Petroleum and Mining: STEPHEN DHIEU DAU.

Minister of Electricity and Dams: DAVID DENG ATHORBEI.

Minister of Gender, Child and Social Welfare: AGNES KWAJE LAUBA.

Minister of Humanitarian Affairs and Disaster Management: JOSEPH LUAL ACUIL.

Minister of Water Resources and Irrigation: PAUL MAYOM AKEC.

Minister of Wildlife Conservation and Tourism: GABRIEL CHANGSON.

Minister of Animal Resources and Fisheries: Dr MARTIN ELIA LOMURO.

Minister of Culture, Youth and Sports: Dr CIRINO HITENG OFUHO.

MINISTRIES

Office of the President: Juba.

Ministry of Agriculture and Forestry: Juba; tel. 249917068933 (mobile); e-mail bedamachar@yahoo.com.

Ministry of Animal Resources and Fisheries: Juba; tel. 24912221935; e-mail wimapa89@yahoo.co.uk.

Ministry of Cabinet Affairs: Juba.

Ministry of Commerce, Industry and Investment: POB 73, Juba; tel. 249914113105 (mobile); e-mail kitoundo@hotmail.com; internet www.commerce-goss.org.

Ministry of Culture, Youth and Sports: Juba.

Ministry of Defence and Veteran Affairs: Juba; tel. 249915485232 (mobile); e-mail kdeimkuol@yahoo.com; internet www.splamilitary.net.

Ministry of Electricity and Dams: Juba.

Ministry of the Environment: Juba.

Ministry of Finance and Economic Planning: Juba; tel. 256477126466 (mobile).

Ministry of Foreign Affairs and International Co-operation: Juba.

Ministry of Gender, Child and Social Welfare: Juba; tel. 249126925801; e-mail mgswragoss@gmail.com.

Ministry of General Education and Instruction: Juba; tel. 249926168090 (mobile); e-mail datjoel@yahoo.com; internet www.moest.gov.sd.

Ministry of Health: Juba; tel. 249917036278 (mobile); e-mail infomohgoss@gmail.com; internet www.mohgoss.com.

Ministry of Higher Education, Science and Technology: Juba.

Ministry of Housing and Physical Planning: Juba.

Ministry of Humanitarian Affairs and Disaster Management: Juba; tel. 249912553790 (mobile); e-mail ajawinsenior@yahoo.com.

Ministry of Information and Broadcasting: Juba; tel. 249922260000; e-mail musabiong@yahoo.ca.

Ministry of the Interior: Juba; tel. 256477103368 (mobile); e-mail pmadol@yahoo.com.

Ministry of Justice: Juba.

Ministry of Labour, Public Service and Human Resource Development: Juba; tel. 249917259719 (mobile).

Ministry of Parliamentary Affairs: Juba; tel. 249912339369 (mobile); e-mail juliaduany@ymail.com.

Ministry of Petroleum and Mining: POB 376, Juba; tel. 249918906406 (mobile); fax 249811829583 (mobile); e-mail megoss@ministryofenergygoss.net; internet www.ministryofenergygoss.net.

Ministry of Roads and Bridges: Juba; tel. 249129187774; e-mail airroadwater@yahoo.com; internet www.mtr-goss.org.

Ministry of Telecommunications and Postal Services: POB 33 Juba; tel. 211977102623 (mobile); fax 211811820188; e-mail Juma.lugga@motps.goss.org; internet www.motps.goss.org/.

Ministry of Transport: Juba.

Ministry of Water Resources and Irrigation: Juba; tel. 249126298074; e-mail alieroka@yahoo.co.uk; internet rwssp-mwrigoss.org.

Ministry of Wildlife Conservation and Tourism: Juba; tel. 249955024191 (mobile); e-mail jameskenyi@yahoo.com.

STATE GOVERNORS

(September 2012)

Central Equatoria: Maj.-Gen. (retd) CLEMENT WANI KONGA (SPLM).

Eastern Equatoria: LOUIS LOBONG LOJORE (SPLM).

Jonglei: KUOL MANYANG JUUK (SPLM).

Lakes: Lt-Gen. CHOL TONG MAYA (SPLM).

Northern Bahr El-Ghazal: PAUL MALONG AWAN ANEI (SPLM).

Unity: Brig. TABAN DENG GAI (SPLM).

Upper Nile: SIMON KON FUJ (SPLM).

Warrap: NYANDENG MALEK DELIECH (SPLM).

Western Bahr El-Ghazal: RIZIK HASSAN ZACHARIAH (SPLM).

Western Equatoria: Col BANGASI JOSEPH BAKOSORO (Ind.).

President and Legislature

PRESIDENT

Election, 11–15 April 2010

Candidate	Votes	% of votes
Lt-Gen. Salva Kiir Mayardit (Sudan People's Liberation Movement)	2,616,613	92.99
Dr Lam Akol Ajawin (Sudan People's Liberation Movement—Democratic Change)	197,217	7.01
Total	2,813,830	100.00

LEGISLATIVE ASSEMBLY

Speaker: JAMES WANI IGGA.

Election 11–15 April 2010

Party	Seats* A	B	C	Total
Sudan People's Liberation Movement	93	25	42	160
Independents	6	—	—	6
Sudan People's Liberation Movement—Democratic Change	2	—	1	3
National Congress Party	1	—	—	1
Total	102	25	43	170

* There are 170 members of the Legislative Assembly of whom 102 (A) are directly elected in single seat constituencies; 25 'party members' (B) are elected on the basis of proportional representation at the state level from separate and closed party lists; and a further 43 women members (C) are elected on the basis of proportional representation at the state level from separate and closed party lists.

Election Commission

National Elections Commission: Juba.

Political Organizations

Sudan People's Liberation Movement (SPLM): Juba; e-mail info@splmtoday.com; internet www.splmtoday.com; Leader Lt-Gen. SALVA KIIR MAYARDIT; Sec.-Gen. PAGAN AMUM.

Sudan People's Liberation Movement—Democratic Change (SPLM—DC): Juba; f. 2009; Leader Dr LAM AKOL AJAWIN.

United Democratic Party: Juba; Leader TONG LUAL AYAT.

Diplomatic Representation

EMBASSIES IN SOUTH SUDAN

China, People's Republic: POB 249, Juba; tel. 256477232333 (mobile); internet ss.chineseembassy.org; Ambassador LI ZHIGUO.

Egypt: Iwzrat St, Plot No. J/119, Cinema Residential Area, Juba; Ambassador MOAYAD FATHALLAH MOHAMMED.

Eritrea: Juba; tel. 249926228425 (mobile); fax 249122488842; e-mail asengal@yahoo.com; Chargé d'affaires ALEM NEGASH.

France: EU Compound, Kololo Rd, Thomping, Juba; tel. 249957127549 (mobile); fax 249955587332 (mobile); internet soudandusud.ambafrance.org; Ambassador CHRISTIAN BADER.

Germany: EU Compound, Kololo Rd, Thomping, Juba; tel. 249956008021 (mobile); Ambassador PETER FELTEN.

Kenya: POB 208, Juba; tel. 249811823664; fax 249811823666; e-mail keconju@yahoo.co.uk; Ambassador CLELAND LESHORE.

Nigeria: Juba; Ambassador DEDAN MADUGU.

United Kingdom: EU Compound, Kololo Rd, Thomping, Juba; tel. 249955584193 (mobile); e-mail ukinsouthsudan@dfid.gov.uk; internet ukinsouthsudan.fco.gov.uk; Ambassador Dr ALASTAIR MCPHAIL.

USA: Juba; e-mail usembassyjuba@state.gov; internet southsudan .usembassy.gov; Ambassador SUSAN DENISE PAGE.

Judicial System

The judicial system of South Sudan comprises a Supreme Court, composed of a President, a Deputy President and five justices; three Courts of Appeal, located in Malakal, Juba and Rumbek, each consisting of a President and two justices; 10 High Courts, one in each state, consisting of a President and one justice; county courts and other courts deemed necessary to be established; and town and rural courts. The President of the Supreme Court of South Sudan is the head of the judiciary and is answerable to the President of the Government of South Sudan for the administration of the judiciary. High Courts are the highest courts at the state level.

Supreme Court: Juba; Pres. CHAN REEC MADUT.

Religion

The majority of the South Sudanese population are Christians or animists.

CHRISTIANITY

Roman Catholic Church

The Roman Catholic Church in Sudan officially remained unified after the secession of South Sudan, although some bishops desired division of the church and the formation of two conferences. For ecclesiastical purposes, South Sudan comprises one archdiocese and six dioceses.

Archbishop of Juba: Most Rev. PAOLINO LUKUDU LORO, Catholic Church, POB 32, Juba; tel. 249811820303; fax 249811820755; e-mail archbishopofjuba@hotmail.com.

ISLAM

Council of Muslims: Juba; Chair. ATIR BIOR.

The Press

NEWSPAPERS

Al-Isteqlal: Juba; f. 2011; daily; Arabic; Man. Editor GAMAL DALMAN.

Al-Mussir: Juba; f. 2011; weekly; Arabic.

The Citizen: Hai Amarat, Airport Road, Juba; tel. 249908760789 (mobile); e-mail thecitizen2006@yahoo.com; f. 2005; daily; Editor-in-Chief NHIAL BOL AKEN.

The Juba Monitor: Juba; f. 2011; Editor-in-Chief ALFRED TABAN.

The Juba Post: Juba; f. 2005; biweekly; Editor-in-Chief MICHAEL KOMA (acting).

The Southern Eye: Tong Ping, Airport Rd, POB 243, Juba; tel. 977100072 (mobile); e-mail southerneyegoss@yahoo.com; internet southerneyeonline.com.

Broadcasting and Communications

TELECOMMUNICATIONS

At the end of 2011 there were five mobile cellular telephone operators in South Sudan.

Gemtel: Juba.

MTN South Sudan: Juba.

Sudatel South Sudan: Juba.

Vivacell: Juba.

Zain South Sudan: Juba.

BROADCASTING

Radio

Radio Miraya: Airport Rd, Juba; internet www.mirayafm.org; operated by the United Nations Mission in South Sudan (UNMISS) in partnership with Fondation Hirondelle.

South Sudan Radio: Juba; Dir-Gen. AROP BAGAT TINGLOTH.

Sudan Catholic Radio Network (SCRN): Juba; seven FM radio stations, at Juba, Malakal, Rumbek, Torit, Yei, Tonj and Nuba Mountains (2010)

Bakhita Radio: Juba; f. 2006; Catholic.

Television

South Sudan TV: Juba; Dir-Gen. AROP BAGAT TINGLOTH.

Finance

BANKING

Established in 2005 as a branch of the Bank of Sudan, the Bank of Southern Sudan operated as the central bank of South Sudan until 9 July 2011. After secession it was formally transformed into the Bank of South Sudan. On 18 July the Bank of South Sudan introduced a new currency, the South Sudan pound, which was to replace the Sudanese pound in South Sudan. In early 2012 there were 14 registered commercial banks in South Sudan.

Central Bank

Bank of South Sudan (BOSS): Juba; tel. 249811821111 (mobile); fax 249811820211 (mobile); e-mail info@bankofsouthernsudan.org; internet www.bankofsouthernsudan.org; f. 2011 to replace the Bank of Southern Sudan; Gov. KORNELIO KORYOM MAYIIK.

Commercial Banks

Buffalo Commercial Bank: BCB Junction, Juba; e-mail info@ buffalocommercialbank.com; internet www.buffalocommercialbank .com; f. 2008; Chair. Dr LUAL ACUEK LUAL DENG; CEO BISWASH GAUCHAN.

Nile Commercial Bank Ltd: Juba; tel. 256477101931 (mobile); f. 2003; Man. Dir AGGREY IDRI.

Trade and Industry

CHAMBER OF COMMERCE

South Sudan Chamber of Commerce, Industry and Agriculture (SSCCIA): adjacent to Summer Palace Hotel, Juba; tel. 211955908673 (mobile); e-mail info@ southsudanchamber-commerce.org; internet southsudanchamber-commerce.org; f. 2003; Chair. BENJAMIN BOL MELL; Sec.-Gen. SIMON AKUEI DENG.

MAJOR COMPANIES

Nile Petroleum Corpn (Nilepet): Juba; f. 2008; Man. Dir MANGOK KHALIL MANGOK KHALIL.

Petronile International: Juba; f. 2011; jt venture co; 51% owned by Nilepet (South Sudan) and 49% owned by Glencore International AG.

Transport

RAILWAYS

South Sudan has 248 km of single track, narrow-gauge railway line from the Sudanese border to Wau terminus. The line, however, has not been operational since 1991. There are proposed extensions from

Wau to Juba, the capital of South Sudan. There are also plans to link Juba with the Kenyan and Ugandan railway networks.

ROADS

South Sudan Road Authority: Juba; f. 2011.

CIVIL AVIATION

Juba Airport is the busiest and most developed international airport in South Sudan, with regular flights to Entebbe, Nairobi, Cairo, Addis Ababa and Khartoum. Other international airports include Malakal, with flights to Addis Ababa and Khartoum; Wau, with a weekly service to Khartoum; and Rumbek, also with weekly flights to Khartoum.

Feeder Airlines: Juba; f. 2007.

Southern Sudan Airlines: Shari El Mina, Juba; f. 2005.

Education

There are nine public universities and 16 private universities in South Sudan, although only five of the public universities were able to admit students in 2011. For the 2011/12 academic year, the four main public universities—Juba, Bahr El-Ghazal, Upper Nile and Rumbek—approved a total intake of 2,722 students, out of just over 4,500 applications, according to the Ministry of Higher Education, Science and Technology.

In October 2011 it was announced that English would become the language of instruction in South Sudanese schools by the end of the year.

Bibliography

Abdel-Rahim, M., *et al. Sudan since Independence*. London, Gower, 1986.

Adar, K. G. *The Sudan Peace Process*. Pretoria, Africa Institute of South Africa, 2005.

Africa Watch. *War in South Sudan: The Civilian Toll*. New York, Africa Watch, 1993.

Alier, A. *Southern Sudan: Too Many Agreements Dishonoured*. Exeter, Ithaca Press, 1990.

Beshir, M. O. *The Southern Sudan: Background to Conflict*. London, C. Hurst, and New York, Praeger, 1968.

Butler, V., Carney, T., and Freeman, M. *Sudan: The Land and the People*. London, Thames & Hudson, 2005.

Collins, R. O. *Shadows in the Grass: Britain in the Southern Sudan 1918–1956*. New Haven, CT, Yale University Press, 1983.

A History of Modern Sudan. Cambridge, Cambridge University Press, 2008.

Daly, M. W., and Sikainga, A. A. *Civil War in the Sudan*. London, British Academic Press, 1993.

Deng, F. M. *War of Visions: Conflict of Identities in the Sudan*. Washington, DC, Brookings Institution, 1995.

Deng, F. M., and Khalil, M. *Sudan's Civil War: The Peace Process Before and Since Machakos*. Pretoria, Africa Institute of South Africa, 2005.

Fluehr-Lobban, C., Fluehr-Lobban, R. A., and Voll, J. *Historical Dictionary of the Sudan*. 2nd edn. Metuchen, NJ, Scarecrow Press, 1992.

Garang, J. *The Call for Democracy in Sudan* (Ed. Khalid, M.). 2nd edn. London, Kegan Paul International, 1992.

Holt, P. M., and Daly, M. W. *The History of the Sudan from the Coming of Islam to the Present Day*. 4th edn. London and New York, Longman, 1988.

Iyob, R., and Khadiagala, G. M. *Sudan: The Elusive Quest for Peace*. Boulder, CO, Lynne Rienner Publishers, 2006.

Johnson, D. H. *The Root Causes of Sudan's Civil Wars*. Revised edn. London, James Currey, 1995.

Keen, D. *The Benefits of Famine: A Political Economy of Famine and Relief in Southwestern Sudan, 1983–1989*. Princeton, NJ, Princeton University Press, 1994.

Khalid, M. *War and Peace in Sudan: A Tale of Two Countries*. London, Kegan Paul International, 2003.

LeRiche, M., and Arnold, M. *South Sudan: From Revolution to Independence*. London, C. Hurst, 2012.

Natsios, A. *Sudan, South Sudan, and Darfur: What Everyone Needs to Know*. New York, Oxford University Press, 2012

Nyaba, P. A. *The Politics of Liberation in South Sudan: An Insider's View*. Kampala, Fountain Publishers, 1997.

O'Ballance, E. *The Secret War in the Sudan 1955–1972*. London, Faber and Faber, 1977.

Oduho, J., and Deng, W. *The Problem of the Southern Sudan*. Oxford, Oxford University Press, 1963.

Petterson, D. *Inside Sudan: Political Islam, Conflict, and Catastrophe*. Philadelphia, PA, Westview, 1999.

Prunier, G. *From Peace to War: The Southern Sudan (1972–1984)*. Hull, University of Hull, 1986.

Rolandsen, O. H. *Guerrilla Government: Political Changes in the Southern Sudan during the 1990s*. Uppsala, Nordic Africa Institute, 2005.

Rone, J., *et al.* (Eds). *Civilian Devastation: Abuses by the Parties in the War in Southern Sudan*. New York, Human Rights Watch, 1994.

Ruay, D. D. A. *The Politics of Two Sudans: The South and the North, 1921–1969*. Uppsala, Nordic Africa Institute, 1994.

Sidahmed, A. S. *Politics and Islam in Contemporary Sudan*. Richmond, Curzon Press, 1996.

Sidahmed, A. S., and Sidahmed, A. *Sudan*. Abingdon, Routledge, 2004.

Sylvester, A. *Sudan under Nimeri*. London, Bodley Head, 1977.

Thomas, G. F. *Sudan: Struggle for Survival, 1984–1993*. London, Darf, 1993.

Voll, J. O. (Ed.). *Sudan: State and Society in Crisis*. Bloomington, IN, Indiana State University Press, 1991.

Woodward, P. *Sudan 1898–1989: The Unstable State*. Boulder, CO, Lynne Rienner Publishers, 1990.

SUDAN

Physical and Social Geography

J. A. ALLAN

THE NILE

The River Nile and its tributaries form the basis of much of the economic activity of Sudan, and of most of the future activity that is now envisaged. The river largely traverses arid deserts and the Nile waters either evaporate or flow until they reach Lake Nubia on the Egyptian border. Prior to the secession of South Sudan, the Republic of Sudan had a total area of 2,505,813 sq km (967,500 sq miles). The area was estimated to have been reduced to 1,861,484 sq km, based upon South Sudan's declaration of its total area. The distances are vast, and the remoteness of places on the Nile system, and those of the rest of the country, explains much of the character of Sudan's land use. The other important factor is climate, which influences vegetation and, more significantly, affects the seasonal flow of the Nile tributaries.

The Blue Nile is the main tributary, both in the volume of water that it carries (four-sevenths of the total average flow of the system) as well as in the area of irrigated land, of which it supports over 40% of the present area and 70% of potential irrigable land. The Blue Nile and other east-bank tributaries are sustained by monsoon rains over the Ethiopian highlands, which cause the river to flood at the end of July, reach a peak in August and remain high through September and the first half of October. The Atbara, another seasonal east-bank tributary, provides a further one-seventh of the flow in the system, and the remaining two-sevenths come from the White Nile. (These figures relate to pre-secession Sudan.) The sustained flow of the White Nile arises first because its main source is Lake Victoria, which regulates the flow, and secondly because the swamps of the Sudd and Machar (in South Sudan) act as a reservoir, absorbing the irregular stream flow while discharging a regular flow, much reduced by evaporation, in the north.

The River Nile is an international river system, and Sudan depends on river flows from eight other states. Sudan does not yet use all of the 18,500m. cu m of annual flow agreed with Egypt in 1959 as its share of the total average flow at Aswan of 84,000m. cu m. (Egypt receives 55,500m. cu m, while 10,000m. cu m are assumed to evaporate annually from Lake Nasser/Nubia.) In anticipation of future additional demand by upstream states such as Ethiopia, and in view of Egypt's rising demand for water, Sudan and Egypt jointly embarked in 1978 on the construction of the Jonglei Canal project, the aim of which was to conserve some 4,000m. cu m of the 33,000m. cu m of water lost annually through evaporation in the Sudd swamp. However, the project was halted by the civil conflict and it was not until 2008 that the Sudanese and Egyptian Governments decided to resume work on the project. The Machar swamps will also yield water at a rate as yet undetermined, but likely to be about 4,000m. cu m per year (3,240m. cu m at Aswan).

PHYSICAL FEATURES AND CLIMATE

Sudan is generally a flat, featureless plain reflecting the proximity to the surface of the ancient Basement rocks of the African continent. The Basement is overlain by the Nubian Sandstone formation in the centre and north-west of the country. These formations hold groundwater bodies of agricultural significance. No point in the country is very high above sea-level. Elevations rise to 3,071 m on Jabel Marrah, an extinct volcano, in west central Sudan near the frontier with Chad. Some idea of the level character of the landscape is provided by the small amount of the fall in the Blue Nile, which starts its 2,000-km flow through Sudan at 500 m above sea-level at the Ethiopian border and formerly flowed past Wadi Halfa (now flooded) at an elevation of 156 m. It now flows into Lake Nubia at 180 m above sea-level. The White Nile, as it emerges from Uganda, falls some 600 m between the border of South Sudan and Uganda and the Sudanese capital, Khartoum, a distance of 1,700 km, but falls only 17 m in the last 700 km from entering the southern clay plains.

Average temperatures and rainfall change steadily from month to month, except where the effect of the Ethiopian highlands disturbs the east–west trend in the climatic belts in the south-east. The north of Sudan is a desert, with negligible rainfall and high average daily temperatures (summer 35°C, winter 20°C). Low temperatures occur only in winter. Rainfall increases steadily south of Khartoum (200 mm per year), but varies from year to year, especially in the north, and is seasonal. The rainy season is progressively shorter towards the north, where it lasts only from July until August. Potential evaporation approaches 3,000 mm per year in the north and is always over 1,400 mm per year.

VEGETATION AND SOILS

The soil resources of Sudan are rich in agricultural potential. Their exploitation, however, depends on the availability of the limiting factor, water, and only a small proportion of the clay plains of central and east Sudan are currently farmed intensively. Recent alluvium provides a basis for productive agriculture in the narrow Nile valley north of Khartoum. Elsewhere, in the west and north the soils are sandy, with little agricultural potential, except in the dry valleys, which generally contain some soil moisture.

Vegetation is closely related to the climatic zones. From the desert in the north vegetation gradually improves through semi-arid shrub to low woodland savannah characterized by acacia and short grasses. Progressively higher rainfall towards the south promotes trees and shrubs as well as herbs, while the more reliably watered rangeland of the Bahr al-Arab provides an important seasonal resource for the graziers from the poor pastures of Darfur and Kordofan.

POPULATION

The population of Sudan was enumerated at 39,154,490 at the census held in April 2008; of this total, 30,894,000 were estimated to be resident in areas not part of the secession state of South Sudan. The population increased at an estimated average annual rate of 2.5% in 2001–10. According to UN estimates, the population was 43,192,000 at mid-2010, giving an estimated population density of 16.9 per sq km. At the 1983 census about 71% of the population resided in rural areas, 18% in urban and semi-urban areas and the remaining 11% were nomadic. The population is concentrated in Khartoum province and the Central Region; in the former population density was 165.6 per sq km at the 1983 census. Agricultural development in the two most populous regions created employment opportunities and this led to the doubling of these populations during 1956–73.

The ethnic origin of the people of Sudan is mixed, and the country is still subject to significant immigration by groups from Nigeria and Chad, such as the Fulani. Arab culture and language predominate in the north, which includes the most populous provinces and Khartoum.

Khartoum had an estimated population of 947,483 at the 1993 census. It is the main administrative, commercial and industrial centre of the country. The neighbouring city of Omdurman had 1,271,403 inhabitants in 1993, thus creating, with Khartoum, a conurbation of some 2.2m. inhabitants. In mid-2011 the UN estimated the population of this conurbation to total about 4.6m. As communications are very poor and since Khartoum is a huge distance away from most other parts of the country, the influence that the capital exerts on the rest of the country is small. The relatively advanced character and general success of much of the irrigated farming on the east-central clay plains has led to a predominance of investment there, and to the misguided impression that the success of the east-central plains could be transferred to other parts of the country where the resources are unfortunately much less favourable. Much of Sudan is so dry for part of each year that the only possible way to use the land and vegetation resources is by grazing, and tribes such as the Bagara traverse the plains and plateaux of Darfur and Kordofan in response to the availability of fodder.

Recent History

DUNCAN WOODSIDE

The British-led military reconquest of the Sudan, formerly an Egyptian territory from the invasion of 1820 until the Mahdist revolt of 1881–85, was completed during 1896–98. A British-dominated Anglo-Egyptian administration governed the territory until the revolt of 1924, after which a system of 'Indirect Rule' through tribal chiefs was introduced, and Egyptian involvement effectively ceased. Nationalist movements, which began to mobilize in the mid-1930s, exerted pressure for increased Sudanese participation in government in preparation for full independence. In 1953 elections were held, resulting in a victory for the National Unionist Party (NUP), the leader of which, Ismail al-Azhari, became the first Sudanese Prime Minister in January 1954. On 19 December 1955 Sudan declared itself to be an independent republic. The United Kingdom and Egypt recognized this independence, which formally took effect on 1 January 1956.

Soon after independence, al-Azhari's Government was replaced by an unstable coalition of the Mahdist-supported Umma Party (UP) and the People's Democratic Party (PDP), the political organ of a rival religious fraternity, the Khatmiyya, with Abdallah Khalil, the UP Secretary-General, as Prime Minister. A military coup in November 1958 by Gen. Ibrahim Abboud won the support of civilian politicians with assurances by the junta that it aimed merely to restore stability. However, the subsequent extent of military involvement in government and allegations of corruption created growing discontent. The Government also pursued a military solution to the rebel uprising in the predominantly Christian south, where its operations against the *Anya Nya* rebels forced thousands of southerners to flee to neighbouring countries. In 1964 Abboud transferred power to a transitional Government, which was formed with representatives from all parties, including, for the first time, the Communist Party of Sudan (CPS) and the Muslim Brotherhood. Following elections held in June 1965, a coalition Government was formed by the UP and the NUP, with the UP's Muhammad Ahmad Mahgoub as Prime Minister and al-Azhari as permanent President of the committee that acted as collective Head of State.

The new Government became increasingly right wing, and in late 1965 the CPS was banned. A split meanwhile developed within the UP, with the more moderate members rallying around the party President, Sadiq al-Mahdi, in opposition to the Prime Minister. Mahgoub resigned in July 1966, and al-Mahdi was elected Prime Minister at the head of another UP-NUP coalition, which collapsed in May 1967. Mahgoub again became Prime Minister. Challenged by worsening violence in the south and growing divisions within the coalition, the Government was overthrown in a bloodless coup, led by Col Gaafar Muhammad Nimeri, in May 1969.

THE NIMERI REGIME, 1969–85

Nimeri's first two years in power were characterized by the adoption of socialist policies and the forging of an alliance between the new military leadership and the CPS. The foundations for a one-party state were laid with the formation of the Sudanese Socialist Union (SSU), and the country was renamed the Democratic Republic of the Sudan. Internal opposition was ruthlessly suppressed. The Government declared its commitment to regional administrative autonomy for the south and created a Ministry for Southern Affairs. However, the announcement in November 1970 that Nimeri, President Anwar Sadat of Egypt and Libyan leader Col Muammar al-Qaddafi had decided to unite their three countries as a single federal state prompted the communists to stage a military coup, led by Maj. Hashim al-Ata, which resulted in the temporary overthrow of Nimeri in July 1971. With popular support, Nimeri was restored to power within three days.

The attempted coup led to a surge in the personal popularity of Nimeri, who won the first presidential election in Sudanese history in October 1971. The SSU became the sole legal political party. The Addis Ababa Agreement, signed in March 1972 between the Government and the *Anya Nya* rebels, appeared to establish the basis for a settlement by introducing regional autonomy for the three southern provinces. A Regional People's Assembly was established in the regional capital of southern Sudan, Juba, with representatives in the National People's Assembly and a Higher Executive Council (HEC) of its own. In the sphere of foreign relations, Nimeri's Government sought to improve its relations with Egypt and in 1974 signed a 10-year agreement providing for political and economic integration. Sudan additionally developed closer ties to the USA, which increased its provision of aid to both countries, especially in the area of security.

Following prolonged discussions about decentralization, a decision to divide the south into three sub-regions to avoid the domination of one ethnic group (the Dinka) was eventually implemented in May 1983, but was opposed by many southerners, who feared it would weaken their collective position *vis-à-vis* the north. A major factor in the deepening crisis was the adoption by the Nimeri regime, after September 1983, of certain aspects of Islamic *Shari'a* law, followed by the introduction, after April 1984, of martial law. Despite official assurances that non-Muslims would not be adversely affected, many southern Sudanese were now alienated to the point of armed insurrection. Commonly known as *Anya Nya II*, the revitalized rebel groups were organized into political and military wings, the Sudan People's Liberation Movement (SPLM) and Sudan People's Liberation Army (SPLA), respectively. During 1983–84 the rebels engaged government forces in a series of battles, especially in Upper Nile and Bahr al-Ghazal.

Meanwhile, Sadiq al-Mahdi, *inter alia*, criticized Nimeri's Islamization policies as a gross distortion of Islamic principles. Relations deteriorated between Nimeri and a faction of the Muslim Brotherhood led by Hassan al-Turabi. In February 1985 Nimeri took action against the Muslim Brotherhood, placing its leaders on trial for sedition and thereby alienated his last vestiges of popular support. Nimeri reacted to this situation by adopting a conciliatory stance. The state of emergency was lifted, and the operation of the special courts was suspended, while an offer was made to revoke the redivision of the south.

MILITARY COUP

Public discontent with Nimeri's regime reached its culmination in March 1985, exacerbated by substantial increases in the price of food and fuel, and Khartoum was immobilized by a general strike. On 6 April, while Nimeri was visiting the USA, he was deposed in a bloodless military coup, led by Lt-Gen. Abd al-Rahman Swar al-Dahab, the Minister of Defence and Commander-in-Chief of the armed forces. A state of emergency was declared, and a Transitional Military Council (TMC) was appointed. A 15-member Council of Ministers, including three non-Muslim southerners, was subsequently announced. Dr Gizuli Dafallah, who had been a prominent organizer of the general strike, was appointed Prime Minister. The Council of Ministers was to be responsible to the TMC during a 12-month transitional period prior to the holding of free elections, scheduled for April 1986. Hundreds of Nimeri's officials were arrested, and the SSU was dissolved.

In response to the coup, the SPLM initially declared a ceasefire, but presented the new regime with a series of demands concerning the Southern Region. Al-Dahab offered various concessions to the south, but the SPLM rejected these terms and resumed hostilities. In an attempt to reach agreement with the SPLM, a conference was held in March 1986 in Addis Ababa, Ethiopia, between the SPLM and the National Alliance for Salvation (NAS), a semi-official alliance of trade unionists and politicians who supported the Government; the SPLM insisted that the retention of *Shari'a* law remained a major obstacle to national unity. Despite these difficulties, al-Dahab promised a return to civilian rule after a 12-month interim period. A transitional Constitution was signed in October 1985; under its provisions, numerous political groupings began to emerge in preparation for the forthcoming general election. In December the name of the country was changed to 'the Republic of Sudan', thus restoring the official designation to its pre-1969 form.

The TMC's foreign policy during its 12-month rule reversed Nimeri's strongly pro-Western stance, seeking to improve relations with Ethiopia, Libya and the USSR, to the concern of Sudan's former allies, Egypt and the USA. A military co-operation agreement was signed with Libya in July 1985, and diplomatic relations were quickly restored between Sudan, Libya and Ethiopia. In November links with Egypt were reaffirmed.

CIVILIAN COALITIONS AND REGIONAL UNREST

More than 40 political parties participated in the general election held in April 1986. Although no single party won an outright majority of seats in the National Assembly, Sadiq al-Mahdi's UP won the largest number (99), followed by the Democratic Unionist Party (DUP), formed in 1968 by a merger of the PDP and the NUP and now led by Osman al-Mirghani (with 63 seats), and the National Islamic Front (NIF) of al-Turabi (with 51 seats). The new Council of Ministers comprised a coalition of the UP and the DUP, with, in addition, four portfolios allocated to southern parties. Sadiq al-Mahdi became Prime Minister and Minister of Defence. The TMC was dissolved in preparation for the return to civilian rule, while Swar al-Dahab relinquished the posts of Head of State (being replaced by a six-member Supreme Council) and of military Commander-in-Chief.

In an attempt to make the new Government acceptable to the southerners, a special portfolio, the Ministry of Peace and Unity, had been created for a member of the NAS, and Col John Garang, leader of the SPLM, had been offered a post in the Council of Ministers. However, the SPLM refused either to recognize or take part in the new Government, and tensions in the south continued to worsen. In July 1986 al-Mahdi and Garang held direct talks for the first time, in Addis Ababa; however, further negotiations, held in August, between the NAS and the SPLM ended abruptly when the SPLM shot down a Sudan Airways aircraft, killing 60 civilians on board. The SPLM launched a new offensive, with the aim of recapturing the four strategic southern towns of Juba, Wau, Malakal and Bentiu.

In July 1987 the Government imposed a 12-month state of emergency, aimed at resolving the country's worsening economic crisis. In April 1988 al-Mahdi requested that the Supreme Council dissolve his coalition Government, following a vote by the National Assembly in favour of the formation of a new 'government of national unity'. Following al-Mahdi's re-election as Prime Minister by the National Assembly later that month, a new 27-member 'Government of National Unity', comprising members of the UP, the DUP, the NIF and a number of southern Sudanese political parties, was announced in May. In February 1989 al-Turabi was appointed Deputy Prime Minister. In March al-Mahdi agreed to form a new, broadly based Government that would begin negotiations with the SPLM. Peace negotiations between a government delegation and the SPLM commenced in Ethiopia in April.

AL-BASHIR SEIZES POWER

On 30 June 1989 a bloodless coup, led by Brig. (later Lt-Gen.) Omar Hassan Ahmad al-Bashir, deposed al-Mahdi's Government and formed a 15-member Revolutionary Command Council for National Salvation (RCC), which declared its primary aim to be the resolution of the southern conflict. Al-Bashir rapidly dismantled the civilian ruling apparatus: the Constitution, National Assembly, and all political parties and trade unions were abolished, and a state of emergency was declared. About 30 members of the former Government were detained, including al-Mahdi, although three of the ex-ministers were included in the new 21-member Cabinet announced in early July. The new Government was generally welcomed as a potentially stabilizing influence in the region.

In February 1991 al-Bashir signed a decree introducing a new penal code, based, like its predecessor, on *Shari'a* law. The code, which was to take effect from 22 March, was not to apply in the three southern regions of Equatoria, Upper Nile and Bahr al-Ghazal. This exemption, however, appeared to cover only five of the code's 186 articles, and it was stated that the code would be applicable to non-Muslim Sudanese residents in the north.

An alleged coup attempt in late August 1991 resulted in the arrest of 10 army officers and a number of civilians. Subsequent official statements alleged that those implicated included members of the National Democratic Alliance (NDA, a grouping formed in 1989 by the SPLA and some of the other former political parties, including the UP and the DUP). The NDA claimed at the end of September 1991 that some 70 people had been arrested and that Sadiq al-Mahdi had been among those interrogated. The subsequent trial by a military court of 15 people accused of involvement in the coup attempt resulted in death sentences for 10 army officers, commuted in December to life imprisonment.

Reports of a split within the SPLA in August 1991 were immediately denied by Garang. Three SPLA field commanders—Dr Riek Machar Teny-Dhurgon, Lam Akol and Kerubino Kuanyin Bol—claimed to have taken over the leadership of the SPLA. The dissidents were reported to favour a policy of secession for the south, whereas the aim of Garang and his supporters, based at Kapoeta, remained a united, secular state. The split was also along ethnic lines, with the Dinka supporting Garang and the Nuer the breakaway faction. Fierce fighting between the two SPLA factions was reported in November and resulted in the massacre of several thousand civilians in the southern towns of Bor and Kongor before a cease-fire was negotiated in mid-December.

Proposals for constitutional reform were announced by al-Bashir on 1 January 1992. A 300-member transitional National Assembly was to be appointed, with full legislative functions and the power to veto decisions of the RCC. The Assembly, which convened for the first time on 24 February, included—as well as all members of the RCC (excluding al-Bashir), state governors, and representatives of the army and police—former members of the banned UP and DUP, and former aides to ex-President Nimeri.

In March 1993 renewed fighting was reported at Kongor between Garang's forces and the 'Forces of Unity' faction of the SPLA, led by William Nyuon. Peace talks between the Government and the faction of the SPLA led by Col Garang resumed in Abuja in April, but little progress was made. Meanwhile, in Nairobi, Kenya, discussions were conducted between a government delegation and SPLA—United, an alliance formed in early April between the Nasir faction, the 'Forces of Unity' and a faction led by Kerubino Kuanyin Bol.

In October 1993 al-Bashir announced political reforms in preparation for presidential and legislative elections to be held in 1994 and 1995, respectively. The RCC was officially dissolved, after it had appointed al-Bashir as President and as head of a new civilian Government. Al-Bashir appointed a new Minister of Defence—a portfolio that he had formerly held himself—and a new Vice-President.

CONFLICT CONTINUES

At the beginning of 1994 the civil war in southern Sudan remained in stalemate. As in previous years, the Government's 1993–94 southern offensive involved the deployment of army and Popular Defence Force (PDF) units from sizeable garrisons in Juba and Wau to locations along the borders with Zaire (now the Democratic Republic of the Congo—DRC) and Uganda. Despite suffering several defeats during 1994, in January 1995 government forces managed to capture a stronghold of a further insurgent group, the South Sudan Independence Movement (SSIM), near the Ethiopian border. With the SSIM now in conflict with the Government, the SSIM commander, Teny-Dhurgon, and Col Garang signed the Lafon Declaration, which provided for a cessation of hostilities and close co-operation between their forces.

In November 1995, having begun a new offensive in late October, Col Garang's SPLA forces were reported to be advancing on the southern town of Juba. The Government declared a mass mobilization, urging all sectors of the population to defend the country. On 11 November the Government claimed that its forces had inflicted a major defeat on the SPLA and on Ugandan and Eritrean forces allied with it. (The Governments of Uganda and Eritrea denied the involvement of their forces in the fighting.) By late 1996 the SPLA claimed to have taken control of all of Western Equatoria and all of the rural regions of Eastern Equatoria.

POST-ELECTION DOMESTIC ISSUES

The first legislative and presidential elections to be held in Sudan since 1989 took place during 6–17 March 1996. Some 5.5m. of Sudan's 10m. eligible voters were reported to have participated in the election of 275 deputies to a new, 400-seat National Assembly. The remaining 125 deputies had been appointed at a national conference in January. In the presidential election al-Bashir obtained 75.7% of the total votes cast, and formally commenced a five-year term of office on 1 April. On the same day al-Turabi was unanimously elected President of the National Assembly. Representatives of opposition groups and parties alleged that electoral malpractice had been widespread and that many voters had been intimidated into participating.

A peace agreement concluded by the Government and the SSIM in February 1996—initially in order to facilitate the provision of emergency food aid to areas of need in southern Sudan—appeared, in April, to culminate in a substantial breakthrough in the southern conflict. On 10 April the Government, the SSIM and the SPLA—United signed an agreement, described as a 'political charter for peace', under which they pledged to preserve Sudan's national unity and to take joint action to develop those areas of the country that had been affected by the civil war. Other opposition groups, however, rejected the charter. The new Cabinet, announced on 21 April, retained the military, Islamic cast of its predecessor.

In April 1997 a further peace agreement was concluded between the Government and six of the southern factions. In this agreement, self-determination was promised for the southern states, as was, after a four-year transitional period, a referendum on independence. The SPLA refused to sign, however, claiming that the pact was devised in such a way as to divide and weaken the southern opposition. In August, in accordance with the terms of the peace treaty, the Southern States Co-ordination Council (SSCC) was established; Teny-Dhurgon was appointed its Chairman. Dr Lam Akol, leader of the SPLA—United, signed a peace agreement with the Government in September and returned to Khartoum in the following month. In early 1998 Teny-Dhurgon announced that the six southern rebel factions that had made peace with the Government had agreed to unify their troops with his Southern Sudan Defence Force (SSDF). Unification of the former factions' troops left two armed organizations, the Sudan People's Armed Forces (SPAF) and the SSDF, operating in the south, which was expected to facilitate the war against the SPLA.

In October 1997 a 277-member constitutional committee was formed to draft a new constitution. This document was approved by the National Assembly in April 1998 and then submitted to al-Bashir. Following a national referendum, held during 1–20 May, it was announced in late June that 96.7% of voters were in favour of the Constitution, which came into force on 1 July 1998. Fighting continued in the south in November, and in that month a state of emergency was declared in Darfur region and in Northern Kordofan.

New legislation approved in November 1998 provided for the establishment of an independent election commission and of a Constitutional Court, and for the legalization of political associations. In January 1999 the age of eligibility to vote was reduced to 17 years. Registration of political parties began in that month; all parties were required to have 100 founding members, none of whom was to have a criminal record. The first registration documents were issued in early February; however, the northern parties affiliated to the NDA were not included. On 9 May al-Bashir granted an amnesty to ex-President Nimeri. Two days later a licence was granted to Nimeri's followers to form a political party, the Alliance of the People's Working Forces. On 22 May Nimeri returned to Khartoum from exile in Egypt. During that month the opposition claimed a series of victories in the south, and on 31 May Col Garang of the SPLA, Sadiq al-Mahdi of the UP and Mubarak al-Mahdi of the NDA met in Kampala, Uganda, to discuss their armed campaign against the Government.

AL-BASHIR ASSUMES GREATER CONTROL

By 2000 it was apparent that al-Bashir remained in firm control of the Government. In December 1999 he had declared a three-month state of emergency and suspended the National Assembly, and in January 2000 he announced the formation of a new Government and appointed new governors in 25 of the 26 states. The state of emergency was extended from three to 12 months in March, and in April it was announced that a presidential election was planned for later that year. On 6 May al-Bashir took action against al-Turabi, who had become increasingly vociferous in his criticism of the Government and demands for a more open political system, by suspending him as Secretary-General of the ruling National Congress Party (NCP). In late June al-Turabi responded to his dismissal by creating a new political party, the Popular National Congress (PNC).

Presidential and legislative elections were held concurrently over a 10-day period in mid-December 2000, although they were boycotted by the main opposition parties. As expected, al-Bashir was re-elected President, securing 86.5% of the votes cast, according to results released by the General Elections Commission (GEC), thus comfortably defeating his nearest rival, former President Nimeri, who obtained 9.6% of the vote. Voting did not take place in three southern states, and opposition leaders dismissed the official turn-out figures. The NCP secured 355 seats in the new 360-member National Assembly; the remaining five seats were taken by small opposition parties. Monitors from the Organization of African Unity (OAU, now the African Union—AU), the Arab League and the Non-aligned Movement endorsed the election. On 3 January 2001 al-Bashir extended the state of emergency for a further year.

On 21 February 2001 al-Turabi was arrested at his home in Khartoum, after it was announced that the PNCP and the SPLM had, two days earlier, signed a memorandum of understanding in Geneva, which appealed for the Sudanese people to participate in 'peaceful popular resistance' against the al-Bashir regime. The following day al-Bashir implemented a major reorganization of the Cabinet and replaced many of the country's state governors. Several new ministries were created, and, although the new 32-member Cabinet was dominated by NCP members, al-Bashir incorporated four members of two minor opposition parties into the Government. Two members of the United Democratic Salvation Front retained their positions in the Cabinet; however, the UP refused to participate in the new administration.

In June 2001 an SPLA offensive resulted in the capture of the strategically important town of Raga in the Bahr al-Ghazal province. In mid-December the state of emergency was extended for a further 12 months. In January 2002 Teny-Dhurgon, the military commander of the Sudan People's Defence Force, announced that the group had merged with the SPLA and that both would conduct joint military operations against the SPAF. In April the consultative council of the National Congress approved resolutions that increased al-Bashir's constitutional powers and strengthened his position against the provincial and national parliaments. Notably, al-Bashir was granted the right to appoint provincial governors, and the two-term limit on the presidential mandate was abolished. Additionally, these changes further isolated al-Turabi by impeding his ability to cultivate parliamentary support and to mount an effective presidential campaign. The amendments were condemned by several opposition parties.

In mid-January 2002 talks sponsored jointly by the USA and Switzerland commenced in Bürgenstock, Switzerland, following which the Sudanese Government and the SPLM agreed to observe a six-month cease-fire, to be supervised by a joint military commission in the central Nuba region in order to facilitate the delivery of vital aid supplies to the area.

In May 2002 the Minister of Finance, Adb al-Rahim Muhammad Hamdi, reportedly resigned owing to ill health. There was, however, speculation that he had been dismissed by al-Bashir following the implementation of several unpopular economic measures. Hamdi was subsequently replaced by Muhammad al-Hasan al-Zubayr. In June three members of the NCP, including the Minister of Transport, Dr Lam Akol, resigned from the party in protest against the increasing dominance of al-Bashir. Akol established a new political party, the Justice Party, in early September and was dismissed from his ministerial post by al-Bashir later that month. Meanwhile, al-Bashir reorganized the Council of Ministers in August, to bring into government eight members of the UP breakaway faction that opposed Sadiq al-Mahdi. Having been placed under a detention order the previous year, in September al-Turabi was removed from house arrest and transferred to prison. In late December Parliament approved al-Bashir's request to extend the state of emergency for another year.

In October 2003 the authorities released al-Turabi and lifted the ban on the PNC and its publications. However, in late March 2004 the Sudanese Government announced that it had uncovered a coup plot and had arrested 10 army officers, 10 police officers and seven PNC members, including al-Turabi; all PNC activities were also suspended. Further arrests followed and the authorities accused al-Turabi of encouraging Darfurian rebels (see below), particularly the Justice and Equality Movement (JEM), to take up arms against the Government.

The strength of al-Bashir's hold on power became increasingly questionable during 2009–11. First, the issuance, in March 2009, of an arrest warrant by the International Criminal Court—(ICC, based in The Hague, Netherlands) against the President for alleged war crimes and crimes against humanity in Darfur further isolated his regime diplomatically, leading moderate elements in the NCP to increasingly question his value. The grassroots membership of the NCP thereby became increasingly marginalized, with al-Bashir arguably placing more reliance than ever on an inner circle of associates. Yet, the secession of South Sudan in 2011, while eliciting praise from the People's Republic of China (Sudan's principal bilateral ally), was received with anger domestically by government hardliners, particularly Nafie Ali Nafie, the NCP's Deputy Chairman for Organizational Affairs and a presidential adviser.

REGIONAL PEACE INITIATIVES

Throughout much of the 1990s the Intergovernmental Authority on Drought and Development (IGADD, now the Intergovernmental Authority on Development—IGAD) sought to broker a settlement between the Sudanese Government and the SPLM. However, by 2000 the IGAD peace process had made little progress. In June 2002 a new round of IGAD-sponsored peace talks between the Government and the SPLM opened in Machakos, Kenya, although fighting between the two sides continued. Nevertheless, a major breakthrough in the conflict was achieved on 20 July, when delegations from the SPLM and the Government signed an accord, the Machakos Protocol, which provided for the holding of a referendum, after a transitional period of six years, on self-determination for the south. The Protocol also stated that Sudan's Constitution would be rewritten to ensure that *Shari'a* law would not be applied to non-Muslim southerners. The Machakos Protocol was not a definitive peace agreement, but rather a framework for future negotiations, and the Government stated that the accord would only be implemented following the cessation of hostilities between the two sides. Government and SPLM delegations reconvened in Machakos in mid-August for talks, and on 17 October the Government and the SPLM agreed to a cease-fire covering the whole of Sudan. In November the second round of talks in Machakos ended with the signing of a memorandum of understanding that proposed a structure for an interim government. The document's main provisions included an agreement for the creation of a directly elected bicameral parliament and a government of national unity, in which the south would have proportional representation. Southerners would also receive a share of senior and mid-level civil service positions.

In September 2003 the Sudanese Government and the SPLM signed an accord in Naivasha, Kenya, which provided for the withdrawal from southern Sudan of 100,000 government troops within two-and-a-half years, in addition to the withdrawal of rebel forces from eastern Sudan within a year. An integrated 'third force', comprising some 40,000 troops, was also to be established and deployed in areas disputed by both sides. During a six-year interim period government and rebel troops were to be treated equally as the Sudan Armed Forces (SAF). On 7 January 2004 the two sides signed an accord on wealth- and revenue-sharing, which also provided for the establishment of two separate banking systems for the north and the south, as well as a new national currency on the signing of a final peace settlement.

In late May 2004 the Sudanese Government and the SPLM signed three protocols that covered power-sharing arrangements—Garang would assume the post of First Vice-President in a proposed 'government of national unity' and would also be appointed President of southern Sudan—and the administration of the three disputed provinces. Other provisions approved the allocation of 50% of Sudan's net revenue (not including petroleum revenues) to the proposed southern government, and both parties agreed that 3% of oil revenues would be given to the province that produced the petroleum with the remainder being divided equally between the Sudanese Government and the SPLM.

THE COMPREHENSIVE PEACE AGREEMENT AND 2005–11 TRANSITION

On 9 January 2005 the Government and the SPLM signed a Comprehensive Peace Agreement (CPA) in Nairobi, thus officially ending the civil war in the south that had lasted for more than two decades, during which at least 2m. people had been killed and more than 4m. displaced. The accord comprised eight protocols, including agreements that political power and Sudan's national wealth would be shared between the national Government and the south; that the SPAF and the SPLA would remain separate forces within the national army, in addition to contributing equally to new Joint Integrated Units (JIU) that would be deployed on both sides of the north–south border, and that all militias would be disbanded within a year; that oil revenues would be shared equally between the north and the south; that the SPLA and other southern groups would hold 30% of government positions in the north, while holding 70% in the south; that the contested regions of the Blue Nile and the Nuba Mountains would be governed by an administration in which 55% of the seats would be taken by government officials and 45% by the SPLM, while the petroleum-rich region of Abeyi would be granted special status under the presidency; that the application of *Shari'a* law would be limited to the north; and that Garang would become Sudan's First Vice-President and would act as President of Southern Sudan and head of the SPLA forces during the six-year period of autonomy, after which a referendum on secession would be held.

The Interim National Constitution was promulgated on 9 July 2005, in accordance with the terms stipulated in the CPA. On 1 August, however, Garang was killed in a helicopter accident while en route to Rumbek, in southern Sudan, from

Uganda. The announcement of Garang's death was followed by several days of rioting in Khartoum, during which more than 130 people were killed. Garang was replaced as leader of the SPLA/SPLM by Commdr Salva Kiir Mayardit, hitherto deputy leader of the organization. Salva Kiir was later appointed First Vice-President in the national Government and assumed the presidency of the new Government of Southern Sudan (GOSS). In September a Government of National Unity was established, which was dominated by the NCP and the SPLM but eventually included some representatives of the NDA; however, the new Government was boycotted by the UP and the PNC. By the end of the year the new National Assembly was also functioning.

In addition to the GOSS, a new Transitional Southern Sudan Legislative Assembly was established and regional administrations were also created. In December 2005 a new Constitution for the south was promulgated. Security remained a difficult issue. In addition to the forces of the SPLA, a number of other rebel groups were known to be active in the south, including the SSDF, which was comprised predominantly from the Nuer people of Upper Nile region. The Ugandan Lord's Resistance Army (LRA) had also carried out attacks in the south. It was suggested that both groups enjoyed the support of the NCP in an attempt to undermine the power base of the SPLA/SPLM. However, since the signing of the CPA, Salva Kiir has reached agreement with the main SSDF leader, Paulino Matip, while the Vice-President of the GOSS, Teny-Dhurgon, met with LRA leader Joseph Kony in an attempt to facilitate peace talks between the LRA and the Ugandan Government. There were also concerns about the SPLA/SPLM's capacity to transform itself from an armed force into a solely political entity; and the repatriation of refugees and internally displaced persons (IDPs) currently in northern Sudan and neighbouring Uganda. In December the office of the United Nations High Commissioner for Refugees (UNHCR) announced that it would begin to repatriate some 500,000 refugees from neighbouring countries; earlier in that month 90,000 refugees had returned to southern Sudan from northern Kenya under UNHCR auspices. In addition, many southerners who were displaced to the north of the country began to return to their homes in the south, although the rate of return was comparatively slow.

The border issue between northern Sudan and the south remains unresolved. In accordance with the CPA, a commission, headed by the former US Ambassador to Sudan, Donald Petterson, decided that Abyei region belonged to southern Sudan, a decision rejected by the Missiriya Arabs, despite the fact that all parties had promised to honour the 'binding and final' agreement. The two other disputed areas of Blue Nile and the Nuba Mountains were less problematic but still presented challenges.

In October 2007 disagreement over a number of divisive issues in the CPA led to the SPLM withdrawing from the Government of National Unity. The main points of contention were the delays in the redeployment of northern troops from the south, border demarcation between north and south, the issue of the disputed area of Abyei, greater transparency on the oil revenues to be shared between north and south, and progress on the postponed national census. The SPLM's withdrawal produced sufficient progress on these issues for it to return to the Government before the end of the year. In April 2008 there was a further crisis over Abyei with a violent clash leading to scores of deaths; once again, however, crisis produced compromise with agreement that the Abyei question be referred to a new international arbitration process at the International Court of Justice (ICJ) in The Hague. Nevertheless, trust between the two parties in the Government remained low.

In February 2009 fighting broke out within a JIU in Malakal (the capital of the contentious, oil-rich Upper Nile State), involving troops from supposedly mixed units of the SAF and SPLA, in which at least 62 people were reportedly killed. The clash in Malakal was just one of several in Southern Sudan during early 2009, with significant fighting also taking place in Jonglei State in January, March and April that year. The clashes in April, ostensibly over cattle, reportedly resulted in more than 1,000 people being killed.

Despite the SPLM's return to the power-sharing Government, major provisions of the CPA remained either unfulfilled or under dispute. In mid-2009 the ICJ had yet to deliver its judgment on the status of oil-rich Abyei. Additionally, although a census belatedly took place in April 2008, the results were disputed by the SPLM. The party had expected the south's population to be at least one-third of Sudan's national population, but the results gave the South 21% out of a final tally of 39.2m. The Southern Sudan Centre for Census and Statistics accused the North's Central Bureau of Statistics of refusing to share information when it tried to verify the latter's data, creating further north–south tension ahead of the planned national polls, which were postponed from July 2009 until February 2010, and subsequently until April 2010. Given its natural southern constituency, under-representation of the south would reduce the SPLM's chances of replacing the NCP as the main national party at the elections. Salva Kiir was confirmed as the SPLM's candidate for the national elections in August 2008.

In addition to the controversial census, one of the few CPA-related achievements in 2008 was the selection of an electoral commission. In a rare instance of unity, the nine-member panel was selected by President al-Bashir, Vice President Ali Osman Taha and GOSS President Salva Kiir, before being approved in November by the national parliament. This followed the adoption in July of an electoral law that guaranteed women 25% of seats in parliament in a voting system based on proportional representation.

THE 2010 ELECTIONS

The registration of more than 16m. voters in late 2009 was accompanied by heightened political tension, as both national and southern Sudanese authorities suppressed peaceful assemblies and intimidated opposition candidates and activists. In the weeks immediately preceding the polls the Government extended national security laws, which drastically restricted the freedom of opposition parties to assemble and campaign. In response to this and other concerns, including the impartiality of the National Elections Commission (NEC), the two main opposition challengers for the presidency—Yasir Saeed Arman of the SPLM and Sadiq al-Mahdi, leader of the Umma National Party—withdrew their candidacies just days before the polls. These boycotts, together with those of smaller parties, including the Sudan Communist Party and the Umma Reform and Renewal Party, brought the credibility of the electoral process into question.

Nevertheless, the first multi-party elections for more than two decades finally took place on 11–15 April 2010. The electorate voted in concurrent presidential, legislative and gubernatorial ballots. As anticipated, incumbent President al-Bashir was re-elected with 68.2% of the vote. In the south, Salva Kiir retained the presidency, securing 93.0% of the ballot. The result of the legislative election was delayed, but it was later announced that the NCP had secured 312 of the 450 seats, of which 132 were elected by proportional representation. The NCP's nearest rival in the ballot was the SPLM, which won a total of 99 seats. Voting in 16 constituencies was postponed, the result in one seat was not released and one seat was declared vacant. Following the announcement of the results, several opposition parties denounced the elections as fraudulent. While observer missions dispatched by the European Union (EU) and the US Carter Center declared that the elections had failed to meet international standards, they refused to corroborate opposition allegations of widespread electoral malpractice.

In mid-June 2010 al-Bashir announced a new 35-member coalition cabinet, which included nine members of the SPLM, two more than required under the terms of the CPA. Lual Achwel Deng of the SPLM, Minister of Foreign Affairs in the previous Government, was appointed as Minister of Petroleum. This represented a conciliatory gesture, designed to placate southern suspicions following the alleged siphoning of oil revenues under the previous Government, and to ensure high-level SPLM involvement in discussions on a post-secession oil-sharing agreement. Meanwhile, President Salva Kiir named the 32 ministers of a new GOSS cabinet. An unequivocal advocate of full independence, Salva Kiir's choice of appointments was a reflection of his determination to achieve this goal. Deng Alor, a former Sudan Minister of Foreign Affairs and a senior member of the SPLM, was appointed as the South Sudan Minister of Regional Co-operation, a key position in managing the referendum preparations. The Secretary-General of the SPLM, Pagan Amum, was named as South Sudan's Minister of Peace and CPA Implementation, giving him a central role in negotiations with the Sudanese Government over issues that must be settled prior to the referendum. Riek Machar, a Nuer, continued as Vice-President, preserving the Dinka-Nuer ethnic balance within the SPLM leadership.

THE 2011 REFERENDUM AND SECESSION OF SOUTH SUDAN

Al-Bashir's Government continued to delay the preparations for the 2011 secession referendum, with many of the crucial prerequisites stipulated by the CPA still not in place by mid-2010. The same critical issues remained unresolved: the demarcation of the North–South border, the post-referendum status of Southern Kordofan and Blue Nile, the formation of referendum commissions for South Sudan and Abyei, and the negotiation of a post-secession oil-sharing agreement. There were also delays in the appointment of joint North-South commissions, to oversee the preparations for the referendum and the polling itself. These commissions had to be established before financial and operational planning, including logistics, education of the electorate and poll personnel, and voter registration, could be executed.

The stability of southern territories was undermined by the emergence of new militias opposed to the GOSS. The SPLM claimed that these militias were being supported by the NCP, as a means of destabilizing the southern government and highlighting that it could not govern itself. The most prominent rebellion was led by Col Galwak Gai, a former SPLM officer who resigned from his post after accusing the SPLM of fraud in the 2010 elections. Meanwhile, the SPLM alleged that a 120-member squadron had been ambushed by the SAF in Bahr al-Ghazal in late April 2010, although this was denied by the SAF. The SPLM also claimed to have captured a member of the SAF during a clash with a force under the command of Col Gai in early June 2010.

However, despite the ongoing bilateral tensions and the amount of secession-related agreements that needed to be concluded, considerable progress towards conducting the long-planned plebiscite took place in the second half of 2010. One of the biggest advances was the appointment of the Southern Sudan Referendum Commission (SSRC), which was headed by Mohammed Khalil Ibrahim, a Muslim lawyer from the north. North-south agreement on the SSRC's composition enabled the practical arrangements for the huge organizational exercise to begin. Voter registration commenced in mid-November, less than two months before the referendum was due to take place, President Kiir insisting that his Government regarded the January 2011 scheduling of the vote as 'sacrosanct'.

However, while the GOSS was steadfast in its commitment to the main referendum, it was, by then, being forced into compromise over the planned simultaneous plebiscite in the disputed Abyei region. Sudan's first Vice-President Ali Osman Taha asserted in October 2010 that it would not be possible to hold the vote in Abyei, in the event that the main referendum took place on schedule. The GOSS eventually accepted this fact, particularly since the two sides had remained unable to agree on who was eligible to vote in the Abyei referendum. Whilst the GOSS insisted that only permanent residents of Abyei should be allowed to participate, Sudan maintained that Arab Misseriya nomads were also eligible, since they migrate into Abyei's territories on a seasonal basis. This lack of agreement generated significant new tensions, with fighting taking place in Abyei in early January 2011 between Ngok Dinka militias and the Misseriya. There were over 30 deaths in this fighting, before representatives of the two communities agreed a settlement (including payments of 'blood money') in mid-January.

Despite the distraction of events in Abyei, voting in the referendum in Southern Sudan itself commenced on 9 January 2011, as scheduled, and was conducted over seven days. In early February it was confirmed by the SSRC that 98.8% of registered voters had chosen independence.

The semi-autonomous region of Southern Sudan officially seceded from Sudan as a whole on 9 July 2011, creating a new nation state, the Republic of South Sudan, exactly six months after the start of the referendum. President al-Bashir became the first Head of State to recognize the new country, formally giving his blessing to South Sudan's right to exist as a sovereign entity on 8 July. Major international states were quick to follow suit, with the US Government and the EU recognizing South Sudan on 9 July, a day that was marked by jubilant celebrations and an official ceremony in its new capital city, Juba.

US President Barack Obama immediately congratulated the new country on achieving its independence; however, perhaps the most significant bilateral recognition of the new nation state came from China, given the People's Republic's long-standing status as an ally of Sudan's ruling NCP and the principal buyer of the country's oil. Prior to independence, the influence of the Chinese Government on President al-Bashir and the NCP—its calculation that its commercial interests were best served by peaceful co-existence between two territories—was significant, confirming to Sudan that it had little option but to accept secession as a *fait accompli*. The Republic of South Sudan became the 193rd member state of the UN on 14 July 2011, after a unanimous vote by the Security Council in favour of the new country's membership the previous day.

POST-SECESSION NEGOTIATIONS AND CONFLICT

Despite South Sudan's extraordinary achievement of independence—and the magnanimous acceptance of this outcome by Sudan's President al-Bashir—nothing could disguise the huge underlying tensions. Secession occurred against a backdrop where the two Governments had failed to agree on almost all outstanding issues, including the status of the disputed Abyei region, the wider demarcation of a border, the sharing of oil revenues and the fate of citizens living in one another's territories. Most portentously of all, however, the long-planned (but loosely-defined) popular consultations on the governance of the disputed states of Southern Kordofan and Blue Nile had yet to yield results. The situation in these two states, which remained part of Sudan, was particularly volatile because of a high preponderance of SPLM-aligned citizens and former SPLA combatants, who had never been fully integrated into the SAF. Even before secession, the uneasy peace was shattered in Southern Kordofan, as a new conflict broke out between the SAF and unintegrated armed elements in the state's Nuba Mountains.

The fighting started in early June 2011, after a dispute about the results of a state governorship election. Incumbent NCP Governor Ahmed Haroun, who had been indicted by the ICC for alleged war crimes in Darfur, was declared the winner by the NEC after the May poll, but the defeated SPLM candidate, Abdelaziz al-Hilu, claimed that the result was marred by fraud. The authorities then demanded that all non-SAF military units disarm. The refusal of the thousands of SPLA soldiers and aligned militia in the state to demobilize precipitated fighting, which, according to the UN, caused more than 70,000 people to flee over the next month. Most of those fleeing were ethnic Nubans, amid a bombing campaign by Sudan's air force. South Sudanese Vice-President Machar claimed that ethnic cleansing was taking place. The AU brokered a preliminary agreement between the NCP and the SPLM over Southern Kordofan in late June, involving pledges to disarm non-SAF elements without the use of force. However, President al-Bashir was subsequently quoted in the state media as asserting that the military campaign in the state would continue.

Although hostilities escalated quickly in Southern Kordofan, the emergence of conflict did not surprise informed analysts. The refusal of SPLA troops and aligned militias to demobilize (albeit in the face of Haroun's hardline reputation), together with the local SPLM's questioning of the NCP's authority, was viewed as a provocation by Sudan's ruling party. Moreover,

Southern Kordofan contains some of the most lucrative oil facilities outside South Sudan, including the Heglig wells, making the NCP particularly intolerant of attempts to undermine its authority in this area.

The armed rebels in Southern Kordofan officially became the Sudan People's Liberation Army North (SPLA-N), while their political wing was named the Sudan People's Liberation Movement North (SPLM-N). This new official politico-military structure professed to have broken off ties with South Sudan's ruling SPLM and the SPLA. Sudan's Government rejected this claim and accused South Sudan of providing material support to the rebels. In turn, the South Sudanese Government insisted that it had no contact with the SPLM-N or the SPLA-N in the post-independence era. The insurgents accused the SAF of indiscriminately bombing civilians. Tens of thousands of people fled rebel-held areas into South Sudan, or sought shelter in the Nuba Mountains. Fighting spread from Southern Kordofan to neighbouring Blue Nile state in September 2011. Predictably, both the SPLM-N and the Sudanese Government blamed each other for the outbreak of hostilities there. The Governor of Blue Nile, Malik Agar, who was also Chairman of the SPLM-N, was removed by the Sudanese Government on 2 September. On the same day fighting began, with the SPLM-N claiming that Agar's residence in Damazin, the state capital, was targeted in an attack by the SAF. The SAF, meanwhile, claimed that armed elements aligned to Agar had attempted to ambush army positions in Damazin on 1 September. Hostilities quickly escalated, resulting in a large-scale cross-state insurgency under the auspices of the SPLA-N. Furthermore, the leaders of this growing rebellion sought support from Darfur's main rebel groups, including the JEM, and SLA factions led, respectively, by Minni Minawi and Abdul Wahid. In November the SPLA-N signed an agreement with these three Darfur factions, thereby forming the Sudan Revolutionary Front (SRF). Agar was appointed as head of the join rebel command, while the JEM, and the two SLA factions were all allocated vice-presidential posts. The movement's stated objective was to overthrow al-Bashir's Government and establish a democratic, secular republic.

While not as severe as the situation in Southern Kordofan and Blue Nile, the Abyei region remained tense in the immediate post-secession period. The SAF had occupied Abyei town in late May 2011, after an alleged attack on one of its military convoys outside the town by the SPLA. Abyei is officially a demilitarized zone. Despite the successful conclusion of South Sudan's main independence referendum, the plebiscite in Abyei was postponed indefinitely, owing to the ongoing failure of the SPLM and the NCP to agree on who would be eligible to vote. The SAF's military occupation from May resulted in the town being 'virtually emptied' of its some 50,000 (largely Ngok Dinka) permanent inhabitants, according to UNHCR. The military takeover had been preceded by intermittent clashes for five months after the January settlement between the pro-SPLM/SPLA Ngok Dinka residents and the Misseriya, which had been used a proxy by the SAF during the 1983–2005 civil war.

Following AU-mediated negotiations, both the SPLM and the NCP accepted in June 2011 the planned deployment of 4,200 peacekeepers to Abyei, under the auspices of a new UN mission, the United Nations Interim Security Force for Abyei (UNISFA). However, although tensions had calmed in Abyei, the key issues of contention between the NCP and SPLM over the future of the region remained unresolved. While the SPLM maintained (in line with the 2005 CPA) that a referendum must be held in Abyei, al-Bashir insisted two days after South Sudan's secession that Abyei must remain part of Sudan. This hardened position on the part of the NCP undermined the prospects for a referendum taking place in Abyei at all.

More generally, with the SPLM and NCP failing to agree on the demarcation of a wider border, it remained possible that conflict could break out anywhere along the 2,100 km that stretches from the Central African Republic in the west and Ethiopia in the east. The other main potential trigger for an eruption of direct north–south conflict was the expiry of an oil-sharing deal. Until 9 July 2011 revenues from the south's oil fields were shared equally between Sudan's central Government and the south. Post-secession, a new agreement would need to be negotiated, predicated either on a diminished share of oil revenues for Sudan, or the replacement of 'revenue sharing' with a system whereby South Sudan would pay fees to Sudan's central Government, in order to use the latter's pipelines to transport oil to Port Sudan on the Red Sea coast. In June al-Bashir threatened to terminate South Sudan's access to Sudan's pipelines, unless a satisfactory agreement was forged.

Negotiations aimed at securing an agreement on oil continued during the second half of 2011 and into 2012. Neither side appeared ready to compromise significantly. Sudan's initial demand was that Juba pay US $22.8 for each barrel of southern oil piped through the north's infrastructure to Port Sudan, a figure that SPLM Secretary-General Amum described in July 2011 as 'daylight robbery'. South Sudan was only prepared to pay $0.7 per barrel, which it underlined was considerably above the $0.4 paid by Chad to Cameroon for what it regarded as a similar pipeline arrangement. However, the Sudanese Government retorted that it had invested heavily in its infrastructure, only for its own production to be slashed by 75% as a result of southern independence, adding that the costs involved in transporting South Sudan's oil were relatively high, while it also claimed entitlement to port storage and loading fees at the point of export. Finally, Sudan pointed to the fact that the agreement between Chad and Cameroon had been reached at a time when oil prices were considerably lower than that prevailing on international markets in 2011. Sudan's negotiators then raised their demand to $36 per barrel, before eventually reducing this slightly, to $32 per barrel. Sudan was also demanding a grant of $7,400m., in order to guarantee pipeline access to the south and to offset the effect of lost oil revenues on its budget. In early 2012 South Sudan was offering grants to Sudan totalling $5,400m. over four years (inclusive of a waiver of payment arrears accrued by Sudan), together with a pipeline fee of $1.00 per barrel of oil; however, the South Sudanese Government insisted that the pipeline fees should be deductible from the grant payment.

The oil impasse reached crisis point in December 2011, when Sudan began to impound southern oil. In January 2012 South Sudan shut down its oil production, claiming that Sudan had stolen oil worth US $815m. Sudan counter-claimed that it was merely impounding oil in order to compensate for South Sudan's alleged non-payment of pipeline fees. As of mid-2012 Juba had yet to resume production, as it sought to persuade the international community—in particular China, the principal buyer of its oil—to intervene and pressure Sudan into adopting a less aggressive negotiating position. The bilateral crisis escalated beyond diplomatic impasse when South Sudan's Government sent its military into the northern reaches of the Heglig oilfields for two days in late March and 10 days in April. Sudan regarded this as a flagrant breach of its sovereignty and a territorial infringement into Southern Kordofan. The international community agreed, with the UN Security Council exerting significant pressure on Kiir to withdraw the SPLA from Heglig, where substantial damage was caused to infrastructure. Sudan claimed that the damage, which suspended approximately one-half of its own (already diminished) oil production, was caused deliberately by the SPLA. South Sudan's military denied this, and instead claimed that the damage had been sustained by Sudan's air force bombing its ground positions in Heglig. UN Resolution 2046 (2012), agreed by on 2 May, condemned South Sudan's occupation of Heglig. However, it also condemned Sudan for launching bombing raids against targets in South Sudan's oil-rich Unity State, which borders Southern Kordofan. The Resolution impelled the two sides to cease fighting within 48 hours and resume AU-sponsored negotiations within two weeks, or face an imposition of multilateral sanctions. It also reiterated demands for a withdrawal of all military forces, except UNISFA peace-keepers, from Abyei.

A few days later, the South Sudanese Government announced that it had withdrawn its police from Abyei. SAF troops initially remained present in Abyei, before withdrawing, according to the UN. However, Sudan insisted that a resumption of serious dialogue could not occur before security issues were dealt with. In particular, it demanded that the SPLA end support for the SPLA-North's insurgency in

Southern Kordofan and Blue Nile. In early April 2012 the SAF had claimed that the SPLA had even been present in Talodi, 100 km northwest of Heglig (i.e. deep inside Southern Kordofan), where it was providing artillery support to the SPLA-North. Khartoum also accused the SPLA of collaborating with the JEM. South Sudan continued to deny these allegations, and countered that Sudan was supporting ongoing rebellions in southern territory, including Upper Nile and Unity States. Resolution 2046 had attempted to address the issue of cross-border support for armed proxies, condemning such alleged activity. The prospects for serious bilateral progress therefore appeared bleak, despite the two sides agreeing in late May to resume their talks in Addis Ababa. Even after Resolution 2046, South Sudan claimed that the SAF was continuing to bomb Unity State.

By that time, the rebel South Sudan Democratic Army (SSDA) was alleged by South Sudan to be the main rebel movement receiving support from the Sudanese Government. Several other renegade factions splintered from the SPLA over the year or so before secession, blighting security in Unity State, Jonglei State, Warrap State and Upper Nile State. Even before the 2012 north–south military escalation, the SPLM consistently alleged that the NCP was supporting a range of dissident movements, in an effort to destabilize the south's ability to govern itself. However, no hard evidence had been presented to confirm these claims against Sudan's Government. President al-Bashir and President Kiir met at the sidelines of an AU Summit in Addis Ababa in mid-July, but no substantive breakthroughs were made, beyond a renewed commitment to talks and repudiation of armed conflict.

THE CONFLICT IN DARFUR

In February 2003 two rebel groups, the Sudan Liberation Movement (SLM), which reportedly comprised as many as 2,500 armed troops, and the JEM, estimated to number several hundred, organized a rebellion against the Government in an attempt to end political oppression and economic neglect in the Darfur region of western Sudan. The Sudanese Government responded by employing pro-Government ethnic Arab militias—the *Janjaweed*—to suppress the revolt, displacing hundreds of thousands of people. International observers reported that the Government's brutal tactics against Darfur's Fur, Masaalit and Zaghawa ethnic groups included targeted killings, mass rapes, the burning of villages and food stocks, and the contamination of water supplies. By 2006 estimates indicated that up to 200,000 had died directly or indirectly as a result of the conflict. Another 250,000 had sought refuge in neighbouring Chad, with a further 2m. displaced in Darfur.

International pressure on the Sudanese Government to take measures to halt the atrocities in Darfur continued in 2004. The USA and the UN stated that they had evidence that the Sudanese Government was providing support to the *Janjaweed* and that the militia forces had carried out summary executions of civilians. On 8 April Chadian-brokered talks resulted in the declaration of a 45-day cease-fire, to be monitored by the AU. However, the agreement collapsed and clashes between rebel fighters and the *Janjaweed* continued. In July Sudan and the UN signed a joint communiqué that committed the former to disarming the *Janjaweed*, improving humanitarian access to Darfur, providing security for the internally displaced and ending impunity for perpetrators of human rights abuses. The UN promised to deliver aid to those in need and to support initiatives for a peace settlement. In mid-July AU-sponsored peace talks between the Sudanese Government and the rebels opened in Addis Ababa. The talks failed after the Government rejected demands by the SLA and the JEM for: the disarmament of the *Janjaweed* and the removal of those *Janjaweed* fighters absorbed by the police and army; the observation of the April cease-fire agreement; the prosecution of the perpetrators of crimes and an inquiry into allegations of genocide; unimpeded humanitarian access for aid agencies; the release of prisoners of war; and a 'neutral' venue for future talks. In late July the US House of Representatives approved a resolution declaring the human rights abuses in Darfur a 'genocide', and on 30 July the UN Security Council adopted Resolution 1556, which demanded that the Sudanese Government end the conflict in Darfur, facilitate the delivery of humanitarian aid, and grant AU peace monitors access to the region. Should the Sudanese Government fail to achieve these goals within 30 days, the UN would take 'further measures' against the country. The Government announced that it 'reluctantly' accepted the UN Resolution, although there were continuing reports of attacks being carried out by the *Janjaweed*. In September the Security Council approved Resolution 1564, which stated that the Council would consider imposing sanctions on Sudan's petroleum industry should the Government fail to act to disarm the *Janjaweed* and to protect civilians from further attacks. Later that month talks were held between the SLA, the JEM and the Government in Abuja, which ended without agreement. The talks resumed the following month, and in November all sides pledged to cease hostilities and the Government agreed to establish a 'no-fly zone' over the region. Nevertheless, during late 2004 AU officials and humanitarian agencies continued to report attacks by forces on both sides of the conflict and several aid agencies temporarily withdrew their staff from the region.

In March 2005 the UN Security Council adopted Resolution 1593, referring the situation in Darfur to the Prosecutor of the ICC. Al-Bashir subsequently vowed not to send any Sudanese national to The Hague for trial, and mass demonstrations were held in the capital against the ICC. In January 2007 the ICC issued indictments against two men, Ahmed Haroun, a Minister of State, and Ali Kushayb, a *Janjaweed* leader; however, al-Bashir repeated his refusal to co-operate. Shortly after being indicted, Haroun was appointed as Sudan's Minister of State for Humanitarian Affairs, subsequently becoming the Governor of Southern Kordofan state in May 2009.

The AU announced in April 2005 that it was to increase its African Mission in Sudan (AMIS) to an authorized strength of 7,731 troops, and in June further talks between the Government and rebels commenced in Abuja, in which a declaration of principles was signed. In the following month the SLA and the JEM agreed to normalize relations following discussions in Tripoli, Libya. A further round of talks in Abuja commenced in mid-September, despite the absence of an SLM faction. Violence continued to escalate, however, and in early October four AU peace-keepers were killed in southern Darfur, prompting the UN to withdraw all non-essential staff from the region. At a meeting in March 2006 the AU agreed to extend the mandate of AMIS to 30 September, while announcing its intention to transfer control of the mission to the UN following the mandate's expiry. The UN Security Council approved Resolution 1672 in late April, imposing sanctions upon four individuals suspected of committing crimes against humanity in Darfur.

Efforts to reach a negotiated peace settlement continued in late April 2006 under AU auspices in Abuja. AU mediators submitted a peace proposal on 30 April, and finally the Government and one of the SLM factions, led by Minni Minawi, agreed to accept the proposal, although the other main SLM leader, Abd al-Wahid Muhammad Nur, and the JEM leader, Khalil Ibrahim, refused to sign the agreement, known as the Darfur Peace Agreement (DPA). Rebel negotiators had insisted on the creation of a national Vice-President's position, but eventually agreed to accept the role of Senior Assistant to the President on Darfur (to be included in the presidency). The Senior Assistant would chair a new Transitional Darfur Regional Authority (TDRA). They had also sought recognition of Darfur as a region rather than as three separate states in the current federal structure. The DPA provided for a referendum in 2008 to decide upon this issue.

It was becoming increasingly clear that AMIS was inadequate, and on 31 August 2006 the UN Security Council approved Resolution 1706, appealing for the UN Mission in Sudan currently deployed in the south of the country to be increased by up to 17,300 military personnel, and for its mandate to be extended to encompass the responsibilities of AMIS in Darfur. However, the Government refused to grant permission for the UN Mission in Sudan to deploy troops in Darfur and, in the wake of the failure of the DPA, the situation in Darfur appeared critical. Relations between the Government and the UN continued to deteriorate, and in October the UN Special Representative for Sudan, Jan Pronk, was expelled from the country following comments on his website regarding defeats of government forces by rebels.

With the situation in Darfur deteriorating in 2007, and the rebels fragmenting into as many as 19 armed factions, in January 2008 a tentative agreement was made with the Government for 3,000 UN troops to give support to AMIS. At the same time Salva Kiir, President of the GOSS, endeavoured to mediate with the rebel groups. Under continuing international pressure, in mid-2007 the Government finally agreed to the establishment of a joint AU-UN hybrid peace-keeping operation in Darfur (UNAMID), which would be composed of 26,000 troops. Disagreements threatened to disrupt the process when, in August, the AU announced that UNAMID peace-keeping forces would comprise only African personnel, safeguarding the AU's lead role in Sudan. UNAMID assumed peace-keeping operations on 31 December but remained severely under-resourced. By late 2008 only 13,000 of the pledged 20,000 peace-keepers were deployed, and the mission continued to lack key equipment.

Progress towards restoring peace was limited, and government-led attacks on civilians and peace-keepers in Darfur continued. However, in February 2008 a legal framework was agreed, which would allow UNAMID peace-keepers to move freely within the country without fear of attacks by government forces. Meanwhile, the humanitarian situation continued to deteriorate, particularly near the border with Chad. In September, under heavy pressure from the international community, the Sudanese Government began a peace initiative for Darfur, the Sudan People's Initiative. The initiative, to be hosted by Qatar, attracted little interest at first, with many opposition groups refusing to participate. While the JEM eventually attended discussions in 2009 in Doha, Qatar, full peace talks remained elusive. Discussions were complicated by the Sudanese Government's decision in March to expel 13 aid agencies, after accusing them of overstepping their humanitarian remit by providing evidence to the ICC. The JEM withdrew from discussions in protest against the Government's decision, which led to a significant reduction in humanitarian aid.

Discussions resumed in May 2009, but were shortly followed by UN claims that the Government had bombed rebel positions around Umm Barra in northern Darfur, in contravention of the terms of a cease-fire and a resolution by the UN Security Council. Despite various efforts by the Sudanese Government to fragment armed opposition in Darfur (attempts that, in some cases, have yielded considerable success in recent years), the JEM consolidated its power in the early months of 2009. Indeed, and with some success, it launched a concerted effort to bring commanders from other armed groups within its fold. Additionally, in a battle close to Umm Barra, the JEM claimed to have defeated forces loyal to ex-rebel leader Minni Minawi, whose SLA faction was co-opted by the Government in a peace deal in 2006.

By the second half of 2009 there appeared to be a relative stabilization of the situation in Darfur, prompting a number of senior diplomats and military officers to declare an imminent end to the conflict. In July, encouraged by an apparent cessation of the co-ordinated campaign against civilians, the US Special Envoy to Sudan, Scott Gration, urged IDPs to start returning to their homes. His words were met with hostility by many IDPs who did not perceive a reduction in the threat to their security. In August the outgoing Nigerian commander of UNAMID, Martin Luther Agwai, declared that the war in Darfur was over, and that the dominant security issues were now banditry and low-intensity engagements. In November Sudan's envoy to the UN, Abdalmahmoud Abdalhaleem, asserted that, since peace was now in sight, the UN should prepare a Darfur exit strategy.

The signing of a cease-fire agreement in mid-February 2010 in N'Djamena, Chad, between the JEM and the Sudanese Government pointed towards a possible revival of the Sudan People's Initiative. The cease-fire agreement included a list of issues to be addressed in future negotiations, including compensation for Darfurians, humanitarian access, and the broad topics of power-sharing and wealth-sharing. However, the JEM acceded to the pact hesitantly, emphasizing that it would withdraw if the Sudanese Government acted in bad faith.

The fragile truce proved to be short-lived. Following a declaration of dissatisfaction with the conduct of the April 2010 elections, the JEM suspended its participation in the Qatari talks and escalated military operations. Fighting consequently intensified in Darfur, and almost 600 people were killed in May, the highest monthly tally since UNAMID deployed peace-keepers in December 2007. Continued sporadic attempts were made to persuade the various rebel factions to enter into negotiations in the later part of 2010 and in 2011. A peace agreement was signed in Doha between the Government and the LJM faction in July 2011. However, this represented only a small component of Darfur's rebels, and conflict with the main factions, particularly the JEM, continued. A renewed coalescence of rebel forces appeared to emerge in November, with the establishment of an alliance between the principal Darfur factions and insurgents in Southern Kordofan and Blue Nile (see Post-secession Negotiations and Conflict).

REBELLION IN THE EAST

As the situation in Darfur deteriorated, so fears grew that rebellion might spread to eastern Sudan. Resentment towards the national Government had increased among the mostly rural population, especially the Rashaida and the Beja communities, which had been severely affected by decades of drought and famine. The success of the SPLA in forcing the Sudanese Government to negotiate, as well as the revolt in Darfur, led some young Beja to launch an armed struggle, helped by the presence of NDA and SPLA forces in eastern Sudan, which had opened up a second front against the Government in the late 1990s.

The Beja Congress, which emerged in the 1960s, was joined in the late 1990s by the Rashaida Free Lions group. The two groups had similar objectives and in 2005 joined forces to form the Eastern Front. The Front's forces were far smaller than those of the SPLA or rebel groups in Darfur, but were active in a region of strategic importance to the national Government. Sudan's sole outlet to the sea was Port Sudan on the Red Sea coast, which was connected to central Sudan by road and rail links, and more recently by an oil pipeline, which was inaugurated in 1999. The Eastern Front perpetrated numerous attacks on roads in the region and on the pipeline, threatening to destabilize Sudan's economy.

In June 2006 representatives from both sides met in Asmara for talks presided over by the Eritrean authorities, and on 19 June the Government and the Eastern Front signed a declaration of principles and agreed a cessation of hostilities. Talks resumed in mid-July, and in October the Eastern Sudan Peace Agreement (ESPA) was signed. Under it, the Eastern Front was given some representation in the Council of Ministers, as well as promises of economic support. In contrast with the situation in Darfur, it appeared that by mid-2007 the ESPA was holding, although progress in implementation remained slow and by 2008 critics in the region were growing in number.

FOREIGN RELATIONS

Since al-Bashir seized power in 1989 Sudan's foreign policy has passed through several phases. Initially, the new regime sought to preserve relations with the West, but as the Government became increasingly determined to spread radical Islamic fundamentalism throughout eastern Africa and the Middle East, the regime experienced periods of increased tension with its neighbours. Sudan provided refuge to a number of radical Islamist groups, including the al-Qa'ida (Base) organization of Osama bin Laden, who was based in Khartoum during 1991–96. This aggressive policy of support of 'Islamization' contributed to the deterioration of relations with neighbouring countries; however, the People's Republic of China, South Africa and Russia all continued to pursue the burgeoning economic opportunities in Sudan. The Government's policies also fostered new links with Middle Eastern countries including Iraq, which supplied arms to the Government and received reciprocal support for its invasion of Kuwait in 1990, and Iran. Meanwhile, the USA condemned the Sudanese Government in the strongest terms for its alleged role in the organization of international terrorism and sought to isolate the country, especially after Sudan was implicated in the attempted assassination of President Muhammad Hosni Mubarak of Egypt in 1995. The USA imposed sanctions on Sudan in 1997, banning imports of Sudanese goods to the USA, and US firms from exporting goods to Sudan.

In the early 2000s, under the new Administration of President George W. Bush, US-Sudanese relations showed modest signs of improvement. Following the suicide attacks on New York and Washington, DC, USA, in September 2001, the Sudanese Government pledged to support the global 'war on terrorism' by providing intelligence about bin Laden and al-Qa'ida, which the USA held responsible for the attacks. US officials welcomed this development, but refused to remove unilateral sanctions, and Sudan continued to be listed by the US Department of State as a sponsor of terrorism. On 21 October 2001 Bush signed the Sudan Peace Act, which provided for punitive financial and diplomatic steps against the Sudanese authorities and for the suspension of aid to areas not under the Government's control, if the USA believed that the Sudanese Government was acting in bad faith at the peace talks. The Act also authorized financial assistance to areas outside government control, including support for civil administration, communications infrastructure, education, health and agriculture. Meanwhile, in its annual *Trends in Global Terrorism* report, the US Administration listed Sudan as a 'state sponsor of terrorism' owing to its links with some hard-line anti-Israeli groups. However, the report also noted that the USA was satisfied with Sudan's anti-terrorism co-operation.

Relations between the two countries became increasingly tense owing to the ongoing crisis in the Darfur region (see above). Nevertheless, on 18 May 2004 the USA removed Sudan from a blacklist of countries deemed not to be co-operating with US anti-terrorism efforts. However, Sudan, which allows terrorist organizations such as the Islamic Resistance Movement (Hamas) and the Palestinian Islamic Jihad to maintain offices in Khartoum, remained on the State Department's list of 'state sponsors of terrorism', inclusion on which also bans arms sales. In late 2004 and early 2005 US-Sudanese relations focused on the implementation of the CPA and attempts to end the fighting in Darfur. In August 2006 the USA and the United Kingdom co-sponsored a draft resolution to the UN Security Council, urging the deployment of a UN peace-keeping force (see above). With frustration growing in the USA over Darfur, in May 2007 President Bush announced new sanctions against Sudan designed to increase the pressure to reach agreement with the UN.

However, the structural underpinnings of relations between Sudan and the USA changed significantly with the election of Barack Obama as the USA's new President in November 2008. With Obama and his new Administration placing less emphasis on aggressive anti-terror activities, al-Bashir's bargaining power with the USA was commensurately reduced, allowing Obama to adopt a more aggressive policy towards Sudan over Darfur. Obama signalled his intent by appointing a number of individuals known for their 'hawkish' stance on Sudan to key foreign policy posts within his Administration. The USA's newly installed ambassador to the UN, Susan Rice, quickly voiced support for the ICC's investigation into alleged war crimes in Darfur. This marked a break with the policy of the Bush Administration, which had distanced itself from the ICC. When the ICC indicted President al-Bashir on seven counts of war crimes and crimes against humanity in March 2009, the Secretary of State, Hillary Clinton, stated that the USA believed the case should be heard.

Although the Obama Administration had previously taken a number of hard-line positions—advocating, for example, the aggressive enforcement of a no-fly zone over the Darfur provinces—from mid-2009 it demonstrated an increasing willingness to engage with the Sudanese Government. In June the USA hosted a conference, attended by members of al-Bashir's ruling NCP and the SPLM, aimed at addressing divisive issues in the CPA (including elections, the secession referendum and boundary demarcation). Following a comprehensive review of US policy towards Sudan, Obama announced a new strategy in October. Although it included a 12-month extension of the sanctions that had been in place since 1997, it avoided recourse to any military intervention and was cautiously welcomed by the NCP, which described it as a strategy of engagement rather than isolation. The policy offered incentives for the Sudanese Government to end the conflict in Darfur and ensure implementation of the stuttering CPA, but threatened tougher steps if it failed to act.

President al-Bashir publically urged President Obama to end US sanctions against Sudan, in a speech in Juba, on 9 July 2011, when the Republic of South Sudan was declared a sovereign nation state, with the blessing of Sudan's central Government. Al-Bashir's position was that Sudan's Government had thereby fulfilled its promise to honour the CPA, leaving it eligible for a termination of US long-term sanctions. Yet, the sanctions remained in place, since many north–south issues (including a post-secession sharing of oil revenues, the status of Abyei and the demarcation of a wider border) remained unresolved (see above). Moreover, the US Government remained concerned about the new conflict in Southern Kordofan. Less than three weeks before the south's secession, Obama condemned 'all acts of violence [in Southern Kordofan], in particular the Sudanese Armed Forces' aerial bombardment of civilians and harassment and intimidation of UN peacekeepers'. The US Government voiced further disapproval when Sudan's air force bombed targets in South Sudan's Unity State in March and April 2012, Secretary of State Hillary Clinton describing these bombings as 'disproportionate force'.

Despite the delicacy of north–south relations, secession by South Sudan resulted in the end of the United Nations Mission in Sudan (UNMIS), the UN's north-south peace-keeping mission (a separate entity to UNAMID). Originally known as the United Nations Advance Mission in Sudan (UNAMIS), the peace-keeping operation was established in 2004, seven months before the CPA. In early 2011 UNMIS maintained a troop strength of nearly 9,300. However, in May Sudan's Minister of Foreign Affairs, Ali Ahmed Karti, told UN Secretary-General Ban Ki-Moon that the country would not permit the presence of UNMIS on its territory, after the 9 July secession date. Although UN spokesperson Hua Jiang announced that 'it is up to the UNSC [Security Council], not the Sudanese Government, to decide whether the UN mission in Sudan continues after the country splits in two', UNMIS' mandate was not replaced when it expired on 9 July. A new mission, the United Nations Mission in the Republic of South Sudan (UNMISS), was established, taking with it most of UNMIS' personnel, but it was given an operational mandate only in the newly independent South Sudan.

Sudan's relations with China, its most powerful bilateral ally, took a new turn in 2007. Since the beginning of the oil development in the 1990s China has been a close commercial partner of Sudan, and an opponent in the Security Council of sanctions over Darfur. However, during 2007 China became more public in its efforts to encourage the Sudanese Government to restore peace in the troubled region. At the start of that year the Chinese President, Hu Jintao, visited Sudan during the course of an African tour, and in May China appointed Liu Giujin as special envoy to Sudan. As a further sign of its concern, China also announced that month that it would send 300 military engineers to assist in Darfur. In response to international pressure, China began to make public requests that the Sudanese Government make a greater effort to negotiate a settlement with the Darfurian rebels.

China's influence was also exerted in an effort to ensure a successful secession by southern Sudan. In mid-2010 China's special envoy to Sudan, Liu Guijin, announced that the People's Republic would respect the outcome of a 'transparent and credible' referendum in southern Sudan, even though a majority of voters were expected to vote in favour of independence. China also lobbied in favour of the vote taking place peacefully and on time. Given China's leverage over the NCP, its position on the referendum was crucial to a successful vote in January 2011, and the subsequent secession of South Sudan on 9 July. President al-Bashir was received by President Hu in China less than two weeks before secession occurred. During the visit, state-owned China National Petroleum Corporation (CNPC) signed an agreement with Sudan's Ministry of Petroleum to 'deepen co-operation'.

Reflecting its desire for continued commercial access to southern oil fields, China had begun to build stronger ties with South Sudan in 2008. In September that year the People's

Republic opened a consulate in Juba, the capital of South Sudan, as GOSS President Salva Kiir received a delegation that included China's Deputy Minister of Foreign Affairs, Zhai Jun. The visit also resulted in China signing a deal providing for financial assistance to South Sudan. The threat of a possible loss of power by the NCP in elections, or a successful secession by the South, motivated China's enhanced relationship with the GOSS. The People's Republic's bilateral dealings with Sudan and South Sudan continued to shift subtly after independence, not only as it was more dependent on the south than the north for its oil supply, but also since southern territories hosted the larger share of Chinese state-owned commercial assets. When Sudan began to impound South Sudan's oil in December 2011, China's ambassador to Khartoum criticized the move as 'very serious and unjustified'. As one of the permanent five powers on the Security Council, China also agreed to the content of UN Resolution 2046, which condemned Sudan and South Sudan for the respective bombings of Unity State and occupation of the Heglig oilfields.

Sudan's relations with Eritrea have been marred by repeated cross-border incidents involving clashes with the Sudanese-supported Eritrean Islamic Jihad (EIJ), which reportedly aims to overthrow the Eritrean Government. Eritrea's support for the NDA also contributed to the tense state of relations between the two countries. The unwillingness of both Governments to compromise undermined several diplomatic efforts to resolve their differences. In January 2000 Sudan and Eritrea finally restored diplomatic relations and agreed to reopen the land route between the two countries and to adopt procedures for issuing cross-border travel permits. In the same month the Eritrean Government ordered the NDA to evacuate the Sudanese embassy in Asmara, which it had been using as a headquarters. In February President al-Bashir and President Issaias Afewerki of Eritrea met in Khartoum and declared that they would not allow opposition groups located in their respective countries to launch cross-border raids. In October Afewerki visited Khartoum where he held talks with al-Bashir, during which both sides agreed to take measures to resolve differences between the two countries in a peaceful manner. Later that month Eritrea sponsored talks between the Sudanese Government and the Asmara-based NDA.

However, efforts at further reconciliation were undermined by the fact that Eritrea continued to provide shelter and support to the NDA. In October 2002 Sudan closed its border with Eritrea following an NDA attack on the town of Hamashkoreb in Kassala state. Eritrea rejected Sudan's accusation that it had been involved in the operation. Nevertheless, Sudan maintained diplomatic relations with Eritrea and allowed the repatriation of tens of thousands of Eritrean refugees from camps in Sudan to continue. In October Sudanese-Eritrean relations were further strained after the Sudanese Government accused Eritrea of participating in the NDA offensive in north-eastern Sudan and of providing support to the SLM/JEM campaign in Darfur. Following these developments, the border was closed and Sudan rejected offers of mediation by the AU. Sudan retaliated by providing aid to the opposition Eritrean National Alliance (ENA), which maintains offices in Khartoum.

During 2003–04 Eritrea repeatedly denied that it had been providing aid to the SLM/JEM rebels in Darfur (see above). Nevertheless, Eritrea hosted a number of SLM representatives who, in January 2004, joined the Asmara-based Beja Congress, which was a member of the NDA. The two groups promised to 'continue their struggle together'. At about the same time Eritrea complained that the Sudanese Government had arrested some of its nationals without charge or trial and had closed several community centres used by Eritreans. In March an estimated 1,700 Eritrean refugees in eastern Sudan returned to Eritrea. The repatriation allowed the Sudanese authorities to close 10 of 18 camps in eastern Sudan. However, some 200,000 Eritrean refugees remained in eastern Sudan. Only some 35,000 of them had signed up for voluntary repatriation in 2004 while more than 29,000 families had applied to remain in Sudan as refugees. Eritrean-Sudanese relations improved in 2006. In June the new Eritrean ambassador presented credentials to al-Bashir in Khartoum, and later in that month the Eritrean Government, having previously supported rebel groups active in the east of Sudan, offered to host talks between the Sudanese Government and the Eastern Front. Following the success of these talks and the signing of the ESPA, relations between the two Governments have moved closer to normalization; in mid-2008 President al-Bashir and President Afewerki signed a new agreement.

Until late 1995 Sudan enjoyed relatively harmonious links with Ethiopia. In September, however, Ethiopia accused Sudan of harbouring three terrorists implicated in the attempted assassination of President Mubarak of Egypt in Addis Ababa in June and announced that it would close some Sudanese diplomatic facilities in the country and all non-governmental organizations (NGOs) connected with Sudan. However, in November 1999 and January 2000 Sudan and Ethiopia conducted talks that resulted in the reopening of their common border. Additionally, the two countries agreed to improve road links, reactivate a joint ministerial committee, and install telephone lines between their respective capitals, while Ethiopia indicated that it would no longer demand the repatriation of those suspected of launching the failed assassination attempt against Mubarak. Bilateral co-operation commissions met regularly to discuss security and economic issues, and in December 2000 Sudan and Ethiopia announced an ambitious long-term rail project. In December 2001 Sudan and Ethiopia agreed to demarcate their border and assess the issues of security, refugees and water management.

In April 2002 Taha visited Ethiopia; at the end of his four-day visit he announced that a 'new era' in relations with Ethiopia had begun, and that the two countries had concluded a preferential trade agreement, as well as accords on the economy, commerce, infrastructure and telecommunications. In January 2003 Sudan delivered its first oil shipment to Ethiopia under an agreement that had been concluded in mid-2002. In June 2003 Sudan and Ethiopia signed an agreement ending a seven-year border dispute. Under the accord, Ethiopia returned small pockets of land to the al-Qadaref region.

The Ethiopian Government in December 2009 claimed that it had foiled a rebel attack aimed at disrupting the elections in that country; the men had apparently been detained while attempting to enter Ethiopia from Sudan. In the wake of these revelations, the Sudanese Government reiterated its commitment to security co-operation with Ethiopia, stating that Sudan would not allow any of its territories to be used by forces opposed to the Ethiopian Government and that the two states would continue to work closely together in monitoring borders.

The Kenyan Government has sought to maintain good relations with all of the opposing forces in Sudan. However, its support of the SPLA frequently has alienated the Sudanese Government. Over the years, there have been numerous accusations that the Government of Kenya and certain Kenya-based NGOs have provided weapons and other military supplies to the SPLA. Moreover, Garang and other senior rebel leaders maintained a strong presence in Nairobi. The UN-administered Operation Lifeline Sudan (OLS), which is headquartered in Nairobi, has transported food relief supplies into southern Sudan. Kenya also has played a major role in peace negotiations between the Sudanese Government and the rebels. During 2002–03 Kenya supported the IGAD-sponsored Sudanese peace talks by providing Gen. Lazaro Sumbeiywo of Kenya as chief negotiator. In July 2002 he concluded the Machakos Protocol that committed the Sudanese Government and the SPLM to a referendum on unity or secession for southern Sudan after a six-year transition period. The subsequent negotiations on the various protocols took place in Naivasha, and the signing of the CPA in Nairobi on 9 January 2005 underscored Kenya's importance as East Africa's diplomatic hub. The Moi Foundation, established by former Kenyan President Daniel arap Moi in 2003, also contributed to the southern Sudanese reconciliation process by sponsoring a conference between Garang and other southern leaders in late April 2005. Following the signing of the CPA, commercial relations between Kenya and southern Sudan expanded rapidly. Relations with Kenya came under strain in late 2008, as Somali pirates hijacked a ship carrying arms from Ukraine. The ship had been bound for the Kenyan port of Mombasa and there were suspicions that the arms on board were for the

GOSS. In this context, Sudan withdrew its ambassador from Kenya in October 2008.

Sudanese-Egyptian relations historically have vacillated between confrontation and co-operation. In June 1995 the Egyptian Government accused Sudan of involvement in an unsuccessful assassination attempt against President Mubarak in Addis Ababa, and relations quickly deteriorated. After a number of conciliatory measures, relations between the two countries had improved markedly by late 1999, when al-Bashir visited Egypt and the two countries agreed to normalize diplomatic relations. In April 2000 al-Bashir visited the Egyptian capital, Cairo, and met with President Mubarak at an Africa-Europe summit. Later that month Egypt appointed a new ambassador to Sudan, for the first time since the assassination attempt on Mubarak in 1995. In September 2000 the Sudanese and Egyptian Ministers of Foreign Affairs held the first session of the Egyptian-Sudanese Commission for 10 years during which the two countries expressed their commitment to further bilateral economic development. In May 2003 Mubarak and al-Bashir held talks in Khartoum, emphasizing their commitment to good relations. Shortly afterwards Garang met with Mubarak in Cairo, and the Secretary-General of the Arab League and former Egyptian Minister of Foreign Affairs, Amr Moussa, led a delegation to southern Sudan to 'build understanding and confidence' with the SPLA leadership. In late May Egypt hosted talks between the SPLA and northern opposition groups not included in the Machakos talks. During a meeting, held in mid-July, of the joint Sudanese-Egyptian higher committee in Khartoum, Taha claimed that relations between the two countries would achieve 'unprecedented progress', partially as a result of the implementation of 19 bilateral co-operation pacts. By 2006 Egypt, together with other Arab states, notably Saudi Arabia, had accepted the CPA and pledged to work with the GOSS to maintain the unity of Sudan. Economic links with Egypt have also been strengthened, while restrictions on movement and trade between the two countries have been tightened. When President al-Bashir was indicted by the ICC on seven counts of war crimes and crimes against humanity in March 2009, Egypt was one of the first countries to show its support for al-Bashir.

Sudan and Libya have traditionally had mixed relations. Having been in dispute during most of the Nimeri era, relations were much closer when al-Mahdi became Prime Minister. In March 1990 the two Governments signed a 'declaration of integration', which provided for the merging of the two countries, but the increasingly Islamic fundamentalist character of the Sudanese regime after 1989 contributed to a cooling of relations. However, the Libyan leader, Col Muammar al-Qaddafi, maintained links with the SPLM and was reported on various occasions to have attempted to mediate between the al-Bashir regime and more hostile neighbouring governments, notably Uganda in 1996. Qaddafi was also involved in attempts to mediate in the Darfur conflict, hosting a meeting between the SLA and JEM in mid-2005 (see above). Thousands of Darfurians have sought refuge in Libya, and Libya has also provided a route for the safe passage of humanitarian aid convoys. In mid-2006 Qaddafi facilitated a resumption in relations between Sudan and Chad, following a dispute in late 2005 (see below). He continued to remain involved in 2007, hosting further talks involving Sudan and Egypt. At the end of 2007 Qaddafi hosted UN-backed talks in Sirte, Libya, between Darfur factions, but a number of the leaders refused to attend and little was achieved. Qaddafi gave strong vocal backing to al-Bashir when Sudan's President was indicted by the ICC. However, he appeared to signal his support for an independent South Sudan when GOSS President Salva Kiir visited Libya in June 2009.

In 2010 there were indications that Sudan's largely cordial relationship with Libya was coming under strain. The discord was prompted by reports that Libya was hosting JEM leader Khalil Ibrahim, after he was denied permission to pass through Chadian territory (see below). Libyan diplomats underlined that the extradition of Ibrahim to Sudan would undermine Libya's impartiality as a mediator in the conflict between Sudan and the JEM. At the end of June the Sudanese Government announced that it was closing its border with Libya in order to protect travellers from rebel attack.

The ongoing crisis in Darfur has also affected Sudan's relations with Chad. Darfur and Chad have long-standing links and both President Hissène Habré and the current President, Idriss Deby Itno, launched coups with Sudanese assistance from bases in Darfur. Deby's seizure of power was supported by both Libya and Sudan, but relations with the latter have deteriorated sharply since late 2005 as the Chadian Government expressed fears that the conflict in Darfur could spread across the border. In December Chad declared 'a state of belligerence' with Sudan, and, in response, Sudan has supported opposition movements operating both within Chad and in Darfur that seek to overthrow Deby. In April 2006 Deby severed relations with Sudan, accusing the Sudanese Government of supporting an attempted coup. However, relations improved in July when the two Governments agreed to withdraw support for rebel groups on both sides of the border. In August, following mediation by Libya, Deby and al-Bashir announced that full diplomatic relations would be restored later in 2006, although in practice relations remained difficult despite meetings in 2007 between the two Presidents. In early 2008 there was a further attack by rebels from eastern Chad on N'Djamena, and President Deby once more blamed Sudan. A meeting was held between him and President al-Bashir in Dakar, Senegal, but relations remained strained.

Sudan and Chad restored diplomatic ties in November 2008, six months after they had been severed. However, in May 2009 Chad accused Sudan of supporting a rebel attack, while Chad admitted launching air attacks on the Sudanese side of the border, in a bid to neutralize Chadian rebels operating from bases in Darfur. When Chad announced that it was sending ground troops into Sudan to confront these rebels, Sudan said that it would destroy any Chadian forces found on its territory. Nevertheless, al-Bashir held talks with Deby in Khartoum in February 2010, and the two Presidents agreed to stop supporting rebel groups as proxy forces, a perennial source of tension between Sudan and Chad. The strong action taken by Chad to repel JEM leader Khalil Ibrahim from the country in May 2010—when the rebel commander and his entourage were denied entry at N'Djamena international airport, and had their Chadian passports destroyed—underlined Deby's commitment to this new agreement.

FOOD AID AND REFUGEE PROBLEMS

The population of Sudan has suffered from both natural disasters and the civil war in recent years. In July 2004 the UN World Food Programme (WFP) commenced the airlifting of enriched food from Addis Ababa to Darfur, where an estimated 1.2m. people required food aid. In many areas the fighting and displacements had drastically reduced harvests and government, militia and rebel forces had looted livestock and food stocks. By early 2005 there were an estimated 5.3m.–6.2m. IDPs in Sudan and some 600,000 Sudanese refugees or asylum seekers in other countries. At that time there were more than 225,900 refugees from other countries in Sudan. By early 2005 the fighting in Darfur had claimed 70,000–140,000 lives, while disease and malnutrition had claimed a further 130,000–260,000 lives; some 30% of Darfur's population had been internally displaced. Throughout 2005–07 conditions for the delivery of relief supplies continued to deteriorate. Attacks against international NGOs increased in frequency and a number of Sudanese NGO personnel were killed in mid-2006, leading to the withdrawal from the country of some NGOs. In addition to worsening conditions, money for relief was increasingly in short supply. On the ground, the number of IDPs requiring assistance continued to grow and there were fears that the camps were becoming semi-permanent with large areas of the countryside being deserted by civilians fleeing the escalating violence. WFP in 2008 halved its distribution of food in Darfur, as a result of the increase in insecurity.

In March 2009 the Sudanese Government forced 13 international aid agencies to leave the country, on the grounds that expelled aid agencies had a political agenda, which included passing false evidence of violations to the ICC. This order coincided with the indictment of President al-Bashir by the ICC on seven counts of war crimes and crimes against humanity. UN agencies were nevertheless permitted to continue operating in the country, in co-operation with local NGOs. However, the dramatic reduction in assistance generated fears of a new exodus of refugees from Sudan to neighbouring Chad. There were reports of clashes between IDPs in refugee camps and Sudan's security forces in the wake of the aid agencies' withdrawal, generating concerns about a fresh radicalization of the displaced population.

In mid-July 2011, less than a week after the Republic of South Sudan seceded and became an independent nation state, Sudan's National Assembly gave preliminary ratification to a bill revoking the Sudanese citizenship rights of southern citizens living in the north. The state news agency reported that people taking citizenship of South Sudan would automatically have their right to be a citizen of Sudan cancelled. Approximately 300,000 southerners migrated back to their homeland in the months prior to secession, with some claiming on arrival that they had returned because they feared post-secession repercussions in the north. However, more than 1m. southerners remained in Sudan in the immediate post-secession period, against a background of limited economic opportunities in their homeland. In March 2012 representatives of Sudan and South Sudan agreed a draft citizenship law, as part of the post-secession negotiations mediated by the AU. The text of the agreement asserted, in part, as follows: 'nationals of each state shall enjoy in the other state . . . freedom of residence, freedom of movement, freedom to undertake economic activity and freedom to acquire and dispose [of] property.' This agreement was to be signed by al-Bashir and Kiir on a visit by the former to Juba in early April 2012, but the SPLA's incursion into Heglig resulted in the cancellation of that state visit. Consequently, an 8 April deadline set by Sudan's Government for South Sudanese citizens to depart northern territory expired without any agreement being secured.

The international community became increasingly concerned about the plight of displaced people in Southern Kordofan and Blue Nile in the second half of 2011 and in 2012. Sudan's continued aerial bombing campaigns had resulted in tens of thousands of people fleeing in both states. Whilst some ended up in refugee camps in South Sudan, others were displaced internally in the two war-blighted northern provinces.

HUMAN RIGHTS ISSUES

According to the US Department of State's 2003 human rights report, Sudan's human rights record remained 'extremely poor', despite improvements in some areas. Security forces and pro-Government militias undertook extra-judicial killings and arbitrarily beat, harassed, arrested, tortured or detained incommunicado opponents or suspected opponents of the al-Bashir regime. Security forces and pro-Government militias also assaulted refugees and raped women abducted during raids. The Civilian Protection Monitoring Team (CPMT), created by an agreement between the Sudanese Government and the SPLA following the 2002 Machakos Protocol, and the Joint Military Commission operating in the Nuba mountains, had some success in monitoring and curbing serious abuses during 2003. However, in Darfur government forces and pro-Government militias committed serious human rights abuses in response to rebel attacks against government troops. Neither the Sudanese Government nor the SPLA respected the conventions of war in the southern insurgency, and neither side took many prisoners—as they regularly executed those who surrendered. Both also failed to co-operate fully with the International Committee of the Red Cross regarding access to or treatment of prisoners of war. Government co-operation with UN-sponsored relief operations in southern Sudan improved significantly as relief flights started operating in early 2004. However, government forces restricted the flow of humanitarian aid to Darfur. Restrictions on press freedom under the National Security Emergency decree increased as the authorities suspended many publications and newspapers during 2003. There were also restrictions on freedom of speech, assembly, association, religion and movement.

In March 2005 the UN resolved to refer allegations of human rights abuses in Darfur to the ICC. Later in that year a sealed list of some 50 names of those suspected of involvement in such crimes was sent to the ICC for investigation and inquiries extended into 2006; two indictments were issued in 2007 (see above). However, the Sudanese Government refused to co-operate with ICC investigators, not least owing to speculation that the list contained the names of senior government officials. In mid-July 2008 Chief Prosecutor of the ICC Luis Moreno Ocampo presented evidence against President al-Bashir in respect of 10 charges of genocide, crimes against humanity and war crimes committed in Darfur from March 2003, and requested the issuance of a warrant for al-Bashir's arrest. According to UN estimates, at mid-2008, 300,000 people had been killed in Darfur since 2003, and a further 2.5m. displaced, as a consequence of attacks on the indigenous population by the Sudanese armed forces and the *Janjaweed*.

In March 2009, having considered the evidence amassed by Chief Prosecutor Ocampo, a panel of three judges at the ICC issued a warrant for al-Bashir's arrest, on seven counts of war crimes and crimes against humanity. A charge of genocide, which had been requested by Ocampo, was not initially included. The Sudanese Government continued to refute the legitimacy of the ICC and its charges, and al-Bashir remained as Head of State. His grip on power initially was seemingly strengthened by widespread anger among Arabs in Sudan, and across much of the Arab world, at his indictment, which was portrayed by the regime as a plot orchestrated by the West against Sudan. In November 2008 Chief Prosecutor Ocampo had applied for arrest warrants for three commanders of rebel groups in Darfur in connection with an attack on AMIS personnel in December 2007 in which 12 of the Mission's troops were killed. In July 2010 the ICC issued a second arrest warrant for President al-Bashir—this time on charges of genocide in connection with crimes committed in the Darfur region.

Renewed protests broke out in Khartoum—and other cities, including Port Sudan and El Obeid, the capital of North Kordofan State—in late June 2012. The demonstrations were initially staged in response to a withdrawal of fuel subsidies and tax increases, amidst an intensifying economic crisis. However, protesters subsequently began overtly to demand regime change, as a degree of popular momentum was generated via communications on social networking sites Facebook and Twitter. The response of the authorities was to order the use of tear gas and rubber bullets against the protesters. Activists were arrested and detained without charge, with some sources reporting that hundreds of people were being arbitrarily detained by the National Intelligence and Security Service. Protests continued in July.

Economy

DUNCAN WOODSIDE

INTRODUCTION

Sudan's economy was dealt a significant (if long anticipated) blow by the secession of the Republic of South Sudan in July 2011. Upon independence, the new nation state assumed control of around 75% of Sudan's oil production, which consequently fell from close to 490,000 barrels per day (b/d) to approximately 120,000 b/d. With oil revenues the essence of Sudan's economy (particularly in terms of the budget and foreign exchange earnings), the secession of the south necessitated significant austerity and increased the urgency of diversifying the country's revenue base, in order to avoid a prolonged fiscal crisis and an escalation of inflation. The country's headline inflation rate was 16.8% year on year in May 2011, while the currency—the Sudanese pound—was trading at 3.50 to the US dollar on the black market in July, compared to an official rate of close to 2.70 to the US dollar. In preparation for the negative effects of secession, the Government had introduced an austerity budget in January, which included a reduction in sugar subsidies, but this was met with protests in the capital, Khartoum. In July the Minister of Finance and National Economy, Ali Mahmood Abd al-Rasool, announced that the Government would have to reduce spending further, just to avoid the budget deficit widening beyond 5.0% of gross domestic product (GDP), compared with an original projection of 3.2% of GDP.

As the first anniversary of South Sudan's independence approached, the state of Sudan's economy had deteriorated even further. The Government announced in May 2012 that the economy had expanded by 2% year on year in the first quarter of 2012, although this appeared unlikely, given the huge plunge in oil output. By mid-2012 the IMF was predicting that real economic output would contract by 7.3% during that year as a whole. The Fund's dire forecast came at the time of a further negative impact to the country's hydrocarbon revenues, due to damage caused to the crucial Heglig oilfields in Southern Kordofan State in April. A temporary occupation of these oilfields by South Sudan, which involved fighting between the two countries' militaries, led to production of 55,000 barrels per day being shut down (approximately one-half of Sudan's post-secession output). Although the Government announced that production had resumed after South Sudan's army withdrew, it remained below capacity. Other statistics were equally alarming. The value of the country's exports fell by 83% in the first quarter of 2012, and inflation was at a rate of more than 20% year on year. The currency, meanwhile, had plunged to new depths on the black market, reaching 6.2 to the US dollar in April 2012, compared with the government-permitted rate of 2.7 to the US dollar.

The continued deterioration of macroeconomic fundamentals necessitated even greater fiscal retrenchment. In late April 2012 the Government dramatically reduced departmental fuel budgets by 50%, while also obliging civil servants to forego two days of wages. Al-Rasool stated that these measures would help to support the army in countering aggression by South Sudan, in a context where around 75% of the central Government's budget was devoted to military spending. He acknowledged in early May that there would need to be further reductions in spending before the end of the year. However, the requirement to stabilize the exchange rate and fiscal accounts needed to be balanced against two key factors. First, massive retrenchment would further constrain economic activity, in a context where the economy was already facing a steep recession. Second, the Government needed to be mindful of the security implications of spending cuts, especially given the popular revolutions in neighbouring Egypt and in Tunisia in early 2011. Reductions in consumer subsidies on fuel and basic food items would be particularly dangerous, in terms of popular reaction.

It therefore remained uncertain as to whether macroeconomic stability could be restored. Much would depend on Sudan mending its damaged political relationships with its neighbour to the south, and with major world powers. With regard to the former, it was crucial that Sudan agree an oil deal with South Sudan. Before secession, Sudan and the then semi-autonomous region of Southern Sudan had shared revenues from southern oilfields equally, but that agreement expired when South Sudan gained independence. With the south dependent on Sudan's pipeline infrastructure in order to deliver its oil to the coast for shipping onto the global market, a new oil agreement would need to involve South Sudan paying transit fees to Sudan's Government. However, in the immediate post-secession period, the two countries had yet to agree such a deal. While Sudan's Government demanded US $22.8 for each barrel of South Sudan's oil piped to Port Sudan, the authorities of South Sudan described this figure as ' daylight robbery'. By January 2012 the two sides' negotiating positions remained far apart, as Sudan's Government by that time was demanding a grant of $7,400m. in compensation for the effect of secession and to guarantee South Sudan access to its pipelines, together with $32.2 for each and every barrel of southern oil transported through its network. South Sudan was prepared to offer a grant of $5,400m. (inclusive of a waiver of alleged payment arrears totalling $2,800m.) over four years. The Government in Juba also offered its counterpart in Khartoum $1.0 for each barrel of oil piped through Sudan, but said this would be deductible from the proposed grant. Frustrated by the failure of South Sudan to provide the oil royalties that the Sudanese authorities felt were due, Sudan's security forces began to impound oil in December 2011, and a month later the South Sudanese Government claimed that $815m. of its oil exports had been stolen by its northern counterpart. As a result, the South suspended oil production in January 2012. Although this deprived South Sudan of its own principal source of revenues, the shutdown—which was still in place at August—also meant that Sudan was unable to secure pipeline royalties, either through the unofficial channels it had used in late 2011, or legitimately, via a bilateral agreement. It was still possible, of course, that the oil impasse could be overcome and a new fee-sharing structure agreed by the two Governments, but until then both sides would be deprived of desperately needed income, compounding their already dire respective fiscal crises.

Beyond the need to co-exist with the south, Sudan's economic health post-secession was hugely dependent on the largesse of the USA and the People's Republic of China. Sudan was lobbying strongly for the USA to lift sanctions and help lead the drive among creditor countries for relief on its US $35,700m. foreign debt burden. However, the prospects for a rapid post-secession termination of sanctions and forgiveness of debt were clouded by the US Government's concerns about the regime's conduct in the troubled Darfur provinces and the outbreak of a new conflict in Southern Kordofan State. Such concerns were compounded by the Sudan Armed Forces' bombing of South Sudan's oil-rich Unity State in March and April 2012, leaving the prospect of debt relief and an end to sanctions as distant as ever. China, however, was better disposed towards providing succour to Sudan, against a background where state-owned China National Petroleum Corpn (CNPC) is a major player in the African nation's oil industry. Prior to secession, China and Sudan signed agreements whereby the former would provide the latter with loans for infrastructure and equipment development. The details of the projects, including finances, remained undisclosed, but China's ongoing commitment to Sudan was crucial to the diminished country's hopes of moving beyond the economic shock caused by secession. In February 2012 China additionally agreed to a five-year moratorium on sovereign debt repayments.

However, the Chinese Government appeared to be becoming increasingly concerned about the viability of its investments. According to an announcement by Sudanese Minister of Finance and National Economy al-Rasool in May 2012, China had stopped funding for 11 development projects. He acknowledged that the suspension was due to his Government's inability to carry on providing oil-based collateral for the funding. A potential new source of international assistance emerged in March, when Qatar's official news agency announced that the Arab state had discussed the details of a US $2,000m. investment in various sectors of Sudan's economy, during a state visit by President Omar al-Bashir to the Qatari capital, Doha. However, at mid-2012 this investment had still to be confirmed.

In terms of employment, Sudan is primarily an agricultural and pastoral country, with about 65% of the economically active population engaged in the agricultural sector—the majority in essentially subsistence production. Industry is largely based around agriculture and the petroleum sector. The vast majority of the population remain below—or struggle just above—the official poverty line, defined as an income of US $1 per day. Although annual per caput income rose from $334 in 1999 to $532 in 2008, this latter figure was still only equivalent to $1.46 per day. In the UN Development Programme's 2011 Human Development Index (which ranks countries according to education, life expectancy and national income), Sudan was placed 169th out of 187 countries, in the least developed category.

A surge in global demand for oil in recent years has generated a significant rise in investment in Sudan, particularly from China and India. Investment in oil facilities, including refining, has been particularly significant. The high demand for oil saw the international price of Brent crude peak at US $147 per barrel in July 2008, compared with a price of below $20 per barrel in the late 1990s. The revenue generated by the increase in international oil prices, which began in earnest in 2004, gave the Sudanese Government funds to spend on other sectors, including agriculture and infrastructure. This resulted in a strong acceleration in the real rate of economic growth, from 5.1% in 2004 to 6.3% in 2005 and 11.3% in 2006, according to the IMF. Overall GDP increased, in real terms, at an average annual rate of 6.3% in 2001–10; growth in 2010 was 4.5%, but was expected to fall to only 0.2% in 2011 and to contract in 2012 (mainly as a result of the loss of the greater part of former state revenue from petroleum).

AGRICULTURE

Approximately one-third of Sudan's pre-secession total area of about 2.5m. sq km is considered to be suitable for some form of agriculture. Of this, about 84m. ha is potential arable land and the remainder pastoral. Only about 15%, however, of the available arable area is cropped, reflecting the critical role of water availability in the development of the sector. The vast majority of settled cultivation has, until recently, been limited to the permanent watercourses of the Blue and White Niles and their tributaries in north-central Sudan. It is these areas that, within the framework of Sudan's 2m. ha of irrigation schemes, have been the focus of modern, commercial agriculture—producing the major export crop, cotton, as well as vital import substitutes such as sugar and wheat.

In contrast, some 60% of Sudan's area is occupied by the 11% of the population (estimated at 43.2m. in 2010) who are fully or partly nomadic—combining cultivation of subsistence crops and some cash crops with seasonal migration, with their herds, along well-defined routes, determined by the location of sources of drinking water during the wet and dry seasons.

The rainlands account for virtually all output of the staple grains—sorghum, millet and wheat—as well as of meat, milk and some vegetable products, and output in normal rainfall years has usually been enough for self-sufficiency. Livestock have also been an important export, as have other rain-fed products such as sesame seed. Sudan exports sorghum to Eritrea, Japan, Saudi Arabia and several European countries. In 2009, according to FAO, sorghum production was an estimated 4.2m. metric tons.

However, chronic drought has had a severe impact on agricultural output in some parts of the country, particularly in the South, where the number of 'severely food insecure people' reached 1.5m. in the first half of 2010, according to the UN Office for the Co-ordination of Humanitarian Affairs. Acute malnutrition rates exceeded the 'emergency threshold' of 15% in some areas. The Government of Southern Sudan (GOSS) was urged by the UN to invest more heavily in agriculture, to ease the suffering of the population. GOSS Vice-President Riek Machar announced in response that the authorities would spend US $35m. on food relief, and pledged long-term investment in agriculture. Also in May 2010 the US Government embarked on a $55m. aid programme, the Food, Agribusiness, and Rural Markets project, to boost Southern Sudan's agricultural sector, with a focus on assisting small-scale farmers in the fertile region of Equatoria to grow crops over a five-year period.

Overall crop production plunged in 2011, reaching only about 50% of the volume of the 2010 harvest, according to FAO, which attributed the poor performance to erratic rainfall and intensified conflict. With regard to the latter, substantial crop-producing areas of Southern Kordofan and Blue Nile states were not harvested, due to the outbreak of a new insurgency and aerial bombing of rebel-held areas by the Sudan Armed Forces. As a result, sorghum prices in Kadugli (the capital of Southern Kordofan) and Damazin (the capital of Blue Nile) more than doubled, according to FAO. Meanwhile, sorghum and millet crops in east and central Sudan, as well as the Darfur regions in the west, were negatively affected by unusual livestock migrations, as pastoralists sought water for their herds, bringing them into conflict with crop growers. FAO's Consolidated Appeal process aimed to restore agricultural production and food access for up to 3.5m. people in Sudan in 2012.

Almost 12% of Sudan's area was classified as forest land before South Sudan gained independence in July 2011, but this proportion fell thereafter, as southern territories are much more fertile than northern areas. Only very small areas are under commercial planting, largely fuel-wood developments in the central region. Exploitation of the natural forest is also predominantly limited to fuel wood, other than gum arabic, which is by far the most important forest product. Until the 1970s Sudan was the world's largest single producer of edible gum, accounting for some 92% of production, but this was reduced to about 80% with the advent of new producers and artificial substitutes and with it the importance of gum in exports. The value of exports of gum arabic amounted to US $107.5m. in 2005 and $50.2m. in 2006.

Of the 2m. ha of land under irrigation, about 50% is in the Gezira scheme, which is located between the Blue and White Niles. First developed by the British in the 1920s, the Gezira became the world's largest farming enterprise under one management—the parastatal Sudan Gezira Board. The remaining irrigated land is also predominantly under publicly administered schemes: the small-scale farmer pump schemes on the Blue, White and main Niles; the New Halfa scheme developed in the 1960s on the Gash river; and the Rahad scheme, on the Blue Nile, inaugurated in 1977. Although these schemes account for over 60% of Africa's total irrigated area, they represent less than 50% of Sudan's estimated potential. In 1994 Sudan embarked on a programme of privatization of irrigation schemes.

The major irrigated crop is cotton. The main types of cotton grown in Sudan are medium-staple Akala variety; long-staple Barakat; and long-medium staple Shambat B. A small amount of rain-fed short-staple cotton is also grown. In 1997 overseas sales of cotton represented 17.8% of the total value of Sudan's exports; however, by 2006 this figure had declined to just 1.5%. In 2010, according to FAO, Sudan produced an estimated 136,000 metric tons of seed cotton.

The development of sugar production began in the 1960s to reduce the cost of Sudan's single most expensive import commodity after petroleum. The largest of the parastatal sugar enterprises, the Kenana Scheme, was officially opened in 1981, and played a major role in eliminating Sudan's sugar import costs in 1986. In early 1999 plans were announced for the construction of a US $500m. sugar production facility in the White Nile region. The majority of the finance was expected to be provided by the Chinese Government. Moreover, Sudan and China agreed to build a sixth sugar plant, which would further increase production. In May 2002 Sudan inaugurated a new facility at the state-owned Sudan Sugar Co in New Halfa, which would increase production to 600 metric tons per day. In

2004 Sudan produced 750,000 tons of sugar, and in May 2005 the Council of Ministers approved a $71m. loan agreement with the Arab Fund for Economic and Social Development to fund the White Nile sugar project, intended to build water pumps and irrigation works. The project was expected to produce 340,000 tons of sugar and 40,000 tons of other cash crops annually. The White Nile region remained the epicentre of Sudan's sugar industry, with three factories in existence in 2009 (and another under construction, in early 2009). In 2005 Sudan exported 5.5m. tons of sugar.

Wheat, Sudan's other major irrigated crop, is also an import substitute, although attempts to increase irrigated domestic production have had very limited success owing to the unsuitability of the climate south of the Egyptian border area. However, some agriculturalists now believe that new strains of wheat are being developed that could prosper even in these hot regions. In July 2005 the Government launched the US $75m. Sondos Agricultural Project, which was to be implemented by Sudan's Eastern Jebel-Awlia firm and the China Engineering Company and would cover 40,500 ha of land across the three states of Khartoum, White Nile and Gezira. The project was intended to expand production of grains, vegetables and livestock, increase job opportunities in agriculture, and promote social development services, in an attempt to enable the country to feed itself.

In the Middle East, the combination of rising oil wealth and fears about the future availability of food supplies has led to renewed interest in Sudan's agricultural potential. There are concerns that these developments might lead to a repeat of the hurried and inappropriate schemes that were established and failed during the 'bread basket' era in the 1970s. Sudan's Ministry of Investment announced in August 2008 that it was seeking US $1,000m. in external funding for 17 agricultural projects. The projects covered nearly 900,000 ha and would involve corn, wheat, vegetables and fruit.

Outsourcing food production by wealthy Middle Eastern states increased in the first half of 2008, as global food and oil prices surged to new highs. High oil prices provided additional income for such states to finance these schemes, while high food prices provided the rationale for guaranteeing supplies from fertile regions. FAO estimates that Sudan possesses fertile land amounting to 105m. ha, yet only 7m. ha were in use in 2008. In March 2009 the Government of Saudi Arabia announced that a consortium of companies would invest in Sudan's agricultural sector. However, the value of the investment was relatively small, at US $40m., and would be split between Sudan and Ethiopia. Three years later, Saudi Arabia announced that it had received approval from Sudan's Government to cultivate 809,000 ha of land in the east of the country, close to Port Sudan, where agricultural produce can quickly be exported across the Red Sea to the Arabian peninsular. Saleh Kamel, the Chairman of the Jeddah Chamber of Commerce, announced in April 2012 that the deal involved the acquisition of the land as a free zone, where activity would not be subject to taxation (or any other Sudanese laws). There was no immediate indication as to the value of the agreement to Sudan's Government, but the flexibility provided to the Saudi side indicated that the deal could provide moderate support to the nation's finances. It had earlier appeared that significant corrections in food prices in the second half of 2008 had tempered the urgency for some countries to outsource food production. Nevertheless, a number of important bilateral deals had been concluded by Sudan. The Governments of the United Arab Emirates (UAE) and Sudan agreed to cultivate 400,000 ha of land in Sudan, while a deal was struck with the Republic of Korea for a project involving 690,000 ha of Sudanese land. In May 2008 Sudan and Egypt were in talks to cultivate wheat covering 800,000 ha of land (520,000 ha of which are in Sudan). The land straddles the Nile and is located in the Arqin area.

In an effort to boost food production in Sudan, following a renewed surge in global prices and popular discontent, Sudanese President Lt-Gen. Omar Hassan Ahmad al-Bashir announced in June 2011 that the country would offer land free of charge for 'vital projects' with 'serious investors', who would need to display commitment to qualify. Although details on how investors would prove their seriousness were not initially forthcoming, sugar and wheat production projects were designated as priority initiatives. Earlier in the year, a reduction of sugar subsidies had contributed to the outbreak of popular protests.

Sudan's Ministry of Agriculture and Irrigation and the Chinese Center of Transfer of Agricultural Technologies reached an agreement to grow cotton in May 2012. Planting would take place in eastern Sudan, while Sudanese technicians and scientists would also be trained under the programme. Also in May, the Iranian Government announced that it would establish a permanent trade office in Sudan and invest in several sectors, including agriculture. The announcement coincided with a visit to the Iranian capital, Tehran, by Sudanese presidential adviser Mustafa Osman Ismail, who declared that Iranian investment in sugar and vegetable oil production in his country would be welcome.

INDUSTRY AND MINERALS

In February 2000 the Sudan authorities officially established the Red Sea Free Trade Zone between Port Sudan and the port of Suwakin, encompassing warehouse, industrial and commercial areas. In October President al-Bashir opened the US $450m. industrial town of Jiad, some 50 km south of Khartoum. The town included factories for manufacturing cables, cars, electricity wires, steel, trucks and pipeline products, together with housing, health and education facilities. However, in February 2002 reports indicated that just seven of the factories in the Red Sea Free Trade Zone were still functioning, and since then the Zone has collapsed. Egypt's Asec Cement started production at a $250m. plant in Al-Takamul in July 2010, with a capacity of 1.6m. metric tons of cement and 1.5m. tons of clinker per year. The plant was expected to halve a deficiency in the cement supply in Sudan, estimated at 3m. tons per year, arising from an oil-financed construction boom in the country. Asec also planned to build a 42-MW power plant to supply the cement factory.

While the overall industrial sector (both heavy and light manufacturing) was still largely underdeveloped by the second decade of the 21st century, the oil sector provided a significant exception. From 1973 a number of international companies began to show an interest in exploring for petroleum, and Chevron of the USA was prepared for production when the resumption of civil war in the south in 1983 halted the project. It was not until the mid-1990s that Sudan began to take steps to commence production, but the hydrocarbon sector developed quickly thereafter. In June 1995 Sudan and China established a joint venture to explore for petroleum. Sudan was to provide 30% of the finance for the company, while China agreed to provide the remaining 70% and to train Sudanese technicians. China subsequently agreed to accord Sudan a grant of US $15m. for the exploitation of its petroleum reserves. In October the Qatar General Petroleum Corporation agreed to participate in a joint venture with Sudan's Concorp to exploit petroleum reserves in central Sudan. China was granted the right to exploit Sudan's largest oilfield, with proven oil reserves of 220m. metric tons, in January 1997, and in March it was awarded a contract to build a refinery in Jaili just north of Khartoum with a capacity of 50,000 b/d. Also in March an agreement was signed with four international companies—from Malaysia, Canada, China and Sudan—allowing for shared petroleum production and the construction of a $1,000m. pipeline to transport petroleum to Port Sudan.

According to the BP Statistical Review of World Energy, proven reserves of petroleum were equivalent to 6,700m. barrels in 2010. In December 2004 the French oil company Total renewed its oil agreement with Sudan that had lapsed in 1985, and began work early in 2008. In February 2005 the Sudanese Government announced that India's ONGC Videsh would build a new $1,200m. oil refinery at Port Sudan that would reportedly have the capacity to produce 100,000 b/d. Port Sudan's existing refinery was more than 40 years old and only had a 25,000 b/d capacity. In the same year Sudan announced the first offshore exploration concession, which was expected to yield significant reserves of natural gas. Work was completed in April 2006 on a new 740-km pipeline to the export terminal at al-Khair, near Port Sudan. In July

CNPC announced that it had completed work to upgrade the production capacity of the al-Jeili refinery from 50,000 b/d to some 100,000 b/d. By 2008 most of the exploration blocks had been allocated, largely to Asian and Arab Gulf companies.

Production developments during 2008 and 2009 in Sudan's oil industry (although not price developments) were largely favourable. According to reports in April 2009, PetroChina was building a refinery in China specifically in order to process Sudan's high-acid crude. Sudan's oil output averaged around 500,000 b/d in 2008, according to the authorities. This was higher than the average 457,000 b/d of output generated in 2007, a year that had seen a large increase from production in 2006 of around 365,000 b/d. The country was targeting a 20% rise in output to 600,000 b/d in 2009, owing in part to an expected increase in production (from 40,000 b/d to 60,000 b/d) by PetroChina at a block in the country's south-west. Conversely, it was reported in April that ONGC Videsh was writing off nearly US $90m. of investment in three oil wells in the Muglad Basin in southern Sudan. The investment in the country's Block 5B had failed to discover sufficient quantities of oil and the company reportedly encountered what it regarded as excessive bureaucratic and security costs.

Japan's Toyota Tsusho Corpn announced in March 2010 that it was in the early stages of consultations to build a US $1,500m. pipeline to transport crude petroleum from South Sudan to a proposed new seaport on the Kenyan island of Lamu. The company stated that it had held initial talks with the Kenyan authorities (which were planning to expand the rudimentary port facilities at Lamu), prior to expected discussions with the GOSS. The plan involved the construction of an 1,400-km pipeline to transport petroleum from Juba, while Lamu would be equipped with an oil jetty and a storage tank. The company proposed that it would own the 450,000-b/d pipeline for 20 years, before it became the property of Kenya and Sudan. However, it was not known how Toyota Tsusho's plans would be received by the GOSS.

Sudan's other known mineral resources include marble, mica, chromite and gypsum. Gold deposits in the Red Sea hills have been known since pharaonic times, and there are uranium reserves on the western borders with Chad and the Central African Republic. Until recently, only the chromite deposits in the Ingessana Hills near the Ethiopian border were exploited on a substantial scale by the state-owned Sudan Mining Co, which produces 10,000–15,000 metric tons per year for export. The known reserves exceed 1m. tons of high-quality chromite. Gold output in Sudan totalled 36.8 metric tons in the first five months of 2011, according to Sudan's Ministry of Minerals. This represented nearly double the gold output recorded in the first 10 months of 2010 (23 tons), according to figures from the same source. Against this background, President al-Bashir informed the country's legislature in April 2011 that he expected the country's total export earnings from gold to increase to US $3,000m. in 2011, from $1,400m. in 2010. Although these government figures were rather higher than independent estimates, the latter at least showed an upward trend, generating some confidence that the loss of oil revenues generated by South Sudan's secession could be partially offset by rising gold exports. British-based consultancy GFMS Ltd, which conducts research into precious metal output around the world, estimated that Sudan produced a total of 10.1 tons of gold in 2010 as a whole, an increase from 4.0 tons in 2009 and 2.7 tons in 2008. Moreover, the 2010 level of output was the highest since 2000, according to GFMS.

Qatar announced in March 2012 that it would invest up to US $2,000m. in Sudan, particularly in sectors such as oil, mining and agriculture. The Qatari News Agency (QNA) reported that the investment would be backed by treasury bonds, after a state visit by President al-Bashir to Doha. However, while the QNA declared that full details of the proposed agreement would be clarified during a visit by a Qatari delegation to Khartoum, no further developments had been reported at mid-2012.

FOREIGN TRADE, BALANCE OF PAYMENTS AND EXCHANGE RATE

In 2009 Sudan's main sources of imports were China (21.9%), Saudi Arabia (7.2%), Egypt (6.1%), India (5.5%) and the UAE (5.3%). China remained Sudan's most important export market, receiving 58.3% of the country's shipments in 2009, most notably, large quantities of oil. Japan (14.7%), Indonesia (8.8%), and India (4.9%) were also significant recipients of Sudanese exports.

Sudan has had a deficit on the current account of its balance of payments since independence in 1956, but the deficits were relatively insignificant until the mid-1970s, when government policies resulted in escalating deficits on the balance of trade and rising debt-service requirements. By 2002 the current account deficit had reached US $1,008m.; however, it was reduced slightly, to $955m., in 2003, and again, to $815m., in 2004. The deficit then increased to some $2,324m. in 2005 and to $5,542m. in 2006, before accelerating further during 2007 to $5,812m., according to the IMF.

Nevertheless, the extended surge in oil prices in the initial months of 2008 gave a boost to exports and reduced the current account deficit in that year to US $5,240m., according to the IMF. However, a significant correction in the oil price left Sudan's current account position exposed once more, particularly as the country continued to rely heavily on imports, while also maintaining a large deficit in the services account.

A severe global economic downturn in late 2008 and 2009 heralded a sharp downturn in investment flows, creating uncertainty as to whether Sudan's capital account could adequately offset a fresh surge in the current account deficit. The negative effect of a global recession on foreign direct investment (FDI) was compounded by the indictment early in 2009 of President al-Bashir by the International Criminal Court, on charges of war crimes and crimes against humanity. Sudan's Minister of Investment George Borin Niami was quoted as acknowledging that investors had 'shied away because of the spectre of indictment'. In response to the deterioration of the balance of payments, the exchange rate came under pressure, depreciating from around 2.05 new Sudanese pounds to US $1 at the beginning of 2008 to 2.40 Sudanese pounds to US $1 by late May 2009. The depreciation of the exchange rate marked a significant—if necessary, in the face of a near-exhaustion of the country's foreign currency reserves—change in policy by Sudan's monetary authorities, which had previously shown a preference for keeping the local currency very closely tied to the US dollar. Alongside the current account deficit, two other factors forced the depreciation of the Sudanese pound. One key factor was a general revival of the US dollar on global currency markets. This revival was driven by a so-called 'flight to safety', particularly when the financial crisis afflicting developed markets in late 2008 drove investors away from assets perceived as being risky and towards what they regarded as the safety of US Treasury bonds. The final key factor undermining the Sudanese pound was high inflation, largely due to a surge in global food prices, which had greater impact in countries where food constitutes a large proportion of consumer purchases.

During the second half of 2009 and the first half of 2010 the central bank once again showed its preference for a 'controlled float', rather than an outright float of the local currency. The central bank announced in June 2010 that it was planning to transfer from an exchange rate regime that tracked only the US dollar, to one tracking a number of currencies, due to the USA's ongoing embargo against Sudan (which included trade and financial sanctions) and a desire to enhance exchange rate stability. In late July the exchange rate was around 2.37 new Sudanese pounds to US $1.

The currency came under pressure in the months ahead of oil-rich South Sudan's secession, amid concerns about the impact of the impending loss of oil revenues on the fiscal and trade accounts. The official exchange rate stood at close to 2.70 new Sudanese pounds to US $1 by the time secession occurred in July 2011, but even this substantially devalued rate was considerably out of line with the parallel market value, which by that time had reached 3.50 new Sudanese pounds to US $1.

Sudan introduced a new currency on 24 July 2011. The new notes featured changed symbols and a downsized map of the country, reflecting the secession of the south. The Bank of Sudan Governor, Mohammad Khair al-Zubair, did not immediately specify how long the old notes would remain valid tender, but declared that the transfer would be effected 'as quickly as possible'. The move attracted complaints from the Government of the newly independent South Sudan, which feared being left with large holdings of an invalid currency. Pagan Amum, the Secretary-General of South Sudan's ruling party, the Sudan People's Liberation Movement, accused Sudan's Government of launching 'economic war' against the new nation.

Sudan's terms of trade, overall balance of payments and exchange rate were all expected to be significantly affected by South Sudan's secession. Export earnings from oil in 2009 totalled US $7,131m., close to 90% of total exports for the year, according to IMF figures. This proportion rose slightly to 92% in 2010 (with oil exports totalling an estimated $9,433m., of total annual shipments of $10,236m.), according to preliminary IMF estimates. Although Sudan recorded a moderate trade surplus in 2010 ($1,086m., according to initial estimates, turning around a 2009 trade deficit of $694m.), a significant deficit was in prospect for the second half of 2011.

Reversing this negative impact to the trade balance would require a tightening of austerity measures (in order to cap imports) and a diversification of the export base. In this latter respect, there were grounds for cautious hope. In the first three months of 2011 non-oil exports increased to US $451.9m., from $338.2m. in the same period of the previous year. Sales of gold were the key driver of this improvement in the first quarter of the year, rising from $169.7m. to $246.9m., according to Sudan's central bank. After central bank figures indicated that gold exports totalled $1,400m. in the 2010 calendar year, the Government targeted a rise of more than 100% for 2011 as a whole, to $3,000m. In a further effort to develop the non-hydrocarbon sector, in July 2011 the central bank announced that it was issuing a tender for the construction of a gold refinery. The Khartoum Gold Refinery commenced operations in May 2012.

The central bank stated in May 2012 that it had been provided with 'a large amount' of foreign currency from overseas, in order to bolster the exchange rate. The source of the funds—and the amount—were not disclosed, so the announcement did little to suppress pessimistic speculation about the local currency. The monetary authority claimed that the new reserves of hard currency would enable it to meet dollar demand until the end of 2012. A day earlier, the central bank had confirmed that it would adjust the official exchange rate from 2.7 to the US dollar, to bring it more in line with the parallel market, where it was trading at close to 6.0 to the dollar. The Deputy Governor of the central bank announced that foreign exchange bureaux would be free to offer rates that they deemed appropriate and added that the bank would consult with commercial lenders in order to establish the new rate. Although he further claimed that the process would eliminate the black market, it was far from certain that this would occur, since the currency's market value could quickly diverge significantly from any new fixed rate, especially given the country's extremely poor post-secession macroeconomic fundamentals.

In an effort to support the balance of payments and the exchange rate, Sudan's authorities have sought to diversify exports. The Government planned to double oil output in 2012, from its initial post-secession level of 120,000 barrels per day, although this appeared unrealistic, in view of the damage caused by north–south fighting in Heglig and ongoing military tensions at various other locations along the oil-rich border. The Sudanese authorities were also seeking to boost gold exports. The central bank announced in May that revenue from gold shipments would reach US $3,000m. in 2012, higher than an earlier target of $2,500m. for the year. In the first six and a half weeks of 2012 alone, Sudan's gold exports reached $400m., as it sold 7.2 metric tons at an average of $55m. per ton, according to government estimates. However, the year-end 2012 projection was unlikely to be met entirely through domestic gold mining, even in view of a further planned increase of indigenous output of the precious metal, after the nation claimed to have produced nearly 36 tons in 2011, compared with just 4 tons in 2009. Indeed, there was widespread scepticism about the reliability of government figures, partly due to the fragmented and primarily artisanal nature of mining in the country. Annual gold sales of $3,000m. in 2012 would surely therefore require the depletion of existing central bank reserves, in exchange for hard currency.

FOREIGN AID

Throughout the post-independence period Sudan's economic well-being depended on ever increasing amounts of foreign aid. During the Cold War the USA became Sudan's largest single donor; other important bilateral donors included Egypt, Libya, the United Kingdom, Kuwait, China and Saudi Arabia. The principal multilateral donors included the World Bank, the European Community (now the European Union, EU) and the IMF. The end of the Cold War coincided with the rise of the al-Bashir regime, and Sudan's economic performance for much of the period that followed was increasingly poor, resulting in international sanctions and isolation, and difficulties with the World Bank and IMF.

The conflict in Sudan's western Darfur provinces from 2003 meant that many countries denied Sudan in terms of bilateral aid. China remained Sudan's primary source of bilateral assistance. Even in the midst of a global recession, Sudan was relying on China for US $4,300m. of loans for infrastructure development (with a focus on roads and railways), according to the Minister of State for Finance and National Economy, Lual Deng, in May 2009. Meanwhile, India was providing $200m.–$300m. in agricultural loans. In March 2008 the Minister of Information and Communication Zahawi Ibrahim Malek urged Western governments to follow China's example, saying that 'instead of criticizing China for helping us, they should be helping us more'. The Organization of the Islamic Conference announced in March 2010 that it had raised $850m. for reconstruction and development projects in Sudan's Darfur provinces, focusing on basic infrastructure requirements, including housing, water and agricultural modernization.

POWER, TRANSPORT AND COMMUNICATIONS

Sudan's electricity sector has been beset by poor infrastructure, frequent outages, and a small customer base. In 2004 Sudan had 728 MW of electric generation capacity, which included roughly equal amounts of thermal (mainly oil) and hydropower capacity. Electricity was transmitted via two interconnected electrical grids; however, these grids cover only a small portion of the country. Regions not covered by the grid rely on small-scale, diesel-fired generators. In total, only an estimated 30% of the country's population has access to electricity. In the 1990s the electricity sector deteriorated as a result of a lack of funding. By 2000 a Rehabilitation and Performance Improvement Programme to upgrade the electricity infrastructure and to improve the adequacy and reliability of the electricity supply had been launched. This programme was supported by a US $10m. loan from the Organization of Petroleum Exporting Countries (OPEC) Fund for International Development and $15m. of funding from Saudi Arabia, Qatar, and other Arab investors. One of the largest projects was the proposed Merowe (or Hamdab) and Kajbar hydroelectric facilities in northern Sudan. The 1,250-MW Merowe facility was to be located 250 miles north of Khartoum at the River Nile's Fourth Cataract. In October 2002 two consortia—China International Water and Electric Corpn (CWE) and China National Water Resources and Hydropower Engineering Corpn; and a joint venture of Consolidated Contractors International Co of Greece and Salini Costruttori of Italy—agreed to build three sections of the civil works portion of the dam, at an estimated cost of $1,900m. In December 2003 the French company Alstom agreed to a $300m. contract to construct the dam, while China's Harbin Power signed an agreement to build seven sub-stations and around 1,000 miles of transmission lines. Egypt has thus far voiced no major objections to the project's planned diversion of River Nile flows. The Kajbar Dam, located at the Nile's Second

Cataract, is currently under construction, and will have a capacity of 300 MW. China was to finance 75% of the project (costing a total of some $200m.), with Sudan providing the remaining 25%. Environmental groups have expressed concern about the Kajbar Dam, citing potential damage to the Nile river's ecosystem and to the culture of the displaced Nubian residents of the area.

The Merowe Dam was to have a generating capacity of 1,250 MW, far surpassing the total generating capacity recorded by the whole country earlier in the decade. The total cost of this upscaled project was estimated at US $2,000m. in early 2008, 40% of which was financed by Sudan's Government and the remainder financed by loans from China and the Middle East. However, in August 2008 the construction of the Merowe Dam encountered opposition, as villagers who had been living close to the dam protested against being relocated. Over 12,000 villagers were reportedly affected by the alleged change of location. Nevertheless, the Merowe Dam was inaugurated in 2009.

The 450-MW Al Fula power plant was inaugurated in March 2010. Located in Northern Kordofan, the plant cost US $680m. and was built by the Shandong Electric Power Construction Corpn of China. In addition to supplying electricity to Northern Kordofan, the plant will also supply Southern Kordofan and Darfur. Accordingly, Sudan's Ministry of Finance and National Economy secured a loan of $274m. from the Export and Import Bank of China, to finance the construction of the transmission lines from the Al Fula plant.

In April 2010 a US $838m. contract was awarded to CWE and China Three Gorges Corpn for the construction of the Upper Atbara Dams Complex in eastern Sudan. Two separate dams—the Rumira Dam and the Bodana Dam, both utilizing the Atbara river—were to be constructed. The work was projected to take more than five years to complete, but would result in a generating capacity of 135 MW. The dam would also be used to irrigate 210,000 ha of land. Meanwhile, Ethiopia was expected to start supplying Sudan with 200 MW of power from its repaired Gilgel Gibe II power plant from September 2010.

Although Sudan still depends heavily on railways for transport, the road network has played an increasingly important role since 1980. More than 48,000 km of tracks are classed as 'motorable'. In February 2004 the Arab Fund for Economic and Social Development granted a loan of $31.5m. to finance the construction of the Gedaref–Doka–Galabat road linking the east of Sudan with Ethiopia. In late May 2005 the Sudan People's Liberation Army (SPLA) leader, John Garang, announced that a project would be started to develop the roads in southern Sudan once the interim period of autonomy in the south had commenced. The project would include the construction of 12 asphalt roads joining the southern towns and linking the south to Uganda, Kenya and the Democratic Republic of the Congo.

In 2002 the total length of railway operated by the Sudan Railways Corpn (SRC) was 5,978 km. The main line runs from Wadi Halfa, on the Egyptian border, to El-Obeid, via Khartoum. Lines from Atbara and Sinnar connect with Port Sudan. There are lines from Sinnar to Damazin on the Blue Nile (227 km) and from Aradeiba to Nyala in the south-western province of Darfur (689 km), with a 445-km branch line from Babanousa to Wau in Bahr El-Ghazal province. The Sudan Gezira Board also operated 1,400 km of railway in 1994, serving the country's cotton plantations. Shortages of spare parts and the impact of import controls on the rehabilitation requirements of track and rolling stock have considerably impeded the country's railway system. The rehabilitation of both lines and rolling stock was announced in September 1997, in order to facilitate the transportation of petroleum. In May 1999 the SRC announced plans to privatize its passenger and cargo services by the end of 2001. Under this proposal, the SRC would retain the responsibility for the management of the rails, the stations and signalling equipment. In April 2001 the IDB announced that it had granted Sudan a loan worth US $10.7m. in order to purchase 180 railway cargo wagons to enhance the railway's transport capabilities. The SRC planned to link el-Obeid with the refinery and to build another line at Sharif field (production area). There also would be a line in the southern White Nile area to link the second refinery with the oil pipeline. The SRC claims that these projects are 'ready for operation'. In 2009 plans were announced for the construction of a 10,000-km transcontinental railway project linking Port Sudan with Dakar, Senegal.

Since the end of the civil war in 2005, there have been efforts to link Sudan and neighbouring Uganda via enhanced transport links. The two countries signed an agreement to develop roads and railways, according to a report in September 2008. This included the finalization of plans to develop the railway between Gulu (in Northern Uganda), Nimule, Juba (the capital of South Sudan) and Wau. It was also agreed that the two countries would accelerate existing plans to resurface and upgrade connecting roads.

Although Sudan has about 4,068 km of navigable river, with some 1,723 km open throughout the year, river transport has, until recently, been minimal. The most frequently used waterway is the 1,435-km section of the White Nile route between Karima and Dongola.

Sudan Airways, the national carrier, is under the control of the Ministry of Transport, Roads and Bridges. At mid-2005 the company had 500 employees and an air fleet that included five Fokker 50 aircraft, two Beech King Air B200s, a Beech King Air C90, and two leased Boeing 737-200s, which are used for flights to Egypt, Kenya, the Persian (Arabian) Gulf and some domestic destinations. The Sudan Airways route network includes 15 domestic destinations, 11 in Saudi Arabia and the Persian Gulf, six in the Middle East, seven in Eastern and Southern Africa, five in Europe, and three in West Africa. It was announced in 2004 that the Government would begin privatization of the company, with 30% of the shares in the new firm being held by the Government, 21% by Sudan's private sector and 49% by foreign investors. Sudan Airways had a US $65m. debt in early 2005; however, in early February Airbus cancelled the $45m. owed to it by the airline. In return, it was agreed that Airbus would win the majority of Sudan Airways' contracts for new aircraft. Over the past few years, air passenger traffic in Sudan has grown at an average annual rate of 49%; however, safety remained an issue and since 2000 there have been at least 26 air accidents. There are 47 charter companies in Sudan (31 for air transport, 11 for air-spraying, and five for servicing the country's oilfields). In June 2005 the Government announced that the initial stages of construction work for a new $530m. international airport 40 km south-west of the capital had been completed. In June 2006 Sudan's Civil Aviation Authority opened the bidding process for the contract to construct core facilities at the airport, including two passenger terminals; the project was expected to be completed in 2012. Also in June 2005, Sudan Airways announced that it had concluded an $82m. contract for the purchase of six Antonov planes from Ukraine, and the construction of a maintenance centre at Khartoum International Airport at a cost of $8.8m. At the end of that month the Civil Aviation Authority allocated $452m. to finance the development and upgrade of 17 airports in the capital cities of the Sudanese states. The EU announced in March 2010 that 'poor safety performance' by airlines based in Sudan had prompted a ban on Sudanese flights entering its airspace.

By 2004 there were more than 1m. main, fixed telephone lines in use in Sudan. A mobile cellular telephone network for Khartoum State was inaugurated in February 1997. By 2004 there were about 1m. SUDATEL mobile cellular telephone subscribers in 17 cities. Despite continued strong subscribership, SUDATEL's profits were reduced in 2008 and the early months of 2009. The company's net profit declined by 39% year on year to US $30.3m. in the first three months of 2009. Revenues contracted by 13.1% year on year, to $157m. for the quarter. A country-wide reduction in liquidity (provoked by a significant negative reversal in oil prices) constrained revenues, while a weak Sudanese pound also undermined the company's performance, as foreign currency-denominated costs rose significantly. The weakening local currency had also undermined performance in 2008 as the company registered a 27% decline in net profit across that calendar year. Sudan invited ZTE Corpn, China's largest telecommunications company, to work with SUDATEL, according to a report in December 2008. In July 2002 SUDATEL awarded the German electrical engineering and electronics company Siemens a contract worth $21.9m. to undertake expansion work on Sudan's fixed-line telephone network. In 2002 Sudan commissioned SR Telecom, a Canadian company, to install a multipoint system for low-density applications. SR Telecom also announced that 85 rural and urban areas would soon be connected to a single grid. In December 2004 Canartel, a consortium led by Emirates Telecommunications Corpn (Etisalat), announced that it would begin to improve Sudan's second nation-wide fixed-line service by providing 500,000 fixed lines during its first year of operation. The number of mobile telephone subscribers rose from 18.1m. in 2010 to 25.1m. in 2011.

Statistical Survey

Source (unless otherwise stated): Department of Statistics, Ministry of Finance and National Economy, POB 735, Khartoum; tel. (183) 777563; fax (183) 775630; e-mail info@mof-sudan.net; internet www.mof-sudan.net; Central Bureau of Statistics, POB 700, Khartoum; tel. (183) 777255; fax (183) 771860; e-mail info@cbs.gov.sd; internet www.cbs.gov.sd.

Note: The Republic of South Sudan achieved independence from Sudan on 9 July 2011 following a referendum held in January at which voters overwhelmingly approved the secession of South Sudan. Unless otherwise indicated, data in this survey refer to pre-secession Sudan. For detailed statistical information on South Sudan, see separate chapter on that country.

Area and Population

AREA, POPULATION AND DENSITY

Area (sq km)	2,505,813*
Population (census results)†	
1 February 1993	24,940,683
22 April 2008	
Males	20,073,977
Females	19,080,513
Total	39,154,490
Population (official estimate at mid-year)	
2009	40,299,000
Density (per sq km) at mid-2009	16.1

* 967,500 sq miles.

† Excluding adjustments for underenumeration, estimated to have been 6.7% in 1993.

Note: Data for South Sudan published by the Republic of South Sudan, National Bureau of Statistics (NBS) in 2011 indicated a residual post-secession total area of 1,861,484 sq km (718,724 sq miles) for Sudan. Of the total enumerated population of 39,154,490 at the time of the 2008 census, according to NBS estimates, 30,894,000 were estimated to be resident in areas not part of the secession state of South Sudan.

POPULATION BY AGE AND SEX

(population at 2008 census)

	Males	Females	Total
0–14	8,718,975	7,964,829	16,683,804
15–64	10,606,796	10,538,986	21,145,782
65 and over	748,206	576,698	1,324,904
Total	20,073,977	19,080,513	39,154,490

PROVINCES

(1983 census, provisional)*

	Area (sq miles)	Population	Density (per sq mile)
Northern	134,736	433,391	3.2
Nile	49,205	649,633	13.2
Kassala	44,109	1,512,335	34.3
Red Sea	84,977	695,874	8.2
Blue Nile	24,009	1,056,313	44.0
Gezira	13,546	2,023,094	149.3
White Nile	16,161	933,136	57.7
Northern Kordofan	85,744	1,805,769	21.1
Southern Kordofan	61,188	1,287,525	21.0
Northern Darfur	133,754	1,327,947	9.9
Southern Darfur	62,801	1,765,752	28.1
Khartoum	10,883	1,802,299	165.6
Eastern Equatoria	46,073	1,047,125	22.7
Western Equatoria	30,422	359,056	11.8
Bahr El-Ghazal	52,000	1,492,597	28.7
Al-Buhayrat	25,625	772,913	30.2
Sobat	45,266	802,354	17.7
Jonglei	47,003	797,251	17.0
Total	967,500	20,564,364	21.3

* In 1991 a federal system of government was inaugurated, whereby Sudan was divided into nine states, which were sub-divided into 66 provinces and 281 local government areas. A constitutional decree, issued in February 1994, redivided the country into 26 states.

PRINCIPAL TOWNS

(population at 1993 census)

Omdurman	1,271,403	Nyala	227,183
Khartoum (capital)	947,483	El-Gezira	211,362
Khartoum North	700,887	Gedaref	191,164
Port Sudan	308,195	Kosti	173,599
Kassala	234,622	El-Fasher	141,884
El-Obeid	229,425	Juba	114,980

Source: UN, *Demographic Yearbook*.

Mid-2011 ('000, including suburbs, UN estimate): Khartoum 4,632,310 (Source: UN, *World Urbanization Prospects: The 2011 Revision*).

BIRTHS AND DEATHS

(annual averages, UN estimates)

	1995–2000	2000–05	2005–10
Birth rate (per 1,000)	38.6	36.5	33.8
Death rate (per 1,000)	12.0	10.3	9.4

Source: UN, *World Population Prospects: The 2010 Revision*.

Life expectancy (years at birth, WHO estimates): 61.1 (males 59.4; females 62.9) in 2010 (Source: World Bank, World Development Indicators database).

ECONOMICALLY ACTIVE POPULATION*
(persons aged 10 years and over, 1983 census, provisional)

	Males	Females	Total
Agriculture, hunting, forestry and fishing	2,638,294	1,390,411	4,028,705
Mining and quarrying	5,861	673	6,534
Manufacturing	205,247	61,446	266,693
Electricity, gas and water	42,110	1,618	43,728
Construction	130,977	8,305	139,282
Trade, restaurants and hotels	268,382	25,720	294,102
Transport, storage and communications	209,776	5,698	215,474
Financing, insurance, real estate and business services	17,414	3,160	20,574
Community, social and personal services	451,193	99,216	550,409
Activities not adequately defined	142,691	42,030	184,721
Unemployed persons not previously employed	387,615	205,144	592,759
Total	4,499,560	1,843,421	6,342,981

* Excluding nomads, homeless persons and members of institutional households.

Mid-2012 (estimates in '000): Agriculture, etc. 7,336; Total 14,800 (Source: FAO).

Health and Welfare

KEY INDICATORS

Total fertility rate (children per woman, 2010)	4.4
Under-5 mortality rate (per 1,000 live births, 2010)	103
HIV/AIDS (% of persons aged 15–49, 2007)	1.4
Physicians (per 1,000 head, 2008)	0.3
Hospital beds (per 1,000 head, 2009)	0.7
Health expenditure (2009): US $ per head (PPP)	159
Health expenditure (2009): % of GDP	7.3
Health expenditure (2009): public (% of total)	27.5
Access to water (% of persons, 2010)	58
Access to sanitation (% of persons, 2010)	26
Total carbon dioxide emissions ('000 metric tons, 2008)	14,051.9
Carbon dioxide emissions per head (metric tons, 2008)	0.3
Human Development Index (2011): ranking	169
Human Development Index (2011): value	0.408

For sources and definitions, see explanatory note on p. vi.

Agriculture

PRINCIPAL CROPS
('000 metric tons)

	2008	2009	2010
Wheat	587	642	403
Rice, paddy	30	23	23
Maize	62	66	35
Millet	721	630	471
Sorghum	3,869	4,192	2,630
Potatoes	284	301	315
Cassava (Manioc)*	10	11	14
Yams*	148	154	193
Sugar cane	7,453	7,527	7,527
Beans, dry	17	12	16*
Broad beans, horse beans, dry	140	113	152
Groundnuts, with shell	716	942	763
Sunflower seed	100	247	200†
Sesame seed	350	318	248
Melonseed*	52	69	52
Seed cotton	107	169	136*
Tomatoes	453	480	504
Pumpkins, squash and gourds*	84	73	79
Aubergines (Eggplants)	235	75	77
Onions, dry*	73	63	68
Garlic	38	25	27
Canteloupes (incl. other melons)*	22	23	24
Watermelons*	107	128	112
Dates	339	422	431
Oranges*	19	21	21
Lemons and limes*	67	80	71
Grapefruits and pomelos*	63	66	54
Guavas, mangoes and mangosteens*	183	186	192
Bananas*	84	89	85

* FAO estimate(s).
† Unofficial figure.

Aggregate production ('000 metric tons, may include official, semi-official or estimated data): Total cereals 5,269 in 2008, 5,552 in 2009, 3,562 in 2010; Total roots and tubers 590 in 2008, 682 in 2009, 785 in 2010; Total vegetables (incl. melons) 2,204 in 2008, 1,905 in 2009, 2,021 in 2010; Total fruits (excl. melons) 1,201 in 2008, 1,374 in 2009, 1,421 in 2010.

Source: FAO.

LIVESTOCK
('000 head, year ending September)

	2008	2009	2010*
Horses*	26	26	26
Asses*	751	751	751
Cattle	41,400	41,563	41,727
Camels	4,400	4,521	4,645
Sheep	51,100	51,555	52,014
Goats	43,100	43,270	43,441
Chickens	41,502	42,400*	43,000

* FAO estimate(s).

Source: FAO.

LIVESTOCK PRODUCTS
('000 metric tons)

	2008	2009	2010*
Cattle meat	1,369	1,442	1,505
Sheep meat	332	335	349
Goat meat	148	150	160
Chicken meat	27	29	29
Cows' milk	5,329	5,366	5,555
Sheep's milk	503	508	452
Goats' milk	1,474	1,493	1,602
Hen eggs*	54	55	56
Wool, greasy*	53	55	55

* FAO estimates.

Source: FAO.

Forestry

ROUNDWOOD REMOVALS
('000 cubic metres, FAO estimates)

	2008	2009	2010
Sawlogs, veneer logs and logs for sleepers	123	123	123
Other industrial wood	2,050	2,050	2,050
Fuel wood	18,326	18,547	18,776
Total	20,499	20,720	20,949

2011: Production assumed to be unchanged from 2010 (FAO estimates).

Source: FAO.

Gum arabic ('000 metric tons, year ending 30 June): 18 in 1996/97; 18 in 1997/98; 28 in 1998/99 (Source: IMF, *Sudan: Statistical Appendix*, July 2000).

Fishing

('000 metric tons, live weight)

	2007	2008*	2009
Capture	65.5*	68.6	71.7
Nile tilapia	22.9	31.9	40.9
Other freshwater fishes	36.9	31.0	25.1
Marine fishes	5.7	5.6	5.6
Aquaculture	2.0*	2.0	2.2*
Total catch	67.5*	70.6	73.9*

* FAO estimate(s).

2010: Catch assumed to be unchanged from 2009 (FAO estimates).

Source: FAO.

Mining

('000 metric tons, unless otherwise stated)

	2008	2009	2010
Crude petroleum ('000 barrels)	168,898	173,453	168,656
Salt (unrefined)	10.6	35.8	141.8
Chromite	27.1	14.1	56.8
Gold ore (kilograms)*	7,508	14,914	26,317

* Figures refer to the metal content of ores.

Source: US Geological Survey.

Industry

PETROLEUM PRODUCTS
(metric tons)

	2008	2009	2010
Motor spirit (petrol)	9,244	9,488	10,593
Naphtha	219	207	180
Jet fuels	836	981	1,059
Kerosene	251	240	196
Gas-diesel (distillate fuel) oils	13,903	19,115	17,489
Residual fuel oils	4,534	2,108	1,732

Source: US Geological Survey.

SELECTED OTHER PRODUCTS
('000 metric tons)

	2006	2007	2008
Wheat flour	1,200	1,245	1,360
Raw sugar	767	743	652
Cement	227	327	340

2002 ('000 metric tons): Refined sugar 674; Vegetable oils 63.

Source: UN Industrial Commodity Statistics Database.

Electric energy (million kWh): 5,021.0 in 2007; 5,506.0 in 2008; 6,372 in 2009.

Finance

CURRENCY AND EXCHANGE RATES

Monetary Units
100 piastres = 1 new Sudanese pound (SDG).

Sterling, Dollar and Euro Equivalents (30 March 2012)
£1 sterling = 4.285 new Sudanese pounds;
US $1 = 2.677 new Sudanese pounds;
€1 = 3.575 new Sudanese pounds;
10 new Sudanese pounds = £2.33 = $3.74 = €2.80.

Average Exchange Rate (new Sudanese pounds per US $)
2009 2.3015
2010 2.3060
2011 2.6666

Note: On 1 March 1999 the Sudanese pound (£S) was replaced by the Sudanese dinar (SDD), equivalent to £S10. The pound was withdrawn from circulation on 31 July 1999. A new Sudanese pound (SDG), equivalent to 100 dinars (and 1,000 old pounds) was introduced on 10 January 2007. The new currency was to circulate along with previous currencies (the old pound had continued to circulate in some regions) for a transitional period, but became the sole legal tender on 1 July 2007.

CENTRAL GOVERNMENT BUDGET
(million new Sudanese pounds)

Revenue*	2008	2009†	2010‡
Tax revenue	7,680	8,619	10,067
Petroleum revenue	17,338	9,519	13,156
Sales to refineries	3,513	2,840	2,792
Export revenues	13,825	6,679	10,364
Other non-petroleum non-tax revenue	833	923	1,258
Total	25,852	19,061	24,481

Expenditure	2008	2009†	2010‡
Current expenditure	24,331	22,073	26,060
Wages	5,951	6,836	7,649
Goods and services	2,919	2,375	2,403
Interest	1,088	1,254	1,364
Subsidies	2,519	712	1,380
Fuel	2,195	447	1,272
Transfers	11,575	9,799	11,874
To South	6,159	4,485	5,464
To North	5,396	5,288	6,353
Other current expenditure	279	1,097	1,390
Capital expenditure	3,838	3,572	3,748
Total	28,169	25,645	29,808

* Excluding grants totalling (million new Sudanese pounds): 572 in 2008; 719 in 2009 (preliminary); 1,061 in 2010 (projection).
† Preliminary.
‡ Projections.

Source: IMF, *Sudan: Second Review Under the 2009–10 Staff-Monitored Program—Staff Report; Staff Supplement; and Statement by the Executive Director for Sudan* (April 2011).

INTERNATIONAL RESERVES
(US $ million at 31 December)

	2008	2009	2010
IMF special drawing rights	—	197.2	193.5
Foreign exchange	1,399.0	897.0	842.8
Total	1,399.0	1,094.2	1,036.2

2011: IMF special drawing rights 192.5.

Source: IMF, *International Financial Statistics*.

MONEY SUPPLY
(million Sudanese dinars at 31 December)

	2009	2010	2011
Currency outside depository corporations	8,066	10,068	12,850
Transferable deposits	9,595	11,593	13,719
Other deposits	10,624	13,800	15,248
Broad money	28,285	35,461	41,817

Source: IMF, *International Financial Statistics*.

COST OF LIVING
(Consumer Price Index for middle income group; base: 2007 = 100)

	2009	2010	2011
Food and beverages	133.1	153.8	185.2
Clothing and footwear	118.3	130.0	152.6
Housing	128.1	140.8	156.3
Household operations	116.4	126.1	151.9
Health care	118.1	124.1	149.1
Transport	107.7	110.3	126.6
Entertainment	109.5	116.7	126.7
Education	119.2	156.5	196.6
All items (incl. others)	127.2	143.7	169.6

NATIONAL ACCOUNTS
(million new Sudanese pounds at current prices)

Expenditure on the Gross Domestic Product

	2007	2008	2009
Government final consumption expenditure	9,635	10,811	12,107
Private final consumption expenditure	85,780	92,073	100,447
Changes in inventories	7,373	5,852	3,038
Gross fixed capital formation	16,170	18,645	26,808
Total domestic expenditure	118,958	127,381	142,400
Exports of goods and services	18,665	25,401	19,120
Less Imports of goods and services	23,607	25,035	25,859
GDP in purchasers' values	114,018	127,747	135,659

Gross Domestic Product by Economic Activity

	2007	2008	2009
Agriculture, hunting, forestry and fishing	32,985	37,481	44,970
Mining and quarrying	17,824	20,064	9,931
Manufacturing	8,782	9,726	11,508
Electricity, gas and water	1,981	2,242	2,513
Construction	4,651	5,239	6,171
Wholesale and retail trade, restaurants and hotels	16,728	18,376	19,706
Transport and communications	13,781	15,046	17,076
Finance, insurance, real estate and business services	7,809	8,961	10,399
Government services	5,944	6,681	7,482
Other services	2,255	2,503	2,729
Sub-total	112,740	126,319	132,485
Less Imputed bank service charge.	1,095	1,126	1,244
Indirect taxes (net)	2,373	2,553	4,418
GDP in purchasers' values	114,018	127,747	135 659

Source: African Development Bank.

BALANCE OF PAYMENTS
(US $ million)

	2008	2009	2010
Exports of goods f.o.b.	11,670.5	8,257.1	11,404.3
Imports of goods f.o.b.	–8,229.4	–8,528.0	–8,839.4
Trade balance	3,441.1	–270.9	2,564.9
Exports of services	492.8	392.0	253.8
Imports of services	–2,619.5	–1,907.1	–2,321.4
Balance on goods and services	1,314.4	–1,786.0	497.3
Other income received	43.4	36.7	137.9
Other income paid	–3,056.5	–2,261.4	–2,609.5
Balance on goods, services and income	–1,698.6	–4,010.7	–1,974.4
Current transfers received	4,023.6	2,973.8	3,360.0
Current transfers paid	–3,638.6	–1,961.5	–1,228.8
Current balance	–1,313.6	–2,998.4	156.8
Direct investment abroad	–89.2	—	—
Direct investment from abroad	2,600.5	1,816.2	2,063.7
Portfolio investment assets	–33.4	20.0	–14.3
Portfolio investment liabilities	–0.1	–0.5	21.4
Other investment assets	–866.5	–860.2	–2,785.7
Other investment liabilities	–101.6	2,250.3	1,365.1
Net errors and omissions	–125.4	–737.1	–859.9
Overall balance	70.8	–509.6	–52.9

Source: IMF, *International Financial Statistics*.

External Trade

PRINCIPAL COMMODITIES
(US $ million)

Imports c.i.f.	2007	2008	2009
Food and live animals	465.4	1,152.5	1,191.7
Cereals and cereal preparations	205.2	569.5	537.4
Unmilled durum wheat	161.2	493.1	386.9
Mineral fuels, lubricants, etc.	32.3	14.3	346.9
Refined petroleum products	32.2	13.8	346.7
Chemicals and related products	1,027.8	395.5	920.6
Medicinal and pharmaceutical products	814.7	216.6	284.6
Basic manufactures	1,017.1	1,352.1	1,807.3
Textiles and textile products (excl. clothing)	152.9	125.3	243.8
Cement	91.5	129.1	109.7
Iron and steel	211.5	768.0	620.3
Machinery and transport equipment	6,264.3	8,774.5	3,254.6
Power generating machinery and equipment	649.7	252.8	317.0
Machinery specialized for particular industries	1,110.5	393.3	520.1
Miscellaneous industrial machinery	260.5	249.6	298.7
Telecommunication and recording equipment	1,310.8	221.1	205.2
Road vehicles	1,043.9	953.9	1,223.2
Passenger vehicles (excl. buses)	301.3	401.9	405.0
Lorries and special purpose vehicles	495.6	327.0	567.9
Miscellaneous manufactured articles	898.1	652.1	817.5
Total (incl. others)	9,853.6	16,416.7	8,589.9

Exports f.o.b.	2006	2008*	2009
Food and live animals	150.8	126.1	298.4
Live animals	109.9	71.5	249.7
Sheep and goats	106.5	50.0	224.2
Sheep	103.2	49.4	220.4
Crude materials (inedible) except fuels	291.2	370.8	281.1
Oil seeds and oleaginous fruit	147.5	173.6	153.8
Sesame seeds	143.7	167.9	147.5
Cotton	71.1	58.3	40.2
Mineral fuels, lubricants, etc.	4,796.1	8,935.4	7,151.8
Petroleum and petroleum products	4,791.7	8,934.0	7,151.8
Machinery and transport equipment	58.3	33.0	46.3
Other commodities and transactions	174.2	3.2	1,279.5
Non-monetary gold, unwrought	148.2		1,278.5
Total (incl. others)	5,478.7	9,500.9	9,079.5

* Data for 2007 were not available.

Source: UN, *International Trade Statistics Yearbook*.

PRINCIPAL TRADING PARTNERS
(US $ million)

Imports c.i.f.	2007	2008	2009
Australia	116.0	287.9	278.3
Canada	136.7	257.0	92.7
China, People's Repub.	1,614.0	1,295.6	1,426.7
Egypt	357.2	422.8	410.3
France (incl. Monaco)	258.3	147.4	113.3
Germany	481.9	119.7	328.4
India	276.6	579.4	548.5
Indonesia	196.0	17.0	46.6
Italy	192.7	124.7	248.5
Japan	744.7	632.1	817.1
Jordan	268.3	126.2	86.2
Kenya	36.8	254.5	63.7
Korea, Repub.	265.3	174.2	205.4
Malaysia	22.1	43.6	52.9
Netherlands	218.9	63.7	90.6
Russia	30.5	738.8	97.3
Saudi Arabia	1,429.6	4,096.6	650.4
Sweden	476.7	64.6	99.1
Switzerland (incl. Liechtenstein)	57.3	16.3	n.a.
Turkey	65.2	80.9	381.0
Ukraine	31.2	621.9	83.3
United Arab Emirates	714.2	499.3	634.0
United Kingdom	564.0	1,075.4	192.0
USA	59.1	43.0	288.3
Total (incl. others)	9,853.6	16,416.7	8,589.9

Exports f.o.b.	2006	2008*	2009
Canada	66.8	0.1	802.1
China, People's Repub.	4,324.3	7,553.5	5,932.2
Egypt	68.6	130.8	93.5
France (incl. Monaco)	15.2	22.8	35.1
Germany	21.3	17.6	9.7
India	22.2	72.6	164.6
Indonesia	5.1	119.1	143.3
Japan	299.0	690.9	213.1
Korea, Repub.	6.5	55.6	7.9
Malaysia	—	107.8	40.6
Saudi Arabia	154.7	114.7	254.4
Singapore	12.2	70.9	94.5
United Arab Emirates	280.5	221.4	951.1
United Kingdom	50.8	7.5	24.0
Yemen	1.2	170.1	24.4
Total (incl. others)	5,478.7	9,500.9	9,079.5

* Data for 2007 were not available.

Source: UN, *International Trade Statistics Yearbook*.

Transport

RAILWAY TRAFFIC

	2007	2008	2009
Passengers carried ('000)	51	91	87
Passenger-km (million)	50	67	62
Freight carried ('000 metric tons)	1,091	1,033	907
Freight ton-km (million)	781	919	800

ROAD TRAFFIC
(motor vehicles in use)

	2000	2001	2002
Passenger cars	46,000	46,400	47,300
Commercial vehicles	60,500	61,800	62,500

Source: UN, *Statistical Yearbook*.

SHIPPING

Merchant Fleet
(registered at 31 December)

	2007	2008	2009
Number of vessels	19	19	18
Displacement (grt)	25,904	25,904	25,072

Source: IHS Fairplay, *World Fleet Statistics*.

International Sea-borne Freight Traffic
(estimates, '000 metric tons)

	1991	1992	1993
Goods loaded	1,290	1,387	1,543
Goods unloaded	3,800	4,200	4,300

Source: UN Economic Commission for Africa, *African Statistical Yearbook*.

CIVIL AVIATION
(traffic on scheduled services)

	2007	2008	2009
Kilometres flown (million)	9	9	9
Passengers carried ('000)	598	618	607
Passenger-km (million)	1,132	1,154	1,111
Total ton-km (million)	146	148	140

Source: UN, *Statistical Yearbook*.

2010: Passengers carried 601,668 (Source: World Bank, World Development Indicators database).

Tourism

	2009	2010	2011*
Foreign visitor arrivals	420,000	495,000	536,000
Tourism receipts (US $ million, excl. passenger transport)	299	94	n.a.

* Provisional.

Source: World Tourism Organization.

Communications Media

	2009	2010	2011
Telephones ('000 main lines in use)	370.4	545.0	483.6
Mobile cellular telephones ('000 subscribers)	15,340	18,093	25,107
Broadband subscribers ('000)	n.a.	13.5	17.4

1996: Daily newspapers 5 (average circulation 737,000 copies).

1997: Radio receivers ('000 in use) 7,550.

1998: Non-daily newspapers 11 (average circulation 5,644,000); Periodicals 54 (average circulation 68,000 copies).

2000: Television receivers ('000 in use) 8,500.

2004: Daily newspapers 22; Non-daily newspapers 3.

2006: Personal computers 4,237,096 (107.1 per 1,000 persons).

2008: Internet users ('000) 4,200.9.

Sources: UNESCO, *Statistical Yearbook*; UN, *Statistical Yearbook*; International Telecommunication Union.

Education

(2008/09 unless otherwise stated)

			Students		
	Institutions*	Teachers	Males	Females	Total
Pre-primary	5,984	20,738	316,792	315,443	632,235
Primary	11,982	123,633	2,539,712	2,204,756	4,744,468
Secondary	3,512	82,665	992,446	845,010	1,837,456
Universities, etc.	n.a.	4,486†	n.a.	n.a.	200,538†

* Figures refer to 1998.

† Estimates for 2000.

Source: UNESCO Institute for Statistics.

Pupil-teacher ratio (primary education, UNESCO estimate): 38.4 in 2008/09 (Source: UNESCO Institute for Statistics).

Adult literacy rate (UNESCO estimates): 71.1% (males 80.1%; females 62.0%) in 2010 (Source: UNESCO Institute for Statistics).

Directory

The Constitution

In early July 2005 the National Assembly approved an interim Constitution as part of the Comprehensive Peace Agreement, which had been signed in January between the Sudanese Government and the Sudan People's Liberation Movement (SPLM). The interim Constitution provided for the establishment of a Government of National Unity, representation in which was to be divided between northerners and southerners, with the former holding 70% of the posts and the latter 30%. Following a transitional period, presidential and legislative elections took place in April 2010, in accordance with the CPA. The President is directly elected for a five-year term, and appoints the Government. The National Assembly comprises 450 members, of whom 270 are directly elected in single seat constituencies, 68 are elected on the basis of proportional representation from party lists, and a further 112 women representatives are elected on the basis of proportional representation.

In accordance with the terms of the CPA, a referendum on the secession of southern Sudan was conducted in January 2011; 98.8% of the population (with a participation rate of 97.6% of the electorate) voted to secede from the north and officially form their own country. On 9 July 2011 the Republic of South Sudan declared independence from Sudan.

The Government

HEAD OF STATE

President: Lt-Gen. Omar Hassan Ahmad al-Bashir (took power as Chairman of the Revolutionary Command Council for National Salvation (RCC) on 30 June 1989; appointed President by the RCC on 16 October 1993; elected President in March 1996; re-elected in December 2000 and in April 2010).

First Vice-President: Ali Osman Muhammad Taha.

Vice-President: Al-Haj Adam Yousef.

COUNCIL OF MINISTERS
(September 2012)

Prime Minister: Lt-Gen. Omar Hassan Ahmad al-Bashir.

Minister of the Presidency: Maj.-Gen. Bakri Hassan Saleh.

Minister of Cabinet Affairs: Ahmed Saad Omar Khadr.

Minister of Defence: Maj.-Gen. Eng. Abd al-Rahim Mohamed Hussein.

Minister of the Interior: Ibrahim Mahmoud Hamed.

Minister of Foreign Affairs: Ali Ahmed Karti.

Minister of Justice: Mohamed Bushara Dousa.

Minister of Finance and National Economy: Ali Mahmood Abd al-Rasool.

Minister of Human Resources Development and Labour: Ishraga Sayed Mahmoud.

Minister of Agriculture and Irrigation: Abd al-Halim Ismail al-Mutaafi.

Minister of Industry: Abdul-Wahab Mohammed Osman.

Minister of Guidance and Endowments: (vacant).

Minister of Culture and Information: Dr Ahmed Bilal Osman.

Minister of Petroleum: Awad Ahmed al-Jaz.

Minister of Higher Education and Scientific Research: Dr Khames Kajo Kundah.

Minister of Public Education: Su'ad Abdel Raziq Mohammed Saeed.

Minister of Water Resources and Electricity: Osama Abdalla Mohamed al-Hassan.

Minister of Minerals: Kamal Abd al-Latif Abdul-Rahim.

Minister of Sciences and Communications: Dr Esha Basheri Mohamed.

Minister of Health: Bahar Idris Abu Gardah.

Minister of Welfare and Social Security: Ustaza Amira al-Fadil Mohamed Ahmed.

Minister of Youth and Sports: Al-Fatih Tag-Alsir Addullah.

Minister of Transport, Roads and Bridges: Dr Ahmed Babiker Nahar.

Minister of Antiquities, Tourism and Wildlife: Mohammed Abdul Kareem al-Hadd.

Minister of the Environment, Forestry and Urban Development: Dr Hassan Abdel Qader Hilal.

Minister of Animal and Fishery Resources and Pastures: Dr Faisal Hassan Ibrahim.

Minister of Commerce: Osman Omer al-Sharif.

In addition, there are 34 State Ministers.

MINISTRIES

Office of the President: Khartoum; internet www.presidency.gov.sd.

Ministry of Agriculture and Irrigation: POB 285, al-Gamaa Ave, Khartoum; tel. (183) 780951; e-mail moafcc@sudanmail.net.

Ministry of Animal and Fishery Resources and Pastures: Khartoum.

Ministry of Antiquities, Tourism and Wildlife: POB 2424, Khartoum; tel. (183) 471329; fax (183) 471437; e-mail admin@sudan-tourism.com.

Ministry of Cabinet Affairs: POB 931, Khartoum; tel. (183) 784205; fax (183) 771331; e-mail info@sudan.gov.sd; internet www.sudan.gov.sd/en.

Ministry of Commerce: Khartoum.

Ministry of Culture and Information: Khartoum.

Ministry of Defence: POB 371, Khartoum; tel. (183) 774910.

Ministry of the Environment, Forestry and Urban Development: POB 300, Khartoum; tel. (183) 462604.

Ministry of Finance and National Economy: POB 735, Khartoum; tel. (183) 777563; fax (183) 775630; e-mail info@mof-sudan.net; internet mof-sudan.com.

Ministry of Foreign Affairs: POB 873, Khartoum; tel. (183) 773101; fax (183) 772941; e-mail ministry@mfa.gov.sd; internet www.sudanmfa.com.

Ministry of Guidance and Endowments: Khartoum.

Ministry of Health: POB 303, Khartoum; tel. (183) 773000; e-mail inhsd@sudanet.net; internet www.fmoh.gov.sd.

Ministry of Higher Education and Scientific Research: POB 2081, Khartoum; tel. (183) 779312; fax (183) 783394; e-mail srp@mohe.gov.sd; internet mohe.gov.sd.

Ministry of Human Resources Development and Labour: Khartoum.

Ministry of Industry: POB 2184, Khartoum; tel. (183) 777830.

Ministry of the Interior: POB 2793, Khartoum; tel. (183) 776554.

Ministry of Justice: POB 302, al-Nil Ave, Khartoum; tel. (183) 774842; fax (183) 771479.

Ministry of Minerals: POB 2087, Khartoum; tel. (183) 775595; fax (183) 775428.

Ministry of Petroleum: Khartoum.

Ministry of Presidential Affairs: Khartoum.

Ministry of Public Education: Khartoum; tel. (183) 772808; e-mail moe-sd@moe-sd.com.

Ministry of Sciences and Communications: Khartoum.

Ministry of Transport, Roads and Bridges: Khartoum.

Ministry of Water Resources and Electricity: POB 878, Khartoum; tel. (183) 783221; fax (183) 773388; e-mail oehamad@hotmail.com.

Ministry of Welfare and Social Security: Khartoum.

Ministry of Youth and Sports: Khartoum.

STATE GOVERNORS
(September 2012)

Blue Nile: Maj.-Gen. AL-HADI BUSHRA.
Central Darfur: YOUSEF TIBIN MUSA ADAM.
East Darfur: ABDUL HAMID MUSA KASHA.
Gadarif: KARAM ALLAH ABBAS (NCP).
Gezira: Dr AL-ZUBEIR BASHIR TAHA (NCP).
Kassala: MOHAMMED YUSUF ADAM BESHIR (NCP).
Khartoum: Dr ABD AL-RAHMAN AL-KHIDIR (NCP).
Northern: FETHI KHALIL MOHAMMED (NCP).
North Darfur: OSMAN MUHAMMAD YUSUF KIBIR (NCP).
North Kordofan: MOATASIM MIRGHANI ZAKI EL-DIN (NCP).
Red Sea: MOHMED TAHEIR AILA (NCP).
River Nile: AL-HADI ABDULLAH MOHAMMED AL-AWWAD (NCP).
Sennar: AHMED ABBAS MOHAMED SAAD AL-THOAM.
South Darfur: HAMAD ISMAIL HAMAD ABU KAREEM (NCP).
South Kordofan: AHMED HAROUN (NCP).
West Darfur: GALO KOMA ATIM (SLJM).
White Nile: YUSUF AHMED EL-SHANBALY.

President and Legislature

PRESIDENT

Election, 11–15 April 2010

Candidate	Votes	% of votes
Omar Hassan Ahmad al-Bashir (National Congress Party)	6,901,694	68.24
Yasir Saeed Arman (Sudan People's Liberation Movement)	2,193,826	21.69
Abdullah Deng Nhial Ayom (Popular Congress Party)	396,139	3.92
Hatim as-Sir Ali Sikunji (Democratic Unionist Party)	195,668	1.93
Others	426,983	4.22
Total	10,114,310	100.00

MAJLIS WATANI
(National Assembly)

Speaker: AHMAD IBRAHIM AL-TAHIR.
Deputy Speakers: ANGELO BEDA, ABDALLAH AL-HARDELLO.

Election, 11–15 April 2010, provisional results

Party	Seats*			
	A	B	C	Total
National Congress Party	180	50	82	312
Sudan People's Liberation Movement	56	17	26	99
Popular Congress Party	—	1	3	4
United Democratic Party	4	—	—	4
Independents	3	—	—	3
Umma Federal Party	2	—	1	3
Sudan People's Liberation Movement—Democratic Change	2	—	—	2
Umma Reform and Renewal Party	2	—	—	2
Democratic Unionist Party—Original	1	—	—	1
Muslim Brotherhood	1	—	—	1
Umma National Party	1	—	—	1
Total	252†	68	112	432†

* There are 450 members of the Majlis Watani of which 270 (A) are directly elected in single seat constituencies; 68 'party members' (B) are elected on the basis of proportional representation at the state level from separate and closed party lists; and a further 112 women members (C) are elected on the basis of proportional representation at the state level from separate and closed party lists.

† Voting in 16 constituencies was postponed, the result in one seat was not released and one seat was declared vacant. Following by-elections held in June 2010 the NCP increased its representation to 323 seats, while the Democratic Unionist Party—Original secured an additional seat. Two seats were taken by minor parties, while four seats remained vacant.

Election Commission

National Elections Commission (NEC): Khartoum; tel. (183) 520282; e-mail info@nec.org.sd; internet www.nec.org.sd; Abd Alla MAULANA AHMED ABD ALLA.

Political Organizations

The right to political association, subject to compliance with the law, was guaranteed in the Constitution approved by referendum in June 1998. (All political organizations had been banned following the military coup of 30 June 1989.) The registration of parties began in January 1999. The following parties are among the most active:

Communist Party of Sudan (CPS): Khartoum; e-mail cpsudan@gmail.com; internet www.midan.net; f. 1946; Gen. Sec. MOHAMED IBRAHIM NUGUD MUNAWAR.

Democratic Unionist Party (DUP): Khartoum; Leader MUHAMMAD OSMAN AL-MIRGHANI.

Free Sudanese National Party (FSNP): Khartoum; Chair. Fr PHILIP ABBAS GHABBUSH.

Independent Democrats: Khartoum; Leader AS-SAMAWITT HUSAYN OSMAN MANSUR.

Islamic-Christian Solidarity: Khartoum; Founder HATIM ABDULLAH AL-ZAKI HUSAYN.

Islamic Revival Movement: Khartoum; Founder SIDDIQ AL-HAJ AL-SIDDIQ.

Islamic Socialist Party: Khartoum; Leader SALAH AL-MUSBAH.

Islamic Ummah Party: Khartoum; Chair. WALI AL-DIN AL-HADI AL-MAHDI.

Justice Party: Khartoum; f. 2002 by fmr members of the NCP.

Moderate Trend Party: Khartoum; Leader MAHMUD JIHA.

Muslim Brotherhood: Khartoum; Islamist fundamentalist; Leader Dr HABIR NUR AL-DIN.

National Congress Party (NCP): Khartoum; successor to National Islamic Front; Pres. Lt-Gen. OMAR HASSAN AHMAD AL-BASHIR; Sec.-Gen. Prof. IBRAHIM AHMAD UMAR.

National Democratic Party: Khartoum; f. 2002 following merger of the Union of Nationalistic Forces, the Communist Party and the National Solidarity Party.

New National Democratic: Leader MUNEER SHEIKH EL-DIN JALAB.

Nile Valley Conference: Khartoum; Founder Lt-Gen. (retd) UMAR ZARUQ.

Popular Congress Party (PCP): Khartoum; f. 2000; Founder HASSAN AL-TURABI.

Popular Masses' Alliance: Khartoum; Founder FAYSAL MUHMAD HUSAYN.

Socialist Popular Party: Khartoum; Founder SAYYID KHALIFAH IDRIS HABBANI.

Sudan Green Party: Khartoum; Founder Prof. ZAKARAIA BASHIR IMAM.

Sudan National Alliance (SNA): f. 1994; Leader ABDEL AZIZ KHALID.

Sudanese Central Movement: Khartoum; Founder Dr MUHAMMAD ABU AL-QASIM HAJ HAMAD.

Sudanese Initiative Party: Khartoum; Leader J'AFAR KARAR.

Sudanese National Party (SNP): Khartoum; Leader HASAN AL-MAHI.

Sudanese Socialist Democratic Union (SSDU): Leader FATIMA AHMED ABDEL MAHMOUD MOHAMED.

Umma National Party (UNP): internet www.umma.org; f. 1945; Mahdist party based on the Koran and Islamic traditions; Chair. Dr UMAR NUR AL-DA'IM; Leader SADIQ AL-MAHDI.

Umma Reform and Renewal Party: Khartoum; f. 2002; Leader MUBARAK AL-FADIL.

Union of Sudan African Parties (USAP): f. 1987; Chair. JOSEPH OKELLO; Sec.-Gen. Prof. AJANG BIOR.

United Democratic Party.

United Democratic Salvation Front (UDSF): Khartoum; political wing of the Sudan People's Defence Force; Chair. Dr GABRIEL CHANGSON CHANG.

In 2003 two rebel groups, the **Sudan Liberation Movement (SLM)** (Leader MINNI ARKUA MINAWI) and the **Justice and Equality Movement (JEM)**, (Leader GIBRIL IBRAHIM) began an armed rebellion in the Darfur region of western Sudan.

At a meeting convened in Asmara, Eritrea, in 2006 the **National Redemption Front (NRF)** was formed by the leader of the JEM, Dr KHALIL IBRAHIM MOHAMED, his counterpart, AHMAD DREIGE of the SFDA, and KHAMIS ABDALLA ABAKAR, the former Deputy Chairman of Abd al-Wahid Muhammad al-Nur's faction of the SLM, and leader of the **Group of 19 (G-19)**. The G-19 emerged as the principal faction of the NRF, originally formed as a group of commanders who defected from al-Nur's faction during the Abuja, Nigeria, negotiations. In December 2006 a group of Arab rebels, opposed to the Sudanese army and the *Janjaweed*, formed an alliance called the **Popular Forces Troops (PFT)**.

Diplomatic Representation

EMBASSIES IN SUDAN

Afghanistan: Madinatol Riyadh, Shareol Moshtal Sq. 10, House No. 81, Khartoum; tel. (183) 221852; fax (183) 222059; e-mail afembsudan@hotmail.com; Chargé d'affaires a.i. KHALILURRAHMAN HANANI.

Algeria: Blvd El-Mechtel Eriad, POB 80, Khartoum; tel. (183) 234773; fax (183) 224190; Ambassador MUHAMMAD YARKI.

Brazil: Kamel Magzob St, House No. 110, Block 21, al-Amarat, POB 8255, Riyadh, 12217 Khartoum; tel. (183) 217079; fax (183) 217049; e-mail ambassador@brasilemb-sd.org; Ambassador ANTONIO CARLOS DO NASCIMENTO PEDRO.

Bulgaria: St 31, House No. 9, Block 10, al-Amarat, POB 1690, 11111 Khartoum; tel. (183) 560106; fax (183) 560107; e-mail bgembsdn@yahoo.co.uk; Chargé d'affaires a.i. SVILEN BOZHANOV.

Chad: St 57, al-Amarat, Khartoum; tel. (183) 471612; Ambassador MAHAMAT ABDERAHIM ACYL.

China, People's Republic: POB 1425, Khartoum; tel. (183) 272730; fax (183) 271138; e-mail ssddssgg@yahoo.com.cn; Ambassador LUO XIAOGUANG.

Congo, Democratic Republic: St 13, Block 12 CE, New Extension, 23, POB 4195, Khartoum; tel. (183) 471125; Chargé d'affaires a.i. BAWAN MUZURI.

Egypt: University St, POB 1126, Khartoum; tel. (183) 777646; fax (183) 778741; e-mail sphinx-egysud@yahoo.com; Ambassador ABDUL-GHAFFAR AL-DEEB.

Eritrea: St 39, House No. 26, POB 1618, Khartoum 2; tel. (183) 483834; fax (183) 483835; e-mail erena@sudanet.net; Ambassador Gen. ISSA AHMED ISSA.

Ethiopia: Plot No. 4, Block 384BC, POB 844, Khartoum; tel. (183) 471379; fax (183) 471141; e-mail eekrt@hotmail.com; Ambassador ATO ALI ABDO.

France: al-Amarat, St 13, Plot No. 11, Block 12, POB 377, 11111 Khartoum; tel. (183) 471082; fax (183) 465928; e-mail cad.khartoum-amba@diplomatie.gouv.fr; internet www.ambafrance-sd.org; Ambassador PATRICK NICOLOSO.

Germany: 53 Baladia St, Block No. 8D, Plot 2, POB 970, Khartoum; tel. (183) 777990; fax (183) 777622; e-mail reg1@khar.auswaertiges-amt.de; internet www.khartum.diplo.de; Ambassador RAINER EBERLE.

Holy See: Kafouri Belgravia, POB 623, Khartoum (Apostolic Nunciature); tel. (183) 330037; fax (183) 330692; e-mail kanuap@yahoo.it; Apostolic Nuncio Most Rev. LEO BOCCARDI (Titular Archbishop of Bitetto).

India: 61 Africa Rd, POB 707, Khartoum II; tel. (183) 574001; fax (183) 574050; e-mail ambassador@indembsdn.com; internet www.indembsdn.com; Ambassador A. K. PANDEY.

Indonesia: St 60, 84, Block 12, ar-Riyadh, POB 13374, Khartoum; tel. (183) 225106; fax (183) 225528; e-mail kbri_khartoum@sudanmail.com; Ambassador Dr M. A. SUJATMIKO.

Iran: Sq. 15, House No. 4, Mogran, POB 10229, Khartoum; tel. (183) 781490; fax (183) 778668; e-mail iransud@yahoo.com; Ambassador REZA AMERI.

Iraq: Sharia ash-Shareef al-Hindi, POB 1969, Khartoum; tel. (183) 271867; fax (183) 271855; e-mail krtemb@iraqmofamail.net; Ambassador Dr SALEH HUSSEIN ALI.

Italy: St 39, Block 61, POB 793, Khartoum; tel. (183) 471615; fax (183) 471217; e-mail ambasciata.khartoum@esteri.it; internet www.ambkhartoum.esteri.it; Ambassador ROBERTO CANTONE.

Japan: St 43, House No. 67, POB 1649, Khartoum; tel. (183) 471601; fax (183) 471600; internet www.sdn.emb-japan.go.jp; Ambassador RYOICHI HORIE.

Jordan: St 33, House No. 13, POB 1379, Khartoum; tel. (183) 483125; fax (183) 471038; Ambassador MUNTHER QUBAAH.

Kenya: Plot No. 516, Block 1 West Giraif, POB 8242, Khartoum; tel. (155) 772800; fax (155) 772802; e-mail kenemb@yahoo.com; Ambassador ROBERT MUTUA NGESU (expelled Nov. 2011).

Korea, Republic: St 1, House No. 2, New Extension, POB 2414, Khartoum; tel. (183) 451136; fax (183) 452822; e-mail ssudan@mofat.go.kr; Ambassador DONG EOK KIM.

Kuwait: Africa Ave, near the Tennis Club, POB 1457, Khartoum; tel. (183) 781525; Ambassador MUNTHIR BADR SALMAN.

Lebanon: St 5, Al-Amarat, Khartoum; tel. (183) 461320; fax (113) 461246; e-mail amliban@hotmail.com; Ambassador SHARBEL STEPHAN.

Libya: 50 Africa Rd, POB 2091, Khartoum; Secretary of People's Bureau (vacant).

Malaysia: St 3, Block 2, al-Amarat, POB 11668, Khartoum; tel. (183) 482763; fax (183) 482762; e-mail malkhtoum@kln.gov.my; internet www.kln.gov.my/web/sdn_khartoum/home; Ambassador Dato' MOHD ASHRI MUDA.

Morocco: St 19, 32, New Extension, POB 2042, Khartoum; tel. (183) 473068; fax (183) 471053; e-mail sifmasoud@sudan.mail.net; Ambassador MUHAMMAD MAA EL-AININE.

Netherlands: St 47, House No. 76, POB 391, Khartoum; tel. (183) 471200; fax (183) 480304; e-mail kha@minbuza.nl; internet www.mfa.nl; Ambassador SUSAN T. BLANKHART.

Nigeria: St 17, Sharia al-Mek Nimr, POB 1538, Khartoum; tel. (183) 779120; fax (183) 771491; e-mail nigeriankhartoum@yahoo.com; Ambassador HALLIRU SODANGI-SHUAIB.

Norway: St 49, House No. 63, POB 13096, Khartoum; tel. (183) 578336; fax (183) 577180; e-mail emb.khartoum@mfa.no; internet www.norway-sudan.org; Ambassador SVEIN SEVJE.

Oman: St 1, New Extension, POB 2839, Khartoum; tel. (183) 471606; fax (183) 471017; Ambassador ABDULLAH BIN-RASHID BIN-ALI AL-MEDELWI.

Pakistan: Dr Mehmood Sharif St, House No. 78, Block 25, POB 1178, Khartoum; tel. (183) 265599; fax (183) 273777; e-mail embkhartoum@yahoo.com; Ambassador MUHAMMAD ALAM BROHI.

Qatar: Elmanshia Block 92H, POB 223, Khartoum; tel. (183) 261113; fax (183) 261116; e-mail qatarembkht@yahoo.com; Ambassador ALI HASSAN ABDULLAH AL-HAMADI.

Romania: Kassala Rd, Plot No. 172–173, Kafouri Area, POB 1494, Khartoum North; tel. (185) 338114; fax (185) 341497; e-mail ambro_khartoum@hotmail.com; Ambassador Dr EMIL GHITULESCU.

Russia: A10 St, B1, New Extension, POB 1161, Khartoum; tel. (183) 471042; fax (183) 471239; e-mail rfsudan@hotmail.com; Ambassador ENVARBIK M. FAZELIYANOV.

Rwanda: Al-Manshia, Block 28G, St 57, House No. 4, Block 10. POB 243, Khartoum; tel. (183) 278842; fax (183) 155174663; e-mail rwaembassy@gmail.com; internet www.sudan.embassy.gov.rw; Chargé d'affaires Maj. JOSEPH RUTABANA.

Saudi Arabia: St 11, New Extension, Khartoum; tel. (183) 741938; Ambassador MOHAMMED IBN ABAS AL-KALABI.

Somalia: St 23–25, New Extension, POB 1857, Khartoum; tel. (183) 744800; Ambassador Prof. MAHDI ABUKAR.

South Africa: St 11, House No. 16, Block B9, al-Amarat, POB 12137, Khartoum; tel. (183) 585301; fax (183) 585082; e-mail khartoum@foreign.gov.za; Ambassador Dr MANELISI GENGE.

South Sudan: Khartoum; Ambassador MAYAN DUT WOL.

Switzerland: St 15, House No. 7, Amarat, POB 1707, Khartoum; tel. (183) 471010; fax (183) 472804; e-mail kha.vertretung@eda.admin.ch; internet www.eda.admin.ch/khartoum; Ambassador LOUIS-JOSÉ TOURON.

Syria: St 3, New Extension, POB 1139, Khartoum; tel. (183) 471152; fax (183) 471066; Ambassador HABIB ALI ABBAS.

Tunisia: St 15, 35, al-Amarat, Khartoum; tel. (183) 487947; fax (183) 487950; e-mail at_khartoum@yahoo.fr; Ambassador ELOUALID DOUDECH.

Turkey: Baladia St, House No. 21, Block 8H, POB 771, Khartoum; tel. (183) 794215; fax (183) 794218; e-mail hartumbe@gmail.com; Ambassador (vacant).

Uganda: POB 2676, Khartoum; tel. (183) 158571; fax (183) 797868; e-mail ugembkht@hotmail.com; Ambassador BETTY AKECH.

United Arab Emirates: St 3, New Extension, POB 1225, Khartoum; tel. (183) 744476; e-mail uaembassy@sudanmail.net; Ambassador HASSAN AHMED SULIEMAN AL-SHIHI.

United Kingdom: St 10, off Baladia St, POB 801, Khartoum; tel. (183) 777105; fax (183) 776457; e-mail media.khartoum@fco.gov.uk; internet www.britishembassy.gov.uk/sudan; Ambassador Dame Dr ROSALIND MARY MARSDEN.

USA: Kilo 10, Soba, off Wad Medani Highway, POB 699, Khartoum; tel. 1-870-2-2000; fax 1-870-2-2012; internet sudan.usembassy.gov; Chargé d'affaires JOSEPH D. STAFFORD, III.

Yemen: St 11, New Extension, POB 1010, Khartoum; tel. (183) 743918; Ambassador SALAH AL-ANSI.

Judicial System

In September 1983 President Nimeri replaced all existing laws with Islamic (*Shari'a*) law. However, following the coup in April 1985, the *Shari'a* courts were abolished, and it was announced that the previous system of criminal courts was to be revived. In 1987 a new legal code, based on a 'Sudanese legal heritage', was introduced. Islamic law was reintroduced in March 1991, but was not applied in the southern states of Equatoria, Bahr al-Ghazal and Upper Nile.

Chief Justice: GALAL EL-DIN MUHAMMAD OSMAN.

Religion

The majority of the population of post-secession Sudan are Muslims.

ISLAM

Islam is the state religion. Sudanese Islam has a strong Sufi element, and is estimated to have more than 15m. adherents.

CHRISTIANITY

Sudan Council of Churches: Inter-Church House, St 35, New Extension, POB 469, Khartoum; tel. (183) 742859; e-mail Ramadan.chan@gmail.com; f. 1967; 12 mem. churches; Chair. Most Rev. EZEKIEL KONDO (Roman Catholic Archbishop of Khartoum); Gen. Sec. Rev. RAMADAN CHAN LIOL.

Roman Catholic Church

Latin Rite

Sudan comprises two archdioceses and seven dioceses. The Roman Catholic Church officially remained undivided following the secession of South Sudan.

Sudan Catholic Bishops' Conference

General Secretariat, POB 6011, Khartoum; tel. (183) 225075.

f. 1971; Pres. Mgr RUDOLF DENG MAJAK (Bishop of Wau); Sec.-Gen. JOHN DINGI MARTIN.

Archbishop of Khartoum: Cardinal GABRIEL ZUBEIR WAKO, Catholic Church, POB 49, Khartoum; tel. (183) 782174; fax (183) 783518; e-mail taban_roko@yahoo.com.uk.

Maronite Rite

Maronite Church in Sudan: POB 244, Khartoum; Rev. Fr YOUSEPH NEAMA.

Melkite Rite

Patriarchal Vicariate of Egypt and Sudan: Greek Melkite Catholic Patriarchate, 16 Sharia Daher, 11271 Cairo, Egypt; tel. (2) 5905790; fax (2) 5935398; e-mail grecmelkitecath_egy@hotmail.com; General Patriarchal Vicar in Egypt and Sudan Mgr (JOSEPH) JULES ZEREY (Titular Archbishop of Damietta); Patriarchal Vicar in Sudan Mgr Exarkhos GEORGE BANNA; , POB 766, Khartoum; tel. (183) 777910.

Syrian Rite

Syrian Church in Sudan: Under the jurisdiction of the Patriarch of Antioch; Protosyncellus Rt Rev. JOSEPH-CLÉMENT HANNOUCHE (Bishop of Cairo).

Orthodox Churches

Coptic Orthodox Church

Metropolitan of Khartoum, Southern Sudan and Uganda: Rt Rev. ANBA DANIAL, POB 4, Khartoum; tel. (183) 770646; fax (183) 785646; e-mail metaous@email-sudan.net.

Bishop of Atbara, Omdurman and Northern Sudan: Rt Rev. ANBA SARABAMON, POB 628, Omdurman; tel. (183) 550423; fax (183) 556973.

Greek Orthodox Church

Metropolitan of Nubia: POB 47, Khartoum; tel. (183) 772973; Archbishop DIONYSSIOS HADZIVASSILIOU.

The Ethiopian Orthodox Church is also active.

The Anglican Communion

Anglicans are adherents of the (Episcopal) Church of the Province of the Sudan. The Province, with 24 dioceses and about 1m. adherents, was established in 1976.

Archbishop in Sudan and Bishop of Juba: Most Rev. DANIEL DENG BUL YAK, ECS Liaison Office, POB 604, Khartoum; tel. (11) 485720; fax (11) 485717; e-mail ecsprovince@hotmail.com; internet www.sudan.anglican.org.

Other Christian Churches

Evangelical Church: POB 57, Khartoum; c. 1,500 mems; administers schools, literature centre and training centre; Chair. Rev. RADI ELIAS.

The Lutheran Church of Sudan: Omdurman Elarda-Markh Studo, POB 12354, Omdurman Khartoum; tel. 912972828 (mobile); e-mail rev_yousifkh@hotmail.com; Bishop AKILLA YOUSIF ELTAHIR; 10,650 mems (2010).

Presbyterian Church: POB 40, Malakal; autonomous since 1956; 67,000 mems (1985); Gen. Sec. Rev. THOMAS MALUIT.

The Africa Inland Church, the Sudan Interior Church and the Sudanese Church of Christ are also active.

The Press

Following the secession of South Sudan, the licences of six newspapers, partially or wholly owned by South Sudanese nationals, were revoked by the Sudanese National Council for Press and Publications, citing a law that bars foreigners from owning newspapers. The list includes: Ajras Al-Hurriya, Khartoum Monitor, Juba Post, Sudan Tribune, Advocate and The Democrat.

DAILIES

Abbar al-Youm: Khartoum; tel. (183) 779396; daily; Editor AHMED AL-BALAL AL-TAYEB.

Al-Anbaa: Khartoum; tel. (183) 466523; f. 1998; Editor-in-Chief NAJIB ADAM QAMAR AL-DIN.

Al-Nasr: Khartoum; tel. (183) 772494; Editor Col YOUNIS MAHMOUD.

Al-Rai al-Akhar: Khartoum; tel. (183) 777934; daily; Editor MOHI AL-DIN TITTAWI.

Al-Rai al-Amm: Khartoum; tel. (183) 778182; fax (183) 772176; e-mail info@rayaam.net; internet www.rayaam.net; daily; Editor SALAH MUHAMMAD IBRAHIM.

Al-Wan: Khartoum; tel. (183) 775036; e-mail alwaan@cybergates.net; daily; independent; pro-Govt; Editor HOUSSEN KHOGALI.

Sudan Mirror: POB 59163, 00200 Nairobi, Kenya; tel. and fax (20) 3876439; e-mail daneiffe@gmail.com; internet www.sudanmirror.co.ke; f. 2003; Dir DANIEL EIFFE.

Sudan Standard: Ministry of Information, Khartoum; daily; English.

PERIODICALS

Al-Guwwat al-Musallaha (The Armed Forces): Khartoum; f. 1969; publs a weekly newspaper and monthly magazine for the armed forces; Editor-in-Chief Maj. MAHMOUD GALANDER; circ. 7,500.

New Horizon: POB 2651, Khartoum; tel. (183) 777913; f. 1976; publ. by the Sudan House for Printing and Publishing; weekly; English; political and economic affairs, devt, home and international news; Editor AL-SIR HASSAN FADL; circ. 7,000.

Sudanow: POB 2651, Khartoum; tel. (183) 777913; f. 1976; publ. by the Sudan House for Printing and Publishing; monthly; English; political and economic affairs, arts, social affairs and diversions; publ. online only since 2010; Editor-in-Chief MOHAMED OSMAN ADAM; circ. 10,000.

NEWS AGENCIES

Sudan News Agency (SUNA): Sharia al-Gamhouria, POB 1506, Khartoum; tel. (183) 775770; e-mail suna@sudanet.net; internet www.suna-sd.net; Dir-Gen. AWAD JADAIN MOHI-EDDIN.

Sudanese Press Agency: Khartoum; f. 1985; owned by journalists.

PRESS ASSOCIATION

Sudanese Media Center (SMC): 21 October St, Khartoum East, Khartoum; tel. (1) 83787604; fax (1) 83787605; e-mail info@smc.sd; internet smc.sd.

Publishers

Ahmad Abd ar-Rahman al-Tikeine: POB 299, Port Sudan.

Al-Ayyam Press Co Ltd: Aboulela Bldg, POB 363, United Nations Sq., Khartoum; f. 1953; general fiction and non-fiction, arts, poetry, reference, newspapers, magazines; Man. Dir BESHIR MUHAMMAD SAID.

Al-Sahafa Publishing and Printing House: POB 1228, Khartoum; f. 1961; newspapers, pamphlets, fiction and govt publs.

Al-Salam Co Ltd: POB 944, Khartoum.

Claudios S. Fellas: POB 641, Khartoum.

Khartoum University Press: POB 321, Khartoum; tel. (183) 776653; f. 1964; academic, general and educational in Arabic and English; Man. Dir ALI EL-MAK.

GOVERNMENT PUBLISHING HOUSE

El-Asma Printing Press: POB 38, Khartoum.

Broadcasting and Communications

TELECOMMUNICATIONS

In 2011 Sudan Telecom provided both fixed-line telephone services and mobile telephone services. In addition, there was one other fixed-line operator and two other mobile operators in the country.

Regulatory Authority

National Telecommunication Corpn: NTC Tower, Buri, North to Manshya Bridge, POB 2869, Khartoum; tel. (183) 484489; fax 0187171140; e-mail customer@ntc.gov.sd; internet www.ntc.gov.sd; Dir-Gen. Dr IZZELDIN KAMIL AMIN.

SERVICE PROVIDERS

Canar Telecommunication (Canartel): Al-Qibla Centre, Block 37, cnr Al-Sahafa and Madani Rds, POB 8182, Khartoum; tel. (15) 5550000; fax (15) 5550055; e-mail support@canar.sd; internet www.canar.sd; f. 2005; operates fixed-line telephone and internet services; CEO ALI AHMED YAROUF.

MTN-Sudan: Manchiya East 60th Ave, Block 64, District 1, POB 34611111, Khartoum; tel. (92) 1111111; e-mail customercare@mtn.sd; internet www.mtn.sd; f. 2005; mobile cellular telephone provider; CEO HASSAN JABER; 1.4m. subscribers (2007).

Sudan Telecom Co (SUDATEL): Sudatel Tower, POB 11155, Khartoum; tel. (183) 797400; fax (183) 782322; e-mail info@sudatel.net; internet www.sudatel.sd; f. 1993; service provider for Sudan; Chair. ABDELAZIZ OSMAN; CEO IMAD ADDIN HUSSEIN AHMED.

Zain: Khartoum; tel. 91230000 (mobile); e-mail info@sd.zain.com; internet www.sd.zain.com; f. 1997 as MobiTel; name changed as above in 2007; provides mobile cellular telephone services; Man. Dir ELFATIH M. ERWA.

BROADCASTING

Radio

Sudan Radio: POB 572, Omdurman; tel. (187) 559315; fax (187) 560566; e-mail info@sudanradio.info; internet www.sudanradio.info; f. 1940; state-controlled service broadcasting daily in Arabic, English, French and Swahili; Dir-Gen. MUTASIM FADUL USUD.

Sudan Radio Service (SRS): Umeme Plaza, Old Naivasha Rd, off Ngong Rd, Dagoretti, POB 4392, 00100 Nairobi, Kenya; tel. (20) 2346218; fax (20) 2346216; e-mail srs@sudanradio.org; internet www.sudanradio.org; f. 2003; by the Education Development Center with support from the United States Agency for International Development; broadcasts in 10 languages including Dinka, Bari, Nuer, Zande, Shilluk, Arabic, Juba-Arabic and English; Chief of Party JON NEWSTROM.

Voice of Sudan: e-mail informationsec@ndasudan.org; active since 1995; run by the National Democratic Alliance; Arabic and English.

Television

An earth satellite station operated on 36 channels at Umm Haraz has much improved Sudan's telecommunications links. A nation-wide satellite network is being established with 14 earth stations in the provinces. There are regional stations at Gezira (Central Region) and Atbara (Northern Region).

Sudan Television: POB 1094, Omdurman; tel. (15) 550022; internet www.sudantv.net; f. 1962; state-controlled; 60 hours of programmes per week; Dir-Gen. MOHAMMED HATEM SULEIMAN.

Finance

(cap. = capital; res = reserves; dep. = deposits; m. = million; brs = branches; amounts in new Sudanese pounds, unless otherwise indicated)

BANKING

All domestic banks are controlled by the Bank of Sudan. Foreign banks were permitted to resume operations in 1976. In December 1985 the Government banned the establishment of any further banks. It was announced in December 1990 that Sudan's banking system was to be reorganized to comply with Islamic principles. In May 2000 the Bank of Sudan issued new policy guidelines under which Sudan's banks were to merge into six banking groups to improve their financial strength and international competitiveness; plans for implementing this merger were ongoing in 2010. In 2009 there were a total of 38 banks in Sudan. Following the secession of South Sudan, a new currency, also called the pound, was introduced in Sudan on 24 July 2011.

Central Bank

Bank of Sudan: Gamhoria St, POB 313, Khartoum; tel. (183) 782246; fax (183) 787226; e-mail sudanbank@sudanmail.net; internet www.bankofsudan.org; f. 1960; bank of issue; cap. and res 274.2m., dep. 8,695.2m. (Dec. 2009); Gov. MOHAMMAD KHAIR AL-ZUBAIR; 13 brs.

Commercial Banks

Al-Baraka Bank: Baraka Tower, Zubeir Pasha St, POB 3583, Khartoum; tel. (183) 785810; fax (183) 778948; e-mail khairy@albarakasudan.com; internet www.albaraka.com.sd; f. 1984; 87.8% owned by Al-Baraka Banking Group (Bahrain); investment and export promotion; cap. SDD 3,353.6m., res SDD 4,042.7m., dep. SDD 37,220.2m. (Dec. 2006); Chair. OSMAN AHMED SULIMAN; Gen. Man. ABDALLAH KHAIRY HAMID; 24 brs.

Al-Shamal Islamic Bank: Al-Shamal Islamic Tower, al-Sayid Abd al-Rahman St, POB 10036, 11111 Khartoum; tel. (183) 779078; fax (183) 772661; e-mail info@alshamalbank.com; internet www.alshamalbank.com; f. 1990; total assets SDD 18,258.0m. (Dec. 2003); Pres. GAFAAR OSMAN FAGIR; Gen. Man. ABDELMONEIM HASSAN SAYED; 17 brs.

Bank of Khartoum: Intersection Gamhouria St and El-Gaser St, POB 1008, Khartoum; tel. 156660000; fax (183) 781120; e-mail info@bok.sd; internet www.bok-sd.com; f. 1913; 60% owned by Dubai Islamic Bank PJSC (United Arab Emirates); absorbed National Export/Import Bank and Unity Bank in 1993; cap. 381m., res 92.9m., dep. 2,818.2m. (Dec. 2009); Chair. Dr KHALID M. ALI AL KAMDA; Gen. Man. FADI SALIM AL-FAQIH; 118 brs.

Blue Nile Mashreg Bank: Barlaman St, POB 984, Khartoum; tel. (183) 776092; fax (183) 782562; e-mail info@bluemashreg.com; internet www.bluemashreg.com; f. 1983; cap. 112.2m., res 173.5m., dep. 618.6m. (Dec. 2011); Chair. MUHAMMAD ISMAIL MOHAMMAD; Gen. Man. ISAM OSMAN MAHGOUB.

Farmers Commercial Bank: POB 11984, Al-Qasr Ave, Khartoum; tel. (183) 774960; fax (183) 773687; e-mail mozarea@alnlilin.com;

internet www.fcbsudan.com; f. 1960 as Sudan Commercial Bank; name changed as above in 1999 following merger with Farmers Bank for Investment and Rural Development; cap. 69.7m., res 13.5m., dep. 377.1m. (Dec. 2009); Chair. AL-TAYB ELOBEID BADR; Pres. SULIMAN HASHIM MOHAMED TOUM; 28 brs.

National Bank of Sudan: Kronfli Bldg, Zubeir Pasha St, POB 1183, Khartoum; tel. (183) 778153; fax (183) 779545; e-mail contactus@nbs.com.sd; internet www.nbs.com.sd; f. 1982; 70% owned by Bank Audi SAL, Lebanon; cap. 150.0m., res 39.3m., dep. 164.9m. (Dec. 2009); Chair. Dr IMAD ITANI; 13 brs in Sudan, 2 abroad.

Omdurman National Bank: Al-Qaser Ave, POB 11522, Khartoum; tel. (183) 770400; fax (183) 777263; e-mail info@omd-bank.com; internet www.omd-bank.com; f. 1993; cap. 523.3m., res 116.9m., dep. 5,597.0m. (Dec. 2009); Gen. Man. ABDEL RAHMAN HASSAN ABDEL RAHMAN; 17 brs; 852 employees.

Sudanese French Bank: Plot No. 6, Block A, Al-Qasr St, POB 2775, Khartoum; tel. (183) 771730; fax (183) 790391; e-mail info@sfbank.net; internet www.sfbank.net; f. 1978 as Sudanese Investment Bank; name changed as above in 1993; cap. 100.1m., res 34.0m., dep. 896.2m. (Dec. 2009); Chair. OSMAN SALMAN MOHAMED NOUR; Gen. Man. MASSAD MOHAMMED AHMED ABDUL KARIM; 20 brs.

Tadamon Islamic Bank: Baladia St, POB 3154, Khartoum; tel. (183) 771505; fax (183) 773840; e-mail info@tadamonbank-sd.com; internet www.tadamonbank-sd.com; f. 1981; cap. 81.5m., res 141.0m., dep. 1,115.9m. (Dec. 2009); Chair. Dr HASSAN OSMAN SAKOTA; Gen. Man. ABBAS ABDALLA ABBAS; 18 brs.

Foreign Banks

Byblos Bank Africa Ltd: 21 al-Amarat St, POB 8121, Khartoum; tel. (183) 566444; fax (183) 566454; e-mail Byblosbankafrica@byblosbank.com; internet www.byblosbank.com.lb; 65% owned by Byblos Bank SAL (Lebanon); f. 2003; cap. 93.3m., res 43.8m., dep. 394.2m. (Dec. 2009); Chair. Dr FRANÇOIS S. BASSIL; Gen. Man. NADIM GHANTOUS.

Faisal Islamic Bank (Sudan) (Saudi Arabia): Faih'a Bldg, Ali al-Latif St, POB 2415, Khartoum; tel. (183) 777920; fax (183) 780193; e-mail fibsudan@fibsudan.com; internet www.fibsudan.com; f. 1977; cap. 110.0m., res 10.4m., dep. 1,800.0m. (Dec. 2009); Chair. Prince MUHAMMAD AL-FAISAL AL-SA'UD; Gen. Man. ALI OMAR IBRAHIM FARAH; 30 brs.

Saudi Sudanese Bank: Baladia St, POB 1773, Khartoum; tel. (183) 780307; fax (183) 781836; e-mail saudi-sud@saudisb.sd; internet www.saudisb.sd; f. 1986; cap. 60.0m., res –49.8m., dep. 372.8m. (Dec. 2009); Chair. FAWZI IBRAHIM MAHMOUD WASSFI; Gen. Man. ABDUL ALIM MOHAMMED ALI (acting); 13 brs.

Sudanese Egyptian Bank (SEB): Ingaz Rd, Elsafia, Khartoum; tel. (183) 745583; fax (183) 745580; e-mail msiralkhatim@sebank.sd; internet www.sebank.sd; f. 2005; total assets 422.6m. (Dec. 2008); Man. Dir AMR BAHAA; 5 brs.

Development Banks

Agricultural Bank of Sudan: Ghoumhoria Ave, POB 1263, Khartoum; tel. (183) 777432; fax (183) 778296; e-mail agribank@yahoo.com; f. 1957; cap. SDD 5,200.0m., res SDD 3,609.4m., dep. SDD 18,864.9m. (Dec. 2003); provides finance for agricultural projects; Pres. AL-SAYID GAFFAR MUHAMMAD AL-HASSAN; Gen. Man. AL-SAYID AL-KINDI MUHAMMAD OSMAN; 40 brs.

Islamic Co-operative Development Bank (ISCOB): Et-Tanmha Tower, Kolyat Eltib St, POB 62, Khartoum; tel. (183) 777789; fax (183) 777715; e-mail info@iscob.com; internet www.iscob.com; f. 1983; cap. and res SDD 3,821.0m., total assets SDD 28,250.4m. (Dec. 2003); Chair. El-Haj ATTA EL-MANAN IDRIS; 6 brs.

El-Nilein Bank: United Nations Sq., POB 1722, Khartoum; tel. (183) 771984; fax (183) 785811; e-mail info@nidbg.com; internet www.nidbg.com; f. 1993 by merger of En-Nilein Bank and Industrial Bank of Sudan; name changed as above in 2007; 99% owned by Bank of Sudan; provides tech. and financial assistance for private sector industrial projects and acquires shares in industrial enterprises; cap. SDD 3,282.6m., res SDD –861.4m., dep. SDD 54,046.9m. (Dec. 2005); Man. Dir MOHAMED ABBAS AGAB; 37 brs.

NIMA Development and Investment Bank: Hashim Hago Bldg, As-Suk al-Arabi, POB 665, Khartoum; tel. (183) 779496; fax (183) 781854; f. 1982 as National Devt Bank; name changed as above 1998; 90% owned by NIMA Groupe, 10% private shareholders; finances or co-finances economic and social devt projects; Dir-Gen. SALIM AS-SAFI HUGIR; 6 brs.

Real Estates Commercial Bank: Baladia St, POB 309, Khartoum; tel. (183) 777917; fax (183) 779465; f. 1967; mortgage bank financing private sector urban housing devt; Chair. Eng. MUHAMMAD ALI EL-AMIN; 6 brs.

STOCK EXCHANGE

Sudanese Stock Exchange: Al-Baraka Tower, 5th Floor, POB 10835, Khartoum; tel. (183) 776235; fax (183) 776134; f. 1995; Chair. HAMZA MUHAMMAD JENAWI; 27 mems.

INSURANCE

African Insurance Co (Sudan) Ltd: New Abu Ella Bldg, Parliament Ave, Khartoum; tel. (183) 173402; fax (183) 177988; f. 1977; fire, accident, marine and motor; Gen. Man. AL-NOMAN AL-SANUSI.

Blue Nile Insurance Co (Sudan) Ltd: Al-Qasr Ave, Blue Nile Insurance Bldg, POB 2215, Khartoum; tel. (183) 170580; fax (183) 172405; internet www.blue-nile-insurance.com; f. 1965; Gen. Man. MUHAMMAD AL-AMIN MIRGHANI.

Foja International Insurance Co Ltd: POB 879, Khartoum; tel. (183) 784470; fax (183) 783248; fire, accident, marine, motor and animal; Gen. Man. MAMOON IBRAHIM ABD ALLA.

General Insurance Co (Sudan) Ltd: El-Mek Nimr St, POB 1555, Khartoum; tel. (183) 780616; fax (183) 772122; f. 1961; Gen. Man. AL-SAMAWL AL-SAYED HAFIZ.

Islamic Insurance Co Ltd: Al-Faiha Commercial Bldg, Ali Abdullatif St, POB 2776, Khartoum; tel. (183) 772656; fax (183) 778959; e-mail islamicins@sudanmail.net; internet www.islamicinsur.com; f. 1979; all classes; CEO Dr KAMAL JADKAREEM.

Khartoum Insurance Co Ltd: Al-Taminat Bldg, Al-Jamhouriya St, POB 737, Khartoum; tel. (183) 778647; f. 1953; Chair. MUDAWI M. AHMAD; Gen. Dir YOUSIF KHAIRY.

Juba Insurance Co Ltd: Al-Baladiya St, Sayen Osnam Al-Amin Bldg, 2nd Floor, POB 10043, Khartoum; tel. (183) 783245; fax (183) 781617; Gen. Man. ABDUL AAL AL-DAWI.

Middle East Insurance Co Ltd: Al-Qasr St, Kuronfuli Bldg, 1st Floor, POB 3070, Khartoum; tel. (183) 772202; fax (183) 779266; f. 1981; fire, marine, motor and general liability; Chair. AHMAD I. MALIK; Gen. Dir ALI MUHAMMAD AHMED EL-FADL.

Sudanese Insurance and Reinsurance Co Ltd: Al-Gamhouria Ave, Nasr Sq., Abd Al-Rahman Makawi Bldg, 3rd Floor, POB 2332, Khartoum; tel. (183) 777796; fax (183) 771820; e-mail info@sudinreco.com; internet www.sudinreco.com; f. 1967; Gen. Man. HASSAN EL-SAYED MUHAMMAD ALI.

United Insurance Co (Sudan) Ltd: United Insurance Tower, 9th and 10th Floors, Parliament St, POB 318, Khartoum; tel. (183) 776630; fax (183) 770783; e-mail info@unitedinsurance.ws; internet www.unitedinsurance.ws; f. 1968; Chair. HASHIM EL-BERIER; Gen. Man. MOHAMAD ABDIN BABIKER.

Trade and Industry

GOVERNMENT AGENCIES

Agricultural Research Corpn (ARC): POB 126, Wadi Medani; tel. (51) 1842226; fax (51) 1843213; e-mail arcdg@sudanmail.net; internet www.arcsudan.sd; f. 1967; Dir-Gen. ADIL OMER SALIH ABDEL RAHIM (acting).

Animal Production Public Corpn: POB 624, Khartoum; tel. (183) 778555; Gen. Man. Dr FOUAD RAMADAN HAMID.

Gum Arabic Co Ltd: POB 857, Khartoum; tel. (183) 462111; fax (183) 467923; e-mail info@gac-arabicgum.com; internet www.gac-arabicgum.com; f. 1969; Chair. ABD EL-HAMID MUSA KASHA; Gen. Man. HASSAN SAAD AHMED.

Industrial Production Corpn: POB 1034, Khartoum; tel. (183) 771278; f. 1976; Dir-Gen. OSMAN TAMMAM.

Cement and Building Materials Sector Co-ordination Office: POB 2241, Khartoum; tel. (183) 774269; Dir T. M. KHOGALI.

Food Industries Corpn: POB 2341, Khartoum; tel. (183) 775463; Dir MUHAMMAD AL-GHALI SULIMAN.

Leather Industries Corpn: POB 1639, Khartoum; tel. (183) 778187; f. 1986; Man. Dir IBRAHIM SALIH ALI.

Oil Corpn: POB 64, Khartoum North; tel. (183) 332044; Gen. Man. BUKHARI MAHMOUD BUKHARI.

Spinning and Weaving General Co Ltd: POB 765, Khartoum; tel. (183) 774306; f. 1975; Dir MUHAMMAD SALIH MUHAMMAD ABDALLAH.

Sudan Tea Co Ltd: POB 1219, Khartoum; tel. (183) 781261.

Sudanese Mining Corpn: POB 1034, Khartoum; tel. (183) 770840; f. 1975; Dir IBRAHIM MUDAWI BABIKER.

Sugar and Distilling Industry Corpn: POB 511, Khartoum; tel. (183) 778417; Man. MIRGHANI AHMAD BABIKER.

Mechanized Farming Corpn: POB 2482, Khartoum; Man. Dir AWAD AL-KARIM AL-YASS.

National Cotton and Trade Co Ltd: POB 1552, Khartoum; tel. (183) 80040; f. 1970; Chair. ABD EL-ATI A. MEKKI; Man. Dir ABD AL-RAHMAN A. MONIEM; Gen. Man. ZUBAIR MUHAMMAD AL-BASHIR.

Port Sudan Cotton Trade Co Ltd: POB 590, Port Sudan; POB 590, Khartoum; Gen. Man. SAÏD MUHAMMAD ADAM.

Public Agricultural Production Corpn: POB 538, Khartoum; Chair. and Man. Dir ABDALLAH BAYOUMO; Sec. SAAD AL-DIN MUHAMMAD ALI.

Public Corpn for Building and Construction: POB 2110, Khartoum; tel. (183) 774544; Dir NAIM AL-DIN.

Public Corpn for Irrigation and Excavation: POB 619, Khartoum; tel. (183) 780167; Gen. Sec. OSMAN AL-NUR.

Public Corpn for Oil Products and Pipelines: POB 1704, Khartoum; tel. (183) 778290; Gen. Man. ABD AL-RAHMAN SULIMAN.

Rahad Corpn: POB 2523, Khartoum; tel. (183) 775175; financed by the World Bank, Kuwait and the USA; Man. Dir HASSAN SAAD ABDALLA.

State Trading Corpn: POB 211, Khartoum; tel. (183) 778555; Chair. E. R. M. TOM.

Automobile Corpn: POB 221, Khartoum; tel. (183) 778555; importer of vehicles and spare parts; Gen. Man. DAFALLA AHMAD SIDDIQ.

Captrade Engineering and Automobile Services Co Ltd: POB 97, Khartoum; tel. (183) 789265; fax (183) 775544; e-mail cap1@sudanmail.net; f. 1925; importers and distributors of engineering and automobile equipment; Gen. Man. ESSAM MOHD EL-HASSAN KAMBAL.

Gezira Trade and Services Co: POB 17, Port Sudan; tel. (311) 825109; fax (311) 822029; e-mail gtsportsudan@hotmail.com; f. 1980; importer of agricultural machinery, spare parts, electrical and office equipment, foodstuffs, clothes and footwear; exporter of oilseeds, grains, hides and skins and livestock; provides shipping insurance and warehousing services; agents for Lloyds and P & I Club; Chair. NASR EL-DIN M. OMER.

Khartoum Commercial and Shipping Co: POB 221, Khartoum; tel. (183) 778555; f. 1982; import, export and shipping services, insurance and manufacturing; Gen. Man. IDRIS M. SALIH.

Silos and Storage Corpn: POB 1183, Khartoum; stores and handles agricultural products; Gen. Man. AHMAD AL-TAIEB HARHOOF.

Sudan Cotton Co Ltd: POB 1672, Khartoum; tel. (183) 775755; fax (183) 770703; e-mail sccl@sudanmail.net; internet www.sudan-cotton.com; f. 1970; exports and markets cotton; Chair. ABBAS ABD AL-BAGI HAMMAD; Dir-Gen. Dr ABDIN MUHAMMAD ALI.

Sudan Gezira Board: POB 884, HQ Barakat Wadi Medani, Gezira Province; tel. 2412; Sales Office, POB 884, Khartoum; tel. (183) 740145; f. 1950; responsible for Sudan's main cotton-producing area; the Gezira scheme is a partnership between the Govt, the tenants and the Board. The Govt provides the land and is responsible for irrigation. Tenants pay a land and water charge and receive the work proceeds. The Board provides agricultural services at cost, technical supervision and execution of govt agricultural policies relating to the scheme. Tenants pay a percentage of their proceeds to the Social Development Fund. The total potential cultivable area of the Gezira scheme is c. 850,000 ha and the total area under systematic irrigation is c. 730,000 ha. In addition to cotton, groundnuts, sorghum, wheat, rice, pulses and vegetables are grown for the benefit of tenant farmers; Man. Dir Prof. FATHI MUHAMMAD KHALIFA.

Sudan Oilseeds Co Ltd: Parliament Ave, POB 167, Khartoum; tel. (183) 780120; f. 1974; 58% state-owned; exporter of oilseeds (groundnuts, sesame seeds and castor beans); importer of foodstuffs and other goods; Chair. SADIQ KARAR AL-TAYEB; Gen. Man. KAMAL ABD AL-HALIM.

Sudan Petroleum Corpn Ltd (Sudapet): POB 2649, Khartoum; tel. (183) 776684; fax (183) 778979; e-mail secretarygeneral@spc.sd; internet www.spc.sd; f. 1998; Chair. Dr AWAD AHMED AL-JAZZ; Sec.-Gen. Dr OMER MOHAMED KHEIR.

DEVELOPMENT CORPORATIONS

Sudan Development Corpn (SDC): 21 al-Amarat, POB 710, Khartoum; tel. (183) 472151; fax (183) 472148; f. 1974 to promote and co-finance devt projects with special emphasis on projects in the agricultural, agri-business and industrial sectors; cap. p.u. US $200m.; Man. Dir ABDEL WAHAB AHMED HAMZA.

Sudan Rural Development Co Ltd (SRDC): POB 2190, Khartoum; tel. (183) 773855; fax (183) 773235; e-mail srdfc@hotmail.com; f. 1980; SDC has 27% shareholding; cap. p.u. US $20m.; Gen. Man. EL-AWAD ABDALLA H. HIJAZI.

Sudan Rural Development Finance Co (SRDFC): POB 2190, Khartoum; tel. (183) 773855; fax (183) 773235; f. 1980; Gen. Man. OMRAN MUHAMMAD ALI.

CHAMBERS OF COMMERCE

Union of Sudanese Chambers of Commerce: POB 81, Khartoum; tel. (183) 772346; fax (183) 780748; e-mail chamber@sudanchamber.org; f. 1908; Pres. AL-TAYEB AHMED OSMAN; Sec.-Gen. IBRAHIM MUHAMMAD OSMAN.

INDUSTRIAL ASSOCIATION

Sudanese Chambers of Industries Association: Africa St, POB 2565, Khartoum; tel. (183) 471716; fax (183) 471720; e-mail info@sudanindustries.org; internet www.sudanindustry.org; f. 1974; Chair. NOUR ELDIN SAEED AL-SAID; Sec.-Gen. Dr EL FATIH ABBAS.

UTILITIES

Public Electricity and Water Corpn: POB 1380, Khartoum; tel. (183) 81021; Dir Dr YASIN AL-HAJ ABDIN.

CO-OPERATIVE SOCIETIES

There are about 600 co-operative societies, of which 570 are officially registered.

Central Co-operative Union: POB 2492, Khartoum; tel. (183) 780624; largest co-operative union operating in 15 provinces.

MAJOR COMPANIES

The following are among the larger companies, either in terms of capital investment or employment.

Aboulela Cotton Ginning Co Ltd: POB 121, Khartoum; tel. (183) 770020; cotton mills.

Bata (Sudan) Ltd: POB 88, Khartoum; tel. (183) 732240; f. 1950; cap. £S 1.7m.; mfrs and distributors of footwear; Man. Dir A. A. ALI; 1,070 employees.

Blue Nile Brewery: POB 1408, Khartoum; f. 1954; cap. £S 734,150; brewing, bottling and distribution of beer; Man. Dirs IBRAHIM ELYAS, HUSSEIN MUHAMMAD KEMAL, OMER AL-ZEIN SAGAYROUN; 336 employees.

Central Desert Mining Co Ltd: POB 20, Port Sudan; f. 1946; cap. £S 150,000; prospecting for and mining of gold, manganese and iron ore; Dirs ABD AL-HADI AHMAD BASHIR, ABOU-BAKR SAID BASHIR; 274 employees.

Cotton Textile Mills Ltd: POB 203, Khartoum; tel. (183) 731414; f. 1976; yarns and fabrics; Man. ABDEL MAROUF ZEIN EL-ABDEEN.

Gabaco (Sudan) Ltd: POB 1155, Khartoum; tel. (183) 780253; f. 1959; cap. £S 15.8m.; distribution of petroleum products; Pres. E. CAMPOLI; Gen. Man. G. BARONIO; 187 employees.

Greater Nile Petroleum Operating Co Ltd (GNPOC): Block No. 4, Plot No. 91, GNPOC Tower, POB 12527, al Mugran District, Khartoum; tel. (187) 0370000; fax (187) 0371919; e-mail info@gnpoc.com; internet www.gnpoc.com; f. 1997; jt venture co 40% owned by CNPC (China), 30% by PETRONAS (Malaysia), 25% by ONGC of India and 5% by SUDAPET (Sudan); Pres. SUN XIANSHENG.

Kenana Sugar Co Ltd: POB 2632, Khartoum; tel. (183) 224703; fax (183) 220563; e-mail info@kenana.com; internet www.kenana.com; f. 1971; financed by Sudanese Govt and other Arab nations; 15,500 employees; Chair. ELZUBAIR AHMED ELHASSA; Man. Dir MOHAMED EL-MARDI EL-NAZIREL-TEGANI.

Libya Oil Sudan Co. Ltd (Oilibya): Shell House, Aboullela Bldg, Parliament Ave, POB 320, Khartoum; tel. (187) 014150; fax (183) 781632; marketing of petroleum products; Gen. Man. LAMINE KABA.

Petrodar Operating Co (PDOC): Petrodar Tower, al Mugran District, POB 11778, Khartoum; tel. (187) 008000; fax (183) 790550; e-mail petrodar@petrodar.com; internet www.petrodar.com; f. 2000; joint venture co 41% owned by CNPC, 40% by Petronas, 8% owned by Sudapet, 6% by Sinopec and 5% by Tri-ocean; Pres. LIU YINGCAI.

White Nile (5B) Petroleum Operating Co Ltd: PETRONAS Complex Nile Ave, POB 8207, Khartoum; tel. (187) 091000; fax (183) 790625; internet www.wnpoc.com.sd; f. 2001; jt venture co 50% owned by PETRONAS (Malaysia) and 50% owned by Sudpet (Sudan).

TRADE UNIONS

Federations

Sudan Workers Trade Unions Federation (SWTUF): POB 2258, Khartoum; tel. (183) 777463; includes 42 trade unions representing c. 1.75m. public service and private sector workers; affiliated to the Int. Confed. of Arab Trade Unions and the Org. of African Trade Union Unity; Pres. IBRAHIM GHANOUR; Gen. Sec. YOUSUF ABU SHAMA HAMED.

Sudanese Federation of Employees and Professionals Trade Unions: POB 2398, Khartoum; tel. (183) 773818; f. 1975; includes 54 trade unions representing 250,000 mems; Pres. IBRAHIM AWADALLAH; Sec.-Gen. KAMAL AL-DIN MUHAMMAD ABDALLAH.

Transport

RAILWAYS

The total length of railway in operation in 2002 was 5,978 route-km. The main line runs from Wadi Halfa, on the Egyptian border, to al-Obeid, via Khartoum. Lines from Atbara and Sinnar connect with Port Sudan. There are lines from Sinnar to Damazin on the Blue Nile (227 km) and from Aradeiba to Nyala in the south-western province of Darfur (689 km), with a 446-km branch line from Babanousa to Wau in Bahr al-Ghazal province. The latter was reopened in 2010, having ceased operations during the civil war. In 2009 plans were announced for the construction of a 10,000-km transcontinental railway project linking Port Sudan with Dakar, Senegal.

Sudan Railways Corpn (SRC): Sudan Railways Corpn Bldg, al-Tabia St, POB 1812, Khartoum; tel. (183) 774009; fax (183) 770652; internet www.sudanrailways.gov.sd; f. 1875; Chair. MOHAMMED AHMED; Gen. Man. HAMZA MOHAMED OSMAN.

ROADS

Roads in Sudan, other than town roads, are only cleared tracks and often impassable immediately after rain. Over 48,000 km of tracks are classed as 'motorable'; there were 3,160 km of main roads and 739 km of secondary roads in 1985. A 484-km highway links Khartoum, Haiya and Port Sudan.

National Transport Corpn: POB 723, Khartoum; Gen. Man. MOHI AL-DIN HASSAN MUHAMMAD NUR.

Public Corpn for Roads and Bridges: POB 756, Khartoum; tel. (183) 770794; f. 1976; Chair. ABD AL-RAHMAN HABOUD; Dir-Gen. ABDOU MUHAMMAD ABDOU.

INLAND WATERWAYS

The total length of navigable waterways served by passenger and freight services is 4,068 km, of which approximately 1,723 km is open all year. From the Egyptian border to Wadi Halfa and Khartoum navigation is limited by cataracts to short stretches, but the White Nile from Khartoum to Juba, in South Sudan, is almost always navigable.

River Navigation Corpn: Khartoum; f. 1970; jtly owned by Govts of Egypt and Sudan; operates services between Aswan and Wadi Halfa.

River Transport Corpn (RTC): POB 284, Khartoum North; operates 2,500 route-km of steamers on the Nile; Chair. ALI AMIR TAHA.

SHIPPING

Port Sudan, on the Red Sea, 784 km from Khartoum, and Suakin are the only commercial seaports.

Axis Trading Co Ltd: POB 1574, Khartoum; tel. (183) 775875; f. 1967; Chair. HASSAN A. M. SULIMAN.

Red Sea Shipping and Services Co: POB 308, Khartoum; tel. (183) 580885; fax (183) 5119090; e-mail redseaco@redsea-sd.com; internet www.redsea-sd.com; Gen. Man. AWAD HAG ALI HAMED.

Sea Ports Corpn: Port Sudan; tel. (311) 822061; fax (311) 822258; e-mail info@sudanports.gov.sd; internet sudanports.gov.sd; f. 1906; Gen. Man. JALAL ELDIN SHILIA.

Sea Pride Enterprise: POB 76, Port Sudan; tel. (311) 820583; fax (311) 825220; e-mail info@spesudan.com; internet www.spesudan.com; f. 1932; fmrly Sea Prince Enterprise; Man. Dir ALNASSER SIDKI.

Sudan Shipping Line Ltd: POB 426, Port Sudan; tel. 2655; POB 1731, Khartoum; tel. (183) 780017; f. 1960; 10 vessels totalling 54,277 dwt operating between the Red Sea and western Mediterranean, northern Europe and United Kingdom; Chair. ISMAIL BAKHEIT; Gen. Man. SALAH AL-DIN OMER AL-AZIZ.

United African Shipping Co: POB 339, Khartoum; tel. (183) 780967; Gen. Man. MUHAMMAD TAHA AL-GINDI.

CIVIL AVIATION

In June 2005 the Government announced that preliminary construction work had been completed for a new international airport at a site 40 km south-west of Khartoum. The airport was expected to open in 2012. In 2010 there were 17 airports in Sudan, of which seven were international airports.

Civil Aviation Authority: Sharia Sayed Abd al-Rahman, POB 430, Khartoum; tel. (183) 787757; fax (183) 779715; e-mail info@caa.gov.sd; internet www.caa-sudan.net; f. 1936; Dir-Gen. ABOU BAKR GAAFAR AHMAD.

Azza Transport: Mak Nimir St, POB 11586, Khartoum; tel. (183) 783761; fax (183) 770408; e-mail info@azzatransport.com; internet www.azzatransport.com; f. 1993; charter and dedicated freight services to Africa and the Middle East; Man. Dir Dr GIBRIL I. MOHAMED.

Badr Airlines: Arkaweet Block 65, Bldg No. 393, POB 6899, Khartoum; tel. 249912327000 (mobile); fax 249155144662 (mobile); e-mail badr@badrairlines.com; internet www.badrairlines.com; operates cargo and passenger air services for humanitarian aid.

Sudan Airways Co Ltd: Sudan Airways Complex, 161 Obeid Khatim St, Riadh Block No. 10, POB 253, Khartoum; tel. (183) 243738; fax (183) 115951; e-mail gm@sudanair.com; internet www.sudanair.com; f. 1947; internal flights and international services to Africa, the Middle East and Europe; Man. Dir ALOBIED FADLULMULA ALI.

Sudanese Aeronautical Services (SASCO): POB 8260, al-Amarat, Khartoum; tel. (183) 7463362; fax (183) 4433362; fmrly Sasco Air Charter; chartered services; Chair. M. M. NUR.

Trans Arabian Air Transport (TAAT): POB 1461, Africa St, Khartoum; tel. (183) 451568; fax (183) 451544; e-mail ftaats@sudanmail.net; f. 1983; dedicated freight services to Africa, Europe and Middle East; Man. Dir Capt. EL-FATI ABDIN.

United Arabian Airlines: POB 3687, Office No. 3, Elekhwa Bldg, Atbara St, Khartoum; tel. (183) 773025; fax (183) 784402; e-mail krthq@uaa.com; f. 1995; charter and dedicated freight services to Africa and the Middle East; Man. Dir M. KORDOFANI.

Tourism

Although tourism in Sudan remains relatively undeveloped, the eastern Red Sea coast and Nile tributaries offer opportunities for water sports. Other attractions include ancient Egyptian remains and the Al-Dinder National Tourist Park, a game reserve established in 1935. In 1991 Sudan's first Marine National Park opened on Sanganeb atoll. There was an estimated total of 536,000 foreign visitor arrivals in Sudan in 2011. Receipts from tourism in 2010 were US $94m.

Public Corpn of Tourism and Hotels: POB 7104, Khartoum; tel. (183) 781764; f. 1977; Dir-Gen. Maj.-Gen. EL-KHATIM MUHAMMAD FADL.

Defence

As assessed at November 2011, the armed forces comprised: army an estimated 105,000; navy an estimated 1,300; air force 3,000. A paramilitary Popular Defence Force included 17,500 active members and 85,000 reserves. Military service is compulsory for males aged 18–30 years and lasts for two years.

Defence Expenditure: Budgeted at an estimated US $1,150m. for 2011.

Chief of Staff of the Air Forces and the Air Defence Forces: Gen. MOHYDEEN AHMED ABDALLA.

Chief of Staff of the Ground Forces: Gen. MUSTAFA OSMAN OBEID.

Chief of Staff of the Marine Forces: Gen. MOHAMED FADL.

Education

The Government provides free primary education from the ages of six to 13 years. Secondary education begins at 14 years of age and lasts for up to three years. According to UNESCO estimates, enrolment at primary schools in 2008/09 was equivalent to 73% of children in the relevant age-group (boys 76%; girls 69%), while in that year enrolment at secondary schools was equivalent to 39% of children in the relevant age-group (boys 41%; girls 36%). There are 26 public universities in Sudan.

Bibliography

Abdel-Rahim, M. *Imperialism and Nationalism in the Sudan: A Study in Constitutional and Political Developments 1899–1956*. Oxford, Oxford University Press, 1969.

Abdel-Rahim, M., *et al. Sudan since Independence*. London, Gower, 1986.

Adar, K. G. *The Sudan Peace Process*. Pretoria, Africa Institute of South Africa, 2005.

Alier, A. *Southern Sudan: Too Many Agreements Dishonoured*. Exeter, Ithaca Press, 1990.

An-Náim, A. A., and Kok, P. N. *Fundamentalism and Militarism: A Report on the Root Causes of Human Rights Violations in the Sudan*. New York, The Fund for Peace, 1991.

Arkell, A. J. *History of Sudan from Earliest Times to 1821*. 2nd edn. London, Athlone Press, 1961.

Asher, M. *Khartoum: The Ultimate Imperial Adventure*. London, Viking, 2005.

Barbour, K. M. *The Republic of the Sudan: A Regional Geography*. London, University of London Press, 1961.

Beasley, I., and Starkey, J. (Eds). *Before the Winds Change: Peoples, Places and Education in the Sudan*. Oxford, Oxford University Press, 1991.

Beshir, M. O. *The Southern Sudan: Background to Conflict*. London, C. Hurst, and New York, Praeger, 1968.

Revolution and Nationalism in the Sudan. New York, Barnes and Noble, 1974.

(Ed.). *Sudan: Aid and External Relations, Selected Essays*. University of Khartoum, Graduate College Publications No. 9, 1984.

Brown, R. P. C. *Public Debt and Private Wealth: Debt, Capital Flight and the IMF in Sudan*. Basingstoke, Macmillan (in association with the Institute of Social Studies), 1992.

Burr, J. M., and Collins, R. O. *Requiem for the Sudan: War, Drought and Disaster Relief on the Nile*. Boulder, CO, Westview Press, 1995.

Revolutionary Sudan: Hassan al-Turabi and the Islamist State, 1989–2000. Leiden, Brill, 2003.

Butler, V., Carney, T., and Freeman, M. *Sudan: The Land and the People*. London, Thames & Hudson, 2005.

Cockett, R. *Sudan: Darfur, Islamism and the World: Darfur and the Failure of an African State*. New Haven, CT, Yale University Press, 2010.

Collins, R. O. *Shadows in the Grass: Britain in the Southern Sudan 1918–1956*. New Haven, CT, Yale University Press, 1983.

A History of Modern Sudan. Cambridge, Cambridge University Press, 2008.

Craig, G. M. (Ed.). *Agriculture of the Sudan*. Oxford, Oxford University Press, 1991.

Daly, M. W. *Imperial Sudan*. New York, Cambridge University Press, 1991.

Darfur's Sorrow: The Forgotten History of a Humanitarian Disaster. Cambridge, Cambridge University Press, 2010.

Deng, F. M. *War of Visions: Conflict of Identities in the Sudan*. Washington, DC, Brookings Institution, 1995.

Deng, F. M., and Khalil, M. *Sudan's Civil War: The Peace Process Before and Since Machakos*. Pretoria, Africa Institute of South Africa, 2005.

Eprile, C. L. *War and Peace in the Sudan 1955–1972*. Newton Abbot, David and Charles, 1974.

Flint, J., and de Waal, A. *Darfur: A Short History of a Long War*. London, Zed Books, 2005.

Fluehr-Lobban, C., Fluehr-Lobban, R. A., and Voll, J. *Historical Dictionary of the Sudan*. 2nd edn. Metuchen, NJ, Scarecrow Press, 1992.

Fukui, K., and Markakis, J. (Eds). *Ethnicity and Conflict in the Horn of Africa*. London, James Currey, 1994.

Gabriel, W. *Islam, Sectarianism and Politics in Sudan since Mahdiyya*. London, C. Hurst, 2003.

Garang, J. *The Call for Democracy in Sudan* (Ed. Khalid, M.). 2nd edn. London, Kegan Paul International, 1992.

Gurdon, C. (Ed.). *The Horn of Africa*. London, University College London Press, 1994.

Hill, R., and Hogg, P. A. *Black Corps d'Elite*. East Lansing, MI, Michigan State University Press, 1995.

Holt, P. M., and Daly, M. W. *The History of the Sudan from the Coming of Islam to the Present Day*. 4th edn. London and New York, Longman, 1988.

Iyob, R., and Khadiagala, G. M. *Sudan: The Elusive Quest for Peace*. Boulder, CO, Lynne Rienner Publishers, 2006.

Johnson, D. H. *The Root Causes of Sudan's Civil Wars*. Revised edn. London, James Currey, 1995.

Karrar, A. S. *The Sufi Brotherhoods in the Sudan*. London, C. Hurst, 1992.

Katsuyoshi, F., and Markakis, J. *Ethnicity and Conflict in the Horn of Africa*. London, James Currey, 1994.

Keen, D. *The Benefits of Famine: A Political Economy of Famine and Relief in Southwestern Sudan, 1983–1989*. Princeton, NJ, Princeton University Press, 1994.

Khalid, M. *War and Peace in Sudan: A Tale of Two Countries*. London, Kegan Paul International, 2003.

Khalifa, M. E. *Reflections on the Sudanese Political System*. Khartoum, Sudan House, 1995.

Mamdani, M. *Saviors and Survivors: Darfur, Politics, and the War on Terror*. New York, Pantheon, 2009.

Niblock, T. *Class and Power in Sudan: The Dynamics of Sudanese Politics 1898–1985*. Albany, NY, State University Press of New York, 1987.

Nyaba, P. A. *The Politics of Liberation in South Sudan: An Insider's View*. Kampala, Fountain Publishers, 1997.

O'Ballance, E. *The Secret War in the Sudan 1955–1972*. London, Faber and Faber, 1977.

O'Fahey, R. S. *Darfur: A History*. London, Hurst, 2007.

Oduho, J., and Deng, W. *The Problem of the Southern Sudan*. Oxford, Oxford University Press, 1963.

Petterson, D. *Inside Sudan: Political Islam, Conflict, and Catastrophe*. Philadelphia, PA, Westview, 1999.

Prendergast, J. *Sudanese Rebels at a Crossroads: Opportunities for Building Peace in a Shattered Land*. Washington, DC, Center of Concern, 1994.

Prunier, G. *From Peace to War: The Southern Sudan (1972–1984)*. Hull, University of Hull, 1986.

Darfur: The Ambiguous Genocide. London, Hurst, 2005.

Reeves, E. *A Long Day's Dying: Critical Moments in the Darfur Genocide*. Toronto, The Key Publishing House, 2007.

Reilly, H. *Seeking Sanctuary: Journeys to Sudan*. Bridgnorth, Eye Books, 2005.

Rolandsen, O. H. *Guerrilla Government: Political Changes in the Southern Sudan during the 1990s*. Uppsala, Nordic Africa Institute, 2005.

Rone, J., *et al.* (Eds). *Civilian Devastation: Abuses by the Parties in the War in Southern Sudan*. New York, Human Rights Watch, 1994.

Ruay, D. D. A. *The Politics of Two Sudans: The South and the North, 1921–1969*. Uppsala, Nordic Africa Institute, 1994.

Santi, P., and Hill, R. (Eds). *The Europeans in the Sudan 1834–1878*. Oxford, Oxford University Press, 1980.

Sidahmed, A. S. *Politics and Islam in Contemporary Sudan*. Richmond, Curzon Press, 1996.

Sidahmed, A. S., and Sidahmed, A. *Sudan*. Abingdon, Routledge, 2004.

Sikainga, A. A. *Slaves into Workers: Emancipation and Labor in Colonial Sudan*. Austin, TX, University of Texas Press, 1996.

Simone, T. A. M. *In Whose Image?* Chicago, IL, University of Chicago Press, 1994.

Sylvester, A. *Sudan under Nimeri*. London, Bodley Head, 1977.

Thomas, G. F. *Sudan: Struggle for Survival, 1984–1993*. London, Darf, 1993.

Voll, J. O. (Ed.). *Sudan: State and Society in Crisis*. Bloomington, IN, Indiana State University Press, 1991.

Woodward, P. *Sudan 1898–1989: The Unstable State*. Boulder, CO, Lynne Rienner Publishers, 1990.

SWAZILAND

Physical and Social Geography

A. MacGREGOR HUTCHESON

The Kingdom of Swaziland is one of the smallest political entities of continental Africa. Covering an area of only 17,363 sq km (6,704 sq miles), it straddles the broken and dissected edge of the South African plateau, surrounded by South Africa on the north, west and south, and separated from the Indian Ocean on the east by the Mozambique coastal plain.

PHYSICAL FEATURES

From the Highveld on the west, averaging 1,050 m to 1,200 m in altitude, there is a step-like descent eastwards through the Middleveld (450 m to 600 m) to the Lowveld (150 m to 300 m). To the east of the Lowveld, the Lebombo Range, an undulating plateau at 450 m–825 m, presents an impressive westward-facing scarp and forms the fourth of Swaziland's north–south aligned regions. Drainage is by four main systems flowing eastwards across these regions: the Komati and Umbeluzi rivers in the north, the Great Usutu river in the centre, and the Ngwavuma river in the south. The eastward descent is accompanied by a rise in temperature and by a decrease in mean annual rainfall from a range of 1,150 mm–1,900 mm in the Highveld to one of 500 mm–750 mm in the Lowveld, but increasing again to about 850 mm in the Lebombo range. The higher parts, receiving 1,000 mm, support temperate grassland, while dry woodland savannah is characteristic of the lower areas.

RESOURCES AND POPULATION

Swaziland's potential for economic development in terms of its natural resources is out of proportion to its size. The country's perennial rivers represent a high hydroelectric potential and their exploitation for irrigation in the drier Middleveld and Lowveld has greatly increased and diversified agricultural production. Sugar, however, is the dominant industry and has traditionally been the principal export commodity. Other major crops include cotton (in terms of the number of producers, this is the most important cash crop), maize, tobacco, rice, vegetables, citrus fruits and pineapples. The well-watered Highveld is particularly suitable for afforestation and over 120,000 ha (more than 100 plantations) have been planted with conifers and eucalyptus since the 1940s, creating the largest man-made forests in Africa. In 1998 there were some 98,000 ha of planted forest in the country.

Swaziland is also rich in mineral wealth. Once a major exporter of iron ore, this industry ceased with the exhaustion of high-grade ores, although considerable quantities of lower-grade ore remain. Coal holds the country's most important mineral potential, with reserves estimated at 1,000m. metric tons in the late 2000s. Coal is currently mined at Maloma, mostly for export, and further reserves have been identified at Lobuka. Other minerals of note are cassiterite (a tin-bearing ore), kaolin, talc, pyrophyllite and silica.

Nearly one-half of the population live in the Middleveld, which contains some of the best soils in the country. This is Swaziland's most densely peopled region, with an average of 50 inhabitants per sq km, rising to more than 200 per sq km in some rural and in more developed areas. The total population of Swaziland (excluding absentee workers) was enumerated at 953,524 at the census of 2007, giving an overall density of 54.9 inhabitants per sq km. According to UN estimates, the population at mid-2011 was 1,220,406, giving a population density of 70.3 per sq km.

A complex system of land ownership, with Swazi and European holdings intricately interwoven throughout the country, is partly responsible for considerable variations in the distribution and density of the population. Only about 40% of the country was under Swazi control at the time of independence in 1968, but this proportion steadily increased in subsequent years, as non-Swazi land and mineral concessions were acquired through negotiation and purchase. The Swazi Nation, to which most of the African population belongs, has now regained all mineral concessions.

Recent History

HUGH MACMILLAN

Swaziland, which began to emerge as a nation in the early 19th century, became a British protectorate following the Anglo-Boer War in 1903, and in 1907 became one of the High Commission Territories. A preoccupation of King Sobhuza II during his 61-year reign, which began in 1921, was the recovery of lands granted to settlers and speculators—and lost to neighbouring countries—in the late 19th century.

Moves towards the restoration of independence in the early 1960s were accompanied by a growth in political activity. The Ngwane National Liberatory Congress (NNLC), an African nationalist party formed in 1962 and led by Dr Ambrose Zwane, advocated independence on the basis of universal adult suffrage and a constitutional monarchy. Royalist interests formed the rival Imbokodvo National Movement, which won all seats in the new House of Assembly in the pre-independence elections in April 1967. The independence Constitution vested legislative authority in a bicameral parliament, with a proportion of its membership nominated by the King. Formal independence followed on 6 September 1968.

The post-independence rule of Sobhuza was characterized by stability and a significant expansion of the economy as investment flowed in, much of it from South Africa. Growing reliance on South African capital, along with Swaziland's membership of the Southern African Customs Union (SACU), restricted the country's economic and political choices. During this period the royal authorities acquired a significant material base in the economy through their control of Tibiyo Taka Ngwane and Tisuka Taka Ngwane, royal corporations that managed the investment of mineral royalties. Politically, the King extended his influence through his indirect control of the country's Tinkhundla (singular: Inkhundla), local authorities, each grouping a small number of chieftaincies. In 1973, in accordance with a resolution of the House of Assembly, Sobhuza decreed a suspension of the Constitution and a formal ban on party political activity. Parliament effectively voted itself out of existence. By the time of Sobhuza's diamond jubilee in 1981, the authority of the Swazi monarchy was absolute. Sobhuza's death in August 1982 precipitated a prolonged and complex power struggle both within the royal family and among contending factions of the Liqoqo, a traditional advisory body. By early 1985, however, supporters of the Regent, Queen Ntombi Latfwala, mother of the 14-year-old heir apparent, Prince Makhosetive, had emerged as the group most likely to ensure an orderly succession and to overcome fractious and corrupt elements within the Liqoqo, the powers of which were substantially curtailed in 1985.

ACCESSION OF MSWATI III

Prince Makhosetive was installed as King Mswati III in April 1986. The young King, or his advisers, moved quickly to assert his authority. The Liqoqo was disbanded in May and the Cabinet reshuffled. In October Sotsha Dlamini, a former assistant commissioner of police, was appointed Prime Minister. In September 1987 the legislature was dissolved in preparation for elections to be held in November, one year ahead of schedule. In November the electoral college duly appointed 40 members of the House of Assembly (none of whom had previously been members). The new House of Assembly and King Mswati each appointed 10 members of the Senate. The low turn-out at the polls for the election of the electoral college was widely interpreted as an indication of dissatisfaction with the Tinkhundla system.

RE-EMERGENCE OF PUDEMO

In July 1989 the King dismissed Sotsha Dlamini for 'disobedience' and replaced him as Prime Minister with Obed Dlamini, a founder member and former Secretary-General of the Swaziland Federation of Trade Unions (SFTU). This appointment was viewed as an attempt to allay labour unrest, which had led to strikes in the banking and transport systems. Until late 1989 open criticism of Mswati's maintenance of autocratic rule had been restricted to sporadic appearances of anti-Liqoqo pamphlets linked to the People's United Democratic Movement (PUDEMO), an organization that had been formed in 1983 during the regency. PUDEMO returned to prominence in 1990 with the distribution of new pamphlets that advocated a constitutional monarchy.

By mid-1991 there appeared to be widespread public support for PUDEMO, and in the second half of the year the organization began to establish civic structures in order to advance its objectives through legal organizations. The most prominent of these were the Swaziland Youth Congress (SWAYOCO) and the Human Rights Association of Swaziland. The King finally agreed to review the Tinkhundla and established a commission, under the chairmanship of Prince Masitsela, which became known as the Vusela ('Greeting') committee, to test opinion on political reforms.

In the second half of 1991 PUDEMO rejected the Vusela process and set out five demands, including the suspension of the state of emergency and the establishment of a constituent assembly to draw up a new constitution. In February 1992 the King announced the establishment of a second committee (Vusela 2) and included a member of PUDEMO among the commissioners.

PRESSURE FOR REFORM

In October 1992 the King approved a number of proposals, which had been submitted by Vusela 2. The House of Assembly (which was to be called the National Assembly) was to be expanded to 65 deputies and the Senate to 30 members. In addition, detention without trial was to cease, and a new constitution, confirming the monarchy, the fundamental rights of the individual and the independence of the judiciary, was to be drafted. PUDEMO announced its opposition to the reforms, and demanded that the Government organize a national convention to determine the country's constitutional future. King Mswati subsequently dissolved parliament and announced that he was to rule by decree, with the assistance of the Cabinet, pending the adoption of the new constitution and the holding of parliamentary elections.

The first round of elections to the expanded National Assembly took place on 25 September 1993. The second round of parliamentary elections, which took place on 11 October, was contested by the three candidates in each Inkhundla who had obtained the highest number of votes in the first poll. In early November the former Minister of Works and Construction, Prince Jameson Mbilini Dlamini, was appointed Prime Minister, and a new Cabinet was formed.

In January 1996 PUDEMO announced a campaign of civil disobedience, and later that month the SFTU initiated an indefinite general strike and there were clashes with the police. The SFTU subsequently suspended its industrial action to allow negotiations with the Government to proceed. In July King Mswati appointed a Constitutional Review Commission, comprising chiefs, political activists and unionists, to draft proposals for a new constitution. At the same time, Dr Barnabas Sibusiso Dlamini, an Executive Director of the IMF and a former Minister of Finance, was appointed Prime Minister.

The draft of the new Constitution was finally presented to the King in April 2001 and published in August of that year. It recommended the extension of the King's powers, the strengthening of traditional structures such as the Tinkhundla and the continuation of the ban on political parties. In December the King announced the appointment of a 15-member body—the Constitution Drafting Committee (CDC). Opposition groups considered this as yet another delaying tactic and accused the Government of manipulating the Commission's report. In February 2002 it was announced that the CDC would be chaired by the King's brother, Prince David Dlamini.

Continued Labour Unrest and Public Discontent

Meanwhile, the Industrial Relations Bill, which had been presented to parliament in 1998, was finally approved by the King in May 2000. Swaziland was threatened with sanctions by the USA, however, when it became clear that the last-minute alterations were unacceptable to both that country and the International Labour Organization (ILO), and changes to the legislation were agreed after talks with ILO in mid-November. These amendments were made against a background of continuous industrial action and popular protest, beginning in September 2000, with strike action against the labour legislation, and intensifying in October, with protests against the eviction from their land by the armed forces of 200 followers of two local chiefs in eastern Swaziland. This was the climax of a protracted dispute between Chief Mliba Fakudze of Macetjeni and Chief Mfutse Dlamini of KaMkhweli, on the one hand, and Prince Maguga Dlamini, an elder half-brother of King Mswati, on the other.

In mid-October 2000 police dispersed a demonstration organized by the Swaziland National Association of Teachers (SNAT) in Mbabane in protest against the evictions, and the Government announced a ban on all trade union meetings in the country and the closure of the University of Swaziland. In response to these measures, the trade unions called a meeting of their members at Nelspruit, South Africa, in early November. The resulting 'Nelspruit Declaration' appealed for the establishment of an interim government outside Swaziland, for strike action in mid-November and for a three-day closure of the Swazi borders at the end of the month. At the time of the strike Mario Bongani Masuku, the President of PUDEMO, was detained, but was released a few days later after court action, while the SFTU leader, Jan Sithole, was placed under police surveillance with his movements restricted. The border blockade at the end of the month received the support of the Congress of South African Trade Unions (COSATU) and was partially successful.

PRESS RELATIONS

Apart from the trade unions, the press continued to be a major focus of opposition and to bear the brunt of government pressure in 1999–2001. The editor of the Sunday edition of *The Times of Swaziland*, Bheki Makhubu, was detained in early October 1999 and charged with defamation under a colonial ordinance, following a series of articles that were critical of King Mswati's choice of Senteni Masango as one of two new royal fiancées.

The press was one of the main targets of a royal decree issued in June 2001, which allowed the Minister of Broadcasting and Information, acting on behalf of the King, to ban newspapers without reason and to deny them the right of appeal to the courts. Other measures in the decree prevented any person or body, including the courts, from challenging the King, and allowed him to appoint and dismiss judges personally and to prevent the courts from considering matters that related to royal prerogatives. The SFTU threatened industrial action and there was a wave of protest from opposition leaders and foreign governments. The Government revoked the decree in July, in response to international diplomatic pressure and the threat of economic sanctions from the USA; a new decree was issued shortly afterwards, which retained certain sections of the original decree, including a provision allowing the detention of Swazi citizens without the option of bail for some offences. In January 2009 it was reported that Mfomfo Nkambule, a former cabinet minister, and a columnist for *The Times of Swaziland*, had, under threat of prosecution, publicly apologized for articles that he had written that were critical of the monarchy. It was disclosed in April that the newspaper had discontinued his column. In 2009–10 there were suggestions that *The Times of Swaziland*, the country's only independent newspaper, was exercising self-censorship in its reports on pro-democracy demonstrations, and there was also evidence that the Government was attempting to censor the internet. In January 2012 Musa Nganglamandla—the editor of the *Swazi Observer*, a newspaper owned by the King—was dismissed after he published an interview with a PUDEMO leader. In the following month it was reported that Nganglamandla had fled to South Africa after his office was searched.

JUDICIAL CRISIS

The monarchy was embroiled in controversy in October 2002 when Lindiwe Dlamini sought a High Court injunction against two royal courtiers, claiming that they had abducted her 18-year-old daughter, Zena Mahlangu, on the instructions of King Mswati. The Chief Justice, Stanley Sapire, issued a court order instructing the woman's captors to release her, only for Mahlangu to announce later that she was not being held against her will and was happy to marry the King. The case was suspended indefinitely, and Sapire resigned in April 2003. The formal marriage of King Mswati to Mahlangu, as his 11th wife, was announced in June 2004.

It was announced at the end of November 2002 that the six South African judges of the Swaziland Court of Appeal, led by Leon Steyn, had resigned in protest against the refusal of the Government to uphold two rulings. The judges of the High Court subsequently announced that they would refuse to sit or set dates for hearings; a strike by members of the legal profession followed. In 2003 the International Bar Association issued a report in which it stated that the ongoing judicial crisis was due to a 'blurring of the lines' between the executive, legislature and judiciary.

Following intervention by the Commonwealth Secretariat, in mid-September 2004 the Government announced the resolution of the judicial crisis and demanded that the Court of Appeal reconstitute itself. In mid-November it was reported that the judges of the Court had returned to work in the belief that their orders had been implemented. After discovering that this was not the case, they announced that they could not resume their duties. Early in 2007 a new Chief Justice, Francis Banda, a Malawian, was appointed, and there were complaints that his appointment on a fixed-term contract undermined the independence of the judiciary. In 2011 there was further controversy when Banda's successor as Chief Justice, Michael Ramodibedi, suspended a judge, Thomas Masuku, who was accused of insulting King Mswati in a court judgment and associating with members of the opposition. Masuku initially refused to accept his suspension, and the Minister of Justice and Constitutional Affairs, David Matse, refused to sign his dismissal letter. However, in October Matse was himself dismissed; he was replaced by Chief Mgwagwa Gamedze.

CONSTITUTIONAL CRISIS AND GENERAL ELECTION

In addition to the legal crisis, the ongoing constitutional crisis created further controversy. On 31 May 2003 King Mswati announced the dissolution of the National Assembly and promised to hold elections in October. The new Constitution was not formally presented to the King until November—after the general election. In what appeared to be a further delaying tactic, it was announced that it would not be published until it had been translated into the national language, siSwati.

The first stage of the general election went ahead on 20 September 2003 and was observed by a number of foreign groups, including the Commonwealth Observer Group (COG). In its final report, the COG entirely rejected the credibility of the electoral process in a country where, it stated, the legislature had no power and political parties were banned. Prior to the second round of voting Mswati dissolved the Cabinet and removed Prime Minister Barnabas Sibusiso Dlamini from office, replacing him with Absolom Themba ('AT') Dlamini, who had served for 10 years as Managing Director of Tibiyo Taka Ngwane, the national development agency.

INTRODUCTION OF THE NEW CONSTITUTION

Constitutional legislation was presented for approval to a joint sitting of the Senate and the National Assembly in June 2005. The document concentrated executive power in the King and preserved the Tinkhundla as the basis of the parliamentary system. The King would have the power to appoint the Prime Minister and the Cabinet, the principal secretaries and the judges. He could also dissolve the legislature. Political parties were not banned, but neither was there any provision for their recognition: indeed, they were not mentioned at all. The bill of rights guaranteed freedoms of speech and assembly, but gave the King the right to abrogate these in the public interest. The King finally signed an amended version of the Constitution on 26 July; *inter alia*, it confirmed the King as absolute monarch, but included a clause that would allow for his removal and replacement by the Queen Mother under certain conditions. The King was immune from prosecution by the courts and members of the royal family were exempt from paying tax. It was announced that the new Constitution would come into effect within six months and that there would then be parliamentary elections.

On 10 February 2006 King Mswati announced to a gathering of 5,000 people at the Ludzidzini royal residence that the new Constitution had entered into force. There was continuing uncertainty, however, as to the position of political parties under the new dispensation. There was evidence that the opposition was divided on how to respond to the new Constitution. The leader of the NNLC, Obed Dlamini, suggested that his party would try to register in order to test the legal position. The leader of PUDEMO, Mario Masuku, indicated that his party rejected the Constitution outright because of the lack of consultation with the opposition on its formulation, the veto over legislation that it appeared to give to the King and the fact that it had been introduced by royal edict, rather than by legislative vote; furthermore, the party refused to participate in any elections organized under the terms of the 'royal Constitution'.

A legal challenge to the Constitution, demanding the publication of evidence of popular support, was mounted by the National Constituent Assembly, a pressure group formed by churches and civic associations, in September 2006. The final response to this petition did not come until May 2008 when the Supreme Court refused to strike down the Constitution.

THE 2008 ELECTIONS

In June 2008 the King announced that the legislature would be dissolved at the end of the month in preparation for a general election later in the year. It was subsequently announced that the elections would take place on 19 September. The status of political parties continued to be obscure and had not yet been tested in the courts. The controversial chairman of the Elections and Boundaries Commission, Chief Gija Dlamini, was quoted as stating that political parties were not banned, but neither were they permitted to compete for office.

Political parties were not allowed to participate in the election campaign and the elections were carried out through the 'traditional' Tinkhundla system, which was rejected by many people, including the supporters of the opposition parties and the trade unions. The pre-election period coincided with the King's 40th birthday celebrations, which were accompanied in early September 2008 by some of the largest demonstrations in Swaziland's history. An estimated 10,000–15,000 people demonstrated in Manzini on 3 September and a similar number protested in Mbabane on the following day. There were two small bomb explosions during the Mbabane demonstration, but these were condemned by the organizers.

The elections took place without incident, but an observer mission, the Commonwealth Expert Team, stated in its report that the elections were 'not entirely credible' because the Constitution banned political parties. It appealed for constitutional changes 'to ensure that Swaziland's commitment to political pluralism is unequivocal'. It was also critical of the Government's near monopoly of control of the media. A later legal challenge to the legitimacy of the constitution of the Swaziland Elections and Boundaries Commission was rejected by the High Court.

On the day after the elections police blocked the road to Oshoek border post, where the South African trade union federation COSATU organized a demonstration on the South African side of the border. PUDEMO President Mario Masuku was detained by the police, and prevented from reaching the border post. On the night of 21 September 2008 there was a bomb explosion at Lozitha bridge, about 1 km from the King's main palace in which two of the people who were placing the bomb were killed and a third man was seriously injured. The injured man, Amos Mbhedzi, a South African citizen and a former member of the armed wing of the African National Congress (ANC—see External Relations), was detained. After many postponements, his trial began in June 2010 and was still ongoing in December 2011.

In November 2008 Masuku was detained and charged with treason and terrorism under a new Terrorism Act, which had been promulgated in August. The Prime Minister, Barnabas Sibusiso Dlamini, who had been reappointed following the elections after five years out of office, had earlier named PUDEMO, SWAYCO and the Swaziland Solidarity Network as 'specified entities' in terms of this act. Anyone found guilty of aiding and abetting such organizations was liable to up to 25 years' imprisonment. In an apparent response to Masuku's detention, Swaziland's rival trade union federations and its banned political parties came together to form the Swaziland United Democratic Front. Masuku was finally brought to court in September 2009, but was acquitted when the case against him was dismissed.

ROYAL EXTRAVAGANCE

In January 2004 the UN's World Food Programme reported that it was feeding 250,000 people in Swaziland—about one-quarter of the population—and in February the King spoke of a humanitarian disaster in the country as a result of famine and HIV/AIDS. Against this backdrop, it was reported in January 2004 that the Government was planning to spend US $14m. on the construction of a palace for each of the King's 11 wives. There were also press reports in April of lavish expenditure on the King's public birthday celebrations in Mbabane.

During 2004–05 there were continued reports of royal extravagance. It was reported that luxury vehicles were being bought for each of the King's wives at a total cost of E5m. In April 2005 there was further criticism of the expenditure of US $1m. on the King's birthday celebrations. Protests regarding the King's birthday celebrations again occurred in 2007, and it was reported that he had married his 13th wife, Phindile Nkambule, and that he had, by that time, fathered 30 children. There were subsequent protests over extravagant plans for the joint celebration in September 2008 of the King's 40th birthday and the 40th anniversary of the country's independence, which were estimated to cost at least E100m. In April 2010 it was reported that King Mswati had acquired a Rolls-Royce Phantom limousine at a cost of E5m. The King's personal wealth at this time was estimated at $100m., subsequently revised upwards to $200m. During 2011 attention was focused on the significant proportion of the national budget that was allocated to the royal family and on King Mswati's trip to London, United Kingdom, in April. He took with him a party of 50 in a chartered jet aircraft, but was forced to alter his accommodation arrangements while in London because of demonstrations against his rule.

In April 2012 it was reported that King Mswati had acquired a DC-9 airliner for his personal use. The Government stated that the plane had been provided as a birthday present to the King by anonymous donors. There was speculation that the plane had in fact been acquired with government funds or that it had been supplied by an Indian company involved in the reopening of the Ngwenya iron ore mine. It was thought that the plane would cost as much as US $5,000 per hour to fly and that it would be expensive to maintain. In the same month it was reported that the Government would not be providing funds for the King's birthday celebrations, but ordinary Swazi citizens were urged to donate cattle for the event. There were again protests in London during May, when King Mswati travelled to the British capital to attend a lunch for crowned heads of state as part of Queen Elizabeth II's diamond jubilee festivities.

RECENT POLITICAL DEVELOPMENTS

Pressure on the Government increased with the establishment in August 2009 of the Swaziland Action Campaign—which became the Swaziland Democracy Campaign (SDC) in February 2010—when a conference bringing together representatives of banned Swaziland political organizations such as PUDEMO and the NNLC, as well as labour organizations such as the SFTU and the Swaziland Federation of Labour, was held in Johannesburg, South Africa, under the chairmanship of the Swaziland Council of Churches. The declared objectives of the SDC included: the democratic election of a national constitutional forum to draft a new constitution; the removal of laws inhibiting free political activity; the release of political prisoners; and guarantees of freedom of the press and the judiciary. The harassment of PUDEMO members, and those affiliated with other opposition groups, continued in 2010. Sipho Jele, a PUDEMO activist, died in detention a few days after his arrest, allegedly for wearing a party t-shirt at a Workers' Day rally in Manzini in May, which was organized by the SFTU and the SNUT. Official claims that he committed suicide were rejected by members of his family, and questioned by an independent pathologist at the inquest into his death. Meanwhile, the royal family was tainted by scandal in August, when the Minister of Justice was arrested and dismissed following an alleged affair with King Mswati's 12th wife, LaDube. According to reports, LaDube was expelled from the royal household in late 2011, allegedly becoming the third of the King's 13 wives to have left or been expelled.

Further pressure was placed on the Government in 2010–11 as a result of a financial crisis that stemmed from the global economic situation, a decline in revenue following the reform of the SACU, an unbudgeted increase in salaries for civil servants in April 2010, and massive expenditure on a new airport (which was widely viewed as another example of royal extravagance). There were also suggestions of high-level corruption. In late 2010 the Government was forced into negotiations with the IMF, which demanded a reduction in the size of the civil service, a wage freeze and further decreases in expenditure. In January 2011 Lutfo Dlamini, the Minister of Foreign Affairs, was arrested and then released, amid rumours that he had been involved in corrupt activities in connection with his role as Ambassador to Kuwait. The Prime Minister, Barnabas Dlamini, took action to prevent the publication of allegations that he and other members of the Council of Ministers had bought government land at a substantial discount. His claims that these transactions were legitimate were undermined when King Mswati announced in June that they had been annulled.

There was increasing international support for the SDC in 2010–11. In early September 2010 the police arrested about 50 opposition activists who were meeting in a Manzini hotel to plan pro-democracy demonstrations for the following day. Foreign activists among those arrested were deported, and the Prime Minister was reported to have threatened international supporters of the democracy movement with torture. On 17 November about 500 demonstrators marched in Mbabane as part of a 'Global Week of Action'. Democracy campaigners were inspired in early 2011 by events in Tunisia and Egypt, where popular protests had unseated the autocratic rulers of those nations, and the Government began to fear contagion. Plans for an 'April 12 Uprising'—coinciding with the 38th anniversary of King Sobhuza's suspension of the democratic Constitution in 1973—first appeared as an anonymous internet campaign. The authorities allowed a demonstration of about 8,000 teachers, students and workers to take place in Mbabane in March 2011, but took determined measures to prevent the 'April 12 Uprising' and the protest action that was planned for 12 –14 April. A massive police presence in Manzini, the arrest of protest leaders, the erection of roadblocks around the city and the diversion of buses transporting demonstrators from other areas, together with the use of tear gas and water cannons by the authorities, ensured that the planned march did not take place. However, the Government's repressive actions, which culminated in a police siege of the SNAT's premises, where up to 500 demonstrators had taken refuge, attracted international attention and condemnation. A spokesperson for the SDC, Mary Da Silva, was beaten and briefly detained while giving an interview to a South African radio station. Maxwell Dlamini, President of the Swaziland National Union of Students, and PUDEMO activist Musa Ngubeni were later charged with the possession of explosives. The charges were widely believed to be unfounded, but Dlamini and Ngubeni were denied bail until February 2012. The two men appeared in court in April, but by May no evidence had been produced against them, and Dlamini reportedly feared that they might be held on bail indefinitely. Amnesty International's annual human rights report, published in May, was strongly critical of the Swazi Government, proclaiming that 'arbitrary and secret detentions, unlawful house arrests and other state of emergency-style measures were used to crush peaceful anti-Government protests over several days.' The report also maintained that the regime had terminated all communications with the democratic movement stating that: 'the Government ignored renewed efforts by civil society organizations to open a dialogue on steps towards multi-party democracy. At the UN Universal Periodic Review hearing on Swaziland in October, the Government rejected recommendations to allow political parties to participate in elections.'

In August 2011 the South African Government granted Swaziland a US $355m. loan, to be disbursed over three years. The country had been unable to meet the IMF's requirement to reduce its budget deficit and the expenditure on civil service salaries, and therefore had been unable to secure assistance from the Fund. Although the South African Government had reportedly demanded political as well as economic reform in return for providing financial support, the SDC and the South Africa-based Swaziland Support Network (SSN) protested against the loan and there were delays in its disbursement. In November the Swazi Government was compelled to raise a large commercial loan to enable it to pay civil servants' salaries, and there was a delay in the payment of wages in December. The IMF argued that reductions in public sector salaries were unnecessary and that a balanced budget could be achieved by decreasing expenditure on the army and the police and by lowering politicians' wages. The opening of the University of Swaziland was delayed for a second time in January 2012 as a result of the Government's failure to provide it with adequate funding.

In May 2012 the results of an unprecedented public opinion survey suggested that 56% of Swaziland's population viewed King Mswati favourably, while 43% were dissatisfied with his rule. Opposition groups appeared to be unable to capitalize on this evidence of waning support for the monarch. In the same month it was reported that PUDEMO had expelled the SSN, which it had formed in 1997, from its offices in Johannesburg, following criticism of PUDEMO by the SSN's leader, Lucky Lukhele. The SSN allegedly had links with the South African Communist Party, and it was suspected that political and personal differences between the leaders of the SSN and PUDEMO may have precipitated this dispute. There were also suggestions that the SSN had exaggerated the prospects for revolutionary change in the country and that it had only limited support within Swaziland.

THE HIV/AIDS CRISIS

Perhaps the greatest single problem confronting Swaziland is the HIV/AIDS pandemic. The UN estimated that 33.4% of Swaziland's adult population (aged between 15 and 49 years) was living with HIV/AIDS in 2005, and in March 2009 it was reported that 42% of Swazi women were living with HIV/AIDS, an increase of 3% since 2006. By 2010 it was estimated that the incidence of HIV/AIDS had declined to 26.1%. In August 2002 the Government announced that antiretrovirals would be made available to pregnant women in order to prevent the transmission of HIV to their children, and that universal provision would be made when sufficient medical and financial resources became available. In June 2003 the King announced the establishment of the Royal Initiative to Combat AIDS.

By 2005 it was estimated that one child in every 15 had been orphaned as a result of HIV/AIDS and that the proportion would reach one child in eight within five years. In August 2007 a new National Health Policy was announced. In June a crisis in food security that threatened 400,000 people was linked not only to a serious drought, but also to the loss of family labour through HIV/AIDS. In 2009 an IMF report estimated that on average 25% of the labour force were absent from work owing to HIV/AIDS-related illness.

A report on the 2007 census indicated that the death rate had increased from 7.6 per 1,000 in 1997 to 18.3 per 1,000 in 2007. It was also reported that the mortality rate for children under 5 years of age was 167 per 1,000. In 2010–11 there were reports that funds for the provision of anti-retroviral drugs and for HIV/AIDS non-governmental organizations were threatened by budget reductions; it was estimated that as many as 65,000 people could die as a result of the shortage of anti-retroviral drugs.

EXTERNAL RELATIONS

After achieving independence in 1968, Swaziland joined a number of international organizations, including the Commonwealth, the UN and the Organization of African Unity (now the African Union). It later also became a member of the Southern African Development Community (SADC). During 2004–05 there were frequent adverse comments in the British and South African press regarding Swaziland's human rights record and its failure to implement democratic reform. These comments focused on royal extravagance and the King's frequent marriages, which were associated in the media with the HIV/AIDS crisis and food shortages. Swaziland was linked with Zimbabwe as a Southern African country with a similar, or even less satisfactory, record of governance and disregard for the rule of law. In view of Swaziland's record on human rights, there was some criticism both inside and outside of Swaziland of the election of King Mswati as Chairman of the SADC troika on politics, defence and security co-operation. In September 2009, however, King Mswati addressed the UN General Assembly and was photographed with US President Barack Obama. In April 2010 the US Embassy issued a statement that was critical of the police action against the pro-democracy demonstrations.

In what was seen as a major blow to Swaziland's international status, the British Government announced in December 2004 that it was to close its High Commission in Mbabane at the end of 2006. It appointed an honorary consul and proceeded to conduct its relations with Swaziland from the High Commission in Pretoria, South Africa. This marked the end of more than a century of direct British representation in the country and was widely regarded as a rebuke to Swaziland's poor record of governance. In a message for the King's 40th birthday, shortly before the general election in 2008, the British High Commissioner to South Africa (and Swaziland), Paul Boateng, stated that 'reform in Swaziland cannot be further delayed'. In 2009–11 there were reports of frequent demonstrations and vigils outside the Swaziland High Commission in London and the Swaziland consulate in Johannesburg.

In September 2011 the release by the WikiLeaks organization of diplomatic cables from the US embassy in Swaziland caused embarrassment to both countries. The US Ambassador had reportedly described King Mswati as 'not intellectually well developed' and under the influence of beliefs in witchcraft and African medicine.

As a small and landlocked country, Swaziland's most important bilateral relationships have been with its two neighbours, South Africa and Mozambique. From the mid-1950s until Swaziland's independence in 1968, South Africa regarded the country as the potential nucleus of a Swazi 'Bantustan' ('homeland'). Conversely, King Sobhuza II harboured the ambition of reclaiming from South Africa areas in the eastern Transvaal and northern Natal that were separated from the Swazi kingdom in the 19th century. The achievement of independence by Mozambique in 1975 created a situation in which the exiled ANC of South Africa was able to use Swaziland as a corridor for the movement of recruits from South Africa and for the infiltration of guerrilla fighters. This posed a threat to South Africa's security and provided the basis for negotiations between the Governments of Swaziland and South Africa about a possible 'land deal'. South Africa offered to transfer to Swaziland the KaNgwane 'Bantustan' in the Transvaal and the Ingwavuma district in northern Natal (the acquisition of the latter area would have afforded Swaziland direct access to the sea) in exchange for the imposition of more stringent restrictions on the activities of the ANC. The first step in these negotiations was the conclusion in February 1982 of a secret security agreement between the two countries. King Sobhuza's death in August removed the only obstacle to an all-out offensive on the ANC, and by the end of that year the first of a series of round-ups and 'deportations' of alleged ANC members had occurred. However, as a result of legal obstacles and strong opposition in South Africa, the proposals for the land transfer were finally abandoned in 1984.

In 1984, within days of the signing of the Nkomati Accord between South Africa and Mozambique, the Swazi Government revealed the existence of its security agreement with South Africa. The systematic suppression of ANC activities intensified, and open collaboration between the two countries led to gun battles in Manzini as speculation increased that this policy was being orchestrated by a South African trade mission that was established in Mbabane earlier that year. In January 1985 the Swazi Prime Minister defended his Government's close relationship with South Africa and implied that the attacks against the ANC would continue. The ANC responded by creating a sophisticated underground network in Swaziland. The conflict escalated in 1986, and armed raids by South African security personnel resulted in a number of ANC deaths in border areas and in Manzini. Increased public outrage at these activities led the Swazi Prime Minister publicly to accuse South Africa of responsibility and to condemn a raid in August as an 'illegal act of aggression', the first open attack on South African policies by a Swaziland Government. The era of political reform within South Africa that followed the release of Nelson Mandela in February 1990 brought a general improvement in relations between the two countries, and in late 1993 formal diplomatic relations were established.

It emerged in February 2001 that King Mswati had still not abandoned his determination to reincorporate parts of the Mpumalanga and KwaZulu/Natal provinces into Swaziland. He declared this intention in a letter to South African President Thabo Mbeki, which he handed to the Deputy President, Jacob Zuma, during a visit by the latter to the kingdom in that month. In June 2003 Prince Khuzulwandle, Chairman of the Swaziland Border Adjustment Committee, criticized Mbeki for refusing to discuss realignments to the border. In November 2006 the Swazi Government announced that it would be taking the border dispute to the International Court of Justice (ICJ) at The Hague, Netherlands. It was not until April 2008 that Mbeki visited Swaziland for the first time as President, after nine years in office. King Mswati was invited to the inauguration of President Zuma in May 2009, in spite of a campaign supported by the SFTU and COSATU appealing for him not be invited in protest against the continued detention of Mario Masuku.

In April 2006 COSATU organized blockades within South Africa at several of the border crossings into Swaziland, including Oshoek and Golela. At the Matsamo border post the South African police opened fire with rubber bullets and injured a number of people. Among those arrested was Joel Nkosi, the First Deputy President of COSATU. (Nkosi and the others were eventually acquitted.) In an indication of the tension between COSATU and the SFTU, SFTU leader Jan Sithole had earlier advised Swazi trade unionists not to participate in these blockades. This tension was reportedly related to an ongoing investigation by COSATU, on behalf of the International Confederation of Free Trade Unions, into alleged irregularities in the affairs of the SFTU. COSATU organized a demonstration at the Oshoek border post on 12 April 2011 to coincide with the planned 'April 12 Uprising'.

In recent years an area of conflict, and co-operation, between Swaziland, South Africa and Mozambique has been the use of the water resources of the Komati river. The apparently excessive use of the river for hydroelectric projects and irrigation schemes in South Africa and Swaziland has severely reduced the flow of water into Mozambique and led that country to take a claim for compensation to the ICJ. In 1995 the Swedish Government provided funds, through the Swedish International Development Agency, for the establishment of the Inkomati Shared River Basin Initiative (ISRBI). This resulted in the presentation by the three countries to the Second World Water Security Forum at The Hague in March 2000 of a proposed scheme for fair and equal access to the water of the river. Mozambique's representative on the ISRBI stated that this plan might encourage the country to withdraw its claim for compensation. Mozambique did not, however, become a signatory to the related Nkomati River Basin Accord until 2002. In the following year the Maguga Dam, the water from which was shared by South Africa and Swaziland on a 60:40 basis, was opened. Mozambique subsequently protested against the reduced flow of the river across its border.

Economy

DONALD L. SPARKS

INTRODUCTION

Swaziland, with a land area of only 17,363 sq km, is the second smallest state in mainland Africa and had a population of 1,386,914 in 2012. In 2011 the kingdom's gross domestic product (GDP) per head was US $5,200, placing it among 54 of the world's 'lower-middle-income' group of countries, according to the World Bank. Swaziland scored poorly on the UN Development Programme's 2011 Human Development Index, ranking 140th out of 183 countries. From 1985–94 Swaziland's GDP recorded impressive average annual growth of 7.3%, the region's highest after Botswana. However, the Swazi economy has proven less robust in recent years. Real GDP growth was 2.4% in 2008, 1.2% in 2009 and 2.0% in 2010, while a decline of 0.2% was recorded in 2011. Swaziland is a small, open economy, and recent lower growth has been due chiefly to the worldwide economic downturn. The poor economic performance of its major trade partner, South Africa, has also played a role. The slump in global demand has resulted in the closure of the Sappi Usutu pulp mill, as well as a loss of perhaps 3,000 jobs in the textile industry. Demand has also fallen for Swaziland's only mineral export, coal. Other factors contributing to this slump include drought, problems associated with the HIV/AIDS pandemic (with an adult HIV/AIDS prevalence rate of 25.9% in 2009, Swaziland has the world's highest rate) and competition from Asian textile producers. Bad weather conditions have had a significant negative impact on farming, affecting at least 25% of the population.

Since independence there has been significant diversification of the economy away from agriculture and mining. Industry and services contributed the largest shares of GDP in 2011, with 50.8% and 41.4%, respectively; agriculture and forestry contributed 7.8%. Despite its relative diversification and wealth, Swaziland has not escaped the extremes of income distribution familiar elsewhere in Africa. The bottom 10% of households received only 1.6% of total income and 69% of the population live below the poverty line. More than two-thirds of the resident population comprises families earning generally poor incomes from smallholder cash cropping or subsistence agriculture on Swazi Nation Land (SNL). Moreover, the condition of the rural poor has been largely unimproved by periods of rapid growth since independence. The 2009/10 household survey, completed in early 2011, reported that the incidence of poverty fell from 69% in 2000/01 to 65% in 2009/10, while the number of people classified as poor fell from 697,000 to 641,000 (based on the poverty threshold of US $2 per day). However, poverty levels are higher in rural areas, and the percentage of those living in poverty in Swaziland is three times as high as in many other developing countries with similar levels of per head GDP (in Egypt, for example, only 19% of the population is considered poor). Nevertheless, the share of households which owned a mobile phone increased from 13% in 2000/01 to 84% in 2009/10, and those which owned a television increased from 31% to 43%. In 2007 the Government approved the Poverty Reduction Strategy and Action Programme with an ambitious goal of reducing poverty by one-half by 2015 and eliminating poverty by 2022. The programme was based upon six foundations: macroeconomic stability and accelerated economy growth; empowering the poor to generate higher incomes; more equitable distribution of the results of growth via fiscal policies; strengthening human capital; improving the poor's quality of life; and improving governance.

The problem of unemployment is serious and growing, especially among young people: 54% of the jobless are under 25 years of age and a further 29% are aged between 25 and 34. The official unemployment rate was 43% in 2011, although the level of disguised or discouraged workers would suggest that the unofficial rate is higher. Large numbers are not registered as unemployed, or do not actively seek work as they believe that the prospect of finding work is so bleak, and are thus not counted in official figures.

Swaziland's development has been dominated in many ways by its neighbour, South Africa, the principal regional economic power. For example, Swaziland receives some 90% of its imports from and sells 60% of its exports to South Africa. South African capital and imports, the South African Currency Union (SACU), the South African labour market and the Common Monetary Area (CMA) have shaped the economy and restricted the scope for an independent economic policy. However, a consistent determination to maintain an investment climate attractive to foreign business and a policy of accepting the dominance of its powerful neighbour brought Swaziland a rate of post-independence capital formation not achieved in most African states. In the late 1980s the kingdom benefited as foreign and South African companies relocated to Swaziland, often to escape anti-apartheid sanctions. In the early 1990s, however, Swaziland experienced the negative repercussions of political uncertainty and economic recession in South Africa. Also, since the mid-1990s, many firms that might have chosen to locate, or relocate, in Swaziland have opted for South Africa, given the political uncertainty and lack of skilled manpower in Swaziland. Swaziland traditionally supplied the South African mines with labour, and those miners' remittances back to Swaziland provided a substantial income base. However, in recent years the number of Swazi miners has declined substantially, along with their remittances. This has been partially balanced by an increasing number of Swazi professionals moving to South Africa and the United Kingdom.

AGRICULTURE AND FORESTRY

Although the agricultural sector (including forestry) accounts for a declining share of GDP (7.8% in 2011, compared with 14.3% in 2004), it remains the backbone of the economy. Agro-industry continues to contribute the majority of manufacturing value added; it provides 70% of employment. Over one-half of the total land area is SNL, where traditional subsistence farming is conducted on land held by the monarchy, access to which is managed by the Swazi aristocracy and local chiefs. However, more than one-half of all SNL is designated as Rural Development Areas, and cash cropping of rain-watered crops, particularly maize and cotton, contributes significantly to total agricultural production when climatic conditions are favourable. The remainder of the land, the Title Deed Land, comprises individual tenure farms, owned by commercial companies, wealthy Swazis and white settlers. The principal agricultural commodities are sugar (of which Swaziland has traditionally been continental Africa's second largest exporter), maize, citrus fruits, pineapples (for canning) and cotton. Livestock-rearing is an important sub-sector of the economy, particularly on SNL, where cattle serve as a store of value, a unit of account, and are used for various cultural purposes (for example, bride price).

Sugar is the dominant agricultural commodity, and Swaziland is the third largest producer in sub-Saharan Africa. According to the Swaziland Sugar Association, it accounts for 60% of agricultural output; 35% of agricultural wage employment; 7% of total exports earnings; 10% of formal sector employment; and 58% of total Swazi exports to the European Union (EU). As the EU moves into sugar production deficit as a result of reduced subsidies, Swaziland can expect to increase its exports to the bloc. The industry consists of four components: miller planters and estates (77%); large growers (17%); medium-sized growers (5%); and small growers (1%). Swaziland is vulnerable to world fluctuations in price: for example, the world price at mid-2007 was actually lower than Swazi production costs (including transportation costs and a stronger rand). Brazilian sugar has also become competitive in the SACU market, causing both South Africa and Swaziland to reduce their prices by 7% in late 2003. Output in 2009/10 was 605,657 metric tons, declining to 582,019 tons in 2010/11. The Swaziland Sugar Association estimated total sugar output of some 650,000 tons in 2011/12, with an expected increase of 150,000 tons within the next five years. There are three sugar mills in the country (Simunye, Mhlume and Umbombo mills), in which the Swazi Nation has substantial shareholdings.

Recent cereal harvests have failed to meet domestic requirements. Maize production has been declining for the past decade, owing to erratic weather conditions, high fuel and other input costs, the decline in advanced agricultural practices and the impact of HIV/AIDS. The UN's World Food Programme estimated that output increased by some 12% in the 2010/11 growing season, to 84,670 tons, due to improved rainfall. None the less, it was forecast that around 220,000 people, about one-fifth of the population, would experience food shortages in 2012.

Supported by the role of cattle as a store of wealth in customary society, the national herd represents a significant environmental problem in terms of the overgrazing of SNL. Frozen and canned meat is exported to the EU under quota.

In 1998 Swaziland had some 98,000 ha of planted forest, representing 6% of the country's total land area. Of the total, more than one-half was devoted to supplying the kingdom's main forestry industry, the Sappi Usutu pulp mill, which produced unbleached wood pulp. The mill, which closed in early 2010, was Swaziland's third largest source of export earnings. The mill's closure (with a loss of 600 jobs) was a result of major forest fires in the area in 2008 and subsequently reduced world-wide demand. In 2004 the People's Republic of China became Swaziland's primary destination for wood pulp exports, surpassing South Africa, Japan, the USA and Europe for the first time.

MINING, MANUFACTURING AND TOURISM

Mining and quarrying have represented a declining proportion of GDP overall since independence, although the kingdom is relatively rich in mineral resources. From 10% in the 1960s, the sector's contribution to GDP fell to a negligible amount by 2010. The sector's poor performance was due to reduced output at the Maloma colliery, to the phasing out of the diamond mine, which closed at the end of 1996, and to the cessation of asbestos mining in 2001. Asbestos was the first mineral product to be exploited in the country on a large scale. The Havelock mine was developed in the 1930s, and it was not until 1962 that it was overtaken by the sugar industry as the territory's leading export earner. Since then, however, the identification of health problems associated with asbestos and the depletion of reserves have resulted in the decline of this sub-sector. The mining sector was expected to receive a boost in 2011/12 with the reopening of the iron ore mine at Ngwenya.

Coal holds the country's most important mineral potential, with reserves estimated at 1,000m. metric tons. Coal production was estimated to have reached a record 550,000 tons in 2004, although that number has been in decline subsequently, with output estimated at 350,000 tons in 2008 and 2009.

Since the late 1980s there has been encouraging diversification of the manufacturing sector, and Swaziland now ranks among some of the most industrialized African economies. Several smaller factories producing knitwear, footwear, gloves, refrigerators, office equipment, beverages, confectionery, pine furniture, safety glass and bricks were established during the investment boom of the 1990s, creating many new jobs.

Swaziland's textile industry has seen significant changes during the past decade. Swaziland was granted provisions by the USA's African Growth and Opportunity Act (AGOA) in 2001, which benefited the local textile industry; under the terms of the Act, Swaziland enjoyed unrestricted access to the US market for the export of textiles and clothes, without having to pay tariffs. Indeed, the garment industry grew rapidly. In 2006 and 2007 Swaziland exported textiles to the USA worth approximately US $135m. Owing to depressed demand in the USA, exports under AGOA between January and October 2009 fell by $16.5m., equivalent to almost 20%. However, Swaziland is a relatively high-cost producer. The average wage in the textile industry is about $200 per month, compared with about $40 per month in southern and eastern Asia, the major competitors. In addition, the World Trade Organization (WTO) agreement on textiles and clothing expired at the end of 2004, and import quotas from other major producers (principally China and Bangladesh) were reduced. Two textile firms (GMS Textiles and First Garments) left Swaziland in 2003. In 2004 and 2005 14 textile factories closed, and the Swaziland Textile Exporters' Association (STEA) estimated that the industry had lost some 15,000 of the 30,000 people employed in the industry. Two major unions signed new contracts, which included wage freezes for the first half of 2005. Natex, one of Swaziland's largest employers and its leading textile producer, which was threatened with closure because of low demand in South Africa and competition from Asia, was bought by Tatex Investment Swaziland of Taiwan in 2002, which invested E180m. in the company.

Swaziland is blessed with an abundance of natural beauty and a fairly well-developed tourism infrastructure (by regional standards). Facilities in the central Ezulwini valley (the heart of the Swazi tourism industry) are dominated by the South African Sun International chain. However, Sun International is disposing of its share and management interest in Swaziland's major hotel group, Swazi Spa. As a result of competition from other casinos nearby, and the global economic downturn, the company's earnings have declined in recent years. In 2007 870,000 tourists visited Swaziland, up from 839,000 in 2005. In 2009 a record 1.3m. visitors came to Swaziland, and, with South Africa successfully hosting the Fédération Internationale de Football Association World Cup in mid-2010, the numbers for 2010 were expected to be even higher. Tourism's contribution to GDP was forecast to rise from 4.3% in 2010 to 4.7% by 2020, with the industry projected to employ 5% of the total work-force by that year.

POWER, TRANSPORT AND COMMUNICATIONS

The country has a comparatively well-developed and well-maintained physical infrastructure, but the Swaziland Electricity Board still imports approximately 70% of its needs (770m. kWh) from South Africa, and the proportion has risen steadily during the recent period of historically low rainfall. However, South Africa's Electricity Supply Commission imposed a load-shedding schedule on Swaziland, which resulted in power cuts early in 2008. In 2012 Swaziland signed an agreement with Equatorial Guinea for a guaranteed supply of crude petroleum at preferred rates. Swaziland consumes some 20m. litres of petrol and diesel each month, almost of all of which is imported from South Africa. After much public discourse, the Government admitted that it had no plans to establish a refinery and that all of the Equato-Guinean crude would be refined in South Africa.

The kingdom's first railway line was built during 1962–64 to connect the Ngwenya iron ore mine in the far west of the country, via the then railhead across the eastern border at Goma, Mozambique, to the port of Maputo and so to its Japanese customers. Long disused west of the Matsapha industrial estate, the line was finally taken up in 1995. A southern link via Lavumisa and connecting to the South African port of Richards Bay was completed in 1978, while a northern link, crossing the border near Mananga and running to the South African town of Komatipoort, was opened in 1986. These lines established a direct link between the eastern Transvaal and the Natal ports, integrating the Swazi lines into the South African network. In 1995 the northern link carried 3.3m. metric tons of transit traffic, which represented 78% of all tonnages hauled by the Swaziland Railway Board. Swaziland is studying the feasibility of linking its rail network to Mpumalanga province in South Africa. This route could compete with existing lines between South Africa and Mozambique, and add alternatives to Durban, South Africa. Swaziland had 301 km of rail lines in 2011. In 1993 Swaziland established an inland container depot, which saw rapid growth (ranging from 10% to 20% annually). The inland port receives imports and moves exports that are transported by rail from Durban.

The kingdom's road network is comparatively well developed. There are an estimated 3,594 km of roads, of which 1,078 km are paved. Road projects have dominated the capital expenditure programmes of recent development plans, and in 1991 work began on the rebuilding of the kingdom's main road artery connecting the capital, Mbabane, to Manzini, via Matsapha. The highway was completed in 1999, behind schedule and well over budget. The Ministry of Public Works and Transport has recently suggested introducing toll roads (as in South Africa) and establishing a roads authority.

By 2006 Swaziland had 25 telephone subscribers per 100 people (compared with the regional average of 19.4), of which there were 22 mobile phone subscribers per 100 people (compared with the regional average of 17.5). The fastest growing service has been the mobile cellular telephone operator MTN Swaziland. MTN began six new transmission facilities at a cost of E32m. in 1999 and increased its coverage from 40% to 65% of the country. By the end of 2002 the number of mobile telephone subscribers exceeded the number of fixed-line telephones. Indeed, by 2010 there were 44,000 land lines in use, compared with 732,700 mobile users. In 2010 there were 90,100 internet users and 2,706 hosts.

TRADE AND BALANCE OF PAYMENTS

The national currency is the lilangeni (plural: emalangeni—E), introduced in 1974. The terms of the Trilateral Monetary Agreement, signed with South Africa and Lesotho to form the CMA in 1986, allowed the Swazi authorities the option of determining the lilangeni's exchange rate independently. Under the amended Multilateral Monetary Agreement (signed in early 1992 to formalize Namibia's de facto membership), this freedom was maintained, but the currency has remained pegged at par to the South African rand. It is generally agreed that this system has served Swaziland well. By June 2006 the exchange rate was US $1 = E6.6, unchanged since the year before, although it depreciated to US $1 = E8.33 in May 2012. SACU (which celebrated its 100th anniversary in 2010) was renegotiated in 2002 and the new agreement guaranteed a duty rate of 17% between Namibia, Botswana, Lesotho and Swaziland (NBLS), reducing the yearly fluctuations of the past. In addition, each SACU member will now receive customs revenues based on its relative share of SACU GDP, of which

Swaziland has 0.9%. None the less, receipts from SACU have played an even more important role since 2007. By 2005 those revenues comprised 62% of the budget, up from 54% in 2004. Customs revenues expanded by 57% in 2006, and equalled a record 27.5% of GDP by 2007 (up from 9% in the previous year). By 2009 SACU receipts amounted to 55.8% of Swaziland's total fiscal revenue. However, revenue from SACU fell by 50% in the 2010/11 fiscal year; the decline was attributed to slackened demand (and thus reduced trade) and a fall in the common external tariff regime from 11.4% in 2008 to 8.1% in 2009. As these rates are higher than WTO averages, further reductions were likely in the near term. Swaziland has called for a review of the revenue distribution formula, and Botswana and South Africa were reportedly also in favour of this move. In early 2011 SACU released a draft report proposing further changes to the revenue distribution formula, one that will favour South Africa even more. If approved, it will be the fifth amendment to the initial agreement of 1910. Swaziland's share of total revenue would contract (over an eight-year adjustment period) from 9.3% in 2012/13 to 3.2% in 2019/20. All the NBLS countries have criticized the recommendations. However, in 2012 Swaziland was awarded an additional E1,000m. as compensation for underpayment during the previous year, boosting government revenue by 68%.

Swaziland has recommitted to negotiating a complete Economic Partnership Agreement with the EU, and signed an interim agreement in late 2007. While the agreement could result in improved access to EU markets, the potential negative effect for Swaziland is increased domestic competition from European imports.

In 2011 the country's exports amounted to US $2,049m., with imports of $2,076m., resulting in a visible trade deficit of $27m. In 2008 the principal source of imports was South Africa (91.8%), which was also the principal market for exports (64.7%); the USA, Kenya and the United Kingdom were also important markets. The principal imports in 2007 were machinery and transport equipment, food and live animals, basic manufactures and mineral fuels and lubricants; the principal exports in 2007 were chemicals and chemical products, and food and live animals. The current account recorded a surplus of $86.4m. in 2005 and of $98.1m. in 2006, but by 2008 the current account recorded a deficit of $232m., increasing to a deficit of $415m. in 2009 and $605m. in 2010.

Besides being a member of SACU, Swaziland is a member of the Southern African Development Community (SADC) and the Common Market for Eastern and Southern Africa (COMESA), but has not elected to join COMESA's free trade area, in common with other CMA members. However, in 2008 SACU members gave Swaziland permission to negotiate with COMESA on a range of issues. The Swaziland Stock Exchange was established in July 1999. It had a capitalization of US $146m. in 2002, and increased the minimum amount of capital requirements for listed companies from E1m. to E5m. in 2003. This requirement is similar to those of other SADC members and was implemented to harmonize regional stock exchange regulations.

PUBLIC FINANCE, DEBT, INFLATION, FOREIGN AID AND INVESTMENT

The budget for fiscal year 2009/10 projected a deficit equivalent to 8% of GDP. In 2010 the Minister of Finance, Majozi Sithole, requested that all government departments reduce their budget applications by 14%. While the decision was taken not to raise income taxes, the levy on casinos was raised from 4.5% to 15%. Tobacco and alcohol taxes were also increased in line with the SADC average. Largely owing to the reduced revenues from SACU and slower GDP growth, in 2010 the Government recorded a deficit of $417,300m. (from revenues of $961,700m. and expenditure of $1,379,000m.). In an effort to reduce the deficit, the Government has launched the Fiscal Adjustment Roadmap (FAR), which aims to reduce spending, improve revenue collection and introduce reforms to boost investment. The FAR could result in public sector job losses of 20% by 2014. If the private sector is not able to absorb these workers (as seems likely to be the case), there could be an exodus of skilled workers to South Africa. Total government revenues in 2011/12 amounted to E7,266m., of which E2,883m. were from SACU receipts. Revenues of E12,230m., including E7,065m. from SACU (see above), were projected for 2012/13.

In 2011 Swaziland had an external debt of US $610.5m., up from $497m. in 2010. Net official development assistance increased from $13m. in 2000 to $63m. in 2007, $69m. in 2008 and $58m. in 2009. In early 2012 South Africa agreed to loan Swaziland $355m., but the loan has not materialized due to the economic and political conditions attached to it. These conditions, which were opposed by the ruling élite, included confidence-building measures on governance, democracy and human rights. Swaziland's inflation rate moves almost in tandem with South Africa (which is the country's major supplier of imports, see above). Inflation peaked at 14.7% in August 2008, and had declined to 4.1% in January 2010, standing at 4.5% for 2010 as a whole. However, significant increases in electricity and water tariffs in 2010 (with further sizeable increases expected in 2011–12), together with a weaker rand and higher oil and food prices, resulted in inflation rising to 6.1% in 2011.

All CMA members keep their interest rates roughly aligned, and the prime lending rate of commercial banks in South Africa and Swaziland was 12.5% in June 2007. The South African Reserve Bank reduced its repurchase rate from 11.5% to 10% in late 2008. The Central Bank of Swaziland followed South Africa's changes. In 2010 the rate was 6.5%. Swaziland's official reserves stood at US $559m. in 2009, $708m. in 2010 and $603m. in 2011.

Net foreign direct investment (FDI) has been erratic in recent years. In 1998 Swaziland attracted a record sum of US $130m. in FDI, which fell to $43m. by 2003, before increasing to $121m. in 2006 and declining again to $37m. in 2007. FDI recovered to $105.8m. in 2008, but declined to $66.0m. in 2009, before increasing to $135.6m. in 2010.

ECONOMIC PROSPECTS

Swaziland faces serious challenges in the near term. It is now ranked as the country with the world's highest percentage of its population infected with HIV/AIDS. Nearly 70% of the population lives below the official poverty line. The Heritage Foundation's 2012 Index of Economic Freedom ranked Swaziland 106th out of 184 countries, placing it in the 'mostly unfree category'. The World Bank's *Ease of Doing Business* index ranked Swaziland 124th out of 183 countries in 2012, owing in large part to the country's poor legal system and obtrusive bureaucracy. Its political system—the sole absolute monarchy remaining in sub-Saharan Africa—is almost at breaking point. Labour productivity is low, unemployment is estimated at a minimum of 43%, labour relations are particularly strained and there is general political instability. Indeed, in March 2011 some 7,000 demonstrators took to the street to protest against planned reductions in public sector jobs and to demand real political and economic reform. The leading political organization, the People's United Democratic Movement, has called for the international community to isolate and ostracize the King. In addition, the country is vulnerable to several internal and external shocks, including the weather, the erosion of trade preferences, an economy that is still not sufficiently diversified or developed, a weak financial sector, and reductions in the SACU revenue stream.

Many had hoped that the King's Millennium Projects, including US $26m. budgeted in 2005 for the airport in the east of the country (the location of which is controversial owing to its lack of proximity to any population centre), and a new conference centre, would stimulate the construction industry in particular and the economy in general. In the event, the IMF and others in the international community expressed concern about these projects, as well as the King's spending excesses (see Recent History).

Despite these significant downsides, there are some areas of optimism. Owing to its strict exchange controls and because of its weak integration into world capital markets, Swaziland escaped the most direct effects of the global financial crisis. Swaziland ranked relatively well under Transparency International's *Corruption Perception Index* of 2012 (95th out of 182 nations), although this was down from 79th in 2009. However, the IMF forecast that real GDP would contract by 2.0% in 2012 following negligible growth of 0.3% in 2011.

Swaziland's economy has undergone many changes during recent years. The most important has been in its relationship with its economically powerful neighbour, South Africa, with which Swaziland's economic future is in many ways linked. None the less, there are a number of social, political and economic areas in which Swaziland will have to make changes independently of that relationship. Most importantly, Swaziland will have to find ways of accommodating a strong and growing desire for political reform in order to establish the domestic and international confidence needed for long-term economic growth and poverty reduction.

Statistical Survey

Source (unless otherwise stated): Central Statistical Office, POB 456, Mbabane; internet www.gov.sz/home.asp?pid=75.

Area and Population

AREA, POPULATION AND DENSITY

Area (sq km)	17,363*
Population (census results)†	
11–12 May 1997	929,718
11 May 2007 (provisional)‡§	
Males	460,498
Females	493,026
Total	953,524
Population (UN estimate at mid-year)‖	
2010	1,186,056
2011	1,203,331
2012	1,220,406
Density (per sq km) at mid-2012	70.3

* 6,704 sq miles.
† Excluding absentee workers.
‡ Source: UN, *Population and Vital Statistics Report*.
§ Population data are *de jure*, although the totals were the subject of some dispute on publication; in early 2009 the Ministry of Economic Planning and Development published the State of Swaziland Population Report, which contained a revised population estimate of 1,018,449 for 2007.
‖ Source: UN, *World Population Prospects: The 2010 Revision*.

POPULATION BY AGE AND SEX
(UN estimates at mid-2012)

	Males	Females	Total
0–14	230,111	226,903	457,014
15–64	353,103	368,059	721,162
65 and over	18,001	24,229	42,230
Total	601,215	619,191	1,220,406

Source: UN, *World Population Prospects: The 2010 Revision*.

ETHNIC GROUPS
(census of August 1986)

Swazi	661,646
Other Africans	14,468
European	1,825
Asiatic	228
Other non-Africans	412
Mixed	2,403
Unknown	77
Total	681,059

REGIONS
(population at census of May 2007, provisional figures)

	Area (sq km)	Population	Density (per sq km)
Hhohho	3,569	263,761	73.9
Manzini	5,945	293,260	49.3
Shiselweni	4,070	202,686	49.8
Lebombo	3,779	193,817	51.3
Total	17,363	953,524	54.9

Source: UN, *2010 World Population and Housing Census Programme*.

PRINCIPAL TOWNS
(population at census of May 1997)

Mbabane (capital)	57,992	Manzini	25,571

Mid-2009 (incl. suburbs, UN estimate): Mbabane 73,815 (Source: UN, *World Urbanization Prospects: The 2009 Revision*).

BIRTHS AND DEATHS
(annual averages, UN estimates)

	1995–2000	2000–05	2005–10
Birth rate (per 1,000)	34.1	31.8	30.1
Death rate (per 1,000)	11.9	15.7	14.9

Source: UN, *World Population Prospects: The 2010 Revision*.

Life expectancy (years at birth): 48.3 (males 48.8; females 47.9) in 2010 (Source: World Bank, World Development Indicators database).

EMPLOYMENT
(persons in paid employment at June)

	2003	2004	2005
Agriculture, hunting, forestry and fishing	21,491	20,804	19,955
Mining and quarrying	1,153	1,407	1,283
Manufacturing	19,485	19,874	20,272
Electricity, gas and water	1,418	1,389	859
Construction	4,824	5,293	5,115
Distribution	9,021	9,988	11,454
Transportation	2,491	2,265	3,007
Finance	6,422	5,202	6,430
Social services	26,758	27,247	27,228
Total employed	93,063	93,469	95,603

Source: IMF, *Kingdom of Swaziland: Selected Issues and Statistical Appendix* (March 2008).

Mid-2012 (estimates in '000): Agriculture, etc. 137; Total labour force 497 (Source: FAO).

Health and Welfare

KEY INDICATORS

Total fertility rate (children per woman, 2010)	3.4
Under-5 mortality rate (per 1,000 live births, 2010)	78
HIV/AIDS (% of persons aged 15–49, 2009)	25.9
Physicians (per 1,000 head, 2004)	0.16
Hospital beds (per 1,000 head, 2006)	2.1
Health expenditure (2009): US $ per head (PPP)	336
Health expenditure (2009): % of GDP	6.7
Health expenditure (2009): public (% of total)	66.5
Access to water (% of persons, 2010)	71
Access to sanitation (% of persons, 2010)	57
Total carbon dioxide emissions ('000 metric tons, 2008)	1,092.8
Carbon dioxide emissions per head (metric tons, 2008)	1.1
Human Development Index (2011): ranking	140
Human Development Index (2011): value	0.522

For sources and definitions, see explanatory note on p. vi.

Agriculture

PRINCIPAL CROPS
('000 metric tons, FAO estimates)

	2008	2009	2010
Maize	64.0	60.8	68.0
Potatoes	6.8	7.1	7.2
Sweet potatoes	2.4	2.5	2.6
Sugar cane	5,000	5,000	5,000
Groundnuts, with shell	3.5	3.7	3.7
Tomatoes	4.1	4.4	4.8
Oranges	41.1	42.0	42.5
Grapefruit and pomelos	35.0	36.0	37.0
Pineapples	24.0	25.0	26.5

Aggregate production ('000 metric tons, may include official, semi-official or estimated data): Total cereals 64.8 in 2008, 61.6 in 2009, 68.9 in 2010; Total roots and tubers 60.8 in 2008, 63.6 in 2009, 64.8 in 2010; Total vegetables (incl. melons) 11.6 in 2008, 11.9 in 2009, 12.5 in 2010; Total fruits (excl. melons) 114.3 in 2008, 117.3 in 2009, 120.7 in 2010.

Source: FAO.

LIVESTOCK
('000 head, year ending September, FAO estimates)

	2008	2009	2010
Horses	1.5	1.5	1.5
Asses	14.8	14.8	14.8
Cattle	600	610	620
Pigs	45	48	50
Sheep	29	35	35
Goats	278	280	280
Chickens	3,300	3,400	3,500

Source: FAO.

LIVESTOCK PRODUCTS
('000 metric tons, FAO estimates)

	2008	2009	2010
Cattle meat	15.2	15.4	15.9
Goat meat	1.9	1.9	1.9
Pig meat	1.7	1.8	1.9
Chicken meat	5.3	5.3	5.4
Cows' milk	40.7	42.0	42.3

Source: FAO.

Forestry

ROUNDWOOD REMOVALS
('000 cubic metres, excl. bark, FAO estimates)

	2008	2009	2010
Sawlogs, veneer logs and logs for sleepers	260	260	260
Other industrial wood	70	70	70
Fuel wood	1,028	1,045	1,063
Total	1,358	1,375	1,393

Source: FAO.

SAWNWOOD PRODUCTION
('000 cubic metres, incl. railway sleepers, FAO estimates)

	1995	1996	1997
Total (all coniferous)	90	100	102

1998–2010: Production assumed to be unchanged from 1997 (FAO estimates).

Source: FAO.

Fishing

(metric tons, live weight)

	1999	2000*	2001*
Capture	70*	70	70
Aquaculture	61	69	72
Common carp	18	20	20
Mozambique tilapia	20	25	25
Redbreast tilapia	12	13	15
North African catfish	5	6	6
Red claw crayfish	6	5	6
Total catch	131*	139	142

* FAO estimate(s).

2002–08 (metric tons, live weight, FAO estimate): Capture 70.

2009–10 (metric tons, live weight, FAO estimates): Capture 70; Aquaculture 73; Total catch 143.

Source: FAO.

Mining

(metric tons, unless otherwise indicated)

	2008	2009	2010
Coal	174,807	129,647	145,903
Ferrovanadium	500	500	500*
Quarrystone ('000 cu m)	241	202	305

* Estimated production.

Source: US Geological Survey.

Industry

SELECTED PRODUCTS

	2006	2007	2008
Raw sugar ('000 metric tons)	623	631	664
Electrical energy (million kWh)	437	454	440

Source: UN Industrial Commodity Statistics Database.

Wood pulp ('000 metric tons, FAO estimates): 160.7 in 2006; 170.4 in 2007; 142.2 in 2008; 102.0 in 2009; 150.0 in 2010 (Source: FAO).

Finance

CURRENCY AND EXCHANGE RATES

Monetary Units
100 cents = 1 lilangeni (plural: emalangeni).

Sterling, Dollar and Euro Equivalents (31 May 2012)
£1 sterling = 13.228 emalangeni;
US $1 = 8.532 emalangeni;
€1 = 10.582 emalangeni;
100 emalangeni= £7.56 = $11.72 = €9.45.

Average Exchange Rate (emalangeni per US $)
2009 8.474
2010 7.321
2011 7.261

Note: The lilangeni is at par with the South African rand.

BUDGET
(million emalangeni, year ending 31 March)

Revenue*	2005/06	2006/07	2007/08
Tax revenue	5,189.5	7,682.8	7,564.9
Taxes on net income and profits	1,267.4	1,534.3	1,644.4
Companies	472.5	560.9	522.1
Individuals	761.7	892.4	1,058.4
Non-resident dividends and interest	33.3	81.0	63.9
Taxes on property	13.3	10.3	18.1
Taxes on goods, services and international trade	3,894.4	6,102.2	5,886.0
Receipts from Southern African Customs Union	3,101.1	5,321.8	4,989.9
Levies on sugar exports	21.1	33.1	32.1
Hotel and gaming taxes	7.8	9.6	13.5
Sales tax	734.9	620.1	725.0
Licences and other taxes	29.4	27.2	30.3
Other taxes	14.4	36.0	16.4
Other current revenue	137.3	172.0	713.5
Property income	53.4	89.6	596.6
Fees, fines and non-industrial sales	83.9	82.3	116.9
Total	5,326.8	7,854.8	8,278.4

Expenditure†	2005/06	2006/07	2007/08
Current expenditure	4,416.3	4,681.3	5,217.3
Wages and salaries	2,443.0	2,588.7	2,750.2
Other purchases of goods and services	995.8	1,202.8	1,343.0
Interest payments	194.4	163.4	211.3
Domestic	31.6	35.3	84.9
Foreign	162.9	128.1	126.4
Subsidies and other current transfers	783.1	726.4	912.8
Capital expenditure	1,409.7	1,436.6	1,732.7
Health	47.8	48.5	69.8
Education	18.9	42.6	82.2
Agriculture	171.6	321.4	587.7
Transport and communications	387.0	632.3	745.6
Other	784.4	391.9	247.4
Total	5,826.0	6,117.9	6,950.0

* Excluding grants received (million emalangeni): 172.2 in 2005/06; 165.6 in 2006/07; 62.8 in 2007/08.

† Excluding net lending (million emalangeni): –68.3 in 2005/06; –55.2 in 2006/07; 43.0 in 2007/08.

Source: IMF, *Kingdom of Swaziland: Selected Issues and Statistical Appendix* (October 2008).

2009/10 (million emalangeni, year ending 31 March): Total revenue (incl. grants) 9,225; Total expenditure (incl. net lending) 9,225 (Source: IMF, *Kingdom of Swaziland: Staff Report for the 2011 Article IV Consultation*—February 2012).

2010/11 (million emalangeni, year ending 31 March, preliminary): Total revenue (incl. grants) 6,944; Total expenditure (incl. net lending) 8,220 (Source: IMF, *Kingdom of Swaziland: Staff Report for the 2011 Article IV Consultation*—February 2012).

2011/12 (million emalangeni, year ending 31 March, projections): Total revenue (incl. grants) 7,212; Total expenditure (incl. net lending) 8,683 (Source: IMF, *Kingdom of Swaziland: Staff Report for the 2011 Article IV Consultation*—February 2012).

INTERNATIONAL RESERVES
(excl. gold, US $ million at 31 December)

	2009	2010	2011
IMF special drawing rights	69.62	68.39	68.18
Reserve position in IMF	10.29	10.11	10.07
Foreign exchange	878.96	677.85	522.25
Total	958.87	756.35	600.51

Source: IMF, *International Financial Statistics*.

MONEY SUPPLY
(million emalangeni at 31 December)

	2009	2010	2011
Currency outside depository corporations	327.63	349.35	357.01
Transferable deposits	2,009.35	2,189.70	2,524.99
Other deposits	5,376.24	5,783.69	5,896.41
Broad money	7,713.23	8,322.74	8,778.41

Source: IMF, *International Financial Statistics*.

COST OF LIVING
(Consumer Price Index; base: 2000 = 100, unless otherwise indicated)

	2006	2007	2008
Food	194.1	228.3	271.5
Clothing	114.6	113.9	116.0
Housing*	101.3	102.5	113.0
All items (incl. others)	147.3	159.2	179.8

* Base 2005 = 100.

2009 (Consumer Price Index; base: 2000 = 100): All items 193.2.

Source: ILO.

NATIONAL ACCOUNTS
(million emalangeni at current prices)

Expenditure on the Gross Domestic Product

	2009	2010*	2011*
Government final consumption expenditure	3,663	4,021	4,413
Private final consumption expenditure	23,622	24,226	25,140
Gross capital formation	2,757	2,758	2,759
Total domestic expenditure	30,042	31,005	32,312
Exports of goods and services	14,875	15,190	14,875
Less Imports of goods and services	18,129	19,217	19,162
GDP at purchasers' values	26,788	26,978	28,025

Gross Domestic Product by Economic Activity

	2009	2010*	2011*
Agriculture, forestry and fishing	1,588	1,630	1,679
Mining	57	73	80
Manufacturing	8,519	9,371	9,840
Electricity, gas and water	188	269	284
Construction	535	519	503
Wholesale and retail trade; restaurants and hotels	2,107	2,166	2,243
Finance, insurance and real estate	1,275	1,507	1,622
Transport and communications	1,446	1,549	1,671
Public administration and defence	3,263	4,258	4,809
Other services	852	389	438
Sub-total	19,830	21,731	23,169
Indirect taxes	7,389	5,721	5,387
Less Imputed bank service charge	431	474	530
GDP at purchasers' values	26,788	26,978	28,025

* Provisional figures.

Source: African Development Bank.

BALANCE OF PAYMENTS
(US $ million)

	2008	2009	2010
Exports of goods f.o.b.	1,568.6	1,660.1	1,805.4
Imports of goods f.o.b.	–1,578.5	–1,781.3	–1,955.2
Trade balance	–9.9	–121.3	–149.9
Exports of services	224.6	200.0	257.5
Imports of services	–650.7	–562.3	–669.6
Balance on goods and services	–435.9	–483.5	–562.0
Other income received	298.0	290.8	212.5
Other income paid	–303.2	–413.4	–438.6
Balance on goods, services and income	–441.1	–606.2	–788.1
Current transfers received	417.7	404.9	482.6
Current transfers paid	–208.0	–213.8	–83.1
Current balance	–231.4	–415.1	–388.6
Capital account (net)	–8.8	–4.0	14.4
Direct investment abroad	7.9	–7.0	–3.9
Direct investment from abroad	105.7	65.7	135.7
Portfolio investment assets	–75.5	122.8	49.7
Portfolio investment liabilities	43.9	–6.6	4.7
Other investment assets	190.1	249.7	–161.6
Other investment liabilities	176.0	48.4	63.3
Net errors and omissions	12.0	–55.0	55.5
Overall balance	219.9	–1.1	–230.9

Source: IMF, *International Financial Statistics*.

External Trade

PRINCIPAL COMMODITIES
(US$ million)

Imports c.i.f.	2005	2006	2007
Food and live animals	230.1	158.8	222.2
Beverages and tobacco	29.9	20.6	26.1
Crude materials (inedible)	26.9	21.2	25.8
Minerals, fuels and lubricants	194.0	180.4	178.5
Chemicals and chemical products	324.4	158.5	166.8
Basic manufactures	323.7	250.5	243.4
Machinery and transport equipment	308.8	279.9	240.6
Miscellaneous manufactures	180.1	134.3	146.8
Total (incl. others)	1,656.1	1,242.4	1,270.1

Exports f.o.b. (incl. re-exports)	2005	2006	2007
Food and live animals	230.5	366.0	230.2
Beverages and tobacco	10.0	16.4	4.8
Crude materials (inedible)	114.3	134.6	85.2
Minerals, fuels and lubricants	8.4	15.1	14.0
Chemicals and chemical products	598.1	638.8	600.9
Basic manufactures	31.1	36.3	31.8
Machinery and transport equipment	57.6	52.7	44.8
Miscellaneous manufactures	222.6	199.0	99.2
Total (incl. others)	1,277.8	1,462.8	1,113.3

Source: UN, *International Trade Statistics Yearbook*.

Total imports (million emalangeni): 10,624 in 2008; 15,094 in 2009; 14,315 in 2010 (Source: African Development Bank).

Total exports (million emalangeni): 12,959 in 2008; 14,067 in 2009; 13,217 in 2010 (Source: African Development Bank).

PRINCIPAL TRADING PARTNERS
(US $ million)

Imports c.i.f.	2005	2006	2007
China, People's Repub.	65.9	24.6	50.8
Germany	1.2	25.4	0.9
Hong Kong	11.8	19.8	2.2
India	0.4	10.7	16.2
Japan	5.8	26.1	30.1
Mozambique	57.3	11.3	17.0
South Africa	1,339.3	995.2	1,033.2
United Kingdom	32.6	8.5	8.5
USA	11.5	10.1	17.4
Zimbabwe	15.8	13.2	4.9
Total (incl. others)	1,656.1	1,242.4	1,270.1

Exports f.o.b.	2005	2006	2007
Australia	441.5	2.3	2.2
Botswana	6.6	13.1	3.3
Italy	0.1	0.4	153.5
Lesotho	8.0	25.6	1.3
Mozambique	96.6	247.4	20.2
Namibia	8.3	11.5	31.1
New Zealand	0.4	22.9	0.9
South Africa	478.8	446.1	888.5
Uganda	0.0	246.7	0.0
United Kingdom	128.4	4.6	1.3
USA	56.2	48.9	1.1
Zimbabwe	0.6	369.0	0.0
Total (incl. others)	1,277.8	1,462.8	1,113.3

Source: UN, *International Trade Statistics Yearbook*.

Total imports (million emalangeni): 10,624 in 2008; 15,094 in 2009; 14,315 in 2010 (Source: African Development Bank).

Total exports (million emalangeni): 12,959 in 2008; 14,067 in 2009; 13,217 in 2010 (Source: African Development Bank).

Transport

RAILWAYS
(traffic)

	2002	2003	2004
Net total ton-km (million)	728	726	710

Source: UN, *Statistical Yearbook*.

ROAD TRAFFIC
(motor vehicles in use at 31 December 2007)

Passenger cars	52,223
Buses and coaches	8,124
Lorries and vans	41,778
Motorcycles and mopeds	3,482

Source: IRF, *World Road Statistics*.

CIVIL AVIATION
(traffic on scheduled services)

	1998	1999	2000
Kilometres flown (million)	1	1	2
Passengers carried ('000)	41	12	90
Passenger-km (million)	43	13	68
Total ton-km (million)	4	1	6

Source: UN, *Statistical Yearbook*.

Tourism

TOURIST ARRIVALS
(at hotels)

Country of residence	2006	2007	2008
Australia	4,192	2,120	2,197
Mozambique	11,702	8,413	12,177
Portugal	8,188	10,674	n.a.
South Africa	130,783	146,605	147,639
United Kingdom	11,948	11,684	9,300
Total (incl. others)	316,082	299,226	323,538

Total tourist arrivals: 909 in 2009.

Tourism receipts (US $ million, excl. passenger transport): 75 in 2006; 32 in 2007; 36 in 2008; 40 in 2009.

Source: World Tourism Organization.

Communications Media

	2008	2009	2010
Telephones ('000 main lines in use)	45.2	45.2	53.0
Mobile cellular telephones ('000 subscribers)	531.6	664.4	725.8
Internet subscribers ('000)	20.0	22.0	n.a.
Broadband subscribers ('000)	0.8	1.5	1.6

Source: International Telecommunication Union.

Personal computers: 42,000 (36.9 per 1,000 persons) in 2006 (Source: International Telecommunication Union).

Radio receivers (year ending 31 March 1998): 155,000 in use (Source: UN, *Statistical Yearbook*).

Television receivers (2002): 32,000 in use (Source: International Telecommunication Union).

Daily newspapers (2004): 2 (estimated circulation 27,000) (Source: UNESCO Institute for Statistics).

Education

(2009/10 unless otherwise indicated)

	Institutions	Teachers	Students
Pre-primary	n.a.	1,924	20,755
Primary	541*	7,462	241,237
Secondary	182*	4,883	88,787
University†	1‡	462§	5,692§

* Figure for 2001/02.

† Figures exclude vocational, technical and teacher-training colleges. In 2000 there were 1,822 students enrolled at these institutions, which numbered 10 in 2003.

‡ Figure for 2000.

§ Figure for 2005/06.

Source: UNESCO Institute for Statistics.

Pupil-teacher ratio (primary education, UNESCO estimate): 32.3 in 2009/10 (Source: UNESCO Institute for Statistics).

Adult literacy rate (UNESCO estimates): 86.8% (males 88.1%; females 87.4%) in 2010 (Source: UNESCO Institute for Statistics).

Directory

The Constitution

A new Constitution entered into force on 7 February 2006, replacing that of October 1978. It vests supreme executive power in the hereditary King (iNgwenyama—the Lion) and succession is governed by traditional law and custom. In the event of the death of the King, the powers of Head of State are transferred to the constitutional dual monarch, the Queen Mother (Ndlovukazi—Great She Elephant), who is authorized to act as Regent until the designated successor, the Crown Prince (Umntfwana), attains the age of 21.

The Parliament of Swaziland consists of the Senate, comprising not more than 31 members, of whom 20 are appointed by the King—at least eight of these are women—and 10 elected by the House of Assembly, one-half of whom are women, and the House of Assembly, which comprises not more than 76 members. Of these, not more than 60 are directly elected from candidates nominated by traditional local councils, known as Tinkhundla, and not more than 10 are appointed by the King, one-half of whom are women. Additionally, one woman is selected from each of the four regions of Swaziland and the Attorney-General is also an ex officio member.

The King appoints the Prime Minister and the Cabinet and has the power to dissolve the bicameral legislature. The Swazi National Council (Sibaya) constitutes the highest policy and advisory council of the nation and functions as the annual general meeting of the nation. A Council of Chiefs, composed of 12 chiefs drawn from the four regions of Swaziland, advises the King on customary issues and any matter relating to chieftancy.

The Constitution affirms the fundamental human rights and freedoms of the individual.

The Government

HEAD OF STATE

King: HM King MSWATI III (succeeded to the throne 25 April 1986).

COUNCIL OF MINISTERS

(September 2012)

Prime Minister: BARNABAS SIBUSISO DLAMINI.

Deputy Prime Minister: THEMBA MASUKU.

Minister of Economic Planning and Development: Prince HLANGUSEMPHI.

Minister of Finance: MAJOZI SITHOLE.

Minister of Foreign Affairs and International Co-operation: MTITI FAKUDZE.

Minister of Public Works and Transport: NTUTHUKO DLAMINI.

Minister of Health: BENEDICT XABA.

Minister of Commerce, Industry and Trade: JABULILE MASHWAMA.

Minister of Housing and Urban Development: Pastor LINDIWE DLAMINI.

Minister of Education and Training: WILSON M. NTJANGASE.

Minister of Agriculture: CLEMENT DLAMINI.

Minister of Tourism and Environmental Affairs: MDUDUZI DLAMINI.

Minister of Labour and Social Security: LUTFO DLAMINI.

Minister of Natural Resources and Energy: Princess TSANDZILE.

Minister of Sports, Culture and Youth Affairs: HLOBSILE NDLOVU.

Minister of Information, Communication and Technology: WINNIE MAGAGULA.

Minister of Home Affairs: PRINCE GCOKOMA.

Minister of Public Service: PATRICK MAGWEBETANE MAMBA.

Minister of Justice and Constitutional Affairs: Chief MGWAGWA GAMEDZE.

Minister of Tinkhundla Administration and Development: ROGERS MAMBA.

MINISTRIES

Office of the Prime Minister: Cabinet Offices, Hospital Hill, POB 395, Swazi Plaza, Mbabane; tel. 24042251; fax 24043943; internet www.gov.sz.

Office of the Deputy Prime Minister: Gwamile St, POB A33, Swazi Plaza, H101, Mbabane; tel. 24042723; fax 24044073.

Ministry of Agriculture: Hospital Hill, opposite Fire and Emergency Services, POB 162, H100, Mbabane; tel. 24042731; fax 24044730; e-mail ps@agriculture.gov.sz.

Ministry of Commerce, Industry and Trade: Interministerial Bldg, Block 8, 1st Floor, Mhlambanyatsi Rd, POB 451, Mbabane; tel. 24043201; fax 24044711; e-mail mcit@gov.sz.

Ministry of Economic Planning and Development: Finance Bldg, 4th and 5th Floors, Lusutfu Rd, POB 602, Mbabane; tel. 24043765; fax 24042157; e-mail ps@planning.gov.sz.

Ministry of Education and Training: Hospital Rd, POB 39, Mbabane; tel. 24042491; fax 24043880; e-mail ps_education@gov.sz.

Ministry of Finance: Mhlambanyatsi Rd, POB 443, Mbabane; tel. 24048148; fax 24043187; e-mail ps@finance.gov.sz.

Ministry of Foreign Affairs: Interministerial Bldg, Block 8, Level 3, Mhlambanyatsi Rd, POB 518, Mbabane; tel. 24042661; fax 24042669; e-mail psforeignaffairs@realnet.co.sz.

Ministry of Health: POB 5, Mbabane; tel. 24042431; fax 24047420; e-mail infohealth@gov.sz.

Ministry of Home Affairs: Home Affairs and Justice Bldg, 1st Floor, Mhlambanyatsi Usuthu Link Rd, POB 432, Mbabane; tel. 24042941; fax 24044303.

Ministry of Housing and Urban Development: Income Tax Bldg, 5th Floor, Mhlambanyatsi Rd, POB 1832, Mbabane; tel. 24046049; fax 24044085; e-mail ps_housing@gov.sz.

Ministry of Information, Communication and Technology: Interministerial Complex, Block 8, 3rd Floor, Mhlambanyatsi Rd, POB 642, Mbabane; tel. 24045826; fax 24041898; e-mail ps_mict@gov.sz.

Ministry of Justice and Constitutional Affairs: Ministry of Justice Bldg, 5th Floor, cnr Mhlambanyatsi and Usuthu Link Rds, POB 924, Mbabane; tel. 24046010; fax 24043533; e-mail ps@justice.gov.sz.

Ministry of Labour and Social Security: Interministerial Office Block, Mhlambanyatsi Rd, POB 198, Mbabane; tel. 24041971; fax 24041966; e-mail deptlab@realnet.sz.

Ministry of Natural Resources and Energy: Income Tax Bldg, 4th Floor, Mhlambanyatsi Rd, POB 57, Mbabane; tel. 24046244; fax 24044851; e-mail nergyswa@realnet.co.sz.

Ministry of Public Service: Finance Bldg, 2nd and 3rd Floors, Mhlambanyatsi Rd, POB 170, Mbabane; tel. 24043521; fax 24045379; e-mail ps_mops@gov.sz.

Ministry of Public Works and Transport: Mhlambanyatsi Rd, POB 58, Mbabane; tel. 24099000; fax 24042364; e-mail nkanmbulep@gov.sz.

Ministry of Sports, Culture and Youth Affairs: Swazi Bank Bldg, 4th Floor, Gwamile St, POB 4843, Mbabane.

Ministry of Tinkhundla Administration and Development: Post and Telecom Bldg, Ground, 1st and 2nd Floors, Sheffield Rd, POB 2701, Mbabane; tel. 24041244; fax 24041012.

Ministry of Tourism and Environmental Affairs: Income Tax Bldg, 2nd Floor, Mhlambanyatsi Rd, POB 2652, Mbabane; tel. 24046162; fax 24045415; e-mail ps_tourism@gov.sz.

Legislature

SENATE

The Senate comprises not more than 31 members, of whom 20 are appointed by the King—at least eight of these are women—and 10 elected by the House of Assembly, one-half of whom are women.

President: GELANE ZWANE.

HOUSE OF ASSEMBLY

The House of Assembly comprises not more than 76 members. Of these, not more than 60 are directly elected from candidates nominated by traditional local councils, known as Tinkhundla, and not more than 10 are appointed by the King, one-half of whom are women. Additionally, one woman is selected from each of the four regions of Swaziland and the Attorney-General is also an ex officio member. The most recent elections to the House of Assembly took place on 19 September 2008.

Speaker: PRINCE GUDUZA.

Election Commission

Elections and Boundaries Commission: POB 4842, Mbabane; tel. 24162813; fax 24161970; five mems; Chair. Chief GIJA DLAMINI.

Political Organizations

Party political activity was banned by royal proclamation in April 1973, and formally prohibited under the 1978 Constitution. Since 1991, following indications that the Constitution was to be revised, a number of political associations have re-emerged. Following the introduction of the new Constitution in February 2006, the legal status of party political activity remained unclear.

African United Democratic Party (AUDP): f. 2006; advocates full democratization of Swaziland; Pres. STANLEY MAUNDZISA; Sec.-Gen. SIBUSISO DLAMINI.

Imbokodvo National Movement (INM): f. 1964 by King Sobhuza II; traditionalist movement, which also advocates policies of devt and the elimination of illiteracy; Leader (vacant).

Ngwane National Liberatory Congress (NNLC): Ilanga Centre, Martin St, Manzini; tel. 25053935; f. 1962 by fmr mems of the SPP; advocates democratic freedoms and universal suffrage, and seeks abolition of the Tinkhundla electoral system; Pres. OBED DLAMINI; Sec.-Gen. DUMISA DLAMINI.

People's United Democratic Movement (PUDEMO): POB 4588, Manzini; tel. and fax 25054181; internet pudemo.org; f. 1983; seeks constitutional limitation of the powers of the monarchy; affiliated orgs include the Human Rights Asscn of Swaziland and the Swaziland Youth Congress (SWAYOCO—Pres. ALEX LANGWENYA; Sec.-Gen. KENNETH KUNENE); Pres. MARIO BONGANI MASUKU; Sec. SIKHUMBUZO PHAKATHI.

Swaziland National Front (SWANAFRO): Mbabane; Pres. ELMOND SHONGWE; Sec.-Gen. GLENROSE DLAMINI.

Diplomatic Representation

EMBASSIES IN SWAZILAND

Mozambique: Princess Dr., POB 1212, Mbabane; tel. 24041296; fax 24048482; e-mail moz.high@swazi.net; Ambassador TIAGO CATIGO RECIBO.

South Africa: The New Mall, 2nd Floor, Dr Sishayi Rd, POB 2507, Mbabane; tel. 24044651; fax 24044335; e-mail sahc@africaonline.co.sz; High Commissioner Dr R. J. M. MAMPANE.

Taiwan (Republic of China): Makhosikhosi St, Mbabane; tel. 24044739; fax 24046688; e-mail rocembassy@africaonline.co.sz; Ambassador TSAI MING-YAW.

USA: Central Bank Bldg, 7th Floor, Mahlokohla St, Mbabane Pl., POB 199, Mbabane; tel. 24046441; fax 24045959; e-mail USEmbassyMbabane@state.gov; internet swaziland.usembassy.gov; Ambassador MAKILA JAMES.

Judicial System

Following the introduction of the new Constitution, the Swaziland Superior Court of Judicature comprised the Supreme Court and the High Court, which replaced the existing Court of Appeal and the High Court. The Supreme Court is headed by the Chief Justice and consists of not fewer than four other Justices of the Supreme Court, and is the final Court of Appeal. The High Court consists of the Chief Justice and not fewer than four Justices of the High Court, and has unlimited original jurisdiction in civil and criminal matters.

Chief Justice of the High Court: MICHAEL MATHEALIRA RAMOLIBELI.

Religion

About 60% of the adult Swazi population profess Christianity. Under the new Constitution, which came into effect on 7 February 2006, Christianity ceased to be recognized as the country's official religion. There was a growing Muslim population, reported to number some 10,000 adherents. Most of the remainder of the population hold traditional beliefs.

CHRISTIANITY

At mid-2000 there were an estimated 153,000 Protestants and 466,000 adherents professing other forms of Christianity.

Council of Swaziland Churches: Mandlenkosi Ecumenical House, 142 Esser St, Manzini; POB 1095, Manzini; tel. 25053697; fax 25055841; e-mail c.o.c@africaonline.co.sz; f. 1976; Chair. Bishop MESHACK MABUZA; Gen. Sec. KHANGEZILE I. DLAMINI; 9 mem. churches incl. Roman Catholic, Anglican, Kukhany'okusha Zion Church and Lutheran.

League of African Churches: POB 230, Lobamba; asscn of 48 independent churches; Chair. SAMSON HLATJWAKO.

Swaziland Conference of Churches: 175 Ngwane St, POB 1157, Manzini; tel. and fax 25055253; e-mail scc@africaonline.co.sz; internet www.swazilandcc.org; f. 1929; Pres. Rev. JOHANNES V. MAZIBUKO; Gen. Sec. Rev. S. F. DLAMINI.

The Anglican Communion

Swaziland comprises a single diocese within the Church of the Province of Southern Africa. The Metropolitan of the Province is the Archbishop of Cape Town, South Africa. The Church had some 40,000 members at mid-2000.

Bishop of Swaziland: Rt Rev. MESHACK BOY MABUZA, Bishop's House, Muir St, POB 118, Mbabane; tel. 24043624; fax 24046759; e-mail anglicanchurch@africaonline.co.sz.

The Roman Catholic Church

The Roman Catholic Church was established in Swaziland in 1913. For ecclesiastical purposes, Swaziland comprises the single diocese of Manzini, suffragan to the archdiocese of Pretoria, South Africa. Some 6% of the total population are adherents of the Roman Catholic Church. The Bishop participates in the Southern African Catholic Bishops' Conference (based in Pretoria, South Africa).

Bishop of Manzini: Rt Rev. LOUIS NCAMISO NDLOVU, Bishop's House, Sandlane St, POB 19, Manzini; tel. 25056900; fax 25056762; e-mail bishop@africaonline.co.sz.

Other Christian Churches

Church of the Nazarene: POB 832, Manzini; tel. 25054732; f. 1910; 7,649 adherents (1994).

The Evangelical Lutheran Church in Southern Africa: POB 117, Mbabane; tel. 24043411; fax 24041847; f. 1902; Bishop JEREMIAH BHEKI MAGAGULA; 2,800 adherents in Swaziland (1994).

Mennonite Central Committee: POB 329, Mbabane; tel. 24042805; fax 24044732; f. 1971; Co-ordinator HLOB'SILE NXUMALO.

The Methodist Church in Southern Africa: POB 42, Mbabane; tel. 26321975; e-mail brianj@bcmc.co.za; internet www.methodist.org.za; f. 1880; Bishop BRIAN C. JENNINGS; 2,578 adherents (1992).

United Christian Church of Africa: POB 1345, Nhlangano; tel. 22022648; f. 1944; Pres. Rev. WELLINGTON B. MKHALIPHI; Founder and Gen. Sec. Dr J. J. NQUKU.

The National Baptist Church, the Christian Apostolic Holy Spirit Church in Zion and the Religious Society of Friends (Quakers) are also active.

BAHÁ'Í FAITH

National Spiritual Assembly: POB 298, Mbabane; tel. 25052689; f. 1960; mems resident in 153 localities.

ISLAM

Ezulwini Islamic Institute: Al Islam Dawah Movement of Swaziland, POB 133, Ezulwini.

The Press

PRINCIPAL NEWSPAPERS

The Swazi News: Sheffield Rd, POB 156, Mbabane; tel. 24041550; fax 24042438; e-mail swazinews@times.co.sz; internet www.times.co.sz; f. 1983; weekly; English; owned by *The Times of Swaziland*; Editor PHEPHISA KHOZA; circ. 28,000.

Swazi Observer: Observer House, 3 West St, POB A385, Swazi Plaza, Mbabane; tel. 24049600; fax 24045503; e-mail info@observer.org.sz; internet www.observer.org.sz; f. 1981; owned by Tibiyo Taka Ngwane; Mon.–Sat.; *Weekend Observer* (Sun.); CEO S. MYZO MAGAGULA; Editor-in-Chief (vacant).

The Times of Swaziland: Sheffield Rd, POB 156, Mbabane; tel. 24042211; fax 24042438; e-mail editor@times.co.sz; internet www.times.co.sz; f. 1897; Mon.–Fri., Sun.; also monthly edn; English; other publs incl. *What's Happening* (tourist interest); Man. Editor MBOGANI MBINGO; circ. 18,000.

PRINCIPAL PERIODICALS

The Nation: Mbabane House, 3rd Floor, Mahlokohla St, POB 4547, Mbabane; tel. and fax 24046611; e-mail thenation@realnet.co.sz; f. 1997; monthly; independent news magazine; Editor BHEKI MAKHUBU.

Swaziview: Mbabane; tel. 24042716; monthly magazine; general interest; circ. 3,500.

UNISWA Research Journal of Agriculture, Science and Technology: Private Bag 4, Kwaluseni; tel. 25274418; fax 25274428; e-mail research@uniswa.sz; internet www.uniswa.sz; 2 a year; publ. of the Faculties of Agriculture, Health Sciences and Science of the Univ. of Swaziland; Chair. Prof. E. M. OSSOM.

Publishers

GBS Printing and Publishing (Pty) Ltd: POB 1384, Mbabane; tel. 25052779.

Longman Swaziland (Pty) Ltd: POB 2207, Manzini; tel. 25053891.

Macmillan Boleswa Publishers (Pty) Ltd: POB 1235, Manzini; tel. 25184533; fax 25185247; e-mail macmillan@africaonline.co.sz; f. 1978; textbooks and general; CEO DUSANKA STOJAKOVIC.

Swaziland Printing & Publishing Co Ltd: POB 28, Mbabane; tel. 24042716; fax 24042710.

Whydah Media Publishers Ltd: Mbabane; tel. 24042716; f. 1978.

Broadcasting and Communications

TELECOMMUNICATIONS

MTN Swaziland: Karl Grant St, POB 5050, H100 Mbabane; tel. 24060000; fax 24046215; e-mail feedback@mtn.co.sz; internet www.mtn.co.sz; f. 1998; jt venture between MTN Group, South Africa, and Swaziland Posts and Telecommunications Corpn; operates mobile cellular telephone network; 213,000 subscribers (2005); Chair. DAVID DLAMINI; CEO AMBROSE DLAMINI.

Swaziland Posts and Telecommunications Corpn (SPTC): Phutfumani Bldg, Mahlokohla St, POB 125, H100 Mbabane; tel. 24052000; fax 24052001; e-mail info@sptc.co.sz; internet www.sptc.co.sz; f. 1983; Acting Man. Dir AMON DLAMINI.

BROADCASTING

Radio

Swaziland Broadcasting and Information Service (SBIS): POB 338, Mbabane; tel. 24042763; fax 24046953; e-mail sbisnews@africaonline.co.sz; f. 1966; broadcasts in English and siSwati; Dir BHEKI GAMA (acting).

Swaziland Commercial Radio (Pty) Ltd: POB 1586, Alberton 1450, South Africa; tel. (11) 24344333; fax (11) 24344777; privately owned commercial service; broadcasts to Southern Africa in English and Portuguese; music and religious programmes; Man. Dir A. DE ANDRADE.

Trans World Radio: POB 64, Manzini; tel. 25052781; fax 25055333; internet www.twr.org; f. 1974; religious broadcasts from five transmitters in 30 languages to Southern, Central and Eastern Africa and to the Far East.

Television

Swaziland Television Authority (Swazi TV): Hospital Hill, POB A146, Swazi Plaza, Mbabane; tel. 24043036; fax 24042093; e-mail info@swazitv.co.sz; internet www.swazitv.co.sz; f. 1978; state-owned; broadcasts seven hours daily in English; CEO BONGANI AUSTIN DLAMINI.

Finance

(cap. = capital; res = reserves; dep. = deposits; m. = million; brs = branches; amounts in emalangeni)

BANKING

In 2010 there were four commercial banks in Swaziland.

Central Bank

Central Bank of Swaziland: POB 546, Mahlokohla St, Mbabane; tel. 24082000; fax 24040013; e-mail info@centralbank.org.sz; internet www.centralbank.org.sz; f. 1974; bank of issue; cap. 21.8m., res 31.4m., dep. 1,388.7m. (March 2006); Gov. MARTIN G. DLAMINI; Dep. Gov. S. G. MDLULI.

Commercial Banks

First National Bank of Swaziland Ltd: Sales House Bldg, 2nd Floor, Swazi Plaza, POB 261, Mbabane; tel. 25184637; fax 24044735; e-mail hnsibande@fnb.co.za; internet www.fnbswaziland.co.sz; f. 1988; fmrly Meridien Bank Swaziland Ltd; wholly owned by FirstRand Bank Holdings Ltd, Johannesburg; cap. and res 61.5m., dep. 484.5m. (June 2002); Chair. Dr D. M. J. VON WISSEL; Man. Dir DAVE WRIGHT; 7 brs.

Nedbank (Swaziland) Ltd: cnr Plaza-Dr Sishayi St and Bypass Rd, POB 68, Mbabane; tel. 24081000; fax 24044060; e-mail info@nedbank.co.sz; internet www.nedbank.co.sz; f. 1974; fmrly Standard Chartered Bank Swaziland Ltd; 23.1% state-owned; cap. 11.9m., res 134.6m., dep. 1,006.2m. (Dec. 2007); Chair. MABILI DLAMINI; Man. Dir FIKILE NKOSI; 6 brs and 1 agency.

Development Banks

Standard Bank Swaziland Ltd: Standard House, 1st Floor, Swazi Plaza, POB A294, Mbabane; tel. 24046587; fax 24045899; e-mail standardbankswaziland@iafricaonline.co.sz; internet www.standardbank.co.sz; f. 1988; fmrly Stanbic Bank Swaziland, present name adopted 1997; merged with Barclays Bank of Swaziland in Jan. 1998; 25% state-owned; cap. 14.6m., res 89.3m., dep. 1,454.3m. (Dec. 2005); Chair. R. J. ROSSOUW (acting); Man. Dir TINEYI MAWOCHA; 10 brs, 1 agency.

Swaziland Development and Savings Bank (SwaziBank—Libhange LeSive): Engungwini Bldg, Gwamile St, POB 336, Mbabane; tel. 24042551; fax 24041214; e-mail swazibank@swazibank.sz; internet www.swazibank.co.sz; f. 1965; state-owned; taken over by central bank in 1995; under independent management since 2000; cap. and res 143.0m., total assets 557.9m. (March 2002); Acting Chair. NOAH M. NKAMBULE; Man. Dir STANLEY M. N. MATSEBULA; 8 brs.

Financial Institution

Swaziland National Provident Fund: POB 1857, Manzini; tel. 25082000; fax 25082001; internet www.snpf.co.sz; f. 1974; provides benefits for employed persons on retirement from regular employment or in the event of becoming incapacitated; employers are required by law to pay a contribution for every eligible staff member; total assets 290m. (June 1996); Chair. MDUDUZI GINA; CEO Prince LONKHOKHELA DLAMINI.

STOCK EXCHANGE

Swaziland Stock Exchange: Capital Markets Development Unit, Infumbe Bldg, 1st Floor, Warner St, POB 546, Mbabane; tel. 24082164; fax 24049493; e-mail info@ssx.org.sz; internet www.ssx.org.sz; f. 1990 as Swaziland Stock Market (SSM); state-owned; Chair. MARTIN G. DLAMINI.

INSURANCE

Between 1974 and 1999 the state-controlled Swaziland Royal Insurance Corpn (SRIC) operated as the country's sole authorized insurance company, although cover in a number of areas not served by SRIC was available from several specialized insurers. In 1999 it was proposed that legislation would be enacted to end SRIC's monopoly and provide for the company's transfer to private sector ownership. The legislation was adopted as the Insurance Act in 2005.

Insurance Companies

Metropolitan Life Swaziland: Mbabane; tel. 24090282; e-mail info@metropolitan.co.sz; internet www.metropolitan.co.sz; f. 2008; Chair. STANLEY MATSEBULA; Man. Dir MUZI DLAMINI.

Swaziland Royal Insurance Corpn (SRIC): SRIC House, Somhlolo Rd, Gilfillan St, POB 917, H100 Mbabane; tel. 24043231; fax 24046415; e-mail sric@sric.sz; internet www.sric.sz; f. 1974; 41% state-owned, 59% owned by Munich-Reinsurance Co of Africa Ltd, Mutual and Fed. Insurance Co of South Africa Ltd, Swiss Re Southern Africa Ltd, S.A. Eagle Insurance Co Ltd, Old Mutual, and Mutual and Federal; Chair. KENNETH MBULI; Gen. Man. ZOMBODZE R. MAGAGULA.

Insurance Association

Insurance Brokers' Association of Swaziland (IBAS): POB 222, Mbabane H100; tel. 24043226; fax 24046412; e-mail mzamo_dlamini@aon.co.sz; f. 1983; Chair. MZAMO ELLIOT DLAMINI; 4 mems.

Trade and Industry

GOVERNMENT AGENCIES

Small Enterprise Development Co (SEDCO): POB A186, Swazi Plaza, Mbabane; tel. 24042811; fax 24040723; e-mail business@sedco.co.sz; internet www.sedco.biz; f. 1970; devt agency; supplies workshop space, training and expertise for 165 local entrepreneurs at eight sites throughout the country; Chair. PHOLILE DLAMINI; CEO DORRINGTON MATIWANE.

Swaziland Investment Promotion Authority (SIPA): Nkhotfotjeni Bldg, 1st Floor, cnr Msakato and Dzeliwe Sts, POB 4194, Mbabane; tel. 24040472; fax 24043374; e-mail info@sipa.org.sz; internet www.sipa.org.sz; f. 1998; Chair. NICK JACKSON; CEO PHIWAYINKOSI GININDZA.

DEVELOPMENT ORGANIZATIONS

National Industrial Development Corpn of Swaziland (NIDCS): POB 866, Mbabane; tel. 24043391; fax 24045619; f. 1971; state-owned; administered by Swaziland Industrial Devt Co; Admin. Dir P. K. THAMM.

Swaziland Coalition of Concerned Civic Organisations (SCCCO): Smithco Industrial Centre, Mswati III Ave, 11th St, Matsapha; POB 4173, Mbabane; tel. and fax 25187688; e-mail webmaster@swazicoalition.org.sz; internet www.swazicoalition.org.sz; f. 2003; promotes constitutional democracy, poverty alleviation, fiscal discipline, economic stability, competitive regional and international trade, social justice, and the rule of law; Sec.-Gen. MUSA HLOPE; 9 mems incl.:

Coordinating Assembly of Non-Governmental Organisations (CANGO): POB A67, Swazi Plaza, Mbabane; tel. 24044721; fax 24045532; e-mail director@cango.org.sz; internet www.cango.org.sz; f. 1983; Exec. Dir EMMANUEL NDLANGAMANDLA; over 70 mem. orgs.

Federation of Swaziland Employers and Chamber of Commerce (FSECC): Emafini Business Center, Malagwane Hill, POB 72, Mbabane; tel. 24040768; fax 24090051; e-mail fsecc@business-swaziland.com; internet www.business-swaziland.com; f. 2003 by merger of Fed. of Swaziland Employers (f. 1964) and Swaziland Chamber of Commerce (f. 1916); CEO ZODWA MABUZA; c. 500 mems (2005).

Swaziland Industrial Development Co (SIDC): Dhlan'Ubeka House, 5th Floor, cnr Mdada and Lalufadlana Sts, POB 866, Mbabane; tel. 24044010; fax 24045619; e-mail info@sidc.co.sz; internet www.sidc.co.sz; f. 1986; 35% state-owned; finances private sector projects and promotes local and foreign investment; cap. E24.1m., total assets E577m. (June 2010); Chair. TIM ZWANE; Man. Dir TAMBO GINA.

Swaki (Pty) Ltd: Liqhaga Bldg, 4th Floor, Nkoseluhlaza St, POB 1839, Manzini; tel. 25052693; fax 25052001; e-mail info@swaki.co.sz; jtly owned by SIDC and Kirsh Holdings; comprises a number of cos involved in manufacturing, services and the production and distribution of food.

Swaziland Solidarity Network (SSN): c/o COSATU House, 3rd Floor, 1–5 Leyds St, Braamfontein, South Africa; POB 1027, Johannesburg 2000, South Africa; tel. (11) 23393621; fax (11) 23394244; e-mail ssnnetwork@gmail.org.za; internet www.swazisolidarity.org; f. 1997; umbrella org. promoting democracy; incorporates mems from Swaziland and abroad incl. PUDEMO, SWAYOCO, and the Swaziland Democratic Alliance (f. 1999); also incl. the African National Congress of South Africa, South African Communist Party and Congress of South African Trade Unions.

Tibiyo Taka Ngwane (Bowels of the Swazi Nation): POB 181, Kwaluseni, Manzini; tel. 25184306; fax 25184399; internet www.tibiyo.com; f. 1968; national devt agency, with investment interests in all sectors of the economy; participates in domestic and foreign jt investment ventures; total assets: E604m. (1999); Chair. Prince LOGCOGCO MANGALISO; Man. Dir ABSALOM THEMBA DLAMINI.

CHAMBERS OF COMMERCE

Sibakho Chamber of Commerce: POB 2016, Manzini; tel. and fax 25057347.

Swaziland Chamber of Commerce and Industry: see Fed. of Swaziland Employers and Chamber of Commerce.

INDUSTRIAL AND TRADE ASSOCIATIONS

National Agricultural Marketing Board: POB 4261, Manzini; tel. 25055314; fax 25054072; internet www.namboard.co.sz; Chair. Dr MICAH B. MASUKU; CEO PHUMELELA SHONGWE.

National Maize Corpn (NMC): 11th St Matsapha Indstrial Sites; tel. 25187432; fax 25184461; e-mail info@nmc.co.sz; internet www.nmc.co.sz; f. 1985; Chair. NATHI GUMEDZE; Acting CEO SIFISO NXUMALO.

Swaziland Citrus Board: Sokhamila Bldg, cnr Dzeliwe and Mdada Sts, POB 343, Mbabane H100; tel. 24044266; fax 24043548; e-mail citrus@realnet.co.sz; f. 1969; Chair. P. S. NODDEBOE.

Swaziland Cotton Board: POB 220, Manzini; tel. and fax 25052775; e-mail dlaminiaa@gov.sz; f. 1967; CEO TOM JELE.

Swaziland Dairy Board: Enguleni Bldg, 3rd Floor, 287 Mahleka St, POB 2975, Manzini; tel. 25058262; fax 25058260; e-mail ceo-swazidairy@africaonline.co.sz; internet swazidairy.org; f. 1971; Gen. Man. N. T. GUMEDE.

Swaziland Sugar Association: 4th Floor, cnr Dzeliwe and Msakato Sts, POB 445, Mbabane; tel. 24042646; fax 24045005; e-mail info@ssa.co.sz; internet www.ssa.co.sz; CEO Dr MICHAEL MATSEBULA.

EMPLOYERS' ORGANIZATIONS

Building Contractors' Association of Swaziland: POB 518, Mbabane; tel. 24040071; fax 24044258; e-mail soconswad@realnet.co.sz.

Swaziland Association of Architects, Engineers and Surveyors: Swazi Plaza, POB A387, Mbabane; tel. 24042227.

Swaziland Institute of Personnel and Training Managers: c/o UNISWA, Private Bag, Kwaluseni; tel. 25184011; fax 25185276.

UTILITIES

Electricity

Swaziland Electricity Company: POB 258, Mbabane; tel. 24094000; fax 24042335; e-mail sifiso.dhlamini@sec.co.sz; internet www.sec.co.sz; statutory body; f. 1963; Chair. S'THOFENI GININDZA; Man. Dir BANELE NYAMANE (acting).

Water

Swaziland Water Services Corpn: Emtfonjeni Bldg, Below Gables Shopping Complex, Ezulwini, MR103, POB 20, Mbabane H100; tel. 24163621; fax 24163617; e-mail headoffice@swsc.co.sz; internet www.swsc.co.sz; state authority; Chair. ESAU N. ZWANE; CEO PETER N. BHEMBE.

MAJOR COMPANIES

Cadbury Swaziland (Pty) Ltd: POB 679, Matsapha M202; tel. 25186168; fax 25186173; f. 1989; mfrs of confectionery; Gen. Man. GREG STOCK.

Mantenga Craft Centre: POB 364, Eveni; tel. 24161136; fax 24161040; internet www.mantengacrafts.com; f. 1975; handicrafts; incorporates 11 shops; Man. Dir DARREN RARAW.

Neopac Swaziland Ltd: Matsapha Industrial Sites, POB 618, Manzini M200; tel. and fax 25184277; e-mail sales@neopac.co.sz; f. 1968; mfrs of corrugated containers for agriculture and industry; Man. Dir WILLIE HORSBURGH.

Ngwane Mills (Pty) Ltd: Matsapha Industrial Sites, POB 1169, Manzini; tel. 25185011; fax 25185112; f. 1992; subsidiary of Namib Management Services, South Africa; wheat and maize millers; exports wheat flour to South Africa; Man. Dir DAWIE FOURIE.

Palfridge Ltd (The Fridge Factory): King Mswati 3rd Ave, SIDC Factory Park, Matsapha Industrial Sites, POB 424, Matsapha; tel. 25184104; fax 25184126; e-mail info@thefridgefactory.com; internet www.thefridgefactory.com; f. 2001; mfrs of domestic, commercial, medical and camping refrigerators and freezers; Chair. COLIN FOSTER; CEO PETER MCCULLOUGH; 500 employees.

Royal Swaziland Sugar Corpn (RSSC): Simunye Sugar Estate, POB 1, Simunye L301; tel. 23134000; fax 23838171; e-mail info@rssc.co.sz; internet www.rssc.co.sz; f. 1977; 53% owned by Tibiyo Taka Ngwane, 25.9% owned by TSB Sugar Int., 6.5% owned by the Govt of Nigeria; mfrs of sugar, and potable alcohol (80% for export); estates at Mhlume and Simunye; incorporates Royal Swazi Distillers (RSD); Chair. ABSALOM THEMBA DLAMINI; Man. Dir NICK JACKSON; c. 3,500 employees.

Sappi Kraft (Pty) Ltd (Sappi Usutu): Bhunya, Private Bag, Mbabane H100; tel. 24026010; fax 24026032; internet www.sappi.com; f. 1961; fmrly Usutu Pulp Co Ltd; subsidiary of Sappi, South Africa; mfrs of unbleached kraft pulp; Pres. I. FORBES; Mill Man. SHANE PERROW; 1,539 employees (2002); c. 70,000 ha of timber plantations.

Spintex Swaziland (Pty) Ltd: Mswati III Ave, POB 6, Matsapha; tel. 25186166; fax 25186038; e-mail spintex@africaonline.co.sz; internet www.spintex.co.sz; f. 1991; mfrs of cotton and poly-cotton combed yarns, sewing thread, core yarns, lycra core yarns and open-end yarns; CEO MANICKUM NAICKER; 400 employees.

Swazi Paper Mills Ltd: Edwaleni Rd, POB 873, Mbabane; tel. 25186024; fax 25186091; e-mail spm@linux.spm.co.sz; internet www.thesharmagroup.com; f. 1987; Swaziland's largest privately owned concern; owned by the Sharma Group; produces paper and paper products; Man. Dir P. SHARMA.

Swazi Timber Products Ltd: 7 Conco St, POB 2313, Manzini M200; tel. and fax 25186291; f. 1987; Man. Dir M. RAMKOLOWAN.

Swaziland Beverages Ltd: POB 100, Matsapha; tel. 25186033; fax 25186309; f. 1976; 40% owned by Tibiyo Taka Ngwane; annual production of 250,000 hl of beer; Group Man. Dir ZAMA KUNENE; 181 employees.

Swaziland Meat Industries Ltd: POB 446, Manzini; tel. 25184165; fax 25184418; e-mail simunyemeats@smi.co.sz; f. 1965; operates an abattoir and deboning plant at Matsapha to process beef for local and export markets; Gen. Man. JONATHAN C. WILLIAMS.

Swaziland Safety Glass: Matsapha Industrial Estate, POB 3058, Manzini; tel. 25085366; fax 25085361; f. 1990; mfrs of glass for transport industry; Man. Dir BRIAN BROOKS.

Swazispa Holdings Ltd: POB 331, Mbabane; tel. 24165000; fax 24161606; e-mail swazisun@sunint.co.za; f. 1962; 50.6% owned by All Saints (Pty) Ltd, 39.7% owned by Tibiyo Taka Ngwane; leisure, casino and hospitality operator with interests in property devt and finance; Chair. DAVID D. DLAMINI; Area Gen. Man. A. C. STEYN; 368 employees.

Ubombo Sugar Ltd: POB 23, Big Bend L311; tel. 23638000; fax 23636330; f. 1958; 60% owned by Illovo Sugar Group (South Africa), 40% owned by Tibiyo Taka Ngwane; produces raw and refined sugar; Man. Dir EDDIE WILLIAMS.

YKK Zippers (Swaziland) (Pty) Ltd: Sobhuza II Ave, Matsapha Industrial Area, Manzini; tel. 25186188; fax 25186130; e-mail enquiries@ykkafrica.com; internet ykkafrica.com; f. 1977; mfrs of zip fasteners; Man. Dir T. SHIMIZU.

TRADE UNIONS

At mid-2005 there were 55 organizations recognized by the Department of Labour. Only non-managerial workers may belong to a union.

Trade Union Federations

Swaziland Amalgamated Trade Unions (SATU): POB 7138, Manzini; tel. 25059544; fax 25052684; f. 2003 by merger of five industrial unions; Sec.-Gen. FRANK NKULULEKO MNCINA; 3,500 mems (2005).

Trade Union Congress Of Swaziland (TUCOSWA): POB 1158, Manzini; tel. 25059514; fax 25059515; e-mail sftu1@swazi.net; f. 2011 following merger of the Swaziland Federation of Labour and the Swaziland Federation of Trade Unions; subsequently joined by the Swaziland National Association of Teachers; deregistered by the Govt in April 2012; Acting Sec.-Gen. MDUDUZI GINA; Pres. BARNES DLAMINI.

Transport

Buses are the principal means of transport for many Swazis. Bus services are provided by private operators; these are required to obtain annual permits for each route from the Road Transportation Board, which also regulates fares.

RAILWAYS

The rail network, which totalled 301 km in 2011, provides a major transport link for imports and exports. Railway lines connect with the dry port at Matsapha, the South African ports of Richards Bay and Durban in the south, the South African town of Komatipoort in the north and the Mozambican port of Maputo in the east. Goods traffic is mainly in wood pulp, sugar, molasses, coal, citrus fruit and canned fruit. In January 2012 Transnet of South Africa announced plans to route a new railway through Swaziland to connect with Richards Bay and a number of ports in Mozambique.

Swaziland Railways: Swaziland Railway Bldg, cnr Johnston and Walker Sts, POB 475, Mbabane; tel. 24047211; fax 24047210; internet www.swazirail.co.sz; f. 1962; Chair. B. A. G. FITZPATRICK; CEO GIDEON J. MAHLALELA.

ROADS

In 2002 there were an estimated 3,594 km of roads, including 1,465 km of main roads and 2,129 km of secondary roads. About 30% of the road network was paved in that year. The rehabilitation of about 700 km of main roads and 600 km of district gravel-surfaced roads began in 1985, financed by World Bank and US loans totalling some E18m. In 1991 work commenced on the reconstruction of Swaziland's main road artery, connecting Mbabane to Manzini, via Matsapha, and in 2001 the Government announced the construction of two main roads in the north of the country, financed by Japanese loans.

Roads Department: Ministry of Public Works and Transport, POB 58, Mbabane; tel. 24042321; fax 24045825; e-mail tshabalalatr@gov.sz; Chief Roads Engineer TREVOR M. TSHABALALA.

SHIPPING

Royal Swazi National Shipping Corpn Ltd: POB 1915, Manzini; tel. 25053788; fax 25053820; f. 1980 to succeed Royal Swaziland Maritime Co; 76% owned by Tibiyo Taka Ngwane; owns no ships, acting only as a freight agent; Gen. Man. M. S. DLAMINI.

CIVIL AVIATION

Swaziland's only airport is at Matsapha, near Manzini, about 40 km from Mbabane. In mid-1997 the Government initiated a three-year programme to upgrade the airport. In early 2003 construction began of an international airport at Sikhupe, in eastern Swaziland. In March 2006 Swaziland Airlink was one of 92 airlines banned from landing at European Union airports owing to safety concerns.

Swaziland Airlink: POB 2042, Matsapha; tel. 25186155; fax 25186148; e-mail info@flyairlink.com; internet www.flyswaziland.com; f. 1999; fmrly Royal Swazi Nat. Airways Corpn; jt venture between SA Airlink, South Africa (40%) and the Govt of Swaziland; scheduled passenger services from Manzini to Johannesburg, South Africa; Chair. SIBUSISO MOTSA.

Tourism

Swaziland's attractions for tourists include game reserves (at Malolotja, Hawane, Mlawula and Mantenga) and magnificent mountain scenery. In 2009 tourist arrivals at hotels totalled 909,000; receipts from tourism amounted to US $40m. in that year.

Hotel and Tourism Association of Swaziland: Oribi Court, 1st Floor, Gwamile St, POB 462, Mbabane; tel. 24042218; fax 24044516; e-mail aliand@realnet.co.sz; internet www.visitswazi.com/tourismassoc; f. 1979.

Swaziland National Trust Commission (SNTC): POB 100, Lobamba; tel. 24161516; fax 24161875; e-mail director@sntc.org.sz; e-mail curator@sntc.org.sz (museums and monuments); internet www.sntc.org.sz; f. 1972; parastatal org. responsible for conservation of nature and cultural heritage (national parks, museums and monuments); CEO T. DLAMINI.

Swaziland Tourism Authority (STA): POB A1030, Swazi Plaza, Mbabane H101; tel. 24049693; fax 24049683; e-mail secretary@tourismauthority.org.sz; internet www.welcometoswaziland.com; f. 2001; CEO ERIC SIPHO MASEKO.

Defence

The Umbutfo Swaziland Defence Force was created in 1973. Compulsory military service of two years was introduced in 1983.

Defence Expenditure: Budgeted at E168m. for 2001/02.

Commander of the Umbutfo Swaziland Defence Force: Maj.-Gen. STANLEY S. DLAMINI.

Deputy Commander of the Umbutfo Swaziland Defence Force: Brig.-Gen. PATRICK V. MOTSA.

Education

Education is not compulsory in Swaziland. Primary education begins at six years of age and lasts for seven years. Secondary education begins at 13 years of age and lasts for up to five years, comprising a first cycle of three years and a second of two years. According to UNESCO estimates, in 2009/10 86% of children in the relevant age-group (males 86%; females 85%) were enrolled at primary schools, while in that year secondary enrolment included 33% of children in the appropriate age-group (males 29%; females 37%). In 2005/06 5,692 students were enrolled at the University of Swaziland, which has campuses at Luyengo and Kwaluseni. However, the university closed in mid-2011 as a result of a lack of funding. There are also a number of other institutions of higher education: in 2000 there were 1,822 students enrolled at 10 vocational, technical and teacher-training colleges. In 2008 1.18% of total government expenditure was allocated to education.

Bibliography

Bischoff, P.-H. *Swaziland's International Relations and Foreign Policy: A Study of a Small African State in International Relations*. Berne, P. Lang, 1990.

Booth, A. R. *Historical Dictionary of Swaziland*. Metuchen, NJ, Scarecrow Press, 1975.

Swaziland: Tradition and Change in a Southern African Kingdom. Boulder, CO, Westview Press, 1983; London, Gower Publishers, 1984.

Booth, M. Z. *Culture and Education: The Social Consequences of Western Schooling in Contemporary Swaziland*. Lanham, MD, University Press of America, 2004.

Daniel, J., and Stephen, M. F. (Eds). *Historical Perspectives on the Political Economy of Swaziland*. Kwaluseni, University of Swaziland, 1986.

Davies, R. H., *et al.* (Eds). *The Kingdom of Swaziland: A Profile*. London, Zed Press, 1985.

Forster, S., and Nsibande, B. S. (Eds). *Swaziland: Contemporary Social and Economic Issues*. Aldershot, Ashgate Publishing Ltd, 2000.

Funnell, D. C. *Under the Shadow of Apartheid: Agrarian Transformation in Swaziland*. Aldershot, Avebury, 1991.

Gillis, D. H. *The Kingdom of Swaziland*. Westport, CT, Greenwood Publishing Group, 1999.

Knox, J. A., Rodríguez Díaz, Nixon, D. J., and Mkhwanazi, M. 'A preliminary assessment of climate change impacts on sugarcane in Swaziland', in *Agricultural Systems*, Vol. 103, Issue 2, 2010.

Konczacki, Z. A., *et al.* (Eds). *Studies in the Economic History of Southern Africa*. Vol. II. London, Cass, 1991.

Matsebula, J. S. *A History of Swaziland*. 2nd edn. Cape Town, Maskew Miller, Longmans, 1988.

Matsebula, M. S. *The Informal Sector: A Historical and Structural Analysis With Special Reference To Swaziland*. Harare, SAPES Books, 1996.

Okpalmba, Chuks, *et al.* (Eds). *Human Rights in Swaziland: The Legal Response*. Kwaluseni, University of Swaziland, 1997.

Organization for Social Science Research in Eastern and Southern Africa (OSSREA). *Democracy, Transformation, Conflict and Public Policy in Swaziland*. Kwaluseni, OSSREA Swaziland Chapter, 2003.

Issues in the Economy and Politics of Swaziland since 1968. Kwaluseni, OSSREA Swaziland Chapter, 2003.

Rose, L. L. *The Politics of Harmony: Land Dispute Strategies in Swaziland*. Cambridge, Cambridge University Press, 1992.

Schwager, D. *Swaziland*. Mbabane, Websters, 1984.

Simelane, H. S. *Colonialism and Economic Change in Swaziland 1940–1960*. Manzini, Jan Publishing Centre, 2003.

Simelane, N. C. (Ed.). *Social Transformation: The Swaziland Case*. Dakar, CODESRIA, 1995.

Tsolo, M., Mogotsi, I., and Motlaleng, G. 'The Impact of European Union-South Africa Trade Development and Cooperation Agreement on Botswana, Lesotho, Namibia and Swaziland', in *Review of Economic and Business Studies*, Vol. 3, Issue 1, 2010.

TANZANIA

Physical and Social Geography

L. BERRY

PHYSICAL FEATURES AND CLIMATE

The 945,087 sq km (364,900 sq miles) of the United Republic of Tanzania (incorporating mainland Tanganyika and a number of offshore islands, including Zanzibar, Pemba, Latham and Mafia) have a wide variety of land forms, climates and peoples. The country includes the highest and lowest points in Africa—the summit of Mt Kilimanjaro (5,892 m above sea-level) and the floor of Lake Tanganyika (358 m below sea-level). The main upland areas occur in a northern belt—the Usambara, Pare, Kilimanjaro and Meru mountains; a central and southern belt—the Southern highlands, the Ugurus and the Ulugurus; and a north–south trending belt, which runs southwards from the Ngorongoro Crater. The highest peaks are volcanic, although block faulting has been responsible for the uplift of the plateau areas. Other fault movements have resulted in the depressed areas of the rift valleys; Lakes Tanganyika, Malawi, Rukwa, Manyara and Eyasi occupy part of the floor of these depressions. Much of the rest of the interior comprises gently sloping plains and plateaux, broken by low hill ranges and scattered isolated hills. The coast includes areas with wide sandy beaches and with developed coral reefs, but these are broken by extensive growth of mangroves, particularly near the mouths of the larger rivers.

With the exception of the high mountain areas, temperatures in Tanzania are not a major limiting factor for crop growth, although the range of altitude produces a corresponding range of temperature regimes from tropical to temperate. Rainfall is variable, both from place to place and time to time, and is generally lower than might be expected for the latitude. About one-fifth of Tanzania can expect with 90% probability more than 750 mm of rainfall annually, and only about 3% normally receives more than 1,250 mm. The central third of the country is semi-arid (less than 500 mm), with evaporation exceeding rainfall in nine months of the year. For much of Tanzania most rain falls in one rainy season, December–May, though two peaks of rainfall in October–November and April–May are found in some areas. Apart from the problem of the long dry season over most parts of the country, there is also a marked fluctuation in annual rainfall from one year to the next, and this may be reflected in the crop production and livestock figures.

The surplus water from the wetter areas drains into the few large perennial rivers. The largest of these, the Rufiji, drains the Southern highlands and much of southern Tanzania. With an average discharge of 1,133 cu m per second, it is one of the largest rivers in Africa, and has major potential for irrigation and hydroelectric power development. The Ruvu, Wami and Pangani also drain to the Indian Ocean. The Pangani has already been developed for hydroelectric power, which supplies Arusha, Moshi, Tanga, Morogoro and Dar es Salaam. Apart from the Ruvuma, which forms the southern frontier, most other drainage is to the interior basins, or to the Lakes Tanganyika, Victoria and Malawi.

The most fertile soils in Tanzania are the reddish-brown soils derived from the volcanic rocks, although elsewhere *mbuga* and other alluvial soils have good potential. The interior plateaux are covered with tropical loams of moderate fertility. The natural vegetation of the country has been considerably modified by human occupation. In the south and west-central areas there are large tracts of woodland covering about 30% of the country, while on the uplands are small but important areas of tropical rain forest. Clearly marked altitudinal variations in vegetation occur around the upland areas and some distinctive mountain flora is found. Tanzania has set aside about one-third of its land for national parks and game and forest reserves.

POPULATION AND RESOURCES

According to the census of 25 August 2002, Tanzania had a population of 34,443,603. In August 2002 some 593,623 people resided in the autonomous Zanzibar region (the islands of Pemba and Zanzibar). According to UN estimates, Tanzania had a population of 47,656,367 in mid-2012, and a population density of 50.4 people per sq km. The highest population densities, reaching over 250 per sq km, occur on the fertile lower slopes of Mt Kilimanjaro and on the shores of Lake Malawi. Most other upland areas have relatively high densities, as does the area south of Lake Victoria known as Sukumaland. Most of the country's inhabitants are of African origin, although people of Indian and Pakistani ancestry comprise a significant component of the urban population. There are more than 120 ethnic groups in Tanzania, of which the largest are the Sukuma and the Nyamwezi. None, however, exceeds 10% of the total population.

Tanzania's mineral resources include diamonds, other gemstones, gold, salt, phosphates, coal, gypsum, kaolin, tin, limestone and graphite, all of which are exploited. There are also reserves of nickel, silver, copper, cobalt, lead, soda ash, iron ore, tungsten, pyrochlore, magnesite, niobium, titanium, vanadium, uranium and natural gas.

Dar es Salaam is the main port, the dominant industrial centre, and the focus of government and commercial activity. Dar es Salaam has been growing at a substantial rate and attempts are being made to decentralize industrial development to other centres. Arusha has also been growing rapidly in recent years, partly because of its importance to tourism.

Recent History

MICHAEL JENNINGS

European interest in the area that now forms the United Republic of Tanzania was attracted in the 17th century by the mercantile opportunities of the Omani-controlled caravan trade from Zanzibar into the eastern Congo and Buganda. British trading interests on the island and its then extensive coastal possessions expanded rapidly after 1841. Zanzibar declared its independence from Oman in 1856, and its mainland areas were acquired by the United Kingdom and Germany in 1886–90, when a British protectorate was established over the islands of Zanzibar and Pemba.

Mainland Tanganyika was declared a German protectorate in 1885. In 1920, following the defeat of Germany in the First World War, Tanganyika was placed under a League of Nations mandate, with the United Kingdom as the administering power, and in 1946 became a UN trust territory, still under British administration. The politicization of indigenous Africans began in 1929, with the formation of the Tanganyika African Association, which evolved in 1954 into the Tanganyika African National Union (TANU), under the leadership of Julius Nyerere.

THE NYERERE PERIOD, 1959–85

TANU won decisive victories in general elections held in Tanganyika in 1959 and 1960, when Nyerere became Chief Minister. Nyerere duly became Prime Minister when internal self-government was granted in May 1961. Full independence followed on 9 December. In January 1962 Nyerere resigned as Prime Minister; he was succeeded by Rashidi Kawawa. In December Tanganyika became a republic, with Nyerere returning to power as the country's first President, having been elected in the previous month. Kawawa became Vice-President.

Zanzibar (together with the neighbouring island of Pemba and several smaller islets), became an independent sultanate in December 1963. The Sultan was overthrown in an armed uprising in January 1964, following which a republic was declared and the Afro-Shirazi Party (ASP) took power. In April an Act of Union between Tanganyika and Zanzibar was signed. The leader of the ASP, Abeid Karume, became the United Republic's First Vice-President, as well as being Chairman of the ruling Supreme Revolutionary Council of Zanzibar. The Union was named Tanzania in October.

A new Constitution, introduced in July 1965, provided for a one-party state (although, until 1977, TANU and the ASP remained the respective official parties of mainland Tanzania and Zanzibar, and co-operated in affairs of state). Nyerere was re-elected as President in September 1965, and subsequently in the 1970, 1975 and 1980 elections. Early in 1967 TANU adopted a programme of socialism and self-reliance, known as the Arusha Declaration. National development was to be based upon that of the rural sector via community (*ujamaa*) villages. Commercial banks and many industries were immediately nationalized. The programme ran into difficulties in the 1970s, facing increased resistance from those being forced into *ujamaa* villages.

In Zanzibar, Karume was assassinated in April 1972. His successor, Aboud Jumbe, reorganized the islands' Government in that month by extending the powers of the ASP. Despite its incorporation into Tanzania, Zanzibar retained a separate administration, which ruthlessly suppressed all opposition.

In February 1977 TANU and the ASP merged to form the Chama Cha Mapinduzi (CCM—Revolutionary Party) In April the National Assembly adopted a permanent Constitution for Tanzania, providing for the election of 10 Zanzibari representatives to the National Assembly. A separate Constitution adopted by Zanzibar in October 1979 made provision for a popularly elected President and a legislative House of Representatives to be elected by delegates of the CCM. A more liberal, Constitution for the islands was introduced in January 1985, providing for the House of Representatives to be directly elected by universal suffrage and for the introduction of a Commonwealth legal system.

In October 1985 Mwinyi was elected as President of Tanzania with 96% of the valid votes cast. Idris Abdul Wakil (formerly Speaker of the Zanzibar House of Representatives) was elected President of Zanzibar to replace Mwinyi. After taking office in November, Mwinyi appointed Joseph Warioba, previously Minister of Justice, as Prime Minister and First Vice-President.

THE MWINYI PRESIDENCY, 1985–95

The change of President coincided with a worsening economic crisis (see below). The new administration was forced to accept a range of policy proposals from the IMF, including greater encouragement to the private sector, and policies on budgeting, agricultural reform and currency valuation to persuade continued aid flows from key donors. In October 1990 Mwinyi was re-elected as sole presidential candidate, and on Zanzibar Dr Salmin Amour, was elected as Wakil's successor

In May 1992 the Constitution was amended to implement a plural political system. The amendment stipulated that all new political organizations should command support in both Zanzibar and mainland Tanzania, and should be free of tribal, religious and racial bias.

THE 'THIRD PHASE' GOVERNMENT

In October 1995 multi-party legislative and presidential elections were held for the first time both in Zanzibar (see below) and throughout the Tanzanian Union. The CCM won 186 of the 232 elective seats in the National Assembly, while the Civic United Front (CUF), a party favouring Zanzibari autonomy (see below), secured 24 seats; NCCR—Mageuzi won 16, and both Chadema and the United Democratic Party (UDP) took three seats. Benjamin Mkapa was elected national President, winning 61.8% of the votes cast. Omar Ali Juma (hitherto the Chief Minister of Zanzibar) was appointed Vice-President. After being appointed to head a special presidential commission on corruption in January 1996, former Prime Minister Joseph Warioba produced his report in December, finding widespread corruption in the public sector.

In early August 1998 a bomb exploded outside the US embassy in Dar es Salaam (concurrently with a similar attack at the US mission in Nairobi, Kenya); 11 people were killed in Dar es Salaam and some 86 were injured. The attacks were believed to have been co-ordinated by international Islamist terrorists led by a Saudi-born dissident, Osama bin Laden. Two suspects were charged with murder by the Tanzanian authorities in mid-September in connection with the Dar es Salaam attack. In May 2001 four men were convicted for the attacks and sentenced to life imprisonment.

THE OCTOBER 2000 ELECTIONS

The National Election Committee (NEC) announced various reforms to guarantee free and fair elections: polling booths were to be introduced to replace voting in the open; and greater efforts would be made to ensure the impartiality of the NEC. However, the CUF complained that some voter registration centres were located in CCM offices and military bases.

At the presidential election, held on 29 October 2000, Mkapa was re-elected, securing 71.7% of the votes cast; Ibrahim Haruna Lipumba, the Chairman of the CUF, secured 16.3%, Mrema 7.8% and John Momose Cheyo, the Chairman of the UDP, 4.2%. The CCM won 244 seats in the National Assembly; the CUF took 15; Chadema, the TLP and the UDP won four, three and two seats, respectively. The polls were declared by international observers to have been freely and fairly conducted, in marked contrast to the controversial events in Zanzibar (see below). In November Mkapa appointed a new national Cabinet, reappointing Sumaye as Prime Minister (official confirmation of the national election results had been delayed until after some Zanzibari constituencies had conducted new polls).

DOMESTIC ISSUES PRIOR TO THE 2005 ELECTIONS

In the run-up to the 2005 elections political attention within the CCM turned to the issue of the successor to Mkapa, who was coming to the end of his two-term limit. The internal campaign to nominate a candidate became increasingly bitter, and exposed serious divisions within the party. Mkapa and former Vice-President Kawawa both indicated their support for Jakaya Mrisho Kikwete, who in the event defeated his nearest rival Dr Salim Ahmed Salim by 1,072 to 476 votes to be chosen as the CCM's candidate. Meanwhile, the opposition remained fragmented across 17 political parties, and made little headway in presenting a serious challenge to the dominance of the CCM (with the exception of Zanzibar, where the CUF maintained a strong presence).

In August 2005 12 of the 18 registered political parties signed a code of conduct for the election campaigning period. The agreement guaranteed equal media space and fair coverage for all candidates and parties, and advised religious leaders not to participate or influence campaigns, and politicians not to use places of worship as venues for rallies or other political events. The Government agreed to ensure that the security services did not use excessive force in the maintenance of order, and not to interfere with rallies and meetings sanctioned by the NEC. Candidates also agreed to campaign in Kiswahili, not in local languages or in English. The NCCR—Mageuzi accused the NEC of being too weak to effectively regulate and control the CCM, but nevertheless signed up to the agreement, leaving the Forum for the Restoration of Democracy as the only registered party refusing to adhere to it. The official presidential and parliamentary election campaign began on 21 August. In September violence connected to campaigning increased in intensity on the mainland, and at the end of the month it was announced that security was being increased across the country in response.

THE KIKWETE ADMINISTRATION

Following the death of Chadema's vice-presidential candidate, Jumbe Rajab Jumbe, five days before the elections, voting was postponed until 14 December 2005. Kikwete won the presidential election with 80.3% of the votes cast. The CCM won an overwhelming majority in the legislative elections, securing 206 of the 232 directly elected seats in the National Assembly. The CUF won 19 seats, Chadema took five seats, and the TLP and UDF each won one seat. Following the allocation of seats reserved for women, presidential nominees and members of the Zanzibar House of Representatives, the CCM received a total of 266 seats, the CUF 28, Chadema 11, and the TLP and UDP one each. Edward Lowassa was appointed as Prime Minister by Kikwete.

Despite his victory, Kikwete struggled to maintain his authority within the increasingly divided CCM. He assumed the presidency of the party in June 2006, and appointed key allies to senior positions within the organization. However, internal divisions remained.

Four opposition parties (the CUF, the TLP, NCCR—Mageuzi and Chadema) formed an unofficial coalition in May 2007. Chadema increased its attacks on the Government over issues of corruption. It demanded inquiries into several ongoing scandals, including that at Tanzania's central bank, and the awarding of several contracts to private investors. Former Chadema leader Bob Makani also launched an attack on former President Mkapa, who refused to comment on allegations of graft during his tenure. However, internal divisions within Chadema surfaced, particularly between Deputy Chairman Chacha Wangwe and the organization's leader, Freeman Mbowe.

Although the Government claimed that it was tackling corruption, legislation approved in 2007, creating a new Prevention and Combating of Corruption Bureau, was criticized for weakening penalties for graft. Corruption scandals undermined the Government, leading to the departure of a number of high-profile officials. In January 2008 central bank Governor Daudi Balai was dismissed for corruption (after having already resigned several weeks earlier and left the country for medical treatment) as part of the External Payments Arrears (EPA) scandal. In February Lowassa resigned as Prime Minister following allegations of fraud relating to energy contracts signed in 2006. In April 2008 the Minister of Infrastructure Development, Andrew Chenge, was implicated in a scandal involving the purchase of radar equipment from British defence firm BAE Systems. He was accused of receiving secret commission payments to a Swiss bank account from BAE.

Amid mounting corruption scandals, President Kikwete moved to restore confidence in the Government with a major cabinet reorganization in which nine ministers lost their positions, including the Minister of Finance, Zakia Meghji, and the Minister of Planning, Economy and Empowerment, Dr Juma Ngasongwa. Mizengo Kayanza Peter Pinda was appointed as Prime Minister, and the number of ministers and deputy ministers in the new Cabinet was reduced from 61 to 47, of whom one-quarter were women.

In mid-2008 Pinda announced a government investigation into abuse of office by former government leaders, including former President Mkapa. An investigation into the EPA scandal, led by Attorney-General Johnson Mwanyika, had recovered around US $46m. out of the $115m. believed to have been siphoned from the central bank. The Government suggested that it would only prosecute those who failed to return the money. However, the opposition demanded that all those named in the official report into the scandal face trial. Chadema took advantage of public anger over corruption in the Tarime by-election, defeating the CCM after a heated political campaign marked by sporadic violence and clashes between rival supporters.

Stung by accusations of insufficient activity in dealing with the EPA scandal, 16 businessmen were arrested in November 2008, having failed to repay the money. In addition, local CCM Treasurer Rajabu Maranda and four officials from the Bank of Tanzania were arrested in connection with the case. Former Finance Minister Basil Pesambili Mramba and the former Energy and Minerals Minister, David Ndhira, also appeared in court in late November accused of abuse of office over the issuing of contracts for auditing Tanzania's gold production. International donors, which had withheld 12% of direct budget support after expressing concern over the slow pace in addressing corruption, announced that month that they would renew full support.

Party Divisions and Reorganizations Prior to the 2010 Elections

Meanwhile, signs emerged of a growing split within the CCM over Kikwete's leadership. At internal party leadership elections in October 2008 several prominent candidates were rejected. Senior CCM officials were reported to be seeking to deny Kikwete the party's nomination. After failing to withdraw the story at the Government's request, the Swahili-language newspaper *Mwana Halisi* was banned for three months, leading to protests against Government attempts to control the press. In mid-November CCM leaders admitted to failures in the leadership election process.

Internal faction disputes continued to undermine CCM unity, which was effectively split between a 'reformist' and anti-corruption group—led by parliamentary Speaker Samuel Sitta—and a 'traditionalist' faction—led by former Prime Minister Lowassa. Open hostility emerged in mid-2008 when Lowassa and his supporters sought to force Sitta to resign as Speaker following his decision to allow several CCM deputies to voice criticisms of the Government in the National Assembly. At a disputatious CCM NEC meeting, Kikwete sought to mediate between the two sides, and secured an agreement to set up a committee to draft guidelines for the conduct of CCM deputies. The decision was lambasted by opposition politicians as an attempt to stifle criticism of the Government. However, the deal failed to end the internal tensions. Former President Mwinyi sought to reconcile the opposing factions before the CCM nomination process for the national elections began in August 2010. Mwinyi, together with former Speaker Pius Msekwa and the former Speaker of the East African Legislative Assembly, Abdulrahman Kinana, established a committee to restore CCM unity and to prevent the party from disintegrating as a result of factional struggles. However, in mid-February the committee reported it had been unable to find a solution, and was given another two months to secure reconciliation between the two warring factions.

In March 2010 the establishment of the Chama Cha Jamii (CCJ) as a new political party was announced. Despite claims that it would include several high-profile CCM members, no major CCM figures defected to the new party. In April two CCM deputies, Fred Mpendazoe Tungu and Sikutu Philipo Chibululu, announced they were joining the party. However, in July the CCJ was deregistered by the Office of the Registrar of Political Parties, and its founders established a further new political party Chama Cha Kijamii, under the chairmanship of Constantine Akitanda. Mpendazoe Tungu was reported to have defected to Chadema.

Nevertheless, with strong support from the rural population in particular, Kikwete was able to impose his authority on the CCM. By June 2010 challenges to Kikwete's leadership from the previous year appeared to have been headed off, and he retained sufficient authority to push for reconciliation on Zanzibar (see below). Chadema had also suffered from internal divisions. At a September 2009 meeting of the party Central Committee, Deputy Sec.-Gen. Zitto Kabwe sought to remove Freeman Mbowe as Chairman. The move was averted only after intervention from a senior party member, determined to preserve party unity. Mbowe subsequently announced he would not stand as Chadema presidential candidate in the 2010 elections.

In July 2009 following the announcement by the Government that it would not sanction *Shari'a* (Islamic law) courts, the National Muslim Council of Tanzania announced it would seek to persuade Muslims to withdraw their support for the CCM in the 2010 elections. Also in July 2009 Transparency International's annual report on corruption announced that Tanzania was the least corrupt East African country. However, its position within the international rankings had fallen and the Government's commitment to tackling graft was questioned by international donors. In August 2009 the Government published its response to the Select Committee report on the Richmond scandal. It announced that it would only seek to prosecute officials named in ongoing court cases connected to the scandal, and exonerated Prevention and Control of Corruption Bureau head Edward Hosea and Mwanyika. Opposition deputies accused the Government of failing to tackle corruption. In March 2010 the US Ambassador to Tanzania called on the Government to expand its efforts against corruption, and to ensure that senior officials and leaders accused of corruption faced trial.

Following the murder of around 45 albinos since 2007 (linked to the trade in body parts for use in some forms of traditional healing and sorcery), in March 2009 Kikwete launched a campaign to identify the culprits. People were called upon to identify the killers anonymously. In late September three men were sentenced to death for the murders, and a further four people were sentenced to death in October following a court case in Shinyanga.

In August 2010 the CCM held primary contests to select candidates to stand in the forthcoming legislative elections. Previously, candidates had been chosen by the party's National Executive Committee. As a result of the primary elections, over 70 incumbents, including some senior CCM figures such as former Prime Minister John Malecela, were deselected. However, amid claims of bribery during the process, the executive committee later overturned some decisions, prompting a number of CCM candidates to join Chadema. Kikwete was selected as the CCM's presidential candidate (by the executive committee rather than popular vote) by a large majority. However, although it appeared that Kikwete had managed to re-establish some authority over the increasingly divided and factious party, his selection merely reflected the lack of a unifying alternative. Later that month concerns were raised over President Kikwete's health following his collapse at the launch of his election campaign.

THE OCTOBER 2010 ELECTIONS AND THE SECOND KIKWETE ADMINISTRATION

Legislative and presidential elections took place on 31 October 2010, with a turn-out of around 43%. In the presidential election, Kikwete was re-elected for a second (and final) term with approximately 62.8% of the votes cast, the lowest percentage received by a CCM presidential candidate and a significant decline from the 80% secured in the 2005 poll. This loss of support reflected Kikwete's weakness, but also the growing strength of Chadema as a national opposition party capable of mobilizing support across the country. Willibrod Peter Slaa, the Secretary-General of Chadema, who received 27.1% of the ballot, demanded a re-run of the elections, citing voting irregularities. However, the NEC found insufficient evidence of serious problems and ruled out new elections. The CCM's support in rural areas appeared strong, while Chadema support was high in towns including Arusha and Mwanza (where Slaa received more votes than Kikwete).

In the parliamentary elections, the CCM won 186 seats (78% of the total), gaining 254 in total when including indirectly elected representatives. Chadema replaced the CUF as the official opposition party, after winning a total of 46 seats to the CUF's 36. NCCR-Mageuzi won four seats, and the TLP and UDP both secured one seat each. Including indirectly elected seats, the results left the CCM with 75% of the parliamentary seats.

Following the elections, protests erupted in Dar es Salaam, Mwanza and Zanzibar over delays in the announcement of the results. In Mwanza police fired tear gas at protesters, and in Dar es Salaam police used water cannons against demonstrators who had blocked roads, alleging vote-rigging in the commercial capital in favour of the ruling CCM. Anti-Government protests organized by the opposition in early 2011 turned violent following police intervention to control the demonstrations. In Arusha in January two Chadema supporters were shot dead by police, and nine people were injured in violence after Chadema chairman Freeman Mbowe was arrested along with 49 party officials. The following week a large protest (reportedly involving tens of thousands of demonstrators) was held to commemorate the deaths of the two Chadema supporters. In May Mbowe was officially charged in connection with the protests.

Despite winning the presidential election, albeit with a reduced majority, power continued to slip away from President Kikwete, as he failed to manage the factions that were splitting the CCM. Corruption issues continued to trouble the Government. In November 2010 Samuel Sitta's re-election to the post of parliamentary Speaker was blocked by the ruling CCM, which stated that it wanted to appoint a woman to the post. However, the move was widely perceived as an attempt to limit debate over, and investigation into, corruption by senior officials and politicians. Sitta, regarded as an anti-corruption campaigner, had allowed debates on the subject in the National Assembly, and had sought to strengthen the institution with respect to holding ministers to account, angering some senior CCM leaders. His removal as Speaker was regarded as further evidence of the ruling CCM's increasing unwillingness to tackle corruption.

In March 2011 the National Assembly adopted the Constitutional Review Act which would allow for consultation on a new draft constitution. The following month the membership was announced of the Constitutional Review Commission (CRC), which was to head the process of drafting a new constitution, to be referred for approval at a referendum in late 2013. Former Prime Minister Joseph Warioba would chair the CRC, with 15 members from Zanzibar and 15 from the mainland. Former Chadema Chairman Edwin Mtei protested that there was an over-representation of Muslims on the committee, and some complained that Zanzibar was disproportionately represented given its much smaller population. However, in general the Commissions's membership prompted few complaints.

In July 2011 a CCM parliamentary deputy, Rostam Aziz, resigned from his seat, and from all party offices. Aziz, who was linked to the faction within the CCM headed by former Prime Minister Edward Lowossa, had been implicated in a number of scandals, although he denied any wrongdoing. His resignation was interpreted by some as part of an effort to remove CCM politicians tainted by corruption allegations as part of the ongoing feud within the CCM for control over the ruling party. CCM retained the seat in the resultant by-election in Igunga. However, the following April the CCM was unexpectedly defeated in a by-election in Arumeru East, when it was second placed with 44% of the votes cast, Chadema taking 54% of the vote. Chadema's success demonstrated the opposition parties' growing strength, especially in urban areas.

Under the leadership of Zitto Kabwe, Chadema was able increasingly effectively to challenge the Government in the National Assembly, achieving some significant victories. In mid-April 2012 the Auditor-General released the annual financial performance report on government ministries, in which a number of ministers were criticized for financial irregularities. At the initiation of Kabwe, Chadema and the CUF, together with deputies from other opposition parties and a small number of CCM politicians, signed a petition demanding that the main six ministers concerned resign. With Kikwete out of the country on official visits, and the ministers refusing to resign, Kabwe introduced a motion of no-confidence in Prime Minister Pinda (against whom there were no allegations of wrong-doing) in an attempt to force the issue. On Kikwete's return, he immediately announced a government reorganization in order to defuse the political crisis, and forced the six ministers to resign: Minister of Finance Mustapha Mkulo, Minister of Energy and Minerals William Ngeleja (who had already been criticized for his poor performance during the 2011 energy crisis), Minister of Transport Omari Nundu, Minister of Health Haji Mponda, Minister of Industry and Trade Cyril Chami, and Minister of Tourism Ezekiel Maige. Replacements were immediately appointed to ensure all resigned.

The Government continued to face protests and strikes from a range of groups. In June 2012 medical doctors staged strike action to demand substantial increases in their pay and allowances. It was reported that Steven Ulimboka, Chairman of the Medical Association of Tanzania, had been abducted, beaten and tortured following the protests. Kikwete strenuously denied allegations that the Government had ordered the attack against Ulimboka.

Meanwhile, in December 2010 BAE Systems was fined £500,000 by a British court over its failure to keep proper records in relation to the Tanzania radar contract, and reached a settlement with the Tanzanian Government to pay £29.5m. It initially argued that it would pay the amount through non-governmental organizations rather than to the Government, attracting complaints from the Tanzanian authorities, which in July 2011 urged the United Kingdom to put pressure on BAE Systems to make the payments directly to the Tanzanian Government. In March 2012 BAE Systems finally announced that it would disburse the money by contributing towards education projects, including the purchase of textbooks.

Concerns over infrastructure and government regulation of potential hazards increased in 2011 and 2012, following a number of tragedies. In February 2011 at least 20 people were killed and more than 100 injured by the explosion of 23 munitions depots in the Gongola Mboto military compound in Dar es Salaam, which raised concerns over the safety of military camps inside the city. In September around 2,000 people died when a ferry capsized while travelling to Pemba from Unguja. The incident highlighted the poor state of regulations over ferries operating between the Zanzibar and the mainland, in particular the serious problem of overcrowding which was believed to have contributed to the disaster. In mid-December more than 20 people died and 5,000 were left homeless in Dar es Salaam, owing to floods caused by unusually heavy rains.

The rapidly growing extractive industries sector resulted in increased tensions between local inhabitants and international mining companies. In May 2011 villagers living near to Barrick Gold's North Mara mine forced their way onto Barrick's premises to protest against fees charged to small-scale miners. The police responded aggressively and shot dead five of the protesters. A few days later, the local CCM deputy and the District Governor were attacked by villagers. Meanwhile, discoveries of onshore and offshore gas deposits in Tanzania promised significant potential for exploitation. New discoveries of gas reserves in March 2012 brought estimated reserves in the country to around 15,000,000m. cu ft, which, according to World Bank estimates, would generate revenue of around US $35,000m. over the next few decades. However, concerns continued over the ability of the Government effectively to manage the sector, with prolonged delays in the approval of a long-promised new Gas Bill.

With heightened security concerns across East Africa (following attacks in Kenya and Uganda), Tanzanian security services remained on high alert for possible international terrorist activity. In June 2012 Emrah Erdogan, a German national suspected of involvement in the attack on a shopping centre in Nairobi in which over 30 people were injured and also believed to have been fighting with the al-Shabaab militia in Somalia, was arrested in Dar es Salaam.

TENSIONS IN ZANZIBAR

From the late 1980s opposition in Zanzibar coalesced around the Kamati ya Mageuzi Huru (Kamahuru), led by Shaaban Mloo, which merged with the mainland-based Chama cha Wananchi to form the CUF in 1992. Former Chief Minister Seif Sharif Hamad was selected as the CUF's presidential candidate. In the October 1995 elections, the CCM secured 26 of the 50 elective seats to the House of Representatives. The CUF took 24 seats, and all those on Pemba. Salmin Amour defeated Hamad in the Zanzibar presidential election, winning 50.2% of votes cast. The CUF refused to accept the election results, and its elected delegates refused to take up their seats in the legislature. An agreement reached in June 1999 soon broke down, with the CUF accusing the CCM of refusing to honour its terms. Armed troops were deployed in August 2000, following clashes between CCM and CUF supporters.

Presidential and legislative elections were held on Zanzibar and Pemba on 29 October 2000, amid widespread accusations of electoral fraud. Voting in 16 of the 50 constituencies was annulled (all areas of strong CUF support) and new elections arranged. Violent clashes between police and opposition supporters took place in the run up to the re-run polls on 5 November. The CCM won 34 seats in the House of Representatives, with 67% of the vote, but the CUF refused to recognize the results, widely seen as rigged in the CCM's favour. Violence continued, with a wave of bomb attacks across the islands. On 27–28 January 2001 clashes between police and demonstrators left at least 40 people dead (including six members of the security forces), and 100 people injured. Over 400 people were arrested and imprisoned. Many CUF supporters fled to Kenya, where by February 636 Zanzibari refugees had claimed asylum. A new agreement signed in October 2001, known as the *muafaka* (peace accord), again broke down, with the CUF accusing the Government of failing to implement the required reforms.

THE 2005 ELECTIONS ON ZANZIBAR AND THEIR AFTERMATH

Violent attacks continued throughout 2005 in the run-up to the October elections, including arson attacks against CCM and CUF offices, and the murder of a CCM official in April. The CUF accused the Government of preventing over 30,000 CUF supporters from registering to vote, and of supporting a local militia in its attacks on CUF supporters. In April the Government banned Hamad from standing in the elections, as he had not resided on Zanzibar for three consecutive years, but this ruling was overturned on appeal. In October police opened fire on a CUF demonstration, wounding 18 and arresting dozens of CUF supporters. Prior to the elections, 30,000 members of the security forces were deployed across Zanzibar in an effort to ensure control.

The elections on Zanzibar took place on 30 October 2005 in comparative calm, and international observers noted the poll on Zanzibar was generally free and fair. Karume was re-elected as President of Zanzibar, winning 53.2% of the votes cast; Hamad won 46.1%. The CCM won 31 seats, and the CUF 18 seats. For several days following the election there were violent clashes between the police and CUF supporters in Stone Town.

The CUF rejected the result, claiming that it had won the election.

Renewed talks on ending the political crisis repeatedly stalled throughout 2007. Although the CUF agreed to a power-sharing deal with the CCM in February 2008, the ruling party rejected the idea in the following month (despite earlier indications of acceptance of the deal), leading to CUF demonstrations against the Government.

In mid-2009 continued protests by the CUF that the Zanzibar Electoral Commission was failing to register its supporters prompted donors to put pressure on the Government to re-establish negotiations. In early November Hamad met with Karume to discuss how to move the reconciliation process forward, and both agreed to the establishment of a unity government. Two days later, at a CUF rally on Unguja, Hamad formally recognized the CCM Government on Zanzibar, and ended the CUF's boycott of the House of Representatives. In January 2010 legislation was approved in the House of Representatives introducing constitutional amendments that would allow for the creation of a government of national unity (GNU). In July the proposal for a GNU was put to a referendum on the islands, in which a majority of 66.4% supported the idea.

THE 2010 ELECTIONS ON ZANZIBAR

In the presidential poll on Zanzibar in October 2010, the CCM's Ali Mohammed Shein secured victory over Hamad by fewer than 4,000 votes in an election regarded by observers as generally free and fair. Shein won 50.1% of the vote and Hamad 49.1%. Under the power-sharing agreement signed in July, a GNU was established, with Shein as Zanzibar President and Hamad as First Vice-President. The GNU was widely seen as an effective stabilizing force, reducing political tensions on the islands. However, while political relations on Zanzibar were improving, those with the mainland were put under increasing strain over discussion of revenue-sharing agreements for oil and gas production. There were also signs of growing tensions between Zanzibaris and mainland Tanzanians living on the islands, after several houses belonging to the latter were burned down in May 2011. An Islamic group known as Uamsho (Awakening) was implicated in riots, attacks on police and the fire-bombing of several churches that took place in May 2012. It was also alleged to have been involved in a number of attacks on bars the previous year.

The CUF suffered a reverse in April 2012, when it was placed third in a by-election in Uzini; the CCM retained its seat, but Chadema was placed second, winning 59 votes more than the CUF. CUF Deputy Secretary-General Mji Mkongwe blamed the influx of mainland Tanzanians and Christians for the defeat, and demanded restrictions on mainland Tanzanians working on the islands. The defeat fuelled ongoing tensions with the CUF, in particular over the succession to CUF Secretary-General and Zanzibar's First Vice-President Hamad. Hamad was forced to state that he had made no decisions as to when he might retire, which was widely regarded as a warning to CUF deputy Hamad Rashid Mohammed, who had begun to promote himself as a likely successor to Hamad's leadership of the party.

FOREIGN RELATIONS

In March 1996 the Presidents of Tanzania, Uganda and Kenya formally inaugurated a commission designed to revive the East African Community (EAC), which had collapsed in its original form in 1977. In 1999 the EAC Treaty was signed by all three leaders, creating a single free trade area, and plans for the creation of a regional legislative assembly and regional court, which came into effect in July 2000. The first meeting of the new East African Council of Ministers was held in Tanzania in January 2001. In March 2004 the three EAC members signed a protocol establishing the East African Customs Union (EACU). The EACU took effect in January 2005. In December 2006 Rwanda and Burundi were accepted as members of the EAC, expanding the bloc to include around 90m. people. In November 2009 EAC leaders signed an agreement permitting free trade, free movement of people across the region, and the right of residence. The last of these principles was considered controversial in Tanzania. In June 2011 the Tanzanian and Ugandan Governments signed a US $1,900m. agreement to develop transport infrastructure, including the construction of a rail link and upgrades to the port at Tanga.

In October 2008 the three main African trading blocks, the EAC, the Southern African Development Community and Common Market for Eastern and Southern Africa, signed an agreement in Kampala to create a single free trade zone of 26 countries. As well as improving African trade within the continent, it was hoped the agreement would lead to a stronger negotiating position with external trading powers.

In September 2010 Somali pirate attacks off the coast of Tanzania escalated, with four in one week, including an attack on a cargo ship some 180 km south-east of Dar es Salaam, the furthest south pirates had ventured to that point. In April 2012 five pirates were arrested near the Songo Songo gas fields, heightening concerns over the security of Tanzania's offshore oil and gas industry.

The People's Republic of China became an increasingly important trade partner from around 2007, and in mid-February 2009 Chinese President Hu Jintao publicly pledged Tanzania US $22m. in aid on an official visit to the country. In August China announced that it was investing $400m. on reviving the Kiwira coal mine. However, hostility towards Chinese immigrants continued to rise. In January 2011 the Deputy Minister of Industry, Trade and Marketing ordered Chinese traders to cease working in a market in Dar es Salaam. Meanwhile, in September 2009 the Republic of Korea (South Korea) announced it had signed a deal with the Tanzanian Government to lease 1,000 sq km to produce food for South Korea.

Relations with donors became increasingly strained, largely due to perceived slow progress in addressing corruption. In July 2011 a group of donors, including the European Union, the United Kingdom, Germany, Japan, the World Bank and the African Development Bank, put pressure on the Government to reveal the outcome of ongoing investigations into a scandal over external payment arrears. However, the USA was also concerned about possible government collusion in Iranian efforts to evade sanctions placed upon Iran's oil export sector. In July 2012 the US Government accused Tanzania of helping Iran to evade oil sanctions by allowing Iranian oil tankers to operate under the Tanzanian flag. The Government denied the allegations, and launched an investigation. The Chair of the US House of Representatives Committee on Foreign Affairs warned that if the accusations were proven to be true the continuation of US bilateral aid programmes would be at threat.

Economy

LINDA VAN BUREN

Revised for this edition by DUNCAN WOODSIDE

INTRODUCTION

With real gross domestic product (GDP) growing by 7.0% in 2010 and by 6.4% in 2011, Tanzania is one of the fastest-growing economies in sub-Saharan Africa. The recent strong performance is largely in line with the previous decade; the country's average annual growth was 7.0% in 2000–08, including 7.5% in 2008, before slowing only modestly, to 5.5% in 2009, when much of the developed world fell into recession, due to the banking crisis in Europe and the USA. After a weak recovery in 2010 and the first half of 2011, the developed world stagnated afresh (and some countries returned to recession) towards the end of 2011 and in the first half of 2012, due to an intensifying sovereign debt crisis in the eurozone, with investors in much of the world constrained by shrinking liquidity and fears about the long-term outlook for global economic growth. Yet, whilst all this impinged on Tanzania's own growth prospects—due largely to the effect on foreign direct investment (FDI)—the negative impact was partially offset by the country's gold mining sector. On the whole, gold prices tend to be elevated during times of global financial stress, due to the commodity's status as a 'safe haven' asset. Major discoveries of natural gas—which resulted in the country's total estimated reserves rising to nearly 30,000,000m. cu ft before mid-2012, compared with 10,000,000m. cu ft in September 2011—also support the growth outlook in Tanzania. In this context, the IMF remained relatively positive in its April 2012 global economic outlook, predicting that the country would experience growth of 6.4%, in real terms, in that year, at the same level as the 2011 rate. The Fund predicted a modest acceleration in real economic growth, to 6.7%, in 2013.

Beyond economic growth, Tanzania's market position is bolstered regionally by a low level of public debt. Total government debt (inclusive of domestic and foreign obligations) stood at around 37% of GDP in the 2010/11 fiscal year (July to the end of June), considerably lower than in many eurozone nations. The country is also perceived to be less corrupt than many other African states; in Transparency International's 2011 Corruption Perceptions Index, Tanzania was ranked 100 of 182 countries. In May 2012 President Jakaya Kikwete dismissed the Minister of Finance, and the Minister of Energy and Minerals, after allegations were presented in parliament about corruption in their ministries.

Although overall economic progress has been strong in recent years, there are significant limitations to Tanzania's current level of economic development. The IMF estimated in January 2012 that GDP per caput was a modest US $550 per annum, due to slow growth before 2000, inflation and rapid population growth. As such, the majority of the population continues to subsist on less than a dollar per day. Furthermore, with a population growth rate of more than 2% per year, GDP growth of at least 8% per year is necessary if Tanzania is to meet its objective of becoming a middle-income country by 2025.

AGRICULTURE

The agricultural sector is the mainstay of Tanzania's economy, providing a livelihood for some 80% of the economically active population and contributing 22% of GDP in 2010. This proportion is declining; agriculture had contributed 47% in 2000 and 30% in 2007. Furthermore, the growth rate in agriculture, at just 3% in 2010, lagged behind all other sectors of the economy. Subsistence farming accounted for about 40% of total agricultural output in 2010. No more than about 8% of the country's land area is cultivated, and only about 3% of the cultivated land is irrigated, yet the growing of field crops heavily dominates the agricultural sector as a whole. The northern and south-western areas of the country are the most fertile, receiving the highest rainfall in most years. The main food crop is maize, which is the staple food in most parts of the country. The staple in the west is green bananas. Other food crops include cassava, paddy rice, sorghum, plantains, sweet potatoes, potatoes, beans and millet. Cash crops include cashew nuts, coffee, groundnuts and cotton from the mainland, and clove stems from Zanzibar. Tea, tobacco and sisal are also produced. In 1999, following intensive efforts to revitalize the cashew nut sector, this tree crop overtook coffee as Tanzania's main agricultural export. In 2006/07 cashew nuts accounted for 5.0% of total exports, while coffee accounted for 3.5%. The 2008/09 budget focused agricultural spending on the Strategic Grain Reserve, fertilizer subsidies, training and research, especially into improved seeds.

In May 2007 a new cashew nut-processing factory was commissioned 60 km west of Dar es Salaam. Cashew nut experts claimed that Tanzania was capable of producing in excess of 300,000 metric tons per year. The 2010/11 budget raised the export levy on raw cashew nuts from 10% to 15%, in order to discourage the export of raw nuts and to encourage local processing to add value before export.

Coffee is grown mainly by some 400,000 smallholders. The main growing area is in the Kilimanjaro region in the north, where the Arabica variety is grown. The centre for the growing of Robusta is west and south of Lake Victoria. Output of green coffee increased from 43,100 metric tons in 2008 to 68,577 tons in 2009. Tanzania's coffee crop in 2010/11 (June 2010–May 2011) was 62% Arabica and 38% Robusta, in volume terms; on global markets, Arabica fetched almost double the price of Robusta. According to the International Coffee Organization (ICO), of which Tanzania is a member, the country exported 726,679 60-kg bags in 2010/11, declining from 963,991 bags in 2008.

Cotton is grown mainly by smallholders, primarily in two adjoining regions to the south of Lake Victoria: Shinyanga and Mwanza. Of Tanzania's 62 ginneries in 2009, 25 were in Shinyanga region, and 23 were in Mwanza region. The production of seed cotton in Tanzania decreased from 376,591 metric tons in 2005/06 to only 230,000 tons in 2006/07 because of severe drought, according to the Tanzania Cotton Board. In 2007/08, despite flooding that delayed planting in June 2007 in some areas and especially drought in other areas, production of seed cotton rose to 320,000 tons. The cotton crop in 2009 declined by 31%, to 254,000 tons, yielding 83,700 tons of cotton lint and 170,000 tons of cottonseed.

The country had 19 tea-processing factories in 2009. The estates were rehabilitated throughout the 1990s, and some now produce organic teas, which command high prices. The revived East African Community (EAC) liberalized the tea sector in the then three member states (Tanzania, Kenya and Uganda), and the 2004 Tanzania budget exempted black tea and packaged tea from value-added tax (VAT) so as to enable Tanzanian tea to compete in the EAC market. Overseas, innovative marketing and participation with fair trade marketing organizations have placed Tanzanian tea in a number of superior international coffee and tea outlets, under branding such as Kibena tea. Tanzania Tea Packers Ltd (Tatepa) has garnered a 70% share of the local market for tea and launched four brands of herbal tea, which also found markets in neighbouring Kenya. The tea sector was expected to receive a boost in the 2012/13 fiscal year, owing to the construction of a new factory with the capacity to process 1.5m. kg of tea per year. The Tanzania Tea Board estimated that production would rise to 36m. kg from an estimated 34m. kg–35m. kg in 2011/12.

In 2011 Tanzania had some 3m. beehives. Honey and beeswax produced by Tabora Beekeepers' Co-operative are exported in small quantities; Zanzibar exports clove honey. Grapes are cultivated in central Tanzania, with output totalling 17,748 metric tons in 2009; some local wine is produced in the area around Dodoma.

Tanzania is one of Africa's largest cattle producers, with an estimated national herd of 19.5m. head in 2010, according to FAO. Tanzania also had 12.9m. goats, 4.2m. sheep and 33.5m. chickens in that year. The country's resources of commercial species of timber, including camphor wood, podo and African mahogany, are exploited. Total roundwood removals amounted to 25.2m. cu m in 2011, according to FAO, most of it used as fuelwood. Tanzania exported 14,208 cu m of sawnwood in 2009 and earned US $39.8m. from exports of all forest products in that year. Fishing, on both a commercial and subsistence basis, contributed an estimated 6% of GDP in 2010. The total fish catch is about 350,000 metric tons per year. Of the total catch in 2010, 87% was freshwater fish, including Nile perch, dagaas and tilapias; other species caught included sardinellas, Indian mackerel and tuna from the Indian Ocean.

INDUSTRY AND POWER

According to estimates by the World Bank, the average annual growth rate of industrial GDP was 3.4% in 1980–90 and 4.4% in 1990–2003, but growth in the sector was estimated at 9.4% in 2008. The industrial sector is based on the processing of local commodities (with agro-industrial companies manufacturing sugar, sisal twine and cigarettes) and on import substitution. However, the Government is seeking to encourage the production of manufactured goods for export, in order to lessen dependence on agricultural commodities. Some industrial goods—textiles, clothing, footwear, tyres, batteries, transformers, switch gear, electric cookers, bottles, cement and paper—are exported to neighbouring countries. Principal manufactures in 2011 were beer, sugar, rope, wheat flour, vegetable oils, animal feeds, iron sheets, rolled steel, paint, batteries, textiles and carpets. Other industrial activities include petroleum-refining, fertilizer production, metal-working, vehicle assembly, fruit-canning, engineering (spares for industrial machinery and for vehicles), railway-wagon assembly, and the manufacture of pulp and paper, paperboard, cement, soft drinks, gunny bags, glassware, ceramics, hoes, pharmaceutical products, oxygen, carbon dioxide, bricks and tiles, light bulbs, electrical goods, wood products, machine tools, footwear, and disposable hypodermic syringes.

From the 1990s the Government expressed its intention to privatize, restructure or dissolve 410 state-owned companies. Of these, 266 had been privatized or disposed of by 2003. The majority were small companies engaged in agro-industrial activities, but mining entities attracted the largest sums of investment money. Management of Tanzania's privatization process has shifted over the years; on 1 January 2008 it was transferred to Consolidated Holding Corporation. Among the companies privatized were the Dar es Salaam Water Supply Authority, the Kagera Sugar Co and Southern Paper Mills (which became Mufindi Paper Mills).

Tanzania's electricity is supplied mainly by the Tanzania Electric Supply Company (TANESCO); the company's own generating facilities are 90% hydroelectric, supplemented by thermal stations. Independent power producers (IPPs) also sell power into the national grid. Of the total Tanzanian national consumption of 4,425.4m. kWh as of 2008, TANESCO supplied about 2,985.3m. kWh, or about 67%, while IPPs supplemented this generating capacity. However, total generating capacity falls well below national demand, resulting in continual power shortages. TANESCO operates six hydroelectric plants, with a combined capacity of 561 MW: Kidatu (204 MW), Kihansi (180 MW), Mtera (80 MW), Pangani Falls (68 MW), Hale (21 MW) and Nyumba ya Mungu (8 MW). In 2011 new plants were under construction at Dar es Salaam (100 MW) and Mwanza (60 MW). Perennially, the lack of a reliable source of electricity to factories has been a key hindrance to the manufacturing sector. The Kikwete Government approved a substantial tariff increase for TANESCO (21.7% on average) that came into effect on 1 January 2008. Nevertheless, in May the IMF repeated the warning that financial viability for TANESCO remained a critical element for establishing a reliable electricity supply to support economic growth. TANESCO's operational cash shortfalls amounted to some Ts. 50,000m. (US $43.55m.) in 2008. Only 14% of Tanzania's population had access to the electricity grid in 2011.

In 2010 the national grid comprised 1,011 MW, of which 55%, or 561 MW, was contributed by hydroelectric power stations. Songas, the Songo Songo gas-to-electricity operation, contributed 200 MW, and Independent Power Tanzania Ltd, a joint venture between Malaysian and Tanzanian investors (see below), contributed 100 MW. TANESCO's new gas-fired plant came on stream in September 2008, adding another 100 MW. Diesel-run generating stations had an installed capacity of 111 MW, but, of this, only about 50 MW was functional. In addition, about 13 MW was imported from Zambia. Of the hydroelectric generating capacity, the largest is the Kidatu hydroelectric complex on the Great Ruaha river, with a capacity of 204 MW. In February 2011 the country recorded a power shortfall of 264 MW, due to the effect of a drought on hydropower generation. State-run Tanzania Electricity Supply Company announced in March 2012 that it would receive a US $165m. loan from HSBC Holdings to construct a 100-MW gas-fired power station in Dar es Salaam, which was already being built by Norway's Jacobsen Elektro. At the same time, it was acknowledged that mobile power firm Aggreko had discontinued output at its two 50-MW plants in the economic capital, due to the authorities' failure to pay $36m. in fees on time. Aggreko commenced generation at the two facilities in October 2011, amid continuing national power shortages. In December TANESCO announced that it was engaged in discussions with a Citigroup-led syndicate of banks, in an effort to secure further funding of $257m., which would be allocated to improvements in power generation.

Despite Tanzania's frequent power cuts, the industrial and manufacturing sectors have performed relatively well since the 2000s, owing to the country's strong overall economic growth. As these sectors have developed, cement demand has risen accordingly. In this context, Portland Cement, the local unit of Germany's HeidelbergCement, announced in May 2012 that it would increase output to 1.4m. metric tons that year, from 1.1m. tons in 2011. As well as strong demand, an increase in the supply of locally-produced clinker, together with an amelioration of the power situation, were expected to drive this output increase. Portland Cement's net profit rose slightly to Ts. 50,600m. in 2011, from Ts. 50,200m. in 2010.

MINERALS

Tanzania's mining sector provided an estimated 6.5% of GDP in 2010. Gold was the leading export earner, providing an estimated 35.6% of total exports in 2010/11. Gold exports earned an estimated US $1,668m. in that year, up from $1,493m. in 2009/10. Tanzania is the third largest gold producer in Africa, after South Africa and Ghana. Proven gold reserves in the Lake Victoria greenstone belt were assessed at up to 40m. troy oz. Investment has been dominated by Canadian mining companies.

Production figures for 2011 remained strong. The country produced 40.4 metric tons of gold during the year as a whole, representing an increase of 13% year on year from 35.6 tons in 2010, according to the central bank, which attributed the improvement to mining companies seeking to exploit elevated prices by bolstering local investment. The average price of gold rose by 28% in 2011, to $1,568 per troy oz. Due to the combination of higher output and strong prices, Tanzania generated a total of US $2,226m. in gold exports during 2011, a rise of 47% year on year, which ensured that gold accounted for 59.1% of the country's total annual exports. However, it was expected that gold production would decline in 2013, due to the expected closures of Resolute's Gold Pride facilities and African Barrick's Tulawaka mine. Although Barrick focused on generating new output from other sources, including its Nyanzaga project, at April 2012 the firm had yet to produce a feasibility study for this latter project, according to the Ministry of Energy and Minerals.

In 2008 output at AngloGold Ashanti's Geita gold mine was 264,000 oz at a total cash cost of US $728 per oz. Drilling information from Nyankanga West and Geita Hill defined an additional 800,000 oz, bringing reserves at Geita to 18m. oz. AngloGold Ashanti planned capital expenditure of $64m. in 2008 but in the out-turn spent only $53m. The $48m. Golden Pride gold mine at Lusu, near Nzega, in central Tanzania, is

100% owned by Resolute Mining Ltd of Australia. This mine had been expected to reach the end of its life in 2009, but the discovery of a new ore zone in 2007 enabled an extension of Golden Pride's life. Resolute Mining formed the Golden Pride East joint venture with Barrick Gold Corpn of Canada to prospect a 350-sq km area in the Nzega Greenstone belt east of the existing Golden Pride mine. Toronto-based Barrick Gold Corpn owned four gold producing operations in Tanzania in 2011: Bulyanhulu, North Mara, Tulawaka and Buzwagi. The $211m. underground gold mine at Bulyanhulu in Kahama district had proven and probable reserves of 12m. oz at 31 December 2008. Output at Bulyanhulu in 2008 was 200,000 oz at a total cash cost of $620 per oz; output in 2009 was projected at up to 290,000 oz at $485–$525 per oz. The North Mara operation lies 100 km east of Lake Victoria and just 20 km south of the Kenyan border. It comprises three open-pit mines: Nyabirama, Nyabigena and Gokona. In 2011 Nyabirama was in production, Nyabigena was in the development phase, and Gokona was 'being prepared for development', according to Barrick. North Mara produced 197,000 oz in 2008. Total cash costs of production in 2008 were $757 per oz. Proven and probable reserves were assessed at 3m. oz of gold as of 31 December 2008. The Tulawaka open-pit gold mine, a joint venture owned 70% by Barrick and 30% by MDN Inc (formerly Northern Mining Explorations Ltd) of Canada, entered production in March 2005 and produced 124,743 oz. Located 120 km west of the Bulyanhulu mine, Tulawaka had proven and probable reserves in excess of 470,000 oz of gold as of 31 December 2006. In 2007 Barrick proceeded with the construction, at a cost of $400m., of the Buzwagi open-pit gold mine, lying 80 km south of the Bulyanhulu gold mine. The Buzwagi mine poured its first gold in May 2009 and was estimated to have produced up to 210,000 oz of gold during 2009, at a total cash cost of between $320 and $335 per oz. Proven and probable reserves at Buzwagi totalled 3.3m. oz of gold, and the lifespan of the mine was projected at 10 years. It also had proven and probable reserves of 118m. lb (53.5m. kg) of copper 'within the gold reserves'.

Tanzania has extensive reserves of precious and semi-precious stones, and new discoveries are continuing to be made, generating a high level of foreign interest, especially in the southern half of the country. The Williamson diamond mine at Mwadui, owned by Petra Diamonds of South Africa (75%) and the Government of Tanzania (25%), covers 146 ha and was reported to be the world's largest diamond mine by area. In 2010 the mine produced 91,901 carats, earning US $14.4m. The Longido ruby mine, established in 1949 after spectacular discoveries, is the largest in the world. The Umba River Valley yields rubies and sapphires, with particular interest in the gem market centring on a fiery reddish-orange sapphire to rival the famous and increasingly scarce paparadzha sapphire of Sri Lanka. Sapphires have been discovered at Songea, and alluvial deposits at Tunduru have yielded sapphires, tourmalines, alexandrites, chrysoberyls and spinels; nine prospecting licences have been granted. Both Songea and Tunduru have been overrun by illegal prospectors. Deposits of tanzanite, a blue semi-precious stone that is found nowhere else in the world, have been exploited by unlicensed miners. Demand for tanzanite rose significantly in the USA from 2005, following aggressive television marketing, but demand weakened in 2008 and 2009 owing to the global economic downturn. In general, exports of diamonds and other gemstones were declining in the late 2000s.

Lake Natron, the most caustic body of water in the world, is a bright orange-red lake in the Rift Valley with large deposits of soda ash for the production of caustic soda. Used in the production of fibreglass and fibre-optics, natural soda ash has advantages over synthetic soda ash. In March 2007 the Kikwete Government announced plans for a US $600m. project to exploit Lake Natron's soda ash potential. Tata Chemicals Ltd of India and Tanzania's National Development Corpn proposed the construction of a soda ash plant on the shores of the lake, complete with a coal-fired power station and housing for up to 1,000 employees, but environmental groups were fiercely opposed to the project. Salt is produced at coastal salt pans and is a potential export. The feasibility of extracting salt from Lake Eyasi, 200 km west of Arusha, was being investigated. Salt output was 135,000 metric tons in 2005. Barrick and Falconbridge Ltd of Canada formed a 50:50 joint venture to develop the 26.4m. tons of nickel sulphide deposits in Kabanga, north-western Tanzania. Xstrata of Switzerland, which acquired Falconbridge in 2006, committed a further $95m. to the project in February 2007 and was to be the operator. The $40m. feasibility study for this project was completed in 2010 and underwent assessment in 2011. In April 2007 the Kikwete Government announced plans to establish a $600m. open-cast colliery, Mchuchuma, producing 1.5m. tons of coal per year. Coal is mined on a smaller scale at Ilima in the Mbeya region. Iron ore is mined at Chunya. Tin is mined on a small scale near the Congolese border. Salt, phosphates, gypsum, kaolin, limestone and graphite are also exploited. Deposits of lead, iron ore, silver, tungsten, pyrochlore, magnesite, copper, cobalt, uranium, niobium, titanium and vanadium have also been identified.

Prospecting for petroleum and natural gas has been continuing for many years. Petroleum has been identified in the Songo Songo island area, off shore from Kilwa, south of Dar es Salaam, but it was the presence of an estimated 42,890m. cu m of natural gas in the area that proved to be of greater interest. Songas Ltd built two gas-processing units on Songo Songo island, as well as a 25-km underwater pipeline to deliver the gas from the island to Somanga, on the mainland, and a 207-km underground pipeline to deliver the gas from Somanga northwards to Dar es Salaam, where it supplies the 122-MW Ubungo power plant (the four turbines of which needed to be converted to run on gas) and the cement plant at Wazo Hill. The scheme entailed several infrastructural developments on Songo Songo island, including the construction of an airstrip. The pipelines were completed in May 2004, and the first gas from Songo Songo arrived in Dar es Salaam in July 2004.

Songo Songo had a projected lifetime of 20 years. There is a much larger offshore gas field at Kimbiji, 40 km south-east of Dar es Salaam, where recoverable reserves were estimated at 130,000m. cu m. Results of petroleum exploration so far have been disappointing, but a number of international companies from Australia, Canada, India, Italy, the Netherlands, Norway, Switzerland, the United Kingdom and the USA have been active, in both on- and offshore areas (in some cases grouped in consortia).

A major boost for Tanzania's natural gas industry came in September 2011, when the Government secured a US $1,000m. loan agreement with the People's Republic of China, in order to construct a 532-km pipeline from Mnazi Bay to Songo Songo and Dar es Salaam, along with processing facilities at Mnazi Bay. The Export-Import Bank of China was to finance most of the construction costs and the pipeline would have a capacity of 784m. cu ft per day of gas, which would be utilized to generate 3,900 MW of electricity, according to the then Minister of Energy and Minerals, William Ngeleja. Construction was initially expected to be finished by March 2013, although the Government acknowledged in June 2012 that work had yet to commence.

The country's estimated recoverable gas reserves rose from 10,000,000m. cu ft in September 2011 to 28,700,000m. in June 2012, according to newly-appointed Minister of Energy and Minerals Sospeter Muhongo. This was due to a series of new discoveries that increased offshore reserves to 21,000,000m. cu ft and onshore deposits to 7,800,000m. cu ft. Norway's state-owned Statoil and Britain's BG Group were among the key players in driving these discoveries. In June 2012 Statoil announced that it had found 3,000,000m. cu ft of gas (equivalent to 530m. barrels of oil) at its Lavani deposit in Indian Ocean waters off the Tanzanian coast, adding to existing discoveries of 6,000,000m. cu ft. This followed an announcement in March that year by BG Group and Ophir that they had found new reserves totalling 3,400,000m. cu ft in their Jordari-1 Well in Block 1, surpassing expectations by 55%. The previous month BG Group stated that it intended to invest US $500m. in exploration in Tanzania during the course of 2012.

A dispute emerged in late 2011 and early 2012 between Tanzania's Government and PanAfrican Energy Tanzania (PAT), the local unit of Canada-listed Orca Exploration. A legislative inquiry alleged that PAT had deprived the

Government of $20.1m in royalties; a claim denied by the company. The inquiry ordered an appraisal of the company's contract, and Ngeleja declared in February 2012 that the State wanted the alleged shortfall to be paid. However, he announced that the Government would not necessarily end the firm's contract. PAT finalized a deal with state-run Tanzania Petroleum Development Corporation (TPDC) in 2001, which involves the former supplying gas to dozens of industrial firms and the national grid.

TPDC announced in March 2012 that it would solicit bids for 16 offshore oil blocks from September that year. The deep sea blocks range from depths of 1,500 metres to 3,000 metres, while they had yielded over 8,000 sq km of three-dimensional seismic data and in excess of 34,000 sq km of two-dimensional data. The bidding process was expected to be completed in 2013, although rising risk appetite in global financial markets presented a potential disadvantage to the auction's prospects. TPDC also announced that Tanzania intended to sell licences for five onshore oil blocs, without specifying a schedule.

TOURISM

During the privatization era Tanzania's tourism sector aroused more investor interest than any other sector except mining. Tourism revenue contributed 14% of GDP and 19% of exports of goods and services in 2009. The sector grew by some 10% annually in the 2000s. According to the Tanzanian Association of Tourism Operators, out of the 281 licensed tour operators in 2007, 247 were Tanzanian, and only 34 were foreign. However, the 34 foreign operators were responsible for between 70% and 80% of the tourist arrivals in the country. In 2010 tourist arrivals totalled 754,000 and receipts from tourism amounted to $1,254m. The sector is co-ordinated by the state-owned Tanzania Tourist Board. Investment was forthcoming from several local and foreign private companies. Most new investment was in the so-called 'northern circuit', linking the Serengeti National Park, the Ngorongoro Crater and Mount Kilimanjaro. Hotel capacity in this area, including Arusha, was about 13,400 beds. The Government intended to encourage the development of tourism in the 'southern circuit', which included the Selous National Park. Other destinations include the soda-rich Lake Natron, where flamingos gather in large numbers, and Lake Eyasi. Zanzibar expanded and upgraded its tourist facilities, in particular through an agreement signed with the Aga Khan Fund for Economic Development to build two new hotels, develop a tourism centre and repair historic buildings in the old capital. Zanzibar's Ras Nungwi peninsula, at the northern end of the island, offers beach-front hotel holidays with water sports and tours to the surrounding area. In June 2008 the Swiss hotel group Mövenpick announced plans to build a 200-room, 100-acre resort and golf course near Arusha, scheduled for completion by 2012.

TRANSPORT AND COMMUNICATIONS

The concentration of Tanzania's population on the periphery of the country, leaving the central part relatively sparsely populated, poses considerable problems in transport and communications. The road network is in a state of poor repair, despite significant investment in the sector.

Tanzania has two distinct railway systems: the Tanzania-Zambia Railway Authority (Tazara) and the Tanzania Railways Corpn (TRC), both of which have been scheduled to be privatized. The Chinese-built 1,860-km Tazara line initially experienced financial and technical problems, together with a lack of equipment and spare parts. Following the political changes that took place in South Africa during the early 1990s, Zambia started to make greater use of the much more reliable southern transport routes, creating new problems for the Tazara line. Tazara was built with a capacity of 5m. metric tons per year yet has carried fewer than 500,000 tons per year since 2000. The other railway, the TRC, operates Tanzania's central railway system, which has two main lines and four branches. The network comprises 2,101 km of main-line track and 405 km of branch-line track.

Precision Air Services Ltd, a joint venture between Kenya Airways (49%) and a private sector Tanzanian businessman (51%), is based in Dar es Salaam. It operates domestic services to 11 Tanzanian cities, including Zanzibar, as well as regional services to the Kenyan cities of Nairobi and Mombasa and to Entebbe in Uganda. The Ministry of Finance announced in February 2012 that the European Investment Bank was to provide a 20-year loan of €50m. to modernize five airports in Tanzania's provinces (Shinyanga and Bukoba in the north-west, and Tabora, Sumbawanga and Kigoma in the west). The developmental focus would be on improving the runways, taxiways, access roads and departure facilities.

The Tanzania Ports Authority (TPA) owns the ports of Dar es Salaam, Tanga and Mtwara, as well as all lake ports in the country. The container portion of TPA, comprising Dar es Salaam and an inland container depot at Ubungo, 15 km from Dar es Salaam, was privatized in 2000, when ownership passed to a consortium including two companies from the Philippines.

Tanzania's land telephone network is extremely limited, and, as in many African countries, development has shifted to mobile cellular systems, which cost much less to build and operate. The number of mobile network subscribers rose from 900,000 in 2003 to 9.3m. in 2008. Mobile cellular telephone services are provided by Zain Tanzania, MIC Tanzania (Mobitel) Ltd, Vodacom (Tanzania) Ltd, and Zanzibar Telecom (Zantel). Tanzania had 520,000 internet users in June 2009. By the end of 2011 the number of mobile network subscribers had reached 25.7m. (47% of the population), a rise of 22% from the level recorded in 2010. In May 2012 the Government announced that tariffs had fallen by 50% over the previous decade, owing to intensifying competition. By that time there were seven cellular providers operating on the Tanzanian market. In terms of market share, South Africa's Vodacom was the biggest local provider at the end of 2011, accounting for an estimated 43% of the market, followed by Bharti Airtel (with 28%), Tigo Tanzania (22%) and Zantel.

EXTERNAL TRADE

The leading visible export is gold, followed by cashew nuts, coffee beans and raw cotton. Gold contributed an estimated 35.6% of visible export revenue in 2010/11. Other exports include fish and prawns, cloves, beans, gemstones, timber, and aromatic oils. Industrial exports include textiles, hides, wattle-bark extract and spray-dried instant coffee. Non-traditional exports developed in the 1990s include fresh fruit, vegetables and cut flowers. Visible exports free-on-board (f.o.b.) grew from US $3,216m. in 2009/10 to $4,683m. in 2010/11, while imports f.o.b. increased from $6,149m. in 2009/10 to an estimated $7,873m. in 2010/11. The resulting 2010/11 trade deficit amounted to $3,190m., with visible exports covering less that 60% of visible imports in that year.

In March 2004 the Presidents of Tanzania, Kenya and Uganda signed a protocol on the creation of a customs union, eliminating most duties on goods within the EAC. The protocol came into force on 1 January 2005.

BALANCE OF PAYMENTS, INTERNATIONAL AID AND PUBLIC FINANCE

Tanzania's current account deficit was an estimated US $2,208m. in 2010/11, but there was an estimated balance of payments surplus of $335m. Gross official foreign reserves stood at an estimated $3,831m. at 31 May 2011, enough to cover 4.7 months' worth of imports of goods and non-factor services. The Government of Benjamin Mkapa rigorously began seeking debt relief from the time it came into office in 1995. By the end of 2004 the Minister of Finance was able to proclaim that 'all Paris Club creditors except Brazil have offered debt relief through partial cancellation (90%) or full cancellation'. The result of these cancellations was that the World Bank estimated the 'present value' of Tanzania's debt in January 2005 at $1,800m. and changed Tanzania's classification to the category of a 'less indebted' country. Nevertheless, Tanzania was listed among the 18 heavily indebted poor countries that were eligible for immediate debt cancellation under the terms of the agreement reached by the Group of Eight leading industrialized nations (G8) in July 2005. The IMF subsequently confirmed that Tanzania was among 19 countries eligible for '100% debt relief' in 2006. Tanzania's public external debt-service paid decreased from $124m. in 2004 to $32m. in 2006, and its debt-service ratio as a percentage of exports of goods and non-factor services declined to just 1% in 2006. Even so, by 31 May 2011 Tanzania's total public sector external debt had risen again, to 35.1% of GDP.

During the 2000s Tanzania began to impress donors with the pace of reform to economic and governance structures, and for its commitment to rooting out graft. In July 2005 Tanzania's debts to the World Bank and the IMF were cancelled. In June 2007 the World Bank committed US $190m. for budgetary support, with the United Kingdom providing $239m. However, in late 2007 the British High Commissioner, speaking as Chair of the group of 14 international donors to Tanzania, voiced concern over the direction of the Government, particularly over its failure to dismiss officials and politicians accused of graft. Nevertheless, Tanzania continued to receive public support from donors. In June 2010 the IMF approved a three-year PSI, in support of Tanzania's new poverty-reduction and growth strategy, *Mkukuta* II.

The 2011/12 national budget appealed for total spending of Ts. 13,525,900m., an increase of 16.5% compared with the Ts. 11,610,000m. requested in the 2010/11 budget. In 2011/12 Ts. 8,600,300m., or 63.6% of the budget, was allocated for recurrent spending and Ts. 4,925,600m. for development. Total tax and non-tax revenue was projected at Ts. 6,776,000m., less than one-half of the proposed spending level. Financing requirements included foreign loans and grants of Ts. 3,923,551m. and non-concessional loans of Ts. 1,271,634m. VAT was reduced from 20% to 18% in the 2009/10 budget, in response to the business sector's complaint that the expense of doing business in Tanzania was higher than in neighbouring Kenya, where VAT was levied at 17%.

CONCLUSION

The Kikwete Government made it clear from the outset that it intended to continue to work in close co-operation with the IMF, the World Bank and bilateral development partners to make *Mkukuta* and *Mkukuta* II succeed in improving the lives of Tanzanians. An inflation rate of 7.5% in 2011 gave no cause for alarm, as the reasons were clear and unavoidable—drought and high prices for imported petroleum products. Favourable weather conditions precipitated good harvests in 2009 and 2010, but low rainfall in late 2010 reduced power supplies from hydroelectric generation sources. Donors and investors continued to show confidence in Tanzania's economic management. Nevertheless, the infrastructure of Tanzania remained weakened by decades of neglect, hindering economic growth, especially in the agricultural sector, in which more than 80% of the Tanzanian people earned their livelihoods, and in industry, starved of reliable electricity supply. The Kikwete Government placed improved export performance prominently in the frame as the preferred engine of growth, and it was apparent that the attraction of foreign investors, particularly in the mining sector, was of increasing importance to the country's prospects, although much more investment would be needed to make significant inroads into the country's widespread poverty. The inability to provide a reliable electricity supply even to the 14% of the population with access to the national grid was a huge shackle on the country's manufacturers. The country has a widespread reputation for excessive bureaucracy, which often deters investment in non-mining sectors of the economy. Furthermore, corruption has been a problem and was the subject of controversy surrounding several investment projects in 2009. Nevertheless, Tanzania continued to win the favour of the IMF in 2012.

Statistical Survey

Sources (unless otherwise stated): Economic and Research Policy Dept, Bank of Tanzania, POB 2939, Dar es Salaam; tel. (22) 2110946; fax (22) 2113325; e-mail info@hq.bot-tz.org; internet www.bot-tz.org; National Bureau of Statistics, POB 796, Dar es Salaam; tel. (22) 2122722; fax (22) 2130852; e-mail dg@nbs.go.tz; internet www.nbs.go.tz.

Area and Population

AREA, POPULATION AND DENSITY

Area (sq km)	945,087*
Population (census results)	
28 August 1988	23,095,882
25 August 2002	
Males	16,829,861
Females	17,613,742
Total	34,443,603
Population (UN estimates at mid-year)†	
2010	44,841,226
2011	46,218,485
2012	47,656,367
Density (per sq km) at mid-2012	50.4

* 364,900 sq miles. Of this total, Tanzania mainland is 942,626 sq km (363,950 sq miles), and Zanzibar 2,461 sq km (950 sq miles).

† Source: UN, *World Population Prospects: The 2010 Revision*.

POPULATION BY AGE AND SEX

(UN estimates at mid-2012)

	Males	Females	Total
0–14	10,772,299	10,604,999	21,377,298
15–64	12,370,319	12,392,345	24,762,664
65 and over	677,204	839,201	1,516,405
Total	23,819,822	23,836,545	47,656,367

Source: UN, *World Population Prospects: The 2010 Revision*.

REGIONS

(at census of 25 August 2002)

	Area (sq km)*	Population	Density (per sq km)
Arusha	36,486	1,288,088	35.3
Dar es Salaam	1,393	2,487,288	1,786.6
Dodoma	41,311	1,692,025	41.0
Iringa	56,864	1,490,892	26.2
Kagera	28,388	2,028,157	71.4
Kigoma	37,037	1,674,047	45.2
Kilimanjaro	13,309	1,376,702	103.4
Lindi	66,046	787,624	11.9
Manyara†	45,820	1,037,605	22.6
Mara	19,566	1,363,397	69.7
Mbeya	60,350	2,063,328	34.2
Morogoro	70,799	1,753,362	24.8
Mtwara	16,707	1,124,481	67.3
Mwanza	19,592	2,929,644	149.5
Pwani	32,407	885,017	27.3
North Pemba‡	574	185,326	322.9
North Unguja‡	470	136,639	290.7
Rukwa	68,635	1,136,354	16.6
Ruvuma	63,498	1,113,715	17.5
Shinyanga	50,781	2,796,630	55.1
Singida	49,341	1,086,748	22.0
South Pemba‡	332	175,471	528.5
South Unguja‡	854	94,244	110.4
Urban West‡	230	390,074	1,696.0
Tabora	76,151	1,710,465	22.5
Tanga	26,808	1,636,280	61.0
Total	883,749	34,443,603	39.0

* Land area only, excluding inland water.

† Before the 2002 census Manyara was included in the region of Arusha.

‡ Part of the autonomous territory of Zanzibar.

PRINCIPAL TOWNS
(estimated population at mid-1988)

Dar es Salaam*	1,360,850	Mbeya	152,844
Mwanza	223,013	Arusha	134,708
Dodoma (capital)*	203,833	Morogoro	117,760
Tanga	187,455	Shinyanga	100,724
Zanzibar	157,634		

* Although Dodoma is officially the administrative capital, Dar es Salaam is still considered the commercial capital, and many government offices remain there.

Source: UN, *Demographic Yearbook*.

Mid-2011 (incl. suburbs, UN estimate): Dodoma (capital) 226,139 (Source: UN, *World Urbanization Prospects: The 2011 Revision*).

BIRTHS AND DEATHS
(annual averages, UN estimates)

	1995–2000	2000–05	2005–10
Birth rate (per 1,000)	41.7	41.7	41.6
Death rate (per 1,000)	14.8	13.5	11.5

Source: UN, *World Population Prospects: The 2010 Revision*.

Life expectancy (years at birth): 57.4 (males 56.5; females 58.3) in 2010 (Source: World Bank, World Development Indicators database).

ECONOMICALLY ACTIVE POPULATION
('000 persons aged 15 years and over, labour force survey, 2006)

	Males	Females	Total
Agriculture, hunting and forestry	6,064.8	7,120.3	13,185.1
Fishing	184.6	25.0	209.6
Mining and quarrying	90.8	14.1	104.9
Manufacturing	332.9	232.2	565.1
Electricity, gas and water supply	13.5	3.5	17.0
Construction	204.8	6.7	211.5
Wholesale and retail trade and restaurants and hotels	907.7	665.0	1,572.7
Hotel and restaurants	98.5	279.0	377.5
Transport, storage and communications	245.0	13.1	258.1
Financial intermediation	11.3	6.2	17.5
Real estate, renting and business activities	69.0	13.0	82.0
Public administration and defence; compulsory social security	157.4	27.3	184.7
Education	126.9	98.7	225.6
Health and social work	46.1	59.1	105.2
Community, social and personal services	88.3	38.2	126.5
Households with employed persons	138.2	563.3	701.5
Total employed	8,779.8	9,164.7	17,944.6
Unemployed	274.3	602.7	877.0
Total labour force	9,054.2	9,767.4	18,821.5

Source: ILO.

Mid-2012 (estimates in '000): Agriculture, etc. 17,805; Total labour force 23,780 (Source: FAO).

Health and Welfare

KEY INDICATORS

Total fertility rate (children per woman, 2010)	5.5
Under-5 mortality rate (per 1,000 live births, 2010)	76
HIV/AIDS (% of persons aged 15–49, 2009)	5.6
Physicians (per 1,000 head, 2004)	0.02
Hospital beds (per 1,000 head, 2010)	7.0
Health expenditure (2009): US $ per head (PPP)	73
Health expenditure (2009): % of GDP	5.5
Health expenditure (2009): public (% of total)	66.1
Access to water (% of persons, 2010)	53
Access to sanitation (% of persons, 2010)	10
Total carbon dioxide emissions ('000 metric tons, 2008)	6,464.9
Carbon dioxide emissions per head (metric tons, 2008)	0.2
Human Development Index (2011): ranking	152
Human Development Index (2011): value	0.466

For sources and definitions, see explanatory note on p. vi.

Agriculture

PRINCIPAL CROPS
('000 metric tons)

	2008	2009	2010
Wheat	92.4	95.0	62.1
Rice, paddy	1,346.3	1,334.0	1,104.9
Maize	3,555.8	3,326.0	4,475.4
Millet*	220.0	205.3	225.0
Sorghum	861.4	709.0	788.8
Potatoes*	675.0	727.4	750.0
Sweet potatoes	1,379.0	1,381.1	1,400.0*
Cassava (Manioc)	5,392.4	5,916.0	4,392.2
Sugar cane	2,595.0*	2,749.0	2,750.0*
Beans, dry*	900.0	949.0	950.0
Cashew nuts, with shell	99.1	74.2	80.0*
Groundnuts, with shell	396.8	385.5	390.0*
Coconuts*	568.5	577.1	590.0
Oil palm fruit*	66.5	68.0	69.5
Seed cotton*	290.0	215.0	315.0
Tomatoes*	192.4	228.2	235.0
Onions, dry*	52.1	52.5	53.0
Bananas	2,947.1	3,219.0	2,924.7
Plantains*	628.5	653.9	660.0
Guavas, mangoes and mangosteens	270.0*	320.0	325.0*
Pineapples*	83.0	84.0	87.5
Coffee, green	58.1	40.0	40.0†
Tea	34.8	33.2	36.0*
Cloves*	8.1	7.5	8.0
Tobacco, unmanufactured	55.4	60.9	65.0*

* FAO estimate(s).
† Unofficial figure.

Aggregate production ('000 metric tons, may include official, semi-official or estimated data): Total cereals 6,102.0 in 2008, 5,698.0 in 2009, 6,687.7 in 2010; Total roots and tubers 7,456.0 in 2008, 8,035.5 in 2009, 6,553.6 in 2010; Total vegetables (incl. melons) 1,623.7 in 2008, 1,783.2 in 2009, 1,913.3 in 2010; Total fruits (excl. melons) 4,233.5 in 2008, 4,581.9 in 2009, 4,309.9 in 2010.

Source: FAO.

LIVESTOCK
('000 head, year ending September)

	2008	2009	2010
Asses*	182	182	182
Cattle	18,800	19,100	19,500*
Pigs*	485	490	495
Sheep*	4,100	4,150	4,200
Goats*	12,800	12,850	12,900
Chickens*	32,500	33,000	33,500

* FAO estimate(s).

Source: FAO.

LIVESTOCK PRODUCTS
('000 metric tons)

	2008	2009	2010
Cattle meat*	285.0	290.0	291.6
Sheep meat*	11.8	11.9	12.1
Goat meat*	32.3	32.4	32.5
Pig meat*	13.8	13.9	14.0
Chicken meat*	50.3	48.2	48.5
Cows' milk	1,500.0	1,604.1	1,650.0*
Goats' milk*	105.5	106.1	108.0
Hen eggs*	37.0	37.4	37.7
Honey*	35.5	33.4	34.1

* FAO estimate(s).

Source: FAO.

Forestry

ROUNDWOOD REMOVALS
('000 cubic metres, excluding bark, FAO estimates)

	2008	2009	2010
Sawlogs, veneer logs and logs for sleepers	317	317	317
Pulpwood	153	153	153
Other industrial wood	1,844	1,844	1,844
Fuel wood	22,352	22,588	22,836
Total	24,666	24,902	25,150

2011: Production assumed to be unchanged since 2010 (FAO estimate).

Source: FAO.

SAWNWOOD PRODUCTION
('000 cubic metres, including railway sleepers, FAO estimates)

	1992	1993	1994
Coniferous (softwood)	26	21	13
Broadleaved (hardwood)	22	18	11
Total	48	39	24

1995–2011: Production assumed to be unchanged from 1994 (FAO estimates).

Source: FAO.

Fishing

('000 metric tons, live weight)

	2008	2009	2010
Capture	326.8	316.2	342.5
Tilapias	35.6	38.7	44.7
Nile perch	94.2	101.1	97.2
Dagaas	13.0	10.3	15.2
Other freshwater fishes	133.3	108.2	119.7
Sardinellas	11.8	14.3	8.0
Aquaculture	0.2*	0.2*	0.5
Total catch	327.0*	316.4*	342.9

* FAO estimate.

Note: Figures exclude aquatic plants ('000 metric tons): 5.3 (FAO estimate) (capture 0.3, aquaculture 5.0) in 2008; 5.8 (FAO estimate) (capture 0.3, aquaculture 5.5) in 2009; 7.3 (FAO estimate) (capture 0.3, aquaculture 7.0) in 2010. Also excluded are crocodiles, recorded by number rather than by weight. The number of Nile crocodiles caught was: 1,784 in 2008; 790 in 2009; 1,796 in 2010.

Source: FAO.

Mining

('000 metric tons, unless otherwise indicated)

	2008	2009	2010
Coal (bituminous)	15.2	—	—
Diamonds ('000 carats)*	237.7	181.9	80.5
Gold (refined, kilograms)	36,434.0	39,112.0	39,448.0
Salt	25.9	28.4	24.3
Gypsum and anhydrite	55.7	8.1	18.6
Limestone, crushed	1,281.8	1,370.9	928.5
Pozzolanic materials	260.4	171.9	45.2
Sand†	8,500.0	8,500.0	8,500.0

* Estimated at 85% gem-quality and 15% industrial-quality stones. Excluding smuggled artisanal production.

† Estimates.

Source: US Geological Survey.

Industry

SELECTED PRODUCTS
(Tanganyika, '000 metric tons, unless otherwise indicated)

	2007	2008	2009*
Refined sugar	285.6	287.1	292.3
Cigarettes (million)	5,821	6,101	5,831
Beer (million litres)	318	294	289
Textiles (million sq m)	169	80	84
Cement	1,632	1,756	1,941
Rolled steel	38	68	83
Iron sheets	36	32	51
Sisal ropes	7.0	7.8	7.9
Paints ('000 litres)	17,451	24,857	25,781

* Provisional figures.

Selected Products for Zanzibar ('000 metric tons, 2008, unless otherwise indicated): Beverages (million litres) 9.4; Animal feeds (metric tons) 0.2; Coconut oil (metric tons) 77; Bread ('000 loaves, 2007) 77; Copra cake (metric tons, 2007) 49.

Electric energy (Tanganyika and Zanzibar, kWh million): 2,199 in 2006; 4,175 in 2007; 4,414 in 2008 (Source: UN Industrial Commodity Statistics Database).

Finance

CURRENCY AND EXCHANGE RATES

Monetary Units

100 cents = 1 Tanzanian shilling.

Sterling, Dollar and Euro Equivalents (30 April 2012)

£1 sterling = 2,550.34 Tanzanian shillings;
US $1 = 1,568.38 Tanzanian shillings;
€1 = 2,072.45 Tanzanian shillings;
10,000 Tanzanian shillings = £3.92 = $6.38 = €4.83.

Average Exchange Rate (Tanzanian shillings per US $)

2009 1,320.31
2010 1,409.27
2011 1,572.12

BUDGET
('000 million shillings, year ending 30 June)*

Revenue†	2010/11	2011/12‡	2012/13§
Tax revenue	5,296	6,371	8,070
Import duties	449	534	648
Value-added tax	1,531	1,932	2,457
Excises	1,052	1,042	1,384
Income tax	1,660	2,143	2,732
Other taxes	604	721	849
Non-tax revenue	443	789	1,007
Total	5,739	7,160	9,077

Expenditure	2010/11	2011/2012‡	2012/13§
Recurrent expenditure	6,690	7,815	9,212
Wages	2,346	2,768	3,147
Interest	353	454	555
Goods, services and transfers	3,991	4,593	5,510
Development expenditure and net lending	2,749	4,357	4,528
Local	985	1,466	2,214
Foreign	1,764	2,891	2,314
Total	9,439	12,172	13,740

* Figures refer to the Tanzania Government, excluding the revenue and expenditure of the separate Zanzibar Government.

† Excluding grants received ('000 million shillings): 1,627 in 2010/11; 2,480 in 2011/12 (projection); 2,009 in 2012/13 (budget figure).

‡ Projections.

§ Budget figures.

Source: IMF, *United Republic of Tanzania: Fourth Review Under the Policy Support Instrument and Request for an Arrangement Under the Standby Credit Facility—Staff Report; Debt Sustainability Analysis; Press Release on the Executive Board Discussion; and Statement by the Alternate Executive Director for The United Republic of Tanzania.* (July 2012).

INTERNATIONAL RESERVES

(excl. gold, US $ million at 31 December)

	2009	2010	2011
IMF special drawing rights	248.8	243.8	240.7
Reserve position in IMF	15.7	15.4	15.4
Foreign exchange	3,205.9	3,645.4	3,470.1
Total	3,470.4	3,904.6	3,726.2

Source: IMF, *International Financial Statistics.*

MONEY SUPPLY

('000 million shillings at 31 December)

	2009	2010	2011
Currency outside depository corporations	1,566.75	1,897.13	2,235.83
Transferable deposits	3,288.92	4,400.03	5,565.55
Other deposits	3,924.47	4,715.50	5,219.94
Broad money	8,780.14	11,012.66	13,021.32

Source: IMF, *International Financial Statistics.*

COST OF LIVING

(Consumer Price Index)

Tanganyika

(base: 2000 = 100)

	2007	2008	2009
Food (incl. beverages)	152.9	172.2	202.4
Fuel, light and water	170.5	188.7	185.6
Clothing (incl. footwear)	120.9	122.6	130.3
Rent	136.0	139.3	156.7
All items (incl. others)	146.2	161.2	180.8

All items: 190.7 in 2010.

Source: ILO.

Zanzibar

(base: 2001 = 100)

	2002	2003
Food (incl. beverages)	106.9	116.7
Fuel, light and water	100.0	106.0
Clothing (incl. footwear)	106.7	128.3
Rent	104.9	118.0
All items (incl. others)	105.2	114.7

2004: Food (incl. beverages) 128.6; All items (incl. others) 124.0.

2005: Food (incl. beverages) 143.7; All items (incl. others) 136.1.

Source: ILO.

NATIONAL ACCOUNTS

('000 million shillings at current prices)

Expenditure on the Gross Domestic Product

	2008	2009	2010*
Government final consumption expenditure	4,321.7	4,926.8	5,208.2
Private final consumption expenditure	16,460.1	18,476.8	20,209.4
Changes in inventories	106.9	152.3	164.8
Gross fixed capital formation	7,274.3	8,021.0	10,177.7
Total domestic expenditure	28,163.0	31,576.9	35,760.1
Exports of goods and services	6,230.7	6,553.2	8,988.3
Less Imports of goods and services	9,612.1	9,917.3	12,455.0
GDP in purchasers' values	24,781.7	28,212.6	32,293.5

Gross Domestic Product by Economic Activity

	2008	2009	2010*
Agriculture, hunting, forestry and fishing	6,671.1	7,344.9	8,241.8
Mining and quarrying	839.5	941.1	1,072.8
Manufacturing	1,936.0	2,434.8	2,899.1
Electricity, gas and water	514.5	584.0	684.8
Construction	1,904.4	2,233.9	2,569.0
Wholesale and retail trade, hotels and restaurants	3,524.9	3,976.9	4,663.6
Transport and communications	1,649.0	2,005.9	2,338.3
Financial intermediation	403.7	477.5	567.8
Real estate, renting and business activities	2,378.5	2,532.8	2,848.9
Public administration and defence	2,026.8	2,282.8	2,579.5
Education	333.1	392.5	455.3
Health and social work	383.4	455.0	532.3
Other community, social and personal service activities	147.2	176.8	202.4
Sub-total	22,712.1	25,838.9	29,655.7
Less Imputed bank service charge	260.0	328.5	358.0
Indirect taxes, less subsidies	2,329.6	2,702.4	2,995.8
GDP in purchasers' values	24,781.7	28,212.6	32,293.5

* Provisional.

BALANCE OF PAYMENTS

(US $ million)

	2008	2009	2010
Exports of goods f.o.b.	3,578.8	3,294.6	4,296.8
Imports of goods f.o.b.	–7,012.3	–5,834.1	–7,125.1
Trade balance	–3,433.5	–2,539.5	–2,828.3
Exports of services	1,998.8	1,854.6	2,091.5
Imports of services	–1,648.9	–1,709.1	–1,849.6
Balance on goods and services	–3,083.6	–2,393.9	–2,586.4
Other income received	110.6	124.7	163.6
Other income paid	–311.2	–361.4	–379.3
Balance on goods, services and income	–3,284.3	–2,630.5	–2,802.1
Current transfers received	689.0	765.4	902.9
Current transfers paid	–79.6	–68.4	–79.0
Current balance	–2,674.8	–1,933.6	–1,978.2
Capital account (net)	537.0	492.8	606.5
Direct investment from abroad	400.0	414.5	433.4
Portfolio investment liabilities	2.9	3.0	3.2
Other investment assets	181.7	–333.8	–75.2
Other investment liabilities	1,036.4	1,492.9	1,226.7
Net errors and omissions	625.1	236.1	132.5
Overall balance	108.3	372.1	348.9

Source: IMF, *International Financial Statistics.*

External Trade

PRINCIPAL COMMODITIES
(US $ million)

Imports c.i.f.	2008	2009	2010
Food and live animals	366.7	402.2	539.0
Cereals and cereal preparations	258.4	281.0	376.2
Wheat and meslin, unmilled	182.0	209.3	291.9
Mineral fuels, lubricants, etc.	2,381.0	1,478.2	2,211.5
Petroleum, petroleum products, etc.	2,359.0	1,467.1	2,196.3
Petroleum products, refined	2,337.7	1,430.2	2,152.9
Animal and vegetable oils, fats and waxes	223.1	130.8	212.0
Fixed vegetable oils and fats	195.0	120.9	203.5
Palm oil	175.5	106.1	173.3
Chemicals and related products	938.2	783.1	1,049.1
Medicinal and pharmaceutical products	145.3	111.0	160.7
Plastics in primary forms	237.6	218.8	351.2
Basic manufactures	1,244.2	1,014.2	1,149.9
Iron and steel	399.9	323.5	347.2
Other metal manufactures	255.5	210.7	228.4
Machinery and transport equipment	2,488.6	2,295.9	2,381.0
Power generating machinery and equipment	170.2	111.2	102.8
Rotating electric plant, and parts thereof	98.3	47.8	59.6
Machinery specialized for particular industries	503.2	477.7	472.0
General industrial machinery, equipment and parts	264.7	285.4	272.8
Telecommunications, sound recording and reproducing equipment	306.2	220.1	176.0
Telecommunication equipment, parts and accessories	286.4	200.5	151.0
Other electrical machinery, apparatus and appliances, and parts	206.5	286.0	249.7
Road vehicles	742.4	755.1	868.7
Passenger motor vehicles, excl. buses	222.5	239.2	300.6
Lorries and special purpose motor vehicles	254.0	243.8	246.3
Vehicles for the transportation of goods or materials	237.9	218.4	221.2
Miscellaneous manufactured articles	312.7	294.9	327.5
Total (incl. others)	8,087.7	6,530.8	8,012.9

Exports f.o.b.	2008	2009	2010
Food and live animals	597.2	571.4	686.9
Fish, crustaceans, molluscs and preparations thereof	140.6	127.8	141.5
Fish, fresh, chilled or frozen	119.3	106.8	121.4
Fish fillets, fresh or chilled	61.3	48.7	44.1
Fish fillets, frozen	55.0	55.8	71.5
Cereals and cereal preparations	63.4	22.8	79.9
Vegetables and fruit	157.8	159.4	229.4
Fruit and nuts, fresh, dried	78.7	64.2	99.0
Cashew nuts, fresh or dried	69.4	90.2	125.1
Coffee, tea, cocoa, spices, and manufactures thereof	188.9	227.0	193.7
Coffee and coffee substitutes	105.9	117.4	118.7
Coffee, not roasted; coffee husks and skins	100.0	111.2	102.3
Spices	14.7	21.2	8.7
Cloves	14.3	18.0	8.5
Beverages and tobacco	189.8	106.7	152.5
Tobacco and tobacco manufactures	180.6	97.9	141.2
Tobacco, wholly or partly stripped	171.6	90.0	111.9
Crude materials, inedible, except fuels	643.1	811.7	1,268.2
Textile fibres (not wool tops) and their wastes (not in yarn)	138.9	125.3	99.7
Raw cotton, excl. linters, not carded or combed	80.9	89.0	72.4
Metalliferous ores and metal scrap	364.3	507.8	971.5
Ores and concentrates of precious metals	349.5	497.7	461.5
Basic manufactures	362.5	259.3	351.9
Non-metallic mineral manufactures	101.6	63.5	79.5
Pearl, precious and semi-precious stones, unworked or worked	73.5	40.3	37.4
Diamonds cut or otherwise worked, but not mounted or set	20.1	18.4	8.6
Gold, non-monetary, unwrought or semi-manufactured	759.4	818.6	966.1
Total (incl. others)	3,121.1	2,982.4	4,050.5

Source: UN, *International Trade Statistics Yearbook*.

PRINCIPAL TRADING PARTNERS
(US $ million)

Imports c.i.f.	2008	2009	2010
Australia	102.8	125.7	161.0
Belgium	142.5	109.7	132.3
China, People's Repub.	721.3	692.1	876.5
France	162.1	112.2	129.0
Germany	220.7	226.8	183.8
India	865.7	772.9	895.0
Indonesia	94.9	109.3	112.5
Italy	95.6	99.6	96.4
Japan	366.8	422.1	568.1
Kenya	430.7	304.5	275.3
Korea, Repub.	86.9	75.6	128.6
Malaysia	163.0	67.8	106.9
Netherlands	213.0	123.3	143.9
Russian Federation	74.3	65.0	101.6
Saudi Arabia	263.4	164.7	199.1
Singapore	441.9	192.0	444.4
South Africa	829.4	686.6	771.7
Sweden	152.0	84.1	61.3
Switzerland-Liechtenstein	139.8	134.6	562.6
Thailand	76.8	71.3	80.4
Turkey	79.6	76.5	59.6
United Arab Emirates	978.9	631.6	672.2
United Kingdom	175.6	183.2	207.9
USA	224.9	141.0	155.9
Total (incl. others)	8,087.7	6,530.8	8,012.9

Exports f.o.b.	2008	2009	2010
Belgium	50.4	81.5	95.8
Burundi	20.6	24.6	56.1
China, People's Repub.	270.4	387.3	656.7
Comoros	50.8	2.3	42.8
Congo, Democratic Repub.	144.6	85.5	156.1
Germany	67.1	57.9	139.3
Hong Kong	13.9	87.4	13.2
India	173.0	187.8	226.5
Italy	67.6	55.0	67.8
Japan	147.8	178.4	217.5
Kenya	252.7	192.9	324.9
Malawi	49.6	25.6	46.3
Mozambique	34.0	22.1	18.5
Netherlands	163.2	182.4	93.3
Rwanda	22.5	15.8	116.8
Saudi Arabia	16.4	31.9	n.a.
South Africa	265.5	187.9	433.7
Switzerland-Liechtenstein	630.0	584.7	710.4
Uganda	59.8	51.7	60.2
United Arab Emirates	68.1	91.4	58.8
United Kingdom	83.9	32.8	34.3
USA	56.8	47.9	48.8
Viet Nam	22.5	29.5	42.5
Zambia	47.1	46.6	60.3
Total (incl. others)	3,121.1	2,982.4	4,050.5

Source: UN, *International Trade Statistics Yearbook*.

Transport

RAILWAYS

	2008	2009	2010
Passengers ('000)	459	443	290
Freight ('000 metric tons)	505	453	256

Source: National Bureau of Statistics, *Tanzania in Figures 2010*.

ROAD TRAFFIC
(estimates, '000 motor vehicles in use)

	1994	1995	1996
Passenger cars	28.0	26.0	23.8
Buses and coaches	78.0	81.0	86.0
Lorries and vans	27.2	27.7	29.7
Road tractors	6.7	6.7	6.6

2007: Passenger cars 171,821; Buses and coaches 27,200; Lorries and vans 103,611; Motorcycles and mopeds 77,371.

Source: IRF, *World Road Statistics*.

SHIPPING

Merchant fleet
(registered at 31 December)

	2007	2008	2009
Number of vessels	53	51	75
Displacement ('000 grt)	38.1	40.6	89.4

Source: IHS Fairplay, *World Fleet Statistics*.

International sea-borne traffic
(port of Dar es Salaam only)

	2007	2008	2009
Vessels docked	3,038	518	2,169
Cargo ('000 metric tons)	7,426	7,167	8,103
Passengers ('000)	714	310	141

2010: Cargo ('000 metric tons) 8,814.

CIVIL AVIATION
(traffic on scheduled services)

	2007	2008	2009
Kilometres flown (million)	6	4	12
Passengers carried ('000)	251	203	684
Passenger-km (million)	252	152	395
Total ton-km (million)	24	15	36

Source: UN, *Statistical Yearbook*.

2010: Passengers carried ('000) 749 (Source: World Bank, World Development Indicators database).

Tourism

FOREIGN VISITOR ARRIVALS
(by country of origin)

	2007	2008	2009
Burundi	11,039	11,721	14,581
Canada	15,198	16,482	14,642
Congo, Democratic Repub.	8,372	7,638	5,879
France	21,314	19,598	20,127
Germany	24,468	27,100	25,508
India	14,042	17,530	17,002
Italy	54,194	49,950	47,804
Kenya	130,823	184,269	177,929
Malawi	19,136	21,459	19,851
Netherlands	18,990	16,945	16,507
Rwanda	14,699	14,394	14,331
South Africa	28,394	28,721	25,586
Spain	11,428	8,470	9,053
Uganda	30,385	31,682	32,826
United Kingdom	55,154	58,245	53,753
USA	58,341	66,953	47,943
Zambia	34,669	37,682	26,999
Total (incl. others)	719,031	770,469	714,367

Tourist arrivals ('000): 754 in 2010.

Tourism receipts (US $ million, excl. passenger transport) 1,160 in 2009; 1,254 in 2010; 1,457 in 2011 (provisional).

Source: World Tourism Organization.

Communications Media

	2009	2010	2011
Telephones ('000 main lines in use)	172.9	174.5	161.1
Mobile cellular telephones ('000 subscribers)	17,469.5	20,983.9	25,666.5
Internet subscribers ('000)	397.5	487.3	n.a.
Broadband subscribers ('000)	2.8	3.2	3.5

Personal computers: 356,000 (9.1 per 1,000 persons) in 2005.

Source: International Telecommunication Union.

Television receivers ('000 in use, 2000): 700.

Radio receivers ('000 in use, estimate, 1997): 8,800 (Source: UNESCO, *Statistical Yearbook*).

Daily newspapers (2004): 14; average circulation ('000 copies, estimate) 60 (Source: UNESCO Institute for Statistics).

Education

(2010 unless otherwise indicated)

	Institutions	Teachers	Students
Primary (state)	15,265	159,081	2,265,000
Primary (private)	551	6,775	39,818
Secondary (state)	3,397	30,252	708,941
Secondary (private)	869	10,265	128,715
Higher (state)*	46†	n.a.	35,718
Higher (private)‡	64†	n.a.	5,275

* Comprising 34 teacher training colleges, 8 full universities and 4 university colleges.

† 2009 figure.

‡ Comprising 43 teacher training colleges, 11 full universities and 10 university colleges.

Pupil-teacher ratio (primary education, UNESCO estimate): 50.8 in 2009/10 (Source: UNESCO Institute for Statistics).

Adult literacy rate (UNESCO estimates): 73.2% (males 79.0%; females 67.5%) in 2010 (Source: UNESCO Institute for Statistics).

Directory

The Constitution

The United Republic of Tanzania was established on 26 April 1964, when Tanganyika and Zanzibar, hitherto separate independent countries, merged. An interim Constitution of 1965 was replaced, on 25 April 1977, by a permanent Constitution for the United Republic. In October 1979 the Revolutionary Council of Zanzibar adopted a separate Constitution, governing Zanzibar's internal administration, with provisions for a popularly elected President and a legislative House of Representatives elected by delegates of the then ruling party. A new Constitution for Zanzibar, which came into force in January 1985, provided for direct elections to the Zanzibar House of Representatives. The provisions below relate to the 1977 Constitution of the United Republic, as subsequently amended.

GOVERNMENT

Legislative power is exercised by the Parliament of the United Republic, which is vested by the Constitution with complete sovereign power, and of which the present National Assembly is the legislative house. The Assembly also enacts all legislation concerning the mainland. Internal matters in Zanzibar are the exclusive jurisdiction of the Zanzibar executive, the Supreme Revolutionary Council of Zanzibar, and the Zanzibar legislature, the House of Representatives.

National Assembly

The National Assembly comprises both directly elected members (chosen by universal adult suffrage) and nominated members (including five members elected from the Zanzibar House of Representatives). The number of directly elected members exceeds the number of nominated members. The Electoral Commission may review and, if necessary, increase the number of electoral constituencies before every general election. The National Assembly has a term of five years.

President

The President is the Head of State, Head of the Government and Commander-in-Chief of the Armed Forces. The President has no power to legislate without recourse to Parliament. The assent of the President is required before any bill passed by the National Assembly becomes law. Should the President withhold his assent and the bill be repassed by the National Assembly by a two-thirds' majority, the President is required by law to give his assent within 21 days unless, before that time, he has dissolved the National Assembly, in which case he must stand for re-election.

The President appoints a Vice-President to assist him in carrying out his functions. The President presides over the Cabinet, which comprises a Prime Minister and other ministers who are appointed from among the members of the National Assembly.

JUDICIARY

The independence of the judges is secured by provisions which prevent their removal, except on account of misbehaviour or incapacity when they may be dismissed at the discretion of the President. The Constitution also makes provision for a Permanent Commission of Enquiry, which has wide powers to investigate any abuses of authority.

CONSTITUTIONAL AMENDMENTS

The Constitution can be amended by an act of the Parliament of the United Republic, when the proposed amendment is supported by the votes of not fewer than two-thirds of all the members of the Assembly.

The Government

HEAD OF STATE

President: Lt-Col (Retd) JAKAYA MRISHO KIKWETE (took office 21 December 2005; re-elected 31 October 2010).

Vice-President: Dr MOHAMED GHARIB BILAL.

CABINET
(September 2012)

President and Commander-in-Chief of the Armed Forces: Lt-Col (Retd) JAKAYA MRISHO KIKWETE.

Prime Minister: MIZENGO KAYANZA PETER PINDA.

Ministers of State in the President's Office: STEPHEN MASATU WASSIRA (Social Relations and Co-ordination), GEORGE MKUCHIKA (Good Governance), CELINA OMPESHI KOMBANI (Public Service Management), MARK JAMES MWANDOSYA (Without Portfolio).

Ministers of State in the Vice-President's Office: SAMIA H. SULUHU (Union Affairs), Dr TEREZYA LUOGA HOVISA (Environment).

Ministers of State in the Prime Minister's Office: HAWA ABDULRAHMAN GHASIA (Regional Administration and Local Governments), WILLIAM LUKUVI (Policy, Co-ordination and Parliamentary Affairs), Dr MARY MICHAEL NAGU (Investment and Empowerment).

Minister of Foreign Affairs and International Co-operation: BERNARD KAMILLIUS MEMBE.

Minister of East African Co-operation: SAMWEL JOHN SITTA.

Minister of Finance and Economic Affairs: Dr WILLIAM MGIMWA.

Minister of Industry, Trade and Marketing: Dr ABDALLAH O. KIGODA.

Minister of Agriculture, Food Security and Co-operatives: Eng. CHRISTOPHER CHIZA.

Minister of Natural Resources and Tourism: KHAMIS SUED KAGASHEKI.

Minister of Water and Irrigation: Prof. JUMANNE ABDALLAH MAGHEMBE.

Minister of Energy and Minerals: Prof. SOSPETER MUHONGO.

Minister of Works: Dr JOHN POMBE JOSEPH MAGUFULI.

Minister of Transport: Dr HARRISON MWAKYEMBE.

Minister of Communication, Science and Technology: Prof. MAKAME MNYAA MBARAWA.

Minister of Health and Social Welfare: Dr HUSSEIN ALI MWINYI.

Minister of Education and Vocational Training: Dr SHUKURU JUMANNE KAWAMBWA.

Minister of Labour and Employment: GAUDENSIA MUGOSI KABAKA.

Minister of Lands, Housing and Human Settlements Development: Prof. ANNA TIBAIJUKA.

Minister of Information, Youth, Culture and Sports: Dr FENELLA E. MUKANGARA.

Minister of Defence and National Service: SHAMSI VUAI NAHODHA.

Minister of Home Affairs: Dr EMMANUEL JOHN NCHIMBI.

Minister of Justice and Constitutional Affairs: MATHIAS MEINRAD CHIKAWE.

Minister of Community Development, Gender and Children: SOPHIA MNYAMBI SIMBA.

Minister of Livestock and Fisheries Development: Dr DAVID MATHAYO DAVID.

There were also 25 deputy ministers.

MINISTRIES

Office of the President: State House, POB 2483, Dar es Salaam; tel. (22) 2116538; fax (22) 2113425; e-mail permsec@estabs.go.tz; internet www.tanzania.go.tz/poffice.htm.

Office of the Vice-President: POB 5380, Dar es Salaam; tel. (22) 2113857; fax (22) 2113856; e-mail makamu@twiga.com; internet www.tanzania.go.tz/vpoffice.htm.

Office of the Prime Minister: POB 3021, Dar es Salaam; tel. (22) 2111249; fax (22) 2117266; e-mail ps@pmo.go.tz; internet www.pmo.go.tz.

Ministry of Agriculture, Irrigation, Food Security and Cooperatives: Kilimo I Building, Temeke, POB 9192, Dar es Salaam; tel. (22) 2862480; fax (22) 2865951; e-mail psk@kilimo.go.tz; internet www.kilimo.go.tz.

Ministry of Communication, Science and Technology: Plot 1168/19, Jamhuri St, POB 2645, Dar es Salaam; tel. (22) 2111254; fax (22) 2112533; e-mail mst@mst.go.tz; internet www.mst.go.tz.

Ministry of Community Development, Gender and Children: Kivukoni Front, POB 3448, Dar es Salaam; tel. (22) 2111459; fax (22) 2110933; e-mail info_wic@uccmail.co.tz; internet www.mcdcg.go.tz.

Ministry of Defence and National Service: POB 9544, Dar es Salaam; tel. (22) 2117153; fax (22) 2116719; internet www.modans.go.tz.

Ministry of East African Co-operation: NSSF Water Front Bldg, 5th Floor, POB 9280, Dar es Salaam; tel. (22) 2126660; fax (22) 2120488; e-mail ps@meac.go.tz; internet www.meac.go.tz.

Ministry of Education and Vocational Training: POB 9121, Dar es Salaam; tel. (22) 2120403; fax (22) 2113271; e-mail psmoevt@moe.go.tz; internet www.moe.go.tz.

Ministry of Energy and Minerals: POB 2000, Dar es Salaam; tel. (22) 2112793; fax (22) 2121606; e-mail info@mem.go.tz; internet www.mem.go.tz.

Ministry of Finance and Economic Affairs: POB 9111, Dar es Salaam; tel. (22) 2111174; fax (22) 2110326; internet www.mof.go.tz.

Ministry of Foreign Affairs and International Co-operation: Kivukoni Front, POB 9000, Dar es Salaam; tel. (22) 2111906; fax (22) 2116600; e-mail nje@foreign.go.tz; internet www.foreign.go.tz.

Ministry of Health and Social Welfare: 36/37 Samore Ave, POB 9083, Dar es Salaam; tel. (22) 2120261; fax (22) 2139951; e-mail moh@moh.go.tz; internet www.moh.gov.tz.

Ministry of Home Affairs: POB 9223, Dar es Salaam; tel. and fax (22) 2119050; e-mail permsec@moha.go.tz; internet www.moha.go.tz.

Ministry of Industry, Trade and Marketing: POB 9503, Dar es Salaam; tel. (22) 2127898; fax (22) 2125832; e-mail tnwinfo@plancom.go.tz; internet www.mitm.go.tz.

Ministry of Information, Culture, Youth Affairs and Sports: Dar es Salaam; internet www.hum.go.tz.

Ministry of Infrastructure Development: Pamba Rd, Tancot House, POB 9144, Dar es Salaam; tel. (22) 2137650; fax (22) 2112751; e-mail permsec@infrastructure.go.tz; internet www.infrastructure.go.tz.

Ministry of Justice and Constitutional Affairs: POB 70069, Dar es Salaam; tel. 2137833; fax (22) 2137831; e-mail katibumkuu@sheria.go.tz; internet www.sheria.go.tz.

Ministry of Labour and Employment: POB 1422, Dar es Salaam; tel. (22) 2120419; fax (22) 2113082; e-mail permsec@kazi.go.tz; internet www.kazi.go.tz.

Ministry of Lands, Housing and Human Settlements Development: Kivukoni Front, Ardhi House, POB 9132, Dar es Salaam; tel. (22) 2121241; fax (22) 2124576; internet www.ardhi.go.tz.

Ministry of Livestock and Fisheries Development: POB 9152, Dar es Salaam; tel. (22) 2861910; fax (22) 2861908; internet www.mifugo.go.tz.

Ministry of Natural Resources and Tourism: POB 9372, Dar es Salaam; tel. (22) 2111061; fax (22) 2110600; e-mail nature.tourism@mnrt.org; internet www.mnrt.org.

Ministry of Transport: Tancot House, cnr Sokoine Dr. and Pamba Rd, POB 9144, Dar es Salaam; tel. (22) 2137650; fax (22) 2112751; e-mail permsec@mot.go.tz; internet www.mot.go.tz.

Ministry of Water: POB 9153, Dar es Salaam; tel. (22) 2452036; fax (22) 2452037; e-mail dppmaj@raha.com; internet www.maji.go.tz.

Ministry of Works: Holland House, Garden Ave, POB 9423, Dar es Salaam; tel. (22) 2111553; fax (22) 2113335; internet www.mow.go.tz.

ZANZIBAR GOVERNMENT OF NATIONAL UNITY
(September 2012)

The Government is formed by members of Chama Cha Mapinduzi (CCM) and the Civic United Front (CUF).

President: Dr Ali Mohammed Shein (CCM).

First Vice-President: Maalim Seif Sharif Hamad (CUF).

Second Vice-President: Seif Ali Iddi (CCM).

Minister of State in the President's Office and Chairman of the Revolutionary Council: Dr Mwinyihaji Makame (CCM).

Minister of State in the President's Office, in charge of Finance, the Economy and Development Planning: Omar Yussuf Mzee (CCM).

Minister of State in the President's Office, in charge of Public Service and Good Governance: Haji Omar Kheri (CCM).

Minister of State in the Vice-President's Office: Fatma Abdulhabib Fereji (CUF).

Minister of State in the Second Vice-President's Office: Mohammed Aboud Mohammed (CCM).

Minister of Constitutional Affairs and Justice: Aboubakar Khamis Bakary (CUF).

Minister of Infrastructure and Communications: Rashid Seif Suleiman (CUF).

Minister of Education and Vocational Training: Ramadhan Abdulla Shaaban (CCM).

Minister of Health: Juma Duni Haji (CUF).

Minister of Social Welfare, Women Development and Children: Zainab Omar Mohammed (CCM).

Minister of Lands, Housing, Water and Energy: Ali Juma Shamhuna (CCM).

Minister of Agriculture and Natural Resources: Mansoor Yussuf Himid (CCM).

Minister of Trade, Industry and Marketing: Nassor Ahmed Mazrui (CUF).

Minister of Livestock and Fisheries: Said Ali Mbarouk (CUF).

Minister of Labour, Economic Empowerment and Co-operatives: Haroun Ali Suleiman (CCM).

Members of the Revolutionary Council and Ministers without Portfolio: Suleiman Othman Nyanga (CCM), Haji Faki Shaali (CUF), Machano Othman Said (CCM).

There were also six deputy ministers.

MINISTRIES

Office of the President: POB 776, Zanzibar; tel. (24) 2230814; fax (24) 2233722.

Office of the Chief Minister: POB 239, Zanzibar; tel. (24) 2311126; fax (24) 233788.

Ministry of Agriculture and Natural Resources: Zanzibar; tel. (24) 232662.

Ministry of Communication and Transport: POB 266, Zanzibar; tel. (24) 2232841.

Ministry of Constitutional Affairs and Justice: Zanzibar.

Ministry of Education and Vocational Training: POB 394, Zanzibar; tel. (24) 232827.

Ministry of Finance and Economic Affairs: Vuga St, POB 1154, Zanzibar; tel. (24) 2231169; fax (24) 2230546; e-mail info@mofeaznz.org; internet www.mofeaznz.org.

Ministry of Health: Zanzibar.

Ministry of Information, Culture and Sport: POB 236, Zanzibar; tel. (24) 232640.

Ministry of Infrastructure and Communications: Zanzibar.

Ministry of Labour, Economic Empowerment and Co-operatives: Zanzibar.

Ministry of Lands, Housing, Water and Energy: Zanzibar.

Ministry of Livestock and Fisheries: Zanzibar.

Minister of Social Welfare, Women Development and Children: POB 884, Zanzibar; tel. (24) 30808.

Ministry of Trade, Industry and Marketing: POB 772, Zanzibar; tel. (24) 232321.

President and Legislature

PRESIDENT

Election, 31 October 2010

Candidate	Votes	% of votes
Lt-Col (Retd) Jakaya Mrisho Kikwete (CCM)	5,276,827	62.83
Dr Willibrod Peter Slaa (Chadema)	2,271,941	27.05
Prof. Ibrahim Haruna Lipumba (CUF)	695,667	8.28
Peter Mziray Kuga (APPT-Maendeleo)	96,933	1.15
Hasim Spunda Rungwe (NCCR—Mageuzi)	26,388	0.31
Muttamwega Bhatt Mgaywa (TLP)	17,482	0.21
Yahmi Nassoro Dovutwa (UPDP)	13,176	0.16
Total	8,398,414*	100.00

* According to results released by the National Election Commission of Tanzania, the total number of valid votes cast was 8,398,394. In addition there were 227,889 spoilt ballots.

NATIONAL ASSEMBLY

Speaker: Anne Makinda.

Election, 31 October 2010

Party	Seats*
Chama Cha Mapinduzi (CCM)	251
Chama Cha Demokrasia na Maendeleo (Chadema)	45
Civic United Front (CUF)	33
National Convention for Construction and Reform (NCCR—Mageuzi)	4
Tanzania Labour Party (TLP)	1
United Democratic Party (UDP)	1
Total	335†

* In addition to the 239 elective seats and 103 special seats, 10 seats are reserved for presidential nominees and five for members of the Zanzibar House of Representatives; the Attorney-General is also an *ex officio* member of the National Assembly.

† Voting in seven constituencies was postponed until 14 November. At elections held on that date the CUF and the CCM each secured three seats, while Chadema took one seat.

ZANZIBAR PRESIDENT

Election, 31 October 2010

Candidate	Votes	% of votes
Dr Ali Mohammed Shein	179,809	50.11
Maalim Seif Sharif Hamad	176,338	49.14
Kassim Ali Bakari	803	0.22
Haji Khamis Haji	525	0.15
Juma Ali Khatib	497	0.14
Said Soud Said	480	0.13
Haji Ambar Khamis	363	0.10
Total	358,815	100.00

ZANZIBAR HOUSE OF REPRESENTATIVES

Speaker: Pandu Ameir Kificho.

Election, 31 October 2010

Party	Seats*
Chama Cha Mapinduzi (CCM)	28
Civic United Front (CUF)	22
Total	50

* In addition to the 50 elective seats, 10 seats are reserved for presidential nominees, 20 for women (on a party basis in proportion to the number of elective seats gained) and one for the Attorney-General.

Election Commissions

National Election Commission of Tanzania (NEC): Posta House, POB 10923, Ghana/Ohio St, 6th and 7th Floor, Dar es Salaam; tel. (22) 2114963; fax (22) 2116740; e-mail info@nec.go.tz; internet www.nec.go.tz; f. 1993; Chair. Lewis M. Makame; Dir of Elections R. R. Kiravu.

Zanzibar Electoral Commission: POB 1001, Zanzibar; tel. (24) 2231489; fax (24) 2233828; e-mail election@zec.go.tz; internet www.zec.go.tz; f. 2007; Chair. Khatib Mwinyi Chande.

Political Organizations

African Progressive Party of Tanzania (APPT-Maendeleo): House No. 294, Wibu St, Kinondoni, POB 31932, Dar es Salaam; tel. 754300302 (mobile); f. 2003; Leader Peter Mziray Kuga; Sec.-Gen. Ahmed Hamad.

Chama Cha Amani na Demokrasia Tanzania (CHADETA): House No. 41, Sadan St Ilala, POB 15809, Dar es Salaam; tel. 744889453 (mobile); granted temporary registration in 2003.

Chama Cha Demokrasia na Maendeleo (Chadema—Party for Democracy and Progress): House No. 170 Ufipa St, POB 31191, Dar es Salaam; tel. (22) 2668866; e-mail info@chadema.or.tz; internet www.chadema.or.tz; supports democracy and social development; Chair. Freeman Mbowe; Sec.-Gen. Willibrod Peter Slaa.

Chama Cha Haki na Usitawi (Chausta—Party for Justice and Development): Drive Inn Oysterbay, POB 5450, Dar es Salaam; tel. 754990228 (mobile); e-mail chausta@yahoo.com; f. 1998; officially regd 2001; Chair. James Mapalala.

Chama Cha Kijamii (CCJ): Kinondoni, Dar es Salaam; f. 2010; Chair. Constantine Akitanda; Sec.-Gen. Renatus Muhabhi.

Chama Cha Mapinduzi (CCM) (Revolutionary Party of Tanzania): Kuu St, POB 50, Dodoma; tel. 2180575; e-mail katibumkuu@ccmtz.org; internet www.ccmtz.org; f. 1977 by merger of the mainland-based Tanganyika African National Union (TANU) with the Afro-Shirazi Party, which operated on Zanzibar and Pemba; sole legal party 1977–92; socialist orientation; Chair. Jakaya Mrisho Kikwete; Vice-Chair. Pius Msekwa, Amani A. Karume; Sec.-Gen. Yusuf Makamba.

Civic United Front (CUF): Mtendeni St at Malindi, POB 3637, Zanzibar; tel. and fax (24) 2237446; e-mail headquarters@cuftz.org; internet www.cuftz.org; f. 1992 by merger of Zanzibar opposition party Kamahuru and the mainland-based Chama Cha Wananchi; commands substantial support in Zanzibar and Pemba, for which it demands increased autonomy; Chair. Prof. Ibrahim Haruna Lipumba; Sec.-Gen. Seif Sharif Hamad.

Democratic Party (DP): Ilala Mchikichini, POB 63102, Dar es Salaam; tel. 713430516; e-mail dp_watanganyika@yahoo.com; f. 2002; Chair. Rev. Christopher Mtikila.

Demokrasia Makini (MAKINI): Mbezi Beach Makonde, nr Nguruko Int. School, POB 75636, Dar es Salaam; tel. 754295670 (mobile); officially regd 2001; Sec.-Gen. Dominick Lyamchai.

Forum for Restoration of Democracy (FORD): 13 Kibambawe St, Kariakoo, POB 15587, Dar es Salaam; tel. 741292271 (mobile); f. 2002; Chair. Ramadhani Mzee; Sec.-Gen. Emmanuel Patuka.

Movement for Democratic Alternative (MDA): Zanzibar; seeks to review the terms of the 1964 union of Zanzibar with mainland Tanzania; supports democratic institutions and opposes detention without trial and press censorship.

National Convention for Construction and Reform (NCCR—Mageuzi): Plot No. 2 Kilosa St, Ilala, POB 72444, Dar es Salaam; tel. (22) 2111484; f. 1992; Chair. James F. Mbatia; Sec.-Gen. Samweli A. Ruhuza.

National League for Democracy (NLD): Plot No. D/73 Sinza, POB 352, Dar es Salaam; tel. 714259442 (mobile); fax (22) 2462180; f. 1993; Chair. Emmanuel J. E. Makaidi; Sec.-Gen. Feruzi Msambichaka.

National Reconstruction Alliance (NRA): Bububu St, Tandika Kilimahewa, POB 100125, Dar es Salaam; tel. 754496724 (mobile); f. 1993; Chair. Rashid Mtuta; Sec.-Gen. Marsheed H. Hemed.

Tanzania Democratic Alliance Party (TADEA): Buguruni Malapa, POB 482, Dar es Salaam; tel. (22) 2865244; f. 1993; Pres. John D. Lifa-Chipaka; Sec.-Gen. Juma Ali Khatib.

Tanzania Labour Party (TLP): Argentina Manzese, POB 7273, Dar es Salaam; tel. (22) 2443237; f. 1993; Chair. Augustine Mrema; Sec.-Gen. John Komba.

Tanzania People's Party (TPP): Mbezi Juu, Kawe, POB 60847, Dar es Salaam; removed from register of political parties 2002; Chair. Alec H. Che-Mponda; Sec.-Gen. Gravel Limo.

United Democratic Party (UDP): Plot No. 34, Block 28, Ilemela St, Mwananyamala, Kinondoni, POB 5918, Dar es Salaam; tel. 784613723 (mobile); f. 1994; Chair. John Momose Cheyo.

Union for Multi-Party Democracy (UMD): House No. 84, Plot No. 630, Block No. 5, Kagera St. Magomeni, POB 2985, Dar es Salaam; tel. 744478153 (mobile); f. 1993; Chair. Salum S. Alli; Sec.-Gen. Ali Mshangama Abdallah.

United People's Democratic Party (UPDP): 46 Kagera St, POB 11746, Dar es Salaam; tel. 754753075 (mobile); e-mail opodsm@yahoo.com; f. 1993; Chair. Yahmi Nassoro Dovutwa; Sec.-Gen. Abdallah Nassoro Ally.

Diplomatic Representation

EMBASSIES AND HIGH COMMISSIONS IN TANZANIA

Algeria: 34 Ali Hassan Mwinyi Rd, POB 2963, Dar es Salaam; tel. (22) 2117619; fax (22) 2117620; e-mail algemb@twiga.com; Ambassador Abdelmoun'aam Ahriz.

Angola: Plot 78, Lugalo Rd, POB 20793, Dar es Salaam; tel. (22) 2117674; fax (22) 2132349; Ambassador Ambrósio Lukoki.

Belgium: 5 Ocean Rd, POB 9210, Dar es Salaam; tel. (22) 2112688; fax (22) 2117621; e-mail daressalaam@diplobel.fed.be; internet www.diplomatie.be/dar-es-salaam; Ambassador Koen Adam.

Burundi: Plot 1007, Lugalo Rd, POB 2752, Upanga, Dar es Salaam; Ambassador (vacant).

Canada: 38 Mirambo St, Garden Ave, POB 1022, Dar es Salaam; tel. (22) 2163300; fax (22) 2116897; e-mail dslam@international.gc.ca; internet www.dfait-maeci.gc.ca/tanzania; High Commissioner Robert Orr.

China, People's Republic: 2 Kajificheni Close at Toure Dr., POB 1649, Dar es Salaam; tel. (22) 2668063; fax (22) 2666353; internet tz.chineseembassy.org; Ambassador Liu Xisheng.

Congo, Democratic Republic: 438 Malik Rd, POB 975, Upanga, Dar es Salaam; tel. (22) 2150282; fax (22) 2153341; Ambassador Juma-Alfani Mpango.

Cuba: Plot 313, Lugalo Rd, POB 9282, Upanga, Dar es Salaam; tel. (22) 2115928; fax (22) 2132338; e-mail embajada@ctvsatcom.net; internet emba.cubaminrex.cu/tanzania; Ambassador Ernesto Gómez Díaz.

Denmark: Ghana Ave, POB 9171, Dar es Salaam; tel. (22) 2165200; fax (22) 2116433; e-mail daramb@um.dk; internet www.ambdaressalaam.um.dk; Ambassador Bjarne Henneberg Sørensen.

Egypt: 24 Garden Ave, POB 1668, Dar es Salaam; tel. (22) 2117622; fax (22) 2112543; e-mail egypt.emb.tz@Cats-net.com; Ambassador Wael Adel Abdel Azeem Nasr.

Finland: cnr Mirambo St and Garden Ave, POB 2455, Dar es Salaam; tel. (22) 2196565; fax (22) 2196573; e-mail sanomat.dar@formin.fi; internet www.finland.or.tz; Ambassador Sinikka Antila.

France: Ali Hassan Mwinyi Rd, POB 2349, Dar es Salaam; tel. (22) 2198800; fax (22) 2198815; e-mail contact@ambafrance-tz.org; internet www.ambafrance-tz.org; Ambassador MARCEL ESCURE.

Germany: Umoja House, Mirambo St/Garden Ave, 2nd Floor, POB 9541, Dar es Salaam; tel. (22) 2117409; fax (22) 2112944; e-mail info@daressalam.diplo.de; internet www.daressalam.diplo.de; Ambassador Dr GUIDO HERZ.

Holy See: Oyster Bay, Plot 146, Haile Selassie Rd, POB 480, Dar es Salaam (Apostolic Nunciature); tel. (22) 2666422; fax (22) 2668059; e-mail nunzio@cats-net.com; Apostolic Nuncio Most Rev. FRANCISCO MONTECILLO PADILLA (Titular Archbishop of Nebbio).

Indonesia: 299 Ali Hassan Mwinyi Rd, POB 572, Dar es Salaam; tel. (22) 2119119; fax (22) 2115849; e-mail kbridsm@raha.com; Ambassador (vacant).

Ireland: 353 Toure Dr., POB 9612, Oyster Bay, Dar es Salaam; tel. (22) 2602355; fax (22) 2602362; e-mail embassydaresalaam@dfa.ie; internet www.embassyofireland.or.tz; Ambassador LORCAN FULLAM.

Italy: Plot 316, Lugalo Rd, Upanga, POB 2106, Dar es Salaam; tel. (22) 2115935; fax (22) 2115938; e-mail segr.dar@esteri.it; internet www.ambdaressalaam.esteri.it; Ambassador PIERLUIGI VELARDI.

Japan: 1018 Ali Hassan Mwinyi Rd, POB 2577, Dar es Salaam; tel. (22) 2115827; fax (22) 2115830; e-mail embassyofjapan_tz@dr.mofa.go.jp; internet www.tz.emb-japan.go.jp; Ambassador MASAKI OKADA.

Kenya: Plot 1858, Oysterbay, Kinondoni, POB 5231, Dar es Salaam; tel. (22) 2668285; fax (22) 2668213; e-mail info@kenyahighcomtz.org; internet www.kenyahighcomtz.org; High Commissioner MUTINDA MUTISO.

Korea, Democratic People's Republic: Plot 5, Ursino Estate, Kawawa Rd, Msasani, POB 2690, Dar es Salaam; tel. (22) 2775395; fax (22) 2700838; Ambassador SOON CHUN LEE.

Korea, Republic: Plot 97, Msese Rd, Kingsway, Kinondoni, POB 1154, Dar es Salaam; tel. (22) 2668788; fax (22) 2667509; e-mail embassy-tz@mofat.go.kr; internet tza.mofat.go.kr; Ambassador (vacant).

Libya: 386 Mtitu St, POB 9413, Dar es Salaam; tel. (22) 2150188; fax (22) 2150068; Secretary of People's Bureau Dr AHMED IBRAHIM EL-ASHHAB.

Malawi: Plot 38, Ali Hassan Mwinyi Rd, POB 7616, Dar es Salaam; tel. (22) 2666284; fax (22) 2668161; e-mail mhc@africaonline.co.tz; High Commissioner (vacant).

Mozambique: 25 Garden Ave, POB 9370, Dar es Salaam; tel. and fax (22) 2124673; fax (22) 2116502; e-mail embamoc.tanzania@minec.gov.mz; High Commissioner ZACARIAS KUPELA.

Netherlands: Umoja House, 4th Floor, Garden Ave, POB 9534, Dar es Salaam; tel. (22) 2110000; fax (22) 2110044; e-mail dar@minbuza.nl; internet tanzania.nlembassy.org; Ambassador Dr KUINDERT ADRIAAN KOEKKOEK.

Nigeria: 83 Haile Selassie Rd, POB 9214, Oyster Bay, Dar es Salaam; tel. (22) 2666000; fax (22) 2668947; e-mail nhc-dsm@raha.com; High Commissioner ISHAYA MAJAMBU.

Norway: 160/50 Mirambo St, POB 2646, Dar es Salaam; tel. (22) 2163100; fax (22) 2163199; e-mail emb.daressalaam@mfa.no; internet www.norway.go.tz; Ambassador INGUNN KLEPSVIK.

Russia: Plot No. 73, Ali Hassan Mwinyi Rd, POB 1905, Dar es Salaam; tel. (22) 2666005; fax (22) 2666818; e-mail embruss@bol.co.tz; Ambassador LEONID SAFANOV.

Rwanda: Plot 32, Ali Hassan Mwinyi Rd, POB 2918, Dar es Salaam; tel. (22) 2120703; fax (22) 2115888; e-mail ambadsm@minaffet.gov.rw; internet www.tanzania.embassy.gov.rw; High Commissioner FATUMA NDANGIZA.

South Africa: Plot 1338/1339, Mwaya Rd, Msaski, POB 10723, Dar es Salaam; tel. (22) 2601800; fax (22) 2600684; e-mail ntombelal@foreign.gov.za; High Commissioner S. G. MFENYANA.

Spain: 99B Kinondoni Rd, POB 842, Dar es Salaam; tel. (22) 2666936; fax (22) 2666938; e-mail embesptz@mail.mae.es; Ambassador JUAN MANUEL GONZÁLEZ DE LINARES PALAU.

Sudan: 'Albaraka', 64 Ali Hassan Mwinyi Rd, POB 2266, Dar es Salaam; tel. (22) 2117641; fax (22) 2115811; e-mail sudan.emb.dar@raha.com; Ambassador Dr YASSIR MOHAMED ALI.

Sweden: Mirambo St and Garden Ave, POB 9274, Dar es Salaam; tel. (22) 2196500; fax (22) 2196503; e-mail ambassaden.dar-es-salaam@foreign.ministry.se; internet www.swedenabroad.se/daressalaam; Ambassador LENNARTH HJELMÅKER.

Switzerland: 79 Kinondoni Rd/Mafinga St, POB 2454, Dar es Salaam; tel. (22) 2666008; fax (22) 2666736; e-mail dar.vertretung@eda.admin.ch; internet www.eda.admin.ch/daressalaam; Ambassador OLIVIER CHAVE.

Syria: 276 Alykhan Rd, Upanga East, POB 2442, Dar es Salaam; tel. (22) 2117656; fax (22) 2115860.

Uganda: Extelcom Bldg, 7th Floor, Samora Ave, POB 6237, Dar es Salaam; tel. (22) 2116754; fax (22) 2112974; e-mail ugadar@intafrica.com; High Commissioner IBRAHIM MUKIIBI.

United Arab Emirates: 2415 Kaunda Drive House, Dar es Salaam; tel. (22) 2669999; fax (22) 2669996; e-mail uaeembassy@bol.co.tz; Ambassador MALALLAH MUBARAK SUWAID AL-AMIRI.

United Kingdom: Umoja House, Garden Ave, POB 9200, Dar es Salaam; tel. (22) 2110101; fax (22) 2110102; e-mail bhc.dar@fco.gov.uk; internet ukintanzania.fco.gov.uk; High Commissioner DIANE LOUISE CORNER.

USA: 686 Old Bagamoyo Rd, Msasani, POB 9123, Dar es Salaam; tel. (22) 2668001; fax (22) 2668238; e-mail embassyd@state.gov; internet tanzania.usembassy.gov; Ambassador ALFONSO E. LENHARDT.

Yemen: 353 United Nations Rd, POB 349, Dar es Salaam; tel. (22) 2117650; fax (22) 2115924; Chargé d'affaires a.i. MOHAMED ABDULLA ALMAS.

Zambia: 5–6 Ohio St/Sokoine Dr. Junction, POB 2525, Dar es Salaam; tel. and fax (22) 2112977; e-mail zhcd@raha.com; High Commissioner DARIUS STRENBECK BUBALA.

Zimbabwe: 2097 East Upanga, off Ali Hassan Mwinyi Rd, POB 20762, Dar es Salaam; tel. (22) 2116789; fax (22) 2112913; e-mail zimdares@cats-net.com; Ambassador EDZAI CHIMONYO.

Judicial System

Permanent Commission of Enquiry: POB 2643, Dar es Salaam; tel. (22) 2113690; fax (22) 2111533; Chair. and Official Ombudsman Prof. JOSEPH F. MBWILIZA; Sec. A. P. GUVETTE.

Court of Appeal

Consists of the Chief Justice and four Judges of Appeal.

Chief Justice of Tanzania: AUGUSTINO RAMADHANI.

Chief Justice of Zanzibar: HAMID MAHMOUD HAMID.

High Court: headquarters at Dar es Salaam, but regular sessions held in all Regions; consists of a Jaji Kiongozi and 29 Judges.

District Courts: situated in each district and presided over by either a Resident Magistrate or District Magistrate; limited jurisdiction, with a right of appeal to the High Court.

Primary Courts: established in every district and presided over by Primary Court Magistrates; limited jurisdiction, with a right of appeal to the District Courts and then to the High Court.

Attorney-General: FREDERICK WEREMA.

Attorney-General of Zanzibar: OMAR MAKUNGU.

Director of Public Prosecutions: ELIEZER FELESHI.

People's Courts were established in Zanzibar in 1970. Magistrates are elected by the people and have two assistants each. Under the Zanzibar Constitution, which came into force in January 1985, defence lawyers and the right of appeal, abolished in 1970, were reintroduced.

Religion

Religious surveys were eliminated from all government census reports after 1967. However, religious leaders and sociologists generally believe that the country's population is 30%–40% Christian and 30%–40% Muslim, with the remainder consisting of practitioners of other faiths, traditional indigenous religions and atheists. Foreign missionaries operate in the country, including Roman Catholics, Lutherans, Baptists, Seventh-day Adventists, Mormons, Anglicans and Muslims.

ISLAM

The Muslim population is most heavily concentrated on the Zanzibar archipelago and in the coastal areas of the mainland. There are also large Muslim minorities in inland urban areas. Some 99% of the population of Zanzibar is estimated to be Muslim. Between 80% and 90% of the country's Muslim population is Sunni; the remainder consists of several Shi'a groups, mostly of Asian descent. A large proportion of the Asian community is Isma'ili.

Ismalia Provincial Church: POB 460, Dar es Salaam.

National Muslim Council of Tanzania: POB 21422, Dar es Salaam; tel. (22) 234934; f. 1969; supervises Islamic affairs on the mainland only; Chair. Sheikh HEMED BIN JUMA BIN HEMED; Exec. Sec. Alhaj MUHAMMAD MTULIA.

Supreme Muslim Council: Zanzibar; f. 1991; supervises Islamic affairs in Zanzibar; Mufti Sheikh HARITH BIN KALEF.

Wakf and Trust Commission: POB 4092, Zanzibar; f. 1980; Islamic affairs; Exec. Sec. YUSUF ABDULRAHMAN MUHAMMAD.

CHRISTIANITY

The Christian population is composed of Roman Catholics, Protestants, Pentecostals, Seventh-day Adventists, members of the Church of Jesus Christ of Latter-day Saints (Mormons) and Jehovah's Witnesses.

Jumuiya ya Kikristo Tanzania (Christian Council of Tanzania): Church House, POB 1454, Dodoma; tel. (26) 2324445; fax (26) 2324352; f. 1934; Chair. Rt Rev. PETER KITULA (Bishop of the African Inland Church); Gen. Sec. Rev. Dr LEONARD AMOS MTAITA.

The Anglican Communion

Anglicans are adherents of the Church of the Province of Tanzania, comprising 16 dioceses.

Archbishop of the Province of Tanzania and Bishop of Dar es Salaam: Most Rev. Dr VALENTINO MOKIWA, POB 1028, Iringa; fax (26) 2702479; e-mail ruaha@maf.or.tz.

Provincial Secretary: Rev. CANON DICKSON CHILONGANI, POB 899, Dodoma; tel. (26) 2321437; fax (26) 2324265; e-mail cpt@maf.org.

Greek Orthodox

Archbishop of East Africa: NICADEMUS OF IRINOUPOULIS (resident in Nairobi, Kenya); jurisdiction covers Kenya, Uganda and Tanzania.

Lutheran

Evangelical Lutheran Church in Tanzania: POB 3033, Boma Rd, Arusha; tel. (27) 2508856; fax (27) 2508858; e-mail elcthq@elct.or.tz; internet www.elct.or.tz; Presiding Bishop ALEX G. MALASUSA; Exec. Sec. AMANI MWENEGOHA; 5.6m. mems (2010).

The Roman Catholic Church

Tanzania comprises five archdioceses and 29 dioceses. Roman Catholics constitute an estimated 28% of the total population.

Tanzania Episcopal Conference

Catholic Secretariat, Mandela Rd, POB 2133, Dar es Salaam; tel. (22) 2851075; fax (22) 2851133; e-mail info@tec.co.tz; internet www.tec.or.tz.

f. 1980; Pres. Mgr JUDE THADDAEUS RUWA'ICHI (Bishop of Dodoma); Sec. Gen. Fr ANTHONY MAKUNDE.

Archbishop of Arusha: Most Rev. JOSAPHAT LOUIS LEBULU, Archbishop's House, POB 3044, Arusha; tel. (27) 2544361; fax (27) 2548004; e-mail angelo.arusha@habari.co.tz.

Archbishop of Dar es Salaam: Cardinal POLYCARP PENGO, Archbishop's House, POB 167, Dar es Salaam; tel. (22) 2113223; fax (22) 2125751; e-mail nyumba@cats-net.com.

Archbishop of Mwanza: Most Rev. JUDE THADAEUS RUWA'ICHI, Archbishop's House, POB 1421, Mwanza; tel. and fax (28) 2501029; e-mail archmwz@mwanza-online.com.

Archbishop of Songea: Most Rev. NORBERT WENDELIN MTEGA, Archbishop's House, POB 152, Songea; tel. (25) 2602004; fax (25) 2602593; e-mail songea-archdiocese@yahoo.com.

Archbishop of Tabora: PAUL R. RUZOKA, Archbishop's House, Private Bag, PO Tabora; tel. (26) 2605608; fax (26) 2604000; e-mail archbishops-office@yahoo.co.uk.

Other Christian Churches

Baptist Mission of Tanzania: POB 9414, Dar es Salaam; tel. (22) 2170130; fax (22) 2170127; f. 1956; Admin. FRANK PEVEY.

Christian Missions in Many Lands (Tanzania): German Branch, POB 34, Tunduru, Ruvuma Region; f. 1957; Gen. Sec. THOMAS MÜHLING.

Moravian Church in Tanzania: POB 747, Mbeya; tel. (25) 2503626; fax (25) 2502155; e-mail mct@moravian.or.tz; internet www.moravian.or.tz; 113,656 mems; Chair. Bishop A. CHEYO; Gen. Sec. Rev. CONRAD NGUVUMALI.

Pentecostal Church: POB 34, Kahama.

Presbyterian Church: POB 2510, Dar es Salaam; tel. (22) 229075.

BAHÁ'Í FAITH

National Spiritual Assembly: POB 585, Dar es Salaam; tel. and fax (22) 2152766; e-mail bahaitz@cats-net.com; internet www.bahai.org; f. 1950; mems resident in 3,000 localities.

OTHER RELIGIONS

Many people follow traditional beliefs. There are also some Hindu communities.

The Press

NEWSPAPERS

Daily

The Citizen: Plot No. 34/35, Mandela Rd, POB 19754, Dar es Salaam; tel. 788455234 (mobile); internet www.thecitizen.co.tz; f. 2004; Man. Editor BAKARI MACHUMU.

Daily News: POB 9033, Dar es Salaam; tel. (22) 2110595; fax (22) 2112881; e-mail newsdesk@dailynews-tsn.com; internet www.dailynews.co.tz; f. 1972; govt-owned; Man. Editor SETHI KAMUHANDA; circ. 50,000.

The Guardian: POB 31042, Dar es Salaam; tel. (22) 275250; fax (22) 273583; e-mail guardian@ipp.co.tz; internet www.ippmedia.com; f. 1994; English and Swahili; Man. Dir KIONDO MSHANA; Man. Editor PASCAL SHIJA.

Kipanga: POB 199, Zanzibar; Swahili; publ. by Information and Broadcasting Services.

Majira: POB 71439, Dar es Salaam; tel. (22) 238901; fax (22) 231104; independent; Swahili; Editor THEOPHIL MAKUNGA; circ. 15,000.

Mwananchi: Plot No. 34/35, Mandela Rd, POB 19754, Dar es Salaam; internet www.mwananchi.co.tz; f. 2000; Swahili; Man. Editor DENNIS MSACKY.

Uhuru: POB 9221, Dar es Salaam; tel. (22) 2182224; fax (22) 2185065; f. 1961; official publ. of CCM; Swahili; Man. Editor SAIDI NGUBA; circ. 100,000.

Weekly

Business Times: POB 71439, Dar es Salaam; tel. (22) 238901; fax (22) 231104; e-mail majira@bcsmedia.com; independent; English; Editor ALLI MWAMBOLA; circ. 15,000.

The Express: POB 20588, Dar es Salaam; tel. (22) 2180058; fax (22) 2182665; e-mail express@raha.com; internet www.theexpress.com; independent; English; Editor FAYAZ BHOJANI; circ. 20,000.

Gazette of the United Republic: POB 9142, Dar es Salaam; tel. (22) 231817; official announcements; Editor H. HAJI; circ. 6,000.

Government Gazette: POB 261, Zanzibar; f. 1964; official announcements.

Kasheshe: POB 31042, Dar es Salaam; Swahili; Editor VENANCE MLAY.

Kiongozi (The Leader): POB 9400, Dar es Salaam; tel. (22) 2851075; fax (22) 2851133; e-mail kiongozinews@yahoo.com; f. 1950; owned by Catholic Publishers Ltd; weekly; Swahili; Roman Catholic; Dir JOSEPH MATUMAINI; circ. 33,500.

Mfanyakazi (The Worker): POB 15359, Dar es Salaam; tel. (22) 226111; Swahili; trade union publ; Editor NDUGU MTAWA; circ. 100,000.

Mwanaspoti: POB 19754, Dar es Salaam; tel. (22) 2150312; fax (22) 2180183; e-mail mwanaspoti@mwanaspoti.co.tz; internet www.mwanaspoti.co.tz.

Mzalendo: POB 9221, Dar es Salaam; tel. (22) 2182224; fax (22) 2185065; e-mail uhuru@udsm.ac.tz; f. 1972; publ. by CCM; Swahili; Man. Editor SAIDI NGABA; circ. 115,000.

Nipashe Jumapili: POB 31042, Dar es Salaam; Swahili.

Sunday News: POB 9033, Dar es Salaam; tel. (22) 2116072; fax (22) 2112881; f. 1954; govt-owned; Man. Editor SETHI KAMUCHANDA; circ. 50,000.

Sunday Observer: POB 31042, Dar es Salaam; e-mail guardian@ipp.co.tz; Man. Dir VUMI URASA; Man. Editor PETER MSUNGU.

PERIODICALS

The African Review: POB 35042, Dar es Salaam; tel. (22) 2410130; e-mail mubakar@udsm.ac.tz; 2 a year; journal of African politics, development and international affairs; publ. by the Dept of Political Science, Univ. of Dar es Salaam; Chief Editor Dr MOHAMMED BAKARI; circ. 1,000.

Eastern African Law Review: POB 35093, Dar es Salaam; tel. (22) 243254; f. 1967; 2 a year; Chief Editor N. N. N. NDITI; circ. 1,000.

Elimu Haina Mwisho: POB 1986, Mwanza; monthly; circ. 45,000.

Habari za Washirika: POB 2567, Dar es Salaam; tel. (22) 223346; monthly; publ. by Co-operative Union of Tanzania; Editor H. V. N. CHIBULUNJE; circ. 40,000.

Jenga: POB 2669, Dar es Salaam; tel. (22) 2112893; fax (22) 2113618; journal of the National Development Corpn; circ. 2,000.

Kweupe: POB 222, Zanzibar; weekly; Swahili; publ. by Information and Broadcasting Services.

Mlezi (The Educator): POB 41, Peramiho; f. 1970; every 2 months; Editor Fr DOMINIC WEIS; circ. 8,000.

Mwenge (Firebrand): POB 1, Peramiho; f. 1937; monthly; Editor JOHN P. MBONDE; circ. 10,000.

Nchi Yetu (Our Country): POB 9142, Dar es Salaam; tel. (22) 2110200; f. 1964; govt publ; monthly; Swahili; circ. 50,000.

Nuru: POB 1893, Zanzibar; f. 1992; bi-monthly; official publ. of Zanzibar Govt; circ. 8,000.

Safina: POB 21422, Dar es Salaam; tel. (22) 234934; publ. by National Muslim Council of Tanzania; Editor YASSIN SADIK; circ. 10,000.

Tantravel: POB 2485, Dar es Salaam; tel. (22) 2111244; fax (22) 2116420; e-mail safari@ud.co.tz; internet www.tanzaniatouristboard.com; f. 1987; quarterly; publ. by Tanzania Tourist Board; Editor GERVAS TATAH MLOLA.

Tanzania Adventist Press: POB 635, Morogoro; tel. and fax (23) 2604374; e-mail reuben.kingamkono@gmail.com; quarterly; Seventh-day Adventist; Editor REUBEN KINGAMKONO; circ. 100,000.

Tanzania Trade Currents: POB 5402, Dar es Salaam; tel. (22) 2850238; fax (22) 2850539; e-mail info@tantrade.or.tz; bi-monthly; publ. by Tanzania Trade Development Authority; circ. 2,000.

Uhuru na Amani: POB 3033, Arusha; tel. (57) 8855; fax (57) 8858; quarterly; Swahili; publ. by Evangelical Lutheran Church in Tanzania; Editor ELIZABETH LOBULU; circ. 15,000.

Ukulima wa Kisasa (Modern Farming): Farmers' Education and Publicity Unit, POB 2308, Dar es Salaam; tel. (22) 2116496; fax (22) 2122923; e-mail fepu@hotmail.co.uk; internet www.kilimo.go.tz; f. 1955; bi-monthly; Swahili; publ. by Ministry of Agriculture, Irrigation, Food Security and Co-operatives; Editor LUCAS NYANGI; circ. 15,000.

Ushirika Wetu: POB 2567, Dar es Salaam; tel. (22) 2184081; e-mail ushirika@covision2000.com; monthly; publ. by Tanzania Federation of Co-operatives; Editor SIMON J. KERARYO; circ. 40,000.

NEWS AGENCY

Press Services Tanzania (PST) Ltd: POB 31042, Dar es Salaam; tel. and fax (22) 2119195.

Publishers

Central Tanganyika Press: POB 1129, Dodoma; tel. (26) 2390015; fax (26) 2324565; e-mail ctp@anglican.or.tz; internet www.anglican.or.tz/ctp.htm; f. 1954; religious; Man. PETER MANG'ATI MAKASSI.

DUP (1996) Ltd: POB 7028, Dar es Salaam; tel. and fax (22) 2410137; e-mail director@dup.udsm.ac.tz; f. 1979; educational, academic and cultural texts in Swahili and English; Dir Dr N. G. MWITTA.

Eastern Africa Publications Ltd: POB 1002 Arusha; tel. (57) 3176; f. 1979; general and school textbooks; Gen. Man. ABDULLAH SAIWAAD.

Inland Publishers: POB 125, Mwanza; tel. (68) 40064; general non-fiction, religion, in Kiswahili and English; Dir Rev. S. M. MAGESA.

Oxford University Press: Maktaba Rd, POB 5299, Dar es Salaam; tel. (22) 229209; f. 1969; literature, literary criticism, essays, poetry; Man. SALIM SHAABAN SALIM.

Tanzania Publishing House: 47 Samora Machel Ave, POB 2138, Dar es Salaam; tel. (22) 2137402; e-mail tphhouse@yahoo.com; f. 1966; educational and general books in Swahili and English; Gen. Man. PRIMUS ISIDOR KARUGENDO.

GOVERNMENT PUBLISHING HOUSE

Government Printer: Office of the Prime Minister, POB 3021, Dar es Salaam; tel. (22) 2860900; fax (22) 2866955; e-mail gptz@pmo.go.tz; Dir KASSIAN C. CHIBOGOYO.

Broadcasting and Communications

REGULATORY AUTHORITY

Tanzania Communications Regulatory Authority (TCRA): Mawasiliano Towers, Plot 2005/5/1, Block C, Sam Nujoma Rd, POB 474, Dar es Salaam; tel. (22) 2199760; fax (22) 2412009; e-mail dg@tcra.go.tz; internet www.tcra.go.tz; f. 1993; licenses postal and telecommunications service operators; manages radio spectrum; acts as ombudsman; Chair. BUXTON CHIPETA; Dir-Gen. Prof. JOHN S. NKOMA.

TELECOMMUNICATIONS

In 2011 there were seven providers of telecommunications services in Tanzania. In December of that year there were 25.7m. subscribers to mobile telephone services and 161,063 subscribers to fixed-line telephone services.

Airtel Tanzania: Airtel House, cnr Ali Hassan Mwinyi and Kawawa Rds, Dar es Salaam; tel. 784103001 (mobile); e-mail info.africa@airtel.com; internet africa.airtel.com/tanzania; f. 2001; fmrly Zain Tanzania, present name adopted 2010; Man. Dir SAM ELANGALLOOR.

Benson Informatics Ltd (BOL): A. H. Mwinyi Rd, Plot No 37, POB 78914, Dar es Salaam; tel. (22) 2666670; fax (22) 2666471; e-mail boldar@bol.co.tz; internet www.bolmobile.co.tz; f. 2000; internet and mobile services provider; CEO NIZAR ABDOU.

MIC Tanzania (Mobitel) Ltd: Lugoda St, POB 2929, Dar es Salaam; tel. 713800800 (mobile); fax (22) 2120474; e-mail mobitel@mobitel.co.tz; internet www.tigo.co.tz; operates mobile cellular telecommunications services through Mobitel network; brand name Tigo; 100% owned by Millicom International Cellular (Luxembourg); Man. Dir MARCELO ALEMAN.

Sasatel: Dar es Salaam; tel. 614200200 (mobile); fax 614200201 (mobile); e-mail customercare@sasatel.co.tz; internet www.sasatel.co.tz; mobile cellular telephone operator.

Tanzania Telecommunications Co Ltd (TTCL): Extelcoms House, Samora Ave, POB 9070, Dar es Salaam; tel. (22) 2142000; fax (22) 2113232; e-mail ttcl@ttcl.co.tz; internet www.ttcl.co.tz; 35% sold to consortium of Detecon (Germany) and Mobile Systems International (Netherlands) in Feb. 2001; operates fixed-line and CDMA network; CEO SAID AMIR SAID.

Vodacom (Tanzania) Ltd: PPF Towers, 14th Floor, Garden Ave/Ohio St, POB 2369, Dar es Salaam; tel. 754705000 (mobile); fax 754704014 (mobile); e-mail feedback@vodacom.co.tz; internet www.vodacom.co.tz; mobile cellular telephone operator; Man. Dir RENE MEZA.

Zanzibar Telecom (Zantel): POB 3459, Zanzibar; tel. (24) 2234823; fax (24) 2234850; e-mail customerservices@zantel.co.tz; internet www.zantel.co.tz; f. 1999; mobile cellular telephone operator for Zanzibar; 18% state-owned, 65% owned by Emirates Telecommunications Corpn (ETISALAT, UAE) and 17% owned by Meeco International; Chair. ESSA AL-HADDAD; CEO ALI BIN JARSH.

BROADCASTING

In 2006 there were 47 radio stations and 29 radio stations licensed to operate in Tanzania.

Radio

Clouds FM: POB 31513, Dar es Salaam; Gen. Man. RUGE MUTAHABA.

Parapanda Radio Tanzania: POB 9191, Dar es Salaam; tel. (22) 2860760; e-mail radiotanzania@raha.com; state-run FM station.

Radio 5 Arusha: POB 11843, Arusha; tel. (27) 8052; fax (27) 4201; e-mail impala@cybernet.co.tz.

Radio FM Zenj 96.8: Zanzibar; f. 2005; owned by Zanzibar Media Corpn; broadcasts to 60% of Zanzibar, to be extended to all of Zanzibar and mainland coast from southern Tanzania to Kenya; Gen. Man. AUSTIN MAKANI.

Radio Kwizera: POB 154, N'Gara; tel. and fax (28) 2226079; e-mail rkngara@jrstz.co.tz; internet www.radiokwizera.org; f. 1995; station's objective is to educate, entertain and inform refugee and local communities, with the aim of bringing about peace and reconciliation; Dir DAMAS S. J. MISSANGA.

Radio One: Mikocheni Light Industrial Area, POB 4374, Dar es Salaam; tel. (22) 275914; fax (22) 2775915; e-mail info@itv.co.tz; internet www.ippmedia.com; wholly owned by IPP Ltd; Man. Dir JOYCE MHAVILLE.

Radio Tanzania Zanzibar: state-owned.

Radio Tumaini (Hope): 1 Bridge St, POB 9916, Dar es Salaam; tel. (22) 2117307; fax (22) 2112594; e-mail tumaini@cats-net.com; internet radiotumaini.tripod.com; broadcasts in Swahili within Dar es Salaam; operated by the Roman Catholic Church; broadcasts on religious, social and economic issues; Dir ESTHER CHILAMBO.

Sauti Ya Tanzania Zanzibar (The Voice of Tanzania Zanzibar): POB 1178, Zanzibar; f. 1951; state-owned; broadcasts in Swahili on three wavelengths; Dir SULEIMAN JUMA.

Tanzania Broadcasting Corporation (TBC): Broadcasting House, Nyerere Rd, POB 9191, Dar es Salaam; tel. (22) 2860760; fax (22) 2865577; e-mail info@tbcorp.org; internet www.tbcorp.org; f. 2008; incorporates Radio Tanzania Dar es Salaam and the national TV network, Televisheni ya Taifa; Dir-Gen. DUNSTAN TIDO MHANDO.

Radio Tanzania Dar es Salaam (RTD): POB 9191, Dar es Salaam; tel. (22) 2860760; fax (22) 2865577; e-mail info@tbcorp.org; internet www.tbcorp.org; f. 1951; state-owned; subsidiary of TBC; domestic services in Swahili; external services in English; Gen. Man. EDDA SANGA.

Television

Dar es Salaam Television (DTV): POB 21122, Dar es Salaam; tel. (22) 2116341; fax (22) 2113112; e-mail franco.dtv@raha.com; f. 1994; Man. Dir FRANCO TRAMONTANO.

Independent Television (ITV): Mikocheni Light Industrial Area, POB 4374, Dar es Salaam; tel. (22) 2775914; fax (22) 2775915; e-mail itv@ipp.co.tz; internet www.ippmedia.com; f. 1994; wholly owned by IPP Ltd; 65% of programmes are locally produced and in Kiswahili; Man. Dir JOYCE MHAVILLE.

Star TV: Post Rd, POB 1732, Mwanza; tel. (28) 2503262; fax (28) 2500713; e-mail marketing@startvtz.com; internet www.startvtz.com; f. 2000.

Tanzania Broadcasting Corporation (TBC): see Radio

Televisheni ya Taifa (TVT): POB 31519, Dar es Salaam; tel. (22) 2700011; fax (22) 2773078; e-mail info@tbcorp.org; internet www.tbc.go.tz; f. 2000; state-owned; subsidiary of TBC since 2008; Gen. Man. CLEMENT MSHANA.

Television Zanzibar: Karume House, POB 314, Zanzibar; tel. and fax (24) 22315951; e-mail karumehouse@tvz.co.tz; internet www.tvz.co.tz; f. 1973; Dir OMAR O. CHANDE.

Finance

(cap. = capital; res = reserves; dep. = deposits; m. = million; brs = branches; amounts in Tanzanian shillings, unless otherwise indicated)

BANKING

In 2010 there were 41 banking institutions in Tanzania: 29 commercial banks, seven regional unit banks and five other financial institutions. Of these, four were fully owned by the Government and the rest were privately owned.

Central Bank

Bank of Tanzania (Benki Kuu Ya Tanzania): 10 Mirambo St, POB 2939, Dar es Salaam; tel. (22) 2110946; fax (22) 2113325; e-mail info@hq.bot-tz.org; internet www.bot-tz.org; f. 1966; bank of issue; cap. 10,000m., res 639,286m., dep. 1,854,572m. (June 2009); Gov. and Chair. Prof. BENNO NDULU; 4 brs.

Principal Banks

Akiba Commercial Bank Ltd: TDFL Bldg, Upanga Rd, POB 669, Dar es Salaam; tel. (22) 2118340; fax (22) 2114173; e-mail akiba@cats-net.com; internet www.acb-bank.com; f. 1997; cap. 8,170.7m., res 4,049.5m., dep. 59,796.2m. (Dec. 2009); Chair. Dr IDRIS RASHIDI; Man. Dir JOHN LWANDE.

Azania Bank Ltd: Mawasiliano Towers, 3rd Floor, Plot No. 2005/5/1/2, Block C, Sinza, Sam Nujoma Rd, POB 32089, Dar es Salaam; tel. (22) 2412025; fax (22) 2412028; e-mail info@azaniabank.co.tz; internet www.azaniabank.co.tz; 55% owned by National Social Security Fund, 31% owned by Parastatal Pension Fund, 9% owned by East African Development Bank, 5% owned by individuals; cap. 10,867.6m., res 918,4m., dep. 120,854.0m (Dec. 2009); Chair. WILLIAM E. ERIO; CEO CHARLES SINGILI; 11 brs.

BancABC (Tanzania) Ltd: Barclays House, 1st Floor, Ohio St, POB 31, Dar es Salaam; tel. (22) 2119303; fax (22) 2112402; e-mail abct@africanbankingcorp.com; internet www.africanbankingcorp.com; wholly owned by African Banking Corpn Holdings Ltd; cap. 5,404m. (Dec. 2003); Man. Dir ISRAEL CHASOSA.

Bank M (Tanzania) Ltd: POB 96, 8 Ocean Rd, Dar es Salaam; tel. (22) 2127825; fax (22) 2127824; e-mail ganpath.pillai@bankm.co.tz; internet www.bankm.co.tz; f. 2007; 19.82% owned by Negus Holdings, 17.65% by Equity & Allied Ltd; cap. 10,502.5m., dep. 97,457.6m. (Dec. 2009); Chair. NIMROD MKONO; CEO SANJEEV KUMAR; 4 brs.

Barclays Bank (Tanzania) Ltd: Barclays House, Ohio St, POB 5137, Dar es Salaam; tel. (22) 2136970; fax (22) 2129750; e-mail kihara.maina@barclays.com; internet www.barclays.com/africa/tanzania; 99.9% owned by Barclays PLC (United Kingdom), 0.1% owned by Ebbgate Holdings Ltd; cap. 18,750m. (Dec. 2003); Man. Dir CHRISTOPHER KIHARA MAINA.

BOA Bank (Tanzania) Ltd: NDC Development House, cnr Kivukoni Front and Ohio St, POB 3054, Dar es Salaam; tel. (22) 2111229; fax (22) 2113740; e-mail eab@eurafricanbank-tz.com; internet www.boatanzania.com; f. 1994 as Eurafrican Bank (Tanzania) Ltd, name changed as above in 2007; 36.68% owned by Bank of Africa Kenya Ltd, 25.01% by Aureos Capital East Africa LLC, 25.01% by Belgian Investment Co; total assets 89,486m. (Dec. 2007); Chair. FULGENCE M. KAZAURA; Man. Dir KOBBY ANDAH.

Citibank Tanzania Ltd: Ali Hassan Mwinyi Rd, POB 71625, Dar es Salaam; tel. (22) 2117575; fax (22) 2113910; 99.98% owned by Citibank Overseas Investment Corpn; Chair. EMEKA EMUWA; CEO JAMAL ALI HUSSEIN.

CRDB Bank: Azikiwe St, POB 268, Dar es Salaam; tel. (22) 2117442; fax (22) 2116714; e-mail crdb@crdbbank.com; internet www.crdbbank.com; f. as Co-operative and Rural Development Bank in 1947, transferred to private ownership and current name adopted 1996; 30% owned by DANIDA Investment; cap. 54,413.3m., res 153,209.5m., dep. 1,625,227.7m. (Dec. 2009); Chair MARTIN J. MMARI; Man. Dir Dr CHARLES S. KIMEI; 56 brs.

Dar es Salaam Community Bank Ltd (DCB): Arnautoglu Bldg, Bibi Titi Mohamed St, POB 19798, Dar es Salaam; tel. (22) 2180253; fax (22) 2180239; e-mail dcb@africaonline.co.tz; f. 2001; cap. 1,796m. (Dec. 2003); Chair. PAUL MILVANGE RUPIA; Man. Dir EDMUND PANCRAS MKWAWA.

Diamond Trust Bank Tanzania Ltd: POB 115, 9th Floor, Harbour View Towers, Dar es Salaam; tel. (22) 2114891; fax (22) 2124244; internet www.dtbafrica.com; f. 1946 as Diamond Jubilee Investment Trust; converted to bank and adopted current name in 1996; 55% owned by Diamond Trust Bank Kenya Ltd, 23% owned by Aga Khan Fund for Economic Development SA (Switzerland); cap. 1,550.6m., res 5,452.9m., dep. 176,827.4m. (Dec. 2009); Chair. ABDUL SAMJI; CEO VIJU CHERIAN.

EXIM Bank (Tanzania) Ltd: NIC Investment House, Samora Ave, POB 1431, Dar es Salaam; tel. (22) 2113091; fax (22) 2119737; e-mail marketing@eximbank-tz.com; internet www.eximbank-tz.com; cap. 12,900m., res 15,452m., dep. 462,039m. (Dec. 2009); Chair. YOGESH MANEK; Man. Dir S. M. J. MWAMBENJA.

FBME Bank Ltd: Samora Ave, POB 8298, Dar es Salaam; tel. (22) 2126000; fax (22) 2126006; e-mail headoffice@fbme.com; internet www.fbme.com; f. 1982; cap. US $43.2m., res US $5.9m., dep. US $1,562.8m. (Dec. 2009); Chair. AYOUB-FARID M. SAAB, FADI M. SAAB; Gen. Man. (Tanzania) JOHN LISTER; 5 brs.

Habib African Bank Ltd: Indira Gandhi/Zanaki St, POB 70086, Dar es Salaam; tel. (22) 2111107; fax (22) 2111014; e-mail hasanrizvi@habibafricanbank.co.tz; f. 1998; cap. 7,475m., dep. 65,236m. (Dec. 2009); Chair. HABIB MOHAMMED D. HABIB; Man. Dir SYED HASAN RIZVI; 2 brs.

I & M Tanzania Ltd Bank Ltd: Jivan Hirji Bldg, Indira Gandhi/Mosque St, POB 1509, Dar es Salaam; tel. (22) 2110212; fax (22) 2118750; e-mail cfunionbank@raha.com; internet www.imbank.com; f. 2002 by merger of Furaha Finance Ltd and Crown Finance & Leasing Ltd; present name adopted 2010; cap. 4m. (Dec. 2006); Chair. SARIT S. RAJA SHAH; CEO SUBRAMANIAN GOPALAN.

International Bank of Malaysia (Tanzania) Ltd: Upanga/Kisutu St, POB 9363, Dar es Salaam; tel. (22) 2110518; fax (22) 2110196; e-mail ibm@afsat.com; Chair. JOSEPHINE PREMLA SIVARETNAM; CEO M. RAHMAT.

International Commercial Bank (Tanzania) Ltd: 1st Floor, Jamhuri St/Morogoro Rd, POB 9362, Dar es Salaam; tel. (22) 2134989; fax (22) 2134286; e-mail enquiry@icbank-tz.com; f. 1998; CEO L. K. GANAPATHIRAMANI; 5 brs.

Kenya Commercial Bank (Tanzania) Ltd: National Audit House, Samora/Ohio St, POB 804, Dar es Salaam; tel. (22) 2115386; fax (22) 2115391; internet www.kcb.co.ke; cap. 6,000m. (Dec. 2003); Chair. PETER MUTHOKA; Man. Dir Dr EDMUND BERNARD MNDOLWA.

Mufindi Community Bank: POB 147, Mafinga; tel. and fax (26) 2772165; e-mail mucoba@africaonline.co.tz; cap. 100m. (Dec. 2003); Chair. ATTILIO MOHELE; Gen. Man. DANY MPOGOLE.

Mwanga Community Bank: Mwanga Township, POB 333, Mwanga, Kilimanjaro; tel. and fax (27) 2754235; Man. Dir CHRIS HALIBUT.

National Microfinance Bank Ltd (NMB): Samora Ave, POB 9213, Dar es Salaam; tel. (22) 2124048; fax (22) 2110077; e-mail ceo@nmbtz.com; internet www.nmbtz.com; f. 1997 following disbandment of the National Bank of Commerce; 51% state-owned, 49% owned by a consortium led by Rabobank Group; Chair. MISHECK NGATUNGA; CEO MARK H. WIESSING; 140 brs.

NBC Ltd (National Bank of Commerce Ltd): NBC House, Sokoine Drive, POB 1863, Dar es Salaam; tel. (22) 2112082; fax (22) 2112887; e-mail nbcltd@nbctz.com; internet www.nbctz.com; f. 1997; 55% owned by ABSA Group Ltd (South Africa), 30% by Govt and 15% by International Finance Corpn; cap. 10,000m., res 154,446m., dep. 1,051,393m. (Dec. 2009); Man. Dir LAWRENCE MAFURU; 56 brs.

NIC Bank Tanzania Ltd: Mezannine Floor, Harbour View Towers, Mission St/Samora Ave, POB 20268, Dar es Salaam; tel. (22) 2118625; fax (22) 2116733; e-mail james.muchiri@nic-bank.com; internet www.nic-bank.com; name changed as above in 2010; 51% owned by National Industrial Credit Bank Ltd (Kenya); Chair. ABDULSULTAN HASHAM JAMAL; Man. Dir JAMES MUCHIRI; 4 brs.

People's Bank of Zanzibar Ltd (PBZ): POB 1173, Stone Town, Zanzibar; tel. (24) 2231119; fax (24) 2231121; e-mail pbzltd@zanlik.com; f. 1966; controlled by Zanzibar Govt; cap. 5,000.0m., res

10,785.2m., dep. 99,480.4m. (Dec. 2009); Chair. ABDUL RAHMAN M. JUMBE; Man. Dirs J. M. AMOUR, N. S. NASSOR; 3 brs.

Stanbic Bank Tanzania Ltd: Sukari House, cnr AH Mwinyi/Kinondoni Rd, POB 72647, Dar es Salaam; tel. (22) 2666430; fax (22) 2666301; e-mail tanzaniainfo@stanbic.com; internet www.stanbic.co.tz; f. 1993; wholly owned by Standard Africa Holdings Ltd; cap. 2,000m., res 871m., dep. 230,804m. (Dec. 2005); Chair ARNOLD B. S. KILEWO; Man. Dir BASHIR AWALE; 10 brs.

Standard Chartered Bank Tanzania Ltd: International House, 1st Floor, cnr Shaaban Robert St and Garden Ave, POB 9011, Dar es Salaam; tel. (22) 2122125; fax (22) 2113770; f. 1992; wholly owned by Standard Chartered Holdings (Africa) BV, Netherlands; cap. 15,032.0m., res 2,525.9m., dep. 713,527.3m. (Dec. 2009); Man. Dir JEREMY AWORI; 7 brs.

Tanzania Development Finance Co Ltd (TDFL): TDFL Bldg, Plot 1008, cnr Upanga Rd and Ohio St, POB 2478, Dar es Salaam; tel. (22) 2116417; fax (22) 2116418; e-mail mail@tdfl.co.tz; f. 1962; owned by Govt (32%), govt agencies of the Netherlands and Germany (5% and 26%, respectively), the Commonwealth Development Corpn (26%) and the European Investment Bank (11%); cap. 3,303m. (Dec. 2001); Chair. H. K. SENKORO; CEO J. MCGUFFOG.

Tanzania Investment Bank (TIB): Bldg No. 3, Mlimani City Office Park, Sam Nujoma Rd, POB 9373, Dar es Salaam; tel. (22) 2411101; fax (22) 2411095; e-mail md@tib.co.tz; internet www.tib.co.tz; f. 1970; 99% govt-owned; cap. 7,641m., res 2,823m., dep. 45,746m. (Dec. 2005); Man. Dir PETER E. M. NONI.

Tanzania Postal Bank (TPB): Extelecoms Annex Bldg, Samora Ave, POB 9300, Dar es Salaam; tel. (22) 2112358; fax (22) 2114815; e-mail md@postalbank.co.tz; internet www.postalbank.co.tz; f. 1991; state-owned; cap. 1,041m. (Dec. 2003); Chair. Prof. LETICIA RUTASHOBYA; Man. Dir and CEO ALPHONSE R. KIHWELE; 4 brs and 113 agencies.

United Bank for Africa Tanzania Ltd: 30C/30D Nyerere Rd, POB 80514, Dar es Salaam; tel. (22) 2863452; fax (22) 2863454; e-mail uba@cats-net.com; Chair. N. N. KITOMARI; Man. Dir AYOBOLA ABIOLA.

BANKING ASSOCIATION

Tanzania Bankers Association: 4th Floor, Sukari House, Ohio/Sokoine Dr., POB 70925, Dar es Salaam; tel. (22) 2127764; fax (22) 2124492; e-mail info@tanzaniabankers.org; internet www.tanzaniabankers.org; f. 1995; Chair. BEN CHRISTIAANSE; Exec. Dir PASCAL L. KAMUZORA.

STOCK EXCHANGE

Dar es Salaam Stock Exchange: Twigga Bldg, 4th Floor, Samora Ave, POB 70081, Dar es Salaam; tel. (22) 2135779; fax (22) 2133849; e-mail info@darstockexchange.com; internet www.dse.co.tz; f. 1998; Chair. PETER MACHUNDE; Chief Exec. Dr HAMISI S. KIBOLA.

INSURANCE

In 2010 there were 23 licensed insurance companies in Tanzania, of which two were fully owned by the government.

African Life Assurance Co Ltd: International House, POB 79651, Dar es Salaam; tel. (22) 2122914; fax (22) 2122917; e-mail charlesw@aflife.co.tz; Chair. CHARLES WASHOMA.

Alliance Insurance Corpn Ltd: 7th Floor, Exim Tower, POB 9942, Dar es Salaam; tel. (22) 2139100; fax (22) 2139098; e-mail admin@alliancetz.com; internet www.alliancetz.com; Chair. SHAFFIN JAMAL; Man. Dir K. V. A. KRISHNAN.

Jubilee Insurance Co of Tanzania Ltd (JICT): 4th Floor, Amani Plaza, Ohio St, POB 20524, Dar es Salaam; e-mail jictz@jubileetanzania.com; internet www.jubileetanzania.com; 40% owned by Jubilee Insurance Kenya, 24% by local investors, 15% by the IFC, 15% by the Aga Khan Fund for Economic Devt, 6% by others; cap. US $2m; Prin. Officer S. RAVI.

National Insurance Corporation of Tanzania Ltd (NIC): POB 9264, Dar es Salaam; tel. (22) 2113823; fax (22) 2113403; e-mail info-nic@nictanzania.com; internet www.nictanzania.co.tz; f. 1963; state-owned; all classes of insurance; Chair. Prof. J. L. KANYWANYI; Man. Dir OCTAVIAN W. TEMU; 30 brs.

Niko Insurance (Tanzania) Ltd: PPF House, 8th Floor, Morogoro Rd/Samora Ave, POB 21228, Dar es Salaam; tel. (22) 2120188; fax (22) 2120193; e-mail info@nikoinsurance.co.tz; internet www.nikoinsurance.co.tz; f. 1998; subsidiary of NICO Holdings Ltd (based in Malawi); Gen. Man. MANFRED Z. SIBANDE.

REGULATORY AUTHORITY

Tanzania Insurance Regulatory Authority (TIRA): Block 33, Plot No. 85/2115, Mtendeni St, POB 9892, Dar es Salaam; tel. (22) 2132537; fax (22) 2132539; e-mail coi@tira.go.tz; internet www.tira.go.tz; f. 2009; Chair. Prof. G. M. FIMBO; Commr of Insurance I. L. KAMUZORA.

Trade and Industry

GOVERNMENT AGENCIES

Parastatal Sector Reform Commission (PSRC): Sukari House, POB 9252, Dar es Salaam; tel. (22) 2115482; fax (22) 2113065; e-mail masalla@raha.com.

Tanzania Investment Centre (TIC): Shaaban Robert St, POB 938, Dar es Salaam; tel. (22) 2116328; fax (22) 2118253; e-mail information@tic.co.tz; internet www.tic.co.tz; f. 1997; promotes and facilitates investment in Tanzania; Chair. E. MTANGO; Exec. Dir RAYMOND MBILINYI (acting).

Tanzania Trade Development Authority (TanTrade): Mwl J. K. Nyerere Fair Grounds, Kilwa Rd, POB 5402, Dar es Salaam; tel. (22) 2850238; fax (22) 2850239; internet www.tantrade.or.tz; f. 2009 to replace the Board of Internal Trade and the Board of External Trade; aims to develop and promote internal and external trade; Chair. SALUM SHAMTE; Dir-Gen. RAMADHAN H. KHALFAN.

CHAMBERS OF COMMERCE

Dar es Salaam Chamber of Commerce: Kelvin House, Samora Machel Ave, POB 41, Dar es Salaam; tel. (754) 270438; fax (22) 2112754; e-mail dcc1919@yahoo.com; f. 1919; Exec. Dir BERNARD MSEKWA.

Tanzania Chamber of Commerce, Industry and Agriculture (TCCIA): 21 Ghana Ave, POB 9713, Dar es Salaam; tel. (22) 2119436; fax (22) 2119437; e-mail info@tccia.com; internet www.tccia.com; f. 1988; Pres. ALOYS MWAMANGA; Exec. Dir DANIEL MACHEMBA (acting).

Zanzibar Chamber of Commerce: POB 1407, Zanzibar; tel. (24) 2233083; fax (24) 2233349.

DEVELOPMENT CORPORATIONS

Capital Development Authority: POB 1, Dodoma; tel. (26) 2324053; fax (26) 2322650; e-mail cda@pmo.com.tz; f. 1973 to develop the new capital city of Dodoma; govt-controlled; Dir-Gen. M. L. KITILLA.

Economic Development Commission: POB 9242, Dar es Salaam; tel. (22) 2112681; f. 1962 to plan national economic development; state-controlled.

National Development Corporation: Kivukoni Front, Ohio St, POB 2669, Dar es Salaam; tel. (22) 2112893; fax (22) 2113618; e-mail epztz@ndctz.com; f. 1965; state-owned; cap. Ts. 30.0m.; promotes progress and expansion in production and investment; Man. Dir GIDEON NASSARI.

Small Industries Development Organization (SIDO): Mfaume/Fire Rd, Upanga, POB 2476, Dar es Salaam; tel. (22) 2151947; fax (22) 2152070; e-mail dg@sido.go.tz; internet www.sido.go.tz; f. 1973; parastatal; promotes and assists development of small-scale enterprises in public, co-operative and private sectors, aims to increase the involvement of women in small businesses; Chair. JAPHET S. MLAGALA; Dir-Gen. MIKE LAISOR.

Sugar Development Corporation: Dar es Salaam; tel. (22) 2112969; fax (22) 230598; Gen. Man. GEORGE G. MBATI.

Tanzania Petroleum Development Corporation (TPDC): POB 2774, Dar es Salaam; tel. (22) 2181407; fax (22) 2180047; internet www.tpdc-tz.com; f. 1969; state-owned; oversees petroleum exploration and undertakes autonomous exploration, imports crude petroleum and distributes refined products; Man. Dir YONA S. M. KILLAGANE.

There is also a development corporation for textiles.

INDUSTRIAL AND TRADE ASSOCIATIONS

Cashewnut Board of Tanzania (CBT): POB 533, Mtwara; tel. (23) 2333303; fax (23) 2333536; e-mail info@cashewnut-tz.org; internet www.cashewnut-tz.org; govt-owned; regulates the marketing, processing and export of cashews; Chair. ANNA M. ABDALLAH; Dir-Gen. A. BENO MHAGAMA.

Confederation of Tanzania Industries (CTI): NIC Investment House, 9th Floor, Samora Ave, POB 71783, Dar es Salaam; tel. (22) 2114954; fax (22) 2115414; e-mail cti@cti.co.tz; internet www.cti.co.tz; f. 1991; Chair. FELIX MOSHA; Exec. Dir CHRISTINE KILINDU.

National Coconut Development Programme: POB 6226, Dar es Salaam; tel. (22) 2700552; fax (22) 275549; e-mail mari@mari.or.tz; f. 1979 to revive coconut industry; processing and marketing via research and devt in disease and pest control, agronomy and farming systems, breeding and post-harvest technology; based at Mikocheni Agricultural Research Inst; Dir Dr ALOIS K. KULLAYA.

Sugar Board of Tanzania: Sukari House, 6th Floor, cnr Ohio St and Sokoine Dr., Dar es Salaam; tel. (22) 2111523; fax (22) 2130598; internet www.sbt.go.tz; f. 2001; Dir-Gen. MATHEW M. KOMBE.

Tanzania Coffee Board (TCB): Kahawa House, POB 732, Moshi; tel. (27) 2752324; fax (27) 2752026; e-mail info@coffeeboard.or.tz; internet www.coffeeboard.or.tz; Chair. EVA HAWA SINARE; Dir-Gen. ADOLPH KUMBURU.

Tanzania Cotton Board: Pamba House, Garden Ave, POB 9161, Dar es Salaam; tel. (22) 2122564; fax (22) 2112894; e-mail info@cotton.co.tz; internet www.cotton.or.tz; f. 1984; regulates, develops and promotes the Tanzanian cotton industry; Chair. Dr FESTUS BULUGU LIMBU; Dir-Gen. MARCO MTUNGA.

Tanzania Exporters' Association: NIC Investment House, 6th Floor, Wing A, Samora Ave, POB 1175, Dar es Salaam; tel. and fax (22) 2125438; e-mail tanexa.exporters@yahoo.com; f. 1994; Exec. Dir MTEMI LAWRENCE NALUYAGA.

Tanzania Horticultural Association (TAHA): Kanisa Rd, House No. 49, POB 16520, Arusha; tel. and fax (27) 2544568; e-mail info@tanzaniahorticulture.com; internet www.tanzaniahorticulture.com; f. 2004; Chair. COLMAN M. NGALO; Exec. Dir JACQUELINE MKINDI.

Tanzania Pyrethrum Board: POB 149, Iringa; f. 1960; Chair. Brig. LUHANGA; CEO P. B. G. HANGAYA.

Tanzania Sisal Board: POB 277, Tanga; tel. and fax (27) 2645060; e-mail tansisal@tsbtz.org; internet www.tsbtz.org; f. 1997; Chair. Prof. JOSEPH SEMBOJA; Dir-Gen. HAMISI MAPINDA.

Tanzania Tobacco Board: POB 227, Mazimbu Rd, Morogoro; tel. (23) 2603364; fax (23) 2604401; Chair. V. KAWAWA; Dir-Gen. FRANK S. URIO.

Tanzania Wood Industry Corporation: POB 9160, Dar es Salaam; Gen. Man. E. M. MNZAVA.

Tea Association of Tanzania: POB 2177, Dar es Salaam; tel. (22) 2122033; e-mail trit@twiga.com; f. 1989; Chair. Dr NORMAN C. KELLY; Exec. Dir DAVID E. A. MGWASSA.

Tea Board of Tanzania: TETEX House, 1st Floor, Pamba Rd, POB 2663, Dar es Salaam; tel. and fax (22) 2114400; e-mail info@teaboardtz.org; internet teaboardtz.org; Chair. ANNE S. MAKINDA; Dir-Gen. Eng. MATHIAS ASSENGA BENEDICT.

Zanzibar State Trading Corporation: POB 26, Zanzibar; internet www.zstczanzibar.com; govt-controlled since 1964; sole exporter of cloves, clove stem oil, chillies, copra, copra cake, lime oil and lime juice; Dir SULEIMAN JONGO.

UTILITIES

Regulatory Authority

Energy and Water Utilities Regulatory Authority (EWURA): 6th Floor, Harbour View Towers, Samora Ave, POB 72175, Dar es Salaam; tel. (22) 2123850; fax (22) 2123180; e-mail info@ewura.go.tz; internet www.ewura.go.tz; f. 2001; technical and economic regulation of the electricity, petroleum, natural gas and water sectors; Chair. SIMON F. SAYORE; Dir-Gen. HARUNA MASEBU.

Electricity

Tanzania Electric Supply Co Ltd (TANESCO): POB 9024, Dar es Salaam; tel. (22) 2451130; fax (22) 2113836; e-mail info@tanesco.com; internet www.tanesco.co.tz; state-owned; placed under private management in May 2002; privatization pending; Chair. Gen. ROBERT MBOMA; Man. Dir WILLIAM MHANDO.

Gas

Enertan Corpn Ltd: POB 3746, Dar es Salaam.

Songas Ltd: cnr Nelson Mandela and Morogoro Rds, POB 6342, Dar es Salaam; tel. (22) 2452160; fax (22) 2452161; internet www.songas.com; f. 1998; Gen. Man. JIM MCCARDLE.

Water

Dar es Salaam Water and Sewerage Authority: POB 1573, Dar es Salaam; e-mail dawasapiu@raha.com; privatization pending.

National Urban Water Authority: POB 5340, Dar es Salaam; tel. (22) 2667505.

Dar es Salaam Water and Sewerage Corporation (DAWASCO): POB 5340, Dar es Salaam; tel. and fax (22) 2110931; internet www.dawasco.com; sole provider of water supply and sewerage services in Dar es Salaam and parts of the coastal region; CEO ALEX KAAYA.

MAJOR COMPANIES

The following are some of the largest companies in terms either of capital investment or employment.

Aluminium Africa Ltd (ALAF): Nyerere Rd, Area Plot No. 18, POB 2070, Dar es Salaam; tel. (22) 2860010; fax (22) 2864690; e-mail alaf@aluminiumafrica.com; internet www.aluminiumafrica.com; f. 1960; mfrs of aluminium circles, corrugated and plain sheets, galvanized corrugated iron sheets, furniture tubes, steel billets, galvanized pipes, cold-rolled steel sheets and coils; Chair. M. P. CHANDARIA; CEO (vacant); 550 employees.

Brooke Bond Liebig Tanzania Ltd: POB 4955, Dar es Salaam; tel. (22) 2863400; fax (22) 2865293; e-mail norman.kelly@unilever.com; wholly owned by Unilever PLC; production and sale of tea; Man. Dir NORMAN KELLY; 6,500 employees.

IPP Ltd: POB 163, Dar es Salaam; tel. (22) 2119349; fax (22) 2119360; e-mail ipp@raha.com; internet www.ippmedia.com; f. 1978; holding co; Exec. Chair. REGINALD A. MENGI; 2,000 employees.

Katani Ltd: POB 123, Tanga; tel. (27) 2644401; fax (27) 2642409; e-mail katani@twiga.com; f. 1997; mfrs of sisal products; Man. Dir SALUM SHAMTE; 2,500 employees.

KJ Motors Ltd: POB 9440, Dar es Salaam; tel. (22) 2863588; fax (22) 2863036; f. 1959; mfrs of light and heavy commercial vehicles, construction equipment and motor cycles; Man. Dir NOORALLY K. J. DHANANI; 400 employees.

Mwanza Textiles Ltd: POB 1344, Mwanza; tel. (068) 40466; f. 1966; spinners, weavers, dyers and printers of cotton; 3,901 employees.

National Chemical Industries: POB 9643, Dar es Salaam; tel. (22) 2135287; fax (22) 2155287; manufacture of industrial chemicals; Man. Dir M. DARESOI; 2,000 employees.

National Milling Corporation (NMC): POB 87, Arusha; tel. (27) 2544959; f. 1968; stores and distributes basic foodstuffs, owns grain milling establishments and imports cereals as required; Chair. T. SIWALE; Gen. Man. JOSHUA MUTINANGI; 1,300 employees.

Sunflag (Tanzania) Ltd: Themi Industrial Area, POB 3123, Arusha; tel. (27) 3739; fax (27) 8210; e-mail info@sunflag-tz.com; internet www.sunflag-tz.com; f. 1965; mfrs of textiles and clothing; Chair. SATYA DEV BHARDWAJ; 2,700 employees.

Tanga Cement Co Ltd: Coco Plaza, 3rd Floor, Toure Dr., POB 78478, Dar es Salaam; tel. (22) 2602784; fax (22) 2602785; e-mail info@simbacement.co.tz; internet www.simbacement.co.tz; subsidiary of Holcim Ltd (Switzerland); mfrs of Portland cement; Chair. Prof. SAMUEL WANGWE (acting); Man. Dir ERIK WESTERBERG; 650 employees.

Tanpack Tissues Ltd: POB 21359, Dar es Salaam; tel. (22) 2773901; fax (22) 2700890; e-mail tanpack@cats-net.com; internet www.chandaria.com; f. 1996; wholly owned by Chandaria Industries Ltd; mfrs of paper and tissue; sales Ts. 2,500m. (2004); Man. Dir MAHESH M. CHANDARIA; Gen. Man. RAJESH SHA; 140 employees.

Tanzania Breweries Ltd (TBL): Ururo St, POB 9013, Dar es Salaam; tel. (22) 2182780; fax (22) 2181458; e-mail info@tbl.co.tz; f. 1960; subsidiary of South African Breweries International; manufacture, bottling and distribution of malt beer; sales Ts. 135,059.05m. (2002); Chair. PAUL L. BOMANI; CEO ROBIN GOETZCHE; 1,266 employees.

Tanzania China Friendship Textile Co.: POB 20842, Dar es Salaam; tel. (22) 2189841; fax (22) 2183689; f. 1966; wholly owned by National Textile Corpn; dyed and printed fabric mfrs; 5,400 employees.

Tanzania Cigarette Co (TCC): POB 40114, Dar es Salaam; tel. (22) 2860150; fax (22) 2865730; e-mail tcc@cats-net.com; f. 1965; 75% owned by JT International; manufacture and marketing of cigarettes; sales US $3,900m. (2003); CEO SIMON MATTA; 700 employees.

Tanzania Distillers Ltd: POB 9412, Dar es Salaam; tel. (22) 2860510; fax (22) 5865202; distillers; CEO N. T. JENKINSON; 78 employees.

Tanzania Portland Cement Co Ltd (Twiga Cement): Wazo Hill, Bagamoyo Rd, POB 1950, Dar es Salaam; tel. (22) 2630130; fax (22) 2630139; e-mail arne.tvedt@tpcc.raha.com; f. 1959; 69.3% owned by HeidelbergCement Group, Germany; mfrs of ordinary Portland cement; capacity: 520,000 metric tons per year; Chair. JEAN-MARC JUNON; Man. Dir KLAUS HVASSING; 390 employees.

TOL Ltd: POB 911, Dar es Salaam; tel. (22) 2860047; fax (22) 2864041; e-mail ccsm@tol.co.tz; f. 1950; 11.4% owned by Govt; manufacture and distribution of industrial and chemical gases; sales Ts. 2,919.8m. (2003); Chair. HAROLD TEMU; 107 employees.

Toyota Tanzania Ltd: 5 Nyerere Rd, POB 9060, Dar es Salaam; tel. (22) 2866815; fax (22) 2866814; e-mail info@toyotatz.com; internet www.toyotatz.com; f. 1825; wholly owned by Karimjee Jivanjee Ltd; distribution of Toyota motor vehicles; Man. Dir MAHMOOD A. KARIMJEE; 300 employees.

CO-OPERATIVES

There are some 1,670 primary marketing societies under the aegis of about 20 regional co-operative unions. The Co-operative Union of Tanzania is the national organization to which all unions belong.

Tanzania Federation of Co-operatives Ltd: Ushirika Bldg, 9th Floor, Lumumba St, POB 2567, Dar es Salaam; tel. (22) 2184084; fax (22) 2184081; e-mail ushirika@ushirika.co.tz; internet www.ushirika.coop; f. 1962; Exec. Sec. WILLIGIS O. MBOGORO; 700,000 mems.

Department of Co-operative Societies: POB 1287, Zanzibar; f. 1952; promotes formation and development of co-operative societies in Zanzibar.

Principal Societies

Kagera Co-operative Union Ltd: POB 5, Bukoba; tel. (28) 2220229; fax (28) 2221168; e-mail kcu@africaonline.co.tz; internet www.kcu-tz.com; 74 affiliated societies; 75,000 mems.

Kilimanjaro Native Co-operative Union (1984) Ltd: POB 3032, Moshi; tel. (27) 2752785; fax (27) 2754204; e-mail kncu@kilinet.co.tz; f. 1984; represents smallholder farmers and coffee producers; 68 regd co-operative societies; Gen. Man. TOBIA MASAKI.

Nyanza Co-operative Union Ltd: POB 9, Mwanza.

TRADE UNIONS

Trade Union Congress of Tanzania (TUCTA): Dar es Salaam; f. 2000; Pres. OMARY AYOUB JUMA; Sec.-Gen. NICHOLAS MGAYA.

Zanzibar Trade Union Congress (ZATUC): Zanzibar; f. 2002; Sec.-Gen. MAKAME LAUNI MAKAME.

Transport

RAILWAYS

In 2010 2,707 km of 1,000-mm-gauge railway track were operated by Reli Assets Holding Co Ltd, which develops, promotes and manages rail infrastructure assets. A new railway project linking Tanga with Musoma on Lake Victoria is currently under consideration. The 1,067-mm-gauge Tazara railway line linking Dar es Salaam with New Kapiri Mposhi, Zambia, has a total length of 1,860 km, of which 969 km are within Tanzania. In 2007 the Tanzania Railways Corpn was privatized under a 25-year lease agreement with the Indian company RITES, and renamed Tanzania Railways Ltd (TRL). However, in 2010, the lease was terminated due to disagreements between the two parties and the Tanzanian Government resumed its control over TRL.

Tanzania Railways Ltd (TRL): POB 468, Dar es Salaam; tel. and fax (22) 2110599; e-mail ccm_shamte@trctz.com; internet www.trctz.com; f. 1977 after dissolution of East African Railways; operates 2,600 km of lines within Tanzania; Chair. J. K. CHANDE; Dir-Gen. LINFORD MBOMA.

Tanzania-Zambia Railway Authority (Tazara): Nyerere Rd, POB 2834, Dar es Salaam; tel. and fax (22) 2862033; e-mail mdhq@tazarasite.com; internet www.tazarasite.com; jtly owned and administered by the Tanzanian and Zambian Govts; operates a 1,860-km railway link between Dar es Salaam and New Kapiri Mposhi, Zambia, of which 975 km are within Tanzania; Man. Dir AKASHAMBATWA MBIKUSITA-LEWANIKA; Regional Man. (Tanzania) ABDALLAH SHEKIMWERI.

ROADS

In 2008 Tanzania had an estimated 87,524 km of classified roads, of which some 7.38% were paved. A 1,930-km main road links Zambia and Tanzania, and there is a road link with Rwanda.

The island of Zanzibar has 619 km of roads, of which 442 km are bituminized, and Pemba has 363 km, of which 130 km are bituminized.

Tanzania National Roads Agency (TANROADS): Airtel House, 3rd Floor, Ali Hassan Mwinyi/Kawawa Rd Junction, POB 11364, Dar es Salaam; tel. (22) 2926001; fax (22) 2926011; e-mail tanroadshq@tanroads.org; internet www.tanroads.org; f. 2000; responsible for the maintenance and development of the trunk and regional road network; Chair. ABEL MWAISUMO; Chief Exec. P. A. L. MFUGALE.

INLAND WATERWAYS

Steamers connect with Kenya, Uganda, the Democratic Republic of the Congo, Burundi, Zambia and Malawi. A rail ferry service operates on Lake Victoria between Mwanza and Port Bell.

SHIPPING

Tanzania's major harbours are at Dar es Salaam (eight deep-water berths for general cargo, three berths for container ships, eight anchorages, lighter wharf, one oil jetty for small oil tankers up to 36,000 gross tons, offshore mooring for oil supertankers up to 100,000 tons, one 30,000-ton automated grain terminal) and Mtwara (two deep-water berths). There are also ports at Tanga (seven anchorages and lighterage quay), Bagamoyo, Zanzibar and Pemba.

Tanzania Ports Authority (TPA): POB 9184, Dar es Salaam; tel. (22) 2116258; fax (22) 2113432; e-mail dp@tanzaniaports.com; internet www.tanzaniaports.com; f. 2005 to replace the Tanzania Harbours Authority, in preparation for privatization; Chair. RAPHAEL MOLLEL; Dir-Gen. EPHRAIM MGAWE.

Chinese-Tanzanian Joint Shipping Co: 31 Kisutu Rd, POB 696, Dar es Salaam; tel. (22) 2113389; fax (22) 2113388; e-mail admin@sinotaship.com; f. 1967; services to People's Republic of China, South-east Asia, Eastern and Southern Africa, Red Sea and Mediterranean ports.

National Shipping Agencies Co Ltd (NASACO): POB 9082, Dar es Salaam; f. 1973; state-owned shipping co; Man. Dir D. R. M. LWIMBO.

Shipping Management Services (SHMASE): POB 5480, Dar es Salaam; tel. (22) 2123796; fax (22) 2123352; e-mail infor@shmase.com; internet www.shmase.com; Man. Dir HASHIM MASHELLE.

Tanzania Coastal Shipping Line Ltd: POB 9461, Dar es Salaam; tel. (22) 237034; fax (22) 2116436; regular services to Tanzanian coastal ports; occasional special services to Zanzibar and Pemba; also tramp charter services to Kenya, Mozambique, the Persian (Arabian) Gulf, Indian Ocean islands and the Middle East; Gen. Man. RICHARD D. NZOWA.

CIVIL AVIATION

There are 53 airports and landing strips. The major international airport is at Dar es Salaam, 13 km from the city centre, and there are also international airports at Kilimanjaro, Mwanza and Zanzibar.

Tanzania Civil Aviation Authority (TCAA): IPS Bldg, cnr Samora Machel Ave and Azikiwe St, POB 2819, Dar es Salaam; tel. (22) 2198100; fax (22) 2844304; e-mail tcaa@tcaa.go.tz; internet www.tcaa.go.tz; f. 2003; replaced Directorate of Civil Aviation (f. 1977); ensures aviation safety and security, provides air navigation services; Dir-Gen. FADHILI MANONGI.

Air Zanzibar: POB 1784, Zanzibar; f. 1990; operates scheduled and charter services between Zanzibar and destinations in Tanzania, Kenya and Uganda.

New ACS Ltd: Peugeot House, 36 Upanga Rd, POB 21236, Dar es Salaam; fax (22) 237017; operates domestic and regional services; Dir MOHSIN RAHEMTULLAH.

Precision Air Services Ltd: Along Nyerere/Pugu Rd, POB 70770, Dar es Salaam; tel. (22) 2860701; fax (22) 2860725; e-mail info@precisionairtz.com; internet www.precisionairtz.com; f. 1993; operates scheduled and charter domestic and regional services; Man. Dir and CEO ALFONSE KIOKO.

Tanzanair: Julius Nyerere Int. Airport, POB 364, Dar es Salaam; tel. (22) 2843131; fax (22) 2844600; e-mail info@tanzanair.com; internet www.tanzanair.com; f. 1969; operates domestic and regional charter services, offers full engineering and maintenance services for general aviation aircraft; agent for sales of Cessna aircraft; Man. Dir JOHN SAMARAS.

Tourism

Mount Kilimanjaro is a major tourist attraction. Tanzania has set aside about one-quarter of its land area for 12 national parks, 17 game reserves, 50 controlled game areas and a conservation area. Other attractions for tourists include beaches and coral reefs along the Indian Ocean coast, and the island of Zanzibar. Visitor arrivals totalled an estimated 754,000 in 2010, and in that year revenue from tourism was an estimated US $1,254m. (excluding passenger transport).

Tanzania Tourist Board: IPS Bldg, 3rd Floor, POB 2485, Dar es Salaam; tel. (22) 2111244; fax (22) 2116420; e-mail safari@ud.co.tz; internet www.tanzaniatouristboard.com; f. 1993; state-owned; supervises the development and promotion of tourism; Man. Dir PETER J. MWENGUO.

Tanzania Wildlife Co Ltd: POB 1144, Arusha; tel. 787787459 (mobile); e-mail info@tanzaniawildlifecompany.com; internet www.tanzaniawildlifecompany.com; f. 1974; organizes hunting, photographic, horseback and adventure safaris; Man. Dir LEON LAMPRECHT.

Zanzibar Tourist Corporation: POB 216, Zanzibar; tel. (24) 2238630; fax (24) 2233417; e-mail ztc@zanzinet.com; internet www.zanzibartouristcorporation.net; f. 1985; operates tours and hotel services; Gen. Man. SABAAH SALEH ALI.

Defence

As assessed at November 2011, the total armed forces numbered 27,000, of whom an estimated 23,000 were in the army, 1,000 in the navy and 3,000 in the air force. Paramilitary forces comprised a 1,400-strong Police Field Force and an 80,000-strong reservist Citizens' Militia. In 2011 a total of 1,064 Tanzanian troops were stationed abroad, of whom 18 were observers.

Defence Expenditure: Budgeted at 415,000m. shillings in 2012.

Commander-in-Chief of the Armed Forces: President JAKAYA MRISHO KIKWETE.

Chief of Defence Forces: Gen. DAVIS MWAMUNYANGE.

Education

In 2004/05 enrolment at pre-primary level was 23% (23% of both boys and girls). Education at primary level is officially compulsory and is provided free of charge. In secondary schools a government-stipulated fee is paid. Villages and districts are encouraged to construct their own schools with government assistance. Almost all primary schools are government-owned. Primary education begins at seven years of age and lasts for seven years. In 2009/10 enrolment at primary level included 92% of pupils in the appropriate age-group (91% of boys; 92% of girls). Secondary education, beginning at the age of 14, lasts for a further six years, comprising a first cycle of four years and a second of two years. Secondary enrolment in 2008/09 was equivalent to 27% of children in the appropriate age-group (males 31%; females 24%), according to UNESCO estimates. Enrolment at tertiary level included just 1% of those in the relevant age-group in 2004/05 (males 2%; females 1%). There are 10 universities, including one on Zanzibar. Tanzania also has a number of vocational training centres and technical colleges. The 2008/09 budget allocated 19.8% of total government expenditure for education.

Bibliography

Admassu Kebede, J. *The Changing Face of Rural Policy in Tanzania.* London, Minerva Press, 2000.

Bagachwa, M. S. D., and Mbelle, A. V. Y. (Eds). *Economic Policy under a Multiparty System in Tanzania.* Dar es Salaam University Press, 1993.

Brennan, J., Burton, A., and Lawi, Y. (Eds). *Dar es Salaam. Histories from an Emerging African Metropolis.* Mkuki na Nyota Publishers, 2007.

Bryceson, D. F. *Liberalizing Tanzania's Food Trade: Public and Private Faces of Urban Marketing Policy 1939–1988.* Geneva, UN Research Institute for Social Development; Tanzania, Mkuki Na Nyota Publishers, 1993.

Buchert, L. *Education in the Development of Tanzania, 1919–1990.* London, James Currey Publishers, 1994.

Campbell, H., and Stein, H. *Tanzania and the IMF: The Dynamics of Liberalization.* Boulder, CO, Westview Press, 1990.

Creighton, C., and Omazi, C. K. (Eds). *Gender, Family and Household in Tanzania.* Brookfield, VT, Ashgate Publishing, 1995.

Fair, L. *Pastimes and Politics.* London, James Currey Publishers, 2001.

Feierman, S. *Peasant Intellectuals: Anthropology and History in Tanzania.* Madison, WI, University of Wisconsin Press, 1990.

Forster, P. G., and Maghimbi, S. (Eds). *The Tanzanian Peasantry: Economy in Crisis.* Aldershot, Avebury, 1992.

The Tanzanian Peasantry: Further Strides. Brookfield, VT, Ashgate Publishing, 1995.

Agrarian Economy, State and Society in Contemporary Tanzania. Brookfield, VT, Ashgate Publishing, 1999.

Gibbon, P. (Ed.). *Liberalized Development in Tanzania: Studies on Accumulation Processes and Local Institutions.* Uppsala, Nordiska Afrikainstitutet, 1995.

Giblin, J. L. *A History of the Excluded: Making Family a Refuge from State in Twentieth Century Tanzania (Eastern African Studies).* Oxford, James Currey Publishers, 2003.

Giblin, J. L., *et al.* (Eds). *In Search of a Nation: Histories of Authority and Dissidence in Tanzania (Eastern African Studies).* Oxford, James Currey Publishers, 2003.

Glassman, J. *War of Words, War of Stones: Racial Thought and Violence in Colonial Zanzibar.* Bloomington, IN, Indiana University Press, 2011.

Havenik, K. J. and Isinika, A. (Eds). *Tanzania in Transition: From Nyerere to Mkapa.* Dar es Salaam, Mkuki na Nyota Publishers, 2010.

Hyden, G., and Mukandala, R. (Eds). *Agencies in Foreign Aid.* London and Basingstoke, Palgrave, 2000.

Kaijage, F., and Tibaijuka, A. *Poverty and Social Exclusion in Tanzania.* Geneva, International Labour Organisation, 1996.

Kikula, I. S. *Policy Implications on Environment: The Case of Villagization in Tanzania.* Uppsala, Nordiska Afrikainstitutet, 1998.

Kimambo, I. N. *Penetration and Protest in Tanzania: The Impact of the World Economy on the Pare, 1860–1960.* London, James Currey Publishers, 1991.

Lange, S. *From Nation-Building to Popular Culture: The Modernization of Performance in Tanzania.* Bergen, CMI, 1995.

Lapperre, P., and Szirmai, A. (Eds). *The Industrial Experience of Tanzania.* London and Basingstoke, Palgrave, 2001.

Legum, C., and Mmari, G. (Eds). *Mwalimu: The Influence of Nyerere.* London, James Currey Publishers, 1995.

Lovejoy, P. E. *Slavery and the Muslim Diaspora: African Slaves in Dar Es-Salaam.* Princeton, NJ, Markus Wiener Publishers, 2003.

Luvanga, N. and Shitundu, J. *The Role of Tourism in Poverty Alleviation in Tanzania.* Dar es Salaam, Mkuki na Nyota Publishers, 2005.

Maddox, G., Giblin, J. L., and Kimambo, I. N. (Eds). *Custodians of the Land: Environment and Hunger in Tanzanian History.* London, James Currey Publishers, 1995; Athens, OH, Ohio University Press, 1996.

Martin, D. *Serengetu Tanzania: Land, People, History.* Harare, APG, 1997.

Mbelle, A., and Mjema, G. D. (Eds). *The Nyerere Legacy and Economic Policy Making in Tanzania.* (2nd edn) Dar es Salaam University Press, 2004.

Mbogoni, L. E. Y. *The Cross Versus the Crescent: Religion and Politics in Tanzania from the 1880s to the 1990s.* Dar es Salaam, Mkuki na Nyota Publishers, 2005.

McHenry, D. E., Jr. *Limited Choices: The Political Struggle for Socialism in Tanzania.* Boulder, CO, Lynne Rienner Publishers, 1994.

Mmuya, M. (Ed.). *Functional Dimensions of the Democratization Process: Tanzania and Kenya.* Dar es Salaam University Press, 1994.

Monson, J. *Africa's Freedom Railway: How a Chinese Development Project Changed Lives and Livelihoods in Tanzania.* Bloomington, IN, Indiana University Press, 2011.

Mukandala, R., and Othman, H. *Liberalization and Politics: The 1990 Election in Tanzania.* Dar es Salaam University Press, 1994.

Mwakikagile, G. *Nyerere and Africa: End of an Era.* Atlanta, GA, Protea Publishing, 2002.

Nyang'oro, J. *JK: A Political Biography of Jakaya Mrisho Kikwete.* Africa World Press, Trenton, NJ, 2011.

Ofcansky, T. P., and Yeager, R. *Historical Dictionary of Tanzania.* Lanham, MD, Scarecrow Press, 1997.

Okema, M. *Political Culture in Tanzania.* Lewiston, Edwin Mellen, 1996.

Othman, H. I. B., and Okema, M. *Tanzania: Democracy in Transition.* Dar es Salaam University Press, 1990.

Pratt, C. *The Critical Phase in Tanzania: Nyerere and the Emergence of a Socialist Strategy.* Cambridge, Cambridge University Press, 2009.

Rosch, P. G. *Der Prozess der Strukturanpassung in Tanzania.* Hamburg, Institut für Afrika-Kunde, 1995.

Sheriff, A. *Slaves, Spices and Ivory in Zanzibar: Integration of an East African Commercial Empire into the World Economy, 1770–1873.* London, James Currey Publishers, 1987.

Shivji, I. G. *Law, State and the Working Class in Tanzania.* London, James Currey Publishers, 1986.

Tanzania: the Legal Foundations of the Union. Dar es Salaam University Press, 1999.

Tripp, A. M. *Changing the Rules.* Berkeley, University of California Press, 1997.

Wange, S. M., *et al.* (Eds). *Traditional Economic Policy and Policy Options in Tanzania.* Dar es Salaam, Mkuki na Nyota Publishers, 1998.

Weiss, B. *Sacred Trees, Bitter Harvests: Globalizing Coffee in Colonial Northwest Tanzania.* Westport, CT, Greenwood Press, 2003.

World Bank. *Tanzania at the Turn of the Century: Background Papers and Statistics (World Bank Country Study).* Washington, DC, World Bank, 2002.

TOGO

Physical and Social Geography

R. J. HARRISON CHURCH

The Togolese Republic, a small state of West Africa (bordered to the west by Ghana, to the east by Benin and to the north by Burkina Faso), covers an area of 56,600 sq km (21,853 sq miles), and comprises the eastern two-thirds of the former German protectorate of Togoland. From a coastline of 56 km on the Gulf of Guinea, Togo extends inland for about 540 km. According to results of the census of November 2010, the population numbered 6,191,155, giving a density of 109.4 persons per sq km (higher than average for West Africa). Northern Togo is more ethnically diverse than the south, where the Ewe predominate. The most numerous ethnic group in 1995 was the Kabré, who represented an estimated 23.7% of the population, when the Ewe accounted for 21.9%. The official languages are French, Ewe and Kabiye. According to the 2010 census, the population of the capital, Lomé, located on the coast, amounted to 837,437.

The coast, lagoons, blocked estuaries and Terre de Barre regions are identical to those of Benin, but calcium phosphate, the only commercially exploited mineral resource, is quarried north-east of Lake Togo. Pre-Cambrian rocks with rather siliceous soils occur northward, in the Mono tableland and in the Togo-Atacora mountains. The latter are, however, still well wooded and planted with coffee and cocoa. To the north is the Oti plateau, with infertile Primary sandstones, in which water is rare and deep down. On the northern border are granite areas, remote but densely inhabited, as in neighbouring Ghana and Burkina Faso. Togo's climate is similar to that of Benin, except that Togo's coastal area is even drier: Lomé had an average annual rainfall of 734 mm in 1999–2000, around one-half of the rainfall recorded in northern regions. Thus Togo, although smaller in area than Benin, is physically, as well as economically, more varied than its eastern neighbour.

Recent History

KATHARINE MURISON

Togoland, of which the Togolese Republic was formerly a part, became a German protectorate in 1894. The territory was occupied by Anglo-French forces in 1914, and was designated a League of Nations mandate in 1919. France was awarded the larger eastern section, while the United Kingdom administered the west. This partition divided the homeland of the Ewe people of the southern part of the territory, and became a continuing source of internal friction. Ewe demands for reunification were intensified during the UN trusteeship system that took effect after the Second World War. In May 1956 a UN-supervised plebiscite in British Togoland produced, despite Ewe opposition, majority support for a merger with the neighbouring territory of the Gold Coast, then a British colony. The region was transferred to the independent state of Ghana in the following year. In October 1956, in a further plebiscite, French Togoland voted to become an autonomous republic within the French Community.

Political life in French Togoland was dominated by the Comité de l'Unité Togolaise (usually known as the Unité Togolaise), led by Sylvanus Olympio, and the Parti Togolais du Progrès, led by Nicolas Grunitzky. Following independence on 27 April 1960, Olympio, a campaigner for Ewe reunification, became President.

In January 1963 Olympio was overthrown and killed in a military coup led by Sgt (later Gen.) Etienne (Gnassingbé) Eyadéma, a Kabiye from the north of the country, who invited Grunitzky to return from exile as head of state. Subsequent efforts by Grunitzky to achieve constitutional multi-party government proved unsuccessful, and in January 1967 Eyadéma, by then army Chief of Staff, assumed power. Political activity remained effectively suspended until the creation in 1969 of the Rassemblement du Peuple Togolais (RPT), which served as a vehicle for integrating the army into political life. Plots to overthrow Eyadéma were suppressed in 1970 and again in 1977, when the exiled sons of ex-President Olympio were accused of organizing a mercenary invasion. The introduction of a new Constitution in 1980 made little impact on Eyadéma's authoritarian style of government. In 1985 the Constitution was amended to allow candidates for election to the Assemblée nationale to be adopted without prior approval by the RPT, which remained the only legal political party.

In September 1986 19 people were detained following an apparent attempted coup, in which some 13 people were killed. In December Eyadéma was re-elected as President, reportedly winning almost 100% of votes cast. At trials in the same month 13 people were sentenced to death, and 14 to life imprisonment, for complicity in the events in September. Gilchrist Olympio, son of the former President, was one of three people sentenced to death *in absentia*. In the aftermath of the alleged coup attempt Eyadéma combined measures to increase his personal security with reforms aimed at apparent political democratization. In October 1987 a national human rights commission, the Commission Nationale des Droits de l'Homme (CNDH), was established, while most of the death sentences imposed in the previous December were commuted.

THE COLLAPSE OF LEGITIMACY

In October 1990 a commission was established to draft a new constitution, to be submitted to a national referendum in December 1991. The constitutional commission presented its draft document, which provided for the establishment of a multi-party political system, in late 1990.

In early 1991 several opposition movements formed a co-ordinating organization, the Front des Associations pour le Renouveau (FAR), to campaign for the immediate introduction of a multi-party political system. Eyadéma subsequently consented to an amnesty for all political dissidents, and agreed to the legalization of political parties and to the organization of a national forum.

The approval of legislation regarding the general amnesty and the legalization of political parties was overshadowed by the discovery, in April 1991, of about 26 bodies in a lagoon in Lomé. Opposition allegations that the bodies were those of demonstrators who had been beaten to death by the security forces were denied by the Government. (In July the CNDH concluded that the security forces had been responsible for the deaths of at least 20 of those whose bodies had been discovered.) Fearing an inter-ethnic conflict between the Kabiye and Ewe ethnic groups, Eyadéma appealed for national unity, and announced that a new constitution would be introduced within one year, and that multi-party legislative elections would be organized.

The FAR was disbanded in April 1991, to allow for the establishment of independent political parties. Yawovi Agboyibo, hitherto leader of the FAR, formed the Comité d'Action pour le Renouveau (CAR), while numerous other movements obtained official status; 10 parties (including the CAR) subsequently formed the Coalition de l'Opposition Démocratique (COD).

A national conference was opened on 8 July 1991, attended by some 1,000 delegates. A resolution by the conference, in mid-July, to declare itself sovereign, to suspend the Constitution and to dissolve the Assemblée nationale prompted the Government to boycott the proceedings for one week. In late July the conference resolved to sequester the assets of the RPT, and to create an authority to control the finances of state and parastatal organizations, with the aim of preventing the transfer of state funds abroad.

On 26 August 1991 Eyadéma, deprived by the national conference of most of his powers, abruptly suspended the conference. Opposition delegates responded by proclaiming a provisional Government under the leadership of Joseph Kokou Koffigoh, a prominent lawyer and the head of the independent Ligue Togolaise des Droits de l'Homme (LTDH). The conference also voted to dissolve the RPT and to form an interim legislature, the Haut Conseil de la République (HCR). Fearing renewed unrest, Eyadéma hastily signed a decree confirming Koffigoh as transitional Prime Minister.

Koffigoh's Council of Ministers, appointed in September 1991, was composed mainly of technocrats who had not previously held political office. The Prime Minister assumed personal responsibility for defence. However, the Kabiye-dominated armed forces looked to Eyadéma for their command. In October a group of soldiers seized control of the offices of the state broadcasting service in Lomé, demanding the resignations of Koffigoh and his Government, but returned to barracks on Eyadéma's orders. One week later, presidential guards attempted to abduct Koffigoh, although Eyadéma again ordered a return to barracks.

CONSTITUTIONAL TRANSITION

In November 1991 the HCR responded to attempts to convene a congress of the RPT by reaffirming the ban on the former ruling party. In December the military captured the Prime Minister. Following negotiations between Eyadéma and Koffigoh, in late December the formation was announced of a 'Government of National Unity', which included two close associates of Eyadéma. The HCR also restored legal status to the RPT.

In July 1992 the Government was reorganized and proposals for a new electoral schedule were announced, beginning with a constitutional referendum in August. The political climate deteriorated shortly after the reshuffle, when a prominent opposition leader, Tavio Ayao Amorin, was killed. In response, a new opposition coalition, the Collectif de l'Opposition Démocratique (COD-2), comprising some 25 political organizations and trade unions, organized a widely observed general strike in Lomé.

The HCR restored a number of powers to the President in August 1992, empowering Eyadéma to preside over the Council of Ministers and to represent Togo abroad, and obliging the Prime Minister to make government appointments in consultation with the Head of State. Moreover, the draft Constitution was amended to permit members of the armed forces seeking election to the new democratic organs of state to retain their commissions.

The transitional Government was dissolved on 1 September 1992, and a new electoral schedule was announced. In mid-September a new transitional Government was formed: Koffigoh remained as Prime Minister, but the most influential posts were allocated to members of the RPT. On 27 September the new Constitution was approved in a referendum by 98.1% of the votes cast (the rate of participation by voters was about 66%). At the end of the month, however, a further rescheduling of the elections was announced. In November a general strike was organized by the COD-2, to support their demands for elections, the neutrality of the armed forces, the formation of a non-military 'peace force', and the bringing to justice of those responsible for the attacks on the HCR. The strike was widely observed, except in the north of Togo (where support for Eyadéma was strongest), and continued for nine months, causing considerable economic disruption.

In January 1993 Eyadéma dissolved the Government, but reappointed Koffigoh as Prime Minister. The President stated that he would appoint a new government of national unity, whose principal task would be the expedited organization of elections. Later in January, representatives of the French and German Governments visited Togo to offer mediation in the political crisis. During their visit at least 20 people were killed when police opened fire on anti-Government protesters. Thousands of Togolese subsequently fled from Lomé, many taking refuge in Benin and Ghana. In February discussions in France, attended by representatives of Eyadéma, the RPT, Koffigoh, the HCR and the COD-2, failed when the presidential delegation left after one day. The formation of a new 'Crisis Government' was announced shortly afterwards; supporters of Eyadéma retained the principal posts.

In July 1993 the Government and the COD-2 agreed on 25 August as the date for the presidential poll. As the election campaign gained momentum during August 1993, opposition demands, supported by the national electoral commission, that the election be postponed intensified, and Edem Kodjo, the leader of the Union Togolaise pour la Démocratie (UTD) and presidential candidate of the COD-2, and Agboyibo effectively withdrew from the election. The COD-2 and Gilchrist Olympio's Union des Forces de Changement (UFC) appealed to their supporters to boycott the poll, and US and German observers withdrew from Togo, alleging irregularities in electoral preparations. As voting began, on 25 August, the Government announced that a coup attempt, plotted by Togolese dissidents in Ghana, had been detected on the eve of polling. Shortly after the poll, it was revealed that at least 15 opposition supporters, arrested in connection with attacks on polling stations in Lomé, had died while in detention. According to official results, Eyadéma was re-elected President by 96.5% of voters. Only about 36% of the electorate voted. Eyadéma was sworn in as President of the Fourth Republic on 24 September.

THE FOURTH REPUBLIC

In January 1994 an armed attack on Eyadéma's official residence was reported. The Government alleged that the attack had been organized by Gilchrist Olympio, with Ghanaian support: this was denied both by Olympio and by the Ghanaian Government. A total of 67 people were officially reported to have died in the violence. It was claimed by the international human rights organization Amnesty International that the armed forces had carried out at least 48 summary executions.

In the elections to the Assemblée nationale, which took place on 6 and 20 February 1994, after several postponements, 347 candidates contested 81 seats. International observers expressed themselves satisfied with the conduct of the elections. The final result revealed a narrow victory for the opposition, with the CAR winning 36 seats and the UTD seven; the RPT obtained 35 seats and two smaller pro-Eyadéma parties won three. During March Eyadéma consulted the main opposition parties on the formation of a new Government. In March the CAR and the UTD reached agreement on the terms of their alliance and jointly proposed the candidacy of Agboyibo for Prime Minister. In March and April the Supreme Court declared the results of the legislative elections invalid in three constituencies (in which the CAR had won two seats and the UTD one) and ordered by-elections. In April Eyadéma nominated Kodjo as Prime Minister. Kodjo accepted the appointment, despite assertions by the CAR that to do so was a violation of the agreement between the party and the UDT. The CAR subsequently announced that it would not participate in an administration formed by Kodjo, who took office on 25 April. It was not until late May that he announced the formation of his Government, which comprised eight members of the RPT and other pro-Eyadéma parties, three members of the UTD, and eight independents.

Political and Constitutional Manoeuvres

In December 1994 the Assemblée nationale declared a general amnesty covering all persons who had been charged with political offences committed before 15 December 1994.

In early 1995 the Government and the major opposition parties reached agreement on equal representation on national, district and local electoral commissions. In November Kodjo implemented a major reorganization of the Council of Ministers. The CAR, which was not represented in the new Government, expressed concern at the level of representation given to supporters of Eyadéma; of the 13 new members, 11 were considered to be close allies of the President.

In April 1996 a CAR deputy resigned from the party, thus reducing its representation in the Assemblée nationale to 33 seats. In May a UTD deputy was dismissed from the party, thus reducing its representation in the Assemblée nationale to five seats. At the by-elections, conducted in August, the RPT won control of the three constituencies being contested. Consequently, the RPT and its political allies were able to command a legislative majority, thus forcing the resignation of the Kodjo administration. On 20 August Eyadéma appointed Kwassi Klutse, hitherto Minister of Planning and Territorial Development, as Prime Minister. Both the CAR and the UTD refused to participate in a proposed government of national unity, and consequently the new Council of Ministers, appointed in late August, comprised almost exclusively supporters of Eyadéma. In October a further CAR deputy left the party, transferring his allegiance to the RPT. In November the Union pour la Justice et la Démocratie, which held two seats in the legislature, announced that it was to merge with the RPT, thus giving the RPT 41 seats and an overall majority.

Electoral Controversies

A presidential election took place on 21 June 1998. On the following day, as early voting figures indicated that Eyadéma might lose the election, the vote count was suspended. On 23 June five of the nine members of the electoral commission resigned, reportedly as a result of intimidation. The vote count was not resumed, and on 24 June the Minister of the Interior and Security declared Eyadéma to have won the election with 52.1% of the vote. European Union (EU) observers expressed serious concern at the suspension of the vote count. Monitors reported that Gilchrist Olympio (who was living in exile in Ghana) had received a greater share of the vote than Eyadéma in much of Lomé and all indications were of a victory for Olympio. Supporters of the UFC staged demonstrations in protest against the announced results, prompting the Government to impose a ban on all organized protests.

In September 1998 Klutse announced his new Council of Ministers. Despite Eyadéma's stated desire for a government of national unity, no opposition figures were willing to be included, and few new appointments were made. In November the Government survived a vote of no confidence tabled by the CAR and the UTD.

Elections to the Assemblée nationale took place on 21 March 1999, but were boycotted by the main opposition parties. The Constitutional Court ruled that the RPT had won 77 seats, and that independent candidates had taken two seats, while fresh elections were scheduled in two constituencies. Turn-out was officially estimated at 66%, although the opposition estimated that it was little more than 10%. In April Klutse tendered his Government's resignation, and in May Eugène Koffi Adoboli, a former UN official, was appointed Prime Minister. In June Adoboli appointed a new Council of Ministers dominated by supporters of Eyadéma.

Discussions took place in Lomé in July 1999 between the Government, the opposition and four international facilitators, representing France, Germany, the EU and La Francophonie. Eyadéma's announcement that he would not stand for re-election, and that new legislative elections would be held in 2000, was widely credited with breaking the deadlock in negotiations. After the opposition had agreed to accept Eyadéma's victory in the presidential election, an accord was signed on 29 July by all the parties involved in negotiations.

In August 1999 the first meeting was held of the 24-member Comité Paritaire de Suivi (CPS) responsible for the implementation of the accord, composed equally of representatives of the opposition and supporters of Eyadéma, and also including a group of intermediaries from the EU. Harry Octavianus Olympio, the cousin of Gilchrist Olympio and the Minister for the Promotion of Democracy and the Rule of Law, was appointed to head the CPS. Agreement on the mechanism for announcing election results was reached in September, and in December agreement was reached on a revised electoral code, providing for the establishment of an independent electoral commission. In April 2000 Eyadéma obliged the Assemblée nationale (which had initially refused to adopt the revised document) to accept the new electoral code.

In August 2000 Adoboli was overwhelmingly defeated in a vote of no confidence in his premiership. (In July 2011 Adoboli and two other former government officials were sentenced to prison terms and fined in connection with the embezzlement of state funds intended for a construction project undertaken during Adoboli's premiership.) In late August 2000 Eyadéma appointed Agbéyomé Kodjo, hitherto President of the Assemblée nationale, as Prime Minister. In January 2001 the Commission Électorale Nationale Indépendante (CENI) announced that legislative elections would be held in October 2001. The CENI also announced that, instead of compiling new voters' lists, the electoral registers from the 1998 presidential election would be used in the forthcoming polls.

In June 2001 Harry Octavianus Olympio was sentenced to 18 months' imprisonment, having been convicted of the illegal possession and manufacture of explosives. In August Agboyibo was gaoled for six months and fined 100,000 francs CFA, having been found guilty on charges of libelling the Prime Minister. Agboyibo had alleged that Kodjo was involved in the organization of an armed militia group when he was director of the port at Lomé in 1998. In October 2001 Eyadéma pardoned Harry Octavianus Olympio. Although an appeal by Agboyibo against his conviction was successful in January 2002, he was immediately rearrested on charges of conspiring to commit violence during the 1998 presidential election campaign.

Meanwhile, in August 2001 the Prime Minister announced that the legislative elections would be further postponed until 2002. In February 2002 the Assemblée nationale approved amendments to electoral legislation and to the remit of the CENI; henceforth all candidates for legislative elections were required to have been continuously resident in Togo for six months prior to elections, with presidential candidates to have been resident for a continuous 12 months. The CENI was also to be reduced in size from 20 to 10 members. The UFC opposed the amendments, which effectively prevented its leader, Gilchrist Olympio, who remained resident in Ghana, from seeking election. In response to the amendments, the EU announced the suspension of financial assistance intended to fund the elections. Five opposition parties accused the Government of breaking the conditions of the accord signed in July 1999, and in March 2002 they rejected an invitation by Kodjo to nominate representatives to the CENI. The Government consequently announced that no date for the legislative elections could be announced until a complete electoral commission had been formed.

Agboyibo was released from prison in March 2002. Eyadéma stated that the release, which he had ordered, was intended to facilitate national reconciliation. The President also ordered that the charges of conspiring to commit violence against Agboyibo be lifted. In May a committee of seven judges (the Comité de Sept Magistrats—C-7), charged with monitoring the electoral process, was appointed, in accordance with a provision of the revised electoral code that permitted the appointment of such a committee in the event that the CENI could not be formed by consensus. The CAR, the Convergence Patriotique Panafricaine (CPP—formed in 1999 by a merger of the UTD and three other parties) and other opposition parties condemned this decision, and announced their intention to boycott any elections organized by the C-7. At the end of May the EU announced that it would not renew funding for the three facilitators it supported, in view of the continued lack of progress towards democracy in Togo.

In June 2002 Eyadéma dismissed Kodjo as Prime Minister, following a dispute within the RPT, appointing Koffi Sama, hitherto Minister of National Education and Research, in his stead. Kodjo subsequently issued a statement criticizing the 'monarchic, despotic' regime of Eyadéma, and—in contrast to his former stated position—appealed for measures to ensure that Eyadéma would be unable to amend the Constitution to stand for a further term of office. The state prosecutor filed a suit against Kodjo on charges of disseminating false information and demeaning the honour of the President; Kodjo subsequently left the country, taking up residence in France. In August Kodjo was expelled from the RPT. Meanwhile, in August four parties, including the CAR, formed an opposition alliance, the Front Uni de l'Opposition (Le Front), headed by Agboyibo.

In September 2002 the authorities announced that the legislative elections would be held on 27 October. In late October nine opposition parties that had declined to participate in the elections formed a new alliance, the Coalition des Forces Démocrates (CFD), chaired, on an interim basis, by Edem Kodjo of the CPP; other members of the grouping included the CAR and the UFC, in addition to a faction of 'renovators' within the RPT (which subsequently became the Pacte Socialiste pour le Renouveau—PSR). Meanwhile, a group of 'constructive' opposition parties (including Harry Octavianus Olympio's Rassemblement pour le Soutien de la Démocratie et du Développement—RSDD), which were prepared to participate in the electoral process and form alliances with the RPT, formed the Coordination des Partis Politiques de l'Opposition Constructive (CPOC). The elections proceeded as scheduled, without the participation of the principal opposition parties. The RPT won 72 of the 81 seats (of which 46 had been secured unopposed) and the RSDD three, while three other parties won a total of five seats, and one independent candidate was elected. The C-7, which now comprised six judges (one member of the committee having resigned), estimated electoral turn-out at 67.4%, although the CFD claimed that no more than 10% of the electorate had voted. Eyadéma reappointed Sama as Prime Minister in November; a new Government was formed in December. All ministers were members of the RPT, with the exception of Harry Octavianus Olympio, who was appointed Minister responsible for Relations with Parliament.

In December 2002 the Assemblée nationale approved several constitutional amendments regarding the eligibility of presidential candidates. The restriction that had limited the President to serving two terms of office was removed, and the age of eligibility was reduced from 45 to 35 years. (It was widely believed that these measures were intended to permit Eyadéma to serve a further term of office, and also to permit the possible candidacy of Eyadéma's son, Faure Gnassingbé.) Candidates were henceforth to be required to hold solely Togolese citizenship, although those holding dual or multiple nationalities were to be permitted to renounce them, prior to seeking election. These measures were vociferously denounced by the extra-parliamentary opposition. In February 2003 the UFC withdrew from the CFD, after other parties within the grouping agreed to appoint representatives to the CENI.

Eyadéma was returned to office in the presidential election, which was held on 1 June 2003, receiving 57.8% of the votes cast. His nearest rivals were Emmanuel Bob Akitani, the First Vice-President of the UFC, with 33.7% of the votes, and Agboyibo, with 5.1%. Gilchrist Olympio's candidacy had been rejected as he did not meet residency requirements. Several of the six defeated candidates, including Bob Akitani, declared that the election had been conducted fraudulently, although observers from the Economic Community of West African States (ECOWAS) and the African Union (AU—formerly the Organization for African Unity—OAU) stated that only minor irregularities had been witnessed. Eyadéma was inaugurated for a further term of office on 20 June. Sama was reappointed as premier on 1 July, apparently with instructions from Eyadéma to form a government of national unity. However, most opposition parties reportedly declined to participate, and the new Government included only two representatives of the 'constructive' opposition, including Harry Octavianus Olympio, who was reappointed as Minister responsible for Relations with Parliament. Faure Gnassingbé received his first ministerial posting, as Minister of Equipment, Mines, Posts and Telecommunications. Olympio resigned in August, expressing dissatisfaction at the post to which he had been appointed. Later in August the RSDD was reportedly expelled from the CPOC. In December local elections were postponed indefinitely.

Democratic Reforms

Discussions between the Government and the EU on the conditions for a resumption of economic co-operation commenced in April 2004 in Brussels, Belgium; the government delegation pledged to implement 22 measures, such as revising the press code, introducing more transparent conditions for fair elections and guaranteeing political parties the freedom to conduct their activities without fear of harassment. Under pressure from the EU to strengthen democracy, President Eyadéma officially opened talks between the Government and opposition parties in May, despite a boycott of the ceremony by the CAR, the UFC and the Convention Démocratique des Peuples Africains—Branche Togolaise (CDPA—BT), which criticized the lack of preparations prior to the discussions; the UFC also deplored the exclusion of its President, Gilchrist Olympio, who, it claimed, had been denied entry into Togo. An EU mission charged with assessing Togo's progress in implementing democratic reforms held meetings with the Government, political leaders, human rights organizations and religious leaders in early June. Later that month Sama commenced a series of separate consultations with leaders of several opposition parties and representatives of civil society organizations. However, following the meetings, the CAR, the UFC and the CDPA—BT criticized Sama's approach and refused to participate in a multi-party commission established in July to consider the revision of the electoral code and the funding of political parties, urging that a more structured framework for the dialogue be formulated. In August it was reported that Olympio had been provided with a Togolese passport and the Assemblée nationale adopted amendments to the press code. The Government, the main opposition parties and a number of civil society associations also agreed on a framework for a new round of national dialogue.

In November 2004 the EU announced a partial resumption of economic co-operation with Togo, expressing satisfaction at the opening of dialogue with opposition parties, the reform of the press code and the release of prisoners. A full restoration of development aid was made conditional on the organization of transparent legislative elections. The inter-Togolese national dialogue resumed in December, although the CAR, the UFC and the CDPA—BT were again critical of procedural aspects of the discussions. Later that month Eyadéma announced that legislative elections would be held during the first quarter of 2005. In January 2005 the Assemblée nationale approved several amendments to the electoral code, notably strengthening the powers of the CENI and increasing its membership to 13, to include two representatives of civil society.

Presidential Succession

On 5 February 2005 Prime Minister Sama announced that President Eyadéma had died while being transported to France for medical treatment. Two hours later the Chief of General Staff of the armed forces, Gen. Zakari Nandja, declared that the Constitution had been suspended and named Faure Gnassingbé as his father's successor. Gnassingbé's appointment as President was in clear contravention of the Constitution, which provided for the assumption of the functions of head of state by the President of the Assemblée nationale for up to 60 days pending an election. However, the military had closed Togo's airports, seaports and land borders immediately after Eyadéma's death, thus preventing the legislative chairman, Ouattara Fambaré Natchaba, from returning to the country from a visit to Europe. Nandja justified Gnassingbé's appointment as being necessary to avoid a power vacuum. The AU denounced the military's installation of Gnassingbé as Head of State as a coup, while the UN, ECOWAS and La Francophonie urged the Togolese authorities to respect the terms of the Constitution. On the following day, amid continuing international condemnation, the Assemblée nationale attempted to legitimize Gnassingbé's assumption of power. Deputies abolished the constitutional provision requiring an election to take place within 60 days of the death of an incumbent President, instead authorizing the new head of state to serve the remainder of his predecessor's term, and amended the electoral code to allow ministers to reassume their mandates as deputies on resigning from the Government (thus rendering them eligible for election to the presidency of the legislature). The Assemblée then voted to remove Natchaba from his post as President of the legislature, electing Gnassingbé in his place.

Gnassingbé was formally sworn in as President of the Republic on 7 February 2005 in a ceremony that was boycotted by diplomats from the UN, the EU, France, Nigeria and the USA. After the Government announced a ban on demonstrations for the duration of a two-month period of mourning for Eyadéma, a coalition of six so-called 'radical' opposition parties, including the CAR, the CDPA—BT and the UFC, instead called a two-day strike in protest against what they also termed a coup, but it was only partially observed. Two days after Gnassingbé's inauguration La Francophonie suspended Togo's membership of the organization, while the Heads of State of nine ECOWAS countries, meeting at an extraordinary summit in Niamey, Niger, agreed that the intervention of the military constituted a coup, threatening to impose sanctions against the new regime if constitutional order was not restored. Protests subsequently broke out in Lomé against Gnassingbé's seizure of power.

ECOWAS continued to exert pressure on Gnassingbé's administration to apply the Constitution as it stood before Eyadéma's death. On 18 February 2005, in a televised speech, Gnassingbé pledged to hold an election within 60 days, but stated his intention to remain in power in the mean time. The Assemblée nationale subsequently reversed the constitutional changes adopted following Eyadéma's death. The day after Gnassingbé's declaration ECOWAS suspended Togo's membership of the Community, imposed an arms embargo on the country, banned its government ministers from travelling in the region and ordered the recall of ambassadors of member states from Lomé. Meanwhile, at least 10,000 people participated in a protest march organized by the opposition in the Lomé district of Bè, while several thousand others attended a rally in support of Gnassingbé outside the presidential palace; the Government had lifted the ban on public demonstrations on the previous day.

On 25 February 2005, following the imposition of sanctions against Togo by the AU, Gnassingbé bowed to international pressure and announced his resignation from the presidency of the Assemblée nationale, and therefore from the presidency of the Republic. He was to be replaced, in an interim capacity, by the Vice-President of the legislature, Abass Bonfoh. Earlier that day Gnassingbé had been acclaimed President of the RPT, at a special congress of the party, and endorsed as the party's candidate for the forthcoming presidential election. ECOWAS rescinded its sanctions against Togo and pledged to assist with election preparations.

In March 2005 the CENI announced that the presidential election would take place on 24 April. The six-party 'radical' opposition coalition subsequently united behind Bob Akitani, of the UFC, as its sole candidate, while Harry Octavianus Olympio, of the RSDD, and Nicolas Lawson, the leader of the Parti du Renouveau et de la Rédemption, were to represent the 'constructive' opposition. As in 2003, Gilchrist Olympio, who returned to Togo in mid-March, was barred from standing owing to his failure to meet the residency requirements.

Tensions mounted in April 2005, as the date of the election approached. Isolated violent incidents were reported across the country at the beginning of the month, with people claiming to have been prevented from registering to vote. The opposition alliance urged the Government and the CENI to postpone the election. The official opening of election campaigning on 8 April was overshadowed by the death of a demonstrator in confrontations between opposition supporters and the security forces. At least seven people were reportedly killed, and around 150 injured, in violent clashes in Lomé between opposition and government supporters on 16 April. On the following day an estimated 30,000 people attended a rally at which Gnassingbé pledged to introduce free primary education and to secure the full restoration of EU development aid, if elected. Lawson withdrew his candidacy on 23 April in protest against alleged irregularities in the electoral process (although his name remained on the ballot).

Voting in the presidential election took place in relatively peaceful conditions in most areas on 24 April 2005, although some violent incidents were reported, and at least three people were believed to have died in clashes between supporters of rival candidates. However, the announcement by the CENI, on 26 April, that preliminary results indicated a clear victory for Gnassingbé provoked widespread rioting, particularly in Lomé and Aného, east of the capital. The security forces quelled the unrest after two days. The six-party opposition coalition later stated that 106 people had been killed in the violence, although the Government estimated the death toll at 22, while thousands of others fled the country for neighbouring Benin and Ghana. Meanwhile, Bob Akitani refused to concede defeat, although ECOWAS observers, while acknowledging that there had been some irregularities, stated that these had not been such as to invalidate the result. The EU had declined to send official monitors owing to concerns regarding the speed with which the election had been organized; however, a confidential EU report on the election that later surfaced apparently revealed that Western diplomats had observed incidents of fraud and intimidation of voters by the security forces. It was alleged that the names of some 900,000 non-existent voters had appeared on the electoral register.

On 3 May 2005 the Constitutional Court declared the official results of the election, proclaiming Gnassingbé President, with 60.2% of the votes cast. Bob Akitani, Gnassingbé's closest rival, was attributed 38.3% of the votes. A turn-out of 63.6% of the electorate was recorded. Gnassingbé was inaugurated on the following day. By this time the office of the UN High Commissioner for Refugees (UNHCR) had registered 22,600 Togolese refugees in Benin and Ghana. In mid-May the LTDH claimed that 790 people had been killed and 4,345 injured between 28 March (when the authorities began updating the electoral register) and 5 May, much higher figures than previous estimates. However, another human rights group, aligned to the Government, reported 58 deaths during this period. Gnassingbé later appointed a national commission of inquiry into the violence, headed by former Prime Minister Koffigoh.

On 19 May 2005 the President of Nigeria, Olusegun Obasanjo, chaired a reconciliation summit in the Nigerian capital, Abuja, under the aegis of ECOWAS and the AU, which was attended by Gnassingbé, Gilchrist Olympio and other opposition leaders, as well as the Heads of State of Benin, Burkina Faso, Gabon, Ghana and Niger. (Bob Akitani was unable to participate owing to ill health.) The talks ended without agreement, however, as the 'radical' opposition alliance continued to reject the legitimacy of Gnassingbé's victory and demanded a full and independent investigation of alleged election irregularities as a precondition for engaging in substantive negotiations on a power-sharing arrangement. None the less, Gnassingbé subsequently held meetings with a number of opposition leaders to discuss the formation of a government of national unity. A split emerged in the six-party coalition, as most members decided to join the talks, while the UFC remained steadfast in its refusal to participate. In late May the AU removed sanctions against Togo, declaring that it considered conditions in Togo to be constitutional. Meanwhile, refugees continued to flee Togo, amid reports that opposition supporters were being arrested or kidnapped by the security forces, and by late May 34,416 had been registered by UNHCR (19,272 in Benin and 15,144 in Ghana). It was estimated that a further 10,000 people had been internally displaced within Togo. In June Gnassingbé created a High Commission for Refugees and Humanitarian Action.

On 8 June 2005 Gnassingbé designated Edem Kodjo, the leader of the moderate opposition CPP, as Prime Minister, replacing Sama. Gnassingbé's talks with five of the 'radical' opposition parties had earlier broken down when the President rejected a series of proposals presented by the parties, including demands for a re-run of the presidential election and increased powers for the Prime Minister. The formation of a 30-member Council of Ministers was announced later that month. The new Government was dominated by the RPT, although some members of the opposition and civil society received posts. Notably, Tchessa Abi of the PSR (part of the 'radical' opposition) was appointed as Keeper of the Seals, Minister of Justice; the other five members of the six-party coalition condemned Abi's acceptance of a ministerial position, deciding to expel the PSR from the coalition. Zarifou Ayéva, the leader of the moderate opposition Parti pour la Démocratie et le Renouveau (PDR), became Minister of State, Minister of Foreign Affairs and African Integration, while a younger half-brother of the President, Kpatcha Gnassingbé, joined the Government as Minister-delegate at the Presidency of the Republic, responsible for Defence and Veterans. In September the UFC expelled Gabrial Sassouvi Dosseh-Anyroh from the party for accepting the position of Minister of Culture, Tourism and Leisure.

Reconciliation Efforts

Efforts to promote national reconciliation and to encourage the return of refugees dominated the new Government's agenda. The return of the refugees was discussed by Gnassingbé and Gilchrist Olympio at a meeting in Rome, Italy, in July 2005, at which the two men also condemned violence and agreed that political prisoners arrested during the electoral process should be released. Earlier that month the Government had announced that some 170 prisoners were to be released, including 48 opposition supporters who had been detained following the electoral violence. By August the number of refugees in Benin exceeded 24,500, although no new arrivals had been registered in Ghana since the end of May and the number of internally displaced people was estimated to have declined from 10,000 to less than 4,000. In September the Government announced the establishment of a commission charged with re-examining Togo's history and making recommendations regarding the proposed rehabilitation of former Togolese leaders and other notable figures, including Sylvanus Olympio, the country's first President. Later that month Gnassingbé stated that he intended to organize legislative elections as quickly as possible, in conditions acceptable to all concerned.

In September 2005 the office of the UN High Commissioner for Human Rights (UNHCHR) released a report stating that 400–500 people had been killed in Togo between 5 February and 5 May and that responsibility for the political violence and human rights violations that occurred during this period lay principally with the security forces, although opposition leaders were also criticized for failing to control militant supporters. The Togolese Government disputed UNHCHR's findings, and in November the national commission of inquiry into the violence reported that 154 people had died.

Representatives of Gnassingbé and Olympio held further talks in Rome in November 2005. Some 460 prisoners were released from detention in Lomé in that month; many of those freed were opposition supporters who had been involved in the post-election unrest.

In March 2006, in an attempt to encourage the return of refugees, the Government abandoned judicial proceedings against alleged perpetrators of acts of violence related to the 2005 election, with the exception of those accused of 'bloody crimes'. Despite repeated government appeals for their return, 19,870 Togolese refugees remained in Benin and 14,100 in Ghana in April, according to UNHCR.

The inter-Togolese national dialogue, which had broken down following the death of Eyadéma, finally resumed in Lomé in April 2006, with the participation of six political parties (the CAR, the CDPA—BT, the CPP, the PDR, the RPT and the UFC), as well as two civil society organizations and the Government; issues to be addressed included the revision of the electoral framework, institutional reform, the restructuring of the security forces and the situation of the refugees. The EU welcomed the renewed dialogue as an important stage in the implementation of the 22 measures agreed in April 2004 for the resumption of full economic co-operation. In July 2006 participants in the dialogue designated the President of Burkina Faso, Blaise Compaoré, to act as a facilitator in future negotiations. Meanwhile, following a meeting in Brussels to consider Togo's progress in strengthening democracy, the EU decided to disburse €15m. (some 10,000m. francs CFA) to the Government in support of further reform.

Following talks, held in the Burkinabè capital, Ouagadougou, under the mediation of Compaoré, on 20 August 2006 the nine participants in the national dialogue formally signed a comprehensive political accord at a ceremony in Lomé. The agreement provided, *inter alia*, for the formation of a government of national unity, the organization of legislative elections by October 2007, the re-establishment of the CENI, the revision of the electoral register, the creation of a commission of inquiry into past political violence and the establishment of a committee charged with accelerating the return of refugees from Benin and Ghana (now estimated to number a total of 16,500).

In mid-September 2006 Agboyibo, who had chaired the board of the national dialogue, was designated Prime Minister. The transitional Council of Ministers, which included members of six political parties, as well as several representatives of civil society, was formed a few days later. The UFC refused to participate in the new administration, rejecting Agboyibo's appointment and complaining that the RPT had secured the most significant portfolios, although the party's Second Vice-President, Amah Gnassingbé, accepted the post of Minister of State on an 'individual basis'. Former Prime Minister Edem Kodjo was appointed Minister of State at the Presidency later that month. In October the Assemblée nationale named the 19 members of the new CENI. Shortly afterwards the CENI proposed that the legislative elections be held on 24 June 2007.

From November 2006 monthly meetings of the nine signatory parties to the August accord were held to monitor the progress of its implementation. These talks were brokered by Compaoré and also attended by representatives of the EU and ECOWAS. The Assemblée nationale adopted amendments to the electoral code in February 2007, notably returning full responsibility for organizing, as well as supervising, elections to the CENI. In May the legislative elections were delayed until 5 August, and in July they were postponed indefinitely owing to ongoing difficulties in finalizing preparations.

Legislative elections of 2007

The legislative elections were finally held on 14 October 2007, with the participation of all the main opposition parties. The RPT secured 50 of the Assemblée nationale's 81 seats, while the UFC won 27 and the CAR the remaining four. Despite opposition complaints of irregularities, international observers (including representatives of the AU, the EU and ECOWAS) declared themselves satisfied with the organization and conduct of the elections, welcoming the high turn-out, which was recorded at 84.9%. In November the EU announced the resumption of full co-operation with Togo; €123m. in development aid was to be provided during 2008–13.

Agboyibo resigned as Prime Minister in November 2007, having completed his mission of organizing the elections. Komlan Mally, hitherto Minister of Towns and Town Planning and a member of the RPT, was appointed Prime Minister in early December. Talks aimed at forming a government of national unity largely failed, however, and the new 21-member Council of Ministers appointed in mid-December did not include any members of the UFC or the CAR. None the less, Léopold Gnininvi, the leader of the CDPA—BT, was appointed to the senior position of Minister of State, Minister of Foreign Affairs and Regional Integration. The President assumed responsibility for the defence portfolio, with the notable departure from the Government of Kpatcha Gnassingbé, hitherto Minister of Defence and Veterans. In July 2008 the UFC nominated Gilchrist Olympio to be its presidential candidate at the election due in 2010.

Mally tendered his resignation in early September 2008, his main achievement in office having been the resumption of co-operation with international creditors. Gnassingbé appointed Gilbert Houngbo, hitherto director of the UN Development Programme's Bureau for Africa, to the premiership. Mally became Minister of State, Minister of Health in Houngbo's new administration, which was formed in mid-September. Responsibility for many of the other principal portfolios remained unchanged, although a new Minister of Foreign Affairs and Regional Integration, Kofi Esaw, previously the Togolese ambassador to Ethiopia, was appointed to replace Gnininvi, who was named Minister of State, Minister of Industry, Crafts and Technological Innovation. Free primary education was introduced in October, fulfilling a pledge that Gnassingbé had made in the 2005 presidential election campaign.

In January 2009 the UFC and the CAR announced the formation of an alliance to contest the 2010 presidential election, with the intention of selecting a joint candidate. A new permanent forum for discussions on constitutional, political and electoral issues was created by presidential decree in February 2009: the Cadre Permanent de Dialogue et de Concertation (CPDC) was to comprise representatives of the Government and parties that either held seats in the Assemblée nationale or had secured at least 5% of the votes cast in the last legislative elections (i.e. the RPT, the UFC and the CAR). However, participants struggled to reach a consensus on matters of institutional reform, particularly the composition of a new CENI. At the beginning of April, in a vote that was boycotted by the UFC and the CAR, the Assemblée nationale extended the tenure of existing CENI members pending agreement on the establishment of a new body.

Kpatcha Gnassingbé was arrested in April 2009 and charged with plotting to overthrow the President. His detention, while attempting to seek asylum at the US embassy in Lomé, followed a raid by the security forces on his house, in which at least two people were reportedly killed. Kpatcha Gnassingbé denied the allegations against him, claiming to have been the victim of an assassination attempt. A total of 10 civilians and 18 soldiers, including five officers, were arrested in connection with the coup plot. Changes to the Council of Ministers and the leadership of the armed forces were effected in May. Brig.-Gen. Essofa Ayéva, hitherto Chief of Staff at the Office of the President, was appointed as Chief of General Staff of the armed forces, replacing Gen. Zakari Nandja, who joined the Government as Minister of State, Minister of Water, Sanitation and Village Hydraulics, while Col Bali Wiyao was named Chief of Staff of the Land Army.

The UFC and the CAR withdrew from the CPDC in mid-June 2009 to protest against the inclusion of smaller political parties and civil society organizations in the dialogue. Later that month, in the absence of UFC and CAR deputies, the Assemblée nationale adopted CPDC-proposed amendments to the electoral code. Following negotiations in early August, mediated by Compaoré, the RPT, the UFC and the CAR reached agreement on matters concerning the CENI and the eligibility of presidential candidates (Gilchrist Olympio having been barred from contesting the 2003 and 2005 elections owing to residency requirements). Later that month the Assemblée nationale elected the new CENI's 17 members, comprising five representatives from the ruling party, five from the parliamentary opposition parties, three from other parties, three from civil society and one from the Government. However, the UFC and the CAR boycotted the election, in September, of Henri Kolani of the PDR as President of the Commission, accusing the PDR of being manipulated by the RPT. Kolani subsequently announced that the presidential election would be held on 28 February 2010, but the UFC and the CAR continued to dispute his authority and in October he was replaced as CENI President by a representative of civil society, Issifou Taffa Tabiou. Meanwhile, a minor government reorganization was effected in September 2009, following the resignation from the Council of Ministers of Gnininvi and the Minister of Higher Education and Research, Messan Adimado Aduayom, also of the CDPA—BT. In mid-February 2010, at the opposition's request, the presidential election was postponed until 4 March. None the less, the UFC and the CAR suspended their participation in the CENI, citing concerns regarding the accuracy of the voters' register; both parties had also expressed discontent at the RPT's insistence that the election be conducted in only one round.

Gnassingbé Re-elected

Seven candidates contested the presidential election on 4 March 2010. With the opposition parties having failed to unite behind a single candidate, Faure Gnassingbé was re-elected by a comfortable margin, winning 60.9% of the valid votes cast, according to official results published by the Constitutional Court on 18 March. His closest challenger, receiving 33.9% of the votes, was Jean-Pierre Fabre, the Secretary-General of the UFC (Gilchrist Olympio having been forced to withdraw his candidacy in January for medical reasons), while the CAR's candidate, Agboyibo, secured only 3.0% of the ballot. A turn-out of 65.7% was recorded. Welcoming the relatively peaceful conditions in which polling had taken place, international observers declared the election to have been largely free and fair, despite opposition allegations of fraud. The opposition organized a series of protests against Gnassingbé's re-election in March and April.

Gnassingbé was sworn in to serve a second presidential term on 3 May 2010. Houngbo was subsequently reappointed as Prime Mister and charged with consulting with all political parties with the aim of forming a broad-based Government. The CAR refused to join the Council of Ministers, but in late May Gilchrist Olympio signed an accord with the RPT on the UFC's participation in Houngbo's new administration. The UFC received seven of the 32 ministerial posts, most notably that of Minister of State, Minister of Foreign Affairs and Co-operation, which was allocated to Elliott Ohin, while the RPT also agreed to implement several political reforms, including the revision of constituency boundaries and of the electoral register.

However, the UFC was deeply divided over the power-sharing agreement: Fabre, who continued to reject Gnassingbé's victory, denounced the accord, and the national bureau suspended Olympio and the seven UFC ministers from membership of the party, claiming not to have been consulted on the decision to join the Government. When the Assemblée nationale approved the new Government's programme in early June 2010, only seven of the UFC's 27 deputies voted in its favour. The split in the UFC was confirmed in August, when the two factions of the party held separate congresses, electing Fabre and Olympio as their respective Presidents; the Olympio faction additionally expelled Fabre and four others from the party for 'indiscipline'. The Government issued a communiqué stating that it recognized Olympio as the leader of the UFC. In September Olympio's UFC elected Kokou Aholou to replace Fabre as the party's leader in the Assemblée nationale, and in the following month Fabre announced the formation of a new party, the Alliance Nationale pour le Changement (ANC). In November, however, the Constitutional Court ruled that Fabre and eight other deputies who had joined the ANC should relinquish their seats in the legislature on the grounds that they had allegedly submitted letters of resignation to the President of the Assemblée nationale, Abass Bonfoh. Although the nine denied having sent such letters and declared their intention to challenge the decision, it was reported that, unlike the 10 other ANC deputies, they had signed an agreement within the UFC, prior to the 2007 legislative elections, whereby they would forfeit their mandate as deputes if they resigned from the party.

Several minor government changes were effected in early 2011. Col Gnama Latta was appointed as Minister of Security and Civil Protection in February, replacing Col Atcha Titikpina, who had recently assumed the post of Chief of General Staff of the armed forces. In March Arthème Kwesi Séléagodji Ahoomey-Zunu, hitherto Secretary-General at the Presidency, was designated Minister of Trade and the Promotion of the Private Sector, following the dismissal of the incumbent, Kokou Gozan, while Tchitchao Tchalim, a judge, was appointed as Keeper of the Seals, Minister of Justice, responsible for Relations with the Institutions of the Republic.

In March 2011 the Council of Ministers adopted draft legislation regulating public demonstrations, which required organizers of demonstrations to obtain the authorization of the Ministry of Territorial Administration, Decentralization and Local Communities, with the penalty for failing to do so being a prison sentence of up to five years. The bill was condemned by the ANC and other opposition parties, grouped in the Front Républicain pour l'Alternance et le Changement (FRAC), which organized protests against the proposals. None the less, the legislation was approved by the Assemblée nationale in May, in a vote boycotted by opposition deputies.

Komlan Mally was dismissed as Minister of Health in June 2011, following several weeks of strike action by health workers demanding improved living and working conditions; he was replaced by Charles Kondi Agba, who had occupied the portfolio previously, notably during Mally's premiership.

In August 2011 police used tear gas to disperse a protest march by journalists against threats allegedly made by the national intelligence agency, the Agence Nationale du Renseignement (ANR), against journalists deemed to be critical of the Togolese authorities. In May 2012, moreover, a US-based press freedom organization, the Committee to Protect Journalists, complained to the Togolese Government regarding three incidents that had occurred since March in which the security forces had allegedly intimidated and obstructed journalists reporting on public protests in Lomé. An attack on a journalist in July prompted similar expressions of concern.

The trial of those accused of involvement in the purported coup attempt of 2009 took place in September 2011. Kpatcha Gnassingbé, the former armed forces Chief of General Staff, Gen. Assani Tidjani (who had only been arrested in July), and the former head of the gendarmerie special forces, Commdt Abi Atti, were convicted of orchestrating the plot and each sentenced to 20 years' imprisonment. Eight co-defendants received lesser prison sentences, while another half-brother of the President, businessman Essolizam Gnassingbé, was acquitted, as were some 20 others. Several suspects claimed to have been tortured by members of the ANR during their detention.

The Government initiated a new multi-party dialogue on institutional and constitutional reforms at the end of September 2011, but the talks were boycotted by the ANC and the CAR. In November the FRAC staged a protest march in Lomé in support of it demands for the reinstatement of the nine opposition deputies removed from their legislative seats in November 2010. The ruling RPT was dissolved at an extraordinary party congress held in April 2012, and replaced by the Union pour la République, a new organization supportive of President Gnassingbé, who was to be its leader.

At the end of May 2012 the Assemblée nationale adopted legislation increasing the number of seats in the legislature from 81 to 91 (with effect from the next elections, due to be held in October) and amending the boundaries of the electoral constituencies. The Government refuted accusations that the changes had been implemented unilaterally, insisting that they were a result of the political dialogue initiated in September 2011. However, in mid-June 2012 the Collectif Sauvons le Togo (CST, 'Let's Save Togo'), a coalition comprising seven opposition movements, including the ANC, and nine civil society groups, organized protests against the reforms, on the grounds that they favoured the ruling party, and in support of demands for the reintroduction of a two-term limit on the presidential mandate, this restriction having been removed from the Constitution in December 2002 (see above). Violent clashes broke out during the three days of protests, as the security forces fired tear gas in an attempt to disperse the demonstrators, with many people on both sides injured (the opposition reported 119 injuries). Following the unrest, which severely disrupted commercial activities in Lomé and resulted in damage to several buildings, three leaders of the CST were briefly detained, and former Prime Minister Agbéyomé Kodjo, the President of the opposition party Organisation pour Bâtir dans l'Union un Togo Solidaire (a member of the CST), was also held for questioning.

Prime Minister Houngbo resigned from office in mid-July 2012, without explanation. Ahoomey-Zunu, hitherto Minister of Trade and the Promotion of the Private Sector and a member of the moderate opposition CPP, replaced Houngbo later that month, and a new Council of Ministers was subsequently appointed. Although several ministers from the outgoing Government retained their posts, the Ministers of Security and Civil Protection and of Territorial Administration, Decentralization and Local Communities were notably dismissed, being succeeded by Col Damehane Yark, previously Chief of Staff of the gendarmerie, and Gilbert Bawara, respectively. Meanwhile, protests by the CST continued in July and August. In mid-July the security forces raided Fabre's home, injuring some of the occupants. Following an official investigation, four police officers were accused of involvement in the attack and were to undergo disciplinary proceedings.

HUMAN RIGHTS ISSUES

In May 1999 Amnesty International published a report detailing numerous abuses of human rights allegedly committed by the security forces in Togo, claiming that hundreds of political opponents of Eyadéma had been killed following the 1998 presidential election. The Government threatened to institute legal proceedings against the organization. Four human rights activists, all members of the opposition CDPA—BT, were detained by the authorities, accused of providing Amnesty with false information. The four men were released on bail in June. In the same month Amnesty accused the Togolese security forces of the detention and torture of one of their members, Amen Ayodole, although the authorities claimed that Ayodole had been detained on suspicion of drugs-smuggling.

In July 1999 a human rights organization in Benin reported that, following the 1998 presidential election in Togo, corpses had been discovered on the beaches of Benin. In late July Eyadéma agreed to the establishment of an international commission of inquiry into the allegations. A UN-OAU joint commission of inquiry was established in June 2000 and published its report in February 2001, concluding that 'systematic violations of human rights' had occurred in Togo in 1998, and that allegations of extra-judicial executions, particularly of opposition party activists, could not be refuted. The commission stated that individuals linked to the security forces appeared to be responsible for the killings, and recommended that the authorities punish those responsible, and that a special rapporteur be appointed to monitor human rights in Togo. However, the Government dismissed the report's conclusions, emphasizing that the commission had been unable to substantiate some of its findings. In March 2001 Prime Minister Agbéyomé Kodjo appeared before UNHCHR to deny the findings of the report.

During its discussions with the EU in April 2004 (see above), the Government pledged to release all political prisoners and guarantee the absence in Togo of extra-judicial executions, torture and other inhumane and degrading acts. In May the Government stated that it had been unable to identify any political prisoners, but was to consult with non-governmental organizations in this regard; the UFC claimed that 11 of its members were in detention, including nine who had been convicted earlier that month of public order offences and illegal possession of weapons. The International Federation of Human Rights Leagues (FIDH), which had visited Togo in February, released a report severely criticizing the Government's human rights record in June; the Government rejected the allegations contained in the report. Seven UFC militants were among some 494 prisoners released in August, having been pardoned by the President, although the authorities denied that they had been political detainees.

Following the presidential election in April 2005, human rights groups expressed serious concerns about human rights in Togo, claiming that the thousands of people leaving the country for Benin and Ghana were fleeing severe harassment from the security forces. In May the FIDH denounced a 'serious and systematic' abuse of human rights in Togo, urging the UN and the AU to conduct an international inquiry into the alleged violations. In mid-June UNHCHR commenced an investigation into allegations of killings, abductions and political persecution. In July the LTDH claimed that it was still receiving complaints of political persecution from opponents of the Government, despite government assurances that it was safe for those who had fled the country to return. The Government dismissed allegations of human rights abuses. Meanwhile, the Government announced plans to release some 170 prisoners, including political detainees; a further 460 prisoners were freed in November. Later in July Amnesty International issued a report denouncing human rights violations allegedly perpetrated by the Togolese security forces and pro-Government militias before and after the presidential election. The Togolese Government condemned the organization's investigation, which was based on testimony from refugees in camps in Benin. UNHCHR's report on pre- and post-election violence and alleged human rights violations, which was published in September (see above), stated that torture and inhumane treatment had been widely used by the security forces during the unrest. In April 2006 Amnesty International released a report criticizing the Government for failing to prosecute those responsible for crimes committed during the

2005 election period and claiming that a culture of impunity had existed in Togo for more than 30 years. In response, the Minister of Justice defended the Government's actions since taking office, stating that people suspected of lesser acts of violence had been freed in the interests of national reconciliation and that the issue of impunity would be addressed by the national dialogue that had resumed that month. Following the signature of a memorandum of understanding with the Togolese Government in July 2006, UNHCHR opened an office in Lomé. Amnesty International issued a further report in January 2007, again urging the Togolese authorities to prosecute those suspected of perpetrating violent crimes in 2005. More than 100 Togolese were reported to have filed cases related to the election violence with the judiciary. The Government insisted that progress was being made in this regard, making reference to the commitment made in the political accord of August 2006 to create a commission to investigate past political violence.

Following the legislative elections in October 2007, Togo's progress in the area of human rights was praised by several international organizations, notably UNHCHR and the EU. In January 2008 UNHCHR's special rapporteur on torture and other cruel, inhuman or degrading treatment or punishment issued a report on a visit to Togo made in April 2007, in which he commended the Government for its commitment to combating torture and ill-treatment and the considerable improvements it had achieved in this regard since 2005, but recommended the implementation of a series of further measures against impunity, including the establishment of effective mechanisms to investigate incidents of torture and to conduct unannounced inspections of places of detention.

Public consultations on the establishment of a 'truth and reconciliation commission' were formally initiated in April 2008, under the chairmanship of the President and with the support of UNHCHR, and completed in September, some 23,000 people having responded to a survey on the form the commission should take. The 11-member Truth, Justice and Reconciliation Commission, comprising religious leaders, academics and traditional chiefs, was inaugurated in May 2009, charged with investigating political violence between 1958 and 2005. In June 2009 the Assemblée nationale unanimously approved the abolition of the death penalty. In February 2011 the EU granted €6m. in support of the development of Togo's civil society organizations and the ongoing activities of the Truth, Justice and Reconciliation Commission, which had recorded more than 20,000 cases of alleged political violence by June that year. Hearings, at which 523 witnesses gave testimony, were conducted later that year, and the Commission submitted its report in April 2012, making 68 recommendations aimed at creating a culture of human rights in Togo, consolidating the rule of law, reconciling Togolese citizens and preventing future conflict. These included ensuring respect for ethnic groups and reforming the electoral system, the judiciary, the law enforcement agencies and the military. The Commission also proposed the establishment of a new body to implement such reforms and the instigation of further investigations with a view to prosecuting perpetrators of the most serious human rights violations.

Meanwhile, in February 2012 the national human rights commission, the CNDH, issued a report on torture allegations made by several of those accused of involvement in a coup plot in 2009 (see above), concluding that, during their detention, the suspects had indeed been subjected to 'acts of physical violence, and inhuman and degrading treatment' by members of the intelligence agency, the ADR. In response, the Government announced that it had requested that the military leadership take disciplinary action against ADR agents implicated in perpetrating the violence.

FOREIGN RELATIONS

The issue of Ewe reunification has at times led to difficult relations with Ghana. Diplomatic relations were suspended in 1982, but by late 1994 relations had improved considerably, and in November full diplomatic relations were formally resumed. In December Togo's border with Ghana, which had been closed since January, was reopened. Thousands of Togolese sought refuge in Benin and Ghana from late April 2005, fleeing the violence that followed the presidential election (see above). By the end of 2005 UNHCR had registered 26,632 Togolese refugees in Benin and 14,136 in Ghana. Following the restoration of stability, many refugees returned to Togo during 2006–08, but at the end of 2011 5,883 still remained in Benin and 1,789 in Ghana. During a visit to Ghana by President Gnassingbé in August 2009, it was agreed to strengthen co-operation in combating cross-border crime and to reconstitute the Ghana-Togo Border Demarcation Commission in 2010. Some 3,600 Ghanaians crossed into northern Togo in April and May 2010, fleeing a violent land dispute between two villages in north-eastern Ghana. By the end of 2010 there were 13,575 Ghanaian refugees in Togo, compared with 8,073 one year earlier; a slight increase, to 13,676, was recorded at the end of 2011.

During the first half of 2011 some 6,200 refugees from Côte d'Ivoire entered Togo (via Ghana or Burkina Faso), having fled violence that followed the Ivorian presidential election in November 2010; 5,374 Ivorian refugees remained in Togo at the end of July 2012, according to UNHCR. In June 2012 Moïse Lida Kouassi, a former Ivorian Minister of Defence and a key ally of erstwhile President of Côte d'Ivoire Laurent Gbagbo (who was himself awaiting trial by the International Criminal Court on charges of crimes against humanity), was detained in Togo—where he had been in exile for some time, despite a long-standing international warrant for his arrest—and extradited to Côte d'Ivoire.

Relations with France improved following the resumption of civil co-operation with Togo in June 1994, and were further strengthened with the election in 1995 of Jacques Chirac as French President. In June 1999 the French Government hosted talks in Paris between the Government and opposition groups, which led to an agreement to hold further talks in Lomé in July. In July Chirac visited Lomé and met the participants in the reconciliation talks. Following Eyadéma's re-election in June 2003, it was reported that France favoured a relaxation of EU sanctions against Togo, on the grounds that the international observers of the polls had not reported any flagrant irregularities, and Chirac subsequently attempted to persuade his European counterparts to resume co-operation with Togo. Chirac urged the Togolese authorities to respect the Constitution following Faure Gnassingbé's installation as President in February 2005, and welcomed Gnassingbé's subsequent decision to stand down. Chirac congratulated Gnassingbé on his victory in the presidential election held in April. During a visit by Gnassingbé to Paris in September 2006, Chirac announced the provision of €5m. to assist the political transition in Togo. A further €3m. was granted by France in July 2007 for the organization of forthcoming legislative elections. Additional aid was disbursed by the EU for this purpose. During a visit to Togo in September 2008, the French Minister-delegate for Co-operation and the French-speaking World, Alain Joyandet, announced that France would grant Togo €140m. during 2008–12 and that aid for 2008 would be doubled to €5m. owing to concerns regarding food insecurity; a debt cancellation agreement was also signed. Relations with France were further strengthened in November, when President Gnassingbé made his second visit to that country since taking office, holding talks with his French counterpart, Nicolas Sarkozy, and other senior officials. In May 2011 the French Government announced that it had agreed to cancel the sovereign debt owed to it by Togo, amounting to €101.1m. France was additionally assisting Togo to pay its domestic debt arrears, granting sums of €3m. and €2m. for this purpose in January and November of that year. (Meanwhile, in June Italy, Sweden and Switzerland also agreed to cancel debt owed by Togo.) Following the suppression of protests against electoral reforms in Togo in June 2012 (see above), the French Government called for civil liberties to be respected and urged dialogue.

Togolese troops have participated in a number of peacekeeping operations. Togo contributed troops to the ECOWAS military mission that was deployed in Côte d'Ivoire from January 2003 and to the UN Operation in Côte d'Ivoire (UNOCI) that succeeded it in April 2004. In September 2003 a contingent of 150 Togolese troops was dispatched to serve in the ECOWAS Mission in Liberia (ECOMIL), which was replaced by the UN Mission in Liberia (UNMIL) in October. In January 2008 it was announced that Togo would contribute 800 troops to the AU/UN hybrid operation in the Darfur region of western Sudan (UNAMID). The participation of 200 Togolese troops in the UN Mission in the Central African Republic and Chad (MINURCAT) was announced in February 2009; MINURCAT completed its mandate in December 2010.

Gnassingbé's assumption of power following the death of his father, Eyadéma, in February 2005 (see above) was condemned by West African countries and the wider international community. Relations with Nigeria were particularly strained that month when the Togolese authorities refused to allow an aeroplane carrying an advance delegation of President Olusegun Obasanjo's aides to land in Lomé ahead of planned talks between an ECOWAS mission and Gnassingbé. However, Obasanjo subsequently assumed a significant role in regional efforts to persuade Gnassingbé to stand down, and later mediated between Gnassingbé and Togolese opposition leaders. Gnassingbé's resignation as Head of State at the end of February, to allow an election to take place, was widely welcomed, and his victory in the poll in April was generally accepted by the international community, despite some concerns over electoral irregularities. At a summit meeting held in Abuja in February 2007, Obasanjo, Gnassingbé and the President of Benin, Boni Yayi, announced the formation of a Co-Prosperity Alliance Zone, aimed at accelerating the integration of their national economies and promoting peace, stability and development in West Africa. Later that month the electricity networks of Benin and Nigeria were officially connected, enabling energy to be supplied from Nigeria to Togo (via Benin) at a lower cost.

Amid mounting concern regarding piracy in the Gulf of Guinea, in September 2011, while addressing the UN General Assembly, the Togolese Prime Minister, Gilbert Houngbo, called for closer international co-operation to combat the problem. In October the UN Security Council adopted a resolution condemning piracy in the Gulf of Guinea, and in the following month UN experts conducted an assessment into the threat, concluding in a report submitted in January 2012 that a failure to act against piracy in the Gulf would be 'catastrophic'. Togo commenced a two-year term as a non-permanent member of the Security Council in January 2012.

Economy

PAUL MELLY

INTRODUCTION

At independence in 1960, Togo's economy, compared with those of most of its neighbours, was relatively advanced and progress continued in the 1970s. However, the 1980s were more difficult, with real gross domestic product (GDP) growth averaging only 0.5% per year, owing to drought, a decline in phosphate output and problems in neighbouring countries. Nevertheless, the 1980s also saw Togo achieve some success in diversifying away from its basic reliance on subsistence and cash crop agriculture and phosphates: the capital, Lomé, was developed as a regional gateway port and a centre for services, such as banking. The country sought to favour private sector business and foreign investment, and develop coastal resort tourism. Yet in the 1990s weaknesses in economic management and widespread human rights abuses, including the security forces' brutal suppression of public protests, led to the breakdown of relations with the donor community; the result was a dramatic slump in external development assistance, while Togo's reputation for harsh authoritarian practices set back investor confidence and the tourism industry. GDP declined at an average annual rate of 9.7% in 1991–93. With limited natural resources, Togo became one of the poorer countries in West Africa. GDP per caput averaged only US $226 in 2004–08, the third lowest level in West Africa—ahead only of Liberia and Niger—according to the IMF.

However, over recent years the country has made significant progress towards recovery. Although per caput GDP was still only US $234 in 2011—well below neighbouring Burkina Faso ($322) and Benin ($360)—Togo has enjoyed solid rates of economic growth. Real GDP has risen by 4% or more in three of the past six years and the partnership with the international donor community has been restored. In 2011 the country successfully completed a three-year IMF programme of stabilization and reform; Lomé is regaining some of its former importance as a gateway port for land-locked West African states. Togo is still categorised by the IMF as a 'fragile' country and longer-term donor and investor confidence is still conditional; however, after a long period of stagnation and decline, the trend is now clearly positive in terms of economic growth and development.

In the years following independence rates of population growth and urbanization continued at a high level, and population density reached 113.7 people per sq km by 2008. By 2011 the total population had reached 6.2m., of whom 43% lived in urban areas. The population grew by an annual average of 2.5% in 2005–10, but the rate of growth is slowing rapidly, to a projected average of just 2% per annum for 2010–15. In most years there is a seasonal migration, of around 100,000 Togolese annually, to neighbouring Ghana and Benin; however, Lomé also attracts seasonal migrant workers from the land-locked Sahelian economies to the north.

Togo is a member of the Union Economique et Monétaire Ouest-Africaine (UEMOA) single currency bloc. As in other member states, the 50% devaluation of the CFA franc in January 1994 bolstered competitiveness and triggered a growth rebound in mining, manufacturing and cash crop agriculture; however, the beneficial impact was largely offset by a lack of investor confidence and donor support, due to the Government's repressive policies. Economic performance was more erratic in the late 1990s, despite ongoing collaboration with the World Bank and the IMF. Relations with international partners improved markedly after the death in 2005 of the dictatorial President Étienne (Gnassingbé) Eyadéma. His son and successor, Faure Gnassingbé, has presided over a significant liberalization, which has improved relations with the European Union (EU) and other key donors, and revived a focus on development and poverty reduction. However, Togo has not yet fully regained the investor confidence it enjoyed in the 1980s and the country remains one of the most fragile economies in West Africa. Real GDP growth has fluctuated; during 2004–08 it increased at an average annual rate of 2.4%, compared with an average of 3.7% per year for the eight-country UEMOA bloc as a whole. However, growth did reach 4.1% in 2006 and, after dipping to 2.3% in 2007, and 2.4% in 2008, it rebounded to 3.4% in 2009. The upward trajectory has continued, with 4% real growth in 2010, 4.1% in 2011 and an estimated 4.4% in 2012. Even so, the rise in output has not always been sufficient to keep pace with the increase in population. None the less, real per caput GDP has been rising steadily since 2008. The global economic crisis depressed export earnings and remittances from expatriate Togolese, but donors responded with an increase in direct budgetary support in 2009 and 2010. This has helped Togo—like many other sub-Saharan countries—sustain growth despite the difficult international environment. The country suffered a sharp rise in consumer price inflation in 2008 as world prices for fuel and food commodities surged. But the tight monetary stance of the UEMOA central bank in Dakar, Senegal, provides an anchor of stability and inflation has fluctuated between only 2% and 4% since 2009.

The key to the restoration of normal relations with donors, particularly the EU—aid from which had been suspended for 15 years—was the holding of parliamentary elections in October 2007 that were adjudged by the international community to have been free and transparent. Relations with the African Development Bank (AfDB), the World Bank and the IMF also improved following the 2007 legislative elections. Togo still faced significant challenges, including massive external debt, a weak financial sector, dilapidated infrastructure and poor social conditions, exacerbated by severe flooding in mid-2008. However, in April the country secured a three-year IMF programme, under which it tightened the management of public finances and began to prioritize public investment and social measures. The Government also began to replace general fuel subsidies with targeted help for the poor. The IMF advised the authorities to prepare the privatization of the four largest state-owned banks, although the implementation of this reform, in 2012, was challenging, with bids for at least one major bank falling short of government expectations, leading to the postponement of the sale.

AGRICULTURE

Agriculture remains the foundation of the economy and the principal source of livelihood: including livestock, forestry and fishing, it accounts for about 45% of GDP. Agriculture accounted for an estimated 53.4% of the economically active population in mid-2010, according to FAO. Favourable weather conditions and government fertilizer subsidies have helped to strengthen farm output. Togo has been an early beneficiary of the multi-donor Global Agriculture and Food Security Program led by the World Bank. In 2010 there was a rise in the output of traditional crops such as yams (0.9%), millet (1.5%) and sorghum (3.2%). The main food crops are cassava (908,800 metric tons in the 2010/11 season), yams (710,500 tons), maize (638,100 tons), millet and sorghum (295,900 tons) and paddy rice (110,100 tons). In non-drought years Togo is self-sufficient in basic foodstuffs. Food supplies are supplemented by artisanal fishing, but with a coastline of only 96 km the total catch (27,000 tons per year, according to FAO) is insufficient to satisfy domestic demand. Livestock is also important, particularly in more arid areas; meat production is around 47,000 tons per year.

Export cash crop production has staged a partial recovery but remains far short of the peaks achieved in the 1990s, when the devaluation of the CFA franc bolstered competitiveness. Although cotton producer prices rose steadily from 2007/08 to 2010/11, production of this key cash crop has fluctuated: cotton output reached 48,800 metric tons in 2007/08, but declined to 31,000 tons and then 27,900 tons over the following two seasons, before rebounding by 69% in 2010/11, to reach 47,000 tons. This fluctuating performance reflects the difficult conditions that have faced Franc Zone cotton farmers, who have suffered from the impact of subsidized US production. Farmers switched to other crops after the parastatal Societé Togolaise du Coton (SOTOCO) fell behind on payments to farmers; in response the IMF persuaded the Government to liquidate SOTOCO in 2008 and replace it with a new joint venture, Nouvelle Société Cotonnière du Togo (NSCT), owned 60% by the Government and 40% by the producers. The rebound in output recorded in 2010/11 suggests that this reform has had a positive impact.

In recent years the coffee sector's performance has been modest, with output fluctuating around the 10,000 metric ton mark: some 9,100 tons was produced in 2008/09, rising to 11,700 tons the following season but then slipping back to 11,500 tons in 2010/11. Cocoa output has followed a similar pattern, climbing sharply to 13,000 tons in 2008/09 and then to 13,100 tons in 2009/10, before falling to 12,500 tons in 2010/11. While increased producer prices have helped drive the modest recovery of cotton and cocoa output, prices for coffee have actually slipped back without significantly affecting output levels. The correlation between price levels and output is not exact for any crop; this may be because other factors such as access to fertilizer or credit at affordable costs can influence farm output. Groundnut production fluctuated markedly in the 1990s, before stabilizing in 2001–05 at an average annual output of 36,821 tons. However, in recent seasons it has picked up steadily, rising from 36,000 tons in 2006/07 to 42,600 tons the following season and to 44,500 tons in 2009/10; output in 2010/11 was estimated at 46,500 tons.

The Government's agricultural development programme has received substantial foreign support, including grants from the European Development Fund (EDF) and France's Fonds d'Aide et de Coopération, for the development of coffee, cocoa and cotton production in the south, the most developed area. Credits have also come from the concessionary lending body of the World Bank, the International Development Association, for rural development projects, intended to increase the area under cultivation and to introduce cotton, maize, sorghum and groundnut crops. The Government also planned to develop irrigated agriculture—rice, sugar cane, fruits and vegetables.

MINING AND POWER

Traditionally, a key element of Togo's exports—and overall economic growth—has come from the mining of phosphates, which were discovered in Togo in 1952. Exports began in 1961. Togo's phosphate deposits are among the richest in the world, with a mineral content of 81%. Reserves of first-grade ore are estimated at 260m. metric tons. There are also more than 1,000m. tons of carbon phosphates, which, although of lower quality, have the advantage of a significantly lower cadmium content (see below). In the early 1990s Togo ranked fifth among the world's producers of calcium phosphates, and they accounted for almost one-half of Togo's domestic export receipts (excluding re-exports) in 1991. They now make a much smaller relative contribution to the country's external account—less than one-tenth of exports in 2010. This is partly because the base of exports is much more diverse, but also because Togolese phosphate sales have suffered from increasing customer concerns over their high cadmium content. The parastatal Office Togolais des Phosphates (OTP) became heavily indebted and, at the end of 2001, was dissolved and replaced by a new management company, International Fertilizers Group-Togo (IFG-TG), which rehabilitated production equipment. Output has declined from 842,500 tons in 2008 to 725,500 tons in 2009, and to 695,100 tons in 2010. The Government attempted to revive the industry through the creation in 2007 of a new sector operator, the 100% state-owned Société Nationale des Phosphates du Togo (SNPT), and a government investment of €18.3m. in production systems in 2009. This was followed in 2010 with the announcement of a further €116m. three-year investment programme. The Government hopes eventually to increase production back to 3m. tons per year—the level of output achieved in the 1980s—by exploiting its hitherto untouched reserves of phosphate carbonate, in partnership with an international investor. The Government believes this could eventually allow Togo to boost production to 6.7m tons per annum.

Togo also possesses reserves of limestone, which is used to produce clinker, an essential ingredient in cement; there is a substantial regional market for clinker, notably in Ghana. Estimated at 175m. metric tons, Togo's limestone deposits have been exploited since 1981. The established operators are West African Cement (Wacem), Indian-owned Diamond Cement and Cimtogo (a subsidiary of HeidelbergCement Group); Chinese group CDI has been commissioned to build a new dry clinker plant for Cimtogo subsidiary Scantogo. Exploitation of reserves of marble at Gnaoulou and Pagola (estimated at 20m. tons) began in 1970 by the Société Togolaise de Marbrerie (later restructured, with Norwegian participation, as the Nouvelle Société Togolaise de Marbrerie et de Matériaux—Nouvelle SOTOMA). A 500m. ton iron ore deposit, with 45% metal content, was discovered in central Togo, and the Indian-funded MM Mining began to develop production at the site in 2010.

In 1999 it was reported that deposits of petroleum and gas had been discovered in Togolese territorial waters by Petroleum Geo-Service of Norway. However, the results from early tests (the first offshore drilling in Togolese territorial waters) proved discouraging. Nevertheless, a two-year exploration deal was signed with Nigeria's Oranto Petroleum in January

2007, and a production-sharing contract for two offshore blocs has also been signed with the Italian company ENI. Togo has declared its intention to join the Extractive Industries Transparency Initiative (EITI), which would bolster its credibility in terms of accountability for the use of mineral revenues. The EITI governing council designated Togo as a candidate country in October 2010, and this gives the country until April 2013 to fulfil the conditions for membership; Togo published its first EITI report—covering revenues in 2010—in April 2012, in the hope of completing the validation process for the initiative before the end of the year.

Economic activity in Togo has for many years been held back by shortages of electricity. Although the country is a partner in the Communauté Électrique du Bénin (CEB), a joint power supply arrangement with Benin, it has also been substantially dependent on imports of power from the Akosombo hydroelectric plant in Ghana and, to a lesser extent, the gas-fired Azito plant in Côte d'Ivoire. One of the main problems has been the extent of reliance on hydro-generation, from Akosombo and from domestic installations at Kpalimé and Nangbeto. The latter, a 65-MW unit on the Mono river, is jointly owned with Benin; it has a maximum capacity of 150m. kWh, and also provides irrigation for 43,000 ha of land. Togolese power imports from Ghana have been around 486m. kWh. However, hydropower supply is vulnerable to periods of low rainfall. For many years Togo had to rely on inadequate thermal generating capacity as a back-up. The security of power supply was much improved in October 2010, with the opening of a 100-MW plant in Lomé, developed by Contour Global-Togo under a 25-year concession to supply all output to CEB. The new plant can operate on diesel or heavy fuel oil, but its main long-term fuel source will be gas, imported from Nigeria through a connection to the West Africa Gas Pipeline developed by a consortium led by Chevron.

The connected electricity grids of Togo and Benin were joined to that of Nigeria in early 2007, and in early 2008 Togo received a loan of 10,000m. francs CFA from the Banque Ouest-Africaine de Développement (BOAD) to improve and extend its electricity grid. In 2005 an estimated 18% of the population had access to electricity, decreasing to 5% in rural areas; per caput consumption of power was 110 kWh, compared with a mere 79 kWh in Benin, but a much more substantial 269 kWh in Ghana. In 2010 fuel imports constituted 9.7% of all merchandise imports by value.

In 2000 the management of the Compagnie Energie Electrique du Togo, which was subsequently renamed Togo Electricité, was ceded to a consortium consisting of Hydro-Québec of Canada and Elyo of France under a 20-year contract; however, the Government was to retain control of the company. The relationship with the consortium deteriorated in 2005 over a contractual dispute, and, in February 2006, the Government cancelled the contract.

INDUSTRY

Togo's manufacturing sector is small and relatively undeveloped. Continued electricity shortages, a weak financial sector and low economic growth hamper its development and performance. Manufacturing was, in the past, centred on the processing of agricultural commodities (palm oil extraction, coffee-roasting, cassava flour-milling, and cotton-ginning) and import substitution of consumer goods—textiles, footwear, beverages, confectionery, salt and tyres. Togotex, a state company that produces cloth from Togolese cotton grown using organic techniques, has plants at Kara and Atakpamé. However, the company faces serious difficulties: in August 2011 workers threatened to commence industrial action, claiming to be owed 140 months of salary arrears.

In order to improve economic efficiency and reduce the fiscal burden of financing unproductive investments, the Government has gradually withdrawn from its dominant role in the productive sectors. It has sold (either wholly or partially) or leased a number of state enterprises to the private sector as well as liquidating the most unprofitable ventures. Togo's business base has also been bolstered by the arrival of companies that moved operations from Côte d'Ivoire because of that country's instability.

SERVICES

Togo's banking system had 11 banks and two other registered finance institutions at the end of 2010, but was in the process of a major overhaul. By the late 2000s the banking system was in a precarious state, heavily burdened by non-performing loans, largely owed by parastatal entities. Therefore, in 2008 the Government recapitalized the five largest banks and transferred the cost of non-performing loans to the state (at a cost of 6.2% of GDP). In March 2010 the Government began to prepare the sale of major stakes in Banque Togolaise pour le Commerce et l'Industrie (formerly BNP Paribas), Banque Internationale pour l'Afrique au Togo (formerly Belgolaise-Fortis), Union Togolaise de Banque (UTB, formerly Crédit Lyonnais), and Banque Togolaise de Développement (BTD). Several international groups submitted expressions of interest; this was not surprising, as bank privatizations in other small Franc Zone economies have proved successful. The Government hoped to attract both foreign and local investors. However, by early September 2012 it had rejected a €7.8m offer from Morocco's Attijariwafa Bank for a 51% stake in UTB, indicating that pre-qualification of bids for stakes in BTCI and BIA would begin later in the month. The banks saw a 24% rise in lending and an 11% rise in deposits in 2010 although they had to maintain a high level of provisioning against bad loans. Microfinance also plays an important role in Togo: some 20 decentralized operations were catering for 630,000 beneficiaries in 2009, lending 61,500m. francs CFA that year—16% of bank lending—while 67,000m. francs CFA in deposits were received (12% of bank deposits). Only 4.3% of the loan portfolio was rated as non-performing.

TRANSPORT, COMMUNICATIONS AND TOURISM

The road network totalled 7,520 km in 2000, of which just under one-third (2,376 km) was paved. The railways, with 519 km of track, are generally in need of modernization, and the lines to Kpalimé and Aného, have been closed to passenger traffic. In 2003 the national railway company, Société Nationale des Chemins de Fer du Togo, was transferred to the private ownership of West African Cement (Wacem). The port of Lomé (Port Autonome de Lomé—PAL) is one of the few natural deep-water harbours on the West African coast, with a 14 m draught. It is one of the main cargo gateways to West Africa, including land-locked Sahelian countries; a major upgrade began, in 2011, to enhance this regional role. The scheme encompasses a new 450-m quay, with 15-m water depth, a new basin, and a container terminal. Lomé Container Terminal (LCT), a consortium of MSC and Getma, is investing €200m. in the project. Another innovation is a 'one-stop-shop' for administrative procedures and the collection of customs dues, to speed up throughput times for inbound freight. Port traffic increased by 9.3% in 2010, with import cargo (68% of the total) reaching 8m. metric tons. Togo's main international airport is at Tokoin, near Lomé; the airport at Niamtougou, in the north, can also handle international flights.

Telecommunications is a growth sector in Togo, as in most of sub-Saharan Africa; the established operators are the state-owned Togo Cellulaire (Togocel) and Atlantique Télécom Togo, which is a subsidiary of the UAE-based Etisalat group; there has been talk of issuing a third GSM licence. Togocel, which had 1.6m. subscribers by 2009 and an 80% market share, has plans to introduce nation-wide wireless broadband. The Export and Import Bank of China loaned state-owned telecommunications provider Togo Télécom US $32m. in 2009 to modernize its network.

Tourism, formerly a major source of foreign exchange, suffered from the political crises of the 1990s. Visitor numbers, which reached a record 143,000 in 1982, declined to a low of 22,244 in 1993. By 2006 the number of foreign tourist arrivals had recovered to reach 94,096. It declined again, to 86,165 the following year and 73,982 in 2008. However, the industry—which directly employs about 2,000 personnel—enjoyed a sharp rebound in 2010, with 202,000 visitors. The Government hopes to diversify Togo's holiday appeal by developing eco-tourism attractions that are closely integrated with local communities. Receipts from tourism (including passenger transport) increased from US $11m. in 2000 to $66m. in

2010. In addition to recreational tourism, efforts have been made to promote Togo as an international conference centre, for which the country is reasonably well equipped.

PUBLIC FINANCE

One of the major objectives of the IMF's Development Plans has been the strengthening of the Government's revenue position. The authorities have had considerable success with this strategy in recent years. In 2004 Togo even recorded a budget surplus equal to 1% of GDP; in subsequent years the budget year has always ended in deficit, but in low single figures, measured as a share of GDP. In 2008 the deficit was just 0.9% of GDP; it rose sharply in 2009, to 5%, as the economy felt the impact of the global economic crisis, but fell back to 3% in 2010. The main reasons for this solid fiscal performance have been careful control of current expenditure and the success of government efforts to bolster revenues. These last rose from an already strong 16.9% of GDP in 2009 to some 18.7% in 2010; this was largely the result of one-off income from the sale of new mineral sector licences, but there was also 7.7% growth in normal fiscal receipts: tax income rose by 7.3% while customs revenue was up by 8%, particularly as a result of tighter controls, greater use of information technology and increased efforts to curb fuel-smuggling. Overall, fiscal receipts were equal to 15.8% of GDP.

Public spending in 2010 reached 21.7% of GDP, an increase of some 4.9% compared with the previous year. However, behind this headline rise was a 27.9% surge in capital expenditure (perhaps reflecting a renewed development effort after the recent receipt of extra donor funds), coupled with a fall of 4.2% of GDP in current expenditure. Seeking to expand decayed public services after several years of declining aid, the Government had recruited many more staff for the health, education and security services; as a result, the public sector salary bill rose by more than one-third in 2009, to consume 37.3% of all budget revenues. However, in 2010 the authorities sought to reassert discipline over staffing costs, and expenditure on wages slipped back by 12.4% to cost only 28% of budget revenues. This reduction of salary outlays freed up resources for the Government to bolster spending on subsidizing the price of energy. The majority of capital spending is funded by aid, with a focus on the rehabilitation of national infrastructure, which was relatively well developed in the 1980s but suffered from the later suspensions of development assistance. Meanwhile, in 2009 the Government embarked on a drive to clear payment arrears to domestic private sector creditors, which is also an effective means of channelling extra liquidity and spending power into the domestic economy. As a result, the deficit on a cash basis, taking account of grant aid receipts, was reduced from 20,800m. francs CFA in 2009 to 13,600m. francs CFA in 2010.

FOREIGN TRADE AND PAYMENTS

Togo's grant aid income grew rapidly between 2007 and 2009, as a result of the resumption of normal donor support after many years when aid was restricted because of Togo's poor record on governance and human rights. In 2009 net grant aid amounted to 64,900m. francs CFA, accounting for 25% of state budget income. In 2010 this slipped back to 56,900m. francs CFA, 19.4% of budget income; however, this may be partly explained by cyclical factors, such as the patterns of funding disbursement for projects and programmes. From 1993 the EU had limited its assistance to 'vital projects' in disease control, sanitation and education, although individual EU member states, notably France, had gradually resumed development aid. Togo had partially offset the reduction in Western and multilateral aid by securing funds from other sources, including the Islamic Development Bank, of which the country became a member in November 1998, and the AfDB. In late 2004 the EU announced a partial resumption of aid to Togo, but the restoration of full support was still blocked by the Government's failure to implement democratic or human rights reforms.

Following the legislative elections in October 2007, the EU resumed full co-operation with Togo and, in March 2008, announced a loan package totalling €123,000m. over five years, to assist with urban development and the improvement of transport and social infrastructure. Also in early 2008 Togo successfully requested a three-year arrangement with the IMF (worth some US $108.4m.) under the Poverty Reduction and Growth Facility (PRGF, later rebranded as the Extended Credit Facility—ECF); this was also a precondition for securing debt relief under the initiative for heavily indebted poor countries (HIPC). In September the IMF disbursed a further $29m. to Togo following a series of misfortunes, including severe flooding and the surge in international prices for food and petroleum. Re-engagement with the IMF was accompanied by a similar improvement in relations with the World Bank, which had suspended disbursements to Togo in 2002, and with the AfDB. By July 2011 the World Bank had committed itself to fund 14 projects, worth a combined $127.9m. Meanwhile, Togo successfully completed its three-year ECF programme, with the IMF approving a sixth and final disbursement of $13.95m. for the first half of 2011.

Like most low-income sub-Saharan countries Togo accumulated a heavy burden of external debt. However, because of its poor relationship with donors and the IMF and World Bank the country lagged behind most of its neighbours in securing large-scale debt relief on these debts through HIPC and the Multilateral Debt Relief Initiative. By the end of 2007 its external debt stood at US $1,968m., of which $1,655m. was long-term public debt. The restoration of normal relations with the Fund, the World Bank, the AfDB and the EU opened the way for Togo finally to benefit from HIPC. After a positive IMF fifth review of its performance under the ECF programme, in 2010, Togo qualified for 'completion point' under the HIPC, which meant that debt relief previously accorded on a provisional basis now became definitive: some $1,800m. of debt was cancelled, equal to 80% of its outstanding value. The aim of HIPC is to reduce debt service costs to a level that is sustainable for Togo and frees up more government money for basic health, education and poverty reduction measures. In 2009 Switzerland, France and Belgium cancelled Togolese debt totalling 150,000m. francs CFA; the full programme of relief reduced debt to members of the 'Paris Club' of foreign government creditors by 95%, and reduced total external debt to only 30% of GDP.

Togo's external current account rose to 6% of GDP in 2010, from 5.6% the previous year. This was mainly due to an increase in the cost of imports, because of high world food and fuel prices, and a 6.6% rise in capital equipment imports, as Togo sought to upgrade its infrastructure. Total imports in 2010 were 645,800m. francs CFA, of which capital equipment accounted for 146,300m. francs CFA; food imports were 69,800m. francs CFA, while fuel costs totalled 62,900m. francs CFA. Freight and insurance charges for external trade (a negative factor in the external accounts) amounted to 76,200m. francs CFA. Nevertheless, exports rose by 3.7%, to reach 442,400m. francs CFA, with increased sales of cotton, coffee and cocoa offsetting a 19.3% decline in phosphate exports. The largest element in the total exports figure was re-exports—essentially to neighbouring countries, for which Togo acts as a trade gateway—which amounted to 75,400m. francs CFA. The main internally produced exports were clinker (42,100m. francs CFA), phosphates (34,300m. francs CFA), cocoa (17,900m. francs CFA), cotton (8,900m. francs CFA) and coffee (7,600m. francs CFA). Overall, exports remain equal to about 68% of import costs. Several other elements in the external accounts were relatively positive: net private transfers actually rose, to 127,900m. francs CFA, despite the recession in Europe, which could have been expected to continue squeezing remittances from the expatriate Togolese community. There was a modest recovery in portfolio investment, to 9,100m. francs CFA, after a withdrawal of funds the preceding year; and foreign direct investment also bounced back, to 10,200m. francs CFA, although this was still well short of the levels seen in 2007 and 2008.

Statistical Survey

Source (except where otherwise indicated): Direction de la Statistique, BP 118, Lomé; tel. 22-21-62-24; fax 22-21-27-75; e-mail dgscn_tg@yahoo.fr; internet www.stat-togo.org.

Area and Population

AREA, POPULATION AND DENSITY

Area (sq km)	56,600*
Population (census results)	
22 November 1981	2,719,567
19 November 2010	
Males	3,009,095
Females	3,182,060
Total	6,191,155
Density (per sq km) at 2010 census	109.4

* 21,853 sq miles.

POPULATION BY AGE AND SEX
(at 2010 census)

	Males	Females	Total
0–14	1,329,502	1,271,195	2,600,697
15–64	1,581,289	1,760,474	3,341,763
65 and over	98,304	150,391	248,695
Total	3,009,095	3,182,060	6,191,155

Ethnic Groups (percentage of total, 1995): Kabré 23.7; Ewe 21.9; Kabiyé 12.9; Watchi 10.1; Guin 6.0; Tem 6.0; Mobamba 4.9; Gourmantché 3.9; Lamba 3.2; Ncam 2.4; Fon 1.2; Adja 0.9; Others 2.9 (Source: La Francophonie).

ADMINISTRATIVE DIVISIONS
(2010 census)

Region	Area (sq km)	Population	Density (per sq km)	Principal city
Centrale	13,317	617,871	46.4	Sokodé
Kara	11,738	769,940	65.6	Kara
Maritime	6,100	2,599,955	426.2	Lomé
Plateaux	16,975	1,375,165	81.0	Atakpamé
Savanes	8,470	828,224	97.8	Dapaong
Total	56,600	6,191,155	109.4	

PRINCIPAL TOWNS
(at 2010 census)

Lomé (capital)	837,437	Atakpamé	69,261
Sokodé	95,070	Dapaong	58,071
Kara	94,878	Tsevie	54,474
Kpalimé	75,084		

BIRTHS AND DEATHS
(annual averages, UN estimates)

	1995–2000	2000–05	2005–10
Birth rate (per 1,000)	38.5	35.9	33.2
Death rate (per 1,000)	12.3	11.7	11.3

Source: UN, *World Population Prospects: The 2010 Revision*.

Life expectancy (years at birth): 56.6 (males 55.1; females 58.1) in 2010 (Source: World Bank, World Development Indicators database).

ECONOMICALLY ACTIVE POPULATION
(census of 22 November 1981)

	Males	Females	Total
Agriculture, hunting, forestry and fishing	324,870	254,491	579,361
Mining and quarrying	2,781	91	2,872
Manufacturing	29,307	25,065	54,372
Electricity, gas and water	2,107	96	2,203
Construction	20,847	301	21,148
Trade, restaurants and hotels	17,427	87,415	104,842
Transport, storage and communications	20,337	529	20,866
Financing, insurance, real estate and business services	1,650	413	2,063
Community, social and personal services	50,750	12,859	63,609
Sub-total	470,076	381,260	851,336
Activities not adequately defined	14,607	6,346	20,953
Total employed	484,683	387,606	872,289
Unemployed	21,666	7,588	29,254
Total labour force	506,349	395,194	901,543

Mid-2012 (estimates in '000): Agriculture, etc. 1,326; Total labour force 2,543 (Source: FAO).

Health and Welfare

KEY INDICATORS

Total fertility rate (children per woman, 2010)	4.1
Under-5 mortality rate (per 1,000 live births, 2010)	103
HIV/AIDS (% of persons aged 15–49, 2009)	3.2
Physicians (per 1,000 head, 2008)	0.05
Hospital beds (per 1,000 head, 2005)	0.9
Health expenditure (2009): US $ per head (PPP)	74
Health expenditure (2009): % of GDP	7.4
Health expenditure (2009): public (% of total)	43.0
Access to water (% of persons, 2010)	61
Access to sanitation (% of persons, 2010)	13
Total carbon dioxide emissions ('000 metric tons, 2007)	1,419.1
Carbon dioxide emissions per head (metric tons, 2007)	0.2
Human Development Index (2011): ranking	162
Human Development Index (2011): value	0.435

For sources and definitions, see explanatory note on p. vi.

Agriculture

PRINCIPAL CROPS
('000 metric tons)

	2008	2009	2010
Rice, paddy	85.5	121.3	110.1
Maize	590.1	651.7	638.1
Millet	47.4	49.1	51.3
Sorghum	211.3	237.7	244.7
Cassava (Manioc)	795.4	895.7	908.8
Taro (Cocoyam)	17.7	19.5	20.2
Yams	648.2	704.4	710.4
Beans, dry	67.3	72.4	76.2
Groundnuts, with shell	42.6	44.5	46.5
Coconuts	15.2*	12.8*	13.4†

—continued	2008	2009	2010
Oil palm fruit†	125	125	125
Seed cotton†	32.5	29.0	33.7
Bananas†	19.5	21.6	24.3
Oranges†	13.5	15.0	13.9
Coffee, green*	8.3	12.2	15.0
Cocoa beans*	111.0	105.0	101.5

* Unofficial figure(s).
† FAO estimate(s).

Aggregate production ('000 metric tons, may include official, semi-official or estimated data): Total cereals 935 in 2008, 1,061 in 2009, 1,046 in 2010; Total roots and tubers 1,466 in 2008, 1,624 in 2009, 1,645 in 2010; Total vegetables (incl. melons) 143 in 2008, 114 in 2009, 149 in 2010; Total fruits (excl. melons) 53 in 2008, 59 in 2009, 63 in 2010.

Source: FAO.

LIVESTOCK
('000 head, year ending September, FAO estimates)

	2008	2009	2010
Cattle	366	378	390
Sheep	2,002	2,054	2,108
Pigs	582	612	646
Goats	1,508	1,517	1,526
Horses	2	2	2
Asses	3	3	3
Chickens	15,300	19,800	21,650

Source: FAO.

LIVESTOCK PRODUCTS
('000 metric tons, FAO estimates)

	2008	2009	2010
Cattle meat	8.5	8.5	8.5
Sheep meat	4.4	4.5	4.5
Goat meat	3.8	3.8	3.8
Pig meat	9.0	9.4	9.4
Chicken meat	20.1	26.0	28.4
Game meat	5.1	5.4	5.8
Cows' milk	9.9	10.2	10.5
Hen eggs	8.7	9.3	9.4

Source: FAO.

Forestry

ROUNDWOOD REMOVALS
('000 cubic metres, excluding bark)

	2003	2004	2005
Sawlogs, veneer logs and logs for sleepers	43	44	86
Other industrial wood	191	210	80
Fuel wood	5,653	4,424	4,424*
Total	5,887	4,678	4,590

* FAO estimate.

2006–11: Production assumed to be unchanged from 2005 (FAO estimates).

Source: FAO.

Fishing

('000 metric tons, live weight)

	2008	2009	2010
Capture	23.5	27.0	27.5
Tilapias	3.5	3.5	3.5
Other freshwater fishes	1.5	1.5	1.5
West African ilisha	0.8	1.0	1.3
Bigeye grunt	1.7	2.4	1.4
Round sardinella	1.8	2.4	2.7
European anchovy	2.7	2.7	5.1
Atlantic bonito	1.2	2.0	0.3
Jack and horse mackerels	0.5	n.a.	—
Jacks, crevalles	3.3	3.7	4.4
Aquaculture	0.1	0.1	0.1
Total catch	23.6	27.1	27.6

Source: FAO.

Mining

('000 metric tons unless otherwise indicated)

	2008	2009	2010
Diamonds (carats)	8,787	125	96
Limestone	1,824	1,704	1,700
Phosphate rock (gross weight)	842	726	720
Phosphate content	303	260	260

Source: US Geological Survey.

Industry

SELECTED PRODUCTS
('000 metric tons unless otherwise indicated)

	2007	2008	2009
Palm oil	7.0*	7.5†	7.8†
Cement	469	360	283
Electric energy (million kWh)	196	123	126

* Unofficial figure.
† FAO estimate.

Palm oil (FAO estimate): 7.4 in 2010.

Sources: FAO; US Geological Survey; UN Industrial Commodity Statistics Database.

Finance

CURRENCY AND EXCHANGE RATES

Monetary Units

100 centimes = 1 franc de la Communauté Financière Africaine (CFA).

Sterling, Dollar and Euro Equivalents (31 May 2012)

£1 sterling = 819.959 francs CFA;
US $1 = 528.870 francs CFA;
€1 = 655.957 francs CFA;
10,000 francs CFA = £12.20 = $18.90 = €15.24.

Average Exchange Rate (francs CFA per US $)

2009 472.19
2010 495.28
2011 471.87

Note: An exchange rate of 1 French franc = 50 francs CFA, established in 1948, remained in force until January 1994, when the CFA franc was devalued by 50%, with the exchange rate adjusted to 1 French franc = 100 francs CFA. This relationship to French currency remained in effect with the introduction of the euro on 1 January 1999. From that date, accordingly, a fixed exchange rate of €1 = 655.957 francs CFA has been in operation.

BUDGET
('000 million francs CFA)

Revenue*	2009	2010	2011†
Tax revenue	229.0	246.6	268.8
Tax administration	105.7	113.4	118.1
Customs administration	123.3	133.2	150.7
Non-tax revenue	23.4	50.2	51.0
Total	252.4	296.9	319.8

Expenditure‡	2009	2010	2011†
Current expenditure	235.0	230.8	292.5
Salaries and wages	94.2	82.6	98.7
Goods and services	64.5	59.5	70.6
Transfers and subsidies	59.2	69.4	109.2
Capital expenditure	82.3	123.6	150.7
Externally financed	44.4	77.3	83.0
Total‡	317.3	354.4	443.3

* Excluding grants received ('000 million francs CFA): 22.8 in 2009; 32.2 in 2010; 57.3 in 2011 (projection).

† Projections.

‡ Including lending minus repayments.

Source: IMF, *Togo: 2011 Article IV Consultation and Sixth Review Under the Extended Credit Facility Arrangement—Staff Report; Public Information Notice and Press Release on the Executive Board Discussion; and Statement by the Executive Director for Togo* (August 2011).

INTERNATIONAL RESERVES
(excluding gold, US $ million at 31 December)

	2009	2010	2011
IMF special drawing rights	92.9	91.4	91.0
Reserve position in IMF	0.5	0.6	0.7
Foreign exchange	609.8	622.9	682.6
Total	703.2	714.9	774.3

Source: IMF, *International Financial Statistics*.

MONEY SUPPLY
('000 million francs CFA at 31 December)

	2009	2010	2011
Currency outside banks	140.3	183.3	193.8
Demand deposits at deposit money banks	224.5	227.4	293.1
Total money (incl. others)	372.9	419.4	497.8

Source: IMF, *International Financial Statistics*.

COST OF LIVING
(Consumer Price Index; base: 2000 = 100)

	2008	2009	2010
Food, beverages and tobacco	138.3	141.7	150.9
Clothing	110.2	109.4	110.2
Housing, water, electricity and gas	121.3	124.9	124.8
All items (incl. others)	127.5	130.0	134.1

2011: Food 153.8; All items (incl. others) 139.0.

Source: ILO.

NATIONAL ACCOUNTS
(million francs CFA at current prices)

Expenditure on the Gross Domestic Product

	2008	2009	2010
Government final consumption expenditure	190,304	211,456	190,229
Private final consumption expenditure	1,215,199	1,236,263	1,338,858
Changes in inventories	47,379	30,083	13,370
Gross fixed capital formation	203,294	248,678	283,250
Total domestic expenditure	1,656,176	1,726,480	1,825,707
Exports of goods and services	508,641	565,007	609,191
Less Imports of goods and services	746,288	797,938	857,013
GDP in purchasers' values	1,418,529	1,493,550	1,577,885

Gross Domestic Product by Economic Activity

	2008	2009	2010
Agriculture, hunting, forestry and fishing	578,603	639,378	642,436
Mining and quarrying	59,114	48,187	41,247
Manufacturing	120,089	118,087	122,733
Electricity, gas and water	38,861	38,937	43,700
Construction	39,382	33,508	53,711
Wholesale and retail trade, restaurants and hotels	131,060	116,032	139,745
Transport and communications	73,285	78,626	91,546
Finance and insurance, real estate and business services	128,519	128,228	147,417
Public administration and defence	103,204	138,932	120,362
Other services	28,653	29,704	30,813
Sub-total	1,300,770	1,369,619	1,433,710
Less Imputed bank service charge.	25,482	26,783	28,412
Indirect taxes, less subsidies	143,240	150,714	172,586
GDP in purchasers' values	1,418,529	1,493,550	1,577,885

Source: African Development Bank.

BALANCE OF PAYMENTS
(US $ million)

	2007	2008	2009
Exports of goods f.o.b.	676.9	852.6	903.0
Imports of goods f.o.b.	–1,072.0	–1,307.2	–1,315.2
Trade balance	–395.1	–454.6	–412.1
Exports of services	236.0	283.1	293.6
Imports of services	–305.5	–359.2	–374.7
Balance on goods and services	–464.5	–530.7	–493.3
Other income received	61.3	81.1	68.4
Other income paid	–91.5	–93.4	–87.4
Balance on goods, services and income	–494.8	–543.1	–512.3
Current transfers received	328.5	385.2	412.9
Current transfers paid	–49.5	–61.4	–77.2
Current balance	–215.8	–219.2	–176.7
Capital account (net)	73.3	655.8	135.2
Direct investment abroad	0.7	13.2	–37.4
Direct investment from abroad	49.2	23.9	48.5
Portfolio investment assets	13.0	–6.8	–1.4
Portfolio investment liabilities	6.3	18.9	–29.2
Financial derivatives (net)	–0.1	—	0.1
Other investment assets	1.1	28.4	–176.8
Other investment liabilities	80.4	–824.4	282.6
Net errors and omissions	16.6	8.0	14.1
Overall balance	24.7	–302.2	59.0

Source: IMF, International Financial Statistics.

External Trade

PRINCIPAL COMMODITIES
(US $ million)

Imports c.i.f.	2004	2005	2007*
Food and live animals	53.2	62.1	83.6
Fish, crustaceans and molluscs and preparations thereof	4.9	8.6	7.8
Fish, fresh, chilled or frozen	4.0	7.5	5.9
Fish, frozen, excl. fillets	3.9	7.2	5.7
Cereals and cereal preparations	26.4	32.7	40.9
Wheat and meslin, unmilled	17.0	21.0	21.8
Mineral fuels, lubricants, etc.	128.2	171.8	212.8
Petroleum products, refined	127.1	170.4	210.3
Animal and vegetable oils, fats and waxes	14.2	10.5	7.6
Chemicals and related products	53.8	47.8	71.5
Medicinal and pharmaceutical products	24.0	30.4	48.6
Basic manufactures	142.8	136.2	190.2

Imports c.i.f.—*continued*	2004	2005	2007*
Textile yarn, fabrics, made-up articles and related products	27.9	26.6	45.5
Cotton fabrics, woven†	11.5	12.6	24.1
Other woven fabrics, 85% plus of cotton, bleached, etc., finished	10.2	10.5	17.3
Non-metallic mineral manufactures	46.5	44.3	74.5
Lime, cement and fabricated construction materials	41.3	39.1	66.4
Cement	39.5	37.3	63.7
Iron and steel	45.4	41.0	37.4
Iron and steel bars, rods, shapes and sections	25.4	23.3	18.2
Machinery and transport equipment	77.1	95.0	111.2
Telecommunications, sound recording and reproducing equipment	6.8	19.2	24.8
Telecommunication equipment, parts and accessories	3.5	16.4	20.9
Road vehicles	35.7	35.1	37.1
Passenger motor vehicles (excl. buses)	11.9	11.2	18.4
Miscellaneous manufactured articles	39.2	35.9	66.7
Total (incl. others)	557.8	592.6	787.1

Exports f.o.b.	2004	2005	2007*
Food and live animals	74.6	62.6	26.7
Cereals and cereal preparations	9.0	8.5	4.5
Coffee, tea, cocoa, spices, and manufactures thereof	28.1	24.8	9.1
Coffee, not roasted; coffee husks and skins	2.8	4.3	3.7
Crude materials, inedible, except fuels	112.7	70.1	61.7
Textile fibres and their waste‡	60.4	31.1	25.5
Cotton	59.6	30.0	25.0
Raw cotton, excl. linters, not carded or combed	49.0	26.6	25.0
Cotton, carded or combed	10.4	3.3	0.0
Crude fertilizers and crude minerals	48.3	35.9	31.4
Crude fertilizers and crude minerals (unground)	48.1	34.9	31.4
Basic manufactures	150.8	141.8	163.7
Non-metallic mineral manufactures	99.1	98.8	122.7
Cement	98.2	98.6	122.6
Iron and steel	41.3	32.4	35.1
Iron and steel bars, rods, shapes and sections	27.7	14.9	14.8
Machinery and transport equipment	5.1	6.8	1.5
Total (incl. others)	389.6	359.9	280.0

* Data for 2006 not available.

† Excluding narrow or special fabrics.

‡ Excluding wool tops and wastes in yarn.

2010 (US $ million): *Imports:* Food and live animals 128.0; Mineral fuels and lubricants 137.7; Animal and vegetable oils, fats and waxes 7.6; Chemicals and related products 112.1; Basic manufactures 231.3; Machinery and transport equipment 229.9; Miscellaneous manufactured articles 95.9; Total (incl. others) 989.5. *Exports:* Food and live animals 52.2; Crude materials, inedible, except fuels 171.9; Basic manufactures 178.0; Machinery and transport equipment 33.4; Total (incl. others) 643.3.

Source: UN, *International Trade Statistics Yearbook*.

PRINCIPAL TRADING PARTNERS

(US $ million)

Imports c.i.f.	2004	2005	2007*
Belgium	26.9	23.2	29.5
Benin	14.8	12.0	9.9
Brazil	14.0	16.1	15.5
Canada	7.4	9.6	10.0
China, People's Repub.	46.5	78.0	124.0
Côte d'Ivoire	33.8	38.3	20.6
France (incl. Monaco)	108.7	104.3	151.1
Germany	18.3	17.3	15.6
Ghana	9.8	8.0	28.4
Hong Kong	14.3	12.1	4.1
India	9.8	14.0	16.6
Indonesia	11.5	5.8	21.4
Italy	20.8	26.4	17.5
Japan	9.1	10.8	13.7
Netherlands	18.7	23.4	87.4
Nigeria	6.3	4.9	12.0
Saudi Arabia	15.0	4.7	0.5
Senegal	4.9	4.6	6.4
South Africa	8.0	11.2	23.6
Spain	16.0	25.0	16.5
Ukraine	12.4	7.6	8.8
United Kingdom	11.4	12.1	6.5
USA	13.5	6.9	33.4
Total (incl. others)	557.8	592.6	787.1

Exports f.o.b.	2004	2005	2007*
Australia	6.5	3.4	0.0
Belgium	10.5	3.2	2.3
Benin	47.5	41.6	30.5
Brazil	4.3	6.3	2.1
Burkina Faso	50.9	66.3	27.3
China, People's Repub.	17.3	7.9	5.1
Côte d'Ivoire	2.6	6.2	9.3
France (incl. Monaco)	15.5	5.0	1.7
Germany	2.0	7.5	0.8
Ghana	46.2	73.0	16.4
India	15.6	21.2	27.4
Indonesia	8.0	1.3	1.9
Italy	3.2	3.1	1.5
Mali	43.5	26.5	19.9
Morocco	3.0	6.5	1.4
Netherlands	15.4	3.9	1.4
New Zealand	7.5	3.1	1.8
Niger	13.1	10.8	35.6
Nigeria	7.3	14.7	0.7
Pakistan	3.5	4.8	0.0
Senegal	14.7	3.2	5.4
Thailand	3.7	1.4	6.5
USA	1.5	4.1	1.6
Total (incl. others)	389.6	359.9	280.0

* Data for 2006 not available.

2010 (US $ million): *Imports:* Belgium 67.3; Benin 5.8; Brazil 10.3; Canada 8.3; China, People's Repub. 162.0; Côte d'Ivoire 32.1; France (incl. Monaco) 174.7; Germany 28.0; Ghana 34.8; India 51.8; Indonesia 20.0; Italy 23.0; Japan 20.9; Malaysia 15.2; Netherlands 37.1; Nigeria 10.9; Senegal 11.2; South Africa 13.1; Spain 12.6; Thailand 40.3; Turkey 13.5; United Arab Emirates 9.4; United Kingdom 8.9; USA 34.2; Total (incl. others) 989.5. *Exports:* Bangladesh 12.1; Benin 89.3; Burkina Faso 76.8; Cameroon 5.2; Chad 4.0; China, People's Repub. 56.6; Côte d'Ivoire 23.7; France (incl. Monaco) 5.5; Ghana 65.9; India 18.2; Indonesia 22.0; Lebanon 8.8; Malaysia 6.0; Mali 20.5; Niger 47.2; Nigeria 34.0; Philippines 7.6; Senegal 5.7; Spain 18.0; Sudan 12.5; Thailand 11.8; Switzerland-Liechtenstein 13.0; Viet Nam 8.9; Total (incl. others) 643.3.

Source: UN, *International Trade Statistics Yearbook*.

Transport

RAILWAYS
(traffic)

	1997	1998	1999
Passengers carried ('000)	152.0	35.0	4.4
Freight carried ('000 metric tons)	250	759	1,090
Passenger-km (million)	12.7	3.4	0.4
Freight ton-km (million)	28.8	70.6	92.4

Source: Société Nationale des Chemins de Fer du Togo, Lomé.

ROAD TRAFFIC
(motor vehicles registered at 31 December)

	1994	1995	1996*
Passenger cars	67,936	74,662	79,200
Buses and coaches	529	547	580
Goods vehicles	31,457	32,514	33,660
Tractors (road)	1,466	1,544	1,620
Motorcycles and scooters	39,019	52,902	59,000

* Estimates.

2007: Passenger cars 10,611; Buses and coaches 193; Lorries and vans 2,219; Motorcycles and scooters 34,246.

Source: IRF, *World Road Statistics*.

SHIPPING

Merchant Fleet
(registered at 31 December)

	2007	2008	2009
Number of vessels	28	50	86
Total displacement ('000 grt)	19.3	74.9	177.8

Source: IHS Fairplay, *World Fleet Statistics*.

International Sea-borne Freight Traffic
('000 metric tons)

Port Lomé	1997	1998	1999
Goods loaded	432.4	794.6	1,021.4
Goods unloaded	1,913.9	1,912.9	1,812.4

Source: Port Autonome de Lomé.

CIVIL AVIATION
(traffic on scheduled services)*

	1999	2000	2001
Kilometres flown (million)	3	3	1
Passengers carried ('000)	84	77	46
Passenger-km (million)	235	216	130
Total ton-km (million)	36	32	19

* Including an apportionment of the traffic of Air Afrique.

Source: UN, *Statistical Yearbook*.

Tourism

FOREIGN TOURIST ARRIVALS*

	2007	2008	2009
Belgium, Luxembourg and the Netherlands	851	708	1,515
Benin	7,037	5,465	12,520
Burkina Faso, Mali and Niger	6,489	5,104	10,258
Côte d'Ivoire	5,348	3,607	6,780
France	18,114	13,480	28,229
Germany	1,115	1,305	3,034
Ghana	2,090	1,795	3,800
Italy	1,167	723	2,286
Nigeria	3,445	3,303	6,873
United Kingdom	1,030	747	1,073
USA	2,200	1,480	4,502
Total (incl. others)	86,165	73,982	149,945

* Arrivals at hotels and similar establishments, by country of residence.

2010: Total tourist arrivals 202,000.

Receipts from tourism (US $ million, excl. passenger transport): 68 in 2009; 66 in 2010.

Source: World Tourism Organization.

Communications Media

	2009	2010	2010
Telephones ('000 main lines in use)	178.7	213.6	240.0
Mobile cellular telephones ('000 subscribers)	2,187.3	2,452.4	3,104.8
Internet subscribers ('000)	59.6	60.6	n.a.
Broadband subscribers ('000)	2.7	3.8	4.8

Television receivers ('000 in use): 150 in 2000.

Radio receivers ('000 in use): 940 in 1997.

Daily newspapers: 1 (average circulation 10,000 copies) in 1999; 1 (average circulation 10,000 copies) in 2000; 1 in 2004.

Book production (number of titles): 5 in 1998.

Personal computers: 185,000 (30.9 per 1,000 persons) in 2005.

Sources: International Telecommunication Union; UNESCO, *Statistical Yearbook*; UNESCO Institute for Statistics; UN, *Statistical Yearbook*.

Education

(2009/10 unless otherwise indicated)

			Students		
	Institutions*	Teachers	Males	Females	Total
Pre-primary	319*	1,646	21,206	21,684	42,890
Primary	4,701*	31,712	677,250	609,403	1,286,653
Secondary	n.a.	11,518†	n.a.	n.a.	482,877
Tertiary†	n.a.	470	n.a.	n.a.	32,502

* 1999/2000 figure.
† 2006/07 figures.

Source: UNESCO Institute for Statistics.

Pupil-teacher ratio (primary education, UNESCO estimate): 40.6 in 2009/10 (Source: UNESCO Institute for Statistics).

Adult literacy rate (UNESCO estimates): 57.1% (males 71.2%; females 43.6%) in 2009 (Source: UNESCO Institute for Statistics).

Directory

The Constitution

The Constitution that was approved in a national referendum on 27 September 1992, and subsequently amended, defines the rights, freedoms and obligations of Togolese citizens, and defines the separation of powers among the executive, legislative and judicial organs of state.

Executive power is vested in the President of the Republic, who is elected, by direct universal adult suffrage, with a five-year mandate. The legislature, the Assemblée nationale, is similarly elected for a period of five years, its 81 members being directly elected by universal suffrage. The President of the Republic appoints a Prime Minister who is able to command a majority in the legislature, and the Prime Minister, in consultation with the President, appoints other government ministers. A Constitutional Court is designated as the highest court of jurisdiction in constitutional matters.

Constitutional amendments, approved by the Assemblée nationale in late December 2002, removed the previous restriction limiting the President to serving two terms of office; reduced the minimum age for presidential candidates from 45 to 35 years; and required presidential candidates holding dual or multiple citizenships to renounce their non-Togolese nationality or nationalities.

The Government

HEAD OF STATE

President: Faure Essozimna Gnassingbé (inaugurated 4 May 2005; re-elected 4 March 2010).

COUNCIL OF MINISTERS
(September 2012)

The Government is formed by the Union pour la République and the Union des Forces de Changement.

Prime Minister: Arthème Kwesi Séléagodji Ahoomey-Zunu.

Minister of State, Minister of Primary and Secondary Education and Literacy: Solitoki Magnim Esso.

Minister of State, Minister of Foreign Affairs and Co-operation: Elliott Ohin.

Minister of the Economy and Finance: Adji Otéth Ayassor.

Minister of Basic Development, Handicrafts, Youth and Youth Employment: Victoire Sidémeho Tomégah-Dogbé.

Minister of Health: Charles Kondi Agba.

Minister of Higher Education and Research: Octave Nicoué Broohm.

Minister of Territorial Administration, Decentralization and Local Communities: Gilbert Bawara.

Keeper of the Seals, Minister of Justice: Tchitchao Tchalim.

Minister of Transport: Dammipi Noupokou.

Minister of Labour, Employment and Social Security: Yacoubou Koumadjo Hamadou.

Minister of Public Works: Ninsao Gnofam.

Minister of Technical Education and Professional Training: Hamadou Brim Bouraïma-Diabacte.

Minister of Post and Telecommunications: Cina Lawson.

Minister of Trade and the Promotion of the Private Sector: Bernadette Essozimna Leguezim-Balouki.

Minister of Industry, the Free Zone and Technological Innovation: François Agbéviadé Galley.

Minister of Security and Civil Protection: Col Damehane Yark.

Minister of the Environment and Forest Resources: Dédé Ahoéfa Ekoué.

Minister of Tourism: Padumhèkou Christophe Tchao.

Minister of Social Affairs and National Solidarity: Afi Ntifa Amenyo.

Minister of Human Rights, the Consolidation of Democracy and Civic Education: Leonardina Rita Doris Wilson-de Souza.

Minister of the Civil Service and Administrative Reform: Kokou Dzifa Adjeoda.

Minister of Sport and Leisure: Bakalawa Fofana.

Minister to the President of the Republic, responsible for Planning, Development and Land Settlement: Mawussi Djossou Semodji.

Minister of the Promotion of Women: Patricia Dagban-Zonvidé.

Minister of Agriculture, Stockbreeding and Fisheries: Col Ouro Koura Agadazi.

Minister of Town Planning and Housing: Komlan Nunyabu.

Minister of Arts and Culture: Fiatuwo Kwadjo Sséssénou.

Minister of Communication: Djimon Oré.

Minister of Water, Sanitation and Rural Water Supply: Bissoune Nabagou.

Minister-delegate to the Minister of Agriculture, Stockbreeding and Fisheries, responsible for Rural Infrastructure: Gourdigou Kolani.

MINISTRIES

Office of the President: Palais Présidentiel, ave de la Marina, Lomé; tel. 22-21-27-01; fax 22-21-18-97; e-mail presidence@republicoftogo.com; internet www.presidencetogo.com.

Office of the Prime Minister: Palais de la Primature, BP 1161, Lomé; tel. 22-21-15-64; fax 22-21-37-53; internet www.primature.gouv.tg.

Ministry of Agriculture, Stockbreeding and Fisheries: 5 ave de Duisburg, BP 385, Lomé; tel. 22-20-40-20; fax 22-20-44-99; internet ministereagriculture.com.

Ministry of Arts and Culture: Lomé.

Ministry of Basic Development, Handicrafts, Youth and Youth Employment: Lomé.

Ministry of the Civil Service and Administrative Reform: angle ave de la Marina et rue Kpalimé, BP 372, Lomé; tel. 22-21-41-83; fax 22-22-56-85; internet fonctionpubliquetogo.com.

Ministry of Communication: BP 40, Lomé; tel. 22-21-29-30; fax 22-21-43-80; e-mail info@republicoftogo.com.

Ministry of the Economy and Finance: CASEF, ave Sarakawa, BP 387, Lomé; tel. 22-21-35-54; fax 22-21-09-05; e-mail eco@republicoftogo.com; internet www.finances.gouv.tg.

Ministry of the Environment and Forest Resources: Lomé; tel. 22-21-56-58; fax 22-21-03-33.

Ministry of Foreign Affairs and Co-operation: pl. du Monument aux Morts, ave Georges Pompidou, BP 900, Lomé; tel. 22-21-29-10; fax 22-21-39-74; e-mail maeirtgce@yahoo.fr; internet www.diplomatie.gouv.tg.

Ministry of Health: rue Branly, BP 386, Lomé; tel. 22-21-35-24; fax 22-22-20-73; internet ministeresante.com.

Ministry of Higher Education and Research: rue Col de Roux, BP 12175, Lomé; tel. 22-22-09-83; fax 22-22-07-83; internet www.ministereeducation.org.

Ministry of Human Rights, the Consolidation of Democracy and Civic Education: BP 1325, Lomé; tel. 22-22-60-63; fax 22-20-07-74; e-mail mdhdcab@yahoo.fr.

Ministry of Industry, the Free Zone and Technological Innovation: Lomé.

Ministry of Justice: ave de la Marina, rue Colonel de Roux, Lomé; tel. 22-21-26-53; fax 22-22-29-06; internet ministerejustice.com.

Ministry of Labour, Employment and Social Security: Lomé.

Ministry of Mines and Energy: Lomé.

Ministry of Post and Telecommunications: ave de Sarakawa, BP 389, Lomé; tel. 22-23-14-00; fax 22-21-68-12; e-mail eco@republicoftogo.com; internet ministeretelecom.com.

Ministry of Primary and Secondary Education and Literacy: BP 398, Lomé; tel. 22-21-20-97; fax 22-21-89-34.

Ministry of the Promotion of Women: Lomé.

Ministry of Public Works: Lomé.

Ministry of Security and Civil Protection: rue Albert Sarraut, Lomé; tel. 22-22-57-12; fax 22-22-61-50; e-mail info@republicoftogo.com.

Ministry of Social Affairs and National Solidarity: Lomé.

Ministry of Sport and Leisure: BP 40, Lomé; tel. 22-21-22-47; fax 22-22-42-28.

Ministry of Technical Education and Professional Training: Lomé.

Ministry of Territorial Administration, Decentralization and Local Communities: Lomé.

Ministry of Tourism: Lomé.

Ministry of Town Planning and Housing: Lomé.

Ministry of Trade and the Promotion of the Private Sector: 1 ave de Sarakawa, face au Monument aux Morts, BP 383, Lomé; tel.

22-21-20-25; fax 22-21-05-72; e-mail ministereducommercetogo@yahoo.fr.

Ministry of Transport: Lomé.

Ministry of Water, Sanitation and Rural Water Supply: Lomé.

President and Legislature

PRESIDENT

Presidential Election, 4 March 2010

Candidate	Valid votes	% of valid votes
Faure Gnassingbé (RPT)	1,242,409	60.89
Jean-Pierre Fabre (UFC)	692,554	33.94
Yawovi Agboyibo (CAR)	60,370	2.96
Agbéyomé Kodjo (OBUTS)	17,393	0.85
Brigitte Kafui Adjamagbo-Johnson (CDPA—BT)	13,452	0.66
Bassabi Kagbara (PDP)	8,341	0.41
Jean Nicolas Messan Lawson (PRR)	6,027	0.30
Total	2,040,546	100.00

LEGISLATURE

Assemblée nationale

Palais des Congrès, BP 327, Lomé; tel. 22-22-57-91; fax 22-22-11-68; e-mail assemblee.nationale@syfed.tg.refer.org.

President: El Hadj ABASS BONFOH.

General Election, 14 October 2007

Party	Votes	% of votes	Seats
Rassemblement du Peuple Togolais (RPT)	922,636	32.71	50
Union des Forces de Changement (UFC)	867,507	30.75	27
Comité d'Action pour le Renouveau (CAR)	192,218	6.81	4
Others	838,484	29.72	—
Total	2,820,845	100.00	81

Election Commission

Commission Électorale Nationale Indépendante (CENI): 198 rue des Echis, BP 7005, Lomé; tel. 22-22-29-51; fax 22-22-39-61; e-mail info@cenitogo.tg; internet www.cenitogo.tg; 19 mems; Pres. ISSIFOU TAFFA TABIOU.

Political Organizations

Alliance Nationale pour le Changement (ANC): Lomé; f. 2010; Leader JEAN-PIERRE FABRE; Sec.-Gen. JEAN-CLAUDE CODJO DÉLAVA.

Comité d'Action pour le Renouveau (CAR): 58 ave du 24 janvier, BP06, Lomé; tel. 22-22-05-66; fax 22-21-62-54; e-mail yagboyibo@bibway.com; moderately conservative; Pres. DODJI APEVON; 251,349 mems (Dec. 1999).

Convention Démocratique des Peuples Africains—Branche Togolaise (CDPA—BT): 5 rue Djidjollé, BP 13963, Lomé; tel. and fax 22-25-38-46; e-mail cdpa-bt.cdpa-bt@orange.fr; internet www.cdpa-bt.net; f. 1991; socialist; Gen. Sec. LÉOPOLD GNININVI; First Sec. Prof. EMMANUEL Y. GU-KONU.

Convergence Patriotique Panafricaine (CPP): BP 12703, Lomé; tel. 22-21-58-43; f. 1999; Pres. EDEM KODJO; First Vice-Pres. JEAN-LUCIEN SAVI DE TOVÉ.

Organisation pour Bâtir dans l'Union un Togo Solidaire (OBUTS): Quartier Djidjole, 686 rue 19 Tosti, Lomé; tel. 22-26-93-41; internet www.obuts.org; f. 2008; Pres. AGBÉYOMÉ KODJO; Sec.-Gen. YAWOVI BOESSI.

Parti Démocratique Panafricain (PDP): Lomé; f. 2005; Pres. BASSABI KAGBARA.

Parti du Renouveau et de la Rédemption (PRR): Lomé; Pres. JEAN NICOLAS MESSAN LAWSON.

Parti des Travailleurs (PT): 49 ave de Calais, BP 13974, Nyékonakpoé, Lomé; tel. 90-13-65-54 (mobile); socialist; Co-ordinating Sec. CLAUDE AMEGANVI.

Union des Forces de Changement (UFC): 59 rue Koudadzé, Lom-Nava, BP 62168, Lomé; tel. and fax 22-31-01-70; e-mail contact-togo@ufctogo.com; internet www.ufctogo.com; f. 1992; social-democratic; Pres. GILCHRIST OLYMPIO; First Vice-Pres. HAMADOU BRIM BOURAÏMA-DIABACTE; Sec.-Gen. Dr PIERRE JIMONGOU.

Union des Libéraux Indépendants (ULI): f. 1993 to succeed Union des Démocrates pour le Renouveau; Leader KWAMI MENSAN JACQUES AMOUZOU.

Union pour la République (UNIR): 572 rue Pydal Tokoin Wuiti, BP 1208, Lomé; tel. 22-26-04-95; fax 22-61-00-33; e-mail rpttogo@yahoo.fr; internet www.rpt.tg; f. 1969 as Rassemblement du peuple togolais; sole legal party 1969–91; name changed as above in 2012; Pres. FAURE GNASSINGBÉ; Sec.-Gen. SOLITOKI ESSO.

Diplomatic Representation

EMBASSIES IN TOGO

Brazil: Cité OUA, près de la Primature, BP 916, Lomé; tel. 22-61-56-58; fax 22-61-56-83; e-mail brasembtogo@helim.tg; Ambassador MIGUEL GUSTAVO DE PAIVA TORRES.

China, People's Republic: 1381 rue de l'Entente, BP 2690, Lomé; tel. 22-22-38-56; fax 22-21-40-75; e-mail chinaemb_tg@mfa.gov.cn; Ambassador WANG ZUOFENG.

Congo, Democratic Republic: Lomé; tel. 22-21-51-55; Ambassador LOKOKA IKUKELE BOMOLO.

Egypt: 1163 rue de l'OCAM, BP 8, Lomé; tel. 22-21-24-43; fax 22-21-10-22; Ambassador MORTADA ALI MOHAMED LASHIN.

France: 13 ave du Golfe, BP 337, Lomé; tel. 22-23-46-00; fax 22-23-46-01; e-mail eric.bosc@diplomatie.fr; internet www.ambafrance-tg.org; Ambassador NICOLAS WARNERY.

Gabon: Lomé; tel. 22-22-18-93; fax 22-22-18-92; Ambassador JOSEPH AIMÉ OBIANG NDOUTOUME.

Germany: blvd de la République, BP 1175, Lomé; tel. 22-23-32-32; fax 22-23-32-46; e-mail amballtogo@cafe.tg; internet www.lome.diplo.de; Ambassador ALEXANDER BECKMANN.

Ghana: 38 rue Moyana, Tokoin-Ouest, BP 92, Lomé; tel. 22-21-31-94; fax 22-21-77-36; e-mail ghmfa01@cafe.tg; Ambassador JOHN MAXWELL KWADJO.

Holy See: BP 20790, Lomé; tel. 22-26-03-06; fax 22-26-68-80; e-mail noncia.tg@gmail.com; Apostolic Nuncio MICHAEL AUGUST BLUME (Titular Archbishop of Alessano).

Korea, Democratic People's Republic: Lomé; Ambassador JONK HAK SE.

Libya: Cite OUA, BP 4872, Lomé; tel. 22-61-47-08; fax 22-61-47-10; Ambassador AHMED BALLUZ.

Nigeria: 311 blvd du 13 janvier, BP 1189, Lomé; tel. and fax 22-21-59-76; Ambassador MATHEW SUNDAY ADOLI.

USA: Blvd Eyadema, BP 852, Lomé; tel. 22-61-54-70; fax 22-61-55-01; e-mail RobertsonJJ2@state.gov; internet togo.usembassy.gov; Ambassador ROBERT E. WHITEHEAD.

Judicial System

Justice is administered by the Constitutional Court, the Supreme Court, two Appeal Courts and the Tribunaux de première instance, which hear civil, commercial and criminal cases. There is a labour tribunal and a tribunal for children's rights. In addition, there are two exceptional courts, the Cour de sûreté de l'Etat, which judges crimes against internal and external state security, and the Tribunal spécial chargé de la répression des détournements de deniers publics, which deals with cases of misuse of public funds.

Constitutional Court: BP 1331, Lomé; tel. 22-61-06-40; fax 22-61-05-45; internet www.courconstitutionnelle.tg; f. 1997; seven mems; Pres. ABOUDOU ASSOUMA.

Supreme Court: BP 906, Lomé; tel. 22-21-22-58; f. 1961; consists of three chambers (judicial, administrative and auditing); Chair. ABALO PIGNAKIWÉ PETCHELEBIA; Attorney-General KOUAMI AMADOS-DJOKO.

Audit Court (Cour des Comptes): Lomé; f. 2009; Pres. LALLE TANKPANDJA.

State Attorney: ATARA NDAKENA.

Religion

It is estimated that about 50% of the population follow traditional animist beliefs, some 35% are Christians and 15% are Muslims.

CHRISTIANITY

The Roman Catholic Church

Togo comprises one archdiocese and six dioceses. An estimated 25% of the total population was Roman Catholic.

Bishops' Conference

Conférence Episcopale du Togo, 561 rue Aniko Palako, BP 348, Lomé; tel. 22-21-22-72; fax 22-22-48-08.

statutes approved 1979; Pres. Most Rev. AMBROISE KOTAMBA DJOLIBA (Bishop of Sokodé).

Archbishop of Lomé: Most Rev. DENIS KOMIVI AMUZU-DZAKPAH, Archevêché, 561 rue Aniko Palako, BP 348, Lomé; tel. 22-21-22-72; fax 22-21-02-46; e-mail archlom@yahoo.cfr.

Protestant Churches

There are about 250 mission centres, with a personnel of some 250, affiliated to European and US societies and administered by a Conseil Synodal, presided over by a moderator.

Directorate of Protestant Churches: 1 rue Maréchal Foch, BP 378, Lomé; Moderator Pastor AGBI-AWUME (acting).

Église Evangélique Luthérienne au Togo: POB 80780, Lome; tel. 22-25-23-51; fax 22-25-32-52; e-mail elca_togo@hotmail.com; Pres. Rev. KOFFI GAWU SALLAH HUKPORTI.

Eglise Evangélique Presbytérienne du Togo: 1 rue Tokmake, BP 2, Lomé; tel. 22-21-46-69; fax 22-22-23-63; e-mail eeptbs@laposte.tg; internet www.eept-online.org; Moderator Rev. IMANUEL KOFFI AWANYOH.

Fédération des Evangéliques du Togo: Lomé; Co-ordinator HAPPY AZIADEKEY.

BAHÁ'Í FAITH

Assemblée Spirituelle Nationale: BP 1659, Lomé; tel. 22-21-21-99; e-mail asnbaha@yahoo.fr; Sec. ALLADOUM NGOMNA; 19,002 adherents (2006).

The Press

DAILIES

Forum de la Semaine: BP 81129, Lomé; tel. 99-53-54-55; fax 22-22-09-51; e-mail forumhebdo7@yahoo.fr; internet www.forumdelasemaine.com; Dir JEAN-BAPTISTE K. D. DZILAN.

Liberté: BP 80744, Lomé; tel. 23-36-88-16; fax 22-22-09-55; internet www.libertetg.com; Dir of Publication ZEUS AZIADOUVO; Editorial Dir MÉDARD AMETEPE.

Togo-Presse: BP 891, Lomé; tel. 22-21-53-95; fax 22-22-37-66; internet www.editogo.tg/presse.php; f. 1961; official govt publ; French, Kabiyé and Ewe; political, economic and cultural; circ. 8,000.

PERIODICALS

L'Alternative: BP 4132, Lomé; tel. 90-09-41-33 (mobile); fax 22-51-86-94; e-mail info@lalternative-togo.com; internet www.lalternative-togo.com; Dir of Publication FERDINAND MENSAH AYITE; Editor-in-Chief MAXIME DOMEGNI.

Carrefour: 596 rue Ablogame, BP 6125, Lomé; tel. 99-44-45-43 (mobile); f. 1991; pro-opposition; weekly; Dir HOLONOU HOUKPATI.

Cité Magazine: 50 ave Pas de Souza, BP 6275, Lomé; tel. and fax 22-22-67-40; e-mail citemag@cafe.tg; internet www.cafe.tg/citemag; monthly; Editor-in-Chief GAËTAN K. GNATCHIKO.

Le Combat du Peuple: 62 rue Blagogee, BP 4682, Lomé; tel. 90-04-53-83 (mobile); fax 22-22-65-89; f. 1994; pro-opposition weekly; Editor LUCIEN DJOSSOU MESSAN; circ. 3,500 (2000).

Le Courrier du Golfe: rue de l'OCAM, angle rue Sotomarcy, BP 660, Lomé; tel. 22-21-67-92.

Crocodile News: 909 rue Kuévidjin, no 27 Bé-Château, BP 61049, Lomé; tel. 99-46-00-36 (mobile); e-mail crocodilenews@yahoo.fr; internet crocodilenews.net; f. 1993; pro-opposition; weekly; Dir of Publication ASSIONGBON FRANCIS PEDRO AMAZUN; circ. 3,500 (2000).

La Dépêche: BP 20039, Lomé; tel. and fax 22-21-09-32; e-mail ladepeche@hotmail.com; f. 1993; 2 a week; Editor ESSO-WE APPOLINAIRE MÈWÈNAMÈSSÈ; circ. 3,000.

L'Etoile du Matin: S/C Maison du journalisme, Casier no 50, Lomé; e-mail wielfridsewa18@hotmail.com; f. 2000; weekly; Dir WIELFRID SÉWA TCHOUKOULI.

Etudes Togolaises (Revue Togolaise des Sciences): Institut National de la Recherche Scientifique, BP 2240, Lomé; tel. 22-21-01-39; fax 22-21-21-59; e-mail inrs@tg.refer.org; f. 1965; 2 a year; scientific review, mainly anthropology.

L'Exilé: Maison du journalisme, Casier no 28, Lomé; e-mail jexil@hotmail.com; f. 2000; weekly; independent; Editor HIPPOLYTE AGBOH.

Game su/Tev Fema: 125 ave de la Nouvelle Marché, BP 1247, Lomé; tel. 22-21-28-44; f. 1997; monthly; Ewe and Kabiyé; govt publ. for the newly literate; circ. 3,000.

Journal Officiel de la République du Togo (JORT): BP 891, Lomé; tel. 22-21-37-18; fax 22-22-14-89; govt acts, laws, decrees and decisions.

Kyrielle: BP 823, Lomé; tel. 99-48-13-69; fax 90-05-38-35; e-mail kyrielljj@yahoo.fr; f. 1999; monthly; culture, sport; Dir CRÉDO TETTEH; circ. 3,000 (2000).

Libre Togovi: BP 81190, Lomé; tel. 90-04-43-36; e-mail libretogovi@mail.com; 2 a week; pro-democracy, opposed to Govt of fmr Pres. Eyadéma; distributed by the Comité Presse et Communication de la Concertation Nationale de la Société Civile.

La Matinée: Tokoin Nkafu, rue Kpoguédé, BP 30368, Lomé; tel. 22-26-69-02; f. 1999; monthly; Dir KASSÉRÉ PIERRE SABI.

Le Miroir du Peuple: 48 rue Defale, BP 81231, Lomé; tel. 99-46-60-24; e-mail nouveau90@hotmail.com; f. 1998; fmrly Le Nouveau Combat; weekly; independent; Dir ELIAS EDOH HOUNKANLY; circ. 1,000 (2000).

Nouvel Echo: BP 3681, Lomé; tel. 99-47-72-40 (mobile); f. 1997; pro-opposition; weekly; Dir ALPHONSE NEVAME KLU; Editor CLAUDE AMEGANVI.

Nouvel Eclat: Lomé; tel. 22-25-51-60; e-mail charlpass@hotmail.com; f. 2000; weekly; Dir CHARLES PASSOU; circ. 2,500 (2000).

La Nouvelle République: Lomé; tel. 99-45-55-43 (mobile); e-mail nouvelle.republique@caramail.com; f. 1999; Dir WIELFRID SÉWA TCHOUKOULI; circ. 2,500 (2000).

Le Regard: BP 81213, Lomé; tel. 90-04-09-09 (mobile); fax 22-26-13-70; e-mail leregard13@caramail.com; f. 1996; weekly; pro-opposition; supports promotion of human rights; Editor ABASS DURMAN MIKAÏLA; circ. 3,000 (2000).

Le Reporter des Temps Nouveaux: Maison du journalisme, Casier no 22, BP 1800, Lomé; tel. and fax 22-26-18-22; e-mail lereporter39@hotmail.com; f. 1998; weekly; independent; political criticism and analysis; Dir AUGUSTIN AMÉGAH; circ. 3,000 (2000).

Le Scorpion—Akéklé: S/C Maison du journalisme, BP 81213, Lomé; tel. 99-44-43-80 (mobile); fax 22-26-13-70; e-mail lescorpion@webmails.com; f. 1998; opposition weekly; Dir DIDIER AGBLETO; circ. 3,500 (2000).

Le Secteur Privé: angle ave de la Présidence, BP 360, Lomé; tel. 22-21-70-65; fax 22-21-47-30; monthly; publ. by Chambre de Commerce et d'Industrie du Togo.

Le Soleil: Lomé; tel. 90-04-41-97 (mobile); fax 90-04-89-10 (mobile); e-mail lesoleil@francemail.com; f. 1999; weekly; Dir YVES LACLÉ; circ. 2,000 (2000).

Témoin de la Nation: Maison du journalisme, Casier no 48, BP 434, Lomé; tel. 22-21-24-92; f. 2000; weekly; Dir ELIAS EBOH.

Tingo Tingo: 44–50 rue Douka, Kotokoucondji, BP 80419, Lomé; tel. and fax 22-22-17-53; e-mail jtingo-tingo@yahoo.fr; f. 1996; weekly; independent; Editor AUGUSTIN ASIONBO; circ. 3,500 (2000).

Togo-Images: BP 4869, Lomé; tel. 22-21-56-80; f. 1962; monthly series of wall posters depicting recent political, economic and cultural events in Togo; publ. by govt information service; Dir AKOBI BEDOU; circ. 5,000.

Togo-Presse: BP 891, Lomé; tel. 22-21-53-95; fax 22-22-37-66; f. 1962; publ. by Govt in French, Ewe and Kabré; political, economic and cultural affairs; Dir WIYAO DADJA POUWI; circ. 5,000 (2000).

L'Union: Lomé; tel. 22-26-12-10; e-mail letambour@yahoo.fr; Dir of Publication ERIC JOHNSON.

PRESS ASSOCIATION

Syndicat National des Journalistes Indépendants du Togo (SYNJIT): Lomé; f. 2011; Sec.-Gen. MAXIME DOMEGNI.

Union des Journalistes Indépendants du Togo: BP 81213, Lomé; tel. 22-26-13-00; fax 22-21-38-21; e-mail maison-du-journalisme@ids.tg; also operates Maison de Presse; Sec.-Gen. CRÉDO ADJÉ K. TÉTTEH.

NEWS AGENCIES

Agence Togolaise de Presse (ATOP): 35 rue des Medias, BP 2327, Lomé; tel. 22-21-24-90; fax 22-22-28-02; e-mail atop.togo@gmail.com; internet www.atoptogo.blogspot.com; f. 1975; Dir-Gen. CLAUDINE ASSIBA AKAKPO.

Savoir News: Lomé; tel. 23-36-40-58; e-mail info@savoirnews.com; internet www.savoirnews.com.

Publishers

Centre Togolais de Communication Evangélique—Editions Haho (CTCE—Editions Haho): 1 rue Sylvanus Olympio, BP 378, Lomé; tel. 22-21-45-82; fax 22-21-29-67; e-mail ctce_ctce@yahoo.fr; f. 1983; general literature, popular science, poetry, school textbooks, Christian interest; Dir TOMPY KUDZO NAKOU.

Editions Akpagnon: BP 3531, Lomé; tel. and fax 22-22-02-44; e-mail yedogbe@yahoo.fr; f. 1978; general literature and non-fiction; Man. Dir YVES-EMMANUEL DOGBÉ.

Editions de la Rose Bleue: BP 12452, Lomé; tel. 22-22-93-39; fax 22-22-96-69; e-mail dorkenoo_ephrem@yahoo.fr; general literature, poetry; Dir EPHREM SETH DORKENOO.

Les Nouvelles Editions Africaines du Togo (NEA-TOGO): 239 blvd du 13 janvier, BP 4862, Lomé; tel. and fax 22-22-10-19; e-mail neatogo@yahoo.fr; general fiction, non-fiction and textbooks; Dir-Gen. KOKOU A. KALIPE; Editorial Dir TCHOTCHO CHRISTIANE EKUE.

Les Presses de l'Université du Lomé: BP 1515, Lomé; tel. 22-25-48-44; fax 22-25-87-84.

Société Nationale des Editions du Togo (EDITOGO): BP 891, Lomé; tel. 22-21-61-06; f. 1961; govt-owned; general and educational; Pres. BIOSSEY KOKOU TOZOUN; Man. Dir WIYAO DADJA POUWI.

Broadcasting and Communications

TELECOMMUNICATIONS

In early 2012 the Togo telecommunications sector comprised one fixed-line operator and two mobile operators. At the end of 2010 there were 56,446 subscribers to fixed–line telephone services and 2.5m. subscribers to mobile telephone services.

Regulatory Authority

Autorité de Réglementation des Secteurs de Postes et de Télécommunications (ART&P): blvd Léopold Sédar Senghor, Tokoin Tamé Côté Est, S.O.S. Village d'Enfants, BP 358, Lomé; tel. 22-23-63-80; fax 22-23-63-94; e-mail artp@artp.tg; internet www.artp.tg; Dir-Gen. PALOUKI MASSINA.

Service Providers

Moov Togo: 225 blvd du 13 janvier, BP 14511, Lomé; tel. 22-20-13-20; fax 22-20-13-23; e-mail moovcontact@moov.tg; internet www.moov.tg; operates mobile cellular telecommunications in 80 localities; Dir-Gen. DJIBRIL OUATTARA.

Togo Télécom: pl. de la Réconciliation, Quartier Atchante, BP 333, Lomé; tel. 22-21-44-01; fax 22-21-03-73; e-mail contact@togotelecom.tg; internet www.togotelecom.tg; Dir-Gen. PÈTCHÈTIBADI BIKASSAM.

Togo Cellulaire—Togocel: Immeubble CFAO, 219 ave du 24 Janvier, BP 924, Lomé; tel. 22-22-66-11; fax 22-22-59-00; e-mail togocel@togocel.tg; internet www.togocel.tg; f. 2001; provides mobile cellular communications services to more than 70% of the territory of Togo; Dir-Gen. AFFOH ATCHA-DEDJI.

BROADCASTING

Haute Autorité de l'Audiovisuel et de la Communication (HAAC): BP 8697, Lomé; tel. 22-50-16-78; fax 22-50-16-80; e-mail infos@haactogo.tg; internet www.haactogo.tg; Pres. BIOSSEY KOKOU TOZOUN.

Radio

Radiodiffusion du Togo (Internationale)—Radio Lomé: BP 434, Lomé; tel. 22-21-24-93; fax 22-21-36-73; e-mail radiolome@radiolome.tg; internet www.radiolome.tg; f. 1953; state-controlled; radio programmes in French, English and vernacular languages; Dir-Gen. WILLIBRONDE TELOU.

Radiodiffusion du Togo (Nationale): BP 21, Kara; tel. 26-60-60-60; f. 1974 as Radiodiffusion Kara (Togo); state-controlled; radio programmes in French and vernacular languages; Dir M'BA KPENOUGOU.

Radio Carré Jeunes: BP 2550, Adidogomé, Lomé; tel. 22-25-77-44; e-mail carrejeunes@yahoo.fr; f. 1999; community radio station; popular education, cultural information; broadcasts in French, Ewe, Kabiyé and other local languages; Dir KOUBATINE MANJAMIE.

Radio de l'Evangile-Jésus Vous Aime (JVA): Klikamé, Bretelle Atikoumé, BP 2313, Lomé; tel. 22-25-44-95; fax 22-25-92-81; e-mail radio.jva@fatad.org; f. 1995; owned by the West Africa Advanced School of Theology (Assemblies of God); Christian; education and development; broadcasts on FM frequencies in Lomé and Agou in French, English and 12 local languages; Dir Pastor DOUTI LALLEBILI FLINDJA.

Radio Kanal FM: Immeuble de CAMPOS, ave Champs de Course, BP 61554, Lomé; tel. 22-21-33-74; fax 22-20-19-68; e-mail kanalfm@cafe.tg; internet www.kanalfm.tg; f. 1997; broadcasts in French and Mina; independent; Dir MODESTE MESSAVUSSU-AKUE.

Radio Maria Togo: BP 30162, 155 de la rue 158, Hédzranawoé, Lomé; tel. 22-26-11-31; fax 22-26-35-00; e-mail info.tog@radiomaria.org; internet www.radiomaria.tg; f. 1997; Roman Catholic; broadcasts in French, English and six local languages; Dir BENU EFOEVI PENOUKOU.

Radio Nana FM: 29 rue Béeniglato, BP 6212, Lomé; tel. 22-20-12-02; e-mail nanafm_tg@yahoo.fr; internet www.nanafm.org; f. 1999; broadcasts in French and Mina; community station; political, economic and cultural information; Dir FERDINAND AFFOGNON.

Radio Nostalgie: 14 ave de la Victoire, Quartier Tokoin-Hôpital, BP 13836, Lomé; tel. 22-22-25-41; fax 22-21-07-82; e-mail nostalgietogo@yahoo.fr; internet www.nostalgie.tg; f. 1995; broadcasts in French, Ewe and Mina; Pres. and Dir-Gen. FLAVIEN JOHNSON.

Radio X-Solaire: Kodjoviakopé; tel. 22-22-30-48; f. 2000; Dir MIWONOVI AKUÉ.

Radio Zion: BP 13853, Kpalimé, Lomé; tel. 24-41-09-15; f. 1999; religious; broadcasts in French, Ewe and Kabiyé; Dir EMMANUEL KOUNOUGNA.

Broadcasts from Radio France Internationale, the British Broadcasting Corpn, Voice of America, Radio Deutsche Welle and Radio Nederland are also received in Togo.

Television

Télévision Togolaise: BP 3286, Lomé; tel. 22-21-53-57; fax 22-21-57-86; e-mail televisiontogolaise@yahoo.fr; internet www.tvt.tg; f. 1973; state-controlled; three stations; programmes in French and vernacular languages; Dir KUESSAN YOVODEVI.

TV2: BP 13100, Agoe; tel. 22-51-49-93; fax 22-54-49-05; e-mail tg_tv2@yahoo.fr; f. 2001; Dir YOUWESSODJO OURO BANG'NA.

TV7: BP 81104, Lomé; tel. 22-21-06-07; Dir JOËL SODJI.

Other television channels include La Chaîne du Futur, TV Jabal Nour al-Islamia and Télé Sport. Many foreign channels, such as TV 5, France 2, France 3, France 24, France 5/Arte, RTI, ORTB, RTS, ORTM, Canal Horizons, Direct 8 and Télésud, are also broadcast to Togo.

Broadcasting Association

Organisation Togolaise des Radios et Télévisions Indépendantes (ORTI): Lomé; tel. 22-21-33-74; e-mail kawokou@syfed.tg.refer.org; Pres. RAYMOND AWOKOU KOUKOU.

Finance

(cap. = capital; res = reserves; dep. = deposits; m. = million; br(s). = branch(es); amounts in francs CFA, unless otherwise indicated)

BANKING

In 2009 there were 11 banks and two other financial institutions in Togo.

Central Bank

Banque Centrale des Etats de l'Afrique de l'Ouest (BCEAO): rue Branly, BP 120, Lomé; tel. 22-21-25-12; fax 22-21-76-02; e-mail ocourrier@lome.bceao.int; internet www.bceao.int; HQ in Dakar, Senegal; f. 1962; bank of issue for the mem. states of the Union Economique et Monétaire Ouest-Africaine (UEMOA, comprising Benin, Burkina Faso, Côte d'Ivoire, Guinea-Bissau, Mali, Niger, Senegal and Togo); cap. 134,120m., res 1,474,195m., dep. 2,124,051m. (Dec. 2009); Gov. KONÉ TIÉMOKO MEYLIET; Dir in Togo KOSSI TÉNOU; br. at Kara.

Commercial Banks

Banque Internationale pour l'Afrique au Togo (BIA—Togo): 13 rue de Commerce, BP 346, Lomé; tel. 22-21-32-86; fax 22-21-10-19; e-mail bia-togo@cafe.tg; internet www.biat.tg; f. 1965; fmrly Meridien BIAO—Togo; 60.2% owned by Banque Belgolaise (Belgium); cap. and res 567m., total assets 51,793m. (Dec. 2003); Pres. VICTOR ALIPUI; Gen. Man. JEAN-PAUL LE CALM; 7 brs.

Banque Togolaise pour le Commerce et l'Industrie (BTCI): 169 blvd du 13 janvier, BP 363, Lomé; tel. 22-21-46-41; fax 22-21-32-65; e-mail btci@btci.tg; internet www.btci.tg; f. 1974; 23.8% owned by Groupe BNP Paribas (France), 24.8% owned by Société Financière pour les Pays d'Outre-mer (Switzerland); cap. 1,700m., res 1,706m., dep. 91,564m. (Dec. 2006); Pres. Barry Moussa Barqué; Dir-Gen. Yao Patrice Kanekatoua; 9 brs.

Ecobank Togo (EBT): 20 rue du Commerce, BP 3302, Lomé; tel. 22-21-72-14; fax 22-21-42-37; e-mail ecobanktg@ecobank.com; internet www.ecobank.com; f. 1988; 80.7% owned by Ecobank Transnational Inc (operating under the auspices of the Economic Community of West African States), 14.0% by Togolese private investors; cap. 5,000.0m., res 7,201.9m., dep. 155,807.2m. (Dec. 2009); Chair. Michel Komlanvi Klousseh; Man. Dir Didier Alexandre Lamine Correa; 3 brs.

Ecobank Transnational Inc: 2 ave Sylvanus Olympio, BP 3261, Lomé; tel. 22-21-03-03; fax 22-21-51-19; e-mail info@ecobank.com; internet www.ecobank.com; f. 1985; holding co for banking cos in Benin, Burkina Faso, Cameroon, Côte d'Ivoire, Ghana, Guinea, Liberia, Mali, Niger, Nigeria, Senegal and Togo, Ecobank Development Corpn and EIC Bourse; cap. and res US $105.5m., total assets $1,523.1m. (Dec. 2003); Chair. Kolapo Lawson; CEO Arnold Ekpe.

Orabank Bank Togo: 11 ave du 24 janvier, BP 325, Lomé; tel. 22-21-62-21; fax 22-21-62-25; e-mail info-tg@orabank.net; internet www.orabank.net; f. 2004; fmrly Financial Bank Togo, present name adopted 2012; 97.38% owned by Oragroup SA; cap. 6,516m. (Dec. 2011); Dir-Gen. Patrick Mestrallet; 8 brs.

Société Interafricaine de Banque (SIAB): 14 ave Sylvanus Olympio, BP 4874, Lomé; tel. 22-21-28-30; fax 22-21-58-29; e-mail info@siabtogo.com; internet www.siabtogo.com; f. 1975; fmrly Banque Arabe Libyenne-Togolaise du Commerce Extérieur; 86% owned by Libyan Arab Foreign Bank, 14% state-owned; cap. and res 181m., total assets 6,999m. (Dec. 2003); Pres. Ayawovi Demba Tignokpa; CEO Rabie Youssef Abushawashi.

Union Togolaise de Banque (UTB): UTB Circulaire, blvd du 13 janvier, Nyékonakpoè, BP 359, Lomé; tel. 22-23-43-00; fax 22-21-22-06; e-mail utbsg@cafe.tg; internet www.utb.tg; f. 1964; 100% state-owned; transfer to majority private ownership proposed; cap. and res −12.3m., total assets 49.0m. (Dec. 2003); Chair. Badawasso Gnaro; Dir-Gen. Yaovi Attigbé Ihou; 11 brs.

Development Banks

Banque Ouest-Africaine de Développement (BOAD): 68 ave de la Libération, BP 1172, Lomé; tel. 22-21-42-44; fax 22-21-72-69; e-mail boadsiege@boad.org; internet www.boad.org; f. 1973; promotes West African economic development and integration; cap. 682,100m., total assets 849,993m. (Dec. 2004); Pres. Christian Adovèlandé.

Banque Togolaise de Développement (BTD): ave des Nîmes X, angle ave N. Grunitzky, BP 65, Lomé; tel. 22-21-36-41; fax 22-21-44-56; e-mail togo_devbank@btd.tg; internet www.btd.tg; f. 1966; f. 43% state-owned, 20% owned by BCEAO, 13% by BOAD; transfer to majority private ownership pending; cap. 3,065m., res 7,591m., dep. 34,514m. (Dec. 2006); Chair. and Pres. Esso Kandja; Dir-Gen. Zakari Darou-Salim; 8 brs.

Savings Bank

Caisse d'Epargne du Togo (CET): 23 ave de Kléber Dadjo, Lomé; tel. 22-21-20-60; fax 22-21-85-83; e-mail cet@ids.tg; internet www.cet.tg; state-owned; privatization proposed; cap. and res 544m., total assets 27,988m. (Dec. 2006); Pres. Djossou Semondji.

Credit Institution

Société Togolaise de Crédit Automobile (STOCA): 3 rue du Mono, BP 899, Lomé; tel. 22-21-37-59; fax 22-21-08-28; e-mail stoca@ids.tg; f. 1962; 93.3% owned by SAFCA; cap. and res −112m., total assets 1,677m. (Dec. 2003); Pres. Diack Diawar; Dir-Gen. Délali Agbale.

Bankers' Association

Association Professionnelle des Banques et Etablissements Financiers du Togo (APBEF): rue Docteur Kaolo-Tokoin Tamé, près de la Résidence du Bénin, BP 4863, Lomé; tel. 22-26-69-13; fax 22-21-85-83; e-mail info@apbeftogo.com; internet apbeftogo.com.

STOCK EXCHANGE

Bourse Régionale des Valeurs Mobilières (BRVM): BP 3263, Lomé; tel. 22-21-23-05; fax 22-21-23-41; e-mail brvm@brvm.org; internet www.brvm.org; f. 1998; national branch of BRVM (regional stock exchange based in Abidjan, Côte d'Ivoire, serving the member states of UEMOA); Man. in Togo Nathalie Bitho Atcholi.

INSURANCE

In 2009 there were 12 insurance companies in Togo.

Allianz Togo: 21 blvd du 13 janvier, angle ave Duisburg, BP 3703, Lomé; tel. 22-21-97-73; fax 22-21-97-75; e-mail allianz.togo@allianz-tg.com; f. 2000; Dir-Gen. Olivier Picard.

Beneficial Life Insurance Togo: BP 1115, Lomé; tel. 22-22-06-07; fax 22-22-06-27; f. 2000; Dir-Gen. Alyson Brown.

Colina Togo: 10 rue du Commerce, BP 1349, Lomé; tel. 22-22-93-65; fax 22-21-73-58; e-mail togo@groupecolina.com; internet www.groupecolina.com; affiliated to Colina SA (Côte d'Ivoire); Dir-Gen. Louis Kakre Badobre.

Compagnie Commune de Réassurance des Etats Membres de la CICA (CICA—RE): 43 ave du 24 janvier, 07 BP 12410, Lomé; tel. 22-23-62-69; fax 22-61-35-94; e-mail cica-re@cica-re.com; f. 1981; reinsurance co-operating in 12 West and Central African states; Pres. Albert Pamsy; Dir-Gen. N'guessan Jean Baptiste Kouame.

Fidelia Assurances: 01 BP 1679, Lomé; tel. 22-20-74-94; fax 22-20-76-16; e-mail fideliaass@helim.tg; f. 2004; Dir-Gen. Akoètè Datè Adamah-Tassah.

Groupement Togolais d'Assurances (GTA): route d'Atakpamé, BP 3298, Lomé; tel. 22-25-60-75; fax 22-25-26-78; e-mail gta@laposte.tg; f. 1974; 62.9% state-owned; non-life insurance; Man. Dir Guy Camara; also **Groupement Togolais d'Assurances Vie**, life insurance; Man. Dir Yao Claude Gbikpi Date.

Nouvelle Société Interafricaine d'Assurances Togo (NSIA Togo): rue Brazza, BP 1120, Lomé; tel. 22-20-81-50; fax 22-20-81-52; e-mail nsia.tg@groupensia.com; f. 2005; Dir-Gen. José Kwassi Symenouh.

Sicar Gras Savoye Togo: 140 blvd du 13 janvier, BP 2932, Lomé; tel. 22-21-35-38; fax 22-21-82-11; e-mail sicargs@sicargs.tg; internet www.grassavoye.com; affiliated to Gras Savoye (France); Dir Guy Bihannic.

Union des Assurances du Togo (UAT): Immeuble BICI, 169 blvd du 13 janvier, BP 495, Lomé; tel. 22-21-10-34; fax 22-21-87-24; e-mail unatinfo@cafe.tg; also **Union des Assurances du Togo—Vie** (UAT—Vie) ; Dir-Gen. Locoh Théophile Kodjo.

Trade and Industry

ECONOMIC AND SOCIAL COUNCIL

Conseil Economique et Social: Lomé; tel. 22-21-53-01; f. 1967; advisory body of 25 mems, comprising five trade unionists, five reps of industry and commerce, five reps of agriculture, five economists and sociologists, and five technologists; Pres. Koffi Gbodzidi Djondo.

GOVERNMENT AGENCIES

Direction Générale des Mines et de la Géologie: BP 356, Lomé; tel. 22-21-30-01; fax 22-21-31-93; organization and administration of mining in Togo; Dir-Gen. Matthias Banimpo Gbengbartane.

Société d'Administration des Zones Franches (SAZOF): 2564 ave de la Chance, BP 3250, Lomé; tel. 22-53-53-53; fax 22-51-43-18; e-mail sazof@zonefranchetogo.tg; internet zonefranchetogo.tg; administers and promotes export processing zones; Dir-Gen. Yazaz Egbaré; Asst Dir-Gen. Atsouvi Yawo Sikpa.

Société Nationale de Commerce (SONACOM): 29 blvd Circulaire, BP 3009, Lomé; tel. 22-21-31-18; f. 1972; cap. 2,000m. francs CFA; importer of staple foods; Dir-Gen. Jean Ladoux.

DEVELOPMENT ORGANIZATIONS

Agricultural development is under the supervision of five regional development authorities, the Sociétés Régionales d'Aménagement et de Développement.

Agence Française de Développement (AFD): 437 ave de Sarakawa, BP 33, Lomé; tel. 22-21-04-98; fax 22-21-79-32; e-mail afdlome@groupe-afd.org; internet www.afd.fr; Country Dir Philippe Collignon.

Association Villages Entreprises: BP 23, Kpalimé; tel. and fax 24-41-00-62; e-mail averafp@hotmail.com; Dir Komi Afelete Julien Nyuiadzi.

France Volontaires: BP 1511, Lomé; tel. 22-21-09-45; fax 22-21-85-04; e-mail afvp@togo-imet.com; internet www.france-volontaires.org; f. 1965; fmrly Association Française des Volontaires du Progrès; name changed as above in 2009; Nat. Del. Marc Lescaudron.

Office de Développement et d'Exploitation des Forêts (ODEF): 59 QAD rue de la Kozah, BP 334, Lomé; tel. 22-21-79-86; fax 22-21-34-91; e-mail kodefly@yahoo.fr; f. 1971; develops and manages forest resources; Man. Dir Edjidomélé Gbadoe.

Recherche, Appui et Formation aux Initiatives d'Autodéveloppement (RAFIA): BP 43, Dapaong; tel. 27-70-80-89; fax 27-70-82-37; f. 1992; Dir Noigue Tambila Lenne.

Service de Coopération et d'Action Culturelle: ave de la Présidence, BP 91, Lomé; tel. 22-23-46-60; fax 22-23-46-75; e-mail scac-lome@tg.refer.org; administers bilateral aid from the French Ministry of Foreign Affairs; Dir ETIENNE CAZIN.

Société d'Appui a la Filière Café-Cacao-Coton (SAFICC): Lomé; f. 1992; development of coffee, cocoa and cotton production.

CHAMBER OF COMMERCE

Chambre de Commerce et d'Industrie du Togo (CCIT): ave de la Présidence, angle ave Georges Pompidou, BP 360, Lomé; tel. 22-21-70-65; fax 22-21-47-30; e-mail ccit@ccit.tg; internet www.ccit.tg; f. 1921; Pres. JONATHAN FIAWOO; br. at Kara.

EMPLOYERS' ORGANIZATIONS

Association des Grandes Entreprises du Togo (AGET): Immeuble UAT, 3e étage, 812 blvd du 13 janvier, Lomé; internet 22-21-95-85; internet www.aget-togo.org; f. 2007; Pres. JOSÉ SYMENOUH; Sec.-Gen. PASCAL COTI.

Conseil National du Patronat du Togo: 60 blvd du Mono, BP 12429, Lomé; tel. 22-21-08-30; fax 22-21-71-11; e-mail cnptogo@gmail.com; internet www.cnp-togo.tg; f. 1963 as Groupement Interprofessionnel des Entreprises du Togo; renamed as above in 1990; Pres. ALBERT KOSSIVI NAKU; Sec.-Gen. MOCKTAR SOW.

Syndicat des Commerçants, Industriels, Importateur et Exportateurs du Togo (SCIMPEXTO): BP 1166, Lomé; tel. 22-22-59-86; Pres. AMA JUSTIN D'ALMEIDA.

Syndicat des Entrepreneurs de Travaux Publics, Bâtiments et Mines du Togo: BP 12429, Lomé; tel. 22-21-19-06; fax 22-21-08-30; Pres. JOSÈPHE NAKU.

UTILITIES

Electricity

Communauté Electrique du Bénin: ave de la Kozah, BP 1368, Lomé; tel. 22-21-61-32; fax 22-21-37-64; e-mail dg@cebnet.org; f. 1968 as a jt venture between Togo and Benin to exploit the energy resources in the two countries; Chairs TCHAMDJA ANDJO, Z. MARIUS HOUNKPATIN; Man. DJIBRIL SALIFOU.

Compagnie Energie Electrique du Togo (CEET): Lomé; tel. 22-20-82-20; e-mail ceet@ceet.tg; internet www.ceet.tg; f. 1963; production, transportation and distribution of electricity; Dir-Gen. GNANDÉ DJÉTÉLI.

Gas

Société Togolaise de Gaz SA (Togogaz): BP 1082, Lomé; tel. 22-21-44-31; fax 22-21-55-30; 71% privatization pending; Dir-Gen. JOËL POMPA.

Water

Société Togolaise des Eaux (TdE): 53 ave de la Libération, BP 1301, Lomé; tel. 22-21-34-81; fax 22-21-46-13; f. 2003 to replace Régie Nationale des Eaux du Togo; production and distribution of drinking water; Pres. MARC AKLESSO AQUITEME.

MAJOR COMPANIES

The following are among the country's largest companies in terms of either capital investment or employment:

Amina Togo SA: 32 blvd de la Paix, BP 10230, Lomé; tel. 22-26-84-04; fax 22-26-92-72; production of synthetic hair; operates in the Export Processing Zone; South Korean-owned; Man. LEE DAE.

Atlantic Produce: Plantes ornamentales, route de Kegue, BP 3170, Lomé; tel. 22-26-31-64; fax 22-26-28-49; exporter of tropical houseplants; Danish-owned; operates in the Export Processing Zone; Man. M. TINGGARRARD.

Brasserie BB Lomé: 169 Agoenyivé route d'Atakpamé, PK 10, BP 896, Lomé; tel. 22-25-39-04; fax 22-25-38-59; e-mail bblome@bblome.com; internet www.bblome.com; f. 1964 as Brasserie du Bénin; cap. 2,500m. francs CFA; 25% owned by Castel, France; mfrs of beer and soft drinks at Lomé and Kara; Man. Dir EMMANUEL DE TAILLY.

Cajou Espoir Tchamba SARL: BP 539, Lomé; tel. 90-04-59-14; Dir-Gen. MAURICE EDORH.

CEREKEM Exotic Togo: BP 2082, Lomé; f. 1987; cap. 400m. francs CFA; agro-industrial complex at Adétikopé for cultivation and processing of aromatic plants; Chair. and Man. Dir OLE RASMUSSEN; 400 employees.

Cotonfil: Cacavéli, BP 1481, Lomé; tel. 22-25-14-45; fax 22-22-38-44; cotton producer; jt Spanish and Togolese ownership; Man. M. MORA.

Industrie Togolaise des Plastiques (ITP): PK 12+, Zone Industrielle du Port de Lomé, BP 9157, Lomé; tel. 22-27-49-83; fax 22-27-15-58; e-mail itp@itp.tg; internet www.itp.tg; f. 1980; 51.7% owned by Groupement Togolaise d'Investissement et de Participation, 15% by WAVIN (Netherlands), 15% by Pumpenboese PB (Germany), 15% by IFU—Danish Fund for Investment in Developing Countries; mfr and marketing of moulded articles, etc.; cap. 1,100m. francs CFA; Pres. MESSANVI CREPPY.

Nouvelle Industrie des Oléagineux du Togo (NIOTO): Zone Industrielle du Port, BP 3086, Lomé; tel. 22-27-23-79; fax 22-27-68-33; e-mail nioto@nioto-togo.com; internet www.nioto-togo.com; f. 1976; cap. 1,000m. francs CFA; affiliate of Groupe Dagris (France); production and marketing of edible plant oils; sales 10,436m. francs CFA (2005); Man. Dir OLIVIER KERGALL; 171 permanent employees (Dec. 2005).

Nouvelle Société Cotonnière du Togo (NSCT): BP 219, Atakpamé; tel. 24-40-01-53; fax 24-40-00-33; f. 2009 to replace the Société Togolaise du Coton (SOTOCO), f. 1974 to promote and develop cotton cultivation; absorbed cotton production and marketing activities of fmr Office des Produits Agricoles du Togo in 2001; 60% state-owned; Dir-Gen. KOKOU K. DJAGNI.

Sagefi: route de l'Aéroport, BP 4566, Lomé; tel. 22-21-55-43; fax 22-21-64-24; f. 1976; mfrs of electronic equipment; Chair. K. HOFFER.

Société des Ciments du Togo (CIMTOGO): Zone Industrielle Portuaire PK 12, BP 1687, Lomé; tel. 22-27-08-59; fax 22-27-71-32; f. 1969; cap. 750m. francs CFA; owned by HeidelbergCement Group (Norway); production and marketing of cement and clinker; Man. Dir ENDRE RYGH.

Société Générale des Moulins du Togo (SGMT): Zone Industrielle Portuaire, BP 9098, Lomé; tel. 22-27-43-77; fax 22-27-74-64; e-mail sgmtsa@yahoo.fr; f. 1971; cap. 300m. francs CFA; flour milling at Lomé; Chair. KOUDJOLOU DOGO; Man. Dir VASKEN BAKALIAN.

Société Industrielle de Coton (SICOT): BP 12465, Lomé; tel. 22-27-00-69; fax 22-27-75-35; ginning and marketing of cotton; Dir-Gen. ENSELME GOUTHON.

Société Nationale pour le Développement de la Palmeraie et des Huileries (SONAPH): Lomé; tel. 22-21-22-32; f. 1968; cap. 1,320m. francs CFA; state-owned; cultivation of palms and production of palm oil and palmettoes; Chair. Dr FOLI AMAIZO BUBUTO; Man. Dir ANANI ERNEST GASSOU.

Société Nouvelle des Phosphates du Togo (SNPT): BP 379, Lomé; tel. 22-22-50-13; fax 22-21-07-18; e-mail snpt@phosphatesdutogo.com; f. 2007 to replace the International Fertilizers Group-Togo (f. 2002); cap. 15,000m. francs CFA; production and marketing of phosphates; Dir-Gen. YAO FLORENT MAGANAWE; 2,500 employees (2002).

Société Togolaise et Danoise de Savons (SOTODAS): Lomé; tel. 22-21-52-03; fax 22-21-52-04; f. 1987; cap. 205m. francs CFA; 40% owned by Domo Kemi (Denmark), 20% by private Togolese interests; mfrs of detergents and cleansers; Man. Dir S. RAZVI.

Société Togolaise de Sidérurgie (STS): Lomé; tel. 22-21-10-16; cap. 700m. francs CFA; steel production; Chair. JOHN MOORE; Man. Dir STANLEY CLEVELAND.

Société Togolaise de Stockage de Lomé (STSL): BP 3283, Lomé; tel. 22-27-50-64; fax 22-21-74-15; f. 1976; cap. 4,000m. francs CFA; exploitation and commercialization of hydrocarbons; Dir-Gen. M. BLAZJENVICZ.

Togotex International: Blvd du 13 Janvier 21, BP 3511, Lomé; tel. 22-21-33-25; fax 22-21-60-49; f. 1990; cap. 2,250m. francs CFA; owned by Cha Chi Ming (Hong Kong); operates textile mills; Pres. CHA CHI MING; Man. Dir VICTOR CHA.

TRADE UNIONS

Collectif des Syndicats Indépendants (CSI): Lomé; f. 1992 as co-ordinating org. for three trade union confederations.

Confédération Générale des Cadres du Togo (CGCT): BP 12837, Lomé; tel. 22-23-13-09; Sec.-Gen. MOLI EPHREM TSIKPLONOU.

Confédération Nationale des Travailleurs du Togo (CNTT): Bourse du Travail, BP 163, 160 blvd du 13 janvier, Lomé; tel. 22-22-02-55; fax 22-21-48-33; f. 1973; Sec.-Gen. AGUI YVES PALANGA; 35,000 mems (2007).

Confédération Syndicale des Travailleurs du Togo (CSTT): 14 rue Van Lare, BP 3058, Lomé; tel. 22-22-11-17; fax 22-22-44-41; e-mail cstt_cstt@yahoo.fr; internet www.csttogo.org; f. 1949, dissolved 1972, re-established 1991; comprises 36 unions and 7 professional federations (Agro-Alimentation, Education, General Employees, Industry, Public Services, Transport, Woodwork and Construction); Sec.-Gen. TÊVI SÉBASTIEN AYIKOÉ; 55,266 mems (2007).

Groupe des Syndicats Autonomes: BP 1728, Lomé; f. 1991; Sec.-Gen. PAP EDOUARD AGLAMEY.

Union Générale des Syndicats Libre du Togo (UGSL): BP 30137, Lomé; tel. 22-25-32-28; Sec.-Gen. MATHIAS HLOMADOR.

Union Nationale des Syndicats Indépendants du Togo (UNSIT): Tokoin-Wuiti, BP 30082, Lomé; tel. 22-21-32-88; fax 22-21-95-66; e-mail unsit@netcom.tg; f. 1991; Sec.-Gen. NORBERT GBIKPI-BENISSAN; 17 affiliated unions; 8,061 mems (2007).

Transport

RAILWAYS

Société Nationale des Chemins de Fer du Togo (SNCT): BP 340, Lomé; tel. 22-21-43-01; fax 22-21-22-19; e-mail togorail@yahoo.com; f. 1900; owned by West African Cement (Wacem) since Jan. 2003; total length 519 km, incl. lines running inland from Lomé to Atakpamé and Blitta (276 km), and Lomé to Tabligbo (77 km); a coastal line, running through Lomé and Aného, was closed to passenger traffic in 1987 (a service from Lomé to Kpalimé—119 km—has also been suspended); passengers carried (1999): 4,400 (compared with 628,200 in 1990); freight handled (2007): 631,798 metric tons; Gen. Man. M. M. REDDY.

ROADS

In 2007 there were an estimated 11,652 km of roads, of which some 21% were paved. The rehabilitation in the late 1990s of the 675-km axis road that links the port of Lomé with Burkina Faso, and thus provides an important transport corridor for land-locked West African countries, was considered essential to Togo's economic competitiveness. Other principal roads run from Lomé to the borders of Ghana, Nigeria and Benin.

Africa Route International (ARI—La Gazelle): Lomé; tel. 22-25-27-32; f. 1991 to succeed Société Nationale de Transports Routiers; Pres. and Man. Dir BAWA S. MANKOUBI.

SHIPPING

The major port, at Lomé, generally handles a substantial volume of transit trade for the land-locked countries of Mali, Niger and Burkina Faso. There is another port at Kpémé for the export of phosphates. At the end of 2009 Togo's merchant fleet comprised 86 vessels, with a total displacement of 177,800 gross registered tons.

Conseil National des Chargeurs Togolais (CNCT): BP 2991, Lomé; tel. 22-23-71-00; fax 22-27-08-40; e-mail cnct@cnct.tg; internet www.cnct.tg; f. 1980; restructured 2001; Dir-Gen. TOÏ GNASSINGBÉ.

Ecomarine International (Togo): Immeuble Ecomarine, Zone Portuaire, BP 6014, Lomé; tel. 22-27-48-04; fax 22-27-48-06; e-mail ecomarine@ecomarineint.com; f. 2001 to develop container-handling facility at Lomé Port; operates maritime transport between Togo, Senegal and Angola; Chair. Alhaji BAMANGA TUKUR.

Port Autonome de Lomé: BP 1225, Lomé; tel. 22-27-47-42; fax 22-27-08-18; e-mail togoport@togoport.tg; internet www.togoport.tg; f. 1968; transferred to private management in Jan. 2002; Pres. ASSIBA AMOUSSOU-GUENOU; Man. Dir Adm. ADEGNON KODJO FOGAN; 1,600 employees (2003).

Société Ouest-Africaine d'Entreprises Maritimes Togo (SOAEM—Togo): Zone Industrielle Portuaire, BP 3285, Lomé; tel. 22-21-07-20; fax 22-21-34-17; f. 1959; forwarding agents, warehousing, sea and road freight transport; Pres. JEAN FABRY; Man. Dir JOHN M. AQUEREBURU.

Société Togolaise de Navigation Maritime (SOTONAM): pl. des Quatre Etoiles, rond-point du Port, BP 4086, Lomé; tel. 22-21-51-73; fax 22-27-69-38; state-owned; privatization pending; Man. PAKOUM KPEMA.

SOCOPAO—Togo: 18 rue du Commerce, BP 821, Lomé; tel. 22-21-55-88; fax 22-21-73-17; f. 1959; freight transport, shipping agents; Pres. GUY MIRABAUD; Man. Dir HENRI CHAULIER.

SORINCO—Marine: 110 rue de l'OCAM, BP 2806, Lomé; tel. 22-21-56-94; freight transport, forwarding agents, warehousing, etc.; Man. AHMED EDGAR COLLINGWOOD WILLIAMS.

Togolaise d'Affrètements et d'Agence de Lignes SA (TAAL): 21 blvd du Mono, BP 9089, Lomé; tel. 22-23-19-00; fax 22-21-06-09; e-mail taalsa@togo-imet.com; internet www.taal.tg; f. 1992; shipping agents, haulage management, crewing agency, forwarding agents; Pres. and Man. Dir PAUL KOKOU EDJAMFEILE.

CIVIL AVIATION

There are international airports at Tokoin, near Lomé (Gnassingbé Eyadéma International Airport), and at Niamtougou. In addition, there are smaller airfields at Sokodé, Sansanné-Mango, Dapaong and Atakpamé.

Africa West Cargo: route de l'Aéroport, Zone Franche Aéroportuaire, BP 10019, Lomé; tel. 22-26-88-10; fax 22-26-17-49; e-mail info@africawestcargo.com; internet www.africawestcargo.com; f. 1997; air freight operator; CEO YANNICK ERBS.

Agence Nationale de l'Aviation Nationale du Togo: BP 2699, Lomé; tel. 22-26-37-40; fax 22-26-08-60; e-mail latta@togo-imet.com; internet www.anac-togo.tg; Dir-Gen. LATTA GNAMA.

ASKY Airlines: BP 2988, Lomé; tel. 22-23-05-10; fax 22-20-89-00; e-mail headoffice@flyasky.com; internet www.flyasky.com; f. 2008; commenced operations in 2010; 25% owned by Ethiopian Airlines; regional services; Chair. GERVAIS KOFFI DJONDO.

Société Aéroportuaire de Lomé-Tokoin (SALT): Aéroport International de Lomé-Tokoin, BP 10112, Lomé; tel. 22-23-60-60; fax 22-26-88-95; e-mail salt@cafe.tg; internet www.salt-togo.com; f. 1987; Dir-Gen. Dr AKRIMA KOGOE.

Tourism

Some 202,000 foreign tourist arrivals were reported in 2010. In that year receipts from tourism totalled US $66m.

Office National Togolais du Tourisme (ONTT): BP 1289, Lomé; tel. 22-21-43-13; fax 22-21-89-27; e-mail angelodjiss@yahoo.fr; internet www.togo-tourisme.com; f. 1963; Dir ANGELO DJISSODEY.

Defence

As assessed at November 2011, Togo's armed forces officially numbered about 8,550 (army 8,100, air force 250, naval force 200). Paramilitary forces comprised a 750-strong gendarmerie. Military service is by selective conscription and lasts for two years. Togo receives assistance with training and equipment from France.

Defence Expenditure: Budgeted at 27,800m. francs CFA in 2011.

Chief of General Staff: Col ATCHA MOHAMMED TITIKPINA.

Chief of Staff of the Land Army: Col BALI WIYAO.

Education

Education is officially compulsory between the ages of six and 15. Primary education is free, begins at six years of age and lasts for six years. It is divided into three cycles, each of two years. Secondary education, beginning at the age of 12, lasts for a further seven years, comprising a first cycle of four years and a second of three years. According to UNESCO estimates, in 2008/09 enrolment at primary schools included 94% of children in the relevant age-group (98% of boys; 89% of girls), while in 2009/10 secondary enrolment was equivalent to 51% of the relevant age-group. Proficiency in the two national languages, Ewe and Kabiyé, is compulsory. Mission schools are important, educating almost one-half of all pupils. In 2006/07 32,502 students were enrolled in institutions providing tertiary education. The Université du Lomé (formerly the University du Bénin) had about 14,000 students in the early 2000s, and scholarships to French universities are available. A second university opened in Kara, in the north of Togo, in early 2004. In 2002 spending on education represented 13.6% of total budgetary expenditure.

Bibliography

Agboyibo, Y. *Combat pour un Togo démocratique: une méthode politique.* Paris, Editions Karthala, 1999.

Ameagbleame, S. *Histoire, littérature et société au Togo.* Frankfurt, IKO Verlag, 1997.

Amenumey, D. *The Ewe Unification Movement: A Political History.* Accra, Ghana University Press, 1989.

Amouzou, E. *Gilchrist Olympio et la lutte pour la libération du Togo.* Paris, L'Harmattan, 2010.

Atisso, F. S. *La problématique de l'alternance politique au Togo.* Paris, L'Harmattan, 2001.

Le Togo sous la dynastie des Gnassingbé. Paris, L'Harmattan, 2012.

Cornevin, R. *Le Togo: des origines à nos jours.* Paris, Académie des sciences d'outre-mer, 1987.

Decalo, S. *Togo.* Paris, ABC-Clio, 1995.

Historical Dictionary of Togo. 3rd edn. Metuchen, NJ, Scarecrow Press, 1996.

Degli, J. Y. *Togo: La Tragédie Africaine.* Ivry-sur-Seine, Editions Nouvelles du Sud, 1996.

Togo: À quand l'alternance politique. Paris, L'Harmattan, 2007.

Delval, R. *Les musulmans au Togo.* Paris, Académie des sciences d'outre-mer, 1984.

Dossouvi Logo, H. *Lutter pour ses droits au Togo.* Paris, L'Harmattan, 2004.

Feuillet, C. *Le Togo 'en général': La Longue Marche de Gnassingbé Eyadéma.* Paris, Afrique Biblio Club, 1976.

François, Y. *Le Togo.* Paris, Editions Karthala, 1993.

Harrison Church, R. J. *West Africa.* 8th edn. London, Longman, 1979.

Houngnikpo, M. C. *Determinants of Democratization in Africa: A Comparative Study of Benin and Togo.* Lanham, MD, University Press of America, 2001.

Napo Kakaye, L. *Histoire politique et aministrative du Togo : Regard sur un nationaliste de la première heure.* Paris, L'Harmattan, 2010.

Nugent, P. *Smugglers, Secessionists and Loyal Citizens on the Ghana–Togo Frontier: the Lie of the Borderlands since 1914.* Oxford, James Currey, 2002.

Schuerkens, U. *Du Togo allemand aux Togo et Ghana indépendants: Changement social sous régime colonial.* Paris, L'Harmattan, 2001.

Scrive, S. *La crise de la démocratie en Afrique: L'exemple du Togo.* Pars, L'Harmattan, 2009.

Stoecker, H. (Ed.). *German Imperialism in Africa.* London, Hurst Humanities, 1987.

Tété-Adjalogo, T. G. *De la colonisation allemande au Deutsche-Togo Bund.* Paris, L'Harmattan, 1998.

Démocratisation à la togolaise. Paris, L'Harmattan, 1998.

Histoire du Togo: La palpitante quête de l'Ablodé (1940–1960). Créteil, NM7, 2000.

*Histoire du Togo: Le coup de force permanent (2006-2011).*Paris, L'Harmattan, 2012.

Toulabor, C. *Le Togo sous Eyadéma.* Paris, Editions Karthala, 1986.

Verdier, R. *Le pays kabiyé Togo.* Paris, Editions Karthala, 1983.

Yagla, O. W. *L'édification de la nation togolaise: naissance d'une conscience nationale dans un pays africain.* Paris, L'Harmattan, 1978.

Les indigènes du Togo à l'assaut du pouvoir colonial, 1920–1958: l'histoire politique d'un peuple africain. Lomé, Nouvelles Editions Africaines du Togo, 1992.

UGANDA

Physical and Social Geography

B. W. LANGLANDS

PHYSICAL FEATURES AND CLIMATE

The Republic of Uganda is located on the eastern African plateau, at least 800 km inland from the Indian Ocean, and has a total area of 241,551 sq km (93,263 sq miles), including 44,228 sq km of inland water. There are several large freshwater lakes, of which Lakes Victoria, Edward and Albert are shared with neighbouring states. These lakes and most of the rivers form part of the basin of the upper (White) Nile, which has its origin in Uganda. At the point where the upper Nile leaves Lake Victoria, it is harnessed for hydroelectricity by the Owen Falls dam.

Of the land area (excluding open water), 84% forms a plateau at 900 m–1,500 m above sea-level, with a gentle downwarp to the centre to form Lake Kyoga. The western arm of the east African rift system accounts for the 9% of the land area at less than 900 m. Some 5% of the land area lies at an altitude of 1,500 m–2,100 m, including (in the eastern and western extremities) the shoulders of rift valley structures, and also the foothills of the mountains referred to below. Mountains of over 2,100 m occupy the remaining 2% of the land area and these lands are above the limit of cultivation. The highest point is Mt Stanley, 5,109 m, in the Rwenzori group on the border with the Democratic Republic of the Congo.

Geologically, the great proportion of the country is made up of Pre-Cambrian material, largely of gneisses and schists into which granites have been intruded. In the west, distinct series of metamorphosed rocks occur, mainly of phyllites and shales, in which mineralized zones contain small quantities of copper, tin, tungsten and beryllium. Deposits of cobalt and nickel have also been identified, and also potentially substantial reserves of gold-bearing ores. Small quantities of gold, tungsten and tin concentrates are currently mined. In the east of the country there are extensive reserves of magnetite, apatite and crystalline limestone. The apatite provides the basis for a superphosphate industry and the limestone for a cement industry.

NATURAL RESOURCES

The economy of Uganda depends upon agriculture and this, in turn, is affected by climate. The country's location gives little variation in temperature throughout the year, affording an equatorial climate modified by altitude. Rainfall is greatest bordering Lake Victoria and on the mountains, where small areas have over 2,000 mm per year. The high ground of the west, the rest of the Lake Victoria zone, and the eastern and north-central interior all have more than 1,250 mm annually. Only the north-east (Karamoja) and parts of the south (east Ankole) have less than 750 mm. However, total amounts of rain are less significant agriculturally than the length of the dry season. For much of the centre and west there is no more than one month with less than 50 mm and this zone is characterized by permanent cropping of bananas for food, and coffee and tea for cash crops. To the south the dry season increases to three months (June–August); in the north it rises to four months (December–March) and in the north-east the dry season begins in October.

Western Uganda, where there is a greater range of different physical conditions, and where population densities are generally below average, shows a diversity of land use, with tropical rainforest, two game parks, ranch lands, fishing, mining and the cultivation of coffee and tea. The north and east is more monotonous, savannah-covered plain with annually sown fields of grain and cotton. Most of the country's coffee comes from the Lake Victoria zone (*Coffea robusta*) and Mt Elgon (*Coffea arabica*). The economy relies heavily upon smallholding peasant production of basic cash crops; however, the discovery of petroleum reserves in the 2000s was expected to result in significant changes to the Ugandan economy.

POPULATION

The latest census, conducted in November 2002, enumerated a population of 24,442,084, giving a density of about 101.2 inhabitants per sq km. According to official estimates, the population had risen to 34,131,400 by mid-2012. The population is predominantly rural; in 2001 only about 13.7% of the populace resided in urban centres. In 2002 the population of Kampala, the capital, was estimated at 1,208,544. The annual birth rate was 44.7 per 1,000 of the population in 2011. Average life expectancy at birth in 2010 was 53.6 years, according to WHO estimates. Demographic patterns have been significantly affected by the high rate of incidence of HIV/AIDS, which, by the early 1990s, had reportedly reached epidemic proportions in parts of Uganda. According to estimates by the World Bank, almost 10% of the adult population were infected with HIV in 1997. By 2009, however, following mass education and prevention campaigns, the percentage of adults living with HIV/AIDS had been reduced to 6.9%.

Recent History

MICHAEL JENNINGS

British colonial activity in Uganda, which commenced after 1860, was consolidated in 1891 by a treaty with the Kabaka (King) of Buganda, the dominant kingdom. In 1894 Buganda was declared a protectorate, and the same status was subsequently conferred on the kingdoms of Bunyoro, Toro, Ankole and Bugosa. For the next 50 years debate over the position of Buganda within a future self-governing state inhibited the creation of a united nationalist movement. In 1954 the Democratic Party (DP) was formed, favouring a unitary independent state of Uganda and opposing the ambitions of the Baganda people, who did not wish Buganda's influence to be diminished after independence. The Uganda National Congress (UNC), meanwhile, advocated greater African control of the economy in a federal independent state. In 1958 seven African members of the protectorate's Legislative Council, including two members of the UNC, joined another faction, led by Dr Milton Obote, to form the Uganda People's Congress (UPC). By 1960 the UPC, the DP (led by Benedicto Kiwanuka) and the Lukiiko (legislature) of Buganda were the principal political forces in Uganda.

In 1961, at the first country-wide election to the Legislative Council, the DP won a majority of the seats. Kiwanuka was appointed Chief Minister, but he proved to be unacceptable to the ruling élite of Buganda. The Kabaka Yekka (KY, or King Alone), a political party representing the interests of the Bugandan Lukiiko, was formed to ally with the UPC against the DP. Uganda was granted self-government in 1962, with Kiwanuka as Prime Minister. At pre-independence elections to a National Assembly, held in April, the UPC won a majority of seats. The UPC-KY coalition formed a Government, led by Obote. The new Constitution provided for a federation of four regions—Buganda, Ankole, Bunyoro and Toro—each with considerable autonomy. In October Uganda became independent, within the Commonwealth, and a year later, on 9 October 1963, the country became a republic, with Mutesa II, the Kabaka of Buganda, as non-executive President.

OBOTE AND THE UPC

During the first years of independence the UPC-KY alliance was placed under increasing strain. By the end of 1964 sufficient KY and DP members of the National Assembly had defected to the UPC for the alliance to be no longer necessary. The UPC had also gained control of all district councils and kingdom legislatures, except in Buganda. The UPC itself, however, was split between conservative, centrist and radical elements of the party. In February 1966 the National Assembly approved a motion demanding an investigation into gold-smuggling, in which Obote, the Minister of Defence, and the second-in-command of the army, Col Idi Amin Dada, were alleged to be involved. Later in that month Obote led a pre-emptive coup against his opponents within the UPC. Five government ministers were arrested, the Constitution suspended, the President deposed and all executive powers transferred to Obote. In April an interim Constitution was introduced, withdrawing regional autonomy and introducing an executive presidency; Obote became Head of State. In May, when the Lukiiko demanded the restoration of Buganda's autonomy, government troops, commanded by Amin, seized the palace of the Kabaka (who escaped abroad) and a state of emergency was imposed in Buganda. A new Constitution was adopted in September 1967, establishing a unitary republic and abolishing traditional rulers and legislatures. National elections were postponed until 1971.

During the late 1960s the Obote regime came to rely increasingly on detention and armed repression by the paramilitary and intelligence services. Estrangement began to develop, however, between Obote and the army. In December 1969 Obote was wounded in an assassination attempt in Kampala; Amin (still commander of the army) immediately fled to a military base in his home area.

THE AMIN REGIME

Amin seized power in January 1971, while Obote was out of the country. In February Amin declared himself Head of State, promising a return to civilian rule within five years. Amin consolidated his military position by massacring troops and police (particularly those of the Langi and Acholi tribes) who had supported the Obote regime. Soon after taking power Amin suspended political activity and most civil rights. The National Assembly was dissolved, and Amin ruled by decree. The jurisdiction of military tribunals was extended to cover the entire population, and several agencies were established to enforce state security. In August 1972 Amin announced the expulsion of all non-citizen Asians (who comprised the majority of the resident Asian population). The order was subsequently extended to include all Asians, and although this was later rescinded, under internal and external pressure, all but 4,000 Ugandan Asians left the country. Most went to the United Kingdom, which severed diplomatic relations and imposed a trade embargo against Uganda. In December all British companies in Uganda were nationalized without compensation.

Former Chief of Staff, David Oyite-Ojok and Yoweri Museveni, a senior officer, led an attempt to oust Amin by invading from Tanzania in September 1972. In retaliation, Amin's air force bombed Tanzanian towns. The Amin regime was supplied with military aid by Libya and the USSR, and by the end of 1972 virtually all Western aid had ceased. No coherent economic development policy existed, and the country's infrastructure deteriorated.

In October 1978 Amin sought to divert the attention of the armed forces from internal divisions (which had led to another abortive coup in August) by invading Tanzania, claiming the rightful possession of the Kagera salient. The attempt was unsuccessful. President Julius Nyerere of Tanzania encouraged political exiles to form a united political front to remove Amin. In January 1979 the Tanzanian armed forces invaded Uganda, assisted by the Uganda National Liberation Army (UNLA) under the command of Oyite-Ojok and Museveni. They met little resistance and captured Kampala in April. Amin fled the country, eventually taking refuge in Saudi Arabia, where he remained until his death in August 2003.

TRANSITIONAL GOVERNMENT

A provisional government, the National Executive Council (NEC), was established in April 1979 from the ranks of the Uganda National Liberation Front (UNLF, a coalition of 18 previously exiled groups), with Dr Yusuf Lule, a former vice-chancellor of Makerere University, as President. When Lule attempted to reshuffle the NEC in June, opposition from within the UNLF forced his resignation. Lule was succeeded by Godfrey Binaisa (a former Attorney-General), who was, in turn, overthrown by the Military Commission of the UNLF in May 1980. The Military Commission was chaired by Paulo Muwanga (an associate of Obote), supported by Oyite-Ojok and with Museveni as Vice-Chairman.

OBOTE AND OKELLO

The elections held in December 1980 were contested by four parties: the UPC, under Obote; the DP, led by Paul Ssemogerere; the Uganda Patriotic Movement (UPM), a regrouping of the radical faction of the UPC, led by Museveni; and the Conservative Party (CP), a successor to the KY. The UPC gained a majority of seats, and Obote was proclaimed President, for the second time, in mid-December.

Dissatisfaction with the conduct and outcome of the elections caused several factions to initiate guerrilla operations. The three main guerrilla movements were the Uganda National Rescue Front (UNRF), comprising supporters of Amin who were active in the West Nile area, the Uganda Freedom Movement (UFM), led by Balaki Kirya and Andrew Kayiira, and the National Resistance Army (NRA), led by Museveni, with the former President, Lule, now in exile, as chairman of its political wing, the National Resistance Movement (NRM). (Following Lule's death in 1985 Museveni became sole leader of the NRM and NRA.)

In July 1985 Obote (a Langi) was overthrown in an Acholi military coup, led by Brig. (later Lt-Gen.) Basilio Okello. (The deposed President was subsequently granted political asylum by Zambia.) A Military Council, headed by Lt-Gen. (later Gen.) Tito Okello, the Commander-in-Chief of the army, was established to govern the country, pending elections to be held a year later. In subsequent months opposition groups, with the exception of the NRA/NRM, accepted positions on the Military Council. An amnesty was declared for exiles who had supported Amin. By late September the NRA controlled much of southern Uganda. Its control of the region's cash crops placed an economic stranglehold on the Kampala Government. A peace accord signed in December 1985 soon broke down, and Museveni returned to south-west Uganda to push for a final offensive.

THE MUSEVENI PRESIDENCY

NRA troops took control of Kampala in January 1986. Museveni was sworn in as President of the country and formed a National Resistance Council (NRC), with both civilian and military members drawn from across the political spectrum. Samson Kisekka was appointed Prime Minister. Elections were postponed for at least three years and the activities of political parties were officially suspended in March. The defeat of Okello's remaining UNLA troops was officially completed by the end of March.

Museveni announced a policy of national reconciliation. He established a commission to investigate breaches of human rights during the regimes of Amin, Obote and Okello. Following an investigation of the activities of the police force, more than 2,500 of its members were dismissed in July 1986. During 1986 the Museveni Government developed a system of resistance committees at local and district level; these were to be partly responsible for the maintenance of security and the elimination of corruption.

In March 1986 an armed movement seeking the overthrow of Museveni, the Uganda People's Democratic Movement (UPDM), was formed, with Obote's former premier, Eric Otema Allimadi, as leader. This, together with raids by remnants of the UNLA, chronic problems with armed cattle-rustlers in the north-east and the lack of any basic infrastructure of law and order, prevented President Museveni from consolidating his control over Uganda. Museveni refused to restore Uganda's traditional monarchies until stability had returned to the country.

The largest uprising in the period immediately following Museveni's accession to power was led by a charismatic cult leader, Alice Lakwena, whose religious sect attracted both peasant farmers from the Acholi tribe and former soldiers of the UNLA. The rebel Holy Spirit Movement, as it became known, was crushed in late 1987 and Lakwena fled to Kenya. However, remaining members of the movement subsequently regrouped themselves as the Lord's Resistance Army (LRA), under the leadership of Joseph Kony, Lakwena's nephew.

In June 1987 an amnesty was declared for insurgents (except those accused of murder or rape), which was subsequently repeatedly extended; by April 1988 Ugandan officials reported that almost 30,000 rebels had surrendered. Peace talks with the armed wing of the UPDM led to agreement in June under the leadership of Lt-Col John Angelo Okello. However, a faction of the Uganda People's Democratic Army regrouped, under the leadership of Odong Latek, and continued to oppose the Government. In mid-1989 the NRC launched a major offensive against guerrilla forces.

Post-election Reforms

In February 1989 the first national election since 1980 was held. The NRC, which had previously comprised only members nominated by the President, was expanded from 98 to 278 members, to include 210 elected representatives. While a total of 20 ministerial posts were reserved for nominated members of the NRC, 50 were allocated to elected members. In October 1989 the NRC approved draft legislation to extend the Government's term of office by five years from January 1990. In May 1991 President Museveni formally invited all *émigré* Ugandan Asians, who had been expelled during the Amin regime, to return.

In December 1992 the constitutional commission recommended continuing the non-party democracy system against the opposition of the UPC and the DP. In April the NRC adopted legislation authorizing the establishment of a Constituent Assembly. In July 1993 legislation was approved that provided for the restoration of each of Uganda's traditional monarchies; these were, however, to be limited to ceremonial and cultural functions.

In October 1993 Lt-Col James Oponyo, the commander of the rebel group the Ugandan People's Army (UPA) in the Teso area in north-eastern Uganda, surrendered to government forces. In January 1994 two other rebel groups, the Ugandan Democratic Alliance (UDA) and the Uganda Federal Army (UFA), also agreed to suspend their guerrilla operations. However, in early 1994 Peter Otai, a former leader of the UPA, established a new rebel group, the Uganda People's Freedom Movement (UPFM).

Political and Constitutional Changes

Elections to the newly created 288-member Constituent Assembly took place in March 1994. Museveni and the NRM won overwhelming support. Although candidates were officially required to stand on a non-party basis, tacit official tolerance of party campaigning was reflected in the leaders of three parties—the DP, the CP and the UPC—being given access to national radio and television during the weeks prior to the election. The NRM and its allies won an estimated 150 of the 214 directly-elected seats, most of which were in Buganda, the Western region and parts of the east, while the opposition (supporters of the UPC and DP) secured most seats in the north and the north-east. The Constituent Assembly, which also comprised nominated representatives of the armed forces, political parties, trade unions and various special interest groups, was empowered to debate, amend and finally to enact the draft constitution. Amendments to the draft required a two-thirds' majority of the Assembly; changes that received majority support but less than two-thirds were to be submitted to referendum. The new Constitution, under the terms of which a national referendum on the future introduction of a multi-party political system was to be staged in 2000, was eventually promulgated in October 1995.

In November 1994 Museveni reorganized the Cabinet, replacing George Adyebo as Prime Minister with Kintu Musoke, hitherto Minister of State for Security, and appointing Dr Speciosa Wandira Kazibwe, the Minister of Women's Affairs and Community Development, as Vice-President. Brig. Moses Ali, a former minister under Amin's regime, rejoined the Cabinet.

In June 1995 the Constituent Assembly rejected the immediate restoration of multi-party democracy. Consequently, candidates at the legislative and presidential elections would be required to seek election without official reference to their respective political affiliations. The Constituent Assembly's decision was strongly opposed by the UPC and other unofficial opposition parties.

The presidential and legislative election dates were postponed several times in 1996. The main challenger to Museveni was Ssemogerere, the leader of the DP. Museveni campaigned with the full backing of the army, police and security forces. The presidential election was held on 9 May; Museveni won convincingly, securing 74.2% of the votes cast (Ssemogerere took 23.7%). The election was declared free and fair by international observers and Museveni immediately declared that he would not restore multi-party democracy for at least five years. Elections to the Parliament (as the NRC had been restyled under the 1995 Constitution), which now consisted of 276 seats, comprising 214 elected and 62 nominated representatives, took place in June. In the same month elections were held for new local councils (to replace the resistance committees).

The referendum on Uganda's non-party system took place on 29 June 2000. Opposition parties boycotted the poll. Electoral monitors from the Organization of African Unity (OAU, now the African Union—AU) declared that the referendum had been conducted fairly and peacefully. The existing system was supported by 90.7% of voters, although the participation rate was only around 45%. The Referendum Act was passed in Parliament, but declared null and void by the Supreme Court in August. The Court ruled that the law had been passed with less than the 93 deputies present required to form a quorum. However, the Parliament reversed this decision at the end of the month, by enacting a validation of the referendum and all other laws passed since October 1996.

Museveni Re-elected

The 2001 presidential election was contested by a number of candidates, the most serious challenger to Museveni being his former physician, Dr Kizza Besigye. Besigye commanded significant support within the Uganda People's Defence Forces (UPDF) in particular, and his criticism of Uganda's continued involvement in the Democratic Republic of the Congo (DRC) also won much popular backing. The campaign was accompanied by violence, and opposition groups complained that state security services targeted their members and supporters for intimidation. On 12 March Museveni was re-elected President with 69% of the votes cast. Besigye won 28%. There were reports of electoral malpractice and intimidation during the poll, but international observers concluded the election was generally free and fair. A number of bombings in the country took place in the immediate aftermath, one in Kampala occurring just after the results were announced. Although no group claimed responsibility, the Government accused Besigye of being linked to the attacks and barred him from leaving the country. Museveni purged the UPDF of Besigye supporters and was sworn in as President in May. Besigye fled to the USA in August. Legislative elections took place on 26 June. The NRM secured more than 70% of seats (the total number of seats having been increased to 292—214 elected and 78 nominated). A new Cabinet appointed in July included 10 ministers who had failed to retain their seats in the elections.

In February 2004 the seven main opposition parties—the DP, the UPC, the CP, the Justice Forum, the National Democratic Forum, the Free Movement and the Reform Agenda—established a coalition known as the Group of Seven (G7). Talks between the G7 and the Government over the transition to multi-party democracy repeatedly broke down. In April the G7 accused the Government of creating around 50 new opposition parties to undermine their members. Throughout 2004 and 2005 opposition politicians regularly denounced the Government for banning rallies and undermining their campaigns. In November 2004 the Constitutional Court overturned legislation preventing parties other than the NRM from contesting elections, and upheld a ruling allowing candidates who lived abroad to lead political parties. Nevertheless, the Government continued to harass opposition politicians. In April 2005 two Forum for Democratic Change (FDC) deputies were accused of murdering a local official three years earlier. In response to what it claimed was a politically motivated trial, the FDC called on donors to suspend aid in protest at government efforts to undermine political opposition. Donors, already concerned at the lack of progress towards multi-party democracy, responded by putting pressure on the Government. In February the Dutch Minister of Development Co-operation, on a visit to Uganda, called on Museveni not to stand for a third term. In March the British Government demanded an easing of restrictions on opposition parties.

The Succession Question

In late May 2003 a number of ministers who had opposed plans to revoke the presidential two-term limit were dismissed from the Cabinet. In September the Cabinet presented proposals for amending the Constitution to the Constitutional Review Commission. In April 2004 Museveni formally retired from the UPDF, having been promoted to the rank of General, in order to comply with legislation barring serving members of the armed forces from active membership of a political party, thereby removing one obstacle to his renewed nomination. In June 2005 Parliament passed legislation officially restoring multi-party democracy and lifting the presidential time limit. On 28 July 92.5% of voters at a national referendum ratified the changes (albeit with a relatively low turn-out of 47%).

The 2006 Elections

In November 2005 Museveni made the long-expected announcement that he would stand in for a third presidential term. On 14 November, three weeks after his return from self-imposed exile, Besigye was arrested and imprisoned on charges of rape and treason. The arrest led to two days of rioting in Kampala, with one opposition supporter shot dead by police. A few days later heavily armed soldiers surrounded the court in which Besigye and 14 co-defendants were attending a bail hearing. Although they were granted bail, Besigye and his co-defendants returned to prison over concerns for their safety should they be released. The UPDF later stated that the soldiers had been present to re-arrest the accused. In December the Electoral Commission announced that Besigye could file his election nomination papers from prison, over-ruling a decision by the Attorney-General that Besigye be denied the opportunity to stand in the election.

International donors became increasingly concerned over the transition to democracy in Uganda, especially following the arrest of Besigye, and allegations of intimidation and violence against opposition supporters and politicians. Several donors reduced or postponed aid payments, or diverted payments away from government agencies.

Presidential and parliamentary elections took place on 23 February 2006. Museveni was re-elected President after securing 59.3% of the votes cast; Besigye, who had been released on bail by the High Court, won 37.4%. Voter turn-out of some 68% was recorded. In the parliamentary elections the NRM was reported to have won 202 seats and its nearest rival, the FDC, 40 seats. The remaining seats were split between the DP (10 seats), the UPC (nine seats), the CP (one seat), the Justice Forum (one seat), and 28 independents. The President's wife, Janet Museveni, was elected to Parliament (which now comprised 319 seats, including 215 directly elected representatives); overall, women made up 19% of deputies. International observers did not challenge the overall result of the elections, although they noted some irregularities—such as Besigye's arrest and the media bias towards Museveni—as well as broader problems with the electoral process.

On 7 March 2006 Besigye filed a petition challenging the election results and alleging significant irregularities in electoral conduct. In April the Supreme Court ruled, by four votes to three, that there was no evidence that the elections had been significantly fraudulent or beset by major irregularities. It did, however, find that names had been struck off the electoral list, evidence of irregularities in the counting of votes, the use of bribery, intimidation and violence, and some examples of multiple voting and ballot-stuffing. Despite this, the Court concluded that the failures had not seriously affected the overall result, and confirmed Museveni's victory. Museveni was sworn in as President in May 2006.

Museveni's Third Term

Although Besigye was acquitted of rape in March 2006, his trial for treason continued. After a ruling in January that he and his co-defendants could not be tried before a court martial, the trial was moved to the High Court. However, the judge charged with hearing the case withdrew in February, and the trial was rescheduled to April. Following the withdrawal of a second judge the trial eventually resumed in June 2007, when Besigye appeared with 10 co-defendants.

Throughout 2006 and 2007 opposition politicians continued to air allegations of intimidation by the Government and the security apparatus, and restrictions were placed on opposition rallies and demonstrations. Questions were also asked over the Government's perceived lack of willingness to ensure the independence of the judiciary. In March 2007, in a repetition of events from November 2005, police and prison guards stormed the High Court to re-arrest nine individuals linked to Besigye (who had been granted bail on charges of treason). The judiciary reacted by holding a three-day strike in protest at what it deemed government interference in the legal system, and opposition supporters marched in Kampala in support of the action. Museveni wrote to Chief Justice Benjamin Odoki apologizing for the confrontation and providing assurances that the Government would ensure that such action was not repeated.

Concerns over growing anti-Asian feelings in Uganda were heightened following riots in mid-April 2007 in which one Asian Ugandan was stoned to death and a Hindu temple was attacked. The riots followed protests organized against the Ugandan-Asian-owned Sugar Corporation of Uganda, which had been awarded substantial forest areas by the Government for cultivating sugar. Police were required to protect over 100 individuals from being attacked by the protesters in Kampala, and two opposition members of Parliament, Beatrice Atim and Hussein Kyanjo, who had organized the protests, were arrested, along with 26 others, on charges of inciting anti-Asian violence. In response to the arrests opposition supporters demonstrated in Kampala; the police used water cannons, tear gas and live ammunition against the protesters.

In October 2007 Uganda hosted the Commonwealth Heads of Government Meeting (CHOGM), which it regarded as an opportunity to restore the reputation of the Government following growing international concerns over Museveni's actions in the lead-up to the 2006 elections. The summit was successful, but questions over contracts and payments over preparations for the meeting were raised by Parliament, and investigated by the Auditor-General, John Muwanga.

In April 2008 concerns over government attempts to limit the freedom of the press were revived when three journalists from *The Independent* magazine were arrested after publishing articles alleging corruption within the armed forces, and accusing the UPDF of committing atrocities in northern Uganda as part of the struggle against the LRA.

In September 2008 Museveni announced during a visit to the United Kingdom that the Government would allow Ugandan Asians expelled by Amin in the late 1970s to hold dual citizenship. Uganda's aspirations to join the growing band of African oil-producing nations were boosted in January 2009 when substantial reserves were discovered in Uganda's Lake

Albert Rift Basin by oil-prospecting companies Heritage Oil and Tullow Oil.

In February 2009 Museveni reorganized the Cabinet, appointing Sydda Bbumba as Minister of Finance, Planning and Economic Development. The Government tabled a bill in March legalizing phone tapping by security services. Opposition deputies criticized the proposed legislation, claiming that the Government would use it to undermine the political opposition. Later that month, Museveni was forced to defend his decision to appoint his wife to a cabinet post, as Minister of State for Karamoja, amid concerns over nepotism within the Government; Museveni's son and brother also held senior government positions. In May the Africa Leadership Institute, a Ugandan organization, issued score cards for all Ugandan officials, grading their performance from triple A to F; according to the reports, 70% did not attend constituency or district local council meetings, and 35% did not have constituency offices or staff. Opposition members performed better on average than those in the Government. Parliament attempted to block the publication of the score cards, and attendance in Parliament reportedly increased following their release.

Tensions between Ronald Muwenda Mutebi, the Kabaka (King) of Uganda, and the Government intensified from mid-2009, with the Kabaka seeking to have more powers restored. The Government's barring of Mutebi from visiting a district within the Bugandan Kingdom prompted riots in Kampala led by supporters of the Kabaka; more than 20 people died in the ensuing unrest. Museveni and Mutebi met following the violence, but little progress was made in resolving underlying tensions. In March 2010 police shot at protesters at the Bugandan royal mausoleum at Kasubi, killing two people. Demonstrators had sought to prevent Museveni making an official visit following a fire that had destroyed the tombs. Another person died in the crowds of mourners that came to visit the mausoleum.

During 2009–10 the issue of homosexuality and rising homophobia in Uganda caused consternation among donor governments. In October 2009 a private member's bill was introduced which sought to increase the punishments for homosexuality, the definition of which was also broadened to include lesbianism. Most controversially, the proposed legislation included provision for the death penalty for the offence of 'aggravated homosexuality'. The 'promotion' of homosexuality was also criminalized; this was interpreted by non-governmental organizations as an attack on organizations campaigning for homosexual rights. The Government was equivocal in its support for the bill, torn between supporting a bill with widespread popular appeal, and the demands of donors that the bill be moderated or abandoned. By May 2010 it appeared that the Government would support the passage of the bill, but would seek to replace the death penalty with a death sentence or voluntary 'treatment' for homosexuality.

In 2010 opposition parties and the ruling NRM began campaigning for the 2011 elections. Within the FDC a struggle for control between Besigye and Maj.-Gen. Gregory Mugisha Muntu emerged in early 2010, with both seeking to secure the opposition coalition (the Inter-Party Organisation for Dialogue) nomination as presidential candidate. However, with the DP continuing to refuse to join the coalition unless its leader, Norbert Mao, was put up as a joint candidate, Besigye was unable to assert his authority within the coalition.

In April 2010 Besigye accused the Government of continuing its campaign to undermine him when he was questioned by police over allegations of inciting violence against government supporters, and of complicity in a corruption scandal. In June Besigye was physically attacked during an opposition rally. The FDC accused the Government of covertly supporting private groups seeking to sabotage opposition rallies with violence. In October treason charges against Besigye, long seen as politically motivated, were finally rejected by the Constitutional Court.

Within the ruling NRM, factional struggles abated in 2010 as the party sought to ensure victory the 2011 elections. No action was taken against several ministers implicated in corruption scandals. A parliamentary report leaked in April 2010 appealed for Vice-President Gilbert Bukenya (who had been removed from the Cabinet in the previous month) and Minister of Foreign Affairs Sam Kutesa to be prosecuted over a scandal involving the procurement of luxury vehicles for the CHOGM in October 2007 (see above) and in June 2011 Bukenya was formally charged with corruption.

The 2011 Elections and Museveni's Fourth Term

In the presidential election held on 18 February 2011, Museveni was re-elected for a fourth term, increasing his share of the vote to 68.4% from 59.3% in 2006. Besigye received 26.0% of the ballot. In the concurrent parliamentary elections, the ruling NRM won 164 of the elected seats, while the FDC took 24, the DP 11, the UPC seven, and the CP and the Justice Forum one each; independents secured 30 elective seats. (The number of seats in Parliament now totalled 375, comprising 238 directly elected representatives and 137 nominated members, including 112 women.) The FDC questioned the results and claimed that electoral fraud had taken place. Besigye appealed for peaceful protests against the results. International observers also raised questions over the electoral process, particularly the distribution of money and gifts by the ruling NRM. However, official reports noted that the elections were an improvement over the 2006 polls, and the results were seen as generally credible, reflecting Museveni's ability to capitalize on opposition disunity to increase his own popularity.

However, throughout the first half of 2011 the Government was confronted by a number of protests organized by the opposition in response to high food and fuel prices. Fearing a popular uprising, inspired by those in the Middle East and North Africa during early 2011, the authorities responded by cracking down on all signs of dissent. In an effort to circumvent government restrictions on protests, opposition parties organized a 'walk-to-work' campaign. Five protests took place between April and May, but they were marred by police violence, arrests of opposition politicians and efforts by the security services to target Besigye, who was injured several times. (During the second protest Besigye was shot in the arm with a rubber bullet, and during the fifth a police officer used pepper spray against him.) Besigye's arrest in late April was televised and widely seen by Ugandans, and in response violent protests erupted in Kampala during which security forces used live ammunition. Two people were killed, 120 were treated in hospital for injuries and around 360 were arrested. In a sign of the Government's growing concern over the level of protests, Museveni announced his intention to secure a new law banning bail for six months for anyone arrested for protesting or economic sabotage. Other opposition leaders were also targeted by the security services: the DP's President, Norbert Mao, was arrested during the walk-to-work protests, and CP leader John Ken Lukyamuzi was placed under house arrest. The police crackdown on opposition protests following the elections had resulted in the death of nine people by May.

Timed to coincide with Museveni's inauguration as President, in May 2011 Besigye returned to Uganda from Kenya following treatment for injuries sustained during the protest in April. Supporters followed his car from the airport to Kampala, and, while the police allowed the march to take place, they later fired tear gas into the crowd.

Also in May 2011 the opposition tried a new strategy and urged its supporters to sound their car horns in protest against rising food and fuel prices, although the police responded with threats of arrest for noise pollution. Citing concerns about Besigye's intention to mobilize his supporters for further protests, the opposition leader was placed under preventive arrest and ordered to remain in his home. Following media coverage of the protests in April and May, Museveni accused several media outlets, including *The Daily Monitor*, NTV and a number of foreign news organizations, of tacitly supporting the protests, labelling them 'enemies of Uganda's recovery'. The Minister of Information and National Guidance, Kabakumba Matsiko, later suggested that new laws could restrict media coverage of the protests.

In early July 2011 another strike was held in protest against price rises caused by Uganda's weak currency, closing down shops across Kampala. Chinese traders, blamed for undercutting Ugandan businesses and importing cheap products, were a particular target of the protests.

In August 2011 charges against Besigye over the protests against the rising cost of living were dropped. However, Museveni became increasingly concerned over the scale of the protests, and the Government sought to clamp down on opposition demonstrations and rallies. In September the Government banned a rally calling for a demonstration to celebrate 'people power'. Museveni suggested that the rally was intended to launch an uprising along Egyptian lines. However, as the economic position worsened, the Ugandan Government continued to face ongoing protests. Businesses closed and boycotted banks, protesting against high interest rates (which rose up to 27% at the start of 2012) for several days in January. Later that month Besigye was arrested again along with other opposition leaders before they could participate in an opposition rally in Kampala to protest against high food prices, corruption and ongoing allegations of fraud in the February 2011 elections. In March 2012 Besigye was arrested once more after a police officer died in clashes when an opposition rally was broken up by security services. In April 2012 the Government banned the opposition group, Action for Change, which had orchestrated many of the demonstrations, on the eve of its latest protest against corruption and high prices.

Meanwhile, in October 2011 Kutesa, the chief whip, John Nasasira, and a junior minister appeared in court on charges of corruption in connection with the 2007 CHOGM summit. (Former Vice-President Gilbert Bukenya had been charged in July 2011 over the scandal of provision of luxury cars for visiting heads of state.) However, just days before his trial was to begin, all charges against Bukenya were dropped. Also in October Parliament voted to suspend all oil deals following allegations that Prime Minister Amama Mbabazi, Kutesa and former energy minister Hilary Onek had all received substantial bribes in connection with the award of contracts to the British-based Tullow Oil. Tullow rejected the claims that it had bribed government ministers, and all ministers similarly rejected the allegations. However, Parliament supported the call to suspend the award of contracts. The action by Parliament suggested the Government's ability to control the legislative body, including its own deputies, was being weakened.

Allegations of corruption led to two more notable resignations in February 2012 when Minister for Gender Syda Bumba and Minister for General Duties Khiddu Makubuya left the Government, following accusations of complicity in a corruption scandal. During investigations both claimed that they had acted with the sanction of Museveni, an allegation Museveni denied.

INTERNAL SECURITY CONCERNS

From the mid-1990s three main rebel groups in northern and western Uganda challenged the Museveni administration. In the north-west were the West Nile Bank Front (WNBF), led by a former Minister of Foreign Affairs, Col Juma Oris, until his death in action in February 1997; and the Allied Democratic Front (ADF), mainly comprising Ugandan Islamists and former soldiers of the defeated UNLA, assisted by exiled Rwandan Hutu militiamen and by former soldiers from Zaire (which in May 1997 became the DRC). Sudanese rebels killed several hundred WNBF rebels in mid-1997, reducing its activities. From mid-1997, the ADF carried out a number of attacks on western Ugandan targets from its bases in the Rwenzori mountains. Libya and Iran were accused of supplying the ADF with military equipment and financial aid. In the north, the LRA (backed by Sudan) became increasingly disruptive in the mid-1990s, killing as many as 10,000 people during 1993–98, and displacing around 220,000 people who sought refuge in protected camps.

The WNBF continued to operate across the Uganda–DRC border, while the ADF launched attacks within Uganda in 1998 and 1999, displacing around 70,000 people in western Uganda by early 1999. The LRA also intensified its campaign. In December Parliament passed a bill granting a general amnesty to all rebels who were prepared to renounce rebellion. An agreement signed in Kenya by the Presidents of Uganda and Sudan that month saw both Governments commit to a cessation of support for rebel groups. Improved relations and co-operation between Uganda and Sudan (see Regional Relations below) resulted in a number of successful UPDF offensives against LRA bases in Sudan in 2002, when Sudan allowed Ugandan troops to operate within its territory.

In 2003 conflict escalated following the UPDF attacks on LRA bases the previous year. The UN estimated that at least 10,000 children had been abducted between 2002 and mid-2004, and the conflict in the north accounted for most of the 1.4m. internally displaced persons (IDPs) in Uganda. Government efforts to defeat the LRA militarily were criticized by international donors, which urged the authorities to seek a negotiated settlement. Despite offers by the administration of a cease-fire and the fact that increasing numbers of LRA fighters were taking advantage of the government amnesty, informal talks failed to make progress and in mid-2005 conflict resumed. Meanwhile, the LRA began to move its military bases from southern Sudan to the DRC, setting up in Garamba National Park.

In October 2005 the International Criminal Court (ICC) at The Hague, Netherlands, issued arrest warrants for Kony and four other LRA commanders (deputy leader Vincent Otti, Raska Lukwiya, Okot Odhiambo and Dominic Ongwen). In November the LRA appealed for peace talks, and the Government announced that it would be willing to meet with the rebels. However, direct talks were repeatedly postponed. In August 2006 the Government and the LRA signed a truce, under the terms of which the LRA agreed to move its fighters to camps in southern Sudan, and in return the Government would end military operations against the rebels.

The Government announced plans to resettle IDPs in northern Uganda, and by January 2007 some 230,000 people had returned to their villages as security conditions in the north improved. However, an estimated 1.2m. people remained in the camps.

Throughout 2006 and 2007 talks repeatedly stalled, with the LRA halting plans to relocate its fighters, and senior army commanders stating that military operations would resume unless progress was made. In mid-April 2007 a new truce was agreed, under the auspices of former Mozambican President Joaquim Chissano, who had been appointed as UN special envoy to mediate between the two sides. However, the LRA again failed to move its soldiers to Ri-Kwangba on the Sudan–DRC border, amid signs of internal divisions within the rebel organization following the execution of deputy leader Vincent Otti by Kony in late 2007. Another senior LRA commander, Opio Makasi, surrendered to the UN in eastern DRC in October. Meanwhile, the LRA relocated its main bases from the DRC to the Central African Republic (CAR).

Museveni invited LRA negotiators to Uganda for talks in November 2007, granting the LRA delegation, led by Martin Ojul, immunity from arrest during the discussions. In March 2008 mediators suggested that a deal could be reached, in which the Government would establish a special tribunal to try the most serious war crimes, with indigenous justice mechanisms used for less serious cases, in return for an LRA surrender. However, the refusal by the ICC to withdraw the arrest warrants against the LRA commanders led to the collapse of talks and the end of the proposed agreement. By June 2008 Kony was reported to be preparing for a return to conflict.

In September 2008 UN and DRC troops began an operation against the LRA. The LRA was reported to have six bases in the DRC, and to be controlling diamond mines in the CAR. In late November Kony once more declared his willingness to sign a peace deal and announced a cease-fire. However, the LRA continued its operations in the DRC, claiming it was attacking former Rwandan Hutu militia. Representatives from the Ugandan Government and the international mediators attended a meeting to sign the agreement, but Kony was once again absent, making allegations of a plot to assassinate him.

In mid-December 2008 the UPDF launched Operation Lightning Thunder in the DRC's Garamba National Park, with support from Congolese and Southern Sudanese troops. Kony escaped, however, and the LRA killed 800 Congolese civilians in revenge attacks forcing Kony to announce that the peace process had collapsed. Later that month the Ugandan Government claimed to have destroyed around 70% of LRA camps in the DRC, although Kony continued to evade capture.

However, in response to the operation, the LRA increased the scale of its attacks on civilians. In late December 2008 the LRA was accused of massacring 45 people in a Catholic church in the DRC, and LRA fighters were believed to be advancing towards the CAR. By the end of January 2009 some 900 Congolese civilians had been killed, and 160 children abducted by the rebels. Despite LRA negotiators meeting with Chissano to appeal for a renewed truce, the LRA continued to attack villages across the region. The CAR Government sent troops to the DRC border in mid-January.

In early March 2009 the Ugandan army announced the capture of a high-ranking LRA member, Thomas Kwoyelo. His trial—Uganda's first war crimes trial against an LRA commander—began in September 2011, but ended after a few days when Kwoyelo was granted an amnesty by the Constitutional Court. The decision came as the joint military operation against the LRA appeared to be under strain. Nationalist Congolese politicians put pressure on the DRC Government to demand that Ugandan troops leave the country. Despite reiterating the joint commitment to persevere with operations against the LRA, in mid-March the Ugandan Government began to withdraw its 300 troops based in the DRC, leaving the Congolese army to continue alone.

From mid-2009 Ugandan armed forces took their military operation against the LRA into the CAR, disrupting the rebel group; several senior LRA commanders were captured or killed. In September Okot Atiak, reported to have led an attack in northern Uganda in 1995 in which more than 200 civilians were killed, was captured; Charles Arop, believed to have organized the attack in eastern DRC in December 2008 in which 143 civilians were killed and 160 children abducted, surrendered; and Bok Abudema was killed in January 2010. Despite these successes, the LRA continued to kill and abduct civilians across a large swathe of northern DRC, the CAR and southern Sudan. In December 2009 UN Human Rights Commissioner Navanethem Pillay accused the LRA of having killed at least 1,200 civilians between September 2008 and June 2009, mostly in the CAR and southern Sudan.

In November 2010 US President Barack Obama announced a 'new' strategy to defeat the LRA, which would focus on protecting civilians, arresting (or eliminating) senior commanders, encouraging the disarmament of LRA fighters and increasing humanitarian assistance for those living in the worst affected areas. In October 2011 the USA announced that it was to send an additional 100 US troops to the region.

In March 2012 'Kony 2012', a video produced by the US organization Invisible Children, attracted world-wide attention for its depiction of the LRA and of Uganda. The film drew widespread criticism for simplifying the conflict, and for the impression that the LRA was still militarily active in Uganda. Prime Minister Amama Mbabazi denounced the film for suggesting that Uganda was still at war. But with more than 80m. people watching the video across the world, the controversy brought the LRA back to international attention.

Having been captured in the Central African Republic in May 2012, senior LRA commander Caesar Acellan's request for an amnesty under the terms of the 2000 Amnesty Law was rejected by the Director of Public Prosecutions, Richard Butera. He argued that Acellan had been captured rather than having handed himself in and was, thus, not entitled to be considered for an amnesty. Acellan was transferred to a Ugandan army base in South Sudan.

From 2010 Uganda faced a new internal security threat arising from its involvement in the African Union military operation in Somalia. On 11 July 2010 two bombs killed at least 74 people in Kampala, and injured about 70 others. Suicide attackers were believed to have detonated their bombs at a rugby club and an Ethiopian restaurant while those attending were watching the Fédération Internationale de Football Association World Cup on television screens. The militant Somali organization al-Shabaab claimed responsibility, citing Uganda's support for the Somali Transitional Federal Government (TFG) and the presence of Ugandan armed forces in Somalia as its reasons for carrying out the attack. In September 2011 two Ugandans who admitted involvement in the 2010 Kampala bombing received prison sentences. Edris Nsubuga had pleaded guilty to planting the explosives, and Muhamoud Mugisha to conspiracy in connection with the attack. Charges against Kenyan human rights activist, Al-Amin Kimathi, who alleged that he had been framed by the Kenyan Government, were dropped. Three others arrested on suspicion of involvement in the 2010 Kampala bombing alleged that they had been illegally transferred from Kenya (where they had been arrested) to Uganda, and had been interrogated by British intelligence agents. In June 2012 the British High Court rejected the case brought by the men in London, although it did not comment on the substance of the allegations. From 2010 Ugandan security services regularly warned of planned terrorist attacks in the country, and arrested several individuals accused of plotting terrorist attacks.

REGIONAL RELATIONS

During the January–February 2008 post-election crisis in Kenya, Museveni played a key role in bringing Kenyan President, Mwai Kibaki, and the leader of Kenya's opposition Orange Democratic Movement, Raila Odinga, to a negotiated settlement.

In March 1996 Museveni, President Daniel arap Moi of Kenya and President Benjamin Mkapa of Tanzania formally inaugurated the secretariat of the permanent tripartite commission for East African co-operation. A treaty for the re-establishment of the defunct East African Community (EAC), providing for the creation of a free trade area and for the establishment of a regional legislative assembly and regional court, was signed in November 1999. In January 2005 the East African Customs Union came into effect. In December 2006 Rwanda and Burundi were accepted as members of the EAC, expanding the bloc to include around 90m. people.

In October 2008 the three main African trading blocs, the EAC, the Southern African Development Community and the Common Market for Eastern and Southern Africa, signed an agreement in Kampala to create a single free trade zone of 26 countries. As well as improving African trade within the continent, it was hoped the agreement would lead to a stronger negotiating position with external trading powers.

In February 2004 Uganda joined four other East African countries in forming the Eastern African Standby Brigade (EASB), which was to form part of the AU's African Standby Force (ASF). The ASF was intended to form the heart of Africa's response to conflict on the continent, and the EASB was one of five regional brigades to be established. In March 2007 Uganda sent 1,700 troops to Somalia as part of an AU peace-keeping force. Uganda also agreed to host a training camp for 2,000 Somali security forces for the Somali TFG. In August 2011 Eritrean President Isaias Afewerki made an official visit to Uganda in order to restore relations between the two countries, following allegations that Eritrea was providing support to the Islamist al-Shabaab militia in Somalia, against which Ugandan forces were fighting. During the early 1990s Uganda was providing support for Laurent-Désiré Kabila, leader of the Alliance des Forces Démocratiques pour la Libération du Congo-Zaïre, which overthrew the Government of President Mobutu Sese Seko in May 1997. However, Kabila's failure to tackle Ugandan rebels in the renamed DRC led to renewed tensions, and Uganda provided support to anti-Kabila rebels in 1998 in co-operation with the Rwandan Government.

In April 2001 the UN reported that Burundi, Rwanda and Uganda were all illegally exploiting mineral reserves in the DRC. Museveni agreed to withdraw troops, but Rwandan armed forces then occupied positions vacated by the UPDF. In April 2002 the two Governments signed a peace treaty in Kigali, and in mid-August the DRC and Uganda signed an agreement leading to the full withdrawal of Ugandan troops from the DRC. In September 2010 a leaked UN report accused Ugandan armed forces of war crimes during their involvement in the DRC between 1993 and 2003.

In December 2006 leaders from the Great Lakes countries signed a security and development agreement in Kenya. A joint military action programme was agreed in April the following year, in which Burundi, the DRC, Rwanda and Uganda agreed joint military action against rebel groups destabilizing the region. In 2008 Ugandan and DRC Governments pursued a joint military campaign against the LRA.

In August 2007 the UN High Commissioner for Refugees (UNHCR) announced that most of the 10,000 refugees from the DRC had returned to their homes. However, relations between Uganda and the DRC became increasingly tense as each sought to establish claims over disputed petroleum reserves in Lake Albert, along the border. Both sides built up troops in the disputed border area, and minor skirmishes took place in August and September (in the former month, a British contractor for the Canadian company Heritage Oil was killed). In early September Museveni and Kabila agreed to withdraw troops, but claims of sovereignty continued to be contested, especially over Rukwanzi island, administered by Uganda until the late 1980s and subsequently settled by Congolese fishermen.

As violence escalated in eastern DRC, the Ugandan Government opened a third refugee camp to accommodate those fleeing the conflict. Since November 2011 around 3,000 Congolese refugees had entered the country. In July 2012 around 600 soldiers from the DRC fled into Uganda after rebels in eastern DRC entered the border town of Bunagana forcing out government troops.

Relations between Sudan and Uganda became tense from the late 1980s, with each accusing the other of harbouring and supporting their respective outlawed rebel soldiers. A brief rapprochement in 1996 was ended when Sudan claimed forces had killed several hundred Ugandan soldiers who had been assisting Sudanese rebels from within Sudan. In December 1999 Presidents Museveni and Omar al-Bashir met in Nairobi and signed a peace agreement. Each country agreed to stop hosting guerrilla groups directed against each other. The two Presidents also agreed to resume full diplomatic relations. In August 2001 al-Bashir announced that his Government would no longer provide support for the LRA, and in 2002 stated that Sudan was to allow the UPDF to deploy forces within its borders in order to pursue operations against the LRA. In March UPDF troops captured all four main LRA bases in Sudan.

Although Uganda accused Sudan of renewing support for the LRA in mid-2003, in October 2005 the UPDF was granted permission by the Sudanese Government to pursue LRA rebels beyond the 62-mile limit accepted in previous negotiations. However, US authorities continued to accuse the Government in Khartoum of providing covert support for the LRA in 2007 and 2008

Relations with Rwanda, which had deteriorated in the early 1990s, improved following the victory in Rwanda of the Front Patriotique Rwandais (FPR) in mid-1994. In August 1998 Uganda and Rwanda jointly deployed troops in the DRC, although tensions subsequently emerged between the two forces (see above). However, this tension eased when both armies withdrew from Kisangani during May 2000, and in July Museveni and Rwandan President Paul Kagame met to discuss relations between their two countries.

In October 2011 the British Prime Minister David Cameron threatened to withdraw a proportion of British aid to Uganda unless it respected gay rights. The threat caused considerable anger in Uganda, which saw the intervention as interfering in domestic politics. However, Uganda's increasingly hardline stance against homosexuality continued to provoke condemnation from the international community, with US President Barack Obama describing the harassment of gay Ugandans as 'odious'.

Economy

LINDA VAN BUREN

Revised for this edition by DUNCAN WOODSIDE

INTRODUCTION

With potential commercially viable reserves in the so-called 'Albertine' *graben* (a *graben* being an elongated block of the earth's crust lying between two faults and displaced downwards) amounting to perhaps as much as 2,000m. barrels, petroleum is set to make an appreciable impact on most of Uganda's economic indicators, particularly government revenue, gross domestic product (GDP) and development expenditure. The IMF in May 2010 described Uganda's oil potential as 'large but temporary', with a life span of 25 years. Future discoveries could extend that life span. Although President Yoweri Museveni predicted in 2002 that exploitation would begin 'by 2009', later forecasts set the beginning of oil exploitation on a commercial scale at 2015. Based on discoveries so far, production would peak in 2016–18, at which time oil would contribute 8% of GDP, and would decline thereafter very gradually. In 2010, while Uganda's private sector oil-exploration partners continued their 'spudding' work (the commencement of drilling operations) in and near Lake Albert and Lake Edward, the Museveni Government was establishing what the IMF described as 'a sound legal and institutional framework for the management and use of oil revenues'. This framework included a transparent regulatory environment, measures to prevent and limit unintended leakages, transport arrangements (including a pipeline extension), and the feasibility of building a refinery in Uganda with an output capacity of 150,000 barrels per day (b/d).

Meanwhile, still in the pre-oil era, the Ugandan economy suffered negative effects from the global economic downturn in 2008 and 2009, but growth remained positive throughout. Real GDP growth slowed from 7.1% in 2008/09 to 5.2% in 2009/10, but it recovered to 6.3% in 2010/11. However, economic growth in 2011 was less robust, slowing in the second half of the year, owing to a withdrawal of fiscal stimulus. Indeed, the Government had increased spending before the February election, which was won easily by incumbent President Museveni. In the final quarter of 2011, the economy shrank by 1.1% year-on-year (after a 4.8% year-on-year increase in the third quarter), owing to monetary and fiscal tightening at home, together with renewed troubles in key European export markets. The industrial sector performed particularly badly in the fourth quarter, contracting by 15% year-on-year, owing largely to rising domestic borrowing costs. The construction market also came under heavy pressure. In an assessment of Uganda's economy in March 2012, the IMF reported that the authorities continued to face significant policy challenges, including high inflation and a substantial current account deficit, both of which required corrective action (i.e. a continuation of high interest rates). In this context, the IMF estimated GDP growth in 2011/12 at a modest 4.3%, although it forecast an increase to 5.5% in 2012/13 and a continued gradual climb to a range of 6.0%–7.0% over the medium-term. However, this was contingent upon a sustained reduction in the inflation rate and a recovery of important export markets, notably the euro zone economy, parts of which fell back into recession in 2012, owing to sovereign debt crises in weaker member economies.

AGRICULTURE

Agriculture is the most important sector in this land-locked country in terms of employment and export revenue. In 2009 agriculture provided a livelihood for about 70% of the population, accounted for 41% of export revenue and contributed 24% of GDP. According to Uganda Bureau of Statistics figures, in 2009 about 11% of total GDP came from the non-monetary sector of the economy, 6% of the total was from agricultural non-monetary activity, and 4% of the total was from food-crop non-monetary activity. However, the sector suffered from the effects of low rainfall and drought in 2010/11 and grew by just

0.9% in that year, compared with 2.4% in 2009/10. Output of cash crops decreased by nearly 16%, while food-crop production grew by only 2.7% and the livestock sector expanded by 3.0%.

Besides coffee, agricultural exports in 2010 included maize, simsim (sesame seeds), cocoa beans, fish and fish products, beans, cowhides and flowers. Simsim exports in 2010/11 increased by 83%, while maize exports grew by 17% (thereby exacerbating shortages on the domestic market and driving up food prices and inflation) and fish exports rose by 16%. Soils are generally fertile, and aside from some parts of the north-east and the north-west, the country has a climate favourable to both field crops and livestock production. Smallholder mixed farming predominates, with estate production confined mainly to tea and sugar cane. In most years there is no shortage of food in Uganda as a whole, but sometimes security issues mean that surpluses cannot always be taken to the areas of greatest need. The most vulnerable area in 2010 was the Karamoja region, in the north-east, where both hunger and malnutrition prevail. The World Food Programme (WFP) lists reasons for this region's vulnerability as gun violence, frequent natural disasters and severe environmental degradation. Key challenges facing Ugandan agriculture in general were lack of access to affordable technology and lack of access to sufficient, reliable and affordable electricity in rural areas, which precludes the development of agro-processing industries and also makes impossible the refrigeration needed to preserve perishables.

Coffee

Coffee is grown by some 2.5m. small-scale farmers. Both Robusta and Arabica are produced, with Robusta accounting for 75% of the total crop by volume in 2010/11. Production of the higher-value Arabica coffee accounted for the remaining 25%. Total production amounted to 3.1m. 60-kg bags in 2010 (October 2009 to September 2010), compared with 2.8m. bags in 2009. In a climate of strong global coffee prices, Uganda's earnings from coffee exports rose by 13.1% in 2010/11, compared with the previous year. The Uganda Coffee Development Authority (UCDA) is responsible for policy-making, as well as for research and development, for promotion, for the co-ordination of marketing,and for quality control. At that time, Uganda was the biggest national coffee exporter in Africa and the ninth largest in the world, according to the International Coffee Organization.

Indications for the 2011/12 coffee crop, appeared favourable. Exports for the period October 2011 to May 2012 totalled 1.74m. 60-kg bags, little changed from the 1.75m. bags shipped during the first eight months of the previous season, owing to strong production in Masaka and in the south-west of the country. At that time, the UCDA announced that it expected annual coffee exports for 2011/12 to register between 3.1m. and 3.2m. bags.

Cotton

In 2010/11 export revenue from cotton rose dramatically to US $67m., compared with $17m. in the previous year. The cotton sector is regulated by the Cotton Development Organization (CDO). The country has 29 ginneries, of which 27 are double-roller gins. A high proportion of Uganda's output is long-staple cotton, which commands a price premium sometimes as high as 20%. The cotton sector is a particular focus of the Government's bid to increase the amount of value added to agricultural products before export. Uganda produced 66,000 metric tons of seed cotton in 2009, yielding 23,000 tons of cotton lint and 40,000 tons of cottonseed. In the local vegetable oil industry, cottonseed oil faces stiff competition from imported palm oil. A growth area within the cotton sector is organic cotton.

Horticulture

Horticulture became significant in Uganda in the late 1990s. Horticultural produce ranges from beans and peas to tomatoes, onions, pimientos, ginger, simsim and vanilla pods. In 2010/11 exports of simsim rose by 83%. Uganda produces some 48 metric tons of vanilla annually. The Kasese Smallholder Income and Investment Programme (KSIIP) seeks to boost the incomes of more than 2,000 small-scale farmers in the western part of Uganda. Their initial focus was on the growing of organic high-quality vanilla pods on the slopes of the Rwenzori Mountains, also known as the Mountains of the Moon; the 'traditionally cured bourbon' vanilla is marketed under the name Vanilla Moon. KSIIP then expanded into the growing of hot peppers, passion fruit and moringa, a tree crop, long ignored but rediscovered in the 21st century as something of a miracle plant. Its nutritious high-protein leaves can be used as food for humans and animals, and the defatted meal can be used to purify drinking water. But the most topical use of moringa is as a biofuel. Uganda exported 4,678 tons of flowers in 2008/09, earning $48.5m. in that year; export revenue from flowers rose to US $49.4m. in 2009/10.

Nation-wide, about 6,000 Ugandans work in the horticultural sector, about 80% of them women. According to FAO, Uganda produced 960,412 metric tons of fresh vegetables and melons in 2009, up from 867,245 tons in 2008. In an effort to add more value locally before export, some vegetables are exported frozen. Limiting factors are high air-freight charges and inadequate storage facilities at Entebbe airport to keep horticultural produce fresh while it awaits air-freight space to Europe. In 2000 the Ugandan Flower Exporters' Association (UFEA) and the Horticultural Exporters' Association (Hortexa) set up Fresh Handling Services Limited to organize the logistics of exporting these perishable commodities to distant markets, especially the Netherlands. Ugandan horticultural exporters pay air-freight costs of US $2.40 per kg, whereas Kenyan and Ethiopian exporters pay $1.70 per kg and $1.50 per kg, respectively. Uganda's flower growers specialize in small roses and, to a lesser extent, chrysanthemums. A new 13-ha joint venture announced in July 2007 between Madhvani of Uganda and Flower Direct of the Netherlands specializes in chrysanthemums. Roses are grown on 142 ha, and chrysanthemums are grown on 32 ha. In 2008 one rose grower alone was exporting 9m. stems per month, representing 35% of the country's rose-export sub-sector. The number of flower-growing companies increased from three in 1993 to 18 in 2007. Of the 18, seven were owned by Ugandans, three were owned jointly by Ugandan and foreign investors, and eight were owned by foreign investors, including three Dutch firms.

Tea

Uganda was the third largest tea producer in Africa in 2009, behind Kenya and Malawi. In addition to its cultivation of tea, the Toro and Mityana Tea Co (a wholly owned subsidiary of the United Kingdom-based company Mitchell Cotts) has branched out into growing lemon grass and rosemary for use in herbal teas and infusions. Other tea producers include Rwenzori Highlands Tea Co, which comprises six tea estates covering over 3,000 ha in western Uganda, along the border with the Democratic Republic of the Congo (DRC). Smallholders, numbering about 1m. and cultivating some 9,500 ha, market their output through the Uganda Tea Growers' Association. The Uganda Tea Authority organizes research into growing methods and oversees the sector, which has benefited from the success of Uganda's economic reform programme, with higher real wages attracting harvest labour. Uganda harvested 41,000 metric tons of tea in 2010. Revenue from tea exports rose from US $50.2m. in 2008/09 to $65.7m. in 2009/10.

Other Crops

Uganda produces some 2.35m. metric tons of sugar cane per annum. Output of sugar was forecast at 350,000 tons in 2011, up from 292,000 tons in 2010. Kakira Sugar Works, part of the Madhvani Group, is the country's largest producer of sugar, with output of some 180,000 tons per annum, more than one-half of the national total. Kinyara Sugar Works, 51% owned by the Rai Group of Mauritius and Kenya, projected that its sugar output would amount to 126,000 tons in 2011, or about 40% of total national production. The Sugar Corporation of Uganda was expecting to produce 54,000 tons in 2011.

Despite declining global demand, production of tobacco leaves rose from 11,333 metric tons in 1998 to a record 36,310 tons in 2002; output in 2010 was 26,000 tons, according to FAO. Tobacco export earnings rose from US $62.6m. in 2008/09 to $78.0m. in 2009/10.

Production of cocoa beans increased from 13,000 metric tons in 2008 to 15,000 tons in 2009, according to FAO, and exports rose from 8,982 tons to 11,881 tons over the same period.

Output of groundnuts in shells was a record 185,000 tons in 2009, but declined to 172,000 tons in 2010. Uganda's staple food crop is matoke, a form of plantain. Output of matoke was an FAO-estimated record 9.51m. tons in 2009, compared with 9.37m. tons in 2008. Also contributing towards national food requirements in 2010 were cassava, sweet potatoes, maize, finger millet, sorghum, potatoes and various pulses (mainly dry beans, pigeon peas and dry cow peas). Both pulses and potatoes are seen as growth sectors among food crops. The International Finance Corpn, an affiliate of the World Bank, provided a US $2.4m. loan to Tilda Uganda Ltd for the development of an integrated rice-growing and -processing facility at Kibimba, in eastern Uganda. The rice mill, with a capacity of 5 tons per hour, processes rice grown locally by smallholders in addition to that cultivated on the main farm. Uganda produced a record 218,000 tons of rice in 2010, up from 178,000 tons in 2008. Maize cultivation is expanding, both for subsistence and as a cash crop, although transport problems and the poor state of rural roads hamper the transit of crops; the 2009 harvest was a record 1.27m. tons. Maize exports rose from 66,670 tons in 2008 to 94,441 tons in 2009, and earned $27m. in 2010/11, a 17% increase over the $23.14m. achieved in 2009/10. Production of soybeans rose reached 175,000 in 2010. Small amounts of ginger, chickpeas, chillies and peppercorns were also produced.

Livestock, Fishing and Forestry

Beef and dairy cattle are kept by smallholders and on large commercial ranches. The country has good-quality pasture, but the prevalence of several endemic diseases and cattle-rustling (the armed theft of cattle) are persistent problems. The total number of cattle was estimated at 7.8m. in 2010. Dairy cattle account for about one-third of the national cattle herd. Goats, pigs, sheep, bees and poultry are also important. Potential has been particularly identified in beekeeping; Uganda had more than 76,000 beehives in 2009, and honey exports could be increased with better marketing overseas.

Although it is land-locked, Uganda has an abundance of lakes and rivers, and fishing is an important rural industry, with considerable scope for further development, particularly in inshore fish farming of eels and freshwater prawns. Uganda has shores on three major lakes: Lake Victoria (Africa's largest), Lake Albert, and Lake Edward. The total catch was an estimated 415,000 metric tons in 2010, of which some 40,000 tons was produced by fish farming. Exports of fish and fish products amounted to 21,502 tons in 2009, and revenue from these exports rose by 16% from US $143.53m. in 2009/10 to $166m. in 2010/11, contributing almost 10% of total exports in the latter year. Ugandan fisheries authorities have complained that while neighbouring Kenya owns only 6% of Lake Victoria compared with the 43% owned by Uganda, Kenya has 16 fish-processing plants on its shore of the lake and earns $200m. a year from the export of Lake Victoria fish.

Forests and woodland cover some 7.5m. ha of the country, although very little of it is regarded as primary forest by the UN. Total roundwood removals amounted to 43.7m. cu m in 2011, of which 39.6m. cu m ended up as wood fuel.

BANKING SECTOR AND MONETARY POLICY

Uganda's banking sector has developed significantly since the turn of the century, largely as a result of the involvement of major foreign operators, most notably Barclays, Standard Chartered and Stanbic, with the latter being the country's largest lender in mid-2012. Credit growth has been very strong in recent years, providing significant assistance to the development of private enterprises in the country. In view of this, the IMF reiterated in October 2011 that the central bank would need to monitor risks to banks' balance sheets in a more stringent way. However, the Bank of Uganda has taken steps to address such risks, including increasing minimum capital requirements. As of March 2011, banks were required to hold a minimum paid-up capital level of Us. 10,000m. (at that time, the equivalent of US $4.2m), before a further increase to Us. 25,000m. by March 2013. The central bank's own data showed a reduction of non-performing loans in Uganda's banking sector from 4.2% of total loans at the end of 2009 to 2.5% in March 2011.

The three major commercial banks cited registered strong profit growth in Uganda during 2011. Standard Chartered Uganda announced in April 2012 that its net profit in 2011 rose to Us. 98,200m., from Us. 73,000m. in 2010, owing largely to an increase in its loan book. Barclays Bank Uganda, meanwhile, saw its net profit in 2011 more than double, to Us. 21,200m., from Us. 9,700m. in 2010. Stanbic, the local unit of South Africa's Standard Bank Group, reported a 69% increase in annual net profit to Us. 121,700m. However, these strong results were tempered somewhat in foreign currency terms, owing to a depreciation of the local currency during 2011. The Ugandan shilling averaged 2,520 to the US dollar during 2011, compared to 2,170 in 2010, a depreciation of 16%. The key factor behind this was inflation, as consumer prices rose 27.0% in 2011, up from a very modest 3.1% in 2010, due largely to rising food prices across the region. Droughts in neighbouring countries, together with export restrictions on maize in Tanzania, put upward pressure on food prices in Uganda. Concerns about Uganda's fiscal situation, caused by excessive government spending during the elections in February 2011, also contributed to the higher inflation rate. The Bank of Uganda was therefore forced to tighten monetary policy, with its key lending rate reaching 23% at the end of 2011, up from 13% in July. Accordingly, banks increased the lending rates they charged to consumers, provoking outcry from much of the country's business community. In January 2012 food traders in Kampala city centre went on strike in protest at the high cost of borrowing. In an attempt to placate borrowers, Prime Minister Amama Mbabazi told the state-aligned *New Vision* newspaper that commercial banks had promised to review their rates in order to reduce the pressure on borrowers. The Bank of Uganda, however, remained determined to reduce inflation and only lowered its key lending rate modestly in the first half of 2012. In June it cut the key lending rate by 1%, taking it to 20%, after two similar reductions earlier in the year. This cautious approach was due to inflation remaining stubbornly high, with consumer price growth running at an annual average of 18.6% in May.

Despite the tightness of monetary policy, investment in Uganda continued to rise in the first few months of 2012. The Uganda Investment Authority announced in May that planned investments more than trebled quarter-on-quarter in the first three months of the year, to US $806m., up from $223.3m. in the fourth quarter of 2011. The principal recipients of investment were the energy, mining, real estate and business service sectors, with the former underpinned by the Government setting aside Us. 215,000m. ($86.6m.) for the planned 700-MW Karuma hydroelectric project. This resulted in domestic sources being the principal contributor to planned investment, with the Government and private local sources accounting for $708m. of pledges in the first three months of 2012, with the next biggest source being Sweden, with $78m.

INDUSTRY

The manufacturing sector is dominated by food-processing and the production of beverages and tobacco products, activities which account for more than 60% of all manufacturing output. Other manufacturing sub-sectors include chemicals, paints, soap and foam products; metals and related products; bricks and cement; textiles, clothing and footwear; and paper products. The Uganda Manufacturers' Association (UMA) has long stressed that manufacturing could expand much faster if it were not for the country's faltering electricity supply. The industrial sector as a whole contributed 23% of GDP in 2009/10 and grew by 7.5% in 2010/11. Manufacturing contributed 7.6% of GDP and expanded by 10.0% in 2009. The Government has sought to encourage private sector investment in a myriad of manufacturing activities, ranging from packaging materials to fish sausages.

The textile industry has suffered from a severe lack of skilled personnel and spare parts as well as from unreliable supplies of electricity. There are four fully integrated textile mills, with a total rated capacity of 66m. linear metres of cloth per year. Yarn is also produced. Uganda's largest textile factory, Southern Range Nyanza Limited, covers 60,000 sq m and is fully integrated, comprising spinning, weaving, dyeing, printing and garmenting operations.

There are two cement plants, at Tororo (near the Kenyan border) and at Hima (about 500 km to the west), with rated annual capacities of 150,000 metric tons and 300,000 tons, respectively. Total domestic requirements are estimated at 650,000 tons per year.

MINERALS

An airborne geophysical survey over 80% of Uganda, the results of which were released in July 2009, found gold deposits not only in Busia and Mubende but also in Busheny, Hoima, Jinja, Kabale, Kabarole, Karamoja, Kibaale, Kisoro, Kitgum, Mbale, Rukungiri and West Nile. In addition, the survey confirmed deposits of other minerals, including cobalt, copper, limestone, phosphate and uranium. Grey Crown Resources describes Uganda's potential mineral wealth as 'vast' and its mining investment incentive programme as 'progressive'. Gold has been confirmed in Ibanda, and exploration is under way in the Buhwezi Plateau by Magnus International Resources Inc of Canada, which also owns gold exploration concessions in Mubende and Lugazi. In April 2009 Australia's Gulf Resources purchased the Namekhala vermiculite mine from British-Australian company Rio Tinto for an undisclosed sum and renamed it East African Vermiculite (EAV). Gulf Resources stated its intention to inject US $500,000 worth of working capital into the operation in the 12 months to April 2010, in order to achieve a sustainable production rate of 8,000 metric tons of vermiculite product per annum. Production commenced in May 2010. The company forecast a production rate of 25,000 tons per annum by 2012.

A 2002/03 evaluation study of Uganda's columbo-tantalite resources identified seven sites in Ntungamo district for further evaluation. They are part of central Africa's 'coltan' belt. A study, financed by the World Bank, was made by US and French consultants on a phosphate fertilizer project using phosphate deposits in the Sukulu hills in eastern Uganda. These deposits have estimated reserves of 30m. metric tons. The study recommended construction of a plant to make single superphosphates, with an initial capacity of 80,000 tons per year. The Madhvani Group, through its Belgian-based subsidiary Nilefos Chemie, announced plans in May 2008 to invest US $535m. to develop the Sukulu phosphate project over the five years to 2013. High-grade iron-ore deposits at Kigezi have not yet been exploited. Haematite iron ore is exploited in Kabale district, in the south-west, to supply domestic iron and steel operations. The concession to mine tungsten at Bjordal, a remote site in the Nyamuliro Wolfram Hills near Kabale, was awarded to the Ugandan company Krone Uganda Limited. Uranium deposits have been identified in six areas and President Museveni has stated that Uganda's uranium could be exploited for local consumption in energy supply. Copper, apatite, tungsten, beryl, columbo-tantalite, gold, bismuth, phosphate, limestone and tin are among the minerals Uganda produced in the past, albeit mostly on a small scale.

HYDROCARBONS

Petroleum exploration proceeded slowly until the 21st century. In 2000 Uganda had no known commercially exploitable oil reserves; however, by 2010, the country had 800m. barrels of proven recoverable oil reserves, with estimated 'potential' reserves of as much as 2,000m. barrels, at a time when exploration was still proceeding. Interest centres on the so-called Albertine *graben*. Uganda shares the Albertine *graben* with the DRC, and once oil was discovered, both countries took a much more fervid interest in defining and protecting their shared borders. The Albertine *graben* on Uganda's western border has two major lakes, Lake Albert and Lake Edward, both of which are also shared with the DRC. Oil has been discovered both in these lakes and on their eastern shores. Uganda's portion of the Albertine *graben* has been divided into 10 exploration areas (EAs), five of which (EAs 1 to 5) have been licensed to oil-exploration companies. By May 2010 a total of 37 exploratory wells had been drilled in Uganda, and 34 of them had encountered hydrocarbons, for a technical success rate of 91.9%. Results have been positive enough that the licensees in EA 1, EA 2 and EA 3A have entered the 'farm-in, farm-out' stage in order to attract the large capital commitment that is needed for the development phase. Interest has been keen among major oil companies such as Total of France and the China National Offshore Oil Corpn.

In July 2007 Tullow Oil, while exploring for oil in Hoima district in western Uganda, chanced unexpectedly upon natural gas. In May 2010 Uganda announced plans for an integrated power project to use gas from the Nzizi discovery in Kaiso-Tonya to generate electricity. In 2010 the Museveni Government established a framework agreement for the management and use of the country's oil revenues, which included creating and implementing a modern, transparent legal and regulatory environment; putting in place measures to prevent and limit unintended leakages such as that which occurred in the Gulf of Mexico in 2010; building secure storage facilities; financing and constructing secure transport arrangements across at least two countries; and the feasibility of building a refinery in Uganda. Such a refinery would allow Uganda to add value close to source and to export not crude petroleum but instead refined petroleum products to the East African region and beyond. The refinery, as proposed in 2010, would have a capacity of 150,000 b/d and would cost US $2,000m. Owing to Uganda's land-locked geographical position, it will require the co-operation of Kenya and Tanzania to allow access to their seaports. In any case, costly and reliable transport arrangements would need to be built with one or both of these countries before oil revenues could begin to flow in.

Tullow Oil agreed a US $2,900m. deal with France's Total and China National Offshore Oil Corporation for the exploitation of its Ugandan fields. This 'farm-down' agreement, which involved the sale by Tullow of 66% of its stakes in Uganda to the French and Chinese companies, followed almost one year of negotiations. Tullow announced that the deal paved the way for a significant increase in production from 2016, in a context where in excess of $10,000m. of investment would be pumped into the various oilfields by the various stakeholders. For its part, France's Total announced in April 2012 that it intended to spend over $300m. during the course of that year on exploring for oil (and starting production) in Uganda.

In October 2011 Uganda's Parliament established a committee to scrutinize alleged corruption in the oil sector, after a lawmaker, Gerald Karuhanga, presented documentation alleging that bribes had been paid by international operators to Prime Minister Amama Mbabazi, former Minister of Foreign Affairs Sam Kutesa and former Minister of Internal Affairs Hilary Onek. Tullow repeatedly stated that it had never been involved in any such activity and claimed, in a statement to the parliamentary committee in April 2012, that the documentary evidence purporting to show bribery had been forged.

Further expansion of Uganda's oil sector appears highly likely. In March 2012 the Uganda Chamber of Mines and Petroleum announced that it would auction four new blocks, together with 10,000 sq km of relinquished acreage. The auctions were tentatively scheduled for early 2013, contingent upon approval by Uganda's Parliament of legislation modernizing the oil sector's regulatory framework. In February 2012 Parliament referred two pieces of proposed legislation, which would introduce new laws for the allocation of oil wells, together with the management of transport, refinement and revenue management, to its Natural Resources Committee. This committee had been due to report back to parliament in April 2012, but in mid-2012 it was still deliberating. Meanwhile, Uganda's oil sector was still being governed by a legal framework established in 1985 (i.e. before the discovery of significant hydrocarbon deposits). In March 2012 Global Witness, a non-governmental organization specializing in the scrutiny of natural resource management in developing countries, raised concerns about Uganda's proposed legislation. It pointed in particular to what it regarded as excessive ministerial control, a lack of commitment to financial transparency and minimal scope for parliamentary scrutiny.

POWER

Uganda has immense hydroelectric potential, most of it not yet exploited. It is thought that the country has at least 3,000 MW of hydroelectric potential, of which less than 10% is exploited. Fewer than 5% of Ugandans are connected to the national electricity grid, and in some parts of the country even large towns have no electricity supply. Power shortages are the major factor hindering Uganda's economic growth and development. In 2007 a poll was conducted to gauge the performance of Uganda's manufacturing sector. Of the 150 companies surveyed, 18 reported that the frequent power shortages were forcing them to contemplate permanent closure. The shortages are exacerbated during periods of drought, as in 2011, since the supply of water to the country's hydroelectric facilities is reduced. This reduction in supply, coupled with growing demand, left Uganda's national grid with a shortfall of almost 200 MW at peak periods in 2011. In June 2011 load-shedding amounted to some 30 hours per week.

Electricity is generated at the Nalubaale (formerly Owen Falls) hydroelectric station at Jinja; its capacity has been extended to 380 MW. A new US $550m., 250-MW dam at Bujagali Falls, near Jinja, was proposed by the Madhvani Group and AES Corpn of the USA; despite objections from environmentalists, promoters of the project won the approval of the Cabinet, of Parliament and of the people living at the proposed site. The project involves the construction of a dam 30 m in height on the Victoria Nile (which began in 2007), 100 km of transmission lines and two sub-stations.

The 240-MW Kiyara Power Station near Jinja, built at a cost of US $230m., became operational in 2000 and produces power both for Uganda and for export to Kenya. The Kiira power plant, formerly known as the Owen Falls extension, contributes 120 MW to the national grid when operating at full capacity, using three 40-MW units. Two more units of 40 MW each have been proposed at Kiira. Construction of the new 700-MW Karuma Falls hydropower scheme, downstream from Bujagali Falls, was due to begin in 2011. However, construction of this new facility was repeatedly delayed. In May 2012 a national newspaper reported that the government committee overseeing the process had yet to appoint a project manager, amid internal wrangling over candidates.

In the feasibility-study stage in 2011 was the new Isimba hydropower project, with a projected capacity of 100 MW; construction was due to commence in 2012. Also proposed in 2010 was the 550–650-MW Ayago scheme, while a 230-MW power plant in Tororo district was due for completion by the end of 2011. In addition, several renewable-energy projects were under construction. One, the 13-MW Bugoye scheme, was completed in October 2009. Four more such projects were stated in June 2010 to be 'near completion': the 18-MW Mpanga, the 10-MW Buseruka, the 6.5-MW Ishasha and the 3.3-MW Nyagak hydropower scheme. The rehabilitation of the Maziba hydropower facility in West Nile was at the feasibility study stage in 2010. Development of a 10-MW project at Kikagati, however, was said in 2010 to have 'stalled due to trans-boundary issues'. Kikagati was one of four proposed mini-hydroelectric facilities with a combined output of 75 MW; the other three were Muzizi, Nshongyenzi and Waki. The Government claimed in 2008 that as much as 25% of the electricity that was being generated in the country was being lost because of theft. A further 13% was lost as a result of the dilapidated state of the electricity distribution system.

The need to increase generation was underscored by increasingly frequent and severe power cuts in late 2011, which were greeted by popular protest in parts of Kampala. In January 2012 the Government removed power subsidies, which it had been paying to generators in order to control retail prices in the sector. It was anticipated that the abolition of these subsidies would provoke an increase in the consumer price of electricity of more than 40%. Energy minister Irene Muloni justified the policy change stating that the Government had spent Us. 1,530,000m ($623.2m.) on such subsidies since 2005, despite the national fiscal accounts being under pressure. She also maintained that such funds would be better spent on enhancing generating capacity. Moreover, the persistent outages meant that there was little point in offering power below market prices, when demand was outstripping supply to such a severe extent.

TRANSPORT AND COMMUNICATIONS

In 2006 the road network comprised 10,800 km of national (trunk) roads, 27,500 km of district roads, 4,300 km of urban roads and some 30,000 km of community roads. In June 2011 about 4% of the roads in Uganda were paved. Described by the Government in that month as 'close to completion' were the Kampala–Gayaza–Zirobwe road, the Soroti–Dokolo–Lira road, and the Matugga–Semuto–Kapeeka road. A number of road-building projects were due to commence in the 2011/12 financial year, including the upgrading to bitumen of the 93-km Moroto–Nakapiripirit road, the 74-km Mukono–Katosi road, the 73-km Hoima–Kaiso–Tonya road, the 66-km Mbarara–Kikagati road, the 37-km Ntungamo–Kakitumba road, and the 35-km Ishaka–Kagamba road. Also to be upgraded to bitumen in 2011/12 were two routes linking Uganda to South Sudan: the Gulu–Atiak–Bibia/Nimule road and the Vurra–Arua–Koboko–Oraba road. Furthermore, the Government vowed to 'accelerate the planning' for the construction of a second bridge across the White Nile at Jinja, at an estimated cost of US $102m. The Kampala Northern Bypass reconstruction was completed in 2010. With $350m. in funding from the People's Republic of China, the Entebbe–Kampala highway, some 37 km in length, was also to be upgraded. Work was expected to start on the project in July 2012.

Uganda Railways Corpn (URC) forms part of the 'northern corridor'. Most Ugandan freight traffic is still transported by road to and from the Kenyan port of Mombasa. The URC carries about 1m. metric tons of freight per year, according to official estimates. In 2004 the Governments of Uganda and Kenya agreed to merge their two railways and offer them for privatization as a single unit. Rift Valley Railways (RVR) consortium, led by South African interests, secured the tender in 2005 and was to manage the line until 2031. In 2006, however, it was reported that RVR had been unable to raise the capital to pay the required fees and was seeking to bring other parties into the consortium. In October 2008 it was announced that Toll Holdings of Australia, through its subsidiary PDL Toll, would take over management of the railways from RVR. In May 2010 proposed railway works included re-opening the Tororo–Gulu–Pakwach railway line and extending it to Nimule and South Sudan; re-opening the Kampala–Kasese railway line; and re-opening the 'Southern Route' (via Tanzania) by reinstating wagon-ferry services on Lake Victoria. In water transport, proposed works included upgrading at Port Bell and Jinja to accommodate multi-purpose vessels and concluding the procurement of a vessel to replace the MV *Kabalega* on the route from Port Bell across Lake Victoria to the Tanzanian lake port of Mwanza.

The main gateway airport is Entebbe International, located 40 km south-west of Kampala. Air Uganda was founded in November 2007 and is 100% owned by the Aga Khan Fund for Economic Development; all its services are regional and connect Entebbe to Dar es Salaam and Zanzibar in Tanzania, to Juba in South Sudan, to Kigali in Rwanda, and to Nairobi and Mombasa in Kenya. Eagle Air Ltd, established in 1994, operates Uganda's only domestic services, in addition to regional routes to Juba and Yei in South Sudan. Domestic routes serve Arua, Moyo, Gulu, Pader, Mbarara and Kihihi, in addition to various national parks.

In 2003 Uganda had 61,000 fixed telephone lines and about 776,200 mobile cellular subscribers; by 2010 the country had 327,100 fixed lines and 12.83m. mobile cellular subscribers. While land lines increased by less than six-fold in seven years, mobile phones increased more than 16-fold. In 2010 Uganda had 3.1m. internet users.

THE EAST AFRICAN COMMUNITY

A treaty for the re-establishment of the East African Community (EAC), providing for the creation of a free trade area and for the development of infrastructure, tourism and agriculture within the community, was ratified in June 2000 by Uganda, Kenya and Tanzania. In 2004 a Protocol was signed for the establishment of a customs union between the three countries. Under the agreement, goods entering the EAC were to be subject to common rules; a common legal, institutional and administrative structure; and a Common External Tariff

(CET). The EAC CET came into effect on 1 January 2005. In addition to the three charter members Uganda, Kenya and Tanzania, the EAC expanded to include Burundi and Rwanda, whose full membership came into effect on 1 July 2009. The initial target date for the launch of the East African Monetary Union, with the East African shilling as a single currency throughout the five member states, was 2012, although this was later deferred to 2015. A sovereign debt crisis in the euro zone in 2011 and 2012, which threatened the continued existence of the EU's single currency, cast significant doubt on the EAC's own plans for monetary union, especially given that the East African bloc's planning for the eventual introduction of a single currency was largely based on the European experience.

PUBLIC FINANCE

The Uganda shilling, has a troubled past, and for years it was virtually worthless. In the 12 months leading up to 27 July 2009, the shilling lost more than one-fifth of its value, depreciating by 22%. Its rate of depreciation slowed to 8% in the year to 5 July 2010, but accelerated to 11% in the year to 4 July 2011, when it weakened from Us. 2,217 = US $1 on 4 July 2010 to Us. 2,525 = $1 at 4 July 2011. By 30 April 2012 the currency had strengthened slightly to $1 = Us. 2,505. Minister of Finance, Planning and Economic Development Maria Kiwanuka presented the 2011/12 budget to Parliament in June 2011. It appealed for total expenditure of Us. 9,811,800m. and forecast total revenue and grants at Us. 8,016,000m., leaving a budgetary deficit of Us. 3,522,100m. excluding grants or Us. 1,795,700m. including grants. Of total spending, Us. 4,965,900m. was recurrent expenditure, and the remaining Us. 4,803,500m. was development expenditure.

BALANCE OF PAYMENTS

Uganda's trade, services and current account balances are perennially in deficit. Export revenue in dollar terms free-on-board (f.o.b.) increased from US $2,329m. in 2009/10 to an estimated $2,413m. in 2010/11, of which coffee exports contributed 13.3%. Import costs, also f.o.b., rose from $4,168m. in 2009/10 to an estimated $4,375m. in 2010/11, of which oil imports accounted for $599m., or 13.7%. The visible trade deficit in 2010/11 was an estimated $1,963m., continuing a trend that shows this shortfall rising steadily every year from 2007/08 through to 2012/13. The current account of the balance of payments carried an estimated deficit in 2010/11 of $1,273m., with this shortfall also demonstrating the same trend. The overall balance of payments, which had recorded a surplus of $91m. in 2009/10, moved into deficit in 2010/11, with an estimated shortfall of $78m. Visible export revenue covered only 55% of import costs in 2010/11.

Gross international reserves at 30 June 2011 stood at US $2,200m., sufficient to cover 4 months' worth of projected imports in 2010/11, a level described by the IMF as 'more than comfortable'. The IMF assessed the present value of Uganda's total external debt at 30 June 2009 at US $2,018,600m., 88% of which was owed to multilateral creditors, mainly the World Bank's International Development Association (IDA). Uganda benefited from the Multilateral Debt Relief Initiative that followed the Group of Eight summit at Gleneagles, United Kingdom, in July 2005.

Statistical Survey

Sources (unless otherwise stated): Uganda Bureau of Statistics, POB 13, Entebbe; tel. (41) 320165; fax (41) 320147; e-mail ubos@infocom.co.ug; internet www.ubos.org; Statistics Department, Ministry of Finance, Planning and Economic Development, POB 8147, Kampala.

Area and Population

AREA, POPULATION AND DENSITY

Area (sq km)	
Land	199,807
Inland water and swamp	41,743
Total	241,551*
Population (census results)	
12 January 1991	16,671,705
12 September 2002	
Males	11,929,803
Females	12,512,281
Total	24,442,084
Population (official projections at mid-year)	
2010	31,784,600
2011	32,939,800
2012	34,131,400
Density (per sq km) at mid-2012	141.3

* 93,263 sq miles.

POPULATION BY AGE AND SEX

('000, official estimates at mid-2012)

	Males	Females	Total
0–14	8,635	8,676	17,311
15–64	7,911	8,447	16,358
65 and over	195	268	463
Total	16,741	17,391	34,131

Note: Totals may not be equal to the sum of components, owing to rounding.

PRINCIPAL ETHNIC GROUPS

(at census of 12 September 2002)*

Acholi	1,145,357	Basoga	2,062,920
Baganda	4,126,370	Iteso	1,568,763
Bagisu	1,117,661	Langi	1,485,437
Bakiga	1,679,519	Lugbara	1,022,240
Banyakole	2,330,212		

* Ethnic groups numbering more than 1m. persons, excluding population enumerated in hotels.

SUB-REGIONS

(population projections at mid-2012)

Region	Area (sq km)	Population	Density (per sq km)
Central	61,403	8,715,800	141.9
Western	55,277	8,487,200	153.5
Northern	85,392	7,972,200	93.4
Eastern	39,479	8,956,200	226.9
Total	241,551	34,131,400	141.3

PRINCIPAL TOWNS

(population according to provisional results of census of 12 September 2002)*

Kampala (capital)	1,208,544	Entebbe	57,518
Gulu	113,144	Kasese	53,446
Lira	89,971	Njeru	52,514
Jinja	86,520	Mukono	47,305
Mbale	70,437	Arua	45,883
Mbarara	69,208	Kabale	45,757
Masaka	61,300	Kitgum	42,929

* According to administrative divisions of 2002.

Mid-2011 ('000, incl. suburbs, UN estimate): Kampala 1,659 (Source: UN, *World Urbanization Prospects: The 2011 Revision*).

BIRTHS AND DEATHS
(annual averages, UN estimates)

	1995–2000	2000–05	2005–10
Birth rate (per 1,000)	48.7	47.9	46.3
Death rate (per 1,000)	18.2	15.8	13.2

Source: UN, *World Population Prospects: The 2010 Revision*.

2011: Birth rate 44.7 per 1,000; Death rate 12.0 per 1,000 (Source: African Development Bank).

Life expectancy (years at birth): 53.6 (males 53.0; females 54.3) in 2010 (Source: World Bank, World Development Indicators database).

EMPLOYMENT
(persons aged 10 years and over, census of 12 September 2002)*

	Males	Females	Total
Agriculture, hunting and forestry	2,545,962	2,649,779	5,195,741
Fishing	102,043	16,743	118,786
Mining and quarrying	13,613	6,127	19,740
Manufacturing	108,653	45,594	154,247
Electricity, gas and water supply	12,860	1,509	14,369
Construction	105,769	2,939	108,708
Wholesale and retail trade, repair of motor vehicles, motorcycles and personal and household goods	191,191	143,145	334,336
Hotels and restaurants	23,741	64,099	87,840
Transport, storage and communications	119,437	5,798	125,235
Financial intermediation; Real estate, renting and business activities	14,539	7,562	22,101
Public administration and defence, compulsory social security	146,319	27,278	173,597
Education	124,167	85,015	209,182
Health and social work	54,327	53,108	107,435
Other community, social and personal service activities	22,736	26,734	49,470
Private households with employed persons	14,019	19,115	33,134
Not classifiable by economic activity	120,219	76,167	196,386
Total employed	3,719,595	3,230,712	6,950,307

* Excluding population enumerated at hotels.

2003 ('000 persons aged 10 years and over): Agriculture, hunting and forestry 6,278.3; Fishing 83.3; Mining and quarrying 27.8; Manufacturing 564.9; Electricity, gas and water supply 9.3; Construction 120.4; Wholesale and retail trade, repair of motor vehicles, motorcycles and personal and household goods 1,074.2; Hotels and restaurants 240.8; Transport, storage and communications 175.9; Real estate, renting and business activities 37.0; Public administration and defence, compulsory social security 74.1; Education 240.8; Health and social work 74.1; Other community, social and personal service activities 148.2; Private households with employed persons 111.1; *Total employed* 9,260.0; Unemployed 346.0; *Total labour force* 9,606.0 (Source: ILO).

Mid-2012 ('000, estimates): Agriculture, etc. 11,621; Total labour force 15,793 (Source: FAO).

Health and Welfare

KEY INDICATORS

Total fertility rate (children per woman, 2010)	6.1
Under-5 mortality rate (per 1,000 live births, 2010)	99
HIV/AIDS (% of persons aged 15–49, 2009)	6.5
Physicians (per 1,000 head, 2005)	0.1
Hospital beds (per 1,000 head, 2010)	0.5
Health expenditure (2009): US $ per head (PPP)	118
Health expenditure (2009): % of GDP	8.5
Health expenditure (2009): public (% of total)	21.8
Access to water (% of persons, 2010)	72
Access to sanitation (% of persons, 2010)	34
Total carbon dioxide emissions ('000 metric tons, 2008)	3,747.7
Carbon dioxide emissions per head (metric tons, 2008)	0.1
Human Development Index (2011): ranking	161
Human Development Index (2011): value	0.446

For sources and definitions, see explanatory note on p. vi.

Agriculture

PRINCIPAL CROPS
('000 metric tons)

	2008	2009	2010
Rice, paddy	178	206	218
Maize	1,266	1,272	1,373*
Millet	783	841	850*
Sorghum	477	497	500*
Potatoes	670	689	695*
Sweet potatoes	2,707	2,766	2,838†
Cassava (Manioc)	5,072	5,179	5,282†
Sugar cane*	2,350	2,350	2,400
Beans, dry	440	452	460*
Cow peas, dry	79	84	85*
Pigeon peas	90	91	93*
Soybeans	178	180	175†
Groundnuts, with shell	173	185	172*
Sesame seed	173	178	170†
Seed cotton*	75	49	82
Onions, dry*	212	184	195
Bananas*	583	592	600
Plantains	9,371	9,512	9,550
Coffee, green	212	196	162†
Tea	43	49	41*
Tobacco, unmanufactured	29	19	26*

* FAO estimate(s).
† Unofficial figure.

Aggregate production ('000 metric tons, may include official, semi-official or estimated data): Total cereals 2,723 in 2008, 2,836 in 2009, 2,963 in 2010; Total roots and tubers 8,449 in 2008, 8,634 in 2009, 8,815 in 2010; Total vegetables (incl. melons) 868 in 2008, 960 in 2009, 986 in 2010; Total fruits (excl. melons) 10,006 in 2008, 10,157 in 2009, 10,204 in 2010.

Source: FAO.

LIVESTOCK
('000 head, year ending September)

	2008	2009	2010
Asses*	18	18	18
Cattle	7,398	7,521†	7,746†
Sheep	1,748	1,800†	1,847†
Goats	8,523	8,720†	8,981†
Pigs	2,186	2,229†	2,297†
Chickens	27,508	31,500†	34,680†

* FAO estimates.
† Unofficial figure.

Source: FAO.

LIVESTOCK PRODUCTS
('000 metric tons, FAO estimates)

	2008	2009	2010
Cattle meat	125	129	130
Sheep meat	9	9	9
Goat meat	31	32	32
Pig meat	108	111	113
Chicken meat	45	46	49
Cows' milk	1,120	1,155	1,190
Hen eggs	23	23	23

Source: FAO.

Forestry

ROUNDWOOD REMOVALS
('000 cubic metres, excl. bark)

	2008	2009	2010
Sawlogs, veneer logs and logs for sleepers*	1,770	1,863	1,973
Other industrial wood†	2,120	2,120	2,120
Fuel wood†	38,468	39,046	39,636
Total	42,358	43,029	43,729

* Unofficial figures.
† FAO estimates.

2011: Production assumed to be unchanged form 2010 (FAO estimates).

Source: FAO.

SAWNWOOD PRODUCTION
('000 cubic metres, incl. railway sleepers)

	2004	2005	2006
Coniferous (softwood)	67	24	24
Broadleaved (hardwood)	197	101	93
Total	264	125	117

2007–11: Figures assumed to be unchanged from 2006 (FAO estimates).

Source: FAO.

Fishing

('000 metric tons, live weight)

	2008*	2009	2010
Capture	403.5	412.0*	413.8
Cyprinids	35.0	52.5*	73.2
Tilapias	150.0	123.0*	83.5
African lungfishes	13.0	10.0*	6.3
Characins	42.0	74.0*	113.4
Nile perch	139.0	131.0*	120.4
Aquaculture	52.3	76.7	95.0*
Total catch	455.8	488.7*	508.8*

* FAO estimate(s).

Note: Figures exclude aquatic animals, recorded by number rather than weight. The number of Nile crocodiles captured was: 290 in 2008; n.a. in 2009; n.a. in 2010.

Source: FAO.

Mining

('000 metric tons unless otherwise indicated)

	2008	2009	2010
Cement (hydraulic)	1,193.4	1,162.2	1,347.3
Tantalum and niobium (columbium) concentrates (kilograms)	80	50	10
Cobalt (metric tons)	663	673	624
Gold (kilograms)	20	—	—
Limestone	520.0	588.9	634.7
Salt (unrefined)*	15	15	15

* Estimates.

Source: US Geological Survey.

Industry

SELECTED PRODUCTS
('000 metric tons unless otherwise indicated)

	2003	2004	2005
Soft drinks (million litres)	78.5	111.5	163.5
Sugar	139.5	189.5	182.9
Soap	101.3	93.4	127.6
Cement	507.1	559.0	692.7
Paint (million litres)	1.9	2.2	8.2
Edible oil and fat	56.0	58.1	43.3
Animal feed	20.9	19.6	17.3
Footwear (million pairs)	3.4	3.6	46.3
Wheat flour	42.2	25.7	20.3
Processed milk (million litres)	14.9	19.6	18.5
Cotton and rayon fabrics (million sq m)	11.1	10.1	13.6
Clay bricks, tiles, etc.	33.3	15.4	36.2
Corrugated iron sheets	39.2	48.8	61.6

Cement ('000 metric tons): 1,162 in 2009; 1,347 in 2010; 1,666 in 2011.

Processed milk (million litres): 1,337 in 2009–10; 1,418 in 2011.

Source: Bank of Uganda.

Electric energy (million kWh): 1,953 in 2007; 2,088 in 2008; 2,186 in 2009 (Source: UN Industrial Commodity Statistics Database).

Finance

CURRENCY AND EXCHANGE RATES

Monetary Units

100 cents = 1 new Uganda shilling.

Sterling, Dollar and Euro Equivalents (30 April 2012)

£1 sterling = 4,074 new Uganda shillings;
US $1 = 2,505 new Uganda shillings;
€1 = 3,311 new Uganda shillings;
10,000 new Uganda shillings = £2.45 = $3.99 = €3.02.

Average Exchange Rate (new Uganda shillings per US $)

2009	2,030.3
2010	2,177.6
2011	2,522.7

Note: Between December 1985 and May 1987 the official exchange rate was fixed at US $1 = 1,400 shillings. In May 1987 a new shilling, equivalent to 100 of the former units, was introduced. At the same time, the currency was devalued by 76.7%, with the exchange rate set at $1 = 60 new shillings. Further adjustments were implemented in subsequent years. Foreign exchange controls were mostly abolished in 1993.

BUDGET

('000 million new shillings, year ending 30 June)

Revenue	2009/10	2010/11	2011/12*
Taxes	4,205.7	5,114.3	6,169.1
Grants	863.0	890.4	1,726.3
Other revenue	113.8	95.1	120.6
Oil revenue	—	1,192.7	—
Total	5,182.6	7,292.5	8,016.0

Expenditure	2009/10	2010/11	2011/12*
Compensation of employees	1,308.4	1,659.5	1,860.4
Interest payments	385.1	423.5	519.6
Non wage expenditure	2,222.3	3,162.1	2,075.4
Statutory expenditure	391.3	712.9	515.9
Development expenditure	2,478.4	2,850.9	4,816.2
Domestic	1,591.4	1,808.9	2,674.3
External	887.0	1,042.0	2,142.0
Statistical discrepancy	45.6	163.6	32.6
Total	6,831.1	8,972.5	9,820.1

* Projections.

INTERNATIONAL RESERVES

(US $ million at 31 December)

	2009	2010	2011
IMF special drawing rights	225.2	220.8	218.4
Foreign exchange	2,769.3	2,485.2	2,399.0
Total	2,994.5	2,706.0	2,617.4

Source: IMF, *International Financial Statistics*.

MONEY SUPPLY

('000 million new shillings at 31 December)

	2009	2010	2011
Currency outside depository corporations	1,329.75	1,776.68	2,091.95
Transferable deposits	3,071.21	4,146.83	4,268.57
Other deposits	2,396.74	3,442.96	4,006.73
Broad money	6,797.70	9,366.47	10,367.25

Source: IMF, *International Financial Statistics*.

COST OF LIVING

(Consumer Price Index for all urban households; base: 2000 = 100)

	2008	2009	2010
Food	171.1	213.9	218.4
Clothing	121.5	131.3	135.1
Rent, fuel and light	181.1	193.2	203.1
All items (incl. others)	158.5	179.2	186.3

2011: Food 289.0; All items (incl. others) 221.0.

Source: ILO.

NATIONAL ACCOUNTS

('000 million new shillings at current prices)

Expenditure on the Gross Domestic Product

	2009	2010	2011
Government final consumption expenditure	3,209	3,555	4,039
Private final consumption expenditure	26,315	32,131	38,736
Increase in stocks	92	101	144
Gross fixed capital formation	7,309	8,528	11,251
Total domestic expenditure	36,925	44,315	54,170
Exports of goods and services	7,229	7,572	9,817
Less Imports of goods and services	10,557	13,304	18,379
GDP in purchasers' values	33,596	38,584	45,607
GDP at constant 2002 prices	19,707	20,933	22,174

Gross Domestic Product by Economic Activity

	2009	2010	2011
Agriculture, hunting, forestry and fishing	7,908	8,114	10,440
Mining and quarrying	84	119	158
Manufacturing	2,595	2,933	3,861
Electricity and water	1,243	1,472	1,461
Construction	4,058	4,620	5,968
Wholesale and retail trade	5,132	6,043	7,873
Hotels and restaurants	1,513	1,772	2,259
Transport, storage and communications	2,120	3,422	2,064
Financial intermediation	1,022	1,160	1,331
Real estate	1,446	1,609	1,814
Business services	503	594	675
Public administration and defence	1,035	1,232	1,563
Education	1,745	1,937	1,894
Health	311	337	335
Other services	737	865	1,054
Sub-total	31,452	36,229	42,750
Less Financial intermediation services indirectly measured	654	765	845
Gross value added at basic prices	30,798	35,464	41,905
Net taxes on products	2,799	3,119	3,702
GDP at market prices	33,596	38,584	45,607

BALANCE OF PAYMENTS

(US $ million)

	2009	2010	2011
Exports of goods f.o.b.	2,326.6	2,164.0	2,576.2
Imports of goods f.o.b.	–3,915.2	–4,540.4	–5,254.9
Trade balance	–1,588.7	–2,376.4	–2,678.6
Exports of services	983.8	1,375.5	1,451.6
Imports of services	–1,417.1	–1,880.1	–2,280.0
Balance on goods and services	–2,021.9	–2,881.0	–3,507.1
Other income received	41.9	21.3	28.1
Other income paid	–418.2	–312.8	–361.8
Balance on goods, services and income	–2,398.3	–3,172.4	–3,840.8
Current transfers received	1,541.2	1,563.0	1,843.6
Current transfers paid	–393.8	–250.0	–278.7
Current balance	–1,250.8	–1,859.4	–2,275.8
Direct investment abroad	—	3.4	—
Direct investment from abroad	841.6	543.9	796.9
Portfolio investment assets	—	—	–0.1
Portfolio investment liabilities	28.7	–110.5	256.8
Financial derivatives liabilities	–6.2	–1.4	5.5
Other investment assets	–1.6	–132.2	154.8
Other investment liabilities	834.3	710.0	482.2
Net errors and omissions	–161.5	593.1	385.9
Statistical discrepancy	—	—	5.6
Overall balance	284.5	–253.1	–188.2

Source: IMF, *International Financial Statistics*.

External Trade

PRINCIPAL COMMODITIES
(distribution by SITC, US $ million)

Imports c.i.f.	2009	2010	2011*
Food and live animals	329.3	333.6	448.5
Cereals and cereal preparations	203.0	187.1	231.1
Mineral fuels, lubricants, etc.	743.7	932.4	1,317.3
Petroleum, petroleum products and related materials	728.6	917.0	1,288.4
Animal and vegetable oils, fats and waxes	139.6	195.4	256.9
Fixed vegetable fats and oils	126.3	179.9	229.0
Chemicals and related products	558.4	574.5	725.5
Medicinal and pharmaceutical products	213.8	204.4	259.2
Basic manufactures	761.5	769.8	809.9
Non-metallic mineral manufactures	158.2	151.2	159.3
Iron and steel	220.0	228.8	271.0
Machinery and transport equipment	1,269.0	1,339.7	1,574.7
Telecommunications and sound recording/reproducing apparatus	229.0	227.9	343.4
Electrical machinery, apparatus, etc.	174.8	145.4	141.7
Road vehicles (incl. air-cushion vehicles) and parts (excl. tyres, engines and electrical parts)	369.7	418.8	499.7
Miscellaneous manufactured articles	314.4	323.0	348.4
Total (incl. others)	4,257.6	4,664.3	5,630.9

Exports f.o.b.	2009	2010	2011*
Food and live animals	633.5	717.9	951.2
Fish, crustaceans, molluscs and preparations thereof	109.2	129.1	136.5
Cereals and cereal preparations	58.3	76.7	69.0
Sugar, sugar preparations and honey	42.8	60.2	81.9
Coffee, tea, cocoa, spices and manufactures	375.3	395.4	593.1
Beverages and tobacco	103.7	101.4	89.6
Tobacco and tobacco manufactures	62.5	68.8	55.2
Crude materials (inedible) except fuels	120.3	106.0	188.4
Textile fibres (not wool tops) and their wastes (not in yarn)	29.9	32.1	91.6
Crude animal and vegetable materials n.e.s.	56.1	52.8	61.0
Mineral fuels, lubricants and related materials	115.9	88.3	124.0
Petroleum, petroleum products and related materials	102.7	75.7	107.7
Animal and vegetable oils, fats and waxes	48.9	54.0	99.9
Chemicals and related products	61.3	53.4	68.6
Basic manufactures	224.5	228.1	308.9
Non-metallic mineral manufactures	85.4	74.1	104.3
Iron and steel	86.2	78.5	103.1
Machinery and transport equipment	205.2	197.4	266.4
Telecommunications and sound recording/reproducing apparatus	62.4	84.9	130.8
Road vehicles (incl. air-cushion vehicles) and parts (excl. tyres, engines and electrical parts)	47.6	51.8	60.8
Miscellaneous manufactured articles	59.2	42.1	55.3
Total (incl. others)	1,567.6	1,618.6	2,159.1

* Provisional.

PRINCIPAL TRADING PARTNERS
(US $ million)

Imports c.i.f.	2008	2009	2010
Bahrain	46.8	18.9	16.7
Belgium	52.8	35.9	34.8
China, People's Republic	365.8	379.2	414.7
France (incl. Monaco)	179.6	158.6	64.5
Germany	88.4	95.9	128.6
Hong Kong	46.9	37.1	35.6
India	470.5	521.1	684.4
Italy	87.5	56.6	69.1
Japan	268.7	270.0	305.5
Kenya	511.3	502.7	511.5
Korea, Republic	47.6	65.2	80.7
Malaysia	146.0	76.9	100.5
Netherlands	75.5	87.3	133.2
Saudi Arabia	115.7	169.5	239.3
Singapore	94.2	89.7	89.9
South Africa	305.2	245.3	250.4
Sweden	96.5	40.3	45.5
Tanzania	55.5	40.8	56.5
Thailand	27.3	39.2	49.0
United Arab Emirates	515.5	416.6	391.0
United Kingdom	137.6	140.3	134.5
USA	117.4	87.0	105.5
Total (incl. others)	4,525.9	4,247.4	4,664.3

Exports f.o.b.	2008	2009	2010
Belgium	63.7	42.0	41.8
Burundi	45.4	55.8	51.3
China, People's Republic	12.8	17.1	22.0
Congo, Democratic Republic	125.0	156.6	184.0
Congo, Republic	22.0	8.3	—
France (incl. Monaco)	33.7	22.7	12.4
Germany	75.0	62.9	73.6
Hong Kong	16.1	16.2	18.9
India	18.7	19.7	13.9
Italy	33.6	31.0	31.4
Kenya	164.6	174.0	190.3
Netherlands	81.8	79.0	89.9
Rwanda	136.9	135.3	149.3
Singapore	26.0	23.5	24.0
South Africa	14.9	23.0	10.3
Spain	26.9	26.0	36.4
Sudan	245.9	184.6	208.6
Switzerland-Liechtenstein	155.7	86.5	57.5
Tanzania	30.5	33.8	37.6
United Arab Emirates	128.1	85.8	120.9
United Kingdom	118.4	52.4	36.9
USA	15.7	37.2	21.4
Total (incl. others)	1,724.3	1,567.6	1,618.6

Source: UN, *International Trade Statistics Yearbook.*

2011 (US $ million, provisional): Total imports 5,630.9; Total exports 2,159.1.

Transport

RAILWAYS
(traffic)

	1994	1995	1996
Passenger-km (million)	35	30	28
Freight ton-km (million)	208	236	187

Freight traffic ('000 ton-km): 212,616 in 2003; 229,439 in 2004; 185,559 in 2005.

ROAD TRAFFIC
(vehicles in use)

	2007	2008	2009
Passenger cars	81,320	90,856	96,575
Buses and coaches	40,471	50,472	63,789
Lorries and vans	79,273	86,818	93,172
Motorcycles	176,516	236,452	292,263

CIVIL AVIATION
(traffic on scheduled services)

	2007	2008	2009
Kilometres flown (million)	3	3	3
Passengers carried ('000)	60	63	64
Passenger-km (million)	346	355	344
Total ton-km (million)	63	61	58

Source: UN, *Statistical Yearbook*.

Passengers carried ('000, Entebbe international airport): 1,111 in 2010; 1,167 in 2011.

Tourism

FOREIGN TOURIST ARRIVALS

Country of residence	2009	2010	2011
Austria	897	20,304	53,820
Germany	6,778	8,650	8,960
India	12,946	16,747	19,419
Kenya	261,329	294,170	344,210
Netherlands	6,017	7,651	8,380
Rwanda	199,530	177,043	266,221
Sudan	15,088	22,909	39,333
Tanzania	48,948	42,289	59,013
United Kingdom	35,716	39,171	37,702
USA	37,971	45,856	47,869
Total (incl. others)	806,655	945,899	1,151,356

Tourism receipts (US $ million): 564 in 2009; 662 in 2010; 805 in 2011.

Communications Media

	2009	2010	2011
Telephones ('000 main lines in use)	233.5	327.1	464.8
Mobile cellular telephones ('000 subscribers)	9,383.7	12,828.3	16,697.0
Internet subscribers ('000)	30.0	134.0	n.a.
Broadband subscribers	6,000	54,800	88,800

Source: International Telecommunication Union.

Personal computers: 500,000 (16.9 per 1,000 persons) in 2006.

Television receivers ('000 in use, 2000): 610.

Radio receivers ('000 in use, 1997): 2,600.

Book production (titles, excl. pamphlets and govt publications, 1996): 288.

Daily newspapers: 2 titles (average circulation 40,000 copies) in 1996; 7 titles in 2004.

Non-daily newspapers: 10 titles in 2004.

Sources: mainly UNESCO, *Statistical Yearbook*; UN, *Statistical Yearbook*; UNESCO Institute for Statistics.

Education

(2009/10 unless otherwise indicated)

	Institutions	Teachers	Students
Pre-primary	n.a	19,844	498,644
Primary	n.a.	172,403	8,374,648
Secondary	n.a.	68,089	1,225,692
Tertiary*	n.a.	3,939	123,887
Teacher-training colleges†	10	n.a.	16,170
Technical schools and institutes†	25	n.a.	7,999
Universities†	18	n.a.	58,823

* 2008/09.
† 2003/04.

Source: mainly UNESCO Institute for Statistics.

Pupil-teacher ratio (primary education, UNESCO estimate): 49 in 2009/10.

Adult literacy rate (UNESCO estimates): 73.2% (males 82.6%; females 64.6%) in 2010 (Source: UNESCO Institute for Statistics).

Directory

The Constitution

In September 1995 a Constituent Assembly (comprising 214 elected and 74 nominated members) enacted a draft Constitution, which was promulgated on 8 October. Amendments to the Constitution, introducing a multi-party political system and removing the two-term limit on the President, were endorsed at a national referendum held on 28 July 2005. Under the amended Constitution, the President (who had an unlimited number of mandates) and the unicameral legislature, the Parliament, were directly elected for a five-year term. Following elections in February 2011, the number of seats in Parliament totalled 375, comprising 238 directly elected representatives and 137 nominated members, including 112 women.

The Government

HEAD OF STATE

President: Gen. (retd) YOWERI KAGUTA MUSEVENI (took office 29 January 1986; elected 9 May 1996, re-elected 12 March 2001, 23 February 2006 and 18 February 2011).

Vice-President: EDWARD KIWANUKA SSEKANDI.

THE CABINET
(September 2012)

Prime Minister: JOHN PATRICK AMAMA MBABAZI.

First Deputy Prime Minister and Minister in Charge of East African Community Affairs: ERIYA KATEGAYA.

Second Deputy Prime Minister and Minister of Public Service: HENRY MUGANWA KAJURA.

Third Deputy Prime Minister and Deputy Leader of Government Business: Gen. MOSES ALI.

Minister of Security: WILSON MURULI MUKASA.

Minister in Charge of the Presidency: FRANK TUMWEBAZE.

Minister for Karamoja: JANET KATAAHA MUSEVENI.

Minister in the Office of the Prime Minister, in charge of General Duties: JOHN MWOONO NASASIRA.

Minister of Disaster Preparedness and Refugees: Dr STEVEN MALLINGA.

Minister of Information and National Guidance: MARY KAROORO OKURUT BUSINGYE.

Minister of Agriculture, Animal Industry and Fisheries: TRESS BUCYANAYANDI.

Minister of Defence: CRISPUS KIYONGA.

Minister of Education and Sports: JESSICA ROSE EPEL ALUPO.

Minister of Energy and Mineral Development: IRENE MULONI.

Minister of Finance, Planning and Economic Development: MARIA KIWANUKA.

Minister of Works and Transport: Eng. JAMES ABRAHAM BYANDAALA.

Minister of Justice and Constitutional Affairs: KAHINDA OTAFIIRE.

Minister of Gender, Labour and Social Affairs: TARSIS KABWEGYERE.

Minister of Trade, Industry and Co-operatives: AMELIA ANNE KYAMBADDE.

Minister of Water and Environment: Prof. EPHRAIM KAMUNTU.

Minister of Lands, Housing and Urban Development: DAUDI MIGEREKO.

Minister of Health: Dr DRADIDI JOYCE CHRISTINE ONDOA.

Minister of Foreign Affairs: SAM KUTESAKAHAMBA.

Minister of Information and Communication Technology: Dr RUHAKANA RUGUNDA.

Minister of Local Government: ADOLF MWESIGYE.

Minister without Portfolio, in charge of Political Mobilization: RICHARD TODWONG.

Minister of Tourism, Wildlife and Heritage: MARIA EMILY LUBEGA MUTAGAMBA.

Minister of Internal Affairs: HILARY ONEK.

In addition to the Cabinet Ministers, there were 48 Ministers of State. The Chief Whip and Attorney-General are also members of the Cabinet.

MINISTRIES

Office of the President: Parliament Bldg, POB 7168, Kampala; tel. (41) 4258441; fax (41) 4256143; e-mail aak@statehouse.go.ug; internet www.statehouse.go.ug.

Office of the Prime Minister: Post Office Bldg, Yusuf Lule Rd, POB 341, Kampala; tel. (41) 4236252; fax (41) 4341139; e-mail ps@opm.go.ug; internet www.opm.go.ug.

Ministry of Agriculture, Animal Industry and Fisheries: POB 102, Entebbe; tel. (41) 4320987; fax (41) 4321255; e-mail mosagr@hotmail.com; internet www.agriculture.go.ug.

Ministry of Communication and Information Communication Technology: NSSF House, Jinja Rd, POB 7817, Kampala; tel. (41) 4236262; fax (41) 4231314; internet www.ict.go.ug.

Ministry of Defence: Bombo, POB 7069, Kampala; tel. (41) 4270331; fax (41) 4245911; e-mail spokesman@defenceuganda.mil.ug; internet www.defence.go.ug.

Ministry of East African Community Affairs: Postel Bldg, 2nd Floor, 67/75 Yusuf Lule Rd, POB 7343, Kampala; tel. (41) 4340100; fax (41) 4237310; e-mail meaca@meaca.go.ug.

Ministry of Education and Sports: Embassy House and Development Bldg, Plot 9/11, Parliament Ave, POB 7063, Kampala; tel. (41) 4234451; fax (41) 42230437; e-mail pro@education.go.ug; internet www.education.go.ug.

Ministry of Energy and Mineral Development: Amber House, Kampala Rd, Kampala; tel. (41) 4311111; fax (41) 4234732; e-mail psmemd@energy.go.ug; internet www.energyandminerals.go.ug.

Ministry of Finance, Planning and Economic Development: Appollo Kaggwa Rd, Plot 2-12, POB 8147, Kampala; tel. (41) 4707000; fax (41) 4230163; e-mail webmaster@finance.go.ug; internet www.finance.go.ug.

Ministry of Foreign Affairs: Embassy House, POB 7048, Kampala; tel. (41) 4345661; fax (41) 4258722; e-mail info@mofa.go.ug; internet www.mofa.go.ug.

Ministry of Gender, Labour and Social Affairs: Plot 2, Lumumba Ave, Simbamanyo House, POB 7136, Kampala; tel. (41) 347854; fax (41) 256374; e-mail ps@mglsd.go.ug; internet www.mglsd.go.ug.

Ministry of Health: Plot 6, Lourdel Rd, Nakasero, POB 7272, Kampala; tel. (41) 4340874; fax (41) 4231584; e-mail info@health.go.ug; internet www.health.go.ug.

Ministry of Information and National Guidance: Kampala.

Ministry of Internal Affairs: Plot 75, Jinja Rd, POB 7191, Kampala; tel. (41) 4231103; fax (41) 4343088; e-mail info@mia.go.ug; internet www.mia.go.ug.

Ministry of Justice and Constitutional Affairs: Plot 1, Parliament Ave, Queens Chambers, POB 7183, Kampala; tel. (41) 4230538; fax (41) 4254829; e-mail mojca@africaonline.co.ug; internet www.justice.go.ug.

Ministry of Lands, Housing and Urban Development: POB 7096, Kampala; tel. (41) 4342931; internet www.mlhud.go.ug.

Ministry of Local Government: Uganda House, 8/10 Kampala Rd, POB 7037, Kampala; tel. (41) 4341224; fax (41) 4258127; e-mail info@molg.go.ug; internet www.molg.go.ug.

Ministry of Public Service: Plot 12, Nakasero Hill Rd, Wandegeya, POB 7003, Kampala; tel. (41) 4250534; e-mail info@publicservice.go.ug; internet www.publicservice.go.ug.

Ministry of Relief and Disaster Preparedness: POB 341, Kampala; tel. (41) 4236967.

Ministry of Security: Kampala.

Ministry of Tourism, Wildlife and Heritage: 6/8 Parliament Ave, POB 7103, Kampala; tel. (41) 4341076; fax (41) 4347286; internet www.mtti.go.ug.

Ministry of Trade, Industry and Co-operatives: 6/8 Parliament Ave, POB 7103, Kampala; tel. (41) 4314000; fax (41) 4347286; e-mail mintrade@mtti.go.ug; internet www.mtti.go.ug.

Ministry of Water and Environment: POB 7096, Kampala; tel. (41) 4342931; e-mail mwle@mwle.go.ug; internet www.mwle.go.ug.

Ministry of Works and Transport: Plot 4/6, Airport Rd, POB 10, Entebbe; tel. (42) 4320101; fax (42) 4321364; e-mail mowt@works.go.ug; internet www.works.go.ug.

President and Legislature

PRESIDENT

Election, 18 February 2011

Candidate	Votes	% of votes
Gen. (retd) Yoweri Kaguta Museveni (NRM)	5,428,368	68.38
Kizza Besigye (FDC)	2,064,963	26.01
Norbert Mao (DP)	147,917	1.86
Olara Otunnu (UPC)	125,059	1.58
Beti Olive Namisango Kamya (UFA)	52,782	0.66
Abed Bwanika (PDP)	51,708	0.65
Jaberi Bidandi Ssali (PPP)	34,688	0.44
Samuel Lubega Walter Mukaaku (Ind.)	32,726	0.41
Total	7,938,211	100.00

PARLIAMENT

Speaker: REBECCA ALITWALA KADAGA.

Deputy Speaker: JACOB OULANYAH.

General Election, 18 February 2011

Party	Directly elected seats	Women members	Total seats
NRM	164	85	249
FDC	24	11	35
DP	11	1	12
UPC	7	3	10
CP	1	—	1
JEEMA	1	—	1
Ind.	30	12	42
Others*	—	—	25
Total	238	112	375

* Comprises 10 nominated representatives from the Uganda People's Defence Forces, five nominated representatives for young people (four from the NRM and one independent), five nominated representatives for people with disabilities (all from the NRM) and five nominated representatives for workers (four from the NRM and one independent).

Election Commission

Electoral Commission: 53–56 Jinja Rd, POB 22678, Kampala; tel. (41) 4337500; fax (41) 4337595; e-mail info@ec.or.ug; internet www.ec.or.ug; f. 1997; independent; Chair. Dr BADRU M. KIGGUNDU.

Political Organizations

Political parties were ordered to suspend active operations, although not formally banned, in March 1986. In mid-2005 legislation was adopted allowing for a return to full multi-party democracy; the legislation was approved by 92.5% of voters in a national referendum held on 28 July 2005. A total of 38 political parties had been officially registered by 2011.

Conservative Party (CP): POB 5145, Kampala; f. 1979; Leader KEN LUKYAMUZI.

Democratic Party (DP): City House, Plot 2/3, William St, POB 7098, Kampala; tel. and fax (41) 4252536; e-mail info@dpuganda.org; internet www.dpuganda.org; f. 1954; main support in southern Uganda; Pres. NORBERT MAO; Vice-Pres. ZACHARY OLUM.

Forum for Democratic Change (FDC): FDC Villas, Entebbe Rd, Plot No. 109, Najjanankumbi, POB 26928, Kampala; tel. (41) 4267920; fax (41) 4267918; e-mail info@fdcuganda.org; internet www.fdcuganda.org; f. 2004 by a merger of the Reform Agenda, the Parliamentary Advocacy Forum and the National Democratic Forum; Leader KIZZA BESIGYE.

Forum for Integrity in Leadership (FIL): Plot 48B, Ntinda Rd, POB 7606, Kampala; Chair. EMMANUEL TUMUSIIME.

Justice Forum (JEEMA): POB 3999, Kampala; Leader MUHAMMAD KIBIRIGE MAYANJA; Sec.-Gen. HUSSEIN KYANJO.

National Resistance Movement (NRM): Plot 10, Kyadondo Rd, POB 7778, Kampala; tel. (41) 346295; e-mail info@nrm.ug; internet www.nrm.ug; f. as National Resistance Movement to oppose the UPC Govt 1980–85; also opposed the mil. Govt in power from July 1985 to Jan. 1986; its fmr mil. wing, the National Resistance Army (NRA), led by Lt-Gen. (later Gen. retd) Yoweri Kaguta Museveni, took power in Jan. 1986; name changed as above on registration in 2003; Chair. YOWERI MUSEVENI; Sec.-Gen. AMAMA MBABAZI.

People's Development Party (PDP): Makerere Hill Rd, Relief Bldg (opp. LDC), POB 25765, Kampala; f. 2007; Pres. Dr ABED BWANIKA.

People's Progressive Party (PPP): Plot 6, Commercial St, Luzira, POB 9252, Kampala; tel. (41) 4505178; internet www.ppp.ug; f. 2004; Chair. JABERI BIDANDI SSALI.

Uganda Federal Alliance (UFA): POB 14196, Kampala; internet www.ugandafederalalliance.com; f. 2010; Leader BETI OLIVE NAMISSANGO KAMYA.

Uganda Patriotic Movement (UPM): POB 2083, Kampala; tel. 752654524 (mobile); fax (41) 4236781; e-mail lubegabyayida@yahoo.com; f. 1980; Nat. Chair. D. A. LUBEGA BYAY; Sec.-Gen. MARIAM SSEMPIJJA.

Uganda People's Congress (UPC): Plot 8–10, Kampala Rd, Uganda House, POB 37047, Kampala; tel. and fax (41) 236748; e-mail upcsecretariat@upcparty.net; internet www.upcparty.net; f. 1960; socialist-based philosophy; ruling party 1962–71 and 1980–85, sole legal political party 1969–71; Pres. OLARA OTUNNU; Sec.-Gen. Rev. Fr JACINTO OGWAL.

The following organizations are in armed conflict with the Government:

Allied Democratic Forces (ADF): active since 1996 in south-eastern Uganda; combines Ugandan Islamic fundamentalist rebels, exiled Rwandan Hutus and guerrillas from the Democratic Republic of the Congo; Pres. Sheikh JAMIL MUKULU.

Lord's Resistance Army (LRA): f. 1987; claims to be conducting a Christian fundamentalist 'holy war' against the Govt; forces est. to number up to 1,500, operating mainly from bases in Sudan; Leader JOSEPH KONY; a breakaway faction (LRA—Democratic) is led by RONALD OTIM KOMAKECH.

Uganda People's Freedom Movement (UPFM): based in Tororo and Kenya; f. 1994 by mems of the fmr Uganda People's Army; Leader PETER OTAI.

West Nile Bank Front (WNBF): operates in northern Uganda.

Diplomatic Representation

EMBASSIES AND HIGH COMMISSIONS IN UGANDA

Algeria: 14 Acacia Ave, Kololo, POB 4025, Kampala; tel. (41) 4232918; fax (41) 4341015; e-mail ambalgka@imul.com; Ambassador ABDERRAHMANE BENMOKHTAR.

Belgium: Rwenzori Towers, 6th Floor, Plot 6, Nakasero Rd, POB 7043, Kampala; tel. (41) 4349559; fax (41) 4347212; e-mail kampala@diplobel.fed.be; internet www.diplomatie.be/kampala; Ambassador ALAIN HANSEN.

China, People's Republic: 37 Malcolm X Ave, Kololo, POB 4106, Kampala; tel. (41) 4259881; fax (41) 4235087; e-mail chinaemb_ug@mfa.gov.cn; internet ug.china-embassy.org; Ambassador SUN HEPING.

Congo, Democratic Republic: 20 Philip Rd, Kololo, POB 4972, Kampala; tel. (41) 4250099; fax (41) 4340140; Ambassador JEAN-CHARLES OKOTO LOLAKOMBE.

Cuba: KAR Dr., 16 Lower Kololo Terrace, POB 9226, Kampala; tel. (41) 4233742; fax (41) 4233320; e-mail ecuba@africaonline.co.ug; Ambassador MARIANO L. BETANCOURT.

Denmark: Plot 3, Lumumba Ave, POB 11243, Kampala; tel. (31) 2263211; fax (31) 2264624; e-mail kmtamb@um.dk; internet www.ambkampala.um.dk; Ambassador DAN E. FREDERIKSEN.

Egypt: 33 Kololo Hill Dr., POB 4280, Kampala; tel. (41) 4254525; fax (41) 4232103; e-mail egyembug@utlonline.co.ug; Ambassador SABRI MAGDI.

Ethiopia: 3L Kitante Close, off Kira Rd, POB 7745, Kampala; tel. (41) 4348340; fax (41) 4341885; Ambassador Ato TERFA MENEGESHA.

France: 16 Lumumba Ave, Nakasero, POB 7212, Kampala; tel. (41) 4304500; fax (41) 4304520; e-mail ambafrance.kampala@diplomatie.gouv.fr; internet www.ambafrance-ug.org; Ambassador ALINE KUSTER-MÉNAGER.

Germany: 15 Philip Rd, Kololo, POB 7016, Kampala; tel. (41) 4501111; fax (41) 4501115; e-mail info@kampala.diplo.de; internet www.kampala.diplo.de; Ambassador KLAUS DIETER DÜXMANN.

Holy See: Chwa II Rd, Mbuya Hill, POB 7177, Kampala (Apostolic Nunciature); tel. (41) 4505619; fax (41) 4441774; e-mail nuntius@imul.com; Apostolic Nuncio PAUL TSCHANG IN-NAM (Titular Archbishop of Amanzia).

India: 11 Kyaddondo Rd, Nakasero, POB 7040, Kampala; tel. (41) 4257368; fax (41) 4254943; e-mail hoc@hicomindkampala.org; High Commissioner S. N. RAY.

Iran: 9 Bandali Rise, Bugolobi, POB 24529, Kampala; tel. (41) 4441689; fax (41) 4443590; Ambassador ALI A. DABIRAN.

Ireland: 25 Yusuf Lule Rd, Nakasero, POB 7791, Kampala; tel. (41) 7713000; fax (41) 4344353; e-mail kampalaembassy@dfa.ie; internet www.embassyofireland.ug; Ambassador ANNE WEBSTER.

Italy: 11 Lourdel Rd, Nakasero, POB 4646, Kampala; tel. (41) 4250442; fax (41) 4250448; e-mail segreteria.kampala@esteri.it; internet www.ambkampala.esteri.it; Ambassador STEFANO ANTONIO DEJAK.

Japan: Plot 8, Kyaddondo Rd, Nakasero, POB 23553, Kampala; tel. (41) 4349542; fax (41) 4349547; e-mail jembassy@jembassy.co.ug; Ambassador KATO KEIICHI.

Kenya: 41 Nakasero Rd, POB 5220, Kampala; tel. (41) 4458235; fax (41) 4458239; e-mail kenyahicom@africaonline.co.ug; High Commissioner Maj.-Gen. (retd) GEOFFREY OKANGA LUKALE.

Korea, Democratic People's Republic: 10 Prince Charles Dr., Kololo, POB 5885, Kampala; tel. (41) 4546033; fax (41) 4450224; Ambassador JONG THAE YANG.

Libya: 26 Kololo Hill Dr., POB 6079, Kampala; tel. (41) 4344924; fax (41) 4344969; Ambassador (vacant).

Netherlands: Rwenzori Courts, 4th Floor, Plot 2, Nakasero Rd, POB 7728, Kampala; tel. (41) 4346000; fax (41) 4231861; e-mail kam@minbuza.nl; internet uganda.nlembassy.org; Ambassador ALPHONS JEAN ANTOINE JOSEPH MARIE GERTRUDE HENNEKENS.

Nigeria: 33 Nakasero Rd, POB 4338, Kampala; tel. (41) 4433691; fax (41) 4432543; e-mail nighicom-sgu@africaonline.co.ug; High Commissioner CORNELIUS OMOLADE OLUWATERU.

Norway: 18B Akii-Bua Rd, Nakasero, POB 22770, Kampala; tel. (41) 7112000; fax (41) 4343936; e-mail emb.kampala@mfa.no; internet www.norway.go.ug; Ambassador BJØRG SCHONHOWD LEITE.

Russia: 28 Malcolm X Ave, Kololo, POB 7022, Kampala; tel. (41) 4433676; fax (41) 4345798; Ambassador SERGEI SHISHKIN.

Rwanda: 2 Nakaima Rd, POB 2468, Kampala; tel. (41) 4344045; fax (41) 4458547; e-mail Ambakampala@minaffet.gov.rw; internet www.uganda.embassy.gov.rw; High Commissioner Maj.-Gen. FRANK MUGAMBAGE.

Saudi Arabia: 3 Okurut Close, Kololo, POB 22558, Kampala; tel. (41) 4340614; fax (41) 4454017; Ambassador AHMAD BIN MUHAMMAD AL-BAHLAL.

South Africa: Plot 15A, Nakasero Rd, POB 22667, Kampala; tel. (41) 4343543; fax (41) 4348216; e-mail kampala.sahc@foreign.gov.za; High Commissioner THANDUYISE HENRY CHILIZA.

South Sudan: Kampala; Ambassador LAURE SAMUEL LOMINSUK.

Sweden: 24 Lumumba Ave, Nakasero, POB 22669, Kampala; tel. (41) 7700800; fax (41) 7700801; e-mail ambassaden.kampala@foreign.ministry.se; internet www.swedenabroad.com/kampala; Ambassador URBAN ANDERSSON.

Tanzania: 6 Kagera Rd, Nakasero, POB 5750, Kampala; tel. (41) 4456272; fax (41) 4343973; High Commissioner LADISLAUS COLUMBAN KOMBA.

United Arab Emirates: Kampala; Ambassador HASSAN MOHAMMED OBAID AL-SUWAIDI.

United Kingdom: Plot 4, Windsor Loop Rd, POB 7070, Kampala; tel. (31) 2312000; fax (41) 4257304; e-mail bhcinfo@starcom.co.ug; internet ukinuganda.fco.gov.uk; High Commissioner ALISON BLACKBURNE.

USA: Plot 1577, Ggaba Rd, POB 7007, Kampala; tel. (41) 4259791; fax (41) 4259794; e-mail kampalawebcontact@state.gov; internet kampala.usembassy.gov; Ambassador SCOTT DELISI.

Zambia: Kampala; High Commissioner JUDITH K. K. KANGOMA KAPIJIMPANGA.

Judicial System

Courts of Judicature: High Court Bldg, POB 7085, Kampala; tel. (41) 4233420; fax (41) 4344116; e-mail info@judicature.go.ug; internet www.judicature.go.ug.

The Supreme Court

Plot 10, Upper Kololo, Seenu Awasthi Terrace, Mengo, Kampala.

Hears appeals from the Court of Appeal. Also acts as a Constitutional Court.

Chief Justice: BENJAMIN ODOKI.

Deputy Chief Justice: L. E. M. MUKASA-KIKONYOGO.

The Court of Appeal: 5 Parliament Ave, Kampala; hears appeals from the High Court; the Court of Appeal consists of the Deputy Chief Justice and no fewer than seven Justices of Appeal, the number thereof being prescribed by Parliament.

The High Court

POB 7085, Kampala; tel. (41) 4233422.

Has full criminal and civil jurisdiction and also serves as a Constitutional Court. The High Court consists of the Principal Judge and 27 Puisne Judges.

Principal Judge: JAMES OGOOLA.

Magistrates' Courts: These are established under the Magistrates' Courts Act of 1970 and exercise limited jurisdiction in criminal and civil matters. The country is divided into magisterial areas, presided over by a Chief Magistrate. Under the Chief Magistrate there are two categories of Magistrates. The Magistrates preside alone over their courts. Appeals from the first category of Magistrates' Court lie directly to the High Court, while appeals from the second categories of Magistrates' Court lie to the Chief Magistrate's Court, and from there to the High Court. There are 27 Chief Magistrates' Courts, 52 Magistrates' Grade I Courts and 428 Magistrates' Grade II Courts.

Religion

Christianity is the majority religion—its adherents constitute approximately 75% of the population. Muslims account for some 15% of the population. A variety of other religions, including traditional indigenous religions, several branches of Hinduism, the Bahá'í Faith and Judaism, are practised freely and, combined, make up around 10% of the population. There are few atheists in the country. In many areas, particularly in rural settings, some religions tend to be syncretistic: deeply held traditional indigenous beliefs are blended into or observed alongside the rites of recognized religions, particularly in areas that are predominantly Christian. Missionary groups of several denominations are present and active in the country, including the Pentecostal Church, the Baptist Church, the Episcopal Church/Church of Uganda, the Church of Christ and the Mormons.

CHRISTIANITY

The Roman Catholic and Anglican Churches claim approximately the same number of followers, accounting for 90% of the country's professed Christians. The Seventh-day Adventist Church, the Church of Jesus Christ of Latter-day Saints (Mormons), the Orthodox Church, Jehovah's Witnesses, the Baptist Church, the Unification Church and the Pentecostal Church, among others, are also active.

The Anglican Communion

Anglicans are adherents of the Church of the Province of Uganda, comprising 29 dioceses. In 2002 there were about 8m. adherents.

Archbishop of Uganda and Bishop of Kampala: Most Rev. HENRY LUKE OROMBI, POB 14123, Kampala; tel. (41) 4270218; fax (41) 4251925; e-mail couab@uol.co.ug.

Greek Orthodox Church

Archbishop of East Africa: NICADEMUS OF IRINOUPOULIS (resident in Nairobi, Kenya); jurisidiction covers Kenya, Tanzania and Uganda.

The Roman Catholic Church

Uganda comprises four archdioceses and 15 dioceses. An estimated 43% of the total population is Roman Catholic.

Uganda Episcopal Conference

Uganda Catholic Secretariat, POB 2886, Kampala; tel. (41) 4510398; fax (41) 4510545.

f. 1974; Pres. Most Rev. JOHN BAPTIST ODAMA (Archbishop of Gulu).

Archbishop of Gulu: Most Rev. JOHN BAPTIST ODAMA, Archbishop's House, POB 200, Gulu; tel. (47) 4132026; fax (47) 4132860; e-mail metrog@archdioceseofgulu.org.

Archbishop of Kampala: CYPRIAN KIZITO LWANGA, Archbishop's House, POB 14125, Mengo, Kampala; tel. (41) 4270183; fax (41) 4345441; e-mail klarchdioc@utlonline.co.ug.

Archbishop of Mbarara: Most Rev. PAUL BAKYENGA, POB 150, Mbarara; tel. (48) 5420052; fax (48) 5421249; e-mail mbarchd@utlonline.co.ug.

Archbishop of Tororo: Most Rev. DENIS KIWANUKA LOTE, Archbishop's House, Plot 17 Boma Ave, POB 933, Mbale; tel. (45) 4433269; fax (45) 4433754; e-mail tororoad@africaonline.co.ug.

ISLAM

Muslims are mainly Sunni, although there are Shi'a followers of the Aga Khan among the Asian community.

The Uganda Muslim Supreme Council: POB 1146, Kampala; tel. (41) 4344499; fax (41) 4256500; Mufti of Uganda Sheikh SHABAN MUBAJJE; Chief Kadi and Pres. of Council HUSAYN RAJAB KAKOOZA.

BAHÁ'Í FAITH

National Spiritual Assembly: Kikaaya Hill Mile 4, Gayaza Rd, Kawempe Division, POB 2662, Kampala; tel. (31) 2262681; e-mail ugandabahai@gmail.com; f. 1951; mems resident in 2,721 localities.

JUDAISM

There is a small Jewish community, the Abayudaya, in central Uganda, with some 600 members and six synagogues.

The Press

DAILY AND OTHER NEWSPAPERS

The Citizen: Kampala; tel. 7846097708 (mobile); internet www.theugandacitizen.com; f. 2007; English.

The Daily Monitor: Plot 29–35, 8th St, POB 12141, Kampala; tel. (41) 7744100; fax (41) 4232369; e-mail editorial@ug.nationmedia.com; internet www.monitor.co.ug; f. 1992; daily; English; Man. Editor DANIEL KALINAKI; circ. 22,000 (Mon.–Sat.), 24,000 (Sun.).

Financial Times: Plot 17/19, Station Rd, POB 31399, Kampala; tel. (41) 4245798; bi-weekly; English; Editor G. A. ONEGI OBEL.

Focus: POB 268, Kampala; tel. (41) 4235086; fax (41) 4242796; f. 1983; publ. by Islamic Information Service and Material Centre; 4 a week; English; Editor HAJJI KATENDE; circ. 12,000.

Guide: POB 5350, Kampala; tel. (41) 4233486; fax (41) 4268045; f. 1989; weekly; English; Editor-in-Chief A. A. KALIISA; circ. 30,000.

Munnansi News Bulletin: POB 7098, Kampala; f. 1980; weekly; English; owned by the Democratic Party; Editor ANTHONY SGEKWEYAMA.

Munno: POB 4027, Kampala; f. 1911; daily; Luganda; publ. by the Roman Catholic Church; Editor ANTHONY SSEKWEYAMA; circ. 7,000.

New Vision: POB 9815, Kampala; tel. (41) 4337000; fax (41) 4232050; e-mail editorial@newvision.co.ug; internet www.newvision.co.ug; f. 1986; official govt newspaper; daily; English; Editor-in-Chief BARBARA KAIJA; Man. Editor BEN OPOLOT; circ. 34,000 (Mon.–Sat.), 42,000 (Sun.).

Bukedde: e-mail bukeddekussande@newvision.co.ug; internet www.bukedde.co.ug; daily; Luganda; Editor GEOFFREY KULUBYA; circ. 16,000.

Etop: e-mail etop@newvision.co.ug; weekly; vernacular; Editor KENNETH OLUKA; circ. 5,000.

Orumuri: tel. (48) 5421265; internet www.orumuri.co.ug; weekly; vernacular; circ. 11,000.

Rupiny: e-mail rupiny@newvision.co.ug; internet www.rupiny.co.ug; weekly; vernacular; Editor NANCY ANEK-OBITA; circ. 5,000.

Ngabo: POB 9362, Kampala; tel. (41) 4242637; f. 1979; daily; Luganda; Editor MAURICE SEKAWUNGU; circ. 7,000.

The Star: POB 9362, Kampala; tel. (41) 4242637; f. 1980; revived 1984; daily; English; Editor SAMUEL KATWERE; circ. 5,000.

Taifa Uganda Empya: POB 1986, Kampala; tel. (41) 4254652; f. 1953; daily; Luganda; Editor A. SEMBOGA; circ. 24,000.

Weekly Topic: POB 1725, Kampala; tel. (41) 4233834; weekly; English; Editor JOHN WASSWA; circ. 13,000.

PERIODICALS

Eastern Africa Journal of Rural Development: Dept of Agricultural Economics and Agribusiness, Makerere University, POB 7062, Kampala; tel. 772616540 (mobile); fax (41) 4530858; e-mail bkiiza@infocom.co.ug; annual; Editor BARNABAS KIIZA; circ. 800.

The Exposure: POB 3179, Kampala; tel. (41) 4267203; fax (41) 4259549; monthly; politics.

The Independent: Kampala; internet www.independent.co.ug; f. 2007; weekly; Editor ANDREW MWENDA.

Leadership: POB 2522, Kampala; tel. (41) 4422407; fax (41) 4421576; f. 1956; 11 a year; English; Roman Catholic; circ. 7,400; Editor Fr CARLOS RODRÍGUEZ.

Mkombozi: c/o Ministry of Defence, Republic House, POB 3798, Kampala; tel. (41) 4270331; f. 1982; military affairs; Editor A. OPOLOTT.

Musizi: POB 4027, Mengo, Kampala; f. 1955; monthly; Luganda; Roman Catholic; Editor F. GITTA; circ. 30,000.

Uganda Confidential: POB 5576, Kampala; tel. (41) 4250273; fax (41) 4255288; e-mail ucl@swiftuganda.com; internet www.swiftuganda.com/~confidential; f. 1990; monthly; Editor TEDDY SSEZI-CHEEYE.

NEWS AGENCY

Uganda News Agency (UNA): POB 7142, Kampala; tel. (41) 4232734; fax (41) 4342259; Dir CRISPUS MUNDUA (acting).

Publishers

Centenary Publishing House Ltd: POB 6246, Kampala; tel. (41) 4241599; fax (41) 4250427; f. 1977; religious (Anglican); Man. Dir Rev. SAM KAKIZA.

Fountain Publishers Ltd: POB 488, Kampala; tel. (41) 4259163; fax (41) 4251160; e-mail fountain@starcom.co.ug; internet www.fountainpublishers.co.ug; f. 1989; general, school textbooks, children's books, academic, scholarly; Man. Dir JAMES TUMUSIIME.

Longman Uganda Ltd: POB 3409, Kampala; tel. (41) 4242940; f. 1965; Man. Dir M. K. L. MUTYABA.

Uganda Printing and Publishing Corporation (UPPC): POB 33, Entebbe; tel. (41) 4220639; fax (41) 4220530; e-mail info@uppc.co.ug; internet www.uppc.co.ug; f. 1993; Man. Dir BAKAAWA ELIZABETH.

Broadcasting and Communications

REGULATORY AUTHORITY

Uganda Communications Commission: UCC House, 42–44 Spring Rd, Bugolobi, POB 7376, Kampala; tel. (41) 4339000; fax (41) 4348832; e-mail ucc@ucc.co.ug; internet www.ucc.co.ug; f. 1998; regulatory body; Exec. Dir GODFREY MUTABAZI.

TELECOMMUNICATIONS

In 2011 there were seven providers of telecommunications services in Uganda.

Airtel Uganda Ltd: Celtel House, 40 Wampewo Ave, Kololo, POB 6771, Kampala; tel. 752230110 (mobile); fax (41) 4230106; e-mail info.africa@airtel.com; internet africa.airtel.com/uganda; f. 1995; fmrly Celtel Uganda, subsequently Zain Uganda, present name adopted 2010; Man. Dir V. G. SOMASEKHAR.

MTN Uganda Ltd: MTN Towers, 22 Hannington Rd, POB 24624, Kampala; tel. and fax (31) 2212333; e-mail mtn@mtn.co.ug; internet www.mtn.co.ug; f. 1998; CEO THEMBA KHUMALO.

Orange Uganda: Plot 28–30, Clement Hill Rd, POB 24144, Kampala; tel. 790000100 (mobile); e-mail care@orange.co.ug; internet www.orange.ug; f. 2009 following acquisition by France Telecom of a 53% stake in the Ugandan mobile phone operator Hits Telecom Uganda Ltd; provides mobile cellular telecommunications services; CEO PHILIPPE LUXCEY.

Uganda Telecom Ltd (UTL): Rwenzori Courts, Plot 2/4A, Nakasero Rd, POB 7171, Kampala; tel. (41) 4333200; fax (41) 4345907; e-mail info@utlonline.co.ug; internet www.utl.co.ug; f. 1998; state-owned; privatization pending; Man. Dir ABDULBASET ELAZZABI.

WARID Telecom: Plot 16A, Clement Hill Rd, POB 70665, Kampala; tel. 700100100 (mobile); fax 200221111; e-mail customercare@waridtel.co.ug; internet waridtel.co.ug; f. 2006; CEO SRIRAM YARLAGADDA.

BROADCASTING

Radio

91.3 Capital FM: POB 7638, Kampala; tel. (41) 4235092; fax (41) 4344556; f. 1993; independent music station broadcasting from Kampala, Mbarara and Mbale; Chief Officers WILLIAM PIKE, PATRICK QUARCOO.

Central Broadcasting Service (CBS): POB 12760, Kampala; tel. (41) 4272993; fax (41) 4340031; f. 1996; independent station broadcasting in local languages and English to most of Uganda; Man. Dir KAAYA KAVUMA.

Radio One: Duster St, POB 4589, Kampala; tel. (41) 4348211; fax (41) 4344385; e-mail info@radioonefm90.com; internet www.radioonefm90.com.

Sanyu Radio: Katto Plaza, Nkrumah Rd, Kampala; f. 1993; independent station broadcasting to Kampala and its environs.

UBC Radio: Plot 17/19, Nile Ave, POB 2038, Kampala; tel. (41) 4257257; fax (41) 4257252; e-mail ubc@ubconline.co.ug; internet ubconline.co.ug; f. 1954; state-controlled; under Uganda Broadcasting Corpn (UBC), formed by merger of Radio Uganda and Uganda Television in 2005; broadcasts in 23 languages, including English and Ugandan vernacular languages, through five stations, Red, Blue, Butebo, Magic and Star FM; Man. Dir PAUL KIHIIKA.

Voice of Toro: POB 2203, Kampala.

Television

Sanyu Television: Naguru; f. 1994; independent station broadcasting to Kampala and its environs.

UBC TV: Plot 17/19, Nile Ave, POB 2038, Kampala; tel. (41) 4257897; fax (41) 4257252; e-mail ubc@ubconline.co.ug; internet ubconline.co.ug; f. 1962; state-controlled commercial service; under Uganda Broadcasting Corpn (UBC), formed by merger of Radio Uganda and Uganda Television in 2005; programmes mainly in English, also in Swahili and Luganda; transmits over a radius of 320 km from Kampala; five relay stations are in operation, others are under construction; Man. Dir PAUL KIHIIKA.

Finance

(cap. = capital; res = reserves; dep. = deposits; m. = million; brs = branches; amounts in new Uganda shillings, unless otherwise indicated)

BANKING

In 2010 there were 22 commercial banks, three credit institutions and three microfinance deposit-taking institutions in Uganda.

Central Bank

Bank of Uganda: 37–43 Kampala Rd, POB 7120, Kampala; tel. (41) 4258441; fax (41) 4230878; e-mail info@bou.or.ug; internet www.bou.or.ug; f. 1966; bank of issue; cap. 20,000m., res 1,099,687m., dep. 5,416,569m. (June 2009); Gov. EMMANUEL TUMUSIIME-MUTEBILE; Dep. Gov. DAVID G. OPIOKELLO (acting).

State Bank

Uganda Development Bank Ltd (UDBL): 15A Clement Hill Rd, Ruth Towers, POB 7210, Kampala; tel. (41) 4355555; fax (41) 4355556; e-mail info@udbl.co.ug; internet www.udbl.co.ug; f. 1972; state-owned; reorg. 2001; CEO GABRIEL OTUDA ETOU.

Commercial Banks

ABC Capital Bank (U) Ltd: Colline House, Plot 4, Pilkington Rd, POB 21091, Kampala; tel. (41) 4345200; fax (41) 4258310; e-mail abc@abccapitalbank.com; f. 2009.

Bank of Africa—Uganda Ltd: Plot 45, Jinja Rd, POB 2750, Kampala; tel. (41) 4302001; fax (41) 4230902; e-mail boa@boa-uganda.com; internet www.boa-uganda.com; f. 1986 as Allied Bank International (Uganda); name changed as above in 2005; 47.7%

owned by Bank of Africa—Kenya, 21.9% by Aureos East Africa Fund, 19.8% by The Netherlands Development Finance Co, 10.6% by Central Holdings Ltd; cap. 7,508m., res 9,599m., dep. 174,631m. (Dec. 2009); Chair. JOHN CARRUTHERS; Man. Dir MICHEL KAHN; 5 brs.

Cairo International Bank: 30 Kampala Rd, POB 7052, Kampala; tel. (41) 4230132; fax (41) 4230130; e-mail moona@cib.co.ug; internet www.cairointernationalbank.co.ug; 44.4% owned by Banque du Caire, 36.1% owned by Kato Aromatics SAE, 6.5% each owned by Bank of Egypt, Bank Misr and Bank of Alexandria; cap. 7,135m. (Dec. 2003); Chair. JOHN ELANGOT; Man. Dir NABIL GHANEM.

Crane Bank Ltd: Crane Chambers, 38 Kampala Rd, POB 22572, Kampala; tel. (41) 4345345; fax (41) 4231578; e-mail cranebank@cranebanklimited.com; internet www.cranebanklimited.com; f. 1995; wholly owned by various private investors; cap. 50,000m., res 9,948m., dep. 418,768m. (Dec. 2009); Chair. J. BIRIBONWA; Man. Dir A. R. KALAN.

DFCU Bank Ltd: Plot 2, Jinja Rd, POB 70, Kampala; tel. (41) 4256891; fax (41) 4231687; e-mail dfcubank@dfcugroup.com; internet www.dfcugroup.com; f. 1984 as Gold Trust Bank Ltd; current name adopted 2000; 60.02% owned by Commonwealth Development Corpn; total assets US $114.3m. (Dec. 2006); Chair. NKOSANA MOYO; Man. Dir GEORGE E. MORTIMER.

Diamond Trust Bank (Uganda) Ltd: Diamond Trust Bldg, Plot 17–19, Kampala Rd, POB 7155, Kampala; tel. (41) 4259331; fax (41) 4342286; e-mail info@dtbuganda.co.ug; internet www.dtbafrica.com; f. 1995; 40% owned by The Diamond Jubilee Investment Trust, 33.3% owned by Aga Khan Fund for Economic Development, 26.7% owned by Diamond Trust Bank Kenya Ltd; cap. 6,000m., res 3,400m., dep. 182,961m. (Dec. 2009); Chair. MAHMOOD MANJI; CEO VARGHESE THAMBI.

Ecobank Uganda Ltd: Plot 4, Parliament Ave, POB 7368, Kampala; tel. (41) 7700231; fax (31) 2266079; e-mail ecobankug@ecobank.com; internet www.ecobank.com; f. 2008; Chair. DAVID TWAHIRWA; Man. Dir OLADELE ADEBIYI ALABI.

Equity Bank Uganda Ltd: Plot 390, Muteesa 1 Rd, Katwe, POB 10184, Kampala; tel. (31) 2262437; fax (31) 2262436; e-mail info@equitybank.co.ug; internet www.equitybank.co.ug; Chair. PETER MUNGA; Exec. Dir APOLLO N. NJOROGE.

Fina Bank Uganda Ltd: Plot 7, Buganda Rd, POB 7323, Kampala; tel. (41) 4237305; fax (41) 4237305; e-mail banking@finabank.co.ug; internet www.finabank.com/ug; f. 2008; Chair. DHANU HANSRAJ CHANDARIA; CEO CHARLES NALYAALI.

Global Trust Bank (U) Ltd: Plot 2A, Kampala Rd, POB 72747, Kampala; tel. (41) 7100700; fax (41) 4254007; e-mail globaltrust@bankglobaltrust.com; internet www.bankglobaltrust.com; f. 2008; Man. Dir MORENIKEJI OLUDOTUN ADEPOJU.

Mercantile Credit Bank Ltd: Plot 10, Old Port Bell Rd, POB 620, Kampala; tel. and fax (41) 4235967; e-mail mcb@afsat.com; cap. 1,000m. (Dec. 2003); Chair. PALLE MOELLER; Man. NELSON LUGOLOBI.

National Bank of Commerce (Uganda) Ltd: Cargen House, Plot 13A, Parliament Ave, POB 23232, Kampala; tel. (41) 2347699; fax (41) 2347701; e-mail nbc@swiftuganda.com; cap. 4,631m. (Dec. 2003); Chair. AMOS NZEYI; Man. Dir G. BANGERA.

Orient Bank Ltd: Orient Plaza, Plot 6/6A, Kampala Rd, POB 3072, Kampala; tel. (41) 4236012; fax (41) 4236066; e-mail mail@orient-bank.com; internet www.orient-bank.com; f. 1993; cap. 5,000m., res 2,440m., dep. 205,920m. (Dec. 2009); Chair. MICHAEL COOK; CEO MAXWELL IBEANUSI; 6 brs.

Post Bank Uganda Ltd: Plot 11/13, Nkrumah Rd, POB 7189, Kampala; tel. (41) 4258551; fax (41) 4347107; e-mail postbank@imul.com; wholly state-owned; cap. 2,000m. (Dec. 2003); Chair. STEPHEN MWANJE.

Development Banks

Capital Finance Corpn Ltd: 4 Pilkington Rd, POB 21091, Kampala; tel. (41) 4345200; fax (41) 4258310; 70% owned by City Credit Bank Ltd; Chair. KEMAL LALANI; Man. Dir and CEO GHULAM HAIDER DAUDANI.

Centenary Rural Development Bank: 7 Entebbe Rd, POB 1892, Kampala; tel. (41) 4251276; fax (41) 4251273; e-mail info@centenarybank.co.ug; internet www.centenarybank.co.ug; cap. 4,020.5m., res 6,675.5m., dep. 448,308.5m. (Dec. 2009); Chair. Dr JOHN DDUMBA SSENTAMU; Man. Dir FABIAN KASI.

Development Finance Co of Uganda Ltd: Rwenzori House, 1 Lumumba Ave, POB 2767, Kampala; tel. (41) 4231215; fax (41) 4259435; e-mail dfcu@dfcugroup.com; internet www.dfcugroup.com; owned by Commonwealth Devt Corpn (60%), Uganda Devt Corpn (18.5%) and International Finance Corpn (21.5%); cap. 3,978m. (Dec. 2003); Chair. WILLIAM S. KALEMA; Man. Dir C. MCCORMACK.

East African Development Bank (EADB): East African Development Bank Bldg, 4 Nile Ave, POB 7128, Kampala; tel. (41) 4230021; fax (41) 4259763; e-mail admin@eadb.org; internet www.eadb.org; f. 1967; majority stake held by the Govts of Kenya, Tanzania and Uganda; provides financial and tech. assistance to promote industrial development within Uganda, Kenya, Rwanda and Tanzania; regional offices in Nairobi (Kenya), Kigali (Rwanda) and Dar es Salaam (Tanzania); cap. US $99.8m., res US $11.1m., dep. US $118.7m. (Dec. 2009); Dir-Gen. APOPO VIVIENNE.

Housing Finance Bank Ltd: Investment House, 25 Kampala Rd, POB 1539, Kampala; tel. (41) 4259651; fax (41) 4341429; internet www.housingfinance.co.ug; f. 1967; 45% owned by Govt, 50% owned by National Social Security Fund, 5% owned by National Housing and Construction Corpn; cap. 61,000.0m., res 6,475.4m., dep. 109,411.7m. (Dec. 2009); Chair. KEITH MUHAKANIZI; Man. Dir NICHOLAS OKWIR.

Foreign Banks

Bank of Baroda (Uganda) Ltd (India): 18 Kampala Rd, POB 7197, Kampala; tel. (41) 4233680; fax (41) 4230781; e-mail bobho@spacenet.co.ug; internet www.bankofbaroda.com; f. 1953; 80% owned by Bank of Baroda (India); cap. 4,000m., res 5,647m., dep. 126,995m. (Dec. 2004); Chair. and Man. Dir M. D. MALLYA; 6 brs.

Barclays Bank of Uganda Ltd (United Kingdom): Barclay House, Plot 4, Hannington Rd, POB 7101, Kampala; tel. (31) 4218300; fax (31) 4259467; e-mail barclays.uganda@barclays.com; internet www.barclays.com; f. 1969; wholly owned by Barclays Bank PLC (United Kingdom); cap. 4,000m., res 15,236m., dep. 328,553m. (Dec. 2005); Chair. GEORGE EGADU; Man. Dir CHARLES ONGWAE; 4 brs.

Citibank (Uganda) Ltd (USA): Plot 4, Centre Court, Ternan Ave, Nakasero, POB 7505, Kampala; tel. (41) 4305500; fax (41) 4340624; internet www.citibank.com/eastafrica/uganda.htm; 99.9% owned by Citicorp Overseas Investment Corpn, 0.1% owned by Foremost Investment; cap. 21,285m. (Dec. 2003); Chair. Prof. J. M. L. SSEBUWUUFU; Man. Dir SHIRISH BHIDE.

Stanbic Bank Uganda Ltd (United Kingdom): Crested Towers, Short Tower, 17 Hannington Rd, POB 7131, Kampala; tel. (31) 4224111; fax (41) 4231116; e-mail ugandainfo@stanbic.com; internet www.stanbicbank.co.ug; f. 1906 as National Bank of India Uganda; adopted present name 199380% owned by Stanbic Africa Holdings Ltd (United Kingdom)merged with Uganda Commercial Bank Ltd 2002; cap. 5,119m., res 67,880m., dep. 1,539,873m. (Dec. 2009); Chair. Dr MARTIN ALIKER; Man. Dir KITILI MBATHI; 2 brs.

Standard Chartered Bank Uganda Ltd (United Kingdom): 5 Speke Rd, POB 7111, Kampala; tel. (41) 44258211; fax (41) 44231473; e-mail scb.uganda@ug.standardchartered.com; internet www.standardchartered.com/ug; f. 1912; wholly owned by Standard Chartered Bank PLC; cap. 4,000m., res 22,806m., dep. 604,380m. (Dec. 2006); Chair. JAMES MULWANA; Man. Dir LAMIN MANJANG; 7 brs.

Tropical Bank (Libya): Plot 27, Kampala Rd, POB 9485, Kampala; tel. (41) 4313100; fax (31) 2264494; e-mail admin@trobank.com; internet www.trobank.com; f. 1972; 99.7% owned by Libyan Arab Foreign Bank; cap. 30,000m., res 8,433m., dep. 125,314m. (Dec. 2009); Chair. GERALD SENDAULA; Man. Dir PRINCE KASSIM NAKIBINGE.

United Bank for Africa (Uganda) Ltd: Spear House, Plot 22, Jinja Rd, POB 7396, Kampala; tel. (41) 7715122; fax (41) 7715117; f. 2008; CEO MARGARET MWANAKATWE; 5 brs.

STOCK EXCHANGE

Uganda Securities Exchange: Workers' House, 2nd Floor, Northern Wing, 1 Pilkington Rd, POB 23552, Kampala; tel. (41) 4343297; fax (41) 4343841; internet www.use.or.ug; f. 1997; Chair. CHARLES MBIRE; Chief Exec. JOSEPH S. KITAMIRIKE.

INSURANCE

In March 2011 there were 22 insurance companies licensed to operate in Uganda.

APA Insurance (Uganda) Ltd: Crown House, 1st Floor, Plot 4A, Kampala Rd, POB 7651, Kampala; tel. (41) 4250087; e-mail apa.uganda@apainsurance.org.

Chartis Uganda Insurance Co Ltd: Plot 60, Bombo Rd, POB 7077, Kampala; tel. (41) 4533781; fax (41) 4541572; e-mail chartisuganda@chartisinsurance.com; internet www.chartisinsurance.com/ug-about-us_918_210594.html; f. 1962; fmrly AIG Uganda Insurance Co Ltd; name changed as above in 2009; Man. Dir ALEX WANJOHI; 3 brs.

East Africa General Insurance Co Ltd: Plot 14, Kampala Rd, POB 1392, Kampala; tel. (31) 22262221; fax (41) 4343234; e-mail vkrishna@eagen.co.ug; internet www.eagen.co.ug; f. 1949; public shareholding co; fire, life, motor, marine and accident; CEO VYASA KRISHNA.

Excel Insurance Co Ltd: Crest House, Plot 2D, Nkurumah Rd, POB 7213, Kampala; tel. (41) 4348595; fax (41) 4342304; e-mail excelins@infocom.co.ug; internet www.excelinsurance.co.ug; Man. Dir JOHN SSENTAMU DDUMBA.

First Insurance Co Ltd: King Fahd Plaza, 2nd Floor, Plot 52, Kampala Rd, POB 5254, Kampala; tel. (41) 4342863; fax (41) 345923.

GoldStar Insurance Co Ltd: Plot 38, Kampala Rd, Crane Chambers, POB 7781, Kampala; tel. (41) 4250110; fax (41) 4254956; e-mail goldstar@goldstarinsurance.com; Man. Dir AZIM THARANI.

Lion Assurance Co Ltd: Tall Tower, 12th Floor, Crested Towers Bldg, POB 7658, Kampala; tel. (41) 4341450; fax (41) 4257027; e-mail insure@lion.co.ug; fmrly Pan World Insurance Co Ltd; Chair. OWEK. GODFREY K. KAVUMA; Gen. Man. GEORGE ALANDE.

National Insurance Corporation: Plot 3, Pilkington Rd, POB 7134, Kampala; tel. (41) 4258001; fax (41) 4259925; e-mail nic@nic.co.ug; internet www.nic.co.ug; f. 1964; 60% owned by IGI PLC, Nigeria; general and life; Chair. REMI OLOWUDE; Man. Dir SAM JEFF NJOROGE.

NICO Insurance (Uganda) Ltd: 3rd Floor, Greenland Towers, Kampala Rd, opposite Bank of Uganda, POB 24256, Kampala; tel. (31) 2264720; fax (31) 2264723; internet www.nicomw.com; subsidiary of NICO Holdings Ltd (based in Malawi); Man. Dir RONALD ZAKE.

Phoenix of Uganda Assurance Co Ltd: Workers House, Northern Wing, 8th Floor, Pilkington Rd, POB 70149, Kampala; tel. (41) 349664; fax (41) 349662; e-mail info@phoenixuganda.com; internet phoenixassurancegroup.com; f. 2003; Chair. MAHEBOOB ALIBHAI; Gen. Man. V. PARTHASARATHI.

Rio Insurance Co Ltd: Plot 20, Kampala Rd, POB 5710, Kampala; tel. (41) 4341264; fax (41) 4235292.

Statewide Insurance Co Ltd (SWICO): Sure House, Plot 1, Bombo Rd, POB 9393, Kampala; tel. (41) 4345996; fax (41) 4343403; e-mail swico@infocom.co.ug; internet www.swico.co.ug; f. 1982; Man. Dir JOSEPH KIWANUKA.

TransAfrica Assurance Co Ltd: Impala House, Plot 13/15, Kimathi Ave, POB 7601, Kampala; tel. (41) 4251411; fax (41) 4254511; e-mail taacl@spacenet.co.ug.

UAP Insurance Co Ltd: Plot 1, Kimathi Ave, POB 7185, Kampala; tel. (41) 4234190; fax (41) 4256388; e-mail uac@starcom.co.ug; internet www.uap.co.ug; Chair. RONALD KALYANGO.

Uganda Co-operative Insurance Ltd: Plot 10, Bombo Rd, POB 6176, Kampala; tel. (41) 4241836; fax (41) 4258231; f. 1982; general; Chair. EPHRAIM KAKURU; Gen. Man. (vacant).

Regulatory Authority

Uganda Insurance Commission: NIC Building Annexe, 3rd Floor, Plot 3, Pilkington Rd, POB 22855; tel. (41) 4346712; fax (41) 4349260; e-mail uic@uginscom.go.ug; Chair. ELIAS B. KASOZI.

Insurance Association

Uganda Insurers' Association: Plot 24A, Acacia Ave, Kololo, POB 8912, Kampala; tel. (41) 4230469; fax (41) 4500944; internet www.uia.co.ug; f. 1965; Chair. SOLOMON RUBONDO.

Trade and Industry

GOVERNMENT AGENCIES

Capital Markets Authority: 8th Floor, Jubilee Insurance Centre, 14 Parliament Ave, POB 24565, Kampala; tel. (41) 4342788; fax (41) 4342803; e-mail info@cmauganda.co.ug; internet www.cmauganda.co.ug; f. 1996 to develop, promote and regulate capital markets sector; Chair. GRACE JETHRO KAVUMA; CEO JAPHETH KATTO.

Enterprise Uganda: 38 Lumumba Ave, Nakasero, POB 24581, Kampala; tel. (41) 4251810; fax (41) 4250968; e-mail info@enterprise.co.ug; internet www.enterprise.co.ug; Exec. Dir CHARLES OCICI.

Export and Import Licensing Division: POB 7000, Kampala; tel. (41) 4258795; f. 1987; advises importers and exporters and issues import and export licences; Prin. Commercial Officer JOHN MUHWEZI.

Privatization Unit: Kampala; f. 2001; oversees privatization programme.

Uganda Advisory Board of Trade: POB 6877, Kampala; tel. (41) 4233311; f. 1974; issues trade licences and services for exporters.

Uganda Export Promotion Board: POB 5045, Kampala; tel. (41) 4230233; fax (41) 4259779; e-mail uepc@starcom.co.ug; internet www.ugandaexportsonline.com; f. 1983; provides market intelligence, organizes training, trade exhibitions, etc.; Exec. Dir FLORENCE KATE.

Uganda Investment Authority (UIA): Investment Centre, TWED Plaza, Plot 22, Lumumba Ave, POB 7418, Kampala; tel. (41) 4301000; fax (41) 4342903; e-mail info@ugandainvest.com; internet www.ugandainvest.com; f. 1991; promotes foreign and local investment, assists investors, provides business information, issues investment licences; Exec. Dir TOM BURINGURIZA (acting).

DEVELOPMENT ORGANIZATIONS

Dairy Development Authority (DDA): Plot 1, Kafu Rd, POB 256, Kampala; tel. (41) 343883; fax (41) 250270; internet www.dda.or.ug; f. 2000.

National Agricultural Research Organisation (NARO): Plot 3, Lugard Ave, POB 295, Entebbe; tel. (41) 320512; fax (41) 321070; e-mail dgnaro@infocom.co.ug; internet www.naro.go.ug; f. 2005.

National Housing and Construction Corpn: Crested Towers, POB 659, Kampala; tel. (41) 4330002; fax (41) 4258708; e-mail sales@nhcc.co.ug; internet www.nhcc.co.ug; f. 1964; govt agent for building works; also develops residential housing; Chair. Dr COLIN SENTONGO; Gen. Man. M. S. KASEKENDE.

Uganda Industrial Development Corpn Ltd: 9–11 Parliament Ave, POB 7042, Kampala; tel. (41) 4234381; fax (41) 4241588; f. 1952; Chair. SAM RUTEGA.

CHAMBER OF COMMERCE

Uganda National Chamber of Commerce and Industry: Plot 1A, Kira Rd, POB 3809, Kampala; tel. (41) 4503024; fax (41) 4230310; e-mail info@chamberuganda.com; internet www.chamberuganda.com; Chair. OLIVE Z. KIGONGO.

INDUSTRIAL AND TRADE ASSOCIATIONS

CMB Ltd (Coffee Marketing Board): POB 7154, Kampala; tel. (41) 4254051; fax (41) 4230790; state-owned; privatization pending; purchases and exports coffee; Chair. Dr DDUMBA SSENTAMU; Man. Dir SAM KIGGUNDU.

Cotton Development Organization: POB 7018, Kampala; tel. (41) 4232968; fax (41) 4232975; Man. Dir JOLLY SABUNE.

Horticultural Exporters' Association of Uganda (HORTEXA): POB 29392, Kampala; tel. (77) 2364389; e-mail hortexa@yahoo.com; f. 1990; Chair. DAVID LULE.

Produce Marketing Board: Plot 15, Clement Hill Rd, POB 3705, Kampala; tel. (41) 232968; fax (41) 232975; internet cdouga.org; Gen. Man. ESTHER KAMPAMPARA.

Uganda Coffee Development Authority (UCDA): Coffee House, Plot 35, Jinja Rd, POB 7267, Kampala; tel. (41) 4256940; fax (41) 4256994; e-mail ucdajc@ugandacoffee.org; internet www.ugandacoffee.org; f. 1991; enforces quality control and promotes coffee exports, maintains statistical data, advises Govt on local and world prices and trains processors and quality controllers; Chair. FABIANO R. TIBEITA; Man. Dir HENRY A. NGABIRANO.

Uganda Flowers Exporters' Association (UFEA): Plot 92, Ssebugwawo Dr., Old Airport, Entebbe, POB 29558, Kampala; tel. (31) 2263320; fax (31) 2263321; e-mail ufea@ufea.co.ug; internet ufea.co.ug; f. 1995; Chair. JACQUE SCHRIER.

Uganda Manufacturers' Association (UMA): Lugogo Show Grounds, POB 6966, Kampala; tel. (41) 4221034; fax (41) 4220285; e-mail administration@uma.or.ug; internet uma.or.ug; f. 1988; promotes mfrs' interests; Chair. KADDU KIBERU.

Uganda National Farmers' Federation: Plot 27, Nakasero Rd, POB 6213, Kampala; tel. (41) 4340249; fax (41) 4230748; internet www.unffe.org; f. 1992 as Uganda National Farmers' Association; Pres. CHARLES OGANG; Sec.-Gen. HENRY MUTEBI KITYO.

Uganda Tea Authority: POB 4161, Kampala; tel. (41) 4231003; state-owned; controls and co-ordinates activities of the tea industry; Gen. Man. MIRIA MARGARITA MUGABI.

Uganda Tea Development Ltd (UTDAL): 821 Rubaga Rd, off Kabaka Anjagala Roundabout, POB 6204, Kampala; tel. (41) 4343633; fax (41) 4343634; e-mail marketing@ugatea.com; internet ugatea.com; f. 2001; Gen. Man. BYARUGABA IGNATIUS.

EMPLOYERS' ORGANIZATION

Federation of Uganda Employers (FUE): Plot 60, Veron House, Ntinda, POB 3820, Kampala; tel. (41) 4220201; fax (41) 4286290; e-mail info@fuemployers.org; internet www.fuemployers.org; f. 1958; Chair. MARTIN KASEKENDE; Exec. Dir ROSEMARY N. SSENABULYA.

UTILITIES

Electricity

Electricity Regulatory Authority (ERA): ERA House, Plot 15, Shimon Rd, Nakasero, POB 10332, Kampala; tel. (41) 4341852; fax (41) 4341624; e-mail era@africaonline.co.ug; internet www.era.or.ug; f. 1999; Chair. RICHARD SANTO APIRE; CEO Eng. Dr F. B. SEBBOWA.

Rural Electrification Agency: 1 Pilkington Rd, Worker's House, 10th Floor, POB 7317, Kampala,; tel. (31) 2264095; fax (41) 4346013; e-mail rea@rea.or.ug; internet www.rea.or.ug; Exec. Dir GODFREY TURYAHIKAYO.

Uganda Electricity Distribution Co Ltd (UEDCL): Nakasero Towers, 6th Floor, 37 Nakasero Rd, Kampala; tel. (31) 2330300; fax (41) 4255600; e-mail contact@uedcl.co.ug; internet www.uedcl.co.ug; f. 2001 as one of the successor bodies of the Uganda Electricity Board; privatized and operations handed over to UMEME Uganda Ltd in 2005 under a 20-year concession agreement; functions as a statutory body overseeing the operations of UMEME Uganda Ltd; Chair. GAD GASAATURA; Man. Dir JOSEPH KATERA.

UMEME Uganda Ltd: Rwenzori House, Plot 1, 2nd Floor, Lumumba Ave, POB 23841, Kampala; tel. (41) 2360600; e-mail info@umeme.co.ug; internet www.umeme.co.ug; f. 2005; develops, operates and maintains the electricity distribution network on behalf of Uganda Electricity Distribution Co Ltd; Chair. PATRICK BITATURE; Man. Dir CHARLES CHAPMAN.

Uganda Electricity Generation Co Ltd: Plot 2–8, Faraday Rd, Ambercourt, POB 1101, Jinja; tel. (43) 4120891; fax (43) 4123064; internet www.uegcl.com; f. 2001 as one of the successor bodies of the Uganda Electricity Board; Chair. SANDY S. TICKODRI-TOGBOA; Man. Dir JOHN MUGYENZI.

Uganda Electricity Transmission Co Ltd: Plot 10, Hannington Rd, POB 7625, Kampala; tel. (41) 7802000; fax (41) 3441789; e-mail transco@uetcl.com; internet www.uetcl.com; f. 2001; as one of the successor bodies of the Uganda Electricity Board; Man. Dir ERIASI KIYEMBA.

Water

National Water & Sewerage Corpn: Plot 39, Jinja Rd, POB 7053, Kampala; tel. (41) 4315100; fax (41) 4234802; e-mail info@nwsc.co.ug; internet www.nwsc.co.ug; f. 1972; serves 22 towns; privatization pending; Chair. CHRISTINE NANDYOSE; Man. Dir ALEX GISAGARA (acting).

MAJOR COMPANIES

The following are some of the largest companies in terms either of capital investment or employment.

African Textile Mills Ltd: POB 242, Mbale; tel. (45) 4234373; fax (45) 4234549; f. 1968; cap. Us. 12,000m.; textile mfrs; operates one mill; Man. Dir J. V. PATEL; 260 employees.

Blenders Uganda Ltd: POB 3515, Kampala; tel. (41) 4259152; fax (41) 4232510; tea- and coffee-blending, packaging and distribution; Gen. Man. DIPAK BANERJEE.

British American Tobacco (BAT) Uganda: Plot 69/71 Jinja Rd, POB 7100, Kampala; tel. (31) 2200100; fax (41) 4256425; f. 1928; 90% owned by BAT (United Kingdom); tobacco mfrs and exporters; Man. Dir JONATHAN D'SOUZA; 650 employees.

East African Breweries Ltd Uganda: POB 7130, PortBell, Luzira, Kampala; tel. (31) 2210011; fax (31) 2233277; internet www.eabl.com; f. 1964 as International Distilleries Uganda Ltd; subsidiary of East African Breweries Ltd (Kenya); production of potable spirits; Man. Dir ALASDAIR MUSSELWHITE; 70 employees.

Hima Cement: Center Court 4, Ternan Ave, POB 7230, Kampala; tel. (31) 2213200; fax (31) 345901; e-mail hima.kampala@hima.lafarge.com; internet www.himacement.com; subsidiary of Bamburi Cement and a member of the Lafarge Group; Chair. RICHARD KEMOLI; Man. Dir HUSSEIN MANSI.

Kilembe Mines Ltd: POB 1, Kilembe; tel. and fax (41) 4234909; internet kilembemines.org; f. 1950; mining of cobalt and copper, generation of hydroelectric power, production of lime, foundry production; 90% govt-owned; Gen. Man. FRED KYAKONYE; 576 employees.

Kinyara Sugar Works Ltd: POB 7474, Kampala; tel. (41) 4236382; fax (41) 4236383; f. 1990; sugar production; 51% owned by Rai Group; Gen. Man. RAMADASAN VEKATRAMAN; 3,700 employees.

Lonrho Motors Uganda Ltd: Plot 45, Jinja Rd, POB 353, Kampala; tel. (41) 4231395; fax (41) 4254388; e-mail toyota@toyotauganda.com; distributors of motor vehicles and parts.

Madhvani International, SA: POB 6361, Kampala; tel. (41) 4259390; fax (41) 4259399; internet www.madhvani-misa.com; f. 1979; involved in the tea, plant-extracts, sugar and chemicals industries; infrastructure devt; maintains interests in East Africa, Europe and India; Pres. NITIN MADHVANI; 13,000 employees.

Kakira Sugar Works Ltd: POB 121, Jinja; tel. (41) 4444000; fax (41) 444336; e-mail kakira@kakirasugar.com; internet www.kakirasugar.com; f. 1985; also operates sugar mills in Rwanda; mfrs of some 100,000 metric tons of sugar annually; Man. Dir MAYUR MADHVANI; 7,000 employees.

Lake Products and Services Ltd: POB 99, Jinja; tel. and fax (43) 4120771; e-mail info@lps-misa.com; internet www.lps-misa.com; f. 2001; production and processing of high-value crops; Gen. Man. NILESH KANABAR.

Mpanga Growers' Tea Factory Ltd: POB 585, Fort Portal; tel. (392) 722441; fax (483) 422441; e-mail mpangatea@iwayafrica.com; internet www.mpangatea.com; Gen. Man. ROGER SIIMA.

Mukwano Industries (Uganda) Ltd: 30 Mukwano Rd, POB 2671, Kampala; tel. (41) 4313313; fax (31) 2313313; e-mail marketing@mukwano.com; internet www.mukwano.com; f. 1984; refining of crude palm and sunflower oils, mfrs of vegetable cooking oils, beverages, soaps, detergents, personal hygiene products and plastics; Man. Dir ALYKHAN KARMALI; 6,000 employees.

Nile Breweries Ltd: M90, Yusuf Lule Rd, Njeru, POB 762, Njeru; tel. (33) 2210009; fax (33) 2240292; internet www.nilebreweries.com; Dir NICK JENKINSON.

Parambot Breweries Ltd: 7 miles Gayaza Rd, POB 6527, Kampala; tel. (39) 2766057; e-mail parambot@parambot.co.ug; internet moonberg.com.

Roko Construction Ltd: Plot 160A Kawempe, POB 172, Kampala; tel. (41) 4567305; fax (41) 4567784; e-mail roko@roko.co.ug; internet www.roko.co.ug; f. 1969; civil engineering and construction; affiliated cos in Rep. of the Congo, Rwanda and Sudan; Man. Dir MARK KOEHLER; 2,038 employees.

Southern Range Nyanza Ltd: POB 1025, Jinja; tel. (43) 4120205; fax (43) 4120241; f. 1949; as Nyanza Textile Industries Ltd (NYTIL); privatized in 1996; owned by Picfare Ltd; went into receivership in May 2000; in 2001 Govt agreed rescue package; textile mfrs; Chair. KISHOR JOBANPUTRA.

Toro and Mityana Tea Co Ltd (TAMTECO): POB 6641, Kampala; tel. (41) 4259885; fax (41) 4243121; e-mail prinsloo@africaonline.co.ug; f. 1980; wholly owned subsidiary of Mitchell Cotts Uganda Ltd (UK) and Probert Investments Inc.; production, processing and export of tea; Man. Dir J. PRINSLOO; 2,500 employees.

Tororo Cement Ltd: Metropole House, 3rd Floor, Entebbe Rd, POB 22753, Kampala; tel. (41) 4344578; fax (41) 4344564; e-mail tcl@tororocement.com; internet www.tororocement.com; f. 1952; as Uganda Cement Industry Ltd; privatized and renamed in 1995; mfrs of cement, construction steel, wire products and iron sheets; Man. Dir B. M. GAGRANI.

Uganda Breweries Ltd: Port Bell, POB 7130, Kampala; tel. (41) 4223201; fax (41) 4221587; produces Bell, Pilsner, Tusker and Guinness beers for the domestic market; 98% owned by East African Breweries Ltd (Kenya); Man. Dir IVO BURATOVICH; 700 employees.

Uganda Clays Ltd: Km 14 Entebbe Rd, POB 3188, Kampala; tel. (41) 4200261; fax (41) 4200167; e-mail uclays@ugandaclays.co.ug; internet www.ugandaclays.co.ug; f. 1950; mfrs of bldg and roofing materials; CEO JOHN WAFULA; 885 employees.

Uganda Grain Milling Co Ltd: POB 895, Jinja; tel. (43) 4120171; fax (43) 4120060; f. 1957; 51% owned by Greenland Investments; production of flour, animal feeds and bread; Exec. Chair. Dr S. KIGUNDU; 600 employees.

CO-OPERATIVES

In 2000 there were 6,313 co-operative societies, grouped in 34 unions. There is at least one co-operative union in each administrative district.

Uganda Co-operative Alliance: Plot 47/49, Nkurumah Rd, Kampala; tel. (41) 4258898; fax (41) 4258556; e-mail ucainfocen@uca.co.ug; internet www.uca.co.ug; co-ordinating body for co-operative unions.

TRADE UNIONS

National Organization of Trade Unions (NOTU): Plot 64, Ntinda Rd, POB 2150, Kampala; tel. (41) 4256295; fax (41) 4259833; e-mail notu@ifocom.co.ug; internet www.notu.or.ug; f. 1973; Chair. OWERE USHER WILSON; Sec.-Gen. PETER CHRISTOPHER WERIKHE; 89,500 mems (2007).

Amalgamated Transport and General Workers' Union: POB 30407, Kampala; tel. (41) 232508; fax (41) 341541; e-mail atgwu@utlonline.co.ug; internet www.atgwu.or.ug; f. 1938; Gen. Sec. OJIAMBO-OCHIENG ROMANO.

Transport

RAILWAYS

In 2002 there were 260 km of track in operation. A programme to rehabilitate the railway network is under way. A 725-km railway project to link Gulu in northern Uganda with Juba, South Sudan, has been under consideration since 2004. There are also plans to upgrade and reopen the 333-km Kampala–Kasese railway line.

Uganda Railways Corporation (URC): Plot 53, 1st Floor, Nasser Rd, POB 7150, Kampala; tel. (41) 4254961; fax (41) 4344405; f. 1977 following the dissolution of East African Railways; management of operations assumed by Rift Valley Railways consortium in Nov. 2006; CEO I. IYAMULEMYE.

ROADS

In 2006 Uganda's road network consisted of approximately 10,800 km of national or trunk roads (of which some 2,200 km were bituminized, the rest being gravel), 27,500 km of district or feeder roads, 4,300 km of urban roads (comprising roads in Kampala City, the 13 municipal councils and the 50 town councils in the country) and 30,000 km of community roads. There are also private roads, some of which are open to the general travelling public. Road transport remains the dominant mode of transport in terms of scale of infrastructure and the volume of freight and passenger movement. The National (Trunk) Road Network carries 80% of Uganda's passenger and freight traffic and includes international routes linking Uganda to neighbouring countries and to the sea (via Kenya and Tanzania), and internal roads linking areas of high population and large administrative and commercial centres. It provides the only form of access to most rural communities. The Government is implementing a programme of continuous upgrading of key gravel roads to bitumen standard.

Uganda National Roads Authority (UNRA): Plot 5, Lourdel Road, Nakasero, POB 28487, Kampala; tel. (31) 2233100; fax (41) 4232807; e-mail roadinfo@unra.go.ug; internet www.unra.go.ug; f. 2006; Exec. Dir Eng. PETER SSEBANAKITTA.

Uganda Road Fund: 5th Floor, Soliz House, Plot 23, Lumumba Ave, POB 7501, Kampala; tel. (41) 4257072; e-mail info@roadfund.ug; internet www.roadfund.ug; f. 2008; Chair. Eng. Dr FRANCIS BAZIRAAKE; Exec. Dir Eng. Dr MICHAEL M. ODONGO.

INLAND WATERWAYS

A rail wagon ferry service connecting Jinja with the Tanzanian port of Tanga, via Mwanza, was inaugurated in 1983, thus reducing Uganda's dependence on the Kenyan port of Mombasa. In 1986 the Uganda and Kenya Railways Corporations began the joint operation of Lake Victoria Marine Services, to ferry goods between the two countries via Lake Victoria.

CIVIL AVIATION

The international airport is at Entebbe, on Lake Victoria, some 40 km from Kampala. There are also several small airfields.

Civil Aviation Authority (CAA): POB 5536, Kampala; Passenger Terminal Bldg, 2nd Floor, Entebbe International Airport; tel. (41) 4352000; fax (41) 4321401; e-mail aviation@caa.co.ug; internet www.caa.co.ug; Man. Dir WENCESLAUS RAMA MAKUZA.

Principal Airlines

Air Uganda (AU): Plot 11/13, Lower Kololo Terrace, POB 36591, Kampala; tel. (41) 4258262; fax (41) 4500932; e-mail info@air-uganda.com; internet www.air-uganda.com; f. 2007; services to Africa; CEO HUGH FRASER.

Eagle Air Ltd: Adam House, Plot 11, Portal Ave, POB 7392, Kampala; tel. (41) 4344292; fax (41) 4344501; e-mail admin@eagleair-ug.com; internet www.eagleair-ug.com; f. 1994; domestic services, charter flights to neighbouring countries; Man. Dir Capt. ANTHONY RUBOMBORA.

Royal Daisy Airlines: Plot 13, Buganda Rd, POB 35177, Kampala; tel. (41) 4256213; fax (41) 4256137; e-mail admin@royaldaisy.com; internet www.royaldaisy.com; f. 2005; Man. Dir and CEO DAISY ROY.

Tourism

Uganda's principal attractions for tourists are the forests, lakes, mountains and wildlife (including its mountain gorillas) and an equable climate. A programme to revive the tourist industry by building or improving hotels and creating new national parks began in the late 1980s. There were 1.15m. tourist arrivals in 2011 (compared with 12,786 in 1983). Revenue from the sector in that year was estimated at US $805m.

Uganda Tourist Board: Impala House, 13/15 Kimatti Ave, POB 7211, Kampala; tel. (41) 4342196; fax (41) 4342188; e-mail utb@visituganda.com; internet www.visituganda.com; Chair. PETER KAMYA; Gen. Man. IGNATIUS NAKISHERO.

Defence

As assessed at November 2011, the Uganda People's Defence Forces (UPDF, formerly the National Resistance Army) was estimated to number 45,000 men, including paramilitary forces (a border defence unit of about 600 men, a police air wing of about 800 men, and around 400 marines and local defence units totalling about 3,000 men). In 2011 a total of 5,208 Ugandan troops were stationed abroad, of whom seven were observers.

Defence Expenditure: Budgeted at Us. 617,000m. in 2012.

Chief of Defence Forces: Gen. ARONDA NYAKARIMA.

Commander of the Air Force: Maj.-Gen. JIM OWOYESIGIRE.

Commander of the Land Forces: Lt-Gen. KATUMBA WAMALA.

Education

Most schools are supported by the Government, although a small proportion are sponsored by missions. Traditionally, all schools have charged fees. In 1997, however, the Government introduced an initiative known as Universal Primary Education (UPE), whereby free primary education was phased in for up to four children per family. In January 2007 the Government initiated free secondary school education in 700 public schools as part of a phased programme to introduce universal free education. Primary education, which is in principle free and compulsory, begins at six years of age and lasts for seven years. Secondary education, beginning at the age of 13, lasts for a further six years, comprising a first cycle of four years and a second of two years. In 2009/10, according to UNESCO, enrolment at primary level included 91% (males 90%; females 92%) of children in the relevant age-group. However, in 2007/08 enrolment at secondary schools included just 22% of children (males 22%; females 21%) in the relevant age-group, while in 2004/05 just 3.5% of those in the relevant age-group (males 4.3%; females 2.7%) were enrolled in tertiary education. In addition to Makerere University in Kampala, there is a university of science and technology at Mbarara, and a small Islamic university is located at Mbale. In 2003/04 58,823 students were enrolled in Ugandan universities. In 2009 spending on education represented 15.6% of total budgetary expenditure.

Bibliography

Ahluwalia, D. P. S. *Plantations and the Politics of Sugar in Uganda.* Kampala, Fountain Publishers, 1995.

Allen, T., and Vlassenroot, K. (Eds). *The Lord's Resistance Army: Myth and Reality.* London, Zed Books, 2010.

Armstrong, J. *Uganda's AIDS Crisis: Its Implications for Development.* Washington, DC, World Bank, 1995.

Barter, J. *Idi Amin (Heroes & Villains).* San Diego, CA, Lucent Books, 2005.

Bigsten, A., and Kayizzi-Mugerwa, S. *Is Uganda an Emerging Economy?* Uppsala, Nordiska Afrikainstitutet, 2001.

Eichstaedt, P. *First Kill Your Family: Child Soldiers of Uganda and the Lord's Resistance Army.* Chicago, IL, Chicago Review Press, 2009.

Hansen, H. B., and Twaddle, M. (Eds). *Uganda Now.* London, James Currey, 1988.

Changing Uganda: The Dilemmas of Structural Management Adjustment and Revolutionary Change. London, James Currey, 1991.

Developing Uganda. Oxford, James Currey, 1998.

Ingham, K. *Obote.* London, Routledge, 1994.

Jones, B. *Beyond the State in Rural Uganda: Development in Rural Uganda.* Edinburgh, Edinburgh University Press, 2011.

Karugire, S. R. *A Political History of Uganda.* London, Heinemann, 1980.

Roots of instability in Uganda. Kampala, Fountain Publrs, 1996.

Kasozi, A. B. K. *Social Origins of Violence in Uganda, 1964–1985.* London, University College London Press, 1995.

Kuteesa, F., Tumusiime-Mutebile, E., Whitworth, A., and Williamson, T. (Eds). *Uganda's Economic Reforms: Insider Accounts.* Oxford, OUP, 2009.

Langseth, P., and Katototbo, J. (Eds). *Uganda: Landmarks in Rebuilding a Nation.* Kampala, Fountain Publrs, 1993.

Lubanga, F., and Villadsen, S.(Eds). *Democratic Decentralisation in Uganda.* Kampala, Fountain Publrs, 1997.

Mamdani, M. *Imperialism and Fascism in Uganda.* London, Heinemann Educational, 1983.

Measures, R., and Walker, T. *Amin's Uganda.* Whitstable, Oyster Press, 2002.

Mukholi, D. *A Complete Guide to Uganda's Fourth Constitution: History, Politics and the Law.* Kampala, Fountain Publrs, 1995.

Museveni, Y. K. *Sowing the Mustard Seed: The Struggle for Freedom and Democracy in Uganda.* London, Macmillan, 1997.

Mutibwa, P. *Uganda since Independence: A Story of Unfulfilled Hopes.* London, Hurst, 1992.

Mwakikagile, G. *Uganda: A Nation in Transition: Post-colonial Analysis.* Dar es Salaam, New Africa Press, 2012.

Nzita, R., and Mbaga-Niwampa. *Peoples and Cultures of Uganda.* 2nd edn. Kampala, Fountain Publrs, 1995.

Oghojafor, K. *Uganda (Countries of the World).* Milwaukee, WI, Gareth Stevens Publishing, 2004.

Okoth, G. P., and Muranga, M. (Eds). *Uganda: A Century of Existence.* Kampala, Fountain Publrs, 1995.

Pirouet, M. L. *Historical Dictionary of Uganda.* Metuchen, NJ, Scarecrow Press, 1995.

Reid, R. J. *Political Power in Pre-Colonial Buganda.* Athens, OH, Ohio University Press, 2003.

Rotberg, R. I. (Ed.). *Uganda (Africa: Continent in the Balance).* Broomall, PA, Mason Crest Publishers, 2005.

Rubongoya, J. B. *Regime Hegemony in Museveni's Uganda: Pax Musevenica.* Basingstoke, Palgrave Macmillan, 2007.

Ruzindana, A., *et al.* (Eds). *Fighting Corruption in Uganda.* Kampala, Fountain Publrs, 1998.

Soghayroun, I. E.-Z. *The Sudanese Muslim Factor in Uganda.* Khartoum, Khartoum University Press, 1981.

Ssekamnsa, I. C. *History and Development of Education in Uganda.* Kampala, Fountain Publrs, 1997.

Tripp, A. M. *Women and Politics in Uganda.* Madison, WI, University of Wisconsin Press, 2000.

Museveni's Uganda: Paradoxes of Power in a Hybrid Regime. Boulder, CO, Lynne Rienner Publishers, 2010.

Whyte, S. R. *Questioning Misfortune.* Cambridge, Cambridge University Press, 1998.

ZAMBIA

Physical and Social Geography

GEOFFREY J. WILLIAMS

PHYSICAL FEATURES

The Republic of Zambia is a land-locked state occupying elevated plateau country in south-central Africa. Zambia has an area of 752,612 sq km (290,585 sq miles). The country is irregularly shaped, and shares a boundary with eight other countries.

The topography of Zambia is dominated by the even skylines of uplifted plantation surfaces. Highest elevations are reached on the Nyika plateau on the Malawi border (2,164 m). Elevations decline westward, where the country extends into the fringe of the vast Kalahari basin. The plateau surfaces are interrupted by localized downwarps (occupied by lakes and swamp areas, such as in the Bangweulu and Lukanga basins) and by the rifted troughs of the mid-Zambezi and Luangwa rivers.

Katangan rocks of upper-Pre-Cambrian age yield the copper ores exploited on the Copperbelt. Younger Karoo sedimentaries floor the rift troughs of the Luangwa and the mid-Zambezi rivers, while a basalt flow of this age has been incised by the Zambezi below the Victoria Falls to form spectacular gorges. Coal-bearing rocks in the Zambezi trough are of this same system. Over the western third of the country there are extensive and deep wind-deposited sands.

The continental divide separating Atlantic from Indian Ocean drainage forms the frontier with the Democratic Republic of the Congo (DRC), then traverses north-east Zambia to the Tanzanian border. Some 77% of the country is drained to the Indian Ocean by the Zambezi river and its two main tributaries, the Kafue and Luangwa, with the remainder being drained principally by the Chambeshi and Luapula via the River Congo to the Atlantic. Rapids occur along most river courses so that the rivers are of little use for transportation.

Zambia's climatic year can be divided into three seasons: a cool dry season (April–August), a hot dry season (August–November) and a warm wet season (November–April). Temperatures are generally moderate. Mean maximum temperatures exceed 35°C only in southern low-lying areas in October, most of the country being in the range 30°C–35°C. July, the coldest month, has mean minima of 5°C–10°C over most of the country, but shows considerable variability. Rainfall is highest on the high plateau of the Northern Province and on the intercontinental divide west of the Copperbelt (exceeding 1,200 mm per year).

The eastern two-thirds of the country has generally poor soils. Soils on the Kalahari Sands of the west are exceptionally infertile, while seasonal waterlogging of soils in basin and riverine flats makes them difficult to use. Savannah vegetation dominates, with miombo woodland extensive over the plateau, and mopane woodland in the low-lying areas. Small areas of dry evergreen forest occur in the north, while treeless grasslands characterize the flats of the river basins.

RESOURCES AND POPULATION

Zambia's main resource is its land, which, in general, is underutilized. Although soils are generally poor, altitudinal modifications of the climate make possible the cultivation of a wide range of crops. Cattle numbers are greatest in the southern and central areas. In the Western Province their numbers are fewer, but their importance to the local economy is even greater. Subsistence farming characterizes most of the country, with commercial farming focusing along the 'line of rail'. Commercial forestry is important on the Copperbelt, where there are extensive softwood plantations, and in the south-west, where hardwoods are exploited. The main fisheries are located on the lakes and rivers of the Northern Province, with the Kafue Flats, Lukanga and Lake Kariba also contributing significantly. Game parks cover some 8% of the country.

For many years, the mining of copper has been the mainstay of Zambia's economy, although its contribution has fluctuated in line with prices on international commodity markets. By 2009 the country was Africa's largest producer, although only the eighth largest in terms of copper output world-wide. Cobalt, a by-product of copper mining, has recently gained in significance, and Zambia has been steadily expanding its cobalt production in an attempt to offset falls in copper output. In 2011 it was the world's second largest producer of cobalt (after the Democratic Republic of the Congo). Coal, of which Zambia has the continent's largest deposits outside South Africa, is mined in the Zambezi valley, although this industry is in need of re-equipment and modernization. Deposits of uranium have been located, and prospects exist for the exploitation of iron ore. No petroleum deposits have yet been located. However, Zambia is rich in hydropower, developed and potential.

According to the preliminary results of the census of October 2010, Zambia's population was 13,046,508, equivalent to 17.9 inhabitants per sq km (rising to 13,883,575 by mid-2012, giving a density of 18.4 inhabitants per sq km, according to UN estimates). Zambia is one of the most urbanized countries in mainland sub-Saharan Africa, with 46.9% of its population in 2000 classified as urban by the African Development Bank. Some 78% of the urban population was, in fact, located in the 10 largest urban areas, all situated on the 'line of rail', extending south from the Copperbelt, through Lusaka, to the Victoria Falls, forming the major focus of Zambia's economic activity. Lusaka, with a population of 1.5m. in 2010, is the largest single urban centre, but the Copperbelt towns together constitute the largest concentration of urban population (47.1% of the total). While the increasing rate of population growth for the country as a whole (2.4% per year in 2001–10) is a problem, the sustained influx to urban areas is even more acute as this growth has not been matched by employment and formal housing provision.

There are no fewer than 73 different ethnic groups among Zambia's indigenous population. Major groups are: the Bemba of the north-east, who are also dominant on the Copperbelt; the Nyanja of the Eastern Province, also numerous in Lusaka; the Tonga of the Southern Province; and the Lozi of the west. Over 80 languages have been identified, of which seven are recognized as 'official' vernaculars. English is the language of government.

Recent History

GREGORY MTHEMBU-SALTER

Zambia's colonial history began in the 1890s, when British troops forced African leaders to accept treaties ceding large land tracts north of the Zambezi river, enabling the British to extend the territory they had earlier annexed south of the river. The first captured territory became known as Southern Rhodesia (now Zimbabwe) and the second as Northern Rhodesia (now Zambia). By the mid-1930s, following earlier discoveries of vast copper deposits, the large-scale mining exploitation of the northern region of Northern Rhodesia, soon known as the Copperbelt, was firmly established. The British colonial authorities granted Northern Rhodesia's prime agricultural land to white farmers, removing Africans to 'native reserves' on inferior land, thus inhibiting the development of African farming—a legacy with which Zambia lives to this day.

Mining helped foster an industrial class-consciousness among Northern Rhodesians, which was both hindered and radicalized by the prohibition of African trade unions by the authorities. Miners, and later other African workers, instead formed 'welfare societies', which by 1951 had emerged as a cohesive, anti-colonial political force, the Northern Rhodesia African National Congress. The Congress unsuccessfully opposed federation with Southern Rhodesia, and in 1953 the colony became part of the Central African Federation (CAF) with Southern Rhodesia and Nyasaland (now Malawi). In 1958 leadership of the Congress passed to Kenneth Kaunda, whose demands for the dissolution of the CAF and the independence of Northern Rhodesia, under the name of Zambia, led to his imprisonment and the banning of the Congress in 1959. On his release, a few months later, Kaunda became leader of the newly formed United National Independence Party (UNIP). In 1962, following a sustained civil disobedience campaign, led by UNIP, the British Government conceded to its demands, introducing a more democratic Constitution for Northern Rhodesia, which was expected to create an African majority in the legislature. UNIP then agreed to participate in the ensuing elections, and formed a coalition Government with the remaining supporters of Congress. The CAF was formally dissolved in December 1963 and Northern Rhodesia became independent as the Republic of Zambia on 24 October 1964, with Kaunda as President.

Kaunda advocated self-reliant black African nationalism, but prospects for the realization of this aim were undermined by the structural dependence of the Zambian economy on the industrial complex of white-ruled southern Africa. The Zambian Government sought to lessen this reliance by investing in import-substitution industries and alternative routes to seaports, such as Dar es Salaam, that did not pass through Southern Rhodesia and South Africa. Southern Rhodesia's unilateral declaration of independence in November 1965, and the subsequent imposition of international sanctions, further stimulated government efforts to reduce Zambia's economic dependence on trade with the country, particularly in relation to fuel, hydroelectric power and rail communications. This proved difficult, however, and there was little substantive change in trade patterns.

UNIP was returned to power at the general election in 1968, but popular support for the party was in decline. Sensing an opportunity, in 1971 Simon Kapwepwe, a former Vice-President of Zambia who had a strong following among the country's numerous Bemba population, left UNIP and formed the United People's Party (UPP), intending to challenge UNIP at the polls. The Government, however, banned the UPP, and in December 1972 Zambia was declared a one-party state. Legislative elections took place in December 1973, and Kaunda was re-elected for a further term of office.

In January 1973 the Government of Rhodesia (formerly Southern Rhodesia) closed the border to all Zambian exports except copper, with a severe impact on the Zambian economy. The Zambian Government's subsequent decision to divert copper exports using routes to Tanzania and Angola led to lower mineral volumes being exported at greater cost, resulting in further economic deterioration; this was compounded, following the outbreak of civil war in Angola in late 1975, by the closure of the Benguela railway, which had provided Zambia with access to the Atlantic. By the end of 1975 there was widespread domestic discontent at high food prices, import restrictions and increasing unemployment. His apparent belief that external forces were exploiting this unrest prompted Kaunda to declare a state of emergency in January 1976.

In 1978 Kapwepwe rejoined UNIP after being courted by Kaunda, who wanted a recognized Bemba leader at a time of acute internal instability. In October rail links with Rhodesia were restored, and an agreement was reached on the shipping of exports via South Africa. From 1977, however, Zambia had openly harboured members of the Zimbabwe African People's Union (ZAPU) wing of the Patriotic Front, and in 1978 and 1979 Rhodesian forces attacked ZAPU bases in Zambia and carried out air raids on Lusaka. Zambia suffered further disruption from Rhodesian bombing until the implementation, in December 1979, of an agreement providing for the internationally recognized independence of Rhodesia, as Zimbabwe, which came into effect in April 1980.

ECONOMIC PROBLEMS AND POLITICAL UNREST

Political dissent increased towards the end of 1980, as economic conditions worsened further. In October several prominent businessmen, government officials and UNIP members allegedly staged a coup attempt. In January 1981 the suspension from UNIP of 17 officials of the Mineworkers' Union of Zambia (MUZ) and the Zambia Congress of Trade Unions (ZCTU) prompted a widely observed strike, and riots.

As the sole candidate, Kaunda easily won the presidential election in October 1983 despite his increasing unpopularity, receiving 93% of the votes cast. In May 1987 Kaunda announced that the economic programme previously agreed with the IMF was to be replaced by a government-devised strategy involving greater state controls, and appointed a new Minister of Finance.

In late October 1988 presidential and legislative elections took place. Kaunda, again the only candidate, received 95.5% of all votes cast in the presidential election. There followed continued unrest among workers and students, and the Government threatened to ban trade unions involved in strike action. Increases in the prices of essential goods in mid-1989 raised political tensions still further, and prompted renewed rioting in the Copperbelt region in July. In June 1990 an announcement that the price of maize meal was to increase by more than 100% was followed by severe rioting in Lusaka, in which at least 30 people were reported to have been killed.

Earlier, in April 1990, and despite the rapidly deteriorating political climate, the UNIP general conference rejected proposals for the introduction of a multi-party political system in Zambia. In May, however, Kaunda announced that a referendum on the issue would be conducted in October of that year, and that proponents of such a system were allowed to campaign and hold public meetings. In early July the Movement for Multi-party Democracy (MMD), an informal alliance of political opponents of the Government, was formed, under the leadership of a former Minister of Finance, Arthur Wina, and the Chairman of the ZCTU, Frederick Chiluba. In addition, the ZCTU demanded an end to the existing state of emergency, the creation of an independent body to monitor the referendum, and equal access to the media for both those supporting and those opposing the introduction of a multi-party system. Although Kaunda's initial response was hostile, in September he proposed abandoning the referendum and instead pressing ahead with the organization of multi-party elections. UNIP quickly endorsed the new proposals and elections were scheduled for October 1991.

CONSTITUTIONAL TRANSITION

In December 1990 Kaunda formally adopted constitutional amendments, approved by the National Assembly earlier that month, which allowed a multi-party system. Shortly afterwards, the MMD was granted official recognition as a political organization; the establishment of a further 11 opposition movements followed in subsequent months. In early 1991 several prominent members of UNIP resigned from the party and declared their support for the MMD, while the ZCTU officially transferred its allegiance to the MMD. In February Kaunda announced that he would permit other members of UNIP to contest the presidential election, despite previous statements to the contrary.

The constitutional commission presented its recommendations in June 1991, but they were immediately rejected by the MMD, which threatened to boycott the elections if the National Assembly accepted the proposals. In July, following intense negotiations, Kaunda conceded to opposition demands that ministers be appointed only from members of the National Assembly and that the proposed establishment of a constitutional court be abandoned; presidential powers to impose martial law were also to be rescinded. On 2 August the National Assembly formally adopted the new draft Constitution, which included these amendments. Later in August Kaunda agreed to permit foreign observers to monitor the forthcoming elections, to counter opposition allegations that UNIP would perpetrate electoral fraud. In a further attempt to increase the distance between party and state, Kaunda announced that leaders of the armed forces were henceforth obliged to retire from membership of UNIP's Central Committee.

In September 1991 the National Assembly was dissolved in preparation for the presidential and legislative elections, which were scheduled for 31 October. On the same day Kaunda formally announced the disassociation of UNIP from the state and banned public sector workers from engaging in party-political activity. While welcoming these developments, international observers expressed concern none the less at UNIP bias in the state-owned media, at open support for the party from parastatal organizations and that the state of emergency remained in force.

THE CHILUBA PRESIDENCY

International observers reported that the elections, which took place on 31 October 1991, were free and fair. In the presidential election Chiluba, who received 75.8% of votes cast, soundly defeated Kaunda, who obtained 24.2% of the vote. In the legislative elections, which were contested by 330 candidates representing six political parties, the MMD again triumphed, securing 125 seats in the National Assembly, while UNIP won just 25 seats; only four members of the previous Government were returned to the National Assembly. On 2 November Chiluba was inaugurated as President; he appointed Levy Mwanawasa, a lawyer, as Vice-President and Leader of the National Assembly, and formed a new 22-member Cabinet. In addition, a minister was appointed to each of the country's nine provinces, which were previously administered by governors. Two days later the Government allowed the state of emergency to lapse. During his first month in office Chiluba began a major restructuring of the civil service and parastatal organizations, replacing Kaunda's appointees with people loyal to himself.

Internal 'Conspiracies' and Official Investigations

In December 1991, following a road accident in which Mwanawasa was severely injured, the Minister without Portfolio, Brig.-Gen. Godfrey Miyanda, was accused of plotting his death. In March 1992, however, following an investigation by British detectives into the circumstances of the accident, Miyanda was exonerated.

In early March 1993 Chiluba declared a state of emergency, following the apparent discovery of documents emanating from UNIP detailing an alleged conspiracy (referred to as the 'Zero Option') to destabilize the Government by inciting unrest and civil disobedience. Prominent members of UNIP, including Kaunda's three sons, were subsequently arrested. Shortly afterwards, the National Assembly approved the state of emergency, which was to remain in force for a further three months. Under pressure from Western governments, however, Chiluba reduced the maximum period of detention without trial from 28 to seven days. Responding to growing domestic and international concern about corruption, Chiluba reorganized his Cabinet in April 1993, but although several ministers were dismissed, those most strongly suspected of corruption—including foreign affairs minister Vernon Mwaanga—were retained. Later that month the state of emergency was lifted.

Political Realignments

In July 1993 UNIP appealed for civil disobedience in protest against economic austerity measures, but was largely ignored by the general population. The persistence of divisions within the MMD was laid bare in August when 15 prominent members left the party. The rebels accused the Government of protecting corrupt cabinet ministers and failing to respond to numerous reports linking senior party officials with the illegal drugs trade. Their opposition to Chiluba's Government was consolidated later in the month by the formation of a new political group, the National Party (NP).

Following continued allegations of his links to illegal drugs-trafficking, Mwaanga resigned in January 1994, while denying any misconduct. In early July Mwanawasa resigned as Vice-President, citing long-standing differences with Chiluba, and was replaced by Miyanda. In the same month former President Kaunda, despite having earlier resigned as leader of UNIP and stating that he was to retire from politics, unexpectedly announced that he might contest the presidential election scheduled to be held in 1996. Then, in June 1995, at an extraordinary congress of UNIP, Kaunda was elected party President by a large majority. Proposed constitutional reforms from the MMD, however, included a clause banning any President from a third term of office and barring candidates from seeking election as President if their parents were not of Zambian origin. (Kaunda's parents were born in Malawi.)

In October 1995 the Minister of Legal Affairs announced that Kaunda had not officially relinquished Malawian citizenship until 1970 and had therefore governed illegally for six years, and that he had not obtained Zambian citizenship through the correct procedures. There followed widespread reports that Kaunda would be deported, but later that month the Government relented and investigations into his citizenship were suspended.

Electoral Controversies

The Government pressed on with its proposed constitutional changes despite the resignation of two ministers over the issue during early 1996, ignoring demands from opposition parties that it negotiate with them on the matter. In May UNIP deputies withdrew from a parliamentary debate on the proposed Constitution, which was subsequently approved by a large majority in the National Assembly. On 28 May the new Constitution, which, as anticipated, contained clauses preventing Kaunda from standing as a presidential candidate, was officially adopted by Chiluba. Donors reduced aid in protest, while Kaunda announced that he would contest the presidency despite the ban. In the same month eight senior UNIP officials, including the party Vice-President, were arrested and charged in connection with a series of bomb attacks against official buildings, which were officially attributed to a clandestine anti-Government organization called 'Black Mamba'.

In August 1996 Chiluba and Kaunda met for discussions in Lusaka, following which the Government made minor concessions regarding the conduct of forthcoming elections, while rejecting UNIP's central demand that the elections be conducted according to the 1991 Constitution. UNIP threatened again to boycott the elections and to organize a campaign of civil disobedience, and soon after a further six political parties also decided on an electoral boycott. Further undermining the credibility of the polls, there was widespread criticism of the voter-registration process, in which fewer than one-half of the estimated 4.6m. eligible voters were listed.

The 1996 Elections

Elections took place on 18 November 1996, with the boycott by the main opposition parties ensuring that Chiluba and the

MMD were returned to power by a large majority. In the presidential election Chiluba defeated the four other candidates, with 72.5% of the valid votes cast. His nearest rival (with only 12.5%) was Dean Mung'omba, who had challenged Chiluba for the MMD leadership in 1995, but had subsequently founded the Zambia Democratic Congress (ZADECO). The MMD secured 131 of the 150 seats in the National Assembly. Of the eight other parties that finally contested the legislative elections, only the NP (five seats), ZADECO (two seats) and Agenda for Zambia (two seats) won parliamentary representation, with independent candidates taking the remaining 10 seats. The rate of voter participation was low. Chiluba was inaugurated for a second presidential term on 21 November 1996.

In early February 1997 a human rights report prepared for the US Department of State condemned police brutality and prison conditions in Zambia, but claimed that there had been no evidence of significant electoral fraud in the 1996 elections. In March 1997 the Government established a permanent commission to investigate human rights violations, but opposition parties refused to participate.

Internal Tensions

In August 1997 the Government accused the opposition of inciting unrest after market-traders rioted when their stalls were destroyed by fire; 56 people were arrested in the disturbances. Later that month Kaunda and Dr Rodger Chongwe, the leader of the Liberal Progressive Front, were shot and wounded when the security forces opened fire on an opposition gathering, following the cancellation of a rally in Kabwe, north of Lusaka. Kaunda's subsequent allegation that the shooting was an assassination attempt organized by the Government was strongly denied by Chiluba. The Government announced in November that all public sector wages would be frozen in 1998 to allow for the financing of major civil service redundancies, as part of its public sector reform programme. In March 1998 the ZCTU organized a general strike in protest, but the action collapsed after the Government threatened the strikers with dismissal. In June 1999 Zambia's industrial relations court ruled that the 1998 wage freeze had been illegal, but the Government ignored the ruling, prompting further strike action from public sector workers.

On 28 October 1997 rebel officers, led by Capt. Stephen Lungu, briefly captured the national television and radio station from where they proclaimed the formation of a military regime. The attempted coup was suppressed within a few hours by regular military units; 15 people, including Lungu, were arrested during the operation and one man was killed. Chiluba declared a state of emergency on 29 October, allowing the detention for 28 days without trial of people suspected of involvement in the attempted coup. Several non-governmental organizations, including the Law Association of Zambia (LAZ), denounced the state of emergency as an abuse of human rights. Mung'omba was among 84 people arrested in the immediate aftermath of the coup attempt, and in November the High Court ordered that he undergo a medical examination to investigate injuries allegedly sustained during interrogation by the police.

On 25 December 1997 Kaunda was arrested under emergency powers and imprisoned. Numerous governments expressed serious concern at Kaunda's detention, and the former President refused food until the end of the month when Julius Nyerere, the former President of Tanzania, visited him. On the following day Kaunda was transferred from prison to house arrest, and then in January 1998 arraigned in court. In mid-February Kaunda was formally notified that he was to stand trial for 'misprision of treason', on the grounds that he had failed to report in advance to the authorities details allegedly known to him of the attempted coup of October 1997. Meanwhile, in late January 1998 the National Assembly voted to extend the state of emergency for a further three months; Chiluba eventually revoked the state of emergency in mid-March, following pressure from external donors. Kaunda was released from detention in early June, after charges against him were withdrawn, apparently owing to lack of evidence. His subsequent resignation as UNIP President in July created a split within the party over the nomination of a replacement. The MMD was also divided over an eventual successor to Chiluba, despite a ban within the party on presidential campaigning, amid suggestions that Chiluba might seek a third term of office in 2001, contrary to the Constitution.

In late March 1999 the High Court delivered its judgment in a case concerning Kaunda's citizenship, declaring him to be stateless. Kaunda appealed to the Supreme Court, and at around the same time survived a reported assassination attempt, when a group of armed men opened fire on his car. In November Chiluba demoted Benjamin Mwila to the Ministry of Energy and Water Development, after increasingly transparent hints from Mwila that he intended to contest the presidency in 2001. Kaunda's son, Maj. Wezi Kaunda, whom he had been grooming to succeed him as UNIP President, was shot dead in early November outside his Lusaka home. Kaunda later alleged the murder had been politically motivated, while police sources stated that Wezi Kaunda had been the victim of an attempted car hijack.

Kenneth Kaunda resigned once again as President of UNIP in late March 2000, and an extraordinary party congress elected Francis Nkhoma as its new leader in mid-May. Another of Kaunda's sons, Tilyenji, was appointed as UNIP's new Secretary-General. Nkhoma was suspended as President by senior UNIP officials in November 2000, although he contested the legality of the suspension, and in January 2001 the UNIP Central Committee returned to the Kaunda dynasty, adopting Tilyenji Kaunda as its President.

Mwila publicly declared his intention to bid for the presidency in May 2000, and was later expelled from the MMD. Mwila's expulsion again raised the issue of Chiluba's intentions regarding the forthcoming presidential election, scheduled to be held in or before November 2001. A constitutional amendment introduced by the Government in 1996 prohibited Chiluba from contesting another election, having already served two terms. However, towards the end of 2000 many MMD cadres began appealing for a further constitutional amendment to allow Chiluba to stand again.

Debate over whether the Constitution should be amended to allow Chiluba to stand for a third term intensified during 2001. Prominent civil society organizations, including trade unions, churches, the LAZ and many smaller bodies in late February adopted the 'Oasis Declaration', which vigorously opposed the proposed third term. The declaration was quickly endorsed by opposition parties. In late March the MMD National Executive Committee (NEC) scheduled a special convention of the party for late April to decide the issue. As the date approached, opposition to the third term within the MMD grew markedly, and in mid-April 50 MMD deputies, including 21 ministers, signed a petition opposing the bid. At the MMD convention at the end of the month, party members opposed to a third term were physically prevented from attending, while pro-third term delegates proceeded to nominate Chiluba as the party's presidential candidate.

On 2 May 2001 Chiluba dismissed all those in his Cabinet who had signed the petition against his re-election bid and the MMD expelled them from the party. Those removed from the MMD contested the legality of their expulsion in the courts, but also established their own political party, the Forum for Democracy and Development (FDD). On 3 May 65 deputies signed a motion to impeach Chiluba for alleged violations of the Constitution. However, the Speaker of the National Assembly, Amusaa Katunda Mwanamwambwa, prevented a parliamentary debate on the motion and as a result the National Assembly failed to convene for five months. In early May Chiluba finally ceded to pressure, and publicly stated that he would not seek a third term in office.

THE MWANAWASA PRESIDENCY

In July 2001 Chiluba selected Levy Mwanawasa as the MMD's presidential candidate, angering aspirational serving MMD cabinet ministers and other influential party members, since Mwanawasa had not been active in politics since the mid-1990s. Despite the tensions, the MMD endorsed Mwanawasa's candidature in August. The FDD held its first national convention in mid-October, electing Christon Tembo as the party President. Tembo and other opposition party leaders then held talks to try to agree on just one candidate from among them to oppose Mwanawasa, but the presidential ambitions of each party leader proved too strong, and the talks failed. In November Chiluba set the election date for late December, and campaigning began in earnest. International observers monitoring poll preparations later noted the substantial deployment of state resources to assist the MMD's campaign.

The elections took place peacefully on 27 December 2001; turn-out was 67% of registered voters. According to the Electoral Commission of Zambia (ECZ), Mwanawasa narrowly won the presidential election—with 29.2% of the votes cast, defeating his closest rival, Anderson Mazoka of the United Party for National Development (UPND), who won 27.2% of the votes—by fewer than 34,000 votes. Mazoka immediately alleged the poll was neither free nor fair, and that the official result should be set aside. In the National Assembly elections, the MMD won 69 seats and opposition parties 80, of which the UPND took 49; one independent was elected. The Constitution allowed Mwanawasa to appoint eight new members to the Assembly, who were then brought into the Government, but—in a first for Zambia—he still lacked a majority in the Assembly. In early February 2002 the European Union (EU) election monitoring team stated the election results were unsafe and alleged a wide range of malpractice, including state media bias and the deliberate failure to supply ballot boxes in marginal constituencies.

Mwanawasa was sworn in as President on 2 January 2002 and a new Government was announced a few days later. Emmanuel Kasonde was appointed as Minister of Finance and Economic Development, and seven ministers from Chiluba's Cabinet were retained, including Enoch Kavindele as Vice-President and Katele Kalumba, who was moved from the Ministry of Finance and Economic Development to the Ministry of Foreign Affairs. Later in January Mwanawasa undertook major changes in the armed forces and intelligence services high command and the senior levels of the civil service, removing Chiluba appointees and replacing them with his own.

A rift between Mwanawasa and Chiluba, who had remained MMD President, became evident soon after Mwanawasa assumed office. Following a ruling by the courts that Chiluba would not be entitled to his benefits package as a former Head of State if he continued in active politics, Chiluba relinquished the MMD presidency in late March 2002. Meanwhile, Mwanawasa continued with his civil service reforms, replacing the heads of the Treasury, the Bank of Zambia, the revenue authority and the privatization agency. In March EU parliamentarians visited Lusaka to discuss the EU's relations with the new Government. The EU later opted to support the new administration, despite its concerns about the election, and in June made substantial new aid pledges.

Following growing demands that he take action against corruption, Mwanawasa called a special sitting of the National Assembly in mid-July 2002, and implicated Chiluba in several major corruption scandals. Mwanawasa also announced the formation of a new anti-corruption task force. In response to a request from Mwanawasa, the Assembly subsequently lifted Chiluba's immunity from prosecution. Chiluba stalled charges being laid against him for several months by applying to the courts for a ruling on the validity of the Assembly's decision, but in February 2003 Chiluba was arrested and charged with over 200 counts of corruption and embezzlement after the Supreme Court ruled in favour of the National Assembly.

As part of a government reorganization, Mwanawasa appointed several opposition party members to his Cabinet in early February 2003. He presented the changes as a bid to unite Zambians, but opposition party leaders complained that the appointments had been made without consultation and that Mwanawasa had, in fact, intended to weaken the opposition.

Inclusive Politics

UNIP announced a formal alliance with the MMD in May 2003, angering many UNIP supporters, although party President Tilyenji Kaunda defended the agreement. At the end of the month Mwanawasa reorganized his Cabinet again, dismissing Kasonde and Kavindele, whom he later accused of corruption. Kavindele was replaced by Nevers Mumba, an evangelical pastor who had previously led an opposition party, the National Citizens' Coalition.

In mid-August 2003, despite several influential MMD members supporting the motion, Mwanawasa survived an attempt by opposition members of the National Assembly to impeach him over the manner of Mumba's appointment and the President's alleged corruption. Mwanawasa removed those implicated from the MMD's NEC soon after. Subsequent victories in 12 parliamentary by-elections by the end of the year gave the MMD its first majority in the National Assembly since Mwanawasa became President. Several of the by-elections had been necessitated by the defection of the UPND incumbents to the MMD. In each case, much to the displeasure of UPND President Mazoka, the deputy who had defected from the UPND became the MMD candidate in the by-election.

In a controversial move, in early 2004 Mwanawasa dismissed the Director of Public Prosecutions (DPP), Mukelabai Mukelabai, for allegedly conducting himself improperly during Chiluba's corruption trial. Mukelabai protested that his removal was illegal, and his petition was subsequently upheld by a legal tribunal, which called for his reinstatement. Ignoring the ruling, Mwanawasa appointed Mukelabai's deputy, Caroline Sokoni, to replace him. Sokoni then abandoned some of the charges against Chiluba and prepared new ones, to which Chiluba again pleaded not guilty. Meanwhile, Mwanawasa dismissed Vice-President Mumba in October, replacing him with Lupando Mwape, a former transport minister.

CONSTITUTIONAL DEBATES

In mid-2005 striking miners at Konkola Copper Mines (KCM—see Economy), the country's largest copper producer, responsible for 70% of national output, rioted after rejecting a 30% wage increase offer; the workers were demanding a 100% salary increase. An explosive device was also set off on KCM property. In July, alleging that the strike and the bomb were the result of political conspiracy, Mwanawasa ordered the arrest of Michael Sata, leader of the Patriotic Front (PF) opposition party, accusing him of involvement. Sata was later arraigned in court on charges including sedition and espionage. The Minister of Mines and Mineral Development, Kaunda Lembalemba, was removed from the Government the following month.

In November 2005 opposition parties and civil society activists grouped under the umbrella of the Oasis Forum (named after the 2001 Oasis Declaration opposing Chiluba's third-term bid) held a public demonstration in Lusaka to call for the adoption of a new constitution before the 2006 elections. The Forum also reiterated demands for the constitution to be adopted by a constituent assembly rather than the National Assembly. A secret ballot of MMD deputies in early 2006 on the constitutional issue indicated that an overwhelming majority of them supported the constitution's adoption by a constituent assembly. In February 2006, to the approval of the Oasis Forum, Mwanawasa reversed his long-standing opposition to the reform, promising that the new constitution would be introduced this way. Mwanawasa insisted, however, that the change must first be approved by a national referendum, and—contrary to the wishes of the Oasis Forum—could not be introduced before the 2006 elections.

MWANAWASA SECURES A SECOND TERM

In March 2006 the three main opposition parties—the UPND, the FDD and UNIP—announced that they would endorse a single presidential candidate to challenge the MMD candidate, under a new grouping styled the United Democratic Alliance (UDA). Zambian opposition parties had tried and failed to achieve similar agreements in past elections, helping to ensure continued victories for the ruling party. Mwanawasa was rushed to London, United Kingdom, for medical treatment on 30 March, after suffering a stroke, raising concerns about whether he would be well enough to stand in the forthcoming elections; however, he soon returned to Zambia, insisting that he was in good health. In May UPND leader Anderson Mazoka died, following a long illness. His death immediately sparked a succession battle within the party, and created uncertainty about who would lead the UDA, since it had previously been assumed this would be Mazoka, as the leader of the largest party within the alliance. A new electoral law was adopted in May that notably failed to incorporate the main demands made of it by opposition parties and the Oasis Forum. Most significantly, the new law made no change to the way in which the President should be elected, retaining the previous requirement of a simple majority rather than the 51% demanded by reformists. In June the UPND selected Hakainde Hichilema (a former managing director of accountancy and financial services provider Grant Thornton Ltd in Zambia) as its new leader. On 26 July Mwanawasa dissolved the National Assembly and announced that the elections would be held on 28 September.

Voting in the presidential election took place as scheduled on 28 September 2006 with a high turn-out, later announced at over 70% by the ECZ. Mwanawasa took 43.0% of the votes cast, a significant improvement on his 2001 showing, and enough to secure him a comfortable victory. Sata was his nearest opponent with 29.4%. While Sata protested that he was the victim of electoral fraud, he did not take his case to court. Hichilema secured 25.3%, suggesting that a united opposition might have defeated Mwanawasa. In the parliamentary elections that were held concurrently, the MMD secured 75 seats, again a sharp increase compared with its 2001 performance, to which were added eight nominated seats, bringing its total to 81. Sata's PF gained 43, the UDA won 26 seats and smaller parties and independents secured the remaining six elected seats, leaving the MMD with an overall majority of just five seats.

Most electoral observers judged the polls to have been free and fair, although the EU observer group stated that there had been insufficient regulation of campaign spending, which had benefited Mwanawasa and the MMD. Mwanawasa was sworn in as President on 4 October 2006. The President's new Cabinet was nearly identical to his previous administration, with the exception of Ronnie Shikapwasha, who was moved from the foreign affairs to the home affairs portfolio. Additionally, Lupando Mwape, who lost his seat at the election, was replaced at the vice-presidency with a veteran politician (and former Minister of Foreign Affairs under Kaunda), Rupiah Banda.

In May 2007 a court in London found Chiluba guilty of conspiring to defraud Zambia of US $46m. via a London account of the Zambia National Commercial Bank (ZNCB), and ordered the former President and his co-conspirators to repay 85% of the money. The case was held in London following a decision by Zambia's Attorney-General in 2006 to launch a civil prosecution case against Chiluba in the United Kingdom, as the Zambian criminal trial against him had stalled. Chiluba, who had refused to testify in the case, denounced the verdict as a conspiracy between Mwanawasa and the British Government, and stated that he would not recognize it.

The Government presented legislation concerning its planned National Constitutional Conference (NCC) to the National Assembly in August 2007, where it was approved despite resistance from the PF. The proposal envisaged that a broadly constituted NCC would make recommendations on a new constitution, which must then be adopted by the National Assembly, as opposed to the PF and Oasis Forum's counter-proposal that a new constitution be adopted by a specially convened constitutional assembly. Of the PF's 43 members of the National Assembly, 27 signalled their intention to participate in the NCC against Sata's wishes. Sata subsequently announced that any member choosing to participate would be expelled from the party. The dissident parliamentarians then brought a case to court and secured an injunction preventing Sata from expelling them.

MWANAWASA'S DEATH AND BANDA'S SUCCESSION

Mwanawasa suffered a stroke while attending the 11th African Union (AU) Summit held in Egypt in July 2008, and was taken to France to receive treatment. He died there on 19 August and Vice-President Rupiah Banda became head of government in an acting capacity. Under the terms of the Zambian Constitution an election was required to be held within 90 days of the death of the President. On 30 October Banda, Sata, Miyanda and Hichilema contested an election, at which Banda received 40.6% of the votes cast. Sata, who had narrowly lost the presidential election to Mwanawasa in 2006, was again placed second, with 38.6% of the total. Hichilema took 20.0% of the vote and Miyanda received 0.8%. Only 45% of the registered electorate participated in the poll. Sata rejected the poll outcome, and stated that he would ask the Supreme Court to demand a recount; however, in March 2009 this request was rejected.

Banda reorganized the Government in mid-November 2008, removing several ministers who had served under Mwanawasa, including Magande, the Minister of Finance and National Planning, who had unsuccessfully challenged Banda for the MMD's presidential nomination prior to the poll. Magande was replaced by Dr Situmbeko Musokotwane, a former economic adviser to Banda. George Kunda, the former Minister of Justice, was appointed to the vice-presidency. Although President of the country, Banda was not yet President of the MMD, and Magande and his supporters began actively to campaign to prevent him from assuming this position. In February 2009, however, the MMD's NEC confirmed Banda as the party President and ruled that he should stand unopposed for the post at the MMD convention in 2010, thus positioning him to be the party's presidential candidate the following year. The NEC's decision emboldened Banda to move against his critics in the party. He swiftly dismissed two junior cabinet ministers and also had them expelled from the MMD, warning that a similar fate would await others in the party who wished to challenge his leadership. In early March 2009 Banda again attacked Magande, claiming to have in his possession a document incriminating Magande in financial impropriety during his tenure as Minister of Finance and National Planning.

Shortly afterwards Banda suffered a setback when in mid-March 2009 the Minister of Communications and Transport, Dora Siliya, who was believed to be a close ally of the President, resigned from office following months of corruption allegations against her in the local press. Banda had strongly defended Siliya, but an independent tribunal ruled that she had broken the law in awarding a US $2m. contract without following tender procedures.

George Mpombo, the Minister of Defence and an influential member of the party, resigned from the Government and the MMD's NEC in July 2009 in protest against the NEC's February decision, and subsequently became an outspoken critic. In October Mpombo publicly accused Banda of being dictatorial, prompting the MMD to suspend Mpombo's party membership, saying he had undermined the party.

In August 2009 the High Court generated headlines worldwide with its decision to acquit Chiluba of all the corruption charges against him. Controversially, Chalwe Muchenga, the Director of Public Prosecutions, elected not to appeal the verdict, prompting allegations from civil society organizations and donors that Banda had lost interest in the struggle against corruption. In a bid to refute the charge, Banda announced a new government anti-corruption policy in September. Chiluba's legal worries, however, were not entirely over. Also in February 2010 the Supreme Court upheld a 2007 decision by the British High Court in London, which found Chiluba and his close allies guilty of stealing US $46m. from the Zambian State. The London High Court had ruled that 85% of the money should be repaid, and the Zambian Supreme Court found that the verdict was valid and could be upheld in Zambia, if the Zambian judicial system so decided. However, in August the Lusaka High Court ruled that the British verdict could not be enforced, and the Government, to the disappointment of anti-corruption campaigners, swiftly announced that it would not appeal against this decision. Chiluba, who declared that he felt vindicated by the Lusaka High Court judgement, subsequently died of a heart attack in June 2011.

The NCC was due to deliver its proposals by July 2009, but failed to do so, prompting Banda to grant it a four-month extension. In September the NCC decided that the power to dissolve the National Assembly should be taken by the Assembly itself, rather than the President. The NCC also agreed that the number of National Assembly members should be nearly doubled, from 158 to 280, which prompted widespread criticism that this would substantially increase public spending while having little positive impact on governance. The NCC also missed its new deadline to submit proposals, notably failing to agree on the key issue of how the President should be elected. Unable to find a resolution, the NCC voted on 19 January 2010 that the issue should be put to a referendum. The Government, however, opposed the decision, arguing that a referendum would be too expensive.

On 15 October 2009 the PF candidate, Geoffrey Mwamba, easily won a by-election in Kasama Central, gaining more than double the number of votes of the MMD candidate. The victory was an apparent vindication of an earlier decision by the PF and UPND to enter into an alliance and field single candidates at by-elections. This was followed by two further by-election victories for the PF-UPND alliance, the first on 19 November 2009 in Solwezi, which had previously been an MMD stronghold, and the second on 30 April 2010 at Mufumbwe. The latter was a close result and the losing MMD candidate appealed against the outcome. There were skirmishes between PF-UPND and MMD supporters before the poll, for which the police blamed the former, arresting 25 of their members including Watson Lumba, who had recently been elected to the National Assembly to represent Solwezi.

The MMD NEC in September 2010 expelled former government ministers Ng'andu Magande and George Mpombo for having publicly criticized Banda. Shortly afterwards, Magande announced his intention to establish a new political party, the National Movement for Progress (NMP), prior to contesting a presidential election in 2011. In February Banda removed the Minister of Works and Supply, Mike Mulongoti, following Mulongoti's announcement that he would contest the MMD's vice-presidency at the party's national convention in April. In the event, the post of vice-president was abolished at the convention, while Banda was re-elected the party leader unopposed, thus preparing for his next presidential bid.

Meanwhile, Sata's presidential aspirations suffered a reverse in January 2011, when the Drug Enforcement Commission (DEC) placed him under investigation for alleged money laundering. Sata immediately accused Banda of manipulating supposedly independent public institutions to exclude him from the contest. In the same month, Florence Mumba, a former Supreme Court judge, resigned as the chairperson of the Electoral Commission of Zambia (ECZ), following public allegations that she had improperly awarded a large tender to international accounting firm KPMG. The allegations were first made by the ECZ director Dan Kalale. Auditor-general Anna Chifungula later judged the KPMG tender to have been awarded improperly, while Mumba protested her innocence and called for a formal investigation by the Anti-corruption Commission.

In mid-October 2010 two Chinese managers at a coal mine in the Southern Province shot and injured at least 11 local workers during a pay strike. The managers were arrested, but were later released on K50m. (US $10,700) bail. In April 2011 the managers were acquitted, following the decision of the state prosecutor to abandon the charges against them, apparently because witnesses had refused to testify. The managers' lawyer had earlier been cited in the press as stating that the Government had secured agreements with the injured miners not to pursue the case, in return for substantial compensation.

SATA'S PRESIDENCY

In March 2011 the PF and UPND ended their alliance, apparently because both party leaders wished to participate in the presidential election, scheduled to be held concurrently with legislative elections on 20 September. The parties did, however, co-operate to defeat a proposed constitutional amendment in the National Assembly on 29 March, with most PF deputies voting against, and UPND members abstaining. The PF had earlier accused the NCC of having become too close to the ruling party. The UPND announced that it had abstained because the legislation failed to replace the 'first-past-the-post' method for electing the President with a system requiring that the winner secure over 50% of the votes.

In July 2011 Banda dissolved the National Assembly, and announced that the presidential and legislative elections would be held on 20 September. A vigorous electoral campaign ensued, with Sata making corruption and the state of the economy his main issues. On 23 September Chief Justice Ernest Sakala declared Sata the winner of the presidential election (which had been contested by 10 candidates), despite the ECZ not having released full results, and he was sworn in later that day. Election monitors from the EU and the Southern African Development Community (SADC) declared the vote free and fair. On 28 September the ECZ confirmed that Sata had won 42.9% of the total votes cast, while Banda had taken 36.2%. Of the other eight candidates only Hichilema (with 18.5%) secured more than 1% of the votes cast. At the legislative elections, the PF won 60 of the 148 seats (voting was not held in two constituencies), the MMD took 55 and the UNDP 28. Independent candidates were elected in three constituencies, while the Alliance for Democracy and Development and the FDD each secured one seat. On 29 September Sata announced the formation of a new Government. Guy Scott was appointed Vice-President, the first white person to hold that position since independence, while other notable new government members included Alexander Chikwanda as Minister of Finance and Chishimba Kambwili as Minister of Foreign Affairs.

The new Government caused consternation among foreign investors by reversing the privatization of Finance Bank Zambia in early October 2011, and that of the country's main telecommunications company, Zamtel, in January 2012. Sata's administration, in addition, initially threatened the introduction of a windfall tax on the mining sector, but later opted instead for an increase in mining royalties to 6% for base metals and to 5% for precious minerals. The Government also introduced new regulations that were designed to prevent mining companies misrepresenting the value and volume of their mineral exports.

Sata's democratic standing was damaged by an announcement by the country's registrar of societies in March 2012 that the MMD would be suspended as a political party, owing to its alleged financial debts, and that all its elected parliamentary seats would be nullified. The Lusaka High Court, however, postponed the motion to deregister the MMD until the hearing of a judicial appeal, and on 26 June ruled that the MMD's suspension was both unreasonable and illegal.

A new law, which was introduced on 18 May 2012, required all domestic transactions to be quoted or paid for in Zambian currency only. The legislation led to an immediate appreciation in the value of the currency, the kwacha, but was criticized by international mining companies, which declared that it would raise operating costs and result in job losses. Also in May, the Government sought the extradition from South Africa of Henry Banda, the son of the former President, on the grounds that he was suspected of fraud. The Government refuted criticism from some civil society groups that Sata was using his anti-corruption policy to target political opponents.

REGIONAL RELATIONS

Relations between Zambia and newly independent Zimbabwe were initially tense, owing to Kaunda's long-standing support for Robert Mugabe's political rival, Joshua Nkomo, although the two countries' shared experience as 'front-line' states opposed to apartheid South Africa did much to improve relations. Nevertheless, Mwanawasa became increasingly agitated with developments in Zimbabwe, and in 2006 he publicly compared Zimbabwe to the sinking ship *Titanic*. Prior to Mwanawasa's appointment as Chairman of SADC in August 2007 the Zambian President attempted to heal the rift between himself and Mugabe, dispatching Vice-President Banda to Harare for talks with the Zimbabwean leader. However, following the controversial presidential election in Zimbabwe in June 2008, which was only contested by Mugabe, Mwanawasa denounced the outcome as undemocratic and unacceptable. Mwanawasa's forthright stance was not endorsed by most other SADC leaders. Banda, by contrast, was supportive of Mugabe, and Sata has been even more so, to the relief of SADC leaders but to the consternation of Zimbabwe's Movement for Democratic Change.

Kaunda assumed a leading role in peace initiatives in southern Africa and supported both the South West Africa

People's Organisation of Namibia (SWAPO), allowing it to operate from Zambian territory, and the African National Congress of South Africa (ANC), which, until its return to South Africa in mid-1990, maintained its headquarters in Lusaka. Owing to Kaunda's support for SWAPO and the ANC, Zambia was frequently subjected to military reprisals by South Africa. However, South African political reforms from 1990 onwards eased relations, and in mid-1993 the South African President, F. W. de Klerk, made an official visit to Zambia (the first by a South African Head of State). The South African Government endorsed Mwanawasa's controversial first election victory and, in return, Mwanawasa supported Thabo Mbeki's proposal for the New Partnership for Africa's Development. Relations between Banda and Jacob Zuma, who was elected President of South Africa in April 2009, appeared warm, with Banda being one of the few African heads of state to attend the World Economic Forum in Cape Town, hosted by Zuma, in June 2009. The South African Government was reported to be concerned at the reversal of the sale of Finance Bank Zambia to South Africa's FirstRand Bank, although there was no formal protest.

The Namibian and Zambian authorities have co-operated since SWAPO came to power to suppress Lozi nationalism. In 1999 Lozi nationalists from the Caprivi strip in Namibia fled to Zambia seeking asylum, but were detained in Lusaka and subsequently returned to Namibia by the Zambian Government. Lozi nationalists clashed with Namibian troops in Caprivi that year, and the Zambia-based Lozi nationalist Imasiku Mutangelwa, the leader of the Barotse Patriotic Front (a militant group based in Zambia), was arrested by the Zambian authorities for allegedly declaring his support for their actions. Mutangelwa had initially sought refuge in the South African High Commission in Lusaka, but the South Africans handed him over to the Zambian police.

Zambia's support for the Governments of Angola and Mozambique during the Kaunda era resulted in retaliatory attacks by União Nacional para a Independência Total de Angola (UNITA) rebels and by Mozambican guerrillas of the Resistência Nacional Moçambicana (Renamo). Renamo attacks ceased after a peace agreement was reached between Renamo and the Government of Mozambique in October 1992. Zambia subsequently contributed 950 troops for a UN peacekeeping force that was deployed in Mozambique. It was frequently alleged by the Angolan Government during the Chiluba presidency that senior members of the Zambian Government were supporting UNITA. Chiluba denied the charges, which were never proved, but it was none the less widely suspected that covert Zambian assistance for UNITA was taking place, even though in early 1996 Zambia contributed some 1,000 troops to the UN Angola Verification Mission. In early 1999 tensions between the two countries peaked when the Angolan Government accused Chiluba's administration of complicity in a mysterious bomb blast that severely damaged the Angolan embassy in Lusaka. The two Governments later signed an agreement aimed at resolving their differences, but the Angolan Government was angered that Chiluba refused to allow its troops to pursue UNITA forces onto Zambian territory, and in December 1999 Angolan military aircraft bombed border areas of Zambia's North-Western Province. The UNITA leader, Jonas Savimbi, was killed in early 2002, and a peace agreement was reached between the Angolan Government and UNITA in April. Following the agreement, relations eased considerably between the two countries as peace largely returned to the border region and the refugees began to go home. Over 20,000 Angolan refugees, however, have declined to return to Angola, and many still remain in camps in Zambia.

The Zambian Government became involved in regional efforts to find a political solution to the conflict in the Democratic Republic of the Congo (DRC), after a rebellion was mounted against its Government in August 1998, and Chiluba was appointed to co-ordinate SADC peace initiatives on the crisis. A summit held in Lusaka in June–July 1999 resulted in a cease-fire document that provided a timetable for the withdrawal of foreign forces from the DRC and for political reform in the country, which was hailed at the time as a major diplomatic achievement by Chiluba. The diplomatic initiative to end the war was subsequently taken by South Africa; Mwanawasa played only a minimal role in later diplomacy. Mwanawasa's relations with Congolese President Joseph Kabila, while cordial, showed little evidence of warmth, but Mwanawasa remained careful not to offend the DRC Government. Meanwhile, Zambia continues to host thousands of Congolese refugees who fled the DRC during the conflict or subsequently, most of whom live in camps assisted by the office of the UN High Commissioner for Refugees. Efforts by that organization at voluntary repatriation have yielded disappointing results, and the majority have remained in Zambia.

Economy

LINDA VAN BUREN

Revised for this edition by OBI IHEME

INTRODUCTION

The Zambian economy has demonstrated significant resilience as the world has begun to recover from the global economic downturn of 2008 and 2009. According to the IMF in its June 2010 review, 'the Zambian economy has performed well in the aftermath of a sharp decline in copper prices in late 2008–early 2009, thanks to prudent macro-economic policies and structural reforms. Growth is high; inflation has moderated; the current account deficit has narrowed; international reserves have strengthened...; and the economic outlook is positive.' The World Bank also praised the country's economic management in April 2011. Generally, the performance of the Zambian economy reflects fluctuations in the global copper market, and the world copper price is not known for its stability, even in the absence of global financial difficulties. The year 2008 turned out to be an *annus horribilis* for many economies around the world, but few more so than Zambia's, and the reasons for this were almost entirely external. The global price for copper decreased by two-thirds in four months, resulting in a heavy reduction in Zambia's terms of trade. Severe declines occurred in Zambia's government revenue, export revenue, balance of payments and currency exchange rate, while inflation rose to 16.6%. Production declined, mines closed (although one important mine opened), more than 12,000 Zambians lost their jobs and investment projects were postponed. These difficulties were further compounded by a poor domestic maize harvest in 2008. Nevertheless, despite the external pressures of the global economic recession of 2008 and 2009, Zambia's economic growth remained strong. According to the IMF, gross domestic product (GDP) grew by 6% in 2008, by 6.4% in 2009 and by 7.6% in 2010. An important factor in this growth rate was that after 2008's disappointing maize crop, 2009 and 2010 saw successive bumper harvests. Increased supply of maize in the country's markets brought prices down and reduced inflation to 9.9% in December 2009 and to 7.7% in September 2010. These reductions resulted mainly from a decrease in food inflation from 8% in December 2009 to 2.8% in September 2010.

Whereas in 1998 73% of all Zambians lived below the poverty line, this figure had been reduced to 59% by 2010. However, even in that year, 80% of rural Zambians still lived in poverty, and the 37% of the population who lived in extreme poverty were mostly located in rural areas. With a GDP per caput of US $1,512 in 2010 according to the IMF, Zambia was ranked above 27 other countries in the world. However, by other benchmarks it fared much worse, with, for example, a life expectancy in 2010 of 42.4 years, the third lowest in the world, according to the UN. Relations between the IMF and the Government remained cordial and in June 2008 the IMF approved a new three-year Poverty Reduction and Growth Facility (PRGF) initially worth $79.2m. The IMF later augmented this PRGF facility (renamed the Extended Credit Facility), increasing it in May 2009 to $329.7m. Actual disbursements under the facility were $10.5m. in June 2008, $160.1m. in May 2009, $81.2m. in December 2009, $27.1m. in June 2010 and $29.3m. in June 2011. Although the 21st century has so far been a period of sustained positive economic growth for Zambia, a higher level of growth—of 7% or more—was required if poverty and joblessness were to be reduced.

Economic growth in Zambia in 2011 was 6.6%, representing a deceleration from 7.6% in 2010, largely because of a poorer performance by the critical mining industry. However, economic performance in the medium term is promising, mainly owing to the expected gains from continued enlargements of the country's main sectors, such as agriculture, construction, manufacturing, transportation and communications, and also to a recovery in the mining sector. Infrastructure developments will also underpin this growth, particularly in the agricultural sector, where improvements are expected that will enable better delivery of products to market. Improved infrastructure is also expected to help the mining sector, with increases in power generation, transmission and distribution (hitherto weak areas that have hampered development in the sector). The Government intends to issue bonds to raise US $700m. to finance these infrastructure investments.

The African Economic Outlook (AEO) projects economic growth of 6.9% for Zambia in 2012, and an increase to a rate of 7.3% in 2013. As the country depends heavily on mining exports, however, the realization of these optimistic forecasts is conditional on continued high demand from its usual export destinations, which is in turn dependent on those countries' economic revivals.

AGRICULTURE

Agriculture accounted for 26% of GDP in 2010 and employed 85% of the economically active population in that year; however, in 2011 the sector's contribution contracted to 21% of GDP. Despite this slowdown, agriculture remains an important sector of the economy. Zambia's topography, with its varied elevation, enables a variety of crops to be grown, although only about 7% of the surface area is under cultivation, while some 40% serves as permanent pasture and 43% is under forest. The Government estimates that, of the country's 60m. ha of arable land, only about 15% is currently being exploited. Maize is the staple food crop of Zambia, consumed in the form of nshima, a porridge-like dish. The national annual requirement for maize was 1.26m. metric tons in 2009. Maize production varies with weather conditions. A poor growing season in 2007/08 coincided with the global economic downturn. However, the 2008/09 season produced a bumper crop of 1.89m. tons, a 31% increase from 2007/08. This was particularly welcome news, as the agriculture sector had experienced negative growth over the previous four years, especially in 2007/08, when the sector contracted by 4%. Zambian farmers harvested a record maize crop of 2.8m. tons in 2010. There has been a drive to diversify the agricultural sector, which has yielded gains in the growth in output of crops other than maize.

Besides maize, Zambia also produces cassava, wheat, millet, vegetables, sugar cane, groundnuts, sweet potatoes, melons, fruits, cotton, sorghum, barley, pulses, soya beans, tobacco, sunflower seeds and paddy rice. Zambia has several hundred large commercial farms, situated mostly near the railway lines, which account for about 45% of the country's agricultural output. In maize, the proportion is smaller; large-scale farms produced only about 12% of the maize crop in 2008/09. The number of smallholders is increasing and stood at about 820,000 in 2011. Most subsistence farmers use traditional methods, without adequate inputs or infrastructural support, although some improvement has taken place through such schemes as a Fertilizer Support Programme (FSP), food-security packs, outgrower programmes and improved access to agricultural credit. Nevertheless, the 2009/10 budget speech lamented that the FSP had 'weaknesses' and that access to credit was still 'limited'. Other constraints itemized were inadequate infrastructure, limited access to inputs and extension services, the high cost of inputs, poor livestock management and a failure to attract adequate private investment into the sector.

Wheat is grown almost exclusively on large commercial farms, usually under irrigation. The country's flour mills require some 140,000 metric tons per year to keep the nation supplied with bread; even in very productive seasons, wheat has to be imported.

The harvest of sugar cane amounted to an average of about 2.5m. metric tons per annum in 2004–08. An expansion brought 2,085 ha of land into irrigated cane production in 2009 and increased the capacity of the sugar factory at Nakambala by 10%. The coffee sector produces Arabica. Output of coffee has been declining: 2004 saw production of 110,000 60-kg bags, but by 2010/11 output had fallen to 21,000 bags. Exports of green coffee declined from 137,333 60-kg bags in 2003/04 (based on a coffee year of June to May) to just 31,463 bags in 2010/11, according to International Coffee Organization figures.

The horticultural sector has experienced strong growth, with the export of fruits, vegetables and flowers to Europe. The sector's interests are overseen by the Zambia Export Growers' Association, which, among other things, lobbies for affordable airfreight charges. Zambia has more than 30 flower farms, covering 135 ha, growing more than 50 varieties of roses and some 20 kinds of summer flowers for export. The chief client is the flower markets of the Netherlands.

About 70% of livestock is owned by traditional farmers. The national cattle herd numbered about 3.0m. head in 2010. A small amount of beef is generally exported. Foot-and-mouth disease constitutes a problem in some areas of the country. The Central Veterinary Research Institute in Chilanga produces livestock vaccines for the local market and for export. Zambeef Products PLC, the largest meat company in Zambia, has an annual turnover of some K200,000m. and employs over 1,400 workers throughout the country. All of its shares are quoted on the Lusaka Stock Exchange (LuSE). Zambeef slaughters 60,000 head of cattle annually, produces 8m. litres of milk, processes 3.5m. chickens, produces over 20m. eggs, tans 60,000 hides for export (earning an annual US $1.2m. in foreign exchange), distributes meat in the Zambian marketplace through 85 outlets and even makes shoes. It also grows maize, wheat, lucerne (alfalfa) and soya beans on 4,200 ha of land, of which 2,700 ha are under irrigation.

Land-locked Zambia has a number of lakes and rivers, particularly Lake Kariba on the southern border with Zimbabwe and those in the Northern Province; these all offer considerable potential for fishing. The total catch was 86,700 metric tons in 2010.

Zambia has 323,000 sq km of forested land, 265,000 sq km of which is open to exploitation. Commercial forestry is important on the Copperbelt, where there are numerous softwood tree plantations, and in the hardwood areas of the south-west, which are rich in African teak. Total roundwood removals amount to more than 10m. cu m per year, but over 9m. cu m is consumed locally in the form of wood fuel.

Even though growth was forecast in the agricultural sector in 2011, it was not expected to equal the average of the previous three years, since late rainfall and poor infrastructure prevented the efficient delivery of products. However, the Government expanded the 2012 budgetary allocation for agriculture by 6.1%, the largest share of which was allocated to the Farmer Input Support Programme, and to buying crops for the country's strategic food reserve. Additionally, irrigation, livestock, fisheries, and aquaculture were also to be developed.

MINING

Zambia's mining and quarrying sector grew by 15.7% during 2009, according to the African Development Bank (AfDB). Currently, Zambia has 6% of the world's copper reserves, is the seventh largest copper producer, with 3.3% of global output, and is the second largest miner of cobalt, with 20% of the world's production. The mining sector contributed 18.8% of GDP in 1990 but just 1.3% in 2009, down from 4.3% in 2008. The sector employed nearly 50,000 people in 2007. Zambia is the largest copper producer in Africa. Copper accounted for about 70% of the country's total export revenue in 2009. The global copper price in 2010 reached a 37-year high, and Zambian copper exports grew to 720,000 metric tons. Copper export receipts were 41% higher in 2010, compared with the previous year. The price of copper in July 2011 was US $9,411 per ton. Exclusive Analysis reported that the country's copper production rose from 260,000 tons in 2002 to about 790,000 tons in 2011, and forecast output of 980,000 tons in 2012. Other minerals exploited include zinc, lead, gold, silver, selenium, marble, emeralds, amethysts, aquamarines, tourmalines and garnets. The AEO projected growth in the mining sector to be 10.6% in 2012 and 10.3% in 2013.

Zambia Consolidated Copper Mines-Investment Holdings (ZCCM-IH) is the government-owned operator of mines, and owns between 10% and 20% of virtually all copper mines. The Government controls some 87% of the company, and 12.4% of the shares are traded on the Lusaka, Euronext and London stock exchanges.

Konkola is potentially the richest of Zambia's copper mines, possessing reserves of 44.3m. metric tons, with a copper content of 3.9%, while reserves at Nchanga have a copper content of 3.8% and those at Mufulira have a content of 3.2%; Nkana is the largest mine, with 95.5m. tons of reserves, but with a copper content of only 2.3%. Konkola Copper Mines PLC (KCM), 51% of which is owned by Vedanta Resources of India and 28.4% by Anglo's Zambia Copper Investments Limited of Bermuda, was already the largest mining company in Zambia when, in 2007, it announced plans to mine even deeper. Vedanta also owns two mines at Nchanga and one at Nampundwe, plus smelters at Nkana and Nchanga. The Konkola Deep Mining Project (KDMP), the largest-ever single mining investment in Zambia, was to cost US $674m. and was to take the mine down to a depth of 1,505 m. The sinking of the main shaft was completed in June 2011, and the mine was expected to enter production by the end of 2011. KDMP was to extend the life of the mine to 2035 and was to increase its throughput from 2m. tons of copper ore to 7.5m. tons per annum. Zambia's Kansanshi, situated near Solwezi, in North-Western Province, is the eighth largest copper mine in the world. The project was expected to last until 2019, and would produce 1.6m. tons of copper, with a by-product of 25,000 oz of gold annually. The total cost of the project was estimated at between $200m. and $300m., and the mine entered production in December 2004, with the creation of 1,300 new jobs. The work-force at Kansanshi as of 31 December 2011 was 1,635, compared with 3,500 at 31 December 2009. Also in North-Western Province, the 1,355-sq km open-pit Lumwana copper mine, 100% owned by Equinox Minerals Limited of Canada and Australia, was expected to produce 172,000 tons of copper metal per year during the first six years of its projected 37-year life. Production began in 2009. In June 2010 Equinox announced plans for a two-phase expansion at Lumwana. Phase 1 would increase throughput from 20m. tons per annum to 24m. tons per annum in 18 months, and Phase 2, pending feasibility study results, would raise throughput from 24m. tons per annum to 35m. tons per annum over a period of 3–4 years at a projected cost of $300m.–$400m. Uranium has also been discovered within Lumwana's copper pitshells.

Zambia Consolidated Copper Mines (B), or 'B Co', comprising the Luanshya and Baluba facilities, shut down in December 2008 when copper prices plunged. In January 2009 the debt-ridden mine returned to the ownership of the Zambian Government. In May the Banda Government sold its 85% stake in the Chambeshi copper mine to China Non-Ferrous Metals (CNFM) for a reported US $50m. In August CNFM announced a $400m. investment that would create 4,000 jobs. The Chibuluma mine assets were sold to a Canadian-South African consortium led by South Africa's Metorex for $17m. The new owners pledged to invest $34m. in the facility, the production capacity of which was described as 480,000 metric tons of ore per year. In 2006 Metorex opened a new mine at Chibuluma South, the first new underground mine to open on the Copperbelt in 30 years. According to Metorex, Chibuluma produced 17,729 tons of copper in 2010.

Private sector investment has been actively in the mining sector. Incentives included a 10% reduction in the corporate tax rate for mining investors and also relief from several other types of tax, such as the withholding tax on dividends, royalties and management fees. The tax on mineral royalties was reduced from 2.0% to 0.6%. The mining corporation tax declined from 35% to 25% for all companies, whereas previously only KCM and Mopani Copper Mines had enjoyed the lower rate. Meanwhile, the global copper price began a sustained rise, owing in large measure to increased demand from the People's Republic of China, which in 2002 had overtaken the USA as the world's largest importer of copper. However, during the 2008–09 global recession copper stocks mounted world-wide; as a result, demand decreased sharply and the global copper price declined by two-thirds. Mining costs that had been comfortably covered by the July 2008 price now exceeded the December price, turning profits into losses and leading some Zambian mines to close in order to stem those losses. Exploration activity dwindled, mining investment projects were shelved and numerous jobs in the sector were lost.

Zambia's first nickel mine began producing ore in 2008, two months ahead of schedule. The Munali nickel-sulphide mine, located some 60 km south of Lusaka, is 100% owned by Albidon Limited of Australia. Munali's first focus is on two ore bodies, Enterprise and Voyager, but drilling in 2008 also explored two nearby areas, Intrepid and Defiant. Zambian output of cobalt rose from 4,414 metric tons in 2007 to 5,700 tons in 2010. Zambia mines gemstones such as emeralds, aquamarines, amethysts and some diamonds. Zambia boasts the world's second largest deposits of emeralds, after Colombia, and Zambian emeralds account for a significant and growing share of the coloured-gem market. Zambian emeralds are valued almost as highly as those from Colombia. Most gemstones are mined on a small scale, but the sector is thought to offer significant potential for growth. Smuggling of gemstones is a major problem.

Marble deposits in Lusaka Province and elsewhere in Zambia range from pure white to pale pink, deep salmon pink and dark green, and some varieties are hard-wearing enough for use in flooring. Zambian granite tends to be dark and suitable for kitchen counters in homes. A rare blue granite has been found near Solwezi. Metorex owns a marble-processing plant in Kabwe. Chilanga Cement, 84.5% of which is owned by Lafarge of France, has plants in Lusaka and Ndola. Petroleum exploration took place after 2000, and in 2006 traces of oil were found in several locations, leading the Government to promulgate a Petroleum Act in 2007 and to offer concessions for exploration. Tenders were invited in June 2009 for 23 blocks; bidding closed in November and concessions were awarded for 11 of the 23 blocks, to eight companies, four of them Zambian, two from the United Kingdom, one from the USA and one from Canada. A second round of bidding was opened in December, and again 23 blocks were offered, comprising the 12 that had not been sold in the first round plus 11 new blocks.

A new 'mining tax regime' came into force on 1 April 2008. Among its main features were an increase in the mineral royalty accruing to the Zambian Government from 0.6% to 3.0%; a rise in the corporate income tax rate from 25% to 30%; and a windfall tax that was to be activated if the global copper price should rise above US $2.50 per lb (in July 2011 the price was $4.28 per lb). Given that the global copper price had been above $3.50 per lb throughout the regime's first four months in power, both the Mwanawasa Government and the IMF were expecting a major revenue boost; however, they were to be sorely disappointed. At its launch, the mining tax regime had been forecast to contribute K917,300m. in the nine months from 1 April to 31 December 2008; however, in the event, the amount collected was just K319,500m. Undoubtedly, significantly lower taxable mining revenue was a contributing factor, but the Banda Government's first budget speech, delivered on 30 January 2009 and covering 2009/10, made no excuses. The reason for the 65% shortfall, Minister of Finance and National Planning Dr Situmbeko Musokotwane admitted, was 'administrative challenges in implementing the regime during the year'. This budget also removed the windfall tax. However, in January 2012 the Government announced that it would seek an increase in copper royalties from 3% to 6%.

The main risk to the mining sector is the paucity of energy supply; growth in mining is expected to be hampered over the next three to five years by production stoppages. Demand for power will exceed supply over the next few years, as more households are connected to the power grid and more mining projects enter into operation. This is despite priority of energy supply already being granted to mining companies.

INDUSTRY

Manufacturing's share of GDP has changed little over the years; it contributed 9.1% of GDP in both 1990 and 2011. Growth in the manufacturing sector was for many years very moderate, rarely achieving a whole percentage point; but in 2007 manufacturing grew by 5.0%, primarily owing to the Government's decision to reduce the duty on imported raw materials. The 2009/10 budget address indicated that the Banda Government intended to continue with this policy. It recognized that 'stimulating growth in the manufacturing sector is a critical element of any diversification drive', that the 'high cost of doing business has been a major impediment' and that Zambia's narrow manufacturing base 'has significantly contributed to its high import bills over the years'. It confirmed that it was to proceed with three 'multi-facility economic zones' at Chambishi, Lusaka East and Lusaka South. Construction at Chambishi began in 2008, with Chinese participation. Development of the 2,100-ha, US $130m. Lusaka South Multi-facility Economic Zone was to take place over five phases, with Phase 1 beginning in 2011; the project was part of the country's Public-Private Partnership scheme.

By 2001 262 companies had been transferred to private sector ownership or had completed the negotiation stage. However, the fact that no further privatizations had been completed by mid-2009 indicated a loss of momentum in the programme. In 2007 the Zambia Development Agency (ZDA) became the country's privatization vehicle. ZDA was tasked with investigating the high cost of doing business in Zambia and with simplifying licensing procedures. In June 2010 a 75% stake in Zambia Telecommunications Co Ltd was privatized. The new owner was Lap Green Networks of Libya.

Nitrogen Chemicals of Zambia Ltd, which had ceased operations in 2008, was relaunched on 1 June 2010, having received a contract from the Banda Government to supply 20,000 metric tons of fertilizers by 31 July.

According to the AEO, the construction sector was forecast to grow by about 17% over 2012–13, which was to be made possible by the anticipated recovery in the mining and quarrying sector, as well as by the growth in public infrastructure spending in the coming years. This was promising news, given the reliance of Zambia's economy on the construction industry, which contributed 21.1% of GDP in 2011.

ENERGY

More than 99% of Zambia's electricity is generated by hydroelectric installations. Electricity shortages affected Zambia repeatedly during 2007–11. The Zambia Electricity Supply Corpn (ZESCO) oversees the country's power generation and distribution. Zambia had 1,670 MW of electric-power capacity in 2007, the year in which national demand rose to meet national supply. Only about 1,200 MW of its installed capacity was available in 2007, compared with demand of 1,450 MW. Load-shedding led to frequent power cuts at peak demand times during 2007–11, while exports continued at off-peak times. According to ZESCO, rehabilitation work in 2007 and 2008 added a further 210 MW to the national grid. Major hydroelectric facilities are at Kafue Gorge, Kariba North and Victoria Falls. ZESCO has long-term plans to add 120 MW at Itezhi-Tezhi, 360 MW through an extension at Kariba North and 750 MW at Kafue Gorge Lower. In June 2010 Zambia had to import 50 MW of power from the Democratic Republic of the Congo (DRC).

Rural electrification is a stated priority, and some extension of the national grid has been achieved, but many areas of rural Zambia still do not have access to mains power supply. ZESCO's customer base was 310,000 in 2007, in a country with a population of well over 11m.; therefore, at that time only 2.8% of Zambians were connected to the national grid. Charcoal and fuel wood remain the main sources of energy supply for cooking and heating purposes for most people in both urban and rural areas.

Zambia's sole remaining colliery, at Maamba, has coal reserves of 78m. metric tons and a life span of more than 70 years.

Power consumption in Zambia is dominated by mining companies, the Government prioritizing their operations above all other industries, and even household consumption, resulting in frequent blackouts. The operation of new power plants will continue, which is expected to increase domestic power production, but some interim measures involve the import of electricity from other southern African countries. For example, in 2009 Zambia imported between 150 MW and 200 MW of electricity from the DRC and Mozambique. Furthermore, in January 2012 ZESCO, presumably in a bid to improve its revenues, announced an increase in electricity prices of between 17% and 33%.

TRANSPORT

Zambia's 15-year Road Sector Investment Programme (ROADSIP), covering the period 1998–2013, entered its second phase (ROADSIP II) in 2004. The objective was to bring 40,113 km into maintainable condition by 2013.Boosted by Danish development assistance, ROADSIP II, which was to cost an estimated US $1,600m., was to focus on improving the high-priority main road between Mongu and Sesheke. This road was to become a key segment in an international corridor linking the DRC to the Namibian port of Walvis Bay. The Tanzania–Zambia Railway Authority (Tazara) railway line leading to Tanzania's Indian Ocean port of Dar es Salaam was built and financed by China with an interest-free loan during the early 1970s. In 2005 the Governments of Tanzania and Zambia agreed to privatize Tazara, with preference given to a Chinese concern that would be chosen by the Chinese Government, but as of mid-2010 the Tazara management had been replaced, staff salaries reportedly had gone unpaid for at least three months, most of the locomotives were inoperative and no further progress towards privatization had been announced. In January 2010 the Chinese Government extended a $39m. loan to Tazara to enable the purchase of six new locomotives and four new wagons and to fund the repair of 120 wagons; however, the Tazara management estimated that it would need $770m. to become commercially viable.

Railways Systems of Zambia is operated by a consortium known as NLPI Limited, comprising mainly South African business interests, under a 20-year concession in exchange for an annual payment to the Zambian Government amounting to US $253m. plus 5% of annual turnover. Zambia's only port, Mpulungu, is on Lake Tanganyika. In 2000 the Government of Frederick Chiluba concessioned Mpulungu harbour, port operations and assets to Mpulungu Harbour Management Ltd for 25 years.

The BotZam Highway links Kazungula with Nata, in Botswana. A new German-financed €8.2m. road bridge across the Zambezi river at Katima Mulilo opened in 2004, facilitating cross-border passage. The 2008/09 budget allocated K1,110,700m. to road construction, rehabilitation and maintenance.

In July 2011 Proflight Zambia was operating domestic flights to 11 destinations. In addition, Zambezi Airlines operates regional services from Lusaka, Livingstone and Ndola to Cape Town and Johannesburg in South Africa, Harare in Zimbabwe, Lubumbashi in the DRC, and Dar es Salaam in Tanzania. The National Airports Corpn Ltd (NACL) operates Lusaka International Airport, in addition to the Ndola, Livingstone and Mfuwe airports. The 2008/09 budget allocated K40,000m. to upgrade the Solwezi and Kasama airports.

TOURISM

The Mwanawasa Government identified tourism as a growth sector. The number of tourist arrivals increased from 668,862 in 2005 to 897,413 in 2007, and tourism receipts rose from

US $98m. in 2005 to $138m. in 2007. The tourism sector, which had been badly affected by the global economic crisis in 2008 (arrivals fell to 811,775 in that year) and 2009, recovered strongly in 2010. Arrivals grew by 25% in that year, after contracting by 13.4% in 2009. Zimbabwe and Zambia boast one of the great tourist attractions of the world in Victoria Falls, on the Zambezi river on their shared border. Until the recent crisis in Zimbabwe, that country attracted a far larger share of the tourists visiting the Falls and had the more highly developed tourism infrastructure. On the Zambian side of the river, the town of Livingstone is the focus of renewed tourism development. Tourist interest in Zambia has expanded beyond Victoria Falls, to the country's game parks. The Tourism Development Credit Facility, launched in 2004, facilitated private sector interest in rapidly building tourism infrastructure such as lodges, guesthouses and camping sites, so that Zambia could capitalize on the boom opportunities. Tourism development in 2011 was focused on the 'Northern Tourism Circuit'. In 2012 the Government also allocated K15,000m. to recapitalize the Zambia Wildlife Authority (ZAWA), in order to improve wildlife resources for tourism.

FOREIGN TRADE AND PAYMENTS

Zambia's policies designed to improve international trade have been promising. The country has implemented a One Stop Border Post with Zimbabwe and one with the DRC, and a Simplified Trade Regime with Malawi. Boosted by copper exports, Zambia's trade balance is usually in surplus. The value of total merchandise exports on a free-on-board (f.o.b.) basis increased by 59% from US $4,319m. in 2009 to an estimated $6,850m. in 2010, mainly due to copper exports, which rose by 71.6% over the same period from $3,179m. to $5,455m. Imports f.o.b. also rose, by 38.7%, from $3,413m. in 2009 to an estimated $4,733m. in 2010. Oil imports accounted for the largest share of the total but not for the largest share of the increase; oil import costs rose by 17.9% from $536m. in 2009 to an estimated $632m. in 2010. The resulting visible trade surplus improved significantly, from $906m. in 2009 to an estimated $2,117m. in 2010.

The current account of the balance of payments recorded a surplus, of US $404m., in 2009. The surplus widened to $614.7m. in 2010 and to $951m. in 2011, equivalent to 5.4% of GDP. This growth was made possible largely because of a rise in mining exports from $5,800m. to $7,000m. Despite an expected increase in metal prices, the surplus on the current account of the balance of payments was forecast by the AEO to fall to 3.6% of GDP in 2012, owing to the lower demand for mining exports arising from the continuing global recession.

GOVERNMENT FINANCE

The 2011 budget, presented to the National Assembly in October 2010 by Musokotwane, appealed for total expenditure of K20,537,400m., while total revenue was forecast at K17,356,800m., leaving a deficit of K3,180,600m. This shortfall was to be financed by borrowing, 62% of it from external sources and the remaining 38% from the domestic market. The 2011 fiscal deficit was 2.6% of GDP, falling below the country's upper limit of 3%. Public spending was reduced from 21.5% of GDP in 2010 to 19.3% of GDP in 2011. Much of the spending in 2011 was on higher-than-expected purchases of maize, and on the organization of elections. Recurrent expenditure fell slightly, from 15.8% of GDP in 2010 to 15.4% in 2011, while the Government's increased infrastructure spending in 2011 pushed capital expenditure slightly higher, from 2.8% of GDP in 2010 to 3.0% of GDP in 2011. According to IMF figures, the budget deficit was projected to increase to K7,983,000m. (expenditure K27,803,000m., revenue K19,820,000m.) in 2012. Increasing tax revenue will be important for maintaining fiscal discipline. Zambia must not only expand the tax base, but also increase taxes from mining companies and use the revenue efficiently, ideally in a manner that promotes further growth, such as on capital investments and social programmes, and must tightly control recurrent expenditures. In 2006, owing to debt relief from the IMF, the World Bank and the African Development Bank, Zambia was able to shed its status as a heavily indebted poor country (HIPC). The IMF, through its Multilateral Debt Relief Initiative (MDRI), in January 2006 announced that Zambia was eligible for 100% debt relief on all debt incurred to the IMF prior to 1 January 2005 that was still outstanding. This MDRI was to have reduced Zambia's total external debt from US $4,500m. at the beginning of 2006 to $635m. However, this figure of $635m. was later revised upward, to $1,019m., to reflect what the 2008/09 budget statement described as 'undelivered HIPC initiative debt relief from some of the bilateral creditors with whom we have not yet reached agreement'. By 31 December 2009 government total external debt stock had risen to $1,587m., equivalent to 12.4% of GDP. With the 2011 budget appealing for domestic borrowing of K1,219,800m. and for some foreign borrowing on non-concessional terms, Zambia's indebtedness was again mounting up. The national currency, the kwacha, weakened against the US dollar by 11.4% in 2010/11, from K2,217.30 = US $1 in July 2010 to K2,510.28 = $1 in July 2011. Overall, the kwacha's depreciation was 5.3% in 2011.

The Government's monetary policy in 2011 successfully targeted low, single-digit inflation—this rose slightly, from 8.5% in 2010 to 8.7% in 2011—and the AEO predicted inflation to reach 8.0% and 8.5%, respectively, in 2012 and 2013. The central bank also ensured in 2011 that easy access to financing for private sector expansion was readily available. Furthermore, in the first half of 2012 the Government made progress towards its scheduled issue later that year of US $500m. of Eurobonds, which attracted significant interest in view of the country's promising economic outlook and strong macroeconomics. These funds were to be used to invest in the country's infrastructure.

FUTURE PROSPECTS

Decades after copper became Zambia's main source of foreign exchange, the economy is still heavily dependent on the commodity. Some significant success has been achieved in encouraging alternative exports, mostly of agricultural commodities, and strenuous efforts are being made to persuade Zambian farmers to cultivate high-value crops such as paprika, cauliflower, artichokes and roses. Trade figures indicate that these non-traditional exports have increased their share of export earnings; however, these activities are still young and fragile, and they face formidable competition in their distant intended markets. The world copper price, long known for its volatility, reached a 37-year high in 2010, easing pressure on Zambia's current account. Every succeeding President has recognized that overdependence on copper renders the Zambian economy vulnerable. Every one of those Presidents has accordingly introduced measures to diversify the economy, but in 2011 the country was still overdependent on copper, and any success in diversification has been much smaller than is needed. Such diversification has proved possible elsewhere in Africa; Uganda reduced its dependence on coffee exports from 97% in the mid-1980s to just 13.5% in 2002. The Banda Government, in its first two budget addresses, promised measures aimed at achieving this long-sought diversification. The Sixth National Development Plan (2011–2015) set the goal of transforming Zambia into a 'prosperous middle-income nation by 2030'. The Plan's launch coincided not only with record global copper prices and improved export volumes, but also with the largest maize harvest in Zambia's history and a boom period in the country's tourism sector. It will be a major challenge to lift 59% of the population out of poverty and 37% out of extreme poverty, but the timing of the Plan's commencement could not have been more auspicious. The Government also began implementing private sector improvement reforms in 2004, as part of its Zambia Private Sector Development Reform Programme (PSDRP), which aimed to create a more conducive business environment, both on the domestic front and for the promotion of exports.

Manufacturing is important to Zambia's long-term diversification; although the sector's contribution to GDP fell from 11.2% in 2006 to 9.1% in 2011, manufacturing output grew by 5% in the latter year, mainly owing to private sector reforms, efficient economic policies and greater investment in the sector, especially in agro-processing.

A major impediment to private sector growth is access to finance, especially for small businesses. However, in November 2011 Zambia's central bank reduced banks' statutory reserve ratio requirement from 8% to 5% in order to liberate the funds of commercial banks' for lending to private enterprises. The Government also lowered the corporate tax rate from 40% to 35%.

Zambia's recent economic and private sector reforms have won approval from international financial and credit institutions. In June 2011 the IMF began discussions with Zambia regarding the introduction of a new Extended Credit Facility following the expiry of the previous arrangement. Also in mid-2011, the World Bank reclassified Zambia as a lower middle-income nation, and both the Standard & Poor's and Fitch credit-rating agencies awarded the country a B+ credit rating.

Statistical Survey

Source (unless otherwise indicated): Central Statistical Office, POB 31908, Lusaka; tel. (21) 1211231; internet www.zamstats.gov.zm.

Area and Population

AREA, POPULATION AND DENSITY

Area (sq km)	752,612*
Population (census results)	
25 October 2000	9,885,591
15 October 2010	
Males	6,454,647
Females	6,638,019
Total	13,092,666
Population (UN estimates at mid-year)†	
2011	13,474,960
2012	13,883,575
Density (per sq km) at mid-2012	18.4

* 290,585 sq miles.

† Source: UN, *World Population Prospects: The 2010 Revision*; estimates not adjusted to take account of 2010 census.

POPULATION BY AGE AND SEX

(UN estimates at mid-2012)

	Males	Females	Total
0–14	3,254,648	3,220,573	6,475,221
15–64	3,517,929	3,467,288	6,985,217
65 and over	188,860	234,277	423,137
Total	6,961,437	6,922,138	13,883,575

Source: UN, *World Population Prospects: The 2010 Revision*.

PROVINCES

(2010 census)

	Area	Population	Density
Central	94,394	1,307,111	13.8
Copperbelt	31,328	1,972,317	63.0
Eastern	69,106	1,592,661	23.0
Luapula	50,567	991,927	19.6
Lusaka	21,896	2,191,225	100.1
Northern*	147,826	1,817,481	12.3
North-Western	125,826	727,044	5.8
Southern	85,283	1,589,926	18.6
Western	126,386	902,974	7.1
Total	752,612	13,092,666	17.4

* Including 711,657 persons enumerated in districts which were separated into the new province of Muchinga in 2011.

PRINCIPAL TOWNS

(population at 2000 census)

Lusaka (capital)	1,084,703	Lundazi	236,833
Kitwe	376,124	Petauke	235,879
Ndola	374,757	Choma	204,898
Chipata	367,539	Solwezi	203,797
Chibombo	241,612	Mazabuka	203,219

Mid-2011 (incl. suburbs, UN estimate): Lusaka 1,802,470 (Source: UN, *World Urbanization Prospects: The 2011 Revision*).

BIRTHS AND DEATHS

(annual averages, UN estimates)

	1995–2000	2000–05	2005–10
Birth rate (per 1,000)	44.6	44.4	44.5
Death rate (per 1,000)	19.6	19.6	16.7

Source: UN, *World Population Prospects: The 2010 Revision*.

Life expectancy (years at birth): 48.5 (males 48.0; females 48.9) in 2010 (Source: World Bank, World Development Indicators database).

EMPLOYMENT

(Usually active population aged 12 years and over at 2000 census)

Agriculture, hunting, forestry and fishing	2,014,028
Mining and quarrying	36,463
Manufacturing	77,515
Electricity, gas and water	11,016
Construction	36,790
Wholesale and retail trade; restaurants and hotels	190,354
Transport, storage and communications	53,736
Financial, insurance, real estate and business services	29,151
Community, social and personal services	363,375
Total	2,812,428

Source: ILO.

2006 (persons in paid employment, labour force survey, January): Agriculture, forestry and fishing 56,139; Mining and quarrying 26,253; Manufacturing 55,709; Electricity and water 12,399; Construction 14,343; Wholesale and retail trade 65,012; Transport and communications 19,378; Finance and insurance 54,032; Public administration 176,062; *Total* 479,327 (Source: IMF, *Zambia: Statistical Appendix*, January 2008).

Mid-2012 ('000, estimates): Agriculture, etc. 3,388; Total labour force 5,466 (Source: FAO).

Health and Welfare

KEY INDICATORS

Total fertility rate (children per woman, 2010)	6.3
Under-5 mortality rate (per 1,000 live births, 2010)	111
HIV/AIDS (% of persons aged 15–49, 2009)	13.5
Physicians (per 1,000 head, 2006)	0.1
Hospital beds (per 1,000 head, 2010)	2.0
Health expenditure (2009): US $ per head (PPP)	90
Health expenditure (2009): % of GDP	6.2
Health expenditure (2009): public (% of total)	58.6
Access to water (% of persons, 2010)	61
Access to sanitation (% of persons, 2010)	48
Total carbon dioxide emissions ('000 metric tons, 2008)	1,888.5
Carbon dioxide emissions per head (metric tons, 2008)	0.2
Human Development Index (2011): ranking	164
Human Development Index (2011): value	0.430

For sources and definitions, see explanatory note on p. vi.

Agriculture

PRINCIPAL CROPS
('000 metric tons)

	2008	2009	2010
Wheat	113.2	195.5	172.3
Rice, paddy	24.0	41.9	51.7
Maize	1,211.6	1,887.0	2,795.5
Millet	33.9	49.0	48.0
Sorghum	10.0	21.8	27.7
Potatoes	10.2	21.3	22.9
Sweet potatoes	106.5	200.5	252.9
Cassava (Manioc)	1,185.6	1,160.9	1,151.7
Sugar cane*	2,050	3,200	4,050
Soybeans (Soya beans)†	13	13	12
Groundnuts, with shell	71	121	164
Sunflower seed	12.7	33.7	26.4
Seed cotton*	168	159	107
Onions, dry*	28.3	28.5	29
Tomatoes*	21.0	25.0	26.0
Tobacco, unmanufactured*	64.1	75.3	89.7

* FAO estimates.
† Unofficial figures.

Aggregate production ('000 metric tons, may include official, semi-official or estimated data): Total cereals 1,394 in 2008, 2,197 in 2009, 3,098 in 2010; Total pulses 24 in 2008, 26 in 2009, 27 in 2010; Total roots and tubers 1,302 in 2008, 1,383 in 2009, 1,428 in 2010; Total vegetables (incl. melons) 370 in 2008, 434 in 2009, 333 in 2010; Total fruits (excl. melons) 111 in 2008–09, 112 in 2010.

Source: FAO.

LIVESTOCK
('000 head, year ending September, FAO estimates)

	2008	2009	2010
Cattle	2,900	2,950	3,000
Sheep	200	210	220
Goats	2,000	2,100	2,200
Pigs	430	450	500
Chickens	31,500	33,000	35,000

Source: FAO.

LIVESTOCK PRODUCTS
('000 metric tons, FAO estimates)

	2008	2009	2010
Cattle meat	59.0	60.0	60.8
Pig meat	14.2	14.7	16.5
Chicken meat	38.5	40.0	42.5
Cows' milk	85.5	87.0	88.5
Hen eggs	42.8	45.0	49.5
Cattle hides	7.7	7.9	8.0

Source: FAO.

Forestry

ROUNDWOOD REMOVALS
('000 cubic metres, FAO estimates)

	2008	2009	2010
Sawlogs, veneer logs and logs for sleepers	245	245	245
Other industrial wood	1,080	1,080	1,080
Fuel wood	8,840	8,978	9,119
Total	10,165	10,303	10,444

2011: Production assumed to be unchanged from 2010 (FAO estimates).

Source: FAO.

SAWNWOOD PRODUCTION
('000 cubic metres, incl. railway sleepers, FAO estimates)

	1995	1996	1997
Coniferous (softwood)	300	230	145
Broadleaved (hardwood)	20	15	12
Total	320	245	157

1998–2011: Figures assumed to be unchanged from 1997 (FAO estimates).

Source: FAO.

Fishing

('000 metric tons, live weight)

	2008	2009	2010
Capture	79.4	84.7	76.4
Dagaas	7.9	10.0	7.8
Other freshwater fishes	71.5	74.7	68.6
Aquaculture	5.6	8.5	10.3
Three-spotted tilapia	2.0	3.1	3.7
Total catch	85.0	93.2	86.7

Note: Figures exclude crocodiles, recorded by number rather than weight. The number of Nile crocodiles caught was: 28,197 in 2008; 43,655 in 2009; 23,717 in 2010.

Source: FAO.

Mining

(estimates)

	2008	2009	2010
Coal ('000 metric tons)	220	200	200
Copper ore ('000 metric tons)*	555	694	820
Cobalt ore (metric tons)*	7,000	4,900	5,700
Amethysts ('000 kilograms)	900	1,400	1,300

* Figures refer to the metal content of ore.

Source: US Geological Survey.

Industry

SELECTED PRODUCTS
('000 metric tons unless otherwise indicated)

	2008	2009	2010
Cement	560	880	1,127
Copper (unwrought): smelter	232	330	490
Copper (unwrought): refined	442	435	530
Cobalt (refined, metric tons)	4,049	1,271	1,092
Raw sugar	207	n.a.	n.a.
Electric energy (million kWh)	9,696	10,308	n.a.

Sources: US Geological Survey; UN Industrial Commodity Statistics Database.

Finance

CURRENCY AND EXCHANGE RATES

Monetary Units
100 ngwee = 1 Zambian kwacha (K).

Sterling, Dollar and Euro Equivalents (31 May 2012)
£1 sterling = 8,285.88 kwacha;
US $1 = 5,344.35 kwacha;
€1 = 6,628.60 kwacha;
10,000 Zambian kwacha = £1.21 = $1.87 = €1.51.

Average Exchange Rate (Zambian kwacha per US $)
2009 5,046.11
2010 4,797.14
2011 4,860.67

Note: On 23 January 2012 it was announced that the kwacha was to be rebased, with existing currency denominations divided by 1,000, with immediate effect

CENTRAL GOVERNMENT BUDGET
(K '000 million)

Revenue	2010	2011*	2012*
Tax revenue	12,700	18,018	17,481
Income tax	6,914	10,655	8,665
Excise taxes	1,377	1,665	1,953
Value-added tax (VAT)	3,160	3,973	4,725
Customs duty	1,250	1,725	2,139
Non-tax revenue	1,109	1,501	2,727
Total†	13,809	19,519	20,208

Expenditure	2010	2011*	2012*
Expense	15,073	18,680	19,382
Compensation of employees	6,325	7,402	9,600
Goods and services	3,272	4,754	3,768
Interest payments	1,370	1,082	1,664
Subsidies	1,897	2,837	1,393
Intergovernmental transfers	1,098	1,433	1,806
Social benefits	194	977	1,047
Other	917	195	104
Net acquisition of non-financial assets	2,512	5,085	7,811
Fiscal Measures	—	—	−843
Total	17,584	23,765	26,350

* Projections.

† Excluding grants received (K '000 million): 1,389 in 2010; 1,450 in 2011 (projection); 1,840 in 2012 (projection).

Source: IMF, *Zambia: Staff Report for the 2012 Article IV Consultation* (July 2012).

INTERNATIONAL RESERVES
(excl. gold, US $ million at 31 December)

	2009	2010	2011
IMF special drawing rights	637.6	625.2	617.8
Foreign exchange	1,254.4	1,468.5	1,706.2
Total	1,892.1	2,093.7	2,324.0

Source: IMF, *International Financial Statistics*.

MONEY SUPPLY
(K '000 million at 31 December)

	2009	2010	2011
Currency outside depository corporations	1,579.6	2,229.5	2,790.3
Transferable deposits	7,517.1	10,039.9	11,535.6
Other deposits	4,700.2	5,647.1	7,478.8
Broad money	13,796.9	17,916.5	21,804.8

Source: IMF, *International Financial Statistics*.

COST OF LIVING
(Consumer Price Index; low-income group; base: 2000 = 100)

	2001	2002	2003
Food (incl. alcohol and tobacco)	118.9	151.1	184.5
Clothing and footwear	120.5	139.4	168.8
Fuel and rent	121.4	145.1	176.5
All items (incl. others)	121.4	148.4	180.1

Food (incl. alcohol and tobacco): 365.5 in 2009; 384.3 in 2010; 403.2 in 2011.

All items: 386.8 in 2009; 419.6 in 2010; 456.0 in 2011.

Source: ILO.

NATIONAL ACCOUNTS
(K '000 million at current prices)

Expenditure on the Gross Domestic Product

	2009	2010*	2011*
Government final consumption expenditure	11,651	12,738	15,410
Private final consumption expenditure	37,532	37,982	45,953
Changes in inventories	946	1,165	1,410
Gross fixed capital formation	12,646	16,553	20,027
Total domestic expenditure	62,775	68,438	82,800
Exports of goods and services	22,624	36,329	43,953
Less Imports of goods and services	20,783	27,101	32,788
GDP in purchasers' values	64,616	77,667	93,964

Gross Domestic Product by Economic Activity

	2009	2010*	2011*
Agriculture, hunting, forestry and fishing	13,461	15,642	18,229
Mining and quarrying	1,682	2,838	3,289
Manufacturing	6,017	6,771	7,611
Electricity, gas and water	1,780	2,202	2,913
Construction	11,819	15,704	20,484
Wholesale and retail trade, restaurants and hotels	11,453	13,043	14,940
Transport and communications	2,355	3,076	3,571
Finance and insurance, real estate and business services	9,206	11,051	12,873
Public administration and defence	1,647	1,733	2,639
Other services	5,002	6,416	7,697
Sub-total	64,423	78,475	94,246
Less Imputed bank service charge	2,922	3,876	4,416
Indirect taxes, less subsidies	3,114	3,068	4,134
GDP in purchasers' values	64,616	77,667	93,964

* Provisional.

Source: African Development Bank.

BALANCE OF PAYMENTS
(US $ million)

	2009	2010	2011
Exports of goods f.o.b.	4,319.1	7,413.6	8,671.8
Imports of goods f.o.b.	−3,413.4	−4,709.9	−6,454.2
Trade balance	905.7	2,703.7	2,217.6
Export of services	240.9	310.9	375.2
Import of services	−705.4	−939.7	−1,193.0
Balance on goods and services	441.2	2,074.9	1,399.7
Other income received	4.5	8.4	11.1
Other income paid	−424.2	−1,371.4	−1,573.5
Balance on goods, services and income	21.5	711.9	−162.7
Current transfers received	255.5	242.4	273.3
Current transfers paid	−37.0	−39.2	−41.5

—continued	2009	2010	2011
Current account	239.9	915.1	69.1
Capital account (net)	237.3	149.7	119.0
Direct investment abroad	−269.6	−1,095.4	−1,150.2
Direct investment from abroad	694.8	1,729.3	1,981.7
Portfolio investment liabilities	−74.9	73.6	47.7
Financial derivatives (net)	219.6	225.7	124.1
Other investment assets	−1,578.0	−3,288.4	−1,654.6
Other investment liabilities	834.3	1,210.3	563.0
Net errors and omissions	−64.4	−66.6	−5.6
Overall balance	239.1	−146.7	94.3

Source: IMF, *International Financial Statistics*.

External Trade

PRINCIPAL COMMODITIES
(US $ million)

Imports c.i.f.	2008	2009	2010
Food and live animals	150.2	145.7	149.0
Crude materials except fuels	592.2	398.5	898.9
Mineral fuels and lubricants	810.7	528.6	616.9
Petroleum and petroleum products	788.4	514.9	597.6
Petroleum oils and oils obtained from bituminous minerals, crude	481.9	430.8	508.8
Chemicals and related products	757.5	709.0	927.0
Medicinal and pharmaceutical products	162.5	157.4	116.3
Basic manufactures	742.2	617.2	869.6
Iron and steel	196.0	148.2	188.8
Machinery and transport equipment	1,644.5	1,085.8	1,528.6
Machinery specialized for particular industries	485.0	318.2	531.9
General industrial machinery, equipment and machine parts	244.5	170.6	225.9
Electrical machinery, apparatus, appliances and electrical parts	196.2	128.8	186.4
Road vehicles	476.4	272.7	361.2
Miscellaneous manufactured articles	214.8	195.9	208.2
Total (incl. others)	5,060.5	3,792.6	5,320.8

Exports f.o.b.	2008	2009	2010
Food and live animals	201.2	220.8	278.3
Beverages and tobacco	79.8	94.1	129.6
Crude materials except fuels	839.7	584.3	620.3
Metalliferous ore and metal scrap	779.2	511.6	526.4
Chemicals and related products	72.3	87.3	138.2
Basic manufactures	3,678.6	3,071.9	5,761.3
Non-ferrous metals	3,275.8	2,890.7	5,416.6
Copper	3,270.9	2,889.0	5,412.8
Machinery and transport equipment	142.6	138.8	136.9
Total (incl. others)	5,098.7	4,312.1	7,200.3

Source: UN, *International Trade Statistics Yearbook*.

PRINCIPAL TRADING PARTNERS
(US $ million)

Imports c.i.f.	2008	2009	2010
China, People's Repub.	227.2	178.0	289.7
Congo, Democratic Repub.	534.7	486.7	1,268.7
Finland	50.6	14.8	36.8
France (incl. Monaco)	40.8	15.5	26.0
Germany	66.7	59.1	54.0
India	191.6	130.9	144.4
Japan	86.7	66.4	84.8
Kenya	80.4	78.0	64.6
Kuwait	513.7	401.0	508.7
Mozambique	53.0	33.9	16.9
Netherlands	34.8	31.0	30.9
South Africa	2,154.0	1,516.0	1,829.5
Sweden	61.6	34.2	48.5
Tanzania	47.6	33.7	40.9
United Arab Emirates	123.5	109.7	116.7
United Kingdom	157.2	136.0	105.9
USA	72.2	50.7	72.5
Zimbabwe	107.1	56.9	72.0
Total (incl. others)	5,060.5	3,792.6	5,320.8

Exports f.o.b.	2008	2009	2010
Belgium	54.8	55.9	72.4
China, People's Repub.	286.9	482.6	1,455.4
Congo, Democratic Repub.	287.1	300.9	333.5
Egypt	384.8	106.5	49.2
France (incl. Monaco)	1.8	2.0	4.8
India	32.6	49.4	19.0
Japan	41.6	2.2	6.9
Korea, Repub.	68.9	77.0	25.4
Malawi	63.0	73.2	102.7
Malaysia	10.8	0.0	0.0
Netherlands	126.6	42.4	44.8
Pakistan	28.9	30.9	2.6
Saudi Arabia	90.5	118.1	23.9
South Africa	528.4	394.7	657.8
Switzerland-Liechtenstein	2,537.3	2,027.2	3,673.5
Tanzania	31.9	34.5	31.8
Thailand	99.8	23.7	5.2
United Arab Emirates	23.7	141.0	176.2
United Kingdom	115.1	87.2	134.8
Zimbabwe	64.1	84.3	120.6
Total (incl. others)	5,098.7	4,312.1	7,200.3

Source: UN, *International Trade Statistics Yearbook*.

Transport

ROAD TRAFFIC
(estimates, '000 motor vehicles in use at 31 December)

	1994	1995	1996
Passenger cars	123	142	157
Lorries and vans	68	74	81

2007: Passenger cars 131; Buses 4; Lorries and vans 76; Motorcycles 7.

2008: Passenger cars 167; Buses 6; Lorries and vans 92; Motorcycles 7.

Source: IRF, *World Road Statistics*.

CIVIL AVIATION
(traffic on scheduled services)

	2006	2007	2008
Kilometres flown (million)	2	2	2
Passengers carried ('000)	59	62	63
Passenger-km (million)	19	20	20
Total ton-km (million)	2	2	2

Source: UN, *Statistical Yearbook*.

Tourism

TOURIST ARRIVALS BY NATIONALITY

	2007	2008	2009
Australia	9,389	14,517	16,316
South Africa	125,231	95,415	84,413
Tanzania	92,732	106,284	81,288
United Kingdom	66,858	46,516	53,370
USA	39,127	33,870	49,451
Zimbabwe	278,010	226,428	171,232
Total (incl. others)	897,413	811,775	709,948

2010: Total tourist arrivals 815,000.

Tourism receipts (US $ million, excl. passenger transport): 148 in 2008; 98 in 2009; 125 in 2010.

Source: World Tourism Organization.

Communications Media

	2009	2010	2011
Telephones ('000 main lines in use)	90.3	118.4	85.7
Mobile cellular telephones ('000 subscribers)	4,406.7	5,447.0	8,164.6
Internet subscribers ('000)	17.8	17.3	n.a.
Broadband subscribers ('000)	10.7	10.3	7.5

Personal computers: 131,000 (11.2 per 1,000 persons) in 2005.

Radio receivers ('000 in use): 1,436 in 1999.

Television receivers ('000 in use): 540 in 2001.

Daily newspapers: 4 (average circulation 55,000 copies) in 2004.

Sources: UNESCO, *Statistical Yearbook*; UNESCO Institute for Statistics; UN, *Statistical Yearbook*; International Telecommunication Union.

Education

(2009/10 unless otherwise indicated)

	Institutions	Teachers	Students
Primary	4,221*	49,987	2,899,131
Secondary	n.a.	29,887	747,935
Tertiary	n.a.	n.a.	24,553†

* 1998 figure.

† 1999/2000 estimate.

Source: UNESCO Institute for Statistics.

Pupil-teacher ratio (primary education, UNESCO estimate): 58.0 in 2009/10 (Source: UNESCO Institute for Statistics).

Adult literacy rate (UNESCO estimates): 71.2% (males 80.7%; females 61.7%) in 2010 (Source: UNESCO Institute for Statistics).

Directory

The Constitution

The Constitution for the Republic of Zambia, which was formally adopted on 28 May 1996 (amending the Constitution of 1991), provides for a multi-party form of government. The Head of State is the President of the Republic, who is elected by popular vote at the same time as elections to the National Assembly. The President's tenure of office is limited to two five-year terms. Foreign nationals and those with foreign parentage are prohibited from contesting the presidency. The legislature comprises a National Assembly of 158 members: 150 are elected by universal adult suffrage, while the remaining eight are nominated by the President. The President appoints a Vice-President and a Cabinet from members of the National Assembly. In September 2009 the National Constitutional Conference approved an increase in the number of members of the National Assembly from 158 to 280. Also approved was a proposal to have 240 of those members elected by simple majority, 30 members elected by proportional representation and a maximum of 10 nominated by the President.

The Constitution also provides for a House of Chiefs numbering 27: four from each of the Northern, Western, Southern and Eastern Provinces, three each from the North-Western, Luapula and Central Provinces and two from the Copperbelt Province. It may submit resolutions to be debated by the Assembly and consider those matters referred to it by the President.

The Supreme Court of Zambia is the final Court of Appeal. The Chief Justice and other judges are appointed by the President. Subsidiary to the Supreme Court is the High Court, which has unlimited jurisdiction to hear and determine any civil or criminal proceedings under any Zambian law.

Note: A constitutional review commission was established in November 2011, which was scheduled to present its draft amendments to the President in September 2012, after which a national referendum on the revised document would be held.

The Government

HEAD OF STATE

President: MICHAEL CHILUFYA SATA (took office 23 September 2011).

THE CABINET
(September 2012)

President: MICHAEL CHILUFYA SATA.

Vice-President: GUY L. SCOTT.

Minister of Justice: WYNTER MUNACAAMBWA KABIMBA.

Minister of Defence: GEOFFREY B. MWAMBA.

Minister of Finance: ALEXANDER BWALYA CHIKWANDA.

Minister of Home Affairs: EDGAR LUNGU.

Minister of Health: DR JOSEPH KASONDE.

Minister of Foreign Affairs: GIVEN LUBINDA.

Minister of Agriculture and Livestock: EMMANUEL T. CHENDA.

Minister of Sports, Youth and Gender: CHISHIMBA KAMBWILI.

Minister of Commerce, Trade and Industry: ROBERT SICHINGA.

Minister of Mines: WILBUR SIMUUSA.

Minister of Labour: FACKSON SHAMENDA.

Minister of Education, Science and Vocational Training: DR JOHN T. N. PHIRI.

Minister of Lands, Energy and Water Development: CHRISTOPHER YALUMA.

Minister of Local Government, Housing, Early Education and Environmental Protection: Prof. NKANDU LUO.

Minister of Community Development, Mother and Child Health: DR JOSEPH KATEMA.

Minister of Chiefs and Traditional Affairs: INONGE WINA.

Minister of Transport, Works, Supply and Communications: WILLIE NSANDA.

Minister of Information and Broadcasting: KENNEDY SAKENI.

Minister of Tourism and the Arts: SYLVIA MASEBO.

There were, in addition, 18 Deputy Ministers.

MINISTRIES

Office of the President: POB 30135, Lusaka 10101; tel. (21) 1260317; fax (21) 1254545; internet www.statehouse.gov.zm.

Office of the Vice-President: Lusaka.

Ministry of Agriculture and Livestock: Mulungushi House, Independence Ave, Nationalist Rd, POB RW50291, Lusaka; tel. (21) 1213551.

Ministry of Chiefs and Traditional Affairs: Lusaka.

Ministry of Commerce, Trade and Industry: 9th and 10th Floor, Nasser Rd, POB 31968, Lusaka 10101; tel. (21) 1228301; fax (21) 1226984; internet www.mcti.gov.zm.

Ministry of Community Development, Mother and Child Health: Fidelity House, POB 31958, Lusaka; tel. (21) 1228321; fax (21) 1225327.

Ministry of Defence: POB 31931, Lusaka; tel. (21) 1252366.

Ministry of Education, Science and Vocational Training: Civic Center Area, Plot 89, cnr Mogadishu and Chimanga Rds, POB 50093, Lusaka 10101; tel. (21) 1250855; fax (21) 1250760; internet www.moe.gov.zm.

Ministry of Finance: Finance Bldg, POB 50062, Lusaka; tel. (21) 1252121; fax (21) 1251078; e-mail info@mofnp.gov.zm; internet www.mofnp.gov.zm.

Ministry of Foreign Affairs and Tourism: POB RW50069, Lusaka; tel. (21) 1252718; fax (21) 1222440.

Ministry of Health: Ndeke House, POB 30205, Lusaka; tel. (21) 1253040; fax (21) 1253344; internet www.moh.gov.zm.

Ministry of Home Affairs: POB 32862, Lusaka; tel. (21) 1213505.

Ministry of Information, Broadcasting and Labour: Independence Ave, POB 51025, Lusaka; tel. and fax (21) 1235410; internet www.mibs.gov.zm.

Ministry of Justice: Fairley Rd, POB 50106, 15101, Ridgeway, Lusaka; tel. (21) 1228522.

Ministry of Lands, Energy and Water Development: POB 50694, Lusaka; tel. (21) 1252288; fax (21) 1250120; internet www.ministryoflands.gov.zm.

Ministry of Local Government, Housing, Early Education and Environmental Protection: Church Rd, POB 50027, Lusaka; tel. (21) 1250528; fax (21) 1252680; e-mail ps@mlgh.gov.zm; internet www.mlgh.gov.zm.

Ministry of Mines: Chilufya Mulenga Rd, POB 31969, 10101 Lusaka; tel. (21) 1235323; fax (21) 1235346.

Ministry of Sports, Youth and Gender: Lechwe House, Freedom Way, POB 32186, Lusaka; tel. (21) 1212020; internet www.mlss.gov.zm.

Ministry of Transport, Works, Supply and Communications: Fairley Rd, POB 50065, Lusaka; tel. (21) 151444; fax (21) 151795; internet www.mct.gov.zm.

President and Legislature

PRESIDENT

Presidential Election, 20 September 2011

Candidate	Votes	% of votes
Michael Chilufya Sata (PF)	1,170,966	42.85
Rupiah Banda (MMD)	987,866	36.15
Hakainde Hichilema (UPND)	506,763	18.54
Charles Milupi (ADD)	26,270	0.96
Others	40,797	1.49
Total	2,732,662	100.00

NATIONAL ASSEMBLY

Speaker: Dr PATRICK MATIBINI.

General Election, 20 September 2011

Party	Seats
Patriotic Front (PF)	60
Movement for Multi-party Democracy (MMD)	55
United Party for National Development (UPND)	28
Independents	3
Alliance for Democracy and Development (ADD)	1
Forum For Democracy and Development (FDD)	1
Total	148*

* Voting in two constituencies did not take place.

House of Chiefs

The House of Chiefs is an advisory body which may submit resolutions for debate by the National Assembly. There are 27 Chiefs, four each from the Northern, Western, Southern and Eastern Provinces, three each from the North-Western, Luapula and Central Provinces, and two from the Copperbelt Province.

Election Commission

Electoral Commission of Zambia (ECZ): Elections House, Haile Selassie Ave, POB 50274, Longacres, Lusaka; tel. (21) 1253155; fax (21) 1253884; e-mail elections@electcom.org.zm; internet www.elections.org.zm; f. 1996; independent; Chair. IRENE C. MAMBILIMA; Dir PRISCILLA MULENGA ISAAC.

Political Organizations

Agenda for Change (AfC): POB 37119, Lusaka; e-mail agenda@zambia.co.zm; internet www.agenda123.com; f. 1995; Pres. Prof. HENRY KYAMBALESA; Nat. Chair. DARROH P. CHOONGA.

Alliance for Democracy and Development (ADD): Plot 6592, Nationalist Rd, opp. UTH Filter Clinic, POB 36792, Lusaka; tel. 977822902 (mobile); e-mail admin@add-zambia.org; f. 2009; Pres. CHARLES MILUPI; Nat. Chair. AMOS NAKALONGA; Sec.-Gen. STAFFORD LIZU (acting).

Citizens Democratic Party (CDP): POB 37277, Lusaka; tel. 975642011 (mobile); fax 967052011 (mobile); e-mail citizens@thecitizensdemocraticparty.com; internet www.thecitizensdemocraticparty.com.

Democratic Party (DP): Plot C4, President Ave (North), POB 71628, Ndola; f. 1991; Pres. EMMANUEL MWAMBA.

Heritage Party (HP): POB 51055, Lusaka; f. 2001 by expelled mems of the MMD; Pres. Brig.-Gen. GODFREY MIYANDA.

Movement for Multi-party Democracy (MMD): POB 30708, Lusaka; tel. (21) 1250177; fax (21) 1252329; e-mail mmd@zamtel.zm; internet www.mmdzam.org; f. 1990; registration suspended in March 2012; Pres. (vacant); Nat. Sec. Maj. RICHARD KACHINGWE.

National Democratic Focus: Lusaka; f. 2006 to contest the presidential election; Acting Chair. NEVERS MUMBA (RP).

All Peoples' Congress Party (APC): Lusaka; f. 2005 by fmr mems of the FDD; Pres. WINRIGHT K. NGONDO.

Party for Unity, Democracy and Development (PUDD): Lusaka; f. 2004 by fmr mems of the MMD; Pres. (vacant).

Reform Party (RP): Lusaka; f. 2005 by fmr mems of the MMD; Pres. NEVERS MUMBA; Nat. Chair. EVA SANDERSON; Sec.-Gen. CLEMENT MICHELO.

Zambia Democratic Conference (ZADECO): Lusaka; f. 1998 as the Zambia Democratic Congress Popular Front by fmr mems of the Zambia Democratic Congress; disbanded in 1999; reformed after 2001 election by fmr mems of the ZAP; Pres. Rev. Dr DAN PULE.

Zambia Republican Party (ZRP): Lusaka; f. 2001 by merger of the Republican Party (f. 2000) and the Zambia Alliance for Progress (f. 1999); Gen. Sec. SILVIA MASEBO; Nat. Chair. BEN KAPITA.

National Leadership for Development (NLD): POB 34161, Lusaka; f. 2000; Pres. Dr YOBERT K. SHAMAPANDE.

National Party (NP): POB 37840, Lusaka 10101; tel. (21) 18491431; e-mail nationalparty1993@yahoo.com; f. 1993; by fmr mems of the MMD; promotes human rights; Pres. Rev. RICHARD KAMBULU; Sec.-Gen. NDANISO BANDA.

National Restoration Party (NAREP): Plot 3065A, Suite B, Fairview, Great East Rd, Lusaka; tel. 966102016 (mobile); e-mail info@newzambia.org; internet www.newzambia.org; f. 2009; Pres. ELIAS CHIPIMO, Jr; Sec.-Gen. MIKE MUYAWALA (acting).

Patriotic Front (PF): Farmers House, POB 320015, Lusaka; tel. 96768080 (mobile); fax (21) 1228661; internet www.pf.com.zm; f. 2001 by expelled mems of the MMD; Pres. MICHAEL CHILUFYA SATA; Sec.-Gen. WYNTER MUNACAAMBWA KABIMBA.

United Democratic Alliance (UDA): Kenneth Kaunda House, Cairo Rd, Lusaka; f. 2006 to contest that year's elections; Nat. Chair. TILYENJI KAUNDA (FDD).

Forum for Democracy and Development (FDD): POB 35868, Lusaka; f. 2001 by expelled mems of the MMD; Pres. EDITH NAWAKWI; Chair. SIMON ZUKAS.

United National Independence Party (UNIP): POB 30302, Lusaka; tel. (21) 1221197; fax (21) 1221327; f. 1959; sole legal party 1972–90; Pres. TILYENJI KAUNDA; Nat. Chair. KEN KAIRA.

United Party for National Development (UPND): POB 33199, Lusaka; internet www.upnd.org; f. 1998; incl. fmr mems of the Progressive People's Party and Zambia Dem. Party; Pres. HAKAINDE HICHILEMA.

Unity Party for Democrats (UPD): POB RW28, Ridgeway, Lusaka; f. 1997; Pres. MATHEW PIKITI.

Zambia Alliance for Progress (ZAP): Lusaka; f. 1999; re-registered as ZAP in 2001 after splitting from Zambia Republican Party; Pres. (vacant).

Diplomatic Representation

EMBASSIES AND HIGH COMMISSIONS IN ZAMBIA

Angola: Plot 108, Great East Rd, Northmead, POB 31595, 10101 Lusaka; tel. (21) 1134764; fax (21) 1221210; Ambassador BALBINA MALHEIROS DIAS DA SILVA.

Botswana: 5201 Pandit Nehru Rd, Diplomatic Triangle, POB 31910, 10101 Lusaka; tel. (21) 1250555; fax (21) 1250804; High Commissioner T. DITLHABI-OLIPHANT.

Brazil: 4 Manenekela Road, Woodlands, Lusaka; tel. (21) 1252171; fax (21) 1253203; e-mail brasemblusaca@iconnect.zm; Ambassador JOSAL LUIZ PELLEGRINO.

Canada: Plot 5199, United Nations Ave, POB 31313, 10101 Lusaka; tel. (21) 1250833; fax (21) 1254176; e-mail lsaka@international.gc.ca; internet www.canadainternational.gc.ca/zambia-zambie; High Commissioner PIERRE-PAUL PERRON.

China, People's Republic: Plot 7430, United Nations Ave, Longacres, POB 31975, 10101 Lusaka; tel. (21) 1251169; fax (21) 1251157; e-mail chinaemb_zm@mfa.gov.cn; Ambassador ZHOU YUXIAO.

Congo, Democratic Republic: Plot 1124, Parirenyatwa Rd, POB 31287, 10101 Lusaka; tel. and fax (21) 1235679; Ambassador JOHNSON WA BINANA.

Cuba: 5574 Mogoye Rd, Kalundu, POB 33132, 10101 Lusaka; tel. (21) 1291308; fax (21) 1291586; e-mail ambassador@iconnect.zm; internet emba.cubaminrex.cu/zambiaing; Ambassador FRANCISCO JAVIER VIAMONTES CORREA.

Denmark: 5219 Haile Selassie Ave, POB 50299, Lusaka; tel. (21) 1254277; fax (21) 1254618; e-mail lunamb@um.dk; internet www.zambia.um.dk; Ambassador THOMAS NEWHOUSE TRIGG SCHJERBECK.

Egypt: Plot 5206, United Nations Ave, Longacres, POB 32428, Lusaka 10101; tel. (21) 1250229; fax (21) 1252213; Ambassador SALAH EL-DIN ABDEL SADEK.

Finland: Haile Selassie Ave, opp. Ndeke House, Longacres, POB 50819, 15101 Lusaka; tel. (21) 1251988; fax (21) 1253783; e-mail pertti.anttinen@formin.fi; internet www.finland.org.zm; Ambassador PERTTI ANTTINEN.

France: Mpile Bldg, 74 Independence Ave, POB 30062, 10101 Lusaka; tel. (21) 1251322; fax (21) 1254475; e-mail cad.lusaka-amba@diplomatie.gouv.fr; internet www.ambafrance-zm.org; Ambassador MARIE-ANNICK BOURDIN.

Germany: Plot 5209, United Nations Ave, POB 50120, 15101 Ridgeway, Lusaka; tel. (21) 1250644; fax (21) 1254014; e-mail info@lusaka.diplo.de; internet www.lusaka.diplo.de; Ambassador FRANK MEYKE.

Holy See: 283 Los Angeles Blvd, POB 31445, 10101 Lusaka; tel. (21) 1251033; fax (21) 1250601; e-mail nuntius@coppernet.zm; Apostolic Nuncio Most Rev. JULIO MURAT (Titular Archbishop of Orange).

India: 1 Pandit Nehru Rd, POB 32111, 10101 Lusaka; tel. (21) 1253159; fax (21) 1254118; e-mail hoc.lusaka@mea.gov.in; internet www.hcizambia.com; High Commissioner ASHOK KUMAR.

Ireland: 6663 Katima Mulilo Rd, Olympia Park, POB 34923, 10101 Lusaka; tel. (21) 1290650; fax (21) 1290482; e-mail iremb@zamnet.zm; internet www.embassyofireland.co.zm; Ambassador TONY COTTER.

Italy: Plot 5211, Embassy Park, Diplomatic Triangle, POB 50497, Lusaka; tel. (21) 1250781; fax (21) 1254929; e-mail ambasciata.lusaka@esteri.it; internet www.amblusaka.esteri.it; Ambassador Dr PIER MARIO DACCO.

Japan: Plot 5218, Haile Selassie Ave, POB 34190, 10101 Lusaka; tel. (21) 1251555; fax (21) 1254425; e-mail jez@zamtel.zm; internet www.zm.emb-japan.go.jp; Ambassador AKIO EGAWA.

Kenya: 5207 United Nations Ave, POB 50298, 10101 Lusaka; tel. (21) 1250722; fax (21) 1253829; e-mail kenhigh@zamnet.zm; High Commissioner LAZARUS O. AMAYO.

Libya: 251 Ngwee Rd, off United Nations Ave, Longacres, POB 35319, 10101 Lusaka; tel. (21) 1253055; fax (21) 1251239; Ambassador KHALIFA OMER SWIEXI.

Malawi: 31 Bishops Rd, Kabulonga, POB 50425, Lusaka; tel. (21) 1265768; fax (21) 1265765; e-mail mhcomm@iwayafrica.com; High Commissioner Dr CHRISSIE MUGHOGHO.

Mozambique: Kacha Rd, Plot 9592, POB 34877, 10101 Lusaka; tel. (21) 1220333; fax (21) 1220345; e-mail embamoc.zambia@minec.gov.mz; High Commissioner MARIA LEOCÁDIA TIVANE MATE.

Namibia: 30B Mutende Rd, Woodlands, POB 30577, 10101 Lusaka; tel. (21) 1260407; fax (21) 1263858; e-mail namibia@coppernet.zm; High Commissioner MARTIN SHALLI.

Netherlands: 5208 United Nations Ave, POB 31905, 10101 Lusaka; tel. (21) 1253819; fax (21) 1253733; e-mail lus@minbuza.nl; internet www.netherlandsembassy.org.zm; Ambassador HARRY MOLENAAR.

Nigeria: 5203 Haile Selassie Ave, Diplomatic Triangle, Longacres, POB 32598, Lusaka; tel. (21) 1229860; fax (21) 1223791; High Commissioner SIFAWU MOMOH.

Norway: cnr Birdcage Walk and Haile Selassie Ave, Plot No. 245/61, Longacres, POB 34570, 10101 Lusaka; tel. (21) 1252188; fax (21) 1253915; e-mail emb.lusaka@mfa.no; internet www.norway.org.zm; Ambassador ARVE OFSTAD.

Russia: Plot 6407, Diplomatic Triangle, POB 32355, 10101 Lusaka; tel. (21) 1252120; fax (21) 1253582; Ambassador BORIS MALAKHOV.

Saudi Arabia: 27BC Leopards Hill Rd, Kabulonga, POB 34411, 10101 Lusaka; tel. (21) 1266861; fax (21) 1266863; e-mail saudiemb@uudial.zm; Ambassador HASSAN ATTAR.

Serbia: Independence Ave 5216, POB 33379, 10101 Lusaka; tel. (21) 1250235; fax (21) 1253889; e-mail serbianemba@zamnet.zm; Chargé d'affaires a.i. MIRKO MANOJLOVIĆ.

Somalia: G3/377A Kabulonga Rd, POB 34051, Lusaka; tel. (21) 1262119; Ambassador (vacant).

South Africa: D26, Cheetah Rd, Kabulonga, Private Bag W369, Lusaka; tel. (21) 1260999; fax (21) 1263001; e-mail sahcadmin@samnet.zm; High Commissioner MOSES MABOKELA CHIKANE.

Sudan: 31 Ng'umbo Rd, Longacres, POB RW179X, 15200 Lusaka; tel. (21) 1252116; fax (21) 1252448; e-mail sudemblsk@hotmail.com; Ambassador SABIT ABBEY ALLEY.

Sweden: Haile Selassie Ave, POB 50264, 10101 Lusaka; tel. (21) 1251711; fax (21) 1254049; e-mail ambassaden.lusaka@foreign.ministry.se; internet www.swedenabroad.com/lusaka; Ambassador LENA NORDSTRÖM.

Tanzania: Ujamaa House, Plot 5200, United Nations Ave, POB 31219, 10101 Lusaka; tel. (21) 1253222; fax (21) 1254861; e-mail tzreplsk@zamnet.zm; High Commissioner GEORGE MWANJABALA.

United Kingdom: Plot 5210, Independence Ave, POB 50050, 15101 Ridgeway, Lusaka; tel. (21) 1423200; fax (21) 1423291; internet ukinzambia.fco.gov.uk; Jt High Commissioner CAROLYN DAVIDSON, THOMAS CARTER.

USA: cnr Independence and United Nations Aves, POB 31617, Lusaka; tel. (21) 1250955; fax (21) 1252225; e-mail irclusaka@state.gov; internet zambia.usembassy.gov; Ambassador MARK CHARLES STORELLA.

Zimbabwe: 11058 Haile Selassie Ave, Longacres, POB 33491, 10101 Lusaka; tel. (21) 1254012; fax (21) 1227474; e-mail zimzam@coppernet.zm; Ambassador LOVEMORE MAZEMO.

Judicial System

The judicial system of Zambia comprises a Supreme Court, composed of a Chief Justice, a Deputy Chief Justice and five Justices; a High Court comprising the Chief Justice and 30 Judges; Senior Resident and Resident Magistrates' Courts, which sit at various centres; and Local Courts, which deal principally with customary law, but which also have limited criminal jurisdiction.

Supreme Court of Zambia

Independence Ave, POB 50067, Ridgeway, Lusaka; tel. (21) 1251330; fax (21) 1251743.

Acting Chief Justice: LOMBE CHIBESAKUNDA.

Acting Deputy Chief Justice: FLORENCE MUMBA.

Supreme Court Judges: E. MUYOVWE, HILDAH CHIBOMBA, G. S. PHIRI, P. MUSONDA (suspended May 2012).

Religion

CHRISTIANITY

Council of Churches in Zambia: CCZ Ecumenical Centre, Plot 377A, Bishops Rd, Kabulonga, POB 30315, Lusaka; tel. (21) 1267738; fax (21) 1267740; e-mail info@ccz.org.zm; internet www.ccz.org.zm; f. 1945; Pres. Rev. MOSES LUCAS MWALE (Brethren in Christ Church); Gen. Sec. SUZANNE MEMBE MATALE; 22 mem. churches and 19 affiliate mem. orgs.

The Anglican Communion

Anglicans are adherents of the Church of the Province of Central Africa, covering Botswana, Malawi, Zambia and Zimbabwe. The Church comprises 15 dioceses, including five in Zambia. There are an estimated 80,000 adherents in Zambia.

Archbishop of the Province of Central Africa and Bishop of Northern Zambia: Rt Rev. ALBERT CHAMA, POB 20798, Kitwe; tel. (21) 2223264; fax (21) 2224778; e-mail dionorth@zamnet.zm.

Bishop of Central Zambia: Rt Rev. DEREK G. KAMUKWAMBA, POB 70172, Ndola; tel. (21) 2612431; fax (21) 2615954; e-mail adcznla@zamnet.zm.

Bishop of Eastern Zambia: Rt Rev. WILLIAM MUCHOMBO, POB 510154, Chipata; tel. and fax (21) 6221294; e-mail dioeastzm@zamnet.zm.

Bishop of Luapula: Rt Rev. ROBERT MUMBI, POB 710210, Mansa, Luapula.

Bishop of Lusaka: Rt Rev. DAVID NJOVU, Bishop's Lodge, POB 30183, Lusaka; tel. (21) 1264515; fax (21) 1262379; e-mail angdiolu@zamnet.zm.

Protestant Churches

At mid-2000 there were an estimated 2.7m. Protestants in Zambia.

African Methodist Episcopal Church: Carousel Bldg, Lumumba Rd, POB 36628, Lusaka; tel. 955708031; fax (21) 1225067; Presiding Elder Rev. PAUL KAWIMBE; 440 congregations, 880,000 mems.

Baptist Church: Lubu Rd, POB 30636, Lusaka; tel. (21) 1253620.

Baptist Mission of Zambia: Baptist Bldg, 3062 Great East Rd, POB 50599, 15101 Ridgeway, Lusaka; tel. (21) 1222492; fax (21) 1227520; internet bmoz.org.

Brethren in Christ Church: POB 630115, Choma; tel. (21) 3320228; fax (21) 3320127; e-mail biccz@zamtel.zm; internet www.bic.org; f. 1906; Bishop Rev. T. HAMUKANG'ANDU; 180 congregations, 19,526 mems.

Evangelical Lutheran Church in Zambia: Plot No. 145-4893, Mpezeni Rd, POB 37701, 10101 Lusaka; tel. 97787584; fax (21) 1224023; e-mail elcza_head@yahoo.com; Senior Pastor Rev. ALFRED CHANA; 2,210 mems (2010).

Reformed Church in Zambia: POB 38255, Lusaka; tel. (21) 1295369; e-mail info@rczsynod.co.zm; internet www.rczsynod.co.zm; f. 1899; African successor to the Dutch Reformed Church mission; Synod Moderator Rev. MOSES LUCAS MWALE; 147 congregations, 400,000 mems.

Seventh-day Adventist Church: Plot 9221, cnr Burma Rd and Independence Ave, POB 36010, Lusaka; tel. and fax (21) 1254036; e-mail lcsdac@zamnet.zm; internet www.lcsdac.net.zm; f. 1905; Pres. Dr CORNELIUS MULENGA MATANDIKO; Sec. HARRINGTON SIMUI AKOMBWA; 534,126 mems.

United Church of Zambia: Synod Headquarters, Nationalist Rd at Burma Rd, POB 50122, Lusaka; tel. (21) 1250641; fax (21) 1252198; e-mail uczsynod@zamnet.zm; f. 1965; Synod Bishop Rev. MUTALE MULUMBWA; Gen. Sec. PEGGY KABONDE; c. 3m. mems.

Other denominations active in Zambia include the Assemblies of God, the Church of Christ, the Church of the Nazarene, the Evangelical Fellowship of Zambia, the Kimbanguist Church, the Presbyterian Church of Southern Africa, the Religious Society of Friends (Quakers) and the United Pentecostal Church. At mid-2000 there were an estimated 2m. adherents professing other forms of Christianity.

The Roman Catholic Church

Zambia comprises two archdioceses and nine dioceses. The number of adherents in the country is equivalent to some 30% of the total population.

Bishops' Conference

Catholic Secretariat, Unity House, cnr Freedom Way and Katunjila Rd, POB 31965, 10201 Lusaka; tel. (21) 1262613; fax (21) 1262658; e-mail zec@zamnet.zm.

f. 1984; Pres. Rt Rev. LUNGU GEORGE COSMOS ZUMAIRE (Bishop of Chipata).

Archbishop of Kasama: Most Rev. IGNATIUS CHAMA, Archbishop's House, POB 410143, Kasama; tel. (21) 4221248; fax (21) 4222202; e-mail archkasa@zamtel.zm.

Archbishop of Lusaka: Most Rev. TELESPHORE GEORGE MPUNDU, 41 Wamulwa Rd, POB 32754, 10101 Lusaka; tel. (21) 1255973; fax (21) 1255975; e-mail adlarch@zamnet.zm.

ISLAM

There are about 10,000 members of the Muslim Association in Zambia.

Supreme Islamic Council of Zambia: Lusaka; Pres. SUZYO ZIMBA.

BAHÁ'Í FAITH

National Spiritual Assembly: Sekou Touré Rd, Plot 4371, Private Bag RW227X, Ridgeway 15102, Lusaka; tel. and fax (21) 1254505; f. 1952; Sec.-Gen. MARGARET K LENGWE; mems resident in 1,456 localities.

The Press

DAILIES

The Post: 36 Bwinjimfumu Rd, Rhodespark, Private Bag E352, Lusaka; tel. (21) 1231092; fax (21) 1229271; e-mail post@post.co.zm; internet www.postzambia.com; f. 1991; privately owned; Editor FRED M'MEMBE; circ. 29,000.

The Times of Zambia: Kabelenga Ave, POB 70069, Ndola; tel. and fax (21) 2614469; e-mail times@zamtel.zm; internet www.times.co.zm; f. 1943; govt-owned; English; Man. Editor GODFREY MALAMA; circ. 25,000.

Zambia Daily Mail: Zambia Publishing Company, POB 31421, Lusaka; tel. (21) 1225131; fax (21) 1225881; internet www.daily-mail.co.zm; f. 1968; govt-owned; English; Man. Editor ISAAC CHIPAMPE; circ. 40,000.

PERIODICALS

The Challenge: Mission Press, Chifubu Rd, POB 71581, Ndola; tel. (21) 2680456; fax (21) 2680484; e-mail info@missionpress.org; internet www.missionpress.org; f. 1999; quarterly; English; social, educational and religious; Roman Catholic; edited by Franciscan friars; Dir Fr MIHA DREVENSEK; circ. 5,000.

Chipembele Magazine: POB 30255, Lusaka; tel. (21) 1251630; fax (21) 1251630; e-mail wecsz@coppernet.zm; internet www.conservationzambia.org; 2 a year; publ. by Wildlife Conservation Soc. of Zambia; circ. 3,000 annually; Editor ADAM GOULDING.

Farming in Zambia: POB 50197, Lusaka; tel. (21) 1213551; f. 1965; quarterly; publ. by Ministry of Agriculture and Livestock; Editor L. P. CHIRWA; circ. 3,000.

Icengelo: Lusaka; internet icengelo.com; Bemba language.

Imbila: POB RW20, Lusaka; tel. (21) 1217254; e-mail mambue2002@zanis.org.zm; f. 1953; monthly; publ. by Zambia Information Services; Bemba; Editor ALFRED M ZULU; circ. 20,000.

Intanda: POB RW20, Lusaka; tel. (21) 1219675; f. 1958; monthly; publ. by Zambia Information Services; Tonga; Editor J. SIKAULU; circ. 6,000.

Konkola: Zambia Consolidated Copper Mines Ltd, PR Dept, POB 71505, Ndola; tel. (21) 2640142; f. 1973 as *Mining Mirror*; monthly; English; Editor G. MUKUWA; circ. 30,000.

The Lowdown: Lusaka; internet www.lowdown.co.zm; f. 1995; monthly; English; Editor HEATHER CHALCRAFT.

Lukanga News: POB 919, Kabwe; tel. (21) 5217254; publ. by Zambia Information Services; Lenje; Editor J. H. N. NKOMANGA; circ. 5,500.

National Mirror: Multimedia Zambia, 15701 Woodlands, POB 320199, Lusaka; tel. (21) 1263864; fax (21) 1263050; f. 1972; fortnightly; news, current affairs and foreign affairs; publ. by Multimedia Zambia; Editor SIMON MWANZA; circ. 40,000.

Ngoma: POB RW20, Lusaka; tel. (21) 1219675; monthly; Lunda, Kaonde and Luvale; publ. by Zambia Information Services; Editor B. A. LUHILA; circ. 3,000.

Speak Out!: POB 70244, Ndola; tel. (21) 2612241; fax (21) 2620630; e-mail speakout@zamnet.zm; f. 1984; six a year; Christian; aimed at youth readership up to 35 years; Man. Editor CONSTANTIA TREPPE; circ. 25,000.

The Sportsman: POB 31762, Lusaka; tel. (21) 1214250; f. 1980; monthly; Man. Editor Sam Sikazwe; circ. 18,000.

Sunday Times of Zambia: Kabelenga Ave, POB 70069, Ndola; tel. (21) 1614469; fax (21) 2617096; e-mail times@zamtel.zm; internet www.times.co.zm/sunday; f. 1965; owned by UNIP; English; Man. Editor Arthur Simuchoba; circ. 78,000.

Workers' Voice: POB 20652, Kitwe; tel. (21) 2211999; f. 1972; fortnightly; publ. by Zambia Congress of Trade Unions.

Youth: POB 30302, Lusaka; tel. (21) 1211411; f. 1974; quarterly; publ. by UNIP Youth League; Editor-in-Chief N. Anamela; circ. 20,000.

Zambia Government Gazette: POB 30136, Lusaka; tel. (21) 1228724; fax (21) 1224486; f. 1911; weekly; English; official notices.

NEWS AGENCY

Zambia News and Information Services (ZANIS): Mass Media Complex, 2nd Floor, Alick Nkhata Rd, POB 50020, Lusaka; tel. (21) 1255255; fax (21) 125163; e-mail zana@zamnet.zm; internet www.zana.gov.zm; f. 2005 through merger of Zambia News Agency (ZANA) and Zambia Information Services (ZIS).

PRESS ASSOCIATIONS

Press Association of Zambia (PAZA): Bishops Rd, Multi-Media Centre, POB 37065, Lusaka; tel. (21) 1263595; fax (21) 1263110; f. 1983; Pres. Andrew Sakala; Vice-Pres. Amos Chanda.

Zambia Media Council (ZAMEC): Lusaka; f. 2012; Chair. Paul Mususu.

Zambia Union of Journalists: POB 30394, Lusaka; tel. (21) 1227348; fax (21) 1221695; e-mail zuj.zambia@yahoo.com; Pres. Anthony Mulowa; Sec.-Gen. Bob Sianjalika.

Publishers

Africa: Literature Centre, POB 21319, Kitwe; tel. (21) 2210765; fax (21) 2210716; general, educational, religious; Dir Jackson Mbewe.

African Social Research: Institute of Economic and Social Research, University of Zambia, POB 32379, Lusaka; tel. (21) 1294131; fax (21) 1253952; social research in Africa; Editor Mubanga E. Kashoki.

Bookworld Ltd: Plot 10552, off Lumumba Rd, POB 31838, Lusaka; tel. (21) 1230606; fax (21) 1230614; e-mail bookworld@realtime.zm; f. 1991.

Daystar Publications Ltd: POB 32211, Lusaka; f. 1966; religious; Man. Dir S. E. M. Pheko.

Directory Publishers of Zambia Ltd: Mabalenga Rd, POB 30963, Lusaka; tel. (21) 1257133; fax (21) 1257137; e-mail dpz@coppernet.zm; f. 1958; trade directories; Gen. Man. W. D. Wratten.

Multimedia Zambia: Woodlands, POB 320199, Lusaka; tel. and fax (21) 1261193; f. 1971; religious and educational books, audio-visual materials; Exec. Dir Eddy Mupeso.

University of Zambia Press (UNZA Press): POB 32379, 10101 Lusaka; tel. (21) 1292269; fax (21) 1253952; f. 1938; academic books, papers and journals.

Zambia Educational Publishing House: Chishango Rd, POB 32708, 10101 Lusaka; tel. (21) 1222324; fax (21) 1225073; f. 1967; educational and general; Man. Dir Beniko E. Mulota.

GOVERNMENT PUBLISHING HOUSES

Government Printer: POB 30136, Lusaka; tel. (21) 1228724; fax (21) 1224486; official documents and statistical bulletins.

Zambia Information Services: POB 50020, Lusaka; tel. (21) 1219673; state-controlled; Dir Benson Sianga.

PUBLISHERS' ASSOCIATION

Booksellers' and Publishers' Association of Zambia: POB 31838, Lusaka; tel. (21) 1222647; fax (21) 1225195; Chair. Ray Munamwimbu; Sec. Basil Mbewe.

Broadcasting and Communications

TELECOMMUNICATIONS

In 2011 there were three providers of mobile telephone services in Zambia. ZAMTEL also provides fixed-line telephone services.

REGULATORY AUTHORITY

Zambia Information and Communications Technology Authority (ZICTA): Plot 3141, cnr Lumumba and Buyantanshi Rds, POB 36871, Lusaka; tel. (21) 1241236; fax (21) 1246701; e-mail info@zicta.zm; f. 1994; fmrly Zambian Communications Authority, present name adopted 2009; Dir-Gen. Margaret Mudenda.

SERVICE PROVIDERS

Airtel Zambia Ltd: Nyerere Rd, Woodlands, POB 320001, Lusaka; tel. (21) 1250707; e-mail customerservice.zm@zain.com; internet africa.airtel.com/zambia; f. 1997 as ZamCell Ltd; fmrly Celtel Zambia, subsequently Zain Zambia, present name adopted 2010; mobile cellular telephone operator; Man. Dir Fayaz King; c. 500,000 subscribers.

MTN (Zambia) Ltd: Plot 1278, Lubuto Rd, Rhodespark, POB 35464, Lusaka; tel. 966750750 (mobile); fax 966257732 (mobile); e-mail mtn@mtnzambia.co.zm; internet www.mtnzambia.co.zm; f. 1997 as Telecel (Zambia) Ltd; acquired by MTN Group, South Africa, in 2005; mobile cellular telecommunications provider; CEO Abdul Ismail; 152,000 subscribers (2006).

Zambia Telecommunications Co Ltd (ZAMTEL): Zamtel House, POB 37000, Lusaka; tel. (21) 1333152; fax (21) 1256622; e-mail zamtel@zamtel.zm; internet www.zamtel.zm; operates fixed-line network and Cell-Z cellular network (f. 1995); Chair. and Acting CEO Dr Mupanga Mwanakatwe.

BROADCASTING

Zambia National Broadcasting Corpn: Mass Media Complex, Alick Nkhata Rd, POB 50015, Lusaka; tel. (21) 1252005; fax (21) 1254013; e-mail lukundosa@yahoo.com; internet www.znbc.co.zm; f. 1961; state-owned; two national radio stations (Radio 1 and Radio 2) and one line-of-rail station (Radio 4); television broadcasts along the line of rail, from Livingstone to Chililabombwe; services in English and seven Zambian languages; Dir-Gen. Joe Chilaizya.

Radio

Breeze FM: POB 511178, Chipata; tel. (21) 6221175; fax (21) 6221823; e-mail news@breezefmchipata.com; internet breezefmchipata.com; f. 2003; Nyanja and English; community-based commercial radio; broadcasts to the Eastern Province; signal is also received in parts of north-west Malawi and border areas of Tete Province in Mozambique; Man. Dir Mike Daka.

Educational Broadcasting Services: Headquarters: POB 50231, Lusaka; tel. (21) 1251724; radio broadcasts from Lusaka; audio-visual aids service from POB 50295, Lusaka; Controller Michael Mulombe.

Radio Chikaya: POB 530290, Lundazi; tel. (6) 480080; e-mail rchikaya@zamtel.zm.

Radio Chikuni: Private Bag E702, POB 660239, Monze; tel. and fax (32) 50708; e-mail chikuni@sat.signis.net; internet www.chikuniradio.org.

Radio Icengelo: Plot 5282, Mwandi Cres., Riverside, POB 20694, Kitwe; tel. (2) 220478; fax (2) 229305; e-mail radioice@mail.zamtel.zm; Man. Rev. Fr Nicholas Mubanga.

Radio Maria Zambia: POB 510307, Chipata; tel. and fax (21) 6221154; e-mail info.zam@radiomaria.org; internet www.radiomaria.org; f. 1999; Dir Mwanza Gabriel Kwaku.

Radio Phoenix: Private Bag E702, Lusaka; tel. (21) 1223581; fax (21) 1226839; e-mail rphoenixinfo@gmail.com; internet www.radiophoenixzambia.com; commercial radio station; Chair. Errol T. Hickey.

Yatsani Radio: Leopards Hill Rd, Bauleni Catholic Church, POB 320147, Lusaka; tel. (21) 1261082; fax (21) 1265842; internet yatsani.com; f. 1999; owned by the Archdiocese of Lusaka; Roman Catholic religious community; broadcasts to Lusaka; Dir Most Rev. Medardo Joseph Mazombwe (Archbishop of Lusaka).

Television

Educational Broadcasting Services: (see Radio).

Muvi Television: Plot No. 17734, Nangwenya Rd, POB 33932, Lusaka; tel. (21) 1253171; fax (21) 1257351; e-mail frontoffice@muvitv.com; internet www.muvitv.com; Man. Dir Steve Nyirenda.

Finance

(cap. = capital; auth. = authorized; res = reserves; dep. = deposits; m. = million; br(s). = branch(es); amounts in kwacha)

BANKING

In 2010 there were 18 commercial banks, 24 microfinance institutions and one development bank in Zambia.

Central Bank

Bank of Zambia: Bank Sq., Cairo Rd, POB 30080, 10101 Lusaka; tel. (21) 1228888; fax (21) 1225652; internet www.boz.zm; f. 1964; bank of issue; cap. 10,020m., res 317,538m., dep. 5,460,206m. (Dec. 2009); Gov. and Chair. Dr MICHAEL M. GONDWE; br. in Ndola.

Commercial Banks

Finance Bank Zambia Ltd: 2101 Chanik House, Cairo Rd, POB 37102, 10101 Lusaka; tel. (21) 1229733; fax (21) 1227290; e-mail fbz@financebank.co.zm; internet www.financebank.co.zm; f. 1986 as Leasing Finance Bank Ltd; name changed as above 1988; cap. 3,630m., res 9,320m., dep. 823,894m. (Dec. 2006); Man. Dir and CEO BARKAT ALI; 33 brs and 10 agencies.

National Savings and Credit Bank: Plot 248B, Cairo Rd, POB 30067, Lusaka; tel. (21) 1227534; fax (21) 1223296; e-mail natsave@zamnet.zm; internet www.natsave.co.zm; f. 1972; state-owned; Chair. FRANK NGAMBI; Man. Dir CEPHAS CHABU.

Zambia National Commercial Bank PLC (ZANACO): POB 33611, Plot 33454 Cairo Rd, Lusaka; tel. (21) 1228979; fax (21) 1223106; e-mail support@zanaco.co.zm; internet www.zanaco.co.zm; f. 1969; 50.8% govt-owned; cap. 11,550m., res 189,142m., dep. 2,296,000m. (Dec. 2009); Chair. Dr MUTUMBA BULL LAWANIKA; Man. Dir MARTYN H. SCHOUTEN; 41 brs.

Foreign Banks

Bank of China (Zambia) Ltd (China): Amandra House, Ben Bella Rd, POB 34550, Lusaka; tel. (21) 1235349; fax (21) 1235350; e-mail service_zm@bank-of-china.com; f. 1997; Chair. PING YUE; Gen. Man. HONG XINSHENG.

Barclays Bank Zambia PLC (United Kingdom): Kafue House, Cairo Rd, POB 31936, Lusaka; tel. (21) 1228858; fax (21) 1226185; e-mail barclays.zambia@barclays.com; internet www.africa.barclays.com; f. 1971; cap. 91,109m., res 247,794m., dep. 2,857,304m. (Dec. 2009); Chair. JACOB SIKAZWE; Man. Dir SAVIOUR CHIBIYA; 5 brs.

Citibank Zambia Ltd (USA): Citibank House, Cha Cha Cha Rd, POB 30037, Southend, Lusaka; tel. (21) 1229025; fax (21) 1226264; internet www.citibank.co.zm; f. 1979; cap. 1,000.0m., res 23,655.7m., dep. 1,100,772.6m. (Dec. 2009); Man. Dir JOYCE-ANN WAINAINA; 1 br.

Ecobank Zambia: 22768 Thabo Mbeki Rd, POB 30705, Lusaka; tel. (21) 1250056; fax (21) 1250171; e-mail ecobankzm@ecobank.com; internet www.ecobank.com; Chair. PETRONELLA N. MWANGALA; Man. Dir CHARITY LUMPA.

Indo-Zambia Bank (IZB): Plot 6907, Cairo Rd, POB 35411, Lusaka; tel. (21) 1224653; fax (21) 1225090; e-mail izb@zamnet.zm; internet www.izb.co.zm; f. 1984; cap. 15,000.0m., res 38,591.9m., dep. 767,161.3m. (March 2010); Chair. ORLENE Y. MOYO; Man. Dir CYRIL PATRO; 9 brs.

Stanbic Bank Zambia Ltd: Woodgate House, 6th Floor, Cairo Rd, POB 32111, Lusaka; tel. (21) 1229285; fax (21) 1225380; e-mail stanbic@zamnet.zm; internet www.stanbicbank.co.zm; f. 1971; wholly owned by Standard Bank Investment Corpn; cap. 7,700m., res 172,526m., dep. 2,160,400m. (Dec. 2009); Chair. V. CHITALU; Man. Dir L. F. KALALA; 7 brs.

Standard Chartered Bank Zambia PLC: Standard House, Cairo Rd, POB 32238, Lusaka; tel. (21) 1229242; fax (21) 1225337; internet www.standardchartered.com/zm; f. 1971; 90% owned by Standard Chartered Holdings (Africa) BV, Netherlands; 10% state-owned; cap. 2,048m., res 23,657m., dep. 2,589,288m. (Dec. 2009); Chair. GEORGE SOKOTA; Man. Dir MIZINGA MELU; 16 brs.

Development Bank

Development Bank of Zambia: Development House, Katondo Rd, POB 33955, Lusaka; tel. (21) 1228576; fax (21) 1222821; e-mail projects@dbz.co.zm; internet www.dbz.co.zm; f. 1973; 99% state-owned; total assets 64,111m. (Dec. 2005); Chair. NAMUKULO MUKUTU; Man. Dir ABRAHAM MWENDA; 2 brs.

Banking Association

Bankers' Association of Zambia: POB 34810, Lusaka; tel. (21) 1234255; fax (21) 1233046; e-mail bazsecretariat@coppernet.zm; Chair. MIZINGA MELU.

STOCK EXCHANGE

Lusaka Stock Exchange (LuSE): Exchange Bldg, 3rd Floor, Central Park, Cairo Rd, POB 34523, Lusaka; tel. (21) 1228391; fax (21) 1225969; e-mail info@luse.co.zm; internet www.luse.co.zm; f. 1994; Chair. FRIDAY NDHLOVU; Gen. Man. BEATRICE NKANZA.

INSURANCE

In 2010 there were 15 licensed insurance companies in Zambia: two reinsurance companies, eight general insurance companies and five long-term insurance companies.

African Life Assurance Zambia: Mukuba Pension House, 4th Floor, Dedan Kimathi Rd, POB 31991; tel. (21) 1225452; fax (21) 1225435; e-mail customercare@african-life.com.zm; f. 2002; life insurance; CEO STEVE WILLIAMS.

Goldman Insurance Ltd: Zambia National Savings and Credit Bank Bldg, 2nd Floor, Cairo Rd, Private Bag W395, Lusaka; tel. (21) 1235234; fax (21) 1227262; e-mail goldman@zamnet.zm; internet www.goldman.co.zm; f. 1992; CEO M. N. RAJU.

Madison Insurance Co Ltd: Plot 255, Kaleya Rd, Roma, POB 37013, Lusaka; tel. (21) 1295311; fax (21) 1295320; internet www.madisonzambia.com; f. 1992; general and micro-insurance; Chair. DAVID A. R. PHIRI; Man. Dir LAWRENCE S. SIKUTWA.

NICO Insurance Zambia Ltd (NIZA): 1131 Parirenyatwa Rd, Fairview, POB 32825, Lusaka; tel. (21) 1222862; fax (21) 1222863; e-mail nicozam@zamnet.zm; internet www.nicomw.com/zambia; f. 1997; subsidiary of NICO Group, Malawi; general insurance; Chair. JOHN MWANAKATWE; Gen. Man. TITUS KALENGA.

Professional Insurance Corpn Zambia Ltd (PICZ): Finsbury Park, Kabwe Roundabout, POB 34264, Lusaka; tel. (21) 1227509; fax (21) 1222151; e-mail customerservice@picz.co.zm; internet www.picz.co.zm; f. 1992; Chair. R. L. MATHANI; Man. Dir ASHOK CHAWLA.

Zambia State Insurance Corpn Ltd: Premium House, Independence Ave, POB 30894, Lusaka; tel. (21) 1229343; fax (21) 1222263; e-mail zsic@zsic.co.zm; internet www.zsic.co.zm; f. 1968; transfer to private sector pending; Chair. ALBERT WOOD; Man. Dir IRENE MUYENGA.

ZIGI Insurance Co Ltd: Mukuba Pension House, 5th Floor, POB 37782, Lusaka; tel. (21) 1226835; fax (21) 1231564; e-mail zigi@zamnet.zm; f. 1998; Chair. and CEO SAVIOUR H. KONIE.

Regulatory Authority

Pensions and Insurance Authority: Private Bag 30X, Ridgeway, Lusaka; tel. (21) 1293533; fax (21) 1293530; e-mail pia@pia.org.zm; internet www.pia.org.zm; f. 2005; Registrar MARTIN LIBINGA.

Trade and Industry

GOVERNMENT AGENCIES

Food Reserve Agency (FRA): Plot 7419, Manda Rd Light Industrial Area, POB 34054, Lusaka; tel. (21) 286097; fax (21) 1286096; e-mail fra@fra.org.zm; internet www.fra.org.zm; f. 1996; Exec. Dir LOVEJOY MALAMBO.

Zambia Development Agency: Privatisation House, Nasser Rd, POB 30819, Lusaka; tel. (21) 1220177; fax (21) 1225270; e-mail info@zda.org.zm; internet www.zda.org.zm; f. 2006 by merger of the Zambia Privatisation Agency, the Zambia Investment Centre, the Export Board of Zambia, the Zambia Export Processing Zones Authority and the Small Enterprises Development Board; operational in July 2007; 262 cos privatized by mid-2006, 22 privatizations pending; Dir-Gen. and CEO ANDREW CHIPWENDE.

Zambia Revenue Authority: Lusaka; internet www.zra.org.zm; f. 1994; Dir-Gen. WISDOM NEKAIRO.

DEVELOPMENT ORGANIZATION

Industrial Development Corpn of Zambia Ltd (INDECO): Indeco House, Buteko Place, POB 31935, Lusaka; tel. (21) 1228026; fax (21) 1228868; f. 1960; auth. cap. K300m.; taken over by the Nat. Housing Authority in May 2005; Chair. R. L. BWALYA; Man. Dir S. K. TAMELÉ.

CHAMBERS OF COMMERCE

Zambia Association of Chambers of Commerce and Industry: Great East Rd, Showgrounds, POB 30844, Lusaka; tel. (21) 1252483; fax (21) 1253020; e-mail secretariat@zacci.co.zm; internet www.zambiachambers.org; f. 1938; Pres. GEOFFREY SAKULANDA; CEO PRISCA M. CHIKWASHI; 16 district chambers, 11 trade assocs, 48 corporate mems.

Member chambers and associations include:

Chamber of Mines of Zambia: POB 22100, Kitwe; tel. (21) 2214122; f. 1941 as Northern Rhodesia Chamber of Mines; replaced by the Copper Industry Service Bureau 1965–2000; represents mining employers; 19 mems; Pres. NATHAN CHISHIMBA; Gen. Man. FREDERICK BANTUBONSE.

Zambia Association of Manufacturers: POB 30036, Lusaka; tel. (21) 1242780; fax (21) 1222912; e-mail babbar@zamnet.zm; f. 1985; Chair. CHANCE KABAGHE; 180 mems.

INDUSTRIAL AND TRADE ASSOCIATIONS

Tobacco Board of Zambia (TBZ): POB 31963, Lusaka; tel. (21) 1288995; fax (21) 1287118; e-mail tbz@zamnet.zm; promotes, monitors and controls tobacco production; CEO AVEN MUVWENDE.

Zambia Farm Employers' Association (ZFEA): Farmers' Village, Lusaka Agricultural and Commercial Showgrounds, POB 30395, Lusaka; tel. (21) 1252649; fax (21) 1252648; e-mail znfu@zamnet.zm; Chair. R. DENLY; 350 mems.

Other associations include: the Bankers' Asscn of Zambia; the Cotton Asscn of Zambia; the Environmental Conservation Asscn of Zambia; the Insurance Brokers' Asscn of Zambia; the Kapenta Fishermen Asscn; the National Aquaculture Asscn of Zambia; the National Council for Construction; the Poultry Asscn of Zambia; the Tobacco Asscn of Zambia; the Wildlife Producers' Asscn of Zambia; the Young Farmers' Clubs of Zambia; the Zambia Asscn of Clearing and Forwarding; the Zambia Asscn of Manufacturers; the Zambia Coffee Growers' Asscn; the Zambia Export Growers' Asscn; and Zambian Women in Agriculture.

EMPLOYERS' ORGANIZATION

Zambia Federation of Employers (ZFE): Electra House, 1st Floor, Cairo Rd, POB 31941, Lusaka; e-mail zfe@zamnet.zm; internet www.zfe.co.zm; f. 1966; Pres. ALFRED MASUPHA.

UTILITIES

Electricity

Copperbelt Energy Corpn PLC (CEC): Private Bag E835, Postnet No. 145, Chindo Rd, Kabulonga, Lusaka; tel. (21) 1261647; fax (21) 1261640; e-mail info@cec.com.zm; internet www.cecinvestor.com; f. 1997 upon privatization of the power div. of Zambia Consolidated Copper Mines; privately owned co supplying power generated by ZESCO to mining cos in the Copperbelt; Exec. Chair. HANSON SINDOWE.

ZESCO (Zambia Electricity Supply Corpn) Ltd: Stand 6949, Great East Rd, POB 33304, Lusaka; tel. (21) 1226084; fax (21) 1222753; e-mail mchisela@zesco.co.zm; internet www.zesco.co.zm; f. 1970; state-owned; Chair. KWALELA LAMASWALA; Man. Dir CYPRIAN CHITUNDU.

MAJOR COMPANIES

The following are among the largest companies in terms either of capital investment or employment.

British American Tobacco (Zambia) PLC: POB 31062, Lusaka; tel. (21) 1272287; fax (21) 1272291; e-mail johan_grobbelaar@bat.com; revenue K67,231m. (2005).

Kafue Textiles (Zambia) Ltd (KTZ): POB 360131, Kafue; tel. (21) 1311501; fax (21) 1311514; f. 1969; subsidiary of MB Int. Ltd; privatized March 2005; mfrs of drills, denims, twills and poplins; dress prints and African prints; industrial and household textiles; Chair. S. C. KOPULANDE; Gen. Man. and CEO J. P. BONDAZ; c. 400 employees.

Konkola Copper Mines PLC (KCM): Stand M/1408, Fern Ave, Private Bag KCM (C) 2000, Chingola; tel. (21) 2350000; e-mail samuel.equamo@kcm.co.zm; internet www.kcm.co.zm; f. 2000; 51% owned by Vedanta Resources, India; 28.4% by Zambia Copper Investments Ltd; and 20.6% by ZCCM Investment Holdings PLC; acquired ZCCM mining operations in 2000; mines at Chingola (Nchanga), Chililabombwe (Konkola) and Nampundwe; smelter and refinery at Kitwe; produces around one-half of national copper output; Chair. NAVIN AGARWAL; CEO JEYAKUMAR JANAKARAJ; 10,500 permanent employees and 2,600 contract employees.

ZCCM—Investment Holdings PLC (ZCCM—IH): Mukuba Pension House, 1st Floor, Plot 5309, Dedan Kimathi Rd, POB 30048, Lusaka 10101; tel. (21) 1221023; fax (21) 1221057; e-mail corporate@zccm-ih.com.zm; internet www.zccm-ih.com.zm; f. 1982 pursuant to privatization of Consolidated Copper Mines and Roan Consolidated Mines Ltd; 87.6% govt owned; Chair. W. D. MUNG'OMBA; CEO MUKELA MUYUNDA.

Lafarge Cement Zambia PLC: 1880 Kafue Rd, POB 32639, Lusaka; tel. (21) 1279029; fax (21) 1278134; e-mail cement.enquiries@lafarge-zm.lafarge.com; f. 1949; privatized in 1994; subsidiary of Lafarge Cement; cement plants at Chilanga and Ndola; manufacture and marketing of cement; Chair. MUNAKUPYA HANTUBA; Man. Dir FOLA ESAN; 445 employees.

Metal Fabricators of Zambia Ltd (ZAMEFA): Cha Cha Cha Rd, POB 90295, Luanshya; tel. (21) 2510453; fax (21) 2512637; e-mail jzulu@zamefa.co.zm; f. 1967; privatized in 1996; 82% owned by Phelps Dodge Int. Corpn, USA; 18% by Zambia Privatisation Trust Fund; mfrs of copper rods, and copper and aluminium wire and cables; CEO LOUIS CORTE; c. 800 employees.

Minestone (Zambia) Ltd: POB 31870, Lusaka; tel. (21) 1228748; fax (21) 1222301; f. 1954; cap. K1.9m.; building, civil and mechanical contractors; Gen. Man. MARK CHISANGA (acting); 3,900 employees.

Mopani Copper Mines PLC (MCM): Central Ave, Kitwe; tel. (21) 2247000; f. 1932; privatized in 2000; 73% owned by Glencore Int. AG, Switzerland; 16.9% by First Quantum Minerals Ltd, Canada; 10% by ZCCM—IH; copper mine, smelter and refinery at Mufuklira; copper mine and cobalt plant at Nkana; annual production: 160,000 tons of copper ore, 2,000 tons of cobalt (2004); Chair. EMMANUEL MUTATI; CEO DANNY CALLOW; 9,600 permanent employees and 6,400 contractors.

National Milling Co Ltd (NMC): POB 31980, Lusaka; tel. (21) 1248045; fax (21) 1242022; e-mail seaboard@seaboardcorp.com; privatized in 1996; acquired by Seaboard Corpn, USA, in 1998; mfrs of maize flour and stockfeeds; Man. Dir DAVID BOSSE; five maize mills.

Nitrogen Chemicals of Zambia Ltd (NCZ): POB 360226, Kafue; tel. (21) 1312279; fax (21) 1321706; e-mail nitrochem@yahoo.com; f. 1967; govt-owned; production of ammonium nitrate for fertilizer and explosives, nitric acid, ammonium sulphate, sulphuric acid, methanol, compound fertilizers and liquid carbon dioxide; revenue US $20.5m. (2008); CEO RICHARD N. SOKO; 509 employees.

Parmalat Zambia: Mungwi Rd, POB 34930, Lusaka; tel. (21) 1286855; fax (21) 1289388; f. 1964 as Dairy Produce Board of Zambia; bought by Bonnita, South Africa, in 1996; acquired by Parmalat Int., Italy, in 1998; producers of milk and mfrs of dairy products and fruit juices; Man. Dir PIET THERON.

Puma Energy Zambia PLC: Mukuba Pension House, Dedani Kamathi Rd, POB 31999, Lusaka; tel. (21) 1228684; fax (21) 1223645; f. 1963; privatized in 1996; fmrly BP Zambia PLC; name changed as above in 2011; 75% owned by Puma Energy (Switzerland); retail and distribution of petroleum products; Chair. JACOB SIKAZWE; Man. Dir FUMU MONDOLOKA; c. 380 employees.

Shoprite Zambia: Manda Hill Shopping Centre, Plot 19255, cnr Great East/Manchinchi Rds, POB 37226, Lusaka; tel. (21) 1255210; fax (21) 1235437; internet www.shoprite.co.zm; f. 1995; wholly owned subsidiary of Shoprite Group, South Africa; supermarket retail and distribution; revenue K276,000,000m. (2002); 1,698 employees (2003).

Zambeef Products PLC: Plot 1164, House No. 1, Nkanchibaya Rd off Addis Ababa Dr., Rhodes Park, Private Bag 17, Woodlands, Lusaka; tel. (21) 1252476; fax (21) 1252496; e-mail info@zambeef.co.zm; internet www.zambeef.com; interests in arable and livestock farming and processing, feedlotting, and retail; group comprises Zamleather Ltd and Zambeef Retailing Ltd subsidiaries; revenue US $43m. (2005); Chair. JACOB MWANZA; CEO FRANCIS GROGAN; 1,531 employees.

Zambezi Sawmills (2005) Ltd: POB 61286, Livingstone; tel. 979070729; internet www.zambezisawmill.com; f. 1911; nationalized in 1968 as Zambezi Sawmills (1968) Ltd; privatized in 1991; production ceased in 1996; went into liquidation in 2001; revived in 2005; Chair. FRED CHUNGA.

Zambia Bata Shoe Company PLC: 6437 Mukwa Rd, Industrial Area, POB 30479, Lusaka; tel. (21) 1244397; fax (21) 1245663; e-mail info@batazambia.com; internet www.batazambia.com; f. 1937; Chair. E. DUTHIE; Man. Dir P. BACHI.

Zambian Breweries PLC: POB 31293, Mungwi Rd, Lusaka; tel. (21) 1244501; fax (21) 1240631; e-mail info.zambrew@zm.sabmiller.com; internet www.sabmiller.com; f. 1951; opened in Lusaka 1966; privatized 1994; subsidiary of SABMiller Africa BV, Netherlands; revenue K107,512m. (2006); brewing, bottling and distribution of beers and soft drinks; Chair. VALENTINE CHITALU; Man. Dir ANELE MALUMO; 1,300 employees.

Zambia Sugar PLC: POB 670240, Mazabuka; tel. (21) 3230666; fax (21) 3230116; e-mail administrator@zamsugar.zm; privatized 1995; 89.7% of Illovo Sugar Ltd, South Africa; accounts for 45% of domestic market; exports 10% of production to the EU; revenue K486,083m. (2005); Chair. FIDELIS BANDA; Man. Dir IAN PARROTT.

CO-OPERATIVE

Zambia Co-operative Federation Ltd: Co-operative House, Cha Cha Cha Rd, POB 33579, Lusaka; tel. 2220157; fax 2222516; f. 1973; agricultural marketing; supply of agricultural chemicals and implements; cargo haulage; insurance; agricultural credit; auditing and accounting; property and co-operative devt; Chair. B. TETAMASHIMBA; Man. Dir G. Z. SIBALE.

TRADE UNIONS

Zambia Congress of Trade Unions (ZCTU): National Center, Solidarity House, POB 31146, Lusaka; tel. (21) 1260016; fax (21) 1266680; e-mail zctu@microlink.zm; f. 1965; Pres. LEONARD HIKAUMBA; Sec.-Gen. ROY MWABA; c. 350,000 mems (2012).

Affiliated Unions

Airways and Allied Workers' Union of Zambia: Lusaka International Airport, 2nd Floor, Terminal Bldg, POB 30175, 10101 Lusaka; Pres. F. MULENGA; Gen. Sec. B. CHINYANTA.

Civil Servants' & Allied Workers' Union of Zambia (CSAWUZ): Plot 5045A, Mumbwa Rd, POB 50160, Lusaka; tel. and fax (21) 1287106; e-mail csuz@zamnet.zm; f. 1975; Pres. DAVY CHIYOBE; Gen. Sec. JOY BEENE; 35,000 mems.

Mineworkers' Union of Zambia (MUZ): POB 20448, Kitwe; tel. (21) 2214022; Pres. CHISIMBA NKOLE; 50,000 mems.

National Union of Building, Engineering and General Workers (NUBEGW): City Sq., Millers Bldg, Plot No. 1094, POB 21515, Kitwe; tel. (21) 2224468; fax (21) 2661119; e-mail nubegw@zamtel.zm; Chair. LUCIANO MUTALE (acting); Gen. Sec. P. N. NZIMA; 18,000 mems.

National Union of Commercial and Industrial Workers (NUCIW): 17 Obote Ave, POB 21735, Kitwe; tel. (21) 2228607; fax (21) 2225211; e-mail nuciw@zamtel.zm; internet nuciw.org; f. 1982; Chair. I. M. KASUMBU; Gen. Sec. JOHN M. BWALYA; 16,000 mems.

National Union of Communication Workers: POB 70751, 92 Broadway, Ndola; tel. (21) 2611345; fax (21) 2614679; e-mail nucw@zamtel.zm; Pres. PATRICK KAONGA; Gen. Sec. CLEMENT KASONDE; 4,700 mems.

National Union of Plantation and Agricultural Workers: POB 80529, Kabwe; tel. (21) 5224548; e-mail nupawhq@yahoo.com; Pres. MUDENDA RISHER; Gen. Sec. MULENGA MUKUKA; 15,155 mems.

National Union of Public Services' Workers (NUPSW): POB 32523, Lusaka; tel. (21) 1227451; fax (21) 1287105; e-mail znslib@zamtel.zm; Gen. Sec. DAVIS J. CHINGONI.

National Union of Transport and Allied Workers (NUTAW): Cha Cha Cha House, Rm 4, 1st Floor, POB 30068, Cario Rd, Lusaka; tel. (21) 1214756; e-mail sapphiri2005@yahoo.com; Pres. PATRICK C. CHANDA; Gen. Sec. SAM A. P. PHIRI.

Railway Workers' Union of Zambia: POB 80302, Kabwe; tel. (21) 5224006; Chair. H. K. NDAMANA; Gen. Sec. BENSON L. NGULA; 10,228 mems.

Zambia Graphical and Allied Workers' Union (ZAGRAWU): POB 290346, Ndola; tel. and fax (21) 2614457; e-mail zatawu@yahoo.com; Gen. Sec. DAVID S. MWABA.

Zambia National Farmers' Union: ZNFU Head Office, Tiyende Pamodzi Rd, opp. Polo Grounds, Farmers' Village, Zambia Agricultural and Commercial Showgrounds, POB 30395, Lusaka; tel. (21) 1252649; fax (21) 1252648; e-mail znfu@zamnet.zm; internet www.znfu.org.zm; Pres. JARVIS ZIMBA.

Zambia National Union of Teachers: POB 31914, Lusaka; tel. (21) 1214623; fax (21) 1214624; e-mail znut@microlink.zm; Chair. RICHARD M. LIYWALII; Gen. Sec. ROY MWABA; 2,120 mems.

Zambia United Local Authorities Workers' Union (ZULAWU): Mugala House, POB 70575, Ndola; tel. (21) 2615022; Gen. Sec. NOEL KALANGU.

Principal Non-affiliated Union

Mine-workers Union of Zambia (MUZ): POB 20448, Kitwe; f. 1967; Pres. CHISHIMBA NKOLE; 40,000 mems.

Transport

RAILWAYS

The total length of railways in Zambia was 2,162 km (including 891 km of the Tanzania–Zambia railway) in 2000. There are two major railway networks: the Zambia Railways network, which traverses the country from the Copperbelt in northern Zambia and links with the National Railways of Zimbabwe to provide access to South African ports, and the Tanzania–Zambia Railway (Tazara) network, linking New Kapiri-Mposhi in Zambia with Dar es Salaam in Tanzania.In August 2010 a 27-km railway line linking Chipata with Mchinji, Malawi, was inaugurated. There were plans to link Mulobezi with the Namibian railway system.

Tanzania–Zambia Railway Authority (Tazara): POB T01, Mpika; Head Office: POB 2834, Dar es Salaam, Tanzania; tel. (21) 4370684; fax (21) 4370228; f. 1975; operates passenger and freight services linking New Kapiri-Mposhi, north of Lusaka, with Dar es Salaam in Tanzania, a distance of 1,860 km, of which 891 km is in Zambia; jtly owned and administered by the Govts of Tanzania and Zambia; Chair. SALIM H. MSOMA; Man. Dir AKASHAMBATWA MBIKUSITA-LEWANIKA.

Zambia Railways Ltd: cnr Buntungwa St and Ghana Ave, POB 80935, Kabwe; tel. (21) 5222201; fax (21) 5224411; f. 1967; Chair. B. NONDE; Man. Dir REGINA MWALE (acting).

ROADS

In 2001 there was a total road network of 91,440 km, including 4,222 km of main roads and 8,948 km of secondary roads. The main arterial roads run from Beitbridge (Zimbabwe) to Tunduma (the Great North Road), through the copper-mining area to Chingola and Chililabombwe (hitherto the Zaire Border Road), from Livingstone to the junction of the Kafue river and the Great North Road, and from Lusaka to the Malawi border (the Great East Road). In 1984 the 300-km BotZam highway linking Kazungula with Nata, in Botswana, was formally opened. A 1,930-km main road (the TanZam highway) links Zambia and Tanzania.

Road Development Agency: POB 50003, Lusaka; tel. (21) 1253801; fax (21) 1253404; e-mail rda_hq@roads.gov.zm; internet www.rda.org.zm; f. 2002; fmrly Dept of Roads; CEO ERASMUS CHILUNDIKA.

CIVIL AVIATION

In 2011 there were four designated international airports in Zambia, at Lusaka, Ndola, Livingstone and Mfuwe.

Department of Civil Aviation: Block 26A, Independence Ave, Ridgeway, POB 5013, Lusaka; tel. (21) 1251861; fax (21) 1251841; e-mail aviation@coppernet.zm; internet www.dca.com.zm.

National Airports Corpn Ltd (NACL): Airport Rd, 10101 Lusaka; tel. (21) 1271313; fax (21) 1271048; e-mail nacl@zamnet.zm; internet www.lun.aero; f. 1973; air cargo services; Man. Dir ROBINSON MISITALA.

Proflight Zambia: Site 15B, Private Hangars, Lusaka International Airport, POB 30536, Lusaka; tel. (21) 1271032; fax (21) 1271139; e-mail reservations@proflight-zambia.com; internet www.proflight-zambia.com; f. 2004; Chair. TONY IRWIN.

Zambezi Airlines: Petroda House, 2nd Floor, Great East Rd, Rhodes Park, POB 35470, Lusaka; tel. (21) 1257606; fax (21) 1257631; e-mail info@flyzambezi.com; internet www.flyzambezi.com; f. 2008; Chair. Dr MAURICE JANGULO; CEO DON MACDONALD.

Tourism

Zambia's main tourist attractions, in addition to the Victoria Falls, are its wildlife, unspoilt scenery and diverse cultural heritage; there are 19 national parks and 36 game management areas. In 2009 709,948 tourists visited Zambia; tourism receipts totalled US $98m. in that year.

Tourism Council of Zambia: 55–56 Mulungushi International Conference Centre, POB 36561, Lusaka; tel. (21) 1291788; fax (21) 1290436; e-mail secretariat.tcz@iconnect.zm; internet www.tcz.org.zm; f. 1997; Exec. Dir VICTOR INAMBWAE.

Zambia National Tourist Board: Century House, Lusaka Sq., POB 30017, Lusaka; tel. (21) 1229087; fax (21) 1225174; e-mail zntb@zambiatourism.org.zm; internet www.zambiatourism.com; Chair. ERROL HICKEY; Man. Dir CHANDA CHARITY LUMPA.

Defence

As assessed at November 2011, Zambia's armed forces officially numbered about 15,100 (army 13,500 and air force 1,600). Paramilitary forces numbered 1,400. Military service is voluntary. There is also a National Defence Force, responsible to the Government. In 2009 some 600 Zambian troops were stationed abroad, attached to UN missions in Africa and Asia; of these, 49 were serving as observers.

Defence Expenditure: Estimated at K1,850,000m. for 2012.

Commander of the Army: Lt-Gen. PAUL MIHOVA.

Commander of the Air Force: Lt-Gen. ANDREW SAKALA.

Education

Primary education, which is compulsory, begins at seven years of age and lasts for seven years. Secondary education, beginning at the age of 14, lasts for a further five years, comprising a first cycle of two years and a second of three years. According to UNESCO estimates, in 2008/09 91% of children (90% of boys; 92% of girls) in the relevant age group attended primary schools, while enrolment at secondary schools included 46% of children (51% of boys; 42% of girls) in the relevant age group. There are two universities: the University of Zambia at Lusaka, and the Copperbelt University at Kitwe, which had a combined total of some 16,655 students in 2010. There are 14 teacher training colleges. The 2011 budgetary allocation for the education sector was equivalent to 18.6% of the overall budget.

Bibliography

Akashambatwa, M. *Milk in a Basket: The Political-Economic Malaise in Zambia.* Lusaka, Zambia Research Foundation, 1990.

Andersson, P., Bigsten, A., and Persson, H. *Foreign Aid, Debt and Growth in Zambia.* Uppsala, Nordiska Africainstitutet, 2001.

Bonnick, G. G. *Zambia Country Assistance Review: Turning an Economy Around.* Washington, DC, World Bank, 1997.

Carmody, B. P. *The Evolution of Education in Zambia.* Lusaka, Bookworld Publrs, 2004.

Chan, S. *Zambia and the Decline of Kaunda 1984–1998.* Lewiston, NY, Edward Mellen Press, 2000.

Crehan, K. *The Fractured Community: Landscapes of Power and Gender in Rural Zambia.* Berkeley, CA, University of California Press, 1997.

Ferguson, J. *Expectations of Modernity.* Berkeley, CA, University of California Press, 1999.

Fraser, A., and Larmer, M. (Eds). *Zambia, Mining, and Neoliberalism: Boom and Bust on the Globalized Copperbelt.* Basingstoke, Palgrave Macmillan, 2011.

Gewald, J-B., Hinfelaar, M., and Macola, G. (Eds). *Living the End of Empire: Politics and Society in Late Colonial Zambia.* Leiden, Brill, 2011.

Grotpeter, J. J., Siegel, B. V., and Pletcher, J. R. *Historical Dictionary of Zambia.* Lanham, MD, Scarecrow Press, 1998.

Hamalengwa, M. *Class Struggle in Zambia, 1884–1989, and the Fall of Kenneth Kaunda, 1990–1991.* Lanham, MD, University Press of America, 1992.

Hill, C. B., and McPherson, M. F. *Promoting and Sustaining Economic Reform in Zambia.* Cambridge, MA, Harvard University Press, 2003.

Ihonvbere, J. O. *Economic Crisis, Civil Society and Democratization: The Case of Zambia.* Trenton, NJ, Africa World Press, 1996.

Larmer, M. *Mineworkers in Zambia: Labour and Political Change in Post-colonial Africa.* London, Tauris Academic Studies, 2006.

Macmillan, H., and Shapiro, F. *Zion in Africa—The Jews of Zambia.* London and New York, I. B. Tauris, 1999.

Makungu, K. *The State of the Media in Zambia: From the Colonial Era to December 2003.* Lusaka, Media Institute of Southern Africa, Zambian Chapter, 2004.

Meebelo, H. S. *Reaction to Colonialism: A Prelude to the Politics of Independence in Northern Zambia, 1839–1939.* International Academic Publrs, 2001.

Moore, H., and Vaughan, M. *Cutting Down Trees: Gender, Nutrition and Agricultural Change in Northern Province, Zambia, 1890–1990.* Zambia, University of Zambia Press, 1994.

Moore, R. C. *The Political Reality of Freedom of the Press in Zambia.* Lanham, MD, University Press of America, 1992.

Mutale, E. *The Management of Urban Development in Zambia.* Aldershot, Ashgate, 2004.

Mwanakatwe, J. M. *End of Kaunda Era.* Lusaka, Multimedia, 1994.

Mwanza, A. M. (Ed.). *The Structural Adjustment Programme in Zambia: Lessons from Experience.* Harare, SAPES Books, 1992.

Noyoo, N. *Social Policy and Human Development in Zambia.* London, Adonis & Abbey Publishers, 2010.

Puta-Chekwe, C. *Getting Zambia to Work.* London, Adonis & Abbey Publishers, 2011.

Rakner, L. *Trade Unions in Processes of Democratisation: A Study of Party Labour Relations in Zambia.* Bergen, Michelsen Institute, 1992.

Saasa, O., and Carlsson, J. *The Aid Relationship in Zambia: A Conflict Scenario.* Uppsala, Nordiska Afrikainstitutet, 1996.

Saasa, O., Wilson, F., and Chingambo, L. *The Zambian Economy in Post-Apartheid Southern Africa: A Critical Analysis of Policy Options.* Lusaka, IAS Consultancy Services, 1992.

Sichone, O., and Chikulo, B. *Democracy in Zambia.* Aldershot, Avebury, 1997.

Van Binsbergen, W. *Tears of Rain: Ethnicity and History in Central Western Zambia.* London, Kegan Paul International, 1992.

Wood, A. P. (Ed.). *Dynamics of Agricultural Policy and Reform in Zambia.* Ames, IO, Iowa State University Press, 1990.

ZIMBABWE

Physical and Social Geography

GEORGE KAY

The Republic of Zimbabwe, covering an area of 390,757 sq km (150,872 sq miles), is land-locked and is bounded on the north and north-west by Zambia, on the south-west by Botswana, by Mozambique on the east and on the south by South Africa. The census of August 2002 enumerated 11,631,657 persons. By mid-2012 the population had increased to 13,013,679, according to UN estimates, giving an average density of 33.3 inhabitants per sq km.

The population of Zimbabwe has altered considerably in recent years. At mid-1980 it was estimated to include some 223,000 persons of European descent and some 37,000 Asians and Coloureds, all of them a legacy of the colonial era. However, the census of 2002 recorded the number of Europeans (whites) at just 46,743 and that number was believed to have declined further to less than 30,000 by 2008. The indigenous inhabitants broadly comprise two ethnic or linguistic groups, the Ndebele and the Shona. The Shona, with whom political power now rests, outnumber the Ndebele by 4:1. There are, in addition, several minor ethnic groups, such as the Tonga, Sena, Hlengwe, Venda and Sotho. The official languages are English, ChiShona and SiNdebele.

In recent years urban growth has proceeded rapidly. The urban poor, operating within the highly competitive 'informal economy', are now a large and increasing part of the urban social structure. During 1982–92 the population of Harare, the capital, grew from 656,000 to 1,189,103, while that of Bulawayo increased from 413,800 to 621,742. At mid-2011, according to UN estimates, the population of Harare (including suburbs) was 1,541,570.

Zimbabwe lies astride the high plateaux between the Zambezi and Limpopo rivers. It consists of four relief regions. The Highveld, comprising land more than 1,200 m above sea-level, extends across the country from south-west to north-east; it is most extensive in the north-east. The Middleveld, land of 900 m–1,200 m above sea-level, flanks the Highveld; it is most extensive in the north-west. The Lowveld, land below 900 m, occupies the Zambezi basin in the north and the more extensive Limpopo and Sabi-Lundi basins in the south and south-east. These three regions consist predominantly of gently undulating plateaux, except for the narrow belt of rugged, escarpment hills associated with faults along the Zambezi trough. The fourth physical region, the eastern highlands, is distinctive because of its mountainous character. Inyangani rises to 2,594 m and many hills exceed 1,800 m.

Temperatures vary by altitude. Mean monthly temperatures range from 22°C in October and 13°C in July on the Highveld to 30°C and 20°C in the low-lying Zambezi valley. Winters are noted for a wide diurnal range; night frosts can occur on the high plateaux and can occasionally be very destructive.

Rainfall is largely restricted to the period November–March and, except on the eastern highlands, is extremely variable; in many regions it is too low for commercial crop production. Mean annual rainfall ranges from 1,400 mm on the eastern highlands, to 800 mm on the north-eastern Highveld and to less than 400 mm in the Limpopo valley. The development of water resources for economic uses is a continually pressing need which, to date, has been met by a major dam-building programme. Underground water resources are limited.

Soils vary considerably. Granite occurs over more than one-half of the country and mostly gives rise to infertile sandy soils; these are, however, amenable to improvement. Kalahari sands are also extensive and provide poor soils. Soil-forming processes are limited in the Lowveld and, except on basalt, soils there are generally immature. Rich, red clays and loams occur on the limited outcrops of Basement Schists, which are also among the most highly mineralized areas of Zimbabwe.

Climatic factors are the chief determinants of agricultural potential and six broad categories of land have been defined largely on bio-climatic conditions: Grade I (1.6% of the country) with good, reliable rainfall—suitable for specialized and diversified farming, including tree crops; Grade II (18.7%) with moderately high rainfall—suitable for intensive commercial crop production with subsidiary livestock farming; Grade III (17.4%) with mediocre rainfall conditions—suitable for semi-extensive commercial livestock farming with supplementary production of drought-resistant crops; Grade IV (33%) with low and unreliable rainfall—suitable for semi-extensive livestock production; Grade V (26.2%) semi-arid country—suitable only for extensive ranching; and Grade VI (3.1%—probably underestimated) which, because of steep slopes, skeletal soils, swamps, etc., is unsuitable for any agricultural use. The seizure of white-owned commercial farms from 2000 adversely affected agricultural production (see Economy).

Zimbabwe possesses a wide variety of workable mineral deposits, which include gold, platinum, asbestos, copper, chrome, nickel, palladium, cobalt, tin, iron ore, limestone, iron pyrites, phosphates and coal. Most mineralization occurs on the Highveld and adjacent parts of the Middleveld.

The socio-economic difficulties of rural African society are compounded by ecological problems. While some extensive areas (notably in remote northern parts of the country) remain sparsely populated, the greater part of the communal lands suffers from overpopulation and overstocking. Deforestation, soil erosion and a deterioration of wildlife and water resources are widespread, and in some areas they have reached critical dimensions. Desertification is a real danger in the semi-arid regions of the country.

Recent History

CHRISTOPHER SAUNDERS

The boundaries of modern Zimbabwe were demarcated after Cecil Rhodes, mine magnate and then Prime Minister of the British Cape Colony, sent whites to settle north of the Limpopo river in 1890. The mineral deposits found there proved much more limited than Rhodes had hoped, but within a decade large areas of land had been seized from the Shona and Ndebele people and occupied by white farmers, mainly from Britain and South Africa. In 1923 the small white population of Southern Rhodesia, as the territory was then known, was accorded self-government. In 1953 Southern Rhodesia was united by the British Government with Northern Rhodesia and Nyasaland (now Zambia and Malawi, respectively) in a Central African Federation, which was opposed by Africans in all three territories. The British Government eventually recognized the strength of African hostility in Northern Rhodesia and Nyasaland, and conceded independence to those territories, breaking up the federation in 1963. Whites in Southern Rhodesia viewed these developments as the outcome of British appeasement, and in 1962 voted into office the newly formed Rhodesian Front (RF), which under Prime Minister Ian Smith in November 1965 declared unilateral independence from Britain. Repressive measures preceding this had seriously weakened the black African nationalist opposition, which in 1963 had split into the Zimbabwe African People's Union (ZAPU), led by Joshua Nkomo, and the breakaway Zimbabwe African National Union (ZANU), led by Rev. Ndabaningi Sithole and subsequently Robert Mugabe. These nationalists embarked upon a 'people's war' to overthrow the Smith regime. ZAPU, based mainly in Zambia, received training and armaments from the USSR. ZANU developed strong links with the Frente de Libertação de Moçambique movement fighting the Portuguese in Mozambique, and with the People's Republic of China.

From 1976 a combined struggle was waged in the name of the Patriotic Front (PF), an uneasy alliance formed by ZAPU and ZANU. In that year Smith was pressured by South Africa to concede the principle of majority rule. Smith and the South African Government then hoped that they could arrange for a moderate black party to take over, with the white minority retaining ultimate control. Such an 'internal settlement' was put in place in early 1979, but with the nationalists excluded from it, the war continued. All parties were then persuaded by the British Government to attend a conference at Lancaster House in London, United Kingdom, to reach an inclusive settlement. At this conference it was agreed that the United Kingdom would again take control of the country for a short period, during which an election would take place, monitored by the United Kingdom and the Commonwealth, after which the country would move to independence. The small white minority was given 20 of the 100 seats in the House of Assembly and the United Kingdom gave only vague assurances of a fund to assist in the redistribution of land. Mugabe was reluctant to sign the agreement, but was pressured to do so by Samora Machel of Mozambique, in whose country ZANU—PF had its military bases. Mugabe, however, correctly anticipated that his party, which had taken the lead in fighting the liberation war, would triumph in the election, held in February 1980. ZANU—PF won 57 of the 80 African seats, taking 63% of the votes, while Nkomo's ZAPU won 20 seats. On 18 April Mugabe became the first Prime Minister of independent Zimbabwe.

Mugabe initially adopted a conciliatory stance. To restore stability, he quickly stressed the need for reconciliation; disavowed rapid change towards his stated socialist goals; emphasized non-alignment in foreign affairs; and included two whites in his Cabinet. Nevertheless, the new Government was faced with formidable problems arising from the ravages of war and the expectations aroused in the struggle against settler rule, especially around land redistribution. The South African Government, which regarded Mugabe as a dangerous radical, waged a campaign of destabilization. Nkomo, who rejected Mugabe's offer of the ceremonial presidency, was soon ousted from the Cabinet, and dissident members of ZAPU's guerrilla army began to perpetrate minor acts of violence in Matabeleland. In response Mugabe used an army brigade, trained by the Democratic People's Republic of Korea (North Korea), to unleash a massive wave of terror in that province, in which perhaps 15,000 people were killed. The full scale of this atrocity was only revealed years later; at the time Mugabe escaped censure for it. Despite this, Nkomo was persuaded to enter into negotiations for a merger with ZANU—PF, and a unity accord was eventually signed in December 1987. Nkomo became one of two Vice-Presidents, but effectively ZAPU was swallowed by ZANU—PF. After an amnesty was proclaimed in April 1988 there was a rapid improvement in political and security conditions in Matabeleland.

By then constitutional changes had moved Zimbabwe closer to becoming a one-party state. The reservation of 20 seats for whites in the House of Assembly and 10 seats in the Senate was abolished in September 1987, and the following month the 80 remaining members of the Assembly elected 20 candidates, all nominated by ZANU—PF, to fill the vacant seats. Parliament also replaced the ceremonial presidency with an executive presidency incorporating the post of Prime Minister. Robert Mugabe was nominated as sole candidate for the office, and on 31 December he was inaugurated as Zimbabwe's first executive President. The Senate was abolished, and the House of Assembly enlarged to 150 seats, some filled by presidential nominees.

As unemployment and prices rose, open public and parliamentary criticism of corrupt government officials mounted. An anti-Government demonstration by students in September 1988 resulted in many arrests. In October a former Secretary-General of ZANU—PF, Edgar Tekere, was expelled from the party for his persistent denunciation of its leadership and policies, including the plans to introduce a one-party state. He then founded the Zimbabwe Unity Movement (ZUM). In July 1989 a rally of ZUM supporters at the University of Zimbabwe was attacked by the police. The Zimbabwe Congress of Trade Unions (ZCTU) issued a statement supporting the students, and its Secretary-General, Morgan Tsvangirai, was arrested and detained for six weeks. In the March 1990 general election, ZANU—PF secured 117 of the 120 elective seats, and ZUM two, while in the election for the presidency, Tekere received 413,840 votes and Mugabe secured 2.03m. votes.

After the Government adopted an Economic Structural Adjustment Programme (ESAP) in 1991, 'Marxism-Leninism' was increasingly replaced in official discourse by references to 'pragmatic socialism' and 'indigenous capitalism'. Vigorous debate followed the expiry of the remaining restrictions of the Lancaster House agreement on 18 April 1990. Constitutional amendments that restored corporal and capital punishment and denied recourse to the courts in cases of compulsory purchase of land by the Government were enacted in April 1991, despite fierce criticism from the judiciary and from human rights campaigners. Amid rising urban discontent fuelled by corruption scandals, declining real wages and the social consequences of the ESAP, the Government was increasingly preoccupied by the land issue, which it continued to regard as the key to retaining its grip on power. A Land Acquisition Act (LAA), adopted in 1992, provided for the compulsory acquisition of land by the state. This brought the Government into conflict with the powerful white-dominated Commercial Farmers' Union (CFU) and Western aid donors. Both groups were angered by the decision in April 1993 to designate 70 commercial white-owned farms for purchase. Many of them were productive holdings, which, it had been understood, were to be exempt from compulsory purchase. The Government eventually allowed appeals in a sufficient number of cases to suggest that an uneasy compromise had been reached, while the CFU announced in September that it would assist in the Government's resettlement programme, and its members were represented on the commission set up in November to make proposals for land tenure reforms. However, in March 1994 it was revealed that the first of the farms acquired under the LAA had been allocated to government minister Witness Mangwende, who had been Minister of

Agriculture when the Act was approved. The scandal escalated when the press revealed that most of the first 98 farms acquired by compulsory purchase had been leased to prominent party figures and civil servants and were not being used for peasant resettlement. The President responded by ordering the cancellation of all relevant leases. In November the High Court ruled against three white farmers who had attempted to prove that the confiscation of their land was unconstitutional; the farmers subsequently lost an appeal to the Supreme Court against the verdict. The United Kingdom, which had granted £40m. for land redistribution since independence, now refused to grant more because of the corruption involved in the process.

In the general election of April 1995, ZANU—PF received more than 82% of the votes and secured 118 of the 120 elective seats (55 of them uncontested), as well as control of 30 nominated and reserved seats. In August the High Court nullified the election result in the bitterly contested Harare South constituency, where more votes were cast than there were registered electors. This lent credence to opposition claims of widespread electoral malpractices. In the presidential election held on 16–17 March 1996, Mugabe won 93% of the votes cast, but only 32% of the eligible electorate voted.

LAND INVASIONS AND ELECTION FRAUD

During 1997 and 1998 the Mugabe administration was increasingly criticized for corruption, arrogance and maladministration. In August 1997 so-called 'war veterans' were awarded substantial benefits that had not been included in the budget, and in October, in an attempt to revive his declining popularity, Mugabe announced that the hitherto slow pace of the national land resettlement programme would be accelerated and white commercial farmers would not receive compensation for confiscated land. He challenged the United Kingdom, in its role as former colonial power, to take responsibility for assisting them, and a list of 1,471 properties to be reallocated forthwith was then published.

Following a South African Development Community (SADC) summit in Harare in August 1998, the Zimbabwe Government dispatched troops and arms to the Democratic Republic of the Congo (DRC) to support the regime of President Laurent-Désiré Kabila against advancing rebel forces. The action was domestically unpopular and placed Zimbabwe's financial and military resources under considerable strain. A cease-fire agreement was signed at Lusaka, Zambia, on 10 July, and troop withdrawals were supposed to follow within the next few months. However, within a few days both the rebels and the allies of the DRC were accused of violating the accord, and the Zimbabwean troops remained in the DRC in support of Kabila. This enabled the Mugabe Government to benefit economically from exploiting the DRC's natural resources, especially diamonds. Following the assassination of Kabila in January 2001 and the succession of his son, Joseph, to the DRC presidency, efforts to agree a solution to the conflict were accelerated, and all countries involved in the conflict agreed to withdraw their forces by May, pending the deployment of a UN force. In October 2002 Zimbabwean troops completed their withdrawal, following a number of positive developments in the peace process in the DRC.

In October 1998 the Government embarked on discussions with a National Constitutional Assembly of opposition interests on proposed changes to the country's Constitution, but Mugabe then unilaterally appointed a commission to make recommendations. The new constitution put to the voters in a referendum in February 2000 was essentially a ZANU—PF document, but 55% of the 26% of the electorate who participated in the polls voted to reject it. The level of participation was highest in urban areas, where support for the Movement for Democratic Change (MDC), which had been formed in September 1999 under the leadership of Tsvangirai, was strong. Mugabe accepted the referendum result, but a state-sponsored campaign of occupations of white-owned farms began, carried out by 'war veterans', many too young to have taken part in the liberation war. The security forces refused to act against the occupiers, and although Mugabe denied that his administration was behind the occupations, he made no secret of his support for them. The invasions became increasingly violent: two farmers were killed in April after Mugabe threatened war against farmers who refused to give up their land voluntarily. He called them 'enemies of the state', and spoke of the third 'Chimurenga' (Shona for struggle). He maintained that 'imperialist forces', the United Kingdom especially, were behind the formation of the MDC, and its supporters were the main targets of the state-sponsored violence.

In the June 2000 parliamentary election, which most international observers concluded had not been free and fair, ZANU—PF won 62 of the 120 contested seats in the House of Assembly. The MDC won 57 seats and subsequently challenged the results in 37 constituencies, on the grounds of either voter intimidation or electoral irregularities. After the election, increasing numbers of white-owned farms were listed for appropriation, until by mid-2001 the CFU, which had offered 1m. ha for resettlement, believed that 95% of all commercial farms, totalling 8.3m. ha, were destined for takeover. As a direct consequence of the continuing land invasions, agricultural production declined sharply, and relatively little new maize or tobacco was planted. By mid-2001 the Government claimed to have little foreign currency, and there was a severe fuel crisis. The manufacturing sector, long in decline, was especially adversely affected; some 400 manufacturers were forced to close their businesses within one year. With an estimated 60% of the work-force unemployed, an estimated 80% of the population now lived below the poverty line. The Government admitted that at least 500,000 metric tons of imported maize would be needed. Yet, new police equipment was imported from Israel, and the Government found almost Z.$1,000m. in unbudgeted funds to give further increases to the so-called war veterans. After the death in June 2001 of their leader, Chenjerai 'Hitler' Hunzvi, notorious for his inflammatory rhetoric, relations between the 'veterans' and the ZANU—PF leadership became even closer. When the Supreme Court ruled that the fast-track land reform programme could only continue if the Government presented a clear plan of action, Mugabe chose to interpret this as an invitation to continue to pursue the policy of seizing commercial farmland, much of which was taken over by members of the ruling élite.

Violence increased before the presidential election in March 2002. MDC supporters were systematically harassed and ill-treated by members of ZANU—PF and war veterans. Tsvangirai and two other senior members of the MDC were arrested and charged with treason for allegedly plotting to assassinate Mugabe. Land owned by white commercial farmers (12 of whom had been killed by mid-2002) continued to be seized. As many of the previously landless people who occupied the land of commercial farmers had no expertise in farming, production declined dramatically, and at least 70,000 farm workers lost their jobs as a consequence of the land reform programme. The politicians and army generals with no experience of farming who received large-scale commercial farms often sold what they found on the farms for massive financial gains. Torture and intimidation of opposition supporters was now widespread. Members of the police and army, and the youth brigades ('green bombers') acted with impunity.

When the presidential election took place, the voting period was extended by one day by the High Court, in response to a request from the MDC, which claimed that the number of polling stations in urban areas, where support for the MDC was strong, had been reduced by some 45%, while those in the Government's rural strongholds had been increased. The MDC alleged that many stations closed early, before numerous voters had been able to cast their ballots, and that a number of its agents had been abducted from polling stations and detained by the police. According to official results, Mugabe won 56.2% of the votes, and Tsvangirai 42.0%. Most observer groups, including that of the Commonwealth, found that conditions had not allowed for a free expression of the will of the electorate, and the South African observer mission gained notoriety for declaring the election 'legitimate'. The Presidents of South Africa, Nigeria and Malawi then attempted to broker talks between ZANU—PF and the MDC, but ZANU—PF would not participate after the MDC challenged the election result in the courts. After the election, another 2,900 white farmers were given a deadline by which to vacate their farms under the LAA. About one-half left their properties, but the rest remained on their farms and awaited the outcome of legal challenges to the legislation. Many of them were then arrested. In September 2002 the House of Assembly adopted an amendment to the LAA, which provided for the eviction of farmers within seven days of being served notice, rather than the 90-day deadline hitherto in force. Although Mugabe announced in early 2003 that his fast-track land redistribution programme was at an end, and instituted an audit of what had been achieved, seizures of white-owned land continued to take place.

Following a new wave of demonstrations in 2003, more MDC supporters were arrested and Tsvangirai was charged with treason for seeking to overthrow the Mugabe regime. While the MDC continued to express its willingness to enter into discussions with ZANU—PF, Mugabe insisted that it must first recognize that his re-election as President was legitimate, and withdraw its legal challenge to the 2002 election. Church leaders attempted to mediate between the two parties, and for a time informal talks took place between Patrick Anthony Chinamasa, the Minister of Justice, for ZANU—PF, and Welshman Ncube, Secretary-General of the MDC, but no significant progress was made. Mugabe insisted that the MDC sever its alleged ties with the West. Tsvangirai continued to be encumbered by his trial on treason charges. As the crisis intensified, Zimbabwe's position on the UN Human Development Index plummeted. Life expectancy, which had been 61 years in 1991, declined to 36 years in 2004, and by then an estimated 6,000 people were dying each week from AIDS-related diseases. Meanwhile, the country's economy contracted at a dramatic rate. Inflation soared to over 600%, and an estimated 75% of the population were now unemployed. Many industries were forced to close, and agricultural production continued to decline. Shortages of foreign currency, fuel, power, basic commodities and food became commonplace. Although the Government blamed drought and even economic sabotage by the opposition, its land redistribution policies were largely responsible for the massive decline of 67% in cereal production since 1999. Stocks of maize held by some commercial farmers were seized, and all maize producers had to sell their grain to the state-owned Grain Marketing Board; maize meal, cooking oil, salt and sugar became increasingly scarce.

In mid-2003 Mugabe announced plans to extend his land policy to the seizure of white-owned mines and industries, and to introduce legislation to force companies to offer one-fifth of their shares to local black investors. Although whites, who had constituted 5% of the total population in 1980, now made up only 0.5% of the population, they owned more than one-half of the companies listed on the Zimbabwe Stock Exchange. Meanwhile, an estimated 500,000 Zimbabweans had left the country, mostly to settle in the United Kingdom, Botswana and South Africa, often illegally in the case of the latter.

In late 2004 internecine conflict within ZANU—PF came to a head over the appointment of a new Vice-President to fill the vacancy created by the death of Simon Muzenda. A group led by Emmerson Mnangagwa, whom many had seen as the heir apparent, and Jonathan Moyo met to try to prevent the elevation of Joyce Mujuru, who had been in the Cabinet since independence and was Mugabe's choice for the post. Moyo was removed from the party's politburo and the Cabinet, however, and Mujuru was appointed Vice-President.

Prior to the March 2005 parliamentary election, many urged the MDC not to participate. The Supreme Court ruled in mid-March that those resident outside Zimbabwe would not be eligible to vote, but after lengthy deliberation, the MDC decided to participate in the ballot. The Government excluded foreign observers considered unsympathetic to its cause, and delayed accrediting other observers until one month before the poll. In that period overt political violence eased and the elections were held in relative calm. SADC and South African observers reported a credible process that 'reflected the will of the Zimbabwean people', but the USA and the European Union (EU), among others, condemned the elections as 'phony'. Many potential voters had been turned away from the polls, and there were gross discrepancies between official figures for the numbers of voters and the results. According to official results, the MDC won 41 of the 120 contested seats (39.5% of the votes cast), 16 fewer than in 2000, but it alleged gross electoral fraud and filed petitions at the Electoral Court challenging the results in 13 constituencies. Nevertheless, MDC members took up their seats in the House of Assembly, and the party welcomed the election of the relatively conciliatory John Nkomo as the new Speaker. ZANU—PF won 78 of the contested seats (59.6% of the vote), but the President could allocate 12 seats in the House of Assembly to candidates of his choosing and other seats were reserved for tribal chiefs, also loyal to Mugabe, so ZANU—PF gained the two-thirds' majority necessary to approve constitutional reforms. When Parliament convened in June 2005, the Government introduced legislation providing for the reintroduction of a second chamber. Meanwhile, it was announced that white farmers who had lost their farms during the resettlement programme would be compensated for the value of assets and improvements, but not for the land itself, which the Government maintained was the responsibility of the United Kingdom. The country's white population had declined from 200,000 in 2000 to around 25,000 at March 2005; of these, some 500 were farmers.

After the election, the economic situation deteriorated further: fuel was again in very short supply, and a devaluation of the currency did not improve matters. In May 2005 the police suddenly began 'Operation Restore Order' and 'Operation Murambatsvina' ('Sweep Away the Rubbish'), in which what were said to be illegal structures, informal shops and markets were bulldozed. The largest market in the country, Mbare in Harare, was entirely demolished, as were many houses. The destruction was carried out in a ruthless fashion, leaving hundreds of thousands of people, almost all of them MDC supporters, homeless. Some were placed in temporary accommodation, others were driven into the countryside. Mugabe claimed that the operation was designed to clean up the cities and end illegal activity, but critics countered that no provision had been made for those left homeless, and many suspected that the destruction was, at least in part, an act of vengeance against those who had voted for the MDC in the March election. The UN Secretary-General dispatched an envoy to report on the situation, who was harshly critical of the evictions, but the Zimbabwean Government claimed that her report was biased and ill-informed. Although the Government suggested that it would build new homes for those made homeless by 'Operation Murambatsvina', no action was taken and the evictions continued.

The MDC proved unable to capitalize on the ongoing crisis. Its appeal for a national strike at the time of the opening of Parliament in June 2005 was not widely observed. Mugabe continued to accuse the MDC of being in league with foreign enemies of the country, and to claim that Zimbabwe's economic problems were a result of sabotage by Western governments opposed to the seizure of white land. Human rights groups charged that the police were implicated in numerous cases of arbitrary actions, assaults and various forms of ill-treatment. Freedom of expression and assembly remained severely curtailed and numerous journalists were arrested for failing to seek accreditation.

In late 2005 the MDC split over the question of participating in the election of members of the new Senate. In that election turn-out was very low and ZANU—PF won 43 of the 50 directly elected seats. Although most members of the MDC, led by Tsvangirai, rejected the idea of participating, a faction led by Gibson Sibanda, the party Vice-President, and Ncube, the Secretary-General, insisted on doing so. Arthur Mutambara, a scientist who returned from exile, took over leadership of the breakaway group. Tsvangirai was able to reassert his leadership over the main body of MDC supporters, and demanded that a commission be established to investigate political and human rights abuses and corruption.

THE CRISIS DEEPENS

By 2006 commercial agricultural production had contracted by 60%–70% since the land redistribution exercise began in 2000. The commercial herd had decreased from 1.2m. cattle to just 150,000, and milk production had halved. In March 2007 Tsvangirai and other leading MDC figures were savagely beaten by the police when trying to hold a prayer rally in Harare; one MDC activist was killed in the incident. Justifying what had happened, Mugabe claimed that the MDC was responsible for a spate of petrol bombings earlier in the month aimed at bringing about regime change. President Thabo Mbeki of South Africa, appointed by SADC as mediator, continued to engage in 'quiet diplomacy' to try to set the scene for free and fairly harmonized presidential and parliamentary elections in 2008. As reports increased of torture, arbitrary killings and intimidation of members of the opposition, Mugabe announced unilaterally that the elections would take place on 29 March 2008. No monitors from Western countries were allowed and the now 4m. Zimbabweans in exile were not permitted to vote.

Following the elections, the Zimbabwe Electoral Commission (ZEC) delayed announcing the official results. It eventually conceded that the faction of the MDC led by Tsvangirai (MDC—T) had secured 99 of the 210 seats in the House of Assembly, ZANU—PF 97 seats and the MDC faction led by Mutambara (MDC—M) 10 seats. However, no immediate announcement was made regarding the outcome of the presidential poll. Widespread irregularities were reported, and observers expressed concern that the delay in releasing official results was allowing the ruling party to manipulate ballot papers. It was only on 2 May that the ZEC released results of the disputed presidential election. According to the Commission, Tsvangirai had secured 47.9% of the votes and Mugabe 43.2%, which meant that a second round of voting had to be conducted. The date for this was eventually set for 27 June. Tsvangirai remained outside the country, fearing for his safety if he returned, and established a number of conditions for his participation in the run-off, including the presence of international peace-keepers, election monitors, free media and an end to violence. He subsequently agreed to participate even though these conditions were not met and returned to Zimbabwe in mid-May, despite a now systematic campaign of retributive violence and terror against MDC supporters by state agents and their allies. The MDC's campaigning was severely restricted, and Tsvangirai was arrested a number of times, but released without charge on each occasion, while the MDC Secretary-General, Tendai Biti, was arrested and charged with election-rigging and other crimes. Election observers from SADC countries only began arriving shortly before the poll.

On 22 June 2008 Tsvangirai withdrew from the run-off, citing the continued violence against his supporters, and took refuge in the Dutch embassy in Harare. SADC later claimed that conditions did not exist for a free and fair election, and similar statements were made by a number of regional heads of state and by the Pan-African Parliament election observer mission. Mbeki, however, remained intent on persuading Mugabe and Tsvangirai to form a government of national unity. Despite increasing international condemnation of events in Zimbabwe, the election proceeded as scheduled and Mugabe secured 90.2% of the valid votes cast, although only 20% of the population voted. He was sworn in for a sixth term as President on 29 June, amid appeals for international intervention. The USA and the United Kingdom announced that they would tighten the targeted sanctions they had imposed since 2003, and promised financial aid if democracy was restored. By then inflation was astronomical and the Zimbabwe dollar effectively worthless. Much of the population was traumatized by the eradication of the rule of law. Whereas in 2000 Zimbabwe had exported tobacco, sugar and maize, it was now the largest beneficiary of food aid in the world.

THE POWER-SHARING EXPERIMENT

Mbeki's continued mediation produced a memorandum of understanding, outlining a framework for formal talks to end the political crisis, which was signed by both Mugabe and Tsvangirai on 21 July 2008; however, the two failed to reach agreement on the composition of a government of national unity. Representatives of ZANU—PF and the two MDC factions met in South Africa later that month to begin negotiations between the two parties. Talks continued regarding a power-sharing deal until on 15 September what was termed the Global Political Agreement (GPA) was signed by Mugabe, Tsvangirai and Mutambara, under which Mugabe would remain President with executive authority and chair a 31-member cabinet and the National Security Council. Tsvangirai would become Prime Minister, also with executive authority, and would chair a council of ministers. The cabinet was to comprise 15 members of ZANU—PF, 13 members of Tsvangirai's MDC faction and three members of Mutambara's. The agreement also provided for the establishment, within two months of the inauguration of a new government, of a select committee to draft a new constitution, which would be subject to approval at a referendum.

The process of setting up the unity government proved problematic. There were continual disagreements between the parties on how to proceed, and the MDC accused ZANU—PF of acting in contravention of the agreement. Farm invasions continued and the MDC appeared powerless to prevent them. On 11 February 2009 Tsvangirai was inaugurated as Prime Minister, and Thokozani Khupe and Mutambara were sworn in as First and Second Deputy Prime Ministers. The original agreement, providing for a 31-member cabinet, was amended to allow ZANU—PF and the MDC—T to share responsibility for the Ministry of Home Affairs. Eventually, 35 ministers were sworn in on 13 February, with ZANU—PF allocated a total of 17 ministers in the new Cabinet. The MDC—T had 15 representatives in the Government, most notably Biti as Minister of Finance, and the MDC—M three portfolios. Shortly before the inauguration ceremony, the designated Deputy Minister of Agriculture, Roy Bennett, of the MDC—T, was arrested and charged with treason. His detention threatened to undermine the projected image of unity within the Government, which was already viewed by many analysts with extreme suspicion.

As the crisis had deepened since 2000, African leaders had failed to criticize Mugabe's lawless and authoritarian rule, although he was removed as chair of the SADC organ on politics, defence and security in 2001. Zimbabwe was also suspended from the Commonwealth, and targeted sanctions were imposed on Mugabe and other leading figures in the Government by the EU and the USA. Nevertheless, Mugabe continued to travel abroad and attend meetings with other African leaders. While continuing to insist that there was no alternative to 'quiet diplomacy', Mbeki frequently showed his partisanship to Mugabe and failed in his statements to distinguish between the principle of land redistribution and the violent means used in Zimbabwe to seize land. Both Mbeki and his successor as South African President, Jacob Zuma, appealed for the sanctions imposed on the country by the West to be lifted. On numerous occasions, Mugabe claimed that the sanctions were responsible for the economic difficulties in which the country found itself, and he blamed the MDC for not getting them lifted, but the EU and the USA refused to withdraw them while Mugabe remained in power. Meanwhile, at times, up to one-half of the country's population depended on international food aid to survive.

Once the unity Government was in place, and the Zimbabwe dollar was replaced by the use of the US dollar and the South African rand, inflation decreased to normal levels and the shops filled with goods, but the hoped-for investment from abroad did not materialize because Mugabe continued to hold power. The exodus of Zimbabweans continued, with South Africa absorbing most of the refugees, thought to number one-quarter of ZImbabwe's population. In October 2009 Tsvangirai declared that the MDC—T had disengaged from the unity Government because of the failure of ZANU—PF to adhere to the GPA and because farm invasions and human rights violations continued to occur, but this disengagement did not last, for the MDC did not see any alternative but to remain in the unity Government. In January 2011 Mutumbara was replaced by Ncube as leader of the MDC—M faction, although the former refused to resign as Second Deputy Prime Minister. The two MDC factions united in support of the election of Lovemore Moyo as Speaker of Parliament in April, preventing the ZANU—PF candidate from being elected.

As the harassment of political opponents increased—Biti's home was fire-bombed and MDC members suffered numerous other acts of violence and intimidation—the process of consulting the people over a new constitution began. Although commissions were appointed to run elections, monitor human rights and open up the media, the MDC could do nothing to stop the political violence directed against it, as Mugabe retained control of most of the levers of state power, and his dictatorial instincts were deeply ingrained. In May 2010 the High Court had dismissed charges against Bennett, but the state then appealed to the Supreme Court and Mugabe continued to refuse to swear him in as a deputy minister. (In March 2011 the Supreme Court upheld the High Court's judgment.) Although the MDC had long demanded that Gideon Gono be removed as Governor of the Reserve Bank, he remained in his post. A body for national healing, though promised, failed to materialize, and many in the rural areas remained traumatized by the violence perpetrated by ZANU—PF and state agents in 2008. The likelihood of another rigged election and increased violence seemed high unless SADC could insist that its election guidelines were followed. To Mugabe's chagrin, President Zuma of South Africa, the facilitator on Zimbabwe, informed a SADC summit meeting in Livingstone, Zambia, in March 2011 that a new constitution must be put in place before any election was held, and this 'roadmap' was accepted by the SADC heads of state when they met in Sandton, South Africa, in June.

Exploitation of the very rich diamond field at Marange in the east of the country resulted in a large new source of revenue (estimated at between US $1,000m. and $2,000m.), although only a small portion of this reached state coffers. The global watchdog body, the Kimberley Process Certification Scheme, initially banned the sale of diamonds from Marange on the grounds that the military, which controlled the field, condoned illegal activity and human rights abuses there. After Mugabe threatened to sell diamonds anyway, the Kimberley Process in mid-2010 allowed the sale of Zimbabwe diamonds under certain conditions, and in mid-2011 the Chairman of the Process unilaterally approved sales from the Marange field. Meanwhile, the Indigenization and Economic Empowerment Act adopted in 2008 required all foreign and white-owned companies worth more than $500,000 to cede at least 51% of their holdings to black Zimbabweans within five years. As the MDC pointed out, this not only severely discouraged any possible foreign direct investment, but led some foreign firms to sell their assets in Zimbabwe. In March 2011 the Government stated that mining firms must submit plans on how they intended to meet the terms of the legislation by the end of September, and in March 2012 the world's second largest platinum-mining company, Impala, agreed to cede 51% of its Zimbabwean business, Zimplats, in line with the Government's policy. The diamond sales and apparent success of the indigenization programme boosted Mugabe and brought new riches to the small élite that surrounded him.

In late August 2011 there was much speculation as to whether the death in a fire of Solomon Mujuru, a former leading army general and husband of Vice-President Joyce Mujuru, would weaken her in the battle between factions in ZANU—PF over the succession to Mugabe, and strengthen the man seen as her main rival, the more hardline Minister of Defence Mnangagwa. Speculation increased about Mugabe's health when, after turning 88, he made yet another visit to Singapore for a medical check-up. A confidential diplomatic cable from 2008 released by the WikiLeaks organization in 2011 indicated that he had prostate cancer and had at most five years to live, but Mugabe naturally denied this. When the United Kingdom's Archbishop of Canterbury led a mission to Harare in late 2011, he gave Mugabe a dossier of incidents of violence committed against Anglicans by the former Bishop of Harare who had been ex-communicated and by the police, but this had little apparent effect.

The UN Commissioner for Human Rights, who visited Zimbabwe in May 2012, allowed her visit to be arranged by the Government, and her calls for adherence to the rule of law went unheeded. The Joint Monitoring and Implementation Committee, which was supposed to be implementing the GPA, achieved little substantial progress; however, in July the Constitution Select Committee of Parliament (COPAC), comprising representatives from the three coalition parties, did finally agree on a draft constitution. Nevertheless, the following month ZANU-PF's politburo stated that the party could not accept certain clauses in the draft that limited the powers of the President. In mid-August it remained to be seen whether SADC would be able to secure all-party agreement to a draft, which would then have to be submitted to the voters in a referendum. SADC continued to insist that a new constitution must be approved before an election could take place, and that such an election must be held in line with SADC's guidelines. Meanwhile, in February 2012 the EU removed some individuals and entities from its sanctions list, but other Western sanctions remained in place, pending an election, which seemed unlikely to take place before mid-2013

Economy

LINDA VAN BUREN

Revised for this edition by OBI IHEME

INTRODUCTION

After nearly a decade of complete macroeconomic collapse in 1999–2008, during which real gross domestic product (GDP) contracted by a cumulative 45%, economic recovery began in Zimbabwe in 2009. Both agriculture and mining exhibited two consecutive years of positive growth, although manufacturing, hindered by electricity shortages and a lack of liquidity, has experienced more sluggish growth. The most positive development for the long-suffering Zimbabwe people was that, due to favourable weather conditions, food crops more than doubled in 2009 and continued their recovery in the harvest seasons of 2010 and 2011. It appeared possible that the Zimbabwean economy had in 2008 finally reached its nadir. If the promises that the Zimbabwe authorities have made are not kept, the downward spiral could resume at any time. However, if those promises are indeed kept, there can only be an improvement.

The African Economic Outlook calculated that Zimbabwe's GDP grew by 6.8% in 2011, a noticeable decrease from the 9.0% growth of 2010. A further decline in growth was expected in 2012, with an anticipated rate of 4.4%, but this was projected to rise to 5.5% in 2013. Zimbabwe's erratic growth and economic slowdown have been caused by many economic difficulties, ranging from problems in accessing finance for business, high interest rates, inconsistent economic policies—especially those related to empowerment of black Zimbabweans and ensuring their economic participation and control through the indigenization of domestic businesses—poor infrastructure, outdated manufacturing technology, and insufficient water and power supplies. Furthermore, although the Government's budgeting principle is a cash budget, Zimbabwe still maintained a deficit of 3.2% of GDP in 2011; nevertheless, this was better than the previous year's deficit of 4.3% of GDP. The figures for 2012 and 2013 are roughly equivalent improvements, being forecast at 2.8% and 3%, respectively. Inflation was expected to increase from the 2010 figure of 3.1% to 5.3% in 2011, and to be 6.5% in 2012 and 6.7% in 2013.

Zimbabwe's economic growth prospects over the next few years rely mainly on agriculture, mining, manufacturing and transport. Tobacco, maize, sugar and cotton are the main cash crops, but the late start of annual rains was widely expected to adversely affect agricultural production in 2012. Mining growth should be positive, given the anticipated return of buoyant commodity prices internationally. Manufacturing is severely hampered by the frequent breakdown of machines, old technologies, high utility costs, inconsistent water and power supplies, and the high cost of accessing an already small capital pool. As such, manufacturing capacity tends to be low, but it has picked up recently, from 43.7% in 2010 to an expected 59% in 2012.

By 2008 the economy of Zimbabwe lay in ruins, with widespread hunger and malnutrition in the country that used to be known as the 'breadbasket of Southern Africa', a cholera epidemic that caused nearly 5,000 deaths, hyperinflation, a worthless currency, unemployment of 95% and business activity at a virtual standstill. Such was the level of hyperinflation in Zimbabwe that the Government of Robert Mugabe issued a new banknote on 19 July 2008, with a face value of Z.$100,000m.; however, its actual value was less than the paper on which it was printed. According to official assessments, the rate of inflation reached 165,000% in February 2008, and broad money supply grew by 51,768.8% in November 2007. With hindsight, the IMF on 11 May 2009 proclaimed that inflation had peaked in September 2008 at 500,000m.%.

Between 31 July 2006 and 31 July 2008 the Zimbabwe dollar had lost the remainder of its purchasing power. On 31 July 2006, the Governor of the Reserve Bank of Zimbabwe (RBZ), Gideon Gono, blamed Zimbabwe's monetary woes on 'three zeroes' and then announced that three zeroes would be removed from the currency to rectify this situation. At the same time, he announced a 60% devaluation of the currency. Gono also announced that old banknotes and bearer cheques would be demonetized on 21 August 2006, leaving anyone holding these old instruments three weeks to present them at banks for conversion to the new banknotes. This devaluation had immediate negative effects: the Zimbabwean people were bewildered and even more mistrusting of the Zimbabwean dollar, and the black market rate for the currency plunged further. One year later nearly all sectors of the economy had ceased to use the Zimbabwe dollar, and Governor Gono's 'three zeroes' had reappeared. On 31 July 2008 the authorities again attempted to deal with hyperinflation by removing a further 10 zeroes from the currency denominations.

However, these measures in fact exacerbated the problem hugely. The viable solution began with the following three steps. First was the signing, on 15 September 2008, of a power-sharing agreement between President Robert Mugabe, of the Zimbabwe African National Union—Patriotic Front (ZANU—PF), and Morgan Tsvangirai, the leader of one faction of the opposition Movement for Democratic Change (MDC—T) (see Recent History). This pact led to the formation of a Government of National Unity, in which Mugabe continued as President and Tsvangirai took up the newly revived post of Prime Minister. This power-sharing agreement raised the prospect of urgently required assistance from the international community.

Second was the adoption by the Zimbabwe Government in February 2009 of hard currencies for all transactions. (This process is known as 'dollarization', a term that is perhaps somewhat confusing in the Zimbabwean context as the currency that was being replaced was the Zimbabwe dollar.) With this dollarization, the Mugabe Government's ruination of the Zimbabwe dollar was complete (although the public had ceased to use the currency some months prior to the decision). All transactions were thenceforth to be denominated in hard currencies, with the South African rand designated on 19 March as the 'reference currency' (although US dollars became ubiquitous almost immediately). With the announcement the Mugabe Government admitted for the first time that the Zimbabwe dollar-denominated currency was 'not functional' and that there was no functioning foreign exchange market for Zimbabwe dollars. The UN quantified the Zimbabwe dollar's final exchange rate as Z.$35,000,000,000,000,000 = US $1. This figure may seem merely academic, but it may well play a part in the eventual dollarization of Zimbabweans' life savings and other assets. It should be noted, however, that according to one clause of the proclamation, the Zimbabwe dollar 'remains legal tender'. This move has brought unofficial estimates of inflation down from an estimated 14,900m.% in 2008 to the single-digit rates listed above. It has also removed a factor that was severely skewing all attempts at quantifying data for statistical purposes.

The third step was the launch in March 2009 of the Short-Term Economic Recovery Programme (STERP I). This 121-page document, covering the period February–December 2009, set out a detailed strategy to begin addressing the dreadful state of the Zimbabwe economy. A further programme, STERP II, was subsequently introduced for the 2010–12 period. The Minister of Finance Tendai Biti, a prominent MDC—T member, was the STERP's most ardent proponent. Perhaps most important of all, the STERP I directed the RBZ to cease engaging in what the IMF termed 'quasi-fiscal activities', namely the uncontrolled printing of banknotes. M3 money-supply grew rapidly during 2005–08, and the velocity of growth in 2008 was 'unprecedented', according to the IMF. These quasi-fiscal activities amounted to US $1,100m. in 2008 alone, equivalent to 36% of GDP.

The humanitarian cost of this type of government economic activity was high. The 2008 harvest of maize, the staple food, was a record low, at scarcely 500,000 metric tons. The UN World Food Programme (WFP) estimated that as many as 5.1m. Zimbabweans would require food assistance in the first quarter of 2009. Zimbabwe's grain requirement amounts to some 2.07m. tons per year, a level which the country historically had often been able to supply. WFP attributed the crisis to bad weather, a shortage of key inputs such as fertilizers and tractors, the crumbling irrigation system and the disincentive effect of the price controls put in place by the Government. However, with no weighting attributed to these factors, the list may mask the fact that one of the four is a greater cause of the food shortages than the others. Good rainfall returned for the next growing season at a time when the monetary situation was stabilized, and the maize crop more than doubled in 2009 (see below). The number of people requiring emergency food assistance fell to 2.8m. per month in 2009 and to 1.5m. per month in the first quarter of 2010.

Zimbabwe has been in continuous arrears with the IMF since February 2001. In December 2003 the Fund took the unprecedented step of initiating compulsory withdrawal procedures against Zimbabwe. The Fund restored Zimbabwe's voting rights and its eligibility to receive lending in February 2010. However, as of mid-2012, no lending had been extended, and it was clear that the IMF would require Zimbabwe to meet a number of criteria before such lending could resume. Zimbabwe at the time was not on the verge of meeting any of those criteria, whic included settling its arrears to the Fund, which in October 2010 amounted to about US $140m. Indeed, Zimbabwe would need to settle its arrears to all its official creditors, of which the IMF was by no means the largest. The country's public sector external debt arrears (excluding arrears owed by parastatals and any outstanding disbursed debt not in arrears) amounted to US $4,769m. in October, of which US $1,190m. was owed to the 'Paris Club' of sovereign creditors, US $507m. to the World Bank and US $409m. to the African Development Bank.

Foreign exchange reserves have been negligible since the beginning of the economic crisis in 1999. The 2011 budget proposed a goal of increasing foreign reserves to a level equivalent to three months' worth of imports of goods and services by the end of 2012, although this was lower than the Southern African Development Community target of six months' worth of imports. Reserves at the end of 2010 were sufficient to cover only 1.4 months' worth of imports. Export volume contracted by 19.3% in 2003 and has been in decline ever since. Exports by value declined from an unofficially estimated US $1,396m. in 2008 to an unofficially estimated US $1,213m. in 2009.

Zimbabwe had the second highest rate of HIV infection in Africa in 2005, and it has been estimated that by 2015 the labour force will be one-sixth smaller than it would have been in the absence of the HIV/AIDS pandemic. Some demographic experts predicted that Zimbabwe could soon reach zero population growth as a result of the AIDS pandemic alone; the simultaneous increase in emigration would only compound the trend. The World Health Organization estimated that in 2009 average life expectancy was just 49 years.

LAND POLICIES AND FOOD INSECURITY

Before independence, whites were allocated 78% of the country's most productive land. The lowest-grade land accounted for 75% of the land allocated to smallholders in the pre-independence era, in what were known as the 'communal areas'. At 1 January 2000 some 11m. black Zimbabweans were still crowded on unproductive communal lands, and 4,500 principally white commercial farmers still owned 11m. ha of prime land.

After independence in 1980, the Mugabe Government reiterated its pre-election pledge to 'resettle' landless Zimbabweans on commercial farmland acquired from willing sellers among the white commercial farmers. Under the 1980 Constitution, the Government was permitted, until 1990, to acquire land compulsorily for purposes of resettlement if it was 'under-utilized'. However, after a whole decade, fewer than 1% of those hoping for resettlement had been resettled. After 1990, expectations were directed towards an acceleration in land reform measures. In March 1992 the Land Acquisition Act was approved, which permitted the compulsory acquisition of land by the state, facilitating the purchase of 5.5m. ha of the 11m. ha of land then still held by white farmers. However, the Act stopped short of detailing the white farmers' guarantee of fair compensation. This matter remained unresolved until President Mugabe, in August 2000, proclaimed that there was to be no compensation unless the United Kingdom wished to compensate these 'British' white farmers (most of whom held Zimbabwean nationality). The British ambassador to Zimbabwe, Deborah Bronnert, stated in May 2012 that she did not think that the United Kingdom would continue paying such compensation, as it had done soon after Zimbabwean independence, when it provided £44m. She reiterated the British Government's view that the land reform was implemented unfairly and ultimately caused the closure of many commercial farms that were providing food for Zimbabwe, which led to the loss of many jobs and negatively affected the economy.

Following the announcement in June 1997 that the National Land Acquisition Committee had concluded its programme of identifying land for reallocation, foreigners and companies were barred from owning land. Nevertheless, by August only 3.4m. ha of land had been acquired in the 17 years since independence, and only about 70,000 families had been resettled—a figure that still constituted scarcely 1% of those hoping for resettlement. Also in August 1997 plans were announced to acquire 1,072 farms, covering 3.2m. ha, to resettle some 100,000 landless peasants; a further 700 farms, covering 1.3m. ha, were to be used for indigenous commercial farming. Controversially, Mugabe proclaimed that farmers would be compensated for the improvements they had made to their farms but not for the land itself. However, under pressure from the IMF, in March 1998 the Mugabe Government made assurances that it would offer full and fair compensation for land seized under the land resettlement programme. In November the Government announced compulsory acquisition orders for a further 841 farms covering 2.24m. ha. In May 1999 the Cabinet approved an Inception Phase Framework Plan to support the resettlement of 77,700 families on 1m. ha by 2001. Of this land, 223,112 ha was to come from 120 farms that were voluntarily offered for sale in 1998, with the balance representing uncontested acquisitions.

In February 2000 'war veterans' began occupying white-owned farms. By April nearly 1,000 farms had been occupied; it was alleged that only some 15% of the squatters were in fact 'war veterans', while the other 85% were unemployed youths paid by Mugabe's ruling party. The tobacco industry was severely disrupted, and by mid-May tourist arrivals had declined to fewer than one-half of the usual levels. In the same month the World Bank halted all funding to Zimbabwe after the Mugabe Government failed to repay a government-guaranteed loan to the electricity parastatal and exceeded the 60-day grace period. In October the World Bank placed Zimbabwe, indefinitely, on non-payment status.

The Confederation of Zimbabwe Industries revealed that more than 400 companies had closed in 2000, with the loss of some 10,000 jobs. Gold, tobacco, maize, wheat and horticultural production was significantly lower. Visible exports declined in terms of both volume and value, and tourism revenue dissipated overnight. The 2000 budgetary deficit, which had been forecast at 3.8% of GDP, expanded to 23% of GDP. Inflation continued to increase. Three-digit inflation, while not unknown in some other African countries, had been unprecedented in Zimbabwe, and it went on to become eventually nine-digit inflation. Hyperinflation created a major and lasting change in the daily lives of the Zimbabwean people. Fuel shortages and electricity cuts also plagued the nation, and the food supply would not stretch from one harvest to the next. In September 2001 the IMF declared Zimbabwe ineligible to use general Fund resources and removed it from the list of countries eligible to borrow resources under the Poverty Reduction and Growth Facility.

In August 2002 the European Union (EU) allocated food aid worth about US $35m. to the Zimbabwean Government. WFP began distributing emergency food aid in Zimbabwe in July; by February 2003 it had distributed 204,000 tons to 4m. people in 49 of the country's 57 districts. This situation was followed by six successive maize harvests of less than one-half of the national annual requirement. When poor harvests continued into 2009, food shortages worsened (see below).

By mid-2012 the ZANU—PF-dominated Government of President Mugabe showed no signs of relenting on the content of its land resettlement policy or in its manner of carrying it out. The ZANU—PF intended to insert a clause into a draft constitution that would require 80% approval in a referendum to amend any land-related issues in the Constitution, which could be interpreted as a way of appeasing and protecting senior ZANU—PF government officials who seized land during Mugabe's land reforms of the early part of the millennium.

NATIONAL INCOME

In 1999 Zimbabwe entered a period of severe economic decline. Real GDP contracted by a cumulative 45% between 1999 and 2008. According to the 2011 budget statement, real GDP increased by 5.7% in 2009 and an estimated 8.1% in 2010, the first economic growth since 1998. In 2009 agriculture was the largest contributor to GDP, at 15.5%, followed by transport and communications (15.2%), manufacturing (14.7%), and tourism (11.0%), according to government figures. Agriculture showed the strongest growth in 2009 and 2010, expanding by 14.9% and an estimated 33.9%, respectively. Manufacturing growth slowed from 10.2% in 2009 to 2.7% in 2010. Also slow to recover was the tourism industry, which suffered from capacity constraints and negative publicity in Zimbabwe's main target tourism markets. The tourism sector grew by only 0.5% in 2010. Official assessments indicated that tourist arrivals amounted to 1.95m. in 2008, 2.02m. in 2009 and an estimated 2.23m. in 2010, with 2.5m. projected for 2011. The sector's earnings were officially quantified at US $294m. in 2008, US $523m. in 2009 and US $770m. in 2010, with US $850m. forecast for 2011. The main source for these 'tourism' arrivals was other African countries, accounting for 89.7% of the total; South Africa provided 72% and Botswana 6%. However, tourists from the most lucrative markets in Europe, North America and Asia were still staying away in 2011.

AGRICULTURE

Zimbabwe has had, and could have again, a diversified and well-developed agricultural sector, in terms of food production, cash crops and livestock, provided the land that has been redistributed to black Zimbabweans can again be used productively. Of the total land area, 8.3% is arable. The principal rainy season is from November to March, and the main harvest is in April and May. The staple food crop is maize, while the principal cash crops are tobacco, sugar and cotton. Other cereal crops grown include wheat, millet, sorghum and barley. In 2011, even though lending from the IMF and the World Bank had not resumed, both institutions expressed their approval of moves by FAO to provide assistance in the form of vital farming inputs, such as fertilizers, pesticides and especially seeds. These inputs, combined with better weather, moderated inflation and the use of stable currencies, contributed to an estimated 33.9% growth rate in agriculture as a whole in 2010.

Driving this high rate of expansion were tobacco, exhibiting 110% growth, sugar (35%), maize (34%) and cotton (23%).

A record tobacco crop of 260m. kg was harvested in 1998. Prior to the troubles of 2000, Zimbabwe had enjoyed a favourable yield, and the area planted under tobacco had set a record in 1998, at 99,293 ha; by 2006 less than 50% of that area, at an FAO-assessed 38,865 ha, was under tobacco. Yield per ha also peaked in 1998, at 2,626.26 kg per ha, but by 2006 tobacco yields were just 1,144 kg per ha. Production of unmanufactured tobacco declined from a peak of 260,000 metric tons in 1998 to just 44,451 tons in 2006. Government data indicated that the tobacco harvest amounted to 59,000 tons in 2009, and 123,500 tons were sold at auction in 2010 at an average price of US $2.88 per kg. In the 2009/10 season about 65,000 ha were planted with tobacco, of which 30,000 ha were under contract farming, 20,000 ha were 'self-financed' using the previous year's tobacco proceeds and 15,000 ha were planted by communal farmers. The tobacco industry continued to recover strongly in 2010, with the sector expanding by 110%. The forecast for 2011 was for the area under tobacco to increase to 90,000 ha and for the tobacco crop to rise to 150,000 tons. However, the tobacco sector is unlikely to reach the peaks it once enjoyed, since global demand for tobacco is on the wane as tobacco consumers in principal markets come under increased pressure to give up smoking.

In the cotton sector, small-scale communal producers account for just over one-half of total production. Cotton production rose from 211,000 metric tons in 2009 to an estimated 260,000 tons in 2010, according to the 2011 budget statement. By mid-November 2010 maize growers had delivered to the Grain Marketing Board 220,910 metric tons of maize in that year, valued at US $60.8m. About 1.8m. ha were planted with maize, compared with 1.5m. ha in 2009. Total sugar output rose from 259,000 metric tons in 2009 to an estimated 350,000 tons in 2010, according to the 2011 budget statement. The sector was boosted by the EU's Programme of Accompanying Measures for Sugar Protocol Countries for 2010, which extended €13.7m. in support of vulnerable small-scale sugar producers in Zimbabwe. Zimbabwe's coffee growers produce mild Arabicas. According to the International Coffee Organization, Zimbabwe's output of coffee beans grew from 23,000 60-kg bags in 2009/10 (the coffee year runs from April to March) to 35,000 bags in 2010/11. Exports, though, declined from 16,186 bags in 2009/10 to 10,236 bags in 2010/11.

According to official assessments, the livestock herd in 2011 was estimated at 5.2m. head of cattle (including 40,000 head of dairy cattle), 3.3m. goats, 391,000 sheep, 202,300 pigs and 22.5m. chickens. In forestry, Zimbabwe's total roundwood removals amount to some 9.1m. cu m annually, about 90% of which goes towards fuelwood. According to FAO, Zimbabwe exported 4,548 cu m of wood in 2008, valued at US $441,000, a small percentage of the pre-2000 annual export volume and value. Land-locked Zimbabwe has few sizeable natural lakes, and most of its fishing potential is in the country's man-made reservoirs, especially Lake Kariba on the Zambezi River. The country's total fish catch is estimated by FAO at some 13,000 metric tons per year. The predominant fish caught are dagaas, which migrate between saltwater and freshwater; dagaas accounted for close to 60% of the total catch in 2009. Only six species, three of them breams, make up 95% of the total fish catch in Zimbabwe.

MINING

Zimbabwe's principal mining commodities are platinum, gold, chrome, nickel, coal and diamonds. Other minerals present include asbestos, copper, iron ore, tin, silver, emeralds, graphite, lithium, granite, cobalt, tungsten, quartz, silica sands, kyanite, vermiculite, corundum, magnesite, kaolin and mica. Mining grew in value terms by 33.3% in 2009 and by an estimated 47% in 2010, according to the 2011 budget statement. The improved economic stabilization from 2009 boosted mining activity significantly. Some mining operations that had closed down in 2008 or had been discontinued began to produce again, while many of the larger mines were conducting feasibility studies with a view to resuming operations.

Zimbabwe has the second largest reserves of platinum in the world, after South Africa. Platinum accounted for an estimated 36% of Zimbabwe's total mineral production in 2010, according to the 2011 budget statement. Production in the first 10 months of 2010 amounted to 5,077 kg and was expected to reach 8,500 kg by the end of that year, a 24% increase compared with the 6,848 kg produced in 2009. The projection for 2011 was 12,000 kg, with investment expansion, mostly at the Unki and Mimosa mines, accounting for the increase. South Africa-based Anglo Platinum's US $600m. Unki mine, near Shurugwe, opened in April 2011. At full production, it was expected to produce 150,000 oz of platinum per annum. Development began in 2003, but was delayed by Zimbabwe's economic collapse. The Mimosa mine, on the Great Dyke mineral belt east of Bulawayo, is owned by Mimosa Investments Ltd of Mauritius (a 50:50 joint venture between Impala Platinum Holdings Ltd of South Africa and Aquarius Platinum Ltd of Australia). The shallow Mimosa mine produced 101,200 oz of platinum in concentrates in 2010.

Gold was the second largest source of revenue in the mining sector in 2010, after platinum. Production in January–September 2010 amounted to 6,284 kg; total output of 8,000 kg was forecast for 2010, rising to 13,000 kg in 2011. Mwana Africa, a pan-African resources company listed on the London Stock Exchange in the United Kingdom, began an 18-month programme to rehabilitate the Freda Rebecca gold mine in 2009. Average monthly production in March–May 2011 was 3,363 oz. Mwana Africa also owned 52.9% of Bindura Nickel Corpn, which was placed under care and maintenance status in November 2008. In July 2011 Mwana Africa was seeking finance with a view to restarting Bindura Nickel's operations in phases, beginning with the Trojan nickel mine. Nickel production was estimated at 9,500 metric tons of contained nickel in 2009. Output of chromium increased from 201,000 tons in 2009 to an estimated 500,000 tons in 2010, according to the 2011 budget statement. Zimbabwe has significant diamond resources. Output was forecast to increase from an estimated 2.7m. carats in 2010 to a projected 4m. carats in 2011, according to government figures. Diamond fields at Chiadzwa entered production in 2010 and accounted for most of the national output in that year. The River Ranch and Murowa diamond mines together produced about 300,000 carats in 2010. A number of obstacles still confronted the diamond sector, including the legal process of awarding concessions, beneficiation, policing and anti-smuggling standards, environmental concerns, and the compensation and relocation of displaced mining communities. However, obtaining certification under the Kimberley Process Certification Scheme was the main obstacle; negotiations were ongoing in mid-2012. Output of coal, which had amounted to some 6m. tons per annum in the 1990s, increased from 1.6m. metric tons in 2009 to an estimated 2m. tons in 2010, with 3m. tons projected for 2011, according to the 2011 budget statement. Zimbabwe's total coal reserves were estimated at 28,000m. tons.

Mining is critical to Zimbabwe's economy, but the industry is under threat from the ruling ZANU—PF's indigenization policy, through which it aims to make indigenous black Zimbabweans at least 51% shareholders of any business in the country. Particularly concerning has been the announcement by the Minister of Youth Development, Indigenization and Empowerment in mid-2012 to transfer complete ownership of all mineral resources to Zimbabweans, which could effectively cripple the industry, given that citizens do not have the funds to purchase such companies, and the vast majority of finance, technical expertise and equipment has been provided by foreign companies. Companies have been threatened that, if they wish to avoid expropriation without compensation, they must comply with the law.

MANUFACTURING

Zimbabwe traditionally produced a wide variety of manufactured products, both for the local market and for export. However, the manufacturing sector came under intense pressure during the economic crisis of 1999 and the subsequent troubles. A severe shortage of fuel in the country from 2005 hindered the movement of manufactured goods, mining equipment and the entire transport sector in general, increasing the cost of conducting business in Zimbabwe significantly, while hyperinflation placed an unsustainable burden on manufacturers.

The manufacturing sector accounted for 11.8% of GDP in 2010, a decline from the 30% annually achieved in 1992–93. Manufacturing output contracted by 3% in 2005 and by an estimated 7% in 2006. A sluggish recovery commenced in 2009, but the sector was hindered by an unreliable electricity supply and a severe lack of medium- and long-term capital with which to source raw materials and replace derelict and obsolete machinery and equipment. The manufacturing sector as a whole grew only by an estimated 2.7% in 2010. The foodstuffs sub-sector grew by just 0.5%, textiles and ginning by 0.4%, chemical and petroleum products by 0.3%, and paper, printing and publishing by 0.2%, according to the 2011 budget statement. The transport equipment, metal and metal products, and clothing and footwear sub-sectors were still experiencing negative growth rates in 2010. Capacity utilization remained at a very low level in 2009–11. The highest level of capacity utilization was in the wood and furniture sub-sector, at an estimated 83% in 2010, followed by tobacco and beverages (59%), clothing and footwear (55%), paper, printing and publishing (43%), and foodstuffs (42%). The lowest level of capacity utilization, at 21%, was in the non-metallic mineral products sub-sector and in the textiles and ginning sub-sector. Official forecasts projected that the manufacturing sector would grow by 5.7% in 2011, despite recurring problems with machines breaking down, out-of-date technology, high utility costs, inconsistent water and power supply, and the high cost of accessing an already small capital pool.

ENERGY

Zimbabwe has a theoretical installed capacity of 1,960 MW; therefore, even if full capacity could be achieved, less than 90% of Zimbabwe's electricity requirements would be met. In reality, capacity utilization levels are extremely low, leading to large-scale load-shedding. Official assessments indicated that in 2010 total generating levels amounted to 1,237 MW, or only 56% of the nation's electricity requirements. In 2010 the Hwange power station generated 547 MW but had a capacity of 920 MW, while the 750-MW Kariba South power station only produced 650 MW. These two power stations are supplemented by the Munyati power station, which generated 40 MW in 2010 out of an installed capacity of 100 MW. The 100-MW Harare and the 90-MW Bulawayo power stations generated no electricity in 2010. The 2010 budget allocated US $20m. to the rehabilitation of Hwange and US $5m. to Kariba South. However, much greater expenditure would be needed to meet the nation's power requirements and to enable the manufacturing sector to recover. In June 2012 Zimbabwe Electricity Supply Authority (ZESA)ZESA signed a US $230m. memorandum of understanding with WAPCO, an Indian power company, to overhaul the three thermal power stations at Bulawayo, Hwange and Munyati. This will be the first significant energy investment in the country since 1982.

INTERNATIONAL TRADE AND BALANCE OF PAYMENTS

Zimbabwe's trade, current and overall balance of payments accounts were all in deficit in 2009 and 2010, as they had been throughout the 1999–2008 economic collapse, and no surpluses were forecast for the near future. RBZ statistics indicated that Zimbabwe's total exports on a free-on-board (f.o.b.) basis increased from US $1,591.3m. in 2009 to an estimated US $2,089.8m. in 2010; they increased even further in 2011, to US $3,670m. Mining exports contributed 65% of the total, followed by tobacco exports (17%), other agricultural exports (9%) and manufacturing exports (8%). Horticultural exports accounted for just 1% of the total; this sector required a functioning support mechanism—in the form of adequate cold storage powered by a reliable electricity grid—in order to achieve the quality demanded in export markets. Until then, the horticultural sector will not reach its considerable earning potential. Of total mineral exports, platinum contributed the largest share, at 45%, followed by gold at 22%, ferrochrome at 18% and diamonds at 11%. Imports, also on an f.o.b. basis, increased from US $3,213.1m. in 2009 to US $3,552.0m. in 2010 and US $6,280m. in 2011. This reflected the country's greater reliance on imported products for domestic consumption, because of the sharp decline in domestic production that has resulted from very poor economic management policies. Major imports included finished manufactures—items that Zimbabwe's manufacturers had provided quite adequately prior to 1999—and oil. The trade balance improved from a deficit of US $1,621.8m. in 2009 to an estimated US $1,462.2m. shortfall in 2010. Visible exports covered just 58.8% of visible imports in 2010. The current account of the balance of payments, excluding official transfers, deteriorated from a deficit of US $927.8m. in 2009 to an estimated shortfall of US $1,041.1m. in 2010. The capital account recovered from a deficit of US $70m. in 2009 to an estimated surplus of US $578.5m. in 2010, boosted by a reversal of the flow of net short-term capital from an outflow of US $925m. in 2009 to an estimated inflow of US $200.9m. in 2010. The overall balance of payments improved from a shortfall of US $1,908m. in 2009 to an estimated deficit of US $462.6m. in 2010. Gross official foreign reserves increased from US $366m. at 31 December 2009, providing import cover of 1.2 months, to an estimated US $420.8m. at 31 December 2010, equivalent to 1.4 months of imports.

Zimbabwe's membership of the Common Market for Eastern and Southern Africa (COMESA), formerly the Preferential Trade Area for Eastern and Southern Africa, has, in theory, provided access to new directions in regional trade. In practice, however, Zimbabwean exporters have not been in a position to benefit from the opportunities of COMESA membership. Zimbabwe had high levels of debt even before the economic collapse of 1999–2008. Official assessments indicated that Zimbabwe's disbursed debt outstanding at 31 October 2010 totalled US $6,929m., of which US $4,769m., more than two-thirds, was in arrears. Of total disbursed outstanding debt, US $1,070m., or 15%, was owed by parastatals, including ZESA supplier credits, National Oil Company of Zimbabwe supplier credits and US $70m. owed by the defunct Air Zimbabwe. Zimbabwe has signed up for COMESA's Simplified Trade Regime, which allows cross-border traders to transport goods of up to US $1,000 in value without paying import duties or facing import quotas. Cross-border trade has become a major source of employment for many Zimbabweans.

LABOUR, WAGES AND INFLATION

Prior to 2000, with the exception of 1988, inflation affected lower-income urban families more than it did higher-income urban families in every year since independence in 1980. By the time high inflation became hyperinflation, everyone was affected at a fundamental level. As the post-2000 crisis deepened and government funds dwindled, the Government resorted to huge increases in the money supply in order to pay its own obligations. This action was the largest single contributory factor to the hyperinflation that ensued. It was reported that the printing of money was accelerated in the first half of 2000 in order to meet the pay increases of civil servants in the months preceding the June election. This sudden, literal increase in the money supply placed great upward pressure on an already excessive inflation rate. This practice continued, and the broad money supply grew by 165% in 2002 and by 207% in the year to 31 March 2003, even according to official assessments. Growth of broad money supply accelerated from 1,638.4% in January 2007 to 51,768.8% in November. Demonetizing the Zimbabwe dollar in February 2009 in favour of hard currencies heralded a swift end to hyperinflation. Consumer price inflation was assessed by the IMF at 6.5% in 2009 and 5.0% in 2010. Unemployment was estimated by the IMF at 95% in June 2010. Salaries had risen hugely in nominal terms during the 1999–2008 economic collapse, but these increases had been denominated in worthless Zimbabwe dollars. During the 2009–12 recovery period wages were paid in hard currency and therefore had spending power, although the Government found it difficult to fund the public sector payroll.

Job creation occurred only in the public and financial sectors, but estimates are that between 1998 and 2010, 180,000 jobs were lost in sectors other than agriculture, while 1m. people entered the work-force. This is an indication that recent estimates regarding the scale of unemployment are credible. The Economist Intelligence Unit reported that inflation from January to April 2012 was 5.7%, and was caused chiefly by a 13.1% increase in housing and utility costs, and a 12.3% price rise of communications. An indicator that official inflation figures may not be accurate is that wages in the tobacco industry, for example, rose by 50% over the last three years. Wage inflation normally causes consumer price inflation, but the officially reported figures do not correspond with wage hikes, which probably means that the Government is under-reporting inflation rates.

FUTURE PROSPECTS

Much progress has been made towards recovering from the complete economic collapse of 1999–2008. The most important steps (see above) culminated in the 'dollarization' of the economy, replacing the worthless Zimbabwe dollar with hard currencies. Until that point, any other remedial actions had been rendered ineffectual, and the country had been operating virtually without a currency. After dollarization, inflation was brought under control, and day-to-day life resumed some of its normality. The agricultural sector, a leading force in the economic recovery, received significant and timely assistance from FAO in the form of inputs such as seeds and fertilizers, enabling it to take advantage of the good weather of 2009–11. Following the improvement in the economic climate, there was also renewed investment in the mining sector, further driving the country's recovery. However, the manufacturing industry struggled to reach its potential, due to erratic power supplies, sub-standard equipment and a dearth of working capital. Much more capital investment would be needed to overcome these obstacles. The 2011 budget statement indicated that US $360m. in support from development partners had been received by October 2010. Minister of Finance Biti estimated that available revenue totalled US $2,700m., whereas the total expenditure required was US $11,300m. However, given the 'absence to recourse of borrowing', proposed spending was subsequently reduced dramatically, to just US $2,700m., equivalent to projected revenues. Biti declared that formulating the budget had been 'an excruciating journey of balancing the unbalanceable'. The economic crisis that Robert Mugabe presided over during 1999–2008 left the country confronting numerous deep-rooted problems. The unity Government remained fragile, and potential donors and lenders were aware that it could fall at any moment. The Zimbabwe dollar, at least nominally, remained legal tender. So much is tentative in Zimbabwe's nascent recovery, and, until investor and lender confidence returns, the country's budgetary requirements will remain 'unbalanceable'.

Economic growth in the coming years will depend largely on the holding of peaceful, free and fair elections. However, Zimbabwe's continued economic recovery also depends on the demand and prices for metal, and the level of winter wheat production. Underpinning all this, the country will need stable economic management and business reforms.

Were ZANU—PF to win the next elections, Zimbabwe would likely increasingly seek aid and trade from Asian countries, in line with their increasingly strident anti-Western rhetoric. Continued progress with Mugabe's indigenization policy, which Tsvangirai supports—particularly the ever-present threat of expropriation without compensation in the mining, financial and other important sectors—will surely dampen enthusiasm for investing in Zimbabwe, especially in the more capital-intensive industries such as mining. Given the importance of mining to Zimbabwe and the relative lack of local capacity and financing, this situation would be even more disastrous for the economy.

However, if the MDC—T were to win, the country would probably try to strengthen its economic relationships with states from the Organisation for Economic Co-operation and Development. This scenario would be expected given the likelihood of renewed economic support by European nations and their allies for the MDC—T under Tsvangirai, who is far more amenable than Mugabe to working with Zimbabwe's traditional trade and donor partners. Confidence would thus be renewed in investors, which would help Zimbabwe's short- to medium-term economic growth and development prospects.

Statistical Survey

Source (unless otherwise stated): Central Statistical Office, Ministry of Finance, Blocks B, E and G, Composite Bldg, cnr Samora Machel Ave and Fourth St, Private Bag 7705, Causeway, Harare; tel. (4) 706681; fax (4) 728529; internet www.mofed.gov.zw.

Area and Population

AREA, POPULATION AND DENSITY

Area (sq km)	390,757*
Population (census results)	
18 August 1997	11,789,274
17 August 2002†	
Males	5,634,180
Females	5,997,477
Total	11,631,657
Population (UN estimates at mid-year)‡	
2010	12,571,454
2011	12,754,376
2012	13,013,679
Density (per sq km) at mid-2012	33.3

* 150,872 sq miles.

† Source: UN, *Population and Vital Statistics Report*.

‡ Source: UN, *World Population Prospects: The 2010 Revision*.

POPULATION BY AGE AND SEX

(UN estimates at mid-2012)

	Males	Females	Total
0–14	2,464,195	2,450,311	4,914,506
15–64	3,724,642	3,827,166	7,551,808
65 and over	238,229	309,136	547,365
Total	6,427,066	6,586,613	13,013,679

Source: UN, *World Population Prospects: The 2010 Revision*.

PRINCIPAL TOWNS

(population at census of August 1992)

Harare (capital)	1,189,103	Chinhoyi (Sinoia)	43,054
Bulawayo	621,742	Hwange (Wankie)	42,581
Chitungwiza	274,912	Marondera (Marandellas)	39,384
Mutare (Umtali)	131,367	Zvishavane (Shabani)	32,984
Gweru (Gwelo)	128,037	Redcliff	29,959
Kwekwe (Que Que)	75,425		
Kadoma (Gatooma)	67,750		
Masvingo	51,743		

Mid-2011 ('000, incl. suburbs, UN estimate): Harare 1,541,570 (Source: UN, *World Urbanization Prospects: The 2011 Revision*).

BIRTHS AND DEATHS
(annual averages, UN estimates)

	1995–2000	2000–05	2005–10
Birth rate (per 1,000)	31.5	29.7	29.4
Death rate (per 1,000)	14.5	17.5	15.1

Source: UN, *World Population Prospects: The 2010 Revision*.

2011: Birth rate 29.0 per 1,000; Death rate 12.7 per 1,000 (Source: African Development Bank).

Life expectancy (years at birth): 49.9 (males 50.7; females 49.0) in 2010 (Source: World Bank, World Development Indicators database).

ECONOMICALLY ACTIVE POPULATION
(sample survey, persons aged 15 years and over, 1999)

	Males	Females	Total
Agriculture, hunting, forestry and fishing	1,215,661	1,584,839	2,800,500
Mining and quarrying	46,946	3,367	50,313
Manufacturing	283,090	94,667	377,757
Electricity, gas and water	10,158	n.a.	10,158
Construction	98,908	6,659	105,567
Trade, restaurants and hotels	154,198	178,341	332,539
Transport, storage and communications	93,289	8,288	101,577
Financing, insurance, real estate and business services	100,425	20,749	121,174
Community, social and personal services	320,020	258,505	578,525
Sub-total	2,322,695	2,155,415	4,478,110
Activities not adequately defined	63,052	124,286	187,338
Total employed	2,385,747	2,279,701	4,665,448
Unemployed	187,142	110,669	297,811
Total labour force	2,572,889	2,390,370	4,963,259

2004 ('000 employees, annual average): Agriculture, hunting, forestry and fishing 154; Mining and quarrying 50; Manufacturing 136; Electricity, gas and water 11; Construction 25; Trade, restaurants and hotels 114; Transport, storage and communications 38; Financing, insurance, real estate and business services 38; Public administration 68; Education 151; Health 26; Domestic 102; Other services 88; *Total employed* 999 (Source: IMF, *Zimbabwe: Selected Issues and Statistical Appendix*—October 2005).

Mid-2012 (estimates in '000): Agriculture, etc. 3,209; Total labour force 5,837 (Source: FAO).

Health and Welfare

KEY INDICATORS

Total fertility rate (children per woman, 2010)	3.3
Under-5 mortality rate (per 1,000 live births, 2010)	80
HIV/AIDS (% of persons aged 15–49, 2009)	14.3
Physicians (per 1,000 head, 2004)	0.2
Hospital beds (per 1,000 head, 2006)	3.0
Health expenditure (2007): US $ per head (PPP)	20
Health expenditure (2007): % of GDP	8.9
Health expenditure (2007): public (% of total)	46.3
Access to water (% of persons, 2010)	80
Access to sanitation (% of persons, 2010)	40
Total carbon dioxide emissions ('000 metric tons, 2008)	9,075.8
Carbon dioxide emissions per head (metric tons, 2008)	0.7
Human Development Index (2011): ranking	173
Human Development Index (2011): value	0.376

For sources and definitions, see explanatory note on p. vi.

Agriculture

PRINCIPAL CROPS
('000 metric tons)

	2008	2009	2010
Wheat	31	40*	42*
Barley*	50	66	67
Maize	496	700†	1,192
Millet	37	40*	51
Sorghum	75	70*	74
Potatoes*	50	47	58
Cassava (Manioc)*	206	216	203
Beans, dry	27*	33*	22
Sugar cane*	3,100	3,100	3,100
Soybeans (Soya beans)	100†	90†	57
Groundnuts, with shell	79†	93†	106
Sunflower seed	23†	15†	12
Oranges*	97	97	49
Bananas*	102	102	92
Coffee, green†	1	1	2
Tea*	19	21	21
Tobacco, unmanufactured	82*	96*	110
Cotton lint*	116	80	38

* FAO estimate(s).
† Unofficial figure(s).

Aggregate production ('000 metric tons, may include official, semi-official or estimated data): 692 in 2008, 919 in 2009, 143 in 2010; Total roots and tubers 260 in 2008, 266 in 2009, 264 in 2010; Total vegetables (incl. melons) 144 in 2008, 185 in 2009; 186 in 2010; Total fruits (excl. melons) 253 in 2008, 252 in 2009, 192 in 2010.

Source: FAO.

LIVESTOCK
('000 head, year ending September)

	2008	2009*	2010*
Horses*	28.0	28.0	28.0
Asses*	112	112	112
Cattle	5,107	5,030	5,040
Sheep	405	380	375
Pigs*	625	630	635
Goats	3,210	2,895	2,703
Chickens*	32,000	32,500	33,000

* FAO estimates.

Source: FAO.

LIVESTOCK PRODUCTS
('000 metric tons, FAO estimates)

	2008	2009	2010
Cattle meat	104.0	104.1	99.6
Goat meat	13.8	12.9	12.9
Pig meat	30.3	31.2	31.2
Chicken meat	61.0	61.9	61.9
Cows' milk	389	389	493
Hen eggs	29	30	30

Source: FAO.

Forestry

ROUNDWOOD REMOVALS
('000 cubic metres, excl. bark, FAO estimates)

	2008	2009	2010
Sawlogs, veneer logs and logs for sleepers	465	445	335
Pulpwood	81	81	8
Other industrial wood	112	112	175
Fuel wood	8,543	8,626	8,709
Total	9,202	9,264	9,227

2011: Production assumed to be unchanged from 2010 (FAO estimates).

Source: FAO.

SAWNWOOD PRODUCTION
('000 cubic metres, incl. railway sleepers, FAO estimates)

	2008	2009	2010
Coniferous (softwood)	254	254	163
Broadleaved (hardwood)	14	14	14
Total	268	268	177

2011: Production assumed to be unchanged from 2010 (FAO estimates).

Source: FAO.

Fishing

('000 metric tons, live weight, FAO estimates)

	2008	2009	2010
Capture	10.5	10.5	10.5
Tilapias	1.0	1.0	1.0
Other freshwater fishes	1.6	1.6	1.6
Dagaas	7.8	7.9	7.9
Aquaculture	2.6	2.7	2.7
Tilapias	2.6	2.7	2.7
Total catch	13.1	13.2	13.2

Note: Figures exclude aquatic animals, recorded by number rather than weight. The number of Nile crocodiles caught was: 81,554 in 2008; 62,101 in 2009; 104,731 in 2010.

Source: FAO.

Mining

('000 metric tons unless otherwise indicated)

	2008	2009	2010*
Asbestos	11	5	2
Chromium ore	442.6	193.7	510.0
Coal	1,947	1,750*	2,400
Cobalt ore (metric tons)†	28	39	60
Copper ore‡	2.8	3.6	4.7
Gold (kilograms)	3,579	4,965	9,100
Iron ore	3	n.a.	n.a.
Limestone	50*	40*	50
Magnesite (metric tons)	2,549	449	n.a.
Nickel ore (metric tons)	6,354	4,858	6,200
Phosphate rock	21.1	20.0*	63.0
Silver (kilograms)	150*	200*	400

* Estimate(s).

† Figures include metal content of compounds and salts and may include cobalt recovered from nickel-copper matte.

‡ Figures refer to the metal content of ores and concentrates.

Source: US Geological Survey.

Industry

SELECTED PRODUCTS
('000 metric tons unless otherwise indicated)

	2008	2009	2010
Coke (metallurgical)	112	43	20*
Cement*	400	700	800
Ferro-chromium	145.4	72.2	146.0*
Crude steel*	10	14	14
Refined copper—unwrought (metric tons)	3,072	4,000*	4,545
Refined nickel—unwrought (metric tons)	13,700*	5,000*	4,039

* Estimate(s).

Source: US Geological Survey.

Raw sugar ('000 metric tons): 446 in 2006; 349 in 2007; 291 in 2008 (Source: UN Industrial Commodity Statistics Database).

Electric energy (net production, million kWh): 8,508 in 2007; 7,990 in 2008; 7,878 in 2009 (Source: UN Industrial Commodity Statistics Database).

Finance

CURRENCY AND EXCHANGE RATES

Monetary Units
100 cents = 1 Zimbabwe dollar (Z.$).

Sterling, US Dollar and Euro Equivalents (31 December 2008)
£1 sterling = Z.$7,143,221.60;
US $1 = Z.$4,900,000.00;
€1 = Z.$6,819,326.81;
Z.$10,000 = £0.0014 = US $0.0020 = €0.0015.

Average Exchange Rate (Z.$ per US dollar)
2008 6,723,052,073

Note: On 1 August 2008 a redenomination of the Zimbabwe dollar was introduced whereby 10,000m. of the former currency was revalued at 1 dollar. In January 2009, in order to address the diminishing value of the national currency, a number of foreign currencies (including the US dollar, the euro, the British pound sterling, the South African rand and the Botswana pula), were also declared legal tender in Zimbabwe. A further massive redenomination of the Zimbabwe dollar was announced in February (whereby 1,000,000m. of the former currency was to be revalued at 1 dollar), but in April of the same year it was announced that legal use of the national currency was to be suspended for at least one year. Foreign currencies (specifically those of Botswana, the Euro Zone, South Africa, the United Kingdom and the USA) are currently in use

BUDGET
(US $ million, estimates)

Revenue*	2008	2009	2010
Tax revenue	128	883	2,074
Personal income tax	22	156	428
Corporate income tax	18	44	256
Other direct taxes	3	21	168
Customs	45	212	340
Excise	6	68	165
Value-added tax	32	367	689
Other taxes	2	14	28
Non-tax revenue	5	51	124
Total	133	934	2,198

Expenditure	2008	2009	2010
Current expenditure	240	1,099	1,809
Salaries and wages	52	419	784
Pensions and benefits	7	98	279
Interest payments	138	198	206
Foreign	137	194	206
Domestic	1	3	0
Grants and transfers	11	123	178
Other current expenditure	32	260	362
Capital expenditure†	17	46	593
Total	257	1,145	2,402

* Excluding budget grants received (US $ million, estimates): 0 in 2008; 41 in 2009; 1 in 2010, and off-budget grants received (excl. food aid, US $ million, estimates): 0 in 2008; 351 in 2009; 630 in 2010.

† Including net lending.

2011 (US $ million, projections): *Revenue:* Tax revenue 2,418; Non-tax revenue 180; Budget grants 3; Total 2,601. Note: Data exclude off-budget grants (excl. food aid) 571. *Expenditure:* Current expenditure 2,372; Capital expenditure (incl. net lending) 811; Total 3,184.

2012 (US $ million, projections): *Revenue:* Tax revenue 2,503; Non-tax revenue 178; Budget grants 3; Total 2,684. Note: Data exclude off-budget grants (excl. food aid) 435. *Expenditure:* Current expenditure 2,451; Capital expenditure (incl. net lending) 718; Total 3,169.

Source: IMF, *Zimbabwe: 2011 Article IV Consultation-Staff Report; Staff Supplement; Public Information Notice on the Executive Board Discussion; and Statement by the Executive Director for Zimbabwe* (June 2011).

INTERNATIONAL RESERVES

(US $ million at 31 December)

	2000	2001	2002
Gold*	45.4	27.5	22.7
IMF special drawing rights	0.2	—	—
Reserve position in IMF	0.4	0.4	0.4
Foreign exchange	192.5	64.3	82.9
Total	238.5	92.2	106.0

* Valued at a market-related price which is determined each month.

2003–11: Reserve position in IMF 0.5.

IMF special drawing rights: 361.3 in 2009; 254.0 in 2010; 252.5 in 2011.
Source: IMF, *International Financial Statistics*.

MONEY SUPPLY

(Z.$ '000 million at 31 December)

	2005	2006	2007
Currency outside banks	9,876	228,064	73,075
Demand deposits at deposit money banks	34,048	404,965	350,999
Total money (incl. others)	44,746	636,799	425,445

Note: The value of the Zimbabwe dollar has not been adjusted retrospectively to reflect subsequent redenominations.

Source: IMF, *International Financial Statistics*.

COST OF LIVING

(Consumer Price Index; base: 2009 = 100)

	2010	2011
Food	104.0	n.a.
All items (incl. others)	103.1	106.6

Source: ILO.

NATIONAL ACCOUNTS

Expenditure on the Gross National Product

(US $ million at current prices)

	2008	2009	2010
Government final consumption expenditure	116.97	802.63	474.98
Private final consumption expenditure	6,621.42	5,689.87	7,680.49
Gross capital formation	313.88	754.94	639.48
Total domestic expenditure	7,052.27	7,247.43	8,794.96
Exports of goods and services	2,331.40	1,591.31	2,655.04
Less Imports of goods and services	3,888.63	3,213.10	4,245.71
GDP in purchasers' values	5,495.04	5,625.68	7,204.30

Source: UN, National Accounts Main Aggregates Database.

Gross Domestic Product by Economic Activity

(Z.$ million, at factor cost)

	2004	2005	2006
Agriculture, hunting, forestry and fishing	3,543	23,494	155,807
Mining and quarrying	5,038	34,722	239,307
Manufacturing	7,774	46,901	282,960
Electricity and water	1,661	6,739	27,343
Construction	666	1,138	15,262
Trade, restaurants and hotels	13,187	47,204	168,978
Transport, storage and communications	6,070	8,244	20,744
Finance, insurance and real estate	3,819	13,095	42,428
Government services	744	2,263	6,885
Other services	4,194	12,324	37,265
Sub-total	46,969	196,124	996,979
Less Imputed bank service charges	330	663	1,331
GDP at factor cost	46,365	195,463	995,648
Indirect taxes, less subsidies	2,688	9,615	34,413
Total	49,053	205,078	1,030,061

Source: African Development Bank.

2008 (US $ million): Agriculture, hunting, forestry and fishing 1,117; Mining, manufacturing and utilities 1,439 (Manufacturing 637); Construction 51; Wholesale, retail trade, restaurants and hotels 1,441; Transport, storage and communications 581; Other services 869; *Total, all industries* 5,498 (Source: UN, National Accounts Main Aggregates Database).

2009 (US $ million): Agriculture, hunting, forestry and fishing 876; Mining, manufacturing and utilities 1,379 (Manufacturing 826); Construction 33; Wholesale, retail trade, restaurants and hotels 616; Transport, storage and communications 854; Other services 1,133; *Total, all industries* 4,889 (Source: UN, National Accounts Main Aggregates Database).

2010 (US $ million): Agriculture, hunting, forestry and fishing 1,483; Mining, manufacturing and utilities 2,158 (Manufacturing 810); Construction 106; Wholesale, retail trade, restaurants and hotels 1,138; Transport, storage and communications 727; Other services 1,263; *Total, all industries* 6,875 (Source: UN, National Accounts Main Aggregates Database).

BALANCE OF PAYMENTS
(US $ million, estimates)

	2008	2009	2010
Exports of goods f.o.b.	1,662	1,616	3,382
Imports of goods f.o.b.	–2,630	–3,213	–5,162
Trade balance	–967	–1,598	–1,779
Non-factor services (net)	–207	–266	–444
Balance on goods and services	–1,174	–1,864	–2,223
Investment income (net)	–477	–442	–486
Balance on goods, services and income	–1,651	–2,306	–2,709
Private transfers (net)	625	879	974
Current balance	–1,026	–1,426	–1,735
Official transfers (net)	73	156	231
Direct investment (net)	44	105	123
Portfolio investment (net)	—	250	63
Long-term capital (net)	–174	–145	–77
Short-term capital (net)	192	241	369
IMF special drawing rights liabilities	—	520	—
Net errors and omissions	–222	395	377
Overall balance	–1,114	96	–649

Source: IMF, *Zimbabwe: 2011 Article IV Consultation—Staff Report; Staff Supplement; Public Information Notice on the Executive Board Discussion; and Statement by the Executive Director for Zimbabwe* (June 2011).

External Trade

PRINCIPAL COMMODITIES
(US $ million)

Imports f.o.b.	2008	2009	2010
Cereals	215.7	220.7	293.2
Maize	169.9	104.9	57.2
Animal, vegetable fats and oils, cleavage products, etc.	47.1	118.5	155.9
Safflower, sunflower/cottonseed oil and fractions	33.3	96.0	96.3
Mineral fuels, oils, distillation products, etc.	320.2	454.2	984.8
Petroleum and related products	266.1	334.8	858.7
Fertilizers	184.5	86.9	151.9
Mixtures of nitrogen, phosphorous and potassium fertilizers	164.6	50.8	64.6
Articles of iron and steel	91.6	110.0	119.8
Structures (rods, angle, plates) of iron and steel	39.3	51.5	24.0
Copper and copper articles	3.2	6.1	22.4
Nickel and nickel articles	108.0	138.7	605.1
Nuclear reactors, boilers, machinery, etc.	299.9	300.8	544.2
Vehicles other than railway, tramway	445.3	533.7	1,088.5
Tractors	74.2	51.8	42.5
Trucks, motor vehicles used for the transport of goods	200.4	269.5	456.6
Total (incl. others)	2,831.8	3,526.8	9,051.5

Exports	2008	2009	2010
Live trees, plants, bulbs, roots, cut flowers etc.	185.8	334.2	9.4
Edible vegetables, roots and tubers	37.3	2.9	1.2
Frozen vegetables	12.3	2.0	0.2
Sugars and sugar confectionery	42.6	78.5	52.5
Cane or beet sugar and chemically pure sucrose, in solid form	39.3	73.5	48.5
Tobacco and manufactured tobacco substitutes	127.4	276.2	478.1
Tobacco and tobacco refuse	99.9	241.8	420.0
Ores, slag and ash	137.3	181.2	310.1
Nickel ores and concentrates	132.7	170.5	269.8
Printed books, newspapers, pictures etc.	64.6	435.5	559.3
Cotton	146.4	114.4	162.5
Raw cotton	88.0	102.4	146.1
Pearls, precious stones, metals, coins, etc.	23.5	129.6	623.4
Gold unwrought or in semi-manufactured forms	8.1	102.1	287.2
Iron and steel	61.4	43.7	204.6
Ferro-alloys	47.5	30.9	194.5
Nickel and nickel articles	166.3	266.3	454.5
Nickel matte and nickel oxide sinters	149.1	251.8	440.7
Unwrought nickel	16.7	14.6	13.7
Electrical, electronic equipment	65.0	26.4	8.8
Vehicles other than railway, tramway	87.4	10.8	9.1
Cars (incl. station wagons)	9.7	1.4	1.8
Optical, photo, technical, medical, etc. apparatus	79.5	0.3	3.8
Furniture, lighting, signs, prefabricated buildings	17.6	15.7	11.5
Total (incl. others)	1,693.9	2,269.0	3,199.2

Source: Trade Map-Trade Competitiveness Map, International Trade Centre, www.intracen.org/marketanalysis.

PRINCIPAL TRADING PARTNERS
(US $ million)

Imports f.o.b.	2008	2009	2010
Botswana	214.8	198.6	243.6
China, People's Repub.	138.1	128.8	556.8
Germany	52.2	38.7	115.8
India	33.4	27.0	86.1
Kuwait	11.1	80.5	317.1
Malawi	24.3	6.7	78.6
Mauritius	5.7	43.5	80.6
Mozambique	81.7	145.1	257.0
Netherlands	15.0	8.3	31.3
South Africa	1,758.9	2,132.2	4,545.2
United Kingdom	67.4	70.7	254.9
USA	113.6	275.1	773.2
Zambia	61.9	91.3	220.6
Total (incl. others)	2,831.8	3,526.8	9,051.5

Exports f.o.b.	2008	2009	2010
Belgium	37.1	61.0	60.4
Botswana	157.0	36.9	28.0
China, People's Repub.	37.5	54.2	237.3
Congo, Democratic Repub.	14.8	14.7	25.0
France (incl. Monaco)	33.2	6.4	14.2
Germany	6.4	8.6	46.7
Italy	48.3	46.5	76.9
Lesotho	1.2	25.6	7.4
Malawi	72.7	29.9	34.6
Mozambique	41.1	98.2	91.9
Netherlands	169.3	187.8	13.3
Russia	4.8	7.7	6.3
Singapore	32.3	22.6	30.5
South Africa	711.3	1,192.2	1,734.5
Switzerland (incl. Liechtenstein)	33.2	169.6	20.0
United Kingdom	57.8	56.7	96.4
USA	20.8	10.0	29.9
Zambia	70.1	82.7	74.2
Total (incl. others)	1,693.9	2,269.0	3,199.2

Source: Trade Map-Trade Competitiveness Map, International Trade Centre, www.intracen.org/marketanalysis.

Transport

RAIL TRAFFIC
(National Railways of Zimbabwe, including operations in Botswana)

	1998	1999	2000
Total number of passengers ('000)	1,787	1,896	1,614
Revenue-earning metric tons hauled ('000)	12,421	12,028	9,422
Gross metric ton-km (million)	9,248	8,962	6,953
Net metric ton-km (million)	4,549	4,375	3,326

ROAD TRAFFIC
('000 motor vehicles in use, estimates)

	1998	1999	2000
Passenger cars	540	555	573
Commercial vehicles	37	38	39

2007 (motor vehicles in use at 31 December): Passenger cars 1,214,137; Buses and coaches 15,566; Vans and lorries 186,790; Motorcycles and mopeds 108,961 (Source: IRF, *World Road Statistics*).

CIVIL AVIATION
(traffic on scheduled services)

	2007	2008	2009
Kilometres flown (million)	11	11	11
Passengers carried ('000)	255	264	262
Passenger-km (million)	711	727	703
Total ton-km (million)	78	81	79

Source: UN, *Statistical Yearbook*.

Passengers carried ('000): 302 in 2010 (Source: World Bank, World Development Indicators database).

Tourism

VISITOR ARRIVALS BY NATIONALITY

	2007	2008	2009
Australia and New Zealand	18,947	20,201	33,041
Botswana	227,777	147,780	183,212
Canada and USA	31,412	37,754	48,809
Malawi	111,177	63,597	108,103
Mozambique	94,290	118,117	110,058
South Africa	1,362,982	936,727	912,244
United Kingdom	22,295	22,778	27,580
Zambia	301,265	346,344	230,198
Total (incl. others)	2,505,988	1,955,597	2,017,264

Tourism receipts (US $ million, excl. passenger transport): 294 in 2008; 523 in 2009; 634 in 2010.

Source: World Tourism Organization.

Communications Media

	2009	2010	2011
Telephones ('000 main lines in use)	385.1	379.0	356.0
Mobile cellular telephones ('000 subscribers)	2,991.0	7,700.0	9,200.0
Internet subscribers ('000)	99.7	121.0	n.a.
Broadband subscribers ('000)	29.1	33.0	34.0

Personal computers: 865,000 (69.4 per 1,000 persons) in 2006.

Radio receivers ('000 in use): 4,488 in 1999.

Television receivers ('000 in use): 410 in 2000.

Daily newspapers: 2 (average circulation 209,000 copies) in 1996; 3 in 2004.

Sources: UNESCO, *Statistical Yearbook*; UNESCO Institute for Statistics; UN, *Statistical Yearbook*; International Telecommunication Union.

Education

(2002/03 unless otherwise indicated)

	Institutions*	Teachers	Students
Pre-primary	n.a.	19,588	448,124
Primary	4,699	64,001†	2,445,520†
Secondary	1,539	33,964	831,488†
Tertiary	n.a.	4,081‡	94,611‡

* 1998 figures.
† 2005/06.
‡ 2009/10.

Source: mainly UNESCO Institute for Statistics.

Pupil-teacher ratio (primary education, UNESCO estimate): 38.2 in 2005/06 (Source: UNESCO Institute for Statistics).

Adult literacy rate (UNESCO estimates): 92.2% (males 94.7%; females 89.9%) in 2010 (Source: UNESCO Institute for Statistics).

Directory

The Constitution

The Constitution of the Republic of Zimbabwe took effect at independence on 18 April 1980. Amendments to the Constitution must have the approval of two-thirds of the members of both the House of Assembly and the Senate. The provisions of the 1980 Constitution (with subsequent amendments) are summarized below. Amendments pertaining to the transitional period were approved in February 2009. These amendments are summarized at the foot of this section.

THE REPUBLIC

Zimbabwe is a sovereign republic and the Constitution is the supreme law.

DECLARATION OF RIGHTS

The declaration of rights guarantees the fundamental rights and freedoms of the individual, regardless of race, tribe, place of origin, political opinions, colour, creed or sex.

THE PRESIDENT

Executive power is vested in the President, and may be exercised by him/her directly or through the Cabinet, a Vice-President, a Minister or a Deputy Minister. The President is Head of State, Head of Government and Commander-in-Chief of the Defence Forces. The President appoints no more than two Vice-Presidents and other Ministers and Deputy Ministers, to be members of the Cabinet. The President holds office for five years and is eligible for re-election.

PARLIAMENT

Legislative power is vested in the Legislature, which consists of the President and a bicameral Parliament, comprising the Senate and the House of Assembly. The Senate comprises 93 members, of whom 60 are directly elected by universal adult suffrage (six are elected in each of the 10 provinces by voters registered in the 60 senatorial constituencies), five are nominated by the President, 10 are provincial governors, two are the President and the Deputy President of the Council of Chiefs and 16 are traditional Chiefs. The life of the Senate is ordinarily to be five years. The House of Assembly comprises 210 members, all of whom are directly elected by universal adult suffrage. The life of the House of Assembly is ordinarily to be five years.

OTHER PROVISIONS

A Public Protector shall be appointed by the President, acting on the advice of the Judicial Service Commission, to investigate complaints against actions taken by employees of the Government or of a local authority.

Chiefs shall be appointed by the President, and shall form a Council of Chiefs from their number in accordance with customary principles of succession.

Other provisions relate to the Judicature, Defence and Police Forces, public service and finance.

TRANSITIONAL AMENDMENTS AND PROVISIONS

Following the unanimous approval of the Zimbabwe Amendment (No. 19) Bill by the House of Assembly and the Senate on 5 February 2009, certain transitional amendments to the Constitution, pertaining to the Interparty Political Agreement signed on 15 September 2008, were adopted. These stated that the President, the Prime Minister and the Cabinet shall all exercise executive authority. The Office of the President shall continue to be occupied by Robert Gabriel Mugabe, who chairs the Cabinet and the National Security Council and formally appoints the Vice-Presidents, the Prime Minister, the Deputy Prime Ministers, ministers and deputy ministers. Following consultation with the Vice-Presidents, the Prime Minister and the Deputy Prime Ministers, he also allocates ministerial portfolios. The Office of the Prime Minister shall be occupied by Morgan Tsvangirai, who chairs the Council of Ministers (which is a subset of the larger Cabinet and which acts as a liaison office) and is Deputy Chairperson of the Cabinet. There shall be two Vice-Presidents nominated by the President and/or the Zimbabwe African National Union—Patriotic Front (ZANU—PF). There shall be two Deputy Prime Ministers, one from the Movement for Democratic Change—Tsvangirai (MDC—T) and one from the Movement for Democratic Change—Mutambara (MDC—M). Provision is made for the nomination of ministers and deputy ministers by ZANU—PF, the MDC—T and the MDC—M. The President shall, at his discretion, appoint five persons to the existing positions of presidential senatorial appointments. An additional six appointed senatorial posts shall be created and filled by persons appointed by the President, four of whom shall be nominated by MDC—T and two by the MDC—M. The Cabinet, inter alia, evaluates and adopts all government policies and the consequential programmes and approves all international agreements. The Council of Ministers, which consists of all ministers from the Cabinet, ensures that the Prime Minister properly discharges his responsibility to oversee the implementation of the work of government and assesses the implementation of decisions made by the Cabinet.

The Government

HEAD OF STATE

President: ROBERT GABRIEL MUGABE (took office 31 December 1987; re-elected March 1990, 16–17 March 1996, 9–11 March 2002 and 27 June 2008).

THE CABINET

(September 2012)

The Cabinet comprises representatives of the Zimbabwe African National Union—Patriotic Front (ZANU—PF), the Movement for Democratic Change—Tsvangirai (MDC—T) and the Movement for Democratic Change—Mutambara (MDC—M).

Vice-President (ZANU—PF): JOHN NKOMO.

Vice-President (ZANU—PF): JOYCE MUJURU.

Prime Minister (MDC—T): MORGAN RICHARD TSVANGIRAI.

First Deputy Prime Minister (MDC—T): THOKOZANI KHUPE.

Second Deputy Prime Minister (MDC—M): ARTHUR MUTAMBARA.

Minister of Agriculture, Mechanisation and Irrigation Development (ZANU—PF): JOSEPH MADE.

Minister of Constitutional and Parliamentary Affairs (MDC—T): ERIC MATINENGA.

Minister of Defence (ZANU—PF): EMMERSON MNANGWAGWA.

Minister of Economic Planning and Development (MDC—T): TAPIWA MASHAKADA.

Minister of Education, Sports and Culture (MDC—M): DAVID COLTART.

Minister of Energy and Power Development (MDC—T): ELTON MANGOMA.

Minister of the Environment and Natural Resources (ZANU—PF): FRANCIS NHEMA.

Minister of Finance (MDC—T): TENDAI BITI.

Minister of Foreign Affairs (ZANU—PF): SIMBARASHE MUMBENGEGWI.

Minister of Health and Child Welfare (MDC—T): HENRY MADZORERA.

Minister of Higher and Tertiary Education (ZANU—PF): I. STANISLAUS GORERAZVO MUDENGE.

Minister of Home Affairs (ZANU—PF): KEMBO MOHADI.

Minister of Home Affairs (MDC—T): THERESA MAKONE.

Minister of Industry and Commerce (MDC—M): WELSHMAN NCUBE.

Minister of Information and Communications Technology (MDC—T): NELSON CHAMISA.

Minister of Justice and Legal Affairs (ZANU—PF): PATRICK ANTHONY CHINAMASA.

Minister of Labour (MDC—T): PAULINE GWANYANYA MPARIWA.

Minister of Lands and Rural Resettlement (ZANU—PF): HERBERT MURERWA.

Minister of Local Government and Urban and Rural Development (ZANU—PF): DR IGNATIUS MORGAN CHIMINYA CHOMBO.

Minister of Media, Information and Publicity (ZANU—PF): WEBSTER SHAMU.

Minister of Mines and Mining Development (ZANU—PF): OBERT MPOFU.

Minister of National Housing and Social Amenities (MDC—T): GILES MUTSEKWA.

Minister of Public Service (MDC—T): LUCIA MATIBENGA.

Minister of Public Works (MDC—T): JOEL GABUZA.

Minister of Regional Integration and International Co-operation (MDC—M): PRISCILLA MISIHAIRABWI.

Minister of Science and Technology (MDC—T): HENERI DZINOTYIWEI.

Minister of Small and Medium Enterprises and Co-operative Development (ZANU—PF): SITHEMBISO NYONI.

Minister of State Enterprises and Parastatals (MDC—T): GORDON MOYO.

Minister of State for National Security in the President's Office (ZANU—PF): SYDNEY SEKERAMAYI.

Minister of State for Presidential Affairs (ZANU—PF): DIDYMUS MUTASA.

Minister of State in the Prime Minister's Office (MDC—T): JAMESON TIMBA.

Minister of State in the Prime Minister's Office (MDC—T): SEKAI MASIKANA HOLLAND.

Minister of Tourism and the Hospitality Industry (ZANU—PF): WALTER MZEMBI.

Minister of Transport and Infrastructural Development (ZANU—PF): NICHOLAS GOCHE.

Minister of Water Resources (MDC—T): SAMUEL SIPEPA NKOMO.

Minister of Women's Affairs, Gender and Community Development (ZANU—PF): OLIVIA MUCHENA.

Minister of Youth Development, Indigenization and Empowerment (ZANU—PF): SAVIOR KASUKUWERE.

In addition, there are 20 deputy ministers, 10 from ZANU—PF, nine from the MDC—T and one from the MDC—M.

The Constitution provides for the Attorney-General to serve as an ex officio member of the Cabinet.

MINISTRIES

Office of the President: Munhumutapa Bldg, Samora Machel Ave, Private Bag 7700, Causeway, Harare; tel. (4) 707091.

Office of the Vice-Presidents: Munhumutapa Bldg, Samora Machel Ave, Private Bag 7700, Causeway, Harare; tel. (4) 707091.

Ministry of Agriculture, Mechanisation and Irrigation Development: Ngungunyana Bldg, 1 Borrowdale Rd, Private Bag 7701, Causeway, Harare; tel. (4) 700596; fax (4) 734646; internet www.moa.gov.zw.

Ministry of Constitutional and Parliamentary Affairs: Harare.

Ministry of Defence: Defence House, cnr Kwame Nkuruma and 3rd Sts, Harare; tel. (4) 700155; fax (4) 727501; internet www.mod.gov.zw.

Ministry of Economic Planning and Development: New Complex Bldg, Government Composite Offices, cnr 3rd St and Samora Machel Ave, Harare; e-mail moed@gta.gov.zw; internet www.mofed.gov.zw.

Ministry of Education, Sports and Culture: Ambassador House, Union Ave, POB CY121, Causeway, Harare; tel. (4) 734051; fax (4) 707599; internet www.moesc.gov.zw.

Ministry of Energy and Power Development: Chaminuka Bldg, Private Bag 7758, Causeway, Harare; tel. (4) 733095; fax (4) 797956; e-mail energy@gta.gov.zw; internet www.energy.gov.zw.

Ministry of the Environment and Natural Resources: Kaguvi Bldg, 12th Floor, cnr 4th St and Central Ave, Private Bag 7753, Causeway, Harare; tel. (4) 701681; fax (4) 252673; e-mail metlib@zarnet.ac.zw; internet www.met.gov.zw.

Ministry of Finance: Blocks B, E and G, Composite Bldg, cnr Samora Machel Ave and Fourth St, Private Bag 7705, Causeway, Harare; tel. (4) 738603; fax (4) 792750; internet www.mofed.gov.zw.

Ministry of Foreign Affairs: Munhumutapa Bldg, Samora Machel Ave, POB 4240, Causeway, Harare; tel. (4) 727005; fax (4) 705161; internet www.zimfa.gov.zw.

Ministry of Health and Child Welfare: Kaguvi Bldg, Fourth St, POB CY198, Causeway, Harare; tel. (4) 730011; fax (4) 729154; internet www.mohcw.gov.zw.

Ministry of Higher and Tertiary Education: Government Composite Bldg, cnr Fourth St and Samora Machel Ave, Union Ave, POB UA275, Harare; tel. (4) 796440; fax (4) 790923; e-mail thesecretary@mhet.ac.zw; internet www.mhet.ac.zw.

Ministry of Home Affairs: Mukwati Bldg, 11th Floor, cnr Fourth St and Livingstone Ave, Private Bag 7703, Causeway, Harare; tel. (4) 703641; fax (4) 707231; e-mail moha@gvt.co.zw; internet www.moha.gov.zw.

Ministry of Industry and Commerce: Mukwati Bldg, Fourth St, Private Bag 7708, Causeway, Harare; tel. (4) 702731; fax (4) 729311; internet www.miit.gov.zw.

Ministry of Information and Communications Technology: Linquenda House, Baker Ave, POB CY825, Causeway, Harare; tel. (4) 703894; fax (4) 707213.

Ministry of Justice and Legal Affairs: New Government Complex, cnr Samora Machel Ave and 4th St, Private Bag 7751, Causeway, Harare; tel. (4) 774620; fax (4) 772999; internet www.justice.gov.zw.

Ministry of Labour: Harare.

Ministry of Lands and Rural Resettlement: Block 2, Makombe Complex, cnr Harare St and Herbert Chitepo, Harare; tel. (4) 797325; internet www.lands.gov.zw.

Ministry of Local Government and Urban and Rural Development: Mukwati Bldg, Fourth St, Private Bag 7755, Causeway, Harare; tel. (4) 7282019; fax (4) 708493; internet www.mlgvturd.gov.zw.

Ministry of Media, Information and Publicity: Harare.

Ministry of Mines and Mining Development: ZIMRE Centre, 6th Floor, cnr Leopold Takawira St and Kwame Nkrumah Ave, Private Bag 7709, Causeway, Harare; tel. (4) 777022; fax (4) 777044; e-mail minsec@technopark.co.zw; internet www.mines.gov.zw.

Ministry of National Housing and Social Amenities: Kaguvi Bldg, 6th Floor, cnr 4th St and Central Ave, Private Bag 7780, Causeway, Harare; tel. (4) 790948.

Ministry of Public Service: Compensation House, cnr Central Ave and Fourth St, Private Bag 7707, Causeway, Harare; tel. (4) 790871; fax (4) 794568; e-mail mpslsw@gta.gov.zw; internet www.pslsw.gov.zw.

Ministry of Public Works: Harare.

Ministry of Regional Integration and International Co-operation: Harare.

Ministry of Science and Technology: Livingstone House, 17th Floor, 48 Samora Machel Avenue, Harare; tel. (4) 727579; fax (4) 734986; internet www.mstd.gov.zw.

Ministry of Small and Medium Enterprises and Co-operative Development: Linquenda House, cnr Nelson Mandela and First Sts, Private Bag 7740, Causeway, Harare; tel. (4) 731003; fax (4) 731879; e-mail info@msmed.gov.zw; internet www.msmed.gov.zw.

Ministry of State Enterprises and Parastatals: Harare.

Ministry of Tourism and the Hospitality Industry: Harare.

Ministry of Transport and Infrastructural Development: Kaguvi Bldg, 4th Central Ave, POB 595, Causeway, Harare; tel. (4) 252396; fax (4) 726661; e-mail angiekaronga@yahoo.co.uk; internet www.transcom.gov.zw.

Ministry of Water Resources: Kurima House, 8th Floor, cnr Nelson Madela Ave and Fourth St, Private Bag CY 7767, Harare; tel. (4) 700596; fax (4) 738165; internet www.water.gov.zw.

Ministry of Women's Affairs, Gender and Community Development: Kaguvi Bldg, 8th Floor, cnr Fourth St and Central Ave, Harare; tel. (4) 708389; internet www.women.gov.zw.

Ministry of Youth Development, Indigenization and Empowerment: ZANU—PF Bldg, Private Bag 7762, Causeway, Harare; tel. (4) 734691; fax (4) 732709; e-mail mydgec@zarnet.ac.zw; internet www.mydgec.gov.zw.

PROVINCIAL GOVERNORS

(September 2012)

Bulawayo: Cain Mathema.

Harare: David Karimanzira.

Manicaland: Christopher Mushohwe.

Mashonaland Central: Martin Dinha.

Mashonaland East: Aeneas Chigwedere.

Mashonaland West: Faber Chidarikire.

Masvingo: Titus Maluleke.

Matabeleland North: Thokozile Mathuthu.

Matabeleland South: Angeline Masuku.

Midlands: Jaison Machaya.

President and Legislature

PRESIDENT

Presidential Election, First Round, 29 March 2008

Candidate	Votes	% of valid votes
Morgan Tsvangirai	1,195,562	47.87
Robert Gabriel Mugabe	1,079,730	43.24
Simba Herbert Makoni	207,470	8.31
Langton Towungana	14,503	0.58
Total	2,497,265	100.00

Presidential Election, Second Round, 27 June 2008, provisional results

Candidate	Votes	% of valid votes
Robert Gabriel Mugabe	2,150,269	90.21
Morgan Tsvangirai*	233,000	9.78
Total†	2,383,629	100.00

* Tsvangirai announced his withdrawal from the second round of voting on 22 June; however, the Zimbabwe Election Commission stated that the Constitution necessitated that the run-off take place and Tsvangirai's name remained on the ballot papers.

† Excludes 131,481 spoiled ballots.

HOUSE OF ASSEMBLY

Speaker: Lovemore Moyo.

General Election, 29 March 2008, provisional results

Party	Votes	% of votes	Seats
MDC—Tsvangirai	1,041,176	42.99	99
ZANU—PF	1,110,649	45.86	97
MDC—Mutambara	202,259	8.35	10
Independents	54,254	2.24	1
Others	13,635	0.56	—
Total	2,421,973	100.00	207*

* Voting was postponed in three constituencies, owing to the deaths of candidates.

SENATE

Speaker: EDNA MADZONGWE.

General Election, 29 March 2008, provisional results

Party	Seats
ZANU—PF	30
MDC—Tsvangirai	24
MDC—Mutambara	6
Total	60*

* In addition to the 60 directly elective seats, five are held by nominees of the President, 10 by provincial governors, two by the President and the Deputy President of the Council of Chiefs and 16 by traditional Chiefs.

Election Commission

Zimbabwe Electoral Commission (ZEC): Century House East, PMB 7782, Causeway, Harare; tel. (4) 759130; fax (4) 781903; e-mail zecpr@gta.gov.zw; internet www.zimbabweelectoralcommission.org; f. 2005; the President appoints eight members, four of whom must be women, and also the Chair. in consultation with the Judicial Service Commission and the Committee on Standing Rules and Orders for a six-year term; superseded and replaced the Electoral Supervisory Commission (abolished Aug. 2005); responsible for establishing constituency boundaries, voter registration and conducting elections; Chair. SIMPSON MTAMBANENGWE.

Political Organizations

Christian Democratic Party: Leader WILLIAM GWATA.

Mavambo Kusile Dawn (MKD): Harare; internet www.mavambokusiledawn.org; f. 2009; Leader SIMBA MAKONI.

Movement for Democratic Change—Mutambara (MDC—M): 11 Creswick Rd, Hillside, Harare; tel. (4) 747071; e-mail a.mutambara@mdczim.com; internet www.mdczim.net; f. 2005; Pres. Prof. WELSHMAN NCUBE.

Movement for Democratic Change—Tsvangirai (MDC—T): Harvest House, 6th Floor, cnr Angwa St and Nelson Mandela Ave, Harare; tel. (4) 770708; fax (4) 780302; e-mail mdcnewsbrief@gmail.com; internet www.mdc.co.zw; f. 2005; allied to Zimbabwe Congress of Trade Unions; Pres. MORGAN TSVANGIRAI; Sec.-Gen. TENDAI BITI.

Mthwakazi Liberation Front: Office 9, Solomon Building, cnr Raymond and Rockey Sts, Yeoville, Johannesburg, South Africa; f. 2010; secessionist movement; Leader PAUL SIWELA.

United People's Party (UPP): f. 2006; Leader DANIEL SHUMBA.

Zimbabwe African National Union—Ndonga (ZANU—Ndonga): POB UA525, Union Ave, Harare; tel. and fax (4) 481180; f. 1977; breakaway faction from ZANU, also includes fmr mems of United African Nat. Council; supports free market economy; Nat. Chair. REKETAI MUSHIWEKUFA SEMWAYO; Sec.-Gen. EDWIN C. NGUWA.

Zimbabwe African National Union—Patriotic Front (ZANU—PF): cnr Rotten Row and Samora Machel Ave, POB 4530, Harare; tel. (4) 753329; fax (4) 774146; f. 1989 by merger of PF—ZAPU and ZANU—PF; Pres. ROBERT GABRIEL MUGABE; Vice-Pres SIMON VENGAYI MUZENDA, JOHN NKOMO; Nat. Chair. SIMON KHAYA MOYO.

Zimbabwe African People's Union (ZAPU): 18 Jason Ziyaphapha Moyo St, Bulwayo; tel. (9) 888850; fax (9) 881378; e-mail info@zapu.org; internet www.zapu.org; f. 1961; merged into ZANU-PF in 1987; re-established 2008; Pres. Dr DUMISO DABENGWA; Sec.-Gen. Dr RALPH MGUNI.

Zimbabwe Development Party: Harare; Leader KISINOTI MUKWAZHE.

Zimbabwe Integrated Programme: f. 1999; seeks economic reforms; Pres. Prof. HENEDI DZINOCHIKIWEYI.

Zimbabwe People's Democratic Party: POB 4001, Harare; e-mail mail@zpdp.org; internet www.zpdp.org; f. 1991; Chair. ISABEL SHANANGURAI MADANGURE; Sec.-Gen. DUDLEY GURA.

Zimbabwe Progressive People's Democratic Party: Harare; Leader TAFIRENYIKA MUDAVANHU.

Zimbabwe Youth in Alliance: Leader MOSES MUTYASIRA.

Diplomatic Representation

EMBASSIES IN ZIMBABWE

Algeria: 8 Pascoe Ave, Belgravia, Harare; tel. (4) 791773; fax (4) 701125; e-mail offambalch@utande.co.zw; internet www.algerianembassy-harare.org; Ambassador LAZHAR SOUALEM.

Angola: 26 Speke Ave, POB 3590, Harare; tel. (4) 770075; fax (4) 770077; Ambassador FILIPE PEDRO HENDRICK VAAL NETO.

Australia: 1 Green Close, Borrowdale, Harare; POB 4541, Harare; tel. (4) 852471; fax (4) 870566; e-mail zimbabwe.embassy@dfat.gov.au; internet www.zimbabwe.embassy.gov.au; Ambassador MATTHEW NEUHAUS.

Austria: 13 Duthie Rd, Alexandra Park, POB 4120, Harare; tel. (4) 702921; fax (4) 705877; e-mail harare-ob@bmeia.gv.at; Ambassador Dr MARIA MOYA-GÖTSCH.

Botswana: 22 Phillips Ave, Belgravia, POB 563, Harare; tel. (4) 729551; fax (4) 721360; Ambassador GLADYS KOKORWE.

Brazil: Old Mutual Centre, 9th Floor, Jason Moyo Ave, POB 2530, Harare; tel. (4) 790740; fax (4) 790754; e-mail brasemb@ecoweb.co.zw; internet www.brazil.org.zw; Ambassador RAUL DE TAUNAY.

Bulgaria: 15 Maasdorp Ave, Alexandra Park, POB 1809, Harare; tel. (4) 730509; fax (4) 732504; e-mail bgembhre@ecoweb.co.zw; Ambassador CHRISTO TEPAVITCHAROV.

Canada: 45 Baines Ave, POB 1430, Harare; tel. (4) 252181; fax (4) 252186; e-mail hrare@international.gc.ca; internet www.canadainternational.gc.ca/zimbabwe; Ambassador LISA STADELBAUER.

China, People's Republic: 30 Baines Ave, POB 4749, Harare; tel. and fax (4) 794155; e-mail chinaemb_zw@mfa.gov.cn; internet www.chinaembassy.org.zw; Ambassador LIN LIN.

Congo, Democratic Republic: 5 Pevensey Rd, Highlands, POB 2446, Harare; tel. (4) 481172; fax (4) 796421; e-mail harare@embadrcongo.co.zw; internet www.embadrcongo.co.zw; Ambassador MAWAMPANGA MWANA NANGA.

Cuba: 5 Phillips Ave, Belgravia, POB A1196, Harare; tel. (4) 790126; fax (4) 707998; e-mail cuba.embassy@cubanembassy.co.zw; internet www.cubadiplomatica.cu/zimbabwe; Ambassador ENRIQUE ANTONIO PRIETO LÓPEZ.

Czech Republic: 4 Sandringham Dr., Alexandra Park, GPO 4474, Harare; tel. (4) 700636; fax (4) 720930; e-mail harare@embassy.mzv.cz; internet www.mzv.cz/harare; Chargé d'affaires LUDĚK ZAHRADNÍČEK.

Egypt: 7 Aberdeen Rd, Avondale, POB A433, Harare; tel. (4) 303445; fax (4) 303115; Ambassador GAMEEL SAEED FAYED.

Ethiopia: 14 Lanark Rd, Belgravia, POB 2745, Harare; tel. (4) 701514; fax (4) 701516; e-mail emb@ecoweb.co.zw; Ambassador ADBI DALAL MOHAMMED.

France: Bank Chambers, 11th Floor, 74–76 Samora Machel Ave, POB 1378, Harare; tel. (4) 703216; fax (4) 730078; e-mail web.harare@diplomatie.gouv.fr; internet www.ambafrance-zw.org; Ambassador FRANÇOIS PONGE.

Germany: 30 Ceres Rd, Avondale, POB A1475, Harare; tel. (4) 308655; fax (4) 303455; e-mail botschaft_harare@gmx.de; internet www.harare.diplo.de; Ambassador Dr ALBRECHT CONZE.

Ghana: 11 Downie Ave, Belgravia, POB 4445, Harare; tel. (4) 700982; fax (4) 707076; e-mail ghanaembassy@zol.co.zw; Ambassador JAMES OKOE NAADJIE.

Greece: 8 Deary Ave, Belgravia, POB 4809, Harare; tel. (4) 793208; fax (4) 703662; e-mail grembha@ecoweb.co.zw; Ambassador MICHAEL KOUKAKIS.

Holy See: 5 St Kilda Rd, Mount Pleasant, POB MP191, Harare (Apostolic Nunciature); tel. (4) 744547; fax (4) 744412; e-mail nunzim@zol.co.zw; Apostolic Nuncio Most Rev. GEORGE KOCHERRY (Titular Archbishop of Othona).

India: 12 Natal Rd, Belgravia, POB 4620, Harare; tel. (4) 795955; fax (4) 722324; e-mail ambassador@embindia.org.zw; Ambassador V. ASHOK.

Indonesia: 3 Duthie Ave, Belgravia, POB CY 69, Causeway, Harare; tel. (4) 251799; fax (4) 796587; e-mail indohar@ecoweb.co

.zw; internet www.indonesia-harare.org; Ambassador EDDY POERWANA.

Iran: 8 Allan Wilson Ave, Avondale, POB A293, Harare; tel. (4) 726942; Ambassador MOHAMMAD POUR-NAJAF.

Italy: 7 Bartholomew Close, Greendale North, POB 1062, Harare; tel. (4) 498190; fax (4) 498199; e-mail ambasciata.harare@esteri.it; internet www.ambharare.esteri.it; Ambassador STEFANO MOSCATELLI.

Japan: Social Security Centre, 4th Floor, cnr Julius Nyerere Way and Sam Nujoma St, POB 2710, Harare; tel. (4) 250025; fax (4) 250111; internet www.zw.emb-japan.go.jp; Ambassador MORITA KOICHI.

Kenya: 95 Park Lane, POB 4069, Harare; tel. (4) 704820; fax (4) 723042; Ambassador Prof. JOHN ABDUBA.

Korea, Democratic People's Republic: 102 Josiah Chinamano Ave, Greenwood, POB 4754, Harare; tel. (4) 724052; Ambassador AN HUI JONG (resident in South Africa).

Kuwait: 1 Bath Rd, Avondale, POB A485, Harare; Ambassador ABDALLAH JUMA ABDALLAH AS-SHARHAN.

Libya: 124 Harare St, POB 4310, Harare; tel. (4) 728381; Ambassador (vacant).

Malawi: 9–11 Duthie Rd, Alexandra Park, POB 321, Harare; tel. (4) 798584; fax (4) 799006; e-mail malahigh@africaonline.co.zw; Ambassador Prof. RICHARD PHOYA.

Malaysia: 40 Downie Ave, Avondale, POB 5570, Harare; tel. (4) 334413; fax (4) 334415; e-mail malharare@kln.gov.my; Ambassador CHEAH CHOONG KIT.

Mozambique: 152 cnr Herbert Chitepo Ave and Leopold Takawira St, POB 4608, Harare; tel. (4) 253871; fax (4) 253875; e-mail emba@embamoc.org.zw; Ambassador VICENTE MEBUNIA VELOSO.

Netherlands: 2 Arden Rd, Highlands, POB HG601, Harare; tel. (4) 776701; fax (4) 776700; e-mail har@minbuza.nl; Ambassador BARBARA JOZIASSE.

Nigeria: 36 Samora Machel Ave, POB 4742, Harare; tel. (4) 253900; fax (4) 253877; e-mail ngrharamb@yahoo.com; internet www.nigeriaharare.co.zw; Ambassador ADEKUNLE OLADOKUN ADEYANJU.

Norway: 5 Lanark Rd, Belgravia, POB A510, Avondale, Harare; tel. (4) 252426; fax (4) 252430; e-mail emb.harare@mfa.no; internet www.norway.org.zw; Ambassador GUNNAR FØRELAND.

Pakistan: 314 Pipendale Rd, Barrowadalf, Harare; tel. (4) 762018; fax (4) 794264; e-mail pahichar@yahoo.com; Ambassador (vacant).

Portugal: 12 Harvey Brown Ave, Milton Park, Harare; tel. (4) 253023; fax (4) 253637; e-mail embport@harare.dgaccp.pt; Ambassador JOÃO DA CÂMARA.

Romania: 105 Fourth St, POB 4797, Harare; tel. (4) 700853; e-mail romemb@cybersatafrica.com; Chargé d'affaires a.i. FLORICĂ BARBU.

Russia: 70 Fife Ave, POB 4250, Harare; tel. (4) 701957; fax (4) 795932; e-mail russianembassy@zol.co.zw; internet www.zimbabwe.mid.ru; Ambassador SERGEI KRYUKOV.

South Africa: 7 Elcombe Rd, Belgravia, POB A1654, Harare; tel. (4) 753147; fax (4) 749657; e-mail admin@saembassy.co.zw; Ambassador VUSI MAVIMBELA.

Spain: 16 Phillips Ave, Belgravia, POB 3300, Harare; tel. (4) 250740; fax (4) 795261; e-mail emb.harare@mae.es; Ambassador (vacant).

Sudan: 4 Pascoe Ave, Harare; tel. (4) 700111; fax (4) 703450; e-mail sudan@africaonline.co.zw; internet www.sudaniharare.org.zw; Ambassador HASSAN AHMED FAGEERI.

Sweden: 32 Aberdeen Rd, Avondale, POB 4110, Harare; tel. (4) 302636; fax (4) 302236; e-mail ambassaden.harare@foreign.ministry.se; internet www.swedenabroad.com/harare; Ambassador ANDERS LIDÉN.

Switzerland: 15 Fleetwood Rd, Alexandra Park, POB 3440, Harare; tel. (4) 745682; fax (4) 745465; e-mail har.vertretung@eda.admin.ch; internet www.eda.admin.ch/harare; Ambassador ALEXANDER WITTWER.

Tanzania: Ujamaa House, 23 Baines Ave, POB 4841, Harare; tel. (4) 792714; fax (4) 792747; e-mail tanrep@icon.co.zw; Ambassador ADADI RAJABU.

United Kingdom: 3 Norfolk Rd, Mount Pleasant, POB 4490, Harare; tel. (4) 338800; fax (4) 338829; e-mail consular.harare@fco.gov.uk; internet ukinzimbabwe.fco.gov.uk/en; Ambassador DEBORAH BRONNERT.

USA: 172 Herbert Chitepo Ave, POB 3340, Harare; tel. (4) 250593; fax (4) 796488; e-mail hararepas@state.gov; internet harare.usembassy.gov; Ambassador BRUCE DAVID WHARTON.

Zambia: Zambia House, cnr Union and Julius Nyerere Aves, POB 4698, Harare; tel. (4) 773777; Ambassador SIPULA KABANJE.

Judicial System

The legal system is Roman-Dutch, based on the system which was in force in the Cape of Good Hope on 10 June 1891, as modified by subsequent legislation.

The Supreme Court

Harare.

Has original jurisdiction in matters in which an infringement of Chapter III of the Constitution defining fundamental rights is alleged. In all other matters it has appellate jurisdiction only. It consists of the Chief Justice, a Deputy Chief Justice and such other judges of the Supreme Court, being not less than two, as the President may deem necessary.

Chief Justice: GODFREY CHIDYAUSIKU.

Deputy Chief Justice: LUKE MALABA.

Other Judges: W. SANDURA, RITA MAKARAU.

The High Court

Harare.

Consists of the Chief Justice, the Judge President, and such other judges of the High Court as may from time to time be appointed.

Judge President: GEORGE CHIWESHE.

Other Judges: SUSAN MAVANGIRA, LAVENDER MAKONI, BEN HLATSHWAYO, NICHOLAS MATHONSI, ANDREW MUTEMA, GARAINESU MAWADZE.

Below the High Court are Regional Courts and Magistrates' Courts with both civil and criminal jurisdiction presided over by full-time professional magistrates. The Customary Law and Local Courts Act, adopted in 1990, abolished the village and community courts and replaced them with customary law and local courts, presided over by chiefs and headmen; in the case of chiefs, jurisdiction to try customary law cases is limited to those where the monetary values concerned do not exceed Z.$1,000 and in the case of a headman's court Z.$500. Appeals from the Chiefs' Courts are heard in Magistrates' Courts and, ultimately, the Supreme Court. All magistrates now have jurisdiction to try cases determinable by customary law.

Attorney-General: JOHANNES TOMANA.

Religion

AFRICAN RELIGIONS

Many Zimbabweans follow traditional beliefs.

CHRISTIANITY

About 55% of the population are Christians.

Zimbabwe Council of Churches: 128 Mbuya Nehanda St, POB 3566, Harare; tel. (4) 772043; fax (4) 773650; e-mail zcc@africaonline.co.zw; f. 1964; Pres. Rt Rev. Dr WILSON SITSHEBO; Gen. Sec. DENSEN MAFIYANI; 24 mem. churches, nine assoc. mems.

The Anglican Communion

Anglicans are adherents of the Church of the Province of Central Africa, covering Botswana, Malawi, Zambia and Zimbabwe. The Church comprises 15 dioceses, including five in Zimbabwe. The current Archbishop of the Province is the Bishop of Northern Zambia.

Bishop of Central Zimbabwe: Rt Rev. ISHMAEL MUKUWANDA, POB 25, Gweru; tel. (54) 21030; fax (54) 21097; e-mail diocent@telconet.co.zw.

Bishop of Harare: Rt Rev. CHAD NICHOLAS GANDIYA, 9 Monmouth Rd, Avondale, Harare; tel. (4) 308042; e-mail diohrecpca@ecoweb.co.zw.

Bishop of Manicaland: JULIUS TAWONA MAKONI, 113 Herbert Chitepo St, Mutare; tel. (20) 64194; fax (20) 63076; e-mail diomani@syscom.co.zw; internet www.anglicandioceseofmanicaland.co.zw.

Bishop of Masvingo: Rt Rev. GODFREY TOANEZVI, POB 1421, Masvingo; tel. (39) 362536; e-mail anglicandiomsv@comone.co.zw.

Bishop of Matabeleland: Rt Rev. CLEOPHAS LUNGA, POB 2422, Bulawayo; tel. (9) 61370; fax (9) 68353; e-mail clunga@aol.com.

The Roman Catholic Church

For ecclesiastical purposes, Zimbabwe comprises two archdioceses and six dioceses. The number of adherents is equivalent to an estimated 10% of the total population.

Zimbabwe Catholic Bishops' Conference (ZCBC)

Catholic Secretariat, Causeway, 29 Selous Ave, POB 8135, Harare; tel. (4) 705368; fax (4) 705369; internet www.zcbc.co.zw.

f. 1969; Pres. Most Rev. ROBERT C. NDLOVU (Archbishop of Harare).

Archbishop of Bulawayo: Most Rev. ALEX THOMAS KALIYANIL, cnr Lobengula St and 9th Ave, POB 837, Bulawayo; tel. (9) 63590; fax (9) 60359; e-mail archdbyo@mweb.co.zw.

Archbishop of Harare: Most Rev. ROBERT C. NDLOVU, Archbishop's House, 66 Fifth St, POB CY330, Causeway, Harare; tel. (4) 727386; fax (4) 721598; e-mail hrearch@zol.co.zw.

Other Christian Churches

At mid-2000 there were an estimated 4.8m. adherents professing other forms of Christianity.

Dutch Reformed Church in Zimbabwe (Nederduitse Gereformeerde Kerk): 35 Samora Machel Ave, POB 503, Harare; tel. (4) 774738; fax (4) 774739; e-mail pvanvuuren@mango.zw; f. 1895; 11 congregations in Zimbabwe and two in Zambia; Chair. Rev. PIETER F. J. VAN VUUREN; Sec. Rev. J. HAASBROEK; 1,245 mems.

Evangelical Lutheran Church: 7 Lawley Rd, POB 2175, Bulawayo; tel. (9) 254991; fax (9) 254993; e-mail elczhead@mweb.co.zw; f. 1903; Sec. Rt Rev. L. M. DUBE; 150,000 mems (2009).

Greek Orthodox Church: POB 2832, Harare; tel. (4) 744991; fax (4) 744928; e-mail zimbabwe@greekorthodox-zimbabwe.org; internet www.greekorthodox-zimbabwe.org; f. 1968; Archbishop SERAPHIM KYKKOTIS.

Methodist Church in Zimbabwe: POB CY71, Causeway, Harare; tel. (4) 250523; fax (4) 723709; e-mail methodistconn@zol.co.zw; f. 1891; Presiding Bishop Rev. SIMBARASHE SITHOLE; Sec. of Conference Rev. AMOS NDHLUMBI.

United Congregational Church of Southern Africa: 40 Jason Moyo St, POB 2451, Bulawayo; tel. (9) 63686; internet www.uccsa.org.za/zimbabwe-synod; Chair. Rev. B. MATHEMA (acting); Sec. Rev. MAJAHA NTHLIZIYO.

United Methodist Church: POB 3408, Harare; tel. (4) 704127; f. 1890; Bishop of Zimbabwe EBEN NHIWATIWA; 45,000 mems.

Among other denominations active in Zimbabwe are the African Methodist Church, the African Methodist Episcopal Church, the African Reformed Church, the Christian Marching Church, the Church of Christ in Zimbabwe, the Independent African Church, the Presbyterian Church (and the City Presbyterian Church), the United Church of Christ, the Zimbabwe Assemblies of God and the Ziwezano Church.

JUDAISM

The Jewish community numbered 897 members at 31 December 1997; by 2006 that number had fallen to around 300.

Zimbabwe Jewish Board of Deputies: POB 1954, Harare; tel. (4) 702507; fax (4) 702506; Pres. P. STERNBERG; Sec. E. ALHADEFF.

BAHÁ'Í FAITH

National Spiritual Assembly: POB GD380, Greendale, Harare; tel. (4) 495945; fax (4) 744611; internet www.bahai.co.zw; Nat. Sec. DEREK SITHOLE; f. 1970; mems resident in 57 clusters.

The Press

DAILIES

In 2011 there were five daily newspapers in Zimbabwe.

The Chronicle: 9th Ave and George Silundika St, POB 585, Bulawayo; tel. (9) 888871; fax (9) 888884; e-mail editor@chronicle.co.zw; internet www.chronicle.co.zw; f. 1894; publ. by govt-controlled co Zimpapers; circulates throughout south-west Zimbabwe; English; Editor ITAI MUSENGEYI; circ. 25,000 (2004).

The Daily News: 18 Sam Nujoma St and cnr Speke Ave, Harare; tel. (4) 753027; fax (4) 753024; internet www.dailynews.co.zw; publ. by Associated Newspapers of Zimbabwe; English; publ. suspended Sept. 2003; Editor NQOBILE NYATHI; CEO SAM SIPEPA NKOMO; Chair. STRIVE MASIYIWA; circ. c. 80,000 (2003).

The Herald: POB 396, Harare; tel. (4) 795771; fax (4) 700305; internet www.herald.co.zw; f. 1891; publ. by govt-controlled co Zimpapers; English; Editor INNOCENT GORE; circ. c. 60,000 (2006).

NewsDay: Harare; tel. (4) 773839; e-mail newsday@zimind.co.zw; internet www.newsday.co.zw; f. 2009; owned by ZimInd Publrs (Pvt) Ltd; Editor-in-Chief VINCENT KAHIYA.

The Zimbabwe Mail: e-mail editor@thezimbabwemail.com; internet www.thezimbabwemail.com; f. 2011; Exec. Chair. LEIGHTON MUSHANINGA; Man. Editor NKULULEKO NDLOVU.

WEEKLIES

Financial Gazette: Coal House, 5th Floor, cnr Nelson Mandela Ave and Leopold Takawira St, Harare; tel. (4) 781571; fax (4) 781578; e-mail schamunorwa@fingaz.co.zw; internet www.fingaz.co.zw; f. 1969; publ. by ZimInd Publrs (Pvt) Ltd; affiliated to the ZANU—PF party; Editor-in-Chief SUNSLEEY CHAMUNORWA; Gen. Man. JACOB CHISESE; circ. c. 40,000 (2004).

Indonsakusa/Ilanga: c/o CNG, POB 6520, Harare; tel. (4) 796855; fax (4) 703873; publ. by Community Newspaper Group (Mass Media Trust); distributed in north and south Matabeleland; circ. c. 10,000.

Kwayedza: POB 396, Harare; tel. (4) 795771; fax (4) 791311; internet www.kwayedza.co.zw; publ. by govt-controlled co Zimpapers; f. 1985; ChiShona; Editor GERVASE M. CHITEWE; circ. c. 15,000 (2003).

Manica Post: POB 960, Mutare; tel. (20) 61212; fax (20) 61149; internet www.manicapost.com; f. 1893; publ. by govt-controlled co Zimpapers; English; Editor PAUL MAMBO; circ. 15,000 (2004).

Mashonaland Guardian/Telegraph: c/o CNG, POB 6520, Harare; tel. (4) 796855; fax (4) 703873; publ. by Community Newspaper Group (Mass Media Trust); distributed in Mashonaland; circ. c. 10,000.

Masvingo Mirror: POB 1214, Masvingo; tel. (39) 64372; fax (39) 64484; independent; Editor NORNA EDWARDS.

Masvingo Star: 2–3 New Market Centre, R. Tangwena Ave, POB 138, Masvingo; tel. and fax (39) 63978; publ. by Community Newspaper Group (Mass Media Trust); English; distributed in Masvingo province; Editor (vacant); circ. c. 10,000.

Midlands Observer: POB 533, Kwekwe; tel. (55) 22248; fax (55) 23985; e-mail nelson_mashiri@yahoo.com; f. 1953; weekly; English; Editor R. JARIJARI; circ. 20,000.

The Standard: 1st Block, 3rd Floor, Ernst and Young Bldg, 1 Kwame Nkrumah Ave, POB 661730, Kopje, Harare; tel. (4) 773930; fax (4) 798897; internet www.thestandard.co.zw; f. 1997; publ. by ZimInd Publrs (Pvt) Ltd; Sun.; Chair. TREVOR NCUBE; Editor NEVANJI MADANHIRE; circ. 42,000 (2004).

Sunday Mail: POB 396, Harare; tel. (4) 795771; fax (4) 700305; internet www.sundaymail.co.zw; f. 1935; publ. by govt-controlled co Zimpapers; English; Chair. THOMAS SITHOLE; Editor WILLIAM CHIKOTO; circ. 110,000 (2004).

Sunday News: POB 585, Bulawayo; tel. (9) 540071; fax (9) 540084; f. 1930; publ. by govt-controlled co Zimpapers; English; Editor BREZHNEV MALABA; circ. 30,000 (2004).

The Times: c/o CNG, POB 6520, Harare; tel. (4) 796855; fax (4) 703873; f. 1897; fmrly *The Gweru Times*; publ. by Community Newspaper Group (Mass Media Trust); distributed in Mashonaland; English; circ. c. 5,000.

uMthunywa (The Messenger): 9th Ave and George Silundika St, POB 585 Bulawayo; tel. (9) 880888; fax (9) 888884; e-mail advertising@chronicle.co.zw; internet www.umthunywa.co.zw; f. 2004; SiNdebele; publ. by govt-controlled co Zimpapers; Editor BHEKITHEMBA J. NCUBE.

The Vanguard: Zimbabwe National Students' Union, 21 Wembley Cres., Eastlea, Harare; tel. (4) 788135; e-mail zinasu@gmail.com; publ. by the Zimbabwe Nat. Students' Union.

Zimbabwe Independent: Zimind Publishers (Pvt) Ltd, Suites 23/24, 1 Union Ave, POB BE1165, Belvedere, Harare; e-mail trevorn@mg.co.za; internet www.theindependent.co.zw; f. 1996; publ. by ZimInd Publrs (Pvt) Ltd; English; Chair. TREVOR NCUBE; Editor DUMISANI MULEYA; circ. 30,500 (2005).

The Zimbabwean: POB 248, Hythe, SO45 4WX, United Kingdom; tel. (23) 8084-8694; e-mail feedback@thezimbabwean.co.uk; internet www.thezimbabwean.co.uk; f. 2005; independent; publ. in the United Kingdom and South Africa; focus on news in Zimbabwe and life in exile; Publr and Editor WILF MBANGA.

Zimbabwean Government Gazette: POB 8062, Causeway, Harare; official notices; Editor L. TAKAWIRA.

PERIODICALS

The Agenda: Information Department, 348 Herbert Chitepo Ave, Harare; tel. (4) 736338; fax (4) 721146; e-mail info@nca.org.zw; internet www.nca.org.zw; f. 1997; publ. by the Nat. Constitutional Assembly; quarterly; civil rights issues.

Chaminuka News: POB 650, Marondera; f. 1988; publ. by Community Newspaper Group (Mass Media Trust); fortnightly; English and ChiShona; distributed in Manicaland and Mashonaland North provinces; Editor M. MUGABE; circ. c. 10,000.

Indonsakusa: Hwange; f. 1988; monthly; English and SiNdebele; Editor D. NTABENI; circ. 10,000.

The Insider: 12 Penwith Court, Jason Moyo St, Bulawayo; tel. (11) 789-739; e-mail charlesrukuni@insiderzim.com; internet www.insiderzim.com; f. 1990; daily; digital newsletter; news and current affairs; Editor and Publr CHARLES RUKUNI.

Masiye Pambili (Let Us Go Forward): POB 591, Bulawayo; tel. (9) 75011; fax (9) 69701; e-mail tcdept@citybyo.co.zw; f. 1964; 2 a year; English; Editor M. Nyoni; circ. 25,000.

Moto (Fire): POB 890, Gweru; tel. (54) 24886; fax (54) 28194; e-mail mot@hnetzim.wn.apc.org; f. 1959; monthly; publ. by govt-controlled co Zimpapers; banned in 1974; relaunched in 1980 as a weekly newspaper, then in magazine format in 1982; Roman Catholic; Editor Sydney Shoko; circ. 22,000.

Mukai-Vukani Jesuit Journal for Zimbabwe: Jesuit Communications, 1 Churchill Ave, Alexandra Park, POB 949, Southerton, Harare; tel. (4) 744571; fax (4) 744284; e-mail owermter@zol.co.zw; internet www.jescom.co.zw; 4–6 a year; Catholic; Editor Fr Oskar Wermter; circ. 2,500.

New Farmer: Herald House, cnr George Sikundika and Sam Nujoma Sts, POB 55, Harare; tel. (4) 708296; fax (4) 702400; e-mail advertising@chronicle.co.zw; internet www.newfarmer.co.zw; f. 2002; publ. by govt-controlled co Zimpapers; weekly; English; Editor George Chisoko.

The Outpost: POB HG106, Highlands; tel. (4) 700171; fax (4) 703631; e-mail theoutpostmag@yahoo.com; f. 1911; publ. of the Zimbabwe Republic Police; monthly; English; Editor Resistant Ncube; circ. c. 45,000 (2012).

Railroader: National Railways of Zimbabwe, cnr Fife St and 10th Ave, POB 596, Bulawayo; tel. (9) 363716; fax (9) 363502; f. 1952; publ. by Nat. Railways of Zimbabwe; monthly; Editor M. Gumede; circ. 10,000.

Southern African Political and Economic Monthly (SAPEM): Southern Africa Political Economy Series Trust, 2–6 Deary Ave, Belgravia, POB MP111, Mt Pleasant, Harare; tel. (4) 252962; fax (4) 252964; f. 1987; monthly; publ. by the SAPES Trust; incorporating *Southern African Economist*; Editor-in-Chief Khabele Matlosa; circ. 16,000.

Trends: 9th Ave and George Silundika St, POB 585 Bulawayo; tel. (09) 880888; fax (09) 888884; e-mail advertising@chronicle.co.zw; internet www.zimtrends.co.zw; f. 2003; publ. by govt-controlled co Zimpapers; monthly; English; leisure and entertainment; Editor Edwin Dube.

The Worker: ZCTU, Chester House, 9th Floor, Speke Ave and Third St, POB 3549, Harare; tel. (4) 794742; fax (4) 728484; e-mail info@zctu.co.zw; publ. by the Zimbabwe Congress of Trade Unions; News Editor Bright Chibvuri.

Zambezia: University of Zimbabwe Publications, POB MP203, Mount Pleasant, Harare; tel. (4) 303211; fax (4) 333407; e-mail uzpub@admin.uz.ac.zw; internet www.uz.ac.zw/publications; publ. by the Univ. of Zimbabwe; 2 a year; humanities and general interest; Editor Dr Zifikile Makwavarara.

Zimbabwe Agricultural Journal: Dept of Research and Specialist Services, 5th St, Extension, POB CY594, Causeway, Harare; tel. (4) 704531; fax (4) 728317; f. 1903; 6 a year; Editor R. J. Fenner; circ. 2,000.

The Zimbabwe Farmer: POB 1683, Harare; tel. (4) 736836; fax (4) 749803; monthly; fmrly *Tobacco News*; present name adopted in 2003; publ. by Thomson Publs; Editor D. Miller; circ. 2,000.

Zimbabwe National Army Magazine: Ministry of Defence, Defence House, cnr Kwame Nkuruma Ave and 3rd St, Harare; tel. (4) 700316; f. 1982; 4 a year; Dir of Communications Col Livingstone Chineka; circ. 5,000.

Zimbabwean Travel: Herald House, cnr George Sikundika and Sam Nujoma Sts, POB 55, Harare; tel. (4) 708296; fax (4) 702400; e-mail advertising@chronicle.co.zw; internet www.zimtravel.com; f. 2003; publ. by govt-controlled co Zimpapers; monthly; English; Editor Nomsa Nkala.

NEWS AGENCY

NewZiana (Pvt) Ltd: Mass Media House, 19 Selous Ave, POB CY511, Causeway, Harare; tel. (4) 251754; fax (4) 794336; internet www.newziana.co.zw; f. 1981 as Zimbabwe Inter-Africa News Agency; present name adopted in 2003; owned by govt-controlled co Multimedia Investment Trust (fmrly Zimbabwe Mass Media Trust); operates 10 community newspapers; CEO Munyaradzi Matanyaire.

Publishers

Amalgamated Publications (Pvt) Ltd: POB 1683, Harare; tel. (4) 736835; fax (4) 749803; f. 1949; trade journals.

The Argosy Press: POB 2677, Harare; tel. (4) 755084; magazine publrs; Gen. Man. A. W. Harvey.

Baobab Books (Pvt) Ltd: POB 567, Harare; tel. (4) 665187; fax (4) 665155; general, literature, children's.

College Press Publishers (Pvt) Ltd: 15 Douglas Rd, POB 3041, Workington, Harare; tel. (4) 754145; fax (4) 754256; f. 1968; educational and general; Man. Dir B. B. Mugabe.

Harare Publishing House: Chiremba Rd, Hatfield, Harare; tel. (4) 570342; f. 1982; Dir Dr T. M. Samkange.

HarperCollins Publishers Zimbabwe (Pvt) Ltd: Union Ave, POB UA201, Harare; tel. (4) 721413; fax (4) 732436; Man. S. D. McMillan.

Longman Zimbabwe (Pvt) Ltd: POB ST125, Southerton, Harare; tel. (4) 62711; fax (4) 62716; f. 1964; general and educational; Man. Dir N. L. Dlodlo.

Munn Publishing (Pvt) Ltd: POB UA460, Union Ave, Harare; tel. (4) 481048; fax (4) 7481081; Man. Dir I. D. Munn.

Southern African Printing and Publishing House (SAPPHO): 109 Coventry Rd, Workington, POB MP1005, Mount Pleasant, Harare; tel. (4) 621681; fax (4) 666061; internet www.zimmirror.co.zw; Editor-in-Chief Dr Ibbo Mandaza.

University of Zimbabwe Publications: University of Zimbabwe, POB MP203, Mount Pleasant, Harare; tel. (4) 303211; fax (4) 333407; e-mail uzpub@admin.uz.ac.zw; internet www.uz.ac.zw/publications; f. 1969; Dir Munani Sam Mtetwa.

Zimbabwe Newspapers (1980) Ltd (Zimpapers): POB 55, Harare; tel. (4) 704088; fax (4) 702400; e-mail theherald@zimpapers.co.zw; internet www.herald.co.zw; f. 1981; 51% state-owned; publ. the newspapers *The Herald, The Sunday Mail, The Manica Post, The Chronicle, The Sunday News, Kwayedza, Umthunywa* and *The Southern Times* (based in Namibia); and magazines incl. *Zimbabwean Travel, Trends Magazine* and *New Farmer Magazine*; Chair. Herbert Nkala; Group CEO Justin Mutasa.

ZPH Publishers (Pvt) Ltd: 183 Arcturus Rd, Kamfinsa, GD510, Greendale, Harare; tel. (4) 497548; fax (4) 497554; e-mail tafi@zph.co.zw; f. 1982 as Zimbabwe Publishing House Ltd; Chair. Blazio G. Tafireyi.

Broadcasting and Communications

TELECOMMUNICATIONS

In 2011 there were three providers of mobile telephone services and one provider of fixed-line telephone services in Zimbabwe.

Econet Wireless Zimbabwe: Econet Park, No. 2 Old Mutare Rd, Msasa, POB BE 1298, Belvedere, Harare; tel. (4) 486121; fax (4) 486120; e-mail enquiry@econet.co.zw; internet www.econet.co.zw; f. 1998; mobile cellular telecommunications operator; Chair. Tawanda Nyambirai; CEO Douglas Mboweni.

Net.One Ltd: POB CY579, Causeway, Harare; tel. (4) 707138; e-mail marketing@netone.co.zw; internet www.netone.co.zw; f. 1998; state-owned; mobile cellular telecommunications operator; Chair. Callistus Ndlovu; CEO Reward Kangai.

Posts and Telecommunication Regulatory Authority (POTRAZ): Block A, Emerald Park, 30 The Chase, Mt Pleasant, POB MP 843, Harare; tel. (4) 333032; fax (4) 333041; e-mail the.regulator@potraz.gov.zw; internet www.potraz.gov.zw; fmrly Post and Telecommunications Corpn; Chair. Davidson Chirombo; Dir-Gen. Charles Manzi Sibanda.

Telecel Zimbabwe: 148 Seke Rd, Graniteside, POB CY232, Causeway, Harare; tel. (4) 748321; fax (4) 748328; e-mail info@telecelzim.co.zw; internet www.telecel.co.zw; f. 1998; 60% owned by Telecel Int. and 40% owned by Empowerment Corpn; mobile cellular telecommunications operator; Chair. James Makamba; Man. Dir Aimable Mpore.

TelOne: Runhare House, 107 K. Nkrumah Ave, POB CY331, Causeway, Harare; tel. (4) 798111; fax (4) 700474; e-mail webmaster@telone.co.zw; internet www.telone.co.zw; state-owned; sole fixed-line telecommunications operator; Man. Dir Hampton Mhlanga.

BROADCASTING

There are four govt-controlled radio stations (National FM, Power FM, Radio Zimbabwe and Spot FM) and one television station. Radio Voice of the People was established as an alternative to state broadcasting. In June 2012 the country's first commercial radio station, Star FM, began broadcasting. An independent radio station, SW Radio Africa, broadcasts to Zimbabwe from London, United Kingdom. Since 2003 Voice of America has broadcast a weekday news and entertainment programme (Studio 7) from the USA in ChiShona, English and SiNdebele.

Regulatory Authority

Zimbabwe Media Commission: Harare; f. 2009 to introduce media reforms; Chair. Godfrey Majonga.

Radio

Feba Radio: 69 Central Ave, POB A300, Avondale, Harare; tel. (4) 708207; e-mail info@feba.co.zw; internet www.feba.co.zw; Nat. Dir KURAI MADZONGA.

Star FM: Harare; f. 2012; broadcasts in Harare and Bulawayo; Gen. Man. ADMIRE TADERERA.

Voice of the People (VOP): POB 5750, Harare; tel. (4) 707123; e-mail voxpop@ecoweb.co.zw; internet www.vopradio.co.zw; f. 2000 by fmr ZBC staff; broadcasts one hour per day; relayed by Radio Netherlands transmitters in Madagascar; news and information in ChiShona, SiNdebele and English; Chair. DAVID MASUNDA; Exec. Dir JOHN MASUKU.

Zimbabwe Broadcasting Corpn: Broadcasting Center, Pocket Hill, POB HG444, Highlands, Harare; tel. and fax (4) 498940; e-mail edward.ndamba@zbc.co.zw; internet www.zbc.co.zw; f. 1957; programmes in English, ChiShona, SiNdebele and 14 minority languages, incl. Chichewa, Venda and Xhosa; broadcasts a general service (mainly in English), vernacular languages service, light entertainment, and educational programmes; Registry Supervisor EDWARD NDAMBA.

Television

Zimbabwe Broadcasting Corpn: (see Radio).

The main broadcasting centre is in Harare, with a second studio in Bulawayo. ZBC-TV is broadcast 24 hours per day, while a second channel (ZBC Channel 2) was launched in May 2010.

Finance

(cap. = capital; res = reserves; dep. = deposits; m. = million; br(s). = branch(es); amounts in Zimbabwe dollars unless otherwise indicated)

BANKING

In 2010 there were 15 commercial banks, six merchant banks, three discount houses and four building societies in Zimbabwe. In August 2012 it was announced that commercial banks and merchant banks operating in Zimbabwe were required to have a minimum capital of US $100m., while discount houses were required to have a minimum capital of US $60m. Institutions were expected to be 100% compliant with these requirements by 30 June 2014.

Central Bank

Reserve Bank of Zimbabwe: 80 Samora Machel Ave, POB 1283, Harare; tel. (4) 703000; fax (4) 707800; e-mail rbzmail@rbz.co.zw; internet www.rbz.co.zw; f. 1964 as Reserve Bank of Rhodesia; bank of issue; cap. 2m., res 89,161,333m., dep. 471,625,968m. (Dec. 2007); Gov. Dr GIDEON GONO.

Commercial Banks

Barclays Bank of Zimbabwe Ltd: Barclays House, cnr First St and Jason Moyo Ave, POB 1279, Harare; tel. (4) 758281; fax (4) 752913; e-mail barmkt@africaonline.co.zw; internet www.barclays.com/africa/zimbabwe; f. 1912; commercial and merchant banking; cap. 1,000m., res 18,123m., dep. 125,836m. (Dec. 2004); Chair. Dr ROBBIE MATONGO MUPAWOSE; 44 brs.

CBZ Bank Ltd (CBZ): Union House, 60 Kwame Nkrumah Ave, POB 3313, Harare; tel. (4) 748050; e-mail info@cbz.co.zw; internet www.cbz.co.zw; state-owned; f. 1981 as Bank of Credit and Commerce Zimbabwe Ltd; renamed Commercial Bank of Zimbabwe Ltd in 1991; present name adopted 2005; Chair. L. ZEMBE; CEO Dr J. P. MANGUDYA; 60 brs.

FBC Bank Ltd: FBC Centre, Marketing and Public Relations Division, 45 Nelson Mandela Ave, POB 1227, Harare; tel. (4) 783204; fax (4) 783440; e-mail info@fbc.co.zw; internet www.fbc.co.zw/bank; f. 1997; cap. 1,000m., res 11,035,000m., dep. 39,946,000m. (Dec. 2007); Chair. DAVID W. BIRCH; Man. Dir JOHN MUSHAYAVANHU.

Kingdom Bank Ltd: 3rd Floor, Karigamombe Centre, 53 Samora Machel Ave, POB CY 3205, Harare; tel. (4) 749400; fax (4) 755201; e-mail kmb@kingdom.co.zw; internet www.kingdom.co.zw; f. 1997; res US $20.4m., dep. US $46.7m. (Dec. 2009); CEO LYNN MUKONOWESHURO.

Stanbic Bank Zimbabwe Ltd: Stanbic Centre, 1st Floor, 59 Samora Machel Ave, POB 300, Harare; tel. (4) 759471; fax (4) 751324; e-mail zimbabweinfo@stanbic.com; internet www.stanbicbank.co.zw; f. 1990 as ANZ Grindlays Bank; acquired by Standard Bank Investment Corpn in 1992; total assets US $201,387 (Dec. 2009); Chair. S. MOYO; Man. Dir JOSHUA TAPAMBGWA; 16 brs.

Standard Chartered Bank Zimbabwe Ltd: Mutual Centre, 2nd Floor, POB 373, Harare; tel. (4) 52852; fax (4) 752609; internet www.standardchartered.com/zw; f. 1983; cap. US $0.8m., res US $26.5m., dep. US $26.5m. (Dec. 2009); Chair. H. P. MKUSHI; CEO WASHINGTON MATSAIRA; 28 brs.

ZB Bank Ltd: ZB House, 10th Floor, 46 Speke Ave, POB 3198, Harare; tel. (4) 757535; fax (4) 757497; e-mail info@zb.co.zw; internet www.zb.co.zw; f. 1951; subsidiary of ZB Financial Holdings Ltd; cap. 102m., res 178,293m., dep. 821,214m. (Sept. 2004); Chair. ZVINECHIMWE RUVINGA CHURU; COO RONALD MUTANDAGAYI; 38 brs.

Development Banks

African Export-Import Bank (Afreximbank): Eastgate Bldg, 3rd Floor, Gold Bridge (North Wing), Second St, POB 1600, Causeway, Harare; tel. (4) 729751; fax (4) 729756; e-mail info@afreximbank.com; internet www.afreximbank.com; Pres. and Chair. J. L. EKRA.

Infrastructure Development Bank of Zimbabwe (IDBZ): 99 Rotten Row, Harare; tel. (4) 750171; fax (4) 774225; e-mail enquiries@zdb.co.zw; internet www.idbz.co.zw; f. 2005, to replace Zimbabwe Development Bank (ZDB); CEO CHARLES CHIKAURA.

Merchant Banks

African Banking Corpn of Zimbabwe Ltd (ABC): ABC House, 1 Endeavour Cres., Mount Pleasant Business Park, Mount Pleasant, POB 2786, Harare; tel. (4) 369260; fax (4) 369939; e-mail abczw@africanbankingcorp.com; internet www.africanbankingcorp.com; f. 1956 as Rhodesian Acceptances Ltd; name changed to First Merchant Bank of Zimbabwe Ltd in 1990; merged with Heritage Investment Bank in 1997; present name adopted in 2002; subsidiary of ABC Holdings Ltd, Botswana; Chair. O. M. CHIDAWU; Man. Dir F. M. DZANYA; 1 br.

MBCA Bank Ltd: Old Mutual Centre, 14th Floor, cnr Third St and Jason Moyo Ave, POB 3200, Harare; tel. (4) 701636; fax (4) 708005; e-mail mbcabank@mbca.co.zw; internet www.mbca.co.zw; f. 1956; a mem of the Nedbank Goup; total assets US $192m. (Jun. 2012); Chair. V. W. ZIREVA; Man. Dir Dr CHARITY C. JINYA.

NMB Bank Ltd: Unity Court, 4th Floor, cnr Union Ave and First St, POB 2564, Harare; tel. (4) 759651; fax (4) 759648; e-mail enquiries@nmbz.co.zw; internet www.nmbz.co.zw; f. 1993; fmrly Nat. Merchant Bank of Zimbabwe; cap. 0.3m., res 8,017m., dep. 51,128m. (Dec. 2006); Chair. TENDAYI MUNDAWARARA; Group CEO JAMES MUSHORE; 10 brs.

Standard Chartered Merchant Bank Zimbabwe Ltd: Standard Chartered Bank Bldg, cnr Second St and Nelson Mandela Ave, POB 60, Harare; tel. (4) 708585; fax (4) 725667; f. 1971; Chair. BARRY HAMILTON; Man. Dir EBBY ESSOKA.

Tetrad Investment Bank: Block 5, 1st Floor, Arundel Office Park, Norfolk Rd, Mt Pleasant, Harare; tel. (4) 704271; fax (4) 338400; internet www.tetrad.co.zw; f. 1995; Chair. A. S. CHATIKOBO; Man. Dir E. E. CHIKAKA.

Discount Houses

African Banking Corpn Securities Ltd: 69 Samora Machel Ave, POB 3321, Harare; tel. (4) 752756; fax (4) 790641; fmrly Bard Discount House Ltd; Chair. N. KUDENGA; Man. Dir D. DUBE.

The Discount Co of Zimbabwe (DCZ): 70 Park Lane, POB 3424, Harare; tel. (4) 705414; fax (4) 731670; Man. Dir PETER MUKUNGA.

Intermarket Discount House: Unity Court, 5th Floor, Union Ave, POB 3290, Harare.

National Discount House Ltd: MIPF House, 5th Floor, Central Ave, Harare; tel. (4) 700771; fax (4) 792927; internet www.ndh.co.zw; Chair. EDWIN MANIKAI; Man. Dir LAWRENCE TAMAYI.

Banking Organizations

Bankers' Association of Zimbabwe (BAZ): Kuwana House, 4th Floor, Union Ave and First St, POB UA550, Harare; tel. (4) 728646; f. 1992; Pres. JOHN MUSHAYAVANHU; Dir SIJABULISO T. BIYAM.

Institute of Bankers of Zimbabwe: Centre Block, Second Floor, Suite 13, 1 Union Ave, POB UA521, Harare; tel. (4) 752474; fax (4) 750281; e-mail info@iobz.co.zw; internet www.iobz.co.zw; f. 1973; Chair. S. MALABA; Pres. STEVE GWASIRA; Dir T. BIYAM; 7,000 mems.

STOCK EXCHANGE

Zimbabwe Stock Exchange: Chiyedza House, 5th Floor, cnr First St and Kwame Nkrumah Ave, POB UA234, Harare; tel. (4) 736861; fax (4) 791045; f. 1946; Chair. G. MHLANGA; CEO EMMANUEL MUNYUKWI.

INSURANCE

Export Credit Guarantee Corpn of Zimbabwe (Pvt): 6 Earles Rd, Alexandra Park, POB CY2995, Causeway, Harare; tel. and fax (4) 744644; e-mail ecgc@telco.co.zw; internet www.ecgc.co.zw; f. 1999 as national export credit insurance agency; also provides export finance guarantee facilities; 100% owned by Reserve Bank of Zimbabwe; Chair. J. A. L. CARTER; Man. Dir RAPHAEL. G. NYADZAYO.

Credit Insurance Zimbabwe (Credsure): Credsure House, 69 Sam Nujoma St, POB CY1584, Causeway, Harare; tel. (4) 706101; fax (4) 706105; e-mail headoffice@credsure.co.zw; export credit insurance; Man. Dir BRIAN HILLEN-MOORE.

Fidelity Life Assurance of Zimbabwe (Pvt) Ltd: 66 Julius Nyerere Way, POB 435, Harare; tel. (4) 750927; fax (4) 751723; f. 1977; 52% owned by Zimre Holdings Ltd; pensions and life assurance; Chair. J. P. MKUSHI; Man. Dir SIMON B. CHAPAREKA.

NICOZ Diamond: Insurance Centre, 30 Samora Machel and Leopold Takawira Ave, POB 1256, Harare; tel. (4) 704911; fax (4) 704134; e-mail enquiries@nicozdiamond.co.zw; internet www.nicozdiamond.co.zw; f. 2003 by merger of National Insurance Co of Zimbabwe and Diamond Insurance of Zimbabwe; Chair. PHINEAS S. CHINGONO; Man. Dir GRACE MURADZIKWA.

Old Mutual PLC: POB 70, Highlands, Harare; tel. (4) 308400; fax (4) 308467; e-mail info@oldmutual.co.zw; internet www.oldmutual.co.zw; f. 1845; life and general insurance, asset management and banking services; Chair. M. J. LEVETT; CEO J. H. SUTCLIFFE.

ZB Life Assurance Ltd: ZB Life Towers, 77 Jason Moyo Ave, POB 969, Harare; tel. (4) 708800; fax (4) 708894; e-mail info@zblife.co.zw; internet www.zb.co.zw/life-assurance.html; f. 1964 as Intermarket Life Assurance; subsidiary of ZB Financial Holdings Ltd, which also owns ZB Reinsurance; Man. Dir AMBROSE G. CHINEMBIRI.

Zimnat Lion Insurance Co Ltd: Zimnat House, cnr Nelson Mandela Ave and Third St, POB CY1155, Causeway, Harare; tel. (4) 707581; fax (4) 793441; e-mail enquiries@zimnatlion.co.zw; internet www.zimnatlion.co.zw; f. 1998 by merger of Zimnat Insurance Co Ltd and Lion of Zimbabwe Insurance; merged with AIG Zimbabwe in 2005; short-term insurance; Chair. NYAJEKA BOTHWELL; Man. Dir ELISHA K. MOYO.

Trade and Industry

GOVERNMENT AGENCIES

Industrial Development Corpn of Zimbabwe (IDC): 93 Park Lane, POB CY1431, Causeway, Harare; tel. (4) 706971; fax (4) 250385; e-mail pr@idc.co.zw; internet www.idc.co.zw; f. 1963; state investment agency; Gen. Man. MICHAEL NDUDZO.

State Enterprises Restructuring Agency (SERA): Cecil House, 1st Floor, cnr Jason Moyo Ave and Third St, Private Bag 7728, Causeway, Harare; tel. (4) 729164; fax (4) 726317; e-mail communications@sera.co.zw; internet www.sera.co.zw; f. 1999 as Privatisation Agency of Zimbabwe; name changed as above in 2005; CEO ANDREW N. BVUMBE.

Zimbabwe Investment Authority (ZIA): Investment House, 109 Rotten Row, POB 5950, Harare; tel. (4) 757931; fax (4) 773843; e-mail info@zia.co.zw; internet www.zia.co.zw; f. 2007 by merger of Zimbabwe Investment Centre and the Export Processing Zones Authority; promotes domestic and foreign investment; CEO RICHARD MBAIWA.

ZimTrade: 904 Premium Close, Mt Pleasant Business Park, POB 2738, Harare; tel. (4) 369330; fax (4) 369244; e-mail info@zimtrade.co.zw; internet www.zimtrade.co.zw; f. 1991; national trade development and promotion org.; Chair. J. SIZIBA; CEO SITHEMBILE PRISCILLA PILIME.

DEVELOPMENT ORGANIZATIONS

Alternative Business Association (ABA): Stand No. 15295, cnr First St and Eighth Cres., Sunningdale, Harare; tel. (4) 589625; fax (4) 799600; f. 1999 to address urban and rural poverty; programme areas include: agriculture, micro-mining, cross-border trade, micro-enterprise devt and micro-finance; Dir ISRAEL MABHOU.

Indigenous Business Development Centre (IBDC): Pocket Bldg, 1st Floor, Jason Moyo Ave, POB 3331, Causeway, Harare; tel. (4) 748345; f. 1990; Pres. BEN MUCHECHE; Sec.-Gen. ENOCH KAMUSHINDA.

Indigenous Business Women's Organisation (IBWO): 73B Central Ave, POB 3710, Harare; tel. (4) 702076; fax (4) 614012; Pres. JANE MUTASA.

Zimbabwe Human Rights NGO Forum: Blue Bridge, 8th Floor, Eastgate, POB 9077, Harare; tel. (4) 250511; fax (4) 250494; e-mail admin@hrforum.co.zw; internet www.hrforumzim.com; f. 1998; provides legal and 'psycho-social' assistance to the victims of organized violence; comprises 16 mem. orgs.

Zimbabwe Women's Bureau: 43 Hillside Rd, POB CR 120, Cranborne, Harare; tel. (4) 747809; fax (4) 707905; e-mail zwbtc@africaonline.co.zw; f. 1978; promotes entrepreneurial and rural community devt; Dir MAVIS MADAURE.

CHAMBERS OF COMMERCE

Manicaland Chamber of Industries: 91 Third St, POB 92, Mutare; tel. (20) 64909; e-mail czimtre@zol.co.zw; f. 1945; Pres. KUMBIRAI KATSANDE; 60 mems.

Mashonaland Chamber of Industries: 31 J. Chinamano Ave, POB 3794, Harare; tel. (4) 772763; fax (4) 750953; f. 1922; Pres. CHESTER MHENDE; 729 mems.

Matabeleland Chamber of Industries: 104 S. Parirenyatwa St, POB 2317, Bulawayo; tel. (9) 60642; fax (9) 60814; e-mail czibyo@zol.co.zw; f. 1931; Pres. Dr RUTH LABODE; 75 mems (2003).

Midlands Chamber of Industries: POB 213, Gweru; tel. (54) 2812; Pres. Dr BILL MOORE; 50 mems.

Zimbabwe National Chamber of Commerce (ZNCC): ZNCC Business House, 42 Harare St, POB 1934, Harare; tel. (4) 749335; fax (4) 750375; e-mail info@zncchq.co.zw; internet www.zncc.co.zw; f. 1983; represents small and medium businesses; Pres. OSWELL BINHA; CEO ANDREW MATIZA; 2,500 mems; 8 brs.

INDUSTRIAL AND TRADE ASSOCIATIONS

Chamber of Mines of Zimbabwe: Stewart House, North Wing, 4 Central Ave, POB 712, Harare; tel. (4) 702841; fax (4) 707983; e-mail info@chamines.co.zw; internet www.chamberofminesofzimbabwe.com; f. 1939 by merger of the Rhodesian Chamber of Mines (Bulawayo) and Salisbury Chamber of Mines; Pres. WINSTON CHITANDO; CEO J. B. R. CHIKOMBERO.

Confederation of Zimbabwe Industries (CZI): 31 Josiah Chinamano Ave, POB 3794, Harare; tel. (4) 251490; fax (4) 252424; e-mail cmsileya@czi.co.zw; internet www.czi.co.zw; f. 1923; Pres. KUMBIRAYI KATSANDE; CEO CLIFFORD M. SILEYA.

Specialized affiliate trade associations include:

CropLife Zimbabwe: POB MP712, Mount Pleasant, Harare; tel. (4) 487211; fax (4) 487242; e-mail graeme.reid@bayer.co.zw; internet www.croplifeafrica.org; fmrly Agricultural Chemical Industry Asscn; Chair. MAX MAKUVISE.

Furniture Manufacturers' Association: c/o CZI, 31 Josiah Chinamano Ave, POB 3794, Harare; Pres. MATT SNYMAN.

Zimbabwe Association of Packaging: 17 Coventry Rd, Workington, Harare; tel. (4) 753800; fax (4) 882020.

Construction Industry Federation of Zimbabwe: Conquenar House, 256 Samora Machel Ave East, POB 1502, Harare; tel. (4) 746661; fax (4) 746937; e-mail cifoz@comone.co.zw; Pres. GILBERT MATIKA; CEO MARTIN CHINGAIRA; c. 460 mems.

Grain Marketing Board (GMB): Dura Bldg, 179–187 Samora Machel Ave, POB CY77, Harare; tel. (4) 701870; fax (4) 251294; e-mail marketing@gmbdura.co.zw; internet www.gmbdura.co.zw; f. 1931; responsible for maintaining national grain reserves and ensuring food security.

Indigenous Petroleum Group of Zimbabwe (IPGZ): Harare; f. 2004 following split from Petroleum Marketers' Asscn of Zimbabwe; Chair. HUBERT NYAMBUYA; represents 68 importers.

Minerals Marketing Corpn of Zimbabwe (MMCZ): 90 Mutare Rd, Msasa, POB 2628, Harare; tel. (4) 487200; fax (4) 487161; e-mail administrator@mmcz.co.zw; internet www.mmcz.co.zw; f. 1982; sole authority for marketing of mineral production (except gold); Chair. J. MACHOBA (acting); Gen. Man. MASIMBA CHANDAVENGERWA (acting).

Petroleum Marketers' Association of Zimbabwe (PMAZ): 142 Samora Machel Ave, Harare; tel. (4) 797556; represents private importers of petroleum-based products; Chair. GORDON MUSARIRA.

Timber Council of Zimbabwe: Conquenar House, 256 Samora Machel Ave, POB 3645, Harare; tel. (4) 746645; fax (4) 746013; Exec. Dir MARTIN DAVIDSON.

Tobacco Association of Zimbabwe (TAZ): Harare; CEO WILFRED NHEMWA.

Tobacco Growers' Trust (TGT): POB AY331, Harare; tel. (4) 781167; fax (4) 781722; f. 2001; manages 20% of tobacco industry foreign exchange earnings on behalf of Reserve Bank of Zimbabwe; affiliated orgs include Zimbabwe Tobacco Asscn and Zimbabwe Farmers' Union; Chair. WILFANOS MASHINGAIDZE; Gen. Man. ALBERT JAURE.

Tobacco Industry and Marketing Board: POB 10214, Harare; tel. (4) 613310; fax (4) 613264; internet www.timb.co.zw; f. 1936; Chair. NJODZI MACHIRORI; CEO ANDREW MATIBIRI.

Tobacco Trade Association: c/o 4–12 Paisley Rd, POB ST180, Southerton, Harare; tel. (4) 773858; fax (4) 773859; e-mail tta@zol.co.zw; f. 1948; represents manufacturers and merchants.

Zimbabwe National Traditional Healers' Association (ZINATHA): Red Cross House, 2nd Floor, Rm 202, 98 Cameron St, POB 1116, Harare; tel. and fax (11) 606771; f. 1980; certifies and oversees traditional healers and practitioners of herbal medicine through the Traditional Medical Practitioners Council; promotes indigenous methods of prevention and treatment of HIV/AIDS; Pres. Prof. GORDON CHAVUNDUKA; 55,000 mems (2004).

Zimbabwe Tobacco Association (ZTA): 108 Prince Edward St, POB 1781, Harare; tel. (4) 796931; fax (4) 791855; e-mail fctobacco@zta.co.zw; internet fctobacco.com; f. 1928; represents growers; Pres. ADRIAN SWALES; CEO RODNEY AMBROSE; c. 5,500 mems.

EMPLOYERS' ASSOCIATIONS

Commercial Farmers' Union (CFU): Agriculture House, cnr Adylinn Rd and Marlborough Dr., Marlborough; POB WGT390, Westgate, Harare; tel. (4) 309800; fax (4) 309849; e-mail aisd3@cfu.co.zw; internet www.cfuzim.org; f. 1942; Pres. CHARLES TAFFS; CEO HENDRIK W. OLIVIER; 1,200 mems.

Cattle Producers' Association (CPA): Agriculture House, cnr Adylinn Rd and Marlborough Dr., Marlborough; POB WGT390, Westgate, Harare; tel. and fax (4) 309837; e-mail livestock@cfuzim.org; Chair. MARYNA ERASMUS.

Crops Association: Agriculture House, cnr Adylinn Rd and Marlborough Dr., Marlborough; POB WGT390, Westgate, Harare; tel. (4) 309843; fax (4) 309850; e-mail copa@cfu.co.zw; comprises the Commercial Oilseeds Producers' Asscn (COPA), the Zimbabwe Cereal Producers' Asscn (ZCPA) and the Zimbabwe Grain Producers' Asscn (ZGPA); Chair. DENNIS LAPHAM; Man. (Crops) GEORGE HUTCHISON; represents c. 800 producers.

National Association of Dairy Farmers: Agriculture House, cnr Adylinn Rd and Marlborough Dr., Marlborough; POB WGT390, Westgate, Harare; tel. (4) 309800; fax (4) 309837; e-mail livestock@cfuzim.org; f. 1953; Chair. PETRUS ERASMUS; CEO ROB J. VAN VUUREN; 174 mems.

Zimbabwe Association of Tobacco Growers (ZATG): Agriculture House, cnr Adylinn Rd and Marlborough Dr., Marlborough; POB WGT390, Westgate, Harare; f. 2001; Pres. JULIUS NGORIMA; CEO CANAAN RUSHIZHA; 1,500 mems.

Zimbabwe Poultry Association (Commercial Poultry Producers' Association): Agriculture House, cnr Adylinn Rd and Marlborough Dr., Marlborough; POB WGT390, Westgate, Harare; tel. (4) 309800; fax (4) 309849; Chair. PETER DRUMMOND; represents c. 200 producers.

Employers' Confederation of Zimbabwe (EMCOZ): Stewart House, 4 Central Ave, 2nd Floor, POB 158, Harare; tel. (4) 739647; fax (4) 739630; e-mail emcoz@emcoz.co.zw; Pres. DAVID GOVERE; Exec. Dir JOHN W. MUFUKARE.

Horticultural Promotion Council (HPC): 12 Maasdorp Ave, Alexandra Park; POB WGT290, Westgate, Harare; tel. (4) 745492; fax (4) 745480; Chief Exec. BASILIO SANDAMU; represents c. 1,000 producers.

Export Flower Growers' Association of Zimbabwe (EFGAZ): 12 Maasdorp Ave, Alexandra Park; POB WGT290, Westgate, Harare; tel. (4) 725130; fax (4) 795303; e-mail exflower@icon.co.zw; Dir MARY DUNPHY; c. 300 mems.

National Employment Council for the Construction Industry of Zimbabwe: St Barbara House, Nelson Mandela Ave and Leopold Takawira St, POB 2995, Harare; tel. (4) 773966; fax (4) 773967; CEO STANLEY R. MAKONI; represents over 19,000 mem. cos (2002).

Timber Producers' Federation (TPF): Fidelity Life Centre, 4th Floor, H. Chitepo St, POB 1736, Mutare; tel. and fax (20) 60959; e-mail lmubaiwa@mweb.co.zw; CEO LOYD MUBAIWA.

Zimbabwe Building Contractors' Association: Caspi House, Block C, 4 Harare St, Harare; tel. (4) 780411; represents small-scale building contractors; CEO CONCORDIA MUKODZI.

Zimbabwe Commercial Farmers' Union (ZCFU): 53 Third St, Mutare; tel. (20) 67163; fmrly Indigenous Commercial Farmers' Union; Pres. TREVOR GIFFORD; Dir JOHN MAUTSA; represents c. 11,000 black farmers (2003).

Zimbabwe Farmers' Union (ZFU): POB 3755, Harare; tel. (4) 704763; fax (4) 700829; Pres. SILAS HUNGWE; Exec. Dir KWENDA DZAVIRA; represents c. 200,000 small-scale black farmers (2002).

Zimbabwe Progressive Farmers' Union: Harare; Pres. NICHOLAS KAPUNGU.

UTILITIES

Electricity

Rural Electrification Agency (REA): Office 720, 7th Floor, Megawatt House, 44 Samora Machel Ave, Private Bag 250A, Harare; tel. (4) 770666; fax (4) 707667; e-mail emidzi@zesa.co.zw; internet www.rea.co.zw; f. 2002; manages the Rural Electrification Fund to expand and accelerate the electrification of rural areas; Chair. Dr SYDNEY ZIKUZO GATA; CEO EMMANUEL MIDZI.

ZESA Holdings (Pvt) Ltd: 25 Samora Machel Ave, POB 377TA, Harare; tel. (4) 774508; fax (4) 774542; e-mail pr@zesa.net; internet www.zesa.co.zw; f. 2002 following restructure of Zimbabwe Electricity Supply Authority; operates one hydroelectric and four thermal power stations; CEO JOSH CHIFAMBA; dependable generation capacity of 1,700 MW.

Zimbabwe Electricity Transmission Co (ZETCO): Electricity Centre, 8th Floor, 25 Samora Machel Ave, POB 1760, Harare; tel. (4) 774508; fax (4) 756179; e-mail zetconews@zetco.co.zw; internet www.zetco.org; f. 2002; develops, operates and maintains transmission infrastructure; Man. Dir (vacant).

Zimbabwe Electricity Regulatory Commission (ZERC): Century Towers, 14th Floor, 45 Samora Machel Ave, POB CY2585, Causeway, Harare; tel. (4) 780010; fax (4) 250696; e-mail admin@zerc.co.zw; internet www.zerc.co.zw; f. 2004 to oversee the unbundling from ZESA of the Zimbabwe Power Co, the Zimbabwe Electricity Transmission Co and the Zimbabwe Electricity Distribution Co; Dir-Gen. MAVIS CHIDZONGA.

Oil

National Oil Company of Zimbabwe (Pvt) Ltd (NOCZIM): NOCZIM House, 100 Leopold Takawira St, POB CY223, Causeway, Harare; tel. (4) 748543; fax (4) 748525; responsible for importing liquid fuels; Chair. CHARLES CHIPATO; Man. Dir ZVINECHIMWE CHURA.

Water

Zimbabwe National Water Authority (ZINWA): POB CY1215, Causeway, Harare; tel. and fax (4) 793139; e-mail mtetwa@utande.co.zw; f. 2001; fmrly Dept of Water, privatized in 2001; construction of dams, water supply, resources planning and protection; Chief Exec. ALBERT MUYAMBO.

MAJOR COMPANIES

African Distillers Ltd (AFDIS): POB WGT900, Westgate, Harare; tel. (4) 308351; fax (4) 308083; e-mail headoffice@afdis.co.zw; internet www.africandistillers.com; f. 1944; mfrs and importers of wines and spirits; Chair. J. S. MUTIZWA; Man. Dir KEN JARVIS.

Almin Metal Industries: POB ST394, Southerton, Harare; tel. (4) 620110-121; fax (4) 620117; e-mail custservice@almin.co.zw; internet www.almin.co.zw; f. 1969; semi-fabricators in non-ferrous metals; Man. Dir MUNASHE NKOMO; 188 employees.

Bindura Nickel Corpn Ltd: 70 Samora Machel Ave; POB 1108, Harare; tel. (4) 704461; fax (4) 725509; f. 1966; 52.9% owned by Anglo American Corpn; mining, smelting and refining of nickel; Chair. GODFREY GREGORY GOMWE; CEO JOE SCHWARZ (acting); 2,800 employees.

Cotton Co of Zimbabwe Ltd (COTTCO): 1 Lytton Rd, Workington, POB 2697, Harare; tel. (4) 771981; fax (4) 753854; e-mail cottco@cottco.co.zw; internet www.thecottoncompany.com; f. 1994; provides services to cotton growers at every stage of the production and sales process; Chair. PATISON SITHOLE.

Dairibord Zimbabwe Ltd (DZL): 1225 Rekayi Tangwena Ave, POB 2512, Harare; tel. (4) 793761; fax (4) 795220; e-mail SamudzimuB@dairibord.co.zw; internet www.dairibord.com; f. 1994; milk processors and mfrs of dairy products and beverages; privatized in 1997; incorporates Lyons, NFB Logistics, and Dairibord Malawi; Man. Dir BENSON P. SAMUDZIMU; 1,530 employees at seven factories.

Delta Corpn Ltd: Sable House, Northridge Close, Northridge Park; POB BW294, Borrowdale, Harare; tel. (4) 883865; fax (4) 883864; internet www.delta.co.zw; f. 1898; brewers and mfrs of soft drinks and agro-industrial products; Chair. CANAAN DUBE; CEO PEARSON GOWERO; 7,115 employees (2005).

Hippo Valley Estates Ltd: POB 1108, Harare; tel. (4) 336802; e-mail amasunda@hippo.co.zw; f. 1956; cap. Z.$192.8m., sales Z.$3,663.4m. (Dec. 2005); production and milling of sugar from cane and other farming operations; Chair. G. G. GOMWE; CEO SYDNEY D. MTSAMBIWA; 4,890 employees (2005).

Hwange Colliery Co Ltd (Wankie Colliery Co Ltd): Coal House, 17 Nelson Mandela Ave, cnr Leopold Takawira St; POB 2870, Harare; tel. (4) 781985; fax (4) 781988; e-mail hccanalyst@zol.co.zw; internet www.hwangecolliery.net; f. 1925; 51% state-owned; coal mining and production of coke and by-products; Chair. FARAI MUTAMANGIRA; Man. Dir FRED MOYO; 3,200 employees.

Lafarge Cement Zimbabwe Ltd: Manresa Works, Arcturus Rd, POB GD160, Greendale, Harare; tel. (4) 491011; fax (4) 491019; e-mail zim.sales@lafarge-zw.lafarge.com; internet www.lafarge.co.zw; f. 1954 as Circle Cement Ltd; name changed as above in 2007; majority owned by Lafarge (France); mfrs and distributors of cement and allied products; Chair. MUCHADEYI ASHTON MASUNDA; Man. Dir ISAIAH BINGWA; 305 employees.

Metallon Gold Zimbabwe: Arundel Office Park, Block 6, 1st Floor, Norfolk Rd, Mt Pleasant, Harare; tel. (4) 338508; CEO COLLEN GURA.

OK Zimbabwe Ltd: OK House, 7 Ramon Rd, Graniteside, POB 3081, Harare; tel. (4) 757311; fax (4) 757028; internet www

.okziminvestor.com; f. 1940; retailers of groceries, clothing, houseware and furniture; Chair. DAVID B. LAKE; CEO VIMBAI W. ZIREVA.

Rio Tinto Zimbabwe Ltd (RioZim): 1 Kenworth Rd, Highlands; POB CY1243, Causeway, Harare; tel. (4) 746614; fax (4) 746267; f. 1956; nickel and copper refining; gold mining; also diamonds and coal prospecting; Chair. M. ERIC KAHARI; CEO JOHN L. NIXON; 1,900 employees.

Murowa Diamonds: Kenilworth Gardens, 1 Kenilworth Rd, Harare; tel. (4) 746614; e-mail info@murowadiamonds.com; internet www.murowadiamonds.com; commenced operations in 2004; 78% owned by Rio Tinto PLC, 22% owned by Riozim Ltd; Man. Dir NEILS KRISTENSEN.

Sable Chemical Industries Ltd: POB 561, Kwekwe; tel. (55) 23601; fax (55) 23611; f. 1965; 51% owned by T. A. Holdings Ltd, 36% owned by Chemplex Corpn, 12% owned by Norsk Hydro; Chair. SHINGAI MUTASA; CEO J. P. MUREHWA; 472 employees.

Zimbabwe Alloys and Smelting Co Pvt Ltd (Zimasco): Pegasus House, 6th Floor, Samora Machel Ave, POB 3110, Harare; tel. (4) 251823; fax (4) 707758; internet www.zimasco.co.zw; f. 1923; chromite mines at Shurugwi and Mutorashanga, smelter at Kwekwe; holding co. Zimasco Consolidated Enterprises (ZCE) is 86.3% owned by Sinosteel Corpn (People's Republic of China) and 13.7% owned by China-Africa Development Fund; Chair. Prof. DENG; CEO SYDWELL JENA; 3,070 employees.

Zimbabwe Fertilizer Co Ltd: 35 Coventry Rd, Workington, POB 385, Harare; tel. (4) 753882; Chair. M. KACHERE; CEO RICHAR DAFANA.

New Zimbabwe Steel (Pvt) Ltd: Private Bag 2, Redcliff; tel. (55) 62401; fax (55) 68666; 36% state-owned, 54% owned by Essar Africa Holdings (Mauritius); fmrly Zimbabwe Iron and Steel Co Ltd and Ziscosteel; ceased operating 2008; relaunched as above 2011; CEO FIRDHOSE COOVADIA.

TRADE UNIONS

Zimbabwe Congress of Trade Unions (ZCTU): Chester House, 9th Floor, Speke Ave and Third St, POB 3549, Harare; tel. (4) 794742; fax (4) 728484; internet www.zctu.co.zw; f. 1981 by merger of the African Trade Union Congress, the Nat. African Trade Union Congress, the Trade Union Congress of Zimbabwe, the United Trade Unions of Zimbabwe, the Zimbabwe Fed. of Labour and the Zimbabwe Trade Union Congress; co-ordinating org. for trade unions; Pres. GEORGE NKIWANE; Sec.-Gen. JAPHET MOYO; c. 70,000 mems (2007).

In 2012 there were 25 affiliated unions. Affiliates with over 3,000 mems include:

Associated Mineworkers of Zimbabwe (AMWZ): St Andrew's House, 4th Floor, Leopold Takawira St and Samora Machel Ave, POB 384, Harare; tel. (4) 700287; fax (4) 706543; e-mail amwz@mweb.co.zw; Nat. Pres. TINAGO EDMUND RUZIVE; 10,000 mems (2002).

Commercial Workers' Union of Zimbabwe (CWUZ): CWUZ House, 15 Sixth Ave, Parktown; POB 3922 Harare; tel. (4) 664701; Pres. TAITUS MAGAYA; Gen. Sec. LOVEMORE MUSHONGA (acting); 22,000 mems (2003).

Communication and Allied Services Workers' Union of Zimbabwe (CASWUZ): Morgan House, 4th Floor, G. Silundika Ave, POB 739, Harare; tel. (4) 794763; e-mail caswuz@africaonline.co.zw; fmrly the Zimbabwe Post and Telecommunication Workers' Union; present name adopted 2002; Gen. Sec. REWARD S. MUSIWOKUWAYA; 5,700 mems (2002).

Federation of Food and Allied Workers' Union of Zimbabwe (FFAWUZ): Gorlon House, 3rd Floor, 7 Jason Moyo Ave, cnr Harare St, POB 4211, Harare; tel. (4) 757600; fax (4) 748482; e-mail ffawuzdick@mweb.co.zw; f. 1962; Gen. Sec. UNGANAI DICKSON TARUSENGA; 8,200 mems (2012).

General Agricultural and Plantation Workers' Union (GAPWUZ): POB 1952, Harare; tel. (4) 734141; fax (4) 797918; e-mail alb@cfu.co.zw; Gen. Sec. GERTRUDE HAMBIRA; 5,000 mems (2002).

National Engineering Workers' Union (NEWU): St Barbara House, cnr Nelson Mandela Ave and Leopold Takawira St, Harare; tel. (4) 759597; fax (4) 759598; e-mail information@newu.org.zw; Pres. ISAAC MATONGO; Gen. Sec. JAPHET MOYO; 9,000 mems (2002).

National Union of Clothing Industry Workers (NUCI): Union House, 139A Lobengula St with 13th Ave, POB RY28, Raylton, Bulawayo; tel. (9) 64432; fax (9) 71089; Gen. Sec. FRED MPOFU; 4,500 mems (2002).

Progressive Teachers' Union of Zimbabwe (PTUZ): 14 McLaren Rd, Milton Park, Harare; POB CR620, Cranborne, Harare; tel. (4) 757746; fax (4) 741937; e-mail ptuz@mweb.co.zw; f. 1997; Pres. TAKAVAFIREI ZHOU; Sec.-Gen. RAYMOND MAJONGWE; 12,000 mems (2002).

Public Service Association: PSA House, 9 Livingstone Ave, POB 179, Harare; tel. (4) 792542; fax (4) 704971; e-mail psahq@mweb.co.zw; f. 1919; Pres. CECILIA ALEXANDER-KHOWA; Exec. Sec. EMMANUEL MUTAKURA TICHAREVA; 12,500 mems (2011).

Civil Service Employees' Association (CSEA): PSA House, 3rd floor, 9 Livingstone Ave, POB CY202, Causeway, Harare; tel. (4) 701123; fax (4) 707208; e-mail civilsea@africaonline.co.zw; f. 1966; represents public sector employees; Pres. MASIMBA KADZIMU; Gen. Sec. GEORGE NASHO WILSON; 5,000 mems (2006).

Zimbabwe Amalgamated Railway Workers' Union (ZARU): Unity House, 13th Ave, Herbert Chitepo St, POB 556, Bulawayo 10; tel. (9) 60948; Gen. Sec. GIDEON P. SHOKO; 7,000 mems (2002).

Zimbabwe Banks and Allied Workers' Union (ZIBAWU): 1 Meredith Dr., Eastlea, POB 966, Harare; tel. (4) 703744; e-mail bankunion@zol.co.zw; Pres. GEORGE KAWENDA; Gen. Sec. COLLEN GWIYO; 4,560 mems (2002).

Zimbabwe Catering and Hotel Workers' Union (ZCHWU): Nialis Bldg, 1st Floor, Manyika, POB 3913, Harare; tel. (4) 753338; 8,500 mems (2002).

Zimbabwe Chemical, Plastics and Allied Workers' Union (ZCPAWU): St Andrew's House, 2nd Floor, Leopold Takawira St and Samora Machel Ave, POB 4810, Harare; tel. (4) 796533; Gen. Sec. F. P. GOMBEDZA; 3,723 mems (2002).

Zimbabwe Construction and Allied Trades Workers' Union (ZCAWU): St Barbara House, Office 306, cnr Nelson Mandela Ave and Leopold Takawira St, POB 1291, Harare; tel. (4) 750159; fax (4) 773967; Gen. Sec. CHARLES GUMBO; 3,000 mems (2002).

Zimbabwe Electricity and Energy Workers' Union (ZEEWU): Crossroads House, 43 Julius Nyere Way, POB 5537, Harare; tel. and fax (4) 724430; e-mail zeewu@comone.co.zw; Pres. ANGELINE CHITAMBO; 3,075 mems (2002).

Zimbabwe Furniture, Timber and Allied Trades Union (ZFTATU): St Andrew's House, 4th Floor, Samora Machel Ave, POB 4793, Harare; tel. (4) 728056; fax (4) 737686; e-mail invioftbb@yahoo.com; Gen. Sec. L. CHISHAKWE; 3,500 mems (2002).

Zimbabwe Graphical Workers' Union (ZGWU): 6 Harare St, POB 494, Harare; tel. (4) 775627; fax (4) 775727; represents employees in the printing and packaging industries; Gen. Sec. MADZIVO CHIMHUKA; 5,000 mems (2005).

Zimbabwe Leather Shoe and Allied Workers' Union (ZLSAWU): POB 4450, Harare; tel. (4) 727925; fax (4) 727926; Gen. Sec. ISIDORE MANHANDO ZINDOGA; 6,745 mems (2002).

Zimbabwe Textile Workers' Union (ZTWU): 50 Jason Moyo Ave, Pockets Bldg, 2nd Floor, South Wing, Hillside, POB 10245, Harare; tel. (4) 770226; fax (4) 758233; e-mail ztwu@mweb.co.zw; Gen. Sec. SILAS KUVEYA; 11,636 mems (2004).

Zimbabwe Tobacco Industry Workers' Union (ZTIWU): St Andrew's House, 2nd Floor, Samora Machel Ave, POB 2757, Harare; tel. (4) 702339; Gen. Sec. ESTEVAO CUMBULANE; 3,000 mems (2002).

Zimbabwe Urban Councils Workers' Union (ZUCWU): POB CY 1859, Causeway, Harare; tel. (4) 729412; f. 1990; represents workers in engineering, housing and community services, health and emergency services, and clerical and treasury services; Pres. SIMON TAYALI; Gen. Sec. MOSES TSHIMKENI-MAHLANGU; 10,200 mems (2003).

Zimbabwe Federation of Trade Unions (ZFTU): Makombe Complex, Causeway, Harare; f. 1996 as alternative to ZCTU; 23 affiliated unions (2006); Gen. Sec. ADAMS VERENGA.

Affiliated unions include:

Zimbabwe Teachers' Union (ZITU): POB GV1, Glen View, Harare; tel. (4) 692454; fax (4) 708929; f. 2002; Gen. Sec. SIMPLISIO K. MATUMBA.

Non-affiliated Unions

Zimbabwe National Students' Union (ZINASU): 53 Hebert Chitepo Ave, Harare; tel. (4) 788135; fax (4) 793246; e-mail zinasu@gmail.com; internet www.zinasu.org; represents students in more than 43 tertiary institutions; Pres. CLEVER BERE; Nat. Co-ordinator BENJAMIN NYANDORO; c. 260,000 mems (2006).

Zimbabwe Nurses' Association (ZINA): 47 Livingstone Ave, POB 2610, Harare; tel. and fax (4) 700479; e-mail zimnurse@mweb.co.zw; f. 1980; Pres. DOREEN CHORUMA; 4,500 mems (2003).

Zimbabwe Teachers' Association (ZIMTA): POB 1440, Harare; tel. (4) 728438; fax (4) 791042; e-mail zimta@telco.co.zw; Pres. TENDAI CHIKOWORE; Sec.-Gen. RICHARD GUNDANE; 55,000 mems (2004).

Transport

RAILWAYS

In 2008 the rail network totalled 2,583 km, of which 313 km was electrified. Trunk lines run from Bulawayo south to the border with Botswana, connecting with the Botswana railways system, which, in turn, connects with the South African railways system; north-west to the Victoria Falls, where there is a connection with Zambia Railways; and north-east to Harare and Mutare connecting with the Mozambique Railways' line from Beira. From a point near Gweru, a line runs to the south-east, making a connection with the Mozambique Railways' Limpopo line and with the Mozambican port of Maputo. A connection runs from Rutenga to the South African Railways system at Beitbridge. A 320-km line from Beitbridge to Bulawayo was opened in 1999. In 2010 plans were announced for the construction of a railway line in northern Zimbabwe running to the border with Zambia, which would eventually be linked with the southern Zambian town of Kafue.

National Railways of Zimbabwe (NRZ): cnr Fife St and 10th Ave, POB 596, Bulawayo; tel. (9) 363716; fax (9) 363502; internet www.nrz.co.zw; f. 1899; reorg. 1967; privatization under way; Chair. KHOTSO DUBE; Gen. Man. Air Commodore MIKE TICHAFA KARAKADZAI.

ROADS

In 2002 the road system in Zimbabwe totalled an estimated 97,267 km; some 18,481 km of the total network was paved. In December 2005 tollgates were introduced at the borders to raise funds to maintain the road network.

CIVIL AVIATION

AirZim operates an effective monopoly over air travel and transport within Zimbabwe. International and domestic air services connect most of the larger towns.

Civil Aviation Authority of Zimbabwe (CAAZ): Harare Int. Airport Terminal, Level 3, New Terminal Bldg, Private Bag CY7716, Causeway, Harare; tel. (4) 585073; fax (4) 585100; e-mail ais@caaz.co.zw; internet www.caaz.co.zw; f. 1999; operates eight airports incl. Harare Int. Airport and Joshua Mqabuko Nkomo Int. Airport (fmrly Bulawayo Airport); CEO DAVID CHAWOTA.

Air Zimbabwe (Pvt) Ltd (AirZim): POB AP1, Harare Airport, Harare; tel. (4) 575111; fax (4) 575068; internet www.airzimbabwe.com; f. 1967; scheduled domestic and international passenger and cargo services to Africa, Australia and Europe; plans were announced in April 2006 to separate operations, creating the new cos Air Zimbabwe Technical, Air Zimbabwe Cargo, Nat. Handling Services and Galileo Zimbabwe, in addition to Air Zimbabwe; Chair. JONATHAN KADZURA; CEO INNOCENT MAVHUNGA (acting).

Tourism

The principal tourist attractions are the Victoria Falls, the Kariba Dam, and the Hwange Game Reserve and National Park. Zimbabwe Ruins, near Fort Victoria, and World's View, in the Matapos Hills, are also of interest. There is climbing and trout-fishing in the Eastern Districts, around Umtali. In 2009 some 2.02m. tourists visited Zimbabwe; revenue from tourism in 2010 totalled an estimated US $634m.

Zimbabwe Tourism Authority (ZTA): Samora Machel Ave, POB CY286, Causeway, Harare; tel. (4) 752570; fax (4) 758826; e-mail info@ztazim.co.zw; internet www.zimbabwetourism.co.zw; f. 1984; promotes tourism domestically and from abroad; Chair. EMMANUEL FUNDIRA; CEO KARIKOGA KASEKE.

Associations licensed by the ZTA include:

Safari Operators' Association of Zimbabwe (SOAZ): 18 Walter Hill Ave, Eastlea, Harare; tel. and fax (4) 702402; e-mail soaz@mweb.co.zw; internet www.soaz.net; f. 1973 as Zimbabwe Association of Tourist and Safari Operators; present name adopted 2006; Chair. EMMANUEL FUNDIRA.

Defence

As assessed at November 2011, total armed forces numbered about 29,000: 25,000 in the army and 4,000 in the air force. Paramilitary forces comprise a police force of 19,500 and a police support unit of 2,300.

Defence Expenditure: Budgeted at US $195m. in 2011.

Commander-in-Chief of the Armed Forces: Pres. ROBERT GABRIEL MUGABE.

Head of the Armed Forces: Lt-Gen. CONSTANTINE CHIWENGA.

Commander of the Zimbabwe National Army: Lt-Gen. PHILLIP V. SIBANDA.

Education

Primary education, which begins at six years of age and lasts for seven years, is free and has been compulsory since 1987. Secondary education begins at the age of 13 and lasts for six years, comprising a first cycle of four years and a second cycle of two years. According to UNESCO estimates, in 2005/06 enrolment at primary schools included 90% of children in the relevant age-group (males 89%; females 91%), while the comparable ratio for secondary enrolment was just 38% of children (males 39%; females 37%) in the same school year. In 2009/10 some 94,611 students were enrolled in tertiary institutions. There are two state-run universities: the University of Zimbabwe, which is located in Harare, and the University of Science and Technology, at Bulawayo. There are also two private universities, Africa University in Mutare and Solusi University in Figtree. Education was allocated Z.$6,800,000m. by the central Government in the budget for 2005, equivalent to 24.7% of total expenditure for that year.

Bibliography

Alexander, J. *The Unsettled Land: State-Making and the Politics of Land in Zimbabwe 1893-2003.* Oxford, James Currey, 2006.

Barclay, P. *Zimbabwe: Years of Hope and Despair.* London, Bloomsbury, 2010.

Bhebe, N., and Ranger, T. (Eds). *Society in Zimbabwe's Liberation War.* Portsmouth, NH, Heinemann, 1993.

Soldiers in Zimbabwe's Liberation War. Portsmouth, NH, Heinemann, 1993.

Blair, D. *Degrees in Violence: Robert Mugabe and the Struggle for Power in Zimbabwe.* London, Continuum International Publishing Group, 2002.

Bond, P., and Manyanya, M. *Zimbabwe's Plunge: Exhausted Nationalism, Neoliberalism and the Struggle for Social Justice.* Scottsville, University of Natal Press; London, Merlin; Harare, Weaver Press, 2002.

Bourne, R. *Catastrophe: What Went Wrong in Zimbabwe?* London, Zed Books, 2011.

Bowyer-Bower, T. A. S., and Stoneman, C. (Eds). *Land Reform in Zimbabwe: Constraints and Prospects.* Aldershot, Ashgate Publishing Ltd, 2000.

Brownell, J. *The Collapse of Rhodesia: Population Demographics and the Politics of Race.* London, I. B. Tauris, 2011.

Chan, S. *Southern Africa: Old Treacheries and New Deceits.* New Haven, CT, Yale University Press, 2011.

Chikuhwa, J. W. *Zimbabwe at the Crossroads.* Bloomington, IN; Milton Keynes, Authorhouse, 2006.

Compagnon, D. *A Predictable Tragedy: Robert Mugabe and the Collapse of Zimbabwe.* Philadelphia, PA, University of Pennsylvania Press, 2011.

Dashwood, H. S. *Zimbabwe: the Political Economy of Transformation.* Toronto, University of Toronto Press, 2000.

De Waal, V. *The Politics of Reconciliation: Zimbabwe's First Decade.* London, Hurst, 1990; Harare, Longman Zimbabwe, 1992.

Goebel, A. *Gender and Land Reform: The Zimbabwe Experience.* Montréal, McGill-Queen's University Press, 2005.

Godwin, P. *The Fear—The Last Days of Robert Mugabe.* London, Picador, 2010.

Hammar, A., Raftopolous, B., and Jensen, S. (Eds). *Zimbabwe's Unfinished Business: Rethinking Land, State and Nation in the Context of Crisis.* Harare, Weaver Press, 2003.

Harold-Barry, D. (Ed.). *Zimbabwe: The Past is the Future.* Harare, Weaver Press, 2004.

Herbst, J. *State Politics in Zimbabwe*. Berkeley, CA, University of California Press; Harare, University of Zimbabwe Publications, 1990.

Kriger, N. *Guerrilla Veterans in Post-war Zimbabwe: Symbolic and Violent Politics, 1980–1987*. Cambridge, Cambridge University Press, 2003.

Mararike, C. G. *Grassroots Leadership: The Process of Rural Development in Zimbabwe*. Harare, University of Zimbabwe Publications, 1995.

Meredith, M. *Mugabe: Power, Plunder, and the Struggle for Zimbabwe's Future*. New York, Public Affairs, 2007.

Moore, D. S. *Suffering for Territory: Race, Place, and Power in Zimbabwe*. Durham, NC, Duke University Press, 2005.

Moyo, J. N. *Voting for Democracy: A Study of Electoral Politics in Zimbabwe*. Harare, University of Zimbabwe Publications, 1992.

Moyo, S. *Economic Nationalism and Land Reform in Zimbabwe*. Harare, Southern African Printing and Publishing House, 1994.

The Land Question in Zimbabwe. Harare, Southern African Printing and Publishing House, 1995.

Mudenge, S. I. G. *A Political History of Munhumutapa, c.1400–1902*. Portsmouth, NH, Heinemann, 1989.

Munkonoweshuro, E. G. *Zimbabwe: Ten Years of Destabilisation: A Balance Sheet*. Stockholm, Bethany Books, 1992.

Ndhlovu, F. *The Politics of Language and Nation Building in Zimbabwe*. New York, NY, Peter Lang, 2009.

Ndhlovu, T. *Zimbabwe: A Decade of Development*. London, Zed Books, 1992.

Ndlovu-Gatsheni, S. J. *Do 'Zimbabweans' Exist? Trajectories of Nationalism, National Identity Formation and Crisis in a Postcolonial State*. New York, NY, Peter Lang, 2009.

Nklwane, S. M. (Ed.). *Zimbabwe's International Borders: A Study in National and Regional Development in Southern Africa*. Harare, University of Zimbabwe Publications, 1997.

Phimister, I. *Wangi Kolia: Coal, Capital and Labour in Colonial Zimbabwe, 1894–1994*. Harare, Baobab Books, 1994.

Pikirayi, I. *The Zimbabwe Culture: Origins and Decline of Southern Zambezian States*. Walnut Creek, CA, AltaMira Press, 2002.

Raftopoulos, B., and Mlambo, A. (Eds). *Becoming Zimbabwe: A History from the Pre-colonial Period to 2008*. Harare, Weaver Press, 2009.

Raftopoulos, B., and Savage, T. (Eds). *Zimbabwe: Injustice and Political Reconciliation*. Cape Town, Institute for Justice and Reconciliation, 2004.

Ranger, T. *The Historical Dimensions of Democracy and Human Rights in Zimbabwe, Vol. 2*. Harare, Zimbabwe University Publications, 2003.

Rasmussen, R. K., and Rubert, S. C. *Historical Dictionary of Zimbabwe*. 2nd edn. Metuchen, NJ, Scarecrow Press, 1991.

Scoones, I. *Zimbabwe's Land Reform: Myths and Realities*. Woodbridge, James Currey, 2010.

Shadur, M. A. *Labour Relations in a Developing Country: A Case Study on Zimbabwe*. Aldershot, Avebury, 1994.

Sibanda, E. M. *The Zimbabwe African People's Union, 1961–87: A Political History of Insurgency in Southern Rhodesia*. Trenton, NJ, Africa World Press, 2005.

Simon, D., Gaitskell, D., and Schumaker, L. (Eds). *Zimbabwe's Crisis*. Abingdon, Routledge, 2006.

Sithole, M. *Democracy and the One-party State in Africa: The Case of Zimbabwe*. Harare, SAPES Books, 1992.

Staunton, I. (Ed.). *Mothers of the Revolution: War Experiences of Thirty Zimbabwean Women*. Harare, Baobab Books, 1991.

Stiff, P. *Cry Zimbabwe: Independence—Twenty Years On*. Johannesburg, Galago Publishing Co, 2002.

Tendi. B-M. *Making History in Mugabe's Zimbabwe: Politics, Intellectuals and the Media*. Oxford, Peter Lang, 2010.

Weiss, R. *Zimbabwe and the New Elite*. London, British Academic Press, 1994.

Whyte, B. *Yesterday, Today and Tomorrow: A 100 Year History of Zimbabwe, 1890–1990*. Harare, David Burke, 1990.

Zvobgo, R. J. *Colonialism and Education in Zimbabwe*. Harare, SAPES Books, 1994.

PART THREE

Regional Information

REGIONAL ORGANIZATIONS

THE UNITED NATIONS

Address: United Nations, New York, NY 10017, USA.

Telephone: (212) 963-1234; **fax:** (212) 963-4879; **internet:** www.un.org.

The United Nations (UN) was founded on 24 October 1945. The organization, which has 193 member states, aims to maintain international peace and security and to develop international co-operation in addressing economic, social, cultural and humanitarian problems. The principal organs of the UN are the General Assembly, the Security Council, the Economic and Social Council, the International Court of Justice and the Secretariat. The General Assembly, which meets for three months each year, comprises representatives of all UN member states. The Security Council investigates disputes between member countries, and may recommend ways and means of peaceful settlement: it comprises five permanent members (the People's Republic of China, France, Russia, the United Kingdom and the USA) and 10 other members elected by the General Assembly for a two-year period. The Economic and Social Council comprises representatives of 54 member states, elected by the General Assembly for a three-year period: it promotes co-operation on economic, social, cultural and humanitarian matters, acting as a central policy-making body and co-ordinating the activities of the UN's specialized agencies. The International Court of Justice comprises 15 judges of different nationalities, elected for nine-year terms by the General Assembly and the Security Council: it adjudicates in legal disputes between UN member states.

Secretary-General: BAN KI-MOON (Republic of Korea) (2007–15).

MEMBER STATES IN AFRICA SOUTH OF THE SAHARA

(with assessments for percentage contributions to UN budget for 2010–12, and year of admission)

Angola	0.010	1976
Benin	0.003	1960
Botswana	0.018	1966
Burkina Faso	0.003	1960
Burundi	0.001	1962
Cameroon	0.011	1960
Cape Verde	0.001	1975
Central African Republic	0.001	1960
Chad	0.002	1960
Comoros	0.001	1975
Congo, Democratic Republic	0.003	1960
Congo, Republic	0.003	1960
Côte d'Ivoire	0.010	1960
Djibouti	0.001	1977
Equatorial Guinea	0.008	1968
Eritrea	0.001	1993
Ethiopia	0.008	1945
Gabon	0.014	1960
The Gambia	0.001	1965
Ghana	0.006	1957
Guinea	0.002	1958
Guinea-Bissau	0.001	1974
Kenya	0.012	1963
Lesotho	0.001	1966
Liberia	0.001	1945
Madagascar	0.003	1960
Malawi	0.001	1964
Mali	0.003	1960
Mauritania	0.001	1961
Mauritius	0.011	1968
Mozambique	0.003	1975
Namibia	0.008	1990
Niger	0.002	1960
Nigeria	0.078	1960
Rwanda	0.001	1962
São Tomé and Príncipe	0.001	1975
Senegal	0.006	1960
Seychelles	0.002	1976
Sierra Leone	0.001	1961
Somalia	0.001	1960
South Africa	0.385	1945
South Sudan	—	2011
Sudan	0.010	1956
Swaziland	0.003	1968
Tanzania	0.008	1961
Togo	0.001	1960
Uganda	0.006	1962
Zambia	0.004	1964
Zimbabwe	0.003	1980

Diplomatic Representation

PERMANENT MISSIONS TO THE UNITED NATIONS

(September 2012)

Angola: 820 Second Ave, 12th Floor, New York, NY 10017; tel. (212) 861-5656; fax (212) 861-9295; e-mail themission@angolaun.org; internet www.angolamissionun.org; Permanent Representative ISMAEL ABRAÃO GASPAR MARTINS.

Benin: 125 East 38th St, New York, NY 10016; tel. (212) 684-1339; fax (212) 684-2058; e-mail beninewyork@gmail.com; Permanent Representative JEAN-FRANCIS RÉGIS ZINSOU.

Botswana: 154 East 46th St, New York, NY 10017; tel. (212) 889-2277; fax (212) 725-5061; e-mail botswana@un.int; Permanent Representative CHARLES THEMBANI NTWAAGAE.

Burkina Faso: 866 United Nations Plaza, Suite 326, New York, NY 10017; tel. (212) 308-4720; fax (212) 308-4690; e-mail bfapm@un.int; internet www.burkina-onu.org; Permanent Representative DER KOGDA.

Burundi: 336 East 45th St, 12th Floor, New York, NY 10017; tel. (212) 499-0001; fax (212) 499-0006; e-mail ambabunewyork@yahoo.fr; Permanent Representative HERMÉNÉGILDE NIYONZIMA.

Cameroon: 22 East 73rd St, New York, NY 10021; tel. (212) 794-2295; fax (212) 249-0533; e-mail cameroon.mission@yahoo.com; Permanent Representative TOMMO MONTHE.

Cape Verde: 27 East 69th St, New York, NY 10021; tel. (212) 472-0333; fax (212) 794-1398; e-mail capeverde@un.int; Permanent Representative ANTONIO PEDRO MONTEIRO LIMA.

Central African Republic: 866 United Nations Plaza, Suite 444, New York, NY 10017; tel. (646) 415-9122; fax (646) 415-9149; e-mail repercaf.ny@gmail.com; internet www.pmcar.org; Permanent Representative CHARLES-ARMEL DOUBANE.

Chad: 129 East 36th St, New York, NY 10017; tel. (212) 986-0980; fax (212) 986-0152; e-mail chadmission@gmail.com; Permanent Representative AHMAD ALLAM-MI.

Comoros: 866 United Nations Plaza, Suite 418, New York, NY 10017; tel. (212) 750-1637; fax (212) 750-1657; e-mail comoros@un.int; Permanent Representative ROUBANI KAAMBI.

Congo, Democratic Republic: 866 United Nations Plaza, Suite 511, New York, NY 10017; tel. (212) 319-8061; fax (212) 319-8232; e-mail drcongo@un.int; Permanent Representative IGNACE GATA MAVITA WA LUFUTA.

Congo, Republic: 14 East 65th St, New York, NY 10065; tel. (212) 744-7840; fax (212) 744-7975; e-mail congo@un.int; Permanent Representative RAYMOND SERGE BALÉ.

Côte d'Ivoire: 800 Second Ave, 5th Floor, New York, NY 10017; tel. (646) 649-5061; fax (646) 781-9974; e-mail cotedivoiremission@yahoo.com; Permanent Representative YOUSSOUFOU BAMBA.

Djibouti: 866 United Nations Plaza, Suite 4011, New York, NY 10017; tel. (212) 753-3163; fax (212) 223-1276; e-mail djibouti@nyct.net; Permanent Representative ROBLE OLHAYE.

Equatorial Guinea: 242 East 51st St, New York, NY 10022; tel. (212) 223-2324; fax (212) 223-2366; e-mail equatorialguineamission@yahoo.com; Permanent Representative ANATOLIO NDONG MBA.

Eritrea: 800 Second Ave, 18th Floor, New York, NY 10017; tel. (212) 687-3390; fax (212) 687-3138; e-mail general@eritrea-unmission.org; internet www.eritrea-unmission.org; Permanent Representative ARAYA DESTA.

Ethiopia: 866 Second Ave, 3rd Floor, New York, NY 10017; tel. (212) 421-1830; fax (212) 756-4690; e-mail ethiopia@un.int; Permanent Representative TEKEDA ALEMU.

Gabon: 18 East 41st St, 9th Floor, New York, NY 10017; tel. (212) 686-9720; fax (212) 689-5769; e-mail info@gabon-un.org; Permanent Representative NELSON MESSONE.

The Gambia: 800 Second Ave, Suite 400F, New York, NY 10017; tel. (212) 949-6640; fax (212) 856-9820; e-mail gambia_un@hotmail.com; internet gambia.un.int; Permanent Representative SUSAN WAFFA-OGOO.

Ghana: 19 East 47th St, New York, NY 10017; tel. (212) 832-1300; fax (212) 751-6743; e-mail ghanaperm@aol.com; Permanent Representative KEN KANDA.

Guinea: 140 East 39th St, New York, NY 10016; tel. (212) 687-8115; fax (212) 687-8248; e-mail missionofguinea@aol.com; Permanent Representative MAMADI TOURÉ.

Guinea-Bissau: 866 United Nations Plaza, Suite 481, New York, NY 10017; tel. (212) 896-8311; fax (212) 896-8313; e-mail guinea-bissau@un.int; Permanent Representative JOÃO SOARES DA GAMA.

Kenya: 866 United Nations Plaza, Rm 304, New York, NY 10017; tel. (212) 421-4740; fax (212) 486-1985; e-mail info@kenyaun.org; Permanent Representative MACHARIA KAMAU.

Lesotho: 204 East 39th St, New York, NY 10016; tel. (212) 661-1690; fax (212) 682-4388; e-mail lesotho@un.int; Chargé d'affaires a.i. MAFIROANE EDMOND MOTANYANE.

Liberia: 866 United Nations Plaza, Suite 480, New York, NY 10017; tel. (212) 687-1033; fax (212) 687-1035; e-mail liberia@un.int; Permanent Representative MARJON V. KAMARA.

Madagascar: 820 Second Ave, Suite 800, New York, NY 10017; tel. (212) 986-9491; fax (212) 986-6271; e-mail repermad@verizon.net; Permanent Representative ZINA ANDRIANARIVELO-RAZAFY.

Malawi: 866 United Nations Plaza, Suite 486, New York, NY 10017; tel. (212) 317-8738; fax (212) 317-8729; e-mail malawinewyork@aol.com; Chargé d'affaires a.i. Brig. GRIFFIN SPOON PHIRI.

Mali: 111 East 69th St, New York, NY 10021; tel. (212) 737-4150; fax (212) 472-3778; e-mail malionu@aol.com; internet www.un.int/mali; Permanent Representative OUMAR DAOU.

Mauritania: 116 East 38th St, New York, NY 10016; tel. (212) 252-0113; fax (212) 252-0175; e-mail mauritaniamission@gmail.com; Permanent Representative AHMED OULD TEGUEDI.

Mauritius: 211 East 43rd St, 15th Floor, Suite 1502, New York, NY 10017; tel. (212) 949-0190; fax (212) 697-3829; e-mail mauritius@un.int; Permanent Representative MILAN JAYA NYAMRAJSINGH MEETARBHAN.

Mozambique: 420 East 50th St, New York, NY 10022; tel. (212) 644-5965; fax (212) 644-5972; e-mail mozambique@un.int; Permanent Representative ANTÓNIO GUMENDE.

Namibia: 360 Lexington Ave, Suite 1502, New York, NY 10017; tel. (212) 685-2003; fax (212) 685-1561; e-mail namibia@un.int; Permanent Representative WILFRIED INOTIRA EMVULA.

Niger: 417 East 50th St, New York, NY 10022; tel. (212) 421-3260; fax (212) 753-6931; e-mail nigermission@ymail.com; Permanent Representative BOUBACAR BOUREIMA.

Nigeria: 828 Second Ave, New York, NY 10017; tel. (212) 953-9130; fax (212) 697-1970; e-mail permny@nigeriaunmission.org; internet nigeriaunmission.org; Permanent Representative U. JOY OGWU.

Rwanda: 370 Lexington Ave, Suite 401, New York, NY 10017; tel. (212) 679-9010; fax (212) 679-9133; e-mail ambanewyork@minaffet.gov.rw; Permanent Representative EUGÈNE-RICHARD GASANA.

São Tomé and Príncipe: (temporarily closed); tel. (202) 415-7606; fax (202) 775-2077; e-mail pmstpun@gmail.com; Chargé d'affaires a.i. ANA PAULA ALVIM.

Senegal: 747 Third Ave, 21st Floor (46th & 47th St), New York, NY 10017; tel. (212) 517-9030; fax (212) 517-3032; e-mail senegal.mission@yahoo.fr; Permanent Representative ABDOU SALAM DIALLO.

Seychelles: 800 Second Ave, Suite 400C, New York, NY 10017; tel. (212) 972-1785; fax (212) 972-1786; e-mail seychelles@un.int; Permanent Representative MARIE-LOUISE POTTER.

Sierra Leone: 245 East 49th St, New York, NY 10017; tel. (212) 688-1656; fax (212) 688-4924; e-mail sierraleone@un.int; Permanent Representative SHEKOU MOMODOU TOURAY.

Somalia: 425 East 61st St, Suite 702, New York, NY 10065; tel. (212) 688-9410; fax (212) 759-0651; e-mail somalia@un.int; Permanent Representative ELMI AHMED DUALE.

South Africa: 333 East 38th St, 9th Floor, New York, NY 10016; tel. (212) 213-5583; fax (212) 692-2498; e-mail pmun.newyork@foreign.gov.za; Permanent Representative BASU SANGQU.

South Sudan: 336 East 45th St, 5th Floor, New York, NY 10017; tel. (917) 601-2376; fax (202) 293-7941; e-mail elgatkuoth@gossmission.org; Permanent Representative FRANCIS M. DENG.

Sudan: 305 East 47th St, 3 Dag Hammarskjöld Plaza, 4th Floor, New York, NY 10017; tel. (212) 573-6033; fax (212) 573-6160; e-mail sudan@sudanmission.org; Permanent Representative DAFFA-ALLA ELHAG ALI OSMAN.

Swaziland: 408 East 50th St, New York, NY 10022; tel. (212) 371-8910; fax (212) 754-2755; e-mail swazinymission@yahoo.com; Permanent Representative ZWELETHU MNISI.

Tanzania: 201 East 42nd St, Suite 425, New York, NY 10017; tel. (212) 697-3612; fax (212) 697-3618; e-mail tzrepny@aol.com; Chargé d'affaires a.i. JUSTIN N. SERUHERE.

Togo: 336 East 45th St, New York, NY 10017; tel. (212) 490-3455; fax (212) 983-6684; e-mail togo@un.int; Permanent Representative KODJO MENAN.

Uganda: 336 East 45th St, New York, NY 10017; tel. (212) 949-0110; fax (212) 687-4517; e-mail ugandaunny@un.int; internet ugandamissionunny.net; Chargé d'affaires a.i. ADONIA AYEBARE.

Zambia: 237 East 52nd St, New York, NY 10022; tel. (212) 888-5770; fax (212) 888-5213; e-mail zambia@un.int; Permanent Representative MWABA PATRICIA KASESE-BOTA.

Zimbabwe: 128 East 56th St, New York, NY 10022; tel. (212) 980-9511; fax (212) 308-6705; e-mail zimnewyork@gmail.com; Permanent Representative CHITSAKA CHIPAZIWA.

OBSERVERS

Intergovernmental organizations, etc., active in the region that participate in the sessions and the work of the UN General Assembly as Observers, maintaining permanent offices at the UN.

African Union: 305 East 47th St, 5th Floor, 3 Dag Hammarskjöld Plaza, New York, NY 10017; tel. (212) 319-5490; fax (212) 319-7135; e-mail aumission_ny@yahoo.com; internet www.africa-union.org; Permanent Observer TÉTE ANTÓNIO.

Asian-African Legal Consultative Organization: 188 East 76th St, Apt 26B, New York, NY 10021; tel. (917) 623-2861; fax (206) 426-5442; e-mail aalco@un.int; Permanent Observer ROY LEE.

Commonwealth Secretariat: 800 Second Ave, 4th Floor, New York, NY 10017; tel. (212) 599-6190; fax (212) 808-4975; e-mail comsec@thecommonwealth.org.

International Committee of the Red Cross: 801 Second Ave, 18th Floor, New York, NY 10017; tel. (212) 599-6021; fax (212) 599-6009; e-mail newyork@icrc.org; Head of Delegation WALTER A. FÜLLEMANN.

International Criminal Court: 866 United Nations Plaza, Suite 476, New York, NY 10017; tel. (212) 486-1362; fax (212) 486-1361; e-mail liaisonofficeny@icc-cpi.int; Head of Liaison Office KAREN ODABA MOSOTI.

International Criminal Police Organization (INTERPOL): One United Nations Plaza, Suite 2610, New York, NY 10017; tel. (917) 367-3463; fax (917) 367-3476; e-mail c.perrin@interpol.int; Special Representative WILLIAM J. S. ELLIOTT (Canada).

International Development Law Organization: 336 East 45th St, 11th Floor, New York, NY 10017; tel. (212) 867-9707; fax (212) 867-9717; e-mail pcivili@idlo.int; Permanent Observer PATRIZIO M. CIVILI.

International Institute for Democracy and Electoral Assistance: 336 East 45th St, 14th Floor, New York, NY 10017; tel. (212) 286-1084; fax (212) 286-0260; e-mail unobserver@idea.int; Permanent Observer MASSIMO TOMMASOLI.

International Olympic Committee: 708 Third Ave, 6th Floor, New York, NY 10017; tel. (212) 209-3952; fax (212) 209-7100; e-mail IOC-UNObserver@olympic.org; Permanent Observer MARIO PESCANTE.

International Organization of La Francophonie (Organisation Internationale de la Francophonie): 801 Second Ave, Suite 605, New York, NY 10017; tel. (212) 867-6771; fax (212) 867-3840; e-mail francophonie@un.int; Permanent Observer FILIPE SAVADOGO.

Inter-Parliamentary Union: 336 East 45th St, 10th Floor, New York, NY 10017; tel. (212) 557-5880; fax (212) 557-3954; e-mail ny-office@mail.ipu.org; Permanent Observer ANDA FILIP.

International Union for Conservation of Nature (IUCN): 551 Fifth Ave, Suites 800 A-B, New York, NY 10176; tel. (212) 346-1163; fax (212) 346-1046; e-mail iucn@un.int; internet www.iucn.org; Permanent Observer NARINDER KAKAR (India).

Organization of Islamic Cooperation: 320 East 51st St, New York, NY 10022; tel. (212) 883-0140; fax (212) 883-0143; e-mail oicny@un.int; internet www.oicun.org; Permanent Observer UFUK GOKCEN.

Partners in Population and Development: 336 East 45th St, 14th Floor, New York, NY 10017; tel. (212) 286-1082; fax (212) 286-0260; e-mail srao@ppdsec.org; internet www.partners-popdev.org; Permanent Observer SETHURAMIAH L.N. RAO.

University for Peace: 551 Fifth Ave, Suites 800 A-B, New York, NY 10176; tel. (212) 346-1163; fax (212) 346-1046; e-mail nyinfo@upeace.org; internet www.upeace.org; Permanent Observer NARINDER KAKAR (India).

The African, Caribbean and Pacific Group of States, the African Development Bank, the Economic Community of West African States, the Intergovernmental Authority on Development, the International Conference on the Great Lakes Region of Africa, the Regional Centre on Small Arms and Light Weapons in the Great Lakes Region, the Horn of Africa and Bordering States and the Southern African Development Community are among several intergovernmental organizations that have a standing invitation to participate as observers but do not maintain permanent offices at the UN.

United Nations Information Centres/Services

Burkina Faso: BP 135, 14 ave de la Grande Chancellerie, Secteur 4, Ouagadougou; tel. 50-30-60-76; fax 50-31-13-22; e-mail unic.ouagadougou@unic.org; internet ouagadougou.unic.org; also covers Chad, Mali and Niger.

Burundi: BP 2160, ave de la Révolution 117, Bujumbura; tel. (2) 225018; fax (2) 241798; e-mail unic.bujumbura@unic.org; internet bujumbura.unic.org.

Cameroon: PB 836, Immeuble Tchinda, rue 2044, Yaoundé; tel. 221-23-67; fax 221-23-68; e-mail unic.yaounde@unic.org; internet yaounde.unic.org; also covers the Central African Republic and Gabon.

Congo, Republic: POB 13210, ave Foch, Case ORTF 15, Brazzaville; tel. 661-20-68; e-mail unic.brazzaville@unic.org; internet brazzaville.unic.org.

Eritrea: Hiday St, Airport Rd, Asmara; tel. (1) 151166; fax (1) 151081; e-mail dpi.er@undp.org; internet asmara.unic.org.

Ghana: POB GP 2339, Gamel Abdul Nassar/Liberia Rds, Accra; tel. (21) 665511; fax (21) 7010943; e-mail unic.accra@unic.org; internet accra.unic.org; also covers Sierra Leone.

Kenya: POB 30552, United Nations Office, Gigiri, Nairobi; tel. (20) 76225421; fax (20) 7624349; e-mail nairobi.unic@unon.org; internet www.unicnairobi.org; also covers Seychelles and Uganda.

Lesotho: POB 301, Maseru 100; tel. (22) 313790; fax (22) 310042; e-mail unic.maseru@unic.org; internet maseru.unic.org.

Madagascar: 159 rue Damantsoa Ankorahotra, Antananarivo; tel. (20) 2233050; fax (20) 2236794; e-mail unic.ant@moov.mg; internet antananarivo.unic.org.

Namibia: Private Bag 13351, 38-44 Stein St, Windhoek; tel. (61) 2046111; fax (61) 2046521; e-mail unic.windhoek@unic.org; internet windhoek.unic.org.

Nigeria: 17 Alfred Rewane (formerly Kingsway) Rd, Ikoyi, Lagos; tel. (1) 7755989; fax (1) 4630916; e-mail lagos@unic.org; internet lagos.unic.org.

Senegal: Immeuble SOUMEX, 3rd Floor, Mamelles, Almadies, Dakar; tel. 869-99-11; fax 860-51-48; e-mail unic.dakar@unic.org; internet dakar.unic.org; also covers Cape Verde, Côte d'Ivoire, The Gambia, Guinea-Bissau and Mauritania.

South Africa: Metro Park Bldg, 351 Schoeman St, POB 12677, Pretoria 0126; tel. (12) 354-8506; fax (12) 354-8501; e-mail unic.pretoria@unic.org; internet pretoria.unic.org.

Sudan: POB 1992, UN Compound, House No. 7, Blk 5, Gamma'a Ave, Khartoum; tel. (183) 783755; fax (183) 773772; e-mail unic.sd@undp.org; internet khartoum.unic.org; also covers Somalia.

Tanzania: POB 9224, International House, 6th Floor, Garden Ave/Shaaban Robert St, Dar es Salaam; tel. (22) 2199326; fax (22) 2667633; e-mail unic.daressalaam@unic.org; internet daressalaam.unic.org.

Togo: 468 angle rue Atimé et ave de la Libération, Lomé; tel. and fax 221-23-06; e-mail unic.lome@unic.org; internet lome.unic.org; also covers Benin.

Zambia: POB 32905, Revenue House, Ground Floor, Cairo Rd (Northend), Lusaka; tel. (21) 1228487; fax (21) 1222958; e-mail unic.lusaka@unic.org; internet lusaka.unic.org; also covers Botswana, Malawi and Swaziland.

Zimbabwe: POB 4408, Sanders House, 2nd Floor, First St/Jason Moyo Ave, Harare; tel. (4) 777060; fax (4) 750476; e-mail unic.harare@unic.org; internet harare.unic.org.

Economic Commission for Africa—ECA

Address: Menelik II Ave, POB 3001, Addis Ababa, Ethiopia.

Telephone: (11) 5517200; **fax:** (11) 5514416; **e-mail:** ecainfo@uneca.org; **internet:** www.uneca.org.

The UN Economic Commission for Africa (ECA) was founded in 1958 by a resolution of the UN Economic and Social Council (ECOSOC). The Commission promotes sustainable socio-economic development in Africa and aims to advance economic integration among African countries, and economic co-operation between Africa and other parts of the world.

MEMBERS

Algeria	Eritrea	Niger
Angola	Ethiopia	Nigeria
Benin	Gabon	Rwanda
Botswana	The Gambia	São Tomé and Príncipe
Burkina Faso	Ghana	Senegal
Burundi	Guinea	Seychelles
Cameroon	Guinea-Bissau	Sierra Leone
Cape Verde	Kenya	Somalia
Central African Republic	Lesotho	South Africa
Chad	Liberia	South Sudan
Comoros	Libya	Sudan
Congo, Democratic Republic	Madagascar	Swaziland
Congo, Republic	Malawi	Tanzania
Côte d'Ivoire	Mali	Togo
Djibouti	Mauritania	Tunisia
Egypt	Mauritius	Uganda
Equatorial Guinea	Morocco	Zambia
	Mozambique	Zimbabwe
	Namibia	

Organization

(September 2012)

COMMISSION

The Commission may only act with the agreement of the government of the country concerned. It is also empowered to make recommendations on any matter within its competence directly to the government of the member or associate member concerned, to governments admitted in a consultative capacity, and to the UN Specialized Agencies. The Commission is required to submit for prior consideration by ECOSOC any of its proposals for actions that would be likely to have important effects on the international economy.

CONFERENCE OF AFRICAN MINISTERS

The Conference, which meets every year, is attended by ministers responsible for finance, planning and economic development, representing the governments of member states, and is the main deliberative body of the Commission. The Commission's responsibility to promote concerted action for the economic and social development of Africa is vested primarily in the Conference, which considers matters of general policy and the priorities to be assigned to the Commission's programmes, considers inter-African and international economic policy, and makes recommendations to member states in connection with such matters.

OTHER POLICY-MAKING BODIES

Five intergovernmental committees of experts attached to the Subregional Offices (see below) meet annually and report to the Commission through a Technical Preparatory Committee of the Whole, which was established in 1979 to deal with matters submitted for the consideration of the Conference.

Seven other committees meet regularly to consider issues relating to the following policy areas: women and development; development information; sustainable development; human development and civil society; industry and private sector development; natural resources and science and technology; and regional co-operation, infrastructure and integration.

SECRETARIAT

The Secretariat provides the services necessary for the meeting of the Conference of Ministers and the meetings of the Commission's subsidiary bodies, carries out the resolutions and implements the programmes adopted there. It comprises the Office of the Executive Secretary and the following divisions: Food Security and Sustainable Development; Governance and Public Administration; ICT, Science and Technology; Economic Development and New Partnership for Africa's Development (NEPAD); Regional Integration and Trade; the African Centre for Gender and Social Development; and the African Centre for Statistics.

Executive Secretary: Dr CARLOS LOPES (Guinea-Bissau).

SUB-REGIONAL OFFICES

The Sub-regional Offices (SROs) aim to enable member states to play a more effective role in the process of African integration and to facilitate the integration efforts of the other UN agencies active in the sub-regions. In addition, the SROs act as the operational arms of ECA at national and sub-regional levels with a view to: ensuring harmony between the objectives of sub-regional and regional programmes and those defined by the Commission; providing advisory services; facilitating sub-regional economic co-operation, integration and development; collecting and disseminating information; stimulating policy dialogue; and promoting gender issues. Under the radical restructuring of ECA, completed in 2006, the SROs were given an enhanced role in shaping the Commission's agenda and programme implementation, and were also designated as privileged partners of the regional economic communities (see below).

Central Africa: POB 14935, Yaoundé, Cameroon; tel. 2222-0861; fax 2223-3185; e-mail sroca@uneca.org; internet new.uneca.org/sro-ca-fr/fr-fr/accueil_sroca.aspx; Officer-in-Charge HACHIM KOUMARÉ.

East Africa: POB 4654, Kigali, Rwanda; tel. 586549; fax 586546; e-mail APedro@uneca.org; Dir ANTONIO M. A. PEDRO.

North Africa: BP 2062 Rabat Ryad, Morocco; tel. (3) 771-78-29; fax (3) 771-27-02; e-mail srdc-na@uneca.org; internet new.uneca.org/sro-na/home_sro_na.aspx; Dir KARIMA BOUNEMRA BEN SOLTANE.

Southern Africa: POB 30647, Lusaka, Zambia; tel. (1) 228502; fax (1) 236949; e-mail srdcsa.uneca@uneca.org; internet new.uneca.org/sro-sa/home_sro_sa.aspx; Dir BEATRICE KIRASO (Uganda).

West Africa: POB 744, Niamey, Niger; tel. 72-29-61; fax 72-28-94; e-mail srdcwest@eca.ne; internet new.uneca.org/sro-wa/home_sro_wa.aspx; Dir EMILE AHOHE.

Activities

The Commission's activities are focused on two pillars: promoting regional integration in support of the visions and priorities of the African Union (AU, formerly the Organization of African Unity—OAU), through research and policy analysis on regional integration issues, capacity building, and the provision of technical assistance to the institutions (including the regional economic communities, see below) underpinning the regional integration agenda; and on meeting emerging global challenges and the special needs of Africa, with particular emphasis on achieving the Millennium Development Goals (MDGs). The Secretariat is guided in its efforts by major regional strategies, including the Abuja Treaty on the establishment of an African Economic Community, signed under the aegis of the OAU in 1991, the UN System-wide Support to the AU and NEPAD (approved in 2006, see below), and the Framework, Roadmap and Architecture for Fast Tracking the Establishment of a Continental Free Trade Area, and an Action Plan for Boosting Intra-African Trade, adopted in January 2012 by AU leaders. The following regional economic communities are regarded as pillars of continental economic integration: the Common Market for Eastern and Southern Africa (COMESA), the East African Community (EAC) and the Southern African Development Community (SADC) (which together form the EAC-COMESA-SADC Tripartite FTA initiative); the Communauté économique des états de l'Afrique centrale (CEEAC), the Economic Community of West African States (ECOWAS), the Intergovernmental Authority on Development (IGAD), and the Union of the Arab Maghreb.

In 2006 ECA initiated a major reform process in order to strengthen its capacity to promote regional integration and to help Africa to meet its particular needs. Greater emphasis was to be placed on knowledge generation and networking, advocacy, advisory services and technical co-operation, as well as co-operation with other regional organizations. A high-level review of the reforms was undertaken in 2009, resulting in further restructuring of some programmes and divisions.

ICT, SCIENCE AND TECHNOLOGY

The ICT (Information and Communications Technology), Science and Technology Division has responsibility for co-ordinating the implementation of the Harnessing Information Technology for Africa project, and for implementing the African Information Society Initiative (AISI), which was founded in 1996 and supports the development of the pan-continental information and communications infrastructure. ECA was given responsibility for the Task Force on e-Government, mandated by the second session of the World Summit on Information Society (WSIS), convened in Tunis, Tunisia, in November 2005. The Commission manages the Information Technology Centre for Africa, established in 1999 (see below), and maintains the Africa Knowledge for Development Networks (accessible at knowledge.africa-devnet.org), an internet-based platform for promoting knowledge sharing on regional economic and social development. In July 2009 the first International Conference on African Digital Libraries and Archives, held under ECA auspices, urged the establishment of an ECA African Digital Library and Archives Programme. In February of that year representatives of UN agencies, NEPAD, the AU, and media executives, convened the first Regional Media Dialogue, in The Vaal, South Africa, at the end of which they adopted a Consensus Declaration and series of recommendations relating to the increasing role of the media in Africa's development. A second Regional Media Dialogue, held in June 2011, in Maseru, Lesotho, adopted the Maseru Declaration, recommending the development of a continent-wide framework for structured engagement with the media. In September 2012 the Division launched a new African Forum for Geospatial Information Systems (GIS), aimed at enhancing the capacity of African media professionals to promote GIS. In October 2011 ECA, with the AU, launched a new Africa Internet Governance Forum (AfIGF), in accordance with the recommendations of the WSIS. ECA hosts the AfIGF's secretariat. The 2012 session of the AfIGF was to be held in October, in Cairo, Egypt. In June of that year a meeting of experts on cyber legislation from member states in eastern, southern and northern Africa, held under the auspices of the ECA, AU, and relevant regional economic communities, adopted the Addis Ababa Declaration on the harmonization of cyber legislation in Africa. During 2012 ECA was providing technical support to the AU in developing a new AU Convention on Cybersecurity.

In August 2012 ECA and the UN Institute for Training and Research launched a series of free internet-based e-Learning courses aimed at supporting the objective of establishing a Continental Free Trade Area by 2017. The Commission supports the Electronic Rural School in Local Languages (ERELA) programme, administered by the Government of Finland with the aim of promoting learning and use of communications technologies in local African mother tongues.

In March 2008 ECA organized a conference entitled Science with Africa to link African science-based organizations and businesses with their global counterparts; the second Science with Africa conference, held in June 2010, adopted a set of recommendations on how African countries might leverage science and technology to carry forwards their development agenda. In September 2012 ECA launched a new Access to Scientific Knowledge in Africa (ASKIA) online portal (accessible at askia.uneca.org/askia), providing scientific and socio-economic information of relevance to scientists, policy-makers, and other researchers in the region.

Since 2007 ECA has organized biennial Technology in Government in Africa (TIGA) awards, with the objective of recognizing the effective use by regional governments and institutions of ICTs for public service delivery. In 2011 ECA, jointly with the Switzerland-based African Innovation Foundation, launched an annual Innovation Prize for Africa (IPA), which aims to reward regional innovation in the areas of science, technology and engineering.

GOVERNANCE AND PUBLIC ADMINISTRATION

The role of ECA's Governance and Public Administration Division is to improve member states' capacity for good governance and development management. The Division provides support for the African Peer Review Mechanism, a NEPAD initiative whereby participating member governments mutually assess compliance with a number of codes, standards and commitments that uphold good governance and sustainable development. The Division also helps civil society organizations to participate in governance; supports the development of private sector enterprises; and helps to improve public administration in member states. To achieve these aims the Division provides technical assistance and advisory services, conducts studies, and organizes training workshops, seminars and conferences at national, sub-regional and regional levels for ministers, public administrators and senior policy-makers, as well as for private and non-governmental organizations. The Commission and the AU jointly provide support to the African Governance Forum (AGF) process, which is implemented through UNDP's Regional Bureau for Africa; such fora have been convened periodically since 1997. AGF VIII, addressing the theme 'Democracy, Elections, and the Management of Diversity in Africa', was to be held in Johannesburg, South Africa, in October 2012. In 2005 the first *African Governance Report (AGR-1)* was published by ECA, monitoring progress towards good governance in 27 countries. *AGR-2*, issued in August 2009, found improvements over the past few years in the observance of human rights and the rule of law, as well as in competitive electoral politics and the scope of political representation, although party and electoral systems were deemed to be weak and poorly structured. Advances were judged to have been made in economic governance, public sector management, private sector development and corporate governance, while weaknesses were highlighted in the management of the tax system and in service delivery, and corruption was cited as a major challenge to achieving sustainable economic progress and development in Africa. *AGR-3*, addressing elections and diversity management in Africa, was to be released in 2013. A *Mutual Review of Development Effectiveness in Africa Report (MRDE)*, jointly compiled by ECA's Governance and Public Administration Division and OECD, is published annually; the Review considers progress achieved hitherto in delivering commitments made by African countries and their development partners, and outlines future key priorities. The 2012 edition was issued in May.

AFRICAN CENTRE FOR GENDER AND SOCIAL DEVELOPMENT

ECA aims to improve the socio-economic prospects of women through the promotion of equal access to resources and opportunities, and equal participation in decision-making. An African Centre for Gender and Development (renamed as above in 2006) was established in 1975 to service all national, sub-regional and regional bodies involved in development issues relating to gender and the advancement of women. The Centre manages the African Women's Development Fund, which was established in June 2000. An African Women's Rights Observatory (AWRO), launched in 1995, monitors gender equality and the advancement of women. An African Gender and Development Index, measuring how far member states had met their commitments towards international agreements on gender equality and women's advancement, was inaugurated in January 2005; the most recent Index, reflecting the state of progress in 2011, was issued in January 2012. The African Women's Decade, covering 2010–20, was launched in October 2010 under the theme 'Grassroots approach to gender equality and women's empowerment'. A Commission on HIV/AIDS and Governance in Africa, with its secretariat based at ECA headquarters, was launched in September 2003. The Commission, an initiative of the UN Secretary-General, was mandated to assess the impact of the HIV/AIDS pandemic on national structures and African economic development and to incorporate its findings in a Final Report; this was issued in October 2005.

FOOD SECURITY AND SUSTAINABLE DEVELOPMENT

ECA's Food Security and Sustainable Development Division aims to strengthen the capacity of member countries to design institutional structures and implement policies and programmes, in areas such as food production, population, environment and human settlements, to achieve sustainable development. It also promotes the use of science and technology in achieving sustainable development. ECA promotes food security in African countries through raising awareness of the relationship between population, food security, the environment and sustainable development; encouraging the advancement of science and technology in member states; and providing policy analysis support and technical advisory services aimed at strengthening national population policies. In March 2010 ECA issued a report urging member countries to build upon the outcomes of the Abuja Food Security Summit, organized by the AU in December 2006, by establishing a common market of strategic food and agricultural commodities. From 2005 ECA increased its work devoted to the changes in climate caused by global warming, and the resulting threat posed by drought, floods and other extreme events. In 2006, with the AU and the AfDB, it established a 10-year Climate for Development in Africa Programme (Clim-Dev Africa) to improve the collection of climate-related data and assist in forecasting and risk management. ECA provides the technical secretariat for Clim-Dev Africa. In December 2007 ECA announced the establishment of an African Climate Policy Centre (ACPC), to help member states to incorporate climate-related concerns in their development policies so as to counter the impact of climate change. The first Climate Change and Development in Africa Conference (CCDA-I) was held in Addis Ababa, Ethiopia, in October 2011. Members were encouraged, inter alia, to incorporate climate change data and analysis in their policy-making decisions, to identify means of increasing agricultural productivity, including water management and soil enrichment, and to develop strategies for low carbon development. CCDA-II was scheduled to be held in October 2012, again in Addis Ababa. In September 2012 a series of ACPC workshops on upgrading hydro-meteorological networks and recovering hydro-meteorological data was launched in Ethiopia; workshops were subsequently to be held in Gambia, Mali, Mozambique and Rwanda.

ECA assists member states in the assessment and use of water resources and the development of river and lake basins common to more than one country. ECA encourages co-operation between countries with regard to water issues and collaborates with other UN agencies and regional organizations to promote technical and economic co-operation in this area. In 1992, on the initiative of ECA, the Interagency Group for Water in Africa (now UN-Water/Africa) was established to co-ordinate and harmonize the water-related activities of the UN and other organizations on the continent. ECA has been particularly active in efforts to promote the integrated development of the water resources of the Zambezi river basin and of Lake Victoria. In December 2003 ECA hosted the Pan-African Implementation and Partnership Conference on Water (PANAFCON). In October 2011—following an invitation by the 17th regular summit of AU heads of state and government, held in late June–early July 2011, inviting African states to work on a common continental position for the UN Conference on Sustainable Development—UNCSD, which took place in Rio de Janeiro, Brazil, in June 2012—ECA organized a UNCSD Africa Regional Preparatory Conference. The October 2011 Conference noted emerging challenges to sustainable development in Africa, including low adaptive capacity to the effects of climate change; increasing severe biodiversity loss, desertification and land degradation, aggravated by the effects of climate change; and rapid urbanization. The conference urged the international community to meet its commitments to the continent in terms of transfer of financial and technological resources, and committed African states to enhancing efforts to improve national governance and development effectiveness, and to formulating national strategies for sustainable development. ECA, in collaboration with other agencies, compiles a Sustainable Development Report on Africa (SDRA); the fourth issue, on the theme 'Managing Africa's natural resource base for sustainable growth and development', was being prepared in 2012.

STATISTICS

The African Centre for Statistics was established in 2006 as a new division of ECA, to encourage the use of statistics in national planning, to provide training and technical assistance for the compilation, analysis and dissemination of statistics, and to prepare members for the 2010 round of population censuses. An Advisory Board on Statistics in Africa, comprising 15 experts from national statistical offices, sub-regional bodies and training institutes, meets annually to advise ECA on statistical developments in Africa and guide its activities. The Statistical Commission for Africa (StatCom-Africa), comprising representatives of national statistical offices, regional and international institutions and development partners, meets every two years as the principal body overseeing statistical development in Africa, with annual working groups monitoring progress and deciding on activities. In January 2012 StatCom-Africa, meeting in Cape Town, South Africa, adopted the Robben Island Declaration on Statistical Development, which aimed to strengthen methods of data collection and analysis, of harmonizing statistics in Africa and upgrading the system of national accounts. ECA assists its member states in population data collection and data processing; analysis of demographic data obtained from censuses or surveys; training demographers; formulation of population policies and integrating population variables in development planning, through advisory missions and through the organization of national seminars on population and development; and in dissemination of demographic information. The first conference of African ministers responsible for civil registration was convened in August 2010, in Addis Ababa, and the second was held in September 2012, in Durban, South Africa.

REGIONAL INTEGRATION, INFRASTRUCTURE AND TRADE

ECA's Regional Integration, Infrastructure and Trade Division comprises sections concerning regional integration; infrastructure and natural resources development; and trade and international negotiations. ECA supports the implementation of the AU's regional integration agenda, through research; policy analysis; strengthening capacity and the provision of technical assistance to the regional economic communities; and working on transboundary initiatives and activities across a variety of sectors. In October 2008 ECA launched an Observatory on Regional Integration in Africa, an internet-based repository of knowledge and information aimed at supporting the activities of policy-makers, member states, regional economic communities, and other stakeholders. The Trade and International Negotiations Section conducts research and outreach activities aimed at ensuring best practice in trade policy development and undertakes research and dissemination activities on bilateral and international trade negotiations (such as the ongoing multilateral trade negotiations under the World Trade Organization) with a view to helping African countries to benefit from globalization through trade. In July 2012 ECA, the AU and the African Development Bank (AfDB) issued their fifth joint *Assessing Regional Integration in Africa* report (ARIA V), which addressed the ongoing process towards establishing, by 2017, an operational Continental Free Trade Area. The African Trade Policy Centre (ATPC), established in 2003, aims to strengthen the human, institutional and policy capacities of African governments to formulate and implement sound trade policies and participate more effectively in international trade negotiations. The Centre takes both a national and regional perspective, and provides a rapid response to technical needs arising from ongoing trade negotiations. In November 2011 the ATPC organized the first Africa Trade Forum (ATF). During ATF II, held in September 2012 on the theme 'Boosting Intra-Africa Trade and Establishing the Continental Free Trade Area', the ATPC launched a new Africa Corridor Management Alliance (ACMA), with the aim of making more efficient the cost of moving goods through Africa's trade and transit corridors, and across international borders. Issues to be addressed by the ACMA included unofficial fees, roadblocks, and corruption; as well as variance in national laws relating to vehicle standards and inspection requirements; inefficient administrative procedures; and delays in the clearance of goods at ports.

ECA and the World Bank jointly co-ordinate the sub-Saharan Africa Transport Programme (SSATP), established in 1987, which aims to facilitate policy development and related capacity-building in the continent's transport sector. In April 2012 ECA formally invited the AU Commission to join the SSATP Board. A meeting of all participants in the programme is held annually. The regional Road Management Initiative (RMI) under the SSATP seeks to encourage a partnership between the public and private sectors to manage and maintain road infrastructure more efficiently and thus to improve country-wide communications and transportation activities. An Urban Mobility component of the SSATP aims to improve sub-Saharan African urban transport services, while a Trade and Transport component aims to enhance the international competitiveness of regional economies through the establishment of more cost-effective services for shippers. The Railway Restructuring element focuses on the provision of financially sustainable railway enterprises. The first session of a forum on Central African regional integration, organized by the ECA SRO for Central Africa, took place in November 2009, in Douala, Cameroon. The second session was held in May–June 2012, also in Douala, on the theme 'Sub-regional Trade and Transport Infrastructure Development in Central Africa'. In November 2005 a meeting of sub-Saharan African ministers of transport, convened in Bamako, Mali, on the fringes of the SSATP Annual General Meeting, adopted a resolution aimed at developing Africa's transport infrastructure, focusing on the importance of incorporating transport issues into poverty reduction strategies, ensuring sustainable financing for Africa's road programmes, and prioritizing road safety issues. The first African Road Safety Conference, held in Accra, Ghana, in February 2007, by African ministers responsible for transport and health, reaffirmed road safety as a key development priority and pledged to set and achieve measurable national targets for road safety and the prevention of traffic injuries in all member states. In November 2011 the second African Road Safety Conference, convened by ECA within the framework of the SSATP, approved an Action Plan, which aimed to halve the number of road crash fatalities by 2020. A meeting of experts convened in September 2011 to review the development of interconnected Trans-African Highways (TAH) reported that by that time the TAH comprised some nine principal axes of roads across the continent, but that about one-quarter of an envisaged final network was yet to be constructed. The meeting recommended the adoption of an inter-governmental agreement on the TAH, and adopted a series of 10 recommendations aimed at accelerating the development of the highways interconnection initiative.

The Division supports efforts to advance the development of Africa's extensive mineral and energy resources, focusing on promoting co-operation, integration and public-private sector partnerships; facilitating policy decisions and dissemination of best practices; and supporting capacity building. The Southern and Eastern African Mineral Centre, established by ECA in Dar-es-Salaam, Tanzania, in 1977, opened its membership to all African states in 2007. The Centre provides data-processing, training, analytical services and research on mineral applications. An international study group to review African mining was convened by ECA for the first time in October 2007. ECA's Energy Programme provides assistance to member states in the development of indigenous energy resources and the formulation of energy policies to extricate member states from continued energy crises. In May 2004 ECA was appointed as the secretariat of a UN-Energy/Africa initiative which aimed to facilitate the exchange of information, good practices and knowledge-sharing among UN organizations and with private sector companies, non-governmental organizations, power utilities and other research and academic institutions. In December 2011 ECA and the AU organized a second conference of African ministers responsible for mineral resources development.

ECONOMIC DEVELOPMENT AND NEPAD

ECA provides guidance to the policy-making organs of the UN and the AU on the formulation of policies supporting the achievement of Africa's development objectives. It contributes to the work of the General Assembly and of specialized agencies by providing an African perspective in the preparation of development strategies. The former UN System-wide Special Initiative on Africa, covering the decade 1995–2006, aimed to mobilize resources and to implement a series of political and economic development objectives; the Initiative was followed by the UN System-wide Support to the AU and NEPAD, launched in 2006. NEPAD was established by the AU in 2001, and ECA was assigned the task of co-ordinating UN support for NEPAD at the regional level. In February 2010 a new NEPAD Planning and Co-ordination Committee (NPCC) was established as a technical body of the AU, to replace the former NEPAD Secretariat, with the aim of improving the implementation of NEPAD projects at country level. In April 2010 ECA and the NPCC concluded a Memorandum of Understanding strengthening collaboration between the two bodies.

Within the Economic Development and NEPAD Division, a Finance, Industry and Investment Section supports members to analyse the challenges of mobilizing domestic and external resources for promoting investment and industrial development. Principal focus areas are foreign aid, debt, private capital flows, and savings and remittances. It also assists member states to implement effective policies and strategies to enhance their investment prospects and competitiveness in the global production system. A Macroeconomic Analysis Section assists member states to improve their capacity to formulate, implement and monitor sound macroeconomic policies and better institutional frameworks, with a view to achieving sustainable development. The Section also focuses on policy advocacy and collaboration with development organizations and institutions, produces publications and provides training, conferences and workshops. It undertakes macroeconomic research and policy analysis in the following areas: macroeconomic modelling and planning; growth strategies; fiscal and monetary policies; and debt management. The Section also prepares background documents for the annual Conference of African Ministers of Finance, Planning, and Economic Development. A separate Section serves to support members reviewing their progress towards and in implementing internationally agreed development objectives, including the MDGs and those defined by the 2001 Brussels Programme of Action for least developed countries. The Section prepares annual reviews and supports capacity building and the sharing of knowledge among African countries.

In October 1999 the first African Development Forum (ADF)—initiated by ECA as a process to formulate an agenda for effective sustainable development in African countries—was organized in Addis Ababa, Ethiopia. Regular ADF meetings are held, each addressing a specific development issue. ADF VII was convened in October 2010, on the theme 'Acting on Climate Change for Sustainable Development in Africa'. The theme of ADF VIII, scheduled to take place in October 2012, was 'Governing and Harnessing Natural Resources for Africa's Development'. In March 2011 ECA launched the Africa Platform for Development Effectiveness (APDEv, accessible at www.africa-platform.org), a multi-stakeholder platform and organizing mechanism for policy-makers in the continent.

In March 2009 the Coalition for Dialogue on Africa (CoDA) was launched, by ECA, the AU and the AfDB, as an independent African forum to serve as an umbrella for all existing fora on Africa. ECA hosts its secretariat. CoDA meetings, including a multi-stakeholder dialogue forum, were convened in Tunis, in November, to consider Africa's recovery from the global economic and financial crisis, and regional integration. In February 2010 CoDA met, again in Tunis, to discuss transforming the Coalition into a fully independent, non-governmental African initiative, with a chief executive; and to develop a work programme. A CoDA policy forum was held in Abidjan, Côte d'Ivoire, in May, on 'Financing Regional Integration in Africa'. Meeting in October 2010, on the sidelines of ADF VII, CoDA urged African leaders to continue to pursue participation multinational negotiations on climate change. A CoDA policy forum on foreign direct investments in land in Africa was convened in Lisbon, Portugal, in June 2011.

In June 2009 ECA and the AU hosted, in Cairo, Egypt, a joint meeting of African ministers of finance and economic affairs, which considered the impact on the region of the global crisis. During that month a joint report of all five UN Regional Commissions, entitled *The Global Economic and Financial Crisis: Regional Impacts, Responses and Solutions*, was launched. In October 2010 ECA, AU and the AfDB established a Joint Secretariat (based at ECA headquarters) to enhance coherence and collaboration in support of Africa's development agenda. In May 2011 ECA launched the *ECA LDC Monitor*, an internet-based tool aimed at assessing economic progress in member Least-Developed Countries. The theme of the 2012 *Economic Report on Africa*, released by ECA in September of that year, was 'Africa's Potential as a Pole of Global Growth'. ECA, the AfDB, OECD and UNDP jointly prepare an annual *African Economic Outlook*: the focus of the 2012 edition, issued in May, was 'Promoting Youth Employment'. Since 2006 ECA and AfDB have organized an annual African Economic Conference (AEC), aimed at enabling an exchange of ideas among economists and policy-makers on development policy. The seventh AEC was to be held in Kigali, Rwanda, in October–November 2012, on the theme 'Fostering Inclusive and Sustainable Development in Africa in an Age of Global Uncertainty'.

ASSOCIATED BODY

Information Technology Centre for Africa (ITCA): POB 3001, Addis Ababa, Ethiopia; tel. (11) 551-4534; fax (11) 551-0512; e-mail itca@uneca.org; internet www.uneca.org/itca; f. 1999 to strengthen the continent's communications infrastructure and promote the use of information and communications technologies in planning and policy-making; stages exhibitions and provides training facilities; Man MAKANE FAYE.

Finance

ECA's proposed regular budget for the two-year period 2012–13, an appropriation from the UN budget, was US $138.3m.

Publications

Africa Climate Policy Bulletin.
African Gender and Development Index.
African Governance Report.
African Review Report on Chemicals.
African Statistical Yearbook.
African Women's Report.
Africa Youth Report.
Assessing Regional Integration in Africa.
ECA Policy Brief.
Eastern Africa News (issued by the SRO for East Africa).
Economic Report on Africa.
Insight ECA-SA (issued by the SRO for Southern Africa).
MDG Report: Assessing Progress in Africa.
Mutual Review of Development Effectiveness in Africa (jointly with OECD).
Sustainable Development Report on Africa (every 2 years).
Country reports, policy and discussion papers, reports of conferences and meetings, training series, working paper series.

United Nations Children's Fund—UNICEF

Address: 3 United Nations Plaza, New York, NY 10017, USA.
Telephone: (212) 326-7000; **fax:** (212) 887-7465; **e-mail:** info@unicef.org; **internet:** www.unicef.org.

UNICEF was established in 1946 by the UN General Assembly as the UN International Children's Emergency Fund, to meet the emergency needs of children in post-war Europe. In 1950 its mandate was expanded to respond to the needs of children in developing countries. In 1953 the General Assembly decided that UNICEF should become a permanent branch of the UN system, with an emphasis on programmes giving long-term benefits to children everywhere, particularly those in developing countries. In 1965 UNICEF was awarded the Nobel Peace Prize.

Organization

(September 2012)

EXECUTIVE BOARD

The Executive Board, as the governing body of UNICEF, comprises 36 member governments from all regions, elected in rotation for a three-year term by ECOSOC. The Board establishes policy, reviews programmes and approves expenditure. It reports to the General Assembly through ECOSOC.

SECRETARIAT

The Executive Director of UNICEF is appointed by the UN Secretary-General in consultation with the Executive Board. The administration of UNICEF and the appointment and direction of staff are the responsibility of the Executive Director, under policy directives laid down by the Executive Board, and under a broad authority delegated to the Executive Director by the Secretary-General. Around 85% of UNICEF staff positions are based in field offices.

Executive Director: ANTHONY LAKE (USA).

UNICEF OFFICES

Regional Office for Eastern and Southern Africa: POB 44145, Nairobi, Kenya 00100; tel. (20) 7621234; fax (20) 7622678; e-mail unicefesaro@unicef.org; internet www.unicef.org/esaro.

Regional Office for West and Central Africa: POB 29720, Dakar-Yoff, Senegal; tel. 33-869-58-58; fax 33-820-89-65; e-mail mdawes@unicef.org; internet www.unicef.org/wcaro.

UNICEF Innocenti Research Centre: Piazza SS. Annunziata 12, 50122 Florence, Italy; tel. (055) 20330; fax (055) 2033220; e-mail florence@unicef.org; internet www.unicef-irc.org; f. 1988; undertakes research in two thematic areas: Social and economic policies and children; and Child protection and implementation of international standards for children; Dir GORDON ALEXANDER.

UNICEF Supply Division: Oceanvej 10–12, 2100 Copenhagen, Denmark; tel. 35-27-35-27; fax 35-26-94-21; e-mail supply@unicef.org; internet www.unicef.org/supply; responsible for overseeing UNICEF's global procurement and logistics operations.

UNICEF New York Supply Centre (USA): UNICEF House, 3 UN Plaza, New York, NY 10017 USA; tel. (212) 35-67-490; fax (212) 35-67-477.

Further strategic supply hubs are located in Dubai, United Arab Emirates; Douala, Cameroon; Colón, Panama; and Shanghai, People's Republic of China.

NATIONAL COMMITTEES

UNICEF is supported by 36 National Committees, mostly in industrialized countries, whose volunteer members raise money through various specific campaigns and activities, including the sale of greetings cards and collection of foreign coins. The Committees also undertake advocacy and awareness campaigns on a number of issues and provide an important link with the general public.

Activities

UNICEF is dedicated to the well-being of children, adolescents and women and works for the realization and protection of their rights within the frameworks of the Convention on the Rights of the Child, which was adopted by the UN General Assembly in 1989, and by 2012 was almost universally ratified, and of the Convention on the Elimination of All Forms of Discrimination Against Women, adopted by the UN General Assembly in 1979. Promoting the full implementation of the Conventions, UNICEF aims to ensure that children worldwide are given the best possible start in life and attain a good level of basic education, and that adolescents are given every opportunity to develop their capabilities and participate successfully in society. The Fund also continues to provide relief and rehabilitation assistance in emergencies. Through its extensive field network in more than 150 developing countries and territories, UNICEF undertakes, in co-ordination with governments, local communities and other aid organizations, programmes in health, nutrition, education, water and sanitation, the environment, gender issues and development, and other fields of importance to children. Emphasis is placed on low-cost, community-based programmes. UNICEF programmes are increasingly focused on supporting children and women during critical periods of their life, when intervention can make a lasting difference. Since the 1950s UNICEF has engaged the services of prominent individuals as Goodwill Ambassadors and Advocates, who can use their status to attract attention to particular causes and support UNICEF's objectives. During 2011 UNICEF advocated for increased focus on children in national development plans and budgets in 102 countries.

The principal themes of UNICEF's medium-term strategic plan for the period 2006–13 are: young child survival and development; basic education and gender equality (including the Fund's continued leadership of the UN Girls' Education Initiative, see below); HIV/AIDS and children (including participation in the Joint UN Programme on HIV/AIDS—UNAIDS—see below); child protection from violence, exploitation and abuse; and policy advocacy and partnerships for children's rights. These priority areas are guided by the relevant UN Millennium Development Goals (MDGs) adopted by world leaders in 2000, and by the 'A World Fit for Children' declaration and plan of action endorsed by the UN General Assembly Special Session on Children in 2002. The 'A World Fit for Children' declaration reaffirmed commitment to the agenda of the 1990 World Summit for Children. The plan of action resolved to work towards the attainment by 2015 of 21 new goals and targets supporting the MDGs in the areas of education, health and the protection of children; these included: a reduction of mortality rates for infants and children under five by two-thirds; a reduction of maternal mortality rates by three-quarters; a reduction by one-third in the rate of severe malnutrition among children under the age of five; and enrolment in primary education by 90% of children. UNICEF issues regular reports that monitor progress in achieving the MDGs. The ninth in the series, entitled *Progress for Children: Achieving the MDGs with Equity (No. 9)*, was published in September 2010. UNICEF supports the 'Global Strategy for Women's and Children's Health', launched by heads of state and government participating in the September 2010 UN Summit on the MDGs; some US $40,000m. has been pledged towards women's and child's health and achieving goals (iv) Reducing Child Mortality and (v) Improving Maternal Health. In 2012 a roadmap was being developed towards the Fund's next medium-term strategic plan, which was to cover the period 2014–17; the new plan was to be passed to the Executive Board for approval in late 2013.

UNICEF estimates that more than 500,000 women die every year during pregnancy or childbirth, largely because of inadequate maternal healthcare, and nearly 4m. newborns die within 28 days of birth. For every maternal death, approximately 30 further women suffer permanent injuries or chronic disabilities as a result of complications during pregnancy or childbirth. Under the Global Partnership for Maternal, Newborn and Child Health, UNICEF works with WHO, UNFPA and other partners in countries with high maternal mortality to improve maternal health and prevent maternal and newborn death through the integration of a continuum of home, community, outreach and facility-based care, embracing every stage of maternal, newborn and child health. UNICEF and partners work with governments and policy-makers to ensure that ante-natal and obstetric care is a priority in national health plans. UNICEF's recent activities in this area have included support for obstetric facilities and training in, and advocacy of, women's health issues, such as ending child marriage, eliminating female genital mutilation/cutting (FGM/C), preventing malaria and promoting the uptake of tetanus toxoid vaccinations and iron and folic acid supplements among pregnant women.

YOUNG CHILD SURVIVAL AND DEVELOPMENT

In 2011 UNICEF allocated some 52% of total programme assistance to young child survival and development. In 2009 UNICEF estimated that around 8.1m. children under five years of age died (compared with some 20m. child mortalities in 1960 and some 13m. in 1990)—mainly in developing countries (three-quarters occurring in the People's Republic of China, the Democratic Republic of the Congo, India, Nigeria, and Pakistan), and the majority from largely preventable causes. UNICEF has worked with WHO and other partners to increase global immunization coverage against the following six diseases: measles, poliomyelitis, tuberculosis, diphtheria, whooping cough and tetanus. In 2003 UNICEF, WHO, the World Bank and other partners established a new Child Survival Partnership, which acts as a forum for the promotion of co-ordinated action in support of efforts to save children's lives in 68 targeted developing countries. UNICEF, WHO, the World Bank and the UN Population Division established an Inter-agency Group for Child Mortality Estimation (IGME) in 2004, to advance work on monitoring progress towards meeting the MDG on reducing child mortality. In September 2012 IGME reported that in 2011 an estimated 6.9m. children died under the age of five years old, compared with around 12m. such deaths in 1990. In September 2005 UNICEF, WHO and other partners launched the Partnership for Maternal, Newborn and Child Health, which aimed to accelerate progress towards the attainment of the MDGs to reduce child and maternal mortality. In 2000 UNICEF, WHO, the World Bank and a number of public- and private-sector partners launched the Global Alliance for Vaccines and Immunization (GAVI), subsequently renamed the GAVI Alliance, which aims to protect children of all nationalities and socio-economic groups against vaccine-preventable diseases. GAVI's strategy includes improving access to sustainable immunization services, expanding the use of existing vaccines, accelerating the development and introduction of new vaccines and technologies and promoting immunization coverage as a focus of international development efforts. In 2006 UNICEF, WHO and other partners launched the Global Immunization Vision and Strategy (GIVS), a global 10-year framework, covering 2006–15, aimed at reducing deaths due to vaccine-preventable diseases by at least two-thirds compared to 2000 levels, by 2015; and increasing national vaccination coverage levels to at least 90%. (In 2009 the global child vaccination coverage rate was estimated at 82%.) From 2006 a Global Immunization Meeting was convened annually by UNICEF, WHO and GAVI Alliance partners; the fifth Meeting, held in February 2010, addressed issues including means of improving routine vaccination and supporting accelerated disease control initiatives; the introduction of new vaccines; and vaccine supply, including the status of pandemic influenza vaccines.

UNICEF works to improve safe water supply, sanitation and hygiene, and thereby reduce the risk of diarrhoea and other water-borne diseases. In partnership with other organizations the Fund supports initiatives to make schools in more than 90 developing countries safer through school-based water, sanitation and hygiene programmes. UNICEF places great emphasis on increasing the testing and protection of drinking water at its source as well as in the home. UNICEF, the World Bank and other partners participate in the Global Public-Private Partnership for Handwashing with Soap, which was established in 2001 with the aim of empowering communities in developing countries to prevent diarrhoea and respiratory infections through the promotion of the practice of thorough hand-washing with soap. In 2006 UNICEF and partners established the Global Task Force on Water and Sanitation with the aim of providing all children with access to safe water, and accelerating progress towards MDG targets on safe drinking water and basic sanitation.

UNICEF-assisted programmes for the control of diarrhoeal diseases promote the low-cost manufacture and distribution of prepackaged salts or home-made solutions. The use of 'oral rehydration therapy' has risen significantly in recent years, and is believed to prevent more than 1m. child deaths annually. During 1990–2000 diarrhoea-related deaths were reduced by one-half. UNICEF also promotes the need to improve sanitation and access to safe water supplies in developing nations in order to reduce the risk of diarrhoea and other water-borne diseases (see 20/20 initiative, below). To control acute respiratory infections, another leading cause of death in children under five in developing countries, UNICEF works with WHO in training health workers to diagnose and treat the associated diseases. At the UN General Assembly Special Session on Children, in 2002, goals were set to reduce measles deaths by 50%. Expanded efforts by UNICEF, WHO and other partners led to a reduction in world-wide measles deaths by 78% between 2000 and 2008. Around 1m. children die from malaria every year, mainly in sub-Saharan Africa. In October 1998 UNICEF, together with WHO, UNDP and the World Bank, inaugurated a new global campaign, Roll Back Malaria, to fight the disease. UNICEF is actively engaged in developing innovative and effective ways to distribute highly-subsidized insecticide-treated mosquito nets at local level, thereby increasing the proportion of children and pregnant women who use them.

According to UNICEF estimates, around 25% of children under five years of age are underweight, while each year malnutrition contributes to more than one-third of the child deaths in that age group and leaves millions of others with physical and mental disabilities. UNICEF supports national efforts to reduce malnutrition, for example, fortifying staple foods with micronutrients, widening women's access to education, improving the nutritional status of pregnant women, strengthening household food security and basic health services, providing food supplies in emergencies, and promoting sound childcare and feeding practices. Since 1991 more than 19,000 hospitals in about 130 countries have been designated 'baby-friendly', having implemented a set of UNICEF and WHO recommendations entitled '10 steps to successful breast-feeding'. The Executive Director of UNICEF chairs the Lead Group of the Scaling Up Nutrition (SUN) initiative, which convened its first meeting in April 2012, and comprises 27 national leaders and agencies jointly providing strategic guidance with a view to improving child and maternal nutrition. SUN, initiated in 2009, and co-ordinated by the UN Secretary-General's Special Representative for Food Security and Nutrition, aims to increase the coverage of interventions that improve nutrition during the first 1,000 days of a child's life (such as exclusive breastfeeding, optimal complementary feeding practices, and provision of essential vitamins and minerals); and to ensure that national nutrition plans are implemented and that government programmes take nutrition into account. The activities of SUN are guided by the Framework for Scaling up Nutrition, which was published in April 2010 and subsequently endorsed by more than 100 partners, including UN agencies, governments, research institutions, and representatives of civil society and of the private sector; and by the SUN Roadmap, finalized in September 2010.

BASIC EDUCATION AND GENDER EQUALITY

In 2011 UNICEF allocated some 21% of total programme assistance to basic education and gender equality. UNICEF considers education to be a fundamental human right, and works to ensure all children receive equal access to quality education. UNICEF participated in and fully supports the objectives and framework for action adopted by the World Education Forum in Dakar, Senegal, in April 2000, including the Education for All initiative. UNICEF was assigned formal responsibility within the initiative for education in emergencies, early childhood care and technical and policy support. UNICEF leads and acts as the secretariat of the United Nations Girls' Education Initiative (UNGEI), which aims to increase the enrolment of girls in primary schools in more than 100 countries. It is estimated that more than 100m. school-age children world-wide, of whom more than one-half are girls, remain deprived of basic education. In May 2010 UNGEI convened the first ever international conference on 'Engendering Empowerment: Education and Equality' ('E4'), in Dakar, Senegal. The E4 conference unanimously adopted the Dakar Declaration on Accelerating Girls' Education and Gender Equality, in which it urged that increased focus should be placed on accelerating access to education for the most socially deprived girls, deemed to be the most disadvantaged group in education.

UNICEF advocates the implementation of the Child Friendly School model, designed to facilitate the delivery of safe, quality education. UNICEF, in partnership with UNESCO, has developed an Essential Learning Package to support countries to reduce disparities in the provision of basic education. The initiative was implemented for the first time by Burkina Faso in 2003, and has since been adopted by a further 11 countries in West and Central Africa.

UNICEF manages a 'Schools for Africa' initiative, which appeals for funds to enable children from disadvantaged backgrounds to enrol at schools and complete their educations. The first phase of the scheme, covering the period 2005–09, sought some US $50m. to benefit 4m. children in six African countries. The second phase, covering 2010–13, aims to raise a further $70m. to benefit vulnerable children in Angola, Burkina Faso, Ethiopia, Madagascar, Malawi, Mali, Mozambique, Niger, Rwanda, South Africa and Zimbabwe.

HIV/AIDS AND CHILDREN

In 2011 UNICEF allocated some 4% of total programme assistance to combating HIV/AIDS. UNICEF is concerned at the danger posed by HIV/AIDS to the realization of children's rights and aims to provide expertise, support, logistical co-ordination and innovation towards ending the epidemic and limiting its impact on children and their mothers. In 2012 it was estimated that 3.4m. children under the age of 15 were living with HIV/AIDS world-wide. During 2011 some 330,000 children under the age of 15 were estimated to have been newly infected with HIV, while 230,000 died as a result of AIDS and AIDS-related illnesses. Around 17m. children world-wide have lost one or both parents to AIDS since the start of the pandemic, and as a result of HIV/AIDS many children have suffered poverty, homelessness, discrimination, and loss of education and other life opportunities. UNICEF's priorities in this area include prevention of infection among young people (through, for example, support for education programmes and dissemination of information through the media), reduction in mother-to-child transmission, care and protection of orphans and other vulnerable children, and care and support for children, young people and parents living with HIV/AIDS. UNICEF works closely in this field with governments and co-operates with other UN agencies in the Joint UN Programme on HIV/AIDS (UNAIDS), which became operational on 1 January 1996. Young people aged 15–24 are reported to account for around 45% of new HIV infections world-wide. IUNICEF advocates Life Skills-Based Education as a means of empowering young people to cope with challenging situations and of encouraging them to adopt healthy patterns of behaviour. In July 2004 UNICEF and other partners produced a *Framework for the Protection, Care and Support of Orphans and Vulnerable Children Living in a World with HIV and AIDS*. In October 2005 UNICEF launched Unite for Children, Unite against AIDS, a campaign that was to provide a platform for child-focused advocacy aimed at reversing the spread of HIV/AIDS amongst children, adolescents and young people; and to provide a child-focused framework for national programmes based on the following four pillars (known as the 'Four Ps'): the prevention of mother-to-child HIV transmission, improved provision of paediatric treatment, prevention of infection among adolescents and young people, and protection and support of children affected by HIV/AIDS. In December 2009 UNICEF issued its fourth *Children and AIDS: A Stocktaking Report*, detailing ongoing progress and challenges. In October 2010 UNICEF issued its first Mother-Baby Pack, containing drugs to prevent mother-to-child transmission of HIV in the poorest households. In June 2011 a high-level meeting on HIV/AIDs convened at UN headquarters launched a global plan towards eliminating new HIV infections among children by 2015. UNICEF supports the Global Plan towards the Elimination of New HIV Infections among Children by 2015 and Keeping Their Mothers Alive, which was endorsed in June 2011 by a UN High Level Meeting on HIV/AIDS.

In 2012 it was estimated that some 91% of children aged 0–14 living with HIV/AIDS globally resided in sub-Saharan Africa. The prevalence of the virus in young people aged 15–24 in the region in 2010 was estimated at 1.4% and 3.3%, for males and females, respectively.

CHILD PROTECTION FROM VIOLENCE, EXPLOITATION AND ABUSE

In 2011 some 10% of total programme resources were allocated to child protection. UNICEF is actively involved in global-level partnerships for child protection, including the Inter-Agency Co-ordination Panel on Juvenile Justice; the Inter-Agency Working Group on Unaccompanied and Separated Children; the Donors' Working Group on Female FGM/C (see above); the Better Care Network; the Study on Violence Against Children; the Inter-Agency Standing Committee (IASC) Task Force on Protection from Sexual Exploitation and Abuse in Humanitarian Crises; and the IASC Task Force on Mental Health and Psychological Support in Emergency Settings.

UNICEF estimates that the births of around 48m. children annually (about 36% of all births) are not registered, and that some 63% of births occuring in South Asia, and 55% of births in sub-Saharan Africa, are unregistered. UNICEF promotes universal registration in order to prevent the abuse of children without proof of age and nationality, for example through trafficking, forced labour, early marriage and military recruitment.

UNICEF estimates that some 158m. children aged from five–14 are engaged in child labour, while around 1.2m. children world-wide are trafficked each year. The Fund, which vigorously opposes the exploitation of children as a violation of their basic human rights, works with the ILO and other partners to promote an end to exploitative and hazardous child labour, and supports special projects to provide education, counselling and care in developing countries. UNICEF co-sponsored and actively participated in the Third Congress Against Commercial Sexual Exploitation of Children, held in Rio de Janeiro, Brazil, in November 2008.

More than 250,000 children are involved in armed conflicts as soldiers, porters and forced labourers. UNICEF encourages ratification of the Optional Protocol to the Convention on the Rights of the Child on the involvement of children in armed conflict, which was adopted by the General Assembly in May 2000 and entered into force in February 2002, and bans the compulsory recruitment of combatants below the age of 18. The Fund also urges states to make unequivocal statements endorsing 18 as the minimum age of voluntary recruitment to the armed forces. UNICEF, with Save the Children, co-chairs the Steering Group of the Paris Principles, which aims to support the implementation of a series of 'Commitments', first endorsed in 2007, to end the recruitment of children, support the release of children from the armed forces and facilitate their reintegration into civilian life. By the end of 2010 95 countries had voluntarily signed up to the Paris Commitments. It is estimated that landmines kill and maim between 8,000 and 10,000 children every year. UNICEF supports mine awareness campaigns, and promotes the full ratification of the Convention on the Prohibition of the Use, Stockpiling, Production and Transfer of Anti-Personnel Mines and on their Destruction, which was adopted in December 1997 and entered into force in March 1999. By September 2012 the Convention had been ratified by 160 countries (most recently by Somalia, in April).

In June 2010 representatives of six central African states, Cameroon, Chad, the Central African Republic, Niger, Nigeria and Sudan, participated in a regional conference, convened in N'Djamena, Chad, under the auspices of UNICEF and the Chad Government, aimed at ending the recruitment and use of children in armed forces. The six participating countries adopted the N'Djamena Declaration, in which they made a commitment to ending the recruitment of child soldiers in the region.

POLICY AND ADVOCACY AND PARTNERSHIPS FOR CHILDREN'S RIGHTS

In 2011 UNICEF allocated some 11% of total programme assistance to policy and advocacy and partnerships for children's rights. UNICEF's annual publication *The State of the World's Children* includes social and economic data relevant to the well-being of children; the theme of the 2012 report, issued in March, was 'Children in an Urban World'. UNICEF's Multiple Indicator Cluster Survey (MICS) method of data collection, initiated in 1995, is a main tool used in measuring progress towards the achievement of the UN MDGs.

Since 2005 young people from the Group of Eight (G8) nations (Canada, France, Germany, Italy, Japan, Russia, the United Kingdom and the USA) and selected emerging countries (including Brazil, China, Egypt, India, Mexico and South Africa) have participated in a Junior 8 (J8) summit, which is organized with support from UNICEF on the fringes of the annual G8 summit. The J8 summits address issues including education, energy, climate change, HIV/AIDS, the global financial crisis, and tolerance. Since 2010 G(irls)20 summits have been convened alongside summits of G20 leaders; the participants represent the G20 countries, and include, also, young female representatives of the African Union and European Union.

UNICEF aims to break the cycle of poverty by advocating for the provision of increased development aid to developing countries, and aims to help poor countries obtain debt relief and to ensure access to basic social services. UNICEF was the leading agency in promoting the 20/20 initiative, which was endorsed at the World Summit for Social Development, held in Copenhagen, Denmark, in March 1995. The initiative encouraged the governments of developing and donor countries to allocate at least 20% of their domestic budgets and official development aid to healthcare, primary education, and low-cost safe water and sanitation.

Through this focus area, UNICEF seeks to work with partners to strengthen capacities to design and implement cross-sectoral social and economic policies, child-focused legislative measures and budgetary allocations that enable countries to meet their obligations under the Convention on the Rights of the Child and the Convention on the Elimination of All Forms of Discrimination against Women. UNICEF has identified the following priority areas of support to 'upstream' policy work: child poverty and disparities; social budgeting; decentralization; social security and social protection; holistic legislative reform for the two Conventions; and the impact of migration on children.

HUMANITARIAN RESPONSE

UNICEF provides emergency relief assistance to children and young people affected by conflict, natural disasters and food crises. In situations of violence and social disintegration the Fund provides support in the areas of education, health, mine-awareness and psychosocial assistance, and helps to demobilize and rehabilitate child soldiers. In 2011 UNICEF responded to 292 humanitarian challenges in 80 countries. The largest humanitarian crisis addressed in that year was the outbreak of severe famine in the Horn of Africa, where some 13m. people were suffering acute hunger, with 750,000 children deemed to be at risk of death. UNICEF, with local partners, provided assistance to more than 241,000 acutely malnourished children in the region; and, in co-ordinated actvities with other international agencies, supported a further 263,000 children. Furthermore, UNICEF facilitated the provision of measles vaccinations to more than 1m. children under 16; provided access to safe water for 3m. Somalis; and supported more than 800,000 people in maintaining good hygiene.

In 1999 UNICEF adopted a Peace and Security Agenda to help guide international efforts in this field. Emergency education assistance includes the provision of 'Edukits' in refugee camps and the reconstruction of school buildings. In the area of health the Fund co-operates with WHO to arrange 'days of tranquillity' in order to facilitate the immunization of children in conflict zones. Psychosocial assistance activities include special programmes to support traumatized children and help unaccompanied children to be reunited with parents or extended families.

In view of heavy rainfall from mid-2012 in (already food-insecure) Niger, which had flooded homes, displacing almost 400,000 people, as well as devastating food crops, UNICEF and other humanitarian partners estimated that around 4m. Nigerian children were malnourished, and that 394,000 children below the age of five would require life-saving treatment before the end of the year for severe acute malnutrition (SAM). By mid-September more than 1.1m. children below the age of five were deemed by UNICEF to be at risk of SAM in Mali, owing to combined drought and food insecurity there, compounded by significant population displacement that had been caused by the eruption earlier in the year of violent conflict in northern areas. At mid-September more than 526,000 Malian children had been given therapeutic care to combat the onset of SAM. In July of that year UNICEF sent some 20,000 water, sanitation and hygiene kits to northern Mali to help address an outbreak of cholera there.

Since 1998 UNICEF's humanitarian response has been structured within a framework of identified Core Commitments for Children in Humanitarian Action (CCCs). Revised CCCs were issued in April 2010 to reflect new humanitarian structures and best practices. The revised CCCs incorporated UNICEF's commitment to working in partnership with international organizations, national authorities and civil society in order to strengthen risk reduction, disaster preparedness and response, and early recovery. During 2005 the UN's Inter-Agency Standing Committee (IASC), concerned with co-ordinating the international response to humanitarian disasters, developed a concept of organizing agency assistance to IDPs through the institutionalization of a 'Cluster Approach', comprising 11 core areas of activity. UNICEF is the lead agency for the clusters on Education (jointly with Save The Children); Nutrition; and Water, Sanitation and Hygiene. In addition, it leads the Gender-based Violence Area of Responsibility sub-cluster (jointly with UNFPA) and the Child Protection Area of Responsibility sub-cluster within the Protection Cluster.

Finance

UNICEF is funded by voluntary contributions from governments and non-governmental and private sector sources. UNICEF's income is divided into contributions for 'regular resources' (used for country programmes of co-operation approved by the Executive Board, programme support, and management and administration costs) and contributions for 'other resources' (for special purposes, including expanding the outreach of country programmes of co-operation, and ensuring capacity to deliver critical assistance to women and children, for example during humanitarian crises). UNICEF's total income in 2011 was US $3,711m., of which $2,260m. (60%) was from governments, $1,089m. (29%) from the private sector and non-governmental organizations, and $362m. (9%) from inter-organizational arrangements. UNICEF's total expenditure in 2011 was $3,819m. Some 57% of the Fund's total programme expenditure in that year was allocated to activities in Africa south of the Sahara, and 4% to interregional projects.

UNICEF, UNDP and UNFPA are committed to integrating their budgets from 2014.

Publications

Progress for Children (in English, French and Spanish).

The State of the World's Children (annually, in Arabic, English, French, Russian and Spanish and about 30 other national languages).

UNICEF Annual Report (in English, French and Spanish).

UNICEF at a Glance (in English, French and Spanish).

UNICEF Humanitarian Action for Children Report (annually).

Reports and studies; series on children and women; nutrition; education; children's rights; children in wars and disasters; working children; water, sanitation and the environment; analyses of the situation of children and women in individual developing countries.

United Nations Development Programme—UNDP

Address: One United Nations Plaza, New York, NY 10017, USA.

Telephone: (212) 906-5300; **fax:** (212) 906-5364; **e-mail:** hq@undp.org; **internet:** www.undp.org.

The Programme was established in 1965 by the UN General Assembly. Its central mission is to help countries to eradicate poverty and achieve a sustainable level of human development, an approach to economic growth that encompasses individual well-being and choice, equitable distribution of the benefits of development, and conservation of the environment. UNDP advocates for a more inclusive global economy. UNDP co-ordinates global and national efforts to achieve the UN Millennium Development Goals, and is contributing to the formulation of a post-2015 UN system-wide development framework.

Organization

(September 2012)

UNDP is responsible to the UN General Assembly, to which it reports through ECOSOC.

EXECUTIVE BOARD

The Executive Board is responsible for providing intergovernmental support to, and supervision of, the activities of UNDP and the UN Population Fund (UNFPA). It comprises 36 members: eight from Africa, seven from Asia and the Pacific, four from eastern Europe, five from Latin America and the Caribbean and 12 from western Europe and other countries. Members serve a three-year term.

SECRETARIAT

Offices and divisions at the Secretariat include: an Operations Support Group; Offices of the United Nations Development Group, the Human Development Report, Development Studies, Audit and Performance Review, Evaluation, and Communications; and Bureaux for Crisis Prevention and Recovery; Partnerships; Development Policy; and Management. Five regional bureaux, all headed by an assistant administrator, cover: Africa; Asia and the Pacific; the Arab states; Latin America and the Caribbean; and Europe and the Commonwealth of Independent States. UNDP's Administrator (the third most senior UN official, after the Secretary-General and the Deputy Secretary-General) is in charge of strategic policy and overall co-ordination of UN development activities (including the chairing of the UN Development Group), while the Associate Administrator supervises the operations and management of UNDP programmes.

Administrator: Helen Clark (New Zealand).

Associate Administrator: Rebeca Grynspan (Costa Rica).

Assistant Administrator and Director, Regional Bureau for Africa: Tegegnework Gettu.

COUNTRY OFFICES

In almost every country receiving UNDP assistance there is an office, headed by the UNDP Resident Representative, who usually also serves as the UN Resident Co-ordinator, responsible for the co-ordination of all UN technical assistance and development activities in that country, so as to ensure the most effective use of UN and international aid resources.

OFFICES OF UN RESIDENT CO-ORDINATORS IN AFRICA SOUTH OF THE SAHARA

Angola: Rua Major Kanhangulo 197, CP 910, Luanda; tel. 222331181; fax 222335609; e-mail registry.ao@undp.org; internet mirror.undp.org/angola; Resident Co-ordinator Maria do Valle Ribeiro.

Benin: Lot 111, Zone Residentielle, BP 506, Cotonou; tel. 31-30-45; fax 31-57-86; e-mail registry.bj@undp.org; internet www.bj.undp.org; Resident Co-ordinator Nardos Bekele-Thomas.

Botswana: UN Place, Khama Crescent, POB 54, Gaborone; tel. 3952121; fax 356093; e-mail undp.bw@undp.org; internet www.unbotswana.org.bw; Resident Co-ordinator Khin-Sandi Lwin.

Burkina Faso: Immeuble des Nations Unies, Koulouba, Secteur 4, 01 BP 575, Ouagadougou 01; tel. 30-67-65; fax 31-04-70; e-mail registry.bf@undp.org; internet www.pnud.bf; Resident Co-ordinator Pascal Karorero.

Burundi: Route de Gatumba, BP 1490, Bujumbura; tel. (2) 301100; fax (2) 301190; e-mail registy.bi@undp.org; internet www.bi.undp.org; Resident Co-ordinator Rosine Sori-Coulibaly.

Cameroon: Immeuble Foul'assi, Nouvelle Route Bastos, Rue 1775, BP 836, Yaoundé; tel. 220-0800; fax 220-0796; e-mail registry.cm@undp.org; internet www.cm.undp.org; Resident Co-ordinator Michel Balima.

Cape Verde: Maison des Nations Unies, Avda OUA, Achada de Santo António, CP 62, Praia; tel. 260-96-12; fax 262-13-52; e-mail anita.pinto@one.un.org; Resident Co-ordinator Petra Lantz de Bernardis.

Central African Republic: ave Boganda, Bangui; tel. 61-19-77; fax 61-17-32; e-mail registry.cf@undp.org; internet www.cf.undp.org; Resident/Humanitarian Co-ordinator Bo Schack.

Chad: ave Colonel D'Ornano, BP 906, N'Djamena; tel. 51-41-00; fax 51-63-30; e-mail registry.td@undp.org; internet www.td.undp.org; Resident Co-ordinator Thomas Gurtner.

Comoros: Hamramba, BP 648, Moroni; tel. 73-15-58; fax 73-15-77; e-mail registry.km@undp.org; internet www.km.undp.org; Resident Co-ordinator Dr Yao Kassankogno.

Congo, Democratic Republic: Immeuble Losonia, blvd du 30 juin, BP 7248, Commune de la Gombe, Kinshasa; tel. (810) 555-3300; fax (810) 555-3305; internet www.cd.undp.org; Resident/Humanitarian Co-ordinator Fidèle Sarassoro (until 30 September 2012), Moustapha Soumaré (designate).

Congo, Republic: ave du Maréchal Foch, BP 465, Brazzaville; tel. 67-75-99; fax 81-16-79; e-mail registry.cg@undp.org; internet www.cg.undp.org; Resident Co-ordinator Lamin Manneh.

Côte d'Ivoire: angle rue Gourgas et ave Marchand, Abidjan-Plateau, 01 BP 1747, Abidjan 01; tel. 20-31-74-00; fax 20-21-13-67; e-mail registry.ci@undp.org; internet www.ci.undp.org; Resident/Humanitarian Co-ordinator Ndolamb Ngokwey.

Djibouti: Lotissement du Héron 52, BP 2001, Djibouti; tel. 354354; fax 350587; e-mail registry.dj@undp.org; internet www.dj.undp.org; Resident Co-ordinator Hodan Haji-Mohamud.

Equatorial Guinea: UNDP Compound, Malabo; tel. (09) 22-75; fax (09) 21-53; e-mail registry.gq@undp.org; Resident Co-ordinator Leo Heileman.

Eritrea: UN Offices, HDAY St, POB 5366, Asmara; tel. (1) 151166; fax (1) 151081; e-mail registry.er@undp.org; internet www.er.undp.org; Resident/Humanitarian Co-ordinator Dr Mamadou Pethe Diallo.

Ethiopia: Africa Hall, Old ECA Bldg, 6th Floor, Menelik II Ave, POB 5580, Addis Ababa; tel. (11) 551-5177; fax (11) 551-4599; e-mail registry.et@undp.org; internet www.et.undp.org; Resident/Humanitarian Co-ordinator Eugene Owusu.

Gabon: BP 2183, Libreville; tel. 73-88-87; fax 73-88-91; e-mail registry.ga@undp.org; internet www.ga.undp.org; Resident Co-ordinator Nadir Hadj-Hammou.

The Gambia: 5 ave Kofi Annan, Cape Point, POB 553, Banjul; tel. 4494760; fax 4494758; e-mail registry.gm@undp.org; internet www.gm.undp.org; Resident Co-ordinator Chinwe Dike.

Ghana: Ring Rd Dual Carriage, nr Police HQ, POB 1423, Accra; tel. (21) 773890; fax (21) 773899; e-mail registry-gh@undp.org; internet www.undp-gha.org; Resident Co-ordinator Ruby Sandhu-Rojon.

Guinea: Maison Commune, rue MA 002, Coléah Corniche Sud, Commune de Matam, BP 222, Conakry; tel. 46-88-98; fax 13-68-64; e-mail registry.gn@undp.org; internet www.gn.undp.org; Resident Co-ordinator Anthony Ohemeng-Boamah.

Guinea-Bissau: Codex 1011, BP 179, Bissau; tel. 320-1368; fax 320-1753; e-mail registry.gw@undp.org; internet www.gw.undp.org; Resident Co-ordinator Gana Fofang.

Kenya: United Nations Avenue, Gigiri, POB 30218, 00100 Nairobi; tel. (20) 7624465; fax (20) 7624661; e-mail registry.ke@undp.org; internet www.ke.undp.org; Resident/Humanitarian Co-ordinator Aeneas Chuma.

Lesotho: UN House, 3rd Floor, Maseru 100; tel. 22313790; fax 22310042; e-mail registry.ls@undp.org; internet www.undp.org.ls; Resident Co-ordinator (and Designated Official for Security) Ahunna Eziakonwa-Onochie.

Liberia: Sekou Toure Ave, Mamba Point, POB 0274, Monrovia 10; tel. 226195; fax 226210; e-mail webmaster.lr@undp.org; internet www.lr.undp.org; Resident/Humanitarian Co-ordinator Moustapha Soumaré.

Madagascar: Maison commune des Nations Unies, rue Dr Raseta, Andraharo, BP 1348, Antananarivo 10147; tel. (20) 2330070; fax (20) 2330042; e-mail registry.mg@unep.org; internet www.snu.mg/pnud; Resident Co-ordinator Fatma Samoura.

Malawi: Plot No 7, Area 40, POB 30135, Lilongwe 3; tel. 773500; fax 774637; e-mail information.mw@undp.org; internet www.undp.org.mw; Resident Co-ordinator Richard Dictus.

Mali: Immeuble Alou Diarra, ACI 2000, BP 120, Bamako; tel. 2022-0181; e-mail registry.ml@undp.org; internet www.ml.undp.org; Resident Co-ordinator MBARANGE GASARABWE.

Mauritania: 203, rue 42–133, Lot K, Lots No. 159–161, BP 620, Nouakchott; tel. (2) 525-24-09; fax (2) 525-26-16; e-mail registry.mr@undp.org; internet www.pnud.mr; Resident Co-ordinator COUMBA MAR GADIO.

Mauritius: Anglo-Mauritius House, 6th Floor, Intendance St, POB 253, Port Louis; tel. 212-3726; fax 208-4871; e-mail registry.mu@undp.org; internet un.intnet.mu; also covers the Seychelles; Resident Co-ordinator LEYLA TEGMO-REDDY.

Mozambique: Avda Kenneth Kaunda, 931, POB 4595, Maputo; tel. (21) 481400; fax (21) 491691; e-mail registry.mz@undp.org; internet www.undp.org.mz; Resident Co-ordinator JENNIFER TOPPING.

Namibia: UN House, 38-44 Stein St, PMB 13329, Windhoek 9000; tel. (61) 2046366; fax (61) 2046203; e-mail registry.namibia@undp.org; internet www.undp.org.na; Resident Co-ordinator MUSINGA BANDORA.

Niger: Maison des Nations Unies, BP 11207, Niamey; tel. 20-73-21-04; fax 20-72-36-30; e-mail registry.ne@undp.org; internet www.pnud.ne; Resident Co-ordinator GARRY CONILLE.

Nigeria: United Nations House, Plot 617/618, Diplomatic Zone, Central Area District, PMB 2851, Garki; tel. (9) 461-8600; fax (9) 461-8546; e-mail registry.ng@undp.org; internet www.ng.undp.org; Resident Co-ordinator DAOUDA TOURE.

Rwanda: BP 445, Kigali; tel. 590400; fax 576263; e-mail registry.rw@undp.org; internet www.undp.org.rw; Resident Co-ordinator OPIA KUMAH.

São Tomé and Príncipe: Avda das Naçoes Unidas, CP 109, São Tomé; tel. 221123; fax 222198; e-mail registry.st@undp.org; internet www.uns.st/undp; Resident Co-ordinator (vacant).

Senegal: Immeuble Wolle Ndiaye, BP 154, Dakar; tel. 859-67-00; e-mail registry.sn@undp.org; internet www.undp.org.sn; Resident Co-ordinator BINTOU DJIBO.

Sierra Leone: United Nations House, 76 Wilkinson Rd, POB 1011, Freetown; tel. (22) 231311; fax (22) 233075; e-mail registry.sl@undp.org; internet www.sl.undp.org; Resident Co-ordinator MICHAEL VON DER SCHULENBURG.

Somalia: tel. (20) 4183642; fax (20) 448439; e-mail registry.so@undp.org; internet www.so.undp.org; Resident/Humanitarian Co-ordinator MARK BOWDEN (outgoing).

South Africa: Metropark Bldg,, 351 Schoeman St, POB 6541, Pretoria 0001; tel. (12) 354-8008; e-mail info@undp.org.za; internet www.undp.org.za; Resident Co-ordinator AGOSTINHO ZACARIAS.

South Sudan: Ministries Rd, POB 410, Juba; e-mail info.ssd@undp.org; internet www.ss.undp.org; Resident Co-ordinator TOBY LANZER.

Sudan: House No 7, Block 5, R.F.E., Gama'a Ave, POB 913, 11111 Khartoum; tel. 1 83 783 820; fax 1 83 783 764; e-mail registry.sd@undp.org; internet www.sd.undp.org; Resident/Humanitarian Co-ordinator GEORG CHARPENTIER.

Swaziland: Lilunga House, 5th Floor, Somhlolo St, POB 261, Mbabane; tel. 4042301; fax 4045341; e-mail registry.sz@undp.org; internet www.undp.org.sz; Resident Co-ordinator MUSINGA ISRAEL DESSALEGNE.

Tanzania: International House, 6th Floor, POB 9182, Dar es Salaam; tel. (22) 2199201; fax (22) 2668749; e-mail registry.tz@undp.org; internet www.tz.undp.org; Resident Co-ordinator (and Designated Official for Security) ALBERIC KACOU.

Togo: 40 ave des Nations Unies, le étage, BP 911, Lomé; tel. 221-20-22; fax 221-16-41; e-mail registry.tg@undp.org; internet www.tg.unpd.org; Resident Co-ordinator KHARDIATA LO N'DIAYE.

Uganda: UN House, 15 Clement Hill Rd, POB 7184, Kampala; tel. (414) 233440; fax (414) 344801; e-mail registry.ug@undp.org; internet www.undp.or.ug; Resident/Humanitarian Co-ordinator THEOPHANE NIKYEMA.

Zambia: Plot No. 11867, Alick Nkhata Ave, Longacres, POB 31966, Lusaka; tel. (1) 250800; e-mail registry.zm@undp.org; internet www.undp.org.zm; Resident Co-ordinator KANNI WIGNARAJA.

Zimbabwe: Takura House, 8th Floor, 67–69 Kwame Nkrumah Ave, POB 4775, Harare; tel. (4) 250606; fax (4) 728695; e-mail registry.zw@undp.org; internet www.undp.org.zw; Resident/Humanitarian Co-ordinator ALAIN NOUDEHOU.

Activities

UNDP describes itself as the UN's global development network, advocating for change and connecting countries to knowledge, experience and resources to help people build a better life. In 2012 UNDP was active in 177 countries. It provides advisory and support services to governments and UN teams with the aim of advancing sustainable human development and building national development capabilities. Assistance is mostly non-monetary, comprising the provision of experts' services, consultancies, equipment and training for local workers. Developing countries themselves contribute significantly to the total project costs in terms of personnel, facilities, equipment and supplies. UNDP also supports programme countries in attracting aid and utilizing it efficiently.

From the mid-1990s UNDP assumed a more active co-ordinating role within the UN system. In 1997 the UNDP Administrator was appointed to chair the UN Development Group (UNDG), which was established as part of a series of structural reform measures initiated by the UN Secretary-General, with the aim of preventing duplication and strengthening collaboration between all UN agencies, programmes and funds concerned with development. The UNDG promotes coherent policy at country level through the system of UN Resident Co-ordinators (see above), the Common Country Assessment mechanism (CCA, a process for evaluating national development needs), and the UN Development Assistance Framework (UNDAF, for planning and co-ordination development operations at country level, based on the CCA). UNDP maintains a series of Thematic Trust Funds to channel support to priority programme activities.

The 2008–13 Strategic Plan emphasized UNDP's 'overarching' contribution to achieving sustainable human development through capacity development strategies, to be integrated into all areas of activity. (The UNDP Capacity Development Group, established in 2002 within the Bureau for Development Policy, organizes UNDP capacity development support at local and national level.) Other objectives identified by the 2008–13 Plan included strengthening national ownership of development projects and promoting and facilitating South-South co-operation.

In 2012 UNDP was working to advance the UN's development agenda through engagement with the MDGs Acceleration Framework (see below); through its participation in the UN Conference on Sustainable Development (UNCSD), which was held in Rio de Janeiro, Brazil, in June; and by contributing to the formulation of a post-2015 system-wide development framework. A new strategic plan was being developed for 2014–17, which aimed to strengthen UNDP's capacity to deliver results. In early January 2012 the UN Secretary-General established a UN System Task Team—led jointly by the UNDP Administrator-General and the UN Under-Secretary-General for Economic and Social Affairs—which was to support system-wide consultations on the advancement of the post-2015 global development agenda. In May and July, respectively, the Co-Chairs and membership were announced of a new High-level Panel of Eminent Persons which was to advise on the pursuit of the post-2015 development agenda. The Panel held its inaugural meeting in late September 2012 and was to present a draft development agenda document to the Secretary-General in the first half of 2013. The Panel was to consult with a working group of experts tasked by UNCSD to formulate a series of Sustainable Development Goals.

A framework to promote a development partnership between African countries and the international community was initiated in 1993 at the Tokyo International Conference on African Development (TICAD). A second conference was convened in 1998, a third in September 2003, and a fourth in May 2008, when a regional action plan, on boosting economic growth; ensuring human security; and adapting to environmental and climate change, was concluded. TICAD V was to take place in June 2013, in Yokohama, Japan. In the interim periods the process is pursued through follow-up meetings, regional forums, trade conferences and seminars. UNDP and the Government of Japan sponsor the Africa-Asia Business Forum (AABF); the fifth AABF took place in June 2009, in Kampala, Uganda. In October 2002 the UN General Assembly recognized the New Partnership for Africa's Development (NEPAD) as the framework for the international community's support of development in Africa. UNDP supported the establishment and operation of a voluntary NEPAD initiative providing for countries to evaluate standards of governance in other participating states, the so-called African Peer Review Mechanism, and manages a trust to support the mechanism. In October 2011 the UNDP Regional Bureau for Africa and NEPAD signed a Memorandum of Understanding on pursuing the following main areas of co-operation: development policy and strategy; governance; capacity development; South-South co-operation and aid effectiveness; knowledge management; environment and climate change; and gender equity and women's empowerment.

UNDP, jointly with the World Bank, leads an initiative on 'additional financing for the most vulnerable', the first of nine activities that were launched in April 2009 by the UN System Chief Executives Board for Co-ordination (CEB), with the aim of alleviating the impact on poor and vulnerable populations of the developing global economic crisis.

MILLENNIUM DEVELOPMENT GOALS

UNDP, through its leadership of the UNDG and management of the Resident Co-ordinator system, has a co-ordinating function as the focus of UN system-wide efforts to achieve the so-called Millennium Development Goals (MDGs), pledged by UN member governments attending a summit meeting of the UN General Assembly in September 2000. The objectives were to establish a defined agenda to reduce poverty and improve the quality of lives of millions of people and to serve as a framework for measuring development. There are eight MDGs, as follows, for which one or more specific targets have been identified:

i) to eradicate extreme poverty and hunger, with the aim of reducing by 50% (compared with the 1990 figure) the number of people with an income of less than US $1 a day and those suffering from hunger by 2015, and to achieve full and productive employment and decent work for all, including women and young people;

ii) to achieve universal primary education by 2015;

iii) to promote gender equality and empower women, in particular to eliminate gender disparities in primary and secondary education by 2005 and at all levels by 2015;

iv) to reduce child mortality, with a target reduction of two-thirds in the mortality rate among children under five by 2015 (compared with the 1990 level);

v) to improve maternal health, specifically to reduce by 75% the numbers of women dying in childbirth and to achieve universal access to reproductive health by 2015 (compared with the 1990 level);

vi) to combat HIV/AIDS, malaria and other diseases, with targets to have halted and begun to reverse the incidence of HIV/AIDS, malaria and other major diseases by 2015 and to achieve universal access to treatment for HIV/AIDS for all those who need it by 2010;

vii) to ensure environmental sustainability, including targets to integrate the principles of sustainable development into country policies and programmes, to reduce by 50% (compared with the 1990 level) the number of people without access to safe drinking water by 2015, and to achieve significant improvement in the lives of at least 100m. slum dwellers by 2020;

viii) to develop a global partnership for development, including an open, rule-based, non-discriminatory trading and financial system, and efforts to deal with international debt, to address the needs of least developed countries and landlocked and small island developing states, to provide access to affordable, essential drugs in developing countries, and to make available the benefits of new technologies.

UNDP plays a leading role in efforts to integrate the MDGs into all aspects of UN activities at country level and to ensure that the MDGs are incorporated into national development strategies. The Programme supports efforts by countries, as well as regions and subregions, to report on progress towards achievement of the goals, and on specific social, economic and environmental indicators, through the formulation of MDG reports. These form the basis of a global report, issued annually by the UN Secretary-General since mid-2002. UNDP also works to raise awareness of the MDGs and to support advocacy efforts at all levels, for example through regional publicity campaigns, target-specific publications and the Millennium Campaign to generate support for the goals in developing and developed countries. UNDP provides administrative and technical support to the Millennium Project, an independent advisory body established by the UN Secretary-General in 2002 to develop a practical action plan to achieve the MDGs. Financial support of the Project is channelled through a Millennium Trust Fund, administered by UNDP. In January 2005 the Millennium Project presented its report, based on extensive research conducted by teams of experts, which included recommendations for the international system to support country level development efforts and identified a series of 'Quick Wins' to bring conclusive benefit to millions of people in the short-term. International commitment to achieve the MDGs by 2015 was reiterated at a World Summit, convened in September 2005. In December 2006 UNDP and the Spanish Government concluded an agreement on the establishment of the MDG Achievement Fund (MDG-F), which aims to support the acceleration of progress towards the achievement of the MDGs and to enhance co-operation at country level between UN development partners. UNDP and the UN Department of Economic and Social Affairs are lead agencies in co-ordinating the work of the Millennium Development Goals Gap Task Force, which was established by the UN Secretary-General in May 2007 to track, systematically and at both international and country level, existing international commitments in the areas of official development assistance, market access, debt relief, access to essential medicines and technology. In November the UN, in partnership with two major US companies, launched an online MDG Monitor (www.mdgmonitor.org) to track progress and to support organizations working to achieve the goals. In September 2010 UNDP launched the MDGs Acceleration Framework, which aimed to support countries in identifying and overcoming barriers to eradicating extreme poverty and achieving sustainable development. The 2012 edition of the *Millennium Development Goals Report*, issued in July of that year, indicated that targets in the areas of poverty, slum dwelling and water had been met three years in advance of 2015.

In January 2004 UNDP launched *Africa 2015*, a campaign, led by well-known personalities, aimed at the continent-wide promotion of all the MDGs, with a special focus on combating poverty and HIV/AIDS. UNDP's Millennium Village Project (MVP), launched in 2006 to support community-based development, was by September being implemented at 15 sites in 10 African countries: Ethiopia, Ghana, Kenya, Malawi, Mali, Nigeria, Rwanda, Senegal, Uganda and Tanzania.

DEMOCRATIC GOVERNANCE

UNDP supports national efforts to ensure efficient and accountable governance, to improve the quality of democratic processes, and to build effective relations between the state, the private sector and civil society, which are essential to achieving sustainable development. As in other practice areas, UNDP assistance includes policy advice and technical support, capacity building of institutions and individuals, advocacy and public information and communication, the promotion and brokering of dialogue, and knowledge networking and sharing of good practices.

UNDP works to strengthen parliaments and other legislative bodies as institutions of democratic participation. It assists with constitutional reviews and reform, training of parliamentary staff, and capacity building of political parties and civil organizations as part of this objective. UNDP undertakes missions to help prepare for and ensure the conduct of free and fair elections. It helps to build the long-term capacity of electoral institutions and practices within a country, for example by assisting with voter registration, the establishment of electoral commissions, providing observers to verify that elections are free and fair, projects to educate voters, and training journalists to provide impartial election coverage.

Within its justice sector programme UNDP undertakes a variety of projects to improve access to justice, in particular for the poor and disadvantaged, and to promote judicial independence, legal reform and understanding of the legal system. UNDP also works to promote access to information, the integration of human rights issues into activities concerned with sustainable human development, and support for the international human rights system.

UNDP is mandated to assist developing countries to fight corruption and improve accountability, transparency and integrity (ATI). It has worked to establish national and international partnerships in support of its anti-corruption efforts and used its role as a broker of knowledge and experience to uphold ATI principles at all levels of public financial management and governance. UNDP publishes case studies of its anti-corruption efforts and assists governments to conduct self-assessments of their public financial management systems.

In March 2002 a UNDP Governance Centre was inaugurated in Oslo, Norway, to enhance the role of UNDP in support of democratic governance and to assist countries to implement democratic reforms in order to achieve the MDGs. In 2012 the Centre's areas of focus were: access to information and e-governance; access to justice and rule of law; anti-corruption; civic engagement; electoral systems and processes; human rights; local governance; parliamentary development; public administration; and women's empowerment. The Democratic Governance Network (DGP-Net) allows discussion and the sharing of information. An iKnow Politics Network, supported by UNDP, aims to help women become involved in politics.

UNDP's Regional Bureau for Africa organizes the Africa Governance Forum (AGF), which has been convened periodically since 1997 to consider aspects of governance and development. The AGF process is supported also by the Economic Commission for Africa and the AU. AGF VIII, addressing the theme 'Democracy, Elections, and the Management of Diversity in Africa', was to be held in Johannesburg, South Africa, in October 2012. UNDP has provided support to South Sudan (which achieved independence from Sudan in July 2011) by embedding professional staff with the South Sudan Government with a view to boosting staff capacity; working alongside the Government as principal development partner; supporting the Government's strategic South Sudan Development Plan; improving access to justice and developing the institutional capacity of rule-of-law institutions; strengthening priority governance structures; promoting community security, economic development; community infrastructure; and through the control of small arms. UNDP has established several legal aid centres in Darfur, western Sudan. During 2008–12 UNDP was implementing a governance programme aimed at strengthening the legislature, the civil service, budgetary planning, local government and judicial reform in the Democratic Republic of the Congo. UNDP, with other partners, supports the Deepening Democracy in Tanzania programme, providing technical and financial assistance to institutions that are essential to strengthening that country's multi-party political system. In November 2011 UNDP helped to organize the Africa Forum on Civil Society and Governance Assessments, in Dakar, Senegal, with participation by more than 120 representatives of civil society, research institutes and development agencies from the region.

POVERTY REDUCTION

UNDP's activities to facilitate poverty eradication include support for capacity building programmes and initiatives to generate sustainable livelihoods, for example by improving access to credit, land and technologies, and the promotion of strategies to improve education and health provision for the poorest elements of populations (especially women and girls). UNDP aims to help governments to reassess their development priorities and to design initiatives for sustainable human development. In 1996, following the World Summit for Social Development, which was held in Copenhagen, Denmark, in March 1995, UNDP launched the Poverty Strategies Initiative (PSI) to strengthen national capacities to assess and monitor the extent of poverty and to combat the problem. All PSI projects were to involve representatives of governments, the private sector, social organizations and research institutions in policy debate and formulation. Following the introduction, in 1999, by the World Bank and IMF of Poverty Reduction Strategy Papers (PRSPs), UNDP has helped governments to draft these documents, and, since 2001, has linked the papers to efforts to achieve and monitor progress towards the MDGs. In 2004 UNDP inaugurated the International Poverty Centre for Inclusive Growth (IPC-IG), in Brasília, Brazil, which fosters the capacity of countries to formulate and implement poverty reduction strategies and encourages South-South co-operation in all relevant areas of research and decision-making. In particular, the Centre aims to assist countries to meet MDGs through research into and implementation of pro-poor policies that encourage social protection and human development, and through the monitoring of poverty and inequality. UNDP's Secretariat hosts the UN Office for South-South Cooperation, which was established, as the Special Unit for South-South Cooperation, by the United Nations General Assembly in 1978.

UNDP country offices support the formulation of national human development reports (NHDRs), which aim to facilitate activities such as policy-making, the allocation of resources, and monitoring progress towards poverty eradication and sustainable development. In addition, the preparation of Advisory Notes and Country Co-operation Frameworks by UNDP officials helps to highlight country-specific aspects of poverty eradication and national strategic priorities. In January 1998 the Executive Board adopted eight guiding principles relating to sustainable human development that were to be implemented by all country offices, in order to ensure a focus to UNDP activities. Since 1990 UNDP has published an annual *Human Development Report*, incorporating a Human Development Index, which ranks countries in terms of human development, using three key indicators: life expectancy, adult literacy and basic income required for a decent standard of living. The Report also includes a Human Poverty Index and a Gender-related Development Index, which assesses gender equality on the basis of life expectancy, education and income. The 2011 edition of the Report, released in November, focused on the need to address in tandem the urgent global challenges of achieving sustainability and equity, and identified policies at global and national level to advance progress. Jointly with the International Labour Organization (ILO) UNDP operates a Programme on Employment for Poverty Reduction, which undertakes analysis and studies, and supports countries in improving their employment strategies. In late March 2012 the first Global Human Development Forum was convened, under UNDP auspices, in Istanbul, Turkey; delegates (comprising experts on development, and representatives of the UN, governments, the private sector and civil society) adopted the Istanbul Declaration, urging that the global development agenda should be redrafted, and calling for concerted global action against social inequities and environmental degradation.

UNDP is committed to ensuring that the process of economic and financial globalization, including national and global trade, debt and capital flow policies, incorporates human development concerns. It aimed to ensure that the Doha Development Round of World Trade Organization (WTO) negotiations should achieve an expansion of trade opportunities and economic growth to less developed countries. With the UN Conference on Trade and Development (UNCTAD), UNDP manages a Global Programme on Globalization, Liberalization and Sustainable Human Development, which aims to support greater integration of developing countries into the global economy. UNDP manages a Trust Fund for the Integrated Framework for Trade-related Technical Assistance to Least Developed Countries, which was inaugurated in 1997 by UNDP, the IMF, the International Trade Centre, UNCTAD, the World Bank and the WTO.

Jointly with the UN Economic Commission for Africa and other agencies, UNDP operates a project on Trade Capacity Development for Sub-Saharan Africa, to help African countries take a greater share of global markets, reinforce African negotiating capacities, and strengthen regional co-operation. In May 2008 UNDP launched a regional initiative to assist African countries in negotiating, managing and regulating large-scale investment contracts, particularly in the exploitation of natural resources, so as to ensure that the host country (and especially its poorest people) receives the maximum benefit.

The *African Human Development Report 2012: Towards a Food-secure Future* was released in May of that year. National Human Development Reports on the Central African Republic and Liberia were also to be issued in 2012.

In 1996 UNDP initiated a process of collaboration between city authorities world-wide to promote implementation of the commitments made at the 1995 Copenhagen summit for social development and to help to combat aspects of poverty and other urban problems, such as poor housing, transport, the management of waste disposal, water supply and sanitation. The World Alliance of Cities Against Poverty was formally launched in 1997, in the context of the International Decade for the Eradication of Poverty. The seventh global Forum of the Alliance took place in February 2010, and the eighth was to convene in Dublin, Ireland, in February 2013.

UNDP sponsors the International Day for the Eradication of Poverty, held annually on 17 October.

ENVIRONMENT AND ENERGY

UNDP plays a role in developing the agenda for international co-operation on environmental and energy issues, focusing on the relationship between energy policies, environmental protection, poverty and development. UNDP promotes development practices that are environmentally sustainable, for example through the formulation and implementation of Poverty Reduction Strategies and National Strategies for Sustainable Development. Together with the UN Environment Programme (UNEP) and the World Bank, UNDP is an implementing agency of the Global Environment Facility (GEF), which was established in 1991 to finance international co-operation in projects to benefit the environment.

UNDP recognizes that desertification and land degradation are major causes of rural poverty and promotes sustainable land management, drought preparedness and reform of land tenure as means of addressing the problem. It also aims to reduce poverty caused by land degradation through implementation of environmental conventions at a national and international level. In 2002 UNDP inaugurated an Integrated Drylands Development Programme which aimed to ensure that the needs of people living in arid regions are met and considered at a local and national level. The Drylands Development Centre implements the programme in 19 African, Arab and West Asian countries. UNDP is also concerned with sustainable management of forestries, fisheries and agriculture. Its Biodiversity Global Programme assists developing countries and communities to integrate issues relating to sustainable practices and biodiversity into national and global practices. Since 1992 UNDP has administered a Small Grants Programme, funded by the GEF, to support community-based initiatives concerned with biodiversity conservation, prevention of land degradation and the elimination of persistent organic pollutants. The Equator Initiative was inaugurated in 2002 as a partnership between UNDP, representatives of governments, civil society and businesses, with the aim of reducing poverty in communities along the equatorial belt by fostering local partnerships, harnessing local knowledge and promoting conservation and sustainable practices.

In December 2005 UNDP (in collaboration with Fortis, a private sector provider of financial services) launched the MDG Carbon Facility, whereby developing countries that undertake projects to reduce emissions of carbon dioxide, methane and other gases responsible for global warming may sell their 'carbon credits' to finance further MDG projects. The first projects under the MDG Carbon Facility were inaugurated in February 2008, in Uzbekistan, the former Yugoslav republic of Macedonia, Yemen and Rwanda.

UNDP supports efforts to promote international co-operation in the management of chemicals. It was actively involved in the development of a Strategic Approach to International Chemicals Management which was adopted by representatives of 100 governments at an international conference convened in Dubai, UAE, in February 2006.

UNDP works to ensure the effective governance of freshwater and aquatic resources, and promotes co-operation in transboundary water management. It works closely with other agencies to promote safe sanitation, ocean and coastal management, and community water supplies. In 1996 UNDP, with the World Bank and the Swedish International Development Agency, established a Global Water Partnership to promote and implement water resources management. UNDP, with the GEF, supports a range of projects which incorporate development and ecological requirements in the sustainable management of international waters. including the Global Mercury Project, a project for improved municipal waste-water management in coastal cities of the African, Caribbean and

Pacific states, a Global Ballast Water Management Programme and an International Waters Learning Exchange and Resources Network.

In Africa UNDP projects concerned with protecting international waters include Large Marine Ecosystem Programmes for the Benguela Current and the Guinea Current, and projects to protect the waters of the Nile, the Senegal and Lake Chad.

CRISIS PREVENTION AND RECOVERY

UNDP is not primarily a relief organization, but collaborates with other UN agencies in countries in crisis and with special circumstances to promote relief and development efforts, in order to secure the foundations for sustainable human development and thereby increase national capabilities to prevent or mitigate future crises. In particular, UNDP is concerned to achieve reconciliation, reintegration and reconstruction in affected countries, as well as to support emergency interventions and management and delivery of programme aid. It aims to facilitate the transition from relief to longer-term recovery and rehabilitation. Special development initiatives in post-conflict countries include the demobilization of former combatants and destruction of illicit small armaments, rehabilitation of communities for the sustainable reintegration of returning populations and the restoration and strengthening of democratic institutions. UNDP is seeking to incorporate conflict prevention into its development strategies. It has established a mine action unit within its Bureau for Crisis Prevention and Recovery in order to strengthen national and local de-mining capabilities including surveying, mapping and clearance of anti-personnel landmines. It also works to increase awareness of the harm done to civilians by cluster munitions, and participated in the negotiations that culminated in May 2008 with the adoption of an international Convention on Cluster Munitions, which in February 2010 received its 30th ratification, enabling its entry into force on 1 August. UNDP also works closely with UNICEF to raise awareness and implement risk reduction education programmes, and manages global partnership projects concerned with training, legislation and the socio-economic impact of anti-personnel devices. In 2005 UNDP adopted an '8-Point Agenda' aimed at improving the security of women and girls in conflict situations and promoting their participation in post-crisis recovery processes. In late 2006 UNDP began to administer the newly established UN Peacebuilding Fund, the purpose of which is to strengthen essential services to maintain peace in countries that have undergone conflict. During 2008 UNDP developed a new global programme aimed at strengthening the rule of law in conflict and post-conflict countries; the programme placed particular focus on women's access to justice, institution building and transitional justice.

In 2006 UNDP launched an Immediate Crisis Response programme (known as 'SURGE') aimed at strengthening its capacity to respond quickly and effectively in the recovery phase following a conflict or natural disaster. Under the programme Immediate Crisis Response Advisors—UNDP staff with special expertise in at least one of 12 identified areas, including early recovery, operational support and resource mobilization—are swiftly deployed, in a 'SURGETeam', to UNDP country offices dealing with crises.

UNDP is the focal point within the UN system for strengthening national capacities for natural disaster reduction (prevention, preparedness and mitigation relating to natural, environmental and technological hazards). UNDP's Bureau of Crisis Prevention and Recovery, in conjunction with the Office for the Co-ordination of Humanitarian Affairs and the secretariat of the International Strategy for Disaster Reduction, oversees the system-wide Capacity for Disaster Reduction Initiative (CADRI), which was inaugurated in 2007, superseding the former United Nations Disaster Management Training Programme. In February 2004 UNDP introduced a Disaster Risk Index that enabled vulnerability and risk to be measured and compared between countries and demonstrated the correspondence between human development and death rates following natural disasters. UNDP was actively involved in preparations for the second World Conference on Disaster Reduction, which was held in Kobe, Japan, in January 2005. Following the Kobe Conference UNDP initiated a new Global Risk Identification Programme. During 2005 the Inter-Agency Standing Committee, concerned with co-ordinating the international response to humanitarian disasters, developed a concept of providing assistance through a 'cluster' approach, comprising core areas of activity (see OCHA). UNDP was designated the lead agency for the Early Recovery cluster, linking the immediate needs following a disaster with medium- and long-term recovery efforts. UNDP was to participate in a series of consultations on a successor arrangement for the Hyogo Framework for Action that were launched in 2012 by the UN International Strategy for Disaster Reduction (UN/ISDR—the focal point of UN disaster planning); it was envisaged that the planned post-Hyogo arrangement would specify measurable outcomes of disaster risk reduction planning, in addition to detailing processes, and that, in view of rapidly increasing urbanization globally, it would have a focus on building safer cities. UNDP hosts the Global Risk Identification Programme (GRIP), initiated in 2007 to support activities world-wide aimed at identifying and monitoring disaster risks. In August 2012 the UNDP Administrator, stating that disaster risk management should become central to development planning, announced that UNDP disaster reduction assistance would be doubled over the next five years.

GRIP has helped Tijuana in Mexico, Kathmandu in Nepal and Maputo in Mozambique to carry out Urban Risk Assessments. The Programme has also supported Laos in completing a National Risk Assessment and finalizing a comprehensive National Hazard Risk Profile, which is to be the basis for the formulation of a national Disaster Risk Management Strategy. Meanwhile, Armenia, Lebanon, Mozambique, Nepal, and Tajikistan have each been helped to complete a Country Situation Analysis and are undertaking National Risk Assessments.

UNDP supports projects in the region financed by the Peacebuilding Fund of the UN Peace-building Support Office, and works closely with the UN Department of Political Affairs in the areas of governance, capacity building for institutions, and conflict prevention. UNDP supports the strengthening of national capacities and institutions with a view to improving security and controlling the proliferation and use of small arms in, *inter alia*, Burundi, the DRC, Liberia, and northern Uganda. In 2012 UNDP was assisting the South Sudan Bureau of Community Security and Small Arms Control (CSAC), a government focal point on small arms control initiatives.

HIV/AIDS

UNDP regards the HIV/AIDS pandemic as a major challenge to development, and advocates making HIV/AIDS a focus of national planning and national poverty reduction strategies; supports decentralized action against HIV/AIDS at community level; helps to strengthen national capacities at all levels to combat the disease; and aims to link support for prevention activities, education and treatment with broader development planning and responses. UNDP places a particular focus on combating the spread of HIV/AIDS through the promotion of women's rights. UNDP is a co-sponsor, jointly with the World Health Organization (WHO) and other UN bodies, of the Joint UN Programme on HIV/AIDS (UNAIDS), which became operational on 1 January 1996. UNAIDS co-ordinates UNDP's HIV and Development Programme. UNDP works in partnership with the Global Fund to Fight HIV/AIDS, Tuberculosis and Malaria, in particular to support the local principal recipient of grant financing and to help to manage fund projects.

UNDP is supporting the implementation of two Global Fund grants, amounting to some US $141.8m., that are aimed at providing access to free HIV/AIDS treatment for 400,000 people in Zambia during 2012–13.

UNDP administers a global programme concerned with intellectual property and access to HIV/AIDS drugs, to promote wider and cheaper access to antiretroviral drugs, in accordance with the agreement on Trade-Related Aspects of Intellectual Property Rights (TRIPS), amended by the WTO in 2005 to allow countries without a pharmaceutical manufacturing capability to import generic copies of patented medicines.

Finance

UNDP and its various funds and programmes are financed by the voluntary contributions of members of the UN and the Programme's participating agencies, cost-sharing by recipient governments and third-party donors. Of UNDP's total provisional programme expenditure of US $4,608m. in 2011, some 28% was allocated to achieving the MDGs and reducing poverty; 26% was allocated to fostering democratic governance; 24% to supporting crisis prevention and recovery; and 12% to managing energy and the environment for sustainable development. Some $1,121m. (24% of total provisional expenditure) was allocated to Africa. For the period 2008–11 total voluntary contributions to UNDP were projected at $20,600m., of which $5,300m. constituted regular (core) resources, $5,000m. bilateral donor contributions, $5,500m. contributions from multilateral partners, and $4,800m. cost-sharing by recipient governments.

UNDP, UNFPA and UNICEF are committed to integrating their budgets from 2014.

Publications

Annual Report of the Administrator.

Choices (quarterly).

Human Development Report (annually).

Poverty Report (annually).

Results-Oriented Annual Report.

Associated Funds and Programmes

UNDP is the central funding, planning and co-ordinating body for technical co-operation within the UN system. A number of associated funds and programmes, financed separately by means of voluntary contributions, provide specific services through the UNDP network. UNDP manages a trust fund to promote economic and technical co-operation among developing countries.

GLOBAL ENVIRONMENT FACILITY (GEF)

The GEF, which is managed jointly by UNDP, the World Bank (which hosts its secretariat) and UNEP, began operations in 1991 and was restructured in 1994. Its aim is to support projects in the six thematic areas of: climate change, the conservation of biological diversity, the protection of international waters, reducing the depletion of the ozone layer in the atmosphere, arresting land degradation and addressing the issue of persistent organic pollutants. Capacity building to allow countries to meet their obligations under international environmental agreements, and adaptation to climate change, are priority cross-cutting components of these projects. The GEF acts as the financial mechanism for the Convention on Biological Diversity and the UN Framework Convention on Climate Change. UNDP is responsible for capacity building, targeted research, pre-investment activities and technical assistance. UNDP also administers the Small Grants Programme of the GEF, which supports community-based activities by local NGOs, and the Country Dialogue Workshop Programme, which promotes dialogue on national priorities with regard to the GEF; by the end of 2011 the Small Grants Programme had co-financed more than 12,000 community projects in 122 countries. In October 2010 donor countries pledged $4,350m. for the fifth periodic replenishment of GEF funds (GEF-5), covering the period 2011–14.

Chair. and CEO: Dr NAOKO ISHII (Japan).

Executive Co-ordinator of UNDP-GEF Unit: YANNICK GLEMAREC; 304 East 45th St, 9th Floor, New York, NY 10017, USA; fax (212) 906-6998; e-mail gefinfo@undp.org; internet www.undp.org/gef/.

MDG ACHIEVEMENT FUND (MDG-F)

The Fund, established in accordance with an agreement concluded in December 2006 between UNDP and the Spanish Government, aims to support the acceleration of progress towards the achievement of the MDGs and to advance country-level co-operation between UN development partners. The Fund operates through the UN development system and focuses mainly on financing collaborative UN activities addressing multi-dimensional development challenges. The Spanish Government provided initial financing to the Fund of nearly €528m., adding some €90m. in September 2008. By 2012 some 128 programmes were under way in 49 countries, in the thematic areas of children and nutrition; climate change; conflict prevention; culture and development; economic governance; gender equality and women's empowerment; and youth employment.

Director of MDG-F Secretariat: SOPHIE DE CAEN (Canada); MDG-F Secretariat, c/o UNDP, One United Nations Plaza, New York, NY 10017, USA; tel. (212) 906-6180; fax (212) 906-5364; e-mail pb.mdgf.secretariat@undp.org; internet www.mdgfund.org.

MONTREAL PROTOCOL

Through its Montreal Protocol/Chemicals Unit UNDP collaborates with public and private partners in developing countries to assist them in eliminating the use of ozone-depleting substances (ODS), in accordance with the Montreal Protocol to the Vienna Convention for the Protection of the Ozone Layer, through the design, monitoring and evaluation of ODS phase-out projects and programmes. In particular, UNDP provides technical assistance and training, national capacity building and demonstration projects and technology transfer investment projects.

UNDP DRYLANDS DEVELOPMENT CENTRE (DDC)

The Centre, based in Nairobi, Kenya, was established in February 2002, superseding the former UN Office to Combat Desertification and Drought (UNSO). (UNSO had been established following the conclusion, in October 1994, of the UN Convention to Combat Desertification in Those Countries Experiencing Serious Drought and/or Desertification, Particularly in Africa; in turn, UNSO had replaced the former UN Sudano-Sahelian Office.) The DDC was to focus on the following areas: ensuring that national development planning takes account of the needs of dryland communities, particularly in poverty reduction strategies; helping countries to cope with the effects of climate variability, especially drought, and to prepare for future climate change; and addressing local issues affecting the utilization of resources.

Officer-in-Charge: ELIE KODSIE; UN Gigiri Compound, United Nations Ave, POB 30552, 00100 Nairobi, Kenya; tel. (20) 7624640; fax (20) 7624648; e-mail ddc@undp.org; internet www.undp.org/drylands.

UNDP-UNEP POVERTY-ENVIRONMENT INITIATIVE (UNPEI)

UNPEI, inaugurated in February 2007, supports countries in developing their capacity to launch and maintain programmes that mainstream poverty-environment linkages into national development planning processes, such as MDG achievement strategies and PRSPs. In May 2007 UNDP and UNEP launched the Poverty-Environment Facility (UNPEF) to co-ordinate, and raise funds in support of, UNPEI. In 2012 UNPEI was supporting programmes in 17 countries, and also providing technical advisory across all regions.

Officer-in-Charge: DAVID SMITH; UN Gigiri Compound, United Nations Avenue, POB 30552, 00100 Nairobi, Kenya; e-mail facility.unpei@unpei.org; internet www.unpei.org.

UNITED NATIONS CAPITAL DEVELOPMENT FUND (UNCDF)

The Fund was established in 1966 and became fully operational in 1974. It invests in poor communities in least developed countries (LDCs) through local governance projects and microfinance operations, with the aim of increasing such communities' access to essential local infrastructure and services and thereby improving their productive capacities and self-reliance. UNCDF encourages participation by local people and local governments in the planning, implementation and monitoring of projects. The Fund aims to promote the interests of women in community projects and to enhance their earning capacities. A Special Unit for Microfinance (SUM), established in 1997 as a joint UNDP/UNCDF operation, was fully integrated into UNCDF in 1999. UNCDF/SUM helps to develop financial services for poor communities and supports UNDP's MicroStart initiative, which supports private sector and community-based initiatives in generating employment opportunities. UNCDF hosts the UN high-level Advisors Group on Inclusive Financial Sectors, established in respect of recommendations made during the 2005 International Year of Microcredit. In November 2008 UNCDF launched MicroLead, a US $26m. fund that was to provide loans to leading microfinance institutions and other financial service providers (MFIs/FSPs) in developing countries; MicroLead was also to focus on the provision of early support to countries in post-conflict situations. In 2010 UNCDF had a programme portfolio with a value of around $200m., in support of initiatives ongoing in 38 LDCs.

UNCDF, jointly with UNDP, organized the UN Conference on Financial Inclusion in Africa, that was convened in Dakar, Senegal, in June 2006. The Conference agreed to establish a network to mobilize resources in order to extend financial services throughout the region.

Executive Secretary a. i.: CHRISTINE ROTH (Senegal); Two United Nations Plaza, 26th Floor, New York, NY 10017, USA; fax (212) 906-6479; e-mail info@uncdf.org; internet www.uncdf.org.

UNITED NATIONS OFFICE FOR SOUTH-SOUTH COOPERATION

The Office was established as the Special Unit for South-South Cooperation in 1978 by the UN General Assembly and is hosted by UNDP. It was renamed, as above, in 2012 in order to strengthen the work of the body within the UN. The Office aims to co-ordinate and support South-South co-operation in the political, economic, social, environmental and technical areas, and to support 'triangular' collaboration on a UN system-wide and global basis. It organizes the annual UN Day for South-South Cooperation (12 September), and manages the UN Trust Fund for South-South Cooperation (UNFSC) and the Perez-Guerrero Trust Fund for Economic and Technical Co-operation among Developing Countries (PGTF), as well as undertaking programmes financed by UNDP.

Director: YIPING ZHOU (People's Republic of China); 304 East 45th St, 12th Floor, New York, NY 11017, USA; tel. (212) 906-6944; fax (212) 906-6352; e-mail ssc.info@undp.org; internet ssc.undp.org.

UNITED NATIONS VOLUNTEERS (UNV)

The United Nations Volunteers is an important source of middle-level skills for the UN development system supplied at modest cost, particularly in the least developed countries (LDCs). Volunteers expand the scope of UNDP project activities by supplementing the work of international and host-country experts and by extending the influence of projects to local community levels. UNV also supports technical co-operation within and among the developing countries by encouraging volunteers from the countries themselves and by forming regional exchange teams comprising such volunteers. UNV is involved in areas such as peace-building, elections, human rights, humanitarian relief and community-based environmental programmes, in addition to development activities.

The UN International Short-term Advisory Resources (UNISTAR) Programme, which is the private sector development arm of UNV, has increasingly focused its attention on countries in the process of economic transition. Since 1994 UNV has administered UNDP's Transfer of Knowledge Through Expatriate Nationals (TOKTEN) programme, which was initiated in 1977 to enable specialists and professionals from developing countries to contribute to development efforts in their countries of origin through short-term technical assignments. In March 2000 UNV established an Online Volunteering Service to connect development organizations and volunteers using the internet; in 2011, 10,910 online volunteers, working on 16,982 assignments, made their skills available through the Online Volunteering Service.

In December 2011 UNV issued the first *State of the World's Volunteerism Report*, on the theme 'Universal Values for Global Well-being'.

During 2011 some 7,303 national and international UNVs were deployed in 162 countries, on 7,708 assignments; some 54% of UNV assignments were undertaken in sub-Saharan Africa in that year.

Executive Co-ordinator: FLAVIA PANSIERI (Italy); POB 260111, 53153 Bonn, Germany; tel. (228) 8152000; fax (228) 8152001; e-mail information@unvolunteers.org; internet www.unv.org.

United Nations Environment Programme—UNEP

Address: POB 30552, Nairobi 00100, Kenya.

Telephone: (20) 621234; **fax:** (20) 623927; **e-mail:** unepinfo@unep.org; **internet:** www.unep.org.

The United Nations Environment Programme was established in 1972 by the UN General Assembly, following recommendations of the 1972 UN Conference on the Human Environment, in Stockholm, Sweden, to encourage international co-operation in matters relating to the human environment.

Organization

(September 2012)

GOVERNING COUNCIL

The main functions of the Governing Council (which meets every two years in ordinary sessions, with special sessions taking place in the alternate years) are to promote international co-operation in the field of the environment and to provide general policy guidance for the direction and co-ordination of environmental programmes within the UN system. It comprises representatives of 58 states, elected by the UN General Assembly, for four-year terms, on a regional basis. The Global Ministerial Environment Forum (first convened in 2000) meets annually as part of the Governing Council's regular and special sessions. The Governing Council is assisted in its work by a Committee of Permanent Representatives.

SECRETARIAT

Offices and divisions at UNEP headquarters include the Offices of the Executive Director and Deputy Executive Director; the Secretariat for Governing Bodies; Offices for Evaluation and Oversight, Programme Co-ordination and Management, Resource Mobilization, and Global Environment Facility Co-ordination; and Divisions of Communications and Public Information, Early Warning and Assessment, Environmental Policy Implementation, Technology, Industry and Economics, Regional Co-operation, and Environmental Law and Conventions.

Executive Director: ACHIM STEINER (Germany).

Deputy Executive Director: AMINA MOHAMED (Kenya).

REGIONAL OFFICES

UNEP maintains six regional offices. These work to initiate and promote UNEP objectives and to ensure that all programme formulation and delivery meets the specific needs of countries and regions. They also provide a focal point for building national, sub-regional and regional partnerships and enhancing local participation in UNEP initiatives. A co-ordination office has been established at headquarters to promote regional policy integration, to co-ordinate programme planning, and to provide necessary services to the regional offices.

Africa: POB 30552, Nairobi, Kenya; tel. (20) 7621234; fax (20) 7624489; e-mail roainfo@unep.org; internet www.unep.org/roa.

UNEP Liaison Office in Addis Ababa: ECA New Bldg, 5th Floor, No. 5SC4-5S25, POB 3001, Addis Ababa, Ethiopia; tel. (1) 5443431; fax (1) 5521633; e-mail unepoffice@uneca.org; internet www.unep.org/roa/addis_ababa_site/index.asp.

OTHER OFFICES

Convention on International Trade in Endangered Species of Wild Fauna and Flora (CITES): 15 chemin des Anémones, 1219 Châtelaine, Geneva, Switzerland; tel. 229178139; fax 227973417; e-mail info@cites.org; internet www.cites.org; Sec.-Gen. JOHN SCANLON (Australia).

Global Programme of Action for the Protection of the Marine Environment from Land-based Activities: GPA Co-ordination Unit, UNEP, POB 30552, 00100 Nairobi, Kenya; tel. (20) 7621206; fax (20) 7624249; internet www.gpa.unep.org.

Secretariat of the Basel, Rotterdam and Stockholm Conventions: 11–13 chemin des Anémones, 1219 Châtelaine, Geneva, Switzerland; tel. 229178729; fax 229178098; e-mail brs@unep.org; internet www.basel.int; www.pic.int; www.pops.int; Exec. Sec. JIM WILLIS (USA).

Secretariat of the Multilateral Fund for the Implementation of the Montreal Protocol: 1800 McGill College Ave, 27th Floor, Montréal, QC, H3A 3J6, Canada; tel. (514) 282-1122; fax (514) 282-0068; e-mail secretariat@unmfs.org; internet www.multilateralfund.org; Chief Officer MARIA NOLAN.

UNEP/CMS (Convention on the Conservation of Migratory Species of Wild Animals) Secretariat: Hermann-Ehlers-Str. 10, 53113 Bonn, Germany; tel. (228) 8152402; fax (228) 8152449; e-mail secretariat@cms.int; internet www.cms.int; Exec. Sec. ELIZABETH MARUMA MREMA.

UNEP Division of Technology, Industry and Economics: 15 rue de Milan, 75441 Paris, Cedex 09, France; tel. 1-44-37-14-50; fax 1-44-37-14-74; e-mail unep.tie@unep.fr; internet www.unep.org/dtie; Dir SYLVIE LEMMET (France).

UNEP International Environmental Technology Centre (IETC): 2–110 Ryokuchi koen, Tsurumi-ku, Osaka 538-0036, Japan; tel. (6) 6915-4581; fax (6) 6915-0304; e-mail ietc@unep.or.jp; internet www.unep.or.jp; Dir PER BAKKEN.

UNEP Ozone Secretariat: POB 30552, Nairobi, Kenya; tel. (20) 762-3851; fax (20) 762-4691; e-mail ozoneinfo@unep.org; internet ozone.unep.org; Exec. Sec. MARCO GONZÁLEZ (Costa Rica).

UNEP Post-Conflict and Disaster Management Branch: 11–15 chemin des Anémones, 1219 Châtelaine, Geneva, Switzerland; tel. 229178530; fax 229178064; e-mail postconflict@unep.org; internet www.unep.org/disastersandconflicts; Chief Officer HENRIK SLOTTE.

UNEP Risoe Centre on Energy, Environment and Sustainable Development: Risoe Campus, Technical University of Denmark, Frederiksborgvej 399, Bldg 142, POB 49, 4000 Roskilde, Denmark; tel. 46-77-51-29; fax 46-32-19-99; e-mail unep@risoe.dtu.dk; internet uneprisoe.org; f. 1990 as the UNEP Collaborating Centre on Energy and Environment; supports UNEP in the planning and implementation of its energy-related policy and activities; provides technical support to governments towards the preparation of national Technology Needs Assessments on climate change adaptation; Head JOHN CHRISTENSEN.

UNEP-SCBD (Convention on Biological Diversity—Secretariat): 413 St Jacques St, Suite 800, Montréal, QC, H2Y 1N9, Canada; tel. (514) 288-2220; fax (514) 288-6588; e-mail secretariat@cbd.int; internet www.cbd.int; Exec. Sec. BRAULIO FERREIRA DE SOUZA DIAS (Brazil).

UNEP Secretariat for the UN Scientific Committee on the Effects of Atomic Radiation: Vienna International Centre, Wagramerstr. 5, POB 500, 1400 Vienna, Austria; tel. (1) 26060-4330; fax (1) 26060-5902; e-mail malcolm.crick@unscear.org; internet www.unscear.org; Sec. Dr MALCOLM CRICK.

Activities

UNEP represents a voice for the environment within the UN system. It is an advocate, educator, catalyst and facilitator, promoting the wise use of the planet's natural assets for sustainable development. It aims to maintain a constant watch on the changing state of the environment; to analyse the trends; to assess the problems using a wide range of data and techniques; and to undertake or support projects leading to environmentally sound development. It plays a catalytic and co-ordinating role within and beyond the UN system. Many UNEP projects are implemented in co-operation with other UN agencies, particularly UNDP, the World Bank group, FAO, UNESCO and WHO. About 45 intergovernmental organizations outside the UN system and 60 international non-governmental organizations (NGOs) have official observer status on UNEP's Governing Council, and, through the Environment Liaison Centre in Nairobi, UNEP is linked to more than 6,000 non-governmental bodies concerned with the environment. UNEP also sponsors international conferences, programmes, plans and agreements regarding all aspects of the environment.

In February 1997 the Governing Council, at its 19th session, adopted a ministerial declaration (the Nairobi Declaration) on UNEP's future role and mandate, which recognized the organization as the principal UN body working in the field of the environment and as the leading global environmental authority, setting and overseeing the international environmental agenda. In June a special session of the UN General Assembly, referred to as 'Rio+5', was convened to review the state of the environment and progress achieved in implementing the objectives of the UN Conference on Environment and Development (UNCED—known as the Earth Summit), that had been held in Rio de Janeiro, Brazil, in June 1992. UNCED had adopted Agenda 21 (a programme of activities to promote sustainable development in the 21st century) and the 'Rio+5' meeting adopted a Programme for Further Implementation of Agenda 21 in order to intensify efforts in areas such as energy, freshwater resources and technology transfer. The meeting confirmed UNEP's essential role in advancing the Programme and as a global authority promoting a coherent legal and political approach to the environmental challenges of sustainable development. An extensive process of restructuring and realignment of functions was subsequently initiated by UNEP, and a new organizational structure reflecting the decisions of the Nairobi Declaration was implemented during 1999. UNEP played a leading role in preparing for the World Summit on Sustainable Development (WSSD), held in August–September 2002 in Johannesburg, South Africa, to assess strategies for strengthening the implementation of Agenda 21. Governments participating in the conference adopted the Johannesburg Declaration and WSSD Plan of Implementation, in which they strongly reaffirmed commitment to the principles underlying Agenda 21 and also pledged support to all internationally agreed development goals, including the UN Millennium Development Goals adopted by governments attending a summit meeting of the UN General Assembly in September 2000. Participating governments made concrete commitments to attaining several specific objectives in the areas of water, energy, health, agriculture and fisheries, and biodiversity. These included a reduction by one-half in the proportion of people world-wide lacking access to clean water or good sanitation by 2015, the restocking of depleted fisheries by 2015, a reduction in the ongoing loss in biodiversity by 2010, and the production and utilization of chemicals without causing harm to human beings and the environment by 2020. Participants determined to increase usage of renewable energy sources and to develop integrated water resources management and water efficiency plans. A large number of partnerships between governments, private sector interests and civil society groups were announced at the conference. The UN Conference on Sustainable Development (UNCSD) (also known as Earth Summit 2012 and as 'Rio+20'), convened in June 2012, again in Rio de Janeiro, determined that UNEP's role should be strengthened as the lead agency in setting the global environmental agenda and co-ordinating UN system-wide implementation of the environmental dimension of sustainable development. The Conference decided to ask the UN General Assembly, during its 67th session (commencing in September 2012), to adopt a resolution that would upgrade UNEP by establishing universal membership of the Governing Council; ensuring increased financial resources to enable the Programme to fulfil its mandate; strengthening UNEP's participation in the main UN co-ordinating bodies; and empowering UNEP to lead efforts to develop UN system-wide strategies on the environment.

In September 2012 the 14th ordinary session of the biennial African Ministerial Conference on the Environment (AMCEN), meeting in Arusha, Tanzania, adopted the Arusha Declaration on Africa's Post Rio+20 Strategy for Sustainable Development, comprising a series of priority programmes and decisions aimed at implementing the UNCSD outcomes continent-wide and stimulating regional sustainable development.

In May 2000 UNEP's first annual Global Ministerial Environment Forum (GMEF), was held in Malmö, Sweden, attended by environment ministers and other government delegates from more than 130 countries. Participants reviewed policy issues in the field of the environment and addressed issues such as the impact on the environment of population growth, the depletion of earth's natural resources, climate change and the need for fresh water supplies. The Forum issued the Malmö Declaration, which identified the effective implementation of international agreements on environmental matters at national level as the most pressing challenge for policy-makers. The Declaration emphasized the importance of mobilizing domestic and international resources and urged increased co-operation from civil society and the private sector in achieving sustainable development. The GMEF has subsequently convened annually, most recently in February 2012.

CLIMATE CHANGE

UNEP worked in collaboration with WMO to formulate the 1992 UN Framework Convention on Climate Change (UNFCCC), with the aim of reducing the emission of gases that have a warming effect on the atmosphere (known as greenhouse gases). (See Secretariat of the UN Framework Convention on Climate Change, below.) In 1998 UNEP and the World Meteorological Organization (WMO) established the Intergovernmental Panel on Climate Change (IPCC, see below), as an objective source of scientific information about the warming of the earth's atmosphere.

UNEP's climate change-related activities have a particular focus on strengthening the capabilities of countries (in particular developing countries) to integrate climate change responses into their national development processes, including improving preparedness for participating in UN Reduced Emissions from Deforestation and Forest Degradation (UN-REDD) initiatives; Ecosystem Based Adaptation; and Clean Tech Readiness.

UN-REDD, launched in September 2008 as a collaboration between UNEP, UNDP and FAO, aims to enable donors to pool resources (through a trust fund established for that purpose) to promote a transformation of forest resource use patterns. In August 2011 UN-REDD endorsed a Global Programme Framework covering 2011–15. Leaders from countries in the Amazon, Congo and Borneo-Mekong forest basins participated, in June 2011, in the Summit of Heads of State and Government on Tropical Forest Ecosystems, held in Brazzaville, Republic of the Congo; the meeting issued a declaration recognising the need to protect forests in order to combat climate change, and to conduct future mutual dialogue. In that month UNEP issued a report focusing on the economic benefits of expanding funding for forests.

UNEP's Technology Needs Assessment and Technology Action Plan aims to support some 35–45 countries with the implementation of improved national Technology Needs Assessments within the framework of the UNFCCC, involving, *inter alia*, detailed analysis of mitigation and adaptation technologies, and prioritization of these technologies. The UNEP Risoe Centre of Denmark supports governments in the preparation of these Assessments.

UNEP's Regional Clean Development Mechanism (CDM) Capacity Building Project for sub-Saharan Africa is being implemented in Ethiopia, Mauritius, Mozambique, Tanzania and Zambia, to attract commercial finance for CDM projects in both the public and private sectors. UNEP, jointly with the World Bank, administers a scheme entitled Carbon Finance for Sustainable Energy in Africa (CF-SEA), identifying CDM investment opportunities and helping to put them into practice; CF-SEA is active in Cameroon, Ghana, Mali, Mozambique and Zambia. In May 2007 UNEP convened an African Bankers Carbon Finance Investment Forum to discuss opportunities for and barriers to using carbon finance to support development in Africa. An Africa Carbon Forum was convened in September 2008, in Dakar, Senegal. In 2009 UNEP established the African Carbon Asset Development Facility, which had, by the end of 2011, approved more than 12 projects.

UNEP encourages the development of alternative and renewable sources of energy, as part of its efforts to mitigate climate change. To achieve this, UNEP has created the Global Network on Energy for Sustainable Development, linking 21 centres of excellence in industrialized and developing countries to conduct research and exchange information on environmentally sound energy technology resources. UNEP's Rural Energy Enterprise Development (REED) initiative (operating within Africa as AREED) helps the private sector to develop affordable 'clean' energy technologies, such as solar crop-drying and water-heating, wind-powered water pumps and efficient cooking stoves. UNEP is a member of the Global Bioenergy Partnership initiated by the G8 group of industrialized countries to support the sustainable use of biofuels. Through its Transport Programme UNEP promotes the use of renewable fuels and the integration of environmental factors into transport planning, leading a world-wide Partnership for Clean Fuels and Vehicles, a Global Fuel Economy Initiative, and a Non Motorised Transport 'Share the Road' scheme. Meanwhile, UNDP's Sustainable Buildings and Construction Initiative promotes energy efficiency in the construction industry. In conjunction with UN-Habitat, UNDP, the World Bank and other organizations and institutions, UNEP promotes environmental concerns in urban planning and management through the Sustainable Cities Programme, and projects concerned with waste management, urban pollution and the impact of transportation systems. In June 2012 UNEP and other partners inaugurated a new Global Initiative for Resource-Efficient Cities, which aimed to lower pollution levels, advance efficiency in the utilization of resources (including through the promotion of energy-efficient buildings), and reduce infrastructure costs in urban areas world-wide with populations in excess of 500,000.

During 2007 UNEP (with WMO and WTO) convened a second International Conference on Climate Change and Tourism, together with two meetings on sustainable tourism development and a conference on global eco-tourism. In June 2009 UNEP and WTO jointly issued a report entitled *Trade and Climate Change*, reviewing the intersections between trade and climate change from the perspectives of: the science of climate change; economics; multilateral efforts to combat climate change; and the effects on trade of national climate change policies.

GREEN ECONOMY

In October 2008, in response to the global economic, fuel and food crises that escalated during that year, UNEP launched the *Green Economy Initiative (GEI)*, also known as the 'Global Green New Deal', which aimed to mobilize and refocus the global economy towards investments in clean technologies and the natural infrastructure (for example the infrastructures of forests and soils), with a view to, simultaneously, combating climate change and promoting employment. The UNEP Executive Director stated that the global crises were in part related to a broad market failure that promoted speculation while precipitating escalating losses of natural capital and nature-based assets, compounded by an over-reliance on finite, often subsidized fossil fuels. The three principal dimensions of the GEI were: the compilation of the *Green Economy* report, to provide an analysis of how public policy might support markets in accelerating the transition towards a low-carbon green economy; the Green Jobs Initiative, a partnership launched by UNEP, the ILO and the International Trade Union Confederation in 2007 (and joined in 2008 by the International Organisation of Employers); and the Economics of Ecosystems and Biodiversity (TEEB) partnership project, focusing on valuation issues. In April 2009 the UN System Chief Executives Board for Co-ordination (CEB) endorsed the GEI as the fourth of nine UN initiatives aimed at alleviating the impact of the global economic crisis on poor and vulnerable populations. UNEP participates in the SEED Initiative, a global partnership for action on sustainable development and the green economy that was launched collaboratively with UNDP and the IUCN at the 2002 WSSD. SEED supports innovative locally driven small-scale businesses that actively work towards providing social and environmental benefits. A Green Economy Coalition was established in 2008 as a loose grouping of UNEP and other UN agencies, research institutes, business interests, trade unions, and NGOs, with the aim of promoting environmental sustainability and social equity.

The 14th session of AMCEN, held in September 2012, recognized the Green Economy as a key means of achieving sustainable development and eradicating poverty in Africa. The participating environment ministers proposed the establishment of a new African Green Economy Partnership, to facilitate co-ordinated support to member states and to promote regional poverty eradication, decent jobs creation, and sustainable development.

In June 2009 UNEP welcomed OECD's 'Green Growth' declaration, which urged the adoption of targeted policy instruments to promote green investment, and emphasized commitment to the realization of an ambitious and comprehensive post-2012 global climate agreement. In January 2012 UNEP, OECD, the World Bank, and the Global Green Growth Institute (established in June 2010 in Seoul, Republic of Korea—South Korea) launched the Green Growth Knowledge Platform. The Platform, accessible at www.greengrowthknowledge.org, aims to advance efforts to identify and address major knowledge gaps in green growth theory and practice, and to support countries in formulating and implementing policies aimed at developing a green economy.

In January 2011 UNEP and the World Tourism Organization launched the Global Partnership for Sustainable Tourism, also comprising other UN agencies, OECD, 18 governments, and other partners, with the aim of guiding policy and developing projects in the area of sustainable tourism, providing a global platform for discussion, and facilitating progress towards a green economy.

UNEP Finance Initiatives (FI) is a programme encouraging banks, insurance companies and other financial institutions to invest in an environmentally responsible way: an annual FI Global Roundtable meeting is held, together with regional meetings. In April 2007 UNEP hosted the first annual Business for Environment (B4E) meeting, on corporate environmental responsibility, in Singapore; the 2012 meeting was held in May, in Berlin, Germany. During 2007 UNEP's Programme on Sustainable Consumption and Production established an International Panel for Sustainable Resource Management (comprising experts whose initial subjects of study were to be the environmental risks of biofuels and of metal recycling), and initiated forums for businesses and NGOs in this field. In May 2011 the International Panel issued a *Decoupling Report* that urged the separation of the global economic growth rate from the rate of natural resource consumption. The report warned that, by 2050, without a change of direction, humanity's consumption of minerals, ores, fossil fuels and biomass were on course to increase threefold. Later in May 2011 the Panel released a report focusing on the need to increase the recycling of metals world-wide.

In February 2009 UNEP issued a report, entitled *The Environmental Food Crisis: Environment's Role in Averting Future Food Crises*, that urged a transformation in the way that food is produced, handled and disposed of, in order to feed the world's growing population and protect the environment.

In 1994 UNEP inaugurated the International Environmental Technology Centre (IETC), based in Osaka, Japan. The Centre promotes and implements environmentally sound technologies for disaster prevention and post-disaster reconstruction; sustainable production and consumption; and water and sanitation (in particular waste-water management and more efficient use of rainwater).

EARLY WARNING AND ASSESSMENT

The Nairobi Declaration resolved that the strengthening of UNEP's information, monitoring and assessment capabilities was a crucial element of the organization's restructuring, in order to help establish priorities for international, national and regional action, and to ensure the efficient and accurate dissemination of information on emerging environmental trends and emergencies.

UNEP's Division of Early Warning and Assessment analyses the world environment, provides early warning information and assesses global and regional trends. It provides governments with data and helps them to use environmental information for decision-making and planning.

UNEP's Global Environment Outlook (GEO) process of environmental analysis and assessment, launched in 1995, is supported by an extensive network of collaborating centres. The fifth 'umbrella' report on the GEO process (*GEO-5*) was issued in June 2012, just in advance of the UN Conference on Sustainable Development. The fifth report assessed progress achieved towards the attainment of some 90 environmental challenges, and identified four objectives—the elimination of the production and use of ozone layer-depleting substances; the removal of lead from fuel; access to improved water supplies; and promoting research into reducing pollution of the marine environment—as the areas in which most progress had been made. Little or no progress, however, was found to have been attained in the pursuit of 24 objectives, including managing climate change, desertification and drought; and deterioration was found to have occurred in the state of the world's coral reefs. In recent years regional and national GEO reports have been issued focusing on Africa, the Andean region, the Atlantic and Indian oceans, Brazil, the Caucasus, Latin America and the Caribbean, North America, and the Pacific; and the following thematic GEO reports have been produced: *The Global Deserts Outlook* (2006) and *The Global Outlook for Ice and Snow* (2007). Various GEO technical reports have also been published.

UNEP's Global International Waters Assessment (GIWA) considers all aspects of the world's water-related issues, in particular problems of shared transboundary waters, and of future sustainable management of water resources. UNEP is also a sponsoring agency of the Joint Group of Experts on the Scientific Aspects of Marine Environmental Pollution and contributes to the preparation of reports on the state of the marine environment and on the impact of land-based activities on that environment. In November 1995 UNEP published a Global Biodiversity Assessment, which was the first comprehensive study of biological resources throughout the world. The UNEP-World Conservation Monitoring Centre (UNEP-WCMC), established in June 2000 in Cambridge, United Kingdom, manages and interprets data concerning biodiversity and ecosystems, and makes the results available to governments and businesses. In October 2008 UNEP-WCMC, in partnership with the IUCN, launched the World Database on Protected Areas (WDPA), an online resource detailing the world's national parks and protected areas; by 2012 images of more than 200,000 sites could be viewed on the site. In 2007 the Centre undertook the 2010 Biodiversity Indicators Programme, with the aim of supporting decision-making by governments so as to reduce the threat of extinction facing vulnerable species. UNEP is a partner in the International Coral Reef Action Network—ICRAN, which was established in 2000 to monitor, manage and protect coral reefs world-wide. In June 2001 UNEP launched the Millennium Ecosystem Assessment, which was completed in March 2005. Other major assessments undertaken include the International Assessment of Agricultural Science and Technology for Development; the Solar and Wind Energy Resource Assessment; the Regionally Based Assessment of Persistent Toxic Substances; the Land Degradation Assessment in Drylands; and the Global Methodology for Mapping Human Impacts on the Biosphere (GLOBIO) project.

In June 2010 delegates from 85 countries, meeting in Busan, South Korea, at the third conference addressing the creation of a new Intergovernmental Science-Policy Platform on Biodiversity and Ecosystem Services (IPBES), adopted the Busan Outcome Document finalizing details of the establishment of the IPBES; the Outcome

Document was subsequently approved by the UN General Assembly. The Platform, inaugurated in April 2012, was to undertake, periodically, assessments, based on current scientific literature, of biodiversity and ecosystem outputs beneficial to humans, including timber, fresh water, fish and climatic stability.

UNEP's environmental information network includes the UNEP-INFOTERRA programme, which facilitates the exchange of environmental information through an extensive network of national 'focal points' (national environmental information centres, usually located in the relevant government ministry or agency). By 2012 177 countries were participating in the network, whereby UNEP promotes public access to environmental information, as well as participation in environmental concerns. UNEP's information, monitoring and assessment structures also serve to enhance early-warning capabilities and to provide accurate information during an environmental emergency.

In June 2008, at a meeting of AMCEN, *Africa: Atlas of Our Changing Environment Features*, compiled by UNEP, was issued, comprising more than 300 satellite images of the continent that demonstrated (through the use of 'before' and 'after' pictures) rapid recent environmental transformation, including the disappearance of glaciers in the Ugandan Rwenzori Mountains, falling water levels in Lake Victoria, and drying-up of Lake Chad. The *Africa Water Atlas*, detailing Africa's vulnerable water resources, was published by UNEP in November 2010.

DISASTERS AND CONFLICTS

UNEP aims to minimise environmental causes and consequences of disasters and conflicts, and supports member states in combating environmental degradation and natural resources mismanagement, deeming these to be underlying risk factors for conflicts and natural hazards. UNEP promotes the integration of environmental concerns into risk reduction policy and practices. In 2011 UNEP targeted activities aimed at reducing conflict and disaster risk at 16 countries, 12 of which had adopted national policies aimed at mitigating post-conflict and post-disaster environmental risks. During 2011 training on environment and disaster risk reduction was conducted in India, Sri Lanka and Thailand.

UNEP undertakes assessments to establish the risks posed by environmental impacts on human health, security and livelihoods, and provides field-based capacity building and technical support, in countries affected by natural disaster and conflict. Since 1999 UNEP has conducted post-crisis environmental assessments in Afghanistan, the Balkans, the Democratic Republic of the Congo, Lebanon, Nigeria (Ogoniland), the Palestinian territories, Rwanda, Sudan, and Ukraine, and in the countries affected by the 2004 Indian Ocean tsunami.

An independent report of the Senior Advisory Group to the UN Secretary General on Civilian Capacity in the Aftermath of Conflict, issued in February 2011, identified natural resources as a key area of focus and designated UNEP as the lead agency for identifying best practices in managing natural resources in support of peace building.

ENVIRONMENTAL GOVERNANCE

UNEP promotes international environmental legislation and the development of policy tools and guidelines in order to achieve the sustainable management of the world environment. It helps governments to implement multilateral environmental agreements, and to report on their results. At a national level it assists governments to develop and implement appropriate environmental instruments and aims to co-ordinate policy initiatives. Training in various aspects of environmental law and its applications is provided. The ninth Global Training Programme on Environmental Law and Policy was conducted by UNEP in November 2009; regional training programmes are also offered. UNEP supports the development of new legal, economic and other policy instruments to improve the effectiveness of existing environmental agreements. It updates a register of international environmental treaties, and publishes handbooks on negotiating and enforcing environmental law. It acts as the secretariat for a number of regional and global environmental conventions (see list above). In June 2011 UNEP launched the Multilateral Environmental Agreements Information and Knowledge Management Initiative, which aimed to expand the sharing of information on more than 12 international agreements relating to the protection of the environment.

In June 2009 the first meeting was convened, in Belgrade, Serbia, of a new Consultative Group of Ministers and High-level Representatives on International Environment Governance; the meeting reviewed UNEP's role and stressed the linkages between sustainable environmental policies and development. From end-June–early July five successive UNEP Executive Directors and other prominent environmentalists met, in Glion, Switzerland, to discuss means of bringing about change in the functioning of the world economy to prioritize a sustainable approach to using and preserving the environment for the benefit of long-term human welfare.

In June 2010 AMCEN adopted the Bamako Declaration, a road map for sustainable development and strengthening the common African negotiating position on climate change and biological diversity; the participating African ministers responsible for the environment urged UNEP and the African Union to support African negotiators in developing a new international regime on access to and benefit sharing of biological diversity.

UNEP is the principal UN agency for promoting environmentally sustainable water management. It regards the unsustainable use of water as one of the most urgent environmental issues, and estimates that two-thirds of the world's population will suffer chronic water shortages by 2025, owing to rising demand for drinking water as a result of growing populations, decreasing quality of water because of pollution, and increasing requirements of industries and agriculture. In 2000 UNEP adopted a new water policy and strategy, comprising assessment, management and co-ordination components. The Global International Waters Assessment (see above) is the primary framework for the assessment component. The management component includes the Global Programme of Action (GPA) for the Protection of the Marine Environment from Land-based Activities (adopted in November 1995), which focuses on the effects of pollution on freshwater resources, marine biodiversity and the coastal ecosystems of small island developing states. UNEP promotes international co-operation in the management of river basins and coastal areas and for the development of tools and guidelines to achieve the sustainable management of freshwater and coastal resources. In 2007 UNEP initiated a South-South Co-operation programme on technology and capacity building for the management of water resources. UNEP provides scientific, technical and administrative support to facilitate the implementation and co-ordination of 13 regional seas conventions and associated regional plans of action. UNEP's Regional Seas Programme aims to protect marine and coastal ecosystems, particularly by helping governments to put relevant legislation into practice.

UNEP was instrumental in the drafting of a Convention on Biological Diversity (CBD) to preserve the immense variety of plant and animal species, in particular those threatened with extinction. The Convention entered into force at the end of 1993; by September 2012 192 states and the European Union (EU) were parties to the CBD. The CBD's Cartagena Protocol on Biosafety (so called as it had been addressed at an extraordinary session of parties to the CBD convened in Cartagena, Colombia, in February 1999) was adopted at a meeting of parties to the CBD in January 2000, and entered into force in September 2003; by September 2012 the Protocol had been ratified by 163 states parties. The Protocol regulates the transboundary movement and use of living modified organisms resulting from biotechnology, in order to reduce any potential adverse effects on biodiversity and human health. It establishes an Advanced Informed Agreement procedure to govern the import of such organisms. In January 2002 UNEP launched a major project aimed at supporting developing countries with assessing the potential health and environmental risks and benefits of genetically modified (GM) crops, in preparation for the Protocol's entry into force. In February the parties to the CBD and other partners convened a conference on ways in which the traditional knowledge and practices of local communities could be preserved and used to conserve highly threatened species and ecosystems. The sixth conference of parties to the CBD, held in April 2002, adopted detailed voluntary guidelines concerning access to genetic resources and sharing the benefits attained from such resources with the countries and local communities where they originate; a global work programme on forests; and a set of guiding principles for combating alien invasive species. In October 2010 the 10th conference of the parties to the CBD, meeting in Nagoya, Japan, approved the Nagoya-Kuala Lumpur Supplementary Protocol to the CBD, with a view to establishing an international regime on access and benefit sharing (ABS) of genetic resources, alongside a strategic 10-year Strategic Plan for Biodiversity, comprising targets and timetables to combat loss of the planet's nature-based resources. The Supplementary Protocol was opened for signature in March 2011, and by September 2012 had been signed by 92 states and ratified by five. The UN Decade on Biodiversity was being celebrated during 2011–20. UNEP supports co-operation for biodiversity assessment and management in selected developing regions and for the development of strategies for the conservation and sustainable exploitation of individual threatened species (e.g. the Global Tiger Action Plan). It also provides assistance for the preparation of individual country studies and strategies to strengthen national biodiversity management and research. UNEP administers the Convention on International Trade in Endangered Species of Wild Flora and Fauna (CITES), which entered into force in 1975 and comprised 176 states parties at September 2012 (Bahrain having ratified the Convention in that month). CITES has special programmes on the protection of elephants, falcons, great apes, hawksbill turtles, sturgeons, tropical timber (jointly with the International Tropical Timber Organization), and big leaf mahogany. Meeting in St Petersburg, Russia, in November 2010, at the International Tiger Forum, the heads of UNODC, the Convention on International Trade in Endangered Species of Wild Fauna and Flora (CITES), the World Customs Organization, INTER-

POL and the World Bank jointly approved the establishment of a new International Consortium on Combating Wildlife Crime (ICCWC), with the aim of combating the poaching of wild animals and illegal trade in wild animals and wild animal products.

In July 2012 a meeting of the CITES Standing Committee adopted measures aimed at halting a recent escalation in the poaching and smuggling of ivory and rhinoceros horn; affected countries were urged to act to control domestic markets and combat the illegal trade.

In December 1996 the Lusaka Agreement on Co-operative Enforcement Operations Directed at Illegal Trade in Wild Flora and Fauna entered into force, having been concluded under UNEP auspices in order to strengthen the implementation of the CBD and CITES in Eastern and Central Africa. UNEP and UNESCO jointly co-sponsor the Great Apes Survival Project (GRASP), which was launched in May 2001. GRASP supports, in 23 'great ape range states' (of which 21 are in Africa and two—Indonesia and Malaysia—in South-East Asia), the conservation of gorillas, chimpanzees, orang-utans and bonobos. GRASP's first intergovernmental meeting, held in Kinshasa, Democratic Republic of the Congo in September 2005, was attended by representatives of governments of great ape habitat states, donor and other interested states, international organizations, NGOs, and private-sector and academic interests. The meeting adopted a Global Strategy for the Survival of Great Apes, and the Kinshasa Declaration pledging commitment and action towards achieving this goal. GRASP, CITES and the World Association of Zoos and Aquariums jointly declared 2009 the Year of the Gorilla. In June 2009 160 government representatives participating in a conference to mark the Year of the Gorilla, convened in Frankfurt, Germany, issued the Frankfurt Declaration to Call for Better Protection of Gorillas.

The Convention on the Conservation of Migratory Species of Wild Animals (CMS, also referred to as the Bonn Convention), concluded under UNEP auspices in 1979, aims to conserve migratory avian, marine and terrestrial species throughout the range of their migration. The secretariat of the CMS is hosted by UNEP. At September 2012 there were 117 states parties to the Convention. A number of agreements and Memoranda of Understanding (MOU) concerning conservation have been concluded under the CMS. An agreement and action plan to protect migratory birds of prey in Africa and Eurasia, supported by UNEP and the CMS, was concluded in October 2008 by 28 countries meeting in Abu Dhabi, United Arab Emirates. Signatory governments committed to protecting the birds from illegal killing (such as poisoning and shooting) and from unsustainable exploitation. A CMS Agreement for the Conservation of Gorillas and their Habitats was concluded, in association with UNEP, UNESCO, GRASP (see above) and the Royal Belgian Institute for Natural Science, in October 2007, and entered into force in June 2008. An Agreement on the Conservation of Albatrosses and Petrels (ACAP) was concluded, under CMS auspices, in 2001 and entered into force in 2004. It is envisaged that the scope of ACAP, currently covering only the Southern Hemisphere, will be extended to include species from the Northern Hemisphere. An MOU concerning Conservation Measures for West African Populations of the African Elephant was concluded under the CMS in November 2005. The first meeting of the 13 signatories to the MOU, convened in Accra, Ghana, in March 2009, agreed to act to halt the depletion of the elephants' natural habitat. Immediately afterwards a joint meeting was held, in Accra, by representatives of the CMS and CITES' Monitoring the Illegal Killing of Elephants (MIKE) programme. In August 2011 CITES established a new trust fund, with the intention of generating $100m. over a three-year period, in support of an African Elephant Action Plan to protect elephant populations, in particular by enhancing law enforcement capacities. In October 2008, convened in Lomé, Togo, the second intergovernmental meeting of the Western African Talks on Cetaceans and their Habitats (WATCH, the first meeting—WATCH I—having been held in October 2007), adopted an MOU on conserving the West African Manatee and Small Whales in Western Africa and Macaronesia, under the auspices of the CMS. The MOU includes two action plans for the conservation of these marine species. MOU have also been concluded under the CMS relating to: Marine Turtles of the Atlantic Coast of Africa, and Marine Turtles and their Habitats of the Indian Ocean and South-East Asia. In August 2012 the conference of parties to the CMS determined to develop a new strategic plan to guide the Convention over the period 2015–23.

In March 2012, following an eight-year process pursued with CMS support, the Niger Government established the 97,000 ha Termit & Tin Toumma National Nature and Cultural Reserve; this now represents the largest single protected area in Africa, and provides, in the form of a variety of habitats, shelter from adverse human intervention to species including Saharan cheetah, Barbary sheep, addax antelopes and dama gazelles.

In October 1994 87 countries, meeting under UN auspices, signed a Convention to Combat Desertification (see UNDP Drylands Development Centre), which aimed to provide a legal framework to counter the degradation of arid regions. An estimated 75% of all drylands have suffered some land degradation, affecting approximately 1,000m. people in 110 countries. UNEP continues to support the implementation of the Convention, as part of its efforts to protect land resources. UNEP also aims to improve the assessment of dryland degradation and desertification in co-operation with governments and other international bodies, as well as identifying the causes of degradation and measures to overcome these.

ECOSYSTEM MANAGEMENT

The Millennium Ecosystem Assessment, a scientific study of the state of 24 ecosystems, that was commissioned by the UN Secretary-General and published in 2001, found that 15 of the ecosystems under assessment were being used unsustainably, thereby inhibiting, particularly in developing countries, the achievement of the UN MDGs of reducing poverty and hunger. UNEP's Ecosystem Management Programme aims to develop an adaptive approach that integrates the management of forests, land, freshwater, and coastal systems, focusing on sustaining ecosystems to meet future ecological needs, and to enhance human well-being. UNEP places particular emphasis on six ecosystem services deemed to be especially in decline: climate regulation; water regulation; natural hazard regulation; energy; freshwater; nutrient cycling; and recreation and ecotourism. Secondary importance is given to: water purification and waste treatment; disease regulation; fisheries; and primary production. UNEP supports governments in building capacity to promote the role of sustainably managed ecosystems in supporting social and economic development; assists national and regional governments in determining which ecosystem services to prioritize; and helps governments to incorporate an ecosystem management approach into their national and developmental planning and investment strategies.

UNEP's Billion Tree Campaign, initiated in February 2007, initially encouraged governments, community organizations and individuals to plant 1,000m. trees before the end of the year, and exceeded that target; by September 2012 some 12,612m. trees had been planted under the continuing campaign.

In September 2011 an independent study, commissioned by UNEP, on the Environmental, Social and Economic Assessment of the Fencing of the Aberdare Conservation Area (ACA) was released. The study found that the enclosure of the ACA, a tropical mountain ecosystem in central Kenya, by a 400-km electrified fence, had improved the livelihoods of millions of people in the area, securing a prime water, forest and biodiversity hotspot, and providing safer living conditions, and better incomes for fence-edge farmers.

HARMFUL SUBSTANCES AND HAZARDOUS WASTE

UNEP administers the Basel Convention on the Control of Transboundary Movements of Hazardous Wastes and their Disposal, which entered into force in 1992 with the aim of preventing the uncontrolled movement and disposal of toxic and other hazardous wastes, particularly the illegal dumping of waste in developing countries by companies from industrialized countries. At September 2012 179 countries and the EU were parties to the Convention.

In 1996 UNEP, in collaboration with FAO, began to work towards promoting and formulating a legally binding international convention on prior informed consent (PIC) for hazardous chemicals and pesticides in international trade, extending a voluntary PIC procedure of information exchange undertaken by more than 100 governments since 1991. The Convention was adopted at a conference held in Rotterdam, Netherlands, in September 1998, and entered into force in February 2004. It aims to reduce risks to human health and the environment by restricting the production, export and use of hazardous substances and enhancing information exchange procedures. UNEP played a leading role in formulating a multilateral agreement to reduce and ultimately eliminate the manufacture and use of Persistent Organic Pollutants (POPs), which are considered to be a major global environmental hazard. The Stockholm Convention on POPs, targeting 12 particularly hazardous pollutants, was adopted by 127 countries in May 2001 and entered into force in May 2004. In May 2009 the fourth conference of parties to the Stockholm Convention agreed on a list of nine further POPs; these were incorporated into the Convention in an amendment that entered into force in August 2010.

In February 2009 140 governments agreed, under the auspices of UNEP, to launch negotiations on the development of an international treaty to combat toxic mercury emissions world-wide. The first session of the intergovernmental negotiating committee on preparing the proposed treaty was convened in June 2010, in Stockholm, Sweden. The second session was held January 2011, in Chiba, Japan, a third took place in October–November, in Nairobi, and a fourth was held in July 2012, in Punta del Este, Uruguay. Pending the adoption of the planned treaty (envisaged for 2013) a voluntary Global Mercury Partnership addresses mercury pollution.

UNEP was the principal agency in formulating the 1987 Montreal Protocol to the Vienna Convention for the Protection of the Ozone Layer (1985), which provided for a 50% reduction in the production of chlorofluorocarbons (CFCs) by 2000. An amendment to the Protocol was adopted in 1990, which required complete cessation of the production of CFCs by 2000 in industrialized countries and by 2010 in developing countries. The Copenhagen Amendment, adopted in 1992, stipulated the phasing out of production of hydrochlorofluorocarbons (HCFCs) by 2030 in developed countries and by 2040 in developing nations. Subsequent amendments aimed to introduce a licensing system for all controlled substances, and imposed stricter controls on the import and export of HCFCs, and on the production and consumption of bromochloromethane (Halon-1011, an industrial solvent and fire extinguisher). In September 2007 the states parties to the Vienna Convention agreed to advance the deadline for the elimination of HCFCs: production and consumption were to be frozen by 2013, and were to be phased out in developed countries by 2020 and in developing countries by 2030. A Multilateral Fund for the Implementation of the Montreal Protocol was established in June 1990 to promote the use of suitable technologies and the transfer of technologies to developing countries, and support compliance by developing countries with relevant control measures. UNEP, UNDP, the World Bank and UNIDO are the sponsors of the Fund, which by February 2012 had approved financing for more than 6,875 projects and activities in 145 developing countries at a cost of more than US $2,800m. The eighth replenishment of the Fund, covering the period 2012–14, raised $400m. in new contributions from donors. In September 2009, following ratification by Timor-Leste, the Montreal Protocol, with 196 states parties, became the first agreement on the global environment to attain universal ratification. UNEP's OzonAction branch promotes information exchange, training and technological awareness, helping governments and industry in developing countries to undertake measures towards the cost-effective phasing-out of ozone-depleting substances.

UNEP encourages governments and the private sector to develop and adopt policies and practices that are cleaner and safer, make efficient use of natural resources, incorporate environmental costs, ensure the environmentally sound management of chemicals, and reduce pollution and risks to human health and the environment. In collaboration with other organizations UNEP works to formulate international guidelines and agreements to address these issues. UNEP also promotes the transfer of appropriate technologies and organizes conferences and training workshops to provide sustainable production practices. Relevant information is disseminated through the International Cleaner Production Information Clearing House. By 2012 UNEP, together with UNIDO, had established 47 National Cleaner Production Centres in developing and transition countries to promote a preventive approach to industrial pollution control. In October 1998 UNEP adopted an International Declaration on Cleaner Production, with a commitment to implement cleaner and more sustainable production methods and to monitor results. In 1997 UNEP and the Coalition for Environmentally Responsible Economies initiated the Global Reporting Initiative, which, with participation by corporations, business associations and other organizations, develops guidelines for voluntary reporting by companies on their economic, environmental and social performance. In April 2002 UNEP launched the 'Life Cycle Initiative', which evaluates the impact of products over their entire life cycle (from manufacture to disposal) and aims to assist governments, businesses and other consumers with adopting environmentally sound policies and practice, in view of the upward trend in global consumption patterns.

In accordance with a decision made by UNEP's Governing Council in February 2002, a Preparatory Committee for the Development of a Strategic Approach to International Chemicals Management was established; the work of the Committee culminated in the first session, held in February 2006, in Dubai, United Arab Emirates, of the International Conference on Chemicals Management (ICCM-1), comprising governments and intergovernmental and non-governmental organizations. ICCM-1 adopted the Strategic Approach to International Chemicals Management (SAICM), a policy framework to promote the sound management of chemicals in support of the objective (determined by the 2002 WSSD) of ensuring that, by 2020, chemicals are produced and used in ways that minimize significant adverse impacts on the environment and human health. ICCM-2, convened in May 2009, in Geneva, reviewed the implementation of the SAICM and adopted 20 indicators to measure its future progress. ICCM-3, held in September 2012, in Nairobi, evaluated data on the 20 indicators. UNEP provides technical support for implementing the Convention on Persistent Organic Pollutants (see above), encouraging the use of alternative pesticides, and monitoring the emission of pollutants through the burning of waste. With UNDP, UNEP helps governments to integrate sound management of chemicals into their development planning. In September 2012 UNEP published the *Global Chemical Outlook*, a report highlighting the effect of chemicals on human health and the environment, and assessing the negative impact on emerging and developing economies.

A Pollutant Release and Transfer Register (PRTR), for collecting and disseminating data on toxic emissions, has been developed in South Africa. The Togolese authorities have prepared a PRTR Feasibility Study, with a view eventually to maintain a national Register.

GLOBAL ENVIRONMENT FACILITY

UNEP, together with UNDP and the World Bank, is an implementing agency of the Global Environment Facility (GEF), established in 1991 to help developing countries, and those undergoing economic transition, to meet the costs of projects that benefit the environment in six specific areas: biological diversity, climate change, international waters, depletion of the ozone layer, land degradation and persistent organic pollutants. Important cross-cutting components of these projects include capacity-building to allow countries to meet their obligations under international environmental agreements (described above), and adaptation to climate change. During 1991–2011 some 522 projects were approved by the GEF to be implemented by UNEP, with a total value amounting to US $1,646m. UNEP services the Scientific and Technical Advisory Panel, which provides expert advice on GEF programmes and operational strategies.

UNEP, together with UNDP and the World Bank, is an implementing agency of the Global Environment Facility (GEF), which was established in 1991. The purpose of the GEF is to help developing countries to meet the costs of projects that benefit the environment in six specific areas: biological diversity, climate change, international waters, depletion of the ozone layer, land degradation and persistent organic pollutants. An important component of these projects is capacity-building to allow countries to meet their obligations under international environmental agreements (described above). UNEP services the Scientific and Technical Advisory Panel, which provides expert advice on GEF programmes and operational strategies. A Western Indian Ocean Marine Highway Development and Coastal and Marine Contamination Prevention project was implemented jointly by UNEP and the World Bank, through the GEF, over the four-year period May 2007–June 2011; the project aimed to improve the efficiency of navigation in, and insodoing protect the environment of, the Western Indian Ocean.

In 2008 the African Rift Geothermal Facility (ARGeo) project, established in 2005 by Djibouti, Eritrea, Ethiopia, Kenya, Tanzania and Uganda to test advanced drilling and seismic systems in eastern Africa, and supported by UNEP through the GEF, reported that geothermal wells in the Rift Valley were capable of producing more than double the energy than had been previously attainable with the use of older technologies. In September 2011 UNEP organized, with the Kenya Government, a high-level meeting of ministers and technical experts of countries participating in the ARGeo project, in order to further the understanding of the objectives of the project and the development of geothermal initiatives in the sub-region.

COMMUNICATIONS AND PUBLIC INFORMATION

UNEP's public education campaigns and outreach programmes promote community involvement in environmental issues. Further communication of environmental concerns is undertaken through coverage in the press, broadcasting and electronic media, publications (see below), an information centre service and special promotional events, including World Environment Day (celebrated on 5 June; slogan in 2012: 'Green Economy: Does It Include You'), the Focus on Your World photography competition, and the awarding of the annual Sasakawa Prize (to recognize distinguished service to the environment by individuals and groups) and of the Champions of the Earth awards (for outstanding environmental leaders from each of UNEP's six regions). An annual Global Civil Society Forum (preceded by regional consultative meetings) is held in association with UNEP's Governing Council meetings. From April 2007 UNEP undertook a two-year programme on strengthening trade unions' participation in environmental processes. UNEP's Tunza programme for children and young people includes conferences, online discussions and publications. UNEP co-operates with the International Olympic Committee, the Commonwealth Games organizing body and international federations for football, athletics and other sports to encourage 'carbon neutral' sporting events and to use sport as a means of outreach.

Finance

Project budgetary resources approved by the Governing Council for UNEP's activities during 2012–13 totalled US $474m. UNEP is allocated a contribution from the regular budget of the United Nations, and derives most of its finances from voluntary contributions to the Environment Fund and to trust funds.

Publications

Annual Report.

CBTF (Capacity Building Task Force on Trade, Environment and Development) Newsletter.

DEWA/GRID Europe Quarterly Bulletin. E+ (Energy, Climate and Sustainable Development).
The Environment and Poverty Times.
Global 500.
Great Apes Survival Project Newsletter.
IETC (International Environmental Technology Centre) Insight.
Life Cycle Initiatives Newsletter.
Our Planet (quarterly).
Planet in Peril: Atlas of Current Threats to People and the Environment.
ROA (Regional Office for Africa) News (2 a year).
Tourism Focus (2 a year).
RRC.AP (Regional Resource Centre for Asia and the Pacific) Newsletter.
Sustainable Consumption Newsletter.
Tunza (quarterly magazine for children and young people).
UNEP Chemicals Newsletter.
UNEP Year Book.
World Atlas of Biodiversity.
World Atlas of Coral Reefs.
World Atlas of Desertification.
Studies, reports (including the *Global Environment Outlook* series), legal texts, technical guidelines, etc.

Associated Bodies

Secretariat of the UN Conference on Sustainable Development (UNCSD): Two UN Plaza, Rm DC2-2220 New York, NY 10017, USA; e-mail uncsd2012@un.org; internet www.uncsd2012.org/rio20/index.html; UNCSD (also known as Rio+20 and as the Earth Summit+20) was convened in Rio de Janeiro, Brazil, on 20–22 June 2012, with participation by more than 100 heads of state and government, and by an estimated 50,000 representatives of international and non-governmental organizations, civil society groups, and the private sector. Rio+20 commemorated the 20th anniversary of the 1992 UN Conference on Environment and Development (UNCED), also held in Rio de Janeiro, and the 10th anniversary of the World Summit on Sustainable Development (WSSD), staged in 2002, in Johannesburg, South Africa. In May 2010 the UN Secretary-General appointed the Under-Secretary-General for Economic and Social Affairs as the Secretary-General of Rio+20. A Conference Secretariat was established within the UN Department of Economic and Social Affairs. Rio+20 aims to assess progress towards, and secure renewed political commitment for sustainable development, with a focus on the following themes: (i) a green economy in the context of sustainable development and poverty eradication, and (ii) the Institutional Framework for Sustainable Development (IFSD). An inclusive preparatory process, involving stakeholders in the Conference, was implemented during 2010–June 2012. The UNCSD Secretariat, with other partners, prepared a series of briefs on Rio+20 issues—such as trade and the green economy; options for strengthening the IFSD; oceans; sustainable cities; green jobs and social inclusion; reducing disaster risk and building resilience; food security and sustainable agriculture; and water—to be made available to policy makers and other interested stakeholders as a basis for discussion. Heads of state and government, and high-level representatives, participating in Rio+20 endorsed an outcome document, entitled 'The Future We Want', which, *inter alia*, reaffirmed commitment to working towards an economically, socially and environmentally sustainable future, and to the eradication of poverty as an indispensable requirement for sustainable development; and deemed the implementation of green economy policy options, in the context of sustainable development and poverty eradication, to be an important tool for achieving sustainable development. The participants determined to strengthen the institutional framework and intergovernmental arrangements for sustainable development; and to establish a high-level intergovernmental forum to promote system-wide co-ordination and coherence of sustainable development policies and to follow up the implementation of sustainable development objectives. The forum was to build on the work of, and eventually replace, the UN Commission on Sustainable Development (see under ECOSOC), which was established in 1993 to oversee integration into the UN's work of UNCED's objectives; it was to meet for the first time in September 2013, at the start of the 68th UN General Assembly. UNSCD approved a set of Sustainable Development Goals (SDGs), setting global targets in sustainable development challenges; it was envisaged that, post-2015, the SDGs would complement the MDGS. A 10-year framework on sustainable consumption and production was also announced, and the Conference decided to develop a new global wealth indicator that was to incorporate more dimensions than Gross National Product (the traditional indicator). The Conference invited all UN agencies and entities to mainstream sustainable development in their mandates, programmes, and strategies. The importance of enhancing the participation of developing countries in international economic decision-making was emphasized.

Secretary-General: SHA ZUKANG (People's Republic of China).

Executive Co-ordinators: H. ELIZABETH THOMPSON (Barbados), BRICE LALONDE (France).

Intergovernmental Panel on Climate Change (IPCC): c/o WMO, 7 bis, ave de la Paix, 1211 Geneva 2, Switzerland; e-mail ipcc-sec@wmo.int; internet www.ipcc.ch; established in 1988 by WMO and UNEP; comprises some 3,000 scientists as well as other experts and representatives of all UN member governments. Approximately every five years the IPCC assesses all available scientific, technical and socio-economic information on anthropogenic climate change. The IPCC provides, on request, scientific, technical and socio-economic advice to the Conference of the Parties to the UN Framework Convention on Climate Change (UNFCCC) and to its subsidiary bodies, and compiles reports on specialized topics, such as *Aviation and the Global Atmosphere*, *Regional Impacts of Climate Change*, and (issued in March 2012) *Managing the Risks of Extreme Events and Disasters to Advance Climate Change Adaptation*. The IPCC informs and guides, but does not prescribe, policy. In December 1995 the IPCC presented evidence to 120 governments, demonstrating 'a discernible human influence on global climate'. In 2001 the Panel issued its *Third Assessment Report*, in which it confirmed this finding and presented new and strengthened evidence attributing most global climate warming over the past 50 years to human activities. The IPCC's *Fourth Assessment Report*, the final instalment of which was issued in November 2007, concluded that increases in global average air and ocean temperatures, widespread melting of snow and ice, and the rising global average sea level, demonstrate that the warming of the climate system is unequivocal; that observational evidence from all continents and most oceans indicates that many natural systems are being affected by regional climate changes; that a global assessment of data since 1970 has shown that it is likely that anthropogenic warming has had a discernable influence on many physical and biological systems; and that other effects of regional climate changes are emerging. The *Fourth Assessment Report* was awarded a share of the Nobel Peace Prize for 2007. In January 2010 the IPCC accepted criticism that an assertion in the 2007 *Report*, concerning the rate at which Himalayan glaciers were melting, was exaggerated, and in February 2010 the Panel agreed that the *Report* had overstated the proportion of the Netherlands below sea level. In late February it was announced that an independent board of scientists would be appointed to review the work of the IPCC. The *Fifth Assessment Report* of the IPCC was to be published in 2014. In May 2011 a meeting of delegates from IPCC member states determined that a 13-member executive committee, under the leadership of the IPCC Chairman, should be established to supervise the day-to-day operations of the Panel and to consider matters requiring urgent action.

Chair.: RAJENDRA K. PACHAURI (India).

Secretariat of the UN Framework Convention on Climate Change (UNFCCC): Haus Carstanjen, Martin-Luther-King-Str. 8, 53175 Bonn, Germany; tel. (228) 815-1000; fax (228) 815-1999; e-mail secretariat@unfccc.int; internet unfccc.int; WMO and UNEP worked together to formulate the Convention, in response to the first report of the IPCC, issued in August 1990, which predicted an increase in the concentration of 'greenhouse' gases (i.e. carbon dioxide and other gases that have a warming effect on the atmosphere) owing to human activity. The UNFCCC was signed in May 1992 and formally adopted at the UN Conference on Environment and Development, held in June. It entered into force in March 1994. It committed countries to submitting reports on measures being taken to reduce the emission of greenhouse gases and recommended stabilizing these emissions at 1990 levels by 2000; however, this was not legally binding. Following the second session of the Conference of the Parties (COP) of the Convention, held in July 1996, multilateral negotiations ensued to formulate legally binding objectives for emission limitations. At the third COP, held in Kyoto, Japan, in December 1997, 38 industrial nations endorsed mandatory reductions of combined emissions of the six major gases by an average of 5.2% during the five-year period 2008–12, to pre-1990 levels. The so-called Kyoto Protocol was to enter into force on being ratified by at least 55 countries party to the UNFCCC, including industrialized countries with combined emissions of carbon dioxide in 1990 accounting for at least 55% of the total global greenhouse gas emissions by developed nations. The fourth COP, convened in Buenos Aires, Argentina, in November 1998, adopted a plan of action to promote implementation of the UNFCCC and to finalize the operational details of the Kyoto Protocol. These included the Clean Development Mechanism, by which industrialized countries may obtain credits towards achieving their reduction targets by assisting developing countries to implement emission-reducing measures, and a system of trading emission quotas. The fifth COP, held in Bonn, Germany, in October–November 1999, and the first session of the sixth COP, convened in The Hague, Netherlands, in November 2000, failed to reach agreement on the implementation of the Buenos Aires plan of action, owing to a lack of consensus on several technical matters, including the formulation of an effective mechanism for ascertaining compliance under the Kyoto Protocol, and adequately defining a provision of the Protocol under which industrialized countries may obtain credits towards achieving their reduction targets in respect of the absorption of emissions resulting from activities in the so-called land-use, land-use change and forestry (LULUCF) sector. Further, informal, talks were held in Ottawa, Canada, in early December. Agreement on implementing the Buenos Aires action plan was finally achieved at the second session of the sixth COP, held in Bonn in July 2001. The seventh COP, convened in Marrakech, Morocco, in October–November, formally adopted the decisions reached in July, and elected 15 members to the Executive Board of the Clean Development Mechanism. In March 2002 the USA (the most prolific national producer of harmful gas emissions) announced that it would not ratify the Kyoto Protocol. The Kyoto Protocol eventually entered into force on 16 February 2005, 90 days after its ratification by Russia. Negotiations commenced in May 2007 on establishing a new international arrangement eventually to succeed the Kyoto Protocol. Participants in COP 13, convened in Bali, Indonesia, in December 2007, adopted the Bali Roadmap, detailing a two-year process leading to the planned conclusion of the schedule of negotiations in December 2009. Further rounds of talks were held during 2008 in Bangkok, Thailand (March–April); Bonn (June); and Accra, Ghana (August). The UN Climate Change Conference (COP 14), convened in Poznań, Poland, in December 2008, finalized the Kyoto Protocol's Adaptation Fund, which was to finance projects and programmes in developing signatory states that were particularly vulnerable to the adverse effects of climate change. Addressing the Conference, the UN Secretary-General urged the advancement of a 'Green New Deal', to address simultaneously the ongoing global climate and economic crises. COP 15 was held, concurrently with the fifth meeting of parties to the Kyoto Protocol, in Copenhagen, Denmark, in December 2009. Heads of state and government and other delegates attending the Conference approved the Copenhagen Accord, which determined that international co-operative action should be taken, in the context of sustainable development, to reduce global greenhouse gas emissions so as to hold the ongoing increase in global temperature below 2°C. It was agreed that enhanced efforts should be undertaken to reduce vulnerability to climate change in developing countries, with special reference to least developed countries, small island states and Africa. Developed countries agreed to pursue the achievement by 2020 of strengthened carbon emissions targets, while developing nations were to implement actions to slow down growth in emissions. A Green Climate Fund (q.v.) was to be established to support climate change mitigation actions in developing countries, and a Technology Mechanism was also to be established, with the aim of accelerating technology development and transfer in support of climate change adaptation and mitigation activities. COP 16, convened, concurrently with the sixth meeting of parties to the Kyoto Protocol, in Cancun, Mexico, in November–December 2010, adopted several decisions (the 'Cancun Agreements'), which included mandating the establishment of a Cancun Adaptation Framework and associated Adaptation Committee, and approving a work programme which was to consider approaches to environmental damage linked to unavoidable impacts of climate change in vulnerable countries, as well as addressing forms of adaptation action, such as: strengthening the resilience of ecological systems; undertaking impact, vulnerability and adaptation assessments; engaging the participation of vulnerable communities in ongoing processes; and valuing traditional indigenous knowledge alongside the best available science. UN system-wide activities to address climate change are co-ordinated by an action framework established by the UN Chief Executives Board for Co-ordination under the UN *Delivering as One* commitment. By September 2012 the Kyoto Protocol had been ratified by 192 states and the European Community, including ratifications by industrialized nations with combined responsibility for 63.7% of greenhouse gas emissions by developed nations in 1990 (although excluding participation by the USA; in December 2011 Canada announced its intention to withdraw from the Protocol). COP 17, held in Durban, South Africa, in November–December 2011 concluded with an agreement on a 'Durban Platform for Enhanced Action'. The Platform incorporated agreements to extend the Kyoto provisions regarding emissions reductions by industrialized nations for a second phase (the commitment period, of either five or eight years, to be determined during 2012), to follow on from the expiry at end-2012 of the first commitment phase, and to initiate negotiations on a new, inclusive global emissions arrangement, to be concluded in 2015, that would come into effect in 2020 with 'legal force'. During the conference sufficient funds were committed to enable the inauguration—in August 2012—of the Green Climate Fund, and a commitment was concluded to establish the Adaptation Committee.

Executive Secretary: CHRISTIANA FIGUERES (Costa Rica).

United Nations High Commissioner for Refugees—UNHCR

Address: CP 2500, 1211 Geneva 2 dépôt, Switzerland.

Telephone: 227398111; **fax:** 227397312; **e-mail:** unhcr@unhcr.org; **internet:** www.unhcr.org.

The Office of the High Commissioner was established in 1951 to provide international protection for refugees and to seek durable solutions to their problems. In 1981 UNHCR was awarded the Nobel Peace Prize.

Organization

(September 2012)

HIGH COMMISSIONER

The High Commissioner is elected by the United Nations General Assembly on the nomination of the Secretary-General, and is responsible to the General Assembly and to the UN Economic and Social Council (ECOSOC).

High Commissioner: ANTÓNIO MANUEL DE OLIVEIRA GUTERRES (Portugal).

Deputy High Commissioner: THOMAS ALEXANDER ALEINIKOFF (USA).

EXECUTIVE COMMITTEE

The Executive Committee of the High Commissioner's Programme (ExCom), established by ECOSOC, gives the High Commissioner policy directives in respect of material assistance programmes and advice in the field of international protection. In addition, it oversees UNHCR's general policies and use of funds. ExCom, which comprises representatives of 66 states, both members and non-members of the UN, meets once a year.

ADMINISTRATION

Headquarters, based in Geneva, Switzerland, include the Executive Office, comprising the offices of the High Commissioner, the Deputy High Commissioner and the two Assistant High Commissioners (for Operations and Protection). The Inspector General, the Director of the UNHCR liaison office in New York, and the Director of the Ethics Office (established in 2008) report directly to the High Commissioner. The principal administrative Divisions cover: International Protection; Programme and Support Management; Emergency Security and Supply; Financial and Administrative Management; Human Resources Management; External Relations; and Information Systems and Telecommunications. A UNHCR Global Service Centre, based in Budapest, Hungary, was inaugurated in 2008 to provide administrative support to the Headquarters. There are five regional bureaux covering Africa, Asia and the Pacific, Europe, the Americas, and North Africa and the Middle East. In 2012 UNHCR employed around 7,190 regular staff, of whom about 85% were working in the field. At that time there were 396 UNHCR offices in 123 countries.

All UNHCR personnel are required to sign, and all interns, contracted staff and staff from partner organizations are required to acknowledge, a Code of Conduct, to which is appended the UN Secretary-General's bulletin on special measures for protection from sexual exploitation and sexual abuse. The post of Senior Adviser to the High Commissioner on Gender Issues, within the Executive Office, was established in 2004.

OFFICES IN AFRICA

Regional Office for Central Africa: BP 7248, Kinshasa, Democratic Republic of the Congo; e-mail codki@unhcr.ch.

Regional Office for West Africa: BP 3125, Dakar, Senegal; e-mail senda@unhcr.ch.

Regional Office for Southern Africa: BP 12506, Pretoria 0001, South Africa; e-mail rsapr@unhcr.ch.

Activities

The competence of the High Commissioner extends to any person who, owing to well-founded fear of being persecuted for reasons of race, religion, nationality or political opinion, is outside the country of his or her nationality and is unable or, owing to such fear or for reasons other than personal convenience, remains unwilling to accept the protection of that country; or who, not having a nationality and being outside the country of his or her former habitual residence, is unable or, owing to such fear or for reasons other than personal convenience, is unwilling to return to it. This competence may be extended, by resolutions of the UN General Assembly and decisions of ExCom, to cover certain other 'persons of concern', in addition to refugees meeting these criteria. Refugees who are assisted by other UN agencies, or who have the same rights or obligations as nationals of their country of residence, are outside the mandate of UNHCR.

In recent years there has been a significant shift in UNHCR's focus of activities. Increasingly UNHCR has been called upon to support people who have been displaced within their own country (i.e. with similar needs to those of refugees but who have not crossed an international border) or those threatened with displacement as a result of armed conflict. In addition, greater support has been given to refugees who have returned to their country of origin, to assist their reintegration, and UNHCR is working to enable local communities to support the returnees, frequently through the implementation of Quick Impact Projects (QIPs). In 2004 UNHCR led the formulation of a UN system-wide Strategic Plan for internally displaced persons (IDPs). During 2005 the UN's Inter-Agency Standing Committee (IASC), concerned with co-ordinating the international response to humanitarian disasters, developed a concept of organizing agency assistance to IDPs through the institutionalization of a 'Cluster Approach', currently comprising 11 core areas of activity (see OCHA). UNHCR is the lead agency for the clusters on Camp Coordination and Management (in conflict situations; the International Organization for Migration leads that cluster in natural disaster situations), Emergency Shelter, and (jointly with OHCHR and UNICEF) Protection.

From the mid-2000s the scope of UNHCR's mandate was widened from the protection of people fleeing persecution and violence to encompass, also, humanitarian needs arising from natural disasters.

In July 2006 UNHCR issued a '10 Point Plan of Action on Refugee Protection and Mixed Migration' (*10 Point Plan*), a framework document detailing 10 principal areas in which UNHCR might make an impact in supporting member states with the development of comprehensive migration strategies. The 10 areas covered by the Plan were as follows: co-operation among key players; data collection and analysis; protection-sensitive entry systems; reception arrangements; mechanisms for profiling and referral; differentiated processes and procedures; solutions for refugees; addressing secondary movements; return of non-refugees and alternative migration options; and information strategy. A revised version of the *10 Point Plan* was published in January 2007. Addressing the annual meeting of ExCom in October 2007 the High Commissioner, while emphasizing that UNHCR was not mandated to manage migration, urged a concerted international effort to raise awareness and comprehension of the broad patterns (including the scale, complexity, and causes—such as poverty and the pursuit of improved living standards) of global displacement and migration. In order to fulfil UNHCR's mandate to support refugees and others in need of protection within ongoing mass movements of people, he urged better recognition of the mixed nature of many 21st century population flows, often comprising both economic migrants and refugees, asylum seekers and victims of trafficking who required detection and support. It was also acknowledged that conflict and persecution—the traditional reasons for flight—were being increasingly compounded by factors such as environmental degradation and the detrimental effects of climate change. A Dialogue on Protection Challenges, convened by the High Commissioner in December 2007, agreed that the *10 Point Plan* should be elaborated further. Regional activities based on the Plan have been focused on Central America, Western Africa, Eastern Africa and Southern Asia; and on countries along the Eastern and South-Eastern borders of European Union member states.

In 2009 UNHCR launched the first annual Global Needs Assessment (GNA), with the aim of mapping comprehensively the situation and needs of populations of concern falling under the mandate of the Office. The GNA was to represent a blueprint for planning and decision-making for UNHCR, populations of concern, governments and other partners. In 2008 a pilot GNA, undertaken in eight countries, revealed significant unmet protection needs including in education, food security and nutrition, distribution of non-food items, health, access to clean water and sanitation, shelter, and prevention of sexual violence.

UNHCR's global strategic priorities for 2012–13 were: to promote a favourable protection environment; to promote fair protection processes and increase levels of documentation; to ensure security from violence and exploitation; to provide basic needs and services; and to pursue durable solutions.

At December 2011 the total global population of concern to UNHCR, based on provisional figures, amounted to 35.4m. At that time the refugee population world-wide totalled 10.4m., of whom 6.1m. were being assisted by UNHCR. UNHCR was also concerned with some 531,907 recently returned refugees, 15.5m. IDPs, 3.2m. returned IDPs, 3.8m. stateless persons, and 895,284 asylum seekers. UNHCR maintains an online statistical population database.

UNHCR is one of the 10 co-sponsors of UNAIDS.

World Refugee Day, sponsored by UNHCR, is held annually on 20 June.

INTERNATIONAL PROTECTION

As laid down in the Statute of the Office, UNHCR's primary function is to extend international protection to refugees and its second function is to seek durable solutions to their problems. In the exercise of its mandate UNHCR seeks to ensure that refugees and asylum seekers are protected against *refoulement* (forcible return), that they receive asylum, and that they are treated according to internationally recognized standards. UNHCR pursues these objectives by a variety of means that include promoting the conclusion and ratification by states of international conventions for the protection of refugees. UNHCR promotes the adoption of liberal practices of asylum by states, so that refugees and asylum seekers are granted admission, at least on a temporary basis.

The most comprehensive instrument concerning refugees that has been elaborated at the international level is the 1951 United Nations Convention relating to the Status of Refugees. This Convention, the scope of which was extended by a Protocol adopted in 1967, defines the rights and duties of refugees and contains provisions dealing with a variety of matters which affect the day-to-day lives of refugees. The application of the Convention and its Protocol is supervised by UNHCR. The Office has actively encouraged states to accede to the Convention (which had 145 parties at September 2012) and the Protocol (146 parties at September 2012). Important provisions for the treatment of refugees are also contained in a number of instruments adopted at the regional level. These include the 1969 Convention Governing the Specific Aspects of Refugee Problems adopted by the Organization of African Unity (now the African Union—AU) member states in 1969, the European Agreement on the Abolition of Visas for Refugees, and the 1969 American Convention on Human Rights. In October 2009 AU member states adopted the AU Convention for the Protection and Assistance of IDPs in Africa, the first legally binding international treaty providing legal protection and support to internally displaced populations. An increasing number of states have also adopted domestic legislation and/or administrative measures to implement the international instruments, particularly in the field of procedures for the determination of refugee status. UNHCR has sought to address the specific needs of refugee women and children, and has also attempted to deal with the problem of military attacks on refugee camps, by adopting and encouraging the acceptance of a set of principles to ensure the safety of refugees. In recent years it has formulated a strategy designed to address the fundamental causes of refugee flows.

UNHCR has been increasingly concerned with the problem of statelessness, where people have no legal nationality, and promotes new accessions to the 1954 Convention Relating to the Status of Stateless Persons and the 1961 Convention on the Reduction of Statelessness. UNHCR maintains that a significant proportion of the global stateless population has not hitherto been systematically identified. In December 2011 UNHCR organized a ministerial meeting, in Geneva, to commemorate the 60th anniversary of the 1951 Refugee Convention and the 50th anniversary of the 1961 Convention on the Reduction of Statelessness, and to reaffirm commitment to the central role played by these instruments. A number of participants at the meeting made pledges to address statelessness, including improving procedures for identifying stateless people on their territories, enhancing civil registration systems, and raising awareness on the options available to stateless people.

ASSISTANCE ACTIVITIES

The first phase of an assistance operation uses UNHCR's capacity of emergency response. This enables UNHCR to address the immediate needs of refugees at short notice, for example, by employing specially trained emergency teams and maintaining stockpiles of basic equipment, medical aid and materials. A significant proportion of UNHCR expenditure is allocated to the next phase of an operation, providing 'care and maintenance' in stable refugee circumstances. This assistance can take various forms, including the provision of food, shelter, medical care and essential supplies. Also covered in many instances are basic services, including education and counselling.

As far as possible, assistance is geared towards the identification and implementation of durable solutions to refugee problems—this being the second statutory responsibility of UNHCR. Such solutions generally take one of three forms: voluntary repatriation, local integration or resettlement in another country. Where voluntary repatriation, increasingly the preferred solution, is feasible, the Office assists refugees to overcome obstacles preventing their return to their country of origin. This may be done through negotiations with governments involved, or by providing funds either for the physical movement of refugees or for the rehabilitation of returnees once back in their own country. Some 531,907 refugees (of whom 291,223 were UNHCR-assisted) repatriated voluntarily to their home countries in 2011. UNHCR supports the implementation of the Guidance Note on Durable Solutions for Displaced Persons, adopted in 2004 by the UN Development Group.

When voluntary repatriation is not an option, efforts are made to assist refugees to integrate locally and to become self-supporting in their countries of asylum. This may be done either by granting loans to refugees, or by assisting them, through vocational training or in other ways, to learn a skill and to establish themselves in gainful occupations. One major form of assistance to help refugees re-establish themselves outside camps is the provision of housing. In cases where resettlement through emigration is the only viable solution to a refugee problem, UNHCR negotiates with governments in an endeavour to obtain suitable resettlement opportunities, to encourage liberalization of admission criteria and to draw up special immigration schemes. During 2011 an estimated 61,995 refugees were resettled under UNHCR auspices.

UNHCR aims to integrate certain priorities into its programme planning and implementation, as a standard discipline in all phases of assistance. The considerations include awareness of specific problems confronting refugee women, the needs of refugee children, the environmental impact of refugee programmes and long-term development objectives. A Policy Development and Evaluation Service reviews systematically UNHCR's operational effectiveness.

SUB-SAHARAN AFRICA

UNHCR has provided assistance to refugees and internally displaced populations in many parts of the continent where civil conflict, violations of human rights, drought, famine or environmental degradation have forced people to flee their home regions. The majority of African refugees and returnees are located in countries that are themselves suffering major economic problems and are thus unable to provide the basic requirements of the uprooted people. In March 2004 a UNHCR-sponsored Dialogue on Voluntary Repatriation and Sustainable Reintegration in Africa endorsed the creation of an international working group—comprising African Governments, UN agencies, the AU and other partners—to support the return and sustainable reintegration of refugees in several African countries, including Angola, Burundi, the Democratic Republic of the Congo (DRC), Eritrea, Liberia, Rwanda, Sierra Leone, Somalia and Sudan. At 31 December 2011 there were an estimated 13.1m. people of concern to UNHCR in sub-Saharan Africa.

The Horn of Africa, afflicted by famine and long-term internal conflict, has suffered large-scale population movements in recent decades. During 1992–mid-2006 more than 1m. Somalis (of whom about 485,000 received UNHCR assistance) returned to their country, having sought sanctuary in neighbouring states following the January 1991 overthrow of the former Somali president Siad Barre. The humanitarian situation in Somalia has remained extremely insecure. There was, at 31 December 2011, a Somalian IDP population totalling an estimated 1.4m. Severe food insecurity in southern areas of Somalia that escalated in 2011—with a state of famine officially declared in two areas from July 2011–early February 2012—exacerbated further the ongoing humanitarian crisis in that country. At September 2011 3.7m. Somalis were estimated to be food-insecure, and many Somali rural households were reported to have migrated in search of food and support towards the conflict-affected Somali capital, Mogadishu, and into neighbouring countries. At that time most of Somalia was designated by the UN at security level 5 ('high'), with Mogadishu and other south-central areas at level 6 ('extreme insecurity'): therefore there was very limited access for humanitarian workers. Following the July 2011 famine declaration UNHCR distributed more than 27,000 emergency assistance packages to 174,000 IDPs in southern Somalia and Mogadishu, and supported nearly 270,000 IDPs throughout the country through the provision of emergency relief items such as blankets, mattresses, kitchen sets, and plastic sheeting. UNHCR maintains a presence in Puntland and in Somaliland, but directs its Somalia programme from Nairobi, Kenya. UNHCR is responsible for co-ordinating the UN's emergency shelter and protection clusters in Somalia, and, with OCHA, co-leads the Puntland IDP Task Force, established in late 2010 with the aim of devising a comprehensive strategy aimed at improving the situation of local IDPs. The Office's priorities within Somalia for 2012 were to protect people of concern within larger mixed migratory flows; to prioritize the most vulnerable asylum seekers in need of resettlement; to provide subsistence allowances to people of concern with urgent needs; to support initiatives aimed at promoting self-reliance and livelihood opportunities; to facilitate access to schools and health facilities; and to reduce xenophobia in host communities towards refugees and asylum seekers.

There was at 31 December 2011 an estimated total Somali refugee population of 1.1m., of whom 517,666 were in Kenya (all assisted by UNHCR) and 204,685 in Yemen (also all UNHCR-assisted). During 2007 Kenya enacted a Refugee Act, in accordance with which it was to assume a more active role in managing the registration and status determination of refugees. In November 2010 UNHCR appealed to the Kenyan authorities to cease the ongoing forcible return to Somalia of up to 8,000 Somali refugees accommodated hitherto in the Mandera camp in northeast Kenya. By September 2012 some 470,000 Somali refugees were accommodated at northeast Kenya's Dadaab complex of camps, comprising the Hagadera, Dagahaley, Ifo, Ifo East, Ifo West and Kambioos camps; Hagadera (with around 135,000 Somali residents) was at that time the largest refugee camp in the world. During September 2012 an outbreak of acute jaundice occurred across all the Dadaab camps. UNHCR continued to protect and assist Somalian refugees during 2012, while also considering possibilities for voluntary repatriation, local integration and resettlement. There were an estimated 300,000 Kenyan IDPs at 31 December 2011.

At 31 December 2011 an estimated 500,014 Sudanese were exiled as refugees, mainly in Chad, Uganda, Kenya, and Ethiopia, owing to a history of civil unrest in southern Sudan and the emergence in early 2003 of a new conflict zone in the western Sudanese province of Darfur (see below). The Ugandan Government, hosting an estimated 18,268 Sudanese refugees at end-2011 (all UNHCR-assisted), has provided new resettlement sites and, jointly with UNHCR and other partners, has developed a Self-Reliance Strategy, which envisages achieving self-sufficiency for the long-term refugee population through integrating services for refugees into existing local structures. In 2006 the Ugandan Government adopted a new Refugee Act that included gender-based persecution as grounds for granting refugee status. At end-2011 there were some 27,776 IDPs in Uganda, and some 95,822 returned Ugandan IDPs. In February 2006 UNHCR and Sudan signed tripartite agreements with Ethiopia, the DRC and the Central African Republic to provide a legal framework for the repatriation of Sudanese refugees remaining in those countries. From 2008 violent attacks committed by Ugandan Lord's Resistance Army rebels on communities in the southern Sudan-DRC-Central African Republic (CAR) border region displaced numerous southern Sudanese people, and forced thousands of displaced DRC villagers northwards into Sudan. At 31 December 2011 some 100,464 Eritreans were sheltering in Sudan, of whom 68,891 were receiving UNHCR assistance.

In August 2011, following the independence in July of South Sudan, the Sudanese Government amended legislation to deprive individuals who acquired South Sudan nationality of Sudanese citizenship. UNHCR expressed concern over the implications of this for significant numbers of people of mixed Sudanese/South Sudanese origin living in border areas. UNHCR's activities in South Sudan in 2012 were to focus on strengthening relevant institutional and legal frameworks; combating sexual and gender-based violence; protecting people at risk of statelessness; and supporting refugees, returnees, IDPs and host communities by targeting assistance at vulnerable families such as female-headed households, and also through the implementation of livelihoods programmes and QIPs. Mounting tensions in the first half of 2012 in disputed border areas between Sudan and South Sudan caused increasing numbers of Sudanese to flee to South Sudan and to Ethiopia. In late June 2012 UNHCR appealed urgently for extra resources to meet an estimated funding requirement of US $219m. to assist some 162,500 Sudanese refugees in South Sudan and 36,500 in Ethiopia.

From April 2003 more than 200,000 refugees from Sudan's western Darfur region sought shelter across the Sudan-Chad border, having fled an alleged campaign of killing, rapes and destruction of property conducted by pro-government militias against the indigenous population. In addition, 2m.–3m. people became displaced within Darfur itself. The Office organized airlifts of basic household items to the camps, aimed to improve and expand refugees' access to sanitation, healthcare and education, to manage supplementary and therapeutic feeding facilities in order to combat widespread malnutrition, to provide psychosocial support to traumatized refugees, and to promote training and livelihood programmes. The Chad-Darfur operation has been hampered by severe water shortages resulting from the arid environment of the encampment areas, necessitating costly UNHCR deliveries of stored water, and by intense insecurity.

A significant deterioration from 2006 in the security situation in the eastern areas of Chad bordering Darfur (where resources were already stretched to the limit), as well as in Darfur itself, led to further population displacement in the region, including the displacement of significant numbers of Chadians. At January 2012 some 39,500 Chadian refugees and Chadians in refugee-like situations were sheltering inside Darfur (of whom just under one-half were UNHCR-assisted), and there were also around 130,000 Chadian IDPs who had fled inwards from the Chad-Sudan border region. At end-December 2011 Chad was hosting 298,391 refugees from Darfur, accommodated in 12 UNHCR camps. UNHCR established a presence within western Darfur in June 2004, and in 2012 the Office was providing protection assistance to around 2.7m. displaced and returned Darfurians, as well as Chadian refugees, in the region. Following the establishment of the AU/UN Hybrid Operation in Darfur (UNAMID) in December 2007, UNHCR opened a liaison office near the UNAMID base in northern Darfur. UNHCR teams have undertaken efforts to train Sudanese managers of camps in Darfur in the areas of protection and human rights. The Office has also established in the area a number of women's centres providing support to survivors of sexual violence, and several centres for IDP youths, as well as rehabilitating conflict-damaged schools. In 2012 a gradual shift in programming from a primarily protection-oriented, camp-based approach to pursuing durable solutions was under way. A continuing volatile security situation in the CAR from 2003 resulted in significant population displacement into southern border areas of Chad; by 2012 more than 70,000 CAR refugees were accommodated by UNHCR in camps there, and at 31 December 2011 there were an estimated 105,206 IDPs inside the CAR.

UNHCR's activities in assisting refugees in West Africa have included a focus on the prevention of sexual and gender-based violence in refugee camps—a regional action plan to combat such violence was initiated in 2002—and collaboration with other agencies to ensure continuity between initial humanitarian assistance and long-term development support. UNHCR provided assistance to 120,000 people displaced by the extreme insecurity that developed in Côte d'Ivoire from September 2002. About 25,000 Côte d'Ivoire refugees fled to southern Liberia, and others sought shelter in Ghana, Guinea and Mali. In addition, between November and January 2003 an estimated 40,000 Liberian refugees in Côte d'Ivoire repatriated, in both spontaneous and partly UNHCR-assisted movements, having suffered harassment since the onset of the conflict. UNHCR initiated a number of QIPs aimed at rehabilitating the infrastructure of communities that were to receive returned Côte d'Ivoire refugees. At 31 December 2011 there were 466,808 IDPs in that country. As a consequence of unrest that erupted in Côte d'Ivoire following a disputed presidential election held in October–November 2010, an estimated 200,000 people became displaced from their homes in western Côte d'Ivoire, and some 150,000 Ivorian nationals fled to Liberia, during December 2010–April 2011. In response to the influx of Côte d'Ivoire refugees into Liberia, UNHCR facilitated the registration of the new refugees and mobilized the delivery of food aid and non-food relief items, as well as material for constructing a campsite. UNHCR planned to support some 55,000 Ivorian refugee returns, and 72,000 IDP returns in Côte d'Ivoire, during 2012.

Violent unrest that erupted in northern Mali in mid-January 2012 had led, by September, to the internal displacement of an estimated 186,000 people (residing in spontaneous settlements or with host communities), and an influx of nearly 280,000 Malian refugees into neighbouring Mauritania (108,953), Burkina Faso (107,929), and Niger (61,406). UNHCR deployed emergency teams to the neighbouring countries, conducted rapid needs assessments, and provided the refugees with family tents and other non-food items. UNHCR was seeking funding of US $153.7m. to fund its protection of the Malian refugees in 2012, in co-ordination with other agencies.

Since 1993 the Great Lakes region of central Africa has experienced massive population displacement, causing immense operational challenges and demands on the resources of international humanitarian and relief agencies. During the late 1990s UNHCR resolved to work, in co-operation with UNDP and WFP, to rehabilitate areas previously inhabited by refugees in central African countries of asylum and undertook to repair roads, bridges and other essential transport infrastructure, improve water and sanitation facilities, and strengthen the education sector. However, the political stability of the Great Lakes region remained extremely uncertain, and, from August 1998, DRC government forces and rebels became involved in a civil war in which the militaries of several regional governments were also implicated. From late 1998 substantial numbers of DRC nationals fled to neighbouring countries (mainly Tanzania and Zambia) or were displaced within the DRC. Meanwhile, the DRC, in turn, was hosting a significant refugee population. In view of the conclusion, in December 2002, of a peace agreement providing for the staging of elections in the DRC after a transition period of 24 months, UNHCR planned for eventual mass refugee returns. The Office, in co-operation with other UN agencies, was to assist efforts to demobilize, disarm and repatriate former combatants. Owing to incessant rebel activity, insecurity continued to prevail, however, during 2003–12, in north-eastern areas of the DRC, resulting in further population displacements. During 2012 militants of the Kivu-based 23 March Movement (known as 'M23') became increasingly active in northeastern DRC, clashing with government forces and causing mass population displacement, and, in late May, UNHCR classified its eastern DRC operation as an emergency. By September it was reported that some 390,000 people had been displaced from their homes in North and South Kivu, and that more than 60,000 people had fled that region into neighbouring Rwanda and Uganda. At that time UNHCR was managing some 31 camps in North Kivu that were hosting more than 127,000 new IDPs; other IDPs were being accommodated by host families. In September 2005 UNHCR and the DRC and Tanzanian Governments signed a tripartite agreement on facilitating refugee returns of DRC refugees from Tanzania, and, during 2005–early 2012 UNHCR assisted 60,000 such returns. The status of Tanzania's Nyaragusu camp, sheltering mainly refugees from the DRC, was under review in 2012. A tripartite agreement on assistance was concluded by the Burundian and Tanzanian Governments and UNHCR in August 2003. In April 2010 the UN High Commissioner for Refugees expressed gratitude to the Tanzanian authorities for offering citizenship to 162,000 long-standing Burundian refugees. In February 2012 the Burundi-Tanzania-UNHCR tripartite commission confirmed that Tanzania's Mtabila camp, hosting 38,378 Burundian refugees, would close at the end of 2012, and that its residents would be repatriated to Burundi during April–November. UNHCR concluded similar tripartite accords in 2003 with the Rwandan Government and other states hosting Rwandan refugees, paving the way subsequently for significant voluntary refugee returns to Rwanda. In 2011 UNHCR assisted a total of 8,254 refugee returns to that country. The major populations of concern to UNHCR in the Great Lakes region at 31 December 2011 were, provisionally, as follows: 1.7m. IDPs, 822,688 returned IDPs and 152,749 refugees in the DRC; 78,796 IDPs in Burundi; 55,325 refugees in Rwanda; and a refugee population of 131,243 in Tanzania, very significantly reduced from 602,088 at end-2004. At the end of 2011 some 131,648 DRC refugees (all of whom were UNHCR-assisted) were sheltering in the Republic of the Congo. Long-standing DRC refugees in the Republic of the Congo are largely self-sufficient, with many refugees working as farmers and fishermen; the Office has aimed to promote the local integration of those unwilling to return to the DRC.

In September 2010 a regional conference on refugee protection and international migration, convened in Dar es Salaam, Tanzania, adopted an action plan to address mixed movements and irregular migration from eastern Africa, the Horn of Africa and the Great Lakes region to southern Africa; this was being implemented during 2011–12.

It was estimated that in all more than 4.3m. Angolans were displaced from their homes during the 1980s and 1990s, owing to long-term civil conflict. Following the signing of the Luanda Peace Agreement in April 2002 between the Angolan Government and rebels of the União National para a Independência Total de Angola, UNHCR made preparations for the voluntary repatriation of a projected 400,000 Angolan refugees sheltering elsewhere in southern Africa. By the end of 2004 the Office had rehabilitated the nine main repatriation corridors into Angola, and by the end of 2005 a total of nearly 4.4m. IDPs, refugees and demobilized fighters had reportedly returned home. UNHCR has assisted the Angolan Government with the development of a Sustainable Reintegration Initiative for returned refugees. From May 2009–early 2011 Angola forcibly returned home some 160,000 DRC refugees. In response to the initial forced repatriations, some 51,000 Angolan refugees were expelled from the DRC to Angola during 2009. An Angola-DRC agreement to suspend the mutual expulsions and enter into consultations, concluded in October 2009, was subsequently not adhered to by the Angolan authorities. At 31 December 2011 an estimated 128,664 Angolans were still sheltering in neighbouring countries, including 78,144 in the DRC and 23,500 in Zambia. HIV/AIDS- and mine-awareness training have been made available by UNHCR at refugee reception centres.

Zimbabwe was the country of origin of the largest number of asylum-seekers world-wide in 2011, with 53,231 new applications made by Zimbabwean nationals in that year.

CO-OPERATION WITH OTHER ORGANIZATIONS

UNHCR works closely with other UN agencies, intergovernmental organizations and non-governmental organizations (NGOs) to increase the scope and effectiveness of its operations. Within the UN system UNHCR co-operates, principally, with the WFP in the distribution of food aid, UNICEF and WHO in the provision of family welfare and child immunization programmes, OCHA in the delivery of emergency humanitarian relief, UNDP in development-related activities and the preparation of guidelines for the continuum of emergency assistance to development programmes, and the Office of the UN High Commissioner for Human Rights. UNHCR also has close working relationships with the International Federation of Red

Cross and Red Crescent Societies and the International Organization for Migration. UNHCR planned to engage with nearly 700 NGOs in 2012–13. In recent years UNHCR has pursued a strategy to engage private sector businesses in supporting its activities through the provision of donations (cash contributions and 'in kind'), of loaned expertise, and of marketing related to designated causes.

TRAINING

UNHCR organizes training programmes and workshops to enhance the capabilities of field workers and non-UNHCR staff, in the following areas: the identification and registration of refugees; people-orientated planning; resettlement procedures and policies; emergency response and management; security awareness; stress management; and the dissemination of information through the electronic media.

Finance

The United Nations' regular budget finances a proportion of UNHCR's administrative expenditure. The majority of UNHCR's programme expenditure (about 98%) is funded by voluntary contributions, mainly from governments. The Private Sector and Public Affairs Service aims to increase funding from non-governmental donor sources, for example by developing partnerships with foundations and corporations. Following approval of the Unified Annual Programme Budget any subsequently identified requirements are managed in the form of Supplementary Programmes, financed by separate appeals. UNHCR's projected funding requirements for 2012 totalled US $3,590.0m.

Publications

Global Trends (annually).

Refugees (quarterly, in English, French, German, Italian, Japanese and Spanish).

Refugee Resettlement: An International Handbook to Guide Reception and Integration.

Refugee Survey Quarterly.

Refworld (annually).

Sexual and Gender-based Violence Against Refugees, Returnees and Displaced Persons: Guidelines for Prevention and Response.

The State of the World's Refugees (every 2 years).

Statistical Yearbook (annually).

UNHCR Handbook for Emergencies.

Press releases, reports.

Statistics

PERSONS OF CONCERN TO UNHCR IN AFRICA SOUTH OF THE SAHARA*

('000 persons, at 31 December 2011, provisional figures)

Host Country	Refugees†	Asylum seekers	Returnees	Others of concern‡
Burundi	35.7	10.1	4.4	80.1
Cameroon	100.4	3.3	—	—
CAR	16.7	2.4	9.0	171.8
Chad	366.5	0.2	0.1	131.0
DRC	152.7	1.1	21.1	2,532.0
Congo, Rep.	141.2	3.0	0.1	0.3
Côte d'Ivoire	24.2	0.7	135.2	594.4
Ethiopia	288.8	1.3	0.0	—
Kenya	566.5	35.3	0.1	320.0
Somalia	2.1	6.0	0.2	1,356.8
South Africa	57.9	219.4	—	—
South Sudan	105.0	0.1	1.0	560.2
Sudan	139.4	6.9	50.1	2,701.8
Tanzania	131.2	0.7	—	162.3
Uganda	139.4	23.5	0.0	125.6

* Figures are provided mostly by governments, based on their own records and methods of estimations. Countries with fewer than 100,000 persons of concern to UNHCR are not listed.

† Includes persons in refugee-like situations.

‡ Mainly internally displaced persons (IDPs) or recently-returned IDPs.

United Nations Peace-keeping

Address: Department of Peace-keeping Operations, Room S-3727-B, United Nations, New York, NY 10017, USA.

Telephone: (212) 963-8077; **fax:** (212) 963-9222; **internet:** www.un.org/Depts/dpko/.

United Nations peace-keeping operations have been conceived as instruments of conflict control. The UN has used these operations in various conflicts, with the consent of the parties involved, to maintain international peace and security, without prejudice to the positions or claims of parties, in order to facilitate the search for political settlements through peaceful means such as mediation and the good offices of the UN Secretary-General. Each operation is established with a specific mandate, which requires periodic review by the UN Security Council. In 1988 the United Nations Peace-keeping Forces were awarded the Nobel Peace Prize.

United Nations peace-keeping operations fall into two categories: peace-keeping forces and observer missions. Peace-keeping forces are composed of contingents of military and civilian personnel, made available by member states. These forces assist in preventing the recurrence of fighting, restoring and maintaining peace, and promoting a return to normal conditions. To this end, peace-keeping forces are authorized as necessary to undertake negotiations, persuasion, observation and fact-finding. They conduct patrols and interpose physically between the opposing parties. Peace-keeping forces are permitted to use their weapons only in self-defence.

Military observer missions are composed of officers (usually unarmed), who are made available, on the Secretary-General's request, by member states. A mission's function is to observe and report to the Secretary-General (who, in turn, informs the Security Council) on the maintenance of a cease-fire, to investigate violations and to do what it can to improve the situation. Peace-keeping forces and observer missions must at all times maintain complete impartiality and avoid any action that might affect the claims or positions of the parties.

The UN's peace-keeping forces and observer missions are financed in most cases by assessed contributions from member states of the organization. In recent years a significant expansion in the UN's peace-keeping activities has been accompanied by a perpetual financial crisis within the organization, as a result of the increased financial burden and some member states' delaying payment. At 31 August 2012 outstanding assessed contributions to the peace-keeping budget amounted to some US $3,090m.

By September 2012 the UN had deployed a total of 67 peace-keeping operations, of which 13 were authorized in the period 1948–88 and 54 since 1988. At 31 August 2012 115 countries were contributing some 96,305 uniformed personnel to 15 ongoing operations, of whom 80,833 were peace-keeping troops, 13,485 police and 1,987 military observers.

AFRICAN UNION (AU)/UN HYBRID OPERATION IN DARFUR—UNAMID

Address: El Fasher, Sudan.

Acting Joint AU-UN Special Representative: AÏCHATOU MINDAOUDOU SOULEYMANE (Niger).

Force Commander: Lt-Gen. PATRICK NYAMVUMBA (Rwanda).

Police Commissioner: JAMES OPPONG-BOANUH (Ghana).

Establishment and Mandate: UNAMID was established by a resolution of the UN Security Council in July 2007, mandated to take necessary action to support the implementation and verification of the Darfur Peace Agreement signed in May 2006 by the Sudanese Government and a rebel faction in Darfur, southern Sudan. UNAMID was also mandated to protect civilians, to provide security for humanitarian assistance, to support an inclusive political process, to contribute to the promotion of human rights and rule of law, and to monitor and report on the situation along the borders with Chad and the Central African Republic. An AU-UN Joint Mediation Support Team for Darfur (JMST) and a Tripartite Committee on UNAMID (including representatives of the UN, AU and Government of Sudan) meet periodically. UNAMID's mandate has subsequently been renewed on an annual basis, most recently until 31 July 2013.

Activities, 2007–10: UNAMID assumed command of the AU Mission in Sudan (AMIS), comprising 10 battalions, in December 2007. In February 2008 UNAMID's Joint Special Representative signed a status of forces agreement with the minister of foreign affairs of Sudan, covering logistical aspects of the mission. In March UNAMID police units conducted their first confidence-building patrols in areas under rebel control in northern Darfur. In May UNAMID's Force Commander condemned aerial attacks against villages in northern Darfur, allegedly by Sudanese forces. Throughout 2008 an estimated 317,000 civilians were newly displaced from their homes in Darfur. A delegation of the UN Security Council visited the region in June and expressed concern at the mission's lack of adequate equipment and troop levels. In July 2008 the UN designated Darfur a 'security phase four' area (a designation that permits the UN to relocate staff temporarily pending an improvement in the security situation). At the end of June 2008 a new joint AU-UN Chief Mediator was appointed, based at UNAMID headquarters in El Fasher. A Joint Support Co-ordination Mechanism (JSCM) Office in Addis Ababa, Ethiopia, comprising liaison officers and communications equipment, was established in November to ensure effective consultation between the UN and AU headquarters. In October 2008 the UN Secretary-General reported that little progress had been achieved in the implementation of the 2006 Darfur Peace Agreement, that violent unrest continued to prevail, and that the conditions in Darfur were not conducive to undertaking a successful peace-keeping operation. From late 2008 activities were undertaken to bring the 10 former AMIS battalions up to full strength in terms of military personnel and equipment. Nevertheless, the Secretary-General reported in February 2009 (at which time the designated security level in Darfur remained at phase four) that UNAMID's operational capabilities continued to be limited by lack of critical and key military enabling equipment, logistical constraints, and the reluctance of many troop- and police-contributing countries to deploy to it well-trained personnel and efficient contingent-owned equipment. In addition, there was concern at restrictions on the movement of troops and on the issuing of visa and vehicle licence applications that were being imposed by the Sudanese authorities. In January 2009 UNAMID, jointly with OHCHR, issued a public report on a law enforcement operation by the Sudan Government in August 2008 against targets in Kalma camp for internally displaced persons (IDPs) in southern Darfur, that had resulted in 33 civilian fatalities and 108 civilian injuries; the report found that the use of force had been indiscriminate and disproportionate, in violation of international law. UNAMID has provided a security presence around Kalma camp. In early 2009 an escalation of violence in the Mahajeriya region of southern Darfur resulted in the displacement of some 46,000 people, the majority of whom moved to the Zam Zam refugee camp near El Fasher. UNAMID undertook to deliver daily water supplies, as well as to conduct protection patrols in and around the camp. The mission also began construction of a community policy centre in the camp. UNAMID provided security and other logistical support to help to ensure the continued distribution of humanitarian assistance following the expulsion from the country, in March, of 13 international non-governmental organizations (NGOs) and the dissolution of three national NGOs by the Sudanese authorities (who claimed that they had collaborated with investigations being conducted by the International Criminal Court). From late 2009 UNAMID provided logistical support to the Government's disarmament, demobilization and rehabilitation programme. In January 2010 the UN Secretary-General reported that the capability of UNAMID batallions in Darfur continued to be a cause of concern, with a number of units not having sufficient major equipment. At that time UNAMID undertook geophysical investigations to locate new water sources around mission camps. UNAMID assisted the former UN Mission in Sudan and the Sudanese authorities with transporting electoral materials to remote locations and with training more than 10,000 local police officers in preparation for the municipal, legislative and presidential elections that were held in April.

In March 2009 an AU High-Level Panel on Darfur (AUPD), led by the former President of South Africa, Thabo Mbeki, was established to address means of securing peace, justice, and reconciliation in Darfur. The panel conducted a series of hearings in Sudan over subsequent months, and, in October, issued a report of its findings and recommendations; a key recommendation was the creation of a hybrid court, comprising both AU and Sudanese judges, to prosecute crimes against humanity committed in Darfur. During October a new AU High-Level Implementation Panel (AUHIP) on Sudan was established, with a mandate to support the implementation of all AUPD recommendations, and to assist the relevant Sudanese parties with the implementation of a Comprehensive Peace Agreement (CPA) concluded in January 2005 (see under UNISFA). In November 2009 an inaugural conference of Darfurian civil society organizations was convened, in Doha, Qatar, in order to strengthen and to further political negotiations to achieve a peace settlement. A second conference was held in July 2010. In February and March 2010, respectively, two rebel groupings that had been operating in Darfur signed framework agreements with the Sudanese Government aimed at resolving the conflict; however, consequent negotiations with the largest rebel group, aimed at securing a cease-fire, stalled in May. During that month violent unrest in Darfur caused nearly 600 fatalities, the highest number since the deployment of the mission. UNAMID strengthened security measures and provided additional medical care in some of the larger IDP camps where inter-tribal conflict was becoming a major security concern. In late July 7,000 people in Kalma camp sought refuge at the UNAMID Community Policing Centre. In the following month UNAMID and the Sudanese Government agreed to establish a joint committee to resolve problems in Kalma, which hosted some 82,000 IDPs. In late August a consultative meeting of representatives of UNAMID, the AU, the USA and the Sudanese President agreed that UNAMID and the Sudanese Government would work closely together to improve the security situation in Darfur and to support stabilization and development of the region. The UN Secretary-General welcomed efforts by the Sudanese authorities to investigate, and restore order in the aftermath of, an attack launched in early September by armed assailants targeting local men attending the market in the Northern Darfur village of Tabarat, causing some 37 fatalities and precipitating the displacement of around 3,000 villagers.

2011–12: In early April 2011 the Sudanese National Electoral Commission initiated preparations for a referendum to be held on the future status of Darfur, and requested material and technical assistance from UNAMID. Towards the end of April the JMST presented a draft peace agreement to the Sudan Government and rebel groupings. The draft agreement was considered by an All-Darfur Stakeholders' Conference, convened, with support from UNAMID, in Doha, Qatar, in late May; participants in the Conference endorsed a communiqué providing for the draft document (the Doha Document for Peace in Darfur—DDPD) to form the basis for achieving a permanent cease-fire and comprehensive Darfurian peace settlement. The DDPD addressed issues including power sharing, wealth sharing, human rights, justice and reconciliation, compensation, returns, and internal dialogue, and provided for the establishment of a Cease-fire Commission, a Darfur Regional Authority, and for a Darfuri to be appointed as the second Vice-President of Sudan. In June the UN Secretary-General welcomed the DDPD as the basis for resolving the Darfur conflict. In mid-July the Sudanese Government and the 'Liberation and Justice Movement', an alliance of rebel groupings, signed an accord on the adoption of the DDPD. Shortly afterwards the two sides also signed a Protocol on the Political Participation of the Liberation and Justice Movement and Integration of its Forces. Meanwhile, UNAMID, a participant in the DDPD Implementation Follow-on Commission, prepared, with civil society representatives, a plan for the dissemination throughout Darfur of information on the Document. In August UNAMID chaired the first meeting of the Cease-Fire Commission established under the provisions of the DDPD.

During late May–early June 2011 UNAMID intervened to assist 11 IDPs at Hassa Hissa camp who had been detained by a gang of youths also sheltering there; although the detainees were eventually released, it was reported in June that 11 IDPs in the area had been killed. At the beginning of May UNAMID and humanitarian agencies active in Darfur launched Operation Spring Basket, aimed at enhancing access to remote parts of Darfur and thereby providing humanitarian aid to around 400,000 beneficiaries. UNAMID continued to implement Quick Impact Projects in Darfur, in support of the education sector, infrastructure and local facilities. UNAMID, where requested, provides logistical and security support to humanitarian agencies assisting returnees to West Darfur. In response to reported cases of crop destruction by nomads in West Darfur, and complaints that returnees from Chad were also contributing to crop destruction, UNAMID liaised in the second half of 2011 with local crop protection committees. The formation in 2011 of a subcommittee comprising UNAMID and Sudanese government security entities led to a significant decrease in restrictions on the movements of UNAMID security patrols in the latter part of the year. There were continued reports of criminal attacks on UN personnel, including the theft of UNAMID vehicles, during 2008–12.

During the first half of 2012 UNAMID undertook 26,995 ground patrols. In early March UNAMID completed an operation to verify positions held by former rebels; information acquired during the verification operation was to be used by the Ceasefire Commission in disarmament, demobilization, and reintegration/integration planning. In June UNAMID and the DDPD signatories agreed to revise the Document's schedule of implementation (extending by one year all previously determined deadlines). During April–June UNAMID provided technical and logistical support towards the convening of 55 workshops aimed at widely disseminating the Doha Document. In July, on the basis of recommendations made by the UN Secretary-General, the Security Council authorized a reconfiguration of UNAMID, entailing a reduction in the mission's numbers to be implemented over a period of 12–18 months. The largest UNAMID presence was to be confined henceforth to areas of Darfur with the highest risk of insecurity. The mission was to make more frequent and longer patrols, with expanded use of temporary operating bases, and was to be more rapidly deployable. The Security Council demanded that all parties to the conflict in Darfur immediately cease acts of violence, and effect a permanent cease-fire and comprehensive peace settlement based on the DDPD.

Operational Strength: From July 2007 UNAMID's authorized strength was set at 19,555 military personnel and 6,432 police; in July 2012 this was reduced to 16,200 military personnel and 4,690 police, to be implemented over 12–18 months. The mission's operational strength at 31 August 2012 comprised 16,521 troops, 265 military observers and 4,821 police (in formed units, each comprising up to 140 personnel); the mission was supported by 452 UN Volunteers and (at 31 July) by 1,096 international civilian personnel and 2,912 local civilian staff.

Finance: The budget for UNAMID amounted to US $1,511.9m. for the period 1 July 2012–30 June 2013, funded from a Special Account comprising assessed contributions from UN member states.

UNITED NATIONS INTERIM SECURITY FORCE FOR ABYEI—UNISFA

Address: Abyei Town, Sudan.

Head of Mission and Force Commander: Lt-Gen. TADESSE WEREDE TESFAY (Ethiopia).

Establishment and Mandate: Following the final conclusion in January 2005 of a Comprehensive Peace Agreement (CPA)—including a Protocol on the Resolution of the Conflict in Abyei Area (the 'Abyei Protocol'), signed in May 2004—between the Sudan Government and opposition Sudan People's Liberation Movement (SPLM), ongoing contention over the competing claims to land ownership in, and the future status of, Abyei presented an impediment to the implementation of the Agreement and to the advancement of stability in the region. From early January 2011, prior to the referendum held in that month on self-determination for South Sudan, heightened tensions and outbreaks of violence were reported in the disputed Abyei region (located at Sudan's border with South Sudan—which eventually gained independence on 9 July 2011). In mid-January and early March the parties to the Comprehensive Peace Agreement agreed on temporary security arrangements for the Abyei region; the ongoing insecurity, however, deteriorated further. Immediately prior to the establishment of UNISFA unrest in Abyei had escalated significantly, displacing around 113,000 people, including most of the civilian inhabitants of the town of Abyei. The 'Temporary Arrangements for the Administration and Security of the Abyei Area'—an accord adopted in mid-June 2011 by the Sudanese Government and rebels, governing the withdrawal of their respective forces from Abyei—facilitated the deployment of the peace-keeping operation. The Temporary Arrangements provided for the establishment of an Abyei Area Administration, to be administered jointly by an SPLM-nominated Chief Administrator and a Government-nominated Deputy, which was mainly to exercise powers determined in the Abyei Protocol to the CPA; responsibility for supervising security and stability, however, was transferred by the Temporary Arrangements to a newly-established Abyei Joint Oversight Committee, comprising members from each party to the conflict, as well as to an AU facilitator.

UNISFA was established by UN Security Resolution 1990 on 27 June 2011, with an initial mandated term of six months. The Force is mandated to protect civilians and humanitarian personnel in Abyei; to facilitate the free movement of humanitarian aid; to monitor and verify the redeployment of government and rebel forces from the Abyei Area; to participate in relevant Abyei Area bodies; to provide demining assistance and advice on technical matters; to strengthen the capacity of the Abyei Police Service; and, as necessary, to provide—in co-operation with the Abyei Police Service—security for the regional oil infrastructure. In December 2011 the UN Security Council expanded UNISFA's mandate to include assisting all parties in ensuring the observance of the Safe Demilitarized Border Zone, and advising, and supporting the operational activities of, the Joint Border Verification and Monitoring Mechanism (the creation of the Zone and Mechanism having been outlined in Agreements concluded in June 2011, see below); facilitating liaison between the parties; and supporting the parties, when requested, in developing effective bilateral management mechanisms along the border. Later in December 2011 the mandate of the mission was extended for a period of five months, and, in May 2012, a further extension of the mandate was authorized, by six months.

Activities: Under the auspices of the 'Friends of Abyei', chaired by the Resident Co-ordinator in Sudan, a planning team, comprising representatives of UN agencies, donor and INGOs, developed during 2011 a humanitarian joint recovery programming strategy for Abyei; it was envisaged that people displaced by the violence in Abyei would only be returned there following the planned withdrawal of forces and the full deployment of UNISFA. At the end of June 2011 the parties to the conflict in Abyei signed an Agreement on Border Security, in which they reaffirmed commitment to a Joint Political and Security Mechanism, established under an agreement concluded in December 2010; and provided for the establishment of a Safe Demilitarized Border Zone, and Joint Border Verification and Monitoring Mechanism, pending the resolution of the status of disputed areas; UNISFA was mandated from December 2011 to provide force protection for Monitoring Mechanism. Since its inauguration UNISFA has conducted regular air and ground patrols, and has established permanent operating bases in Abyei Town, Agok, and Diffra. In February 2012 South Sudan and Sudan signed a Memorandum of Understanding on non-aggression and co-operation, committing each state to respecting the other's sovereignty and territorial integrity. In the following month the UN Secretary-General reported that the security situation in Abyei remained tense, owing to the continued presence—in violation of the June 2011 Agreement on Border Security—of unauthorized Sudanese armed forces, South Sudanese police, and rebels in the area; as well as owing to ongoing large-scale nomadic migration, and IDP returns. In April 2012, as tensions continued and violent clashes mounted, the UN Security Council demanded that Sudan and South Sudan redeploy their forces from Abyei; that the two sides withdraw forces from their joint border and cease escalating cross-border violence with immediate effect, with the support of UNISFA and through the establishment of a demilitarized border zone; that Sudanese rebels should vacate oil-fields in Heglig (Sudan); that Sudan should cease aerial bombardments of South Sudan; and that a summit should be convened between the two states to resolve outstanding concerns. During April the African Union High-Level Implementation Panel (AUHIP) on Sudan (established in October 2009 and mandated to assist the relevant Sudanese parties with the implementation of the January 2005 CPA), presented to both parties a draft Joint Decision for Reduction of Tension, providing for the immediate cessation of hostilities between the two states, and the withdrawal of armed forces of each state from the territory of the other. At the end of April 2012 and in early May, respectively, South Sudan and Sudan agreed to abide by a seven-point Roadmap for Action by Sudan and South Sudan, approved in late April by the African Union (AU) Peace and Security Council. The AU Roadmap provided for: (i) the immediate cessation of all hostilities; (ii) the unconditional withdrawal of all armed forces to their respective sides of the border; (iii) the activation, within one week from the adoption of the Roadmap, of all necessary border security mechanisms; (iv) cessation of harbouring of, and support to, rebel groups active against the other state; (v) the activation of an ad hoc Committee to investigate complaints made by one party against the other; (vi) immediate cessation of hostile propaganda and inflammatory statements in the media, and against property, cultural and religious symbols belonging to the nationals of the other state; and (vii) implementation of pending aspects of the June 2011 Temporary Arrangements for the Administration and Security of the Abyei Area, most particularly the redeployment of all Sudanese and South Sudanese forces out of Abyei. In accordance with its commitment to the Roadmap, South Sudan withdrew its forces from Abyei in early May 2012, with logistical support and protection from UNISFA; and, also with mission assistance, Sudan withdrew its military and most police from the area at, respectively, the end of May and beginning of June. However, by September a presence of up to 150 Sudanese police, equipped with small arms, remained in Abyei, guarding infrastructures at the Diffra oil fields, in contravention of the June 2011 Agreement. During mid-2012 UNISFA pursued contact with local community leaderships, and worked to promote inter-community dialogue.

Operational Strength: At 31 August 2012 UNISFA comprised 3,830 troops and 137 military observers; it was supported by two UN Volunteers, and (as 31 July) by 73 international civilian staff members and by 43 local civilian personnel.

Finance: The approved budget for the operation for the two-year period 1 July 2012–30 June 2013 was US $269.2m.

UNITED NATIONS MISSION IN LIBERIA—UNMIL

Address: Monrovia, Liberia.

Special Representative of the UN Secretary-General and Head of Mission: KARIN LANDGREN (Sweden).

Force Commander: Lt-Gen. MUHAMMAD KHALID (Pakistan).

Police Commissioner: JOHN NIELSEN (USA).

Establishment and Mandate: UNMIL was authorized by the UN Security Council in September 2003 to support the implementation of the cease-fire accord agreed in June and the Comprehensive Peace Agreement concluded in August by the parties to the conflict in

Liberia. UNMIL was mandated to assist with the development of an action plan for the disarmament, demobilization, reintegration and, where appropriate, repatriation of all armed groups and to undertake a programme of voluntary disarmament; to protect civilians and UN personnel, equipment and facilities; to support humanitarian and human rights activities; to support the implementation of national security reforms; and, in co-operation with ECOWAS and other partners, to assist the National Transitional Government (inaugurated in mid-October) with the training of a national police force and the restructuring of the military. Troops were also to assist with the rehabilitation of damaged physical infrastructure, in particular the road network. On 1 October UNMIL assumed authority from an ECOWAS-led multinational force in Liberia (the ECOWAS Mission in Liberia—ECOMIL), which had been endorsed by the Security Council in August; ECOMIL's 3,600 troops were reassigned to UNMIL, which then had an authorized maximum strength of 15,000 military personnel.

Activities, 2003–05: In 2004 UNMIL's civil affairs component assessed the functional capacities of public administration structures, including government ministries, in order to assist the National Transitional Government in re-establishing authority throughout Liberia. UNMIL was to support the National Transitional Government in preparing the country for national elections, which were expected to be held in October 2005. In December 2003 the programme for disarmament, demobilization, rehabilitation and reintegration (DDRR) officially commenced when the first cantonment site was opened. However, the process was disrupted by an unexpectedly large influx of former combatants and a few days later the process was temporarily suspended. In mid-January 2004 an agreement was concluded by all parties on necessary prerequisites to proceeding with the programme, including the launch of an information campaign, which was to be co-ordinated and organized by UNMIL, and the construction of new reception centres and cantonment sites. The DDRR process resumed, under UNMIL command, in mid-April. A training programme for the country's new police service was inaugurated in July and the first UN-trained police officers were deployed at the end of the year. By July 2007 some 3,500 officers had graduated from the UN training programme. In August 2004 UNMIL launched a further vocational training scheme for some 640 former combatants to learn building skills. By the end of October, when the disarmament phase of the DDRR programme was officially terminated, more than 96,000 former combatants, including 10,000 child soldiers, had handed over their weapons. Some 7,200 commenced formal education. At the same time, however, UNMIL troops were deployed throughout the country to restore order, after an outbreak of sectarian hostilities prompted widespread looting and destruction of property and businesses. In early December the Special Representative of the UN Secretary-General (SRSG) hosted a meeting of the heads of all West African peace-keeping and political missions, in order to initiate a more integrated approach to achieving stability and peace throughout the region.

During 2005 UNMIL continued to work to integrate ex-combatants into society through vocational training schemes, and to support community rehabilitation efforts, in particular through the funding of Quick Impact Projects. By August an estimated 78,000 former combatants had participated in rehabilitation and reintegration schemes, funded bilaterally and by a Trust Fund administered by the UN Development Programme. A programme to enrol 20,000 disarmed combatants in formal education was initiated in November. UNMIL provided technical assistance to the National Elections Commission, which, in April, initiated a process of voter registration in preparation for presidential and legislative elections. UNMIL was also concerned with maintaining a peaceful and secure environment for the electoral campaigns and polling days and undertook a large-scale civic education campaign in support of the democratic election process. In October UNMIL, with the Transitional Government, established a Joint National Security Operations Centre. The elections were held, as scheduled, in October, with a second-round presidential poll in November.

2006–12: In 2006 UNMIL determined to strengthen its focus on the rule of law, economic recovery and good governance. It also pledged to support the new Government in efforts to remove UN sanctions against sales of rough diamonds and to become a member of the Kimberley Process Certification Scheme by providing air support for surveillance and mapping activities in mining areas. Throughout 2006 and 2007 UNMIL personnel undertook projects to rehabilitate and construct roads and bridges, police stations, courtrooms and educational facilities. The mission also initiated, with the support of other UN agencies, a scheme to create employment throughout the country. In March 2007 UNMIL initiated a Sports for Peace programme to promote national reconciliation. In late April the UN Security Council removed the embargo against sales of diamonds from Liberia, and in the following month UNMIL transferred control of the regional diamond certification office to the national authorities.

In September 2006 the UN Security Council endorsed a recommendation by the Secretary-General that a consolidation, drawdown and withdrawal plan for UNMIL should be developed and implemented; the consolidation phase was completed in December 2007. In August 2007 the UN Secretary-General recognized the efforts of the new Government in consolidating peace and promoting economic recovery in the country. In the following month the Security Council endorsed a plan to reduce UNMIL's military component by 2,450 troops between October and September 2008, and to reduce the number of police officers by 498 in the period April 2008–December 2010. In April 2008 the SRSG reported that greater progress was needed in the training and restructuring of Liberia's security forces to enable the proposed drawdown of UNMIL personnel and transfer of responsibility to proceed. In September 2008 the Security Council approved an increase of 240 in the authorized number of personnel deployed as part of UNMIL's police component, to provide strategic advice and expertise in specialized files and operational support to regular policing activities. UNMIL continued to monitor and control security incidents, local demonstrations, cross-border activities and drugs-trafficking. In June 2009 the UN Secretary-General issued a special report recommending a further reduction of UNMIL's military component, of some 2,029 troops, in the period October 2009–May 2010, and that UNMIL's mandate be revised to enable the mission to support the authorities in preparing for presidential and legislative elections to be held in late 2011. In accordance with a UN Security Council resolution adopted in September 2009, UNMIL, the UN country team in Liberia, the Liberian National Electoral Commission, and other stakeholders subsequently developed a multi-sector electoral assistance project, with a view to supporting the planned election. In July 2009 an UNMIL training programme for the new Armed Forces of Liberia was initiated. The Liberian Government officially assumed responsibilities for the development of the Armed Forces of Liberia in January 2010. In February UNMIL troops intervened to restore order in Lofa County, in north-western Liberia, following widespread inter-ethnic violence, during which four people died and several churches and mosques were set on fire. In September the SRSG reported that the security situation in the country was stable, but remained fragile. She observed that the country required greater national reconciliation and more progress towards resolving issues concerning access to land, strengthening public confidence in the justice system and developing an independent security sector. The third stage of UNMIL's drawdown was completed, as planned, in May. In February 2011 formal responsibility for guarding the Special Court for Sierra Leone was transferred from UNMIL to the Sierra Leone police force. In September 2010 the UN Security Council authorized UNMIL to assist the Liberian Government with staging the 2011 elections, through the provision of logistical support, co-ordination of international electoral assistance, and support for Liberian institutions and political parties in creating an atmosphere conducive to the conduct of peaceful elections.

Following the successful staging of legislative and presidential elections in October–November 2011, the UN Secretary-General sent a technical assessment mission to Liberia in February 2012 to assess progress made in achieving the mission's strategic objectives, and to evaluate the capacity of national security institutions and their ability to operate independently of UNMIL. The mission found that the security situation in Liberia remained fragile, and that there remained high levels of violent crime, and marked vulnerability of women and girls to sexual violence. Causes that were cited included an inadequate justice system and other weak state institutions; large numbers of unemployed, unskilled ex-combatants; ethnic divisions; and disputes over land ownership. In April 2012 the UN Secretary-General recommended a gradual reduction of UNMIL's strength, by around 4,200 troops, to be implemented in three phases during 2012–15. It was envisaged that thereafter a residual presence of about 3,750 troops would remain. Meanwhile, over that period, the mission was gradually to reconfigure, consolidating its presence in the capital, Monrovia, and in the Liberia–Côte d'Ivoire border area. The mission was also to develop a more mobile posture and a quick reaction capability. It was envisaged that the Liberian security forces would be fully operational by 2015. In September 2012 the UN Security Council extended UNMIL's mandate until September 2013, and authorized the implementation of the first phase of the proposed reduction (by 1,900) in the mission's strength, to be implemented over the period October 2012–September 2013. UNMIL was to continue to support the Liberian Government's efforts towards consolidating peace and stability and protecting civilians; and was also to support the Government in facilitating the transfer of full responsibility for security to the national police force, by strengthening the Police's ability to manage personnel, and improving training programmes.

The impact on Liberia of violent unrest in neighbouring Côte d'Ivoire during late 2010–early 2011, including an influx into Liberia of Ivorian combatants, represented a major security threat to Liberia in 2011, which the Liberian authorities and UNMIL worked to address. In July 2011 UNMIL destroyed a cache of weaponry and ammunition believed to have been hidden by Côte d'Ivoire combatants. From May that year the Liberian military, supported by UNMIL, increased its presence along the Liberia-Côte d'Ivoire border, and UNMIL and UNOCI intensified inter-mission co-operation, including undertaking joint border patrols under the so-called 'Operation Mayo'. In June UNMIL and UNOCI conducted a joint assessment mission in western Côte d'Ivoire. In 2011–12 UNMIL also conducted operations along Liberia's borders with Guinea and Sierra Leone, with the Liberian Government and the Guinean and Sierra Leone authorities. UNMIL strengthened its monitoring in 2011 of electoral, legal, political, public information, security and human rights matters prior to the elections conducted in October–November. Equal airtime was given by UNMIL Radio to all participating parties. The mission also co-ordinated international assistance to the electoral process through a Donor Co-ordination Group.

In June 2012 the heads of UNMIL and UNOCI, and government representatives from Liberia and Côte d'Ivoire, held a quadripartite meeting, in Abidjan, Côte d'Ivoire, on developing a strategy to enhance joint border security, following a fatal attack on UNOCI troops, and other fatal incidents, perpetrated in the border area during that month. Liberia closed the border, excepting for humanitarian purposes, from July. In September the UN Security Council urged UNMIL and UNOCI further to develop their inter-mission collaboration.

Operational Strength: At 31 August 2012 UNMIL comprised 7,541 troops, 131 military observers, and 1,321 police officers, supported by 223 UN Volunteers, and (as at 31 July) by 468 international civilian personnel and 993 local civilian staff.

Finance: The General Assembly appropriation to the Special Account for UNMIL amounted to US $518.1m. for the period 1 July 2012–30 June 2013.

UNITED NATIONS MISSION IN SOUTH SUDAN—UNMISS

Address: Juba, Sudan.

Special Representative of the Secretary-General: HILDE JOHNSON (Norway).

Force Commander: Maj.-Gen. MOSES BISONG OBI (Nigeria).

Establishment and Mandate: UNMISS was established in July 2011 upon the independence of South Sudan. The mission succeeded the former UN Mission in the Sudan (UNMIS). UNMISS is mandated to support the consolidation of peace, thereby fostering longer-term state-building and economic development; to support the South Sudan authorities with regard to conflict prevention, mitigation, and the protection of civilians; and to develop the new Government's capacity to provide security, to establish the rule of law, and to strengthen the security and justice sectors.

Activities: From July 2011 UNMISS liaised with the South Sudan Government and provided good offices to facilitate inclusive consultative processes involving all the stakeholders invested in nation-building. The mission responded to a request by the South Sudan authorities to support the development of a national security strategy; assisted, with UNDP, the South Sudan Disarmament, Demobilization and Reintegration Commission in preparing a disarmament, demobilization and reintegration (DDR) policy; and cleared and opened (by November) some 121 km of road, through its Mine Action Service. During August–September the UNMISS Human Rights Division (HRD) undertook a fact-finding operation. UNMISS also supported the new Government's ratification of principal international human rights treaties, and monitored the harmonization of the national legislative framework with international human rights standards. In early August UNMISS and the Government of South Sudan signed a status-of-forces agreement guaranteeing the mission's freedom of movement throughout the new country; during the second half of 2011, however, UNMISS reported several restrictions on its movements. Planned deployments under UNMISS to Lord's Resistance Army (LRA)-affected areas were doubled, in comparison with deployments mandated under UNMIS. From the inception of UNMISS its forces were deployed mainly in response to violent unrest in Jonglei State, which persisted into 2012. Further UNMISS deployments in the second half of 2011 included deterrence operations in Western Equatoria, and a mission to support the integration of rebel forces in Pibor. UNMISS police activities focused on training and advising the new South Sudan Police Service.

From January 2012 relations between South Sudan and Sudan deteriorated significantly, owing to factors including the disputed delineation of the two countries' joint border; mutual accusations of support for anti-government rebel militia groups; control over the territory of Abyei (in Sudan, see under UNMISS); and the dependence at that time of landlocked South Sudan (which had significant oilfields) on the use of Sudanese infrastructure—a pipeline and Port Sudan—for the export of petroleum. South Sudanese oil production was suspended in that month, pending a resolution of the logistical issues relating to its exportation. In February South Sudan and Sudan signed a Memorandum of Understanding on non-aggression and co-operation, committing each state to respecting the other's sovereignty and territorial integrity. In early April an African Union High-Level Implementation Panel (AUHIP) on Sudan (established in October 2009), that was facilitating discussions between the two sides, presented to both parties a draft Joint Decision for Reduction of Tension, providing for the immediate cessation of hostilities between the two states, and the withdrawal of armed forces of each state from the territory of the other. Shortly afterwards the UN Security Council made several demands of both parties, including that they redeploy their forces from forward positions and end cross-border violence with immediate effect; that Sudan should cease aerial bombardments of South Sudan; that South Sudan and Sudan should redeploy forces from Abyei; and that a summit should be convened between the two states to resolve outstanding concerns. In mid-April an UNMISS support base was among buildings damaged by an aerial bombardment by Sudanese forces of Mayom, in Unity State, South Sudan, which resulted in several fatalities in that settlement. In early and late May, respectively, South Sudan and Sudan withdrew their forces from Abyei, in accordance with a seven-point Roadmap for Action by Sudan and South Sudan that was approved in late April by the AU Peace and Security Council (see under the UN Interim Security Force for Abyei). In early July the UN Security Council extended the mission's mandate until 15 July 2013. In late September South Sudan and Sudan reached agreement on reviewing effective mechanisms for metering supplies of petroleum, and determined to establish a committee, under AU auspices, that would review oil sector-related payments and technical matters, as a means of avoiding future disputes and enabling the resumption of South Sudanese petroleum production. In 2012 the UNMISS HRD continued to monitor the observance of human rights in the emerging nation, as well as reporting on potential threats against the civilian population and violations of international humanitarian law. The HRD also undertook capacity building activities, in collaboration with the Southern Sudan Human Rights Commission and other partners. UNMISS contributed to the construction of a DDR transitional facility, which opened in Wau, in August, to support—through the provision of skills training—the reintegration into society of demobilized ex-combatants.

UNMISS, although not mandated to pursue militants of the Lord's Resistance Army (LRA—active in parts of South Sudan, as well as of Uganda, the CAR and Democratic Republic of the Congo), supports the AU-Regional Task Force (AU-RTF), launched in March 2012 to combat the LRA. At September the activities of one UNMISS battalion were focused on assisting the local population in the LRA-affected areas of Ezo, Tambura and Yambio.

In 2012 UNMISS co-operated with UNISFA and UNAMID to support the migration of pastoralists in the sensitive South Sudan–Sudan border area. UNMISS provides administrative and logistical support to UNISFA through its logistics hub, based in Wau, and a liaison office in Juba.

Operational Strength: At 31 August 2012 UNMISS comprised 5,975 troops, 130 military liaison officers and 528 police officers; it was supported by 336 UN Volunteers and (as at 31 July) by 802 international and 1,388 local civilian personnel.

Finance: The budget for the mission amounted to US $876.2m. for the period 1 July 2012–30 June 2013, funded from a Special Account comprising assessed contributions from UN member states.

UNITED NATIONS OPERATION IN CÔTE D'IVOIRE—UNOCI

Address: Abidjan, Côte d'Ivoire.

Special Representative of the Secretary-General and Head of Mission: ALBERT (BERT) GERARD KOENDERS (Netherlands).

Force Commander: Maj.-Gen. MUHAMMAD IQBAL ASI (Pakistan).

Police Commissioner: Maj.-Gen. JEAN MARIE BOURRY (France).

Establishment and Mandate: UNOCI was authorized by the UN Security Council in February 2004 and began operations in early April. It was mandated to observe and monitor the implementation of the Linas-Marcoussis Accord, signed by the parties to the conflict in Côte d'Ivoire in January 2003, and hitherto supported by the UN Mission in Côte d'Ivoire (MINUCI), forces of the Economic Community of West African States—ECOWAS and French peace-keeping troops. UNOCI was authorized also to assist with the disarmament, demobilization and reintegration of rebel groups, to protect civilians and UN personnel, institutions and equipment, and to support ongoing humanitarian and human rights activities. With a contingent of the French *'Licorne'* peace-keeping force, UNOCI was to monitor a so-called Zone of Confidence separating the two areas of the country under government and rebel control.

Activities, 2003–04: In July 2003 all parties, attending a meeting of West African heads of state that had been convened by the UN Secretary-General and the President of Ghana, endorsed the Accra III Agreement identifying means of implementing the Linas-Marcoussis Accord. UNOCI was to participate in a tripartite monitoring group, together with ECOWAS and the African Union, to oversee progress in implementing the agreement. In mid-August UNOCI launched a radio station, in accordance with its mandate, to assist the process of national reunification, and in the following month established some secure transit routes between the areas under government and rebel control in order to facilitate travel and enable family reunions. None the less, by October UNOCI officials expressed concern at ongoing violations of human rights and a deterioration in security, as well as a lack of progress in implementing provisions of the peace accords.

In early November 2004 government troops violated the cease-fire and the Zone of Confidence by launching attacks against rebel Forces Nouvelles in the north of the country. An emergency session of the UN Security Council, convened following an escalation of the hostilities and a fatal air strike on a French peace-keeping unit, urged both sides to refrain from further violence. Security further deteriorated in the south of the country when French troops destroyed the government air force, prompting rioting in the capital, Abidjan, and violence directed towards foreign nationals. UNOCI assisted with the evacuation of foreign workers and their families and provided secure refuge for other personnel. In mid-November the Security Council imposed an immediate embargo on the sale or supply of armaments to Côte d'Ivoire and demanded a cessation of hostilities and of the use of media broadcasts to incite hatred and violence against foreigners. UNOCI was to monitor the terms of the resolution and to broadcast its own messages of support for the peace process. By the end of that month reports indicated that the security situation had improved and that some of the estimated 19,000 who fled the country to Liberia had started to return. In addition, conditions in the northern city of Bouaké were improving as water and electricity supplies were restored. In December UNOCI funded three Quick Impact Projects, in order to highlight the humanitarian aspect of the mission, and commenced joint patrols with government forces to uphold security in Abidjan.

2005–11: In February 2005 the UN Security Council demanded that all parties co-operate with UNOCI in compiling a comprehensive list of armaments under their control as preparation for implementing a programme of disarmament, demobilization and reintegration. In March UNOCI increased its presence in western regions of the country owing to an increase in reported violent incidents. In the following month UNOCI troops were deployed to the border regions with Liberia and Ghana in order to support implementation of the UN-imposed arms embargo. UNOCI troops also monitored the withdrawal of heavy weaponry by both government forces and the Forces Nouvelles. In June UN representatives condemned the massacre of almost 60 civilians in Duékoué, in the west of the country, and urged that an inquiry be held into the incident. UNOCI reinforcements were sent to restore stability in the area and undertook joint patrols with local forces. Later in that month the UN Security Council authorized an increase in UNOCI's military and civilian police components, as well as the redeployment of troops from other missions in the region in order to restore security in the country. In July UN troops, investigating reports of violent attacks by rebel groups, were prevented from entering two towns north of Abidjan. UNOCI later complained at further reported obstruction of human rights and civilian police teams. In spite of persisting concerns regarding the political and human rights situation in the country, UNOCI continued to provide logistical and technical assistance to the independent national electoral commission in preparing for elections, scheduled to be held in October; however, these were later postponed. A Transitional Government of National Unity was formed in December. In early 2006 UN property and personnel were subjected to hostile attacks during a period of unrest by groups protesting against a report of an International Working Group, co-chaired by the SRSG, that had recommended the dissolution of the national assembly (the mandate of which had already expired). Several hundred humanitarian personnel were evacuated from the country. At the end of February UNOCI initiated a large-scale operation to provide security for school examinations, to be held in the north of the country for the first time in three years. In June the Security Council authorized an increase in the mission's force strength by 1,025 military personnel and 475 police officers needed to strengthen security throughout the country and undertake disarmament operations. In October UNOCI conducted joint border patrols with UN forces in Liberia to monitor movements of combatants and weapons. In January 2007 the Security Council formally enlarged UNOCI's mandate to co-ordinate with UNMIL to monitor the arms embargo and to conduct a voluntary repatriation and resettlement programme for foreign ex-combatants. The Council's resolution also defined UNOCI's mandate as being to monitor the cessation of hostilities and movements of armed groups; to assist programmes for the disarmament, demobilization and reintegration of all combatants; to disarm and dismantle militias; to support population identification and voter registration programmes; to assist the reform of the security sector and other activities to uphold law and order; to support humanitarian assistance and the promotion of human rights; and to provide technical support for the conduct of free and fair elections no later than 31 October. A new political agreement to work towards national reconciliation was signed by leaders of the opposing parties in Ouagadougou, Burkina Faso, in March. According to the Ouagadougou Agreement the Zone of Confidence was to be dismantled and replaced by a UN-monitored 'green line'. UNOCI organized a series of meetings to ensure the support of traditional leaders for the peace process. In June UNOCI condemned a rocket attack on a plane carrying the country's Prime Minister. The process of disarmament was officially launched at the end of July; it was, however, hindered by underfunding of the arrangements for the reintegration of former militia members. In August 2008 UNOCI, in collaboration with UNDP, initiated a scheme of 'micro projects' to help to reduce poverty and youth unemployment and facilitate the reintegration of ex-combatants.

The redeployment of UNOCI troops from the former Zone of Confidence was completed by late July 2008, when the last observation post was officially closed. In April UNOCI announced that the presidential election was scheduled to be held later in that year on 30 November. UNOCI personnel were assisting in the rehabilitation of polling stations and in supporting the independent electoral commission. In July the SRSG met with the country's President to confirm UN support for the electoral process and plans to implement security arrangements. The process of voter identification and registration was formally inaugurated in mid-September, with UNOCI to provide transport and other logistical assistance in support of the electoral and registration processes. The electoral preparations, however, were disrupted by severe logistical problems, and in November the election was officially postponed. A new timetable, providing for the election to be held in November 2009 and for voter identification and registration processes to be concluded by 30 June, was announced in May; the election was, however, subsequently postponed once again, until 2010, owing to delays in preparing and publishing the provisional electoral list. The list was eventually issued in November 2009. In January 2010, however, a parallel list was found to be in existence, prompting the Côte d'Ivoire President in February to dissolve both the electoral commission and the national Government, in order to maintain the credibility of the process; a new electoral commission and Government were appointed at the end of that month. None the less, the consequent national tension and outbreak of violence caused the electoral process to remain stalled.

In view of a deterioration in the security situation in Guinea in late 2009 UNOCI forces intensified at that time air and ground patrols of the Côte d'Ivoire–Guinea border area.

During 2010 UNOCI developed, jointly with the Côte d'Ivoire military and French *'Licorne'* force, a co-ordinated plan for helping ensure the security of the planned election. In September an agreement on a final voters list was concluded by the leaders of the three main political parties, and this list was officially certified by the SRSG on 24 September. At the end of September the UN Security Council approved a temporary increase of UNOCI's authorized military and police personnel from 8,650 to 9,150, to be deployed with immediate effect. The first round of the long planned presidential election was held on 31 October, and, following certification of the results of the first round by the SRSG on 12 November, a second electoral round was contested by the two first round forerunners on 28 November. (The incumbent President, Laurent Gbagbo, had received the most votes at the first round, but by a margin that did not constitute an outright victory.) At the beginning of December the electoral commission, supported by the UN, confirmed that Gbagbo's opponent, Alassane Ouattara, had won the presidential election; on the following day, however, the national constitutional council rejected the final results, declaring Gbagbo to be the winner. International opinion, including the UN, African Union and ECOWAS, continued to endorse Ouattara as the rightfully elected new Ivorian President, and the UN Secretary-General and French Government rejected demands by Gbagbo, who refused to concede defeat to Ouattara, that UNOCI and *Licorne* troops should leave Côte d'Ivoire. From mid-December serious violent unrest erupted, with numerous fatalities, as well as obstructions to the movement and activities of UNOCI peace-keepers, and attacks on UN personnel and on the UNOCI headquarters, reported during late 2010–early 2011. In mid-January 2011 the Security Council authorized the deployment of an additional 2,000 military personnel to UNOCI, until end-June 2011; and extended, until end-June 2011, the temporary additional military and police capabilities authorized in September 2010.

On 30 March 2011 the UN Security Council adopted Resolution 1975, urging all Ivorian parties to respect the will of the electorate and therefore to acknowledge the election of Ouattara as Côte d'Ivoire President. Resolution 1975 emphasized that UNOCI might use 'all necessary measures' in executing its mandate to protect civilians under threat of attack. On the following day forces loyal to Ouattara advanced on Abidjan, while UNOCI peacekeepers took control of the capital's airport. In early April UNOCI and *Licorne* forces directed fire at pro-Gbagbo heavy artillery and armoured vehicles. On 9 April UNOCI troops fired on pro-Gbagbo forces, in response to a reported Gbagbo-sanctioned attack on Ouattara at an Abidjan hotel. UNOCI and *Licorne* air strikes were undertaken on the following day against pro-Gbagbo heavy weaponry, reportedly inflicting significant damage on the presidential palace. On 11 April forces loyal to Ouattara arrested Gbagbo, with assistance from *Licorne*; Gbagbo and his entourage were then placed under UNOCI guard. Ouattara was eventually inaugurated as President in May.

During the first half of May 2011 the UN Secretary-General dispatched an assessment mission to examine, and make a number of recommendations on, the situation in Côte d'Ivoire. The Secretary-General subsequently recommended that UNOCI play a greater role in helping the national authorities to stabilize the security situation, with a particular focus on Abidjan and western (including border) areas. Accordingly, UNOCI was to increase joint patrols with the Côte d'Ivoire military and police; and was to facilitate the resumption of law enforcement responsibilities by the police and gendarmerie; to deter the activities of militias; and to assist in the protection of civilians. UNOCI was also to continue to collect, secure and dispose of weaponry; and to assist in demining activities. It was recommended that UNOCI, in close co-operation with UNMIL, should enhance its support to the Côte d'Ivoire and Liberian authorities to monitor and address cross-border security challenges, and should increase patrols of the Côte d'Ivoire-Liberia border area (under the so-called 'Operation Mayo'); in June UNOCI and UNMIL conducted a joint assessment mission in western Côte d'Ivoire. It was recommended following the May assessment that UNOCI should provide assistance for the development of a UN justice support programme; support the capacity development for the police, gendarmerie and corrections officers; deploy an expert to work with the authorities on security sector reform; assist the Government in developing a new national programme for demobilization, disarmament and reintegration of combatants, and dismantling of militias, that would be tailored to the post April 2011 context; continue to support the registration and profiling of former combatants; support the organization and conduct of the legislative elections; and strengthen its human rights monitoring activities. UNOCI provided logistical and security support to facilitate the conduct of legislative elections that were held in Côte d'Ivoire in December 2011.

2012: In February 2012 the SRSG determined that the December 2011 electoral process had been 'free, fair, just and transparent' in 193 of the 204 parliamentary constituencies that had been polled; results in the remaining constituencies had, however, been found by the Constitutional Court to be irregular, and had consequently been annulled. The elections in these constituencies were repeated at the end of February 2012. In late March, having considered the findings of an assessment mission sent to Côte d'Ivoire in February, the UN Secretary-General recommended a reduction in UNOCI's authorized strength, and decided that the mission should adjust the scope of its deployment to cover more remote areas and to intensify its engagement with local communities. From April UNOCI began the rehabilitation of nine of its 20 disarmament, demobilization and reintegration sites (each with a capacity of 500 people), to assist the Ivorian authorities in disarming a further 40,000 former combatants. In June the heads of UNOCI and UNMIL, and government representatives from Côte d'Ivoire and Liberia, held a quadripartite meeting, in Abidjan, Côte d'Ivoire, on developing a strategy to enhance joint border security, following a fatal attack on UNOCI troops, and other fatal incidents, recently perpetrated in the border area.

Operational Strength: At 31 August 2012 UNOCI had an operational strength of 9,398 troops, 192 military observers and 1,364 police officers; it was supported by 189 UN Volunteers, and (at 31 July) by 408 international and 768 local civilian personnel.

Finance: The General Assembly appropriated US $600.2m. to finance the mission during the period 1 July 2012–30 June 2013.

UNITED NATIONS ORGANIZATION STABILIZATION MISSION IN THE DEMOCRATIC REPUBLIC OF THE CONGO—MONUSCO

Address: Kinshasa, Democratic Republic of the Congo.

Liaison offices are situated in Kigali (Rwanda) and Pretoria (South Africa). A logistics base is located in Entebbe, Uganda.

Special Representative of the UN Secretary-General and Chief of Mission: ROGER MEECE (USA).

Force Commander: Lt-Gen. CHANDER PRAKASH (India).

Police Commissioner: ABDALLAH WAFY (Niger).

Establishment and Mandate: On 1 July 2010 MONUSCO succeeded the former United Nations Mission in the Democratic Republic of the Congo (MONUC), which had been established by the UN Security Council in August 1999 and had been operational until the end of June 2010. MONUSCO was inaugurated—to reflect a new phase in the ongoing peace process in the Democratic Republic of the Congo (DRC)—as a consequence of the adoption, in late May 2010, of Security Council Resolution 1925. Resolution 1925 emphasized that the DRC regime (which had reportedly requested the full withdrawal of the UN peace-keeping presence) should bear primary responsibility for maintaining security and promoting peace-building and development in the country, and authorized MONUSCO's deployment until, initially, 30 June 2011 (the mandate was subsequently extended, most recently until 30 June 2013). MONUSCO was to comprise, initially, a maximum of 19,815 military personnel, 760 military observers, 391 police personnel and 1,050 members of formed police units, with future reconfigurations to be determined as the situation evolved on the ground. The mission was to use all necessary means to carry out its mandate, which focused on protecting civilians and humanitarian personnel, as well as protecting UN staff, facilities, installations and equipment; supporting the DRC regime in efforts towards stabilizing the country and consolidating peace, including supporting its International Security and Stabilization Support Strategy (ISSSS), helping with strengthening the capacity of the military and with police reforms, developing and implementing a multi-year joint UN justice support programme, consolidating state authority in areas freed from the control of armed militia, providing technical and logistics support for local and national elections at the request of the Government, and monitoring the arms embargo against rebel militia active in the DRC; providing human rights training to DRC government officials, security service personnel, journalists, and civil society organizations; and advancing child protection, combating sexual violence, and promoting the representation of women in decision-making roles. MONUSCO was to focus its military forces in eastern areas of the DRC, while maintaining a reserve force that could be deployed elsewhere at short notice. MONUSCO screens DRC battalion commanders for human rights violations prior to the provision of logistical and other support.

Activities: From mid-2010 MONUSCO implemented several Quick Impact Projects, including the establishment of new press and vocational training centres and the rehabilitation of play areas and schools. The mission continued to support the Government's disarmament, demobilization and rehabilitation initiative, and through its regional radio network the mission aimed to encourage defections from the Lord's Resistance Army (LRA) rebel group. In late July MONUSCO established a mobile base in Beni, North Kivu province, in order to enhance security for humanitarian personnel working to provide essential medical and food assistance to an estimated 90,000 people who had been temporarily displaced by an escalation of fighting in that area between the national armed forces and the Ugandan rebel group, the Allied Democratic Forces. In the following month three peace-keepers were killed in an attack on their base in Kirumba, North Kivu. In September MONUSCO initiated special patrols in North Kivu to enhance civilian protection following a series of violent attacks, including mass rapes, by illegal armed groups. During 2010–12 MONUSCO worked to launch community alert networks aimed at enhancing the protection of civilians; under the community alert system, settlements in isolated areas were enabled to request, through mission community liaison assistants, intervention to deter threatened attacks. MONUSCO also provided technical advice, logistical support, and police electoral security training, during the preparation for legislative and presidential elections that were held in November–December 2011, as well as providing security patrols before, during and after the electoral process. (The outcome of the presidential election was disputed.) During 2011 MONUSCO documented several hundred reported violations of human rights linked to the electoral process, affecting, in particular, political opposition supporters, journalists and human rights defenders.

During 2011 MONUSCO conducted 46 joint protection team missions with DRC armed forces, in North and South Kivu, Equateur, Ituri and Haut Uélé and Katanga. In late April MONUSCO implemented Operation Easter Shield, aimed an enhancing civilian protection and facilitating the delivery of humanitarian assistance in the northeastern Doruma area (bordering South Sudan), following reports of LRA attacks there. MONUSCO also undertook road rehabilitation activities in north-eastern DRC in 2011.

MONUSCO and the national armed forces launched the joint military operations 'Amani Kamilifu' and 'Radi Strike' in, respectively, February and March 2012, targeting militants in the Kivu provinces. MONUSCO undertook several military operations in the first half of 2012 to protect civilians in LRA-affected areas, and supported an initiative of the national armed forces to encourage LRA members to defect and to enter a disarmament, demobilization, repatriation, resettlement and reintegration (DDRRR) process. The mission was to assist a newly-created AU-Regional Task Force, mandated to combat the LRA, through the provision of logistical support to the Force's Dungu (Haut-Uele) Joint Intelligence and Operations Centre. Militants of the newly-formed Kivus-based 23 March Movement (known as 'M23') became increasingly active from May 2012, clashing with government forces and causing mass population displacement. In response to reports in mid-2012 of systematic targeted massacres of civilians by armed groups at that time in North Kivu, the UN Joint Human Rights Office in the DRC (UNJHRO)—comprising representatives of MONUSCO and UNHCR—conducted several missions to affected areas to interview witnesses and verify the crimes. In late June the UN Security Council expressed great concern at the deteriorating humanitarian situation in eastern DRC and at the ongoing human rights abuses against civilians, as well as at pervasive sexual violence, arbitrary arrests, extrajudicial executions, and conscription of child and youth combatants (by M23, *inter alia*), and urged the UN presence, the DRC authorities and other relevant bodies to provide security, medical, humanitarian, and other support to victims. MONUSCO and partners were undertaking efforts at that time to provide training to the DRC security forces in child/youth protection and protection from sexual and gender-based violence, as well as in human rights. In late June the Security Council also requested MONUSCO to undertake by early 2013 a strategic review—identifying a clear strategy and schedule for its implementation—of the DRC Government's ISSSS (the framework, developed in 2008–09, for establishing sustainable national security forces, and for consolidating state authority in eastern DRC). In late August 2012 the Special Representative of the Secretary-General expressed deep concern over alleged further systematic massacres of civilians undertaken in early August, in Masisi, North Kivu. During May–August UNJHRO verified 45 attacks on some 30 communities in the Masisi area. In September MONUSCO, as part of its work to support the DDRRR process, was implementing a Quick Impact Project to construct a vocational training centre for former combatants, in Kasindi, North Kivu. During January–September 2012 more than 2000 ex-combatants were disarmed under the DDRRR programme.

During late 2011 MONUSCO, with the UN DRC country team, finalized the 2011–13 UN Transitional Framework for the DRC, defining areas of collaboration between MONUSCO and other UN agencies.

Operational Strength: At 31 August 2012 MONUSCO comprised 17,000 troops, 703 military observers and 1,374 police officers (including formed police units), supported by 573 UN Volunteers and (at 31 July 2012) by 953 international and 2,859 local civilian personnel.

Finance: The budget for the mission amounted to US $1,402.3m. for the period 1 July 2012–30 June 2013, funded from a Special Account comprising assessed contributions from UN member states.

United Nations Peace-building

Address: Department of Political Affairs, United Nations, New York, NY 10017, USA.

Telephone: (212) 963-1234; **fax:** (212) 963-4879; **internet:** www.un.org/Depts/dpa/.

The Department of Political Affairs provides support and guidance to UN peace-building operations and political missions working in the field to prevent and resolve conflicts or to promote enduring peace in post-conflict societies.

The World Summit of UN heads of state held in September 2005 approved recommendations made by the UN Secretary-General in his March 2005 report entitled 'In Larger Freedom: Towards Development, Security and Human Rights for All' for the creation of an intergovernmental advisory Peace-building Commission. In December the UN Security Council and General Assembly authorized the establishment of the Commission; it was inaugurated, as a special subsidiary body of both the Council and Assembly, in June 2006. A multi-year standing peace-building fund, financed by voluntary contributions from member states and mandated to support post-conflict peace-building activities, was established in October 2006. A Peace-building Support Office was established within the UN Secretariat to administer the fund, as well as to support the Commission. In 2012 the Peace-building Commission was actively concerned with the situation in six African countries: Burundi, Central African Republic, Guinea, Guinea-Bissau, Liberia and Sierra Leone.

OFFICE OF THE SPECIAL REPRESENTATIVE OF THE UN SECRETARY-GENERAL FOR WEST AFRICA—UNOWA

Address: BP 23851 Dakar-Ponty, 5 ave Carde, Immeuble Caisse de sécurité sociale, Dakar, Senegal.

Telephone: (221) 849-07-29; **fax:** (221) 842-50-95.

Special Representative of the UN Secretary-General: SAID DJINNIT (Algeria).

Establishment and Mandate: UNOWA was established, with an initial three-year mandate, from January 2002, to elaborate an integrated approach by the United Nations to the prevention and management of conflict in West Africa; and to promote peace, security and development in the sub-region. (UNOWA's mandate has subsequently been renewed, most recently for a further three years until December 2013.) In pursuit of these objectives, the Special Representative of the Secretary-General (SRSG) meets regularly with the leaders of UN regional and political offices in West Africa.

Activities: UNOWA supports the development of a regional harmonized approach to disarmament, demobilization and reintegration in West Africa, and its projects have included an initiative to address cross-border challenges, such as mercenaries, child-soldiers and small arms proliferation. UNOWA also aims to support and facilitate a sub-regional approach to issues that impact stability in West Africa, in particular electoral processes and the transfer of power. UNOWA works with the Economic Community of West African States (ECOWAS), whose projects embrace security sector reform (identified as a key priority for the sub-region), small arms, transborder co-operation, etc. A trilateral partnership between UNOWA, the European Union and ECOWAS has also been established. In July 2009 UNOWA, with the UN Office on Drugs and Crime, the UN Department of Peace-keeping Operations and INTERPOL, inaugurated a West Africa Coast Initiative (WACI) to support the ECOWAS Regional Action Plan, which aimed to counter the problem of illicit drugs trafficking, organized crime, and drug abuse in West Africa. WACI provides advice, equipment, technical assistance and specialized training, and supports the establishment of Transnational Crime Units in each country. UNOWA, with the UN Office for the Co-ordination of Humanitarian Affairs (OCHA), has worked to address economic, political, security and humanitarian problems that confront the populations of certain border areas in West Africa through the development of integrated, multi-agency strategies in respect of four border clusters: Guinea/Côte d'Ivoire/Liberia/Sierra Leone (Guinea Forestière); Mali/Burkina Faso/Côte d'Ivoire/Ghana; Mauritania/Mali/Niger; and Senegal/The Gambia/Guinea-Bissau. UNOWA works closely with OCHA in strengthening the UN's regional humanitarian response. It is also concerned to promote respect for human rights and to support the full consideration of gender issues in conflict management and peace-building activities.

In May 2011 UNOWA organized a Regional Conference on Elections and Stability in West Africa, in Praia, Cape Verde; the Conference adopted the Praia Declaration on Elections and Stability in West Africa, identifying practical recommendations for improving electoral processes in the region. A round table meeting was convened in September, in New York, USA, by UNOWA and the International Peace Institute, further to discuss issues raised by the Conference. In the following month UNOWA supported the organization by the West African Human Rights Defenders Network of a panel discussion on the role of civil society organizations in elections; as a consequence of the panel discussion, civil society organizations in the subregion adopted a roadmap for the implementation of the Praia Declaration.

In early December 2011 UNOWA, jointly with OHCHR, ECOWAS, the African Union, the Mano River Union and the Organisation Internationale de la Francophonie, convened a Regional Conference on Impunity, Justice and Human Rights in West Africa, in Bamako, Mali; the Conference adopted the Bamako Declaration and a strategic framework, outlining recommendations aimed at strengthening good governance and the rule of law, in order to promote stability and development in West Africa. A Regional Forum on Media, Peace and Security in West Africa, organized by UNOWA, together with ECOWAS and the Francophonie, in Abidjan, Côte d'Ivoire, in June 2012, with participation by representatives of government, regional and international organizations, and by media professionals, adopted a set of recommendations on the role of the media in peace and security, with a view to fostering mutual capacity-building and collaboration among regional stakeholders.

In February 2012 the UN Security Council requested the UN Secretary-General to support, through UNOWA and UNOCA, states and sub-regional organizations in convening a joint Summit on combating maritime piracy in the Gulf of Guinea.

Following the overthrow of the legitimate governments of Mali and Guinea-Bissau in, respectively, March and April 2012, the SRSG devoted his good offices to promoting a return to civilian rule and constitutional order in those countries (in the case of Guinea-Bissau he acted in co-operation with the SRSG to that country). UNOWA continued to work at supporting the consolidation of democratic processes and institutions throughout the region, with a particular focus on Guinea, Senegal and Togo; and at managing election-related tensions in the region.

The SRSG serves as chairman of the Cameroon-Nigeria Mixed Commission, which has met regularly since December 2002, and hosts high level meetings of the heads of UN peace missions in West Africa.

Operational Strength: At 31 July 2012 UNOWA comprised one military adviser, and (as at 30 June) 21 international civilian and 18 local civilian personnel.

UNITED NATIONS OFFICE IN BURUNDI—BNUB

Address: BP 6899, Gatumba Rd, Bujumbura, Burundi.

Telephone: 22205165; **internet:** binub.unmissions.org.

Special Representative of the UN Secretary-General and Head of Office: PARFAIT ONANGA-ANYANGA (Gabon).

Establishment and Mandate: The United Nations Office in Burundi (Bureau des Nations Unies au Burundi—BNUB) was established on 1 January 2011, as a successor to the UN Integrated Office in Burundi (BINUB), which had operated in the country since 2007. BNUB represented a commitment by the UN to maintaining a scaled-down presence in the country, for an initial 12-month period, in order to support the country's progress towards peace consolidation and long-term development. BNUB mandate was to support the efforts of the Burundi Government to strengthen the independence, capacities and legal frameworks of key national institutions, in accordance with international standards and principles; to facilitate political dialogue and broad-based participation in political life; to support efforts to fight impunity, in particular through the establishment of transitional justice mechanisms to strengthen national unity, and to promote justice and reconciliation within Burundi's society, and to provide operational support to the functioning of these bodies; to promote and protect human rights, and strengthen national capacities in that area; to ensure that all strategies and policies with respect to public finance and the economic sector, in particular the next Poverty Reduction Strategy Paper (PRSP), have a focus on peace-building, equitable growth, and addressing the needs of the most vulnerable population; and to provide support to Burundi's 2011 chairmanship of the East African Community, as well as providing advice, as requested, on regional integration issues. The Office was to work to ensure effective co-ordination among UN agencies in Burundi.

In December 2011 the UN Security Council extended the mandate of BNUB until 15 February 2013, emphasizing, in so doing, that significant challenges remained in areas including human rights, democratic governance, civilian protection, combating corruption, security sector reform, and promoting economic development.

Operational Strength: At 31 July 2012 BNUB comprised one military adviser, one police officer, and six UN Volunteers; at 30 June the mission was supported by 55 international and 66 local civilian staff.

UNITED NATIONS INTEGRATED PEACE-BUILDING OFFICE IN SIERRA LEONE—UNIPSIL

Address: Cabenda Hotel, 14 Signal Hill Rd, POB 5, Freetown, Sierra Leone.

Telephone: (76) 692810; **internet:** unipsil.unmissions.org.

Executive Representative of the UN Secretary-General and Head of Mission: JENS ANDERS TOYBERG-FRANDZEN (Denmark).

Establishment and Mandate: The Office was established on 1 October 2008, in accordance with UN Security Council Resolution 1829 (4 August 2008), as a successor to the United Nations Integrated Office in Sierra Leone (UNIOSIL). UNIOSIL had been established in January 2006 following the expiry of the mandate of the large UN peace-keeping operation in Sierra Leone, UNAMSIL, and assisted the Government of Sierra Leone to consolidate peace and to build the capacity of national institutions to support democracy and economic and social development. The key elements of UNIPSIL's mandate were to support the Government of Sierra Leone: to identify and resolve tensions and areas of potential conflict; to monitor and promote human rights, democratic institutions and the rule of law, including efforts to counter transnational organized crime and drugs-trafficking; to consolidate good governance reforms, in particular anti-corruption bodies; to support decentralization; and to co-ordinate with and support the work of the Peace-building Commission, as well as the implementation of a Peace-building Co-operation Framework. UNIPSIL was to work closely with the Economic Community of West African States (ECOWAS), the Mano River Union, other international partners and other UN missions in the region. The head of UNIPSIL, the Executive Representative of the UN Secretary-General, also serves as the Resident Representative of the UN Development Programme and as the UN Resident and Humanitarian Co-ordinator. In December 2008 UNIPSIL, with all other UN agencies and programmes working in Sierra Leone, as well as the African Development Bank, adopted a Joint Vision to co-ordinate facilities and services in order to help to consolidate a sustainable peace in the country.

In 2012 UNIPSIL was supporting the dissemination of a Declaration signed in May by all registered political parties in Sierra Leone, as well as by other major stakeholders, committing all signatories to conducting free, fair and peaceful presidential and legislative elections (scheduled for November).

Operational Strength: At 31 July 2012 UNIPSIL comprised seven police personnel and eight UN Volunteers; it was supported by 36 international civilian and 34 local civilian personnel (as at 30 June).

UNITED NATIONS INTEGRATED PEACE-BUILDING OFFICE IN THE CENTRAL AFRICAN REPUBLIC—BINUCA

Address: BP 3338, PK 4 ave Boganda, Bangui, Central African Republic.

Telephone: 21-61-70-98; **internet:** binuca.unmissions.org.

Special Representative of the UN Secretary-General and Head of Office: MARGARET VOGT (Nigeria).

Establishment and Mandate: The United Nations Integrated Peace-building Office in the CAR (BINUCA) was inaugurated on 1 January 2010, replacing the UN Peace-building Office in the CAR (BONUCA), which was established in February 2000, following the withdrawal of the UN Peace-keeping Mission in the Central African Republic (MINURCA). BINUCA is mandated to support national and local efforts to develop governance reforms and electoral processes; to support the completion of disarmament, demobilization and reintegration programme activities; to help to restore state authority in the provinces; to promote respect for human rights and the rule of law; to support the UN Mission in the CAR and Chad (MINURCAT); and to ensure that child protection measures are observed. Successive extensions of BINUCA's mandate were approved by the Security Council in December 2010 and December 2011 (the former by one year, and the latter until 31 January 2013).

Operational Strength: At 31 July 2012 BINUCA comprised two military observers, two police and five UN Volunteers; in addition, it was supported by 65 international civilian and 85 local civilian personnel (as at 30 June 2012).

UNITED NATIONS INTEGRATED PEACE-BUILDING OFFICE IN GUINEA-BISSAU—UNIOGBIS

Address: UN Bldg, CP 179, Rua Rui Djassi, Bissau, Guinea-Bissau.

Telephone: 20-36-18; **fax:** 20-36-13; **internet:** uniogbis.unmissions.org.

Special Representative of the UN Secretary-General and Head of Office: JOSEPH MUTABOBA (Rwanda).

Establishment and Mandate: Established to assist the Peace-building Commission in its multi-dimensional engagement with Guinea-Bissau, the United Nations Integrated Peace-building Office in Guinea-Bissau (UNIOGBIS) first became operational in January 2010, succeeding the UN Peace-building Office in Guinea-Bissau (UNOGBIS). UNOGBIS had not been preceded by a UN peace-keeping mission.

Activities: From 2003 the work of UNOGBIS, which preceded UNIOGBIS, focused on transition to civilian rule in the aftermath of a military coup that took place in that year. UNOGBIS was mandated by the UN Security Council to promote national reconciliation, respect for human rights and the rule of law; to support national capacity for conflict prevention; to encourage reform of the security sector and stable civil-military relations; to encourage government efforts to suppress trafficking in small arms; and to collaborate with a 'comprehensive peace-building strategy' to strengthen state institutions and mobilize international resources. In December 2007 the UN Security Council authorized a revised mandate for UNOGBIS to support efforts by the Guinea-Bissau authorities to counter illegal drugs-trafficking. UNOGBIS undertook training of electoral agents and journalists in preparation for legislative elections, conducted in November 2008, and co-ordinated the activities of international observers monitoring the voting. In June 2009 the UN Security Council endorsed the establishment of UNIOGBIS, which succeeded UNOGBIS from 1 January 2010. From mid-2010 UNIOGBIS facilitated the preparation of meetings of security and defence forces, as part of a National Reconciliation Conference process. It also worked to enhance the co-ordination and effectiveness of international assistance to further defence and security sector reform, co-operated with the UN Mine Action Service to assess the country's weapons and ammunition stockpiles, and supported the national authorities to combat human trafficking, drugs trafficking and other areas of organized crime. During 2011 UNIOGBIS, with UNDP, provided support to the organizing committee of the National Reconciliation Conference process. The Office also supported the ongoing constitutional review process, and provided technical and financial assistance to the National Technical Independent Mixed Commission, responsible for the selection of police officers. In September a model police station, established with support from UNIOGBIS, was inaugurated in Bissau; 12 further model police stations were planned. In early May 2012 the Special Representative of the UN Secretary-General (SRSG) expressed strong concern at the impact on civilian living standards of a political crisis that had emerged following a military coup in the previous month against the legitimate Guinea-Bissau authorities. The SRSG, in co-operation with the SRSG to West Africa (see UNOWA), devoted his good offices following the April coup to promoting a return to civilian rule and constitutional order in Guinea-Bissau.

Operational Strength: At 31 July 2012 UNIOGBIS comprised 17 police officers, one military adviser and seven UN Volunteers; in addition, there were 61 international civilian and 52 local civilian personnel (as at 30 June).

UNITED NATIONS POLITICAL OFFICE FOR SOMALIA—UNPOS

Address: UNPOS Public Information Office, POB 48246-00100, Nairobi, Kenya.

Telephone: (20) 7622131; **fax:** (20) 7622697; **e-mail:** unpos_pio@un.org; **internet:** unpos.unmissions.org.

Special Representative of the UN Secretary-General and Head of Office: AUGUSTINE P. MAHIGA (Tanzania).

Establishment and Mandate: The United Nations Political Office for Somalia (UNPOS) was established in 1995 with the objective of assisting the Secretary-General to advance peace and reconciliation in the country by utilizing its contacts with Somali leaders and civic organizations. Owing to the security situation in that country, UNPOS was administered from offices in Nairobi, Kenya. UNPOS provides good offices, co-ordinates international political support and financial assistance to peace and reconciliation initiatives, and monitors and reports on developments in the country. In 2002–04 UNPOS supported the Somali National Reconciliation Conference that was organized in Nairobi under the auspices of the Inter-governmental Authority on Development, and worked with international partners to facilitate agreement among Somali leaders on a transitional administration. By early 2005 the Conference had established a broad-based Transitional Federal Government, which was able to relocate to Somalia from its temporary base in Kenya. The UN Security Council consequently authorized UNPOS to promote reconciliation through dialogue between Somali parties; to assist efforts to address the 'Somaliland' issue; to co-ordinate the support of Somalia's neighbours and other international partners for the country's peace process; and to assume a leading political role in peace-building initiatives. In January 2012 the Special Representative of the Secretary-General (SRSG), with several core UNPOS staff members, relocated from Nairobi to the Somali capital, Mogadishu; the last SRSG to be based in Mogadishu had departed there in 1995. An UNPOS Public Information Office remained in Nairobi.

Activities: In spite of an outbreak of hostilities in May 2006, the Transitional Federal Institutions continued to function during that year and to co-operate with the UN's Special Representative to pursue peace negotiations. In May 2008 the Special Representative chaired inter-Somali peace negotiations, held in Djibouti. An agreement was reached in June, and formally signed in August, on the cessation of hostilities and the establishment of a Joint Security Committee and a High Level Committee on political issues. In March 2009 UNPOS organized a meeting, in Djibouti, with representatives of the Somali business community. A committee was established to develop and implement a strategy to support entrepreneurs. From mid-2009 UNPOS, with AMISOM and key members of the transitional Government and the international community acting in Somalia, met as a revised Joint Security Committee. In April 2010 UNPOS signed a Memorandum of Understanding with IGAD and AMISOM, in order to strengthen co-ordination of activities between the organizations in support of the peace process. In early 2011 UNPOS supported a consensus-building process to enable the transitional period of government to conclude, as determined under the Djibouti Peace Agreement, in August. In June the Special Representative facilitated the signing of the so-called Kampala Accord by the President and Speaker of the Transitional Federal Parliament providing for the establishment of a new interim administration to undertake the tasks necessary to end the transitional phase (with a presidential election and election for a new Parliamentary Speaker to take place around August 2012). In September 2011 the Special Representative helped to organize, in the Somali capital Mogadishu, a High Level Consultative Meeting on Ending Transition, attended by high level representatives of the Transitional Federal Institutions, the regional administrations serving Galmudug and Puntland, and other international partners. The meeting endorsed a roadmap for the forthcoming 12-month period, with UNPOS to administer the implementation of various mechanisms identified in the document. In June 2012 two UNPOS personnel were elected as non-voting members of a newly established Technical Selection Committee tasked with vetting prospective parliamentary candidates. The election of the Parliamentary Speaker was held in late August 2012, while presidential elections were staged in the first half of September, leading to the inauguration of the new Somali President, Hassan Sheikh Mohamud, in mid-September. Towards the end of September UNPOS organized a workshop on women and elections; it was reported that only 15% of the members of the new Somali legislature were female. The mission maintains a small Human Rights Unit, with offices located in Mogadishu, Garowe, and Hargeisa (Somalia), and at the Nairobi, Kenya headquarters. The following were identified as thematic areas of priority for the Unit during 2012–13: protecting human rights in situations of violence and insecurity; combating impunity and strengthening accountability, rule of law, and democratic institutions; and combating discrimination, particularly against IDPs, women and children.

Operational Strength: At 31 July 2012 UNPOS was composed of three military advisers; there were, in addition, 55 international civilian and 34 local civilian personnel (as at 30 June).

UNITED NATIONS REGIONAL OFFICE FOR CENTRAL AFRICA—UNOCA

Address: BP 23773, Cité de la Démocratie, Villas 55–57, Libreville, Gabon.

Telephone: (241) 741-401; **fax:** (241) 741-402.

Special Representative of the UN Secretary-General: ABOU MOUSSA (Chad).

Establishment and Mandate: UNOCA—covering the 10 member states of the Communauté économique des états de l'Afrique centrale (CEEAC): Angola, Burundi, Cameroon, Central African Republic (CAR), Chad, Democratic Republic of the Congo (DRC), Republic of the Congo, Equatorial Guinea, Gabon, and São Tomé and Príncipe—was inaugurated in March 2011, having been established through an exchange of letters, finalized in August 2010, between the UN Secretary-General and the UN Security Council. UNOCA is mandated to extend the UN's good offices and other assistance to regional states and organizations in support of preventive diplomacy and the consolidation of peace. The Office is also mandated to work closely with UN and other entities to address cross-border challenges, such as organized crime, trafficking in arms, and the activities of armed groups (including the Lord's Resistance Army—LRA). In August 2012 the UN Security Council extended UNOCA's mandate until 28 February 2014.

Activities: UNOCA's priority areas of activity include: supporting conflict mediation, and, where requested, assisting with the peaceful conduct of elections in the region; facilitating cohesion in the general work of the UN in the region, including in partnership with other agencies, such as UNDP, UNODC, UN Women and OHCHR; promoting activities in partnership with the private sector and civil society networks; co-ordinating UN efforts in the region against armed groups; undertaking studies on regional challenges and threats; providing technical assistance aimed at advancing early warning and mediation capabilities; helping to build the capacity of CEEAC; promoting the formulation of a regional integrated approach to addressing cross-border insecurity; and combating maritime insecurity in the Gulf of Guinea.

In February 2012 the UN Security Council requested the UN Secretary-General to support, through UNOCA and UNOWA, states and sub-regional organizations in organizing a joint Summit to be held on combating maritime piracy in the Gulf of Guinea.

In June 2012 a Regional Strategy to Address the Threat and Impact of the Activities of the LRA—developed by UNOCA to address the challenges posed by the LRA to civilians residing in the CAR, DRC, South Sudan, and in Uganda—was endorsed by the Security Council. The Strategy has the following priority objectives: (i) supporting the full operationalization and implementation of the ongoing AU regional co-operation initiative against the LRA; (ii) enhancing efforts to protect civilians; (iii) expanding ongoing disarmament, demobilization, repatriation, resettlement and reintegration activities across all LRA-affected areas; (iv) supporting a co-ordinated humanitarian and child protection response in these areas; and (v) assisting governments combating the LRA in the areas of peace-building, human rights, rule of law and development. The Council requested the UN Secretary-General to report back in a single document before the end of November on progress being made by UNOCA, by the Regional Strategy, and by other actors in the region, towards combating the LRA.

Operational Strength: At 31 July 2012 the Office comprised one military adviser, supported (as at 30 June) by 18 international civilian and seven local civilian personnel.

World Food Programme—WFP

Address: Via Cesare Giulio Viola 68, Parco dei Medici, 00148 Rome, Italy.

Telephone: (06) 65131; **fax:** (06) 6513-2840; **e-mail:** wfpinfo@wfp.org; **internet:** www.wfp.org.

WFP, the principal food assistance organization of the United Nations, became operational in 1963. It aims to alleviate acute hunger by providing emergency relief following natural or man-made humanitarian disasters, and supplies food assistance to people in developing countries to eradicate chronic undernourishment, to support social development and to promote self-reliant communities.

Organization

(September 2012)

EXECUTIVE BOARD

The governing body of WFP is the Executive Board, comprising 36 members, 18 of whom are elected by the UN Economic and Social Council (ECOSOC) and 18 by the Council of the Food and Agriculture Organization (FAO). The Board meets four times each year at WFP headquarters.

SECRETARIAT

WFP's Executive Director is appointed jointly by the UN Secretary-General and the Director-General of FAO and is responsible for the management and administration of the Programme. Around 90% of WFP staff members work in the field. WFP administers some 87 country offices, in order to provide operational, financial and management support at a more local level, and maintains six regional bureaux, located in Bangkok, Thailand (for Asia), Cairo, Egypt (for the Middle East, Central Asia and Eastern Europe), Panama City, Panama (for Latin America and the Caribbean), Johannesburg, South Africa (for Southern Africa), Kampala, Uganda (for Central and Eastern Africa), and Dakar, Senegal (for West Africa).

Executive Director: Ertharin Cousin (USA).

Activities

WFP is the only multilateral organization with a mandate to use food assistance as a resource. It is the second largest source of assistance in the UN, after the World Bank Group, in terms of actual transfers of resources, and the largest source of grant aid in the UN system. WFP handles more than one-third of the world's food assistance. WFP is also the largest contributor to South–South trade within the UN system, through the purchase of food and services from developing countries (at least three-quarters of the food purchased by the Programme originates in developing countries). WFP's mission is to provide food assistance to save lives in refugee and other emergency situations, to improve the nutrition and quality of life of vulnerable groups and to help to develop assets and promote the self-reliance of poor families and communities. WFP aims to focus its efforts on the world's poorest countries and to provide at least 90% of its total assistance to those designated as 'low-income food-deficit'. At the World Food Summit, held in November 1996, WFP endorsed the commitment to reduce by 50% the number of undernourished people, no later than 2015. During 2011 WFP food assistance, distributed through development projects, emergency operations (EMOPs) and protracted relief and recovery operations (PRROs), benefited some 99.1m. people, including 82.9m. women and children, and 15.1m. IDPs, in 75 countries. Total food deliveries in 2011 amounted to 3.6m. metric tons.

WFP rations comprise basic food items (staple foods such as wheat flour or rice; pulses such as lentils and chickpeas; vegetable oil fortified with vitamins A and D; sugar; and iodized salt). Where possible basic rations are complemented with special products designed to improve the nutritional intake of beneficiaries. These include fortified blended foods, principally 'Corn Soya Blend', containing important micronutrients; 'Super Cereals'; ready-to-use foods, principally peanut-based pastes enriched with vitamins and minerals trade-marked as 'Plumpy Doz' and 'Supplementary Plumpy', which are better suited to meeting the nutritional needs of young and moderately malnourished children; high energy biscuits, distributed in the first phases of emergencies when cooking facilities may be scarce; micronutrient powder ('sprinkles'), which can be used to fortify home cooking; and compressed food bars, given out during disaster relief operations when the distribution and preparation of local food is not possible. Some 11.1m. children were in receipt of special nutrition support in 2011. The Programme's food donations must meet internationally agreed standards applicable to trade in food products. In May 2003 WFP's Executive Board approved a policy on donations of genetically modified (GM) foods and other foods derived from biotechnology, determining that the Programme would continue to accept donations of GM/biotech food and that, when distributing it, relevant national standards would be respected. It is WFP policy to buy food as near to where it is needed as possible, with a view to saving on transport costs and helping to sustain local economies. From 2008 targeted cash and voucher schemes started to be implemented, as a possible alternative to food rations (see below). There were some 4.4m. beneficiaries of cash and voucher programmes in 2011. During 2011 WFP and several corporate partners started to implement pilot schemes in targeted areas in Bangladesh and Indonesia under a new Project Laser Beam (PLB) initiative, aimed at addressing child malnutrition. With other UN agencies, governments, research institutions, and representatives of civil society and of the private sector, WFP supports the Scaling up Nutrition (SUN) initiative, which was initiated in 2009, under the co-ordination of the UN Secretary-General's Special Representative for Food Security and Nutrition, with the aim of increasing the coverage of interventions that improve nutrition during the first 1,000 days of a child's life (such as exclusive breastfeeding, optimal complementary feeding practices, and provision of essential vitamins and minerals); and ensuring that nutrition plans are implemented at national level, and that government programmes take nutrition into account.

WFP aims to address the causes of chronic malnourishment, which it identifies as poverty and lack of opportunity. It emphasizes the role played by women (who are most likely to sow, reap, harvest and cook household food) in combating hunger, and endeavours to address the specific nutritional needs of women, to increase their access to food and development resources, and to promote girls' education. WFP estimates that females represent four-fifths of people engaged in farming in Africa and three-fifths of people engaged in farming in Asia, and that globally women are the sole breadwinners in one-third of households. Increasingly WFP distributes food assistance through women, believing that vulnerable children are more likely to be reached in this way. In September 2012 WFP, FAO, IFAD and UN Women launched 'Accelerating Progress Toward the Economic Empowerment of Rural Women', a five-year initiative that was to be implemented initially in Ethiopia, Guatemala, Kyrgyzstan, Liberia, Nepal, Niger and Rwanda. The Programme also focuses resources on supporting the nutrition and food security of households and communities affected by HIV/AIDS, and on promoting food security as a means of mitigating extreme poverty and vulnerability and thereby combating the spread and impact of HIV/AIDS. In February 2003 WFP and the Joint UN Programme on HIV/AIDS (UNAIDS) concluded an agreement to address jointly the relationship between HIV/AIDS, regional food shortages and chronic hunger, with a particular focus on Africa, Southeast Asia and the Caribbean. In October of that year WFP became a co-sponsor of UNAIDS. WFP also urges the development of new food assistance strategies as a means of redressing global inequalities and thereby combating the threat of conflict and international terrorism.

WFP is a participant in the High Level Task Force (HLTF) on the Global Food Security Crisis, which was established by the UN Secretary-General in April 2008 with the aim of addressing the global impact of soaring levels of food and commodity prices, and of formulating a comprehensive framework for action. WFP participated in the High-Level Conference on World Food Security and the Challenges of Climate Change and Bioenergy that was convened by FAO in June. At that time WFP determined to allocate some US $1,200m. in extra-budgetary funds to alleviate hunger in the worst-affected countries. In January 2009 the HLTF participated in a follow-up high-level meeting convened in Madrid, Spain, and attended also by 62 government ministers and representatives from 126 countries. The meeting agreed to initiate a consultation process with regard to the establishment of a Global Partnership for Agriculture, Food Security and Nutrition. During 2009 the long-standing Committee on World Food Security (CFS), open to member states of WFP, FAO and IFAD, underwent reform, becoming a central component of the new Global Partnership; thereafter the CFS was tasked with influencing hunger elimination programmes at global, regional and national level, taking into account that food security relates not just to agriculture but also to economic access to food, adequate nutrition, social safety nets and human rights. WFP participated in a World Summit on Food Security, organized by FAO, in Rome, in November 2009, which aimed to secure greater coherence in the global governance of food security and set a 'new world food order'. WFP, with FAO, IFAD and other agencies, contributes to the Agriculture Market Information System, established in 2011 to improve transparency in agricultural markets and contribute to stabilizing food price volatility.

WFP, with FAO and IFAD, leads an initiative on ensuring food security by strengthening feeding programmes and expanding support to farmers in developing countries, the second of nine activities that were launched in April 2009 by the UN System Chief Executives Board for Co-ordination (CEB), with the aim of alleviating the impact on poor and vulnerable populations of the developing global economic crisis. WFP also solely leads an initiative on emergency activities to meet humanitarian needs and promote security, the seventh of the CEB activities launched in April 2009.

In June 2008 WFP's Executive Board approved a strategic plan, covering the period 2008–13, that shifted the focus of WFP's activities from the supply of food to the supply of food assistance, and provided a new institutional framework to support vulnerable populations affected by the ongoing global food crisis and by possible future effects of global climate change. The five principal objectives of the 2008–13 plan were: saving lives and protecting livelihoods in emergencies; preparing for emergencies; restoring and rebuilding lives after emergencies; reducing chronic hunger and undernutrition everywhere; and strengthening the capacity of countries to reduce hunger. The plan emphasized prevention of hunger through early warning systems and analysis; local purchase of food; the maintenance of efficient and effective emergency response systems; and the use of focused cash and voucher programmes (including electronic vouchers) to ensure the accessibility to vulnerable people in urban environments of food that was locally available but, owing to the high level of market prices and increasing unemployment, beyond their financial means. It was envisaged that the cash and voucher approach would reduce the cost to WFP of transporting and storing food supplies, and would also benefit local economies (both being long-term WFP policy objectives). Vouchers are considered to be relatively easy to monitor, and also may be flexibly increased or reduced depending upon the severity of an emergency situation.

WFP has developed a range of mechanisms to enhance its preparedness for emergency situations (such as conflict, drought and other natural disasters) and to improve its capacity for responding effectively to crises as they arise. Through its Vulnerability Analysis and Mapping (VAM) project, WFP aims to identify potentially vulnerable groups by providing information on food security and the capacity of different groups for coping with shortages, and to enhance emergency contingency-planning and long-term assistance objectives. VAM produces food security analysis reports, guidelines, reference documents and maps. In 2011 VAM launched an online Food and Commodity Price Data Store relating to data on the most commonly consumed staples in 1070 markets in 68 countries. In 2012 VAM field units were operational in 43 countries world-wide. The key elements of WFP's emergency response capacity are its strategic stores of food and logistics equipment (drawn from 'stocks afloat': ships loaded with WFP food supplies that can be re-routed to assist in crisis situations; development project stocks redesignated as emergency project contingency reserves; and in-country borrowing from national food reserves enabled by bilateral agreements); stand-by arrangements to enable the rapid deployment of personnel, communications and other essential equipment; and the Augmented Logistics Intervention Team for Emergencies (ALITE), which undertakes capacity assessments and contingency-planning. When engaging in a crisis WFP dispatches an emergency preparedness team to quantify the amount and type of food assistance required, and to identify the beneficiaries of and the timescale and logistics (e.g. means of transportation; location of humanitarian corridors, if necessary; and designated food distribution sites, such as refugee camps, other emergency shelters and therapeutic feeding centres) underpinning the ensuing EMOP. Once the EMOP has been drafted, WFP launches an appeal to the international donor community for funds and assistance to enable its implementation. WFP special operations are short-term logistics and infrastructure projects that are undertaken to facilitate the movement of food aid, regardless of whether the food is provided by the Agency itself. Special operations typically complement EMOPs or longer rehabilitation projects.

During 2000 WFP led efforts, undertaken with other UN humanitarian agencies, for the design and application of local UN Joint Logistics Centre facilities, which aimed to co-ordinate resources in an emergency situation. In 2001 a UN Humanitarian Response Depot was opened in Brindisi, Italy, under the direction of WFP experts, for the storage of essential rapid response equipment. In that year the Programme published a set of guidelines on contingency planning. Since 2003 WFP has been mandated to provide aviation transport services to the wider humanitarian community. During 2005 the UN's Inter-Agency Standing Committee (IASC), concerned with co-ordinating the international response to humanitarian disasters, developed a concept of organizing agency assistance to IDPs through the institutionalization of a 'Cluster Approach', currently comprising 11 core areas of activity. WFP was designated the lead agency for the clusters on Emergency Telecommunications (jointly with OCHA and UNICEF) and Logistics. During January 2008–June 2009 WFP implemented a special operation to improve country-specific communications services in order to enhance country-level cluster capacities. A review of the humanitarian cluster approach, undertaken during 2010, concluded that a new cluster on Food Security should be established. The new cluster, established accordingly in 2011, is led jointly by WFP and FAO, and aims to combine expertise in food aid and agricultural assistance in order to boost food security and to improve the resilience of food-insecure disaster-affected communities.

WFP aims to link its relief and development activities to provide a continuum between short-term relief and longer-term rehabilitation and development. In order to achieve this objective, WFP aims to promote capacity-building elements within relief operations, e.g. training, income-generating activities and environmental protection measures; and to integrate elements that strengthen disaster mitigation into development projects, including soil conservation, reafforestation, irrigation infrastructure, and transport construction and rehabilitation. In all its projects WFP aims to assist the most vulnerable groups (such as nursing mothers and children) and to ensure that beneficiaries have an adequate and balanced diet. Through its development activities, WFP aims to alleviate poverty in developing countries by promoting self-reliant families and communities. No individual country is permitted to receive more than 10% of the Programme's available development resources. WFP's Food-for-Assets development operations pay workers living in poverty with food in return for participation in self-help schemes and labour-intensive projects, with the aim of enabling vulnerable households and communities to focus time and resources on investing in lasting assets with which to raise themselves out of poverty (rather than on day-to-day survival). Food-for-Assets projects provide training in new techniques for achieving improved food security (such as training in new agricultural skills or in the establishment of home gardening businesses); and include, for example, building new irrigation or terracing infrastructures; soil and water conservation activities; and allocating food rations to villagers to enable them to devote time to building schools and clinics. In areas undermined by conflict WFP offers food assistance as an incentive for former combatants to put down their weapons and learn new skills. In 2011 some 21.3m. people were in receipt of food from WFP as an incentive to build assets, attend training, strengthen resilience to shocks and preserve livelihoods. WFP focuses on providing good nutrition for the first 1,000 days of life, from the womb to two years of age, in order to lay the foundations for a healthy childhood and adulthood. WFP's *1,000 days plus* approach supports children over the age of two through school feeding activities, which aim to expand educational opportunities for poor children (given that it is difficult for children to concentrate on studies without adequate food and nutrition, and that food-insecure households frequently have to choose between educating their children or making them work to help the family to survive), and to improve the quality of the teaching environment. During 2011 school feeding projects benefited 23.2m. children. As an incentive to promote the education of vulnerable children, including orphans and children with HIV/AIDS, and to encourage families to send their daughters to school, WFP also implements 'take-home ration' projects, under which it provides basic food items to certain households, usually including sacks of rice and cans of cooking oil. WFP's Purchase for Progress (P4P) programme, launched in September 2008, expands the Programme's long-term 'local procurement' policy, enabling smallholder and low-income farmers in developing countries to supply food to WFP's global assistance operations. Under P4P farmers are taught techniques and provided with tools to enable them to compete competitively in the market-place. P4P also aims to identify and test specific successful local practices that could be replicated to benefit small-scale farmers on a wider scale. During 2008–13 P4P initiatives were being piloted in 21 countries, in Africa, Latin America and Asia. By 2012 WFP had established links under P4P with more than 1,000 farmers' organizations representing more than 1.1m. farmers world-wide. In September 2009 WFP, the Global Alliance for Improved Nutrition and other partners launched Project Laser Beam (PLB), a five-year public-private partnership aimed at eradicating eradicating child malnutrition; PLB initially undertook pilot projects in Bangladesh and India.

Since 1999 WFP has been implementing PRROs, where the emphasis is on fostering stability, rehabilitation and long-term development for victims of natural disasters, displaced persons and refugees. PRROs are introduced no later than 18 months after the initial EMOP and last no more than three years. When undertaken in collaboration with UNHCR and other international agencies, WFP has responsibility for mobilizing basic food commodities and for related transport, handling and storage costs.

In November 2011 WFP and the Brazilian authorities inaugurated a Centre of Excellence Against Hunger, in Brasília, Brazil, which aimed to utilize techniques used in a long-term Brazilian initiative known as 'Fome Zero' (Zero Hunger) to support other countries in ending malnutrition and hunger. The Centre is a global reference point on school meals, nutrition and food security. In 2012 its activities were focused on 18 countries, in Africa, Asia and Latin America and the Caribbean.

In 2011 the five sub-regions of sub-Saharan Africa represented the main regional focus of WFP relief activities; during that year operational expenditure there amounted to US $2,180.9m. (58% of WFP's total annual operational expenditure), including $1,762.6m. for relief operations and $316m. for development projects. During 2008–13 WFP's new P4P programme (see above) was being piloted in Burkina Faso, the Democratic Republic of the Congo (DRC), Ethiopia, Ghana, Kenya, Liberia, Malawi, Mali, Mozambique, Rwanda, Sierra Leone, Sudan, Tanzania, Uganda and Zambia.

Drought-affected communities in the Horn of Africa are a particular focus of WFP's sub-Saharan Africa activities. By mid-2011, as a result of crop failure and livestock loss following two consecutive seasons of poor rainfall, a severe drought prevailed in the Horn of Africa, with southern Somalia, in particular, a focus of humanitarian emergency. The situation in Somalia was exacerbated by the long-term lack of effective government there, the inaccessibility of extensive rebel-controlled areas, and high food prices which had further limited access to adequate nutrition. An estimated 3.7m. southern Somalis were estimated to be suffering food insecurity at that time—with the rate of acute malnutrition reaching 30% in some areas—and, over the period July 2011–early February 2012, the UN declared a state of famine in two southern Somali regions. It was reported in July 2011 that many Somali rural households were migrating in search of food and support to the conflict-affected Somali capital, Mogadishu, as well as into neighbouring countries. During July 2011–December 2012 an EMOP was being undertaken which aimed to provide 239,820 metric tons of food assistance to 3.9m. beneficiaries in Somalia. Over the period January 2009–December 2011 some 130,271 Eritrean, Somali and Sudanese refugees sheltering in Ethiopia benefited from an $83.9m. PRRO. From 2009–13 WFP was implementing a country development programme, costing $106.3m., that was to support annually about 650,000 Kenyan primary school children in food-insecure areas and to assist annually around 78,000 food-insecure Kenyans affected by HIV/AIDS to graduate from food support. A one-year emergency operation in South Sudan for 2012 aimed to supply 152,243 metric tons of food aid to 2.7m. food-insecure and conflict-affected beneficiaries at a cost of $78.7m.

In 2010 and, again, from early 2012, the Sahel region of West Africa (including parts of Niger, Mali, Mauritania, Burkina Faso, Chad, Gambia, northern Nigeria and Senegal) was affected by severe drought, causing acute food insecurity. In early 2012, in response, WFP aimed to provide emergency food assistance to some 3.3m. beneficiaries in Niger, 750,000 in Mali, and 400,000 Mauritanians. The situation in northern areas of Mali was exacerbated from March by violent conflict, causing some 200,000 people to be displaced from their homes and a further 160,000 to seek shelter in neighbouring countries (Burkino Faso, Mauritania, Niger). An EMOP 'Assistance to Refugees and IDPs Affected by Insecurity in Mali' was under way during June–December 2012, and was to support some 550,000 people. A $46.4m. country development programme being implemented in Niger during 2009–13, and targeting 1.3m. beneficiaries, was to increase access to basic education, especially for girls; to strengthen the prevention and mitigation of food insecurity during lean periods; and to contribute to improving the health and nutritional status of patients living with HIV/AIDS and TB. From mid-2012 heavy rainfall in Niger devastated food crops, further disrupting food security there.

In September 2012 WFP launched an EMOP, with a projected cost of US $81m., to provide high energy biscuits and then emergency food rations—or, in areas with functioning food markets, cash or vouchers—to some 1.2m. people affected by ongoing conflict in the DRC provinces of North Kivu, South Kivu, North Katanga, Maniema and Province Orientale.

Finance

The Programme is funded by voluntary contributions from donor countries, intergovernmental bodies such as the European Commission, and the private sector. Contributions are made in the form of commodities, finance and services (particularly shipping). Commitments to the International Emergency Food Reserve (IEFR), from which WFP provides the majority of its food supplies, and to the Immediate Response Account of the IEFR (IRA), are also made on a voluntary basis by donors. WFP's projected budget for 2012 amounted to some US $5,484.4m. Contributions by donors were forecast at $3,750m.

Publications

Food and Nutrition Handbook.
School Feeding Handbook.
World Hunger Series.
Year in Review.

Food and Agriculture Organization of the United Nations—FAO

Address: Viale delle Terme di Caracalla, 00100 Rome, Italy.

Telephone: (06) 5705-1; **fax:** (06) 5705-3152; **e-mail:** fao-hq@fao.org; **internet:** www.fao.org.

FAO, the first specialized agency of the UN to be founded after the Second World War, aims to alleviate malnutrition and hunger, and serves as a co-ordinating agency for development programmes in the whole range of food and agriculture, including forestry and fisheries. It helps developing countries to promote educational and training facilities and to create appropriate institutions.

Organization

(September 2012)

CONFERENCE

The governing body is the FAO Conference of member nations. It meets every two years, formulates policy, determines the organization's programme and budget on a biennial basis, and elects new members. It also elects the Director-General of the Secretariat and the Independent Chairman of the Council. Regional conferences are also held each year.

COUNCIL

The FAO Council is composed of representatives of 49 member nations, elected by the Conference for rotating three-year terms. It is the interim governing body of FAO between sessions of the Conference, and normally holds at least five sessions in each biennium. There are eight main Governing Committees of the Council: the Finance, Programme, and Constitutional and Legal Matters Committees, and the Committees on Commodity Problems, Fisheries, Agriculture, Forestry, and World Food Security.

HEADQUARTERS

At 1 July 2012 there were 1847 FAO professional staff and 1729 support staff, of whom about 55% were based at headquarters. FAO maintains five regional offices (see below), 10 sub-regional offices, five liaison offices (in Yokohama, Japan; Washington, DC, USA: for liaison with North America; Geneva, Switzerland, and New York, USA: liaison with the UN; and Brussels, Belgium: liaison with the European Union), and some more than 130 country offices. The Office of the Director-General includes the Office of Evaluation; Office of the Inspector-General; Legal Office; Ethics Office; Office of Corporate Communications; External Relations Office; and Office of Strategy, Planning and Resources Management. Work is undertaken by the following departments: Agriculture and Consumer Protection; Economic and Social Development; Fisheries and Aquaculture; Forestry; Natural Resources Management and Environment; Corporate Services, Human Resources and Finance; and Technical Co-operation.

Director-General: Dr José Graziano da Silva (Brazil).

REGIONAL OFFICES

Africa: POB 1628, Accra, Ghana; tel. (21) 675000; fax (21) 668427; e-mail fao-raf@fao.org; internet www.fao.org/world/regional/raf/index_en.asp; a biennial Regional Conference for Africa (ARC) is convened (most recently in April 2012, in Brazzaville, Republic of the Congo); Regional Rep. Maria Helena de Morais Semedo; Sub-Regional Rep. for West Africa Musa Saihou Mbenga.

Sub-regional Office for Central Africa: POB 2643, Libreville, Gabon; fax 740035; e-mail FAO-SFC@fao.org; internet www.fao.org/africa/central; Sub-regional Rep. Thombiano Lamourdia.

Subregional Office for Eastern Africa: CMC Rd, nr ILRI, Kebele 12/13, Bole Sub City, Gurd SholaAddis Ababa, Ethiopia; tel. (11) 6478888; fax (11) 647 8800; e-mail FAO-SFE@fao.org; internet www.fao.org/africa/sfe/en.

Sub-regional Office for Southern Africa: POB 3730, Harare, Zimbabwe; tel. (4) 253657; fax (4) 703497; e-mail FAO-SFS@fao.org; internet www.fao.org/world/subregional/safr; Sub-regional Rep. Gaoju Han.

Activities

FAO aims to raise levels of nutrition and standards of living by improving the production and distribution of food and other commodities derived from farms, fisheries and forests. FAO's ultimate objective is the achievement of world food security, 'Food for All'. The organization provides technical information, advice and assistance by disseminating information; acting as a neutral forum for discussion of food and agricultural issues; advising governments on policy and planning; and developing capacity directly in the field.

In November 1996 FAO hosted the World Food Summit, which was held in Rome and was attended by heads of state and senior government representatives of 186 countries. Participants approved the Rome Declaration on World Food Security and the World Food Summit Plan of Action, with the aim of halving the number of people afflicted by undernutrition, then estimated to total 828m. world-wide, by no later than 2015. A review conference to assess progress in achieving the goals of the summit, entitled World Food Summit: Five Years Later, held in June 2002, reaffirmed commitment to this objective, which is also incorporated into the UN Millennium Development Goals (MDGs). During that month FAO announced the formulation of a global 'Anti-Hunger Programme', which aimed to promote investment in the agricultural sector and rural development, with a particular focus on small-scale farmers, and to enhance food access for those most in need, for example through the provision of school meals, schemes to feed pregnant and nursing mothers and food-for-work programmes. FAO hosts the UN System Network on Rural Development and Food Security, comprising some 20 UN bodies, which was established in 1997 as an inter-agency mechanism to follow-up the World Food Summits.

In November 1999 the FAO Conference approved a long-term Strategic Framework for the period 2000–15, which emphasized national and international co-operation in pursuing the goals of the 1996 World Food Summit. The Framework promoted interdisciplinarity and partnership, and defined three main global objectives: constant access by all people to sufficient, nutritionally adequate and safe food to ensure that levels of undernourishment were reduced by 50% by 2015 (see above); the continued contribution of sustainable agriculture and rural development to economic and social progress and well-being; and the conservation, improvement and sustainable use of natural resources. It identified five corporate strategies (each supported by several strategic objectives), covering the following areas: reducing food insecurity and rural poverty; ensuring enabling policy and regulatory frameworks for food, agriculture, fisheries and forestry; creating sustainable increases in the supply and availability of agricultural, fisheries and forestry products; conserving and enhancing sustainable use of the natural resource base; and generating knowledge. In October 2007 the report of an Independent External Evaluation (IEE) into the role and functions of FAO recommended that the organization elaborate a plan for reform to ensure its continued efficiency and effectiveness. In November 2008 a Special Conference of member countries approved a three-year Immediate Plan of Action to reform the governance and management of the organization based on the recommendations of the IEE. In June 2012 the FAO Council endorsed a proposal of the Organization's Director-General to reallocate budgetary savings towards strengthening country offices, increasing strategic planning capacity, and funding more interdisciplinary activities.

In December 2007 FAO inaugurated an Initiative on Soaring Food Prices (ISFP) to help to boost food production in low-income developing countries and improve access to food and agricultural supplies in the short term, with a view to countering an escalation since 2006 in commodity prices. (During 2006–08 the Food Price Index maintained by FAO recorded that international prices for many basic food commodities had increased by around 60%, and the FAO Cereal Price Index, covering the prices of principal food staples such as wheat, rice and maize, recorded a doubling in the international price of grains over that period.) In April 2008 the UN Secretary-General appointed FAO's Director-General as Vice-Chairman of a High Level Task Force (HLTF) on the Global Food Security Crisis, which aimed to address the impact of the ongoing soaring levels of food and fuel prices and formulate a comprehensive framework for action. In June FAO hosted a High Level Conference on World Food Security and the Challenges of Climate Change and Bioenergy. The meeting adopted a Declaration on Food Security, urging the international donor community to increase its support to developing countries and countries with economies in transition. The Declaration also noted an urgent need to develop the agricultural sectors and expand food production in such countries and for increased investment in rural development, agriculture and agribusiness. In January 2009 a follow-up high level meeting was convened in Madrid, Spain, and attended by 62 government ministers and representatives from 126 countries. The meeting agreed to initiate a consultation process with regard to the establishment of a Global Partnership for Agriculture, Food Security and Nutrition to strengthen international co-ordination and governance for food security. During 2009 the long-standing Committee on World Food Security (CFS), open to member states of FAO, WFP and IFAD, underwent reform, becoming a central component of the new Global Partnership; thereafter the CFS was tasked with influencing hunger elimination programmes at global, regional and national level, taking into account that food security relates not just to agriculture but also to economic access to food, adequate nutrition, social safety nets and human rights. The CFS appoints the steering committee of the High Level Panel of Experts on Food Security and Nutrition (HLPE), established in October 2009.

In May 2009 the EU donated €106m. to FAO, to support farmers and improve food security in 10 developing countries in Africa, Asia and the Caribbean that were particularly badly affected by the recently emerged global food crisis. Addressing the World Grain Forum, convened in St Petersburg, Russia, in June 2009, the FAO Director-General demanded a more effective and coherent global governance system to ensure future world food security, and urged that a larger proportion of development aid should be allocated to agriculture, to enable developing countries to invest in rural infrastructures. During June it was estimated that, in 2009, the number of people world-wide suffering chronic, daily hunger had risen to an unprecedented 1,020m., of whom an estimated 642m. were in Asia and the Pacific; 265m. in sub-Saharan Africa; 53m. in Latin America and the Caribbean; and 42m. in the Middle East and North Africa. Around 15m. people resident in developed countries were estimated at that time to be afflicted by chronic hunger. The *OECD-FAO Agricultural Outlook 2009–18*, issued in June 2009, found the global agriculture sector to be showing more resilience to the ongoing world-wide economic crisis than other sectors, owing to the status of food as a basic human necessity. However, the report warned that the state of the agriculture sector could become more fragile if the ongoing global downturn were to worsen. In July the FAO Director-General welcomed the L'Aquila Joint Statement on Global Food Security (promoting sustainable agricultural development), and the Food Security Initiative with commitments of US $20,000m., that were approved in that month by G8 leaders.

In mid-October 2009 a high-level forum of experts was convened by FAO to discuss policy on the theme 'How to Feed the World in 2050'. In November 2009 FAO organized a World Summit on Food Security, in Rome, with the aim of achieving greater coherence in the global governance of food security and setting a 'new world food order'. Leaders attending the Summit issued a declaration in which they adopted a number of strategic objectives, including: ensuring urgent action towards achieving World Food Summit objectives/the UN MDG relating to reducing undernutrition; promoting the new Global Partnership for Agriculture, Food Security and Nutrition and fully committing to reform of the CFS; reversing the decline in national and international funding for agriculture, food security and rural development in developing countries, and encouraging new investment to increase sustainable agricultural production; reducing poverty and working towards achieving food security and access to 'Food for All'; and confronting proactively the challenges posed by climate change to food security. The Summit determined to base its pursuit of these strategic objectives on the following *Five Rome Principles for Sustainable Global Food Security*: (i) investment in country-owned plans aimed at channelling resources to efficient results-based programmes and partnerships; (ii) fostering strategic co-ordination at national, regional and global level to improve governance, promote better allocation of resources, avoid duplication of efforts and identify response gaps; (iii) striving for a comprehensive twin-track approach to food security comprising direct action to combat hunger in the most vulnerable, and also medium- and long-term sustainable agricultural, food security, nutrition and rural development programmes to eliminate the root causes of hunger and poverty, including through the progressive realization of the right to adequate food; (iv) ensuring a strong role for the multilateral system by sustained improvements in efficiency, responsiveness, co-ordination and effectiveness of multilateral institutions; and (v) ensuring sustained and substantial commitment by all partners to investment in agriculture and food security and nutrition, with provision of necessary resources in a timely and reliable fashion, aimed at multi-year plans and programmes. The FAO Director-General welcomed a new 'Zero Hunger Challenge' initiative announced by the UN Secretary-General in June 2012, which aimed to eliminate malnutrition through measures such as boosting the productivity of smallholders, creating sustainable food systems, and reducing food wastage.

FAO, with WFP and IFAD, leads an initiative to strengthen feeding programmes and expand support to farmers in developing countries, the second of nine activities that were launched in April 2009 by the UN System Chief Executives Board for Co-ordination (CEB), with the aim of alleviating the impact on poor and vulnerable populations of the developing global economic crisis.

With other UN agencies, FAO attended the Summit of the World's Regions on Food Insecurity, held in Dakar, Senegal, in January 2010. The summit urged that global governance of food security should integrate players on every level, and expressed support for the developing Global Partnership for Agriculture, Food Security and Nutrition.

In February 2011 the FAO Food Price Index, at 238 points, recorded the highest levels of global food prices since 1990, with prices having risen in each consecutive month during July 2010–February 2011 (and having, in December 2010, exceeded the previous peak reached during mid-2008). The Cereal Price Index also recorded in February 2011 the highest price levels since mid-2008. FAO maintains, additionally, a Dairy Price Index, an Oils/Fats Price Index, a Meat Price Index and a Sugar Price Index. In August 2012 the Food Price Index averaged 213 points, unchanged from July.

In June 2011 agriculture ministers from G20 countries adopted an action plan aimed at stabilizing food price volatility and agriculture, with a focus on improving international policy co-ordination and agricultural production; promoting targeted emergency humanitarian food reserves; and developing, under FAO auspices, an Agricultural Market Information System (AMIS) to improve market transparency and help stabilize food price volatility.

FAO's annual *State of Food Insecurity in the World* report (see below), compiled in 2011 with help from IFAD and WFP, maintained that volatile and high food prices were likely to continue, rendering poorer consumers, farmers and nations more vulnerable to poverty and hunger.

In May 2012 the CFS endorsed a set of landmark Voluntary Guidelines on the Responsible Governance of Tenure of Land, Fisheries and Forests in the Context of National Food Security, with the aim of supporting governments in safeguarding the rights of citizens to own or have access to natural resources. In June, in the context of the UN Conference on Sustainable Development, convened during that month in Rio de Janeiro, Brazil, FAO released a study that advocated for the promotion of energy-smart systems for food production and usage.

World Food Day, commemorating the foundation of FAO, is held annually on 16 October. In May 2010 FAO launched an online petition entitled the *1billionhungry project*, with the aim of raising awareness of the plight of people world-wide suffering from chronic hunger.

AGRICULTURE AND CONSUMER PROTECTION

The Department of Agriculture and Consumer Protection has the following divisions: Animal Production and Health; Nutrition and Consumer Protection; Plant Production and Protection; Rural Infrastructure and Agro-Industries; and the Joint FAO/IAEA Division of Nuclear Techniques in Food and Agriculture.

FAO's overall objective is to lead international efforts to counter hunger and to improve levels of nutrition. Within this context FAO is concerned to improve crop and grassland productivity and to develop sustainable agricultural systems to provide for enhanced food security and economic development. It provides member countries with technical advice for plant improvement, the application of plant biotechnology, the development of integrated production systems and rational grassland management. There are groups concerned with the main field cereal crops, i.e. rice, maize and wheat, which *inter alia* identify means of enhancing production, collect and analyse relevant data and promote collaboration between research institutions, government bodies and other farm management organizations. In 1985 and 1990 FAO's International Rice Commission endorsed the use of hybrid rice, which had been developed in the People's Republic of China, as a means of meeting growing demand for the crop, in particular in the Far East, and has subsequently assisted member countries to acquire the necessary technology and training to develop hybrid rice production. In Africa FAO has collaborated with the West African Rice Development Association to promote and facilitate the use of new rice varieties and crop management practices. FAO actively promotes the concept of Conservation Agriculture, which aims to minimize the need for mechanical soil tillage or additional farming resources and to reduce soil degradation and erosion.

FAO is also concerned with the development and diversification of horticultural and industrial crops, for example oil seeds, fibres and medicinal plants. FAO collects and disseminates data regarding crop trials and new technologies. It has developed an information processing site, Ecocrop, to help farmers identify appropriate crops and environmental requirements. FAO works to protect and support the sustainable development of grasslands and pasture, which contribute to the livelihoods of an estimated 800m. people world-wide.

FAO's plant protection service incorporates a range of programmes concerned with the control of pests and the use of pesticides. In February 2001 FAO warned that some 30% of pesticides sold in developing countries did not meet internationally accepted quality standards. In November 2002 FAO adopted a revised International Code of Conduct on the Distribution and Use of Pesticides (first adopted in 1985) to reduce the inappropriate distribution and use of pesticides and other toxic compounds, particularly in developing countries. In September 1998 a new legally binding treaty on trade in hazardous chemicals and pesticides was adopted at an international conference held in Rotterdam, Netherlands. The so-called Rotterdam Convention required that hazardous chemicals and pesticides banned or severely restricted in at least two countries should not be exported unless explicitly agreed by the importing country. It also identified certain pesticide formulations as too dangerous to be used by farmers in developing countries, and incorporated an obligation that countries halt national production of those hazardous compounds. The treaty entered into force in February 2004. FAO co-operates with UNEP to provide secretariat services for the Convention. FAO has promoted the use of Integrated Pest Management (IPM) initiatives to encourage the use, at local level, of safer and more effective methods of pest control, such as biological control methods and natural predators.

FAO hosts the secretariat of the International Plant Protection Convention (first adopted in 1951, revised in 1997) which aims to prevent the spread of plant pests and to promote effective control measures. The secretariat helps to define phytosanitary standards, promote the exchange of information and extend technical assistance to contracting parties (177 at September 2012).

FAO is concerned with the conservation and sustainable use of plant and animal genetic resources. It works with regional and international associations to develop seed networks, to encourage the use of improved seed production systems, to elaborate quality control and certification mechanisms and to co-ordinate seed security activities, in particular in areas prone to natural or man-made disasters. FAO has developed a World Information and Early Warning System (WIEWS) to gather and disseminate information concerning plant genetic resources for food and agriculture and to undertake periodic assessments of the state of those resources. FAO is also developing, as part of the WIEWS, a Seed Information Service to extend information to member states on seeds, planting and new technologies. In June 1996 representatives of more than 150 governments convened in Leipzig, Germany, at an International Technical Conference organized by FAO to consider the use and conservation of plant genetic resources as an essential means of enhancing food security. The meeting adopted a Global Plan of Action, which included measures to strengthen the development of plant varieties and to promote the use and availability of local varieties and locally adapted crops to farmers, in particular following a natural disaster, war or civil conflict. In November 2001 the FAO Conference adopted the International Treaty on Plant Genetic Resources for Food and Agriculture (also referred to as the Seed Treaty), with the aim of providing a framework to ensure access to plant genetic resources and to related knowledge, technologies, and—through the Treaty's Benefit-sharing Fund (BSF)—funding. The Seed Treaty entered into force in June 2004, having received the required number of ratifications, and, by September 2012, had 127 states parties. The BSF assists poor farmers in developing countries with conserving, and also adapting to climate change, their most important food crops; in 2011 the Fund supported 11 high-impact projects for small-scale farmers in four regions. It was hoped that international donors would raise US $116m. for the BSF by 2014. By 2012 around 1,750 gene banks had been established world-wide, storing more than 7m. plant samples.

FAO's Animal Production and Health Division is concerned with the control and management of major animal diseases, and, in recent years, with safeguarding humans from livestock diseases. Other programmes are concerned with the contribution of livestock to poverty alleviation, the efficient use of natural resources in livestock production, the management of animal genetic resources, promoting the exchange of information and mapping the distribution of livestock around the world. In 2001 FAO established a Pro-Poor Livestock Policy Initiative to support the formulation and implementation of livestock-related policies to improve the livelihood and nutrition of the world's rural poor, with an initial focus on the Andean region, the Horn of Africa, West Africa, South Asia and the Mekong.

The Emergency Prevention System for Transboundary Animal and Plant Pests and Diseases (EMPRES) was established in 1994 to strengthen FAO's activities in the prevention, early warning, control and, where possible, eradication of pests and highly contagious livestock diseases (which the system categorizes as epidemic diseases of strategic importance, such as rinderpest or foot-and-mouth; diseases requiring tactical attention at international or regional level, e.g. Rift Valley fever; and emerging diseases, e.g. bovine spongiform encephalopathy—BSE). EMPRES has a desert locust component, and has published guidelines on all aspects of desert locust monitoring. A web-based EMPRES Global Animal Disease Information System (EMPRES-i) aims to support veterinary services through the timely release of disease information to enhance early warning and response to transboundary animal diseases, including emergent zoonoses. FAO assumed responsibility for technical leadership and co-ordination of the Global Rinderpest Eradication Programme (GREP), which had the objective of eliminating that disease by 2011; in June 2011 the FAO Conference adopted a resolution declaring global freedom from rinderpest. The FAO and the World Organisation for Animal Health (OIE) adopted two resolutions during 2011 relating to the destruction/safe storage of remaining stocks of rinderpest virus and on banning the use of the live virus in research. In June 2012 a conference convened in Bangkok, Thailand, under the auspices of the FAO, OIE and Thai Government, endorsed a new Global Foot and Mouth Disease Control Strategy. In November 1997 FAO initiated a Programme Against African Trypanosomiasis, which aimed to counter the disease affecting cattle in almost one-third of Africa. In November 2004 FAO established a specialized Emergency Centre for Transboundary Animal Disease Operations (ECTAD) to enhance FAO's role in assisting member states to combat animal disease outbreaks and in co-ordinating international efforts to research, monitor and control transboundary disease crises. In May 2004 FAO and the OIE signed an agreement to clarify their respective areas of competence and improve co-operation, in response to an increase in contagious transboundary animal diseases (such as foot-and-mouth disease and avian influenza, see below). The two bodies agreed to establish a global framework on the control of transboundary animal diseases, entailing improved international collaboration and circulation of information. In early 2006 FAO, OIE and the World Health Organization (WHO) launched a Global Early Warning and Response System for Major Animal Diseases, including Zoonoses (GLEWS), in order to strengthen their joint capacity to detect, monitor and respond to animal disease threats. In October 2006 FAO inaugurated a new Crisis Management Centre (CMC) to co-ordinate (in close co-operation with OIE) the organization's response to outbreaks of H5N1 and other major emergencies related to animal or food health.

In September 2004 FAO and WHO declared an ongoing epidemic in certain East Asian countries of the H5N1 strain of highly pathogenic avian influenza (HPAI) to be a 'crisis of global importance': the disease was spreading rapidly through bird populations and was also transmitting to human populations through contact with diseased birds (mainly poultry). In that month FAO published *Recommendations for the Prevention, Control and Eradication of Highly Pathogenic Avian Influenza in Asia*. In April 2005 FAO and OIE established an international network of laboratories and scientists (OFFLU) to exchange data and provide expert technical advice on avian influenza. In the following month FAO, with WHO and OIE, launched a global strategy for the progressive control of the disease. In November a conference on Avian Influenza and Human Pandemic Influenza, jointly organized by FAO, WHO and OIE and the World Bank, issued a plan of action identifying a number of responses, including: supporting the development of integrated national plans for H5N1 containment and human pandemic influenza preparedness and response; assisting countries with the aggressive control of H5N1 and with establishing a more detailed understanding of the role of wild birds in virus transmission; nominating rapid response teams of experts to support epidemiological field investigations; expanding national and regional capacity in surveillance, diagnosis, and alert and response systems; expanding the network of influenza laboratories; establishing multi-country networks for the control or prevention of animal transboundary diseases; expanding the global antiviral stockpile; strengthening veterinary infrastructures; and mapping a global strategy and work plan for co-ordinating antiviral and influenza vaccine research and development. In June 2006 FAO and OIE convened a scientific conference on the spread and management of H5N1 that advocated early detection of the disease in wild birds, improved biosecurity and hygiene in the poultry trade, rapid response to disease outbreaks, and the establishment of a global tracking and monitoring facility involving participation by all relevant organizations, as well as by scientific centres, farmers' groupings, bird-watchers and hunters, and wildlife and wild bird habitat conservation bodies. The conference also urged investment in telemetry/satellite technology to improve tracking capabilities. International conference and pledging meetings on the disease were convened in Washington, DC, USA, in October 2005, Beijing, China, in January 2006, Bamako, Mali, in December and in New Delhi, India, in December 2007. In August 2008 a new strain of HPAI not previously recorded in sub-Saharan Africa was detected in Nigeria. In October the sixth international ministerial conference on avian influenza was convened in Sharm el-Sheikh, Egypt. FAO, with WHO, UNICEF, OIE, the World Bank and the UN System Influenza Co-ordinator, presented a new strategic framework, within the concept of 'One World, One Health', to improve understanding and co-operation with respect to emerging infectious diseases, to strengthen animal and public health surveillance and to enhance response mechanisms. During 2003–end-2011 outbreaks of H5N1 were recorded in 63 countries and territories, and some 250m. domestic and wild birds consequently died or were culled.

In December 2011 the conference of parties to the CMS officially ratified the establishment of a Scientific Task Force on Wildlife and

Ecosystem Health, with FAO participation, reflecting a shift in focus from the isolated targeting avian influenza towards a 'One Health' policy of caring for the health of animals, humans, and the ecosystems that support them; a Task Force on Avian Influenza and Wild Birds, established under the CMS in August 2005, was to continue as a core focus area within the larger Scientific Task Force.

In April 2009, in response to a major outbreak in humans of the swine influenza variant pandemic (H1N1) 2009, the FAO Crisis Management Centre mobilized a team of experts to increase animal disease surveillance and maintain response readiness to protect the global pig sector from infection with the emerging virus. In early May FAO, OIE, WHO and WTO together issued a statement stressing that pork products handled in accordance with hygienic practices could not be deemed a source of infection.

In December 1992 FAO, with WHO, organized an International Conference on Nutrition, which approved a World Declaration on Nutrition and a Plan of Action, aimed at promoting efforts to combat malnutrition as a development priority. Since the conference, more than 100 countries have formulated national plans of action for nutrition, many of which were based on existing development plans such as comprehensive food security initiatives, national poverty alleviation programmes and action plans to attain the targets set by the World Summit for Children in September 1990. FAO promotes other efforts, at household and community level, to improve nutrition and food security, for example a programme to support home gardens. It aims to assist the identification of food-insecure and vulnerable populations, both through its *State of Food Insecurity in the World* reports and taking a lead role in the development of Food Insecurity and Vulnerability Information and Mapping Systems (FIVIMS), a recommendation of the World Food Summit. In 1999 FAO signed a Memorandum of Understanding with UNAIDS on strengthening co-operation to combat the threat posed by the HIV/AIDS epidemic to food security, nutrition and rural livelihoods. FAO is committed to incorporating HIV/AIDS into food security and livelihood projects, to strengthening community care and to highlighting the importance of nutrition in the care of those living with HIV/AIDS.

FAO is committed to promoting food quality and safety in all different stages of food production and processing. It supports the development of integrated food control systems by member states, which incorporate aspects of food control management, inspection, risk analysis and quality assurance. The joint FAO/WHO Codex Alimentarius Commission, established in 1962, aims to protect the health of consumers, ensure fair trade practices and promote the co-ordination of food standards activities at an international level. The Commission maintains databases of standards for food additives, and for maximum residue levels of veterinary drugs maximum and pesticides. In January 2001 a joint team of FAO and WHO experts issued a report concerning the allergenicity of foods derived from biotechnology (i.e. genetically modified—GM—foods). In July the Codex Alimentarius Commission agreed the first global principles for assessing the safety of GM foods, and approved a series of maximum levels of environmental contaminants in food. In June 2004 FAO published guidelines for assessing possible risks posed to plants by living modified organisms. In July 2001 the Codex Alimentarius Commission adopted guidelines on organic livestock production, covering organic breeding methods, the elimination of growth hormones and certain chemicals in veterinary medicines, and the use of good quality organic feed with no meat or bone meal content. In January 2003 FAO organized a technical consultation on biological risk management in food and agriculture which recognized the need for a more integrated approach to so-called biosecurity, i.e. the prevention, control and management of risks to animal, human and plant life and health. FAO has subsequently developed a *Toolkit*, published in 2007, to help countries to develop and implement national biosecurity systems and to enhance biosecurity capacity. In July 2012 the Codex Alimentarius Commission agreed a set of maximum residue limits in animal tissues for the veterinary growth promoting drug Ractopamine.

FAO aims to assist member states to enhance the efficiency, competitiveness and profitability of their agricultural and food enterprises. FAO extends assistance in training, capacity-building and the formulation of agribusiness development strategies. It promotes the development of effective 'value chains', connecting primary producers with consumers, and supports other linkages within the agribusiness industry. Similarly, FAO aims to strengthen marketing systems, links between producers and retailers and training in agricultural marketing, and works to improve the regulatory framework for agricultural marketing. FAO promotes the use of new technologies to increase agricultural production and extends a range of services to support mechanization, including training, maintenance, testing and the promotion of labour saving technologies. Other programmes are focused on farm management, post-harvest management, food and non-food processing, rural finance, and rural infrastructure. FAO helps reduce immediate post-harvest losses, with the introduction of improved processing methods and storage systems. FAO participates in PhAction, a forum of 12 agencies that was established in 1999 to promote post-harvest research and the development of effective post-harvest services and infrastructure.

FAO's Joint Division with the International Atomic Energy Agency (IAEA) is concerned with the use of nuclear techniques in food and agriculture. It co-ordinates research projects, provides scientific and technical support to technical co-operation projects and administers training courses. A joint laboratory in Seibersdorf, Austria, is concerned with testing biotechnologies and in developing non-toxic fertilizers (especially those that are locally available) and improved strains of food crops (especially from indigenous varieties). In the area of animal production and health, the Joint Division has developed progesterone-measuring and disease diagnostic kits. Other sub-programmes of the Joint Division are concerned with soil and water, plant breeding and nutrition, insect pest control and food and environmental protection.

NATURAL RESOURCES MANAGEMENT AND ENVIRONMENT

The Natural Resources Management and Environment Department comprises divisions of climate, energy and tenure; and land and water.

FAO is committed to promoting the responsible and sustainable management of natural resources and other activities to protect the environment. FAO assists member states to mitigate the impact of climate change on agriculture, to adapt and enhance the resilience of agricultural systems to climate change, and to promote practices to reduce the emission of greenhouse gases from the agricultural sector. In recent years FAO has strengthened its work in the area of using natural biomass resources as fuel, both at grassroots level and industrial processing of cash crops. In 2006 FAO established the International Bioenergy Platform to serve as a focal point for research, data collection, capacity-building and strategy formulation by local, regional and international bodies concerned with bioenergy. FAO also serves as the secretariat for the Global Bioenergy Partnership, which was inaugurated in May 2006 to facilitate the collaboration between governments, international agencies and representatives of the private sector and civil society in the sustainable development of bioenergy.

FAO aims to enhance the sustainability of land and water systems, and as a result to secure agricultural productivity, through the improved tenure, management, development and conservation of those natural resources. The organization promotes equitable access to land and water resources and supports integrated land and water management, including river basin management and improved irrigation systems. FAO has developed AQUASTAT as a global information system concerned with water and agricultural issues, comprising databases, country and regional profiles, surveys and maps. AquaCrop, CropWat and ClimWat are further productivity models and databases which have been developed to help to assess crop requirements and potential yields. Since 2003 FAO has participated in UN Water, an inter-agency initiative to co-ordinate existing approaches to water-related issues. In August 2012 FAO launched an initiative entitled 'Coping with water scarcity: An action framework for agriculture and food security', which aimed to support the improved management of water resources in agricultural production, including through the development of irrigation schemes, the recycling and re-using of waste water, and the implementation of measures to reduce water pollution.

In December 2008 FAO organized a Ministerial Conference on Water for Agriculture and Energy in Africa: 'the Challenges of Climate Change', in Sirte, Libya, which was attended by representatives of 48 African member countries and other representatives of international, regional and civil organizations.

Within the FAO's Natural Resources Management and Environment Department is a Research and Extension Division, which provides advisory and technical services to support national capacity-building, research, communication and education activities. It maintains several databases which support and facilitate the dissemination of information, for example relating to proven transferable technologies and biotechnologies in use in developing countries. The Division advises countries on communication strategies to strengthen agricultural and rural development, and has supported the use of rural radio. FAO is the UN lead agency of an initiative, 'Education for Rural People', which aims to improve the quality of and access to basic education for people living in rural areas and to raise awareness of the issue as an essential element of achieving the MDGs. The Research and Extension Division hosts the secretariat of the Global Forum on Agricultural Research, which was established in October 1996 as a collaboration of research centres, non-governmental and private sector organizations and development agencies. The Forum aims to strengthen research and promote knowledge partnerships concerned with the alleviation of poverty, the increase in food security and the sustainable use of natural resources. The Division also hosts the secretariat of the Science Council of the Consultative Group on International Agricultural Research (CGIAR), which, specifically, aims to enhance and promote the quality, relevance and impact of science within the network of CGIAR research centres and to mobilize global scientific expertise.

In September 2009 FAO published, jointly with the Centre for Indigenous People's Nutrition and Environment (CINE—based in McGill University, Montreal, Canada) a report entitled *Indigenous People's Food Systems: The Many Dimensions of Culture, Diversity and Environment for Nutrition and Health*, which aimed to demonstrate the wealth of knowledge on nutrition retained within indigenous communities world-wide.

FISHERIES AND AQUACULTURE

FAO's Fisheries and Aquaculture Department comprises divisions of fisheries and aquaculture policy and economics; and fisheries and aquaculture resources use and conservation.

FAO aims to facilitate and secure the long-term sustainable development of fisheries and aquaculture, in both inland and marine waters, and to promote its contribution to world food security. In March 1995 a ministerial meeting of fisheries adopted the Rome Consensus on World Fisheries, which identified a need for immediate action to eliminate overfishing and to rebuild and enhance depleting fish stocks. In November the FAO Conference adopted a Code of Conduct for Responsible Fishing (CCRF), which incorporated many global fisheries and aquaculture issues (including fisheries resource conservation and development, fish catches, seafood and fish processing, commercialization, trade and research) to promote the sustainable development of the sector. In February 1999 the FAO Committee on Fisheries adopted new international measures, within the framework of the Code of Conduct, in order to reduce over-exploitation of the world's fish resources, as well as plans of action for the conservation and management of sharks and the reduction in the incidental catch of seabirds in longline fisheries. The voluntary measures were endorsed at a ministerial meeting, held in March and attended by representatives of some 126 countries, which issued a declaration to promote the implementation of the Code of Conduct and to achieve sustainable management of fisheries and aquaculture. Several international plans of action (IPOA) have been elaborated within the context of the CCRF: the IPOA for Conservation and Management of Sharks (IPOA-Sharks, 1999); the IPOA for the Management of Fishing Capacity (IPOA-Capacity, 1999); the IPOA for Reducing Incidental Catch of Seabirds in Longline Fisheries ((IPOA-Seabirds, 1999); and the IPOA to Prevent, Deter and Eliminate Illegal, Unreported and Unregulated Fishing (IPOA-IUU, 2001). FAO has prepared guidelines to support member countries with implementing IPOAs and has encouraged states to develop national plans of action to complement the international plans. FishCode, an interregional assistance programme, supports developing countries in implementing the CCRF.

In 2001 FAO estimated that about one-half of major marine fish stocks were fully exploited, one-quarter under-exploited, at least 15% over-exploited, and 10% depleted or recovering from depletion. IUU was estimated to account for up to 30% of total catches in certain fisheries. In October FAO and the Icelandic Government jointly organized the Reykjavík Conference on Responsible Fisheries in the Marine Ecosystem, which adopted a declaration on pursuing responsible and sustainable fishing activities in the context of ecosystem-based fisheries management (EBFM). EBFM involves determining the boundaries of individual marine ecosystems, and maintaining or rebuilding the habitats and biodiversity of each of these so that all species will be supported at levels of maximum production. In March 2005 FAO's Committee of Fisheries adopted voluntary guidelines for the so-called eco-labelling and certification of fish and fish products, i.e. based on information regarding capture management and the sustainable use of resources. In March 2007 the Committee agreed to initiate a process of negotiating an internationally-binding agreement to deny port access to fishing vessels involved in IUU activities; the eventual 'Agreement on Port State Measures to Prevent, Deter and Eliminate Illegal, Unreported and Unregulated Fishing' was endorsed by the Conference in November 2009. In recent years FAO has focused on 'flag state performance', and since 2008 has worked on developing criteria for assessing the performance of flag states, and on means of preventing vessels from flying the flags of irresponsible states. An expert consultation on flag state performance was convened in June 2009; and a technical consultation on flag state performance was initiated at FAO Headquarters in May 2011, and was resumed in March 2012.

FAO undertakes extensive monitoring, publishing every two years *The State of World Fisheries and Aquaculture*, and collates and maintains relevant databases. It formulates country and regional profiles and has developed a specific information network for the fisheries sector, GLOBEFISH, which gathers and disseminates information regarding market trends, tariffs and other industry issues. FAO aims to extend technical support to member states with regard to the management and conservation of aquatic resources, and other measures to improve the utilization and trade of products, including the reduction of post-harvest losses, preservation marketing and quality assurance. FAO promotes aquaculture (which contributes almost one-third of annual global fish landings) as a valuable source of animal protein and income-generating activity for rural communities. It has undertaken to develop an ecosystem approach to aquaculture (EAA) and works to integrate aquaculture with agricultural and irrigation systems. In February 2000 FAO and the Network of Aquaculture Centres in Asia and the Pacific (NACA) jointly convened a Conference on Aquaculture in the Third Millennium, which was held in Bangkok, Thailand, and attended by participants representing more than 200 governmental and non-governmental organizations. The Conference debated global trends in aquaculture and future policy measures to ensure the sustainable development of the sector. It adopted the Bangkok Declaration and Strategy for Aquaculture Beyond 2000. In September 2010 FAO and NACA convened the Global Conference on Aquaculture 2010, in Phuket, Thailand, on the theme 'Farming the Waters for People and Food'; the Global Conference adopted a set of recommendations on further advancing aquaculture.

In April 2012 FAO and the New Partnership for Africa's Development (NEPAD) jointly launched the NEPAD FAO Fish Programme (NFFP), which aimed to boost fisheries development, and improve the livelihoods of fishers in Africa.

FORESTRY

FAO's Forestry Department comprises divisions of forest economics, policy and products; and forest assessment, management and conservation.

FAO is committed to the sustainable management of trees, forests and forestry resources. It aims to address the critical balance of ensuring the conservation of forests and forestry resources while maximising their potential to contribute to food security and social and economic development. In March 2009 the Committee on Forestry approved a new 10-year FAO Strategic Plan for Forestry, replacing a previous strategic plan initiated in 1999. The new plan, which was 'dynamic' and was to be updated regularly, covered the social, economic and environmental aspects of forestry. The first World Forest Week was held in March 2009 and the second in October 2010. 2011 was declared the International Year of Forests by the UN General Assembly.

FAO assists member countries to formulate, implement and monitor national forestry programmes, and encourages the participation of all stakeholders in developing plans for the sustainable management of tree and forest resources. FAO also helps to implement national assessments of those programmes and of other forestry activities. At a global level FAO undertakes surveillance of the state of the world's forests and publishes a report every two years. A separate *Forest Resources Assessment* is published every five years; the latest (for 2010) was initiated in March 2008. FAO is committed to collecting and disseminating accurate information and data on forests. It maintains the Forestry Information System (FORIS) to make relevant information and forest-related databases widely accessible.

In September 2008 FAO, with UNEP and UNDP, launched the UN Collaborative Programme on Reducing Emissions from Deforestation and Forest Degradation in Developing Countries (UN-REDD), with the aim of enabling donors to pool resources (through a trust fund established for that purpose) to promote a transformation of forest resource use patterns. In August 2011 UN-REDD endorsed a Global Programme Framework covering 2011–15.

FAO is a member of the Collaborative Partnership on Forests, an informal, voluntary arrangement among 14 agencies with significant forestry programme, which was established in April 2004 on the recommendation of the UN's Economic and Social Council. FAO organizes a World Forestry Congress, generally held every six years; the 13th Congress was convened in Buenos Aires, Argentina, in October 2009.

ECONOMIC AND SOCIAL DEVELOPMENT

The Economic and Social Development Department comprises divisions of Agricultural Development; Economics; Statistics; Trade and Markets; and Gender, Equity and Rural Employment.

FAO provides a focal point for economic research and policy analysis relating to food security and sustainable development. It produces studies and reports on agricultural development, the impact of development programmes and projects, and the world food situation, as well as on commodity prices, trade and medium-term projections. It supports the development of methodologies and guidelines to improve research into food and agriculture and the integration of wider concepts, such as social welfare, environmental factors and nutrition, into research projects. In November 2004 the FAO Council adopted a set of voluntary Right to Food Guidelines, and established a dedicated administrative unit, that aimed to 'support the progressive realization of the right to adequate food in the context of national food security' by providing practical guidance to countries in support of their efforts to achieve the 1996

World Food Summit commitment and UN MDG relating to hunger reduction. FAO's Statistical Division assembles, analyses and disseminates statistical data on world food and agriculture and aims to ensure the consistency, broad coverage and quality of available data. The Division advises member countries on enhancing their statistical capabilities. It maintains FAOSTAT (accessible at faostat.fao.org) as a core database of statistical information relating to nutrition, fisheries, forestry, food production, land use, population, etc. In 2004 FAO developed a new statistical framework, CountrySTAT, to provide for the organization and integration of statistical data and metadata from sources within a particular country. By 2012 CountrySTAT systems had been developed in 25 developing countries. FAO's internet-based interactive World Agricultural Information Centre (WAICENT) offers access to agricultural publications, technical documentation, codes of conduct, data, statistics and multimedia resources. FAO compiles and co-ordinates an extensive range of international databases on agriculture, fisheries, forestry, food and statistics, the most important of these being AGRIS (the International Information System for the Agricultural Sciences and Technology) and CARIS (the Current Agricultural Research Information System). In June 2000 FAO organized a high-level Consultation on Agricultural Information Management (COAIM), which aimed to increase access to and use of agricultural information by policy-makers and others. The second COAIM was held in September 2002 and the third meeting was convened in June 2007.

In September 2012 FAO, IFAD, WFP and UN Women launched 'Accelerating Progress Toward the Economic Empowerment of Rural Women', a five-year initiative that was to be implemented initially in Ethiopia, Guatemala, Kyrgyzstan, Liberia, Nepal, Niger and Rwanda.

FAO's Global Information and Early Warning System (GIEWS), which become operational in 1975, maintains a database on and monitors the crop and food outlook at global, regional, national and sub-national levels in order to detect emerging food supply difficulties and disasters and to ensure rapid intervention in countries experiencing food supply shortages. It publishes regular reports on the weather conditions and crop prospects in sub-Saharan Africa and in the Sahel region, issues special alerts which describe the situation in countries or sub-regions experiencing food difficulties, and recommends an appropriate international response. FAO has also supported the development and implementation of Food Insecurity and Vulnerability Information and Mapping Systems (FIVIMS) and hosts the secretariat of the inter-agency working group on development of the FIVIMS. In October 2007 FAO inaugurated an online Global Forum on Food Security and Nutrition, to contribute to the compilation and dissemination of information relating to food security and nutrition throughout the world. In December 2008 a regular report issued by GIEWS identified 33 countries as being in crisis and requiring external assistance, of which 20 were in Africa, 10 in Asia and the Near East and three in Latin America and the Caribbean. All countries were identified as lacking the resources to deal with critical problems of food insecurity, including many severely affected by the high cost of food and fuel. The publication *Crop Prospects and Food Situation* reviews the global situation, and provides regional updates and a special focus on countries experiencing food crises and requiring external assistance, on a quarterly basis. *Food Outlook*, issued in June and November, analyses developments in global food and animal feed markets.

In March 2012 GIEWS published a special report on the food production situation in Syria; the report recommended—in view of ongoing violent conflict in that country—that the food security situation should be closely monitored and that a detailed assessment of requirements should be drafted.

In February 2012 GIEWS produced a special report on the food production situation in South Sudan (which became an independent state in July 2011), based on the findings of an FAO/WFP Crop and Food Security Assessment mission that took place in October–November 2011. In April 2012 a special report on Ethiopia was issued, also based on the findings of an October–November FAO/WFP Assessment Mission. The regular publication *Sahel Report* assesses the weather and crop situation in that region on a monthly basis during the growing season (July–October).

TECHNICAL CO-OPERATION

The Technical Co-operation Department has responsibility for FAO's operational activities, including policy and programme development assistance to member countries; the mobilization of resources; investment support; field operations; emergency operations and rehabilitation; and the Technical Co-operation Programme.

FAO provides policy advice to support the formulation, implementation and evaluation of agriculture, rural development and food security strategies in member countries. It administers a project to assist developing countries to strengthen their technical negotiating skills, in respect to agricultural trade issues. FAO also aims to co-ordinate and facilitate the mobilization of extrabudgetary funds from donors and governments for particular projects. It administers a range of trust funds, including a Trust Fund for Food Security and Food Safety, established in 2002 to generate resources for projects to combat hunger, and the Government Co-operative Programme. FAO's Investment Centre, established in 1964, aims to promote greater external investment in agriculture and rural development by assisting member countries to formulate effective and sustainable projects and programmes. The Centre collaborates with international financing institutions and bilateral donors in the preparation of projects, and administers cost-sharing arrangements, with, typically, FAO funding 40% of a project. The Centre is a co-chair (with the German Government) of the Global Donor Platform for Rural Development, which was established in 2004, comprising multilateral, donor and international agencies, development banks and research institutions, to improve the co-ordination and effectiveness of rural development assistance.

FAO's Technical Co-operation Programme, which was inaugurated in 1976, provides technical expertise and funding for small-scale projects to address specific issues within a country's agriculture, fisheries or forestry sectors. An Associate Professional Officers programme co-ordinates the sponsorship and placement of young professionals to gain experience working in an aspect of rural or agricultural development.

FAO's Special Programme for Food Security (SPFS), initiated in 1994, assists low-income countries with a food deficit to increase food production and productivity as rapidly as possible, primarily through the widespread adoption by farmers of improved production technologies, with emphasis on areas of high potential. Within the SPFS framework are national and regional food security initiatives, all of which aim towards the MDG objective of reducing the incidence of hunger by 50% by 2015. The SPFS is operational in more than 100 countries. The Programme promotes South-South co-operation to improve food security and the exchange of knowledge and experience. Some 40 bilateral co-operation agreements are in force, for example, between Gabon and China, Egypt and Cameroon, and Viet Nam and Benin. In 2012 some 66 countries were categorized formally as 'low-income food-deficit'.

FAO organizes an annual series of fund-raising events, 'TeleFood', some of which are broadcast on television and the internet, in order to raise public awareness of the problems of hunger and malnutrition. Since its inception in 1997 public donations to TeleFood have exceeded some US $29m. (2012), financing more than 3,200 'grassroots' projects in 130 countries. The projects have provided tools, seeds and other essential supplies directly to small-scale farmers, and have been especially aimed at helping women.

The Technical Co-operation Division co-ordinates FAO's emergency operations, concerned with all aspects of disaster and risk prevention, mitigation, reduction and emergency relief and rehabilitation, with a particular emphasis on food security and rural populations. FAO works with governments to develop and implement disaster prevention policies and practices. It aims to strengthen the capacity of local institutions to manage and mitigate risk and provides technical assistance to improve access to land for displaced populations in countries following conflict or a natural disaster. Other disaster prevention and reduction efforts include dissemination of information from the various early-warning systems and support for adaptation to climate variability and change, for example by the use of drought-resistant crops or the adoption of conservation agriculture techniques. Following an emergency FAO works with governments and other development and humanitarian partners to assess the immediate and longer-term agriculture and food security needs of the affected population. It has developed an Integrated Food Security and Humanitarian Phase Classification Scheme to determine the appropriate response to a disaster situation. Emergency co-ordination units may be established to manage the local response to an emergency and to facilitate and co-ordinate the delivery of inter-agency assistance. In order to rehabilitate agricultural production following a natural or man-made disaster FAO provides emergency seed, tools, other materials and technical and training assistance. During 2005 the UN's Inter-Agency Standing Committee, concerned with co-ordinating the international response to humanitarian disasters, developed a concept of providing assistance through a 'cluster' approach, comprising core areas of activity. FAO was designated the lead agency for the then Agriculture cluster. A review of the humanitarian cluster approach, undertaken during 2010, concluded that a new cluster on Food Security should be established, replacing the Agriculture cluster. The new cluster, established accordingly in 2011, is led jointly by FAO and WFP, and aims to combine expertise in agricultural assistance and food aid in order to boost food security and to improve the resilience of food-insecure disaster-affected communities. FAO also contributes the agricultural relief and rehabilitation component of the UN's Consolidated Appeals Process (CAP), which aims to co-ordinate and enhance the effectiveness of the international community's response to an emergency; during 2011 FAO received US $200m. in funding in response to its appeals under the 2011 CAP process. In April 2004 FAO established a Special Fund for Emergency and Rehabilitation Activities to enable it to respond promptly to a humanitarian crisis before making an emergency appeal for additional resources.

During 2008–mid-2012 projects (providing fertilizers, seeds and other support necessary to ensure the success of harvests) were undertaken in more than 90 countries under the framework of the Initiative on Soaring Food Prices (see above); some US $314m. in project funding had been provided by the EU Food Facility, while other projects (to the value of $37m.) were implemented through FAO's Technical Co-operation Programme.

FAO has worked extensively, alongside other international partners, within Somalia to monitor and improve the food security situation in that country, which has suffered large-scale humanitarian crises resulting from civil conflict and natural disasters. By mid-2011, as a result of crop failure and livestock loss following two consecutive seasons of poor rainfall, a severe drought prevailed in the Horn of Africa, with southern Somalia, in particular, a focus of humanitarian emergency. The situation in Somalia was exacerbated by the long-term lack of effective government there, the inaccessibility of extensive rebel-controlled areas, and high food prices which had further limited access to adequate nutrition. An estimated 3.7m. southern Somalis were estimated to be suffering food insecurity at that time, and, over the period July 2011–early February 2012 the UN declared a state of famine in two southern Somali regions. It was estimated at that time that around 80% of Somalis relied on agriculture for their livelihoods. FAO Somalia's activities include supporting long-term initiatives aimed at improving the country's agriculture sector; crisis mitigation and natural disaster response; and using information systems (Somali Water and Land Information Management System and the Food Security and Nutrition Analysis Unit) and analysing data to inform decision-making and response planning for humanitarian interventions. An international meeting on the crisis in the Horn of Africa, organized by FAO in late July 2011, adopted a programme aimed at preventing humanitarian disaster and building long-term regional food security. In 2012 FAO was working through its Food Security and Nutrition Analysis Unit for Somalia (FSNAU) to improve food security analysis and monitoring activities in that country, and FAO was also providing continued support to Somalia Water and Land Information Management (SWALIM)—an information service serving the Somali authorities, and also UN agencies, non-governmental organizations and development agencies active in Somalia, through the provision of increased access to drought and flood information and improved early warning systems. Under the UN's 2012 Consolidated Appeals Process (CAP) FAO requested some US $180.8m. to fund the following projects in Somalia: Capacity building for effective implementation and co-ordination of Cluster activities; Emergency crisis response—livelihood support to fishing coastal communities in crisis; Strengthening food security and nutrition analysis; Livelihood support for agropastoral communities in famine, humanitarian emergency and acute food and livelihood crisis; Information and tools for early warning and emergency preparedness; Integrated approach to protecting the livelihood assets of pastoral communities in famine, humanitarian emergency and acute food and livelihood crisis; Livelihood, nutrition and food security support for agricultural communities in famine, humanitarian emergency and acute food and livelihood crisis in; Support to communities and institutions in disaster risk reduction, resilience building and emergency preparedness; and Integrated assistance to voluntary returns in south and central Somalia (jointly implemented with UNHCR).

FAO requested US $41m. under the UN CAP for 2012 to finance the following projects in Sudan (where agricultural livelihoods and food security had been undermined by protracted conflict): Support for the restoration and maintenance of the food and livelihood security of vulnerable households (IDPs, refugees, returnees and host communities) in Darfur; Co-ordination of interventions and capacity building of food security and livelihoods sector partners in crisis-affected areas of the Sudan; and Emergency and early recovery support to restore and improve the food and livelihood security of vulnerable households in the Three Protocol Areas and Eastern Sudan. FAO also appealed under the 2012 CAP for $23m. to fund the following three projects in South Sudan (which had achieved independence from Sudan in July 2011): Enhancing the food security of returnees, IDPs and vulnerable host communities through the provision of appropriate production inputs, technologies and services; Enhancing the income security of returnees, IDPs, women and demobilized ex-combatants through support to market-oriented agricultural production and processing; and supporting a Food Security and Livelihood Cluster Co-ordination mechanism for effective emergency planning and response.

Under the UN CAP for 2012 FAO appealed for US $23m. to fund project activities in Niger, where in recent years recurrent drought and locust outbreaks, changes in climatic conditions, and population movements had severely undermined agricultural production and food security. In September 2012 FAO reported that widespread breeding of desert locusts was under way in northern desert areas, central pasture areas, and parts of southern Niger, and forecast that, as vegetation dried, locust bands and swarms would emerge in Niger and Mali from October, posing a potential threat to crops and pastures, and therefore necessitating the urgent implementation of control measures. Breeding was reported still to be in progress, on a smaller scale, in Mauritania and Chad.

Following rains in southwestern Libya and southeastern Algeria (the location of locust breeding grounds) in early October 2011, and a disruption to normal ground survey activities during 2011 in Libya owing to violent insecurity there, an outbreak of desert locusts occurred in southwestern areas of Libya from January 2012. From late May, as vegetation that had been supporting bands and swarms of locusts dried out, a migration south was reported into areas of Niger and Mali that had experienced recent rainfall; the arrival of the locusts posed a severe threat to crops in those countries as well as to crop production in Chad. The 40th session of the FAO Desert Locust Control Committee, meeting in June, convened a group of experts to draft an action plan on addressing the immediate locust threat posed to Chad, Mali and Niger. Some US $10m. was requested to fund the activities of national locust control units in the Sahel area and to enable the Commission for Controlling the Desert Locust in the Western Region and FAO to co-ordinate sub-regional operations.

Under the 2012 CAP FAO also requested US $215m. to help vulnerable communities in the Democratic Republic of the Congo restore agricultural livelihoods, thereby generating income, promoting peace building and increasing local resilience. Some $32m. was requested to fund projects to strengthen early warning systems and to provide agricultural inputs to smallholders in Zimbabwe (where erratic climatic conditions, high prevalence of HIV/AIDS, and successive economic crises had exacerbated hunger and poverty), with a view to increasing the production of smallholder farmers beyond subsistence level. Further requests by FAO under the 2012 CAP included $20m. to finance activities aimed at assisting vulnerable pastoral communities in arid and semi-arid areas of Kenya to combat the effects of ongoing drought, and better prepare for future drought conditions; $18m. to strengthen food security in Chad; $8m. to help drought-affected communities in Djibouti; $5m. to support conflict-affected farmers in Central African Republic; and $4m. to fund four projects in Liberia, where an influx of refugees from Côte d'Ivoire during 2011 had impacted the food security of host communities; futhermore, $7m. was requested to help restore the agriculture-based livelihoods of conflict-affected people in Côte d'Ivoire.

FAO Statutory Bodies and Associated Entities

(based at the Rome headquarters, unless otherwise indicated)

African Commission on Agricultural Statistics: c/o FAO Regional Office for Africa, POB 1628, Accra, Ghana; e-mail Eloi.OuedraogoATfao.org; f. 1961 to advise member countries on the development and standardization of food and agricultural statistics; 22nd session: Nov.–Dec. 2011, in Addis Ababa, Ethiopia; 37 member states.

African Forestry and Wildlife Commission: c/o FAO Regional Office for Africa, POB 1628, Accra, Ghana; e-mail foday.bojang@fao.org; f. 1959 to advise on the formulation of forest policy and to review and co-ordinate its implementation on a regional level; to exchange information and advise on technical problems; 19th session: Feb. 2014, Namibia; 42 member states.

Agricultural Market Information System (AMIS): AMIS Secretariat, FAO, Viale delle Terme di Caracalla, 00153 Rome, Italy; tel. (6) 5705-2057; fax (6) 5705-3152; e-mail amis-secretariat@fao.org; internet www.amis-outlook.org; f. 2011 to improve transparency in agricultural markets and contribute to stabilizing food price volatility; a partnership of FAO, the International Food Policy Research Institute, IFAD, OECD, UNCTAD, the World Bank, WFP, WTO, and the UN High Level Task Force on the Global Food Security Crisis (f. 2008).

Codex Alimentarius Commission (Joint FAO/WHO Food Standards Programme): e-mail codex@fao.org; internet www.codexalimentarius.org; f. 1962 to make proposals for the co-ordination of all international food standards work and to publish a code of international food standards; Trust Fund to support participation by least-developed countries was inaugurated in 2003; there are numerous specialized Codex committees, e.g. for food labelling, hygiene, additives and contaminants, pesticide and veterinary residues, milk and milk products, and processed fruits and vegetables; and an intergovernmental task force on antimicrobial resistance; 184 member states and the EU; 208 observers (at September 2012).

Commission for Controlling the Desert Locust in the Central Region: c/o FAO Regional Office for the Near East, POB 2223, Cairo, Egypt; e-mail eclo@fao.org; internet www.fao.org/ag/locusts/en/info/info/index.html; covers northeastern Africa and the Middle East; reported in September 2012 that limited expansion of the locust population might occur in Red Sea coastal areas of Yemen that had received recent rainfall; 28th session: November 2012, Jeddah, Saudi Arabia; 16 member states.

Commission for Controlling the Desert Locust in the Western Region: 30 rue Asselah Hocine, BP 270, Algiers, Algeria; e-mail clcpro@fao.org; internet www.clcpro-empres.org; f. 2002; covers northwestern Africa; has implemented a preventive control programme to strengthen locust surveillance and control in member countries (first phase: 2006–11; second phase 2011–14); and has advocated to help member countries establish autonomous national locust control units; works closely with EMPRES; 6th session: March 2012, Tunis, Tunisia; 10 member states.

Committee for Inland Fisheries and Aquaculture of Africa (CIFAA): c/o FAO Regional Office for Africa, POB 1628, Accra, Ghana; internet www.fao.org/fishery/rfb/cifaa; f. 1971 to promote improvements in inland fisheries and aquaculture in Africa; the 16th session of CIFAA, convened in November 2010, in Maputo, Mozambique, proposed that the role of the Committee should be re-examined; consequently, a working group was established to make recommendations on the future direction of the Committee, and, in March 2012, an FAO-New Partnership for Africa seminar was held in Cape Town, South Africa, to discuss the review of CIFAA; 38 member states.

Emergency Prevention System for Transboundary Animal and Plant Pests and Diseases (EMPRES): e-mail vincent.martin@fao.org; internet www.fao.org/ag/againfo/programmes/en/empres.html; f. f. 1994 to strengthen FAO's activities in prevention, early warning, control and eradication of pests and highly contagious livestock diseases; maintains an internet-based EMPRES Global Animal Disease Information System (EMPRES-i, accessible at empres-i.fao.org/eipws3g).

FAO Desert Locust Control Committee: f. 1955 as a primary forum bringing together locust-affected countries, international donors and other agencies, to advise FAO on the management of desert locusts; 40th session: June 2012, Rome.

Fishery Committee for the Eastern Central Atlantic: f. 1967 to promote improvements in inland fisheries in the Eastern Central Atlantic area between Cape Spartel (Morocco) and the Congo River; 20th session: March 2012, in Rabat, Morocco; 33 member states and the EU.

Governing Body of the International Treaty on Plant Genetic Resources (Seed Treaty): e-mail pgrfa-treaty@fao.org; internet www.planttreaty.org; f. 2004 to oversee the implementation of the Seed Treaty; fourth session: March 2011, Nusa Dua, Bali; 126 member states and the EU (at September 2012).

International Rice Commission (IRC): internet www.fao.org/ag/irc; f. 1949 to promote national and international action on production, conservation, distribution and consumption of rice, except matters relating to international trade; supports the International Task Force on Hybrid Rice, the Working Group on Advanced Rice Breeding in Latin America and the Caribbean, the Inter-regional Collaborative Research Network on Rice in the Mediterranean Climate Areas, and the Technical Co-operation Network on Wetland Development and Management/Inland Valley Swamps; in July 2012 27 experts from 22 IRC member countries convened a Global Rice Roundtable, in Le Corum, Montpelier, France, to consider possible future directions of the IRC; 62 member states (accounting for around 93% of global rice production).

South West Indian Ocean Fisheries Commission: c/o FAO Sub-regional Office for Southern Africa, POB 3730, Harare, Zimbabwe; internet www.fao.org/fishery/rfb/swiofc/en; f. 2004 to promote the sustainable development and utilization, through proper management, of living marine resources; 12 member states.

Finance

FAO's Regular Programme, which is financed by contributions from member governments, covers the cost of FAO's Secretariat, its Technical Co-operation Programme (TCP) and part of the cost of several special action programmes. The regular budget for the two-year period 2012–13 totalled US $1,006m. Much of FAO's technical assistance programme and emergency (including rehabilitation) support activities are funded from extra-budgetary sources, predominantly by trust funds that come mainly from donor countries and international financing institutions; voluntary donor contributions to FAO were projected at around $1,400m. in 2011–13.

Publications

Commodity Review and Outlook (annually).
Crop Prospects and Food Situation (5/6 a year).
Desert Locust Bulletin.
Ethical Issues in Food and Agriculture.
FAO Statistical Yearbook (annually).
FAOSTAT Statistical Database (online).
Food Outlook (2 a year).
Food Safety and Quality Update (monthly; electronic bulletin).
Forest Resources Assessment.
The State of Agricultural Commodity Markets (every 2 years).
The State of Food and Agriculture (annually).
The State of Food Insecurity in the World (annually).
The State of World Fisheries and Aquaculture (every 2 years).
The State of the World's Forests (every 2 years).
Unasylva (quarterly).
Yearbook of Fishery Statistics.
Yearbook of Forest Products.
Commodity reviews, studies, manuals. A complete catalogue of publications is available at www.fao.org/icatalog/inter-e.htm.

International Bank for Reconstruction and Development—IBRD (World Bank)

Address: 1818 H St, NW, Washington, DC 20433, USA.
Telephone: (202) 473-1000; **fax:** (202) 477-6391; **e-mail:** pic@worldbank.org; **internet:** www.worldbank.org.

The IBRD was established in December 1945. Initially it was concerned with post-war reconstruction in Europe; since then its aim has been to assist the economic development of member nations by making loans where private capital is not available on reasonable terms to finance productive investments. Loans are made either directly to governments, or to private enterprises with the guarantee of their governments. The World Bank, as it is commonly known, comprises the IBRD and the International Development Association (IDA). The affiliated group of institutions, comprising the IBRD, IDA, the International Finance Corporation (IFC), the Multilateral Investment Guarantee Agency (MIGA) and the International Centre for Settlement of Investment Disputes (ICSID, see below), is referred to as the World Bank Group.

Organization

(September 2012)

Officers and staff of the IBRD serve concurrently as officers and staff in IDA. The World Bank has offices in New York, Brussels, Paris (for Europe), Frankfurt, London, Geneva and Tokyo, as well as in more than 100 countries of operation. Country Directors are located in some 30 country offices.

BOARD OF GOVERNORS

The Board of Governors consists of one Governor appointed by each member nation. Typically, a Governor is the country's finance minister, central bank governor, or a minister or an official of comparable rank. The Board normally meets once a year.

EXECUTIVE DIRECTORS

The general operations of the Bank are conducted by a Board of 25 Executive Directors. Five Directors are appointed by the five members having the largest number of shares of capital stock, and the rest are elected by the Governors representing the other members. The President of the Bank is Chairman of the Board.

PRINCIPAL OFFICERS

The principal officers of the Bank are the President of the Bank, three Managing Directors, two Senior Vice-Presidents and 25 Vice-Presidents.

President and Chairman of Executive Directors: Dr Jim Yong Kim (USA).

Vice-President, Africa: Makhtar Diop (Senegal).

Activities

The World Bank's primary objectives are the achievement of sustainable economic growth and the reduction of poverty in developing countries. In the context of stimulating economic growth the Bank promotes both private sector development and human resource development and has attempted to respond to the growing demands by developing countries for assistance in these areas. In September 2001 the Bank announced that it was to become a full partner in implementing the UN Millennium Development Goals (MDGs), and was to make them central to its development agenda. The objectives, which were approved by governments attending a special session of the UN General Assembly in September 2000, represented a new international consensus to achieve determined poverty reduction targets. The Bank was closely involved in preparations for the International Conference on Financing for Development, which was held in Monterrey, Mexico, in March 2002. The meeting adopted the Monterrey Consensus, which outlined measures to support national development efforts and to achieve the MDGs. During 2002/03 the Bank, with the IMF, undertook to develop a monitoring framework to review progress in the MDG agenda. The first *Global Monitoring Report* was issued by the Bank and the IMF in April 2004.

In October 2007 the Bank's President defined the following six strategic themes as priorities for Bank development activities: the poorest countries; fragile and post-conflict states; middle-income countries; global public goods; the Arab world; and knowledge and learning. In May 2008 the Bank established a Global Food Crisis Response Programme (GFRP, see below) to assist developing countries affected by the escalating cost of food production. In December the Bank resolved to establish a new facility to accelerate the provision of funds, through IDA, for developing countries affected by the global decline in economic and financial market conditions. The Bank participated in the meeting of heads of state and government of the Group of 20 (G20) leading economies, that was held in Washington, DC, USA, in November 2008 to address the global economic situation, and pursued close collaboration with other multinational organizations, in particular the IMF and OECD, to analyse the impact of the ongoing economic instability. During early 2009 the Bank elaborated its operational response to the global economic crisis. Three operational platforms were devised to address the areas identified as priority themes, i.e. protecting the most vulnerable against the effects of the crisis; maintaining long-term infrastructure investment programmes; and sustaining the potential for private sector-led economic growth and employment creation. Consequently, a new Vulnerability Financing Facility was established, incorporating the GFRP and a new Rapid Social Response Programme, to extend immediate assistance to the poorest groups in affected low- and middle-income countries. Infrastructure investment was to be supported through a new Infrastructure Recovery and Assets Platform, which was mandated to release funds to secure existing infrastructure projects and to finance new initiatives in support of longer-term economic development. Private sector support for infrastructure projects, bank recapitalization, microfinance, and trade financing was to be led by IFC.

The Bank's efforts to reduce poverty include the compilation of country-specific assessments and the formulation of country assistance strategies (CASs) to review and guide the Bank's country programmes. In 1998/99 the Bank's Executive Directors endorsed a Comprehensive Development Framework (CDF) to effect a new approach to development assistance based on partnerships and country responsibility, with an emphasis on the interdependence of the social, structural, human, governmental, economic and environmental elements of development. The CDF, which aimed to enhance the overall effectiveness of development assistance, was formulated after a series of consultative meetings organized by the Bank and attended by representatives of governments, donor agencies, financial institutions, non-governmental organizations, the private sector and academics. In December 1999 the Bank introduced a new approach to implement the principles of the CDF, as part of its strategy to enhance the debt relief scheme for heavily indebted poor countries (HIPCs, see below). Applicant countries were requested to formulate, in consultation with external partners and other stakeholders, a results-oriented national strategy to reduce poverty, to be presented in the form of a Poverty Reduction Strategy Paper (PRSP). In cases where there might be some delay in issuing a full PRSP, it was permissible for a country to submit a less detailed 'interim' PRSP (I-PRSP) in order to secure the preliminary qualification for debt relief. The approach also requires the publication of annual progress reports. In 2001 the Bank introduced a new Poverty Reduction Support Credit to help low-income countries to implement the policy and institutional reforms outlined in their PRSP. Increasingly, PRSPs have been considered by the international community to be the appropriate country-level framework to assess progress towards achieving the MDGs.

The Bank's poverty reduction strategy for Africa, where an estimated 45% of the population are affected by poverty, involves projects that aim to alleviate the adverse effects of structural adjustment programmes; that assist governments to assess and monitor poverty; and that increase food security. In March 1996 a new programme to co-ordinate development efforts in Africa was announced by the UN Secretary-General. The World Bank was to facilitate the mobilization of the estimated US $25,000m. required to achieve the objectives of the UN System-wide Special Initiative on Africa over a 10-year period. In addition, the Bank was to provide technical assistance to enable countries to devise economic plans (in particular following a period of civil conflict), agricultural development programmes and a common strategy for African countries to strengthen the management capacities of the public sector. In 1987 the Bank established a Special Programme of Assistance for sub-Saharan Africa (SPA, renamed the Strategic Partnership with Africa in 1997), which aimed to increase concessional lending to heavily-indebted and impoverished African countries, mainly by the co-ordination of international aid contributions and to co-financing mechanisms. Only IDA member countries implementing a policy adjustment programme, with a debt-service ration of more than 30%, were to be eligible for SPA funds. In September 2005 the Bank's Board of Directors approved an African Action Plan to identify specific development objectives for the region, based on results-orientated, country-specific projects. The Plan, which was updated in March 2007, defined the following themes as areas for action: strengthening the private sector; increasing the economic empowerment of women; building skills for competitiveness in the global economy; raising agricultural productivity; improving access to and reliability of clean energy; expanding and upgrading road networks and transit corridors; increasing access to safe water and sanitation; and strengthening national health systems to combat malaria and HIV/AIDS. In March 2011 the Bank's Executive Directors approved a successor strategy for the five year period July 2011 to June 2016, entitled 'Africa's future and World Bank support to it'. The plan was the result of an extensive consultation process, conducted in 2010. Bank operations in support of development in Africa under the new strategy were to be organized according to the following two pillars: competitiveness and employment; and vulnerability and resilience. The Bank aimed to establish greater partnerships with the private sector, development bodies and civil society in order to formulate and implement more effective development operations. In July 2011 the Bank announced an allocation of some $500m. to support areas of the Horn of Africa affected by a severe drought. In September, following preliminary needs assessments conducted by Bank experts in Djibouti, Ethiopia, Kenya,Uganda, and refugee camps in Somalia the Bank formulated a three-phase response plan, committing $1,872m. to addressing the crisis. Some $288m. was to be available until 30 June 2012 to provide immediate relief from drought and resulting food shortages, $384m. was to fund economic recovery efforts in the period up to 30 June 2014, and $1,200m. was committed to enhancing resilience to drought and other natural disasters in the longer-term.

In 1991 the African Capacity Building Foundation was established by the World Bank, the African Development Bank and UNDP, with the aim of encouraging indigenous research and managerial capabilities, by supporting or creating institutions for training, research and analysis. From 1999 the Bank has supported the Partnership for Capacity Building in Africa (PACT), for which it committed US $150m. over a five-year period. It also supports various schemes under the Knowledge Partnerships for Africa initiative. The Bank, with IDA and IFC, supports the Chad/Cameroon Petroleum Development and Pipeline Project, which was approved in June 2000 to develop Chad's oil fields and undertake construction of a 1,070km connecting pipeline to Cameroon's Atlantic coast. In addition, the Bank supports the Nile Basin Initiative which aims to promote co-operation among basin states of the Nile to achieve sustainable socio-economic development through the equitable use of its water resources. Other regional initiatives supported by the Bank include Early Childhood Development in Africa and the Sub-Saharan Africa Transport Policy Programme. It also focuses on efforts to prevent conflict and assist post-conflict recovery, for example the Multi-Country Demobilization and Reintegration Programme in the Greater Great Lakes Region. In March 2006 the Bank inaugurated an Africa Catalytic Growth Fund to foster investment in infrastructure and support ongoing government programmes to achieve the MDGs.

FINANCIAL OPERATIONS

IBRD capital is derived from members' subscriptions to capital shares, the calculation of which is based on their quotas in the IMF. At 30 June 2011 the total subscribed capital of the IBRD was US $193,732m., of which the paid-in portion was $11,720m. (6.1%); the remainder is subject to call if required. Most of the IBRD's lendable funds come from its borrowing, on commercial terms, in world capital markets, and also from its retained earnings and the flow of repayments on its loans. IBRD loans carry a variable interest rate, rather than a rate fixed at the time of borrowing.

IBRD loans usually have a 'grace period' of five years and are repayable over 15 years or fewer. Loans are made to governments, or must be guaranteed by the government concerned, and are normally made for projects likely to offer a commercially viable rate of return. In 1980 the World Bank introduced structural adjustment lending, which (instead of financing specific projects) supports programmes and changes necessary to modify the structure of an economy so that it can restore or maintain its growth and viability in its balance of payments over the medium term.

The IBRD and IDA together made 362 new lending and investment commitments totalling US $43,005.6m. during the year ending 30 June 2011, compared with 354 (amounting to $58,747.1m.) in the previous year. During 2010/11 the IBRD alone approved commitments totalling $26,737.2m. (compared with $44,197.4m. in the previous year). Total disbursements by the IBRD in the year ending 30 June 2011 amounted to $21,879m.

In September 1996 the World Bank/IMF Development Committee endorsed a joint initiative to assist HIPCs to reduce their debt burden to a sustainable level, in order to make more resources available for poverty reduction and economic growth. A new Trust Fund was established by the World Bank in November to finance the initiative. The Fund, consisting of an initial allocation of US $500m. from the IBRD surplus and other contributions from multilateral creditors, was to be administered by IDA. Of the 41 HIPCs identified by the Bank, 33 were in sub-Saharan Africa. In April 1997 the World Bank and the IMF announced that Uganda was to be the first beneficiary of the initiative, enabling the Ugandan Government to reduce its external debt by some 20%, or an estimated $338m. In early 1999 the World Bank and IMF initiated a comprehensive review of the HIPC initiative. By April meetings of the Group of Seven industrialized nations (G7) and of the governing bodies of the Bank and IMF indicated a consensus that the scheme needed to be amended and strengthened, in order to allow more countries to benefit from the initiative, to accelerate the process by which a country may qualify for assistance, and to enhance the effectiveness of debt relief. In June the G7 and Russia (known as the G8), meeting in Cologne, Germany, agreed to increase contributions to the HIPC Trust Fund and to cancel substantial amounts of outstanding debt, and proposed more flexible terms for eligibility. In September the Bank and IMF reached an agreement on an enhanced HIPC scheme. During the initial phase of the process to ensure suitability for debt relief, each applicant country should formulate a PRSP, and should demonstrate prudent financial management in the implementation of the strategy for at least one year, with support from IDA and IMF. At the pivotal 'decision point' of the process, having thus developed and successfully applied the poverty reduction strategy, applicant countries still deemed to have an unsustainable level of debt were to qualify for interim debt relief from the IMF and IDA, as well as relief on highly concessional terms from other official bilateral creditors and multilateral institutions. During the ensuing 'interim period' countries were required successfully to implement further economic and social development reforms, as a final demonstration of suitability for securing full debt relief at the 'completion point' of the scheme. Data produced at the decision point was to form the base for calculating the final debt relief (in contrast to the original initiative, which based its calculations on projections of a country's debt stock at the completion point). In the majority of cases a sustainable level of debt was targeted at 150% of the net present value (NPV) of the debt in relation to total annual exports (compared with 200%–250% under the original initiative). Other countries with a lower debt-to-export ratio were to be eligible for assistance under the scheme, providing that their export earnings were at least 30% of GDP (lowered from 40% under the original initiative) and government revenue at least 15% of GDP (reduced from 20%). In March 2005 the Bank and the IMF implemented a new Debt Sustainability Framework in Low-income Countries to provide guidance on lending to low-income countries and to improve monitoring and prevention of the accumulation of unsustainable debt. In June finance ministers of the G8 proposed providing additional resources to achieve the full cancellation of debts owed by eligible HIPCs to assist those countries to meet their MDG targets. Countries that had reached their completion point were to qualify for immediate assistance. In July the heads of state and government of G8 countries requested that the Bank ensure the effective delivery of the additional funds and provide a framework for performance measurement. In September the Bank's Development Committee and the International Monetary and Financial Committee of the IMF endorsed the proposal, subsequently referred to as the Multilateral Debt Relief Initiative (MDRI). The Committees agreed to protect the financial capability of IDA, as one of the institutions (with the IMF and African Development Bank) which was to meet the additional cancellation commitments, and to develop a monitoring programme. At July 2011 assistance committed under the HIPC initiative amounted to an estimated $76,000m. (in 2010 NPV terms), of which the World Bank Group had committed $14,900m. At that time the estimated costs of the MDRI amounted to $52,500m. in nominal value terms, of which the Bank's share amounted to an estimated $35,300m. By September 2012 34 countries had reached completion point under the enhanced HIPC initiative, of which 28 were in sub-Saharan Africa (Benin, Burkina Faso, Burundi, Cameroon, Central African Republic, Côte d'Ivoire, Democratic Republic of the Congo, Republic of Congo, Ethiopia, The Gambia, Ghana, Guinea, Guinea-Bissau, Liberia, Madagascar, Malawi, Mali, Mauritania, Mozambique, Niger, Rwanda, São Tomé and Príncipe, Senegal, Sierra Leone, Tanzania, Togo, Uganda and Zambia).

The Bank has been active in supporting countries in the region to deal with the immense challenges of the HIV/AIDS epidemic, for example through the formulation of national AIDS programmes. A multisectoral campaign team for Africa (ACTafrica) has been established to support the Bank's HIV/AIDS strategy. In September 2000 a new Multi-Country HIV/AIDS Programme for Africa (MAP) was launched, in collaboration with UNAIDS and other major donor agencies and non-governmental organizations. Some US $500m. was allocated for the first phase of the initiative and was used to support projects in seven countries. In February 2002 the Bank approved an additional $500m. for a second phase of MAP, which was envisaged to assist HIV/AIDS schemes in a further 12 countries, as well as regional activities. In June 2004 the Bank approved a Treatment Acceleration Programme, with funds of $60m., to support activities in Burkina Faso, Ghana, Mozambique. In November 2001 the Bank appointed its first Global HIV/AIDS Adviser. In November 2004 the Bank launched an AIDS Media Center to improve access to information regarding HIV/AIDS, in particular to journalists in developing countries. In July 2009 the Bank published a report, with UNAIDS, concerned with the impact of the global economic crisis on HIV prevention and treatment programmes.

In March 2007 the Board of Executive Directors approved an action plan to develop further its Clean Energy for Development Investment Framework, which had been formulated in response to a request by the G8 heads of state, meeting in Gleneagles, United Kingdom, in July 2005. The action plan focused on efforts to improve access to clean energy, in particular in sub-Saharan Africa; to accelerate the transition to low carbon-emission development; and to support adaptation to climate change. In October 2008 the Bank Group endorsed a new Strategic Framework on Development and Climate Change, which aimed to guide the Bank in supporting the efforts of developing countries to achieving growth and reducing poverty, while recognizing the operational challenges of climate change. In June 2010 the Bank appointed a Special Envoy to lead the Bank's representation in international discussions on climate change. In February 2012 the Bank supported the establishment of a Global Partnership for Oceans.

In February 2012 the Bank opened a new Global Centre on Conflict, Security and Development in Nairobi, Kenya, in order to enhance its support for the poorest people living in some 30 countries considered 'fragile' or affected by conflict. The Centre was to help co-ordinate development efforts in those countries, to improve the efficiency of financial support, and to serve as a focus for experts and practitioners to share knowledge and experience.

TECHNICAL ASSISTANCE AND ADVISORY SERVICES

In addition to providing financial services, the Bank also undertakes analytical and advisory services, and supports learning and capacity-building, in particular through the World Bank Institute, the Staff Exchange Programme and knowledge-sharing initiatives. The Bank has supported efforts, such as the Global Development Gateway, to disseminate information on development issues and programmes, and, since 1988, has organized the Annual Bank Conference on Development Economics (ABCDE) to provide a forum for the exchange and discussion of development-related ideas and research. In September 1995 the Bank initiated the Information for Development Programme (InfoDev) with the aim of fostering partnerships between governments, multilateral institutions and private-sector experts in order to promote reform and investment in developing countries through improved access to information technology.

The provision of technical assistance to member countries has become a major component of World Bank activities. The economic and sector work (ESW) undertaken by the Bank is the vehicle for considerable technical assistance and often forms the basis of CASs and other strategic or advisory reports. In addition, project loans and credits may include funds earmarked specifically for feasibility studies, resource surveys, management or planning advice, and training. The World Bank Institute has become one of the most important of the Bank's activities in technical assistance. It provides training in national economic management and project analysis for government officials at the middle and upper levels of responsibility. It also runs overseas courses aiming to build up local training capability, and administers a graduate scholarship programme. Technical assistance (usually reimbursable) is also extended to countries that do not need Bank financial support, e.g. for training and transfer of technology. The Bank encourages the use of local consultants to assist with projects and stimulate institutional capability.

The Project Preparation Facility (PPF) was established in 1975 to provide cash advances to prepare projects that may be financed by the Bank. In 1992 the Bank established an Institutional Development Fund (IDF), which became operational on 1 July; the purpose of the Fund was to provide rapid, small-scale financial assistance, to a maximum value of US $500,000, for capacity building proposals. In 2002 the IDF was reoriented to focus on good governance, in particular financial accountability and system reforms.

ECONOMIC RESEARCH AND STUDIES

In the 1990s the World Bank's research, conducted by its own research staff, was increasingly concerned with providing information to reinforce the Bank's expanding advisory role to developing countries and to improve policy in the Bank's borrowing countries. The principal areas of current research focus on issues such as maintaining sustainable growth while protecting the environment and the poorest sectors of society, encouraging the development of the private sector, and reducing and decentralizing government activities.

The Bank chairs the Consultative Group on International Agricultural Research (CGIAR), which was founded in 1971 to raise financial support for international agricultural research work for improving crops and animal production in developing countries; it supports 15 research centres.

CO-OPERATION WITH OTHER ORGANIZATIONS

The World Bank co-operates with other international partners with the aim of improving the impact of development efforts. It collaborates with the IMF in implementing the HIPC scheme and the two agencies work closely to achieve a common approach to development initiatives. The Bank has established strong working relationships with many other UN bodies, in particular through a mutual commitment to poverty reduction objectives. In May 2000 the Bank signed a joint statement of co-operation with OECD. The Bank holds regular consultations with other multilateral development banks and with the European Union with respect to development issues. The Bank-NGO Committee provides an annual forum for discussion with non-governmental organizations (NGOs). Strengthening co-operation with external partners was a fundamental element of the Comprehensive Development Framework, which was adopted in 1998/99 (see above). In 2001/02 a Partnership Approval and Tracking System was implemented to provide information on the Bank's regional and global partnerships. In June 2007 the World Bank and the UN Office on Drugs and Crime launched a joint Stolen Asset Recovery (StAR) initiative, as part of the Bank's new Governance and Anti-Corruption (GAC) strategy. In April 2009 the G20 recommended that StAR review and propose mechanisms to strengthen international co-operation relating to asset recovery. The first global forum on stolen asset recovery and development was convened by StAR in June 2010.

In 1997 the Bank, in partnership with the IMF, UNCTAD, UNDP, the World Trade Organization (WTO) and the International Trade Commission, established an Integrated Framework for Trade-related Assistance to Least Developed Countries, at the request of the WTO, to assist those countries to integrate into the global trading system and improve basic trading capabilities. Also in 1997 a Partnerships Group was established to strengthen the Bank's work with development institutions, representatives of civil society and the private sector. The Group established a new Development Grant Facility, which became operational in October, to support partnership initiatives and to co-ordinate all of the Bank's grant-making activities. The Bank establishes and administers trust funds, open to contributions from member countries and multilateral organizations, NGOs, and private sector institutions, in order to support development partnerships. By 30 June 2011 the Bank had a portfolio of 1,038 active trust funds, with assets of some US $29,100m.

In June 1995 the World Bank joined other international donors (including regional development banks, other UN bodies, Canada, France, the Netherlands and the USA) in establishing a Consultative Group to Assist the Poorest (CGAP), which was to channel funds to the most needy through grass-roots agencies. An initial credit of approximately US $200m. was committed by the donors. The Bank manages the CGAP Secretariat, which is responsible for the administration of external funding and for the evaluation and approval of project financing. The CGAP provides technical assistance, training and strategic advice to microfinance institutions and other relevant bodies. As an implementing agency of the Global Environment Facility (GEF) the Bank assists countries to prepare and supervise GEF projects relating to biological diversity, climate change and other environmental protection measures. It is an example of a partnership in action which addresses a global agenda, complementing Bank country assistance activities. A new international partnership, the African Stockpiles Programme, was initiated in June 2004 with the aim of disposing of an estimated 50,000 metric tons of obsolete pesticides throughout the region. The Bank was to manage the Programme's Multi-Donor Trust Fund and to host the unit acting as a secretariat for the Programme's Steering Committee. Ethiopia, Mali, Morocco, Niger, South Africa, Tanzania and Tunisia were to be the first participants in the project, which was anticipated to last for 12–15 years at a cost of US $250m. In 2004/05 two multi-donor trust funds were established, with total committed funds of $508m., to support reconstruction and development needs in Sudan. In the following financial year a multi-donor trust fund was established to finance a study into the feasibility of transferring water from the Red Sea to the Dead Sea. Other funds administered by the Bank include the Global Program to Eradicate Poliomyelitis, launched during the financial year 2002/03, the Least Developed Countries Fund for Climate Change, established in September 2002, an Education for All Fast-Track Initiative Catalytic Trust Fund, established in 2003/04, and a Carbon Finance Assistance Trust Fund, established in 2004/05. In 2006/07 the Bank established a Global Facility for Disaster Reduction and Recovery. In September 2007 the Bank's Executive Directors approved a Carbon Partnership Facility and a Forest Carbon Partnership Facility to support its climate change activities. In May 2008 the Bank inaugurated the Global Food Crisis Response Programme (GFRP) to provide financial support, with resources of some $1,200m., to help meet the immediate needs of countries affected by the escalating cost of food production and by food shortages. Grants and loans were to be allocated on the basis of rapid needs assessments, conducted by the Bank with the FAO, the WFP and IFAD. As part of the facility a Multi-Donor Trust Fund established to facilitate co-ordination among donors and to leverage financial support for the rapid delivery of seeds and fertilizer to small-scale farmers. In April 2009 the Bank increased the resources available under the GFRP to $2,000m. By mid-2011 $1,500m. had been approved under the GFRP for initiatives in 40 countries, of which $1,155m. had been disbursed. In early November 2011 the Bank's President urged the forthcoming summit meeting of the G20 to address issues relating to food shortages and food price volatility.

The Bank has worked with FAO, WHO and the World Organisation of Animal Health (OIE) to develop strategies to monitor, contain and eradicate the spread of highly pathogenic avian influenza. In September 2005 the Bank organized a meeting of leading experts on the issue and in November it co-sponsored, with FAO, WHO and OIE, an international partners' conference, focusing on control of the disease and preparedness planning for any future related influenza pandemic in humans. In January 2006 the Bank's Board of Directors approved the establishment of a funding programme (the Global Program for Avian Influenza Control and Human Pandemic Preparedness and Response—GPAI), with resources of up to US $500m., to assist countries to combat the disease. Later in that month the Bank co-sponsored, with the European Commission and the People's Republic of China, an International Ministerial Pledging Conference on Avian and Human Pandemic Influenza (AHI), convened in Beijing. Participants pledged some $1,900m. to fund disease control and pandemic preparedness activities at global, regional and country levels. Commitments to the AHI facility amounted to $126m. at January 2009. In June the Bank approved an additional $500m. to expand the GPAI in order to fund emergency operations required to prevent and control outbreaks of the new swine influenza variant pandemic (H1N1).

EVALUATION

The Independent Evaluation Group is an independent unit within the World Bank. It conducts Country Assistance Evaluations to assess the development effectiveness of a Bank country programme, and studies and publishes the results of projects after a loan has been fully disbursed, so as to identify problems and possible improvements in future activities. In addition, the department reviews the Bank's global programmes and produces the *Annual Review of Development Effectiveness*. In 1996 a Quality Assurance Group was established to monitor the effectiveness of the Bank's operations and performance. In March 2009 the Bank published an Action Plan on Aid Effectiveness, based on the Accra Agenda for Action that had been adopted in

September 2008 during the Third High Level Forum on Aid Effectiveness, held in Ghana.

In September 1993 the Bank established an independent Inspection Panel, consistent with the Bank's objective of improving project implementation and accountability. The Panel, which became operational in September 1994, was to conduct independent investigations and report on complaints from local people concerning the design, appraisal and implementation of development projects supported by the Bank. By the end of 2011 the Panel had received 77 formal requests for inspection.

IBRD INSTITUTIONS

World Bank Institute (WBI): founded in March 1999 by merger of the Bank's Learning and Leadership Centre, previously responsible for internal staff training, and the Economic Development Institute (EDI), which had been established in 1955 to train government officials concerned with development programmes and policies. The new Institute aimed to emphasize the Bank's priority areas through the provision of training courses and seminars relating to poverty, crisis response, good governance and anti-corruption strategies. The Institute supports a Global Knowledge Partnership, which was established in 1997 to promote alliances between governments, companies, other agencies and organizations committed to applying information and communication technologies for development purposes. Under the EDI a World Links for Development programme was also initiated to connect schools in developing countries with partner establishments in industrialized nations via the internet. In 1999 the WBI expanded its programmes through distance learning, a Global Development Network, and use of new technologies. A new initiative, Global Development Learning Network (GDLN), aimed to expand access to information and learning opportunities through the internet, video conferences and organized exchanges. The WBI had also established 60 formal partnership arrangements with learning centres and public, private and non-governmental organizations to support joint capacity building programmes; many other informal partnerships were also in place. During 2009/10 new South-South Learning Middle-income country (MIC)–OECD Knowledge Exchange facilities were established. At 2012 the WBI was focusing its work on the following areas: fragile and conflict-affected states; governance; growth and competitiveness; climate change; health systems; public-private partnerships in infrastructure; and urban development; Vice-Pres. SANJAY PRADHAN (India); publs *Annual Report*, *Development Outreach* (quarterly), other books, working papers, case studies.

International Centre for Settlement of Investment Disputes (ICSID): founded in 1966 under the Convention of the Settlement of Investment Disputes between States and Nationals of Other States. The Convention was designed to encourage the growth of private foreign investment for economic development, by creating the possibility, always subject to the consent of both parties, for a Contracting State and a foreign investor who is a national of another Contracting State to settle any legal dispute that might arise out of such an investment by conciliation and/or arbitration before an impartial, international forum. The governing body of the Centre is its Administrative Council, composed of one representative of each Contracting State, all of whom have equal voting power. The President of the World Bank is (*ex officio*) the non-voting Chairman of the Administrative Council. At the end of August 2012 402 cases had been registered with the Centre, of which 249 had been concluded and 153 were pending consideration. At that time 147 countries had signed and ratified the Convention to become ICSID Contracting States; Sec.-Gen. MEG KINNEAR (Canada).

Publications

Abstracts of Current Studies: The World Bank Research Program (annually).
African Development Indicators (annually).
Annual Report on Operations Evaluation.
Annual Report on Portfolio Performance.
Annual Review of Development Effectiveness.
Doing Business (annually).
Global Commodity Markets (quarterly).
Global Development Finance (annually).
Global Economic Prospects (annually).
ICSID Annual Report.
ICSID Review—Foreign Investment Law Journal (2 a year).
Joint BIS-IMF-OECD-World Bank Statistics on External Debt (quarterly).
News from ICSID (2 a year).
Poverty Reduction and the World Bank (annually).
Poverty Reduction Strategies Newsletter (quarterly).
Research News (quarterly).
Staff Working Papers.
The World Bank and the Environment (annually).
World Bank Annual Report.
World Bank Atlas (annually).
World Bank Economic Review (3 a year).
World Bank Research Observer.
World Development Indicators (annually).
World Development Report (annually).

Statistics

IBRD LOANS APPROVED IN AFRICA SOUTH OF THE SAHARA, JULY 2010–JUNE 2011
(US $ million)

Country	Purpose	Amount
Seychelles . .	Second development policy loan	9.0
Swaziland . .	Local government development	27.0
	Health services investment	20.0

Source: World Bank, *Annual Report 2011*.

International Development Association—IDA

Address: 1818 H Street, NW, Washington, DC 20433, USA.
Telephone: (202) 473-1000; **fax:** (202) 477-6391; **internet:** www.worldbank.org/ida.

The International Development Association began operations in November 1960. Affiliated to the IBRD, IDA advances capital to the poorer developing member countries on more flexible terms than those offered by the IBRD.

Organization

(September 2012)

Officers and staff of the IBRD serve concurrently as officers and staff of IDA.

President and Chairman of Executive Directors: DR JIM YONG KIM (USA).

Activities

IDA assistance is aimed at the poorer developing countries (i.e. those with an annual GNP per capita of less than US $1,175 were to qualify for assistance in 2011/12) in order to support their poverty reduction strategies. Under IDA lending conditions, credits can be extended to countries whose balance of payments could not sustain the burden of repayment required for IBRD loans. Terms are more favourable than those provided by the IBRD; credits are for a period of 35 or 40 years, with a 'grace period' of 10 years, and carry no, or very low, interest and service charges. From 1 July 2011 the maturity of credits was to be 25 or 40 years, with a grace period of five or 10 years. In 2012 81 countries were eligible for IDA assistance, including 10 small-island economies with a GNP per head greater than $1,175, but which would otherwise have little or no access to Bank funds, and 16 so-called 'blend borrowers' which are entitled to borrow from both IDA and the IBRD.

IDA's total development resources, consisting of members' subscriptions and supplementary resources (additional subscriptions and contributions), are replenished periodically by contributions from the more affluent member countries. In December 2007 an agreement was concluded to replenish IDA resources by some US $41,600m., for the period 1 July 2008–30 June 2011, of which $25,100m. was pledged by 45 donor countries. In March 2010 negotiations on the 16th replenishment of IDA funds (IDA16) commenced, in Paris, France. Participants determined that the overarching theme of IDA16 should be achieving development results, and the following areas of focus be 'special themes': gender; climate change; fragile and conflicted affected states; and crisis response. Replenishment meetings were subsequently held in Bamako, Mali, in June, and in Washington, DC, USA, in October. An agreement was concluded in December, at a meeting convened in Brussels, Belgium. The IDA16 replenishment amounted to $49,300m., to cover the period 1 July 2011–30 June 2014, of which $26,400m. was committed by 51 donor countries.

During the year ending 30 June 2011 new IDA commitments amounted to US $16,269m. for 230 projects, compared with $14,550m. for 190 projects in the previous year. Of total IDA assistance during 2010/11 $7,004m. (43%) was for Africa and $6,340m. (39%) for South Asia. In that financial year some 42% of lending was for infrastructure projects (including energy and mining, transportation, water sanitation and flood protection, and information and communications and technologies sectors), 23% for law, justice and public administration and 20% for social sector projects.

In December 2008 the Bank's Board of Executive Directors approved a new IDA facility, the Financial Crisis Response Fast Track Facility, to accelerate the provision of up to US $2,000m. of IDA15 resources to help the poorest countries to counter the impact of the global economic and financial crisis. The first operations approved under the Facility, in February 2009, were for Armenia (amounting to $35m.) and the Democratic Republic of Congo ($100m.) in support of employment creation and infrastructure development initiatives and meeting the costs of essential services. In December the Board of Executive Directors approved a pilot Crisis Response Window to deploy an additional $1,300m. of IDA funds to support the poorest countries affected by the economic crisis until the end of the IDA15 period (30 June 2011). The new facility was proposed during a mid-term review of IDA15, held in November, with the aim of assisting those countries to maintain spending on sectors critical to achieving the Millennium Development Goals. Permanent funding for the Crisis Response Window, which additionally was to assist low-income countries manage the impact of natural disasters, was agreed as part of the IDA16 replenishment accord in December 2010. In mid-2011 $250m. was allocated from the Crisis Response Window to provide relief and longer-term rehabilitation assistance to areas of the Horn of Africa affected by a severe drought. In September the World Bank announced that $30m. of those funds were to be disbursed through UNHCR in order to improve basic facilities in settlements occupied by persons displaced as a result of the drought. In December the World Bank's Board of Executive Directors approved the establishment of an Immediate Response Mechanism in order to accelerate the provision of assistance to IDA-eligible countries following a natural disaster or economic crisis.

IDA administers a Trust Fund, which was established in November 1996 as part of a World Bank/IMF initiative to assist heavily indebted poor countries (HIPCs). In September 2005 the World Bank's Development Committee and the International Monetary and Financial Committee of the IMF endorsed a proposal of the Group of Eight (G8) industrialized countries to cancel the remaining multilateral debt owed by HIPCs that had reached their completion point under the scheme (see IBRD). In December IDA convened a meeting of donor countries to discuss funding to uphold its financial capability upon its contribution to the so-called Multilateral Debt Relief Initiative (MDRI). The scheme was approved by the Board of Executive Directors in March 2006 and entered into effect on 1 July. By September 2012 34 countries had reached completion point, of which 28 were in sub-Saharan Africa.

Publication

Annual Report.

Statistics

IDA CREDITS APPROVED IN SUB-SAHARAN AFRICA, 1 JULY 2010–30 JUNE 2011
(US $ million)

Country	Purpose	Amount
Angola	Water sector institutional development	120.0
Benin	Community-driven development (additional financing)	12.0
	Agricultural productivity and diversification credit/grant	6.0/25.0
	Protected areas conservation management	5.0
	Sixth poverty reduction developmental policy grant	22.0
	Emergency urban environment credit	50.0
Burkina Faso	Transport sector (additional financing)	115.0
	Competitiveness and enterprise development (additional financing)	20.0
	Economic growth support in the Bagre region	115.0
	Mineral sector development	33.0
	Health sector support and multi-sectoral HIV/AIDS grant (additional financing)	36.0
Burundi	Emergency energy recovery	15.4
	Fourth economic reform development support grant	25.0
	Financial and private sector development (additional financing)	8.0
	Road sector development	19.0
Cameroon	Urban and water development support (additional financing)	28.7
	Sanitation improvements	30.0
Cape Verde	Sixth poverty reduction support development policy credit	10.0
	Road sector support (additional financing)	10.0
Central African Republic	Third economic management and governance reform development policy grant	8.8
	Emergency urban infrastructure rehabilitation and maintenance (additional financing) credit/grant	7.5/16.4
	Agro-pastoral recovery credit/grant	13.1/10.7
Chad	Second local development programme support adaptable credit/grant	13.8/11.3
	Urban development (additional financing) credit/grant	15.1/12.3
Comoros	Economic governance and financial management assistance	1.8
Congo, Democratic Republic	Mining sector technical assistance grant	50.0
	Malaria control emergency recovery grant	80.0
	Emergency social action (additional financing)	6.8
	Core public management technical assistance grant	29.9
	Health sector rehabilitation	30.0
	High-priority roads re-opening and maintenance (additional financing)	63.3
Congo, Republic	Support to economic diversification	10.0
Djibouti	Rural community development and water mobilization	5.8

Country—*continued*	Purpose	Amount
Ethiopia	Agricultural growth specific investment credit/grant	108.4/41.6
	Protection of basic services investment and maintenance credit/grant (additional financing)	173.4/246.6
	Irrigation and draining (additional financing)	60.0
The Gambia	Growth and competitiveness	12.0
Ghana	Oil and gas sector capacity building technical assistance credit	38.0
	Seventh poverty reduction support credit	215.0
	Local government capacity building support	175.0
	Skills and technology development in selected economic sectors	70.0
	Second land administration specific investment credit	50.0
	Third agriculture development policy credit	57.0
Guinea	Re-engagement and reform of public sector governance and services	78.0
Guinea-Bissau	Emergency electricity and water rehabilitation	12.7
	Biodiversity conservation	1.9
	Emergency electricity and water rehabilitation (additional financing)	2.2
	Third economic governance reform grant	6.4
Kenya	Coastal development	35.0
	HIV/AIDS prevention and mitigation (additional financing)	55.0
	Informal settlements improvements	100.0
	Transport sector support	300.0
Lesotho	Integrated transport project credit/grant (additional financing)	8.5/6.5
	Third poverty reduction support credit/grant	1.6/16.4
Liberia	Third re-engagement and reform support development grant	11.0
	Electricity systems enhancement	10.0
	Economic governance and institutional reform (additional financing)	7.0
	Monrovia emergency urban sanitation investment credit	4.0
	Road asset management	67.7
Madagascar	Third environmental support specific investment credit/grant (additional financing)	42.0
Malawi	Irrigation rural livelihoods and agricultural development (additional financing)	12.7
	Mining sector governance and growth	25.0
	Financial sector technical assistance	28.2
	Second national water development specific investment credit/grant (additional financing)	95.0/25.0
	Energy sector support investment credit/grant	19.3/65.4
Mali	Rural community development (additional financing)	11.2
	Fifth poverty reduction support development policy credit	70.0
	Governance and budget decentralization technical assistance credit	12.0
	Urban local government	70.0
Mauritania	Education sector and skills development	16.0
	Second mining sector technical assistance credit (additional financing)	7.1
Mozambique	Health commodity distribution programme	39.0
	Second Maputo municipal development adaptable programme credit	50.0
	Spatial development planning	20.0
	Water services and institutional support (additional financing)	37.0
	Seventh poverty reduction support development policy credit	85.0
	Sustainable irrigation development in Sofala, Manica and Zambezia provinces	70.0
	Roads and bridges management and maintenance (additional financing)	41.0
	Education sector support	71.0
Niger	Second HIV/AIDS support specific investment credit	20.0
	Urban water and sanitation services	90.0
	Safety-net systems support	70.0
	Second growth policy reform credit	52.0
Nigeria	First Lagos state development policy credit	200.0
	Strengthening industry competitiveness and growth for employment	160.0
	Partnership for polio eradication (additional financing)	60.0
	Public–private partnership investment in core infrastructures	115.0
Rwanda	Seventh poverty reduction support credit/grant	34.4/70.0
	Third community living standards development policy grant	6.0
	Skills development	30.0
	Transport sector development (additional financing)	11.0
São Tomé and Príncipe	Public resource management and governance reform	4.2
Senegal	Public financial management	15.0
	Fifth poverty reduction support policy credit	42.0
	Tertiary education governance and financing for results	101.3
Sierra Leone	Fourth governance reform and growth development policy credit	10.0
	Financial sector development plan	4.0
	Extractive industries technical assistance grant (additional financing)	4.0
	Rural and private sector development (additional financing)	20.0
Tanzania	'Backbone' power transmission investment credit	150.0
	Eighth poverty reduction support development policy credit	115.0
	Zanzibar urban infrastructure and services	38.0
	National statistical system development	30.0
	Energy development and access expansion (additional financing)	27.9
	Transport sector support (additional financing)	59.0
Togo	Private sector development	13.0
	Fourth economic recovery and governance development policy grant	28.0
	Agriculture sector support	9.0
	Access to urban infrastructure and services	15.0
Uganda	Eighth poverty reduction support development policy credit	100.0
	Transport sector development (additional financing)	75.0
	Electricity sector development	120.0
	Financial sector development	50.0

Country—*continued*	Purpose	Amount
Zambia	Increased access to electricity services (additional financing)	20.0
	Road rehabilitation and maintenance (additional financing)	15.0
	Malaria prevention and treatment (additional financing)	30.0
	Second poverty reduction support development policy credit	30.0
	Irrigation systems development and support	115.0
Regional	Agricultural productivity credit/grant	45.0/45.0
	Central African 'backbone' communications infrastructure and technology phase II grant	14.9
	West Africa regional communications infrastructure	56.6
	EAC financial sector development and regionalization	16.0
	ACBF regional capacity building	25.0
	West Africa agricultural productivity credit/grant	36.0/47.8
	West Africa regional fisheries management	6.0
	Central African 'backbone' adaptable programme credit	15.0
	Lake Victoria environmental management credit/grant	15.0/15.0
	Regional trade facilitation credit/grant	20.0/7.5
	West Africa regional communications infrastructure	92.0
	East Africa trade and transport facilitation (additional financing)	30.0
	ECOWAS transport and transit facilitation (additional financing)	112.0
	Regional and domestic power markets (additional financing)	283.0
	West Africa regional fisheries (additional financing)	2.0
	West Africa Power Pool credit/grant	25.9/16.0
	Central African 'backbone' credit/grant	17.5/22.5

Source: World Bank, *Annual Report 2011*.

International Finance Corporation—IFC

Address: 2121 Pennsylvania Ave, NW, Washington, DC 20433, USA.

Telephone: (202) 473-3800; **fax:** (202) 974-4384; **e-mail:** information@ifc.org; **internet:** www.ifc.org.

IFC was founded in 1956 as a member of the World Bank Group to stimulate economic growth in developing countries by financing private sector investments, mobilizing capital in international financial markets, and providing technical assistance and advice to governments and businesses.

Organization

(September 2012)

IFC is a separate legal entity in the World Bank Group. Executive Directors of the World Bank also serve as Directors of IFC. The President of the World Bank is *ex officio* Chairman of the IFC Board of Directors, which has appointed him President of IFC. Subject to his overall supervision, the day-to-day operations of IFC are conducted by its staff under the direction of the Executive Vice-President. The senior management team includes 10 Vice-Presidents responsible for regional and thematic groupings. At the end of June 2011 IFC had 3,354 staff members, of whom 54% were based in field offices in 86 countries.

PRINCIPAL OFFICERS

President: Dr Jim Yong Kim (USA).

Executive Vice-President: Jin-Yong Cai (People's Republic of China) (from 1 Oct. 2012).

Vice-President, Sub-Saharan Africa, Latin America and the Caribbean, Western Europe: Bernie Sheahan (acting).

OFFICES IN AFRICA SOUTH OF THE SAHARA

Head Office: 14 Fricker Rd, Illovo 2196, Johannesburg, South Africa; tel. (11) 731-3000; fax (11) 268-0074; e-mail ifcjohannesburg@ifc.org; also serves, Botswana, Lesotho, Malawi, Swaziland, Zambia and Zimbabwe; Country Man. Saleem Karimjee.

Regional Head Office: Commercial Bank of Africa (CBA) Bldg, Mara/Ragai Rd, Upper Hill, POB 30577–00100, Nairobi, Kenya; tel. (20) 2759000; fax (20) 2759210; also serves Burundi, Djibouti, Eritrea, Rwanda, Somalia, Sudan, and Uganda; Dir Jean-Philippe Prosper.

Regional Head Office: rue Aime Cesaire x Impasse FN Prolongee, Fann Residence, BP 3296, Dakar, Senegal; tel. (33) 859-7100; fax (33) 849-7144; also serves Cape Verde, Gambia, Guinea Bissau, Mali and Mauritania; Dir Yolande Duhem.

Burkina Faso: 179 ave du President Saye Zerbo, Zone des Ambassades, Kouloubа, 01 BP 622, Ougadougou; tel. 50-49-63-51; Senior Investment Officer Jeremie Bernard Dumon.

Cameroon: Citigroup Bldg, 96 Flatters St, Suite 305, POB 4616, Douala; tel. 3350-4000; fax 3342-8014; also serves Chad, Republic of Congo, Equatorial Guinea and Gabon; Country Man. Henri Rabarijohn.

Central African Republic: rue des Missions, POB 819, Bangui; tel. 21-61-61-38; fax 21-61-60-87; Resident Rep. Justin Kouakou.

Congo, Democratic Republic: 4847 Wagenia Ave, Kinshasa, Gombe; tel. 817005215; fax 8807817; Country Co-ordinator Jean-Philippe Mukuaki.

Côte d'Ivoire: angle rues Booker Washington/Jacques Aka, BP 1850, Abidjan 01; tel. 22-40-04-00; fax 22-44-44-83; Resident Rep. Cassandra Colbert.

Ethiopia: c/o World Bank, Africa Ave, Bole Rd, POB 5515, Addis Ababa; tel. (11) 5176000; fax (11) 6627717; Resident Rep. Adamou Labara.

Ghana: House No.1, Central Link St, South Legon; POB CT2638, Cantonments, Accra; tel. (21) 7012170; fax (21) 509069; e-mail ifcaccra@ifc.org; also serves, Benin, Guinea, Niger and Togo; Country Man. Mary-Jean Lindile Moyo.

Liberia: Bright Bldg, UN Drive, Mamba Point, Sekou Toure Ave and Gibson St, Monrovia; tel. (6) 930916; Resident Rep. Frank Ajibola Ajilore.

Madagascar: rue Andriamifidy, Anosy, Antananarivo 101; tel. (20) 2326000; fax (20) 2233338; also serves Comoros, Mauritius and Seychelles; Country Man. Kailash Ramnauth (acting).

Mozambique: 160 Jose Craveirinha St, POB 4053, Maputo; tel. 21483000; fax 21496247; also serves Angola; Country Man. Jumoke Jakun-Dokunmu.

Nigeria: Maersk House, Plot 121 Louis Solomon Close, off Ahmadu Bellow Way, Victoria Island, Lagos; tel. (1) 279-9400; fax (1) 279-3618; Country Man. Solomon Quaynor.

Rwanda: SORAS Building, blvd de la Revolution, 4th floor, POB 609, Kigali; tel. 591-350; fax 570-405; Senior Operations Officer Ignace Rusenga Mihigo Bacyaha.

Sierra Leone: Bishop House, 13 Lamina Sankoh St, Freetown; tel. (22) 220480; fax (22) 228555; Senior Country Officer Mary Agboli.

Tanzania: 50 Mirambo St, Dar es Salaam; Senior Investment Officer Dan Kasirye.

Zambia: Pyramid Plaza, 746B Church Rd, Box 35410, Lusaka; tel. (21) 252811; fax (21) 254283; Senior Investment Officer Sylvain Kakou.

Activities

IFC aims to promote economic development in developing member countries by assisting the growth of private enterprise and effective capital markets. It finances private sector projects, through loans, the purchase of equity, quasi-equity products, and risk management services, and assists governments to create conditions that stimulate the flow of domestic and foreign private savings and investment. IFC may provide finance for a project that is partly state-owned, provided that there is participation by the private sector and that the project is operated on a commercial basis. IFC also mobilizes additional resources from other financial institutions, in particular through syndicated loans, thus providing access to international capital markets. IFC provides a range of advisory services to help to improve the investment climate in developing countries and offers technical assistance to private enterprises and governments. In 2008 IFC formulated a policy document to help to increase its impact in the three-year period 2009–11. The IFC Road Map identified five strategic 'pillars' as priority areas of activity: strengthening the focus on frontier markets (i.e. the lowest-income countries or regions of middle-income countries, those affected by conflict, or underdeveloped industrial sectors); building long-term partnerships with emerging 'players' in developing countries; addressing climate change and securing environmental and social sustainability; promoting private sector growth in infrastructure, health and education; and developing local financial markets. From late 2008 IFC's overriding concern was to respond effectively to the difficulties facing member countries affected by the global economic and financial crisis and to maintain a sustainable level of development. In particular it aimed to preserve and create employment opportunities, to support supply chains for local businesses, and to provide credit.

To be eligible for financing projects must be profitable for investors, as well as financially and economically viable; must benefit the economy of the country concerned; and must comply with IFC's environmental and social guidelines. IFC aims to promote best corporate governance and management methods and sustainable business practices, and encourages partnerships between governments, non-governmental organizations and community groups. In 2001/02 IFC developed a Sustainability Framework to help to assess the longer-term economic, environmental and social impact of projects. The first Sustainability Review was published in mid-2002. In 2002/03 IFC assisted 10 international banks to draft a voluntary set of guidelines (the Equator Principles), based on IFC's environmental, social and safeguard monitoring policies, to be applied to their global project finance activities. In September 2009 IFC initiated a Performance Standards Review Process to define new standards to be applied within the Equator Principles framework. At January 2012 73 financial institutions had signed up to the Equator Principles.

In November 2004 IFC announced the establishment of a Global Trade Finance Programme (GTFP), with initial funding of some US $500m., which aimed to support small-scale importers and exporters in emerging markets, and to facilitate South–South trade in goods and services, by providing guarantees for trade transactions, as well as extending technical assistance and training to local financial institutions. Additional funding of $500m. was approved in January 2007, and in October 2008, by which time there were 147 confirming banks from 70 countries participating in the initiative and 126 issuing banks in 66 countries. In December, as part of a set of measures to support the global economy, the Board of Directors approved an expansion of the GTFP, doubling its funding to $3,000m. Other initiatives included the establishment of an Infrastructure Crisis Facility to provide investment for existing projects affected by a lack of private funding, and a new Bank Capitalization Fund (to be financed, up to $3,000m., with the Japan Bank for International Co-operation) to provide investment and advisory services to banks in emerging markets. In May 2009 IFC established an Asset Management Company, as a wholly owned subsidiary, to administer the Capitalization Fund. In February of that year IFC inaugurated a Microfinance Enhancement Facility, with a German development bank, to extend credit to microfinancing institutions and to support lending to low-income borrowers, with funds of up to $500m. IFC committed $1,000m. in funds to a new Global Trade Liquidity Program (GTLP), which was inaugurated by the World Bank Group in April, with the aim of mobilizing support of up to $50,000m. in trade transactions through financing extended by governments, other development banks and the private sector. In October IFC established a Debt and Asset Recovery Program to help to restore stability and growth by facilitating loan restructuring for businesses and by investing in funds targeting distressed assets and companies. IFC pledged to contribute $1,550m. to the Program over a three-year period, and aimed to mobilize resources through partnerships with other international financial institutions and private sector companies.

IFC's authorized capital is US $2,450m. At 30 June 2011 paid-in capital was $2,369m. The World Bank was originally the principal source of borrowed funds, but IFC also borrows from private capital markets. IFC's net income amounted to $1,579m. (after a $600m. grant transfer to IDA), compared with $1,746m. in 2009/10 (after a $600m. transfer to IDA). In December 2008 the Board of Directors approved a Sovereign Funds Initiative to enable IFC to raise and manage commercial capital from sovereign funds. In July 2010 the Board of Directors recommended a special capital increase of $130m., to raise authorized capital to $2,580m. The increase required the approval of the Board of Governors.

In the year ending 30 June 2011 project financing approved by IFC amounted to US $18,660m. for 518 projects in 102 countries (compared with $18,041m. for 528 projects in the previous year). Of the total approved in 2010/11, $12,186m. was for IFC's own account, while $6,474m. was in the form of loan syndications and parallel loans, underwriting of securities issues and investment funds and funds mobilized by the IFC Asset Management Company. Generally, IFC limits its financing to less than 25% of the total cost of a project, but may take up to a 35% stake in a venture (although never as a majority shareholder). Disbursements for IFC's account amounted to $6,715m. in 2010/11.

In 2010/11 IFC approved commitments totalling US $2,150m. for projects in 32 countries in sub-Saharan Africa, compared with $2,428m. in the previous year. An additional $589m. was mobilized during 2010/11 in the form of loan participation, parallel loans and structured finance. IFC's strategic priorities for the region are: to accelerate and deepen support to small and medium-sized enterprises (SMEs); to catalyze and conclude large investment projects; and to bolster reform of the investment climate. In particular, IFC was concerned with the needs of countries emerging from conflict and with the promotion of projects that support cross-border trade and investment. IFC aims significantly to increase its investment in and advisory services to agribusiness operations in order to improve efficiency and counter the escalating cost of food production. In 2008 IFC inaugurated a five-year programme to address the specific economic recovery needs of conflict-affected states in Africa, with an initial focus on Liberia, the Democratic Republic of the Congo, Sierra Leone and the Central African Republic. In May 2009 IFC pledged an additional $1,000m. in funding to the region in support of an international initiative, the Joint Action Plan for Africa, to promote trade, to strengthen the financial sector and to increase lending for infrastructure, agribusiness and SMEs in the region affected by the global financial crisis.

IFC's Advisory Services are a major part of the organization's involvement with member countries to support the development of private enterprises and efforts to generate funding, as well as to enhance private sector participation in developing infrastructure. Advisory services cover the following five main areas of expertise: the business enabling environment (i.e improving the investment climate in a country); access to financing (including developing financing institutions, improving financial infrastructure and strengthening regulatory frameworks); infrastructure (mainly encouraging private sector participation); environment and social sustainability; and corporate advice (in particular in support of small and medium-sized enterprises—SMEs). In December 2008 the Board of Directors determined to provide additional funding to IFC advisory services in order to strengthen the capacity of financial institutions and governments to respond to the crisis in the global financial markets. At 30 June 2011 there were 642 active Advisory Service projects with a value of US $820m. Total expenditure on Advisory Services during that year amounted to $206.7m. IFC manages, jointly financed with the World Bank and MIGA, the Foreign Investment Advisory Service (FIAS), which provides technical assistance and advice on promoting foreign investment and strengthening the country's investment framework at the request of governments. Under the Technical Assistance Trust Funds Program (TATF), established in 1988, IFC manages resources contributed by various governments and agencies to provide finance for feasibility studies, project identification studies and other types of technical assistance relating to project preparation. In 2004 a Grassroots Business Initiative was established, with external donor funding, to support businesses that provide economic opportunities for disadvantaged communities in Africa, Latin America, and South and Southeast Asia. Since 2002 IFC has administered an online SME Toolkit to enhance the accessibility of business training and advice. By 2011 the service was available in 16 languages.

In April 1989 IFC (with UNDP and the African Development Bank—ADB) initiated the African Management Services Company (AMSCo): its aim is to help find qualified senior executives from around the world to work with African companies, assist in the training of local managers, and provide supporting services. IFC's Africa Enterprise Fund (AEF), which began operations in 1988, provides financial assistance to SMEs, typically in the tourism, agribusiness and small-scale manufacturing sectors. Most projects cost less than US $5m., with IFC financing in the range of $100,000 to $1.5m. The Enterprise Support Services for Africa (ESSA) was initiated by IFC in 1995 to provide post-investment operational advice, including the development and strengthening of management information systems and technical capacity, to SMEs in the sub-Saharan region. In 1998/99 ESSA was expanded to be available throughout sub-Saharan Africa as part of the APDF. In the same year IFC approved the establishment of an African Infrastructure Fund, which commenced work evaluating investment in 1999/2000. In April 2005 IFC inaugurated the Private Enterprise Partnership (PEP)-Africa, as a successor to the Africa Project Development Facility, which had been operational since 1986. The new facility aimed to enhance its effectiveness in supporting and developing local business capacity. It was to support a new SME Entrepreneurship Development Initiative and to help to develop a network of SME Solution Centers. In addition, PEP-Africa aimed to provide technical assistance to regional member states, in particular on issues relating to the investment. During 2010/11 25% of IFC Advisory Services was allocated to sub-Saharan Africa.

Since 2004 IFC has presented an annual Client Leadership Award to a chosen corporate client who most represents IFC values in innovation, operational excellence and corporate governance.

Publications

Annual Report.

Doing Business (annually).

Emerging Stock Markets Factbook (annually).

Lessons of Experience (series).

Outcomes (quarterly).

Results on the Ground (series).

Review of Small Businesses (annually).

Sustainability Report (annually).

Other handbooks, discussion papers, technical documents, policy toolkits, public policy journals.

Multilateral Investment Guarantee Agency—MIGA

Address: 1818 H Street, NW, Washington, DC 20433, USA.

Telephone: (202) 473-6163; **fax:** (202) 522-2630; **internet:** www.miga.org.

MIGA was founded in 1988 as an affiliate of the World Bank. Its mandate is to encourage the flow of foreign direct investment to, and among, developing member countries, through the provision of political risk insurance and investment marketing services to foreign investors and host governments, respectively.

Organization

(September 2012)

MIGA is legally and financially separate from the World Bank. It is supervised by a Council of Governors (comprising one Governor and one Alternate of each member country) and an elected Board of Directors (of no less than 12 members).

President: Dr Jim Yong Kim (USA).

Executive Vice-President: Izumi Kobayashi (Japan).

Activities

The convention establishing MIGA took effect in April 1988. Authorized capital was US $1,082m., although the convention provided for an increase of capital stock upon the admission of new members. In April 1998 the Board of Directors approved an increase in MIGA's capital base. A grant of $150m. was transferred from the IBRD as part of the package, while the capital increase (totalling $700m. callable capital and $150m. paid-in capital) was approved by MIGA's Council of Governors in April 1999. A three-year subscription period then commenced, covering the period April 1999–March 2002 (later extended to March 2003). At 30 June 2011 110 countries had subscribed $749.9m. of the general capital increase. At that time total subscriptions to the capital stock amounted to $1,912.8m., of which $364.9m. was paid-in.

MIGA guarantees eligible investments against losses resulting from non-commercial risks, under the following main categories:

(i) transfer risk resulting from host government restrictions on currency conversion and transfer;

(ii) risk of loss resulting from legislative or administrative actions of the host government;

(iii) repudiation by the host government of contracts with investors in cases in which the investor has no access to a competent forum;

(iv) the risk of armed conflict and civil unrest;

(v) risk of a sovereign not honouring a financial obligation or guarantee.

Before guaranteeing any investment, MIGA must ensure that it is commercially viable, contributes to the development process and is not harmful to the environment. During the fiscal year 1998/99 MIGA and IFC appointed the first Compliance Advisor and Ombudsman to consider the concerns of local communities directly affected by MIGA- or IFC-sponsored projects. In February 1999 the Board of Directors approved an increase in the amount of political risk insurance available for each project, from US $75m. to $200m. During 2003/04 MIGA established a new fund, the Invest-in-Development Facility, to enhance the role of foreign investment in attaining the Millennium Development Goals. In 2005/06 MIGA supported for the first time a project aimed at selling carbon credits gained by reducing greenhouse gas emissions; it provided $2m. in guarantee coverage to the El Salvador-based initiative. In April 2009 the Board of Directors approved modifications to MIGA's policies and operational regulations in order to enhance operational flexibility and efficiency, in particular in the poorest countries and those affected by conflict. In November 2010 the Council of Governors approved amendments to MIGA's convention (the first since 1988) to broaden the eligibility for investment projects and to enhance the effectiveness of MIGA's development impact.

During the year ending 30 June 2011 MIGA issued 50 investment insurance contracts for 38 projects with a value of US $2,100m. (compared with 28 contracts amounting to $1,500m. in 2009/10). Since 1990 the total investment guarantees issued amounted to some $24,500m., through 1,030 contracts in support of 651 projects.

MIGA works with local insurers, export credit agencies, development finance institutions and other organizations to promote insurance in a country, to ensure a level of consistency among insurers and to support capacity-building within the insurance industry. MIGA also offers investment marketing services to help to promote foreign direct investment in developing countries and in transitional economies, and to disseminate information on investment opportunities. MIGA maintains an internet service (www.pri-center.com), providing access to political risk management and insurance resources, in order to support those objectives. In early 2007 MIGA's technical assistance services were amalgamated into the Foreign Advisory Investment Service (FIAS, see IFC), of which MIGA became a lead partner, along with IFC and the World Bank. During 2000/01 an office was established in Paris, France, to promote and co-ordinate European investment in developing countries, in particular in Africa and Eastern Europe. In March 2002 MIGA opened a regional office, based in Johannesburg, South Africa. In September a new regional office was inaugurated in Singapore, in order to facilitate foreign investment in Asia. A Regional Director for Asia and the Pacific was appointed, for the first time, in August 2010 to head a new Asian Hub, operating from offices in Singapore, Hong Kong SAR and the People's Republic of China.

Publications

Annual Report.

MIGA News (online newsletter; every 2 months).

World Investment and Political Risk (annually).

Other guides, brochures and regional briefs.

International Fund for Agricultural Development—IFAD

Address: Via Paolo di Dono 44, 00142 Rome, Italy.

Telephone: (06) 54591; **fax:** (06) 5043463; **e-mail:** ifad@ifad.org; **internet:** www.ifad.org.

IFAD was established in 1977, following a decision by the 1974 UN World Food Conference, with a mandate to combat hunger and eradicate poverty on a sustainable basis in the low-income, food-deficit regions of the world. Funding operations began in January 1978.

Organization

(September 2012)

GOVERNING COUNCIL

Each member state is represented in the Governing Council (the Fund's highest authority) by a Governor and an Alternate. Sessions are held annually with special sessions as required. The Governing Council elects the President of the Fund (who also chairs the Executive Board) by a two-thirds majority for a four-year term. The President is eligible for re-election.

EXECUTIVE BOARD

Consists of 18 members and 18 alternates, elected by the Governing Council, who serve for three years. The Executive Board is responsible for the conduct and general operation of IFAD and approves loans and grants for projects; it holds three regular sessions each year. An independent Office of Evaluation reports directly to the Board.

The governance structure of the Fund is based on the classification of members. Membership of the Executive Board is distributed as follows: eight List A countries (i.e. industrialized donor countries), four List B (petroleum-exporting developing donor countries), and six List C (recipient developing countries), divided equally among the three Sub-List C categories (i.e. for Africa, Europe, Asia and the Pacific, and Latin America and the Caribbean).

President and Chairman of Executive Board: KANAYO F. NWANZE (Nigeria).

Activities

IFAD provides financing primarily for projects designed to improve food production systems in developing member states and to strengthen related policies, services and institutions. In allocating resources IFAD is guided by: the need to increase food production in the poorest food-deficit countries; the potential for increasing food production in other developing countries; and the importance of improving the nutrition, health and education of the poorest people in developing countries, i.e. small-scale farmers, artisanal fishermen, nomadic pastoralists, indigenous populations, rural women, and the rural landless. All projects emphasize the participation of beneficiaries in development initiatives, both at the local and national level. Issues relating to gender and household food security are incorporated into all aspects of its activities. IFAD is committed to achieving the Millennium Development Goals (MDGs), pledged by governments attending a special session of the UN General Assembly in September 2000, and, in particular, the objective to reduce by 50% the proportion of people living in extreme poverty by 2015. In 2001 the Fund introduced new measures to improve monitoring and impact evaluation, in particular to assess its contribution to achieving the MDGs.

In May 2011 the Executive Board adopted IFAD's Strategic Framework for 2011–15, in which it reiterated its commitment to improving rural food security and nutrition, and enabling the rural poor to overcome their poverty. The 2011–15 Strategic Framework was underpinned by five strategic objectives: developing a natural resource and economic asset base for poor rural communities, with improved resilience to climate change, environmental degradation and market transformation; facilitating access for the rural poor to services aimed at reducing poverty, improving nutrition, raising incomes and building resilience in a changing environment; supporting the rural poor in managing profitable, sustainable and resilient farm and non-farm enterprises and benefiting from decent employment opportunities; enabling the rural poor to influence policies and institutions that affect their livelihoods; and enabling institutional and policy environments that support agricultural production and the related non-farm activities.

From 2009 IFAD implemented a new business model, with the direct supervision of projects, and maintaining a stable presence in countries of operations, as its two main pillars. Consequently, by 2011 the Fund directly supervised some 93% of the projects it was funding, compared with 18% in 2007.

IFAD is a participant in the High Level Task Force (HLTF) on the Global Food Security Crisis, which was established by the UN Secretary-General in April 2008 and aims to address the impact of soaring global levels of food and fuel prices and to formulate a comprehensive framework for action. In June IFAD participated in the High-Level Conference on World Food Security and the Challenges of Climate Change and Bioenergy, convened by FAO in Rome, Italy. The meeting adopted a Declaration on Food Security, which noted an urgent need to develop the agricultural sectors and expand food production in developing countries and countries with economies in transition, and for increased investment in rural development, agriculture and agribusiness. In January 2009 the HLTF participated in a follow-up high level meeting convened in Madrid, Spain, which agreed to initiate a consultation process with regard to the establishment of a Global Partnership for Agriculture, Food Security and Nutrition. During 2009 the long-standing Committee on World Food Security (CFS), open to member states of IFAD, FAO, and WFP, underwent reform, becoming a central component of the new Global Partnership; thereafter the CFS was tasked with influencing hunger elimination programmes at global, regional and national level, taking into account that food security relates not just to agriculture but also to economic access to food, adequate nutrition, social safety nets and human rights. IFAD contributes, with FAO, WFP and other agencies, to a new Agricultural Market Information System (AMIS), which was agreed by a meeting of agriculture ministers from G20 countries, held in June 2011 to increase market transparency and to address the stabilization of food price volatility. In October IFAD and WFP helped FAO to compile its annual *State of Food Insecurity in the World* report, which maintained that volatile and high food prices were likely to continue, rendering poorer consumers, farmers and states more vulnerable to poverty and hunger. IFAD welcomed a commitment made, in May 2012, by G8 heads of state and government and leaders of African countries, to supporting a New Alliance for Food Security and Nutrition; the Alliance was to promote sustainable and inclusive agricultural growth over a 10-year period.

IFAD, with FAO and WFP, leads an initiative on ensuring food security by strengthening feeding programmes and expanding support to farmers in developing countries, the second of nine activities that were launched in April 2009 by the UN System Chief Executives Board for Co-ordination (CEB), with the aim of alleviating the impact on poor and vulnerable populations of the developing global economic crisis.

In September 2012 IFAD, FAO, WFP and UN Women launched 'Accelerating Progress Toward the Economic Empowerment of Rural Women', a five-year initiative that was to be implemented initially in Ethiopia, Guatemala, Kyrgyzstan, Liberia, Nepal, Niger and Rwanda.

In March 2010 the Executive Board endorsed a new IFAD Climate Change Strategy, under which the Fund aimed to create a climate-smart portfolio, and to support smallholder farmers increase their resilience to climate change. During 2011 an Adaptation for Smallholder Agriculture Programme (ASAP) was developed; under ASAP finance for climate adaptation initiatives was to be integrated into IFAD-supported investments.

IFAD is a leading repository of knowledge, resources and expertise in the field of rural hunger and poverty alleviation. In 2001 it renewed its commitment to becoming a global knowledge institution for rural poverty-related issues. Through its technical assistance grants, IFAD aims to promote research and capacity-building in the agricultural sector, as well as the development of technologies to increase production and alleviate rural poverty. In recent years IFAD has been increasingly involved in promoting the use of communication technology to facilitate the exchange of information and experience among rural communities, specialized institutions and organizations, and IFAD-sponsored projects. Within the strategic context of knowledge management, IFAD has supported initiatives to establish regional electronic networks, such as Electronic Networking for Rural Asia/Pacific (ENRAP, conducted over three phases during the period 1998–2010), and FIDAMERICA in Latin America and the Caribbean (conducted over four phases during 1995–2009), as well as to develop other lines of communication between organizations, local agents and the rural poor.

IFAD is empowered to make both loans and grants. Loans are available on highly concessionary, hardened, intermediate and ordinary terms. Highly concessionary loans carry no interest but have an annual service charge of 0.75% and a repayment period of 40 years; loans approved on hardened terms carry no interest charge, have an annual service charge of 0.75%, and are repaid over 20 years; intermediate loans are subject to a variable interest charge, equivalent to 50% of the interest rate charged on World Bank loans, and are repaid over 20 years; and ordinary loans carry a variable interest charge equal to that levied by the World Bank, and are repaid over 15–18 years. New Debt Sustainability Framework (DSF) grant financing was introduced in 2007 in place of highly concessional loans for heavily indebted poor countries (HIPCs). In 2011 highly concessionary loans represented some 50.1% of total lending in that year, DSF grants 22.8%, intermediate loans 14.5%, ordinary loans 9.2%, and hardened loans 3.4%. Research and technical assistance grants are awarded to projects focusing on research and training, and for project preparation and development. In order to increase the impact of its lending resources on food production, the Fund seeks as much as possible to attract other external donors and beneficiary governments as cofinanciers of its projects. In 2011 external cofinancing accounted for some 18.8% of all project funding, while domestic contributions, i.e. from recipient governments and other local sources, accounted for 37.9%.

The IFAD Indigenous Peoples Assistance Facility was created in 2007 to fund microprojects that aim to build upon the knowledge and natural resources of indigenous communities and organizations. Under IFAD's Policy on Engagement with Indigenous Peoples, adopted by the Executive Board in September 2009, an Indigenous Peoples' Forum was established in February 2011; this was to convene every two years, from 2013. Prior to the inaugural session of the Forum regional consultations were being undertaken in 2012 in Africa, Asia, the Pacific, and Latin America and the Caribbean. In September 2010, the Executive Board approved the establishment of a new Spanish Food Security Cofinancing Facility Trust Fund (the 'Spanish Trust Fund'), which is used to provide loans to IFAD borrower nations. On 31 December 2010 the Spanish Government provided, on a loan basis, €285.5m. to the Spanish Trust Fund.

In November 2006 IFAD was granted access to the core resources of the HIPC Trust Fund, administered by the World Bank, to assist in financing the outstanding debt relief on post-completion point countries participating in the HIPC debt relief initiative (see under IBRD). By December 2011 36 of 39 eligible countries had passed their decision points, thereby qualifying for HIPC debt relief assistance from IFAD, and 32 countries had reached completion point, thereby qualifying for full and irrevocable debt reduction.

IFAD's development projects usually include a number of components, such as infrastructure (e.g. improvement of water supplies, small-scale irrigation and road construction); input supply (e.g. improved seeds, fertilizers and pesticides); institutional support (e.g. research, training and extension services); and producer incentives (e.g. pricing and marketing improvements). IFAD also attempts to enable the landless to acquire income-generating assets: by increasing the provision of credit for the rural poor, it seeks to free them from dependence on the capital market and to generate productive activities.

In addition to its regular efforts to identify projects and programmes, IFAD organizes special programming missions to selected countries to undertake a comprehensive review of the constraints affecting the rural poor, and to help countries to design strategies for the removal of these constraints. In general, projects based on the recommendations of these missions tend to focus on institutional improvements at the national and local level to direct inputs and services to small farmers and the landless rural poor. Monitoring and evaluation missions are also sent to check the progress of projects and to assess the impact of poverty reduction efforts.

The Fund supports projects that are concerned with environmental conservation, in an effort to alleviate poverty that results from the deterioration of natural resources. In addition, it extends environmental assessment grants to review the environmental consequences of projects under preparation. IFAD administers the Global Mechanism of the 1996 Convention to Combat Desertification in those Countries Experiencing Drought and Desertification, particularly in Africa. The Mechanism mobilizes and channels resources for the implementation of the Convention, and IFAD is its largest financial contributor. IFAD is an executing agency of the Global Environmental Facility, specializing in the area of combating rural poverty and environmental degradation.

During 2011 IFAD approved lending for five projects in the Eastern and Southern Africa region and nine in Western and Central Africa, involving loans amounting to US $223.6m. (or 23.5% of total lending in that year) and $173.1m. (18.2%) respectively. At end-2011 52 programmes and projects were ongoing in 17 countries in Eastern and Southern Africa, and 52 programmes and projects were ongoing in 23 countries in Western and Central Africa.

During 1998 the Executive Board endorsed a policy framework for the Fund's provision of assistance in post-conflict situations, with the aim of achieving a continuum from emergency relief to a secure basis from which to pursue sustainable development. In July 2001 IFAD and UNAIDS signed a Memorandum of Understanding on developing a co-operation agreement.

During the late 1990s IFAD established several partnerships within the agribusiness sector, with a view to improving performance at project level, broadening access to capital markets, and encouraging the advancement of new technologies. Since 1996 it has chaired the Support Group of the Global Forum on Agricultural Research (GFAR), which facilitates dialogue between research centres and institutions, farmers' organizations, non-governmental bodies, the private sector and donors. In October 2001 IFAD became a co-sponsor of the Consultative Group on International Agricultural Research (CGIAR). In 2006 IFAD reviewed the work of the International Alliance against Hunger, which was established in 2004 to enhance co-ordination among international agencies and non-governmental organizations concerned with agriculture and rural development, and national alliances against hunger. In November 2009 IFAD and the Islamic Development Bank concluded a US $1,500m. framework cofinancing agreement for jointly financing priority projects during 2010–12 in many of the 52 countries that had membership of both organizations.

Finance

In accordance with the Articles of Agreement establishing IFAD, the Governing Council periodically undertakes a review of the adequacy of resources available to the Fund and may request members to make additional contributions. In February 2012 a target of US $1,500m. was set for the ninth replenishment of IFAD funds, covering the period 2013–15; it was announced in September 2012 that this target had been achieved. The provisional budget for administrative expenses for 2012 amounted to $144.1m., while some $12m. was budgeted in that year to the Fund's capital budget.

Publications

Annual Report.
IFAD Update (2 a year).
Rural Poverty Report.
Staff Working Papers (series).

Statistics

PROJECTS IN AFRICA SOUTH OF THE SAHARA APPROVED IN 2011

Country	Purpose	Loan amount (SDRm.*)
Central African Republic	Reviving food crops and small livestock production in the savannah	3.5
Congo, Republic	Agricultural value chains development	6.2
Côte d'Ivoire	Agricultural development and marketing	14.5
Ethiopia	Rural financial intermediation—phase II	31.3
Ghana	Rural enterprise project—phase III	19.7
Lesotho	Smallholder agricultural development	3.2
Liberia	Smallholder tree crop revitalization in Lofa	10.5
Malawi	Sustainable agricultural production	14.7
Mauritania	Poverty reduction in Aftout South and Karakoro—phase II	5.6
Niger	Food security and development support in the Maradi Region	14.3
Rwanda	Rural income through exports	11.6
Senegal	Agricultural development and rural entrepreneurship	20.2
Sierra Leone	Smallholder commercialization	50.0
Sudan	Seed development project	6.4
Zambia	Smallholder productivity promotion	15.5

* The average value of the SDR—Special Drawing Right—in 2011 was US $1.57868.

International Monetary Fund—IMF

Address: 700 19th St, NW, Washington, DC 20431, USA.

Telephone: (202) 623-7000; **fax:** (202) 623-4661; **e-mail:** publicaffairs@imf.org; **internet:** www.imf.org.

The IMF was established at the same time as the World Bank in December 1945, to promote international monetary co-operation, to facilitate the expansion and balanced growth of international trade and to promote stability in foreign exchange.

Organization

(September 2012)

Managing Director: CHRISTINE LAGARDE (France).

First Deputy Managing Director: DAVID LIPTON (USA).

Deputy Managing Directors: NAOYUKI SHINOHARA (Japan), NEMAT SHAFIK (Egypt/United Kingdom/USA), MIN ZHU (People's Republic of China).

Director, African Department: ANTOINETTE MONSIO SAYEH (Liberia).

BOARD OF GOVERNORS

The highest authority of the Fund is exercised by the Board of Governors, on which each member country is represented by a Governor and an Alternate Governor. The Board normally meets annually. The voting power of each country is related to its quota in the Fund. An International Monetary and Financial Committee (IMFC, formerly the Interim Committee) advises and reports to the Board on matters relating to the management and adaptation of the international monetary and financial system, sudden disturbances that might threaten the system and proposals to amend the Articles of Agreement.

BOARD OF EXECUTIVE DIRECTORS

The 24-member Board of Executive Directors is responsible for the day-to-day operations of the Fund. The USA, United Kingdom, Germany, France and Japan each appoint one Executive Director. There is also one Executive Director from the People's Republic of China, Russia and Saudi Arabia, while the remainder are elected by groups of the remaining countries.

REGIONAL REPRESENTATION

There is a network of regional offices and Resident Representatives in more than 90 member countries. In addition, special information and liaison offices are located in Tokyo, Japan (for Asia and the Pacific), in New York, USA (for the United Nations), and in Europe (Paris, France; Geneva, Switzerland; Belgium, Brussels; and Warsaw, Poland, for Central Europe and the Baltic states).

Activities

The purposes of the IMF, as defined in the Articles of Agreement, are:

(i) To promote international monetary co-operation through a permanent institution which provides the machinery for consultation and collaboration on monetary problems;

(ii) To facilitate the expansion and balanced growth of international trade, and to contribute thereby to the promotion and maintenance of high levels of employment and real income and to the development of members' productive resources;

(iii) To promote exchange stability, to maintain orderly exchange arrangements among members, and to avoid competitive exchange depreciation;

(iv) To assist in the establishment of a multilateral system of payments in respect of current transactions between members and in the elimination of foreign exchange restrictions which hamper the growth of trade;

(v) To give confidence to members by making the general resources of the Fund temporarily available to them, under adequate safeguards, thus providing them with the opportunity to correct maladjustments in their balance of payments, without resorting to measures destructive of national or international prosperity;

(vi) In accordance with the above, to shorten the duration of and lessen the degree of disequilibrium in the international balances of payments of members.

In joining the Fund, each country agrees to co-operate with the above objectives. In accordance with its objective of facilitating the expansion of international trade, the IMF encourages its members to accept the obligations of Article VIII, Sections two, three and four, of the Articles of Agreement. Members that accept Article VIII undertake to refrain from imposing restrictions on the making of payments and transfers for current international transactions and from engaging in discriminatory currency arrangements or multiple currency practices without IMF approval. At the end of 2011 some 90% of members had accepted Article VIII status.

In 2000/01 the Fund established an International Capital Markets Department to improve its understanding of financial markets and a separate Consultative Group on capital markets to serve as a forum for regular dialogue between the Fund and representatives of the private sector. In mid-2006 the International Capital Markets Department was merged with the Monetary and Financial Systems Department to create the Monetary and Capital Markets Department, with the intention of strengthening surveillance of global financial transactions and monetary arrangements. In June 2008 the Managing Director presented a new Work Programme, comprising the following four immediate priorities for the Fund: to enable member countries to deal with the current crises of reduced economic growth and escalating food and fuel prices, including efforts by the Fund to strengthen surveillance activities; to review the Fund's lending instruments; to implement new organizational tools and working practices; and to advance further the Fund's governance agenda.

The deceleration of economic growth in the world's major economies in 2007 and 2008 and the sharp decline in global financial market conditions, in particular in the second half of 2008, focused international attention on the adequacy of the governance of the international financial system and of regulatory and supervisory frameworks. The IMF aimed to provide appropriate and rapid financial and technical assistance to low-income and emerging economies most affected by the crisis and to support a co-ordinated, multinational recovery effort. The Fund worked closely with the Group of 20 (G20) leading economies to produce an Action Plan, in November 2008, concerned with strengthening regulation, transparency and integrity in financial markets and reform of the international financial system. In March 2009 the IMF released a study on the 'Impact of the Financial Crisis on Low-income Countries', and in that month convened, with the Government of Tanzania, a high-level conference, held in Dar es Salaam, to consider the effects of the global financial situation on African countries, as well as areas for future partnership and growth. Later in that month the Executive Board approved a series of reforms to enhance the effectiveness of the Fund's lending framework, including new conditionality criteria, a new flexible credit facility and increased access limits (see below).

In April 2009 a meeting of G20 heads of state and government, convened in London, United Kingdom, determined to make available substantial additional resources through the IMF and other multinational development institutions in order to strengthen global financial liquidity and support economic recovery. There was a commitment to extend US $250,000m. to the IMF in immediate bilateral financial contributions (which would be incorporated into an expanded New Arrangements to Borrow facility) and to support a general allocation of special drawing rights (SDRs), amounting to a further $250,000m. It was agreed that additional resources from sales of IMF gold were to be used to provide $6,000m. in concessional financing for the poorest countries over the next two to three years. The G20 meeting also resolved to implement several major reforms to strengthen the regulation and supervision of the international financial system, which envisaged the IMF collaborating closely with a new Financial Stability Board. In September G20 heads of state and government endorsed a Mutual Assessment Programme, which aimed to achieve sustainable and balanced growth, with the IMF providing analysis and technical assistance. In January 2010 the IMF initiated a process to review its mandate and role in the 'post-crisis' global economy. Short-term priorities included advising countries on moving beyond the policies they implemented during the crisis; reviewing the Fund's mandate in surveillance and lending, and investigating ways of improving the stability of the international monetary system; strengthening macro-financial and cross-country analyses, including early warning exercises; and studying ways to make policy frameworks more resilient to crises. In November 2011 G20 heads of state and government, meeting in Cannes, France, agreed to initiate an immediate review of the Fund's resources, with a view to securing global financial stability which had been undermined by high levels of debt in several euro area countries. In December European Union heads of state and government agreed to allocate to the IMF additional resources of up to $270,000m. in the form of bilateral loans.

A joint meeting of the IMFC, G20 finance ministers and governors of central banks, convened in April 2012, in Washington, DC, USA, welcomed a decision in March by euro area member states to strengthen European firewalls through broader reform efforts and the availability of central bank swap lines, and determined to enhance IMF resources for crisis prevention and resolution, announcing commitments from G20 member states to increasing, by more than US $430,000m., resources to be made available to the IMF as part of a protective firewall to serve the entire IMF membership. Additional resources pledged by emerging economies (notably by the People's Republic of China, Brazil, India, Mexico and Russia) at a meeting of G20 heads of state and government held in June, in Los Cabos, Baja California Sur, Mexico, raised the universal firewall to $456,000m.

In August 2009 the Fund's Board of Governors approved the new general allocation of SDRs, amounting to SDR 161,200m., which became available to all members, in proportion to their existing quotas, from 28 August. A further SDR 21,400m. (equivalent to US $33,000m.) became available on 9 September under a special allocation provided for by the Fourth Amendment to the Articles of Agreement, which entered into force in the previous month having been ratified by members holding 85% of the total voting power.

In September 2011 the IMF joined other international financial institutions active in the Middle East and North Africa region to endorse the so-called Deauville Partnership, established by the G8 in May to support political and economic reforms being undertaken by several countries, notably Egypt, Jordan, Morocco and Tunisia. The Fund was committed to supporting those countries to maintain economic and financial stability, and to promote inclusive growth.

QUOTAS

MEMBERSHIP AND QUOTAS IN AFRICA SOUTH OF THE SAHARA

(million SDR*)

Country	September 2012
Angola	286.3
Benin	61.9
Botswana	87.8
Burkina Faso	60.2
Burundi	77.0
Cameroon	185.7
Cape Verde	9.6
Central African Republic	55.7
Chad	66.6
Comoros	8.9
Congo, Democratic Republic	533.0
Congo, Republic	84.6
Côte d'Ivoire	325.2
Djibouti	15.9
Equatorial Guinea	52.3
Eritrea	15.9
Ethiopia	133.7
Gabon	154.3
The Gambia	31.1
Ghana	369.0
Guinea	107.1
Guinea-Bissau	14.2
Kenya	271.4
Lesotho	34.9
Liberia	129.2
Madagascar	122.2
Malawi	69.4
Mali	93.3
Mauritania	64.4
Mauritius	101.6
Mozambique	113.6
Namibia	136.5
Niger	65.8
Nigeria	1,753.2
Rwanda	80.1
São Tomé and Príncipe	7.4
Senegal	161.8
Seychelles	10.9
Sierra Leone	103.7
Somalia	44.2
South Africa	1,868.5
South Sudan	123.0
Sudan	169.7
Swaziland	50.7
Tanzania	198.9
Togo	73.4
Uganda	180.5
Zambia	489.1
Zimbabwe	353.4

* The Special Drawing Right (SDR) was introduced in 1970 as a substitute for gold in international payments, and was intended eventually to become the principal reserve asset in the international monetary system. Its value (which was US $1.54074 at 24 September 2012, and averaged $1.57868 in 2011) is based on the currencies of the five largest exporting countries. Each member is assigned a quota related to its national income, monetary reserves, trade balance and other economic indicators; the quota approximately determines a member's voting power and the amount of foreign exchange it may purchase from the Fund. A member's subscription is equal to its quota. Quotas are reviewed at intervals of not more than five years, to take into account the state of the world economy and members' different rates of development. In December 2010 the Board of Governors concluded the 14th General Review, with an agreement to increase quotas by 100%, to realign quota shares to ensure greater representation of emerging economies and to preserve the basic votes share of low-income countries. The reforms required approval by member states constituting 85% of total quotas in order to enter into effect. At 24 September 2012 109 countries accounting for 66.58% of the Fund's voting power had accepted the amendment. A Quota and Voice Reform agreement, concluded in March 2008 to increase quotas by a total of SDR 20,800m. for 54 member countries, entered into effect in March 2011. At 24 September 2012 total quotas in the Fund amounted to SDR 238,116.4m.

RESOURCES

Members' subscriptions form the basic resource of the IMF. They are supplemented by borrowing. Under the General Arrangements to Borrow (GAB), established in 1962, the Group of Ten industrialized nations (G10—Belgium, Canada, France, Germany, Italy, Japan, the Netherlands, Sweden, the United Kingdom and the USA) and Switzerland (which became a member of the IMF in May 1992 but which had been a full participant in the GAB from April 1984) undertake to lend the Fund as much as SDR 17,000m. in their own currencies to assist in fulfilling the balance of payments requirements of any member of the group, or in response to requests to the Fund from countries with balance of payments problems that could threaten the stability of the international monetary system. In 1983 the Fund entered into an agreement with Saudi Arabia, in association with the GAB, making available SDR 1,500m., and other borrowing arrangements were completed in 1984 with the Bank for International Settlements, the Saudi Arabian Monetary Agency, Belgium and Japan, making available a further SDR 6,000m. In 1986 another borrowing arrangement with Japan made available SDR 3,000m. In May 1996 GAB participants concluded an agreement in principle to expand the resources available for borrowing to SDR 34,000m., by securing the support of 25 countries with the financial capacity to support the international monetary system. The so-called New Arrangements to Borrow (NAB) was approved by the Executive Board in January 1997. It was to enter into force, for an initial five-year period, as soon as the five largest potential creditors participating in NAB had approved the initiative and the total credit arrangement of participants endorsing the scheme had reached at least SDR 28,900m. While the GAB credit arrangement was to remain in effect, the NAB was expected to be the first facility to be activated in the event of the Fund's requiring supplementary resources. In July 1998 the GAB was activated for the first time in more than 20 years in order to provide funds of up to US $6,300m. in support of an IMF emergency assistance package for Russia (the first time the GAB had been used for a non-participant). The NAB became effective in November, and was used for the first time as part of an extensive programme of support for Brazil, which was adopted by the IMF in early December. (In March 1999, however, the activation was cancelled.) In November 2008 the Executive Board initiated an assessment of IMF resource requirements and options for supplementing resources in view of an exceptional increase in demand for IMF assistance. In February 2009 the Board approved the terms of a borrowing agreement with the Government of Japan to extend some SDR 67,000m. (some $100,000m.) in supplemental funding, for an initial one-year period. In April G20 heads of state and government resolved to expand the NAB facility, to incorporate all G20 economies, in order to increase its resources by up to SDR 367,500m. ($500,000m.). The G20 summit meeting held in September confirmed that it had contributed the additional resources to the NAB. In April 2010 the IMF's Executive Board approved the expansion and enlargement of NAB borrowing arrangements; these came into effect in March 2011, having completed the ratification process. By July

2012 38 members or state institutions were participating in the NAB, and had committed SDR 369,997m. in supplementary resources.

FINANCIAL ASSISTANCE

The Fund makes resources available to eligible members on an essentially short-term and revolving basis to provide members with temporary assistance to contribute to the solution of their payments problems. Before making a purchase, a member must show that its balance of payments or reserve position makes the purchase necessary. Apart from this requirement, reserve tranche purchases (i.e. purchases that do not bring the Fund's holdings of the member's currency to a level above its quota) are permitted unconditionally. Exchange transactions within the Fund take the form of members' purchases (i.e. drawings) from the Fund of the currencies of other members for the equivalent amounts of their own currencies.

With further purchases, however, the Fund's policy of conditionality means that a recipient country must agree to adjust its economic policies, as stipulated by the IMF. All requests other than for use of the reserve tranche are examined by the Executive Board to determine whether the proposed use would be consistent with the Fund's policies, and a member must discuss its proposed adjustment programme (including fiscal, monetary, exchange and trade policies) with IMF staff. New guidelines on conditionality, which, *inter alia*, aimed to promote national ownership of policy reforms and to introduce specific criteria for the implementation of conditions given different states' circumstances, were approved by the Executive Board in September 2002. In March 2009 the Executive Board approved reforms to modernize the Fund's conditionality policy, including greater use of pre-set qualification criteria and monitoring structural policy implementation by programme review (rather than by structural performance criteria).

Purchases outside the reserve tranche are made in four credit tranches, each equivalent to 25% of the member's quota; a member must reverse the transaction by repurchasing its own currency (with SDRs or currencies specified by the Fund) within a specified time. A credit tranche purchase is usually made under a 'Stand-by Arrangement' with the Fund, or under the Extended Fund Facility. A Stand-by Arrangement is normally of one or two years' duration, and the amount is made available in instalments, subject to the member's observance of 'performance criteria'; repurchases must be made within three-and-a-quarter to five years. An Extended Arrangement is normally of three years' duration, and the member must submit detailed economic programmes and progress reports for each year; repurchases must be made within four-and-a-half to 10 years. In October 1994 the Executive Board approved an increase in members' access to IMF resources, on the basis of a recommendation by the then Interim Committee. The annual access limit under IMF regular tranche drawings, Stand-by Arrangements and Extended Fund Facility credits was increased from 68% to 100% of a member's quota, with the cumulative access limit set at 300%. In March 2009 the Executive Board agreed to double access limits for non-concessional loans to 200% and 600% of a member's quota for annual and cumulative access respectively. In 2010/11 regular funding arrangements approved (and augmented) amounted to SDR 129,628m. (compared with SDR 74,175m. in the previous financial year, SDR 66,736m. in 2008/09, and SDR 1,333m. in 2007/08).

In October 1995 the Interim Committee of the Board of Governors endorsed recent decisions of the Executive Board to strengthen IMF financial support to members requiring exceptional assistance. An Emergency Financing Mechanism was established to enable the IMF to respond swiftly to potential or actual financial crises, while additional funds were made available for short-term currency stabilization. The Mechanism was activated for the first time in July 1997, in response to a request by the Philippines Government to reinforce the country's international reserves, and was subsequently used during that year to assist Thailand, Indonesia and the Republic of Korea. It was used in 2001 to accelerate lending to Turkey. In September 2008 the Mechanism was activated to facilitate approval of a Stand-by Arrangement amounting to SDR 477.1m. for Georgia, which urgently needed to contain its fiscal deficit and undertake rehabilitation measures following a conflict with Russia in the previous month. In November the Board approved a Stand-by Arrangement of SDR 5,169m., under the Emergency Financing Mechanism procedures, to support an economic stabilization programme in Pakistan, one for Ukraine, amounting to SDR 11,000m., and another of SDR 10,538m. for Hungary, which constituted 1,015% of its quota, to counter exceptional pressures on that country's banking sector and the Government's economic programme. An arrangement for Latvia, amounting to SDR 1,522m., was approved in the following month. In May 2010 the Board endorsed a three-year Stand-by Arrangement for Greece amounting to SDR 26,400m., accounting for some 2,400% of that country's new quota (under the 2008 quota reform). The Arrangement was approved under the Emergency Financing Mechanism, as part of a joint financial assistance package with the euro area countries, which aimed to alleviate Greece's sovereign debt crisis and to support an economic recovery and reform programme. In July 2011 the Fund completed a fourth review of the country's economic performance under the Stand-by Arrangement, enabling a further disbursement of SDR 2,900m. In March 2012, following the cancellation of the Stand-by Arrangement, the Executive Board approved an allocation of SDR 23,800m. to be distributed over four years under the Extended Fund Facility—representing access to IMF resources amounting to 2,159% of Greece's quota—in support of the country's ongoing economic adjustment programme; some SDR 1,400m, was to be disbursed immediately. An allocation of SDR 19,465.8m., to be distributed over three years, was approved in December 2010 for Ireland, in conjunction with a euro area assistance programme for that country aimed at supporting the restoration of stability in its financial sector. In May 2011 the Fund allocated SDR 23,742m. to Portugal, again in tandem with a wider euro area package of assistance that was supporting the Portuguese Government's ongoing economic adjustment programme.

In October 2008 the Executive Board approved a new Short-Term Liquidity Facility (SLF) to extend exceptional funds (up to 500% of quotas) to emerging economies affected by the turmoil in international financial markets and economic deceleration in advanced economies. Eligibility for lending under the new Facility was to be based on a country's record of strong macroeconomic policies and having a sustainable level of debt. In March 2009 the Executive Board decided to replace the SLF with a Flexible Credit Line (FCL) facility, which, similarly, was to provide credit to countries with very strong economic foundations, but was also to be primarily considered as precautionary. In addition, it was to have a longer repayment period (of up to five years) and have no access 'cap'. The first arrangement under the FCL was approved in April for Mexico, making available funds of up to SDR 31,528m. for a one-year period. In August 2010 the duration of the FCL, and credit available through it, were increased, and a new Precautionary Credit Line (PCL) was established for member states with sound economic policies that had not yet meet the requirements of the FCL. Three FCL arrangements, amounting to SDR 68,780m., were approved in 2010/11, accounting for around 53% of Fund lending commitments in that year. (A further FCL was approved in that financial year, but was subsequently cancelled.)

In January 2006 a new Exogenous Shocks Facility (ESF) was established to provide concessional assistance to economies adversely affected by events deemed to be beyond government control, for example commodity price changes, natural disasters, or conflicts in neighbouring countries that disrupt trade. Loans under the ESF were to be offered on the same terms as those of the Poverty Reduction and Growth Facility (PRGF) for low-income countries without a PRGF in place. In September 2008 modifications to the ESF were approved, including a new rapid-access component (to provide up to 25% of a country's quota) and a high-access component (to provide up to 75% of quota). These came into effect in late November. Malawi was the first country to draw on the new ESF, with a loan of SDR 52.1m. approved in December, to support balance of payments adjustments required by an increase in fuel and commodity prices in the first half of the year. Other commitments under the ESF were approved for Senegal (SDR 48.5m.) and Comoros (SDR 2.2m.) in December, Ethiopia (SDR 33.4m.) in January 2009, the Democratic Republic of the Congo (SDR 133.3m.) in March, Tanzania (SDR 218.8m.) in May, Mozambique (SDR 113.6m.) in July and Ethiopia (SDR 153.8m.) in August.

In January 2010 the Fund introduced new concessional facilities for low-income countries as part of broader reforms to enhance flexibility of lending and to focus support closer to specific national requirements. The three new facilities aimed to support country-owned programmes to achieve macroeconomic positions consistent with sustainable poverty reduction and economic growth. They carried zero interest rate, although this was to be reviewed every two years. An Extended Credit Facility (ECF) succeeded the existing PRGF to provide medium-term balance of payments assistance to low-income members. ECF loans were to be repayable over 10 years, with a five-and-a-half-year grace period. A Standby Credit Facility (SCF) replaced the high-access component of the Exogenous Shocks Facility (see above) in order to provide short-term balance of payments financial assistance, including on a precautionary basis. SCF loans were to be repayable over eight years, with a grace period of four years. A new Rapid Credit Facility was to provide rapid financial assistance to members requiring urgent balance of payments assistance, under a range of circumstances. Loans were repayable over 10 years, with a five-and-a-half-year grace period. A Post-Catastrophe Debt Relief (PCDR) Trust was established in June 2010 to enable the Fund—in the event of a catastrophic disaster—to provide debt relief to any vulnerable low-income eligible member state in order to free up resources to meet exceptional balance of payments needs.

In May 2001 the Executive Board decided to provide a subsidized loan rate for emergency post-conflict assistance for PRGF-eligible countries, in order to facilitate the rehabilitation of their economies and to improve their eligibility for further IMF concessionary arrangements. In January 2005 the Executive Board decided to extend the subsidized rate for natural disasters.

During 2010/11 members' purchases from the general resources account amounted to SDR 26,616m., compared with SDR 21,087m. in the previous year. Outstanding IMF credit at 30 April 2011 totalled SDR 70,421m., compared with SDR 46,350m. in 2009/10.

During the financial year 2009/10 a Stand-by Arrangement was approved for Angola (in November 2009, amounting to SDR 859m.) and an Extended Fund Facility was approved for the Seychelles (in December 2009, amounting to SDR 20m.).

IMF participates in the initiative to provide exceptional assistance to heavily indebted poor countries (HIPCs), in order to help them to achieve a sustainable level of debt management. The initiative was formally approved at the September 1996 meeting of the Interim Committee, having received the support of the 'Paris Club' of official creditors, which agreed to increase the relief on official debt from 67% to 80%. In all 41 HIPCs were identified, of which 33 were in sub-Saharan Africa. Resources for the HIPC initiative were channelled through the PRGF Trust. In early 1999 the IMF and the World Bank initiated a comprehensive review of the HIPC scheme, in order to consider modifications of the initiative and to strengthen the link between debt relief and poverty reduction. A consensus emerged among the financial institutions and leading industrialized nations to enhance the scheme, in order to make it available to more countries, and to accelerate the process of providing debt relief. In September the IMF Board of Governors expressed its commitment to undertaking an off-market transaction of a percentage of the Fund's gold reserves (i.e. a sale, at market prices, to central banks of member countries with repayment obligations to the Fund, which were then to be made in gold), as part of the funding arrangements of the enhanced HIPC scheme; this was undertaken during the period December 1999–April 2000. Under the enhanced initiative it was agreed that countries seeking debt relief should first formulate, and successfully implement for at least one year, a national poverty reduction strategy (see above). In May 2000 Uganda became the first country to qualify for full debt relief under the enhanced scheme. In September 2005 the IMF and the World Bank endorsed a proposal of the Group of Eight (G8) nations to achieve the cancellation by the IMF, IDA and the African Development Bank of 100% of debt claims on countries that had reached completion point under the HIPC initiative, in order to help them to achieve their Millennium Development Goals. The debt cancellation was to be undertaken within the framework of a Multilateral Debt Relief Initiative (MDRI). The IMF's Executive Board determined, additionally, to extend MDRI debt relief to all countries with an annual per caput GDP of US $380, to be financed by IMF's own resources. Other financing was to be made from existing bilateral contributions to the PRGF Trust Subsidy Account. In December the Executive Board gave final approval to the first group of countries assessed as eligible for 100% debt relief under the MDRI, including 17 countries that had reached completion point at that time, as well as Cambodia and Tajikistan. The initiative became effective in January 2006 once the final consent of the 43 contributors to the PRGF Trust Subsidy Account had been received. By the end of 2011 a further 15 countries had qualified for MDRI relief. As at July the IMF had committed some $6,500m. in debt relief under the HIPC initiative, of a total of $76,000m. pledged for the initiative (in 2010 net present value terms); at that time the cost to the IMF of the MDRI amounted to some $3,900m. (in nominal value terms). In June 2010 the Executive Board approved the establishment of a Post-Catastrophe Debt Relief Trust (PCDR Trust) to provide balance of payments assistance to low-income members following an exceptional natural disaster.

SURVEILLANCE

Under its Articles of Agreement, the Fund is mandated to oversee the effective functioning of the international monetary system. Accordingly, the Fund aims to exercise firm surveillance over the exchange rate policies of member states and to assess whether a country's economic situation and policies are consistent with the objectives of sustainable development and domestic and external stability. The Fund's main tools of surveillance are regular, bilateral consultations with member countries conducted in accordance with Article IV of the Articles of Agreement, which cover fiscal and monetary policies, balance of payments and external debt developments, as well as policies that affect the economic performance of a country, such as the labour market, social and environmental issues and good governance, and aspects of the country's capital accounts, and finance and banking sectors. In April 1997 the Executive Board agreed to the voluntary issue of Press Information Notices (PINs) following each member's Article IV consultation, to those member countries wishing to make public the Fund's views. Other background papers providing information on and analysis of economic developments in individual countries continued to be made available. The Executive Board monitors global economic developments and discusses policy implications from a multilateral perspective, based partly on World Economic Outlook reports and Global Financial Stability Reports. In addition, the IMF studies the regional implications of global developments and policies pursued under regional fiscal arrangements. The Fund's medium-term strategy, initiated in 2006, determined to strengthen its surveillance policies to reflect new challenges of globalization for international financial and macroeconomic stability. In June 2007 the Executive Board approved a Decision on Bilateral Surveillance to update and clarify principles for a member's exchange rate policies and to define best practice for the Fund's bilateral surveillance activities. In October 2008 the Board adopted a Statement of Surveillance Priorities, based on a series of economic and operational policy objectives, for the period 2008–11. The need to enhance surveillance and economic transparency was a priority throughout 2009 as the Fund assessed the global economic and financial crisis and its own role in future crisis prevention. The IMF, with the UN Department for Economic and Social Affairs, leads an initiative to strengthen monitoring and analysis surveillance, and to implement an effective warning system, one of nine initiatives that were endorsed in April 2009 by the UN System Chief Executives Board for Co-ordination (CEB), with the aim of alleviating the impact of the global crisis on poor and vulnerable populations. In September 2010 the Executive Board decided that regular financial stability assessments, within the Financial Sector Assessment Programme framework (see below), were to be a mandatory exercise for 25 jurisdictions considered to have systemically important financial sectors.

In April 1996 the IMF established the Special Data Dissemination Standard (SDDS), which was intended to improve access to reliable economic statistical information for member countries that have, or are seeking, access to international capital markets. In March 1999 the IMF undertook to strengthen the Standard by the introduction of a new reserves data template. By December 2011 69 countries had subscribed to the Standard. The financial crisis in Asia, which became apparent in mid-1997, focused attention on the importance of IMF surveillance of the economies and financial policies of member states and prompted the Fund further to enhance the effectiveness of its surveillance through the development of international standards in order to maintain fiscal transparency. In December 1997 the Executive Board approved a new General Data Dissemination System (GDDS), to encourage all member countries to improve the production and dissemination of core economic data. The operational phase of the GDDS commenced in May 2000. By August 2012 105 countries were participating in the GDDS. The Fund maintains a Dissemination Standards Bulletin Board, which aims to ensure that information on SDDS subscribing countries is widely available.

In April 1998 the then Interim Committee adopted a voluntary Code of Good Practices on Fiscal Transparency: Declaration of Principles, which aimed to increase the quality and promptness of official reports on economic indicators, and in September 1999 it adopted a Code of Good Practices on Transparency in Monetary and Financial Policies: Declaration of Principles. The IMF and World Bank jointly established a Financial Sector Assessment Programme (FSAP) in May 1999, initially as a pilot project, which aimed to promote greater global financial security through the preparation of confidential detailed evaluations of the financial sectors of individual countries. In September 2009 the IMF and World Bank determined to enhance the FSAP's surveillance effectiveness with new features, for example introducing a risk assessment matrix, targeting it more closely to country needs, and improving its cross-country analysis and perspective. As part of the FSAP Fund staff may conclude a Financial System Stability Assessment (FSSA), addressing issues relating to macroeconomic stability and the strength of a country's financial system. A separate component of the FSAP are Reports on the Observance of Standards and Codes (ROSCs), which are compiled after an assessment of a country's implementation and observance of internationally recognized financial standards.

TECHNICAL ASSISTANCE

Technical assistance is provided by special missions or resident representatives who advise members on every aspect of economic management, while more specialized assistance is provided by the IMF's various departments. In 2000/01 the IMFC determined that technical assistance should be central to the IMF's work in crisis prevention and management, in capacity-building for low-income countries, and in restoring macroeconomic stability in countries following a financial crisis. Technical assistance activities subsequently underwent a process of review and reorganization to align them more closely with IMF policy priorities and other initiatives.

Since 1993 the IMF has delivered some technical assistance, aimed at strengthening local capacity in economic and financial management, through regional centres. The first, established in that year, was a Pacific Financial Technical Assistance Center, located in Fiji. A Caribbean Regional Technical Assistance Centre (CARTAC), located in Barbados, began operations in November 2001. In October 2002 an East African Regional Technical Assistance Centre (East AFRITAC), based in Dar es Salaam, Tanzania, was inaugurated and a second AFRITAC was opened in Bamako, Mali, in May 2003, to cover the West African region. In October 2004 a new technical assistance centre for the Middle East (METAC) was inaugurated, based in

Beirut, Lebanon. A regional technical assistance centre for Central Africa, located in Libreville, Gabon, was inaugurated in 2006/07. The fourth AFRITAC, located in Port Louis, Mauritius, serving Southern Africa and the Indian Ocean, was inaugurated in October 2011. A Regional Technical Assistance Centre for Central America, Panama and the Dominican Republic (CAPTAC-DR), was inaugurated in June 2009, in Guatemala City, Guatemala. In September 2002 the IMF signed a Memorandum of Understanding with the African Capacity Building Foundation to strengthen collaboration, in particular within the context of a new IMF Africa Capacity-Building Initiative.

The IMF Institute, which was established in 1964, trains officials from member countries in macroeconomic management, financial analysis and policy, balance of payments methodology and public finance. The IMF Institute also co-operates with other established regional training centres and institutes in order to refine its delivery of technical assistance and training services. The IMF is a co-sponsor, with the Austrian authorities, the EBRD, OECD and WTO, of the Joint Vienna Institute, which was opened in the Austrian capital in October 1992 and which trains officials from former centrally-planned economies in various aspects of economic management and public administration. In May 1998 an IMF-Singapore Regional Training Institute (an affiliate of the IMF Institute) was inaugurated, in collaboration with the Singaporean Government, in order to provide training for officials from the Asia-Pacific region. In 1999 a Joint Regional Training Programme, administered with the Arab Monetary Fund, was established in the United Arab Emirates. During 2000/01 the Institute established a new joint training programme for government officials of the People's Republic of China, based in Dalian, Liaoning Province. A Joint Regional Training Centre for Latin America became operational in Brasília, Brazil, in 2001. In July 2006 a Joint India-IMF Training Programme was inaugurated in Pune, India.

Publications

Annual Report.
Balance of Payments Statistics Yearbook.
Civil Society Newsletter (quarterly).
Direction of Trade Statistics (quarterly and annually).
Emerging Markets Financing (quarterly).
F & D—Finance and Development (quarterly).
Financial Statements of the IMF (quarterly).
Global Financial Stability Report (2 a year).
Global Monitoring Report (annually, with the World Bank).
Government Finance Statistics Yearbook.
Handbook on Securities Statistics (published jointly by IMF, BIS and the European Central Bank).
IMF Commodity Prices (monthly).
IMF Financial Activities (weekly, online).
IMF in Focus (annually).
IMF Research Bulletin (quarterly).
IMF Survey (monthly, and online).
International Financial Statistics (monthly and annually).
Joint BIS-IMF-OECD-World Bank Statistics on External Debt (quarterly).
Quarterly Report on the Assessments of Standards and Codes.
Staff Papers (quarterly).
World Economic Outlook (2 a year).
Other country reports, regional outlooks, economic and financial surveys, occasional papers, pamphlets, books.

United Nations Educational, Scientific and Cultural Organization—UNESCO

Address: 7 place de Fontenoy, 75352 Paris 07 SP, France.
Telephone: 1-45-68-10-00; **fax:** 1-45-67-16-90; **e-mail:** bpi@unesco.org; **internet:** www.unesco.org.

UNESCO was established in 1946 'for the purpose of advancing, through the educational, scientific and cultural relations of the peoples of the world, the objectives of international peace and the common welfare of mankind'.

Organization

(September 2012)

GENERAL CONFERENCE

The supreme governing body of the Organization, the Conference meets in ordinary session once in two years and is composed of representatives of the member states. It determines policies, approves work programmes and budgets and elects members of the Executive Board.

EXECUTIVE BOARD

The Board, comprising 58 members, prepares the programme to be submitted to the Conference and supervises its execution; it meets twice a year.

SECRETARIAT

The organization is headed by a Director-General, appointed for a four-year term. There are Assistant Directors-General for the main thematic sectors, i.e education, natural sciences, social and human sciences, culture, and communication and information, as well as for the support sectors of external relations and co-operation and of administration.

Director-General: IRINA BOKOVA (Bulgaria).

CO-OPERATING BODIES

In accordance with UNESCO's constitution, national Commissions have been set up in most member states. These help to integrate work within the member states and the work of UNESCO. Most member states also have their own permanent delegations to UNESCO. UNESCO aims to develop partnerships with cities and local authorities.

FIELD CO-ORDINATION

UNESCO maintains a network of offices to support a more decentralized approach to its activities and enhance their implementation at field level. Cluster offices provide the main structure of the field co-ordination network. These cover a group of countries and help to co-ordinate between member states and with other UN and partner agencies operating in the area. In 2012 there were 27 cluster offices covering 148 states. In addition 21 national offices serve a single country, including those in post-conflict situations or economic transition and the nine most highly populated countries. The regional bureaux (see below) provide specialized support at a national level.

REGIONAL BUREAUX

Regional Bureau for Education in Africa (BREDA): 12 ave L. S. Senghor, BP 3311, Dakar, Senegal; tel. 849-23-23; fax 823-86-23; e-mail dakar@unesco.org; internet www.dakar.unesco.org; Dir ANN THERESE NDONG-JATTA.

Regional Bureau for Science and Technology in Africa: POB 30592, Nairobi, Kenya; tel. (20) 7621-234; fax (20) 7622-750; e-mail nairobi@unesco.org; internet www.unesco-nairobi.org; f. 1965 to execute UNESCO's regional science programme, and to assist in the planning and execution of national programmes; Dir JOSEPH M. G. MASSAQUOI.

Activities

In the implementation of all its activities UNESCO aims to contribute to achieving the UN Internationally Agreed Development Goals, and the UN Millennium Development Goal (MDG) of halving levels of extreme poverty by 2015, as well as other MDGs concerned with education and sustainable development. UNESCO was the lead agency for the International Decade for a Culture of Peace and Non-violence for the Children of the World (2001–10). In November 2007 the General Conference approved a medium-term strategy to guide UNESCO during the period 2008–13. UNESCO's central mission as defined under the strategy was to contribute to building peace, the alleviation of poverty, sustainable development and intercultural dialogue through its core programme sectors (Education; Natural Sciences; Social and Human Sciences; Culture; and Communication and Information). The strategy identified five 'overarching objectives' for UNESCO in 2008–13, within this programme framework: Attaining quality education for all; Mobilizing scientific knowledge and science policy for sustainable development; Addressing emerging ethical challenges; Promoting cultural diversity and intercultural dialogue; and Building inclusive knowledge societies through information and communication.

The 2008–13 medium-term strategy reaffirmed the organization's commitment to prioritizing Africa and its development efforts. In particular, it was to extend support to countries in post-conflict and disaster situations and strengthen efforts to achieve international targets and those identified through the New Partnership for Africa's Development (NEPAD, see under African Union). A further priority for UNESCO, to be implemented through all its areas of work, was gender equality. Specific activities were to be pursued in support of the welfare of youth, least developed countries and small island developing states.

EDUCATION

UNESCO recognizes education as an essential human right, and an overarching objective for 2008–13 was to attain quality education for all. Through its work programme UNESCO is committed to achieving the MDGs of eliminating gender disparity at all levels of education and attaining universal primary education in all countries by 2015. The focus of many of UNESCO's education initiatives are the nine most highly-populated developing countries (Bangladesh, Brazil, the People's Republic of China, Egypt, India, Indonesia, Mexico, Nigeria and Pakistan), known collectively as the E-9 ('Education-9') countries.

UNESCO leads and co-ordinates global efforts in support of 'Education for All' (EFA), which was adopted as a guiding principle of UNESCO's contribution to development following a world conference, convened in March 1990. In April 2000 several UN agencies, including UNESCO and UNICEF, and other partners sponsored the World Education Forum, held in Dakar, Senegal, to assess international progress in achieving the goal of Education for All and to adopt a strategy for further action (the 'Dakar Framework'), with the aim of ensuring universal basic education by 2015. The Dakar Framework, incorporating six specific goals, emphasized the role of improved access to education in the reduction of poverty and in diminishing inequalities within and between societies. UNESCO was appointed as the lead agency in the implementation of the Framework, focusing on co-ordination, advocacy, mobilization of resources, and information-sharing at international, regional and national levels. It was to oversee national policy reforms, with a particular focus on the integration of EFA objectives into national education plans. An EFA Global Action Plan was formulated in 2006 to reinvigorate efforts to achieve EFA objectives and, in particular, to provide a framework for international co-operation and better definition of the roles of international partners and of UNESCO in leading the initiative. UNESCO's medium-term strategy for 2008–13 committed the organization to strengthening its role in co-ordinating EFA efforts at global and national levels, promoting monitoring and capacity-building activities to support implementation of EFA objectives, and facilitating mobilization of increased resources for EFA programmes and strategies (for example through the EFA-Fast Track Initiative, launched in 2002 to accelerate technical and financial support to low-income countries). An EFA Global Monitoring Report is released annually; the 2012 edition, on the theme 'Youth and Skills: Putting Education to Work', was to be published in October. In September 2012 the UN Secretary-General launched 'Education First', a new initiative aimed at increasing access to education, and the quality thereof, world-wide.

UNESCO advocates 'Literacy for All' as a key component of Education for All, regarding literacy as essential to basic education and to social and human development. UNESCO is the lead agency of the UN Literacy Decade (2003–12), which aims to formulate an international plan of action to raise literacy standards throughout the world and to assist policy-makers to integrate literacy standards and goals into national education programmes. The Literacy Initiative for Empowerment (LIFE) was developed as an element of the Literacy Decade to accelerate efforts in some 35 countries where illiteracy is a critical challenge to development. UNESCO is also the co-ordinating agency for the UN Decade of Education for Sustainable Development (2005–14), through which it aims to establish a global framework for action and strengthen the capacity of education systems to incorporate the concepts of sustainable development into education programmes. In 2014 UNESCO was to organize, with the Government of Japan, a UNESCO World Conference on Education for Sustainable Development, to assess the implementation of the UN Decade. The April 2000 World Education Forum recognized the global HIV/AIDS pandemic to be a significant challenge to the attainment of Education for All. UNESCO, as a co-sponsor of UNAIDS, takes an active role in promoting formal and non-formal preventive health education. Through a Global Initiative on HIV/AIDS and Education (EDUCAIDS) UNESCO aims to develop comprehensive responses to HIV/AIDS rooted in the education sector, with a particular focus on vulnerable children and young people. An initiative covering the 10-year period 2006–15, the Teacher Training Initiative in sub-Saharan Africa, aims to address the shortage of teachers in that region (owing to HIV/AIDS, armed conflict and other causes) and to improve the quality of teaching.

A key priority area of UNESCO's education programme is to foster quality education for all, through formal and non-formal educational opportunities. It assists members to improve the quality of education provision through curricula content, school management and teacher training. UNESCO aims to expand access to education at all levels and to work to achieve gender equality. In particular, UNESCO aims to strengthen capacity-building and education in natural, social and human sciences and promote the use of new technologies in teaching and learning processes. In May 2010 UNESCO, jointly with ITU, established a Broadband Commission for Digital Development, to comprise high level representatives of governments, industry and international agencies concerned with the effective deployment of broadband networks as an essential element of economic and social development objectives; the Commission's first report, *State of Broadband 2012: Achieving Digital Inclusion for All*, was released in September 2012.

The Associated Schools Project (ASPnet—comprising more than 9,000 institutions in 180 countries in 2012) has, since 1953, promoted the principles of peace, human rights, democracy and international co-operation through education. It provides a forum for dialogue and for promoting best practices. At tertiary level UNESCO chairs a University Twinning and Networking (UNITWIN) initiative, which was established in 1992 to establish links between higher education institutions and to foster research, training and programme development. A complementary initiative, Academics Across Borders, was inaugurated in November 2005 to strengthen communication and the sharing of knowledge and expertise among higher education professionals. In October 2002 UNESCO organized the first Global Forum on International Quality Assurance, Accreditation and the Recognition of Qualifications to establish international standards and promote capacity-building for the sustainable development of higher education systems.

Within the UN system UNESCO is responsible for providing technical assistance and educational services in the context of emergency situations. This includes establishing temporary schools, providing education for refugees and displaced persons, as well as assistance for the rehabilitation of national education systems. In Palestine, UNESCO collaborates with UNRWA to assist with the training of teachers, educational planning and rehabilitation of schools. In February 2010 UNESCO agreed to form an International Co-ordination Committee in support of Haitian culture, in view of the devastation caused by an earthquake that had struck that country in January, causing 230,000 fatalities and the destruction of local infrastructure and architecture.

In February 2010 a high-level meeting on Education for All, comprising ministers of education and international co-operation, and representatives from international and regional organizations, civil society and the private sector, was held to assess the impact on education of the ongoing global economic crisis, and to consider related challenges connected to social marginalization.

NATURAL SCIENCES

The World Summit on Sustainable Development, held in August–September 2002, recognised the essential role of science (including mathematics, engineering and technology) as a foundation for achieving the MDGs of eradicating extreme poverty and ensuring environmental sustainability. UNESCO aims to promote this function within the UN system and to assist member states to utilize and foster the benefits of scientific and technical knowledge. A key objective for the medium-term strategy (2008–13) was to mobilize science knowledge and policy for sustainable development. Throughout the natural science programme priority was to be placed on Africa, least developed countries and small island developing states. The Local and Indigenous Knowledge System (LINKS) initiative aims to strengthen dialogue among traditional knowledge holders, natural and social scientists and decision-makers to enhance the conservation of biodiversity, in all disciplines, and to secure an active and equitable role for local communities in the governance of resources. In June 2012, in advance of the UN Conference on Sustainable Development ('Rio+20'), which was convened later in that month, UNESCO, with the International Council of Scientific Unions and other partners, participated in a Forum on Science, Technology and Innovation for Sustainable Development, addressing the role to be played by science and innovation in promoting sustainable development, poverty eradication, and the transition to a green economy.

In November 1999 the General Conference endorsed a Declaration on Science and the Use of Scientific Knowledge and an agenda for action, which had been adopted at the World Conference on Science, held in June–July 1999, in Budapest, Hungary. By leveraging scientific knowledge, and global, regional and country level science networks, UNESCO aims to support sustainable development and the sound management of natural resources. It also advises governments on approaches to natural resource management, in particular the collection of scientific data, documenting and disseminating good practices and integrating social and cultural aspects into management structures and policies. UNESCO's Man and the Biosphere Programme supports a world-wide network of biosphere reserves (comprising 599 biosphere reserves in 117 countries in 2012), which aim to promote environmental conservation and research, education and training in biodiversity and problems of land use (including the fertility of tropical soils and the cultivation of sacred sites). The third World Congress of Biosphere Reserves, held in Madrid, Spain, in February 2008, adopted the Madrid Action Plan, which aimed to promote biosphere reserves as the main internationally-designated areas dedicated to sustainable development. UNESCO also supports a Global Network of National Geoparks (91 in 27 countries in September 2012) which was inaugurated in 2004 to promote collaboration among managed areas of geological significance to exchange knowledge and expertise and raise awareness of the benefits of protecting those environments. Member geoparks must have effective management structures that facilitate sustainable development, with a particular emphasis on sustainable tourism. UNESCO organizes regular International Geoparks Conferences; the fifth was held in May 2012, in Unzen Volcanic Area Global Geopark, Japan.

UNESCO promotes and supports international scientific partnerships to monitor, assess and report on the state of Earth systems. With the World Meteorological Organization and the International Council of Science, UNESCO sponsors the World Climate Research Programme, which was established in 1980 to determine the predictability of climate and the effect of human activity on climate. UNESCO hosts the secretariat of the World Water Assessment Programme (WWAP), which prepares the periodic *World Water Development Report*. UNESCO is actively involved in the 10-year project, agreed by more than 60 governments in February 2005, to develop a Global Earth Observation System of Systems (GEOSS). The project aims to link existing and planned observation systems in order to provide for greater understanding of the earth's processes and dissemination of detailed data, for example predicting health epidemics or weather phenomena or concerning the management of ecosystems and natural resources. From 2005 UNESCO's Intergovernmental Oceanographic Commission (UNESCO-IOC) developed a Tsunami Early Warning and Mitigation System in the North-eastern Atlantic, the Mediterranean and Connected Seas (NEAMTWS), which was to conduct its first tsunami training exercise (NEAM-Wave12) in November 2012. UNESCO-IOC serves as the Secretariat of the Global Ocean Observing System. The International Geoscience Programme, undertaken jointly with the International Union of Geological Sciences (IUGS), facilitates the exchange of knowledge and methodology among scientists concerned with geological processes and aims to raise awareness of the links between geoscience and sustainable socio-economic development. The IUGS and UNESCO jointly initiated the International Year of Planet Earth (2008).

UNESCO is committed to contributing to international efforts to enhance disaster preparedness and mitigation. Through education UNESCO aims to reduce the vulnerability of poorer communities to disasters and improve disaster management at local and national levels. It also co-ordinates efforts at an international level to establish monitoring networks and early-warning systems to mitigate natural disasters, in particular in developing tsunami early-warning systems in Africa, the Caribbean, the South Pacific, the Mediterranean Sea and the North East Atlantic similar to those already established for the Indian and Pacific oceans. Other regional partnerships and knowledge networks were to be developed to strengthen capacity-building and the dissemination of information and good practices relating to risk awareness and mitigation and disaster management. Disaster education and awareness were to be incorporated as key elements in the UN Decade of Education for Sustainable Development (see above). UNESCO is also the lead agency for the International Flood Initiative, which was inaugurated in January 2005 at the World Conference on Disaster Reduction, held in Kobe, Japan. The Initiative aims to promote an integrated approach to flood management in order to minimize the damage and loss of life caused by floods, mainly with a focus on research, training, promoting good governance and providing technical assistance. The fifth International Conference on Flood Management was convened in Tsukuba, Japan, in September 2011.

A priority of the natural science programme has been to promote policies and strengthen human and institutional capacities in science, technology and innovation. At all levels of education UNESCO aims to enhance teaching quality and content in areas of science and technology and, at regional and sub-regional level, to strengthen co-operation mechanisms and policy networks in training and research. With the International Council of Scientific Unions and the Third World Academy of Sciences, UNESCO operates a short-term fellowship programme in the basic sciences and an exchange programme of visiting lecturers.

UNESCO is the lead agency of the New Partnership for Africa's Development (NEPAD) Science and Technology Cluster and the NEPAD Action Plan for the Environment.

SOCIAL AND HUMAN SCIENCES

UNESCO is mandated to contribute to the world-wide development of the social and human sciences and philosophy, which it regards as of great importance in policy-making and maintaining ethical vigilance. The structure of UNESCO's Social and Human Sciences programme takes into account both an ethical and standard-setting dimension, and research, policy-making, action in the field and future-oriented activities. One of UNESCO's so-called overarching objectives in the period 2008–13 was to address emerging ethical challenges.

A priority area of UNESCO's work programme on Social and Human Sciences has been to promote principles, practices and ethical norms relevant for scientific and technological development. The programme fosters international co-operation and dialogue on emerging issues, as well as raising awareness and promoting the sharing of knowledge at regional and national levels. UNESCO supports the activities of the International Bioethics Committee (IBC—a group of 36 specialists who meet under UNESCO auspices) and the Intergovernmental Bioethics Committee, and hosts the secretariat of the 18-member World Commission on the Ethics of Scientific Knowledge and Technology (COMEST), established in 1999, which aims to serve as a forum for the exchange of information and ideas and to promote dialogue between scientific communities, decision-makers and the public.

The priority Ethics of science and technology element aims to promote intergovernmental discussion and co-operation; to conduct explorative studies on possible UNESCO action on environmental ethics and developing a code of conduct for scientists; to enhance public awareness; to make available teaching expertise and create regional networks of experts; to promote the development of international and national databases on ethical issues; to identify ethical issues related to emerging technologies; to follow up relevant declarations, including the Universal Declaration on the Human Genome and Human Rights (see below); and to support the Global Ethics Observatory, an online world-wide database of information on applied bioethics and other applied science- and technology-related areas (including environmental ethics) that was launched in December 2005 by the IBC.

UNESCO itself provides an interdisciplinary, multicultural and pluralistic forum for reflection on issues relating to the ethical dimension of scientific advances, and promotes the application of international guidelines. In May 1997 the IBC approved a draft version of a Universal Declaration on the Human Genome and Human Rights, in an attempt to provide ethical guidelines for developments in human genetics. The Declaration, which identified some 100,000 hereditary genes as 'common heritage', was adopted by the UNESCO General Conference in November and committed states to promoting the dissemination of relevant scientific knowledge and co-operating in genome research. In October 2003 the General Conference adopted an International Declaration on Human Genetic Data, establishing standards for scientists working in that field, and in October 2005 the General Conference adopted the Universal Declaration on Bioethics and Human Rights. At all levels UNESCO aims to raise awareness and foster debate about the ethical implications of scientific and technological developments and promote exchange of experiences and knowledge between governments and research bodies.

UNESCO recognizes that globalization has a broad and significant impact on societies. It is committed to countering negative trends of social transformation by strengthening the links between research and policy formulation by national and local authorities, in particular concerning poverty eradication. In that respect, UNESCO promotes the concept that freedom from poverty is a fundamental human right. In 1994 UNESCO initiated an international social science research programme, the Management of Social Transformations (MOST), to promote capacity-building in social planning at all levels of decision-making. In 2003 the Executive Board approved a continuation of the programme but with a revised strategic objective of strengthening links between research, policy and practice. In 2008–13 UNESCO aimed to promote new collaborative social science research programmes and to support capacity building in developing countries.

UNESCO aims to monitor emerging social or ethical issues and, through its associated offices and institutes, formulate preventative action to ensure they have minimal impact on the attainment of UNESCO's objectives. As a specific challenge UNESCO is committed to promoting the International Convention against Doping in Sport, which entered into force in 2007. UNESCO also focuses on the educational and cultural dimensions of physical education and sport and their capacity to preserve and improve health.

Fundamental to UNESCO's mission is the rejection of all forms of discrimination. It disseminates information aimed at combating racial prejudice, works to improve the status of women and their access to education, promotes equality between men and women, and raises awareness of discrimination against people affected by HIV/AIDS, in particular among young people. In 2004 UNESCO inaugurated an initiative to enable city authorities to share experiences and collaborate in efforts to counter racism, discrimination, xenophobia and exclusion. As well as the International Coalition of Cities against Racism, regional coalitions were to be formed with more defined programmes of action. The African coalition was inaugurated in September 2006, in Nairobi, Kenya. An International Youth Clearing House and Information Service (INFOYOUTH) aims to increase and consolidate the information available on the situation of young people in society, and to heighten awareness of their needs, aspirations and potential among public and private decision-makers. Supporting efforts to facilitate dialogue among different cultures and societies and promoting opportunities for reflection and consideration of philosophy and human rights, for example the celebration of World Philosophy Day, are also among UNESCO's fundamental aims.

CULTURE

In undertaking efforts to preserve the world's cultural and natural heritage UNESCO has attempted to emphasize the link between culture and development. In December 1992 UNESCO established the World Commission on Culture and Development, to strengthen links between culture and development and to prepare a report on the issue. The first World Conference on Culture and Development was held in June 1999, in Havana, Cuba. In November 2001 the General Conference adopted the UNESCO Universal Declaration on Cultural Diversity, which affirmed the importance of intercultural dialogue in establishing a climate of peace. UNESCO's medium-term strategy for 2008–13 recognized the need for a more integrated approach to cultural heritage as an area requiring conservation and development and one offering prospects for dialogue, social cohesion and shared knowledge.

UNESCO aims to promote cultural diversity through the safeguarding of heritage and enhancement of cultural expressions. In January 2002 UNESCO inaugurated the Global Alliance on Cultural Diversity, to promote partnerships between governments, non-governmental bodies and the private sector with a view to supporting cultural diversity through the strengthening of cultural industries and the prevention of cultural piracy. In October 2005 the General Conference approved an International Convention on the Protection of the Diversity of Cultural Expressions. It entered into force in March 2007 and the first session of the intergovernmental committee servicing the Convention was convened in Ottawa, Canada, in December.

UNESCO's World Heritage Programme, inaugurated in 1978, aims to protect historic sites and natural landmarks of outstanding universal significance, in accordance with the 1972 UNESCO Convention Concerning the Protection of the World Cultural and Natural Heritage, by providing financial aid for restoration, technical assistance, training and management planning. The medium-term strategy for 2008–13 acknowledged that new global threats may affect natural and cultural heritage. It also reinforced the concept that conservation of sites contributes to social cohesion. During mid-2012–mid-2013 the 'World Heritage List' comprised 962 sites globally, of which 745 had cultural significance, 188 were natural landmarks, and 29 were of 'mixed' importance. In addition to numerous nature reserves and national parks, examples in Africa include: the royal palaces of Abomey (Benin); the rock-hewn churches at Lalibela (Ethiopia); forts, castles and Ashanti traditional buildings in Ghana; Lamu Old Town (Kenya); the Royal Hill of Ambohimanga (Madagascar); the old town of Djenné and the Bandiagara cliffs of the Dogon people (Mali); four old trading towns in Mauritania; the Sukur Cultural Landscape (Nigeria); Robben Island and the Mapungubwe Cultural Landscape (South Africa); the pyramids at Gebel Barkal and other archaeological sites in the Napatan region (Sudan); the stone town of Zanzibar (Tanzania); and Great Zimbabwe National Monument. UNESCO also maintains a list of World Heritage in Danger; during mid-2012–mid-2013 this numbered 38 sites, including the Niokolo-Koba National Park in Senegal, the ruins of Kilwa Kisiwani and Songo Mnara ports in Tanzania, the tombs of Buganda Kings at Kasubi, Uganda, and (newly inscribed in June 2012, owing to ongoing conflict in northern Mali) the city of Timbuktu and the Tomb of Askia (dating from 1495, and situated in Gao, Mali).

UNESCO supports the safeguarding of humanity's non-material 'intangible' heritage, including oral traditions, music, dance and medicine. An Endangered Languages Programme was initiated in 1993. By 2012 the Programme estimated that, of some 6,700 languages spoken world-wide, about one-half were endangered. It works to raise awareness of the issue, for example through publication of the *Atlas of the World's Languages in Danger of Disappearing,* to strengthen local and national capacities to safeguard and document languages, and administers a Register of Good Practices in Language Preservation. In October 2003 the UNESCO General Conference adopted a Convention for the Safeguarding of Intangible Cultural Heritage, which provided for the establishment of an intergovernmental committee and for participating states to formulate national inventories of intangible heritage. The Convention entered into force in April 2006 and the intergovernmental committee convened its inaugural session in November. The second session was held in Tokyo, Japan, in September 2007. A Representative List of the Intangible Cultural Heritage of Humanity, inaugurated in November 2008, comprised, in 2012, 232 elements ('masterpieces of the oral and intangible heritage of humanity') deemed to be of outstanding value; these included: Chinese calligraphy; falconry; several dances, such as the tango, which originated in Argentina and Uruguay, and the dances of the Ainu in Japan; the chant of the Sybil on Majorca, Spain; and the Ifa Divination System (Nigeria). The related List of Intangible Cultural Heritage in Need of Urgent Safeguarding comprised 27 elements in 2012, such as the Naqqāli form of story-telling in Iran, the Saman dance in Sumatra, Indonesia, and the Qiang New Year Festival in Sichuan Province, China. UNESCO's culture programme also aims to safeguard movable cultural heritage and to support and develop museums as a means of preserving heritage and making it accessible to society as a whole.

In November 2001 the General Conference authorized the formulation of a Declaration against the Intentional Destruction of Cultural Heritage. In addition, the Conference adopted the Convention on the Protection of the Underwater Cultural Heritage, covering the protection from commercial exploitation of shipwrecks, submerged historical sites, etc., situated in the territorial waters of signatory states. UNESCO also administers the 1954 Hague Convention on the Protection of Cultural Property in the Event of Armed Conflict and the 1970 Convention on the Means of Prohibiting and Preventing the Illicit Import, Export and Transfer of Ownership of Cultural Property. In 1992 a World Heritage Centre was established to enable rapid mobilization of international technical assistance for the preservation of cultural sites. Through the World Heritage Information Network (WHIN), a world-wide network of more than 800 information providers, UNESCO promotes global awareness and information exchange.

UNESCO aims to support the development of creative industries and or creative expression. Through a variety of projects UNESCO promotes art education, supports the rights of artists, and encourages crafts, design, digital art and performance arts. In October 2004 UNESCO launched a Creative Cities Network to facilitate public and private sector partnerships, international links, and recognition of a city's unique expertise. In 2012 the following cities were participating in the Network: Aswan (Egypt), Icheon (Republic of Korea), Kanazawa (Japan) and Santa Fe (Mexico) (UNESCO Cities of Craft and Folk Art); Berlin (Germany), Buenos Aires (Argentina), Graz (Austria), Montreal (Canada), Nagoya and Kobe (Japan), Seoul (Republic of Korea), Shanghai and Shenzhen (China), Saint-Etienne (France) (UNESCO Cities of Design); Chengdu (China), Östersund (Sweden), Popayan (Colombia) (UNESCO Cities of Gastronomy); Dublin (Republic of Ireland), Edinburgh (United Kingdom), Iowa City (USA), Melbourne (Australia), Reykjavik (Iceland) (UNESCO Cities of Literature); Bologna (Italy), Ghent (Belgium), Glasgow (United Kingdom), Seville (Spain) (UNESCO Cities of Music); Bradford (United Kingdom), Sydney (Australia) (UNESCO Cities of Film); and Lyon (France) (UNESCO City of Media Arts). UNESCO is active in preparing and encouraging the enforcement of international legislation on copyright, raising awareness on the need for copyright protection to uphold cultural diversity, and is contributing to the international debate on digital copyright issues and piracy.

Within its ambition of ensuring cultural diversity, UNESCO recognizes the role of culture as a means of promoting peace and dialogue. Several projects have been formulated within a broader concept of Roads of Dialogue. In Central Asia a project on intercultural dialogue follows on from an earlier multi-disciplinary study of the ancient Silk Roads trading routes linking Asia and Europe, which illustrated many examples of common heritage. Other projects include a study of the movement of peoples and cultures during the slave trade, a Mediterranean Programme, the Caucasus Project and the Arabia Plan, which aims to promote world-wide knowledge and understanding of Arab culture. UNESCO has overseen an extensive programme of work to formulate histories of humanity and regions, focused on ideas, civilizations and the evolution of societies and cultures. These have included the *General History of Africa, History of Civilizations of Central Asia,* and *History of Humanity*. UNESCO endeavoured to consider and implement the findings of the Alliance of Civilizations, a high-level group convened by the UN Secretary-General that published a report in November 2006. UNESCO signed a Memorandum of Understanding with the Alliance during its first forum, convened in Madrid, Spain, in January 2008.

UNESCO was designated as the lead UN agency for organizing the International Year for the Rapprochement of Cultures (2010). In February 2010, at the time of the launch of the International Year, the UNESCO Director-General established a High Panel on Peace and Dialogue among Cultures, which was to provide guidance on means of advancing tolerance, reconciliation and balance within societies world-wide.

COMMUNICATION AND INFORMATION

UNESCO regards information, communication and knowledge as being at the core of human progress and well-being. The Organization advocates the concept of knowledge societies, based on the principles of freedom of expression, universal access to information and knowledge, promotion of cultural diversity, and equal access to quality education. In 2008–13 it determined to consolidate and implement this concept, in accordance with the Declaration of Principles and Plan of Action adopted by the second phase of the World Summit on the Information Society (WSIS) in November 2005. UNESCO was to host the WSIS+10 Review meeting, in February 2013 (the first WSIS phase having taken place in December 2003), in Paris, on the theme 'Towards Knowledge Societies for Peace and Sustainable Development'.

A key strategic objective of building inclusive knowledge societies was to be through enhancing universal access to communication and information. At national and global levels UNESCO promotes the rights of freedom of expression and of access to information. It promotes the free flow and broad diffusion of information, knowledge, data and best practices, through the development of communications infrastructures, the elimination of impediments to freedom of expression, and the development of independent and pluralistic media, including through the provision of advisory services on media legislation, particularly in post-conflict countries and in countries in transition. UNESCO recognizes that the so-called global 'digital divide', in addition to other developmental differences between countries, generates exclusion and marginalization, and that increased participation in the democratic process can be attained through strengthening national communication and information capacities. UNESCO promotes policies and mechanisms that enhance provision for marginalized and disadvantaged groups to benefit from information and community opportunities. Activities at local and national level include developing effective 'infostructures', such as libraries and archives and strengthening low-cost community media and information access points, for example through the establishment of Community Multimedia Centres (CMCs). Many of UNESCO's principles and objectives in this area are pursued through the Information for All Programme, which entered into force in 2001. It is administered by an intergovernmental council, the secretariat of which is provided by UNESCO. UNESCO also established, in 1982, the International Programme for the Development of Communication (IPDC), which aims to promote and develop independent and pluralistic media in developing countries, for example by the establishment or modernization of news agencies and newspapers and training media professionals, the promotion of the right to information, and through efforts to harness informatics for development purposes and strengthen member states' capacities in this field. In March 2012 the IPDC approved funding for 85 new media development projects in developing and emerging countries world-wide. In 2011, on the basis of discussions held at the 2010 session of the Internet Governance Forum (established by the second phase of the WSIS to support the implementation of the Summit's mandate) UNESCO published a report entitled 'Freedom of Connection-Freedom of Expression: the Changing Legal and Regulatory Ecology Shaping the Internet'. UNESCO has engaged with the Freedom Online Coalition, launched in December 2011 by the first Freedom Online Conference, held in The Hague, Netherlands, with the objective of facilitating global dialogue regarding the role of governments in furthering freedom on the internet. The second Freedom Online Conference was convened in Nairobi, Kenya, in September 2012, by which time the Freedom Online Coalition had 17 member states.

UNESCO supports cultural and linguistic diversity in information sources to reinforce the principle of universal access. It aims to raise awareness of the issue of equitable access and diversity, encourage good practices and develop policies to strengthen cultural diversity in all media. In 2002 UNESCO established Initiative B@bel as a multidisciplinary programme to promote linguistic diversity, with the aim of enhancing access of under-represented groups to information sources as well as protecting underused minority languages. In December 2009 UNESCO and the Internet Corporation for Assigned Names and Numbers (ICANN) signed a joint agreement which aimed to promote the use of multilingual domain names using non-Latin script, with a view to promoting linguistic diversity. UNESCO's Programme for Creative Content supports the development of and access to diverse content in both the electronic and audiovisual media. The Memory of the World project, established in 1992, aims to preserve in digital form, and thereby to promote wide access to, the world's documentary heritage. Documentary material includes stone tablets, celluloid, parchment and audio recordings. By 2012 245 inscriptions had been included on the project's register; three inscriptions originated from international organizations: the Archives of the ICRC's former International Prisoners of War Agency, 1914–23, submitted by the ICRC, and inscribed in 2007; the League of Nations Archives, 1919–46, submitted by the UN Geneva Office, and inscribed in 2009; and the UNRWA Photo and Film Archives of Palestinian Refugees' Documentary Heritage, submitted by UNRWA, and also inscribed in 2009. In September 2012 UNESCO organized an International Conference on the 'Memory of the World in the Digital Age: Digitization and Preservation', in Vancouver, Canada. UNESCO also supports other efforts to preserve and disseminate digital archives and, in 2003, adopted a Charter for the Preservation of Digital Heritage. In April 2009 UNESCO launched the internet based World Digital Library, accessible at www.wdl.org, which aims to display primary documents (including texts, charts and illustrations), and authoritative explanations, relating to the accumulated knowledge of a broad spectrum of human cultures.

UNESCO promotes freedom of expression, of the press and independence of the media as fundamental human rights and the basis of democracy. It aims to assist member states to formulate policies and legal frameworks to uphold independent and pluralistic media and infostructures and to enhance the capacities of public service broadcasting institutions. In regions affected by conflict UNESCO supports efforts to establish and maintain an independent media service and to use it as a means of consolidating peace. UNESCO also aims to develop media and information systems to respond to and mitigate the impact of disaster situations, and to integrate these objectives into wider UN peace-building or reconstruction initiatives. UNESCO is the co-ordinating agency for 'World Press Freedom Day', which is held annually on 3 May; it also awards an annual World Press Freedom Prize. A conference convened in Tunis, Tunisia, in celebration of the May 2012 World Press Freedom Day—held on the theme 'New Voices: Media Freedom Helping to Transform Societies', with a focus on the transition towards democracy in several countries of North Africa and the Middle East—adopted the Carthage Declaration, urging the creation of free and safe environments for media workers and the promotion of journalistic ethics. The Declaration also requested UNESCO to pursue implementation of the UN Plan of Action on the Safety of Journalists and the Issue of Impunity, which had been drafted with guidance from UNESCO, and endorsed in April by the UN System Chief Executives Board for Co-ordination. UNESCO maintains an Observatory on the Information Society, which provides up-to-date information on the development of new ICTs, analyses major trends, and aims to raise awareness of related ethical, legal and societal issues. UNESCO promotes the upholding of human rights in the use of cyberspace. In 1997 it organized the first International Congress on Ethical, Legal and Societal Aspects of Digital Information ('INFOethics').

UNESCO promotes the application of information and communication technology for sustainable development. In particular it supports efforts to improve teaching and learning processes through electronic media and to develop innovative literacy and education initiatives, such as the ICT-Enhanced Learning (ICTEL) project. UNESCO also aims to enhance understanding and use of new technologies and support training and ongoing learning opportunities for librarians, archivists and other information providers.

Finance

UNESCO's activities are funded through a regular budget provided by contributions from member states and extrabudgetary funds from other sources, particularly UNDP, the World Bank, regional banks and other bilateral Funds-in-Trust arrangements. UNESCO co-operates with many other UN agencies and international non-governmental organizations.

UNESCO's Regular Programme budget for the two years 2012–13 was US $685.7m.

In response to a decision, in late October 2011, by a majority of member states participating in the UNESCO General Conference to admit Palestine as a new member state, the USA decided to withhold from UNESCO significant annual funding.

Publications

(mostly in English, French and Spanish editions; Arabic, Chinese and Russian versions are also available in many cases)

Atlas of the World's Languages in Danger of Disappearing (online).

Copyright Bulletin (quarterly).

Encyclopedia of Life Support Systems (online).

Education for All Global Monitoring Report.
International Review of Education (quarterly).
International Social Science Journal (quarterly).
Museum International (quarterly).
Nature and Resources (quarterly).
The New Courier (quarterly).
Prospects (quarterly review on education).
UNESCO Sources (monthly).
UNESCO Statistical Yearbook.
UNESCO World Atlas of Gender Equality in Education.
World Communication Report.
World Educational Report (every 2 years).
World Heritage Review (quarterly).
World Information Report.
World Science Report (every 2 years).
Books, databases, video and radio documentaries, statistics, scientific maps and atlases.

Specialized Institutes and Centres

Abdus Salam International Centre for Theoretical Physics: Strada Costiera 11, 34151 Trieste, Italy; tel. (040) 2240111; fax (040) 224163; e-mail sci_info@ictp.it; internet www.ictp.it; f. 1964; promotes and enables advanced study and research in physics and mathematical sciences; organizes and sponsors training opportunities, in particular for scientists from developing countries; aims to provide an international forum for the exchange of information and ideas; operates under a tripartite agreement between UNESCO, IAEA and the Italian Government; Dir FERNANDO QUEVEDO (Guatemala).

International Bureau of Education (IBE): POB 199, 1211 Geneva 20, Switzerland; tel. 229177800; fax 229177801; e-mail doc .centre@ibe.unesco.org; internet www.ibe.unesco.org; f. 1925, became an intergovernmental organization in 1929 and was incorporated into UNESCO in 1969; the Council of the IBE is composed of representatives of 28 member states of UNESCO, designated by the General Conference; the Bureau's fundamental mission is to deal with matters concerning educational content, methods, and teaching/learning strategies; an International Conference on Education is held periodically; Dir CLEMENTINA ACEDO (Venezuela); publs *Prospects* (quarterly review), *Educational Innovation* (newsletter), educational practices series, monographs, other reference works.

UNESCO Institute for Information Technologies in Education: 117292 Moscow, ul. Kedrova 8, Russia; tel. (495) 129-29-90; fax (495) 129-12-25; e-mail liste.info.iite@unesco.org; internet www.iite .unesco.org; the Institute aims to formulate policies regarding the development of, and to support and monitor the use of, information and communication technologies in education; it conducts research and organizes training programmes; Chair BERNARD CORNU.

UNESCO Institute for Life-long Learning: Feldbrunnenstr. 58, 20148 Hamburg, Germany; tel. (40) 448-0410; fax (40) 410-7723; e-mail uil@unesco.org; internet www.unesco.org/uil/index.htm; f. 1951, as the Institute for Education; a research, training, information, documentation and publishing centre, with a particular focus on adult basic and further education and adult literacy; Dir ARNE CARLSEN.

UNESCO Institute for Statistics: CP 6128, Succursale Centre-Ville, Montréal, QC, H3C 3J7, Canada; tel. (514) 343-6880; fax (514) 343-5740; e-mail uis.information@unesco.org; internet www.uis .unesco.org; f. 2001; collects and analyses national statistics on education, science, technology, culture and communications; Dir HENDRIK VAN DER POL (Netherlands).

UNESCO Institute for Water Education: Westvest 7, 2611 AX Delft, Netherlands; tel. (15) 2151715; fax (15) 2122921; e-mail info@ unesco-ihe.org; internet www.unesco-ihe.org; f. 2003; activities include education, training and research; and co-ordination of a global network of water sector organizations; advisory and policy-making functions; setting international standards for postgraduate education programmes; and professional training in the water sector; Rector ANDRÁS SZÖLLÖSI-NAGY.

UNESCO International Centre for Technical and Vocational Education and Training: UN Campus, Hermann-Ehlers-Str. 10, 53113 Bonn, Germany; tel. (228) 8150-100; fax (228) 8150-199; e-mail unevoc@unesco.org; internet www.unevoc.unesco.org; f. 2002; promotes high-quality lifelong technical and vocational education in UNESCO's member states, with a particular focus on young people, girls and women, and the disadvantaged; Head SHYAMAL MAJUMDAR (India).

UNESCO International Institute for Capacity Building in Africa (UNESCO–IICBA): ECA Compound, Africa Ave, POB 2305, Addis Ababa, Ethiopia; tel. (11) 5445284; fax (11) 514936; e-mail info@unesco-iicba.org; internet www.unesco-iicba.org; f. 1999 to promote capacity building in the following areas: teacher education; curriculum development; educational policy, planning and management; and distance education; Dir ARNALDO NHAVOTO.

UNESCO International Institute for Educational Planning (IIEP): 7–9 rue Eugène Delacroix, 75116 Paris, France; tel. 1-45-03-77-00; fax 1-40-72-83-66; e-mail info@iiep.unesco.org; internet www .unesco.org/iiep; f. 1963; serves as a world centre for advanced training and research in educational planning; aims to help all member states of UNESCO in their social and economic development efforts, by enlarging the fund of knowledge about educational planning and the supply of competent experts in this field; legally and administratively a part of UNESCO, the Institute is autonomous, and its policies and programme are controlled by its own Governing Board, under special statutes voted by the General Conference of UNESCO; a satellite office of the IIEP is based in Buenos Aires, Argentina; Dir KHALIL MAHSHI (Jordan).

World Health Organization—WHO

Address: 20 ave Appia, 1211 Geneva 27, Switzerland.
Telephone: 227912111; **fax:** 227913111; **e-mail:** info@who.int; **internet:** www.who.int.

WHO, established in 1948, is the lead agency within the UN system concerned with the protection and improvement of public health.

Organization

(September 2012)

WORLD HEALTH ASSEMBLY

The Assembly meets in Geneva, once a year. It is responsible for policy-making and the biennial programme and budget; appoints the Director-General; admits new members; and reviews budget contributions. The 65th Assembly was convened in May 2012.

EXECUTIVE BOARD

The Board is composed of 34 health experts designated by a member state that has been elected by the World Health Assembly to serve on the Board; each expert serves for three years. The Board meets at least twice a year to review the Director-General's programme, which it forwards to the Assembly with any recommendations that seem necessary. It advises on questions referred to it by the Assembly and is responsible for putting into effect the decisions and policies of the Assembly. It is also empowered to take emergency measures in case of epidemics or disasters. Meeting in November 2011 the Board agreed several proposals on reforms to the Organization aimed at improving health outcomes, achieving greater coherence in global health matters, and promoting organizational efficiency and transparency.

Chairman: Dr MIHALY KÖKÉNY (Hungary).

SECRETARIAT

Director-General: Dr MARGARET CHAN (People's Republic of China).

Deputy Director-General: Dr ANARFI ASAMOA-BAAH (Ghana).

Assistant Directors-General: Dr BRUCE AYLWARD (Canada) (Polio, Emergencies and Country Collaboration), FLAVIA BUSTREO (Italy) (Family, Women's and Children's Health), OLEG CHESTNOV (Russia) (Non-communicable Diseases and Mental Health), Dr CARISSA F. ETIENNE (Dominica) (Health Systems and Services), KEIJI FUKUDA (USA) (Health Security and Environment), MOHAMED ABDI JAMA (Somalia) (General Management), MARIE-PAULE KIENY (France) (Innovation, Information, Evidence and Research), HIROKI NAKATANI (Japan) (HIV/AIDS, TB, Malaria and Neglected Tropical Diseases).

PRINCIPAL OFFICES

Each of WHO's six geographical regions has its own organization, consisting of a regional committee representing relevant member states and associate members, and a regional office staffed by experts in various fields of health.

International Health Regulations Coordination—WHO Lyon Office: 58 ave Debourg, 69007 Lyon, France; tel. 4-72-71-64-70; fax 4-72-71-64-71; e-mail ihrinfo@who.int; internet www.who.int/ihr/lyon/en/index.html; supports (with regional offices) countries in strengthening their national surveillance and response systems, with the aim of improving the detection, assessment and notification of events, and responding to public health risks and emergencies of international concern under the International Health Regulations.

WHO Centre for Health Development: I. H. D. Centre Bldg, 9th Floor, 5–1, 1-chome, Wakinohama-Kaigandori, Chuo-ku, Kobe, Japan; tel. (78) 230-3100; fax (78) 230-3178; e-mail wkc@wkc.who.int; internet www.who.or.jp; f. 1995 to address health development issues; Dir ALEX ROSS (USA).

Activities

WHO is the UN system's co-ordinating authority for health (defined as 'a state of complete physical, mental and social well-being and not merely the absence of disease and infirmity'). WHO's objective is stated in its constitution as 'the attainment by all peoples of the highest possible level of health'. The Organization's core functions, outlined in its 11th programme of work covering 2006–15, are to provide leadership on global public health matters, in partnership, where necessary, with other agencies; to help shape the global health research agenda; to articulate ethical and evidence-based policy options; to set, and monitor the implementation of, norms and standards; to monitor and assess health trends; and to provide technical and policy support to member countries. Aid is provided in emergencies and natural disasters.

In its work WHO adheres to a six-point agenda covering: promoting development; fostering health security; strengthening health systems; harnessing research, information and evidence; enhancing partnerships; and improving performance.

WHO has developed a series of international classifications, including the *International Statistical Classification of Disease and Related Health Problems (ICD)*, providing an etiological framework of health conditions, and currently in its 10th edition; and the complementary *International Classification of Functioning, Disability and Health (ICF)*, which describes how people live with their conditions.

WHO keeps diseases and other health problems under constant surveillance, promotes the exchange of prompt and accurate information and of notification of outbreaks of diseases, and administers the International Health Regulations (the most recently revised version of which entered into force in June 2007). It sets standards for the quality control of drugs, vaccines and other substances affecting health. It formulates health regulations for international travel.

It collects and disseminates health data and carries out statistical analyses and comparative studies in such diseases as cancer, heart disease and mental illness.

It receives reports on drugs observed to have shown adverse reactions in any country, and transmits the information to other member states.

It promotes improved environmental conditions, including housing, sanitation and working conditions. All available information on effects on human health of the pollutants in the environment is critically reviewed and published.

A global programme of collaborative research and exchange of scientific information is carried out in co-operation with about 1,200 national institutions. Particular stress is laid on the widespread communicable diseases of the tropics, and the countries directly concerned are assisted in developing their research capabilities. Co-operation among scientists and professional groups is encouraged. The organization negotiates and sustains national and global partnerships. It may propose international conventions and agreements. The organization promotes the development and testing of new technologies, tools and guidelines. It assists in developing an informed public opinion on matters of health.

In the implementation of all its activities WHO aims to contribute to achieving by 2015 the UN Millennium Development Goals (MDGs) that were agreed by the September 2000 UN Millennium Summit. WHO has particular responsibility for the MDGs of: reducing child mortality, with a target reduction of two-thirds in the mortality rate among children under five; improving maternal health, with a specific goal of reducing by 75% the numbers of women dying in childbirth; and combating HIV/AIDS, malaria and other diseases. In addition, it directly supports the following Millennium 'targets': halving the proportion of people suffering from malnutrition; halving the proportion of people without sustainable access to safe drinking water and basic sanitation; and providing access, in co-operation with pharmaceutical companies, to affordable, essential drugs in developing countries. Furthermore, WHO reports on 17 health-related MDG indicators; co-ordinates, jointly with the World Bank, the High-Level Forum on the Health MDGs, comprising government ministers, senior officials from developing countries, and representatives of bilateral and multilateral agencies, foundations, regional organizations and global partnerships; and undertakes technical and normative work in support of national and regional efforts to reach the MDGs.

The 2006–15 11th General Programme of Work defined a policy framework for pursuing the principal objectives of building healthy populations and combating ill health. The Programme took into account: increasing understanding of the social, economic, political and cultural factors involved in achieving better health and the role played by better health in poverty reduction; the increasing complexity of health systems; the importance of safeguarding health as a component of humanitarian action; and the need for greater co-ordination among development organizations. It incorporated four interrelated strategic directions: lessening excess mortality, morbidity and disability, especially in poor and marginalized populations; promoting healthy lifestyles and reducing risk factors to human health arising from environmental, economic, social and behavioural causes; developing equitable and financially fair health systems; and establishing an enabling policy and an institutional environment for the health sector and promoting an effective health dimension to social, economic, environmental and development policy. WHO is the sponsoring agency for the Health Workforce Decade (2006–15).

Strengthening national health services has been one of WHO's primary tasks in Africa south of the Sahara. Integrated health systems are being developed to provide services related to medical care, rehabilitation, family health, communicable disease control, environmental health, health education, and health statistics. By providing educators and fellowships and by organizing training courses, support is given to national programmes aimed at preparing health workers best suited to local needs and resources. Specialists and advisory services are provided to assist in planning the health sector, which in most African countries forms an integral part of the overall plan for socio-economic development.

During 2005 the UN's Inter-Agency Standing Committee (IASC), concerned with co-ordinating the international response to humanitarian disasters, developed a concept of organizing agency assistance to IDPs through the institutionalization of a 'Cluster Approach', comprising 11 core areas of activity. WHO was designated the lead agency for the Health Cluster. The 65th World Health Assembly, convened in May 2012, adopted a resolution endorsing WHO's role as Health Cluster lead and urging international donors to allocate sufficient resources towards health sector activities during humanitarian emergencies.

WHO, with ILO, leads the Social Protection Floor initiative, the sixth of nine activities that were launched in April 2009 by the UN System Chief Executives Board for Co-ordination (CEB), with the aim of alleviating the impact on poor and vulnerable populations of the global economic downturn. In October 2011 a Social Protection Floor Advisory Group, launched in August 2010 under the initiative, issued a report entitled *Social Protection Floor for a Fair and Inclusive Globalization*, which urged that basic income and services should be guaranteed for all, stating that this would promote both stability and economic growth globally.

COMMUNICABLE DISEASES

WHO identifies infectious and parasitic communicable diseases as a major obstacle to social and economic progress, particularly in developing countries, where, in addition to disabilities and loss of productivity and household earnings, they cause nearly one-half of all deaths. Emerging and re-emerging diseases, those likely to cause epidemics, increasing incidence of zoonoses (diseases or infections passed from vertebrate animals to humans by means of parasites, viruses, bacteria or unconventional agents), attributable to factors such as environmental changes and changes in farming practices, outbreaks of unknown etiology, and the undermining of some drug therapies by the spread of antimicrobial resistance, are main areas of concern. In recent years WHO has noted the global spread of communicable diseases through international travel, voluntary human migration and involuntary population displacement.

WHO's Communicable Diseases group works to reduce the impact of infectious diseases world-wide through surveillance and response; prevention, control and eradication strategies; and research and product development. The group seeks to identify new technologies and tools, and to foster national development through strengthening health services and the better use of existing tools. It aims to strengthen global monitoring of important communicable disease problems, and to create consensus and consolidate partnerships around targeted diseases and collaborates with other groups at all stages to provide an integrated response. In 2000 WHO and several partner institutions in epidemic surveillance established the Global Outbreak Alert and Response Network (GOARN). Through the Network WHO aims to maintain constant vigilance regarding outbreaks of disease and to link world-wide expertise to provide an immediate response capability. From March 2003 WHO, through the Network, was co-ordinating the international investigation into the global spread of Severe Acute Respiratory Syndrome (SARS), a previously unknown atypical pneumonia. From the end of that year WHO was monitoring the spread through several Asian countries of the virus H5N1 (a rapidly mutating strain of zoonotic highly pathogenic avian influenza—HPAI) that was transmitting to human populations through contact with diseased birds, mainly poultry. It was feared that H5N1 would mutate into a form transmissable from human to human. In March 2005 WHO issued a *Global Influenza Preparedness Plan*, and urged all countries to develop national influenza pandemic preparedness plans and to stockpile antiviral drugs. In May, in co-operation with FAO and the World Organisation for Animal Health (OIE), WHO launched a Global Strategy for the Progressive Control of Highly Pathogenic Avian Influenza. A conference on Avian Influenza and Human Pandemic Influenza that was jointly organized by WHO, FAO, OIE and the World Bank in November 2005 issued a plan of action identifying a number of responses, including: supporting the development of integrated national plans for H5N1 containment and human pandemic influenza preparedness and response; assisting countries with the aggressive control of H5N1 and with establishing a more detailed understanding of the role of wild birds in virus transmission; nominating rapid response teams of experts to support epidemiological field investigations; expanding national and regional capacity in surveillance, diagnosis, and alert and response systems; expanding the network of influenza laboratories; establishing multi-country networks for the control or prevention of animal transboundary diseases; expanding the global antiviral stockpile; strengthening veterinary infrastructures; and mapping a global strategy and work plan for co-ordinating antiviral and influenza vaccine research and development. An International Pledging Conference on Avian and Human Influenza, convened in January 2006 in Beijing, People's Republic of China, and co-sponsored by the World Bank, European Commission and Chinese Government, in co-operation with WHO, FAO and OIE, requested a minimum of US $1,200m. in funding towards combating the spread of the virus. By 10 August 2012 a total of 608 human cases of H5N1 had been laboratory confirmed, in Azerbaijan, Bangladesh, Cambodia, China, Djibouti, Egypt, Indonesia, Iraq, Laos, Myanmar, Nigeria, Pakistan, Thailand, Turkey and Viet Nam, resulting in 359 deaths. Cases in poultry had become endemic in parts of Asia and Africa, and outbreaks in poultry had also occurred in some European and Middle Eastern countries.

In April 2009 GOARN sent experts to Mexico to work with health authorities there in response to an outbreak of confirmed human cases of a new variant of swine influenza A(H1N1) that had not previously been detected in animals or humans. In late April, by which time cases of the virus had been reported in the USA and Canada, the Director-General of WHO declared a 'public health emergency of international concern'. All countries were instructed to activate their national influenza pandemic preparedness plans (see above). At the end of April the level of pandemic alert was declared to be at phase five of a six-phase (phase six being the most severe) warning system that had been newly revised earlier in the year. Phase five is characterized by human-to-human transmission of a new virus into at least two countries in one WHO region. On 11 June WHO declared a global pandemic (phase six on the warning scale, characterized by human-to-human transmission in two or more WHO regions). The status and development of pandemic influenza vaccines was the focus of an advisory meeting of immunization experts held at the WHO headquarters in late October. In June 2010 the WHO Director-General refuted allegations, levelled by a British medical journal and by the Parliamentary Assembly of the Council of Europe, regarding the severity of pandemic (H1N1) 2009 and the possibility that the Organization had, in declaring the pandemic, used advisers with a vested commercial interest in promoting pharmaceutical industry profitability. In August 2010 the WHO Director-General declared that transmission of the new H1N1 virus had entered a post-pandemic phase.

One of WHO's major achievements was the eradication of smallpox. Following a massive international campaign of vaccination and surveillance (begun in 1958 and intensified in 1967), the last case was detected in 1977 and the eradication of the disease was declared in 1980. In May 1996 the World Health Assembly resolved that, pending a final endorsement, all remaining stocks of the variola virus (which causes smallpox) were to be destroyed on 30 June 1999, although 500,000 doses of smallpox vaccine were to remain, along with a supply of the smallpox vaccine seed virus, in order to ensure that a further supply of the vaccine could be made available if required. In May 1999, however, the Assembly authorized a temporary retention of stocks of the virus until 2002. In late 2001, in response to fears that illegally held virus stocks could be used in acts of biological terrorism (see below), WHO reassembled a team of technical experts on smallpox. In January 2002 the Executive Board determined that stocks of the virus should continue to be retained, to enable research into more effective treatments and vaccines. World Health Assemblies (most recently in May 2011) have affirmed that the remaining stock of variola virus should be destroyed following the completion of the ongoing research. The state of variola virus research was to be reviewed in 2014, by the 67th World Health Assembly, which was to discuss nominating a deadline for the destruction of the remaining virus stocks.

In 1988 the World Health Assembly launched the Global Polio Eradication Initiative (GPEI), which aimed, initially, to eradicate poliomyelitis by the end of 2000; this target was subsequently extended to 2013 (see below). Co-ordinated periods of Supplementary Immunization Activity (SIA, facilitated in conflict zones by the negotiation of so-called 'days of tranquility'), including National Immunization Days (NIDs), Sub-National Immunization Days (SNIDs), mop-up campaigns, VitA campaigns (Vitamin A is administered in order to reduce nutritional deficiencies in children and thereby boost their immunity), and Follow up/Catch up campaigns, have been employed in combating the disease, alongside the strengthening of routine immunization services. Since the inauguration of the GPEI WHO has declared the following regions 'polio-free': the Americas (1994); Western Pacific (2000); and Europe (2002). Furthermore, type 2 wild poliovirus has been eradicated globally (since 1999), although a type 2 circulating vaccine-derived poliovirus (cVDPV) was reported to be active in northern Nigeria during 2006–early 2010. In January 2004 ministers of health of affected countries, and global partners, meeting under the auspices of WHO and UNICEF, adopted the Geneva Declaration on the Eradication of Poliomyelitis, in which they made a commitment to accelerate the drive towards eradication of the disease, by improving the scope of vaccination programmes. Significant progress in eradication of the virus was reported in Asia during that year. In sub-Saharan Africa, however, an outbreak originating in northern Nigeria in mid-2003—caused by a temporary cessation of vaccination activities in response to local opposition to the vaccination programme—had spread, by mid-2004, to 10 previously polio-free countries. These included Côte d'Ivoire and Sudan, where ongoing civil unrest and population displacements impeded control efforts. During 2004–05 some 23 African governments, including those of the affected West and Central African countries, organized, with support from the African Union, a number of co-ordinated mass vaccination drives, which resulted in the vaccination of about 100m. children. By mid-2005 the sub-regional epidemic was declared over; it was estimated that since mid-2003 it had resulted in the paralysis of nearly 200 children. In Nigeria itself, however, the number of confirmed wild poliovirus cases had by 2006 escalated to 1,122 from 202 in 2002. In February 2007 the GPEI launched an intensified eradication effort aimed at identifying and addressing the outstanding operational, technical and financial barriers to eradication. The May 2008 World Health Assembly adopted a resolution urging all remaining polio-affected member states to ensure the vaccination of every child during each SIA. By the end of 2008, having received independent advice that the intensified eradication effort initiated in 2007 had demonstrated that the remaining challenges to eradication were surmountable, the GPEI endorsed a strategic plan covering the period 2009–13 (replacing a previous plan for 2004–08), with the aim of achieving the interruption of type 1 wild poliovirus transmission in India, and the cessation of all prolonged outbreaks in Africa by the end of 2009; the interruption of all poliovirus transmission in Afghanistan, India and Pakistan, of type 1 wild poliovirus transmission in Nigeria, and of all wild poliovirus transmission elsewhere in Africa, by end-2010; the interruption of type 3 wild poliovirus transmission in Nigeria by end-2011; and the eradication of new cVDPVs within six months of detection by end-2013. During 2009, however, polio outbreaks, which were subsequently eradicated, occurred in 10 of 15 previously polio-free countries in Africa. In June 2010 a new strategic plan, covering 2010–12, was launched, incorporating the following targets: cessation in mid-2010 of all polio outbreaks with onset in 2009; cessation by end-2010 of all re-established wild poliovirus transmission; cessation by end-2011 of all transmission in at least two of the four countries designated at that time as polio-endemic (i.e. Afghanistan, India, Nigeria, and Pakistan); and the cessation by end-2012 of all transmission. Some 650 polio cases were confirmed world-wide in 2011, of which 340 were in the then four polio-endemic countries (Pakistan, 198 cases; Afghanistan, 80 cases; Nigeria, 61 cases; and India one case), and 310 cases were recorded in non-endemic countries (including 132 cases in Chad and 93 cases in Democratic Republic of the Congo). (In 1988, in comparison, 35,000 cases had been confirmed in 125 countries, with the actual number of cases estimated at around 350,000.) India was declared to be no longer polio-endemic in February 2012.

WHO's Onchocerciasis Control Programme in West Africa (OCP), active during 1974–2002, succeeded in eliminating transmission in 10 countries in the region, excepting Sierra Leone, of onchocerciasis ('river blindness', spread by blackflies, and previously a major public health problem and impediment to socio-economic development in

West Africa). It was estimated that under the OCP some 18m. people were protected from the disease, 600,000 cases of blindness prevented, and 25m. ha of land were rendered safe for cultivation and settlement. The former headquarters of the OCP, based in Ouagadougou, Burkina Faso, was transformed into a Multi-disease Surveillance Centre. In January 1996 another initiative, the African Programme for Onchocerciasis Control (APOC), covering 19 countries outside West Africa, became operational, with funding co-ordinated by the World Bank and with WHO as the executing agency.

WHO is committed to the elimination of leprosy (the reduction of the prevalence of leprosy to less than one case per 10,000 population). The use of a highly effective combination of three drugs (known as multi-drug therapy—MDT) resulted in a reduction in the number of leprosy cases world-wide from 10m.–12m. in 1988 to 192,246 registered cases in January 2011. In 2010 some 228,474 cases were detected globally. The number of countries having more than one case of leprosy per 10,000 had declined to four by January 2007 (Brazil, Democratic Republic of the Congo, Mozambique and Nepal), compared with 122 in 1985. The country with the highest prevalence of leprosy cases in 2007 was Brazil (3.21 per 10,000 population) and the country with the highest number of cases was India (139,252). The Global Alliance for the Elimination of Leprosy was launched in November 1999 by WHO, in collaboration with governments of affected countries and several private partners, including a major pharmaceutical company, to support the eradication of the disease through the provision of free MDT treatment; WHO has supplied free MDT treatment to leprosy patients in endemic countries since 1995. In June 2005 WHO adopted a Strategic Plan for Further Reducing the Leprosy Burden and Sustaining Leprosy Control Activities, covering the period 2006–10 and following on from a previous strategic plan for 2000–05. In 1998 WHO launched the Global Buruli Ulcer Initiative, which aimed to co-ordinate control of and research into Buruli ulcer, another mycobacterial disease. In July of that year the Director-General of WHO and representatives of more than 20 countries, meeting in Yamoussoukro, Côte d'Ivoire, signed a declaration on the control of Buruli ulcer. In May 2004 the World Health Assembly adopted a resolution urging improved research into, and detection and treatment of, Buruli ulcer.

The Special Programme for Research and Training in Tropical Diseases, established in 1975 and sponsored jointly by WHO, UNDP and the World Bank, as well as by contributions from donor countries, involves a world-wide network of some 5,000 scientists working on the development and application of vaccines, new drugs, diagnostic kits and preventive measures, and applied field research on practical community issues affecting the target diseases.

The objective of providing immunization for all children by 1990 was adopted by the World Health Assembly in 1977. Six diseases (measles, whooping cough, tetanus, poliomyelitis, tuberculosis and diphtheria) became the target of the Expanded Programme on Immunization (EPI), in which WHO, UNICEF and many other organizations collaborated. As a result of massive international and national efforts, the global immunization coverage increased from 20% in the early 1980s to the targeted rate of 80% by the end of 1990. In 2006 WHO, UNICEF and other partners launched the Global Immunization Vision and Strategy (GIVS), a global 10-year framework, covering 2006–15, aimed at reducing deaths due to vaccine-preventable diseases by at least two-thirds compared to 2000 levels, by 2015; and increasing national vaccination coverage levels to at least 90%. In 2010 the global child vaccination coverage rate was estimated at 85%.

In June 2000 WHO released a report entitled 'Overcoming Antimicrobial Resistance', in which it warned that the misuse of antibiotics could render some common infectious illnesses unresponsive to treatment. At that time WHO issued guidelines which aimed to mitigate the risks associated with the use of antimicrobials in livestock reared for human consumption.

HIV/AIDS, TB, MALARIA AND NEGLECTED DISEASES

Combating the human immunodeficiency virus/acquired immunodeficiency syndrome (HIV/AIDS), tuberculosis (TB) and malaria are organization-wide priorities and, as such, are supported not only by their own areas of work but also by activities undertaken in other areas. TB is the principal cause of death for people infected with the HIV virus and an estimated one-third of people living with HIV/AIDS globally are co-infected with TB. In July 2000 a meeting of the Group of Seven industrialized nations and Russia, convened in Genoa, Italy, announced the formation of a new Global Fund to Fight AIDS, TB and Malaria (as previously proposed by the UN Secretary-General and recommended by the World Health Assembly).

The HIV/AIDS epidemic represents a major threat to human well-being and socio-economic progress. Some 95% of those known to be infected with HIV/AIDS live in developing countries, and AIDS-related illnesses are the leading cause of death in sub-Saharan Africa. It is estimated that more than 25m. people world-wide died of AIDS during 1981–2008. WHO supports governments in developing effective health sector responses to the HIV/AIDS epidemic through enhancing their planning and managerial capabilities, implementation capacity, and health systems resources. The Joint UN Programme on HIV/AIDS (UNAIDS) became operational on 1 January 1996, sponsored by WHO and other UN agencies; the UNAIDS secretariat is based at WHO headquarters. Sufferers of HIV/AIDS in developing countries have often failed to receive advanced antiretroviral (ARV) treatments that are widely available in industrialized countries, owing to their high cost. In May 2000 the World Health Assembly adopted a resolution urging WHO member states to improve access to the prevention and treatment of HIV-related illnesses and to increase the availability and affordability of drugs. A WHO-UNAIDS HIV Vaccine Initiative was launched in that year. In June 2001 governments participating in a special session of the UN General Assembly on HIV/AIDS adopted a Declaration of Commitment on HIV/AIDS. WHO, with UNAIDS, UNICEF, UNFPA, the World Bank, and major pharmaceutical companies, participates in the 'Accelerating Access' initiative, which aims to expand access to care, support and ARVs for people with HIV/AIDS. In March 2002, under its 'Access to Quality HIV/AIDS Drugs and Diagnostics' programme, WHO published a comprehensive list of HIV-related medicines deemed to meet standards recommended by the Organization. In April WHO issued the first treatment guidelines for HIV/AIDS cases in poor communities, and endorsed the inclusion of HIV/AIDS drugs in its *Model List of Essential Medicines* (see below) in order to encourage their wider availability. The secretariat of the International HIV Treatment Access Coalition, founded in December of that year by governments, non-governmental organizations, donors and others to facilitate access to ARVs for people in low- and middle-income countries, is based at WHO headquarters. In September 2006, Brazil, Chile, France, Norway and the United Kingdom launched UNITAID, an international drug purchase facility aiming to provide sustained, strategic market intervention, with a view to reducing the cost of medicines for priority diseases and increasing the supply of drugs and diagnostics. In July 2008, UNITAID created the Medicines Patent Pool; the Pool, a separate entity, was to focus on increasing access to HIV medicines in developing countries. The Pool is funded by UNITAID, under a five-year arrangement. By the end of 2010 an estimated 6.6m. people in developing and middle-income countries were receiving appropriate HIV treatment, compared with 4m. at end-2008. In May 2011 the 64th World Health Assembly adopted a new Global Health Sector Strategy on HIV/AIDS, covering 2011–15, which aimed to promote greater innovation in HIV prevention, diagnosis, treatment, and the improvement of care services to facilitate universal access to care for HIV patients. WHO supports the following *Three Ones* principles, endorsed in April 2004 by a high-level meeting organized by UNAIDS, the United Kingdom and the USA, with the aim of strengthening national responses to the HIV/AIDS pandemic: for every country there should be one agreed national HIV/AIDS action framework; one national AIDS co-ordinating authority; and one agreed monitoring and evaluation system.

In December 2011 the UN General Assembly adopted a Political Declaration on HIV/AIDS, outlining 10 targets to be attained by 2015: reducing by 50% sexual transmission of HIV; reducing by 50% HIV transmission among people who inject drugs; eliminating new HIV infections among children, and reducing AIDS-related maternal deaths; ensuring that at least 15m. people living with HIV are receiving ARVs; reducing by 50% TB deaths in people living with HIV; reaching annual global investment of at least US $22,000m. in combating AIDS in low- and medium-resource countries; eliminating gender inequalities and increasing the capacity of women and girls to self-protect from HIV; promoting the adoption of legislation and policies aimed at eliminating stigma and discrimination against people living with HIV; eliminating HIV-related restrictions on travel; strengthening the integration of the AIDS response in global health and development efforts.

At December 2011 an estimated 23.5m. people in sub-Saharan Africa were estimated to have HIV/AIDS, of whom around 1.7m. were newly affected during that year. An estimated 1.2m. adults and children died of AIDS in that year. More people were living with HIV/AIDS in South Africa than in any other country world-wide (an estimated 5.6m., with an estimated national prevalence rate of 17%, at end-2010), while, in 2009, the national adult prevalence rates were 25.9% in Swaziland, 24.8% in Botswana, and 23.6% in Lesotho, and exceeded 10% in Malawi, Mozambique, Namibia, Zambia and Zimbabwe.

In 1995 WHO established a Global Tuberculosis Programme to address the challenges of the TB epidemic, which had been declared a global emergency by the Organization in 1993. According to WHO estimates, one-third of the world's population carries the TB bacillus. In 2009 this generated 9.4m. new active cases (1.1m. in people co-infected with HIV), and killed 1.7m. people (0.4m. of whom were also HIV-positive). Some 22 high-burden countries account for four-fifths of global TB cases. The largest concentration of TB cases is in South-East Asia. WHO provides technical support to all member countries, with special attention given to those with high TB prevalence, to establish effective national tuberculosis control programmes. WHO's strategy for TB control includes the use of the expanded DOTS (direct observation treatment, short-course) regime, involving the following five tenets: sustained political commitment to increase human and financial resources and to make TB control in endemic countries a nation-wide activity and an integral part of the national health system; access to quality-assured TB sputum microscopy; standardized short-course chemotherapy for all cases of TB under proper case-management conditions; uninterrupted supply of quality-assured drugs; and maintaining a recording and reporting system to enable outcome assessment. Simultaneously, WHO is encouraging research with the aim of further advancing DOTS, developing new tools for prevention, diagnosis and treatment, and containing new threats (such as the HIV/TB co-epidemic). Inadequate control of DOTS in some areas, leading to partial and inconsistent treatments, has resulted in the development of drug-resistant and, often, incurable strains of TB. The incidence of so-called Multidrug Resistant TB (MDR-TB) strains, that are unresponsive to at least two of the four most commonly used anti-TB drugs, has risen in recent years, and WHO estimates that about four-fifths are 'super strains', resistant to at least three of the main anti-TB drugs; an estimated 3.3% of new TB cases were reported to be MDR in 2009. MDR-TB cases occur most frequently in Eastern Europe, Central Asia, China, and India; it was reported in 2010 that in certain areas of the former Soviet Union up to 28% of all new TB cases were MDR. WHO has developed DOTS-Plus, a specialized strategy for controlling the spread of MDR-TB in areas of high prevalence. By August 2010 59 countries had reported at least one case of Extensive Drug Resistant TB (XDR-TB), defined as MDR-TB plus resistance to additional drugs. XDR-TB is believed to be most prevalent in Eastern Europe and Asia. In 2007 WHO launched the Global MDR/XDR Response Plan, which aimed to expand diagnosis and treatment to cover, by 2015, some 85% of TB patients with MDR-TB.

The 'Stop TB' partnership, launched by WHO in 1999, in partnership with the World Bank, the US Government and a coalition of non-governmental organizations, co-ordinates the Global Plan to Stop TB, which represents a roadmap for TB control covering the period 2006–15. The Global Plan aims to facilitate the achievement of the MDG of halting and beginning to reverse by 2015 the incidence of TB by means of access to quality diagnosis and treatment for all; to supply ARVs to 3m. TB patients co-infected with HIV; to treat nearly 1m. people for MDR-TB (this target was subsequently altered by the 2007 Global MDR/XDR Response Plan, see above); to develop a new anti-TB drug and a new vaccine; and to develop rapid and inexpensive diagnostic tests at the point of care. A second phase of the Global Plan, launched in late 2010 and covering 2011–15, updated the Plan to take account of actual progress achieved since its instigation in 2006. The Global TB Drug Facility, launched by 'Stop TB' in 2001, aims to increase access to high-quality anti-TB drugs for sufferers in developing countries. In 2007 'Stop TB' endorsed the establishment of a new Global Laboratory Initiative with the aim of expanding laboratory capacity.

In December 2010 WHO endorsed a new rapid nucleic acid amplification test (NAAT) that provided an accurate diagnosis of TB in around 100 minutes; it was envisaged that NAAT, by eliminating the current wait of up to three months for a TB diagnosis, would greatly enhance management of the disease and patient care.

In October 1998 WHO, jointly with UNICEF, the World Bank and UNDP, formally launched the Roll Back Malaria (RBM) programme. The disease acutely affects at least 350m.–500m. people, and kills an estimated 1m. people, every year. Some 85% of all malaria cases occur in sub-Saharan Africa. It is estimated that the disease directly causes 18% of all child deaths in that region. The global RBM Partnership, linking governments, development agencies, and other parties, aims to mobilize resources and support for controlling malaria. The RBM Partnership Global Strategic Plan for the period 2005–15, adopted in November 2005, lists steps required to intensify malaria control interventions with a view to attaining targets set by the Partnership for 2010 and 2015 (the former targets include: ensuring the protection of 80% of people at risk from malaria and the diagnosis and treatment within one day of 80% of malaria patients, and reducing the global malaria burden by one-half compared with 2000 levels; and the latter: achieving a 75% reduction in malaria morbidity and mortality over levels at 2005). WHO recommends a number of guidelines for malaria control, focusing on the need for prompt, effective antimalarial treatment, and the issue of drug resistance; vector control, including the use of insecticide-treated bednets; malaria in pregnancy; malaria epidemics; and monitoring and evaluation activities. WHO, with several private and public sector partners, supports the development of more effective anti-malaria drugs and vaccines through the 'Medicines for Malaria' venture.

Joint UN Programme on HIV/AIDS (UNAIDS): 20 ave Appia, 1211 Geneva 27, Switzerland; tel. 227913666; fax 227914187; e-mail communications@unaids.org; internet www.unaids.org; established in 1996 to lead, strengthen and support an expanded response to the global HIV/AIDS pandemic; activities focus on prevention, care and support, reducing vulnerability to infection, and alleviating the socio-economic and human effects of HIV/AIDS; launched the Global Coalition on Women and AIDS in Feb. 2004; guided by UN Security Council Resolution 1308, focusing on the possible impact of AIDS on social instability and emergency situations, and the potential impact of HIV on the health of international peace-keeping personnel; by the UN Millennium Development Goals adopted in Sept. 2000; by the Declaration of Commitment on HIV/AIDS agreed in June 2001 by the first-ever Special Session of the UN General Assembly on HIV/AIDS, which acknowledged the AIDS epidemic as a 'global emergency'; and the Political Declaration on HIV/AIDS, adopted by the June 2006 UN General Assembly High Level Meeting on AIDS; launched the Global Coalition on Women and AIDS in Feb. 2004; co-sponsors: WHO, UN Women, UNICEF, UNDP, UNFPA, UNODC, the ILO, UNESCO, the World Bank, WFP, UNHCR; Exec. Dir MICHEL SIDIBÉ (Mali).

NON-COMMUNICABLE DISEASES AND MENTAL HEALTH

The Non-communicable Diseases (NCDs) and Mental Health group comprises departments for the surveillance, prevention and management of uninfectious diseases, and departments for health promotion, disability, injury prevention and rehabilitation, substance abuse and mental health. Surveillance, prevention and management of NCDs, tobacco, and mental health are organization-wide priorities.

Addressing the social and environmental determinants of health is a main priority of WHO. Tobacco use, unhealthy diet and physical inactivity are regarded as common, preventable risk factors for the four most prominent NCDs: cardiovascular diseases, cancer, chronic respiratory disease and diabetes. It is estimated that the four main NCDs are collectively responsible for an estimated 35m. deaths—60% of all deaths—globally each year, and that up to 80% of cases of heart disease, stroke and type 2 diabetes, and more than one-third of cancers, could be prevented by eliminating shared risk factors, the main ones being: tobacco use, unhealthy diet, physical inactivity and harmful use of alcohol. WHO envisages that the disease burden and mortality from these diseases will continue to increase, most rapidly in Africa and the Eastern Mediterranean, and that the highest number of deaths will occur in the Western Pacific region and in South-East Asia. WHO aims to monitor the global epidemiological situation of NCDs, to co-ordinate multinational research activities concerned with prevention and care, and to analyse determining factors such as gender and poverty. The 53rd World Health Assembly, convened in May 2000, endorsed a Global Strategy for the Prevention and Control of NCDs. In May 2008 the 61st World Health Assembly endorsed a new Action Plan for 2008–13 for the Global Strategy for the Prevention and Control of NCDs, based on the vision of the 2000 Global Strategy. The Action Plan aimed to provide a roadmap establishing and strengthening initiatives on the surveillance, prevention and management of NCDs, and emphasized the need to invest in NCD prevention as part of sustainable socio-economic development planning.

The sixth Global Conference on Health Promotion, convened jointly by WHO and the Thai Government, in Bangkok, Thailand, in August 2005, adopted the Bangkok Charter for Health Promotion in a Globalized World, which identified ongoing key challenges, actions and commitments.

In May 2004 the World Health Assembly endorsed a Global Strategy on Diet, Physical Activity and Health; it is estimated that more than 1,000m. adults world-wide are overweight, and that, of these, some 300m. are clinically obese. WHO has studied obesity-related issues in co-operation with the International Association for the Study of Obesity (IASO). The International Task Force on Obesity, affiliated to the IASO, aims to encourage the development of new policies for managing obesity. WHO and FAO jointly commissioned an expert report on the relationship of diet, nutrition and physical activity to chronic diseases, which was published in March 2003.

WHO's programmes for diabetes mellitus, chronic rheumatic diseases and asthma assist with the development of national initiatives, based upon goals and targets for the improvement of early detection, care and reduction of long-term complications. WHO's cardiovascular diseases programme aims to prevent and control the major cardiovascular diseases, which are responsible for more than 14m. deaths each year. It is estimated that one-third of these deaths could have been prevented with existing scientific knowledge. The programme on cancer control is concerned with the prevention of cancer, improving its detection and cure, and ensuring care of all cancer patients in need. In May 2004 the World Health Assembly adopted a resolution on cancer prevention and control, recognizing an increase in global cancer cases, particularly in developing countries, and stressing that many cases and related deaths could be prevented. The resolution included a number of recommendations for the improvement of national cancer control programmes. In May 2009 WHO and the IAEA launched a Joint Programme on Cancer Control, aimed at enhancing efforts to fight cancer in the developing world. WHO is a co-sponsor of the Global Day Against Pain, which is held annually on 11 October. The Global Day highlights the need for improved pain management and palliative care for sufferers of diseases such as cancer and AIDS, with a particular focus on patients living in low-income countries with minimal access to opioid analgesics, and urges recognition of access to pain relief as a basic human right.

The WHO Human Genetics Programme manages genetic approaches for the prevention and control of common hereditary diseases and of those with a genetic predisposition representing a major health factor. The Programme also concentrates on the further development of genetic approaches suitable for incorporation into health care systems, as well as developing a network of international collaborating programmes.

WHO works to assess the impact of injuries, violence and sensory impairments on health, and formulates guidelines and protocols for the prevention and management of mental problems. The health promotion division promotes decentralized and community-based health programmes and is concerned with developing new approaches to population ageing and encouraging healthy lifestyles and self-care. It also seeks to relieve the negative impact of social changes such as urbanization, migration and changes in family structure upon health. WHO advocates a multi-sectoral approach—involving public health, legal and educational systems—to the prevention of injuries, which represent 16% of the global burden of disease. It aims to support governments in developing suitable strategies to prevent and mitigate the consequences of violence, unintentional injury and disability. Several health promotion projects have been undertaken, in collaboration between WHO regional and country offices and other relevant organizations, including: the Global School Health Initiative, to bridge the sectors of health and education and to promote the health of school-age children; the Global Strategy for Occupational Health, to promote the health of the working population and the control of occupational health risks; Community-based Rehabilitation, aimed at providing a more enabling environment for people with disabilities; and a communication strategy to provide training and support for health communications personnel and initiatives. In 2000 WHO, UNESCO, the World Bank and UNICEF adopted the joint Focusing Resources for Effective School Health (FRESH Start) approach to promoting life skills among adolescents.

WHO supports the UN Convention, and its Optional Protocol, on the Rights of Persons with Disabilities, which came into force in May 2008, and seeks to address challenges that prevent the full participation of people with disabilities in the social, economic and cultural lives of their communities and societies; at that time the WHO Director-General appointed a Taskforce on Disability to ensure that WHO was reflecting the provisions of the Convention overall as an organization and in its programme of work.

In February 1999 WHO initiated the ongoing programme, 'Vision 2020: the Right to Sight', which aimed to eliminate avoidable blindness (estimated to be as much as 80% of all cases) by 2020. Blindness was otherwise predicted to increase by as much as twofold, owing to the increased longevity of the global population.

The Tobacco or Health Programme aims to reduce the use of tobacco, by educating tobacco-users and preventing young people from adopting the habit. In 1996 WHO published its first report on the tobacco situation world-wide. According to WHO, about one-third of the world's population aged over 15 years smoke tobacco, which causes nearly 6m. deaths each year (through lung cancer, heart disease, chronic bronchitis and other effects); in 2012 WHO estimated that tobacco would lead to more than 8m. deaths annually by 2030. In 1998 the 'Tobacco Free Initiative', a major global anti-smoking campaign, was established. In May 1999 the World Health Assembly endorsed the formulation of a Framework Convention on Tobacco Control (FCTC) to help to combat the increase in tobacco use (although a number of tobacco growers expressed concerns about the effect of the convention on their livelihoods). The FCTC entered into force in February 2005. The greatest increase in tobacco use is forecast to occur in developing countries. In 2008 WHO published a comprehensive analysis of global tobacco use and control, the *WHO Report on the Global Tobacco Epidemic*, which designated abuse of tobacco as one of the principal global threats to health, and predicted that during the latter part of the 21st century the vast majority of tobacco-related deaths would occur in developing countries. The Report identified and condemned a global tobacco industry strategy to target young people and adults in the developing world, and it detailed six key proven strategies, collectively known as the 'MPOWER package', that were aimed at combating global tobacco use: monitoring tobacco use and implementing prevention policies; protecting people from tobacco smoke; offering support to people to enable them to give up tobacco use; warning about the dangers of tobacco; enforcing bans on tobacco advertising, promotion and sponsorship; and raising taxes on tobacco. The MPOWER package provided a roadmap to support countries in building on their obligations under the FCTC. The FCTC obligates its states parties to require 'health warnings describing the harmful effects of tobacco use' to appear on packs of tobacco and their outside packaging, and recommends the use of warnings that contain pictures. WHO provides technical and other assistance to countries to support them in meeting this obligation through the Tobacco Free Initiative. WHO encourages governments to adopt tobacco health warnings meeting the agreed criteria for maximum effectiveness in convincing consumers not to smoke: these appear on both the front and back of a cigarette pack, should cover more than half of the pack, and should contain pictures.

WHO's Mental Health and Substance Abuse department was established in 2000 from the merger of formerly separate departments to reflect the many common approaches in managing mental health and substance use disorders.

WHO defines mental health as a 'state of well-being in which every individual realizes his or her own potential, can cope with the normal stresses of life, can work productively and fruitfully, and is able to make a contribution to her or his community'. WHO's Mental Health programme is concerned with mental health problems that include unipolar and bipolar affective disorders, psychosis, epilepsy, dementia, Parkinson's disease, multiple sclerosis, drug and alcohol dependency, and neuropsychiatric disorders such as post-traumatic stress disorder, obsessive compulsive disorder and panic disorder. Although, overall, physical health has improved, mental, behavioural and social health problems are increasing, owing to extended life expectancy and improved child mortality rates, and factors such as war and poverty. WHO aims to address mental problems by increasing awareness of mental health issues and promoting improved mental health services and primary care. In October 2008 WHO launched the so-called mental health Gap Action Programme (mhGAP), which aimed to improve services addressing mental, neurological and substance use disorders, with a special focus on low and middle income countries. It was envisaged that, with proper care, psychosocial assistance and medication, many millions of patients in developing countries could be treated for depression, schizophrenia, and epilepsy; prevented from attempting suicide; and encouraged to begin to lead normal lives. A main focus of mhGAP concerns forging strategic partnerships to enhance countries' capacity to combat stigma commonly associated with mental illness, reduce the burden of mental disorders, and promote mental health. WHO is a joint partner in the Global Campaign against Epilepsy: Out of the Shadows, which aims to advance understanding, treatment, services and prevention of epilepsy world-wide.

The Substance Abuse programme addresses the misuse of all psychoactive substances, irrespective of legal status and including alcohol. WHO provides technical support to assist countries in formulating policies with regard to the prevention and reduction of the health and social effects of psychoactive substance abuse, and undertakes epidemiological surveillance and risk assessment, advocacy and the dissemination of information, strengthening national and regional prevention and health promotion techniques and strategies, the development of cost-effective treatment and rehabilitation approaches, and also encompasses regulatory activities as required under the international drugs-control treaties in force. In May 2010 WHO endorsed a new global strategy to reduce the harmful use of alcohol; this promoted measures including taxation on alcohol, minimizing outlets selling alcohol, raising age limits for those buying alcohol, and the employment of effective measures to deter people from driving while under the influence of alcohol.

In June 2010 WHO launched the Global Network of Age-Friendly Cities, as part of a broader response to the ageing of populations world-wide. The Network aims to support cities in creating urban environments that would enable older people to remain active and healthy.

FAMILY AND COMMUNITY HEALTH

WHO's Family and Community Health group addresses the following areas of work: child and adolescent health, research and programme development in reproductive health, making pregnancy safer and men's and women's health. Making pregnancy safer is an organization-wide priority. The group's aim is to improve access to sustainable health care for all by strengthening health systems and fostering individual, family and community development. Activities include newborn care; child health, including promoting and protecting the health and development of the child through such approaches as promotion of breast-feeding and use of the mother-baby package, as well as care of the sick child, including diarrhoeal and acute respiratory disease control, and support to women and children in difficult circumstances; the promotion of safe motherhood and maternal health; adolescent health, including the promotion and development of young people and the prevention of specific health problems; women, health and development, including addressing issues of gender, sexual violence, and harmful traditional practices; and human reproduction, including research related to contraceptive technologies and effective methods. In addition, WHO aims to provide technical leadership and co-ordination on reproductive health and to support countries in their efforts to ensure that people: experience healthy sexual development and maturation; have the capacity for healthy, equitable and responsible relationships; can achieve their reproductive intentions safely and healthily; avoid illnesses, diseases and injury related to sexuality and reproduction; and receive appropriate counselling, care and rehabilitation for diseases and conditions related to sexuality and reproduction.

WHO supports the 'Global Strategy for Women's and Children's Health', launched by heads of state and government participating in the September 2010 UN Summit on the MDGs; some US $40,000m. has been pledged towards women's and child's health and achieving goals (iv) Reducing Child Mortality and (v) Improving Maternal Health. In May 2012 the World Health Assembly adopted a resolution on raising awareness of early marriage (entered into by more than 30% of women in developing countries) and adolescent pregnancy, and the consequences thereof for young women and infants.

In September 1997 WHO, in collaboration with UNICEF, formally launched a programme advocating the Integrated Management of Childhood Illness (IMCI). IMCI recognizes that pneumonia, diarrhoea, measles, malaria and malnutrition cause some 70% of the approximately 11m. childhood deaths each year, and recommends screening sick children for all five conditions, to obtain a more accurate diagnosis than may be achieved from the results of a single assessment. WHO encourages national programmes aimed at reducing childhood deaths as a result of diarrhoea, particularly through the use of oral rehydration therapy and preventive measures. In November 2009 WHO and UNICEF launched a Global Action Plan for the Prevention and Control of Pneumonia (GAPP), which aimed to accelerate pneumonia control through a combination of interventions of proven benefit. Accelerated efforts by WHO to promote vaccination against measles through its Measles Initiative (subsequently renamed the Measles and Rubella Initiative), established in 2001, contributed to a three-quarters reduction in global mortality from that disease over the period 2000–10. In April 2012 WHO and other partners launched a global strategy that aimed to eliminate measles deaths and congenital rubella syndrome.

SUSTAINABLE DEVELOPMENT AND HEALTHY ENVIRONMENTS

The Sustainable Development and Healthy Environments group focuses on the following areas of work: health in sustainable development; nutrition; health and environment; food safety; and emergency preparedness and response. Food safety is an organization-wide priority.

WHO promotes recognition of good health status as one of the most important assets of the poor. The Sustainable Development and Healthy Environment group seeks to monitor the advantages and disadvantages for health, nutrition, environment and development arising from the process of globalization (i.e. increased global flows of capital, goods and services, people, and knowledge); to integrate the issue of health into poverty reduction programmes; and to promote human rights and equality. Adequate and safe food and nutrition is a priority programme area. WHO collaborates with FAO, WFP, UNICEF and other UN agencies in pursuing its objectives relating to nutrition and food safety. It has been estimated that 780m. people world-wide cannot meet basic needs for energy and protein, more than 2,000m. people lack essential vitamins and minerals, and that 170m. children are malnourished. In December 1992 WHO and FAO hosted an international conference on nutrition, at which a World Declaration and Plan of Action on Nutrition was adopted to make the fight against malnutrition a development priority. Following the conference, WHO promoted the elaboration and implementation of national plans of action on nutrition. WHO aims to support the enhancement of member states' capabilities in dealing with their nutrition situations, and addressing scientific issues related to preventing, managing and monitoring protein-energy malnutrition; micronutrient malnutrition, including iodine deficiency disorders, vitamin A deficiency, and nutritional anaemia; and diet-related conditions and NCDs such as obesity (increasingly affecting children, adolescents and adults, mainly in industrialized countries), cancer and heart disease. In 1990 the World Health Assembly resolved to eliminate iodine deficiency (believed to cause mental retardation); a strategy of universal salt iodization was launched in 1993. In collaboration with other international agencies, WHO is implementing a comprehensive strategy for promoting appropriate infant, young child and maternal nutrition, and for dealing effectively with nutritional emergencies in large populations. Areas of emphasis include promoting healthcare practices that enhance successful breast-feeding; appropriate complementary feeding; refining the use and interpretation of body measurements for assessing nutritional status; relevant information, education and training; and action to give effect to the International Code of Marketing of Breast-milk Substitutes. The food safety programme aims to protect human health against risks associated with biological and chemical contaminants and additives in food. With FAO, WHO establishes food standards (through the work of the Codex Alimentarius Commission and its subsidiary committees) and evaluates food additives, pesticide residues and other contaminants and their implications for health. The programme provides expert advice on such issues as food-borne pathogens (e.g. listeria), production methods (e.g. aquaculture) and food biotechnology (e.g. genetic modification). In July 2001 the Codex Alimentarius Commission adopted the first global principles for assessing the safety of genetically modified (GM) foods. In March 2002 an intergovernmental task force established by the Commission finalized 'principles for the risk analysis of foods derived from biotechnology', which were to provide a framework for assessing the safety of GM foods and plants. In the following month WHO and FAO announced a joint review of their food standards operations. In February 2003 the FAO/WHO Project and Fund for Enhanced Participation in Codex was launched to support the participation of poorer countries in the Commission's activities. WHO supports, with other UN agencies, governments, research institutions, and representatives of civil society and of the private sector, the initiative on Scaling up Nutrition (SUN), which was initiated in 2009, under the co-ordination of the UN Secretary-General's Special Representative for Food Security and Nutrition, with the aim of increasing the coverage of interventions that improve nutrition during the first 1,000 days of a child's life (such as exclusive breastfeeding, optimal complementary feeding practices, and provision of essential vitamins and minerals); and ensuring that nutrition plans are implemented at national level, and that government programmes take nutrition into account. The activities of SUN are guided by the Framework for Scaling up Nutrition, which was published in April 2010; and by the SUN Roadmap, finalized in September 2010.

WHO's programme area on environmental health undertakes a wide range of initiatives to tackle the increasing threats to health and well-being from a changing environment, especially in relation to air pollution, water quality, sanitation, protection against radiation, management of hazardous waste, chemical safety and housing hygiene. In 2008 it was estimated that some 1,200m. people world-wide had no access to clean drinking water, while a further 2,600m. people are denied suitable sanitation systems. WHO helped launch the Water Supply and Sanitation Council in 1990 and regularly updates its *Guidelines for Drinking Water Quality*. In rural areas the emphasis continues to be on the provision and maintenance of safe and sufficient water supplies and adequate sanitation, the health aspects of rural housing, vector control in water resource management, and the safe use of agrochemicals. In urban areas assistance is provided to identify local environmental health priorities and to improve municipal governments' ability to deal with environmental conditions and health problems in an integrated manner; promotion of the 'Healthy City' approach is a major component of the programme. Other programme activities include environmental health information development and management, human resources development, environmental health planning methods, research and work on problems relating to global environment change, such as UV-radiation. The WHO Global Strategy for Health and Environment, developed in response to the WHO Commission on Health and Environment which reported to the UN Conference on Environment and Development in June 1992, provides the framework for programme activities. In May 2008 the 61st World Health Assembly adopted a resolution urging member states to take action to address the impact of climate change on human health.

In sub-Saharan Africa, where conditions are considered to be the worst in the world, it is estimated that more than one-half of the population lack safe drinking water and that around three-fifths are living without adequate sanitation, contributing to the problems of endemic malnutrition and diarrhoeal diseases. In August 2008 WHO, UNEP and the Gabonese Government jointly organized a conference of African health and environment ministers, with the aim of enhancing regional political commitment towards reducing environmental threats to health.

Through its International EMF Project WHO is compiling a comprehensive assessment of the potential adverse effects on human health deriving from exposure to electromagnetic fields (EMF). In May 2011 the International Agency for Research on Cancer, an agency of WHO, classified radiofrequency EMF as possibly carcinogenic to humans, on the basis of an increased risk of glioma (malignant brain cancer) associated with the use of wireless phones.

WHO's work in the promotion of chemical safety is undertaken in collaboration with the ILO and UNEP through the International Programme on Chemical Safety (IPCS), the Central Unit for which is located in WHO. The Programme provides internationally evaluated scientific information on chemicals, promotes the use of such information in national programmes, assists member states in establishment of their own chemical safety measures and programmes, and helps them strengthen their capabilities in chemical emergency preparedness and response and in chemical risk reduction. In 1995 an Inter-organization Programme for the Social Management of Chemicals was established by UNEP, the ILO, FAO, WHO, UNIDO and OECD, in order to strengthen international co-operation in the field of chemical safety. In 1998 WHO led an international assessment of the health risk from bendocine disruptors (chemicals which disrupt hormonal activities).

Since the major terrorist attacks perpetrated against targets in the USA in September 2001, WHO has focused renewed attention on the potential malevolent use of bacteria (such as bacillus anthracis, which causes anthrax), viruses (for example, the variola virus, causing smallpox) or toxins, or of chemical agents, in acts of biological or chemical terrorism. In September 2001 WHO issued draft guidelines entitled 'Health Aspects of Biological and Chemical Weapons'.

Within the UN system, WHO's Department of Emergency and Humanitarian Action co-ordinates the international response to emergencies and natural disasters in the health field, in close co-operation with other agencies and within the framework set out by the UN's Office for the Co-ordination of Humanitarian Affairs. In this context, WHO provides expert advice on epidemiological surveillance, control of communicable diseases, public health information and health emergency training. Its emergency preparedness activities include co-ordination, policy-making and planning, awareness-building, technical advice, training, publication of standards and guidelines, and research. Its emergency relief activities include organizational support, the provision of emergency drugs and supplies and conducting technical emergency assessment missions. The Division's objective is to strengthen the national capacity of member states to reduce the adverse health consequences of disasters. In responding to emergency situations, WHO always tries to develop projects and activities that will assist the national authorities concerned in rebuilding or strengthening their own capacity to handle the impact of such situations. WHO appeals through the UN's inter-agency Consolidated Appeals Process (CAP) for funding for its emergency humanitarian operations.

HEALTH TECHNOLOGY AND PHARMACEUTICALS

WHO's Health Technology and Pharmaceuticals group, made up of the departments of essential drugs and other medicines, vaccines and other biologicals, and blood safety and clinical technology, covers the following areas of work: essential medicines—access, quality and rational use; immunization and vaccine development; and world-wide co-operation on blood safety and clinical technology. Blood safety and clinical technology are an organization-wide priority.

In January 1999 the Executive Board adopted a resolution on WHO's Revised Drug Strategy which placed emphasis on the inequalities of access to pharmaceuticals, and also covered specific aspects of drugs policy, quality assurance, drug promotion, drug donation, independent drug information and rational drug use. Plans of action involving co-operation with member states and other international organizations were to be developed to monitor and analyse the pharmaceutical and public health implications of international agreements, including trade agreements. In April 2001 experts from WHO and the World Trade Organization participated in a workshop to address ways of lowering the cost of medicines in less developed countries. In the following month the World Health Assembly adopted a resolution urging member states to promote equitable access to essential drugs, noting that this was denied to about one-third of the world's population. WHO participates with other partners in the 'Accelerating Access' initiative, which aims to expand access to antiretroviral drugs for people with HIV/AIDS.

WHO reports that 2m. children die each year of diseases for which common vaccines exist. In September 1991 the Children's Vaccine Initiative (CVI) was launched, jointly sponsored by the Rockefeller Foundation, UNDP, UNICEF, the World Bank and WHO, to facilitate the development and provision of children's vaccines. The CVI has as its ultimate goal the development of a single oral immunization shortly after birth that will protect against all major childhood diseases. An International Vaccine Institute was established in Seoul, South Korea, as part of the CVI, to provide scientific and technical services for the production of vaccines for developing countries. A comprehensive survey, *State of the World's Vaccines and Immunization*, was published by WHO, jointly with UNICEF, in 1996; revised editions of the survey were issued in 2003 and 2010. In 1999 WHO, UNICEF, the World Bank and a number of public and private sector partners formed the Global Alliance for Vaccines and Immunization (GAVI), which aimed to expand the provision of existing vaccines and to accelerate the development and introduction of new vaccines and technologies, with the ultimate goal of protecting children of all nations and from all socio-economic backgrounds against vaccine-preventable diseases.

WHO supports states in ensuring access to safe blood, blood products, transfusions, injections, and healthcare technologies.

INFORMATION, EVIDENCE AND RESEARCH

The Information, Evidence and Research group addresses the following areas of work: evidence for health policy; health information management and dissemination; and research policy and promotion and organization of health systems. Through the generation and dissemination of evidence the Information, Evidence and Research group aims to assist policy-makers assess health needs, choose intervention strategies, design policy and monitor performance, and thereby improve the performance of national health systems. The group also supports international and national dialogue on health policy.

WHO co-ordinates the Health InterNetwork Access to Research Initiative (HINARI), which was launched in July 2001 to enable relevant authorities in developing countries to access biomedical journals through the internet at no or greatly reduced cost, in order to improve the world-wide circulation of scientific information; by 2012 more than 8,500 journals and 7,000 e-books were being made available to health institutions in more than 100 countries.

In 2004 WHO developed the World Alliance on Patient Safety, further to a World Health Assembly resolution in 2002. Since renamed WHO Patient Safety, the programme was launched to facilitate the development of patient safety policy and practice across all WHO member states.

In 2003 WHO launched a virtual Healthy Academy which, in 2012, was providing 15 eLearning courses, on topics such as HIV/AIDS; malaria; oral health; and safer food. In May 2005 the World Health Assembly adopted a resolution asking WHO to extend the accessibility of the Health Academy, and urging WHO to support member states in integrating 'eHealth' into national health systems and services.

Finance

WHO's regular budget is provided by assessment of member states and associate members. An additional fund for specific projects is provided by voluntary contributions from members and other sources, including UNDP and UNFPA.

A regular budget of US $4,804m. was proposed for the two years 2012–13, of which some 29.3%, or $1,409m., was provisionally allocated to Africa.

Publications

Bulletin of WHO (monthly).

Eastern Mediterranean Health Journal (annually).

International Classification of Functioning, Disability and Health—ICF.

International Pharmacopoeia.

International Statistical Classification of Disease and Related Health Problems.

International Travel and Health.

Model List of Essential Medicines (every two years).

Pan-American Journal of Public Health (annually).

3 By 5 Progress Report.

Toxicological Evaluation of Certain Veterinary Drug Residues in Food (annually).

Weekly Epidemiological Record (in English and French, paper and electronic versions available).

WHO Drug Information (quarterly).

WHO Global Atlas of Traditional, Complementary and Alternative Medicine.

WHO Model Formulary.

WHO Report on the Global Tobacco Epidemic.

World Health Report (annually, in English, French and Spanish).

World Cancer Report.

World Malaria Report (with UNICEF).

Zoonoses and Communicable Diseases Common to Man and Animals.

Technical report series; catalogues of specific scientific, technical and medical fields available.

Other UN Organizations Active in the Region

INTERNATIONAL RESIDUAL MECHANISM FOR CRIMINAL TRIBUNALS (MICT)

The Residual Mechanism was established by Security Council Resolution 1966 (December 2010) to undertake some essential functions of the International Tribunal for the Former Yugoslavia (ICTY) and of the International Criminal Tribunal for Rwanda (ICTR) pending and after their planned closure. The Residual Mechanism comprises a branch that is based in Arusha, Tanzania (MICT Arusha Branch, which commenced operations on 1 July 2012), and a branch based in The Hague, Netherlands (to be operational from 1 July 2013). In January 2012 the UN Secretary-General appointed John Hocking, the ICTY Registrar, to be concurrently Registrar of the Mechanism, and in February Theodor Meron, the ICTY President, and Hassan Bubacar Jallow, the ICTR Prosecutor, were appointed to be, respectively, President and Prosecutor of the Residual Mechanism. The Mechanism was to operate for an initial period of four years from the first commencement date (1 July 2012). It was to conduct any appeals against Tribunal judgements filed following its entry into operation.

President of the Residual Mechanism: THEODOR MERON (Poland).

Prosecutor of the Residual Mechanism: HASSAN BUBACAR JALLOW (The Gambia).

Registrar of the Residual Mechanism: JOHN HOCKING (Australia).

INTERNATIONAL CRIMINAL TRIBUNAL FOR RWANDA—ICTR

Address: Registry: Arusha International Conference Centre, POB 6016, Arusha, Tanzania.

Telephone: (212) 963-2850; **fax:** (212) 963-2848; **e-mail:** ictr-press@un.org; **internet:** www.ictr.org.

In November 1994 the Security Council adopted Resolution 955, establishing the ICTR to prosecute persons responsible for genocide and other serious violations of humanitarian law that had been committed in Rwanda and by Rwandans in neighbouring states. Its temporal jurisdiction was limited to the period 1 January to 31 December 1994. UN Secretary Council Resolution 977, adopted in February 1995, determined that the seat of the Tribunal would be located in Arusha, Tanzania. The Tribunal consists of 11 permanent judges, of whom nine sit in four trial chambers and two sit in the seven-member appeals chamber that is shared with the ICTY and based at The Hague. A high security UN Detention Facility, the first of its kind, was constructed within the compound of the prison in Arusha and opened in 1996. In August 2002 the UN Security Council endorsed a proposal by the ICTR President to elect a pool of 18 ad litem judges to the Tribunal with a view to accelerating its activities. In October 2003 the Security Council increased the number of ad litem judges who may serve on the Tribunal at any one time from four to nine. The first plenary session of the Tribunal was held in The Hague in June 1995; formal proceedings at its permanent headquarters in Arusha were initiated in November. The first trial of persons charged by the Tribunal commenced in January 1997, and sentences were imposed in July. In September 1998 the former Rwandan Prime Minister, Jean Kambanda, and a former mayor of Taba, Jean-Paul Akayesu, both Hutu extremists, were found guilty of genocide and crimes against humanity; Kambanda subsequently became the first person ever to be sentenced under the 1948 Convention on the Prevention and Punishment of the Crime of Genocide. In October 2000 the Tribunal rejected an appeal by Kambanda. In November 1999 the Rwandan Government temporarily suspended co-operation with the Tribunal in protest at a decision of the appeals chamber to release an indicted former government official owing to procedural delays. (The appeals chamber subsequently reversed this decision.) In 2001 two ICTR investigators employed on defence teams were arrested and charged with genocide, having been found to be working at the Tribunal under assumed identities. Relations between the Rwandan Government and the ICTR deteriorated again in 2002, with the then Chief Prosecutor accusing the Rwandan authorities of failing to facilitate the travel of witnesses to the Tribunal and withholding access to documentary materials, and counter-accusations by the Rwandan Government that the Tribunal's progress was too slow, that further suspected perpetrators of genocide had been inadvertently employed by the Tribunal and that Rwandan witnesses attending the Tribunal had not received sufficient protection. Reporting to the UN Security Council in July, the then Chief Prosecutor alleged that the Rwandan refusal to co-operate ensued from her recent decision to indict former members of the Tutsi-dominated Rwanda Patriotic Army for human rights violations committed against Hutus in 1994. In January 2004 a former minister of culture and education, Jean de Dieu Kamuhanda, was found guilty on two counts of genocide and extermination as a crime against humanity. In the following month Samuel Imanishimwe, a former military commander, was convicted on seven counts of genocide, crimes against humanity and serious violations of the Geneva Conventions. In December 2008 Théoneste Bagosora, Aloys Ntabakuze and Anatole Nsengiyumva, former high-ranking military commanders, were found guilty of genocide, crimes against humanity and war crimes, and were each sentenced to life imprisonment. In May 2012 Callixte Nzabonimana, a former Minister of Youth, was convicted of genocide, conspiracy and incitement to commit genocide, and extermination as a crime against humanity, and sentenced to life imprisonment. By September 2012 the Tribunal had delivered judgments against 72 accused, of whom 10 were acquitted, and 17 were appealing their convictions. Trial proceedings relating to one case (that of Augustin Ngirabatware, a former Minister of Planning, indicted on six charges concerning genocide, and rape and extermination as crimes against humanity) were ongoing at that time, while one indictee was awaiting trial; two cases were being tried in France under French national jurisdiction and a further eight cases had been referred (during 2011–12) to be tried in the Rwandan national court system. Nine fugitives wanted by the Tribunal remained at large. On 1 July 2012 the International Residual Mechanism for Criminal Tribunals (MICT) Arusha Branch began to take over outstanding essential functions of the Tribunal; all ICTR responsibilities were to be transferred to MICT by 31 December 2014.

The ICTR has been supported by teams of investigators and human rights experts working in the field to collect forensic and other evidence in order to uphold indictments. Evidence of mass graves resulting from large-scale unlawful killings has been uncovered.

President of the ICTR: VAGN JOENSEN (Denmark).

ICTR Prosecutor: HASSAN BUBACAR JALLOW (The Gambia).

ICTR Registrar a.i.: PASCAL BESNIER (France).

OFFICE FOR THE CO-ORDINATION OF HUMANITARIAN AFFAIRS—OCHA

Address: United Nations Plaza, New York, NY 10017, USA.

Telephone: (212) 963-1234; **fax:** (212) 963-1312; **e-mail:** ochany@un.org; **internet:** unocha.org.

The Office was established in January 1998 as part of the UN Secretariat, with a mandate to co-ordinate international humanitarian assistance and to provide policy and other advice on humanitarian issues. It administers the Humanitarian Early Warning System, as well as Integrated Regional Information Networks (IRIN), to monitor the situation in different countries, and a Disaster Response System. A complementary service, Reliefweb, which was launched in 1996, monitors crises and publishes information on the internet.

OCHA facilitates the inter-agency Consolidated Appeals Process (CAP), which aims to organize a co-ordinated response to resource mobilization following humanitarian crises. CAP appeals for 2012, seeking an estimated US $7,700m. in total, were issued in December 2011; the largest appeals were for Somalia ($1,522m.), Sudan ($1,066m.), Kenya ($764m.), South Sudan ($763m.) and Democratic Republic of the Congo ($719m.).

Under-Secretary-General for Humanitarian Affairs and Emergency Relief Co-ordinator: VALERIE AMOS (United Kingdom).

Inter-Agency Secretariat of the International Strategy for Disaster Reduction—UN/ISDR: International Environment House II, 7–9 Chemin de Balexert, 1219 Châtelaine, Geneva 10, Switzerland; tel. 229178908; fax 229178964; e-mail isdr@un.org; internet www.unisdr.org; operates as secretariat of the International Strategy for Disaster Reduction (ISDR), adopted by UN member states in 2000 as a strategic framework aimed at guiding and co-ordinating the efforts of humanitarian organizations, states, intergovernmental and non-governmental organizations, financial institutions, technical bodies and civil society representatives towards achieving substantive reduction in disaster losses, and building resilient communities and nations as the foundation for sustainable development activities; UN/ISDR promotes information sharing to reduce disaster risk, and serves as the focal point providing guidance for the implementation of the Hyogo Framework for Action (HFA), adopted in 2005 as a 10-year plan of action for protecting lives and livelihoods against disasters; in early 2012 UN/ISDR initiated consultations on formulating a blueprint on a post-2015 diaster risk reduction framework in advance of the third World Conference on Disaster Reduction that was scheduled to be held in 2015, in Japan; UN/ISDR implements a 'Making Cities Resilient' campaign in view in increasing urbanization world-wide; Head,

Special Representative of the UN Secretary-General for Disaster Risk Reduction MARGARETA WAHLSTRÖM.

UN WOMEN—UNITED NATIONS ENTITY FOR GENDER EQUALITY AND THE EMPOWERMENT OF WOMEN

Address: 304 East 45th St, 15th Floor, New York, NY 10017, USA.

Telephone: (212) 906-6400; **fax:** (212) 906-6705; **internet:** www.unwomen.org.

UN Women was established by the UN General Assembly in July 2010 in order to strengthen the UN's capacity to promote gender equality, the empowerment of women, and the elimination of discrimination against women and girls. It commenced operations on 1 January 2011, incorporating the functions of the Office of the Special Adviser on Gender Issues and Advancement of Women, the Division for the Advancement of Women of the Secretariat, the United Nations Development Fund for Women (UNIFEM) and the International Research and Training Institute for the Advancement of Women (INSTRAW).

Executive Director and Under-Secretary-General: MICHELLE BACHELET (Chile).

UNITED NATIONS OFFICE ON DRUGS AND CRIME—UNODC

Address: Vienna International Centre, POB 500, 1400 Vienna, Austria.

Telephone: (1) 26060-0; **fax:** (1) 26060-5866; **e-mail:** unodc@unodc.org; **internet:** www.unodc.org.

The Office was established in November 1997 (as the UN Office of Drug Control and Crime Prevention) to strengthen the UN's integrated approach to issues relating to drug control, crime prevention and international terrorism. It comprises two principal components: the United Nations Drug Programme and the United Nations Crime Programme.

Executive Director: YURI FEDOTOV (Russia).

OFFICE OF THE UNITED NATIONS HIGH COMMISSIONER FOR HUMAN RIGHTS—OHCHR

Address: Palais Wilson, 52 rue de Paquis, 1201 Geneva, Switzerland.

Telephone: 229179290; **fax:** 229179022; **e-mail:** infodesk@ohchr.org; **internet:** www.ohchr.org.

The Office is a body of the UN Secretariat and is the focal point for UN human-rights activities. Since September 1997 it has incorporated the Centre for Human Rights. The High Commissioner is the UN official with principal responsibility for UN human rights activities.

High Commissioner: NAVANETHEM PILLAY (South Africa).

UNITED NATIONS HUMAN SETTLEMENTS PROGRAMME—UN-HABITAT

Address: POB 30030, Nairobi, Kenya.

Telephone: (20) 621234; **fax:** (20) 624266; **e-mail:** infohabitat@unhabitat.org; **internet:** www.unhabitat.org.

UN-Habitat was established, as the United Nations Centre for Human Settlements, in October 1978 to service the intergovernmental Commission on Human Settlements. It became a full UN programme on 1 January 2002, serving as the focus for human settlements activities in the UN system.

Regional Office for Africa and the Arab States: POB 30030, Nairobi, Kenya 00100; tel. (20) 623221; fax (20) 623904; e-mail roaas@unhabitat.org; internet www.unhabitat.org/roaas.

Executive Director: JOAN CLOS (Spain).

UNITED NATIONS CONFERENCE ON TRADE AND DEVELOPMENT—UNCTAD

Address: Palais des Nations, 1211 Geneva 10, Switzerland.

Telephone: 229171234; **fax:** 229070057; **e-mail:** info@unctad.org; **internet:** www.unctad.org.

UNCTAD was established in 1964. It is the principal organ of the UN General Assembly concerned with trade and development, and is the focal point within the UN system for integrated activities relating to trade, finance, technology, investment and sustainable development. It aims to maximize the trade and development opportunities of developing countries, in particular least-developed countries, and to assist them to adapt to the increasing globalization and liberalization of the world economy. UNCTAD undertakes consensus-building activities, research and policy analysis and technical co-operation.

Secretary-General: DR SUPACHAI PANITCHPAKDI (Thailand).

UNITED NATIONS POPULATION FUND—UNFPA

Address: 605 Third Ave, New York, NY 10158, USA.

Telephone: (212) 297-5000; **fax:** (212) 370-0201; **e-mail:** hq@unfpa.org; **internet:** www.unfpa.org.

Created in 1967 as the Trust Fund for Population Activities, the UN Fund for Population Activities (UNFPA) was established as a Fund of the UN General Assembly in 1972 and was made a subsidiary organ of the UN General Assembly in 1979, with the UNDP Governing Council (now the Executive Board) designated as its governing body. In 1987 UNFPA's name was changed to the United Nations Population Fund (retaining the same acronym).

Executive Director: BABATUNDE OSOTIMEHIN (Nigeria).

Regional Office for Africa: 7 Naivasha Rd, Sunninghill, Johannesburg 2157, South Africa; tel. (11) 603-5300; fax (11) 603-5380; e-mail aro.info@unfpa.org; sub-regional offices are located in Johannesburg and in Dakar, Senegal.

UN Specialized Agencies

INTERNATIONAL CIVIL AVIATION ORGANIZATION—ICAO

Address: 999 University St, Montréal, QC H3C 5H7, Canada.

Telephone: (514) 954-8219; **fax:** (514) 954-6077; **e-mail:** icaohq@icao.org; **internet:** www.icao.int.

ICAO was founded in 1947, on the basis of the Convention on International Civil Aviation, signed in Chicago, in 1944, to develop the techniques of international air navigation and to help in the planning and improvement of international air transport.

Secretary-General: RAYMOND BENJAMIN (France).

Eastern and Southern Africa Office: Limuru Rd, Gigiri, POB 46294, Nairobi, Kenya; tel. (20) 7622395; fax (20) 7623028; e-mail icaoesaf@icao.int; internet www.icao.int/esaf.

Western and Central African Office: 15 blvd de la République, BP 2356, Dakar, Senegal; tel. 839-2424; fax 823-3259; e-mail icaowacaf@dakar.icao.int; internet www.icao.int/wacaf.

INTERNATIONAL LABOUR ORGANIZATION—ILO

Address: 4 route des Morillons, 1211 Geneva 22, Switzerland.

Telephone: 227996111; **fax:** 227988685; **e-mail:** ilo@ilo.org; **internet:** www.ilo.org.

ILO was founded in 1919 to work for social justice as a basis for lasting peace. It carries out this mandate by promoting decent living standards, satisfactory conditions of work and pay and adequate employment opportunities. Methods of action include the creation of international labour standards; the provision of technical co-operation services; and training, education, research and publishing activities to advance ILO objectives.

Director-General: JUAN O. SOMAVÍA (Chile).

Regional Office for Africa: BP 2788, Africa Hall, 6th Floor, Menelik II Ave, Addis Ababa, Ethiopia; tel. (11) 544-4480; fax (11) 544-5573; e-mail addisababa@ilo.org.

INTERNATIONAL MARITIME ORGANIZATION—IMO

Address: 4 Albert Embankment, London, SE1 7SR, United Kingdom.

Telephone: (20) 7735-7611; **fax:** (20) 7587-3210; **e-mail:** info@imo.org; **internet:** www.imo.org.

The Inter-Governmental Maritime Consultative Organization (IMCO) began operations in 1959, as a specialized agency of the UN to facilitate co-operation among governments on technical matters affecting international shipping. Its main aims are to improve the safety of international shipping, and to control pollution caused by ships. IMCO became IMO in 1982.

A high-level sub-regional meeting of states from the Western Indian Ocean, the Gulf of Aden and Red Sea areas, held under IMO auspices in Djibouti, in January 2009, adopted a code of conduct for regional co-operation on enhancing maritime security and combating piracy in the region. In December 2009 the IMO Assembly adopted a resolution supporting UN Security Council efforts to combat piracy, and also adopted a revised code of practice for investigating crimes of piracy and armed robbery against ships.

Secretary-General: KOJI SEKIMIZU (Japan).

INTERNATIONAL TELECOMMUNICATION UNION—ITU

Address: Place des Nations, 1211 Geneva 20, Switzerland.

Telephone: 227305111; **fax:** 227337256; **e-mail:** itumail@itu.int; **internet:** www.itu.int.

Founded in 1865, ITU became a specialized agency of the UN in 1947. It acts to encourage world co-operation for the improvement and use of telecommunications, to promote technical development, to harmonize national policies in the field, and to promote the extension of telecommunications throughout the world. ITU helped to organize the World Summit on the Information Society, held, in two phases, in 2003 and 2005, and supports follow-up initiatives. ITU has assumed responsibility for issues relating to cybersecurity.

Secretary-General: HAMADOUN TOURÉ (Mali).

UNITED NATIONS INDUSTRIAL DEVELOPMENT ORGANIZATION—UNIDO

Address: Vienna International Centre, Wagramerstr. 5, POB 300, 1400 Vienna, Austria.

Telephone: (1) 260260; **fax:** (1) 2692669; **e-mail:** unido@unido.org; **internet:** www.unido.org.

UNIDO began operations in 1967 and became a specialized agency in 1985. Its objectives are to promote sustainable and socially equitable industrial development in developing countries and in countries with economies in transition. It aims to assist such countries to integrate fully into global economic system by mobilizing knowledge, skills, information and technology to promote productive employment, competitive economies and sound environment.

Director-General: KANDEH YUMKELLA (Sierra Leone).

UNIVERSAL POSTAL UNION—UPU

Address: CP 13, 3000 Bern 15, Switzerland.

Telephone: 313503111; **fax:** 313503110; **e-mail:** info@upu.int; **internet:** www.upu.int.

The General Postal Union was founded by the Treaty of Berne (1874), beginning operations in July 1875. Three years later its name was changed to the Universal Postal Union. In 1948 UPU became a specialized agency of the UN. It aims to develop and unify the international postal service, to study problems and to provide training.

Director-General: EDOUARD DAYAN (France).

WORLD INTELLECTUAL PROPERTY ORGANIZATION—WIPO

Address: 34 chemin des Colombettes, 1211 Geneva 20, Switzerland.

Telephone: 223389111; **fax:** 227335428; **e-mail:** wipo.mail@wipo.int; **internet:** www.wipo.int.

WIPO was established in 1970. It became a specialized agency of the UN in 1974 concerned with the protection of intellectual property (e.g. industrial and technical patents and literary copyrights) throughout the world. WIPO formulates and administers treaties embodying international norms and standards of intellectual property, establishes model laws, and facilitates applications for the protection of inventions, trademarks etc. WIPO provides legal and technical assistance to developing countries and countries with economies in transition and advises countries on obligations under the World Trade Organization's agreement on Trade-Related Aspects of Intellectual Property Rights (TRIPS).

Director-General: FRANCIS GURRY (Australia).

WORLD METEOROLOGICAL ORGANIZATION—WMO

Address: 7 bis, ave de la Paix, 1211 Geneva 2, Switzerland.

Telephone: 227308111; **fax:** 227308181; **e-mail:** wmo@wmo.int; **internet:** www.wmo.int.

WMO was established in 1950 and was recognized as a Specialized Agency of the UN in 1951, aiming to improve the exchange of information in the fields of meteorology, climatology, operational hydrology and related fields, as well as their applications. WMO jointly implements, with UNEP, the UN Framework Convention on Climate Change. In June 2011 the 16th World Meteorological Congress endorsed a new Global Framework for Climate Services.

Secretary-General: MICHEL JARRAUD (France).

WORLD TOURISM ORGANIZATION—UNWTO

Address: Capitán Haya 42, 28020 Madrid, Spain.

Telephone: (91) 5678100; **fax:** (91) 5713733; **e-mail:** omt@unwto.org; **internet:** www.world-tourism.org.

The World Tourism Organization was established in 1975 and was recognized as a Specialized Agency of the UN in December 2003. It works to promote and develop sustainable tourism, in particular in support of socio-economic growth in developing countries.

Secretary-General: TALEB RIFAI (Jordan).

Special High Level Appointments of the UN Secretary-General

Joint UN-AU Chief Mediator for Darfur, a. i.: AÏCHATOU MINDAOUDOU SOULEYMANE (Niger).

Special Adviser and Mediator in the Border Dispute between Equatorial Guinea and Gabon: NICOLAS MICHEL (Switzerland).

Special Adviser on Africa: MAGED ABDELAZIZ (Egypt).

Special Adviser on Legal Issues related to Piracy off the Coast of Somalia: JACK LANG (France).

Special Envoy for HIV/AIDS in Africa: ASHA-ROSE MIGIRO (Tanzania).

Special Envoy for Sudan and South Sudan: HAILE MENKERIOS (South Africa).

Special Envoy on the Great Lakes Region: OLUSEGUN OBASANJO (Nigeria).

Further Special Representatives and other high-level appointees of the UN Secretary-General are listed in entries on UN peace-keeping and peace-building missions.

Affiliated Body

SPECIAL COURT FOR SIERRA LEONE

Address: Jomo Kenyatta Rd, New England, Freetown, Sierra Leone.

Telephone: (22) 297000; **fax:** (22) 297001; **e-mail:** scsl-mail@un.org; **internet:** www.sc-sl.org.

The Court was established in January 2002 by agreement of the UN and the government of Sierra Leone, pursuant to a UN Security Council resolution of August 2000 to establish an independent Special Court to prosecute those 'bearing the greatest responsibility for committing violations against humanitarian law' since 20 November 1996. The Court is funded entirely by voluntary contributions. The Court indicted in total some 13 people, although two indictments were withdrawn in December 2003 following the deaths of two of the accused, and, following the death of another of the accused, a further indictment was terminated in May 2007. Trial proceedings commenced in June 2004. Three cases involving eight defendants have been completed. In April 2006 the Special Court for Sierra Leone and the ICC concluded a memorandum of understanding in accordance with which the Special Court was to use the courtroom and detention facilities of the ICC for the planned trial of Charles Taylor, the former President of Liberia, who had been indicted in March 2003 on 17 counts (subsequently reduced to 11) of crimes against humanity and violations of international law, relating to his 'acts or omissions' in relation to the activities of the rebel forces of the Sierra Leone Revolutionary United Front. Taylor, who had been arrested in Nigeria and transferred to the Special Court in March 2006, was taken to the ICC's detention centre in The Hague, the Netherlands, in June of that year. Taylor's trial commenced in June 2007. It was adjourned shortly afterwards and reconvened in January 2008. In February 2009 the Prosecution formally closed its case. The Defence case was conducted during July 2009–March 2011. In late April 2012 Taylor was found guilty of aiding and abetting the crimes on which he had been indicted, while acquitted of bearing criminal responsibility and 'joint enterprise' in the commission of the crimes; he was sentenced, in May, to 50 years' imprisonment. Taylor was the first former head of state to be found guilty of charges relating to war crimes by an international court. In June formal notice was filed with the Court of Taylor's intention to appeal the verdict.

President of the Court: SHIREEN AVIS FISHER (USA).

Chief Prosecutor: BRENDA HOLLIS (USA).

Registrar: BINTA MANSARAY (Sierra Leone).

AFRICAN DEVELOPMENT BANK—AfDB

Address: Statutory Headquarters: rue Joseph Anoma, 01 BP 1387, Abidjan 01, Côte d'Ivoire.

Telephone: 20-20-44-44; **fax:** 20-20-49-59; **e-mail:** afdb@afdb.org; **internet:** www.afdb.org.

Address: Temporary Relocation Agency: 15 ave du Ghana, angle des rues Pierre de Coubertin et Hedi Nouira, BP 323, 1002 Tunis Belvédère, Tunisia.

Telephone: (71) 103-900; **fax:** (71) 351-933.

Established in 1964, the Bank began operations in July 1966, with the aim of financing economic and social development in African countries. The Bank's headquarters are officially based in Abidjan, Côte d'Ivoire. Since February 2003, however, in view of ongoing insecurity in Côte d'Ivoire, the Bank's operations have been conducted, on a long-term temporary basis, from Tunis, Tunisia.

AFRICAN MEMBERS

Algeria
Angola
Benin
Botswana
Burkina Faso
Burundi
Cameroon
Cape Verde
Central African Republic
Chad
Comoros
Congo, Democratic Republic
Congo, Republic
Côte d'Ivoire
Djibouti
Egypt
Equatorial Guinea
Eritrea
Ethiopia
Gabon
The Gambia
Ghana
Guinea
Guinea-Bissau
Kenya
Lesotho
Liberia
Libya
Madagascar
Malawi
Mali
Mauritania
Mauritius
Morocco
Mozambique
Namibia
Niger
Namibia
Rwanda
São Tomé and Príncipe
Senegal
Seychelles
Sierra Leone
Somalia
South Africa
South Sudan
Sudan
Swaziland
Tanzania
Togo
Tunisia
Uganda
Zambia
Zimbabwe

There are also 24 non-African members.

Organization

(September 2012)

BOARD OF GOVERNORS

The highest policy-making body of the Bank, which also elects the Board of Directors and the President. Each member country nominates one Governor, usually its Minister of Finance and Economic Affairs, and an alternate Governor or the Governor of its Central Bank. The Board meets once a year. The 2012 meeting was convened in Arusha, Tanzania, in May–June.

BOARD OF DIRECTORS

The Board, elected by the Board of Governors for a term of three years, is responsible for the general operations of the Bank and meets on a weekly basis. The Board has 20 members.

OFFICERS

The President is responsible for the organization and the day-to-day operations of the Bank under guidance of the Board of Directors. The President is elected for a five-year term and serves as the Chairperson of the Board of Directors. The President oversees the following senior management: Chief Economist; Vice-Presidents of Finance, Corporate Services, Country and Regional Programmes and Policy, Sector Operations, and Infrastructure, Private Sector and Regional Integration; Auditor General; General Counsel; Secretary-General; and Ombudsman. Bank field offices are located in around 30 member countries under a strategy of decentralization. In January 2011 a Permanent Committee on the Review and Implementation of the Decentralization was established. In accordance with a Roadmap on Decentralization, adopted by the Board of Directors in April 2011, and covering the period 2011–16, greater responsibility for portfolio management was to be transferred to the Bank's field offices; the Bank's presence in Fragile States was to be enhanced, through the extension of the field office network to Burundi, Central African Republic, Liberia (which was inaugurated in September 2012), South Sudan and Togo; and five regional resource centres were to be established with the aim of consolidating regional capacity. The Bank also plans to establish three external representation offices: for the Americas, to be based in Washington, DC, USA (by the end of 2012); for Asia, to be based in Tokyo, Japan (also 2012); and for Europe, to be based in Brussels, Belgium (from 2013).

Executive President and Chairperson of Board of Directors: DONALD KABERUKA (Rwanda).

FINANCIAL STRUCTURE

The African Development Bank (AfDB) Group of development financing institutions comprises the African Development Fund (ADF) and the Nigeria Trust Fund (NTF), which provide concessionary loans, and the AfDB itself. The Group uses a unit of account (UA), which, at December 2011, was valued at US $1.53257.

The capital stock of the Bank was at first exclusively open for subscription by African countries, with each member's subscription consisting of an equal number of paid-up and callable shares. In 1978, however, the Governors agreed to open the capital stock of the Bank to subscription by non-regional states on the basis of nine principles aimed at maintaining the African character of the institution. The decision was finally ratified in May 1982, and the participation of non-regional countries became effective on 30 December. It was agreed that African members should still hold two-thirds of the share capital, that all loan operations should be restricted to African members, and that the Bank's President should always be a national of an African state. In May 1998 the Board of Governors approved an increase in capital of 35%, and resolved that the non-African members' share of the capital be increased from 33.3% to 40%. In May 2010 the Board of Governors approved a general capital increase of 200%. At 31 December 2011 the Bank's authorized capital was UA 66,054.5m. (compared with UA 67,687.5m. at the end of 2010); subscribed capital at the end of 2011 was UA 37,322.0m. (of which the paid-up portion was UA 3,289.1m.)

Activities

At the end of 2011 the Bank Group had approved total lending of UA 67,949m. since the beginning of its operations in 1967. In 2011 the Group approved 184 lending operations amounting to UA 5,720.3m., compared with UA 4,099.8m. in the previous year. Of the total amount approved in 2011 UA 4,128.0m. was for loans and grants, UA 1,350.9m. for heavily indebted poor countries (HIPC) debt relief, UA 53.4m. for equity participation and UA 188.1m. for special funds. Of the total loans and grants approved in 2011, UA 1,572.3m. (38%) was for infrastructure projects (of which UA 1,005.4m. was for transportation); UA 853.2m. (21%) was for multisector projects; and UA 802.3m. (19%) for projects in the finance sector. Some 24% of Bank Group loan and grant approvals in 2011 were allocated to countries in West Africa, 21.9% to North Africa, 14.8% to East Africa, 11% to Central Africa, and 9.8% to Southern Africa.

In 2006 the Bank established a High Level Panel of eminent personalities to advise on the Bank's future strategic vision. The Panel issued its report, 'Investing in Africa's future—The AfDB in the 21st Century', in February 2008. In May the Bank's President announced that the new medium-term strategy for 2008–12 was to focus on the achievement of the Millennium Development Goals (MDGs) and on shared and sustainable economic growth. It envisaged a significant increase in Bank operations and in its institutional capacity. A Roadmap on Development Effectiveness was approved by the Board in March 2011, focusing on areas deemed most likely to bring about transformational change, including strengthening transparency and accountability; and accelerating decentralization. In mid-2008 the Bank established an African Food Crisis Response initiative to extend accelerated support to members affected by the sharp increase in the cost of food and food production. The initiative aimed to reduce short-term food poverty and malnutrition, with funds of some UA 472.0m., and to support long-term sustainable food security, with funding of UA 1,400m. In February 2009 the Bank hosted a meeting of the heads of multilateral development banks and of the IMF to discuss recent economic developments, the responses of each institution and future courses of action. In March the Bank's Board of Directors endorsed four new initiatives to help to counter the effects of the crisis: the establishment of an Emergency Liquidity Facility, with funds of some US $1,500m., to assist members with short-term financing difficulties; a new Trade Finance Initiative, with funds of up to $1,000m., to provide credit for trade financing operations; a Framework for the Accelerated Resource Transfer of ADF Resources; and enhanced policy advisory support. The Bank also agreed to contribute $500m. to a multinational Global Trade Liquidity Program, which commenced operations in mid-2009. In September the Bank initiated a consultative process for a sixth general capital increase. An increase of 200% was endorsed by a committee of the governing body representing the Bank's shareholders, meeting in April 2010, in order to enable the Bank to sustain its increased level of lending. The capital increase was formally approved by the Board of Governors in May.

In November 2008 the Bank hosted a special conference of African ministers of finance and central bank governors to consider the impact on the region of the contraction of the world's major economies and the recent volatility of global financial markets. The meeting determined to establish a Committee of African Finance Ministers and Central Bank Governors, comprising 10 representatives from each Bank region, with a mandate to examine further the impact of the global financial crisis on Africa, to review the responses by member governments, and to develop policy options. The so-called Committee of Ten (C10) convened for its inaugural meeting in Cape Town, South Africa, in January 2009. In March the C10 adopted a paper outlining the major concerns of African countries in preparation for the meeting of heads of state of the Group of 20 (G20) leading economies, held in London, United Kingdom, in early April. The third meeting of the Committee, held in Abuja, Nigeria, in July, reviewed economic indicators and developments since the G20 meeting and appealed for all commitments to low-income countries pledged at the summit to be met. The Committee also issued a series of messages for the next G20 summit meeting, held in Pittsburgh, USA, in September, including a request for greater African participation in the G20 process and in international economic governance. The fourth meeting of the C10, convened in February 2010, determined that it should meet formally two times a year, with other informal meetings and meetings of deputies to be held in between; the Secretariat of the Committee was to be provided by the AfDB.

In May 2011 the Group of Eight (G8) industrialized nations, in collaboration with regional and international financial institutions and the governments of Egypt and Tunisia, established a Deauville Partnership to support political and economic reforms being undertaken by several countries in North Africa and the Middle East, notably Egypt, Jordan, Morocco and Tunisia. The AfDB supported the establishment of the Partnership and was to chair a Co-ordination Platform. In September Kuwait, Qatar, Saudi Arabia, Turkey and the UAE joined the Partnership.

Since 1996 the Bank has collaborated closely with international partners, in particular the World Bank, in efforts to address the problems of HIPCs (see IBRD). Of the 41 countries identified as potentially eligible for assistance under the scheme, 33 were in sub-Saharan Africa. Following the introduction of an enhanced framework for the initiative, the Bank has been actively involved in the preparation of Poverty Reduction Strategy Papers, that provide national frameworks for poverty reduction programmes. In April 2006 the Board of Directors endorsed a new Multilateral Debt Relief Initiative (MDRI), which provided for 100% cancellation of eligible debts from the ADF, the IMF and the International Development Association to secure additional resources for countries to help them attain their MDGs. ADF's participation in the MDRI, which became effective in September, was anticipated to provide some UA 5,570m. (US $8,540m.) in debt relief.

The Bank contributed funds for the establishment, in 1986, of the Africa Project Development Facility, which assists the private sector in Africa by providing advisory services and finance for entrepreneurs: it was managed by the International Finance Corporation (IFC), until replaced by the Private Enterprise Partnership for Africa in April 2005. In 1989 the Bank, in co-ordination with IFC and the UN Development Programme (UNDP), created the African Management Services Company (AMSCo), which provides management support and training to private companies in Africa. The Bank is one of three multilateral donors, with the World Bank and UNDP, supporting the African Capacity Building Foundation, which was established in 1991 to strengthen and develop institutional and human capacity in support of sustainable development activities. The Bank hosts the secretariat of an Africa Investment Consortium, which was inaugurated in October 2005 by several major African institutions and donor countries to accelerate efforts to develop the region's infrastructure. An Enhanced Private Sector Assistance Initiative was established, with support from the Japanese Government, in 2005 to support the Bank's strategy for the development of the private sector. The Initiative incorporated an Accelerated Cofinancing Facility for Africa and a Fund for African Private Sector Assistance. In October 2010 the Board of Directors agreed to convert the Fund into a multi-donor trust fund.

In November 2006 the Bank Group, with the UN Economic Commission for Africa (ECA), organized an African Economic Conference (AEC), which has since become an annual event. The sixth AEC was held in Addis Ababa, Ethiopia, in October 2011, on the theme 'Green Economy and Structural Transformation in Africa', and the seventh was to be convened in October–November 2012 in Kigali, Rwanda. In September 2011 the Bank organized a regional meeting on peace-building and state-building in Africa, in preparation for the Fourth High Level Forum on Aid Effectiveness, which was held in Busan, Republic of Korea, in November–December.

In March 2000 African ministers of water resources endorsed an African Water Vision and a Framework for Action to pursue the equitable and sustainable use and management of water resources in Africa in order to facilitate socio-economic development, poverty alleviation and environmental protection. An African Ministers' Council on Water (AMCOW) was established in April 2002 to provide the political leadership and focus for implementation of the Vision and the Framework for Action. AMCOW requested the Bank to establish and administer an African Water Facility Special Fund, in order to provide the financial requirements for achieving their objectives; this became operational in December. In March the Bank approved a Rural Water Supply and Sanitation Initiative to accelerate access in member countries to sustainable safe water and basic sanitation, in order to meet the requirements of several MDGs. In March 2008 the Bank hosted the first African Water Week, organized jointly with AMCOW, on the theme of 'Accelerating Water Security for the Socio-economic Development of Africa'. The Bank co-ordinated and led Africa's regional participation in the Sixth World Water Forum, which was held in Marseilles, France, in March 2012. The Bank was actively involved in preparing for the fourth Africa Carbon Forum, which was convened in Addis Ababa, Ethiopia, in April 2012 (previous fora having been held in September 2008, March 2010 and July 2011).

The Bank hosts the secretariat of the Congo Basin Forest Fund, which was established in June 2008, as a multi-donor facility, with initial funding from Norway and the United Kingdom, to protect and manage the forests in that region.

Through the Migration and Development Trust Fund, launched in 2009, the Bank supports the development of financial services for migrant workers, and facilitates channelling remittances towards productive uses in workers' countries of origin.

The Bank provides technical assistance to regional member countries in the form of experts' services, pre-investment feasibility studies, and staff training. Much of this assistance is financed through bilateral trust funds contributed by non-African member states. The Bank's African Development Institute provides training for officials of regional member countries in order to enhance the management of Bank-financed projects and, more broadly, to strengthen national capacities for promoting sustainable development. The Institute also manages an AfDB/Japan Fellowship programme that provides scholarships to African students to pursue further education. A Joint Africa Institute, established jointly by the Bank, the World Bank and the IMF, was operational from November 1999–end-2009, offering training opportunities and strengthening capacity building. In 1990 the Bank established the African Business Round Table (ABR), which is composed of the chief executives of Africa's leading corporations. The ABR aims to strengthen Africa's private sector, promote intra-African trade and investment, and attract foreign investment to Africa. The ABR is chaired by the Bank's Executive President. In 2008 the Bank endorsed a Governance Strategic Directions and Action Plan as a framework for countering corruption and enhancing democratic governance in Africa in the period 2008–12.

In 1990 a Memorandum of Understanding (MOU) for the Reinforcement of Co-operation between the Organization of African Unity, now African Union (AU), the UN Economic Commission for Africa and the AfDB was signed by the three organizations. A joint secretariat supports co-operation activities between the organizations. In March 2009 a new Coalition for Dialogue on Africa (CoDA) was inaugurated by the Bank, the ECA and the AU. In 1999 a Co-operation Agreement was formally concluded between the Bank and the Common Market for Eastern and Southern Africa (COMESA). In March 2000 the Bank signed an MOU on its strategic partnership with the World Bank. Other MOUs were signed during that year with the United Nations Industrial Development Organization, the World Food Programme, and the Arab Maghreb Union. In September 2008 the Bank supported the establishment of an African Financing Partnership, which aimed to mobilize private sector resources through partnerships with regional development finance institutions. The Bank hosts the secretariat of the Partnership. It also hosts the secretariat of the Making Finance Work for Africa Partnership, which was established, by the G8, in October 2007, in order to support the development of the financial sector in the sub-Saharan region. In December 2010 the Bank signed an MOU with the Islamic Development Bank to promote economic development in common member countries through co-financing and co-ordinating projects in priority areas. It signed an MOU with the European Bank for Reconstruction and Development (EBRD) in September 2011. The Bank is actively involved in the New Partnership for Africa's Development (NEPAD), established in 2001 to promote sustainable development and eradicate poverty throughout the region. Since 2004 it has been a strategic partner in NEPAD's African Peer Review Mechanism. In 2011 the Bank supported the development of a Program for Infrastructure Development in Africa (PIDA), as a joint initiative with NEPAD and the AU.

AFRICAN DEVELOPMENT BANK

The Bank makes loans at a variable rate of interest, which is adjusted twice a year, plus a commitment fee of 0.75%. Lending approved amounted to UA 3,689.4m. for 59 operations in 2011, including resources allocated under the HIPC debt relief initiative, the Post-conflict Country Facility (see below), and equity participations, compared with UA 2,581.1m., again for 59 operations, in the previous year. Lending for private sector projects amounted to UA 868.9m. in 2011. Since October 1997 new fixed and floating rate loans have been made available.

AFRICAN DEVELOPMENT FUND

The ADF commenced operations in 1974. It grants interest-free loans to low-income African countries for projects with repayment over 50 years (including a 10-year grace period) and with a service charge of 0.75% per annum. Grants for project feasibility studies are made to the poorest countries.

In May 1994 donor countries withheld any new funds owing to dissatisfaction with the Bank's governance. In May 1996, following the implementation of various institutional reforms to strengthen the Bank's financial management and decision-making capabilities and to reduce its administrative costs, an agreement was concluded on the seventh replenishment of ADF resources. In December 2004 donor countries pledged some US $5,400m. for the 10th replenishment of the ADF covering the three-year period 2005–07; it was agreed that poverty reduction and the promotion of sustainable growth would remain the principal objectives of the Fund under ADF-10. In December 2007 donor countries committed $8,900m. to replenish the Fund for the period 2008–10 (ADF-11), during which there was to be a focus on infrastructure, governance and regional integration. The funding arrangements for ADF-11 allocated UA 408m. to a new Fragile States Facility to support the poorer regional member countries, in particular those in a post-conflict or transitional state. The Facility was to incorporate the Post-Conflict Country Facility, which was established in 2003 to help certain countries to clear their arrears and accelerate their progress within the HIPC process. An agreement was concluded by donors in October 2010 to increase contributions to the Fund by 10.6%, to some $9,350m., under ADF-12, covering the period 2011–13. ADF-12 was to support ongoing institutional reform and capacity building, as well as efforts to stimulate economic growth in Africa's lowest income countries. Operational priorities included climate change adaptation and mitigation measures, regional economic integration, and private sector development.

In 2011 lending under the ADF amounted to UA 1,831.9m. for 87 projects, compared with UA 1,456.7m. for 65 projects in the previous year.

NIGERIA TRUST FUND

The Agreement establishing the NTF was signed in February 1976 by the Bank and the Government of Nigeria. The Fund is administered by the Bank and its loans are granted for up to 25 years, including grace periods of up to five years, and carry 0.75% commission charges and 4% interest charges. The loans are intended to provide financing for projects in co-operation with other lending institutions. The Fund also aims to promote the private sector and trade between African countries by providing information on African and international financial institutions able to finance African trade.

Operations under the NTF were suspended in 2006, pending a detailed assessment and consideration of the Fund's activities which commenced in November. The evaluation exercise was concluded in July 2007 and an agreement was reached in November to authorize the Fund to continue activities for a further 10-year period. Three operations, amounting to UA 10.9m., were approved in 2011.

Publications

Annual Report.
Annual Development Effectiveness Review.
AfDB Business Bulletin (10 a year).
AfDB Statistics Pocketbook.
AfDB Today (every 2 months).
African Competitiveness Report.
African Development Report (annually).
African Development Review (3 a year).
African Economic Outlook (annually, with OECD).
African Statistical Journal (2 a year).
Annual Procurement Report.
Economic Research Papers.
Gender, Poverty and Environmental Indicators on African Countries (annually).
OPEV Sharing (quarterly newsletter).
Quarterly Operational Summary.
Selected Statistics on African Countries (annually).
Summaries of operations and projects, background documents, Board documents.

Statistics

SUMMARY OF BANK GROUP OPERATIONS
(millions of UA)

	2010	2011	Cumulative total*
AfDB approvals†			
Number	59	59	1,318
Amount	2,581.13	3,689.43	36,008.07
Disbursements	1,339.85	1868.79	20,541.59
ADF approvals†			
Number	65	87	2,474
Amount	1,456.72	1,831.86	25,540.06
Disbursements	1,165.84	1,296.65	16,098.51
NTF approvals			
Number	2	3	85
Amount	29.53	10.88	382.21
Disbursements	5.02	8.67	235.74
Special Funds‡			
Number	13	35	108
Amount approved	32.38	188.12	329.23
Group total†			
Number	139	184	3,985
Amount approved	4,099.75	5,720.29	67,949.00
Disbursements	2,510.70	3,174.11	38,744.62

* Since the initial operations of the three institutions (1967 for AfDB, 1974 for ADF and 1976 for NTF).

† Approvals include loans and grant operations, private and public equity investments, emergency operations, HIPC debt relief, loan reallocations and guarantees, the Post-Conflict Country Facility and the Fragile States Facility.

‡ Includes the African Water Fund, the Rural Water Supply and Sanitation Initiative, the Global Environment Facility, the Congo Basin Forest Fund, the Fund for African Private Sector Assistance, and the Migration and Development Trust Fund.

BANK GROUP APPROVALS BY SECTOR, 2011

Sector	Number of projects	Amount (millions of UA)
Agriculture and rural development	11	145.6
Social	27	451.3
Education	6	39.0
Health	2	56.0
Other	19	356.3
Infrastructure	36	1,572.3
Water supply and sanitation	5	139.1
Energy supply	12	420.1
Communication	1	7.6
Transportation	18	1,005.4
Finance	11	802.3
Multisector	47	853.2
Industry, mining and quarrying	2	293.7
Environment	1	9.6
Total (loans and grants)	135	4,128.0
HIPC debt relief	7	1,350.9
Equity participations	7	53.4
Special funds	35	188.1
Other approvals	49	1,592.6
Total approvals	184	5,720.3

Source: African Development Bank, *Annual Report 2011*.

AFRICAN UNION—AU

Address: Roosevelt St, Old Airport Area, POB 3243, Addis Ababa, Ethiopia.

Telephone: (11) 5517700; **fax:** (11) 5517844; **e-mail:** webmaster@africa-union.org; **internet:** au.int.

In May 2001 the Constitutive Act of the African Union entered into force. In July 2002 the African Union (AU) became fully operational, replacing the Organization of African Unity (OAU), which had been founded in 1963. The AU aims to support unity, solidarity and peace among African states; to promote and defend African common positions on issues of shared interest; to encourage human rights, democratic principles and good governance; to advance the development of member states by encouraging research and by working to eradicate preventable diseases; and to promote sustainable development and political and socio-economic integration, including co-ordinating and harmonizing policy between the continent's various 'regional economic communities' (see below).

MEMBERS*

Algeria	Eritrea	Nigeria
Angola	Ethiopia	Rwanda
Benin	Gabon	São Tomé and Príncipe
Botswana	The Gambia	Senegal
Burkina Faso	Ghana	Seychelles
Burundi	Guinea	Sierra Leone
Cameroon	Guinea-Bissau	Somalia
Cape Verde	Kenya	South Africa
Central African Republic	Lesotho	South Sudan‡
Chad	Liberia	Sudan
Comoros	Libya	Swaziland
Congo, Democratic Republic	Madagascar†	Tanazania
Congo, Republic	Malawi	Togo
Côte d'Ivoire	Mali†	Tunisia
Dijbouti	Mauritania†	Uganda
Egypt	Mauritius	Zambia
Equatorial Guinea	Mozambique	Zimbabwe
	Namibia	
	Niger	

* The Sahrawi Arab Democratic Republic (SADR–Western Sahara) was admitted to the OAU in February 1982, following recognition by more than one-half of the member states, but its membership was disputed by Morocco and other states which claimed that a two-thirds' majority was needed to admit a state whose existence was in question. Morocco withdrew from the OAU with effect from November 1985, and has not applied to join the AU. The SADR ratified the Constitutive Act in December 2000 and is a full member of the AU.

† Mauritania's participation in the activities of the AU was suspended in August 2008, following the overthrow of its constitutional Government in a military coup d'état. In March 2009 Madagascar's participation in the activities of the AU was suspended, following the forced resignation of its elected President and transfer of power to the military. Mali was suspended from AU participation after the overthrow of that country's Government by a military coup in March 2012, and, in April, Guinea-Bissau was also suspended following a military coup, pending the restoration of constitutional order.

‡ South Sudan (which became independent on 9 July 2011) was admitted as a member of the AU in August 2011.

Note: The Constitutive Act stipulates that member states in which Governments accede to power by unconstitutional means are liable to suspension from participating in the Union's activities and to the imposition of sanctions by the Union.

Organization

(September 2012)

ASSEMBLY

The Assembly, comprising member countries' heads of state and government, is the supreme organ of the Union and meets at least once a year (with alternate sessions held in Addis Ababa, Ethiopia) to determine and monitor the Union's priorities and common policies and to adopt its annual work programme. Resolutions are passed by a two-thirds' majority, procedural matters by a simple majority. Extraordinary sessions may be convened at the request of a member state and on approval by a two-thirds' majority. A chairperson is elected at each meeting from among the members, to hold office for one year. The Assembly ensures compliance by member states with decisions of the Union, adopts the biennial budget, appoints judges of the African Court of Human and Peoples' Rights, and hears and settles disputes between member states. The first regular Assembly meeting was held in Durban, South Africa, in July 2002, and a first extraordinary summit meeting of the Assembly was convened in Addis Ababa in February 2003. The 19th ordinary session of the Assembly took place in Addis Ababa, in July 2012, on the theme 'Boosting Intra-African Trade'. The location of the 19th session was to have been Lilongwe, Malawi, but was moved, owing to the Malawi Government's refusal to host President al-Bashir of Sudan, who had been indicted by the International Criminal Court on genocide charges.

Chairperson: (2012/13) Yayi Boni (Pres. of Benin).

EXECUTIVE COUNCIL

Consists of ministers of foreign affairs and others and meets at least twice a year (in February and July), with provision for extraordinary sessions. The Council's Chairperson is the minister of foreign affairs (or another competent authority) of the country that has provided the Chairperson of the Assembly. Prepares meetings of, and is responsible to, the Assembly. Determines the issues to be submitted to the Assembly for decision, co-ordinates and harmonizes the policies, activities and initiatives of the Union in areas of common interest to member states, and monitors the implementation of policies and decisions of the Assembly.

PERMANENT REPRESENTATIVES COMMITTEE

The Committee, which comprises Ambassadors accredited to the AU and meets at least once a month. It is responsible to the Executive Council, which it advises, and whose meetings, including matters for the agenda and draft decisions, it prepares.

COMMISSION

The Commission is the permanent secretariat of the organization. It comprises a Chairperson (elected for a four-year term of office by the Assembly), Deputy Chairperson and eight Commissioners (responsible for: peace and security; political affairs; infrastructure and energy; social affairs; human resources, science and technology; trade and industry; rural economy and agriculture; and economic affairs) who are elected on the basis of equal geographical distribution. Members of the Commission serve a term of four years and may stand for re-election for one further term of office. Further support staff assist the smooth functioning of the Commission. The Commission represents the Union under the guidance of, and as mandated by, the Assembly and the Executive Council, and reports to the Executive Council. It deals with administrative issues, implements the decisions of the Union, and acts as the custodian of the Constitutive Act and Protocols, and other agreements. Its work covers the following domains: control of pandemics; disaster management; international crime and terrorism; environmental management; negotiations relating to external trade; negotiations relating to external debt; population, migration, refugees and displaced persons; food security; socio-economic integration; and all other areas where a common position has been established by Union member states. It has responsibility for the co-ordination of AU activities and meetings.

Chairperson: Dr Nkosazana Dlamini-Zuma (South Africa) (from 16 Oct. 2012).

SPECIALIZED TECHNICAL COMMITTEES

There are specialized committees for monetary and financial affairs; rural economy and agricultural matters; trade, customs and immigration matters; industry, science and technology, energy, natural resources and environment; infrastructure; transport, communications and tourism; health, labour and social affairs; and education, culture and human resources. These have responsibility for implementing the Union's programmes and projects.

PAN-AFRICAN PARLIAMENT

The Pan-African Parliament comprises five deputies (including at least one woman) from each AU member state, presided over by an elected President assisted by four Vice-Presidents. The President and Vice-Presidents must equitably represent the central, northern, eastern, southern and western African states. The Parliament convenes at least twice a year; an extraordinary session may be called by a two-thirds' majority of the members. The Parliament currently has only advisory and consultative powers. Its eventual evolution into an institution with full legislative authority is planned. The Parliament is headquartered at Midrand, South Africa.

President: Bethel Nnaemeka Amadi (Nigeria).

AFRICAN COURT OF JUSTICE AND HUMAN RIGHTS

An African Court of Human and Peoples' Rights (ACHPR) was created following the entry into force in January 2004 of the Protocol to the African Charter on Human and Peoples' Rights Establishing the ACHPR (adopted in June 1998). In February 2009 a protocol (adopted in July 2003) establishing an African Court of Justice entered into force. The Protocol on the Statute of the African Court of Justice and Human Rights, aimed at merging the ACHPR and the African Court of Justice, was opened for signature in July 2008, and had, by September 2012, been ratified by three states.

PEACE AND SECURITY COUNCIL

The Protocol to the Constitutive Act of the African Union Relating to the Peace and Security Council of the African Union entered into force on 26 December 2003; the 15-member elected Council was formally inaugurated in May 2004. It acts as a decision-making body for the prevention, management and resolution of conflicts.

ECONOMIC, SOCIAL AND CULTURAL COUNCIL

The Economic, Social and Cultural Council (ECOSOCC), inaugurated in March 2005, was to have an advisory function and to comprise representatives of civic, professional and cultural bodies at national, regional and diaspora levels. Its main organs were to be: an elected General Assembly; Standing Committee; Credential Committee; and Sectoral Cluster Communities. It is envisaged that the Council will strengthen the partnership between member governments and African civil society. The General Assembly. was inaugurated in September 2008. The Sectoral Cluster Communities were to be established to formulate opinions and influence AU decision-making in the following 10 areas: peace and security; political affairs; infrastructure and energy; social affairs and health; human resources, science and technology; trade and industry; rural economy and agriculture; economic affairs; women and gender; and cross-cutting programmes.

NEW PARTNERSHIP FOR AFRICA'S DEVELOPMENT (NEPAD)

NEPAD Planning and Co-ordination Agency (NPCA): POB 1234, Halfway House, Midrand, 1685 South Africa; tel. (11) 256-3600; fax (11) 206-3762; e-mail media@nepad.org; internet www.nepad.org; f. Feb. 2010, as a technical body of the AU, to replace the former NEPAD Secretariat, with the aim of improving the country-level implementation of projects; NEPAD was launched in 2001 as a long-term strategy to promote socio-economic development in Africa; adopted Declaration on Democracy, Political, Economic and Corporate Governance and the African Peer Review Mechanism in June 2002; the July 2003 AU Maputo summit decided that NEPAD should be integrated into AU structures and processes; a special 'Brainstorming on NEPAD' summit, held in Algiers, Algeria in March 2007, issued a 13-point communiqué on the means of reforming the Partnership; a further Review Summit on NEPAD, convened in Dakar, Senegal, in April 2008, reaffirmed the centrality of NEPAD as the overarching developmental programme for Africa; the UN allocated US $12.6m. in support of NEPAD under its 2012–13 budget; CEO Dr Ibrahim Assane Mayaki.

PROPOSED INSTITUTIONS

In 2012 three financial institutions, for managing the financing of programmes and projects, remained to be established: an African Central Bank; an African Monetary Fund; and an African Investment Bank.

Activities

From the 1950s various attempts were made to establish an inter-African organization. In November 1958 Ghana and Guinea (later joined by Mali) drafted a Charter that was to form the basis of a Union of African States. In January 1961 a conference was held at Casablanca, Morocco, attended by the heads of state of Ghana, Guinea, Mali, Morocco, and representatives of Libya and of the provisional government of the Algerian Republic (GPRA). Tunisia, Nigeria, Liberia and Togo declined the invitation to attend. An African Charter was adopted and it was decided to institute an African Military Command and an African Common Market. Between October 1960 and March 1961 three conferences were held by French-speaking African countries: at Abidjan, Côte d'Ivoire; Brazzaville, Republic of the Congo (ex-French); and Yaoundé, Cameroon. None of the 12 countries that attended these meetings had been present at the Casablanca Conference. These conferences led to the signing, in September 1961, at Tananarive, Madagascar, of a charter establishing the Union africaine et malgache, later the Organisation commune africaine et mauricienne (OCAM). In May 1961 a conference was held at Monrovia, Liberia, attended by the heads of state or representatives of 19 countries: Cameroon, Central African Republic, Chad, Congo Republic (ex-French), Côte d'Ivoire, Dahomey, Ethiopia, Gabon, Liberia, Madagascar, Mauritania, Niger, Nigeria, Senegal, Sierra Leone, Somalia, Togo, Tunisia and Upper Volta. Meeting again (with the exception of Tunisia and with the addition of the ex-Belgian Congo Republic) in January 1962 at Lagos, Nigeria, they established a permanent secretariat and a standing committee of ministers of finance, and accepted a draft charter for an Organization of Inter-African and Malagasy States.

It was the Conference of Addis Ababa, convened in 1963, which finally brought together African states despite the regional, political and linguistic differences that divided them. The ministers of foreign affairs of 32 African states attended the Preparatory Meeting held in mid-May: Algeria, Burundi, Cameroon, Central African Republic, Chad, Congo (Brazzaville—now Republic of the Congo), Congo (Léopoldville—now Democratic Republic of the Congo, DRC), Côte d'Ivoire, Dahomey (now Benin), Ethiopia, Gabon, Ghana, Guinea, Liberia, Libya, Madagascar, Mali, Mauritania, Morocco, Niger, Nigeria, Rwanda, Senegal, Sierra Leone, Somalia, Sudan, Tanganyika (now Tanzania), Togo, Tunisia, Uganda, the United Arab Republic (Egypt) and Upper Volta (now Burkina Faso). The topics discussed by the meeting were: (i) the creation of an Organization of African States; (ii) co-operation among African states in the following fields: economic and social; education, culture and science; collective defence; (iii) decolonization; (iv) apartheid and racial discrimination; (v) the effects of economic grouping on the economic development of Africa; (vi) disarmament; (vii) the creation of a Permanent Conciliation Commission; and (viii) Africa and the United Nations. The Heads of State Conference that opened on 23 May 1963 drew up the Charter of the Organization of African Unity, which was then signed by the heads of 30 states on 25 May. The Charter was essentially functional and reflected a compromise between the concept of a loose association of states favoured by the Monrovia Group and the federal idea supported by the Casablanca Group, in particular by Ghana. In May 1994 the Abuja Treaty Establishing the African Economic Community (AEC, signed in June 1991) entered into force.

An extraordinary summit meeting, convened in September 1999, in Sirte, Libya, at the request of the then Libyan leader Col al-Qaddafi, determined to establish an African Union, based on the principles and objectives of the OAU and AEC, but furthering African co-operation, development and integration. Heads of state declared their commitment to accelerating the establishment of regional institutions, including a pan-African parliament, a court of human and peoples' rights and a central bank, as well as the implementation of economic and monetary union, as provided for by the Abuja Treaty Establishing the AEC. In July 2000 at the annual OAU summit meeting, held at Lomé, Togo, 27 heads of state and government signed the draft Constitutive Act of the African Union, which was to enter into force one month after ratification by two-thirds of member states' legislatures; this was achieved on 26 May 2001. The Union was inaugurated, replacing the OAU, on 9 July 2002, at a summit meeting of heads of state and government held in Durban, South Africa, after a transitional period of one year had elapsed since the endorsement of the Act in July 2001. During the transitional year, pending the transfer of all assets and liabilities to the Union, the OAU Charter remained in effect. A review of all OAU treaties was implemented, and those deemed relevant were retained by the AU. The four key organs of the AU were launched in July 2002. Morocco is the only African country that is not a member of the AU. The AU aims to strengthen and advance the process of African political and socio-economic integration initiated by the OAU. The Union operates on the basis of both the Constitutive Act and the Abuja Treaty.

The AU has the following areas of interest: peace and security; political affairs; infrastructure and energy; social affairs; human resources, science and technology; trade and industry; rural economy and agriculture; and economic affairs. In July 2001 the OAU adopted a New African Initiative, which was subsequently renamed the New Partnership for Africa's Development (NEPAD). NEPAD, which was officially launched in October, represents a long-term strategy for socio-economic recovery in Africa and aims to promote the strengthening of democracy and economic management in the region. The heads of state of Algeria, Egypt, Nigeria, Senegal and South Africa played leading roles in its preparation and management. In June 2002 NEPAD heads of state and government adopted a Declaration on Democracy, Political, Economic and Corporate Governance and announced the development of an African Peer Review Mechanism (APRM—whose secretariat was to be hosted by the UN Economic Commission for Africa). Meeting during that month the Group of Seven industrialized nations and Russia (the G8) welcomed the formation of NEPAD and adopted an Africa Action Plan in support of the initiative. The inaugural summit of the AU Assembly, held in Durban, South Africa, in July 2002, issued a Declaration on the Implementation of NEPAD, which urged all member states to adopt the Declaration on Democracy, Political, Economic and Corporate Governance and to participate in the peer review process. By 2012 some 15 nations had completed the APRM process. NEPAD focuses on the following sectoral priorities: infrastructure (covering information and communication technologies, energy, transport, water and sanitation); human resources development; agriculture; culture; science and technology; mobilizing resources; market access; and the environment. It implements action plans concerned with capacity building, the environment, and infrastructure. The summit meeting of the AU Assembly convened in Maputo, Mozambique, in July 2003 determined that NEPAD should be integrated into AU structures and processes. In March 2007 a special NEPAD summit held in Algiers, Algeria, issued a 13-point communiqué on the best means of achieving this objective without delay. The centrality of NEPAD as the overarching developmental programme for Africa was reaffirmed by a further summit meeting, convened in Dakar, Senegal, in April 2008, which also published a number of further key decisions aimed at guiding the future orientation of the Partnership. In February 2010 African leaders approved the establishment of the NEPAD Planning and Co-ordination Agency (NPCA), a technical body of the AU, to replace the former NEPAD Secretariat, with the aim of improving the implementation of projects at country level. The Chairperson of the African Union Commission (AUC) exercises supervisory authority over the NPCA. NEPAD's Programme for Infrastructure Development in Africa (PIDA), of which the African Development Bank is executing agency, aims to develop the continental energy, ICT, transport and transboundary water resources infrastructures. Some 80 programmes and projects aimed at regional integration, with a particular focus on developing the continental infrastructure, were being undertaken in the context of an AU/NEPAD African Action Plan (AAP) covering the period 2010–15.

The eighth AU Assembly, held in January 2007 in Cairo, Egypt, adopted a decision on the need for a 'Grand Debate on the Union Government', concerned with the possibility of establishing an AU Government as a precursor to the eventual creation of a United States of Africa. The ninth Assembly, convened in July 2007 in Accra, Ghana, adopted the Accra Declaration, in which AU heads of state and government expressed commitment to the formation of a Union Government of Africa and ultimate aim of creating a United States of Africa, and pledged, as a means to this end, to accelerate the economic and political integration of the African continent; to rationalize, strengthen and harmonize the activities of the regional economic communities; to conduct an immediate audit of the organs of the AU ('Audit of the Union'); and to establish a ministerial committee to examine the concept of the Union Government. A panel of eminent persons was subsequently established to conduct the proposed institutional Audit of the Union; the panel became operational at the beginning of September, and presented its review to the 10th Assembly, which was held in January–February 2008 in Addis Ababa. A committee comprising 10 heads of state was appointed to consider the findings detailed in the review.

In March 2005 the UN Secretary-General issued a report on the functioning of the United Nations which included a clause urging donor nations to focus particularly on the need for a 10-year plan for capacity-building within the AU. The UN System-wide Support to the AU and NEPAD was launched in 2006, following on from the UN System-wide Special Initiative on Africa, which had been undertaken over the decade 1996–2005.

In May 2012, with a view to increasing the involvement in the African development agenda of people of African origin living beyond the continent, the AU hosted the first Global African Diaspora Summit, in Midrand, South Africa.

PEACE AND SECURITY

The Protocol to the Constitutive Act of the African Union Relating to the Establishment of the Peace and Security Council, adopted by the inaugural AU summit of heads of state and government in July 2002, entered into force in December 2003, superseding the 1993 Cairo Declaration on the OAU Mechanism for Conflict Prevention, Management and Resolution. The Protocol provides for the development of a collective peace and security framework (known as the African Peace and Security Architecture—APSA). This includes a 15-country Peace and Security Council, operational at the levels of heads of state and government, ministers of foreign affairs, and permanent representatives, to be supported by a five-member advisory Panel of the Wise, a Continental Early Warning System, an African Standby Force (ASF) and a Peace Fund (superseding the OAU Peace Fund, which was established in June 1993). In March 2004 the Executive Council elected 15 member states to serve on the inaugural Peace and Security Council. The activities of the Peace and Security Council include the promotion of peace, security and stability; early warning and preventive diplomacy; peace-making mediation; peace support operations and intervention; peace-building activities and post-conflict reconstruction; and humanitarian action and disaster management. The Council was to implement the common defence policy of the Union, and to ensure the implementation of the 1999 OAU Convention on the Prevention and Combating of Terrorism (which provided for the exchange of information to help counter terrorism and for signatory states to refrain from granting asylum to terrorists). Member states were to set aside standby troop contingents for the planned ASF, which was to be mandated to undertake observation, monitoring and other peace-support missions; to deploy in member states as required to prevent the resurgence or escalation of violence; to intervene in member states as required to restore stability; to conduct post-conflict disarmament and demobilization and other peace-building activities; and to provide emergency humanitarian assistance. The Council was to harmonize and co-ordinate the activities of other regional security mechanisms. An extraordinary AU summit meeting, convened in Sirte, Libya, in February 2004, adopted a declaration approving the establishment of the multinational ASF, comprising five regional brigades—the Central African Multinational Force (FOMAC), the Eastern Africa Standby Force (EASF), the ECOWAS Standby Force (ESF), the North African Regional Capability (NARC), and the SADC Standby Brigade (SADCBRIG)—to be deployed in African-led peace support operations. A Policy Framework Document on the establishment of the ASF and the Military Staff Committee was approved by the third regular summit of AU heads of state, held in July 2004. It is envisaged that the ASF, which is composed of rapidly deployable multidimensional military, police and civilian capabilities, will become fully operational by 2015. In October 2010 the ASF conducted an exercise known as 'AMANI AFRICA', with pan-continental participation, in Addis Ababa, Ethiopia. A roadmap on achieving the full operationalization of the ASF was under development in 2012.

The extraordinary OAU summit meeting convened in Sirte, Libya, in September 1999 determined to hold a regular ministerial Conference on Security, Stability, Development and Co-operation in Africa (CSSDCA): the first CSSDCA took place in Abuja, Nigeria, in May 2000. The CSSDCA process provides a forum for the development of policies aimed at advancing the common values of the AU and AEC in the areas of peace, security and co-operation. In December 2000 OAU heads of state and government adopted the Bamako Declaration, concerned with arresting the circulation of small arms and light weapons (SALW) on the continent. It was envisaged that the Central African Convention for the Control of SALW, their Ammunition, Parts and Components that can be used for their Manufacture, Repair or Assembly (Kinshasa Convention), adopted by central African states in April 2010, would contribute to the AU's SALW control capacity. In September 2011 AU member states, met in Lomé, Togo, to debate a draft strategy on SALW control and to elaborate an African Common Position on an Arms Trade Treaty (ATT) in advance of the UN Conference on an ATT, which took place in July 2012. In May 2012 an African Regional Consultation on the ATT was organized at AU headquarters by the Regional Centre for Peace and Disarmament in Africa (UNREC, a subsidiary of the UN Office for Disarmament Affairs).

In May 2003 the AU, UNDP and UN Office for Project Services agreed a US $6.4m. project entitled 'Support for the Implementation of the Peace and Security Agenda of the African Union'. In June of that year a meeting of the G8 and NEPAD adopted a Joint Africa/G8 Plan to enhance African capabilities to undertake Peace Support Operations. Within the framework of the Plan, a consultation between the AU, the NEPAD Secretariat, the G8, the African regional economic communities, as well as the European Union (EU) and UN and other partners, was convened in Addis Ababa in April 2005. In September 2002 and October 2004 the AU organized high-level intergovernmental meetings on preventing and combating terrorism in Africa. An AU Special Representative on Protection of Civilians in Armed Conflict Situations in Africa was appointed in September 2004.

In January 2005 the AU Non-Aggression and Common Defence Pact was adopted to promote co-operation in developing a common defence policy and to encourage member states to foster an attitude of non-aggression. The Pact, which entered into force in December 2009, establishes measures aimed at preventing inter- and intra-state conflicts and arriving at peaceful resolutions to conflicts. It also sets out a framework defining, *inter alia,* the terms 'aggression' and 'intervention' and determining those situations in which intervention may be considered an acceptable course of action. As such, the Pact stipulates that an act, or threat, of aggression against an individual member state is to be considered an act, or threat, of aggression against all members states.

In recent years the AU has been involved in peace-making and peace-building activities in several African countries and regions.

In April 2003 the AU authorized the establishment of a 3,500-member African Mission in Burundi (AMIB) to oversee the implementation of cease-fire accords in that country, support the disarmament and demobilization of former combatants, and ensure favourable conditions for the deployment of a future UN peacekeeping presence. In June 2004 AMIB was terminated and its troops 'rehatted' as participants in the then newly authorized UN Operation in Burundi (ONUB, which was terminated in 2006).

The July 2003 Maputo Assembly determined to establish a post-conflict reconstruction ministerial committee on Sudan. The first meeting of the committee, convened in March 2004, resolved to dispatch an AU team of experts to southern Sudan to compile a preliminary assessment of that region's post-conflict requirements; this was undertaken in late June. In early April, meeting in N'Djamena, Chad, the Sudan Government and other Sudanese parties signed, under AU auspices, a Humanitarian Cease-fire Agreement providing for the establishment of an AU-led Cease-fire Commission and for the deployment of an AU military observer mission (the AU Mission in the Sudan—AMIS) to the western Sudanese region of Darfur, where widespread violent unrest (including reportedly systematic attacks on the indigenous civilian population by pro-government militias), resulting in a grave humanitarian crisis, had prevailed since early 2003. Following the adoption in late May 2004 of an accord on the modalities for the implementation of the Humanitarian Cease-fire Agreement (also providing for the future deployment of an armed protection force as an additional component of AMIS, as requested by a recent meeting of the Peace and Security Council), the Cease-fire Commission was inaugurated at the end of that month and, at the beginning of June, the Commission's headquarters were opened in El Fasher, Sudan; some 60 AMIS military observers were dispatched to the headquarters during that month. In early July the AU Assembly agreed to increase the strength of AMIS to 80 observers. From mid-2004 the AU mediated contact between the parties to the conflict in Darfur on the achievement of a negotiated peace agreement. AMIS's military component, agreed in May 2004, initially comprising 310 troops from Nigeria and Rwanda and mandated to monitor the cease-fire and protect the Mission, began to be deployed in August. In October the Peace and Security Council decided to expand AMIS into a full peace-keeping operation, eventually to comprise 3,300 troops, police and civilian support staff. The mission's mandate was enhanced to include promoting increased compliance by all parties with the cease-fire agreement and helping with the process of confidence-building; responsibility for monitoring compliance with any subsequent agreements; assisting IDP and refugee returns; and contributing to the improvement of the security situation throughout Darfur. In April 2005 the Peace and Security Council authorized the further enhancement of AMIS to comprise, by the end of September, some 6,171 military personnel, including up to 1,560 civilian police personnel. A pledging conference for the mission, convened in April, resulted in commitments from AU partners and some member states totalling US $291.6m.; the promised funding included $77.4m. from the EU and $50m. from the USA. In January 2005 a Comprehensive Peace Agreement (CPA)—including a Protocol on the Resolution of the Conflict in Abyei Area (the 'Abyei Protocol'), signed in May 2004—was finalized between the Sudan Government and opposition Sudan People's Liberation Movement (SPLM); continuing contention, however, over competing claims to land ownership in, and the future status of, the Abyei region (located at Sudan's border with South Sudan) hindered the Agreement's implementation. In March 2006 the Peace and Security Council agreed, in principle, to support the transformation of AMIS into a UN operation. In late April, following talks in Abuja, Nigeria, AU mediators submitted a proposed peace agreement to representatives of the Sudanese Government and rebel groups; the so-called Darfur Peace Agreement (DPA) was signed on 5 May by the Sudanese Government and the main rebel grouping (the Sudan Liberation Movement).

In August 2006 the UN Security Council expanded the mandate of UNMIS to provide for its deployment to Darfur, in order to enforce a cease-fire and support the implementation of DPA. The Council also requested the UN Secretary-General to devise jointly with the AU, in consultation with the parties to the DPA, a plan and schedule for a transition from AMIS to a sole UN operation in Darfur. The Sudanese Government, however, initially rejected the concept of an expanded UN peace-keeping mission, on the grounds that it would compromise national sovereignty. Eventually, in late December, the UN, AU and Sudanese Government established a tripartite mechanism which was to facilitate the implementation of a UN-formulated three-phase approach, endorsed by the AU Peace and Security Council in November, that would culminate in a hybrid AU/UN mission in Darfur. In January 2007 UNMIS provided AMIS with supplies and extra personnel under the first ('light') phase of the approach; the second ('heavy') phase, finalized in that month, was to involve the delivery of force enablers, police units, civilian personnel and mission support items. UNMIS continued to make efforts to engage the non-signatories of the DPA in the political process in Darfur. In June the AU and UN special representatives for Darfur defined a political road-map to lead eventually to full negotiations in support of a peaceful settlement to the sub-regional conflict. In August the first AU/UN-chaired 'pre-negotiation' discussions with those rebel groups in Darfur that were not party to the DPA approved an agreement on co-operation in attempting to secure a settlement.

In June 2007 the Sudanese Government agreed to support unconditionally the deployment of the Hybrid UN/AU Operation in Darfur (UNAMID); UNAMID was authorized by the UN Security Council in the following month, with a mandated force ceiling of up to 26,000 troops and police officers, supported by 5,000 international and local civilian staff, and a mandate to take necessary action to support the implementation and verification of the May 2006 Darfur Peace Agreement. UNAMID was also mandated to protect civilians, to provide security for humanitarian assistance, to support an inclusive political process, to contribute to the promotion of human rights and rule of law, and to monitor and report on the situation along the borders with Chad and the Central African Republic (CAR). An AU-UN Joint Mediation Support Team for Darfur (JMST) and a Tripartite Committee on UNAMID (including representatives of AU, the UN and Government of Sudan), meet periodically. UNAMID assumed command of AMIS (then comprising 10 battalions) in December 2007. In February 2008 UNAMID's Joint Special Representative signed a status of forces agreement with the minister of foreign affairs of Sudan, covering logistical aspects of the mission. In March UNAMID police units conducted their first confidence-building patrols in areas under rebel control in northern Darfur. In May UNAMID's Force Commander condemned aerial attacks against villages in northern Darfur, allegedly by Sudanese forces.

At the end of June 2008 a new joint AU-UN Chief Mediator was appointed, based at UNAMID headquarters in El Fasher. A Joint Support Co-ordination Mechanism (JSCM) Office in Addis Ababa, comprising liaison officers and communications equipment, was established in November to ensure effective consultation between AU headquarters and the UN. In October 2008 the UN Secretary-General reported that little progress had been achieved in the implementation of the 2006 Darfur Peace Agreement and that violent unrest continued to prevail, and that the conditions in Darfur were not conducive to undertaking a successful peace-keeping operation. From 2008 activities were under way to bring the 10 former AMIS battalions up to full strength in terms of military personnel and equipment. Nevertheless, the UN Secretary-General reported in February 2009 that UNAMID's operational capabilities continued to be limited by lack of critical and key military enabling equipment, logistical constraints, and the reluctance of many troop- and police-contributing countries to deploy to it well-trained personnel and efficient contingent-owned equipment. In January 2010 the UN Secretary-General reported that the capability of UNAMID battalions in Darfur continued to be a cause of concern, with a number of units not having sufficient major equipment.

In March 2009 an AU High-Level Panel on Darfur (AUPD), led by the former President of South Africa, Thabo Mbeki, was established to address means of securing peace, justice, and reconciliation in Darfur. The panel conducted a series of hearings in Sudan over subsequent months, and, in October, issued a report of its findings and recommendations; a key recommendation was the creation of a hybrid court, comprising both AU and Sudanese judges, to prosecute crimes against humanity committed in Darfur. During October a new AU High-Level Implementation Panel (AUHIP) on Sudan was established, with a mandate to support the implementation of all AUPD recommendations, and to assist the relevant Sudanese parties with the implementation of the January 2005 CPA. In November 2009 an inaugural conference of Darfurian civil society organizations was convened, in Doha, Qatar, in order to strengthen and to further political negotiations to achieve a peace settlement. A second conference was held in July 2010. In February and March 2010, respectively, two rebel groupings that had been operating in Darfur signed framework agreements with the Sudanese Government aimed at resolving the conflict; however, consequent negotiations with the largest rebel group, aimed at securing a cease-fire, stalled in May. During that month violent unrest in Darfur caused nearly 600 fatalities, the highest number since the deployment of the mission. UNAMID strengthened security measures and provided additional medical care in some of the larger IDP camps. In late August a consultative meeting of representatives of UNAMID, the AU, the USA and the Sudanese President agreed that UNAMID and the Sudanese Government would work closely together to improve the security situation in Darfur and to support stabilization and development of the region.

In April 2011 the Sudanese National Electoral Commission initiated preparations for a referendum to be held on the future status of Darfur, and requested material and technical assistance from UNAMID. Towards the end of April the JMST presented a draft peace agreement to the Sudan Government and rebel groupings. The agreement was considered by an All-Darfur Stakeholders' Conference, convened, with support from UNAMID, in Doha, Qatar, in late May; participants in the Conference endorsed a communiqué providing for the draft document (the Doha Document for Peace in Darfur—DDPD) to form the basis for achieving a permanent cease-fire and comprehensive Darfurian peace settlement. The DDPD addressed issues including power sharing, wealth sharing, human rights, justice and reconciliation, compensation, returns, and internal dialogue, and provided for the establishment of a Cease-fire Commission, a Darfur Regional Authority, and for a Darfuri to be appointed as the second Vice-President of Sudan. In June the UN Secretary-General welcomed the DDPD as the basis for resolving the Darfur conflict. In mid-July the Sudanese Government and the 'Liberation and Justice Movement', an alliance of rebel groupings, signed an accord on the adoption of the DDPD. Shortly afterwards the two sides also signed a Protocol on the Political Participation of the Liberation and Justice Movement and Integration of its Forces. Meanwhile, UNAMID, a participant in the DDPD Implementation Follow-on Commission, prepared, with civil society representatives, a plan for the dissemination throughout Darfur of information on the Document. In August UNAMID chaired the first meeting of the

Cease-Fire Commission established under the provisions of the DDPD. The formation in 2011 of a subcommittee comprising UNAMID and Sudanese government security entities led to a significant decrease in restrictions on the movements of UNAMID security patrols in the latter part of the year. There were continued reports of criminal attacks on UN personnel, including the theft of UNAMID vehicles, during 2008–12. In early March 2012 UNAMID completed an operation to verify positions held by former rebels; information acquired during the verification operation was to be used by the Cease-fire Commission in disarmament, demobilization, and reintegration/integration planning. In July 2012, on the basis of recommendations made by the UN Secretary-General, the UN Security Council authorized a reconfiguration of UNAMID, entailing a reduction in the mission's numbers to a maximum of 16,200 military personnel and 2,310 police, to be implemented over a period of 12–18 months. The largest UNAMID presence was to be confined henceforth to areas of Darfur with the highest risk of insecurity. The mission was to make more frequent and longer patrols, with expanded use of temporary operating bases, and was to be more rapidly deployable. The Security Council demanded that all parties to the conflict in Darfur immediately cease acts of violence, and effect a permanent cease-fire and comprehensive peace settlement based on the DDPD.

UNAMID's operational strength at 31 August 2012 comprised 16,521 troops, 265 military observers and 4,821 police officers. At September 2012 UNAMID was being led by the acting Joint AU-UN Special Representative, Aïchatou Mindaoudou Souleymane (who was concurrently the AU-UN Chief Mediator for Darfur).

From January 2011, when a referendum was held on future self-determination for South Sudan, violent tensions escalated significantly in Abyei, and had, by July, when South Sudan's independence was achieved, displaced around 113,000 people. In July UNSMIS was succeeded by a new UN mission, the UN Mission in South Sudan (UNMISS). A further UN mission, the UN Interim Security Force for Abyei (UNISFA) was established in June. The 'Temporary Arrangements for the Administration and Security of the Abyei Area'—an accord adopted in mid-June by the Sudanese Government and rebels, governing the withdrawal of their respective forces from Abyei—vested responsibility for supervising security and stability in the region in an Abyei Joint Oversight Committee, comprising members from each party to the conflict, and also in an AU Facilitator. From January 2012 relations between South Sudan and Sudan deteriorated significantly, owing to factors including the disputed delineation of the two countries' joint border, mutual accusations of support for anti-government rebel militia groups, South Sudan's dependency on the use of Sudanese infrastructure (a pipeline and Port Sudan) for the export of petroleum, and sovereignty over Abyei. In February the two countries signed a Memorandum of Understanding on non-aggression and co-operation, committing each state to respecting the other's sovereignty and territorial integrity. In early April AUHIP, facilitating discussions between the two sides, presented to both parties a draft Joint Decision for Reduction of Tension, providing for the immediate cessation of hostilities between the two states, and the withdrawal of armed forces of each state from the territory of the other. In late April the AU Peace and Security Council approved a seven-point Roadmap for Action by Sudan and South Sudan, aimed at normalizing relations between the two states. The Roadmap provided for: (i) the immediate cessation of all hostilities; (ii) the unconditional withdrawal of all armed forces to their respective sides of the border; (iii) the activation, within one week from the adoption of the Roadmap, of all necessary border security mechanisms; (iv) cessation of harbouring of, and support to, rebel groups active against the other state; (v) the activation of an ad hoc Committee to investigate complaints made by one party against the other; (vi) immediate cessation of hostile propaganda and inflammatory statements in the media, and against property, cultural and religious symbols belonging to the nationals of the other state; and (vii) implementation of pending aspects of the June 2011 Temporary Arrangements for the Administration and Security of the Abyei Area, most particularly the redeployment, within two weeks, of all Sudanese and South Sudanese forces out of Abyei. In late April 2012 the AU Commission welcomed South Sudan's acceptance of the Roadmap, and in early May the Sudan Government approved the document. In accordance with its commitment to the Roadmap, South Sudan withdrew its forces from Abyei in early May 2012, with logistical support from UNISFA; and, at the end of May, UNISFA confirmed that Sudan had also withdrawn its military from the area. By the beginning of June Sudan had withdrawn most of its police; a small Sudanese police presence remained, however, to guard infrastructures at the Diffra oil fields, in violation of the June 2011 Agreement. In late September South Sudan and Sudan reached agreement on reviewing effective mechanisms for metering supplies of petroleum, and determined to establish a committee, under AU auspices, that would review oil sector-related payments and technical matters, as a means of avoiding future disputes and enabling the resumption of South Sudanese petroleum production.

Meeting in January 2006 the Peace and Security Council accepted in principle the future deployment of an AU Peace Support Mission in Somalia, with a mandate to support that member country's transitional federal institutions; meanwhile, it was envisaged that an IGAD peace support mission (IGASOM, approved by IGAD in January 2005 and endorsed by that month's AU summit) would be stationed in Somalia. In mid-March 2006 the IGAD Assembly reiterated its support for the deployment of IGASOM, and urged the UN Security Council to grant an exemption to the UN arms embargo applied to Somalia in order to facilitate the regional peace support initiative. At a consultative meeting on the removal of the arms embargo, convened in mid-April, in Nairobi, Kenya, representatives of the Somali transitional federal authorities presented for consideration by the AU and IGAD a draft national security and stabilization plan. It was agreed that a detailed mission plan should be formulated to underpin the proposed AU/IGAD peace missions. In January 2007 the Peace and Security Council authorized the deployment of the AU Mission in Somalia (AMISOM), in place of the proposed IGASOM. AMISOM was to be deployed for an initial period of six months, with a mandate to contribute to the political stabilization of Somalia. It was envisaged that AMISOM would evolve into a UN operation focusing on the post-conflict restoration of Somalia. In the following month the UN Security Council endorsed AMISOM and proposed that it should eventually be superseded by such a UN operation. AMISOM became operational in May 2007. In mid-September 2009 the AU strongly condemned terrorist attacks that were perpetrated against the AMISOM headquarters in Mogadishu, Somalia, killing more than 20 people, including the Deputy Force Commander of the Mission, and injuring a further 40. In October 2010 Flt Lt Jerry Rawlings, the former President of Ghana, was appointed as the AU High Representative on Somalia. AMISOM reached its then mandated strength of 8,000 troops in November 2010. In the following month the UN Security Council, concerned at continuing unrest and terrorist attacks, extended AMISOM's mandate until 30 September 2011 and requested the AU to increase the mission's numbers to 12,000. AMISOM's mandate was extended further, in September 2011, until 31 October 2012. In so doing, the UN Security Council requested the AU urgently to increase the mission's strength to the then mandated level of 12,000. In late February 2012 the Security Council voted unanimously to enhance the mission further, to comprise 17,700 troops, and to expand its areas of operation. At that time the Council also banned trade in charcoal with Somalia, having identified that commodity as a significant source of revenue for militants. In January 2012 the Peace and Security Council adopted a Strategic Concept for future AMISOM Operations

In February 2008 the AU welcomed the efforts of African leaders, including the outgoing chairperson of the AU Assembly, President Kufuor of Ghana, and the former UN Secretary-General, Kofi Annan, to secure a peaceful outcome to the political crisis and violent unrest that had erupted in Kenya following the disputed outcome of a presidential election staged in December 2007. In March 2008 the Pan-African Parliament sent an observer mission to monitor the legislative and presidential elections that were held concurrently in Zimbabwe. In February 2009 the Assembly welcomed ongoing political progress in Zimbabwe and demanded the immediate suspension of international sanctions against that country.

In November 2008 the AU and International Conference on the Great Lakes Region jointly convened, in Nairobi, Kenya, with participation by the UN Secretary-General, a regional summit on ongoing heightened insecurity in eastern regions of the DRC. Meeting on the sidelines of the July 2012 Assembly summit, the Presidents of the DRC and Rwanda agreed in principle to the deployment in eastern DRC of an international force with a mandate to suppress armed rebels active in that area; the two leaders were to convene again in the following month to discuss the details of the proposed force. Meanwhile the AU Commission Chairperson stated the willingness of the AU to contribute to such a force.

In November 2011 the Peace and Security Council authorized an AU Regional Cooperation Initiative for the Elimination of the Lord's Resistance Army (AU RCI-LRA), with three components: (i) a Joint Coordination Mechanism, based in Bangui, CAR, and chaired by the AU Commissioner for Peace and Security, with participation by the defence ministers of LRA-affected countries, and responsibility for strategic co-ordination with all affected states and actors; (ii) a 5,000-strong Regional Task Force (RTF), comprising national contingents from LRA-affected countries, headquartered in Yambio, South Sudan, with four liaison officers based at a Joint Intelligence and Operations Centre, in Dungu, DRC; and (iii) a Joint Operations Centre, reporting to the RTF Commander, and comprising 30 officers engaged in integrated planning and monitoring activities. The AU RCI-LRA was officially launched in March 2012. (The LRA is active in parts of Uganda, the CAR, DRC and South Sudan.)

In August 2008, following the overthrow of its constitutional Government in a military *coup d'état*, Mauritania was suspended from participating in the activities of the AU. Guinea was suspended from the AU during December 2008–December 2010, also following a *coup d'état*; Guinea's membership suspension was lifted in view of presidential elections held in 2010. In March 2009 the AU suspended Madagascar from participation in its activities, following the forced resignation of the elected President, Mark Ravalomanana, and transfer of power to the military. In February 2010 Niger was suspended from participation in AU activities, following a *coup d'état*; Niger's membership suspension was lifted in March 2011, following the successful organization, in October 2010, of a referendum on a new constitution, and of legislative and presidential elections in early 2011.

In early 2011 the Peace and Security Council held a series of meetings to consider ongoing unrest in Côte d'Ivoire, where the security situation had deteriorated following the refusal of the outgoing President Laurent Gbagbo to acknowledge the outcome of presidential elections held in 2010, and consequently to cede power. In late January 2011 the Council, meeting at the level of heads of state and government, determined to establish a High-level Panel on Côte d'Ivoire. The Panel, which was inaugurated at the end of that month, included five African leaders, the AU Chairperson, and the President of the ECOWAS Commission. Meeting in mid-March 2011 the Peace and Security Council decided that an AU High Representative should be appointed to pursue a peaceful resolution of the Côte d'Ivoire political crisis, through the implementation of peace proposals developed by the High-level Panel. The legitimately elected President, Alassane Ouattara, was eventually inaugurated in May 2011.

Following the overthrow of the legitimate Government of Mali by the military in March 2012 that country was suspended from participation in AU activities. The AU Commission, recalling the 'fundamental principle of the intangibility of borders inherited by the African countries at their accession to independence' expressed its 'total rejection' of a unilateral declaration, made in early April by separatist militants of the National Movement for the Liberation of Azawad (MNLA), who, supported by Islamist forces, had just seized land in the Kidal, Gao and Tombouctou regions of northern Mali, that this was, henceforth, to be known as the independent entity of Azawad. The Commission affirmed the AU's full support for efforts being undertaken by ECOWAS to protect Mali's unity and territorial integrity, both through mediation and through the envisaged deployment there of the ECOWAS Standby Force Mission in Mali—MICEMA. It was reported in mid-June that the AU had requested the UN Security Council to draft a resolution endorsing military intervention against the militants in northern Mali. In July the Security Council adopted a resolution expressing its readiness to consider mandating ECOWAS to authorize the deployment of MICEMA, and requesting additional information on the objectives and modalities of the proposed mission. In early September the Peace and Security Council expressed deep concern at the occupation of northern Mali by terrorist and militant groups, and condemned violations of human rights being committed there, while welcoming an initiative of the African Commission on Human and People's Rights to investigate the situation. The Council strongly condemned the activities of the Movement for Oneness and Jihad in West Africa, and condemned its reported presence in northern Mali. In April 2012 Guinea-Bissau was also suspended from the AU, following a military coup, pending the restoration of constitutional order.

The EU assists the AU financially in the areas of: peace and security; institutional development; governance; and regional economic integration and trade. In June 2004 the European Commission activated for the first time its newly-established Africa Peace Facility (APF), which aims to contribute to the African peace and security agenda, including, since 2007, conflict prevention, post-conflict stabilization, and accelerating decision making and co-ordination processes. During 2007–12 APF funds were chanelled as follows: €607m. to peace support operations (the Fund's core area of activity); €100m. towards the operationalization of the African Peace and Security Architecture and Africa-EU dialogue; €20m. for unforeseen contingencies; and €15m. towards early response. A €300m. replenishment of the APF, to cover 2011–13, was agreed in August 2011. It was announced in March 2012 that €11.4m. would be allocated through the APF over the period 1 February 2012–31 January 2014 towards the training of the ASF, and towards the establishment of an African e-library comprising documentation of relevance to the Force.

Since October 2007 APF and UN funding have jointly financed the deployment of UNAMID (with the APF financing of UNAMID and AUHIP totalling €305m). AMISOM was allocated €208m. in APF funding during 2007–12. The APF has, furthermore, channelled more than €90m. towards peace support operations in the CAR, including support for the deployment, since July 2008, of the Mission for the Consolidation of Peace in the CAR—MICOPAX, which, under the auspices of the Communauté économique des états de l'Afrique centrale, superseded the Multinational Force in the Central African Republic (established in 2002). MICOPAX has a military strength of around 520 troops, and a civilian component that includes a police unit of 150 officers.

INFRASTRUCTURE, ENERGY AND THE ENVIRONMENT

Meeting in Lomé, Togo, in July 2001, OAU heads of state and government authorized the establishment of an African Energy Commission (AFREC), with the aim of increasing co-operation in energy matters between Africa and other regions. AFREC was launched in February 2008. It was envisaged at that time that an African Electrotechnical Standardization Commission (AFSEC) would also become operational, as a subsidiary body of AFREC.

In 1964 the OAU adopted a Declaration on the Denuclearization of Africa, and in April 1996 it adopted the African Nuclear Weapons Free Zone Treaty (also known as the 'Pelindaba Treaty'), which identifies Africa as a nuclear weapons-free zone and promotes co-operation in the peaceful uses of nuclear energy.

In 1968 OAU member states adopted the African Convention on the Conservation of Nature and Natural Resources. The Bamako Convention on the Ban of the Import into Africa and the Control of Transboundary Movement and Management of Hazardous Wastes within Africa was adopted by OAU member states in 1991 and entered into force in April 1998.

In June 2010 a consultative meeting was convened between the AU, COMESA, IGAD, and other regional partners, aimed at advancing co-ordination and harmonization of their activities governing the environment. It was envisaged that the AU should facilitate the development of a comprehensive African Environmental Framework, to guide pan-continental and REC environmental activities. At that time the AU was in the process of integrating two regional fora—the African Ministerial Conference on Water (AMCOW) and the African Ministerial Conference on the Environment (AMCEN)—into its structures, as specialized institutes.

The 17th regular summit of AU heads of state and government, held in late June–early July 2011, adopted a decision inviting member states to work on a common African position for the landmark United Nations Conference on Sustainable Development—UNCSD (also referred to as Rio+20), which was to be held in Rio de Janeiro, Brazil, in June 2012. Consequently an Africa Regional Preparatory Conference for UNCSD was convened, under the auspices of ECA, in October 2011. The Conference noted emerging challenges to continental sustainable development, including low adaptive capacity to the effects of consequences of climate change; increasing severe biodiversity loss, desertification and land degradation, aggravated by the effects of climate change; and rapid urbanization. The conference urged the international community to meet its commitments to the continent in terms of transfer of financial and technological resources, and committed African states to enhancing efforts to improve national governance and development effectiveness, and to developing national strategies for sustainable development.

In February 2007 the first Conference of African Ministers responsible for Maritime Transport was convened to discuss maritime transport policy in the region. A draft declaration was submitted at the Conference, held in Abuja, Nigeria, outlining the AU's vision for a common maritime transport policy aimed at 'linking Africa' and detailing programmes for co-operation on maritime safety and security and the development of an integrated transport infrastructure. The subsequently adopted Abuja Maritime Transport Declaration formally provided for an annual meeting of maritime transport ministers, to be hosted by each region in turn in a rotational basis. In July 2009 the AU Assembly decided to establish an African Agency for the Protection of Territorial and Economic Waters of African Countries. In June 2011 a task force was inaugurated to lead the development and implementation of a new '2050 Africa's Integrated Maritime Strategy' (2050 Aim-Strategy); the Strategy was to address maritime challenges affecting the continent, including the development of aquaculture and offshore renewable energy resources; unlawful activities, such as illegal fishing, acts of maritime piracy (particularly in the Gulfs of Aden and Guinea), and trafficking in arms and drugs; and environmental pressures, such as loss of biodiversity, degradation of the marine environment, and climate change. The first Conference of African Ministers responsible for Maritime-related Affairs was held in April 2012, alongside a workshop on developing the 2050 AIM-Strategy.

In January 2012 the Executive Council endorsed a new African Civil Aviation Policy (AFCAP); and also endorsed the African Action Plan for the UN 2011–20 Decade of Action on Road Safety.

POLITICAL AND SOCIAL AFFAIRS

The African Charter on Human and People's Rights, which was adopted by the OAU in 1981 and entered into force in October 1986, provided for the establishment of an 11-member African Commission on Human and People's Rights, based in Banjul, The Gambia. A Protocol to the Charter, establishing an African Court of People's and Human Rights, was adopted by the OAU Assembly of Heads of State in June 1998 and entered into force in January 2004. In February 2009 a protocol (adopted in July 2003) establishing an African Court of Justice entered into force. The Protocol on the Statute of the African Court of Justice and Human Rights, aimed at merging the African

Court of Human and Peoples' Rights and the African Court of Justice, was opened for signature in July 2008. A further Protocol, relating to the Rights of Women, was adopted by the July 2003 Maputo Assembly. The African Charter on the Rights and Welfare of the Child was opened for signature in July 1990 and entered into force in November 1999. A Protocol to the Abuja Treaty Establishing the AEC relating to the Pan-African Parliament, adopted by the OAU in March 2001, entered into force in December 2003. The Parliament was inaugurated in March 2004 and was, initially, to exercise advisory and consultative powers only, although its eventual evolution into an institution with full legislative powers is envisaged. In March 2005 the advisory Economic, Social and Cultural Council was inaugurated.

In April 2003 AU ministers of labour and social affairs requested the AU Commission to develop, in consultation with other stakeholders, a pan-African Social Policy Framework (SPF). The SPF, finalized in November 2008, identified the following thematic social issues: population and development; social protection; labour and employment; education; health; HIV/AIDS, TB, malaria and other infectious diseases; the family; children, adolescents and youth; migration; agriculture, food and nutrition; ageing; disability; gender equality and women's empowerment; culture; urban development; environmental sustainability; the impact of globalisation and trade liberalization; and good governance, anti-corruption and rule of law. The following areas of focus: drug abuse and crime prevention; civil conflict; foreign debt; and sport were given special consideration under the Framework. Recommendations were outlined in the SPF that were aimed at supporting AU member states in formulating and implementing national social policies.

The July 2002 inaugural summit meeting of AU heads of state and government adopted a Declaration Governing Democratic Elections in Africa, providing guidelines for the conduct of national elections in member states and outlining the AU's electoral observation and monitoring role. In April 2003 the AU Commission and the South African Independent Electoral Commission jointly convened an African Conference on Elections, Democracy and Governance. In February 2012 a new African Charter on Democracy, Elections and Governance entered into force, having been ratified at that time by 15 AU member states.

In recent years several large population displacements have occurred in Africa, mainly as a result of violent conflict. In 1969 OAU member states adopted the Convention Governing the Specific Aspects of Refugee Problems in Africa, which entered into force in June 1974 and had been ratified by 45 states at June 2012. The Convention promotes close co-operation with UNHCR. The AU maintains a Special Refugee Contingency Fund to provide relief assistance and to support repatriation activities, education projects, etc., for displaced people in Africa. In October 2009 AU member states participating in a regional Special Summit on Refugees, Returnees and IDPs in Africa, convened in Kampala, Uganda, adopted the AU Convention for the Protection and Assistance of IDPs in Africa, the first legally binding international treaty providing legal protection and support to people displaced within their own countries by violent conflict and natural disasters; the Convention had received four ratifications by September 2012. The AU aims to address pressing health issues affecting member states, including the eradication of endemic parasitic and infectious diseases and improving access to medicines. An African Summit on HIV/AIDS, TB and other related Infectious Diseases was convened, under OAU auspices, in Abuja in March 2001 and, in May 2006, an AU Special Summit on HIV/AIDS. TB and Malaria was convened, also in Abuja, to review the outcomes of the previous Summit. The 2006 Special Summit adopted the Abuja Call for Accelerated Action on HIV/AIDS, TB and Malaria, and, in September of that year AU ministers of health adopted the Maputo Plan of Action for the operationalisation of the Continental Policy Framework for Sexual and Reproductive Health, covering 2007–10, aimed at advancing the goal of achieving universal access to comprehensive sexual and reproductive health services in Africa; in July 2010 the Plan was extended over the period 2010–15. In January 2012 the 18th AU Assembly meeting decided to revitalize AIDS Watch Africa (AWA), an advocacy platform established in April 2001, and hitherto comprising several regional heads of states, to be henceforth an AU Heads of State and Government Advocacy and Accountability Platform with continent-wide representation. AWA's mandate was to be extended to cover, also, TB and malaria. In March 2012 NEPAD and UNAIDS signed an agreement on advancing sustainable responses to HIV/AIDS, health and development across Africa. An AU Scientific, Technical and Research Commission is based in Lagos, Nigeria.

In July 2004 the Assembly adopted the Solemn Declaration on Gender Equality in Africa (SDGEA), incorporating a commitment to reporting annually on progress made towards attaining gender equality. The first conference of ministers responsible for women's affairs and gender, convened in Dakar, Senegal, in October 2005, adopted the Implementation Framework for the SDGEA, and Guidelines for Monitoring and Reporting on the SDGEA, in support of member states' reporting responsibilities.

The seventh AU summit, convened in Banjul, The Gambia, in July 2006, adopted the African Youth Charter, providing for the implementation of youth policies and strategies across Africa, with the aim of encouraging young African people to participate in the development of the region and to take advantage of increasing opportunities in education and employment. The Charter outlined the basic rights and responsibilities of youths, which were divided into four main categories: youth participation; education and skills development; sustainable livelihoods; and health and well-being. The Charter, which entered into force in August 2010, also details the obligations of member states towards young people.

In December 2007 the AU adopted a Plan of Action on Drug Control and Crime Prevention covering the period 2007–12, and determined to establish a follow-up mechanism to monitor and evaluate its implementation. In March 2009 the AU and UNODC (which in October 2008 had published a report identifying the expanding use in recent years of West Africa as a transit route for narcotics being illegally traded between Latin America and Europe) launched a joint initiative to support the Plan. The AU-UNODC co-operation aimed to strengthen the policy-making, norm-setting and capacity building capabilities of the AU Commission and sub-regional organizations (notably ECOWAS).

AU efforts to combat human trafficking are guided by the 2006 Ouagadougou Action Plan to Combat Trafficking in Human Beings. In June 2009 the AU launched AU COMMIT, a campaign aimed at raising the profile of human trafficking on the regional development agenda. It was estimated at that time that nearly 130,000 people in sub-Saharan Africa and 230,000 in North Africa and the Middle East had been recruited into forced labour, including sexual exploitation, as a result of trafficking; many had also been transported to Western Europe and other parts of the world.

TRADE, INDUSTRY AND ECONOMIC CO-OPERATION

In October 1999 a conference on Industrial Partnerships and Investment in Africa was held in Dakar, Senegal, jointly organized by the OAU with UNIDO, the ECA, the African Development Bank and the Alliance for Africa's Industrialization. In June 1997 the first meeting between ministers of the OAU and the EU was convened in New York, USA. In April 2000 the first EU-Africa summit of heads of state and government was held in Cairo, under the auspices of the EU and OAU. The summit adopted the Cairo Plan of Action, which addressed areas including economic integration, trade and investment, private-sector development in Africa, human rights and good governance, peace and security, and development issues such as education, health and food security. The second EU-Africa summit meeting was initially to have been held in April 2003 but was postponed, owing to disagreements concerning the participation of President Mugabe of Zimbabwe, against whom the EU had imposed sanctions. In February 2007 the EU and the AU began a period of consultation on a joint EU-Africa Strategy, aimed at outlining a long-term vision of the future partnership between the two parties. The Strategy was adopted by the second EU-Africa Summit, which was convened, finally, in December 2007, in Lisbon, Portugal (with participation by President Mugabe). The third EU-Africa Summit, held in November 2010, in Tripoli, Libya, confirmed commitment to the Strategy and adopted an action plan on co-operation, covering 2011–13. A fourth EU-Africa Business Forum was convened alongside the November 2010 summit. A Joint Africa-EU Task Force meets regularly, most recently in March 2012, to consider areas of co-operation.

Co-operation between African states and the People's Republic of China is undertaken within the framework of the Forum on China-Africa Co-operation (FOCAC). The first FOCAC ministerial conference was held in October 2000; the second in December 2003; the third (organized alongside a China-Africa leaders' summit) in November 2006; the fourth in November 2009; and the fifth in July 2012. During the fifth FOCAC the Chinese President announced strengthened China-Africa co-operation in the following priority areas: support for sustainable development in Africa, including investment in the development of trans-national and trans-regional infrastructure, agricultural technology, manufacturing, and small and medium-sized enterprises; implementation of an 'African Talents Program', which was to provide skills training; capacity building in meteorological infrastructure, in the protection and management of forests, and in water supply projects; and the implementation of a new 'Initiative on China-Africa Cooperative Partnership for Peace and Security'. Africa–USA trade is underpinned by the US African Growth and Opportunity Act (AGOA), adopted in May 2000 to promote the development of free market economies in Africa. Regular Africa-EU and Africa-South America ('ASA') summits are convened. The second ASA summit, convened by the AU and Union of South American Nations—UNASUR in Porlamar, Margarita Island, Venezuela, in September 2009, adopted the Margarita Declaration and Action Plan, covering issues of common concern, including combating climate change, and developing an alternative financial mechanism to address the global economic crisis. The third ASA summit took place in May 2012, in Malabo, Equatorial Guinea.

The AU aims to reduce obstacles to intra-African trade and to reverse the continuing disproportionate level of trade conducted by many African countries with their former colonial powers. In June 2005 an AU conference of Ministers of Trade was convened, in Cairo, to discuss issues relating to the development of Trade in Africa, particularly in the context of the World Trade Organization's (WTO) Doha Work Programme. The outcome of the meeting was the adoption of the Cairo Road Map on the Doha Work Programme, which addressed several important issues including the import, export and market access of agricultural and non-agricultural commodities, development issues and trade facilitation.

The 1991 Abuja Treaty Establishing the AEC initially envisaged that the Economic Community would be established by 2028, following a gradual six-phase process involving the co-ordination, harmonization and progressive integration of the activities of all existing and future sub-regional economic unions. (The AU recognizes the following eight so-called 'regional economic communities', or RECs, in Africa: the Common Market for Eastern and Southern Africa—COMESA, the East African Community—EAC and the Southern African Development Community—SADC, which together comprise the EAC-COMESA-SADC Tripartite FTA initiative; the Communauté économique des états de l'Afrique centrale—CEEAC, the Economic Community of West African States—ECOWAS, the Intergovernmental Authority on Development—IGAD, and the Union of the Arab Maghreb. The subsidiary RECs are: the Communauté économique et monétaire de l'Afrique centrale—CEMAC, the Community of Sahel-Saharan States—CEN-SAD, the Economic Community of the Great Lakes Countries, the Indian Ocean Commission—IOC, the Mano River Union, the Southern African Customs Union, and the Union économique et monétaire ouest-africaine—UEMOA.) The inaugural meeting of the AEC took place in June 1997. In July 2007 the ninth AU Assembly adopted a Protocol on Relations between the African Union and the RECs, aimed at facilitating the harmonization of policies and ensuring compliance with the schedule of the Abuja Treaty.

In January 2012 the 18th summit of AU leaders endorsed a new Framework, Roadmap and Architecture for Fast Tracking the Establishment of a Continental Free Trade Area (CFTA), and an Action Plan for Boosting Intra-African Trade. The summit determined that the implementation of the CFTA process should follow these milestones: the finalization by 2014 of the EAC-COMESA-SADC Tripartite FTA initiative; the completion during 2012–14 of other REC FTAs; the consolidation of the Tripartite and other regional FTAs into the CFTA initiative during 2015–16; and the establishment of an operational CFTA by 2017. The January 2012 summit invited ECOWAS, CEEAC, CEN-SAD and the Union of the Arab Maghreb to draw inspiration from the EAC-COMESA-SADC Tripartite initiative and to establish promptly a second pole of regional integration, thereby accelerating continental economic integration. In the context of UNCSD, held later in that year, the summit recognized the need to strengthen the AU's institutional framework for sustainable development, deeming that promoting the transition to 'green' and 'blue' economies would accelerate continental progress towards sustainable development.

In February 2008 the AU Assembly endorsed the AU Action Plan for the Accelerated Industrial Development of Africa (AIDA), which had been adopted in September 2007 by the first extraordinary session of the Conference of African Ministers of Industry. The Action Plan details a set of programme and activities aimed at stimulating a competitive and sustainable industrial development process.

A roadmap and plan of action for promoting microfinance in Africa was finalized in 2009, and is under consideration.

The AU leadership participated in the summit meeting of G8 heads of state and government that was convened in Huntsville, Canada, in June 2010; the summit also included an African Outreach meeting with the leaders of Algeria, Ethiopia, Malawi, Nigeria, Senegal and South Africa.

In October 2010 the AU, ECA and African Development Bank established a Joint Secretariat to enhance coherence and collaboration in support of Africa's development agenda.

RURAL ECONOMY AND AGRICULTURE

In July 2003 the second Assembly of heads of state and government adopted the Maputo Declaration on Agriculture and Food Security in Africa, focusing on the need to revitalize the agricultural sector and to combat hunger on the continent by developing food reserves based on African production. The leaders determined to deploy policies and budgetary resources to remove current constraints on agricultural production, trade and rural development; and to implement the Comprehensive Africa Agriculture Programme (CAADP). The CAADP, which is implemented through NEPAD, focuses on the four pillars of sustainable land and water management; market access; food supply and hunger; and agricultural research. CAADP heads of state have agreed the objective of allocating at least 10% of national budgets to investment in agricultural productivity. The CAADP aims by 2015 to achieve dynamic agricultural markets between African countries and regions; good participation in and access to markets by farmers; a more equitable distribution of wealth for rural populations; more equitable access to land, practical and financial resources, knowledge, information, and technology for sustainable development; development of Africa's role as a strategic player in the area of agricultural science and technology; and environmentally sound agricultural production and a culture of sustainable management of natural resources.

In December 2006 AU leaders, convened at a Food Security Summit in Abuja, adopted a declaration of commitment to increasing intra-African trade by promoting and protecting as strategic commodities at the continental level cotton, legumes, maize, oil palm, rice and beef, dairy, fisheries and poultry products; and promoting and protecting as strategic commodities at the sub-regional level cassava, sorghum and millet. The AU leaders also declared a commitment to initiating the implementation of the NEPAD Home-grown School Feeding Project, the African Regional Nutrition Strategy, the NEPAD African Nutrition Initiative, and the NEPAD 10-Year Strategy for Combating Vitamin and Mineral Deficiency.

In December 2006 the AU adopted the Great Green Wall of the Sahara and Sahel Initiative (GGWSSI), comprising a set of cross-sectoral actions and interventions (including tree planting) that were aimed at conserving and protecting natural resources, halting soil degradation, reducing poverty, and increasing land productivity in some 20 countries in the Sahara and Sahel areas.

The AU's Programme for the Control of Epizootics (PACE) has co-operated with FAO to combat the further spread of the Highly Pathogenic Avian Influenza (H5N1) virus, outbreaks of which were reported in poultry in several West African countries in the 2000s; joint activities have included establishing a regional network of laboratories and surveillance teams and organizing regional workshops on H5N1 control.

In April 2009 AU ministers responsible for agriculture met to address the challenges to the continent posed by high food prices, climate change and the ongoing global financial and economic crisis. In July 2009 the 13th regular session of the Assembly issued a Declaration on Land Issues and Challenges in Africa, and the Sirte Declaration on Investing in Agriculture for Economic Growth and Food Security. The Sirte Declaration urged member states to review their land sector policies, and determined to undertake studies on the establishment of an appropriate institutional framework, and to launch an African Fund for Land Policy, in support of these efforts. The meeting also urged the establishment of a 'South to South Forum for Agricultural Development in Africa', recommitted to the Maputo Declaration, and urged member states to expand efforts to accelerate the implementation of the CAADP.

In January 2011 the Executive Council endorsed the Accelerated African Agribusiness and Agro-Industries Development Initiative (3ADI), which had been launched at a high-level conference on the development of agribusiness and agro-industries in Africa, convened in Abuja, Nigeria, in March 2010. The framework for the implementation of the 3ADI is the Strategy for the Implementation of the AU Plan of Action for the Accelerated Industrial Development of Africa (AIDA), adopted by African ministers responsible for industry, in October 2008; the Ministerial Action Plan for the Least Developed Countries (LDCs), adopted in December 2009 by LDC ministers responsible for industry and trade; and the Abuja Declaration on Development of Agribusiness and Agro-industries in Africa, adopted by the March 2010 Abuja high-level conference. The initiative aims to mobilize private sector investment, from domestic, regional and international sources, in African agribusiness and agro-industrial development, with the long-term objective of achieving, by 2020, highly productive and profitable agricultural value chains.

The First Conference of African Ministers of Fisheries and Aquaculture (CAMFA) was convened in September 2010, in Banjul, The Gambia. In January 2011 the Executive Council urged member states to adopt and integrate ecosystem approaches in their national and regional fisheries management plans; to strengthen measures to address Illegal, Unreported and Unregulated (IUU) fishing; and to eliminate barriers to intra-regional trade in fish and fishery products.

HUMANITARIAN RESPONSE

In December 2005 a ministerial conference on disaster reduction in Africa, organized by the AU Commission, adopted a programme of action for the implementation of the Africa Regional Strategy for Disaster Risk Reduction (2006–15), formulated in the context of the Hyogo Framework of Action that had been agreed at the World Conference on Disaster Reduction held in Kobe, Japan, in January 2005. A second ministerial conference on disaster reduction, convened in April 2010, urged all member states, and the RECs, to take necessary measures to implement the programme of action. In August 2010 the AU and OCHA signed an agreement detailing key areas of future co-operation on humanitarian issues, with the aim of strengthening the AU's capacity in the areas of disaster preparedness and response, early warning, co-ordination, and protection of civilians affected by conflict or natural disaster.

Finance

The 2012 budget, adopted by the Executive Council in December 2011, totalled US $274.9m., comprising an operational budget of $114.8m. and a programme budget $159.3m. Some 75% of the operational budget is financed by contributions from Algeria, Egypt, Libya, Nigeria and South Africa. Around 90% of programme budgetary funding derives from the AU's development partners.

Specialized Agencies

African Academy of Languages (ACALAN): BP 10, Koulouba-Bamako, Mali; tel. 2023-84-47; fax 2023-84-47; e-mail acalan@acalan.org; internet www.acalan.org; f. 2006 to foster continental integration and development through the promotion of the use—in all domains—of African languages; aims to restore the role and vitality of indigenous languages (estimated to number more than 2,000), and to reverse the negative impact of colonialism on their perceived value; implements a Training of African Languages Teachers and Media Practitioners Project; a core programme is the promotion of the Pan-African Masters and PhD Program in African Languages and Applied Linguistics (PANMAPAL), inaugurated in 2006 at the University of Yaoundé 1 (Cameroon), Addis Ababa University (Ethiopia), and at the University of Cape Town (South Africa); identified in 2009 some 41 'Vehicular Cross-Border Languages'; Vehicular Cross-Border Language Commissions were to be established for 12 of these: Beti-fang and Lingala (Central Africa); Kiswahili, Somali and Malagasy (East Africa); Standard modern Arab and Berber (North Africa); Chichewa/Chinyanja and Setswana (Southern Africa); and Hausa, Mandenkan and Fulfulde (West Africa); in Dec. 2011 organized a workshop on African languages in cyberspace; ACALAN is developing a linguistic Atlas for Africa; Exec. Dir Dr SOZINHO FRANCISCO MATSINHE.

African Civil Aviation Commission (AFCAC): 1 route de l'Aéroport International LSS, BP 2356, Dakar, Senegal; tel. 859-88-00; fax 820-70-18; e-mail secretariat@afcac.org; internet www.afcac.org; f. 1969 to co-ordinate civil aviation matters in Africa and to co-operate with ICAO and other relevant civil aviation bodies; promotes the development of the civil aviation industry in Africa in accordance with provisions of the 1991 Abuja Treaty; fosters the application of ICAO Standards and Recommended Practices; examines specific problems that might hinder the development and operation of the African civil aviation industry; 53 mem states; promotes co-ordination and better utilization and development of African air transport systems and the standardization of aircraft, flight equipment and training programmes for pilots and mechanics; organizes working groups and seminars, and compiles statistics; Sec.-Gen. IYABO SOSINA.

African Telecommunications Union (ATU): ATU Secretariat, POB 35282 Nairobi, 00200 Kenya; tel. (20) 4453308; fax (20) 4453359; e-mail sg@atu-uat.org; internet www.atu-uat.org; f. 1999 as successor to Pan-African Telecommunications Union (f. 1977); promotes the rapid development of information communications in Africa, with the aim of making Africa an equal participant in the global information society; works towards universal service and access and full inter-country connectivity; promotes development and adoption of appropriate policies and regulatory frameworks; promotes financing of development; encourages co-operation between members and the exchange of information; advocates the harmonization of telecommunications policies; 46 national mems, 18 associate mems comprising fixed and mobile telecoms operators; Sec.-Gen. ABDOULKARIM SOUMAILA.

Pan-African Institute of Education for Development (IPED): 49 ave de la Justice, BP 1764, Kinshasa I, Democratic Republic of the Congo; tel. (81) 2686091; fax (81) 2616091; internet iped-auobs.org; f. 1973, became specialized agency in 1986, present name adopted 2001; undertakes educational research and training, focuses on co-operation and problem-solving, acts as an observatory for education; responsible for Education Management Information Systems (EMIS) under the Second Decade for Education for Africa (2006–15); publs *Bulletin d'Information* (quarterly), *Revue africaine des sciences de l'éducation* (2 a year), *Répertoire africain des institutions de recherche* (annually).

Pan-African News Agency (PANAPRESS): BP 4056, ave Bourguiba, Dakar, Senegal; tel. 869-12-34; fax 824-13-90; e-mail panapress@panapress.com; internet www.panapress.com; f. 1979 as PanAfrican News Agency, restructured under current name in 1997; regional headquarters in Khartoum, Sudan; Lusaka, Zambia; Kinshasa, Democratic Republic of the Congo; Lagos, Nigeria; Tripoli, Libya; began operations in May 1983; receives information from national news agencies and circulates news in Arabic, English, French and Portuguese; publs *Press Review*, *In-Focus*.

Pan-African Postal Union (PAPU): POB 6026, Arusha, Tanzania; tel. (27) 2543263; fax (27) 2543265; e-mail sg@papu.co.tz; internet www.upap-papu.org; f. 1980 to extend members' co-operation in the improvement of postal services; 43 mem. countries; Sec.-Gen. RODAH MASAVIRU; publ. *PAPU News*.

Supreme Council for Sport in Africa (SCSA): POB 1363, Yaoundé, Cameroon; tel. 223-95-80; fax 223-45-12; e-mail scsa_yaounde@yahoo.com; f. 1966; co-ordinating authority and forum for the development and promotion of sports in Africa; hosts All Africa Games, held every four years; mems: sports ministers from 53 countries; Sec.-Gen. MVUZO MBEBE (South Africa); publ. *Newsletter* (monthly).

COMMON MARKET FOR EASTERN AND SOUTHERN AFRICA—COMESA

Address: COMESA Centre, Ben Bella Rd, POB 30051, 101101 Lusaka, Zambia.

Telephone: (1) 229725; **fax:** (1) 225107; **e-mail:** info@comesa.int; **internet:** www.comesa.int.

The COMESA treaty was signed by member states of the Preferential Trade Area for Eastern and Southern Africa (PTA) in November 1993. COMESA formally succeeded the PTA in December 1994. COMESA aims to strengthen the process of regional economic and social development that was initiated under the PTA, with the ultimate aim of merging with the other regional economic communities of the African Union.

MEMBERS

Burundi	Malawi
Comoros	Mauritius
Congo, Democratic Republic	Rwanda
Djibouti	Seychelles
Egypt	South Sudan*
Eritrea	Sudan
Ethiopia	Swaziland
Kenya	Uganda
Libya	Zambia
Madagascar	Zimbabwe

* South Sudan, which achieved independence on 9 July 2011, was admitted to COMESA in October of that year.

Organization

(September 2012)

AUTHORITY

The Authority of the Common Market is the supreme policy organ of COMESA, comprising heads of state or government of member countries. The inaugural meeting of the Authority took place in Lilongwe, Malawi, in December 1994. The 15th summit meeting was held in October 2011, in Lilongwe, Malawi, on the theme 'Harnessing Science and Technology for Development'. The 16th summit was to take place in November 2012.

COUNCIL OF MINISTERS

Each member government appoints a minister to participate in the Council. The Council monitors COMESA activities, including supervision of the Secretariat, recommends policy direction and development, and reports to the Authority.

A Committee of Governors of Central Banks advises the Authority and the Council of Ministers on monetary and financial matters.

COURT OF JUSTICE

The sub-regional Court is vested with the authority to settle disputes between member states and to adjudicate on matters concerning the interpretation of the COMESA treaty. The Court is composed of seven judges, who serve terms of five years' duration. The Court was restructured in 2005 to comprise a First Instance division and an Appellate division.

SECRETARIAT

COMESA's Secretariat comprises the following divisions: Administration; Budget and finance; Gender and social affairs; Infrastructure development; Investment promotion; Private sector development; and Trade customs and monetary affairs. There are also units at the Secretariat dealing with legal and institutional affairs, and climate change.

Secretary-General: SINDISO NWENGYA (Zimbabwe).

Activities

COMESA aims to promote economic and social progress, co-operation and integration, and eradicate poverty, in member states. A strategic plan, endorsed by the COMESA Authority at its 14th summit meeting convened in August 2010, governs COMESA's medium-term goals and activities during the period 2011–15, prioritizing integration; enhancing productive capacity for global competitiveness; infrastructure development; cross-cutting issues such as gender and social development, climate change, statistics, peace and security, knowledge-based capacity and human capital; co-operation and partnership; and institutional development. COMESA supports capacity building activities and the establishment of other specialized institutions (see below).

From COMESA's establishment there were concerns on the part of member states, as well as other regional non-member countries, in particular South Africa, of adverse rivalry between COMESA and the SADC and of a duplication of roles. In 1997 Lesotho and Mozambique terminated their membership of COMESA owing to concerns that their continued participation in the organization was incompatible with their SADC membership. Tanzania withdrew from COMESA in September 2000, reportedly also in view of its dual commitment to that organization and to SADC. In June 2003 Namibia announced its withdrawal from COMESA. The summit meeting of COMESA heads of state or government held in May 2000 expressed support for an ongoing programme of co-operation by the Secretariats of COMESA and SADC aimed at reducing the duplication of roles between the two organizations, and urged further mutual collaboration. A co-ordinating task force was established in 2001, and was joined by the EAC (becoming the COMESA-EAC-SADC Task Force) in 2005, as the EAC became involved in the REC co-operation programme. The Regional Trade Facilitation Programme covering southern and eastern Africa, and based in Pretoria, South Africa, provides secretariat services to the Task Force.

TRADE, CUSTOMS AND MONETARY AFFAIRS

In May 1999 COMESA established a Free Trade Area (FTA) Committee to facilitate and co-ordinate preparations for the creation of the common market envisaged under the COMESA treaty. An extraordinary summit of COMESA heads of state or government, held in October 2000, inaugurated the FTA, with nine initial members: Djibouti, Egypt, Kenya, Madagascar, Malawi, Mauritius, Sudan, Zambia and Zimbabwe. Burundi and Rwanda became members of the FTA in January 2004, and Swaziland undertook in April to seek the concurrence of the Southern African Customs Union, of which it is also a member, to allow it to participate in the FTA. Trading practices within the FTA have been fully liberalized, including the elimination of non-tariff barriers, thereby enabling the free internal movement of goods, services and capital. The COMESA Customs Union (CU), with a common external tariff (CET) set at 0% for capital goods and raw materials, 10% for intermediate goods and 25% for finished products, was launched at the 13th annual summit meeting of the Authority, in June 2009. It was envisaged that the Customs Union would be fully operational in 2012. A Protocol establishing the COMESA Fund, which assists member states in addressing structural imbalances in their economies, came into effect in November 2006. COMESA plans to form an economic community (entailing monetary union and the free movement of people between member states) by 2014. In May 2007 the Authority endorsed the establishment of an 'Aid for Trade' unit in the COMESA Secretariat, which was to assist countries with the identification and implementation of projects aimed at removing trade-related supply constraints. A COMESA Competition Commission, based in Blantyre, Malawi, was inaugurated in December 2008. In June 2009 a regional payments and settlement system (REPSS), headquartered in Lusaka, Zambia, was launched.

Under the COMESA Regional Economic and Trade Integration Program (CRETIP), implemented during September 2006–September 2010, COMESA received US assistance towards the implementation of programmes promoting COMESA–USA trade, regional trade, and the institutional strengthening of the COMESA Secretariat. In August 2007 COMESA appointed a Special Representative to the Middle East to establish partnerships with that region and to promote trade opportunities.

In October 2008 the first tripartite COMESA-EAC-SADC summit was convened, in Kampala, Uganda, to discuss the harmonization of policy and programme work by the three RECs. Leaders of the 26 countries attending the Kampala summit approved a roadmap towards the formation of a common FTA and the eventual establishment of a single African Economic Community (a long-term objective of AU co-operation). A COMESA-EAC-SADC Joint Competition Authority was established at the tripartite summit. At the second tripartite summit, held in June 2011, in Johannesburg, South Africa, negotiations were initiated on the establishment of the proposed COMESA-EAC-SADC Tripartite FTA. In January 2012 AU leaders endorsed a new Framework, Roadmap and Architecture for Fast Tracking the Establishment of a Continental FTA (referred to as CFTA), and an Action Plan for Boosting Intra-African Trade, which planned for the consolidation of the COMESA-EAC-SADC Tripartite FTA with other regional FTAs into the CFTA initiative during 2015–16; and the establishment of an operational CFTA by 2017. COMESA has co-operated with other sub-regional organizations to finalize a common position on co-operation between African ACP countries and the European Union (EU) under the Cotonou Agreement (concluded in June 2000, see the chapter on the EU). The COMESA Customs Bond Guarantee Scheme facilitate the movement of goods through the region, and provides the necessary customs security and guarantee to transit countries.

In September 2012 a pilot version of a new COMESA Virtual Trade Facilitation System (CVTFS) was launched for the Djibouti–Addis Ababa–Khartoum and Juba trade corridors, with the aim of co-ordinating information exchange, and monitoring the movement of goods-in-transit, to promote trade efficiency and competitiveness.

AGRICULTURE

A regional food security programme aims to ensure continuous adequate food supplies. COMESA works with private sector interests through the African Union (AU) Comprehensive African Agricultural Development Programme (CAADP) to improve agricultural performance. The CAADP undertook efforts in 2008 to strengthen regional capacity to address food insecurity, promoting robust markets and long-term competitiveness. COMESA maintains a Food and Agricultural Marketing Information System (FAMIS), providing up-to-date data on the sub-regional food security situation. In 1997 COMESA heads of state advocated that the food sector be supported by the implementation of an irrigation action plan for the region. The organization supports the establishment of common agricultural standards and phytosanitary regulations throughout the region in order to stimulate trade in food crops. In March 2005 more than 100 standards on quality assurance, covering mainly agricultural products, were adopted. Meeting for the first time in November 2002, COMESA ministers of agriculture determined to formulate a regional policy on genetically modified organisms. At their second meeting, held in October 2004, ministers of agriculture agreed to prioritize agriculture in their development efforts, and—in accordance with a Declaration of the AU—the objective of allocating at least 10% of national budgets to agriculture and rural development. In September 2008 COMESA ministers of agriculture launched the Alliance for Commodity Trade in Eastern and Southern Africa (ACTESA), with the aim of integrating small farmers into national, regional and international markets. ACTESA became a specialized agency of COMESA in June 2009. In March 2010 COMESA and ACTESA signed an agreement aimed at accelerating the implementation of regional initiatives in agriculture, trade and investment.

CLIMATE CHANGE ADAPTATION AND ENVIRONMENT

Following a recommendation by the AU, in January 2007, that climate change adaptation strategies should be integrated into African national and sub-regional development planning and activities, COMESA launched a Climate Change Initiative, which aims to improve economic and social resilience to the impacts of climate change. In July 2010 COMESA, the EAC and SADC adopted a five-year Tripartite Programme on Climate Change Adaptation and Mitigation in the COMESA-EAC-SADC region. A tripartite agreement for the implementation of the Programme was signed by the three parties in July 2012.

In June 2010 a consultative meeting was convened between COMESA, the AU, IGAD, and other regional partners, aimed at advancing co-ordination and harmonization of their activities related to the environment.

INVESTMENT PROMOTION AND PRIVATE SECTOR DEVELOPMENT

The COMESA Regional Investment Agency (RIA), based in Cairo, Egypt, was inaugurated in June 2006, its founding charter having been adopted in June 2005 by the 10th summit meeting of the Authority. An Agreement on the establishment of a COMESA Common Investment Area (CCIA) was adopted by the Authority at its May 2007 summit meeting.

In February 2000 a COMESA economic forum was convened in Cairo, Egypt. A COMESA Business Council was inaugurated in 2003, with a mandate to provide a policy and advocacy platform for regional private sector interests. The seventh COMESA Business Forum was organized in October 2011, in Lilongwe, Malawi, on the sidelines of the 15th summit of the Authority. The COMESA RIA sponsors annual investment fora: the fourth forum was convened in Dubai, United Arab Emirates, in March 2011. In August 2012 the COMESA Business Council, jointly with the Kenyan authorities, organized the first COMESA Sustainable Tourism Development Forum, on the theme 'Shaping the Future of Tourism in COMESA'.

In June 2012 COMESA the first meeting of COMESA ministers of science, technology and innovation decided to establish an Innovation Council, which was to adopt knowledge practices from around the world to assist member states in the research and development of information technology. The second such meeting was convened in September 2012.

In February 2010 COMESA and ECOWAS concluded a Memorandum of Understanding aimed at enhancing private sector development in their regions, and at advancing pan-African economic integration.

INFRASTRUCTURE DEVELOPMENT

An Eastern Africa Power Pool (EAPP) has been established by COMESA, comprising Burundi, Democratic Republic of the Congo, Djibouti, Ethiopia, Kenya, Sudan, Tanzania and Uganda. COMESA and the Southern African Development Community (SADC) have the joint objective of eventually linking the EAPP and the Southern Africa Power Pool. COMESA maintains a priority list of regional infrastructure projects, and, in 2008, launched an interactive database recording the status of the projects. In March 2009 a new Regional Association of Energy Regulators for Eastern and Southern Africa was launched.

A COMESA Telecommunications Company (COMTEL) was registered in May 2000. In January 2003 the Association of Regulators of Information and Communication for Eastern and Southern Africa was launched, under the auspices of COMESA. COMESA is developing a regional e-Government programme, providing for the greater dissemination of government information through, for example, the internet, mobile telephones and radios; it was envisaged that e-Government activities would promote civic engagement and make government operations more transparent and accountable.

Organization-wide initiatives to facilitate travel in the region include a scheme for third-party motor vehicle insurance, a road customs declaration document, and a system of regional travellers cheques.

GENDER AND SOCIAL AFFAIRS

A new Gender and social affairs division of the COMESA Secretariat was established in 2008, with the aim of facilitating increased involvement by COMESA in areas related to social development, including health, education, youth affairs, and migration and labour. During 2012 a COMESA Social Charter was being drafted, which was to support the incorporation of social dimensions into the regional integration agenda, through the identification of economic- and social rights-related benchmarks. The new Charter was to provide a regional platform for the promotion of the AU Commission's 2008 pan-African Social Development Framework (q.v.); and was to help guide the formulation of member states' national development strategies.

A joint COMESA-EAC-IGAD observer mission was dispatched to monitor presidential and legislative elections that took place in Uganda in February 2011. COMESA also sent an observer mission to monitor the conduct of the presidential, legislative and local government elections that were held in late September in Zambia.

REGIONAL SECURITY

In May 1999 the COMESA Authority resolved to establish a Committee on Peace and Security comprising ministers of foreign affairs from member states. It was envisaged that the Committee would convene at least once a year to address matters concerning regional stability. (Instability in certain member states was regarded as a potential threat to the successful implementation of the FTA.) The Committee met for the first time in 2000. It was announced in September 2002 that the COMESA Treaty was to be amended to provide for the establishment of a formal conflict prevention and resolution structure to be governed by member countries' heads of state. COMESA participates, with other regional economic communities (RECs) in the AU's Continental Early Warning System, and has, since 2008, taken part in joint technical meetings and training sessions in this respect. In June 2009 COMESA inaugurated the regional COMWARN early warning system, which was to monitor indicators of vulnerability to conflict in member states. The seventh meeting of the Committee, held in November 2006, recommended the establishment of a COMESA Committee of Elders, which was to undertake preventive peace-building assignments; the Committee of Elders held its inaugural meeting in December 2011. The seventh meeting of COMESA ministers of foreign affairs also decided that COMESA's peace and security activities should focus in particular on the economic dimensions of conflicts.

Finance

COMESA is financed by member states.

Publications

Annual Report of the Council of Ministers.
Asycuda Newsletter.
COMESA Journal.
COMESA Trade Directory (annually).
COMESA Trade Information Newsletter (monthly).
e-comesa (monthly newsletter).
Demand/supply surveys, catalogues and reports.

COMESA Institutions

African Trade Insurance Agency (ATI): POB 10620, 00100-GPO, Nairobi, Kenya; tel. (20) 27269999; fax (20) 2719701; e-mail info@ati-aca.org; internet www.ati-aca.org; f. 2001 to promote trade and investment activities throughout the region; mems: 13 African countries; CEO GEORGE O. OTIENO.

Alliance for Commodity Trade in Eastern and Southern Africa (ACTESA): Corporate Park, Alick Nkhata Rd, Lusaka, 10101 Zambia; tel. 211-253572; e-mail info@actesacomesa.org; internet www.actesacomesa.org; f. 2008, became a specialized agency of COMESA in June 2009; aims to integrate small farmers into national, regional and international markets; CEO Dr CHUNGU MWILA.

COMESA Bankers Association: Private Bag 271, Kapeni House, 1st Floor, Blantyre, Malawi; tel. and fax (1) 674236; e-mail info@comesabankers.org; internet www.comesabankers.org; f. 1987 as the PTA Association of Commercial Banks; name changed as above in 1994; aims to strengthen co-operation between banks in the region; organizes training activities; conducts studies to harmonize banking laws and operations; implements a bank fraud prevention programme; mems: 55 commercial banking orgs in Burundi, Egypt, Eritrea, Ethiopia, Kenya, Malawi, Rwanda, Sudan, Swaziland; Exec. Sec. ERIC C. CHINKANDA (acting).

COMESA Leather and Leather Products Institute (LLPI): POB 2358, 1110 Addis Ababa, Ethiopia; tel. (11) 4390928; fax (11) 4390900; e-mail comesa.llpi@ethionet.et; internet www.comesa-llpi.org/index.php; f. 1990 as the PTA Leather Institute; mems: 17 COMESA mem. states; Chair. WILSON MAZIMBA.

COMESA Regional Investment Authority (COMESA-RIA): 3 Salah Salem Rd, Nasr City, Cairo, Egypt; tel. (2) 405-5428; fax (2) 405-5421; e-mail info@comesaria.org; internet www.comesaria.org; Man. HEBA SALAMA.

Compagnie de réassurance de la Zone d'échanges préférentiels (ZEP-RE) (PTA Reinsurance Co): ZEP-RE Place, Longonot Rd, Upper Hill, POB 42769, 00100 Nairobi, Kenya; tel. (20) 2738221; fax (20) 2738444; e-mail mail@zep-re.com; internet www.zep-re.com; f. 1992 (began operations on 1 Jan. 1993); provides local reinsurance services and training to personnel in the insurance industry; total assets US $103.1m. (2010); Chair. Dr MICHAEL GONDWE; Man. Dir RAJNI VARIA.

East African Power Pool (EAPP): Bole Sub City, Gulz Aziz Bldg, Addis Ababa Ethiopia; tel. (11) 6183694; fax (11) 6183694; e-mail eapp@eappool.org; internet www.eappool.org/eng/about.html; in Feb. 2005 energy ministers from Burundi, DRC, Egypt, Ethiopia, Kenya, Rwanda and Sudan signed the Inter-Governmental Memorandum of Understanding on the establishment of the Eastern Africa Power Pool (EAPP); EAPP was adopted by COMESA as a specialized institution in 2006; Tanzania and Libya joined in 2010 and 2011, respectively; Exec. Sec. JASPER ODUOR.

Eastern and Southern African Trade and Development Bank: NSSF Bldg, 22nd/23rd Floor, Bishop's Rd, POB 48596, 00100

Nairobi, Kenya; tel. (20) 2712250; fax (20) 2711510; e-mail official@ptabank.org; internet www.ptabank.org; f. 1983 as PTA Development Bank; aims to mobilize resources and finance COMESA activities to foster regional integration; promotes investment and co-financing within the region; in Jan. 2003 the US dollar replaced the UAPTA (PTA unit of account) as the Bank's reporting currency; shareholders: 15 COMESA mem. states, the People's Republic of China, Somalia, Tanzania and the African Development Bank; total assets US $1,055.9m. (Dec. 2010); Pres. and CEO ADMASSU Y. TADESSE (Ethiopia).

Federation of National Associations of Women in Business in Eastern and Southern Africa (FEMCOM): Off Queens Drive, Area 6, Plot No. 170, POB 1499, Lilongwe, Malawi; tel. (1) 205-908; e-mail info@femcomcomesa.org; internet www.femcomcomesa.org; f. 1993; autonomous secretariat launched in 2009; aims to promote programmes that integrate women into regional trade and development activities, with a particular focus on the areas of agriculture, fishing, energy, communications, industry, mining, natural resources, trade, services, and transport; has chapters in all COMESA mem. states; Exec. Dir KATHERINE ICHOYA.

COMMONWEALTH

Address: Commonwealth Secretariat, Marlborough House, Pall Mall, London, SW1Y 5HX, United Kingdom.

Telephone: (20) 7747-6500; **fax:** (20) 7930-0827; **e-mail:** info@commonwealth.int; **internet:** www.thecommonwealth.org.

The Commonwealth is a voluntary association of 53 independent states (at September 2012), comprising about one-quarter of the world's population. It includes the United Kingdom and most of its former dependencies, and former dependencies of Australia and New Zealand (themselves Commonwealth countries). All Commonwealth countries accept Queen Elizabeth II as the symbol of the free association of the independent member nations and as such the Head of the Commonwealth.

MEMBERS IN AFRICA SOUTH OF THE SAHARA

Botswana	Mauritius	South Africa
Cameroon	Mozambique	Swaziland
The Gambia	Namibia	Tanzania
Ghana	Nigeria	Uganda
Kenya	Rwanda	Zambia
Lesotho	Seychelles	
Malawi	Sierra Leone	

Note: In March 2002 Zimbabwe was suspended from participation in meetings of the Commonwealth. Zimbabwe announced its withdrawal from the Commonwealth in December 2003. Rwanda was admitted to membership of the Commonwealth in November 2009. In 2012 the Commonwealth was considering possible future membership for South Sudan, which attained independence in July 2011.

United Kingdom Overseas Territories

British Indian Ocean Territory
St Helena, Ascension, Tristan da Cunha

Organization

(September 2012)

The Commonwealth is not a federation: there is no central government nor are there any rigid contractual obligations such as bind members of the United Nations (UN).

Commonwealth members subscribe to the ideals of the Declaration of Commonwealth Principles unanimously approved by a meeting of heads of government in Singapore in 1971. Members also approved the Gleneagles Agreement concerning apartheid in sport (1977); the Lusaka Declaration on Racism and Racial Prejudice (1979); the Melbourne Declaration on relations between developed and developing countries (1981); the New Delhi Statement on Economic Action (1983); the Goa Declaration on International Security (1983); the Nassau Declaration on World Order (1985); the Commonwealth Accord on Southern Africa (1985); the Vancouver Declaration on World Trade (1987); the Okanagan Statement and Programme of Action on Southern Africa (1987); the Langkawi Declaration on the Environment (1989); the Kuala Lumpur Statement on Southern Africa (1989); the Harare Commonwealth Declaration (1991); the Ottawa Declaration on Women and Structural Adjustment (1991); the Limassol Statement on the Uruguay Round of multilateral trade negotiations (1993); the Millbrook Commonwealth Action Programme on the Harare Declaration (1995); the Edinburgh Commonwealth Economic Declaration (1997); the Fancourt Commonwealth Declaration on Globalization and People-centred Development (1999); the Coolum Declaration on the Commonwealth in the 21st Century: Continuity and Renewal (2002); the Aso Rock Commonwealth Declaration and Statement on Multilateral Trade (2003); the Malta Commonwealth Declaration on Networking for Development (2005); the Munyonyo Statement on Respect and Understanding (2007); the Marlborough House Statement on Reform of International Institutions (2008); the Commonwealth Climate Change Declaration (2009); and the Perth Declaration on Food Security Principles (2011).

In October 2011 Commonwealth heads of government agreed that a non-binding Charter of the Commonwealth, embodying the principles contained in previous declarations, should be drawn up. Meeting in September 2012, on the sidelines of the 67th UN General Assembly session, in New York, USA, Commonwealth ministers of foreign affairs approved a draft of the new Charter; the draft was to be submitted for endorsement by the next meeting of Commonwealth heads of government.

MEETINGS OF HEADS OF GOVERNMENT

Commonwealth Heads of Government Meetings (CHOGMs) are private and informal and operate not by voting but by consensus. The emphasis is on consultation and exchange of views for co-operation. A communiqué is issued at the end of every meeting. Meetings are normally held every two years in different capitals in the Commonwealth. The 2011 meeting was convened in Perth, Australia, at the end of October. The 2013 meeting was to be held, in November, in Colombo, Sri Lanka; and Mauritius was to host the 2015 meeting.

OTHER CONSULTATIONS

The Commonwealth Ministerial Action Group on the Harare was formed in 1995 to support democracy in member countries (see Activities, below). It comprises a group of nine ministers of foreign affairs, with rotating membership.

A Commonwealth Eminent Persons Group was inaugurated in July 2010 to make recommendations on means of raising the profile of the Commonwealth, strengthening its networks, and increasing its impact.

Since 1959 Commonwealth finance ministers have met in the week prior to the annual meetings of the IMF and the World Bank. Ministers responsible for civil society, education, the environment, foreign affairs, gender issues, health, law, tourism and youth also hold regular meetings.

Biennial conferences of representatives of Commonwealth small states are convened.

Senior officials—cabinet secretaries, permanent secretaries to heads of government and others—meet regularly in the year between meetings of heads of government to provide continuity and to exchange views on various developments.

COMMONWEALTH SECRETARIAT

The Secretariat, established by Commonwealth heads of government in 1965, operates as an intergovernmental organization at the service of all Commonwealth countries. It organizes consultations between governments and runs programmes of co-operation. Meetings of heads of government, ministers and senior officials decide these programmes and provide overall direction. A Board of Governors, on which all eligible member governments are represented, meets annually to review the Secretariat's work and approve its budget. The Board is supported by an Executive Committee which convenes four times a year to monitor implementation of the Secretariat's work programme. The Secretariat is headed by a secretary-general, elected by heads of government.

In 2002 the Secretariat was restructured, with a view to strengthening the effectiveness of the organization to meet the priorities determined by the meeting of heads of government held in Coolum, Australia, in March 2002. Under the reorganization the number of deputy secretaries-general was reduced from three to two. Certain work divisions were amalgamated, while new units or sections, concerned with youth affairs, human rights and good offices, were created to strengthen further activities in those fields. Accordingly, the Secretariat's divisional structure is as follows: Legal and constitutional affairs; Political affairs; Corporate services; Communications and public affairs; Strategic planning and evaluation; Economic affairs; Governance and institutional development; Social transformation programmes; Youth affairs (from 2004); and Special advisory services. (Details of some of the divisions are given under Activities, below.) In addition there is a unit responsible for human rights, and an Office of the Secretary-General.

The Secretariat's Strategic Plan for 2008–12, approved by the Board of Governors in May 2008, set out two main, long-term objectives for the Commonwealth. The first, 'Peace and Democracy', was to support member countries in preventing or resolving conflicts, to strengthen democracy and the rule of law, and to achieve greater respect for human rights. The second, 'Pro-Poor Growth and Sustainable Development', was to support policies for economic growth and sustainable development, particularly for the benefit of the poorest people, in member countries. Four programmes were to facilitate the pursuit of the first objective: Good Offices for Peace; Democracy and Consensus Building; Rule of Law; and Human Rights. The second objective was to be pursued through the following four programmes: Public Sector Development; Economic Development; Environmentally Sustainable Development; and Human Development.

A successor Strategic Plan, to cover the period January 2013–June 2016, was under development in 2012. It was envisaged that the new Plan, aimed at creating a more dynamic, contemporary organization, would have a stronger focus on promoting the relative strengths of the Secretariat, and would focus on advancing strategic partnerships with other international actors to improve the application of Commonwealth values and developmental priorities.

Secretary-General: Kamalesh Sharma (India).

Deputy Secretaries-General: Mmasekgoa Masire-Mwamba (Botswana), Ransford Smith (Jamaica).

Assistant Secretary-General for Corporate Affairs: Stephen Cutts (United Kingdom).

Activities

PROMOTING DEMOCRACY, HUMAN RIGHTS AND DEVELOPMENT

In October 1991 heads of government, meeting in Harare, Zimbabwe, issued the Harare Commonwealth Declaration, in which they reaffirmed their commitment to the Commonwealth Principles declared in 1971, and stressed the need to promote sustainable development and the alleviation of poverty. The Declaration placed emphasis on the promotion of democracy and respect for human rights and resolved to strengthen the Commonwealth's capacity to assist countries in entrenching democratic practices. In November 1995 Commonwealth heads of government, convened in New Zealand, formulated and adopted the Millbrook Commonwealth Action Programme on the Harare Declaration, to promote adherence by member countries to the fundamental principles of democracy and human rights (as proclaimed in the 1991 Declaration). The Programme incorporated a framework of measures to be pursued in support of democratic processes and institutions, and actions to be taken in response to violations of the Harare Declaration principles, in particular the unlawful removal of a democratically elected government. A Commonwealth Ministerial Action Group on the Harare Declaration (CMAG) was established in December 1995 to implement this process and to assist the member country involved to comply with the Harare principles. In March 2002 Commonwealth leaders expanded CMAG's mandate to enable the Group to consider action against serious violations of the Commonwealth's core values perpetrated by elected administrations as well as by military regimes. In October 2011 the Perth summit of Commonwealth leaders agreed a series of reforms aimed at strengthening the role of CMAG in addressing serious violations of Commonwealth political values; these included clearer guidelines and time frames for engagement when the situation in a country causes concern, with a view to shifting from a reactive to a more proactive role.

The October 2011 heads of government reconstituted CMAG's membership to comprise over the next biennium the ministers responsible for foreign affairs of Australia, Bangladesh, Canada, Jamaica, the Maldives (suspended from the Group in February 2012), Sierra Leone, Tanzania, Trinidad and Tobago, and Vanuatu.

In response to the earthquake and tsunami that devastated coastal areas of several Indian Ocean countries in late December 2004, the Commonwealth Secretary-General appealed for assistance from Commonwealth Governments for the mobilization of emergency humanitarian relief. In early January 2005 the Secretariat dispatched a Disaster Relief Co-ordinator to the Maldives to assess the needs of that country and to co-ordinate ongoing relief and rehabilitation activities, and later in that month the Secretariat sent emergency medical doctors from other member states to the Maldives. In mid-January, meeting during the fifth Summit of the Alliance of Small Island States, in Port Louis, Mauritius, the Secretaries-General of the Commonwealth, the Caribbean Community and Common Market (CARICOM), the Pacific Islands Forum and the Indian Ocean Commission determined to take collective action to strengthen the disaster-preparedness and response capacities of their member countries in the Caribbean, Pacific and Indian Ocean areas.

In March 2002, meeting in Coolum, near Brisbane, Australia, Commonwealth heads of government adopted the Coolum Declaration on the Commonwealth in the 21st Century: Continuity and Renewal, which reiterated commitment to the organization's principles and values. Leaders at the meeting condemned all forms of terrorism and endorsed a Plan of Action for combating international terrorism, establishing a Commonwealth Committee on Terrorism, convened at ministerial level, to oversee the implementation of the Plan. The leaders welcomed the Millennium Development Goals (MDGs) adopted by the UN General Assembly; requested the Secretary-General to constitute an expert group on implementing the objectives of the Fancourt Commonwealth Declaration on Globalization and People-Centred Development (see Economic Co-operation, below); pledged continued support for small states; and urged renewed efforts to combat the spread of HIV/AIDS. They also endorsed a Commonwealth Local Government Good Practice Scheme, to be managed by the Commonwealth Local Government Forum (established in 1995). The heads of government adopted a report on the future of the Commonwealth drafted by the High Level Review Group. The document recommended strengthening the Commonwealth's role in conflict prevention and resolution and support of democratic practices; enhancing the 'good offices' role of the Secretary-General; better promoting member states' economic and development needs; strengthening the organization's role in facilitating member states' access to international assistance; and promoting increased access to modern information and communications technologies.

In concluding the 2003 meeting heads of government issued the Aso Rock Commonwealth Declaration, which emphasized their commitment to strengthening development and democracy, and incorporated clear objectives in support of these goals. Priority areas identified included efforts to eradicate poverty and attain the MDGs, to strengthen democratic institutions, empower women, promote the involvement of civil society, combat corruption and recover assets (for which a working group was to be established), facilitate finance for development, address the spread of HIV/AIDS and other diseases, combat illicit trafficking in human beings, and promote education. The leaders also adopted a separate statement on multilateral trade, in particular in support of the stalled Doha Round of World Trade Organization (WTO) negotiations.

The 2007 meeting of Commonwealth heads of government, convened in Kampala, Uganda, in November, issued the Munyonyo Statement on Respect and Understanding, which commended the work of the Commonwealth Commission on Respect and Understanding (established in 2005) and endorsed its recently published report entitled *Civil Paths to Peace* aimed at building tolerance and understanding of diversity.

In November 2009 Commonwealth heads of government, meeting in Trinidad and Tobago, welcomed recent progress in the discussion of border disputes between Belize and Guatemala, and between Guyana and Venezuela. They expressed support for negotiations on the reunification of Cyprus, initiated in 2008, and welcomed the recent agreement on power-sharing in Zimbabwe. They urged the renewal of commitment to the non-proliferation of nuclear weapons at the next Non-Proliferation Treaty review conference (convened in May 2010), and the pursuit of negotiations on a comprehensive Arms Trade Treaty (on conventional weapons) at a global conference that was held in July 2012. Heads of government also urged the conclusion of a UN treaty on international terrorism and discussed combating piracy and human trafficking. In July 2010, in view of a decision of the 2009 heads of government meeting, a new Commonwealth Eminent Persons Group (EPG) was inaugurated, with a mandate to make recommendations on means of strengthening the organization. During June 2010 the Commonwealth Secretariat hosted the first biennial conference of small states, and the second was convened in September 2012 (see under Economic Affairs Division).

The summit of heads of government held in Perth, Australia, in October 2011, issued the Perth Declaration on Food Security Principles, reaffirming the universal right to safe, sufficient and nutritious food. The summit agreed that a Charter of the Commonwealth, proposed by the EPG, should be drafted, embodying the principles contained in previous declarations; and that the appointment of a Commonwealth Commissioner for Democracy, Rule of Law and Human Rights, also recommended by the EPG, should be considered.

Political Affairs Division: assists consultation among member governments on international and Commonwealth matters of common interest. In association with host governments, it organizes the meetings of heads of government and senior officials. The Division services committees and special groups set up by heads of government dealing with political matters. The Secretariat has observer status at the UN, and the Division manages a joint office in New York to enable small states, which would otherwise be unable to afford facilities there, to maintain a presence at the UN. The Division monitors political developments in the Commonwealth and international progress in such matters as disarmament and the Law of the Sea. It also undertakes research on matters of common interest to member governments, and reports back to them. The Division is involved in diplomatic training and consular co-operation.

In 1990 Commonwealth heads of government mandated the Division to support the promotion of democracy by monitoring the preparations for and conduct of parliamentary, presidential or other elections in member countries at the request of national governments. In May 2010 a new Commonwealth Network of National Election Management Bodies was inaugurated; the Network aims to enhance collaboration among institutions, thereby boosting standards. Commonwealth groups were dispatched to observe legislative elections held in Lesotho in May 2012, and in Papua New Guinea, in June.

In September 2012 a Commonwealth Secretariat pre-election fact finding team visited Sierra Leone to evaluate ongoing preparations for presidential and legislative elections scheduled to be held in mid-November. Commonwealth groups were to observe the Sierra Leone polls, as well as parliamentary elections to be held in Ghana, in early December.

Under the reorganization of the Secretariat in 2002 a Good Offices Section was established within the Division to strengthen and support the activities of the Secretary-General in addressing political conflict in member states and in assisting countries to adhere to the principles of the Harare Declaration. The Secretary-General's good offices may involve discreet 'behind the scenes' diplomacy to prevent or resolve conflict and assist other international efforts to promote political stability.

Human Rights Unit: undertakes activities in support of the Commonwealth's commitment to the promotion and protection of fundamental human rights. It develops programmes, publishes human rights materials, co-operates with other organizations working in the field of human rights, in particular within the UN system, advises the Secretary-General, and organizes seminars and meetings of experts. It also provides training for police forces, magistrates and government officials in awareness of human rights. The Unit aims to integrate human rights standards within all divisions of the Secretariat.

Legal and Constitutional Affairs Division: promotes and facilitates co-operation and the exchange of information among member governments on legal matters and assists in combating financial and organized crime, in particular transborder criminal activities. It administers, jointly with the Commonwealth of Learning (see below), a distance training programme for legislative draftsmen and assists governments to reform national laws to meet the obligations of international conventions. The Division organizes the triennial meeting of ministers, Attorneys General and senior ministry officials concerned with the legal systems in Commonwealth countries. It has also initiated four Commonwealth schemes for co-operation on extradition, the protection of material cultural heritage, mutual assistance in criminal matters and the transfer of convicted offenders within the Commonwealth. It liaises with the Commonwealth Magistrates' and Judges' Association, the Commonwealth Legal Education Association, the Commonwealth Lawyers' Association (with which it helps to prepare the triennial Commonwealth Law Conference for the practising profession), the Commonwealth Association of Legislative Counsel, and with other international non-governmental organizations. The Division provides in-house legal advice for the Secretariat. The *Commonwealth Law Bulletin*, published four times a year, reports on legal developments in and beyond the Commonwealth. The *Commonwealth Human Rights Law Digest* (three a year) contains details of decisions relating to human rights cases from across the Commonwealth.

ECONOMIC AND ENVIRONMENTAL CO-OPERATION

In May 1998 the Commonwealth Secretary-General appealed to the Group of Eight industrialized nations (G8) to accelerate and expand the initiative to ease the debt burden of the most heavily indebted poor countries (HIPCs—see World Bank and the IMF). In October Commonwealth finance ministers reiterated their appeal to international financial institutions to accelerate the HIPC initiative. The meeting also issued a Commonwealth Statement on the global economic crisis and endorsed proposals to help to counter the difficulties experienced by several countries. These measures included a mechanism to enable countries to suspend payments on all short-term financial obligations at a time of emergency without defaulting, assistance to governments to attract private capital and to manage capital market volatility, and the development of international codes of conduct regarding financial and monetary policies and corporate governance. In March 1999 the Commonwealth Secretariat hosted a joint IMF-World Bank conference to review the HIPC scheme and initiate a process of reform. In November Commonwealth heads of government, meeting in South Africa, declared their support for measures undertaken by the World Bank and IMF to enhance the HIPC initiative. At the end of an informal retreat the leaders adopted the Fancourt Commonwealth Declaration on Globalization and People-Centred Development, which emphasized the need for a more equitable spread of wealth generated by the process of globalization, and expressed a renewed commitment to the elimination of all forms of discrimination, the promotion of people-centred development and capacity building, and efforts to ensure that developing countries benefit from future multilateral trade liberalization measures. In June 2002 the Commonwealth Secretary-General urged more generous funding of the HIPC initiative. Meetings of ministers of finance from Commonwealth member countries participating in the HIPC initiative are convened twice a year, as the Commonwealth Ministerial Debt Sustainability Forum. The Secretariat aims to assist HIPCs and other small economies through its Debt Recording and Management System (DRMS), which was first used in 1985 and updated in 2002; at September 2012 the DRMS had 61 participating states. In July 2005 the Commonwealth Secretary-General welcomed an initiative of the G8 to eliminate the debt of those HIPCs that had reached their completion point in the process, in addition to a commitment substantially to increase aid to Africa.

In February 1998 the Commonwealth Secretariat hosted a meeting of intergovernmental organizations to promote co-operation between small island states and the formulation of a unified policy approach to international fora. A second meeting was convened in March 2001, where discussions focused on the forthcoming WTO ministerial meeting and OECD's Harmful Tax Competition Initiative. In September 2000 Commonwealth ministers of finance, meeting in Malta, reviewed the OECD initiative and agreed that the measures, affecting many member countries with offshore financial centres, should not be imposed on governments. The ministers mandated the involvement of the Commonwealth Secretariat in efforts to resolve the dispute; a joint working group was subsequently established by the Secretariat with the OECD. In April 2002 a meeting on international co-operation in the financial services sector, attended by representatives of international and regional organizations, donors and senior officials from Commonwealth countries, was held under Commonwealth auspices in Saint Lucia. In September 2005 Commonwealth finance ministers, meeting in Barbados, considered new guidelines for Public Financial Management Reform.

In November 2005 Commonwealth heads of government issued the Malta Declaration on Networking the Commonwealth for Development, expressing their commitment to making available to all the benefits of new technologies and to using information technology networks to enhance the effectiveness of the Commonwealth in supporting development. The meeting endorsed a new Commonwealth Action Programme for the Digital Divide and approved the establishment of a special fund to enable implementation of the programme's objectives. Accordingly a Commonwealth Connects programme was established in August 2006 to develop partnerships and help to strengthen the use of and access to information technology in all Commonwealth countries; a Commonwealth Connects web portal—www.commonwealthconnects.org—was launched at the October 2011 heads of government summit. The 2005 Heads of Government Meeting also issued the Valletta Statement on Multilateral Trade, emphasizing their concerns that the Doha Round of WTO negotiations proceed steadily, on a development-oriented agenda, to a successful conclusion and reiterating their objectives of achieving a rules-based and equitable international trading system. A separate statement drew attention to the specific needs and challenges of small states and urged continued financial and technical support, in particular for those affected by natural disasters.

The Commonwealth Climate Change Action Plan, adopted by heads of government in November 2007, acknowledged that climate change posed a serious threat to the very existence of some small island states within the Commonwealth, and to the low-lying coastal areas of others. It offered unqualified support for the UN Framework Convention on Climate Change, and recognized the need to overcome technical, economic and policy-making barriers to reducing carbon emissions, to using renewable energy, and to increasing energy efficiency. The Plan undertook to assist developing member states in international negotiations on climate change; to support improved land use management, including the use of forest resources; to investigate the carbon footprint of agricultural exports from member countries; to increase support for the management of natural disasters in member countries; and to provide technical assistance to help least developed members and small states to assess the implications of climate change and adapt accordingly. A high-level meeting on climate finance, convened in London, in January 2011, determined to establish a working group to advance climate-related Commonwealth initiatives; and to integrate work on climate-related finance mechanisms into the next (January 2013–June 2016) Strategic Plan.

In June 2008 the Commonwealth issued the Marlborough House Statement on Reform of International Institutions, declaring that ongoing global financial turbulence and soaring food and fuel prices highlighted the poor responsiveness of some international organizations mandated to promote economic stability, and determining to identify underlying principles and actions required to reform the international system. In November 2009 heads of government reiterated the need for reform in the UN system, demanding greater representation for developing countries in international economic decision making, with particular reference to the IMF and the World Bank. They expressed concern that many Commonwealth countries were falling behind the MDG targets, and resolved to strengthen existing networks of co-operation: in particular, they undertook to take measures to improve the quality of data used in policy making, and to strengthen the links between research and policy making. A new Commonwealth Partnership Platform Portal was to provide practical support for sharing ideas and best practices. Heads of government also undertook to promote investment in science, technology and innovation.

Economic Affairs Division: organizes and services the annual meetings of Commonwealth ministers of finance and the ministerial group on small states and assists in servicing the biennial meetings of heads of government and periodic meetings of environment ministers. It engages in research and analysis on economic issues of interest to member governments and organizes seminars and conferences of government officials and experts. The Division actively supports developing Commonwealth countries to participate in the Doha Round of multilateral trade negotiations and is assisting the ACP group of countries to negotiate economic partnership agreements with the European Union. It continues to help developing countries to strengthen their links with international capital markets and foreign investors. The Division also services groups of experts on economic affairs that have been commissioned by governments to report on, among other things, protectionism; obstacles to the North-South negotiating process; reform of the international financial and trading system; the debt crisis; management of technological change; the impact of change on the development process; environmental issues; women and structural adjustment; and youth unemployment. A separate section within the Division addresses the specific needs of small states and provides technical assistance. The work of the section covers a range of issues including trade, vulnerability, environment, politics and economics. In 2000 a Commonwealth Secretariat/World Bank Joint Task Force on Small States finalized a report entitled *Small States: Meeting Challenges in the Global Economy*. A review of the report was issued in 2005. In June 2010 the first Commonwealth Biennial Small States Conference was convened, in London, comprising representatives of small states from the Africa, Asia-Pacific and Caribbean regions. In January 2011 a new Commonwealth Small States Office was inaugurated in Geneva, Switzerland; the Office was to provide subsidized office space for the Geneva-based diplomatic missions of Commonwealth small states, and business facilities for both diplomatic personnel and visiting delegations from small member states. The second Commonwealth Biennial Global Small States Conference was held in London in September 2012. Participating representatives of small states discussed the development of sustainable economies, job creation and improving livelihoods, agreeing that 'green growth' might act as a vehicle for progress. The Economic Affairs Division also co-ordinates the Secretariat's environmental work and manages the Iwokrama International Centre for Rainforest Conservation and Development.

The Division supported the establishment of a Commonwealth Private Investment Initiative (CPII) to mobilize capital, on a regional basis, for investment in newly privatized companies and in small and medium-sized businesses in the private sector. The first phase of the CPII commenced in 1995, and the second phase, with a particular focus on small and medium-sized businesses, was initiated in 2005, and is ongoing. The first regional fund under the CPII, the Commonwealth Africa Investment Fund (Comafin), was operational during the period July 1996–end-December 2006, and made 19 investments (of which three were subsequently written off) to assist businesses across nine sectors in seven countries in sub-Saharan Africa. A Pan-Commonwealth Africa Partners Fund was launched in 2002, which aimed to help existing businesses expand to become regional or pan-African in scope. In 1997 an investment fund for the Pacific Islands (known as the Kula Fund) was launched; a successor fund (Kula Fund II), with financing of some US $20m., was launched in October 2005, with the aim of injecting capital into the smaller Pacific Island countries. A $200m. South Asia Regional Fund (SARF) was established in October 1997. In 1998 the Tiona Fund for the Commonwealth Caribbean was inaugurated, at a meeting of Commonwealth finance ministers; this was subsequently absorbed into the Caribbean Investment Fund (established in 1993 by member states of the Caribbean Community and Common Market—CARICOM). A $380m. Africa Fund was launched in November 2009.

SOCIAL WELFARE

Social Transformation Programmes Division: consists of three sections concerned with education, gender and health.

The **Education Section** arranges specialist seminars, workshops and co-operative projects, and commissions studies in areas identified by ministers of education, whose meetings it also services. Its areas of work include improving the quality of and access to basic education; strengthening science, technology and mathematics education in formal and non-formal areas of education; improving the quality of management in institutions of higher learning and basic education; improving the performance of teachers; strengthening examination assessment systems; and promoting the movement of students between Commonwealth countries. The Section also promotes the elimination of gender disparities in education, support for education in difficult circumstances, such as areas affected by conflict or natural disasters, and mitigating the impact of HIV and AIDS on education. It attempts to address the problems of scale particular to smaller member countries, and encourages collaboration between governments, the private sector and other non-governmental organizations. A meeting of Commonwealth ministers of education, held at the end of August 2012, in Port Louis, Mauritius, discussed means of achieving education-related MDGs by 2015 and considered priorities for the Commonwealth's contribution to a post-2015 development framework. The meeting was synchronized with parallel fora for Commonwealth teachers, post-secondary and tertiary education leaders, young people, and stakeholders.

The **Gender Affairs Section** is responsible for the implementation of the Commonwealth Plan of Action for Gender Equality, covering the period 2005–15, which succeeded the Commonwealth Plan of Action on Gender and Development (adopted in 1995 and updated in 2000). The Plan of Action supports efforts towards achieving the MDGs, and the objectives of gender equality adopted by the 1995 Beijing Declaration and Platform for Action and the follow-up Beijing+5 review conference, held in 2000, and Beijing+10 in 2005. Gender equality, poverty eradication, promotion of human rights, and strengthening democracy are recognized as intrinsically inter-related, and the Plan has a particular focus on the advancement of gender mainstreaming in the following areas: democracy, peace and conflict; human rights and law; poverty eradication and economic empowerment; and HIV/AIDS.

The **Health Section** organizes ministerial, technical and expert group meetings and workshops, to promote co-operation on health matters, and the exchange of health information and expertise. The Section commissions relevant studies and provides professional and technical advice to member countries and to the Secretariat. It also supports the work of regional health organizations and promotes health for all people in Commonwealth countries. The Commonwealth's five priority areas of focus with regard to health are: e-health; health worker migration; HIV/AIDS; maternal and child health; and non-communicable diseases (NCDs). A Commonwealth Advisory Committee on Health advises the Secretariat on public health matters. The first meeting of a Commonwealth Advisory Group on NCDs was held in November 2008 in Toronto, Canada.

Youth Affairs Division: established within the Secretariat in 2002, reporting directly to a Deputy Secretary-General, and acquired divisional status in 2004. The Division administers the Commonwealth Youth Programme (CYP), which was initiated in 1973 to promote the involvement of young people in the economic and social development of their countries. The CYP is funded by dedicated voluntary contributions from governments. The Programme's activities are in three areas: Youth Enterprise and Sustainable Livelihoods; Governance, Development and Youth Networks; and Youth Work Education and Training. Regional centres are located in Zambia (for Africa), India (for Asia), Guyana (for the Caribbean), and Solomon Islands (for the Pacific). The Programme administers a Youth Study Fellowship scheme, a Youth Project Fund, a Youth Exchange Programme (in the Caribbean), and a Youth Development Awards Scheme. It also holds conferences and seminars, carries out research and disseminates information. The CYP Diploma in Youth Development Work is offered by partner institutions in 45 countries, primarily through distance education. The Commonwealth Youth Credit Initiative, initiated in 1995, provides funds and advice for young entrepreneurs setting up small businesses. A Plan of Action for Youth Empowerment, covering the period 2007–15, was approved by the sixth meeting of Commonwealth ministers responsible for youth affairs, held in Nassau, Bahamas, in May 2006. The Commonwealth Youth Games are normally held at four-yearly intervals (2015: Samoa). The eighth Commonwealth Youth Forum was convened in Freemantle, Australia, in October 2011. In September 2012 a Commonwealth Pacific Youth Leadership and Integrity Conference was convened in Honiara, Solomon Islands. A new pan-Commonwealth Student Association was launched in August of that year.

TECHNICAL ASSISTANCE

Commonwealth Fund for Technical Co-operation (CFTC): f. 1971 to facilitate the exchange of skills between member countries and to promote economic and social development; it is administered by the Commonwealth Secretariat and financed by voluntary subscriptions from member governments. The CFTC responds to requests from member governments for technical assistance, such as the provision of experts for short- or medium-term projects, advice on economic or legal matters, and training programmes. Public sector development, allowing member states to build on their capacities, is the principal element in CFTC activities. This includes assistance for improvement of supervision and combating corruption; improving economic management, for example by advising on exports and investment promotion; strengthening democratic institutions, such as electoral commissions; and improvement of education and health policies. The CFTC also administers the Langkawi awards for the study of environmental issues, which is funded by the Canadian Government; the CFTC's annual budget amounts to around £29m, supplemented by external resources through partnerships.

CFTC activities are mainly implemented by the following divisions:

Governance and Institutional Development Division: strengthens good governance in member countries, through advice, training and other expertise in order to build capacity in national public institutions. The Division administers the Commonwealth Service Abroad Programme (CSAP), which is funded by the CFTC. The Programme extends short-term technical assistance through highly qualified volunteers. The main objectives of the scheme are to provide expertise, training and exposure to new technologies and practices, to promote technology transfers and sharing of experiences and knowledge, and to support community workshops and other local activities.

Special Advisory Services Division: provides advice and technical assistance in four principal areas: debt management; economic and legal services; enterprise and agriculture; and trade.

Finance

Member governments meet the costs of the Secretariat through subscriptions on a scale related to income and population.

Publications

Advisory (annual newsletter of the Special Advisory Services Division).

Global (electronic magazine).

Commonwealth News (weekly e-mail newsletter).

Report of the Commonwealth Secretary-General (every 2 years).

Small States Digest (periodic newsletter).

Numerous reports, studies and papers (catalogue available).

Commonwealth Organizations

(in the United Kingdom, unless otherwise stated)

The two principal intergovernmental organizations established by Commonwealth member states, apart from the Commonwealth Secretariat itself, are the Commonwealth Foundation and the Commonwealth of Learning. In 2012 there were nearly 90 other professional or advocacy organizations bearing the Commonwealth's name and associated with or accredited to the Commonwealth, a selection of which are listed below.

PRINCIPAL INTERGOVERNMENTAL ORGANIZATIONS

Commonwealth Foundation: Marlborough House, Pall Mall, London, SW1Y 5HY; tel. (20) 7930-3783; fax (20) 7839-8157; e-mail geninfo@commonwealth.int; internet www.commonwealthfoundation.com; f. 1966; intergovernmental body promoting people-to-people interaction, and collaboration within the non-governmental sector of the Commonwealth; supports non-governmental organizations, professional associations and Commonwealth arts and culture; awards an annual Commonwealth Writers' Prize; funds are provided by Commonwealth govts; Chair. SIMONE DE COMARMOND (Seychelles); Dir VIJAY KRISHNARAYAN (Trinidad and Tobago); publ. *Commonwealth People* (quarterly).

Commonwealth of Learning (COL): 1055 West Hastings St, Suite 1200, Vancouver, BC V6E 2E9, Canada; tel. (604) 775-8200; fax (604) 775-8210; e-mail info@col.org; internet www.col.org; f. 1987 by Commonwealth Heads of Government to promote the devt and sharing of distance education and open learning resources, including materials, expertise and technologies, throughout the Commonwealth and in other countries; implements and assists with national and regional educational programmes; acts as consultant to international agencies and national governments; conducts seminars and studies on specific educational needs; core financing for COL is provided by Commonwealth governments on a voluntary basis; COL has an annual budget of approx. C $12m; Pres. and CEO Prof. ASHA KANWAR (India); publ. *Connections*.

The following represents a selection of other Commonwealth organizations:

ADMINISTRATION AND PLANNING

Commonwealth Association for Public Administration and Management (CAPAM): L'Esplanade Laurier, 300 Laurier Ave West, West Tower, Room A1245, Ottawa, ON K1A 0M7, Canada; tel. (416) 996-5026; fax (416) 947-9223; e-mail capam@capam.org; internet www.capam.org; f. 1994; aims to promote sound management of the public sector in Commonwealth countries and to assist those countries undergoing political or financial reforms; an international awards programme to reward innovation within the public sector was introduced in 1997, and is awarded every 2 years; more than 1,200 individual mems and 80 institutional memberships in some 80 countries; Pres. PAUL ZAHRA (Malta); Exec. Dir and CEO DAVID WAUNG.

Commonwealth Association of Planners: c/o Royal Town Planning Institute in Scotland, 18 Atholl Crescent, Edinburgh, EH3 8HQ; tel. (131) 229-9628; fax (131) 229-9332; e-mail annette.odonnell@rtpi.org.uk; internet www.commonwealth-planners.org; aims to develop urban and regional planning in Commonwealth countries, to meet the challenges of urbanization and the sustainable development of human settlements; Pres. CHRISTINE PLATT (South Africa); Sec.-Gen. CLIVE HARRIDGE (United Kingdom).

Commonwealth Local Government Forum: 16A Northumberland Ave, London, WC2N 5AP; tel. (20) 7389-1490; fax (20) 7389-1499; e-mail info@clgf.org.uk; internet www.clgf.org.uk; works to promote democratic local government in Commonwealth countries, and to encourage good practice through conferences, programmes, research and the provision of information; regional offices in Fiji, India and South Africa.

AGRICULTURE AND FORESTRY

Commonwealth Forestry Association: Crib, Dinchope, Craven Arms, Shropshire, SY7 9JJ; tel. (1588) 672868; fax (870) 0116645; e-mail cfa@cfa-international.org; internet www.cfa-international.org; f. 1921; produces, collects and circulates information relating to world forestry and promotes good management, use and conservation of forests and forest lands throughout the world; mems: 1,200; Chair. JOHN INNES (Canada); Pres. JIM BALL (United Kingdom); publs *International Forestry Review* (quarterly), *Commonwealth Forestry News* (quarterly), *Commonwealth Forestry Handbook* (irregular).

Royal Agricultural Society of the Commonwealth: Royal Highland Centre, Ingleston, Edinburgh, EH28 8NF; tel. (131) 335-6200; fax (131) 335-6229; e-mail rasc@commagshow.org; internet www.commagshow.org; f. 1957 to promote development of agricultural shows and good farming practice, in order to improve incomes and food production in Commonwealth countries.

Standing Committee on Commonwealth Forestry: Forestry Commission, 231 Corstorphine Rd, Edinburgh, EH12 7AT; tel. (131) 314-6405; fax (131) 316-4344; e-mail jonathan.taylor@forestry.gsi.gov.uk; internet www.cfc2010.org; f. 1923 to provide continuity between Confs, and to provide a forum for discussion on any forestry matters of common interest to mem. govts which may be brought to the Cttee's notice by any mem. country or org.; 54 mems; June 2010 Conference: Edinburgh, United Kingdom; Sec. JONATHAN TAYLOR.

BUSINESS

Commonwealth Business Council: 18 Pall Mall, London, SW1Y 5LU; tel. (20) 7024-8200; fax (20) 7024-8201; e-mail info@cbcglobal.org; internet www.cbcglobal.org; f. 1997 by the Commonwealth Heads of Government Meeting to promote co-operation between governments and the private sector in support of trade, investment and development; the Council aims to identify and promote investment opportunities, in particular in Commonwealth developing countries, to support countries and local businesses to work within the context of globalization, to promote capacity building and the exchange of skills and knowledge (in particular through its Information Communication Technologies for Development programme), and to encourage co-operation among Commonwealth members; promotes good governance; supports the process of multilateral trade negotiations and other liberalization of trade and services; represents the private sector at government level; Dir-Gen. and CEO Sir ALAN COLLINS.

EDUCATION AND CULTURE

Association of Commonwealth Universities (ACU): Woburn House, 20-24 Tavistock Sq., London, WC1H 9HF; tel. (20) 7380-6700; fax (20) 7387-2655; e-mail info@acu.ac.uk; internet www.acu.ac.uk; f. 1913; promotes international co-operation and understanding; provides assistance with staff and student mobility and development programmes; researches and disseminates information about universities and relevant policy issues; organizes major meetings of Commonwealth universities and their representatives; acts as a liaison office and information centre; administers scholarship and fellowship schemes; operates a policy research unit; mems: c. 500 universities in 36 Commonwealth countries or regions; Sec.-Gen. Prof. JOHN WOOD; publs include *Yearly Review*, *Commonwealth Universities Yearbook*, *ACU Bulletin* (quarterly), *Who's Who of Executive Heads: Vice-Chancellors, Presidents, Principals and Rectors*, *International Awards*, student information papers (study abroad series).

Commonwealth Association of Museums: R.R.1, De Winton, Alberta, T0L 0X0, Canada; tel. and fax (403) 938-3190; e-mail irvinel@fclc.com; internet www.maltwood.uvic.ca/cam; f. 1985; professional asscn working for the improvement of museums throughout the Commonwealth; encourages links between museums and assists professional development and training through distance learning, workshops and seminars; general assembly held every three or four years; mems in 38 Commonwealth countries; Pres. Prof. LOIS IRVINE.

Commonwealth Association of Science, Technology and Mathematics Educators (CASTME): 7 Lion Yard, Tremadoc Rd, London, SW4 7NQ; tel. (20) 7819-3936; e-mail castme@lect.org; internet www.castme.org; f. 1974; special emphasis is given to the social significance of education in these subjects; organizes an Awards Scheme to promote effective teaching and learning in these subjects, and biennial regional seminars; Chair. COLIN MATHESON; publ. *CASTME Journal* (3 a year).

Commonwealth Council for Educational Administration and Management: POB 1891, Penrith, NSW 2751, Australia; tel. (2) 4732-1211; fax (2) 4732-1711; e-mail admin@cceam.org; internet www.cceam.org; f. 1970; aims to foster quality in professional development and links among educational administrators; holds national and regional conferences, as well as visits and seminars; mems: 24 affiliated groups representing 3,000 persons; Pres. Prof. FRANK CROWTHER; publ. *International Studies in Educational Administration* (2 a year).

Commonwealth Education Trust: New Zealand House, 6th Floor, 80 Haymarket, London, SW1Y 4TE; tel. (20) 7024-9822; fax (20) 7024-9833; e-mail info@commonwealth-institute.org; internet www.commonwealtheducationtrust.org; f. 2007 as the successor trust to the Commonwealth Institute; funds the Centre of Commonwealth Education, established in 2004 as part of Cambridge University; supports the Lifestyle of Our Kids (LOOK) project initiated in 2005 by the Commonwealth Institute (Australia); Chief Exec. JUDY CURRY.

Institute of Commonwealth Studies: South Block, 2nd Floor, Senate House, Malet Street, London, WC1E 7HU; tel. (20) 7862-8844; fax (20) 7862-8813; e-mail ics@sas.ac.uk; internet commonwealth.sas.ac.uk; f. 1949 to promote advanced study of the Commonwealth; provides a library and meeting place for postgraduate students and academic staff engaged in research in this field; offers postgraduate teaching; Dir Prof. PHILIP MURPHY; publs *Annual Report*, *Collected Seminar Papers*, *Newsletter*, *Theses in Progress in Commonwealth Studies*.

HEALTH AND WELFARE

Commonwealth Medical Trust (COMMAT): BMA House, Tavistock Sq., London, WC1H 9JP; tel. (20) 7272-8492; fax (1689) 890609; e-mail office@commat.org; internet www.commat.org; f. 1962 (as the Commonwealth Medical Association) for the exchange of information; provision of techical co-operation and advice; formulation and maintenance of a code of ethics; promotes the Right to Health; liaison with WHO and other UN agencies on health issues; meetings of its Council are held every three years; mems: medical asscns in Commonwealth countries; Dir MARIANNE HASLEGRAVE.

Commonwealth Nurses' Federation: c/o Royal College of Nursing, 20 Cavendish Sq., London, W1G 0RN; tel. (20) 7647-3593; fax (20) 7647-3413; e-mail jill@commonwealthnurses.org; internet www.commonwealthnurses.org; f. 1973 to link national nursing and midwifery asscns in Commonwealth countries; aims to influence health policy, develop nursing networks, improve nursing education and standards, and strengthen leadership; inaugural Conference held in March 2012 (in London); Exec. Sec. JILL ILIFFE.

Commonwealth Organization for Social Work: Halifax, Canada; tel. (902) 455-5515; e-mail moniqueauffrey@eastlink.ca; internet www.commonwealthsw.org; promotes communication and collaboration between social workers in Commonwealth countries; provides network for information and sharing of expertise; Sec.-Gen. MONIQUE AUFFREY (Canada).

Commonwealth Pharmacists Association: 1 Lambeth High St, London, SE1 7JN; tel. (20) 7572-2216; fax (20) 7572-2504; e-mail admin@commonwealthpharmacy.org; internet www.commonwealthpharmacy.org; f. 1970 (as the Commonwealth Pharmaceutical Association) to promote the interests of pharmaceutical sciences and the profession of pharmacy in the Commonwealth; to maintain high professional standards, encourage links between members and the creation of nat. asscns; and to facilitate the dissemination of information; holds conferences (every four years) and regional meetings; mems: pharmaceutical asscns from over 40 Commonwealth countries; Pres. RAYMOND ANDERSON (United Kingdom); publ. *Quarterly Newsletter*.

Commonwealth Society for the Deaf (Sound Seekers): 34 Buckingham Palace Rd, London, SW1W 0RE; tel. (20) 7233-5700; fax (20) 7233-5800; e-mail sound.seekers@btinternet.com; internet www.sound-seekers.org.uk; f. 1959; undertakes initiatives to establish audiology services in developing Commonwealth countries, including mobile clinics to provide outreach services; aims to educate local communities in aural hygiene and the prevention of ear infection and deafness; provides audiological equipment and organizes the training of audiological maintenance technicians; conducts research into the causes and prevention of deafness; Chief Exec. GARY WILLIAMS; publ. *Annual Report*.

Royal Commonwealth Ex-Services League: Haig House, 199 Borough High St, London, SE1 1AA; tel. (20) 3207-2413; fax (20) 3207-2115; e-mail mgordon-roe@commonwealthveterans.org.uk; internet www.commonwealthveterans.org.uk; links the ex-service orgs in the Commonwealth, assists ex-servicemen of the Crown who are resident abroad; holds conferences every four years; 56 mem. orgs in 48 countries; Grand Pres. HRH The Duke of EDINBURGH; publ. *Annual Report*.

Sightsavers (Royal Commonwealth Society for the Blind): Grosvenor Hall, Bolnore Rd, Haywards Heath, West Sussex, RH16 4BX; tel. (1444) 446600; fax (1444) 446688; e-mail info@sightsavers.org; internet www.sightsavers.org; f. 1950 to prevent blindness and restore sight in developing countries, and to provide education and community-based training for incurably blind people; operates in collaboration with local partners in some 30 developing countries, with high priority given to training local staff; Chair. Lord NIGEL CRISP; Chief Exec. Dr CAROLINE HARPER; publ. *Sight Savers News*.

INFORMATION AND THE MEDIA

Commonwealth Broadcasting Association: 17 Fleet St, London, EC4Y 1AA; tel. (20) 7583-5550; fax (20) 7583-5549; e-mail cba@cba.org.uk; internet www.cba.org.uk; f. 1945; general conferences are held every two years (2012: Brisbane, Australia, in April); mems: c. 100 in more than 50 countries; Pres. MONEEZA HASHMI; Sec.-Gen. SALLY-ANN WILSON; publs *Commonwealth Broadcaster* (quarterly), *Commonwealth Broadcaster Directory* (annually).

Commonwealth Journalists Association: c/o Canadian Newspaper Association, 890 Yonge St, Suite 200, Toronto, ON M4W 3P4, Canada; tel. (416) 575-5377; fax (416) 923-7206; e-mail cantleyb@commonwealthjournalists.com; internet www.commonwealthjournalists.com; f. 1978 to promote co-operation between journalists in Commonwealth countries, organize training facilities and conferences, and foster understanding among Commonwealth peoples; Pres. RITA PAYNE (United Kingdom); publ. *Newsletter* (3 a year).

CPU Media Trust (Association of Commonwealth Newspapers, News Agencies and Periodicals): e-mail webform@cpu.org.uk; internet www.cpu.org.uk; f. 2008 as a 'virtual' organization charged with carrying on the aims of the Commonwealth the Commonwealth Press Union (CPU, f. 1950, terminated 2008); promotes the welfare of the Commonwealth press; Chair. GUY BLACK.

LAW

Commonwealth Lawyers' Association: c/o Institute of Advanced Legal Studies, 17 Russell Sq., London, WC1B 5DR; tel. (20) 7862-8824; fax (20) 7862-8816; e-mail cla@sas.ac.uk; internet www.commonwealthlawyers.com; f. 1983 (fmrly the Commonwealth Legal Bureau); seeks to maintain and promote the rule of law throughout the Commonwealth, by ensuring that the people of the Commonwealth are served by an independent and efficient legal profession; upholds professional standards and promotes the availability of legal services; organizes the biannual Commonwealth Law Conference; Chair. LAURENCE WATT; publs *The Commonwealth Lawyer*, *Clarion*.

Commonwealth Legal Advisory Service: c/o British Institute of International and Comparative Law, Charles Clore House, 17 Russell Sq., London, WC1B 5DR; tel. (20) 7862-5151; fax (20) 7862-5152; e-mail contact@biicl.org; internet www.biicl.org;

f. 1962; financed by the British Institute and by contributions from Commonwealth govts; provides research facilities for Commonwealth govts and law reform commissions; publ. *New Memoranda* series.

Commonwealth Legal Education Association: c/o Legal and Constitutional Affairs Division, Commonwealth Secretariat, Marlborough House, Pall Mall, London, SW1Y 5HX; tel. (20) 7747-6415; fax (20) 7004-3649; e-mail clea@commonwealth.int; internet www.clea-web.com; f. 1971 to promote contacts and exchanges and to provide information regarding legal education; Pres. DAVID MACQUOID-MASON; Gen. Sec. SELINA GOULBOURNE; publ. *Commonwealth Legal Education Association Newsletter* (3 a year).

Commonwealth Magistrates' and Judges' Association: Uganda House, 58–59 Trafalgar Sq., London, WC2N 5DX; tel. (20) 7976-1007; fax (20) 7976-2394; e-mail info@cmja.org; internet www.cmja.org; f. 1970 to advance the administration of the law by promoting the independence of the judiciary, to further education in law and crime prevention and to disseminate information; confs and study tours; corporate membership for asscns of the judiciary or courts of limited jurisdiction; assoc. membership for individuals; Pres. Hon. Mrs Justice NORMA WADE-MILLER; Sec.-Gen. Dr KAREN BREWER; publs *Commonwealth Judicial Journal* (2 a year), *CMJA News*.

PARLIAMENTARY AFFAIRS

Commonwealth Parliamentary Association: Westminster House, Suite 700, 7 Millbank, London, SW1P 3JA; tel. (20) 7799-1460; fax (20) 7222-6073; e-mail hq.sec@cpahq.org; internet www.cpahq.org; f. 1911 to promote understanding and co-operation between Commonwealth parliamentarians; organization: Exec. Cttee of 35 MPs responsible to annual Gen. Assembly; 176 brs in national, state, provincial and territorial parliaments and legislatures throughout the Commonwealth; holds annual Commonwealth Parliamentary Confs and seminars; also regional confs and seminars; Chair. Sir ALAN HASELHURST; Sec.-Gen. Dr WILLIAM F. SHIJA; publ. *The Parliamentarian* (quarterly).

SCIENCE AND TECHNOLOGY

Commonwealth Association of Architects: POB 1166, Stamford, PE2 2HL; tel. and fax (1780) 238091; e-mail info@comarchitect.org; internet www.comarchitect.org; f. 1964; aims to facilitate the reciprocal recognition of professional qualifications; to provide a clearing house for information on architectural practice; and to encourage collaboration. Plenary conferences every three years; regional conferences are also held; 38 societies of architects in various Commonwealth countries; Pres. MUBASSHAR HUSSAIN; Exec. Dir TONY GODWIN; publs *Handbook, Objectives and Procedures: CAA Schools Visiting Boards, Architectural Education in the Commonwealth* (annotated bibliography of research), *CAA Newsnet* (2 a year), a survey and list of schools of architecture.

Commonwealth Engineers' Council: c/o Institution of Civil Engineers, One Great George St, London, SW1P 3AA; tel. (20) 7222-7722; e-mail secretariat@ice.org.uk; internet www.cec.ice.org.uk; f. 1946; links and represents engineering institutions across the Commonwealth, providing them with an opportunity to exchange views on collaboration and mutual support; holds international and regional conferences and workshops; mems: 45 institutions in 44 countries; Sec.-Gen. NEIL BAILEY.

Commonwealth Telecommunications Organization: 64-66 Glenthorne Rd, London, W6 0LR; tel. (20) 8600-3800; fax (20) 8600-3819; e-mail info@cto.int; internet www.cto.int; f. 1967 as an international development partnership between Commonwealth and non-Commonwealth governments, business and civil society organizations; aims to help to bridge the digital divide and to achieve social and economic development by delivering to developing countries knowledge-sharing programmes in the use of information and communication technologies in the specific areas of telecommunications, IT, broadcasting and the internet; CEO Prof. TIM UNWIN; publs *CTO Update* (quarterly), *Annual Report*, *Research Reports*.

Conference of Commonwealth Meteorologists: c/o International Branch, Meteorological Office, FitzRoy Rd, Exeter, EX1 3PB; tel. (1392) 885680; fax (1392) 885681; e-mail commonwealth@metoffice.gov.uk; internet www.commonwealthmet.org; links national meteorological and hydrological services in Commonwealth countries; conferences held every four years.

SPORT AND YOUTH

Commonwealth Games Federation: 138 Piccadilly, 2nd Floor, London, W1J 7NR; tel. (20) 7491-8801; fax (20) 7409-7803; e-mail info@thecgf.com; internet www.thecgf.com; the Games were first held in 1930 and are now held every four years; participation is limited to competitors representing the mem. countries of the Commonwealth; 2014 games: Glasgow, United Kingdom; mems: 72 affiliated bodies; Pres. HRH Prince IMRAN (Malaysia); CEO MICHAEL HOOPER.

Commonwealth Youth Exchange Council: 7 Lion Yard, Tremadoc Rd, London, SW4 7NQ; tel. (20) 7498-6151; fax (20) 7622-4365; e-mail ival@cyec.org.uk; internet www.cyec.org.uk; f. 1970; promotes contact between groups of young people of the United Kingdom and other Commonwealth countries by means of educational exchange visits, provides information for organizers and allocates grants; provides host governments with technical assistance for delivery of the Commonwealth Youth Forum, held every two years; since July 2011 administers the Commonwealth Teacher Exchange Programme; mems: 222 orgs, 134 local authorities, 88 voluntary bodies; Chief Exec. V. S. G. CRAGGS; publs *Contact* (handbook), *Exchange* (newsletter), *Final Communiqués* (of the Commonwealth Youth Forums), *Safety and Welfare* (guidelines for Commonwealth Youth Exchange groups).

RELATIONS WITHIN THE COMMONWEALTH

Commonwealth Countries League: 37 Priory Ave, Sudbury, HA0 2SB; tel. (20) 8248-3275; e-mail info@ccl-int.org; internet www.ccl-int.org; f. 1925; aims to secure equality of liberties, status and opportunities between women and men and to promote friendship and mutual understanding throughout the Commonwealth; promotes women's political and social education and links together women's organizations in most countries of the Commonwealth; an education sponsorship scheme was established in 1967 to finance the secondary education of bright girls from lower income backgrounds in their own Commonwealth countries; the CCL Education Fund was sponsoring more than 300 girls throughout the Commonwealth (2012); Exec. Chair. MARJORIE RENNIE; publs *News Update* (3 a year), *Annual Report*.

Commonwealth War Graves Commission: 2 Marlow Rd, Maidenhead, SL6 7DX; tel. (1628) 634221; fax (1628) 771208; internet www.cwgc.org; casualty and cemetery enquiries; e-mail casualty.enq@cwgc.org; f. 1917 (as Imperial War Graves Commission); responsible for the commemoration in perpetuity of the 1.7m. members of the Commonwealth Forces who died during the wars of 1914–18 and 1939–45; provides for the marking and maintenance of war graves and memorials at some 23,000 locations in 150 countries; mems: Australia, Canada, India, New Zealand, South Africa, United Kingdom; Pres. HRH The Duke of KENT; Dir-Gen. ALAN PATEMAN-JONES.

Council of Commonwealth Societies: c/o Royal Commonwealth Society, 25 Northumberland Ave, London, WC2N 5AP; tel. (20) 7766-9206; fax (20) 7930-9705; e-mail ccs@rcsint.org; internet www.rcsint.org/day; f. 1947; provides a forum for the exchange of information regarding activities of member orgs which promote understanding among countries of the Commonwealth; co-ordinates the distribution of the Commonwealth Day message by Queen Elizabeth II, organizes the observance of and promotes Commonwealth Day, and produces educational materials relating to the occasion; seeks to raise the profile of the Commonwealth; mems: 30 official and unofficial Commonwealth orgs; Chair. Lord ALAN WATSON.

Royal Commonwealth Society: 25 Northumberland Ave, London, WC2N 5AP; tel. (20) 7766-9200; fax (20) 7930-9705; e-mail info@thercs.org; internet www.thercs.org; f. 1868; to promote international understanding of the Commonwealth and its people; organizes meetings and seminars on topical issues, projects for young people, a youth leadership programme, and cultural and social events; Pres. Baroness PRASHAR; Dir Dr DANNY SRISKANDARAJAH; publs *RCS Exchange* (3 a year), conference reports.

Royal Over-Seas League: Over-Seas House, Park Place, St James's St, London, SW1A 1LR; tel. (20) 7408-0214; fax (20) 7499-6738; e-mail info@rosl.org.uk; internet www.rosl.org.uk; f. 1910 to promote friendship and understanding in the Commonwealth; club houses in London and Edinburgh; membership is open to all British subjects and Commonwealth citizens; Dir-Gen. Maj.-Gen. RODDY PORTER; publ. *Overseas* (quarterly).

Victoria League for Commonwealth Friendship: 55 Leinster Sq., London, W2 4PW; tel. (20) 7243-2633; fax (20) 7229-2994; e-mail enquiries@victorialeague.co.uk; internet www.victorialeague.co.uk; f. 1901; aims to further personal friendship among Commonwealth peoples and to provide hospitality for visitors; maintains Student House, providing accommodation for students from Commonwealth countries; has branches elsewhere in the UK and abroad; Chair. LYN D. HOPKINS; Gen. Man. DOREEN HENRY; publ. *Annual Report*.

ECONOMIC COMMUNITY OF WEST AFRICAN STATES—ECOWAS

Address: ECOWAS Executive Secretariat, 101 Yakubu Gowon Crescent, PMB 401, Asokoro, Abuja, Nigeria.

Telephone: (9) 3147647; **fax:** (9) 3147646; **e-mail:** info@ecowas.int; **internet:** www.ecowas.int.

The Treaty of Lagos, establishing ECOWAS, was signed in May 1975 by 15 states, with the object of promoting trade, co-operation and self-reliance in West Africa. Outstanding protocols bringing certain key features of the Treaty into effect were ratified in November 1976. Cape Verde joined in 1977. A revised ECOWAS treaty, designed to accelerate economic integration and to increase political co-operation, was signed in July 1993.

MEMBERS

Benin	Ghana	Niger
Burkina Faso	Guinea	Nigeria
Cape Verde	Guinea-Bissau	Senegal
Côte d'Ivoire	Liberia	Sierra Leone
The Gambia	Mali	Togo

Organization

(September 2012)

AUTHORITY OF HEADS OF STATE AND GOVERNMENT

The Authority is the supreme decision-making organ of the Community, with responsibility for its general development and realization of its objectives. The Chairman is elected annually by the Authority from among the member states. The Authority meets at least once a year in ordinary session. The 41st ordinary session was convened at the end of June 2012, in Yammasoukro, Côte d'Ivoire.

COUNCIL OF MINISTERS

The Council consists of two representatives from each member country; the chairmanship is held by a minister from the same member state as the Chairman of the Authority. The Council meets at least twice a year, and is responsible for the running of the Community.

ECOWAS COMMISSION

The ECOWAS Commission, formerly the Executive Secretariat, was inaugurated in January 2007, following a decision to implement a process of structural reform taken at the January 2006 summit meeting of the Authority. Comprising a President, a Vice-President and seven Commissioners, the Commission is elected for a four-year term, which may be renewed once only.

President: KADRÉ DÉSIRÉ OUÉDRAOGO (Burkina Faso).

TECHNICAL COMMITTEES

There are nine technical committees, formerly specialized technical commissions, which prepare Community projects and programmes in the following areas:

(i) Administration and Finance;

(ii) Agriculture, Environment and Water Resources;

(iii) Communication and Information Technology;

(iv) Human Development and Gender;

(v) Infrastructure;

(vi) Legal and Judicial Affairs;

(vii) Macro-economic Policy;

(viii) Political Affairs, Peace and Security; and

(ix) Trade, Customs and Free Movement of Persons.

ECOWAS PARLIAMENT

The inaugural session of the 120-member ECOWAS Parliament, based in Abuja, Nigeria, was held in November 2000. The January 2006 summit meeting of the Authority determined to restructure the Parliament, in line with a process of wider institutional reform. The number of seats was reduced from 120 to 115 and each member of the Parliament was to be elected for a four-year term (reduced from five years). The second legislature was inaugurated in November 2006. There is a co-ordinating administrative bureau, comprising a speaker and four deputy speakers, and there are also eight standing committees (reduced in number from 13) covering each of the Parliament's areas of activity.

Speaker: IKE EKWEREMADU (Nigeria).

ECOWAS COURT OF JUSTICE

The Court of Justice, established in January 2001, is based in Abuja, and comprises seven judges who serve a five-year renewable term of office. At the January 2006 summit meeting the Authority approved the creation of a Judicial Council, comprising qualified and experienced persons, to contribute to the establishment of community laws. The Authority also approved the inauguration of an appellate division within the Court. The judges will hold (non-renewable) tenure for four years.

President: NANA AWA DABOYA (Togo).

Activities

ECOWAS aims to promote co-operation and development in economic, social and cultural activities, to raise the standard of living of the people of the member countries, to increase and maintain economic stability, to improve relations among member countries and to contribute to the progress and development of Africa. ECOWAS is committed to abolishing all obstacles to the free movement of people, services and capital, and to promoting: harmonization of agricultural policies; common projects in marketing, research and the agriculturally based industries; joint development of economic and industrial policies and elimination of disparities in levels of development; and common monetary policies.

Initial slow progress in achieving many of ECOWAS's aims was attributed *inter alia* to the reluctance of some governments to implement policies at the national level and their failure to provide the agreed financial resources; to the high cost of compensating loss of customs revenue; and to the existence of numerous other intergovernmental organizations in the region (in particular the Union économique et monétaire ouest-africaine—UEMOA, which replaced the francophone Communauté économique de l'Afrique de l'ouest in 1994). In respect of the latter obstacle to progress, however, ECOWAS and UEMOA resolved in February 2000 to create a single monetary zone (see below). In October ECOWAS and the European Union (EU) held their first joint high-level meeting, at which the EU pledged financial support for ECOWAS's economic integration programme, and in April 2001 it was announced that the IMF had agreed to provide technical assistance for the programme.

A revised treaty for the Community was drawn up by an ECOWAS Committee of Eminent Persons in 1991–92, and was signed at the ECOWAS summit conference that took place in Cotonou, Benin, in July 1993. The treaty designated the achievement of a common market and a single currency as economic objectives, while in the political sphere it envisaged the establishment of an ECOWAS parliament, an economic and social council, and an ECOWAS court of justice to enforce Community decisions (see above). The treaty also formally assigned the Community with the responsibility of preventing and settling regional conflicts. At a summit meeting held in Abuja, in August 1994, ECOWAS heads of state and government signed a protocol agreement for the establishment of a regional parliament. The meeting also adopted a Convention on Extradition of non-political offenders. The new ECOWAS treaty entered into effect in August 1995, having received the required number of ratifications. A draft protocol providing for the creation of a mechanism for the prevention, management and settlement of conflicts, and for the maintenance of peace in the region, was approved by ECOWAS heads of state and government in December 1999. In December 2000 Mauritania, a founding member, withdrew from the Community.

In May 2002 the ECOWAS Authority met in Yamoussoukro, Côte d'Ivoire, to develop a regional plan of action for the implementation of the New Partnership for Africa's Development (NEPAD). In January 2006 the Authority, meeting in Niamey, Niger, commended the recent establishment of an ECOWAS Project Development and Implementation Unit, aimed at accelerating the implementation of regional infrastructural projects in sectors such as energy, telecommunications and transport. Also at that meeting the Authority approved further amendments to the revised ECOWAS treaty to provide for institutional reform.

Meeting in Abuja, in June 2007, the Authority adopted a long-term ECOWAS Strategic Vision, detailing the proposed establishment by 2020 of a West African region-wide borderless, stateless space and single economic community. In January 2008 the Authority adopted a comprehensive strategy document proposing a number of initiatives and programmes aimed at reducing poverty in West Africa. The Authority also approved the establishment of a statistics development support fund, and the ECOWAS Common Approach on Migration.

TRADE AND MONETARY UNION

Under the founding ECOWAS treaty elimination of tariffs and other obstructions to trade among member states, and the establishment of a common external tariff, were planned over a transitional period of 15 years, from 1975. At the 1978 Conference of Heads of State and Government it was decided that from May 1979 no member state might increase its customs tariff on goods from another member. This was regarded as the first step towards the abolition of customs duties within the Community. During the first two years import duties on intra-community trade were to be maintained, and then eliminated in phases over the next eight years. Quotas and other restrictions of equivalent effect were to be abolished in the first 10 years. It was envisaged that in the remaining five years all differences between external customs tariffs would be abolished.

In 1980 ECOWAS heads of state and government decided to establish a free trade area for unprocessed agricultural products and handicrafts from May 1981. Tariffs on industrial products made by specified community enterprises were also to be abolished from that date, but implementation was delayed by difficulties in defining the enterprises. From 1 January 1990 tariffs were eliminated on 25 listed items manufactured in ECOWAS member states. Over the ensuing decade, tariffs on other industrial products were to be eliminated as follows: the 'most-developed' countries of ECOWAS (Côte d'Ivoire, Ghana, Nigeria and Senegal) were to abolish tariffs on 'priority' products within four years and on 'non-priority' products within six years; the second group (Benin, Guinea, Liberia, Sierra Leone and Togo) were to abolish tariffs on 'priority' products within six years, and on 'non-priority' products within eight years; and the 'least-developed' members (Burkina Faso, Cape Verde, The Gambia, Guinea-Bissau, Mali and Niger) were to abolish tariffs on 'priority' products within eight years and on 'non-priority' products within 10 years. By December 2000 only Benin had removed tariffs on all industrial products.

In 1990 ECOWAS heads of state and government agreed to adopt measures that would create a single monetary zone and remove barriers to trade in goods that originated in the Community. ECOWAS regards monetary union as necessary to encourage investment in the region, since it would greatly facilitate capital transactions with foreign countries. In September 1992 it was announced that, as part of efforts to enhance monetary co-operation and financial harmonization in the region, the West African Clearing House was to be restructured as the West African Monetary Agency (WAMA). As a specialized agency of ECOWAS, WAMA was to be responsible for administering an ECOWAS exchange rate system (EERS) and for establishing the single monetary zone. In July 1996 the Authority agreed to impose a common value-added tax (VAT) on consumer goods, in order to rationalize indirect taxation and to stimulate greater intra-Community trade. In August 1997 ECOWAS heads of state and government authorized the introduction of a regional travellers' cheque scheme. (The scheme was formally inaugurated in October 1998, and the cheques, issued by WAMA in denominations of a West African Unit of Account and convertible into each local currency at the rate of one Special Drawing Right—SDR—see IMF—entered into circulation on 1 July 1999.) In December 1999 the ECOWAS Authority determined to pursue a 'Fast Track Approach' to economic integration, involving a two-track implementation of related measures. In April 2000 seven, predominantly anglophone, ECOWAS member states—Cape Verde, The Gambia, Ghana, Guinea, Liberia, Nigeria and Sierra Leone—issued the 'Accra Declaration', in which they agreed to establish a second West African monetary union (the West African Monetary Zone—WAMZ) to co-exist initially alongside UEMOA, which unites eight, mainly francophone, ECOWAS member states. As preconditions for adopting a single currency and common monetary and exchange rate policy, the member states of the second West African monetary union were (under the supervision of a newly established ECOWAS Convergence Council, comprising member states' ministers of finance and central bank governors) to attain a number of convergence criteria, including: a satisfactory level of price stability; sustainable budget deficits; a reduction in inflation; and the maintenance of an adequate level of foreign exchange reserves. The two complementary monetary unions were expected to harmonize their economic programmes, with a view to effecting an eventual merger, as outlined in an action plan adopted by ECOWAS and UEMOA in February 2000. The ECOWAS Authority summit held in December 2000, in Bamako, Mali, adopted an Agreement Establishing the WAMZ, approved the establishment of a West African Monetary Institute to prepare for the formation of a West African Central Bank (WACB), and determined that the harmonization of member countries' tariff structures should be accelerated to facilitate the implementation of the planned customs union. In December 2001 the Authority determined that the currency of the WAMZ (and eventually the ECOWAS-wide currency) would be known as the 'eco' and authorized the establishment during 2002 of an exchange rate mechanism. This was achieved in April. Meeting in November 2002 the heads of state and government determined that a forum of WAMZ ministers of finance should be convened on a regular basis to ensure the effective implementation of fiscal policies. In May 2004 ECOWAS and UEMOA signed an agreement that provided for the establishment of a Joint Technical Secretariat to enhance the co-ordination of their programmes.

Owing to slower-than-anticipated progress in achieving the convergence criteria required for monetary union, past deadlines for the inauguration of the WAMZ and launch of the 'eco' were not met. In May 2009 the Convergence Council adopted a new roadmap towards realizing the single currency for West Africa by 2020. Under the roadmap (of which an updated version was released in March 2010), the harmonization of the regulatory and supervisory framework for banking and other financial institutions, the establishment of the payment system infrastructure for cross-border transactions and of the payment system infrastructure in Guinea, The Gambia and Sierra Leone, and also the ongoing integration of regional financial markets, were all to be finalized during 2009–early 2013. The roadmap envisaged that, by 2014, ratification of the legal instruments for the creation of the WAMZ would have been achieved, and that during 2014 the WACB, WAMZ Secretariat and West African Financial Supervisory Agency would be established. The WAMZ monetary union was finally to enter into effect before or at the start of 2015, with the 'eco' scheduled to enter into circulation in January 2015. In October 2011 the Convergence Council adopted supplementary acts to facilitate the process of establishing the single currency. The documents included: the Guideline on the Formation of a Multi-year Programme on Convergence with ECOWAS; and the Draft Supplementary Act on Convergence and Macroeconomic Stability Pact among Member States, the latter constituting a formal commitment by signatories to ensure economic policy co-ordination, to strengthen economic convergence and to increase macroeconomic stability.

In January 2006 the Authority approved the implementation of a four-band common external tariff (CET) that was to align the WAMZ tariff structure with that of UEMOA, as follows: a 0% tariff would be applied to social goods (for example, educational and medical equipment); 5% would be levied on raw materials and most agricultural inputs; 10% on intermediate goods and rice; and 20% on finished consumer products. At the inaugural meeting of the Joint ECOWAS–UEMOA Management Committee of the ECOWAS CET, convened in July 2006, members agreed on a roadmap for implementing the uniform tariff system. The roadmap also outlined the legal framework for the introduction of the CET. In December 2011 a meeting of the Joint Committee agreed on a timetable for concluding the draft CET, in order to be able to present it for adoption by the ECOWAS Council of Ministers during 2012.

In December 1992 ECOWAS ministers agreed on the institutionalization of an ECOWAS trade fair, in order to promote trade liberalization and intra-Community trade. The first trade fair was held in Dakar, Senegal, in 1995; the seventh was to be held in Accra, Ghana, in October–November 2012. In September 2011 an ECOWAS Investment Forum was held in Lagos, Nigeria (following an inaugural event held in Brussels, Belgium, in the previous year), during which member states were called upon to implement measures to reduce risk and improve investor confidence and the business climate. A further Investment Forum was staged in Accra, Ghana, in August 2012. ECOWAS business fora are organized periodically (the fourth, with a focus on ICT, was scheduled to be held in late 2012 in The Gambia). A feasibility study for the establishment of an ECOWAS Investment Guarantee/Reinsurance Agency was under consideration in 2012.

An extraordinary meeting of ministers of trade and industry was convened in May 2008 to discuss the impact on the region of the rapidly rising cost at that time of basic food items. In December the ECOWAS Authority warned that the ongoing global financial crisis might undermine the region's economic development, and called for a regional strategy to minimize the risk. In late June 2012 the Authority endorsed measures aimed at finding a durable resolution to the ongoing food security crisis in the Sahel region, that had been agreed by an ECOWAS-UEMOA-Permanent Inter-State Committee on Drought Control in the Sahel high-level meeting convened earlier in that month; these included the development of a regional food reserve. The Authority also urged the international community to mobilize resources required to support affect communities in the Sahel, and welcomed a new Partnership for Resilience in the Sahel initiative, launched earlier in that month by the EU.

TRANSPORT AND COMMUNICATIONS

In 1979 ECOWAS heads of state signed a Protocol relating to free circulation of the region's citizens and to rights of residence and establishment of commercial enterprises. The first provision (the right of entry without a visa) came into force in 1980. An optional ECOWAS travel certificate, valid for travel within the Community in place of a national passport, was established in July 1985. The second provision of the 1979 Protocol, allowing unlimited rights of residence, was signed in 1986 (although Nigeria indicated that unskilled workers and certain categories of professionals would not be allowed to stay for an indefinite period) and came into force in 1989. The third provision, concerning the right to establish a commercial enterprise in another member state was signed in 1990.

In July 1992 the ECOWAS Authority formulated a Minimum Agenda for Action for the implementation of Community agreements regarding the free movement of goods and people, for example the removal of non-tariff barriers, the simplification of customs and transit procedures and a reduction in the number of control posts on international roads. However, implementation of the Minimum Agenda was slow. In April 1997 Gambian and Senegalese finance and trade officials concluded an agreement on measures to facilitate the export of goods via Senegal to neighbouring countries, in accordance with ECOWAS protocols relating to inter-state road transit arrangements. An Inter-state Road Transit Authority has been established. A Brown Card scheme provides recognized third-party liability insurance throughout the region. In January 2003 Community heads of state and government approved the ECOWAS passport; by 2011 the passport was being issued by Benin, Guinea, Liberia, Niger, Nigeria and Senegal.

In February 1996 ECOWAS and several private sector partners established ECOAir Ltd, based in Abuja, Nigeria, which was to develop a regional airline. In December 2007, following a recommendation by the Authority, a new regional airline, ASKY (Africa Sky) was established, which initiated operations in January 2010. A regional shipping company, ECOMARINE, commenced operations in February 2003. In October 2011 West African ministers of transported concluded a series of measures to establish a common regulatory regime for the airline industry in order to improve the viability of regional airlines and to support regional integration.

An ECOWAS programme for the development of an integrated regional road network comprises: the Trans-West African Coastal Highway, linking Lagos, Nigeria, with Nouackchott, Mauritania (4,767 km), and envisaged as the western part of an eventual Pan-African Highway; and the Trans-Sahelian Highway, linking Dakar, Senegal, with N'Djamena, Chad (4,633 km). By 2006 about 83% of the coastal route was reportedly complete, and by 2001 about 87% of the trans-Sahelian route had reportedly been built. It was reported in January 2009 that construction companies were tendering to complete the Nigerian section of the Coastal Highway. In 2003 the African Development Bank agreed to finance a study on interconnection of the region's railways.

In August 1996 the initial phase of a programme to improve regional telecommunications was reported to have been completed. A second phase of the programme (INTELCOM II), which aimed to modernize and expand the region's telecommunications services, was initiated by ECOWAS heads of state in August 1997. A West African Telecommunications Regulators' Association was established, under the auspices of ECOWAS, in September 2000. The January 2006 summit meeting of the Authority approved a new Special Fund for Telecommunications to facilitate improvements to cross-border telecommunications connectivity. In May ECOWAS ministers of information and telecommunications agreed guidelines for harmonizing the telecommunications sector. In January 2007 ECOWAS leaders adopted a regional telecommunications policy and a regulatory framework that covered areas including interconnection to ICT and services networks, license regimes, and radio frequency spectrum management. A common, liberalized ECOWAS telecommunications market is envisaged. In October 2008 ECOWAS ministers responsible for telecommunications and ICT adopted regional legislation on combating cybercrime. In October 2011 ECOWAS ministers of ICT and telecommunications, meeting in Yamoussoukro, Côte d'Ivoire, adopted a series of priority projects to be undertaken in the next five years, including the elaboration of a regulation on access to submarine cable landing stations and national rights of way. The meeting recommended the establishment of a Directorate of Telecoms-ICT and Post sectors by late 2012, in order to improve ECOWAS's operational capacity and to enhance the planning and monitoring of these sectors at the Community level.

ECONOMIC AND INDUSTRIAL DEVELOPMENT

In June 2010 the Council of Ministers adopted the West African Common Industrial Policy (WACIP), and a related action plan and supplementary acts. WACIP aimed to diversify and expand the regional industrial production base by supporting the creation of new industrial production capacities as well as developing existing capacities. WACIP envisaged the expansion of intra-ECOWAS trade from 13% to 40% by 2030, through enhancing skills, industrial competitiveness and quality infrastructure, with a particular focus on the areas of information, communications and transport.

TIn September 2008 the inaugural meeting was convened of an ECOWAS–People's Republic of China economic and trade forum, which aimed to strengthen bilateral relations and discuss investment possibilities in the development of infrastructure, financial services, agriculture and the exploitation of natural resources. A second forum was convened in March 2012, in Accra, Ghana.

In November 1984 ECOWAS heads of state and government approved the establishment of a private regional investment bank, Ecobank Transnational Inc. ECOWAS has a 10% share in the bank, which is headquartered in Lomé, Togo.

In September 1995 Nigeria, Ghana, Togo and Benin resolved to develop a gas pipeline to connect Nigerian gas supplies to the other countries. In August 1999 the participating countries, together with two petroleum companies operating in Nigeria, signed an agreement on the financing and construction of the 600-km West African Gas Pipeline, which was to extend from the Nigerian capital, Lagos, to Takoradi, Ghana. It became operational in late 2007. The implementation of a planned energy exchange scheme, known as the West African Power Pool Project (WAPP), is envisaged as a means of efficiently utilizing the region's hydro-electricity and thermal power capabilities by transferring power from surplus producers to countries unable to meet their energy requirements. An ECOWAS Energy Protocol, establishing a legal framework for the promotion of long-term co-operation in the energy sector, was adopted in 2003. In May of that year the Community decided to initiate the first phase of WAPP, to be implemented in Benin, Côte d'Ivoire, Ghana, Niger, Nigeria and Togo, at an estimated cost of US $335m. In January 2005 the Authority endorsed a revised masterplan for the implementation of WAPP, which was scheduled to be completed by 2020. In July 2005 the World Bank approved a $350m. facility to support the implementation of WAPP, which became fully operational in January 2006.

In November 2008 the Authority approved the establishment of a Regional Centre for Renewable Energy and Energy Efficiency (ECREEE), to be based in Praia, Cape Verde, and also endorsed the establishment of an ECOWAS Regional Electricity Regulatory Authority, to be based in Accra. The Authority also adopted a joint ECOWAS/UEMOA action plan on priority regional infrastructure projects. ECREEE was inaugurated in 2009, and a Secretariat was established in July 2010. In September 2011 the ECOWAS Commission signed a €2.3m. grant contract with the EU for an ECREEE project on energy efficiency in West Africa.

In April 2009 ministers responsible for the development of mineral resources endorsed an ECOWAS Directive on the Harmonization of Guiding Principles and Policies in the Mining Sector. An ad hoc committee to monitor the implementation of the Directive convened in May 2011.

REGIONAL SECURITY

The revised ECOWAS treaty, signed in July 1993, incorporates a separate provision for regional security, requiring member states to work towards the maintenance of peace, stability and security. In December 1997 an extraordinary meeting of ECOWAS heads of state and government was convened in Lomé, Togo, to consider the future stability and security of the region. It was agreed that a permanent mechanism should be established for conflict prevention and the maintenance of peace. ECOWAS leaders also reaffirmed their commitment to pursuing dialogue to prevent conflicts, co-operating in the early deployment of peace-keeping forces and implementing measures to counter trans-border crime and the illegal trafficking of armaments and drugs.

In December 1999 ECOWAS heads of state and government, meeting in Lomé, Togo, approved a draft protocol to the organization's treaty, providing for the establishment of a Permanent Mechanism for the Prevention, Management and Settlement of Conflicts and the Maintenance of Peace in the Region, and for the creation of a Mediation and Security Council, to comprise representatives of 10 member states, elected for two-year terms. The Council was to be supported by an advisory Council of Elders (also known as the Council of the Wise), comprising 32 eminent statesmen from the region; this was inaugurated in July 2001. In January 2003 the Council of Elders was recomposed as a 15-member body with a representative from each member state. In December 2006 a Technical Committee of Experts on Political Affairs, Peace and Security was established as a subsidiary body of the Mediation and Security Council.

An ECOWAS Warning and Response Network (ECOWARN) asseses threats to regional security. In June 2004 the Community approved the establishment of the ECOWAS Standby Force (ESF), comprising 6,500 troops, including a core rapid reaction component, the ECOWAS Task Force, numbering around 2,770 soldiers (deployable within 30 days). The ECOWAS Defence and Security Commission approved the operational framework for the ESF in April 2005. A training exercise for the logistics component of the ESF was conducted, in Ouagadougou, Burkina Faso, in June 2009.

In January 2005 the Authority authorized the establishment of a humanitarian depot, to be based in Bamako, Mali, and a logistics depot, to be based in Freetown, Sierra Leone, with a view to expanding regional humanitarian response capacity. In December 2009 the Sierra Leone Government allocated land for the construction of the planned Freetown depot, and, in February 2011, ECOWAS signed Memoranda of Understanding with WFP and with the Government of Mali relating to the planned creation of the Bamako ECOWAS Humanitarian Depot, which, once established, was to provide storage for food and non-food items, and for emergency equipment. An ECOWAS Emergency Response Team (EERT) was established in 2007.

In October 1998 the ECOWAS Authority determined to implement a renewable three-year moratorium on the import, export or manufacture of small armaments in order to enhance the security of the sub-region. In March 1999 the Programme of Co-ordination and Assistance for Security and Development (PCASED) was launched to complement the moratorium. The moratorium was renewed for a further three years in July 2001. (In 2004 ECOWAS announced its intention to transform the moratorium into a convention and PCASED was decommissioned.) In June 2006 the Authority adopted the ECOWAS Convention on Small Arms and Light Weapons, their Ammunitions and other Materials, with the aim of regulating the importation and manufacture of such weapons. The ECOWAS Small Arms Control Programme (ECOSAP) was inaugurated in that month. Based in Bamako, Mali, ECOSAP aims to improve the capacity of national and regional institutions to reduce the proliferation of small weapons across the region. During 1999 ECOWAS member states established the Intergovernmental Action Group Against Money Laundering in Africa (GIABA), which was mandated to combat drugs-trafficking and money laundering throughout the region; a revised regulation for GIABA adopted by the Authority in January 2006 expanded the Group's mandate to cover regional responsibility for combating terrorism. Representatives from ECOWAS member states met in Ouagadougou, Burkina Faso, in September 2007 to draft a new West African strategy for enhanced drug control. In October 2008—during a High-level Conference on Drugs Trafficking as a Security Threat to West Africa, convened by ECOWAS jointly with the UN Office on Drugs and Crime (UNODC) and the Cape Verde Government, in Praia, Cape Verde—the Executive Director of UNODC warned that West Africa was at risk of becoming an epicentre for drugs-trafficking, representing a serious threat to public health and security in the region. He proposed the establishment of a West African intelligence-sharing centre, and urged the promotion of development and the strengthening of the rule of law as a means of reducing regional vulnerability to drugs and crime. At the Conference ECOWAS adopted a Political Declaration on Drugs Trafficking and Organized Crime in West Africa, and approved an ECOWAS Regional Response Plan. In April 2009 ECOWAS ministers with responsibility for issues relating to trafficking in persons adopted a policy aimed at establishing a legal mechanism for protecting and assisting victims of trafficking. In July 2009 ECOWAS, UNODC, other UN agencies, and INTERPOL launched the West Africa Coast Initiative (WACI), which aimed to build national and regional capacities to combat drugs trafficking and organized crime in, initially, four pilot post-conflict countries: Côte d'Ivoire, Guinea-Bissau, Liberia and Sierra Leone. In February 2010 the pilot countries signed the 'WACI-Freetown Commitment', endorsing the implementation of the initiative, and agreeing to establish specialized transnational crime units on their territories. WACI activities were to be expanded to Guinea during 2012. In March 2010 ECOWAS, the African Union, the International Organization for Migration and UNODC launched an initiative to develop a roadmap for implementing in West Africa the Ouagadougou Action Plan to Combat Trafficking in Human Beings (adopted by the AU in 2006).

In October 2006 it was reported that ECOWAS planned to introduce a series of initiatives in each of the member states under a Peace and Development Project (PADEP). The Project intended to foster a 'culture of peace' among the member states of ECOWAS, strengthening social cohesion and promoting economic integration, democracy and good governance.

In March 2008 an ECOWAS Network of Electoral Commissions, comprising heads of member states' institutions responsible for managing elections, was established with the aim of ensuring the transparency and integrity of regional elections and helping to entrench a culture of democracy.

In February 2005 ECOWAS briefly suspended Togo's membership of the Community and imposed an arms embargo on that country and a travel ban on its leaders, owing to the unconstitutional installation of a new President; the sanctions against Togo were reversed when the illegal appointment was withdrawn at the end of the month. In May, in response to unrest in Togo following the allegedly fraudulent election there of Faure Gnassingbé as President, ECOWAS organized a 'mini-summit' meeting, attended by Gnassingbé himself and the leader of the opposition Union des forces de changement, at the conclusion of which, in a communiqué, the Community urged the establishment of a government of national unity in Togo.

In October 2011 ECOWAS dispatched a 150-member observer mission to monitor presidential and legislative elections in Liberia. An enlarged mission, comprising 200 observers, returned to the country in November in order to monitor the second round of voting in the presidential poll. In February 2012 ECOWAS heads of state and government authorized a Joint AU–ECOWAS high-level mission to Senegal, in order to promote political dialogue and to ensure peaceful, fair and transparent forthcoming elections. An observer mission was dispatched to Senegal in late February to monitor the presidential poll.

Meeting in late June 2012 the Authority expressed concern at the rise in terrorist activities in the Sahel region, and also in Nigeria.

Piracy in the Gulf of Guinea: In April 2011 ECOWAS initiated a series of regional measures to combat the increased incidence of piracy, in co-operation with the Communauté économique des états de l'Afrique centrale (CEEAC—Economic Community of Central African States). In October the UN Security Council adopted Resolution 2018 which urged ECOWAS, the CEEAC and the Gulf of Guinea Commission to develop a comprehensive regional action plan against piracy and armed robbery at sea. In June 2012 the Authority expressed concern at increased acts of piracy, illegal trafficking activities (relating to drugs, weapons and human beings), and environmental degradation, in the Gulf of Guinea.

Côte d'Ivoire: The President of the ECOWAS Commission participated in an AU High-level Panel appointed in January 2011 to address ongoing unrest in Côte d'Ivoire, where the security situation had deteriorated following the refusal of the outgoing President Laurent Gbagbo to acknowledge the outcome of presidential elections held in 2010, and consequently to cede power. The legitimately elected President, Alassane Ouattara, was eventually inaugurated in May 2011. In September the President of the Commission led an ECOWAS delegation to Côte d'Ivoire to assess that country's post-conflict humanitarian and economic needs. The President appointed Oluwole Coker as his Special Representative to Côte d'Ivoire in order to facilitate the provision and distribution of ECOWAS assistance. In the same month five ECOWAS heads of state met to consider the deteriorating security situation along the borders between Côte d'Ivoire and Liberia.

Guinea: Guinea's membership of ECOWAS was suspended in January 2009, following a *coup d'état* in December 2008. The inaugural meeting of an International Contact Group on Guinea (ICG-G), co-chaired by ECOWAS and the AU Commission, and also comprising representatives of other regional and international organizations, was held in February 2009. Meeting in October, in its eighth session, the ICG-G strongly condemned brutal acts perpetrated by armed troops in Guinea against women and other unarmed civilians in late September. The ICG-G also invited ECOWAS, with support from partners, to establish an international observer and protection mission to contribute to the establishment of an atmosphere of security in Guinea. An extraordinary summit of the ECOWAS Authority, held in mid-October, urged the establishment of a transitional regime in Guinea. In June 2010 the Mediation and Security Council expressed satisfaction with progress being made towards the restoration of democracy in Guinea, where a presidential election was being held, in two rounds, in June and November. In March 2011 the Authority ended Guinea's membership suspension.

Guinea-Bissau: In March 2009 ECOWAS Chiefs of Defence agreed to deploy a multidisciplinary group to monitor and co-ordinate security sector reforms in Guinea-Bissau, following the assassinations of the military Chief of Staff and President of that country at the beginning of the month. The ECOWAS Chiefs of Defence also demanded a review of ECOWAS legislation on conflict prevention and peace-keeping. In November 2010 ECOWAS and the Comunidade dos Países de Língua Portuguesa (CPLP) adopted an ECOWAS-CPLP roadmap on reform of the defence and security sector in Guinea-Bissau. In March 2012 an 80-member ECOWAS observation mission monitored the first round of a presidential election held in Guinea-Bissau following the death in office, in January, of the president. In mid-April, before the planned second round of the Guinea-Bissau presidential election, scheduled for later in that month, a military junta usurped power by force and established a Transitional National Council (TNC), comprising military officers and representatives of political parties that had been in opposition to the legitimate government. The ECOWAS Commission strongly condemned the military coup and denounced the establishment of the TNC. An ECOWAS high-level delegation visited Guinea-Bissau in mid-April to hold discussions with the military leadership. An extraordinary summit meeting of ECOWAS heads of state and government convened in late April decided to deploy troops from the ESF to Guinea-Bissau in support of a swift restoration of constitutional order. Sanctions, including economic measures and targeted individual penalties, were to be imposed if the military continued to obstruct the democratic process. The summit meeting urged the military leadership to release civilians who had been detained during the coup and to ensure the safety of officials from the former legitimate administration. The meeting stipulated that democratic elections should be held in Guinea-Bissau within 12 months. A seven-nation Contact Group on Guinea-Bissau (comprising Benin, Cape Verde, The Gambia, Guinea, Senegal and Togo, and chaired by Nigeria) was established by the extraordinary summit, with a mandate to follow up its decisions. At the end of April diplomatic, economic and financial sanctions were imposed on military leaders and their associates in Guinea-Bissau, in view of the failure at that time of talks between the Contact Group and Guinea-Bissau stakeholders to secure an arrangement for restoring constitutional rule within a 12-month period. A 620-strong ESF contingent was deployed in Guinea-Bissau in May. At the end of June the ECOWAS Authority endorsed new transitional organs established in Guinea Bissau and withdrew the sanctions that had been imposed in April.

Mali: In mid-March 2012 the President of the ECOWAS Commission led a fact-finding mission to Mali, in view of escalating unrest in northern areas of that country arising from attacks by separatist militants of the National Movement for the Liberation of Azawad (MNLA). The Commission condemned all acts of violence committed by the MNLA. In late March ECOWAS heads of state and government convened an extraordinary summit to discuss the recent illegal overthrow, by the Comité National de Redressement pour la Démocratie et la Restauration de l'Etat (CNRDRE), of the legitimate government of Mali's elected President Amadou Touré, and also to address the separatist violence ongoing in the north of the country. The regional leaders suspended Mali from participating in all decision-making bodies of ECOWAS pending the restoration of constitutional order, and imposed sanctions (including a ban on travel and an assets freeze) on members of the CNRDRE and their associates. The summit appointed President Blaise Compaoré of Burkina Faso as ECOWAS mediator, with a mandate to facilitate dialogue between the legitimate Mali Government and the CNRDRE regime on achieving a return to civilian rule, and also on means of terminating the northern rebellion. Meanwhile, in early April, MNLA rebels, assisted by Islamist forces, seized land in the Kidal, Gao and Tombouctou regions of northern Mali, unilaterally declaring this to be the independent entity of Azawad. At that time the Commission denounced a 'Declaration of Independence by the MNLA for the North of Mali', reminding all militants that Mali is an 'indivisible entity', and stating that ECOWAS would be prepared to use all necessary measures, including force, to ensure Mali's territorial integrity. An emergency meeting of ECOWAS Joint Chiefs of Defence Staff, held in early April, adopted preparatory measures for the rapid deployment of the ESF to Mali if necessary. On 6 April representatives of the CNRDRE and the ECOWAS mediation team, under the chairmanship of Compaoré, signed an accord that was intended to lead to a return to full constitutional rule; the accord entailed the appointment of a new interim president, who was to lead a transitional administration pending the staging of democratic elections. Accordingly, an interim president, Dioncounda Traoré, was sworn in on 12 April, and ECOWAS sanctions against Mali were withdrawn. The CNRDRE, however, subsequently appeared to influence the political process: in late April Traoré announced a new government, which included three posts held by military officers and no ministers from the former Touré government.

An extraordinary summit meeting of ECOWAS heads of state and government convened in late April 2012 decided to deploy troops from the ESF to Mali to support a swift restoration of constitutional order. Sanctions, including economic measures and targeted individual penalties, were to be imposed if the military continued to obstruct the democratic process. The summit meeting urged military leaders in both countries to release civilians who had been detained during the coup and to ensure the safety of officials from the former legitimate administration. The meeting stipulated that democratic elections should be held in Mali within 12 months. It was reported that the ESF presence in Mali (the ESF Mission in Mali—MICEMA) would number at least 3,000. Meeting in early May an extraordinary summit of the Authority condemned violent clashes that had erupted in Bamako, the Malian capital, from the end of April, and welcomed the availability of the President of Nigeria, Goodluck Jonathan, to assist, as 'Associate Mediator', Compaoré in pursuing a negotiated resolution to the conflict in northern Mali. Later in May the President of the Commission condemned a violent assault on Traoré, the interim Malian President, by opponents protesting against the length of his term of office. At the end of that month the President of the Commission reaffirmed support to the transitional authorities and warned that sanctions would be imposed on those deemed to be disrupting the transitional process. ECOWAS heads of state and government attending a consultative meeting on the situation in Mali that was organized in early June, in Lomé, Togo, on the sidelines of the 16th UEMOA summit, strongly condemned acts of rape, robbery, and killing, and the desecration of cultural sites, allegedly being perpetrated by armed groups in northern Mali. The meeting instructed the ECOWAS Commission to continue with preparations for the deployment of MICEMA in Mali, and urged the Community and the AU to seek UN Security Council approval for the operation.

Meeting in late June 2012 the Authority reaffirmed all previous decisions on Mali, and noted with deep concern that terrorist groups—such as Boko Haram, al-Shabaab ('The Youth'), al-Qa'ida au Maghreb islamique, and the Unity Movement for Jihad in West Africa—were aiming to establish a safe haven in the north of the country. The Authority decided to send a technical assessment mission to Mali to prepare for the deployment of MICEMA. In early July a committee of ECOWAS culture experts urged the Mali separatists to respect and ensure the preservation of the cultural heritage under occupation in Timbuktu, Gao and Kidal. Shortly afterwards the UN Security Council adopted a resolution expressing its readiness to consider mandating ECOWAS to authorize the deployment of MICEMA; the Council requested additional information on the objectives and modalities of the planned mission. In mid-September ECOWAS Chiefs of Defence Staff met to finalize a road-map for MICEMA's deployment.

Niger: In October 2009 Niger's ECOWAS membership was suspended, following the refusal of that country's authorities to respond to a request by ECOWAS to postpone a controversial presidential election. ECOWAS condemned a *coup d'état* which took place in Niger in February 2010. In June 2010 the Mediation and Security Council expressed satisfaction with progress being made towards the restoration of democracy in Niger, where, in April, a 12-month timetable outlining the return to democratic rule had been adopted by the military regime. A meeting of the Authority in March 2011 ended Niger's membership suspension.

Past Peace-keeping Operations

ECOMOG: The ECOWAS Cease-fire Monitoring Group (ECOMOG) was established in 1990, when it was dispatched to Liberia in an attempt to enforce a cease-fire between conflicting factions there and to help restore public order. It remained in that country until October 1999, undertaking roles including disarmament of rebel soldiers, maintaining security during presidential and legislative elections, and restructuring the national security forces. In August 1997 ECOMOG was mandated by ECOWAS heads of state and government to monitor a cease-fire in Sierra Leone negotiated with the dissident Armed Forces Revolutionary Council (ARFC), which had removed the president, Ahmed Tejan Kabbah, from office earlier in that year. ECOMOG was also mandated to upholding international sanctions against the new authorities. In February 1999 ECOMOG troops assumed control of Freetown from ARFC and the rebel Revolutionary United Front (RUF) control. Following the return of Kabbah in March, it was agreed that ECOMOG forces, then numbering some 10,000, were to remain in the country in order to ensure the full restoration of peace and security, to assist in the restructuring of the armed forces and to help to resolve the problems of the substantial numbers of refugees and internally displaced persons. ECOMOG's mandate in Sierra Leone was further adapted, following the signing of a political agreement in July, to support the consolidation of peace in that country and national reconstruction. In October a new UN mission, UNAMSIL, assumed many of the functions then being performed by ECOMOG, and the ECOMOG contingent was withdrawn in April 2000. During February–June 1999 a 600-strong ECOMOG Interposition Force was deployed to Guinea-Bissau to help uphold a cease-fire agreement between government and rebel factions in that country, to supervise the border region with Senegal and to facilitate the delivery of humanitarian assistance.

ECOMIL: The ECOWAS Mission in Liberia (ECOMIL) was authorized in July 2003 to protect civilians following political disturbances in the Liberian capital, Monrovia. The 3,500 ECOMIL troops transferred to a UN-mandated mission in October.

ECOMICI: In September 2002 an extraordinary summit meeting of ECOWAS heads of state and government was convened in Accra, Ghana, to address the violent unrest that had erupted in Côte d'Ivoire during that month. The meeting condemned the attempt to overthrow democratic rule and constitutional order and established a high-level contact group, comprising the heads of state of Ghana, Guinea-Bissau, Mali, Niger, Nigeria and Togo, to prevail upon the rebel factions to end hostilities, and to negotiate a general framework for the resolution of the crisis. The contact group helped to mediate a cease-fire in the following month; this was to be monitored by an ECOWAS Mission in Côte d'Ivoire (ECOMICI), which was also to be responsible for ensuring safe passage for deliveries of humanitarian assistance. In March 2003, following the conclusion in January by the parties to the conflict of a peace agreement, signed at Marcoussis, France, ECOWAS chiefs of staff endorsed the expansion of ECOMICI from 1,264 to a maximum of 3,411 troops, to monitor the implementation of the peace agreement in co-operation with the UN Mission in Côte d'Ivoire (MINUCI), and French forces. In April 2004 authority was transferred from ECOMICI and MINUCI to the newly established UN Operation in Côte d'Ivoire (UNOCI). In mid-June ECOWAS heads of state and government convened at a summit to address means of reviving the implementation of the stalled Marcoussis peace accord. A high-level meeting of ECOWAS heads of state and government, other African leaders, the Chairperson of the AU, and the parties to the Côte d'Ivoire conflict, held in Accra in late July, affirmed that a monitoring mechanism, comprising representatives of ECOWAS, the AU, Côte d'Ivoire and the UN, should produce regular reports on progress towards peace in Côte d'Ivoire.

AGRICULTURE AND THE ENVIRONMENT

The Community enforces a certification scheme for facilitating the monitoring of animal movement and animal health surveillance and protection in the sub-region. In February 2001 ECOWAS ministers of agriculture adopted an action plan for the formulation of a common agricultural policy, as envisaged under the ECOWAS treaty. An ECOWAS Regional Agricultural Policy (ECOWAP) was endorsed by the January 2005 Authority summit. In January 2006 the Authority approved an action plan for the implementation of ECOWAP. The Policy was aimed at enhancing regional agricultural productivity with a view to guaranteeing food sufficiency and standards. In October 2011 a high-level consultative meeting of ECOWAS and FAO officials determined that ECOWAP was the most effective means of countering the effects of food price increases and volatility.

ECOWAS promotes implementation of the UN Convention on Desertification Control and supports programmes initiated at national and sub-regional level within the framework of the treaty. Together with the Permanent Inter-State Committee on Drought Control in the Sahel, ECOWAS has been designated as a project leader for implementing the Convention in West Africa. Other environmental initiatives include a regional meteorological project to enhance meteorological activities and applications, and in particular to contribute to food security and natural resource management in the sub-region. ECOWAS pilot schemes have formed the basis of integrated control projects for the control of floating (or invasive aquatic) weeds in five water basins in West Africa, which had hindered the development of the local fishery sectors. A rural water supply programme aims to ensure adequate water for rural dwellers in order to improve their living standards. The first phase of the project focused on schemes to develop village and pastoral water points in Burkina Faso, Guinea, Mali, Niger and Senegal, with funds from various multilateral donors.

In September 2009 a regional conference, convened in Lomé, Togo, to address the potential effects of rapid climate change on regional stability, issued the Lomé Declaration on Climate Change and Protection of Civilians in West Africa, and recommended the establishment of a fund to support communities suffering the negative impact of climate change. In March 2010 ECOWAS ministers responsible for agriculture, environment and water resources adopted a Framework of Strategic Guidelines on the Reduction of Vulnerability and Adaptability to Climate Change in West Africa, outlining the development of regional capacities to build up resilience and adaptation to climate change and severe climatic conditions. ECOWAS supports the development and implementation by member states of Nationally Appropriate Mitigation Actions (NAMAs).

SOCIAL PROGRAMME

The following organizations have been established within ECOWAS: the Organization of Trade Unions of West Africa, which held its first meeting in 1984; the West African Universities' Association, the ECOWAS Youth and Sports Development Centre (EYSDC), the ECOWAS Gender Development Centre (EGDC), and the West African Health Organization (WAHO), which was established in 2000 by merger of the West African Health Community and the Organization for Co-ordination and Co-operation in the Struggle against Endemic Diseases. ECOWAS and the European Commission jointly implement the West African Regional Health Programme, which aims to improve the co-ordination and harmonization of regional health policies, with a view to strengthening West African integration. In December 2001 the ECOWAS summit of heads of state and government adopted a plan of action aimed at combating trafficking in human beings and authorized the establishment of an ECOWAS Criminal Intelligence Bureau. In March 2009 ECOWAS ministers of education, meeting in Abuja, Nigeria, identified priority activities for advancing the regional implementation of regional activities relating to the AU-sponsored Second Decade of Education in Africa (2006–15). In the following month ECOWAS ministers responsible for labour and employment adopted a regional labour policy. In February 2012 the ECOWAS Commission and the International Labour Organization determined to collaborate in order to address the challenges of child labour in West Africa. The Commission resolved to harmonize national action plans relating to child labour and to formulate a regional strategy. Since 2010 the EYSDC has organized the biennial 'ECOWAS Games' (September 2010: Abuja, Nigeria; June 2012: Accra, Ghana; 2014: Côte d'Ivoire).

Specialized Agencies

ECOWAS Bank for Investment and Development (EBID): BP 2704, 128 blvd du 13 janvier, Lomé, Togo; tel. 22-21-68-64; fax 22-21-86-84; e-mail bidc@bidc-ebid.org; internet www.bidc-ebid.org; f. 2001, replacing the former ECOWAS Fund for Co-operation, Compensation and Development; comprises two divisions, a Regional Investment Bank and a Regional Development Fund; Pres. BASHIR M. IFO.

West African Monetary Agency (WAMA): 11–13 ECOWAS St, PMB 218, Freetown, Sierra Leone; tel. 224485; fax 223943; e-mail wamao@amao-wama.org; internet www.amao-wama.org; f. 1975 as West African Clearing House; agreement founding WAMA signed by governors of ECOWAS central banks in March 1996; administers transactions between its eight member central banks in order to promote sub-regional trade and monetary co-operation; administers ECOWAS travellers' cheques scheme. Mems: Banque Centrale des Etats de l'Afrique de l'Ouest (serving Benin, Burkina Faso, Côte d'Ivoire, Guinea-Bissau, Mali, Niger, Senegal, Togo) and the central banks of Cape Verde, The Gambia, Ghana, Guinea, Liberia, Nigeria and Sierra Leone; Dir-Gen. Prof. MOHAMED BEN OMAR NDIAYE; publ. *Annual Report*.

West African Monetary Institute (WAMI): Gulf House, Tetteh Quarshie Interchange, Cantonments 75, Accra, Ghana; tel. (30) 2743801; fax (30) 2743807; e-mail info@wami-imao.org; internet www.wami-imao.org; f. by the ECOWAS Authority summit in December 2000 to prepare for the establishment of a West African Central Bank, currently scheduled for 2014; Dir-Gen. TEI KITCHER (acting).

West African Health Organization (WAHO): 01 BP 153 Bobo-Dioulasso 01, Burkina Faso; tel. and fax (226) 975772; e-mail wahooas@fasonet.bf; internet www.wahooas.org; f. 2000 by merger of the West African Health Community (f. 1978) and the Organization for Co-ordination and Co-operation in the Struggle against Endemic Diseases (f. 1960); aims to harmonize member states' health policies and to promote research, training, the sharing of resources and diffusion of information; Dir-Gen. Dr PLACIDO MONTEIRO CARDOSO (Guinea-Bissau); publ. *Bulletin Bibliographique* (quarterly).

West African Power Pool (WAPP): 06 BP 2907, Zone des Ambassade, PK 6 Cotonou, Benin; tel. 21-37-41-95; fax 21-37-41-96; e-mail info@ecowapp.org; internet www.ecowapp.org; f. 1999; new organization approved as a Specialized Agency in Jan. 2006; inaugural meeting held in July 2006; aims to facilitate the integration of the power systems of member nations into a unified regional electricity market; Gen. Sec. AMADOU DIALLO; publ. *WAPP Newsletter* (intermittent).

Finance

Under the revised treaty, signed in July 1993, ECOWAS was to receive revenue from a community tax, based on the total value of imports from member countries. In July 1996 the summit meeting approved a protocol on a community levy, providing for the imposition of a 0.5% tax on the value of imports from a third country. In August 1997 the Authority of Heads of State and Government determined that the community levy should replace budgetary contributions from member states as the organization's principal source of finance. The protocol came into force in January 2000, having been ratified by nine member states, with the substantive regime entering into effect on 1 January 2003. The January 2006 meeting of the Authority approved a budget of US $121m. for the operations of the Community in that year.

Publications

Annual Report.
Contact.
ECOWAS National Accounts.
ECOWAS News.
ECOWAS Newsletter.
West African Bulletin.

EUROPEAN UNION—EU

Presidency of the Council of the European Union: Cyprus (July–December 2012); Ireland (January–June 2013); Lithuania (July 2013–December 2013).

President of the European Council: HERMAN VAN ROMPUY (Belgium).

High Representative of the Union for Foreign Affairs and Security Policy: CATHERINE ASHTON (United Kingdom).

SUB-SAHARAN AFRICA

The first Africa-EU summit, representing the institutionalization of Africa-EU dialogue, was convened in April 2000, in Cairo, Egypt. The second summit was held in December 2007, in Lisbon, Portugal (having been postponed from 2003 owing to concerns over the participation of President Mugabe of Zimbabwe, see below). The 2007 Lisbon summit adopted a Joint Africa-EU Strategy as a vision and road map, providing an overarching long-term framework for future political co-operation, to be implemented through successive short-term action plans. The First Action Plan of the Joint Strategy identified eight areas for strategic partnership during 2008–10: peace and security; democratic governance and human rights; trade, regional integration and infrastructure; achievement of the UN Millennium Development Goals; energy; climate change; migration, mobility and employment; and science, information society and space. The third Africa-EU summit, with the theme of 'investment, economic growth and job creation' was held in Tripoli, Libya, in November 2010. An action plan for 2011–13 was adopted, focusing on the following principal areas of co-operation: peace and security; democratic governance and human rights; regional integration, trade and infrastructure; the UN's eight Millennium Development Goals; energy; climate change and the environment; migration, mobility and employment; and science, the information society and space.

In June 2004 the European Commission activated for the first time its newly established Africa Peace Facility (APF), which provided €12m. in support of African Union (AU) humanitarian and peace-monitoring activities in Darfur (Sudan). In 2007 the EU and the AU agreed to expand the APF to cover the prevention of conflict and post-conflict stabilization, and to facilitate decision-making and co-ordination. APF funds were allocated accordingly: €600m. for Peace Support Operations, the principal focus of the APF; €100m. to aid capacity-building efforts, specifically in the context of the African Peace and Security Architecture (APSA) and Africa-EU dialogue; €15m. to support the Early Response Mechanism; and €40m. for contingencies.

Allocations by the European Commission Humanitarian Aid Office (ECHO) towards sub-Saharan Africa in 2010 included €131m. to distribute food and aid the implementation of other life-saving activities (for example, in the areas of sanitation, hygiene and shelter) in Sudan, €47m. to help refugees in the Democratic Republic of the Congo, €38m. to support vulnerable refugee populations, to combat a cholera epidemic and to aid drought in the Sahel region in Chad, and €96m. to provide support to populations affected by drought in the Horn of Africa (Djibouti, Ethiopia, Kenya, Somalia and Uganda). In January–September 2011 the EU also contributed some €160m. in emergency funding to help those affected by the continuing severe drought throughout the Horn of Africa region.

During 2002 the European Council condemned the worsening human rights situation in Zimbabwe, and imposed a range of targeted sanctions, including a travel ban on and freezing of the assets of certain members of the leadership, an arms embargo, and the suspension of development aid. Sanctions relating to Zimbabwe have been extended repeatedly on an annual basis. In September 2009 an EU delegation visited Zimbabwe for the first time since the imposition of sanctions, and indicated that further progress was needed to end human rights violations there. The majority of the sanctions were extended in February 2010 and February 2011. In February 2012 the EU welcomed developments towards the formation of a Government of National Unity, and agreed to remove sanctions from 51 people and 20 entities with immediate effect.

The EU, together with, *inter alia*, the UN Secretary-General, US President Barack Obama, the IMF and the Economic Community of West African States (ECOWAS), recognized Alassane Ouattara as the legitimate victor of a run-off election to decide the presidency of Côte d'Ivoire in November 2010; however, in early December the country's constitutional council released results indicating that incumbent President Laurent Gbagbo had won the election. Widespread disruption and violence followed the disputed elections. In mid-January 2011 the EU imposed sanctions against Côte d'Ivoire, which were subsequently strengthened at the end of that month. Ouattara was officially sworn in as President in May. In July the EU adopted five programmes, which allocated some €125m. to Côte d'Ivoire to support vocational training, road maintenance, health and the management of public finances, and to strengthen civil society organizations.

The EU maintains several missions in Africa. During June–September 2003 an EU military operation, codenamed Artemis, was conducted in the Democratic Republic of the Congo (DRC). In June 2005 1,400 EUSEC RD Congo peace-keepers were dispatched to attempt to curb ongoing ethnic violence in the DRC; the mandate of EUSEC RD Congo was scheduled to terminate in 2012. In October 2007 the Council approved a EUFOR operation (EUFOR Chad/CAR), comprising 3,300 troops, to support a UN mission in eastern Chad and north-eastern Central African Republic (MINURCAT) in efforts to improve security in those regions, where more than 200,000 people from the Darfur region of western Sudan had sought refuge from violence in their own country. The force began deployment in early 2008. In March 2009 EUFOR Chad/CAR's mandate expired and MINURCAT assumed the EU force's military and security responsibilities. In December 2008 Operation EU NAVFOR Somalia—Operation Atalanta, the EU's first maritime military operation, reached its initial operational capacity; Operation EU NAVFOR Somalia was established in support of UN Security Council resolutions aimed at deterring and repressing acts of piracy and armed robbery in waters off the coast of Somalia, and protecting vulnerable vessels in that area (including vessels delivering humanitarian aid to displaced persons in Somalia). The mandate of EU NAVFOR Somalia was due to expire in December 2012, subsequently extended to December 2014. In February 2010 the Council of the European Union established the EU Training Mission for Somalia (EUTM Somalia), to help strengthen the Somali transitional federal Government, in particular through providing military training to 2,000 security force recruits; EUTM Somalia became operational in April. An EU mission in support of security sector reform in Guinea-Bissau was established in February 2008, and its mandate expired in September 2010.

In 2012 the EU launched three new civilian missions in Africa. In mid-June 2012 the Council of the EU approved the establishment of EUAVSEC South Sudan, to strengthen airport security in South Sudan over a period of 19 months. The establishment of EUCAP SAHEL Niger, with an initial two-year mandate, was approved by the Council in mid-July, as a training, advisory and assistance mission aimed at augmenting the capacity of Niger's security forces to combat terrorism and organized crime. The third, EUCAP NESTOR, was established in mid-July, with a two-year mandate, to develop the maritime capacity of five countries in the Horn of Africa and the Western Indian Ocean. The mission aims to support the rule of law in Somalia and the maritime capacity of Djibouti, Kenya and the Seychelles, and eventually Tanzania, and thus complements EU NAVFOR Somalia and EUTM Somalia.

There are EU Special Representatives to the African Union and for the Great Lakes Region.

AFRICAN, CARIBBEAN AND PACIFIC (ACP) COUNTRIES

In June 2000, meeting in Cotonou, Benin, heads of state and of government of the EU and African, Caribbean and Pacific (ACP) countries concluded a new 20-year partnership accord between the EU and ACP states. The EU-ACP Partnership Agreement, known as the Cotonou Agreement, entered into force on 1 April 2003 (although many of its provisions had been applicable for a transitional period since August 2000), following ratification by the then 15 EU member states and more than the requisite two-thirds of the ACP countries. Previously, the principal means of co-operation between the Community and developing countries were the Lomé Conventions. The First Lomé Convention (Lomé I), which was concluded at Lomé, Togo, in February 1975 and came into force on 1 April 1976, replaced the Yaoundé Conventions and the Arusha Agreement. Lomé I was designed to provide a new framework of co-operation, taking into account the varying needs of developing ACP countries. The Second Lomé Convention entered into force on 1 January 1981 and the Third Lomé Convention on 1 March 1985 (trade provisions) and 1 May 1986 (aid). The Fourth Lomé Convention, which had a 10-year commitment period, was signed in December 1989: its trade provisions entered into force on 1 March 1990, and the remainder entered into force in September 1991.

The Cotonou Agreement was to cover a 20-year period from 2000 and was subject to revision every five years. A financial protocol was attached to the Agreement, which indicated the funds available to the ACP through the European Development Fund (EDF), the main instrument for Community aid for development co-operation in ACP countries. The ninth EDF, covering the initial five-year period from March 2000, provided a total budget of €13,500m., of which €1,300m. was allocated to regional co-operation and €2,200m. was for the new investment facility for the development of the private sector. In addition, uncommitted balances from previous EDFs amounted to a further €2,500m. The new Agreement envisaged a more participatory approach with more effective political co-operation to encourage good governance and democracy, increased flexibility in the provision of aid to reward performance, and a new framework for economic and trade co-operation. Its objectives were to alleviate poverty, contribute to sustainable development and integrate the ACP economies into the global economy. Negotiations to revise the Cotonou Agreement were initiated in May 2004 and concluded in February 2005. The political dimension of the Agreement was broadly strengthened and a reference to co-operation in counter-terrorism and the prevention of the proliferation of weapons of mass destruction was included. The revised Cotonou Agreement was signed on 24 June 2005.

Under the provisions of the new accord, the EU was to finalize free trade arrangements (replacing the previous non-reciprocal trade preferences) with the most-developed ACP countries during 2000–08; these would be structured around a system of six regional free trade zones, and would be designed to ensure full compatibility with World Trade Organization (WTO) provisions. Once in force, the agreements would be subject to revision every five years. The first general stage of negotiations for the Economic Partnership Agreements (EPAs), involving discussions with all ACP countries regarding common procedures, began in September 2002. The regional phase of EPA negotiations to establish a new framework for trade and investment commenced in October 2003. Negotiations had been scheduled for completion in mid-2007 to allow for ratification by 2008, when the WTO exception for existing arrangements expired. However, the negotiation period was subsequently extended. Some 36 ACP states have signed full or interim EPAs, covering the liberalization of goods and agricultural products. The EPAs have attracted some criticism for their focus on trade liberalization and their perceived failure to recognize the widespread poverty of ACP countries.

In March 2010 negotiations were concluded on the second revision of the Cotonou Agreement, which sought to take into account various factors, including the increasing importance of enhanced regional co-operation and a more inclusive partnership in ACP countries; the need for security; efforts to meet the Millennium Development Goals; the new trade relationship developed following the expiry of trade preferences at the end of 2007; and the need to ensure the effectiveness and coherence of international aid efforts. The second revised Cotonou Agreement was formally signed in Ouagadougou, Burkina Faso, in June 2010, and entered into effect, on a provisional basis, at the beginning of November.

Meanwhile, the EU had launched an initiative to allow free access to the products of the least-developed ACP nations by 2005. Stabex and Sysmin, instruments under the Lomé Conventions designed to stabilize export prices for agricultural and mining commodities, respectively, were replaced by a system called FLEX, introduced in 2000, to compensate ACP countries for short-term fluctuations in export earnings. In February 2001 the EU agreed to phase out trade barriers on imports of everything but military weapons from the world's 48 least-developed countries, 39 of which were in the ACP group. Duties on sugar, rice, bananas and some other products were to remain until 2009 (these were withdrawn from October of that year). In May 2001 the EU announced that it would cancel all outstanding debts arising from its trade accords with former colonies of member states.

One major new programme set up on behalf of the ACP countries and financed by the EDF was Pro€Invest, which was launched in 2002, with funding of €110m. over a seven-year period. In October 2003 the Commission proposed to incorporate the EDF into the EU budget (it had previously been a fund outside the EU budget, to which the EU member states made direct voluntary contributions). The cost-sharing formula for the 25 member states would automatically apply, obviating the need for negotiations about contributions for the 10th EDF. The Commission proposal was endorsed by the European Parliament in April 2004. Despite the fears of ACP countries that the enlargement of the EU could jeopardize funding, the 10th EDF was agreed in December 2005 by the European Council and provided funds of €22,682m. for 2008–13.

On 1 July 1993 the EC introduced a regime to allow the preferential import into the Community of bananas from former French and British colonies in the Caribbean. This was designed to protect the banana industries of ACP countries from the availability of cheaper bananas, produced by countries in Latin America. Latin American and later US producers brought a series of complaints before the WTO, claiming that the EU banana import regime was in contravention of free trade principles. The WTO upheld their complaints on each occasion leading to adjustments of the complex quota and tariffs systems in place. Following the WTO authorization of punitive US trade sanctions, in April 2001 the EU reached agreement with the USA and Ecuador on a new banana regime. Under the new accord, the EU was granted the so-called Cotonou waiver, which allowed it to maintain preferential access for ACP banana exports, in return for the adoption of a new tariff-only system for bananas from Latin American countries from 1 January 2006. The Latin American producers were guaranteed total market access under the agreement and were permitted to seek arbitration if dissatisfied with the EU's proposed tariff levels. Following the WTO rejection of EU proposals for tariff levels of €230 and €187 per metric ton (in comparison with existing rates of €75 for a quota of 2.2m. tons and €680 thereafter), in November 2005 the EU announced that a tariff of €176, with a duty-free quota of 775,000 metric tons for ACP producers, would be implemented on 1 January 2006. In late 2006 Ecuador initiated a challenge to the EU's proposals at the WTO. Twelve other countries subsequently initiated third-party challenges to the proposals at the WTO, in support of the challenge by Ecuador. In April 2008 the WTO upheld the challenge by Ecuador, and ordered the EU to align its tariffs with WTO regulations. In December 2009 representatives from the EU and Latin American countries initialled the Geneva Agreement on Trade in Bananas (GATB), which aimed to end the dispute. Under the Agreement, which made no provision for import quotas, the EU was gradually to reduce its import tariff on bananas from Latin American countries, from €176 per metric ton to €114 per ton by 2017. In March 2010 The EU also approved the implementation of Banana Accompanying Measures, which aimed to mobilize €190m. to support the 10 main ACP banana-exporting countries in adjusting to the anticipated increase in market competition from Latin America during 2010–13. (ACP countries would continue to benefit from duty- and quota-free access to EU markets.) For their part, Latin American banana-producing countries undertook not to demand further tariff reductions; and to withdraw several related cases against the EU that were pending at the WTO. In response to the Agreement, the US authorities determined to settle ongoing parallel complaints lodged with the WTO against the EU relating to bananas.

Following a WTO ruling at the request of Brazil, Australia and Thailand in 2005 that the EU's subsidized exports of sugar breached legal limits, reform of the EU's sugar regime was required by May 2006. Previously, the EU purchased fixed quotas of sugar from ACP producers at two or three times the world price, the same price that it paid to sugar growers in the EU. In November 2005 the EU agreed to reform the sugar industry through a phased reduction of its prices for white sugar of 36% by 2009 (which was still twice the market price in 2005). Compensation to EU producers amounted to €6,300m. over the four years beginning in January 2006, but compensation to ACP producers was worth just €40m. in 2006. Development campaigners and impoverished ACP countries, notably Jamaica and Guyana, condemned the plans.

In June 1995 negotiations opened with a view to concluding a wide-ranging trade and co-operation agreement with South Africa, including the eventual creation of a free trade area (FTA). The accord was approved by heads of state and of government in March 1999, after agreement was reached to eliminate progressively, over a 12-year period, the use of the terms 'port' and 'sherry' to describe South African fortified wines. The accord provided for the removal of duties from about 99% of South Africa's industrial exports and some 75% of its agricultural products within 10 years, while South Africa was to liberalize its market for some 86% of EU industrial goods (with protection for the motor vehicle and textiles industries), within a 12-year period. The accord also introduced increased development assistance for South Africa after 1999. The long-delayed agreement was finally signed in January 2002, allowing South African wines freer access to the EU market. Under the terms of the agreement, South Africa was allowed to export 42m. litres of wine a year duty-free to the EU, in exchange for abandoning the use of names such as 'sherry', 'port', 'ouzo' or 'grappa'. In March 1997 the Commission approved a Special Protocol for South Africa's accession to the Lomé Convention, and in April South Africa attained partial membership. Full membership was withheld, as South Africa was not regarded as, in all respects, a developing country, and was therefore not entitled to aid provisions. The EU and South Africa launched a strategic partnership in November 2006. In May 2007 the two sides agreed an Action Plan, which aimed to develop political dialogue and increase co-operation on a range of economic, social and other issues. The first EU-South Africa summit meeting was held in Bordeaux, France, in July 2008.

In May 2003 Timor-Leste joined the ACP and the ACP-EC Council of Ministers approved its accession to the ACP-EC Partnership Agreement. Cuba, which had been admitted to the ACP in December 2000, was granted observer status. Cuba withdrew its application to join the Cotonou Agreement in July 2003.

FRANC ZONE

Address: c/o Direction de la Communication (Service de Presse), Banque de France, 48 rue Croix-des-Petits-Champs, 75049, Paris Cedex 01, France.

Telephone: 1-42-92-39-08; **fax:** 1-42-92-39-40; **e-mail:** infos@banque-france.fr; **internet:** www.banque-france.fr/en/eurosystem-international/franc-zone-and-development-financing.html.

MEMBERS*

Benin	French Overseas Territories
Burkina Faso	Gabon
Cameroon	Guinea-Bissau
Central African Republic	Mali
Chad	Niger
Comoros	Senegal
Republic of the Congo	Togo
Côte d'Ivoire	
Equatorial Guinea	

* Prior to 1 January 2002, when the transition to a single European currency (euro) was finalized (see below), the Franc Zone also included Metropolitan France, the French Overseas Departments (French Guiana, Guadeloupe, Martinique and Réunion), the French Overseas Collectivité Départementale (Mayotte) and the French Overseas Collectivité Territoriale (St Pierre and Miquelon). The French Overseas Territory (French Polynesia) and the French Overseas Countries (New Caledonia and the Wallis and Futuna Islands) have continued to use the franc CFP (franc des Comptoirs français du Pacifique, 'French Pacific franc').

Apart from Guinea and Mauritania (see below), all of the countries that formerly comprised French West and Equatorial Africa are members of the Franc Zone. The former West and Equatorial African territories are still grouped within the two currency areas that existed before independence, each group having its own variant on the CFA, issued by a central bank: the franc de la Communauté Financière d'Afrique ('franc CFA de l'Ouest'), issued by the Banque centrale des états de l'Afrique de l'ouest—BCEAO, and the franc Coopération financière en Afrique centrale ('franc CFA central'), issued by the Banque des états de l'Afrique centrale—BEAC.

The following states withdrew from the Franc Zone during the period 1958–73: Guinea, Tunisia, Morocco, Algeria, Mauritania and Madagascar. Equatorial Guinea, formerly a Spanish territory, joined the Franc Zone in January 1985, and Guinea-Bissau, a former Portuguese territory, joined in May 1997.

The Comoros, formerly a French Overseas Territory, did not join the Franc Zone following its unilateral declaration of independence in 1975. However, the franc CFA was used as the currency of the new state and the Institut d'émission des Comores continued to function as a Franc Zone organization. In 1976 the Comoros formally assumed membership. In July 1981 the Banque centrale des Comores replaced the Institut d'émission des Comores, establishing its own currency, the Comoros franc.

The Franc Zone operates on the basis of agreements concluded between France and each group of member countries, and the Comoros. The currencies in the Franc Zone were formerly linked with the French franc at a fixed rate of exchange. However, following the introduction of the euro (European single currency) in January 1999, within the framework of European economic and monetary union, in which France was a participant, the Franc Zone currencies were effectively linked at fixed parity to the euro (i.e. parity was based on the fixed conversion rate for the French franc and the euro). From 1 January 2002, when European economic and monetary union was finalized and the French franc withdrawn from circulation, the franc CFA, Comoros franc and franc CFP became officially pegged to the euro, at a fixed rate of exchange. (In accordance with Protocol 13 on France, appended to the 1993 Maastricht Treaty on European Union, France was permitted to continue issuing currencies in its Overseas Territories—i.e. the franc CFP—following the completion of European economic and monetary union.) All the convertability arrangements previously concluded between France and the Franc Zone remained in force. Therefore, Franc Zone currencies are freely convertible into euros, at the fixed exchange rate, guaranteed by the French Treasury. Each group of member countries, and the Comoros, has its own central issuing bank, with overdraft facilities provided by the French Treasury. (The issuing authority for the French Overseas Territories is the Institut d'émission d'outre-mer, based in Paris, France.) Monetary reserves are held mainly in the form of euros. The BCEAO and the BEAC are authorized to hold up to 35% of their foreign exchange holdings in currencies other than the euro. Franc Zone ministers of finance normally meet twice a year to review economic and monetary co-operation. The meeting is normally attended by the French Minister of Co-operation and Francophony.

During the late 1980s and early 1990s the economies of the African Franc Zone countries were adversely affected by increasing foreign debt and by a decline in the prices paid for their principal export commodities. The French Government, however, refused to devalue the franc CFA, as recommended by the IMF. In 1990 the Franc Zone governments agreed to develop economic union, with integrated public finances and common commercial legislation. In April 1992, at a meeting of Franc Zone ministers, a treaty on the insurance industry was adopted, providing for the establishment of a regulatory body for the industry, the Conférence Intrafricaine des Marchés d'Assurances (CIMA), and for the creation of a council of Franc Zone ministers responsible for the insurance industry, with its secretariat in Libreville, Gabon. (A code of conduct for members of CIMA entered into force in February 1995.) At the meeting held in April 1992 ministers also agreed that a further council of ministers was to be created with the task of monitoring the social security systems in Franc Zone countries. A programme drawn up by Franc Zone finance ministers concerning the harmonization of commercial legislation in member states through the establishment of l'Organisation pour l'Harmonisation en Afrique du Droit des Affaires (OHADA) was approved by the Franco-African summit in October. A treaty to align corporate and investment regulations was signed by 11 member countries in October 1993.

In August 1993, in view of financial turmoil related to the continuing weakness of the French franc and the abandonment of the European exchange rate mechanism, the BCEAO and the BEAC determined to suspend repurchasing of francs CFA outside the Franc Zone. Effectively this signified the temporary withdrawal of guaranteed convertibility of the franc CFA with the French franc. Devaluations of the franc CFA and the Comoros franc (by 50% and 33.3%, respectively) were implemented in January 1994. Following the devaluation the CFA countries embarked on programmes of economic adjustment, designed to stimulate growth and to ensure eligibility for development assistance from international financial institutions. France established a special development fund of FFr 300m. to alleviate the immediate social consequences of the devaluation, and announced substantial debt cancellations. The IMF, which had strongly advocated a devaluation of the franc CFA, and the World Bank approved immediate soft-credit loans, technical assistance and cancellations or rescheduling of debts. In January 1996 Afristat, a research and training institution based in Bamako, Mali, commenced activities to support national statistical organizations in participating states in order to strengthen their economic management capabilities. The IMF and the World Bank have continued to support economic development efforts in the Franc Zone. France provides debt relief to Franc Zone member states eligible under the World Bank's initiative for heavily indebted poor countries (HIPCs). The Franc Zone was admitted in June 2012 as an observer to the Financial Action Task Force on Money Laundering.

In February 2000 the Union économique et monétaire ouest-africaine (UEMOA) and the Economic Community of West African States (ECOWAS) adopted an action plan for the creation of a single West African Monetary Zone and consequent replacement of the franc Communauté financière africaine by a single West African currency (see below).

In accordance with an agreement concluded between the Banque de France and the French Government in March 1994, and subsequently revised in June 2011, the Banque's Franc Zone and Development Financing Studies Division acts as the secretariat for six-monthly meetings of Franc Zone ministers of finance; conducts studies on Franc Zone economies; and produces, in conjunction with the BCEAO, the BEAC and the Banque centrale des Comoros, the *Rapport Annuel de la Zone Franc*. The 2010 report found that, in the aftermath of the global economic downturn that commenced in 2008, economic growth of 4.3% was recorded in the UEMOA area in 2010, compared with 3.0% in 2009 (attributable in particular to good agricultural sector performance, and public investment in infrastructure); and economic growth of 4.3% was also recorded in the CEMAC region in that year, recovering from 1.8% in 2009. Owing to the impact of a rise in foreign direct investment flows, and of debt cancellation under the Multilateral Debt Relief Initiative endorsed in September 2005 by the World Bank and IMF, the balance of payments positions of UEMOA, CEMAC and the Comoros were reported to show substantial surpluses in 2010.

CURRENCIES OF THE FRANC ZONE

1 franc CFA = €0.00152. CFA stands for Communauté financière africaine in the West African area and for Coopération financière en Afrique centrale in the Central African area. Used in the monetary areas of West and Central Africa, respectively.

1 Comoros franc = €0.00201. Used in the Comoros, where it replaced the franc CFA in 1981.

1 franc CFP = €0.00839. CFP stands for Comptoirs français du Pacifique. Used in New Caledonia, French Polynesia and the Wallis and Futuna Islands.

WEST AFRICA

Union économique et monétaire ouest-africaine (UEMOA): BP 543, Ouagadougou 01, Burkina Faso; tel. 31-88-73; fax 31-88-72; e-mail commission@uemoa.int; internet www.uemoa.int; f. 1994; promotes regional monetary and economic convergence, and envisages the eventual creation of a sub-regional common market. A preferential tariff scheme, eliminating duties on most local products and reducing by 30% import duties on many Union-produced industrial goods, became operational on 1 July 1996; in addition, from 1 July, a community solidarity tax of 0.5% was imposed on all goods from third countries sold within the Union, in order to strengthen UEMOA's capacity to promote economic integration. (This was increased to 1% in December 1999.) In June 1997 UEMOA heads of state and government agreed to reduce import duties on industrial products originating in the Union by a further 30%. An inter-parliamentary committee, recognized as the predecessor of a UEMOA legislature, was inaugurated in Mali in March 1998. In September Côte d'Ivoire's stock exchange was transformed into the Bourse regionale des valeurs mobilières, a regional stock exchange serving the Union, in order to further economic integration. On 1 January 2000 internal tariffs were eliminated on all local products (including industrial goods) and a joint external tariff system, in five bands of between 0% and 20%, was imposed on goods deriving from outside the new customs union. Guinea-Bissau was excluded from the arrangement owing to its unstable political situation. The UEMOA member countries also belong to ECOWAS and, in accordance with a decision taken in April 2000, aim to harmonize UEMOA's economic programme with that of a planned second West African monetary union (the West African Monetary Zone—WAMZ), to be established by the remaining—mainly anglophone—ECOWAS member states by January 2015 (as currently scheduled). A merger of the two complementary monetary unions, and the replacement of the franc Communauté financière africaine by a new single West African currency (the 'eco', initially to to be adopted by the WAMZ), is eventually envisaged. In January 2003 member states adopted a treaty on the establishment of a UEMOA parliament. During 2006–10 UEMOA implemented a regional economic programme aimed at developing regional infrastructures. UEMOA adopted in March 2009 a Regional Initiative for Sustainable Energy, aiming to meet all regional electricity needs by 2030. A subsidiary mortgage refinancing institution (Caisse Régionale de Refinancement Hypothécaire de l'UEMOA—CRRH-UEMOA) was established in July 2010. The 16th summit of UEMOA heads of state and government was held in Lomé, Togo, in June 2012. Mems: Benin, Burkina Faso, Côte d'Ivoire, Guinea-Bissau, Mali, Niger, Senegal and Togo; Pres. CHEIKH HADJIBOU SOUMARÉ (Senegal).

Banque centrale des états de l'Afrique de l'ouest (BCEAO): ave Abdoulaye Fadiga, BP 3108, Dakar, Senegal; tel. 839-05-00; fax 823-93-35; e-mail webmaster@bceao.int; internet www.bceao.int; f. 1962; central bank of issue for the mems of UEMOA; total assets 8,370.1m. francs CFA (31 Dec. 2009); mems: Benin, Burkina Faso, Côte d'Ivoire, Guinea-Bissau, Mali, Niger, Senegal and Togo; Gov. TIEMOKO MEYLIET KONE (Côte d'Ivoire); publs *Annual Report, Notes d'Information et Statistiques* (monthly), *Annuaire des banques, Bilan des banques et établissements financiers* (annually).

Banque ouest-africaine de développement (BOAD): 68 ave de la Libération, BP 1172, Lomé, Togo; tel. 221-42-44; fax 221-52-67; e-mail boadsiege@boad.org; internet www.boad.org; f. 1973 to promote the balanced development of mem. states and the economic integration of West Africa; a Guarantee Fund for Private Investment in West Africa, established jtly by BOAD and the European Investment Bank in Dec. 1994, aims to guarantee medium- and long-term credits to private sector businesses in the region; in April 2012, jointly with CDC Climat and Proparco (see Agence française de développement), BOAD launched the Fonds carbone pour l'Afrique (FCA), aimed at financing a green economy in West Africa; auth. cap. 1,050,000m. francs CFA (30 June 2010); mems: Benin, Burkina Faso, Côte d'Ivoire, Guinea-Bissau, Mali, Niger, Senegal, Togo; Pres. CHRISTIAN ADOVELANDE (Benin); publs *Rapport Annuel*, *BOAD en Bref* (quarterly).

Bourse Régionale des Valeurs Mobilières (BRVM): 18 rue Joseph Anoma, BP 3802, Abidjan 01, Côte d'Ivoire; tel. 20-32-66-85; fax 20-32-66-84; e-mail brvm@brvm.org; internet www.brvm.org; f. 1998; regional electronic stock exchange; Dir-Gen. JEAN-PAUL GILLET.

CENTRAL AFRICA

Communauté économique et monétaire de l'Afrique centrale (CEMAC): BP 969, Bangui, Central African Republic; tel. and fax 21-61-47-81; fax 21-61-21-35; e-mail secemac@cemac.int; internet www.cemac.int; f. 1998; formally inaugurated as the successor to the Union douanière et économique de l'Afrique centrale (UDEAC, f. 1966) at a meeting of heads of state held in Malabo, Equatorial Guinea, in June 1999; aims to promote the process of sub-regional integration within the framework of an economic union and a monetary union; CEMAC was also to comprise a parliament and sub-regional tribunal; UDEAC established a common external tariff for imports from other countries and administered a common code for investment policy and a Solidarity Fund to counteract regional disparities of wealth and economic development; mems: Cameroon, Central African Republic, Chad, Republic of the Congo, Equatorial Guinea, Gabon; Pres. ANTOINE NTSIMI (Cameroon).

At a summit meeting in December 1981, UDEAC leaders agreed in principle to form an economic community of Central African states (Communauté économique des états de l'Afrique centrale—CEEAC), to include UDEAC members and Burundi, Rwanda, São Tomé and Príncipe and Zaire (now Democratic Republic of the Congo). CEEAC began operations in 1985.

Banque de développement des états de l'Afrique centrale (BDEAC): place du Gouvernement, BP 1177, Brazzaville, Republic of the Congo; tel. 281-18-85; fax 281-18-80; e-mail bdeac@bdeac.org; internet www.bdeac.org; f. 1975; auth. cap. 250,000m. francs CFA (30 Sept. 2011) (BDEAC's auth. cap. was increased by 100% in 2010); shareholders: Cameroon, Central African Republic, Chad, Republic of the Congo, Gabon, Equatorial Guinea, AfDB, BEAC, France, Germany and Kuwait; Pres. MICHAËL ADANDÉ.

Banque des états de l'Afrique centrale (BEAC): 736 ave Mgr François Xavier Vogt, BP 1917, Yaoundé, Cameroon; tel. 223-40-30; fax 223-33-29; e-mail beac@beac.int; internet www.beac.int; f. 1973 as the central bank of issue of Cameroon, the Central African Republic, Chad, Republic of the Congo, Equatorial Guinea and Gabon; a monetary market, incorporating all national financial institutions of the BEAC countries, came into effect on 1 July 1994; cap. 88,000m. francs CFA (Dec. 2009); Gov. LUCAS ABAGA NCHAMA (Equatorial Guinea); publs *Rapport Annuel*, *Etudes et statistiques* (monthly).

CENTRAL ISSUING BANKS

Banque centrale des Comores: place de France, BP 405, Moroni, Comoros; tel. (773) 1814; fax (773) 0349; e-mail bancecom@snpt.km; internet www.bancecom.com; f. 1981; Gov. ABOUDOU MOHAMED CHAFIOUN.

Banque centrale des états de l'Afrique de l'ouest: see above.

Banque des états de l'Afrique centrale: see above.

Institut d'émission d'outre-mer (IEOM): 5 rue Roland Barthes, 75012 Paris Cedex 12, France; tel. 1-53-44-41-41; fax 1-43-47-51-34; e-mail direction@iedom-ieom.fr; internet www.ieom.fr; f. 1966; issuing authority for the French Overseas Territories; Dir-Gen. NICOLAS DE SEZE.

FRENCH ECONOMIC AID

France's connection with the African Franc Zone countries involves not only monetary arrangements, but also includes comprehensive French assistance in the forms of budget support, foreign aid, technical assistance and subsidies on commodity exports.

Official French financial aid and technical assistance to developing countries is administered by the following agencies:

Agence française de développement (AFD): 5 rue Roland Barthes, 75598 Paris Cedex 12, France; tel. 1-53-44-31-31; fax 1-44-87-99-39; e-mail com@afd.fr; internet www.afd.fr; f. 1941; fmrly the Caisse française de développement—CFD; French development bank that lends money to member states and former member states of the Franc Zone and several other states, and executes the financial operations of the FSP (see below). Following the devaluation of the franc CFA in January 1994, the French Government cancelled some FFr 25,000m. in debt arrears owed by member states to the CFD. The CFD established a Special Fund for Development and the Exceptional Facility for Short-term Financing to help to alleviate the immediate difficulties resulting from the devaluation. Serves as the secretariat for the Fonds français pour l'environnement mondial (f. 1994). Has, together with private shareholders, an interest in the development investment company PROPARCO (f. 1977). Since 2000 the AFD has been implementing France's support of the World Bank's HIPC initiative; Pres. PIERRE-ANDRÉ PERISSOL; CEO DOV ZERAH.

Fonds de Solidarité Prioritaire (FSP): c/o Ministry of Foreign and European Affairs, 37 quai d'Orsay, 75351 Paris, France; tel. 1-43-17-53-53; fax 1-43-17-52-03; internet www.diplomatie.gouv.fr; f. 2000, taking over from the Fonds d'aide et de coopération (f. 1959) the administration of subsidies from the French Government to 54 countries of the Zone de solidarité prioritaire; FSP is administered by the French Ministry of Foreign and European Affairs, which allocates budgetary funds to it.

INTERGOVERNMENTAL AUTHORITY ON DEVELOPMENT—IGAD

Address: Ave Georges Clemenceau, BP 2653, Djibouti.

Telephone: 354050; **fax:** 356994; **e-mail:** igad@igad.org; **internet:** www.igad.org.

The Intergovernmental Authority on Development (IGAD), established in 1996 to supersede the Intergovernmental Authority on Drought and Development (IGADD, founded in 1986), aims to co-ordinate the sustainable socio-economic development of member countries, to combat the effects of drought and desertification, and to promote regional food security.

MEMBERS*

Djibouti	Kenya	South Sudan	Uganda
Ethiopia	Somalia	Sudan	

* In April 2007 Eritrea suspended its IGAD membership; the IGAD Council of Ministers has subsequently engaged with Eritrea to promote its return to the organization. South Sudan was admitted as the seventh member of the organization in November 2011.

Organization

(September 2012)

ASSEMBLY

The Assembly, consisting of heads of state and of government of member states, is the supreme policy-making organ of the Authority. It holds a summit meeting at least once a year. The chairmanship of the Assembly rotates among the member countries on an annual basis.

COUNCIL OF MINISTERS

The Council of Ministers is composed of the minister of foreign affairs and one other minister from each member state. It meets at least twice a year and approves the work programme and the annual budget of the Secretariat.

COMMITTEE OF AMBASSADORS

The Committee of Ambassadors comprises the ambassadors or plenipotentiaries of member states to Djibouti. It convenes as regularly as required to advise and assist the Executive Secretary concerning the interpretation of policies and guidelines and the realization of the annual work programme.

SECRETARIAT

The Secretariat, the executive body of IGAD, is headed by the Executive Secretary, who is appointed by the Assembly for a term of four years, renewable once. In addition to the Office of the Executive Secretary, the Secretariat comprises the following three divisions: Agriculture and Environment; Economic Co-operation; and Political and Humanitarian Affairs, each headed by a director. A workshop was convened in September 2011 to discuss the future organizational restructuring of IGAD.

Executive Secretary: Mahboub Maalim (Kenya).

Activities

IGADD was established in 1986 by Djibouti, Ethiopia, Kenya, Somalia, Sudan and Uganda, to combat the effects of aridity and desertification arising from the severe drought and famine that has periodically affected the Horn of Africa. Eritrea became a member of IGADD in September 1993, following its proclamation as an independent state. In April 1995, at an extraordinary summit meeting held in Addis Ababa, Ethiopia, heads of state and of government resolved to reorganize and expand the Authority. In March 1996 IGAD was endorsed to supersede IGADD, at a second extraordinary summit meeting of heads of state and of government, held in Nairobi, Kenya. The meeting led to the adoption of an agreement for a new organizational structure and the approval of an extended mandate to co-ordinate and harmonize policy in the areas of economic co-operation and political and humanitarian affairs, in addition to its existing responsibilities for food security and environmental protection.

IGAD aims to achieve regional co-operation and economic integration. To facilitate this, IGAD assists the governments of member states to maximize resources and co-ordinates efforts to initiate and implement regional development programmes and projects. In this context, IGAD promotes the harmonization of policies relating to agriculture and natural resources, communications, customs, trade and transport; the implementation of programmes in the fields of social sciences, research, science and technology; and effective participation in the global economy. Meetings between IGAD ministers of foreign affairs and the IGAD Partners' Forum (IPF), comprising the grouping's donors, are convened periodically to discuss issues such as food security and humanitarian affairs. In October 2001 delegates from IGAD and representatives of government and civil society in member states initiated a process to establish an IGAD-Civil Society Forum; the founding assembly of the Forum was convened in Nairobi, in July 2003. In August 2008 a meeting was held with the UN Development Programme (UNDP) on mobilizing resources and capacity building for the regional organization. Negotiations were conducted during 2008 on formulating a regional Integration Plan to cover all sectors of IGAD's activity. In February 2009 the IGAD Executive Secretary chaired a technical meeting, in Djibouti, which aimed to chart a road map for future integration.

In October 2003 the 10th IGAD summit meeting ratified a decision of the eighth summit, held in November 2000, to absorb the Harare, Zimbabwe- and Nairobi-based Drought Monitoring Centre (an initiative of 24 eastern and southern African states inaugurated in 1989 under the auspices of UNDP and the World Meteorological Organization) as a specialized institution of IGAD; the Centre was renamed the IGAD Climate Prediction and Applications Centre (ICPAC). In April 2007 ICPAC was fully integrated into IGAD.

A Protocol establishing the Inter-parliamentary Union of IGAD (IPU-IGAD), signed in February 2004 by the participants in the first meeting of regional speakers of parliament, entered into force in November 2007; IPU-IGAD was to be based in Addis Ababa.

In January 2008 the IGAD Regional AIDS Partnership Program (IRAPP) was launched, with a particular focus on protecting mobile communities (for example pastoralists, internally displaced persons, and refugees) at risk of HIV/AIDS. IRAPP was implementing a common regional strategic plan for combating HIV/AIDS, targeting cross-border and mobile populations, over the period 2011–16. Jointly with the World Bank the IGAD Secretariat is developing a mechanism for monitoring the occurrence of HIV/AIDS in member states.

In June 2006 IGAD launched the IGAD Capacity Building Program Against Terrorism (ICPAT), a four-year programme based in Addis Ababa, which aimed to combat the reach of international terrorism through the enhancement of judicial measures and inter-departmental co-operation, improving border control activities, supporting training and information-sharing, and promoting strategic co-operation. In April 2009 a meeting of IGAD justice ministers, organized by ICPAT, approved a draft IGAD Convention on Extradition, and also a draft Convention on Mutual Legal Assistance. In October 2011 a new IGAD Security Sector Program (ISSP) was launched, focusing on initiatives in the areas of counter-terrorism; organized crime; maritime security; and capacity building of security institutions.

A draft framework for an IGAD Gender Peer Review Mechanism is under consideration; it is envisaged that the Mechanism would be a means of addressing the issue of violence against women in the region as well as other matters relating to women's progress. In December 2009 the first IGAD Women's Parliamentary Conference, convened in Addis Ababa, adopted a declaration on the Enhancement of Women's Participation and Representation in Decision-Making Positions. In April 2011 IGAD convened a conference on women and peace, considering the engagement of women in peace-building and security initiatives in the region.

In October 2011 IGAD was granted observer status at the UN General Assembly.

FOOD SECURITY AND ENVIRONMENTAL PROTECTION

IGAD seeks to achieve regional food security, the sustainable development of natural resources and environmental protection, and to encourage and assist member states in their efforts to combat the consequences of drought and other natural and man-made disasters. The region suffers from recurrent droughts, which severely impede crop and livestock production. Natural and man-made disasters increase the strain on resources, resulting in annual food deficits. About 80% of the IGAD sub-region is classified as arid or semi-arid, and some 40% of the region is unproductive, owing to severe environmental degradation. Activities to improve food security and preserve natural resources have included: the introduction of remote-sensing services; the development of a Marketing Information System and of a Regional Integrated Information System (RIIS); the establishment of training and credit schemes for fishermen; research into the sustainable production of drought-resistant, high-yielding crop varieties; transboundary livestock disease control and vaccine production; the control of environmental pollution; the promotion of alternative sources of energy in the home; the management of integrated water resources; the promotion of community-based land husbandry; training programmes in grain marketing; and the implementation of the International Convention to Combat Desertification. IGAD's Livestock Marketing Information System (LMIS) aims to improve food security in the sub-region.

In June 2008 the IGAD Assembly, meeting in a climate of escalating global food prices and shortfalls in regional imports of foodstuffs, issued a Declaration on the Current High Food Price Crisis, in which it resolved to pursue policies aimed at improving sustainable food production; urged IGAD's partners to support regional agricultural development programmes; determined to enhance the regional drought, climate change monitoring, and early warning mechanisms; and announced that a regional emergency reserve fund would be established. In addition the Authority decided to establish a ministerial task force to assess regional emergency food aid requirements with a view to launching an international appeal for assistance. In July an IGAD meeting on regional food security and risk management, held in Nairobi, Kenya, addressed means of improving social protection and disaster risk management strategies and policies. In December 2009 IGAD and the World Food Programme (WFP) concluded a Memorandum of Understanding (MOU) aimed at enhancing mutual co-operation with a view to improving food and nutrition security in the IGAD region. An executive body, technical committee and co-ordination office were to be established to facilitate the implementation of the MOU.

In November 2011 IGAD and partner countries held a consultative meeting entitled 'Ending Drought Emergencies in the Horn of Africa', in response to ongoing severe drought and an ensuing food security crisis, that had resulted in some 13m. people in the region requiring food assistance. The meeting determined the institutional arrangements for implementing a Horn of Africa Disaster Resilience and Sustainability Initiative: Ending Drought Emergencies, which had been launched by regional heads of state in September. The meeting also agreed to establish an IGAD Platform, intended as an enhanced partnership with donors facilitating long-term investment—particularly in regional arid and semi-arid lands—to end the recurrence of drought emergencies.

IGAD adopted an Environment and Natural Resources Strategy in April 2007, identifying a number key strategic objectives that were to guide future sub-regional environmental programmes. In June 2010 a consultative meeting was convened between IGAD, the African Union (AU), the Common Market for Eastern and Southern African (COMESA), and other regional partners, aimed at advancing the coordination and harmonization of their activities governing the environment.

ECONOMIC CO-OPERATION

The Economic Co-operation division concentrates on the development of a co-ordinated infrastructure for the region, in particular in the areas of transport and communications, to promote foreign, cross-border and domestic trade and investment opportunities. IGAD seeks to harmonize national transport and trade policy and thereby to facilitate the free movement of people, goods and services. The improvements to infrastructure also aim to facilitate more timely interventions in conflicts, disasters and emergencies in the sub-region. Projects under way include: the construction of missing segments of the Trans-African Highway and the Pan African Telecommunications Network; the removal of barriers to trade and communications; improvements to ports and inland container terminals; and the modernization of railway and telecommunications services. In November 2000 the IGAD Assembly determined to establish an integrated rail network connecting all member countries. In addition, the heads of state and government considered the possibility of drafting legislation to facilitate the expansion of intra-IGAD trade. The development of economic co-operation has been impeded by persisting conflicts in the sub-region (see below). In August 2010 an IGAD Business Forum was held, in Kampala, Uganda.

POLITICAL AND HUMANITARIAN AFFAIRS

The field of political and humanitarian affairs focuses on conflict prevention, management and resolution through dialogue. The division's primary aim is to restore peace and stability to member countries affected by conflict, in order that resources may be diverted for development purposes. Efforts have been pursued to strengthen capacity for conflict prevention and to relieve humanitarian crises. The ninth IGAD summit meeting, held in Khartoum, Sudan, in January 2002, adopted a protocol to IGAD's founding agreement establishing a conflict early warning and response mechanism (CEWARN). CEWARN, which is based in Addis Ababa, Ethiopia, collects and analyses information for the preparation of periodic early warning reports concerning the potential outbreak of violent conflicts in the region. In February 2006 IGAD convened a ministerial conference on refugees, returnees and internally displaced persons, to consider means of addressing the burden posed by population displacement in member states; at that time it was estimated that 11m. people had been forcibly displaced from their homes in the region. In May 2008 IGAD, the AU and the International Organization for Migration (IOM) jointly organized a workshop, held in Addis Ababa, on inter-state and intra-regional cooperation on migration; an IGAD Regional Consultative Process (IGAD-RCP) on migration was launched, with the aim of building member countries' management capacities. In February 2012 a meeting of the IGAD-RCP considered the possibility of developing a regional action plan for Diaspora engagement in development. IGAD contributes to efforts to raise awareness of the AU's 2006 Ouagadougou Action Plan to Combat Trafficking in Human Beings, and supports the AU COMMIT campaign, launched in June 2009 to combat human trafficking.

The Executive Secretary of IGAD participated in the first summit meeting of all East African heads of state and government, convened in April 2005 in Addis Ababa; the meeting agreed to establish an Eastern African Standby Brigade (EASBRIG). EASBRIG, the development of which is co-ordinated by IGAD, will form the regional component of the AU African Standby Force. In November 2009 EASBRIG undertook a field training exercise ('Exercise Amani Carana') in Djibouti.

In 2008 a new IGAD Peace and Security Strategy was devised. In August IGAD chaired the first meeting of the steering committee on Conflict Prevention Management and Resolution (CPMR), comprising IGAD, COMESA and the East African Community (EAC), which aimed to promote a co-ordinated approach to peace and security in the region. In September 2012 IGAD launched a new regional strategy for conflict early-warning and response, facilitating information-sharing among member states and joint action against emerging conflict.

Kenya: At the beginning of February 2008 IGAD heads of state and government convened in Addis Ababa, on the sidelines of the 10th Assembly of the AU, to discuss the violent unrest that had erupted in Kenya in the aftermath of that country's December 2007 disputed general election; following the meeting an IGAD ministerial delegation was dispatched to Kenya as a gesture of regional solidarity with the Kenyan people and with a peace initiative led by the former UN Secretary-General, Kofi Annan. IGAD sent an observer mission to monitor the national referendum on a new draft constitution held in Kenya in August 2010.

Somalia: In May–August 2000 a conference aimed at securing peace in Somalia was convened in Arta, Djibouti, under the auspices of IGAD. The conference appointed a transitional Somali legislature, which then elected a transitional national president. The eighth summit of IGAD heads of state and government, held in Khartoum, in November, welcomed the conclusion in September of an agreement on reconciliation between the new Somali transitional administration and a prominent opposition alliance, and determined that those member countries that neighboured Somalia (the 'frontline states' of Djibouti, Ethiopia and Kenya) should co-operate in assisting the process of reconstruction and reconciliation in that country. The summit appointed a special envoy to implement IGAD's directives concerning the Somali situation. In January 2002 the ninth IGAD summit meeting determined that a new conference for promoting reconciliation in Somalia (where insecurity continued to prevail) should be convened, under IGAD's auspices. The leaders also issued a statement condemning international terrorism and urged Somalia, in particular, to make a firm commitment to eradicating terrorism. The second Somalia reconciliation conference, initiated in October, in Eldoret, Kenya, under IGAD auspices, issued a Declaration on Cessation of Hostilities, Structures and Principles of the Somalia National Reconciliation Process, as a basis for the pursuit of a peace settlement. In February 2003 the conference was relocated to Nairobi, Kenya. In January 2004 the Nairobi conference determined to establish a new parliament; this was inaugurated in August. In January 2005 IGAD heads of state and government authorized the deployment of a Peace Support Mission to Somalia (IGASOM) to assist the transitional federal authorities there, pending the subsequent deployment of an AU peace force; this arrangement was endorsed in the same month by the AU. In mid-March 2006 the IGAD Assembly reiterated its support for the planned deployment of IGASOM, and urged the UN Security Council to grant an exemption to the UN arms embargo applied to Somalia in order to facilitate the regional peace support initiative. At a consultative meeting on the removal of the arms embargo, convened in mid-April, in Nairobi, representatives of the Somali transitional federal authorities presented for consideration by IGAD and the AU a draft national security and stabilization plan. It was agreed that a detailed mission plan should be formulated to underpin the proposed IGAD/AU peace missions. In January 2007 the AU Peace and Security Council authorized the deployment of the AU Mission in Somalia (AMISOM) in place of the proposed IGASOM.

An extraordinary meeting of the IGAD Council of Ministers, held in New York, USA, in September 2008, noted with serious concern the ongoing escalation in acts of piracy in waters off the Somalian coast, and urged the international community to take co-ordinated action to safeguard maritime safety in the region. In December a new IGAD Facilitator for the Somali peace process was appointed. Meeting in May 2009 an extraordinary session of the IGAD Council of Ministers urged the UN Security Council to impose (except for humanitarian personnel) a no-fly zone over Somalia and blockades on identified Somali seaports, and also to impose targeted sanctions against all those providing assistance to extremists—including foreign forces—who were continuing to attack AMISOM and otherwise to destabilize that country. A further extraordinary meeting of IGAD leaders, convened in June 2009, on the sidelines of the AU summit, in Sirte, Libya, noted with deep concern the continuing poor security situation in Somalia; urged the UN Security Council to consider enabling front-line states to deploy troops to Somalia if necessary; committed IGAD member states individually and collectively to establishing an internal mechanism to effect the sanctions called for in May and to enact legislation aimed at combating piracy; and directed the IGAD Secretariat to accord full support to the grouping's Facilitator for the Somali peace process. In mid-September IGAD, the UN, the European Union (EU), the League of Arab States and the respective Governments of Norway and the USA issued a joint statement strongly condemning suicide car bomb attacks that were perpetrated by Islamic extremists against the AMISOM headquarters in Mogadishu, Somalia, killing more than 20 people, including the Deputy Force Commander of the Mission. The January 2010 IGAD extraordinary summit gathering determined to send a ministerial delegation to selected partner countries and organizations to solicit their support for the Somali transitional federal authorities; and welcomed the imposition by the UN Security Council in December 2009 of punitive sanctions against the Eritrean political and military leadership, who were found to have provided political, financial and logistical support to armed groups engaged in undermining the reconciliation process in Somalia, and to have acted aggressively towards Djibouti. The Kampala Accord, signed in June 2011 by the President of the Somali transitional federal authorities and the Speaker of the transitional legislature, and related Roadmap on its implementation, outlined a schedule for national elections, and determined that the IGAD and EAC heads of state, with UN and AU co-operation, should establish a political bureau to oversee and advance the Somali peace process. The January 2012 extraordinary session of the Authority endorsed a new IGAD Somalia Inland Strategy and Action Plan to Prevent and Counter Piracy. In September IGAD congratulated Hassan Sheikh Mohamud and the people of Somalia on his peaceful election as president of a new federal government.

Sudan: In September 1995 negotiations between the Sudanese Government and opposition leaders were initiated, under the auspices of IGAD, with the aim of resolving the conflict in southern Sudan; these were subsequently reconvened periodically. In March 2001 IGAD's mediation committee on southern Sudan, chaired by (then) President Daniel arap Moi of Kenya, publicized a seven-point plan for a peaceful settlement of the conflict. In June, at a regional summit on the situation in Sudan convened by IGAD, it was agreed that a permanent negotiating forum comprising representatives of the parties to the conflict would be established at the Authority's secretariat. In July 2002 the Sudanese Government and the main rebel grouping in that country signed, under IGAD auspices, in Machakos, Kenya, a protocol providing for a six-year period of autonomy for southern Sudan to be followed by a referendum on self-determination, and establishing that northern Sudan would be governed in accordance with *Shari'a* law and southern Sudan by a secular judicial system. Peace negotiations subsequently continued under IGAD auspices. A cease-fire agreement was concluded by the parties to the conflict in October, to which an addendum was adopted in February 2003, recommending the deployment of an IGAD verification and monitoring team to oversee compliance with the agreement. In September of that year the parties to the conflict signed an accord on interim security arrangements. During 2003–04 IGAD mediated several further accords that paved the way for the conclusion, in January 2005, of a final Comprehensive Peace Agreement (CPA). An extraordinary session of the IGAD Council of Ministers, convened in January 2010, in Addis Ababa, expressed concern regarding the ongoing status of the implementation of the CPA and directed the IGAD Secretariat to develop programmes and seminars aimed at promoting a culture of peace in Sudan. An extraordinary summit meeting of the IGAD Assembly, held in March, *inter alia* emphasized the centrality of IGAD's role in the full implementation of the CPA; directed the IGAD Secretariat to open immediately a liaison office in Juba, Sudan, to follow up the implementation of the CPA; directed the IGAD Secretariat to accept an invitation to observe the April 2010 Sudanese elections; and directed the IGAD Secretariat to convene, in collaboration with the IPF and the parties to the CPA, an international Donors' Conference for Sudan. The IGAD monitoring team dispatched to observe the presidential and legislative elections in Sudan, in April, found them to be 'credible', while noting that technical problems had occurred and that the electoral authorities had been overwhelmed by the magnitude of their task. Following the referendum on self-determination for South Sudan, held in January 2011, and South Sudan's consequent attainment of independence in July, the new nation was admitted to IGAD in November 2011. The 20th extraordinary session of the Authority, held in January 2012, noted with concern deteriorating relations between Sudan and South Sudan, and strongly urged both states to refrain from actions that might undermine the resolution of outstanding issues under the CPA. In February the IGAD Executive Secretary reiterated the position of the AU that a warrant issued in November 2011 by the Kenyan High Court for the arrest of Sudanese President Omar Al-Bashir—indicted by the International Criminal Court on charges of including crimes against humanity and genocide—contravened the interests of peace, stability and economic development in the region, and risked undermining the peace process being undertaken by IGAD in Sudan. In April 2012 the IGAD Executive Secretariat issued a statement expressing deep concern at escalating conflict between Sudan and South Sudan, urging the two sides to adhere to a Memorandum of Understanding signed in February on non-aggression and co-operation, and fully supporting the ongoing mediation efforts of an AU High Level and Implementation Panel.

Publications

Annual Report.

IGAD News (2 a year).

Proceedings of the Summit of Heads of State and Government; Reports of the Council of Ministers' Meetings.

Specialized Institutions

Conflict Early Warning and Response Mechanism (CEWARN): off Bole Medhanialem Rd (behind the Millennium Hall), Bole Sub City, Addis Ababa, Ethiopia; tel. (11) 6530977; fax (11) 6614489; internet www.cewarn.org; f. 2002; aims to prevent and mitigate violent conflict in the IGAD member states; has hitherto directed particular attention to cross-border pastoralist and related conflicts; works through a network of Conflict Early Warning and Response Units (CEWERUs), national research institutes (NRIs), and field monitors; focuses its activities in the following geographical clusters: Karamoja Cluster (covering cross-border areas of Ethiopia, Kenya, Sudan and Uganda), Somali Cluster (cross-border areas of Ethiopia, Kenya and Somalia), and Dikhil Cluster (cross-border areas of Djibouti and Ethiopia); in accordance with the new regional strategy for conflict early-warning and response launched by IGAD in September 2012, CEWARN was to be strengthened to address a broader range of national and trans-boundary security factors, such as: competition for natural resources and land, migration, displaced populations, internal and international boundaries, climate, environment, ethnicity and religion, and economic variations.

IGAD Climate Prediction and Applications Centre (ICPAC): POB 10304, Nairobi, Kenya; tel. (20) 3878340; fax (20) 2878343; e-mail director@icpac.net; internet www.icpac.net; f. 1989 as the Drought Monitoring Centre and subsequently renamed; became an IGAD specialized institution in 2007; aims to enhance sub-regional and national capacities to utilize climate knowledge for the provision of climate information and prediction, and early warning, and for advancing sustainable development; mems: Burundi, Djibouti, Eritrea, Ethiopia, Kenya, Rwanda, Sudan, Somalia, Tanzania, Uganda.

Other IGAD specialist institutions are: the IGAD Capacity Building Program against Terrorism (ICPAT), the IGAD Regional HIV and AIDS Partnership Program (IRAPP), and the IGAD Livestock Policty Initiative (IGAD-LPI).

INTERNATIONAL CRIMINAL COURT

Address: Maanweg 174, 2516 AB The Hague, Netherlands.
Telephone: (70) 5158515; **fax:** (70) 5158555; **e-mail:** otp.informationdesk@icc-cpi.int; **internet:** www.icc-cpi.int.

The International Criminal Court (ICC) was established by the Rome Statute of the International Criminal Court, adopted by 120 states participating in a UN Diplomatic Conference in July 1998. The Rome Statute (and therefore the temporal jurisdiction of the ICC) entered into force on 1 July 2002, 60 days after ratification by the requisite 60th signatory state in April. The ICC is a permanent, independent body, in relationship with the UN, that aims to promote the rule of law and punish the most serious international crimes. The Rome Statute reaffirmed the principles of the UN Charter and stated that the relationship between the Court and the UN system should be determined by a framework relationship agreement between the states parties to the Rome Statute and the UN General Assembly: under the so-called negotiated relationship agreement, which entered into force in October 2004, upon signature by the Court's President and the Secretary-General of the UN, there was to be mutual exchange of information and documentation to the fullest extent and co-operation and consultation on practical matters, and it was stipulated that the Court might, if deemed appropriate, submit reports on its activities to the UN Secretary-General and propose to the Secretary-General items for consideration by the UN.

The Court comprises the Presidency (consisting of a President and first and second Vice-Presidents), Chambers (including a Pre-Trial Chamber, Trial Chamber and Appeals Chamber) with 18 permanent judges, Office of the Prosecutor (comprising the Chief Prosecutor and up to two Deputy Prosecutors), and Registry. The judges must each have a different nationality and equitably represent the major legal systems of the world, a fair geographical distribution, and a fair proportion of men and women. They are elected by the Assembly of States Parties to the Rome Statute from two lists, the first comprising candidates with established competence in criminal law and procedures and the second comprising candidates with established competence in relevant areas of international law, to terms of office of three, six or nine years. The President and Vice-Presidents are elected by an absolute majority of the judges for renewable three-year terms of office. The Chief Prosecutor is elected by an absolute majority of states parties to the Rome Statute to an unrenewable nine-year term of office. The first judges were elected to the Court in February 2003, the first Presidency in March, and the first Chief Prosecutor in April.

The Court has established a Victims Trust Fund to finance compensation, restitution or rehabilitation for victims of crimes (individuals or groups of individuals). The Fund is administered by the Registry and supervised by an independent board of directors. In August 2012 the ICC issued its first decision on reparations for victims, in relation to the conviction in March of that year of Thomas Lubanga (see Situation in the Democratic Republic of the Congo). At August 2012 the Fund's reserve for reparations totalled €1.2m. The Court had received more than 8,000 applications for reparations by that time.

By September 2012 16 cases in seven situations had been brought before the Court. Three situations were being addressed by the Court that had been referred to it by states party to the Rome Statute relating to occurrences on their territories; two situations were being pursued that had been referred by the UN Security Council; and investigations *proprio motu* were being conducted into situations in Kenya and Côte d'Ivoire (see below).

In mid-July 2012, at the request of the Government of Mali, the Court launched a preliminary examination of 'the situation in Mali'—relating to atrocities allegedly perpetrated since January of 2012 by armed militants in northern areas of that country—to determine whether the ongoing situation met criteria stipulated under the Rome Statute for launching a formal investigation.

Situation in Uganda: referred to the Court in January 2004 by the Ugandan Government; the Chief Prosecutor agreed to open an investigation into the situation in July 2004; relates to the long-term unrest in the north of the country; in October 2005 the Court unsealed warrants of arrest (issued under seal in July) against five commanders of the Ugandan Lord's Resistance Army (LRA), including the LRA leader, Joseph Kony; in July 2007 the Court's proceedings against one of the named commanders were terminated on the grounds that he had been killed during LRA rebel activities in August 2006; the other four suspects remained at large at September 2012.

Situation in the Democratic Republic of the Congo (DRC): referred in April 2004 by the DRC Government; the Chief Prosecutor agreed to open an investigation into the situation in June 2004; relates to alleged war crimes; in March 2006 Thomas Lubanga Dyilo, a DRC militia leader, was arrested by the Congolese authorities and transferred to the Court, thereby becoming the first ICC indictee to be captured; Lubanga was charged with conscripting child soldiers, a sealed warrant for his arrest having been issued in February; in July 2007 warrants of arrest were issued for the DRC rebel commanders Germain Katanga and Mathieu Ngudjolo Chui; Katanga was transferred into the custody of the Court in October 2007 and Ngudjolo Chui in February 2008; in April 2008 the Court unsealed a warrant of arrest for the rebel leader Bosco Ntaganda, relating to the exploitation of children under the age of 15 as soldiers during 2002–03; a second warrant for Ntaganda, expanding upon the original charges, was issued in July 2012; in July 2012 a warrant was issued for the arrest of Sylvestre Mudacumura, the commander of the Democratic Forces for the Liberation of Rwanda, relating to war crimes (specifically: cruel treatment; attacking civilians; mutilation; outrages against personal dignity; rape; torture; murder; destruction of property; and pillaging) allegedly committed over the period 20 Jan. 2009–end-Sept. 2010; Lubanga's trial—the first conducted by the Court—commenced in January 2009; the Prosecution concluded its presentation of its case in the trial of Lubanga in July 2009; Lubanga was found guilty in March 2012, in the first verdict given by the Court, and in July of that year he was sentenced to 14 years' imprisonment; the trial in the case of Katanga and Ngudjolo Chui (the Court's second trial) commenced in November 2009; in December 2011 charges relating to crimes against humanity and other war crimes were withdrawn against Callixte Mbarushimana, an alleged rebel leader who had been arrested by the French authorities in October 2010 and transferred to the custody of the Court in January 2011; Ntaganda remained at large at September 2012.

Situation in the Central African Republic (CAR): referred in January 2005 by the CAR Government; the Chief Prosecutor agreed to open an investigation into the situation in May 2005; relates to war crimes and crimes against humanity allegedly committed during the period October 2002–March 2003; in May 2008 the Court issued a warrant of arrest for Jean-Pierre Bemba Gombo, the leader of the Mouvement du Libération du Congo (the 'Banyamulenge'); Bemba Gombo was transferred into the custody of the Court in July 2008, and his trial commenced in November 2010.

Situation in Darfur, Sudan: referred to the Court in March 2005 by the UN Security Council on the basis of the recently issued report of an International Commission of Inquiry on Darfur; the Chief Prosecutor agreed to open an investigation into the situation in June 2005; relates to the situation prevailing in Darfur since 1 July 2002; the UN Secretary-General handed the Chief Prosecutor a sealed list of 51 names of people identified in the report as having committed crimes under international law; in April 2007 the Court issued warrants for the arrests of Ahmad Harun, a former Sudanese government minister, and Ali Kushayb, a leader of the Sudanese Janjaweed militia, who were both accused of perpetrating war crimes and crimes against humanity; both remained at large at September 2012; in July 2008 the Chief Prosecutor presented evidence that Sudan's President Omar al-Bashir had been responsible for committing alleged war crimes, including crimes against humanity and genocide, in Darfur; an arrest warrant for President al-Bashir was issued by the Court in March 2009; a second arrest warrant for President al-Bashir was issued in July 2010, charging him with genocide against three ethnic groups in Darfur; al-Bashir had not surrendered to the Court at September 2012; in May 2009 a summons was issued against the militia leader Bahr Idriss Abu Garda, who appeared voluntarily before the Court later in that month; the Pre-Trial Chamber examining the Garda case declined, in February 2010, to confirm the charges against him; in June 2010 Abdallah Banda Abakaer Nourain and Saleh Mohammed Jerbo Jamus surrendered voluntarily to the Court, having been accused, with Abu Garda, of attacking the Haskanita African Union (AU) camp in September–October 2007 and causing the deaths of 12 peace-keeping troops deployed to the former AU Mission in Sudan; on 1 March 2012 the Court issued an arrest warrant for the Sudanese Minister of Defence, Abdelrahim Mohamed Hussein, for crimes against humanity and war crimes committed during August 2003–March 2004, when he was the country's Minister for the Interior, as detailed in the case of Harun and Kushayb (see above).

Situation in Kenya: in November 2009 the Presidency of the Court decided to assign the situation in Kenya (relating to violent unrest following the December 2007 presidential elections there) to a Pre-Trial Chamber; in July 2009 the International Commission of Inquiry on Post-Election Violence (known also as the Waki Commission), which had been established by the Kenyan Government in February 2008, presented the Court Prosecutor with documentation, supporting materials, and a list of people suspected of being implicated in the violent unrest; on 31 March 2010 Pre-Trial Chamber II granted the Prosecution authorization to open an investigation *proprio motu* into the situation of Kenya; in March 2011 the ICC issued summonses for six Kenyans alleged to be criminally responsible for crimes against humanity, and in April the six accused presented voluntarily to the Court; charges against four of the six: William Samoei Ruto, Joshua Arap Sang, Francis Kirimi Muthaura, and Uhuru Muigai Kenyatta were confirmed in January 2012; it was announced in July 2012 that trial proceedings against the four men would commence in April 2013.

Situation in Libya: referred to the Court in February 2011 by the UN Security Council; in the following month the Prosecutor agreed to open an investigation into the situation in Libya since February 2011; in late June 2011 the Court issued arrest warrants against the Libyan leader Col Muammar al-Qaddafi, Saif al-Islam (his son), and Abdullah al-Senussi (his former Head of Military Intelligence), regarding crimes against humanity (murder and persecution) committed in Libya—through the state apparatus and security forces—from 15 February until at least 28 February; in September 2011 the ICC Prosecutor requested INTERPOL to issue a Red Notice for the arrest of the three Libyan indictees; Col Qaddafi was killed during fighting with opposition forces on 20 October; in late November Saif al-Islam was detained in southern Libya; al-Senussi was detained by Mauritanian security forces in mid-March 2012 and was extradited to Libya in September; despite the ICC indictments the Libyan authorities have expressed their intention of bringing al-Islam and al-Senussi to trial within Libya on charges relating to their conduct under the al-Qaddafi regime, and in May 2012 the Libyan National Transitional Council presented a formal challenge to the ICC concerning the admissibility of the Court's case against the two men, on the grounds that the Libyan national judicial system was itself actively investigating their alleged crimes.

Situation in Côte d'Ivoire: in early October 2011 an ICC Pre-Trial Chamber agreed, at the request of the Prosecutor, to commence an investigation into alleged crimes committed in Côte d'Ivoire between 28 November 2010 and 12 April 2011, during a period of civil unrest resulting from disputed presidential election results, and to consider also any crimes that may be committed in the future in the context of this situation; in late November 2011 the former president, Laurent Gbagbo, who had been in Ivorian custody since April, was transferred to the Court to face charges of crimes against humanity; in February 2012 the Court expanded the scope of the Côte d'Ivoire investigation also to include crimes within the jurisdiction of the Court allegedly committed during the period 19 September 2002–28 November 2010.

The Office of the Prosecutor also receives communications from civilian individuals and organizations relating to alleged crimes that come under the Court's jurisdiction; by 31 May 2011 9,214 such communications had been received since July 2002.

The Court also conducts an Outreach Programme, which pursues activities (through community, legal, academic, and media divisions) aimed at raising awareness and understanding of the Court's mandate in the communities most affected by the situations and cases being addressed (i.e. currently in the CAR, Darfur—Sudan, the DRC, and Uganda). During 1 October 2009–1 October 2010 more than 46,499 individuals participated in 422 Outreach Programme activities.

By September 2012 121 states had ratified the Rome Statute.

THE JUDGES
(September 2012)

	Term ends*
President: Sang-Hyun Song (Republic of Korea)	2015
First Vice-President: Sanji Mmasenono Monageng (Botswana)	2018
Second Vice President: Cuno Jakob Tarfusser (Italy)	2018
Hans-Peter Kaul (Germany)	2015
Akua Kuenyehia (Ghana)	2015
Erkki Kourula (Finland)	2015
Anita Ušacka (Latvia)	2015
Ekaterina Trendafilova (Bulgaria)	2015
Joyce Aluoch (Kenya)	2018
Christine van den Wyngaert (Belgium)	2018
Silvia Alejandra Fernández de Gurmendi (Argentina)	2018
Kuniko Ozaki (Japan)	2018
Miriam-Defensor Santiago (Philippines)	2021
Howard Morrison (United Kingdom)	2021
Anthony T. Carmona (Trinidad and Tobago)	2021
Olga Herrera Carbuccia (Dominican Republic)	2021
Robert Fremr (Czech Republic)	2021
Chile Eboe-Osuji (Nigeria)	2021

* Each term ends on 10 March of the year indicated.

Chief Prosecutor: Fatou B. Bensouda (The Gambia).

Registrar: Silvana Arbia (Italy).

Finance

The proposed budget for the International Criminal Court for 2012 amounted to €111m.

Publication

ICC Weekly Update (electronic publication).

Booklets, factsheet, official records.

ISLAMIC DEVELOPMENT BANK

Address: POB 5925, Jeddah 21432, Saudi Arabia.

Telephone: (2) 6361400; **fax:** (2) 6366871; **e-mail:** idbarchives@isdb.org; **internet:** www.isdb.org.

The Bank was established following a conference of Ministers of Finance of member countries of the then Organization of the Islamic Conference (now Organization of Islamic Cooperation—OIC), held in Jeddah in December 1973. Its aim is to encourage the economic development and social progress of member countries and of Muslim communities in non-member countries, in accordance with the principles of the Islamic *Shari'a* (sacred law). The Bank formally opened in October 1975. The Bank and its associated entities—the Islamic Research and Training Institute, the Islamic Corporation for the Development of the Private Sector, the Islamic Corporation for the Insurance of Investment and Export Credit, and the International Islamic Trade Finance Corporation—constitute the Islamic Development Bank Group.

MEMBERS

There are 56 members.

Organization

(September 2012)

BOARD OF GOVERNORS

Each member country is represented by a governor, usually its Minister of Finance, and an alternate. The Board of Governors is the supreme authority of the Bank, and meets annually. The 37th meeting was held in Khartoum, Sudan, in March–April 2012. The 38th meeting was scheduled to be convened in Dushanbe, Tajikistan, in May 2013.

BOARD OF EXECUTIVE DIRECTORS

The Board consists of 18 members, half of whom are appointed by the eight largest subscribers to the capital stock of the Bank; the remaining eight are elected by Governors representing the other subscribers. Members of the Board of Executive Directors are elected for three-year terms. The Board is responsible for the direction of the general operations of the Bank.

ADMINISTRATION

President of the Bank and Chairman of the Board of Executive Directors: Dr AHMAD MOHAMED ALI AL-MADANI (Saudi Arabia).

Vice-President Corporate Services and Acting Vice-President Co-operation and Capacity Development, Acting Chief Economist: Dr AHMET TIKTIK (Turkey).

Vice-President Finance: Dr ABDULAZIZ BIN MOHAMED BIN ZAHIR AL HINAI (Oman).

Vice-President Operations: BIRAMA BOUBACAR SIDIBE (Mali).

REGIONAL OFFICES

Kazakhstan: 050000 Almati, Aiteki bi 67; tel. (727) 272-70-00; fax (727) 250-13-03; e-mail idbroa@isdb.org; Dir HISHAM TALEB MAAROUF.

Malaysia: Menara Bank, Pembangunan Bandar Wawasan, Level 13, Jalan Sultan Ismail, 508250 Kuala Lumpur; tel. (3) 26946627; fax (3) 26946626; e-mail ROKL@isdb.org.

Morocco: Km 6.4, Ave Imam Malik Route des Zaers, POB 5003, Rabat; tel. (3) 7757191; fax (3) 7757260; Dir ABDERRAHAM EL-GLAOUI.

Senegal: 18 blvd de la République, Dakar; tel. (33) 889-1144; fax (33) 823-3621; e-mail RODK@isdb.org; Dir SIDI MOHAMED OULD TALEB.

FINANCIAL STRUCTURE

The Bank's unit of account is the Islamic Dinar (ID), which is equivalent to the value of one Special Drawing Right (SDR) of the IMF (average value of the SDR in 2011 was US $1.57868). In May 2006 the Bank's Board of Governors approved an increase in the authorized capital from ID 15,000m. to ID 30,000m. An increase in subscribed capital, from ID 15,000m. to ID 16,000m. was approved by the Board of Governors in June 2008. In June 2010 the Board of Governors approved a further increase in subscribed capital to ID 18,000m. At 25 November 2011 total committed subscriptions amounted to ID 17,782.6m.

Subscriptions
(million Islamic Dinars, as at 25 November 2011)

Afghanistan	9.93	Maldives	9.23
Albania	9.23	Mali	18.19
Algeria	459.22	Mauritania	9.77
Azerbaijan	18.19	Morocco	91.69
Bahrain	25.88	Mozambique	9.23
Bangladesh	182.16	Niger	24.63
Benin	20.80	Nigeria	1,384.00
Brunei	45.85	Oman	50.92
Burkina Faso	24.63	Pakistan	459.22
Cameroon	45.85	Palestine	19.55
Chad	9.77	Qatar	1,297.50
Comoros	4.65	Saudi Arabia	4,249.60
Côte d'Ivoire	4.65	Senegal	52.80
Djibouti	4.96	Sierra Leone	4.96
Egypt	1,278.67	Somalia	4.96
Gabon	54.58	Sudan	83.21
The Gambia	9.23	Suriname	9.23
Guinea	45.85	Syria	18.49
Guinea-Bissau	4.96	Tajikistan	4.96
Indonesia	406.48	Togo	4.96
Iran	1,491.20	Tunisia	19.55
Iraq	48.24	Turkey	1,165.86
Jordan	78.50	Turkmenistan	4.96
Kazakhstan	19.29	Uganda	24.63
Kuwait	985.88	United Arab Emirates	1,357.20
Kyrgyzstan	9.23	Uzbekistan	4.80
Lebanon	9.77	Yemen	92.38
Libya	1,704.46		
Malaysia	294.01		

Activities

The Bank adheres to the Islamic principle forbidding usury, and does not grant loans or credits for interest. Instead, its methods of project financing are: provision of interest-free loans, mainly for infrastructural projects which are expected to have a marked impact on long-term socio-economic development; provision of technical assistance (e.g. for feasibility studies); equity participation in industrial and agricultural projects; leasing operations, involving the leasing of equipment such as ships, and instalment sale financing; and profit-sharing operations. Funds not immediately needed for projects are used for foreign trade financing. Under the Bank's trade financing operations funds are used for importing commodities for development purposes (i.e. raw materials and intermediate industrial goods, rather than consumer goods), with priority given to the import of goods from other member countries. In 2005 the Bank initiated a consultation process, led by a commission of eminent persons, to develop a new long-term strategy for the Bank. A document on the AH 1440 (2020) Vision was published in March 2006. It recommended that the Bank redefine its mandate and incorporate a broad focus on comprehensive human development, with priority concerns to be the alleviation of poverty and improvements to health, education and governance. The new strategy also envisaged greater community involvement in Bank operations and more support given to local initiatives. In October 2008 the Bank organized a forum to consider the impact of the international economic and financial crisis on the Islamic financial system. The meeting resolved to establish a Task Force for Islamic Finance and Global Financial Stability, which met for the first time in January 2009, in Kuala Lumpur, Malaysia. In May the Board of Executive Directors agreed to double ordinary capital resources operations over a three-year period in order to support economic recovery in member countries. In the following month the Board of Governors approved the measure, along with others in support of mitigating the effects of the global financial crisis. During that year the Bank resolved to accelerate implementation of a major reform programme to enhance its relevance and impact in member countries, in accordance with the AH 1440 (2020) Vision. The Bank also adopted a Thematic Strategy for Poverty Reduction and Comprehensive Human Development to focus efforts to achieve the Vision's objectives.

By 25 November 2011 the Bank had approved a total of ID 25,526.7m. (equivalent to some US $37,350.5m.) for project financing since operations began in 1976, including ID 264.1m. ($371.7m.) for technical assistance, in addition to ID 28,491.6m. ($39,951.7m.) for foreign trade financing, and ID 556.0m. ($723.4m.) for special assistance operations, excluding amounts for cancelled operations. Total net approved operations amounted to ID 54,574.3m. ($79,025.5m.) at that time.

During the Islamic year 1432 (7 December 2010–25 November 2011) the Bank approved a net total of ID 6,973.0m., for 398 operations, compared with ID 4,550.3m. for 367 operations in the previous year. Of the total approved in AH 1432 ID 239.6m. was approved for 40 loans, supporting projects concerned with the education and health sectors, infrastructural improvements, and agricultural developments. The Bank approved 98 technical assistance operations during that year in the form of grants and loans, amounting to ID 22.5m. Trade financing approved amounted to ID 2,056.2m. for 77 operations. During AH 1432 the Bank's total disbursements totalled ID 3,347.8m., bringing the total cumulative disbursements since the Bank began operations to ID 36,626.2m.

During AH 1427 the Bank's export financing scheme was formally dissolved, although it continued to fund projects pending the commencement of operations of the International Islamic Trade Finance Corporation (ITFC). The Bank also finances other trade financing operations, including the Islamic Corporation for the Development of the Private Sector (ICD, see below), the Awqaf Properties Investment Fund and the Treasury Department. In addition, a Trade Co-operation and Promotion Programme supports efforts to enhance trade among OIC member countries. In June 2005 the Board of Governors approved the establishment of the ITFC as an autonomous trade promotion and financing institution within the Bank Group. The inaugural meeting of the ITFC was held in February 2007. In May 2006 the Board of Governors approved a new fund to reduce poverty and support efforts to achieve the UN Millennium Development Goals, in accordance with a proposal of the OIC. It was inaugurated, as the Islamic Solidarity Fund for Development, in May 2007, and became operational in early 2008. By the end of the Islamic year 1432 capital contributions to the Fund amounted to US $1,633m., of a total of $2,639m. that had been pledged by 43 countries.

In AH 1407 (1986/87) the Bank established an Islamic Bank's Portfolio for Investment and Development (IBP) in order to promote the development and diversification of Islamic financial markets and to mobilize the liquidity available to banks and financial institutions. During AH 1428 resources and activities of the IBP were transferred to the newly established ITFC. The Bank's Unit Investment Fund (UIF) became operational in 1990, with the aim of mobilizing additional resources and providing a profitable channel for investments conforming to *Shari'a*. The initial issue of the UIF was US $100m., which was subsequently increased to $325m. The Fund finances mainly private sector industrial projects in middle-income countries and also finances short-term trade operations. The Bank also mobilizes resources from the international financial markets through the issuance of the International Islamic Sukuk bond. In October 1998 the Bank announced the establishment of a new fund to invest in infrastructure projects in member states. The Bank committed $250m. to the fund, which was to comprise $1,000m. equity capital and a $500m. Islamic financing facility. In January 2009 the Bank launched a second phase of the infrastructure fund. In November 2001 the Bank signed an agreement with Malaysia, Bahrain, Indonesia and Sudan for the establishment of an Islamic financial market. In April 2002 the Bank, jointly with governors of central banks and the Accounting and Auditing Organization for Islamic Financial Institutions, concluded an agreement, under the auspices of the IMF, for the establishment of an Islamic Financial Services Board. The Board, to be located in Kuala Lumpur, Malaysia, was intended to elaborate and harmonize standards for best practices in the regulation and supervision of the Islamic financial services industry.

The Bank's Special Assistance Programme was initiated in AH 1400 to support the economic and social development of Muslim communities in non-member countries, in particular in the education and health sectors. It also aimed to provide emergency aid in times of natural disasters, and to assist Muslim refugees throughout the world. Operations undertaken by the Bank are financed by the Waqf Fund (formerly the Special Assistance Account). By the end of the Islamic year 1432 some ID 556.0m. (US $723.4m.) had been approved under the Waqf Fund Special Assistance Programme for 1,415 operations. Other assistance activities include scholarship programmes, technical co-operation projects and the sacrificial meat utilization project (see below). In addition the Bank supports recovery, rehabilitation and reconstruction efforts in member countries affected by natural disasters or conflict.

In October 2002 the Bank's Board of Governors, meeting in Burkina Faso, adopted the Ouagadougou Declaration on the co-operation between the Bank group and Africa, which identified priority areas for Bank activities, for example education and the private sector. The Bank pledged US $2,000m. to finance implementation of the Declaration over the five year period 2004–08. A successor initiative, the IDB Special Programme for the Development of Africa, was endorsed at a summit meeting of the OIC held in March 2008. The Bank committed $4,000m. to the Programme for the next five-year period, 2008–12. By the end of the Islamic year 1432 $3,980m. had been approved under the Programme, of which $1,400m. had been disbursed. During the Islamic year 1431 the Bank initiated a Membership Country Partnership (MCP) Strategy to strengthen dialogue with individual member countries and to contribute more effectively to their medium- and long-term development plans. By the end of AH 1432 five MCPs were being implemented, in Indonesia, Mali, Mauritania, Turkey and Uganda, and one had been completed for Pakistan.

In June 2008 the Board of Governors inaugurated the Jeddah Declaration Initiative, with an allocation of US $1,500m. in funds over a five-year period, to assist member countries to meet the escalating costs of food and to attain greater food security. In November 2009 the Bank concluded a co-financing agreement with IFAD, with funds of up to $1,500m., to support priority projects concerned with food security and rural development in the poorest member countries in Africa and Asia. The agreement was signed by the presidents of the two organizations in February 2010. During 2011 the Bank contributed to the preparation of an Action Plan on Food Price Volatility and Agriculture, which was adopted by heads of state and government of the Group of 20 industrialized and emerging economies (G20) in November. The Bank also contributed, through participation in a working group and high-level panel, to the elaboration of a G20 Multilateral Development Bank Infrastructure Action Plan. In April the Bank collaborated with the World Bank Group to inaugurate an Arab Financing Facility for Infrastructure in roder to support national and cros-border infrastructure development, in particular through use of public–private partnerships. In September the Bank participated in a meeting of ministers of finance of the Group of Eight industrialized nations (G8) and high-level representatives of international financial institutions active in the Middle East and North Africa region to further support of the so-called Deauville Partnership, which had been established in May in order to assist countries in the region undergoing social and economic transformations. The Bank was a founding member of the new Co-ordination Platform to facilitate and promote collaboration among the institutions extending assistance under the Partnership.

In AH 1404 (1983/84) the Bank established a scholarship programme for Muslim communities in non-member countries to provide opportunities for students to pursue further education or other professional training. The programme also assists 12 member countries on an exceptional basis. By the end of the Islamic year 1432 6,794 people had graduated and 4,977 were undertaking studies under the scheme. The Merit Scholarship Programme, initiated in AH 1412 (1991/92), aims to develop scientific, technological and research capacities in member countries through advanced studies and/or research. A total of 760 scholarships had been awarded by the end of AH 1432. In AH 1419 (1998/99) a Scholarship Programme in Science and Technology for IDB Least Developed Member Countries became operational for students in 20 eligible countries. By the end of the Islamic year 1432 404 students had received scholarships under the programme. The Bank awards annual prizes for science and technology to promote excellence in research and development and in scientific education.

The Bank's Programme for Technical Co-operation aims to mobilize technical capabilities among member countries and to promote the exchange of expertise, experience and skills through expert missions, training, seminars and workshops. In December 1999 the Board of Executive Directors approved two technical assistance grants to support a programme for the eradication of illiteracy in the Islamic world, and one for self-sufficiency in human vaccine production. The Bank also undertakes the distribution of meat sacrificed by Muslim pilgrims. The Bank was the principal source of funding of the International Centre for Biosaline Agriculture, which was established in Dubai, UAE, in September 1999.

BANK GROUP ENTITIES

International Islamic Trade Finance Corporation: POB 55335, Jeddah 21534, Saudia Arabia; tel. (2) 6361400; fax (2) 6371064; e-mail info@isdb.org; internet www.itfc-idb.org; f. 2007; commenced operations Jan. 2008; aims to promote trade and trade financing in Bank member countries, to facilitate access to public and private capital, and to promote investment opportunities; during the Islamic year 1432 the ITFC approved US $3,033m. for 66 trade financing operations; auth. cap. $3,000m.; subs. cap. $750m. (Nov. 2011); CEO Dr WALID AL-WOHAIB.

Islamic Corporation for the Development of the Private Sector (ICD): POB 54069, Jeddah 21514, Saudi Arabia; tel. (2) 6441644; fax (2) 6444427; e-mail icd@isdb.org; internet www.icd-idb.org; f. 1999; to identify opportunities in the private sector, provide financial products and services compatible with Islamic law, mobilize additional resources for the private sector in member countries, and encourage the development of Islamic financing and capital markets; approved 22 projects amounting to US $364.8m. in the Islamic year 1432; the Bank's share of the capital is 50%, member countries 30% and public financial institutions of member countries 20%; auth. cap. $2,000m., subs. cap. $1,000m. (Sept. 2012); mems: 51 countries, the Bank, and 5 public financial institutions; CEO and Gen. Man. KHALID M. AL-ABOODI.

Islamic Corporation for the Insurance of Investment and Export Credit (ICIEC): POB 15722, Jeddah 21454, Saudi Arabia; tel. (2) 6445666; fax (2) 6379504; e-mail idb.iciec@isdb.org.sa; internet www.iciec.com; f. 1994; aims to promote trade and the flow of investments among member countries of the OIC through the provision of export credit and investment insurance services; a representative office was opened in Dubai, UAE, in May 2010; auth. cap. increased from ID 150m. to ID 400m. in July 2011; mems: 40 mem. states and the Islamic Development Bank (which contributes two-thirds of its capital); Gen. Man. Dr ABDEL RAHMAN A. TAHA.

Islamic Research and Training Institute: POB 9201, Jeddah 21413, Saudi Arabia; tel. (2) 6361400; fax (2) 6378927; e-mail irti@isdb.org; internet www.irti.org; f. 1982 to undertake research enabling economic, financial and banking activities to conform to Islamic law, and to provide training for staff involved in development activities in the Bank's member countries; the Institute also organizes seminars and workshops, and holds training courses aimed at furthering the expertise of government and financial officials in Islamic developing countries; Dir-Gen. Dr AZMI OMAR (Malaysia); publs *Annual Report*, *Islamic Economic Studies* (2 a year), various research studies, monographs, reports.

Publication

Annual Report.

Statistics

Operations approved, Islamic year 1432
(7 December 2010–25 November 2011)

Type of operation	Number of operations	Amount (million Islamic Dinars)
Total project financing	272	3,255.5
Project financing	174	3,233.0
Technical assistance	98	22.5
Trade financing operations*	77	2,056.2
Special assistance operations	49	9.6
Total†	398	5,321.3

* Including operations by the ITFC, the ICD, the UIF, Treasury operations, and the Awqaf Properties Investment Fund.
† Excluding cancelled operations.

Distribution of project financing and technical assistance by sector, Islamic year 1432
(7 December 2010–25 November 2011)

Sector	Number of operations	Amount (million Islamic Dinars)	%
Agriculture	29	422.1	15.5
Education	38	219.2	8.0
Energy	15	782.5	28.7
Finance	50	147.4	5.4
Health	21	202.2	7.4
Industry and mining	5	15.5	0.6
Information and communications	4	35.1	1.3
Public administration	1	0.2	0.0
Transportation	13	505.1	18.5
Water, sanitation and urban services	22	397.6	14.6
Total*	198	2,727.1	100.0

* Excluding cancelled operations.

Source: Islamic Development Bank, *Annual Report 1432 H.*

ORGANIZATION OF ISLAMIC COOPERATION—OIC

Address: Medina Rd, Sary St, POB 178, Jeddah 21411, Saudi Arabia.

Telephone: (2) 690-0001; **fax:** (2) 275-1953; **e-mail:** info@oic-oci.org; **internet:** www.oic-oci.org.

The Organization was formally established, as the Organization of the Islamic Conference, at the first conference of Muslim heads of state convened in Rabat, Morocco, in September 1969; the first conference of Muslim foreign ministers, held in Jeddah in March 1970, established the General Secretariat; the latter became operational in May 1971. In June 2011 the 38th ministerial conference agreed to change the name of the Organization, with immediate effect, to the Organization of Islamic Cooperation (abbreviated, as hitherto, to OIC).

MEMBERS

Afghanistan	Indonesia	Qatar
Albania	Iran	Saudi Arabia
Algeria	Iraq	Senegal
Azerbaijan	Jordan	Sierra Leone
Bahrain	Kazakhstan	Somalia
Bangladesh	Kuwait	Sudan
Benin	Kyrgyzstan	Suriname
Brunei	Lebanon	Syria*
Burkina Faso	Libya	Tajikistan
Cameroon	Malaysia	Togo
Chad	Maldives	Tunisia
Comoros	Mali	Turkey
Côte d'Ivoire	Mauritania	Turkmenistan
Djibouti	Morocco	Uganda
Egypt	Mozambique	United Arab Emirates
Gabon	Niger	Uzbekistan
The Gambia	Nigeria	Yemen
Guinea	Oman	
Guinea-Bissau	Pakistan	
Guyana	Palestine	

* In August 2012 Syria was suspended from participation in the activities of the OIC and also from all its subsidiary organs and specialized and affiliated institutions, in view of the Syrian Government's violent suppression of opposition elements and related acts of violence against civilian communities.

Note: Observer status has been granted to Bosnia and Herzegovina, the Central African Republic, Russia, Thailand, the Muslim community of the 'Turkish Republic of Northern Cyprus', the Moro National Liberation Front (MNLF) of the southern Philippines, the UN, the African Union, the Non-Aligned Movement, the League of Arab States, the Economic Cooperation Organization, the Union of the Arab Maghreb and the Cooperation Council for the Arab States of the Gulf. The revised OIC Charter, endorsed in March 2008, made future applications for OIC membership and observer status conditional upon Muslim demographic majority and membership of the UN.

Organization

(September 2012)

SUMMIT CONFERENCES

The supreme body of the Organization is the Conference of Heads of State ('Islamic summit'), which met in 1969 in Rabat, Morocco, in 1974 in Lahore, Pakistan, and in January 1981 in Mecca, Saudi Arabia, when it was decided that ordinary summit conferences would normally be held every three years in future. An extraordinary summit conference was convened in Doha, Qatar, in March 2003, to consider the situation in Iraq. A further extraordinary conference, held in December 2005, in Makkah (Mecca), Saudi Arabia, determined to restructure the OIC. The 11th ordinary Islamic summit was convened in Dakar, Senegal, in March 2008. An extraordinary summit was convened in August 2012, in Makkah, with a focus on the ongoing violent conflict in Syria. The summit conference troika comprises member countries equally representing the OIC's African, Arab and Asian membership.

CONFERENCE OF MINISTERS OF FOREIGN AFFAIRS

Conferences take place annually, to consider the means of implementing the general policy of the Organization, although they may also be convened for extraordinary sessions. The ministerial conference troika comprises member countries equally representing the OIC's African, Arab and Asian membership.

SECRETARIAT

The executive organ of the organization, headed by a Secretary-General (who is elected by the Conference of Ministers of Foreign Affairs for a five-year term, renewable only once) and four Assistant Secretaries-General (similarly appointed).

Secretary-General: Prof. Dr Ekmeleddin Ihsanoglu (Turkey).

At the summit conference in January 1981 it was decided that an International Islamic Court of Justice should be established to adjudicate in disputes between Muslim countries. Experts met in January 1983 to draw up a constitution for the court; however, by 2012 it was not yet in operation.

EXECUTIVE COMMITTEE

The third extraordinary conference of the OIC, convened in Mecca, Saudi Arabia, in December 2005, mandated the establishment of the Executive Committee, comprising the summit conference and ministerial conference troikas, the OIC host country, and the OIC Secretariat, as a mechanism for following up resolutions of the Conference.

STANDING COMMITTEES

Al-Quds Committee: f. 1975 to implement the resolutions of the Islamic Conference on the status of Jerusalem (Al-Quds); it meets at the level of foreign ministers; maintains the Al-Quds Fund; Chair. King Muhammad VI of Morocco.

Standing Committee for Economic and Commercial Co-operation (COMCEC): f. 1981; Chair. ABDULLAH GÜL (Pres. of Turkey).

Standing Committee for Information and Cultural Affairs (COMIAC): f. 1981; Chair. MACKY SALL (Pres. of Senegal).

Standing Committee for Scientific and Technological Co-operation (COMSTECH): f. 1981; Chair. ASIF ALI ZARDARI (Pres. of Pakistan).

Other committees include the Islamic Peace Committee, the Permanent Finance Committee, the Committee of Islamic Solidarity with the Peoples of the Sahel, the Eight-Member Committee on the Situation of Muslims in the Philippines, the Six-Member Committee on Palestine, the Committee on UN reform, and the ad hoc Committee on Afghanistan. In addition, there is an Islamic Commission for Economic, Cultural and Social Affairs, and there are OIC Contact Groups on Bosnia and Herzegovina, Iraq, Kosovo, Jammu and Kashmir, Myanmar (formed in 2012), Sierra Leone, and Somalia. A Commission of Eminent Persons was inaugurated in 2005.

OIC Independent Human Rights Commission (IPHRC): f. 2012 to promote the civil, political, social and economic rights enshrined in the covenants and declarations of the OIC, and in universally agreed human rights instruments, in conformity with Islamic values; inaugural session convened in Jakarta, Indonesia (February 2012); second session convened (in August) in Ankara, Turkey, with a focus on the human rights situations in Mali, Myanmar (with regard to the Rohingya Muslim minority), Palestine, and Syria; OIC human rights instruments include: the Shari'a-based Cairo Declaration on Human Rights in Islam (1990) and Covenant of the Rights of the Child in Islam (2005); IPHRC comprises 18 commissioners, equally representing Africa, Asia and the Middle East.

Activities

The Organization's aims, as proclaimed in the Charter (adopted in 1972, with revisions endorsed in 1990 and 2008), are:

(i) To promote Islamic solidarity among member states;

(ii) To consolidate co-operation among member states in the economic, social, cultural, scientific and other vital fields, and to arrange consultations among member states belonging to international organizations;

(iii) To endeavour to eliminate racial segregation and discrimination and to eradicate colonialism in all its forms;

(iv) To take necessary measures to support international peace and security founded on justice;

(v) To co-ordinate all efforts for the safeguard of the Holy Places and support of the struggle of the people of Palestine, and help them to regain their rights and liberate their land;

(vi) To strengthen the struggle of all Muslim people with a view to safeguarding their dignity, independence and national rights;

(vii) To create a suitable atmosphere for the promotion of co-operation and understanding among member states and other countries.

The first summit conference of Islamic leaders (representing 24 states) took place in 1969 following the burning of the al-Aqsa Mosque in Jerusalem. At this conference it was decided that Islamic governments should 'consult together with a view to promoting close co-operation and mutual assistance in the economic, scientific, cultural and spiritual fields, inspired by the immortal teachings of Islam'. Thereafter the foreign ministers of the countries concerned met annually, and adopted the Charter of the Organization of the Islamic Conference in 1972.

At the second Islamic summit conference (Lahore, Pakistan, 1974), the Islamic Solidarity Fund was established, together with a committee of representatives that later evolved into the Islamic Commission for Economic, Cultural and Social Affairs. Subsequently, numerous other subsidiary bodies have been set up (see below).

ECONOMIC CO-OPERATION

A general agreement on economic, technical and commercial co-operation came into force in 1981, providing for the establishment of joint investment projects and trade co-ordination. This was followed by an agreement on promotion, protection and guarantee of investments among member states. A plan of action to strengthen economic co-operation was adopted at the third Islamic summit conference in 1981, aiming to promote collective self-reliance and the development of joint ventures in all sectors. The fifth summit conference, held in 1987, approved proposals for joint development of modern technology, and for improving scientific and technical skills in the less developed Islamic countries. In 1994 the 1981 plan of action was revised to place greater emphasis on private sector participation in its implementation. In October 2003 a meeting of COMCEC endorsed measures aimed at accelerating the hitherto slow implementation of the plan of action. A 10-year plan of action for fostering member states' development and strengthening economic and trade co-operation was launched in December 2005.

In 1991 22 OIC member states signed a Framework Agreement on a Trade Preferential System among the OIC Member States (TPS-OIC); this entered into force in 2003, following the requisite ratification by more than 10 member states, and was envisaged as representing the first step towards the eventual establishment of an Islamic common market. A Trade Negotiating Committee (TNC) was established following the entry into force of the Framework Agreement. The first round of trade negotiations on the establishment of the TPS-OIC, concerning finalizing tariff-reduction modalities and an implementation schedule for the Agreement, was held during April 2004–April 2005, and resulted in the conclusion of a Protocol on the Preferential Tariff Scheme for TPS-OIC (PRETAS). In November 2006, at the launch of the second round of negotiations, ministers adopted a roadmap towards establishing the TPS-OIC; the second round of negotiations ended in September 2007 with the adoption of rules of origin for the TPS-OIC. PRETAS entered into force in February 2010. By mid-2012 the Framework Agreement had been ratified by 28 OIC member states, and PRETAS had 15 ratifications.

In March 2008 the summit adopted a five-year Special Programme for the Development of Africa, covering the period 2008–12, which aimed to promote the economic development of OIC African member states and to support these countries in achieving the UN Millennium Development Goals.

The first OIC Anti-Corruption and Enhancing Integrity Forum was convened in August 2006 in Kuala Lumpur, Malaysia. The 13th Trade Fair of the OIC member states was staged in Sharjah, Saudi Arabia, in April 2011. The second OIC Tourism Fair was to take place in Cairo, Egypt, in December 2012. The seventh World Islamic Economic Forum was convened in Astana, Kazakhstan, in June 2011. In November 2009 a COMCEC Business Forum was held, in Istanbul, Turkey. An International Islamic Business and Finance Summit has been organized annually since 2009, in Kazan, Russia, by the OIC and the Russian Government; 'KAZANSUMMIT 2012' was convened in May 2012.

In March 2012 OIC ministers responsible for water approved the OIC Water Vision 2025, providing a framework for co-operation in maximizing the productive use of, and minimizing the destructive impact of, members' water resources. In May 2012 the fifth Islamic Conference of Environment Ministers, convened in Astana, adopted an Islamic Declaration on Sustainable Development. An OIC Green Technology Blue Print was under development in 2012.

CULTURAL AND TECHNICAL CO-OPERATION

The Organization supports education in Muslim communities throughout the world, and was instrumental in the establishment of Islamic universities in Niger and Uganda. It organizes seminars on various aspects of Islam, and encourages dialogue with the other monotheistic religions. Support is given to publications on Islam both in Muslim and Western countries. In June 1999 an OIC Parliamentary Union was inaugurated; its founding conference was convened in Tehran, Iran. An inaugural Conference of Muslim Women Parliamentarians was convened in January 2012, in Palembang, Indonesia.

The OIC organizes meetings at ministerial level to consider aspects of information policy and new technologies. An OIC Digital Solidarity Fund was inaugurated in May 2005. Participation by OIC member states in the Fund was promoted at the 11th OIC summit meeting in March 2008, and the meeting also requested each member state to establish a board to monitor national implementation of the Tunis Declaration on the Information Society, adopted by the November 2005 second phase of the World Summit on the Information Society. The first OIC Conference on Women was held in November 2006, on the theme 'The role of women in the development of OIC member states'. In January 2009 the OIC and the League of Arab States signed an agreement providing for the strengthening of co-operation and co-ordination in the areas of politics, media, the economy, and in the social and scientific spheres. In August 2011 the OIC organized a Decorative Arts and Calligraphy Exhibition, at its headquarters in Jeddah.

HUMANITARIAN ASSISTANCE

Assistance is given to Muslim communities affected by violent conflict and natural disasters, in co-operation with UN organizations, particularly UNCHR. It was announced in August 2010 that an OIC Emergency Fund for Natural Disasters would be established, to assist survivors of any natural disaster occurring in future in a Muslim country. The first conference of Islamic humanitarian organizations was convened by the OIC in March 2008, and a second conference, bringing together 32 organizations, took place in April 2009. The third conference of Islamic humanitarian organizations, held in March 2010, established a working group to draft a plan aimed at strengthening co-operation between the OIC and other humanitarian organizations active in Afghanistan, Gaza, Darfur, Iraq, Niger, Somalia, and Sudan; and also approved the formation of a joint commission which was to study the structure and mechanism of co-operation and co-ordination between humanitarian organizations. The fourth conference was convened in June 2011, with the theme 'Civil Society Organizations in the Muslim World: Responsibilities and Roles'. In May 2012 the first Conference on Refugees in the Muslim World was convened by the OIC, UNHCR and the Turkmen Government, in Aşgabat, Turkmenistan.

The OIC has established trust funds to assist vulnerable people in Afghanistan, Bosnia and Herzegovina, and Sierra Leone. Humanitarian assistance has in past years been provided by OIC member states has included aid to the Muslim population affected by the conflict in Chechnya; to victims of conflict in Darfur, southern Sudan; to Indonesia following the tsunami disaster in December 2004; and to Pakistan following the major earthquake there in October 2005.

The drought-prone countries of the Sahel region (Burkina Faso, Cape Verde, Chad, The Gambia, Guinea, Guinea-Bissau, Mali, Mauritania, Niger and Senegal) receive particular attention. In early September 2012 the OIC Secretary-General launched an urgent appeal for Niger and Senegal, as a response to the damage and loss of life caused by sudden heavy rainfall and flooding in August.

In August 2011 OIC governments pledged US $350m. in aid to combat famine in Somalia, where some 3.7m. people were reported at that time to be at risk of starvation. The OIC Secretary-General urged donor nations to help to rehabilitate Somalia's infrastructure and agricultural production with a view to improving the long-term prospects for food security. In early October 2011 the OIC convened a conference on the theme 'Water for Life in Somalia', with participation by 32 non-governmental humanitarian relief agencies; the conference adopted a declaration pledging to drill 682 boreholes in 11 provinces of Somalia, with a view to alleviating the acute shortage of water that had contributed to the famine.

POLITICAL CO-OPERATION

In June 2011 OIC foreign ministers adopted the Astana Declaration on Peace, Co-operation and Development, in which they recognized emerging challenges presented by unfolding significant political developments in the Middle East and North Africa (the so-called 'Arab Spring') and appealed for engagement in constructive dialogue towards peaceful solutions. The Declaration expressed grave concern at the then ongoing conflict in Libya, and at the humanitarian consequences thereof. The foreign ministers also adopted the OIC Action Plan for Cooperation with Central Asia, which aimed to establish centres of excellence with a view to encouraging scientific innovation; and to promote job training and public-private partnership; to promote a reduction in the incidence of HIV/AIDS, polio, malaria and TB in the region; to build cultural understanding; and to combat trafficking in human beings and in illegal drugs. The OIC gives support to member countries in regaining or maintaining political stability. During 2011, for example, it participated in International Contact Groups on Afghanistan, Libya, and Somalia, co-operating with the UN and other international organizations and national governments in supporting efforts to restore constitutional rule in those countries. In early April 2012 the OIC Secretary-General expressed 'total rejection' of the proclamation by militants in northern Mali of an independent homeland of 'Azawad'. A delegation of the OIC was dispatched to observe legislative elections held in Algeria, in May of that year. In June the Secretary-General strongly condemned bomb attacks perpetrated by the Islamist group Boko Haram against churches in northern Nigeria, and subsequent reprisal attacks against Muslims and mosques, which had resulted in dozens of fatalities, and appealed for calm and restraint in the region. In September the Secretary-General strongly condemned the killing of the US Ambassador to Libya, as well as three officials, at the US Consulate in the Libyan town of Benghazi, initially reported to have been carried out by objectors to a film produced in the USA that had offended Muslim religious sentiment. The Secretary-General also expressed grave concern at a similar attack at that time against the US Embassy in Cairo, Egypt, and urged restraint, while describing the offending film as a 'deplorable act of incitement'. The Secretary-General stated that issues pertaining to both the freedom of religion and freedom of expression ought to be addressed through structured engagement, referring to UN Human Rights Council Resolution 16/18 and the Istanbul Process for Combating Intolerance and Discrimination Based on Religion or Belief (see under Supporting Muslim Minorities and Combating Anti-Islamic Feeling).

Combating Terrorism: In December 1994 OIC heads of state adopted a Code of Conduct for Combating International Terrorism, in an attempt to control Muslim extremist groups. The code commits states to ensuring that militant groups do not use their territory for planning or executing terrorist activity against other states, in addition to states refraining from direct support or participation in acts of terrorism. An OIC Convention on Combating International Terrorism was adopted in 1998. In September 2001 the OIC Secretary-General strongly condemned major terrorist attacks perpetrated against targets in the USA. Soon afterwards the US authorities rejected a proposal by the Taliban regime that an OIC observer mission be deployed to monitor the activities of the Saudi Arabian-born exiled militant Islamist fundamentalist leader Osama bin Laden, who was accused by the US Government of having co-ordinated the attacks from alleged terrorist bases in the Taliban-administered area of Afghanistan. An extraordinary meeting of OIC ministers of foreign affairs, convened in early October, in Doha, Qatar, to consider the implications of the terrorist atrocities, condemned the attacks and declared its support for combating all manifestations of terrorism within the framework of a proposed collective initiative co-ordinated under the auspices of the UN. The meeting, which did not pronounce directly on the recently-initiated US-led military retaliation against targets in Afghanistan, urged that no Arab or Muslim state should be targeted under the pretext of eliminating terrorism. In February 2002 the Secretary-General expressed concern at statements of the US administration describing Iran and Iraq (as well as the Democratic People's Republic of Korea) as belonging to an 'axis of evil' involved in international terrorism and the development of weapons of mass destruction. In April OIC ministers of foreign affairs convened an extraordinary session on terrorism, in Kuala Lumpur, Malaysia. The meeting issued the Kuala Lumpur Declaration, which reiterated member states' collective resolve to combat terrorism, recalling the organization's 1994 code of conduct and 1998 convention to this effect; condemned attempts to associate terrorist activities with Islam or any other particular creed, civilization or nationality, and rejected attempts to associate Islamic states or the Palestinian struggle with terrorism; rejected the implementation of international action against any Muslim state on the pretext of combating terrorism; urged the organization of a global conference on international terrorism; and urged an examination of the root causes of international terrorism. The meeting adopted a plan of action on addressing the issues raised in the declaration. Its implementation was to be co-ordinated by a 13-member committee on international terrorism. Member states were encouraged to sign and ratify the Convention on Combating International Terrorism in order to accelerate its implementation. In June 2002 ministers of foreign affairs issued a declaration reiterating the OIC call for an international conference to be convened, under UN auspices, in order clearly to define terrorism and to agree on the international procedures and mechanisms for combating terrorism through the UN. In May 2003 the 30th session of the Conference of Ministers of Foreign Affairs, entitled 'Unity and Dignity', issued the Tehran Declaration, in which it resolved to combat terrorism and to contribute to preserving peace and security in Islamic countries. The Declaration also pledged its full support for the Palestinian cause and rejected the labelling as 'terrorist' of those Muslim states deemed to be resisting foreign aggression and occupation.

Supporting Muslim Minorities and Combating Anti-Islamic Feeling: In December 1995 OIC ministers of foreign affairs determined that an intergovernmental group of experts should be established to address the situation of minority Muslim communities residing in non-OIC states. The OIC committee of experts responsible for formulating a plan of action for safeguarding the rights of Muslim communities and minorities met for the first time in 1998. In June 2001 the OIC condemned attacks and ongoing discrimination against the Muslim community in Myanmar. In October 2005 the OIC Secretary-General expressed concern at the treatment of Muslims in the southern provinces of Thailand. The first tripartite meeting between the OIC, the Government of the Philippines and Muslim separatists based in the southern Philippines took place in November 2007, and in April 2009 the OIC Secretary-General announced the appointment of an OIC special envoy to assist in negotiating a peaceful solution to the conflict in the southern Philippines.

In January 2006 the OIC strongly condemned the publication in a Norwegian newspaper of a series of caricatures of the Prophet Muhammad that had originally appeared in a Danish publication in September 2005 and had caused considerable offence to many Muslims. An Islamic Observatory on Islamophobia was established in September 2006; the Observatory has released periodic reports on intolerance against Muslims. In December 2007 the OIC organized the first International Conference on Islamophobia, aimed at addressing concerns that alleged instances of defamation of Islam appeared to be increasing world-wide (particularly in Europe). Responding to a reported rise in anti-Islamic attacks on Western nations, OIC leaders denounced stereotyping and discrimination, and urged the promotion of Islam by Islamic states as a 'moderate, peaceful and tolerant religion'. In June 2011 the OIC Secretary-General issued a statement strongly condemning 'attacks on Islam and insult and vilification of the Prophet Muhummad and his wives' by the right-wing Dutch politician Geert Wilders. The Secretary-General stated in June 2012 that Islamophobia was being exploited in electoral campaigns in Europe, citing the campaigns for the French presidential election held in April–May.

In March 2011 the UN Human Rights Council adopted by consensus a resolution (A/HRC/Res/16/18), that had been presented on behalf of the OIC, on 'Combating intolerance, negative stereotyping, and stigmatization of, and discrimination, incitement to violence and violence against, persons based on religion or belief'. Resolution 16/18 called on UN member states to ensure, *inter alia*, that public officials avoid discriminating against individuals on the basis of religion or belief; that citizens might manifest their religion; that religious profiling be avoided; and that places of worship be protected. Previous related draft resolutions proposed by the OIC had focused on combating 'defamation of religions', and had been rejected by human rights organizations and by some UN member states on grounds related to the right to freedom of expression. In July 2011 the OIC and the USA jointly launched the Istanbul Process for Combating Intolerance and Discrimination Based on Religion or Belief, and, in December, a joint OIC-USA Conference on Addressing the Istanbul Process was convened in Washington, DC, USA.

Reform of the OIC: In March 1997, at an extraordinary meeting of heads of state and of government, held in Islamabad, Pakistan, an Islamabad Declaration was adopted, which pledged to increase co-operation between members of the OIC. In November 2000 OIC heads of state attended the ninth summit conference, held in Doha, Qatar, and issued the Doha Declaration, which reaffirmed commitment to the OIC Charter and undertook to modernize the organization. The 10th OIC summit meeting, held in October 2003, in Putrajaya, Malaysia, issued the Putrajaya Declaration, in which Islamic leaders resolved to enhance Islamic states' role and influence in international affairs. The leaders adopted a plan of action that entailed: reviewing and strengthening OIC positions on international issues; enhancing dialogue among Muslim thinkers and policy-makers through relevant OIC insitutions; promoting constructive dialogue with other cultures and civilizations; completing an ongoing review of the structure and efficacy of the OIC Secretariat; establishing a working group to address means of enhancing the role of Islamic education; promoting among member states the development of science and technology, discussion of ecological issues, and the role of information communication technology in development; improving mechanisms to assist member states in post-conflict situations; and advancing trade and investment through data-sharing and encouraging access to markets for products from poorer member states. In January 2005 the inaugural meeting of an OIC Commission of Eminent Persons was convened in Putrajaya. The Commission was mandated to make recommendations in the following areas: the preparation of a strategy and plan of action enabling the Islamic community to meet the challenges of the 21st century; the preparation of a comprehensive plan for promoting enlightened moderation, both within Islamic societies and universally; and the preparation of proposals for the future reform and restructuring of the OIC system. In December the third extraordinary OIC summit, convened in Mecca, Saudi Arabia, adopted a Ten-Year Programme of Action to Meet the Challenges Facing the Ummah (the Islamic world) in the 21st Century, a related Mecca Declaration and a report by the Commission of Eminent Persons. The summit determined to restructure the OIC, and mandated the establishment of an Executive Committee, comprising the summit conference and ministerial conference troikas (equally reflecting the African, Arab and Asian member states), the OIC host country, and the OIC Secretariat, to implement Conference resolutions.

The 11th OIC heads of state summit meeting, held in Dakar, Senegal, in March 2008, endorsed a revised OIC Charter.

Finance

The OIC's activities are financed by mandatory contributions from member states.

Subsidiary Organs

Islamic Centre for the Development of Trade: Complexe Commercial des Habous, ave des FAR, BP 13545, Casablanca, Morocco; tel. (522) 314974; fax (522) 310110; e-mail icdt@icdt-oic.org; internet www.icdt-oic.org; f. 1983 to encourage regular commercial contacts, harmonize policies and promote investments among OIC mems; Dir-Gen. Dr El Hassane Hzaine; publs *Tijaris: International and Inter-Islamic Trade Magazine* (bi-monthly), *Inter-Islamic Trade Report* (annually).

Islamic Jurisprudence (Fiqh) Academy: POB 13917, Jeddah, Saudi Arabia; tel. (2) 667-1664; fax (2) 667-0873; internet www.fiqhacademy.org.sa; f. 1982; Gen. Sec. Maulana Khalid Saifullah Rahmani.

Islamic Solidarity Fund: c/o OIC Secretariat, POB 1997, Jeddah 21411, Saudi Arabia; tel. (2) 698-1296; fax (2) 256-8185; e-mail info@isf-fsi.org; internet www.isf-fsi.org; f. 1974 to meet the needs of Islamic communities by providing emergency aid and the finance to build mosques, Islamic centres, hospitals, schools and universities; Exec. Dir Ibrahim bin Abdallah al-Khozaim.

Islamic University in Uganda: POB 2555, Mbale, Uganda; tel. (35) 2512100; fax (45) 433502; e-mail info@iuiu.ac.ug; internet www.iuiu.ac.ug/; f. 1988 to meet the educational needs of Muslim populations in English-speaking African countries; second campus in Kampala; mainly financed by OIC; Rector Dr Ahmad Kawesa Sengendo.

Islamic University of Niger: BP 11507, Niamey, Niger; tel. 20-72-39-03; fax 20-73-37-96; e-mail unislam@intnet.ne; internet www.universite_say.ne/; f. 1984; provides courses of study in *Shari'a* (Islamic law) and Arabic language and literature; also offers courses in pedagogy and teacher training; receives grants from Islamic Solidarity Fund and contributions from OIC member states; Rector Prof. Abdeljaouad Sekkat.

Islamic University of Technology (IUT): Board Bazar, Gazipur 1704, Dhaka, Bangladesh; tel. (2) 9291254; fax (2) 9291260; e-mail vc@iut-dhaka.edu; internet www.iutoic-dhaka.edu; f. 1981 as the Islamic Centre for Technical and Vocational Training and Resources, named changed to Islamic Institute of Technology in 1994, current name adopted in 2001; aims to develop human resources in OIC mem. states, with special reference to engineering, technology, and technical education; 145 staff and 800 students; library of 30,450 vols; Vice-Chancellor Prof. Dr M. Imtiaz Hossain; publs *Journal of Engineering and Technology* (2 a year), *News Bulletin* (annually), *News Letter* (6 a year), annual calendar and announcement for admission, reports, human resources development series.

Research Centre for Islamic History, Art and Culture (IRCICA): POB 24, Beşiktaş 34354, İstanbul, Turkey; tel. (212) 2591742; fax (212) 2584365; e-mail ircica@ircica.org; internet www.ircica.org; f. 1980; library of 60,000 vols; Dir-Gen. Prof. Dr Halit Eren; publs *Newsletter* (3 a year), monographical studies.

Statistical, Economic and Social Research and Training Centre for Islamic Countries (SESRIC): Kudüs Cad. No. 9, Diplomatik Site, 06450, Ankara, Turkey; tel. (312) 4686172; fax (312) 4673458; e-mail oicankara@sesric.org; internet www.sesric.org; became operational in 1978; has a three-fold mandate: to collate, process and disseminate socio-economic statistics and information on, and for the utilization of, its member countries; to study and assess economic and social developments in member countries with the aim of helping to generate proposals for advancing co-operation; and to organize training programmes in selected areas; the Centre also acts as a focal point for technical co-operation activities between the OIC system and related UN agencies; and prepares economic and social reports and background documentation for OIC meetings; Dir-Gen. Dr Savaş Alpay (Turkey); publs *Annual Economic Report on the OIC Countries*, *Journal of Economic Cooperation and Development* (quarterly), *Economic Cooperation and Development Review* (semi-annually), *InfoReport* (quarterly), *Statistical Yearbook* (annually), *Basic Facts and Figures on OIC Member Countries* (annually).

Specialized Institutions

International Islamic News Agency (IINA): King Khalid Palace, Madinah Rd, POB 5054, Jeddah 21422, Saudi Arabia; tel. (2) 665-8561; fax (2) 665-9358; e-mail iina@islamicnews.org; internet www.iinanews.com; f. 1972; distributes news and reports daily on events in the Islamic world, in Arabic, English and French; Dir-Gen. Erdem Kok.

Islamic Educational, Scientific and Cultural Organization (ISESCO): BP 2275 Rabat 10104, Morocco; tel. (37) 566052; fax (37) 566012; e-mail cid@isesco.org.ma; internet www.isesco.org.ma; f. 1982; Dir-Gen. Dr Abdulaziz bin Othman Altwaijri; publs *ISESCO Newsletter* (quarterly), *Islam Today* (2 a year), *ISESCO Triennial*.

Islamic Broadcasting Union (IBU): POB 6351, Jeddah 21442, Saudi Arabia; tel. (2) 672-1121; fax (2) 672-2600; e-mail ibu@ibuj.org; internet www.ibuj.org; f. 1975; Dir-Gen. Mohamed Salem Walad Boake.

Affiliated Institutions

International Association of Islamic Banks (IAIB): King Abdulaziz St, Queen's Bldg, 23rd Floor, Al-Balad Dist, POB 9707, Jeddah 21423, Saudi Arabia; tel. (2) 651-6900; fax (2) 651-6552; f. 1977 to link financial institutions operating on Islamic banking principles; activities include training and research; mems: 192 banks and other financial institutions in 34 countries.

Islamic Chamber of Commerce and Industry: POB 3831, Clifton, Karachi 75600, Pakistan; tel. (21) 5874910; fax (21) 5870765; e-mail icci@icci-oic.org; internet www.iccionline.net/en/icci-en/index.aspx; f. 1979 to promote trade and industry among member states; comprises nat. chambers or feds of chambers of commerce and industry; Pres. SALEH ABDULLAH KAMEL; Sec.-Gen. Dr BASSEM AWADALLAH.

Islamic Committee for the International Crescent: POB 17434, Benghazi, Libya; tel. (61) 9095824; fax (61) 9095823; e-mail info@icic-oic.org; internet www.icic-oic.org; f. 1979 to attempt to alleviate the suffering caused by natural disasters and war; Pres. ALI MAHMOUD BUHEDMA.

Islamic Solidarity Sports Federation: POB 5844, Riyadh 11442, Saudi Arabia; tel. (1) 480-9253; fax (1) 482-2145; e-mail issf@awalnet.net.sa; f. 1981; organizes the Islamic Solidarity Games (2005: Jeddah, Saudi Arabia, in April; the next Games were to have been held in April 2010, in Tehran, Iran, but were postponed); Sec.-Gen. Dr MOHAMMAD SALEH QAZDAR.

Organization of Islamic Capitals and Cities (OICC): POB 13621, Jeddah 21414, Saudi Arabia; tel. (2) 698-1953; fax (2) 698-1053; e-mail oiccmak@oicc.org; internet www.oicc.org; f. 1980; aims to preserve the identity and the heritage of Islamic capitals and cities; to achieve and enhance sustainable development in member capitals and cities; to establish and develop comprehensive urban norms, systems and plans to serve the growth and prosperity of Islamic capitals and cities and to enhance their cultural, environmental, urban, economic and social conditions; to advance municipal services and facilities in the member capitals and cities; to support member cities' capacity-building programmes; and to consolidate fellowship and co-ordinate the scope of co-operation between members; comprises 157 capitals and cities as active members, eight observer members and 18 associate members, in Asia, Africa, Europe and South America; Sec.-Gen. OMAR KADI.

Organization of the Islamic Shipowners' Association: POB 14900, Jeddah 21434, Saudi Arabia; tel. (2) 663-7882; fax (2) 660-4920; e-mail mail@oisaonline.com; internet www.oisaonline.com; f. 1981 to promote co-operation among maritime cos in Islamic countries; in 1998 mems approved the establishment of a new commercial venture, the Bakkah Shipping Company, to enhance sea transport in the region; Sec.-Gen. Dr ABDULLATIF A. SULTAN.

World Federation of Arab-Islamic Schools: 2 Wadi el-Nile St, Maadi, Cairo, Egypt; tel. (2) 358-3278; internet www.wfais.org; f. 1976; supports Arab-Islamic schools world-wide and encourages co-operation between the institutions; promotes the dissemination of the Arabic language and Islamic culture; supports the training of personnel.

SOUTHERN AFRICAN DEVELOPMENT COMMUNITY—SADC

Address: SADC HQ, Plot No. 54385, Private Bag 0095, Gaborone, Botswana.

Telephone: 3951863; **fax:** 3972848; **e-mail:** registry@sadc.int; **internet:** www.sadc.int.

The first Southern African Development Co-ordination Conference (SADCC) was held at Arusha, Tanzania, in July 1979, to harmonize development plans and to reduce the region's economic dependence on South Africa. In August 1992 the 10 member countries of the SADCC signed the Treaty establishing the Southern African Development Community (SADC), which replaced SADCC upon its entry into force in October 1993. The Treaty places binding obligations on member countries, with the aim of promoting economic integration towards a fully developed common market. The Community Tribunal, envisaged in the Treaty, was inaugurated in 2005. The Protocol on Politics, Defence and Security Co-operation, regulating the structure, operations and functions of the Organ on Politics, Defence and Security, established in June 1996 (see under Regional Security), entered into force in March 2004. A troika system, comprising the current, incoming and outgoing SADC chairpersonship, operates at the level of the summit, Council of Ministers and Standing Committee of Officials, and co-ordinates the Organ on Politics, Defence and Security. Other member states may be co-opted into the troika as required. A system of SADC national committees, comprising representatives of government, civil society and the private sector, oversees the implementation of regional programmes at country level and helps to formulate new regional strategies. In recent years SADC institutions have undergone a process of intensive restructuring.

MEMBERS

Angola	Malawi	South Africa
Botswana	Mauritius	Swaziland
Congo, Democratic Republic	Mozambique	Tanzania
Lesotho	Namibia	Zambia
Madagascar*	Seychelles	Zimbabwe

* In March 2009 Madagascar was suspended from meetings of SADC, pending its return to constitutional normalcy, following the forced resignation of the elected President and transfer of power to the military.

Organization

(September 2012)

SUMMIT MEETING

The meeting is held at least once a year and is attended by heads of state and government or their representatives. It is the supreme policy-making organ of SADC and is responsible for the appointment of the Executive Secretary. A report on the restructuring of SADC, adopted by an extraordinary summit held in Windhoek, Namibia, in March 2001, recommended that biannual summit meetings should be convened. The 2011 regular SADC summit meeting was convened in Luanda, Angola, in August. An extraordinary summit meeting was held in June 2012, in Luanda.

COUNCIL OF MINISTERS

Representatives of SADC member countries at ministerial level meet at least once a year.

INTEGRATED COMMITTEE OF MINISTERS

The Integrated Committee of Ministers (ICM), which is responsible to the Council of Ministers, meets at least once a year and comprises at least two ministers from each member state. The ICM facilitates the co-ordination and harmonization of cross-sectoral areas of regional integration; oversees the activities of the Community Directorates; and provides policy guidance to the Secretariat. The ICM formulated and supervises the implementation of the Regional Indicative Strategic Development Plan (RISDP—see below).

STANDING COMMITTEE OF OFFICIALS

The Committee, comprising senior officials, usually from the ministry responsible for economic planning or finance, acts as the technical advisory body to the Council. It meets at least once a year. Members of the Committee also act as a national contact point for matters relating to SADC.

SECRETARIAT

Executive Secretary: TOMÁS AUGUSTO SALOMÃO (Mozambique).

The Secretariat comprises permanently staffed Directorates covering the following priority areas of regional integration: Trade, Industry, Finance and Investment; Infrastructure and Services; Food, Agriculture and Natural Resources; Social and Human Development and Special Programmes; and Policy, Planning and Resource Mobilization.

SADC TRIBUNAL

The establishment of the SADC Tribunal was provided for under the Treaty establishing the SADC and facilitated by a protocol adopted in 2000. The Windhoek, Namibia-based 10-member Tribunal was inaugurated in November 2005 and is mandated to arbitrate in the case of disputes between member states arising from the Treaty.

Activities

In July 1979 the first Southern African Development Co-ordination Conference (SADCC) was attended by delegations from Angola, Botswana, Mozambique, Tanzania and Zambia, with participation by representatives from donor governments and international agencies. In April 1980 a regional economic summit conference was held in Lusaka, Zambia, and the Lusaka Declaration, a statement of strategy entitled 'Southern Africa: Towards Economic Liberation', was approved, with the aim of reducing regional economic dependence on South Africa, then in its apartheid period. The 1986 SADCC summit meeting recommended the adoption of economic sanctions against South Africa but failed to establish a timetable for doing so.

In January 1992 a meeting of the SADCC Council of Ministers approved proposals to transform the organization (by then expanded to include Lesotho, Malawi, Namibia and Swaziland) into a fully integrated economic community, and in August the Treaty establishing SADC was signed. Post-apartheid South Africa became a member of SADC in August 1994, thus strengthening the objective of regional co-operation and economic integration. Mauritius became a member in August 1995. In September 1997 SADC heads of state agreed to admit the Democratic Republic of the Congo (DRC) and Seychelles as members of the Community; Seychelles withdrew, however, in July 2004. In August 2005 Madagascar was admitted as a member.

A task force to co-ordinate a programme of co-operation between SADC and the Common Market for Eastern and Southern Africa (COMESA) was established in 2001, and in 2005 the East African Community (EAC) became incorporated into the process, which was led thereafter by the COMESA-EAC-SADC Task Force. In October 2008 the first tripartite COMESA-EAC-SADC summit was convened, in Kampala, Uganda, to discuss the harmonization of policy and programme work by the three regional economic communities (RECs). The Kampala summit approved a roadmap towards the formation of a single free trade area and the eventual establishment of a single African Economic Community (a long-term objective of African Union (AU) co-operation). At the second tripartite summit, held in June 2011, in Johannesburg, South Africa, negotiations were initiated on the establishment of the proposed COMESA-EAC-SADC Tripartite Free Trade Area. In January 2012 AU leaders endorsed a new Framework, Roadmap and Architecture for Fast Tracking the Establishment of a Continental FTA (referred to as CFTA), and an Action Plan for Boosting Intra-African Trade, which planned for the consolidation of the COMESA-EAC-SADC Tripartite FTA with other regional FTAs into the CFTA initiative during 2015–16; and the establishment of an operational CFTA by 2017. In July 2010 the SADC, COMESA and the EAC adopted a tripartite five-year Programme on Climate Change Adaptation and Mitigation in the COMESA-EAC-SADC region. A tripartite agreement for the implementation of the Programme was signed by the three parties in July 2012.

In September 1994 the first conference of ministers of foreign affairs of SADC and the European Union (EU) was held in Berlin, Germany, instigating the so-called Berlin Initiative on SADC-EU Dialogue. The participants agreed to establish working groups to promote closer trade, political, regional and economic co-operation. In particular, a declaration issued from the meeting specified joint objectives, including a reduction of exports of weapons to southern Africa and of the arms trade within the region, promotion of investment in the region's manufacturing sector and support for democracy at all levels. A second SADC-EU ministerial conference, held in Namibia in October 1996, endorsed a Regional Indicative Programme (RIP) to enhance co-operation between the two organizations over the next five years. The third ministerial conference under the Berlin Initiative took place in Vienna, Austria, in November 1998. In September 1999 SADC signed a co-operation agreement with the US Government, which incorporated measures to promote US investment in the region, and commitments to support HIV/AIDS assessment and prevention programmes and to assist member states to develop environmental protection capabilities. The fourth SADC–EU ministerial conference, convened in Gaborone, in November 2000, adopted a joint declaration on the control of small arms and light weapons in the SADC region. The fifth SADC-EU ministerial conference was held in Maputo, Mozambique, in November 2002. In July SADC and the EU approved a roadmap to guide future co-operation, and in October of that year an EU-SADC ministerial 'double troika' meeting took place in The Hague, Netherlands, to mark 10 years of dialogue between the two organizations under the Berlin Initiative. At the meeting both SADC and the EU reaffirmed their commitment to reinforcing co-operation with regard to peace and security in Africa. In November 2006, at an EU-SADC double troika meeting held in Maseru, Lesotho, SADC representatives agreed to the development of institutional support to the member states through the establishment of a Human Rights Commission and a new SADC Electoral Advisory Council (SEAC). SEAC became operational in April 2011. The 14th SADC-EU double troika ministerial conference under the Berlin initiative, convened in Brussels, Belgium, in November 2008, discussed, *inter alia*, the ongoing global financial crisis and means of addressing volatility in commodity prices and food insecurity in southern Africa. The ongoing EU-SADC Investment Promotion Programme (ESIPP) aims to mobilize foreign capital and technical investment in southern Africa. SADC has co-operated with other sub-regional organizations to finalize a common position on co-operation between African ACP countries and the EU under the Cotonou Agreement (concluded in June 2000, see chapter on the EU).

In July 1996 the SADC Parliamentary Forum was inaugurated, with the aim of promoting democracy, human rights and good governance throughout the region. In September 1997 SADC heads of state endorsed the establishment of the Forum as an autonomous institution. A regional women's parliamentary caucus was inaugurated in April 2002.

The August 2004 summit meeting of heads of state and government, held in Grand Baie, Mauritius, adopted a new Protocol on Principles and Guidelines Governing Democratic Elections, which advocated: full participation by citizens in the political process; freedom of association; political tolerance; elections at regular intervals; equal access to the state media for all political parties; equal opportunity to exercise the right to vote and be voted for; independence of the judiciary; impartiality of the electoral institutions; the right to voter education; the respect of election results proclaimed to be free and fair by a competent national electoral authority; and the right to challenge election results as provided for in the law. Regional elections are monitored by SADC Election Observation Missions (SEOMs); in 2012 SEOMs were dispatched to oversee legislative elections in Lesotho (in May), and in Angola (in August).

At the summit meeting of heads of state and government held in Maseru, Lesotho, in August 2006, a new Protocol on Finance and Investment was adopted. Amendments to SADC protocols on the Tribunal, trade, immunities and privileges, transport, communications and meteorology, energy and mining, combating illicit drugs and education and training were also approved at the meeting. The summit emphasized the need to scale up implementation of SADC's agenda for integration, identifying the RISDP (see below) and the Strategic Indicative Plan for the Organ (SIPO) as the principal instruments for achieving this objective. In pursuit of this aim, the summit established a task force—comprising ministers responsible for finance, investment, economic development, trade and industry—charged with defining the measures necessary for the eradication of poverty and how their implementation might be accelerated.

In accordance with a decision of an extraordinary summit meeting convened in March 2001, SADC's institutions were extensively restructured during 2001–03, with a view to facilitating the more efficient and effective application of the objectives of the organization's founding Treaty and of the SPA. The March 2001 summit meeting endorsed a Common Agenda for the organization, which covered the promotion of poverty reduction measures and of sustainable and equitable socio-economic development, promotion of democratic political values and systems, and the consolidation of peace and security. Furthermore, the establishment of an integrated committee of ministers was authorized; this was mandated to formulate and oversee a Regional Indicative Strategic Development Plan (RISDP), intended as the key policy framework for managing, over a period of 15 years, the SADC Common Agenda. A draft RISDP was approved by the summit meeting convened in Dar es Salaam, Tanzania, in August 2003. In April 2006 SADC adopted the Windhoek Declaration on a new relationship between the Community and its international co-operating partners. The declaration provides a framework for co-operation and dialogue between SADC and international partners, facilitating the implementation of the SADC Common Agenda. A Consultative Conference on Poverty and Development, organized by SADC and attended by its international co-operating partners, was convened in April 2008, in Port Louis, Mauritius.

A high-level meeting concerned with integrating the objectives of the New Partnership for Africa's Development (NEPAD) into SADC's regional programme activities was convened in August 2004. In December 2008 SADC and NEPAD launched a joint business hub, aimed at consolidating regional private sector investment.

An SADC Vision 2050 was under development in 2012.

REGIONAL SECURITY

In November 1994 SADC ministers of defence, meeting in Arusha, Tanzania, approved the establishment of a regional rapid-deployment peace-keeping force, which could be used to contain regional conflicts or civil unrest in member states. An SADC Mine Action Committee is maintained to monitor and co-ordinate the process of removing anti-personnel land devices from countries in the region. The summit meeting of heads of state and government held in August 2007 authorized the establishment of the SADC Standby Brigade (SADCBRIG), with the aim of ensuring collective regional security and stability. SADCBRIG is a pillar of the African Union's African

Standby Force (ASF). SADC's Regional Peacekeeping Training Centre (SADC-RPTC) was established in June 1999 and since August 2005 has been directed by the SADC Secretariat.

In June 1996 SADC heads of state and government, meeting in Gaborone, Botswana, inaugurated an Organ on Politics, Defence and Security (OPDS), with the aim of enhancing co-ordination of national policies and activities in these areas. The stated objectives of the body were, *inter alia*, to safeguard the people and development of the region against instability arising from civil disorder, inter-state conflict and external aggression; to undertake conflict prevention, management and resolution activities, by mediating in inter-state and intra-state disputes and conflicts, pre-empting conflicts through an early warning system and using diplomacy and peace-keeping to achieve sustainable peace; to promote the development of a common foreign policy, in areas of mutual interest, and the evolution of common political institutions; to develop close co-operation between the police and security services of the region; and to encourage the observance of universal human rights, as provided for in the charters of the UN and the Organization of African Unity (OAU—now AU). The extraordinary summit held in March 2001 determined to develop the OPDS as a substructure of SADC, with subdivisions for defence and international diplomacy, to be chaired by a member country's head of state, working within a troika system. A Protocol on Politics, Defence and Security Co-operation—to be implemented by an Inter-state Politics and Diplomacy Committee—regulating the structure, operations and functions of the Organ, was adopted and opened for signature in August 2001 and entered into force in March 2004.

The March 2001 extraordinary SADC summit adopted a Declaration on Small Arms, promoting the curtailment of the proliferation of and illicit trafficking in light weapons in the region. A Protocol on the Control of Firearms, Ammunition and Other Related Materials was adopted in August of that year. In July SADC ministers of defence approved a draft regional defence pact, providing for a mechanism to prevent conflict involving member countries and for member countries to unite against outside aggression. In January 2002 an extraordinary summit of SADC heads of state, held in Blantyre, Malawi, adopted a Declaration against Terrorism.

An extraordinary SADC summit meeting convened in March 2007, in Dar es Salaam, Tanzania, mandated the OPDS to assess the political and security situations in the Democratic Republic of the Congo (DRC) and Lesotho (see below). The ministerial committee of the OPDS troika stressed to the summit the need for SADC support to the ongoing post-conflict reconstruction process in the DRC. An extraordinary meeting of the ministerial committee of the OPDS troika convened in October of that year resolved to mobilize humanitarian assistance for eastern areas of the DRC in view of an escalation in the violent unrest there, with a particular focus on assisting internally displaced civilians. In November 2008 SADC convoked an extraordinary summit of heads of state or government in response to mounting insecurity in eastern DRC. The summit determined to assist the government of the DRC, if necessary by sending a regional peace-keeping force to the province of North Kivu. In February 2009 it was reported that SADCBRIG was ready to intervene if required in the DRC situation. A large team of SADC observers, comprising more than 200 representatives of Community member states, was sent to monitor the presidential and legislative elections that were held in the DRC in November 2011. In August 2012 SADC heads of state or government urged Rwanda to denounce militants of the Kivu-based 23 March Movement (known as 'M23'), which during 2012 had became highly active in northeastern DRC, clashing with government forces and causing mass population displacement. The SADC determined that a Community mission of security experts should be dispatched to Rwanda to assess the situation; the mission was sent, accordingly, in that month, and reported back to SADC ministers of defence. A meeting of the OPDS ministerial troika, convened in early September 2012, urged the parties to the conflict in eastern DRC to seek a negotiated resolution. The OPDS troika also urged co-operation between SADC and the International Conference of the Great Lakes Region in facilitating dialogue over the eastern DRC crisis.

In April 2007 the OPDS ministerial troika, in respect of a mandate issued by the extraordinary SADC summit convened in Dar es Salaam in the previous month, issued an assessment report on the impasse between Lesotho's ruling party, opposition parties and other stakeholders following unsatisfactory legislative elections held in February of that year. In mid-June an eminent person mission aimed at facilitating the post-electoral political dialogue in Lesotho was inaugurated, on the recommendation of the assessment report. In June 2008 an emergency summit meeting of the OPDS troika, convened in Swaziland, considered the unstable political situation in Malawi and offered to facilitate dialogue between the opposing parties.

In August 2001 SADC established a task force, comprising representatives of five member countries, to address the ongoing political crisis in Zimbabwe. The Community sent two separate observer teams to monitor the controversial presidential election held in Zimbabwe in March 2002; the SADC Council of Ministers team found the election to have been conducted freely and fairly, while the Parliamentary Forum group was reluctant to endorse the poll. Having evaluated both reports, the Community approved the election. An SADC Council of Ministers group was convened to observe the parliamentary elections held in Zimbabwe in March 2005; however, the Zimbabwean Government refused to invite a delegation from the SADC Parliamentary Forum. The Zimbabwean Government claimed to have enacted electoral legislation in accordance with the provisions of the August 2004 SADC Protocol on Principles and Guidelines Governing Democratic Elections (see above). The extraordinary summit meeting of SADC heads of state and government, convened in Dar es Salaam, Tanzania, in March 2007, to address the political, economic, and security situation in the region, declared 'solidarity with the government and people of Zimbabwe' and mandated then President Thabo Mbeki of South Africa to facilitate dialogue between the Zimbabwean government and opposition. Mbeki reported to the ordinary SADC summit held in August of that year that restoring Zimbabwe's capacity to generate foreign exchange through balance of payments support would be of pivotal importance in promoting economic recovery and that SADC should assist Zimbabwe with addressing the issue of international sanctions.

In early March 2008 an SADC election observer team was sent to monitor preparations for and the conduct of presidential and national and local legislative elections that were staged in Zimbabwe at the end of that month. In mid-April, at which time the Zimbabwe Electoral Commission had failed to declare the results of the presidental election, prompting widespread international criticism, SADC convened an extraordinary summit to address the electoral outcome. The OPDS presented to the summit a report by the observer team on the presidential and legislative elections which claimed that the electoral process had been acceptable to all parties. The summit urged the Zimbabwe Electoral Commission to verify and release the results of the elections without further delay and requested President Mbeki of South Africa to continue in his role as Facilitator of the Zimbabwe Political Dialogue. In June an emergency meeting of the OPDS troika, at the level of heads of state, was convened following an announcement by the main opposition candidate, Morgan Tsvangirai, that he was withdrawing from a forthcoming second round of voting in the presidential election owing to an escalation of violence against opposition supporters in that country. In July Mugabe and the leaders of the two main opposition parties signed a Memorandum of Understanding, brokered by President Mbeki, confirming their commitment to pursuing dialogue and forming an inclusive government. An agreement (the Global Political Agreement—GPA) to share executive responsibilities in a government of national unity was concluded and signed in September. In December 2008 SADC launched a new Zimbabwe Humanitarian and Development Assistance Framework (ZHDAF), and in January 2009 it established an All Stakeholders Working Committee to implement the ZHDAF. The extraordinary SADC summit convened in March commended political progress recently achieved in Zimbabwe, and established a committee to co-ordinate SADC support, and to mobilize international support for, Zimbabwe's recovery process. The SADC summit held in September urged the termination of all forms of international sanctions against Zimbabwe. It was reported in that month that Zimbabwe had withdrawn from participation in the SADC Tribunal. Responsibility for managing the ZHDAF was transferred to the Zimbabwe Government in December 2009. The June 2012 emergency SADC summit meeting urged President Zuma of South Africa, the current SADC Facilitator of the Zimbabwe Political Dialogue, and the parties to the GPA, to develop an implementation mechanism and establish a schedule for the implementation of a 'Road Map to Zimbabwe Elections' which had been agreed by Zimbabwean stakeholders in April 2011.

The March 2009 extraordinary summit strongly condemned the unconstitutional actions that led to the forced resignation during that month of the elected President of Madagascar, Mark Ravalomanana, and ensuing transfer of power to the military in that country; the summit suspended Madagascar from participation in the activities of the Community and urged the immediate restoration of constitutional order. In June SADC appointed a Community mediator in the Madagascar consitutional crisis. Negotiations subsequently facilitated by the mediator, under SADC auspices, in Maputo, Mozambique, led, in August, to the conclusion of an agreement on the establishment of a power-sharing administration in Madagascar; the power-sharing accord was not, however, subsequently implemented. In March 2011 SADC mediators proposed a new 'Roadmap Out of the Crisis' for Madagascar, again envisaging a power-sharing interim government; this was approved by SADC heads of state and government at a summit convened in June 2011, and was signed by 10 of 11 Malagasy stakeholders in September. An SADC Liaison Office in Madagascar was established in November to support the implementation of the Roadmap. The extraordinary SADC summit convened in June 2012 mandated the Community's mediator and the OPDS ministerial troika to facilitate dialogue between the main Malagasy stakeholders as a matter of urgency in order to ensure the full implementation of the Roadmap. In August an SADC delegation visited Madagascar to hold consultations with stakeholders, including the signatories of the roadmap, the prime minister of the transitional administration, the military leadership, church leaders, and representatives of the international community. It was announced in that month that the first round of a presidential election would be held in May 2013, with the second round to take place in July, alongside parliamentary elections.

TRADE, INDUSTRY AND INVESTMENT

Under the Treaty establishing SADC, efforts were to be undertaken to achieve regional economic integration. The Directorate of Trade, Industry, Finance and Investment aims to facilitate such integration, and poverty eradication, through the creation of an enabling investment and trade environment in SADC countries. Objectives include the establishment of a single regional market; the progressive removal of barriers to the movement of goods, services and people; and the promotion of cross-border investment. SADC supports programmes for industrial research and development and standardization and quality assurance, and aims to mobilize industrial investment resources and to co-ordinate economic policies and the development of the financial sector. In August 1996, at a summit meeting held in Lesotho, SADC member states signed the Protocol on Trade, providing for the establishment of a regional free trade area (FTA), through the gradual elimination of tariff barriers. (Angola and the DRC are not yet signatories to the Protocol.) In October 1999 representatives of the private sector in SADC member states established the Association of SADC Chambers of Commerce, based in Mauritius. The Protocol on Trade entered into force in January 2000, and an Amendment Protocol on Trade came into force in August, incorporating renegotiated technical details on the gradual elimination of tariffs, rules of origin, customs co-operation, special industry arrangements and dispute settlement procedures. The implementation phase of the Protocol on Trade commenced in September. In accordance with a revised schedule, some 85% of intra-SADC trade tariffs were withdrawn by 1 January 2008. The SADC Free Trade Area was formally inaugurated, under the theme 'SADC FTA for Growth, Development and Wealth Creation', at the meeting of heads of state and government, held in Sandton, South Africa, in August 2008; Angola, the DRC, Malawi and Seychelles, however, had not implemented all requirements of the Protocol on Trade and were not yet participating in the FTA. According to the schedule, reaffirmed at the EU–SADC ministerial meeting in 2006, an SADC customs union was to be implemented by 2010 (however, this deadline was not achieved), a common market by 2015, monetary union by 2016, and a single currency was to be introduced by 2018. Annual meetings are convened to review the work of expert teams in the areas of standards, quality, assurance, accreditation and metrology. At an SADC Extraordinary Summit convened in October 2006 it was determined that a draft roadmap was to be developed to facilitate the process of establishing a customs union. In November 2007 the Ministerial Task Force on Regional Economic Integration approved the establishment of technical working groups to facilitate the development of policy frameworks in legal and institutional arrangements; revenue collection, sharing and distribution; policy harmonization; and a common external tariff. A strategic forum of the Ministerial Task Force, to review the regional economic integration agenda, was convened in February 2010, in Johannesburg, South Africa, immediately prior the Task Force's ninth meeting.

The mining sector contributes about 10% of the SADC region's annual GDP. The principal objective of SADC's programme of action on mining is to stimulate increased local and foreign investment in the sector, through the assimilation and dissemination of data, prospecting activities, and participation in promotional fora. In December 1994 SADC held a mining forum, jointly with the EU, in Lusaka, Zambia, with the aim of demonstrating to potential investors and promoters the possibilities of mining exploration in the region. A second mining investment forum was held in Lusaka in December 1998; and a third ('Mines 2000'), also in Lusaka, in October 2000. In April 2006 SADC and the EU launched a new initiative, in the framework of the EU-SADC Investment Promotion Programme, to facilitate European investment in some 100 mining projects in southern Africa. Other objectives of the mining sector are the improvement of industry training, increasing the contribution of small-scale mining, reducing the illicit trade in gemstones and gold, increasing co-operation in mineral exploration and processing, and minimizing the adverse impact of mining operations on the environment. In February 2000 a Protocol on Mining entered into force, providing for the harmonization of policies and programmes relating to the development and exploitation of mineral resources in the region. SADC supports the Kimberley Process Certification Scheme aimed at preventing illicit trade in illegally mined rough diamonds. (The illicit trade in so-called 'conflict diamonds' and other minerals is believed to have motivated and financed many incidences of rebel activity in the continent, for example in Angola and the DRC.)

In July 1998 a Banking Association was officially constituted by representatives of SADC member states. The Association was to establish international banking standards and regional payments systems, organize training and harmonize banking legislation in the region. In April 1999 governors of SADC central banks determined to strengthen and harmonize banking procedures and technology in order to facilitate the financial integration of the region. Efforts to harmonize stock exchanges in the region were also initiated in 1999.

The summit meeting of heads of state and government held in Maseru, Lesotho, in August 2006 adopted a new Protocol on Finance and Investment. The document, regarded as constituting the main framework for economic integration in southern Africa, outlined, *inter alia*, how the region intended to proceed towards monetary union, and was intended to complement the ongoing implementation of the SADC Protocol on Trade and targets contained in the RISDP.

INFRASTRUCTURE AND SERVICES

An SADC Regional Infrastructure Development Master Plan (RIDMP), intended to be the basis for infrastructure-related co-operation and planning until 2027, was under development in 2012.

The Directorate of Infrastructure and Services focuses on transport, communications and meteorology, energy, tourism and water. At SADC's inception transport was regarded as the most important area to be developed, on the grounds that, as the Lusaka Declaration noted, without the establishment of an adequate regional transport and communications system, other areas of co-operation become impractical. The SADC Protocol on Transport, Communications and Meteorology, adopted in August 1996, provides, *inter alia*, for an integrated regional transport policy, an SADC Regional Trunk Road Network (RTRN), and harmonized regional policies relating to maritime and inland waterway transport; civil aviation; regional telecommunications; postal services; and meterology. An Integrated Transport Committee, and other sub-committees representing the sectors covered by the Protocol, have been established. In January 1997 the Southern African Telecommunications Regional Authority (SATRA), a regulatory authority, was established. In March 2001 the Association of Southern African National Road Agencies (ASANRA) was created to foster the development of an integrated regional road transportation system.

SADC development projects have aimed to address missing links and over-stretched sections of the regional network, as well as to improve efficiency, operational co-ordination and human resource development, such as management training projects. Other objectives have been to ensure the compatibility of technical systems within the region and to promote the harmonization of regulations relating to intra-regional traffic and trade. SADC's road network, whose length totals more than 1m. km, constitutes the regions's principal mode of transport for both freight and passengers and is thus vital to the economy. Unsurfaced, low-volume roads account for a substantial proportion of the network and many of these are being upgraded to a sealed standard as part of a wider strategy that focuses on the alleviation of poverty and the pursuit of economic growth and development. In July 1999 a 317-km rail link between Bulawayo, Zimbabwe, and the border town of Beitbridge, administered by SADC as its first build-operate-transfer project, was opened.

SADC policy guidelines on 'making information and communications technology a priority in turning SADC into an information-based economy' were adopted in November 2001. Policy guidelines and model regulations on tariffs for telecommunications services have also been adopted. An SADC Regional Information Infrastructure (SRII) was adopted in December 1999, with the aim of linking member states by means of high capacity digital land and submarine routes. In May 2010 SADC ministers responsible for telecommunications, postal services and ICT adopted a regional e-SADC Strategy Framework, which aimed to utilize ICT for regional socio-economic development and integration. Proposed priorities for the period 2011–12 under the e-SADC initiative included creating national and regional internet exchange points; harmonizing cyber security regulatory frameworks in member countries; and implementing a regional project aimed at improving interconnection of the electronic, physical and financial postal networks. An SADC Digital Broadcasting Migration Forum, convened in Luanda, Angola, in October 2011, to review an SADC Roadmap for Digital Broadcasting Migration, confirmed 31 December 2013 as the SADC Analogue Switch Off (ASO) date, marking the transition from analogue to digital broadcasting. A further Forum, to monitor progress of ASO, was held in August 2012, with two more such fora to take place in 2013. In September 2011 SADC endorsed the inaugural Southern Africa Internet Governance Forum (SAIGF), hosted by the South African Government, in Pretoria, and jointly convened by NEPAD and other agencies.

The SADC Drought Monitoring Centre organizes an annual Southern African Regional Climate Outlook Forum (SARCOF), which assesses seasonal weather prospects. SARCOF-16 was convened in Harare, Zimbabwe, in August 2012.

Areas of activity in the energy sector include: joint petroleum exploration, training programmes for the petroleum sector and studies for strategic fuel storage facilities; promotion of the use of coal; development of hydroelectric power and the co-ordination of SADC generation and transmission capacities; new and renewable sources of energy, including pilot projects in solar energy; assessment of the environmental and socio-economic impact of wood-fuel scarcity and relevant education programmes; and energy conservation. In July 1995 SADC energy ministers approved the establishment of the Southern African Power Pool (SAPP), whereby all member states were to be linked into a single electricity grid. Utilities participating in SAPP aim to provide to consumers in the region an economical and reliable electricity supply. SADC and COMESA have the joint objective of eventually linking SAPP and COMESA's Eastern Africa Power Pool. In July 1995 ministers also endorsed a protocol to promote greater co-operation in energy development within SADC, providing for the establishment of an Energy Commission, responsible for 'demand-side' management, pricing, ensuring private sector involvement and competition, training and research, collecting information, etc.; the protocol entered into force in September 1998. In September 1997 heads of state endorsed an Energy Action Plan to proceed with the implementation of co-operative policies and strategies in four key areas of energy: trade; information exchange; training and organizational capacity building; and investment and financing. There are two major energy supply projects in the region: utilities from Angola, Botswana, the DRC, Namibia and South Africa participate in the Western Power Corridor project, approved in October 2002, while a Zambia–Tanzania Inter-connector project was under development in 2012. In July 2007 it was announced that a Regional Petroleum and Gas Association (REPGA) would be established, with the aim of promoting a common investment destination with harmonized environmental standards.

The tourism sector operates within the context of national and regional socio-economic development objectives. It comprises four components: tourism product development; tourism marketing and research; tourism services; and human resources development and training. SADC has promoted tourism for the region through trade fairs and investment fora. In September 1997 the legal charter for the establishment of the Regional Tourism Organization for Southern Africa (RETOSA), administered jointly by SADC regional national tourism authorities and private sector operators, was signed by ministers of tourism. RETOSA assists member states to formulate tourism promotion policies and strategies. The development is under way of a region-wide common visa (UNI-VISA) system, aimed at facilitating tourism.

In June 2005 the SADC Council of Ministers endorsed the Transfrontier Conservation Area (TFCA) 2010 Development Strategy, aimed at establishing and promoting TFCAs, conservation parks straddling international borders, as premier regional tourist and investment destinations. Phase 1 of the Strategy, up to 2010, focused on the following TFCAs: Ais/Richtersveld (in Namibia and South Africa), Kgalagadi (Botswana, Namibia and South Africa), Limpopo-Shashe (Botswana, South Africa, Zimbabwe), the Great Limpopo Transfrontier Park (GLTP) (Mozambique, South Africa, Zimbabwe), Lubombo (Mozambique, South Africa, Swaziland), Maloti-Drakensburg (Lesotho, South Africa), and Kavango-Zambezi (envisaged as the largest conservation area in the world, straddling the borders of Angola, Botswana, Namibia, Zambia and Zimbabwe); while Phase 2 ('Beyond 2010') focused on Iona-Skeleton Coast (Angola, Namibia), Liuwa Plain-Kamela (Zambia, Angola), Lower Zambezi-Mana Pools (Zambia, Zimbabwe), Malawi-Zambia, Niassa-Selous (a woodland ecosystem) (Mozambique and Tanzania), Mnazi Bay-Quirimbas (Mozambique and Tanzania), and Chimanimani (Zimbabwe, Mozambique).

SADC aims to promote equitable distribution and effective management of the region's water resources, around 70% of which are shared across international borders. A Protocol on Shared Watercourse Systems entered into force in April 1998, and a Revised Protocol on Shared Watercourses came into force in September 2003. An SADC Regional Water Policy was adopted in August 2005 as a framework for providing the sustainable and integrated development, protection and utilization of national and transboundary water resources.

A first Regional Strategic Action Plan (RASP I) on Integrated Water Resources Development and Management was implemented during 1999–2004; RASP II was undertaken in 2005–10; and RASP III was ongoing during 2011–15, covering three strategic areas: water governance; infrastructure development; and water management.

FOOD, AGRICULTURE AND NATURAL RESOURCES

The Directorate of Food, Agriculture and Natural Resources aims to develop, co-ordinate and harmonize policies and programmes on agriculture and natural resources with a focus on sustainability. The Directorate covers the following sectors: agricultural research and training; inland fisheries; forestry; wildlife; marine fisheries and resources; food security; livestock production and animal disease control; and environment and land management. According to SADC figures, agriculture contributes one-third of the region's gross national product (GNP), accounts for about one-quarter of total earnings of foreign exchange and employs some 80% of the labour force. The principal objectives in this field are regional food security, agricultural development and natural resource development.

The Southern African Centre for Co-operation in Agricultural Research (SACCAR), was established in Gaborone, in 1985. It aims to strengthen national agricultural research systems, in order to improve management, increase productivity, promote the development and transfer of technology to assist local farmers, and improve training. Examples of activity include: a sorghum and millet improvement programme; a land and water management research programme; a root crop research network; agroforestry research, implemented in Malawi, Tanzania, Zambia and Zimbabwe; and a grain legume improvement programme, comprising separate research units for groundnuts, beans and cowpeas. SADC's Plant Genetic Resources Centre, based near Lusaka, Zambia, aims to collect, conserve and utilize indigenous and exotic plant genetic resources and to develop appropriate management practices. In November 2009 scientists from SADC member states urged the Community to strengthen and support regional capacity to screen for and detect genetically modified organisms (GMOs), with a view to preventing the uncontrolled influx into the region of GMO products; the results of a survey conducted across the region, released in February 2011, concluded that most Southern African countries lacked sufficient technological capacity to screen for and detect GMOs.

SADC aims to promote inland and marine fisheries as an important, sustainable source of animal protein. Marine fisheries are also considered to be a potential source of income of foreign exchange. In May 1993 the first formal meeting of SADC ministers of marine fisheries convened in Namibia, and it was agreed to hold annual meetings. Meeting in May 2002 ministers of marine fisheries expressed concern about alleged ongoing illegal, unregulated and unreported (IUU) fisheries activities in regional waters. The development of fresh water fisheries is focused on aquaculture projects, and their integration into rural community activities. The SADC Fisheries Protocol entered into force in September 2003. Environment and land management activities have an emphasis on sustainability as an essential quality of development. SADC aims to protect and improve the health, environment and livelihoods of people living in the southern African region; to preserve the natural heritage and biodiversity of the region; and to support regional economic development on a sustainable basis. There is also a focus on capacity building, training, regional co-operation and the exchange of information in all areas related to the environment and land management. SADC operates an Environmental Exchange Network and implements a Land Degradation and Desertification Control Programme. Projects on the conservation and sustainable development of forestry and wildlife are under implementation. An SADC Protocol on Forestry was signed in October 2002, and in November 2003 the Protocol on Wildlife Conservation and Law Enforcement entered into force.

Under the food security programme, the Regional Early Warning System (REWS) aims to anticipate and prevent food shortages through the provision of information relating to the food security situation in member states. As a result of frequent drought crises, SADC member states have agreed to inform the food security sector of their food and non-food requirements on a regular basis, in order to assess the needs of the region as a whole. A programme on irrigation development and water management aims to reduce regional dependency on rain-fed agricultural production, while a programme on the promotion of agricultural trade and food safety aims to increase intra-regional and inter-regional trade with a view to improving agriculture growth and rural incomes. An SADC extraordinary summit on agriculture and food security, held in May 2004 in Dar es Salaam, Tanzania, considered strategies for accelerating development in the agricultural sector and thereby securing food security and reducing poverty in the region. In July 2008 the inaugural meeting was convened of a Task Force of ministers of trade, finance and agriculture, which was established by SADC heads of government earlier in that year in response to rising food prices and production costs. The Task Force agreed upon several measures to improve the food security situation of the SADC region, including increased investment in agriculture and the establishment of a Regional Food Reserve Facility. It also directed the SADC secretariat to develop a regional policy on the production of biofuels. The first Food, Agriculture and Natural Resources cluster ministerial meeting was held in November 2008, in Gaborone, to assess the regional food security situation in view of the ongoing global food security crisis.

The Livestock Sector Unit of the Directorate of Food, Agriculture and Natural Resource co-ordinates activities related to regional livestock development, and implements the Promotion of Regional INTegration (PRINT) livestock sector capacity-strengthening programme; the SADC foot-and-mouth disease (FMD) Programme; and the SADC Transboundary Animal Diseases (TADs) project, which aims to strengthen capacity (with a special focus on Angola, Malawi, Mozambique, Tanzania, and Zambia) to control TADs such as FMD, rinderpest, contagious bovine pleuropneumonia, African swine fever, Newcastle disease, avian influenza, Rift Valley Fever, and lumpy skin disease.

In early June 2012 SADC member states, meeting in Gaborone, Botswana, adopted common regional priorities and policy in the areas of environment and development in advance of the UN Conference on Sustainable Development (Rio+20), which was convened in Rio de Janeiro, Brazil, later in that month.

SOCIAL AND HUMAN DEVELOPMENT AND SPECIAL PROGRAMMES

SADC helps to supply the region's requirements in skilled manpower by providing training in the following categories: high-level managerial personnel; agricultural managers; high- and medium-level technicians; artisans; and instructors. Human resources development activities focus on determining active labour market information systems and institutions in the region, improving education policy analysis and formulation, and addressing issues of teaching and learning materials in the region. SADC administers an Intra-regional Skills Development Programme, and the Community has initiated a programme of distance education to enable greater access to education, as well as operating a scholarship and training awards programme. In July 2000 a Protocol on Education and Training, which was to provide a legal framework for co-operation in this sector entered into force. An extra-ordinary meeting of ministers of higher education and training, held in June 2012, in Johannesburg, South Africa, considered means of redressing the comparatively poor level of enrolment in higher education in the SADC region, noting that higher education tends to be the cornerstone of national innovation, socio-economic and human development; the meeting established an SADC Technical Committee on Higher Education and Training and Research and Development and mandated the Committee to formulate a regional strategic plan on higher education and training. In September 1997 SADC heads of state, meeting in Blantyre, Malawi, endorsed the establishment of a Gender Department within the Secretariat to promote the advancement and education of women. A Declaration on Gender and Development was adopted. SADC leaders adopted an SADC Protocol on Gender Equality in August 2008.

An SADC Protocol on Combating Illicit Drugs entered into force in March 1999. In October 2000 an SADC Epidemiological Network on Drug Use was established to enable the systematic collection of narcotics-related data. SADC operates a regional drugs control programme, funded by the EU.

In August 1999 an SADC Protocol on Health was adopted. In December 1999 a multisectoral sub-committee on HIV/AIDS (which are endemic in the region) was established. In August 2000 the Community adopted a set of guidelines to underpin any future negotiations with major pharmaceutical companies on improving access to and reducing the cost of drugs to combat HIV/AIDS. In July 2003 an SADC special summit on HIV/AIDS, convened in Maseru, Lesotho, and attended by representatives of the World Bank, UNAIDS and WHO, issued the Maseru Declaration on HIV/AIDS, identifying priority areas for action, including prevention, access to testing and treatment, and social mobilization. The implementation of the priority areas outlined in the Maseru Declaration is co-ordinated through an SADC Business Plan on HIV/AIDS (currently in a phase covering the period 2010–15), with a focus on harmonizing regional guidelines on mother-to-child transmission and anti-retroviral therapy; and on issues relating to access to affordable essential drugs, including bulk procurement and regional production. The SADC summit held in September 2009 urged member states to intensify their efforts to implement the Maseru Declaration. An SADC Model Law on HIV/AIDS was adopted by the SADC Parliamentary Forum in 2008; the Forum is implementing a Strategic Framework for HIV/AIDS during 2010–15. The SADC aims to achieve, by 2015, an 'HIV-Free Generation' and no new infections. Since 2008 SADC has celebrated an annual Healthy Lifestyles Day, during the last week in February (25 February in 2012). SADC is implementing a Strategic Plan for the Control of TB In the SADC Region, 2007–15, which aims to address challenges posed by the emergence of Multidrug Resistant TB (MDR-TB) and Extensive Drug Resistant TB (XDR-TB) strains. SADC supports the Southern Africa Roll Back Malaria Network (SARN), which was established in November 2007. SADC member states met in October 2011 to address the elimination of malaria from the region by 2015.

SADC seeks to promote employment and harmonize legislation concerning labour and social protection. Activities include: the implementation of International Labour Standards; the improvement of health and safety standards in the workplace; combating child labour; and the establishment of a statistical database for employment and labour issues. In February 2007 a task force was mandated to investigate measures for improving employment conditions in member countries.

Following the ratification of the Treaty establishing the Community, regional socio-cultural development was emphasized as part of the process of greater integration. Public education initiatives have been undertaken to encourage the involvement of people in the process of regional integration and development, as well as to promote democratic and human rights' values. Two SADC Artists AIDS Festivals have been organized, the first in Bulawayo, Zimbabwe, in August 2007; and the second in Lilongwe, Malawi, in December 2009. The first SADC Poetry Festival was convened in November 2009, in Windhoek, Namibia, with the second held in August 2010, in Gaborone. The creation of an SADC Culture Trust Fund is planned.

Finance

SADC's administrative budget for 2012–13 amounted to US $78.4m., to be financed by contributions from member states (45%) and by international co-operating partners (55%). Madagascar, suspended from meetings of the SADC in 2009 pending its return to constitutional normalcy, has subsequently entered into arrears (owing contributions of $1.8m. in 2012).

Publications

SACCAR Newsletter (quarterly).
SADC Annual Report.
SADC Energy Bulletin.
SADC Food Security Update (monthly).
SADC Today (six a year).

Associated Bodies

Regional Tourism Organisation of Southern Africa (RETOSA): POB 7381, Halfway House, 1685 Midrand, South Africa; tel. (11) 3152420; fax (11) 3152422; e-mail retosa@iafrica.com; internet www.retosa.co.za; f. 1997 to assist SADC member states with formulating tourism promotion policies and strategies; the establishment of a regional tourist visa (UNI-VISA) system aimed at facilitating the the movement of international visitors through the region; RETOSA is administered by a Board comprising representatives of national tourism authorities in SADC member states and private sector umbrella bodies in the region.

SADC Parliamentary Forum: 578 Love St, off Robert Mugabe Ave, Windhoek, Namibia; tel. (61) 2870000; fax (61) 254642; e-mail info@sadcpf.org; internet www.sadcpf.org; f. 1996 to promote democracy, human rights and good governance throughout the SADC region, ensuring fair representation for women; endorsed in Sept. 1997 by SADC heads of state as an autonomous institution; a training arm of the Forum, the SADC Parliamentary Leadership Centre, was established in 2005; the Forum frequently deploys missions to monitor parliamentary and presidential elections in the region (most recently to observe legislative elections held in Lesotho in May 2012 and in Angola in late August 2012); adopted, in March 2001, Electoral Norms and Standards for the SADC Region; from the 2000s expanded the scope of its electoral activities beyond observation to guiding the pre- and post-election phases; under the Forum's third Strategic Plan, covering 2011–15, a review of election observation activities and of the 2001 Norms and Standards was to be implemented; programmes are also undertaken in the areas of democracy and governance; HIV/AIDS and public health; regional development and integration; gender equality and empowerment; ICTs; and parliamentary capacity development; the Forum is funded by member parliaments, governments and charitable and international organizations; mems: national parliaments of SADC countries, representing more than 3,500 parliamentarians; Sec.-Gen. Dr ESAU CHIVIYA.

OTHER REGIONAL ORGANIZATIONS

Agriculture, Food, Forestry and Fisheries

(for organizations concerned with agricultural commodities, see Commodities)

African Agricultural Technology Foundation: POB 30709, Nairobi 00100, Kenya; tel. (20) 4223700; fax (20) 4223701; e-mail aatf@aatf-africa.org; internet www.aatf-africa.org; f. 2002; aims to facilitate and promote public/private partnerships for the access and delivery of agricultural technologies for use by resource poor smallholder farmers; Exec. Dir DENIS TUMWESIGYE KYETERE (Uganda).

African Feed Resources Network (AFRINET): c/o ASARECA, POB 765, Entebbe, Uganda; tel. (41) 320212; fax (41) 321126; e-mail asareca@imul.com; f. 1991 by merger of two African livestock fodder and one animal nutrition research networks; aims to co-ordinate research in all aspects of animal feeding and to strengthen national programmes to develop solutions for inadequate livestock food supplies and poor quality feeds; mems: in 34 countries; publ. *AFRINET Newsletter* (quarterly).

African Timber Organization (ATO): BP 1077, Libreville, Gabon; tel. 732928; fax 734030; e-mail oab-gabon@internetgabon.com; f. 1976 to enable members to study and co-ordinate ways of ensuring the optimum utilization and conservation of their forests; mems: 13 African countries; publs *ATO Information Bulletin* (quarterly), *International Magazine of African Timber* (2 a year).

Association for the Advancement of Agricultural Science in Africa (AAASA): POB 30087, Addis Ababa, Ethiopia; tel. (1) 44-3536; f. 1968 to promote the development and application of agricultural sciences and the exchange of ideas; to encourage Africans to enter training; holds several seminars each year in different African countries; mems: individual agricultural scientists, research institutes in 63 countries; publs *Journal* (2 a year), *Newsletter* (quarterly).

CAB International (CABI): Nosworthy Way, Wallingford, Oxon, OX10 8DE, United Kingdom; tel. (1491) 832111; fax (1491) 829292; e-mail enquiries@cabi.org; internet www.cabi.org; f. 1929 as the Imperial Agricultural Bureaux (later Commonwealth Agricultural Bureaux), current name adopted in 1985; aims to improve human welfare world-wide through the generation, dissemination and application of scientific knowledge in support of sustainable development; places particular emphasis on sustainable agriculture, forestry, human health and the management of natural resources, with priority given to the needs of developing countries; a separate microbiology centre, in Egham, Surrey (UK), undertakes research, consultancy, training, capacity-building and institutional development measures in sustainable pest management, biosystematics and molecular biology, ecological applications and environmental and industrial microbiology; compiles and publishes extensive information (in a variety of print and electronic forms) on aspects of agriculture, forestry, veterinary medicine, the environment and natural resources, and Third World rural development; maintains regional centres in the People's Republic of China, India, Kenya, Malaysia, Pakistan, Switzerland, Trinidad and Tobago, and the USA; mems: 45 countries and territories; Chair. JOHN RIPLEY (United Kingdom); CEO Dr TREVOR NICHOLLS (United Kingdom).

Desert Locust Control Organization for Eastern Africa (DLCOEA): POB 4255, Addis Ababa, Ethiopia; tel. (1) 461477; fax (1) 460296; e-mail dlc@ethionet.et; internet www.dlcoea.org.et; f. 1962 to promote effective control of desert locust in the region and to conduct research into the locust's environment and behaviour; also assists member states in the monitoring, forecasting and extermination of other migratory pests; mems: Djibouti, Eritrea, Ethiopia, Kenya, Somalia, Sudan, Tanzania, Uganda; Dir GASPAR ATTMAN MALLYA; Co-ordinator JAMES M. GATIMU; publs *Desert Locust Situation Reports* (monthly), *Annual Report*, technical reports.

Indian Ocean Tuna Commission (IOTC): POB 1011, Victoria, Mahé, Seychelles; tel. 4225494; fax 4224364; e-mail iotc.secretary@iotc.org; internet www.iotc.org; f. 1996 as a regional fisheries organization with a mandate for the conservation and management of tuna and tuna-like species in the Indian Ocean; mems: Australia, Belize, People's Republic of China, the Comoros, European Union, Eritrea, France, Guinea, India, Indonesia, Iran, Japan, Kenya, Republic of Korea, Madagascar, Malaysia, Maldives, Mauritius, Mozambique, Oman, Pakistan, Philippines, Seychelles, Sudan, Sri Lanka, Tanzania, Thailand, United Kingdom, Vanuatu; co-operating non-contracting parties: Senegal, South Africa; Exec. Sec. ALEJANDRO ANGANUZZI (Argentina).

International Crops Research Institute for the Semi-Arid Tropics (ICRISAT): Patancheru, Andhra Pradesh 502 324, India; tel. (40) 30713071; fax (40) 30713074; e-mail icrisat@cgiar.org; internet www.icrisat.org; f. 1972 to promote the genetic improvement of crops and for research on the management of resources in the world's semi-arid tropics, with the aim of reducing poverty and protecting the environment; research covers all physical and socio-economic aspects of improving farming systems on unirrigated land; maintains regional centres in Nairobi, Kenya (for eastern and southern Africa) and in Niamey, Niger (for western and central Africa); Dir-Gen. Dr WILLIAM D. DAR (Philippines); publs *ICRISAT Report* (annually), *Journal of Semi-Arid Tropical Agricultural Research* (2 a year), information and research bulletins.

International Food Policy Research Institute (IFPRI): 2033 K St, NW, Washington, DC 20006, USA; tel. (202) 862-5600; fax (202) 467-4439; e-mail ifpri@cgiar.org; internet www.ifpri.org; f. 1975; co-operates with academic and other institutions in further research; develops policies for cutting hunger and malnutrition; committed to increasing public awareness of food policies; participates in the Agricultural Market Information System (f. 2011); Dir-Gen. SHENGGEN FAN (People's Republic of China).

International Service for National Agricultural Research (ISNAR): IFPRI, ISNAR Division, ILRI, POB 5689, Addis Ababa, Ethiopia; tel. (11) 646-3215; fax (11) 646-2927; e-mail kasenso-okeyere@cgiar.org; internet www.ifpri.org/divs/isnar.htm; fmrly based in The Hague, Netherlands, the ISNAR Program relocated to Addis Ababa in 2004, as a division of IFPRI; Dir KWADWO ASENSO-OKEYERE.

International Institute of Tropical Agriculture (IITA): Oyo Rd, PMB 5320, Ibadan, Oyo State, Nigeria; tel. (2) 7517472; fax (2) 2412221; e-mail iita@cgiar.org; internet www.iita.org; f. 1967; principal financing arranged by the Consultative Group on International Agricultural Research—CGIAR and several NGOs for special projects; research programmes comprise crop management, improvement of crops and plant protection and health; conducts a training programme for researchers in tropical agriculture; maintains a virtual library and an image database; administers Research Stations, Research Sites, and Regional Administrative Hubs in 41 African countries; Dir-Gen. Dr NTERANYA SANGINGA (Democratic Repub. of the Congo); publs *Annual Report*, *R4DReview*, *MTP Fact Sheets*, *BOT Newsletter* (quarterly), technical bulletins, research reports.

International Livestock Research Institute (ILRI): POB 30709, Nairobi 00100, Kenya; tel. (20) 4223000; fax (20) 4223001; e-mail ilri-kenya@cgiar.org; internet www.ilri.org; f. 1995 to supersede the International Laboratory for Research on Animal Diseases and the International Livestock Centre for Africa; conducts laboratory and field research on animal health and other livestock issues, focusing on the following global livestock development challenges: developing vaccine and diagnostic technologies; conservation and reproductive technologies; adaptation to and mitigation of climate change; addressing emerging diseases; broadening market access for the poor; sustainable intensification of smallholder crop-livestock systems; reducing the vulnerability of marginal systems and communities; carries out training programmes for scientists and technicians; maintains a specialized science library; Dir-Gen. JIMMY SMITH (Guyana); publs *Annual Report*, *Livestock Research for Development* (newsletter, 2 a year).

International Red Locust Control Organization for Central and Southern Africa (IRLCO-CSA): POB 240252, Ndola, Zambia; tel. (2) 651251; fax (2) 650117; e-mail locust@zamnet.zm; f. 1971 to control locusts in eastern, central and southern Africa; also assists in the control of African army-worm and quelea-quelea; mems: 6 countries; Dir MOSES M. OKHOBA; publs *Annual Report*, *Quarterly Report*, *Monthly Report*, scientific reports.

International Scientific Council for Trypanosomiasis Research and Control: c/o AU Interafrican Bureau for Animal Resources, POB 30786, Nairobi, Kenya; tel. (20) 338544; fax (20) 332046; e-mail ibar.office@au-ibar.org; internet www.au-ibar.org; f. 1949 to review the work on tsetse and trypanosomiasis problems carried out by organizations and workers concerned in laboratories and in the field; to stimulate further research and discussion and to promote co-ordination between research workers and organizations in the different countries in Africa, and to provide a regular opportunity for the discussion of particular problems and for the exposition of new experiments and discoveries; holds a General Conference (last held Sept. 2011: Bamako, Mali); Sec. Dr JAMES WABACHA.

Arts and Culture

Afro-Asian Writers' Association: 18 Ismail Abou el-Fotouh St, Veiny Sq., in front of Misr International Hospital, Dokki, Cairo, Egypt; tel. (2) 37600549; fax (2) 37600548; f. 1958; mems: writers' orgs in 51 countries; Chair. MOHAMED MAGDY MORGAN; publs *Lotus Magazine of Afro-Asian Writings* (quarterly in English, French and Arabic), *Afro-Asian Literature Series* (in English, French and Arabic).

Organization of World Heritage Cities: 15 rue Saint-Nicolas, Québec, QC G1K 1M8, Canada; tel. (418) 692-0000; fax (418) 692-5558; e-mail secretariat@ovpm.org; internet www.ovpm.org; f. 1993 to assist cities inscribed on the UNESCO World Heritage List to implement the Convention concerning the Protection of the World Cultural and Natural Heritage (1972); promotes co-operation between city authorities, in particular in the management and sustainable development of historic sites; holds an annual General Assembly, comprising the mayors of member cities; mems: 238 cities world-wide; Sec.-Gen. DENIS RICARD; publ. *OWHC Newsletter* (2 a year, in English, French and Spanish).

Pan-African Writers' Association (PAWA): PAWA House, Roman Ridge, POB C456, Cantonments, Accra, Ghana; tel. (21) 773062; fax (21) 773042; e-mail pawahouse@gmail.com; f. 1989 to link African creative writers, defend the rights of authors and promote awareness of literature; mems: 52 national writers' associations on the continent; Sec.-Gen. ATUKWEI OKAI (Ghana).

Commodities

Africa Rice Center (AfricaRice): 01 BP 2031, Cotonou, Benin; tel. 21-35-01-88; fax 21-35-05-56; e-mail AfricaRice@cgiar.org; internet www.africarice.org/; f. 1971 (as the West Africa Rice Development Association—WARDA, present name adopted in 2009); participates in the network of agricultural research centres supported by the Consultative Group on International Agricultural Research (CGIAR); aims to contribute to food security and poverty eradication in poor rural and urban populations, through research, partnerships, capacity strengthening and policy support on rice-based systems; promotes sustainable agricultural development based on environmentally sound management of natural resources; maintains research stations in Nigeria and Senegal; provides training and consulting services; from 2007 expanded scope of membership and activities from West African to pan-African; mems: 24 African countries; Dir-Gen. Dr PAPA ABDOULAYE SECK (Senegal); publs *Program Report* (annually), *Participatory Varietal Selection* (annually), *Rice Interspecific Hybridization Project Research Highlights* (annually), *Inland Valley Newsletter*, *ROCARIZ Newsletter*, training series, proceedings, leaflets.

African Groundnut Council (AGC): C43, Wase Satellite Town, Rjiyar Zaki, Kano, Kano State, Nigeria; tel. (1) 8970605; e-mail info@afgroundnutcouncil.org; f. 1964 to advise producing countries on marketing policies; mems: The Gambia, Mali, Niger, Nigeria, Senegal, Sudan; Exec. Sec. ELHADJ MOUR MAMADOU SAMB (Senegal); publ. *Groundnut Review*.

African Oil Palm Development Association (AFOPDA): 15 BP 341, Abidjan 15, Côte d'Ivoire; tel. 21-25-15-18; fax 20-25-47-00; f. 1985; seeks to increase production of, and investment in, palm oil; mems: Benin, Cameroon, Democratic Republic of the Congo, Côte d'Ivoire, Ghana, Guinea, Nigeria, Togo.

African Petroleum Producers' Association (APPA): POB 1097, Brazzaville, Republic of the Congo; tel. 665-38-57; fax 669-99-13; e-mail appa@appa.int; internet appa.int; f. 1987 by African petroleum-producing countries to reinforce co-operation among regional producers and to stabilize prices; council of ministers responsible for the hydrocarbons sector meets twice a year; holds regular Congress and Exhibition: March 2010, Kinshasa, Democratic Republic of the Congo; mems: Algeria, Angola, Benin, Cameroon, Democratic Republic of the Congo, Republic of the Congo, Côte d'Ivoire, Egypt, Equatorial Guinea, Gabon, Libya, Nigeria; Exec. Sec. GABRIEL DANSOU LOKOSSOU; publ. *APPA Bulletin* (2 a year).

Alliance of Cocoa Producing Countries (COPAL): National Assembly Complex, Tafawa Balewa Sq., POB 1718, Lagos, Nigeria; tel. (9) 8141735; fax (9) 8141734; e-mail info@copal-cpa.org; internet www.copal-cpa.org; f. 1962 to exchange technical and scientific information, to discuss problems of mutual concern to producers, to ensure adequate supplies at remunerative prices and to promote consumption; organizes a Research Conference (Oct. 2012: Yaoundé, Cameroon); mems: Brazil, Cameroon, Côte d'Ivoire, Dominican Republic, Gabon, Ghana, Malaysia, Nigeria, São Tomé and Príncipe, Togo; Sec.-Gen. NANGA COULIBALY.

Common Fund for Commodities (CFC): POB 74656, 1070 BR, Amsterdam, Netherlands; tel. (20) 5754949; fax (20) 6760231; e-mail managing.director@common-fund.org; internet www.common-fund.org; f. 1989 as the result of an UNCTAD negotiation conference; finances commodity development measures including research, marketing, productivity improvements and vertical diversification, with the aim of increasing the long-term competitiveness of particular commodities; paid-in cap. US $181m.; mems: 105 countries and 10 institutional mems; Man. Dir (also Chief Exec.) ALI MCHUMO.

East Africa Tea Trade Association: Tea Trade Centre, Nyerere Ave, Mombasa, Kenya; tel. (41) 2228460; fax (41) 2225823; e-mail info@eatta.com; internet www.eatta.com; f. 1957; brings together producers, brokers, buyers and packers; Chair. PETER KIMANGA; Man. Dir. EDWARD K. MUDIBO.

Gas Exporting Countries Forum: POB 23753, Tornado Tower, 47-48th Floors, West Bay, Doha, Qatar; tel. 44048410; fax 44048416; e-mail gecfsg@gmail.com; internet www.gecf.org; f. 2001 to represent and promote the mutual interests of gas exporting countries; aims to increase the level of co-ordination among member countries and to promote dialogue between gas producers and consumers; a ministerial meeting is convened annually; the seventh ministerial meeting, convened in Moscow, Russia, in Dec. 2008, agreed on a charter and a permanent structure for the grouping; mems: Algeria, Bolivia, Egypt, Equatorial Guinea, Iran, Libya, Nigeria, Oman, Qatar, Russia, Trinidad and Tobago, Venezuela; observers: Kazakhstan, Netherlands, Norway; Sec.-Gen. LEONID BOKHANOVSKIY.

Inter-African Coffee Organization (IACO) (Organisation Inter-Africaine du Café—OIAC): BP V210, Abidjan, Côte d'Ivoire; tel. 20-21-61-31; fax 20-21-62-12; e-mail sg@iaco-oiac.org; internet www.iaco-oiac.org; f. 1960 to adopt a common policy on the marketing and consumption of coffee; aims to foster greater collaboration in research technology transfer through the African Coffee Research Network (ACRN); seeks to improve the quality of coffee exports, and implement poverty reduction programmes focusing on value added product (VAP) and the manufacturing of green coffee; mems: 25 coffee-producing countries in Africa; Sec.-Gen. JOSEFA LEONEL CORREIA SACKO (Angola).

International Cocoa Organization (ICCO): Commonwealth House, 1–19 New Oxford St, London, WC1A 1NU, United Kingdom; tel. (20) 7400-5050; fax (20) 7421-5500; e-mail info@icco.org; internet www.icco.org; f. 1973 under the first International Cocoa Agreement, 1972; the ICCO supervises the implementation of the agreements, and provides member governments with up-to-date information on the world cocoa economy; the sixth International Cocoa Agreement (2001) entered into force in October 2003; the seventh International Cocoa Agreement was signed in June 2010 and was to enter into force in October 2012; mems: 13 exporting countries and 28 importing countries; and the EU; Exec. Dir a.i. Dr JEAN-MARC ANGA (Côte d'Ivoire); publs *Quarterly Bulletin of Cocoa Statistics*, *Annual Report*, *World Cocoa Directory*, *Cocoa Newsletter*, studies on the world cocoa economy.

International Coffee Organization (ICO): 22 Berners St, London, W1T 3DD, United Kingdom; tel. (20) 7612-0600; fax (20) 7612-0630; e-mail info@ico.org; internet www.ico.org; f. 1963 under the International Coffee Agreement, 1962, which was renegotiated in 1968, 1976, 1983, 1994 (extended in 1999), 2001 and 2007; aims to improve international co-operation and provide a forum for intergovernmental consultations on coffee matters; to facilitate international trade in coffee by the collection, analysis and dissemination of statistics; to act as a centre for the collection, exchange and publication of coffee information; to promote studies in the field of coffee; and to encourage an increase in coffee consumption; mems: 36 exporting countries and 6 importing countries, plus the European Union; Chair. of Council HENRY NGABIRANO (Uganda); Exec. Dir ROBÉRIO SILVA (Brazil).

International Energy Forum (IEF): POB 94736, Diplomatic Quarter, Riyadh 11614, Saudi Arabia; tel. (1) 4810022; fax (1) 4810055; e-mail info@ief.org; internet www.ief.org; f. 1991; annual gathering of ministers responsible for energy affairs from states accounting for about 90% of global oil and gas supply and demand; the IEF is an intergovernmental arrangement aimed at promoting dialogue on global energy matters among its membership; the annual IEF is preceded by a meeting of the International Business Energy Forum (IEBF), comprising energy ministers and CEOs of leading energy companies; 13th IEF and fifth IEBF: March 2012, Kuwait; mems: 89 states, including the mems of OPEC and the International Energy Agency; Sec.-Gen. ALDO FLORES-QUIROGA.

International Grains Council (IGC): 1 Canada Sq., Canary Wharf, London, E14 5AE, United Kingdom; tel. (20) 7513-1122;

fax (20) 7513-0630; e-mail igc@igc.int; internet www.igc.int; f. 1949 as International Wheat Council, present name adopted in 1995; responsible for the administration of the International Grains Agreement, 1995, comprising the Grains Trade Convention (GTC) and the Food Aid Convention (FAC, under which donors pledge specified minimum annual amounts of food aid for developing countries in the form of grain and other eligible products); aims to further international co-operation in all aspects of trade in grains, to promote international trade in grains, and to achieve a free flow of this trade, particularly in developing member countries; seeks to contribute to the stability of the international grain market; acts as a forum for consultations between members; provides comprehensive information on the international grain market (with effect from 1 July 2009 the definition of 'grain' was extended to include rice); mems: 25 countries and the EU; Exec. Dir ETSUO KITAHARA; publs *World Grain Statistics* (annually), *Wheat and Coarse Grain Shipments* (annually), *Report for the Fiscal Year* (annually), *Grain Market Report* (monthly), *IGC Grain Market Indicators* (weekly), *Rice Market Bulletin* (weekly).

International Rubber Research and Development Board (IRRDB): POB 10150, 50908 Kuala Lumpur, Malaysia; tel. (3) 42521612; fax (3) 42560487; e-mail sec_gen@theirrdb.org; internet www.irrdb.com; f. 1960 following the merger of International Rubber Regulation Committee (f. 1934) and International Rubber Research Board (f. 1937); mems: 19 natural rubber research institutes; Sec. Dr ABDUL AZIZ B. S. A. KADIR (Malaysia).

International Rubber Study Group: 111 North Bridge Rd, 23-06 Peninsula Plaza, Singapore 179098; tel. 68372411; fax 63394369; e-mail irsg@rubberstudy.com; internet www.rubberstudy.com; f. 1944 to provide a forum for the discussion of problems affecting synthetic and natural rubber and to provide statistical and other general information on rubber; mems: Cameroon, Côte d'Ivoire, the EU, India, Japan, Nigeria, Russia Singapore and Sri Lanka; Sec.-Gen. Dr STEPHEN V. EVANS; publs *Rubber Statistical Bulletin* (every 2 months), *Rubber Industry Report* (every 2 months), *Proceedings of International Rubber Forums* (annually), *World Rubber Statistics Handbook*, *Key Rubber Indicators*, *Rubber Statistics Yearbook*, *Outlook for Elastomers* (annually).

International Sugar Organization: 1 Canada Sq., Canary Wharf, London, E14 5AA, United Kingdom; tel. (20) 7513-1144; fax (20) 7513-1146; e-mail exdir@isosugar.org; internet www.isosugar.org; administers the International Sugar Agreement (1992), with the objectives of stimulating co-operation, facilitating trade and encouraging demand; aims to improve conditions in the sugar market through debate, analysis and studies; serves as a forum for discussion; holds annual seminars and workshops; sponsors projects from developing countries; mems: 84 countries producing some 83% of total world sugar; Exec. Dir Dr PETER BARON; publs *Sugar Year Book*, *Monthly Statistical Bulletin*, *Market Report and Press Summary*, *Quarterly Market Outlook*, seminar proceedings.

International Tea Committee Ltd (ITC): 1 Carlton House Terrace, London, SW1Y 5DB, United Kingdom; tel. (20) 7839-5090; e-mail info@inttea.com; internet www.inttea.com; f. 1933 to administer the International Tea Agreement; now serves as a statistical and information centre; in 1979 membership was extended to include consuming countries; producer mems: national tea boards or asscns in Bangladesh, People's Republic of China, India, Indonesia, Kenya, Malawi, Sri Lanka and Tanzania; consumer mems: Tea Asscn of the USA Inc., Irish Tea Trade Asscn, and the Tea Asscn of Canada; assoc. mems: Netherlands Ministry of Agriculture, Nature and Food Quality and United Kingdom Dept for Environment Food and Rural Affairs, and national tea boards/asscns in 10 producing and 4 consuming countries; Chief Exec. MANUJA PEIRIS; publs *Annual Bulletin of Statistics*, *Monthly Statistical Summary*.

International Tobacco Growers' Association (ITGA): Av. Gen. Humberto Delgado 30A, 6001-081 Castelo Branco, Portugal; tel. (272) 325901; fax (272) 325906; e-mail itga@tobaccoleaf.org; internet www.tobaccoleaf.org; f. 1984 to provide a forum for the exchange of views and information of interest to tobacco producers; holds annual meeting; mems: 23 countries producing over 80% of the world's internationally traded tobacco; Chief Exec. ANTÓNIO ABRUNHOSA (Portugal); publs *Tobacco Courier* (quarterly), *Tobacco Briefing*.

International Tropical Timber Organization (ITTO): International Organizations Center, 5th Floor, Pacifico-Yokohama, 1-1-1, Minato-Mirai, Nishi-ku, Yokohama 220-0012, Japan; tel. (45) 223-1110; fax (45) 223-1111; e-mail itto@itto.or.jp; internet www.itto.int; f. 1985 under the International Tropical Timber Agreement (1983); subsequently a new treaty, ITTA 1994, came into force in 1997, and this was replaced by ITTA 2006, which entered into force in Dec. 2011; provides a forum for consultation and co-operation between countries that produce and consume tropical timber, and is dedicated to the sustainable development and conservation of tropical forests; facilitates progress towards 'Objective 2000', which aims to move as rapidly as possible towards achieving exports of tropical timber and timber products from sustainably managed resources; encourages, through policy and project work, forest management, conservation and restoration, the further processing of tropical timber in producing countries, and the gathering and analysis of market intelligence and economic information; mems: 25 producing and 36 consuming countries and the EU; Exec. Dir EMMANUEL ZE MEKA (Cameroon); publs *Annual Review and Assessment of the World Timber Situation*, *Tropical Timber Market Information Service* (every 2 weeks), *Tropical Forest Update* (quarterly).

Kimberley Process: internet www.kimberleyprocess.com; launched following a meeting of southern African diamond-producing states, held in May 2000 in Kimberley, South Africa, to address means of halting the trade in 'conflict diamonds' and of ensuring that revenue derived from diamond sales would henceforth not be used to fund rebel movements aiming to undermine legitimate governments; in Dec. of that year a landmark UN General Assembly resolution was adopted supporting the creation of an international certification scheme for rough diamonds; accordingly, the Kimberley Process Certification Scheme (KPCS), detailing requirements for controlling production of and trade in 'conflict-free' rough diamonds, entered into force on 1 Jan. 2003; it was estimated in 2012 that participating states accounted for 99.8% of global rough diamond production; a review of the core objectives and definitions of the Process was being undertaken during 2012–13; participating countries, with industry and civil society observers, meet twice a year; working groups and committees also convene frequently; implementation of the KPCS is monitored through 'review visits', annual reports, and through ongoing exchange and analysis of statistical data; mems: 49 participating states and the EU; the following 3 participating states were (in 2012) inactive mems: Côte d'Ivoire (barred by UN sanctions from trading in rough diamonds), Taiwan (yet to achieve the minimum requirements set by the KPCS), and Venezuela (voluntary suspension of exports and imports of rough diamonds in place); trade in diamonds from the Republic of the Congo was suspended from the KPCS during 2004–07; observers incl. the World Diamond Council; chaired, on a rotating basis, by participating states (2012: USA).

Organization of the Petroleum Exporting Countries (OPEC): 1010 Vienna, Helferstorferstr. 17; tel. (1) 211-12-279; fax (1) 214-98-27; e-mail prid@opec.org; internet www.opec.org; f. 1960 to unify and co-ordinate mems' petroleum policies and to safeguard their interests generally; holds regular conferences of mem countries to set reference prices and production levels; conducts research in energy studies, economics and finance; provides data services and news services covering petroleum and energy issues; mems: Algeria, Angola, Ecuador, Iran, Iraq, Kuwait, Libya, Nigeria, Qatar, Saudi Arabia, United Arab Emirates, Venezuela; Sec.-Gen. ABDULLA SALEM EL-BADRI (Libya); publs *Annual Report*, *Annual Statistical Bulletin*, *OPEC Bulletin* (10 year), *OPEC Review* (quarterly), *Monthly Oil Market Report*, *World Oil Outlook* (annually).

World Diamond Council: 580 Fifth Ave, 28th Floor, New York, NY 10036, USA; tel. (212) 575-8848; fax (212) 840-0496; e-mail worlddiamondcouncil@gmail.com; internet www.worlddiamondcouncil.com; f. 2000, by a resolution passed at the World Diamond Congress, convened in July by the World Federation of Diamond Bourses, with the aim of promoting responsibility within the diamond industry towards its stakeholders; lobbied for the creation of a certification scheme to prevent trade in 'conflict diamonds', and became an observer on the ensuing Kimberley Process Certification Scheme, launched in January 2003; has participated in review visits to Kimberley Process participating countries; in Oct. 2002 approved—and maintains—a voluntary System of Warranties, enabling dealers, jewellery manufacturers and retailers to pass on assurances that polished diamonds derive from certified 'conflict-free' rough diamonds, with the aim of extending the effectiveness of the Kimberley Process beyond the export and import phase; meets annually; mems: more than 50 diamond and jewellery industry orgs; Pres. ELI IZHAKOFF.

Development and Economic Co-operation

African Capacity Building Foundation (ACBF): ZB Life Towers, 7th Floor, cnr Jason Moyo Ave/Sam Nujoma St, POB 1562, Harare, Zimbabwe; tel. (4) 702931; fax (4) 702915; e-mail root@acbf-pact.org; internet www.acbf-pact.org; f. 1991 by the World Bank, UNDP, the African Development Bank, African governments and bilateral donors; aims to build sustainable human and institutional capacity for sustainable growth, poverty reduction and good governance in Africa; mems: 44 African and non-African govts, the World Bank, UNDP, AfDB, the IMF; Exec. Sec. Dr FRANNIE A. LÉAUTIER.

African Training and Research Centre in Administration for Development (Centre Africain de Formation et de Recherche Administratives pour le Développement—CAFRAD): POB 1796, Tangier, 90001 Morocco; tel. (661) 307269; fax (539) 325785; e-mail cafrad@cafrad.org; internet www.cafrad.org; f. 1964 by agreement between Morocco and UNESCO; undertakes research into administrative problems in Africa and documents results; provides a consultation service for governments and organizations; holds workshops to train senior civil servants; prepares the Biennial Pan-African Conference of Ministers of the Civil Service; mems: 37 African countries; Chair. MOHAMED SAÂD EL-ALAMI; Dir-Gen. Dr SIMON MAMOSI LELO; publs *African Administrative Studies* (2 a year), *Research Studies*, *Newsletter* (internet), *Collection: Etudes et Documents, Répertoires des Consultants et des institutions de formation en Afrique*.

Afro-Asian Rural Development Organization (AARDO): No. 2, State Guest Houses Complex, Chanakyapuri, New Delhi 110 021, India; tel. (11) 24100475; fax (11) 24672045; e-mail aardohq@nde .vsnl.net.in; internet www.aardo.org; f. 1962 to act as a catalyst for the co-operative restructuring of rural life in Africa and Asia and to explore opportunities for the co-ordination of efforts to promote rural welfare and to eradicate hunger, thirst, disease, illiteracy and poverty; carries out collaborative research on development issues; organizes training; encourages the exchange of information; holds international conferences and seminars; awards 150 individual training fellowships at 12 institutes in Bangladesh, Egypt, India, Japan, Republic of Korea, Malaysia, Nigeria, Taiwan and Zambia; mems: 15 African countries, 14 Asian countries, 1 African associate; Sec.-Gen. WASSFI HASSAN EL-SREIHIN (Jordan); publs *Afro-Asian Journal of Rural Development* (2 a year), *Annual Report*, *AARDO Newsletter* (2 a year).

Arab Bank for Economic Development in Africa (Banque arabe pour le développement économique en Afrique—BADEA): Sayed Abdar-Rahman el-Mahdi St, POB 2640, Khartoum 11111, Sudan; tel. (1) 83773646; fax (1) 83770600; e-mail badea@badea.org; internet www.badea.org; f. 1973 by Arab League; provides loans and grants to sub-Saharan African countries to finance development projects; paid-up cap. US $2,800m. (Dec. 2010); during 2010 the Bank approved project loans totalling $192.0m., and technical assistance for feasibility studies and institutional support grants amounting to $8.0m; by the end of 2010 total net commitments (incl. technical assistance) approved since funding activities began in 1975 totalled $3,092.8m; during 2010 the Bank contributed $13.9m. to the heavily indebted poor countries initiative, bringing the cumulative total to $186.3m. since the scheme commenced in 1997; Chair. YOUSSOUF IBRAHEM AL-BASSAM (Saudi Arabia); Dir-Gen. ABDELAZIZ KHELEF (Algeria); publs *Annual Report*, *Co-operation for Development* (quarterly), Studies on Afro-Arab co-operation.

Centre on Integrated Rural Development for Africa (CIRDAFRICA): Nigeria; f. 1979 (operational 1982) to promote integrated rural development through a network of national institutions; to improve the production, income and living conditions of small-scale farmers and other rural groups; to provide tech. support; and to foster the exchange of ideas and experience; financed by mem. states and donor agencies; mems: 17 African countries; Dir Dr ABDELMONEIM M. ELSHEIKH; publ. *CIRDAfrica Rural Tribune* (2 a year).

Club du Sahel et de l'Afrique de l'Ouest (Sahel and West Africa Club): c/o OECD, 2 rue André Pascal, 75775 Paris, France; tel. 1-45-24-89-87; fax 1-45-24-90-31; e-mail swac.contact@oecd.org; internet www.westafricaclub.org; f. 1977 as Club du Sahel, current name and structure adopted in April 2001; an informal discussion forum for exchange of ideas and experience between OECD donor agencies and African recipients; aims to create, promote and facilitate links between the countries of OECD and West Africa, and between the private and public sectors in order to improve the efficiency of development aid; mems: 9 national and international orgs, 3 observers; Dir LAURENT BOSSARD.

Coalition for Dialogue on Africa (CoDA): POB 3001, Addis Ababa, Ethiopia; tel. (11) 15443277; fax (11) 15443715; e-mail coda@uneca.org; internet www.uneca.org/coda; f. 2009; brings together African stakeholders and policy-makers; policy-oriented, working in collaboration with regional and international organizations to address issues relating to security, peace, governance and development; sponsored by, but not a programme of, the AU Commission, the UN Economic Commission for Africa and the AfDB; Chair. FESTUS MOGAE.

COMESA-EAC-SADC Tripartite Secretariat: 1st Floor Bldg 41, CSIR Campus, Meiring Naude Rd, Brummeria, Pretoria, 0001 South Africa; e-mail info@comesa-eac-sadc-tripartite.org; internet www .comesa-eac-sadc-tripartite.org; tripartite COMESA -EAC-SADC co-operation, aiming to advance regional integration through the harmonization of the trade and infrastructure development programmes of these AU regional economic communities (RECs), was initiated in 2005 (a COMESA-SADC task force having been active during 2001–05); a Tripartite Task Force—led by the Secretaries-General of COMESA and the EAC, and the Executive Secretary of SADC—has convened regularly thereafter; a five-year Tripartite Programme on Climate Change Adaptation and Mitigation was adopted in July 2010; the first Tripartite Summit, organized in October 2008, in Kampala, Uganda, approved a roadmap towards the formation of a single free trade area (FTA) and the eventual establishment of a single African Economic Community; at the second Tripartite summit, held in June 2011, in Johannesburg, South Africa, negotiations were initiated on the establishment of the proposed COMESA-EAC-SADC Tripartite FTA; in accordance with a Framework, Roadmap and Architecture for Fast Tracking the Establishment of a Continental FTA (referred to as CFTA), and an Action Plan for Boosting Intra-African Trade, adopted by AU leaders in January 2012, the COMESA-EAC-SADC Tripartite FTA was to be finalized by 2014 and, during 2015–16, consolidated with other regional FTAs into the CFTA initiative, with the aim of establishing by 2017 an operational CFTA.

Communauté économique des états de l'Afrique centrale (CEEAC) (Economic Community of Central African States): BP 2112, Libreville, Gabon; tel. (241) 44-47-31; fax (241) 44-47-32; e-mail secretariat@ceeac-eccas.org; internet www.ceeac-eccas.org; f. 1983, operational 1 January 1985; aims to promote co-operation between member states by abolishing trade restrictions, establishing a common external customs tariff, linking commercial banks, and setting up a development fund, over a period of 12 years; works to combat drug abuse and to promote regional security; has since July 2008 deployed the Mission for the Consolidation of Peace in the CAR—MICOPAX; a CEEAC Parliament was inaugurated in Malabo, Equatorial Guinea, in April 2010; mems: 10 African countries; Sec.-Gen. NASSOUR GUELENGDOUSKSIA OUAIDO.

Community of Sahel-Saharan States (Communauté des états Sahelo-Sahariens—CEN-SAD): Place d'Algeria, POB 4041, Tripoli, Libya; tel. (21) 361-4832; fax (21) 334-3670; e-mail info@cen-sad.org; internet www.uneca.org/cen-sad; f. 1998; fmrly known as COMESSA; aims to strengthen co-operation between signatory states in order to promote their economic, social and cultural integration and to facilitate conflict resolution and poverty alleviation; partnership agreements concluded with many orgs, including the AU, UN and ECOWAS; mems: Benin, Burkina Faso, Central African Republic, Chad, Côte d'Ivoire, Djibouti, Egypt, Eritrea, The Gambia, Ghana, Guinea-Bissau, Liberia, Libya, Mali, Morocco, Niger, Nigeria, Senegal, Sierra Leone, Somalia, Sudan, Togo, Tunisia; Sec.-Gen. Dr MOHAMMED AL-MADANI AL-AZHARI (Libya).

Conseil de l'Entente (Entente Council): 01 BP 3734, angle ave Verdier/rue de Tessières, Abidjan 01, Côte d'Ivoire; tel. 20-33-28-35; fax 20-33-11-49; e-mail fegece@conseil-entente.org; f. 1959 to promote economic development in the region; the Council's Mutual Aid and Loan Guarantee Fund (Fonds d' entraide et de garantie des emprunts) finances development projects, including agricultural projects, support for small and medium-sized enterprises, vocational training centres, research into new sources of energy and building of hotels to encourage tourism; a Convention of Assistance and Co-operation was signed in Feb. 1996; holds annual summit; mems: Benin, Burkina Faso, Côte d'Ivoire, Niger, Togo; publ. *Rapport d'activité* (annually).

Conseil Ouest et Centre Africain pour le Recherche et le Développement Agricoles (West and Central African Council for Agricultural Research and Development): BP 48, Dakar, Senegal; tel. 33-869-9618; fax 33-869-9631; e-mail secoraf@coraf.org; internet www.coraf.org; f. 1987; aims to achieve a sustainable reduction of poverty through agricultural development and growth in West and Central Africa; Chair. Prof. EMMANUEL OWUSU-BENNOAH.

East African Community (EAC): AICC Bldg, Kilimanjaro Wing, 5th Floor, POB 1096, Arusha, Tanzania; tel. (27) 2504253; fax (27) 2504255; e-mail eac@eachq.org; internet www.eac.int; f. 2001, following the adoption of a treaty on political and economic integration (signed in November 1999) by the heads of state of Kenya, Tanzania and Uganda, replacing the Permanent Tripartite Commission for East African Co-operation (f. 1993) and reviving the former East African Community (f. 1967; dissolved 1977); initial areas for co-operation were to be trade and industry, security, immigration, transport and communications, and promotion of investment; further objectives were the elimination of trade barriers and ensuring the free movement of people and capital within the grouping; a customs union came into effect on 1 Jan. 2005; a Court of Justice and a Legislative Assembly have been established; in April 2006 heads of state agreed that negotiations on a common market would commence in July; the Protocol on the Establishment of the EAC Common Market entered into force on 1 July 2010; negotiations on the establishment of an East African Monetary Union were initiated in 2011; Rwanda and Burundi formally became members of the Community on 1 July 2007; South Sudan (which achieved independence in July 2011) has applied for membership; an East African Legislative Assembly and an East African Court of Justice were both inaugurated in 2001; has participated, since 2005, to advance regional co-operation through the COMESA-EAC-SADC Tripartite, with a view to advancing regional co-operation; Sec.-Gen. RICHARD SEZIBERA (Rwanda).

Economic Community of the Great Lakes Countries (Communauté économique des pays des Grands Lacs—CEPGL): POB 58, Gisenyi, Rwanda; tel. 61309; fax 61319; f. 1976 main organs: annual Conference of Heads of State, Council of Ministers of Foreign Affairs, Permanent Executive Secretariat, Consultative Commission, Security Commission, three Specialized Technical Commissions; there are four specialized agencies: a development bank, the Banque de Développement des Etats des Grands Lacs (BDEGL) at Goma, Democratic Republic of the Congo; an energy centre at Bujumbura, Burundi; the Institute of Agronomic and Zootechnical Research, Gitega, Burundi; and a regional electricity company (SINELAC) at Bukavu, Democratic Republic of the Congo; mems: Burundi, Democratic Republic of the Congo, Rwanda; Exec. Sec. HERMAN TUYAGA (Burundi); publs *Grands Lacs* (quarterly review), *Journal* (annually).

Gambia River Basin Development Organization (Organisation pour la mise en valeur du fleuve Gambie—OMVG): BP 2353, 13 passage Leblanc, Dakar, Senegal; tel. 822-31-59; fax 822-59-26; e-mail omvg@omvg.sn; f. 1978 by Senegal and The Gambia; Guinea joined in 1981 and Guinea-Bissau in 1983. A masterplan for the integrated development of the Kayanga/Geba and Koliba/Corubal river basins has been developed, encompassing a projected natural resources management project; a hydraulic development plan for the Gambia river was formulated during 1996–98; a pre-feasibility study on connecting the national electric grids of the four member states has been completed, and a feasibility study for the construction of the proposed Sambangalou hydroelectric dam, was undertaken in the early 2000s; maintains documentation centre; Exec. Sec. JUSTINO VIEIRA.

Group of 15 (G15): G15 Technical Support Facility, 1 route des Morillons, CP 2100, 1218 Grand Saconnex, Geneva, Switzerland; tel. 227916701; fax 227916169; e-mail tsf@g15.org; internet www.g15.org; f. 1989 by 15 developing nations during the ninth summit of the Non-Aligned Movement; retains its original name although current membership totals 17; convenes biennial summits to address the global economic and political situation and to promote economic development through South-South co-operation and North-South dialogue; mems: Algeria, Argentina, Brazil, Chile, Egypt, India, Indonesia, Iran, Jamaica, Kenya, Malaysia, Mexico, Nigeria, Senegal, Sri Lanka, Venezuela, Zimbabwe; Head of Office AUDU A. KADIRI.

Group of 77 (G77): c/o UN Headquarters, Rm NL-2077, New York, NY 10017, USA; tel. (212) 963-0192; fax (212) 963-1753; e-mail secretariat@g77.org; internet www.g77.org; f. 1964 by the 77 signatory states of the 'Joint Declaration of the Seventy-Seven Countries' (the G77 retains its original name, owing to its historic significance, although its membership has expanded since inception); first ministerial meeting, held in Algiers, Algeria, in Oct. 1967, adopted the Charter of Algiers as a basis for G77 co-operation; subsequently G77 Chapters were established with liaison offices in Geneva (UNCTAD), Nairobi (UNEP), Paris (UNESCO), Rome (FAO/IFAD), Vienna (UNIDO), and the Group of 24 (G24) in Washington, DC (IMF and World Bank); as the largest intergovernmental organization of developing states in the United Nations the G77 aims to enable developing nations to articulate and promote their collective economic interests and to improve their negotiating capacity with regard to global economic issues within the UN system; in Sept. 2006 G77 ministers of foreign affairs, and the People's Republic of China, endorsed the establishment of a new Consortium on Science, Technology and Innovation for the South (COSTIS); a chairperson, who also acts as spokesperson, co-ordinates the G77's activities in each Chapter; the chairmanship rotates on a regional basis between Africa, Asia, and Latin America and the Caribbean; the supreme decision-making body of the G77 is the South Summit, normally convened at five-yearly intervals (2005: Doha, Qatar; the third Summit was scheduled to be convened in Africa, during 2012); the annual meeting of G77 ministers of foreign affairs is convened at the start (in September) of the regular session of the UN General Assembly; periodic sectoral ministerial meetings are organized in preparation for UNCTAD sessions and prior to the UNIDO and UNESCO General Conferences, and with the aim of promoting South-South co-operation; other special ministerial meetings are also convened from time to time; the first G77 Ministerial Forum on Water Resources was convened in February 2009, in Muscat, Oman; mems: 132 developing countries.

Indian Ocean Commission (IOC) (Commission de l'Océan Indien—COI): Blue Tower, 13th Floor, BP 7, Ebene, Mauritius; tel. 402-6100; fax 465-6798; e-mail secretariat@coi-ioc.org; internet www.coi-ioc.org; f. 1982 to promote regional co-operation, particularly in economic development; projects include tuna-fishing development, protection and management of environmental resources and strengthening of meteorological services; tariff reduction is also envisaged; in Oct. 2011 the Council of Ministers determined to establish an Anti-Piracy Unit within the secretariat; organizes an annual regional trade fair; mems: the Comoros, France (representing the French Overseas Department of Réunion), Madagascar, Mauritius, Seychelles; Sec.-Gen. JEAN-CLAUDE DE L'ESTRAC (Mauritius); publ. *La Lettre de l'Océan Indien*.

Indian Ocean Rim Association for Regional Co-operation (IOR–ARC): Nexteracom Tower 1, 3rd Floor, Ebene, Mauritius; tel. 454-1717; fax 468-1161; e-mail iorarcsec@iorarc.org; internet www.iorarc.org; the first intergovernmental meeting of countries in the region to promote an Indian Ocean Rim initiative was convened in March 1995; charter to establish the Asscn was signed at a ministerial meeting in March 1997; aims to promote the sustained growth and balanced devt of the region and of its mem. states and to create common ground for regional economic co-operation, *inter alia* through trade, investment, infrastructure, tourism, and science and technology; 13th meeting of the Working Group of Heads of Missions held in April 2012 (Pretoria, South Africa); mems: Australia, Bangladesh, India, Indonesia, Iran, Kenya, Madagascar, Malaysia, Mauritius, Mozambique, Oman, Singapore, South Africa, Sri Lanka, Tanzania, Thailand, United Arab Emirates and Yemen. Dialogue Partner countries: People's Republic of China, Egypt, France, Japan, United Kingdom. Observers: Indian Ocean Research Group (IORG) Inc., Indian Ocean Tourism Org; Sec.-Gen. K. V. BHAGIRATH.

Lake Chad Basin Commission (LCBC): BP 727, N'Djamena, Chad; tel. 52-41-45; fax 52-41-37; e-mail lcbc@intnet.td; internet www.cblt.org; f. 1964 to encourage co-operation in developing the Lake Chad region and to promote the settlement of regional disputes; work programmes emphasize the regulation of the utilization of water and other natural resources in the basin; the co-ordination of natural resources development projects and research; holds annual summit of heads of state; mems: Cameroon, Central African Republic, Chad, Niger, Nigeria; Exec. Sec. MUHAMMAD SANI ADAMU; publ. *Bibliographie générale de la CBLT* (2 a year).

Liptako-Gourma Integrated Development Authority (LGA): POB 619, ave M. Thevenond, Ouagadougou, Burkina Faso; tel. (3) 30-61-48; f. 1970; scope of activities includes water infrastructure, telecommunications and construction of roads and railways; in 1986 undertook study on development of water resources in the basin of the Niger river (for hydroelectricity and irrigation); mems: Burkina Faso, Mali, Niger; Chair. SEYDOU BOUDA (Mali).

Mano River Union: Private Mail Bag 133, Delco House, Lightfoot Boston St, Freetown, Sierra Leone; tel. (22) 226883; e-mail sg@manoriveruniononline.org; internet www.manoriveruniononline.org; f. 1973 to establish a customs and economic union between member states to accelerate development via integration; a common external tariff was instituted in 1977. Intra-union free trade was officially introduced in May 1981, as the first stage in progress towards a customs union. A non-aggression treaty was signed by heads of state in 1986. The Union was inactive for three years until mid-1994, owing to regional conflict and disagreements regarding funding. In Jan. 1995 a Mano River Centre for Peace and Development was established, to provide a permanent mechanism for conflict prevention and resolution, and monitoring of human rights violations, and to promote sustainable peace and development. A new security structure was approved in 2000. In Aug. 2001 ministers of foreign affairs, security, internal affairs, and justice, meeting as the Joint Security Committee, resolved to deploy joint border security and confidence-building units, and to work to re-establish the free movement of people and goods; implements programmes in the following areas: institutional revitalisation, restructuring and development; peace and security; economic development and regional integration; and social development; mems: Guinea, Liberia, Sierra Leone; Sec.-Gen. Dr HADJA SARAN DARABA KABBA.

Niger Basin Authority (Autorité du Bassin du Niger): BP 729, Niamey, Niger; tel. 20724395; fax 20724208; e-mail sec-executif@abn.ne; internet www.abn.ne; f. 1964 (as River Niger Commission; name changed 1980) to harmonize national programmes concerned with the River Niger Basin and to execute an integrated development plan; compiles statistics; regulates navigation; runs projects on hydrological forecasting, environmental control; infrastructure and agro-pastoral development; mems: Benin, Burkina Faso, Cameroon, Chad, Côte d'Ivoire, Guinea, Mali, Niger, Nigeria; Exec. Sec. Maj.-Gen. COLLINS REMY UMUNAKWE IHEKIRE; publ. *NBA-INFO* (quarterly).

Nile Basin Initiative: POB 192, Entebbe, Uganda; tel. (41) 321424; fax (41) 320971; e-mail nbisec@nilebasin.org; internet www.nilebasin.org; f. 1999; aims to achieve sustainable socio-economic development through the equitable use and benefits of the Nile Basin water resources and to create an enabling environment for the implementation of programmes with a shared vision. Highest authority is the Nile Basin Council of Ministers (Nile-COM); other activities undertaken by a Nile Basin Technical Advisory Committee (Nile-TAC); mems: Burundi, Democratic Republic of the Congo,

Egypt, Eritrea, Ethiopia, Kenya, Rwanda, Sudan, Tanzania, Uganda; Chair. CHARITY K. NGILU (Kenya).

OPEC Fund for International Development: Postfach 995, 1010 Vienna, Austria; tel. (1) 515-64-0; fax (1) 513-92-38; e-mail info@ofid.org; internet www.ofid.org; f. 1976 by mem. countries of OPEC, to provide financial co-operation and assistance in support of social and economic development in low-income countries, and to promote co-operation between OPEC countries and other developing states; in 2011 new approvals amounted to US $758.5m., of which 49% was for Africa, 31% for Asia, 15% for Latin America and the Caribbean, and 5% for Europe; Dir-Gen. SULEIMAN J. AL-HERBISH (Saudi Arabia); publs *Annual Report*, *OPEC Fund Newsletter* (3 a year).

Organization for the Development of the Senegal River (Organisation pour la mise en valeur du fleuve Sénégal—OMVS): c/o Haut-Commissariat, 46 rue Carnot, BP 3152, Dakar, Senegal; tel. 859-81-81; fax 864-01-63; e-mail omvssphc@omvs.org; internet www.omvs.org; f. 1972 to promote the use of the Senegal river for hydroelectricity, irrigation and navigation; the Djama dam in Senegal provides a barrage to prevent salt water from moving upstream, and the Manantali dam in Mali is intended to provide a reservoir for irrigation of about 375,000 ha of land and for production of hydroelectricity and provision of year-round navigation for ocean-going vessels. In 1997 two companies were formed to manage the dams: Société de gestion de l'énergie de Manantali (SOGEM) and Société de gestion et d'exploitation du barrage de Djama (SOGED); mems: Guinea, Mali, Mauritania, Senegal; High Commissioner MOHAMED SALEM OULD MERZOUG (Mauritania).

Organization for the Management and Development of the Kagera River Basin (Organisation pour l'aménagement et le développement du bassin de la rivière Kagera—OBK): BP 297, Kigali, Rwanda; tel. (7) 84665; fax (7) 82172; f. 1978; envisages joint development and management of resources, including the construction of an 80-MW hydroelectric dam at Rusumo Falls, on the Rwanda-Tanzania border, a 2,000-km railway network between the four member countries, road construction (914 km), and a telecommunications network between member states; mems: Burundi, Rwanda, Tanzania, Uganda.

Pan-African Institute for Development (PAID): BP 1756, Ouagadougou 01, Burkina Faso; tel. 5036-4807; fax 5036-4730; e-mail ipdaos@fasonet.bf; internet www.ipd-aos.org; f. 1964; gives training to people from African countries involved with development at grassroots, intermediate and senior levels; emphasis is given to: development management and financing; agriculture and rural development; issues of gender and development; promotion of small and medium-sized enterprises; training policies and systems; environment, health and community development; research, support and consultancy services; and specialized training. There are four regional institutes: Central Africa (Douala, Cameroon), Sahel (Ouagadougou, Burkina Faso), West Africa (Buéa, Cameroon), Eastern and Southern Africa (Kabwe, Zambia) and a European office in Geneva; publs *Newsletter* (2 a year), *Annual Progress Report*, *PAID Report* (quarterly).

Partners in Population and Development (PPD): IPH Bldg, 2nd Floor, Mohakhali, Dhaka 1212, Bangladesh; tel. (2) 988-1882; fax (2) 882-9387; e-mail partners@ppdsec.org; internet www.partners-popdev.org; f. 1994; aims to implement the decisions of the International Conference on Population and Development, held in Cairo, Egypt in 1994, in order to expand and improve South-South collaboration in the fields of family planning and reproductive health; administers a Visionary Leadership Programme, a Global Leadership Programme, and other training and technical advisory services; mems: 24 developing countries; Exec. Dir Dr JOE THOMAS.

Permanent Interstate Committee on Drought Control in the Sahel (Comité permanent inter états de lutte contre la sécheresse au Sahel—CILSS): POB 7049, Ouagadougou 03, Burkina Faso; tel. 50-37-41-25; fax 50-37-41-32; e-mail cilss.se@cilss.bf; internet www.cilss.bf; f. 1973; works in co-operation with UNDP Drylands Development Centre; aims to combat the effects of chronic drought in the Sahel region, by improving irrigation and food production, halting deforestation and creating food reserves; initiated a series of projects to improve food security and to counter poverty, entitled Sahel 21; the heads of state of all members had signed a convention for the establishment of a Fondation pour le Développement Durable du Sahel; maintains Institut du Sahel at Bamako (Mali) and centre at Niamey (Niger); mems: Burkina Faso, Cape Verde, Chad, The Gambia, Guinea-Bissau, Mali, Mauritania, Niger, Senegal; Pres. BA MAMADOU MBARE (Mauritania); Exec. Sec. ALHOUSSEÏNI BRETAUDEAU (The Gambia); publ. *Reflets Sahéliens* (quarterly).

United Nations African Institute for Economic Development and Planning (IDEP) (Institut africain de développement économique et de planification): rue du 18 Juin, BP 3186, Dakar, Senegal; tel. 823-10-20; fax 822-29-64; e-mail unidep@unidep.org; internet www.unidep.org; f. 1963 by UN ECA to train economic development planners, conduct research and provide advisory services; has library of books, journals and documents; mems: 53 mem. states; Dir ADEBAYO OLUKOSHI.

World Economic Forum: 91–93 route de la Capite, 1223 Cologny/Geneva, Switzerland; tel. 228691212; fax 227862744; e-mail contact@weforum.org; internet www.weforum.org; f. 1971; the Forum comprises commercial interests gathered on a non-partisan basis, under the stewardship of the Swiss Government, with the aim of improving society through economic development; convenes an annual meeting in Davos, Switzerland; organizes the following programmes: Technology Pioneers; Women Leaders; and Young Global Leaders; and aims to mobilize the resources of the global business community in the implementation of the following initiatives: the Global Health Initiative; the Disaster Relief Network; the West-Islamic World Dialogue; and the G20/International Monetary Reform Project; the Forum is governed by a guiding Foundation Board; an advisory International Business Council; and an administrative Managing Board; regular mems: representatives of 1,000 leading commercial companies in 56 countries world-wide; selected mem. companies taking a leading role in the movement's activities are known as 'partners'; Chair. KLAUS SCHWAB.

Economics and Finance

African Insurance Organization (AIO): 30 ave de Gaulle, BP 5860, Douala, Cameroon; tel. 33-42-01-63; fax 33-43-20-08; e-mail info@africaninsurance.net; internet www.african-insurance.org; f. 1972 to promote the expansion of the insurance and reinsurance industry in Africa, and to increase regional co-operation; holds annual conference, periodic seminars and workshops, and arranges meetings for reinsurers, brokers, consultant and regulators in Africa; has established African insurance 'pools' for aviation, petroleum and fire risks, and created asscns of African insurance educators, supervisory authorities and insurance brokers and consultants; Sec.-Gen. P. M. G. SOARES; publ. *African Insurance Annual Review*.

African Reinsurance Corporation (Africa-Re): Africa Re House, Plot 1679, Karimu Kotun St, Victoria Island, PMB 12765, Lagos, Nigeria; tel. (1) 2626660; fax (1) 2663282; e-mail info@africa-re.com; internet www.africa-re.com; f. 1976; its purpose is to foster the development of the insurance and reinsurance industry in Africa and to promote the growth of national and regional underwriting capacities; auth. cap. US $100m., of which the African Development Bank holds 10%; mems: 41 countries, 5 development finance institutions, and some 110 insurance and reinsurance companies; Chair. MUSA AL-NAAS; Man. Dir and CEO CORNEILLE KAREKEZI; publ. *The African Reinsurer* (annually).

African Rural and Agricultural Credit Association (AFRACA): ACK Garden House, 2nd Floor, POB 41378–00100, Nairobi, Kenya; tel. (20) 2717911; fax (20) 2710082; e-mail afraca@africaonline.co.ke; internet www.afraca.org; f. 1977 to develop the rural finance environment by adopting and promoting policy frameworks and assisting sustainable financial institutions to increase outreach; 86 mems in 27 African countries, including central, commercial and agricultural banks, micro-finance institutions, and national programmes working in the area of agricultural and rural finance in the continent; Chair. JULES ASSANGO BONDOMBE; publs *Afraca Workshop Reports*, *Rural Finance Reports*.

Association of African Central Banks (AACB): Ave Abdoulaye Fadiga, BP 3108, Dakar, Senegal; tel. 839-05-00; fax 839-08-01; e-mail akangni@bceao.int; internet www.aacb.org; f. 1968 to promote contacts in the monetary and financial sphere, in order to increase co-operation and trade among member states; aims to strengthen monetary and financial stability on the African continent; since 2002 administers an African Monetary Co-operation Programme; mems: 40 African central banks representing 47 states; Chair. Dr PERKS LIGOYA; Exec. Sec. SAMUEL MÉANGO.

Association of African Development Finance Institutions (AADFI): Immeuble AIAFD, blvd Latrille, rue J61, Cocody Deux Plateaux, Abidjan 0, Côte d'Ivoire; tel. 22-52-33-89; fax 22-52-25-84; e-mail info@adfi-ci.org; internet www.aadfi.org; f. 1975; aims to promote co-operation among financial institutions in the region in matters relating to economic and social development, research, project design, financing and the exchange of information; mems: 92 in 43 African and non-African countries; Chair. PETER M. NONI; Sec.-Gen. JOSEPH AMIHERE; publs *Annual Report*, *AADFI Information Bulletin* (quarterly), *Finance and Development in Africa* (2 a year).

East African Development Bank: 4 Nile Ave, POB 7128, Kampala, Uganda; tel. (417) 112900; fax (41) 259763; e-mail info@eadb.org; internet www.eadb.org; f. 1967 by the former East African Community to promote regional development within Kenya, Tanzania and Uganda, which each hold 24.07% of the equity capital; Kenya, Tanzania and Uganda each hold 27.2% of the equity capital; the remaining equity is held by the African Development Bank

(6.8%), Rwanda (4.3%) and other institutional investors; Dir-Gen. VIVIENNE YEDA APOPO.

Equator Principles Association: tel. (1621) 853-900; fax (1621) 731-483; e-mail secretariat@equator-principles.com; internet www.equator-principles.com; f. July 2010; aims to administer and develop further the Equator Principles, first adopted in 2003, with the support of the International Finance Corporation, as a set of industry standards for the management of environmental and social risk in project financing; a Strategic Review conference was convened in Beijing, People's Republic of China, in Dec. 2010; 70 signed-up Equator Principles Financial Institutions (EPFIs); Administrators JOANNA CLARK, SAMANTHA HOSKINS.

Financial Action Task Force (FATF) (Groupe d'action financière—GAFI): 2 rue André-Pascal, 75775 Paris Cedex 16, France; tel. 1-45-24-79-45; fax 1-44-30-61-37; e-mail contact@fatf-gafi.org; internet www.fatf-gafi.org; f. 1989, on the recommendation of the Group of Seven industrialized nations (G7), to develop and promote policies to combat money laundering and the financing of terrorism; formulated a set of recommendations (40+9) for countries world-wide to implement; established partnerships with regional task forces in the Caribbean, Asia-Pacific, Central Asia, Europe, East and South Africa, the Middle East and North Africa and South America; mems: 34 state jurisdictions, the European Commission, and the Cooperation Council for the Arab States of the Gulf; observers: India, Basel Committee on Banking Supervision, Eurasian Group (EAG) on combating money laundering and financing of terrorism; Pres. BJØRN SKOGSTAD AAMO (Italy); Exec. Sec. RICK MCDONELL; publs *Annual Report*, *e-Bulletin*.

Financial Stability Board: c/o BIS, Centralbahnplatz 2, 4002 Basel, Switzerland; tel. 612808298; fax 612809100; e-mail fsb@bis.org; internet www.financialstabilityboard.org; f. 1999 as the Financial Stability Forum, name changed in April 2009; brings together senior representatives of national financial authorities, international financial institutions, international regulatory and supervisory groupings and committees of central bank experts and the European Central Bank; aims to promote international financial stability and strengthen the functioning of the financial markets; in March 2009 agreed to expand its membership to include all Group of 20 (G20) economies, as well as Spain and the European Commission; in April 2009 the meeting of G20 heads of state and government determined to re-establish the then Forum as the Financial Stability Board, strengthen its institutional structure (to include a plenary body, a steering committee and three standing committees concerned with Vulnerabilities Assessment; Supervisory and Regulatory Co-operation; and Standards Implementation) and expand its mandate to enhance its effectiveness as an international mechanism to promote financial stability; the Board was to strengthen its collaboration with the International Monetary Fund, and conduct joint 'early warning exercises'; in Dec. 2009 the Board initiated a peer review of implementation of the Principles and Standards for Sound Compensation Practices; in Nov. 2010 determined to establish six FSB regional consultative groups; Chair. MARK CARNEY (Canada).

Fonds Africain de Garantie et de Co-opération Economique (FAGACE) (African Guarantee and Economic Co-operation Fund): 01 BP 2045 RP, Cotonou, Benin; tel. 30-03-76; fax 30-02-84; e-mail fagace_dg@yahoo.fr; internet www.le-fagace.org; commenced operations in 1981; guarantees loans for development projects, provides loans and grants for specific operations and supports national and regional enterprises; mems: 13 African countries; Dir-Gen. HENRI MARIE JEANNENEY DONDRA.

Intergovernmental Group of 24 (G24) on International Monetary Affairs and Development: 700 19th St, NW, Rm 3-600 Washington, DC 20431, USA; tel. (202) 623-6101; fax (202) 623-6000; e-mail g24@g24.org; internet www.g24.org; f. 1971; aims to co-ordinate the position of developing countries on monetary and development finance issues; operates at the political level of ministers of finance and governors of central banks, and also at the level of government officials; mems (Africa): Algeria, Côte d'Ivoire, DRC, Egypt, Ethiopia, Gabon, Ghana, Nigeria, South Africa; (Latin America and the Caribbean): Argentina, Brazil, Colombia, Guatemala, Mexico, Peru, Trinidad and Tobago and Venezuela; (Asia and the Middle East): India, Iran, Lebanon, Pakistan, Philippines, Sri Lanka and Syrian Arab Republic; the People's Republic of China has the status of special invitee at G24 meetings; G77 participant states may attend G24 meetings as observers.

Islamic Financial Services Board: Sasana Kijang, Level 5, Bank Negara Malaysia, 2 Jalan Dato Onn, 50840 Kuala Lumpur, Malaysia; tel. (3) 91951400; fax (3) 91951405; e-mail ifsb_sec@ifsb.org; internet www.ifsb.org; f. 2002; aims to formulate standards and guiding principles for regulatory and supervisory agencies working within the Islamic financial services industry; mems: 187 mems, incl. 53 regulatory and supervisory authorities, 8 orgs (including the World Bank, International Monetary Fund, Bank for International Settlements, Islamic Development Bank, Asian Development Bank) and 126 firms and industry asscns; Sec.-Gen. JASEEM AHMED.

West African Bankers' Association (WABA): 11–13 Ecowas St, PM Bag 1012, Freetown, Sierra Leone; tel. (22) 226752; fax (22) 229024; e-mail aabosi@waba-abao.org; internet www.wabaonline.org; f. 1981; aims to strengthen links between banks in West Africa, to enable exchange of information, and to contribute to regional economic development; holds annual general assembly; mems: 217 commercial banks in 15 West African countries; Sec.-Gen. AGBAI ABOSI; publ. *West African Banking Almanac*.

Education

Association for the Development of Education in Africa: c/o Temporary Relocation Agency, 13 ave du Ghana, BP 323, 1002 Tunis, Tunisia; tel. 71-10-39-00; e-mail adea@afdb.org; internet www.adeanet.org; f. 1988 as Donors to African Education, adopted present name in 1995; aims to enhance collaboration in the support of African education; promotes policy dialogue and undertakes research, advocacy and capacity-building in areas of education in sub-Saharan Africa through programmes and working groups comprising representatives of donor countries and African ministries of education; Exec. Sec. AHLIN BYLL-CATARIA.

Association of African Universities (AAU) (Association des universités africaines): POB 5744, Accra-North, Ghana; tel. (21) 774495; fax (21) 774821; e-mail info@aau.org; internet www.aau.org; f. 1967 to promote exchanges, contact and co-operation among African university institutions and to collect and disseminate information on research and higher education in Africa; mems: 272 in 46 countries; Pres. a.i. GEORGE ALBERT MAGOHA (Kenya); Sec.-Gen. Prof. OLUGBEMIRO JEGEDE (Nigeria); publs *AAU Newsletter* (3 a year), *Directory of African Universities* (every 2 years).

Pan-African Association for Literacy and Adult Education: Rue 10, Bldg. 306, POB 21783, Ponty, Dakar, Senegal; tel. 825-48-50; fax 824-44-13; e-mail anafa@sentoo.sn; f. 2000 to succeed African Asscn for Literacy and Adult Education (f. 1984); Co-ordinator Dr LAMINE KANE.

Southern and Eastern Africa Consortium for Monitoring Educational Quality: e-mail info@sacmeq.org; internet www.sacmeq.org; f. 1995; aims to undertake integrated research and training activities in order to develop the capacities of education planners to enhance the evaluation and monitoring of the condition of schools and the quality of education; receives technical assistance from UNESCO International Institute for Educational Planning (IIEP); mems: Ministries of Education in 15 countries of the region; Dir a.i. Dr DEMUS MAKUWA.

West African Examinations Council (WAEC) (Conseil des examens de l'Afrique orientale): POB GP125, Accra, Ghana; tel. (30) 2248967; fax (30) 2222905; e-mail waechqrs@africaonline.com.gh; internet www.waecheadquartersgh.org; f. 1952; administers prescribed examinations in mem. countries; aims to harmonize examinations procedures and standards. Offices in each mem. country and in London, United Kingdom; mems: The Gambia, Ghana, Liberia, Nigeria, Sierra Leone; Chair. Prof. PIUS A. I. OBANYA; Registrar Dr IYI J. UWADIAE.

Environmental Conservation

African Conservation Foundation: POB 189, Buéa, Cameroon; e-mail info@africanconservation.org; internet www.africanconservation.org; f. 1999 as an Africa-wide network for information exchange and capacity building towards environmental conservation; aims to improve management and utilization of natural resources to reconcile development needs in the region with biodiversity conservation; Dir AREND DE HAAS; Country Dir LOUIS NKEMBI.

Conservation International: 2011 Crystal Drive, Suite 500, Arlington, VA 22202, USA; tel. (703) 341-2400; internet www.conservation.org; f. 1987; aims to demonstrate to governments, institutions and corporations that sustainable global development is necessary for human well-being, and provides strategic, technical and financial support to partners at local, national and regional level to facilitate balancing conservation actions with development objectives and economic interests; focuses on the following priority areas: biodiversity hotspots (34 threatened habitats: 13 in Asia and the Pacific; eight in Africa; five in South America; four in North and Central America and the Caribbean; and four in Europe and Central Asia) that cover just 2.3% of the Earth's surface and yet hold at least 50% of plant species and some 42% of terrestrial vertebrate species); high biodiversity wilderness areas (five areas retaining at least 70% of their original vegetation: Amazonia; the Congo Basin; New Guinea; North American deserts—covering northern parts of Mexico and southwestern areas of the USA; and the Miomo-Mopane woodlands and savannas of southern Africa); and oceans and seascapes; organized Summit for Sustainability in Africa in May 2012, in Gaborone, Botswana; maintains offices in more than 30 countries world-wide; partners: governments, businesses, local communities, non-profit orgs and universities world-wide; Chair. and CEO PETER SELIGMANN.

Consortium for Ocean Leadership: 1201 New York Ave, NW, Suite 420, Washington, DC 20005, USA; tel. (202) 232-3900; fax (202) 462-8754; e-mail info@oceanleadership.org; internet www.oceanleadership.org; f. 2007, following the merger of the Consortium for Oceanographic Research and Education (CORE, f. 1999) and the Joint Oceanographic Institutions (JOI); aims to promote, support and advance the science of oceanography; Pres. ROBERT B. GAGOSIAN.

Global Coral Reef Monitoring Network: POB 772, Townsville MC 4810, Australia; tel. (7) 4721-2699; fax (7) 4772-2808; e-mail clive.wilkinson@rrrc.org.au; internet www.gcrmn.org; f. 1994, as an operating unit of the International Coral Reef Initiative; active in more than 80 countries; aims include improving the management and sustainable conservation of coral reefs, strengthening links between regional organizations and ecological and socioeconomic monitoring networks, and disseminating information to assist the formulation of conservation plans; Global Co-ordinator Dr CLIVE WILKINSON (Australia); publ. *Status of Coral Reefs of the World*.

International Coral Reef Initiative: c/o Australia/Great Barrier Reef Marine Park Authority (GBRMPA), 2–68 Flinders St, POB 1379, Townsville, QLD, 4810, Australia; e-mail icri@gbrmpa.gov.au; internet www.icriforum.org; f. 1994 at the first Conference of the Parties of the Convention on Biological Diversity; a partnership of governments, non-governmental organizations, scientific bodies and the private sector; aims to highlight the degradation of coral reefs and provide a focus for action to ensure the sustainable management and conservation of these and related marine ecosystems; in 1995 issued a Call to Action and a Framework for Action; the Secretariat is co-chaired by a developed and a developing country, on a rotational basis among mem. states (2012–13, Australia and Belize); Co-Chair. MARGARET JOHNSON (Australia), BEVERLEY WADE (Belize).

International Renewable Energy Agency: C67 Office Bldg, Khalidiyah (32nd) St, POB 236, Abu Dhabi, United Arab Emirates; tel. (2) 4179000; internet www.irena.org; f. 2009 at a conference held in Bonn, Germany; aims to promote the development and application of renewable sources of energy; to act as a forum for the exchange of information and technology transfer; and to organize training seminars and other educational activities; inaugural Assembly convened in April 2011; mems: 100 states and the EU; at September 2012 a further 58 countries had signed but not yet ratified the founding agreement or had applied to become full mems; Dir-Gen. ADNAN Z. AMIN (Kenya).

IUCN—International Union for Conservation of Nature: 28 rue Mauverney, 1196 Gland, Switzerland; tel. 229990000; fax 229990002; e-mail press@iucn.org; internet www.iucn.org; f. 1948, as the International Union for Conservation of Nature and Natural Resources; supports partnerships and practical field activities to promote the conservation of natural resources, to secure the conservation of biological diversity as an essential foundation for the future; to ensure the equitable and sustainable use of the earth's natural resources; and to guide the development of human communities towards ways of life in enduring harmony with other components of the biosphere, developing programmes to protect and sustain the most important and threatened species and ecosystems and assisting governments to devise and carry out national conservation strategies; incorporates the Species Survival Commission (SSC), a science-based network of volunteer experts aiming to ensure conservation of present levels of biodiversity; compiles annually updated Red List of Threatened Species, comprising in 2011 some 59,508 species, of which 19,265 were threatened with extinction; maintains a conservation library and documentation centre and units for monitoring traffic in wildlife; mems: more than 1,000 states, government agencies, non-governmental organizations and affiliates in some 140 countries; Pres. ASHOK KHOSLA (India); Dir-Gen. JULIA MARTON-LEFÈVRE (USA); publs *World Conservation Strategy*, *Caring for the Earth*, *Red List of Threatened Plants*, *Red List of Threatened Species*, *United Nations List of National Parks and Protected Areas*, *World Conservation* (quarterly), *IUCN Today*.

Wetlands International: POB 471, 6700 AL Wageningen, Netherlands; tel. (318) 660910; fax (318) 660950; e-mail post@wetlands.org; internet www.wetlands.org; f. 1995 by merger of several regional wetlands organizations; aims to protect and restore wetlands, their resources and biodiversity through research, information exchange and conservation activities; promotes implementation of the 1971 Ramsar Convention on Wetlands; Chair. JAN ERNST DE GROOT (Netherlands); CEO JANE MADGWICK.

WWF International: 27 ave du Mont-Blanc, 1196 Gland, Switzerland; tel. 223649111; fax 223648836; e-mail info@wwfint.org; internet www.wwf.panda.org; f. 1961 (as World Wildlife Fund), name changed to World Wide Fund for Nature in 1986, current nomenclature adopted 2001; aims to stop the degradation of natural environments, conserve bio-diversity, ensure the sustainable use of renewable resources, and promote the reduction of both pollution and wasteful consumption; addresses six priority issues: forests, freshwater, marine, species, climate change, and toxics; has identified, and focuses its activities in, 200 'ecoregions' (the 'Global 200'), believed to contain the best part of the world's remaining biological diversity; actively supports and operates conservation programmes in more than 90 countries; mems: 54 offices, 5 associate orgs, c. 5m. individual mems world-wide; Pres. YOLANDA KAKABADSE (Ecuador); Dir-Gen. JAMES P. LEAPE; publs *Annual Report*, *Living Planet Report*.

Government and Politics

Accord de Non-agression et d'Assistance en Matière de Défence (ANAD) (Non-Aggression and Defence Aid Agreement): 08 BP 2065, Abidjan 08, Côte d'Ivoire; tel. 20-21-88-33; fax 20-33-86-13; e-mail colpape@aviso.ci; f. 1977 to serve as a framework for sub-regional co-operation in conflict prevention and resolution; adopted a draft protocol for the establishment of a regional peace-keeping force and a fund to promote peace and security in April 1999; mems: Benin, Burkina Faso, Côte d'Ivoire, Mali, Mauritania, Niger, Senegal, Togo.

African Association for Public Administration and Management (AAPAM): Britak Centre, Ragati and Mara Rds, POB 48677, 00100 GPO, Nairobi, Kenya; tel. (20) 2730555; fax (22) 310102; e-mail aapam@aapam.org; internet www.aapam.org; f. 1971 to promote good practices, excellence and professionalism in public administration through training, seminars, research, publications; convenes regular conferences to share learning experiences among members, and an annual Roundtable Conference; funded by membership contributions, government and donor grants; mems: 500 individual, 50 corporate; Pres. ABDON AGAW JOK NHIAL (South Sudan); Sec.-Gen. Dr YOLAMU R. BARONGO (Uganda); publs *Newsletter* (quarterly), *Annual Seminar Report*, *African Journal of Public Administration and Management* (2 a year), books.

African Parliamentary Union: BP V314, Abidjan, Côte d'Ivoire; tel. 20-30-39-70; fax 20-30-44-05; e-mail upa1@aviso.ci; internet www.african-pu.org; f. 1976 (as Union of African Parliaments); holds annual conference (2012: Kigali, Rwanda, in Nov.); mems: 40 parliaments; Chair, ANGEL SERAFIN SERICHE DOUGAN MALABO (Equatorial Guinea); Sec.-Gen. N'ZI KOFFI.

Afro-Asian Peoples' Solidarity Organization (AAPSO): 89 Abdel Aziz Al-Saoud St, POB 11559-61 Manial El-Roda, Cairo, Egypt; tel. (2) 3636081; fax (2) 3637361; e-mail aapso@idsc.net.eg; internet www.aapsorg.org; f. 1958; acts among and for the peoples of Africa and Asia in their struggle for genuine independence, sovereignty, socio-economic development, peace and disarmament; mems: national committees and affiliated organizations in 66 countries and territories, assoc. mems in 15 European countries; Sec.-Gen. NOURI ABDEL RAZZAK HUSSEIN (Iraq); publs *Solidarity Bulletin* (monthly), *Socio-Economic Development* (3 a year).

Club of Madrid: Carrera de San Jerónimo 15, 3A planta, 28014 Madrid, Spain; tel. (91) 1548230; fax (91) 1548240; e-mail clubmadrid@clubmadrid.org; internet www.clubmadrid.org; f. 2001, following Conference on Democratic Transition and Consolidation; forum of former Presidents and Prime Ministers; aims to strengthen democratic values and leadership; maintains office in Brussels, Belgium; 87 mems. from 60 countries; Pres. WIM KOK (Netherlands); Sec.-Gen. CARLOS WESTENDORP (Spain).

Comunidade dos Países de Língua Portuguesa (CPLP) (Community of Portuguese-Speaking Countries): rua de S. Mamede (ao Caldas) 21, 1100-533 Lisbon, Portugal; tel. (21) 392-8560; fax (21) 392-8588; e-mail comunicacao@cplp.org; internet www.cplp.org; f. 1996; aims to produce close political, economic, diplomatic and cultural links between Portuguese-speaking countries and to strengthen the influence of the Lusophone Commonwealth within the international community; deployed an observer mission to oversee presidential elections held in Timor-Leste in May 2007; in Nov. 2010 adopted, jointly with ECOWAS, the CPLP-ECOWAS road map on reform of the defence and security sector in Guinea-Bissau; mems: Angola, Brazil, Cape Verde, Guinea-Bissau, Mozambique, Portugal, São Tomé and Príncipe, Timor-Leste; assoc. observers: Equatorial Guinea, Mauritius, Senegal; Exec. Sec. DOMINGOS SIMÕES PEREIRA (Guinea-Bissau).

Gulf of Guinea Commission (Commission du Golfe de Guinée—CGG): f. 2001 to promote co-operation among mem. countries, and the peaceful and sustainable development of natural resources in the sub-region; mems: Angola, Cameroon, the Republic of the Congo, Equatorial Guinea, Gabon, Nigeria, São Tomé and Príncipe; in 2012 plans were under way to formulate, in partnership with ECOWAS and CEEAC, a regional strategy aimed at curbing piracy in the Gulf of Guinea, building on a UN assessment mission undertaken in Nov. 2011; Exec. Sec. MIGUEL TROVOADA (São Tomé and Príncipe).

International Conference on the Great Lakes Region, (ICGLR) (Conference Internationale sur la region des grands lacs): POB 7076, Bujumbura, Burundi; e-mail secretariat@icglr.org; internet www.icglr.org; f. 2006 following the signing of the Security, Stability and Development Pact for the Great Lakes Region at the second summit meeting of the International Conference on the Great Lakes Region, held in December, in Nairobi, Kenya; the UN Security Council proposed in 2000 the organization of a Great Lakes Conference to initiate a process that would bring together regional leaders to pursue agreement on a set of principles and to articulate programmes of action to help end the cycle of regional conflict and establish durable peace, stability, security, democracy and development in the whole region; runs the Special Fund for Reconstruction and Development (SFRD) which is hosted and managed by the African Development Bank (AfDB); the first summit meeting of the Conference was convened in Dar es Salaam, Tanzania, in November 2004; executive secretariat created in May 2007; mems: Angola, Burundi, Central African Republic, Democratic Republic of the Congo, Republic of the Congo, Kenya, Rwanda, Sudan, Tanzania, Uganda, Zambia; Exec. Sec. Prof. ALPHONSE LUMU NTUMBA LUABA.

International Institute for Democracy and Electoral Assistance (IDEA): Strömsborg, 103 34 Stockholm, Sweden; tel. (8) 698-3700; fax (8) 20-2422; e-mail info@idea.int; internet www.idea.int; f. 1995; aims to promote sustainable democracy in new and established democracies; works with practitioners and institutions promoting democracy in Africa, Asia, Arab states and Latin America; 27 mem. states and one observer; Sec.-Gen. VIDAR HELGESEN (Norway).

Inter-Parliamentary Union (IPU): 5 chemin du Pommier, CP 330, 1218 Le Grand-Saconnex/Geneva, Switzerland; tel. 229194150; fax 229194160; e-mail postbox@mail.ipu.org; internet www.ipu.org; f. 1889 to promote peace, co-operation and representative democracy by providing a forum for multilateral political debate between representatives of national parliaments; mems: national parliaments of 162 sovereign states; 10 assoc. mems; Pres. ABDELWAHAD RADI (Morocco); Sec.-Gen. ANDERS B. JOHNSSON (Sweden); publs *Chronicle of Parliamentary Elections* (annually), *The World of Parliaments* (quarterly), *World Directory of Parliaments* (annually).

North Atlantic Treaty Organization (NATO): blvd Léopold III, 1110 Brussels, Belgium; tel. (2) 707-41-11; fax (2) 707-45-79; e-mail natodoc@hq.nato.int; internet www.nato.int; NATO implements the objectives of the Atlantic Alliance, which was established on the basis of the 1949 North Atlantic Treaty and aims to provide common security for its members through co-operation and consultation in political, military and economic fields, as well as scientific, environmental, and other non-military aspects; the highest authority of the Alliance is the North Atlantic Council, which meets at the level of permanent representatives of member countries, ministers of foreign affairs, defence ministers, or heads of state or government; in June 2005 the NAC agreed to provide logistical support to the African Union (AU) peace-keeping mission in Darfur, western Sudan (AU Mission in Sudan—AMIS), airlifting supplementary AU peace-keepers into the region; no NATO combat troops, however, were to be deployed to Darfur; NATO established a Senior Military Liaison Officer team, in Addis Ababa, Ethiopia, to liaise with the AU; in June 2006 the AU requested enhanced NATO assistance for AMIS, including the certification of troops allocated to the mission, and support in the establishment of a joint operations centre; in November NATO ministers extended its support for proposals by the AU and UN to undertake a hybrid peace-keeping mission in Darfur; NATO support to AMIS was concluded on 31 December 2007 when the mission was transferred to the UN/AU operation; in June 2007 NATO agreed to support the AU Mission in Somalia (AMISOM) by providing strategic airlifts for deployment of personnel and equipment; during October–December 2008 NATO implemented Operation Allied Provider, which was mandated to protect ships chartered by the World Food Programme to deliver humanitarian aid to Somalia, and to conduct patrols to deter piracy and other criminal acts against merchant shipping in the high risk areas in the Gulf of Aden; NATO resumed its counter-piracy operations in that region in March 2009, under Operation Allied Protector, which was superseded, in August, by Operation Ocean Shield; mems: 28 states; Sec.-Gen. ANDERS FOGH RASMUSSEN (Denmark).

Organisation Internationale de la Francophonie (La Francophonie): 19-21 ave Bosquet, 75007 Paris, France; tel. 1-44-11-12-50; fax 1-44-11-12-80; e-mail oif@francophonie.org; internet www.francophonie.org; f. 1970 as l'Agence de coopération culturelle et technique; promotes co-operation among French-speaking countries in the areas of education, culture, peace and democracy, and technology; implements decisions of the Sommet francophone; technical and financial assistance has been given to projects in every member country, mainly to aid rural people; mems: 56 states and govts; 19 countries with observer status; Sec.-Gen. ABDOU DIOUF (Senegal); publ. *Journal de l'Agence de la Francophonie* (quarterly).

Industrial and Professional Relations

African Regional Organization of ITUC (ITUC-Africa): route Internationale d'Atakpamé, POB 44101, Lomé, Togo; tel. and fax 225-61-13; e-mail info@ituc-africa.org; internet www.ituc-africa.org; f. 2007; mems: 13m. workers in 44 countries; Pres. MODY GUIRO; Gen. Sec. KWASI ADU-AMANKWAH.

Organisation of African Trade Union Unity (OATUU): POB M386, Accra, Ghana; tel. (21) 508855; fax (21) 508851; e-mail oatuu@ighmail.com; f. 1973 as a single continental trade union org., independent of international trade union organizations; has affiliates from all African trade unions. Congress, the supreme policy-making body, is composed of four delegates per country from affiliated national trade union centres, and meets at least every four years; the General Council, composed of one representative from each affiliated trade union, meets annually to implement Congress decisions and to approve the annual budget; mems: trade union movements in 53 independent African countries; Sec.-Gen. Gen. HASSAN A. SUNMONU (Nigeria); publ. *The African Worker*.

Pan-African Employers' Confederation (PEC): c/o Mauritius Employers' Federation (MEF), Ebene Cyber City Ebene, Mauritius; tel. 466-3600; fax 465-8200; e-mail mefmim@intnet.mu; internet www.pec-online.org; f. 1986 to link African employers' organizations and represent them at the AU, UN and the ILO; mems: representation in 39 countries on the continent; Pres. THABO MAKEKA; Sec.-Gen. AZAD JEETUN (Mauritius).

Law

African Intellectual Property Organization (Organisation Africaine de la Propriété Intellectuelle—OAPI): 158 pl. de la prefecture, Yaoundé, Cameroon; tel. 22-20-57-00; fax 22-20-57-00; e-mail oapi@oapi.int; internet www.oapi.int; f. 1962; supports the technological development of member states and promotes the application of patent rights; mems: 16 African states; Dir-Gen. PAULIN EDOU EDOU.

African Society of International and Comparative Law (ASICL): Private Bag 520, Kairaba Ave, KSMD, Banjul, The Gambia; tel. 375476; fax 375469; e-mail africansociety@aol.com; f. 1986; promotes public education on law and civil liberties; aims to provide a legal aid and advice system in each African country, and to facilitate the exchange of information on civil liberties in Africa; publs *Newsletter* (every 2 months), *African Journal of International and Comparative Law* (3 a year).

Asian-African Legal Consultative Organization (AALCO): 29-C, Rizal Marg, Diplomatic Enclave, Chanakyapuri, New Delhi 110057, India; tel. (11) 24197000; fax (11) 26117640; e-mail mail@aalco.int; internet www.aalco.int; f. 1956 to consider legal problems referred to it by member countries and to serve as a forum for Afro-Asian co-operation in international law, including international trade law, and economic relations; provides background material for conferences, prepares standard/model contract forms suited to the needs of the region; promotes arbitration as a means of settling international commercial disputes; trains officers of member states; has permanent UN observer status; has established four International Commercial Arbitration Centres in Kuala Lumpur, Malaysia; Cairo, Egypt; Lagos, Nigeria; and Tehran, Iran; mems: 47 countries; Sec.-Gen. Prof. Dr RAHMAT BIN MOHAMAD (Malaysia).

East African Court of Justice: AICC Bldg, Kilimanjaro Wing, 6th Floor, POB 1096, Arusha, Tanzania; tel. (27) 2504253; fax (27) 2504255; e-mail eacj@eachq.org; internet www.eacj.org/index.php; f. 2001; organ of the East African Community (EAC), established under the Treaty for the Establishment of the EAC with responsibility for ensuring compliance with the Treaty; Registrar Dr JOHN RUHANGISA.

East African Legislative Assembly: POB 1096, AICC Bldg, Arusha, Tanzania; tel. (27) 2504253; internet www.eala.org; f. 2001; established under the EAC's founding Treaty as the legislative organ of the Community; Speaker MARGARET NANTONGO ZZIWA (Uganda).

Inter-African Union of Lawyers (IAUL) (Union interafricaine des avocats): BP14409, Libreville, Gabon; tel. 76-41-44; fax 74-54-01; f. 1980; holds congress every three years; publ. *L'avocat africain* (2 a year).

International Criminal Police Organization (INTERPOL): 200 quai Charles de Gaulle, 69006 Lyon, France; tel. 4-72-44-70-00; fax 4-72-44-71-63; e-mail info@interpol.int; internet www.interpol.int; f. 1923, reconstituted 1946; aims to promote and ensure mutual assistance between police forces in different countries; co-ordinates activities of police authorities of member states in international affairs; works to establish and develop institutions with the aim of preventing transnational crimes; centralizes records and information on international criminals; operates a global police communications network linking all member countries; maintains a Global Database on Maritime Piracy; holds General Assembly annually; mems: 190 countries; Sec.-Gen. RONALD K. NOBLE (USA); publ. *Annual Report*.

International Development Law Organization (IDLO): Viale Vaticano, 106 00165 Rome, Italy; tel. (06) 40403200; fax (06) 40403232; e-mail idlo@idlo.int; internet www.idlo.int; f. 1983; aims to promote the rule of law and good governance in developing countries, transition economies and nations emerging from conflict and to assist countries to establish effective infrastructure to achieve sustainable economic growth, social development, security and access to justice; activities include Policy Dialogues, Technical Assistance, Global Network of Alumni and Partners, Training Programs, Research and Publications; maintains Country Offices for Afghanistan, Kenya, Kyrgyzstan, South Sudan, Somalia (based in Nairobi) and Tajikistan; mems: 27 mems (26 states and the OPEC Fund for International Development); Dir-Gen. IRENE KHAN.

West African Bar Association: 1 Lafia Close, off Ilorin St, Area 8, Garki,, Abuja, Nigeria; fax (229) 21305271; e-mail info@wabalaw.org; internet wabalaw.org; f. 2004; Sec.-Gen. OLAWOLE FAPOHUNDA.

Medicine and Health

Organisation panafricaine de lutte contre le SIDA (OPALS): 15–21 rue de L'École de Médecine, 75006 Paris, France; tel. 1-43-26-72-28; fax 1-43-29-70-93; internet www.opals.asso.fr; f. 1988; disseminates information relating to the treatment and prevention of AIDS; provides training of medical personnel; promotes co-operation between African medical centres and specialized centres in the USA and Europe; Pres. Prof. MARC GENTILINI; Sec.-Gen. Prof. DOMINIQUE RICHARD-LENOBLE; publ. *OPALS Liaison*.

Organization for Co-ordination in the Struggle against Endemic Diseases in Central Africa (Organisation de coordination pour la lutte contre les endémies en Afrique Centrale—OCEAC): BP 288, Yaoundé, Cameroon; tel. 23-22-32; fax 23-00-61; e-mail contact@oceac.org; internet www.oceac.org; f. 1965 to standardize methods of controlling endemic diseases, to co-ordinate national action, and to negotiate programmes of assistance and training on a regional scale; mems: Cameroon, Central African Republic, Chad, Republic of the Congo, Equatorial Guinea, Gabon; Exec. Sec. Dr JEAN JACQUES MOKA; publ. *Bulletin de Liaison et de Documentation* (quarterly).

Posts and Telecommunications

Internet Corporation for Assigned Names and Numbers (ICANN): 4676 Admiralty Way, Suite 330, Marina del Rey, CA 90292-6601, USA; tel. (310) 823-9358; fax (310) 823-8649; e-mail icann@icann.org; internet www.icann.org; f. 1998; non-profit, private sector body; aims to co-ordinate the technical management and policy development of the Internet in relation to addresses, domain names and protocol; supported by an At-Large Advisory Committee (representing individual users of the Internet), a Country Code Names Supporting Organization (ccNSO), a Governmental Advisory Committee, a Generic Names Supporting Organization (GNSO), and a Security and Stability Advisory Committee; through its Internet Assigned Numbers Authority (IANA) department ICANN manages the global co-ordination of domain name system roots and Internet protocol addressing; at 30 June 2011 there were 310 top-level domains (TLDs), 30 of which were in non-Latin scripts, and the most common of which were generic TLDs (gTLDs) (such as .org or .com) and country code TLDs (ccTLDs); in June 2011 ICANN adopted an expanded gTLD programme, under which applications were to be accepted from 2012 from qualified orgs wishing to register domain names of their choosing, including the possibility of Internationalized Domain Names (IDNs) incorporating non-Latin character sets (Arabic, Chinese and Cyrillic), with a view to making the Internet more globally inclusive; details of the first 1,930 filed applications were published in June 2012 ('app' being the most popular), in advance of a seven-month objection period; the International Chamber of Commerce International Centre for Expertise was to administer the objections process; Pres. and CEO AKRAM ATALLAH (Lebanon).

Regional African Satellite Communications System (RASCOM): 2 ave Thomasset, BP 3528, Abidjan 01, Côte d'Ivoire; tel. (225) 20223683; fax (225) 20223676; e-mail rascomps@rascom.org; internet www.rascom.org; f. 1992; aims to provide telecommunications facilities to African countries and supports a regional satellite communication system; mems: 45 countries; Dir-Gen. JONES A. KILLIMBE.

Southern African Telecommunications Association (SATA): Av. Martires de Inhaminga 170-3, POB 2677, Maputo, Mozambique; tel. 21302194; fax 21431288; e-mail jacob.munodawafa@sata-sec.net; internet www.sata-sec.net; f. 1980, present name adopted 1999, following the Southern Africa Development Community (SADC) Treaty and the provisions of the SADC Protocol on Transport, Communications and Meteorology; aims to improve regional co-operation among mems of the SADC and to address common issues in the telecommunications industry; mems: 15 regional telecommunications cos; Exec. Sec. JACOB MUNODAWAFA.

Press, Radio and Television

African Union of Broadcasting (AUB): 101 rue Carnot, BP 3237, Dakar, Senegal; tel. 821-16-25; fax 822-51-13; internet www.aub-uar.org/eng/; f. 1962 as Union of National Radio and Television Organizations of Africa (URTNA), new org. f. Nov. 2006; co-ordinates radio and television services, including monitoring and frequency allocation, the exchange of information and coverage of national and international events among African countries; mems: 48 orgs and 6 assoc. members; Pres. TEWFIK KHELLADI (Algeria), LAWRENCE ADDO-YAO ATIASE (Ghana).

Federation of African Journalists (FAJ): c/o East African Journalists' Association Secretariat, BP 4099, Djibouti; e-mail omar@nusoj.org; f. 2008; defends the freedom of the press, and addresses professional issues affecting journalists; supports a network encompassing the West African Journalists Association, the Southern African Journalists Association, the Eastern African Journalists Association, the Association of Media Professionals Unions of Central Africa, and the Network of North African Journalists; Pres. OMAR FARUK OSMAN NUR (Somalia).

Southern African Broadcasting Association (SABA): Postnet Suite 210, P/Bag X9, Melville 2109, Johannesburg, South Africa; tel. (11) 7144918; fax (11) 7144868; e-mail sabasg@telkomsa.net; f. 1993; promotes quality public broadcasting; facilitates training of broadcasters at all levels; co-ordinates broadcasting activities in the SADC region; organizes radio news exchange service; produces television and radio programmes; mems: corpns in more than 20 countries; Sec.-Gen. ARLINDO LOPES (Mozambique).

Religion

All Africa Conference of Churches (AACC): Waiyaki Way, POB 14205, 00800 Westlands, Nairobi, Kenya; tel. (20) 4441483; fax (20) 4443241; e-mail secretariat@aacc-ceta.org; internet www.aacc-ceta.org; f. 1963; an organ of co-operation and continuing fellowship among Protestant, Orthodox and independent churches and Christian Councils in Africa; 10th Assembly: Kampala, Uganda, in June 2013; mems: 173 churches and affiliated Christian councils in 40 African countries; Pres. Archbishop VALENTINE MOKIWA (Tanzania); Gen. Sec. Rev. Dr ANDRÉ KARAMAGA (Rwanda); publs *ACIS/APS Bulletin*, *Tam Tam*.

World Council of Churches (WCC): 150 route de Ferney, Postfach 2100, 1211 Geneva 2, Switzerland; tel. 227916111; fax 227910361; e-mail info@wcc-coe.org; internet www.wcc-coe.org; f. 1948 to promote co-operation between Christian Churches and to prepare for a clearer manifestation of the unity of the Church; activities are grouped under the following programmes: The WCC and the ecumenical movement in the 21st century; Unity, mission, evangelism and spirituality; Public witness: addressing power, affirming peace; Justice, *diakonia* and responsibility for creation; Education and ecumenical formation; and Inter-religious dialogue and co-operation; mems: 349 Churches in more than 110 countries; Gen. Sec. Dr OLAV FYKSE TVEIT (Norway); publs *Current Dialogue* (2 a year), *Ecumenical News International* (weekly), *Ecumenical Review* (quarterly), *International Review of Mission* (quarterly), *WCC News* (quarterly), *WCC Yearbook*.

Science

Association for the Taxonomic Study of the Flora of Tropical Africa (Association pour l'Etude Taxonomique de la Flore d'Afrique Tropicale—AETFAT): c/o Herbarium, Royal Botanic Gardens, Kew, Surrey, TW9 3AR, United Kingdom; e-mail aetfat-sec@kew.org; internet www.kew.org/aetfat/index.html; f. 1951 to facilitate co-operation and liaison between botanists engaged in the study of the flora of tropical Africa south of the Sahara including Madagascar; holds Congress every three years (April 2010: Antananarivo, Madagascar); maintains a library; mems: c. 800 botanists in 63 countries; Sec.-Gen. Dr SYLVAIN RAZAFIMANDIMBISON; publs *AETFAT Bulletin* (annually), *Proceedings*.

International Council for Science (ICSU): 5 rue Auguste Vacquerie, 75116 Paris, France; tel. 1-45-25-03-29; fax 1-42-88-94-31; e-mail secretariat@icsu.org; internet www.icsu.org; f. 1919 as International Research Council; present name adopted 1998; revised statutes adopted 2011; incorporates national scientific bodies and International Scientific Unions, as well as 19 Interdisciplinary Bodies (international scientific networks established to address specific areas of investigation); through its global network coordinates interdisciplinary research to address major issues of relevance to both science and society; advocates for freedom in the conduct of science, promotes equitable access to scientific data and information, and facilitates science education and capacity-building; General Assembly of representatives of national and scientific members meets every three years to formulate policy. Interdisciplinary Bodies and Joint Initiatives: Future Earth; Urban Health and Well-being; Committee on Space Research (COSPAR); Scientific Committee on Antarctic Research (SCAR); Scientific Committee on Oceanic Research (SCOR); Scientific Committee on Solar-Terrestrial Physics (SCOSTEP); Integrated Research on Disaster Risk (IRDR); Programme on Ecosystem Change and Society (PECS); DIVERSITAS; International Geosphere-Biosphere Programme (IGBP); International Human Dimensions Programme on Global Environmental Change (IHDP); World Climate Research Programme (WCRP); Global Climate Observing System (GCOS); Global Ocean Observing System (GOOS); Global Terrestrial Observing System (GTOS); Committee on Data for Science and Technology (CODATA); International Network for the Availability of Scientific Publications (INASP); Scientific Committee on Frequency Allocations for Radio Astronomy and Space Science (IUCAF); World Data System (WDS); mems: 120 national mems from 140 countries, 31 Int. Scientific Unions; Pres. LEE YUAN-TSEH (Taiwan); publs *Insight* (quarterly), *Annual Report*.

Scientific, Technical and Research Commission of African Unity (OAU/STRC): Nigerian Ports Authority Bldg, PMB 2359, Marina, Lagos, Nigeria; tel. (1) 2633359; fax (1) 2636093; e-mail oaustrcl@hyperia.com; f. 1965 to succeed the Commission for Technical Co-operation in Africa (f. 1954); implements priority programmes of the African Union relating to science and technology for development; supervises the Inter-African Bureau for Animal Resources (Nairobi, Kenya), the Inter-African Bureau for Soils (Lagos, Nigeria) and the Inter-African Phytosanitary Commission (Yaoundé, Cameroon) and several joint research projects; provides training in agricultural management, and conducts pest control programmes; services various inter-African committees of experts, including the Scientific Council for Africa; publishes and distributes specialized scientific books and documents of original value to Africa; organizes training courses, seminars, symposia, workshops and technical meetings; Exec. Sec. Dr MBAYE NDOYE.

Southern and Eastern African Mineral Centre (SEAMIC): POB 9573, Dar es Salaam, Tanzania; tel. (22) 2650-347; fax (22) 2650-319; e-mail seamic@seamic.org; internet www.seamic.org; f. 1977 to promote socio-economic and environmentally responsible mineral sector development in the region; sponsored by mem. states; provides advisory and consultancy services in exploration geology, geophysics, geochemistry, mining and mineral processing; archives and processes geoinformation data; organizes training courses in the areas of geoinformatics; provides minerals related specialized laboratory services; mems: Angola, Comoros, Ethiopia, Kenya, Mozambique, Tanzania, Sudan, Uganda (membership limited to eastern and southern African countries until May 2007; subsequently opened to all African countries); Dir-Gen. KETEMA TADESSE; publ. *Seamic Newsletter* (2 a year).

United Nations University Institute for Natural Resources in Africa (UNU/INRA): ISSER Bldg Complex, Annie Jiagge Rd, University of Ghana, Legon; Private Mail Bag, Kotoka International Airport, Accra, Ghana; tel. (21) 500396; fax (21) 500792; e-mail inra@unu.edu; internet inra.unu.edu; f. 1986 as a research and training centre of the United Nations University (Tokyo, Japan); operational since 1990; aims at human resource development and institutional capacity building through co-ordination with African universities and research institutes in advanced research, training and dissemination of knowledge and information on the conservation and management of Africa's natural resources and their rational utilization for sustainable devt; INRA has a mineral resources unit (MRU) at the University of Zambia in Lusaka; Dir Dr ELIAS TAKOR AYUK; MRU Co-ordinator Prof. STEPHEN SIMUKANGA.

Social Sciences

African Centre for Applied Research and Training in Social Development (ACARTSOD): Africa Centre, Wahda Quarter, Zawia Rd, POB 80606, Tripoli, Libya; tel. (21) 4835103; fax (21) 4835066; e-mail info@acartsod.net; internet www.acartsod.net; f. 1977 under the joint auspices of the ECA and OAU (now AU) to promote and co-ordinate applied research and training in social devt, and to assist in formulating national development strategies; Exec. Dir Dr AHMED SAID FITURI.

Council for the Development of Social Science Research in Africa (CODESRIA): Ave Cheikh, Anta Diop X Canal IV, BP 3304, CP 18524, Dakar, Senegal; tel. 825-98-22; fax 825-12-89; internet www.codesria.org; f. 1973; promotes research, organizes conferences, working groups and information services; mems: research institutes and university faculties and researchers in African countries; Exec. Sec. Dr EBRIMA SALL; publs *Africa Development* (quarterly), *CODESRIA Bulletin* (quarterly), *Index of African Social Science Periodical Articles* (annually), *African Journal of International Affairs* (2 a year), *African Sociological Review* (2 a year), *Afrika Zamani* (annually), *Identity, Culture and Politics* (2 a year), *Afro Arab Selections for Social Sciences* (annually), directories of research.

International African Institute (IAI): School of Oriental and African Studies, Thornhaugh St, Russell Sq., London, WC1H 0XG, United Kingdom; tel. (20) 7898-4420; fax (20) 7898-4419; e-mail iai@soas.ac.uk; internet www.internationalafricaninstitute.org; f. 1926 to promote the study of African peoples, their languages, cultures and social life in their traditional and modern settings; organizes an international seminar programme bringing together scholars from Africa and elsewhere; links scholars in order to facilitate research projects, especially in the social sciences; Chair. Prof. V. Y. MUDIMBE; Hon. Dir Prof. PHILIP BURNHAM; publs *Africa* (quarterly), *Africa Bibliography* (annually).

International Peace Institute: 777 United Nations Plaza, New York, NY 10017-3521, USA; tel. (212) 687-4300; fax (212) 983-8246; e-mail ipi@ipinst.org; internet www.ipacademy.org; f. 1970 (as the International Peace Academy) to promote the prevention and settlement of armed conflicts between and within states through policy research and development; educates government officials in the procedures needed for conflict resolution, peace-keeping, mediation and negotiation, through international training seminars and publications; off-the-record meetings are also conducted to gain complete understanding of a specific conflict; Chair. RITA E. HAUSER; Pres. TERJE ROD-LARSEN.

Southern African Research and Documentation Centre (SARDC): POB 5690, Harare, Zimbabwe; tel. (4) 791141; fax (4) 791271; e-mail sardc@sardc.net; internet www.sardc.net; f. 1987; aims to enhance and disseminate information on political, economic, cultural and social developments in southern Africa; Exec. Dir PHYLLIS JOHNSON.

Third World Forum: 39 Dokki St, POB 43, Orman Giza, Cairo, Egypt; tel. (2) 7488092; fax (2) 7480668; e-mail 20sabry2@gega.net; internet www.forumtiersmonde.net; f. 1975 to link social scientists and others from the developing countries, to discuss alternative development policies and encourage research; maintains regional offices in Egypt, Mexico, Senegal and Sri Lanka; mems: individuals in more than 50 countries.

Social Welfare and Human Rights

African Commission on Human and Peoples' Rights: 31 Bijilo Annex Layout, POB 673, Banjul, The Gambia; tel. 4410505; fax 4410504; e-mail au-banjul@africa-union.org; internet www.achpr.org; f. 1987; mandated to monitor compliance with the African Charter on Human and People's Rights (ratified in 1986); investigates claims of human rights abuses perpetrated by govts that have ratified the Charter (claims may be brought by other African govts, the victims themselves, or by a third party); meets twice a year for 15 days in March and Oct; mems: 11; Exec. Sec. Dr MARY MABOREKE.

Global Migration Group: c/o UNICEF, 3 United Nations Plaza, New York, NY 10017, USA; tel. and fax (212) 906-5001; internet www.globalmigrationgroup.org; f. 2003, as the Geneva Migration Group; renamed as above in 2006; mems: ILO, IOM, UNCTAD, UNDP, United Nations Department of Economic and Social Affairs (UNDESA), UNFPA, OHCHR, UNHCR, UNODC, and the World Bank; holds regular meetings to discuss issues relating to int. migration, chaired by mem. orgs on a six-month rotational basis.

International Federation of Red Cross and Red Crescent Societies (IFRC): 17 chemin des Crêts, Petit-Saconnex, CP 372, 1211 Geneva 19, Switzerland; tel. 227304222; fax 227330395; e-mail secretariat@ifrc.org; internet www.ifrc.org; f. 1919 to prevent and alleviate human suffering and to promote humanitarian activities by national Red Cross and Red Crescent societies; conducts relief operations for refugees and victims of disasters, co-ordinates relief supplies and assists in disaster prevention; pan-African conferences of national Red Cross and Red Crescent societies are convened every four years under the joint auspices of the IFRC and the host government (eighth conference: Oct. 2012, in Addis Ababa, Ethiopia); Pres. TADATERU KONOÉ (Japan); Sec.-Gen. BEKELE GELETA

(Canada/Ethiopia); publs *Annual Report*, *Red Cross Red Crescent* (quarterly), *Weekly News*, *World Disasters Report*, *Emergency Appeal*.

International Organization for Migration (IOM): 17 route des Morillons, CP 71, 1211 Geneva 19, Switzerland; tel. 227179111; fax 227986150; e-mail info@iom.int; internet www.iom.int; f. 1951 as Intergovernmental Committee for Migration; name changed in 1989; a non-political and humanitarian organization, activities include the handling of orderly, planned migration to meet the needs of emigration and immigration countries and the processing and movement of refugees, displaced persons, etc., in need of international migration services; mems: 120 states; observer status is held by 20 states and 71 intergovernmental and non-governmental organizations; Dir-Gen. WILLIAM LACY SWING (USA); publs include *International Migration* (quarterly), *Migration* (quarterly, in English, French and Spanish), *World Migration Report* (every 2 years, in English).

Médecins sans frontières (MSF): 78 rue de Lausanne, CP 116, 1211 Geneva 21, Switzerland; tel. 228498400; fax 228498404; internet www.msf.org; f. 1971; independent medical humanitarian org. composed of physicians and other members of the medical profession; aims to provide medical assistance to victims of war and natural disasters; operates longer-term programmes of nutrition, immunization, sanitation, public health, and rehabilitation of hospitals and dispensaries; awarded the Nobel Peace Prize in 1999; mems: 23 asscns in more than 60 countries world-wide; Pres. Dr UNNI KRISHNAN KARUNAKARA; Sec.-Gen. KRIS TORGESON; publ. *Activity Report* (annually).

Shack/Slum Dwellers International (SDI): POB 14038, Mowbray 7705 Cape Town, South Africa; tel. (21) 689-9408; fax (21) 689-3912; e-mail sdi@courc.co.za; internet www.sdinet.co.za; f. 1996; a transnational network of local shack/slum dweller orgs; mems: community-based orgs in 33 countries; Pres. ARPUTHAM JOCKIN.

Union Africaine de la Mutualité (African Union of Mutuals): Rue Aram, Lot 14, Secteur 7, Hay Riad, Rabat, Morocco; tel. and fax (5) 37570988; internet www.am.org.ma; f. 2007; promotes co-operation among African companies concerned with health care and social insurance; mems: in 18 African countries; Pres. ABDELMOULA ABDELMOUMNI.

Sport and Recreations

Confederation of African Football (Confédération africaine de football—CFA): 3 Abdel Khalek Sarwat St, El Hay El Motamayez, POB 23, 6th October City, Egypt; tel. (2) 38371000; fax (2) 38370006; e-mail info@cafonline.com; internet www.cafonline.com; f. 1957; promotes football in Africa; organizes inter-club competitions and Cup of Nations; General Assembly held every two years; mems: national asscns in 54 countries; Pres. ISSA HAYATOU (Cameroon); Sec.-Gen. HICHAM EL AMRANI (Morocco) (acting); publ. *CAF News* (quarterly).

International Cricket Council: POB 500070, St 69, Dubai Sports City, Emirates Rd, Dubai, UAE; tel. (4) 382-8800; fax (4) 382-8600; e-mail enquiry@icc-cricket.com; internet www.icc-cricket.com; f. 1909 as the governing body for international cricket; holds an annual conference; mems: Australia, Bangladesh, England, India, New Zealand, Pakistan, South Africa, Sri Lanka, West Indies, Zimbabwe, and 23 associate and 13 affiliate mems; Pres. SHARAD PAWAR; CEO HAROON LORGAT.

International Federation of Association Football (Fédération internationale de football association—FIFA): FIFA-Str. 20, POB 8044, Zürich, Switzerland; tel. 432227777; fax 432227878; e-mail media@fifa.org; internet www.fifa.com; f. 1904 to promote the game of association football and foster friendly relations among players and national asscns; to control football and uphold the laws of the game as laid down by the International Football Association Board; to prevent discrimination of any kind between players; and to provide arbitration in disputes between national asscns; organizes World Cup competition every four years (2014: Brazil); the FIFA Executive Committee—comprising the Federation's President, eight vice-presidents and 15 members—meets at least twice a year; in May 2011 FIFA provisionally suspended, with immediate effect, one of the Federation's vice-presidents and a member of the Executive Committee in relation to alleged violations of the Federation's code of ethics relating to the election to the FIFA presidency held on 1 June 2011; mems: 208 national asscns, 6 continental confederations; Pres. JOSEPH (SEPP) BLATTER (Switzerland); Sec.-Gen. JÉRÔME VALCKE (France); publs *FIFA News* (monthly), *FIFA Magazine* (every 2 months) (both in English, French, German and Spanish), *FIFA Directory* (annually), *Laws of the Game* (annually), *Competitions' Regulations* and *Technical Reports* (before and after FIFA competitions).

International Hockey Federation: 61 rue du Valentin, Lausanne, Switzerland; tel. 216410606; fax 216410607; e-mail info@fih.ch; internet www.fih.ch; f. 1924; mems: 127 national asscns; Pres. LEANDRO NEGRE (Spain); CEO KELLY G. FAIRWEATHER (South Africa).

International Olympic Committee (IOC): Château de Vidy, 1007 Lausanne, Switzerland; tel. 216216111; fax 216216216; internet www.olympic.org; f. 1894 to ensure the regular celebration of the Olympic Games; the IOC is the supreme authority on all questions concerning the Olympic Games and the Olympic movement; Olympic Games held every four years (summer games 2012: London, United Kingdom, 2016: Rio de Janeiro, Brazil; winter games 2014: Sochi, Russia; youth games 2014: Nanjing, People's Republic of China); mems: 115 representatives; Pres. Dr JACQUES ROGGE (Belgium); publ. *Olympic Review* (quarterly).

International Rugby Board: Huguenot House, 35-38 St Stephen's Green, Dublin 2, Ireland; tel. (1) 240-9200; fax (1) 240-9201; e-mail irb@irb.com; internet www.irb.com; f. 1886; serves as the world governing and law-making body for the game of rugby union; supports education and development of the game and promotes it through regional and world tournaments; since 1987 has organized a Rugby World Cup every four years (2011: New Zealand); holds General Assembly every two years; mems: 97 national unions as full mems, 20 assoc. mems and six regional asscns; Chair. BERNARD LAPASSET; Acting CEO ROBERT BROPHY.

Technology

African Organization of Cartography and Remote Sensing: 5 route de Bedjarah, BP 102, Hussein Dey, Algiers, Algeria; tel. (21) 23-17-17; fax (21) 23-33-39; e-mail sg2@oact.dz; f. 1988 by amalgamation of African Association of Cartography and African Council for Remote Sensing; aims to encourage the development of cartography and of remote sensing by satellites; organizes conferences and other meetings, promotes establishment of training institutions; maintains four regional training centres (in Burkina Faso, Kenya, Nigeria and Tunisia); mems: national cartographic institutions of 24 African countries; Sec.-Gen. ANWER SIALA.

African Regional Centre for Technology: Imm. Fahd, 17th Floor, blvd Djilly Mbaye, BP 2435, Dakar, Senegal; tel. 823-77-12; fax 823-77-13; e-mail arct@sonatel.senet.net; f. 1977 to encourage the development of indigenous technology and to improve the terms of access to imported technology; assists the establishment of national centres; mems: govts of 31 countries; Exec. Dir. Dr OUSMANE KANE; publs *African Technodevelopment*, *Alert Africa*.

Regional Centre for Mapping of Resources for Development (RCMRD): POB 632, 00618 Ruaraka, Nairobi, Kenya; tel. (20) 8560227; fax (20) 8561673; e-mail rcmrd@rcmrd.org; internet www.rcmrd.org; f. 1975; present name adopted 1997; provides services for the professional techniques of map-making and the application of satellite and remote sensing data in resource analysis and development planning; undertakes research and provides advisory services to African governments; mems: 18 signatory govts; Dir-Gen. Dr HUSSEIN O. FARAH.

Regional Centre for Training in Aerospace Surveys (RECTAS) (Centre Regional de Formations aux Techniques des leves aerospatiaux): PMB 5545, Ile-Ife, Nigeria; tel. (803) 384-0581; e-mail info@rectas.org; internet www.rectas.org; f. 1972; provides training, research and advisory services in aerospace surveys and geoinformatics; administered by the ECA; mems: 8 govts; Exec. Dir Prof. ISI IKHUORIA.

Tourism

African Tourism Organization: POB 605, Banjul, The Gambia; tel. 8806047; internet www.african-tourism.org; e-mail ato@african-tourism.org; f. 2002 in response to a World Tourism Consultative meeting in Dakar, Senegal; liaises with travel and tourism industries in Sub-Saharan Africa and a wide network of partners with a focus on responsible and sustainable tourism development; aims to combat human trafficking, sex tourism and exploitation through advocacy networks, awareness-building activities, data collection and dissemination, and capacity building at national and regional levels.

Trade and Industry

African Organization for Standardization (ARSO): POB 57363-00200, Nairobi, Kenya; tel. (20) 224561; fax (20) 218792; e-mail info@arso-oran.org; internet www.arso-oran.org; f. 1977 to promote standardization, quality control, certification and metrology in the African region, to formulate regional standards, and to co-ordinate participation in international standardization activities; mems: 27 African states; Pres. JOSEPH IKEMEFUNA ODUMODU (Nigeria); Sec.-Gen. HERMOGENE NSENGIMANA; publs *ARSO Bulletin* (2 a year), *ARSO Catalogue of Regional Standards* (annually), *ARSO Annual Report*.

African Regional Intellectual Property Organization (ARIPO): POB 4228, Harare, Zimbabwe; tel. (4) 794065; fax (4) 794072; e-mail mail@aripo.org; internet www.aripo.org; f. 1976; grants patents, registers industrial designs and marks, and promotes devt and harmonization of laws concerning industrial property; mems: Botswana, The Gambia, Ghana, Kenya, Lesotho, Liberia, Malawi, Mozambique, Namibia, Rwanda, Sierra Leone, Somalia, Sudan, Swaziland, Tanzania, Uganda, Zambia and Zimbabwe; Dir-Gen. G. H. SIBANDA; publs *ARIPO Magazine* (every 2 months), *Journal* (every 2 months).

African Water Association (Association Africaine de l'Eau): 05 BP 1910, Abidjan 05, Côte d'Ivoire; tel. 21-24-14-43; fax 21-24-26-29; e-mail contact@afwa-hq.org; internet www.afwa-hq.org; f. 1980; facilitates co-operation between public and private bodies concerned with water supply and sewage management in Africa; promotes the study of economic, technical and scientific matters relating to the industry; congress held every two years (16th Congress: Marrakesh, Morocco, Feb. 2012); mems: 70 water and sanitation utilities in 36 countries; Sec.-Gen. SYLVAIN USHER; publ. *AFWA News Magazine* (quarterly).

Federation of West African Chambers of Commerce and Industry (FEWACCI): Aviation House 204, POB CT 5875, Accra, Ghana; tel. (21) 763720; internet www.fewacci.org; f. 1975 to bring together the National Chambers of Commerce of ECOWAS mem. states; Pres. WILSON ATTA KROFAH; CEO CHERNO SALLOW.

Southern African Customs Union: Private Bag 13285, Windhoek, Namibia; tel. (61) 243950; fax (61) 245611; e-mail info@sacu.int; internet www.sacu.int; f. 1969; provides common pool of customs, excise and sales duties, according to the relative volume of trade and production in each country; goods are traded within the union free of duty and quotas, subject to certain protective measures for less developed mems; the South African rand is legal tender in Lesotho, Namibia and Swaziland; the Customs Union Commission meets quarterly in each of the mems' capital cities in turn; mems: Botswana, Lesotho, Namibia, South Africa, Swaziland; Exec. Sec. TSWELOPELE CORNELIA MOREMI.

Union of Producers, Conveyors and Distributors of Electric Power in Africa (UPDEA): 01 BP 1345, Abidjan 01, Côte d'Ivoire; tel. 20-20-60-53; fax 20-33-12-10; e-mail secgen@updea-africa.org; internet www.updea-africa.org; f. 1970 to study tech. matters and to promote efficient devt of enterprises in this sector; operates training school in Côte d'Ivoire; mems: 53 cos in 42 countries; Pres. EDWARD NJOROGE; Sec.-Gen. ABEL DIDIER TELLA; publs *UPDEA Information* (quarterly), technical papers.

World Trade Organization: Centre William Rappard, 154 rue de Lausanne, 1211 Geneva 21, Switzerland; tel. 227395111; fax 227314206; e-mail enquiries@wto.org; internet www.wto.org; f. Jan. 1995 as the successor to the General Agreement on Tariffs and Trade (GATT); aims to encourage development and economic reform among developing countries and countries with economies in transition participating in the international trading system; monitors trade policies and handles trade disputes; since 2009, aims to strengthen co-operation with the ILO, the IMF, the World Bank, and OECD in the interest of future economic development, and as a response to the global financial crisis; mems: 157 countries (at Aug. 2012), incl. 36 in Africa South of the Sahara; Comoros, Equatorial Guinea, Ethiopia, Liberia, Seychelles and Sudan are Observers; since the accession of Russia to the WTO, all participants in the BRICS informal grouping of large emerging economies, comprising Brazil, Russia, India, People's Republic of China, and South Africa (which together accounted for some 20% of global GDP in 2011), are mems of the org; Dir-Gen. PASCAL LAMY (France); publs *Annual Report* (2 volumes), *World Trade Report*, *International Trade Statistics*.

Transport

African Airlines Association: POB 20116, Nairobi 00200, Kenya; tel. (20) 2320144; fax (20) 6001173; e-mail afraa@afraa.org; internet www.afraa.org; f. 1968 to give African air companies expert advice in technical, financial, juridical and market matters; to improve air transport in Africa through inter-carrier co-operation; and to develop manpower resources; mems: 34 national carriers, representing 80% of African airlines; Pres. SIZA MZIMELA; Sec.-Gen. ELIJAH CHINGOSHO; publs *Newsletter*, reports.

Agency for the Safety of Air Navigation in Africa and Madagascar (ASECNA) (Agence pour la Sécurité de la Navigation Aérienne en Afrique et Madagascar): 32–38 ave Jean Jaurès, BP 3144, Dakar, Senegal; tel. 849-66-00; fax 823-46-54; e-mail contact@asecna.aero; internet www.asecna.aero; f. 1959 under Article 2 of the Dakar Convention; organizes air-traffic communications in mem. states; co-ordinates meteorological forecasts; provides training for air-traffic controllers, meteorologists and airport fire-fighters; ASECNA is under the authority of a cttee comprising Ministers of Civil Aviation of mem. states; mems: Benin, Burkina Faso, Cameroon, Central African Repub., Chad, Comoros, Repub. of the Congo, Côte d'Ivoire, Equatorial Guinea, Gabon, Guinea Bissau, Madagascar, Mali, Mauritania, Niger, Senegal, Togo; Dir-Gen. AMADOU OUSMANE GUITTEYE.

Youth and Students

Pan-African Youth Union (Union pan-africaine de la jeunesse): Khartoum, Sudan; tel. 8037038097 (mobile); internet panafricanyouthunion.org; f. 1962; aims to encourage the participation of African youth in socio-economic and political development and democratization; organizes conferences and seminars, youth exchanges and youth festivals; 2011 Congress: Khartoum, Sudan, in Dec.; mems: youth groups in 52 African countries and liberation movements; Pres. ANDILE LUNGISA (South Africa) (2012–14); publ. *MPJ News* (quarterly).

WFUNA Youth Network: c/o WFUNA, 1 United Nations Plaza, Room DC1-1177, New York, NY 10017, USA; tel. (212) 963-5610; fax (212) 963-0447; e-mail youth@wfuna.org; internet www.wfuna.org/youth; f. 1948 by the World Federation of United Nations Associations (WFUNA) as the International Youth and Student Movement for the United Nations (ISMUN), independent since 1949; an international non-governmental organization of students and young people dedicated especially to supporting the principles embodied in the United Nations Charter and Universal Declaration of Human Rights; encourages constructive action in building economic, social and cultural equality and in working for national independence, social justice and human rights on a world-wide scale; organizes periodic regional WFUNA International Model United Nations (WIMUN) conferences; maintains regional offices in Austria, France, Ghana, Panama and the USA; mems: asscns in over 100 mem. states of the UN.

MAJOR COMMODITIES OF AFRICA

Note: For each of the commodities in this section, there is a statistical table relating to recent levels of production. Each production table shows estimates of output for the world and for Africa (including North Africa, a region not covered by this Survey). In addition, the table lists the main African producing countries and, for comparison, the leading producers from outside the continent.

ALUMINIUM AND BAUXITE

Aluminium (known as aluminum in the USA and, generally, Canada) is the most abundant metallic element in the earth's crust, comprising about 8% of the total. However, it is much less widely used than steel, despite having about the same strength and only half the weight. Aluminium has important applications as a metal because of its lightness, ease of fabrication and other desirable properties. Other products of alumina (aluminium oxide trihydrate, into which bauxite, the commonest aluminium ore, is refined) are materials in refractories, abrasives, glass manufacture, other ceramic products, catalysts and absorbers. Alumina hydrates are used for the production of aluminium chemicals, as fire retardants in carpet-backing, and as industrial fillers in plastics and related products.

The major markets for aluminium are in transportation, packaging, building and construction, electrical and other machinery and equipment, and consumer durables. Transportation was estimated to have accounted for about one-third, and containers and packaging for about 26%, of all US aluminium end-use in 2009, for example. Although the production of aluminium is energy-intensive, its light weight results in a net saving, particularly in the transportation industry, where the use of the metal as a substitute for steel, in particular in the manufacture of road motor vehicles and components, is well established. Aluminium is valued by the aerospace industry for its weight-saving characteristics and for its low cost relative to alternative materials. Aluminium-lithium alloys command considerable potential for use in this sector, although the traditional dominance of aluminium in the aerospace industry has been challenged since the 1990s by 'composites' such as carbonepoxy, a fusion of carbon fibres and hardened resins, the lightness and durability of which can exceed that of many aluminium alloys.

Bauxite is the principal aluminium ore. Nepheline syenite, kaolin, shale, anorthosite and alunite are all potential alternative sources of alumina, but these are not currently economic to process. Of all bauxite mined, approximately 85% is converted to alumina (Al_2O_3) for the production of aluminium metal. The developing countries, in which at least 70% of known bauxite reserves are located, supply some 60% of the ore required. According to the US Geological Survey (USGS), 32% of potential world bauxite resources lie in Africa, 23% in Oceania, 21% in Latin America and the Caribbean, and 18% in Asia. Total world bauxite production in 2011 was estimated at 220,000 metric tons by the USGS, compared with 209,000 tons in 2010. Australia was by far the largest producer, providing 67,000 tons, or 30%, of the 2011 total, followed by the People's Republic of China (21%), Brazil (14%), India (9%), Guinea (8%) and Jamaica (5%).

The industry is structured in three stages: bauxite mining, alumina refining, and smelting. While the high degree of 'vertical integration' (i.e. the control of successive stages of production) in the industry means that a significant proportion of trade in bauxite and alumina is in the form of intra-company transfers, and the increasing tendency to site alumina refineries near to bauxite deposits has resulted in a shrinking bauxite trade, there is a growing free market in alumina, serving the needs of the increasing number of independent (i.e. non-integrated) smelters.

The alumina is separated from the ore by the Bayer process. After mining, bauxite is fed direct to process if mine-run material is adequate (as in Jamaica), or else it is crushed and beneficiated. Where the ore 'as mined' presents handling problems, or weight reduction is desirable, it may be dried prior to shipment.

At the alumina plant the ore is slurried with spent-liquor direct, if the soft Caribbean type is used, or, in the case of other types, it is ball-milled to reduce it to a size that will facilitate the extraction of the alumina. The bauxite slurry is then digested with caustic soda to extract the alumina from the ore while leaving the impurities as an insoluble residue. The digest conditions depend on the aluminium minerals in the ore and the impurities. The liquor, with the dissolved alumina, is then separated from the insoluble impurities by combinations of sedimentation, decantation and filtration, and the residue washed to minimize the soda losses. The clarified liquor is concentrated and the alumina precipitated by seeding with hydrate. The precipitated alumina is then filtered, washed and calcined to produce alumina. The ratio of bauxite to alumina is approximately 1.95:1.

The smelting of the aluminium is generally by electrolysis in molten cryolite. Owing to the high consumption of electricity by this process, alumina is usually smelted in areas where low-cost electricity is available. However, most of the electricity now used in primary smelting in the Western world is generated by hydroelectricity—a renewable energy source.

The recycling of aluminium is economically, as well as environmentally, desirable, as the process uses only 5% of the electricity required to produce a similar quantity of primary aluminium. Aluminium recycled from scrap accounted for approximately one-third of the total annual world output of primary aluminium in 2008, according to the International Aluminium Institute (IAI), which also reckoned that three-quarters of the aluminium produced since the 19th century was still in use. With the added impetus of environmental concerns, considerable growth occurred world-wide in the recycling of used beverage cans (UBC) during the 1990s and 2000s. The IAI reckoned that in 2007 some 69% of UBC globally were being collected for recycling, making this the world's most recycled container (the industry was aiming for a recycling rate of 75% by 2015).

At the end of the 20th century world markets for finished and semi-finished aluminium products were dominated by six Western producers—Alcan (Canada), Alcoa, Reynolds, Kaiser (all USA), Pechiney (France) and algroup (formerly Alusuisse, of Switzerland). From 2000 the picture began to change dramatically, through mergers and the emergence of new international players from Russia and the People's Republic of China. In mid-2000 Alcoa merged with Reynolds. In October Alcan took over algroup; a tripartite merger proposal from the previous year, which had also included Pechiney, was effectively achieved in 2003. Concerns regarding the safeguarding of competition were met by divestment of some of the new group's rolled aluminium assets into a new group, Novelis, in 2005; two years later Novelis was bought by India's Hindalco, which thus became the world's largest aluminium rolling company and one of Asia's biggest producers of primary aluminium. Meanwhile, in 2002, after the purchase of Germany's VAW, Norway's Norsk Hydro became the world's third largest integrated aluminium concern. (Hydro separated out its fertilizer business in 2005 and its petroleum and gas concerns, through a merger with Norway's Statoil, in 2007.) The level of dominance of the six major Western producers was already being challenged by a significant geographical shift in the location of alumina and aluminium production to countries where cheap power is available, such as Australia, Brazil, Norway, Canada and Venezuela. In the Persian (Arabian) Gulf, Bahrain and Dubai (United Arab Emirates), with the advantage of low energy costs, also produce primary aluminium. From the mid-1990s Russia emerged as a significant force in the world aluminium market, and in 2000 the country's principal producers, together with a number of plants located in other former Soviet states, joined together to form the Russian Aluminium Co (RUSAL). In March 2007 United Company RUSAL was formed by RUSAL's merger with Russia's second largest aluminium producer, Siberian-Urals Aluminium Company (SUAL), and the alumina assets of Switzerland's Glencore International AG. At mid-2009 United Company RUSAL claimed to be the world's largest aluminium company, accounting for almost 12% of world output of primary aluminium and 15% of global alumina production. In late 2007 the multinational mining concern Rio Tinto purchased Canada's Alcan Inc.—like United Company RUSAL, Rio Tinto Alcan, as the Rio Tinto division formed by the purchase was named (administratively, still based in Canada, although the aluminium and bauxite subdivision is based in Australia), also claims to be the world's biggest aluminium company. In February 2008 China's principal aluminium producer, Aluminium Corpn of China (Chinalco), and the USA's Alcoa jointly purchased a 12% stake in Rio Tinto in a move that was perceived as intended to obstruct an attempt by the Anglo-Australian company BHP Billiton, the world's largest mining company (and the sixth largest primary aluminium producer), to take over Rio Tinto. In June 2009 Rio Tinto ended moves towards greater integration with Chinalco (or, more specifically, its listed subsidiary, Chalco) amid some recriminations.

In 2011, according to USGS estimates, world output of primary aluminium totalled 44.1m. metric tons–compared with some 40.8m. tons in 2010, when eastern Asia accounted for 40.3% of the global total (39.7% by China alone, but with some production in Indonesia and a little in Japan), with an additional 5.6% in Oceania (mainly Australia, but also New Zealand). North America provided 11.5% of world production in that year, Russia and the other Soviet successor states 11.2%, Europe 10.2%, the Middle East and North Africa 8.3%, Latin America (mainly Brazil, but also Venezuela and some from Argentina) 5.6%, sub-Saharan Africa (South Africa, Mozambique,

Cameroon and some from Nigeria) 3.6% and South Asia (India) 3.6%. In 2011 the USGS estimated that China alone provided 41% of world primary aluminium production, followed by Russia (9%), Canada (7%), the USA (5%), Australia (4%), the United Arab Emirates (4%) and Brazil (3%).

China displaced the USA as the most significant country for the international aluminium industry in the 2000s, accounting for about one-third of both consumption and production globally by 2009. The USA was for many years the world's principal producing country, but in 2001 US output of primary aluminium was surpassed by that of Russia and China. From 2002 Canadian production also exceeded that of the USA. In 2011 production of primary aluminium by China was estimated to be some nine times that by the USA.

In 2011, according to the USGS, Guinea possessed about 26% of the world's known bauxite reserves. The country is the world's leading exporter of bauxite, mainly because other producers export more refined aluminium. Formerly ranking second in the world, after Australia, in terms of ore production, Guinea's output was also now outstripped by that of China, Brazil and, from 2007, India. Exports of aluminium ore and concentrate dominate the Guinean economy. In 2008 exports of bauxite, concentrate and aluminium hydroxide, together valued at US $740m., contributed 52% of Guinea's total revenue from foreign sales. In 2010 bauxite was mined locally by Alumina Co of Guinea (ACG), Compagnie des Bauxites de Guinée (CBG) and Compagnie des Bauxites de Kindia (CBK). ACG and CBK were wholly owned by United Company RUSAL, while CBG was operated as a joint venture by the Government (49%) and Halco Mining Inc. (itself a joint venture, formed by Alcan Inc.—now Rio Tinto Alcan—Alcoa World Alumina LLC and Dadco Group). CBG accounted for 73% of bauxite production capacity, but United Company RUSAL's ACG operated an alumina refinery near its Friguia mine. In 2005 the Government concluded an agreement with Canada's Global Alumina Corpn Ltd (GAC) that provided for the development of a bauxite mine and the construction of an alumina refinery in Boké; the project, which was a joint venture with BHP Billiton, Dubai Aluminium Co (Dubal) and Mubadala Development Co (these last two both of the United Arab Emirates), was delayed by both economic and political uncertainties, and any completion was unlikely before 2014. At mid-2012, the Government was reported to be prepared to sign a US $6,000m.-agreement in September with China Power Investment Corpn to develop a mine and refinery, with associated infrastructure, in Boffa—work might even begin in 2012. The military coup at the end of 2008 had installed a regime determined to dismantle the patronage networks of the late, long-serving President Conté, and all mining contracts were reviewed. (RUSAL operation of the Friguia refinery was challenged, while its operation and that of the mines was severely disrupted, the refinery also suffering from strike action by workers from April 2012.) Several candidates in the 2010 presidential election reiterated such promises during the campaign, adding some uncertainty to mining sector investment, which was perpetuated to an extent by continuing tension in the country in 2011, although, contingent on the restoration of political stability, international interest remained strong. Alumina production in Guinea was less affected than mine production, with production falling from 593 metric tons in 2008 to 530 tons in 2009, and recovering to 597 tons in 2010. The new mining code in September 2011 came at a time when commodity prices were less strong, so the increase in the government stake in all mining contracts gave pause to potential investors and at mid-2012 it remained to be seen whether the sector would suffer or if any changes in ownership would result.

Cameroon traditionally receives bauxite from Guinea for its smelter, but has its own extensive bauxite deposits, estimated at some 1,200m. metric tons. However, these await commercial exploitation. Compagnie Camérounaise de l'Aluminium, in which Rio Tinto Alcan and the Government have shares, produces primary aluminium at Edéa. In July 2009 Rio Tinto Alcan agreed to construct another aluminium plant in Cameroon, powered by a new hydroelectric station, at Kribi, on the southern coast, where a deep-water port would also be built. Production capacity was expected to be 400,000 tons, with work beginning on the plant by the end of 2011 and aluminium production expected by 2016. A project that was expected to come online earlier, in around 2013, involved the exploitation of local bauxite from the Minim-Martap and Ngaoundal deposits. The bauxite and alumina complex would be linked by rail to the coast, and the Government would need to invest in significant infrastructure work, especially roads to link the deposits. The joint venture involved was between Dubal, Hindalco (India) and Hydromine (USA). Meanwhile, according to the USGS, Cameroon produced 73,000 tons of primary aluminium in 2009, down 20% on the previous year, as the smelter reduced its output given the adverse world economic conditions, but this recovered slightly to 76,000 tons in 2010.

Malawi's reserves of bauxite, located at Mulanje and estimated at 29m. metric tons in the mid-1990s, remain unexploited, although South Africa's Gondo Resources was criticized for an alleged lack of progress. At mid-2012 one of the main impediments to establishing a bauxite industry in the country remained the availability of power, for which an electricity grid connection with Mozambique was the main hope.

Ghana's bauxite reserves have been estimated at 780m. metric tons. The country's bauxite production fell to only 490,000 tons in 2009, from 796,000 tons in 2008, because of problems with the railway line for shipments and given world-wide economic conditions since August 2008, which had also affected the country's smelter; recovery in 2010 was limited, production rising to 512,000 tons. Although Ghana lacks an alumina refinery, imported alumina was processed at a smelter at Tema, operated by the Volta Aluminium Co (Valco). The smelter was closed down in 2008 (operation had been intermittent since 2003, and in particular since 2007, owing to severe power shortages resulting from the effect of drought on the hydroelectric supply), when it was acquired in its entirety by the Government. The smelter, one of the largest in Africa, had a capacity of some 200,000 tons, and at its peak had absorbed 65% of the country's electricity consumption. Valco eventually resumed some production in January 2011. In the mid-2000s both Alcan (now Rio Tinto Alcan—see above) and Alcoa were interested in developing various aspects of an integrated aluminium industry in Ghana, which had long been an ambition of the Government. In pursuit of that aim, the authorities welcomed the February 2010 sale by Rio Tinto Alcan of its bauxite interests in the Ghana Bauxite Co to the Bosai Minerals Group of China. Bosai expressed support for Ghana's long-sought integrated aluminium industry, but it was unclear how feasible a proposal that was, given anxieties about energy provision. In September 2010 the Chinese company promised a US $1,200m. investment in reviving the country's bauxite industry.

Sierra Leone, meanwhile, displaced Ghana as Africa's second largest bauxite producer in 2006, when it produced 1.1m. metric tons of bauxite; output was 1.2m. tons in 2007, dipping as low as 0.8m. tons by 2009, but recovering to an estimated 1.1m. tons in 2010. The country had no processing facilities for the ore. However, the country has estimated bauxite reserves of more than 100m. tons. Exploitation of the Mokanji deposits, in the Southern province, began in 1964, but was interrupted from early 1995 by guerrilla insurgency. A local holding company, Titanium Resources Group Ltd, relaunched production at the Sierra Minerals Ltd Mokanji mine, near Moyamba, in early 2006; the mine was sold to the Dutch-based integrated aluminium company Vimetco in July 2008; and in May 2011 Vimetco transferred formal ownership to a sister company, Alum SA, of Romania.

South Africa, which has no significant bauxite reserves, produces primary aluminium from imported alumina. In 2012 BHP Billiton operated the country's two smelters at Richards Bay (Hillside, accounting for 88% of capacity, and Bayside). Primary aluminium production in South Africa fell back steadily from 931,000 tons in 2006 to 811,000 tons in 2008 and then more slowly down to an estimated 800,000 tons in 2011, owing to problems with electricity supply. Power supply reliability prompted Rio Tinto in 2009 to suspend indefinitely any planning for a new smelter at Coega. The value of South Africa's exports of primary aluminium amounted to US $1,464m. in 2009 (2.7% of total exports).

A major aluminium smelter project (Mozal) in Mozambique was formally inaugurated in 1998, although the country is not a significant producer of bauxite (an estimated 5,000 metric tons in 2010, almost one-half the total of even three years previously)—Zimbabwe's E. C. Meikles (Pty) Ltd undertakes small, but expanding, bauxite-mining activities in Manica province. The Mozal smelter, located near Maputo and owned by a consortium including BHP Billiton, represented the largest single investment project in Mozambique, with an estimated cost of about US $1,300m. The first aluminium was cast at the smelter in 2000. Using alumina from Australia, the smelter increased its output to 266,000 tons in 2001, compared with 54,000 tons in 2000. By 2006 and 2007 Mozambique was producing 564,000 tons per year. Output dipped in 2008, but recovered thereafter, reaching an estimated 560,000 tons by 2011. BHP Billiton had intended to raise Mozal's annual capacity, but the achievement of this aim depended on the company's ability to conclude long-term contracts for energy supplies with South African utility Eskom Holdings Ltd. In the event, power shortages in South Africa contributed to depressed output in Mozambique in 2008, as well as a delay to BHP Billiton's planned expansion, especially given the international financial crisis and consequent recession from the second half of the year. Mozambique remains Africa's second largest producer of aluminium, after South Africa, and exports its output to Europe. In 2010 exports of aluminium, valued at $1,160m., contributed 52% of Mozambique's total export revenue (down from 62% in 2008).

In 2006 RUSAL (now United Company RUSAL—see above) purchased a 77.5% interest in Aluminium Smelter Co of Nigeria (ALSCON), in which the Nigerian Government holds a 15% stake and Ferrostaal AG one of 7.5%. Thus reconstituted, ALSCON began renovation of its smelter at Akwa Ibom, which had shut down in 2000 owing to the high cost of production and inadequate power supplies and transport infrastructure. Production recommenced in February 2008 (11,000 metric tons of aluminium were produced in that year, and 13,000 tons in 2009) and, despite the constraints of the international economic recession and security problems, reached 21,000 tons in 2010. In 2011 there was some controversy about the sale price of the privatization of ALSCON, following the investigations of a parliamentary inquiry, and in July 2012 the Supreme Court declared the sale to RUSAL illegal, although the Russian company insisted that the ruling was against the privatization agency and that its ownership was not in question.

Production of Bauxite
(crude ore, '000 metric tons)

	2009	2010*
World total (excl. USA)	209,000	220,000
Sub-Saharan Africa*	16,924	19,136
Leading sub-Saharan African producers		
Ghana	440	512
Guinea†	15,600	17,400
Sierra Leone	757	1,089
Leading non-African producers		
Australia	65,231	68,414
Brazil	25,628	28,100
China, People's Repub.*	40,000	44,000
India	16,000	18,000
Jamaica†‡	7,817	8,540
Kazakhstan	5,130	5,310
Russia	5,775	5,475
Suriname	4,000	4,000
Venezuela*	2,500	2,500

* Estimated production.
† Dried equivalent of crude ore.
‡ Kiln-dried ore for export plus bauxite processed for conversion to alumina domestically.

Source: US Geological Survey.

In 2007 the average settlement price for aluminium (unalloyed primary ingots, high grade—minimum 99.7% purity) traded on the London Metal Exchange (LME) increased by 2.8%, compared with the previous year, to US $2,639 per metric ton. During 2007 aluminium traded within a range of $2,317–$2,953 per ton. Prices fluctuated throughout the year, but, generally, were lower in the second half of the year than in the first. Chinese consumption remained a key market influence in 2007. In January–May, according to analysts, Chinese utilization rose by 47%, while consumption world-wide in the same period grew at a substantially lower rate of 10.5%. LME inventories of aluminium rose steadily in January–May, totalling 833,525 tons at the end of that period. In June, however, they declined to 823,625 tons. By the end of September stocks had risen to 937,400 tons, but they fell in October, to 918,250 tons at the end of that month. At the end of 2007 LME stocks of aluminium totalled 929,450 tons.

In 2008 the average LME price for aluminium per metric ton was US $2,573, part of a dramatic escalation in commodity prices until the onset of global economic anxieties in the second half of the year. By July 2008 the monthly average price of aluminium traded on the LME had soared to a record $3,380 per ton. Stocks of the metal held by the LME, meanwhile, had risen to more than 1.1m. tons by the end of May, compared with 956,475 tons at the end of January. The general trend in the prices of base metals was downward, but aluminium prices were supported by a continued decline in the value of the US dollar and by concern about possible shortages. However, weak demand in the West and the generally weak economic context world-wide caused the average monthly aluminium price to collapse, falling below $1,800 per ton by February 2009.

In 2009 the average LME aluminium price was US $1,665 per metric ton. In the first quarter an average price of only $1,360 per ton was recorded, but there was some recovery thereafter. Although demand in the USA, Japan and Europe remained weak, and stocks continued to increase, aluminium prices rose later in 2009 because there were expectations of recovering demand, as well as a resurgence in Chinese growth. There was a realization that many of the stocks were committed, aluminium production had lessened, and car-makers had returned to the market. In July prices exceeded $1,800 per ton for the first time since the previous November, and they then spiked beyond $2,000 per ton: the average quarterly price for October–December was $2,003 per ton. LME stocks were put at 4.6m. tons in July 2009, having doubled since the end of 2008.

In 2010 the average price for aluminium on the LME was US $2,173 per metric ton. After early rises at the beginning of the year, the average price fell back into February before beginning to recover in the latter part of that month. Prices peaked in April, with a monthly average of $2,317 per ton, and then in October, at $2,347 per ton. The lowest prices were in June, which recorded a monthly average price of $1,931 per ton. LME stocks were put at just above 4.4m. tons in mid-August 2010.

In 2011 the average settlement price for aluminium on the LME was US $2,401 per metric ton. Average monthly prices rose steadily at the beginning of the year, to peak at $2,678 per ton in April, but then fell back slowly. By the last quarter of the year, in common with trends in other commodities, the average price was $2,094 per ton. LME stocks were put at 4.6m. tons in mid-June.

In the first seven months of 2012 the average price for aluminium on the LME was down to US $2,051 per metric ton, indicating concern about US and even Chinese economic performance and the ongoing European sovereign debt crisis, which lowered optimism and commodity prices. Average monthly prices in the first quarter were up on late 2011, but had declined generally, if more slowly by mid-year. The average monthly price in July was down to $1,876 per ton. LME stocks were put at 4.9m. tons in mid-August.

The IAI, based in London, United Kingdom, is a global forum of producers of aluminium dedicated to the development and wider use of the metal. In 2012 the IAI had 28 member companies, representing every part of the world, including Russia and China, and responsible for more than 80% of global primary aluminium production and a significant proportion of the world's secondary output.

CASSAVA (Manioc, Tapioca, Yuca) (*Manihot esculenta*)

Cassava is a perennial woody shrub, up to 5 m in height, which is cultivated mainly for its enlarged starch-rich roots, although the young shoots and leaves of the plant are also edible. The plant can be harvested at any time from seven months to three years after planting. A native of South and Central America, cassava is now one of the most important food plants in all parts of the tropics (except at the highest altitudes), having a wide range of adaptation for rainfall (500–8,000 mm per year). Cassava is also well adapted to low-fertility soils, and grows where other crops will not. It is produced mainly on marginal agricultural land, with virtually no input of fertilizers, fungicides or insecticides.

The varieties of the plant fall into two broad groups, bitter and sweet cassava, formerly classed as two separate species, *Manihot utilissima* and *M. dulcis* or *aipi*. The roots of the sweet variety are usually boiled and then eaten. The roots of the bitter variety are either soaked, pounded and fermented to make a paste (such as 'fufu' in West Africa), or given an additional roasting to produce 'gari'. They can also be made into flour and starch, or dried and pelletized as animal feed.

The cassava plant contains two toxic substances, linamarin and lotaustralin, in its edible roots and leaves, which release the poison hydrocyanic acid, or cyanide, when plant tissues are damaged. Sweet varieties of cassava produce as little as 20 mg of acid per kg of fresh roots, whereas bitter varieties may produce more than 1,000 mg per kg. Although traditional methods of food preparation are effective in reducing cyanogenic content to harmless levels, if roots of bitter varieties are under-processed and the diet lacks protein and iodine (as occurs during famines and wars), cyanide poisoning can cause fatalities. Despite the disadvantages of the two toxins, some farmers prefer to cultivate the bitter varieties, possibly because the cyanide helps to protect the plant from potential pests, and possibly because the texture of certain food products made from bitter varieties is preferred to that of sweet cassavas.

Cassava, which was introduced to Africa from South America in the 16th century, is the most productive source of carbohydrates and produces more calories per unit of land than any cereal crop. Although the nutrient content of the roots consists almost entirely of starch, the leaves are high in vitamins, minerals and protein and, processed as meal or eaten as a fresh vegetable ('saka saka'), provide a useful source of nutrition in many parts of Africa, especially in the Democratic Republic of the Congo (DRC), the Congo basin generally, Sierra Leone, Malawi, Mozambique, Niger, Tanzania and Uganda. A plot of cassava may be left unattended in the ground for two years after maturity without deterioration of the roots. As the plant is also resistant to prolonged drought it is valued as a famine reserve. The roots are highly perishable after harvest, however, and if not consumed immediately must be processed (into flour, starch, pellets, etc.).

While the area under cassava has expanded considerably through the 2000s, there is increasing concern that the rapid expansion of cassava root planting may threaten the fertility of the soil and subsequently other crops. Under cropping systems where no fertilizer is used, cassava is the last crop in the succession because of its particular adaptability to infertile soils and its high nutrient use-efficiency in yield terms (although there is now evidence to suggest that cassava yields increase with the use of fertilizer). Soil fertility is not threatened by cassava itself, but rather by cultivation systems that dispense with fertilizers.

Production of Cassava
('000 metric tons)

	2009	2010
World total*	235,040	230,266
Sub-Saharan Africa*	120,434	121,661
Leading African producers		
Angola	12,828	13,859
Congo, Dem. Repub.	15,055	15,050
Ghana	12,231	13,504
Mozambique*	5,672	5,700
Nigeria	36,804	37,504
Tanzania	5,916	4,392
Uganda	5,179	5,282†
Leading non-African producers		
Brazil	24,404	24,524
Cambodia	3,497	4,247
China, People's Repub.*	4,506	4,684
India	9,623	8,060
Indonesia	22,039	23,918
Thailand	30,088	22,006
Viet Nam	8,557	8,522

* FAO estimates.
† Unofficial estimate.
Source: FAO.

As a staple source of carbohydrates in the tropics, cassava is an essential part of the diet of about 600m. people. In 2010 it was harvested from 12.0m. ha in sub-Saharan Africa (cassava is not grown in North Africa), and it may provide more than one-half of the calorific requirements of about 500m. people in the continent. The area in Africa from which cassava was harvested in 2010 amounted to about 64% of the area harvested world-wide in that year, and Africa's output accounted for more than one-half (53%) of estimated world production. Most of the African crop is produced by subsistence farmers and is traded domestically: only a small quantity enters world trade, mainly dried or as cassava starch. The expansion of production from the mid-1980s was driven by demand for food consumption. Attempts undertaken in a number of African countries to increase the use of cassava as a feedstuff have met with only limited success, owing to cassava chips and pellets' uncompetitiveness relative to imported feedstuffs.

Pests and diseases can cause yield losses of up to one-half the cassava crop in Africa. From the early 1970s African production was seriously undermined by mealybug infestation. Indigenous to South America, the mealybug (*Phenacoccus manihoti*) encountered few natural enemies in Africa, and by about 1992 had infested almost all African cassava-growing areas. In 1981 the parasitic wasp *Epidinocarsis lopezi* was introduced into Nigeria from Paraguay to attack the mealybug, and by 1990 it was successfully established in 25 African countries. The introduction of natural enemies, such as *E. lopezi*, has brought about a 95% reduction in mealybug damage to cassava crops. The green spider mite (*Mononychellus tanajoa*), another threat to cassava cultivation, has also been successfully combated by the introduction of a natural enemy, the phytoseiid mite (*Typhlodromalus aripo*), which by 1997 had established a presence over 400,000 sq km in West Africa and in 1999 was reported to have reduced the presence of the green spider mite by up to 70% in some regions. Overall, there was reported to have been a 50% reduction in green spider mite damage to cassava crops owing to the introduction of natural predators. Current major threats include the variegated grasshopper, *Zonocerus variegatus*, and African cassava leaf mosaic disease (CMD), which, like the green spider mite, deprives the plant of chlorophyll and causes low yields. Pest and diseases, in combination with poor husbandry, have in the past led to substantial yield losses in African cassava crops. To combat these losses, in addition to the measures described above, the International Institute of Tropical Agriculture (IITA) has conducted numerous projects, including programmes to develop (for resistance to pests and diseases) new (in some cases high-yielding) varieties of cassava in Africa's cassava belt. Notably, distribution of cassava varieties resistant to CMD brought the most recent outbreak of the disease (which began in Uganda in the 1990s) under control by 2006 and led to a recovery of cassava crops to pre-epidemic levels within five years. Countries in which the IITA led or participated in ongoing cassava-related projects in mid-2012 included Benin, Burundi, the DRC, Kenya, Malawi, Mozambique, Nigeria, Rwanda, Sierra Leone, Tanzania, Uganda and Zimbabwe.

In recent years there has been interest in the utilization of cassava as an industrial raw material as well as a food crop. Cassava has the potential to become a basic energy source for ethyl alcohol (ethanol), a substitute for petroleum. 'alcogas' (a blend of cassava alcohol and petrol) can be mixed with petrol to provide motor fuel, while the high-protein residue from its production can be used for animal feed. The possibility of utilizing cassava leaves and stems (which represent about 50% of the plant and are normally discarded) as cattle-feed concentrates has also been receiving scientific attention.

In 2000 the average price of hard cassava pellets (f.o.b. Bangkok, Thailand) was US $55 per metric ton. In 2001 an average price of $59 per ton was recorded and in 2002 the average price rose to $66 per ton. Further increases, to, respectively, $71.9 per ton and $78 per ton, were recorded in 2003 and 2004. An average price of $111 per ton was recorded in 2005, and the average price rose further, to $109 per ton, in 2006. In January–April 2007 the average price of hard cassava pellets of Thai origin was $113 per ton. In 1999 the average international price of cassava (tapioca) starch (f.o.b. Bangkok) was $181 per ton, the lowest price since 1993. This price declined further throughout 2000, to an average of $157.4 per ton. In 2001 an average price of $173.8 per ton was recorded, and in 2002 the average price increased to $184.6 per ton. After falling to $172.7 per ton in 2003, the average international price of cassava starch recovered to $188.2 per ton in 2004. A substantial increase, of more than one-third, to $252 per ton, was recorded in the Bangkok price of cassava starch in 2005, but the price decreased slightly in 2006, to $221.7 per ton. The average price of cassava starch of Thai origin rose by some 13% in 2007, to $250.5 per ton, and more dramatically into 2008, even surpassing $400 per ton for a time. The FAO put the average price for 2008 as a whole at $383.6 per ton—this being dragged down by the collapse in commodity prices later in the year, which continued into 2009 and held that annual average to $281.3 per ton. In January–October the average cassava starch price had reached $496.0 per ton, and the trend was rising. According to the listing of weekly export prices (f.o.b. Bangkok) by the Thai Tapioca Starch Association, tapioca starch prices had risen steadily through 2007, from $245 per metric ton to $355 per ton, continuing to rise into 2008, to peak at $440 per ton. Some authorities have argued that the general commodity price rise, and its reversal later in 2008, with the international financial crisis and the onset of recession, had obscured the general crisis in food supplies, particularly in the developing world. Certainly the pressure on prices seemed to be upward from 2009. The weekly price at the start of the year was $280 per ton and, although it dipped to $240 per ton for much of February, it then rose steadily, to end the year at $395 per ton, continuing the upward trend into 2010. The cassava starch price then reached a record high in the week beginning 10 August 2010, at $630 per metric ton. The surge in food commodity prices came amid fears of inflation arising from economic stimulus spending in the developed world, and, for cassava in particular, because of a fall in Thailand's crop, as a result of a bug infestation from 2009, as well as adverse weather conditions. In 2010 average weekly prices for cassava starch had fallen to $545 per ton in mid-October, but then rose again to stabilize at $580 per ton in December and into the first week of January 2011. The price then fell, though no lower than $560 per ton, before rising back to $590 per ton from the end of March to the beginning of May, and after another fall stabilizing through July. Prices downwards again in August, ending the month at $440 per ton, the lowest level since March 2010. Cassava starch prices in December 2011 were 21% lower than in December 2010, but there was a rising trend in the third quarter of 2012.

CHROMIUM

Chromium, historically used as an alloying element, is a hard, lustrous metal, the name of which derives from the Greek *kroma* (colour). It is only obtained from chromite (the name applied both to the metal-bearing mineral and to the ore containing that mineral—the terms chromite ore, chromium ore and chrome ore are used interchangeably). About 91% of total demand for chromite is from the metallurgical industry, some 5% from the chemical industry and about 4% from the refractory and foundry industries. For the metallurgical industry, most chromite ore is smelted in an electric arc furnace to produce ferrochromium. Within this industry the major use of chromium remains as an alloying element—it is essential to the composition of stainless steel, which is valued for its toughness and resistance to most forms of corrosion. Chromium chemicals are also used for wood preservation, dyeing and tanning. Chrome plating is a popular way of enhancing the appearance of motor vehicles, kitchen appliances, etc. Chromite is also used as a refractory mineral.

The US Geological Survey (USGS) estimated world reserves to be at least 480m. metric tons of shipping-grade chromite ore in 2011, including Kazakhstan's 220m. tons, South Africa's 200m. tons, India's 54m. tons and the USA's 620,000 tons. What the USGS describes as the world's resources of shipping-grade chromite ore (i.e. not only economic reserves) are reckoned to be greater than 12,000m. tons, 95% located in southern Africa and Kazakhstan. South Africa is the leading producer and, in the 2000s, generally accounted for about two-fifths of world chromite ore supplies—an estimated 46% in 2011 (of a total of some 24m. tons). The country is also the world's dominant ferrochromium producer, accounting for a record 3.6m. tons, or 41% of estimated world output, in 2010. In 2008 Zimbabwe contributed 1.8% of estimated world ferrochromium production;

output halved in the following year, when it accounted for 1.0% of the world total, but more than doubled in 2010, to 1.7% of world output. South African charge-grade, high-carbon ferrochromium (which has a chromium content of 52%–55%) has been replacing the more expensive high- and low-carbon ferrochromiums (which have a chromium content of 60%–70%) since the development, during 1965–75, of the argon-oxygen decarbonizing process. South Africa's ferrochromium sector has also benefited historically from its access to inexpensive supplies of electrical power, and from low labour costs, but in the 2000s was bedevilled by power supply problems.

Production of Chromium Ore
('000 metric tons, gross weight)

	2009	2010
World total*	19,500	23,700
Sub-Saharan Africa	7,914	11,458
Sub-Saharan African producers		
Madagascar	60*	105
South Africa	7,561	10,871
Sudan*	14	57
Zimbabwe	279	425
Leading non-African producers		
Albania	289	290
Brazil	365	370
China, People's Repub.*	200	200
Finland	247	245
India	3,760	3,800
Iran	255	250*
Kazakhstan	3,544	3,829
Oman	636	802
Pakistan	90	257
Russia	416	400*
Turkey	1,574	1,700*

* Estimated production.

Source: US Geological Survey.

Strong demand for ferrochromium in the late 1980s, together with conditions of under-supply, generated an expansion of capacity both in South Africa and Zimbabwe. However, the potentially damaging effects of international boycotts and trade bans, and of civil disturbances, on South Africa's ferrochrome industry led, in the 1980s, to the development of new production capacity, generally close to ore deposits, in Brazil, Finland, Greece, India, Sweden and Turkey. After 1993 the implementation of political change in South Africa acted to consolidate the country's pre-eminence in international ferrochromium markets. South Africa's is the world's leading producer of ferrochromium and, in the mid-2000s, the fourth largest exporter of chromite ore, after—in order of rank—India, Kazakhstan and Turkey (South Africa is the largest producer of chromite ore, but processes much of its production). Together, these countries met some 70% of the annual import requirements of the world's principal importer of chromite ore, the People's Republic of China. From 2000 ferrochromium plants were increasingly developed in South Africa's Bushveld Complex—more than 80% of the world's chromite ore resources are located in southern Africa, associated with the Complex and the Great Dyke of Zimbabwe—while ferrochromium producers also sought to make greater use of chromite ore generated as a by-product of platinum mining. According to the USGS, South African production of chromite ore peaked at 9.7m. metric tons in 2008, fell to 7.6m. tons in 2009, and then rose again, to 10.9m. tons in 2010 and an estimated 11.0m. tons in 2011, while its production of ferrochromium peaked at 3.6m. tons in 2007, but then fell to 3.3m. tons in 2008 and 2.3m. tons in 2009, before recovering to an estimated 3.6m. tons in 2010. The value of exports of chromite in 2010 amounted to US $322m., and of ferrochromium to $3,170m. South Africa exported only 18% of its chromite ore production in that year, but 86% of ferrochromium; domestic consumption of chromium ore had been challenged by Chinese demand and problems with electricity for the ferrochromium industry. The inadequacy of transport infrastructure, as well as electricity supply, and concerns about the environmental impact of chromite ore mining confronted the industry from the mid-2000s. The largest chromite and ferrochromium producer in South Africa, and the world, is Xstrata, which runs the Project Lion ferrochrome facility. In 2006 Tata Iron and Steel Co Ltd of India had decided to proceed with the construction of a smelter at Richards Bay, Kwazulu-Natal. The plant commenced operations in 2008, and was seeking ore from southern Africa; 14% of its electricity supply was co-generated by use of the smelter's gas emissions as fuel. Samancor Chrome, South Africa's second chromite ore and ferrochromium producer, was also expanding its ferrochrome production facilities from 2006, as part of its pursuit of an increase greater than 100% in its ferrochrome capacity, to 2.7m. tons, by 2015; global economic problems caused it to suspend many activities in late 2008 until February 2009. The company operated two mining complexes and four ferrochromium plants. Activity increased again from late in 2009, as world conditions improved.

Zimbabwe's ferrochromium industry was beset into the 2000s by problems arising from the currency exchange rate, by inadequate power supplies and by deficiencies in rail transportation. In 2006 Ruscole Investments was formed by Zimbabwe Mining Development Corpn (ZMDC) and a Russian concern in order to explore for chromite ore on the Great Dyke of Zimbabwe. A similar exploration enterprise focused on the Ngezi area of the Great Dyke was formed by ZMDC, Norinco International Co-operation Ltd and Zimbabwe Defence Industries in the same year. Chinese companies have also invested in the industry. Global economic conditions from 2008 contributed further to the downward trend of chromite ore output (less than 0.3m. metric tons in 2009, compared with 0.5m. tons one year earlier and even 0.8m. tons four years earlier), but recovery had set in by 2010 (over 0.4m. tons). Ferrochrome output fell by about one-half in 2009, to some 72,000 tons, but production had resumed in April at the main Zimbabwe Mining and Smelting Co (Zimasco) plant, and the Government's mid-year ban on the export of chromite ore was effectively over by the end of the year, as the industry recovered; national output rose to some 150,000 tons in 2010.

Of the other two chromite producers in Africa, neither has a ferrochromium industry. Sudan is increasing its relatively minor production (more strongly from 2010, after a dip in 2009), while Madagascar reopened its Bemanevika mine (with a remaining estimated production life of 15 years) in 2009, so output recovered from the 60,000 tons low point of that year. In 2010 Nigeria found that its chromite deposits in the Anka area of Zamfara state were exploitable, and production was expected to increase.

In 2004, according to South African industry sources, world demand for ferrochromium rose to some 5.5m. metric tons, compared with about 5.2m. tons in 2003. Growth in demand in 2004 was a consequence of continued growth in global, in particular Chinese, output of stainless steel, which accounts for some 80% of ferrochromium consumption world-wide (China's stainless steel production exceeded that of the USA in 2004, and by 2011 produced five times as much as the Americas as a whole). The average price received for ferrochromium in 2004, again according to South African industry sources, was 68 US cents per lb, compared with 46 cents per lb in 2003. During 2004 prices for ferrochromium rose to their highest levels for 10 years. According to the South African mines ministry, in 2005 the average world price for ferrochrome was 70 cents per lb. In 2006 the average price declined by about 11%, to 63 cents per lb. Prices for chrome, along with those for other commodities, rose into the first quarter of 2008, before collapsing with the onset of the global economic downturn later in the year. Poor prices continued into 2009: for example, ferrochromium contract prices between South African producers and European steel-makers in the first quarter of 2009 averaged only 79 cents per lb, compared with US $1.85 per lb even in the last quarter of 2008. However, despite increasing ore production capacity around the world, continued anxiety about South Africa's power supply problems pushed the prices back up, the European benchmark price for ferrochrome rising from 89 cents per lb in the third quarter of 2009 and $1.03 per lb in the final quarter. Despite a dip in the first three months of 2010 ($1.01 per lb), the second-quarter average reached $1.36 per lb, after which prices dropped slightly, standing at $1.25 per lb in the first quarter of 2011. The second-quarter average for 2011 rose dramatically, as it had one year earlier (although not as high as some had forecast), to $1.35 per lb, but the average fell back to $1.20 per lb in the third and fourth quarters, as producers reduced output dramatically in response to the unreliability of the energy supply and world economic anxieties. The contract price fell to an average $1.15 per lb in the first quarter of 2012, but recovered to $1.35 per lb in the second quarter and remained firm, if lower, into the second half of the year; the cost of ferrochrome on international markets was not expected to increase significantly while Europe addressed its sovereign debt problems. The rising cost of ferrochrome production in South Africa, because of shortages and cost of energy, meant that exports of chromite ore—notably to China—were increasing to the detriment of ferrochrome. Manufacturers were changing some facilities to ferromanganese production instead, because that used less power.

COBALT

Cobalt is usually mined as a by-product of another metal; in the case of African cobalt, this is principally copper, although cobalt is also produced from nickel-copper-cobalt ores in Botswana and Zimbabwe and from platinum ores in South Africa. It is rarely mined as the primary product of an ore, and is found in very weak concentration, generally 0.1%–0.5%. The ore must be crushed and ground after mining, and subjected to a flotation process to obtain the concentrate. In the mid-1990s it was predicted that a new method of extraction, known as pressure acid leaching, would substantially increase the rate of recovery of cobalt as a by-product when laterite nickel ore is treated. In the first decade of the 2000s, however, this process was still not widely applied.

In 2010, according to the Cobalt Development Institute (CDI), the principal uses of cobalt were in the manufacture of rechargeable batteries (30%); in superalloys (19%—mainly for aircraft engines); for hard and wear-resistant materials (13%); as catalysts (9%); in ceramics, enamels, pigments and colours (9%); for magnets (7%); for tyre adhesives, soaps and driers in paint or ink (5%); for hardfacing and other alloys (5%); and for feedstuffs, electrolysis, recording, etc. (3%). In 2011 the CDI cited chemical applications as accounting for 54% of cobalt use, and metallurgical applications 46% (including 19% for superalloys), whereas in 1998 metallurgy had absorbed 60% of cobalt, superalloys alone 28%. Rechargeable batteries had accounted for 40% of the increase in cobalt demand, batteries being the largest single end-use sector, accounting for more than one-quarter of consumption (about one-half on batteries for mobile telephones and one-third for laptop computers in 2007). The USA is the world's principal consumer of cobalt. The US aerospace industry, for instance, consumed about 58% of all superalloys produced worldwide.

In 2011 the Democratic Republic of the Congo (DRC) possessed almost one-half of the world's identified economic cobalt reserves (45%, according to estimates by the US Geological Survey—USGS). These reserves, associated with the country's copper deposits, also have the highest grade of the metal, with up to six metric tons of cobalt produced with every 100 tons of copper. In 2011 production of mined cobalt by the DRC totalled an estimated 52,000 metric tons, compared with 47,400 tons in 2010, a figure that had risen from 25,400 tons in 2007; mined output had been 27,100 tons in 2006 and 24,500 tons in 2005. Meanwhile, production of refined cobalt in 2006 was estimated to have declined to the historically low level of 550 tons, it having been some years since refined cobalt output had amounted to anything like the 2,149 tons of 2002. Government limits on the export of unprocessed ore, however, helped a strong recovery to 4,182 tons by 2010. The mining, marketing and export of cobalt from the DRC was conducted by a state monopoly, La Générale des Carrières et des Mines (Gécamines), but from 2008 a refinery of Katanga Mining also operated, so although Gécamines only produced an estimated 300 tons of refined cobalt, overall production in the DRC reached 1,049 tons in that year, and 2,950 tons in 2009, including a recovery of one-half as much again by Gécamines. Since the return of relative stability to the main mining areas of Katanga province in 2004, foreign investors have been actively reassessing a number of existing joint ventures with Gécamines, while proposals for new cobalt projects have proceeded apace. Between 2010 and 2014 there were plans for several new projects, including two new mines, two new refineries, and enhanced capacity at several refining and processing facilities. In recent years artisanal miners have been responsible for much of the DRC's mined output of cobalt ore production, gathering by hand cobalt-rich ores containing the mineral heterogenite. Many of these ores have been exported, via intermediaries and illegally, in particular to India and China. Much of China's cobalt refining industry is supplied with Congolese ore or semi-processed cobalt. The DRC's cobalt unprocessed ores and concentrate exports to China, declined from the mid-2000s, while those of semi-refined output rose. In 2006 revenue from cobalt exports contributed 16% of the total value of the DRC's merchandise exports, compared with 13% in 2005 and 22% in 2004. In 2008 cobalt exports accounted for 38% of the DRC's total exports of $6,590m., owing to the sharp increase in commodity prices into the middle of that year.

Production of Cobalt Ore
(cobalt content, metric tons)

	2009	2010*
World total	72,100	89,500
Sub-Saharan Africa	41,354	56,004
Sub-Saharan African producers		
Botswana	270	325
Congo, Dem. Repub.*	35,500	47,400
Madagascar*	—	700
South Africa*	610	1,800
Zambia*	4,900	5,700
Zimbabwe	74	79
Leading non-sub-Saharan African producers		
Australia*	4,340	3,850
Brazil*	1,200	1,600
Canada	3,919	4,568†
China, People's Repub.*	6,000	6,500
Cuba*	3,500	3,600
Indonesia	1,200	1,600
Morocco*	2,200	2,200
New Caledonia	719	1,000
Philippines*	1,500	2,200
Russia*	6,100	6,200

* Estimated production.
† Preliminary figure.

Source: US Geological Survey.

Since the early 1980s Zambia has promoted the expansion of its cobalt production in an attempt to offset declines in copper output. In 2009 the country's mined output of cobalt ore amounted to only 4,900 metric tons, in the latest of successive production declines since a 2003 peak of 11,000 tons. World demand was recovering into 2010, although a Zambian refinery had been closed in late 2008. However, USGS estimates had output in 2010 back up to 5,700 tons, with a similar level estimated for 2011. Zambia remains a significant producer of refined cobalt, being until 2008 the largest in Africa and the third in the world (after China and Finland), but with output falling to an estimated 1,506 tons in 2009 (owing to production being lowered in the face of world recession) compared with a peak of 6,620 tons in 2003, it even fell to second place in sub-Saharan Africa—China, Finland, Canada, Australia, Norway, the DRC, Russia, Belgium and Morocco all recording greater refinery production. A resumption of refinery activity in 2010 put Zambia back into third place internationally for refined cobalt production, at 5,026 tons, after China and Finland. Companies active in the mining and refining of cobalt in Zambia included Mopani Copper Mines PLC, Chambishi Metals PLC, Konkola Copper Mines PLC and Metorex. Exports of cobalt ores, concentrates, mattes, etc. earned some US $319m. in 2008 (6.3% of total merchandise exports), at the end of the commodity price boom and the start of world recession late in the year; ores and concentrates accounted for only about 8% of such exports. With refining production closing down, exports of ores and concentrates (mainly to China) increased and, when the industry began to recover in 2010, they accounted for 37% of total cobalt exports; in that year cobalt exports earned $311m. (4.3% of total exports).

Elsewhere in Africa, according to the USGS, cobalt was being produced as a by-product at nine South African platinum-group metal mines and one nickel mine in 2006. In addition, two South African mining companies were producing refined cobalt as a by-product of domestic platinum mining and refining. South African production of cobalt ore totalled an estimated 600 tons in 2007, unchanged compared with the previous year, but fell back to 590 tons in 2008, before recovering to 610 tons in 2009 and increasing to 1,800 tons in 2010. Output of refined metal is more significant; it totalled an estimated 307 tons in 2007—just short of 2004 production of 309 tons—compared with 267 tons in 2006 and 268 tons in 2005. Refinery production was put at 244 tons in 2008 and 238 tons in 2009, but new capacity and an improved world economic outlook saw production leap to 833 tons in 2010. In 1992 the Ugandan Government initiated a project to extract cobalt from stockpiles of cobaltiferous concentrate at the old Kilembe copper-cobalt mine, in south-western Uganda (where operations ceased in 1977). An extraction plant was subsequently operated at Kilembe by Kasese Cobalt Co Ltd (KCCL), a joint venture between state-owned Kilembe Mines Ltd and Canada's Banff Resources Ltd. In 2002 MFC Bancorp Ltd acquired control of Banff's Ugandan cobalt interests. In 2004 MFC Bancorp was reported to have distributed its cobalt assets, including its stake in KCCL, into Blue Earth Refineries Inc. of Hong Kong. Output rose steadily after a suspension of operations in 2003, from 436 tons of refined metal in 2004 to 698 tons in 2007; given the contraction in the world economy in the second half of the year, 663 tons were produced in 2008, with 673 tons in 2009 and 624 tons in 2010. The Kilembe stockpile was expected to be exhausted in 2013. In 2010, according to data cited by the USGS, Ugandan cobalt exports contributed 1.1% of total export revenue. In 2007 production of cobalt ore by Botswana totalled an estimated 242 tons, compared with 303 tons in 2006 and 326 tons in 2005. Botswanan production rose to a reported 337 tons in 2008, but fell to 270 tons in 2009, before recovering to 325 tons in 2010. Botswana tends to export cobalt to Norway and Zimbabwe for refining. In 2006, having completed a feasibility study initiated in 2003 LionOre International Ltd of Botswana (a majority stake in which was acquired by Norilsk Nickel of Russia in 2007) decided to proceed with the construction of a refinery for the production, among other metals, of cobalt carbonate at Tati Nickel Mining Co (Pty) Ltd's facilities. In August 2011, however, the Norilsk Nickel management announced the cancellation of the Activox refinery project, owing to escalating costs and interruptions to power supply in the area. Botswana's neighbour Zimbabwe produced 79 tons of cobalt ore in 2010, up from 74 tons in 2009, after a steady fall since the 110 tons of 2006. In 2007 Canada's Dynatec Corpn reportedly planned to initiate the Ambatovy nickel laterite project (owned by Dynatec, Sumitomo Corpn and Korea Resources Corpn) east of Antananarivo, Madagascar; Sherritt acquired Dynatec later that year, becoming the operator of Ambatovy, and construction work began thereafter. Some production began in 2010, with 700 tons, but escalating costs slowed down completion of what would become one of the world's biggest nickel laterite mines; an operating licence was granted in September 2012. Nickel-cobalt deposits were first identified in north-western Tanzania in the early 1990s, and have since been the object of detailed exploration. Cobalt reserves, estimated initially at about 20,000 tons, remained unexploited there as of 2010, as did reserves identified in Côte d'Ivoire.

Traditional cobalt-mining may eventually be complemented, and perhaps superseded, by the wide-scale retrieval of manganese nodules from the world's seabeds. It is estimated that the cobalt content of each nodule is about 0.25%, although nodules recovered from the Pacific Ocean in 1983 had a cobalt content of 2.5%. Ferromanganese crusts, containing extractable cobalt, have been identified at relatively shallow depths within the USA's exclusive economic zones, which extend 370 km (200 nautical miles) into US coastal waters. Research into the potential exploitation of cobalt-bearing nodules continued throughout the 1990s and 2000s. Some of the most valuable were considered to be those in the Pacific Ocean around the Cook Islands, where estimates of the cobalt resource were placed as high as 32m. metric tons. Nodules off Namibia were thought to have a lesser, though still significant, cobalt content. However, the full exploitation of seabed resources such as these is thought likely to remain impracticable for many years to come.

From 1999 WMC Resources Ltd of Australia (fully owned by BHP Billiton Ltd from 2005) offered cobalt for sale via the internet, through its Cobalt Open Sales System (COSS). COSS brought a degree of transparency to the market for cobalt and the price of contracts concluded via COSS were generally accepted as an important indicator of the prevailing price situation for cobalt world-wide. Very strong Chinese demand for cobalt, as well as a strong overall demand for cobalt for rechargeable batteries and superalloys, have been the main factors influencing a steady price increase from the mid-2000s. In 2006 the price for cobalt sold via COSS (Falconbridge 1 inch x 1 inch cut electrolytic cathodes, 99.8% grade) more than doubled, rising from US $12.50 per lb in February to $30 per lb in November, while displaying a low level of volatility. In 2007 continued strong demand combined with a shortfall of cobalt ore and concentrate from the DRC was reflected in record prices for the metal. The lowest price for cobalt sold via COSS—$24 per lb—was recorded in January, and the highest—$43 per lb—in December, following a short-lived easing of prices in September. In the first quarter of 2008 the price of cobalt rose from $45 per lb (January) to $52.25 per lb (March). Subsequently, however, in July the price declined to $42 per lb. In common with other commodities, cobalt prices fell in the later months of the year. At the end of the year BHP Billiton suspended the COSS. However, although useful, it had not necessarily been the most significant indicator: during some periods of 2005, for example, contracts concluded by Russia's Norilsk Nickel for sales of cobalt to North American destinations were regarded as the key determinant of the prevailing price situation for the metal. The main price reference was generally regarded as the London *Metal Bulletin* free-market quotation (average bid/offer). The price series for high grade (HG—minimum cobalt content of 99.8%) recorded a fall from a peak of US $51.25 per lb in March–April 2008 to only $17.50 per lb at the beginning of 2009, then a recovery mainly in the second half of the year to close at $21 per lb. The low grade (LG—minimum cobalt content of 99.3%) series paralleled the fluctuation: $48.63 in March–April 2008, to $11.5 per lb at the beginning of 2009 and $20 per lb at the end. The 2009 annual average HG price was $17.36 per lb and the LG price $15.89 per lb. The global drop in demand for cobalt because of economic recession was masked by initially sustained Chinese requirements, which dropped off later than in the West, and by the recovery in prices through 2009. However, the last-quarter rally of the cobalt price was not only attributable to returning consumer confidence, but to the imminent launch of a cobalt contract on the London Metal Exchange (LME—see below). The average price in 2010 was $20.56 per lb (HG) and $18.74 per lb (LG), with prices drifting down after April. The average price in 2011 was $17.60 per lb (HG) and $16.44 per lb (LG); prices traded in a narrow range a little higher than the average until August–September, weakening thereafter. The year ended with an average price for HG cobalt of $14.70 per lb and for LG of $13.98 per lb.

Under the new LME contract, cobalt was traded in lots consisting of four 250-kg drums (one metric ton) of minimum 99.3% cobalt, delivered by brand, with impurities identified, to warehouses in Baltimore (USA), Rotterdam (Netherlands) and Singapore. Trading was by 'open outcry' ring trading, as well as electronically and by telephone. The prices determined in the ring were intended to be used by the industry as a reference price. It remained unclear whether the market would adapt in the long term to this type of regulated pricing model for trading 'spot' and future contracts, but early interest was strong. The LME cobalt futures contract began trading in February 2010, with futures prompt dates from three months: the LME official price (cash buyer) on 1 June, therefore, was US $38,350 per metric ton, and on 1 September $40,500 per ton. The average cobalt price for 2010, as from 24 May, when the quotation first traded, was some $38,690 per ton ($17.55 per lb). The monthly price averaged some $31,700 per ton over 2011, reaching a high of $38,850 per ton on 1 August and collapsing to a low of $28,000 per ton on 1 November. Prices into the first quarter of 2012 remained above $30,000 per ton, but did not exceed $34,000 per ton, and weakened later in the year. On 3 September the cash price was $29,000 per ton (some $13.15 per lb).

The CDI, an association of producers, users and traders of cobalt, was founded in 1982, and in 2012 comprised 44 members from 18 countries.

COCOA (*Theobroma cacao*)

The cacao or cocoa tree, up to 14 m tall, originated in the tropical forests of South America. The first known cocoa plantations were in southern Mexico around AD 600. Cocoa first came to Europe in the 16th century. The Spanish and Portuguese introduced cocoa into Africa—on the islands of Fernando Póo (now Bioko), in Equatorial Guinea, and São Tomé and Príncipe—at the beginning of the 19th century. At the end of the century the tree was established on the African mainland, first in Ghana and then in other West African countries.

Cocoa is now widely grown in the tropics, usually at altitudes less than 300 m above sea-level, where it needs a fairly high rainfall and good soil. The cocoa tree has a much shallower tap root than, for example, the coffee bush, making cocoa more vulnerable to dry weather. Cocoa trees can take up to four years from planting before producing sufficient fruit for harvesting. They may live to 80 years or more, although the fully productive period is usually about 20 years. The tree is highly vulnerable to pests and diseases, and it is also very sensitive to climatic changes. Its fruit is a large pod, about 15–25 cm in length, which at maturity is yellow in some varieties and red in others. The ripe pods are cut from the tree, where they grow directly out of the trunk and branches. When opened, cocoa pods disclose a mass of seeds (beans) surrounded by white mucilage. After harvesting, the beans and mucilage are scooped out and fermented. Fermentation lasts several days, allowing the flavour to develop. The mature fermented beans, dull red in colour, are then dried, ready to be bagged as raw cocoa which may be further processed or exported.

Cultivated cocoa trees may be broadly divided into three groups. All West African cocoas belong to the Amazonian Forastero group, which now accounts for more than 80% of world cocoa production. It includes the Amelonado variety, suitable for chocolate manufacturing, grown in Ghana, Côte d'Ivoire and Nigeria. Criollo cocoa is not widely grown and is used only for luxury confectionery. The third group is Trinitario, which comprises about 15% of world output and is cultivated mainly in Central America and the northern regions of South America.

The cocoa production chain is extremely labour-intensive: the International Cocoa Organization (ICCO) estimated that in the 2000s some 3m. smallholders accounted for 90% of output worldwide. Large-scale plantations are found only in Brazil and Indonesia. The cocoa-processing industry, meanwhile, is highly concentrated. In the few years up to 2010 the ICCO reckoned that the three major companies (Archer Daniels Midland, Barry Callebaut and Cargill) processed about 40% of global cocoa production. Most cocoa processing takes place in importing countries, mainly in the USA and the Netherlands, although processing capacity was established in West Africa during the 1960s and processed products now account for a significant part of the value of cocoa exports. The processes include shelling, roasting and grinding the beans. The primary product of grinding is chocolate liquor, a part of which is sold directly to chocolate manufacturers; the remainder is then processed further, in order to extract both a fat—cocoa butter—and chocolate powder. Almost half of each bean after shelling consists of cocoa butter. Cocoa powder for use as a beverage is largely fat-free. Cocoa is a mildly stimulating drink, because of its caffeine content, and, unlike coffee and tea, is highly nutritious.

The most important use of cocoa liquor is for the manufacture of chocolate, of which it is the main ingredient. About 90% of all cocoa liquor produced is used in chocolate-making, for which extra cocoa butter is added, as well as other substances such as sugar and, in the case of milk chocolate, milk. Cocoa butter is also used in cosmetic products, while the by-products of cocoa beans—the husks and shells—are used to make fertilizers and animal feed. Proposals initially announced in 1993 (and subsequently amended in 1997) by the consumer countries of the European Union (EU), permitting chocolate manufacturers in member states to add as much as 5% vegetable fats to cocoa solids and cocoa fats in the manufacture of chocolate products, were perceived by producers as potentially damaging to the world cocoa trade. In 1998 it was estimated that the implementation of this plan could reduce world demand for cocoa beans by 130,000–200,000 metric tons annually. In July 1999, despite protests from Belgium, which—with France, Germany, Greece, Italy, Luxembourg, the Netherlands and Spain—prohibited the manufacture or import of chocolate containing non-cocoa-butter vegetable fats, the European Commission cleared the way to the abolition of this restriction throughout the EU countries, which took effect in June 2000. The implementation of the new regulations by all member states ensued in 2003. Producers identified another, potentially more damaging, threat when, in March 2007, the US Chocolate Manufacturers Association, following a similar request at the end of 2006 from the Grocery Manufacturers of America, began to lobby the US Food and Drug Administration (FDA) to change the legal definition of chocolate, in order to allow them to substitute at will vegetable fats and oils for cocoa butter in products labelled as chocolate. In response, the FDA initiated a public consultation. In order to allay consumers' concerns, in June 2007 the FDA provisionally assured that 'cacao fat, as one of the signature characteristics of the product, will remain a principal component of standardized chocolate'. Meanwhile, an EU study that evaluated the new European regulations, published in June 2006, found that the annual rate of growth of net cocoa imports had increased to 3.5% by 2005, despite a saturated market for chocolate products. The study attributed this growth mainly to an increase in consumer demand for products with a high cocoa content. According to a report published by the ICCO in June 2008, changes in consumption behaviour had had a significant impact on demand for cocoa beans in terms of both quality and quantity. Between 2001/02 and 2006/07 world cocoa consumption expanded at an average annual rate of 3.8%. In 2006/07 consumption increased by 2.5%, compared with the previous season. A significant part of the increase resulted from higher consumption in Europe (where it rose by 21%), where consumers were increasingly inclined to purchase organic, fine-flavour and high cocoa-content products. In particular, the growing demand for products with a high cocoa content was influenced by research findings on the beneficial health properties of cocoa, and led in turn to increased demand for cocoa beans of superior quality—which command higher prices. In the same year global consumption of dark chocolate was estimated to constitute 5%–10% of the total consumption of chocolate bars, with the highest share (20%) in continental Europe, particularly in the Netherlands, France, Belgium and Switzerland. A Euromonitor report, covering 2003–08, had the average annual increase in the consumption of single-origin chocolate at more than 20%, of certified organic chocolate at almost 20% and dark chocolate at over 15%. Concerns about food safety and environmental issues had prompted an increase in demand for organic chocolate, the share of which in global production was, however, still estimated at less than 0.5% of output world-wide in 2005. According to the ICCO, such changes in the pattern of consumption were primarily of benefit to the economies of those countries recognized by the International Cocoa Council (ICC) as exporters of premium cocoa (Colombia, Costa Rica, Dominica, the Dominican Republic, Ecuador, Grenada, Indonesia, Jamaica, Madagascar, Papua New Guinea, Peru, Saint Lucia, São Tomé and Príncipe, Trinidad and Tobago, and Venezuela). At the same time as the expansion of existing, saturated markets, increased consumption in Russia and in emerging and newly industrialized markets, in particular in Asia, has sustained demand for bulk cocoa. However, premium chocolate manufacturers proved less resilient during the world-wide economic recession beginning in late 2008 than the mass-market producers, although the latter too were affected.

A combination of growing consumer concerns about poverty in less developed countries and a more organized fair-trade movement has established steady growth in sales of fair-trade products since the early 1990s. Sales of cocoa labelled 'fair trade' increased from 700 metric tons in 1996 to 5,657 tons in 2005, equivalent to annual growth of 23%. By 2011 the ICCO still estimated that the share of fair-trade cocoa represented less than 0.5% of global production. In 2005 83% of sales of fair-trade cocoa world-wide were distributed among only six countries: the United Kingdom (40%), Germany and France (13% each), Austria, Italy and Switzerland (6% each).

In 2010, according to FAO, the most important producing area in the world was Africa, which accounted for 65% of total output, followed by South-East Asia and Oceania, at 21%, and Latin America and the Caribbean, at 14%. In 2009 Africa accounted for 68% of foreign sales of cocoa beans world-wide, by volume, South-East Asia and Oceania 17%, and Latin America and the Caribbean 7% (the balance includes re-exports). According to ICCO figures, the largest single producer of cocoa beans in 2011/12 (the cocoa year runs October–September), despite problems early in the 2000s, remained Côte d'Ivoire, with a forecast 1.41m. metric tons (down from 1.51m. tons in 2010/11), followed by Ghana with 890,000 tons (down from 1.03m. tons), Indonesia with 500,000 tons (up from 440,000 tons), Nigeria with 220,000 tons (240,000 tons), Cameroon with 210,000 tons (229,000 tons), Brazil with 190,000 tons (200,000 tons) and Ecuador with 175,000 tons (161,000 tons). World output of cocoa beans, according to FAO, was 4.23m. tons in 2008, 4.14m. tons in 2009 and 4.23m. tons in 2010. ICCO figures for production tend to be lower: world production was put at 3.64m. tons in 2009/10, an estimated 4.31m. tons in 2010/11 and a projected 3.99m. tons in 2011/12. Since two-fifths of the processing (grinding) of cocoa beans does not take place in the country of origin, the Netherlands is the world leader, accounting for an estimated 13.7% of the world total of 3.92m. tons in 2010/11, followed by Germany (11.2%), the USA (10.2%), Côte d'Ivoire (9.2%—down from second place and 11.0% the previous year), Malaysia (7.8%), Brazil (6.1%), Ghana (5.9%) and Indonesia (4.8%). Overall, Europe accounted for 41% of grindings, the Americas 22%, Asia and Oceania 20% and Africa 17%. Global consumption of chocolate products is dominated by the European Union (EU—53%); and by Northern America (26%).

Production of Cocoa Beans
('000 metric tons)

	2009	2010
World total	4,201	4,188
Sub-Saharan Africa*	2,698	2,667
Leading African producers		
Cameroon	235	264
Côte d'Ivoire	1,223	1,242
Ghana	711	632
Nigeria	364	360*
Togo†	105	102
Leading non-African producers		
Brazil	218	235
Colombia	49	40
Dominican Republic	55	58
Ecuador	121	132
Indonesia	810	845
Mexico	60*	27
Papua New Guinea†	59	39
Peru	37	47

* FAO estimate(s).
† Unofficial figures.

Source: FAO.

Cocoa is the most valuable agricultural export commodity in West Africa. Recorded world exports of cocoa beans leapt by 27% in 2004, dipped the following year and then rose to a record 3.03m. tons in 2006, before declining steadily to total 2.73m. metric tons in 2008 (the lowest figure in five years); world exports rose to 3.00m. tons in 2009, but fell back to 2.70m. tons in 2010, of which sub-Saharan African countries accounted for 60%. The world's leading exporters of cocoa beans in 2010 were Côte d'Ivoire (790,912 tons—down on the previous year, but above the 2008 total, the lowest figure for the 2000s), Indonesia (432,437 tons), Ghana (281,437 tons), Nigeria (226,634 tons) and Cameroon (193,881 tons); the next largest African exporter was Togo (82,100 tons), after Ecuador. In 2008 the number of cocoa farms in West Africa was estimated at 1.2m.–1.5m., with an average size of 3–5 ha, employing 10.5m. workers in total. Côte d'Ivoire has been the leading producer in both regional and world terms since it overtook Ghana in 1977. According to FAO, in 2010 Côte d'Ivoire still accounted for about 30% of global output of cocoa and for 29% of international cocoa exports. Since 2002 fluctuations in international cocoa bean prices have to a large extent been determined by developments in the civil conflict in Côte d'Ivoire. According to the ICCO, Côte d'Ivoire is the leading grinding country among cocoa-producing countries, and in 2011/12 it was the third most important grinding country in the world, after the Netherlands and Germany—though it still accounted for some 11% annually of global grinding of cocoa beans. The Ivorian cocoa industry suffered disruptions to the processing and export supply chain in the first half of 2011, owing to political instability, but increased investment in grindings capacity by the leading multinationals helped to resume the impetus towards Côte d'Ivoire's soon becoming the world's leading grinding country. Côte d'Ivoire's first cocoa transformation plant, SUCSO, opened in the port of San Pedro in late 2007, and was expected to produce 15,000 tons of chocolate bars per year. Cocoa superseded coffee as Côte d'Ivoire main cash crop at the beginning of the 1980s. In 2011 an estimated 34% of the country's export revenue was derived from cocoa and cocoa preparations. Government measures implemented in August 1999 to liberalize the country's cocoa sector included the abolition of the state cocoa board, with the consequent removal of guaranteed prices. In November, however, the impact on Ivorian cocoa growers of sharply lower world cocoa prices (see below) prompted the Government to reintroduce a minimum price mechanism and buffer stock arrangements. In 2001 prices paid to farmers reached record high levels. However, the outbreak of civil conflict in 2002 isolated cocoa-growing areas from the government-held coastal region and caused the flight of thousands of immigrant workers from plantations. Cocoa production totalled 1.4m. tons in the 2003/04 season, but fell to 1.3m. tons in 2004/05. In 2004 the buying season was delayed as farmers refused to accept very low price levels (300 francs CFA per kg, compared with 704 francs CFA per kg in 2002), and the buying season did not begin until late November. Output rose to 1.4m. tons in 2005/06, but fell back to 1.2m. tons in 2006/07 as a result of the smuggling of an estimated 300,000 tons of Ivorian cocoa out of the country—especially to Ghana, where prices paid were considerably higher—and of adverse weather conditions. Cocoa production recovered to 1.4m. tons in 2007/08 (ICCO figures), due to government efforts to prevent smuggling, but fell back to 1.2m. tons in 2008/09 and 2009/10, rising to a peak of 1.5m. tons in 2010/11, with 1.4m. tons predicted for 2011/12. That would represent one-half of the African total and 35% of global output.

Cocoa is traditionally Ghana's most important cash crop, occupying more than one-half of all the country's cultivated land. In the mid-1960s Ghana was the world's leading producer, accounting for more than one-third of world production. From the mid-1970s to the mid-1990s, however, Ghana's cocoa production underwent a sharp decline. This contraction of the country's cocoa industry has been attributed to growing competition from Côte d'Ivoire and mismanagement. The decline was exacerbated by the smuggling of cocoa to neighbouring countries, where higher prices were obtainable. The spread of plant diseases, particularly black pod and swollen shoot, have also inhibited recovery. Ghana endeavoured to revive cocoa production through programmes of replanting and the introduction of disease-resistant varieties, together with pest control, and improved facilities for transport and storage. From July 1993 the Ghana Cocoa Board (COCOBOD) was deprived of its monopoly. Nevertheless, in 1998 the Government restated its intention to resist pressure from the IMF and the World Bank to liberalize the external marketing of cocoa, which was still carried out exclusively by the Government and, in 2001, it began to license private cocoa-exporting companies. From the mid-1990s the recovery of Ghana's cocoa sector commenced, assisted to some extent, from 2002, by political instability in Côte d'Ivoire. The 2004 cocoa harvest, of 736,911 tons, was the largest ever recorded in Ghana, staying at that level for two more years, until prolonged adverse weather conditions from 2007. According to FAO, Ghana's share of world exports declined from 17% in 2008 to 10% in 2010. ICCO figures had production rising from 632,000 tons in 2009/10 to 1.25m. tons in 2010/11, then 890,000 tons forecast for 2011/12 (22% of global production). Although cocoa was overtaken in 1992 by gold as Ghana's main export commodity, it regained its pre-eminence in 2003–06, only to be displaced again thereafter. In 2011, when substantial petroleum exports began, sales of cocoa beans and cocoa products still accounted for 11% of Ghana's export revenue. Ghana has also invested considerably in processing facilities in recent years, as part of an attempt to add value to its exports. Between 2004/05 and 2010/11 Ghanaian grindings of cocoa beans almost tripled, from 80,000 tons to a forecast 235,000 tons, while the country's share of world grindings rose from 2.4% to 5.9%.

Among the smaller African producers, cocoa exports are a significant component of the economies of Cameroon (where they contributed about 31% of total export revenue in 2009, but only 16% in 2010 owing to the beginning of petroleum production) and São Tomé and Príncipe (where they contributed 68% of total export revenue in 2009); cocoa exports remain important to but by no means dominate in Togo. Although cocoa is still the main export crop in Nigeria (which itself is Africa's third largest producer), its significance to the economy has been eclipsed by petroleum, and the same applies to Equatorial Guinea.

World prices for cocoa are highly sensitive to changes in supply and demand, making its market position volatile. Negotiations to secure international agreement on stabilizing the cocoa industry began in 1956. Full-scale cocoa conferences, under UN auspices, were held in 1963, 1966 and 1967, but all proved abortive. A major difficulty was the failure to agree on a fixed minimum price. In 1972 the fourth UN Cocoa Conference took place in Geneva and resulted in the first International Cocoa Agreement (ICCA), adopted by 52 countries, although the USA, the world's principal cocoa importer at that time, did not participate. The ICCA took formal effect in October 1973. It operated for three quota years and provided for an export quota system for producing countries, a fixed price range for cocoa beans and a buffer stock to support the agreed prices. In accordance with the ICCA, the ICCO, based in London, was established in 1973. By October 2010 the membership of the 2001 ICCA (see below) comprised 44 countries (15 exporting members, 29 importing members), representing about 85% of world cocoa production and some 60% of world cocoa consumption. EU is also an intergovernmental party to the 2001 Agreement—its 27 members, together with Russia and Switzerland, comprise the importing membership. However, the USA, a leading importer of cocoa, is not a member, nor is Indonesia, which is now the third largest producer in the world. Membership of the 2010 ICCA at June 2012 included Indonesia among the 11 exporting members; the 28 importing members included the 27 EU members and Switzerland, as before, but not Russia (nor, still, the USA). The governing body of the ICCO is the ICC, established to supervise implementation of the ICCA. The ICC is also based in London (consideration of plans to relocate to Abidjan, Côte d'Ivoire, was postponed to 2015, pending security considerations).

A second ICCA operated during 1979–81. It was followed by an extended agreement, which was in force in 1981–87. A fourth ICCA took effect in 1987. During the period of these ICCAs the effective operation of cocoa price stabilization mechanisms was frequently impeded by a number of factors, principally by crop and stock surpluses, which continued to overshadow the cocoa market in the early 1990s. In addition, the achievement of ICCA objectives was affected by the divergent views of producers and consumers, led by Côte d'Ivoire, on one side, and by the USA, on the other, as to appropriate minimum price levels. Disagreements also developed regarding the allocation of members' export quotas and the conduct of price support measures by means of the buffer stock (which ceased to operate during 1983–88), and subsequently over the disposal of unspent buffer stock funds. The effectiveness of financial operations under the fourth ICCA was severely curtailed by the accumulation of arrears of individual members' levy payments, notably by Côte d'Ivoire and Brazil. The fourth ICCA was extended for a two-year period from October 1990, although the suspension of the economic clauses relating to price-support operations rendered the agreement ineffective in terms of exerting any influence over cocoa market prices.

Preliminary discussions on a fifth ICCA, again held under UN auspices, ended without agreement in May 1992, when consumer members, while agreeing to extend the fourth ICCA for a further year (until October 1993), refused to accept producers' proposals for the creation of an export quota system as a means of stabilizing prices, on the grounds that such arrangements would not impose sufficient limits on total production to restore equilibrium between demand and supply. Additionally, no agreement was reached on the disposition of cocoa buffer stocks, then totalling 240,000 metric tons. In March 1993 ICCO delegates abandoned efforts to formulate arrangements whereby prices would be stabilized by means of a stock-withholding scheme. At a further negotiating conference in July, however, terms were finally agreed for a new ICCA, to take effect from October, subject to its ratification by at least five exporting countries (accounting for at least 80% of total world exports) and by importing countries (representing at least 60% of total imports). Unlike previous commodity agreements sponsored by the UN, the fifth ICCA aimed to achieve stable prices by regulating supplies and promoting consumption, rather than through the operation of buffer stocks and export quotas.

The fifth ICCA, operating until September 1998, entered into effect in February 1994. Under the new agreement, buffer stocks totalling 233,000 metric tons that had accrued from the previous ICCA were to be released on the market at the rate of 51,000 tons annually over a maximum period of four-and-a-half years, beginning in the 1993/94 crop season. At a meeting of the ICCO held in October 1994 it was agreed that, following the completion of the stocks reduction programme, the extent of stocks held should be limited to the equivalent of three months' consumption. ICCO members also assented to a voluntary reduction in output of 75,000 tons annually, beginning in 1993/94 and terminating in 1998/99. Further measures to achieve a closer balance of production and consumption, under which the level of cocoa stocks would be maintained at 34% of world grindings during the 1996/97 crop year, were introduced by the ICCO in September 1996. The ICCA was subsequently extended until September 2001. In April 2000 the ICCO agreed to implement measures to remedy low levels of world prices, which were to centre on the elimination of sub-grade cocoa in world trade: these cocoas were viewed by the ICCO as partly responsible for the downward trend in prices. In mid-July Côte d'Ivoire, Ghana, Nigeria and Cameroon disclosed that they had agreed to destroy a minimum of 250,000 tons of cocoa at the beginning of the 2000/01 crop season, with a view to assisting prices to recover and to 'improving the quality of cocoa' entering world markets.

A sixth ICCA was negotiated, under the auspices of the UN, in February 2001. Like its predecessor, the sixth ICCA aimed to achieve stable prices through the regulation of supplies and the promotion of consumption, but it also incorporated into its objectives the development of a sustainable cocoa economy. The Agreement took provisional effect on 1 October 2003, for an initial five-year period; it was twice extended for two years, latterly from 1 October 2010. In December, in accordance with its provisions, the ICC established a Consultative Board on the World Cocoa Economy, a private sector board with a mandate to 'contribute to the development of a sustainable cocoa economy; identify threats to supply and demand and propose action to meet the challenges; facilitate the exchange of information on production, consumption and stocks; and advise on other cocoa-related matters within the scope of the Agreement'. In November 2005, on its ratification by the Dominican Republic, the sixth ICCA entered definitively into force (this was the first time that an ICCA had ever entered definitively into force). The Agreement remained open to new signatories until 2010, and was extended to the point at which the next Agreement was due to enter into force.

A seventh ICCA was signed in Geneva on the last day of the UN Cocoa Conference of 21–25 June 2010. It was opened for signature on 1 October for two years (subsequently extended to 2026). In July 2011 Costa Rica became the third signatory to the document, after Switzerland and the EU. Previous agreements had been for five years, with extensions possible. The new document built on the strengths of the 2001 Agreement, improving product quality and co-operation between exporters and importers, emphasizing improved incomes for farmers and other producer benefits, and aiming for sustainability in the cocoa economies. The 2010 Agreement, unlike the previous five-year accords, was to be in effect for 10 years, provisionally from 1 October 2012, with the possibility of two four-year extensions, recognizing the perceived success of the current regime.

International prices for cocoa were generally very low until the early 2000s. In 2002, however, the average of the ICCO's daily prices (based on selected quotations from the London and New York markets) rebounded by almost 63%, compared with the low of the previous year, to reach $1,778 per ton. In 2003 the ICCO's average daily price fell slightly, by 1.3%, to $1,755 per ton. A more substantial decline, of 11.8%, was recorded in 2004, when the ICCO's daily quotation averaged $1,548 per ton. In 2005 the average quotation fell marginally, by 0.6%, compared with the previous year, to $1,538 per ton. The ICCO's average daily price recovered by 3.5% in 2006, to $1,592 per ton. The average daily price increased substantially, by 22.6%, to $1,952 per ton in 2007, and again, by 32.0%, to $2,577 per ton in 2008. Global economic concerns, which had depressed cocoa quotations in the second half of 2008 and had affected all commodity prices, were pronounced into the first half of 2009, despite continued expectation of a production deficit. Nevertheless, the average price for 2009 was $2,889 per ton, the price having risen considerably later in the year (the final quarter average was $3,418 per ton). After a monthly peak of $3,525 per ton in January 2010, prices fell back somewhat from earlier heights and fluctuated downwards, in particular from September, but still recorded an average of $3,133 per ton over the year. In 2011 assurance of sufficient supply to meet demand had eased the price by the middle of 2011 (from a monthly peak of $3,472 per ton in February), although concerns remained of a cocoa deficit in the longer term, despite the expected beginnings of recovery in Côte d'Ivoire's production; the average price for the year was $2,980 per ton. In the first seven months of 2012 the average of the ICCO daily prices had fallen still lower, to $2,317 per ton, as uncertain macroeconomic factors in the USA and, in particular, Europe countered the fears of a production deficit; monthly averages were fairly consistent, between a high of $2,359 per ton (March) and a low of $2,264 per ton (June).

The Cocoa Producers' Alliance (COPAL), with headquarters in Lagos, Nigeria, had 10 members in 2012, including Cameroon, Côte d'Ivoire, Gabon, Ghana, Nigeria, São Tomé and Príncipe, and Togo. COPAL was formed in 1962 with the aim of preventing excessive price fluctuations by regulating the supply of cocoa. Members of COPAL currently account for about three-quarters of world cocoa production, with its seven African members providing some 69%. COPAL has acted in concert with successive ICCAs.

The principal centres for cocoa-trading in the industrialized countries are the London Cocoa Terminal Market, in the United Kingdom, and the New York Coffee, Sugar and Cocoa Exchange, in the USA.

COFFEE (*Coffea*)

The coffee plant is an evergreen shrub or small tree, generally 5–10 m in height, indigenous to Asia and tropical Africa. Wild trees grow to 10 m, but cultivated shrubs are usually pruned to a maximum of 3 m. The dried seeds (beans) are roasted, ground and brewed in hot water to provide one of the most popular of the world's non-alcoholic beverages. Coffee is drunk in every country in the world, and its consumers comprise an estimated one-third of the world's population. Although it has little nutrient value, coffee acts as a mild stimulant, owing to the presence of caffeine, an alkaloid also present in tea and cocoa.

There are about 40 species of *Coffea*, most of which grow wild in the eastern hemisphere. The two species of economic importance are *C. arabica* (native to Ethiopia), which in the mid-2000s accounted for about 60%–65% of world production, and *C. canephora* (the source of Robusta coffee), which accounted for almost all of the remainder. Arabica coffee is more aromatic, but Robusta, as the name implies, is a stronger plant. Coffee grows in the tropical belt, between 20°N and 20°S, and from sea-level to as high as 2,000 m above. The optimum growing conditions are found at 1,250–1,500 m above sea-level, with an average temperature of around 17°C and an average annual rainfall of 1,000–1,750 mm. Trees begin bearing fruit three to five years after planting, depending upon the variety, and give their maximum yield (up to 5 kg of fruit per year) from the sixth to the 15th year. Few remain profitable beyond 30 years.

Arabica coffee trees are grown mostly in the American tropics and supply the largest quantity and the best quality of coffee beans. In Africa and Asia Arabica coffee is vulnerable in lowland areas to a serious leaf disease, and consequently cultivation has been concentrated on highland areas. Some highland Arabicas, such as those grown in Kenya, have a high reputation for quality.

The Robusta coffee tree, grown mainly in East and West Africa, and in the Far East, has larger leaves than Arabica but the beans are generally smaller and of lower quality and price. However, Robusta coffee has a higher yield than Arabica as the trees are more resistant to disease and it can be grown at lower elevations—from 500 m to 1,500 m above sea level—than Arabicas. Robusta is also more suitable for the production of soluble ('instant') coffee and is favoured by multinational roasters and instant coffee manufacturers on account of its low cost. In the mid-2000s four main roasting companies (Kraft Foods, Nestlé, Procter & Gamble, and Sara Lee) purchased more than 50% of global Robusta coffee output. Soluble coffee accounts for more than one-fifth of world coffee consumption. About 60% of African coffee is of the Robusta variety.

Each coffee berry, green at first but red when ripe, usually contains two beans (white in Arabica, light brown in Robusta), which are the commercial product of the plant. To produce the best quality Arabica beans—known in the trade as 'mild' coffee—the berries are opened by a pulping machine and the beans fermented briefly in water before being dried and hulled into green coffee. Much of the crop is exported in green form. Robusta beans are generally prepared by dry-hulling. Roasting and grinding are usually undertaken in the importing countries, for economic reasons and because roasted beans rapidly lose their freshness when exposed to air.

Apart from beans, coffee produces a few minor by-products. When the coffee beans have been removed from the fruit, what remains is a wet mass of pulp and, at a later stage, the dry material of the 'hull' or fibrous sleeve that protects the beans. Coffee pulp is used as cattle feed, the fermented pulp makes a good fertilizer, and coffee bean oil is an ingredient in soaps, paints and polishes.

More than one-half of the world's coffee is produced on smallholdings of less than 5 ha. In most producing countries, and especially in Africa, coffee is almost entirely an export crop, with little domestic consumption. Green coffee accounts for some 96% of all the coffee that is exported, with soluble and roasted coffee comprising the balance. Tariffs on green/raw coffee are usually low or non-existent, but those applied to soluble coffee may be as high as 30%. The USA is the largest single importer (24% of the world total in 2011/12, according to the US Department of Agriculture—USDA), although its volume of coffee purchases was overtaken in 1975 by the combined imports of the (then) nine countries of the European Community (EC, now the European Union—EU—the 27 members of which imported 46% of the world total in 2011/12). Sub-Saharan Africa has no significant importers; the continent's largest exporter, and the ninth in the world in 2011/12, was Ethiopia (3.6% of global exports), followed by Uganda, which it had displaced as Africa's principal exporter two years previously, according to USDA. The International Coffee Organization (ICO) had Uganda selling more abroad again in 2011/12, with 2.8% of global exports.

After petroleum, coffee is the major raw material in world trade, and the single most valuable agricultural export of the tropics. Of the estimated total world crop of coffee beans in 2011/12, Latin American and Caribbean countries accounted for 59.2% (Brazil alone contributed 33.1% of the world total). Africa, which formerly ranked second, was overtaken in 1992/93 by Asian producers. In 2011/12 African producers accounted for 12.7% of the estimated world coffee crop, compared with 23.4% for countries in eastern Asia and Oceania. India harvested a further 4.1% of the world coffee crop in the same year; the only other producer in South Asia was Sri Lanka, not a member of the ICO. (The above shares have been calculated on the basis of data released by the ICO. Non-members of the ICO accounted for 0.5% of the world coffee crop in 2011/12.) The largest single producer after Brazil is Viet Nam (15.2% of world production), followed by Indonesia (6.3%) and Colombia (5.9%). Forecasts for 2012/13 reckoned on a higher harvest, primarily because it was the higher yield year in the biennial Arabica cycle for the important Brazilian crop.

Production of Green Coffee Beans
('000 bags, each of 60 kg, coffee years)

	2010/11	2011/12
World total	134,386	131,253
Sub-Saharan Africa*	16,304	16,691
Leading African producers		
Cameroon	608	1,083
Congo, Dem. Repub.	300	1,056
Côte d'Ivoire	982	1,600
Ethiopia	7,500	6,500
Kenya	658	680
Madagascar	529	597
Tanzania	800	534
Uganda	3,290	3,212

—continued	2010/11	2011/12
Leading non-African producers		
Brazil	48,095	43,484
Colombia	8,523	7,800
Honduras	4,326	4,500
India	5,033	5,333
Indonesia	9,129	8,250
Mexico	4,850	4,300
Peru	4,069	5,443
Viet Nam	19,467	20,000

* Excluding Equatorial Guinea, which, with other non-members of the ICO, is included in the world total.

Source: International Coffee Organization.

In every year during 1970–90, except in 1974 and 1984, Côte d'Ivoire was Africa's leading coffee producer, and coffee was the country's leading cash crop. Since 1980 cocoa has overtaken coffee as its most important export crop—in 2009, according to trade statistics compiled by the UN, exports of coffee accounted for 2.1% of the country's total export revenue. Despite a programme of replanting in the 1990s, more than 60% of Côte d'Ivoire's coffee trees were reported in 2005 to be over 30 years old. Higher prices for coffee contributed to a very substantial increase in Ivorian production from 1995, reaching some 379,000 metric tons in 1999/2000. Production then declined steadily, to as low as 101,460 tons by 2005/06. Recovery was slow, disrupted by the continued political and military crisis in the country, which affected the maintenance of coffee plantations. Production had risen to 143,820 tons by 2008/09, falling to only 58,920 by 2010/11, before recovering slowly to some 96,000 tons in 2011/12. As a result, the country was not a major exporter in that year.

The African countries that have traditionally been most dependent on coffee as a source of foreign exchange are Burundi and Uganda. In 2002 coffee sales accounted for three-quarters of Burundi's total export revenue. The proportion varied, depending on international coffee prices, but in 2011 it was 60%. According to the UN, in Uganda coffee provided about 18% of export earnings in 2010. The country was traditionally Africa's leading exporter of coffee, but only the continent's second largest producer (192,700 metric tons in 2011/12). Ethiopia has emerged as the major regional producer of Arabicas, accounting in 2011/12 for almost two-fifths of total African output of coffee. Despite high domestic consumption and widespread smuggling, coffee accounted for 62% of Ethiopia's total export earnings in 1991, and for 71% in 1997/98. The contribution of coffee to total export earnings had declined by the early 2000s, representing only about 39% in 2002 and falling to 23% by 2009; it was 32% in 2011, reflecting rising international prices. Ethiopia vies with Uganda to be Africa's leading exporter. Meanwhile, Ethiopia's coffee production peaked in 2007/08, fell back in 2008/09, and then recovered to successive records, reaching some 450,000 tons in 2010/11 (compared with 166,000 tons in 2000/01), before slipping back to 390,000 tons in 2011/12. The coffee sector in Rwanda, which contributed more than 60% of export revenue in 1991, was severely affected by civil war, and in 1994 the bulk of the crop was lost. Rwanda's coffee output in 1997 was the smallest since 1974, and it declined still further in 1998. Output recovered in the early 2000s. In 2004/05 Rwanda's production—which consists mainly of Arabicas—rose by more than 70%, to some 27,000 metric tons, approaching pre-conflict levels and the most reached in the decade. The biennial peak was 22,000 tons in 2008/09, but reached only 19,000 tons in 2010/11, with a low of 13,800 tons in 2011/12. Coffee, which still contributed about 56% of Rwanda's total export earnings in 1999, was overtaken by tea as the major cash crop in 2000. Depending on the relative international prices as well as production, coffee and tea was each in some years the leading agricultural export; by 2011 a steady improvement in coffee exports meant that they accounted for 18% of total exports, compared with tea at 13% (both exceeded by tin, since the previous year, at 24%).

Among other African countries where coffee is an important export are Cameroon (where exports of coffee accounted for 2.4% of total export revenue in 2005, although this had fallen to less than 1.0% by 2011), the Central African Republic (2.2% in 2009), Kenya (4.0% in 2010) and Tanzania (3.1% in 2011). In 2011/12, according to the ICO, Kenya displaced Tanzania as Africa's fourth largest exporter (after Uganda, Ethiopia and Côte d'Ivoire), and they were followed by Cameroon and Guinea. Madagascar is not a significant exporter, but it is Africa's seventh largest producer. The Democratic Republic of the Congo recorded significant official output in 2011/12, making it the continent's sixth largest producer. Angola was formerly the world's leading exporter of Robusta coffee, but production during 1975–95 was severely disrupted by civil conflict. Although recovery began in the mid-1990s, followed by restructuring and privatization, the full rehabilitation of Angola's coffee industry depended on an enduring political and military settlement, and even then was expected to span many years. According to the ICO, post-war coffee production peaked in 2002/03, at some 3,400 tons, with the next biennial peak at only 2,300 tons; 2009/10 recorded the lowest output of the decade, barely at an estimated 800 tons but, after a peak of 2,100 tons in 2010/11, 1,740 tons was achieved in 2011/12.

Effective international attempts to stabilize coffee prices began in 1954, when a number of producing countries made a short-term agreement to fix export quotas. After three such agreements, a five-year International Coffee Agreement (ICA), covering both producers and consumers and introducing a quota system, was signed in 1962. This led to the establishment in 1963 of the ICO, with its headquarters in London, United Kingdom. Successive ICAs took effect in 1968, 1976, and 1983. The system of export quotas to stabilize prices was eventually abandoned in July 1989, contributing to a crisis in coffee prices as over-supply undermined market stability (see below). In October 1993 the USA withdrew from the ICO (it did not rejoin it until 2005), which was increasingly perceived at that time to have been eclipsed by the Association of Coffee Producing Countries (ACPC—see below). In 1994 the ICO agreed provisions for a new ICA, again with primarily consultative and administrative functions, to operate for a five-year period, until September 1999. In November of that year it was agreed to extend this limited ICA until September 2001. A successor ICA took effect provisionally in October 2001, and definitively in May 2005. By May 2007 the new ICA had been endorsed by 74 of the 77 members (45 exporting countries, 32 importing countries) of the International Coffee Council (ICC), the highest authority of the ICO. Among the principal objectives of the 2001 ICA were the promotion of international co-operation with regard to coffee, and the provision of a forum for consultations, both intergovernmental and with the private sector, with the aim of achieving a reasonable balance between world supply and demand in order to guarantee adequate supplies of coffee at fair prices for consumers, and markets for coffee at remunerative prices for producers. A seventh ICA, agreed between the 77 members of the ICC, was formally adopted in September 2007. The new agreement reiterated the objectives contained in the sixth ICA, emphasizing the need to support the advancement of a sustainable coffee economy to benefit small-scale farmers. It established in particular a Consultative Forum of Coffee Sector Finance that was to facilitate access to financial and market information in the coffee sector, and a Promotion and Market Development Committee that was to co-ordinate information campaigns, research and studies. At July 2012, the ICO consisted of 37 exporting members and six importing members (32 importing nations in all, because one member was the 27-country EU); a further 12 countries had signed the seventh ICA but had not yet completed all membership procedures.

During each ICA up to and including the one implemented in 1994, contention arose over the allocation of members' export quotas, the operation of price support mechanisms, and, most importantly, illicit sales by some members of surplus stocks to non-members of the ICO (notably to the USSR and to countries in Eastern Europe and the Middle East). These 'leaks' of low-price coffee, often at less than one-half of the official ICA rate, also found their way to consumer members of the ICO through free ports, depressing the general market price and making it more difficult for exporters to fulfil their quotas. The issue of coffee export quotas had become further complicated in the 1980s, as consumers in the main importing market, the USA, and, to a lesser extent, in the EC came to prefer the milder Arabica coffees grown in Central America at the expense of the Robustas exported by Brazil and the main African producers. Disagreements over a new system of quota allocations, taking account of coffee by variety, had the effect of undermining efforts in 1989 to preserve the economic provisions of the ICA, pending the negotiation of a new agreement. The ensuing deadlock between consumers and producers, as well as among the producers themselves, led in July to the collapse of the quota system and the suspension of the economic provisions of the ICA. The administrative clauses of the agreement, however, continued to operate and were subsequently extended until October 1993, pending an eventual settlement of the quota issue and the entry into force of a successor ICA.

With the abandonment of the ICA quotas, coffee prices fell sharply in world markets, and were further depressed by a substantial accumulation of coffee stocks held by consumers. The response by some Latin American producers was to seek to revive prices by imposing temporary suspensions of exports; this strategy, however, merely increased losses of coffee revenue. By early 1992 there had been general agreement among the ICO exporting members that the export quota mechanism should be revived. However, disagreements persisted over the allocation of quotas, and in April 1993 it was announced that efforts to achieve a new ICA with economic provisions had collapsed. In the following month Brazil and Colombia, the two largest coffee producers at that time, were joined by some Central American producers in a scheme to limit their coffee production and exports in the 1993/94 coffee year. Although world consumption of coffee exceeded the level of shipments, prices were severely depressed by surpluses of coffee stocks totalling 62m. bags (each of 60 kg), with an additional 21m. bags held in reserve by consumer countries. Prices, in real terms, stood at historic 'lows'.

In September 1993 the Latin American producers announced the formation of an Association of Coffee Producing Countries (ACPC) to implement an export-withholding, or coffee-retention, plan. In the following month the Inter-African Coffee Organization (IACO, see below), whose membership includes Côte d'Ivoire, Kenya and Uganda, agreed to join the Latin American producers in a new plan to withhold 20% of output whenever market prices fell below an agreed limit. With the participation of Asian producers, a 28-member ACPC was formally established. Angola and Zaire (now the Democratic Republic of the Congo) were subsequently admitted to membership. With headquarters in London, United Kingdom, its signatory member countries numbered 28 in 2001, 14 of which were ratified. Production by the 14 ratified members in 1999/2000 accounted for 61.4% of coffee output world-wide.

The ACPC coffee-retention plan came into operation in October 1993 and gradually generated improved prices; by April 1994 market quotations for all grades and origins of coffee had achieved their highest levels since 1989. Ultimately, however, in spite of this initial success, the ACPC was unable—even with the support of non-members—to bring about lasting price stability by pursuing coffee/export-retention strategy. In September 2001 the ICO daily composite indicator price reached a low point unseen for decades, averaging 41.17 US cents per lb—the average for the whole year was 45.59 cents per lb, compared with an average of 64.24 cents per lb for the whole of 2000, itself the lowest annual average since 1973. In October 2001 the ACPC announced that it would dissolve itself in January 2002. The Association's relevance had been increasingly compromised by the failure of some of its members to comply with the retention plan in operation at that time, and by some members' inability to pay operating contributions to the group owing to the depressed state of the world market for coffee. Meanwhile, in May 2001 the collapse in the price of coffee had been described as the most serious crisis in a global commodity market since the 1930s, with prices at their lowest level ever in real terms. The collapse of the market was regarded, fundamentally, as the result of an ongoing increase in world production at twice the rate of growth in consumption, this over-supply having led to an overwhelming accumulation of stocks. In this connection, some observers highlighted the role of Viet Nam, which had substantially increased its production and exports of coffee in recent years: by mid-2000 Viet Nam had overtaken Indonesia to become the world's leading supplier of Robusta coffee, and was rivalling Colombia as the second largest coffee-producing country overall.

In early July 2001 the price of the Robusta coffee contract for September delivery fell below US $540 per metric ton, marking a record 30-year 'low'. At about the same time the ICO recorded its lowest composite price ever, at 43.80 US cents per lb. Despite a recovery beginning in October, the average composite price recorded by the ICO for 2001 was 45.60 cents per lb, 29% lower than the average composite price (64.25 cents per lb) recorded in 2000. In 2001 coffee prices were at their lowest level since 1973 in nominal terms, and at a record low level in real terms. Although prices began to recover slowly, the low returns for producers in the early 2000s created what was sometimes called the 'coffee crisis'. In 2005 the average composite price recorded by the ICO, at 89.36 US cents per lb, was 43.8% higher than in 2004, with the price of Robustas recovering strongly. In its review of the 2004/05 crop year the ICO noted that the crisis in the coffee economy of exporting countries had abated somewhat. The ICO composite indicator price continued its steady recovery through the mid-2000s, regaining the levels of the mid-1990s by 2008: 124.25 cents per lb.

In common with other commodities, coffee prices were stronger in the first half of 2008, before economic uncertainties set in, although the ICO also attributed the upward trend in its composite average price to a 4% reduction in coffee supply in the second half of 2007, when exports from both Kenya—which consist exclusively of Arabicas—and Uganda were affected by social and political unrest in Kenya. According to the ICO, the composite average price for February 2008, at 138.82 US cents per lb, was the highest since June 1997, but the year ended with an average price of only 103.07 cents per lb in December. The annual average ICO composite price for 2009 was 115.67 cents per lb, indicating a gradual if erratic recovery of prices through the year, after the lows of late 2008. That the 2009 average price had not fallen by more than 6.9% on the previous year's price was largely a result of the strength of the Arabica price. The Colombian Mild price remained particularly strong into 2010, and the Robusta price stabilized, so that the monthly averages for the ICO composite price, from December 2009, consistently remained above the levels seen since October 2008. Prices surged up in July 2010, for all the four main coffee groups, driven by tight supplies and the efforts of major producers to replenish stocks and that general trend continued into 2011. By October, however, all prices were in decline, mainly because of anxiety about the global economy. (The ICO implemented a change in the criteria for its pricing from March 2011, so data are not strictly comparable.) Monthly average prices (daily weighted average) reached had peaked in April 2011, the composite price reaching 231.24 cents per lb, although the peak for the more resilient Robusta price being in the following month slowed the decline overall. Prices had fallen to their lowest point since two years previously in June 2012 (145.31 cents per lb) before making a small recovery in July. The average July 2012 price for Colombian Milds was 202.56 cents per lb (down 28.6% on the 2011 average), for Other Milds 190.45 cents per lb (29.7%), Brazilian Naturals 175.98 cents per lb (28.9%) and Robustas 107.06 cents per lb (2.0%), giving an ICO composite price of 159.07 cents per lb (24.4% lower than the average for 2011).

The IACO was formed in 1960, with its headquarters in Abidjan, Côte d'Ivoire. In 2012 the IACO represented 25 producer countries, all of which, except Equatorial Guinea and Liberia, were also members of the ICO. The aim of the IACO is to study common problems and to encourage the harmonization of production.

COPPER

The ores containing copper are mainly copper sulphide or copper oxide. They are mined both underground and by open-cast or surface mining. After break-up of the ore body by explosives, the lumps of ore are crushed, ground and mixed with reagents and water in the case of sulphide ores, and then subjected to a flotation process by which copper-rich minerals are extracted. The resulting concentrate, which contains about 30% copper, is then dried, smelted and cast into anode copper, which is further refined to about 99.98% purity by electrolysis (chemical decomposition by electrical action). The cathodes are then cast into convenient shapes for working or are sold as such. Oxide ores, less important than sulphides, are treated in ways rather similar to the solvent extraction process described below.

Two alternative processes of copper extraction, both now in operation in Zambia, have been developed in recent years. The first of these techniques, and as yet of minor importance in the industry, is known as 'Torco' (treatment of refractory copper ores) and is used for extracting copper from silicate ores that were previously not treatable.

The second, and relatively low-cost, technique is the solvent extraction process. This is suited to the treatment of very low-grade oxidized ores and is currently being used on both new ores and waste dumps that have accumulated over previous years from conventional copper working. The copper in the ore or waste material is dissolved in acid, and the copper-bearing leach solution is then mixed with a special organic-containing chemical reagent that selectively extracts the copper. After allowing the two layers to separate, the layer containing the copper is separated from the acid leach solution. The copper is extracted from the concentrated leach solution by means of electrolysis to produce refined cathodes.

Copper is ductile, resists corrosion and is an excellent conductor of heat and electricity. Its industrial uses are mainly in the electrical industry (about 60% of copper is made into wire for use in power cables, telecommunications, domestic and industrial wiring) and the building, engineering and chemical industries. Bronzes and brasses are typical copper alloys used for both industrial and decorative purposes. There are, however, substitutes for copper in almost all of its industrial uses, and in recent years aluminium has presented a challenge in the electrical and transport industries.

According to the International Copper Study Group (ICSG), mined production of copper world-wide increased steadily in the second half of the 2000s, reaching 15.9m. tons in 2009, 16.0m. tons in 2010 and a provisional 16.0m. tons in 2011. Using ICSG figures, the US Geological Survey (USGS) stated that the largest single producer in 2011 was Chile, which alone accounted for 34% of global output, followed by Peru (8%), the People's Republic of China (7%) and the USA (7%). Australia (6%), Zambia (4%), Russia (4%) and Indonesia (4%) were also important producers. Regionally, Latin America and the Caribbean mined the bulk of world copper (46% in 2009), followed by eastern Asia and Oceania (22%). Africa provided only 8% of world mine output of copper in 2010, but 55% of its total was from one country, Zambia.

The major copper-importing countries are China, the member states of the European Union (EU), Japan and the USA. According to the ICSG, world-wide usage of refined copper peaked in 2007 at 18.2m. metric tons, decreasing by 1.0% in 2008, recovering slightly in 2009, then strongly, to 19.4m. tons in 2010 and 19.9m. tons in 2011 (provisional figure). Refined production, including secondary output (recovery from scrap), continued to increase in 2009, though more slowly, to 18.2m. tons, but more strongly thereafter, to 19.0m. tons in 2010 and a provisional 19.7m. tons in 2011. Consequently, in 2011 the ICSG reckoned that a copper deficit of 238,000 tons was achieved, down from 434,000 tons in 2010, but still far from the surpluses of the two years before that. Identified stocks of refined copper throughout the world had fallen by 177,000 tons during 2010, but rose slightly, by 6,000 tons in 2011, to total 1.2m. tons at the end of the year.

Proven world reserves of copper were estimated by the USGS at 690m. metric tons in 2011. In that year about 2.9% of the world's total reserves were located in Zambia, where copper production is the mainstay of the economy, and copper sales at one time accounted for some 85% of export earnings. In the late 1990s, however, owing to the low price of copper on the world market, the contribution of the metal to export revenues declined substantially. In 2002 sales of refined copper (unwrought) were estimated to have accounted for only about 50% of total export earnings. In 2006 the value of copper and cobalt exports was reported to have risen threefold, compared with 2005, as a consequence of higher prices on international metal markets. In 2007 copper alone accounted for 71% of total export earnings, according to UN figures, and in 2008 the proportion was still 64%. By 2010, however, copper provided 78% of Zambian exports. Among the companies active in Zambia's copper sector in that year were, notably, Equinox Minerals Ltd of Australia, with its 20m.-ton (ore) annual capacity Lumwana mine (Malundwe pit), First Quantum Minerals Ltd of Canada, with its recently expanded capacity at the Kansanshi mine, and Mopani Copper Mines PLC (MCM), a consortium comprising Glencore International AG of Switzerland (73.1%), First Quantum Minerals Ltd (16.9%) and Zambia Consolidated Copper Mines Investment Holdings PLC (ZCCM-IH—10%). ZCCM-IH is the main government holding company in the national copper industry. Zambian mined copper production had dipped in 2000, and it remained steady in 2003, but generally it increased each year of the 2000s, to reach an estimated 697,000 tons by 2009; mine output fell back slightly in 2010, but rose to an estimated 715,000 tons in 2011. Output from smelters (primary metal) in 2006 totalled 290,000 tons, having risen every year of the 2000s, but smelter production amounted to only 224,000 tons in 2007 and 232,000 in 2008, before surging to 334,000 tons in 2009 and 490,000 tons in 2010. Estimated production of copper by refineries (primary metal), meanwhile, steadily recovered from only 399,000 tons in 2005 to levels not seen since the early 1990s: notably, 430,000 tons in 2007; output was 415,000 tons in 2008 and 405,000 tons in 2009, rising to a high of 530,000 tons in 2010. Production of refined copper in Zambia had entered a gradual decline in the mid-1980s; dwindling ore grades, high extraction costs, transport problems, shortages of foreign exchange, equipment and skilled labour, lack of maintenance and labour unrest combined to make the copper industry seem an unstable basis for the Zambian economy. However, following a change of government in 1991, a number of remedial measures were implemented. Before being overtaken by Canada in 1983, Zambia ranked second only to Chile among the world's copper exporters, but it was also behind Peru in 2010. Zambian copper exports are predominantly in refined but unwrought form.

Even before the Zairean (Congolese) civil conflict, which began in 1993 and was renewed in 1998, led to the suspension of much of the country's normal mining activity—in 1999 La Générale des Carrières et des Mines (Gécamines), the state-owned minerals enterprise, was reported to be operating at only 5%–10% of its production capacity—the copper industry in what is now the Democratic Republic of the Congo (DRC) had become increasingly vulnerable to competition from other producers, such as Chile, which have established new open-cast, low-cost mines. The DRC had placed greater emphasis on efforts to increase refined production capacity, and in the late 1980s about one-half of the country's copper exports were in the form of refined copper leach cathodes and blister copper. The country remains Africa's second copper producer and exporter. The DRC's estimated production of mined copper fell to about 21,000 metric tons in both 2000 and 2001, but recovered steadily thereafter, amounting to 148,099 tons in 2007, compared with 144,285 tons in 2006, before surging to 233,742 tons in 2008, 309,751 tons in 2009, some 343,000 tons in 2010 and an estimated 440,000 tons in 2011. Smelter output of copper (primary metal) totalled an estimated 10,000 tons in 2005 and 2006, compared with 20,000 in 2004 and 8,000 tons in 2003, but during 2007 activity upgraded smelter production into output of refined copper, which amounted to 6,897 tons in that year, 38,632 tons in 2008, 154,671 tons in 2009 and an estimated 235,204 tons in 2010. At US $257m. in 2006, the value of the DRC's copper exports accounted for 11.1% of the value of all merchandise exports, compared with 5.5% in 2005 and 3.1% in 2004; in 2008 copper accounted for 35% of total exports of $6,590m. (second only to cobalt, on 38%).

South Africa is the continent's other main producer, although from the 1980s copper output was affected by declining grades of ore, leading to mine closures and a reduction in the level of operations. In 2007 South Africa's mined production of copper totalled an estimated 97,000 metric tons, up from just less than 90,000 tons in the previous few years, rising to a reported 108,700 tons in 2008 and 107,600 tons in 2009, but falling back further to 102,600 tons in 2010. South African smelter production peaked one year earlier than mine output, at an estimated 111,900 tons of primary copper in 2007, falling back to 75,900 tons by 2010, while refinery production followed a similar pattern, falling from 113,166 tons in 2007 to 82,202 tons by 2010. In 2006 South Africa exported a total of 24,000 metric tons of copper (including cathode, blister and concentrate), worth some R1,064m. Compared with 2005, South African copper exports were 20% lower in terms of quantity; in terms of value, however, they increased by 62%, reflecting the extraordinary increase in the average price of copper on international markets. South African copper exports earned US $183m. in 2008.

Namibia derived more than 10% of its total export revenue from copper in the late 1980s, although by 1997 this proportion had declined to less than 4%. Mining operations recovered in the early 2000s, but mining production declined through the mid-2000s to reach only an estimated 6,262 metric tons in 2006, although it then recovered to 6,580 tons in 2007 and 7,471 tons in 2008. However, flooding at one mine and then the global economic climate meant that by the end of 2008 Weatherly International PLC, the operator of the Namibian copper mining industry, had closed all mining activities in the country; the mines only reopened at the beginning of 2011, with output of 5,000 tons expected for the year. Smelter production, too, had declined, reaching 16,271 tons in 2008, but remained in operation in 2009–10 processing imported concentrates (some 20,000 tons in 2010). In Botswana copper and nickel are mined at Selebi-Phikwe, and high-grade copper ore deposits have also been identified in the Ghanzi area. Selebi-Phikwe was expected to remain productive into 2012. The main copper producer is the Tati Nickel Mining Co (Phoenix and Selkirk Mines, near Francistown). Mine output had declined by almost 4%, to 27,700 tons, in 2009, but rose strongly to some 31,000 tons in 2010; smelter production (copper content of matte exported) rose from a 2007 low of less than 20,000 tons to 24,382 tons in 2009, with about 24,000 tons expected again the following year. In 2010 exports of copper-nickel matte contributed about 11% of Botswana's total export revenue. In 2006, in response, partly, to the high price of copper on international markets, Wambao Shinex of China (51%) and Zimbabwe Mining Development Corpn (49%) formed Zimbao Mining Ventures, in order to assess the potential for reopening Zimbabwe's Mhangura and Sanyati copper mines and the country's smelter and refining complex at Lomangundi. Copper mine production (copper content of concentrates) recovered slowly until 2008, when reported production was 2,827 tons, but then rose to 3,572 tons in 2009 and an estimated 4,000 tons in 2010. Refined copper production, however, fell from about 7,000 tons annually in the mid-2000s to some 3,000 tons annually in 2008 and 2009, before rising to an estimated 5,000 tons in 2010. From 2007 Mauritania was producing in excess of 30,000 tons of copper in concentrates per year, with output rising to 37,000 tons by 2010, from the Guelb Moghrein mine, 250 km north-east of Nouakchott. In 2010 Tanzanian production of concentrates and bullion leapt from a low of 2,319 tons to a figure far in excess of earlier years, at 5,326 tons.

Production of Copper Ore
(copper content, '000 metric tons)

	2009	2010
World total*	15,900	16,000
Sub-Saharan Africa*	1,183	1,250
Leading sub-Saharan African producers		
Congo, Dem. Repub.	310	380*
South Africa	108	103
Zambia	697	690
Leading non-African producers		
Australia*	854	870
Canada	495	525
Chile	5,394	5,419
China, People's Repub.*	1,070	1,200
Indonesia	999	872
Kazakhstan	406	380
Peru	1,276	1,247
Poland	439	425
Russia*	676	703
USA	1,180	1,110

* Estimate(s).

Source: US Geological Survey.

There is no international agreement between producers and consumers governing the stabilization of supplies and prices. Although most of the world's supply of primary and secondary copper is traded directly between producers and consumers, prices quoted on the London Metal Exchange (LME) and the New York Commodity Exchange (COMEX) provide the principal price-setting mechanism for world copper trading.

In 2007 the average settlement price of Grade 'A' copper (minimum purity 99.9935%) traded on the LME reached the height of US $7,126 per metric ton. During the year prices ranged between $5,226 and $8,301 per ton. World stocks of refined copper fell back over the year, ending at 1.03m. tons, although this level was a recovery from earlier in the year.

The average LME copper price for 2008 was US $6,952 per metric ton, owing to the collapse in commodity prices in the last months of the year. During the first four months of 2008 the price of copper traded on the LME rose steadily, from an average of $7,601 per ton in January to an average of $8,685 per ton in April. In May, however, the average price of copper declined to $8,397 per ton. The average price of copper recorded in the first quarter of 2008, at $7,763 per ton, was 7.2% higher than that recorded in the final quarter of 2007 and more than 30% higher than that recorded in the corresponding period of 2007. Daily prices ranged from $6,666 to $8,885 per ton in January–May 2008. Although not as high in real terms as in 1974, the international price of copper remained at a high level until September 2008. Copper prices had peaked in April, with a record high of $8,985 per ton, but fears of a global recession gained ground thereafter, particularly from October, when prices plummeted. In November prices were their lowest in three years. At the end of the year, international stocks had increased somewhat, to 1.16m. tons.

In 2009 the average settlement price of copper on the LME was down to US $5,164 per metric ton, because of continuing low prices at the beginning of the year, which offset the later recovery. In fact, the average price over the first four months of 2009 was only $3,673 per ton, compared with $7,361 per ton in the corresponding period in 2010. Generally, prices recovered, strengthened and remained generally high into the first quarter of 2010. World stocks of refined copper ended 2009 23% up on one year earlier, at 1.43m. tons.

In 2010 the average LME copper price 46.0% higher than in the previous year, at US $7,535 per metric ton, and prices further strengthened into 2011, to reach $8,828 per ton over the year. Prices were stronger at the beginning of the year, the last quarter recording an average price of $7,514 per ton, according to the LME price cited by the World Bank, but the first quarter of 2012 reached back up to $8,138 per ton. Again prices fell through the year, given uncertainty about the global economy, and the average for January–July was $8,029 per ton, with the July price at $7,584 per ton. Refined copper stocks at the end of April 2012 were 1.10m. tons (17% down on one year previously).

The ICSG, initially comprising 18 producing and importing countries, was formed in 1992 to compile and publish statistical information and to provide an intergovernmental forum on copper. In 2012 ICSG members and observers totalled 22 countries, plus the EU, accounting for more than 80% of world trade in copper. The ICSG, which is based in Lisbon, Portugal, does not participate in trade or exercise any form of intervention in the market.

COTTON (*Gossypium*)

This is the name given to the hairs which grow on the epidermis of the seed of the plant genus *Gossypium*. The most important of the four species cultivated for fibre is *G. hirsutum*, upland cotton, which originated in Mexico and now accounts for about 90% of the cotton harvest. *G. barbadense*, is the extra long staple cotton, originating in Peru and accounting for a further 5%–8%; it is generally known by a number of names, such as Pima, American or Creole cotton and, with a reputation for quality, Egyptian and Sea Island cotton. The two Old World commercial species are *G. arboreum*, the tree cotton of South Asia, and *G. herbaceum* or Levant cotton. The initial development of the cotton fibres takes place within a closed pod, called a boll, which, after a period of growth lasting about 50 days (depending upon climatic conditions), opens to reveal the familiar white tufts of cotton hair. After the seed cotton has been picked, the cotton fibre, or lint, has to be separated from the seeds by means of a mechanical process known as ginning. Depending upon the variety and growing conditions, it takes about three metric tons of seed cotton to produce one ton of raw cotton fibre. After ginning, a fuzz of very short cotton hairs remains on the seed. These are called linters, and may be removed and used in the manufacture of paper, cellulose-based chemicals, explosives, etc. The remaining cottonseed can have an oil extracted, the residual meal or cake being used for animal feed, etc.

About one-half of all cotton produced world-wide is used in the manufacture of clothing, about one-third is used for household textiles, and the remainder for numerous industrial products (tarpaulins, rubber reinforcement, abrasive backings, filters, high-quality papers, etc.).

The official cotton 'season' (for trade purposes) runs from 1 August to 31 July of the following year. Quantities are measured in both metric tons and bales; for statistical purposes, one bale of cotton is 226.8 kg (500 lb) gross or 217.7 kg (480 lb) net.

Production of Cotton
('000 metric tons, USDA estimates)

	2010/11	2011/12*
World total	25,342	26,709
Sub-Saharan Africa	973	1,207
Leading sub-Saharan African producers		
Benin	65	76
Burkina Faso	142	152
Côte d'Ivoire	74	98
Mali	103	185
Nigeria	103	71
Tanzania	60	69
Zimbabwe	109	114
Leading non-African producers		
Australia	914	1,067
Brazil	1,960	1,894
China, People's Repub.	6,641	7,924
India	5,748	5,770
Pakistan	1,881	2,308
USA	3,942	3,391
Uzbekistan	893	914

* Preliminary.

Source: US Department of Agriculture (USDA).

The price of a particular type of cotton depends upon its availability relative to demand and upon characteristics related to yarn quality and suitability for processing. These include fibre length, fineness, cleanliness, strength and colour. The most important of these is length. Generally speaking, the length of the fibre determines the quality of the yarn produced from it, with the longer fibres being preferred for the finer, stronger and more expensive yarns.

Cotton is the world's leading textile fibre. However, with the increased use of synthetics, cotton's share in the world's total consumption of fibre declined from 48% in 1988 to only about 40% in 2007. About one-third of the decline in its market share was attributed to increases in the real cost of cotton relative to prices of competing fibres, and the remaining two-thirds to other factors, for example greater use of chemical fibre filament yarn (yarn that is not spun but is extruded in a continuous string) in domestic textiles such as carpeting. The break-up of the Council for Mutual Economic Assistance (the trade grouping of the former communist bloc) in 1990, and of the USSR in 1991, led to substantial reductions in cotton consumption in those countries and also contributed to cotton's declining share of the world fibre market. Officially enforced limits on the use of cotton in the People's Republic of China (which now generally accounts for about two-fifths of cotton consumption world-wide—38% in 2011/12) also had an impact on the international market. According to data compiled by the US Department of Agriculture (USDA), consumption of cotton world-wide dipped slightly (by less than 1%) in 2007/08, after expanding steadily during the 2000s hitherto, reaching a record peak of 26.95m. metric tons in 2006/07. However, 2008/09 saw the greatest contraction in cotton consumption since the Second World War (some 11%). From 2008 the cotton industry was not only suffering the impact of the global financial and economic crisis, but was also encountering more specific challenges from a global commodity price crisis and problems in the cotton futures market, so although consumption recovered in 2009/10, from 23.99m. tons to 25.81m. tons, it declined thereafter, to 24.96m. tons in 2010/11 and 22.95m. tons in 2011/12. A recovery was expected in 2012/13. After China, the world's main consumer is India (19% of all cotton use in 2011/12), followed by Pakistan (10%), Turkey (5%), Brazil (4%), the USA (3%) and Bangladesh (3%).

The world's largest cotton producers are China (27% of global production in 2011/12), India (22%), the USA (9%), Pakistan (9%) and Brazil (7%), according to USDA. China is also the world's largest importer of cotton, accounting for an exceptionally high 55% of the international market's total in 2011/12 (owing to high domestic prices—expected to be back at a more usual level of 35% in 2012/13). Bangladesh and Turkey vie for second place—the former purchasing more from abroad in 2010/11 and 2011/12 (and being expected to do so again in 2012/13), but not in 2009/10. In 2011/12 Bangladesh accounted for 7% of world imports and Turkey 5%. Indonesia, Viet Nam and Thailand came next. Pakistan had, meanwhile, fallen out of the ranks of the principal importers by 2010 (problems with its domestic production having forced it into this status earlier in the 2000s), but it was expected to regain the position of fourth largest importer in 2012/13. Importing countries have large textile industries, much of them geared towards exports. The world's principal exporter is the USA, which sold a low 26% of cotton exported globally in 2011/12. Although in 2008/09 the demands of India's domestic market and falling production meant that the country came in fourth place among the principal cotton exporters, it was usually the world's second largest seller of cotton, and was comfortably so in the next three years (achieving a strong 23% of global exports in 2011/12). The next most important exporters are Brazil (11% in 2010/11), Australia (10%) and Uzbekistan (6%).

Cotton is a major source of income and employment for many developing countries, both as a primary product and, increasingly, through sales of yarn, fabrics and finished goods. The countries of francophone West Africa are, generally, significant exporters of cotton. Cotton is usually the principal commercial crop, in terms of foreign exchange earnings, in Benin, Burkina Faso, the Central African Republic, Chad, Mali, Mozambique, Sudan and Togo. It is also important in Senegal, although less than in the 20th century, and Tanzania. In the early 2000s more than 90% of cotton entering the world market from sub-Saharan Africa came from the francophone countries of the CFA franc zone, in which the total area under cotton cultivation was about 2.3m. ha.

The largest producer and exporter of cotton in sub-Saharan Africa—indeed, in the whole continent from 2008/09, owing to poor harvests in Egypt—is usually Burkina Faso, although a reported 79% increase in the 2011/12 harvest put Mali ahead in that year (making that country the world's 14th largest producer). Burkina Faso was the 16th largest producer in the world in 2011/12, when the country's output was 152,000 metric tons of cotton, and it exported 130,600 tons that year, a little behind Mali. In 2011/12 the largest sub-Saharan producers, after Mali and Burkina Faso, were Zimbabwe, then Benin and Nigeria, Cameroon and Zambia, followed by Tanzania. The next largest African producers were Sudan, Uganda, Malawi, Togo, Chad and Mozambique. For many years in the 20th century Sudan was the largest cotton producer in sub-Saharan Africa. However, from the 1970s the industry was adversely affected by domestic difficulties resulting from climatic factors, an inflexible, government-dictated marketing policy and crop infestation by whitefly. The area under cotton cultivation in Sudan had declined dramatically by the late 1990s. It was not until the early 2000s that improved levels of output seemed likely to be sustained; Sudan increased its output fourfold between 2009 and 2012, becoming the seventh largest exporter in 2011/12, although it remained a minor producer.

Although co-operation in cotton affairs has a long history, there have been no international agreements governing the cotton trade. Proposals to link producers and consumers in price-stabilization arrangements have been opposed by the USA (the world's largest cotton exporter), and by Japan and the European Union (EU).

Liverpool, United Kingdom, is the historic centre of cotton-trading activity, and international cotton prices are still collected by organizations located in Liverpool. However, almost no US cotton has been imported through Liverpool in the 2000s, and consumption in the textile industry in the United Kingdom has fallen to negligible levels. The price for Memphis cotton, from the USA, quoted in international markets (e.g. by the World Bank) was c.i.f. Northern European ports, of which Bremen, Germany, is the most important, until the beginning of October 2008, when it became cost and freight (C/F), as traded in the Far East. The Cotton Outlook (Cotlook) 'A' index likewise changed, long since from Liverpool quotations, then in August 2004 from c.i.f. Northern Europe to C/F Far East. The cotton quality base for both indexes is middling upland cotton, 1–3/32 inch.

The average price for Memphis Territory cotton in North Europe (compiled on the basis of daily prices) was put at US $1,613 per metric ton over 2008, although the price had reached much higher before the collapse in commodity prices generally in the last months of the year, with the onset of global economic uncertainty arising from the international financial crisis of that year. Prices began to recover in 2009, although the average for the year was down to $1,453 per ton. However, in January–June 2010 the average price had risen as high as $1,910 per ton, exceeding the $2,000 mark in the sixth month of the year (at $2,027 per ton). According to FAO, and also based on calendar years, the weighted average of official weekly prices for cotton that comprise the Cotlook 'A' index was 57.68 US cents per lb in 2006. In 2007 the average weekly Cotlook 'A' index recovered to 60.29 cents per lb and in 2008 it reached 64.46 cents per lb (ranging between 82.81 cents per lb in March, before the impact of the crisis in cotton futures, to 45.46 cents per lb by December). In 2009 official weekly cotton prices averaged only 56.83 cents per lb, but that concealed a range between 42.61 cents per lb (March) and 74.69 cents per lb (December), prices rising steadily from June. Prices dipped slightly in January 2010 (72.04 cents per lb), rising in March and remaining fairly steady through until August, when the prices rose steadily until March 2011 (198.96 cents per lb—up from 81.76 per lb the previous March). By mid-2010, meanwhile, the fall in world cotton stocks (the first significant drop since they increased by about one-third in 2004/05), as supplies remained tight, not only maintained prices at high levels but also created problems for indexing. From 22 June the usual Cotlook 'A' index was suspended, owing to a lack of quotations on offers, and the new 'A' forward index was then relied on. FAO cites the Cotlook 'A' index based on the weighted average of weekly official prices announced by traders: it rose from 56.83 cents per lb in 2009 to 93.14 cents per lb in 2010 and 137.99 cents per lb in 2011. The average monthly price had fallen by 56% from a March 2011 peak to 88.35 cents per lb by the end of the year; cotton prices were tending downwards in the first half of 2012, although some upward pressure was expected later in the year.

In March 2003 the World Trade Organization (WTO) established a panel to rule on a claim by Brazil that subsidies and other measures enjoyed by US producers, users and exporters of cotton had harmed its interests. The US Cotton Farm Program had reportedly been represented by Brazil and by some other countries as inconsistent with the USA's obligations in respect of the WTO, and as the most important factor in the fall in world cotton prices from the mid-1990s—to the point at which, in 2001/2002, the Cotlook 'A' index was at its lowest level for 30 years. Some analysts, however, contended that the decline in the world price of cotton could not be attributed solely or even mainly to the subsidization of US (and EU and Chinese) output, but that it was instead the consequence of a combination of structural changes, such as competition from synthetics, affecting the production and consumption of cotton; the appreciation of the US dollar, which had depressed nominal prices of cotton; the extent of China's net trade in cotton; and a number of unusual factors that affected world cotton output in 2001/02. Brazil was the sole initiator of a legal process at the WTO, but, as noted above, it was not the only critic of the subsidizing of cotton production in the USA and elsewhere. A number of West and Central African countries have argued that they ought to be compensated, within the framework of the international regulation of trade, for financial losses incurred as a result of the subsidizing of US, EU and Chinese cotton production. The cost of producing cotton in West and Central Africa is among the lowest in the world, and African producers would be able to compete strongly with their US, EU and Chinese counterparts were it not for subsidies, which, they have argued, aggravated the fall in the world price of cotton detailed above. In a review of studies of the effects of subsidies on the world market for cotton, FAO stated in the early 2000s that current levels of EU output of cotton could be imported at one-third of the cost of production, and that in some years in the USA the cost of subsidies to cotton producers was greater than the total value of world exports of cotton at prevailing prices. In September 2004 the WTO panel that investigated the US–Brazil dispute ruled overwhelmingly in Brazil's favour. In March 2005, following an appeal by the USA, the panel's ruling was upheld in respect of all critical points of the dispute. As a consequence, the USA would be obliged to bring the subsidies found to be at fault into compliance with its WTO obligations. In July 2007 a WTO panel ruled that the USA had not fully complied with the 2005 ruling, and this interim judgment was confirmed in December 2007. The USA appealed against the decision, but Brazil's case was again upheld, in June 2008. In March 2009 Brazil claimed the right to impose retaliatory sanctions against the USA, although their nature and extent were disputed. In April 2010 Brazil agreed to suspend its WTO-sanctioned programme of retaliatory tariffs and removal of patent protections, when the US Administration offered concessions on an export loan guarantee scheme, pending negotiations to resolve the dispute within the framework of amending the USA's Farm Bill, which was due for renewal by Congress in 2012. At mid-2012, however, Brazil claimed that it could see no sign of the new legislative proposals making the US cotton regime compliant with international trade rules. Crucially, the WTO had given Brazil the right to 'cross-retaliate' across other sectors, by lifting intellectual property protections on a wide range of US goods, which could prove a costly as well as controversial measure (the WTO has granted the right only twice before, although it had never been exercised).

The International Cotton Advisory Committee (ICAC), an intergovernmental body, established in 1939, with its headquarters in Washington, DC, USA, publishes statistical and economic information and provides a forum for consultation and discussion among its 41 members (July 2012).

DIAMONDS

Diamonds are a crystalline form of carbon, and are the hardest naturally occurring substance. They are of two categories: gem qualities (among the most prized gemstones used in jewellery), which are superior in terms of colour or quality; and industrial quality, about one-half of the total by weight, which are used for high-precision machining or crushed into an abrasive powder called boart (bort). The primary source of diamonds is a rock known as kimberlite, occurring in volcanic pipes, which may vary in area from a few hectares to more than 100 ha, and volcanic fissures, which are considerably smaller. Among the indicator minerals for kimberlite are chrome diopside, pyrope garnet, ilmenite and zircon. Few kimberlites contain diamonds, and in ore that does, the ratio of diamond to waste is about one part per 20m. There are four methods of diamond mining, of which open-cast mining is the commonest; diamonds are also recovered by underground, alluvial and, increasingly, offshore mining. The diamond is separated from its ore by careful crushing and gravity concentration, which maximizes the diamond's high specific gravity in a process called dense media separation.

The size of diamonds and other precious stones is measured in carats. One metric carat is equal to 0.2 gram, so one ounce avoirdupois equals 141.75 carats.

Diamonds can also be formed artificially, although these are usually very small. Synthetic diamonds form the bulk of industrial use (99%), although since the end of the 20th century production of gem-quality synthetic diamonds of appreciable size has been possible. However, synthetic gemstone diamonds amount to only a few thousand carats per year (compared with some 90m. carats of natural gemstones); many of the so-called fancy diamonds, which are coloured other than clear through yellow to brown, are synthetic—only 0.01% of natural diamonds are fancy. Production of synthetic diamonds, almost all of which are destined for industrial use, usually amounts to between 25 and 30 times the output of natural diamonds annually: 4,380m. carats in 2010, compared with 144m. carats of natural diamonds (44% industrial), according to the US Geological Survey (USGS). (Figures from 2008 were distorted by the impact of global economic conditions, with reduced demand contributing to the fall in output.) The People's Republic of China is, overwhelmingly, the principal producer of synthetic diamonds (91% of 2010 production; the USA produces 2.1% and nine other countries the rest—these USGS figures exclude production by Germany and the Republic of Korea). In Africa, only South Africa produces synthetic diamonds (1.4% in 2010). The principal market for synthetic diamonds remains the USA. Synthetic diamonds are produced by simulating geological formation under high-pressure, high-temperature (HPHT) conditions, or by chemical vapour deposition (CVD). Although the largest volume of diamond production and commerce is for industrial purposes, the gemstone market accounts for some 90% of the value traded. Sub-Saharan Africa, therefore, which produces about one-half (62% in 2010) of the world's natural diamonds is the vital region in the diamond commodity market.

Africa is the major producing region for natural diamonds, although Australia joined the ranks of the major producers in 1983, and the Argyle open-cast diamond mine, in Western Australia, became the world's largest producing mine and the main source of industrial diamonds—output is predominantly of industrial-grade diamonds, with some lower-quality gem diamonds and a few pink diamonds. In 1998 Australian diamond production represented almost one-third of world output by volume, but in the 2000s its pre-eminence was increasingly challenged by Botswana, the Democratic Republic of the Congo (DRC) and Russia, reflecting a sharp decline in output at Argyle, which was obliged to enlarge in order to access deeper ores. In 2010 Russia accounted for about 23% (22% of gem diamonds and 24% of industrial diamonds) of world-wide natural diamond production, by volume; Botswana accounted for 22% (31% of gemstones and 11% industrial) and the DRC 19% (7% and 35%). Angola is the world's fourth largest producer (10% of world production) and Canada the fifth (8%), the former almost (91%) and the latter entirely because of gemstone production; Australia, by contrast, retained sixth place overwhelmingly through industrial diamond output (16% of the industrial total, even though output was continuing to decline), its gemstone production having collapsed in 2007 (sinking to an estimated 100,000 carats in 2010, or 1.4% of the 2006 total). In 2010 Africa accounted for 62% of gem diamond production and 58% of natural industrial diamond production.

The continent's wealth in natural diamonds accounts for the dominance in the international trade of the great South African mining and trading house of De Beers. Founded in the late 19th century, De Beers Consolidated Mines Ltd controlled 90% of world diamond production by the beginning of the 1900s and proceeded to dominate the international trade in diamonds for the rest of that century. The company maintained a cartel by persuading or coercing independent producers to sell through its single marketing channel, while underpinning its control of supply by stockpiling. The Diamond Corporation, formed in 1930 by the major diamond producers, acted as the single channel through which most of the world's rough diamond production would be sold. To stabilize the market, the corporation put surplus output into reserve, to be sold at a time when conditions were favourable. The corporation was one of a group of companies, based in London, United Kingdom, that constituted the Central Selling Organisation (CSO). Until the 1990s the CSO dealt with about 90% of the world natural diamond trade, but De Beers' monopoly was challenged by Russian and Canadian interests, as well as its loss of control of Australian output. Competition authorities were also increasingly critical of the De Beers system, with its Russian deals attracting legal complications in Europe into the 2000s. Finally, in mid-2000 De Beers announced the abandonment of its monopoly of world diamond supply, in favour of adopting a more profitable demand-led business model; the 'historical' diamond stockpile had been sold off within four years. The successor to the CSO, the Diamond Trading Company (DTC), is still the leading marketing channel for natural diamonds, accounting for 40%–50% of the international trade in the 2000s. The parent company has been a Swiss-domiciled corporation, De Beers Centenary AG, since 1990, with De Beers Consolidated Mines retaining only the South African interests. De Beers still dominates the main national diamond ventures, joint ventures with the respective Governments, in Botswana and Namibia.

Production of Uncut Diamonds
(gem and industrial stones, million metric carats)

	2009	2010
World total	131.0	144.0
Sub-Saharan Africa	73.8	86.8
Leading sub-Saharan African producers		
Angola	13.8	13.8*
Botswana*	31.0	32.0
Congo, Dem. Repub.	15.3	27.7
Namibia	1.2	1.2*
South Africa*	6.1	8.9
Zimbabwe*	0.9	0.9
Other leading producers		
Australia	10.9	10.0
Canada	10.9	11.8
China, People's Repub.*	1.1	1.1
Russia*	32.8	32.8

* Estimate(s).

Source: US Geological Survey.

In terms of value, Botswana now ranks as the world's largest producer of diamonds, which are the country's principal source of export earnings, normally accounting for up to three-quarters of export receipts and for as much as one-half of government revenues. In 2011 the value of Botswana's exports (f.o.b.) of diamonds, at US $4,448.5m., represented 76% of the total value of the country's merchandise exports. In 2007 the diamond sector alone accounted for some 27% of the country's gross domestic product (GDP). The main mines are Orapa (where national diamond production began in 1971—annual production of 12m.–13m. carats) and Jwaneng (11m.–12m. carats—considered the world's richest diamond mine, based on the value of recovered diamonds), as well as the Letlhakane and Damtshaa mines (1m. carats and 700,000 carats). The mines are all open-cast, but the feasibility of underground mining at Jwaneng was to being explored. Most diamond-mining operations in Botswana are conducted by the Debswana Diamond Co (Pty) Ltd, which is owned equally by the Botswana Government and De Beers Centenary AG. Debswana is expected to be able to maintain diamond output at its 2002 level until around 2030, although production dipped during the global economic contraction of 2008–09; the company also announced investment of up to US $3,000m. over 15 years to extend the life of the Jwaneng mine, which provided 70% of Debswana revenue. A new sales agreement with the Government announced in September 2011 consolidated the company's position and also provided for the DTC to move its hitherto London-based sales and aggregation functions to the country from 2013. More than three-quarters (78%) of Botswana's natural diamond production in 2010 consisted of gemstones.

About 90% of diamond output in the DRC (80% in 2010), which is mainly derived from alluvial mining operations in Kasai Oriental, consists of industrial diamonds, of which the DRC (then Zaire) was the world's principal producer until it was overtaken by Australia in 1986. During 1993–96 the DRC's combined output of industrial and gem diamonds exceeded that of Botswana; however, as much as 50% of its production of gem- or near-gem-quality stones was smuggled out of the country. In the 2000s, apart from 2000 and 2002, the DRC has again been the world's leading producer of industrial natural diamonds, although Russia was estimated to have exceeded it in 2009; an increase of 52% in industrial diamond production in 2010 put the country firmly back into first place and USGS estimated similar output and position for 2011. The Société Minière de Bakwanga (MIBA), in which the Government has an 80% share, holds the DRC diamond monopoly; MIBA accounted for 27% of annual capacity until the mid-2000s, the rest being artisanal. Since 2001, after some engagement with Zimbabwean military and Israeli interests, MIBA has operated an open-bidding and free-market sales and export system. Artisanal production has been boosted by greater domestic political stability and by the implementation of the Kimberley Process (see below). The main MIBA site is at Mbuyi-Mayi. Owing to worker unrest—over not being paid and suspicions of embezzlement by government figures—and world economic problems, MIBA ceased operations in November 2008, but it resumed mining in 2011, although it remained in need of investment. Meanwhile, almost all DRC diamond mining depended on artisanal production, although this fell off in 2008–09. In 2008 the value of the DRC's foreign sales of diamonds, at an estimated US $702m., represented about 11% of its total export revenue (down from 14% the previous year and almost 61% in 2003).

The USGS put South African production in 2006 and 2007 at a similar level, if down from 2006, but dropping further in 2008 and, more dramatically, in 2009, only to recover in 2010 (some 39% of the total being gemstones); the USGS estimated similar levels of production in 2011. De Beers Consolidated Mines Ltd contributed about 96% of South Africa's diamond production in terms of volume in 2006. The next largest producers were Petra Diamonds and Trans Hex, complemented by stated-owned Alexkor, some small companies and individual operations. According to official sources, South Africa usually exports more rough diamonds than it produces domestically because of the re-export of imported diamonds supplied by the DTC to its clients—'sightholders'—and of diamonds imported by dealers and cutters. The country is the only African producer of synthetic diamonds, providing some 60m. carats annually, according to the USGS. South Africa sold overseas worked and unworked diamonds (not mounted or set) worth US $2,249.1m. in 2011, representing some 2.4% of total exports,up on the $1,304.2m. of two years previously, as natural diamond output recovered.

Angola's diamond output, which totalled 2.4m. carats in 1974, subsequently fell sharply, as a consequence of the civil war. Official diamond production began to revive after 1990, rising from 1m. carats in 1993 to 3.8m. carats in 1996, before declining to 3.3m. carats in 1997 and to about 3.0m. carats in 1998, reflecting continued internal political conflict. Production recovered substantially thereafter, and totalled more than 5m. carats in 2001, when diamonds contributed 10.4% of the country's total export earnings. Diamond production was fairly stable into the mid-2000s, generally with a rising trend thereafter (9.7m. carats in 2007, slipping back to 8.9m. carats in 2008, but recovering to 13.8m. tons in 2009 with a similar level estimated for 2010—91% gemstones), but the share in export revenues declined as petroleum became more important. In 2010 exports of diamonds accounted for 1.9% of Angola's export earnings. The dominant national companies are the result of restructuring of the industry that began in 2000, under international pressure over 'conflict diamonds' (see below). The state-owned Empresa Nacional de Diamantes de Angola (Endiama), hitherto Angola's national mining organization, became the main prospecting company, usually in joint ventures with foreign operators, while a new state diamond company, Sociedade de Comercialização de Diamantes (Sodiam), was formed. All marketing was transferred to the newly created Angolan Selling Corpn (Ascorp), in which Sodiam held a 51% interest. The Sociedade Mineira de Catoca Ltda (SMC), a joint venture of Endiama, Russia's Almazy Rossii-Sakha Co (Alrosa), Odebrecht Mining Services Inc. of Brazil and the Leviev Group of Israel, was the country's largest diamond producer, with output from its Catoca kimberlite mine reportedly amounting to 5m.–5.5m. carats annually.

Guinea replaced Namibia as the continent's fifth largest producer of diamonds in 2008, although the spike in production was not maintained in 2009 and 2010. Most Guinean production, principally of gemstones, is alluvial and artisanal. The dramatic rise in registered production and export from 2007 and in 2008 was considered indicative more of the failings of the certification process for 'conflict diamonds' than of greater industry in the mining sector. Namibian production, also mainly of gem-quality, suffers from high recovery costs, and the country has extensive offshore deposits. In 1994 the Namibian Government and De Beers established the Namdeb Diamond Corpn (Pty) Ltd. Namdeb, owned 50% by De Beers and 50% by the Government, was Namibia's leading producer. In 2005, according to the Bank of Namibia, the diamond sector accounted for 41% of Namibia's total export earnings and contributed 10% of the country's GDP. The sector's GDP contribution fell slightly, to 8.6%, in 2006. In 2008 diamonds accounted for 16% of exports.

Other than the DRC, Angola, Guinea and the Republic of the Congo, African countries whose diamond industries became tainted by the trade in also became embroiled in 'conflict diamonds' were Sierra Leone, Côte d'Ivoire and Liberia. The Central African Republic was bedevilled more by the loss of diamond revenues to smuggling, as artisanal production was sold abroad illegally, but it hoped to benefit from certification. However, countries such as Tanzania also have strong and non-controversial production. Indeed, the Mwadui diamond pipe in Tanzania was one of the world's largest producing pipes, covering an area of 146 ha. Tanzania's diamond output was 838,000 carats in 1971, but production later declined, owing to deterioration in diamond grades, technical engineering problems and difficulties in maintaining the mines. By the late 1980s exports from Mwadui had effectively ceased. Following extensive rehabilitation, mining at Mwadui, and exports, recommenced in 1995. The country's main producer recently has been the Williamson mine—mainly gem-quality stones. Tanzania exported diamonds with a value of US $19.7m. in 2005, a fall of 41% compared with 2004, and the decline continued steadily into 2010. Ghana, which once had a flourishing diamond sector, regained fairly steady production for most of the 2000s. Lesotho has a small industry, as does Zimbabwe, while Mauritania and Mozambique both have hopes of benefiting from the exploitation of diamond reserves.

In the 1990s the increasing role of the world diamond trade in the financing of guerrilla insurgencies in Africa, with particular reference to Angola, Sierra Leone and the DRC, prompted the UN Security Council in June 1998 to adopt a resolution (No. 1173) requiring that international markets ensure that illicitly exported diamonds from these areas did not enter world trade. These 'conflict diamonds' were defined as diamonds that had been either mined or stolen by rebels in opposition to the legitimate government of a country. According to estimates by De Beers, about 3.7% of world diamond production in 1999, with a value of US $255m., could be attributed to areas (principally in Angola and Sierra Leone) under guerrilla control.

Although considerable technical difficulties exist in the identification of diamonds originating in conflict areas, De Beers, as the principal conduit for African diamond sales, implemented a range of measures to comply with Resolution 1173. The company, which had in the mid-1980s discontinued purchases from Sierra Leone and Liberia (into which a large proportion of Sierra Leone's diamond output was smuggled), announced in October 1999 that it had suspended all diamond purchases in Angola, and that no diamonds of Angolan origin would be purchased by any of its offices world-wide. In order to eliminate risks that illicit Angolan diamonds might be mixed with officially marketed diamonds, De Beers subsequently suspended all purchases of diamonds originating in West and Central Africa, other than those produced in its own mines, and announced that it was restricting 'outside' purchases to diamonds of Russian and Canadian origin. In 2000 the company introduced documentation guaranteeing customers that none of its marketed diamonds emanated from conflict areas of Africa, while the report of a UN sanctions committee explicitly cited the Presidents of Togo and Burkina Faso, as well as Belgian, Bulgarian and Ukrainian officials, who were all accused of involvement in the illicit diamond trade and of providing military assistance to the União Nacional para a Independência Total de Angola (UNITA). As a result, the Diamond High Council in Antwerp, Belgium, entered into an origin-verification agreement with the Angolan Government, which also initiated the restructuring of its national industry. In December 2002, following the death of the leader of UNITA, Jonas Savimbi, the UN Security Council voted to end the sanctions that it had applied to UNITA's diamond mining and selling operations; none the less, it was widely recognized that UNITA continued to dispose of large quantities of 'conflict diamonds'.

Despite the efforts to stem the trade in 'conflict diamonds', outlets for smuggled stones continued to operate, principally in Antwerp, in Mumbai (Bombay), India, and in Tel-Aviv, Israel, while illicit output from guerrilla-controlled regions of Angola was marketed under false certification provided mainly by outlets in Côte d'Ivoire, Guinea and Liberia. In May 2000 southern African producing countries initiated what was termed the Kimberley Process, with the objective of ending the commercialization of 'conflict diamonds'. Endorsed in December by the UN General Assembly, and subsequently expanded to involve, as of May 2012, 50 participants representing 76 countries (including the European Union, whose members count as a single participant), the Kimberley Process has established the Kimberley Process Certification Scheme (KPCS), which has since 1 January 2003 imposed strict standards on all of its participants in respect of trade in rough diamonds. In July 2000 representatives of the World Federation of Diamond Bourses and the International Diamond Manufacturers Association resolved to implement a certification system that would allow rough diamonds to be monitored direct from mines to trading centres. At the same time the World Diamond Council (WDC) was established in order to implement and monitor the certification system. In October 2002 the WDC adopted a resolution in favour of the implementation of a system of warranties that would endorse each transaction of rough diamonds in trading centres world-wide. The WDC scheme was designed to complement the international certification scheme then under development by the Kimberley Process. Both the UN Security Council (in 2003) and the UN General Assembly (in 2000—see above—and 2004) have adopted resolutions supporting the Kimberley Process. In 2007, according to the WDC, 99.8% of rough diamonds were certified under the KPCS. In recent years, however, both the UN and some non-governmental organizations have documented anomalies within the Kimberley Process, alleging a failure to address non-compliance, and with some in 2010, for instance, urging a widening of the definition of 'conflict diamonds'. In December 2011 one organization, Global Witness, even withdrew from the KPCS, alleging the system was not working.

Rough diamonds, of which there are currently more than 5,000 categories, were traditionally sold by the CSO in mixed packages 10 times each year at regular sales, known as 'sights', in London, Johannesburg, South Africa, and Lucerne, Switzerland. Gems accounted for about 20% of total sales by weight, but, it was estimated, more than 90% by value. After being sold by the CSO, gem diamonds were sent to be cut and polished in preparation for jewellery manufacture. The leading cutting centres were in Antwerp, Mumbai, New York, USA, and Tel-Aviv; this last opened an exchange for 'raw', or uncut, diamonds in 1993, with the intention of lessening the dependence of Israeli cutters on allocations from the CSO and purchases from the small, independent diamond exchange in Antwerp. However, by 2003 it was reported that 92% of the world's diamonds were cut and polished in Surat, India; higher grade diamonds tended to be dealt with in the older centres. Antwerp is the leading trading bourse.

As there are so many varieties of diamond, changes to prices (quoted in US dollars) effected by the CSO and its successor, the DTC, represent averages only. There are wide discrepancies in price, depending on such factors as rarity, colour and quality. The sales turnover of US $3,417m. recorded in 1992 by the CSO represented a six-year 'low', then rising variably to a record $4,834m. in 1996, despite the termination of marketing arrangements with the Argyle diamond mine in Australia and the impact of direct sales by Russia. By 1998, owing to the financial crisis in Russia and Asia, sales turnover stood at only $3,350m., its lowest level since 1987. This reflected the weakness of demand from Japan and East Asia, which traditionally account for about 40% of world diamond sales. However, sales turnover achieved a strong recovery in 1999, advancing by 57% on the 1998 total to a record $5,240m., reflecting the onset of economic recovery in Japan and East Asia and continued strong demand in the USA—which in that year overtook Japan as the principal market for gem diamonds, accounting for almost one-half of world diamond jewellery sales. In 2000 De Beers' sales turnover rose by 8%, to a new level of $5,670m. In 2001, however, sales by the DTC totalled only $4,450m., a decline of 21.5% compared with 2000. The decline was attributed to slow growth in the global economy, especially in the USA. The DTC's sales then increased, reaching $5,695m. by 2004, this growth being attributed to improving economic conditions in the major diamond-consuming countries—in particular in the USA, which accounted for more than one-half of all sales of diamond jewellery world-wide in 2004. The value of sales rose by almost 15% in 2005, to $6,539m. In 2006, a decline of some 6%, to $6,150m., was registered in the value of sales by the DTC. This new decline in 2006 was attributed to the reduced availability of Russian diamonds, and to the impact on pipeline demand of a lack of liquidity, pressure on margins and higher financing costs in the wholesale market for rough diamonds. In 2007, mainly as a result of the ongoing gradual reduction in supplies from Russia's Alrosa, the value of the DTC's sales declined by a further 3.7%, to $5,920m. The value steadied in 2008, increasing slightly to $5,930m., despite the onset of the global economic crisis and ensuing market volatility that extended into 2009. It was in 2009 that the impact of recession became apparent, with DTC sales falling to $3,240m., a level unseen since the 1980s. However, sales made a healthy recovery in the first half of 2010, particularly in Asian markets, with retail sales coming in more strongly in the second half of the year. According to De Beers, the effective 2010 price was 27% higher than in the year previously, and DTC sales rose to some $5,080m. Strong performance lasted into the first half of 2011, weakening thereafter as confidence in a global economic recovery subsided, but DTC sales reached $6,470m., with the rough diamond price up by a reported further 29%. Another indicator of price is the unit value of South African diamond exports (according to UN figures), which were US $123.6 per carat in 2009, $186.5 per carat in 2010 and $286.3 per carat in 2011.

GOLD

Gold minerals commonly occur in quartz, and are also found in alluvial deposits and in rich, thin underground veins. In South Africa gold occurs in sheets of low-grade ore (reefs) which may be at great depths below ground level. Gold is associated with silver, which is its commonest by-product. Uranium oxide is another valuable by-product, particularly in the case of South Africa. Depending upon its associations, gold is separated by cyaniding, or else is concentrated and smelted.

Gold, silver and platinum are customarily measured in troy weight. A troy pound (now obsolete) contains 12 ounces, each of 480 grains. One troy oz is equal to 31.1 grams (1 kg = 32.15 troy oz), compared with the avoirdupois oz of 28.3 grams.

In modern times the principal function of gold has been as bullion in reserve for bank notes issued. Since the early 1970s, however, the USA has actively sought to 'demonetize' gold and so make it simply another commodity. This objective was later adopted by the IMF, which has attempted to end the position that gold occupied for many years in the international monetary system (see below).

Gold reserves were discovered near Johannesburg, South Africa, in 1884, and their exploitation formed the basis of the country's subsequent economic prosperity. For more than 100 years South Africa was the world's leading gold producer. In 2007, however, the country relinquished primacy to the People's Republic of China, where output had been rising steadily since 1999. China's position was confirmed in 2008 (when it accounted for 12% of world production), in which year the USA also exceeded South African production. In 2009 the South Africa was just ahead of the USA, but behind Australia; South Africa still accounted for 8.5% of world production and 43.8% of African production. In the same year the continued contractions in African output meant that the continent remained in third place among the largest gold-producing regions for a second successive year, the continent of Asia accounting for about one-quarter of mined global gold, and Latin America and Africa each accounting for about one-fifth. South Africa achieved its peak gold production in 1970, mining some 1,000 metric tons in that year. From the mid-1980s in particular the South African gold industry was adversely affected by the rising costs of extracting generally declining grades of ore from ageing and increasingly marginal (low-return) mines. Additionally, the level of world gold prices was not sufficiently high to stimulate the active exploration and development of new mines. The share of gold in South Africa's export revenue accordingly declined. and in 1989 the commercial profitability of South African gold production was for the first time exceeded by profits from mining activities other than gold. In 1996 South Africa's gold production fell to less than 500 tons for the first time since 1956. Output continued to fall until 2002, although the recovery in production in that year was slight. The decline resumed thereafter and in 2006, for the first time since 1925, South Africa produced less than 300 tons of gold: 295.7 tons. Production fell—by 8.7%—for a fifth consecutive year in 2007, to total 269.9 tons (China produced 280.5 tons in the same year). According to analysts, the fall in South Africa's output in 2007 was principally due to lower grades of ore having been mined. An additional factor behind the decline was the introduction towards the end of the year of new safety procedures that forced the temporary closure of some production facilities. With regard to production *per se*, 2007 remained characterized by the dominant trend of recent years: the inability of increases in output at some mines to counterbalance declines recorded at others. A production decline of almost 14% on the previous year reduced South Africa's 2008 mine output to 233.3 tons (a 13% fall in Australian production for the same year allowed the USA to become the world's second largest gold producer, just ahead of South Africa). This was the lowest level of gold production since the South African national strike of 1922, when the fall in production was of the same order—similar falls had not otherwise been recorded since the Second Boer War (1899–1901). Having provided two-thirds of mined production of gold in 1970, South Africa's contribution in 2008 fell to below one-10th for the first time in more than a century. Safety, power and other infrastructural issues, and skills shortages all remained problems for the industry. New projects could not offset the major contractions in output. A further 6.0% contraction in output took the 2009 total to 219.8 tons, which had the country ahead of the USA again, but behind Australia as well as China. However, the fall in production was less than the annual average over the decade, and most prospects for the South African gold sector were steady at best, given the high cost of deep mining, as well as issues with organized labour and power supply. In 2010 output fell by 7.7%, to 202.9 tons, which was less than one-half the total a decade earlier; production was slightly exceeded by Russia's, so South Africa fell to fifth place among the world's major gold mining countries, and it remained in that position in 2011, after production declined by 2.5%, taking it to 197.9 tons.

The relative decline of South Africa's position in world gold markets has been accompanied by substantial increases in output as new capacity has been brought into production around the world. With more than 1,200 gold mines reportedly in operation in 2005, China consistently increased its output of gold after 1999 (when a 1.5% decline in production was believed to represent the first reverse in national annual output for about 20 years) and had then all but doubled output by 2009, from 162.8 metric tons to 324.0 tons; in 2010 China produced 350.9 tons of gold and in 2011 some 371.0 tons. In Asia as a whole gold production in 2011 declined, with most other producers recording small contractions and Indonesia, the continent's second gold miner, at only four-fifths of the level produced two years earlier. Latin America and the former USSR also reached new highs with continued expansion, while a slight weakening in Australian production was reflected in the total for Oceania.

From 2009 rising gold production elsewhere in Africa began to compensate for the continuing contraction in South African mining of the metal. Ghana, formerly a significant African producer of gold, had from 1990 begun to reverse a long period of decline, and by the end of the decade was secure in its position as the second largest producer on the continent (16% of African production in 2011). Output increased considerably in most years during the 1990s, as a result of the rehabilitation of the country's gold industry. In the early 2000s, however, production declined, heavily in 2004, and Ghanaian output, at only 57.6 metric tons, sank to its lowest level since 1997. Thereafter, it recorded successive increases in output, to reach 92.4 tons in 2010, the major mines to contribute being Newmont's Ahafo and the Tarkwa open-pit mine, but the main input being the higher grade ore from mid-sized mines. Production eased slightly in 2011, to 91.0 tons. In 2011 exports of gold accounted for about 26% of Ghana's total export revenue, which was down from 64% in the previous year, despite continuing strength in the international commodity price, because significant hydrocarbons exports began in the latter year.

Gold production in Mali increased substantially during 1997–2002 (the country was Africa's third largest producer in 2000–03 and 2006–10), reflecting the exploitation of deposits at Sadiola Hill, with a projected capacity of 11 metric tons per year, but this was followed by a decline of some 15% in 2003. In 2004 Mali's output fell by a further 16.1%, to 39.6 tons. Reduced production in 2004 was attributed to the exploitation of lower ore grades at the Morila mine (extraction was expected to come only from stockpile milling from 2009). In 2005, however, output recovered by almost 18%, to 46.7 tons. Gold production rose again, by 21.8%, to 56.9 tons, in 2006. Output declined to 51.9 tons in 2007 and to 47.0 tons in 2008. Maturing resources at a number of mines were among the reasons for the decline in these two years, according to analysts. Accordingly, production rose to 48.9 tons in 2009. However, increasing production at the new Syama and Tabakoto mines in 2010 failed to offset falls in the country's four largest operations, and national output fell to 44.7 tons, and only rose marginally in 2011, to 45.8 tons (allowing Tanzania to exceed it). Most mining operations were located in the south of the country, so activity was little affected by the political upheavals in 2012. In 2010 gold was overwhelmingly Mali's most important source of export revenue, accounting for 79% of the country's total export earnings.

Tanzania's first large-scale gold mine commenced operations in 1998. Production began in 2000 at another Tanzanian mine, the Geita project, which is the largest producer of gold in East Africa; and in 2001 at Bulyanhulu. In 2002 a fourth large-scale, modern mine commenced production. Tanzania recorded an increase of almost 87% in its output in 2000, and in 2001 production almost doubled. Production thus rose from 17.2 metric tons in 2000 to a peak of 49.3 tons in 2005, before falling back almost to 2001 levels in 2008—when output was 35.6 tons—owing to labour disputes, problems with the encroachment of artisanal miners and low-grade resources. However, Tanzanian production increased by 14.9%, to 40.9 tons, in 2009, then rising to 44.6 tons in 2010 and 45.8 tons in 2011. The country challenged Mali for third place among African producers and succeeded in 2004, 2005 and 2011.

Burkinabè production had risen from an average of some 1.5 metric tons annually in the first half of the decade to 2.1 tons in 2006, and 2.9 tons in 2007. From 2008 five large-scale mines came into production in Burkina Faso, and in 2010 it displaced Guinea as Africa's fifth largest producer. Gold output went up to 6.9 tons in 2008, and to 13.8 tons in 2009, before almost doubling, to 25.3 tons, in 2010; in mid-2010 the Inata mine of Avocet Mining and the Essakane mine of IAMGOLD began commercial production, alone contributing almost one-third of Burkinabè output in that year and accounting for most of the boost in 2011 production, which reached 34.0 tons. The impact on national exports was apparent even in 2008, when the contribution of gems and precious metals (overwhelmingly gold) went from 2% in the previous year to one-quarter, reaching 69% in 2010.

Output in Guinea rose by almost 65% in 1998 with the entry into production of the Siguiri mine, operated by Ashanti Goldfields. The Siguiri mine accounted for more than one-half of Guinea's total output of gold in 1999. Falls in production at Siguiri and Guinea's two other main mining operations meant that the country recorded a decline on the record output of 2008, 23.9 metric tons (when gold sales abroad accounted for 32% of total exports), meaning that national production had fallen to 19.8 tons by 2011, and the country fell from Africa's fifth largest gold producer to its eighth largest (exceeded in the last year by the rising production of Sudan and the Democratic Republic of the Congo—DRC). In Zimbabwe, gold had been overtaken in 1980 by tobacco as the country's major source of foreign exchange. The gold-mining industry then contracted substantially as a result of closures and rationalization. In 2004, after many years of decline, output increased by almost 18%, to 24.3 metric tons, but in 2005 production again began to fall, descending to its lowest level—19.5 tons—for 15 years. Zimbabwe's gold sector suffered from its political problems, and in particular from insufficient capital, inadequate infrastructure and power shortages, as well as hyperinflation and foreign exchange controls. Contracting output had fallen as low as 8.9 tons by 2008, taking Zimbabwean gold production to its lowest level in 90 years. However, a new economic recovery programme helped gold production to improve somewhat in 2009, to 9.8 tons, and more strongly in 2010 and 2011, to 16.3 tons and 16.6 tons, respectively.

A number of countries other than Burkina Faso also began to emerge as significant producers of gold in the 21st century. Sudan in the early 2000s typically still produced three or four metric tons annually (after a peak of 5.9 tons in 2000), dipping to a low of 2.7 tons in 2008, but some the high commodity price encouraged a 'gold rush' thereafter, and production leapt from 4.0 tons in 2009 to 10.1 tons in 2010 and 22.5 tons in 2011, putting the country in sixth place among African producers. Gold output in the DRC rose more steadily through the 2000s, although actual, as opposed to licit, production and export figures remain opaque. According to Gold Fields Mineral Services Ltd, output reached 10.0 tons in 2009 and then leapt to 17.0 tons in 2010 and 22.5 tons in 2011, the last figure matching Sudan. In 2011 Ethiopian production too increased dramatically, up 74% to 11.5 tons. All three countries relied on artisanal output for increases in production. In Eritrea, where production was put at some 0.5 tons in earlier years, gold output rose to 12.8 tons in 2011 as the Bisha mine came into production (although the gold-rich cap of the copper-zinc deposit will probably be exhausted in 2013).

A strong 2009 performance in West Africa, Côte d'Ivoire, had helped to offset production failings in a number of established African gold-mining countries, but in 2010 Ivorian production fell back from a peak of 8.6 tons to 7.3 tons, although the new Tongon mine poured its first gold in November, and the increasing production from it more than offset interruptions to supply from other mines owing to civil unrest in 2011, with national output reaching a record 13.3 tons for the year. Mauritania's output went from less than 1.0 tons annually to 1.9 tons in 2007, 6.8 tons in 2008, 8.4 tons in 2009, 9.1 tons in 2010 and 8.7 tons in 2011. Commercial production at the Sabodala open-pit mine in Senegal began promptly in 2009, taking that country's gold output from 0.1 tons annually to 5.2 tons in 2009, before falling slightly, to 4.3 tons, by 2011. In Egypt, not in the sub-Saharan region, the Sukari mine made the country a new addition to the listings of gold producers in Africa in 2010 and 2011, with output of 4.7 tons and 6.3 tons, respectively. The smaller African producers, such as Niger, also made a significant contribution to the continent's total output, at 24.4 tons in 2011.

Production of Gold Ore
(metric tons, gold content)

	2010	2011
World total	2,740.5	2,818.4
Africa	530.3	580.9
Leading African producers		
Ghana	92.4	91.0
Guinea	20.8	19.8
Mali	44.7	45.8
South Africa	202.9	197.9
Tanzania	44.6	49.6
Leading non-African producers		
Argentina	63.5	59.3
Australia	260.8	258.3
Brazil	68.0	67.5
Canada	103.5	107.7
China, People's Repub.	350.9	371.0
Indonesia	140.1	111.0
Mexico	79.4	86.6
Papua New Guinea	69.7	62.4
Peru	184.8	188.0
Russia	203.4	211.9
USA	230.0	232.8
Uzbekistan	71.0	71.4

Source: Gold Fields Mineral Services Ltd.

World supply of gold in 2011 was characterized by continuing strong mine production (up 2.8%, to 2,818 metric tons, but the gains across all regions experienced in the previous year, for the first time since 1988, were not repeated, with the largest increase in Africa, up 9.5%), a fall of 3.4% on scrap (down to 1,661 tons, despite higher gold prices) and hedging activity shifting to the supply side (net official sales remained on the demand side for a second year, which before 2010 had last been seen in 1988). Mine production accounted for 63% of the gold supply in 2011, and scrap for 37%. Demand, meanwhile, recorded a slight rise as higher net official sector purchases more than offset the falling back in fabrication and so-called world investment (the sum of implied net investment—which suffered a collapse—physical bar and all coins), as well as the absence of net de-hedging. Jewellery demand fell by less than expected, while physical bar investment recorded further strong growth. Investment demand remained the principal driver of the gold price in 2011, as well as the sovereign debt problems in Europe fuelling fears about world economic recovery and encouraging investors to the traditional haven of gold. As a general rule, when fears of recession recede, gold prices are likely to fall. Despite high prices, jewellery still accounted for about one-half (48%) of end-use gold consumption in 2011, according to the *Gold Survey 2012* of Gold Fields Mineral Services Ltd, and identifiable investment for 41% (the main component was physical bar investment, which surged again, by 37%, to a new record of 1,209 tons). Electronics was the most important industrial use of gold (8% of global end-use in 2011).

As a portable real asset which is easily convertible into cash, gold is widely esteemed as a store of value. Another distinguishing feature of gold is that new production in any one year is very small in relation to existing stocks. Much of the world's gold is in private bullion stocks, held for investment purposes, or is hoarded as a 'hedge' against inflation. Private investment stocks of gold throughout the world are estimated at 15,000–20,000 metric tons, much of it held in East Asia and India.

During the 19th century gold was increasingly adopted as a monetary standard, with prices set by governments. In 1919 the Bank of England allowed some South African gold to be traded in London, United Kingdom, 'at the best price obtainable'. The market was suspended in 1925–31, when sterling returned to a limited form of the gold standard, and again in 1939–54. In 1934 the official price of gold was fixed at US $35 per troy oz and, by international agreement, all transactions in gold had to take place within narrow margins around that price. In 1960 the official gold price came under pressure from market demand. As a result, an international gold 'pool' was established in 1961 at the initiative of the USA. Originally a consortium of leading central banks with the object of restraining the London price of gold in case of excessive demand, it later widened into an arrangement by which eight central banks agreed that all purchases and sales of gold should be handled by the Bank of England. However, growing private demand for gold continued to exert pressure on the official price, and the gold 'pool' was ended in 1968, in favour of a two-tier price system. Central banks continued to operate the official price of $35 per troy oz, but private markets were permitted to deal freely in gold. However, the free market price did not rise significantly above the official price.

In August 1971 the USA announced that it would cease dealing freely in gold to maintain exchange rates for the dollar within previously agreed margins. This 'floating' of the dollar against other major currencies continued until December, when it was agreed to raise the official gold price to US $38 per oz. Gold prices on the free market rose to $70 per oz in August 1972. In February 1973 the US dollar was devalued by a further 10%, the official gold price rising to $42.22 per oz. Thereafter the free market price rose even higher, reaching $127 per oz in June 1973. In November it was announced that the two-tier system would be terminated, and from 1974 governments were permitted to value their official gold stocks at market prices.

In 1969 the IMF introduced a new unit for international monetary dealings, the special drawing right (SDR), with a value of US $1.00, and the first allocation of SDRs was made on 1 January 1971. The SDR was linked to gold at an exchange rate of SDR 35 per troy oz. When the US dollar was devalued in December 1971 the SDR retained its gold value and a new parity with the US dollar was established. A further adjustment was made following the second dollar devaluation, in February 1973. In July 1974 the direct link between the SDR and the US dollar was ended, and the SDR was valued in terms of a weighted 'basket' of national currencies. At the same time the official gold price of SDR 35 per troy oz was retained as the IMF's basis for valuing official reserves.

In 1976 the membership of the IMF agreed on proposals for far-reaching changes in the international monetary system. These reforms, which were implemented on a gradual basis during 1977–81, included a reduction in the role of gold in the international system and the abolition of the official price of gold. A principal objective of the IMF plan was achieved in April 1978, when central banks were able to buy and sell gold at market prices. The physical quantity of reserve gold held by the IMF and member countries' central banks as national reserves has subsequently fallen (see below). The USA still maintains the largest national stock of gold, although the volume of its reserves has been substantially reduced in recent years. At the end of 1949 US gold reserves were 701.8m. oz, but since the beginning of the 1980s the level has been in the range of 261.4m.–264.6m. oz. At the end of 2011 the total gold reserves held by members of the IMF, including international financial organizations but excluding countries not reporting, amounted to 883.73m. oz (27,487 metric tons), of which the USA had 29.6% and Germany 12.4%; the IMF, the ECB and the Bank for International Settlements, based in Switzerland, held a further 110.44m. oz (3,435 tons).

In June 1996 the Group of Seven major industrialized countries (G7) considered proposals by the United Kingdom and the USA whereby the IMF would release for sale US $5,000m.–$6,000m. of its $40,000m. gold reserves to finance debt-relief for the world's poorest countries, principally in Africa. The plan, which was opposed by Germany on the grounds that it could prompt demands for similar gold sales by its central bank, remained the subject of discussion within the IMF during 1997. In the spring of 1999 the G7 endorsed a revised proposal whereby the IMF would sell about 10% of its holdings of gold to provide debt-relief for 36 of the world's poorest countries. Under the plan, the proceeds of the IMF disposals would be invested and the resulting revenue used to amortize IMF loans to the designated countries. However, in response to concerns that these disposals by the IMF and central banks would depress world gold prices further and seriously affect gold-producing countries, the IMF announced in September that the operation was to be restricted at the time to 'off-market' sales to members having repayment obligations. Between December 1999 and April 2000 13m. oz of gold were 'sold' to Brazil and Mexico at prevailing market prices, and the profit on the sales was placed in special accounts designated for debt-relief. Brazil and Mexico then immediately returned the same gold to the IMF, at the same price that they had paid for it, in order to settle debt repayments falling due.

During 1996 substantial amounts of gold bullion, jointly exceeding 500 metric tons, were sold by the central banks of Belgium and the Netherlands, and the Swiss National Bank announced its intention to allocate part of its gold reserves to fund a new humanitarian foundation. In July 1997 the Reserve Bank of Australia announced that it had disposed of more than two-thirds of its bullion holdings (reducing its reserves from 247 tons to 80 tons) over the previous six months. In October a Swiss government advisory group recommended the sale of more than one-half of Switzerland's gold reserves, and in December the Government of Argentina disclosed that it had sold the bulk of its gold reserves during a seven-month period earlier in the year. During 1997 loans to the market of official stocks of gold were carried out by the central banks of Germany, the Netherlands and Switzerland, and in March 1998 Belgium's central bank disposed of one-half of its gold reserves. In April 1999 the Government of Switzerland implemented constitutional changes that removed the requirement for gold to support the national currency. In May the British Government announced that it intended to reduce its gold reserves by 415 tons, to 300 tons, over several years, including the offering for sale of 125 tons in the year to March 2000. The initial disposal, of 25 tons, followed in July 1999, and the second auction of British gold reserves, again offering 25 tons, took place in September. In response to concerns that the official sector's unco-ordinated gold sales were depressing gold prices, later that month the European Central Bank (ECB), in a joint statement with the central banks of Switzerland and 13 members of the European Union (Sweden, the United Kingdom and the 11 countries then in the euro zone), announced a five-year moratorium on new sales of gold held in official reserves. Total gold reserves held by the 15 signatory banks totalled 16,336 metric tons, accounting for around 48% of global gold reserves. The agreement—referred to as the Central Bank Gold Agreement (CBGA) and also known as the Washington Agreement on gold—allowed impending sales that had already been decided to proceed, although total sales were not to exceed 400 tons per year over the five-year period. The announcement also stated that gold would remain an important element of global monetary reserves. The European agreement was generally welcomed for removing uncertainty from the gold market, although the permitted rate of sales (400 tons per year) was more than 100% greater than the average net sales by the signatory countries in 1989–98. In March 2004 the renewal of the CBGA was announced, to cover the five-year period from September 2004 to September 2009, without the United Kingdom but with Greece as a new signatory. The second CBGA ended the moratorium on sales not already decided, and annual sales quotas were raised to 500 tons in order to take into account the consolidation of the price of gold that had occurred. Slovenia became a signatory of the second CBGA in December 2006, immediately prior to its adoption of the euro as its currency. Cyprus and Malta likewise became CBGA signatories on adopting the euro in January 2008, as did Slovakia in January 2009. The third CBGA entered effect at the end of September 2009, with the same signatories as those to the second agreement. Under the new CBGA, covering the five-year period to 2014, the cap on annual sales was again reduced to 400 tons (with the signatories noting that the intention of the IMF to sell 403 tons of gold could be accommodated within the overall quotas). At the end of 2011 gold reserves held by the CBGA signatories amounted to 12,264 tons.

The unit of dealing in international gold markets is the 'good delivery' gold bar, weighing about 400 oz (12.5 kg). The principal centres for gold trading are London, Hong Kong and Zürich, Switzerland. The dominant markets for gold futures (buying and selling for future delivery) are the New York Commodity Exchange (COMEX) in the USA and the Tokyo Commodity Exchange (TOCOM) in Japan.

Gold Prices on the London Bullion Market
(afternoon 'fixes', US $ per troy oz)

	Average	Highest	Lowest
2000	279.11	312.70 (7 Feb.)	263.80 (27 Oct.)
2009	972.35	1,212.50 (2 Dec.)	810.00 (15 Jan.)
2010	1,224.52	1,421.00 (9 Nov.)	1,058.00 (5 Feb.)
2011	1,571.52	1,895.00 (5–6 Sept.)	1,319.00 (28 Jan.)

A small group of dealers meets twice on each working day (morning and afternoon) to 'fix' the price of gold in the London Bullion Market, and the table above is based on the second of these daily 'fixes'. During any trading day, however, prices may fluctuate above or below these levels. In 1999 the average London gold price was only US $278.6 per oz—5.3% below the 1998 average and the lowest annual level, in nominal terms, since 1978. In real terms (i.e. taking inflation into account), the average price of gold in 1999, measured in US dollars, was the lowest since 1972. In 2000 a slightly higher average price—in nominal terms—of $279.1 (£187.04) was recorded for gold traded on the London market. In 2001, at $271.0 per oz, the average price, even in nominal terms, was the lowest recorded since 1978—and 3% lower than the average price registered in 2000. In 2002, at $309.7 (£206.1) per oz, the average London gold price was 14% higher than the average price recorded in 2001. However, although this was, in percentage terms, the greatest year-on-year increase since 1987, and the greatest increase within a single year since 1979, commentators noted that, in real terms, the average price of gold in 2002 was at its lowest level since 1972. In 2003 the average price of gold, at $363.3 (£222.2) per oz, was 17.3% higher than the average price recorded in 2002, the year-on-year increase thus overtaking that recorded in 2002 as the highest since 1987. Price volatility subsided during 2004 and the first half of 2005, while the average price rose—particularly influenced towards the end of 2005 by global economic and inflation anxieties prompted by the increase in petroleum prices.

In 2006 the average London price of gold, expressed in US dollars, increased dramatically, by 35.8%, to US $603.8 per oz. In nominal terms the average price was at its highest level since the $614.5 registered in 1980, while in real terms it was the highest price recorded since 1989. Price volatility, at 24%, was exceptional, reaching its highest level for 26 years and almost double that recorded for 2005. The intra-year gain, however, was more modest, and, at 19.2%, just below the 2005 intra-year rise. Analysts noted that comparable increases in the price of gold were registered in other currencies. None the less, the rise in the average price was significantly higher when expressed in terms of the South African rand and the Japanese yen. The indications were that the decline in the value of the US dollar had contributed to a change in the attitude of official financial institutions towards gold in recent years. For the first time since the mid-1990s countries outside the CBGA group emerged as net buyers of the metal, while the ECB announced that the sales quota for the second CBGA was unlikely to be reached.

In 2007, expressed in US dollars, the average London price of gold rose by 15%, to a record US $695.39 per oz—some 13% higher than the nominal average price of $614.50 recorded in 1980. In real terms, the average price recorded in 2007 was the highest since 1988, although less than one-half of that registered in 1980. During 2007 the London afternoon gold fix ranged between $841.1 per oz (November) and $608.4 per oz (January). Price volatility, at 16%, was considerably lower than the level recorded in 2006, while the intra-year gain, at 30.3%, was substantially higher. Analysts noted that, expressed in terms of the euro, the Australian dollar, the Turkish lira and the Indian rupee, the increase in the price of gold was far more subdued than when expressed in US dollars, while in terms of the Japanese yen and the Indonesian rupiah increases comparable with those recorded in terms of the US dollar occurred. In terms of the South African rand, the increase in the price of gold was more marked. In terms of other currencies generally, the intra-year gain in the price of gold was lower than that recorded in terms of the US dollar—only in terms of the Indonesian rupiah was the intra-year gain, at 36.2%, higher. Analysts identified a surge in investor demand for gold towards the end of the year as the key factor behind the increase in the London price in 2007: the price of gold rose by almost $170 per oz in September–November. At the same time, however, a solid base had been established earlier by strong demand from the jewellery fabrication sector and a relatively low level of supply from scrap.

In 2008 the average London gold price reached a new record level of US $871.96 per oz, as well as reaching a new record daily high of $1,011.25 per oz in March (although, in real terms, these records still did not exceed 1980 prices). The year-on-year increase in the annual average gold price was 25.4%, but the intra-year rise (i.e. the difference between prices at the beginning of the year and at the end) was a much more modest 2.7%. Prices in other currencies, particularly those of producer countries, recorded larger changes. The South African rand price rose by 46.0% year-on-year and 41.1% intra-year in 2008. Prices in Japanese yen, particularly, and Chinese yuan recorded intra-year declines. The year was noteworthy for the extreme price volatility (32% on the London price for the year, with 45% in the final quarter of the year), with the March high followed by further price spikes in July, September and December. In common with other commodities, gold experienced soaring prices in the first quarter of the year, followed by falls with the onset of apprehension about global economic recession. Prices fell most dramatically from July into September, recovered strongly and then collapsed into October, followed by a resurgence from the end of the year. The typical alignment of the gold price with petroleum prices was less apparent from October 2008, as the financial crisis prompted many investors to seek refuge in gold.

In 2009 the average annual gold price rose for the eighth consecutive year, despite a weak start, and in the final quarter prices surged to new heights. The average price year-on-year increased by 11.5%, but the intra-year rise was a strong 24.4%. Price volatility, however, was down. Non-US dollar prices tended to show stronger gains year-on-year (except for the yen and, to a lesser extent, the yuan), but intra-year changes were generally less varied, the notable exceptions being in terms of the Australian and South African currencies, which recorded small devaluations in the average gold price. Prices were driven up mainly by investment (which, if broadly defined, exceeded jewellery demand for the first time since 1980), including net official purchases of gold, although jewellery demand recovered into 2010. The new nominal record price over 2009 was US $972.35 per oz, the daily high also reaching a new nominal record on 3 December (morning fix basis), at $1,218.25 per oz. The prices underwent a short, sharp correction at the end of the year, continuing into 2010—falling to $1,058 per oz in early February.

In 2010 the average annual gold price rose for the ninth consecutive year, growth that continued into 2011 as recovering demand atypically combined with economic uncertainty pushed the price to new records. The average price year-on-year increased by a strong 25.9%, while the intra-year rise was much the same, at 25.3%, indicating the remorseless uninterrupted nature of the rise, in particular from February 2010. Price volatility was restrained. Non-US dollar prices tended to show weaker gains, in particular among producers, certainly year-on-year (except in the case of the euro), but also intra-year (except for not only the euro price but also the Turkish and Russian currencies). The euro prices were driven up by the euro zone's sovereign debt problems. The new nominal record price over 2010 was US $1,224.52 per oz, the daily high also reaching a new nominal record on 7 December (morning fix basis), at $1,426.00 per oz. The gold price continued to climb in 2011, rising through successive nominal records and exceeding $1,800.00 per oz in August (peaking for the first eight months of the year at $1,886 per oz on 23 August, morning fix); the lowest price of January–August 2011 was on 28 January ($1,316.00 per oz, morning fix).

In 2011 the average annual gold price rose for the 10th consecutive year, although price volatility increased in the middle of the year and prices recorded some broad swings from mid-September. The average price year-on-year, therefore, increased by a strong 28.3%, but the intra-year rise was lower, at 10.3%. Non-US dollar prices tended to show weaker gains year-on-year, in particular among producers (except among the Turkish, Vietnamese and Indian currencies), but intra-year trends were more variable. The euro prices were still influenced by the sovereign debt crisis. The new nominal record price over 2011 was US $1,571.52 per oz, the daily high also reaching a new nominal record on 5 September (morning fix basis), at $1,896.50 per oz. After some price volatility, the gold price bull run continued into 2012, peaking at some $1,788 per oz in the morning fix on 29 February. Prices weakened thereafter. According to the World Bank, the average London gold price for the first seven months of 2012 was $1,643 per oz (compared with $1,569 per oz over 2011).

The World Gold Council (WGC), founded in 1987, is an international association of gold-producing companies which aims to promote gold as a financial asset and to increase demand for the metal. The WGC, based in London, had 23 corporate members in 2012, and a number of associate members.

GROUNDNUT, PEANUT, MONKEY NUT, EARTH NUT

(*Arachis hypogaea*)

This is not a true nut, although the underground pod, which contains the kernels, forms a more or less dry shell at maturity. The plant is a low-growing annual herb introduced from South America, and resembles the indigenous African Bambarra groundnut (*Vigna subterranea*), which it now outnumbers.

Each groundnut pod contains between two and four kernels, enclosed in a reddish skin. The kernels are highly nutritious because of their high content of both protein (about 30%) and oil (40%–50%). In tropical countries the crop is grown partly for domestic consumption and partly for export. Whole nuts of selected large dessert types, with the skin removed, are eaten raw or roasted. Peanut butter is made by removing the skin and germ and grinding the roasted nuts. The most important commercial use of groundnuts is the extraction of oil. Groundnut oil is used as a cooking and salad oil, as an ingredient in margarine, and, in the case of lower-quality oil, in soap manufacture. According to the US Department of Agriculture (USDA), the world's most produced vegetable oils are palm oil and soybean oil, then rapeseed oil and sunflowerseed oil, and distantly followed by palm kernel oil, cottonseed oil and groundnut oil (then coconut oil and olive oil). Consumption followed a similar pattern, but in terms of world exports palm oil was by far the most important vegetable oil, with groundnut oil eighth of the nine listed by USDA in 2011/12. Oilseed production, however, in volume terms, is dominated by soybean, followed by rapeseed, cottonseed, sunflowerseed and groundnut, then palm kernel and copra.

Production of Groundnuts
(in shell; '000 metric tons)

	2009	2010
World total	36,570	37,954
Sub-Saharan Africa*	9,980	10,082
Leading sub-Saharan African producers		
Burkina Faso	331	340
Cameroon†	475	460
Chad*	413	394
Congo, Dem. Repub.	371	371

—continued	2009	2010
Ghana	485	531
Guinea†	277	292
Malawi	275	297
Mali	300	314
Niger	253	406
Nigeria	2,969	2,636
Senegal	1,033	1,287
Sudan	942	763
Tanzania	385	300
Other leading producers		
Argentina	605	611
China, People's Repub.	14,765	15,709
India	5,510	5,640
Indonesia	778	779
Myanmar†	1,362	1,341
USA	1,675	1,886
Viet Nam	525	486

* FAO estimates.
† Unofficial figures.

Source: FAO.

An oilcake, used in animal feeding, is manufactured from the groundnut residue left after oil extraction. However, trade in this groundnut meal is limited by health laws in some countries, as groundnuts can be contaminated by a mould which generates toxic and carcinogenic metabolites, the most common and most dangerous of which is aflatoxin B_1. The European Community (EC, now the European Union—EU) has banned imports for use as animal feed of oilcake and meal which contain more than 0.03 mg of aflatoxin per kg. The meal can be treated with ammonia, which both eliminates the aflatoxin and enriches the cake. Groundnut shells, which are usually incinerated or simply discarded as waste, can be converted into a low-cost organic fertilizer, which has been produced since the early 1970s.

Since the late 20th century more than 90% of the world's groundnut output has come from developing countries. Groundnuts are the most important of Africa's oilseeds and form the chief export crop of The Gambia and, traditionally, Senegal (which still exports groundnut oil in reasonable quantities). However, according to USDA, sub-Saharan Africa's exports accounted for less than 4% of the world total (20% of world production) in 2011/12; little more than 1% of African production was exported in that year. The People's Republic of China and Argentina were the world's leading exporters (35% and 25% of total world exports, respectively), followed by India and the USA; the largest sub-Saharan African exporter, Malawi, lay in ninth place, followed by The Gambia. Malawi has been the region's largest exporter since 2007/08 and, in 2011/12, it accounted for 1% of world exports; Ghana, South Africa and Tanzania were the next largest exporters in Africa and the world. Mali, Sudan, Mozambique, Zimbabwe and Zambia sold some produce abroad, while Senegalese exports had become negligible. The EU was the world's largest importer (34% of the world total in 2011/12), followed by Indonesia (14%) and Mexico (8%). USDA put the world's largest individual producer of peanut as China (45% of the world total in 2011/12), followed by India (16%), the USA (5%), Nigeria (4%), Myanmar (4%) and Indonesia (3%); Senegal, normally among the six leading producers, saw output almost halve that year, so its production was exceeded by Sudan. The next largest sub-Saharan African producers, in descending order, were Chad, Ghana, the Democratic Republic of the Congo (DRC), Burkina Faso, Mali, Malawi, Guinea, Cameroon, Côte d'Ivoire, Uganda, Central African Republic (CAR), Benin, Mozambique and Niger, The Gambia, South Africa, Tanzania, Zambia, Zimbabwe and Togo.

In 2005 exports of groundnut products contributed just 1.3% of The Gambia's total revenue from exports (including re-exports). This poor performance was partially due to a reduced crop in that year, but was compounded by disruption to the processing of the groundnuts caused by transport difficulties, and also by changes in licensing requirements which left one company as the sole operator. In 2004 groundnuts had contributed 13.3% of total revenue from exports, and 12.0% in 2006 (shelled groundnuts earned US $4.3m. and groundnut oil $3.6m.), but only 0.6% in 2007, after production declined by 37%, to 72,557 metric tons. By 2009 exports of groundnuts and products earned 16% of total exports. According to FAO, The Gambia remained Africa's largest exporter in both 2006 and 2007. Malawi, hitherto an erratic but often strong exporter, achieved similar levels of exports in 2007, selling 16,985 tons of shelled nuts abroad (compared with some 17,000 from The Gambia), but that was after sales of just 3,778 tons in 2006. In 2008 FAO had Malawi's exports falling back to 14,270 tons, while Gambian sales abroad were unofficially put slightly up at some 18,000 tons (an estimated 25% of sub-Saharan African exports), but, according to USDA figures, Malawi became the region's principal exporter of groundnuts thereafter; however, groundnuts only provided 1.5% of total Malawian exports in 2009, earning US $18m., and less than 1% the following year. Except when affected by drought, Sudan and South Africa are also important suppliers, and in 2002 South Africa accounted for 10.5% of groundnut exports world-wide (exports declined steadily thereafter, accounting for only 0.8% of global exports by 2008, despite a recovery). South Africa was among the smaller exporters in 2011/12. Most of Sudan's production is used domestically, and it became generally the largest producer in Africa after Nigeria, although Senegal surpassed it from 2009/10. Niger and Mali, formerly significant exporters, ceased to feature in the international groundnut trade to any great extent in the 1990s, largely as a consequence of the Sahel drought. However, measures to revive the groundnut export sector in Mali were proceeding in the late 1990s, by which time subsistence output had recovered strongly. In 2002 Mali was reported to have exported groundnuts for the first time in more than 10 years; it maintained a steady level up to the end of the decade, but was surpassed by Ghana and Tanzania. Efforts to establish commercial production in Uganda had, by 2007, enjoyed negligible success, although cultivation was well established at subsistence level—a strong harvest kept the domestic market well supplied. Groundnut harvests in southern Africa, notably in Mozambique, South Africa and Zimbabwe, could also be affected by drought, as during the second half of the 1980s. Subsistence-level production recovered strongly in Zimbabwe in the late 1990s, but Zimbabwe's trade in groundnuts remained minimal in the 2000s. Mozambique, by contrast, recovered a varying level of exports. Ghana became a fairly strong exporter in the second half of the first decade of the 21st century, but of the traditional groundnut states of West Africa, Nigeria had become less relevant to the international market because of its burgeoning internal market, while Senegal has suffered the collapse of its overseas trade owing to political upheaval, although it was attempting a recovery. Both remained significant growers.

In the 2000s prices for groundnut oil have generally been more volatile than those for groundnuts. The average import price of groundnut oil (any origin, c.i.f.) at the port of Rotterdam, in the Netherlands, declined from US $788 per metric ton in 1999 to $680 per ton by 2001, rising only slightly in 2002. From late 2002 the average price of groundnut oil rose precipitously, reaching an average $845 per ton over the last month of the year. In March 2003 an average price of $1,195 per ton was recorded, and in July this rose further, to $1,397 per ton. For the whole of 2003 an average price of $1,243 per ton was recorded. In 2004 the average import price of groundnut oil at Rotterdam eased somewhat, to $1,161 per ton, and in 2005 it was $1,060 per ton. The average import price fell considerably, by about 9%, to $970 per ton in 2006. This decline was succeeded, in 2007, by a dramatic increase, of almost 40%, in the average import price at Rotterdam, to about $1,352 per ton. In the first half of 2008 and into the third quarter the average import price of groundnut oil continued to rise steadily, from $1,861 per ton in January, to $2,328 per ton in April–June, and $2,417 per ton in the third quarter. Over the year the average import price was $2,105 per ton—in common with other international commodity prices, groundnut oil prices had begun to slide steeply from October with the onset of the global financial crisis. The Rotterdam average import price then fell steadily each month up to September 2009, when it reached $1,120 per ton, although the rate of decline since May had slowed. The average price for October was a little higher, but then fell back to $1,116 per ton in November, before beginning a steadier recovery into the first quarter of the next year. The average import price for groundnut oil over the whole of 2009, therefore, was only $1,184 per ton, but this recovered to $1,404 per ton over 2010 and $1,985 per ton over 2011. Figures for the first months of 2012 were not available, but at the end of 2011 prices were on a rising trend ($2,245 per ton in the final quarter), and the average monthly price in July 2012 was $2,468 per ton, down from $2,520 per ton in June.

Meanwhile, in 2000 the average import price of groundnuts at Rotterdam rose slightly, from US $836 per metric ton in 1999 to $838 per ton. The import price declined slightly in 2001, and more substantially in 2002, to $751 per ton. From late 2002 the import price at Rotterdam rose steeply, in March 2003 achieving an average price of $1,000 per ton, and the monthly average remained at, or very close to, that level until July, when it fell slightly. For the whole of 2003 an average price of $976 per ton was recorded. A slight decline in the average annual price was recorded in 2004, and a more substantial one in 2003 (to $888 per ton), followed, in 2006, by an increase of 2%, to $906 per ton. Like that of the oil, the average import price of groundnuts at Rotterdam rose very considerably in 2007, by 40%, to $1,268 per ton for the year. The rate of increase stabilized towards the end of the year, steadying, on a monthly basis, at $1,700 per ton in December 2007 and in January 2008, dipping in February, then steadying again at $1,795 per ton (March–May), before rising to a peak of $1,850 per ton in July. Prices then began to decline, although an average Rotterdam price of $1,644 per ton was recorded for the whole of 2008. By December the price had fallen to $1,282 per ton, and the decline continued into 2009, to a low point of $1,108 per ton in March. The average import price then recovered, variably, but stabilized up at $1,160 per ton for most of the second half of the year, but rising in December and the first two months of the following year—the average Rotterdam import price for groundnuts for the whole of 2009 was $1,160 per ton. After dipping for March–April 2010, average monthly import prices for groundnuts tended upwards, giving an average price at Rotterdam for that year of $1,284 per ton and for 2011 of $2,086 per ton. The average price for January–July 2012 was some $2,632 per ton; prices were weaker in the second quarter, although the May price of $2,800 per ton matched the average for the first quarter, but the monthly averages fell to $2,250 per ton in June and $2,175 per ton in July.

The African Groundnut Council was founded in 1964 to advise its member producing countries (The Gambia, Mali, Niger, Nigeria, Senegal and Sudan) on marketing policies. It is based in Kano, Nigeria (having relocated from Lagos in 2005), and has a sales promotion office in Geneva, Switzerland. Western Europe, particularly France, has traditionally been the principal market for African groundnuts.

IRON ORE

The main economic iron ore minerals are magnetite and haematite, which are used almost exclusively to produce pig-iron and direct-reduced iron (DRI). These comprise the principal raw materials for the production of crude steel. Most iron ore is processed after mining to improve its chemical and physical characteristics and is often agglomerated by pelletizing or sintering. The transformation of the ore into pig-iron is achieved through reduction by coke in blast furnaces; the proportion of ore to pig-iron yielded is usually about 1.5 or 1.6:1. Pig-iron is used to make cast iron and wrought iron products, but most of it is converted into steel by removing most of the carbon content. From the 1990s processing technology was being developed in the use of high-grade ore to produce DRI, which, unlike the iron used for traditional blast furnace operations, requires no melting or refining. Particular grades of steel (e.g. stainless) are made by the addition of ferro-alloys such as chromium, nickel and manganese.

Iron is, after aluminium, the second most abundant metallic element in the earth's crust, and its ore volume production is far greater than that of any other metal. Some ores contain 70% iron, while a grade of only 25% is commercially exploitable in certain areas. As the basic feedstock for the production of steel, iron ore is a major raw material in the world economy and in international trade. Mining the ore usually involves substantial long-term investment, so about 60% of trade is conducted under long-term contracts, and the mine investments are financed with some financial participation from consumers.

Iron ore is widely distributed throughout Africa, with several countries having substantial reserves of high-grade deposits (60%–68% iron). One of the world's largest unexploited iron ore deposits (with estimated resources of more than 560m. metric tons, with a metal content of 64%) is located at Bélinga, in north-east Gabon. In 2006 the Gabon Government allocated rights pertaining to the development of these deposits to a group led by China National Machinery and Equipment Import and Export Corpn (CMEC). In May 2008 La Compagnie Minière de Bélinga, whose shareholders included the Republic of Gabon (25%), CMEC and Panzhihua Iron and Steel Group, signed a convention governing the Bélinga project with the Gabonese Government. Construction of facilities, including a mine, transport infrastructure and a hydroelectric dam, was expected to last four years, and CMEC anticipated that it would invest some US $5,000m. in the project. Annual output from the Bélinga project was ultimately expected to reach 20m.–30m. tons of ore. The project had caused considerable concern over transparency and possible corruption, but it was for environmental reasons that the Chinese bank backing CMEC suspended funding and, in August 2012, the Government announced that it might not grant the concession until 2014, after a reassessment of the deposit. In Senegal, the Government agreed in 2007 that the development of the country's Falémé iron ore project would be undertaken by the multinational conglomerate ArcelorMittal, despite a challenge from South Africa's Kumba Resources Ltd (KRL), which had undertaken the prefeasibility study and hoped to develop the mine. The mine was to be linked to a new port near Dakar by a 750-km railway, and would exploit 750m. tons of iron ore in four deposits at a full production rate of 25m. tons annually. Production was scheduled to begin in 2011, after capital expenditure of US $2,200m. However, in June 2011 the project had still not managed to get under way, reportedly because of the Government's reservations about the project and its refusal to build the necessary infrastructure, but late in the year the Government, starting proceedings against ArcelorMittal at the International Chamber of Commerce, accused the company of reneging on its commitments. Côte d'Ivoire's as yet unexploited resources of iron ore were estimated at 3,000m. tons (40% iron) in 2003; Tata Steel signed a joint-venture agreement at the end of 2007 with the government-owned Société pour le Développement Minier de la Côte d'Ivoire, as a precursor to exploratory and feasibility work on the Mount Nimba deposit. The Mount Nimba iron ore reserves, estimated at 1,000m. tons, extended into two other countries, Liberia and Guinea; the Côte d'Ivoire mine had been expected to be in production in 2010, although the world-wide economic problems from late 2008 delayed a number of projects, and 2014 seemed a more realistic date, by which time it was hoped that a railway to a new port at San Pedro would have been built. ArcelorMittal began iron ore production at the Liberia site in September 2011 (see below), while the first iron ore mine in Guinea commenced operations in mid-2012. Other iron ore reserves in Guinea include the Pic du Fon deposit, totalling an estimated 1,200m. tons, at Simandou, one of the world's few remaining unexploited iron ore resources. In 2006 a subsidiary of United Kingdom-based Rio Tinto, SIMFER SA (in which the International Finance Corpn—IFC held a share of 5%), was awarded a concession to develop the Simandou iron ore project. The IFC was to play a supportive role in respect of the conduct of various studies—feasibility, environmental, transport, etc.—connected with the project. Production was not expected to begin until 2013, once the associated infrastructure was in place. In 2009 the Government detached the rights to the northern half of the project, eventually awarding them to the Swiss company BSG Resources Ltd, which subsequently ceded majority control to Vale of Brazil. In 2011 Rio Tinto secured its part of the concession by agreeing the terms of the development, including a greater share of the project for the Government of Guinea (up from 20% to 35%), and projected the first shipments of iron ore for early 2015. Meanwhile, in 2009 Xstrata of Switzerland announced investment of US $50m. in exploration of the Zanaga iron ore deposits in the Republic of the Congo.

The continent's leading producer of iron ore is South Africa. The US Geological Survey (USGS) estimated South African iron ore production to be stable, at some 42m. metric tons, gross weight, in 2007 and rising to 49m. in 2008, 55m. in 2009 and 59m. in 2010, with the estimate for 2011 falling back to 55m. tons. South Africa's export sales rose by 3% in 2006, to reach 27.4m. tons, 65% of which was destined for Pacific Rim countries. In 2008 iron ore sales abroad earned US $2,450m., putting them behind platinum group metals, gold and coal in the ranking of South African mineral exports. However, the country also has a significant processing and steel industry: iron and steel together accounted for 12% of all South Africa's exports in 2008. In 2011 iron ore exports earned $9,002m., 10% of total exports and only behind platinum group metals in value. The country's two principal iron ore concerns, Kumba Iron Ore (KIO) and Assmang, both continued to invest in iron ore production in South Africa. KIO depended on its massive Sishen mine, which it planned to expand further, while Assmang's declining production at Beeshoek was offset by its new mine at Khumani, at which it had begun operations in 2008. Highveld is also an important iron ore miner, and there are two other, smaller operations.

Production of Iron Ore
(iron content, '000 metric tons, estimates)

	2009	2010*
World total	1,090,000	1,280,000
Sub-Saharan Africa	41,496	44,466
Sub-Saharan African producers		
Mauritania	6,680	7,150
Nigeria	16	16
South Africa†	34,800	37,300
Leading non-African producers		
Australia	228,000	271,000
Brazil	199,200	240,000
Canada*	20,000	23,300
China, People's Repub.*	280,000	332,000
India*	144,000	147,000
Russia*	53,200	58,500
Sweden	11,500	16,400
Ukraine*	36,600	43,000
USA	16,600	31,300

* Estimated production.

† Includes magnetite ore ('000 metric tons): 4,725 in 2009; 5,474 in 2010 (estimate).

Source: US Geological Survey.

Among the African producers of iron ore, the country most dependent on the mineral as a source of foreign exchange is Mauritania, which still derived 45% of its total export earnings from shipments of iron ore in 2010 (compared with 65% in 2005, because petroleum production began in 2006, as well as the increase in copper and gold exports), despite a contraction owing to global economic conditions. The Société Nationale Industrielle et Minière (SNIM), which has sole responsibility for iron ore production and beneficiation, operated a mining centre at the northern town of Zouérate, three open-pit iron ore mines (at Guelb El Rhein, Kedia d'Idjill and M'Haoudat) and transport infrastructure including a railway linking the mining centre with port facilities at Nouadhibou. In 2007 a joint venture between SNIM and Sphere Investments Ltd was still developing a mine at Guelb el Aouj, but partners for development proved elusive, as a Saudi company dropped and then, in 2008, a Qatari company. The coup in Mauritania may have contributed to the decision, but such politics did not prevent other investments, such as that intended by ArcelorMittal in the El Agareb deposit near Zouérate. Investment in existing sources of output was expected to maintain output in 2011 at the 2010 level.

The exploitation of iron ore deposits in Nigeria, unofficially estimated in 1999 to exceed 3,000m. metric tons, commenced in 1986, but output has been at negligible levels since the late 1990s. In 1980 deposits estimated at 20m. tons of ore (50% iron) were identified in the west of Zambia, but these remained unexploited almost 30 years later. In 2000 Tanzania's National Development Corpn was attempting to attract investment in the development of ore reserves estimated at 45m. tons (52% iron) at Liganga. Tanzania's other iron ore resources reportedly include deposits in the Uluguru Mountains, estimated at 8m. tons (40% iron). Zimbabwean production, exceeding 350m. tons in some years until 2005, declined thereafter, and was put at just 50m. tons in 2007 and one-half that in 2008, ending that year.

Iron ore mining in Angola was beset by civil conflict and abandoned in 1975. Angola holds considerable ore production stockpiles, but the resumption of export trade in the ore depends on the eventual rehabilitation of the 520-km rail link between mines at Cassinga and the coast. The Marampa mine in Sierra Leone has been inactive since the mid-1980s, although plans exist for the eventual resumption of operations to extract its ore deposits, which have an iron content of 69%. In 2004 Liberia was reported to have agreed terms for the transport of abandoned stockpiles of iron ore totalling 800,000 metric tons to the People's Republic of China. Additional quantities of abandoned Liberian ore were reportedly available for purchase. Also in 2004 the Liberian Government was reportedly involved in talks with a venture seeking to reopen Liberia's Yekepa iron ore mine, which had ceased operations in 1992. Mittal Steel (now part of ArcelorMittal) signed an agreement with the Liberian Government in 2005 in order to access the Mount Nimba iron ore reserves in western Liberia (see above). Infrastructure for the project was expected to cost about US $900m.; output began in late 2011. Cline Mining Corpn of Canada reportedly acquired the Bekipsa iron ore deposit in Madagascar in 2004.

In 2010, on the basis of data compiled by the UN Conference on Trade and Development (UNCTAD) Trust Fund Project on Iron Ore Information, two-thirds of world exports of iron ore were provided by Australia (38%) and Brazil (28%), followed by India (9%), South Africa (5%) and Canada (3%). Exports increased by 11% in that year, as the world recovered from the effects of recession. World imports in 2010 increased by 12% on the previous year, with demand from China dipping slightly (by 1.7%, to 619m. metric tons) after eight years of successive, significant increases in purchases of ore. Between 2001 and 2010 four countries—China, Japan, the Republic of Korea (South Korea) and Germany—had consistently accounted for more than two-thirds of all world imports of iron ore; over that period, however, China's share in the world total had gone from 19% to 59%, while Japan's share went from 26% to 13%, South Korea's from 9% to 5% and Germany's from 8% to 4%. In regional terms, the Americas were the largest contributor to total world exports of iron ore in 2006, followed by Oceania; Africa was the least significant exporter. Iron ore exports globally doubled between 1999 and 2008, mainly owing to increased demand from China, which was the leading importer of iron ore. The largest iron ore companies in the world are Vale, Rio Tinto and BHP Billiton, which accounted for 35.4% of global iron ore production in 2009, up slightly on the year before. The three companies are even more significant in export markets, controlling 61% of the world seaborne trade of iron ore.

Until 2009 world reference prices for iron ore were decided annually at a series of meetings between producers and purchasers (the steel industry accounts for about 95% of all iron ore consumption), but when China failed to agree prices with major producers, and with 'spot' prices for iron ore soaring in the latter half of that year when miners were still selling at prices agreed in March, the system effectively collapsed in 2010. The USA and the republics of the former USSR, although major steel producers, rely on domestic ore production and had taken little part in the price negotiations. It was generally accepted that, because of its diversity in form and quality, iron ore was ill-suited to price stabilization through an international buffer stock arrangement. Given the complexity of the old pricing system, a general trend can be indicated from the prices cited by the World Bank. The average 'spot' price (cost and freight) to China of iron ore of any origin in 2009 was US $80.0 per metric ton, rising to $145.9 per ton in 2010 and $167.8 per ton in 2011. Prices remained high for much of 2011, but fell towards the end of the year. Chinese demand remained the principal determinant of prices in the international iron ore trade, although fears about prospects for growth in the world economy, in particular because of the European sovereign debt crisis, kept prices volatile into 2012. The average 'spot' price was $138.9 per ton in the first seven months of 2012, dropping to $127.9 per ton by July. As outlined above, the 40-year-old annual series of benchmark negotiations to determine iron ore prices finally ended in early 2010. Even the commercially dominant Chinese steel companies, as well as the Japanese and European steel industry organizations, could not resurrect the process, which was replaced by a general model of quarterly semi-negotiated prices. Criticism of the new system in the iron ore market concerns the inherent uncertainties and the lack of transparency, according to the UNCTAD Trust Fund Project on Iron Ore Information: price settlements were no longer announced and the published 'spot' prices were still not fully reliable. Less clarity and greater volatility were also encouraged by the pressure on supply, expected up to 2015, given the length of time new capacity takes to come into production. In response to the changing conditions, in 2009 an Iron Ore and Steel Derivatives Association was formed, as an independent grouping of principals, brokers and clearers; in August 2011 it had 39 members.

The Association of Iron Ore Exporting Countries (Association des pays exportateurs de minerai de fer—APEF) was established in 1975 to promote close co-operation among members, to safeguard their interests as iron ore exporters, to ensure the orderly growth of international trade in iron ore, and to secure 'fair and remunerative' returns from its exploitation, processing and marketing. In 1995 APEF, which also collects and disseminates information on iron ore from its secretariat in Geneva, Switzerland, had nine members, including Algeria, Liberia, Mauritania and Sierra Leone. UNCTAD compiles statistics on iron ore production and trade, and has established a permanent international forum for discussion of the industry's problems.

MAIZE (Indian Corn, Mealies) (*Zea mays*)

Maize is one of the world's three principal cereal crops, with wheat and rice. Originally from America, maize has been dispersed to many parts of the world. The principal varieties are dent maize (which has large, soft, flat grains) and flint maize (which has round, hard grains). Dent maize is the predominant type world-wide, but flint maize is widely grown in southern Africa. Maize may be white or yellow (there is little nutritional difference), but the former is preferred for human consumption in Africa. Maize is an annual crop, planted from seed, and matures within three to five months. It requires a warm climate and ample water supplies during the growing season. Genetically modified varieties of maize, with improved resistance to pests, are now being cultivated, particularly in the USA and also in Argentina and the People's Republic of China. However, further development of genetically modified maize may be slowed by consumer resistance in importing countries and doubts about its environmental impact.

Maize is an important foodstuff in regions such as sub-Saharan Africa and the tropical zones of Latin America, where the climate precludes the extensive cultivation of other cereals. It is, however, inferior in nutritive value to wheat, being especially deficient in lysine, and tends to be replaced by wheat in diets when the opportunity arises. In many African countries the grain is ground into a meal, mixed with water, and boiled to produce a gruel or porridge. In other areas it is made into (unleavened) corn bread or breakfast cereals. Maize is also the source of an oil used in cooking.

Production of Maize
('000 metric tons)

	2009	2010
World total*	819,210	840,308
Sub-Saharan Africa*	51,187	56,115
Leading sub-Saharan African producers		
Ethiopia	3,933	3,897
Kenya	2,439	3,222
Malawi	3,583	3,419
Nigeria	7,339	7,306
South Africa	12,050	12,815
Tanzania	3,324	4,736
Zambia	1,887	2,795
Leading non-African producers		
Argentina	13,121	22,677
Brazil	50,720	55,395
Canada	9,561	11,715
China, People's Repub.	164,108	177,541
France	15,288	13,975
India	16,680	14,060
Indonesia	17,630	18,328
Mexico	20,143	23,302
Ukraine	10,486	11,953
USA	332,549	316,165

* FAO estimates.

Source: FAO.

The high starch content of maize makes it highly suitable as a compound feed ingredient, especially for pigs and poultry. Animal feeding is the main use of maize in the USA, Europe and Japan, and large amounts are also used for feed in developing countries in Far East Asia, Latin America and, to some extent, in North Africa. Maize has a variety of industrial uses, including the preparation of ethyl alcohol (ethanol), which may be added to petrol to produce a blended motor fuel. Maize is also a source of dextrose and fructose, which can be used as artificial sweeteners, many times sweeter than sugar. The amounts of maize used for these purposes depend, critically, on its price to the users relative to that of petroleum, sugar and other potential raw materials. Maize cobs, previously discarded as a waste product, may be used as feedstock to produce various chemicals (e.g. acetic acid and formic acid).

Since 2000 global production has averaged about 670m. metric tons annually. From 2006 the world maize crop grew steadily, to reach a record 827m. tons in 2008, before falling back slightly, to 819m. tons, in 2009 and rising in 2010, to a new record of 840m. tons (FAO figures). The USA is by far the largest producer, with annual harvests of, on average, about 270m. tons in 2000–07; the 2006 harvest of 270m. tons increasing to 331m. tons in 2007, before contracting to 307m. tons in 2008, and then rising to 333m. tons in 2009 and 316m. in 2010. (In years of drought or excessive heat, however, US output can fall significantly: in 1995, for example, the maize crop totalled only 188m. tons.) In the crop year 2011/12 US output accounted for 38% of global maize production, according to the US Department of Agriculture (USDA). China, whose maize output has been expanding rapidly, is the second largest producer—its harvest averaged about 133m. tons annually in 2000–08, reaching a peak of 166m. tons in the final year of that series, but falling slightly in 2009 to 164m. tons before rising to 178m. tons in 2010 (FAO figures). China's production, however, is mainly destined for the domestic market, whereas US output makes the country the world's largest exporter by far (a low and declining 44% of global exports in 2011/12). Argentina (20% in 2011/12), Ukraine (13%) and Brazil (9%) follow; Ukraine emerged in a clear fourth place in 2008/09 and displaced Brazil as the world's third largest exporter in 2011/12.

Apart from in Egypt, most maize in Africa is grown south of the Sahara. The sub-Saharan region's production averaged about 43m. tons annually in 2000–10, varying according to patterns of rainfall, but reaching some 56m. tons in 2010. USDA had maize production continuing to rise into 2012. Maize is not grown under irrigation in most of sub-Saharan Africa, as scarce water supplies are reserved instead for export crops with a higher value. Yields are therefore low. In many countries in the region commercial farming is hindered by the lack of foreign exchange to buy essential equipment, as well as fuels and fertilizers. In addition, transport difficulties make marketing expensive and uncertain. In much of Africa maize is a subsistence crop.

The world's principal maize importer is Japan. However, the volume of Japanese imports remained stable through the 2000s, as the domestic livestock industry was rationalized to compete with imported meat. Japanese imports of maize totalled about 16.1m. metric tons in 2011/12. Rapidly growing livestock industries elsewhere in East Asia made the region the major world market for maize, although in terms of individual countries Mexico sometimes challenges the Republic of Korea (South Korea) for the title of second largest importer—as in 2011/12, when the latter bought 8.0m. tons. Feed users in South Korea are willing to substitute other grains for maize, particularly feed wheat, when prices are attractive, with the effect that maize imports can be variable. Taiwan bought 4.4m. tons of maize from abroad in 2011/12, while imports by the European Union (EU) together declined to 3.5m. tons. Meanwhile, rising import levels by Egypt, which purchased 6.0m. tons of maize from abroad in 2011/12, made it the world's third largest maize importer in that year.

Maize imports by sub-Saharan Africa vary from around 1m. metric tons annually in years of good crops to far higher amounts after droughts. In 1992/93, for example, these imports exceeded 8m. metric tons, most of which entered through South African ports, either for that country's own use or for onward transport overland to neighbouring countries. In 2011/12, according to USDA, sub-Saharan African imports of maize totalled 2.0m. tons which, although up on the previous year, was far less than the 2005/06 peak of 3.1m. tons.

South Africa, which grows both white corn (for human consumption) and yellow corn (for animal feed), is traditionally the region's largest producer (although Nigeria exceeded South African production in 2007). It was formerly an exporter of both types (except in years of severe drought), but market deregulation in 1997 altered the economic basis of commercial maize production. In the absence of government support, domestic maize is not competitive with imported maize in the feed mills of the coastal regions, with the result that sowings, particularly of yellow corn, have fallen. White corn production usually exceeds local food requirements, the surplus being exported to neighbouring food-deficit countries. South African production increased by almost 80% in 2008 (wiping out the bulk of imports). USDA figures had South African production reaching more than 13m. metric tons by 2009/10, although it fell back somewhat in the following year, to 11m. tons, before rising to almost 12m. tons in 2011/12. South Africa was a significant exporter in the 1980s, when annual sales, mostly of white maize, sometimes exceeded 3m. tons. Owing to lower output, exports in the second half of the 1990s averaged only about 1.3m. tons per year. In 2004/05–2007/08 South African exports averaged about 1.2m. tons annually. In the last few years of the decade exports were generally a little over 2m. tons annually, reaching 2.8m. tons in 2010/11 but only 1.7m. tons in 2011/12. Maize is the main staple food in Zimbabwe. Its maize crop, like that of South Africa, is often affected by drought. Traditionally, after good harvests the country was able to export its surplus of maize. In 2000 the country still exported 107,000 tons of maize, mainly to other sub-Saharan countries, but thereafter, however, Zimbabwe's agricultural sector was severely disrupted by the deteriorating economic, social and political situation in the country. Exports ceased, and imports were necessary to sustain supplies in most years after 2001. Output fell as low 525,000 tons in 2008/09, according to USDA, although it then began to recover, still held back by continuing low yields, and reached some 1.0m. tons in 2010/11 (one-half the 2000/01 harvest) and 1.4m. tons in 2011/12. Maize is also Kenya's main food crop. Output is erratic, depending strongly on weather conditions, and tends to conform to a boom-and-bust pattern. Imports are required in most seasons, especially when, as in recent years, the subsistence needs of refugee camps add to domestic food requirements. Substantial growth in maize production was registered in the mid-2000s. Production began to decline dramatically in 2007, owing to the failure of the rains in the northern Rift Valley region, where the growing areas are concentrated: USDA had it falling to 2.1m. tons in 2008/09, with a small recovery in the next year and 3.4m. tons in 2010/11, although only 2.7m. tons in 2011/12, with little more forecast for 2012/13. Maize is one of Nigeria's main subsistence crops, and is traded locally—mainly outside of the official market economy. In the past, an important end-use of maize in Nigeria was for brewing of beer, but since a ban on imports of barley and barley malt was revoked in 1998 breweries have used less maize. Nigerian production rose steadily from the beginning of the 2000s, to peak at 7.1m. tons in 2007 (FAO), eclipsing South Africa, which had had a poor harvest, as the region's major producer in that year. However, after a dip in output, it remained the region's second producer, reaching some 7.5m. tons in 2008 and 7.3m. tons in both 2009 and 2010; USDA assessed Nigerian output as rising, from a dip to 6.5m. tons in 2007/08, to 9.0m. tons in 2009/10, followed by a dip to 8.8m. tons and then 9.3m. tons in 2011/12, with a higher estimate for the next year. The potential for output growth had been hindered by marketing difficulties and shortages of essential agricultural inputs, such as fertilizers, but newly introduced maize varieties have helped improve yields. In 2011/12 the top eight maize producing countries of sub-Saharan Africa were: South Africa, firmly in first place; Nigeria; Ethiopia, where production had improved to a record 5.4m. tons (from 3.1m. tons in 2000/01); Tanzania 3.6m. tons (down 24% on the previous year, but still up from the 2.0m. tons in 2000/01), Malawi 3.9m. tons (from 2.5m. tons); steady Kenya 2.7m. tons; Zambia 3.0m. tons (up from 0.8m. tons 10 years earlier); and Mozambique 2.2m. tons (up from 1.0m. tons in 2000/01).

One of the most notable differences between maize production in developed and developing countries is in yields. In the USA, the continual development of new hybrids and the availability of adequate fertilizer and water supplies have resulted in a substantial increase in yields, interrupted only by the occasional years of drought. Yields exceed 8 metric tons per ha in good years, and in 2010/11, according to USDA, they were 9.2 tons per ha. South Africa usually achieved yields of more than 2.5 tons per ha but, from 2008 spiked over 4.0 tons per ha for two years (3.6 tons per ha in 2011/12). Yields of at least 2 tons per ha were previously the norm in Zimbabwe, although they have declined to below 1 ton per ha in the 2000s (USDA figures indicated some recovery from 2009). In much of West and Central Africa, however, yields of 1 ton per ha are normal. Although hybrid forms of maize suited to African conditions are being developed, their adoption is hindered in many countries by low producer prices, inefficient marketing arrangements, and, above all, the inability of producers to obtain regular supplies of fertilizers at economic prices. The average yield in sub-Saharan Africa in 2011/12 had reached 1.8 tons per ha, compared with a world average of 5.2 tons per ha.

Export prices of maize are mainly influenced by the level of supplies and demand in the USA, and the intensity of competition between the exporting countries. Record quotations were achieved in April 1996, when the price of US No. 2 Yellow Corn (f.o.b. Gulf ports) reached US $210 per metric ton. The quotation subsequently declined, however. In each of the five years in 2000–04 an increase in the quotation was recorded, the average price rising to $88.4 per ton in 2000, $89.6 per ton in 2001, $99.2 per ton in 2002, $105.2 per ton in 2003 and $111.7 in 2004. In 2005, the average export price declined to $98.5 per ton. However, the price began to rise again in 2006, when it was $122.1 per ton. This has been attributed largely to the increased use of maize for the production of ethanol in the USA and Europe. Prices continued to increase in 2007, to $162.7 per ton, rising to $223.1 in 2008, as global stocks fell to a 24-year low at the end of the 2007/08 crop year, despite a 9.5% increase in global production and a 24% increase in US output. The global recession that had gained momentum by the end of 2008 restrained prices in 2009, so that the average US No. 2 Yellow Corn price for the year fell to $165.5. In 2010 the price rose to an annual average of $185.9 per ton, although this relatively modest increase disguises the surge in the price from the last quarter of the year, which was to give an annual average in 2011 of $291.7 per ton, although prices fell in the second half of the year and, in particular, in the last few months. The average monthly maize price in mid-2011 was higher, atypically, than the price for the lower-protein class of wheat (Soft Red Winter), prompting some Asian countries to substitute it for maize as feed. The price inversion was caused by restricted US maize supplies being accompanied by high domestic demand in the world's leading producer, while wheat exports from the Black Sea region had recovered. The average for the first seven months of 2012 was $282.4 per ton, but for June it stood at $267.3 per ton, because high corn prices had encouraged further planting in Argentina and Brazil. However, drought in the USA—in common with other extreme weather and its effect generally on food commodity prices from mid-2012—pushed maize prices up dramatically in July, to a monthly average of $333.1 per ton, as anxiety about supply heightened.

Maize and grain prices were also generally projected to increase in line with the expanding market for ethanol, which is closely linked to the price of petroleum. New energy legislation in 2007, in both the European Union and the USA, stipulated the greater use of biofuels for motor vehicles. According to the World Bank, the share of global maize production used for ethanol increased from 2.5% in 2000 to 11.0% in 2007, and the trend remained evident thereafter. However, maize-based ethanol production remained a heavily subsidized industry in the USA, and it remained a costly and relatively inefficient substitute for its sugar-based equivalent (see below). Critics remained sceptical regarding the long-term prospects for the industry, especially as sugar-based ethanol was already being produced more cheaply in Latin America.

MANGANESE

This metal is obtained from various ores containing such minerals as hausmannite, manganite and pyrolusite. The ore is usually washed or hand-sorted and then smelted to make ferromanganese (80% manganese), in which form it is chiefly used to alloy into steel, manganese steel being particularly hard and tough. Almost 95% of manganese produced is thus used in the manufacture of steel, which, on average, consumes about 6 kg of manganese per metric ton. Electrolytic manganese is used to make stainless steel and in the aluminium industry. Minor uses of manganese as oxides are in dry-cell batteries, paints and varnishes, and in ceramics and glass-making. Manganese is the world's fourth most consumed metal by weight.

According to the International Manganese Institute, in 2009 manganese ore (wet) production world-wide totalled 38.40m. metric tons (down 16% from 45.51m. tons in 2008), with a manganese content of 11.32m. tons (down from 14.41m. tons). The largest producer was the People's Republic of China (2.7m. tons of manganese units, or 24% of the world total), followed by South Africa (1.9m. tons, or 17%) and Australia (1.8m. tons, also 17%). Brazil and Gabon each accounted for 9% of global production, and India 8%. In the same year, 15m. tons of manganese ore entered international trade, China alone accounting for 60% of world imports. Australia, Brazil, Gabon and South Africa together accounted for 74% of the seaborne supply of manganese ore. Ghana and India, meanwhile, are no longer significant exporters. The Institute put wet production world-wide at 48m. tons in 2011, to push output of metal content up 9% to 15.8m. tons; according to figures from the US Geological Survey (USGS), South Africa accounted for 24% of the manganese produced, China 20%, Australia 17% and Gabon 11%.

In 2011 world reserves of manganese were estimated by the USGS at 630m. metric tons, of which about 24% was located in South Africa, 22% in Ukraine and 17% in Brazil. About 75% of the world's identified manganese resources, estimated at 4,000m. tons in 2008, were in South Africa. In 2006, according to the South African Department of Minerals and Energy (DME), South Africa's output of manganese ore increased by 13%, to 5.2m. tons (gross weight), while the country's exports of manganese ore rose by 34.3%, to total 2.8m. tons—more than those of any other country. Export earnings were reported to have fallen fractionally in 2006, however, by 0.1%, to R1,519m., owing to the significantly lower price obtainable in 2006 compared with the previous year. According to the USGS, production of manganese ore rose to 6.0m. tons in 2007 (equivalent to a metal content of 2.6m. tons, which figure rose to an estimated 3.0m. tons in 2008). In 2006 a number of companies operating within the framework of the Government's Black Economic Empowerment programme were awarded exploration licences for the Kalahari Manganese Field (KMF), where production had hitherto been dominated by two companies—Assmang and Samancor. Investor interest in the new prospectors prompted the Industrial Development Corpn to invest in Kalahari Resources, a company owned by a group of black investors. Transport infrastructure was to be expanded in anticipation of the increased production from the KMF that new exploration was expected to generate. South Africa's share of the world manganese ore export market increased to 21.3% in 2006, compared with 19.7% in 2005, despite attempts by the Government to promote greater local beneficiation of ore into value-added products—South Africa's traditional policy has been to maximize export revenues by shipping as much manganese as possible in processed ferro-alloy form. Nevertheless, the country's share of the high carbon ferromanganese market also increased in 2006, to 32%, compared with 22% in 2005. At the same time, however, South Africa's share of the silicomanganese export market declined steeply, from 20% to 7.9%. In production terms, South African ferromanganese had exceeded a 2004 peak by 2007 (rising to an 698,654 tons, gross weight), while silicomanganese had recovered strongly (302,000 tons). The world economic downturn resulting from the international financial crisis in the second half of 2008 severely affected industrial demand and, consequently, the South African manganese industry. Output of ferromanganese and silicomanganese both fell immediately, so the year ended down on the previous one, continuing to contract into 2009 (to 260,000 tons of ferromanganese and 110,000 tons of silicomanganese), but ore production took longer to decelerate, with the 2008 total reaching a record 6.8m. tons (gross weight) or 2.9m. tons (metal content), before falling to some 4.6m. tons or 1.9m. tons, respectively, in 2009. The USGS had ferromanganese and silicomanganese production both more than doubling in 2010 (to 530,000 tons and 230,000 tons, respectively), while ore output recovered to 7.2m. tons (gross weight) or 2.9m. tons (metal content—with 3.4m. tons estimated for 2011).

Gabon, Africa's second major producer, had estimated reserves of manganese totalling 21m. metric tons in 2011. Output of manganese ore from Gabon's Moanda mine, which is operated by Compagnie Minière de l'Ogooué (Comilog), a subsidiary of France's Eramet SA, reached 3.0m. tons in 2006, compared with about 2.9m. tons in 2005. Moanda ore production achieved the planned 3.3m. tons (gross weight) in 2007 and in 2008, which amounted to a manganese content of 1.5m. tons, and according to press reports, in 2011 Comilog production exceeded the 2008 record with 3.5m. tons. All exports reportedly passed through Owendo Port, near Libreville, the opening of which, in 1988, greatly facilitated Gabon's manganese exports. However, further increases in production from Moanda were limited by the capacity of the railway link to the coast, which Eramet was committed to upgrading. In 2009 Eramet reported the beginning of construction work on a metallurgical complex at Moanda, with the intention of producing up to 20,000 tons of manganese and 65,000 tons of silicomanganese annually from late 2012 or early 2013, but problems with such development work hit company profits in early 2012. Chinese companies were also hoping to exploit manganese near Ndjole. Exports of manganese contributed 2.9% of Gabon's total export revenue in 2009, petroleum having become the most important export (the country's timber resources also earn more than manganese). Plans exist to produce ferromanganese in Gabon; at present, however, electricity production is not adequate to achieve this aim, although the Government's Grand Poubara hydroelectric project was expected to begin producing power in July 2013. In Gabon, too, manganese production fell from late 2008, with ore output dipping to 881,000 tons in 2009 (57% of the 2007 peak—metal content), but it recovered to 1.4m. tons in 2010 and 1.5m. tons in 2011.

Ghana, Africa's third most important producer, has benefited from government measures to revive manganese operations, assisted by loan finance from the World Bank. In 2006, out of total production amounting to about 1.7m. metric tons, Ghana exported 52% to Ukraine's Privat Group, 37% to China and the remainder to Norway. China has traditionally purchased exports of manganese carbonate ore from Ghana, but Chinese demand for manganese metal increased in 2007. Ukraine's Privat Group took over the management of Ghana Manganese Co Ltd in 2006. Production figures remained strong at 1.2m. tons in 2007 and 1.3m. tons in 2008, but prices fell with the international economy, and production followed—to some 1.0m. tons annually (350,000 tons metal content). Burkina Faso has deposits of manganese ore sufficient to establish it as a minor regional producer. These reserves, located at Tambao and estimated at 19m. tons, contain an average ore content of 50% manganese. A joint venture between the Government and Canadian interests to develop these resources was formed in 1995, but this was suspended in the late 1990s. The development of the project had been impeded by the high cost of overland transport relative to the value of raw manganese ore. The Burkinabè Government formally awarded the contract to mine the deposit and develop the accompanying infrastructure in the north of the country to Pan African Minerals in August 2012. Chinese interests were involved in the mining concession at Kiere, which began production in 2010. In 1994 manganese production resumed in Namibia after a lapse of almost 30 years. The Ofjosondu mine was reactivated for production of medium-grade ore having a relatively low phosphorus content. Its initial annual output was projected at about 100,000 tons. Operations were suspended in 1998, owing to financial difficulties, but resumed in 2001. The Democratic Republic of the Congo, once a significant source of manganese exports, has mined only on a sporadic basis since 1980. In Côte d'Ivoire, a new mine operated by Taurian Resources began production in 2007, but a mine opened in Zambia in March of the same year was closed by the Government in May for environmental and safety reasons. A new mine was planned in Cameroon in 2010, according to the USGS, but commencement of operations there was delayed as a result of global economic conditions.

Production of Manganese Ore
(manganese content, '000 metric tons)

	2009	2010
World total	10,800	14,200
Sub-Saharan Africa*	3,132	4,666
Leading African producers		
Gabon	881	1,416
Ghana†	351	350
South Africa	1,900†	2,900
Leading non-African producers		
Australia†	2,140	3,100
Brazil	778	780‡
China, People's Repub.†	2,400	2,600
India	980	1,000
Kazakhstan†	520	640
Mexico	119	175
Ukraine†	316	540

* Figures are the sum of output in the listed countries. Small quantities of manganese ore, included in the world total, are also produced in Burkina Faso, Côte d'Ivoire, Namibia and Zambia. Some ore may also have been produced in Sudan.
† Estimate(s).
‡ Preliminary figure.

Source: US Geological Survey.

Extensive accumulations of manganese in marine environments have been identified. The characteristic occurrences are as nodules on deep ocean floors and as crusts on sea mounts at shallower depths. Both forms are oxidic and are often termed 'ferromanganese' because they generally contain iron and manganese. The main commercial interest in both types of deposit derives from the copper, nickel and cobalt contents also present, which represent large resources of these metals. Attention was focused initially on nodules, of which the Pacific Ocean encompasses the areas with the densest coverage and highest concentration of potentially economic metals. However, the exploitation of nodules has, to date, been impeded by legal, technical and economic factors.

In 2005, according to estimates by the USGS, the average price of metallurgical-grade ore containing 48% manganese was about US $4.39 per metric ton unit. The price of manganese in ore in 2005 was 43.9 US cents per lb, compared with 28.9 cents per lb in 2004. In 2004 the international benchmark price for metallurgical-grade ore increased by 16% compared with the previous year. On an f.o.b. basis per metric ton unit for delivery during the annual contract year, the agreed price (contracted between BHP Billiton Ltd and major Japanese consumers) was $2.46 for ore from the Groote Eylandt mine in Australia. The rise in manganese ore prices was mainly due to higher demand for manganese ferro-alloys from the steel industry, in combination with restricted supply and higher transportation costs. Prices of ferromanganese alloys reached record levels in 2004. The benchmark international price for manganese that was negotiated for the 2005 contract year was reportedly a record 63% higher than that which took effect on 1 April 2004. On an f.o.b. basis per metric ton unit for delivery during the annual contract year in 2005, the agreed price (contracted between BHP Billiton Ltd and major Japanese consumers) was $3.99 for ore from the Groote Eylandt mine. Export volumes of ferromanganese generally reflect world trends in steel production. In recent decades Japanese industrial consumers have exerted the strongest influence on the international benchmark price of manganese through the annual contracts that they conclude with its producers. Settlements between other consumers are generally based on the South Africa/Japan and Australia/Japan models.

As noted above, steel production accounts for more than 90% of world demand for manganese. In 2006 output of crude steel worldwide rose by 10% compared with 2005, China having registered an increase of 21% in its production. This trend continued in the first half of 2007, Chinese steel production remaining the main determinant of demand for manganese ore and alloys. In 2006, nevertheless, output of manganese ore continued to grow at a rate exceeding demand and by the end of the year the market was in over-supply. Global production capacity for manganese ore reportedly remained unchanged in that year, mainly as a result of steps taken by the Chinese authorities to discourage excessive output and exports of alloys and steel. By the end of the first quarter of 2007 the balance had been redressed to the extent that the market had fallen into deficit, shortages of ore and alloys causing prices to soar. Overproduction of manganese ore had caused the average' spot' price to decline to US $3 per metric ton unit (mtu) in 2006, compared with an average of $3.5 per mtu in 2005. However, by the end of March 2007 'spot' prices had stabilized and begun to rise. World raw steel production was estimated to have increased by 7% in 2007 but by less than 2% in 2008, as commodity prices rose to a mid-2008 peak before falling with the global financial crisis and the onset of recession. With uncertainty about future demand for iron and steel, major producers attempted to shift manganese contracts from an annual to a quarterly basis from 2008—prices dropped dramatically in October and again in the first quarter of 2009. The average monthly price for manganese ore, as cited by UNCTAD, ranged from $7.25 per mtu in January 2008 to $17.50 per mtu in August, before falling back, particularly in October, and stabilizing at some $15.00 per mtu in November and December. Looking at the average annual indicator price cited by UNCTAD (for metallurgical manganese ore, 48%/50% maximum manganese 0.1%, f.o.b.), it was stable in the early 2000s at just under US $200 per mtu, but rose to $327.06 per mtu in 2005, $259.79 per mtu in 2006, $356.94 per mtu in 2007 and an astonishing $1,410.49 per mtu in 2008. The average annual indicator price fell to $546.36 per mtu in 2009—the monthly average had peaked at $1,750.00 per mtu in June 2008, then falling steadily to $1,500.00 per mtu in November and December, and to only $862.50 per mtu in January 2009. The monthly average was some $650.00 per mtu in February–April, and it declined further thereafter, to a low point of $351.50 per mtu in June. A recovery, generally, ended the year with a December average indicator price of $640.00 per mtu, with the rise continuing into 2010 and the price reaching a monthly average $750.00 per mtu in February–April and peaking at $862.50 in June and July. The average for the year was $771.72 per mtu, although it fell over the 12 months from August 2010, with a November–April period of stability at a monthly average price of $700.00 per mtu; by July 2011 the average manganese price per mtu was down to $540.00, a level maintained until the end of the year. For 2011 overall the average annual manganese price was $603.33 per mtu, while the average price for the first eight months of 2012 fell further, to $476.00 per mtu ($463.00 per mtu each month until June, then $520.00 per mtu in July and $510.00 per mtu in August).

MILLET AND SORGHUM

Millet and sorghum are often grouped together in economic analyses of world cereals, not because of any affinity between the two grains—in fact they are quite dissimilar—but because in many developing countries both are subsistence crops that are little traded. Figures for the production of the individual grains should be treated only as broad estimates in most cases. Data cover only crops harvested for grain.

Data on millet relate mainly to the following: cat-tail millet (*Pennisetum glaucum* or *P. typhoides*), also known as bulrush millet, pearl millet or, in India and Pakistan, as 'bajra'; finger millet (*Eleusine coracana*), known in India as 'ragi'; common or bread millet (*Panicum miliaceum*), also called 'proso'; foxtail millet (*Setaria italica*), or Italian millet; and barnyard millet (*Echinochloa crus-galli*), also often called Japanese millet.

Production of Millet
('000 metric tons)

	2009	2010
World total	26,525	31,583
Sub-Saharan Africa	14,766	15,253
Leading sub-Saharan African producers		
Burkina Faso	971	1,148
Chad*	550	600
Ethiopia	560	524
Mali	1,390	1,373
Niger	2,678	3,843
Nigeria	4,885	4,125
Senegal	810	813
Sudan	630	471

—continued	2009	2010
Uganda	841	850*
Leading non-African producers		
China, People's Repub.	1,226	1,260†
India	8,780	13,290
Nepal	293	300
Pakistan	293	346
Russia	265	133

* FAO estimate(s).
† Unofficial figure.

Production of Sorghum
('000 metric tons)

	2009	2010
World total	56,490	55,722
Sub-Saharan Africa	21,009	20,399
Leading sub-Saharan African producers		
Burkina Faso	1,521	1,990
Ethiopia	2,804	2,971
Mali	1,466	1,257
Niger	739	1,305
Nigeria	5,271	4,784
Sudan	4,192	2,630
Leading non-African producers		
Argentina	1,471	3,629
Australia	2,692	1,598
Brazil	1,854	1,532
China, People's Repub.	1,677	1,729*
India	7,250	6,700
Mexico	6,108	6,940
USA	9,728	8,779

* Unofficial figure.

Source: FAO.

Sorghum statistics refer mainly to the several varieties of *Sorghum vulgare*, known by various names such as great millet, Guinea corn, kafir or kafircorn (*caffrorum*), milo (in the USA and Argentina), feterita, durra, jowar, sorgo or maicillo. Other species included in the table are Sudan grass (*S. sudanense*) and Columbus grass or sorgo negro (*S. almum*). The use of grain sorghum hybrids has resulted in a considerable increase in yields in recent years.

Millet and sorghum are cultivated particularly in semi-arid areas where there is too little rainfall to sustain maize and the temperature is too high for wheat. These two cereals constitute the staple diet of people over large areas of Africa, India, the People's Republic of China and parts of the former USSR. They are usually consumed as porridge or unleavened bread. Both grains have good nutritional value, but are less palatable than wheat, and tend to be replaced by the latter when circumstances permit. In many African countries sorghum is used to make beer. Sorghum is also produced and used in certain countries in the western hemisphere (particularly Argentina, Mexico and the USA), where it is used mainly as an animal feed, although the high tannin content of some varieties lowers their value as a feed grain.

World production of millet averaged almost 31m. metric tons annually in 2000–10, and sub-Saharan Africa generally accounted for more than one-half (only 48% in 2010, owing to a surge in non-African production). The region's major producers are Nigeria, Niger and Mali. World production of sorghum averaged about 58m. metric tons annually in 2000–10, and sub-Saharan Africa has generally accounted for about 40% of the total (37% in 2010). The region's major producers are Nigeria, Sudan, Ethiopia and Burkina Faso.

Millet and sorghum are grown largely for human consumption, but are gradually being replaced by wheat and rice as those cereals become more widely available. Only low-grade sorghum is used for animal feed in Africa, but some is used for starch when maize is in short supply. Apart from food and animal feed requirements, sorghum is used in a number of countries in Asia and Africa for the production of beers and other alcoholic liquors.

World trade in sorghum ranges between 5m. and 10m. metric tons per year, but has in the mid-2000s tended to be closer to the lower end of this range, reflecting the small volume of exportable supplies (around 6.1m. tons in 2010). The principal exporters are the USA (which in the 2000s has, on average, accounted for more than four-fifths of total world exports—76% in 2010—and holds the greater part of world sorghum stocks) and Argentina (27% in 2010). China, South Africa, Sudan, Brazil and Thailand are occasional exporters. Japan is one of the principal sorghum markets (buying 24% of world imports in 2010), although its imports have declined in recent years. Mexico's annual sorghum purchases averaged more than 2m. tons annually in the mid-2000s (2.3m. tons in 2010, or 33% of world imports), but they vary, as they depend upon the size of the domestic crop and on the relative prices of sorghum and maize. Annual imports of sorghum by sub-Saharan Africa averaged some 950,000 tons in 2005–10. In 2005 sub-Saharan Africa's imports of sorghum rose to 661,173 tons, their highest level since 1992; imports increased again in 2006, to 864,258 tons, but fell back to 589,553 tons in 2007, before rising to 1.0m. tons in 2008 and in 2009, then falling back to 1.0m. tons in 2010.

Export prices for sorghum tend closely to follow those of maize—sorghum is generally slightly cheaper, although for most of the 2000s until January 2008 it was a little more expensive (until the spike and then crash in commodity prices). The price of US No. 2 Yellow Sorghum (f.o.b. US Gulf Ports) reached US $200 per metric ton in May 1996, but had fallen to an average of $89 per ton, about $3 per ton less than the average export price of maize (f.o.b. US Gulf ports), by the end of 1999. The average prices of sorghum (milo) and of maize rose steadily through to 2004, when they almost matched over the year, at about $112 per ton. An average price of $101 per ton was recorded for sorghum in 2005, followed by substantial annual average increases, to $130 per ton in 2006, $172 per ton in 2007 and $214 per ton in 2008. During the first half of 2008 the average monthly price of sorghum had increased very considerably, from $226 per ton in January to $277 per ton in June. Over the same period the average monthly price of maize overtook that of sorghum, rising from $203 per ton in January to $294 per ton in June—an increase of about 45%. The fall in commodity prices in the second half of the year, particularly in the last quarter, hit both grains, but sorghum more steeply: the average price for the year of maize was $223 per ton. Fluctuating grain prices in 2009 resulted in an average price over the year of $151 per ton for sorghum and $166 per ton for maize. In December sorghum was briefly again the more expensive of the two grains, but in 2010 the average US export price for yellow milo was $165 per ton, compared with $186 per ton for maize. The average price for 2011 reached $269 per ton for sorghum, while maize rose slightly less strongly to $292 per ton; the average price for maize peaked in the first quarter of the year, whereas the sorghum price peaked later, in the third quarter. Apart from a brief strengthening of grain prices early in 2012, generally the downward trend continued and, in May, the average price of yellow sorghum stood at $217 per ton, compared with $269 per ton for maize (the maize price, according to the World Bank, rallied in July, but sorghum prices were not available).

Very little millet enters international trade (357,320 metric tons in 2010, worth some US $121m., according to FAO), and no reliable export price series can be established.

OIL PALM (*Elaeis guineensis*)

This tree is native to West Africa, and grows wild in tropical forests along the coast of that region. The palm fruit is a red colour, about the size of a big plum, and grows in large clusters that can contain hundreds of fruit and usually weigh between 40 and 50 kg. The entire fruit is of use commercially; palm oil is made from its pulp, and palm kernel oil from the seed. Palm oil is a versatile product and, because of its very low acid content (4%–5%), it is almost all used in food. It is used in margarine and other edible fats; as a 'shortener' for pastry and biscuits; as an ingredient in ice cream and chocolate; and in the manufacture of soaps and detergents. Palm kernel oil, which is similar to coconut oil, is also used for making soaps and fats. The sap from the stems of the tree can be used to make palm wine, an intoxicating beverage. Most processing is done near where the oil palms are harvested, so the production figures cited tend to be for palm oil and for palm kernels, the latter giving an indication of the number of fruit harvested—for every 100 kg of palm fruit bunches, 22 kg of palm oil and 1.6 kg of palm kernel oil can typically be produced.

Palm oil can be produced virtually through the year once the palms have reached oil-bearing age, which takes about five years. The palms continue to bear oil for 30 years or more and the yield far exceeds that of any other oil plant, with one ha of oil palms producing as much oil as six ha of groundnuts or 10–12 ha of soybeans. However, it is an intensive crop, needing considerable investment and skilled labour.

During the 1980s palm oil accounted for more than 15% of world production of vegetable oils, second only to soybean oil. Largely driven by high levels of demand in Asia, especially in the People's Republic of China, palm oil production increased considerably, to account for almost one-third of world vegetable oils (32% in 2011/12, according to the US Department of Agriculture—USDA, compared with 27% soybean oil and 16% rapeseed oil). In world markets for vegetable oils, the dominance of palm oil was even more marked: in 2011/12 palm oil accounted for 61% of all exports of vegetable oils globally. In that year the equivalent of 78% of palm oil production world-wide entered international markets. The main producers of palm oil are, overwhelmingly, Indonesia and Malaysia, which accounted, respectively, for almost 51% and for 36% of world output in 2011/12, followed by Thailand (3%), Colombia (2%) and Nigeria (2%). Indonesia replaced Malaysia as the world's leading individual producer in 2005/06, while in the following year Thailand definitively replaced Nigeria in third place; in 2011/12 Colombia even took fourth place from Nigeria. Indonesia and Malaysia likewise dominate export markets, with Papua New Guinea and Thailand being in distant third and fourth places in 2011/12 (the latter displacing Benin from the year before). India, China and the member countries of the European Union (EU) are the chief importers. The principal consumers are India (15% of world domestic consumption in 2011/12) and Indonesia (14%), the latter surpassing China (12%) for a second year, followed by the member countries of the European Union (EU), Malaysia, Pakistan, Nigeria, Egypt, Thailand, the USA and Bangladesh.

In Africa a large proportion of oil palms still grow in wild groves, and the bulk of oil production is for local consumption. In export terms, Africa has since 1980 accounted for less than 3% of world trade in palm oil, and in 2011/12 sub-Saharan African exports comprised 2.1% of the world market. Benin was by far the largest African exporter in that year. Nigeria had been the world's leading producer of palm oil until overtaken by Malaysia in 1971. The loss of Nigeria's market dominance was, in part, a result of civil war and the authorities' failure to replace old, unproductive trees. From the early 1980s, however, measures were taken to revive palm oil output and to enhance the efficiency and capacity of associated mills and refineries. Foreign investment was encouraged, as was the transfer of inefficiently managed state-owned plantations to private ownership. A ban by the Nigerian Government on palm oil imports, in force since 1986, was partially relaxed in 1990, as domestic output (of which an estimated 70% came from smallholder producers) was able to satisfy only two-thirds of annual demand. Nigeria's reliance on imports subsequently grew, and increases in domestic production now tend to be used for import substitution rather than to boost exports. Nigeria is the world's fifth largest producer of palm oil, but mainly participates in the international trade as an importer. Many of Africa's largest producers are not significant exporters of palm oil, using it instead in manufacturing, whether for domestic consumption or export at that stage.

Production of Palm Kernels
('000 metric tons, USDA oilseed estimates)

	2010/11	2011/12
World total	12,547	13,095
Africa	1,049	1,049
Leading African producers		
Cameroon	70	70
Congo, Dem. Repub.	55	55
Côte d'Ivoire	76	76
Ghana	36	36
Guinea	53	53
Nigeria	670	670
Leading non-African producers		
Colombia	85	100
Indonesia	6,200	6,700
Malaysia	4,522	4,500
Papua New Guinea	135	137
Thailand	260	310

Source: US Department of Agriculture (USDA).

Production of Palm Oil
('000 metric tons, USDA estimates)

	2010/11	2011/12
World total	47,948	49,967
Sub-Saharan Africa	1,873	1,873
Leading sub-Saharan African producers		
Angola	58	58
Cameroon	190	190
Congo, Dem. Repub.	185	185
Côte d'Ivoire	300	300
Ghana	120	120
Guinea	50	50
Nigeria	850	850

—continued	2010/11	2011/12
Leading non-African producers		
Colombia	775	885
Ecuador	460	500
Indonesia	23,600	25,400
Malaysia	18,211	18,000
Papua New Guinea	500	510
Thailand	1,288	1,546

Source: USDA.

Benin is not now a major producer of palm oil, but is an entrepôt for surrounding countries and, therefore, Africa's largest exporter. In Benin, where the oil palm was traditionally a staple crop of the national economy, oil palm plantations and natural palm groves covered some 450,000 ha in the 1990s, but only an estimated 26,000 ha in 2010 (FAO figure), albeit increasing since the nadir of the early 2000s. In 2006 sales abroad of oilseeds and products (mainly palm and palm-kernel oil) had begun to recover, and in 2009 they contributed about 4% of Benin's total export earnings (palm oil exports fell by 46% in 2010, before rising by 35% the next year). Benin was an important exporter of palm oil in the late 2000s, but much was the production of neighbouring countries; it accounted for 43% of sub-Saharan African exports in 2011/12, according to USDA. Côte d'Ivoire had become Africa's principal palm oil producer-exporter in the mid-2000s, but the country certainly no longer attained the rank of fourth largest exporter in the world as it did throughout most of the 1990s. More than one-half of Côte d'Ivoire's palms were planted in 1965–70 and passed their peak of productivity by the end of the 1990s. Management and financial difficulties during the 1990s, as well as declining world prices for palm oil, led to the scaling-down of a replanting programme. However, following the revival in prices during 1997 and 1998, when Côte d'Ivoire had recourse to imports from Malaysia in order to satisfy domestic demand, plans were announced in 1999 to increase production, although these were interrupted by civil conflict. In 2011 Côte d'Ivoire was the world's ninth largest producer-exporter of palm oil. The palm oil sector in Cameroon similarly experienced delays in the implementation of replanting. The state-owned SOCAPALM was transferred to private ownership (90%) in 1999 and renamed PALMCAM/SOGEPAR. Uganda received international aid to develop a palm oil sector, and was a significant exporter for a time in the 2000s. However, Ghana and Kenya were the next largest exporters of palm oil after Benin and Côte d'Ivoire in 2011/12. In 2010/11 Angola, Cameroon and Nigeria were listed by USDA as minor exporters of palm oil; Togo, Tanzania, South Africa and the Democratic Republic of the Congo exported minimal amounts. Other African producers, notably Liberia, lacked sufficient refinery capacity to process their palm oil output, while Sierra Leone and São Tomé and Príncipe exported unprocessed palm kernels. Much production among the smaller producers was to satisfy domestic demand, such as the output of Guinea, sub-Saharan Africa's seventh largest producer but not an exporter.

Internationally, palm oil is faced with sustained competition from the other major edible lauric oils—soybean, rapeseed and sunflower oils—and these markets are subject to a complex and changing interaction of production, stocks and trade. Two main distinguishing features have traditionally characterized palm oil relative to its competitors: a very high trade-to-production ratio—far greater than that of comparable crops; and the geographical concentration of both production and trade, for both of which Indonesia and Malaysia account for approximately 90%. Palm oil has enjoyed a long-term price advantage over its principal competitor, soybean oil, which has enabled it to achieve a very high degree of market penetration. It is only recently—since about 1999—that the prices recorded for palm oil have consistently exceeded the long-term trend, reflecting new demand for feedstocks for biodiesel production. Even so palm oil is the lowest-priced vegetable oil, and it is, in the opinion of many market analysts, the most competitive biodiesel feedstock. However, its utilization for this purpose has remained very low compared with, in particular, rapeseed oil, which enjoys a high level of subsidization in the member states of the EU, where it is the principal biodiesel feedstock. The average import price (c.i.f. North West Europe) of Malaysian crude palm oil (5% bulk) recovered from a 2000s low in 2001 each year until 2004, but then declined by about one-10th in 2005, to US $422.1 per metric ton, before recovering to $478.3 per ton in 2006. The average annual price then almost doubled in two years, reaching $780 per ton in 2007 and $948 per ton in 2008. The average monthly price of palm oil rose above $800 per ton in June 2007 (it had been rising steadily since September 2006), and thereafter increased in each subsequent month of 2007, until November, with an average only slightly down in December, at $950 per ton. The upward trend continued until March 2008, when the average monthly price peaked at $1,249 per ton. The palm oil import price then remained fairly stable until June, but, as the financial crisis and fears of world-wide recession made their impact on commodities, the price then sank to as low as $488 per ton by November (a fall of 60% since June). There was a slow recovery in the price until May 2009, but even thereafter the prices did not fall back to the level of the first quarter, giving an average palm oil import price over the year of $683 per ton. Prices rose steadily from September 2009 until March 2010, and remained generally stable until a decline in the second half of 2011, with the result that the average price for 2010 was $901 per ton and that for 2011 was $1,125 per ton. The average price in January–July 2012 was $1,086 per ton, with prices strongest early in the year; the average monthly price for June was $999 per ton, although for July it recovered to $1,015 per ton.

PETROLEUM

Crude oils, from which petroleum fuel is derived, consist essentially of a wide range of hydrocarbon molecules which are separated by distillation in the refining process. Refined oil is treated in different ways to make the different varieties of fuel. More than four-fifths of total world oil supplies are used as fuel for the production of energy in the form of power or heating.

Petroleum, together with its associated mineral fuel, natural gas, is extracted both from onshore and offshore wells in many areas of the world. The dominant producing region is the Middle East, whose proven reserves in December 2011 accounted for 48.1% of known world deposits of crude petroleum and natural gas liquids. The Middle East accounted for 32.6% of estimated world output in 2011. Africa (including North Africa) contained 17,563m. metric tons of proven reserves (8.0% of the world total) at the end of 2011, and accounted for 10.4% (417.4m. tons) of estimated world production in that year.

From storage tanks at the oilfield wellhead, crude petroleum is conveyed, frequently by pumping for long distances through large pipelines, to coastal depots where it is either treated in a refinery or delivered into bulk storage tanks for subsequent shipment for refining overseas. In addition to pipeline transportation of crude petroleum and refined products, natural (petroleum) gas is, in some areas, also transported through networks of pipelines. Crude petroleum varies considerably in colour and viscosity, and these variations are a determinant both of price and of end-use after refining.

In the refining process, crude petroleum is heated until vaporized. The vapours are then separately condensed, according to their molecular properties, passed through airless steel tubes and pumped into the lower section of a high cylindrical tower, as a hot mixture of vapours and liquid. The heavy unvaporized liquid flows out at the base of the tower as a 'residue' from which is obtained heavy fuel and bitumen. The vapours passing upwards then undergo a series of condensation processes that produce 'distillates', which form the basis of the various petroleum products.

The most important of these products is fuel oil, composed of heavy distillates and residues, which is used to produce heating and power for industrial purposes. Products in the kerosene group have a wide number of applications, ranging from heating fuels to the powering of aviation gas turbine engines. Gasoline (petrol) products fuel internal combustion engines (used mainly in road motor vehicles), and naphtha, a gasoline distillate, is a commercial solvent that can also be processed as a feedstock. Propane and butane, the main liquefied petroleum gases, have a wide range of industrial applications and are also used for domestic heating and cooking.

Petroleum is the leading raw material in international trade. World-wide demand for this commodity totalled an estimated 88.0m. barrels per day (b/d) in 2011. The world's 'published proven' reserves of petroleum and natural gas liquids at 31 December 2011 were estimated to total 234,251m. metric tons, equivalent to 1,652,611m. barrels (1 metric ton is equivalent to approximately 7.3 barrels, each of 42 US gallons or 34.97 imperial gallons, i.e. 159 litres).

Production of Crude Petroleum
('000 metric tons, including natural gas liquids and oil from shale, estimates)

	2010	2011
World total	3,945,409	3,995,621
Africa	478,549	417,395
Leading African producers		
Algeria	75,501	74,311
Angola	91,973	85,242
Chad	6,403	5,971
Congo, Repub.	15,085	15,230
Egypt	35,031	35,151
Equatorial Guinea	13,566	12,474
Gabon	12,483	12,233
Libya	77,444	22,432
Nigeria	117,239	117,441
Sudan	22,905	22,314
—continued		
Leading non-African producers		
Brazil	111,707	114,554
Canada	164,369	172,629
China, People's Repub.	203,014	203,646
Iran	207,100	205,847
Iraq	121,447	136,936
Kazakhstan	81,647	82,373
Kuwait	122,689	140,041
Mexico	146,280	145,113
Norway	98,562	93,446
Qatar	65,685	71,053
Russia	505,130	511,420
Saudi Arabia	466,554	525,800
United Arab Emirates	131,420	150,094
United Kingdom	62,963	52,003
USA	339,915	352,273
Venezuela	142,537	139,643

Source: BP, *Statistical Review of World Energy 2012*.

Nigeria's first petroleum discovery was made in the Niger Delta region in 1956, and exports began in 1958. Production and exports increased steadily until output was disrupted by the outbreak of civil war in 1967. After the end of hostilities, in 1970, Nigeria's petroleum production greatly increased, and it became the country's major industry. After Libya restricted output in 1973, Nigeria became Africa's leading petroleum-producing country. Being of low sulphur content and high quality, Nigerian petroleum is much in demand on the European market. Nigeria's proven reserves were estimated to be 5,020m. metric tons at 31 December 2011. A member of the Organization of the Petroleum Exporting Countries (OPEC, see below), Nigeria's production quota was 1.7m. b/d at August 2011. The state petroleum enterprise, the Nigerian National Petroleum Corpn (NNPC), operates refinery facilities at Port Harcourt (I and II), Kaduna and Warri. According to the Energy Information Administration (EIA) of the US Department of Energy, Nigeria's 'nameplate' annual refinery capacity amounts to about 2.9m. b/d. However, Nigerian petroleum industry sources estimated that in 2010 only 1.7m.–2.1m. b/d were actually produced, owing to deficient management, and fire and theft, compounded by the frequent unavailability of sufficient supplies of crude after attacks on the country's oil infrastructure (see below). Indeed, production has remained at these levels for the past 10 years. Since an amnesty was declared in late 2009 between militants and the Government—militants exchanged weapons for money and training opportunities—attacks have declined and companies have been able to rebuild infrastructure. Despite a significant rise in operational capacity, according to the EIA, to between 60% and 75% by early 2011, Nigeria still depends on imports to meet national demand for petroleum products. In 2010 imports of refined fuel products reached US $7,900m. As part of a wider process of reform of the country's petroleum sector, which was still under way in mid-2011, the Government planned to address the shortcomings of the refining sector through a programme of privatization and by removing subsidies that encouraged producers of crude petroleum to supply foreign refineries at the expense of local ones. It was reported in mid-2012 that President Goodluck Johnson and his Cabinet had approved the Petroleum Industry Bill, which aims for transparency in the sector and includes tax and royalty reforms. It is hoped the bill will help the petroleum sector increase output to 4m. b/d. However, the bill had yet to be approved by the country's legislature, and analysts predicted there would need to be concessions before it passed into law. None the less, industry analysts believe the bill will strengthen the sector. In 2010, of crude exports totalling some 1.8m. b/d (about 93m. tons), 43% was destined for the USA, 20% for European markets (including 5% for Spain, 4% for Netherlands and 3% for each of Germany and France), 14% for India, 8% for Brazil, and 3% for South Africa. Asia as a whole imported some 17% of Nigerian crude oil. In 2010, at $72,300m., the value of exports of crude petroleum accounted for about 97% of the estimated total value of exports. According to data published by the IMF, petroleum contributed 66.9% of federal government revenue and 63.8% of consolidated government revenue in 2009.

Equitable distribution of Nigeria's oil wealth has been negligible, and in spite of the country's high ranking among the world's major exporters of petroleum, more than half of the country's population were reported to live in relative poverty in 2004, according to the IMF. The country is targeting reducing that figure to around 20% by 2015. The operations of multinational oil companies—notably Royal Dutch/Shell—in the Niger Delta have increasingly become the focus of local politically- and environmentally-motivated opposition. This is frequently expressed in acts of sabotage carried out against pipelines and other oil infrastructure, and in the kidnapping of expatriate oil workers in the Delta. The Movement for the Emancipation of the Niger Delta is prominent among groups that have claimed responsibility for kidnappings and acts of sabotage in recent years. In 2010 the explosion at BP's Deepwater Horizon petroleum exploration platform in the Gulf of Mexico and the resulting environmental catastrophe there refocused international attention on environmental damage due to oil production/exploration in other locations, including the Niger Delta, where heavy contamination has occurred regularly for 50 years, and where there were, according to the Nigerian National Oil Spill Detection and Response Agency, more than 2,400 oil spills between 2006 and 2010. In December 2011 Royal Dutch/Shell's Bonga field experienced its worst spill for a decade, affecting 150km–200km of Nigeria's coastline. In mid-2012 it was reported that the Nigerian National Oil Spill Detection and Response Agency had recommended a fine of some US $5,000m., equivalent to some $125,000 per barrel spilled.

Angola, which joined OPEC as its 12th member in January 2007, made its first petroleum discovery in 1955 near Luanda. However, Cabinda province has a major offshore deposit, in production since 1968, which now forms the basis of the country's oil industry. Output from Cabinda was briefly disrupted by the country's civil war, but has proceeded uninterrupted since 1977 and has risen steadily since 1982. Since the late 1980s production of crude petroleum has risen more than fourfold. According to the EIA, output will increase further in 2007–12, as a number of deep-water offshore projects are brought into operation. Thereafter, in 2015, on the basis of existing production, some experts have forecast that Angolan production will peak. In 2008 Angola obtained 96.5% of its total foreign earnings from crude petroleum. Angola's proven oil reserves were assessed at 1,822m. metric tons at 31 December 2011. Domestic consumption of crude petroleum has been forecast to increase in coming years, but is at present sufficiently low to allow most of the country's output to be exported. About 45% of Angola's crude exports in 2010 were sent to the People's Republic of China, of which it was the second largest crude supplier in 2010, after Saudi Arabia. Around 23% of Angola's crude oil exports went to the USA in that year, making it one of the largest suppliers of oil to that country. In 2010, according to US Department of Energy data, Chinese imports of Angolan crude averaged 790,000 b/d, while US imports of Angolan crude averaged some 400,000 b/d. European, Latin American and other Asian countries, in particular India, Taiwan, France, South Africa and Canada, were also major buyers of Angolan crude. Plans exist to augment the annual capacity of Angola's sole refinery, at Luanda, which stood at about 2m. tons in 2010. The national oil company, Sociedade Nacional de Combustíveis de Angola (SONANGOL), is constructing a new refinery, SonaRef, at the coastal city of Lobito. The new refinery, with planned daily capacity of 200,000 barrels, will be able to process heavy crudes such as those produced from Angola's Kuito and Dalia fields. However, in mid-2011 it was reported that the project had been delayed because of a shortfall in financing caused by the withdrawal of SINOPEC, China's state petroleum company which was the partner in the scheme. None the less, the facility's construction continues, although the completion date has been pushed back to 2015. Along with SINOPEC, other international oil companies that were reported to be active in Angola's oil industry in 2010, via joint ventures or production-sharing agreements with SONANGOL, included BP, Chevron, Eni, Total, ExxonMobil, and China National Offshore Oil Corpn (CNOOC).

The Republic of the Congo, with proven recoverable reserves estimated at 274m. metric tons in December 2011, commenced onshore petroleum production in 1957. Subsequent expansion, however, has been in operations off shore, where major new deposits, discovered in 1992, began to augment the country's petroleum output from 1996. Further significant offshore discoveries have been made since 1998. Output declined overall between 2000 and 2005 as a result of maturing oilfields and delays in bringing new projects into operation, but increased in 2006. There was a reverse in 2007, however, when output totalled 11.7m. tons, compared with 14.3m. tons in 2006. In 2008 production recovered by 6.0%, to 12.2m. tons, and a further increase, to an estimated 14.2m. tons, was recorded in 2009. Production in 2010 was estimated at 15.1m. tons, while in 2011 production rose by 1%, to an estimated 15.2m. tons. The Congo ranked as the fourth largest producer in sub-Saharan Africa, after Nigeria, Angola and Sudan, in 2011. In 2008 a joint petroleum venture formed by Total Exploration and Production Congo (53.5%), Chevron Overseas (Congo) Ltd (31.5%) and the state-owned Société Nationale des Pétroles du Congo (SNPC, 15%) commenced production at Moho-Bilondo, the Congo's first deep-water oilfield. Output from Moho-Bilondo, where initial annual capacity reportedly amounted to more than 30m. barrels, was expected to account for almost one-third of total national output by 2010. Meanwhile, Total estimated that a further US $10,000m. would be needed to develop the Moho-Bilondo Nord project, located off shore and part of the greater Moho-Bilondo development. The same company expected production at this facility to commence sometime between 2015 and 2017. Chevron, together with a number of partners, was reportedly engaged in early 2007 in the development of resources uncovered by the Lianzi-1 exploration well—located within the Zone of Common Interest established by Angola and the Congo in 2003—where a significant discovery was made in 2004. In 2006 the Congo's exports totalled some 12m. tons. Most foreign sales were to Asian destinations, with China accounting for about one-half. In 2010, according to the USGS, the petroleum sector was estimated to have accounted for some 89% of the Congo's exports and for about 79% of government revenues. In 2007 imports of petroleum products were also reported to have represented about one-third of total imports. The state-owned Congolaise de Raffinage operates a petroleum refinery with annual capacity of 10.5m. tons (as of 2007) at Pointe-Noire. Output of refined products was reported to have declined by almost 30%, to 2.5m. barrels, in 2008, owing to maintenance and renovation work at the refinery. Once the renovation process had been completed, the refinery was expected to begin to process crude from Moho-Bilondo, thereby reducing the Congo's reliance on imported petroleum products. Congolaise de Raffinage usually also processes some Angolan production, in addition to domestic crude. In late 2011 the Government instructed petroleum companies currently engaged in exploration activities in the country to develop oil fields located off shore, in the hope that increased production would offset declining output at exiting fields. A tender process was expected to commence in 2012.

In Gabon, whose recoverable reserves were estimated at 504m. metric tons at 31 December 2011 (the fourth largest in sub-Saharan Africa), the exploitation of petroleum deposits began in 1956, and, as in the Republic of the Congo, increased as offshore fields were brought into production. Output from most of the country's 122 oilfields has now reportedly peaked—although efforts to prolong their productivity by supplementary drilling are ongoing. June 2011 saw the Government's establishment of a national oil company—Gabon Oil Company—aimed at increasing the state's involvement in the petroleum sector by investing in future projects. In 2008 Total S. A.—via Total Gabon S. A. and its subsidiary, Total Participations Pétrolières Gabon—pursued petroleum production and exploration activities in Gabon, including the launch of redevelopment work at the offshore Anguille oilfield. A second phase of the project was scheduled to begin in 2009. Annual production from Anguille is expected to reach about 11m. barrels by 2014. Likewise via subsidiaries—VAALCO Gabon (Etame) Inc. and VAALCO Production (Gabon)—US-based VAALCO Energy Inc. produced petroleum from oilfields located in the offshore Etame Marin Block in 2008, selling its output to Total Oil Trading S. A. Domestic consumption of petroleum is very low, so Gabon exports some 90% of its crude, mostly to the USA and Europe. In 2010, according to the USGS, sales of petroleum and petroleum products accounted for about 75% of total export revenue. The most important export destinations for Gabon's surplus crude in 2006 were the USA, Europe (in particular France), China and India. The value of crude exports to the USA reportedly amounted to US $2,100m. in 2009, representing about 96% of the value of Gabon's total exports to that country. Sales of petroleum products to the USA generated a further $3.7m. in export revenue. In 2010, according to the USGS, crude petroleum contributed 40% of Gabon's GDP (compared with 51% in 2008) and 60% of government revenues. A member of OPEC until its withdrawal from the Organization in December 1996, Gabon's output accounted for just 1.4% of OPEC's total output in that year. In addition to the Government's stake of 25%, Société Gabonnaise de Raffinage (Total Gabon S. A.) holds a 58% share in Gabon's sole oil refinery, at Sogara, the annual capacity of which was 8m. barrels in 2008. Output of petroleum products at Sogara totalled 6m. barrels in each year in 2005–08, according to data cited by the USGS.

Cameroon, which is virtually self-sufficient in oil and petroleum products, derived about 50% of its export income from this source in 2010, according to the USGS. In 2009 the country's proven reserves were estimated at about 55m. metric tons. The country has reportedly been well explored for additional reserves. Some 85% of the Chad–Cameroon petroleum pipeline (see below) is located in Cameroon, and the country derives additional revenue in transit fees from Chadian exports. Société Nationale de Raffinage (SONARA) operates Cameroon's sole oil refinery, with a capacity of about 45,000 b/d, at the port of Limbé. In 2008 CityView Corpn Ltd of Australia announced plans to purchase a refinery with annual capacity of some 20m. barrels from the United Kingdom's Tagore Investments S. A. Once installed, capacity would be raised to about 37m. barrels per year. In late 2010 it was announced that BowLeven, of the United Kingdom, would be increasing its efforts to explore the offshore MLHP 5 block. In 2009 Cameroon's production of crude petroleum amounted to some 30m. barrels. Output of refined petroleum products was reportedly steady at 12m. barrels in each year in 2005–09.

The Democratic Republic of the Congo (DRC) entered offshore petroleum production in 1975, operating from oilfields near the Atlantic coast and at the mouth of the Congo River. These deposits became depleted at the end of the 1980s (estimates of its proven reserves fell from 13.2m. metric tons in 1989 to 7.6m. tons in 1990). However, the level of these reserves was substantially replenished during 1991, raising estimates to 25.6m. tons for each of the subsequent seven years. In 2010 production of crude was estimated at 8.6m. barrels; production declined by 8.5% compared with the previous year, according to USGS figures. Although the DRC has an annual refinery capacity of 850,000 tons, its exceptionally heavy-grade petroleum cannot be processed locally and the country cannot therefore consume its own output. According to the USGS, imports of petroleum products accounted for almost 14% of all imports in 2009. In the same year petroleum exploration licences were halted until the country had adopted new petroleum legislation. However, by mid-2010 the Government had awarded blocks to companies from the British Virgin Islands, South Africa, the United Kingdom and Bermuda.

In Equatorial Guinea the offshore Zafiro oilfield, discovered north-west of Bioko by ExxonMobil and Ocean Energy, commenced production in late 1996. (The Ceiba and Alba fields also contain significant reserves.) Output subsequently advanced very rapidly, reaching some 9m. metric tons by 2001, and has contributed greatly to the country's economic growth. In 2002 the Government created a national oil company, GEPetrol, primarily in order to manage its stakes in a number of production-sharing agreements with foreign interests. Although petroleum production is expected to decline in the short term, recent discoveries of rich hydrocarbon areas—once developed—could help to reverse this trend. Indeed the Aseng and Alen oil and gas-condensate fields were expected to revive production of natural gas liquids, with the latter anticipated to begin operations in late 2013. (The Aseng field began operations in November 2011.) In 2011 production totalled an estimated 12.5m. tons, and Equatorial Guinea ranked as the fifth largest producer in sub-Saharan Africa. Reserves were estimated at 231m. tons at the end of 2011. In 2009 preliminary IMF data indicated that petroleum exports totalled US $8,386m., contributed 59% towards government revenue, and also accounted for 59% of the country's GDP. According to the IMF, 98% of Equatorial Guinea's export earnings derive from crude oil, which, together with liquefied natural gas, contributes more than 90% of government revenue. Most of the country's production is sold on European, US and Asian markets. At around 70,000 b/d, exports of crude to the USA represented 29% of Equatorial Guinea's total crude exports in 2010. Other destinations included Spain (14% of the total), Italy (13%), Canada (10%), China (7%) and Brazil (6%). All of Equatorial Guinea's production of crude oil is exported. Local demand is met by imports of refined products. As in Nigeria (see above), the equitable distribution of Equatorial Guinea's oil wealth has been negligible—it has frequently been alleged that the Government has misappropriated much of the revenue generated by the resource. In 2007, however, Equatorial Guinea was accepted as a Candidate country of the Extractive Industries Transparency Initiative, a coalition of governments, companies, civil society groups, investors and international organizations that aims to improve transparency and accountability in the extractive industries. As of mid-2012 Equatorial Guinea had not yet met all necessary requirements to be considered a fully compliant member country.

Côte d'Ivoire, with estimated proven reserves of 13.7m. metric tons in 2008, and Benin, whose proven reserves were estimated at 1.1m. tons in 1998, are among the other smaller sub-Saharan offshore producers. Deposits of an estimated 52m.–58m. tons of petroleum have been identified off the coast of Senegal, but the development of these reserves (which are overwhelmingly of heavy oil) is not economically feasible at present.

At 31 December 2011 the proven petroleum reserves of Chad were assessed at 216m. metric tons. According to the USGS, revenue from petroleum increased significantly in 2011, to some US $2,000m. (compared with $1,300m. in 2010), as oil prices rose in that year. Petroleum output in 2011 was estimated to have amounted to 6.0m. tons, compared with 6.4m. tons in 2010 and 6.2m. tons in 2009. Among the main producers in 2011 was Esso Exploration and Production Chad, Inc.—Esso Chad. However, its production decreased to 115,000 b/d in 2011, compared with 122,500 b/d in the previous year. The exploitation of reserves in the Doba Basin region in south-western Chad commenced in mid-2003. Output from the Doba Basin's fields is conveyed by a 1,070-km pipeline, through Cameroon, to the Atlantic coast. In order to obtain funding to secure a stake in the Chad/Cameroon Petroleum Development and Pipeline Project (CCPDP), Chad became the first country to conclude a loan agreement with the World Bank with terms governing the way in which oil revenues should be spent. Some 80% was to be targeted at such sectors as health, education and rural development, and environmental protection projects were also to benefit. The remaining 20% was to be distributed for government expenditure and as a supplement payable to the Doba region. In early 2006 a dispute with the World Bank arose after the Government voted to allocate more than 20% of its oil revenue to the general budget. In response, the World Bank suspended loans to Chad and froze its oil revenue account. The dispute was resolved in mid-2006, when the Government agreed that it would allocate 70% of its oil revenues to development projects; the balance would be available for government expenditure. The Government of Chad has declared the goals of assuming control of as much as 60% of the country's oil industry and, possibly, of assuming membership of the ExxonMobil-led consortium that controls the CCPDP. The Société des Hydrocarbures du Tchad, the country's first national oil company, was created in 2006 in order to pursue these objectives. In late 2008 China National Petroleum Corpn (CNPC) International Ltd, with the Government of Chad, initiated the construction of a petroleum refinery close to N'Djamena. CNPC and the Government were to hold, respectively, stakes of 60% and 40% in the 53,000 b/d facilty. The first phase was completed in June 2011, with the arrival of crude oil announced soon after. This phase included the construction of an oil refinery with capacity of 1m. tons and a 311-km pipeline. In 2009 and 2010, CNPC made discoveries of further reserves in the Mimosa and Ronier areas of the Bongor Basin.

In 1998 Sudan, a relatively minor producer with estimated proven reserves of some 360m. metric tons in that year, finalized an agreement with four foreign companies to construct a 1,600-km pipeline to convey output from western Sudan to a terminal at Bachair, south of Port Sudan. The pipeline, with the capacity to carry 450,000 b/d, was inaugurated in mid-1999, and petroleum production has since risen rapidly to total an estimated 22.3m. tons in 2011, compared with 22.9m. tons in 2010 and 23.4m. tons in 2009. Owing to limited resources, the Sudan National Petroleum Corpn (SUDAPET) has frequently collaborated in joint exploration and production venture with foreign companies, retaining minority stakes in these projects. Among the foreign companies active in Sudan's oil sector are CNPC, Oil and Natural Gas Corpn of India and Petronas of Malaysia. Activity in the petroleum industry in the south of the country has been complicated by conflicting claims to ownership of resources by northern and southern authorities—NILEPET is the southern counterpart of SUDAPET. Sudan's refining facilities are state-owned, with the Khartoum oil refinery (the location of 36m. barrels, or 80%, of national refining capacity) being operated as a joint venture between a Sudanese government vehicle and CNPC. A smaller facility is operated at Port Sudan. In 2010, according to the USGS, the value of Sudan's exports of crude petroleum represented 82% of the total value of the country's foreign sales. Exports of petroleum products were reported to have contributed an additional 4%. According to data cited by the EIA, Sudan's exports of crude in 2011 were almost exclusively to Asian markets, with China being the destination for some 220,000 b/d (66% of the total), Malaysia taking about 30,000 b/d (9%) and Japan some 25,000 b/d (8%). Other destinations included India and Singapore (4% each). Sudan's proven reserves were estimated at 904m. tons at the end of 2011. The manner in which both the production of and exploration for petroleum in Sudan have hitherto been conducted has allegedly involved the Government in human rights abuses, including the forced evacuation of populations living in the vicinity of oilfields. In late 2006 the USA banned US individuals and organizations from investing in Sudan's petroleum and petrochemical industries, a measure that was intended, partly, to counter the alleged use of petroleum-derived revenues to fund the Darfur conflict.

At the time of the official declaration of independence of South Sudan from the Republic of Sudan on 9 July 2011, it was unclear how the northern and southern regions would handle the division of petroleum resources: the southern region produces most of the area's petroleum, but all of the refineries are located in the north, as is the main port. According to the EIA, the South Sudan authorities announced plans to build refining capacity in the south and a 3,600-km pipeline to Lamu port in Kenya in anticipation of the eventual secession. In December 2011 the Government of Sudan prevented South Sudanese crude from leaving Port Sudan. Some shipments were subsequently released, but it remained unclear whether the exported crude originated in the Republic of Sudan or South Sudan. Moreover, other disputed shipments in early 2012 continued to damage relations between the two countries. Meanwhile, in January South Sudan halted all production of crude after it could not agree a deal with its northern neighbour regarding payment for rights to export its crude through Sudan. Following border fighting that damaged production infrastructure, and a continuing failure to reach an agreement, production was expected to resume no earlier than December 2012. The unresolved status of the oil-rich border area of Abyei continues to jeopardize the security of the petroleum sector.

According to the Oil and Gas Journal, South Africa's proven reserves of petroleum were estimated at about 15m. barrels at the beginning of 2011. According to the EIA, all of the country's reserves were located off shore in the Bredasdorp basin and off the west coast, close to the border with Namibia. Crude output in 2010 amounted to some 1.4m. barrels, according to the USGS. About two-thirds of domestic demand for crude is met by imports, mainly from Saudi Arabia, Iran, Nigeria and Angola. At about 35m. tons, South Africa's annual refining capacity is surpassed within Africa only by that of Egypt. Durban, Cape Town and Sasolburg are the locations of the most important refining facilities.

With the development of two oilfields—Jubilee and Tweneboa—off the Ghanaian coast, containing reserves estimated at 3,000m. barrels, Ghana was set to join the list of petroleum-producing countries in sub-Saharan Africa in 2011/12. The Jubilee field began operations in late 2010. IMF data published in June 2011 suggested that revenues from the petroleum sector could contribute some 3%–4% of GDP annually in the first three years of production (the anticipated period of peak output). Production was expected to peak in August 2011 at around 115,000 b/d. Cumulative government revenues from oil and gas could, according to the IMF analysis, amount to US $12,000m. over the production period 2012–30.

Among other sub-Saharan African countries where petroleum reserves are known or believed to exist, but which do not yet produce, are Guinea, Mozambique, Swaziland, Eritrea, São Tomé and Príncipe, and Tanzania. Exploration has also taken place, or is under way, in Ethiopia, Namibia, Kenya, Madagascar and Zimbabwe.

International petroleum prices are strongly influenced by OPEC, founded in 1960 to co-ordinate the production and marketing policies of those countries whose main source of export earnings is petroleum. OPEC had 12 members in 2011. Nigeria joined OPEC in 1971; the other African members are Algeria, Angola and Libya (Gabon having terminated its membership in 1997).

The (then) four African members of OPEC (Algeria, Gabon, Libya and Nigeria) formed the African Petroleum Producers' Association (APPA) in 1987. Angola, Benin, Cameroon, Chad, the DRC, the Republic of the Congo, Côte d'Ivoire, Egypt, Equatorial Guinea, Ghana, Mauritania, South Africa and Sudan subsequently joined the association, in which Tunisia has observer status. Apart from promoting co-operation among regional producers, the APPA, which is based in Brazzaville, Republic of the Congo, co-¬operates with OPEC in stabilizing oil prices.

Price History of the OPEC 'Basket' of Crude Oils
(US $ per barrel)

	Average	Highest month(s)	Lowest month(s)
2001	23.12	26.10 (June)	17.53 (Dec.)
2002	24.36	28.39 (Dec.)	18.33 (Jan.)
2003	28.10	31.54 (Feb.)	25.34 (April)
2004	36.05	45.37 (Oct.)	29.56 (Feb.)
2005	50.54	57.88 (Sept.)	40.24 (Jan.)
2006	61.08	68.89 (July)	54.97 (Oct.)
2007	69.08	88.84 (Nov.)	50.79 (Jan.)
2008	94.45	131.22 (July)	38.60 (Dec.)
2009	61.06	76.29 (Nov.)	41.41 (Feb.)
2010	77.45	88.56 (Dec.)	72.51 (July)
2011	107.46	118.09 (April)	92.83 (Jan.)

Source: OPEC, *Annual Reports*.

The average price of the OPEC reference 'basket' (ORB) of crude oils recovered in July 2011—following two months of decline—as markets stabilized and the US dollar weakened, to reach US $111.62 per barrel—an increase of $2.58 (2.4%) compared with June. The average Brent price likewise increased during July, by $2.85 (2.5%), to $116.89 per barrel. The average price of West Texas Intermediate (WTI) was $97.14, $0.93 (1%) higher than in June. The price range for the month narrowed, reflecting a more stable environment. Data reflected a spur in Japanese demand, as reconstruction plans following the earthquake, tsunami and nuclear accident earlier in the year necessitated increased imports of oil. Meanwhile, high unemployment, high gasoline prices and a slowing of the economy weakened US demand for oil. Demand in Europe was also down, although not as markedly as in the previous two months. Consumption in the Netherlands, Spain and France was particularly subdued as consumers were deterred by high transport fuel prices. Rapidly developing economies—especially China and India—helped to offset lower demand elsewhere, but overall demand was down over the course of July. Prices of the ORB fell sharply once again in early August, as concerns regarding euro zone debt undermined macroeconomic confidence. On 8 August the ORB price stood at $102.37 per barrel.

In August 2011 the average price of the ORB fell by US $5.30 (4.7%), compared with that for July, to $106.32 per barrel. This was the largest decline in percentage terms since May 2010. The average price of Brent crude also fell, by $6.42 (5.5%), to $110.46 per barrel. The largest decline compared with July was recorded by WTI, the average price of which fell by $10.84 (11.2%), to $86.30 per barrel. Prices fell sharply at the beginning of the month as a result of continued concerns regarding credit and the US economy—GDP data released in the first half of 2011 were more disappointing than expected—but recovered later in the month following supply disruptions in the North Sea and the US Gulf, the latter as a result of seasonal storms. All components within the ORB declined in August, with African grades recording the most significant losses. The rebound in prices towards the end of the month was partly offset by expectations that Libya would resume production in the near future. Lower demand in the USA had been reported in 2011—in June a year-on-year decline in consumption of 1.3% was registered—attributed to higher fuel prices and improved vehicle fuel efficiency. China showed a year-on-year growth in consumption of 2.3% in July—despite the end of a government programme of vehicle incentives, which led to a downward revision in gasoline consumption for the third quarter of 2011. Demand in Brazil was better than expected in the same month.

Compared with August, the average price of the ORB increased in September 2011 by US $1.29 (1.2%), reaching $107.61 per barrel. The average price of Brent crude also rose over the same period, by $2.67 (2.4%), to $113.13 per barrel. The average price of WTI declined, albeit slightly, by $0.70 (less than 0.1%), to $85.60 per barrel. The ORB's wide range of prices during September was attributed to economic uncertainty in Europe, precipitated by the sovereign debt crisis in Greece. Following a decline in the ORB price in August, recovery in September was driven primarily by Ecuador's Oriente crude, the price of which increased by 6.0% during the course of the month. Meanwhile, the prices for African light crudes such as Algeria's Saharan Blend and Nigeria's Bonny Light remained strong as a result of high demand in Asia and the continued absence from the market of Libya's light crude. None the less, the price recovery slowed towards the end of the month. Demand for petroleum was expected to decline as the global economy continued to struggle: economic growth in the USA was slowing, while the unemployment rate in that country remained high. Moreover, debt problems in the euro zone, delays in Japan's reconstruction plan and lower demand in India as a result of disappointing automobile sales and GDP figures contributed to the negative outlook.

The average price of the ORB declined again in October 2011, compared with the previous month, by 1.2%, to US $106.29 per barrel. The average price of Brent crude fell by 3.3%, or $3.69, to $109.44 per barrel. However, the average WTI price in October recorded a slight increase, of 1.0%, to reach $86.45 per barrel. The 'basket' price fell to less than $100 in the first week of October, the first time it had done so since February. However, it recovered in the latter part of the month as a result of optimism for a possible solution to the European debt crisis. The significant decline in Brent crudes, particularly in North Africa and the Middle East, was attributed to the return of Libyan petroleum exports, a return to production of the Buzzard North Sea oil field (following an unscheduled halt) and increased production in West Africa. Meanwhile, in spite of the demand for fuel products over the winter period, consumption of petroleum in those countries was expected to remain subdued in the final quarter of 2011 owing to uncertainty in the EU and torpid economic growth elsewhere. Moreover, Chinese demand for petroleum was also weakening, though non-OECD countries offset this, in particular Thailand and India.

In November 2011 the average price of the ORB increased by 3.6%, or US $3.79, to reach $110.08 per barrel. The average price of Brent crude increased slightly—1.1% ($1.22)—to reach $110.66 per barrel. WTI recorded the largest increase in its average price, reaching $97.11 per barrel, a figure which represented a rise of 12.3%, or $10.66, compared with the previous month. In November 2011 the year-on-year average price for the 'basket' was some 40% higher than it was at the same point in 2010. The growth in prices overall was attributed to optimism that Greece and Italy—and the EU in general—were close to resolving their debt problems; increased prices were also attributed to more promising economic data from the USA. The improved performance of Middle Eastern crudes was aided by good refining margins in the Dubai/Oman market. With around 50% of petroleum consumption related to transportation fuel, vehicle manufacture is an important indicator for oil demand. It was reported in late 2011 that slowing demand in China in the second half of the year could be associated with lower exports, higher petroleum prices and the country ending incentives for new car purchases. However, it was reported that in November that Asian demand in general was strong, especially for heating fuels.

In the final month of 2011 the average price of the ORB fell by 2.5%, or US $2.74, compared with November, to $107.34 per barrel. Over the same period Brent crude also declined, the price of which averaged $107.86 per barrel, which was $2.80, or 2.5%, lower than a month earlier. The average price of WTI, however, remained strong in December, increasing by $1.47, or 1.5%, to reach $98.58 per barrel. The lower prices recorded for every component of the 'basket' (except WTI) was attributed to continued challenges in Europe, including its debt crisis and a poorly performing euro; while lower prices were also attributed to worries over economic growth in Europe and China, specifically over the possibility of poor market sentiment spreading, and then undermining economies in the rest of the world. None the less, towards the end of December the average price of the 'basket' began to recover, aided by political instability in the Middle East, specifically anti-government protests in Syria, where analysts expected supply to drop significantly. While demand continued to be negatively affected by global economic troubles, it was proving more resilient compared with 2009. Indeed, it was reported that non-OECD countries' demand would grow in 2012, albeit not as rapidly as in previous years. However, demand in OECD countries was expected to contract, partly as a result of expected higher petroleum prices in 2012. Meanwhile, supply of crude for December 2011 was at its highest level since October 2008.

In January 2012 the average price of the ORB recovered, increasing by US $4.42 (4.1%), compared with the previous month, to reach $111.76 per barrel. Brent crude also recovered in January, increasing by $2.72 (2.5%), to average $110.58 per barrel. The average price of WTI remained strong, increasing by $1.72 (1.7%). Its average price for January was $100.30 per barrel. Continuing instability in the Middle East, coupled with a continuing improvement in economic data concerning the USA, accounted for higher prices during the month, according to industry analysts. However, stronger growth was constrained by ongoing concerns in Europe, where a number of countries' credit ratings were downgraded. The development was expected to hinder demand in the region. Venezuela's Merey crude was the best performer in January, with its average price increasing by over 6%. Middle East-grade crudes also performed strongly, particularly Iran Heavy and Kuwait Export. Growth in demand in 2012 was expected to be concentrated in China, India, Latin America and the Middle East, while poorly performing economies in the OECD were expected to erode demand in those countries. The suspended operations of Japanese nuclear power plants, however, were expected to result in increased demand for petroleum products in order to increase electricity production from conventional plants. Moreover, new vehicle sales in Japan increased by some 36% compared with the previous month. US petroleum demand remained subdued in January, in spite of strong year-on-year vehicle sales (sales growth was the highest since the Government introduced its vehicle incentives scheme in 2009).

There was a significant increase in the average price of the ORB in February 2012. It reached US $116.48 per barrel, which represented an increase of $5.72 (5.1%) compared with January. Brent crude also rose steeply, its average price reaching $119.56 per barrel—an increase of $8.98 (8.1%). The average price of WTI increased by $2.05, or 2.0%, to $102.35 per barrel. Speculative action in the crude futures market and positive progress in the Greek financial position were credited with the higher prices over the month. Speculation was believed to have heightened fears of disruptions to supply. The price of all components in the 'basket' improved in February, with Bonny Light crude showing the largest growth in dollar terms; it grew by $9.28, compared with the average price in January. In contrast to the previous month, Venezuelan Merey was the worst performer in dollar terms, growing by just $1.49. The poor performance of Merey was attributed to a near-collapse in the fuel oil market. Global demand for petroleum in 2012 was again expected to remain at the same level as the previous year, given the negative outlook for the world economy and high prices. Meanwhile, the USA continued to consume less petroleum in February. The contraction was attributed to poor economic growth and particularly high prices for transportation and industrial fuel. However, demand outlook remained positive as a result of further increases in new vehicle sales (the best growth since February 2008).

The price of the ORB rose once again in March 2012, to average US $122.97 per barrel. This represented an increase of $5.49, or 4.7%, compared with the previous month, and was the highest monthly average since July 2008. Brent crude was a strong performer in March, with its average price growing by $5.77 (4.8%). It averaged $125.33 per barrel for the month. The average price of WTI in March was $106.31 per barrel, representing an increase of $3.96 (3.9%) compared with February. Prices were driven higher by problems with supply in the North Sea and East Africa, and improving economic data in the USA and China. Ongoing problems in the euro zone and higher prices for refined products did not negatively affect the price of crudes during the month. Crudes including Bonny Light, Es Sider, Girassol and Saharan Blend performed well as a result of the supply disruptions in some of the biggest North Sea fields. Meanwhile, Venezuelan Merey was the worst performer again, growing at a much lower rate than any other component in the 'basket', which was around 5% in March. Production in Saudi Arabia was described as 'record-breaking' by analysts, but there were suggestions and some evidence of stock-builds. Compared with the previous month, demand in March was largely unchanged.

Following three consecutive months of price increases, there was some relief for consumers in April 2012, as the average price of the ORB declined by US $4.79 (3.9%), to $118.18 per barrel. The average price of Brent crude decreased to $119.71 per barrel, which represented a fall of $5.62 (4.5%), compared with March. WTI declined by $2.96 (2.8%) over the same period. It averaged $103.35 per barrel for the month. The decline in all components in the 'basket' was attributed to the start of the low demand season. Rising global supply and the subsequent rise in inventories had kept prices from rising inexorably. The price declines were recorded by North African and West African crudes. Meanwhile, Middle Eastern grades such as Murban and Qatar Marine also showed significant losses compared with their average prices in March. It was reported that the US economy had stabilized, which, coupled with the ongoing suspension of operations of Japanese nuclear power plants, had arrested the decline in OECD demand in the short term. However, in April petroleum consumption in Europe declined for the eighth consecutive month. Increased production and the resultant oversupply contributed to lower prices during the month. Production in OECD countries increased by around 1% in April, compared with production in March, while non-OECD supply was forecast to grow by 0.6m. b/d in 2012, compared with just 0.1m. b/d in 2011.

In May 2012 the average price of the ORB saw significant losses. Compared with the previous month, the price declined by US $10.11 (8.6%), to $108.07 per barrel. The fall in prices was the largest since December 2008. The average price of Brent crude decreased by $9.44 (7.9%), to $110.27 per barrel. The average price of WTI fell below the $100 per barrel level again, declining by $8.90 (8.6%), to settle at $94.45 per barrel. The significant declines in all components in the 'basket' were ascribed to disappointing data from the world's leading economies, a broad sell-off in petroleum markets, record levels of stock and the ongoing crisis in the euro zone. All components in the 'basket' declined by around 8–10%, a figure twice as high as losses sustained in April. Ecuador's Oriente and Venezuelan Merey lost $11.61 and $8.65 of their value per barrel, respectively; while the latter fell below the $100 per barrel benchmark. Growth in demand was hampered by a slowdown in Chinese manufacturing in May. Meanwhile, some analysts predicted that the start of the driving season in the USA would be affected by declining fuel prices, as consumers waited for the price to 'bottom out'. However, high prices had already negatively affected consumption there, with year-on-year figures suggesting a contraction of some 6% in March 2012. Other analysts predicted a recovery in US fuel demand in the short term, but the negative outlook for 2012 overall remained. In the first two weeks of June the average price of the ORB had dropped further, to $97.34 per barrel.

In June 2012 the average price of the ORB declined once again. In fact, the decline accelerated, falling by US $14.09 (13.0%), compared with the previous month, to average $93.98 per barrel for the month. It had been 18 months since the price had averaged less than $100 per barrel. The average price of Brent crude decreased by $15.08 (13.7%) over the same period; it averaged $95.19 per barrel in June. In that month the average price of WTI also fell, though compared with all the components in the 'basket' its decline was the least significant in dollar terms. For June it averaged $82.33 per barrel, which represented a decline of $12.12 (12.8%) compared with May. The main factors contributing to the decline in prices across the board were sell-offs in the petroleum markets and oversupply of crudes. It was reported that losses in the Asian or Dubai/Oman-related components in the 'basket' were mitigated by a somewhat stronger market for sour grades in the region, particularly in China, where significant expansion was envisaged. The slowdown in the OECD economies continued to dampen demand in June, with forecast demand in 2012 unchanged from the previous month. Japan's increased consumption of fuel oil was the exception, though that would change should Japan's nuclear power plants resume operations. It was forecast that non-OECD growth in production would be driven by Brazil, Colombia and Kazakhstan, whereas declining production in OECD countries would be attributed most keenly to Mexico, Norway and the United Kingdom.

The average price of the ORB recovered in July 2012, following three consecutive months of decline; it increased by US $5.57 (5.9%) compared with June, averaging $99.55 per barrel for the month. The price of Brent crude rose in July by $7.40 (7.8%) to average $102.59 per barrel. The average price of WTI increased by $5.46 (6.6%) over the same period, reaching $87.79 per barrel. The overall increase in price in July was attributed to production problems in the North Sea as a result of brief strikes in Norway, and better-than-expected economic data coming out of China and the USA. All basket components increased over the month by around $5–$8, with Urals recording the most significant rise. World demand showed signs of stabilizing. The heat, summer driving season and the ongoing closure of Japan's nuclear power plants supported this trend. It was reported in August that demand in the USA and Japan was rising. Meanwhile, seasonal flooding in India led to a rise in power-generator usage, which in turn increased consumption of diesel fuel. However, demand in Europe remained subdued, and was expected to remain so in the short term, or as long as the region's debt problems continued to affect industrial activity. In the second week of August the ORB had reached $108.36, which represented an increase of close to $9 compared with July's average.

PLATINUM

Platinum is one of a group of six related metals known as the platinum-group metals (PGM), which also includes palladium, rhodium, ruthenium, iridium and osmium. In nature, platinum is usually associated with the sulphides of iron, copper and nickel. Depending on the relative concentration of the PGM and copper and nickel in the deposit, platinum is either the major product or a by-product of base metal production. PGM are highly resistant to corrosion, and do not oxidize in air. They are also extremely malleable and have a high melting point, giving them a wide range of industrial uses.

Although widely employed in the petroleum-refining and petrochemical sectors, the principal industrial use for platinum is in catalytic converters in motor vehicles (which reduce pollution from exhaust emissions), which, from 2004, generally accounted for about one-half of global platinum consumption (an estimated 41.8% in 2011, as the motor trade recovered but remained sluggish, and with an increase in jewellery demand). Most Western countries and many others have implemented legislation to neutralize vehicle exhaust gases, and this necessitates the fitting of catalytic converters, using platinum, rhodium and palladium, to vehicles. In 1989 the Council of (Environment) Ministers of the European Community (subsequently the European Union—EU) decided to oblige vehicle manufacturers within the Community to fit three-way catalytic converters as compulsory features, first in smaller passenger cars and then in larger vehicles and heavy lorries (trucks), in 1992–95. The resultant increase in demand for automotive emission control catalysts (autocatalysts) generated a rising trend in the consumption of platinum, rhodium and palladium during the 1990s. Stricter EU limits on emissions took effect in 2000, and further restrictions were gradually introduced subsequently. In the USA regulations to reduce emissions of exhaust gases required full compliance by vehicle manufacturers from 2001. The increasing use of autocatalysts, principally by US and European motor vehicle manufacturers, was reflected in a strong advance in autocatalyst demand for platinum into the 2000s, from 1.8m. oz in 1999 to 4.1m. oz in 2007. Autocatalyst demand for platinum fell slightly in 2008 (palladium was increasingly being favoured as an alternative to platinum, particularly in North America), to 3.6m. oz, although recovery of platinum from autocatalyst scrap continued to rise in that year, reaching 998,000 oz (compared with 520,000 oz in 1999). In 2009 autocatalyst demand fell to only 2.6m. oz, and recovery from autocatalyst scrap declined too, for the first time, to 780,000 oz. Economic expansion was more settled into 2010 and in the following year, so autocatalyst demand increased to 3.0m. oz by 2011, while recovery increased to 978,000 oz. Almost one-half of platinum use in autocatalysts is accounted for by Europe (49% in 2011), followed by North America (14%) and Japan (10%). Palladium use in autocatalysts (62.7% of palladium consumption in 2011) was increasing more rapidly than that of platinum, in particular in North America, while in the longer term new technologies in motor vehicles threatened the need for autocatalysts.

Alloyed platinum is very heavy and hard. Platinum's white colour makes it popular for jewellery, which accounts for the other principal source of consumption (30.0%, or 2.2m. oz, in 2011, as jewellery demand tried to recover from higher prices and its belated reaction to recession). The largest single source of platinum demand in 2004–08 was for use in European autocatalysts, but at the beginning of the decade Japan was the world's main consumer of platinum, its jewellery industry absorbing 1.2m. oz in 1999 (19% of total global demand) and a further 1.1m. oz in 2000. However, Japanese demand for platinum jewellery fell steadily through the 2000s, from 2001 Chinese jewellery demand being greater (peaking at 1.7m. oz in 2002, and falling as low as 835,000 oz in 2006, before recovering). In 2009, after a 73% increase on the previous year, jewellery demand from China was again the largest single source of global total platinum demand (25%), displacing European autocatalysts (19%), but elevated stocks and rising prices saw the status quo ante return. In 2011 European autocatalyst accounted for 21% of global demand and Chinese jewellery for 20%. Industrial and other miscellaneous applications account for the balance of platinum consumption; these uses include platinum for minting coins and small bars purchased as an investment, petroleum refining, production of nitric acid, glass manufacture, electrical applications and dentistry. From the 1990s demand by industrial consumers raised international demand for platinum steadily. Demand of 6.3m. oz in 2000 rose to a peak of 7.9m. oz by 2007, falling to 6.4m. oz by 2009, mainly on account of the impact of world-wide economic recession on the automotive industry; total international demand recovered to 6.8m. oz in 2010 and 7.2m. oz in 2011. Supply, which had dipped slightly in 2000 (to 5.7m. oz), increased thereafter until 2006 (8.2m. oz), before dipping slightly and stabilizing in 2007 and 2008 at just less than 8.1m. oz; it fell to 7.3m. oz in 2009 and recovered to 7.7m. oz in 2010 and 8.0m. oz in 2011. The most powerful driver of platinum supply was South African mined output of the metal, which rose from 3.9m. oz in 2000 (3.4% down on 1999) to 5.4m. oz in 2006, falling back to 4.6m. oz by 2009; South African mine production then began to recover, increasing to almost 4.8m. oz in 2010 and 4.7m. oz in 2011.

World production of PGM generally is dominated by South Africa, which traditionally accounted for about three-quarters of supplies of platinum—the proportion has declined in recent years (60% of total world supply in 2011, but 74% of global mined production)—and approximately one-third of supplies of palladium to the international market (31% of total supply and 39% of mined production). Russia has accounted for, on average, about 40% of the world's palladium supplies in the 2000s (32% of total supply and 40% of mined production in 2011). In 2005 official data relating to Russian PGM were declassified. Russian platinum production in that year was reported to have totalled an estimated peak of 960,000 oz, but had fallen to 785,000 oz by 2010, before recovering to 818,000 oz in 2011. Russia is the world's largest producer of mined palladium and the second largest of platinum. Canada was usually the third largest producer of platinum, mined as a by-product of nickel production, but in 2009 it was displaced by Zimbabwe. The next largest platinum producer was the USA. The world's four leading platinum-mining companies in 2011 were Anglo Platinum Ltd of South Africa, Impala Platinum Holdings Ltd (Implats) of South Africa, Lonmin of the United Kingdom and South Africa and MMC Norilsk Nickel of Russia (these same four dominated palladium output, with Norilsk Nickel foremost, and Lonmin edged ahead of by Stillwater Mining of the USA).

Zimbabwe, the only other significant African platinum producer apart from South Africa, has significant deposits of PGM. In 2011 Zimbabwe was the world's third largest platinum producer—in that year, the 10th successive year of increased output, a record 341,000 oz were mined (5.3% of world mine production). There are two mines for PGM: the Mimosa mine, which is operated as a joint venture between Aquarius Platinum and Impala Platinum of South Africa; and the Ngezi mine, which is operated by Zimplats. In 2011 a new mine, Unki, operated by Anglo Platinum, began production and boosted Zimbabwe's output by 19%. In 2004 draft legislation governing the mining sector recommended that indigenous ownership should rise to 20% within two years, to 25% within seven years and to 30% within 10 years of the legislation's enactment. In late 2007 Zimbabwe's parliament approved an Indigenization and Economic Empowerment bill that proposed the transfer of 51% of all foreign-owned companies in the country to Zimbabwe nationals (specifically 'any person who before the 18th April 1980 was disadvantaged by unfair discrimination on the grounds of his or her race, and any descendant of such person'), and the legislation received presidential assent in March 2008. While it remained unclear to what extent, if at all, the provisions of the new law would be applied in practice, Zimbabwe's PGM producers were reported to have made arrangements for this transfer by, for example, relinquishing resources in exchange for what were termed empowerment credits. In March 2011 the Government gazetted details on compliance with the indigenization legislation within six months, but, although the prices of shares in the companies affected suffered, the exact outcome following negotiation between the stakeholders remained uncertain into 2012. In the long term the Government also favoured the construction of a refinery in the country, but how that would be financed and operated given the perceived 'asset grab' against the major multinational companies, and with the power problems in southern Africa, remained problematic. PGM occur as trace element by-products associated with nickel production in Botswana, but the country produces more palladium. Elsewhere in Africa, there are known or probable deposits of platinum in Ethiopia, Kenya and Sierra Leone. Minor producers outside Africa, North America and Russia include, notably, China, Colombia, Australia, Spain and Finland. In 1999 it was reported that significant deposits of PGM had been identified in Mongolia, but no exploitation was developed in the 2000s.

Whereas PGM are produced in Canada and Russia as by-products of copper and/or nickel mining, PGM in South Africa are produced as the primary products, with nickel and copper as by-products. Another fundamental difference between the platinum deposits in South Africa and those in Russia and Canada is the ratio of platinum to palladium. In South Africa the percentage of platinum contained in PGM has, to date, exceeded that of palladium, although the ratio tended to favour palladium in new mines that were brought into production from the early 1990s (see below). In Russia, Canada and the USA there is a higher proportion of palladium than platinum.

South African production capacity was substantially increased in 1993, following the completion of a number of expansion projects that had been under development since the mid-1980s. However, the level of world platinum prices, together with rises in production costs, led to the subsequent postponement or cancellation of several of these projects and to the closure of unprofitable operations. From the mid-1990s, none the less, improved productivity in the platinum industry, together with the prospect of increasing demand for PGM and continued uncertainty regarding Russian exports, encouraged South African producers to undertake a number of new expansion programmes. South Africa's platinum sales (mine production) increased annually in 2000–06, but declined in 2007–09 and, slightly, in 2011. Analysts attributed the reversals recorded in South Africa's production of both platinum and palladium in 2007 to, in large measure, the stricter enforcement of safety procedures at mines, as part of an attempt by the Government to reduce fatalities in all of the country's mining industries. Into 2011, therefore, interventions in support of safety regulations, as well as industrial action and interruptions to the electricity supply, had an effect on mine output. In 2011 South Africa's exports (f.o.b.) of platinum (unwrought, powder, or semi-manufactured) contributed US $10,991m., or 11.8%, of the country's total export earnings.

Prices for Platinum
(London Platinum and Palladium Market, afternoon 'fixes', US $ per troy oz)

	Average	Highest	Lowest
2000	544.1	622 (13 Dec.)	414 (6 Jan.)
2009	1,203.5	1,494 (3 Dec.)	918 (15 Jan.)
2010	1,609.4	1,786 (9 Nov.)	1,475 (5 Feb.)
2011	1,721.9	1,887 (22 Aug.)	1,354 (29 Dec.)

International commodity prices for platinum (and palladium) are based on the afternoon 'fix' on the London Platinum and Palladium Market (LPPM) in the United Kingdom, cited in US dollars per troy ounce. A twice-daily quotation of platinum prices began in London in 1973 (the main London and Zurich, Switzerland, dealers agreeing certain common standards in 1979), but the system was only formalized as the LPPM in 1987, with quotations upgraded to full fixings in 1989. In that year the nominal London platinum price was US $507.3 per oz, a level that was not exceeded until 2000 (in real terms, the 1989 price was not exceeded until 2004). At the end of 2004 the London price of platinum was $861 per oz. Over 2004 the average price of platinum was $845.8 per oz. The average price for 2005 was $896.6 per oz, after strong growth in the second half of the year: in late October the highest price for platinum in 25 years—more than $940 per oz—was recorded; and in December the price of platinum rose above $1,000 per oz. Platinum continued to perform strongly thereafter, achieving an average price of $1,142.6 per oz over 2006 and a record $1,302.8 per oz in 2007. This last was the highest level, in real terms, for 27 years.

In January–March 2008, in response to concerns regarding the level of South African production, but in line with other commodity prices, the London price of platinum rose dramatically, reaching a new record high of US $2,273 per oz on 4 March. A sharp correction ensued, however: on 20 March the afternoon fix for platinum was $1,830.0 per oz. Although the record daily high of March was not equalled, the average monthly London price reached a record $2,054.7 per oz in May (compared with $2,046.5 per oz for March); however, it declined sharply in August–November amid fears of global recession and, particularly, the dramatic fall in demand from the automotive industry. The year-on-year change in the platinum price from 2007, in US dollars, was an increase of 21% (the change was less pronounced in other currencies, except for the South African rand—in which it was 38%); the average annual London price for platinum in 2008 was $1,577.5 per oz, in nominal terms a record and in real terms not bettered since 1980. None the less, the December price, the lowest of the year, was just $834.8 per oz (the year had started with a January price of $1,585.8 per oz). Price volatility, therefore, was put at 45%, while the intra-year change in prices recorded a decline of 42%.

By March 2009 the London platinum price had recovered to more than US $1,100 per oz, owing to reductions in mine production, steadier jewellery demand and investor gains. Volatility over the year decreased markedly on 2008 (27%, compared with 45%), although still historically high. Although annual average for 2009, at $1,203.5 per oz, was considerably down on the previous year, much of this was because of the distortion of the 2008 price spike. Generally, the platinum price rally by the end of the year marked a 58% intra-year gain, in US dollar terms (for rands, the intra-year gain was less marked), with a similar pattern in non-dollar prices. The price rally continued into 2010 and, after spiking in April above levels not seen since July 2008,prices remained above $1,500.0 per oz from late July and into September.

The London platinum price began 2010 rising to a 17-month high on 20 January, but by the first week of February had fallen to what would prove to be the low point of the year. The early rally was a result of rising confidence in the recovery of automobile sales, as well as the introduction of a new platinum exchange-traded fund in the USA. Platinum is both an investment and an industrial metal, and can be variously affected by the competing demand levels. During 2010 economic anxieties remained, although the November fall in prices was also attributable to the growing appreciation of the fundamental platinum surplus. The London price fell from more than US $1,780 per oz in the first half of November to $1,637 on 17 November alone. A strong recovery towards the end of the year continued into 2011.

The London price for platinum began 2011 by rising to its highest since July 2008, at US $1,863 per oz on 9 February. Prices were volatile in the first three-quarters of the year, however, falling below $1,700 per oz in late June and reaching a new daily high of $1,899 per oz (morning fix) on 23 August. Platinum prices fell in late September and, despite a recovery in the following two months, were falling into 2012. Concern about the European sovereign debt crisis affected prices, given the importance of Europe's automobile market to platinum demand, and by 2012 doubts about the Chinese economy were having an impact on expectations for jewellery demand. The average price for 2011 overall was a record $1,722 per oz, 7% higher than the year previously. However, the London price was little more than $1,400 per oz by the beginning of 2012, although this marked an upward trend from the final fix of 2011, which had been below that level. Prices went above $1,700 per oz in late February 2012 ($1,729 per oz for the afternoon fix of 23 February was the high point for the first eight months of the year). The London price reached a low of $1,390 per oz for the afternoon of 3 August, but then strengthened to above $1,600 per oz in September. Economic concerns tended to prevail over platinum as a precious metal, and the metal came to be seen as undervalued by comparison with gold, despite strong supply.

The London price of palladium started the 2000s with a record average annual price of US $680.3 per oz, almost double the price in the previous year—the average price for the 1990s was $165.5 per oz (ranging between a low of $88.1 per oz in 1992 and a high of $357.7 in 1999). In real terms, the 2000 price remained unequalled for the rest of the decade (the 2008 price was only 41% of the real 2000 value). Palladium prices then fell to $200.6 per oz by 2003, the lowest nominal annual price of the decade (the lowest real price was in 2005), only resuming any significant climb in 2006 (up 59% on the previous year), when the nominal average London price was $320.0 per oz. The palladium price rise rose to $354.8 per oz in 2007, but fell to $352.3 per oz in 2008. The price had been driven as high as $582.0 per oz in early March 2008, mainly, as with platinum, because of anxieties about South African supplies following the January electricity crisis, but the price fell sharply in the latter part of the year with the onset of the global financial crisis and the collapse in the market for autocatalysts. A price of $164.0 per oz in early December was of a level not seen since July 2003. Palladium prices recovered steadily thereafter, echoing platinum prices until July, then rallying more strongly and almost doubling over 2009 as a whole, from $188.4 per oz in January to $372.2 per oz in December, to average the year at $263.2 per oz. The price recovery continued into 2010, again doubling year-on-year, to $525.5 per oz. As with platinum, the palladium price started strongly, fell in early February, rallied in April and then slumped in May before firming thereafter, in particular from mid-August, ending 2010 on a nine-year high at $797 per oz. The average palladium price for 2011 rose more strongly than the platinum price, reaching $733.6 per oz, with a high of $858 per oz (afternoon fix) on 21 February, but the collapse in the price from September took it to a low of $549 per oz on 5 October. Prices in the last quarter of 2011 recovered more strongly, if erratically, than platinum prices, continuing the rise into the following year. The daily London palladium price in the first eight months of 2012 peaked at $722 per oz on 29 February (afternoon fix), softening to a low of $564 per oz in late July, then tending upwards and remaining above $600 per oz from the last 10 days of August.

RICE (*Oryza*)

Rice is an annual grass belonging to the same family as (and having many similar characteristics to) small grains such as wheat, oats, rye and barley. It is principally the semi-aquatic nature of rice that distinguishes it from other grain species, and this is an important factor in determining its place of origin. In Africa and Asia unmilled rice is referred to as 'paddy', although 'rough' rice is the common appellation in the West. After removal of the outer husk, it is called 'brown' rice. After the grain is milled to varying degrees to remove the bran layers, it is called 'milled' rice. Since rice loses 30%–40% of its weight in the milling process, most rice is traded in the milled form to save shipping expenses.

There are two cultivated species of rice, *Oryza sativa* and *O. glaberrima*. Originating in tropical Asia, *O. sativa* is widely grown in tropical and semi-tropical areas, while the cultivation of the native *O. glaberrima* is limited to the high rainfall zone of West Africa. In Africa rice is grown mainly as a subsistence crop, principally by smallholder farmers of whom a disproportionate number are women. Methods of cultivation differ from region to region and yields tend to be low by world standards. Rice is a staple food in several African countries, including Côte d'Ivoire, The Gambia, Guinea, Guinea-Bissau, Liberia, Madagascar, Senegal and Sierra Leone. In West African countries generally rice is a staple food of 40% of the population. As a consequence of population growth and increased dietary preference for rice, sub-Saharan African demand for consumption increased rapidly in the late 20th century, outstripping supply, and by the end of the first decade of the 21st century demand had reached 20m. metric tons (milled rice) annually (22.55m. tons in 2011/12, according to the US Department of Agriculture—USDA). In 2011/12 sub-Saharan African consumption exceeded domestic production by 9.89m. tons (milled rice).

Production of Paddy Rice
('000 metric tons)

	2009	2010
World total	684,595	696,324
Sub-Saharan Africa*	17,782	18,597
Leading sub-Saharan African producers		
Guinea	1,456	1,499
Madagascar	4,540	4,738
Mali	1,951	2,308
Nigeria	3,403	3,219
Sierra Leone	888	1,027
Tanzania	1,334	1,105
Leading non-African producers		
Bangladesh	47,724	50,061
Brazil	12,651	11,236
China, People's Repub.	196,681	197,212
India	133,700	143,963
Indonesia	64,399	66,469
Japan†	10,593	10,600
Myanmar	32,682	33,205*
Pakistan	10,325	7,235
Philippines	16,266	15,772
Thailand	32,116	31,597
USA	9,972	11,027
Viet Nam	38,950	39,989

* FAO estimate(s).
† Unofficial figures.
Source: FAO.

World rice production is dominated by the Asian region (East, South and South-East Asia produced about 90% of the world's total in 2011/12). African rice production increased steadily from the 1970s, as a consequence of expanded cultivation and improved yields, to total more than 17m. metric tons at the end of the 1990s. However, increased dependence on imports helped reduce domestic production, although it began to recover from 2006, reaching 13.03m. tons by 2010/11, falling to 12.66m. tons in 2011/12. Nevertheless, sub-Saharan African output accounted for only some 2.7% of total world output in the latter year (compared with 4.9% of global domestic consumption). As the bulk of rice production is consumed mainly in the producing countries, international trade until very recently usually accounted for just 3%–5% of world output. Since the early 2000s the quantity of rice traded has risen to 6%–7% of the total produced world-wide—still a very small proportion (USDA put all imports at 7.1% of global production in 2011/12). The market is subject to great volatility and fluctuating prices. A little more than 1% of the African rice crop enters international trade, and more than 90% of African rice exports have traditionally been supplied by Egypt, the continent's largest producer. Sub-Saharan Africa is a substantial net importer of rice, although the volume growth in imports was held in check by the impact of higher world rice prices on the depleted foreign exchange reserves of many African importing countries: imports peaked at 8.3m. tons in 2004/05 before falling back to 7.6m. tons the following year, only to rise steadily thereafter, reaching a new record of 9.72m. in 2010/11; imports eased to 9.70m. tons in 2011/12, and were forecast by USDA to decline slightly again in 2012/13, but the impact of international prices remained to be seen. The major African importers include Nigeria, Côte d'Ivoire, South Africa, Senegal, Ghana, Mozambique and Cameroon. In fact, by the turn of the first decade of the 21st century Nigeria was the world's largest importer, accounting for 2.45m. tons or 7% of the total in international trade in 2011/12 (the next largest importer was Iran, with 1.90m. tons). Madagascar, the world's largest consumer of rice in per caput terms, has yet quite to achieve its goal of self-sufficiency in rice, although steadily improving harvests from 2002/03 put this aim within reach, with milled rice production peaking at 3.06m. tons in 2010/11 (USDA put the shortfall at the level of 100,000 tons). Certainly, the country began to oust Nigeria from its position as sub-Saharan Africa's largest rice producer in the mid-2000s, and seemed to have consolidated that lead at the end of the decade, with some 0.44m. tons on Nigeria's total of 2.62m. tons of milled rice. However, in 2011/12 milled production fell back to 2.88m. tons in Madagascar, compared with a rise to 2.71m. tons in Nigeria; if USDA forecasts for 2012/13 were accurate, those continuing trends appeared likely to put Nigeria back in position as the principal sub-Saharan producer (without reducing the scale of its imports). In 2010 Madagascar harvested rice from an estimated 1.81m. ha. Nigeria had about 1.79m. ha under rice in the same year, Guinea an estimated 864,300 ha, Tanzania an estimated 720,000 ha, Sierra Leone 549,022 and Mali 471,800 ha. Rice was harvested from 8.87m. ha in sub-Saharan Africa in 2010, according to FAO.

Most of the varieties of rice cultivated in Africa originated in Asia and are relatively new to the region, so suitable high-yielding varieties (HYV) have only recently begun to be propagated. The development of HYV is among the activities of the Africa Rice Center (AfricaRice), formed by the producing countries in 1971 as the West Africa Rice Development Association (WARDA, which acronym it retained until 2009). The grouping had 24 members in 2012: most recently, Egypt joined in 2008, Gabon in 2009 and Madagascar in 2010. From the beginning of 2005 the organization transferred its operations to Cotonou, Benin, from its headquarters in Bouaké, Côte d'Ivoire, owing to ongoing political instability in the latter country. Its research staff are also based in Côte d'Ivoire, Nigeria, Senegal and Tanzania, conducting scientific research on crop improvement and providing technical assistance, with the aim of advancing the region towards eventual self-sufficiency in rice production. Since 2000 several New Rice for Africa (NERICA) cultivation projects have been initiated. The NERICA varieties have been developed by what is now AfricaRice, and it is hoped that their adaptation to West African growing conditions will increase their yields by at least 25%, compared with conventional rice crops.

The world's leading exporter of rice is Thailand (31% of total world exports in 2010/11). The average export price of Thai milled white rice ('Thai 100% B second grade', f.o.b. Bangkok) strengthened steadily from 2002, when it had fallen to was US $177.4 per metric ton, to reach $334.5 per ton in 2007. At $334.5 per ton, the average export price of Thai milled white rice was 7.5% higher in 2007 than in 2006. From September 2007 the average monthly price rose remorselessly, from $332.8 per ton to an unprecedented peak of $962.6 per ton in May 2008—a price that was 150% higher than that recorded in January. Market observers placed the extraordinarily high levels to which international prices of rice rose in the first half of 2008 in the context of a rising trend in the prices of basic food commodities—in particular wheat, soya, maize, rape and palm oil—that had been apparent for two years, prompted to a large extent by the inability, owing to such factors as accelerated urbanization and crop losses attributed to climate change, of supply to keep pace with increasing demand for food that proceeded from a generally higher standard of living in developing countries—especially in Asia. A high level of speculative investment in agricultural commodities also contributed, because they had come to be viewed as a refuge from rising inflation and the weakness of the US dollar (for a three-month period in the first half of 2008 rice reportedly became the agricultural 'market of choice' for speculative funds). Additionally, despite rising world production, high prices for rice stemmed from export curbs or other restrictions imposed by some major rice-exporting countries—including China, India, Egypt and Viet Nam—as part of attempts to restrain domestic consumer price inflation, or to placate social unrest, as in the Philippines or Thailand. Such policies—with some countries reducing exports and others increasing imports—are of particular significance because of the small proportion of world rice production that enters world trade. Given the continuation of such restrictions, notably in India, rice prices remained firm after the general commodity price correction in the second half of 2008. The annual average price of Thai milled white rice in 2008 was more than double that in 2007, and although it had fallen back to a monthly average of $582.0 by December, this remained much higher than prices in the early months of 2008. The annual average price for 2009 was $583.5 per ton, with the year ending with the average December price for Thai rice being up at $618.0, only for a decline to set in during the first half of 2010. Prices recovered somewhat in August, with some quotations stabilizing and Vietnamese prices responding to government attempts to stimulate them. The overall annual average of Thai milled white rice (100% B second grade) in 2010 was down $520.0 per ton, recovering to $566.2 per ton in 2011 and $585.9 per ton in January–July 2012. In 2010 and 2011 record consumption was matched by record production, but increased purchases from Bangladesh and Indonesia in the latter year drove up the need for exports. In 2012/13, for the first time in six years, USDA expected global consumption to exceed production, with a disappointing monsoon in India in 2012 and a relatively small US crop, but the upward pressure on prices in mid-2012 had more to do with a general trend in food commodities, with ample stocks expected to compensate for production limitations.

SISAL (*Agave sisalana*)

Sisal, which is not indigenous to Africa, was introduced to Tanganyika (now mainland Tanzania) from Mexico at the end of the 19th century. The leaf tissue of this plant yields hard, flexible fibres suitable for making rope and twine, cord matting, padding and upholstery. In 2010 sisal accounted for an estimated 91% of world production of sisal, henequen and similar hard fibres. Traditionally, about three-quarters of sisal consumption has been for agricultural twine. World output of sisal and other hard fibres generally declined owing to competition from nylons and petroleum-based synthetics (in particular polypropylene harvest twine, which is stronger than sisal and less labour-intensive to produce), although the intensity of the competition and the success of hard fibres depend on fluctuations in the price of petroleum. However, from 2003 world volumes of sisal production have recovered steadily, to reach 383,895 metric tons in 2009 (compared with 407,540 in 2000), before falling back to 361,307 tons in 2010 (plus an estimated 34,210 tons of other agave fibres).

Production of Sisal
(metric tons)

	2009	2010
World total	383,895	361,307
Sub-Saharan Africa	58,500	74,604
Leading sub-Saharan African producers		
Kenya	19,048	23,924
Madagascar*	13,061	17,600
Tanzania	23,800	30,000*
Leading non-African producers		
Brazil	280,004	246,535
China, People's Repub.*	16,500	15,500
Mexico*	11,128	9,400

* FAO estimate(s).

Source: FAO.

In 1970 Tanzania, whose sisal is generally regarded as being of the best quality, was overtaken as the world's leading producer by Brazil (which accounted for 68% of world production in 2010). The nationalization of more than one-half of Tanzania's sisal estates in 1976, together with low prices, inefficient management and lack of equipment and spare parts, contributed to the decline of the Tanzanian crop. From the 1980s, however, the Government sought to revive the industry by returning some state-owned estates to private or co-operative ownership, and in 1998 it completed the transfer of its sisal estates and factories to a consortium of European and Tanzanian entrepreneurs from the private sector. Tanzania was, generally, the world's second largest and Africa's largest sisal producer (8% of global and 40% of sub-Saharan production in 2010), although Kenya exceeded it in 2003 and 2004. Kenyan exports, however, exceeded Tanzania's from 2004 (until export volumes fell to nothing in 2009, according to FAO). In 2006 Malagasy sisal exports also exceeded those of Tanzania. According to FAO, Tanzania's annual exports of sisal were stable at some 12,000–13,000 metric tons in the early 2000s, but then fluctuated widely, from 12,041 tons in 2004, to a peak 38,545 tons in 2005, then 10,067 tons in 2006 and just 7,101 tons in 2007, before recovering to 13,786 tons in 2008. The decline of the sisal sector in Tanzania spurred the development of production in Kenya to the extent that the country was able to compete strongly with both Brazil and Tanzania, even though, having no processing industry, it has never exported sisal products. However, Kenyan production peaked, at some 87,000 tons, as long ago as 1974, averaged some 25,000 tons in 2002–07 (up from some 17,000 tons at the beginning of the decade) and declined to an estimated 19,048 tons by 2009, recovering by 26% in 2010. Kenya's annual exports of sisal and henequen have, on average, totalled almost 18,000 tons in the 2000s, making the country the world's second largest exporter, after Brazil (except when displaced by Tanzania in 2005 and when sisal exports collapsed completely in 2008). The contribution of exports of sisal to Kenya's total export earnings is less than 1%, however. Madagascar, Africa's third largest and generally the world's fourth largest producer (China exceeded it in 2009), surpassed Tanzania's exports in 2006 and almost matched them in 2007 (both countries accounted for almost 9% of world exports in 2007), only to fall to just less than 4,000 tons in 2008, while Tanzanian exports almost doubled. Prospects remain overshadowed by the longer-term outlook for sisal. According to FAO, annual world demand for sisal (and henequen) declined from some 800,000 tons in the early 1970s to only slightly more than 300,000 tons in the mid-1990s. Over the same period consumption of sisal in the manufacture of agricultural twine fell from 230,000 tons to only 130,000 tons. However, by the 2000s there were greater hopes for the future of natural fibres, given the price of petroleum and greater demand for sustainable products.

Sisal producers operate a quota system, in an attempt to improve the pricing structure of the crop. East African sisal rose each year from 2003. The average import price of ungraded East African sisal (f.o.b. European ports) reached US $958 per metric ton in 2007 and $1,087 per ton in 2008. Monthly prices per ton in 2008 were stable at $1,075 in January–June and peaked at $1,213 in July–September, before suffering the impact of the commodity price crash later in the year brought about by the global financial crisis: monthly average prices dropped to $900 per ton in October and November, and to $850 in December. The sisal price continued its fall into 2009, falling to $650 per ton over July, but averaging the year at $773 per ton. The annual average price recovered in 2010 to $1,010 per ton and in January–September 2011 to $1,313 per ton (the last available monthly price recorded by FAO was the highest, in September, at $1,650 per ton). According to FAO, the import price of East African 3L grade sisal (c.i.f. European ports) declined from a peak US $1,493 per metric ton in 2006 to $1,032 per ton (f.o.b. European ports) in 2007, despite a recovery in prices in the second half of the year. The 3L grade price trajectory in 2008 (the average annual price was $1,159 per ton) was similar to that for ungraded East African sisal over the same period, rising from a monthly average of $1,200 per ton at the beginning of the year to $1,258 per ton in July–September, and then falling to finish the year at $895 per ton. The 2009 price overall fell to $823 per ton (the lowest annual average since 2003), recovering to $1,111 per ton in 2010 and $1,413 per ton in January–September 2011. From July 2009 the monthly average price strengthened steadily until October 2010, rising again from December to reach $1,750 per ton by September 2011. The UN Conference on Trade and Development (UNCTAD) cited prices into 2012, such as the average for East African ungraded and no. 3 sisal (f.o.b.), which rose from US $629 per metric ton in 2000 to a peak of $1,077 per ton in 2008, falling back to $771 per ton in 2009, then recovering strongly to $1,010 per ton in 2010 and reaching a new record in 2011 of $1,323 per ton. Monthly prices rose steadily from a post-2008 nadir of $650 per ton in July and August 2009 to $850 per ton by January 2010, $1,150 per ton by January 2011 and $1,475 per ton in January 2012 (the same price for two months before and one month after). Average monthly prices dropped for the first time since July 2009 in March 2012, to $1,375 per ton, but then recovered, reaching $1,480 per ton in July and (estimated) August. As of December 2005 prices for sisal were at their highest level (in nominal terms) since 1974, although in real terms they remained below the levels of the 1970s and 1980s.

In 2006, according to FAO, imports of raw sisal fibres by China accounted for about 45% of global imports, compared with only about 9% in 2001. Chinese imports in 2006 thus exceeded those by the member states of the European Union, which together accounted for about 24% of the total imported world-wide. However, Chinese exports collapsed to negligible levels in 2007, leaving Morocco as the leading importer (23% of global imports), as well as other North African and Middle Eastern countries (notably Algeria and Syria), and Mexico, India, Indonesia and the Philippines. In 2008 Morocco remained the largest single importer of sisal (31% of all sisal imports world-wide), followed by the Philippines, Indonesia and Nigeria. In the same year the USA was the major market for sisal manufactures, accounting for about 46% of world imports totalling 80,300 tons.

SUGAR

Sugar is a sweet crystalline substance, which may be derived from the juices of various plants. Chemically, the basis of sugar is sucrose, one of a group of soluble carbohydrates which are important sources of energy in the human diet. It can be obtained from trees, including the maple and certain palms, but virtually all manufactured sugar comes from two plants, sugar beet (*Beta vulgaris*), and sugar cane, a giant perennial grass of the genus *Saccharum*.

Sugar cane, found in tropical areas, grows to a height of up to 5 m. The plant is native to Polynesia, but its distribution is now widespread. It is not necessary to plant cane every season as, if the root of the plant is left in the ground, it will grow again in the following year. This practice, known as 'ratooning', may be continued for as long as three years, when yields begin to decline. Cane is ready for cutting 12–24 months after planting, depending on local conditions. More than one-half of the world's sugar cane is still cut by hand, but rising costs are hastening the change to mechanical harvesting. The cane is cut as close as possible to the ground, and the top leaves, which may be used as cattle fodder, are removed.

After cutting, the cane is loaded by hand or by machine into lorries (trucks) or trailers and towed directly to a factory for processing. Sugar cane deteriorates rapidly after it has been cut and should be processed as soon as possible. At the factory the cane passes first through shredding knives or crushing rollers, which break up the hard rind and expose the inner fibre, and then to squeezing rollers, where the crushed cane is subjected to high pressure and sprayed with water. The resulting juice is heated and lime is added for clarification and the removal of impurities. The clean juice is then concentrated in evaporators. This thickened juice is next boiled in steam-heated vacuum pans until a mixture or 'massecuite' of sugar crystals and 'mother syrup' is produced. The massecuite is then spun in centrifugal machines to separate the sugar crystals (raw cane sugar) from the residual syrup (cane molasses).

After the milling of sugar, the cane has dry fibrous remnants known as bagasse, which is usually burned as fuel in sugar mills. Bagasse can also be pulped and used for making fibreboard, particle board and most grades of paper. As the costs of imported wood pulp have risen, cane-growing regions have turned increasingly to the manufacture of paper from bagasse. In view of rising energy costs, some countries (such as Cuba) have encouraged the use of bagasse as fuel for electricity production in order to conserve foreign exchange expended on imports of petroleum. Another by-product, cachaza, has been utilized as an animal feed.

The production of beet sugar follows the same process as sugar from sugar cane, except that the juice is extracted by osmotic diffusion. Its manufacture produces white sugar crystals that do not require further refining. In most producing countries it is consumed domestically, and a fall in the production of beet sugar by the European Union (EU), which only accounted for about 10% of total world sugar output in 2011/12, has meant that it has become a net importer of white refined sugar. Beet sugar accounted for 22% of estimated world sugar production in 2011/12, according to the US Department of Agriculture (USDA). The production data in the first table, therefore, is for sugar cane, covering all crops harvested, except crops grown explicitly for feed. The second table covers the production of raw sugar by the centrifugal process (including beet sugar). While global output of non-centrifugal sugar (i.e. produced from sugar cane which has not undergone centrifugation) is not insignificant, it tends to be destined for domestic consumption. The main producer of non-centrifugal sugar is India, but countries such as Brazil and Colombia are also significant producers.

Most of the raw cane sugar produced in the world is sent to refineries outside the country of origin, unless the sugar is for local consumption. Cuba, Thailand, Brazil and India are among the few cane-producers that export part of their output as refined sugar. The refining process further purifies the sugar crystals and eventually results in finished products of various grades, such as granulated, icing or castor sugar. The ratio of refined to raw sugar is usually about 0.9:1.

As well as providing sugar, quantities of cane are grown in some countries for seed, feed, fresh consumption, the manufacture of alcohol and other uses. Molasses may be used as cattle feed or fermented to produce alcoholic beverages for human consumption, such as rum, a distilled spirit manufactured in Caribbean countries. Sugar cane juice may be used to produce ethyl alcohol (ethanol). This chemical can be utilized, either exclusively or mixed with petroleum derivatives, as a fuel for motor vehicles. The steep rise in the price of petroleum after 1973 made the large-scale conversion of sugar cane into ethanol economically attractive (particularly to developing countries), especially as sugar, unlike petroleum, is a renewable source of energy. Several countries developed ethanol production by this means in order to reduce petroleum imports and to support cane growers. Ethanol-based fuel, a type of biofuel that generates fewer harmful exhaust hydrocarbons than petroleum-based fuel, may be known as 'gasohol', 'alcogas', 'green petrol' or, as in Brazil, simply as alcohol. Brazil was the pioneer in this field, establishing in 1975, in the wake of the first global oil crisis, the largest ethanol-based fuel production programme—PROALCOOL—in the world. Public subsidies and tax concessions encouraged farmers to plant more sugar cane, investors to construct more distilleries, and designers to blueprint cars fuelled exclusively by ethanol. By the early 1980s almost every new car sold in Brazil was fuelled exclusively by ethanol. In the 1990s, however, a shortage of ethanol, in conjunction with lower world petroleum prices and the Government's withdrawal of ethanol subsidies, resulted in a sharp fall in Brazil's output of such vehicles. Research to improve efficiency in ethanol production continued none the less, so that by the time petroleum prices reached new heights, in the mid-2000s, the production cost of ethanol had been reduced by two-thirds. Most Brazilian filling stations now offer as vehicle fuels, in addition to gasoline (petrol), a choice of pure ethanol or a blend of gasoline and 20% ethanol. By 2010 more than 90% of new cars sold in the country were so-called 'flex-fuel' models (first introduced in 2003), and by 2011 flex-fuel vehicles were expected to account for almost 50% of the light vehicles fleet. Moreover, Brazil was becoming a significant exporter of ethanol, as interest in biofuel increased world-wide—in 2007 Brazil exported 20% of its production, accounting for almost one-half of world exports. Although Asian attempts to establish 'gasohol' production were less successful (e.g. in the Philippines and Papua New Guinea), other Latin American countries were encouraged by free trade agreements with the USA, where the Energy Independence and Security Act of 2007 requires the greater use of biofuel. The EU also adopted similar legislation in 2007. Global output of ethanol (including ethanol derived from crops other than sugar, such as maize) had already increased by 70% in 2000–06, from 30,000m. litres to 51,000m. litres, while production in 2010 was expected to reach some 103,000m. litres—equivalent to 2% of world petroleum consumption. Since 2006 the USA had been the largest producer of ethanol (48% in 2010), followed by Brazil (38%). In 2010 the USA became a net ethanol exporter and in 2011 displaced Brazil as the world's largest exporter; however, concessionary US tax arrangements lapsed at the end of the year, while the Brazilian currency had been devalued, so the status quo ante was expected to return in 2012. Sugar cane cultivation is projected to expand in line with ethanol production, as it is the most cost-effective feedstock for biofuel production, and as demand is expected to increase by 80% between 2010 and 2015.

In Africa ethanol has been blended with gasoline (petrol) for use in fuel for motor vehicles in Kenya, Malawi and Zimbabwe, but Zimbabwe is the only one of those countries to have required it, legally, to be used. In 2008 the World Bank estimated that Mozambique, Tanzania and other African countries had large cultivable areas that could be used for sugar cane ethanol production without directly displacing food crop production.

By the mid-2000s the promotion of biofuels was becoming increasingly controversial. In April 2008 a report compiled by the World Bank argued that the drive for biofuels by the US and European governments had been the most important factor responsible for the rapid increase in the prices of internationally traded food commodities since 2002. In the same month a UN report warned that unchecked expansion of the production of biofuel jeopardized food security in developing countries, not only by raising food prices, but also by making 'substantial demands on the world's land and water resources at a time when demand for both food and forest products is also rising rapidly'. The UN urged governments to put in place regulations to manage the growth of the biofuel industry.

Production of Sugar Cane
('000 metric tons)

	2009	2010
World total	1,686,891	1,711,087
Sub-Saharan Africa	76,681	59,797
Leading sub-Saharan African producers		
Kenya	5,611	5,710
Mauritius	4,667	4,366
South Africa	18,655	16,016
Sudan	7,527	6,728
Swaziland*	5,000	5,000
Zambia*	3,200	3,500
Zimbabwe*	3,100	3,100
Other leading producers		
Argentina*	25,580	25,000
Australia	30,284	31,457
Brazil	691,606	717,462
China, People's Repub.	116,251	111,454
Colombia*	38,500	38,500
India	285,029	292,300
Mexico	49,493	50,422
Pakistan	50,045	49,373
Philippines*	32,500	34,000
Thailand	66,816	68,808

* FAO estimates.

Source: FAO.

From the last part of the 20th century sugar encountered increased competition from other sweeteners, including maize-based products, such as isoglucose (a form of high-fructose corn syrup—HFCS), and chemical additives, such as saccharine, aspartame (APM) and xylitol. Aspartame (APM) was the most widely used high-intensity artificial sweetener in the early 1990s, its market dominance then came under challenge from sucralose, which is about 600 times as sweet as sugar (compared with 200–300 times for other intense sweeteners) and is more resistant to chemical deterioration than APM. In 1998 the US Government approved the domestic marketing of sucralose, the only artificial sweetener made from sugar. Sucralose was stated to avoid many of the taste problems associated with other artificial sweeteners. From the late 1980s research was conducted in the USA to formulate means of synthesizing thaumatin, a substance derived from the fruit of the West African katemfe plant, *Thaumatococcus daniellii*, which is about 2,500 times as sweet as sugar. As of 2005, the use of thaumatin had been approved in the EU, Israel and Japan, while in the USA its use as a flavouring agent had been endorsed. By 2011 sugar use was rising because of health concerns about other sweeteners—for example, sugar producers attempted to preserve this advantage in the US courts by preventing the Corn Refiners Association from renaming HFCS 'corn sugar'.

Production of sugar cane is dominated by the countries of Latin America and the Caribbean, which grow about one-half of the world total: 54% in 2010, according to FAO (South America 48%, Central America 6% and the Caribbean a little more than 1%). South Asia grew 20% of the world's sugar cane, eastern Asia and Oceania 18% and Africa 5%. The area under sugar cane cultivation in the whole of Latin America and the Caribbean more than doubled in 40 years. The area from which sugar cane was harvested increased from 4.6m. ha in 1968 to 12.1m. ha in 2010 (FAO), as part of an attempt to satisfy greater domestic consumption and to diversify from predominant industries (such as coffee and cocoa), but this figure conceals important sub-regional variations. In Central America the area harvested increased by 76% between 1968 and 2010, to 1.2m. ha, meaning that in importance to sugar production it displaced the Caribbean, where the area harvested fell by 59% over the same period (to 0.6m. ha). In South America, however, the area harvested for sugar cane increased more than fourfold between 1968 and 2010, from 2.4m. ha to 10.2m. ha. Moreover, South America enjoyed productive yields, whereas the Caribbean yield was the lowest in the world. In 2010 South America, followed by Oceania, had the highest average yields. Latin America and the Caribbean also dominate world trade in sugar. According to USDA, exports of (centrifugal) sugar from Latin American and Caribbean countries contributed 53% of total world sales abroad in 2011/12, compared with 28% from (eastern and southern) Asia and Oceania, notably Thailand and Australia (major producers such as India and China being net importers). The main importing region was Asia and Oceania (35% in 2011/12, mainly Indonesia and China—not India in that year), followed by the Middle East (21%), Africa (excluding Egypt—17%), Europe (Western Europe—mainly the EU—8%; and Eastern Europe—mainly Russia—4%) and the USA and Canada (10%).

Sugar cane production in sub-Saharan Africa accounts for only a small share of global output (3.5% in 2010). However, the rate of growth of Africa's sugar output increased between the mid-1990s and the mid-2000s. Expansion in production responds to an increase in regional sugar consumption, but is also a consequence of national sugar expansion programmes that aimed to boost exports—a number of African sugar-producing least developed countries (LDCs) gained duty- and quota-free access to the EU sugar market from 1 October 2009, under the EBA (Everything But Arms) regulation (see below). According to preliminary figures from USDA, in 2010/11 Africa—i.e. continental Africa, excluding Egypt—increased sugar production by almost 2% on the previous year, although sugar exports fell by a little more than 3%. In 2012/13 USDA expected African centrifugal sugar production to rise from 8.2m. metric tons to 8.5m. tons, while hitherto falling exports would rise from 3.3m. tons to 3.9m. tons. In South Africa falls in production were recorded in four successive years to 2011/12, but a rise was forecast for 2012/13; likewise, exports, which reached a low of 330,000 tons in 2011/12, were expected to increase again in 2012/13. Meanwhile, those falling sales abroad meant that South Africa was only just ahead of Swaziland, Zambia and Sudan in 2011/12, and remained behind Mauritius for a second year. Traditionally, South Africa is the principal producer (24% of production in 2011/12) and exporter (12%—down from 25% only two years before) of sugar in Africa. In the mid-1990s South Africa had ranked as the world's seventh largest sugar exporter. With regard to the domestic market, however, the South African sugar industry has encountered increased competition from neighbouring countries, most notably Swaziland, as a result of free trade agreements in the context of the Southern African Customs Union (SACU) and the Southern African Development Community.

Sugar is the staple product in the economies of Mauritius and Réunion, although output is vulnerable to climatic conditions, as both islands are subject to cyclones. In Mauritius, where it was estimated that more than 75% (72,750 ha) of cultivated land was devoted to sugar production in the late 1990s, sugar sales accounted for about 13% of the island's revenue from exports in 2011. Increasingly, the island was exporting refined sugar, and in July 2010 it was reported that a deal with the EU would enable the country to raise exports from 78,000 metric tons in 2009 to 320,000 tons in that year; USDA certainly reported an increase in refined sugar exports from 10,000 tons in 2009/10 to 200,000 tons in the following year, with a corresponding decline in raw exports. In Réunion 56% of the island's cropland was planted with sugar cane in 2008, while sales of sugar provided 50.4% of export income in 2005. The expansion of sugar output, however, was subsequently impeded by unfavourable weather, and by the pressure on agricultural land use from the increasing demands of road construction and housing.

Mozambique's sugar industry, formerly the country's primary source of foreign exchange, has begun to surmount the effects of many years of disruption and neglect. Considerable Mauritian and South African investment following the resolution of internal civil conflict made possible the rehabilitation both of cane-growing and of four of the country's six sugar complexes. Production of raw centrifugal sugar increased rapidly after the conclusion of the peace agreement, rising from 39,000 metric tons in 1998 to about 265,000 tons in 2005, its highest level for 30 years, according to the National Sugar Institute. USDA put centrifugal sugar production in Mozambique as rising steadily through 2008/09, at some 250,000 tons, to 2011/12 production of 350,000 tons, with a similar forecast for 2012/13. The country became a net importer of sugar in 2002, and signed the sugar protocol between the EU and sugar producers of the African, Caribbean and Pacific (ACP) group in 2005, but rising production as a result of increased investment in the second half of the decade restored the country as a net exporter. In 2009/10 Mozambique sugar exports (raw sugar) rose 17% to 303,000 tons, with 250,000 tons sold abroad in 2010/11 (and forecast for 2012/13) and 230,000 tons in 2011/12. South Africa is another important preferential export market, favourable prices being regulated under SACU. In 2010 sugar was Malawi's third most important agricultural export commodity (after tobacco and tea), providing 6.5% of revenue from foreign sales; the differing fortunes of commodity prices mean the country's most valuable agricultural export after tobacco varies between sugar, tea and coffee. Tanzania sought to develop its sugar sector during the 1990s, with the aim of reducing reliance on imports from Malawi and Zambia. In 2000 the Government banned the import of sugar into all but the country's three largest ports, in an attempt to suppress the widespread smuggling of cheaper foreign sugar into Tanzania. Output of centrifugal sugar cane was put by USDA at a peak of 308,000 tons in 2010/11 and estimated at back above 300,000 tons for 2012/13, after a dip back below in 2011/12. Although domestic demand for raw sugar, at some 480,000 tons annually, outstrips production, Tanzania exports about 40,000 tons of sugar each year to the EU and had expanded its sugar industry to take advantage of improved EU market access under the EBA regulation. Uganda increased production too, steadily through the 2000s: from 130,000 tons in 1999/2000 to 350,000 tons annually in 2010/11 and 2011/12. Zambia and Zimbabwe have also launched rehabilitation and expansion programmes: Zambia succeeded in improving sugar production from about 200,000 tons at the beginning of the decade to a record 435,000 tons in 2011/12 (output was expected to slip back in 2012/13), and Zambian exports increased impressively, to reach 308,000 tons in 2011/12. Zimbabwe's annual production of more than 500,000 tons in the first half of the decade, however, fell steadily below that amount in the second half, reaching 259,000 tons in 2009/10; output rose thereafter, to 372,000 tons in 2011/12 and a forecast of 430,000 tons for 2012/13. In 2011/12 Ethiopian production was reckoned still to be steady at some 290,000 tons, with rising domestic consumption having put an end to exports in 2007. Kenya's output of raw centrifugal sugar increased steadily from the mid-2000s, reaching 550,000 tons in 2009/10, with a dip to 524,000 in 2010/11 and 490,000 tons in 2011/12, but a further increase expected in 2012/13, to 550,000 tons, which would make the country sub-Saharan Africa's fourth largest producer after South Africa, Sudan and Swaziland, but a negligible exporter.

In Sudan one of the world's largest single sugar projects was inaugurated in 1981 at Kenana, on the eastern bank of the White Nile, south of Khartoum. The Kenana Sugar Co (in which the governments of Sudan, Kuwait and Saudi Arabia are the major shareholders), comprising an estate and processing facilities, was instrumental in the elimination of the drain on reserves of foreign exchange of sugar, which was, until the mid-1980s, Sudan's costliest import item after petroleum. However, the subsequent imposition by the Sudanese authorities of a regional quota distribution system led to supply shortages and high prices, and during the 1990s the renewal of Sudan's sugar sector was further impeded by drought, inadequate investment and technical and management problems. In 1999 plans were announced for the construction of a second growing and refining facility in the White Nile region, north of the Kenana site. Sudanese centrifugal sugar production grew fairly steadily through the 2000s, dipping in 2009/10 but recovering strongly, to reach 850,000 tons in 2010/11 and in 2011/12. A significant increase in purchases from abroad from 2008/09 made Sudan a net importer, but its exports are of refined sugar and remain important. Sudan was not only sub-Saharan Africa's second largest producer of centrifugal sugar, but its largest exporter of refined sugar. Sugar cane grows wild throughout Nigeria, but domestic production has not been developed and the country's sugar industry depends on imports, mainly from Brazil, Guatemala and the EU. In 2005 one sugar refinery was reported to be in operation in Nigeria. Since the 1990s the country has consistently been a significant importer of raw sugar. In 2011/12 imports of sugar totalled 1.5m. tons (the country exported 200,000 tons of refined sugar).

The first International Sugar Agreement (ISA) was negotiated in 1958, and its economic provisions operated until 1961. A second ISA did not come into operation until 1969. It included quota arrangements and associated provisions for regulating the price of sugar traded on the open market, and established the International Sugar Organization (ISO) to administer the agreement. However, the USA and the six original members of the European Community (EC, now EU) did not participate in the ISA, and, following its expiry in 1974, it was replaced by a purely administrative interim agreement, which remained operational until the finalization of a third ISA, which took effect in 1978. The new agreement's implementation was supervised by an International Sugar Council (ISC), which was empowered to establish price ranges for sugar-trading and to operate a system of quotas and special sugar stocks. Owing to the reluctance of the USA and EC countries (which were not a party to the agreement) to accept export controls, the ISO ultimately lost most of its power to regulate the market, and since 1984 the activities of the organization have been restricted to recording statistics and providing a forum for discussion between producers and consumers. Subsequent ISAs, without effective regulatory powers, have been in operation since 1985.

Production of Centrifugal Sugar
(raw value, '000 metric tons)

	2010/11	2011/12
World total*	161,642	170,967
Sub-Saharan Africa	7,764	7,736
Leading sub-Saharan African producers		
Kenya	524	490
Mauritius	480	470
South Africa	1,985	1,885
Sudan	850	850
Swaziland	602	650
Zambia	410	435
Leading non-African producers		
Australia	3,700	3,900
Brazil	38,350	36,150
China, People's Repub.	11,199	12,324
European Union	15,667	17,461
India	26,574	28,830
Mexico	5,495	5,194
Pakistan	3,920	4,320
Russia	2,996	5,500
Thailand	9,6630	10,415
USA	7,104	7,521

* Including beet sugar production ('000 metric tons): 31,843 in 2010/11 (China, People's Repub. 863; EU 15,392; USA 4,226); 37,683 in 2011/12 (China, People's Repub. 1,100; EU 17,170; USA 4,309).

Source: USDA.

Special arrangements for the sugar trade were incorporated into the successive Lomé Conventions that were in operation from 1975 between the EU and a group of African, Caribbean and Pacific (ACP) countries. A special protocol on sugar, forming part of each Convention, required the EU to import specified quantities of raw sugar annually from ACP countries. In June 1998, however, the EU indicated its intention to phase out preferential sugar prices paid to ACP countries within three years. Under the terms of the Cotonou Agreement, a successor to the fourth Lomé Convention covering the period 2000–2020, the protocol on sugar was to be maintained initially, but would become subject to review within the framework of negotiations for new trading arrangements (negotiations for more WTO-compatible Economic Partnership Agreements—EPAs began in 2002). In 2001 the EU Council adopted the EBA (Everything but Arms) regulation, whereby the least developed countries were granted unlimited duty-free access to the EU for all goods except arms and ammunition. EBA was to apply to sugar from October 2009. Meanwhile, in September 2007 the EU Council of Ministers criticized the protocol on sugar on the grounds that it was not compatible with EU sugar reforms (themselves undertaken in response to upheld complaints before the WTO by Australia, Brazil and Thailand about export subsidies for the ACP countries) and did not take into account the specific needs of different ACP regions. The EU offered duty- and quota-free access to the ACP countries after 2015, in compensation for the loss of subsidies and quotas. A transitional period from October 2009 until September 2015 was to effect the progressive removal of reciprocal trade barriers. However, there was concern that the benefits that ACP countries were intended to derive from unlimited access to the EU market would be undermined by falling sugar prices. It was also uncertain whether some countries that had refused to embrace the EPA arrangements, such as Malawi, would be allowed to continue trading under EBA in order to take advantage of unrestricted access to the EU market sooner (i.e. from 2009 instead of 2015), while sugar prices were still guaranteed to be maintained at a relatively high level.

In tandem with world output of cane and beet sugars, stock levels (of centrifugal sugar) are an important factor in determining the prices at which sugar is traded internationally. These stocks, which were at relatively low levels in the late 1980s, increased significantly in the 1990s, although not, according to USDA data, in each successive trading year (September–August). In 2006/07, when world production of sugar totalled 164m. tons and world consumption 151m. tons, world sugar stocks increased to some 40m. tons. World stocks of sugar increased to 41m. tons in 2007/08, in which year world production amounted to 166m. tons and consumption to 155m. tons. In 2008/09, on the basis of the decline in world production to 144m. tons and reasonably stable consumption at 154m. tons, USDA assessed that stocks fell sharply, to 28m. tons. In 2009/10, with an increase in world production to 154m. tons and steady consumption of 156m. tons, USDA had stocks strengthening slightly, to almost 30m. tons. The strengthening of stocks was put at an additional 1m. tons per year through into the forecast for 2012/13 (33m. tons), given rising production of 162m. tons (with consumption up to 156m. tons) in 2010/11 and an estimated 171m. tons in 2011/12 (160m. tons).

After reasonably steady sugar prices during 2005 (the average ISA daily prices—sugar in bulk, f.o.b. Caribbean ports—for the year was 9.88 US cents per lb), in 2006 they displayed a high level of volatility. Overall, the average ISA daily price rose by 49%, to 14.75 cents per lb, in 2006. In 2007 prices declined by 32%, compared with 2006, to 10.07 cents per lb. This decline in prices was largely attributed to continued substantial excess of supply, and was exacerbated by the weakness of the US dollar. According to the ISO, prices in real terms were too low to cover production costs. However, the relative weakness of sugar prices, compared with those of other agricultural commodities, subsequently spurred speculative investment, and sugar prices recovered in 2008 to peak at 14.51 cents per lb in August. The average ISA daily price was 12.80 cents per lb for that year, rising to 18.14 cents per lb in 2009, because of the basic underlying deficit in the world sugar market and because of the impact of high petroleum prices on demand for ethanol. Average monthly prices in 2009 recorded a steady increase until September, rising from 12.49 cents per lb in January and staying above 22.00 cents per lb at the end of the year. A jump back up in December, to 23.23 cents per lb, marked the start of a speculative rise in the price in the course of January 2010, with an average of 26.46 cents per lb over the month, a 30-year high. After a small decline in February prices fell considerably, recording a 43% decline by May, as the markets adjusted to better-than-expected production in India and Brazil. Prices rose steadily from June, with their general level being sustained by the production shortfall, and reached a new 30-year monthly peak in January 2011 of 29.61 cents per lb. The average price for 2010 was 21.28 cents per lb and 26.00 cents per lb in 2011. The price had slipped in February 2011 and then declined steadily, to 26% below the January peak by May (22.00 cents per lb), but rose to a monthly average of 28.22 cents per lb in July, before declining to 23.04 cents per lb by December. The average price for the first six months of 2012 was 22.64 cents per lb, ranging from a monthly high of 24.12 cents per lb in February steadily down to 20.47 cents per lb by July. Increased production globally was accompanied by lower consumption, while a likely contraction in EU exports into 2013 would be offset by increased exports by Brazil and Thailand.

The World Bank records three sugar prices, to reflect the major markets. The world price that it quotes is the ISA daily price for raw sugar (f.o.b., stowed at greater Caribbean ports), but using different measurements to the prices cited above: the average price for 2009 was 40.00 US cents per kg, for 2010 it was 46.93 cents per kg, for 2011 it was 57.32 cents per kg and for the first seven months of 2012 the average was 49.98 cents per kg. From mid-2011 the average ISA daily price gradually declined, from 60.72 cents per kg in the third quarter of the year to 47.05 cents per kg in the second quarter of 2012. The average monthly price by June was 45.13 cents per kg, although it recovered to 50.44 cents per kg in July. The US price, under nearby futures contract (c.i.f.), recorded similar but more pronounced fluctuations: 54.88 cents per kg in 2009, 79.25 cents per kg in 2010, 83.92 cents per kg in 2011 and 70.02 cents per kg in January–July 2012. An average US price of 86.72 cents per kg in April–June 2011 fell to 63.06 cents per kg in June 2012, with a limited recovery to 63.23 cents per kg in July. The increasingly anachronistic EU-negotiated import price for raw, unpackaged sugar from African, Caribbean and Pacific (ACP) countries under the Lomé Conventions (c.i.f., European ports) recorded a continuing decline from an annual average of 52.44 cents per kg in 2009 to 44.18 cents per kg in 2010, but rose slightly, to 45.46 cents per kg, in 2011; the average price of 42.06 cents per kg in January–July 2012, reflecting the steady decline since the second half of 2011. The price had fallen to a monthly average of 40.14 cents per kg by July 2012.

On the basis of data for 2009, the 86 members of the ISO (including 17 sub-Saharan African countries) together contributed 83% of world sugar production and 95% of world exports of sugar; ISO members additionally accounted for 69% of global sugar consumption and 47% of world imports. At mid-2012 the ISO had 87 members (Indonesia joined in 2011), including both the EU and its 27 member states. The ISO is based in London, United Kingdom.

TEA (*Camellia sinensis*)

Tea is a beverage made by infusing in boiling water the dried young leaves and unopened leaf-buds of the tea plant, an evergreen shrub or small tree. Black and green tea are the most common finished products. The former accounts for the bulk of the world's supply, and is associated with machine manufacture and, generally, the plantation system, which guarantees an adequate supply of leaf to the factory. The latter, produced mainly in the People's Republic of China and Japan, is grown mostly on smallholdings, and much of it is consumed locally. There are two main varieties of tea, the China and the Assam, although hybrids may be obtained, such as Darjeeling. In this survey, wherever possible, data on production and trade relate to made tea, i.e. dry, manufactured tea. Where figures have been reported in terms of green (unmanufactured) leaf, appropriate allowances have been made to convert the reported amounts to the approximate equivalent weight of made tea.

Total recorded tea exports by producing countries achieved successive records in each of the years 1983–90. World exports (excluding transactions between former Soviet republics) declined in 1991 and 1992, but then fluctuated until volumes began to increase again from 1995, reaching a new record in 1998, then easing in 1999, before recording successive records in 2000–02 (1,436,678 metric tons in 2002). Exports fell to 1,391,800 tons in 2003, but in the following five years foreign sales of tea world-wide increased to successive new record levels, reaching 1,653,062 tons by 2008. Foreign sales of tea world-wide were estimated to have contracted in 2009, by 2.9%, to 1,605,102 tons, but they recovered strongly in 2010, to a new record of 1,741,805 tons, before falling back slightly in 2011, to 1,718,839 tons. The major exporting countries in 2011 were Kenya, China, Sri Lanka and India; an estimated 41% of tea production world-wide was exported. Global production of tea reached an unprecedented level in 1998 (3,026,340 tons), with record crops in all of the major producing countries (India, China, Sri Lanka and Kenya). From 2000 world output increased steadily every year up to and including 2011, exceeding 3m. tons of tea for a second time in 2001. Production almost reached 3.5m. in 2005, continuing to increase and rising to 4,217,143 tons in 2011, a rise of 1.3% on the previous year. China, meanwhile, achieved successive years of record production throughout the 2000s (consistently over 1996–2011, in fact, exceeding 1m. tons for the first time in 2006), with the estimated rise in 2011 at 5.1% (Chinese production more than doubled between 2001 and 2010). National records were achieved in Sri Lanka in 2000, 2002, 2005, 2008 and 2010; in Kenya in 2001, 2004, 2007 and 2010; and in India each year of 2004–07 and, according to preliminary figures, 2011. In 2011 China and India's joint tea output accounted for an estimated 60% of global production—China's output represented an estimated 37% of production world-wide, while that of India accounted for 23%. The growth in world production during 2011 was largely attributable to record harvests in China and India offsetting contractions elsewhere, notably in Africa, which had performed particularly strongly in the previous year.

India (the world's largest consumer) and Sri Lanka were traditionally the two leading tea exporters, with approximately equal sales. During the 1960s these two countries together exported more than two-thirds of all the tea sold by producing countries, but their joint foreign sales gradually declined; during the 1970s until they came to constitute less than one-half of world exports (in 2010 the proportion was estimated at 28%). Over the years Sri Lankan sales came to exceed those of India by a comfortable margin (Indian exports have been far exceeded by those of Sri Lanka throughout the 2000s—and, indeed, by those of China). From 1990 until 1995, when it was displaced by Kenya, Sri Lanka ranked as the main exporting country. Exports by Sri Lanka again took primacy in 1997, when Kenya's tea sales declined sharply. Sri Lanka remained the principal tea exporter in 1998 until 2003. In 2004–05, however, Kenya again overtook Sri Lanka as the main tea exporting country. In 2004 Kenya's shipments rose sharply, by about 24% compared with 2003, to some 332,502 metric tons, and in 2005 the country's foreign sales rose by a further 5%, to 348,276 tons. In 2006, albeit by a small margin, Sri Lanka regained the rank of principal exporting country, Kenyan sales having declined by 10%. Kenya's foreign sales recovered strongly thereafter, however, propelling the country into the first place among tea exporters world-wide. A ballooning of exports in 2010 took its total to 441,021 metric tons, or 25% of the world total, a proportion that was retained in 2011 even though sales abroad fell slightly to 421,272 tons; also in 2011 China accounted for just over 19% of world exports, with Sri Lanka on 18% and India on 10%. Kenya's exports in 2011 were equivalent to 89% of the combined foreign sales of India and Sri Lanka. Exports by India have been surpassed by those of China (whose sales include a large proportion of green tea) in every year since 1996; in 2009 China became Asia's largest tea exporter for the first time in centuries. A newer challenge to the four principal exporters has come from Viet Nam, which has been the world's fifth largest seller of tea on the international market since 2000, increasing its exports every year except 2003, 2005 and 2008 to reach a third successive peak in 2011 of some 143,000 tons (8% of total global exports), which was still almost double the volumes sold of Asia's next largest exporter, Indonesia (75,000 tons, 4%). Meanwhile, in 2010 Argentina had exceeded Indonesian sales to become the world's sixth largest exporter for the first time; in 2011 exports of 86,197 tons gave the country a 5% share in the international market.

Exports of tea by African producers accounted for about one-quarter of world trade during the early 1990s, and the proportion rose to about 30% at the end of that decade—a record shipment of 389,499 was achieved in 1998. Although by 2000 the share of African teas in the world tea trade had declined, with shipments falling to 351,673 tons, by 2004 foreign sales of African teas had recovered to 481,403 tons, accounting for 31% of the world total. Foreign sales of tea by African countries increased further in 2005, to 486,224 tons, but fell back again, to 451,731 tons, in 2006. African exports recovered strongly in 2007, to a new record of 506,886 tons, and rose further in 2008, to 534,466 tons, before declining to 505,368 tons in 2009. In 2010 African tea exports surged to a record 619,255 tons (36% of world trade), mainly as a result of Kenyan sales, and continent-wide exports fell back only slightly in 2011, to 583,849 tons (34% of world trade).

Production of Made Tea
('000 metric tons)

	2010	2011
World total	4,162.5	4,217.1
Africa	606.8	569.3
Leading African producers		
Kenya	399.0	377.9
Malawi	51.6	47.1
Rwanda	22.2	23.5
Tanzania	31.6	32.8
Uganda	56.5	44.0
Zimbabwe	14.3	12.0
Leading non-African producers		
Argentina	90.0	93.0
China, People's Repub.[1]	1,475.1	1,550.0
India[2]	966.4	988.3
Indonesia[3]	129.2	123.7
Japan[4]	83.0	78.0
Sri Lanka	331.4	328.4
Turkey	148.0	145.0
Viet Nam[5]	170.0	178.0

[1] Mainly green tea (about 1,046,382 tons in 2010).
[2] Including a small quantity of green tea (about 10,600 tons in 2010).
[3] Including green tea (about 33,200 tons in 2010).
[4] Almost all green tea (about 92,500 tons in 2010).
[5] Including green tea (about 76,000 tons in 2010).

Source: International Tea Committee, *Annual Bulletin of Statistics 2011.*

Prior to its reversal in 1997, Kenya was one of the fastest growing exporters, ranking fourth in the world during 1975–92, third in 1993, and second in 1994, when its tea exports exceeded those of China. Kenya was the principal world exporter of tea in 1995 and 1996, but not then again until 2004, when the country was the world's largest exporter of tea by a considerable margin, its foreign sales having risen by almost 24% compared with 2003. Kenya retained the rank of leading exporter in 2005, but was overtaken by Sri Lanka in 2006, when its tea exports declined. Kenya re-established primacy from 2007, when its foreign sales of tea rose and reached 383,444 tons in 2008; Kenya easily maintained its position in 2009, with 342,482 tons, and consolidated it in 2010, with a surging 441,021 tons, followed by 421,272 tons in 2011. In the 1990s and 2000s the conservation of tea supplies by India, in order to satisfy rising domestic consumption, enabled Kenya to replace India as the United Kingdom's principal supplier. In 1999 Kenya provided 50% of British tea imports (by volume), but the proportion declined in 2000 to only about 35%. In 2001–04 Kenya supplied between 43% and 46% annually of all tea imported into the United Kingdom, and thereafter generally more than one-half. Kenya's tea sales provided 23% of its total export receipts in 2010, making tea the country's most valuable export crop. In that year about 171,900 ha in Kenya were planted with tea, an increase of 43% since 2000.

Malawi, with an estimated 18,600 ha under tea in 2009, is generally considered to be Africa's second largest producer and exporter of tea, although Ugandan production surpassed that of Malawi in 2008 and 2010–11, with Ugandan exports exceeding Malawi each year of 2008–10, but not in 2011 (according to preliminary figures). Malawian exports in 2011 totalled 44,893 metric tons, accounting for 7.7% of all African tea exports in that year. In 2010 exports of tea accounted for 7.6% of Malawi's total export earnings. Tea was the country's second most valuable export crop after tobacco for a second consecutive year, ahead of sugar. A great increase in Ugandan exports from 2007 challenged Malawi's position as Africa's second tea exporter. Prior to the regime of Idi Amin and the nationalization of tea plantations in 1972, Uganda had been second only to neighbouring Kenya among African producers. Uganda's tea exports were negligible by the early 1980s, but, following agreements between tea companies and the subsequent Ugandan governments, exports were resumed. There has been a sustained recovery since 1990, when sales of tea totalled only 4,760 tons. In 1994 Uganda's exports of tea reached their highest annual total since 1977. Exports in subsequent years advanced strongly, reaching 34,069 tons in 2003. Fluctuations in export volumes over the mid-2000s was succeeded by a significant expansion in 2007, when Uganda's foreign sales of tea rose by one-third, compared with the previous year, to 43,638 tons. Despite a dip in export volumes in 2008, with 42,385 tons, Ugandan sales abroad exceeded those of Malawi, and this position was maintained up to and including 2010, when exports amounted to 50,834 tons (8.2% of the

African total). In that year tea exports contributed 4.2% of the country's total exports, according to the UN. In 2011, however, according to preliminary figures, exports fell back to some 40,000 tons, less than Malawi. Still in East Africa, during the 1980s Tanzania's exports of tea ranged between 10,000 tons and 15,000 tons annually. These sales advanced significantly during the 1990s, moving from 20,511 tons in 1995 to 22,462 tons in 2000. In 2007 Tanzania's exports of tea rose to 29,125 tons, but they fell back to 24,766 tons in 2008 and to 21,512 tons in 2009, before rallying to 25,388 tons in 2010 and 27,114 tons in 2011. Foreign sales of tea contributed 1.7% of Tanzania's estimated total revenue from exports in 2005. Zimbabwe was Africa's fifth largest exporter of tea in 1999–2004, but ranked sixth in 2005–11. In 2008, at 5,654 tons, Zimbabwe's tea shipments were about one-half the level in 2006, and about one-third that in 2000; however, they recovered to 7,541 tons in 2009 and 8,498 tons in 2010, before falling back to 6,800 tons in 2011. Historically, however, tea has not been a significant cash crop in Zimbabwe—in 2000 it accounted for only about 1% of the country's total export earnings. Tea has traditionally made a significant contribution to the export earnings of Burundi and Rwanda, however, whose foreign sales were estimated at 5,400 tons and 24,500 tons, respectively, in 2011 (the latter country was Africa's fifth largest exporter). Since 1997 Rwanda's tea industry has recovered from the disruption caused by civil unrest during 1993–96. In 2008 surging international commodity prices sent exports of tea to 32% of all exports, up from 17% in the previous year, but the share then fell back, to 13% in 2011. Tea provided 9% of total export earnings in Burundi in 2010.

For many years the United Kingdom was the largest single importer of tea. From the late 1980s consumption and imports expanded significantly in developing countries (notably in countries of the Middle East) and, particularly, in the USSR, which in 1989 overtook the United Kingdom as the world's principal tea importer. However, internal factors following the break-up of the USSR in 1991 caused a sharp decline in tea imports by its successor republics; as a result, the United Kingdom regained its position as the leading tea importer in 1992. In 1993 the former Soviet republics (whose own tea production had fallen sharply) once more displaced the United Kingdom as the major importer, but in 1994 the United Kingdom was again the principal importing country. Since 1999, however, imports by the former USSR have exceeded those of the United Kingdom by a substantial and, generally, increasing margin. In 2011 world tea imports for consumption (i.e. net of re-exports) amounted to 1.61m. tons, down negligibly on the previous year's record, according to provisional figures. Russia imported an estimated 174,000 metric tons of tea, accounting for 11% of the world market, followed by the United Kingdom, with 128,065 tons (8%), the USA (126,771 tons, also 8%) and Pakistan (126,170 tons, 8%). Other major importers of tea in 2011 were Egypt, Iran, Morocco and Dubai (United Arab Emirates).

Much of the tea traded internationally is sold by auction, principally in the exporting countries. Until declining volumes brought about their termination in June 1998 (Kenya having withdrawn in 1997, and a number of other exporters, including Malawi and Tanzania, having established their own auctions), the weekly London auctions in the United Kingdom had formed the centre of the international tea trade. At the London auctions, five categories of tea were offered for sale: 'low medium' (based on a medium Malawi tea), 'medium' (based on a medium Assam and Kenyan tea), 'good medium' (representing an above-average East African tea), 'good' (referring to teas of above-average standard) and (from April 1994) 'best available'. At the end of June 1998, with the prospect of a record Kenyan crop, the quotation for 'medium' tea at the final London auction was £980 per ton. Based on country of origin, the highest priced tea at London auctions during 1989–94 was that from Rwanda, which realized an average of £1,613 per ton in the latter year. The quantity of tea sold at these auctions declined from 43,658 tons in 1990 to 11,208 tons in 1997.

The main tea auctions in Africa are the weekly sales at Mombasa, Kenya. In contrast to London, volumes traded at the Mombasa auctions moved generally upward during the 1990s, and Mombasa is now one of the world's major centres for the international tea trade. The tea sold at Mombasa is mainly from Kenya, but smaller amounts from Tanzania, Uganda and other African producers are also traded. Total annual sales at the Mombasa auctions had increased to 221,601 tons by 2000. A record volume of trade was achieved in 2003, 2004 and 2005, but in 2006 the volume contracted by 8.2%, from 306,833 tons in 2005, to 281,651 tons. In 2007 the volume of tea traded in Mombasa more than recovered, increasing by 22.2% on the previous year, to a new record of 344,307 tons—76% of which was Kenyan. In 2008 302,888 tons of tea (227,645 tons Kenyan) were traded in Mombasa. Meanwhile, average prices per metric ton in Mombasa reached US $2,000 in 1997, dipped, and reached $2,020 in 2000, but fell to only $1,490 by 2002. The average price of teas traded at Mombasa showed a slow recovery thereafter, to $1,550 per ton by 2004, but dropped again in 2005, to $1,470 per ton. The average Mombasa price in 2006 was $1,930 per ton, but it fell again in 2007, to $1,660 per ton over the year. Prices rose markedly in 2008, reaching an average over the year of $2,180 per ton, with a monthly peak in August ($2,600 per ton) but with prices falling as low as $1,700 per ton in November. The Mombasa price recovered strongly in the first half of 2009, continuing to rise in July and August, to reach a monthly average of $2,970 per ton in September and an average for the year of $2,290 per ton, which exceeded the 2008 annual average. The average Mombasa auction price for the first seven months of 2010 was up again, at $2,586 per ton, although prices had been highest in the first quarter and had actually fallen as low as $2,235 per ton in June, before recovering slightly in July. There is also a small tea auction in Limbe, Malawi, but the volume of tea traded in 2008 was only 14,960 tons (down from 17,609 tons in 2007), although this recovered to 17,295 tons in 2009. The average annual price of tea traded at Limbe in 2006 was $1,229 per ton, in 2007 $1,051 per ton, in 2008 $1,372 per ton and $1,583 per ton in 2009.

An International Tea Agreement (ITA), signed in 1933 by the governments of India, Ceylon (now Sri Lanka) and the Netherlands East Indies (now Indonesia), established the International Tea Committee (ITC), based in London, as an administrative body. Although ITA operations ceased after 1955, the ITC has continued to function as a statistical and information centre. In 2012 there were eight producer/exporter members (the tea boards or associations of Bangladesh, India, Indonesia, Kenya, Malawi, Sri Lanka and Tanzania, and the China Chamber of Commerce of Import and Export of Foodstuffs, Native Produce and Animal By-products), three consumer members, 24 associate members and 41 corporate members.

In 1969 the FAO Consultative Committee on Tea (renamed as the Intergovernmental Group on Tea in 1970) was formed, and an exporters' group, meeting under this committee's auspices, set voluntary export quotas in an attempt to avert an overall long-term decline in the real price of tea. These succeeded in raising prices for two consecutive years, but arrangements subsequently collapsed as (mainly) African countries—Kenya in particular—opposed efforts to restrict their rapidly increasing production. The regulation of tea prices is in any case complicated by the perishability of the commodity, which impedes the effective operation of a buffer stock. India, while opposed to the revival of a formal ITA to regulate supplies and prices, has advocated greater co-operation between producers to regulate the market.

TOBACCO (*Nicotiana tabacum*)

Tobacco originated in South America and was used in rituals and ceremonials or as a medicine; it was smoked and chewed for centuries before its introduction into Europe, the Middle East, Africa and South Asia in the 16th century. The generic name *Nicotiana* denotes the presence of the alkaloid nicotine in its leaves. The most important species in commercial tobacco cultivation is *N. tabacum*. Another species, *N. rustica*, is widely grown, but on a smaller scale, to yield cured leaf for snuff or simple cigarettes and cigars.

Production of Tobacco
(unmanufactured, farm sales weight, '000 metric tons)

	2009	2010
World total	7,085	7,038
Sub-Saharan Africa	609	689
Leading sub-Saharan African producers		
Malawi	208	220
Mozambique	63	86*
Tanzania	55	50*
Uganda	19	26*
Zambia*	75	90
Zimbabwe	96*	110
Leading non-African producers		
Argentina	136*	137
Brazil	863	788
China, People's Repub.	3,068	3,006
India	620	756*
Indonesia	177	122
Italy	98	89
Korea, Democratic Repub.*	73	79
Pakistan	105	119
Thailand	62	59
Turkey	85	55
USA	373	326

* FAO estimate(s).

Source: FAO.

Commercially grown tobacco (from *N. tabacum*) can be divided into four major types—flue-cured, air-cured (including burley, cigar, light and dark), fire-cured and sun-cured (including oriental)—depending on the procedures used to dry or 'cure' the leaves. Each system imparts specific chemical and smoking characteristics to the cured leaf, although these may also be affected by other factors, such as the type of soil on which the crop is grown, the type and quantity of fertilizer applied to the crop, the cultivar used, the spacing of the crop in the field and the number of leaves left at topping (the removal of the terminal growing point). Each type is used, separately or in combination, in specific products (e.g. flue-cured in Virginia cigarettes). All types are grown in Africa.

As in other major producing areas, local research organizations in Africa have developed new cultivars with specific desirable chemical characteristics, disease-resistance properties and improved yields. The principal tobacco research centres are in Zimbabwe, Malawi and South Africa. In recent years efforts have been made to develop low-cost sources of tobacco in Tanzania and, more recently, in Swaziland and Mozambique.

In Malawi, South Africa and, to a lesser extent, in Zambia and Tanzania, tobacco is grown mainly as a direct-labour crop on large farms, some capable of producing as much as 250 metric tons of cured leaf per year. In other parts of Africa, however, tobacco is a smallholders' crop, with each farmer cultivating, on average, 1 or 2 ha of tobacco as well as essential food crops and, usually, other cash crops. Emphasis has been placed on improving yields by the selection of cultivars, by the increased use of fertilizers, by the reduction of crop loss (through the use of crop chemicals) and by reducing hand-labour requirements through the mechanization of land-preparation and the use of crop chemicals. Where small farmers are responsible for producing the crop, harvesting remains a manual operation, as the area under tobacco and their limited financial means preclude the adoption of mechanical harvesting devices.

The principal type of tobacco commercially cultivated in Africa is flue-cured, of which Malawi and Zimbabwe are the dominant regional producers. The tobacco sector formerly normally accounted for about 47% of Zimbabwe's total agricultural earnings, and as recently as 2002 it provided 31% of the country's total export revenue. In 2004, however, tobacco was the source of only about 13.5% of the total. The Zimbabwean tobacco crop, of which 98% has traditionally been exported, is highly regarded for its quality and flavour, and its marketability has been assisted by its relatively low tar content. Nevertheless, depressed conditions in international tobacco markets in the early 1990s encouraged some Zimbabwean growers to switch to cotton cultivation. During the 1990s Zimbabwe officially encouraged small-scale producers of burley and flue-cured tobaccos. In 1999, however, Zimbabwean tobacco plantings declined by about 8%, reflecting an accumulation in the stocks held by manufacturers world-wide. Subsequently the country's tobacco sector has been overshadowed by the programme of land reform pursued by the Government. In 2004 the Zimbabwe tobacco sector was reported to have lost, in the four years after 2000, 50% of the expansion that it had achieved in 1990–2000. Output was reported by FAO to have reached an all-time low of about 44,000 metric tons in 2006, compared with about 260,000 tons in 1998, despite an increase in the number of tobacco farmers to 12,700 in 2004 (from 8,531 in 2000 and 1,493 in 1990). According to the US Department of Agriculture (USDA), the number of farmers engaged in tobacco production in 2005 exceeded 30,000. The area planted to tobacco halved between 2002 and 2004, falling from 81,000 ha to 40,000 ha, while the average yield per hectare was reported to have fallen from 2,509 kg in 2000 to 1,558 kg in 2004. The increase in the number of farmers reflects an officially encouraged transfer away from the large-scale, estate-based cultivation of tobacco to a smallholder-based sector. As a consequence of land reform, many former estate cultivators of tobacco are reported to have relocated to countries such as Zambia and Mozambique and to have resumed large-scale tobacco cultivation there. Furthermore, some predicted that small-scale production would have an adverse effect on quality (about 50% of the 2005 crop was expected to comprise low-grade tobacco leaf). Additional factors in the decline in production have been the under-utilization of irrigation and curing capacity, and farmers' loss of access to finance despite the extension of contract cultivation (a system under which buyers supply production inputs—seeds, fertilizers, etc.) to 60% of the tobacco crop in 2006. In 2006 tobacco sales accounted for only 12.9% of the country's contracted export revenues. Zimbabwe reportedly accounted for about 2.7% of global exports of tobacco in 2006, compared with some 20% in the late 1990s. Nevertheless, output recovered somewhat in 2007, to 79,000 tons, and the country exported 65,511 tons of unmanufactured tobacco (2.5% of world exports), earning some US $245m. FAO imputed recovering harvests of 81,952 tons in 2008 and 96,367 tons in 2009, although sales abroad were reported to have fallen to 59,103 tons in 2008 (although export earnings were only down 1% to US $242.2m.). The Zimbabwe Tobacco Industry Marketing Board reported an average auction price for tobacco of $2,010 per ton in 2004, compared with $2,160 per ton ($2.16 per kg) in 2003. In April 2005 Zimbabwean tobacco farmers were reported to have refused to sell tobacco at auction owing to the low price—45 US cents per kg—offered. In 2005, according to industry sources, an average auction price of $1.61 per kg was recorded. However, farmers reportedly remained dissatisfied with payments made in Zimbabwe dollars, with some seeking payment in foreign currency. In April 2006 a bonus scheme was introduced to encourage early deliveries to auctions by tobacco growers. This bonus was in addition to a 65% subsidy termed the Tobacco Performance, Research and Development Facility. The two programmes together constituted a 95% subsidization of tobacco prices. By 2009 tobacco sales were being paid for in foreign currency, which helped maintain prices and improve prospects. In 2008, before the fears of world-wide economic recession towards the end of the year, commodity prices had been high, and in Zimbabwe the average was more than $3 per kg. At mid-2009 the average price in Zimbabwe remained above $2.90 per kg, while into the next year robust prices were accompanied by strong production. The 2010 auctions (February–September) reported the highest output since 2003 and, on the basis of seed sold, expectations of a further 50% increase in production in the following year. The average price peaked at $3.47 per kg in late March, although it was back down to $2.90 per kg in August. The recovering tobacco industry, therefore, contributed 26% of Zimbabwe's gross domestic product in 2009, compared with 12% in 2008. Sales of tobacco accounted for 13% of the country's export earnings in 2010. In August 2011 it was reported that the industry had fallen short of its targeted expansion in sales by 17%, but its volumes were still up 11% and receipts up 4%; weather conditions had been against fulfilment of the highest hopes for the crop. Chinese buyers were increasingly important, accounting for some 40% of sales, matching the share going to Europe. At mid-2011 average prices were reported to be up by about 5% on the previous year, to $3.00 per kg. In September 2012 it was reported that tobacco sales were up by about 9% on the previous year, at the end of August, earning an average price of $3.66 per kg, compared with $2.74 per kg at the end of August 2011.

Malawi is reckoned to be the most tobacco-dependent economy in the world. In the mid-1990s Malawi obtained as much as 70% of its export revenue from tobacco, exporting more than 98% of the mainly flue-cured, fire-cured and burley varieties that it produced. Thereafter, output, especially of burley tobacco, of which Malawi formerly supplied about one-fifth of world output, declined (although it remained the world's largest producer in 2010). From the early 2000s, however, Malawi was reported to have benefited indirectly from the problems of the tobacco sector in Zimbabwe, and to have attracted increased investment from multinational tobacco companies. In 2010 the country earned 55% of the value of its total exports from tobacco and tobacco products. Three-quarters of employment was reckoned to depend on the tobacco industry. Small-scale tobacco growers in Malawi, backed by the Government and some independent sources, asserted in the 2000s that the national auction system employed for tobacco has been manipulated by international buyers who, by establishing what amounts to a cartel, have artificially depressed tobacco prices to their own advantage. According to Malawi's Tobacco Control Commission, burley tobacco auctioned in Malawi in 2006 achieved an average price of US $0.91 per kg, compared with $0.99 per kg in 2005 and $1.09 per kg in 2004. The recorded prices achieved thus fell below those recommended by the Government in April 2006—$1.1 per kg for low-grade tobacco and $1.7 per kg for top-grade. It was claimed that the auction price offered to small-scale tobacco producers in Malawi was insufficient to meet their production costs—it reportedly costs a Malawian grower $1.00 on average to produce one kilo of leaf. According to the Tobacco Control Commission, low auction prices resulted from a calculated decision among buyers, in order to buy tobacco cheaply, not to compete against one another. Large-scale growers, meanwhile, deal directly with buyers, growing their crops under contract and receiving a price ($1.06 per kg in 2006) that is fixed in advance of the selling season. Low prices were also attributed to over-supply of tobacco in 2006. In 2007 tobacco output increased slightly, to an estimated 118,000 tons, compared with 115,000 tons in 2006. At the opening of the 2007 auction season in April considerably higher prices, of $1.60–$1.70 per kg, were recorded, encouraged by Government-set minimums. According to data from the Tobacco Control Commission, auction sales of burley almost doubled in volume in 2008 (albeit from an historic low in 2007, but exceeding the decade's previous best figure, in 2000), taking the average price to $2.37 per kg, compared with $1.73 per kg in the previous year and a price low in 2006 of little more than 90 US cents per kg. In the mean time, a 2006 sales peak of flue-cured tobacco had coincided with a low in the price—which averaged $1.55 per kg in that year—but sales volumes fell back in 2007 and only slightly improved in 2008, while the average price per kg went from $1.92 in 2007 to $2.82 in 2008. In the latter year, of total tobacco sales at auction in Malawi of some 194,708 tons, burley accounted for 87% and flue-cured for 12%. In 2009 higher tobacco production (19% on the previous year) went some way to offsetting the lower prices (about 23% down). Production was down in 2010 (having risen in 2008 and 2009), in reaction to the lower prices the year before, and because of drier weather, but prices were reported to have recovered somewhat in the 2010 auction season, when tobacco was reported to be selling for an average $1.99 per kg. According to FAO, although exports volumes in 2010 reduced by 21%, earnings increased by 15%, reflecting better prices. In 2011, however, with prices falling, earnings were reported to be as much as 70% down on what they were one year earlier, provoking deadly civil unrest in July. In August prices were reported to have improved slightly and firmed, but they remained lower than in 2010: burley was selling for about $1.10 per kg at auction and $2.10 per kg on contract, while flue-cured was averaging $1.67 per kg at auction. The collapse in sales provoked the authorities to blame the cartel of international buyers, while they blamed the Government's failure to ensure the quality of the leaf. Attention was focused on the widespread practice of smuggling, and the sale of Malawian tobacco in Zambia and Zimbabwe, where prices were better, leaving the Government deprived of revenue. The industry managed to increase sales by some 11% in 2012, however, with prices at about $2.13 per kg (more than double the prices the year before), according to reports, at the end of the tobacco season in July.

Tanzania contributes a small but significant quantity of flue-cured tobacco to the world market, and in 2009 exports of tobacco contributed 3.2% the country's total; lower prices meant the contribution of tobacco to total exports fell to 2.2% in 2010. In 2010 Mozambique, a country that had benefited from the emigration of Zimbabwean agricultural investment, almost matched Zambian production, and it continued to exceed Tanzanian tobacco output; Mozambique's export performance was more varied, although it was sub-Saharan Africa's third largest exporter after Malawi and Zimbabwe in 2010, followed by Tanzania and Zambia. Tobacco production in Nigeria is fairly static, and its flue-cured crop is entirely reserved for local consumption. Kenya has greatly increased its output of flue-cured leaf since commencing tobacco exports in 1984, and tobacco cultivation has recently been increasing in importance in Uganda, as part of a government programme to offset declining earnings from coffee. Exports of tobacco contributed about 4% of Uganda's total export earnings in 2010. There are also small exports of flue-cured tobacco from Sierra Leone. Nigeria, Malawi and South Africa account for the African crop of sun- and air-cured types of tobacco. Modest quantities of oriental tobacco are cultivated in Malawi and South Africa. Côte d'Ivoire also produces some tobacco.

About two-fifths of world tobacco production are traded internationally. Until 1993, when it was overtaken by Brazil, the USA was the world's principal tobacco-exporting country. Since 1993 Brazil has consolidated its position as the world's leading exporter of tobacco, largely at the expense of the USA and Zimbabwe. Brazil's share of global exports of unmanufactured tobacco increased in volume from 13% in 1993 to about one-quarter in the mid-2000s (25% in 2009). According to the UN Conference on Trade and Development (UNCTAD), tobacco prices soon recovered from the commodity slump of late 2008 and early 2009, when the average price for unmanufactured tobacco (US import unit value) over August 2008 to July 2009 was US $3,988 per metric ton. The average annual price for 2008 as a whole was $3,589 per ton; in 2009 it was $4,235 per ton, in 2010 $4,313 per ton and in 2011 $4,475 per ton. In April 2011 the monthly average peaked again, at $4,577 per ton, having risen sharply over the previous two months, as commodity prices world-wide rose, but it fell back to as low as $4,390 per ton in June, before peaking again in September at $4,595 per ton; the US import unit value then gradually declined to an estimated $4,283 per ton in June and July 2012 (having started the year with a January average of $4,415 per ton).

The International Tobacco Growers' Association (ITGA), with headquarters in Portugal, was formed in 1984 by growers' groups in Argentina, Brazil, Canada, Malawi, the USA and Zimbabwe. The ITGA's member countries numbered 25 in 2012, accounting for more than 80% of the world's internationally traded tobacco. African members of the ITGA in 2012 comprised Kenya, Malawi, South Africa, Tanzania, Uganda, Zambia and Zimbabwe. The ITGA provides a forum for the exchange of information among tobacco producers, conducts research and publishes studies on tobacco issues.

URANIUM

Uranium occurs in a variety of ores, often in association with other minerals, such as gold, phosphate and copper, and may be mined by open-cast, underground or *in situ* leach methods, depending on the circumstances. The concentration of uranium that is needed to form an economic mineral deposit varies widely, depending upon its geological setting and physical location. Average ore grades at operating uranium mines vary from 0.03% U to as high as 15% U, but are most frequently less than 1% U. South Africa produces uranium concentrates as a by-product of the mining of gold and copper, and possesses uranium conversion and enrichment facilities. Both copper-mining and the exploitation of phosphates by wet (phosphoric acid-yielding) processes offer a more widespread potential for by-product uranium production.

Uranium is principally used as a fuel in nuclear reactors for the production of electricity. There were 433 commercial nuclear reactors operable in 30 countries world-wide at 1 August 2012, generating almost 14% of the world's electricity; 65 more reactors were under construction, with 160 more in planning. Enriched uranium is used as fuel in most nuclear power stations and in the manufacture of nuclear weapons. With regard to the latter, however, the abandonment of East–West confrontation and the conclusion of a series of nuclear disarmament treaties between the USA and Russia (and other former Soviet republics) has led to the ongoing release from military stockpiles of substantial quantities of uranium for civil energy programmes. In 2011, according to data cited by the World Nuclear Association (WNA), the world's known recoverable resources of uranium (defined as reasonably assured resources plus estimated additional resources, recoverable up to a cost of US $130 per kg) totalled about 5.33m. metric tons of metal content (31% in Australia, 12% in Kazakhstan; Russia and Canada each had 9% of world resources, followed by Niger on 8% and South Africa, Brazil and Namibia each on 5%).

Because of uranium's strategic military value, there was intense prospecting activity in the 1940s and 1950s, but the market was later depressed as government purchasing programmes ceased. Uranium demand fell in the late 1960s and early 1970s, until industrialized countries responded to the 1973–74 petroleum crisis by intensifying their civil nuclear power programmes. Anticipated strong demand for rapidly expanding nuclear power further improved the uranium market until the early 1980s, when lower-than-expected growth in electricity consumption forced nuclear power programmes to be restricted, leaving both producers and consumers with high levels of accumulated stocks requiring liquidation. A number of mining operations were also scaled down or closed. The market was further depressed in the aftermath of the accident in 1986 at the Chornobyl (Chernobyl) nuclear plant in Ukraine (then part of the USSR). Following nine consecutive years of reduced output, uranium production achieved modest advances in each year during 1995–97. In 1998 and 1999, however, world mine production declined, increasing fairly steadily from 2000 (apart from a pause in 2002) until 2005, when it reached 41,719 tons. Mined production of uranium declined in 2006, to 39,444 tons, but increased thereafter, reaching 51,450 tons by 2009 and then 54,660 tons in 2010 and 54,610 tons in 2011, the latter figure marking the first contraction in mined output in five years. Production from world uranium mines, however, in 2011 was sufficient to meet about 85% of annual requirements for power generation. Secondary sources provide the balance of required uranium.

Production of Uranium
(uranium content of ores, metric tons)

	2010	2011
World total	54,660	54,610
Africa	9,947	9,037
African producers		
Malawi	670	846
Namibia	4,496	3,258
Niger	4,198	4,351
South Africa	583	582
Leading non-African producers		
Australia	5,900	5,983
Canada	9,783	9,145
Kazakhstan	17,803	19,451
Russia	3,562	2,993
USA	1,660	1,537
Uzbekistan	2,874	3,000

Source: World Nuclear Association.

A leap in production meant that Kazakhstan replaced Canada as the world's main source of mined uranium from 2009, accounting for almost 36% of world uranium output in 2011, and it is expected to remain the leading producer in the immediate future. After a second year of declining output, Canada still accounted for 17% of mined production in 2011, the next largest producers being Australia, Niger, Namibia, Uzbekistan and Russia. Niger has Africa's largest known recoverable resources (estimated at some 421,000 metric tons), followed by South Africa (279,100 tons) and Namibia (261,000 tons). Uranium production has been an important component of the South African mining industry since uranium extraction began in 1951, with output reaching a record 6,146 tons in 1980. South Africa's production has subsequently declined sharply, and has been overtaken by that of Namibia, Niger and, in 2010, Malawi. Deliveries of ore from the world's largest open-pit uranium mine, at Rössing in Namibia, began in 1976. In 2003 output was a not untypical 2,036 tons, but it rose very substantially, by 49%, in 2004, to 3,038 tons. In 2008 the Rössing mine, the source of almost four-fifths of Namibia's uranium output, was the world's third largest uranium mine in production, contributing 8% of total world supplies. In 2006, following two years of growth, Namibia's output of uranium retreated to 3,067 tons, and the opening of a new mine at the end of that year (it was slow to achieve planned production levels) did not prevent a further contraction of output in 2007, to 2,879 tons. However, the works to expand Rössing, as well as rising extraction at the new Langer Heinrich mine, boosted Namibian production by 52% to 4,366 tons of uranium in 2008, then 4,626 tons in 2009 and 4,496 tons in 2010. The country having firmly, therefore, taken back fourth place in terms of the largest world producers, labour unrest and flooding combined to lower production in 2011, to 3,258 tons, allowing Niger's production to surpass it. New capacity, however, was expected to increase output fourfold by 2014. Exports of ores and concentrates of uranium and thorium contributed 9% of Namibia's total revenue from exports in 2007, rising to 16% in 2008.

Uranium exploration in Niger started in the 1950s, around the Aïr mountains near Agadez, with production commencing at the Arlit mine in 1971. Niger's other main uranium mine, where operations commenced in 1978, is at Akouta. France purchases most of Niger's uranium production, with the remainder taken by German, Japanese and Spanish customers. Like Namibia, Niger was compelled in the early 1990s to restructure and streamline its uranium operations, and output has subsequently risen. From 2002 production remained above 3,000 tons of uranium annually, with a peak of 3,434 tons in 2006 and a low of 3,032 tons in 2008; thereafter output rose steadily, to 4,351 tons by 2011, when the country became the world's fourth largest producer. In 2008, according to trade data cited by the UN, exports of uranium ore, valued at US $289m., contributed 58% of Niger's total export earnings, owing to rising commodity prices, but in 2011 the corresponding figures were $669m., or 69% of total exports. The Nigerien Government's target was to increase its annual uranium production to 10,500 tons early in the 2010s. Gabon, which commenced uranium production in 1958, possesses six identified deposits containing sufficient reserves to support 30 years' output at production rates achieved during the mid-1990s. However, the depressed level of uranium prices in the late 1990s, with little prospect of recovery in the short term, prompted French interests, exploiting the deposits in conjunction with the Government of Gabon, to terminate uranium-mining operations there from early 1999, leaving Namibia, Niger and South Africa as the only regional producers for the next 10 years. Reclamation work at Gabon's Mounana uranium mine was reported to have been completed in 2004, and survey activities by a consortium of Canadian companies was ongoing in 2010. A uranium mine in Malawi only began production in 2009, but it increased output sixfold in 2010, to exceed South African production, a position maintained in 2011 with a further 26% increase in output. By 2010, with sales abroad worth US $114m., uranium or thorium ores and concentrates already provided 11% of total Malawian exports.

Uranium has also been found, but has been hitherto unexploited, in Botswana (production is planned from 2014), the Central African Republic (a mine opened in 2010, with full production expected from 2014), Chad, the Democratic Republic of the Congo, Guinea, Madagascar, Mali, Mauritania, Nigeria, Somalia, Tanzania (production is expected at several sites within four years of 2012), Togo and Zambia (an Australian company is investigating uranium recovery at a copper mine).

The market for uranium is small, comprising only about 100 buyers world-wide, according to industry sources. Marginal trading, to which 'spot' prices for uranium apply, accounts for only a small proportion of the total quantity of the metal traded, but 'spot' prices nevertheless provide a reference price for long-term contracts concluded between miners and utilities. According to the WNA, very high prices for uranium in the 1970s were succeeded by very low prices in the early 1990s, to the extent that 'spot' prices fell below the cost of production in most mines. In 1996 'spot' prices reportedly recovered to the extent that most mines were able to produce at a profit. That recovery, however, was succeeded by a further decline which lasted until late 2003. Prices began to rise thereafter, and interest in uranium-mining accordingly increased. According to the Euratom Supply Agency (ESA), the weighted 'spot' price of uranium delivered to European Union (EU) utility companies rose to $12.51 per lb in 2004, from $9.46 per lb in 2003. The price of uranium then rose sharply, doubling in 2007 alone, to $64.21 per lb. According to industry sources, the price rises that have occurred since late 2003 have been due to the weakness of the US dollar relative to the currencies of the major uranium-producing countries; disruptions to the uranium supply chain; lower commercial inventories; Russia's withdrawal from the market for uranium concentrates; and rising demand. The average 'spot' price reached $66.86 per lb in 2008, a price that would have been higher but for the general collapse in commodity prices in the final months of the year, brought about by the global financial crisis. Uranium prices were reported to have continued falling until April 2009, but then recovered somewhat, but the average price for 2009 was only $41.83 per lb over the year, or €77.96 per kg, rising to €79.48 per kg in 2010 and a remarkable €107.43 per kg in 2011. The ESA's index based on the average price of deliveries of natural uranium under multi-annual contracts smoothed out price spikes such as in 2008 or the market caution in 2009, so it has recorded a general upward tendency in prices since 2004: most recently, US $29.88 per lb, or €55.70 per kg, in 2009; €61.68 per kg in 2010; and €83.45 per kg in 2011. In 2008 the ESA announced a new price series, historical average uranium prices in the so-called MAC-3 index, based on the prices of the natural uranium delivered under long-term contracts concluded during the previous three years: US $34.06 per lb, or €63.49 per kg, in 2009; €78.12 per kg in 2010; and €100.02 per kg in 2011. Nuclear energy was attracting renewed interest from decision-makers as they strove to develop energy policies that would respond to both rising fossil fuel prices and concerns about climate change, although the accident at the Fukushima nuclear reactor in north-east Japan following the earthquake and tsunami of February 2011 unsettled public acceptance.

The WNA, which succeeded the Uranium Institute in 2001, is a global industrial organization that seeks to promote the peaceful use of nuclear power world-wide as a sustainable source of energy. The WNA concerns itself with all stages of the nuclear fuel cycle, including the mining of uranium, its enrichment, the manufacture of nuclear plants and the safe disposal of spent fuel.

ESA, established in 1960 under the EC Euratom Treaty, operates in areas connected with atomic energy, including research, the formulation of safety standards, and the peaceful uses of nuclear energy. Its main duty is to co-ordinate the supply of nuclear fuels (source materials and special fissile materials) in the EU, while ensuring a regular and equitable supply of ores and nuclear fuels to all users.

WHEAT (*Triticum*)

The most common species of wheat (*Triticum vulgare*) includes hard, semi-hard and soft varieties which have different milling characteristics but which, in general, are suitable for bread-making. Another species, *T. durum*, is grown mainly in semi-arid areas, including North Africa and the Mediterranean. This wheat is very hard and is suitable for the manufacture of semolina. In North Africa, in addition to being used for making local bread, semolina is the basic ingredient of pasta and couscous. A third species, spelt (*T. spelta*), is also included in production figures for wheat. It is grown in very small quantities in parts of Europe and is used mainly as animal feed.

Although a most adaptable crop, wheat does not thrive in hot and humid climates. Africa's wheat production is mainly concentrated in a narrow strip along the Mediterranean coast from Morocco to Tunisia, in the Nile valley, and in parts of South Africa. Zimbabwe, Kenya, Ethiopia and Sudan also grow limited quantities, but very little is grown in West Africa. In contrast with some developing countries of Asia, the potential of improved wheat varieties has yet to be realized in much of Africa, especially south of the Sahara. One reason is the undeveloped state of the transport systems in many countries in the region, which hinders both the distribution of production inputs (e.g. seeds and fertilizers) and the marketing of farmers' surplus produce. Until recently, many governments have also been unwilling to pay sufficiently attractive producer prices to encourage farmers to grow wheat for marketing.

World wheat production declined during the 1990s, albeit only marginally, at an average rate of less than 0.1% a year. The fall was largely due to the sharp decline in agricultural output in the former USSR, excluding which the trend in world production growth was upward. Wheat production is highly variable from year to year. Part of the variation is attributable to weather conditions, particularly rainfall, in the main producing areas, but national policies on support for producers have also been a major influence. In the 1990s several major wheat-producing countries, including leading exporters, pursued policies of market deregulation, and began to remove the links between producers' support and the financial returns from particular commodities. This encouraged their farmers more readily to switch between crops according to expected relative market returns. After 1996, for example, when wheat was in short supply on world markets, output was stimulated in many growing areas, and a record 613m. metric tons was harvested in 1997. Production then remained below that level (reaching a low of some 560m. tons in 2003) until a new record level of 632m. tons in 2004, although it lapsed to 627m. tons in 2005 and to 605m. tons in 2006. FAO figures suggested a small recovery in output in 2007, to 613m. tons, then a dramatic increase to new records of 683m. tons in 2008 and 687m. tons in 2009, before contracting to 654m. tons in 2010. At August 2012 US Department of Agriculture (USDA) figures, which use local marketing years, put total world production in 2006/07 at 596m. tons, rising to 612m. tons in 2007/08, a record 683m. tons in 2008/09 and 686m. tons in 2009/10, before declining to 652m. tons in 2010/11; a recovery to a record 695m. tons took place in 2011/12, but the return of dry conditions in Russia contributed to a smaller world harvest being forecast for 2012/13 (although stocks were high). The largest producer of wheat in the world is the European Union (EU—20% of the world total in 2011/12), followed by East Asia (17%), South Asia (17%) and the countries of the former USSR (16%), the last region still recovering from the devastation caused by the 2010 drought and fires that reduced the Russian harvest by almost one-third. By far the largest individual wheat producers internationally in 2011/12 were the People's Republic of China (17%), which accounted for most of the East Asian production, India (12%), Russia (8%) and the USA (8%).

Wheat production in sub-Saharan Africa, according to USDA rose to 6.1m. metric tons in both 2008/09 and 2009/10, up from 5.5m. tons in 2007/08; wheat output dipped to 5.2m. tons in 2010/11, but recovered to 6.1m. tons in 2011/12 and was expected to maintain 6.0m. tons in the following year. Wheat is principally grown in the south and east of the region, often at high altitudes where conditions are less humid. South Africa was traditionally the main regional producer, with output of about 2.0m. tons annually in the first decade of the 2000s, but it was surpassed by Ethiopia in 2003/04, hitherto the second largest regional producer. In 2011/12 Ethiopia harvested a record 3.1m. tons of wheat (60% of the sub-Saharan total), up from 2.9m. tons the year before and with a forecast for the same level (but 51%) the following year; by comparison, South Africa's production in 2011/12 was 1.9m. tons (31%), up from 1.4m. tons in the previous year, with 1.8m. tons forecast for 2012/13. Ethiopia, however, grows for a domestic market, while South Africa is the more important exporter of wheat (300,000 tons in 2011/12—31% of the sub-Saharan total), although on a small scale compared with major producers elsewhere in the world. The continent's principal exporter, on paper, was Nigeria (460,000 tons in 2011/12), which grew very little, but had taken on a similar role to Côte d'Ivoire as a re-exporter for West Africa; since the mid-2000s Côte d'Ivoire has registered steadily increasing export volumes (150,000 tons by 2011/12). In some other wheat-producing countries (e.g. Tanzania and Zimbabwe) the crop is grown mainly on large commercial farms and, with the benefit of irrigation, usually yields well. Efforts to produce wheat in tropical countries such as the Democratic Republic of the Congo (DRC) and Nigeria have shown mixed results. In the case of the DRC, production declined at least partially because of the prevalence of civil unrest rather than purely agricultural considerations. Production in the 2000s was generally about 10,000 tons (as it was in 2011/12), with an atypical spike to 18,000 tons in 2002/03. In Nigeria output of wheat was generally about 100,000 tons annually (according to USDA). Tanzanian production was about 80,000 tons per year in the 2000s, but dipped to 62,000 in 2010/11 and then rose to 95,000 tons in 2011/12 (with a similar forecast for the following year). Zimbabwean wheat output fell from a peak of 325,000 tons in 2001/02 to 90,000 tons in 2003/04, 135,000 tons in 2006/07 and the next year, and 38,000 tons in 2008/09; Zimbabwe produced only 12,000 tons of wheat in 2009/10 and 18,000 tons annually in 2010/11 and 2011/12 (with the same forecast for 2012/13). Such levels were little more than those in Lesotho, which, although a much smaller country, was an elevated country with a suitable climate; the kingdom produced 10,000 tons of wheat in 2009/10 (higher than the mere 5,000 tons two years earlier, but much less than the 23,000 tons at the beginning of the decade), 20,000 tons in 2010/11 and 16,000 tons in 2011/12. Eritrea grew some 15,000 tons of wheat in 2011/12. Zambian production rose from 60,000 tons in 2000/01 to 195,000 tons in 2009/10, USDA put the total at 172,000 tons in the next two years, with 237,000 tons expected in the following two years. Kenyan production, which had only been 100,000 tons in 2000/01, reached peaks of 300,000 tons in 2002/03 and 2006/07, but was generally between 220,000 and 225,000 tons in the later years of the decade; 250,000 tons was cited for 2010/11, 200,000 tons expected for 2011/12 and the mid-point of those figures forecast for 2012/13. The only other sub-Saharan grower of wheat of any significance was Sudan; it had achieved a production peak of 642,000 tons in 2008/09, which fell to 403,000 tons in 2009/10 and only 291,000 tons in 2010/11, before rising to 324,000 in 2011/12 and a forecast of 480,000 tons in 2012/13 (most of Sudan's wheat-growing areas are outside what became South Sudan in July 2011). FAO marked Rwanda as increasing its wheat production in the decade, in particular the later years, reaching 77,193 tons in 2010, up from 21,942 tons in 2005 and only 6,444 tons in 2000.

World consumption, which has, in the long term, been increasing at a similar rate to production, varies much less from year to year than the wheat harvest. Wheat food use has been expanding at the expense of rice: its growth is associated with rising consumer incomes and an increasing number of fast-food outlets. Substantial amounts of wheat are used for animal feed in Europe and, when prices are favourable, in North America. Substantial quantities were also used for feed in the 1980s in the what was then the USSR, but this volume decreased sharply in response to the diminution in livestock numbers. Some wheat is used for feed in Japan, while the Republic of Korea (South Korea) imports wheat for feed when prices are low in comparison with those of coarse grains such as sorghum and maize (corn). According to USDA, domestic consumption of wheat was highest in the EU until 2010/11, when East Asia just exceeded it for the first time, widening the margin in 2011/12, when it accounted for 20% of the world total of 688m. metric tons, followed by the EU on 18% and South Asia on 17%. Most of the countries in such regions are also producers.

On average, 72% of world wheat production is used for human food, and 15%–20% for animal feed. Feed use is variable, depending on the amount of sub-standard wheat produced each season, and also on the relationship between wheat prices and those of feed grains, especially maize. Of the total quantity of wheat consumed annually as food, developing countries account for about 70%. North Africa is an important wheat-consuming region (the Middle East and North Africa is, by far, the largest wheat importing region of the world), but in sub-Saharan Africa consumption is mostly restricted to the larger towns and cities. Wheat use in the region amounts to about 3% of the world total.

Wheat is the principal cereal in international trade. FAO assessed international trade in wheat at about 133m. metric tons in 2007, the fourth successive year of increase, with a dip to 131m. tons in 2008 and a powerfully resurgent 149m. tons in 2009. USDA figures had world trade in wheat, flour and products peaking in 2008/09, before falling back for two years, largely owing to global economic problems and high prices dampening consumption; continued uncertainty, in particular in Europe, was expected to reverse the 2011/12 recovery in 2012/13. The downward tendency was emphasized by government policies—to counter high prices, for instance—such as the decision by the Government of India in 2009 to restrict wheat exports. In 2010 the drought in Russia further restricted supplies to the world market, and this situation was repeated less dramatically in 2012. The largest importing region, by far, was the Middle East and North Africa (32% of world imports in 2011/12), followed by South-East Asia (12%) and sub-Saharan Africa (as defined by USDA, all African states except the five Mediterranean littoral countries—12%), East Asia (11%) and South America (9%). According to USDA data, amounts exported in 2004/05–2007/08 ranged between 109m. tons and 117m. tons annually, rising in the following year to 143m. tons, before falling to 136m. tons in 2009/10 and 134m. tons in 2010/11; exports in 2011/12 reached 152m. tons, but in the following year were expected to return to some 136m. tons. The main exporter in 2009/10 was still the USA (18% of the world total), whose share had declined from about 30% of the total in the first half of the 1990s to about 24% in 2005/06. In 2010/11, however, dramatically increased US exports, up by almost one-half, and the collapse in Russian exports (to 4m. tons, from 19m. tons the previous year) led to a surge in the US share of world exports back up to 27%. In 2011/12 the USA provided 19% of world exports, Australia 15% and Russia 14%. Other major exporters were Canada, the EU, Argentina and Kazakhstan (Ukrainian exports had not recovered in the same way as Russia's had). EU imports had declined substantially since the early 2000s, owing to the introduction of a system of import quotas designed to curb purchases of cheap Ukrainian and Russian wheat. Developed countries were formerly the principal consumers of wheat, but the role of developing countries as importers has been steadily increasing and they now regularly account for approximately two-thirds of world imports.

The majority of Africa's imports are accounted for by North Africa, where, according to USDA data, Egypt was again the world's largest wheat-importing country in 2011/12: the country's annual imports rose from 7.3m. tons in 2006/07 to more than 10.0m. tons annually from 2009/10, reaching 11.7m. tons in 2011/12, although they were expected to fall back to 9.0m. tons in 2012/13. Algeria, in particular, and Morocco are also consistently major importers of wheat. Imports by sub-Saharan Africa totalled a high 17.8m. tons in 2011/12, still less than three-quarters of the level in North Africa. Most countries in the region import at least small amounts (often including wheat or flour supplied as food aid), the main markets being Nigeria and Sudan. Central America and the Caribbean, North Africa and, usually, South-East Asia are the only regions to export less wheat than sub-Saharan Africa.

Production of Wheat
('000 metric tons)

	2009	2010
World total*	686,636	653,655
Sub-Saharan Africa*	6,053	6,031
Leading sub-Saharan African producers		
Ethiopia	2,638	3,076
Kenya	219	512
Nigeria*	50	51
Rwanda	72	77
South Africa	1,958	1,430
Sudan	642	403
Tanzania	92	100
Zambia	195	172
Leading non-African producers		
Australia	21,656	22,138
Canada	26,848	23,167
China, People's Repub.	115,115	115,181
France	38,332	40,787
Germany	25,192	24,107

—continued	2009	2010
India	80,680	80,800
Iran	13,485	15,029
Kazakhstan	17,052	9,638
Pakistan	24,033	23,311
Russia	61,740	41,508
Turkey	20,600	19,660
Ukraine	20,886	16,851
USA	60,366	60,062

* FAO estimates.

Source: FAO.

The export price (f.o.b. Gulf ports) of US No. 2 Hard Red Winter, one of the most widely traded wheat varieties, averaged US $119 per metric ton in 2000, rising to $151 per ton by 2002. Prices fluctuated thereafter, the average price falling in 2005 to $158 per ton. In 2006 the average price jumped to $200 per ton, and thereafter the price continued to rise substantially, reaching $264 per ton in 2007 to $345 per ton in 2008. Average monthly prices in 2008 attained a record $482 per ton in March, in line with other international commodity prices, but had fallen as low as $235 per ton by December. In 2009 the average export price of US No. 2 Hard Red Winter wheat was $236 per ton, ranging between a high of $270 in June and a low of $201 in September. The average price in 2010 was $241 per ton. Prices fell as low as $183 per ton by June (the lowest monthly price in more than four years, since March 2006), but jumped to $304 per ton by September, forced up by anxiety about the drought in Russia and other countries of the former USSR, notably Kazakhstan and Ukraine—in particular given the devastating fires in central Russia in the intense summer heat of that year. Average prices for US No. 2 Hard Red Winter rose above $300 per ton by the end of 2010 ($320 per ton in December) and had remained so until December 2011, when the monthly average fell to $289 per ton. The average price was $330 per ton over 2011. Although Black Sea exports from Russia, Kazakhstan and Ukraine had returned to the market in 2011, helping keep prices below the monthly average peak of $362 per ton in February, prices remained below $300 per ton from December until July and August 2012. The lowest monthly average in the first half of 2012 was $276 per ton in April, but the price was back up to $350 per ton for July, with more than $360 per ton expected for August. The average price for January–July 2012 was $305 per ton.

Since 1949 nearly all world trade in wheat has been conducted under the auspices of successive international agreements, administered by the International Wheat Council (IWC) in London, United Kingdom. The early agreements involved regulatory price controls and supply and purchase obligations, but such provisions became inoperable in more competitive market conditions, and were abandoned in 1972. The IWC subsequently concentrated on providing detailed market assessments to its members and encouraging them to confer on matters of mutual concern. A new Grains Trade Convention, which entered into force in July 1995, gave the renamed International Grains Council (IGC) a wider mandate to consider all coarse grains as well as wheat (rice was added to the definition of grains from 1 July 2009). This facilitates the provision of information to member governments, and enhances their opportunities to hold consultations. In addition, links between governments and industry are strengthened at an annual series of grain conferences sponsored by the IGC. In mid-2012 the IGC consisted of 26 members, including the EU. African members comprised Algeria, Côte d'Ivoire, Egypt, Kenya, Morocco, South Africa and Tunisia.

Since 1967 a series of Food Aid Conventions (FACs), linked to the successive Wheat and Grains Trade Conventions, have ensured continuity of supplies of food aid in the form of cereals to needy countries. Under the last FAC, negotiated in 1999, the donor countries (including the member states of the EU) pledged to supply a minimum of some 5m. metric tons of food aid annually to developing countries, with priority given to least developed countries and other low-income food-importing countries. Aid was provided mostly in the form of cereals, and all aid given to least developed countries was in the form of grants. The FAC sought to improve the effectiveness, and increase the impact, of food aid by improved monitoring and consultative procedures. In mid-2004 FAC members undertook a renegotiation of the 1999 FAC in order 'to strengthen its capacity to meet identified needs when food aid is the appropriate response'. However, it was decided that this renegotiation should await the conclusion of discussions on trade-related food aid issues in agriculture negotiations at the World Trade Organization. In the meantime, it was agreed to extend the FAC, 1999, for two years from July 2005; further, one-year extensions were agreed subsequently and it only finally expired on 30 June 2012. In December 2010 formal negotiations on the future of the FAC had commenced, so the extensions were to give the discussions a fair chance of fruition. A new Food Assistance Convention was adopted in London on 25 April 2012, and was open for signature from 11 June to the 34 signatories and the EU. It was expected to come into force on 1 January 2013 (if ratified by five signatories—at July 2012, only Japan and the EU had done so), and from that date would be open to other signatories. Rather than focusing only on certain specified food items (expressed in wheat-equivalent tons), the new instrument focused on 'nutritious food', leaving it up to the parties to express commitments in wheat tons or monetary terms, as part of the mechanisms for information sharing and registration of undertakings.

ACKNOWLEDGEMENTS

We gratefully acknowledge the assistance of the following organizations in the preparation of this section: Centro Internacional de Agricultura Tropical; De Beers; Food and Agricultural Organization of the United Nations (FAO); Gold Fields Mineral Services Ltd; International Cocoa Organization; International Coffee Organization; International Copper Study Group; International Cotton Advisory Committee; International Monetary Fund; International Aluminium Institute; International Rice Research Institute; International Tea Committee; International Tobacco Growers' Association; Johnson Matthey PLC; US Department of Agriculture (USDA); US Department of Energy; US Geological Survey, US Department of the Interior; World Nuclear Association.

CALENDARS

The Islamic Calendar

The Islamic era dates from 16 July 622, which was the beginning of the Arab year in which the *Hijra* ('flight' or migration) of the prophet Muhammad (the founder of Islam), from Mecca to Medina (in modern Saudi Arabia), took place. The Islamic or *Hijri* Calendar is lunar, each year having 354 or 355 days, the extra day being intercalated 11 times every 30 years. Accordingly, the beginning of the *Hijri* year occurs earlier in the Gregorian Calendar by a few days each year. Dates are reckoned in terms of the *anno Hegirae* (AH) or year of the Hegira (*Hijra*). The Islamic year AH 1434 began on 14 November 2012.

The year is divided into the following months:

1. Muharram	30 days	7. Rajab	30 days
2. Safar	29 days	8. Shaaban	29 days
3. Rabia I	30 days	9. Ramadan	30 days
4. Rabia II	29 days	10. Shawwal	29 days
5. Jumada I	30 days	11. Dhu'l-Qa'da	30 days
6. Jumada II	29 days	12. Dhu'l-Hijja	29 or 30 days

The *Hijri* Calendar is used for religious purposes throughout the Islamic world.

PRINCIPAL ISLAMIC FESTIVALS

New Year: 1st Muharram. The first 10 days of the year are regarded as holy, especially the 10th.

Ashoura: 10th Muharram. Celebrates the first meeting of Adam and Eve after leaving Paradise, also the ending of the Flood and the death of Hussain, grandson of the prophet Muhammad. The feast is celebrated with fairs and processions.

Mouloud (Birth of Muhammad): 12th Rabia I.

Leilat al-Meiraj (Ascension of Muhammad): 27th Rajab.

Ramadan (Month of Fasting).

Id al-Fitr or Id al-Saghir or Küçük Bayram (The Small Feast): Three days beginning 1st Shawwal. This celebration follows the constraint of the Ramadan fast.

Id al-Adha or Id al-Kabir or Büyük Bayram (The Great Feast, Feast of the Sacrifice): Four days beginning on 10th Dhu'l-Hijja. The principal Islamic festival, commemorating Abraham's sacrifice and coinciding with the pilgrimage to Mecca. Celebrated by the sacrifice of a sheep, by feasting and by donations to the poor.

Islamic Year	1433	1434	1435
New Year	26 Nov. 2011	14 Nov. 2012	4 Nov. 2013
Ashoura	5 Dec. 2011	23 Nov. 2012	13 Nov. 2013
Mouloud	4 Feb. 2012	23 Jan. 2013	13 Jan. 2014
Leilat al-Meiraj	16 June 2012	5 June 2013	26 May 2014
Ramadan begins	19 July 2012	8 July 2013	28 June 2014
Id al-Fitr	18 Aug. 2012	7 Aug. 2013	28 July 2014
Id al-Adha	25 Oct. 2012	14 Oct. 2013	4 Oct. 2014

Note: Local determinations may vary by one day from those given here.

The Ethiopian Calendar

The Ethiopian Calendar is solar, and is the traditional calendar of the Ethiopian Church. New Year (1st Maskarem) usually occurs on 11 September Gregorian. The Ethiopian year 2005 began on 12 September 2012.

The year is divided into 13 months, of which 12 have 30 days each. The 13th and last month (Paguemen) has five or six days, the extra day occurring in leap years. The months are as follows:

1. Maskarem	5. Tir	10. Sene
2. Tikimit	6. Yekatit	11. Hamle
3. Hidar	7. Megabit	12. Nahasse
4. Tahsas	8. Maiza	13. Paguemen
	9. Ginbat	

The Ethiopian Calendar is used for most purposes, religious and secular, in Ethiopia.

RESEARCH INSTITUTES

ASSOCIATIONS AND INSTITUTIONS STUDYING AFRICA

ARGENTINA

Facultad de Filosofía y Letras, Sección Interdisciplinaria de Estudios de Asia y Africa: Universidad de Buenos Aires, Moreno 350, 1002 Buenos Aires; tel. and fax (11) 4345-8196; f. 1982; research and lectures; Dir Prof. MARISA PINEAU; publs include *Temas de Africa y Asia* (2 a year).

AUSTRALIA

Australian Institute of International Affairs: 32 Thesiger Court, Deakin, ACT 2600; tel. (2) 6282-2133; fax (2) 6285-2334; e-mail ceo@aiia.asn.au; internet www.aiia.asn.au; f. 1933; 1,800 mems; brs in all States; Pres. JOHN MCCARTHY; Exec. Dir MELISSA H. CONLEY TYLER; publs include *Australian Journal of International Affairs* (5 a year).

Indian Ocean Research Group (IORG): POB 884, Cottesloe, WA 6011; e-mail rumley8@gmail.com; internet www.iorgroup.org; f. 2002; Chair. Prof. DENNIS RUMLEY; publ. *Journal of the Indian Ocean Region* (2 a year).

AUSTRIA

Afro-Asiatisches Institut in Wien (Afro-Asian Institute in Vienna): 1090 Vienna, Türkenstr. 3; tel. (1) 310-51-45-311; fax (1) 310-51-45-312; e-mail office@aai-wien.at; internet www.aai-wien.at; f. 1959; cultural and other exchanges between Austria and African and Asian countries; assistance to students from Africa and Asia; economic and social research; lectures, seminars; Rector Dr RAINER PORSTNER; Gen. Sec. GERHARD LANG.

Österreichische Forschungsstiftung für Internationale Entwicklungshilfe (ÖFSE) (Austrian Foundation for International Development Research): 1090 Vienna, Sensengasse 3; tel. (1) 317-40-10; fax (1) 317-40-15; e-mail office@oefse.at; internet www.oefse.at; f. 1967; documentation and information on devt aid and developing countries, particularly in relation to Austria; Chair. Dr ANDREAS NOVY; Man. Dir Dr WERNER RAZA; library of 45,000 vols and 130 periodicals; publs include *Ausgewählte neue Literatur zur Entwicklungspolitik* (2 a year), *Österreichische Entwicklungspolitik* (annually).

Österreichische Gesellschaft für Aussenpolitik und die Vereinten Nationen (ÖGAVN) (Foreign Policy and United Nations Association of Austria): 1010 Vienna, Hofburg/Stallburg, Reitschulgasse 2/2; tel. (1) 535-46-27; fax (1) 532-26-05; e-mail office@oegavn.org; internet www.oegavn.org; f. 1945; lectures, discussions; c. 600 mems; Pres. Dr WOLFGANG SCHÜSSEL; publ. *Österreichisches Jahrbuch für Internationale Politik* (annually).

BELGIUM

Académie Royale des Sciences d'Outre-Mer/Koninklijke Academie voor Overzeese Wetenschappen: ave Louise 231, 1050 Brussels; tel. (2) 538-02-11; fax (2) 539-23-53; e-mail kaowarsom@skynet.be; internet www.kaowarsom.be; f. 1928 as Institut Royal Colonial Belge; name changed as above in 1959; promotion of scientific knowledge of overseas areas, especially those with special devt problems; 127 mems, 61 assoc. mems, 100 correspondence mems; Pres. STANNY GEERTS; Perm. Sec. Prof. DANIELLE SWINNE; publ. *Bulletin des Séances* (4 a year).

Bibliothèque Africaine: 15 rue des Petites Carmes, 1000 Brussels; tel. (2) 501-80-98; fax (2) 501-37-36; e-mail biblio@diplobel.fed.be; internet www.diplomatie.be; f. 1885; library of 225,000 vols; large collections in the fields of African history, ethnography, economics, politics; Dir MICHEL ERKENS.

Centre International des Langues et des Traditions d'Afrique (CILTADE): ave des Clos 30, 1348 Louvain-la-Neuve; tel. (1) 045-06-65; fax (32) 45-56-85; e-mail nzuji@acla.ucl.ac.be; Sec.-Gen. Dr CLÉMENTINE MADIYA FAÏK-NZUJI.

Fondation pour Favoriser les Recherches Scientifiques en Afrique: 1 rue Defacqz, BP 5, 1050 Brussels; tel. (2) 269-39-05; f. 1969 to conduct scientific research in Africa with special reference to environmental management and conservation; Dir Dr A. G. ROBYNS; publs *Exploration des Parcs Nationaux, Etudes du Continent Africain*.

Institut d'Etudes du Développement: Université catholique de Louvain, Dépt des sciences de la population et du développement, 1 place Montesquieu, 1348 Louvain-La-Neuve; tel. (32) 47-40-41; fax (32) 47-29-52; e-mail vandenbossche@dvlp.ucl.ac.be; internet www.uclouvain.be; f. 1961; Pres. JEAN-MARIE WAUTELET.

Institut voor Ontwikkelingsbeleid en beheer—Institute of Development Policy and Management: University of Antwerp, Prinsstraat 13, B-2000 Antwerp; tel. (3) 265-57-70; fax (3) 265-57-71; e-mail iob@ua.ac.be; internet www.ua.ac.be/iob; f. 1965; conducts postgraduate study courses; library and documentation centre (50,000 vols); Chair. TOM DE HERDT; publs research reports and papers.

Institut Royal des Relations Internationales, EGMONT: rue de Namur 69, 1000 Brussels; tel. (2) 223-41-14; fax (2) 223-41-16; e-mail info@egmontinstitute.be; internet www.egmontinstitute.be; f. 1947; research in international relations, economics, law and politics; archives and library of 16,500 vols and 600 periodicals; Dir-Gen. MARC TRENTESEAU; publs include *Studia Diplomatica* (bimonthly).

Koninklijk Museum voor Midden-Afrika/Musée royal de l'Afrique centrale: Leuvensesteenweg 13, 3080 Tervuren; tel. (2) 769-52-11; fax (2) 769-52-42; e-mail info@africamuseum.be; internet www.africamuseum.be; f. 1897; collections of prehistory, ethnography, nature arts and crafts; geology, mineralogy, palaeontology; zoology (entomology, ornithology, mammals, reptiles, etc.); history; economics; library of 90,000 vols and 4,500 periodicals; Dir GUIDO GRYSEELS; publs include *Annales du Musée Royal de l'Afrique Centrale*.

Société Belge d'Etudes Géographiques (Belgian Society for Geographical Studies): de Croylaan 42, 3001 Heverlee (Leuven); tel. (16) 32-24-45; fax (16) 32-29-80; f. 1931; centralizes and coordinates geographical research in Belgium; 395 mems; Pres. JACQUES CHARLIER; Sec. H. VAN DER HAEGEN; publ. *Bulletin* (2 a year).

BRAZIL

Centro de Estudos Africanos (African Studies Centre): University of São Paulo, Av. Prof. Luciano Gualberto 315, sala 1087, 05508-900 São Paulo, SP; tel. (11) 3091-3744; fax (11) 3032-9416; e-mail cea@usp.br; internet www.fflch.usp.br/cea; f. 1969; co-ordinating unit for all depts with African interests; specialist studies in sociology, international relations and literature concerning Africa; library; Dirs Prof. KABENGELE MUNANGA, Prof. CARLOS SERRANO; publ. *Africa* (annually).

Centro de Estudos Afro-Asiáticos (CEAA) (Afro-Asian Studies Centre): Praça Pio X 7, 9°, 20040-020, Rio de Janeiro, RJ; tel. (21) 2233-9294; fax (21) 2518-2798; e-mail ceaa@candidomendes.edu.br; internet www.candidomendes.br/ceaa; f. 1973; instruction and seminars; library; Dir Prof. Dr BELUCE BELLUCCI; publ. *Estudos Afro-Asiáticos*.

Centro de Estudos Afro-Orientais (CEAO) (Afro-Oriental Studies Centre): Praça Inocêncio Galvão, 42, Largo Dois de Julho, 40060-055 Salvador-BA; tel. (71) 3322-6742; fax (71) 3322-8070; e-mail ceao@ufba.br; internet www.ceao.ufba.br; f. 1959; African and Afro-Oriental Studies; library; Dir Prof. PAULA CRISTINA DA SILVA BARRETO; publ. *Afro-Ásia* (irregular).

Núcleo de Estudos Afro-Asiáticos (Afro-Asian Studies Unit): State University of Londrina, CP 6001, CEP 86051-990 Londrina, PR; tel. (43) 3371-4599; fax (43) 3371-4679; e-mail neaa@uel.br; internet www2.uel.br/neaa; f. 1985; seminars and lectures; Dir Prof. ELENA MARIA ANDREI; publ. *Africa Asia* (annually).

CANADA

Canadian Association of African Studies (CAAS): 4–17E Old Arts Bldg, University of Alberta, Edmonton, AB T6G 2E6; fax (780) 492-9125; e-mail caas@ualberta.ca; internet www.arts.ualberta.ca/~caas; f. 1970; Pres. JOSÉ C. CURTO; publs *CAAS Journal* (English and French—3 a year), *CAAS Newsletter* (online; English and French—irregular).

Canadian Council for International Co-operation: 450 Rideau St, Suite 200, Ottawa, ON K1N 5Z4; tel. (613) 241-7007; fax (613) 241-5302; e-mail info@ccic.ca; internet www.ccic.ca; f. 1968; information and training centre for international devt and forum for voluntary agencies; 100 mems; Chair. JIM CORNELIUS; CEO JULIA SÁNCHEZ; publs include *Au Courant* (2 a year).

Canadian International Council: 45 Willcocks St, Box 210, Toronto, ON M5S 1C7; tel. (416) 946-7209; fax (416) 946-7319; e-mail info@opencanada.org; internet www.onlinecic.org; f. 1928; research in international relations; library of 8,000 vols; Chair. JIM BALSILLIE; Pres. Dr JENNIFER A. JEFFS; publs include *International Journal* (quarterly).

Centre for African Studies: Dalhousie University, Dept of International Development Studies, Henry Hicks Administration Bldg,

Halifax, NS B3H 4H6; tel. (902) 494-3814; fax (902) 494-2105; e-mail ulickit@dal.ca; f. 1975; Dir Prof. THERESA ULICKI; publs include *Dalhousie African Studies* series, *Dalhousie African Working Papers* series, *Briefing Papers on the African Crisis*.

The Harriet Tubman Institute For Research On The Global Migrations Of African Peoples: 321 York Lanes, York University 4700 Keele St., Toronto, ON M3J 1P3; tel. (416) 736-2100; fax (416)-650-8173; e-mail tubman@yorku.ca; internet diaspora.homelinux .net; f. 2007; studies the global diaspora of Africans and their descendants; Dir PAUL E. LOVEJOY.

Institute for the Study of International Development (ISID): Room 126, Peterson Hall, 3460 McTavish St, Montréal, QC H3A 1X9; tel. (514) 398-3507; fax (514) 398-8432; e-mail info.isid@mcgill.ca; internet www.mcgill.ca/isid; Found. Dir Prof. PHILIP OXHORN; Exec. Dir ROBIN MCLAY; publs include *Labour, Capital and Society* (English and French—2 a year), discussion papers.

International Development Research Centre: POB 8500, Ottawa, ON K1G 3H9; tel. (613) 236-6163; fax (613) 238-7230; e-mail info@idrc.ca; internet www.idrc.ca; f. 1970 by the Govt with the mission to support research in developing countries to promote growth and development; regional offices in Kenya, Senegal, Egypt, Singapore, Uruguay and India; Pres. DAVID M. MALONE; publs include *IDRC Bulletin* (English and French—monthly).

PEOPLE'S REPUBLIC OF CHINA

Centre for International Studies: 22 Xianmen Dajie, POB 7411, Beijing; tel. (10) 63097083; fax (10) 63095802; f. 1982; conducts research on international relations and problems; organizes academic exchanges; Dir-Gen. ZHANG YIJUN.

China Institute of Contemporary International Relations: 2A Wanshousi, Haidian, Beijing 100081; tel. (10) 8418640; fax (10) 8418641; e-mail contact@cicir.ac.cn; internet www.cicir.ac.cn; f. 1980; research on international devt and peace issues; Pres. CUI LIRU; publ. *Contemporary International Relations* (monthly).

Institute of West Asian and African Studies: Chinese Academy of Social Sciences, 3 Zhangzhizhong Rd, Beijing 100007; tel. (10) 64039165; fax (10) 64035718; e-mail iwaas@public.fhnet.cn.net; internet iwaas.cass.cn; f. 1961; 40 full-time research fellows; library of 40,000 vols; Dir-Gen. YANG GUANG; publ. *West Asia and Africa* (Chinese, with summary in English—6 a year).

CZECH REPUBLIC

Ústav mezinárodních vztahů (Institute of International Relations): Nerudova 3, 118 50 Prague 1; tel. 251108111; fax 251108222; e-mail iir@iir.cz; internet www.iir.cz; f. 1957; Dir Dr Ing. PETR DRULÁK; publs include *Mezinárodní politika / International Politics* (in Czech—monthly), *Mezinárodní vztahy / International Relations* (in Czech—quarterly), *Perspectives—The Central European Review of International Affairs* (in English—2 a year).

DENMARK

Danish Institute for International Studies: Strandgade 56, 1401 Copenhagen K; tel. 32-69-87-87; fax 45 32-69-87-00; e-mail diis@diis.dk; internet www.diis.dk; f. 2003; independent research institution engaged in research in international affairs; Chair. of Board Prof. LAURIDS S. LAURIDSEN; Dir NANNA HVIDT; publs include *Den Ny Verden* (quarterly).

FINLAND

Aasian ja Afrikan kielten ja kulttuurien laitos (Institute for Asian and African Studies): Faculty of Arts, University of Helsinki, Unioninkatu 38A, POB 59, 00014 University of Helsinki; tel. (9) 19122224; fax (9) 19122094; e-mail maria.colliander@helsinki.fi; internet www.helsinki.fi/hum/aakkl; f. 1974; fmrly Unit for East Asian Languages and Altaic Studies; Institute Head LARS-FOLKE LANDGRÉN.

FRANCE

Académie des Sciences d'Outre-mer: 15 rue La Pérouse, 75116 Paris; tel. 1-47-20-87-93; fax 1-47-20-89-72; e-mail bibliotheque@ academiedoutremer.fr; internet www.academiedoutremer.fr; f. 1922; 275 mems, of which 200 mems are attached to sections on geography, politics and administration, law, economics and sociology, science and medicine, education; library of 70,000 vols and 2,500 periodicals; Pres. DENIS SADDA; Perm. Sec. PIERRE GÉNY; publs include *Mondes et Cultures* (quarterly).

Les Afriques dans le Monde (LAM): 11 allée Ausone, Domaine universitaire, 33607 Pessac; tel. 5-56-84-42-82; fax 5-56-84-43-24; e-mail infolam@sciencespobordeaux.fr; internet www.cean .sciencespobordeaux.fr; f. 2011; formed through merger of the Centre d'Etude d'Afrique Noire (CEAN) and the Centre d'Etudes et de Recherches sur les Pays d'Afrique Orientale (CREPAO); Dir RENÉ OTAYEK.

Centre d'Etudes Juridiques et Politiques du Monde Africain (CEJPMA): Université de Paris I, 9 rue Malher, 75181 Paris Cedex 04; tel. 1-44-78-33-25; fax 1-44-78-33-39; e-mail politique.africaine@ univ-paris1.fr; internet mald.univ-paris1.fr/centres/cejpma.htm; Dir RICHARD BANÉGAS.

Centre d'Etudes des Mondes Africains (CEMAf): Centre Malher, 9 rue Malher, 75181 Paris Cedex 04; tel. 1-44-78-33-34; e-mail daronian@univ-paris1.fr; internet www.cemaf.cnrs.fr; f. 1962; Man. ANGÉLIQUE MALEC.

Centre d'Etudes et de Recherches sur le Développement International (CERDI): Université d'Auvergne, 65 blvd François Mitterrand, BP 320, 63009 Clermont-Ferrand Cedex 1; tel. 4-73-17-74-00; fax 4-73-17-74-28; e-mail cerdi@u-clermont1.fr; internet www .cerdi.org; f. 1976; Dir PATRICK PLANE.

Centre de Recherches Africaines (CRA): 9 rue Malher, 75181 Paris Cedex 04; tel. 1-44-78-33-40; fax 1-44-78-33-33; e-mail cra@ univ-paris1.fr; an institute of the University of Paris I; Dir PIERRE BOILLEY.

Institut Français des Relations Internationales (Ifri): 27 rue de la Procession, 75740 Paris Cedex 15; tel. 1-40-61-60-00; fax 1-40-61-60-60; e-mail ifri@ifri.org; internet www.ifri.org; f. 1979; international politics and economy, security issues, regional studies; library of 32,000 vols and 250 periodicals; Pres. ANDRÉ LÉVY-LANG; Dir-Gen. Prof. THIERRY DE MONTBRIAL; publs *Politique Etrangère* (quarterly), *Ramses* (annually), *Notes de l'Ifri*, *Cahiers et Conférences de l'Ifri*, *Travaux et Recherches de l'Ifri*, *Publications du CFE à l'Ifri*, *Cahiers du Centre Asie Ifri*.

Institut de Recherche pour le Développement (IRD): Le Sextant, 44 blvd de Dunkerque, CS 90009, 13002 Marseille Cedex 02; tel. 4-91-99-92-00; fax 4-91-99-92-22; e-mail dic@paris.ird.fr; internet www.ird.fr; f. 1943, reorg. 1982 and 1998; self-financing; centres, missions and rep. offices in Benin, Bolivia, Brazil, Burkina Faso, Cameroon, Côte d'Ivoire, Chile, Ecuador, Egypt, French Guiana, Guinea, Indonesia, Kenya, Madagascar, Mali, Mexico, New Caledonia, Niger, Peru, Senegal, South Africa, Thailand, Tunisia and Viet Nam; Pres. MICHEL LAURENT.

Musée de l'Homme: Palais de Chaillot, 17 place du Trocadéro, 75116 Paris; tel. 1-44-05-72-72; e-mail liongau@mnhn.fr; internet www.mnhn.fr; f. 1878; library of 250,000 vols (c. 30,000 on Africa), 5,000 periodicals and c. 300,000 photographic images; ethnography, physical anthropology, prehistory; also a research and education centre; Dirs Profs ZEEV GOURARIER (Musée de l'Homme), FRANÇOIS SÉMAH (Prehistory), SERGE BAHUCHET (Mankind and Society).

Société des Africanistes (CSSF): Musée du quai Branly, 222, rue de l'Université, 75007 Paris; tel. 1-56-61-71-17; e-mail africanistes@ yahoo.fr; internet www.mae.u-paris10.fr/africanistes/index; f. 1930; 350 mems; Pres. ELISÉE COULIBALY; publ. *Journal des Africanistes* (2 a year).

Société Française d'Historie d'Outre-mer: 15 rue Catulienne, 93200 Saint-Denis; fax 1-45-82-62-99; e-mail sfhom4@yahoo.fr; internet sfhom.free.fr; f. 1913; 500 mems; Pres. HÉLÈNE D'ALMEIDA-TOPOR; Sec.-Gen. JOSETTE RIVALLAIN; publ. *Revue Française d'Histoire d'Outre-mer* (2 a year).

GERMANY

Deutsche Gesellschaft für Auswärtige Politik eV (German Council on Foreign Relations): Rauchstr. 17/18, 10787 Berlin; tel. (30) 2542310; fax (30) 25423116; e-mail info@dgap.org; internet www .dgap.org; f. 1955; promotes research on problems of international politics; library of 79,500 vols; 2,300 mems; Pres. Dr AREND OETKER; Exec. Vice-Pres. FRITJOF VON NORDENSKJÖLD; Dir Research Inst. Prof. Dr EBERHARD SANDSCHNEIDER; publs *Internationale Politik* (monthly), *Internationale Politik: Transatlantic Edition* (quarterly), *Die Internationale Politik* (annually).

GIGA Institute of African Affairs: Neuer Jungfernstieg 21, 20354 Hamburg; tel. (40) 42825523; fax (40) 42825511; e-mail iaa@ giga-hamburg.de; internet www.giga-hamburg.de/iaa; f. 1963; research, transfer of knowledge, library; library of 52,000 vols and 250 periodicals; Dir Dr ANDREAS MEHLER; publs include *Africa Spectrum*, *GIGA Focus Afrika*, *GIGA Working Paper Series*.

IFO—Institut für Wirtschaftsforschung (Institute for Economic Research): Poschingerstr. 5, 81679 Munich; tel. (89) 92240; fax (89) 985369; internet www.cesifo-group.de; f. 1949; library of 80,000 vols; Pres. Prof. Dr HANS-WERNER SINN.

Informationsstelle Südliches Afrika eV (Information Centre on Southern Africa): Königswintererstr. 116, 53227 Bonn; tel. (228) 464369; fax (228) 468177; e-mail issa@comlink.org; internet www .issa-bonn.org; f. 1971; research, documentation, and information on southern Africa; Editor (Afrika Süd) HEIN MÖLLERS; publs include *Afrika Süd* (6 a year).

Institut für Afrikanistik: Leipzig University, Beethovenstr. 15, 04107 Leipzig; tel. (341) 9737030; fax (341) 9737048; e-mail mgrosze@rz.uni-leipzig.de; internet www.uni-leipzig.de/~afrika; Man. Dir Prof. Dr HELMUT ASCHE.

HUNGARY

Magyar Tudományos Akadémia Világgazdasági Kutató Intézete (Institute for World Economics of the Hungarian Academy of Sciences): 1014 Budapest, Országház u. 30; tel. (1) 224-6700; fax (1) 224-6765; e-mail vki@vki.hu; internet www.vki.hu; f. 1965; library of 103,000 vols; Dir INOTAI ANDRÁS.

INDIA

Centre for African Studies: University of Mumbai, Vidyanagari Kalina Campus, Santacruz (East), Mumbai 400 098; tel. (22) 26526091, ext. 329; fax (22) 26526893; internet www.mu.ac.in; f. 1971; Dir Dr APARAJITA BISWAS; publ. *African Currents* (2 a year).

Centre for African Studies: Jawaharlal Nehru University, New Delhi 110 067; tel. (11) 26738718; fax (11) 26704607; e-mail akdubey@mail.jnu.ac.in; internet www.jnu.ac.in; f. 1969; interdisciplinary centre for study of Africa; Dir Prof. AJAY KUMAR DUBEY.

African Studies Association of India (ASA): Centre for African Studies, School of International Studies, Jawaharlal Nehru University, New Mehrauli Rd, New Delhi 110 067; tel. and fax (11) 26704607; fax 26741551; e-mail office@africanstudies.in; internet www.africanstudies.in; f. 2003 to foster and promote the study, knowledge and understanding of African affairs in India and Indian affairs in Africa through research and studies; Pres. APARAJITA BISWAS; Chair. SHASHANK; Gen. Sec. Prof. AJAY DUBEY; publs incl. *Africa Review* and *Insight on Africa*.

Centre for Development Studies: Prasanth Nagar Rd, Ulloor, Thiruvananthapuram 695 011; tel. (471) 2448881; fax (471) 2447137; e-mail somannair@cds.ac.in; internet www.cds.edu; f. 1971; instruction and research in disciplines relevant to economic devt; library of 125,000 vols; Dir Dr K. NARAYANAN NAIR.

Centre for West Asian and African Studies: School of International Studies, Jawaharlal Nehru University, New Mehrauli Rd, New Delhi 110 067; tel. (11) 26742676; fax (11) 26742580; Chair. Dr AJAY K. DUBEY.

Department of African Studies: Faculty of Social Sciences, University of Delhi, Delhi 110 007; tel. and fax (11) 27666673; e-mail depttafrica@yahoo.com; f. 1955; Head of Dept Dr SURESH KUMAR; publs include *Indian Journal of African Studies, Documentation on Africa*.

Indian Council for Cultural Relations: Azad Bhavan, Indraprastha Estate, New Delhi 110 002; tel. (11) 23370229; fax (11) 23378639; e-mail iccr@vsnl.com; internet www.iccrindia.net; f. 1950; Pres. KARAN SINGH; Dir-Gen. VIRENDRA GUPTA; publ. *Africa Quarterly*.

Indian Council of World Affairs: Sapru House, Barakhamba Rd, New Delhi 110 001; tel. (11) 23317246; fax (11) 23310638; e-mail dg@icwa.in; internet www.icwa.in; f. 1943; independent institution for the study of Indian and international issues; library of 125,000 books, 384 periodicals, 700,000 press clippings, also UN documents and microfiches; 2,480 mems; Pres. M. H. ANSARI; Dir-Gen. SUDHIR T. DEVARE; publs include *India Quarterly*.

Indian Society for Afro-Asian Studies: 297 Saraswati Kunj, Indraprastha Ext., Mother Dairy Rd, New Delhi 110 092; tel. (11) 22722801; fax (11) 22725024; e-mail isaas@vsnl.com; f. 1980; conducts research and holds seminars and confs; Pres. LALIT BHASIN; Gen. Sec. Dr DHARAMPAL; publs include *Indian Review of African Affairs* (6 a year).

IRAN

Institute for Political and International Studies: Shaheed Bahonar Ave, Shaheed Aghaii Ave, POB 19395-1793, Tajrish, Tehran; tel. (21) 22802641; fax (21) 22802649; e-mail mousavi@ipis.ir; internet www.ipis.ir; f. 1983; research and information on international relations, foreign policy, economics, culture and law; library of 22,000 vols; Dir-Gen. Dr MOSTAFA DOLATYAR; publs include *Iranian Journal of International Affairs* (quarterly).

ISRAEL

Harry S. Truman Research Institute for the Advancement of Peace: The Hebrew University of Jerusalem, Mt Scopus, Jerusalem 91905; tel. 25882300; fax 25828076; e-mail truman@savion.huji.ac.il; internet truman.huji.ac.il; f. 1965; conducts a broad range of research relating to the advancement of peace in the Middle East and the non-Western world, including Africa, Asia and Latin America; Chair. WILLIAM A. BROWN; Academic. Dir STEVEN KAPLAN.

Institute of Asian and African Studies: Hebrew University, Mount Scopus, Jerusalem 91905; tel. (2) 5883516; fax (2) 5883658; internet asiafrica.huji.ac.il; f. 1926 as the Institute of Oriental Studies; incorporates Max Schloessinger Memorial Foundation; studies of medieval and modern languages, culture and history of Middle East, Asia and Africa; Dir Prof. MEIR M. BAR-ASHER; Sec. YEHUDIT MAGEN; publs incl. Max Schloessinger Memorial Series, Collected Studies in Arabic and Islam Series, Jerusalem Studies in Arabic and Islam , translation series and studies in classical Islam and Arabic language and literature, Hebrew University Armenian Series.

International Institute—Histadrut: Bet Berl 44905, Kfar Saba; tel. 97612323; fax 97456962; e-mail info@peoples.org.il; internet www.peoples.org.il; f. 1958 to train leadership for trade unions, co-operatives, community orgs, women's and youth groups, etc. in developing countries; library of 35,000 vols; Dir-Gen. MOLY OREN; Dep. Dir-Gen. MICHAEL FROHLICH.

Moshe Dayan Center for Middle Eastern and African Studies, Shiloah Institute: Tel Aviv University, Ramat-Aviv, Tel-Aviv 69978; tel. 36409646; fax 36415802; e-mail dayancen@post.tau.ac.il; internet www.dayan.org; f. 1959; Dir Prof. EYAL ZISSER; publs include *Current Contents of Periodicals on the Middle East* (6 a year), *Middle East Contemporary Survey* (annually), *The Moshe Dayan Center Bulletin* (2 a year).

ITALY

The Bologna Center, Paul H. Nitze School of Advanced International Studies, The Johns Hopkins University: Via Belmeloro 11, 40126 Bologna; tel. (051) 2917811; fax (051) 228505; e-mail registrar@jhubc.it; internet www.jhubc.it; f. 1955; graduate studies in international affairs; Dir KENNETH H. KELLER; publs include occasional papers series.

Istituto Italiano per l'Africa e l'Oriente (IsIAO): Via Ulisse Aldrovandi 16, 00197 Rome; tel. (06) 328551; fax (06) 3225348; e-mail info@isiao.it; internet www.isiao.it; f. 1906; Chair. Prof. GHERARDO GNOLI; Dir-Gen. GIANCARLO GARGARUTI; publ. *Africa* (quarterly).

Istituto per gli Studi di Politica Internazionale (ISPI): Palazzo Clerici, Via Clerici 5, 20121 Milan; tel. (02) 8633131; fax (02) 8692055; internet www.ispionline.it; f. 1934 for the promotion of the study of international relations; conducts research, documentation and training; Pres. BORIS BIANCHERI; CEO Dr GIOVANNI ROGGERO FOSSATI; publs include *Relazioni Internazionali* (6 a year).

JAPAN

Ajia Keizai Kenkyusho (IDE—JETRO) (Institute of Developing Economies, Japan External Trade Organization): 3-2-2, Wakaba, Mihama-ku, Chiba-shi, Chiba 261-8545; tel. (4) 3299-9536; fax (4) 3299-9726; e-mail info@ide.go.jp; internet www.ide.go.jp; f. 1960; library of 557,000 vols; Chair. OSAMU WATANABE; Pres. TAKASHI SHIRAISHI; publs *Ajia Keizai* (Japanese, monthly), *The Developing Economies* (English, quarterly), *Africa Report* (Japanese, biannually).

Nihon Afurika Gakkai (Japan Association for African Studies): c/o Dogura and Co Ltd, 1-8, Nishihanaikecho, Koyama, Kita-ku, Kyoto 603-8148; tel. (75) 451-4844; fax (75) 441-0436; e-mail AEI04761@nifty.com; internet wwwsoc.nii.ac.jp/africa; f. 1964; promotes multidisciplinary African studies; Pres. MITSUO ICHIKAWA; publs *Afurika Kenkyu / Journal of African Studies* (2 a year), *Kaiho* (annually).

Nihon Kokusai Mondai Kenkyusho (Japan Institute of International Affairs): 11th Floor, Kasumigaseki Bldg, 3-2-5, Kasumigaseki, Chiyoda-ku, Tokyo 100-6011; tel. (3) 3503-7261; fax (3) 3503-7292; e-mail jiiajoho@jiia.or.jp; internet www.jiia.or.jp; f. 1959; Pres. YOSHIJI NOGAMI; Exec. Dir HUZIWARA MINORU; publs include *Kokusai Mondai* (International Affairs, monthly), *Japan Review of International Affairs* (quarterly).

Research Institute for the Study of Languages and Cultures of Asia and Africa: Tokyo University of Foreign Studies, 3-11-1, Asahi-cho, Fuchu, Tokyo 183-8534; tel. (42) 330-5601; fax (42) 330-5610; e-mail editcom@aa.tufs.ac.jp; internet www.aa.tufs.ac.jp; f. 1964; library of c. 91,000 vols; Dir Prof. HIROHIDE KURIHARA; publs *Newsletter* (3 a year), *Journal of Asian and African Studies* (2 a year).

MAURITANIA

Strategic Centre for the Security of the Sahel-Sahara: Nouakchott; e-mail contact@centre4s.org; internet www.centre4s.org; Founder AHMEDOU OULD ABDALLAH.

MEXICO

Asociación Latinoamericana de Estudios de Asia y Africa (Latin American Asscn for Asian and African Studies): El Colegio de México, Camino al Ajusco 20, Pedregal de Santa Teresa, CP 10740, Magdalena Contreras, México DF; tel. (55) 5449-3021; fax (55) 5645-4584; e-mail aalada@colmex.mx; internet ceaa.colmex.mx/aladaa; f. 1976; promotes African and Asian studies in Latin America; 450

mems; Sec.-Gen. Prof. LUIS MESA DELMONTE; publs newsletters and proceedings.

Centro de Estudios de Asia y Africa (CEAA) (Centre for Asian and African Studies): El Colegio de México, Camino al Ajusco 20, Pedregal de Santa Teresa, CP 10740, Magdalena Contreras México DF; tel. (55) 5449-3025; fax (55) 5645-0464; e-mail ceaa@colmex.mx; internet ceaa.colmex.mx; f. 1964; postgraduate studies and research; library; Dir Prof. BENJAMÍN PRECIADO SOLÍS; publs include *Estudios de Asia y Africa* (quarterly).

THE NETHERLANDS

Afrika-Studiecentrum (African Studies Centre): Wassenaarseweg 52, 2333 AK, Leiden ; POB 9555, 2300 RB, Leiden; tel. (71) 5273372; fax (71) 5273344; e-mail asc@ascleiden.nl; internet www.ascleiden.nl; f. 1948 to carry out research on sub-Saharan Africa in the social sciences, and to disseminate information on African affairs; library of 55,000 vols and 450 periodicals; Chair. E. M. A. SCHMITZ; Dir Prof. Dr A. J. DIETZ; publs include *African Dynamics* (2 a year), *Afrika-Studiecentrum Series* (2–3 titles a year) and *African Studies Abstracts Online* (quarterly).

Institute of Social Studies (ISS): Kortenaerkade 12, 2518 AX, The Hague; POB 29776, 2502 LT, The Hague; tel. (70) 4260460; fax (70) 4260799; e-mail information@iss.nl; internet www.iss.nl; f. 1952; postgraduate instruction, research and consultancy in devt studies; Pres. Prof. Dr J. A. VAN GINKEL; Rector Prof. L. DE LA RIVE BOX; publs *Development and Change* (quarterly), *Development Issues*, working papers.

Netherlands-African Business Council: Prinses Beatrixlaan 614, 2595 BM, The Hague; tel. (70) 3043618; fax (70) 3043620; e-mail info@nabc.nl; internet www.nabc.nl; f. 1946; trade and investment promotion for sub-Saharan Africa; Chair. KEES VAN HEIJST; Man. Dir BOB VAN DER BIJL.

Netherlands Institute for Southern Africa (NiZA): Prins Hendrikkade 33, POB 10707, 1001 ES, Amsterdam; tel. (20) 5206210; fax (20) 5206249; e-mail niza@niza.nl; internet www.niza.nl; f. 1997; promotes democracy in southern Africa; publs *Zuidelijk Afrika*, *NiZA Informatie* (quarterly), *Niza Cahiers* and reports of seminars and conferences.

NIGERIA

Institute of African Studies: University of Ibadan, Ibadan; tel. (2) 8101100; e-mail dvcadmin@mail.ui.edu.ng; internet www.ui.edu.ng; Dir Prof. M. OMIBIYI-OBIDIKE.

NORWAY

Norsk Utenrikspolitisk Institutt (Norwegian Institute of International Affairs): C. J. Hambros plass 2D, POB 8159 Dep, 0033 Oslo; tel. 22994000; fax 22362182; e-mail info@nupi.no; internet www.nupi.no; f. 1959; information and research in international relations; Pres. KJETIL STULAND; Dir JAN EGELAND; publs include *Hvor Hender Det* (weekly), *Internasjonal Politikk* (quarterly), *Nordisk Østforum* (quarterly), *Forum for Development Studies* (2 a year), *NUPI Notat* and *NUPI Rapport* (research reports).

PAKISTAN

Pakistan Institute of International Affairs: Aiwan-e-Sadar Rd, POB 1447, Karachi 74200; tel. (21) 5682891; fax (21) 5686069; internet www.piia.org.pk; e-mail info@piia.org.pk; f. 1947 to study international affairs and to promote the study of international politics, economics and law; over 600 mems; library of c. 28,000 vols; Chair. Dr MASUMA HASAN; Hon. Sec. SYED ABDUL MINAM JAFRI; publs include *Pakistan Horizon* (quarterly).

POLAND

Departament Studiów i Planowania (MSZ) (Dept of Studies and Planning, Ministry of Foreign Affairs): 00-950 Warsaw, ul. Warecka 1A; tel. (22) 8263021; fax (22) 8263026; f. 1947; library of 125,000 vols; Dir Dr HENRYK SZLAJFER; publs include *Sprawy Międzynarodowe* (quarterly, in Polish and English), *Zbiór Dokumentów* (quarterly, in Polish, French, English and German), occasional papers (in English).

Institute of Oriental Studies, Department of African Languages and Cultures, University of Warsaw: 00-927 Warsaw, Krakowskie Przedmieście 26/28; tel. (22) 5520517; fax (22) 8263683; e-mail afrykanistyka.orient@uw.edu.pl; internet www.orient.uw.edu.pl/en/afrykanistyka; f. 1950; postgraduate studies and research in linguistics, literature, history, sociology and ethnology; Head of Dept Prof. Dr NINA PAWLAK; publ. *Studies of the Department of African Languages and Cultures*.

Instytut Studiów Regionalnych i Globalnych (Institute of Regional and Global Studies): 00-324 Warsaw, Karowa 20; tel. and fax (22) 5523237; e-mail ikr@uw.edu.pl; internet isrig.wgsr.uw.edu.pl; undergraduate and postgraduate studies; interdisciplinary research on developing countries; Dir Prof. Dr MIROSŁAWA CZERNY; publs include *Africana Bulletin* (annually, in French and English), *Afryka, Azja, Ameryka Łacińska* (annually, with summaries in English).

PORTUGAL

Centro de Estudos Africanos (African Studies Centre): Faculty of Letters, University of Lisbon, Cidade Universitária, 1600-214 Lisbon; tel. (21) 7920000; fax (21) 7960063; e-mail ceafrica@fl.ul.pt; internet www.fl.ul.pt/unidades/centros/ceafrica; literary studies and documentation centre; Dir Prof. ISABEL CASTRO HENRIQUES.

Centro de Estudos Africanos (African Studies Centre): Instituto Superior de Ciências do Trabalho e da Empresa (ISCTE), Av. das Forças Armadas, 1649-026 Lisbon; tel. (21) 7903067; fax (21) 7955361; e-mail cea@iscte.pt; internet cea.iscte.pt; f. 1990; research and postgraduate courses in African Studies; Pres. JOSÉ MANUEL ROLO CORREIA; Dir Prof. CLARA CARVALHO; publ. *Cadernos de Estudos Africanos*.

Centro de Estudos Africanos da Universidade do Porto (CEAUP) (African Studies Centre of the University of Porto): University of Porto, Via Panorâmica s/n, 4150-564 Porto; tel. and fax (22) 6077141; e-mail ceaup@letras.up.pt; internet www.africanos.eu; f. 1997; research and postgraduate courses in African Studies; Pres. Prof. MANUEL LARANJEIRA RODRIGUES DE AREIA; Dir ISABEL GALHANO RODRIGUES; publ. *Africana Studia*.

Centro de Estudos Sobre África e do Desenvolvimento (Centre of African and Development Studies): Instituto Superior de Economia e Gestão, Rua Miguel Lupi 20, 1249-078 Lisbon; tel. (21) 3925983; fax (21) 3976271; e-mail cesa@iseg.ult.pt; internet pascal.iseg.utl.pt/~cesa; f. 1982; conducts research and holds seminars; Pres. Prof. Dr JOCHEN OPPENHEIMER; Dir JOANA HELENA MARIA FAJARDO PACHECO PEREIRA LEITE; publs occasional papers.

Centro de Intervenção para o Desenvolvimento Amílcar Cabral (CIDAC) (Amílcar Cabral Information and Documentation Centre): Rua Pinheiro Chagas, 77-2° esq., 1069-069 Lisbon; tel. (21) 3172860; fax (21) 3172870; internet www.cidac.pt; Pres. ANA SOARES BARBOSA BÉNARD DA COSTA.

Instituto de Estudos Estratégicos e Internacionais (IEEI): Largo de S Sebastião, 8 Paço do Lumiar, 1600-762 Lisbon; tel. (21) 0306700; fax (21) 7593983; e-mail ieei@ieei.pt; internet www.ieei.pt; f. 1980; Pres. ALVARO VASCONCELOS; Dir LUÍS PAIS ANTUNES; publs include *Estratégia, Lumiar Briefs*.

Instituto de Investigação Científica Tropical (IICT) (Institute for Tropical Scientific Research): Rua da Junqueira 86, 1300-344 Lisbon; tel. (21) 3616340; fax (21) 3631460; e-mail iict@iict.pt; internet www2.iict.pt; f. 1883; comprises departments of social sciences and natural sciences, colonial archives and a documentation centre, dealing mainly with lusophone African countries; Pres. JORGE BRAGA DE MACEDO; publs include monographs, serials and maps.

RUSSIA

Institute for African Studies: 123001 Moscow, 30/1 Spiridonovka; tel. (495) 690-63-85; fax (495) 697-19-54; e-mail info@inafr.ru; internet www.inafran.ru; Dir ALEKSEI M. VASSILIEV; publ. *Vostok (Oriens—6 a year)*.

Institute of Asian and African Studies: ul. Mokhovaya 11, 125009 Moscow; tel. (495) 629-43-49; fax (495) 629-74-91; e-mail office@iaas.msu.ru; internet www.iaas.msu.ru; f. 1956 as Institute for Oriental Languages, renamed as above 1972; comprises three sections: philology, history, and social and economic studies, and research centres incl. Centre for Arabic and Islamic Studies and Centre of Judaica; 250 mems; Pres. Prof. MIKHAIL S. MEYER.

Institute of World Economy and International Relations Russian Academy of Sciences (IMEMO RAN): 117997 Moscow, ul. Profsoyuznaya 23; tel. (499) 120-43-32; fax (499) 120-65-75; e-mail imemoran@imemo.ru; internet www.imemo.ru; f. 1956; Dir ALEXANDER DYNKIN; publs include *Mirovaya Economika I Mezhdunarodnye Otnosheniya* (monthly).

Moscow State Institute of International Relations (MGIMO): 117454 Moscow, Vernadskogo pr. 76; tel. (495) 434-91-58; fax (495) 434-90-66; internet www.mgimo.ru; f. 1944; library of 718,000 vols; Rector ANATOLII V. TURKUNOV; publ. *Moscow Journal of International Law*.

Moscow State University Institute of Asian and African Studies: 125009 Moscow, Mokhovaja 11; tel. (095) 629-43-49; fax (095) 629-74-91; e-mail office@iaas.msu.ru; internet www.iaas.msu.ru; f. 1956; Pres. M. S. MEYER.

SAUDI ARABIA

King Faisal Centre for Research and Islamic Studies: POB 5149, Riyadh 11543; tel. (1) 4652255; fax (1) 4659993; e-mail info@kfcris.com; internet www.kfcris.com; f. 1983; advances research and studies into Islamic civilization; provides grants for research and organizes symposia, lectures and confs on Islamic matters; library of over 30,000 vols and periodicals; Chair. TURKI AL-FAISAL; Dir-Gen. Dr ZEID AL-HUSAIN; publ. *Newsletter* and *Islamic Civilization Magazine* (quarterly, electronic).

SENEGAL

Council for the Development of Social Science Research in Africa (CODESRIA): ave Cheikh Anta Diop, angle Canal IV, BP 3304, Dakar; tel. 33-825-98-22; fax 33-824-12-89; e-mail codesria@codesria.sn; internet www.codesria.org; f. 1973; pan-African org., focusing on the social sciences; Pres. SAM MOYO; Exec. Sec. Dr EBRIMA SALL; publs include *Africa Development* (quarterly), *African Sociological Review* (biannually), *African Journal of International Affairs* (biannually), *CODESRIA Bulletin* (quarterly), *Journal of Higher Education in Africa* (biannually), *Africa Media Review* (quarterly), *Africa Review of Books* (biannually), *The African Anthropologist* (biannually), *Afrika Zamani* (biannually) and *Identity, Culture and Politics: An Afro-Asian Dialogue* (biannually).

Institut Africain de la Gouvernance: Sotrac Mermoz Sipres 32, Dakar; tel. 30-102-94-88; fax 33-824-67-06; internet www.iag-agi.org; f. 2003; Pres. OUSMANE SY.

SOUTH AFRICA

Africa Institute of South Africa: 1 Embassy House, cnr Bailey Lane and Edmond St, Arcadia, Pretoria; tel. (12) 3049700; fax (12) 3213164; e-mail humbulani@ai.org.za; internet www.ai.org.za; f. 1960; undertakes research and collects and disseminates information on all aspects of continental Africa and its offshore islands, with particular focus on politics, economics and devt issues; library of c. 66,500 vols and periodicals; Chair. Dr BEKI HLATSWAYO; CEO Dr M. P. MATLOU; publs include *Africa Insight* (quarterly).

Centre for African Studies: Harry Oppenheimer Institute Building, 3rd Floor, University of Cape Town, Private Bag, Rondebosch 7701; tel. (21) 6502308; fax (21) 6503579; e-mail cas-africas@uct.ac.za; internet www.africanstudies.uct.ac.za; f. 1976; incorporates the Harry Oppenheimer Inst. for African Studies; promotes comparative study of Africa and research; offers multi-disciplinary courses at postgraduate level; Dir Assoc. Prof. HARRY GARUBA; publs include *Social Dynamics* (2 a year).

Centre for Southern African Studies: University of the Western Cape, Private Bag X17, Bellville 7535; tel. (21) 959-2911; fax (21) 959-3627; internet www.uwc.ac.za; Dir Prof. L. THOMPSON.

Human Sciences Research Council (HSRC): 134 Pretorius St, Private Bag X41, Pretoria; tel. (12) 3022000; fax (12) 3022001; internet www.hsrc.ac.za; f. 1968; conducts large-scale, policy-relevant, social-scientific projects for public sector users, non-governmental organizations and international development agencies; CEO Dr OLIVE SHISANA; Chair. PHUMELELE NZIMANDE (acting).

Institute for Advanced Social Research: University of the Witwatersrand, 1 Jan Smuts Ave, Private Bag 3, Wits 2050, Johannesburg; tel. (11) 7162414; fax (11) 7168030; f. 1973; Dir Prof. CHARLES VAN ONSELEN.

Institute for the Study of Man in Africa (ISMA): Rm 2B17, University of the Witwatersrand Medical School, York Rd, Parktown, Johannesburg 2193; tel. (11) 7172203; fax (11) 6434318; e-mail 055JSK@chiron.wits.ac.za; internet www.wits.ac.za/isma; f. 1960 to perpetuate the work of the late Prof. Raymond A. Dart on the study of man in Africa, past and present; serves as a centre of anthropological and related field work; publs include the Raymond Dart series and occasional papers.

National Research Foundation: Meiring Naudé Rd, Brummeria, POB 2600, Pretoria; tel. (12) 4814000; fax (12) 3491179; e-mail info@nrf.ac.za; internet www.nrf.ac.za; f. 1999; govt agency, responsible for supporting and promoting research; Chair. Prof. BELINDA BOZZOLI; Pres. and CEO Dr ALBERT VAN JAARSVELD.

South African Institute of Race Relations: 2 Clamart Rd, Richmond, Johannesburg; tel. (11) 4827221; fax (11) 4033671; e-mail sairr@sairr.org.za; internet www.sairr.org.za; f. 1929; research, education, publishing; library; 4,313 mems, 600 affiliated bodies; Chair. CHARLES SIMKIN; Pres. Prof. JONATHAN JANSEN; Dir J. KANE-BERMAN; publs include *Fast Facts* (monthly), *Frontiers of Freedom* (quarterly), *South Africa Survey* (annually).

SPAIN

Cátedra UNESCO de Estudios Afroiberoamericanos: Departamento de Fundamentos de Economía, Facultad de Ciencias Económicas, Universidad de Alcalá, 28801 Alcalá de Henares; tel. (91) 8855233; fax (91) 8854239; e-mail luis.beltran@uah.es; internet www2.uah.es/estudiosafroiberoamericanos; f. 1994; promotes and co-ordinates co-operation with African universities and research centres; organizes conferences, seminars, lectures, exhibitions and courses, as well as publishing books and promoting scholarly exchanges, on African influences in Iberian America; Chair. Dr LUIS BELTRÁN.

Colegio Mayor Universitario Nuestra Señora de Africa: Avda Ramiro de Maeztu s/n, Ciudad Universitaria, 28040 Madrid; tel. (1) 5540104; fax (1) 5540401; e-mail info.africa@fundacioncolegiosmayores.org; internet www.fundacioncolegiosmayores.org/Plano_afri.asp; f. 1964; attached inst. of the Complutense Univ. of Madrid and the Spanish Ministry of Foreign Affairs; linguistic studies and cultural activities; Dir BASILIO RODRÍGUEZ CAÑADA.

Fundación Sur (South Foundation): Gaztambide 31, 28015 Madrid; tel. (1) 915441818; fax (1) 915497789; e-mail correo@africafundacion.org; internet www.africafundacion.org; f. 1980; seminars and lectures; specialized library of 20,000 vols and periodicals; Dir-Gen. JOSÉ JULIO MARTÍN-SACRISTÁN NÚÑEZ; Chief Librarian RAFAEL SÁNCHEZ SANZ; publs include *Noticias de Africa* (monthly), *Cuadernos*.

Mundo Negro: Arturo Soria 101, 28043 Madrid; tel. (1) 914152412; fax (1) 5192550; e-mail mundonegro@combonianos.com; internet www.mundonegro.com; f. 1960; holds lectures; library and museum; Dir ROBERTO MISAS RÍOS; publ. *Mundo Negro* (monthly).

SWEDEN

Institutet för Internationell Ekonomi (Institute for International Economic Studies): Stockholm University, 106 91 Stockholm; tel. (8) 164377; fax (8) 161443; e-mail christina.loennblad@iies.su.se; internet www.iies.su.se; attached to Stockholm Univ; f. 1962; Dir Prof. HARRY FLAM.

Nordiska Afrikainstitutet (The Nordic Africa Institute): POB 1703, 751 47 Uppsala; tel. (18) 562200; fax (18) 562290; e-mail nai@nai.uu.se; internet www.nai.uu.se; f. 1962; documentation, information and research centre for contemporary African affairs, publication work, lectures and seminars; library of 64,000 vols and 400 periodicals; Dir CARIN NORBERG; publs include *Current African Issues*, *News from the Nordic Africa Institute*, seminar proceedings, research reports, discussion papers, annual report.

Utrikespolitiska Institutet (Swedish Institute of International Affairs): Drottning Kristinas väg 37, POB 27035, 102 51 Stockholm; tel. (8) 51176800; fax (8) 51176899; e-mail info@ui.se; internet www.ui.se; f. 1938; promotes studies of international affairs; library of c. 240,000 vols and 400 periodicals; Pres. MATS BERGQUIST; Dir ANNA JARDFELT MELVIN; publs include *Världspolitikens Dagsfrågor*, *Världens Fakta*, *Internationella Studier*, *Länder i fickformat*, *Yearbook*, conference papers, research reports (in English).

SWITZERLAND

Institut de Hautes Etudes Internationales et du Développement (IHEID): rue de Lausanne 132, CP 136, 1211 Geneva 21; tel. (22) 9085700; fax (22) 9085710; e-mail info@graduateinstitute.ch; internet graduateinstitute.ch; f. 2008; a centre of higher education and research into devt problems of Africa, Latin America, Asia and Eastern Europe; conducts courses, seminars and practical work; Dir PHILIPPE BURRIN; publs include *Revue Internationale de Politique de Développement*, *Itinéraires*.

UNITED KINGDOM

African Studies Association of the United Kingdom: Royal African Society, 36 Gordon Sq., London, WC1H 0PD; tel. (20) 3073-8335; fax (20) 3073-8340; e-mail asa@soas.ac.uk; internet www.asauk.net; f. 1963 to advance academic studies relating to Africa by providing facilities for the interchange of information and ideas; holds inter-disciplinary confs and symposia; 575 mems; Pres. Prof. MEGAN VAUGHAN; Hon. Sec. Dr NICI NELSON.

Centre for the Study of African Economies (CSAE): Dept of Economics, University of Oxford, Manor Rd Bldg, Manor Rd, Oxford, OX1 3UQ; tel. (1865) 271084; fax (1865) 281447; e-mail csae.enquiries@economics.oxford.ac.uk; internet www.csae.ox.ac.uk; Dir Prof. PAUL COLLIER; publ. *Journal of African Economies* (quarterly).

Centre of African Studies: Alison Richard Building, 7 West Road, Cambridge, CB3 9DT; tel. and fax (1223) 334396; e-mail centre@african.cam.ac.uk; internet www.african.cam.ac.uk; f. 1965; attached inst. of the Univ. of Cambridge; Dir HARRI ENGLUND.

Centre of African Studies: University of London, School of Oriental and African Studies, Thornhaugh St, Russell Sq., London, WC1H 0XG; tel. (20) 7898-4370; fax (20) 7898-4369; e-mail cas@soas.ac.uk; internet www.soas.ac.uk/cas; f. 1965; co-ordinates interdisciplinary study, research and discussion on Africa; Chair. Dr CHEGE GITHIORA.

Centre of African Studies: University of Edinburgh, Chrystal MacMillan Bldg, 15A George Sq., Edinburgh, EH8 9LD, Scotland; tel. (131) 650-3878; fax (131) 650-6535; e-mail african.studies@ed.ac.uk; internet www.cas.ed.ac.uk; f. 1962; postgraduate studies; Dir Prof.

PAUL NUGENT; publs include occasional paper series and annual conference proceedings.

Centre of West African Studies: The University of Birmingham, School of History and African Studies, Edgbaston, Birmingham, B15 2TT; tel. (121) 4145128; fax (121) 4143228; e-mail CWAS@bham.ac.uk; internet www.historycultures.bham.ac.uk/cwas; Dir Dr REGINALD CLINE-COLE.

Department of Development and Economic Studies: University of Bradford, Bradford, West Yorkshire, BD7 1DP; tel. (1274) 233980; fax (1274) 235280; e-mail bcid@bradford.ac.uk; internet www.brad.ac.uk/acad/bcid; f. 1969; undergraduate economics and postgraduate devt degrees, professional training, research and consultancy in economic and social policy; an attached inst. of the Univ. of Bradford; Head of Centre PATRICK RYAN; publs include research papers.

Institute of Commonwealth Studies (ICS): Senate House, 2nd Floor, South Block, Malet St, London WC1E 7HU; tel. (20) 7862-8844; fax (20) 7862-8820; e-mail ics@sas.ac.uk; internet commonwealth.sas.ac.uk; f. 1949; promotes advanced study of the Commonwealth and its member nations; provides a library and meeting place for postgraduate students and academic staff engaged in research in this field; offers postgraduate teaching; library of 200,000 vols and archive of over 200 collections; Dir Prof. PHILIP MURPHY.

Institute of Development Studies: University of Sussex, Brighton, East Sussex, BN1 9RE; tel. (1273) 606261; fax (1273) 621202; e-mail ids@ids.ac.uk; internet www.ids.ac.uk; f. 1966; research, training, postgraduate teaching, advisory work, information services; Dir Prof. LAWRENCE HADDAD; publ. *IDS Bulletin* (quarterly).

International African Institute (IAI): School of Oriental and African Studies, Thornhaugh St, Russell Sq., London, WC1H 0XG; tel. (20) 7898-4420; fax (20) 7898-4419; e-mail iai@soas.ac.uk; internet internationalafricaninstitute.org; f. 1926 to promote the study of African peoples, their languages, cultures and social life in their traditional and modern settings; holds seminars and conducts projects; Chair. Prof. V. Y. MUDIMBE; publs include *Africa* (quarterly), *Africa Bibliography* (annually), monograph and reprint series.

Leeds University Centre for African Studies: University of Leeds, Leeds, West Yorkshire, LS2 9JT; tel. (113) 3435069; e-mail african-studies@leeds.ac.uk; internet www.leeds.ac.uk/lucas; f. 1964; a liaison unit for all depts with African interests; organizes public seminars and conferences and a book donation scheme for African university theatre arts departments; Dir Prof. JANE PLASTOW; publ. *Leeds African Studies Bulletin* (annually).

Overseas Development Institute (ODI): 111 Westminster Bridge Rd, London, SE1 7JD; tel. (20) 7922-0300; fax (20) 7922-0399; e-mail odi@odi.org.uk; internet www.odi.org.uk; f. 1960 as a research centre and forum for the discussion of devt issues and problems; publishes its research findings in books and working papers; Dirs Lord ADAIR TURNER, SIMON MAXWELL; publs include *Development Policy Review* (quarterly), *Disasters* (quarterly).

Progressio: Unit 3, Canonbury Yard, 190 A New North Rd, London, N1 7BJ; tel. (20) 7354-0883; fax (20) 7359-0017; e-mail enquiries@progressio.org.uk; internet www.progressio.org.uk; f. 1940; fmrly the Catholic Institute for International Relations (CIIR); information and analysis of socio-economic, political, church and human rights issues in the developing countries; Exec. Dir CHRISTINE ALLEN; publs include specialized studies on southern Africa and EU development policy.

Royal African Society: 36 Gordon Sq., London, WC1H 0PD; tel. (20) 3073-8335; fax (20) 3073-8340; e-mail ras@soas.ac.uk; internet www.royalafricansociety.org; f. 1901; 1,000 mems; Chair. Lord MARK MALLOCH-BROWN; Exec. Dir RICHARD DOWDEN; Sec. GEMMA HAXBY; publ. *African Affairs* (quarterly).

Royal Institute of International Affairs: Chatham House, 10 St James's Sq., London, SW1Y 4LE; tel. (20) 7957-5700; fax (20) 7957-5710; e-mail contact@chathamhouse.org.uk; internet www.chathamhouse.org.uk; f. 1920; independent body, which aims to promote the study and understanding of international affairs; over 300 corporate mems; library of 160,000 vols and 650 periodicals; Chair. Dr DEANNE JULIUS; Dir Dr ROBIN NIBLETT; publs include *International Affairs* (5 a year), *The World Today* (monthly).

School of International Development: University of East Anglia, Norwich, NR4 7TJ; tel. (1603) 592329; fax (1603) 451999; e-mail dev.general@uea.ac.uk; internet www.uea.ac.uk/dev; Dean Dr BRUCE LANKFORD.

School of Oriental and African Studies: Thornhaugh St, Russell Sq., London, WC1H 0XG; tel. (20) 7637-2388; fax (20) 7436-3844; e-mail study@soas.ac.uk; internet www.soas.ac.uk; f. 1916; a school of the Univ. of London; Dir Prof. PAUL WEBLEY; Registrar and Sec. DONALD BEATON; 220 teachers, incl. 44 professors; 3,220 students; publs *The Bulletin*, *Calendar*, *Annual Report*, *Journal of African Law*.

School of Oriental and African Studies Library: Thornhaugh St, Russell Sq., London, WC1H 0XG; tel. (20) 7898-4163; fax (20) 7898-4159; e-mail libenquiry@soas.ac.uk; internet www.soas.ac.uk/library; f. 1916; 1.2m. vols and pamphlets; 4,500 current periodicals, 50,000 maps, 6,300 microforms, 2,800 MSS and private papers collections, extensive missionary archives, all covering Asian and African languages, literatures, philosophy, religions, history, law, cultural anthropology, art and archaeology, social sciences, geography and music; Dir of Library and Information Services JOHN ROBINSON.

UNITED STATES OF AMERICA

Africa Action: 1634 Eye St, NW, 810, Washington, DC 20006; tel. (202) 546-7961; fax (202) 546-1545; e-mail info@africaaction.org; internet www.africaaction.org; f. 2001 by merger of the Africa Fund, the Africa Policy Information Center and the American Committee on Africa; supports political, economic and social justice in Africa and, through the provision of information and analysis, aims to encourage positive US and international policies on African issues; Chair. EMIRA WOODS; Exec. Dir GERALD LEMELLE.

Africa-America Institute: 420 Lexington Ave, Suite 1706, New York, NY 10170; tel. (212) 949-5666; fax (212) 682-6174; e-mail aainy@aaionline.org; internet www.aaionline.org; f. 1953; organizes training programmes and offers devt assistance; maintains reps in 21 African countries; also sponsors confs and seminars; Chair. KOFI APPENTENG; Pres. and CEO MORA MCLEAN.

Africa Center for Strategic Studies: National Defense University, 300 Fifth Ave, Bldg 62, Fort McNair, Washington, DC 20319-5066; tel. (202) 685-7300; fax (202) 685-3210; e-mail isacoffj@ndu.edu; internet www.africacenter.org; supports the devt of US strategic policy towards Africa by providing academic programmes, fostering awareness of and dialogue on US strategic priorities and African security issues; Dir WILLIAM M. BELLAMY.

African Development Foundation: 1400 I St, NW, 10th Floor, Washington, DC 20005-2248; tel. (202) 673-3916; fax (202) 673-3810; e-mail info@adf.gov; internet www.adf.gov; f. 1984; an independent agency of the US Federal Govt focused on community-based devt; focuses on marginalized, underserved populations and participatory community development; Chair. JACK LESLIE; Pres. and CEO LLOYD O. PIERSON; publs include online news sources *ADF e-news* (monthly) and *The ADF Approach* (quarterly).

African Studies Association of the US: c/o African Studies Asscn, Rutgers, The State University, 54 Joyce Kilmer Ave, Piscataway, NJ 08854-8045; tel. (732) 932-8173; fax (732) 445-1366; e-mail asaed@rci.rutgers.edu; internet www.africanstudies.org; f. 1957; 2,700 mems; collects information on Africa; Pres. JUDITH BYFIELD; Exec. Dir KAREN JENKINS; publs *African Studies Review* (3 a year), *African Issues*, *ASA News*, *History in Africa* (annually).

African Studies Center: Boston University, 232 Bay State Rd, Boston, MA 02215; tel. (617) 353-7303; fax (617) 353-4975; e-mail africa@bu.edu; internet www.bu.edu/africa; f. 1953; research and teaching on archaeology, African languages, anthropology, economics, history, geography and political science of Africa; library of 125,000 vols and document titles, 1,000 periodicals and an extensive collection of non-current newspapers and periodicals; Dir Prof. TIMOTHY LONGMAN; publs include *International Journal of African Historical Studies* (3 a year), working papers, discussion papers.

African Studies Center: Center for International Programs, Michigan State University, East Lansing, MI 48824; tel. (517) 353-1700; fax (517) 432-1209; e-mail africa@msu.edu; internet www.africa.msu.edu; f. 1960; Dir Dr JAMES A. PRITCHETT; offers instruction in 30 African languages; library of over 200,000 vols; online resources include database of 11,000 films and videos on Africa; publs include *African Rural and Urban Studies* (3 a year), *Northeast African Studies* (3 a year).

African Studies Program: Ohio University, Yamada Int. House, Athens, OH 45701; tel. (740) 593-1834; fax (740) 593-1837; e-mail african.studies@ohio.edu; internet www.african.ohio.edu; African politics, education, economics, geography, community health, anthropology, languages, literature, philosophy and history; Dir Prof. STEPHEN HOWARD.

Institute for the African Child: Ohio University, Yamada Int. House, Athens, OH 45701; tel. (740) 593-1834; fax (740) 593-1837; e-mail african.studies@ohio.edu; internet www.afrchild.ohio.edu; f. 1998; Dir Prof. STEVE HOWARD.

African Studies Program: Princeton University, 323 Aaron Burr Hall, Princeton, NJ 08544; tel. (609) 258-9400; fax (609) 258-3988; e-mail raguas@princeton.edu; f. 1961; Dir DANIEL I. RUBENSTEIN.

African Studies Program: University of Wisconsin-Madison, 205 Ingraham Hall, 1155 Observatory Dr., Madison, WI 53706; tel. (608) 262-2380; fax (608) 265-5851; e-mail publications@africa.wisc.edu; internet africa.wisc.edu; study courses; library of over 220,000 vols; Chair. Prof. GAY SEIDMAN; publs include *News and Notes* (biannually), *African Economic History* (annually), *Ghana Studies* (annually), *Mande Studies* (annually), occasional papers and African texts and grammars.

African Studies Program: Paul H. Nitze School of Advanced International Studies, Johns Hopkins University, 1740 Massachusetts Ave, NW, Washington, DC 20036-1983; tel. (202) 663-5676; fax (202) 663-5683; e-mail africanstudies@jhu.edu; internet www.sais-jhu.edu/africa; Dir PETER M. LEWIS; publ. *SAIS African Studies Library Series*.

African Studies and Research Program: Dept of African Studies, Howard University, Washington, DC 20059; tel. (202) 238-2328; fax (202) 238-2326; e-mail rcummings@howard.edu; f. 1953; Chair. MBYE B. CHAM; publs include monographs and occasional papers.

Africare: Africare House, 440 R St, NW, Washington, DC 20001; tel. (202) 462-3614; fax (202) 387-1034; e-mail info@africare.org; internet www.africare.org; f. 1970; supports programmes in health and HIV/AIDS, food security and agriculture, water and sanitation, emergency humanitarian assistance, environmental management, as well as private sector devt; Chair. W. FRANK FOUNTAIN; Pres. DARIUS MANS; publs include *Newsletter* (2 a year).

Association of African Studies Programs: Dept of African and African-American Studies, 214A Willard Bldg, Penn State University, University Park, PA 16802; tel. (814) 863-4243; internet aaas.la.psu.edu; mems represent more than 40 centres of African studies at US colleges and univs; Interim Head PAUL TAYLOR; publ. *Newsletter* (2 a year).

Brookings Institution: 1775 Massachusetts Ave, NW, Washington, DC 20036-2188; tel. (202) 797-6000; fax (202) 797-6004; internet www.brookings.edu; f. 1916; research, education, and publishing in economics, govt and foreign policy; organizes confs and seminars; library of c. 75,000 vols and 700 periodicals; Pres. STROBE TALBOTT; Man. Dir WILLIAM ANTHOLIS; publs include *The Brookings Review* (quarterly), *Brookings Papers on Economic Activity* (2 a year), *Brookings Trade Forum* (2 a year).

Center for African Studies: Stanford University, 417 Galvez Mall, Encina Hall West, Room 216, Stanford, CA 94305-6045; tel. (650) 723-0295; fax (650) 723-3010; e-mail africanstudies@stanford.edu; internet africanstudies.stanford.edu; f. 1963; African languages, society, culture, foreign policy and social and behavioural sciences; holds research confs; offers jt degree in African studies for students enrolled in professional schools; Dir Prof. JEREMY M. WEINSTEIN; Assoc. Dir LAURA HUBBARD.

Center for African Studies: 427 Grinter Hall, University of Florida, Gainesville, FL 32611; tel. (352) 392-2183; fax (352) 392-2435; e-mail villalon@africa.ufl.edu; internet web.africa.ufl.edu; encourages research projects and sponsors lectures, exhbns and confs; library of 50,000 vols, 500 periodical titles, 40,000 maps; Dir ABRAHAM GOLDMAN; Assoc. Dir TODD H. LEEDY; publ. *African Studies Quarterly*.

Center for African Studies: University of Illinois at Urbana-Champaign, 210 International Studies Bldg, 910 South Fifth St, Champaign, IL 61820; tel. (217) 333-6335; fax (217) 244-2429; e-mail african@illinois.edu; internet www.afrst.uiuc.edu; f. 1970; Acting Dir and Assoc. Dir MAIMOUNA BARRO; publ. *Habari Newsletter*.

Center for International Studies: Massachusetts Institute of Technology, Bldg E40-400, 1 Amherst St, Cambridge, MA 02139; tel. (617) 253-8093; fax (617) 253-9330; e-mail cis-info@mit.edu; internet web.mit.edu/cis; f. 1951; Dir RICHARD J. SAMUELS; publ. *Newsletter* (2 a year).

Council on Foreign Relations, Inc: 58 East 68th St, New York, NY 10065; tel. (212) 434-9400; fax (212) 434-9800; e-mail communications@cfr.org; internet www.cfr.org; f. 1921; 3,010 mems; library of 10,000 vols, 221 periodicals and databases; Pres. RICHARD N. HAASS; publs include *Foreign Affairs* (bimonthly) and *Backgrounders*.

Human Rights Watch: 350 Fifth Ave, 34th Floor, New York, NY 10118-3299; tel. (212) 290-4700; fax (212) 736-1300; e-mail africa@hrw.org; internet www.hrw.org; Chair. JAMES F. HOGE, Jr; Exec. Dir KENNETH ROTH.

Institute of African Affairs: Duquesne University, 600 Forbes Ave, Pittsburgh, PA 15282; tel. (412) 434-6000; fax (412) 434-5146; f. 1957; research into uncommon languages of sub-Saharan Africa; library of 9,000 vols; Dir Rev. JOSEPH L. VARGA; publ. *African Reprint Series*.

Institute of World Affairs (IWA): 1928 Beulah Rd, Vienna, VA 22182; tel. (202) 744-7755; fax (703) 255-6578; e-mail hgregorian@iwa.org; internet www.iwa.org; f. 1924; conducts seminars on international issues; Chair. (acting) and Pres. GERALDINE S. KUNSTADTER; publ. *IWA International* (irregular).

James S. Coleman African Studies Center: 10244 Bunche Hall, University of California, Los Angeles, CA 90095-1310; tel. (310) 825-3686; fax (310) 206-2250; e-mail africa@international.ucla.edu; internet www.international.ucla.edu/africa; f. 1959; centre for coordination of and research on Africa in the social sciences, the arts, humanities, the sciences and public health; and for multi-disciplinary graduate training in African studies; Dir FRANÇOISE LIONNET; publs include *African Arts* (quarterly), *African Studies Center Newsletter* (2 a year), *UFAHAMU* (quarterly).

John L. Warfield Center for African and African-American Studies: University of Texas, Jester Center A232A, Austin, TX 78712; tel. (512) 471-1784; fax (512) 471-1798; e-mail jonijones@mail.utexas.edu; internet www.utexas.edu/cola/centers/caaas; f. 1969; Dir JONI L. JONES; publs working papers and reprint series (irregular).

Library of International Relations: Chicago-Kent College of Law, Illinois Institute of Technology, 565 West Adams St, Chicago, IL 60661-3691; tel. (312) 906-5600; fax (312) 906-5679; internet www.infoctr.edu; f. 1932; financed by voluntary contributions; stimulates interest and research in international problems; conducts seminars and offers special services to businesses and academic institutions; library of 520,000 items; Pres. HOKEN SEKI; Dir MICKIE A. VOGES; publ. *Newsletter* (5 a year).

Princeton Institute for International and Regional Studies: Aaron Burr Hall, Princeton University, Princeton, NJ 08544-1022; tel. (609) 258-4851; fax (609) 258-3988; e-mail piirs@princeton.edu; internet www.princeton.edu/~piirs; f. 2003; Dir MARK R. BEISSINGER; Assoc. Dir SUSAN F. BINDIG; publ. *World Politics* (quarterly).

Program of African and Asian Languages: Northwestern University, 4–400 Kresge Hall, 1880 Campus Drive, Evanston, IL 60208-2209; tel. (847) 491-5288; fax (847) 467-1097; e-mail r.susan@northwestern.edu; internet www.cas.northwestern.edu/paal; f. 1973; Dir LICHENG GU.

Program of African Studies: Northwestern University, 620 Library Place, Evanston, IL 60208-4110; tel. (847) 491-7323; fax (847) 491-3739; e-mail african-studies@northwestern.edu; internet www.northwestern.edu/african-studies; f. 1948; supported by various private and govt grants for research in Africa and the USA, as well as by university; awards undergraduate minor and graduate certificate of African studies to students enrolled at Northwestern University; sponsors fellowship awards for African students pursuing doctoral studies at Northwestern University; also sponsors brief residencies for students and practitioners of the African humanities; Dir Prof. RICHARD JOSEPH; publs include *PAS Newsletter*, *PAS Working Paper* series, conference proceedings.

Schomburg Center for Research in Black Culture: 515 Malcolm X Blvd, New York, NY 10037; tel. (212) 491-2200; e-mail scgenref@nypl.org; internet www.nypl.org/locations/schomburg; f. 1972; a research unit of the New York Public Library; contains more than 150,000 volumes and 85,000 microforms; Dir KHALIL GIBRAN MUHAMMAD.

TransAfrica Forum: 1426 21st St, NW, 2nd Floor, Washington, DC 20036; tel. (202) 223-1960; fax (202) 223-1966; e-mail info@transafricaforum.org; internet www.transafricaforum.org; f. 1981; Chair. DANNY GLOVER; Pres. NICOLE C. LEE, Jr.

Woodrow Wilson School of Public and International Affairs (African Studies Program): Bendheim Hall, Princeton University, Princeton, NJ 08540; tel. (609) 258-5633; fax (609) 258-5974; internet wws.princeton.edu; Dean CHRISTINA H. PAXSON; Program Dir Prof. JEFFREY HERBST.

VATICAN CITY

Pontificio Instituto di Studi Arabi e d'Islamistica (PISAI): Viale di Trastevere 89, 00153 Rome; tel. (06) 58392611; fax (06) 5882595; e-mail info@pisai.it; internet www.pisai.it; f. 1949; library of 31,500 vols; Dir P. MIGUEL ANGEL AYUSO GUIXOT; publs include *Encounter* (monthly), *Islamochristiana* (annually), *Etudes arabes* (annually).

SELECT BIBLIOGRAPHY (BOOKS)

See also bibliographies at end of relevant chapters in Part Two.

Abbink, J., and Hesseling, G. *Election Observation and Democratization in Africa*. London, Palgrave Macmillan, 1999.

Abdulahi, A. *Governance and Internal Wars in Sub-Saharan Africa: Exploring the Relationship*. London, Adonis & Abbey Publishers, 2007.

Achebe, C. *Africa: Altered States, Ordinary Miracles*. London, Portobello Books Ltd, 2008.

Adamoleku, L. (Ed.). *Public Administration in Africa*. Boulder, CO, Westview Press, 1999.

Adams, W. M. *The Physical Geography of Africa*. Oxford, Oxford University Press, 1999.

Adandé, A. (Ed.). *Intégration régionale, démocratie et panafricanisme: paradigmes anciens, nouveaux défis*. Dakar, CODESRIA, 2007.

Addison, T. (Ed.). *From Conflict to Recovery in Africa*. Oxford, Oxford University Press, 2003.

Adebajo, A., and Rashid, I. (Eds). *West Africa's Security Challenges: Building Peace in a Troubled Region*. Boulder, CO, Lynne Rienner Publishers, 2004.

Adebajo, A., and Whiteman, K. (Eds). *The EU and Africa: From Eurafrique to Afro-Europa*. New York, Columbia University Press, 2012.

Adedeji, A. *South Africa and Africa: Within or Apart?* London, Zed Publishing/African Centre for Strategic Studies and Development, 1996.

Adepoju, A. (Ed.). *Family, Population and Development in Africa*. London, Zed Publishing, 1997.

Adesina, J. (Ed.). *Social Policy in Sub-Saharan African Context: In Search of Inclusive Development*. London, Palgrave Macmillan, 2007.

Adu Boahen, A. *African Perspectives on Colonialism*. Baltimore, MD, Johns Hopkins University Press, 1992.

Adu Boahen, A. (Ed.). *UNESCO General History of Africa*. Berkeley, CA, University of California Press, 1993.

African Centre for Monetary Studies. *Debt Conversion Schemes in Africa*. Oxford, James Currey Publishers, 1992.

Agyeman, O. *Africa's Persistent Vulnerable Link: Global Politics*. New York, New York University Press, 2001.

The Failure of Grassroots Pan-Africanism: The Case of the All-African Trade Union Federation. Lanham, MD, Lexington Books, 2003.

Ajayi, J. F. A., and Crowder, M. *History of West Africa*. Cambridge, Cambridge University Press, 1976.

Ake, C. *Democracy and Development in Africa*. Washington, DC, Brookings, 1996.

Akeya Agnango, G. (Ed.). *Issues and Trends in Contemporary African Politics*. New York, Peter Lang, 2003.

Akyuz, Y., and Gore, C. *African Development in a Comparative Perspective*. Oxford, James Currey Publishers, 2000.

Alao, A. *Natural Resources and Conflict in Africa: The Tragedy of Endowment*. Rochester, NY, University of Rochester Press, 2007.

Ali, T. M., and Matthews, R. O. *Civil Wars in Africa: Roots and Resolution*. Montréal, QC, McGill-Queen's University Press, 1999.

Amoah, M. *Nationalism, Globalization, and Africa*. London, Palgrave Macmillan, 2011.

Anseeuw, W., and Alden, C. (Eds). *The Struggle over Land in Africa: Conflicts, Politics & Change*. Cape Town, HSRC Press, 2010.

Anshan, L. *A History of Overseas Chinese in Africa to 1911*. New York, Diasporic Africa Press, 2012.

Appiah, K. *In My Father's House: A Statement of African Ideology*. Oxford, Oxford University Press, 1992.

Arnold, G. *A Guide to African Political and Economic Development*. London, Frank Cass, 2001.

Africa: A Modern History. Southend-on-Sea, Atlantic, 2006.

Aryeetey, E., and Nissanke, M. *Financial Integration and Development: Liberalization and Reform in Sub-Saharan Africa*. London, Routledge, 1998.

Asante, M. K. *The History of Africa: The Quest for Eternal Harmony*. London, Routledge, 2007.

Asante, S. K. *Regionism and Africa's Development*. London, Palgrave Macmillan, 1997.

Asiwaju, A. I., and de Leeuw, M. E. J. A. (Eds). *Border Region Development in Africa: Focus on Eastern and Southern Sub-Regions*. Nagoya, United Nations Centre for Regional Development, 1998.

Assensoh, A. B., and Alex-Assensoh, Y. M. *African History and Politics*. London, Palgrave Macmillan, 2003.

Ayittey, G. B. N. *Africa in Chaos*. London, Palgrave Macmillan, 1998.

Africa Unchained. New York, Palgrave Macmillan, 2005.

Bach, D. *State and Society in Francophone Africa since Independence*. London, Palgrave Macmillan, 1995.

Regionalisation in Africa. Oxford, James Currey Publishers, 1999.

Baker, B. *Security in Post-Conflict Africa: The Role of Nonstate Policing*. Boca Raton, FL, CRC Press, 2009.

Bakut, B. T., and Dutt, S. *Africa at the Millennium*. London, Palgrave Macmillan, 2000.

Banham, M. (Ed.). *Southern Africa*. Oxford, James Currey Publishers, 2004.

Bardhan, P. *International Trade, Growth and Development*. Malden, MA, Blackwell Publishing, 2002.

Barratt Brown, M. *Africa's Choices after Thirty Years of the World Bank*. Boulder, CO, Westview Press, 1997.

Barrett, C. B., Little, P., and Carter, M. (Eds). *Understanding and Reducing Persistent Poverty in Africa*. London, Routledge, 2007.

Bart, F., and Lenoble-Bart, A. *Afrique des réseaux et mondialisation*. Paris, Editions Karthala, 2003.

Bassey, C., and Oshita, O. (Eds). *Conflict Resolution, Identity Crisis, and Development in Africa*. Lagos, Malthouse Press, 2007.

Basu, A., *et al. Foreign Direct Investment in Africa: Some Case Studies*. Washington, DC, IMF Publications, 2002.

Bayart, J.-F. *The State in Africa: The Politics of the Belly*. 2nd edn. Cambridge, Polity Press, 2009.

Bayart, J.-F., *et al. The Criminalisation of the State in Africa*. Bloomington, IN, Indiana University Press, 1999.

Beauchamp, C. *Démocratie, Culture et Développement en Afrique noire*. Paris, L'Harmattan, 1997.

Beinart, W., and McGregor, J. A. (Eds). *Social History and African Environments*. Athens, OH, Ohio University Press, 2003.

Belshaw, D., and Livingstone, I. *Renewing Development in Sub-Saharan Africa*. London, Routledge, 2001.

Ben Hammouda, H. *Afrique: Pour un nouveau contrat de développement*. Paris, L'Harmattan, 2000.

Ben Hammouda, H., and Kasse, M. *L'avenir de la zone franc*. Paris, Editions Karthala, 2001.

Berger, I., and White, E. F. *Women in Sub-Saharan Africa: Restoring Women to History*. Bloomington, IN, Indiana University Press, 1999.

Berkeley, B. *The Graves are Not Yet Full: race, tribe and power in the heart of Africa*. Oxford, Basic Books, 2003.

Bernault, F. *Démocraties ambigues en Afrique Centrale: Congo-Brazzaville, Gabon 1940–65*. Paris, Editions Karthala, 1996.

Berry, S. *No Condition is Permament: The Social Dynamics of Agrarian Change in Sub-Saharan Africa*. Madison, WI, University of Wisconsin Press, 1993.

Berthélemy, J.-C. *Will There Be New Emerging Market Economies in Africa by the Year 2020?* Washington, DC, IMF Publications, 2002.

Bhalla, S. S. *Imagine There's No Country: Poverty, Inequality and Growth in the Era of Globalization*. Washington, DC, Institute for International Economics, 2002.

Binns, T., Dixon, A., and Nel, E. *Africa: Diversity and Development*. Abingdon, Routledge, 2012.

Birmingham, D. *The Decolonization of Africa*. Athens, OH, Ohio University Press, 1996.

Birmingham, D., and Martin, P. *History of Central Africa: The Contemporary Years since 1960*. London, Longman, 1998.

Bond, G. *Aids in Africa and the Caribbean*. Boulder, CO, Westview Press, 2002.

Contested Terrains and Constructed Categories: Contemporary Africa in Focus. Boulder, CO, Westview Press, 1997.

Boulden, J. *Dealing with Conflict in Africa.* London, Palgrave Macmillan, 2004.

Bratton, M., and Van de Walle, N. *Democratic Experiments in Africa: Regime Transitions in Comparative Perspective.* Cambridge, Cambridge University Press, 1997.

Brauer, J., and Hartley, K. *The Economics of Regional Security.* London, Routledge, 2000.

Brautigam, D. *The Dragon's Gift: The Real Story of China in Africa.* New York, Oxford University Press, 2010.

Bridges, R. *Imperialism, Decolonization and Africa.* London, Palgrave Macmillan, 1999.

Broadman, H. G. *Africa's Silk Road: China and India's New Economic Frontier.* Washington, DC, World Bank Publications, 2007.

Broch-Due, V. *Violence and Belonging.* London, Routledge, 2004.

Brownbridge, M., and Harvey, C. *Banking in Africa.* Oxford, James Currey Publishers, 1998.

Brune, S., *et al. Africa and Europe: Relations of Two Continents in Transition.* Hamburg, LIT Verlag, 1994.

Van Buuren, M., *et al* (Eds). *State Recognition and Democratization in Sub-Saharan Africa: A New Dawn for Traditionalist Authorities?* London, Palgrave Macmillan, 2007.

Calamitsis, E. A. *Adjustment and Growth in Sub-Saharan Africa.* Washington, DC, IMF Publications, 2000.

Calderisi, R. *The Trouble with Africa: Why Foreign Aid Isn't Working.* New York, Palgrave Macmillan, 2006.

Cambridge University Press. *Cambridge History of Africa.* Cambridge, Cambridge University Press, 1986.

Carey, K., Gupta, S., and Jacoby, U. *Sub-Saharan Africa: Forging New Trade Links with Asia.* Washington, DC, IMF Publication Services, 2007.

Carmody, P. *Neoliberalism, Civil Society and Security in Africa.* London, Palgrave Macmillan, 2007.

The New Scramble for Africa. Cambridge, Polity Press, 2011

Chabal, P. *Africa Works: Disorder as Political Instrument.* Oxford, James Currey Publishers, 1999.

Africa: The Politics of Suffering and Smiling. London, Zed Books, 2009.

Chabal, P., and Deloz, J.-P. *L'Afrique est partie!* Paris, Economica, 1999.

Chabal, P., *et al. A History of Postcolonial Lusophone Africa.* London, Hurst and Company, 2002.

Chafer, T., and Cumming, G. (Eds). *From Rivalry to Partnership?: New Approaches to the Challenges of Africa.* London, Ashgate Publishing, 2011.

Charton, H., and Médard, C. (Eds). *L'Afrique Orientale Annuaire 2005.* Paris, L'Harmattan, 2007.

Chazan, N., *et al. Politics and Society in Contemporary Africa.* Boulder, CO, Lynne Rienner Publishers, 1999.

Cheru, F., and Obi, C. (Eds). *The Rise of China and India in Africa: Challenges, Opportunities and Critical Interventions.* London, Zed Books, 2010.

Chiwandamira, L., and Makaula, M. (Eds). *Perspectives on African Governance.* Cape Town, Institute for Democracy in South Africa, 2006.

Choucane-Verdier, A. *Libéralisation financière et croissance économique: le cas de l'Afrique subsaharienne.* Paris, L'Harmattan, 2001.

Chrétien, J.-P. *The Great Lakes of Africa: 2,000 years of history.* New York, Zone, 2003.

Christiaensen, L., and Demery, L. *Down to Earth: Agriculture and Poverty Reduction in Africa.* Washington, DC, World Bank Publications, 2007.

Christopher, A. J. *Atlas of Changing Africa.* London, Routledge, 2000.

Clapham, C. *Africa and the International System: The Politics of State Survival.* Cambridge, Cambridge University Press, 1996.

Clapp, J. *Adjustment and Agriculture in Africa.* London, Palgrave Macmillan, 1997.

Clarke, J. F. *Political Reform in Francophone Africa.* Boulder, CO, Westview Press, 1996.

Cleaver, K. M., and Graeme Donovan, W. *Agriculture, pauvreté et réforme des politiques en Afrique Sub-saharienne.* Guinea, Editions Ganndal, 2000.

Club du Sahel. *Preparing for the Future—A Vision of West Africa in the Year 2020.* Paris, OECD, 1999.

Cohen, A. *Custom and Politics in Urban Africa.* London, Frank Cass, 2003.

Cole, R., and De Blij, H. J. *Survey of Sub-Saharan Africa: A Regional Geography.* New York, Oxford University Press Inc, 2006.

Coleman, J. S. *Nationalism and Development in Africa: Selected Essays.* Berkeley, CA, University of California Press, 1994.

Collins, R. O., and Burns, J. M. *A History of Sub-Saharan Africa.* Cambridge, Cambridge University Press, 2007.

Collins, R. O., Burns, J. M., and Ching, E. (Eds). *Historical Problems of Imperial Africa.* Princeton, NJ, Markus Wiener, 1994.

Constantin, F., and Coulon, C. *Réligion et transition démocratique en Afrique.* Paris, Editions Karthala, 1997.

Cooper, F. *Africa Since 1940: The Past of the Present.* Cambridge, Cambridge University Press, 2002.

Decolonization and African Society. Cambridge, Cambridge University Press, 1996.

Coquery-Vidrovitch, C. *African Women: A Modern History.* Boulder, CO, Westview Press, 1997.

Africa: Endurance and Change South of the Sahara. Berkeley, CA, University of California Press, 1998.

History of African Cities South of the Sahara. Princeton, NJ, Markus Wiener, 2006.

Cowan, M., and Laakso, L. *Multiparty Elections in Africa.* Oxford, James Currey Publishers, 2002.

Cross, C., *et al* (Eds). *Views on Migration in Sub-Saharan Africa: Proceedings of an African Migration Alliance Workshop.* Cape Town, Human Sciences Research Council Press, 2006.

Cruise O'Brien, D., *et al* (Eds). *Contemporary West African States.* Cambridge, Cambridge University Press, 1990.

Curtin, P., *et al. African History.* London, Longman, 1995.

Dago, F. *Politics, Economics and Development in Sub-Saharan Africa.* Twickenham, Athena Press, 2004.

D'Almeida Topor, H., Coquery-Vidrovitch, C., and Georg, O. (Eds). *Les jeunes en Afrique.* Paris, L'Harmattan, 1992.

Daumont, R., *et al. Banking in Sub-Saharan Africa: What went wrong?* Washington, DC, IMF Institute, 2004.

David, J. (Ed.). *Africa and the War on Terrorism.* London, Ashgate Publishing, 2007.

Davids, Y., *et al. Measuring Democracy and Human Rights in Southern Africa.* Uppsala, Nordic Africa Institute, 2002.

Davidson, B. *Africa in History: Themes and Outlines.* London, Simon and Schuster, 1995.

Let Freedom Come. Boston, MA, Little, Brown & Co, 1989.

The Black Man's Burden: Africa and the Curse of the Nation-State. Oxford, James Currey Publishers, 1992.

African Civilization Revisited. Trenton, NJ, Africa World Press, 1993.

De Waal, A. *Famine Crimes: Politics and the Disaster Relief Industry in Africa.* Oxford, James Currey Publishers, 1997.

Debrun, X., Masson, P. R., and Pattillo, C. A. *Monetary Union in West Africa: Who Might Gain, Who Might Lose, and Why?* Washington, DC, IMF Publication Services, 2003.

Decalo, S. *Coups and military rule in Africa: Motivations and Constraints.* Newhaven, CT, Yale University Press, 1990.

Deng, F. M., and Lyons, T. *Africa Reckoning: A Quest for Good Governance.* Washington, DC, Brookings Institution Press, 1998.

Dessart, M. A. *Capacity Building, Governance and Economic Reform in Africa.* Washington, DC, IMF Publication Services, 2002.

Diamond, L., and Plattner, M. F. (Eds). *Nationalism, Ethnic Conflict and Democracy.* Baltimore, MD, Johns Hopkins University Press, 1997.

Diawara, M. *In Search of Africa.* Cambridge, MA, Harvard University Press, 1998.

Dibie, R. (Ed.). *Non-governmental Organizations and Sustainable Development in sub-Saharan Africa.* Lanham, MD, Lexington Books, 2007.

Diop, M.-C., and Diouf, M. *Les Figures du politique en Afrique: Des pouvoirs hérités aux pouvoirs élus.* Paris, Éditions Karthala, 1999.

Diouf, M. *L'Afrique dans la mondialisation.* Paris, L'Harmattan, 2002.

Doo Kinge, M. *Quelle démocratie en Afrique?* Dakar, Nouvelles Editions Africaines de Senegal, 1999.

Dowden, R. *Africa: Altered States, Ordinary Miracles.* London, Portobello Books, 2007.

Dussey, R. *L'Afrique face au sida.* Abidjan, Editions Bognini, 1995.

Ecker, O. *Economics of Micronutrient Malnutrition: The Demand for Nutrients in Sub-Saharan Africa.* New York, Peter Lang, 2009.

Ehui, F. T. *L'Afrique noire: de la superpuissance au sous-développement.* Abidjan, Nouvelles Editions Ivoiriennes, 2002.

Elbadawi, I., and Ndula, B. *Economic Development in SubSaharan Africa. Proceedings of the Eleventh World Congress of the*

International Economic Association, Tunis. London, Palgrave Macmillan, 2001.

Ellis, S. *Africa Now: People, Policies, Institutions*. Oxford, James Currey Publishers, 1996.

Engel, U., and Gomes Porto, J. *Africa's New Peace and Security Architecture (Global Security in a Changing World)*. London, Ashgate Publishing, 2010.

Engelhard, P. *L'Afrique: Plaidoyer pour une nouvelle économie*. Senegal, Enda tiers-monde.

Englebert, P. *State Legitimacy and Development in Africa*. Boulder, CO, Lynne Rienner Publishers, 2000.

Estache, A., and Wodon, Q. *Infrastructure and Poverty in Sub-Saharan Africa*. Washington, DC, World Bank Publications, 2007.

Europa Publications. *A Political Chronology of Africa*. London, Europa Publications, 2001.

Eyene-Mba, J. *Afrique sur le chemin de la croissance et de l'évolution*. Paris, L'Harmattan, 2003.

Fage, J. (updated by Tordoff, W.). *A History of Africa*. London, Frank Cass, 2001.

Falola, T. *Nationalism and African Intellectuals*. Rochester, NY, University of Rochester Press, 2001.

Falola, T., and Usman, A. (Eds). *Movements, Borders, and Identities in Africa*. Rochester, NY, University of Rochester Press, 2009.

Ferguson, J. *Global Shadows: Africa in the Neoliberal World Order*. Durham, NC, Duke University Press, 2006.

Finaldi, G. M. *Italian National Identity in the Scramble for Africa*. New York, Peter Lang, 2009.

Forest People's Programme. *From Principles to Practice*. 2003.

Francis, D. J. *Uniting Africa: Building Regional Peace and Security Systems*. London, Ashgate Publishing, 2006.

French, H. W. *A Continent for the Taking: The Tragedy and Hope of Africa*. New York, Alfred A. Knopf, 2004.

Freund, B. *The Making of Contemporary Africa*. London, Palgrave Macmillan, 1998.

Fuller, B. *Government Confronts Culture: The Struggle for Local Democracy in Southern Africa*. London, Garland Science, 1999.

Funke, N. *The New Partnership for Africa's Development (NEPAD): Opportunities and Challenges*. Washington, DC, IMF Institute, 2003.

Futurs africains. *Afrique 2025*. Paris, Editions Karthala, 2003.

Gebissa, E. *Leaf of Allah: Khat and Agricultural Transformation*. Oxford, James Currey Publishers, 2005.

Geda, A. *Finance and Trade in Africa*. London, Palgrave Macmillan, 2002.

Ghaia, D. *Renewing Social and Economic Progress in Africa*. London, Palgrave Macmillan, 2000.

Gikandi, S. *Encyclopaedia of African Literature*. London, Routledge, 2003.

Gilbert, E., and Reynolds, J. *Africa in World History (2nd Edition)*. Harlow, Prentice Hall, 2007.

Gooneratne, W., and Mbilinyi, M. (Eds). *Reviving Local Self-reliance: People's Responses to the Economic Crisis in Eastern and Southern Africa*. Nagoya, United Nations Centre for Regional Development, 1992.

Gordon, A. A., and D. L. (Eds). *Understanding Contemporary Africa*. Boulder, CO, Lynne Rienner Publishers, 2001.

Grosh, B., and Mukandala, R. *State-Owned Enterprises in Africa*. Boulder, CO, Lynne Rienner Publishers, 1994.

Gulliver, P. H. (Ed.). *Tradition and Transition in East Africa*. London, Routledge, 2004.

Gunning, J. W., and Oostendorp, R. *Industrial Change in Africa*. London, Palgrave Macmillan, 2001.

Guyer, J. *Money Matters: Instability, Values and Social Payments in the Modern History of West African Communities*. Portsmouth, NH, Heinemann, 1994.

Gyimah-Boadi, E. *Democratic Reform in Africa: The Quality of Progress*. Boulder, CO, Lynne Rienner Publishers, 2004.

Harbeson, J. W. *Africa in World Politics: The African State System in Flux*. Boulder, CO, Westview Press, 1999.

Harbeson, J. W., Rothchild, D., and Chazan, N. (Eds). *Civil Society and the State in Africa*. Boulder, CO, Lynne Rienner Publishers, 1994.

Harel, X, and Hofnung, T. *Le scandale des biens mal acquis. Enquête sur les milliards volés de la Françafrique*. Paris, La Découverte, 2011.

Hargreaves, J. D. *Decolonization in Africa*. London, Longman, 2003.

Harris, G. (Ed.). *Achieving Security in Sub-Saharan Africa: Cost Effective Alternatives to the Military*. Pretoria, Institute for Security Studies, 2004.

Harrison, G. *Issues in the Contemporary Politics of Sub-Saharan Africa*. London, Palgrave Macmillan, 2002.

The World Bank and Africa. London, Routledge, 2004.

Hastings, A. *The Construction of Nationhood: Ethnicity, Religion and Nationalism*. Cambridge, Cambridge University Press, 1997.

Havinden, M., and Meredith, D. *Colonialism and Development: Britain and its Tropical Colonies*. London, Routledge, 1993.

Havnevik, K., *et al*. (Eds). *African Agriculture and the World Bank: Development or Impoverishment?* Uppsala, Nordic Africa Institute, 2007.

Herbst, J. *States and Power in Africa: Comparative Lessons in Authority and Control*. Princeton, NJ, Princeton University Press, 2000.

Herbst, J., and Mills, G. *The Future of Africa: A New Order in Sight?* Oxford, Oxford University Press, 2003.

Hiscox, M. J. *International Trade and Political Conflict: Commerce, Coalitions and Mobility*. Princeton, NJ, Princeton University Press, 2002.

Honohan, P., and Beck, T. *Making Finance Work for Africa*. Washington, DC, World Bank Publications, 2007.

Hope, Christopher. *Brothers under the Skin: Travels in Tyranny*. London, Macmillan, 2003.

Hope, K. R., and Chikulo, B. C. *Corruption and Development in Africa*. London, Palgrave Macmillan, 1999.

Hopkins, A. G. *An Economic History of West Africa*. Cambridge, Cambridge University Press.

Houngnikpo, M. C. *L'Illusion démocratique en Afrique*. Paris, L'Harmattan, 2004.

Howe, H. M. *Ambiguous Order: Military Forces in African States*. Boulder, CO, Lynne Rienner Publishers, 2005.

Huband, M. *The Skull beneath the Skin: Africa and the Cold War*. Boulder, CO, Westview Press, 2002.

Hugon, P. *La zone franc à l'heure de l'Euro*. Paris, Editions Karthala, 1999.

Hyden, G., and Bratton, M. (Eds). *Governance and Politics in Africa*. Boulder, CO, Lynne Rienner Publishers, 1992.

Iliffe, J. *Africans: The History of a Continent*. Cambridge, Cambridge University Press, 1995.

Institute of African Studies. *African Perspectives: Selected Works*. Pretoria, Centre for Development Analysis, 1993.

Jackson, R., and Rosberg, C. *Personal Rule in Black Africa*. Berkeley, CA, University of California Press, 1982.

Jackson, T. *Management and Change in Africa*. London, Frank Cass, 2004.

Jamieson, D. T., *et al*. (Eds). *Disease and Mortality in Sub-Saharan Africa*. 2nd edn. Washington, DC, World Bank Publications, 2006.

Janis, M. *Africa After Modernism: Transitions in Literature, Media, and Philosophy*. London, Routledge, 2007.

Joseph, R. (Ed.). *State, Conflict and Democracy in Africa*. Boulder, CO, Lynne Rienner Publishers, 1992.

Kabbaj, O. *The Challenge of African Development*. Oxford, Oxford University Press, 2003.

Kamate, E. *Quel développement pour l'Afrique?* Mali, Editions Jamana, 1997.

Kane, I., and Mbelle, N. *Towards a People-Driven African Union: Current Obstacles and New Opportunities*. Oxford, Oxfam Publishing/Open Society Institute's Africa Governance Monitoring and Advocacy Project/African Network on Debt and Development, 2007.

Kayizzi-Mugerwa, S. *The African Economy*. London, Frank Cass, 1998.

Kayizzi-Mugerwa, S., *et al*. *Towards a New Partnership with Africa*. Uppsala, Nordic Africa Institute, 2000.

Keller, E. J., and Rothchild, D. *Africa in the New International Order: Rethinking State Sovereignty and Regional Security*. Boulder, CO, Lynne Rienner Publishers, 1996.

Kidanu, A., and Kumssa, A. (Eds). *Social Development in Africa*. Nairobi, United Nations Centre for Regional Development Africa Office, 2001.

Kieh, G. K., and Agbese, P. O. (Eds). *Reconstituting the State in Africa*. London, Palgrave Macmillan, 2007.

Kingma, K. *Demobilization in Sub-Saharan Africa*. London, Palgrave Macmillan, 2000.

Kiros, T. (Ed.). *Explorations in African Political Thought*. London, Frank Cass, 2001.

Koser, K. (Ed.). *New African Diasporas*. London, Routledge, 2003.

Kouvouama, A. *Modernité africaine: Les figures du politique et du religieux.* Congo, Editions Paari, 2002.

Kroslak, D. *France's Role in the Rwandan Genocide.* London, Hurst Publishers, 2007.

Kumssa, A., and Khan, H. A. (Eds). *Transnational Economies and Regional Economic Development Strategies: Lessons from Five Low-income Developing Countries.* Nagoya, United Nations Centre for Regional Development, 1996.

Kwaa Prah, K. *The State of the Nation.* Cape Town, Centre for Advanced Studies of African Society, 2008.

Lamphear, J. *African Military History.* London, Ashgate Publishing, 2007.

Lata, L. *Peacekeeping As State Building: Current Challenges for the Horn of Africa.* Trenton, NJ, Africa World Press, 2011.

Lawrence, P., and Thirtle, C. *Africa and Asia in Comparative Economic Perspective.* London, Palgrave Macmillan, 2001.

Le Vine, V. T. *Politics in Francophone Africa.* Boulder, CO, Lynne Rienner Publishers, 2007.

Lebeau, Y., Niane, B., Piriou, A., and de Saint Marie, M. *Etat et acteurs émergents en Afrique.* Paris, Editions Karthala, 2003.

Leonard, D. K., and Straus, S. *Africa's Stalled Development: International Causes and Cures.* Boulder, CO, Lynne Rienner Publishers, 2003.

Levitt, J. I. *Illegal Peace in Africa: An Inquiry into the Legality of Power Sharing with Warlords, Rebels, and Junta.* Cambridge, Cambridge University Press, 2012.

Lewis, P. *Africa: Dilemmas of Development and Change.* Boulder, CO, Westview Press, 1998.

Lugan, B. *Décolonisez l'Afrique!* Paris, Editions Ellipses, 2011.

Lumumba-Kasongo, T. *The Dynamics of Political and Economic Relations between Africa and the Foreign Powers: A Study in International Relations.* Westport, CT, Praeger, 1998.

Political Re-Mapping of Africa: Transnational Ideology and Re-definition of Africa in World Politics. Lanham, MD, University Press of America, 1993.

The Rise of Multipartyism and Democracy in the Context of Contemporary Global Change: the Case of Africa. Westport, CT, Praeger, 1998.

Japan-Africa Relations. New York, Palgrave Macmillan, 2010.

Lundahl, M. (Ed.). *From Crisis to Growth in Africa.* London, Frank Cass, 2001.

Lynn, M. *Commerce and Economic Change in West Africa.* Cambridge, Cambridge University Press, 1997.

Magyar, K. P., and Conteh-Morgan, E. *Peacekeeping in Africa.* London, Palgrave Macmillan, 1998.

Mahadevan, V. *Contemporary African Politics and Development: A Comprehensive Bibliography, 1981–1990.* Boulder, CO, Lynne Rienner Publishers, 1995.

Mailafia, O. O. *Europe and Economic Reform in Africa.* London, Frank Cass, 1997.

Makhan, V. *Economic Recovery in Africa.* London, Palgrave Macmillan, 2002.

Makinda, S. M., and Wafula Okumu, F. (Eds). *The African Union: Challenges Of Globalization, Security, And Governance.* London, Routledge, 2009.

Mamdami, M., and Wamba dia Wamba, E. *African Studies in Social Movements and Democracy.* Dakar, CODESRIA, 1995.

Mangala, J. *New Security Threats and Crises in Africa: Regional and International Perspectives.* London, Palgrave Macmillan, 2011.

Manning, P. *Francophone Sub-Saharan Africa 1880–1995.* Cambridge, Cambridge University Press, 1999.

Martin, D.-C. *Nouveaux langages du politique en Afrique orientale.* Paris, Editions Karthala, 1998.

Masson, P., *et al. Monetary Union in West Africa (ECOWAS).* Washington, DC, IMF Publications, 2001.

Mazrui, A., and Mazrui, A. M. *The Power of Babel: Language and Governance in the African Experience.* Oxford, James Currey, 1998.

Mazumdar, D., and Mazaher, A. *The African Manufacturing Firm.* London, Routledge, 2003.

McAleese, D., *et al. Africa and the European Community after 1992.* Washington, DC, Economic Development Institute of the World Bank, 1993.

McDonald, D. (Ed.). *On Borders: Perspectives on Internal Migration in Southern Africa.* New York, St Martin's Press, 2000.

McEvedy, C. *The Penguin Atlas of African History.* London, Penguin Books, 1987.

McIntyre, W. D. *British Decolonization, 1946–1997.* London, Palgrave Macmillan, 1998.

Medard, J.-F. (Ed.). *Etats d'Afrique Noire: Formation, mécanismes et crises.* Paris, Editions Karthala, 1994.

Mehler, A., Melber, H., and van Walraven, K. (Eds). *Africa Yearbook: Politics, Economy and Society South of the Sahara 2006.* Leiden, Brill, 2007.

Melber, H., *et al. The New Partnership for African Development (NEPAD): African Perspectives.* Uppsala, Nordic Africa Institute, 2002.

Meredith, M. *The Fate of Africa: A History of the Continent Since Independence.* Revised edn. New York, Public Affairs, 2011.

Merlin, P. *L'Afrique peut gagner.* Paris, Editions Karthala, 2001.

Middleton, J. (Ed.). *Encyclopaedia of Africa South of the Sahara.* New York, Scribners, 1997.

Migani, G. *La France et l'Afrique sub-saharienne, 1957–1963.* New York, Peter Lang, 2008.

Mikell, G. (Ed.). *African Feminism: The Politics of Survival in Sub-Saharan Africa.* Philadelphia, PA, University of Pennsylvania Press, 1997.

Mlambo, N. *Violent Conflicts, Fragile Peace: Perspectives on Africa's Security Problems.* London, Adonis & Abbey Publishers, 2007.

Monga, C. *The Anthropology of Anger: Civil Society and Democracy in Africa.* Boulder, CO, Lynne Rienner Publishers, 1996.

Mortimore, M. *Adapting to Drought: Farmers, Famines, and Desertification in West Africa.* Cambridge, Cambridge University Press, 1990.

Moser, G. G., *et al. Economic Growth and Poverty Reduction in Sub-Saharan Africa.* Washington, DC, IMF Publications, 2001.

Moss, T. J. *African Development: Making Sense of the Issues and Actors.* Boulder, CO, Lynne Rienner Publishers, 2007.

Mouandjo Lewis, P. *Crise et croissance en Afrique.* Paris, L'Harmattan, 2002.

Konaté, M. *L'Afrique noire est-elle maudite?* Paris, Fayard, 2010.

Moyo, B. *Africa in Global Power Play: Debates, Challenges and Potential Reforms.* London, Adonis & Abbey Publishers, 2007.

Moyo, D. *Dead Aid: Why Aid is Not Working and How There is Another Way for Africa.* London, Penguin, 2009.

Muchie, M. (Ed.). *The Making of the African Nation: Pan-Africanism and the African Renaissance.* London, Adonis & Abbey Publishers, 2005.

Murithi, T. *The African Union: Pan-Africanism, Peacebuilding and Development.* London, Ashgate Publishing, 2005.

Ndulu, B. J., *et al. The Political Economy of Economic Growth in Africa, 1960–2000.* Cambridge, Cambridge University Press, 2007.

Ndulo, M., and Grieco, M. *Failed and Failing States: The Challenges to African Reconstruction.* Cambridge, Cambridge Scholars Publishing, 2010.

Nehma, A., and Tiyambe Zeleza., P. (Eds). *The Roots of African Conflicts: The Causes and Costs.* Oxford, James Currey, 2008.

The Resolution of African Conflicts: The Management of Conflict Resolution and Post-Conflict Reconstruction. Oxford, James Currey, 2008

Nohlen, D., *et al.* (Eds). *Elections in Africa: A Data Handbook.* Oxford, Oxford University Press, 1999.

Nordic Africa Institute. *Regionalism and Regional Integration in Africa.* Uppsala, Nordic Africa Institute, 2001.

Nugent, P. *Africa Since Independence.* London, Palgrave Macmillan, 2004.

Obudho, R. A. *Small Urban Centres in Africa: A Bibliographical Survey.* Nagoya, United Nations Centre for Regional Development, 1995.

OECD. *Regional Integration in Africa.* Paris, OECD, 2002.

Towards a Better Regional Approach to Development in West Africa: Conclusions of the Special Event of Sahel and West Africa Club. Paris, OECD, 2002.

Aid Activities in Africa 2002. Paris, OECD, 2004.

Privatisation in Sub-Saharan Africa: Where Do We Stand? Paris, OECD, 2004.

La téléphonie mobile en Afrique: qui sont ces investisseurs? Paris, OECD, 2009.

OECD Development Centre. *African Economic Outlook 2009.* Paris, OECD.

Conflict and Growth in Africa. Paris, OECD, 1999.

Reform and Growth in Africa. Paris, OECD, 2000.

Emerging Africa. Paris, OECD, 2002.

Business for Development 2008: Promoting Commercial Agriculture in Africa. Paris, OECD, 2008.

Ohaegbelum, F. U. *U.S. Policy in Postcolonial Africa: Four Case Studies in Conflict Resolution*. New York, Peter Lang, 2004.

Okafor, O. C. *The African Human Rights System, Activist Forces and International Institutions*. Cambridge, Cambridge University Press, 2007.

Okoth, G. P. (Ed.). *Africa at the Beginning of the 21st Century*. Nairobi, University of Nairobi Press, 2000.

Oliver, R. *The African Experience*. London, Weidenfeld & Nicolson, 1991.

Oliver, R., and Fage, J. D. *A Short History of Africa*. London, Penguin Books, 1988.

Olowu, D., and Sako, S. (Eds). *Better Governance and Public Policy*. Bloomsfield, CT, Kumarian Press, 2003.

Olukoshi, A. *The Politics of Opposition in Contemporary Africa*. Uppsala, Nordic Africa Institute, 1998.

Olukoshi, A., and Laakso, L. (Eds). *Challenges to the Nation-State in Africa*. Uppsala, Nordic Africa Institute, 1996.

Oyejide, A., Ndulu, B., and Greenaway, D. *Regional Integration and Trade Liberalization in Subsaharan Africa*. London, Palgrave Macmillan, 1999.

Pakenham, T. *The Scramble for Africa*. London, 1991.

Parker, J., and Rathbone, R. *African History: A Very Short Introduction*. Oxford, Oxford University Press, 2007.

Pathe Gueye, S. *Du bon usage de la démocratie en Afrique*. Dakar, Nouvelles Editions Africaines du Sénégal (NEAS), 2003.

Patterson, A. S. *The African State and the AIDS Crisis*. London, Ashgate Publishing, 2005.

The Politics of AIDS in Africa. Boulder, CO, Lynne Rienner Publishers, 2006.

Paulson, J. A. *African Economies in Transition*. London, Palgrave Macmillan, 1999.

Pfister, R. *Apartheid South Africa and African States: From Pariah to Middle Power, 1961-1994 (International Library of African Studies, Vol. 14)*. London, I. B. Tauris, 2005.

Philips, J. E. (Ed.). *Writing African History*. Rochester, NY, University of Rochester Press, 2006.

Pitcher, M. A. *Party Politics and Economic Reform in Africa's Democracies*. Cambridge, Cambridge University Press, 2012.

Poku, N. *AIDS in Africa: How the Poor are Dying*. Cambridge, Polity Press, 2006.

Poku, N., and Mdee, A. *Politics in Africa: A New Introduction*. London, Zed Books, 2011.

Prendergast, J. *Frontline Diplomacy: Humanitarian Aid and Conflict in Africa*. Boulder, CO, Lynne Rienner Publishers, 1996.

Prunier, G. *Africa's World War: Congo, the Rwandan Genocide, and the Making of a Continental Catastrophe*. Oxford, Oxford University Publishing, 2011.

Quantin, P. (Ed.). *Voter en Afrique: comparaisons et différenciations*. Paris, L'Harmattan, 2004.

Radelet, S. *Emerging Africa: How 17 Countries Are Leading the Way*. Washington, DC, Center for Global Development, 2010.

Raine, S. *China's African Challenges*. London, International Institute For Strategic Studies, 2009.

Rankhumise, S. P., and Mahlako, A. (Eds). *Defence, Militarism, Peace Building and Human Security in Africa*. Pretoria, Africa Institute of South Africa, 2005.

Reader, J. *Africa: A Biography of the Continent*. London, Penguin Books, 1998.

Reid, R. J. *A History of Modern Africa: 1800 to the Present*. Chichester, Wiley-Blackwell, 2011.

Reno, W. *Warlord Politics and African States*. Boulder, CO, Lynne Rienner Publishers, 1999.

Reynolds, A. *Electoral Systems and Democratization in Southern Africa*. Oxford, Oxford University Press, 1999.

Rimmer, D. *Africa Thirty Years On*. Oxford, James Currey, 1991.

Roberts, A. (Ed.). *The Colonial Moment in Africa: Essays on the Movement of Minds and Materials*. Cambridge, Cambridge University Press, 1990.

Robinson, D. *Muslim Societies in African History*. Cambridge, Cambridge University Press, 2004.

Rotberg, R. I. (Ed.). *Battling Terrorism in the Horn of Africa*. Washington, DC, Brookings Institution Press and the World Peace Foundation, 2005.

Roy, J.-L. *Une nouvelle Afrique*. Mali, Le Figuier, 1999.

Ruben N'Dongo, M. *L'Afrique sud-saharienne du XXème siecle*. Paris, L'Harmattan, 1997.

Rukato, H. *Future Africa: Prospects for Democracy and Development under NEPAD*. Trenton, NJ, Africa World Press, 2009.

Sachs, J. *The End of Poverty*. London, Allen Lane, 2005.

Salih, M. A. (Ed.). *African Political Parties: Evolution, Institutionalisation and Governance*. Sterling, VA, Pluto Press, 2003.

African Parliaments: Between Governance and Government. Cape Town, Human Sciences Research Council Press, 2006.

Sall, A. (Ed.). *Africa 2025: What possible futures for sub-Saharan Africa?* Pretoria, Unisa Press, 2003.

Sarris, A., and Morrison, J. (Eds). *Food Security in Africa: Market and Trade Policy for Staple Foods in Eastern and Southern Africa*. Cheltenham, Edward Elgar Publishing, 2010.

Saul, J. S. *Decolonization and Empire: Contesting the Rhetoric and Reality of Resubordination in Southern Africa*. London, The Merlin Press, 2007.

Saunders, C, Dzinesa, G., and Nagar, D. (Eds). *Region-building in Southern Africa: Progress, Problems and Prospects*. London, Zed Books, 2012.

Saxena, S. C. *Politics in Africa*. Delhi, Kalinga Publications, 1993.

Schraeder, P. *African Politics and Society: A Mosaic in Transformation*. Boston, MA, Wadsworth, 2003.

Schwab, P. *Africa: A Continent Self Destructs*. London, Palgrave Macmillan, 2003.

Scoones, M., and Wolmer, W. *Pathways of Change in Africa*. Oxford, James Currey, 2002.

Seck, C. S. *Afrique: Le spectre de l'échec*. Paris, L'Harmattan, 2001.

Sherwood, M., and Adi, H. *Pan-African History*. London, Frank Cass, 2003.

Shillington, K. *Encyclopedia of African History*. London, Frank Cass, 2004.

Shorter, A. *East African Societies*. London, Frank Cass, 2004.

Sindayigaya, J.-M. *Mondialisation: Le nouvel esclavage de l'Afrique*. Paris, L'Harmattan, 2000.

Skard, T. *Continent of Mothers, Continent of Hope: Understanding and Promoting Development in Africa Today*. London, Zed Books, 2003.

Smith, A. D. *State and nation in the Third World: the Western state and African nationalism*. Brighton, Wheatsheaf Books, 1983.

Smith, M. S. *Beyond the 'African Tragedy': Discourses on Development and the Global Economy*. London, Ashgate Publishing, 2006.

Soares, B. (Ed.). *Islam and Muslim Politics in Africa*. London, Palgrave, 2007.

Sorensen, J. *Disaster and Development in the Horn of Africa*. London, Palgrave Macmillan, 1995.

Souare, I. K. *Africa in the United Nations System, 1945–2005*. London, Adonis & Abbey Publishers, 2006.

Souare, I. K. (Ed.). *Electoral Violence and Post-Electoral Arrangements in Africa (African Renaissance, Vol. 5, Nos 3–4)*. London, Adonis & Abbey Publishers, 2009.

Southall, R., and Melber, H. (Eds). *Legacies of Power: Leadership Change and Former Presidents in African Politics*. Cape Town, Human Sciences Research Council Press, 2006.

Stock, R. *Africa South of the Sahara*. London, Frank Cass, 1995.

Subramanian, A. *Africa's Trade Revisited*. Washington, DC, IMF Publications, 2001.

Suttner, R. (Ed.). *Africa in the New Millennium*. Uppsala, Nordic Africa Institute, 2001.

Taylor, I., and Williams, P. (Eds). *Africa in International Politics*. London, Routledge, 2004.

Thomas, C., and Wilkin, P. (Eds). *Globalization, Human Security and the African Experience*. Boulder, CO, Lynne Rienner Publishers, 1999.

Thomson, A. *An Introduction to African Politics*. London, Routledge, 2004.

Tiyambe Z., Paul, and Eyoh, D. (Eds). *Encyclopaedia of Twentieth-Century African History*. London, Routledge, 2003.

Tordoff, W. *Government and Politics in Africa*. Basingstoke, Macmillan, 1997.

Totte, M., Dahou, T., and Billaz, R. *La décentralisation en Afrique de l'Ouest*. Paris, Editions Karthala, 2003.

Tranfo, L. *Africa: La transizione tra sfruttamento e indifferenza*. Bologna, EMI, 1995.

Tvedt, T. *The River Nile in the Post-Colonial Age*. London, I. B. Tauris, 2009.

Twaddle, M. *The Making of Modern Africa: 1787 to the Present*. Oxford, Oxford University Press, 2004.

Udogu, E. I. *African Renaissance in the Millennium: The Political, Social and Economic Discourses on the Way Forward.* Lanham, MD, Lexington Books, 2007.

United Nations Centre for Regional Development. *Regional Development Policy Analysis: Issues in Food Security, Resource Management and Democratic Empowerment in Eastern and Southern Africa.* Nagoya, UNCRD, 1996.

The Role of Nongovernmental Organizations in Fostering Good Governance and Development at the Local Level in Africa. Nagoya, UNCRD.

Decentralization in Africa (Regional Development Dialogue, Vol. 29, No. 2). Nagoya, UNCRD, 2008.

Regional Development Policy and Practice in Africa (Regional Development Dialogue, Vol. 28, No. 1). Nagoya, UNCRD, 2007.

Local Governance and Poverty Alleviation in Africa (Regional Development Dialogue, Vol. 25, No. 1). Nagoya, UNCRD, 2004.

Utas, M. (Ed.). *African Conflicts and Informal Power: Big Men and Networks.* London, Zed Books, 2012.

Van de Walle, N. *African Economies and the Politics of Permanent Crisis, 1979–1999.* Cambridge, Cambridge University Press, 2001.

Villalon, L., and Huxtable, P. (Eds). *The African State at a Critical Juncture: Between Disintegration and Reconfiguration.* Boulder, CO, Lynne Rienner Publishers, 1998.

Wallerstein, I. *Africa: The Politics of Independence and Unity.* Lincoln, NE, University of Nebraska Press, 2006.

Weinreb, A., and Trinitapoli, J. *Religion and AIDS in Africa.* New York, OUP, 2012

White, L. *Speaking with Vampires: Rumor and History in Colonial Africa.* Berkeley, CA, University of California Press, 2000.

White, O. *Children of the French Empire.* Oxford, Oxford University Press, 1999.

Widner, J. (Ed.). *Economic Change and Political Liberalization in Sub-Saharan Africa.* Baltimore, MD, Johns Hopkins University Press, 1994.

Williams, M. D. J. *Broadband for Africa: Developing Backbone Communications Networks.* Washington, DC, World Bank Publications, 2010.

Williams, P. D. *War and Conflict in Africa.* Cambridge, Polity Press, 2011.

Wills, A. J. *An Introduction to the History of Central Africa.* Oxford, Oxford University Press, 1985.

Wiseman, J. A. (Ed.). *Democracy and Political Change in Sub-Saharan Africa.* London, Frank Cass, 1995.

Wohlgemuth, L., *et al. Institution Building and Leadership in Africa.* Uppsala, Nordic Africa Institute, 1998.

Wood, G., and Brewster, C. *Industrial Relations in Africa.* London, Palgrave Macmillan, 2007.

World Bank. *Africa Development Indicators 2010.* Washington, DC, World Bank, 2010.

Can Africa Claim the 21st Century? Washington, DC, World Bank, 2000.

Will the Euro Create a Bonanza for Africa? Washington, DC, World Bank, 1999.

The Africa Multi-Country AIDS Program 2000–2006: Results of the World Bank's Response to a Development Crisis. Washington, DC, World Bank, 2007.

World Economic Forum. *The Africa Competitiveness Report 2009.* Oxford, Oxford University Press, 2009.

Yalae, P. *The Road to a New Africa: An Essay to the African People.* New York, Random House Ventures, 2003.

Young, C. *The African Colonial State in Comparative Perspective.* New Haven, CT, Yale University Press, 1994.

Young, T. (Ed.). *Readings in African Politics.* Bloomington, IN, Indiana University Press, 2003.

Zartman, W., *et al. Europe and Africa: The New Phase.* Boulder, CO, Lynne Rienner Publishers, 1992.

Zeilig, L. *Revolt and Protest: Student Politics and Activism in Sub-Saharan Africa.* London, I. B. Tauris, 2007.

Zell, H. M. (Ed.). *The African Studies Companion: A Guide to Information Resources.* Glais Bheinn, Hans Zell Publishing Consultants, 2003.

Zossou, G. *Au nom de l'Afrique.* Paris, L'Harmattan, 2000.

SELECT BIBLIOGRAPHY (PERIODICALS)

Africa: Istituto Italiano per l'Africa e l'Oriente, Via Ulisse Aldrovandi 16, 00197 Rome, Italy; tel. (06) 328551; fax (06) 3225348; e-mail info@isiao.it; internet www.isiao.it; f. 1946; Dir Prof. Gianluigi Rossi; in English, French and Italian; quarterly.

Africa: International African Institute, School of Oriental and African Studies, Thornhaugh St, Russell Sq., London, WC1H 0XG, England; tel. (20) 7898-4420; fax (20) 7898-4419; e-mail iai@soas.ac.uk; internet www.internationalafricaninstitute.org; f. 1928; study of African societies and culture; Editors Prof. Karin Barber, Dr David Pratten; quarterly; also annual bibliography.

Africa Confidential: 73 Farringdon Rd, London, EC1M 3JQ, England; tel. (20) 7831-3511; fax (20) 7831-6778; e-mail editorial@africa-confidential.com; internet www.africa-confidential.com; f. 1960; political and economic news and analysis; Editor Patrick Smith; fortnightly.

Africa Contemporary Record: Africana Publishing Co, Holmes & Meier Publishers, Inc, POB 943, Teaneck, NJ 07666, USA; tel. (201) 833-2270; fax (201) 833-2272; e-mail info@holmesandmeier.com; annual documents, country surveys, special essays, indices; Publr Miriam Holmes; Editor Colin Legum.

Africa Development: Council for the Development of Social Science Research in Africa (CODESRIA), ave Cheikh Anta Diop X, Canal IV, BP 3304, Dakar 18524, Senegal; tel. 33-825-9822; fax 33-824-1289; e-mail codesria@codesria.sn; internet www.codesria.org; f. 1976; in French and English; Editor-in-Chief Alexander Bangirana; quarterly.

Africa Education Review: Routledge, Taylor & Francis, 4 Park Sq., Milton Park, Abingdon, Oxfordshire, OX14 4RN, England; internet www.tandf.co.uk/journals/RAER; f. 1972 as Educare; Editor Prof. Kuzvinetsa P. Dzvimbo; 3 a year.

Africa Energy Intelligence: 142 rue Montmartre, 75002 Paris, France; tel. 1-44-88-26-10; fax 1-44-88-26-15; e-mail info@africaintelligence.com; internet www.africaintelligence.com; f. 1983; French and English edns; Editor-in-Chief Philippe Vasset; fortnightly.

Africa Health: Vine House, Fair Green, Reach, Cambridge, CB5 0JD, England; tel. (1638) 743633; fax (1638) 743998; e-mail info@fsg.co.uk; internet www.africa-health.com; f. 1978; Editor Bryan Pearson; 6 a year.

Africa Insight: Africa Institute of South Africa, POB 630, Pretoria 0001, South Africa; tel. (12) 3286970; fax (12) 3238153; e-mail beth@ia.org.za; internet www.ai.org.za/africa_insight.asp; f. 1971; Editor Elizabeth Le Roux; quarterly.

Africa Mining Intelligence: 142 rue Montmartre, 75002 Paris, France; tel. 1-44-88-26-10; fax 1-44-88-26-15; e-mail info@indigo-net.com; internet www.africaintelligence.com; f. 1983; global mining information on exploration, contracts, legislation, corporate strategy and project funding, etc; French and English edns; Editor-in-Chief Gaëlle Arenson; fortnightly.

Africa Renewal/Afrique Renouveau: Africa Section, DPI Rm M-16031, United Nations, New York, NY 10017, USA; tel. (212) 963-6857; fax (212) 963-4556; e-mail africarenewal@un.org; internet www.un.org/ecosocdev/geninfo/afrec; Man. Editor Ernest Harsch; Editor-in-Chief Masimba Tafirenyika; in English and French; quarterly.

The Africa Report: 57 bis rue d'Auteuil, 75016 Paris, France; tel. 1-44-30-19-60; fax 1-44-30-19-55; e-mail editorial@the africareport.com; internet www.theafricareport.com; Editor-in-Chief Patrick Smith; Man. Editor Nicholas Norbrook.

Africa Research Bulletin: Blackwell Publishing Ltd, 9600 Garsington Rd, Oxford, OX4 2DQ, England; tel. (1865) 776868; fax (1865) 714591; e-mail editors@africaresearch.co.uk; internet www.wiley.com/bw/journal.asp?ref=0001-9852&site=1; f. 1964; separate bulletins on political and economic topics; Editors Virginia Baily, Veronica Hoskins; monthly.

Africa Spectrum: GIGA Institut für Afrika-Studien, Neuer Jungfernstieg 21, 20354 Hamburg, Germany; tel. (40) 42825522; fax (40) 42825511; e-mail afrika-spectrum@giga-hamburg.de; internet hup.sub.uni-hamburg.de/giga/afsp; f. 1966; articles in English; Man. Editors Dr Andreas Mehler, Henning Melber; 3 a year.

Africa Today: AMC House, 2nd Floor, 12 Cumberland Ave, London, NW10 7QL, England; tel. (20) 8838-5900; e-mail publisher@africatoday.com; internet www.africatoday.com; Publr Kayode Soyinka; monthly.

Africa Today: 221 Woodburn Hall, Indiana University, Bloomington, IN 47405, USA; tel. (812) 855-9449; fax (812) 855-8507; e-mail afrtoday@indiana.edu; internet inscribe.iupress.org/loi/aft; Editors Eileen Julien, Maria Grosz-Ngaté, Patrick McNaughton, Samuel Obeng.

Africa Week: Trans Africa Publishing Co Ltd, 14–15 Colman House, Empire Sq., High St, London, SE20 7EX, England; POB 50010, London, SE6 2WJ, England; tel. (20) 8285-1675; fax (87) 0429-2026; e-mail info@africaweekmagazine.com; internet www.africaweekmagazine.com; Editor Desmond Davies.

African Administrative Studies: Centre africain de formation et de recherche administratives pour le développement (CAFRAD), blvd Mohammed V, Pavillon International, BP 310, Tangier, 90001 Morocco; tel. (3) 9322707; fax (3) 9325785; e-mail cafrad@cafrad.org; internet www.cafrad.org; 2 a year.

African Affairs: Royal African Society, 36 Gordon Sq., London, WC1H 0PD, England; tel. (20) 3073-8335; fax (20) 3073-8340; e-mail ras@soas.ac.uk; internet www.royalafricansociety.org; f. 1901; social sciences and history; Editors Dr Rita Abrahamsen, Dr Sara Rich Dorman; quarterly.

African Agenda: Third World Network-Africa, 9 Ollennu St, East Legon, POB AN19452, Accra, Ghana; tel. (21) 511189; fax (21) 5111888; e-mail communications@twnafrica.org; internet www.twnafrica.org; f. 1994; analysis of economic and social issues.

African Arts: James S. Coleman African Studies Center, 10363 Bunche Hill, Box 951319, University of California, Los Angeles, CA 90095-1310, USA; tel. (310) 825-3686; fax (310) 206-2250; e-mail afriartsedit@international.ucla.edu; internet www.mitpressjournals.org/loi/afar; f. 1967; Editors Marla C. Berns, Allen F. Roberts, Mary Nooter Roberts, Doran H. Ross, Steven Nelson; quarterly.

African and Black Diaspora: 4 Park Sq., Milton Park, Abingdon, Oxon, OX14 4RN, England; tel. (20) 7017-6000; fax (20) 7017-6336; e-mail tf.enquiries@tandf.co.uk; internet www.tandf.co.uk/journals/rabd; f. 2008; locates the movement of African-descended populations in the context of globalized and transnational spaces; Editors Dr Fassil Demissie, Dr Sandra Jackson; 2 a year.

The African Book Publishing Record: De Gruyter Saur, Mies-van-der-Rohe-Str. 1, 80807 München, Germany; tel. (89) 769020; fax (89) 76902150; e-mail info@degruyter.com; internet www.degruyter.de/journals/abpr; f. 1975; bibliographic listings, book reviews, articles and information on book trade activities in Africa; Editor Cécile Lomer; quarterly.

African Business: 7 Coldbath Sq., London, EC1R 4LQ, England; tel. (20) 7841-3210; fax (20) 7841-3211; e-mail editorial@africasia.com; internet www.africasia.com; f. 1966; economics, business, commerce and finance; Editor Anver Versi; monthly.

African Farming and Food Processing: Alain Charles Publishing Ltd, University House, 11–13 Lower Grosvenor Pl., London, SW1W 0EX, England; tel. (20) 7834-7676; fax (20) 7973-0076; e-mail post@alaincharles.com; internet www.alaincharles.com; f. 1980; 6 a year.

African Finance Journal: POB 3628, Bellville 7536, South Africa; tel. (21) 9146778; fax (21) 9144438; e-mail info@africagrowth.com; internet www.africagrowth.com/afj.htm; f. 1999; finance, accounting and economics; Exec. Editor Nicholas Biekpe; 2 a year.

African Historical Review: Routledge, Taylor & Francis, 4 Park Sq., Milton Park, Abingdon, Oxfordshire, OX14 4RN, England; tel. www.tandf.co.uk/journals/RAHR; fmrly Kleio: A Journal of Historical Studies from Africa; Editors Greg Cuthbertson, Paul Landau, Henriëtte Lubbe, Russel Russel; 2 a year.

African Identities: 4 Park Sq., Milton Park, Abingdon, Oxon, OX14 4RN, England; tel. (20) 7017-6000; fax (20) 7017-6336; internet www.tandf.co.uk/journals/cafi; f. 2003; social, political and cultural expressions of African identity; Editor Pal Ahluwalia; 4 a year.

African Journal of AIDS Research: Centre for AIDS Development, Research and Evaluation, Institute of Social and Economic Research, Rhodes University, POB 94, Grahamstown 6140, South Africa; tel. (46) 6038553; fax (46) 6223948; e-mail ajar@ru.ac.za; internet www.nisc.co.za; f. 2002; Editor-in-Chief Dr Kevin Kelly; 4 a year.

African Journal on Conflict Resolution: ACCORD, Private Bag X018, Umhlanga Rocks 4320, South Africa; tel. (31) 5023908; fax (31) 5024160; e-mail info@accord.org.za; internet www.accord.org.za/publications/ajcr; f. 1999; conflict transformation in Africa; Editor-in-Chief VASU GOUNDEN; Editors JANNIE MALAN, JAKES GERWEL, TOR SELLSTRÖM; annually.

African Journal of Economic Policy: Trade Policy Research and Training Programme, Dept of Economics, University of Ibadan, Ibadan, Nigeria; tel. 8023258013; e-mail asbanky@yahoo.com; internet ajol.info/index.php/ajep; f. 1994; Man. Editor ADEMOLA OYEJIDE.

African Journal of Health Sciences: Kenya Medical Research Institute, POB 54840, 00200 Nairobi, Kenya; tel. (20) 2722541; fax (20) 2720030; e-mail dkoech@kemri.org; internet www.kemri.org; f. 1994; Editor-in-Chief Dr DAVY K. KOECH; quarterly.

African Journal of International Affairs: ave Cheikh Anta Diop X, Canal IV, BP 3304, Dakar, Senegal; tel. 33-825-9822; fax 33-824-1289; e-mail codesria@codesria.sn; internet www.codesria.org/spip.php?rubrique44; f. 1998; Editor-in-Chief ADEBAYO OLUKOSHI; 2 a year.

African Journal of International Affairs & Development: POB 30678, Ibadan, Nigeria; tel. (2) 8101963; fax (2) 8104165; e-mail collegepresspublishers@yahoo.com; internet www.inasp.org.uk/ajol/journals/ajiad; Editor Dr JIDE OWOEYE; 2 a year.

African Journal of International and Comparative Law: Edinburgh University Press, 22 George Sq., Edinburgh, EH8 9LF, Scotland; tel. (131) 650-4218; fax (131) 650-3286; e-mail rachel.murray@bristol.ac.uk; internet www.euppublishing.com/journal/ajicl; Editors Prof. RACHEL MURRAY, Dr KOFI OTENG KUFUOR.

African Journal of Political Science: 195 Beckett St, Arcadia, Pretoria, South Africa; POB 13995, The Tramshed 0126; tel. (12) 3430409; fax (12) 3443622; e-mail program@aaps.org.za; internet ajol.info/index.php/ajps; articles in English and French; Editor MUSA ABUTUDU (acting); 2 a year.

African Publishing Review: Immeuble Roume, 7e étage, blvd Roume, BP 3429, Abidjan 01, Côte d'Ivoire; tel. 20-21-18-01; fax 20-21-18-03; e-mail apnetes@yahoo.com; internet www.freewebs.com/africanpublishers; English and French edns; Editors SARAH GUMBIE (English), ALICE MOUKO-MINKALA (French); 6 a year.

African Review: Dept of Political Science and Public Administration, University of Dar es Salaam, POB 35042, Dar es Salaam, Tanzania; tel. (22) 2410130; fax (22) 2410395; e-mail politics@ucc.ac.tz; internet www.udsm.ac.tz; f. 1971; Editor Prof. DAUDI MUKANGARA; 2 a year.

African Review of Business and Technology: Alain Charles Publishing Ltd, University House, 11–13 Lower Grosvenor Pl., London, SW1W 0EX, England; tel. (20) 7834-7676; fax (20) 7973-0076; e-mail post@alaincharles.com; internet www.alaincharles.com; f. 1966; Editor ANDREW CROFT; 11 a year.

African Security: Taylor & Francis, Inc, 325 Chestnut St, Suite 800, Philadelphia, PA 19106, USA; internet www.tandf.co.uk/journals/uafs; Editor JAMES J. HENTZ; quarterly.

African Security Review: Institute for Security Studies, POB 1787, Brooklyn Sq. 0075, Tshwane, South Africa; tel. (12) 3469500; fax (12) 3469570; e-mail rsigsworth@issafrica.org; internet www.issafrica.org; African human security issues; Editor ROMI SIGSWORTH; 4 a year.

African Studies: 4 Park Sq., Milton Park, Abingdon, Oxon, OX14 4RN, England; tel. (20) 7017-6000; fax (20) 7017-6336; internet www.tandf.co.uk/journals/CAST; f. 1921; social and cultural studies of southern Africa; Editors Prof. ELIZABETH GUNNER, Dr BRIDGET KENNY; Prof. Prof. SHAHID VAWDA; 3 a year.

African Studies Review: 706 Herter Hall, 161 Presidents Dr., University of Massachusetts, Amherst, MA 01003, USA; tel. (413) 545-2065; fax (413) 545-9494; e-mail asr@anthro.umass.edu; internet www.umass.edu/anthro/asr; f. 1957; Editors ROWLAND FAULKINGHAM, MITZI GOHEEN; 3 a year.

Africana Bulletin: Institute of Developing Countries, Faculty of Geography and Regional Studies, University of Warsaw, Krakowskie Przedmieście 30, 00-927 Warsaw 64, Poland; tel. (22) 5520638; fax (22) 5521521; e-mail africana@uw.edu.pl; f. 1964; articles in English and French; Editor Dr BOGDAN STEFAŃSKI; annually.

Africanus: Unisa Press, Periodicals, POB 392, Unisa 0003, South Africa; tel. (12) 4292953; fax (12) 4293449; e-mail unisa-press@unisa.ac.za; internet www.unisa.ac.za; f. 1972; devt issues; Editor FRIK DE BEER; 2 a year.

Afriche e Orienti: 24 Via S. Mamolo, 40136 Bologna, Italy; e-mail africheorienti@hotmail.it; internet www.comune.bologna.it/iperbole/africheorienti; f. 1999; immigration, development, co-operation, multiculturalism and human rights in Africa and the Mediterranean; Editor MARIO ZAMPONI; quarterly.

Afrika Süd: Informationsstelle Südliches Afrika eV, Königswinterer-str. 116, 53227 Bonn, Germany; tel. (228) 464369; fax (228) 468177; e-mail issa@comlink.org; internet www.issa-bonn.org; f. 1971; politics, economics, social and military affairs of southern Africa and German relations with the area; Editor HEIN MÖLLERS; 6 a year.

Afrika und Übersee, Sprachen-Kulturen: Asien-Afrika-Institut, Abteilung für Afrikanistik und Äthiopistik, Edmund-Siemers-Allee 1, 20146 Hamburg, Germany; tel. (40) 428384874; fax (40) 428385675; e-mail AfrikaundUebersee@uni-hamburg.de; f. 1910; African linguistics and cultures; in German, English and French; Editors E. DAMMANN, L. GERHARDT, H. MEYER-BAHLBURG, L. M. REH, S. UHLIG, J. ZWERNEMANN; 2 a year.

Afrique Agriculture: BP 90146, 57004 Metz, Cedex 1, France; tel. 3-87-69-18-18; fax 3-87-69-18-14; f. 1975; bimonthly.

Afrique-Asie: 3 rue de l'Atlas, 75019 Paris, France; tel. 1-40-22-06-72; fax 1-45-23-28-02; e-mail africasi@wanadoo.fr; internet www.afrique-asie.fr; Dir MAJED NEHMÉ; monthly.

Afrique Contemporaine: c/o Agence Française de Développement, 5 rue Roland-Barthes, 75598 Paris Cédex 12, France; e-mail afrique-contemporaine@afd.fr; f. 1962; political, economic and sociological studies; Editor-in-Chief JEAN-BERNARD VÉRON; quarterly.

Afrique Expansion: Bureau 401, 1255 rue University, Montréal, QC, H3B 3B6, Canada; tel. (514) 393-8059; fax (514) 393-9024; e-mail info@afriqueexpansion.com; internet www.afriqueexpansion.com; building and construction; Editor-in-Chief DIDIER OTI.

Afrique Magazine: 31 rue Poussin, 75016, Paris, France; tel. 1-53-84-41-81; fax 1-53-84-41-96; e-mail redaction@afriquemagazine.com; internet www.afriquemagazine.com; African current affairs; Editor JÉRÔME BOURGEOIS; monthly.

Afryka, Azja, Ameryka Łacińska: Institute of Regional and Global Studies, Faculty of Geography and Regional Studies, University of Warsaw, 00-927 Warsaw, Krakowskie Przedmieście 30, Poland; tel. (2) 5520624; f. 1974; in Polish, with English summary; Editor BOGUMILA LISOCKA-JAEGERMANN; annually.

Agrekon: Arcadia, Pretoria 0001; tel. www.tandf.co.uk/journals/RAGR; a journal of the Agricultural Economics Association of South Africa; Editor A. JOOSTE; quarterly.

Annales Aequatoria: Centre Aequatoria, Maison MSC, BP 779, 3ème rue, Limete, Kinshasa 1, Democratic Republic of the Congo; e-mail vinck.aequatoria@skynet.be; internet www.aequatoria.be; f. 1980; central African culture, languages and history; Editor HONORÉ VINCK; annually.

El Arbol del Centro: Centro Cultural Español de Malabo, Carretera del Aeropuerto, Malabo, Equatorial Guinea; tel. (09) 2186; fax (09) 3275; e-mail ccem@wanadoo.gq; f. 2005; Equato-Guinean social and cultural review; Spanish; Editor GLORIA NISTAL; quarterly.

BBC Focus on Africa Magazine: Bush House, Strand, London, WC2B 4PH, England; tel. (20) 7557-2906; fax (20) 7379-0519; e-mail focus.magazine@bbc.co.uk; internet www.bbc.co.uk/focusonafricamagazine; Editor NICK ERICSSON; 4 a year.

Botswana Notes and Records: The Botswana Society, POB 71, Gaborone, Botswana; tel. 3919675; e-mail botsoc@info.bw; internet www.botsoc.org.bw; f. 1969; Editor CHRISTIAN JOHN MAKGALA; annually.

Bulletin of the School of Oriental and African Studies: School of Oriental and African Studies, Thornhaugh St, Russell Sq., London, WC1H 0XG, England; tel. (20) 7898-4064; fax (20) 7898-4849; e-mail bulletin@soas.ac.uk; internet uk.cambridge.org/journals/bso; f. 1917; Editor ULRICH PAGEL; 3 a year.

Business Monitor International: Mermaid House, 3rd Floor, 2 Puddle Dock, London, EC4V 3DS, England; tel. (20) 7248-0468; fax (20) 7248-0467; e-mail mbrooks@businessmonitor.com; internet www.businessmonitor.com; f. 1984; political and economic brief with macroeconomic forecasts covering sub-Saharan Africa; Editors LIZ MARTINS, JAMES LORD; weekly, monthly and quarterly publs.

Cahiers d'Etudes Africaines: 54 blvd Raspail, 75006 Paris, France; tel. 1-49-54-25-10; fax 1-49-54-26-92; e-mail Cahiers-Afr@ehess.fr; internet etudesafricaines.revues.org; f. 1960; in French and English; Editor-in-Chief JEAN-LOUP AMSELLE; quarterly.

Canadian Journal of African Studies (CJAS): c/o Roger Riendeau, Man. Editor, Innis College, University of Toronto, 2 Sussex Ave, Toronto, ON M5S 1J5, Canada; e-mail roger.riendeau@utoronto.ca; internet ejournals.library.ualberta.ca/index.php/cjas-rcea; f. 1967; in French and English; Editor-in-Chief CHRIS YOUÉ; Editors JOEY POWER, ABDOULAYE GUEYE; 3 a year.

Communicatio: 4 Park Sq., Milton Park, Abingdon, Oxon, OX14 4RN, England; tel. (20) 7017-6000; fax (20) 7017-6336; e-mail tf.enquiries@tandf.co.uk; internet www.tandf.co.uk/journals/rcsa; f. 1975; South African journal for communication theory and research; Editor Prof. PEITER J. FOURIE; 3 a year.

Communications Africa: Alain Charles Publishing Ltd, 27 Wilfred St, London, SW1E 6PR, England; tel. (20) 7834-7676; fax (20) 7973-0076; e-mail post@alaincharles.com; internet www.alaincharles

.com; f. 1991; telecommunications, broadcasting and information technology; in French and English; Editor ANDREW CROFT; 6 a year.

The Courier: 45 rue de Trèves, 1040 Brussels, Belgium; tel. (2) 237-43-92; fax (2) 280-14-06; e-mail info@acp-eucourier.info; internet www.acp-eucourier.info; affairs of the African, Caribbean and Pacific countries and the European Union; English, French, Spanish and Portuguese edns; Editor-in-Chief HEGEL GOUTIER; 6 a year.

Critical Arts: 4 Park Sq., Milton Park, Abingdon, Oxon, OX14 4RN, England; tel. (20) 7017-6000; fax (20) 7017-6336; e-mail authorqueries@tandf.co.uk; internet www.tandf.co.uk/journals/rcrc; f. 1980; north-south media and cultural studies; Editor KEYAN TOMASELLI; 4 a year.

Development Policy Review: Overseas Development Institute, III Westminster Bridge Rd, London, SE1 7JD, England; tel. (20) 7922-0300; fax (20) 7922-0399; e-mail dpr@odi.org.uk; internet www.odi.org.uk; f. 1982; Editor DAVID BOOTH; 6 a year.

Development Southern Africa: 4 Park Sq., Milton Park, Abingdon, Oxon, OX14 4RN, England; tel. (20) 7017-6000; fax (20) 7017-6336; e-mail enquiry@tandf.co.uk; internet www.tandf.co.uk/journals/CDSA; debates among devt specialists, policy decision makers, scholars and students in the wider professional fraternity and especially in southern Africa; Editor MARIÉ KIRSTEN; 5 a year.

English Academy Review: 4 Park Sq., Milton Park, Abingdon, Oxon, OX14 4RN, England; tel. (20) 7017-6000; fax (20) 7017-6336; e-mail tf.enquiries@tandf.co.uk; internet www.tandf.co.uk/journals/racr; f. 1983; promoting effective English as a vital resource and respecting Africa's diverse linguistic ecology; Editor-in-Chief MICHAEL WILLIAMS; 2 a year.

English Studies in Africa: 4 Park Sq., Milton Park, Abingdon, Oxon, OX14 4RN, England; tel. (20) 7017-6000; fax (20) 7017-6336; e-mail tf.enquiries@tandf.co.uk; internet www.tandf.co.uk/journals/reia; f. 1959; study of world literature in English within African contexts; Editor MICHAEL TITLESTAD; biannually.

Ethiopian Review: POB 98499, Atlanta, GA 30539, USA; tel. (404) 325-8411; e-mail EthRev@aol.com; internet www.ethiopic.com/ethrev.htm; Editor ELIAS KIFLE; monthly.

Heritage of Zimbabwe: History Society of Zimbabwe, POB CY 35, Causeway, Zimbabwe; tel. (4) 339175; e-mail mjksec@honeyb.co.zw; f. 1956; history of Zimbabwe and adjoining territories; Editor MICHAEL J. KIMBERLEY; annually.

Horn of Africa Bulletin: Life and Peace Institute, Eddagatan 12, SE 753 16 Uppsala, Sweden; tel. (18) 660132; fax (18) 693059; e-mail info@life-peace.org; internet www.life-peace.org; f. 1989; Editor SHAMSIA RAMADHAN; bi-monthly.

Indian Ocean Newsletter: 142 rue Montmartre, 75002 Paris, France; tel. 1-44-88-26-10; fax 1-44-88-26-15; e-mail info@indigo-net.com; internet www.africaintelligence.com; f. 1981; articles on politics, power-brokers, business networks, regional diplomacy and business intelligence in the Horn of Africa, East Africa, southern Africa and the islands of the Indian Ocean; French and English edns; Editor-in-Chief FRANCIS SOLER; fortnightly.

Indilinga: African Journal of Indigenous Knowledge Systems: POB 13789, Cascades, Pietermaritzburg 3202, South Africa; tel. (31) 9077000; fax (31) 9073011; e-mail nmkabela@hotmail.com; internet www.indilinga.org.za; f. 2002; issues relating to the transmission of local or traditional knowledge; Editor-in-Chief QUEENETH MKABELA; 1–2 a year.

International African Bibliography: De Gruyter Saur, Mies-van-der-Rohe-Str. 1, 80807 München, Germany; tel. (89) 769020; fax (89) 76902150; e-mail info@degruyter.com; internet www.saur.de; bibliographic listings; publ. in asscn with The Centre of African Studies, Univ. of London; Editor DAVID HALL; quarterly.

International Development Policy Series: 20 rue Rothschild, CP 136, 1211 Geneva 21, Switzerland; tel. (22) 9084364; fax (22) 9086273; e-mail marie.thorndahl@graduateinstitute.ch; internet poldev.revues.org; f. 2010; Editor-in-Chief Prof. GILLES CARBONNIER; 2 a year.

International Journal of African Historical Studies: African Studies Center, Boston University, 232 Bay State Rd, Boston, MA 02215, USA; tel. (617) 353-7306; fax (617) 353-4975; e-mail ascpub@bu.edu; internet www.bu.edu/africa/publications/ijahs; f. 1968 as African Historical Studies; Editor MICHAEL DIBLASI; 3 a year.

International Journal of African Renaissance Studies: 4 Park Sq., Milton Park, Abingdon, Oxon, OX14 4RN, England; tel. (20) 7017-6000; fax (20) 7017-6336; e-mail tf.enquiries@tandf.co.uk; internet www.tandf.co.uk/journals/rars; f. 2006; resource utilization and development; Editor MILDRED TROUILLOT; biannually.

Jeune Afrique L'Intelligent: Groupe Jeune Afrique, 57 bis rue d'Auteuil, 75016 Paris, France; tel. 1-44-30-19-60; fax 1-44-30-19-30; e-mail redactionweb@jeuneafrique.com; internet www.jeuneafrique.com; f. 1960; Editor-in-Chief BÉCHIR BEN YAHMED; weekly.

Journal of African Business: Taylor & Francis, Inc, 325 Chestnut Street, Suite 800, Philadelphia, PA 19106, USA; internet www.tandf.co.uk/journals/wjab; official journal of the International Academy of African Business and Development; Editor SIMON P. SIGUÉ; 3 a year.

Journal of African Cultural Studies: 4 Park Sq., Milton Park, Abingdon, Oxon, OX14 4RNP, England; tel. 7017-6000; fax 7017-6336; e-mail tf.enquiries@tandf.co.uk; internet www.tandf.co.uk/journals/rjac; f. 1988; literature, performance arts, visual arts, music, media, sociolinguistics and gender; Editor Dr CHEGE GITHIORA; biannually.

Journal of African Economies: Oxford University Press, Great Clarendon St, Oxford, OX2 6DP, England; tel. (1865) 353907; fax (1865) 353485; e-mail jnl.info@oup.co.uk; internet jae.oupjournals.org; f. 1992; Editor MARCEL FAFCHAMPS; quarterly.

Journal of African Elections: EISA, POB 740, Auckland Park 2006, South Africa; tel. (11) 3816000; internet www.eisa.org.za/EISA/publications/jae.htm; f. 1992; Editors DENIS KADIMA, NOAM PINES.

Journal of African History: School of Oriental and African Studies, Thornhaugh St, Russell Sq., London, WC1H 0XG, England; tel. (20) 7637-2388; fax (20) 7436-3844; e-mail akyeamp@fas.harvard.edu; internet journals.cambridge.org; f. 1960; Editors EMMANUEL K. AKYEAMPONG, ANDREAS ECKERT, JUSTIN WILLIS, LYNN M. THOMAS; 3 a year.

Journal des Africanistes: Société des Africanistes, Musée du Quai Branly, 222 rue de l'Université,75007 Paris, France; tel. 1-46-69-26-27; e-mail africanistes@yahoo.fr; internet africanistes.revues.org; f. 1931 as Journal de la Société des Africanistes; some articles in English; 2 a year.

Journal of Asian and African Studies (JAAS): SAGE Publications Ltd, 1 Oliver's Yard, 55 City Rd, London, EC1Y 1SP, England; tel. (20) 7324-8500; fax (20) 7324-8600; internet jas.sagepub.com; f. 1965; Editor NIGEL C . GIBSON.

Journal of Contemporary African Studies: 4 Park Sq., Milton Park, Abingdon, Oxon, OX14 4RNPP, England; tel. (20) 7017-6000; fax (20) 7017-6336; e-mail tf.enquiries@tandf.co.uk; internet www.tandf.co.uk/journals/cjca; economics, political science, international affairs, military strategy, modern history, law, sociology, education, industrial relations, urban studies, demography, social anthropology, literature, devt studies and related fields; Man. Editor Prof. ROGER SOUTHALL; quarterly.

The Journal of Development Studies: 4 Park Sq., Milton Park, Abingdon, Oxon, OX14 4RN, England; tel. (20) 7017-6000; fax (20) 7017-6336; e-mail info@frankcass.com; internet www.tandf.co.uk/journals; f. 1964; Man. Editors OLIVER MORRISSEY, Dr RICHARD PALMER-JONES, KEN SHADLEN, HOWARD WHITE, OLIVER MORRISSEY; 12 a year.

Journal of Eastern African Studies: 4 Park Sq., Milton Park, Abingdon, Oxon, OX14 4RN, England; tel. (20) 7017-6000; fax (20) 7017-6336; e-mail jeas@sant.ox.ac.uk; internet www.tandf.co.uk/journals/rjea; f. 2007; Editors Prof. DAVID M. ANDERSON, Dr HASAN WARIO ARERO; quarterly.

Journal Estudios de Asia y África: El Colegio de México, Camino al Ajusco No 20, Pedregal de Santa Teresa, 10740 Tlalpan, Mexico; tel. (55) 5449-3000; fax (55) 5645-0464; e-mail rcornejo@colmex.mx; internet ceaa.colmex.mx/revista/INDEX.html; f. 1966; Editor-in-Chief ROMER CORNEJO BUSTAMANTE; 3 a year.

The Journal of Imperial and Commonwealth History: 4 Park Sq., Milton Park, Abingdon, Oxon, OX14 4RN, England; tel. (20) 7017-6000; fax (20) 7017-6336; e-mail tf.enquiries@tandf.co.uk; internet www.tandf.co.uk/journals/fich; f. 1972; Editors Prof. STEPHEN HOWE, Prof. PHILIP MURPHY; quarterly.

Journal for Islamic Studies: Dept of Religious Studies, Room 5.38, Leslie Social Science Bldg, Upper Campus, University of Cape Town, Private Bag, Rondebosch 7701, South Africa; tel. (21) 6503889; fax (21) 6897575; e-mail Nabowayah.Kafaar@uct.ac.za; internet www.cci.uct.ac.za/publications/jis/overview; Editor-in-Chief SA'DIYYA SHAIKH; 1 a year.

Journal of Islamic Studies: Oxford Centre for Islamic Studies, George St, Oxford, OX1 2AR, England; tel. (1865) 278730; fax (1865) 248942; e-mail islamic.studies@oxcis.ac.uk; internet www.oxfordjournals.org/islamj; all aspects of Islam; Editor Dr FARHAN AHMAD NIZAMI; 3 a year.

Journal of Literary Studies: 4 Park Sq., Milton Park, Abingdon, Oxon, OX14 4RN, England; tel. (20) 7017-6000; fax (20) 7017-6336; e-mail tf.enquiries@tandf.co.uk; internet www.tandf.co.uk/journals/rjls; f. 1985; provides a forum for the discussion of literary theory, methodology, research and related matters; Editors ANDRIES OLIPHANT, RORY RYAN; in English and Afrikaans; quarterly.

Journal of Modern African Studies: Cambridge University Press, The Edinburgh Bldg, Shaftesbury Rd, Cambridge, CB2 2RU, England; tel. (1223) 312393; fax (1223) 315052; e-mail journals@cambridge.org; internet journals.cambridge.org/moa; f. 1962; articles and book reviews ranging widely over developments in modern

African society and politics; Editor Prof. CHRISTOPHER CLAPHAM; quarterly.

Journal of the Musical Arts in Africa: South Africa; internet www.tandf.co.uk/journals/RMAA; publ. by NISC (Pty) Ltd in association with the South African College of Music; Editor-in-Chief ANRI HERBST.

The Journal of Peasant Studies: 4 Park Sq., Milton Park, Abingdon, Oxfordshire, OX14 4RN, England; tel. (20) 7017-6000; fax (20) 7017-6336; e-mail tf.enquiries@tandf.co.uk; internet www.tandf.co.uk/journals/jps; f. 1973; Editor SATURNINO (JUN) BORRAS, Jr; quarterly.

Journal of Religion in Africa: The Mirfield Centre, Stocksbank Rd, Mirfield, West Yorkshire, WF14 0BW, England; tel. (1924) 481914; e-mail jraedit@aol.com; internet www.brill.nl/jra; f. 1967; Exec. Editors BRAD WEISS, ADELINE MASQUELIER; quarterly.

Journal of Social Development in Africa: School of Social Work, University of Zimbabwe, Private Bag 66022, Kopje, Harare, Zimbabwe; tel. and fax (4) 751903; e-mail sswprinc@mweb.co.zw; 2 a year; Editor Prof. RODRECK MUPEDZISWA.

Journal of Southern African Studies: Old School, Swine, Hull, HU11 4JE, England; tel. and fax (1482) 811227; e-mail jsas@stoneman.karoo.co.uk; internet www.tandfonline.com/toc/cjss20/current; f. 1974; Editors Dr JOOST FONTEIN, Dr DONAL LOWRY, Dr MORRIS SZEFTEL, Dr LYN SCHUMAKER; quarterly.

Journal for the Study of Religion: Dept of Religious Studies, Room 5.40, Leslie Social Science Bldg, Upper Campus, University of Cape Town, Private Bag, Rondebosch 7701, South Africa; tel. (21) 6503452; fax (21) 6897575; e-mail davidc@iafrica.com; Editor Prof. DAVID CHIDESTER; Administrator ELAINE NOGUEIRA; 2 a year.

Language Matters: 4 Park Sq., Milton Park, Abingdon, Oxon, OX14 4RN, England; tel. (20) 7017-6000; fax (20) 7017-6336; e-mail tf.enquiries@tandf.co.uk; internet www.tandf.co.uk/journals/rlms; f. 1970; multilingualism in Africa; Editor LAWRIE BARNES; 2 a year.

La Lettre d'Afrique Expansion: 17 rue d'Uzès, 75002 Paris, France; tel. 1-40-13-33-81; fax 1-40-41-94-95; f. 1984; business affairs; Editor HASSAN ZIADY; weekly.

La Lettre du Continent: 142 rue Montmartre, 75002 Paris, France; tel. 1-44-88-26-13; fax 1-44-88-26-15; e-mail lc@indigo-net.com; internet www.africaintelligence.fr; f. 1985; political power and business networks in francophone Africa; Editor ANTOINE GLASER; fortnightly.

Liberian Studies Journal: Liberian Studies Association, Fayetteville State University, POB 14613, Fayetteville, NC 28301-4297, USA; internet www.onliberia.org/lsa_journal.htm; f. 1968; Editor Dr AMOS J. BEYAN; 2 a year.

Marchés Tropicaux et Mediterranéens: 5 rue de Charonne, 75011 Paris, France; tel. 1-43-18-87-00; fax 1-43-18-87-02; e-mail moreux@wanadoo.fr; internet www.marches-tropicaux.com; f. 1945; current affairs, mainly economics; Editor-in-Chief ANAÏS DUBOIS; weekly.

New Africa Analysis: Studio 6, The Grange, Neasden Lane, London, NW10 1QB, England; tel. (20) 8150-8283; fax (1895) 471028; e-mail editor@newafricaanalysis.co.uk; internet newafricaanalysis.co.uk; f. 2008; Editor CHARLES DAVIES; monthly.

New African: 7 Coldbath Sq., London, EC1R 4LQ, England; tel. (20) 7841-3210; fax (20) 7841-3211; e-mail editorial@africasia.com; internet www.africasia.com/newafrican; f. 1966; politics and general interest; Editor BAFFOUR ANKOMAH; monthly.

Newslink Africa: 15 Kensington High St, London, W8 5NP, England; tel. (20) 7376-1996; fax (20) 7938-4168; e-mail ishamlalpuri@gmail.com; internet www.adlinkint-newslinkafri.com; business and devt issues; Editor SHAMLAL PURI; weekly.

Nigrizia-Il Mensile dell'Africa e del Mondo Nero: Vicolo Pozzo 1, 37129 Verona, Italy; tel. (45) 8092390; fax (45) 8092391; e-mail redazione@nigrizia.it; internet www.nigrizia.it; f. 1883; Dir RENATO KIZITO SESANA; monthly.

Nordic Journal of African Studies: University of Helsinki, POB 59, 00014 Helsinki, Finland; tel. (9) 19122677; fax (9) 19122094; e-mail axel.fleisch@helsinki.fi; internet www.njas.helsinki.fi; f. 1992; Editor Prof. AXEL FLEISCH; 4 a year.

Optima: POB 61587, Marshalltown 2107, South Africa; tel. (11) 6385189; fax (11) 6382557; internet www.angloamerican.co.uk; f. 1951; political, economic, social, cultural and scientific aspects of South and southern African devt; Editor NORMAN BARBER; 2 a year.

Politikon: South African Journal of Political Studies: Routledge, Taylor & Francis, 4 Park Sq., Milton Park, Abingdon, Oxfordshire, OX14 4RN, England; tel. (20) 7017-6000; fax (20) 7017-6636; internet www.tandf.co.uk/journals/titles/13629395.asp; f. 1974; primarily South African politics; Editor Dr MEENAL SHRIVASTAVA; 3 a year.

Politique Africaine: Centre d'étude d'Afrique noire, Institut d'études politiques de Bordeaux, Domaine universitaire 11, allée Ausone, 33607 Pessac, France; tel. 5-56-84-82-28; fax 5-56-84-68-44; e-mail politique-africaine@sciencespobordeaux.fr; internet www.politique-africaine.com; f. 1981; political science and international relations; Editor-in-Chief VINCENT FOUCHER; quarterly.

Red Cross, Red Crescent: BP 372, 1211 Geneva 19, Switzerland; tel. (22) 7304222; fax (22) 7530395; e-mail rcrc@ifrc.org; internet www.redcross.int; English, French and Spanish edns; Editors JEAN-FRANÇOIS BERGER, ROSEMARIE NORTH; quarterly.

Research in African Literatures: Ohio State University, 361 Dulles Hall, 230 W 17th Ave, Columbus, OH 43210, USA; tel. (812) 855-9449; fax (812) 855-8507; e-mail ral@osu.edu; internet www.iupjournals.org; f. 1970; Editor KWAKU LARBI KORANG; quarterly.

Research Review: Institute of African Studies, POB 73, University of Ghana, Legon, Ghana; tel. (21) 502397; fax (21) 513389; e-mail iaspubs@ug.edu.gh; internet www.ug.edu.gh; f. 1965; Editor Prof. M. E. KROPP DAKUBU; 2 a year.

Review of African Political Economy: 4 Park Sq., Milton Park, Abingdon, Oxfordshire, OX14 4RN, England; tel. (20) 7017-6000; fax (20) 7017-6336; e-mail tf.enquiries@tandf.co.uk; internet www.tandf.co.uk/journals/crea; f. 1974; Chair. of Editorial Working Group JANET M. BUJRA; quarterly.

Revue Française d'Etudes Politiques Africaines: Société Africaine d'Edition, BP 1877, Dakar, Senegal; f. 1966; political; Editors PIERRE BIARNÈS, PHILIPPE DECRAENE; monthly.

Revue de l'Ocean Indien: rue H. Rabesahala, BP 46, Antsakaviro, 101 Antananarivo, Madagascar; tel. 22536; fax 34534; e-mail roi@dts.mg; internet www.madatours.com/roi; f. 1980; Editor GEORGES RANAIVASOA; quarterly.

Revue Tiers Monde: Institut d'Etude du Développement Economique et Social, 45 bis ave de la Belle Gabrielle, 94736 Nogent sur Marne Cédex, France; tel. 1-43-94-72-26; fax 1-43-94-72-44; e-mail tiermond@univ-paris1.fr; internet www.univ-paris1.fr/index.php?id=110718; f. 1960; devt issues; Editor-in-Chief YANN LÉZÉNÈS; quarterly.

Safundi: Routledge, Taylor & Francis, 4 Park Sq., Milton Park, Abingdon, Oxfordshire, OX14 4RN, England; tel. (20) 7017-6000; fax (20) 7017-6636; e-mail tf.enquiries@tandf.co.uk; internet www.tandf.co.uk/journals/rsaf; f. 2000; topics related to South Africa and the USA; Founding Editor Dr ANDREW OFFENBURGER; Editors RITA BARNARD, ANDREW VAN DER VLIES; quarterly.

Scrutiny 2: 4 Park Sq., Milton Park, Abingdon, Oxon, OX14 4RN, England; tel. (20) 7017-6000; fax (20) 7017-6336; e-mail tf.enquiries@tandf.co.uk; internet www.tandf.co.uk/journals/rscr; f. 1996; theoretical and practical concerns in English studies in southern Africa, particularly tertiary education; Man. Editor DEIRDRE BYRNE; 2 a year.

Serving in Mission Magazine: SIM International Communication, 1838 Gold Hill Rd, Fort Mill, SC 29708, USA; tel. (803) 802-7300; fax (803) 548-0885; e-mail magazine.editor@sim.org; internet www.sim.org; f. 1958; edns also publ. in Australia, New Zealand, South Africa, Republic of Korea, Singapore, Switzerland, United Kingdom and USA; French, German, Italian, Korean and Mandarin edns; Editorial Dir CAROL WILSON; quarterly.

Social Dynamics: 4 Park Sq., Milton Park, Abingdon, Oxfordshire, OX14 4RN, England; tel. (20) 7017-6000; fax (20) 7017-6336; e-mail tf.enquiries@tandf.co.uk; internet www.tandf.co.uk/journals/rsdy; f. 1975; humanities and social sciences; Editors KYLIE THOMAS, LOUISE GREEN; 3 a year.

South African Historical Journal: Unisa Press, POB 392, Muckleneuk, Pretoria 0003, South Africa; tel. (12) 4292953; fax (12) 4293221; e-mail tf.enquiries@tandf.co.uk; internet www.tandf.co.uk/journals/RSHJ; Co-ordinating Editors ARIANNA LISSONI, MUCHAPARARA MUSEMWA, THULA SIMPSON, SANDRA SWART; quarterly.

South African Review of Sociology: 4 Park Sq., Milton Park, Abingdon, Oxon, OX14 4RN, England; tel. (20) 7017-6000; fax (20) 7017-6336; internet www.tandf.co.uk/journals/rssr; South African sociology; Editors SHIREEN ALLY, Dr MARCELLE DAWSON, MARCELLE DAWSON, Dr BRIDGET KENNY, Dr LUKE SINWELL; 3 a year.

Southern Africa Monitor: Business Monitor International, Mermaid House, 4th Floor, Queen Victoria Street, London, EC4V 4AB, England; tel. (20) 7246-1403; fax (20) 7248-0467; e-mail marketing@meamonitor.com; internet www.meamonitor.com; f. 1996; business; Editors LISA LEWIN, EDWARD EMERSON; monthly.

Southern Africa Monthly Regional Bulletin (MRB): 920 M St, SE, Washington, DC 20003, USA; tel. (202) 546-0676; fax (202) 543-7957; e-mail southscan@allafrica.com; f. 1992; political, security and economic issues within the Southern African Development Community; Publr DAVID COETZEE.

Southern Africa Report: 23 Wellington Rd, Parktown, Johannesburg, 2000, South Africa; tel. (11) 486 9517; e-mail administrator@southernafricareport.com; internet www.southernafricareport.com; f. 1983; current affairs and financial newsletter; Publr DAVID NIDDRIE; Editors KARIMA BROWN, VUKANI MDE; 50 a year.

Southern African Linguistics and Applied Language Studies: 4 Park Sq., Milton Park, Abingdon, Oxon, OX14 4RN, England; tel. (20) 7017-6000; fax (20) 7017-6336; e-mail tf.enquiries@tandf.co.uk; internet www.tandf.co.uk/journals/rall; f. 1983; the core areas of linguistics, both theoretical (e.g. syntax, phonology, semantics) and applied (e.g. sociolinguistic topics, language teaching, language policy) in all the languages of southern Africa, including English and Afrikaans; Editor-in-Chief Prof. JACOBUS A. NAUDÉ; quarterly.

Southscan: 920 M St, SE, Washington, DC 20003, USA; tel. (202) 248-3120; fax (202) 546-0676; e-mail southscan@allafrica.com; f. 1986; political and economic affairs in South Africa and the other countries of the Southern African Development Community; Publr DAVID COETZEE; fortnightly.

Studia Africana: Centor d'estudis Africans, Mare de Déu del Pilar 15 pral., 08003 Barcelona, Spain; tel. (93) 3194008; fax (93) 3194008; e-mail cea@pangea.org; internet www.estudisafricans.org; Editor ALBERT ROCA.

Third World Quarterly: Dept of Geography, Royal Holloway College, Egham, Surrey, TW20 0EX, England; e-mail editor@thirdworldquarterly.com; fax (20) 8947-1243; internet www.tandf.co.uk/journals/CTWQ; f. 1979; Editor SHAHID QADIR; 10 a year.

This Is Africa: A Global Perspective: Number One, Southwark Bridge, London, SE1 9HL, England; tel. (20) 7775 6373; e-mail thisisafrica@ft.com; internet www.thisisafricaonline.com; Editor LANRE AKINOLA; 4 a year.

Vostok / Oriens (The East): Afro-Aziatskiye Obtchestva, Istoria i Sovremenost, Institut Vostokovedeniya, Institut Afriki, Rossiyskaya Akad. Nauk, Moscow 107031, 12 Rozhdestvenka St, Russia; tel. (495) 625-51-46; e-mail vostok.o@yandex.ru; internet www.vostokoriens.ru; f. 1955; text in Russian, summaries in English; Editor-in-Chief Dr VITALII NAUMKIN; 6 a year.

West Africa Review: POB 7152, Endicott, NY 13760, USA; e-mail subscriptions@africaknowledgeproject.org; internet www.westafricareview.com; f. 1999; Man. Editor NKIRU NZEGWU; 2 a year.

INDEX OF REGIONAL ORGANIZATIONS

(Main reference only)

A

B

C

J

K

L

M

N

O